2 (before a superlative *adj* or *own*) in the fullest sens… *best quality* ○ *the very first to arrive* ○ *six o'clock at the* … ○ *your very own cheque-book.* **3** exactly: *sitting in the* … *seat.*

start of compound(s) section

□ **ˌvery high ˈfrequency** (*abbr* **VHF**) radio frequenc… 300 megahertz.

compound of headword, showing stress pattern

NOTE ON USAGE: **1 Very much** is used to modify ve… *likes Beethoven very much.* ○ *We have enjoyed staying* … *very much.* **2 Much** or **very much** can modify past par… *She is (very) much loved by everyone.* ○ **3 Very** is used to modify adjectives and past participles used as adjectives: *She is very talented.* ○ *I am very tired.* ○ *They were very interested.*

…on a particular point of grammar

grammatical information on adjectives

very[2] /ˈverɪ/ *adj* [attrib] **1** itself, himself, etc and no other; actual; truly such: *This is the very book I want!* ○ *At that very moment the phone rang.* ○ *You're the very man I want to see.* ○ *These pills are the very thing for your cold.* **2** extreme: *at the very end/beginning.* **3** (used to emphasize a *n*): *He knows our very thoughts*, ie our thoughts themselves, even our innermost thoughts. ○ *The very idea* (ie The idea alone, quite apart from the reality) *of going abroad delighted him.* ○ *The very idea/thought!* ie That is an impractical or improper suggestion. ○ *Sardine tins can be the very devil* (ie very difficult) *to open.* **4** (idm) **under/before one's very eyes** ⇨ EYE[1]

extra note on grammar or usage

cross-reference to entry where idiom is defined

Very light /ˈverɪ laɪt/ coloured signal flare fired at night, eg as a sign of distress from a ship.

label showing specialist subject area(s)

vesicle /ˈvesɪkl/ *n* (*anatomy or biology*) **1** small hollow bladder or cavity in the body of a plant or an animal. **2** blister.

derivative, with pronunciation

start of derivative(s) section

▷ **vesicular** /vəˈsɪkjʊlə(r)/ *adj* [usu attrib] of or characterized by the formation of vesicles: *swine vesicular disease.*

vespers /ˈvespəz/ *n* [pl] church service or prayers in the evening; evensong. Cf MATINS.

cross-reference to related headword

Vespucci /veˈspu:tʃɪ/ Amerigo (1451-1512), Italian (Florentine) explorer. He made several voyages to the New World for the king of Portugal and claimed to have been the first to sight the mainland of S America in 1497. It is possible that the name America comes from his first name.

vessel /ˈvesl/ *n* **1** (*fml*) ship or boat, esp a large one: *ocean-going vessels* ○ *cargo vessels.* Cf CRAFT 2. **2** (*fml*) any hollow container, esp one used for holding liquids, eg a cask, bowl, bottle or cup. **3** tube-like structure in the body of an animal or a plant, conveying or holding blood or other fluid: *blood-vessels.*

American English equivalent

vest[1] /vest/ *n* **1** (a) (*Brit*) (*US* **undershirt**) garment worn under a shirt, etc next to the skin: *thermal, cotton, string, etc vests.* (b) special (usu sleeveless) garment covering the upper part of the body: *a bullet-proof vest.* **2** (*US*) = WAISTCOAT.

cross-reference to headword where meaning is given

letters showing closely related meanings within numbered sense

□ **ˌvest-ˈpocket** *adj* [attrib] (*esp US*) small enough to fit in a waistcoat pocket: *a ˌvest-pocket ˈcamera.*

example showing stress variation in context

vest[2] /vest/ *v* **1** [Tn·pr usu passive] ~ **sth in sb/sth**; ~ **sb/sth with sth** (*fml*) give sth as a firm or legal right to sb/sth; confer sth on sb/sth: *the powers vested in a priest* ○ *Authority is vested in the people* ○ *vest sb with authority, rights in an estate, etc* ○ *Parliament is vested with the power of making laws.* **2** [Tn] (*arch or religion*) put on (ceremonial garments). **3** (idm) **have a vested interest (in sth)** expect to benefit (from sth): *You have a vested interest in Tim's resignation*, eg because you may get his job.

information on the right preposition(s) to use with a headword

start of idiom(s) section

vestibule /ˈvestɪbju:l/ *n* **1** (*fml*) lobby or entrance hall, eg where hats and coats may be left: *the vestibule of a theatre, hotel, etc.* **2** (*US*) enclosed space between passenger coaches on a train: [attrib] *vestibule train.*

one-word synonym to supplement definition

vestige /ˈvestɪdʒ/ *n* **1** small remaining part of what once existed; trace: *Not a vestige of the abbey remains.* **2** (esp in negative sentences) not even a small amount: *not a vestige of truth/common sense in the report.* **3** (*anatomy*) organ, or part of one, which is a survival of sth that once existed at an earlier stage of evolution: *man's vestige of a tail.*

extra note on grammar or usage

▷ **vestigial** /veˈstɪdʒɪəl/ *adj* remaining as a vestige.

For a fuller description of how the dictionary is organized, see **Using the Dictionary – a Guide to the Entries**, pages ix–xxxviii.

OXFORD ADVANCED LEARNER'S ENCYCLOPEDIC DICTIONARY

OXFORD UNIVERSITY PRESS

Oxford University Press, Walton Street, Oxford OX2 6DP

Oxford New York
Athens Auckland Bangkok Bombay
Calcutta Cape Town Dar es Salaam Delhi
Florence Hong Kong Istanbul Karachi
Kuala Lumpur Madras Madrid Melbourne
Mexico City Nairobi Paris Singapore
Taipei Tokyo Toronto

and associated companies in
Berlin Ibadan

OXFORD and OXFORD ENGLISH are
trade marks of Oxford University Press

This book is an expanded and updated version of A S Hornby's
Oxford Advanced Learner's Dictionary 4/e (1989),
chief editor A P Cowie

First published (as *Oxford Advanced Learner's Dictionary, Encyclopedic Edition*) 1992
Hardback: Second impression 1993
Paperback: Third impression 1995

ISBN 0 19 431313 1 (hardback)
ISBN 0 19 431310 7 (paperback)

Text capture and processing by Oxford University Press and
Compulexis; phototypesetting by Pindar Graphics, Scarborough
Printed and bound in Hong Kong

CONTENTS

Editor Jonathan Crowther
Phonetics Editor Dr Susan Ramsaran, University of London
Deputy Editor Helen Warren
US Consultant Richard Yorkey, Professor Emeritus, St Michael's College, Winooski, Vermont

Specialist Advisers

David Blackwell (*Music*)
Dr Keith Brown (*Linguistics*)
Lisa Chaney (*Art*)
Bill Coumbe (*Computing*)
Derek Heater (*History*)
Margaret Hebblethwaite (*Religion, the Bible*)
Peter Mellet (*Chemistry*)
Anthony Orhnial (*Economics*)
David Parkinson (*Cinema*)
Dr Stephen Ridd (*Philosophy, Mythology, Archaeology*)
Michael Storm (*Geography, Geology*)
Michael Wardle (*Mathematics*)
Dr Charles Webster (*Medicine*)
Michael Wilkinson (*Physics*)
Dr Kendal Williams (*Biology, Botany, Zoology*)

ACKNOWLEDGEMENTS

The publishers are grateful to the following for permission to reproduce illustrations used in this dictionary, identified in each case by the dictionary entry at which they occur:

The Bridgeman Art Library: George Romney, Sir John Everett Millais; City of Salford Art Gallery and Museum: L S Lowry; The Daily Mirror: Andy Capp; The Epstein Archive, The Henry Moore Centre for the Study of Sculpture, Leeds City Art Galleries: Jacob Epstein (photo by Hans Wild); Gimpel Fils Gallery: Barbara Hepworth; © 1989 Grandma Moses Properties Co, New York: Grandma Moses; The Henry Moore Foundation: Henry Moore; Michael Holford: Bayeux tapestry; The Hulton Picture Company: Woody Allen, Alexander Graham Bell, Ingrid Bergman/ Humphrey Bogart (© Warner Brothers), Laurel and Hardy, Martin Luther King; Images Colour Library: the Cerne Giant; The Kobal Collection: the Marx Brothers; Mansell Collection: Thomas Edison, Florence Nightingale; Mary Evans Picture Library: George Cruickshank, Charles Dickens, Kate Greenaway, Sherlock Holmes, William Shakespeare, Stanley and Livingstone, Sir John Tenniel, Oscar Wilde; The Metropolitan Museum of Art, New York: Robert Motherwell (© DACS 1991); Musée d'Orsay, Paris (Photographie Giraudon): Alfred Sisley; Museum of Fine Arts, Boston (gift of Mrs Rachel Warren Barton and the Emily L Ainsley Fund): John Singer Sargent; National Galleries of Scotland: Sir Henry Raeburn; The Trustees, The National Gallery, London: John Constable, Thomas Gainsborough, William Hogarth, J M W Turner; National Gallery of Art, Washington DC (Rosenwald Collection): Mary Cassatt; National Portrait Gallery, London: Jane Austen, the Brontë sisters, Lord Byron, Sir Joshua Reynolds, Mary Shelley, Percy Bysshe Shelley; Newcastle upon Tyne City Libraries and Arts, Thomas Bewick; The Peter Roberts Collection, c/o Neill Bruce: Henry Ford; Rex Features: Louis Armstrong, Charlie Chaplin, Concorde, Statue of Liberty, Stonehenge: Royal Commission on the Historical Monuments of England: art deco; The Trustees of the Science Museum: the Wright brothers; the Tate Gallery, London: William Blake, Sir Edward Burne-Jones, David Hockney, Holman Hunt, Augustus John, Gwen John, Paul Nash, Ben Nicholson, Sidney Nolan, Jackson Pollock (© 1991 Pollock-Krasner Foundation/ARS, New York), Sir Stanley Spencer (reproduced by permission of the Stanley Spencer Estate), George Stubbs, James Whistler; © 1971 Helen Thurber and Rosemary A Thurber: James Thurber (from *Men, Women and Dogs*, published in the USA by Harcourt Brace Jovanovich Inc, and in the UK by Hamish Hamilton); United Feature Syndicate Inc: Peanuts; University of Liverpool Art Gallery and Collection: John James Audubon; The Board of Trustees of the Victoria and Albert Museum: Aubrey Beardsley, William Morris, Dante Gabriel Rossetti; Frederick Warne & Co: Beatrix Potter; Windsor Castle Royal Library: Thomas Rowlandson (© 1991 Her Majesty the Queen); D Yarwood: Dress (from *English Costume*, Batsford, 1952).

The drawings and maps in the dictionary are the work of the following illustrators:

David Haldane, JoneSewell and Associates, Richard Lewington, Martin Lonsdale/ Hardlines, Vanessa Luff, David More/Linden Artists, Coral Mula, Oxford Illustrators, John Storey, Michael Woods, Oxford University Press Technical Graphics Department.

Jacket photograph: Jon Davison

FOREWORD

This book grew out of a realization that there is a need among foreign learners of English at an advanced level – in universities and elsewhere – for a dictionary that gives full and detailed information on English lexis, grammar and usage within a controlled defining vocabulary, but at the same time offers wider reference coverage than other such dictionaries currently available. It has been adapted from A S Hornby's *Oxford Advanced Learner's Dictionary 4/e* (chief editor A P Cowie), with new material consisting of additional vocabulary appropriate at this level – including more entries for scientific, technical and computing terms and the expansion of many existing entries – but also many encyclopedic entries, especially of a literary, geographical and biographical nature. The number of illustrations has also been greatly increased, many half-tones being included in addition to drawings, diagrams and maps.

A noteworthy feature of the dictionary is the many specially written articles on British life and institutions and the equally numerous 'mini-notes' added to dictionary entries, which explain the particular connotations certain words have for British people in addition to their basic dictionary meaning(s). In these we have attempted to get 'under the skin' of the language for those foreign learners of English who wish to know more of our culture. Here, as elsewhere throughout the dictionary, the bias is deliberately towards British English and British culture, though as in the *Oxford Advanced Learner's Dictionary* (OALD) itself we have been at pains to indicate the major differences between British and American English and between British and American life and institutions. A similar emphasis may also be seen in the choice of encyclopedic entries, where we have focused more on the needs of the intended user as we perceive them than on comprehensiveness of information (beyond the scope of a book of this size).

Although OALD formed the basis for this new volume and virtually nothing in OALD was omitted in the preparation of it, space unfortunately does not allow individual acknowledgement here of all those who worked on that dictionary, under Tony Cowie's editorship. Special mention must however be made of certain specific contributions to the present book. Michael Dibdin played a major part in the early formulation of editorial policy; John Ayto and Edwin Carpenter between them undertook the bulk of the drafting of new material; Susan Ramsaran, following on her work on OALD itself, supplied the phonetic transcriptions for all the additional headwords; Adrian Room planned and wrote the special articles and mini-notes referred to above; and Richard Yorkey gave much valuable advice on aspects of American life covered in these. Helen Warren steered the project through a critical period and assembled the team of specialist advisers who checked the text. Catherine Blackie researched the photographs selected for inclusion and Eunice Gill gave considerable help in the preparation and editing of the maps.

Great care has been taken to ensure that all the encyclopedic entries are accurate at the time of going to press. In today's rapidly changing world certain types of information, especially geographical and political, can date with unforeseen suddenness. We can only ask readers to be tolerant in cases where subsequent events may have rendered any such entries incomplete.

Jonathan Crowther
Editor

NOTES ON USAGE

The following list includes all the words or phrases in the dictionary which are dealt with in the many notes on usage throughout the book (⇨ Guide to Entries 18.1). The notes are of various kinds. They may for example clarify points of grammar, as in the note at **as**, where the use of *as, like* and *as if* is explained, or distinguish the meanings of a group of words which are semantically related, as in the note at **rob**, where the verbs *rob, steal* and *burgle* are compared.

Users of the dictionary will find at the entries for each of the words listed below a reference to the usage note in which it is dealt with, eg, at **achievement**, ⇨ Usage at ACT[1]. If the reference is simply ⇨ Usage, the usage note follows the entry in which the reference occurs.

a
a-
about
above
achievement
act
action
affect
after
afternoon
afterwards
aged
albeit
all
alley
almost
alone
already
also
alter
altercation
although
among
ancient
and
anti-
antique
apparatus
appear
appliance
argument
arrange
as
as if
ask
as well
attractive
avenue
bake
balance
bang
bank
bash
bathroom
be (contracted forms)
beach
bear (born or borne)
bear
beat
beautiful
become
been (Cf 'gone')
before
beg
begin
behind
beseech
between
bi-
big
blunder
body
boil
bony
bootleg
border
born
borne
both
bounce
boundary
break
bring about
Britain
Britisher
British Isles
Briton
broad
broil
bump
burgle
by myself, etc
call in on
call on
calm
can
care
care (about)
care (for)
care for
care to do
cargo
carry
cart (*v*)
cause (*n*)
cause (*v*)
certain
chair (= chairperson)
chairman
championship
chance (*n*)
chance (*v*)
change
charge
chat
choose
chop
chortle
Christendom
Christian
Christianity
Christian name
chubby
chuckle
church (use with or without definite article)
citizen
clip
close (*v*)
closed
coach
coast
college (used with or without definite article)
come and see, etc
come and stay
command
competition
compose, composed of
comprise
comprised of
condense
consist of
constitute
contemporary
contest
continual
continuous
contracted forms of the verb 'be'
contracted, negative and question forms of the verb 'have'
conversation
cook
cost
could, could have
counter-
country
creep
cry
cry (out)
current
cut
dart
data
dealer
decree
deed
deep
deep-fry
defect
defrost
demonstration
depth
device
dictate
different from/than/to
dimension
dinner
direct
dis-
discussion
disinterested
display
drag
draw
dream (alternative regular and irregular past tense and past participle forms)
drip
drive
drop by
drop in on
due to
each, each (one) of
earth
educate
effect
eg
elder
elderly
emaciated
employment
empty
entreat
error
-ess
-ette
evening
event
every, every (one) of
excursion
excuse
Excuse me
expect
exploit
expressway
factory
fair (*adj*)
fair (*n*)
fairly
family name
farther
fat
fault
feat
fee
feel
female
feminine
fewer
fight
first, firstly
first floor
first name
fish, fishes (alternative plurals)
fit
flabby
flammable
flog
floor (first, second floor)
floor
fly
fog
footpath
force
forename
forward, forwards
frankly
freeway
freeze
freight
frontier
frown
frozen
fry
full
funfair
further
gadget
gallop
game
gawp
gaze
GB
generally
Gents, the
get
giggle
given name
go
go and see, etc
go and stay
go by
gone
good-looking
goods
gossip (*v* and *n*)
go to see
great
Great Britain
grill
grimace
ground floor
ground
ground(s)
hack
half
handsome
happen
happen (syntax)
hardly
haul
have (contrast with 'have got')
have (contracted, negative and question forms of the verb 'have')
have got
have got to
have to, not have to
haze
healthy
hear
height
he/she
he or she
high
highway
hire (out)
hit
hobble
holiday
hope
hopefully
hospital (use with or without definite article)
however
human
human being
humanity
human race
hump
hunt
hunter
hunting
huntsman
hurt
I beg your pardon
-ic
-ical
ice
icy
ie
if
if ... not
il-
ill
im-
implement
implore
in-
in front of
incident
income
inflammable
injure
innumerable
instruct
instrument
interest
interested
interlude
intermission
interval
invaluable
ir-
-ise
Islam
-ist
-ite
-ize
jab
Jew, Jewry
job
jog
journey
Judaism
jump
justification
kind of
knock
labour
Ladies, the
lady
land
landlord
lane
large
last (*adj*)
last (*v*)
last, the (*adj*)
late
lately
latest, the
latter
lavatory
lay

leak
leap
lease
leave
left-overs
length
less
less
lessee
lessor
let
let (out)
lie (lie down)
lie (say sth untrue)
like (would you like?)
like (*prep*)
like (*v*)
limp
listen
little
lock
lonely
lonesome
long
long time, a
loo
look
loose
loosen
lug
lunch
lurk
machine
make
male
man
-man
mankind
masculine
match
may, may have
melt
merchant
might
mill
mist
mistake
modern
modify
morning
motive
motorway
much
Muhammedanism
Muslim
must, must have, must not, mustn't
name
namely
nation
near, nearby, near(by), near (to)
nearest (to)
nearly
need, needn't, need to
neuter
new
next, next (to)
night
nil
nip
non-
non-flammable
not ... either
nothing
not long ago
nought
nudge
numberless
O
obese
obviously
occasion
occupation
occupied
occur
occurrence
old
older
on
one
ooze
opportunity
opt (for)
ordain
order
organize
ought to, oughtn't to, ought to have
over
overweight
owing to
own, on my, etc
pack
package
packaging
packet
parcel
pardon?
Pardon me
pare
path
pause
pay
peddle
peer
people
peoples
person, persons
-person
personally
pick
piece
pirate (*v*)
place
plan (*v*)
plant
plod
plump
podgy
poke
poorly
power
prepositions used with 'night'
prescribe
presently
pretty (*adj*)
pretty (*adv*)
price
principal
principle
prison (use with or without definite article)
prod
profession
proved, proven (alternative past tense and past participle forms)
prowl
prune
public convenience
pull
push
quarrel
quarter
quiet
quite
race (*n*)
race (*v*)
rand (variant pronunciations)
rare
rather
re-
really
reason
recent
recently
recess
recount/re-count
recover/re-cover
reflexive verbs (stress)
relation
relations
relationships
relic
remainder, the
remains
remnants
rent (*n*)
rent (out)
request
residue
rest
rest, the
rest-room
ride
road
roast
rob
room
row
run (Cf walk)
run (of illegal goods)
run (of liquids)
sadly
sail (in)
salary
sauté
saw
say
scamper
scarce
scarcely
scatter
school (use with or without definite article)
Scotch
Scots
Scotsman/-woman
Scottish
scowl
scrawny
scream
scurry
scuttle
seaside, the
seat
second floor
second(ly)
see
seem
seep
select
sell
sensible
sensitive
seriously
shall
shamble
shave
shaved, shaven (alternative past tense and past participle forms)
s/he
shoot
shooting
shore
should, shouldn't, should have
shout
show (*n*)
shower
shuffle
shut
sick
sidle
signs of the zodiac
silent
Sincerely, Sincerely yours, Yours sincerely
skinny
skulk
slash
slender
slim
slink
slosh
small
smell
smirk
smog
smuggle
sneak
sneer
snicker
snigger
sob
soil
solitary
somebody (use of pronouns after 'somebody')
Sorry?
sort of
sound
space
spatter
speak
splash
splatter
sport
spray
spring
sprinkle
sprint
stab
stagger
stair
staircase
stare
start
state
stay
steal (take without permission)
steal (move stealthily)
steam (*n*)
steam (*v*)
steer
step(s)
still
stomp
stout
street
strength
strew
strike
stumble
stump
subject
supper
sure
surname
take
take care of
take place
talk
tall
task
taste
tea
teach
tear
tell
tell (give an order)
tenancy
tenant
thankfully
thaw
the (pronunciation of definite article with abbreviations)
thin
third(ly)
though
time (prepositions of time)
tiptoe
to begin with
toil
toilet
too
tool
tour
tournament
tow
track
trade
trade exhibition/show/fair
trader
trail
train (*v*)
tramp
travel (*v*)
travel(s) (*n*)
trim
trip
trot
trudge
try and see, etc
tubby
turn
UK
un-
underweight
uninterested
United Kingdom
university (use with or without definite article)
unless
unloose
unloosen
used to
vacant
vacation
valuable
valueless
vary
vend
verbs with alternative regular and irregular past tense and past participle forms
very, very much
vigour
visit (with)
viz
vomit
voyage
waddle
wages
wail
wait
wait and see, etc
want
-ward, -wards
washroom
water
WC
wear
weep
well
what
whether
which
whimper
whiz
who
whole
whom
wide
width
will
wish
With best wishes
words ending in -us, -a, -um, -on
work
works
worthless
would
Would you like?
wound
yell
yet
Yours (ever, faithfully, sincerely, truly)
zero
zip
zodiac
zoom

ARTICLES

The following topics relating to British life and institutions are treated in special articles throughout the dictionary (⇨ Guide to Entries 18.2). The user will find them at or near their alphabetical position except where otherwise specified.

accent and dialect
accommodation
advertising
animals
architecture
aristocratic titles
armed forces
banks and building societies
charities
Christmas
Church of England
class
clothes
clubs
countryside
crime
drink
drugs
eating out (at **eat**)
electricity and gas
emergency services
employment
England
entertaining
environment
ethnic minorities
family
finance
food
gambling
gardens
government
greetings cards
health
hobbies
holidays
house and home
humour
industry
Ireland
language
law
leisure
libraries
London
magazines
museums and galleries
music
names
national symbols
newspapers
nuclear power
nursery rhymes
oil
parliament
performing arts
police
politics
Post Office
post-school education
protest movements
publishing
punishment
radio
railways
religion
retirement
rivers and canals
roads
royal family
schools
Scotland
sea
the season
services
shops
social conventions (at **convention**)
social security
sports and games
superstition
taboo words
taxation
technology
telephone
television
town and country
trade unions
voluntary organizations
Wales
water
weather
weddings
women
youth movements

'MINI-NOTES'

The following dictionary entries contain 'mini-notes' — short extra paragraphs giving information on the special connotations these words have for native speakers of English. These notes are headed by the symbol 📖.

age
animal
apple
bell
bible
bicycle
birthday
black
blond
bonfire
bungalow
bus
ceremony
cigarette
coffee
comic
constituency
county
crescent
day
decade
deck
deer
desert
detective
diet
dragon
drunk
election
equator
Europe
explore
fancy
flower
folk
fun
gaol
giant
god
heaven
hell
highway
hike
hockey
hymn
identity
lawn
monk
monster
motor
moustache
nut
parrot
pillar
pirate
port
prayer
prize
queue
rat
recorder
reservoir
rum
sauce
scooter
slum
snow
soap
spinach
spire
suburb
swan
tea
teddy bear
teens
tweed
valley
vicar
white

USING THE DICTIONARY
A GUIDE TO THE ENTRIES

ENTRIES AND HEADWORDS

Each entry is a block of information introduced by a headword, which is made prominent by bold print and set out slightly from the main body of text:

> **dictionary** /ˈdɪkʃənrɪ; *US* -nerɪ/ *n* **(a)** book that lists and explains the words of a language, or gives translations of them into one or more other languages, ...

One of the aims of this dictionary is to help the user to understand how longer words (ie derivatives and compounds) are formed from shorter words (or parts of words). The various smaller elements involved are themselves listed as headwords, and the first section below explains the different types of headword and, where appropriate, how they can be combined.

1 TYPES OF HEADWORD

1.1 Simple words. Most headwords in this dictionary are simple words, or 'roots'. A root is the smallest vocabulary item that can occur independently with a meaning of its own. Thus *lady, child, thank* and *happy* are all roots. Roots can be contrasted with derivatives (eg *thankful, happiness*), formed by adding affixes (*-ful, -ness*) to roots, and with compounds (eg *childbirth*) in which two roots are joined together. As a rule, derivatives and compounds are not placed in entries of their own in this dictionary (⇨ 16, 17).

1.2 Homographs. Homographs are separate roots which happen to share the same spelling. They differ completely in meaning, and they may differ in grammatical use as well. Examples of homographs are *bow* (a type of weapon) and *bow* (to bend the head or body), which apart from the differences of meaning and grammar are also pronounced differently. Homographs are given separate numbered entries, as follows:

> **bow**[1] /bəʊ/ *n* ...
> **bow**[2] /baʊ/ *v* ...

1.3 Affixes. Meaningful elements such as *-ish, -ment* and *-ly* cannot be used independently. These are affixes, used to form derivatives such as *clownish, astonishment* and *bravely*. To help users to understand how affixes (ie prefixes and suffixes) in their various meanings are used to form derivatives, the dictionary lists them as headwords, indicates the classes of words they can be attached to, supplies definitions, and gives examples of the derivatives formed:

> **-ship** *suff* (with *ns* forming *ns*) **1** state of being; status; office: *friendship* ○ *ownership* ...
> **-ish** *suff* **1** (with *ns* forming *adjs* and *ns*) (language or people) of the specified nationality: *Danish* ○ *Irish* ...

1.4 Combining forms. These are important elements in the creation of technical or scientific words. They may occur at the beginning of a word (as *bio-* does in *biodegradable*) or at the end (as *-cide* does in *suicide*). Like a root (a simple word), a combining form can be made into a larger word by adding an affix (eg *neur-* + *-al*), or by joining it to another combining form (eg *biblio-* + *-phile*); but unlike a root, a combining form cannot occur alone. Entries for combining forms contain definitions and illustrate the types of word that can be formed:

> **electr(o)-** *comb form* of electricity: *electrocardiogram* ○ *electrolysis*.
> **-mania** *comb form* (forming *ns*) madness or abnormal behaviour of a particular type: *kleptomania* ○ *nymphomania*.

1.5 Abbreviations. The dictionary contains many common abbreviations of simple words (Cf *pint, pt; Captain, Capt*), compounds (Cf *tuberculin-tested, TT*) and phrases (Cf *World Wide Fund for Nature, WWF*). All abbreviations are entered as headwords in the dictionary, with alternative forms, pronunciations and examples as appropriate:

> **t** (*US* **tn**) *abbr* ton(s); tonne(s): *5t* (ie tonnes) *of wheat per acre.*
> **PA** /ˌpiː ˈeɪ/ *abbr* **1** (*infml*) personal assistant: *She works as PA to the managing director*. ...

As well as being headwords in their own right, abbreviations appear in the entries for the full words which they represent, after the part of speech label and any accompanying grammatical information:

> **volt** ... *n* (*abbr* **v**) unit of electrical force, ...
> **postscript** ... *n* ~ **(to sth) 1** (*abbr* **PS**) ...

1.6 Dummy entries. When an irregular past tense, plural, etc is so different from the headword to which it relates that the dictionary user may not connect the two, a 'dummy' entry is provided for the irregular form. A dummy entry is one which contains no definitions or examples but is intended simply to refer the user to a normal main entry, thus:

took *pt* of TAKE[1].
mice *pl* of MOUSE.

(For other uses of the dummy entry ⇨ (2.1, 2.3, 2.4.)

2 ALTERNATIVE FORMS AND SYNONYMS OF THE HEADWORD

2.1 Alternative written forms. When a word can be spelt in two or more different ways (eg **facia, fascia**) and there are no differences of pronunciation or grammar, the most usual spelling is given as the headword, and the alternative form (or forms) are given immediately after the headword, thus:

facia (also **fascia**) /ˈfeɪʃə/ *n* ...

However, if the form chosen as the headword and its alternative(s) are so different in spelling that the user is unlikely to trace the one from the other(s), dummy entries (⇨ 1.6), are given for the alternatives:

bo'sn, bos'n = BOATSWAIN.
bo'sun = BOATSWAIN.

2.2 US equivalents. Differences between British and American equivalents present special problems for the foreign learner. Sometimes the difference is one of spelling alone. In such cases, the US form follows the British one (given as the headword) but precedes the pronunciation:

humour (*US* **humor**) /ˈhju:mə(r)/...

If the difference is one of pronunciation as well as spelling, each written form is followed by the appropriate phonetic spelling:

aluminium /ˌæljʊˈmɪnɪəm/ (*US* **aluminum** /əˈlu:mɪnəm/) ...

2.3 US synonyms of British words. A particular word (eg *nappy*) which is limited to British English may have a synonym (in this case *diaper*) which is restricted to US English. In such cases, the British word will be treated in a full entry, with the US word placed near the beginning in brackets:

nappy ... (*US* **diaper**) piece of towelling cloth or similar ...

A dummy entry for the US word directs the dictionary user back to this entry:

diaper ... **2** [C] (*US*) = NAPPY.

If a word is used in both British and US English, but has a synonym which is only British or only US, the former is treated in a full entry, and the synonym is labelled '(*Brit* also ...)' or '(*US* also ...)':

parcel /ˈpɑ:sl/ *n* **1** (*US* also **package**) ...

If a word is British only, but its US equivalent can be used by British as well as US speakers, both words are given a special label:

rubber[1] /ˈrʌbə(r)/ *n* **1** [U] ... **2** [C] (*Brit*) (also *esp US* **eraser**) ...

2.4 Other synonyms. A number of words, especially the names of substances, animals, plants and trees, have quite widely used synonyms. (In some cases the synonym may be a compound.) One word is treated in a full entry and the equivalents are entered prominently after the phonetic spelling:

bilberry /ˈbɪlbrɪ; *US* -berɪ/ (also **blaeberry, whortleberry**) *n* ...

If the synonyms are more than four entries away alphabetically from the headword (as in both cases here), they are given dummy entries (⇨ 1.6) at their own alphabetical places, and the user is referred to the entry where the definition is to be found:

blaeberry /ˈbleɪbrɪ; *US* -berɪ/ *n* = BILBERRY.
whortleberry /ˈwɜ:tlberɪ; *US* ˈhwɜ:rtlberɪ/ *n* = BILBERRY.

2.5 Compounds which include an equivalent word. Sometimes a simple word is also the first part of a compound with the same meaning as that simple word: cf *wellington, wellington boot; bowler, bowler hat.* Pairs such as these are treated in the entry for the simple word, thus:

wellington /ˈwelɪŋtən/ *n* (also ˌ**wellington** ˈ**boot**, ...) ...
bowler[2] /ˈbəʊlə(r)/ *n* (also ˌ**bowler** ˈ**hat**, ...) ...

PRONUNCIATION

3 SOUNDS AND SPELLING

3.1 Phonetic alphabet. Any single letter of the English alphabet can often be pronounced in different ways. For example, the letter *a* is pronounced differently in *hat, pass, came, water, dare, ago.* Phonetic spelling is a way of writing a word so that one symbol always represents only one sound. Two words may be spelt differently in ordinary spelling; but if they sound the same then the phonetic spelling is the same. For example, **key** and **quay** have the same phonetic spelling /kiː/. Each headword is followed by a phonetic spelling separated from the rest of the text by / /. Inside the back cover of the dictionary there is a list of all the letters (phonetic symbols) used in the phonetic spelling. Phonetic symbols are given at other places within the entry (⇨ 3.4, 6.1) where the user needs to know there is a change in pronunciation.

3.2 Models of pronunciation. A British English pronunciation is given for each word and, in those cases where there is a marked difference, the American version is also shown (⇨ 5.5). The British English form is that which has been called Received Pronunciation (RP) or General British. Where there is a choice between several acceptable forms, that form is selected which is likely to be easiest for users of this dictionary.

3.3 Linking 'r'. In spoken British English an *r* at the end of a written word (either as the final letter or in an *-re* ending as in *fire*) is not sounded unless another word that begins with a vowel sound immediately follows. For example, the *r* is not heard in *His car was sold* but it is heard in *His car isn't old.* To show this, words which end in *r* or *re* have /(r)/ at the end of the phonetic spelling in the dictionary, for example **car** /kɑː(r)/ (Cf 5.5.3).

3.4 How an inflection is pronounced. An inflection is the suffix added to the end of a word when it is used in a particular grammatical form, for example in the plural (*cups, skies*), in the past tense (*pointed, smiled*), in the comparative (*finer, wilder*). The pronunciation of these inflections follows a set of rules described below. Phonetic spelling is only given in the entry for inflected forms if they do not follow these rules, eg the plural of *basis*: *bases* /ˈbeɪsiːz/ or the comparative of *young*: *younger* /ˈjʌŋɡə(r)/.

3.4.1 -s and -es. The plural of nouns, and the third person singular present tense of verbs:

- If the final sound of the noun's singular or the verb's root form is a *vowel* or /b, d, ɡ, v, ð, m, n, ŋ, l/, the ending is formed by adding the sound /-z/. For example, *city* /ˈsɪtɪ/, *cities* /ˈsɪtɪz/; *ring* /rɪŋ/, *rings* /rɪŋz/.
- If the final sound of the noun's singular or the verb's root form is /p, t, k, f, θ/, the ending is formed by the addition of /-s/. For example, *work* /wɜːk/, *works* /wɜːks/.
- If the final sound of the noun's singular or the verb's root form is /s, z, ʃ, ʒ, tʃ, dʒ/, the ending is formed by the addition of /-ɪz/. For example, *match* /mætʃ/, *matches* /ˈmætʃɪz/.

3.4.2 -d and -ed. The past tense and past participle of verbs:

- If the final sound of the verb's root form is a *vowel* or /b, ɡ, v, ð, z, ʒ, dʒ, m, n, ŋ, l/, the past tense and the past participle are formed by the addition of /-d/. For example *hurry* /ˈhʌrɪ/, *hurried* /ˈhʌrɪd/; *judge* /dʒʌdʒ/, *judged* /dʒʌdʒd/.
- If the final sound of the verb's root form is /p, k, f, θ, s, ʃ, tʃ/, the past tense and the past participle are formed by the addition of /-t/. For example *stop* /stɒp/, *stopped* /stɒpt/.
- If the final sound of the verb's root form is /t, d/, the past tense and the past participle are formed by the addition of /-ɪd/. For example *paint* /peɪnt/, *painted* /ˈpeɪntɪd/.

3.4.3 -r and -er. The comparative and superlative of adjectives and adverbs:

- The comparative of adjectives or adverbs with only one syllable is formed by the addition of /-ə(r)/ to the final sound of the root word. For example *high* /haɪ/, *higher* /ˈhaɪə(r)/; *wild* /waɪld/, *wilder* /ˈwaɪldə(r)/.
- The superlative of these adjectives and adverbs is formed by the addition of /-ɪst/ to the final sound of the root word. For example *green* /ɡriːn/, *greenest* /ˈɡriːnɪst/; *fast* /fɑːst/, *fastest* /ˈfɑːstɪst/.

3.5 A note on the pronunciation of combining forms. It often happens, especially in the case of initial combining forms (⇨ 1.4), that more than one pronunciation occurs according to the sound of the remainder of the word. For instance **bio-**, **bi-** may have the following different forms: in *biochemistry* /ˌbaɪəʊˈkemɪstrɪ/, *biology* /ˌbaɪˈɒlədʒɪ/, *biopsy* /ˈbaɪɒpsɪ/, *bioscope* /ˈbaɪəskəʊp/. For this reason, each combining form given in the dictionary has examples, and the user should refer to the entries for these examples for information about the pronunciation in each individual case.

4 STRESS

4.1 Stress marks. When a word has more than one syllable, one of them is spoken with more force than the rest. This force is called stress, and the syllable which is stressed is shown with the stress mark /ˈ/ before it in the dictionary. For example, *any* /ˈenɪ/ has a stress on the first syllable; *depend* /dɪˈpend/ has a stress on the second syllable.

In some words, usually long ones, other syllables may also be spoken with more force than the rest, but with a stress that is not as strong as for those syllables marked /ˈ/. The stress mark /ˌ/ is used to show this. So, /ˈ/ is used to show the strongest or *primary* stress, and /ˌ/ is used to show the *secondary* stress (which is less strong), as in *pronunciation* /prəˌnʌnsɪˈeɪʃn/.

4.2 How context affects stress patterns. English tends to space strong stresses at intervals in speech, particularly avoiding the occurrence of two strong stresses in adjacent syllables. So, for example, the second syllable of *fourteen* is stressed in *There are fourteen* /ˌfɔːˈtiːn/ but in the phrase *fourteen years* the stressing is /ˌfɔːtiːn ˈjɪəz/. This type of 'stress shift' applies to all classes of full words (ie noun, verb, adjective or adverb). Another example would be *ˌrecomˈmend* but *ˌrecommend ˈseveral*. It should be understood that any word which is shown in the dictionary as having a secondary stress before a later primary stress, may lose the primary stress when the following word begins with a strongly stressed syllable. This applies to phrasal verbs (as *ˌcome ˈround* but *he'll ˌcome round ˈsoon*) and also to compounds (⇨ 6.2.2), eg *ˌshort-ˈlived*, where the stress shift in *a ˌshort-lived ˈtriumph* is not shown explicitly in the example in the dictionary.

The learner will hear similar shifting in some words which have a single stress, for example *chamˈpagne* but *ˌchampagne ˈcocktail*, *iˈdea* but *the ˌidea ˈpleases me*, and the adjective *comˈpact* /kəmˈpækt/ but *compact disc* /ˌkɒmpækt ˈdɪsk/.

4.3 Stress in examples. It is a feature of this dictionary that stress is marked on many examples where it is felt that this might be useful extra information. For example, under **hang**[1], the phrasal verbs **hang aˈbout/aˈround** and **hang ˈon** are shown with primary stress on the particles *about*, *around* and *on*. When an example follows in which the stressing would usually alter in normal speech, the changed stress is explicitly marked, as in *unemployed people hanging about (the ˈstreets)* and *ˌHang on ˈtight*.

5 VARIANT PRONUNCIATIONS

5.1 British variants. Different speakers may choose different pronunciations of the same word, for example *again* /əˈgen/ or /əˈgeɪn/; *exquisite* /ˈekskwɪzɪt/ or /ɪkˈskwɪzɪt/; *telegraph* /ˈtelɪgrɑːf/ or /ˈtelɪgræf/. The dictionary shows variant pronunciations in cases where two acceptable versions of a word are used by speakers of RP English. The different status of variants is indicated as follows:

1 separation by a comma, eg **again** /əˈgen, əˈgeɪn/ (where the variants are almost equal in frequency);

2 with the gloss *also*, eg **amenity** /əˈmiːnətɪ, *also* əˈmenətɪ/ (where the second form is common but not equal to the first);

3 with the gloss *or, rarely*, eg **despicable** /dɪˈspɪkəbl *or, rarely*, ˈdespɪkəbl/ (where the second form is old-fashioned or otherwise restricted in usage).

In each case the first form listed is the one which speakers are advised to use, though the first variant is always a version that is common and acceptable wherever RP is spoken. Sometimes a rarer RP version is the common US version, as in the case of *poor*. Although /pʊə(r)/ may be heard in Britain, /pɔː(r)/ is the most common RP pronunciation. Accordingly, the entry under **poor** reads /pɔː(r); *US* pʊər/.

5.2 Strong and weak forms. The words listed below all have two or more different pronunciations: a *strong* form and one or more *weak* forms. It is the weak forms that occur most frequently in connected speech. For example, *from* is /frəm/ in *He ˌcomes from ˈSpain*.

The strong form occurs when a word is said in isolation or when it is given special emphasis in connected speech. For example *from* is /frɒm/ in *This ˌpresent's not ˈfrom John; it's ˈfor him*. In addition, when prepositions and auxiliary verbs come at the end of a phrase or clause they generally take their strong form, whether or not they are stressed. For example, *ˌWhere do you ˈcome from?* has /frɒm/ (not /frəm/).

Since in ordinary speech weak forms account for 95% of the occurrences of a grammatical word (ie one which is *not* a noun, an adjective, an adverb or a main verb), the dictionary lists the weak before the strong form which, for some words, may have a special meaning. For example, under **and** the more common forms /ən, ənd/ are listed before the less frequent /ænd/. When an additional weak form exists that occurs in a limited context (for example /n/ for **and**), the dictionary user is referred to the list below where that form is given with appropriate comment.

		Weak Forms	Strong Form	Notes on the weak form
Determiners				
	a	/ə/	/eɪ/	
	an	/ən/	/æn/	
	some	/səm/	/sʌm/	/səm/ is used only when *some* means 'an unspecified amount or number of'.
	the	/ðə, ðɪ/	/ðiː/	/ðə/ before consonants; /ðɪ/ before vowels.
Conjunctions				
	and	/ən, ənd, n/	/ænd/	/n/ may be used after /t, d, f, v, θ, ð, s, z, ʃ, ʒ/.
	as	/əz/	/æz/	
	but	/bət/	/bʌt/	

	Weak Forms	Strong Form	Notes on the weak form
than	/ðən/	/ðæn/	
that	/ðət/	/ðæt/	Also used when *that* is a relative pronoun.
Prepositions			
at	/ət/	/æt/	
for	/fə(r), fr/	/fɔ:(r)/	/fr/ is optional before vowels.
from	/frəm/	/frɒm/	
of	/əv/	/ɒv/	
to	/tə, tʊ/	/tu:/	/tə/ is not used before vowels.
Pronouns			
he	/hɪ, i:, ɪ/	/hi:/	These are optional; /i:, ɪ/ are not used to begin a sentence.
her	/hə, ɜ:(r), ə(r)/	/hɜ:(r)/	These are optional; /ɜ:(r), ə(r)/ are not used to begin a sentence.
him	/ɪm/	/hɪm/	/ɪm/ is optional.
his	/ɪz/	/hɪz/	/ɪz/ is not used to begin a sentence and is optional elsewhere.
me	/mɪ/	/mi:/	/mɪ/ is optional.
she	/ʃɪ/	/ʃi:/	/ʃɪ/ is optional.
them	/ðəm/	/ðem/	
us	/əs/	/ʌs/	
we	/wɪ/	/wi:/	/wɪ/ is optional.
you	/jʊ/	/ju:/	/jʊ/ is optional.
Verbs			
am	/m, əm/	/æm/	
are	/ə(r)/	/ɑ:(r)/	
be	/bɪ/	/bi:/	/bɪ/ is optional.
can	/kən/	/kæn/	
could	/kəd/	/kʊd/	
do	/də, dʊ/	/du:/	/də/ is not used before vowels.
does	/dəz/	/dʌz/	
had	/həd, əd, d/	/hæd/	Auxiliary use only; /həd/ is used to begin a sentence; /d/ is an optional form after vowels.
has	/həz, əz, z, s/	/hæz/	Auxiliary use only; /həz/ is used to begin a sentence; /əz/ after /s, z, ʃ, ʒ, tʃ, dʒ/; /s/ after /p, t, k, f, θ/; /z/ elsewhere.
have	/həv, əv, v/	/hæv/	Auxiliary use only; /həv/ is used to begin a sentence; /v/ is an optional form after vowels.
is	/z, s/	/ɪz/	/z, s/ are not used to begin or end a sentence or after /s, z, ʃ, ʒ, tʃ, dʒ/; /s/ is used after /p, t, k, f, θ/; /z/ elsewhere.
must	/məst/	/mʌst/	
shall	/ʃəl/	/ʃæl/	
should	/ʃəd/	/ʃʊd/	
was	/wəz/	/wɒz/	
were	/wə(r)/	/wɜ:(r)/	
will	/əl, l/	/wɪl/	/əl, l/ are not used to begin or end a sentence.
would	/wəd, əd/	/wʊd/	/əd/ is not used to begin or end a sentence.

5.3 Contractions. A contraction is a shortened form used either in speech or in writing. In speech some words combine together to form contractions. These are represented in writing that reproduces spoken language (eg drama, personal letters, direct speech in novels and short stories), by omitting one or two letters and replacing the letters that are omitted by an apostrophe (').

Written contractions are used to represent the weak forms of spoken *has*, *is*, *will* and *would*, for example: *the train's come* (= *train has*), *what's that* (= *what is*), *John'll come* (= *John will*), *that'd help* (= *that would*).

In speech there is an area of overlap between weak forms and contractions. Weak forms (eg the weak forms of *be* and *have*) are used throughout connected speech in close proximity to a wide range of vocabulary. When personal pronouns are combined with the auxiliary verbs *be* and *have*, the auxiliaries take their weak forms. These are spoken as weak forms and may be written as contractions.

However, strict speech contractions involve the loss of a syllable whilst the remaining syllable contains some vowel other than /ə/. This applies to certain auxiliary verbs which have special pronunciations when they are combined with *not*. For example, *can* /kæn/ but *can't* /kɑ:nt/; *do* /du:/ but *don't* /dəʊnt/. These are not weak forms and may be stressed. When unstressed they retain the vowel of the form listed.

For the convenience of the dictionary user, the list below gives examples of some weak forms as well as contractions.

Verb + not

aren't	/ɑ:nt/	are not; am not	*mayn't*	/ˈmeɪənt/	may not
can't	/kɑ:nt/	cannot	*mightn't*	/ˈmaɪtnt/	might not
couldn't	/ˈkʊdnt/	could not	*mustn't*	/ˈmʌsnt/	must not
daren't	/deənt/	dare not	*needn't*	/ˈni:dnt/	need not
didn't	/ˈdɪdnt/	did not	*oughtn't*	/ˈɔ:tnt/	ought not
doesn't	/ˈdʌznt/	does not	*shan't*	/ʃɑ:nt/	shall not
don't	/dəʊnt/	do not	*shouldn't*	/ˈʃʊdnt/	should not
hasn't	/ˈhæznt/	has not	*wasn't*	/ˈwɒznt/	was not
haven't	/ˈhævnt/	have not	*weren't*	/wɜ:nt/	were not
hadn't	/ˈhædnt/	had not	*won't*	/wəʊnt/	will not
isn't	/ˈɪznt/	is not	*wouldn't*	/ˈwʊdnt/	would not

Personal pronoun + Verb

I'm	/aɪm/	I am	*she'll*	/ʃi:l/	she will
I've	/aɪv/	I have	*she'd*	/ʃi:d/	she would; she had
I'll	/aɪl/	I shall/will	*it's*	/ɪts/	it is; it has
I'd	/aɪd/	I would; I had	*it'll*	/ˈɪtl/	it will
you're	/jʊə(r)/	you are	*we're*	/wɪə(r)/	we are
you've	/ju:v/	you have	*we've*	/wi:v/	we have
you'll	/ju:l/	you will	*we'll*	/wi:l/	we shall/will
you'd	/ju:d/	you would; you had	*we'd*	/wi:d/	we would; we had
he's	/hi:z/	he is; he has	*they're*	/ðeə(r)/	they are
he'll	/hi:l/	he will	*they've*	/ðeɪv/	they have
he'd	/hi:d/	he would; he had	*they'll*	/ðeɪl/	they will
she's	/ʃi:z/	she is; she has	*they'd*	/ðeɪd/	they would; they had

5.4 How foreign words are pronounced in English. There are many words of foreign origin in English. Nearly all of these have been completely assimilated into the language, with purely English sounds and stress patterns, eg *mutton* /ˈmʌtn/ or more recently *café* /ˈkæfeɪ/. However, some foreign words and phrases commonly used by English speakers and included in the dictionary are still felt to be foreign. They are nevertheless pronounced with English sounds, eg *à la carte* /ˌɑ: lɑ: ˈkɑ:t/, *table d'hôte* /ˌtɑ:bl ˈdəʊt/. Most of these are borrowings from French, where a difficulty arises in anglicizing the pronunciation of the French nasalized vowels (unknown in English), as in *salon, en route.* Native speakers of English use different pronunciations in such cases, ranging from totally anglicized forms to a more or less successful imitation of the French. This dictionary gives completely anglicized forms, eg /ˈsælɒn/, /ˌɒn ˈru:t/.

Similarly, in the case of the relatively few words borrowed from other languages, eg (from Germanic languages) *angst, sauerkraut, smorgasbord*; (other Romance languages) *adagio, ballerina, hacienda, patio*; (Middle and Far Eastern languages) *harem, sheikh, guru, kimono*, the most commonly used anglicized pronunciation is given in the dictionary.

The anglicized pronunciation is likewise given for all the non-English proper names (of people, places, etc) appearing as headwords in the dictionary.

5.5 The pronunciation of American English.

5.5.1 American variations. The model for American English pronunciation is one which is widely acceptable in the USA and has been called General American. Whenever Americans pronounce a word in a very different way from British speakers the dictionary gives the phonetic spelling of the American pronunciation after the British one, for example:

half /hɑ:f; *US* hæf/...
address[1] /əˈdres; *US* ˈædres/...

If only part of the pronunciation changes, only that part is given for the American pronunciation, in order to save space, for example:

attitude /ˈætɪtju:d; *US* -tu:d/...

5.5.2 Use of phonetic symbols. American English forms are shown with the same phonetic symbols as are used for British English. However, particularly in the case of vowels, the same symbol will often mean somewhat different qualities in the British and American varieties. For example, in American English the /ɒ/ in *hot* is similar to the British English /ɑ:/ sound, and the /ʌ/ of *cut* is similar to a stressed /ə/ sound.

5.5.3 American /r/. An important difference between British and American pronunciation, which is not shown in the dictionary, is the use of the /r/ sound in American English in words where British English does not use it, for example in the words *arm* and *star*. The British pronunciations of these words are /ɑ:m/ and /stɑ:(r)/ (Cf 3.3); the American pronunciations are /ɑ:rm/ and /stɑ:r/. The rule to follow in the case of the /r/ sound in American English is to sound the /r/ whenever it occurs in the spelling of a word.

One common vowel variant that is not shown in the dictionary is the unstressed vowel of the second syllable of a word such as *happy* /ˈhæpɪ/. This vowel is regularly shown as /ɪ/. For most American and some British speakers, the quality of this short vowel is somewhat closer to /i:/, particularly before a following vowel, as in *happier*. Since in such contexts either quality is acceptable and the length is always short, the dictionary always shows /ɪ/ in such words.

6 PRONUNCIATION OF DERIVATIVES AND COMPOUNDS

6.1 Derivatives. Many derivatives are formed by adding a suffix to the end of a word (⇨16). These derivatives are pronounced by simply saying the suffix after the word. For example, the adverb *slowly* /ˈsləʊlɪ/ is pronounced by joining the suffix *-ly* /lɪ/ to the word *slow* /sləʊ/.

However, whenever there may be doubt about how a suffix or a derivative is pronounced, the phonetic spelling is given. For example *mouthful* /-fʊl/, *regretful* /-fl/. Also, if a change of stress is caused by adding a suffix to a word, then the pronunciation of the derivative is given in full, eg *arithmetic* /əˈrɪθmətɪk/, *arithmetical* /ˌærɪθˈmetɪkl/, *arithmetician* /əˌrɪθməˈtɪʃn/.

6.2 Compounds.

6.2.1 Assimilation. The pronunciation of a compound is not shown after the compound itself. This is because the pronunciation of the two parts appears elsewhere in the dictionary. However, the user should note that in speech adjacent sounds influence each other and the pronunciation of the root word may change slightly in one of two different ways:

1. It may result in the replacement of a particular sound by a different one. Note that within a compound these alterations commonly occur. For example, /t/ at the end of *boat* may be replaced by /p/ before /m/ as in *boatman* /ˈbəʊpmən/ (cf *slot-machine* /ˈslɒpməʃi:n/), or /d/ by /g/ before /k/ as in *headquarters* /hegˈkwɔ:təz/. Although these are not shown in the dictionary, they follow the same regular pattern.
2. Instead of being replaced, some sounds are often omitted entirely. This applies especially to /t/ and /d/ when surrounded by other consonants, eg *postmark* /ˈpəʊstmɑ:k/ is often /ˈpəʊsmɑ:k/, *windscreen* /ˈwɪndskri:n/ may be pronounced /ˈwɪnskri:n/.

Such changes in pronunciation may occur whenever these sounds are adjacent in speech. In the case of a headword eg *landscape* the sound /d/ is often omitted although the fuller version is always shown in the dictionary.

Variations of types 1 and 2 occur within the speech of any native speaker of English. It is not possible to predict exactly when they will be encountered, but these variant forms tend to be used more frequently as the speed or the informality of speech increases.

6.2.2 Stress in compounds. Compounds have their own stress patterns which may be different from the normal pattern of the two separate parts. When an adjective modifies a noun, the noun usually has the primary stress, for example *ˌsilver ˈfish*. When an adjective and noun combine to form a compound noun, the compound may be spoken with the strong stress on the first word, for example *ˈsilver-fish* (an insect). This second stress pattern is also especially common when two nouns form a two-word or hyphenated compound, for example: *ˈghost-writer, ˈbus-stop, ˈfield sports.* To help the dictionary user, the stress is explicitly marked on all compounds.

6.3 Idioms. Idioms, like compounds, have their own special stress patterns. One of the words in any idiom is always spoken with more force than in other words. This stressed word is often the last full word (⇨ 4.2), for example: *rain cats and ˈdogs.* In some idioms, however, a grammatical word (⇨ 5.2) carries the main stress, for example: *There's nothing ˈfor it.* For the sake of clarity, the main stress is marked in each idiom printed in bold type under the heading '(idm)' in the dictionary, except for those few idioms that fall into two categories, namely those where the placing of the main stress can vary (like *to cap it all*) and those which are grammatically incomplete without variable additions (like *be a good thing (that)...*).

GRAMMAR

7 PARTS OF SPEECH

7.1 Part of speech labels. A number of standard abbreviations indicating the appropriate part of speech (ie grammatical class) are used throughout the dictionary. The labels, with the parts of speech they represent, are:

adj (adjective), *adv* (adverb), *aux v* (auxiliary verb), *conj* (conjunction), *det* (determiner), *interj* (interjection), *n* (noun), *prep* (preposition), *pron* (pronoun), *v* (verb).

More complex labels are produced by adding such modifiers as *rel* (relative) and *possess* (possessive), thus: *rel pron, rel adv, possess det, possess pron,* etc. (For a full list of the abbreviations used in the dictionary see the list inside the back cover.) All these additional parts of speech labels are defined at their point of entry in the appropriate place in the dictionary.

Part of speech labels are not normally given for proper names (of people, places, etc) appearing as headwords in the dictionary, nor for compounds that consist of more than one word.

7.2 Position. A part of speech label is provided for each headword and derivative, and for every compound that is written as one word or hyphenated. It is placed immediately after the pronunciation, if this is given, or next to the derivative or compound if not:

irregular /ɪˈregjʊlə(r)/ *adj* ...
▷**irregular** *n* ...
irregularity /ɪˌregjʊˈlærətɪ/ *n* ...
irregularly *adv*.

race[1] ... *n* ...
□ˈ**racecard** *n* ...
ˈ**racecourse** *n* ...

Additional labels are provided when the headword or derivative is used in different ways with no change of meaning:

chauvinist /ˈʃəʊvɪnɪst/ *n, adj* ...

8 IRREGULAR WRITTEN FORMS

8.1 Past tense and past participle forms of verbs.

- If a final consonant is doubled when forming the past tense and past participle, the doubling is shown in **bold** print:

bob[1] /bɒb/ *v* (-**bb**-) ...

- If a verb has one or two irregular forms, the form or forms are given in full:

catch[1] /kætʃ/ *v* (*pt, pp* **caught** /kɔːt/) ...
see[1] /siː/ *v* (*pt* **saw** /sɔː/, *pp* **seen** /siːn/) ...

- If both the past tense and past participle are irregular, but a final consonant is doubled in forming the present participle (*-ing* form), that doubling is shown, thus:

begin /bɪˈgɪn/ *v* (-**nn**-; *pt* **began** /bɪˈgæn/, *pp* **begun** /bɪˈgʌn/) ...

8.2 Plural forms of nouns. These are indicated wherever necessary, either because simple addition of *-s* or *-es* is not correct, or where there may be some doubt.

- The plural forms of nouns ending in *-o* (whether *-s, -es* or both) are always shown:

mango /ˈmæŋgəʊ/ *n* (*pl* ~**es** or ~**s**) ...

- When the form of a countable noun is unchanged in the plural, this is indicated as follows:

grouse /graʊs/ *n* (*pl* unchanged) ...

- When the formation of the plural affects the spelling or pronunciation of the headword, the plural spelling and pronunciation are given in full:

child /tʃaɪld/ *n* (*pl* **children** /ˈtʃɪldrən/) ...

- Other irregular forms are either represented by the last two syllables, preceded by a hyphen:

synthesis /ˈsɪnθəsɪs/ *n* (*pl* **-theses** /-siːz/) ...

or are given in full, with alternatives where appropriate:

basis /ˈbeɪsɪs/ *n* (*pl* **bases** /ˈbeɪsiːz/) ...

8.3 Comparative and superlative forms of adjectives and adverbs. Whenever an adjective (or an adverb) forms its comparative and superlative by adding *-er* and *-est*, or *-r* and *-st*, those endings are shown, as follows:

cheap /tʃiːp/ *adj* (**-er, -est**) ...
safe /seɪf/ *adj* (**-r , -st**) ...

If a final consonant is doubled before the comparative or superlative ending, this doubling is shown in the entry:

hot /hɒt/ *adj* (**-tter**, **-ttest**) ...

Irregular forms of an adjective are given in full at the entry for that adjective (though their special meanings, idioms, etc may be given in separate entries, eg at **worse**, **worst**, etc):

bad /bæd/ *adj* (**worse** /wɜːs/, **worst** /wɜːst/) ...

9 GRAMMATICAL PATTERNS AND CODES

9.1 Verbs.

9.1.1 Verb patterns and codes. Foreign learners of English often have great difficulty in deciding which sentence constructions, or patterns, a verb can be used in. (They may know that *I liked to help him* and *I liked helping him* are both correct, but be unaware that with the verb *dislike* only the second pattern is possible.) In this dictionary much help in dealing with this problem is provided in the form of example sentences. At the first meaning for the verb *bear*, for instance, the pattern 'transitive verb + direct object noun' is illustrated by *The document bore his signature.* But the **bear**[2] entry (like other verb entries) also contains a reference to the pattern itself, in the form of a code. The code for the pattern just given is [Tn], in which T = transitive verb and n = noun.

9.1.2 The positions of codes. If a verb has only one meaning, or several meanings all with the same pattern(s), the pattern or patterns are placed after the part of speech label:

re-echo ... *v* [I] echo again and again ...
bequeath ... *v* [Tn, Dn·n, Dn·pr] ... **1** ... **2** ...

But if the various meanings of a verb correspond to different patterns (or sets of patterns), the codes are placed after the sense numbers, as follows:

sell ... *v* ... **1** [I, Ipr, Tn, Tn·pr, Dn·n, Dn·pr] ... **2** [Tn] ... **3** [Tn] ... **4** [I, Ipr, In/pr] ...

The verb pattern scheme described below (⇨ 9.1.4) shows that certain verb patterns (eg [Tn], [Tn·pr], [Tni], etc) regularly have corresponding passive constructions. Users can assume that when any of those patterns are referred to in an entry *without any further label* a passive is possible. However, if an individual verb or meaning is an exception to the rule for a pattern (eg because it is usually or especially used in the passive, or not used in the passive at all), additional labels are used, as follows:

shape[2] ... *v* ... **4** [Tn esp passive] ...

When all the patterns to which a verb or meaning belongs are restricted in one of these ways, the label precedes the patterns:

breed ... *v* ... **3** [esp passive: Tn, Tn·pr, Cn·n/a, Cn·t] ...

9.1.3 The meanings of codes. Thirty-two patterns (with matching codes) are used in the dictionary to account for the various ways in which verbs can be used. The codes can be read by the dictionary user on two levels:

- The SIMPLE level. A code such as [Dn·pr] (as in *He gave the book to John*) is designed to suggest to the learner 'double-transitive verb + noun + prepositional phrase', ie the parts of speech (or phrase or clause types) of which the pattern is composed. These indications will be sufficient for many learners. Moreover, the meanings of the letters (n = noun, a = adjective, etc) can be easily learnt, so that within a short time the learner should be able to recall patterns simply by looking at their codes. (Dictionary users who wish to be reminded of the meaning of a code at this basic level should refer to the quick guide inside the back cover.)

- The STRUCTURAL level. The codes are also designed to indicate the structural elements which the patterns contain (ie whether they have one or more objects, a complement, an adjunct, etc). The 'D' in the code [Dn·pr], for example, means that the verb is followed by a direct object and an indirect object. The dot in the code shows the division between these elements. (In the example *He gave the book to John*, '*the book*' is the direct object and '*to John*' the indirect object.) The structural level is important for teachers and more advanced learners because it enables them to distinguish between sentences which are superficially the same. (*She liked him to play the piano* is [Tnt], *She inspired him to play the piano* is [Cn·t], *She told him to play the piano* is [Dn·t]).

The following table shows what elements are indicated at the structural level by the capital letters L, I, T, C and D:

L = LINKING verb (followed by a COMPLEMENT, an element which provides more information about the subject of the sentence).
I = INTRANSITIVE verb (NOT followed by a COMPLEMENT or an OBJECT, though it may be followed by an ADJUNCT, an element which tells us about the time, place, manner, etc of the action of the verb).
T = TRANSITIVE verb (followed by a DIRECT OBJECT, an element which often refers to the person or thing affected by the action of the verb).

C = COMPLEX-TRANSITIVE verb (followed by a DIRECT OBJECT and a COMPLEMENT, an element which provides more information about the direct object). Note: in the code, a dot divides the direct object from the complement.
D = DOUBLE-TRANSITIVE verb (followed by a DIRECT OBJECT and an INDIRECT OBJECT, an element which refers to a person who receives something or benefits from an action). Note: in the code, a dot divides the direct from the indirect object.

9.1.4 Verb pattern scheme. At the top of each of the following tables, a full explanation of the pattern is given, thus:

[Tt]

subject	transitive verb	direct object: non-finite clause (*to*-infinitive)

These explanations are followed by examples and notes. Reference is made in the notes to the possibility or otherwise of a passive construction for that pattern.

[La]

subject	linking verb	subject complement: adjective (phrase)
1 The lesson	**was**	interesting.
2 The damage	**appears** (to be)	serious.
3 The soup	**tasted**	delicious.
4 The beach	**looked**	deserted.
5 The game	**became**	more exciting.
6 The actors	**got**	ready.
7 The milk	**went**	sour.
8 The cinemas	**remained**	open all week.
9 To go further	**was**	impossible.
10 To give time to the project	**became**	more difficult.

(a) The complement is an adjective or adjective phrase which describes some quality or feature of the subject (Cf Cn·a).
(b) The verbs *appear*, *seem* and *prove* may be followed by *to be*.
(c) When the subject is a *that*-clause or a *to*-infinitive clause, and the verb is *be*, *appear* or *become*, *it* can be introduced at the beginning and the subject moved to the end. This pattern is preferred when the subject is relatively long compared with the complement:

- To go further **was** impossible.
- It **was** impossible to go further.

- To give time to the project **became** more difficult.
- It **became** more difficult to give time to the project.

[Ln]

subject	linking verb	subject complement: noun (phrase)
1 David	**is**	my younger brother.
2 That	**appears** (to be)	the best answer.
3 Jeffries	**sounds**	just the man we're looking for.
4 Frank	**became**	a teacher.
5 This	**proved** (to be)	a good investment.
6 The boys	**remained**	the best of friends.
7 To stay out of sight	**seemed** (to be)	the wisest thing to do.

(a) The complement is a noun or noun phrase, and it refers to the role, occupation, etc of the subject (Cf Cn·n).
(b) The verbs *appear*, *seem* and *prove* may be followed by *to be*.
(c) When the subject is a *to*-infinitive clause and the verb is *be*, *seem* (*to be*), *appear* (*to be*) or *become*, *it* can be introduced at the beginning and the subject moved to the end. This pattern is preferred when the subject is relatively long compared with the complement.

- To stay out of sight **seemed** (to be) the wisest thing to do.
- It **seemed** the wisest thing to do to stay well out of sight.

[I]

subject	intransitive verb	adjunct: (adverb (phrase) of time, manner, etc)
1 The moon	**rose**	early.
2 The clothes-line	**sagged**.	
3 Veronica	is **reading**.	
4 John and Jane	are **arguing**	again.
5 The door	**opened**.	
6 Oil and water	don't **mix**.	

(a) In this pattern, the verb is not followed by an object, a complement or a closely linked adjunct (Cf Ipr). Optional adverbs of time, manner, result, etc *can* be used (eg *early*).

(b) Some verbs can be used in this pattern and the [Tn] pattern without a change of subject (or of verb meaning):

- Veronica is **reading**. [I]
- Veronica is **reading** a fairy story. [Tn]

(c) Some verbs can be used in this pattern (with *and* linking two nouns as the subject) and in a corresponding [Ipr] pattern (with *with* following the verb):

- Oil and water don't **mix**. [I]
- Oil doesn't **mix with** water. [Ipr]

[Ipr]

subject	intransitive verb	adjunct: prepositional phrase
1 Helen	is **coming**	**to** dinner.
2 The minister	**referred**	**to** the importance of exports.
3 Mother	can't **cope**	**with** the extra visitors.
4 People	are **complaining**	**about** the traffic.
5 You	can't **rely**	**on** Martin.
6 Oil	doesn't **mix**	**with** water.

(a) Here, the verb is closely linked in grammar and meaning to a prepositional phrase. The exact choice of preposition is shown in **bold print** in the above table and in dictionary entries (Cf Tn·pr).

(b) After some verbs, the prepositional phrase cannot be removed without producing nonsense (*) or changing the meaning of the verb:

- The minister **referred to** the importance of exports.
- *The minister **referred**.

Prepositional phrases which are fixed in this way are shown in entries in **bold print**:

refer ... [Ipr ...] ~ **to sb/sth** ...

(c) After other verbs, the prepositional phrase can be removed freely:

- Mother can't **cope with** the extra visitors.
- Mother can't **cope**.

In such cases, the prepositional phrase is shown like this:

cope ... [I, Ipr] ~ **(with sb/sth)** ...

(d) After some verbs, a *to*-infinitive or *-ing* form can be added to the prepositional phrase:

- You can't **rely on** Martin.
- You can't **rely on** Martin to help.

This addition to the pattern is shown thus:

rely ... [Ipr ...] ~ **on/upon sb/sth (to do sth)** ...

(e) Some verbs used in this pattern can be made passive. The noun or noun phrase following the preposition in the active pattern becomes the subject of the passive one:

- The minister **referred to** the importance of exports.
- The importance of exports was **referred to** (by the minister).

This possibility is illustrated in the entries by examples.

[Ip]

subject	intransitive verb	adjunct: adverbial particle
1 A tiger	has **got**	**out**.
2 A visitor	**came**	**in**.
3 The noise	**faded**	**away**.
4 The house	has **warmed**	**up**.
5 The train	**whistled**	**past**.
6 We'll have to	**toss**	**up**.

(a) Here, the verb is closely linked to an adverbial particle. The exact choice of particle is shown in **bold print** in the above table and in dictionary entries (Cf Tn·p).

(b) After some verbs, the particle cannot be removed without changing the meaning of the verb or producing nonsense (*):

- A tiger has **got out**.
- *A tiger has **got**.

(c) After other verbs, the particle can be deleted freely:

- The noise **faded away**. [Ip]
- The noise **faded**. [I]

In such cases the particle is shown thus:

fade ... [I, Ip] **(away)** ...

(d) Idiomatic combinations such as **dry up** (= become unable to speak), **blaze away** (= fire continuously), which also fit this pattern, are treated separately in this dictionary (⇨ 15 PHRASAL VERBS).

[In/pr]

subject	intransitive verb	adjunct: noun (phrase)/prepositional phrase
1 The book	**cost** (me)	ten dollars.
2 The room	**measures**	10 metres across.
3 The meeting	**lasted**	(**for**) three hours.
4 The sea front	**extends**	(**for**) three miles.

(a) Here, the verb is closely linked to a noun (phrase) or prepositional phrase which indicates 'extent' (eg how much the subject costs, what it measures, how long it lasts).

(b) The correct choice of preposition is *for* or *by*. This is shown in the dictionary as follows:

last ... [In/pr] ~ **(for) sth** ...

[It]

subject	intransitive verb	adjunct: non-finite clause (*to*-infinitive)
1 Jane	**hesitated**	to phone the office.
2 We all	**longed**	to get away for a family holiday.
3 I	wouldn't **care**	to have a fight with him.
4 They	wouldn't **condescend**	to speak to ordinary mortals.

(a) Here, an intransitive verb is closely linked to a *to*-infinitive clause.

(b) Verbs in this pattern cannot be made passive.

[Tn]

subject	transitive verb	direct object: noun (phrase)/pronoun
1 George	was **watching**	television.
2 Veronica	is **reading**	a fairy story.
3 The company	**paid**	a colossal sum.
4 Peter	doesn't **owe**	anything.
5 A small boy	**opened**	the door.

(a) The direct object is a noun (eg *television*), noun phrase (eg *the door*) or pronoun (eg *anything*) (Cf Dn·n).

(b) For verbs used in this pattern and the [I] pattern without a change of subject or meaning, see [I], note (b).

(c) Most verbs in this pattern can be made passive, with the object of the active pattern becoming the subject of the passive one:

- A small boy **opened** the door.
- The door was **opened** (by a small boy).

Exceptions are shown in dictionary entries thus: [Tn no passive].

[Tn·pr]

subject	transitive verb	direct object	adjunct: prepositional phrase
1 The teacher	**referred**	the class	**to** a passage in the textbook.
2 The waiter	**served**	Sarah	**with** a double helping.
3 The Council	have **cleared**	the pavements	**of** rubbish.
4 The lecturer	**confused**	your name	**with** mine.
5 The visiting speaker	**thanked**	the Chairman	**for** his kind remarks.

(a) In this pattern, the verb is closely linked in grammar and meaning to a prepositional phrase. The exact choice of preposition is shown in **bold print** in the above table and in dictionary entries (Cf Ipr).

(b) After some verbs, the prepositional phrase cannot be removed without producing nonsense (*) or changing the meaning of the verb:

- The teacher **referred** the class **to** a passage in the textbook.
- *The teacher **referred** the class.

Prepositional phrases which are fixed in this way are shown in the dictionary in **bold print**:

refer ... [Tn·pr ...] ~ **sb/sth to sb/sth**

(c) After other verbs, the prepositional phrase can be removed without changing the meaning of the verb:

- The visiting speaker **thanked** the Chairman **for** his kind remarks. [Tn·pr]
- The visiting speaker **thanked** the Chairman. [Tn]

In those cases, the prepositional phrase is shown thus:

thank ... [Tn, Tn·pr] ~ **sb (for sth)** ...

(d) Most verbs in this pattern can be made passive. The direct object of an active verb becomes the subject of the same verb in the passive:

- The Council have **cleared** the pavements **of** rubbish.
- The pavements have been **cleared of** rubbish (by the Council).

Exceptions are shown in dictionary entries thus: [Tn·pr no passive].

[Tn·p]

subject	transitive verb	direct object	adjunct: adverbial particle
1 Bill	**has**	a blue shirt	**on**.
2 The frost	has **killed**	the buds	**off**.
3 The nurse	**shook**	the medicine	**up**.
4 Sally	is **tidying**	her room	**up**.

(a) In this pattern, the verb is closely linked to an adverbial particle. The exact choice of particle is shown in **bold print** in the above table and in dictionary entries (Cf Ip).

(b) After some verbs, the particle cannot be removed without changing the meaning of the verb or producing nonsense (*):

- Bill **has** a blue shirt **on**.
- Bill **has** a blue shirt.

(c) After other verbs, the particle can be deleted freely:

- Sally is **tidying** her room **up**. [Tn·p]
- Sally is **tidying** her room. [Tn]

In those cases the particle is shown thus:

tidy ... [Tn, Tn·p ...] ~ **sth (up)** ...

(d) Idiomatic combinations such as **blow sth up** (= explode sth), **whip sb up** (= excite sb), which also fit this pattern, are treated separately in this dictionary (⇨ 15 PHRASAL VERBS).

(e) When the direct object is a pronoun, it precedes the particle:

The nurse **shook** it **up**.

When it is a short noun phrase or a noun (see examples in the table), it can usually either precede or follow the particle:

- The frost has **killed** the buds **off**.
- The frost has **killed off** the buds.

When the direct object is a long noun phrase, it usually follows the particle:

- Bill **has on** a blue shirt and a pair of jeans.

(f) Most verbs in this pattern can be made passive. The direct object of an active verb becomes the subject of the same verb in the passive:

- The frost has **killed** the buds **off**.
- The buds have been **killed off** (by the frost).

Exceptions are shown in dictionary entries thus: [Tn·p no passive].

[Tf]

subject	transitive verb	direct object: *that*-clause
1 The employers	**announced**	that the dispute had been settled.
2 The department	**proposed**	that new salary scales should be introduced.
3 Doctors	had **noted**	that the disease was spreading.
4 Officials	**believe**	that a settlement is possible.
5 We	**consider**	that Frank has been badly treated.
6 The weathermen	**forecast**	that more snow is on the way.

(a) In this pattern, the direct object is a *that*-clause (Cf Dn·f, Dpr·f).

(b) The conjunction *that* can sometimes be omitted. When it can, *that* is usually shown in brackets in the first (or only) example sentence in entries:

consider ... *We consider (that) Frank has been badly treated.*

(c) Some verbs used in this pattern can be made passive. (Note the construction with *it*).

- Officials **believe** that a settlement is possible.
- It is **believed** (by officials) that a settlement is possible.

Exceptions are shown in dictionary entries thus: [Tf no passive].

[Tw]

subject	transitive verb	direct object: finite clause/non-finite clause
1 The class	doesn't **know**	what time it has to be in school/what time to be in school.
2 The students	haven't **learnt**	which tutors they can rely on/which tutors to rely on.
3 Bill	**discovered**	who he had to give the money to/who to give the money to.
4 We	hadn't **decided**	what we ought to do next/what to do next.

(a) In this pattern, the direct object is a finite or non-finite clause beginning with

EITHER (i) A '*wh*-element', which can be a pronoun (*who(m), whose, which, what*), a determiner + noun (*what time, which tutors*, etc) or an adverb (*why* (finite clauses only), *when, where, how*);

OR (ii) One of the conjunctions *if* (finite clauses only) or *whether* (Cf Dn·w, Dpr·w).

(b) Some verbs used in this pattern can be made passive. (Note the construction with *it*).

- We hadn't **decided** what we ought to do next/what to do next.
- It hadn't been **decided** (by us) what we ought to do next/what to do next.

Exceptions are shown in dictionary entries thus: [Tw no passive].

[Tt]

subject	transitive verb	direct object: non-finite clause (*to*-infinitive)
1 Tom	**loves**	to do the household chores.
2 Bill	**liked**	to arrive early for meetings.
3 Mary	**hates**	to drive in the rush-hour.
4 The laboratories	**failed**	to produce useful results.
5 Jane	**wants**	to finish the job by tomorrow.
6 Peter	**expects**	to be promoted soon.
7 I	**remembered**	to post your letters.
8 The children	will still **need**	to be looked after.

(a) In this pattern, the direct object is a non-finite clause consisting of or containing a *to*-infinitive (Cf Dn·t, Dpr·t).

(b) After *remember* and *forget*, the contrast between the *to*-infinitive and the *-ing* form corresponds to a difference of meaning:

- I **remembered** to post your letters. [Tt] (= 'I didn't forget to post them.')
- I **remembered** posting your letters. [Tg] (= 'I recalled having posted them.')

(c) For *need, require, want* see [Tg], note (c).

(d) Verbs in this pattern cannot be made passive.

[Tnt]

subject	transitive verb	direct object: non-finite clause (noun (phrase)/pronoun + *to*-infinitive)
1 Tony	**prefers**	his wife/her to do the housework.
2 The boss	**liked**	the staff/them to arrive early for work.
3 Julia	**hates**	her husband/him to lose his temper.
4 The teacher	**wants**	her class/them to finish the job by Wednesday.
5 I	**expect**	the parcel/it to arrive tomorrow.

(a) In this pattern, the direct object is a non-finite clause consisting of a *to*-infinitive introduced by a noun or noun phrase (eg *his wife, the staff*) or a pronoun (eg *her, them*). The noun (phrase) or pronoun is the subject of the whole non-finite clause.

(b) Some verbs in this pattern can be made passive. The subject of the non-finite clause becomes the subject of the whole passive sentence:

- I **expect** the parcel to arrive tomorrow.
- The parcel is **expected** to arrive tomorrow.

Exceptions are shown in dictionary entries thus: [Tnt no passive].

[Tg]

subject	transitive verb	direct object: non-finite clause (*-ing* form)
1 Peter	**enjoys**	playing football.
2 John	**prefers**	walking to the office.
3 Jill	**hates**	working in the garden.
4 Fred	**started**	arguing.
5 This airline	will **finish**	operating next year.
6 The laboratories	**ceased**	producing useful results.
7 I	**remembered**	posting your letters.
8 The children	will still **need**	looking after.

(a) In this pattern, the direct object is a non-finite clause consisting of, or containing, an *-ing* form.

(b) For *remember* and *forget*, see [Tt], note (b).

(c) After *need, require* and *want* (as in *This shirt wants washing*), the *-ing* form of the verb can be replaced by the passive *to*-infinitive:

- The children will still **need** looking after. [Tg]
- The children will still **need** to be looked after. [Tt]

(d) This pattern has no corresponding passive construction.

[Tsg]

subject	transitive verb	direct object: non-finite clause (personal pronoun/noun (phrase)/possessive + *-ing* form)
1 I	don't **like**	him/John interrupting all the time.
2 Jill	**hates**	him/her husband coming home late.
3 We	**anticipated**	her/Mary('s) taking over the business.
4 Our parents	**dislike**	us/our working late at night.
5 The employers	**resented**	the staff('s)/their being consulted.

(a) In this pattern, the direct object is a non-finite clause consisting of the *-ing* form of a verb introduced EITHER by a personal pronoun or noun (phrase) (eg *him*, *her*, *us*; *John*, *the staff*) OR by a possessive form (eg *his*, *her*, *our*; *John's*, *the staff's*). The introductory pronoun, noun, etc is the subject of the whole non-finite clause.

(b) The possessive form at the beginning of the direct object is more formal than a noun (phrase) or pronoun. It is not likely to be used when the verb itself is fairly informal:

- (*)I don't **like** John's interrupting all the time.

(c) The verbs in this pattern cannot normally be made passive.

[Tng]

subject	transitive verb	direct object: non-finite clause (noun (phrase)/pronoun + *-ing* form)
1 We	**watched**	the men destroying the furniture.
2 The porter	**heard**	someone slamming the door.
3 The children	**saw**	the cat stealing the meat.
4 The rescuers	**felt**	John losing his grip of the rope.
5 He	**noticed**	a child entering the courtyard.

(a) In this pattern, the direct object is a non-finite clause, in which a noun (eg *John*), noun phrase (eg *the cat*) or pronoun (eg *someone*) introduces the *-ing* form of the verb. Neither the noun nor the pronoun can be in the possessive form (as they can in the [Tsg] pattern). Compare:

- We **watched** the men/*men's destroying the furniture. [Tng]
- We **resented** the men/men's destroying the furniture. [Tsg]

(b) Most verbs in this pattern are 'perception' verbs. Of these, *see*, *hear*, *feel*, *watch*, *notice*, *overhear* and *observe* are also used in the [Tni] pattern:

- The rescuers **felt** John losing his grip of the rope. [Tng]
- The rescuers **felt** John lose his grip of the rope. [Tni]

Using the 'bare' infinitive here [Tni] implies that John fully lost his hold of the rope while the rescuers were in contact with him. The *-ing* form [Tng] does not imply this.

(c) Verbs in this pattern can be made passive. The noun (phrase) or pronoun introducing the *-ing* form becomes the subject of the whole passive sentence:

- The children **saw** the cat stealing the meat.
- The cat was **seen** stealing the meat (by the children).

Exceptions are shown in dictionary entries thus: [Tng no passive].

[Tni]

subject	transitive verb	direct object: non-finite clause (noun (phrase)/pronoun + 'bare' infinitive)
1 We	**watched**	the men destroy the furniture.
2 The porter	**heard**	someone slam the door.
3 The children	**saw**	the cat steal the meat.
4 The rescuers	**felt**	John lose his grip of the rope.
5 He	**noticed**	a child enter the courtyard.

(a) In this pattern, the direct object is a non-finite clause, in which a noun (eg *John*), noun phrase (eg *the cat*) or pronoun (eg *someone*) introduces a 'bare' infinitive (the infinitive without *to*).

(b) All the verbs used in this pattern are verbs of perception. They are *watch, hear, see, feel, notice, overhear* and *observe*. All are used in the [Tng] pattern also (see [Tng], note (b)).

(c) Except for *watch* and *notice*, verbs in this pattern can be made passive. The noun (phrase) or pronoun introducing the bare infinitive becomes the subject of the whole passive sentence, while the bare infinitive itself (eg *slam, steal*) becomes the *to*-infinitive (eg *to slam, to steal*):

- The porter **heard** someone slam the door.
- Someone was **heard** to slam the door (by the porter).

Exceptions are shown in dictionary entries thus: [Tni no passive].

[Cn·a]

subject	complex-transitive verb	direct object	object complement: adjective (phrase)
1 I	**imagined**	him	much taller than that.
2 Jane	**prefers**	her coffee	black.
3 Peter	**has**	a tooth	loose.
4 The experts	**confessed**	themselves	baffled.
5 The fridge	**keeps**	the beer	cool.
6 The teacher	**made**	the lesson	interesting.
7 The mayor	**declared**	the meeting	open.

(a) In this pattern, the object complement is an adjective or adjective phrase which describes a feature or quality of the direct object (Cf La).

(b) Many verbs in this pattern can be made passive. The direct object of an active verb becomes the subject of the same verb in the passive:

- The teacher **made** the lesson interesting.
- The lesson was **made** interesting (by the teacher).

Exceptions are shown in dictionary entries thus: [Cn·a no passive].

[Cn·n]

subject	complex-transitive verb	direct object	object complement: noun (phrase)
1 We	**made**	Frank	chairman.
2 The club	**elected**	Mr Jones	membership secretary.
3 We	**declare**	Holroyd	the winner.
4 The court	**considered**	Smith	a trustworthy witness.
5 The rebels	are **holding**	her	prisoner.

(a) In this pattern, the object complement is a noun or noun phrase which indicates the role, name, status, etc of the direct object (Cf Ln).

(b) Many verbs used in this pattern can be made passive. The direct object of an active verb becomes the subject of the same verb in the passive:

- The court **considered** Smith a trustworthy witness.
- Smith was **considered** a trustworthy witness (by the court).

Exceptions are shown in dictionary entries thus: (Cn·n no passive].

[Cn·n/a]

subject	complex-transitive verb	direct object	object complement: *as* + noun (phrase)/ adjective (phrase)
1 Fellow-sportsmen	**regard**	him	**as** a world-class player.
2 Doctors	**recognize**	Johnson	**as** a leading authority.
3 The police	didn't **accept**	the story	**as** genuine.
4 The club	won't **appoint**	a teenager	**as** the committee treasurer.

(a) In this pattern, the object complement tells us how the direct object is regarded, judged, etc, or what he, she or it is chosen to act or serve as.

(b) The first word in the complement is always *as*. It is shown in dictionary entries like this:

regard ... [Cn·n/a] ~ **sb/sth as sth** ...

(c) A passive construction is possible for all verbs in this pattern except *have*. The direct object of an active verb becomes the subject of the same verb in the passive:

- The police didn't **accept** the story **as** genuine.
- The story wasn't **accepted as** genuine (by the police).

[Cn·t]

subject	complex-transitive verb	direct object	object complement: non-finite clause (*to*-infinitive)
1 The reporter	**pressed**	her	to answer his questions.
2 The thief	**forced**	Jane	to hand over the money.
3 The extra money	**helped**	John	to be independent.
4 An official	**declared**	the place	to be free of infection.

(a) In this pattern, the object complement is a *to*-infinitive, either alone or as part of a longer clause. It tells us what the object is made or helped to do or be.

(b) The verbs in this pattern can be made passive. The direct object of an active verb becomes the subject of the same verb in the passive:

- An official **declared** the place to be free of infection.
- The place was **declared** to be free of infection (by an official).

Exceptions are shown in dictionary entries thus: [Cn·t no passive].

[Cn·g]

subject	complex-transitive verb	direct object	object complement: non-finite clause (*-ing* form)
1 This remark	**set**	everyone	thinking.
2 The look on Bill's face	**had**	me	trembling with fear
3 The policeman	**got**	the traffic	moving.
4 The smoke	**started**	her	coughing.
5 We	**left**	the children	playing in the garden.
6 The driver	**kept**	his engine	running.

(a) In this pattern, the object complement is the *-ing* form of a verb, either alone (eg *thinking*) or as part of a longer clause (eg *playing in the garden*). It tells us what the object is made to do or is kept doing.

(b) Only the verbs shown in the table are used in this pattern. Of these, *set*, *have*, *get* and *start* are 'causative' verbs (ie verbs meaning 'cause something to happen').

(c) Except for *have* and *start*, the verbs can be made passive. The direct object of an active verb becomes the subject of the same verb in the passive:

- The policeman **got** the traffic moving.
- The traffic was **got** moving (by the policeman).

[Cn·i]

subject	complex-transitive verb	direct object	object complement: non-finite clause ('bare' infinitive)
1 His tutor	**made**	him	work.
2 We	**had**	Jane	run through the procedure again.
3 Mother	won't **let**	the children	play in the road.
4 Stephen	**helped**	us	organize the party.

(a) In this pattern, the object complement is the 'bare' infinitive (the infinitive without *to*), either alone (eg *work*) or as part of a larger clause (eg *play in the road*). It tells us what the object is made or allowed to do.

(b) Only the verbs shown in the table are used in this pattern.

(c) The verbs *make* and *help* can be made passive, but when they are, they are followed by a *to*-infinitive as in pattern [Cn·t]:

- He was **made** to work (by his tutor).
- We were **helped** to organize the party (by Stephen).

The other verbs shown here cannot be made passive. This restriction is shown in dictionary entries thus: [Cn·i no passive].

[Dn·n]

subject	double-transitive verb	indirect object	direct object: noun (phrase)
1 The Queen	**awarded**	the pilot	a gallantry medal.
2 The waiter	**poured**	Sarah	a glass of water.
3 Henri	**taught**	the children	French.
4 Christina	will **lend**	us	her flat.
5 The department	has **offered**	Mary	a job.
6 I	will **make**	everyone	some fresh coffee.
7 Father	**bought**	Emma	a white cat.

(a) This pattern has an indirect object (without a preposition) followed by a direct object. Both can consist of a noun or noun phrase. The indirect but not the direct object can also be a personal pronoun (Cf Tn).

(b) When the indirect object refers to someone who *receives* something, this pattern can usually be changed to the [Dn·pr] pattern with *to*:

- Henri **taught** the children French. [Dn·n]
- Henri **taught** French **to** the children. [Dn·pr]

In dictionary entries, this possibility is shown thus:

teach ... [... Dn·n, Dn·pr ...] ~ **sth (to sb)** ...

(c) When the indirect object refers to someone who is expected to *benefit* from the action of the verb, the [Dn·n] pattern can be changed to the [Dn·pr] pattern with *for*:

- I will **make** everyone some fresh coffee. [Dn·n]
- I will **make** fresh coffee **for** everyone. [Dn·pr]

In dictionary entries, this possibility is shown thus:

make ... [... Dn·n, Dn·pr ...] ~ **sth (for sb)** ...

(d) For reasons why the [Dn·pr] pattern (with *to* or *for*) may be preferred to the [Dn·n] pattern, see [Dn·pr], note (c).

(e) Most verbs in this pattern can be made passive, with the *indirect* object becoming the subject:

- The Queen **awarded** the pilot a gallantry medal.
- The pilot was **awarded** a gallantry medal (by the Queen).

Exceptions are shown in dictionary entries thus: [Dn·n no passive].

A passive in which the *direct* object becomes subject is rare:

- A gallantry medal was **awarded** the pilot (by the Queen).

[Dn·pr]

subject	double-transitive verb	direct object	indirect object: *to*/*for* + noun (phrase)/pronoun
1 The Queen	**awarded**	the medal	**to** a helicopter pilot.
2 The waiter	**poured**	a glass of water	**for** Sarah.
3 Henri	**taught**	French	**to** the children.
4 Christina	will **lend**	the flat	**to** us.
5 The department	has **offered**	the job	**to** Mary.
6 I	will **make**	fresh coffee	**for** everyone.
7 Father	**bought**	the white cat	**for** Emma.

(a) In this pattern, the indirect object is placed at the end. It consists of *to* or *for* and a noun (eg *Sarah*), noun phrase (eg *the children*) or pronoun (eg *us*, *everyone*).

(b) When introduced by *to*, the indirect object refers to a person or people *receiving* something (see [Dn·n], note (b)). When introduced by *for*, it refers to a person or people intended to *benefit* (see [Dn·n], note (c)). The correct choice of preposition is shown in entries like this:

award ... [... Dn·n, Dn·pr ...] ~ **sth (to sb)** ...
buy ... [... Dn·n, Dn·pr ...] ~ **sth (for sb)** ...

(c) When the *indirect* object provides new information (eg in answer to a question), this pattern is preferred to [Dn·n], and the main stress falls on the last noun or pronoun.
Who did Henri **teach** French **to**?

- Henri **taught** French **to** the ˈchildren. [Dn·pr]

But when the *direct* object refers to information that is new, [Dn·n] is preferred:
What did Henri **teach** the children?

- Henri **taught** the children ˈFrench. [Dn·n]

(d) Most verbs in this pattern can be made passive, with the *direct* object of the active pattern becoming the subject of the passive one:

- Father **bought** the white cat **for** Emma.
- The white cat was **bought for** Emma (by Father).

Exceptions are shown in dictionary entries thus: [Dn·pr no passive].

[Dn·f]

subject	double-transitive verb	indirect object	direct object: *that*-clause
1 Colleagues	**told**	Paul	that the job wouldn't be easy.
2 The manager	**informed**	the audience	that the show had been cancelled.
3 Police	**warned**	drivers	that the roads were icy.
4 We	**persuaded**	the survivors	that they weren't in any danger.

(a) This pattern has an indirect object without *to* and a direct object consisting of a *that*-clause (Cf Tf). The indirect object refers to the person or people addressed by the subject.

(b) Some verbs in this pattern can be made passive, with the *indirect* object of the active pattern becoming the subject of the passive one:

- Colleagues **told** Paul that the job wouldn't be easy.
- Paul was **told** (by colleagues) that the job wouldn't be easy.

Exceptions are shown in dictionary entries thus: [Dn·f no passive].

[Dpr·f]

subject	double-transitive verb	indirect object: *to* + noun (phrase)	direct object: *that*-clause
1 The employers	**announced**	**to** journalists	that the dispute had been settled.
2 The consultant	**recommended**	**to** the employers	that new salary scales should be introduced.
3 The garage	**explained**	**to** customers	that the spare parts had not been delivered.

(a) This pattern has an indirect object with *to* and a direct object consisting of a *that*-clause (Cf Tf). The indirect object refers to the person or people addressed by the subject.

(b) Some verbs in this pattern can be made passive. (Note the construction with *it*).

- The garage **explained** to customers that the spare parts had not been delivered.
- It was **explained** to customers (by the garage) that the spare parts had not been delivered.

Exceptions are shown in dictionary entries thus: [Dpr·f no passive].

[Dn·w]

subject	double-transitive verb	indirect object	direct object: finite clause/ non-finite clause
1 A friendly guard	**showed**	the prisoner	how he could escape/how to escape.
2 Experience	hasn't **taught**	Martha	whom she can trust/ whom to trust.

subject	double-transitive verb	indirect object: *to* + noun (phrase)/ pronoun	direct object: finite clause/ non-finite clause
3 The organizers	didn't **tell**	the children	whether they should bring a picnic lunch/ whether to bring a picnic lunch.
4 The porter	**reminded**	guests	where they should leave their luggage/where to leave their luggage.

(a) In this pattern, the direct object is a finite or non-finite clause beginning with
EITHER (i) A '*wh*-element', which can be a pronoun (*who(m), whose, which, what*), or a determiner + noun (*which roads, what time*), or an adverb (*why* (finite clauses only), *when, where, how*);
OR (ii) One of the conjunctions *if* (finite clauses only) *or whether* (Cf Tw).

(b) Some verbs used in this pattern can be made passive, with the *indirect* object of the active pattern becoming the subject of the passive one:

- A friendly guard **showed** the prisoner how he could escape/how to escape.
- The prisoner was **shown** how he could escape/how to escape (by a friendly guard).

Exceptions are shown in dictionary entries thus: [Dn·w no passive].

[Dpr·w]

subject	double-transitive verb	indirect object: *to* + noun (phrase)/ pronoun	direct object: finite clause/ non-finite clause
1 We	**explained**	**to** the staff	how they should handle complaints/how to handle complaints.
2 You	should **indicate**	**to** the team	where they are to assemble/ where to assemble.

(a) This pattern has an indirect object with *to* and a direct object consisting of a finite or non-finite *wh*-clause (Cf Tw). The indirect object refers to the person or people addressed by the subject.

(b) Some verbs in this pattern can be made passive. (Note the construction with *it*).

- It was **explained to** the staff how they should handle complaints/how to handle complaints.

Exceptions are shown in dictionary entries thus: [Dpr·w no passive].

[Dn·t]

subject	double-transitive verb	indirect object	direct object: non-finite clause (*to*-infinitive)
1 We	**told**	Peter	to see a doctor.
2 His teacher	**advised**	him	to take up the piano.
3 The court	**forbade**	the father	to see his children.
4 John and Mary	**encouraged**	Simon	to stay.

(a) In this pattern, the direct object is a non-finite clause, consisting of or containing a *to*-infinitive (Cf Tt).

(b) Some verbs used in this pattern can be made passive, with the *indirect* object of the active pattern becoming the subject of the passive one:

- John and Mary **encouraged** Simon to stay.
- Simon was **encouraged** to stay (by John and Mary).

Exceptions are shown in dictionary entries thus: [Dn·t no passive].

[Dpr·t]

subject	double-transitive verb	indirect object: *to* + noun (phrase)/ pronoun	direct object: non-finite clause (*to*-infinitive)
1 She	**gestured**	**to** the children	to stand up.
2 Fred	**signalled**	**to** the waiter	to bring another chair.
3 Stephen	**shouted**	**to** the chairman	to let someone else speak.
4 A policeman	**motioned**	**to** us	to move to the side of the road.

(a) This pattern has an indirect object with *to* and a direct object consisting of or containing a *to*-infinitive (Cf Tt). The indirect object refers to the person or people to whom the subject is calling or signalling.

(b) The verbs in this pattern cannot usually be made passive.

9.2 Nouns.

9.2.1 Noun classes. Foreign learners of English often have difficulty in using English nouns correctly. This may be because of the agreement between noun and verb (Cf *The furniture is old/The news is unreliable*), or because of the rules which govern the proper choice of determiners (Cf *not much furniture, not much news, not many tables*). To help with these problems, a scheme of noun classes (represented in the entries by codes) has been devised for this dictionary, which reflects the grammatical differences.

9.2.2 Codes and their positions. Each class in the scheme is represented in the dictionary entries by an easily understood code in square brackets, eg [C] (= 'countable noun'). If a noun has only one meaning, or several meanings all of which belong to the same noun class, the code or codes are placed after the part of speech label:

continuity ... *n* [U] **1** ... **2** ... **3** ... **4** ...

But if a noun in its various senses may belong to more than one class, the labels are placed after the sense numbers, as appropriate:

check[3] ... *n* **(a)** [C] pattern of crossed lines (often in different colours) forming squares ... **(b)** [U] cloth with this pattern ...

A particular noun or meaning of a noun may require more than one class. In such cases the labels are placed within the same set of brackets, separated by a comma:

recurrence [C, U] (instance of) recurring; repetition.

No code is given if a noun (in all its various meanings) belongs to the countable ([C]) class.

9.2.3 Noun class scheme. Details of the various classes, with their codes, are given below. (For a quick guide, users should look inside the back cover of the dictionary.)

• [C] Countable nouns. These are used in the singular and plural forms with *is/are*, etc: *The picture is dusty/The pictures are dusty*. They can be used with *a/an* in the singular and *many/few* in the plural: *A complaint was made.* ○ *There were many/few complaints.*

• [U] Uncountable (or mass) nouns. These are used in the singular form only, with *is*, etc: *The heat is unbearable*. They can be used without a determiner, as in *Butter is cheap*, and can also be preceded by *much/little*: *Can we expect much support?* ○ *There was very little support for the plan.*

• [CGp] Countable group nouns. These nouns can be used in both the singular and plural forms, with matching verbs: *The committee has met/The committees have met.* But when used in the singular form, a CGp noun can agree with a plural verb as well, thus suggesting the individuals that make up a group rather than the group itself. Cf *The committee have not yet chosen their chairman/The committee has not yet chosen its chairman.*

• [Gp] Group nouns. These are mostly place names such as *Whitehall, the Kremlin*, etc, used to refer to groups of people who govern, manage, etc in those places. They are used in the singular form only, but they can agree with a singular or a plural verb: *The Kremlin are studying the President's letter.* ○ *Whitehall was quick to react.*

• [sing *v*] Plural nouns with singular verbs. Nouns such as *measles, mumps*; *billiards, bowls*; *physics, linguistics* have no singular form but take a singular verb: *Measles is contagious.* ○ *Physics is a compulsory subject. Measles, mumps*, etc can be used with *the* or with *a lot of/much/less*: *She's caught (the) mumps.* ○ *There's a lot of measles about.*

• [pl *v*] Singular nouns with plural verb. Nouns such as *police, clergy*, etc have no plural form but take a plural verb: *The police have not arrested anyone.* ○ *The clergy have all signed the petition.* Such nouns can be used with *many/few/several*: *Many police were on duty that night.* ○

Several staff have resigned. Also in this class are nouns formed from adjectives, eg *the wounded, the injured, the sick.*

- [sing or pl *v*] Plural nouns with singular or plural verb. These have a plural form but may agree with either a singular or a plural verb: *The barracks was/were badly damaged in the explosion.* ○ *The firm's headquarters is/are in Manchester.*

- [pl] Plural nouns. Nouns in this class are plural in form and agree with a plural verb: *Your trousers are torn.* ○ *These premises are vacant.* ○ *Earnings have risen sharply.* Some (like *shorts, braces; pliers, scissors*) can be used with *a pair of/pairs of*: *I've laddered my new (pair of) tights.* ○ *Fetch some pliers/a pair of pliers.*

- [sing] Singular nouns. Nouns in this class are singular in form and agree with a singular verb. They are normally used with *a/an*: *We'll have to have a quick think.* ○ *There was an abundance of fruit and vegetables.*

9.2.4 Fixed forms of nouns. Sometimes a noun in a particular sense can occur only with the definite or indefinite article. If it is used with the definite article it will be in either the singular or plural form – not both. In addition to the article (sometimes instead of it), the noun can have a capital letter. These are fixed forms of nouns, and to help the user to recognize them, they are shown in **bold** print after the sense number and before any grammatical code and/or stylistic label:

> **scene** ... *n* ... **7 the scene** [sing] ... (*infml*) the current situation in a particular area of activity or way of life ...
> **shame** ... *n* ... **4 a shame** [sing] (*derog infml*) ...

9.3 Attributive and predicative uses of adjectives. Most adjectives can be used either before a noun or after the verb *to be*, as in *a serious affair/The affair was serious.* The terms 'attributive' and 'predicative' are used to refer to these functions, abbreviated in this dictionary to [attrib] and [pred]. These labels are not used in entries in which the adjective in its various senses can occur in both positions. When, however, it is restricted in one or more of its meanings to attributive or predicative position, the appropriate label is given:

> **bare**[1] ... *adj* ... **3** [attrib] only just sufficient; basic: *the bare necessities of life* ...
> **ablaze** ... *adj* [pred] **1** ... *The whole building was soon ablaze.* **2** ... *The palace was ablaze with lights.*

Nouns are sometimes used in attributive position, as in *a stone wall, a marble column.* All such uses are labelled [attrib]:

> **iron** ... *n* **1** ... *as hard as iron* ○ [attrib] *iron ore* ...

10 COMPLEMENTATION

10.1 Fixed or optional. Many nouns, adjectives and verbs (⇨ 9.1) are incomplete and ungrammatical without a following prepositional phrase or non-finite construction. These fixed elements are called the 'complementation' of the noun, adjective, etc. In other cases, the complementation is optional (but highly predictable). The obligatory type can be seen in *That's tantamount to treason* and *The idea never occurred to me*, and the optional type in *He can't cope (with the extra work)* and *They've already protested (to the authorities).* In this dictionary, complementation is shown by means of a pattern in **bold** print after the grammatical code(s):

> **tantamount** /ˈtæntəmaʊnt/ *adj* [pred] ~ **to sth** ...

10.2 Brackets and obliques. The absence of brackets shows that complementation is fixed; the use of brackets indicates that it is optional:

> **occur** /əˈkɜː(r)/ *v* ... **2** [Ipr] ~ **to sb** ...
> **cope** /kəʊp/ *v* [I, Ipr] ~ **(with sb/sth)** ...

A choice between alternatives is shown by means of an oblique stroke, as here between two non-finite clauses:

> **happy** /ˈhæpɪ/ *adj* ~ **(doing sth/to do sth)** ...

In this part of an entry, as elsewhere, **sb** = somebody and **sth** = something. The use of '**...**' after a preposition shows that a noun must be used there, but one which refers to a place:

> **depart** /dɪˈpɑːt/ *v* [I, Ipr] ~ **(from ...)** ...

10.3 A and B. Sometimes a verb or noun can be followed by alternative phrases which are related in structure and meaning. For example, *supply books to the students* is closely related to *supply the students with books.* These connected patterns are shown thus:

> **supply** /səˈplaɪ/ *v* ... [Tn, Tn·pr] ~ **sth (to sb)**; ~ **sb (with sth)** ...

However, when two things (or two people) are referred to in BOTH of the alternative phrases (as in the example *sprinkle pepper on one's food/sprinkle one's food with pepper*), **A** and **B** are used to prevent confusion:

> **sprinkle** /ˈsprɪŋkl/ *v* [Tn, Tn·pr] ~ **A (on/onto/over B)**; ~ **B (with A)** ...

MEANING AND USAGE

11 STYLE AND FIELD

11.1 The problems of the learner. It is often as difficult for foreign learners to decide how to use English words appropriately as it is to be sure about their meanings. They may not be aware, for instance, that *wireless* is an old-fashioned (and chiefly British) word, now almost entirely replaced by *radio*, or that to call a woman *petite* or *slender* implies an approving attitude towards her – in contrast with *skinny*, which suggests criticism or dislike. To help learners with these difficulties, a number of labels are used in the dictionary to denote the stylistic values of words or the technical fields in which they are used. Style and field labels are of six major types, described below in sections 11.3–11.8. (See also inside the back cover of the dictionary for a list of abbreviations of labels, etc.)

11.2 Position of labels. Style and field labels are printed in *italics* and placed in round brackets after the grammatical codes and/or complementation:

> **bags**[1] ... *n* [pl] (*infml*) trousers: *Oxford bags.*

When different stylistic values are attached to different meanings of a word, idiom, etc, the appropriate labels are positioned as follows:

> **fabulous** ... *adj* ... **2** (*infml*) wonderful ... **3** [attrib] (*fml*) appearing in fables ...

Two or more labels may be combined, usually in the order of the major types 'currency', 'region', etc as arranged below. Whether used singly or in combination, labels may be modified by *esp* ('especially'), *usu* ('usually'), *sometimes*, etc:

> **bally** ... *adj, adv* (*dated Brit sl*) ... *It's a bally nuisance!*
>
> **baggage** ... *n* ... **3** [C] (*dated infml joc*) lively or mischievous girl ...
>
> ˈ**cheer-leader** *n* (*esp US*) person who leads the cheering by a crowd...

11.3 Currency. Not all words and meanings treated in this dictionary are in general present-day use. Certain words (eg *court* (verb), *gramophone*) are still used by some older speakers but not by the majority of younger ones. These are words passing out of use, and they are labelled (*dated*). Other words (eg *thou* for 'you' or *knave* in the sense of 'dishonest man'), though found in books written in the first half of this century or earlier, have now passed out of use altogether. These are labelled *arch* (= 'archaic').

Note that when the object, institution, etc being referred to is out of date, rather than the word used to refer to it, this is shown by including 'formerly' in the definition:

> ˈ**battering-ram** *n* large heavy log with an iron head formerly used in war for breaking down walls, etc.

11.4 Region. A number of words and senses are restricted to (or especially restricted to) one country or area. The largest regionally-restricted groups of words are represented below, with the appropriate labels. Other abbreviations used to denote place of origin are (*S African*) for 'South African', (*Austral*) for 'Australian' and (*NZ*) for 'New Zealand'. All other regional labels are spelt out in full.

- (*Brit*) denotes specifically British words and senses, eg *banger* ('sausage'), *suspender* ('device for supporting stockings'), *vest* ('garment worn under a shirt, etc').
- (*US*) indicates words and senses used specifically in the United States, eg *suspenders* ('braces'), *vest* ('waistcoat').
- (*Scot*) denotes Scottish words and meanings, eg *bairn* ('child'), *ben* ('mountain peak'), *loch* ('lake').
- (*dialect*) refers to words and senses that are restricted to particular regions of the British Isles not including Scotland and Ireland, eg *beck* ('stream'), *parky* ('cold').

11.5 Register. Certain words must be used with particular care because they reflect a special relationship between speakers (which could vary from very distant to very close) or a special occasion or setting (which could vary from an official ceremony to a relaxed meeting between friends). Labels used to indicate such factors are described below in an order which goes from least formal to most formal.

- (⚠) denotes words or senses likely to be thought offensive or shocking or indecent (though not necessarily by everyone or on every occasion), eg *wop*, *nigger*, *Christ!*; *fuck*, *prick*, *shit*, *piss*. Foreign learners should exercise great care in using these words. They should also note that words such as *wop* and *nigger* are generally used with the deliberate aim of giving offence (Cf (*offensive*) at 11.6).
- (*sl*) indicates 'slang' words and senses, ie inventive and often colourful items generally used in a very informal spoken context. Such items usually belong to, or originate in, the language of a particular social or occupational group (eg soldiers, nurses, prisoners). Examples include: *the nick* ('prison'), *the fuzz* ('police'), *scarper* ('go away').
- (*infml*) denotes 'informal' words and senses, ie those indicating a close personal relationship and an unofficial occasion or setting, eg *pinch* ('steal'), *brolly* ('umbrella'), *dad*, *granny*.

• (*fml*) denotes 'formal' words and meanings, ie those chosen when speaking or writing in a serious or an official context to someone who is not a close friend or relation, eg *warrant* ('deserve'), *countenance* ('support or approve'), *acquiesce in* ('accept without protest').

• (*rhet*) 'Rhetorical' items are associated with writing or speech on serious or elevated themes, especially on very formal occasions (eg public meetings, state ceremonies). The use of such words elsewhere suggests a self-consciously pompous speaker or writer. Examples include *tribulation* ('event that causes suffering'), *alas* (expression of sorrow).

11.6 Evaluation. The use of certain words or phrases implies a particular attitude (disapproving, approving, ironic, etc) towards the person, thing or action referred to. The following categories are recognized in this dictionary:

• (*derog*) 'Derogatory' words, etc imply that one disapproves of or scorns the person or thing referred to or described by those words, eg *puerile, skulk, swagger*.

• (*approv*) 'Approving' words, etc imply the opposite of derogatory ones; they suggest approval of or admiration for the thing or person referred to or described, eg *petite, slender, bonny*.

• (*offensive*) This label denotes words used to address or refer to people, usually with the deliberate intention of offending them, especially on account of their race or religion. Words such as *dago, wop, nigger* are almost always used offensively in this way; words such as *arsehole* and *prick* are often found shocking, but they need not be used as terms of abuse (Cf (⚠) at 11.5).

• (*euph*) 'Euphemistic' words, etc are ones chosen to refer to something unpleasant or painful in a pleasant (because more indirect) way, eg *pass away* ('die'), *senior citizen* ('old age pensioner').

• (*ironic*) This label denotes words, often used within a longer phrase, that are intended to convey a sense opposite to the apparent sense, eg *fine* (as in *a fine mess*), *lovely* (as in *a lovely black eye*).

• (*fig*) A 'figurative' sense of a word is a non-literal (often metaphorical) sense which can still be related by native speakers to an original literal one. (Where there has been such a link in the past, but it is no longer perceived, the label is not used.) An example sentence which shows the connection (at **cheer**[1]) is: (*fig*) *Flowers always cheer a room up*. This can be related to a previous literal example: *Bring her a present – that'll cheer her up*.

• (*joc*) 'Jocular' words and phrases are intended to be funny, whether grim or innocent humour is meant, eg *push up the daisies, Alma Mater, nothing daunted, put one's foot in it*.

• (*sexist*) This label denotes words and phrases that express a (sometimes unconscious) discriminatory or patronizing attitude towards someone of the opposite sex. They are almost always words, etc used by men about or to women, and can be used to express approval in a 'man-to-man' context, eg *chick, the weaker sex, a bit of skirt/crumpet/stuff, an easy lay*.

11.7 Technical fields. This dictionary contains a large number of words and senses which are normally confined to technical use. Our policy has been to limit coverage to those words, etc which, though they would be used as technical terms by the specialists concerned, are nevertheless likely to be encountered by the well-read layman. The labels used here are mostly self-explanatory. The following examples show only a small part of the range:

acinus (*botany*)
basilica (*architecture*)
carbon cycle (*physics*)
chiaroscuro (*art*)
continuity (*cinema or TV*)
cursor (*computing*)
enzyme (*chemistry*)
habeas corpus (*law*)
mastectomy (*medical*)
septum (*anatomy*)
subjunctive (*grammar*)
vivace (*music*)

The dictionary also includes thousands of 'encyclopedic' entries covering a wide range of subject areas. These are not explicitly labelled when the entries themselves clearly indicate the field or fields to which they belong.

11.8 Sayings and catchphrases. These labels denote a variety of longer phrases and sentences, which often have meanings quite different from those of their parts and are used to perform various functions.

• (*saying*) 'Sayings' are fixed phrases or sentences used to make comments, give advice, issue warnings, etc. They often reflect traditional values and rules, eg *too many cooks spoil the broth*; *a stitch in time saves nine*.

• (*catchphrase*) 'Catchphrases' often originate with public figures, popular entertainers, etc and help to identify them. Later, they may pass into general use, and acquire other meanings and functions, eg *the buck stops here*; *if you can't beat them, join them*.

11.9 Proprietary names. Some words in common use in speech and writing are registered trademarks belonging to manufacturing companies. Such words, eg *Jacuzzi*, *Aqualung*, are given the label (*propr*) ('proprietary term') in the dictionary.

12 DEFINITIONS

12.1 Definitions: phrase and single word. Definitions usually consist of a phrase which is equivalent in meaning to the headword (and is sometimes substitutable for it in a particular context):

representative ... *adj* **1** ... (**a**) serving to show or portray a class or group ...
sack[3] ... *v* [Tn] steal or destroy property in (a captured town, etc).

If a one-word definition (ie a synonym) exists for a headword in a particular sense, this is placed immediately after the phrase definition, thus:

safe[1] ... *adj* ... **1** ... protected from danger and harm; secure ... **4** (**a**) [usu attrib] (of a person) unlikely to do dangerous things; cautious ...

Sometimes, such words can replace the headword in a given context (cf *safe from attack*, *secure from attack*; *a safe driver*, *a cautious driver*). But learners should beware of substituting a word given as a one-word definition without first checking the entry for the word itself. They will often find that words closely related in meaning may differ in grammar (*This driver is safe* is less normal than *This driver is cautious*) or in style (*secure* is more formal than *safe* in sense **1**).

12.2 Sense divisions. In entries with more than one meaning, the meanings are usually arranged in sections introduced by numbers or letters. The use of numbers normally indicates that the senses are fairly distant in relation to each other; this is often further reflected in differences of grammar and/or style:

pack[1] ... *n* ... **4** [CGp] ... (*derog*) number of people or things ...: *a pack of fools/thieves* ○ *a pack of lies*. **5** [C] ... complete set of 52 playing cards. **6** [C] (only in compounds) thing placed on the body for a period of time ...: *a ˈface-pack* ○ *an ˈice-pack*.

The use of letters suggests a closer relationship, as for example when a noun such as *ham*, *beer* or *wine* denotes (a) the food or drink itself, (b) a particular type or brand and (c) a measured quantity:

beer ... *n* **1** (**a**) [U] alcoholic drink made from malt and flavoured with hops, etc: *a barrel, bottle, glass of beer* ... (**b**) [C] type of beer: *beers brewed in Germany*. (**c**) [C] glass of beer: *Two beers, please.*

Sometimes, two closely related meanings are combined in one definition, for example when referring to a process or action and an individual instance of that process or action:

embezzlement ... *n* [C, U] (instance of) embezzling ...

12.3 Indicating subjects and objects in definitions. Dictionary entries show whether the *object* of a verb can be a person or a thing or both by the use of '(sb)', '(sth)', and occasionally '(oneself)', '(itself)', in the definitions:

chauffeur ... *v* [Tn] drive (sb) as a chauffeur.
cheapen ... *v* ... **2** [Tn] make (oneself/sth) less worthy of respect ...

When it is necessary to show whether the *subject* is a person or type of thing, the convention is this:

drop[2] ... **3** [I, Ipr] (of people and animals) collapse from exhaustion ...
drive[1] ... **3** [Tn, Tn·pr, Tn·p] (of wind or water) carry (sth) along ...

12.4 Types of subject or object. Sometimes the choice of subject or object is limited to one specific noun. This too will be placed in brackets:

come in (**a**) (of the tide) move towards the land.

In other cases, the user can choose from a range of subject or object nouns: for example, one can *bait* (in the sense of 'torment') a variety of animals. In cases like this, the general type of person, animal or thing may be indicated in brackets:

bait *v* ... **2** ... (**a**) torment (a chained animal) by making dogs attack it ...

(For ways of indicating, in example phrases, the *specific* nouns, adjectives, etc which the user can choose when writing or speaking ⇨ 13.3).

12.5 Glosses. Sometimes the meaning of an example may differ in some special way from the definition which it illustrates. This special sense may be a figurative extension (⇨ 11.6) of the meaning that has been given in the definition and illustrated by an earlier example. In these cases, a gloss is provided either within or at the end of the example which has the special meaning:

come ... **2** ... travel (a specified distance): *We've come fifty miles since lunch.* ○ (*fig*) *This company has come a long way* (ie made a lot of progress) *in the last five years.*

Sometimes the definition is a very general one, so that a number of distinct glosses are needed to explain individual examples:

> **balanced** *adj* ... keeping or showing a balance: *a balanced state of mind*, ie a stable one in which no single emotion is too strong ○ *a balanced decision*, ie one reached after comparing all the arguments ...

13 EXAMPLES

13.1 The user's needs. Examples in this dictionary are designed to meet several learning needs. They help learners to understand the meanings of words, they provide models for them to imitate when writing or speaking, and they illustrate the grammatical patterns in which words are used. Examples are of two main types: sentence examples and phrase examples.

13.2 Sentence examples. Examples which are complete sentences are chiefly helpful in giving the user a clearer impression of a word's meaning and use than a definition is able to do. For example:

> **come out** ... **(f)** ... *The full story came out at the trial.*

Here light is thrown on the meaning of *come out* ('be revealed') by its context *at the trial*. In another example, the meaning of *come off* is made clear by its contrast with *fixed on permanently*:

> **come off (a)** ... *'Does this knob come off?' 'No, it's fixed on permanently.'*

Sentence examples are also an important way of indicating grammatical patterns, and as far as possible each common verb pattern is exemplified (⇨ 9.1). Sometimes examples are divided by an oblique stroke, or have a part in round brackets, to show alternative patterns in a single sentence:

> **bake** ... *v* ... [... Dn·n, Dn·pr] ... *I'm baking Alex a birthday cake/baking a birthday cake for Alex.*
>
> **contract**[2] ... *v* ... [Ipr, It] ... *Having contracted (with them) to do the repairs, we cannot withdraw now.*

13.3 Phrase examples with collocations. Phrase examples also help to clarify meaning, but they are chiefly helpful in showing, or suggesting, the kinds of words that regularly combine (or 'collocate') with the headword. (This information is of particular value to the writer or translator.) Three conventions are used in phrases to show which words collocate with the headword, and how wide the range of choice is:

- A phrase example may show a list of words separated by commas (but without *etc*):

  come forward present oneself: *come forward with help, information, money.*

Here the nouns *help*, etc are not closely related in meaning; the list is 'open-ended' and so can suggest other choices, eg *assistance, proposals, cash.*

- Other phrase examples have a list ending in *etc*:

  cheap ... *adj* ... **5** ... *a cheap gibe, joke, remark, retort, etc.*

Here the choice is again fairly open but the words are more closely related, showing that, for instance, *cheap crack* and *cheap insult* are possible collocations.

- Other examples show a few words divided by an oblique stroke (/). Here the words may be related or not, but the choice is limited, and foreign learners would be wise to restrict themselves to the collocations shown:

  besetting *adj* ... *a besetting difficulty/fear/sin.*

  bet *n* ... *place/put a bet on a horse.*

  ˈcheck-up *n* ... *go for/have a check-up.*

SPECIAL TYPES OF WORDS AND PHRASES

14 IDIOMS

14.1 Problems of meaning and form. An idiom is a phrase whose meaning is difficult (often impossible) to recognize from the familiar meanings of the words it contains. For example, the phrase *get sth off one's chest* means 'say something that one has wanted to say for a long time'. Of equal difficulty for foreign learners, though, is the fact that idioms either have a fixed form, or are changeable in quite unpredictable ways. In *show one's teeth*, for instance, nothing can be substituted for *show* or *teeth*. In the quite separate idiom *draw sb's/sth's teeth*, however, *fangs* can be used in place of *teeth* (though *draw* is unchangeable). It is important to show possible variation clearly; and in this dictionary an oblique stroke (/) is used to mark alternatives, while brackets are used to show when a word or phrase can be omitted altogether:

> **make one's/sb's ˈflesh crawl/creep**
> **make/pull ˈfaces/a ˈface (at sb)**

14.2 Choice of 'key' word. Idioms are listed and defined at the entry for the first 'full' word (noun, verb, adjective or adverb) which they contain. Thus *a big cheese* is defined at **big** (not **cheese**), and *(as) different as chalk and/from cheese* at **different** (not **chalk** or **cheese**). Idioms appear in the last or, with some verbs, next to last numbered section of the entry for their key word (**big**, **different**, etc), headed by the abbreviation '(idm)'.

15.3 Commonly used words. The words *bad, be, break, bring, come, cut, do, fall, get, give, go, good, have, hold, keep, lay, let, look, make, play, put, run, see, set, stand, take, throw, turn* and *work* are used in so many idioms that to include them as key words would result in very long lists of idioms at **bad**, **break**, **bring**, etc and make individual idioms difficult to find. Instead, a few specimen idioms only are given in the entries for each of these words, and the user is referred to the entries for the nouns and adjectives, etc that occur in the idioms containing them.

14.4 Idioms consisting of grammatical words. Idioms which consist entirely of such 'grammatical' words (Cf 'full' words ⇨ 14.2) as *be, may, it, oneself*, etc are normally treated in the entry for the first of these words that occurs in the idiom. Thus, **be oneself** and **be that as it may** both appear in the entry for **be**[1], and nowhere else.

14.5 Alphabetical arrangement. In each entry in which they appear, idioms are arranged in strict alphabetical order, ignoring only *a/an, the*; *sb, sth* and possessive forms (*one's, sb's, his*, etc); and words in brackets or after obliques.

14.6 Cross-reference. To help any user who may have difficulty in identifying the first full word in an idiom, every idiom containing two (or more) such words has a cross-reference at the entry for each full word other than the first one. At each cross-reference the user is directed to the entry where the idiom is fully treated. Thus, in the case of **laugh in sb's face**, the user will find the idiom listed alphabetically at **face**, but with a cross-reference to the entry for **laugh**:

> **face**[1] ... (idm) ... **laugh in sb's face** ⇨ LAUGH.

15 PHRASAL VERBS

15.1 Verbs with prepositions and particles. Verbs of many types combine freely with prepositions (*go into the garden, hang one's coat on a peg, make a figure out of clay*) and adverbial particles (*run away, send the goods back, beat the eggs up*). Combinations such as these represent 'literal' meanings of the verbs and of the prepositions and particles, and they are illustrated in the numbered sections of the verbs, prepositions, etc concerned, as, for example, at **come**:

> **come** /kʌm/ *v* ... **1** (**a**) ... *She comes to work by bus.* ○ *Are you coming out for a walk?*

Many apparently similar combinations, though, have meanings which are more difficult to relate to those of their component words. In *He came at me with a knife, come at* means 'attack', not 'advance towards'; in *Long hair for men came in while I was at school, come in* means 'become fashionable', not 'enter'. In these examples, *come at* and *come in* are idiomatic combinations (or 'phrasal verbs'), and they are treated in this dictionary in a special way.

15.2 Arrangement. Phrasal verbs are listed in bold print in a numbered section headed '(phr v)' and positioned immediately after the idioms section (if there is one). They are listed alphabetically according to the preposition(s) or particle(s) they contain, thus:

> **check**[1] ... **6** (phr v) **check in (at ...)**; **check into** ... **check sth in** ... **check sth off** ... **check (up) on sb** ... **check (up) on sth** ... **check out (of ...)** ... **check sth out** ...

15.3 The grammar of phrasal verbs. The forms in bold print in which phrasal verbs are presented in the dictionary (eg **come by sth**, **take sth in**) are designed to show the grammatical patterns in which they are used. There are six types of phrasal verb. These can be further divided into those *without* a direct object (Group A) and those *with* a direct object (Group B):

A Group WITHOUT a direct object (**sb** or **sth** is ABSENT altogether from the bold form, as in 1, or it appears at the END, as in 2 and 3).

1 Type with an adverbial particle, eg **come down** collapse: *The ceiling came down.*

2 Type with a preposition, eg **come by sth** receive sth by chance: *How did you come by that scratch?* (NOT *How did you come that scratch by?*)

3 Type with an adverbial particle and a preposition, eg **come down on sb** criticize sb severely: *Don't come down on her too hard.*

B Group WITH a direct object (**sb** or **sth** is in the MIDDLE of the bold form, as in 1, 2 and 3, and possibly *also* at the END, as in 2 and 3).

1 Type with an adverbial particle, **take sth in** understand sth: *I can't take this information in.* (ALSO *I can't take in this information.*)

2 Type with a preposition, eg **take sth off sth** deduct money from sth: *They've taken 50 pence off the price.*

3 Type with an adverbial particle and a preposition, eg **take sth out on sb** make sb suffer for sth for which he is not responsible: *Don't take your frustrations out on me.* (ALSO *Don't take out your frustrations on me.*)

(For a full description of these types, see the *Oxford Dictionary of Current Idiomatic English*, Vol. I, pp xxxiv–lvii.)

16 DERIVATIVES

16.1 Position. A derivative is formed from a simple word (root) by the addition of a prefix (eg *assign*: *reassign*) or suffix (eg *resign*: *resignation*). Sometimes a word moves from one grammatical class to another without any such addition (eg **head** (*n*): **head** (*v*); **welcome** (*adj*): **welcome** (*n*)). Derivatives formed with a suffix or with a change of grammatical class only – the latter are called 'zero-derivatives' – are usually set out following the numbered sub-sections of the headword and preceded by the symbol ▷.

cheap ... *adj* ...
▷**cheap** *adv* ...
cheaply *adv* ...
cheapness *n* ...

16.2 Derivatives as headwords. When there is no connection of meaning between a simple word and a more complex one similar to it in form, the latter is treated as a separate entry:

scarce ... *adj* ... not available in sufficient quantities ...
scarcely ... *adv* barely; not quite ...

In cases, too, where the difference in spelling between a simple word and its derivative is such that the dictionary user may not connect the two, the derivative is entered as a separate headword:

satisfy ... *v* ... **example** ... *n* ...
satisfaction ... *n* ... **exemplary** ... *adj* ...

16.3 Derivatives of derivatives. Often, derivatives are formed not from the headword itself but from one or other of its derivatives. *Maniacal*, for instance, is formed from *maniac* (not *mania*), and *maniacally* from *maniacal*. In cases like these, the derivatives are 'run on' (ie not placed at the beginning of a new line in the dictionary):

mania ... *n* ...
▷**maniac** ... *n* ... **maniacal** ... *adj* ... **maniacally** ... *adv*.

16.4 Defining derivatives. When the meaning of a derivative is not straightforwardly related to that of its root (or of another derivative), the various meanings are all given:

contort ... *v* ... (cause sth to) twist out of its natural shape ...
▷ **contortion** ... *n* ... contorting or being contorted (esp of the face or body) ... **contortionist** ... person who is skilled in contorting his body.

In the many cases where the connection is straightforward, however, the derivatives are not defined. (Thus, at the entry for **chauvinism**, **chauvinist** is defined, but not **chauvinistic** or **chauvinistically**.) Note, though, that the part of speech and other grammatical information are always given.

16.5 Zero-derivatives. When a zero-derivative (⇨ 16.1) is formed from a headword, it is shown in full and listed alphabetically in the derivative section of the entry (⇨ **cheap** *adv* at 16.1). Consider, though, **alcoholic** *adj* and **alcoholic** *n*. Here the zero-derivative noun is identical in form to a word that is itself a derivative (the adjective). In such a case, the noun is not shown in full, but represented by a run-on dash, followed by a new part of speech label and a definition:

alcohol ... *n* ...
▷**alcoholic** ... *adj* of or containing alcohol ... — *n* person who drinks too much alcohol ...

17 COMPOUNDS

17.1 Position. A compound is made up of two or more simple words functioning as a single unit (ie it cannot be interrupted by another word). It may be written as one piece (eg *fireman*, *rattlesnake*) or with a hyphen (eg *check-out*, *king-size*). But some compounds appear as separate words (eg *barley sugar*, *traffic warden*). In this dictionary, compounds do not normally appear as separate entries but are included in the entry for the first element in each case (thus, **check-list** appears at **check**[1] and **doorknob** at **door**). This is helpful because it brings close together items which are often related in meaning. At the same time, reference to individual compounds is made easier by grouping them in a section at the end of the entry (indicated by the symbol □), with each compound starting a new line at the left-hand margin:

cut[1] ... *v* ...
□ˈ**cutaway** *n* ...
ˈ**cut-back** *n* ...
ˌ**cut** ˈ**glass** ...
ˈ**cut-off** *n* ...

17.2 Compounds as headwords. Some compounds are treated in entries of their own. These include items such as *hocus-pocus* and *hurly-burly* (whose first elements do not occur as separate words); technical terms (eg *Bailey bridge*) whose first parts are not listed as headwords in the dictionary; and some loan-words (eg *fait accompli*, *faux pas*). A larger group consists of compounds which cannot be understood from the meanings of their parts (eg *barnstorm*, meaning 'travel quickly through rural areas making political speeches, etc').

17.3 Derivatives of compounds. Sometimes derivatives are formed from compounds, either by the addition of a suffix or simply by a change of class (⇨ 16.5). In such cases, the derivatives are run on, with a dash in place of any zero-derivative:

□ˈ**baby carriage** (*US*) = PRAM ...
ˈ**baby-sit** *v* ... be a baby-sitter: *She regularly baby-sits for us.* ˈ**baby-sitter** *n* (*infml*) ... person who looks after a child for a short time while the parents are out.

□ˈ**press-gang** *n* ... (**b**) group who force others to do sth. — *v* [Tn] force (sb) into service ...

EXTRA INFORMATION

18 INFORMATION OUTSIDE THE MAIN ENTRIES

The dictionary includes a large amount of additional information of various kinds outside the standard dictionary entries themselves but referred to in them. The different types of information are listed below.

18.1 Usage notes. These are paragraphs in which special problems to do with the grammar or meaning of English words and phrases are clarified. They are separated from the main dictionary text by a line of space above and below, and have the heading NOTE ON USAGE. The dictionary user is referred to these usage notes in the entries for each word dealt with in them, eg, at **dictate**, ⇨ Usage at DECREE, where the words **decree, dictate, ordain** and **prescribe** are compared and contrasted. A complete list of words treated in usage notes is given at the front of the dictionary.

18.2 Articles. These give specially extended treatment to major aspects of British life and institutions, such as accent and dialect, the environment, and schools. They appear in shaded 'boxes' alphabetically positioned throughout the dictionary, and the user is referred to them from relevant dictionary entries or from other articles, eg, at **the National Health Service** (a compound at **national**), ⇨ articles at HEALTH, SOCIAL SECURITY. A list of all the articles is given at the front of the dictionary.

18.3 'Mini-notes'. These are short extra paragraphs at individual dictionary entries giving information on the special connotations that particular words and expressions have for native speakers of English in addition to their specific dictionary meaning. They are headed by the symbol 🕮.

18.4 Illustrations. These complement the text of the dictionary and take the form of drawings (or diagrams), half-tones and maps. The dictionary user is referred to them from relevant entries, eg, at **plus-fours** (a compound at **plus**), ⇨ illus at DRESS, and at **Nepal**, ⇨ map at INDIA.

18.5 Appendices. These present information at the back of the dictionary in the form of lists, tables, etc under such headings as common forenames, numerical expressions, irregular verbs and punctuation. A complete list of the appendices is given at the front of the dictionary, and the dictionary user is referred to the relevant appendix from individual entries wherever such a reference is appropriate.

A, a

A, a[1] /eɪ/ *n* (*pl* **A's, a's** /eɪz/) **1** the first letter of the English alphabet: *'Ann' begins with (an) A/'A'.* **2** (*music*) the sixth note in the scale of C major; the note to which orchestras tune. **3** academic mark indicating the highest standard of work: *get (an) A/'A' in biology.* **4** (used to designate a range of standard paper sizes): [attrib] *an A4 folder,* ie 297 x 210 mm. **5** (idm) **A1** /ˌeɪ ˈwʌn/ (*infml*) excellent; first rate: *an ˌA1 ˈdinner* ○ *I'm feeling A1,* ie very well. **from A to B** from one place to another: *I don't care what a car looks like as long as it gets me from A to B.* **from A to Z** from beginning to end; thoroughly: *know a subject from A to Z.*
□ **A-OK** /ˌeɪ əʊˈkeɪ/ *adj* [usu pred] (*US infml*) emphatically OK. Cf OKAY.
A-road /ˈeɪ rəʊd/ *n* (*Brit*) major road, less important than a motorway but usu wider and straighter than a B-road: *There's a good A-road going North — the A1.*
ˈA-side *n* (music recorded on the) first or main side of a single-play gramophone record.

a[2] /ə; *strong form* eɪ/ (also **an** /ən; *strong form* æn/) *indef art* (The form *a* is used before consonant sounds and the form *an* before vowel sounds. Both are used before [C], [Cgp] or [sing] *ns* that have not previously been made specific.) **1** one: *a man, hotel, girl, committee, unit, U-turn* (Cf *some men, hotels, girls, etc*) ○ *an egg, aunt, uncle, hour, X-ray, MP, L-plate* (Cf *some eggs, aunts, uncles, hours, etc*) ○ *I can only carry two at a time.* ○ *There's a book on the table — is that the one you want?* **2** (used with an abstract *n* that is restricted by the phrase which follows it): *There was still an abundance of food when we arrived.* ○ *We're looking for someone with a good knowledge of German.* **3** any; every: *A horse is a quadruped.* (Cf *Horses are quadrupeds.*) ○ *An owl can see in the dark.* (Cf *Owls can see*...). **4** one single: *He didn't tell us a thing about his holiday.* **5** (used with *ns* followed by *of* + *possess det* + *n* + *'s*): *a friend of my father's,* ie one of my father's friends ○ *a habit of Sally's,* ie one of Sally's habits. **6** (used in front of two *ns* seen as a unit): *a cup and saucer* ○ *a knife and fork.* **7** to or for each; per: *£2 a gallon* ○ *800 words a day* ○ *50p a pound.* **8** (*often derog*) person like (sb): *My boss is a little Napoleon.* **9** (used with sb's name to show that the speaker does not know the person): *Do we know a Tim Smith?* ○ *A Mrs Green is waiting to see you.* ○ *A Doctor Simpson telephoned.* **10** (used to show membership of a class): *My mother is a solicitor.* ○ *My father is a Fulham supporter.* ○ *It was a Volvo, not a Saab.* **11** painting, sculpture, etc by: *The painting my grandfather gave me turned out to be a Constable.*

NOTE ON USAGE: Note that the sound of the first letter of an abbreviation, not its spelling, determines the form and pronunciation of the article before it: *an MP* ○ *an SRN* ○ *a UHF radio* ○ *the* /ðɪ/ *NSPCC* ○ *the* /ðə/ *USA.*

A *abbr* **1** ampere(s): *13A,* eg on a fuse. **2** answer. Cf Q. **3** (in academic degrees) Associate of: *ARCM,* ie Associate of the Royal College of Music. Cf F 2.
A /eɪ/ *symb* (*Brit*) (of roads) major: *the A40 to Oxford* ○ *an A-road.* Cf B.
a- *pref* **1** (with *ns, adjs* and *advs*) not; without: *atheist* ○ *atypical* ○ *asexually.* ⇨ Usage at UN-. **2** (with *vs* forming *adjs*) in the state or process of: *awake* ○ *asleep* ○ *ablaze* ○ *adrift.*
AA /ˌeɪ ˈeɪ/ *abbr* **1** Alcoholics Anonymous, a society for alcoholics (ALCOHOL) who want to cure themselves of alcoholism. ⇨ article at VOLUNTARY. **2** (*Brit*) Automobile Association: *members of the AA.* ⇨ article at EMERGENCY.
AAA /ˌeɪ eɪ ˈeɪ/ *abbr* **1** (also **the three A's**) (*Brit*) Amateur Athletic Association. **2** (*US*) American Automobile Association.
Aaron /ˈeərən/ (in the Old Testament) brother of *Moses, who according to tradition founded the Jewish priesthood.
AB /ˌeɪ ˈbiː/ *abbr* **1** (*Brit*) able-bodied seaman. **2** (*US*) Bachelor of Arts.
aback /əˈbæk/ *adv* (phr v) **take sb aback** ⇨ TAKE.
abacus /ˈæbəkəs/ *n* (*pl* **-cuses** /-kəsɪz/) frame with beads that slide along parallel rods, used for teaching numbers to children, and (in some countries) for counting.
abaft /əˈbɑːft; *US* əˈbæft/ *adv* (*nautical*) in or towards the stern half of a ship.
▷ **abaft** *prep* (*nautical*) nearer to the stern than (sth); behind: *abaft the mainmast.*
abandon /əˈbændən/ *v* **1 (a)** [Tn] go away from (a person or thing or place) not intending to return; forsake; desert: *a baby abandoned by its parents* ○ *an abandoned car, dwelling, fort, village* ○ *give orders to abandon ship,* ie to leave a sinking ship. **(b)** [Tn, Dn·pr] ~ **sth/sb (to sb)** leave sth/sb to be taken (by sb): *They abandoned their lands and property to the invading forces.* **2** [Tn] give up completely (esp sth begun): *abandon a project, plan, scheme, etc* ○ *urge people who smoke to abandon the habit* ○ *He abandoned all hope,* ie stopped hoping. ○ *The match was abandoned because of bad weather.* **3** [Tn·pr] ~ **oneself to sth** (*fml*) yield completely to (an emotion or impulse): *He abandoned himself to despair.*
▷ **abandon** (also **abandonment**) *n* [U] freedom from worry or inhibitions: *dance with wild/gay abandon.*
abandoned *adj* [usu attrib] (of people or behaviour) wild or immoral.
abandonment *n* [U] **1** abandoning: *her abandonment of the idea.* **2** = ABANDON *n.*
abase /əˈbeɪs/ *v* [Tn] ~ **oneself/sb** lower oneself/sb in dignity; degrade oneself/sb. ▷ **abasement** *n* [U].
abashed /əˈbæʃt/ *adj* [pred] ~ **(at/by sth)** embarrassed; ashamed: *His boss's criticism left him feeling rather abashed.*
abate /əˈbeɪt/ *v* [I, Tn] (of wind, noise, pain, etc) make or become less: *The ship sailed when the storm had abated.* ○ *People are campaigning to abate the noise in our cities.* ▷ **abatement** *n* [U].
abattoir /ˈæbətwɑː(r); *US* ˌæbəˈtwɑːr/ *n* = SLAUGHTERHOUSE (SLAUGHTER).
abbess /ˈæbes/ *n* woman who is head of a convent or nunnery.
abbey /ˈæbɪ/ *n* **1** [C] building(s) in which monks or nuns live as a community under an abbot or abbess. **2** [CGp] the whole number of monks or nuns in an abbey. **3** [C] church or house that was formerly an abbey: *Westminster Abbey.*
Abbey Theatre /ˌæbɪ ˈθɪətə(r)/ **the Abbey Theatre** theatre in Dublin, Ireland, founded in 1904, where many famous Irish plays (eg by *Synge and *O'Casey) were first performed.
abbot /ˈæbət/ *n* man who is head of a monastery or abbey.
abbr (also **abbrev**) *abbr* abbreviated; abbreviation.
abbreviate /əˈbriːvɪeɪt/ *v* [Tn, Tn·pr] ~ **sth (to sth)** shorten (a word, phrase, etc), esp by omitting letters: *In writing, the title 'Doctor' is abbreviated to 'Dr'.*
▷ **abbreviation** /əˌbriːvɪˈeɪʃn/ *n* **1** [U] abbreviating or being abbreviated. **2** [C] shortened form of a word, phrase, etc: *'Sept' is an abbreviation for 'September'.* ○ *'GB' is the abbreviation of/for 'Great Britain'.*
ABC /ˌeɪ biː ˈsiː/ *n* [sing] **1** (Roman) alphabet, ie all the letters from A to Z: *Does the boy know his ABC?* **2** simplest and most basic facts about a subject: *the ABC of gardening.* **3** (idm) **easy as ABC** ⇨ EASY[1].
ABC /ˌeɪ biː ˈsiː/ *abbr* **1** American Broadcasting Company: *watch ABC.* ⇨ article at TELEVISION. **2** Australian Broadcasting Commission.
abdicate /ˈæbdɪkeɪt/ *v* **1** [I] resign from or formally renounce the throne: *King Edward VIII abdicated in 1936.* **2** [Tn] (*fml*) formally relinquish (power, a high official position, etc): *He's abdicated all responsibility in the affair.* ▷ **abdication** /ˌæbdɪˈkeɪʃn/ *n* [C, U].
abdomen /ˈæbdəmən/ *n* **1** part of the body below the chest and diaphragm, containing the stomach, bowels and digestive organs. Cf INTESTINE. **2** rearmost section of an insect, a spider or a crustacean: *head, thorax and abdomen.* ⇨ illus at INSECT.
▷ **abdominal** /æbˈdɒmɪnl/ *adj* in, of or for the abdomen: *abdominal pains* ○ *an abdominal operation.* **abdominally** /æbˈdɒmɪnəlɪ/ *adv.*
abduct /əbˈdʌkt, æb-/ *v* [Tn] take (sb) away illegally, using force or deception; kidnap. ▷ **abduction** /əbˈdʌkʃn, æb-/ *n* [U, C]. **abductor** *n.*
abeam /əˈbiːm/ *adv* (*nautical*) on a line at right angles to the length of a ship or an aircraft: *The lighthouse was abeam of the ship.*
Abel /ˈeɪbl/ (in the Old Testament) son of *Adam and *Eve, who was killed by his elder brother *Cain.
Abelard /ˈæbəlɑːd/ Peter (1079-1142), French theologian and philosopher who was accused of heresy for his religious theories. He is best remembered for his love affair with his pupil Héloïse, whom he secretly married. Her uncle had him castrated, and he became a monk.
Aberdeen Angus /ˌæbədiːn ˈæŋgəs/ Scottish breed of black cattle reared for their meat: *an Aberdeen Angus bull.*
aberrant /æˈberənt/ *adj* not following the normal or correct way: *aberrant behaviour.*
aberration /ˌæbəˈreɪʃn/ *n* **1 (a)** [U] deviation from what is accepted as normal or right: *steal sth in a moment of aberration.* **(b)** [C] moral or mental lapse; temporary loss of memory: *Owing to a strange mental aberration he forgot his own name.* **2** [C] fault or defect: *an aberration in the computer.* **3** [C] (defect in a lens or mirror that causes a) distortion of an image. **4** [C] apparent change in the position of a star, planet, etc in the sky, caused by the motion of the earth.
abet /əˈbet/ *v* (**-tt-**) **1 (a)** [Tn, Tn·pr] ~ **sb (in sth)** help or encourage sb to commit an offence or do sth wrong: *He was abetted in these illegal activities by his wife.* **(b)** [Tn] encourage (a crime, etc): *You are abetting theft.* **2** (idm) **aid and abet** ⇨ AID. ▷ **abetter,** (*esp law*) **abettor** *ns.*
abeyance /əˈbeɪəns/ *n* [U] (idm) **be in abeyance; fall/go into abeyance (a)** (of a right, rule, problem, etc) be suspended temporarily; not be in force or use for a time: *The question is in abeyance,* ie left unanswered, eg until more information is obtained. ○ *This law falls into abeyance when the country's security is threatened.* **(b)** (*law*) (of a right, a title, ownership, etc) be not yet legally decided.
abhor /əbˈhɔː(r)/ *v* (**-rr-**) [Tn] feel hatred and disgust for (sb/sth); detest: *abhor terrorism, terrorists.*
▷ **abhorrence** /əbˈhɒrəns; *US* -ˈhɔːr-/ *n* [U] hatred and disgust: *have an abhorrence of war.*
abhorrent /əbˈhɒrənt; *US* -ˈhɔːr-/ *adj* ~ **(to sb)** disgusting; hateful: *Violence is abhorrent to his gentle nature.*
abide /əˈbaɪd/ *v* (*pt, pp* **abided**; in sense 3 **abode** /əˈbəʊd/) **1** [Tn] (esp with *can/could,* in negative sentences or questions) tolerate (sb/sth); endure;

bear: *I can't abide that man.* ○ *How could you abide such conditions?* **2** [Ipr] ~ **by sth** act in accordance with sth; be faithful to sth: *abide by* (ie keep) *a promise* ○ *abide by* (ie observe) *an agreement, verdict, ruling, etc* ○ *You'll have to abide by* (ie accept) *the referee's decision.* **3** [Ipr] (*arch*) remain; continue; stay: *abide at a place* ○ *abide with sb.*

▷ **abiding** *adj* enduring; permanent: *an abiding friendship, hatred, mistrust, etc.*

ability /əˈbɪlətɪ/ *n* **1** [U] capacity or power to do sth physical or mental: *a machine with the ability to cope with large loads* ○ *He has the ability to do the work.* **2** (**a**) [U] cleverness; intelligence: *a woman of great ability.* (**b**) [U, C] talent: *have a great musical ability* ○ *We found him work more suited to his abilities.* **3** (idm) **to the best of one's ability** ⇨ BEST[3].

ab initio /ˌæb ɪˈnɪʃɪəʊ/ (*Latin*) from the beginning: *The entire process must be repeated ab initio.*

abject /ˈæbdʒekt/ *adj* **1** (of conditions) wretched; hopeless: *living in abject poverty/misery.* **2** (of people, their actions or behaviour) lacking all pride; contemptible; despicable: *an abject coward* ○ *an abject* (ie very humble) *apology.* ▷ **abjectly** *adv.*

abjure /əbˈdʒʊə(r)/ *v* [Tn] (*fml*) promise or swear to give up (a claim, an opinion, a belief, etc); renounce formally: *abjure one's religion.* ▷ **abjuration** /ˌæbdʒʊəˈreɪʃn/ *n* [U, C].

ablation /əˈbleɪʃn/ *n* [U] **1** removal of body tissue by means of surgery. **2** melting of the front part of a space vehicle caused by friction as it re-enters the earth's atmosphere: *Ablation is normally prevented by a heat shield.*

ablative /ˈæblətɪv/ *n* (usu *sing*) (*grammar*) special form of a noun, a pronoun or an adjective used (in some inflected languages) to indicate or describe esp the agent or instrument of an action.

▷ **ablative** *adj* of or in the ablative.

ablaut /ˈæblaʊt/ *n* [U] (*linguistics*) systematic way in which vowels change in related forms of a word, esp in Indo-European languages (eg *drive, drove, driven*).

ablaze /əˈbleɪz/ *adj* [pred] **1** burning; on fire: *set sth ablaze* ○ *The whole building was soon ablaze.* **2** ~ (**with sth**) (*fig*) (**a**) very bright; glittering: *The palace was ablaze with lights.* (**b**) very excited: *His face was ablaze with anger.*

able[1] /ˈeɪbl/ *adj* **be** ~ **to do sth** (used as a *modal v*) have the power, means or opportunity to do sth: *The child is not yet able to write.* ○ *Will you be able to come?* ○ *You are better able to do it than I (am).*

able[2] /ˈeɪbl/ *adj* (**-r**, **-st** /ˈeɪblɪst/) having knowledge or skill; competent; capable: *an able worker* ○ *the ablest/most able student in the class.*

▷ **ably** /ˈeɪblɪ/ *adv* in an able manner: *They have done their work very ably.*

□ ˌ**able-ˈbodied** /-ˈbɒdɪd/ *adj* healthy, fit and strong.

ˌ**able(-ˌbodied) ˈseaman** (*abbr* **AB**) sailor who is trained and fit for all duties. ⇨ App 4.

-able, -ible /-əbl/ *suff* **1** (with *ns* forming *adjs*) having or showing the quality of: *fashionable* ○ *comfortable.* **2** (with *vs* forming *adjs*) (**a**) that may or must be: *eatable* ○ *payable* ○ *reducible.* (**b**) apt to: *changeable* ○ *perishable.*

▷ **-ability, -ibility** (forming uncountable *ns*): *profitability* ○ *reversibility.*

-ably, -ibly (forming *advs*): *noticeably* ○ *incredibly.*

ablution /əˈbluːʃn/ *n* (usu *pl*) (*fml or joc*) ceremonial washing of the body, hands, sacred vessels, etc: *perform one's ablutions,* ie wash oneself.

ABM /ˌeɪ biː ˈem/ *abbr* anti-ballistic-missile.

abnegation /ˌæbnɪˈgeɪʃn/ *n* [U] (*fml*) **1** denial or renunciation (of a doctrine). **2** (also ˌ**self-abneˈgation**) self-sacrifice.

abnormal /æbˈnɔːml/ *adj* different, esp in an undesirable way, from what is normal, ordinary or expected: *abnormal specimens, weather conditions, behaviour* ○ *be physically/mentally abnormal.* ▷ **abnormality** /ˌæbnɔːˈmælətɪ/ *n* [U, C]. **abnormally** /æbˈnɔːməlɪ/ *adv*: *abnormally large feet.*

Abo /ˈæbəʊ/ *n* (*pl* ~**s**) (⚠ *Austral sl offensive*) = ABORIGINAL.

aboard /əˈbɔːd/ *adv part, prep* on or into a ship, an aircraft, a train or (*esp US*) a bus: *We went/climbed aboard.* ○ *Welcome aboard!* ○ *All aboard!* ie The ship, etc is about to depart. ○ *He was already aboard the ship.*

abode[1] /əˈbəʊd/ *n* [sing] (*fml or rhet or joc*) **1** house; home: *one's place of abode,* ie where one lives ○ *Welcome to our humble abode!* **2** (idm) **no fixed abode/address** ⇨ FIX[1].

abode[2] *pt, pp* of ABIDE 3.

abolish /əˈbɒlɪʃ/ *v* [Tn] end the existence of (a custom, an institution, etc): *Should the death penalty be abolished?*

▷ **abolition** /ˌæbəˈlɪʃn/ *n* [U] abolishing or being abolished: *the abolition of slavery, hanging.* **abolitionist** /ˌæbəˈlɪʃənɪst/ *n* person who favours abolition, esp of capital punishment.

A-bomb /ˈeɪ bɒm/ *n* = ATOMIC BOMB (ATOMIC).

abominable /əˈbɒmɪnəbl; *US* -mən-/ *adj* **1** ~ (**to sb**) (*fml*) causing disgust; detestable: *Your behaviour is abominable to me.* **2** (*infml*) very unpleasant: *abominable weather, food, music.* ▷ **abominably** /əˈbɒmɪnəblɪ; *US* -mən-/ *adv.*

□ **Abominable Snowman** = YETI.

abominate /əˈbɒmɪneɪt; *US* -mən-/ *v* [Tn] feel hatred or disgust for (sth/sb); detest; loathe: *I abominate fascism.*

▷ **abomination** /əˌbɒmɪˈneɪʃn; *US* -mən-/ *n* **1** [U] feeling of disgust and extreme hatred: *hold sth in abomination.* **2** [C] act, habit, person or thing that is hated: *That new concrete building is an abomination.*

aboriginal /ˌæbəˈrɪdʒənl/ *adj* (esp of people) inhabiting a land from a very early period, esp before the arrival of colonists: *aboriginal inhabitants, plants.*

▷ **aboriginal** *n* **1** aboriginal inhabitant. **2** (also **Aboriginal**) aboriginal inhabitant of Australia.

aborigines /ˌæbəˈrɪdʒəniːz/ *n* [pl] aboriginal inhabitants, esp (**Aborigines**) those of Australia.

▷ **aborigine** /ˌæbəˈrɪdʒənɪ/ *n* (*infml*) aboriginal inhabitant.

abort /əˈbɔːt/ *v* **1** (*medical*) (**a**) [Tn] cause (sb/sth) to undergo abortion: *abort an expectant mother, a deformed foetus, the pregnancy.* (**b**) [I] undergo abortion; miscarry: *She aborted after four months.* **2** [I, Tn] (cause sth to) end prematurely and unsuccessfully: *abort a space mission,* ie cancel it in space, usu because of mechanical trouble ○ *abort a computer program.*

▷ **aborted** *adj* **1** undeveloped. **2** (*biology*) rudimentary: *Thorns are aborted branches.*

abortion /əˈbɔːʃn/ *n* **1** (**a**) [U] (esp deliberately induced) expulsion of a foetus from the womb before it is able to survive, esp in the first 28 weeks of pregnancy: *Many people are anti-abortion.* (**b**) [C] operation to terminate a pregnancy: *She had an abortion.* Cf MISCARRIAGE 1. **2** [C] project or action that has failed completely.

▷ **abortionist** /əˈbɔːʃənɪst/ *n* person who performs abortions, esp illegally.

abortive /əˈbɔːtɪv/ *adj* coming to nothing; unsuccessful: *an abortive attempt, coup, mission* ○ *plans that proved abortive.* ▷ **abortively** *adv.*

abound /əˈbaʊnd/ *v* **1** [I] be very plentiful; exist in great numbers: *Oranges abound here all the year round.* **2** [Ipr] ~ **in/with sth** have sth in great numbers or quantities: *The river abounds in/with fish.*

about[1] /əˈbaʊt/ *adv* **1** (also *esp US* **around**) a little more or less than; a little before or after; approximately: *It costs about £10.* ○ *He's about the same height as you.* ○ *She drove for about ten miles.* ○ *They waited for about an hour.* **2** (*infml*) nearly: *I'm (just) about ready.* **3** (*infml*) (in understatements): *I've had just about enough,* ie quite enough. ○ *He's been promoted, and about time too,* ie it ought to have happened earlier. **4** (idm) **that's about ˈit/the ˈsize of it** (*infml*) that is how I see it or assess it.

about[2] /əˈbaʊt/ *adv part* (in senses 1, 2 and 3 *esp Brit*; in these senses also, *esp US,* **around**) **1** (**a**) (indicating movement) here and there, in many directions; all around: *The children were rushing aˈbout.* ○ *The boys were climbing about on the rocks.* (**b**) (indicating position) here and there (in a place): *books lying about on the ˈfloor* ○ *people sitting about on the ˈgrass.* **2** in circulation; moving around: *There was nobody aˈbout,* ie Nobody was to be seen. ○ *There's a lot of ˈflu about,* ie Many people have flu. ○ *He'll soon be aˈbout again,* eg after an illness. **3** somewhere near; not far off: *She's ˈsomewhere about.* **4** facing around: *put the ship aˈbout,* ie so as to face in the opposite direction ○ *It's the wrong way aˈbout.* ○ *Aˌbout ˈturn!* ie Turn to face the opposite way (as a military command).

□ aˌ**bout-ˈturn** (*US* aˌ**bout-ˈface**) *n* **1** turn made so as to face the opposite direction. **2** (*fig*) complete change of opinion, policy, etc: *These new measures indicate an about-turn in government policy.*

about[3] /əˈbaʊt/ *prep* (in senses 1, 2 and 5 *US* **around**; *Brit* also **around** in these senses) **1** (**a**) (indicating movement) here and there in (a place); in many directions in: *walking about the town* ○ *travelling about the world* ○ *Look aˈbout you.* (**b**) (indicating position, state, etc) here and there in (a place); at points throughout: *papers strewn about the room.* **2** near to (a place); not far off from: *She's somewhere about the place.* ○ *I dropped the key somewhere about here.* **3** on the subject of (sb/sth); in connection with; concerning or regarding: *a book about flowers* ○ *Tell me about it.* ○ *What is he so angry about?* ○ *He is careless about his personal appearance.* ⇨ Usage. **4** concerned or occupied with (sth): *And while you're aˈbout it...,* ie while you're doing that... ○ *Mind what you're about,* ie Be careful. **5** at a time near to; at approximately: *He arrived (at) about ten o'clock.* **6** (idm) **be about to do sth** intend to do sth immediately; be on the point of doing sth: *As I was about to say when you interrupted me...* ○ *We're about to start.* ○ *I'm not about to admit defeat,* ie I have no intention of doing so. **how/what about...?** (**a**) (used when asking for information or to get sb's opinion): *What about his qualifications* (ie Is he qualified) *for the job?* (**b**) (used when making a suggestion): *How about going to France for our holidays?*

NOTE ON USAGE: Both **about** and **on** can mean 'on the subject of'. A book, film or lecture **on** Chinese art, education or prehistory suggests a serious, academic presentation. A book, discussion or TV programme **about** China, schools or dinosaurs is of more general interest and more informal.

above[1] /əˈbʌv/ *adv* **1** at or to a higher point; overhead: *My bedroom is immediately above.* ○ *Put the biscuits on the shelf above.* ○ *Seen from above, the fields looked like a geometrical pattern.* ○ *A voice called down to us from above.* **2** earlier or further back (in a book, an article, etc): *in the above paragraph* ○ *As was stated above...* ○ *See above, page 97.* **3** (*rhet*) in or to heaven: *the powers above* ○ *blessings from above* ○ *gone above.* Cf BELOW, UNDER, UNDERNEATH.

□ ˌ**above-ˈmentioned**, ˌ**above-ˈnamed** *adjs* mentioned or named earlier (in this book, article, etc). Cf UNDERMENTIONED.

above[2] /əˈbʌv/ *prep* **1** (**a**) higher than (sth): *The sun rose above the horizon.* ○ *The water came above our knees.* ○ *We were flying above the clouds.* (Cf *We were flying over/across the Sahara.*). (**b**) higher in rank, position, importance, etc than (sb/sth): *A captain in the Navy ranks above a captain in the Army.* ○ *She married above her,* ie married sb from a higher social class than herself. **2** greater in number, price, weight, etc than (sth): *The temperature has been above the average recently.* ○ *There's nothing in this shop above/over a dollar.* ○ *It weighs above/over ten tons.* ○ *Applicants must be above/over the age of 18.* **3** (*fml*) more than (sb/sth): *Should a soldier value honour above life?* **4** beyond the reach of (sth), because too good, great, etc: *He is above suspicion,* ie is not suspected because he is completely trusted. ○ *Her behaviour was above/*

beyond reproach. **5** too good, etc for (sth): *She wouldn't lie — she's above that.* ○ *She is above deceit*, ie is not deceitful. ○ *Although she's the manager, she's not above asking* (ie she isn't too proud to ask) *for advice from her staff.* **6** upstream from (a place): *the waterfall above the bridge.* **7** (idm) **above ˈall** most important of all; especially: *He longs above all (else) to see his family again.* **aˈbove oneself** too pleased with oneself; conceited; arrogant. Cf BELOW, UNDER, UNDERNEATH.

□ **above-board** *adv, adj* ⇨ ABOVE BOARD (BOARD[1]).

NOTE ON USAGE: **1** When they indicate a position higher than something, **above** and **over** can often be used in the same way: *They built a new room above/over the garage.* **2** When there is movement across something, only **over** can be used: *She threw the ball over the fence.* ○ *jump over the stream.* **3 Over** can also mean 'covering': *Pull the sheet over the body.* ○ *Throw the water over the flames.* **4 Over** and **above** can mean 'more than' in number, measurement, etc. **Above** is generally used in relation to a minimum or standard: *2000 ft above sea-level* ○ *above average intelligence/height* ○ *two degrees above zero* ○ *He's over fifty.* ○ *She's been here over two hours.*

abracadabra /ˌæbrəkəˈdæbrə/ *n, interj* meaningless word said as a supposedly magic formula esp by conjurors while performing magic tricks: *'Abracadabra,' said the conjuror as he pulled the rabbit from the hat.*

abrade /əˈbreɪd/ *v* [Tn] wear away (skin, fabric, rock, etc) by rubbing; scrape off.

Abraham /ˈeɪbrəhæm/ (in the Old Testament) ancestor of the Jewish nation. God promised to give him and his descendants the land of *Canaan to live in, and tested his obedience by asking him to kill his son *Isaac.

abrasion /əˈbreɪʒn/ *n* **1** [U] scraping or wearing away; rubbing off. **2** [C] damaged area, esp of the skin, caused by rubbing, etc.

abrasive /əˈbreɪsɪv/ *adj* **1** that scrapes or rubs sth away; rough: *abrasive substances, surfaces, materials.* **2** (*fig*) tending to hurt other people's feelings; harsh and offensive: *an abrasive person, personality, tone of voice.*

▷ **abrasive** *n* [U, C] substance used for grinding or polishing surfaces.

abreast /əˈbrest/ *adv* **1** ~ **(of sb/sth)** side by side (with sb/sth) and facing the same way: *cycling two abreast* ○ *The boat came abreast of us and signalled us to stop.* **2** (idm) **be/keep abreast of sth** be or remain up to date with or well-informed about sth: *You should read the newspapers to keep abreast of current affairs.*

abridge /əˈbrɪdʒ/ *v* [Tn] make (a book, etc) shorter, esp by using fewer words; condense: *an abridged edition/version of 'War and Peace'.*

▷ **abridgement** (also **abridgment**) *n* **1** [U] shortening of a book, etc. **2** [C] book, etc that has been abridged.

abroad /əˈbrɔːd/ *adv* **1** in or to a foreign country or countries; away from one's own country: *be, go, live, travel abroad* ○ *visitors (who have come) from abroad*, ie from another country. **2** being circulated widely: *There's a rumour abroad that...*, ie People are saying that.... **3** (*arch or rhet*) out of doors: *Have you ventured abroad yet today?*

abrogate /ˈæbrəgeɪt/ *v* [Tn] (*fml*) cancel, repeal or annul (sth): *abrogate a law, custom, treaty.* ▷ **abrogation** /ˌæbrəˈgeɪʃn/ *n* [U, C].

abrupt /əˈbrʌpt/ *adj* **1** sudden and unexpected: *a road with many abrupt turns* ○ *an abrupt ending, change, departure.* **2** (**a**) (of speech, etc) not smooth; disconnected; disjointed: *short abrupt sentences* ○ *an abrupt style of writing.* (**b**) (of behaviour) rough; curt: *He has an abrupt manner*, ie makes no attempt to be polite. **3** (of a slope) very steep. ▷ **abruptly** *adv.* **abruptness** *n* [U].

abscess /ˈæbses/ *n* swollen part of the body in which a thick yellowish liquid (called *pus*) has collected: *abscesses on the gums.*

abscissa /æbˈsɪsə/ *n* (*mathematics*) the horizontal or *x*-co-ordinate in a rectangular Cartesian co-ordinate system. Cf ORDINATE. ⇨ illus at CARTESIAN.

abscission /æbˈsɪʃn, -ˈsɪʒn/ *n* [U] (*botany*) natural process by which leaves, flowers, etc become separated from and fall off plants.

abscond /əbˈskɒnd/ *v* **1** [I, Ipr] ~ **(from...)** go away suddenly and secretly, esp in order to avoid arrest: *He absconded from the country.* **2** [Ipr] ~ **with sth** go away taking sth to which one has no right: *He absconded with £8 000 stolen from his employer.*

abseil /ˈæbseɪl/ *v* [I, Ipr, Ip] (in mountaineering) descend a steep slope or vertical rock face by using a double rope that is fixed at a higher point: *abseil down the mountain.*

▷ **abseil** *n* act of abseiling.

absence /ˈæbsəns/ *n* **1** ~ **(from...)** (**a**) [U] being away: *His repeated absence (from school) is worrying.* ○ *It happened during/in your absence.* ○ *In the absence of the manager* (ie While he is away) *I shall be in charge.* ○ *during his absence in America*, ie while he was there ○ (*saying*) *Absence makes the heart grow fonder*, ie Being separated from people one loves often makes one love them more. (**b**) [C] occasion or time of being away: *numerous absences from school* ○ *throughout his long absence* ○ *after an absence of three months.* Cf PRESENCE. **2** [U] lack; non-existence: *the absence of definite proof.* **3** (idm) **ˌabsence of ˈmind** failure to think about what one is doing; absent-mindedness. **conspicuous by one's absence** ⇨ CONSPICUOUS. **leave of absence** ⇨ LEAVE[2].

absent[1] /ˈæbsənt/ *adj* **1** ~ **(from sth)** (**a**) not present (at sth); at another place (than...): *be absent from school, a meeting, work* ○ *absent friends.* (**b**) not existing; lacking: *Love was totally absent from his childhood.* **2** showing that one is not really thinking about what is being said or done around one: *an absent expression, look, etc.*

□ **ˌabsent-ˈminded** *adj* with one's mind on other things; forgetful: *become absent-minded with age.* **ˌabsent-ˈmindedly** *adv.* **ˌabsent-ˈmindedness** *n* [U].

absent[2] /əbˈsent/ *v* [Tn, Tn·pr] ~ **oneself (from sth)** (*fml*) not be present (at sth); stay away (from sth): *He deliberately absented himself from the meeting.*

absentee /ˌæbsənˈtiː/ *n* person who is absent.

▷ **absenteeism** /ˌæbsənˈtiːɪzəm/ *n* [U] frequent absence from school or work, esp without good reason.

□ **ˌabsentee ˈballot** (*US*) voting in advance by people (**absentee voters**) who will be away on the day of an election.

ˌabsentee ˈlandlord person who does not live at and rarely visits the property he lets.

absinthe (also **absinth**) /ˈæbsɪnθ/ *n* [U] bitter green alcoholic drink made with wormwood and other herbs.

absolute /ˈæbsəluːt/ *adj* **1** (**a**) complete; total: *have absolute trust in a person* ○ *tell the absolute truth* ○ *absolute ignorance, silence* ○ *You're an absolute fool!* (**b**) certain; undoubted: *have absolute proof* ○ *It's an absolute fact.* **2** unlimited; unrestricted; unqualified: *absolute power.* **3** having unlimited power; despotic: *an absolute ruler.* **4** not relative; independent: *There is no absolute standard for beauty.*

▷ **the absolute** *n* [sing] (*philosophy*) that which is regarded as existing independently of anything else.

□ **ˌabsolute ˈalcohol** = ETHANOL.

ˌabsolute maˈjority majority over all rivals combined; more than half.

ˌabsolute ˈpitch = PERFECT PITCH (PERFECT[1]).

ˌabsolute ˈtemperature temperature measured from absolute zero.

ˌabsolute ˈzero lowest temperature that is theoretically possible. ⇨ App 10.

absolutely /ˈæbsəluːtlɪ/ *adv* **1** completely: *It's absolutely impossible.* ○ *You're absolutely right.* **2** unreservedly; unconditionally: *I absolutely refuse.* ○ *He believes absolutely that....* **3** not relatively; in an absolute(4) sense: *The term is being used absolutely.* **4** (used to give emphasis) positively: *It's absolutely pouring down.* ○ *He did absolutely no work*, ie no work at all. **5** /ˌæbsəˈluːtlɪ/ (*infml*) (used in answer to a question or as a comment) yes; certainly; quite so: *'Don't you agree?' 'Oh, absolutely!'*

absolution /ˌæbsəˈluːʃn/ *n* [U] (esp in the Christian Church) formal declaration by a priest that a person's sins have been forgiven: *grant sb absolution* ○ *pronounce absolution.*

absolutism /ˈæbsəluːtɪzəm/ *n* [U] (*politics*) (**a**) principle that those responsible for government should have unlimited power. (**b**) government with unlimited power. ▷ **absolutist** *n.*

absolve /əbˈzɒlv/ *v* [Tn, Tn·pr] ~ **sb (from/of sth)** **1** (*fml esp law*) clear sb (of guilt); declare sb free (from blame, a promise, a duty, etc): *The court absolved the accused man (from all responsibility for her death).* **2** give absolution to sb: *absolve repentant sinners.*

absorb /əbˈsɔːb/ *v* [Tn] **1** (**a**) take (sth) in; suck up: *absorb heat* ○ *Fish absorb oxygen through their gills.* ○ *Dry sand absorbs water.* ○ *Aspirin is quickly absorbed by/into the body.* ○ (*fig*) *Clever children absorb knowledge easily.* (**b**) include (sth/sb) as part of itself or oneself; incorporate; merge with: *The larger firm absorbed the smaller one.* ○ *The surrounding villages have been absorbed by/into the growing city.* **2** reduce the effect of (an impact, a difficulty, etc): *Buffers absorbed most of the shock.* **3** hold the attention or interest of (sb) fully: *His business absorbs him.*

▷ **absorbed** *adj* with one's attention fully held: *absorbed in her book.*

absorbent /-ənt/ *n, adj* (substance) that is able to take in moisture, etc: *absorbent cotton wool.*

absorbing *adj* holding the attention fully: *an absorbing film.*

absorption /əbˈsɔːpʃn/ *n* [U] ~ **(by/in sth)** absorbing or being absorbed: *His work suffered because of his total absorption in sport.*

abstain /əbˈsteɪn/ *v* [I, Ipr] ~ **(from sth)** **1** keep oneself from doing or enjoying sth, esp from taking alcoholic drinks; refrain. **2** decline to use one's vote: *At the last election he abstained (from voting/the vote).*

▷ **abstainer** *n* person who abstains: *a total abstainer*, ie one who never takes alcoholic drinks.

abstemious /əbˈstiːmɪəs/ *adj* not taking much food or drink; not self-indulgent; moderate: *an abstemious person, meal* ○ *abstemious habits.* ▷ **abstemiously** *adv.* **abstemiousness** *n* [U].

abstention /əbˈstenʃn/ *n* (**a**) [U] ~ **(from sth)** abstaining, esp not using one's vote at an election. (**b**) [C] instance of this: *five votes in favour of the proposal, three against and two abstentions.*

abstinence /ˈæbstɪnəns/ *n* [U] ~ **(from sth)** abstaining, esp from food or alcoholic drinks: *total abstinence* ○ *The nuns had taken a vow of abstinence.* ▷ **abstinent** /ˈæbstɪnənt/ *adj* [usu pred].

abstract[1] /ˈæbstrækt/ *adj* **1** existing in thought or as an idea but not having a physical or practical existence: *We may talk of beautiful things, but beauty itself is abstract.* ○ *He has some abstract* (ie vague, impractical) *notion of wanting to change the world.* **2** (of art) not representing objects in a realistic way but expressing the artist's ideas and feelings about certain aspects of them: *an abstract painting, painter.* Cf CONCRETE[1] 1.

□ **ˌabstract exˈpressionism** type of painting which originated in the USA in the late 1940s, in which the application of paint to canvas is done to illustrate the painter's feelings rather than to represent a particular subject. The paintings often give the impression of a random pattern of marks. Painters associated with the school include Jackson *Pollock, Robert *Motherwell and Mark *Rothko. Cf ACTION PAINTING (ACTION).

ˌabstract ˈnoun noun that refers to an abstract quality or state, eg *goodness* or *freedom.*

abstract[2] /ˈæbstrækt/ *n* **1** abstract idea or quality. **2** example of abstract art: *a painter of abstracts.* **3** short account of the contents of a book, etc;

summary: *an abstract of a lecture.* **4** (idm) **in the ˈabstract** in a theoretical way: *Consider the problem in the abstract,* ie as if it had no relation to any specific object, person, fact, etc.

abstract[3] /əbˈstrækt/ *v* **1** [Tn, Tn·pr] ~ **sth (from sth)** remove sth; separate sth (from sth): *abstract metal from ore.* **2** [Tn] make a written summary of (a book, etc).

abstracted /æbˈstræktɪd/ *adj* thinking of other things; not paying attention. ▷ **abstractedly** *adv.*

abstraction /əbˈstrækʃn/ *n* **1** [U] ~ **of sth (from sth)** removing; taking away. **2** [C] abstract idea: *lose oneself in abstractions,* ie become unrealistic in one's thinking. **3** [U] absent-mindedness.

abstruse /əbˈstru:s/ *adj* difficult to understand. ▷ **abstrusely** *adv.* **abstruseness** *n* [U].

absurd /əbˈsɜ:d/ *adj* **1** unreasonable; not sensible: *What an absurd suggestion!* ○ *It was absurd of you to suggest such a thing.* **2** foolish in a funny way; ridiculous: *That uniform makes them look absurd.* ○ *the Theatre of the Absurd.* ▷ **absurdity** *n* [U, C]. **absurdly** *adv.*

abundance /əˈbʌndəns/ *n* [U, sing] quantity that is more than enough; plenty: *There was good food in abundance/an abundance of good food at the party.*

abundant /əˈbʌndənt/ *adj* **1** more than enough; plentiful: *an abundant supply of fruit* ○ *We have abundant proof of his guilt.* **2** [pred] ~ **in sth** having plenty of sth; rich in sth: *a land abundant in minerals.*

▷ **abundantly** *adv* plentifully: *be abundantly supplied with fruit* ○ *He's made his views abundantly* (ie very) *clear.*

abuse[1] /əˈbju:z/ *v* [Tn] **1** make bad or wrong use of (sth): *abuse one's authority, sb's hospitality, the confidence placed in one.* **2** treat (sb) badly; exploit: *a much abused wife.* Cf MISUSE. **3** speak insultingly to or about (sb); attack in words.

abuse[2] /əˈbju:s/ *n* **1** (a) [U] wrong or bad use or treatment of sth/sb: *drug abuse* ○ *child abuse.* (b) [C] ~ **of sth** wrong or bad use of sth: *an abuse of trust, privilege, authority.* **2** [C] unjust or corrupt practice: *put a stop to political abuses.* **3** [U] insulting words; offensive or coarse language: *hurl (a stream of) abuse at sb* ○ *The word 'bastard' is often used as a term of abuse.*

abusive /əˈbju:sɪv/ *adj* (of speech or a person) criticizing harshly and rudely; insulting: *abusive language, remarks, etc* ○ *He became abusive,* ie began uttering angry insults, curses, etc. ▷ **abusively** *adv.*

abut /əˈbʌt/ *v* (-tt-) [Ipr] ~ **on/against sth** (of land or a building) have a common boundary or side with sth; adjoin sth: *His land abuts on the motorway.* ○ *Their house abuts against ours.*

abutment /əˈbʌtmənt/ *n* (*engineering*) structure that bears the weight of a bridge or an arch.

abysmal /əˈbɪzməl/ *adj* **1** (*infml*) extremely bad: *live in abysmal conditions* ○ *His manners are abysmal.* **2** extreme; utter: *abysmal ignorance.* ▷ **abysmally** *adv.*

abyss /əˈbɪs/ *n* hole so deep that it seems to have no bottom: (*fig*) *an abyss of ignorance, despair, loneliness, etc.*

AC (also **ac**) /ˌeɪ ˈsi:/ *abbr* alternating current. Cf DC 3.

a/c *abbr* (*commerce*) account (current): *charge to a/c 319054* ○ *a/c payee only,* ie on a cheque, written to show that it must be paid into the account of the person to whom it is made out, and cannot be exchanged for cash.

acacia /əˈkeɪʃə/ *n* any of several trees with yellow or white flowers, esp one from which gum arabic is obtained.

academic /ˌækəˈdemɪk/ *adj* **1** [attrib] of (teaching or learning in) schools, colleges, etc: *the ˌacademic ˈyear,* ie the total time within a year when teaching is done in schools, etc, usu starting in September or October ○ *ˌacademic ˈfreedom,* ie liberty to teach and discuss educational matters without interference from politicians, etc. **2** [attrib] scholarly; not technical or practical: *academic subjects.* **3** of theoretical interest only: *a matter of academic concern* ○ *The question is purely academic,* ie not relevant to practical affairs but still interesting.

▷ **academic** *n* teacher at a university, college, etc; professional scholar.

academically /-klɪ/ *adv.*

academician /əˌkædəˈmɪʃn; *US* ˌækədəˈmɪʃn/ *n* member of an academy(3b).

Académie française /əˌkædəmɪ frɑ:nˈsez/ **the Académie française** French literary academy founded in 1635 in order to control the development of the French language, esp by compiling and revising a dictionary. Membership is limited to 40 and is an honour given to important writers.

academy /əˈkædəmɪ/ *n* **1** [C] school for special training: *an aˌcademy of ˈmusic* ○ *a ˈnaval/ˈmilitary academy.* **2** [C] (in Scotland) secondary school. **3** (a) **the Academy** [Gp] *Plato's school of philosophy, named after the garden near Athens where he taught. (b) (usu **Academy**) [C] society of distinguished scholars or artists; society for cultivating art, literature, etc, of which membership is an honour: *The Royal Academy (of Arts).*

□ **Aˌcademy Aˈward** any of the annual awards for achievement in the cinema given by the US Academy of Motion Picture Arts and Sciences. Cf OSCAR.

Acadian /əˈkeɪdɪən/ *n, adj* (any of the inhabitants) of a former French colony in eastern N America, in the area of present-day *Nova Scotia, some of whose descendants now live in *Louisiana, USA. Cf CAJUN.

acanthus /əˈkænθəs/ *n* [U, C] **1** Mediterranean plant with large prickly leaves. **2** carved representation of the leaf of this plant, used as a decoration (eg on ancient Greek columns).

a cappella /ˌɑ: kəˈpelə/ *adj, adv* (of choral music) without accompaniment.

ACAS /ˈeɪkæs/ *abbr* (*Brit*) Advisory, Conciliation and Arbitration Service, for helping with negotiation during industrial disputes. ⇨ article at TRADE UNION.

accede /əkˈsi:d/ *v* [I, Ipr] ~ **(to sth)** (*fml*) **1** (a) take office: *accede to the chancellorship.* (b) become monarch: *Queen Victoria acceded to the throne in 1837.* **2** agree (to a request, proposal, etc).

accelerando /ækˌseləˈrændəʊ/ *adv, adj* (*music*) with gradually increasing speed.

▷ **accelerando** *n* (*pl* ~**s** or **-di**) piece of music (to be) played in this way. Cf RALLENTANDO.

accelerate /əkˈseləreɪt/ *v* **1** [Tn] make (sth) move faster or happen earlier; increase the speed of: *accelerating the rate of growth.* **2** [I] move or happen more quickly: *The car accelerated as it overtook me.* Cf DECELERATE.

▷ **acceleration** /əkˌseləˈreɪʃn/ *n* [U] **1** making or being made quicker; increase in speed: *an acceleration in the rate of economic growth.* **2** (of a vehicle) ability to gain speed: *a car with good acceleration.*

accelerator /əkˈseləreɪtə(r)/ *n* **1** device for increasing speed, esp the pedal in a car, etc that controls the speed of the engine. ⇨ illus at CAR. **2** (*physics*) apparatus for causing charged particles to move at high speeds. **3** (*chemistry*) substance that causes a chemical reaction to happen more quickly.

accent /ˈæksent, ˈæksənt/ *n* **1** [C] emphasis given to a syllable or word by means of stress or pitch: *In the word 'today' the accent is on the second syllable.* **2** [C] mark or symbol, usu above a letter, used in writing and printing to indicate such emphasis or the quality of a vowel sound. **3** [C, U] national, local or individual way of pronouncing words: *speak English with a foreign accent* ○ *have an American accent* ○ *a voice without (a trace of) accent.* Cf BROGUE, DIALECT. ⇨ article. **4** [C usu *sing,* U] special emphasis given to sth: *In all our products the accent is on quality.*

▷ **accent** /ækˈsent/ *v* [Tn] **1** pronounce (a word or syllable) with emphasis. **2** write accents on (words, etc).

accentuate /əkˈsentʃʊeɪt/ *v* [Tn] make (sth) very noticeable or prominent; emphasize: *The tight jumper only accentuated his fat stomach.* ▷ **accentuation** /əkˌsentʃʊˈeɪʃn/ *n* [U].

accept /əkˈsept/ *v* **1** (a) [Tn] take (sth offered) willingly: *accept a gift, a piece of advice, an apology.* (b) [I, Tn] say yes to (an offer, invitation, etc): *She offered him a lift and he accepted (it).* ○ *He proposed marriage and she accepted (him).* (c) [Tn] receive (sth/sb) as adequate or suitable: *Will you accept a cheque?* ○ *The machine only accepts 10p coins.* ○ *The college I applied to has accepted me.* **2** [Tn] be willing to agree to (sth): *accept the judge's decision* ○ *I accept the proposed changes.* **3** [Tn] take upon oneself (a responsibility, etc): *He accepts blame for the accident,* ie agrees that it was his fault. ○ *You must accept the consequences of your action.* **4** [Tn, Tf, Tw, Cn·n/a] ~ **sth (as sth)** take sth as true; believe sth: *I cannot accept that he is to blame.* ○ *We do not accept your explanation/what you have said.* ○ *Can we accept his account as the true version?* ○ *It is an accepted fact,* ie sth that everyone thinks is true. **5** [Tn] treat (sb/sth) as welcome: *He was never really accepted by his classmates.*

acceptable /əkˈseptəbl/ *adj* ~ **(to sb)** **1** (a) worth accepting: *Is the proposal acceptable to you?* (b) welcome: *A cup of tea would be most acceptable.* **2** tolerable: *an acceptable risk, sacrifice, profit margin.* ▷ **acceptability** /əkˌseptəˈbɪlətɪ/ *n* [U]. **acceptably** /-blɪ/ *adv.*

acceptance /əkˈseptəns/ *n* **1** [C, U] (act of) accepting or being accepted: *Since we sent out the invitations we've received five acceptances and one refusal.* **2** [U] favourable reception; approval: *The new laws gained widespread acceptance.* **3** [C] (*commerce*) (a) agreement to pay a bill. (b) bill accepted in this way.

acceptor /əkˈseptə(r)/ *n* (*physics*) atom or molecule able to receive an extra electron.

access /ˈækses/ *n* [U] **1** ~ **(to sth)** means of approaching or entering (a place); way in: *The only access to the farmhouse is across the fields.* ○ *The village is easy/difficult of access,* ie easy/difficult to reach. **2** ~ **(to sth/sb)** opportunity or right to use sth or approach sb: *get access to classified information* ○ *Students must have access to a good library.* ○ *Only high officials had access to the president.* **3** ~ **(to sb)** divorced parent's legal right to see his or her children when the other parent has been given the right to look after them: *Will the judge grant him access (to his daughter)?*

▷ **access** *v* [Tn] (*computing*) get information from or put information into (a computer file): *She accessed three different files to find the correct information.* ○ *The files were accessed every day to keep them up to date.*

□ **ˈaccess road** **1** (*esp US*) = SLIP-ROAD (SLIP[2]). **2** road giving access to a place, site, etc.

ˈaccess time (*computing*) time taken to obtain information stored in a computer.

accessible /əkˈsesəbl/ *adj* ~ **(to sb)** that can be reached, used, etc: *a beach accessible only from the sea* ○ *documents not accessible to the public.* ▷ **accessibility** /əkˌsesəˈbɪlətɪ/ *n* [U].

accession /ækˈseʃn/ *n* ~ **(to sth)** **1** [U] reaching a rank or position: *celebrating the queen's accession (to the throne).* **2** (a) [C] thing added, esp a new item in a library, museum, etc: *recent accessions to the art gallery.* (b) [U] action of being added: *the accession of new members to the party.*

▷ **accession** *v* [Tn] record the addition of (a new item) to a library, museum, etc.

accessory /əkˈsesərɪ/ *n* **1** (usu *pl*) (a) thing that is a useful or decorative extra but that is not essential; minor fitting or attachment: *bicycle accessories,* eg lamp, pump, etc. (b) small article of (esp women's) dress, eg a belt, handbag, etc. **2** (also **accessary**) ~ **(to sth)** (*law*) person who helps another in a crime: *He was charged with being an accessory to murder.* **3** (idm) **accessory before/after the fact** (*law*) person who, although not present when a crime is committed, helps the person committing it beforehand/afterwards.

▷ **accessory** *adj* additional; extra.

acciaccatura /əˌtʃækəˈtʊərə/ *n* additional note played or sung as quickly as possible before a main note of a melody or sounded with it. ⇨ illus at GRACE-NOTE (GRACE). Cf APPOGGIATURA, GRACE-NOTE (GRACE).

Accent and Dialect

Although the words 'accent' and 'dialect' are often used interchangeably, in linguistics a clear distinction is made between accent as the particular features of a person's pronunciation, and dialect, meaning a variety of a language with particular vocabulary and grammar. Dialects may be regionally or socially based.

In Britain, Received Pronunciation (RP) originated as the social accent spoken, with comparatively little regional variation, by the educated upper classes, particularly in the public schools. Because there was very little regional variation amongst speakers of RP it was used by BBC announcers and newsreaders from the early days of broadcasting, since it could be understood in all parts of the country. Today, the BBC and educated speakers in general show far more regional variation than previously and there are many modified forms of RP. Especially among younger people, regionally marked accents are now increasingly preferred to RP, and the language of broadcasters and actors recorded even a few decades ago often sounds rather stilted and formal to the modern ear.

It is often assumed that regional dialects are gradually disappearing. In fact, although rural dialects are dying out in Britain, urban dialects are spoken by increasing numbers of people and are frequently heard on radio and television. Urban areas whose dialects are readily recognized by the population as a whole are London (especially the Cockney dialect of east London), Liverpool (Scouse), Tyneside in the north-east of England (Geordie) and Birmingham (Brummie). One of the most widely recognized rural dialects is that of the West Country, spoken in Devon and Cornwall.

Cockneys are renowned for their distinctive and colourful speech, with use of rhyming slang ('apples and pears' for 'stairs'), dropping of initial 'h' (''ouse' for 'house'), weakened vowel sounds ('mite' for 'mate'), and the substitution of some consonants, such as 'w' for final 'l' ('new' for 'kneel'), or 'f' for 'th' ('fink' for 'think').

Scouse has an accent typified by flat vowel sounds, nasal consonants, and a 'querulous' intonation. Geordie has a 'slurred' pronunciation giving such forms as 'worra' for 'what a' and 'gorra' for 'got a'.

In the West Country, speech is typically 'burred', with prominent 'r' sounds, 'z' for 's' (as exemplified in 'Zummerzet', ie 'Somerset', the popular name for such speech) and dialect forms, such as 'I be' for 'I am', 'her says to we' for 'she said to us', etc.

The Scots, Welsh and Irish have distinctive dialects, with many regional words and phrases. Scottish speech is often indicated in literature by the use of words and phrases such as 'aye' for 'yes', 'wee' for 'little', 'I dinna ken' for 'I don't know', 'mon', for 'man', 'laddie' for 'boy', 'lassie' for 'girl', 'bairns' for 'children' and 'ye' for 'you'. Broad (ie extreme) Scots speech may be almost unintelligible to a person from southern England.

Welsh and Irish speech are both noted for their musical or 'lilting' intonation, so that an Irish person's statement may sound like a question to an English listener. Welsh speech is popularly typified in such stock words and phrases as 'boyo' for 'man', 'look you' for 'do you see', and 'there is cold it is' for 'it is cold'. Irishness is often indicated by such expressions as 'begorra' for 'by God', 'would you be after wanting' for 'do you want', and by repetition of final phrases such as 'at all, at all'.

Many immigrants in Britain come from countries where English is spoken as a first or second language and they retain their variety of English. This is true for example of people from the Caribbean or the Indian subcontinent.

US English differs from British English in many items of vocabulary, in certain spelling conventions and, more generally, in pronunciation. Thus American 'sidewalk' is used for British 'pavement', 'elevator' for 'lift', 'flat' for 'puncture', 'apartment' for 'flat', while 'colour', 'kerb', 'tyre', 'grey', 'licence', for example, are spelt 'color', 'curb', 'tire', 'gray', 'license', in US English. There are also differences in grammatical usage, such as US 'gotten' for British 'got'. A distinctive feature of American pronunciation is the burred 'r' in words such as 'port' and 'more', while this letter is silent in the British equivalent (though the Scots pronounce it). Many Americans pronounce words such as 'bath' and 'path' with a short 'a', whereas British RP has a long vowel. Again, Americans tend to enunciate the individual syllables of words such as 'voluntarily', whereas the British 'swallow' many syllables in such cases. The stressed or accented syllable in US English words may also differ from that in the same words in British English.

The USA can be regarded as having three distinct dialects: those of New England and the South, and General (or Midwestern) American. The language of New England has a characteristic 'twang' and has retained some of the features of British English, such as the long 'a' in words like 'bath', and the silent 'r' in 'port'. The English of the southern states is famous for its marked 'drawl', and is said to have developed from a blend of the English spoken by the original British colonists and that of the black slaves.

accident /ˈæksɪdənt/ *n* **1** [C] event that happens unexpectedly and causes damage, injury, etc: *be killed in a car/road accident* ○ *I had a slight accident at home and broke some crockery.* ○ *He's very late — I do hope he hasn't met with an accident.* ○ [attrib] *accident insurance.* **2** [U] chance; fortune: *By accident of birth* (ie Because of where he happened to be born) *he is entitled to British citizenship.* **3** (idm) **ˌaccidents ˌwill ˈhappen** (*saying*) some unfortunate events must be accepted as inevitable. **by accident** as a result of chance or mishap: *I only found it by accident.* **a chapter of accidents** ⇨ CHAPTER. **without ˈaccident** safely.

□ **ˈaccident-prone** *adj* [usu pred] more than usually likely to have accidents.

accidental /ˌæksɪˈdentl/ *adj* happening unexpectedly or by chance: *a verdict of accidental death* ○ *an accidental meeting with a friend.*

▷ **accidental** *n* (*music*) any of various signs used in written or printed music to show that a note is sharp, flat or natural.

accidentally /-təlɪ/ *adv.*

acclaim /əˈkleɪm/ *v* **1** (**a**) [Tn] welcome (sb/sth) with shouts of approval; applaud loudly: *acclaim the winner of a race.* (**b**) [esp passive: Tn, Cn·n/a] ~ **sb/sth (as sth)** acknowledge the greatness of sb/sth: *a much acclaimed performance* ○ *It was acclaimed as a great discovery.* **2** [Cn·n] (*fml*) hail or salute (sb) as sth: *They acclaimed him king.*

▷ **acclaim** *n* [U] enthusiastic welcome or approval; praise: *The book received great critical acclaim.*

acclamation /ˌækləˈmeɪʃn/ *n* **1** [U] loud and enthusiastic approval (of a proposal, etc): *elected by acclamation*, ie without voting. **2** [C usu *pl*] shouting to honour or welcome sb: *the acclamations of the crowd.*

acclimatize, -ise /əˈklaɪmətaɪz/ (also *esp US* **acclimate** /ˈæklɪmeɪt, əˈklaɪmət/) *v* [I, Ipr, Tn, Tn·pr] ~ **(oneself/sb/sth) (to sth)** get (oneself, animals, plants, etc) used to a new climate or a new environment, new conditions, etc; become or make accustomed (to sth): *It takes many months to acclimatize/become acclimatized to life in a tropical climate.* ▷ **acclimatization, -isation** /əˌklaɪmətaɪˈzeɪʃn; *US* -tɪˈz-/ *n* [U].

acclivity /əˈklɪvətɪ/ *n* (*fml*) upward slope. Cf DECLIVITY.

accolade /ˈækəleɪd; *US* ˌækəˈleɪd/ *n* **1** praise; approval: *To be chosen to represent their country is the highest accolade for most athletes.* **2** ceremonial tap on the shoulder with the flat part of a sword, given when a knighthood is conferred.

accommodate /əˈkɒmədeɪt/ *v* **1** [Tn] provide lodging or room for (sb): *This hotel can accommodate up to 500 guests.* **2** [Tn·pr] ~ **sth to sth** change or adjust sth so that it fits or harmonizes with sth else: *I will accommodate my plans to yours.* **3** (*fml*) (**a**) [Tn, Tn·pr] ~ **sb (with sth)** grant or supply (sth) to sb: *The bank will accommodate you with a loan.* (**b**) [Tn] do (sb) a favour; oblige: *I shall endeavour to accommodate you whenever possible.* **4** [Tn] (*fml*) cater for (sth/sb); take into consideration: *accommodate the special needs of minority groups.*

▷ **accommodating** *adj* (of a person) easy to deal with; willing to help; obliging.

accommodation /əˌkɒməˈdeɪʃn/ *n* **1** (**a**) [U] (*Brit*) room(s), esp for living in; lodgings: *find suitable, cheap, temporary, permanent, etc accommodation* ○ *Hotel accommodation is scarce.* ○ *Wanted, accommodation for a young married couple.* ⇨ article. (**b**) **accommodations** [pl] (*US*) lodgings; room(s) and food. **2** [U] ~ **(of sth to sth)** (*fml*) process of adapting; adjustment: *arrange the accommodation of my plans to yours.* **3** [C] (*fml*) convenient arrangement; compromise: *The two sides failed to agree on every point but came to an accommodation.*

□ **accommoˈdation address** address often used on letters to or by sb who is unable or unwilling to give a permanent address.

accommoˈdation ladder ladder hung from the side of a ship to reach small boats.

accompaniment /əˈkʌmpənɪmənt/ *n* **1** thing that naturally or often goes with another thing: *White wine provided the perfect accompaniment to the meal.* **2** (*music*) part played by an instrument or orchestra to support a solo instrument or voice or a choir: *singing with (a) piano accompaniment.*

accompanist /əˈkʌmpənɪst/ *n* person who plays a musical accompaniment.

accompany /əˈkʌmpənɪ/ *v* (*pt, pp* **-ied**) **1** [Tn] walk or travel with (sb) as a companion or helper; escort: *I must ask you to accompany me to the police station.* ○ *He was accompanied on the expedition by his wife.* ○ *Warships will accompany the convoy.* **2** [esp passive: Tn, Tn·pr] ~ **sth (by/with sth)** (**a**) be present or occur with sth: *fever accompanied with delirium* ○ *strong winds accompanied by heavy rain.* (**b**) provide sth in addition to sth else;

Accommodation

When British people are away from their own house, or have no home of their own, there are various kinds of places to stay in.

For holiday-makers who can afford it, and for people travelling on business, a hotel is usually the first choice. Most towns have one or more hotels, while some of the most luxurious and expensive hotels are in the country and are often large country-houses that have been converted. Many country inns also offer overnight accommodation.

A cheaper kind of accommodation, especially for holiday-makers, is a guest-house. This is normally a large private house and is run as a small family hotel. 'Bed and breakfast' ('B and B') is usually in a smaller house where the owners let one or two bedrooms to overnight visitors. Houses that provide bed and breakfast accommodation for longer stays are sometimes called boarding-houses. They are often found at seaside resorts.

A popular kind of accommodation is a self-catering holiday cottage. This is a house, often in the country, where a family or group of people can stay for a week or two at a time, cooking their own meals and paying rent to the owner. An alternative, especially in seaside resorts, is a holiday flat. (Cf article at HOLIDAY.)

Elderly people who can no longer live in their own home often live in a retirement or residential home (also called an old people's home or rest-home). Many such homes are comfortable and resemble country hotels, with attractive gardens, but others are dreary and have few comforts.

Young people who leave home to work or study often stay in lodgings called 'digs'. In many cases, this is a bed-sitting-room (or 'bed-sit') in a private house. Students, however, often live in college hostels or halls of residence, which many people prefer if they enjoy the company of others.

The owner of a guest-house or boarding-house is often called a landlady. In the past, landladies have had a reputation for being unfriendly and inhospitable. This is mainly because some of them enforced strict rules, especially about being punctual for meals and the noise made by children, etc. Most modern landladies, however, are efficient but friendly people, enforcing a minimum of rules.

Many people in Britain have no home at all, with the number of homeless in the late 1980s double that of ten years earlier. This increase is mainly due to changes in the way social security benefits are paid, periods of rapid increase in house prices, and a sharp decline in the number of council houses being built. Local authorities have an obligation to provide accommodation for homeless families in their area and many families are housed in bed-and-breakfast accommodation until permanent housing for them can be found. The homeless also include young people who have run away from home or a children's home, elderly people who have no family, and the mentally disturbed, all forced to live wherever they can. This often means 'living rough', begging or travelling by day and sleeping in the open or in doorways at night. The big cities, especially London, have a large number of such homeless people. One part of London's South Bank area has come to be called 'Cardboard City' because of the many people living there in huts made from cardboard boxes.

There are some free hostels for the young homeless, but these are for short stays. The charity Shelter works on behalf of the homeless, and the Salvation Army, a religious charity, offers them food and shelter.

In the USA, the problem of homelessness is just as serious, with many people sleeping under freeways, in makeshift shanties and 'tent cities', in their cars, or, as in Britain, in empty packing cartons. In the late 1980s. it was estimated that there were around 2 million homeless in the USA.

supplement sth: *Each application should be accompanied by a stamped addressed envelope.* **3** [Tn, Tn·pr] ~ **sb (at/on sth)** (*music*) play an accompaniment for sb: *The singer was accompanied at/on the piano by her sister.*

accomplice /əˈkʌmplɪs; *US* əˈkɒm-/ *n* person who helps another to do sth wicked or illegal: *The police arrested him and his two accomplices.*

accomplish /əˈkʌmplɪʃ; *US* əˈkɒm-/ *v* [Tn] **1** succeed in doing (sth); complete successfully; achieve: *accomplish one's aim, a task* ○ *a man who will never accomplish anything.* **2** (idm) **an accomplished ˈfact** thing that has been done and is no longer worth arguing about because it cannot be changed.

▷ **accomplished** *adj* **1** ~ **(in sth)** skilled: *an accomplished dancer, cook, poet, etc* ○ *be accomplished in music.* **2** well trained or educated in social skills such as conversation, art, music, etc: *an accomplished young lady.*

accomplishment /əˈkʌmplɪʃmənt; *US* əˈkɒm-/ *n* **1** [U] successful completion: *celebrate the accomplishment of one's objectives.* **2** [C] thing achieved. **3** [C] skill that can be learnt, esp in the social arts: *Dancing and singing were among her many accomplishments.*

accord[1] /əˈkɔːd/ *n* **1** peace treaty; agreement: *an accord between countries/with another country.* **2** (idm) **in accord (with sth/sb)** agreeing (with sth/sb); in harmony: *Such an act would not be in accord with our policy.* ○ *They live in perfect accord with each other.* **of one's own acˈcord** without being asked or forced; voluntarily: *He joined the army of his own accord.* **with ˌone acˈcord** everybody agreeing; unanimously: *With one accord they all stood up and cheered.*

accord[2] /əˈkɔːd/ *v* **1** [Ipr] ~ **with sth** (*fml*) (of a thing) agree or be in harmony with sth; correspond with sth: *His behaviour does not accord with his principles.* ○ *What you say does not accord with the previous evidence.* **2** [Dn·n, Dn·pr] ~ **sth to sb** (*fml*) give or grant sth to sb: *accord sb permission/accord permission to sb* ○ *The tribute accorded him was fully deserved.*

accordance /əˈkɔːdəns/ *n* (idm) **in accordance with sth** in agreement or harmony with sth: *in accordance with sb's wishes* ○ *act in accordance with custom, the regulations, the law.*

according /əˈkɔːdɪŋ/ **1 according to** *prep* (**a**) as stated by (sb) or in (sth): *According to John you were in Edinburgh last week.* ○ *You've been in prison six times according to our records.* (**b**) in a manner that is consistent with (sth): *act according to one's principles* ○ *Everything went according to plan.* ○ *The work was done according to her instructions.* (**c**) in a manner or degree that is in proportion to (sth): *salary according to qualifications and experience* ○ *Arrange the exhibits according to size.* **2 according as** *conj* (*fml*) in a manner or to a degree that varies as: *Everyone contributes according as he is able.* **3** (idm) **according to Hoyle** ⇨ HOYLE.

▷ **accordingly** *adv* **1** in a manner that is suggested by what is known or has been said: *I've told you what the situation is; you must act accordingly.* **2** for that reason; therefore.

accordion /əˈkɔːdɪən/ *n* (also **piano accordion**) portable musical instrument with a bellows, metal reeds and a keyboard. ⇨ illus at CONCERTINA.

accost /əˈkɒst; *US* əˈkɔːst/ *v* [Tn] (**a**) approach and speak to (sb) boldly: *She was accosted by a complete stranger.* (**b**) (of a prostitute) solicit (sb).

account[1] /əˈkaʊnt/ *n* **1** (*abbr* **a/c**) statement of money paid or owed for goods or services: *send in/render an account* ○ *keep the accounts*, ie keep a detailed record of money spent and received ○ *The accounts show a profit of £9 000.* **2** (*commerce*) (**a**) (*abbr* **a/c**) arrangement made with a bank, firm, etc allowing credit for financial or commercial transactions (used esp as in the expressions shown): *have an account at/with that bank*, ie keep money there and use its facilities ○ *open/close an account* ○ *pay money into/draw money out of an account* ○ *I have £200 in my account.* ○ *Will you pay cash or shall I charge it to your account* (eg at a shop or restaurant)*?* (**b**) (esp in advertising) work (to be) done for a particular customer: *The agency has lost two of its most important accounts.* **3** report; description: *She gave the police a full account of the incident.* ○ *Don't believe the newspaper account (of what happened).* ○ *Keep an account of your daily activities.* **4** (idm) **by/from all accounts** according to what has been said or reported: *I've never been there but it is, by all accounts, a lovely place.* **by one's own account** according to what one says oneself. **call sb to account** ⇨ CALL[2]. **give a good, poor, etc account of oneself** do or perform well, badly, etc esp in a contest: *Our team gave a splendid account of themselves to win the match.* **leave sth out of account/consideration** ⇨ LEAVE[1]. **of great, small, no, some, etc acˈcount** of great, small, etc importance: *a man of no account.* **on account** (**a**) as a payment in advance of a larger one: *I'll give you £20 on account.* (**b**) to be paid for later: *buy sth on account.* **on account of sth; on this/that account** because of sth; for this/that reason: *We delayed our departure on account of the bad weather.* **on no account; not on any account** not for any reason: *Don't on any account leave the prisoner unguarded.* **on one's own acˈcount** (**a**) for one's own benefit and at one's own risk: *work on one's own account.* (**b**) on one's own behalf: *I was worried on my own account, not yours.* **on sb's account** for sb's sake: *Don't change your plans on my account.* **put/turn sth to good acˈcount** use (money, talents, etc) well and profitably: *He turned his artistic gifts to good account by becoming a sculptor.* **render an account of oneself, etc** ⇨ RENDER. **settle one's/an account (with sb)** ⇨ SETTLE[2]. **square one's account/accounts with sb** ⇨ SQUARE[3]. **take account of sth; take sth into account** include sth in one's assessment, etc; make allowances for sth; consider sth: *When judging his performance, don't take his age into account.*

account[2] /əˈkaʊnt/ *v* **1** [Cn·a] regard (sb/sth) as; consider: *In English law a man is accounted innocent until he is proved guilty.* **2** [Ipr] ~ **(to sb) for sth** give a satisfactory record of (money, etc in one's care): *We must account (to our employer) for every penny we spend during a business trip.* **3** (idm) **there's no accounting for taste** (*saying*) it is impossible to explain why people have different likes and dislikes. **4** (phr v) **account for sth** be the explanation of sth; explain the cause of sth: *His illness accounts for his absence.* ○ *Please account for your disgraceful conduct.* **account for sth/sb** destroy sth or kill sb: *Our anti-aircraft guns*

accounted for five enemy bombers.
▷ **accounting** *n* [U] practice, skill or profession of keeping financial accounts; accountancy.
accountable /əˈkaʊntəbl/ *adj* [pred] ~ **(to sb) (for sth)** required or expected to give an explanation for one's actions, etc; responsible: *Who are you accountable to in the organization?* ○ *He is mentally ill and cannot be held accountable for his actions.*
accountant /əˈkaʊntənt/ *n* person whose profession is to keep or inspect financial accounts.
▷ **accountancy** /əˈkaʊntənsɪ/ *n* [U] profession of an accountant.
accoutrements /əˈku:trəmənts/ (*US* **accouterments** /*US* əˈku:tərmənts/) *n* [pl] **1** equipment; trappings. **2** soldier's equipment other than weapons and clothes.
accredit /əˈkredɪt/ *v* **1** [Tn·pr usu passive] ~ **sth to sb**/~ **sb with sth** attribute (a saying, etc) to sb; credit sb with (a saying, etc): *He is accredited with having first introduced this word into the language.* **2** [Tn·pr] ~ **sb to/at...**; ~ **sb to sb** (*fml*) send or appoint sb (esp an ambassador) as the official representative to a foreign government, etc: *He was accredited to/at Madrid/accredited to the Spanish king.* **3** [Tn] gain belief or influence for (advice, an adviser, a statement, etc).
▷ **accredited** *adj* [usu attrib] **1** officially recognized: *our accredited representative.* **2** generally accepted or believed: *the accredited theories.* **3** certified as being of a prescribed quality.
accretion /əˈkri:ʃn/ *n* **1** [U] **(a)** growth or increase by means of gradual additions. **(b)** the growing of separate things into one. **2** [C] **(a)** added matter that causes such growth. **(b)** thing formed by the addition of such matter: *a chimney blocked by an accretion of soot.*
accrue /əˈkru:/ *v* [I, Ipr] ~ **(to sb) (from sth)** come as a natural increase or advantage, esp financial; accumulate: *the power and wealth which accrued to the prince* ○ *Interest will accrue if you keep your money in a savings account.* ▷ **accrual** *n* [U, C].
accumulate /əˈkju:mjʊleɪt/ *v* **1** [Tn] gradually get or gather together an increasing number or quantity of (sth); get (sth) in this way: *accumulate books, a library* ○ *accumulate enough evidence to ensure his conviction* ○ *By investing wisely she accumulated a fortune.* ○ *My savings are accumulating interest.* **2** [I] increase in number or quantity: *Dust and dirt soon accumulate if a house is not cleaned regularly.* ▷ **accumulation** /əˌkju:mjʊˈleɪʃn/ *n* [U, C]: *the accumulation of money, knowledge, experience* ○ *an accumulation of unwanted rubbish.*
accumulative /əˈkju:mjʊlətɪv; *US* -leɪtɪv/ *adj* growing steadily by a series of additions; resulting from accumulation; cumulative: *accumulative interest* ○ *the accumulative effects of eating too much.*
accumulator /əˈkju:mjʊleɪtə(r)/ *n* **1** (*Brit*) storage battery that can be recharged, eg for a motor vehicle. **2** (*esp Brit*) bet placed on a series of sporting events, esp horse races, with the winnings from each being staked on the next. **3** device in a computer that stores and progressively adds numbers.
accuracy /ˈækjərəsɪ/ *n* [U] precision or exactness, esp resulting from careful effort: *predict sth with great accuracy* ○ *It is impossible to say with any (degree of) accuracy how many are affected.*
accurate /ˈækjərət/ *adj* **1** free from error: *an accurate clock, map, weighing machine* ○ *accurate statistics, measurements, calculations, etc* ○ *His description was accurate.* **2** careful and exact: *take accurate aim* ○ *Journalists are not always accurate (in what they write).* ▷ **accurately** *adv.*
accursed /əˈkɜ:sɪd/ *adj* **1** [usu attrib] (*infml*) hateful; detestable; annoying: *those accursed neighbours of ours* ○ *this accursed weather.* **2** (*dated*) under a curse.
accusation /ˌækju:ˈzeɪʃn/ *n* **1** [U] accusing or being accused: *prevent the accusation of an innocent person.* **2** [C] statement accusing a person of a fault, wrongdoing or crime: *Accusations of corruption have been made/brought/laid against him.*
accusative /əˈkju:zətɪv/ *n* (usu *sing*) (*grammar*) special form of a noun, a pronoun or an adjective used (in some inflected languages) when it is the direct object of a verb.
▷ **accusative** *adj* of or in the accusative: *The accusative forms of the pronouns 'I', 'we' and 'she' are 'me', 'us' and 'her'.*
accusatorial /əˌkju:zəˈtɔ:rɪəl/ *adj* (of a legal system) in which the roles of prosecutor and judge are kept separate. Cf INQUISITORIAL.
accuse /əˈkju:z/ *v* [Tn, Tn·pr] ~ **sb (of sth)** say that sb has done wrong, is guilty (of sth) or has broken the law: *accuse sb of cheating, cowardice, theft.*
▷ **accusatory** /əˈkju:zətərɪ; *US* -tɔ:rɪ/ *adj* of or indicating an accusation: *accusatory remarks, glances.*
the accused *n* (*pl* unchanged) person charged in a criminal case: *The accused was/were acquitted of the charge.*
accuser *n.*
accusingly /əˈkju:zɪŋlɪ/ *adv* in an accusing manner: *look, point, etc accusingly at sb.*
accustom /əˈkʌstəm/ *v* [Tn·pr] ~ **oneself/sb/sth to sth** make oneself, etc used to sth: *He quickly accustomed himself to this new way of life.*
▷ **accustomed** *adj* **1** [attrib] usual; habitual: *He took his accustomed seat by the fire.* **2** [pred] ~ **to sth** used to sth: *I soon got accustomed to his strange ways.* ○ *He quickly became accustomed to the local food.* ○ *My eyes slowly grew accustomed to the gloom.* ○ *This is not the kind of treatment I am accustomed to,* ie not the kind I usually receive.
ace /eɪs/ *n* **1** playing-card with a large single spot, usu having the highest or lowest value in card games: *the ace of spades.* **2** (*infml*) person who is an expert at some activity: *a World War 1 flying ace,* ie a pilot who shot down many enemy aircraft ○ [attrib]: *an ace pilot, footballer, marksman, etc.* **3** (in tennis) stroke, esp a service, that is too good for the opponent to return. **4** (idm) **(have) an ˈace up one's sleeve**; *US* **(have) an ace in the hole** (*infml*) (have) sth effective kept secretly in reserve. **black as the ace of spades** ⇨ BLACK[1]. **play one's ˈace** use one's best resource. **within an ace of sth/doing sth** very near to (doing) sth: *He came/was within an ace of death/being killed.*
acerbic /əˈsɜ:bɪk/ *adj* (*fml*) (esp of speech or manner) harsh and sharp: *an acerbic remark, tone, etc.* ▷ **acerbity** /əˈsɜ:bətɪ/ *n* [U, C].
acetate /ˈæsɪteɪt/ *n* **1** [U, C] (*chemistry*) compound derived from acetic acid. **2** [C] (also **acetate silk**) fabric made from cellulose acetate.
acetic /əˈsi:tɪk/ *adj* of or like vinegar.
□ **aˌcetic ˈacid** acid in vinegar that gives it its characteristic taste and smell.
acetone /ˈæsɪtəʊn/ (also **propanone** /ˈprəʊpəˌnəʊn/) *n* [U] (*chemistry*) colourless liquid with a strong smell used as a solvent and as a raw material for making plastics.
acetylene /əˈsetɪli:n/ *n* [U] (*chemistry*) colourless gas that burns with a bright flame, used in cutting and welding metal.
acetylsalicylic acid /ˌæsətaɪlˌsæləsɪlɪk ˈæsɪd, əˌsi:təlsæləˌsɪlɪk ˈæsɪd/ = ASPIRIN a.
ache /eɪk/ *n* (often in compounds) continuous dull pain: *ˈbackache* ○ *ˈearache* ○ *a ˈheadache* ○ *ˈstomach-ache* ○ *ˈtoothache* ○ *a ˈtummy-ache* ○ *My body was all aches and pains.* ○ *He has an ache in his/the chest.*
▷ **ache** *v* **1** [I] suffer from a continuous dull pain: *My head aches/is aching.* ○ *I'm aching all over.* ○ (*fig*) *It makes my heart ache* (ie makes me sad) *to see her suffer.* **2** [Ipr, It] ~ **for sb/sth** have a longing for sb/sth or to do sth: *He was aching for home/to go home.*
achy /ˈeɪkɪ/ *adj* (*infml*) full of or suffering from aches.
Acheron /ˈækərɒn/ (in Greek mythology) one of the rivers of the underworld.
achieve /əˈtʃi:v/ *v* [Tn] **1** gain or reach (sth), usu by effort, skill, courage, etc: *achieve success, one's ambition, notoriety, peace of mind.* **2** get (sth) done; accomplish or complete: *I've achieved only half of what I'd hoped to do.*
▷ **achievable** *adj* (of an objective) that can be achieved.
achievement *n* **1** [U] action of achieving: *celebrate the achievement of one's aims.* **2** [C] thing done successfully, esp with effort and skill: *the greatest scientific achievement of the decade.* ⇨ Usage at ACT[1].
Achilles /əˈkɪli:z/ *n* **1** (in Greek legend) Greek hero of the *Trojan War, whose story is told in the **Iliad*. When he was a baby his mother, holding him by the heel, put him in the river *Styx, whose water made him invulnerable, except in the heel. He died after being shot in the heel by *Paris. **2** (idm) **an/one's Achilles' ˈheel** weak or vulnerable point; fault, esp in sb's character, which can lead to his downfall: *Vanity is his Achilles' heel.*
□ **Aˌchilles' ˈtendon** tendon attaching the calf muscles to the heel.
achromatic /ˌeɪkrəʊˈmætɪk, ækrəˈmætɪk/ *adj* **(a)** without colour. **(b)** that can transmit light without separating it into the colours of which it is made up: *an achromatic lens/prism/telescope.*
achy ⇨ ACHE.
acid[1] /ˈæsɪd/ *n* **1** [U, C] (*chemistry*) any of a class of substances that either neutralize and are neutralized by alkalis, and contain hydrogen that can be replaced by a metal to form a salt, or are proton donors. The main types are sour and are able to corrode and dissolve metals. Common types of acid include hydrochloric acid, nitric acid and sulphuric acid: *Some acids burn holes in wood.* Cf ALKALI. **2** [C] any sour substance. **3** [U] (*sl*) = LSD. ⇨ article at DRUG. **4** (idm) **the ˈacid test** test that gives conclusive proof of the value or worth of sth/sb: *The acid test of a good driver is whether he remains calm in an emergency.* **put the acid on sb** (*Austral sl*) try to obtain a loan, favour, etc from sb.
▷ **acidic** /əˈsɪdɪk/ *adj* **1** of or like an acid. **2** (*chemistry*) having the essential properties of an acid. Cf ALKALINE (ALKALI).
acidosis /ˌæsɪˈdəʊsɪs/ *n* [U] condition of having too much acid in the blood or body tissues.
□ **ˌacid ˈrain** rainwater that is made acid by chemical substances (esp from factories) becoming dissolved in it, and that damages trees, crops, etc. ⇨ article at ENVIRONMENT.
acid[2] /ˈæsɪd/ *adj* **1** having a bitter sharp taste; sour: *A lemon is an acid fruit.* ○ *Vinegar has an acid taste.* **2** (*fig*) severe; sarcastic: *an acid wit* ○ *His remarks were rather acid.* **3** (*chemistry*) = ACIDIC (ACID[1]).
▷ **acidify** /əˈsɪdɪfaɪ/ *v* (*pt, pp* **-ied**) [I, Tn] (cause sth to) become acid.
acidity /əˈsɪdətɪ/ *n* [U] state or quality of being acid: *suffer from acidity of the stomach.*
acidly *adv* sarcastically.
acidulous /əˈsɪdjʊləs; *US* -ɪdʒʊl-/ *adj* rather sharp or bitter in taste or manner.
▷ **acidulated** /əˈsɪdjʊleɪtɪd; *US* -ɪdʒʊl-/ *adj* made slightly acid.
acinus /ˈæsɪnəs/ *n* (*pl* **-ni** /-naɪ/) (*botany*) any of the small parts that form the fruit of certain plants, eg the blackberry, raspberry, etc.
acknowledge /əkˈnɒlɪdʒ/ *v* **1** [Tn, Tf, Tw, Cn·a, Cn·t] accept the truth of (sth); admit (sth): *acknowledge the need for reform* ○ *a generally acknowledged fact* ○ *He acknowledged it to be true/that it was true.* ○ *They refused to acknowledge defeat/that they were defeated/themselves beaten.* **2** [Tn] report that one has received (sth): *acknowledge (receipt of) a letter.* **3** [Tn] express thanks for (sth): *acknowledge help* ○ *His services to the country were never officially acknowledged.* **4** [Tn] show that one has noticed or recognized (sb) by a smile, nod of the head, greeting, etc: *I was standing right next to her, but she didn't even acknowledge me/my presence.* **5 (a)** [Cn·n/a, Cn·t] ~ **sb (as sth)** accept sb (as sth): *Stephen acknowledged Henry as* (ie recognized his claim to be) *his heir.* ○ *He was generally acknowledged to be the finest poet in the land.* **(b)** [Tn] accept or recognize (sth): *The country acknowledged his*

claim to the throne.

▷ **acknowledgement** (also **acknowledgment**) *n* **1** [U] act of acknowledging: *We are sending you some money in acknowledgement of your valuable help.* **2** [C] (**a**) letter, etc stating that sth has been received: *I didn't receive an acknowledgement of my application.* (**b**) thing given or done in return for a service, etc: *These flowers are a small acknowledgement of your great kindness.* **3** [C, U] statement (in a book, etc) of an author's thanks to other people or writings that have helped him: *Her theory was quoted without (an) acknowledgement.*

acme /ˈækmɪ/ *n* (*usu sing*) highest stage of development; point of perfection: *reach the acme of success.*

acne /ˈæknɪ/ *n* [U] inflammation of the oil-glands of the skin, producing red pimples on the face and neck: *Many adolescents suffer from/have acne.*

acolyte /ˈækəlaɪt/ *n* **1** person who helps a priest in certain church services. **2** assistant; apprentice; faithful follower.

Aconcagua /ˌækənˈkægwə; *US* -ˈkɑːgwə/ mountain in the *Andes of Argentina (6 960 m, 22 834 ft), the second highest in S America. It is an extinct volcano.

aconite /ˈækənaɪt/ *n* **1** [C, U] perennial plant with yellow or blue flowers and a poisonous root. **2** [U] drug made from this plant.

acorn /ˈeɪkɔːn/ *n* **1** fruit of the oak-tree, with a cup-like base. ⇨ illus at TREE. **2** (idm) **big, etc oaks from little acorns grow** ⇨ OAK.

acoustic /əˈkuːstɪk/ *adj* **1** (**a**) of sound or the sense of hearing: *an acoustic mine*, ie one that can be exploded by sound-waves transmitted under water. (**b**) of acoustics. **2** [usu attrib] (of a musical instrument) not electric: *an acoustic guitar.* ⇨ illus at MUSIC.

▷ **acoustic** *n* [sing] = ACOUSTICS 1: *The hall has a fine acoustic.*

acoustically *adv*: *The hall is excellent acoustically.*

acoustics *n* **1** [pl] (also **acoustic** [sing]) qualities of a room, hall, etc that make it good or bad for carrying sound: *The acoustics of this concert hall are excellent.* **2** [sing *v*] scientific study of sound.

acquaint /əˈkweɪnt/ *v* [Tn·pr] ~ **sb/oneself with sth** make sb/oneself familiar with or aware of sth: *Please acquaint me with the facts of the case.* ○ *The lawyer acquainted himself with the details of his client's business affairs.*

▷ **acquainted** *adj* [pred] **1** ~ **with sth** familiar with sth: *Are you acquainted with the works of Shakespeare?* ○ *You will soon become fully acquainted with the procedures.* **2** ~ (**with sb**) knowing sb personally: *I am not acquainted with the lady.* ○ *We are/became acquainted.* ○ *Let's get better acquainted.*

acquaintance /əˈkweɪntəns/ *n* **1** [U] ~ **with sth/sb** (often slight) knowledge of sth/sb: *He has some little acquaintance with the Japanese language.* **2** [C] person whom one knows but who is not a close friend: *He has a wide circle of acquaintances.* ○ *She's an old acquaintance*, ie I've known her for a long time. **3** (idm) **have a nodding acquaintance with sb/sth** ⇨ NOD. **make sb's acquaintance/make the acquaintance of sb** get to know sb; meet sb personally: *I made his acquaintance at a party.* **on (further) acˈquaintance** when known for a (longer) period of time: *His manner seemed unpleasant at first, but he improved on further acquaintance.* **scrape an acquaintance with sb** ⇨ SCRAPE[1].

acquiesce /ˌækwɪˈes/ *v* [I, Ipr] ~ (**in sth**) (*fml*) accept sth without protest; offer no opposition (to a plan, conclusion, etc): *Her parents will never acquiesce in such an unsuitable marriage.*

▷ **acquiescence** /ˌækwɪˈesns/ *n* [U].

acquiescent /-ˈesnt/ *adj* ready to acquiesce: *an acquiescent nature* ○ *She is too acquiescent*, ie too ready to comply.

acquire /əˈkwaɪə(r)/ *v* **1** [Tn] (**a**) gain (sth) by one's own ability, efforts or behaviour: *acquire a good knowledge of English, an antique painting, a taste for brandy, a reputation for dishonesty.* (**b**) obtain (sth); be given (sth): *My sister couldn't take her desk with her to the new house: that's how I came to acquire it.* ○ *We've just acquired a dog.* **2** (idm) **an acquired ˈtaste** thing that one learns to like gradually: *Abstract art is an acquired taste.*

□ **acˌquired characteˈristic** feature of an organism that is caused by the effects of its environment and has not been inherited genetically.

acˌquired imˌmune deˈficiency syndrome (*medical*) ⇨ AIDS.

acquisition /ˌækwɪˈzɪʃn/ *n* **1** [U] action of acquiring: *the acquisition of antiques, knowledge, a fortune.* **2** [C] thing acquired, esp sth useful: *the library's most recent acquisitions*, ie books it has obtained recently ○ *The school has a valuable new acquisition* (ie a valuable new teacher) *in Mr Smith.*

acquisitive /əˈkwɪzətɪv/ *adj* (*often derog*) keen to acquire things, esp material possessions: *an acquisitive collector.* ▷ **acquisitively** *adv.* **acquisitiveness** *n* [U].

acquit /əˈkwɪt/ *v* (**-tt-**) **1** [Tn, Tn·pr] ~ **sb (of sth)** declare sb to be not guilty (of a crime, etc); free or clear sb (of blame, responsibility, etc): *The jury acquitted him of (the charge of) murder.* Cf CONVICT. **2** [Tn] ~ **oneself well, badly, etc** behave or perform in a specified way: *He acquitted himself bravely in the battle.*

▷ **acquittal** /əˈkwɪtl/ *n* (*law*) **1** [C] judgement that a person is not guilty of the crime with which he has been charged: *There were three convictions and two acquittals in court today.* **2** [U] being acquitted: *Lack of evidence resulted in their acquittal.*

Acre /ˈeɪkə(r)/ seaport in northern Israel that was first captured by the Christians during the First *Crusade in 1104, and was the last Christian stronghold to be recaptured by the Muslims, in 1291.

acre /ˈeɪkə(r)/ *n* **1** measure of land, 4 840 square yards or about 4 050 square metres: *a three-acre wood.* ⇨ App 9, 10. **2** field; piece of land: *rolling acres of farm land.*

▷ **acreage** /ˈeɪkərɪdʒ/ *n* [U] area of land measured in acres: *What is the acreage of the farm?*

acrid /ˈækrɪd/ *adj* **1** having a strongly bitter smell or taste: *acrid fumes from burning rubber* ○ *Vinegar smells acrid.* **2** bitter in temper or manner; caustic: *an acrid dispute.* ▷ **acridity** /əˈkrɪdətɪ/ *n* [U].

acrimony /ˈækrɪmənɪ; *US* -məʊnɪ/ *n* [U] bitterness of manner or words: *The dispute was settled without acrimony.*

▷ **acrimonious** /ˌækrɪˈməʊnɪəs/ *adj* (esp of quarrels) bitter: *an acrimonious meeting, discussion, atmosphere.* **acrimoniously** *adv.*

acrobat /ˈækrəbæt/ *n* person, esp at a circus, who performs difficult or unusual physical acts (eg somersaults, walking on the hands or walking on a rope).

▷ **acrobatic** /ˌækrəˈbætɪk/ *adj* of or like an acrobat: *acrobatic feats, skills.* **acrobatically** *adv.* **acrobatics** *n* **1** [pl] acrobatic acts: *perform/do acrobatics* ○ *Her acrobatics were greeted with loud applause.* **2** [sing *v*] art of performing these: *Acrobatics takes a long time to learn.*

acronym /ˈækrənɪm/ *n* word formed from the initial letters of a group of words, eg *UNESCO* /juːˈneskəʊ/, ie United Nations Educational, Scientific and Cultural Organization.

acropolis /əˈkrɒpəlɪs/ *n* (**a**) [C] citadel or upper fortified part of an ancient Greek city. (**b**) **the Acropolis** [sing] the one in Athens, containing the *Parthenon and other buildings mostly dating from the 5th century BC.

across[1] /əˈkrɒs; *US* əˈkrɔːs/ *adv part* **1** from one side to the other side: *Can you swim across?* ○ *Will you row me across?* ○ *I helped the blind man across.* ○ *Come across to my office this afternoon.* **2** on the other side: *We leave Dover at ten and we should be across in France by midnight.* **3** from side to side: *The river is half a mile across*, ie wide.

□ **across from** *prep* (*esp US*) opposite (sth): *Just across from our house there's a school.*

across[2] /əˈkrɒs; *US* əˈkrɔːs/ *prep* **1** from one side to the other side of (sth): *walk across the street* ○ *row sb across a lake.* **2** on the other side of (sth): *We shall soon be across the Channel.* ○ *He shouted to me from across the room.* ○ *My house is just across the street.* **3** extending from one side to the other side of (sth): *a bridge across the river* ○ *Draw a line across the page.* **4** so as to cross or intersect (sth): *He sat with his arms across his chest.*

acrostic /əˈkrɒstɪk; *US* -ˈkrɔːs-/ *n* poem or word-puzzle in which the first, or the first and last, letters of the lines form a word or words.

acrylic /əˈkrɪlɪk/ *adj* of a synthetic material made from an organic acid and used for making dress fabrics, etc.

▷ **acrylic** *n* [U, C] acrylic fibre, plastic or resin.

ACT /ˌeɪ siː ˈtiː/ *abbr* Australian Capital Territory.

act[1] /ækt/ *n* **1** (**a**) [C] thing done; deed: *It is an act of kindness/a kind act to help a blind man across the street.* ○ *This dreadful murder is surely the act of a madman.* (**b**) (**the**) **Acts** (**of the Apostles**) [pl] book of the New Testament that follows the Gospels and gives an account of the missionary work of the *Apostles. ⇨ Usage. ⇨ App 5. **2** [C] any of the main divisions of a play or an opera: *a play in five acts* ○ *The hero dies in Act 4, Scene 3.* **3** [C] any of a series of short performances in a programme; piece of entertainment: *a circus act* ○ *a song and dance act.* **4** [C] decree or law made by a legislative body: *an Act of Parliament* ○ *Parliament has passed an act which makes such sports illegal.* ⇨ article at LAW. **5** [C] (*infml*) way of behaving which is not genuine, but which is adopted for the effect it will have on others; pretence (used esp as in the expressions shown): *Don't take her seriously — it's all an act.* ○ *She's just putting on an act*, ie only pretending. **6** (idm) **an ˌact of ˈGod** (*law*) event caused by uncontrollable natural forces, eg a storm, a flood, an earthquake or a volcanic eruption: *insure against all loss or damage including that caused by an act of God.* **a balancing act** ⇨ BALANCE[2]. **be/get ˈin on the act** (*infml*) be/become involved in a particular activity, esp for one's own benefit or profit: *She has made a lot of money from her business and now her family want to get in on the act too.* **do a disappearing act** ⇨ DISAPPEAR. (**catch sb**) **in the** (**very**) **act** (**of doing sth**) (discover sb) while he is doing sth, esp sth wrong: *I caught her in the act (of reading my letters).* ○ *In the act of bending down, he slipped and hurt his back.* **read the Riot Act** ⇨ READ.

NOTE ON USAGE: **1** An **act** or **action** can be good or bad. The words are close in meaning and sometimes identical: *a generous act/action* ○ *the acts/actions of a monster.* When speaking about general behaviour, **actions** is used: *He is impulsive in his actions.* An **act** is often specified: *Helping the homeless is an act of mercy.* **Deed** is more formal and often refers to major acts: *be guilty of many foul deeds* ○ *He spent his whole life doing good deeds.* **2 Exploit**, **feat** and **achievement** are all desirable or noteworthy actions. Both **feat** and **achievement** emphasize the difficulty of accomplishing something mental or physical: *Coming top in the exam was quite an achievement.* ○ *The new bridge is a feat of engineering.* **Exploit** relates to the performance of a physical action or series of actions which are often brave or daring: *The travellers wrote an account of their dangerous exploits in the Andes.*

act[2] /ækt/ *v* **1** [I] (**a**) do sth; perform actions: *The time for talking is past; we must act at once.* ○ *The girl's life was saved because the doctors acted so promptly.* ○ *You acted* (ie behaved) *wisely by/in ignoring such bad advice.* (**b**) do what is expected of one as a professional or an official person: *The police refused to act without more evidence.* **2** (**a**) [I] perform a part in a play or film; be an actor or actress: *Have you ever acted?* ○ *She acts well.* (**b**) [Ln, Tn] take the part of (a character in a play or film): *Who is acting (the part of) Hamlet?* (**c**) [Ln, I] pretend by one's behaviour to be a certain person or type of person: *He's not really angry — he's just* *acting (the stern father).* **3** (idm) **act/play the fool** ⇨ FOOL[1]. **act/play the goat** ⇨ GOAT. **4** (phr v) **act as sb/sth** perform the role or function of sb/sth: *I don't understand their language; you'll have to act as interpreter.* **act for/on behalf of sb** perform sb's duties, etc on his behalf; represent sb: *During her illness her solicitor has been acting for her in her business affairs.* **act on sth (a)** take action in accordance with or as a result of sth: *Acting on information received, the police raided the club.* **(b)** have an effect on sth: *Alcohol acts on the brain.* **act sth out** act a part, usu in a real-life situation and for some purpose: *She acted out the role of wronged lover to make him feel guilty.* **act up** (*infml*) cause pain or annoyance by functioning badly: *My sprained ankle has been acting up badly all week.* ○ *The car's acting up again.*

▷ **acting** *n* [U] (art or occupation of) performing in plays, films, TV, etc: *She did a lot of acting while she was at college.*

Actaeon /æk'ti:ən/ (in Greek mythology) hunter who was punished for seeing the goddess *Artemis bathing by being changed into a stag and killed by his own hounds.

acting /'æktɪŋ/ *adj* [attrib] doing the duties of another person for a time: *the acting manager, headmistress, etc.*

actinide /'æktɪnaɪd/ *n* (*chemistry*) any of a series of 16 radioactive metallic elements with increasing atomic numbers from actinium (atomic number 89) to rutherfordium (104).

actinism /'æktɪnɪzəm/ *n* [U] property of short-wave radiation that produces chemical changes, as in photography.

actinium /æk'tɪnɪəm/ *n* [U] (*symb* **Ac**) radioactive metallic element that is found in pitchblende.

actinometer /ˌæktɪ'nɒmɪtə(r)/ *n* instrument for measuring the strength of radiation, esp of the sun's rays.

action /'ækʃn/ *n* **1** [U] **(a)** process of doing sth; using energy or influence; activity: *I only like films that have got plenty of action.* ○ *The time has come for action.* ○ *a man of action*, ie one who achieves much by being decisive and energetic. **(b)** [C] thing done; deed; act: *Her quick action saved his life.* ○ *You must judge a person by his actions, not by what he says.* ⇨ Usage at ACT[1]. **2** [U] events in a story or play: *The action is set in France.* **3** [sing] ~ **on sth** effect that one substance has on another: *The action of salt on ice causes it to melt.* **4** [U] fighting in battle between troops, warships, etc: *killed in action* ○ *the destruction caused by enemy action* ○ *He saw* (ie was involved in) *action in North Africa.* **5** [C] legal process; lawsuit: *He brought an action against her*, ie sought judgement against her in a lawcourt. **6** [C] **(a)** way of functioning, esp of a part of the body: *study the action of the liver.* **(b)** way of moving, eg of an athlete, or of a horse when jumping: *a fast bowler with a fine action.* **(c)** mechanism of an instrument, esp of a gun, piano or clock. **7** (idm) ˌ**actions speak** ˌ**louder than** '**words** (*saying*) what a person actually does means more than what he says he will do. **course of action** ⇨ COURSE. **in** '**action** in operation or engaging in a typical activity: *I've heard she's a marvellous player but I've never seen her in action.* **into** '**action** into operation or a typical activity: *put a plan into action* ○ *At daybreak the troops went into action*, ie started fighting. **out of** '**action** no longer able to operate or function; not working: *This machine is out of action.* ○ *The enemy guns put many of our tanks out of action.* ○ *I've been out of action for several weeks with a broken leg.* **a piece/slice of the** '**action** (*infml*) involvement in some enterprise, esp in order to get a share of the profits: *I'm only putting money into this scheme if I get a slice of the action.* **swing into action** ⇨ SWING[1]. **take** '**action** do sth in response to what has happened: *Immediate action must be taken to stop the fire spreading.* **take evasive action** ⇨ EVASIVE. **where the** '**action is** (*infml*) any place where life is thought to be busy, enjoyable, profitable, etc: *Life in the country can be dull — London is where all the action is.*

▷ **actionable** *adj* giving sufficient cause for a lawsuit: *Be careful what you say — your remarks may be actionable.*

□ '**action group** group formed to take active measures, esp in politics.

'**action painting** method of painting in which the artist puts the paint on randomly, eg by throwing or splashing it. It is used in abstract expressionism.

'**action point** note or proposal made eg at a meeting about a specified task that needs to be done.

ˌ**action** '**replay** running again, often in slow motion, of part of a film showing a specific incident, esp in a sports match.

'**action stations** positions to which soldiers, etc go when fighting is expected to begin: (*fig*) *Action stations, I can hear the boss coming!*

activate /'æktɪveɪt/ *v* [Tn] **1** make (sth) active: *The burglar alarm was activated by mistake.* **2** (*chemistry*) supply enough energy for (a reaction) to proceed. ▷ **activation** /ˌæktɪ'veɪʃn/ *n* [U].

active /'æktɪv/ *adj* **1 (a)** (in the habit of) doing things; energetic: *Although he's quite old he's still very active.* ○ *lead an active life*, ie one full of activity ○ *She takes an active part* (ie is energetically involved) *in local politics.* **(b)** quick; lively: *have an active brain.* **2** functioning; in operation: *an active volcano*, ie one that erupts occasionally. **3** having an effect; not merely passive: *the active ingredients* ○ *active resistance.* **4** radioactive. **5** (*grammar*) of the form of a verb whose grammatical subject is the person or thing that performs the action, as in *He was driving the car* and *The children ate the cake.* Cf PASSIVE.

▷ **active** *n* [sing] (also **active voice**) (*grammar*) active(5) forms of a verb: *In the sentence 'She cleaned the car' the verb is in the active.* Cf PASSIVE VOICE (PASSIVE).

actively *adv*: *actively involved in the project* ○ *Your proposal is being actively considered.*

activeness *n* [U].

□ '**active list** list of officers available for military service.

active '**service** (*US* also **active** '**duty**) full-time service in the armed forces, esp during a war: *be on active service.*

active voice = ACTIVE *n.*

activist /'æktɪvɪst/ *n* person who takes or supports vigorous action, esp for a political cause.

activity /æk'tɪvətɪ/ *n* **1** [U] **(a)** being active or lively. **(b)** busy or energetic action: *The house has been full of activity all day.* **2** [C esp *pl*] specific thing or things done; action; occupation: *outdoor, recreational, sporting, classroom activities* ○ *Her activities include tennis and painting.* ○ *Sailing is an activity I much enjoy.* **3** [U] average number of atoms disintegrating in a substance in a given unit of time; radioactivity.

actor /'æktə(r)/ *n* person who acts on the stage, on TV or in films.

□ **the Actors' Studio** experimental theatre workshop founded in 1947 in New York by Elia *Kazan, Cheryl Crawford and Robert Lewis. It trained actors in the method school (METHOD), based on the theory of *Stanislavsky.

actress /'æktrɪs/ *n* **1** woman actor. **2** (idm) **as the** ˌ**actress said to the** '**bishop** (*infml catchphrase*) (used for suggesting that what has been said has a second, usu indecent, meaning).

actual /'æktʃʊəl/ *adj* existing in fact; real: *What were his actual words?* ○ *The actual cost was much higher than we had expected.* ○ *He looks younger than his wife, but in actual fact he's a lot older.* ⇨ Usage at NEW.

▷ **actually** /'æktʃʊlɪ/ *adv* **1** really; in fact: *What did he* '*actually say?* ○ *Actually, I'm busy at the moment — can I phone you back?* ○ *the political party actually in power.* **2** though it may seem strange; even: *He actually expected me to pay for his ticket.* ○ *She not only entered the competition — she actually won it!*

actuality /ˌæktʃʊ'ælətɪ/ *n* **1** [U] actual existence; reality. **2 actualities** [pl] existing conditions; facts.

actuary /'æktʃʊərɪ; *US* -tʃʊerɪ/ *n* expert who calculates insurance risks and premiums (by studying rates of mortality and frequency of accidents, fires, thefts, etc). ▷ **actuarial** /ˌæktʃʊ'eərɪəl/ *adj.*

actuate /'æktʃʊeɪt/ *v* [Tn] (*fml*) **1** make (a machine, an electrical device, etc) move or work; make (a process) begin. **2** cause (sb) to act; motivate: *He was actuated solely by greed.*

acuity /ə'kju:ətɪ/ *n* [U] (*fml*) sharpness (esp of thought or the senses); acuteness.

acumen /'ækjʊmen, *also* ə'kju:mən/ *n* [U] ability to understand and judge things quickly and clearly; shrewdness: *business acumen* ○ *have/show/display great political acumen.*

acupuncture /'ækjʊpʌŋktʃə(r)/ *n* [U] (*medical*) method of pricking the tissues of the human body with fine needles in order to relieve pain or as a local anaesthetic.

▷ **acupuncturist** *n* expert in acupuncture.

acute /ə'kju:t/ *adj* (**-r**, **-st**) **1** very great; severe: *suffer acute hardship* ○ *There's an acute shortage of water.* **2 (a)** (of feelings or the senses) keen; sharp; penetrating: *suffer acute pain, embarrassment, remorse, etc* ○ *Dogs have an acute sense of smell.* **(b)** shrewd; perceptive: *He is an acute observer.* ○ *Her judgement is acute.* **3** (of an illness) coming quickly to the most severe or critical stage: *acute appendicitis* ○ *an acute patient*, ie one whose illness has reached this stage. Cf CHRONIC. ▷ **acutely** *adv*: *I am acutely aware of the difficulty we face.* **acuteness** *n* [U].

□ **acute** '**accent** mark over a vowel (´) as over *e* in *café.*

acute '**angle** angle of less than 90°. ⇨ illus at ANGLE.

-acy ⇨ -CY.

AD /ˌeɪ 'di:/ *abbr* in the year of Our Lord; of the Christian era (Latin *anno domini*): *in (the year)* ˌ*55 A'D/*ˌ*AD 5'5.* Cf BC 1.

ad /æd/ *n* (*infml*) = ADVERTISEMENT (ADVERTISE): *put an ad in the local paper.*

adage /'ædɪdʒ/ *n* traditional saying; proverb.

adagio /ə'dɑ:dʒɪəʊ/ *adj, adv* (*music*) in slow time; slowly.

▷ **adagio** *n* (*pl* **-gios**) (part of a) piece of music (to be) played in this way.

the entrance hall at Osterley Park, designed by Robert and James Adam

Adam[1] /'ædəm/ *n* **1** (in the Bible) the first man, created by God from the dust. With *Eve he lived in the Garden of *Eden until they disobeyed God by eating the fruit of the Tree of Knowledge, for which God expelled them into the world. **2** (idm) **not know sb from Adam** ⇨ KNOW.

□ ˌ**Adam's** '**ale** (*dated rhet*) water.

ˌ**Adam's** '**apple** part at the front of the neck, especially prominent in men, that moves up and down when one speaks. ⇨ illus at THROAT.

Adam[2] /'ædəm/ Robert (1728-92), Scottish architect who, with his brother James (1730-94), created a new neoclassical decorative style in British domestic architecture and furniture. ⇨ illus.

▷ **Adam** *adj* [usu attrib] of this style in architecture and furniture: *an Adam fireplace.*

adamant /ˈædəmənt/ *adj* (esp of a person or his manner) firmly or stubbornly determined; unwilling to be persuaded: *an adamant refusal* ○ *She was quite adamant that she would not come.* ○ *On this point I am adamant,* ie my decision will not change. ▷ **adamantly** *adv.*

adapt /əˈdæpt/ *v* **1** (**a**) [Tn, Tn·pr, Tnt] ~ **sth** (**for sth**) make sth suitable for a new use, situation, etc; modify sth: *This machine has been specially adapted for use underwater.* ○ *These styles can be adapted to suit individual tastes.* (**b**) [Tn, Tn·pr] ~ **sth** (**for sth**) (**from sth**) alter or modify (a text) for television, the stage, etc: *This novel has been adapted for radio* (ie translated and changed so that it can be presented on the radio) *from the Russian original.* **2** [I, Ipr, Tn·pr] ~ (**oneself**) (**to sth**) become adjusted to new conditions, etc: *Our eyes slowly adapted to the dark.* ○ *She adapted (herself) quickly to the new climate.*

▷ **adaptable** *adj* (**a**) (*approv*) able to adapt oneself/itself: *He is not very adaptable,* ie does not adapt easily to new circumstances, etc. (**b**) able to be adapted. **adaptability** /əˌdæptəˈbɪlətɪ/ *n* [U].

adaptation /ˌædæpˈteɪʃn/ *n* ~ (**of sth**) (**for/to sth**) **1** [U] (*esp biology*) action or process of adapting or being adapted. **2** [C] thing made by adapting sth else, esp a text for production on the stage, radio, etc: *an adaptation for children of a play by Shakespeare.*

adaptor *n* **1** device that connects pieces of equipment that were not originally designed to be connected. **2** type of plug that enables several electrical appliances to be connected to one socket. **3** (also **adapter**) person who adapts sth.

ADC /ˌeɪ diː ˈsiː/ *abbr* aide-de-camp.

add /æd/ *v* **1** [Tn, Tn·pr] ~ **sth** (**to sth**) put sth together with sth else so as to increase the size, number, amount, etc: *Whisk the egg and then add the flour.* ○ *He added his signature (to the petition).* ○ *If the tea is too strong, add some more water.* ○ *Many words have been added to this edition of the dictionary.* ○ *This was an added* (ie an extra, a further) *disappointment.* **2** [Tn, Tn·pr, Tn·p] ~ **A to B**; ~ **A and B** (**together**) put (numbers or amounts) together to get a total: *If you add 5 and 5 (together), you get 10.* ○ *Add 9 to the total.* Cf SUBTRACT. **3** [Tn, Tn·pr, Tf] ~ **sth** (**to sth**) continue to say sth; make (a further remark): *I have nothing to add to my earlier statement.* ○ *'And don't be late,' she added.* ○ *As a postscript to his letter he added that he loved her.* **4** (idm) **add ˌfuel to the ˈflames** do or say sth that makes people react more strongly or fiercely. **add ˌinsult to ˈinjury** make a relationship with another person even worse by offending him as well as actually harming him. **5** (phr v) **add sth in** include sth; put or pour sth in. **add sth on** (**to sth**) include or attach sth: *add on a 10% service charge.* **add to sth** increase sth: *The bad weather only added to our difficulties.* ○ *The house has been added to* (ie New rooms, etc have been built on to it) *from time to time.* **add up** (*infml*) seem reasonable or consistent; make sense: *His story just doesn't add up — he must be lying.* **add** (**sth**) **up** calculate the total of (two or more numbers or amounts): *The waiter can't add up.* ○ *Add up all the money I owe you.* **add up to sth** (**a**) amount to sth: *These numbers add up to 100.* (**b**) (*infml*) be equivalent to sth; indicate sth: *These clues don't really add up to very much,* ie give us very little information.

addendum /əˈdendəm/ *n* (*pl* **-da** /-də/) **1** [C] thing that is to be added. **2 addenda** [sing or pl *v*] material added at the end of a book.

adder /ˈædə(r)/ *n* small poisonous snake; viper.

addict /ˈædɪkt/ *n* **1** person who is unable to stop taking drugs, alcohol, etc: *a heroin addict.* **2** person who is strongly interested in sth: *a chess, TV, football addict.*

▷ **addicted** /əˈdɪktɪd/ *adj* [pred] ~ (**to sth**) **1** unable to stop taking or using sth as a habit: *become addicted to drugs, alcohol, tobacco, etc.* **2** strongly interested in sth as a hobby or pastime: *be addicted to TV soap operas.*

addiction /əˈdɪkʃn/ *n* [U, C] ~ (**to sth**) condition of taking drugs, etc habitually and being unable to stop doing so without suffering adverse effects: *heroin addiction* ○ *overcome one's addiction to alcohol.*

addictive /əˈdɪktɪv/ *adj* causing addiction: *addictive drugs* ○ *Coffee is addictive in a mild way.*

Addison[1] /ˈædɪsn/ Joseph (1672-1719), English essayist and dramatist who co-operated with *Steele on the *Spectator* and was active in politics. As a dramatist he is best known for his tragedy *Cato.*

Addison[2] /ˈædɪsn/ Thomas (1793-1860), English physician who was the first to describe the condition named after him as Addison's disease.

□ **ˈAddison's disease** disease caused by the failure of the adrenal glands. It is marked by extreme weakness, loss of weight, progressive anaemia and a bluish-brown colouring of the skin.

addition /əˈdɪʃn/ *n* **1** [U] adding, esp calculating the total of two or more numbers. **2** [C] ~ (**to sth**) person or thing added or joined: *Such an outfit would be a useful addition to my wardrobe.* ○ *They've just had an addition to the family,* ie another child. ○ *Ann will be a very useful addition to our team.* **3** (idm) **in addition** (**to sth**) as an extra person, thing or circumstance: *In addition (to the names on the list) there are six other applicants.*

▷ **additional** /-ʃənl/ *adj* added; extra; supplementary: *additional charges, candidates, supplies.* **additionally** /-ʃənəlɪ/ *adv.*

additive /ˈædɪtɪv/ *n* substance added in small amounts for a special purpose: *chemical additives in food* ○ *food additives,* ie to add colour or flavour to the food or to preserve it.

▷ **additive** *adj* involving addition.

addle /ˈædl/ *v* **1** [Tn] confuse (sth/sb); muddle: *My brain feels addled.* **2** (**a**) [I] (of an egg) become rotten and not produce a chick. (**b**) [Tn] cause (an egg) to become rotten: *addled eggs.*

address[1] /əˈdres; *US* ˈædres/ *n* **1** details of where a person lives, works or can be found, and where letters, etc may be delivered: *Tell me if you change your address.* ○ *My home/business address is 3 West St, Oxford.* **2** speech made to an audience. **3** (*computing*) part of a computer instruction that specifies where a piece of information is stored. **4** (idm) **a form of address** ⇨ FORM[1].

address[2] /əˈdres/ *v* **1** [Tn, Tn·pr] ~ **sth** (**to sb/sth**) write on (a letter, parcel, etc) the name and address of the person, firm, etc that it is to be delivered to: *The card was wrongly addressed to (us at) our old home.* **2** [Tn] make a speech to (a person or an audience), esp formally: *The chairman will now address the meeting.* **3** [Tn·pr] ~ **sth to sb/sth** direct (a remark or written statement) to sb/sth: *Please address all complaints to the manager.* **4** [Cn·n/a] ~ **sb as sth** use (a particular name or title) in speaking or writing to sb: *Don't address me as 'Colonel': I'm only a major.* **5** [Tn·pr] ~ **oneself to sth** (*fml*) direct one's attention to (a problem); tackle sth: *It is time we addressed ourselves to the main item on the agenda.* **6** [Tn] take aim at (the ball) in golf. **7** [Tn] (*computing*) store or retrieve (a piece of information) by using an address[1](3).

▷ **addressee** /ˌædreˈsiː/ *n* person to whom a letter, etc is addressed.

adduce /əˈdjuːs; *US* əˈduːs/ *v* [Tn] (*fml*) put (sth) forward as an example or as proof: *I could adduce several reasons for his strange behaviour.*

-ade *suff* (with countable *ns* forming uncountable *ns*) drink made from or tasting of the specified fruit: *orangeade.*

Aden /ˈeɪdn/ capital (since 1967) of the People's Democratic Republic of *Yemen (South Yemen) and now part of the *Yemen Republic. As a port situated at the entrance to the *Red Sea it has been a trading centre since Roman times. Between 1839 and 1967 it was a British possession. ⇨ map at ARABIAN PENINSULA.

adenoids /ˈædɪnɔɪdz; *US* -dən-/ *n* [pl] (*anatomy*) excessive growth of spongy tissue between the back of the nose and the throat, often making breathing and speaking difficult: *have one's adenoids out,* ie by a surgical operation ○ (*infml*) *She's got adenoids,* ie is suffering from an inflammation of the adenoids.

▷ **adenoidal** /ˌædɪˈnɔɪdl/ *adj* **1** of the adenoids. **2** affected by diseased adenoids: *an adenoidal child, voice.*

adept /ˈædept, əˈdept/ *adj* ~ (**in sth**); ~ (**at/in doing sth**) expert or skilful in (doing) sth: *She's adept at growing roses.*

▷ **adept** *n* ~ (**at/in sth**) person who is skilful (in sth): *He's an adept in carpentry.*

adequate /ˈædɪkwət/ *adj* ~ (**to/for sth**) satisfactory in quantity or quality; sufficient: *take adequate precautions* ○ *Our accommodation is barely adequate.* ○ *Their earnings are adequate (to their needs).* ○ *Your work is adequate but I'm sure you could do better.* ○ *She has adequate grounds for a divorce.* ▷ **adequacy** /ˈædɪkwəsɪ/ *n* [U]. **adequately** *adv*: *Are you adequately insured?*

adhere /ədˈhɪə(r)/ *v* (*fml*) **1** [I, Ipr] ~ (**to sth**) remain attached (to sth); stick (as if) by means of glue or suction: *Paste is used to make one surface adhere to another.* **2** [Ipr] ~ **to sth** (**a**) give support to sth; remain faithful to sth: *adhere to one's opinions, a promise, a political party.* (**b**) act in accordance with sth; follow sth: *adhere to one's principles, a treaty, a schedule, the rules.*

adherent /ədˈhɪərənt/ *n* supporter of a party or doctrine: *The movement is gaining more and more adherents.*

▷ **adherent** *adj* ~ (**to sth**) sticking; adhering: *an adherent surface.* **adherence** /-rəns/ *n* [U] ~ (**to sth**): *their strict adherence to their religion.*

adhesion /ədˈhiːʒn/ *n* **1** [U] ~ (**to sth**) being or becoming attached (to sth). **2** [U] ~ (**to sth**) (*fml*) support (for a plan, an ideology, a political party, etc). **3** (*medical*) (**a**) [U] unnatural growing together of body tissues that are normally separate, as a result of inflammation or injury. (**b**) [C] tissue formed in this way: *painful adhesions caused by a wound that is slow to heal.*

adhesive /ədˈhiːsɪv/ *adj* that can adhere; causing things to adhere; sticky: *the adhesive side of a stamp* ○ *adhesive tape/plaster.*

▷ **adhesive** *n* [C, U] substance that makes things stick: *quick-drying adhesives.* Cf CEMENT 2, GLUE.

ad hoc /ˌæd ˈhɒk/ *adj, adv* (*Latin*) **1** (made or arranged) for a particular purpose only; special(ly): *appoint an ad hoc committee to deal with the affair.* **2** (in a way that is) not planned in advance; informal(ly): *Problems were solved on an ad hoc basis.* ○ *Points of policy are decided ad hoc.*

adieu /əˈdjuː; *US* əˈduː/ *interj, n* (*pl* **adieus** or **adieux** /əˈdjuːz; *US* əˈduːz/) (*arch or fml*) **1** goodbye: *Bidding them adieu we departed.* **2** (idm) **make one's aˈdieus** say goodbye.

ad infinitum /ˌæd ˌɪnfɪˈnaɪtəm/ (*Latin*) without limit; for ever: *I don't want to go on working here ad infinitum.*

adipose /ˈædɪpəʊs/ *adj* [usu attrib] of animal fat; fatty: *a layer of adipose tissue under the skin.* ▷ **adiposity** /ˌædɪˈpɒsətɪ/ *n* [U].

Adirondack Mountains /ˌædɪˈrɒndæk maʊntɪnz/ **the Adirondack Mountains** (also **the Adirondacks**) mountain range in New York State, USA, an area of great natural beauty, with lakes, waterfalls and forests.

adit /ˈædɪt/ *n* (in mining) horizontal entrance or passage dug into a hillside so that coal or minerals can be reached.

Adj *abbr* Adjutant.

adjacent /əˈdʒeɪsnt/ *adj* ~ (**to sth**) situated near or next to sth; close or touching: *We work in adjacent rooms.* ○ *My room is adjacent to his.* ▷ **adjacency** /-snsɪ/ *n* [U]. **adjacently** *adv.*

□ **adjacent ˈangles** (*geometry*) angles that share a common line. ⇨ illus at ANGLE.

adjective /ˈædʒɪktɪv/ *n* (*grammar*) word that indicates a quality of the person or thing referred to by a noun, eg *old, rotten, foreign* in *an old house, rotten apples, foreign names.*

▷ **adjectival** /ˌædʒekˈtaɪvl/ *adj* of or like an adjective: *an adjectival phrase/clause.*

adjectivally /ˌædʒekˈtaɪvəlɪ/ *adv.*

adjoin /əˈdʒɔɪn/ *v* [I, Tn] be next or nearest to and joined with (sth): *We heard laughter in the adjoining room.* ○ *The playing-field adjoins the school.*

adjourn /əˈdʒɜːn/ *v* **1 (a)** [Tn usu passive] stop (a meeting, etc) for a time; postpone: *The trial was adjourned for a week/until the following week.* **(b)** [I] (of people at a meeting, in court, etc) stop proceedings and separate: *The court will adjourn for lunch.* ○ *Let's adjourn until tomorrow.* **2** [Ipr] ~ **to...** (of people who have come together) go to another place: *After dinner we all adjourned to the lounge.*

▷ **adjournment** *n* [C, U]: *The judge granted us a short adjournment.* **adˈjournment debate** *(Brit)* debate in the House of Commons on the motion that the House should be adjourned, used as an opportunity to raise various matters.

adjudge /əˈdʒʌdʒ/ *v (fml)* **1** (also **adjudicate**) [Tf, Cn·a, Cn·t] declare officially or decide by law: *The court adjudged that she was guilty.* ○ *The court adjudged her (to be) guilty.* **2** [Tn·pr] ~ **sth to sb** award sth to sb: *The court adjudged legal damages to her.*

adjudicate /əˈdʒuːdɪkeɪt/ *v* **1 (a)** [I, Ipr] act as judge in a court, tribunal, contest, etc: *Would you please adjudicate on who should get the prize?* **(b)** [Tn] judge and give a decision on (sth): *adjudicate sb's claim for damages.* **2** [Tf, Cn·a, Cn·t] = ADJUDGE 1.

▷ **adjudication** /əˌdʒuːdɪˈkeɪʃn/ *n* [U].

adjudicator *n* judge, esp in a competition.

adjunct /ˈædʒʌŋkt/ *n* **1** ~ **(to/of sth)** thing that is added or attached to sth else but is less important and not essential. **2** *(grammar)* adverb or adverbial phrase added to a clause or sentence to modify the meaning of the verb.

adjure /əˈdʒʊə(r)/ *v* [Dn·t] *(fml)* command or request (sb) earnestly or solemnly: *I adjure you to tell the truth before this court.* ▷ **adjuration** /ˌædʒʊəˈreɪʃn/ *n* [U, C].

adjust /əˈdʒʌst/ *v* **1** [Tn] **(a)** put (sth) into the correct order or position; arrange: *She carefully adjusted her clothes and her hair before going out.* **(b)** alter (sth) by a small amount so that it will fit or be right for use; regulate: *adjust the rear mirror, the focus of a camera, the sights of a gun* ○ *The brakes need adjusting.* ○ *Please do not adjust your set,* eg as a warning on a TV screen that the controls do not need to be changed. **2** [I, Ipr, Tn, Tn·pr] ~ **(sth/oneself) (to sth)** become or make suited (to new conditions); adapt: *former soldiers who have difficulty in adjusting to civilian life* ○ *The body quickly adjusts (itself) to changes in temperature.* **3** [Tn] decide (the amount to be paid out for loss or damages) when settling an insurance claim.

▷ **adjustable** *adj* that can be adjusted: *adjustable seat-belts.*

adjustment *n* [C, U] (act of) adjusting: *I've made a few minor adjustments to the seating plan.* ○ *Some adjustment of the lens may be necessary.*

adjutant /ˈædʒʊtənt/ *n* army officer responsible for administrative work in a battalion.

□ ˌ**Adjutant** ˈ**General** high-ranking administrative officer in the army.

ˈ**adjutant bird** type of large Indian stork.

Adler /ˈɑːdlə(r)/ Alfred (1870-1937), Austrian psychologist and psychiatrist, an associate of *Freud. Unlike Freud he believed that the need for power was a basic motivation in human behaviour. He developed the concept of the 'inferiority complex' (INFERIOR).

ad lib /ˌæd ˈlɪb/ *adj (infml)* (esp of speaking and performing in public) without preparation; spontaneous: *give an ad lib* (ie improvised) *performance.*

▷ **ad lib** *adv (infml)* **1** without preparation; spontaneously: *I had forgotten to bring my notes and had to speak ad lib.* **2** as one pleases; without restraint; freely: *We were told to help ourselves to the food ad lib.*

ad lib *v* **(-bb-)** [I] *(infml)* speak or act without preparation, esp when performing in public; improvise: *The actress often forgot her lines but was very good at ad libbing.*

Adm *abbr* Admiral: *Adm (Richard) Hill.*

adman /ˈædmæn/ *n* (*pl* **admen** /ˈædmen/) *(infml)* person who produces commercial advertisements.

admass /ˈædmæs/ *n* [sing] *(dated Brit)* section of the public that is thought to be easily influenced by advertising and the media.

admin /ˈædmɪn/ *n* [U] *(infml)* = ADMINISTRATION 2: *The professor's time is entirely taken up with admin, so he can't do any research work.*

administer /ədˈmɪnɪstə(r)/ *v* **1 (a)** [Tn, Dn·pr] ~ **sth (to sb)** *(fml)* hand out or give sth formally; provide: *administer punishment, justice, comfort* ○ *administer relief to famine victims* ○ *administer the last rites to a dying man* ○ *administer an oath to sb,* ie hear him swear it officially. **(b)** [Tn] put (sth) into operation; apply: *administer the law.* **2** [Tn] control the affairs of (a business, etc); manage: *administer a charity, a trust fund, an estate* ○ *administer* (ie govern) *a country.*

administration /ədˌmɪnɪˈstreɪʃn/ *n* **1** [U] ~ **(of sth)** administering; giving: *be responsible for the administration of justice, the law, charitable aid, an oath, a remedy.* **2** [U] management of public or business affairs: *He works in hospital administration.* ○ *Head teachers are more involved in administration than in teaching.* **3** (often **the Administration**) [C] (part of the Government that manages public affairs during the) period of office of a US president: *during the Kennedy administration* ○ *Successive administrations have failed to solve the country's economic problems.*

administrative /ədˈmɪnɪstrətɪv; *US* -streɪtɪv/ *adj* of or involving the management of public or business affairs: *an administrative post, problem* ○ *Her duties are purely administrative.* ▷ **administratively** *adv*: *administratively complicated.*

administrator /ədˈmɪnɪstreɪtə(r)/ *n* **1 (a)** person responsible for managing (esp business) affairs. **(b)** person able to manage well: *She's an excellent administrator.* **2** *(law)* person appointed to manage the property of others.

admirable /ˈædmərəbl/ *adj* deserving or causing admiration; excellent: *an admirable performance* ○ *His handling of the situation was admirable.* ▷ **admirably** /-əblɪ/ *adv.*

admiral /ˈædmərəl/ *n* **(a)** naval officer of high rank, specifically (in the British Royal Navy) any of the four grades Admiral of the Fleet, Admiral, Vice Admiral and Rear Admiral. **(b) Admiral** naval officer of the second highest rank: *Admiral Wilson.* ⇨ App 4.

▷ **admiralty** /-əltɪ/ *n* **the Admiralty (a)** [Gp] former British government department that administered the Royal Navy. **(b)** [sing] government building in London where the Admiralty offices were, now the headquarters of the Civil Service. ˌ**Admiralty** ˈ**Arch** triumphal arch in London near the Admiralty, built as a memorial to Queen *Victoria.

□ ˌ**Admiral of the** ˈ**Fleet** (*US* ˌ**Fleet** ˈ**Admiral**) commander-in-chief of the Navy.

the ˌ**Admiral's** ˈ**Cup** prize given to the winner of a British yachting contest consisting of four races and held every two years.

admiration /ˌædməˈreɪʃn/ *n* **1** [U] feeling of respect, warm approval or pleasure: *Her handling of the crisis fills me with admiration.* ○ *I have great admiration for his courage.* ○ *They looked in silent admiration at the painting.* **2** [sing] person or thing that is admired: *He was the admiration of his whole family.* **3** (idm) **a mutual admiration society** ⇨ MUTUAL.

admire /ədˈmaɪə(r)/ *v* **1** [Tn, Tn·pr, Tsg] ~ **sb/sth (for sth)** regard sb/sth with respect, pleasure, satisfaction, etc: *They admired our garden.* ○ *I admire him for his success in business.* **2** [Tn] express admiration of (sb/sth): *Aren't you going to admire my new hat?*

▷ **admirer** *n* **(a)** person who admires sb/sth: *I am not a great admirer of her work.* **(b)** man who admires and is attracted to a woman: *She has many admirers.*

admiring *adj* showing or feeling admiration: *give sb/receive admiring glances* ○ *be welcomed by admiring fans.* **admiringly** *adv.*

admissible /ədˈmɪsəbl/ *adj* **1** *(law)* that can be allowed: *admissible evidence.* **2** *(fml)* worthy of being accepted or considered: *Such behaviour is not admissible among our staff.* ▷ **admissibility** /ədˌmɪsəˈbɪlətɪ/ *n* [U]. **admissibly** /-blɪ/ *adv.*

admission /ədˈmɪʃn/ *n* **1** [U] ~ **(to/into sth)** entering or being allowed to enter a building, society, school, etc: *Admission (to the club) is restricted to members only.* ○ *Admission to British universities depends on examination results.* ○ *A week after his admission into the army, he fell ill.* ○ *Do they charge for admission?* ○ *How does one gain admission to the State Apartments?* **2** [U] money charged for being admitted to a public place: *You have to pay £2 admission.* **3** [C] ~ **(of sth)**; ~ **(that...)** statement acknowledging the truth of sth; confession: *an admission that one has lied* ○ *Her resignation amounts to an admission of failure.* **4** (idm) **by/on one's own adˈmisssion** as one has oneself admitted: *He is a coward by his own admission.*

admit /ədˈmɪt/ *v* **(-tt-) 1** [Tn, Tn·pr] ~ **sb/sth (into/to sth) (a)** allow sb/sth to enter: *That man is not to be admitted.* ○ *Each ticket admits two people to the party.* ○ *The small window admitted very little light.* **(b)** accept sb into a hospital as a patient, or into a school, etc as a pupil: *The school admits sixty new boys and girls every year.* ○ *He was admitted to hospital with minor burns.* **2** [Tn] (of an enclosed space) have room for (sb/sth): *The theatre admits only 250 people.* **3** [Ipr, Tn, Tf, Tnt, Tg] ~ **to sth/doing sth** recognize or acknowledge sth as true, often reluctantly; confess sth: *George would never admit to being wrong.* ○ *The prisoner has admitted his guilt.* ○ *I admit my mistake/that I was wrong.* ○ *I admit (that) you have a point.* ○ *He admitted having stolen the car.* ○ *It is now generally admitted to have been* (ie Most people agree and accept that it was) *a mistake.* **4** [Ipr] ~ **of sth** *(fml)* allow the possibility of sth; leave room for sth: *His conduct admits of no excuse.* ○ *The plan does not admit of improvement,* ie cannot be improved. **5** (idm) **be admitted to sb's presence** *(fml)* be allowed to enter the room, etc where sb (esp sb important) is.

▷ **admitted** *adj* [attrib] as one has admitted oneself to be: *an admitted liar.* **admittedly** *adv* (esp in initial position) as is or must be admitted: *Admittedly, he didn't know that at the time.* ○ *Admittedly, I've never actually been there.*

admittance /ədˈmɪtns/ *n* [U] **1** allowing sb or being allowed to enter (esp a private place); right of entry: *No admittance — keep out!* ○ *I was refused admittance to the house.* **2** ease with which an alternating current can flow through an electric circuit. Cf IMPEDANCE.

admixture /ædˈmɪkstʃə(r)/ *n (fml)* **(a)** [C] thing added, esp as a minor ingredient. **(b)** [U] process of adding this.

admonish /ədˈmɒnɪʃ/ *v (fml)* **1** [Tn, Tn·pr] ~ **sb (for/against sth)** give a mild but firm warning or scolding to sb: *The teacher admonished the boys for being lazy.* **2** [Dn·t] advise or urge (sb) seriously: *She admonished us to seek professional help.*

▷ **admonishment, admonition** /ˌædməˈnɪʃn/ *ns* [U, C] *(fml)* warning.

admonitory /ədˈmɒnɪtrɪ; *US* -tɔːrɪ/ *adj (fml)* admonishing: *an admonitory letter, tone of voice.*

ad nauseam /ˌæd ˈnɔːzɪæm/ *(Latin)* to an excessive or sickening extent: *play the same four records ad nauseam,* ie again and again so that it becomes irritating.

ado /əˈduː/ *n* [U] trouble; fuss; unnecessary activity (used esp as in the expressions shown): *Without more/much/further ado, we set off.* ○ *It was all much ado about nothing.*

adobe /əˈdəʊbɪ/ *n* [U] **1** brick made of clay and straw and dried in the sun: [attrib] *adobe houses.* **2** clay from which this type of brick is made.

adolescence /ˌædəˈlesns/ *n* [U] time in a person's life between childhood and mature adulthood: *during (one's) adolescence.*

▷ **adolescent** /ˌædəˈlesnt/ *adj* of or typical of

adolescence: *adolescent boys, crises, attitudes.* — *n* young person between childhood and adulthood (ie roughly between the ages of 13 and 17).

Adonis /əˈdəʊnɪs/ *n* **1** (in Greek mythology) beautiful young man who was loved by *Aphrodite. **2** (*fig*) any handsome young man.

adopt /əˈdɒpt/ *v* **1** [Tn, Tn·pr] ~ **sb (as sth)** take sb into one's family, esp as one's child or heir: *Having no children of their own they decided to adopt an orphan.* ○ *Paul's mother had him adopted because she couldn't look after him herself.* ○ *He is their adopted son.* Cf FOSTER 2. **2** [Tn·pr] ~ **sb as sth** choose sb as a candidate or representative: *She has been adopted as Labour candidate for York.* **3** [Tn] take over and have or use (sth) as one's own: *adopt a name, a custom, an idea, a style of dress* ○ *adopt a hard line towards terrorists* ○ *her adopted country*, ie not her native country but the one in which she has chosen to live. **4** [Tn] accept (eg a report or recommendation); approve: *Congress has adopted the new measures.*

▷ **adoption** /əˈdɒpʃn/ *n* [C, U] (act of) adopting or being adopted: *offer a child for adoption* ○ *her adoption as Labour candidate for York* ○ *the country of her adoption* ○ *This textbook has had adoptions* (ie been officially chosen for special study) *in many countries.*

adoptive *adj* [usu attrib] related by adoption: *his adoptive parents.*

adorable /əˈdɔːrəbl/ *adj* very attractive; delightful; lovable: *What an adorable child!* ○ *Your dress is absolutely adorable.* ○ *My darling, you are adorable.* ▷ **adorably** /-əblɪ/ *adv.*

adore /əˈdɔː(r)/ *v* **1** [Tn] **(a)** love deeply and respect (sb) highly: *He adores his wife and children.* **(b)** worship (God). **2** [Tn, Tg] (*infml*) (not used in the continuous tenses) like (sth) very much: *adore ice-cream, Paris, skiing* ○ *I simply adore that dress!*

▷ **adoration** /ˌædəˈreɪʃn/ *n* [U] great love or worship: *be filled with adoration* ○ *They knelt in adoration of their gods.* **the ˌAdoration of the ˈMagi** visit of the three Kings to worship the infant Jesus, described in St Matthew's Gospel. It has been the subject of many paintings since early Christian times.

adoring /əˈdɔːrɪŋ/ *adj* [usu attrib] showing great love: *his adoring grandmother* ○ *give sb an adoring look.* **adoringly** *adv.*

adorn /əˈdɔːn/ *v* [Tn, Tn·pr] ~ **sth/sb/oneself (with sth)** add beauty or ornament to sth/sb/oneself: *admire the paintings that adorn the walls* ○ *The dancer was adorned with flowers.*

▷ **adornment** *n* **1** [U] act of adorning: *a simple dress without adornment.* **2** [C] thing that adorns; ornament: *Many adornments were carved on the temple walls.*

ADP /ˌeɪ diː ˈpiː/ *abbr* automatic data processing (by computers).

adrenal /əˈdriːnl/ *adj* (*anatomy*) close to the kidneys.

□ **aˈdrenal gland** (*anatomy*) either of the two ductless glands above the kidney that produce adrenalin.

adrenalin /əˈdrenəlɪn/ *n* [U] (*medical*) **(a)** hormone produced by the adrenal glands that increases the heart rate and stimulates the nervous system, causing a feeling of excitement. **(b)** this substance prepared synthetically for medical use.

Adriatic Sea /ˌeɪdrɪætɪk ˈsiː/ **the Adriatic Sea** (also **the Adriatic**) area of the Mediterranean Sea that is situated between Italy to the west and the former Yugoslavia and Albania to the east.

adrift /əˈdrɪft/ *adj* [pred] **1 (a)** (esp of a boat) driven by wind and water and out of control; drifting: *cut a boat adrift from its moorings* ○ *The survivors were adrift on a raft for six days.* **(b)** (*fig*) having no purpose; aimless: *young people adrift in our big cities* ○ *turn sb adrift*, ie send sb away without help or support. **2** (*infml*) **(a)** unfastened; loose: *Part of the car's bumper had come adrift.* **(b)** out of order; wrong: *Our plans went badly adrift.*

adroit /əˈdrɔɪt/ *adj* ~ **(at/in sth)** skilful; clever: *the minister's adroit handling of the crisis* ○ *He soon became adroit at steering the boat.* Cf MALADROIT.

▷ **adroitly** *adv.* **adroitness** *n* [U].

adsorb /ədˈsɔːb/ *v* [Tn] (usu of a solid) attract and hold (a gas or liquid) to its surface: *Iron adsorbs oxygen.* ▷ **adsorbent** /-ənt/ *adj.* **adsorption** /ədˈsɔːpʃn/ *n* [U].

ADT /ˌeɪ diː ˈtiː/ *abbr* (in Canada, Puerto Rico and Bermuda) Atlantic Daylight Time.

adulation /ˌædjʊˈleɪʃn; *US* ˌædʒʊˈl-/ *n* [U] excessive admiration or praise; flattery: *the fans' adulation of their favourite pop stars.* ▷ **adulatory** *adj.*

adult /ˈædʌlt, *also* əˈdʌlt/ *adj* **1 (a)** grown to full size or strength: *adult monkeys.* **(b)** intellectually and emotionally mature: *His behaviour is not particularly adult.* **2** (*law*) old enough to vote, marry, etc.

▷ **adult** *n* adult person or animal: *These films are suitable for adults only.* ○ *The bear was a fully grown adult.* ○ [attrib] *adult education*, ie for those over the usual school age.

adulthood *n* [U] state of being adult: *reach adulthood.*

adulterate /əˈdʌltəreɪt/ *v* [Tn] make (sth) poorer in quality by adding another substance: *adulterated milk*, eg with water added. ▷ **adulteration** /əˌdʌltəˈreɪʃn/ *n* [U].

adultery /əˈdʌltərɪ/ *n* [U] voluntary sexual intercourse between a married person and sb who is not that person's husband or wife: *commit adultery.*

▷ **adulterer** /əˈdʌltərə(r)/ (*fem* **adulteress** /əˈdʌltərɪs/) *n* person who commits adultery.

adulterous /əˈdʌltərəs/ *adj* of or involving adultery: *have an adulterous affair with sb.*

adumbrate /ˈædʌmbreɪt/ *v* [Tn] (*fml*) **1** indicate (sth) faintly or in outline. **2** suggest (esp a coming event) in advance; foreshadow. ▷ **adumbration** /ˌædʌmˈbreɪʃn/ *n* [U, C].

advance[1] /ədˈvɑːns; *US* -ˈvæns/ *n* **1** [C usu *sing*] forward movement: *The enemy's advance was halted.* **2 (a)** [U] progress: *the continued advance of civilization.* **(b)** [C] ~ **(in sth)** improvement: *recent advances in medical science.* **3** [C] ~ **(on sth)** increase in price or amount: *'Any advance on* (ie Who will offer more than) *£20?' called the auctioneer.* ○ *Share prices showed significant advances today.* **4** [C] money paid before it is due, or for work only partially completed; loan: *The bank gave/made her an advance of £500.* ○ *She asked for an advance on her salary.* **5 advances** [pl] ~ **(to sb)** attempts to establish a friendly or an amorous relationship or a business agreement: *He made advances to her.* ○ *She rejected his advances.* **6** (idm) **in advance (of sth)** beforehand; ahead in time: *The rent must be paid in advance.* ○ *Send your luggage on in advance.* ○ *It's impossible to know in advance what will happen.* ○ *Galileo's ideas were well in advance of the age in which he lived.*

▷ **advance** *adj* [attrib] **1** going before others: *the advance party*, ie a group (of explorers, soldiers, etc) sent on ahead. **2** done or provided in advance: *give sb advance warning/notice of sth* ○ *make an advance booking*, ie reserve a hotel room, a seat in a theatre, etc before the time when it is needed ○ *an advance copy of a new book*, ie one supplied before publication.

advance[2] /ədˈvɑːns; *US* -ˈvæns/ *v* **1 (a)** [I, Ipr, In/pr] ~ **(on/towards sb/sth)** come or go forward: *The mob advanced towards/on us shouting angrily.* ○ *Our troops have advanced two miles.* **(b)** [I] (*fig*) make progress: *advance in one's career* ○ *Has civilization advanced during this century?* **2** [Tn] move or put (sb/sth) forward: *The general advanced his troops at night.* ○ *He advanced his queen to threaten his opponent's king*, ie in a game of chess. Cf RETREAT 1. **3** [Tn] help the progress of (sth); promote (a person, plan, etc): *Such conduct is unlikely to advance your interests.* **4** [Tn] (*fml*) make or present (a claim, suggestion, etc): *Scientists have advanced a new theory to explain this phenomenon.* **5** [Dn·n, Dn·pr] ~ **sth (to sb)** pay (money) before it is due to be paid; lend (money): *The bank advanced me £2000.* ○ *He asked his employer to advance him a month's salary.* **6** [Tn, Tn·pr] bring (an event) to an earlier date: *The date of the meeting was advanced from 10 to 3 June.* Cf POSTPONE 1. **7 (a)** [Tn] increase (a price). **(b)** [I] (of prices, costs, etc) rise: *Property values continue to advance rapidly.*

▷ **advanced** *adj* **1** far on in life or progress: *be advanced in years* ○ *She died at an advanced age.* **2** not elementary: *advanced studies.* **3** new and not yet generally accepted: *have advanced ideas.*

□ **advanced ˈcredit** (also **advanced ˈstanding**) (*US*) credit given by one college for courses taken at another.

Adˈvanced level (also **A level** /ˈeɪ levl/) (in Britain) further examination taken after the General Certificate of Secondary Education, usually in two or three subjects only. Cf A/S LEVEL, S LEVEL, GENERAL CERTIFICATE OF SECONDARY EDUCATION (GENERAL).

Adˌvanced ˈPassenger Train (*abbr* **APT**) British experimental high-speed electric train.

advancement /ədˈvɑːnsmənt; *US* -ˈvænsmənt/ *n* [U] **1** process of advancing; furthering: *the advancement of learning.* **2** promotion in rank or status: *The job offers good opportunities for advancement.*

advantage /ədˈvɑːntɪdʒ; *US* -ˈvæn-/ *n* **1 (a)** [C] ~ **(over sb)** condition or circumstance that gives one superiority or success (esp when competing with others): *gain an advantage over an opponent* ○ *He has the advantage of a steady job.* ○ *Her French upbringing gives her certain advantages over other students in her class.* **(b)** [U] benefit; profit: *There is little advantage in buying a dictionary if you can't read.* **2** [sing] (in tennis) first point scored after deuce: [attrib] *Becker reached advantage point several times before losing the game.* **3** (idm) **have the advantage of sb** be in a better position than sb, esp in knowing sth that he does not know: *You have the advantage of me, I'm afraid*, eg said when a stranger addresses one by name. **take advantage of sth/sb (a)** make use of sth well, properly, etc: *They took full advantage of the hotel's facilities.* **(b)** make use of sb/sth unfairly or deceitfully to get what one wants; exploit sb/sth: *She took advantage of my generosity*, ie took more than I had intended to give. ○ *He's using his charm to try to take advantage of her*, ie seduce her. **to adˈvantage** in a way that shows the best aspects of sth: *The picture may be seen to (its best) advantage against a plain wall.* **to sb's advantage** with results which are profitable or helpful to sb: *The agreement is/works to our advantage.* **turn sth to one's (own) adˈvantage** cause (a situation or an event) to lead to personal profit; make the most of sth.

▷ **advantage** *v* [Tn] (*fml*) be beneficial to (sb); profit.

advantageous /ˌædvənˈteɪdʒəs/ *adj* ~ **(to sb)** profitable; beneficial. **advantageously** *adv.*

advection /ædˈvekʃn/ *n* [U] transfer of heat by the horizontal flow of air: *the advection of warm air from tropical areas through wind movements.* Cf CONVECTION.

advent /ˈædvənt/ *n* [sing] **1 the ~ of sth/sb** the approach or arrival of (an important person, event, etc): *With the advent of the new chairman, the company began to prosper.* **2 Advent (a)** the period (with four Sundays) before Christmas, when Christians prepare for the celebration of Christ's birth: [attrib] *Advent hymns.* ⇨ article at CHRISTMAS. **(b)** (*Bible*) the coming of Christ to earth.

▷ **Adventist** /ˈædvəntɪst, *also* ədˈventɪst/ *n* member of various religious groups believing that Christ's second coming is very near. The largest is the Seventh-day Adventists, founded in 1860.

□ **ˈAdvent calendar** pictorial calendar for the period of Advent, esp one for children, with flaps to be opened each day revealing pictures.

ˌAdvent ˈSunday Sunday nearest 30 November, marking the beginning of Advent.

adventitious /ˌædvenˈtɪʃəs/ *adj* **1** (*fml*) not planned; accidental: *an adventitious occurrence.* **2** (*biology*) (of a plant or animal part) occurring in an unusual position: *Ivy has adventitious roots growing from its stems.*

adventure /ədˈventʃə(r)/ *n* **1** [C] unusual,

Advertising

Almost everyone in Britain and North America is exposed daily to advertising, in the press, on television and on hoardings. Newspapers, magazines and television companies are dependent on advertising for a large part of their income. Glossy magazines and the supplements to Sunday newspapers frequently contain full-page colour advertisements of different kinds, with the product or service often carefully aimed at a particular type of reader (according to age, social status, profession, sex, etc). In Britain, about 64 per cent of total advertising expenditure is on advertising in the press and 30 per cent on television advertising.

National newspapers concentrate more on specialized advertising, especially for business and professional people, while local papers frequently have a high proportion of advertisements devoted to the sale of cars and houses. All newspapers have a section called 'classified ads' where small advertisements or announcements are listed under various headings. Free newspapers, which are delivered weekly to most homes, have the highest advertising content of all newspapers.

One of the most powerful and pervasive types of advertising is that of television, and slogans used in television commercials often become popular catchphrases. All the independent channels in Britain, ITV, Channel 4 and the satellite stations include commercial breaks in their schedules, both between programmes and during them. Similar commercial advertising is carried by the independent radio stations. BBC television and radio (and in the USA, CBC and PBS), however, carry no advertising.

Manufacturers often use other methods of promotion to advertise their products. Sometimes leaflets with details of a particular product are inserted in a magazine or newspaper, or posted to a person's home. Free samples of new products are often also delivered. A firm may telephone people at home to tell them about a product or service, perhaps with a special 'introductory offer' to persuade them to buy. As more of these direct marketing and telephone 'shots' are used both in Britain and the USA, many people regard them as a nuisance and ask for their names to be taken off the mailing lists, which are often sold by one company to another.

In towns, advertisements are seen on almost every street, both in individual shops and on hoardings and posters. Stores place eye-catching notices in the window to tempt people in, and advertisements are put on buses and taxis, and inside trains on the London Underground.

Many large companies sponsor popular events as well as individual athletes or players, using the opportunity to advertise their name prominently at the sports ground or on the individual's sportswear or equipment. Tobacco companies frequently use this method.

Advertising on British television is subject to strict regulations. It is limited to 7½ minutes an hour between 6.00 and 11.00 pm and advertising breaks may not be inserted in certain kinds of programmes, such as schools broadcasts. No advertising of a political nature is allowed, and advertisements for cigarettes and betting are also prohibited. On the other hand, cigars and alcoholic drinks are heavily promoted on television. On independent radio, advertising is restricted to a maximum of 9 minutes per hour. Recent changes in the law mean that some professional groups that were previously not allowed to advertise their services, may do so. These include solicitors and family doctors in Britain and lawyers in the USA.

In Britain advertising in the press, the cinema and on posters is controlled by the Advertising Standards Authority, which aims to ensure that advertisements are 'legal, decent, honest and truthful'. The public has the right to complain to the authority about any advertisement. The Independent Broadcasting Authority (IBA) is responsible for controlling advertising on television.

exciting or dangerous experience or undertaking: *have an adventure* ○ *her adventures in Africa.* **2** [U] excitement associated with danger, taking risks, etc: *a love/spirit/sense of adventure* ○ *a life full of adventure* ○ [attrib] *adventure stories.*

▷ **adventurer** /əd'ventʃərə(r)/ (*fem* **adventuress** /əd'ventʃərɪs/) *n* **1** person who seeks adventures. **2** (*often derog*) person who is ready to take risks or act dishonestly, immorally, etc in seeking personal gain.

adventurous *adj* **1** eager for or fond of adventure: *adventurous children.* **2** full of danger and excitement: *an adventurous holiday.* **adventurously** *adv.*

□ **ad'venture playground** playground containing objects and structures of wood, metal, etc for children to play with, in or on.

adverb /'ædvɜːb/ *n* (*grammar*) word that adds more information about place, time, circumstance, manner, cause, degree, etc to a verb, an adjective, a phrase or another adverb: *In 'speak kindly', 'incredibly deep', 'just in time' and 'too quickly', 'kindly', 'incredibly', 'just' and 'too' are all adverbs.*

▷ **adverbial** /æd'vɜːbɪəl/ *adj* of, like or containing an adverb: *'Very quickly indeed' is an adverbial phrase.* **adverbially** /æd'vɜːbɪəlɪ/ *adv.*

adversary /'ædvəsərɪ; *US* -serɪ/ *n* opponent in a contest; enemy: *He defeated his old adversary.*

adverse /'ædvɜːs/ *adj* [usu attrib] **1** (**a**) not favourable; contrary: *adverse winds, weather conditions, circumstances.* (**b**) hostile; opposing: *adverse criticism* ○ *an adverse reaction to the proposals.* **2** harmful: *the adverse effects of drugs.* ▷ **adversely** *adv*: *His health was adversely affected by the climate.*

adversity /əd'vɜːsətɪ/ *n* **1** [U] unfavourable conditions; trouble: *remain cheerful in adversity* ○ *face adversity with courage.* **2** [C] unfortunate event or circumstances: *She overcame many adversities.*

advert /'ædvɜːt/ *n* (*Brit infml*) = ADVERTISEMENT 2 (ADVERTISE).

advertise /'ædvətaɪz/ *v* **1** [Tn] make (sth) generally or publicly known: *advertise a meeting, a concert, a job* ○ *It may be safer not to advertise your presence.* **2** [I, Tn] praise (sth) publicly in order to encourage people to buy or use it: *advertise on TV, in a newspaper* ○ *advertise soap, one's house, one's services.* **3** [Ipr] ~ **for sb/sth** ask for sb/sth by placing a notice in a newspaper, etc: *I must advertise for a new secretary.*

▷ **advertisement** /əd'vɜːtɪsmənt; *US* ˌædvər'taɪzmənt/ *n* **1** [U] action of advertising: [attrib] *the advertisement page.* **2** [C] (also **advert, ad**) ~ (**for sb/sth**) public notice offering or asking for goods, services, etc: *If you want to sell your old sofa, why not put an advertisement in the local paper?*

advertiser *n* **1** person who advertises. **2 Advertiser** title of various local newspapers, esp in Britain: *the Durham Advertiser.*

advertising *n* [U] **1** action of advertising: [attrib] *a national advertising campaign.* **2** business that deals with the publicizing of goods, esp to increase sales: *He works in advertising.* ○ *Cigarette advertising should be banned.* ○ [attrib] *advertising revenue.* ⇨ article. **the ˌAdvertising 'Standards Authority** (*abbr* **ASA**) independent organization that checks standards of advertising in Britain, aiming to make sure that all advertisements are truthful and legal.

advice /əd'vaɪs/ *n* [U] **1** opinion given about what to do or how to behave: *act on/follow/take sb's advice*, ie do what sb suggests ○ *You should take legal advice*, ie consult a lawyer. ○ *My advice to you would be to wait.* ○ *If you take my advice you'll see a doctor.* ○ *Let me give you a piece/a bit/a few words/a word of advice....* **2** (*esp commerce*) formal note giving information about a transaction, etc: *We received advice that the goods had been dispatched.* ○ [attrib] *an advice note.*

advisable /əd'vaɪzəbl/ *adj* [usu pred] worth recommending as a course of action; sensible: *Do you think it advisable to wait?* ▷ **advisability** /ədˌvaɪzə'bɪlətɪ/ *n* [U].

advise /əd'vaɪz/ *v* **1** [Ipr, Tn, Tn·pr, Tf, Tw, Tg, Dn·f, Dn·w, Dn·t] ~ (**sb**) **against sth/doing sth**; ~ **sb** (**on sth**) give advice to sb; recommend: *The doctor advised (me to take) a complete rest.* ○ *They advised her against marrying quickly.* ○ *She advises the Government on economic affairs.* ○ *We advised that they should start early/advised them to start early.* ○ *I'd advise taking a different approach.* ○ *You would be well advised* (ie sensible) *to stay indoors.* ○ *Can you advise (me) what to do next?* **2** [Tn, Tn·pr, Dn·f, Dn·w] ~ **sb** (**of sth**) (*esp commerce*) inform or notify sb: *Please advise us of the dispatch of the goods/when the goods are dispatched.*

▷ **advisedly** /əd'vaɪzɪdlɪ/ *adv* (*fml*) after careful thought; deliberately: *I use these words advisedly.*

adviser (also *esp US* **advisor**) *n* ~ (**to sb**) (**on sth**) person who gives advice, esp sb who is regularly consulted: *serve as special adviser to the President.*

advisory /əd'vaɪzərɪ/ *adj* having the power to advise; giving advice: *an advisory committee, body, role.*

advocacy /'ædvəkəsɪ/ *n* [U] **1** ~ (**of sth**) giving of support (to a cause, etc): *She is well known for her advocacy of women's rights.* **2** (*law*) profession or work of an advocate(2a).

advocate /'ædvəkeɪt/ *v* [Tn, Tf, Tg, Tsg] speak publicly in favour of (sth); recommend; support: *I advocate a policy of gradual reform.* ○ *Do you advocate banning cars in the city centre?*

▷ **advocate** /'ædvəkət/ *n* **1** ~ (**of sth**) person who supports or speaks in favour of a cause, policy, etc: *a lifelong advocate of disarmament.* **2** (**a**) person who pleads on behalf of another, esp a lawyer who presents a client's case in a lawcourt. Cf BARRISTER, SOLICITOR, article at LAW. (**b**) (*Scot*) = BARRISTER. Cf LORD ADVOCATE (LORD). **3** (idm) **devil's advocate** ⇨ DEVIL[1].

advt *abbr* advertisement.

adze (*US* **adz**) /ædz/ *n* tool like an axe with a blade at right angles to the handle used for cutting or shaping large pieces of wood.

Aegean Sea /ɪˌdʒiːən 'siː/ **the Aegean Sea** (also **the Aegean**) area of the Mediterranean Sea between Greece and Turkey.

aegis /'iːdʒɪs/ *n* (idm) **under the aegis of sb/sth** with the protection or support of sb/sth, esp a public institution. In Greek mythology, the Aegis was the indestructible shield of the god Zeus, which symbolized divine protection: *Medical supplies are being flown in under the aegis of the Red Cross.*

Aelfric /ˈælfrɪk/ (c 955-1010), English monk and the best-known prose writer in Old English literature. His most famous work is the *Catholic Homilies*.

Aeneas /ɪˈni:əs/ (in Greek and Roman legend) Trojan leader, who after the defeat of Troy wandered for a long time, finally reaching Italy. The Romans regarded him as the founder of their state. He is the hero of the *Aeneid*, and also appears in the *Iliad*.

Aeneid /ˈi:ni:ɪd/ **the Aeneid** Latin epic poem by *Virgil describing the travels and adventures of the Trojan hero *Aeneas after the Greeks had destroyed *Troy.

aeolian (*US* **eolian**) /i:ˈəʊlɪən/ *adj* (*fml or geology*) of, caused by or carried by the wind: *aeolian rock formations.*

□ **aeˌolian ˈharp** musical instrument that makes sounds when the wind blows over its strings.

aeon (also **eon**) /ˈi:ən/ *n* period of time so long that it cannot be measured: *The earth was formed aeons ago.*

aerate /ˈeəreɪt/ *v* [Tn] **1** add carbon dioxide to (a liquid) under pressure: *aerated water.* **2** expose (sth) to the chemical action of air: *aerate the soil by digging it.* ▷ **aeration** /eəˈreɪʃn/ *n* [U].

aerial[1] /ˈeərɪəl/ (*US* **antenna**) *n* one or more wires or rods for sending or receiving radio waves. ⇨ illus at HOME.

aerial[2] /ˈeərɪəl/ *adj* **1** from aircraft or the air: *aerial bombardment, photography, reconnaissance.* **2** existing or suspended in the air: *an aerial railway.* **3** (*arch*) of or like air.

aerie = EYRIE.

aero- *comb form* of air or aircraft: *aerodynamic* ○ *aerospace.*

aerobatics /ˌeərəˈbætɪks/ *n* **1** [pl] spectacular feats performed with aircraft, esp as part of a display, eg flying upside-down or in loops: *The aerobatics were the best part of the show.* **2** [sing *v*] art of performing these: *Aerobatics is a dangerous sport.* ▷ **aerobatic** *adj.*

aerobe /ˈeərəʊb/ *n* micro-organism that needs oxygen or air to live and grow.

▷ **aerobic** /eəˈrəʊbɪk/ *adj* **1** using oxygen from the air: *aerobic respiration.* **2** (of exercises) designed to increase the amount of oxygen taken into the body.

aerobics /-bɪks/ *n* [pl] very energetic aerobic exercises.

aerodrome /ˈeərədrəʊm/ *n* (*dated esp Brit*) small airport or airfield, used mainly by private aircraft.

aerodynamics /ˌeərəʊdaɪˈnæmɪks/ *n* [pl, usu sing *v*] science dealing with the forces acting on solid bodies (eg aircraft or bullets) moving through air. ▷ **aerodynamic** *adj.*

aerofoil /ˈeərəfɔɪl/ (*US* **airfoil** /ˈeəfɔɪl/) *n* structure (eg an aircraft wing) shaped so that it produces a lifting force as it moves forward through the air.

aeronautics /ˌeərəˈnɔ:tɪks/ *n* [pl, usu sing *v*] scientific study or practice of flying and navigating aircraft. ▷ **aeronautic, aeronautical** /-ˈnɔ:tɪkl/ *adjs*: *aeronautical engineering, skills.*

aeroplane /ˈeərəpleɪn/ (*US* **airplane** /ˈeərpleɪn/) *n* aircraft that is heavier than air, with wings and one or more engines.

aerosol /ˈeərəsɒl; *US* -sɔ:l/ *n* **1** very small solid or liquid particles suspended in a gas. **2** (**a**) substance (eg scent, paint, insecticide) sealed in a container with gas under pressure, with a device for releasing it as a fine spray. Scientists now believe that the type of gas typically used in such containers accumulates in the earth's upper atmosphere and damages the ozone layer (OZONE): [attrib] *an aerosol can.* ⇨ illus at CAN. (**b**) such a container: *Deodorants are available as aerosols or roll-ons.*

aerospace /ˈeərəʊspeɪs/ *n* [U] **1** the earth's atmosphere and the space beyond it. **2** technology of aircraft, spacecraft, etc that operate in this: [attrib] *the aerospace industry.*

Aeschylus /ˈi:skələs/ (c 525-456 BC), Greek dramatist regarded as one of the founders of Greek tragedy. He wrote over 80 plays, of which only seven survive (eg *Prometheus Bound* and the *Oresteia* trilogy). They are filled with deep religious feeling and emphasize the power of destiny and of the gods.

Aesculapius /ˌi:skjʊˈleɪpɪəs/ Latin name for Asclepius, the god of medicine and healing in Greek mythology.

▷ **Aesculapian** *adj* (*fml*) of medicine or doctors.

Aesop /ˈi:sɒp/ (early 6th century BC), Greek teller of moral stories, said to have been a slave and to have been deformed.

□ **ˌAesop's ˈFables** collection of stories about animals which behave in a human way. Each story teaches a moral lesson. Traditionally they are said to have been told by Aesop, although many are far older.

aesthete /ˈi:sθi:t/ (*US* also **esthete** /ˈesθi:t/) *n* (*sometimes derog*) person who has or claims to have a fine appreciation of art and beauty.

aesthetic /i:sˈθetɪk/ (*US* also **esthetic** /esˈθetɪk/) *adj* [usu attrib] **1** (**a**) concerned with beauty and the appreciation of beauty: *aesthetic standards* ○ *an aesthetic sense.* (**b**) appreciating beauty and beautiful things: *an aesthetic person.* **2** pleasing to look at; artistic; tasteful: *aesthetic design* ○ *Their furniture was more aesthetic than practical.*

▷ **aesthetically** (*US* also **es-**) /-klɪ/ *adv*: *aesthetically pleasing.*

aestheticism /i:sˈθetɪsɪzəm/ (*US* also **es-**) *n* [U] belief that art should be appreciated simply as art and should serve no other purpose, whether political, moral, social or religious. It is generally expressed by the phrase 'art for art's sake', and was first formulated by the philosopher *Kant. It was also emphasized by *Goethe and *Schiller, and was introduced to Britain by the poet *Coleridge and the historian and philosopher *Carlyle.

aesthetics (*US* also **es-**) *n* [sing *v*] branch of philosophy dealing with the principles of beauty and artistic taste.

□ **the Aesˈthetic movement** literary and artistic movement which developed in England in the 1880s and which was devoted to 'art for art's sake'. It was greatly influenced by *Ruskin and Walter *Pater. Its followers, who included Oscar *Wilde and Aubrey *Beardsley, carried their devotion to extravagant lengths, often wearing unusual clothes and speaking and behaving in an unnatural way.

aestivation (*US* **estivation**) /ˌi:stɪˈveɪʃn; *US* ˌestəˈveɪʃn/ *n* [U] **1** (*zoology*) state of inactivity in which certain animals spend prolonged periods of drought or heat. Feeding, breathing, movement and other bodily activities are greatly slowed down. Cf HIBERNATION. **2** (*botany*) arrangement of the petals and sepals of a flower bud before it opens out.

aetiology (*US* also **etiology**) /ˌi:tɪˈɒlədʒɪ/ *n* [U] **1** study of causes and reasons. **2** (*medicine*) study of the causes or origin of disease: *the aetiology of malaria.*

afar /əˈfɑ:(r)/ *adv* **1** at or to a distance: *lights visible afar off.* **2** (idm) **from aˈfar** from a long distance away: *news from afar.*

affable /ˈæfəbl/ *adj* **1** polite and friendly: *affable to everybody* ○ *an affable reply.* **2** easy to talk to: *He found her parents very affable.* ▷ **affability** /ˌæfəˈbɪlətɪ/ *n* [U]. **affably** /-əblɪ/ *adv.*

affair /əˈfeə(r)/ *n* **1** [sing] thing (to be) done; concern; matter: *It's not my affair*, ie I am not interested in or responsible for it. **2 affairs** [pl] (**a**) personal business matters: *put one's affairs in order.* (**b**) matters of public interest: *current/foreign/world affairs* ○ *affairs of state.* **3** [C esp *sing*] (**a**) event; happening: *We must try to forget this sad affair.* ○ *The press exaggerated the whole affair wildly.* (**b**) event or series of events connected with a particular person, thing or place: *the Suez affair.* (**c**) organized social event: *The wedding was a very grand affair.* **4** [C] (*infml*) (following an *adj*) thing described in a specified way: *Her hat was an amazing affair of ribbons and feathers.* **5** [C] sexual relationship between people who are not married to each other: *She's having an affair with her boss.* **6** (idm) **a state of affairs** ⇨ STATE.

affect[1] /əˈfekt/ *v* [Tn] **1** have an influence on (sb/sth); produce an effect on: *The tax increases have affected us all.* ○ *The change in climate may affect your health*, ie be bad for you. ○ *Their opinion will not affect my decision.* **2** (of disease) attack (sb/sth); infect: *Cancer had affected his lungs.* **3** cause (sb) to have feelings of sadness or sympathy; touch: *We were deeply affected by the news of her death.*

▷ **affecting** moving or touching: *an affecting appeal for help.* **affectingly** *adv.*

NOTE ON USAGE: **Affect** is a verb meaning 'have an influence on': *Alcohol affects drivers' concentration.* **Effect** is a noun meaning 'result or influence': *Alcohol has a very bad effect on drivers.* It is also a (formal) verb meaning 'accomplish': *They effected their escape in the middle of the night.*

affect[2] /əˈfekt/ *v* **1** [Tn] (*often derog*) make an obvious show of using, wearing or liking (sth): *affect bright colours, bow ties* ○ *He affects a pretentious use of language*, ie tries to impress people by using obscure words, etc. **2** (**a**) [Tn, Tt] pretend to have or feel (sth): *affect not to know sth/affect ignorance of sth* ○ *She affected a foreign accent.* (**b**) [Ln] (*fml*) pretend to be (sth); pose as: *She affects the helpless female.*

▷ **affected** /əˈfektɪd/ *adj* not natural or genuine; pretended; artificial: *an affected politeness, cheerfulness, etc* ○ *a highly affected style of writing* ○ *Do try not to be so affected.*

affect[3] /ˈæfekt/ *n* (*psychology*) feeling, mood or desire, esp one leading to an action.

▷ **affective** /ˈæfektɪv/ *adj* (*psychology*) of feeling or mood: *affective disorders.*

affectation /ˌæfekˈteɪʃn/ *n* **1** [C, U] (instance of) unnatural behaviour, manner of speaking, etc, intended to impress others: *His little affectations irritated her.* ○ *I detest all affectation.* **2** [C] ~ (**of sth**) pretence; deliberate display (of sth that is not truly felt): *an affectation of interest, indifference, etc.*

affection /əˈfekʃn/ *n* **1** [U, C usu *pl*] ~ (**for/towards sb/sth**) feeling of fondness; love: *He felt great affection for his sister.* ○ *The old king was held in great affection.* ○ *I tried to win her affection(s).* **2** [C] (*dated*) disease or diseased condition: *an affection of the throat.*

affectionate /əˈfekʃənət/ *adj* ~ (**towards sb**) showing fondness (for sb); loving: *an affectionate child* ○ *affectionate kisses, words, smiles* ○ *He is very affectionate towards his children.* ▷ **affectionately** *adv*: *He patted her affectionately on the head.* ○ *Yours affectionately*, ie used at the end of a letter to a close relative or friend.

affiance /əˈfaɪəns/ *v* [usu passive: Tn, Tn·pr] ~ **sb** (**to sb**) (*dated or fml*) promise sb in marriage: *He is affianced to the princess*, ie engaged to marry her.

affidavit /ˌæfɪˈdeɪvɪt/ *n* (*law*) written statement that can be used as evidence in court, made by sb who swears that it is true: *swear/make/take/sign an affidavit.*

affiliate /əˈfɪlɪeɪt/ *v* [usu passive: Tn, Tn·pr] ~ **sb/sth** (**to/with sb/sth**) attach (a person, a society, an institution, etc) to a larger organization: *We are affiliated with the national group.* ○ *The College is affiliated to the University.*

▷ **affiliate** /əˈfɪlɪət/ *n* affiliated person, institution, etc: [attrib] *affiliate members.*

affiliation /əˌfɪlɪˈeɪʃn/ *n* **1** [U] affiliating or being affiliated. **2** [C] link or connection made by affiliating: *The society has many affiliations throughout the country.*

□ **affiliˈation order** (*law*) order compelling the father of an illegitimate child to help to support it.

affinity /əˈfɪnətɪ/ *n* **1** [U, C] ~ (**with sb/sth**); ~ (**between A and B**) structural resemblance or similarity of character; relationship: *There is (a) close affinity between Italian and Spanish.* ○ *Early man shows certain affinities with the ape.* **2** [C] ~

(**to/for sb/sth**); ~ (**between A and B**) strong liking for or attraction to sb/sth: *They share a special affinity.* ○ *She has a strong affinity for Beethoven.* **3** [C] ~ (**with sb**) (*law*) relationship, esp by marriage: *He was not an impartial witness because of his affinity with the accused.* **4** [C] ~ (**for sth**) (*chemistry*) tendency of certain substances to combine with others: *the affinity of salt for water.*

affirm /əˈfɜːm/ *v* **1** [Tn, Tf, Dn·pr, Dpr·f] ~ **sth** (**to sb**) state sth as the truth; assert sth: *She affirmed her innocence.* ○ *He affirmed that he was responsible.* Cf DENY. **2** [I] (*law*) make a solemn declaration in court instead of swearing an oath.
▷ **affirmation** /ˌæfəˈmeɪʃn/ *n* **1** [C, U] (act of) affirming: *The poem is a joyous affirmation of the power of love.* **2** [C] (**a**) thing that is affirmed. (**b**) (*law*) solemn declaration made in court instead of an oath.

affirmative /əˈfɜːmətɪv/ *adj* (of words, etc) expressing agreement; indicating 'yes': *an affirmative reply, nod, reaction.* Cf NEGATIVE.
▷ **affirmative** *n* **1** word or statement that expresses agreement. **2** (idm) **in the afˈfirmative** (*fml*) expressing agreement: *He answered in the affirmative,* ie said 'yes'.
affirmatively *adv.*

affix[1] /əˈfɪks/ *v* [Tn, Tn·pr] ~ **sth** (**to/on sth**) (*fml*) **1** stick, fasten or attach sth: *affix a stamp to an envelope* ○ *affix a seal on a document.* **2** add sth in writing: *affix one's signature to a contract.*

affix[2] /ˈæfɪks/ *n* (*grammar*) letter or group of letters added to the beginning or the end of a word to change its meaning or the way it is used; prefix or suffix, eg *un-*, *-esque* and *-less* in *unkind, picturesque* and *hopeless.*

afflict /əˈflɪkt/ *v* [usu passive: Tn, Tn·pr] ~ **sb/sth** (**with sth**) cause trouble, pain or distress to sb/sth: *She is afflicted with* (ie suffers from) *arthritis.* ○ *Severe drought has afflicted the countryside.*
▷ **affliction** /əˈflɪkʃn/ *n* (*fml*) **1** [U] pain; suffering; distress: *help people in affliction.* **2** [C] thing that causes suffering: *Blindness can be a terrible affliction.*

affluence /ˈæfluəns/ *n* [U] abundance of money, goods or property; wealth: *live in/live a life of affluence* ○ *He quickly rose to affluence,* ie became wealthy.

affluent /ˈæfluənt/ *adj* rich; prosperous: *affluent circumstances* ○ *an affluent lifestyle* ○ *His parents were very affluent.*
□ ˌ**affluent soˈciety** social system in which there is widespread material wealth.

afford /əˈfɔːd/ *v* **1** [no passive: Tn, Tt] (usu with *can, could* or *be able to*) have enough money, time, space, etc for (a specified purpose): *They walked because they couldn't afford (to take) a taxi.* ○ *You can't afford* (ie are not in a position to spend) *£90.* ○ *I'd love to go on holiday but I can't afford the time.* ○ *We would give more examples if we could afford the space.* **2** [no passive: Tn, Tt] (usu with *can* or *could*) be able to do sth without risk to oneself: *I mustn't annoy my boss because I can't afford to lose my job,* ie must not take the risk of losing my job. ○ *You can ill afford to criticize others when you behave so badly yourself.* **3** [Tn, Dn·n, Dn·pr] ~ **sth** (**to sb**) (*fml*) provide sth; give sth: *The tree afforded (us) welcome shade.* ○ *Television affords pleasure to many.*

afforest /əˈfɒrɪst; US əˈfɔːr-/ *v* [Tn] plant (areas of land) with trees to form a forest. ▷ **afforestation** /əˌfɒrɪˈsteɪʃn; US əˌfɔːr-/ *n* [U].

affray /əˈfreɪ/ *n* (usu *sing*) (*fml or law*) disturbance of the peace caused by fighting or rioting in a public place: *The men were charged with causing an affray.*

affront /əˈfrʌnt/ *n* (usu *sing*) ~ (**to sb/sth**) deliberately insulting or disrespectful remark, action, etc, esp in public: *His speech was an affront to all decent members of the community.*
▷ **affront** /əˈfrʌnt/ *v* [Tn usu passive] insult (sb) deliberately and openly; offend. **affronted** *adj* ~ (**at/by sth**) offended: *He felt deeply affronted at her rudeness.*

Afghan /ˈæfɡæn/ *n* **1** (**a**) [C] native or inhabitant of Afghanistan. (**b**) [U] language of Afghanistan; Pushtu. **2** [C] = AFGHAN HOUND: *three large Afghans.* **3 afghan** [C] type of loose sheepskin coat, often embroidered.
▷ **Afghan** (also **Afghani** /æfˈɡɑːnɪ; US æfˈɡænɪ/) *adj* of Afghanistan, its people or their language.
ˌ**Afghan ˈhound** tall breed of dog with long silky hair.

Afghanistan

Afghanistan /æfˈɡænɪstɑːn; US æfˈɡænəstæn/ mountainous country in central Asia; pop approx 15 513 000; official language Pushtu; capital Kabul; unit of currency afghani (= 100 puls). It was part of the Indian *Moghul empire until the mid 18th century, when it became independent. In 1979 it was invaded by the Soviet Union. During the period of Soviet occupation, which lasted until 1989, over 3 million people left as refugees. A civil war followed. It is a Muslim country, and its main occupation is agriculture. ⇨ map.

aficionado /əˌfɪsjəˈnɑːdəʊ, *also* əˌfɪʃj-/ *n* (*pl* ~**s**) (*Spanish*) person who is very enthusiastic about a particular sport or pastime: *an aficionado of bullfighting.*

afield /əˈfiːld/ *adv* (idm) **far/farther/further aˈfield** far, etc away, esp from home; to or at a distance: *Some villagers have never been further afield than the neighbouring town.* ○ *To find the causes of the problem we need look no further afield than our own department.*

aflame /əˈfleɪm/ *adj* [pred] **1** (red as if) in flames; burning: *The whole building was soon aflame.* ○ *Her cheeks were aflame.* ○ *The autumn woods were aflame with colour.* **2** very excited: *aflame with desire.*

AFL-CIO /ˌeɪ ef ˈel ˌsiː aɪ ˈəʊ/ *abbr* (*US*) American Federation of Labor and Congress of Industrial Organizations.

afloat /əˈfləʊt/ *adj* [pred] **1** floating in water or air: *The boat stuck on a sandbank but we soon got it afloat again.* ○ *The ship was listing badly but still kept afloat.* **2** at sea; on board ship: *enjoy life afloat.* **3** out of debt or difficulties: *The firm managed to stay afloat during the recession.* **4** functioning: *get a new business afloat,* ie start it. **5** (of rumours) being generally talked about; circulating: *There's a story afloat that he'll resign.*

afoot /əˈfʊt/ *adj* [pred] being prepared or progressing: *There's mischief afoot,* ie being planned. ○ *There's a scheme afoot to put a motorway through the park.*

aforementioned /əˌfɔːˈmenʃənd/ (also **aforesaid** /əˈfɔːsed/, **said**) *adj* [usu attrib] (*fml*) (esp in legal documents) mentioned or referred to earlier: *The aˌforementioned (ˈperson/ˈpersons) was/were acting suspiciously.*

aforethought /əˈfɔːθɔːt/ *adj* (idm) **with malice aforethought** ⇨ MALICE.

a fortiori /ˌeɪ ˌfɔːtɪˈɔːraɪ/ (*Latin*) for this stronger reason: *If he can afford a luxury yacht, then a fortiori he can afford to pay his debts.*

afraid /əˈfreɪd/ *adj* [pred] **1** (**a**) ~ (**of sb/sth**); ~ (**of doing sth/to do sth**) frightened: *Don't be afraid.* ○ *There's nothing to be afraid of.* ○ *Are you afraid of snakes?* ○ *He's afraid of going out/to go out alone at night.* ○ *Don't be afraid* (ie Don't hesitate) *to ask for help if you need it.* (**b**) ~ **of doing sth**/~ **that...** worried or anxious about (the possible result of sth): *I didn't mention it because I was afraid of upsetting him/afraid (that) I might upset him.* ○ *He's afraid of losing customers/that he might lose customers.* (**c**) ~ **for sth/sb** frightened or worried about things that may put sth/sb in danger: *parents afraid for (the safety of) their children.* **2** (idm) **be afraid of one's own shadow** be very timid. **I'm afraid (that...)** (usu without *that*, used to express politely a piece of information that may be unwelcome) I am sorry to say: *I'm afraid we can't come.* ○ *I can't help you, I'm afraid.* ○ *'Have we missed the train?' 'I'm afraid so.'* ○ *'Have you any milk?' 'I'm afraid not.'*

afresh /əˈfreʃ/ *adv* again, esp from the very beginning: *Let's start afresh.* ○ *The work will have to be done afresh.*

Africa /ˈæfrɪkə/ **1** second largest of the world's continents; area 30 319 000 sq km (11 707 000 sq miles); pop approx 537 000 000. It contains 53 independent countries (including island nations), and is divided almost exactly in two by the equator. Much of the northern half is covered by the *Sahara desert. Egypt in the north-east was one of the world's earliest centres of civilization. Most of the continent (with the exception of Ethiopia and Liberia) was divided up and colonized by European countries in the second half of the 19th century. Since the Second World War most African countries have gained independence. ⇨ maps at ALGERIA, NAMIBIA, NIGERIA, TANZANIA, ZAIRE. **2** (idm) **darkest Africa** ⇨ DARK.
▷ **African** /ˈæfrɪkən/ *adj* of Africa or its people or languages. — *n* African person, esp a dark-skinned one. ˌ**African ˈmarigold** annual garden plant with orange or yellow flowers. ˌ**African ˈviolet** E African plant with purple, pink or white flowers, often grown indoors in Britain.
□ **the African National Congress** (*abbr* **ANC**) Black nationalist movement in South Africa founded in 1912 to campaign for political rights for Blacks. It was banned in 1960 and its leader Nelson *Mandela was imprisoned 1964-89.

Afrikaans /ˌæfrɪˈkɑːns/ *n* [U] language developed from Dutch, spoken in S Africa.

Afrikaner /ˌæfrɪˈkɑːnə(r)/ *n* white S African, usu of Dutch descent, whose native language is Afrikaans.

Afro /ˈæfrəʊ/ *adj* (of hair-style) very curly, thick and long, like the hair of some Blacks. ⇨ illus at HAIR.

Afro- *comb form* African; of Africa: *Afro-Asian,* ie of Africa and Asia ○ *the Afro-Caribbean peoples.*

Afro-American /ˌæfrəʊ əˈmerɪkən/ *adj* of American Blacks or their culture.
▷ ˌ**Afro-Aˈmerican** *n* American of African descent.

aft /ɑːft; US æft/ *adv* **1** in, near or towards the stern of a ship or the tail of an aircraft. **2** (idm) **fore and aft** ⇨ FORE.

after[1] /ˈɑːftə(r); US ˈæf-/ *adv* **1** later (in time): *The day after, he apologized.* ○ *It reappeared long/soon after.* ○ *They lived happily ever after.* **2** behind (in place): *She followed on after.* Cf BEFORE[1]. ⇨ Usage at BEFORE[2].
□ ˈ**afterglow** *n* [U] glow in the sky sometimes seen after sunset, caused by tiny particles of dust in the upper atmosphere scattering the light from the sun.

after[2] /ˈɑːftə(r); US ˈæf-/ *prep* **1** (**a**) later than (sth): *leave after lunch, shortly after six, the day after tomorrow, the week after next* ○ (*US*) *half after seven in the morning,* ie 7.30 am. (**b**) **sth** ~ **sth** (indicating much repetition): *day after day/week after week/year after year/time after time,* ie very often ○ *He fired shot after shot,* ie many shots. Cf BEFORE[2] 1. ⇨ Usage at BEFORE[2]. **2** behind (sb/sth): *Shut the door after you when you go out.* **3** next to and following (sb/sth) in order, arrangement or importance: *C comes after B in the alphabet.* ○ *Your name comes after mine on the list.* ○ *His book is the best on the subject after mine.* ○ *After you,* ie Please enter before me, serve yourself first, etc. ○ *After you with the salt.* ⇨ Usage at BEFORE². **4** because of (sth); following: *After what he did to my family, I hate him.* ○ *After your conduct last time, did you expect to be invited again?* **5** in pursuit of or in search of (sb/sth): *We ran after the thief.* ○ *The police are after him.* ○ *She's after* (ie She wants) *a job in publishing.* **6** about (sb/sth); concerning: *They inquired after you,* ie asked how you were. **7** in spite of (sth): *After everything I've done for him, he still ignores me.* **8** in the style of; in imitation of: *a painting after Rubens* ○ *draw up a constitution after the American model* ○ *We've named the baby after you,* ie given him your first name in honour of you. **9** (idm) **ˌafter ˈall** (**a**) in spite of what has been said, done or expected: *So you've come after all!* ○ *After all, what does it matter?* (**b**) it should be remembered: *He should have offered to pay — he has plenty of money, after all.*

□ **ˈafterbirth** *n* [sing] placenta and foetal membrane discharged from the womb after childbirth.

ˈafter-damp *n* [U] poisonous mixture of gases, including carbon monoxide, formed after the explosion of firedamp (a mixture of air and methane) in a coal-mine.

ˈafterlife *n* [sing] existence that is thought by some to follow death: *Do you believe in an afterlife?*

ˈaftershave *n* [U, C] lotion used on the face after shaving: *He uses aftershave.* ○ [attrib] *aftershave lotion.*

after³ /ˈɑːftə(r); *US* ˈæf-/ *conj* at or during a time later than (sth): *I arrived after he (had) left.* ○ *We'll arrive after you've left.* Cf BEFORE³.

after⁴ /ˈɑːftə(r); *US* ˈæf-/ *adj* [attrib] **1** later; following: *in after years.* **2** nearer the stern of a ship: *the ˈafter cabins.*

▷ **ˈaftermost** *adj* furthest aft.

□ **ˈafter-care** *n* [U] attention or treatment given to a person who has just left hospital, prison, etc: [attrib] *ˌafter-care ˈservices.*

ˈafter-effect *n* effect that occurs afterwards, eg a delayed effect of a drug used medically; effect that occurs after its cause has gone: *suffer from/feel no unpleasant after-effects.*

ˈafter-image *n* sensation retained by one of the senses, esp the eye, after the original stimulus has stopped.

ˈafter-taste *n* [sing] **1** taste that stays after eating or drinking sth: *wine which leaves an unpleasant after-taste (in the mouth).* **2** (*fig*) impression or feeling that stays in the mind.

ˈafterthought *n* thing that is thought of or added later: *Just as an afterthought — why not ask Jim?* ○ *The film was made first and the music was added as an afterthought.* ○ *Mary was a bit of an afterthought — her brothers and sisters are all much older than her.*

aftermath /ˈɑːftəmæθ; *Brit also* -mɑːθ/ *n* (usu *sing*) circumstances that follow and are a consequence of an event, etc (esp an unpleasant one): *the rebuilding which took place in the aftermath of the war.*

afternoon /ˌɑːftəˈnuːn; *US* ˌæf-/ *n* [U, C] time from midday or lunch-time to about 6 pm or sunset (if this is earlier): *in/during the afternoon* ○ *this/yesterday/tomorrow afternoon* ○ *every afternoon* ○ *on Sunday afternoon* ○ *on the afternoon of 12 May* ○ *one afternoon last week* ○ *She goes there two afternoons a week.* ○ [attrib] *an afternoon sleep, performance, train* ○ *afternoon tea.* ⇨ Usage at MORNING.

▷ **afternoons** *adv* in the afternoons as a practice or habit: *Afternoons, he works at home.*

afters /ˈɑːftəz; *US* ˈæf-/ *n* [pl] (*Brit infml*) (usu sweet) course following the main course of a meal: *What's for afters?* ○ *We had fruit salad for afters.* Cf DESSERT, PUDDING 1.

afterwards /ˈɑːftəwədz; *US* ˈæf-/ (*US* also **afterward**) *adv* at a later time: *Let's go to the theatre first and eat afterwards.* Cf BEFORE¹. ⇨ Usage at BEFORE².

Ag *symb* silver.

again /əˈgen, əˈgeɪn/ *adv* **1** once more; another time: *Try again.* ○ *Say that again, please.* ○ *Here comes Joe, drunk again.* ○ *Do call again.* ○ *Don't do that again.* ○ *This must never happen again.* **2** as before; to or in the original place or condition: *He was glad to be home again.* ○ *Back again already?* ○ *You'll never get the money back again.* ○ *You'll soon be well again.* ○ *I'm glad he's himself/his old self again,* ie that he has returned to his normal state again after a shock, an illness, etc. **3** (**a**) likewise; furthermore: *Again, we have to consider the legal implications.* (**b**) on the other hand: *I might, and (there/then) again I might not.* **4** in addition: *I'd like as many/much again,* ie twice as many/much. ○ *half as much again,* ie one-and-a-half times as much. **5** (idm) **aˌgain and aˈgain** repeatedly: *I've told you again and again not to do that.* **here we go again** ⇨ GO¹. **sb/sth rides again** ⇨ RIDE².

against /əˈgenst, əˈgeɪnst/ *prep* **1** in opposition to (sb/sth): *We were rowing against the current.* ○ *Are most people against the proposal?* ○ *That's against the law.* ○ *She was married against her will.* ○ *His age is against him,* ie is a disadvantage to him. **2** in contact with (sb/sth); into collision with: *Put the piano there, with its back against the wall.* ○ *He was leaning against a tree.* ○ *The rain beat against the car windscreen.* **3** in contrast to (sth): *silhouetted against the sky* ○ *The skier's red clothes stood out clearly against the snow.* ○ (*fig*) *The salaries here are low (as) against the rates elsewhere.* **4** in preparation for (sth); in anticipation of: *protect plants against frost* ○ *take precautions against fire* ○ *an injection against rabies.* **5** opposite (sth), so as to cancel or lessen: *allowances to be set against income.* **6** in return for (sth): *What's the rate of exchange against the dollar?* ○ *Tickets are issued only against payment of the full fee.* **7** (idm) **as against sth** ⇨ AS.

Aga Khan /ˌɑːgə ˈkɑːn/ (hereditary title of the) spiritual leader of most of the Ismaili Muslims.

Agamemnon /ˌægəˈmemnɒn/ (in Greek legend) king of *Mycenae (and, in later legend, of Argos), brother of *Menelaus. In *Homer's **Iliad* he is the leader of the Greek forces in the *Trojan war. Aeschylus's play *Agamemnon* tells how he was murdered by his wife *Clytemnestra and her lover when he returned from Troy.

agape¹ /ˈægəpɪ/ *n* [U] **1** Christian love, esp in contrast to sexual love. **2** feast held by early Christians to commemorate the *Last Supper and celebrate Christian love.

agape² /əˈgeɪp/ *adj* [pred] ~ (**with sth**) (of the mouth) wide open, esp with wonder: *He watched with mouth agape.*

agar-agar /ˌeɪgɑːr ˈeɪgɑː(r); *US* ˌɑːgɑːr ˈɑːgɑːr/ (also **agar**) *n* [U] **1** any of various types of SE Asian seaweed. **2** jelly-like substance extracted from this, used in food, as a laxative, and for growing bacteria on in laboratories.

agaric /ˈægərɪk, *also* əˈgærɪk/ *n* type of fungus having a stalk and a cap with gills underneath. The group includes the common mushroom and poisonous types such as the fly agaric.

agate /ˈægət/ *n* [U, C] type of very hard semi-precious stone with bands or patches of colour: *a brooch made of agate* ○ [attrib] *an agate ring.*

agave /əˈgeɪvɪ, əˈgɑːvɪ/ *n* tall tropical plant with spiny leaves which flowers only once. Some types are used as a source of fibre, esp sisal, or of alcoholic drinks, such as the Mexican spirit mescal.

age¹ /eɪdʒ/ *n* **1** [C, U] length of time that a person has lived or a thing has existed: *What age is he?* ○ *He's six years of age/six years old.* ○ *Their ages are two and ten.* ○ *At what age did she retire?* ○ *I left school at the age of 18.* ○ *When I was your age…* ○ *We have a son your age.* ○ *He lived to a great age.* ○ *Geologists have calculated the age of the earth.* ○ [attrib] *Anyone can enter the contest — there's no age limit,* ie no one will be regarded as too old or too young. ⇨ App 9. **2** [U] latter part of life; old age: *the wisdom that comes with age* ○ *His face was wrinkled with age.* ○ *Fine wine improves with age.* Cf YOUTH 1, 2. **3** [C] (**a**) period of history with special characteristics or events: *the Elizabethan Age,* ie the time of Queen Elizabeth I of England ○ *the modern age, the nuclear age, the age of the microchip.* (**b**) (*geology*) period of time in the earth's history: *the Ice Age.* **4** [C usu *pl*] (*infml*) very long time: *I waited (for) ages/an age.* ○ *It took (us) ages to find a place to park.* **5** (idm) **ˌage before ˈbeauty** (*saying often ironic*) younger people must give way to older people. **the age/years of discretion** ⇨ DISCRETION. **at a tender age/of tender age** ⇨ TENDER¹. **the awkward age** ⇨ AWKWARD. **ˌbe/ˌcome of ˈage** reach the age at which one has an adult's legal rights and obligations. **ˌbe your ˈage** (*infml*) (esp imperative) behave as sb of your age should and not as though you were much younger. **feel one's age** ⇨ FEEL. **in this day and age** ⇨ DAY. **ˌlook one's ˈage** seem as old as one really is: *She doesn't look her age at all,* ie appears much younger than she really is. (**be**) **of an ˈage** having reached an age when one should do sth: *He's of an age when he ought to settle down.* **of an ˈage with sb** of the same age as sb. **ˌover ˈage** too old. **ˌunder ˈage** not old enough; not yet adult: *You shouldn't sell cigarettes to teenagers who are under age/to under-age teenagers.*

📖 In English people are described as being 'young', 'middle-aged' or 'old' (more politely 'elderly'). A 'young' person is usually aged between about 20 and about 40, a 'middle-aged' person between about 40 and about 64, and an 'old' person about 65 or over. 'Old age pensioners' (OAPs), also called 'senior citizens', are retired people who receive a state pension. Terms relating to age can be misleading. For example, a 'young girl' or 'young boy' is not necessarily a child. Similarly, grown men are often collectively referred to as 'the boys' or 'the lads', especially in an informal context, and women may be called 'girls', though many object to this. From middle age onwards people are often quite sensitive about their age and for this reason it is generally considered impolite to ask middle-aged people how old they are.

□ **ˈage-group** (also **ˈage-bracket**) *n* (people in a) period of life between two (often specified) ages: *mix with (people in) one's own age-group* ○ *Only people in the age-bracket 20-30 need apply.*

ˈagelong *adj* [usu attrib] existing for a very long time: *man's agelong struggle for freedom.*

ˌage of conˈsent age at which sb, esp a girl, is considered old enough to consent to sexual intercourse.

ˌage-ˈold *adj* [usu attrib] having existed for a very long time: *ˌage-old ˈcustoms, ˈceremonies, etc.*

age² /eɪdʒ/ *v* (*pres p* **ageing** or **aging**, *pp* **aged** /eɪdʒd/) **1** (**a**) [I] grow old; show signs of growing old: *He's aged a lot recently.* ○ *She's aging gracefully.* (**b**) [Tn] cause (sb) to become old: *Worry aged him rapidly.* ○ *I found her greatly aged.* **2** (**a**) [I] become mature: *allow wine to age.* (**b**) [Tn] cause or allow (sth) to mature.

▷ **aged** *adj* **1** /eɪdʒd/ [pred] of the age of: *The boy was aged ten.* **2** /ˈeɪdʒɪd/ [attrib] very old: *an aged man.* ⇨ Usage at OLD.

the aged /ˈeɪdʒɪd/ *n* [pl] very old people: *caring for the sick and the aged.*

ageing (also **aging**) *n* [U] **1** process of growing old. **2** changes that occur as the result of time passing.

-age *suff* (with *ns* and *vs* forming *ns*) **1** state or condition of: *bondage.* **2** set or group of: *baggage* ○ *a/the peerage.* **3** action or result of: *breakage* ○ *wastage.* **4** cost of: *postage* ○ *porterage.* **5** place where: *anchorage* ○ *orphanage.* **6** quantity or measure of: *mileage* ○ *dosage.*

ageism (also **agism**) /ˈeɪdʒɪzəm/ *n* [U] (*derog*) (practice of) treating people unfairly or unjustly because of their age.

ageless /ˈeɪdʒlɪs/ *adj* **1** never growing old or appearing to grow old: *Her beauty seems ageless.* **2** eternal: *the ageless mystery of the universe.*

agency /ˈeɪdʒənsɪ/ *n* **1** (**a**) business or place of business providing a (usu specified) service: *an employment, a travel, an advertising, a secretarial, etc agency* ○ *Our company has agencies all over the world.* (**b**) (*esp US*) government office providing a specific service: *Central Intelligence Agency.* **2** (idm) **by/through the agency of sth/sb** (*fml*) as a result of the action of sth/sb: *rocks worn smooth through the agency of water* ○ *He obtained his position by/through the agency of friends.*

agenda /əˈdʒendə/ *n* (list of) matters of business to be discussed at a meeting, etc: *What is the next item on the agenda?* ○ *The agenda for the meeting is as follows....*

agent /ˈeɪdʒənt/ *n* **1** person who acts for, or manages the affairs of, other people in business, politics, etc: *an insurance agent* ○ *a travel agent* ○ *our agents in the Middle East.* **2** (**a**) person who does sth or causes sth to happen: *the agent of his own ruin.* (**b**) force or substance that produces an effect or change: *cleaning, oxidizing agents* ○ *Yeast is the raising agent in bread.* **3** = SECRET AGENT (SECRET): *an enemy agent.*

agent provocateur /ˌæʒɒn prəˌvɒkəˈtɜ:(r)/ (*pl* **agents provocateurs** /ˌæʒɒn prəˌvɒkəˈtɜ:(r)/) (*French*) person employed to help in catching suspected criminals by tempting them to act illegally.

agglomerate /əˈglɒməreɪt/ *v* [I, Tn] (cause sth to) become collected into a mass.
▷ **agglomerate** /əˈglɒmərət/ *n* [U] (*geology*) fragments of (esp volcanic) rock fused together in a mass.
agglomerate *adj* formed or growing into a mass.
agglomeration /əˌglɒməˈreɪʃn/ *n* **1** [U] action of agglomerating. **2** [C] (esp untidy) collection of objects: *an ugly agglomeration of new buildings.*

agglutinate /əˈglu:tɪneɪt; *US* -tən-/ *v* [I, Tn] join together as with glue; combine. ▷ **agglutination** /əˌglu:tɪˈneɪʃn; *US* -təˈn-/ *n* [U]. **agglutinative** /əˈglu:tɪnətɪv; *US* -təneɪtɪv/ *adj*: *Agglutinative languages combine parts of words into long sequences to form sentences.*

aggrandize, -ise /əˈgrændaɪz/ *v* [Tn] (*fml*) increase the power, rank, wealth or importance of (a person or country). ▷ **aggrandizement, -isement** /əˈgrændɪzmənt/ *n* [U]: *His sole aim is personal aggrandizement.*

aggravate /ˈægrəveɪt/ *v* [Tn] **1** make (a disease, a situation, an offence, etc) worse or more serious: *He aggravated his condition by leaving hospital too soon.* **2** (*infml*) irritate (sb); annoy: *He aggravates her just by looking at her.*
▷ **aggravating** *adj* (*infml*) irritating; annoying: *Constant interruptions are very aggravating when you're trying to work.*
aggravation /ˌægrəˈveɪʃn/ *n* **1** [U] making more serious; irritation. **2** [C] thing that annoys: *minor aggravations.*

aggregate[1] /ˈægrɪgeɪt/ *v* **1** [I, Tn, Tn·pr] ~ **sb (to sth)** (*fml*) be formed or bring sb into an assembled group or amount: *aggregating riches* ○ *aggregate sb to a political party.* **2** [Tn] (*infml*) amount to (a total): *The television audience aggregated 30 millions.* ▷ **aggregation** /ˌægrɪˈgeɪʃn/ *n* [U, C].

aggregate[2] /ˈægrɪgət/ *n* **1** [C] total amount; mass or amount brought together: *the complete aggregate of unemployment figures.* **2** [U] (*geology*) mass of minerals formed into one type of rock. **3** [U] materials (sand, gravel, etc) that are mixed with cement and water to make concrete. **4** (idm) **in the ˈaggregate** added together; collectively: *The tax increases will, in the aggregate, cause much hardship.* **on ˈaggregate** taken as a whole: *Our team scored the most goals on aggregate.*
▷ **aggregate** *adj* [attrib] total; combined: *the aggregate sum, amount, profit, etc.*

aggression /əˈgreʃn/ *n* **1** [C, U] (instance of) unprovoked attacking or hostility by one country against another: *an act of open aggression.* **2** [U] (*psychology*) hostile feelings or behaviour: *She was always full of aggression as a child.*

aggressive /əˈgresɪv/ *adj* **1** (**a**) (of people or animals) apt or ready to attack; offensive; quarrelsome: *dogs trained to be aggressive* ○ *Aggressive nations threaten world peace.* (**b**) (of things or actions) for or of an attack; offensive: *aggressive weapons.* **2** (*often approv*) forceful; self-assertive: *A good salesman must be aggressive if he wants to succeed.* ▷ **aggressively** *adv.* **aggressiveness** *n* [U].

aggressor /əˈgresə(r)/ *n* person or country that attacks first, without being provoked: *armed aggressors* ○ [attrib] *the aggressor nation.*

aggrieved /əˈgri:vd/ *adj* ~ (**at/over sth**) made to feel resentful (because of unfair treatment, etc): *feel much aggrieved at losing one's job* ○ *I was aggrieved to find that someone had used my toothbrush.* ○ *the aggrieved party*, eg in a legal case.

aggro /ˈægrəʊ/ *n* [U] (*Brit sl*) violent aggressive behaviour intended to cause trouble: *Don't give me any aggro or I'll call the police!*

aghast /əˈgɑ:st; *US* əˈgæst/ *adj* [pred] ~ (**at sth**) filled with horror or amazement: *He stood aghast at the terrible sight.*

agile /ˈædʒaɪl; *US* ˈædʒl/ *adj* able to move quickly and easily; active; nimble: *as agile as a monkey* ○ (*fig*) *an agile mind/brain.* ▷ **agilely** *adv.* **agility** /əˈdʒɪlətɪ/ *n* [U].

Agincourt /ˈæʒɪŋkɔ:(r), ˈædʒɪŋkɔ:t/ village in NW France, scene of a battle (1415) in the *Hundred Years War, when a small invading English army, led by *Henry V, defeated a much larger French force. The English were then able to occupy Normandy.

aging ⇨ AGE.

agitate /ˈædʒɪteɪt/ *v* **1** [Tn] cause anxiety to (a person, his feelings, etc); disturb; excite: *She was agitated by his sudden appearance at the party.* **2** [Ipr] ~ **for/against sth** argue publicly or campaign for/against sth: *agitate for tax reform* ○ *agitate against nuclear weapons.* **3** [Tn] stir or shake (a liquid) briskly: *Agitate the mixture to dissolve the powder.*
▷ **agitated** *adj* troubled or excited: *Don't get all agitated!*
agitation /ˌædʒɪˈteɪʃn/ *n* **1** [U] disturbed state of mind or feelings; anxiety: *She was in a state of great agitation.* **2** (**a**) [C, U] public discussion for or against sth: *women leading the agitation for equal rights.* (**b**) [U] serious public concern or unrest connected with such discussion.
agitator *n* **1** person who stirs up public opinion, esp on a political matter. **2** device for shaking or mixing a liquid.

agitprop /ˈædʒɪtprɒp/ *n* [U] Russian Communist propaganda, usu in the form of literature, music or art.

aglow /əˈgləʊ/ *adv, adj* [pred] glowing; shining with warmth and colour: *Christmas trees aglow with coloured lights.* ○ (*fig*) *happy children's faces all aglow.*

AGM /ˌeɪ dʒi: ˈem/ *abbr* (*esp Brit*) annual general meeting: *report to the AGM.*

agnail /ˈægneɪl/ *n* = HANGNAIL.

Agnes /ˈægnɪs/ Saint (died c 304 AD), patron saint of young virgins, martyred at the age of 13. In *Keats's poem 'The Eve of St Agnes', a young girl is told the legend that on the evening before St Agnes's day (21 January) young girls may have visions of their future husbands.

agnostic /ægˈnɒstɪk/ *n* person who believes that nothing can be known about the existence of God or of anything except material things.
▷ **agnostic** *adj* holding this belief.
agnosticism /ægˈnɒstɪsɪzəm/ *n* [U]. Cf ATHEISM.

Agnus Dei /ˌægnəs ˈdeɪi:, *in singing* ˌɑ:njəs/ **1** part of the Roman Catholic Mass beginning with the Latin words *Agnus Dei* (meaning 'Lamb of God'). **2** figure of a lamb with a cross or flag, used as a symbol of Christ.

ago /əˈgəʊ/ *adv* (used after the word or phrase it modifies, esp with the simple past tense, not with the perfect tense) gone by; in the past: *ten years ago* ○ *not long ago* ○ *It happened a few minutes ago.* ○ *How long ago is it that you last saw her?* ○ *It was seven years ago that my brother died.* ⇨ Usage at RECENT.

agog /əˈgɒg/ *adj* [pred] eager; excited: *agog with curiosity* ○ *be agog for news/to hear the news* ○ *He was all agog at the surprise announcement.*

agonize, -ise /ˈægənaɪz/ *v* [I, Ipr] ~ (**about/over sth**) suffer great anxiety or worry intensely (about sth): *We agonized for hours about which wallpaper to buy.*
▷ **agonized, -ised** *adj* expressing agony: *an agonized look, scream.*
agonizing, -ising *adj* causing agony: *an agonizing pain, delay, decision.* **agonizingly, -isingly** *adv*: *agonizingly slow.*

agony /ˈægənɪ/ *n* **1** [U, C] extreme mental or physical suffering: *The wounded man was in agony.* ○ *They suffered the agony of watching him burn to death.* ○ *She was in an agony of indecision.* ○ *He suffered agonies of remorse.* **2** (idm) **pile on the agony** ⇨ PILE[3]. **prolong the agony** ⇨ PROLONG.
□ **ˈagony aunt** (*Brit infml or joc*) person who writes replies to letters printed in an agony column(2).
ˈagony column (*Brit infml or joc*) **1** = PERSONAL COLUMN (PERSONAL). **2** part of a newspaper or magazine for letters from readers writing for advice about personal problems.

agoraphobia /ˌægərəˈfəʊbɪə/ *n* [U] abnormal fear of being in open spaces.
▷ **agoraphobic** /-ˈfəʊbɪk/ *n, adj* (person) suffering from this fear.

AGR /ˌeɪ dʒi: ˈɑ:(r)/ *abbr* advanced gas-cooled (nuclear) reactor.

agrarian /əˈgreərɪən/ *adj* [usu attrib] (of the cultivation or ownership) of land: *agrarian laws, problems, reforms.*

agree /əˈgri:/ *v* **1** [I, Ipr, It] ~ (**to sth**) say 'yes'; say that one is willing; consent (to sth): *I asked for a pay rise and she agreed.* ○ *Is he going to agree to our suggestion?* ○ *He agreed to let me go home early.* Cf REFUSE[2]. **2** (**a**) [I, Ipr, It, Tf, Tw] ~ (**with sb**) (**about/on sth**); ~ (**with sb**) (**about sb**); ~ (**with sth**) be in harmony (with sb); have or form a similar opinion (as sb): *When he said that, I had to agree.* ○ *Do you agree with me about the need for more schools?* ○ *We couldn't agree on a date/agree when to meet.* ○ *I agree with his analysis of the situation.* ○ *We agreed to start early.* ○ *Do we all agree that the proposal is a good one?* Cf DISAGREE. (**b**) [Tn] reach the same opinion on (sth): *Can we agree a price?* ○ *They met at the agreed time.* **3** [Tn] accept (sth) as correct; approve: *The tax inspector agreed the figures.* ○ *Next year's budget has been agreed.* **4** [I, Ipr] ~ (**with sth**) be consistent (with sth); match: *The two accounts do not agree.* ○ *Your account of the affair does not agree with mine.* Cf DISAGREE. **5** [I, Ip] ~ (**together**) be happy together; enjoy each other's company: *Brothers and sisters never seem to agree.* Cf DISAGREE. **6** [I, Ipr] ~ (**with sth**) (*grammar*) correspond (with a word or phrase) in number, person, etc: *The verb agrees with its subject in number and person.* Cf DISAGREE. **7** (idm) **aˌgree to ˈdiffer** accept differences of opinion, esp in order to avoid further argument: *We must agree to differ on this.* **be agreed (on/about sth); be agreed (that...)** (with *it* or a plural subject) have reached an agreement: *Are we all agreed on the best course of action?* ○ *It was agreed that another meeting was necessary.* **ˌcouldn't agree (with sb) ˈmore** agree completely with sb: *'The scheme's bound to fail.' 'I couldn't agree more!'* **8** (phr v) **agree with sb** (esp in negative sentences or questions) suit sb's health or digestion: *The humid climate didn't agree with him.* ○ *I like mushrooms but unfortunately they don't agree with me*, ie they make me ill if I eat them.

agreeable /əˈgri:əbl/ *adj* **1** pleasing; giving pleasure: *agreeable weather* ○ *agreeable company* ○ *I found him most agreeable.* **2** [pred] ~ (**to sth**) ready to agree: *If you're agreeable to our proposal, we'll go ahead.* ○ *I'll invite her, if you're agreeable to her coming.*
▷ **agreeably** /-əblɪ/ *adv* pleasantly: *agreeably surprised.*

agreement /əˈgri:mənt/ *n* **1** [C] arrangement, promise or contract made with sb: *Please sign the agreement.* ○ *An agreement with the employers was* *finally worked out.* ○ *They have broken the agreement between us.* **2** [U] harmony in opinion or feeling: *The two sides failed to reach agreement.* ○ *There is little agreement as to what our policy should be.* ○ *Are we in agreement about the price?* **3** [U] (*grammar*) having the same number, gender, case or person: *agreement between subject and verb.* **4** (idm) **a gentleman's agreement** ⇨ GENTLEMAN.

agribusiness /ˈæɡrɪbɪznɪs/ *n* **1** [U] agriculture as a modern commercial enterprise, esp using advanced technology. **2** [C] group of industries concerned with agriculture (eg suppliers of seed and manufacturers of agricultural chemicals and farm machinery).

Agricola /əˈɡrɪkələ/ Gnaeus Julius (40-93 AD), Roman senator and general, and governor of Britain from 78 AD. He led the Roman army into Scotland, where he built a number of forts and defeated the Highland tribes.

agriculture /ˈæɡrɪkʌltʃə(r)/ *n* [U] science or practice of cultivating the land and rearing animals; farming. Agriculture began about 9 000 years ago during the *Neolithic period, with a gradual change from a way of life in which people obtained food by gathering roots, berries, etc and hunting animals, to one in which they kept animals and planted crops. Farming methods developed at different rates throughout the world and still vary greatly from place to place. In Britain, the biggest changes in farming methods came in the 18th century, when much open land was turned into private fields and new agricultural machinery was introduced. In the 20th century, increased use of chemicals, more sophisticated farm machinery and methods of breeding animals, improved methods of transport, etc have increased the amount of food farms can produce, but over-intensive farming has also caused soil erosion, destruction of habitats for wild animals and pollution of the environment.
▷ **agricultural** /ˌæɡrɪˈkʌltʃərəl/ *adj*: *agricultural land, workers, machinery.* **agricultural credits** [pl] money borrowed for agricultural purposes, usu by mortgaging farm land. **agriculturally** *adv.* **agriculturist** /ˌæɡrɪˈkʌltʃərɪst/ *n.*

agrimony /ˈæɡrɪmənɪ/ *n* [U] plant of the rose family with long spikes of small yellow flowers.

Agrippa /əˈɡrɪpə/ Marcus Vipsanius (64/3-12 BC), leading supporter of the Roman emperor *Augustus in the defeat of *Mark Antony. He was commander of the western and eastern provinces of the Roman empire, and played an important part in restoring and improving the city of Rome, building public baths, aqueducts and sewers.

agr(o)- *comb form* of soil: *agriculture* ○ *agronomy.*

agronomy /əˈɡrɒnəmɪ/ *n* [U] science of controlling the soil to produce crops. ▷ **agronomist** /əˈɡrɒnəmɪst/ *n.*

aground /əˈɡraʊnd/ *adv, adj* [pred] (of ships) touching the bottom in shallow water: *The tanker was/went/ran aground.*

ague /ˈeɪɡjuː/ *n* [U] (*arch*) recurring fever (eg malaria) with alternate cold, shivering and sweating stages.

AH /ˌeɪ ˈeɪtʃ/ *abbr* of the Muslim era; used to show the year in the Muslim calendar, calculated from the *Hegira, Muhammad's flight from Mecca in 622 AD (Latin *anno Hegirae*). Cf AD, BC.

ah /ɑː/ *interj* (used to express surprise, delight, admiration, sympathy, etc): *Ah, ˈthere you are.* ○ *Ah, good, here's the bus.* ○ *Ah, what a lovely baby!* ○ *Ah well, never mind.*

aha /ɑːˈhɑː/ *interj* (used esp to express surprise or triumph): *Aha, so that's where she hides her money!*

ahead /əˈhed/ *adv* ~ (**of sb/sth**) further forward in space or time: *He ran ahead.* ○ *The way ahead was blocked by fallen trees.* ○ *The time to relax is when we're ahead,* eg in advance of our working schedule.
□ **ahead of** *prep* **1** further forward in space or time than (sb/sth); in front of: *Directly ahead of us is the royal palace.* ○ *London is about five hours ahead of New York.* ○ *Ahead of us lay ten days of intensive training.* **2** in the lead over (sb/sth); further advanced than: *She was always well ahead of the rest of the class.* ○ *His ideas were (way) ahead of his time.*

ahem /əˈhəm/ *interj* (used in writing to indicate the noise made when clearing the throat, esp to get sb's attention, express disapproval or gain time): *Ahem, might I make a suggestion?*

ahimsa /əˈhɪmsɑː/ *n* [U] (in Hinduism, Buddhism and Jainism) belief in and teaching of respect for all living things and avoidance of violence of any kind.

ahoy /əˈhɔɪ/ *interj* (cry used by seamen to call attention): *Ahoy there!* ○ *Land/Ship ahoy!* ie There is land/a ship in sight.

AI /ˌeɪ ˈaɪ/ *abbr* **1** artificial insemination. **2** artificial intelligence.

AID /ˌeɪ aɪ ˈdiː/ *abbr* artificial insemination by donor.

aid /eɪd/ *n* **1** [U] help: *with the aid of a friend* ○ *legal aid* ○ *She came quickly to his aid,* ie to help him. **2** [C] thing or person that helps: *a ˈhearing aid* ○ *ˈteaching aids* ○ *visual ˈaids,* eg pictures, films, etc used in teaching. **3** [U] food, money, etc sent to a country to help it: *How much overseas/foreign aid does Britain give?* ○ [attrib] *medical ˈaid programmes.* **4** (idm) **in aid of sth/sb** in support of sth/sb: *collect money in aid of charity.* **what's (all) this, etc in aid of?** (*infml*) what is the purpose of this, etc?: *Now then, what's all this crying in aid of?*
▷ **aid** *v* **1** [Tn, Tn·pr, Tnt] ~ **sb (in/with sth)** (*fml*) help sb. **2** (idm) **ˌaid and ˈabet** (*esp law*) encourage or help (sb) in some criminal activity.

aide /eɪd/ *n* **1** = AIDE-DE-CAMP. **2** (*esp US*) assistant: *the chief aides to the President.*

aide-de-camp /ˌeɪd də ˈkɒm; *US* ˈkæmp/ (also **aide**) *n* (*pl* **aides-de-camp** /ˌeɪd də ˈkɒm/) (*abbr* **ADC**) naval or military officer who acts as assistant to a senior officer.

aide-mémoire /ˌeɪd memˈwɑː(r)/ *n* (*pl* **aides-mémoire** /ˌeɪd memˈwɑː(r)/) document, book, etc used to remind sb of sth.

AIDS (also **Aids**) /eɪdz/ *abbr* (*medical*) acquired immune deficiency syndrome, a disease caused by a virus that weakens the body's resistance to infection: *an Aids victim* ○ *Aids is a fatal disease.* Cf HIV.

aikido /aɪˈkiːdəʊ/ *n* [U] Japanese sport based on a form of self-defence in which the attacker's energy is used against him without injuring him.

ail /eɪl/ *v* [Tn] (*arch*) trouble (sb) in body or mind (used esp as in the expression shown): *What ails you?*
▷ **ailing** *adj* unwell; ill: *My wife is ailing.* ○ (*fig*) *the ailing economy.*

aileron /ˈeɪlərɒn/ *n* hinged part of the wing of an aircraft, used to control its balance while it is flying. ⇨ illus at AIRCRAFT.

ailment /ˈeɪlmənt/ *n* illness, esp a slight one: *He's prone to minor ailments.*

aim[1] /eɪm/ *v* **1** (**a**) [I, Ipr, Tn, Tn·pr] ~ **(sth) (at sth/sb)** point or direct (a weapon, blow, missile, etc) towards an object: *You're not aiming straight.* ○ *He aimed (his gun) at the target, fired and missed it.* ○ *The punch was aimed at his opponent's head.* (**b**) [I, Ipr] ~ **(at/for sth)** direct one's efforts (in the specified direction): *He has always aimed high,* ie been ambitious. ○ *She's aiming at* (ie trying to win) *a scholarship.* (**c**) [Tn·pr] ~ **sth at sb** direct (a comment, criticism, etc) at sb: *My remarks were not aimed at you.* **2** [Ipr, It] ~ **at doing sth** intend or try to do sth: *We must aim at increasing/to increase exports.*

aim[2] /eɪm/ *n* **1** [U] action of pointing or directing a weapon or missile at a target: *My aim was accurate.* ○ *Take careful aim (at the target) before firing.* ○ *He missed his aim,* ie did not hit the target. **2** [C] purpose; intention: *What are the social and moral aims of the society?* ○ *He has only one aim in life — to become rich.*

aimless /ˈeɪmlɪs/ *adj* having no purpose: *aimless wanderings* ○ *lead an aimless life.* ▷ **aimlessly** *adv*: *drift aimlessly from job to job.* **aimlessness** *n* [U].

ain't /eɪnt/ *contracted form* (*non-standard or joc*) **1** am/is/are not: *Things ain't what they used to be.* **2** has/have not: *You ain't seen nothing yet.*

air[1] /eə(r)/ *n* **1** [U] mixture of gases surrounding the earth and used by all land animals and plants for respiration. The average composition of dry air at sea-level is: nitrogen 78.08%, oxygen 20.95%, argon 0.93%, carbon dioxide 0.03%, neon 0.0018%, helium 0.0005%, krypton 0.0001% and xenon 0.00001%. It also contains small amounts of water vapour, hydrocarbons, hydrogen peroxide, sulphur compounds, ammonia and dust particles: *Let's go out for some fresh air.* **2** [U] (**a**) the earth's atmosphere; open space in this: *the birds of the air* ○ *be in the open air.* (**b**) the earth's atmosphere as the place where aircraft fly: *send goods by air* ○ *travel by air,* ie in an aircraft ○ *The site of the old fort is clearly visible from the air.* ○ [attrib] *air travel, transport, traffic, freight.* **3** [C] impression given; appearance or manner: *smile with a triumphant air* ○ *do things with an air,* ie confidently ○ *The place has an air of mystery (about it),* ie looks mysterious. **4** [C] (*dated*) melody; tune: *Bach's Air on the G String.* **5** [C] (*dated*) light wind; breeze. **6** (idm) **ˌairs and ˈgraces** (*derog*) affected manner intended (usu unsuccessfully) to make one appear a very refined person. **a breath of fresh air** ⇨ BREATH. **castles in the air** ⇨ CASTLE. **a change of air/climate** ⇨ CHANGE[2]. **clear the air** ⇨ CLEAR[3]. **give oneself/put on ˈairs** behave in an unnatural or affected way in order to impress others. **hot air** ⇨ HOT. **in the ˈair** (**a**) in circulation; current: *There's (a feeling of) unrest in the air.* (**b**) uncertain; undecided: *Our plans are still (up) in the air.* **in the open air** ⇨ OPEN[1]. **light as air/as a feather** ⇨ LIGHT[3]. **ˌon/ˌoff the ˈair** broadcast(ing)/not broadcast(ing) on radio or television: *This channel comes on the air every morning at 7 am.* ○ *We'll be off the air for the summer and returning for a new series in the autumn.* **ˌtake the ˈair** (*dated or fml*) go out of doors in order to enjoy the fresh air. **tread on air** ⇨ TREAD. **vanish, etc into thin air** ⇨ THIN. **with one's nose in the air** ⇨ NOSE[1].
□ **ˈair base** place from which military aircraft operate.
ˈair-bed *n* mattress that can be filled with air.
ˈair-bladder *n* (in animals and plants) bladder filled with air.
ˈair brake brake worked by air pressure.
ˈair-brick *n* type of brick with holes in it to allow air to pass through it for ventilation.
ˈairbrush *n* device used, esp by commercial artists, for spraying paint by means of compressed air.
ˈAirbus *n* (*propr*) aircraft operating regularly and often over short or medium distances.
ˌAir Chief ˈMarshal (*Brit*) second highest rank in the Royal Air Force.
ˌair ˈcommodore (*Brit*) officer of the Royal Air Force next below Air Vice-Marshal.
ˈair-conditioning *n* [U] system controlling the humidity and temperature of the air in a room or building. **ˈair-conditioned** *adj*: *an air-conditioned office* ○ *Is the house air-conditioned?* **air-conditioner** *n.*
ˌair-ˈcooled *adj* cooled by a current of air: *an ˌair-cooled ˈengine.*
ˈaircrew *n* [CGp] crew of an aircraft.
ˈair-cushion *n* **1** cushion that can be filled with air. **2** layer of air supporting eg a hovercraft.
ˈairfield *n* area of open level ground equipped with hangars and runways for (esp military) aircraft.
ˈairfoil *n* (*US*) = AEROFOIL.
ˈair force [CGp] branch of the armed forces that uses aircraft for attack and defence: *the Royal Air Force* ○ [attrib] *air force officers.* ⇨ article at ARMED FORCES.
ˈairframe *n* main body of an aircraft, without its engine(s).
ˈairglow *n* [U] radiation from the upper atmosphere that can be detected at night as a faint glow in the sky.
ˈairgun *n* (also **ˈair rifle**) gun that fires pellets by means of compressed air.
ˈair hostess stewardess in a passenger aircraft.
ˈair letter single sheet of light paper folded to form

a letter that may be sent cheaply by airmail.

ˈ**airlift** *n* transport of supplies, troops, etc by aircraft, esp in an emergency or when other routes are blocked: *an emergency airlift of food to the famine-stricken areas.* — *v* [Tn] transport (people, supplies, etc) in this way: *Civilians trapped in the beleaguered city have been airlifted to safety.*

ˈ**airline** *n* [CGp] company or service providing regular flights for public use: [attrib] *an airline pilot.* ˈ**airliner** *n* large passenger aircraft.

ˈ**airlock** *n* **1** stoppage in the flow of liquid in a pump or pipe, caused by a bubble of air. **2** compartment with an airtight door at each end, providing access to a pressurized chamber.

ˈ**airmail** *n* [U] mail carried by air: *send a letter (by) airmail* ○ [attrib] *an airmail envelope* ○ *an airmail edition*, eg of a newspaper or magazine, printed on special light paper. — *v* [Tn] send (sth) by airmail.

ˈ**airman** /-mən/ *n* (*pl* ˈ**airmen** /-mən/) **1** pilot or member of the crew of an aircraft. **2** (*Brit*) member of the Royal Air Force, esp below the rank of a commissioned officer. ➪ App 4.

ˌ**Air** ˈ**Marshal** (*Brit*) third highest rank in the Royal Air Force. ➪ App 4.

ˈ**airmiss** near collision between two aircraft in flight.

ˈ**airplane** *n* (*US*) = AEROPLANE.

ˈ**air pocket** partial vacuum in the air causing aircraft in flight to drop suddenly.

ˈ**airport** *n* large area where civil aircraft land and take off, usu with facilities for passengers and goods, and customs.

ˈ**air pump** device for pumping air into or out of sth.

ˈ**air raid** attack by aircraft dropping bombs: *Many civilians were killed in the air raids on London.* ○ [attrib] *an air-raid warning, shelter.*

air rifle = AIRGUN.

ˌ**air-sea** ˈ**rescue** (organization for the) rescue of people from the sea using aircraft.

ˈ**airship** *n* aircraft filled with gas and driven by engines. Airships developed from balloons. They are longer and can be steered instead of having to drift with the wind. The first was built in 1852 by the Frenchman Henri Giffard. The most famous designer was the German Count von Zeppelin, whose airships were used in passenger services, and for bombing during the First World War. A series of crashes in the 1930s, in which many people were killed, stopped interest in their use until the 1970s and 1980s, when helium was used as the lifting gas instead of hydrogen, which can catch fire.

ˈ**airsick** *adj* feeling sick as a result of travelling in an aircraft. ˈ**airsickness** *n* [U].

ˈ**airspace** *n* [U] part of the earth's atmosphere above a country and legally controlled by that country: *a violation of British airspace by foreign aircraft*, ie flying over Britain without permission.

ˈ**air speed** speed of an aircraft relative to the air through which it is moving. Cf GROUND SPEED (GROUND[1]).

ˈ**air-stream** *n* current of air, esp at high altitude as it affects flying aircraft, etc.

ˈ**airstrip** (also **landing-field, landing-strip**) *n* strip of ground cleared for aircraft to land and take off.

ˈ**air terminal** building in a town providing transport to and from an airport.

ˈ**airtight** *adj* not allowing air to enter or escape.

ˌ**air-to-**ˈ**air** *adj* [usu attrib] from one aircraft to another in flight: *an air-to-air missile.*

ˌ**air traffic con**ˈ**troller** person at an airport who gives radio instructions to pilots wishing to take off or land. ˌ**air traffic con**ˈ**trol** organization within which such a person works.

ˌ**Air Vice** ˈ**Marshal** (*Brit*) fourth highest rank in the Royal Air Force. ➪ App 4.

ˈ**air-waves** *n* [pl] radio waves.

ˈ**airway** *n* **1** ventilating passage in a mine. **2** route regularly followed by aircraft. **3** passage for air into the lungs: *a blocked airway* ○ *Make sure the airway is clear.*

ˈ**airwoman** *n* (*pl* **-women**) **1** woman pilot or member of the crew of an aircraft. **2** (*Brit*) member of the Women's Royal Air Force, esp below the rank of commissioned officer.

ˈ**airworthy** *adj* (of aircraft) fit to fly; in good working order. **airworthiness** *n* [U].

air[2] /eə(r)/ *v* [Tn] **1** (**a**) put (clothing, etc) in a warm place or the open air in order to make it completely dry. (**b**) let air into (a room, etc) to cool or freshen it. **2** express (an idea, a complaint, etc) publicly: *air one's views, opinions, grievances, etc* ○ *He likes to air his knowledge*, ie let others see how much he knows. ▷ **airing** /ˈeərɪŋ/ *n* [sing]: *give the blanket a good airing*, ie expose it to fresh air or warmth ○ *(fig) give one's views an airing*, ie express them to others.

□ ˈ**airing cupboard** heated cupboard in which to keep sheets, towels, etc.

airborne /ˈeəbɔːn/ *adj* (**a**) [attrib] transported by the air: *airborne seeds.* (**b**) [pred] (of aircraft) in the air after taking off: *Smoking is forbidden until the plane is airborne.* (**c**) [attrib] (of troops) specially trained for operations using aircraft: *an airborne division.*

aircraft

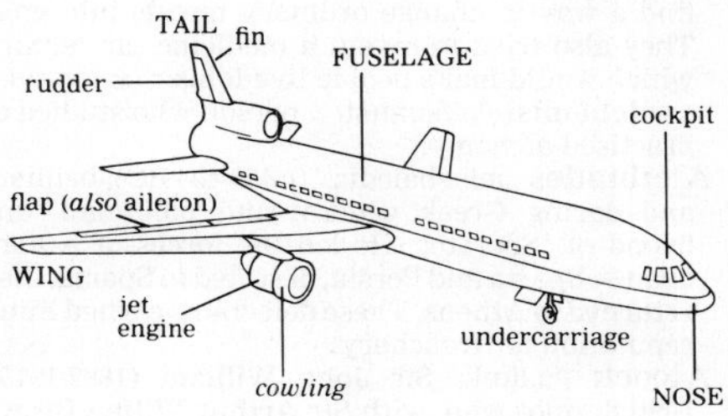

aircraft /ˈeəkrɑːft/ *n* (*pl* unchanged) any machine or structure that can fly in the air and is regarded as a vehicle or carrier. ➪ illus.

□ ˈ**aircraft-carrier** *n* ship that carries aircraft and is used as a base for landing and taking off.

ˈ**aircraftman** /-mən/ *n* (*pl* **-men** /-mən/) (*Brit*) lowest rank in the Royal Air Force.

ˈ**aircraftwoman** *n* (*pl* **-women** /-wɪmɪn/) (*Brit*) lowest rank in the Women's Royal Air Force.

airless /ˈeəlɪs/ *adj* **1** not having enough fresh air; stuffy: *an airless room.* **2** without a breeze; calm and still: *It was a hot, airless evening.*

airy /ˈeərɪ/ *adj* (**-ier, -iest**) **1** having plenty of fresh air moving about; well-ventilated: *The office was light and airy.* **2** [usu attrib] (**a**) light as air: *airy silk gauze.* (**b**) (*fig*) without substance; not sincere: *an airy promise*, ie one that is unlikely to be kept. (**c**) carefree and light-hearted: *an airy manner* ○ *an airy disregard for the law.*

▷ **airily** /ˈeərəlɪ/ *adv* in a carefree light-hearted manner: *'I don't care,' he said airily.*

□ ˌ**airy-**ˈ**fairy** *adj* (*infml derog*) not practical or realistic: *airy-fairy notions* ○ *The scheme seems a bit airy-fairy to me.*

aisle /aɪl/ *n* **1** side passage in a church that is divided by a row of pillars from the nave. ➪ illus at CHURCH. **2** passage between rows of seats in a church, theatre, railway carriage, etc. **3** (idm) **knock them in the aisles** ➪ KNOCK[2]. **rolling in the aisles** ➪ ROLL.

aitch /eɪtʃ/ *n* **1** the letter H. **2** (idm) **drop one's aitches** ➪ DROP[2].

aitchbone /ˈeɪtʃbəʊn/ *n* (**a**) rump-bone of an animal. (**b**) piece of beef cut from the part above this bone.

ajar /əˈdʒɑː(r)/ *adj* [pred] (of a door) slightly open: *The door was/stood ajar.* ○ *leave the door ajar.*

Ajax /ˈeɪdʒæks/ (in Greek legend) Greek hero who fought in the *Trojan war. Said to be second only to *Achilles in prowess, he committed suicide when Achilles' armour was given to *Odysseus.

aka *abbr* (*esp US*) also known as: *Antonio Fratelli, aka 'Big Tony'.*

Akbar /ˈækbɑː(r)/ Jalaludin Muhammad (1542-1605), *Moghul emperor of India who spread the Moghul empire over most of India and was the first ruler to unite the whole subcontinent into a single system.

akimbo /əˈkɪmbəʊ/ *adv* (idm) **with arms akimbo** ➪ ARM. ➪ illus at ARM.

akin /əˈkɪn/ *adj* [pred] ~ (**to sth**) similar; related: *He felt something akin to pity.* ○ *Pity and love are closely akin.*

-al *suff* **1** (with *ns* forming *adjs*) of or concerning: *magical* ○ *verbal.* **2** (with *vs* forming *ns*) process or state of: *recital* ○ *survival.*

▷ **-ally** (with sense 1 forming *advs*): *sensationally.*

alabaster /ˈæləbɑːstə(r); *US* -bæs-/ *n* [U] soft (usu white) stone, like marble in appearance, often carved to make ornaments.

▷ **alabaster** *adj* [usu attrib] (**a**) of alabaster: *an alabaster vase.* (**b**) white or smooth like alabaster: *her alabaster complexion.*

à la carte /ˌɑː lɑː ˈkɑːt/ (of a restaurant meal) ordered as separate items from a menu, not at a fixed price for the complete meal: *We only have an à la carte menu.* Cf TABLE D'HÔTE.

alacrity /əˈlækrətɪ/ *n* [U] (*fml or rhet*) prompt and eager readiness: *He accepted her offer with alacrity.*

Aladdin /əˈlædɪn/ **1** (in oriental legend) boy who finds a magic lamp containing a spirit (or *genie*) who will come out whenever the lamp is rubbed and obey the lamp-owner's commands. His story forms the basis of a popular British Christmas pantomime. **2** (idm) **an A**ˌ**laddin's** ˈ**cave** place filled with many precious, beautiful or desirable things.

Alamo /ˈæləməʊ/ **the Alamo** fortified religious settlement in Texas which was attacked by Mexican forces in 1836 during the war for Texan independence from Mexico. All its defenders, including Davy *Crockett, were killed.

à la mode /ˌɑː lɑː ˈməʊd/ **1** fashionable. **2** (*US*) (of food) served with ice-cream: *apple pie à la mode.*

Alaric /ˈælərɪk/ (c 370–410 AD), king of the *Visigoths, a Germanic people who invaded Italy and in 410 captured and destroyed Rome.

alarm /əˈlɑːm/ *n* **1** [C] (**a**) warning sound or signal: *give/raise/sound the alarm.* (**b**) apparatus that gives such a warning: *Where's the fire alarm?* **2** [C] = ALARM CLOCK. **3** [U] fear and excitement caused by the expectation of danger: *This news fills me with alarm.* ○ *He jumped up in alarm.* ○ *There's no cause for alarm.* **4** (idm) **a false alarm** ➪ FALSE.

▷ **alarm** *v* [Tn] give a warning or feeling of danger to (a person or an animal); frighten; disturb: *I don't want to alarm you, but there's a strange man in your garden.* ○ *Alarmed by the noise, the birds flew away.* **alarmed** *adj* [pred] ~ (**at/by sth**) anxious or afraid: *I'm rather alarmed (to hear) that you're planning to leave the company.* **alarming** *adj* causing fear; disturbing: *an alarming increase in the number of burglaries* ○ *The report is most alarming.* **alarmingly** *adv*: *Prices have increased alarmingly.*

alarmist *n* (*derog*) person who alarms others unnecessarily or excessively. - *adj*: *alarmist warnings, forecasts, etc* ○ *We mustn't be alarmist.*

□ **a**ˈ**larm clock** (also **alarm**) clock with a device that can be set to ring at a particular time, esp to wake sleepers: *set the alarm (clock) for six o'clock.*

alas /əˈlæs/ *interj* (*dated or rhet*) (expressing sorrow or regret): *Alas, they've all sold out, madam.*

Alaska /əˈlæskə/ largest and least populated state of the USA, separated from the rest of the USA by Canada. Much of the land is mountainous and there are coastlines on the Arctic Ocean, Bering Sea and North Pacific. The capital city is Juneau. Alaska's economy is based largely on fishing and important mineral resources, including coal, copper and platinum. ▷ **Alaskan** *adj, n.* ➪ map at UNITED STATES OF AMERICA.

albacore /ˈælbəkɔː(r)/ *n* type of large edible tuna fish.

Alban /ˈɔːlbən/ Saint (c 300 AD), first British person to be killed for his Christian faith. He lived in a town now called St Albans in memory of him; it is in Hertfordshire.

Albania /ælˈbeɪnɪə/ country in SE Europe, bordering Greece and the former Yugoslavia; pop approx 3 331 000; official language Albanian;

Albania

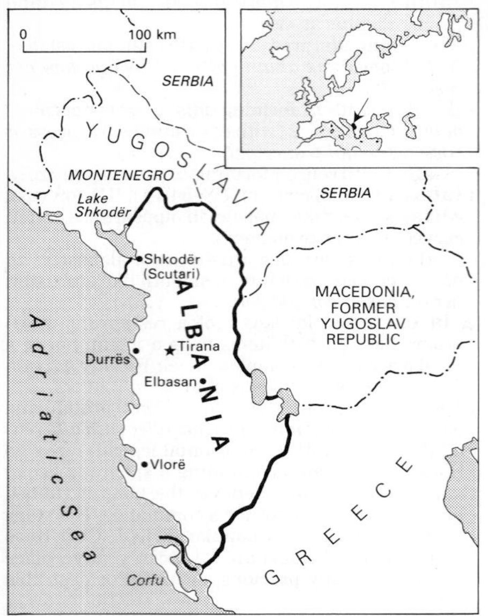

capital Tirana; unit of currency lek (= 100 qintars). For many years part of the Turkish empire, it became independent in 1912, first as a republic and then as a monarchy. After the Second World War a Communist regime took over, which virtually isolated Albania from the rest of the world until in 1991 a multi-party government began a programme of economic and political reform. ⇨ map.
▷ **Albanian** /-ɪən/ *adj* of Albania. — *n* **1** [C] native or inhabitant of Albania. **2** [U] Albanian language, part of the *Indo-European language group.

albatross /ˈælbətrɒs; *US also* -trɔ:s/ *n* **1** large white sea-bird with long wings, common in the Pacific and Southern Oceans. **2** (in golf) score of three strokes less than average (*par*) at a hole. Cf EAGLE 2, BIRDIE 2, PAR[1] 3.

albedo /ælˈbi:dəʊ/ *n* (*pl* ~**s**) (*physics*) fraction of light reflected from a surface.

Albee /ˈælbi:, ˈɔ:lbi:/ Edward Franklin (1928-), American playwright whose best-known work is *Who's Afraid of Virginia Woolf?*, about a quarrelling married couple.

albeit /ˌɔ:lˈbi:ɪt/ *conj* (*dated or fml*) although: *I tried, albeit unsuccessfully, to contact him.* ⇨ Usage at ALTHOUGH.

Albert /ˈælbət/ Prince (1819-61), prince of Saxe-Coburg-Gotha, husband of Queen *Victoria of Britain. His official title was Prince Consort. He took an active role in encouraging new enterprises in business, science and technology, and the arts, and was one of the main sponsors of the Great Exhibition of 1851, which displayed the products of British industry. He died of typhoid.

Albert Hall /ˌælbət ˈhɔ:l/ **the Albert Hall** large circular concert hall in London, where most of the BBC promenade concerts (PROMENADE) are held. It was built in 1871, and commemorates Prince Albert.

Albigenses /ˌælbɪˈdʒensi:z/ *n* [pl] members of a strict 12th- to 13th-century Christian sect of southern France, who regarded the material world as evil and hated the Church. They were named after the French city of Albi.

albino /ælˈbi:nəʊ; *US* -ˈbaɪ-/ *n* (*pl* ~**s**) person or animal born with no colouring pigment in the skin and hair (which are white) and the eyes (which are pink): [attrib] *an albino rabbit.*
▷ **albinism** /ˈælbɪnɪzəm/ *n* [U] condition of being an albino.

Albion /ˈælbɪən/ **1** (*arch*) England or Britain. **2** (idm) **perfidious Albion** ⇨ PERFIDIOUS (PERFIDY).

album /ˈælbəm/ *n* **1** book in which a collection of photographs, autographs, postage stamps, etc can be kept. **2** long-playing record with several items by the same performer: *This is one of the songs from/on her latest album.* Cf SINGLE n 5.

albumen /ˈælbjʊmɪn; *US* ælˈbju:mən/ *n* [U] **1** white of egg. ⇨ illus at EGG. **2** (*botany*) substance found in many seeds, esp the eatable part.

albumin /ˈælbjʊmɪn; *US* ælˈbju:mɪn/ *n* [U] protein found in egg-white, milk, blood and some plants.

Alcaeus /ælˈsi:əs/ (born c 600 BC), Greek lyric poet who wrote love-songs, drinking-songs, and also political poems.

Alcaic /ælˈkeɪɪk/ *adj* of a type of ancient Greek and Latin poetry (first used by Alcaeus) in which each verse consists of four lines containing four beats each.
▷ **Alcaics** *n* [pl] Alcaic poetry.

Alcatraz /ˌælkəˈtræz, *also* ˈælkətræz/ island in San Francisco Bay, California, USA. Until 1963 there was a prison on it.

alchemy /ˈælkəmɪ/ *n* [U] medieval form of chemistry. It was based on the belief that substances could be changed ('transmuted') into other substances. In particular, alchemists tried to find a way to change ordinary metals into gold. They also tried to invent a medicine (an 'elixir') which would make people live longer or for ever.
▷ **alchemist** /ˈælkəmɪst/ *n* person who studied or practised alchemy.

Alcibiades /ˌælsɪˈbaɪədi:z/ (c 450-404 BC), brilliant and daring Greek general and politician, and friend of *Socrates. He led the forces of Athens against Sparta and Persia, deserted to Sparta, then returned to Athens. These defections earned him a reputation for treachery.

Alcock /ˈɔ:lkɒk/ Sir John William (1892-1919), British pilot who, with Sir Arthur Witten Brown (1886-1948), made the first flight across the Atlantic Ocean, in 1919.

alcohol /ˈælkəhɒl; *US* -hɔ:l/ *n* **1** [U] **(a)** colourless liquid that can cause drunkenness, contained in drinks such as beer, wine, brandy and whisky. **(b)** this liquid used as a solvent and fuel. **2** [U] drinks containing this: *prohibit the sale of alcohol* ○ *I never touch* (ie drink drinks that contain) *alcohol.* **3** [U, C] chemical compound of the same type as alcohol.
▷ **alcoholic** /ˌælkəˈhɒlɪk; *US* -ˈhɔ:l-/ *adj* **1** of or containing alcohol: *ˌalcoholic ˈdrinks* ○ *Home-made wine can be very alcoholic.* **2** [attrib] caused by drinking alcohol: *be in an ˌalcoholic ˈstupor.* — *n* person who drinks too much alcohol or suffers from alcoholism.
alcoholism /-ɪzəm/ *n* [U] (disease caused by) continual heavy drinking of alcohol; addiction to alcohol.

Alcott /ˈɔ:lkɒt/ Louisa May (1832-88), American novelist best known for *Little Women*, a largely autobiographical book about a 19th-century New England family.

alcove /ˈælkəʊv/ *n* small space in a room, etc formed by part of the wall being set back; recess: *The bed fits neatly into the alcove.*

Alcuin /ˈælkwɪn/ (c 735-804), English scholar who became *Charlemagne's religious and educational adviser, and organized education throughout his empire. He developed the style of handwriting which formed the basis for the commonest sort of printed letters.

Aldebaran /ælˈdebərən/ very large bright red star in the constellation *Taurus.

aldehyde /ˈældɪhaɪd/ *n* any of a group of chemical compounds made by the partial oxidation of alcohols. They are used in making resins, dyes, etc.

alder /ˈɔ:ldə(r)/ *n* tree of the birch family, usu growing in marshy places.

alderman /ˈɔ:ldəmən/ *n* (*pl* **-men** /mən/) **1** (*Brit*) (esp formerly) member of a county or borough council, next in rank below the mayor. **2** (*US*) (in some cities) member of the city council, representing a particular part of the city. ▷ **aldermanic** /ˌɔ:ldəˈmænɪk/ *adj.*

Aldermaston /ˈɔ:ldəmɑ:stən/ village in Berkshire, England. Near it is the United Kingdom Atomic Energy Research Establishment. For several years from the late 1950s there were annual marches between London and Aldermaston to protest against nuclear weapons. ⇨ article at PROTEST.

Alderney /ˈɔ:ldənɪ/ **1** most northerly of the main *Channel Islands. **2** [C] breed of cattle, originally from Alderney, reared for its milk.

Aldwych Theatre /ˌɔ:ldwɪtʃ ˈθɪetə(r)/ **the Aldwych Theatre** theatre in the *West End of London, famous for the 'Aldwych farces', a series of comedy plays written by Ben Travers and performed there in the 1920s and early 1930s.

ale /eɪl/ *n* **1** **(a)** [U, C] (used esp in compounds and phrases) (type of) strong beer, usu sold in bottles: *We sell a wide range of ales and stouts.* ⇨ article at DRINK. **(b)** [C] glass of ale: *Two light ales, please.* **2** [U] (*dated or dialect*) beer: *a pint of ale.* **3** (idm) **Adam's ale** ⇨ ADAM[1]. **cakes and ale** ⇨ CAKE.
□ **ˈalehouse** *n* (*pl* **-houses** /-haʊzɪz/) (*arch*) inn or tavern.

aleatory /ˌælɪˈeɪtərɪ; *US* ˈeɪlɪətɔ:rɪ/ *adj* **1** (*fml*) depending on chance. **2** (of music) made up of elements chosen at random.

alert /əˈlɜ:t/ *adj* ~ **(to sth)** attentive and quick to think or act: *be alert to possible dangers* ○ *The alert listener will have noticed the error.* ○ *Although he's over eighty his mind is still remarkably alert.*
▷ **alert** *n* **1** (usu *sing*) (time of) special watchfulness before or during an attack: *The troops were placed on full alert.* **2** warning given to prepare for danger or an attack: *give/receive the alert.* **3** (idm) **on the aˈlert (against/for sth)** watchful and prepared: *Police warned the public to be on the alert for suspected terrorists.*
alert *v* **1** [Tn] warn (soldiers, etc) to watch for danger and be ready to act: *Why weren't the police alerted?* **2** [Tn·pr] ~ **sb to sth** make sb aware of sth: *alert staff to the crisis facing the company.*
alertly *adv.*
alertness *n* [U].

A level /ˈeɪ levl/ (*infml*) = ADVANCED LEVEL (ADVANCE): *When are you taking A level/your A levels?* ○ *How many A levels have you got?* Cf O LEVEL, GCSE. ⇨ article at SCHOOL.

Alexander the Great /ˌælɪgˌzɑ:ndə ðə ˈgreɪt; *US* -ˌzæn-/ (356-323 BC), king of *Macedon 336-323 BC, son of *Philip of Macedon. After he became king, he invaded and defeated the Persian empire. He took his armies further and further eastwards, until eventually the territory he controlled extended to India. His huge empire did not long survive his death, but he is usu regarded as the greatest general of the ancient world. In his lifetime people thought of him as a god.

Alexandra Palace /ˌælɪgzɑ:ndrə ˈpælɪs; *US* -zæn-/ large public building in north London, used mainly for exhibitions and concerts. It formerly housed BBC television studios.

Alexandria /ˌælɪgˈzɑ:ndrɪə; *US* -ˈzæn-/ city and chief port of Egypt. Founded by *Alexander the Great in 332 BC, it was a major cultural centre of the ancient world, with famous libraries. For over 1 000 years it was the capital of Egypt.

alfalfa /ælˈfælfə/ *n* [U] (*US*) = LUCERNE.

Alfred the Great /ˌælfrɪd ðə ˈgreɪt/ (849-99 AD), king of *Wessex 871-99. As military leader he defeated the Danish invaders, saving the west of England from falling under their control. He founded a navy to protect the coastline. He introduced several important legal reforms, encouraged the spread of education (himself translating several Latin works into English) and inaugurated the Anglo-Saxon Chronicle.

alfresco /ælˈfreskəʊ/ *adj, adv* in the open air: *an alfresco lunch* ○ *lunching alfresco.*

algae /ˈældʒi:, *also* ˈælgaɪ/ *n* [pl] (*sing* **alga** /ˈælgə/) very simple plants with no true stems or leaves, found chiefly in water.

algebra /ˈældʒɪbrə/ *n* [U] branch of mathematics in which letters and symbols are used to represent quantities. ▷ **algebraic** /ˌældʒɪˈbreɪɪk/ *adj.* **algebraically** /-klɪ/ *adv.*

Algeria /ælˈdʒɪərɪə/ country in N Africa, on the Mediterranean coast, consisting mainly of desert;

North Africa

pop approx 23 841 000; official language Arabic; capital Algiers; unit of currency dinar (= 100 centimes). From the mid 19th century it was a French colony, but following a long war of independence in the 1950s it became self-governing in 1962. Its main exports are oil and natural gas. ⇨ map (NORTH AFRICA). ▷ **Algerian** *adj, n.*

ALGOL (also **Algol**) /ˈælgɒl/ *abbr* (*computing*) algorithmic oriented language, a high-level programming language.

Algonquian /ælˈgɒŋkwɪən/ (also **Algonkian** /-kɪən/) *n* **1** [C] member of any of a group of N American Indian peoples of the Middle West of the USA and southern central and eastern Canada. **2** [U] any of the languages spoken by these peoples.

▷ **Algonquian** (also **Algonkian**) *adj* of these people or their languages.

Algonquin /ælˈgɒŋkwɪn/ *n* **1** [C] member of a N American Indian people of the regions around Ontario and Quebec, Canada. **2** [U] language of this people.

▷ **Algonquin** *adj* of this people or their language.

algorithm /ˈælgərɪðəm/ *n* (*esp computing*) set of rules or procedures that must be followed in solving a problem.

Alhambra /ælˈhæmbrə/ fortified palace near Granada in southern Spain, built in the 13th and 14th centuries by the Arab occupiers of Spain. It is an outstanding example of Moorish architecture.

Ali /ˈɑːlɪ/ Muhammad (1942-), American boxer who became world heavyweight champion in 1964 and regained the title twice afterwards, in 1974 and 1978. He was famous for his speed and skill, and also for his colourful flamboyant character. His original name was Cassius Clay, but he changed it to Muhammad Ali when he became a Muslim.

alias /ˈeɪlɪəs/ *n* name by which a person is called at other times or in other places; false name: *The criminal Mick Clark has/uses several aliases.*

▷ **alias** *adv* also (falsely) called: *Mick Clark, alias Sid Brown, is wanted for questioning by the police.*

Ali Baba /ˌælɪ ˈbɑːbɑː/ (in oriental legend) poor woodcutter who discovered the magic words 'Open Sesame!', which opened the door of a cave in which a gang of forty thieves hid their stolen treasure. The story forms the basis of a popular British Christmas pantomime. Cf OPEN SESAME (OPEN[1]).

alibi /ˈælɪbaɪ/ *n* **1** (*law*) formal statement or evidence that a person was in another place at the time of a crime: *The suspects all had good alibis for the day of the robbery.* **2** (*infml*) excuse of any kind: *Late again, Richard? What's your alibi this time?*

Alice in Wonderland /ˌælɪs ɪn ˈwʌndəlænd/ children's book (1865) written by Lewis *Carroll, which tells the story of the dream adventure of a young girl, Alice. She meets many strange creatures, including animals that speak (a white rabbit, a caterpillar, a mock turtle, etc) and characters from playing-cards (the Queen of Hearts). She also changes size several times as a result of eating or drinking sth. The full title of the book is *Alice's Adventures in Wonderland.* Carroll later wrote a second book about Alice's adventures, *Through the Looking-Glass.* ⇨ illus at TENNIEL.

alien /ˈeɪlɪən/ *n* **1** (*fml or law*) person who is not a naturalized citizen of the country in which he is living. **2** being from another world.

▷ **alien** *adj* **1** (a) foreign: *an alien land.* (b) unfamiliar; strange: *an alien environment* ○ *alien customs.* **2** [pred] ~ **to sth/sb** contrary to sth; hateful to sb: *Such principles are alien to our religion.* ○ *Cruelty was quite alien to his nature/to him.*

alienate /ˈeɪlɪəneɪt/ *v* **1** [Tn, Tn·pr] ~ **sb (from sb/sth)** cause sb to become unfriendly or indifferent; estrange sb: *The Prime Minister's policy alienated many of her followers.* ○ *Many artists feel alienated from society,* ie feel they do not belong to it or have been rejected by it. **2** [Tn] (*law*) transfer the ownership of (property) from one person to another.

▷ **alienation** /ˌeɪlɪəˈneɪʃn/ *n* [U] ~ **(from sb/sth)** alienating or being alienated; estrangement: *His criminal activities led to complete alienation from his family.* ○ *Mental illness can create a sense of alienation from the real world.*

alight[1] /əˈlaɪt/ *adj* [pred] on fire; lit: *A cigarette set the dry grass alight.* ○ *Her dress caught alight in the gas fire.* ○ (*fig*) *Their faces were alight with joy.*

alight[2] /əˈlaɪt/ *v* (*fml*) **1** [I, Ipr] ~ **(from sth)** get down from a horse or vehicle: *Passengers should never alight from a moving bus.* Cf DISMOUNT 1. **2** [I, Ipr] ~ **(on sth)** (of a bird) come down from the air and settle: *The sparrow alighted on a nearby branch.* **3** [Ipr] ~ **on sth** find sth by chance: *My eye alighted on a dusty old book at the back of the shelf.*

align /əˈlaɪn/ *v* **1** (a) [Tn, Tn·pr] ~ **sth (with sth)** place or arrange (a thing or things) in a straight line: *a row of trees aligned with the edge of the road.* (b) [Tn] put (the parts of a machine) into the correct position in relation to each other: *align the wheels of a car.* **2** [Tn·pr] ~ **oneself with sb** join sb as an ally; come into agreement with sb: *The Communist Party has aligned itself with the Socialists.*

▷ **alignment** *n* [U, C] **1** arrangement in a straight line: *The sights of the gun must be in alignment with the target.* **2** (esp political) arrangement in groups: *the alignment of Japan with the West.* **3** (idm) **out of alignment** not in line.

alike /əˈlaɪk/ *adj* [pred] like one another; similar: *These two photographs are almost alike.* ○ *The twins don't look at all alike.* ○ *All music is alike to him,* ie He cannot tell one kind from another.

▷ **alike** *adv* in the same way: *treat everybody exactly alike* ○ *The climate here is always hot, summer and winter alike.*

alimentary /ˌælɪˈmentərɪ/ *adj* of food and digestion.

□ **ˌalimentary caˈnal** tubular passage between the mouth and the anus through which food passes as it is digested.

alimony /ˈælɪmənɪ; *US* -məʊnɪ/ *n* [U] allowance that a court may order a man to pay to his wife or former wife before or after a legal separation or divorce. Cf MAINTENANCE 2.

aliphatic /ˌælɪˈfætɪk/ *adj* (of chemical compounds) in which carbon atoms form open chains and non-aromatic rings.

alive /əˈlaɪv/ *adj* [pred] **1** living; not dead: *She was still alive when I reached the hospital.* ○ *Many people are still buried alive after the earthquake.* **2** active; lively: *You seem very much alive today.* **3** in existence; continuing: *Newspaper reports kept interest in the story alive.* **4** (idm) **aˌlive and ˈkicking** (*infml*) still living, in good health and active: *You'll be glad to hear that Bill is alive and kicking.* **(be) alive to sth** aware of or responsive to sth: *He is fully alive to the possible dangers.* **(be) alive with sth** full of (living or moving things): *The lake was alive with fish.* **ˌlook aˈlive** hurry up; be brisk: *Look alive! You'll miss the bus.*

alkali /ˈælkəlaɪ/ *n* [C, U] (*chemistry*) any of a class of substances (eg caustic soda and ammonia) that either neutralize acids and form caustic or corrosive solutions in water or are proton acceptors. Cf ACID[1] 1. ▷ **alkaline** *adj*: *alkaline soil.* Cf ACID[2] 3. **alkalinity** /ælkəˈlɪnɪtɪ/ *n* [U].

all[1] /ɔːl/ *indef det* **1** (used with plural *ns*; the *n* may be preceded by *the, this/that/these/those, my, his, her,* etc or a cardinal number) the whole number of: *All horses are animals, but not all animals are horses.* ○ *All the people you invited are coming.* ○ *All my plants have died.* ○ *All five men are hard workers.* **2** (used with uncountable *ns*; the *n* may be preceded by *the, this/that* or *my, his, her,* etc) the whole amount of: *All wood tends to shrink.* ○ *You've had all the fun and I've had all the hard work.* ○ *All this mail must be answered.* **3** (used with singular *ns* denoting a period of time) (for) the whole duration of: *He's worked hard all year/month/week/day,* ie throughout the year, etc. ○ *She was abroad all last summer.* ○ *We were unemployed (for) all that time.* ○ *He has lived all his life in London.* ⇨ Usage. **4** the greatest possible: *with all speed/haste/dispatch* ○ *in all honesty/frankness/sincerity,* ie speaking with the greatest honesty, etc. **5** any whatever: *Beyond all doubt* (ie There can't be any doubt that) *changes are coming.* ○ *He denied all knowledge of the crime.* **6** (idm) **and all ˈthat (jazz, rubbish, etc)** (*infml*) and other similar things: *I'm bored by history — dates and battles and all that stuff.* **for all** ⇨ FOR[1]. **not all that good, well, etc** not particularly good, well, etc: *He doesn't sing all that well.* **not as bad(ly), etc as all ˈthat** not to the extent implied: *They're not as rich as all that.*

□ **ˌAll ˈFools' Day** = APRIL FOOL'S DAY (APRIL).

ˈall-night *adj* [attrib] lasting, functioning, etc throughout the night: *an all-night party, café, vigil.*

ˌAll ˈSaints' Day (also **ˌAll ˈHallows' Day**) 1 November.

ˌAll ˈSouls' Day 2 November.

ˈall-time *adj* [attrib] of all recorded time: *one of the all-time great tennis players* ○ *an all-time* (ie unsurpassed) *record* ○ *Profits are at an all-time low,* ie lower than they have ever been.

NOTE ON USAGE: **All** and **half** can be used with countable and uncountable nouns. **Both** is used only with plural countable nouns and refers to two in number. **1** All three can come before a noun, often with a determiner (eg *the, this, my*). **Half** must be followed by a determiner: *He's been here all (the) week.* ○ *Half this money is yours.* ○ *Both (our) cars are Fords.* ○ *Both (the/his) parents are teachers.* **2 All** and **both** can come after a noun or pronoun: *The spectators all booed the teams.* ○ *His parents are both teachers.* ○ *We all/both arrived late.* **3 All, both** and **half** are used with **of** followed by a noun or a pronoun: *All/Half (of) the milk had been drunk.* ○ *Both (of) his brothers are lawyers.* ○ *All/Both/Half of us wanted to leave early.*

all[2] /ɔːl/ *indef pron* **1** the whole number or amount. **(a)** ~ **(of sb/sth)** (referring back): *We had several bottles of beer left — all (of them) have disappeared.* ○ *I invited my five sisters but not all (of them) can come.* ○ *Some of the food has been eaten, but not all (of it).* **(b)** ~ **of sb/sth** (referring forward): *All of the mourners were dressed in black/They were all dressed in black.* ○ *All of the toys were broken/They were all broken.* ○ *Take all of the wine/Take it all.* ○ *All of this is yours/This is all yours.* **2** (followed by a relative clause, often without *that*) the only thing; everything: *All I want is peace and quiet.* ○ *He took all there was/all that I had.* **3** (idm) **all in ˈall** when everything is considered: *All in all it had been a great success.* **all or ˈnothing** (of a course of action) requiring all one's efforts: *It's all or nothing — if we don't score now we've lost the match.* **and ˈall** also; included; in addition: *The wind blew everything off the table, tablecloth and all.* **(not) at all** in any way; to any extent: *I didn't enjoy it at all.* ○ *There was nothing at all to eat.* ○ *Are you at all worried about the forecast?* **in all** altogether; as a total: *There were twelve of us in all for dinner.* ○ *That's £5.40 in all.* **ˌnot at ˈall** (used as a polite reply to an expression of thanks). **one's ˈall** everything one has; life: *They gave their all* (ie fought and died) *in the war.*

all[3] /ɔːl/ *indef adv* **1** completely: *She was dressed all in white,* ie All the clothes she was wearing were white. ○ *She lives all alone/all by herself.* ○ *The coffee went all over my trousers.* **2** (*infml*) very: *She was all excited.* ○ *Now don't get all upset about it.* **3** (used with *too* and *adjs* or *advs*) more than is desirable: *The end of the holiday came all too soon.* **4** (in sports and games) to each side: *The score was four all.* **5** (idm) **all aˈlong** (*infml*) all the time; from the beginning: *I realized I had had it in my pocket all along.* **all but** almost: *The party was all but over when we arrived.* ○ *It was all but impossible to climb back into the boat.* **all ˈin** physically tired; exhausted: *At the end of the race he felt all in.* **all of sth** (of size, height, distance, etc) probably more than; fully: *It was all of two miles to the beach.* **all ˈone** forming a complete unit: *We don't have a separate dining-room — the living area is all one.* **all over (a)** everywhere: *We looked all over for the ring.* ○ *I'm aching all over after the match.* **(b)** what one would expect of the person specified: *That sounds like my sister all over.* **all ˈright** (also (*infml*) **alˈright**) **(a)** as desired; satisfactor(il)y: *Is the coffee all right?* ○ *Are you getting along all right in your new job?* **(b)** safe and well: *I hope the children are all right.* **(c)** only just good enough: *This homework is all right but you could do better.* **(d)** (expressing agreement to do what sb has asked): *'Will you post this for me?' 'Yes, all right.'* **(e)** (expressing absolute certainty): *That's the man I saw in the car all right.* **all the better, harder, etc** so much better, harder, etc: *We'll have to work all the harder with two members of staff away ill.* **ˌall ˈthere** (*infml*) completely sane; mentally alert: *He behaves very oddly at times — I don't think he's quite all there.* **be all about sb/sth** have sb/sth as its subject matter or main point of interest: *The news is all about the latest summit meeting.* **be all for sth/doing sth** believe strongly that sth is desirable: *She's all for more nursery schools being built.* **be all ˈone to sb** (of two or more choices) be a matter of indifference to sb: *It's all one to me whether we eat now or later.* **be all over ...** become known by everyone in (a place): *News of the holiday was all over the school within minutes.* **be all ˈover sb** (*infml*) show excessive affection for or enthusiasm about sb when in his company: *You can see he's infatuated by her — he was all over her at the party.* **be all up (with sb)** (*infml*) be the end (for sb): *It looks as though it's all up with us now,* ie we're ruined, have no further chances, etc.

□ **ˌall-ˈclear** *n* **the all-clear** (usu *sing*) signal that danger is over.

ˌall-ˈin *adj* including everything: *an ˌall-in ˈprice,* ie with no extras. **ˈall-in wrestling** type of wrestling in which there are few or no restrictions.

ˈall out using all possible strength and resources: *The team is going all out to win the championship.* ○ [attrib] *make an all-out attempt to meet a deadline.*

ˌall-ˈpurpose *adj* having many different uses: *an ˌall-purpose ˈworkroom.*

ˌall-ˈround *adj* [attrib] **1** not specialized; general: *a good ˌall-round eduˈcation.* **2** (of a person) with a wide range of abilities: *an ˌall-round ˈsportsman.* **all-rounder** *n* person with a wide range of abilities.

ˈall-star *adj* [attrib] including many famous actors: *an all-star cast.*

all- *pref* (forming compound *adjs* and *advs*) **1** entirely: *an all-electric kitchen* ○ *an all-American show.* **2** in the highest degree: *all-important* ○ *all-powerful* ○ *all-merciful.*

Allah /ˈælə/ *n* name of God among Muslims and among Arabs of all faiths.

allay /əˈleɪ/ *v* [Tn] (*fml*) make (sth) less; relieve: *allay trouble, fears, suffering, doubt, suspicion.*

allegation /ˌælɪˈgeɪʃn/ *n* **1** act of alleging. **2** statement made without proof: *These are serious allegations.*

allege /əˈledʒ/ *v* [Tf, Cn·n/a, Cn·t only passive] (*fml*) state (sth) as a fact but without proof; give as an argument or excuse: *The prisoner alleges that he was at home on the night of the crime.* ○ *He alleged illness as the reason for his absence.* ○ *We were alleged to have brought goods into the country illegally.*

▷ **alleged** *adj* [attrib] stated without being proved: *the alleged culprit,* ie the person said to be the culprit. **allegedly** /əˈledʒɪdlɪ/ *adv*: *The novel was allegedly written by a computer.*

Alleghenies /ˌælɪˈgeɪnɪz/ **the Alleghenies** (also **the Allegheny Mountains**) range of mountains forming part of the *Appalachians in the eastern USA.

allegiance /əˈliːdʒəns/ *n* [U] (*fml*) ~ **(to sb/sth)** support of or loyalty to a government, ruler, cause, etc: *swear (an oath of) allegiance to the Queen.*

allegory /ˈælɪgərɪ; *US* ˈælɪgɔːrɪ/ *n* [U, C] (style of a) story, painting or description in which the characters and events are meant as symbols of purity, truth, patience, etc. ▷ **allegorical** /ˌælɪˈgɒrɪkl; *US* ˌælɪˈgɔːrəkl/ *adj.* **allegorically** *adv.*

allegretto /ˌælɪˈgretəʊ/ *adj, adv* (*music*) fairly fast and lively.

▷ **allegretto** *n* (*pl* ~**s**) piece of music (to be) played in this way.

allegro /əˈleɪgrəʊ/ *adj, adv* (*music*) in quick time; fast and lively.

▷ **allegro** *n* (*pl* ~**s**) piece of music (to be) played in this way.

alleluia /ˌælɪˈluːjə/ (also **hallelujah**) *n, interj* (song or shout expressing) praise to God.

Woody Allen

Allen /ˈælən/ Woody (real name Allen Stewart Konigsberg, 1935-), US film director, writer and actor whose films, (eg *Play It Again Sam, Annie Hall* and *Manhattan*) are noted for their off-beat New York humour and their exploration of modern American neuroses. ⇨ illus.

allergy /ˈælədʒɪ/ *n* ~ **(to sth)** medical condition that produces an unfavourable reaction to certain foods, pollens, insect bites, etc: *have an allergy to certain milk products.*

▷ **allergic** /əˈlɜːdʒɪk/ *adj* **1** [pred] ~ **(to sth)** having an allergy: *I like cats but unfortunately I'm allergic to them.* **2** caused by an allergy: *an allergic rash.* **3** [pred] ~ **to sth** (*joc infml*) having a strong dislike of sth: *I'm allergic to hard work!*

alleviate /əˈliːvɪeɪt/ *v* [Tn] make (sth) less severe; ease: *The doctor gave her an injection to alleviate the pain.* ○ *They alleviated the boredom of waiting by singing songs.* ▷ **alleviation** /əˌliːvɪˈeɪʃn/ *n* [U].

alley /ˈælɪ/ *n* **1** (also **ˈalley-way**) narrow passage, esp between or behind houses or other buildings, usu for pedestrians only. **2** path bordered by trees or hedges in a garden or park. ⇨ Usage at ROAD. **3** long narrow area in which games like tenpin bowling and skittles are played.

alliance /əˈlaɪəns/ *n* **1** [U] action or state of being joined or associated: *States seek to become stronger through alliance.* **2** [C] union or association formed for mutual benefit, esp between families (by marriage), countries or organizations: *enter into/break off an alliance with a neighbouring state.* **3** (idm) **in alliance (with sb/sth)** united; joined together: *We are working in alliance with our foreign partners.*

allied ⇨ ALLY.

alligator /ˈælɪgeɪtə(r)/ *n* **1** [C] reptile of the crocodile family found esp in the rivers and lakes of tropical America and China. **2** [U] its skin made into leather: [attrib] *an alligator handbag.*

alliteration /əˌlɪtəˈreɪʃn/ *n* [U] occurrence of the

same letter or sound at the beginning of two or more words in succession, as in *sing a song of sixpence* or *as thick as thieves.* ▷ **alliterative** /əˈlɪtrətɪv; *US* əˈlɪtəreɪtɪv/ *adj.* **alliteratively** *adv.*

allocate /ˈæləkeɪt/ *v* [Tn, Dn·n, Dn·pr] ~ **sth (to sb/sth)** allot or assign sth (to sb/sth) for a special purpose: *allocate funds for repair work* ○ *He allocated each of us our tasks/allocated tasks to each of us.*

▷ **allocation** /ˌæləˈkeɪʃn/ *n* **1** [U] action of allocating. **2** [C] amount (of money, space, etc) allocated: *We've spent our entire allocation for the year.*

allogamy /əˈlɒgəmɪ/ *n* [U] (*botany*) fertilization of a plant with pollen from another plant. Cf AUTOGAMY.

allot /əˈlɒt/ *v* (-tt-) [Tn, Dn·n, Dn·pr] ~ **sth (to sb/sth)** give (time, money, duties, etc) as a share of what is available; apportion sth: *How much cash has been allotted?* ○ *We did the work within the time they'd allotted (to) us.* ○ *Who will she allot the easy jobs to?*

▷ **allotment** *n* **1** [U] action of allotting. **2** [C] amount or portion allotted. **3** [C] (*esp Brit*) small piece of land that is rented by a private individual (usu from the local council) for growing vegetables, fruit, flowers, etc. Allotments are usu grouped together. They were started during the First World War. ⇨ article at GARDEN.

allotropy /əˈlɒtrəpɪ/ *n* [U] (*chemistry*) ability of certain chemical elements to exist in more than one form in a given state: *Sulphur and phosphorus exhibit allotropy.*

▷ **allotrope** /ˈælətrəʊp/ *n* (*chemistry*) any of the allotropic forms in which a particular chemical element can exist: *Diamond and graphite are allotropes of carbon.*

allotropic /ˌæləˈtrɒpɪk/ *adj*: *Solid sulphur exists in several different allotropic forms.*

allow /əˈlaʊ/ *v* **1** (a) [Tnt] permit (sb/sth) to do sth: *My boss doesn't allow me to use the telephone.* ○ *Passengers are not allowed to smoke.* ○ (*fig*) *She allowed her mind to wander.* (b) [Tn] let (sth) be done or happen: *Photography is not allowed in this theatre.* ○ *We don't allow smoking in our house.* (c) [Tn esp passive] (usu negative) permit (sb/sth) to go in: *Dogs not allowed/No dogs allowed*, ie It is not permitted to bring dogs into this park, building, etc. **2** [Dn·n, Dn·pr] ~ **sth to sb** let sb have sth: *This diet allows you one glass of wine a day.* ○ *How much holiday are you allowed?* ○ *I'm not allowed visitors.* ○ *The garage allowed me £500 on my old car*, ie as a discount on the price of a new one. ○ (*fig*) *He allows his imagination full play*, ie does not try to control it. **3** [Tn, Tn·pr] ~ **sth (for sb/sth)** provide sth or set sth aside for a purpose or in estimating sth: *allow four sandwiches for each person* ○ *You must allow three metres for a long-sleeved dress.* ○ *I should allow an hour to get to London.* **4** (a) [Tn, Tf] (*law*) agree that (sth) is true or correct: *The court allowed my appeal.* ○ *He allowed that I had the right to appeal.* (b) [Tf, Tnt] (*fml*) accept (sth); admit: *Even if we allow that the poet was mad...* ○ *Many allow him to be the leading artist in his field.* **5** (phr v) **allow for sb/sth** include sb/sth in one's calculations: *It will take you half an hour to get to the station, allowing for traffic delays.* **allow sb in, out, up, etc** permit sb to enter, leave, get up, etc: *She won't allow the children in(to the house) until they've wiped their shoes.* ○ *The patient was allowed up* (ie permitted to get out of bed) *after 10 days.* **allow of sth** (*fml*) permit sth; leave room for sth: *The facts allow of only one explanation.*

▷ **allowable** *adj* that is or can be allowed by law, the rules, etc: *allowable expenses.*

allowance /əˈlaʊəns/ *n* **1** [C, U] amount of sth, esp money, allowed or given regularly: *an allowance of £15 per day* ○ *be paid a clothing/subsistence/travel allowance*, ie money to be spent on clothes, etc ○ *I didn't receive any allowance from my father.* ○ *a luggage allowance*, ie amount of luggage a passenger can take free, esp on an aeroplane. **2** [C] sum of money deducted; discount: *get an allowance for your old car, fridge, cooker* ○ *tax allowance*, ie money deducted from income before the current rate of tax is imposed. **3** (idm) **make (an) allowance for sth** consider sth when making a decision, etc. **make allowances for sb** regard sb as deserving to be treated differently from others for some reason: *You must make allowances for him because he has been ill.*

alloy[1] /ˈælɔɪ/ *n* [C, U] **1** metal formed of a mixture of metals or of metal and another substance. The physical properties of an alloy are often very different from those of the original substances (eg aluminium alloys are much stronger than aluminium and are more resistant to heat): *Brass is an alloy of copper and zinc.* ○ *Brass and bronze are alloys.* ○ [attrib]: *alloy steel.* **2** inferior metal mixed with one of greater value, esp gold or silver.

alloy[2] /əˈlɔɪ/ *v* [Tn] **1** mix (sth) with metal(s) of lower value. **2** (*fig fml*) weaken or spoil (sth) by sth that reduces value or pleasure: *happiness that no fear could alloy.*

allspice /ˈɔːlspaɪs/ (also **pimento**) *n* [U] spice made from the dried berries of the pimento, a West Indian tree. It is commonly used in baking, and is supposed to taste like a mixture of cinnamon, nutmeg and cloves.

allude /əˈluːd/ *v* [Ipr] ~ **to sb/sth** (*fml*) mention sb/sth briefly or indirectly: *You alluded to certain developments in your speech — what exactly did you mean?*

allure /əˈlʊə(r)/ *v* [Tn, Tnt] (*fml or rhet*) tempt or attract (sb) by the expectation of gaining sth: *Many settlers were allured by promises of easy wealth.*

▷ **allure** *n* [C, U] attractiveness; charm: *the false allure of big-city life.*

allurement *n* [C, U].

alluring *adj* attractive; charming: *an alluring smile, prospect, promise.*

allusion /əˈluːʒn/ *n* ~ **(to sb/sth)** indirect reference: *Her poetry is full of obscure literary allusions.* ○ *He resents any allusion to his baldness.*

▷ **allusive** *adj* /əˈluːsɪv/ containing allusions: *Her allusive style is difficult to follow.*

alluvium /əˈluːvɪəm/ *n* [U] material (eg earth, sand, gravel, silt), often very fertile or rich in minerals, left by rivers or floods, esp at the mouth of a river. Cf DELTA.

▷ **alluvial** /əˈluːvɪəl/ *adj* [usu attrib] made up of alluvium: *alluvial deposits, soil, mud, etc* ○ *an alluvial plain* ○ *an alluvial fan*, ie a fan-shaped deposit of alluvium found when a narrow river enters a large valley or plain, esp from a mountainous region. Cf FLOOD-PLAIN (FLOOD).

ally /əˈlaɪ/ *v* (*pt, pp* **allied**) [Ipr, Tn·pr] ~ **(sb/oneself) with/to sb/sth** join or become joined with sb/sth by treaty, marriage, etc: *Britain has allied itself with other western powers for trade and defence.*

▷ **allied** /ˈælaɪd, *also* əˈlaɪd/ *adj* **1** ~ **(to sth)** connected; similar: *a union of ˈallied trades* ○ *The increase in violent crimes is alˈlied to the rise in unemployment.* **2 Allied** /ˈælaɪd/ [attrib] of the Allies (ALLY *n* 2): *the Allied advance* ○ *the Allied forces.*

ally /ˈælaɪ/ *n* **1** [C] person, country, etc joined with another in order to give help and support. **2 the Allies** [pl] those countries which fought with Britain in each of the two World Wars.

Ally Pally /ˌælɪ ˈpælɪ/ (*infml*) nickname for *Alexandra Palace in London.

Alma Mater /ˌælmə ˈmɑːtə(r)/ **1** (*fml or joc*) university or school at which one was or is being taught. **2** (*US*) school song or anthem.

almanac (also **almanack**) /ˈɔːlmənæk; *US also* ˈæl-/ *n* **1** annual book or calendar of months and days, giving information about the sun, moon, tides, anniversaries, etc. Some books of this type also include predictions. Cf OLD MOORE'S ALMANACK. **2** book published annually giving statistical information on various subjects, eg sport, the theatre, etc. Cf WHITAKER'S ALMANACK, WISDEN.

almighty /ɔːlˈmaɪtɪ/ *adj* **1** having all power; powerful beyond measure: *God Almighty/Almighty God.* **2** [attrib] (*infml*) very great: *an almighty crash, nuisance, row.*

▷ **the Almighty** *n* [sing] God.

almond /ˈɑːmənd/ *n* **1** type of tree with pink flowers related to the plum and peach. **2** nut inside the stone-fruit of this tree: [attrib] *almond oil/essence.* ⇨ illus at NUT.

□ ˌ**almond-ˈeyed** *adj* having narrow oval eyes.

ˌ**almond ˈpaste** edible paste made from finely ground almonds.

almoner /ˈɑːmənə(r); *US* ˈælm-/ *n* **1** (formerly) official who distributed money and gave help to the poor. **2** (*Brit* also **medical social worker**) social worker attached to a hospital.

almost /ˈɔːlməʊst/ *adv* **1** (used before *advs, ns, adjs, vs, dets* and *prons*) nearly; not quite: *It's a mistake they almost always make.* ○ *It's almost time to go.* ○ *Dinner's almost ready.* ○ *He slipped and almost fell.* ○ *He's almost six feet tall.* ○ *Almost anything will do.* **2** (used before *no, nobody, none, nothing, never*) virtually; practically: *Almost no one* (ie Hardly anyone) *believed him.* ○ *The speaker said almost nothing* (ie scarcely anything) *worth listening to.*

NOTE ON USAGE: **Almost, nearly, scarcely** and **hardly** are adverbs and can be used with verbs, adverbs, adjectives and nouns. **1 Almost** and **nearly** are usually used in positive sentences: *She fell and almost/nearly broke her neck.* ○ *He nearly/almost always arrives late.* **2 Almost** can be used with negative words. In these cases it can be replaced with **hardly** or **scarcely:** *He ate almost nothing* (= *He ate hardly anything*). ○ *There's almost no space to sit* (= *There's hardly any space to sit*). **3 Hardly** is generally preferred to **almost** + a negative verb: *She sang so quietly that I could hardly hear her* (not *I almost couldn't hear*). **4** In sentences indicating one thing happening immediately after another, **hardly** and **scarcely** can be placed at the beginning of the sentence and then subject and verb are inverted: *Hardly/Scarcely had we arrived, when it began to rain.*

alms /ɑːmz/ *n* [pl] (*dated*) money, clothes, food, etc given to poor people: *He gave alms to beggars in the street.* ○ *They had to beg alms (of others) in order to feed their children.*

□ ˈ**almshouse** *n* (*Brit*) house, founded by gifts of charity, where poor (usu old) people may live without paying rent.

aloe /ˈæləʊ/ *n* **1** [C] type of plant that grows in southern Africa and has thick pointed leaves from which a bitter juice is obtained. **2 aloes** [sing *v*] (also **bitter aloes**) juice of the aloe plant used in medicine.

aloft /əˈlɒft; *US* əˈlɔːft/ *adv* **1** up in the air; overhead: *flags flying aloft* ○ *The balloons were already aloft.* **2** above the deck or in the rigging of a ship: *He went aloft to check the sails.*

alone /əˈləʊn/ *adj* [pred], *adv* **1** (a) without any companions: *I don't like going out alone after dark.* ○ *She lives all alone in that large house.* ○ (*fig*) *She stands alone* (ie is without equal) *among modern sculptors.* (b) without the help of other people or things: *It will be difficult for one person alone.* ○ *She raised her family quite alone.* ○ *I prefer to work on it alone.* Cf LONE, LONELY 1. ⇨ Usage. **2** (following a *n* or *pron*) only; exclusively: *The shoes alone cost £100.* ○ (*saying*) *Time alone will tell.* ○ *He will be remembered for that one book alone.* ○ *You alone can help me.* **3** (idm) **go it aˈlone** (attempt to) carry out a task or start a difficult project without help from anyone: *He decided to go it alone and start his own business.* **leave/let sb/sth alone** not take, touch or interfere with sb/sth; not try to influence or change sb/sth: *She's asked to be left alone but the press keep pestering her.* ○ *I've told you before — leave my things alone!* **leave/let well alone** ⇨ WELL[3]. **let alone** without considering: *There isn't enough room for ˈus, let alone six dogs and a cat.* ○ *I haven't decided on the ˈmenu yet, let alone bought the food.* **not be alone in doing sth** be one of several people who think, feel, etc sth: *He is not alone in believing* (ie Other people agree with him) *that it may lead to war.*

NOTE ON USAGE: **1 Alone** and **solitary** describe a person or thing that is separate from others. A person may prefer to be alone/solitary and these words do not suggest unhappiness. **Alone** is not used before a noun: *I look forward to being alone in the house.* ○ *Our house stands alone at the end of the lane.* ○ *She goes for long solitary walks.* In this sense **on my**, **our**, **etc own** or **by myself**, **ourselves**, **etc** are often used in informal speech instead of **alone:** *She's going on holiday on her own this year.* **2 Lonely** and, in US English, **lonesome** suggests that someone does not want to be alone and is unhappy: *He was very lonely at first when he moved to London.* ○ *She led a solitary existence but was seldom lonely.* **3 Lonely** and **solitary** can describe out-of-the-way places where people rarely go: *a lonely/solitary cottage on the moors.*

along /əˈlɒŋ; *US* əˈlɔːŋ/ *prep* **1** from one end to or towards the other end of (sth): *walk along the street* ○ *go along the corridor.* **2** close to or parallel with the length of (sth): *Flowers grow along the side of the wall.* ○ *You can picnic along the river bank.*
▷ **along** *adv part* **1** onward; forward: *The policeman told the crowds to move along.* ○ *Come along or we'll be late.* **2** in one's or sb's company: (*infml*) *Come to the party and bring some friends along.* ○ *He took his dog along (with him) to work.* ○ *I'll be along* (ie I will come and join you) *in a few minutes.* **3** (idm) **along with sth** in addition to sth: *Tobacco is taxed in most countries, along with alcohol.*
□ **alongside** /əˈlɒŋsaɪd; *US* əlɔːŋˈsaɪd/ *adv* close to the side of a ship, pier, etc: *a boat moored alongside.* — *prep* beside (sth): *The car drew up alongside the kerb.*

aloof /əˈluːf/ *adj* [usu pred] ~ (**from sb/sth**) **1** cool and remote in character; unconcerned: *I find her very aloof and unfriendly.* ○ *Throughout the conversation he remained silent and aloof.* **2** (idm) **keep/hold/stand aloof from sb/sth** take no part in sth; show no friendship towards sb: *He stood aloof from the crowd.* ▷ **aloofness** *n* [U].

alopecia /ˌæləˈpiːʃə/ *n* [U] (*medical*) absence of hair from parts of the body where it normally grows; baldness.

aloud /əˈlaʊd/ *adv* **1** in a voice loud enough to be heard, not silently or in a whisper: *He read his sister's letter aloud.* **2** loudly, so as to be heard at a distance: *She called aloud for help.* **3** (idm) **think aloud** ⇨ THINK[1].

alp /ælp/ *n* **1** (**a**) [C] high mountain, esp in Switzerland and neighbouring countries. (**b**) **the Alps** [pl] largest European mountain range, extending over 1 000 km (650 miles) from the Mediterranean coast of France through Switzerland, N Italy, Germany, Austria and Yugoslavia to W Hungary. Many of its mountains are over 4 000 m (13 000 ft), the highest being *Mont Blanc. **2** [C] pasture-land on the side of a mountain, esp in Switzerland, to which animals are driven in summer. Cf ALPINE.

alpaca /ælˈpækə/ *n* (**a**) [C] type of S American llama with long wool. (**b**) [U] (cloth made from) its wool: [attrib] *an alpaca coat.*

alpenstock /ˈælpənstɒk/ *n* long stick with an iron tip, used in climbing mountains.

alpha /ˈælfə/ *n* **1** the first letter in the Greek alphabet (Α, α). **2** first-class mark in an examination or for a piece of work in school: *Jane got an alpha plus for her last essay.* **3** (idm) ˌ**Alpha and ˈOmega** the beginning and the end.
□ ˈ**alpha particle** positively charged helium nucleus, a combination of two neutrons and two protons. Alpha particles are emitted in radioactivity or other nuclear reactions.
ˌ**alpha radiˈation** emission of alpha rays.
ˈ**alpha ray** fast-moving stream of alpha particles.

alphabet /ˈælfəbet/ *n* set of letters or symbols in a fixed order, used when writing a language. The earliest alphabet with both consonants and vowels was developed in Greece about 750 BC: *There are 26 letters in the English alphabet.*
▷ **alphabetical** /ˌælfəˈbetɪkl/ *adj* in the order of the alphabet: *Put these words in alphabetical order.* **alphabetically** /-klɪ/ *adv*: *books arranged alphabetically by author.*
alphabetize, -ise /ˈælfəbetaɪz/ *v* [Tn] arrange (words, etc) in alphabetical order. **alphabetization**, **-isation** /ˌælfəˌbetaɪˈzeɪʃn; *US* -tɪˈz-/ *n* [U].

Alpha Centauri /ˌælfə senˈtɔːrɪ/ bright star in the constellation Centaurus. It is the second closest star to the Earth, being 4.3 light-years away.

alphanumeric /ˌælfənjuːˈmerɪk; *US* -nuː-/ (also **alphameric** /ˌælfəˈmerɪk/) *adj* (of a set of symbols) consisting of both letters and numbers: *alphanumeric characters.*

alphorn /ˈælphɔːn/ (also **alpenhorn** /ˈælpənhɔːn/) *n* very long wooden horn that plays only a few notes, used, esp formerly, in the Swiss Alps for calling cattle home.

alpine /ˈælpaɪn/ *adj* (**a**) of or found in high mountains, esp the Alps: *alpine flowers* ○ *an alpine climate.* (**b**) **Alpine** of the Alps: *Alpine ski resorts.*
▷ **alpine** *n* plant that grows best in mountain regions.

already /ɔːlˈredɪ/ *adv* **1** (used esp with perfect tenses of a *v*) before now or before a stated or suggested time in the past: *I've already seen that film, so I'd rather see another one.* ○ *The teacher was already in the room when I arrived.* ○ *She had already left when I phoned.* **2** (used in negative sentences or questions, to show surprise) as soon or as early as this: *Have your children started school already?* ○ *Is it 10 o'clock already?* ○ *You're not leaving us already, are you?*

NOTE ON USAGE: **Yet** and **already** are both used when talking about the possible completion of an action by or before a particular time. They are mostly used with the perfect tenses (in US usage also with the simple past). **Yet** is only used in negative statements and in questions: *'It's time to go.' 'I'm not ready yet.'* ○ *Are you out of bed yet?* **Already** emphasizes the completion of an action. It is usually used in positive statements: *By midday they had already travelled 200 miles.* **Already** can be used in questions to express surprise: *Have you finished lunch already? It's only 12 o'clock!*

alright /ɔːlˈraɪt/ *adv* (*non-standard or infml*) = ALL RIGHT (ALL[3]).

Alsace /ælˈsæs/ region of NE France, west of the Rhine river, famous for its white wine.

Alsace-Lorraine /ˌælsæs ləˈreɪn/ area of NE France controlled by Germany from 1871 to 1919 and from 1940 to 1944.

Alsatian /ælˈseɪʃn/ *n* (also **German shepherd dog**, **German shepherd**) type of large smooth-haired dog like a wolf, often trained to help the police, to guard property, etc, or kept as a pet. ⇨ illus at DOG.

also /ˈɔːlsəʊ/ *adv* (not used with negative *vs*) in addition; besides; too: *She speaks French and German and also a little Russian.* ○ *He is young and good-looking, and also very rich.* ○ *I teach five days a week and I also teach evening classes.* ○ *She not only plays well, but also writes music.*
□ ˈ**also-ran** *n* **1** (in racing) horse or dog not among the first three to finish. **2** (*fig*) person who fails to gain success or distinction: *I'm afraid John is one of life's also-rans.*

NOTE ON USAGE: **Also**, **too** and **as well** indicate that the word or part of the sentence that they are specially linked to has been added to something previously mentioned. They differ in degree of formality and position in the sentence. **Also** is more formal and usually comes before the main verb (but after 'be' if this is the main verb): *I've met Jane and I've also met her mother.* ○ *He speaks French and he also writes it.* ○ *She was rich. She was also selfish.* **Too** and **as well** are less formal and usually come at the end of the clause: *I've read the book and I've seen the film as well/too.* In negative sentences, **not...either** is used to indicate addition: *They haven't phoned and they haven't written either.*

altar /ˈɔːltə(r)/ *n* **1** (in Christian churches) table on which bread and wine are consecrated in the Communion service. The altar is usu situated at the east end of the church and is separated from the area where the congregation sit. ⇨ illus at CHURCH. **2** table or raised flat-topped platform on which offerings are made to a god: (*fig*) *He's willing to sacrifice all his ideals on the altar of ambition*, ie ignore his ideals because he is ambitious. **3** (idm) **lead sb to the altar** ⇨ LEAD[3].
□ ˈ**altar boy** boy who acts as an attendant to a priest in (esp Roman Catholic) church services.
ˈ**altar-piece** *n* painting or sculpture placed behind an altar.

altazimuth /ælˈtæzɪməθ/ *n* type of telescope that can be moved both horizontally and vertically. Cf AZIMUTH.

alter /ˈɔːltə(r)/ *v* **1** [I, Tn] (cause sth/sb to) become different; change in character, position, size, shape, etc: *I didn't recognize him because he had altered so much.* ○ *She had to alter her clothes after losing weight.* ○ *The plane altered course.* ○ *That alters things*, ie makes the situation different. ⇨ Usage at CHANGE[1]. **2** [Tn] (*euph esp US*) remove the testicles or ovaries of (an animal).
▷ **alterable** /ˈɔːltərəbl/ *adj* that can be altered.
alteration /ˌɔːltəˈreɪʃn/ *n* **1** [U] changing; making a change: *How much alteration will be necessary?* **2** [C] act or result of changing: *We are making a few alterations to the house.*

altercation /ˌɔːltəˈkeɪʃn/ *n* [C, U] (*fml*) (act of) quarrelling or arguing noisily. ⇨ Usage at ARGUMENT.

alter ego /ˌæltər ˈegəʊ; *US* ˈiːgəʊ/ (*pl* **alter egos**) (*Latin*) intimate friend; person very like oneself: *He's my alter ego — we go everywhere together.*

alternate[1] /ɔːlˈtɜːnət; *US* ˈɔːltərnət/ *adj* [usu attrib] **1** (of two things) happening or following one after the other: *a pattern of alternate circles and squares* ○ *alternate triumph and despair.* **2** every second: *on alternate days*, eg on Monday, Wednesday, Friday, etc. **3** (of leaves growing on both sides of a stem) not opposite each other. ▷ **alternately** *adv.*
□ **alˌternate ˈangles** (*mathematics*) angles like those in the Z shape formed when one line intersects two others.

alternate[2] /ˈɔːltəneɪt/ *v* **1** [Tn, Tn·pr] ~ **A and B**/ ~ **A with B** cause (things or people) to occur or appear one after the other; arrange by turns: *Most farmers alternate their crops.* ○ *He alternated kindness with cruelty*, ie was kind, then cruel, then kind again, etc. ○ *She alternated boys and girls round the table.* **2** [Ipr] ~ **with sth**; ~ **between A and B** occur in turn; consist of two different things in turn: *Rainy days alternated with dry ones.* ○ *The weather alternated between rain and sunshine.* ○ *Their work alternates between London and New York*, ie is first in London, then in New York, then back in London, etc.
▷ **alternation** /ˌɔːltəˈneɪʃn/ *n* [U, C] regular change from one thing, situation, etc to another, then back to the first again; alternating. ˌ**alternation of geneˈrations** the occurrence of two or more distinct forms within the life cycle of an organism. It is found in most plants (eg ferns) and certain lower animals (eg jellyfish) and involves regular alternations between sexual and asexual generations.
alternator /ˈɔːltəneɪtə(r)/ *n* machine that produces an alternating current by means of a coil that rotates in the field of a magnet or electromagnet, used esp in motor-vehicle engines.
□ ˌ**alternating ˈcurrent** (*abbr* **AC**) electric current that reverses its direction at regular intervals. Cf DIRECT CURRENT (DIRECT[1]).

alternative /ɔːlˈtɜːnətɪv/ *adj* [attrib] **1** available in place of sth else; other: *find alternative means of transport* ○ *Have you got an alternative suggestion?* ○ *The alternative book to study for the examination is 'War and Peace'.* **2** [usu attrib] (of lifestyles, art, culture, etc) away from the accepted or established form, practice, etc; unconventional: *alternative comedians.* Cf FRINGE 3. **3** (idm) **the**

alˌ**ternative so**ˈ**ciety** people who prefer not to live according to the conventional standards of social behaviour.

▷ **alternative** *n* **1** freedom to choose between two or more possibilities: *You have the alternative of marrying or remaining a bachelor.* ○ *Caught in the act, he had no alternative but to confess.* **2** one of two or more possibilities: *One of the alternatives open to you is to resign.*

alternatively *adv* as an alternative: *We could take the train or alternatively go by car.*

□ **al**ˌ**ternative** ˈ**medicine** methods of treating illness, injuries, etc that are not regarded by Western doctors as part of conventional treatment. They include acupuncture and homoeopathy. Many of them are becoming more popular in the West and are gaining some official recognition.

the Alˌ**ternative** ˈ**Service Book** book of prayers in modern style, which can be used in the Church of England instead of the *Book of Common Prayer.

although (*US* also **altho**) /ɔːlˈðəʊ/ *conj* **1** in spite of the fact that; even if: *Although he had only entered the contest for fun, he won first prize.* **2** and yet; nevertheless; but: *He said they were married, although I'm sure they aren't.*

NOTE ON USAGE: **1 Although** and **(even) though** can be used at the beginning of a sentence or a clause with a verb. **Though** is less formal: *Although/Though/Even though we all tried our best, we lost the game.* ○ *We lost the game although/though/even though we tried our best.* **2 However** can be used to give a similar meaning, but must begin a new sentence: *We all tried our best. However, we lost the game.* **3 Though** and **however** can come at the end of a sentence: *We all tried our best. We lost the game, though/however.* **4 (Al)though** (or more formal **albeit**) can come before an adjective, adverb or adverbial phrase: *Her appointment was a significant, (al)though/albeit temporary success.* ○ *He performed the task well, (al)though/albeit slowly.*

altimeter /ˈæltɪmiːtə(r); *US* ˌælˈtɪmətər/ *n* instrument used esp in aircraft to measure and show the height above sea-level.

altitude /ˈæltɪtjuːd; *US* -tuːd/ *n* **1** height above sea-level: *What is the altitude of this village?* ○ *We are flying at an altitude of 20 000 feet.* **2** (often *pl*) place or area high above sea-level: *It is difficult to breathe at these altitudes.* **3** (*astronomy*) distance of a star or planet above the horizon, measured as an angle.

□ ˈ**altitude sickness** nausea, exhaustion, breathlessness, etc caused by low atmospheric pressure and lack of oxygen at high altitudes.

Altman /ˈɔːltmən/ Robert (1925-), American film director. His first major success was the comedy *M.A.S.H.*, and he is noted for his ironic portrayals of American social life (eg *Nashville* and *A Wedding*).

alto /ˈæltəʊ/ *n* (*pl* **~s**) (*music*) **1** = CONTRALTO. **2** (boy singer with a) voice of the lowest pitch for an unbroken male voice. **3** part written for the alto voice: [attrib] *the alto clef.* **4** musical instrument with the second highest pitch in its group: *an alto-saxophone.*

altocumulus /ˌæltəʊˈkjuːmjələs/ *n* (*pl* **-li** /-laɪ/) mass of rounded white or grey clouds similar to cumulus but at a higher level. Such clouds are usu a sign of good weather.

altogether /ˌɔːltəˈgeðə(r)/ *adv* **1** entirely; completely: *I don't altogether agree with you.* ○ *I am not altogether happy about the decision.* **2** including everything: *You owe me £68.03 altogether.* **3** considering everything; on the whole: *The weather was bad and the food dreadful. Altogether the holiday was very disappointing.*

▷ **altogether** *n* (idm) **in the alto**ˈ**gether** (*infml*) without clothes on; naked.

altostratus /ˌæltəʊˈstreɪtəs/ *n* (*pl* **-ti** /-taɪ/) mass of clouds occurring at medium height. Such clouds usu consist of a greyish layer covering much of the sky and are often a sign of rain coming.

altruism /ˈæltruːɪzəm/ *n* [U] **1** principle of considering the welfare and happiness of others before one's own; unselfishness. Cf EGOISM 2. **2** (*biology*) behaviour by an animal that reduces its own chances of survival while increasing those of another member of the same species (eg when a female puts herself in danger to save her young).

▷ **altruist** /ˈæltruːɪst/ *n* unselfish person.

altruistic /ˌæltruːˈɪstɪk/ *adj*: *altruistic behaviour.*

altruistically /-klɪ/ *adv.*

alum /ˈæləm/ *n* [U] white mineral salt used in medicine and in dyeing.

aluminium /ˌæljʊˈmɪnɪəm/ (*US* **aluminum** /əˈluːmɪnəm/) *n* [U] (*symb* **Al**) chemical element, light silvery-white metal. It is the most common metal in the earth's crust, occurring mainly in bauxite. Aluminium does not corrode and is used (usu alloyed with another metal for strength) in cooking utensils, window frames, electrical apparatus and aircraft construction: [attrib] *aluminium window frames* ○ *aluminium foil*, ie used esp for wrapping food in. ⇨ App 11.

alumna /əˈlʌmnə/ *n* (*pl* **-nae** /-niː/) (*US*) female former student of a school, college or university.

alumnus /əˈlʌmnəs/ *n* (*pl* **-ni** /-naɪ/) (*US*) male former student of a school, college or university.

alveolar /ælˈvɪələ(r), ˌælvɪˈəʊlə(r)/ *adj, n* (*phonetics*) (of a) consonant made with the tongue touching the bony ridge behind the upper front teeth, eg /t/ or /d/. ⇨ illus at THROAT.

alveolus /ˌælvɪˈəʊləs; *US* ælˈviːələs/ *n* (*pl* **-li** /-laɪ/) **1** (*biology*) (usu *pl*) any of the tiny air pockets in the lungs of mammals, from which oxygen passes into the blood and through which carbon dioxide is removed from it. **2** (*esp biology*) small hole (eg a tooth socket or a cell in a honeycomb).

always /ˈɔːlweɪz/ *adv* **1** at all times; without exception: *I always think of her in that dress.* ○ *He nearly always wears a bow tie.* ○ *She has always loved gardening.* **2** repeatedly; regularly: *The postman always calls at 7.30.* ○ *We're nearly always at church on Sundays.* **3** (usu with the continuous tenses) again and again; persistently: *He was always asking for money.* ○ *Why are you always biting your nails?* **4** (with *can/could*) if everything else fails; whatever the circumstances may be: *You could always use a dictionary.* ○ *They can always go to a bank if they need more money.* **5** (idm) **always supposing (that)...** if a specified condition is fulfilled: *I'm going to university, always supposing I pass my exams.* **as** ˈ**always** in a way that is expected because it usu happens like that: *As always he was late and had to run to catch the bus.*

alyssum /ˈælɪsəm/ *n* [U] garden plant with small (usu white or yellow) flowers.

Alzheimer's disease /ˈæltshaɪməz dɪziːz/ *n* [U] incurable disease, occurring in middle age or later, in which the brain degenerates, so that functions such as memory, reasoning, speech, etc gradually fail.

AM /ˌeɪ ˈem/ *abbr* **1** (*radio*) amplitude modulation. Cf FM 2. **2** (*US*) Master of Arts. Cf MA.

Am *symb* americium.

am ⇨ BE.

am (*US* **AM**) /ˌeɪ ˈem/ *abbr* before noon (Latin *ante meridiem*): *at 10 am*, ie in the morning. Cf PM.

amalgam /əˈmælgəm/ *n* **1** [U] alloy of mercury with another metal: *The dentist used amalgam to fill my teeth.* **2** [C] mixture or blend: *a subtle amalgam of spices.*

amalgamate /əˈmælgəmeɪt/ *v* [I, Ipr, Tn, Tn·pr] ~ **(sb/sth) (with sb/sth)** (cause people or things to) combine or unite: *Our local brewery has amalgamated with another firm.* ○ *The boys' and girls' schools have (been) amalgamated to form a new comprehensive.*

▷ **amalgamation** /əˌmælgəˈmeɪʃn/ *n* **(a)** [U] mixing or uniting: *Amalgamation was the only alternative to going bankrupt.* **(b)** [C] instance of this: *We've seen two amalgamations in one week.*

amanuensis /əˌmænjʊˈensɪs/ *n* (*pl* **-ses** /-siːz/) (*dated or fml*) person who writes from dictation or copies what sb else has written.

amaryllis /ˌæməˈrɪlɪs/ *n* **(a)** plant, originally from southern Africa, with large lily-like white or red flowers growing from a bulb. **(b)** any of various related plants.

amass /əˈmæs/ *v* [Tn] gather together or collect (sth), esp in large quantities: *amass a fortune* ○ *They amassed enough evidence to convict him on six charges.*

amateur /ˈæmətə(r)/ *n* **1** person who practises a sport or artistic skill without receiving money for it: *The tournament is open to amateurs as well as professionals.* ○ *Although he's only an amateur he's a first-class player.* ○ [attrib] *an amateur photographer, golfer, boxer, etc* ○ *amateur dramatics, wrestling, etc.* Cf PROFESSIONAL *n.* **2** (*usu derog*) person who is unskilled or inexperienced in an activity: *I shouldn't employ them — they're just a bunch of amateurs.*

▷ **amateurish** /ˈæmətərɪʃ/ *adj* (*often derog*) inexpert; unskilled. **amateurishly** /ˈæmətərɪʃlɪ/ *adv.*

amateurism /ˈæmətərɪzəm/ *n* [U].

Amati /əˈmɑːtɪ/ family of violin-makers who lived in Cremona, Italy in the 16th and 17th centuries: *playing an Amati*, ie a violin, cello, etc made by a member of the Amati family.

amatory /ˈæmətərɪ; *US* -tɔːrɪ/ *adj* (*fml or joc*) relating to or inspired by sexual love: *amatory literature, adventures.*

amaze /əˈmeɪz/ *v* [Tn esp passive] fill (sb) with great surprise or wonder: *He amazed everyone by passing his driving test.* ○ *We were amazed at/by the change in his appearance.* ○ *She was amazed/It amazed her that he was still alive.* ▷ **amazement** *n* [U]: *He looked at me in amazement.* ○ *I heard with amazement that....* **amazing** *adj* (*usu approv*): *an amazing speed, player, feat* ○ *I find it amazing that you can't swim.* **amazingly** *adv*: *She's amazingly clever.*

Amazon /ˈæməzən; *US* -zɒn/ **the Amazon** S American river, 6 750 km (4 080 miles) long, flowing from the Andes mountains into the Atlantic Ocean on the northern coast of Brazil. It carries more water than any other river in the world. The forests which surround it are the home of many American Indian peoples. The river was named by Spanish explorers who believed that the female warriors called Amazons lived there: [attrib] *the Amazon rain forests.* ▷ **Amazonian** /ˌæməˈzəʊnɪən/ *adj*: *Amazonian Indians.*

amazon /ˈæməzən; *US* -zɒn/ *n* **1** tall strong athletic woman. **2 Amazon** (in Greek mythology) member of a race of female warriors. They appear in many legends, including those of the labours of *Hercules and the Trojan war, where their queen Penthesilea was killed by *Achilles. ▷ **amazonian** /ˌæməˈzəʊnɪən/ *adj.*

ambassador /æmˈbæsədə(r)/ *n* **1** diplomat sent from one country to another either as a permanent representative or on a special mission: *the British Ambassador to Greece.* Cf CONSUL 1, HIGH COMMISSIONER (HIGH[1]). **2** authorized representative or messenger.

▷ **ambassadorial** /æmˌbæsəˈdɔːrɪəl/ *adj.*

ambassadress /æmˈbæsədrɪs/ *n* **1** (*dated*) female ambassador. **2** ambassador's wife.

□ **ambassador-at-large** *n* (*pl* **-dors-at-large**) (*esp US*) ambassador to more than one country, often on a specific mission.

amber /ˈæmbə(r)/ *n* **1** [U] **(a)** hard clear yellowish-brown gum used for making ornaments or jewellery. Amber is the fossil resin of prehistoric trees and often contains the bodies of insects trapped before it hardened. Much amber is found on the southern shores of the Baltic Sea: [attrib] *an amber necklace.* **(b)** its colour. **2** [C] yellow traffic-light seen between red and green.

ambergris /ˈæmbəgriːs; *US* -grɪs/ *n* [U] wax-like substance present in the intestines of sperm-whales and found floating in tropical seas, used as a fixative in perfumes.

ambi- *comb form* referring to both of two: *ambidextrous* ○ *ambivalent.*

ambidextrous /ˌæmbɪˈdekstrəs/ *adj* able to use the left hand or the right hand equally well.

ambience (also **ambiance**) /ˈæmbɪəns/ *n*

environment; atmosphere of a place: *We've tried to create the ambience of a French bistro.*

ambient /ˈæmbɪənt/ *adj* [attrib] (*fml*) of air, etc on all sides; surrounding: *ambient pressure, temperature.*

ambiguity /ˌæmbɪˈgju:ətɪ/ *n* **(a)** [U] presence of more than one meaning: *Much British humour depends on ambiguity.* **(b)** [C] instance of this: *She was quick to notice the ambiguities in the article.*

ambiguous /æmˈbɪgjʊəs/ *adj* **1** having more than one possible meaning: *'Look at those pretty little girls' dresses' is ambiguous, because it is not clear whether the girls or the dresses are 'pretty'.* **2** uncertain in meaning or intention: *an ambiguous smile, glance, gesture, etc.* ▷ **ambiguously** *adv.* **ambiguousness** *n* [U].

ambit /ˈæmbɪt/ *n* [sing] bounds, scope or extent (of power, authority, etc): *That falls outside the ambit of our authority.*

ambition /æmˈbɪʃn/ *n* ~ **(to be/do sth) 1 (a)** [U, C] strong desire to achieve sth: *filled with ambition to become famous, rich, powerful, etc.* **(b)** [C] particular desire of this kind: *have great ambitions.* **2** [C] object of this desire: *achieve/realize/fulfil one's ambitions.*

ambitious /æmˈbɪʃəs/ *adj* **1** ~ **(to be/do sth); ~ (for sth)** full of ambition, esp for success or money: *an ambitious young manager* ○ *ambitious to succeed in life* ○ *ambitious for one's children.* **2** showing or requiring ambition: *ambitious plans to complete the project ahead of schedule.* ▷ **ambitiously** *adv.*

ambivalent /æmˈbɪvələnt/ *adj* having or showing mixed feelings about a certain object, person or situation: *an ambivalent attitude towards one's best friend's wife.* ▷ **ambivalence** *n* [U]. **ambivalently** *adv.*

amble /ˈæmbl/ *v* [I, Ipr, Ip] **1** (of a person) ride or walk at a slow, leisurely pace: *He came ambling down the road.* ○ *We ambled along for miles.* **2** (of a horse) move slowly, lifting the two feet on one side together.

▷ **amble** *n* [sing] slow, leisurely pace: *walk at an amble.*

Ambrose /ˈæmbrəʊz/ Saint (c 339-397 AD), Bishop of Milan and one of the earliest Christian writers on theology. He also wrote several hymns.

ambrosia /æmˈbrəʊzɪə; *US* -əʊʒə/ *n* [U] **1** (in Greek mythology) food of the gods. Cf NECTAR 2. **2** thing that tastes or smells delicious.

ambulance /ˈæmbjʊləns/ *n* vehicle equipped to carry sick or injured people to hospital, etc.

ambulatory /ˈæmbjʊlətrɪ; *US* ˈæmbjʊlətɔ:rɪ/ *adj* **1** (*fml*) of or designed for walking. **2** (also **ambulant**) (*medical*) able to walk; not having to stay in bed: *ambulatory patients.*

▷ **ambulatory** *n* place for walking, esp an aisle or a cloister in a church or monastery.

ambulant /ˈæmbjʊlənt/ *adj* **1** (*fml*) moving about from place to place. **2** (*medical*) = AMBULATORY 2.

ambush /ˈæmbʊʃ/ *n* **1** [U] (of troops, police, etc) waiting in a hidden position to make a surprise attack: *lie/wait in ambush.* **2** [C] **(a)** surprise attack from a hidden position: *They laid an ambush for the enemy patrol.* **(b)** people making such an attack. **(c)** place from which it is made.

▷ **ambush** *v* [Tn] make a surprise attack on (sb) from a hidden position: *ambush an enemy patrol.*

ameba (*US*) = AMOEBA.

ameliorate /əˈmi:lɪəreɪt/ *v* [I, Tn] (*fml*) (cause sth to) become better: *ameliorate conditions, circumstances, living standards, etc.* ▷ **amelioration** /əˌmi:lɪəˈreɪʃn/ *n* [U].

amen /ɑ:ˈmen, eɪˈmen/ *interj, n* (used esp at the end of a prayer or hymn) so be it; may it be so: *The choir sang the amens beautifully.* ○ *Amen to that,* ie I certainly agree with that.

amenable /əˈmi:nəbl/ *adj* **1** ~ **(to sth)** (of people) willing to be influenced or controlled (by sth): *amenable to kindness, advice, reason* ○ *I find him amenable to argument.* **2** ~ **to sth (a)** (of people) subject to the authority of sth: *amenable to the law.* **(b)** (of cases, situations, etc) that can be tested by sth: *This case is not amenable to the normal rules.*

amend /əˈmend/ *v* **1** [Tn] correct an error in (sth); make minor improvements in; change slightly: *amend a document, proposal, law.* **2** [I, Tn] (*fml*) (cause sth to) become better; improve: *You must amend your behaviour.*

▷ **amendment** *n* **1** [C] ~ **(to sth)** minor alteration or addition to a document, etc: *Parliament debated several amendments to the bill.* **2** [U] amending: *passed without amendment.* **3 Amendment** [C] major change to the US Constitution that must be proposed by Congress and agreed to by three-quarters of the states. Only 25 Amendments have been accepted since the first ten Amendments that form the *Bill of Rights were passed in 1791: *plead the Fifth Amendment,* ie claim the constitutional right not to say anything in court that might make one seem guilty.

amends /əˈmendz/ *n* [pl] (idm) **make amends (to sb) (for sth)** compensate sb (for an insult or injury given in the past): *How can I ever make amends for ruining their party?*

amenity /əˈmi:nətɪ, *also* əˈmenətɪ/ *n* **1** [C often *pl*] feature or facility of a place that makes life there easy or pleasant: *People who retire to the country often miss the amenities of a town,* eg libraries, cinemas, etc. ○ *A sauna in the hotel would be a useful amenity.* **2** [U] (*fml*) pleasantness: *He immediately noticed the amenity of his new surroundings.*

amenorrhoea (*also esp US* **amenorrhea**) /əˌmenəˈri:ə, eɪ-/ *n* [U] (*medical*) abnormal stopping or absence of menstrual bleeding.

America /əˈmerɪkə/ **1** (also **the Americas**) land mass in the Western hemisphere consisting of the two continents *North America and *South America, joined together by *Central America. The name is thought to come from that of Amerigo Vespucci (1451-1512), an Italian who claimed to have been the first European to find S America. Cf COLUMBUS. **2** = UNITED STATES OF AMERICA.

□ **the Aˌmerica's ˈCup** international yachting trophy originally won by the yacht *America* in 1851 and held by the New York Yacht Club until 1983 when it was won by an Australian yacht. The competition to win the cup is held every few years.

American /əˈmerɪkən/ *adj* **1** of the United States of America or its inhabitants or of American English: *an American city* ○ *American films* ○ *unfamiliar American expressions.* Cf UN-AMERICAN. **2** of the whole land mass of America (North, South and Central America) or any of its parts.

▷ **American** *n* **1** [C] person born or living in North, South or Central America. **2** [C] citizen of the USA. **3** [U] (also **Aˌmerican ˈEnglish**) the English language as spoken and written in the USA. Differences between British and American English include spelling (British *colour,* American *color),* vocabulary (British *pavement,* American *sidewalk*), pronunciation (wrath: British /rɒθ/, American /ræθ/), and grammar (British *I've just eaten,* American *I just ate*). Nevertheless, British and American speakers can usu understand each other without difficulty.

Americana /əˌmerɪˈkɑ:nə/ *n* [pl] objects (eg relics, documents, etc) connected with America, esp with the USA: *a collector of Americana.*

Americanism /-nɪzəm/ *n* word or phrase used in American English but not in standard English in Britain.

Americanize, -ise *v* [Tn] make (sth/sb) American in form or character: *After two years in New York she's become completely Americanized.* **Americanization, -isation** /əˌmerɪkənaɪˈzeɪʃn; *US* -nɪˈz-/ *n* [U]: *the Americanization of our way of life.*

□ **the Aˌmerican Civil ˈWar** war (1861-65) between the northern US states (called 'the Union') and the southern US states (the 'Confederate' states), fought over the issue of the southern states' right to decide their own policies, esp in relation to slavery and secession from the Union. The northern states won.

the Aˌmerican ˈdream (*esp ironic or joc*) all the things that inhabitants of the USA supposedly want very much and consider to be characteristic of a perfect society, esp wealth and social equality.

Aˌmerican ˈeagle = BALD EAGLE (BALD).

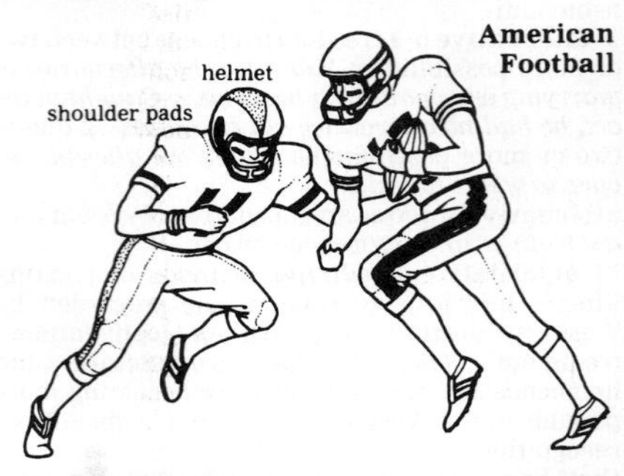

American ˈfootball form of football played esp in the USA between two teams of 11 players, with an oval ball and an H-shaped goal, on a field marked with parallel lines. The object of the game is to move the ball over the opponents' goal-line by carrying or throwing it. Strategy and tactics are carefully planned in both attack and defence, and the game is violent enough to require the players to wear helmets and thick padded protective clothing. ⇨ App 9. ⇨ illus. ⇨ article at SPORT.

American ˈIndian (also **Amerindian, Native American**) any of the original inhabitants of North, Central and South America, characterized by straight black hair and yellow-brown skin. They probably crossed the Bering Strait from Asia to America at the end of the last Ice Age. *Columbus later called them Indians because he discovered America while looking for a route to India. They were badly treated and often killed by British, French and Spanish settlers.

the Aˌmerican ˈLegion association of former American soldiers of both World Wars. Cf THE BRITISH LEGION (BRITISH).

Aˌmerican ˈorgan = MELODEON 1.

the Aˈmerican plan system of hotel charges including room, meals and service.

the Aˌmerican Revoˈlution (*esp US*) = THE WAR OF AMERICAN INDEPENDENCE (WAR).

americium /ˌæməˈrɪsɪəm, -ˈrɪʃɪəm/ *n* [U] (*symb* **Am**) (*chemistry*) radioactive metallic element made artificially from plutonium and used in industrial measuring equipment, radiography, etc.

Amerindian /ˌæməˈrɪndɪən/ *n* = AMERICAN INDIAN (AMERICAN).

amethyst /ˈæmɪθɪst/ *n* [C, U] purple or violet precious stone, a variety of quartz: [attrib] *an amethyst bracelet.*

Amharic /æmˈhærɪk/ *adj, n* (of the) official language of Ethiopia, spoken by about 9 million people in the north of the country. It is a *Semitic language.

amiable /ˈeɪmɪəbl/ *adj* showing and inspiring friendliness; pleasant and good-tempered: *an amiable character, mood, conversation.* ▷ **amiability** /ˌeɪmɪəˈbɪlətɪ/ *n* [U]. **amiably** *adv.*

amicable /ˈæmɪkəbl/ *adj* showing friendliness; without hostility: *An amicable settlement was reached.* ▷ **amicability** /ˌæmɪkəˈbɪlətɪ/ *n* [U]. **amicably** *adv*: *They lived together amicably for several years.*

amid /əˈmɪd/ (also **amidst** /əˈmɪdst/) *prep* (*dated or fml*) in the middle of (sth); among: *Amid all the rush and confusion she forgot to say goodbye.*

amidships /əˈmɪdʃɪps/ (also **midships**) *adv* half-way between the bows and stern of a ship: *go/stand amidships* ○ *You'll find your cabin amidships.*

amino acid /əˌmi:nəʊ ˈæsɪd/ (*chemistry*) any of a group of organic compounds that occur naturally in all plants and animals and form the basic components of protein.

amir = EMIR.

Amis /ˈeɪmɪs/ Kingsley (1922-), English author, most of whose novels (eg *Lucky Jim* and *Jake's Thing*) satirize modern life and behaviour from an increasingly conservative and hostile viewpoint. He has also written several volumes of poetry.

Amish /ˈeɪmɪʃ, ˈɑ:m-/ *n* **the Amish** [pl *v*] US Christian sect with very strict rules of life (eg refusing to do military service or hold any sort of public office). They live in their own communities, working mainly as farmers and using old-fashioned farming methods and machinery. ▷ **Amish** *adj*.

amiss /əˈmɪs/ *adj* [pred], *adv* (*dated*) **1** wrong(ly); inappropriate(ly): *Something seems to be amiss — can I help?* **2** (idm) **(not) come/go aˈmiss** (not) be unwelcome or unsuitable: *A new pair of shoes wouldn't come amiss.* **take sth aˈmiss** be offended by sth: *Would she take it amiss if I offered to help?*

amity /ˈæmətɪ/ *n* [U] friendly relationship between people or countries: *live in amity with one's neighbours.*

ammeter /ˈæmɪtə(r)/ *n* instrument that measures electric current in amperes.

ammo /ˈæməʊ/ *n* [U] (*infml*) = AMMUNITION 1.

ammonia /əˈməʊnɪə/ *n* [U] **1** colourless gas with a strong smell, soluble in water and alcohol. It is industrially produced from nitrogen and hydrogen. It becomes a liquid when compressed and cooled. It is used for making fertilizers and explosives and in industrial refrigerators. **2** (also **liquid ammonia**) ammonia gas that has been liquified by compression and cooling.

ammonite /ˈæmənaɪt/ *n* fossil of a shell, with a coiled shape.

ammunition /ˌæmjʊˈnɪʃn/ *n* [U] (abbr **ammo**) **1** supply of bullets, bombs, grenades, etc fired from weapons or thrown: *They had to meet the attack with very little ammunition.* **2** (*fig*) facts and reasoning used in trying to win an argument: *This letter gave her all the ammunition she needed.*

amnesia /æmˈni:zɪə; *US* -ˈni:ʒə/ *n* [U] partial or total loss of memory.

amnesty /ˈæmnəstɪ/ *n* general pardon, esp for offences against the State: *An amnesty has been declared.* ○ *The rebels returned home under a general amnesty.*

Amnesty International /ˌæmnəstɪ ˌɪntəˈnæʃnəl/ organization that campaigns for human rights around the world, and particularly for the freeing of people imprisoned because of their political, religious, etc beliefs.

amniocentesis /ˌæmnɪəʊsenˈti:sɪs/ *n* (*pl* **-teses** /-ˈti:si:z/) (*medical*) removal of a sample of amniotic fluid from the womb in order to obtain information about a developing baby (eg if it is male or female or has any genetic abnormalities).

amniotic fluid /ˌæmnɪɒtɪk ˈflu:ɪd/ [U] fluid that surrounds and protects a developing baby in the womb.

amoeba (*US* **ameba**) /əˈmi:bə/ *n* (*pl* **~s** or **~e** /-bi:/) microscopic organism consisting of a single cell, found in water and soil, which changes shape constantly.

▷ **amoebic** /əˈmi:bɪk/ *adj* of or caused by amoebae: *amoebic dysentery.*

amok /əˈmɒk/ (also **amuck** /əˈmʌk/) *adv* (idm) **run amok** rush about in a wild and angry frenzy: *The tiger escaped from the zoo and ran amok for hours.*

among /əˈmʌŋ/ (also **amongst** /əˈmʌŋst/) *prep* (followed by a plural *n* or *pron* or a group *n*) **1** surrounded by (sb/sth): *work among the poor, the sick, the elderly, etc* ○ *He found it amongst a pile of old books.* **2** in the number of (sth); included in: *I was among the last to leave.* ○ *Among those present were the Prime Minister and her husband.* ○ *He was only one amongst many who needed help.* **3** (in parts) to each member of (a group): *distribute the books among the class.* **4** between: *Politicians are always arguing amongst themselves.* ○ (*saying*) *There is honour among thieves.*

NOTE ON USAGE: **1 Among** is used of people or things considered as a group: *Share out the books among the class.* ○ *They talked among themselves while they waited.* ○ *standing among the crowd at the football match.* **2 Between** is used of people or things, either two in number or more than two considered individually: *one book between two (pupils).* ○ *She divided her possessions equally between her four children.* ○ *They hung flags across the street between the houses.* ○ *There's a lot of disagreement between the two main political parties on this issue.* (Compare: *There's a lot of disagreement among politicians on this issue.*)

amontillado /əˌmɒntɪˈlɑ:dəʊ/ *n* [U] type of pale, fairly dry sherry.

amoral /ˌeɪˈmɒrəl; *US* ˌeɪˈmɔ:rəl/ *adj* not based on moral standards; not following any moral rules. Cf IMMORAL.

amorous /ˈæmərəs/ *adj* readily showing or feeling love; relating to (esp sexual) love: *amorous looks, letters, poetry, experiences* ○ *He became quite amorous at the office party.* ▷ **amorously** *adv*: *gazing amorously into her eyes.* **amorousness** *n* [U]: *a reputation for amorousness.*

amorphous /əˈmɔ:fəs/ *adj* [usu attrib] **1** having no definite shape or form; not organized: *amorphous blobs of paint* ○ *an amorphous collection of jumpers and socks.* **2** (*chemistry*) not having a definite crystalline structure.

amortize, -ise /əˈmɔ:taɪz; *US* ˈæmərtaɪz/ *v* [Tn] (*law*) end (a debt) by making regular payments into a special fund. ▷ **amortization, -isation** /əˌmɔ:tɪˈzeɪʃn; *US* ˌæmərtɪ-/ *n* [U].

amount /əˈmaʊnt/ *v* [Ipr] **~ to sth 1** add up to or total sth: *The cost amounted to £250.* ○ *Our information doesn't amount to much,* ie We have very little information. **2** be equal to or the equivalent of sth: *It all amounts to a lot of hard work.* ○ *What you say amounts to a direct accusation.* **3** (idm) **amount to/come to/be the same thing** ⇨ SAME[1].

▷ **amount** *n* **~ (of sth)** (used esp with [U] *ns*) **1** total sum or value: *a bill for the full amount* ○ *Can you really afford this amount?* **2** quantity: *a large amount of work, money, furniture* ○ *Food was provided in varying amounts.* ○ *No amount of encouragement would make him jump,* ie Despite much encouragement he refused to jump. **3** (idm) **any amount of sth** a large quantity of sth: *He can get any amount of help.*

amour /əˈmʊə(r)/ *n* (*joc or rhet*) (esp secret) love affair: *Have you heard about his latest amour?*

amour propre /ˌæmʊə ˈprɒprə/ (*French*) self-respect; self-esteem: *Try not to offend his amour propre.*

amp /æmp/ *n* (*infml*) = AMPERE.

ampere /ˈæmpeə(r); *US* ˈæmpɪər/ (also **amp**) *n* (*abbr* **A**) unit for measuring electric current. ⇨ App 12.

▷ **amperage** /ˈæmpərɪdʒ/ *n* [U] strength of electric current measured in amperes.

ampersand /ˈæmpəsænd/ *n* sign (&) meaning 'and': *Ampersands are often used in names of companies, eg Brown, Brown & Watkins.*

amphetamine /æmˈfetəmi:n/ *n* [C, U] (*medical*) (any of several types of) synthetic drug used esp as a stimulant. People can become addicted to them if they use them repeatedly. ⇨ article at DRUG.

amphi- *comb form* **1** both; of both kinds: *amphibian.* **2** around: *amphitheatre.*

amphibian /æmˈfɪbɪən/ *n* **1** animal able to live both on land and in water: *Frogs and newts are amphibians.* **2** aircraft that can take off from or alight on either land or water. **3** vehicle that can move over land or water.

amphibious /æmˈfɪbɪəs/ *adj* **1** living or operating both on land and in water: *amphibious vehicles.* **2** [usu attrib] involving both sea and land forces: *amphibious operations.*

amphitheatre (*US* **-ter**) /ˈæmfɪθɪətə(r)/ *n* **1** oval or circular unroofed building with rows of seats rising in steps all round an open space, used for presenting entertainments. The first amphitheatres were built by the ancient Romans and used for gladiator fights, wild-beast shows, mock sea-battles, etc. The most famous was the *Colosseum in Rome. **2** similar but semi-circular arrangement of seats inside a building used for eg lectures. **3** level area surrounded by hills.

amphora /ˈæmfərə/ *n* (*pl* **-ae** /-fəri:/) bottle-like container with a narrow neck and two handles, used by the ancient Greeks and Romans for wine and oil.

ample /ˈæmpl/ *adj* **1** (more than) enough: *ample time to get to the station* ○ *A small piece of cake will be ample, thank you.* ○ *£5 will be ample for my needs.* **2** abundant; plentiful: *a man of ample strength* ○ *The director of the company receives an ample salary.* **3** large in size; spacious; extensive: *an ample bosom* ○ *There's ample room for the children on the back seat.* ○ *The election was given ample coverage on TV.* ▷ **amply** /ˈæmplɪ/ *adv*: *amply fed, furnished, provided for, rewarded.*

amplify /ˈæmplɪfaɪ/ *v* (*pt, pp* **-fied**) [Tn] **1** increase (sth) in size or strength: *amplify the sound, electric current, signal.* **2** add details to (a story, etc); make fuller: *We must ask you to amplify your statement.* ▷ **amplification** /ˌæmplɪfɪˈkeɪʃn/ *n* [U].

amplifier *n* device for amplifying (esp sounds or radio signals).

amplitude /ˈæmplɪtju:d; *US* -tu:d/ *n* [U] **1** (*fml*) breadth; largeness; abundance. **2** (*physics*) maximum extent to which a particular vibration, oscillation, radio wave, etc differs from the average.

□ **ˈamplitude modulation** (*abbr* **AM**) method of radio broadcasting in which the radio signal alters the strength of the carrier wave. Cf FREQUENCY MODULATION (FREQUENCY).

ampoule (*US* also **ampule**) /ˈæmpu:l/ *n* (*medical*) small sealed glass container holding a drug under sterile conditions.

amputate /ˈæmpjʊteɪt/ *v* [I, Tn] cut off (a diseased or an injured limb) by surgical operation: *Her arm is so badly injured they will have to amputate (it).* ▷ **amputation** /ˌæmpjʊˈteɪʃn/ *n* [U, C].

amputee /ˌæmpjʊˈti:/ *n* person who has had a limb amputated.

Amsterdam /ˌæmstəˈdæm/ capital and largest city of the *Netherlands. It is a major port and contains many canals.

amuck = AMOK.

amulet /ˈæmjʊlɪt/ *n* piece of jewellery, etc worn as a charm[1](2) against evil.

Amundsen /ˈɑ:mənsn/ Roald (1872-1928), Norwegian explorer who in 1911 led the first expedition to reach the South Pole, beating Captain *Scott's expedition by a few weeks.

amuse /əˈmju:z/ *v* [Tn] **1** make (sb) laugh or smile: *Everyone was amused at/by the story about the dog.* ○ *My funny drawings amused the children.* ○ *We were amused to learn that....* **2** make time pass pleasantly for (sb): *These toys will help to keep the baby amused.* ○ *They amused themselves by looking at old photographs.*

▷ **amusement 1** [C] thing that makes time pass pleasantly: *I would never choose to watch cricket as an amusement.* ○ *The hotel offers its guests a wide variety of amusements.* **2** [U] state of being amused: *She could not disguise her amusement at his mistake.* ○ *To my great amusement his false beard fell off.* ○ *I only do it for amusement,* ie not for any serious purpose. **aˈmusement arcade** room or hall containing coin-operated machines for playing games. **aˈmusement park** open area with swings, roundabouts, shooting galleries, etc where one can amuse oneself.

amusing *adj* causing laughter or smiles; enjoyable: *an amusing story, story-teller* ○ *Our visits to the theatre made the holiday more amusing.*

an ⇨ A[2].

-an ⇨ -IAN.

-ana ⇨ -IANA.

Anabaptist /ˌænəˈbæptɪst/ *n* member of any of various Protestant religious groups, esp in the 16th century, which believed that only adults should be baptized.

anabolic steroid /ˌænəbɒlɪk ˈsterɔɪd, -ˈstɪərɔɪd/ hormone that increases the size of muscles. Synthetic forms are sometimes taken by athletes to improve their performance.

anachronism /əˈnækrənɪzəm/ *n* **1** mistake of placing sth in the wrong historical period: *It would be an anachronism to talk of Queen Victoria watching television.* **2** thing dated wrongly in this way: *Modern dress is an anachronism in productions of Shakespeare's plays.* **3** person, custom or idea regarded as out of date: *The monarchy is seen by some as an anachronism in present-day society.* ▷ **anachronistic** /əˌnækrəˈnɪstɪk/ *adj.*

anacoluthon /ˌænəkəˈlu:θɒn/ *n* (*pl* ~**s** or **-tha** /-θə/) sentence in which a new grammatical construction is begun before a previous one is finished (eg '*I thought you said — oh well, it doesn't matter*').

anaconda /ˌænəˈkɒndə/ *n* large snake of tropical S America that crushes its victims to death.

anaemia (*US* **anemia**) /əˈni:mɪə/ *n* [U] (*medical*) condition of the blood caused by a lack of red corpuscles, making the person look pale. It can be brought about by blood loss, or by insufficient iron, a substance which helps the body to make the red corpuscles.

▷ **anaemic** (*US* **anemic**) /əˈni:mɪk/ *adj* **1** suffering from or showing the symptoms of anaemia: *She looks anaemic in my opinion.* **2** (*fig*) lacking vigour; weak: *an anaemic performance.*

anaesthesia /ˌænɪsˈθi:zɪə/ (*US* **anesthesia** /-ˈθi:ʒə/) *n* [U] state of being unable to feel (pain, heat, cold, etc).

▷ **anaesthetic** (*US* **anesthetic**) /ˌænɪsˈθetɪk/ *n* [C, U] substance or process that produces anaesthesia. The modern surgical use of anaesthetics dates from the 1840s, when doctors and dentists began to use gases such as ether and nitrous oxide to produce unconsciousness during operations. Today anaesthesia is produced by breathing in various gases, by injection, or by spraying the skin. It has made possible the huge increase in the range of surgical operations over the past 150 years: *be under (an) anaesthetic* ○ *give sb a general anaesthetic,* ie cause sb to lose consciousness ○ *a local anaesthetic* (ie one affecting part of the body) *for the removal of a tooth.* — *adj* producing anaesthesia.

anaesthetist (*US* **anesthetist**) /əˈni:sθətɪst/ *n* person trained to administer anaesthetics.

anaesthetize, -ise (*US* **anesthetize**) /əˈni:sθətaɪz/ *v* [Tn] administer an anaesthetic to (sb); deprive of sensation. **anaesthetization, -isation** (*US* **anesthetization**) /əˌni:sθətaɪˈzeɪʃn/ *n* [U].

anagram /ˈænəgræm/ *n* word or phrase made by rearranging the letters of another word or phrase: *'Cart-horse' is an anagram of 'orchestra'.* ○ *This crossword is full of anagrams.*

anal /ˈeɪnl/ *adj* of the anus: *the anal region.*

□ ˌ**anal reˈtentive** (*psychology*) (of a person) unusually fussy about tidiness, etc (supposedly because of certain aspects of one's toilet-training in early childhood).

analgesia /ˌænælˈdʒi:zɪə; *US* -ʒə/ *n* [U] (*medical*) loss of ability to feel pain while still conscious.

▷ **analgesic** /ˌænælˈdʒi:sɪk/ *adj, n* (having the effects of a) substance that relieves pain: *Aspirin is a mild analgesic.*

analogous /əˈnæləgəs/ *adj* ~ (**to/with sth**) partially similar or parallel; offering an analogy: *The two processes are not analogous.* ○ *The present crisis is analogous with the situation immediately before the war.* ▷ **analogously** *adv.*

analogue (*US* **analog**) /ˈænəlɒg; *US* -lɔ:g/ *n* thing that is similar to another thing: *A vegetarian gets protein not from meat but from its analogues.*

□ ˌ**analogue comˈputer** computer using physical quantities, eg voltage, weight, length, etc, to represent numbers: *A slide-rule is a simple analogue computer.* Cf DIGITAL COMPUTER (DIGIT).

analogy /əˈnælədʒɪ/ *n* **1** [C] ~ (**between sth and sth**) partial similarity between two things that are compared: *point to analogies between the two events* ○ *The teacher drew an analogy between the human heart and a pump.* **2** [U] ~ (**with sth**) process of reasoning based on such similarity: *My theory applies to you and by analogy to others like you.* **3** [U] way in which words change their form because of their similarity to other words. ▷ **analogical** /ˌænəˈlɒdʒɪkl/ *adj.*

analyse (*US* **analyze**) /ˈænəlaɪz/ *v* [Tn] **1** separate (sth) into its parts in order to study its nature or structure: *analyse the sample and identify it* ○ *By analysing the parts of the sentence we learn more about English grammar.* **2** examine and explain (sth): *We must try to analyse the causes of the strike.* **3** = PSYCHOANALYSE.

analysis /əˈnæləsɪs/ *n* (*pl* **-yses** /-əsi:z/) **1** [U, C] study of sth by examining its parts and their relationship: *Textual analysis identified the author as Shakespeare.* ○ *Close analysis of sales figures shows clear regional variations.* **2** [C] statement of the result of this: *present a detailed analysis of the situation.* **3** [U] = PSYCHOANALYSIS. **4** [C, U] (*chemistry*) (act of) separating a compound substance into the individual simple substances of which it is made up, or of finding out what those simple substances are. **5** [U] (*mathematics*) method of solving problems using mainly algebra and calculus. **6** (idm) **in the** ˌ**last**/ˌ**final aˈnalysis** after all due consideration: *In the final analysis I think our sympathy lies with the heroine of the play.*

▷ **analytic** /ˌænəˈlɪtɪk/, **analytical** /-kl/ *adjs* of or using analysis: *analytical geometry.* **analytically** /-klɪ/ *adv.*

analyst /ˈænəlɪst/ *n* **1** person skilled in making (esp chemical) analyses. **2** = PSYCHOANALYST.

anapaest /ˈænəpi:st/ (*US* **anapest** /-pest/) *n* metrical foot in poetry consisting of two short or unstressed syllables followed by one long or stressed syllable. ▷ **anapaestic** /ˌænəˈpi:stɪk/ (*US* **anapestic** /-ˈpestɪk/) *adj*: *'Like the ˈleaves of the ˈforest when ˈsummer is ˈgreen' has an anapaestic rhythm.*

anaphora /əˈnæfərə/ *n* [U] (*grammar*) use of a word to refer back to or replace a word previously used, eg *do* in *If you don't want to iron my shirt I'll do it.* ▷ **anaphoric** /ˌænəˈfɒrɪk/ *adj.*

anarchy /ˈænəkɪ/ *n* [U] **1** absence of government or control in society; lawlessness: *The overthrow of the regime was followed by a period of anarchy.* **2** disorder; confusion: *In the absence of their teacher the class was in a state of anarchy.*

▷ **anarchic** /əˈnɑ:kɪk/, **anarchical** /-ɪkl/ *adjs.*

anarchism /ˈænəkɪzəm/ *n* [U] political theory that laws and government should be abolished.

anarchist *n* person who believes in anarchism.

anathema /əˈnæθəmə/ *n* **1** [U, C] detested person or thing: *Racial prejudice is (an) anathema to me.* **2** [C] formal declaration of the Christian Church, excommunicating sb or condemning sth as evil.

▷ **anathematize, -ise** /əˈnæθəmətaɪz/ *v* [I, Tn] curse (sb/sth).

Anatolia /ˌænəˈtəʊlɪə/ peninsula between the Mediterranean Sea in the south, the Aegean Sea in the west, and the Black Sea in the north, forming the most westerly part of Asia. In historical times it was known as Asia Minor. Today it is occupied by Turkey. ▷ **Anatolian** *adj, n.*

anatomy /əˈnætəmɪ/ *n* **1** [U] scientific study of the structure of animal bodies: *We have to do anatomy next term.* **2** [C] bodily structure of an animal or plant: *the anatomy of the frog.* **3** [C] (*joc*) human body: *Various parts of his anatomy were clearly visible.*

▷ **anatomical** /ˌænəˈtɒmɪkl/ *adj.* **anatomically** /-klɪ/ *adv.*

anatomist /əˈnætəmɪst/ *n* person who studies anatomy.

ANC *abbr* African National Congress.

-ance, -ence *suff* (with *vs* forming *ns*) action or state of: *assistance* ○ *resemblance* ○ *confidence.*

ancestor /ˈænsestə(r)/ *n* **1** (*fem* **ancestress** /-trɪs/) any of the people from whom sb is descended, esp those more remote than his grandparents; forefather: *His ancestors had come to England as refugees.* Cf DESCENDANT (DESCEND). **2** (*fig*) early form of a machine or structure which later became more developed; forerunner: *The ancestor of the modern bicycle was called a penny farthing.*

▷ **ancestral** /ænˈsestrəl/ *adj* belonging to or inherited from one's ancestors: *her ancestral home.*

ancestry /ˈænsestrɪ/ *n* line of ancestors: *a distinguished ancestry.*

anchor /ˈæŋkə(r)/ *n* **1** heavy metal device attached to a rope, chain, etc and used to moor a ship or boat to the sea-bottom or a balloon to the ground: *They brought the boat into the harbour and dropped (the) anchor.* **2** (*fig*) person or thing that gives stability or security. **3** (idm) **at ˈanchor** moored by the anchor: *We lay at anchor outside the harbour.* **bring (a ship)/come to ˈanchor** stop sailing and lower the anchor. **cast anchor** ⇨ CAST[1]. **ride at anchor** ⇨ RIDE[2]. **slip anchor** ⇨ SLIP[2]. **weigh anchor** ⇨ WEIGH.

▷ **anchor** *v* [I, Tn] lower an anchor; make (sth) secure with an anchor: *We anchored (our boat) close to the shore.*

anchorage /ˈæŋkərɪdʒ/ *n* **1** [C] place where ships, etc may anchor safely. **2** [U] money charged for anchoring.

□ ˈ**anchor man** /mæn/ **1** person who co-ordinates the work of a group, esp that of interviewers and reporters in a radio or television broadcast. **2** strong member of a sports team who has a vital part to play: *The anchor man in a relay team runs last.*

anchorite /ˈæŋkəraɪt/ *n* hermit or religious recluse.

▷ **anchoress** /ˈæŋkərɪs/ *n* female anchorite.

anchovy /ˈæntʃəvɪ; *US* ˈæntʃəʊvɪ/ *n* small fish of the herring family with a strong taste: [attrib] ˌ*anchovy* ˈ*paste.*

ancien régime /ˌɒnsjæn reɪˈʒi:m/ (*pl* **anciens régimes** /ˌɒnsjæn reɪˈʒi:m/) (*French*) **1** French political and social system before the Revolution of 1789. **2** (*usu derog*) any outdated or former political and social system.

ancient /ˈeɪnʃənt/ *adj* **1** belonging to times long past: *ancient civilizations.* **2** (*usu joc*) very old: *I feel pretty ancient when I see how the younger generation behaves.* ⇨ Usage at OLD.

▷ **the ancients** *n* [pl] people who lived in ancient times, esp the Greeks and Romans.

□ ˌ**ancient ˈhistory** history of the Greek and Roman civilizations.

ˌ**ancient ˈlights** legal right to receive light through one's window if it has been unobstructed for a long time (so that eg other people may not put up a building which obstructs one's window).

ˌ**ancient ˈmonument** (*Brit*) old building, etc recognized by the Government as worth preserving.

ancillary /ænˈsɪlərɪ; *US* ˈænsələrɪ/ *adj* ~ (**to sth**) helping in a subsidiary way: *ancillary staff, duties, roads, industries.*

-ancy, -ency *suff* (with *ns, adjs* and *vs* forming *ns*) state or quality of: *complacency* ○ *irrelevancy* ○ *presidency.*

and /ənd, ən, *also* n, *esp after* t, d; *strong form* ænd/ *conj* (used to connect words of the same part of speech, phrases or clauses) **1** also; in addition to: *bread and butter* ○ *slowly and carefully* ○ *able to read and write* ○ *one woman, two men and three children* ○ *shutting doors and opening windows* (When *and* connects two *ns* standing for things or people that are closely linked, a determiner is not normally repeated before the second *n*, eg *a knife and fork, my father and mother,* but *a knife and a spoon, my father and my uncle.*). **2** added to; plus: *5 and 5 makes 10* (When numbers are said, *and* is used between the hundreds and any digits that follow, eg *two thousand, two hundred and sixty four,* ie 2 264. The use of *and* in expressions of time, eg *five and twenty past two,* ie twenty-five past two, is now dated.). **3** then; following this: *She came in and sat down.* ○ *I pulled the trigger and the gun went off.* **4** as a result of this: *Work hard and* (ie If you work hard) *you will pass your examinations.* ○ *Arrive late once more and* (ie If you arrive late once more) *you're fired.* **5** then again; repeatedly; increasingly: *We walked for miles and miles.* ○ *They talked for hours and hours.* ○ *Your work is getting better and better.* ○ *He tried and tried but without success.* **6** contrasting with (different kinds of the same thing): *Don't worry — there are rules and rules,* ie Some rules are more important, more easy to ignore, etc than others.

□ **and/or** (*infml*) together with or as an alternative to: *Bring wine and/or chocolates.*

Andy Capp

NOTE ON USAGE: In informal English **and** can be used after a few verbs (eg **go**, **come**) instead of **to.** It indicates purpose: *Will you go and fetch me a screwdriver, please?* ○ *Can I come and look at your work?* ○ *We stayed and had a drink.* ○ *He stopped and bought some flowers.* When used with **try** and in the phrase *wait and see* only the base form of the verb is possible: *Try and improve.* ○ *We'll try and get one tomorrow.* ○ *'What's for dinner?' 'Wait and see.'*

Andalusia /ˌændəˈlu:sɪə; *US* ˌændəˈlu:ʒə/ southernmost and largest region of Spain, with both Atlantic and Mediterranean coastlines. ▷ **Andalusian** *adj, n.*

Andaman and Nicobar Islands /ˈændəmən ənd ˈnɪkəbɑ:r aɪləndz/ two groups of islands (more than 200 in all) in the Bay of Bengal. They belong to India.

andante /ænˈdæntɪ/ *adj, adv* (*music*) (to be played) at a moderately slow pace.

▷ **andante** *n* piece of music (to be) played in this way.

andantino /ˌændænˈti:nəʊ; *US* ˌɑ:ndɑ:n-/ *adj, adv* (to be played) slightly faster than andante. — *n* (*pl* ~**s**) piece of music (to be) played in this way.

Andersen /ˈændəsn/ Hans Christian (1805-75), Danish author best known for his fairy-tales for children (eg 'The Snow Queen', 'The Ugly Duckling', 'The Emperor's New Clothes' and 'The Little Mermaid').

Anderson[1] /ˈændəsn/ Elizabeth Garrett (1836-1917), British doctor who campaigned for women to be allowed to train as doctors.

Anderson[2] /ˈændəsən/ Lindsay (1923-), British film director. His style is marked by social observation and satire, most notably in *If*..., a savage attack on the British public school system.

Andes /ˈændi:z/ **the Andes** [pl] mountain range that extends along the Pacific coast of S America. ▷ **Andean** /ˈændiən/ *adj.*

andiron /ˈændaɪən/ (also **firedog**) *n* iron support (usu one of a pair) for holding logs in a fireplace.

Andorra /ænˈdɔ:rə/ small independent principality in the Pyrenees between France and Spain; pop approx 49 000; official language Catalan; capital Andorra la Vella; unit of currency franc (= 100 centimes) and peseta (= 100 centimos). The main industry is tourism. ⇨ map at SPAIN.

Andrea del Sarto /ˌændreɪə del ˈsɑ:təʊ/ (1486-1530), Italian painter of the Renaissance period. He is best known for his religious paintings, particularly a series of frescos on the life of John the Baptist in a Florence church.

Andrew /ˈændru:/ Saint (1st century AD), one of Christ's twelve apostles, a fisherman and brother of *Peter. He is the patron saint of Scotland. ⇨ article at NATIONAL.

Androcles /ˈændrəkli:z/ (in Roman legend) slave who removed a thorn from the paw of a lion which later spared his life when Androcles was thrown into the arena to be attacked by lions. G B *Shaw's play *Androcles and the Lion* is based on this story.

androgen /ˈændrədʒən/ *n* [C, U] male sex hormone that causes certain male sexual characteristics (eg facial hair and a deep voice) to develop and then maintains them.

androgynous /ænˈdrɒdʒɪnəs/ *adj* **1** having both male and female characteristics; hermaphrodite: *pop-stars dressing up in androgynous styles.* **2** (*botany*) (of a plant) having both stamens and pistils in the same flower.

android /ˈændrɔɪd/ *n* (in science fiction) robot made to look like a human being.

Andromache /ænˈdrɒməkɪ/ (in Greek legend) wife of the Trojan hero *Hector, who was captured by the Greeks after Hector's death. She is the subject of plays by *Euripides and *Racine.

Andromeda /ænˈdrɒmɪdə/ **1** (in Greek mythology) woman who was chained to a rock to be eaten by a sea-monster after her mother had angered the sea-god *Poseidon. She was rescued by *Perseus, whom she later married. **2** (*astronomy*) large constellation in the northern hemisphere.

□ **the An'dromeda galaxy** spiral-shaped nebula in the Andromeda constellation, about 2.2 million light-years away from the earth.

Andy Capp /ˌændɪ ˈkæp/ character in a strip cartoon in the *Daily Mirror* newspaper, representing a comic exaggeration of the supposed behaviour of a typical British working-class man. ⇨ illus. ⇨ article at CLASS.

anecdote /ˈænɪkdəʊt/ *n* short, interesting or amusing story about a real person or event. ▷ **anecdotal** /ˌænekˈdəʊtl/ *adj*: *anecdotal memoirs.*

anechoic /ˌænɪˈkəʊɪk/ *adj* [usu attrib] (esp of a room) not producing an echo.

anemia, anemic (*US*) = ANAEMIA, ANAEMIC.

anemometer /ˌænɪˈmɒmɪtə(r)/ (also **wind-gauge**) *n* instrument for measuring the force of the wind, and sometimes also its direction.

anemone /əˈnemənɪ/ *n* small wild or garden plant with white, red or purple star-shaped flowers.

aneroid barometer /ˌænərɔɪd bəˈrɒmɪtə(r)/ instrument that measures air-pressure by the action of air on the outside of a box containing a vacuum.

anesthesia, anesthetic (*US*) = ANAESTHESIA, ANAESTHETIC.

aneurysm (also **aneurism**) /ˈænjʊərɪzəm/ *n* place where a blood vessel has become swollen.

anew /əˈnju:; *US* əˈnu:/ *adv* (*usu rhet*) in a new or different way; again: *Our efforts must begin anew.*

angel

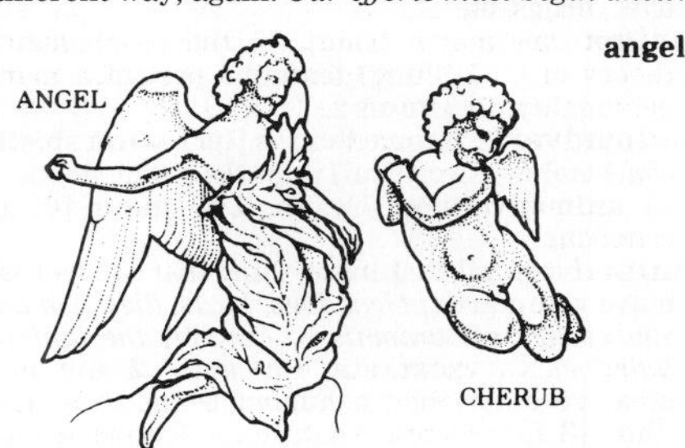

angel /ˈeɪndʒl/ *n* **1** (esp in Christian belief) messenger or attendant of God: *Angels are usually shown in pictures dressed in white, with wings.* ⇨ illus. **2** beautiful, innocent or kind person: *Mary's three children are all angels — not like mine.* ○ *Be an angel and make me a cup of tea.* ○ *He sings like an angel,* ie very sweetly. **3** (idm) **fools rush in where angels fear to tread** ⇨ FOOL. **a ministering angel** ⇨ MINISTER[2]. **on the side of the angels** ⇨ SIDE[1].

▷ **angelic** /ænˈdʒelɪk/ *adj* of or like an angel: *an angelic smile, voice, face.* **angelically** /-klɪ/ *adv*: *The children behaved angelically.*

□ **ˈangel cake** light pale sponge cake, made with egg whites.

ˈangel-fish *n* (*pl* unchanged) tropical fish with wing-like fins, commonly kept in aquariums.

angelica /ænˈdʒelɪkə/ *n* [U] (**a**) sweet-smelling plant used in cooking and in medicine. (**b**) stalks of this plant that have been boiled in sugar.

Angelico /ænˈdʒelɪkəʊ/ Fra (1387-1455), Italian painter best known for his religious works (eg the frescos in the convent of San Marco, Florence, and the *Scenes from the Lives of St Stephen and St Lawrence* in the Vatican).

angelus /ˈændʒɪləs/ *n* [sing] (also **Angelus**) **1** (in the Roman Catholic Church) prayer to the Virgin Mary. **2** bell rung at morning, noon and sunset, calling people to say this prayer.

anger /ˈæŋgə(r)/ *n* [U] **1** strong feeling of displeasure and hostility: *filled with anger at the way he had been tricked* ○ *speak in anger about the plight of poor people* ○ *It was said in a moment of anger.* **2** (idm) **more in sorrow than in anger** ⇨ SORROW.

▷ **anger** *v* [Tn] fill (sb) with anger; make angry: *He was angered by the selfishness of the others.*

Angevin /ˈændʒəvɪn/ *adj* of the ruling dynasty of Anjou, an ancient region of W France, and esp those members of it who became the *Plantagenet kings of England.

angina pectoris /ænˌdʒaɪnə ˈpektərɪs/ (also **angina**) *n* [U] (*medical*) disease of the heart which results in sharp pains in the chest after exertion.

Angkor /ˈæŋkɔ:(r)/ capital of the ancient kingdom of *Khmer (in present-day Cambodia), famous for its temples, esp the 12th-century Angkor Wat.

Angle /ˈæŋgl/ *n* member of a Germanic people who came from Denmark to England in the 5th century AD and settled mainly in the north and east of the country. Cf ANGLO-SAXON.

angle

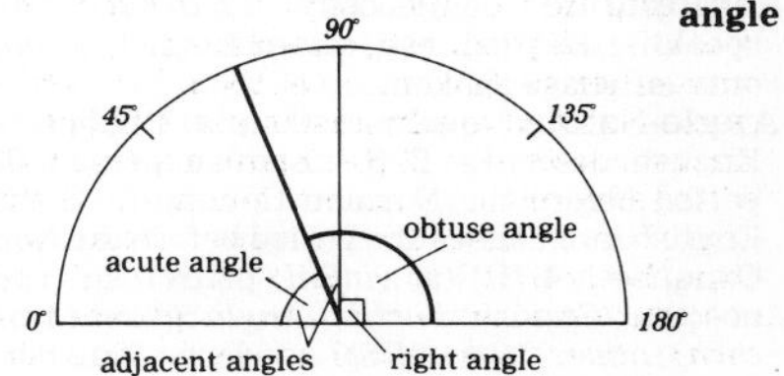

angle[1] /ˈæŋgl/ *n* **1** space between two lines or surfaces that meet: *an angle of 45°.* ⇨ illus. **2** point of view: *Seen from this angle the woman in the picture is smiling.* ○ (*fig*) *Try looking at the affair from a different angle.* **3** corner (of a building or an object): *She hit her knee against the angle of the bed.* **4** (idm) **at an ˈangle** not straight up; sloping: *The famous tower of Pisa leans at an angle.*

▷ **angle** *v* **1** [Tn] move or place (sth) in a slanting position: *Try angling the camera for a more interesting picture.* **2** [Tn, Tn·pr] ~ **sth (at/to/towards sb)** present (information, etc) from a particular point of view: *This programme is angled at young viewers.*

□ **ˈangle bracket** ⇨ BRACKET 2.

angle[2] /ˈæŋgl/ *v* **1** [I] (usu **go angling**) fish with line and hook: *angling for trout.* **2** [Ipr] ~ **for sth** (*infml*) try and obtain sth by hinting: *angle for compliments, an invitation, a free ticket.*

▷ **angler** /ˈæŋglə(r)/ *n* person who goes angling. Cf FISHERMAN.

angling *n* [U] art or sport of fishing with a line and hook: *Angling is his main hobby.*

Anglesey /ˈæŋgəlsɪ/ island off the north-west coast of Wales. ⇨ map at UNITED KINGDOM.

Anglican /ˈæŋglɪkən/ *n, adj* (member) of the Church of England or of another Church with the same beliefs and forms of worship: *the Anglican prayer-book.* ⇨ article at CHURCH OF ENGLAND.

▷ **Anglicanism** /ˈæŋglɪkənɪzəm/ *n* [U] beliefs and forms of worship of the Anglican Church.

□ ˌ**Anglican Comˈmunion** the Church of England and other Christian Churches around the world, mainly in English-speaking countries, that share its beliefs and forms of worship and are formally linked with it.

Anglicize, -ise /ˈæŋglɪsaɪz/ *v* [Tn] make (sb/sth) English or like English: *Anglicized pronunciation.* ▷ **Anglicism** /ˈæŋglɪsɪzəm/ *n* typically English way of saying sth; English word or phrase used by speakers of another language: *The French language contains many Anglicisms, such as 'le weekend'.*

Anglo- *comb form* English or British: *Anglo-American* ○ *Anglophobia.*

Anglo-American /ˌæŋgləʊ əˈmerɪkən/ *n* American person descended from an English family.

▷ **Anglo-American** *adj* of or concerning England and America: *the Anglo-American agreement.*

Anglo-Catholic /ˌæŋgləʊ ˈkæθəlɪk/ *n, adj* (member) of the section of the Church of England that stresses its unbroken connection with the early Christian Church and objects to being called Protestant. ▷ **Anglo-Catholicism** /ˌæŋgləʊ kəˈθɒləsɪzəm/ *n* [U].

Anglo-French /ˌæŋgləʊ ˈfrentʃ/ *adj* English and French: *a joint Anglo-French project.*

▷ **Anglo-French** *n* [U] variety of French used in medieval England.

Anglo-Indian /ˌæŋgləʊ ˈɪndɪən/ *n, adj* **1** (person) of mixed British and Indian blood. **2** (*dated*) (person) of British birth but having lived for a long time in India.

Anglo-Norman /ˌæŋgləʊ ˈnɔːmən/ *n* **1** [C] medieval descendant of the Normans who settled in England in 1066. **2** [U] = ANGLO-FRENCH.

Anglophile /ˈæŋgləʊfaɪl/ *n* person who loves England or English things.

Anglophobe /ˈæŋgləʊfəʊb/ *n* person who hates or fears England or English things.

Anglophobia /ˌæŋgləʊˈfəʊbɪə/ *n* [U] (esp excessive) hatred or fear of England or English things.

anglophone /ˈæŋgləʊfəʊn/ *n, adj* (person) speaking English, esp where English is not the only language spoken.

Anglo-Saxon /ˌæŋgləʊ ˈsæksn/ *n* **1** [C] person of English descent. **2** [C] English person of the period before the Norman Conquest. **3** [U] the English language of the period before the Norman Conquest. **4** [U] **(a)** (*infml*) plain (esp crude or obscene) English: *hurling Anglo-Saxon insults at each other.* **(b)** (*US*) modern English. ▷ **Anglo-Saxon** *adj.*

Angola /æŋˈgəʊlə/ country on the west coast of Africa; pop approx 10 303 000; official language Portuguese; capital Luanda; unit of currency kwanza (= 100 lweis). It was ruled by Portugal until 1975 when, after extensive fighting, it achieved independence. This was followed by a long civil war which continued in the 1990s despite a free election and peace talks. Its main exports are oil, coffee and diamonds. ⇨ map at NAMIBIA. ▷ **Angolan** *adj, n.*

angora /æŋˈgɔːrə/ *n* **1** [C] long-haired breed of cat, goat or rabbit. **2** [U] yarn or material made from the hair of angora goats or rabbits.

angry /ˈæŋgrɪ/ *adj* (**-ier, -iest**) **1** ~ (**with sb**) (**at/about sth**) filled with anger: *angry at being delayed/about the delay* ○ *I was angry with myself for making such a stupid mistake.* ○ (*fig*) *The sea/sky looks angry*, ie stormy, threatening. **2** (of a wound) painful; inflamed. ▷ **angrily** /-əlɪ/ *adv.*

□ ˌ**angry young** ˈ**man 1** any of a group of young British writers of the 1950s (eg John *Osborne and Alan Sillitoe) who criticized the British ruling class and the social conventions of the time. **2** any young man, esp an intellectual, who disagrees strongly with existing moral, social and political attitudes and tries to change them.

angst /æŋst/ *n* [U] (*German*) feeling of anxiety, guilt or remorse, esp about the state of the world.

angstrom /ˈæŋstrəm/ *n* (*symb* Å) unit of length equal to one hundred-millionth of a metre, used, esp formerly, in measuring the wavelength of radiation.

Anguilla /æŋˈgwɪlə/ island in the Caribbean, the most northerly of the *Leeward Islands. It is a British colony. ⇨ map at CARIBBEAN.

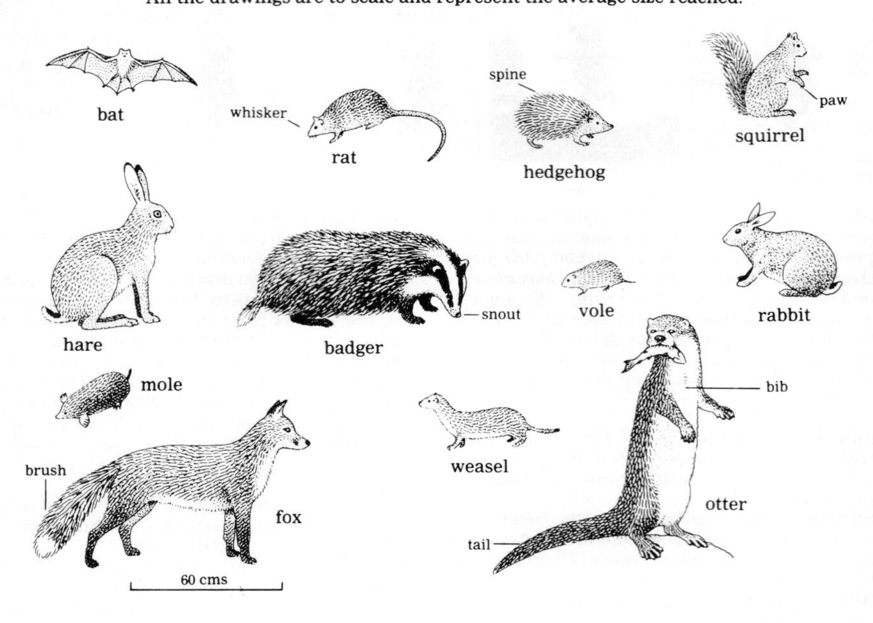

anguish /ˈæŋgwɪʃ/ *n* [U] severe physical or mental pain: *I was in anguish until I knew she was still alive.*

▷ **anguished** *adj* feeling or expressing anguish: *an anguished heart* ○ *anguished cries.*

angular /ˈæŋgjʊlə(r)/ *adj* **1** having angles or sharp corners. **2** (of people) thin and bony. **3** (of a person's character or manner) stiff and awkward: *an angular posture, gait, stride.* **4** measured by the angle: *angular distance*, ie the distance between two objects measured as an angle from a given point. ▷ **angularity** /ˌæŋgjʊˈlærətɪ/ *n* [U, C].

□ ˌ**angular mo**ˈ**mentum** momentum of sth caused by its rotation round an axis.

ˌ**angular ve**ˈ**locity** speed of sth rotating round an axis.

anhydrous /ænˈhaɪdrəs/ *adj* (*chemistry*) containing no water.

aniline /ˈænɪliːn; *US* ˈænəlɪn/ *n* [U] oily liquid obtained chemically from coal tar, used in making dyes, drugs, etc.

anima /ˈænɪmə/ *n* [sing] (in the psychological theory of C G *Jung) feminine part of a man's personality. Cf ANIMUS 2.

animadvert /ˌænɪmædˈvɜːt/ *v* [Ipr] ~ (**on sb/sth**) (*fml*) make (esp critical) remarks about sb/sth.

▷ **animadversion** /-ˈvɜːʃn; *US* -ʒn/ *n* [C, U] criticism.

animal /ˈænɪml/ *n* **1** living thing that can feel and move voluntarily: *Men, dogs, birds, flies, fish and snakes are all animals.* ○ [attrib] *the* ˈ*animal kingdom.* Cf VEGETABLE, MINERAL. **2** any such creature other than a human being. ⇨ article, illus. **3** four-footed creature as distinct from a bird, a fish or an insect. **4** wild or brutish person. **5** (idm) **there is** ˌ**no such** ˈ**animal** (*infml saying*) such a (type of) thing does not exist.

▷ **animal** *adj* [attrib] characteristic of animals: *animal needs*, eg food and drink ○ *animal desires*, ie sexual desires.

□ ˌ**animal** ˈ**husbandry** the care and management of cattle, sheep, horses, etc.

ˌ**animal** ˈ**magnetism 1** (formerly) hypnotism. **2** physical attraction in animals.

ˌ**animal** ˈ**spirits** natural enjoyment of life.

📖 Animals have been used in fairy tales and fables to represent human qualities and weaknesses, and specific characteristics are still associated with certain animals. For example, the lion is supposed to be brave, the owl wise and the fox sly. Animal names have also been used to describe people in unfavourable terms. A person can be called an ass or a donkey (stupid), a bitch or a cat (malicious), a goose (silly), a monkey (mischievious), a mouse (timid), a pig (greedy), a rat (disloyal), a shark (a swindler), a sheep (easily led), or a snake (deceitful).

animalcule /ˌænɪˈmælkjuːl/ *n* microscopically small animal.

animate[1] /ˈænɪmət/ *adj* living; having life: *The dog lay so still it scarcely seemed animate.*

animate[2] /ˈænɪmeɪt/ *v* **1** [Tn] give life to (sth/sb); make lively: *A smile animated her face.* **2** [Tn, Tn·pr] ~ **sb** (**to/with sth**) inspire or motivate sb: *animate sb to greater efforts, with a desire to succeed* ○ *Animated by fresh hope, he started again.* **3** [Tn] produce (sth) as an animated cartoon.

▷ **animated** *adj* **1** lively: *an animated discussion* ○ *I had rarely seen him so animated.* **2** given the appearance of movement: *animated drawings.* **animatedly** *adv.* ˌ**animated car**ˈ**toon** = CARTOON 2.

animation /ˌænɪˈmeɪʃn/ *n* [U] **1** liveliness; vivacity: *We could see how excited he was by the animation in his face.* **2** technique of making animated cartoons. Cf SUSPENDED ANIMATION (SUSPEND).

animator *n* person who makes animated cartoons.

animism /ˈænɪmɪzəm/ *n* [U] belief that all natural objects and phenomena (eg trees, stones, the wind, etc) have souls.

animosity /ˌænɪˈmɒsətɪ/ *n* [C, U] ~ (**against/towards sb/sth**); ~ (**between A and B**) (instance of) strong dislike or of hostility: *He felt no animosity towards his critics.* ○ *I could sense the animosity between them.*

animus /ˈænɪməs/ *n* [U] **1** animosity shown in speech or action. **2** (in the psychological theory of C G *Jung) masculine part of a woman's personality.

anion /ˈænaɪən/ *n* ion with a negative charge. Cf CATION.

anise /ˈænɪs/ *n* plant with sweet-smelling seeds.

aniseed /ˈænɪsiːd/ *n* [U] seed of anise, used for flavouring liqueurs and sweets.

Animals

The importance of animals in British life is reflected in many ways. In the past, landowners liked to be portrayed with their dogs and horses and many such pictures can be seen in art galleries and country houses. Animals are used frequently in advertising, especially on television. The Royal Society for the Prevention of Cruelty to Animals (RSPCA) is one of the largest charities in Britain and it is not unusual for people to leave their money to it or other animal causes when they die.

Dogs and cats are the most popular pets, and about half the households in the country own one or the other. There is no official national register of either animal, although dog-owners were required to possess a licence until the 1980s. Attacks by dogs on children, as well as the increase in abandoned dogs and strays, have since led to demands for licences to be reintroduced. Other creatures frequently kept as pets include goldfish, budgerigars and, for children, small animals such as rabbits, mice and hamsters. Pigeons are kept for racing and exhibiting by breeders ('pigeon fanciers'), and greyhounds and whippets are bred for racing.

Labradors, collies, Alsatians, spaniels and terriers are all popular as pet dogs, and foxhounds and beagles are used in hunting. In the USA, the most popular breeds are cocker spaniels, labradors, poodles and golden retrievers. In most states, owners have to buy an annual licence to keep a dog.

Guide-dogs are used for work with blind people, and both the police and the army use dogs as trackers and in combating crime. 'Sniffer' dogs are used to detect concealed drugs and explosives.

Many people specialize in breeding particular types of dog for show. Cruft's Dog Show is an annual event, held in London until 1990 and in Birmingham since 1991. Prizes are awarded to dogs in many different classes as well as to one supreme champion, the 'dog of the year'.

Horses play an important part in British life. The British Horse Society, which exists to promote the art of riding, has 51 000 members. Ponies and donkeys are popular with children. Pony-trekking is a popular sport in hilly country and donkey rides on the beach are a feature of many seaside resorts. Many young riders compete in gymkhanas.

More generally, horses are familiar both on the racecourse and in hunting, while popular contests and ceremonial events such as the Royal Windsor Horse Show, the Royal Tournament, the Badminton Horse Trials, the Horse of the Year Show and Trooping the Colour also feature horses prominently. Apart from the famous horse-races, such as the Grand National and the Derby, there is racing at courses throughout the country almost every day of the year.

Hunting, in which riders and foxhounds chase foxes across open country, has drawn increasing opposition in recent years. To those who hunt, it is an exciting and convivial sport, displaying in the picturesque setting of the English countryside much of the traditional colour and glamour preserved in sporting prints, with the red jackets (called 'coats of hunting pink') worn by the hunt master and his assistants. To many animal lovers, however, the chase and killing of a fox is no sport at all or, as Oscar Wilde put it, 'the English country gentleman galloping after a fox—the unspeakable in full pursuit of the uneatable'. As a result, many hunting events have been sabotaged by anti-hunt protesters in recent years. There is similar opposition to hare coursing and otter hunting, both done on foot using hounds, and to rabbit, grouse and pheasant shooting, which are essentially forms of hunting without the chase. Even fishing is opposed by some. (Cf article at PROTEST.)

Anti-hunt protesters are part of a more general movement in support of animal rights that has emerged recently in Britain and the USA. The movement's main aim is to ban the cruel treatment of animals, both in laboratory experiments using beagles, rabbits, monkeys, etc, and in factory farming, in which hens, pigs and calves are kept in overcrowded pens and cages. The irresponsible and neglectful treatment of animals by some farmers and pet owners is also the concern of the RSPCA (SPCA in the USA).

Both Britain and the USA have seen the rise of outspoken campaigns against whaling and the fur industry, while at another level there is considerable opposition to the slaughtering of animals for food and an increase in the number of people who are vegetarians.

There is also controversy about keeping animals in zoos. Among the best-known zoos in Britain are the London Zoo in Regent's Park and Whipsnade Wild Animal Park, Bedfordshire, where animals are kept in a near-natural environment. Popular American zoos include Lincoln Park, Chicago, the San Diego Zoo, California, and the National Zoological Park, Washington DC. Many American zoos have colourful specialized attractions, such as elephant shows and 'Gorilla Worlds'. The San Diego Zoo, for example, includes a large aviary constructed over natural canyons.

ankh /æŋk/ *n* ancient Egyptian symbol of eternal life, consisting of a cross with a loop on top.

ankle /ˈæŋkl/ *n* **1** joint connecting the foot with the leg. **2** thin part of the leg between this joint and the calf: [attrib] ˈ*ankle socks*, ie short socks covering the ankles but no higher. ⇨ illus at FOOT.
▷ **anklet** /ˈæŋklɪt/ ornamental chain, ring or band worn round the ankle.

ankylosis /ˌæŋkɪˈləʊsɪs/ *n* [U] stiffening of a joint in the body usu due to disease of the joint.

annals /ˈænlz/ *n* [pl] story of events year by year; historical records: *a name that will go down in the annals*, ie be recorded in history ○ *the Annals of the Society*.
▷ **annalist** /ˈænəlɪst/ *n* person who writes annals.

Anne[1] /æn/ (1665-1714), queen of Britain 1702-14. Daughter of *James II, she was the last of the *Stuart monarchs. While she was on the throne the union between England and Scotland was finalized. She was the last monarch to veto a law passed by parliament. ⇨ App 3. Cf QUEEN ANNE (QUEEN).

Anne[2] /æn/ Saint (1st century BC), mother of the *Virgin Mary and patron saint of Brittany and Canada.

anneal /əˈni:l/ *v* [Tn] make (metals, glass, etc) tough by cooling slowly after heating.

annelid /ˈænəlɪd/ *n* any of a large group of segmented worms (eg earthworms and leeches).

Anne of Cleves /ˌæn əv ˈkli:vz/ (1515-57), fourth wife of *Henry VIII of England, whom she married in 1540. He did not like her, and divorced her after six months.

annex /əˈneks/ *v* **1** [Tn] take possession of (a territory, etc): *annex a neighbouring state*. **2** [Tn, Tn·pr] ~ **sth (to sth)** add or join sth to a larger thing: *A new wing has been annexed to the hospital.*
▷ **annexation** /ˌænekˈseɪʃn/ *n* (**a**) [U] act of annexing. (**b**) [C] instance of this; that which is annexed.

annexe (also *esp US* **annex**) /ˈæneks/ *n* ~ **(to sth) 1** building added to a larger one; building providing additional accommodation: *The hotel was full so we had to sleep in the annexe.* **2** addition, eg to a document.

annihilate /əˈnaɪəleɪt/ *v* [Tn] destroy (sb/sth) completely: *The enemy was annihilated.*
▷ **annihilation** /əˌnaɪəˈleɪʃn/ *n* [U] complete destruction: *A full-scale nuclear war could lead to the annihilation of the human race.*

anniversary /ˌænɪˈvɜ:sərɪ/ *n* yearly return of the date of an event; celebration of this: *the hundredth anniversary of the composer's death* ○ *our wedding anniversary* ○ [attrib] *an anniversary dinner*.

Anno Domini /ˌænəʊ ˈdɒmɪnaɪ/ *adv* (*abbr* **AD**) (*Latin*) (used, esp in its abbreviated form, for giving dates of the Christian era) in the year of Our Lord.
▷ **Anno Domini** *n* [U] (*joc*) old age: *I can't run up the stairs like I used to — it's Anno Domini catching up with me!*

annotate /ˈænəteɪt/ *v* [Tn] add notes to (a book, manuscript, text, etc) giving explanation or comment: *annotated by the author*.
▷ **annotation** /ˌænəˈteɪʃn/ *n* **1** [U] action or process of annotating. **2** [C] note or comment added to a text: *annotations in the margin*.

announce /əˈnaʊns/ *v* **1** [Tn, Tf, Tw, Dn·pr, Dpr·f, Dpr·w] make (sth) known publicly: *They announced their engagement to the family.* ○ *The Prime Minister announced that she would resign.* ○ *Have they announced when the race will begin?* **2** [Tn] make known the presence or arrival of (sb/sth): *Would you announce the guests as they come in?* **3** [Tn] introduce (a speaker, singer, etc) on radio, TV, etc.
▷ **announcement** *n* statement in spoken or written form that makes sth known: *The announcement of the royal birth was broadcast to the nation.* ○ *Announcements of births, marriages and deaths appear in some newspapers.*
announcer *n* person who announces speakers, singers, programmes, etc, esp on radio or TV.

annoy /əˈnɔɪ/ *v* [Tn] **1** cause slight anger to (sb); irritate: *His constant sniffing annoys me.* ○ *It annoys me when people forget to say thank you.* ○ *I was annoyed by his insensitive remarks.* **2** cause trouble or discomfort to (sb); harass: *Stop annoying your mother.* ○ *The mosquitoes annoyed me so much I couldn't sleep.*
▷ **annoyance** /-əns/ *n* **1** [U] being annoyed: *a look of annoyance* ○ *much to our annoyance*. **2** [C] thing that annoys: *One of the annoyances of working here is the difficulty of parking near the office.*
annoyed *adj* ~ **(with sb) (at/about sth)**; ~ **(that.../to do sth)** rather angry: *He got very annoyed with me about my carelessness.* ○ *I'm extremely annoyed at the way he always stares at me in the office.* ○ *Will she be annoyed that you forgot to phone?* ○ *I was annoyed to find they had left without me.*
annoying *adj* causing slight anger or irritation: *This interruption is very annoying.* ○ *How annoying, I've left my wallet at home!*

annual /ˈænjʊəl/ *adj* [usu attrib] **1** happening

every year: *annual event, meeting, report, show, visit.* **2** calculated for the year: *an annual income, production, rainfall, subscription* ○ *the annual subscription.* **3** lasting for one year: *the annual course of the sun.*

▷ **annual** *n* **1** plant that completes its life-cycle within one year. **2** book or periodical that is published once a year, having the same title each time but different contents.

annually *adv*: *The exhibition is held annually.*

□ **ˌannual ˌgeneral ˈmeeting** yearly meeting of members (of a club, etc) or shareholders of a company, esp for holding elections and reporting on the year's events.

ˌannual ˈring layer of new wood produced each year by a tree, and seen in a cross-section of the trunk. The number of layers can be counted to find out how old the tree is, and the rings can be studied in other ways (eg to investigate climate in former times). ⇨ illus at DENDROCHRONOLOGY.

annuity /əˈnju:ətɪ; *US* -ˈnu:-/ *n* **1** fixed sum of money paid to sb yearly, usu for the remaining part of his lifetime: *receiving a modest annuity.* **2** form of insurance that provides such a regular annual income.

▷ **annuitant** /əˈnju:ɪtənt; *US* -ˈnu:-/ *n* person who receives an annuity.

annul /əˈnʌl/ *v* (**-ll-**) [Tn] declare (sth) no longer valid; abolish; cancel: *annul an agreement/a contract/a law/a marriage.* ▷ **annulment** *n* [C, U].

annular /ˈænjʊlə(r)/ *adj* shaped like a ring: *The annular markings on a tree indicate its age.*

□ **ˌannular eˈclipse** eclipse of the sun by the moon when a ring of sunlight can be seen round the moon.

annunciation /əˌnʌnsɪˈeɪʃn/ *n* **the Annunciation** [sing] (*religion*) (festival held on 25 March to commemorate) the announcement to Mary that she was to be the mother of Christ.

annus mirabilis /ˌænəs mɪˈrɑ:bəlɪs/ (*Latin*) wonderful year; year in which marvellous or exceptional things happen.

anode /ˈænəʊd/ *n* **1** positive electrode by which an electric current enters a device. Cf CATHODE. **2** positive terminal of a battery.

▷ **anodize, -ise** /ˈænədaɪz/ *v* [Tn] coat (a piece of metal) with a protective surface by passing an electric current through it.

anodyne /ˈænədaɪn/ *n, adj* **1** (drug) that can relieve pain. **2** (thing) that can relieve or soothe mental distress.

anoint /əˈnɔɪnt/ *v* **1** [Tn, Tn·pr] ~ **sb (with sth)** apply oil or ointment to sb (esp as a religious ceremony): *The priest anointed the baby's forehead.* **2** [Cn·n] show that (sb) has taken high office by doing this: *The high priest anointed him king.*

anomaly /əˈnɒməlɪ/ *n* **1** thing that is different from what is normal; irregularity; inconsistency: *the many anomalies in the tax system.* **2** (*astronomy*) angle between a planet, the sun and the point at which the planet is closest to the sun (its *perihelion*).

▷ **anomalistic** /əˌnɒməˈlɪstɪk/ *adj* of an anomaly(2). **aˌnomalistic ˈmonth** period of time (about 27.5 days) taken for the moon to go round the earth, measured from the point when it is nearest to the earth (its *perigee*). **aˌnomalistic ˈyear** period of time taken for the earth to go round the sun, measured from the time when it is nearest to the sun (its *perihelion*).The period is about 365 days, 6 hours, 13 minutes and 53 seconds.

anomalous /əˈnɒmələs/ *adj* different from what is normal; irregular: *She is in an anomalous position as the only part-time worker in the firm.* **anomalously** *adv.*

anon /əˈnɒn/ *adv* (*dated or joc*) **1** soon: *See you anon.* **2** (idm) **ever and anon** ⇨ EVER.

anon /əˈnɒn/ *abbr* (usu at the end of a piece of writing, etc) (by an) anonymous (author).

anonymity /ˌænəˈnɪmətɪ/ *n* [U] state of being anonymous.

anonymous /əˈnɒnɪməs/ *adj* **1** with a name that is not known or not made public: *an anonymous donor, buyer, benefactor, etc* ○ *The author wishes to remain anonymous.* **2** written or given by sb who does not reveal his name: *an anonymous letter, message, gift, phone call.* ▷ **anonymously** *adv.*

anopheles /əˈnɒfɪli:z/ *n* mosquito of the type that spreads malaria and other infections.

anorak /ˈænəræk/ *n* (usu waterproof) hooded jacket worn as a protection against rain, wind and cold.

anorexia /ˌænəˈreksɪə/ *n* [U] (*medical*) **1** loss of the wish to eat. **2** (also **anorexia nervosa** /nɜ:ˈvəʊsə/) mental illness that causes abnormal fear of eating and thus leads to dangerous loss of weight. Cf BULIMIA.

▷ **anorexic** /ˌænəˈreksɪk/ (also **anorectic** /-ˈrektɪk/) *n, adj* (person who is) suffering from anorexia nervosa.

anosmia /æˈnɒzmɪə/ *n* [U] lack or loss of the sense of smell.

A N Other /ˌeɪ ˌen ˈʌðə(r)/ (*esp Brit*) (used to name a person who has not yet been chosen, esp as a member of a sports team).

another /əˈnʌðə(r)/ *indef det* **1** an additional (person or thing): *Would you like another cup of tea?* ○ *She's going to have another baby.* ○ *In another two weeks it'll be finished.* **2** a different (person or thing): *We can do it another time.* ○ *She's got another boy-friend.* ○ *That's quite another matter.* ○ *This pen doesn't work — can you give me another one?* **3** a similar (person or thing): *Can he be another Einstein?* **4** (idm) **another place** ⇨ PLACE[1]. **that's another story** ⇨ STORY[1].

▷ **another** *indef pron* **1** an additional person or thing: *Can I have another?* ○ *Not another!* ○ *Suddenly the letters started arriving — another of them came today.* **2** a different person or thing: *I don't like this room — let's ask for another.* **3** a similar person or thing: *Shakespeare is the greatest English writer - will there ever be such another?*

Anouilh /ˌænu:ˈi:/ Jean (1910-87), French playwright whose best-known works include *Becket* (about the conflict between *Henry II and Thomas *Becket), *Antigone* and *The Waltz of the Toreadors.*

ans *abbr* answer.

Anschluss /ˈænʃlʊs; *US* ˈɑ:nʃlʊs/ **the Anschluss** [sing] (*German*) the German take-over of Austria in 1938.

Anselm /ˈænselm/ Saint (c1030-1109), Italian-born philosopher and theologian who became Archbishop of Canterbury in 1093. He was later exiled after disagreements with *Henry I.

answer[1] /ˈɑ:nsə(r); *US* ˈænsər/ *n* ~ **(to sb/sth) 1** thing said, written or done as a response or reaction; reply: *The answer he gave was quite surprising.* ○ *Have you had an answer to your letter?* ○ *I rang the bell but there was no answer.* **2** solution to a problem, difficulty, etc: *This could be the answer to all our problems.* ○ *Who knows the answer to this question?* ○ *The answer to 3 x 17 is 51.* **3** (idm) **a dusty answer** ⇨ DUSTY. **have/know all the answers** (*often derog*) know a great deal about sth: *He thinks he knows all the answers.* **in answer (to sth)** as a reply: *The doctor came at once in answer to my phone call.*

answer[2] /ˈɑ:nsə(r); *US* ˈænsər/ *v* **1** [I, Tn, Tf, Dn·n] say, write or do sth in response to (sb/sth): *Think carefully before you answer.* ○ *answer the question, the teacher, the invitation* ○ *answer the door*, ie open the door after sb has knocked or rung the bell ○ *answer the telephone*, ie pick up the receiver and speak to the person who is calling ○ *My prayers have been answered*, ie I have got what I wanted. ○ *Nobody answered my call for help.* ○ (*fml*) *How do you answer the charge?* ○ *She answered that she preferred to eat alone.* ○ *Can you answer me this?* Cf REPLY. **2** [Tn] be suitable for (sth); satisfy: *answer sb's purpose/needs/requirements.* **3** (idm) **answer to the description (of sb/sth)** correspond to or match the description (of sb/sth): *The photograph answers to the description of the wanted man.* **answer to the name of sth** (*infml or joc*) (esp of a pet animal) have the name of sth; be called sth: *My dog answers to the name of Spot.* **4** (phr v) **answer back** defend oneself against sth written or said about one: *It's wrong of the press to publish articles attacking the Queen when she can't answer back.* **answer (sb) back** speak rudely or cheekily (to sb), esp when being criticized oneself: *He's a rude little boy, always answering his mother back.* **answer for sb/sth (a)** be responsible for or blamed for sth: *He has a lot to answer for.* ○ *You will have to answer for your crimes one day.* **(b)** speak on behalf of sb or in support of sth: *I agree but I can't answer for my colleagues.* ○ *Knowing her well I can certainly answer for her honesty*, ie can guarantee that she is honest. **answer to sb (for sth)** be responsible to sb: *Who do you answer to in your new job?* ○ *You will answer to me for any damage to the car.* **answer to sth** be controlled by sth: *The plane answered smoothly to the controls.*

▷ **answerable** /ˈɑ:nsərəbl/ *adj* **1** that can be answered. **2** [pred] ~ **to sb (for sth)** responsible to sb: *I am answerable to the company for the use of this equipment.*

answerphone /ˈɑ:nsəfəʊn; *US* ˈæns-/ *n* (also **answering machine**) device that automatically answers telephone calls and records any message left by the caller.

ant /ænt/ *n* **1** small insect that lives in highly organized social groups. Within these groups there are different types of ant, each with special duties, eg fertile females (queens), winged males and wingless sterile female workers. There are over 10 000 species of ants. **2** (idm) **have ants in one's pants** (*infml*) be very restless or excited about sth.

□ **ˈant-eater** *n* any of various types of animal that feed on ants and termites.

ˈanthill *n* mound of earth, etc formed by ants over their nest.

-ant, -ent *suff* **1** (with *vs* forming *adjs*) that is or does (sth): *significant* ○ *different.* **2** (with *vs* forming *ns*) person or thing that: *inhabitant* ○ *deterrent.*

antacid /æntˈæsɪd/ *n* [C, U], *adj* (substance) that prevents or reduces acidity in the stomach: *I need an/some antacid to cure my indigestion.*

antagonism /ænˈtægənɪzəm/ *n* [C, U] ~ **(against/for/to/towards sb/sth);** ~ **(between A and B)** (instance of) active opposition or hostility, esp between two people: *The antagonism he felt towards his old enemy was still very strong.* ○ *You could sense the antagonism between them.*

antagonist /ænˈtægənɪst/ *n* person who actively opposes sb/sth; adversary.

antagonistic /ænˌtægəˈnɪstɪk/ *adj* ~ **(to/towards sb/sth)** showing or feeling antagonism; hostile: *He's always antagonistic towards new ideas.* ▷ **antagonistically** /-klɪ/ *adv.*

antagonize, -ise /ænˈtægənaɪz/ *v* [Tn] arouse hostility in (sb); annoy: *It would be dangerous to antagonize him.*

Antarctic /ænˈtɑ:ktɪk/ *adj* of the regions around the South Pole. ⇨ illus at GLOBE.

Antarctica

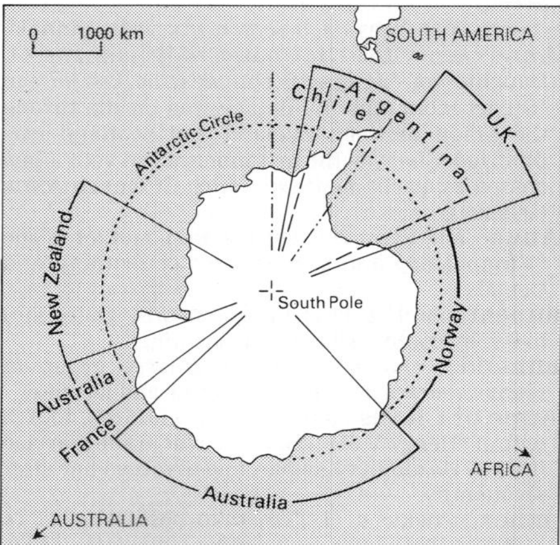

▷ **the Antarctic** *n* [sing] the regions around the South Pole.
□ **the Antarctic ˈCircle** the line of latitude 66° 30′ S. ⇨ illus at GLOBE.

Antarctica /ænˈtɑːktɪkə/ continent round the South Pole, situated mainly within the Antarctic Circle and almost entirely covered by ice. Beneath the ice are large mineral deposits (eg iron, coal and oil). Parts of it are claimed by Britain, France, Australia, New Zealand and Norway, but there is no permanent human population. Its use and the exploitation of its resources are strictly controlled by international treaty. ⇨ map.

ante /ˈæntɪ/ *n* stake in poker², etc that a player must make before receiving new cards: *raise/up the ante*, ie increase one's stake.
▷ **ante** *v* **1** [Tn] make (sth) as an ante. **2** (phr v) **ante up** (*esp US*) make a stake or payment.

ante- *pref* (with *ns, adjs* and *vs*) (of time or position) before; in front of: *ante-room* ○ *antenatal* ○ *antedate*. Cf POST-, PRE-.

ante-bellum /ˌæntɪˈbeləm/ *adj* [usu attrib] of the period before a war, esp the *American Civil War: *a fine ante-bellum mansion.*

antecedent /ˌæntɪˈsiːdnt/ *n* **1** [C] (*fml*) thing or circumstance that is or comes before another. **2** [C] (*grammar*) word or phrase to which a following word, esp a relative pronoun, refers: *'Which proves I'm right' is not clear unless we know the antecedent of 'which'.* **3 antecedents** [pl] person's ancestors or past life.
▷ **antecedence** *n* [U] (*fml*) priority.
antecedent *adj* ~ **(to sb/sth)** (*fml*) previous.

antechamber /ˈæntɪtʃeɪmbə(r)/ *n* (*fml*) = ANTE-ROOM.

antedate /ˌæntɪˈdeɪt/ (also **pre-date**) *v* [Tn] **1** put an earlier date on (a document, letter, etc) than the one at the time of writing: *an antedated cheque.* **2** be before (sth/sb) in time: *This event antedates the discovery of America by several centuries.* Cf POST-DATE.

antediluvian /ˌæntɪdɪˈluːvɪən/ *adj* **1** of the time before Noah's Flood. **2** (*infml or joc*) completely out of date; old-fashioned: *His ideas are positively antediluvian!*

antelope /ˈæntɪləʊp/ *n* (*pl* unchanged or ~**s**) any of various types of animal resembling a deer, with thin legs and able to run very fast, found esp in Africa.

antenatal /ˌæntɪˈneɪtl/ *adj* [usu attrib] **(a)** existing or occurring before birth; pre-natal: *Antenatal complications can affect a baby's health.* **(b)** for pregnant women: *antenatal clinics.* Cf POSTNATAL.
▷ **antenatal** *n* medical examination of a pregnant woman.

antenna /ænˈtenə/ *n* **1** (*pl* **-nae** /-niː/) either of a pair of flexible sensitive organs on the heads of insects, crustaceans, etc; feeler. ⇨ illus at BUTTERFLY. **2** (*pl* ~**s**) (*US*) = AERIAL¹.

antepenultimate /ˌæntɪpɪˈnʌltɪmət/ *adj* third from last: *The main stress in 'photography' falls on the antepenultimate syllable.*

anterior /ænˈtɪərɪə(r)/ *adj* [usu attrib] (*fml*) coming before in position or time; nearer the front. Cf POSTERIOR.

ante-room /ˈæntɪrʊm, -ruːm/ (also **antechamber**) *n* room leading into a larger or more important room; waiting-room.

anthelion /æntˈhiːlɪən, ænˈθiːlɪən/ (*pl* ~**s** or ~**ia** /-lɪə/) shiny white spot sometimes seen in the sky opposite the sun, eg against a patch of cloud.

anthem /ˈænθəm/ *n* **1** short musical composition, usu for a choir and an organ, to be sung in religious services, often with words taken from the Bible. Cf MOTET. **2** = NATIONAL ANTHEM (NATIONAL).

anther /ˈænθə(r)/ *n* (*botany*) part of the stamen of a flower that contains the pollen.

anthology /ænˈθɒlədʒɪ/ *n* collection of poems or pieces of prose on the same subject or by the same writer: *an anthology of love poetry.*
▷ **anthologist** /ænˈθɒlədʒɪst/ *n* person who compiles an anthology.

anthracite /ˈænθrəsaɪt/ *n* [U] very hard form of coal that burns with little smoke or flame.

anthrax /ˈænθræks/ *n* [U] infectious, often fatal, disease of sheep and cattle that can be transmitted to people.

anthrop(o)- *comb form* of human beings: *anthropomorphic* ○ *anthropology.*

anthropoid /ˈænθrəpɔɪd/ *adj* man-like in form: *anthropoid ancestors of modern man.*
▷ **anthropoid** *n* any of a group of apes that have no tails and resemble man, eg the chimpanzee or the gorilla.

anthropology /ˌænθrəˈpɒlədʒɪ/ *n* [U] study of mankind, esp of its origins, development, customs and beliefs. Physical anthropology is the study of the structure and evolution of human beings. Social anthropology is the study of the social organization and cultural systems of human groups. Cf ETHNOLOGY, SOCIOLOGY.
▷ **anthropological** /ˌænθrəpəˈlɒdʒɪkl/ *adj.*
anthropologist /ˌænθrəˈpɒlədʒɪst/ *n* student of or expert in anthropology.

anthropomorphic /ˌænθrəpəˈmɔːfɪk/ *adj* treating gods, animals, etc as human in form and personality. ▷ **anthropomorphism** /ˌænθrəpəˈmɔːfɪzəm/ *n* [U].

anti /ˈæntɪ/ *prep* in opposition to (sb/sth); against: *They're completely anti the new proposals.* Cf PRO¹.

anti- (also **ant-**) *pref* (used widely with *ns* and *adjs*) **1** opposed to; against: *anti-aircraft* ○ *anti-personnel.* Cf PRO-. **2** opposite of: *anti-hero* ○ *anticlimactic.* **3** preventing: *antiseptic* ○ *antifreeze* ○ *antacid.*

NOTE ON USAGE: **Anti-** and **counter-** both have the meaning of 'opposed to'. **Anti-** suggests an attitude of opposition: *anti-war literature* ○ *the anti-nuclear campaign*; while **counter-** refers to an action taken to prevent or respond to something: *counter-espionage activities* ○ *counter-revolution.*

anti-aircraft /ˌæntɪ ˈeəkrɑːft; *US* -kræft/ *adj* designed to destroy enemy aircraft: *anti-aircraft guns, missiles, etc.*

antiballistic missile /ˌæntɪbəlɪstɪk ˈmɪsaɪl; *US* ˈmɪsl/ rocket designed to attack ballistic missiles in the air or in space.

antibiotic /ˌæntɪbaɪˈɒtɪk/ *n, adj* (substance, eg penicillin) that can destroy or prevent the growth of bacteria.

antibody /ˈæntɪbɒdɪ/ *n* protein formed in the blood in response to harmful bacteria, etc, which it then attacks and destroys: *Our bodies produce antibodies to counteract disease.*

antic /ˈæntɪk/ *n* (usu *pl*) absurd or exaggerated movement or behaviour intended to amuse people: *laughing at the clown's silly antics.*

Antichrist /ˈæntɪkraɪst/ great enemy of Christ, who was expected by early Christians to appear just before the end of the world, and to be defeated by Christ.

anticipate /ænˈtɪsɪpeɪt/ *v* **1** [Tn, Tf, Tg, Tsg] expect (sth): *Do you anticipate (meeting) any trouble?* ○ *We anticipate that demand is likely to increase.* **2** [Tn, Tf, Tw] see (what is going to happen or what needs to be done) and act accordingly: *She anticipates all her mother's needs.* ○ *Anticipating that it would soon be dark, they all took torches.* ○ *A good general can anticipate what the enemy will do.* **3** [Tn, Tsg] (*fml*) do (sth) before it can be done by sb else; forestall (sb/sth): *When Scott reached the South Pole he found Amundsen had anticipated him.* ○ *Earlier explorers probably anticipated Columbus's discovery of America.* ○ *We anticipated their (making a) complaint by writing a full report.* **4** [Tn, Tsg] (*fml*) deal with or use (sth) before the right or natural time: *anticipate one's income*, ie spend money before receiving it. ▷ **anticipatory** /ænˌtɪsɪˈpeɪtərɪ/ *adj* (*fml*): *anticipatory precautions.*

anticipation /ænˌtɪsɪˈpeɪʃn/ *n* [U] action or state of anticipating: *A tennis player shows good anticipation by moving quickly into position.* ○ *In anticipation of bad weather they took plenty of warm clothes.*

anticlimax /ˌæntɪˈklaɪmæks/ *n* disappointing end to a series of events which had seemed likely to become more interesting, exciting or impressive: *The holiday itself was rather an anticlimax after all the excitement of planning it.* ▷ **anticlimactic** /ˌæntɪklaɪˈmæktɪk/ *adj* (*fml*).

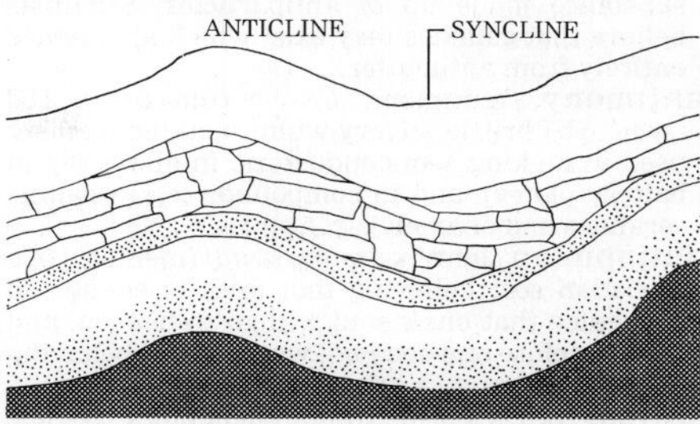

anticline /ˈæntɪklaɪn/ *n* geological structure in which layers of rock are folded into an arch or a dome. ⇨ illus. Cf SYNCLINE.

anticlockwise /ˌæntɪˈklɒkwaɪz/ (also *esp US* **counter-clockwise**) *adv, adj* in the direction opposite to the movements of the hands of a clock: *Turn the key antiˈclockwise/in an ˌanticlockwise diˈrection.* Cf CLOCKWISE (CLOCK¹).

anticoagulant /ˌæntɪkəʊˈægjʊlənt/ *n* [C, U] drug that prevents blood from clotting or slows the rate at which it clots.

anticyclone /ˌæntɪˈsaɪkləʊn/ *n* area in which atmospheric pressure is high, producing fine and settled weather, with an outward flow of air. Cf DEPRESSION.

anti-depressant /ˌæntɪdɪˈpresnt/ *n, adj* (drug) that reduces depression(1): *She's been taking/on anti-depressants since her baby died.*

antidote /ˈæntɪdəʊt/ *n* ~ **(against/for/to sth) 1** substance that acts against the effects of a poison or disease: *an antidote against snake-bites, malaria, food poisoning.* **2** (*fig*) anything that counteracts sth unpleasant: *The holiday was a marvellous antidote to the pressures of office work.*

antifreeze /ˈæntɪfriːz/ *n* [U] substance added to water to lower its freezing point, eg as used in the radiator of a motor vehicle.

antigen /ˈæntɪdʒən/ *n* [U] (*medical*) substance (eg a bacterium) which causes the body to produce antibodies.

Antigone /ænˈtɪgənɪ/ (in Greek mythology) daughter of *Oedipus, who, against the orders of her uncle, buried her dead brother Polynices, after he had led an enemy attack on their city. Her uncle Creon ordered her to be buried alive for this, but she killed herself before the sentence could be carried out.

Antigua and Barbuda /ænˌtiːgə ən bɑːˈbjuːdə/ country, made up of three islands, that is part of the *Leeward Islands in the West Indies; pop approx 85 000; official language English; capital St John's; unit of currency dollar (= 100 cents). The islands gained independence from Britain in 1981. ⇨ map at CARIBBEAN.

anti-hero /ˈæntɪ hɪərəʊ/ *n* (*pl* ~**es**) central character in a story or drama who lacks the qualities usu associated with a hero, such as courage and dignity.

antihistamine /ˌæntɪˈhɪstəmiːn/ *n* [C, U] (*medical*) any of a variety of drugs used to treat allergies (eg hay fever).

antiknock /ˌæntɪˈnɒk/ *n* [U] substance added to motor fuel to prevent or reduce knock²(4) in the engine.

Antilles /ænˈtɪliːz/ **the Antilles** group of islands in the West Indies, consisting of the **Greater Antilles** (Cuba, Jamaica, Hispaniola and Puerto Rico) and the **Lesser Antilles** (including the Virgin Islands, the Leeward Islands and the Windward Islands, Trinidad and Tobago, Barbados and the isles off the coast of *Venezuela). ⇨ map at WEST INDIES.

antilogarithm /ˌæntɪˈlɒgərɪðəm; *US* -ˈlɔːg-/ (also **antilog** /ˈæntɪlɒg; *US* -lɔːg/) *n* (*mathematics*) number to which a logarithm belongs: *1 000, 100 and 10 are the antilogarithms of 3, 2 and 1.*

antimacassar /ˌæntɪməˈkæsə(r)/ *n* cloth put over the back of a chair to keep it clean or as an ornament.

antimatter /ˈæntɪmætə(r)/ *n* [U] hypothetical substance made up of antiparticles. Scientists believe that galaxies may exist which are formed entirely from antimatter.

antimony /ˈæntɪmənɪ; *US* ˈæntɪməʊnɪ/ *n* [U] (*symb* **Sb**) brittle silvery-white metallic element used in making semiconductors, in alloys (eg in battery plates), and in compounds (eg in paints, ceramics and enamels). ⇨ App 11.

antinomian /ˌæntɪˈnəʊmɪən/ *n, adj* (member) of a Christian sect believing that faith is enough to guarantee that one's soul will go to heaven, and that therefore one need not worry about behaving in a moral way. ▷ **antinomianism** *n* [U].

antiparticle /ˈæntɪpɑ:tɪkl/ *n* elementary particle that has the same mass as an ordinary electron, proton, etc but an opposite electric charge or magnetic movement.

antipathy /ænˈtɪpəθɪ/ *n* ~ (**to/towards/against sb/sth**); ~ (**between A and B**) (**a**) [U] strong or deep dislike: *She felt no antipathy towards younger women.* (**b**) [C] instance or object of this: *He showed a marked antipathy to foreigners.*
▷ **antipathetic** /ˌæntɪpəˈθetɪk/ *adj* ~ (**to/towards sb/sth**) showing or feeling antipathy.

anti-personnel /ˌæntɪ ˌpɜ:səˈnel/ *adj* (of bombs, explosives, etc) designed to kill or injure people, not to destroy property, vehicles, etc.

antiperspirant /ˌæntɪˈpɜ:spərənt/ *n* [C, U] substance that prevents or reduces perspiration, esp under the arms.

antiphon /ˈæntɪfən, -fɒn/ *n* hymn in which short verses or phrases are sung alternately by two sections of a choir.
▷ **antiphonal** /ænˈtɪfənl/ *adj* sung or played alternately, like an antiphon. **antiphonally** *adv* /-fənəlɪ/.

antipodes /ænˈtɪpədi:z/ *n* [pl] **1** places on opposite sides of the earth to each other. **2 the Antipodes** the Australasian regions in relation to Europe.

antipyretic /ˌæntɪpaɪˈretɪk/ *n, adj* (drug) that relieves or reduces fever.

antiquarian /ˌæntɪˈkweərɪən/ *adj* [usu attrib] of, for or concerning the study, collection or sale of antiques, esp old or rare books: *an antiquarian bookseller.*
▷ **antiquarian** *n* = ANTIQUARY.

antiquary /ˈæntɪkwərɪ; *US* ˈæntɪkwerɪ/ (also **antiquarian**) *n* person who studies, collects or sells antiques.

antiquated /ˈæntɪkweɪtɪd/ *adj* **1** (*usu derog*) (of things) out of date, obsolete. **2** (of people, ideas, etc) old-fashioned.

antique /ænˈti:k/ *adj* **1** (**a**) belonging to the distant past, esp ancient Greek and Roman times. (**b**) existing since old times. **2** valuable because of age and rarity. ⇨ Usage at OLD.
▷ **antique** *n* object, eg a piece of furniture or a work of art, that is old and valuable, esp one that is of interest to collectors: [attrib] *an antique shop*, ie one that sells antiques.

antiquity /ænˈtɪkwətɪ/ *n* **1** [U] ancient times, esp before the Middle Ages: *the heroes of antiquity.* **2** [U] great age: *Athens is a city of great antiquity.* **3** [C usu *pl*] object that dates from ancient times: *a museum full of Greek and Roman antiquities*, eg coins, pottery, sculptures.

antirrhinum /ˌæntɪˈraɪnəm/ (also **snapdragon**) *n* (*botany*) type of garden flower with bag-shaped petals which open when pressed.

antiscorbutic /ˌæntɪskɔ:ˈbju:tɪk/ *n, adj* (drug, etc) that prevents or cures scurvy.

anti-Semite /ˌæntɪ ˈsi:maɪt; *US* ˈsem-/ *n* person who hates Jews. ▷ **anti-Semitic** /ˌæntɪ sɪˈmɪtɪk/ *adj*. **anti-Semitism** /ˌæntɪ ˈsemɪtɪzəm/ *n* [U].

antiseptic /ˌæntɪˈseptɪk/ *n* [C, U] substance that destroys harmful micro-organisms, esp bacteria, or prevents their growth. Antiseptics are used to treat minor wounds: *Have you got any antiseptic for this cut?*
▷ **antiseptic** *adj* **1** preventing infection by destroying bacteria. **2** thoroughly clean and free from bacteria: *an ˌantiseptic ˈbandage.*

antiserum /ˈæntɪsɪərəm/ *n* (*pl* **-ra** /-rə/ or ~**s**) [C, U] blood serum containing antibodies, injected to treat specific diseases.

antisocial /ˌæntɪˈsəʊʃl/ *adj* **1** opposed or harmful to the laws and customs of an organized community: *It is antisocial to leave one's litter in public places.* **2** avoiding the company of others; unsociable: *ˌantisocial beˈhaviour* ○ *It's rather antisocial of you not to come to the party.*

antistatic /ˌæntɪˈstætɪk/ *adj* [usu attrib] that reduces the effects of static electricity: *ˌantistatic ˈfluid.*

antistrophe /ænˈtɪstrəfɪ/ *n* second of three parts of a choral ode sung by the chorus in ancient Greek drama. Cf EPODE, STROPHE.

anti-tank /ˌæntɪˈtæŋk/ *adj* [attrib] designed to destroy enemy tanks: *ˌanti-tank ˈmissiles.*

antithesis /ænˈtɪθəsɪs/ *n* (*pl* **-ses** /ænˈtɪθəsi:z/) **1** (**a**) [C usu *sing*] ~ (**of/to sth/sb**) direct opposite: *Slavery is the antithesis of freedom.* (**b**) [U] ~ (**of sth to sth**); ~ (**between A and B**) contrast; opposition: *The style of his speech was in complete antithesis to mine.* **2** [C, U] contrast of ideas marked by the choice and arrangement of words: *'Give me liberty, or give me death' is an example of antithesis.* ▷ **antithetic** /ˌæntɪˈθetɪk/, **antithetical** /-ɪkl/ *adjs*. **antithetically** /-klɪ/ *adv*.

antitoxin /ˌæntɪˈtɒksɪn/ *n* [C, U] substance that acts against a poisonous substance and prevents it from having a harmful effect.

anti-trust /ˌæntɪˈtrʌst/ *adj* [attrib] (*US*) (of a law) intended to control or remove monopolies or unfair trading practices which restrict free competition between businesses.

antler /ˈæntlə(r)/ *n* branched horn of a stag or of some other deer: *a fine pair of antlers.* ⇨ illus at DEER. ▷ **antlered** *adj*.

Antonine Wall /ˌæntənaɪn ˈwɔ:l/ **the Antonine Wall** Roman wall about 59 km (37 miles) long across southern Scotland. It was built about 140 AD for the Roman emperor Antoninus Pius, to mark the northern frontier of the Roman province of Britain and as a defence against the northern tribes.

Antonioni /ˌæntəʊnɪˈəʊnɪ/ Michelangelo (1912-), Italian film director. In films like *L'avventura* and *Blow-up* (in English) he examines the suffocation of human emotion and communication by the modern world.

antonym /ˈæntənɪm/ *n* word that is opposite in meaning to another: *'Old' has two possible antonyms: 'young' and 'new'.* Cf SYNONYM.

anus /ˈeɪnəs/ *n* (*pl* ~**es**) (*anatomy*) opening at the end of the alimentary canal, through which waste matter passes out of the body. ⇨ illus at DIGESTIVE SYSTEM. ▷ **anal** /ˈeɪnl/ *adj*.

anvil /ˈænvɪl/ *n* **1** iron block on which a smith shapes heated metal by hammering it. **2** (*anatomy*) one of the bones in the ear. ⇨ illus at EAR.

anxiety /æŋˈzaɪətɪ/ *n* **1** (**a**) [U] troubled feeling in the mind caused by fear and uncertainty about the future: *We waited for news with a growing sense of anxiety.* ○ *He caused his parents great anxiety by cycling long distances alone.* (**b**) [C] instance of such a feeling: *The anxieties of the past week had left her exhausted.* ○ *The doctor's report removed all their anxieties.* **2** [U] ~ **for sth/to do sth** strong desire or eagerness for sth/to do sth: *anxiety to please.*

anxious /ˈæŋkʃəs/ *adj* **1** ~ (**about/for sb/sth**) feeling anxiety; worried; uneasy: *an anxious mother* ○ *I am very anxious about my son's health.* ○ *He was anxious for his family, who were travelling abroad.* **2** [attrib] causing anxiety: *We had a few anxious moments before landing safely.* **3** ~ **for sth/(for sb) to do sth/that...** strongly wishing sth; eager for sth: *anxious for their safety* ○ *anxious to meet you/for his brother to meet you* ○ *They were anxious that aid should be sent promptly.* ▷ **anxiously** *adv*.

any[1] /ˈenɪ/ *indef det* **1** (used in negative sentences and in questions; after *if/whether*; after *hardly, never, without*, etc; and after such *vs* as *prevent, ban, avoid, forbid*) (**a**) (used with [U] *ns*) an unspecified amount of: *I didn't eat any meat.* ○ *Do you know any French?* ○ *There was hardly any free time.* ○ *We did the job without any difficulty.* ○ *To avoid any delay please phone your order direct.* ○ *It didn't seem to be any distance* (ie It seemed a very short distance) *to the road.* (**b**) (used with plural [C] *ns*) an unspecified number of (people or things): *I haven't read any books by Tolstoy.* ○ *Are there any stamps in that drawer?* ○ *I wonder whether Mr Black has any roses in his garden?* ○ *You can't go out without any shoes.* ○ *They bought a dog to prevent any burglaries.* Cf SOME[1]. **2** (**a**) (used with singular [C] *ns*) one out of a number, (the particular choice being unimportant): *Take any book you like.* ○ *Give me a pen — any pen will do.* ○ *Phone me any day next week.* (**b**) (used with singular [C] *ns* in negative sentences or sentences implying doubt or negation; also used after *if, whether*) a; one: *Hasn't it got any tail?* ○ *I can't see any door in this room.* **3** every; no matter which: *Any fool could tell you that.* ○ *You'll find me here at any hour of the day.* ○ *Any train from this platform stops at Gatwick.* ○ *They want any money you can spare.* **4** (used in negative sentences and after *if, whether*) a normal; an ordinary: *This isn't any old bed — it belonged to Shakespeare.* ○ *If it were any ordinary paint you would need two coats.* ○ *She isn't just any woman — she's the Queen.*
□ **ˈany time** whatever time you like: *Come round any time.*

any[2] /ˈenɪ/ *indef pron* **1** (used in negative sentences and in questions; after *if/whether*; and after *hardly, never, without*, etc) an unspecified amount or number. (**a**) (referring back): *I can't give you any.* ○ *Have you got any?* (**b**) (referring forward): *She didn't spend any of the money.* ○ *If he had read any of those books he would have known the answer.* ○ *He returned home without any of the others.* **2** one single example: *If you recognize ˈany of the people in the photograph, tell us.* Cf SOME[3]. **3** (idm) **sb isn't ˈhaving any** (*infml*) sb isn't interested or does not agree: *I tried to get her to talk about her divorce but she wasn't having any.*

any[3] /ˈenɪ/ *indef adv* (used with *faster, slower, better*, etc, in questions and after *if, whether*) to any degree; at all: *I can't run any faster.* ○ *Is your father any better at all?* ○ *If it were any further we wouldn't be able to get there.* ○ *I can't afford to spend any more on food.* ○ *The children didn't behave any too well*, ie They behaved rather badly.
□ **any ˈmore** (*US* **anymore**) any further; now, or any longer starting from now: *She doesn't live here any more.*

anybody /ˈenɪbɒdɪ/ (also **anyone**) *indef pron* **1** any person: *Did anybody see you?* ○ *Hardly anybody came.* ○ *Anybody who saw the accident should phone the police.* ○ *He left without speaking to anyone else.* **2** one person out of many (the choice being unimportant): *Anybody will tell you where the bus stop is.* ○ *Ask anyone in your class.* **3** (in negative sentences) any person of importance: *She wasn't anybody before she got that job.*

anyhow /ˈenɪhaʊ/ *indef adv* **1** carelessly; unsystematically: *The books were lying on the shelves just/all anyhow.* ○ *He made notes anyhow across the page.* **2** (also **anyway**) whatever the facts may be; in spite of this; at least: *It's too late now, anyhow.* ○ *Anyhow, you can try.*

anyone /ˈenɪwʌn/ *indef pron* = ANYBODY.

anyplace (*US*) = ANYWHERE.

anything /ˈenɪθɪŋ/ *indef pron* **1** any thing: *Did she tell you anything interesting?* ○ *There's never anything worth watching on TV.* ○ *If you remember anything at all, please let us know.* **2** any thing of importance: *Is there anything* (ie any truth) *in these rumours?* **3** something (its exact nature being unimportant): *I'm very hungry — I'll eat anything.* ○ *Anything will do to sleep on.* **4** (idm) **anything but** definitely not: *The hotel was anything but satisfactory.* **anything like sb/sth** (*infml*) in any way similar(ly): *He isn't anything like my first boss.* ○ *The film wasn't anything like as good as ET.* **like ˈanything** (*infml*) very much; very quickly, loudly, successfully, etc: *The thief* *ran like anything when he heard the alarm.* **or anything** (*infml*) (used to refer to similar examples) or another thing similar to that mentioned: *If you want to call a meeting or anything, put up a notice.*

anyway /ˈeniweɪ/ *indef adv* = ANYHOW 2.

anywhere /ˈeniweə(r); *US* -hweər/ (*US* also **anyplace**) *indef adv* **1** in, at or to any place: *I can't see it anywhere.* ○ *If you want to go anywhere else, let me know.* **2** one place out of many (the choice being unimportant): *Put the box down anywhere.* ○ *We can go anywhere you like.*

▷ **anywhere** *indef pron* any place: *I haven't anywhere to stay.* ○ *Do you know anywhere (where) I can buy a second-hand typewriter?*

Anzac /ˈænzæk/ *n* **1** soldier in the Australian and New Zealand Army Corps, which fought during the First World War in Europe and the Middle East. **2** any Australian or New Zealand soldier.

□ ˈ**Anzac Day** 25 April, the day in Australia and New Zealand when the dead of both world wars are remembered, commemorating the landing of the Anzacs in *Gallipoli in 1915.

aorist /ˈeərɪst/ *n* **(a) the aorist** [sing] past tense of the verb in certain languages, esp ancient Greek, which does not distinguish between completed and continuous actions. **(b)** [C] verb in this tense.

aorta /eɪˈɔːtə/ *n* main artery through which blood is carried from the left side of the heart. ⇨ illus at HEART.

apace /əˈpeɪs/ *adv* (*dated or rhet*) quickly: *Work is proceeding apace.*

Apache /əˈpætʃɪ/ *n* (*pl* unchanged or ~**s**) member of a N American Indian people of the south-western USA. The Apache were, in the late 19th century, the last American Indian group to be conquered by the US cavalry. They now live on reservations in Arizona: [attrib] *Apache warriors.*

apart /əˈpɑːt/ *adv* **1** to or at a distance: *The two houses stood 500 metres apart.* ○ *The employers and the unions are still miles apart,* ie are far from agreement. **2** to or on one side; aside: *She keeps herself apart from* (ie does not mix with) *other people.* **3** separate(ly): *You never see them apart these days.* ○ *He was standing with his feet wide apart.* ○ *These pages are stuck together — I can't pull them apart.* **4** into pieces: *I'm sorry, the cup just came/fell apart in my hands.* **5** (idm) **be poles apart** ⇨ POLE[1]. **joking apart** ⇨ JOKE. **put/set sb/sth apart (from sb/sth)** make sb/sth appear superior or unique: *His use of language sets him apart from most other modern writers.* **a race apart** ⇨ RACE. **take sb/sth apart** criticize sb/sth severely: *He took my essay apart but I found his criticism helpful.* **take sth apart** separate sth into pieces: *John enjoys taking old clocks apart.* **tell/know A and B apart** distinguish two people or things; recognize the difference between two people or things. **worlds apart** ⇨ WORLD.

□ **apart from** (also *esp US* **aside from**) *prep* **1** independently of (sth); except for: *Apart from his nose (Cf His nose apart) he's quite good-looking.* **2** in addition to (sth): *Apart from the injuries to his face and hands, he broke both legs.*

apartheid /əˈpɑːthaɪt, -heɪt/ *n* [U] (in S Africa) (official government policy of) racial segregation, separating whites and non-whites.

apartment /əˈpɑːtmənt/ *n* (*abbr* **apt**) **1** (*US*) = FLAT[1]. **2** set of rooms, usu furnished and rented, esp for a holiday. **3** (often *pl*) single room in a house, esp a large or famous one: *You can visit the whole palace except for the private apartments.*

□ **aˈpartment block** (*Brit*) (*US* **aˈpartment house**) block of flats.

apathy /ˈæpəθɪ/ *n* [U] ~ (**towards sb/sth**) lack of interest, enthusiasm or concern; indifference: *Extreme poverty had reduced them to a state of apathy.*

▷ **apathetic** /ˌæpəˈθetɪk/ *adj* showing or feeling apathy. **apathetically** /-klɪ/ *adv.*

apatite /ˈæpətaɪt/ *n* [U] mineral consisting mainly of calcium and phosphorus. It is found in limestone and igneous rocks and is used in fertilizers. The enamel of teeth is composed mainly of apatite.

apes

ape /eɪp/ *n* **1** any of the four (usu tailless) primates (gorilla, chimpanzee, orang-utan, gibbon) most closely related to man. ⇨ illus. **2** (idm) **go ape** (*sl*) start behaving crazily.

▷ **ape** *v* [Tn] imitate (sb/sth); mimic.

□ ˈ**ape-man** *n* extinct creature intermediate between ape and man.

Apennines /ˈæpənaɪnz/ **the Apennines** [pl] mountain range, extending from NW Italy to the southern tip of the country.

aperient /əˈpɪərɪənt/ *n* [C, U], *adj* (*fml*) (medicine that is) laxative.

aperiodic /ˌeɪˌpɪərɪˈɒdɪk/ *adj* **1** (*fml*) not occurring regularly. **2** (*physics*) not having regular vibrations or oscillations (eg of an instrument with a pointer).

aperitif /əˈperətɪf; *US* əˌperəˈtiːf/ *n* alcoholic drink taken as an appetizer before a meal.

aperture /ˈæpətʃə(r)/ *n* **1** narrow opening. **2** (size of an) adjustable opening for letting light into a camera or some other optical instrument: *What aperture are you using?*

Apex (also **APEX**) /ˈeɪpeks/ *abbr* Advance Purchase Excursion, a system of cheap air fares for reservations made a specified time in advance: [attrib] *APEX fares.*

apex /ˈeɪpeks/ *n* (*pl* ~**es** or **apices** /ˈeɪpɪsiːz/) top or highest point: *the apex of a triangle* ○ (*fig*) *At 41 he'd reached the apex of his career.*

aphasia /əˈfeɪzɪə; *US* -ʒə/ *n* [U] (*medical*) partial or total loss of ability to speak or understand spoken language, caused by damage to the brain.

▷ **aphasic** *n, adj* (person) suffering from aphasia.

aphelion /æˈfiːlɪən, æpˈhiːlɪən/ *n* (*pl* **-ia**) point in the orbit of a planet, comet, etc when it is furthest from the sun. Cf PERIHELION.

aphid /ˈeɪfɪd/ *n* very small insect that sucks the juices from plants, harming them.

aphis /ˈeɪfɪs/ *n* (*pl* **aphides** /ˈeɪfɪdiːz/) aphid, esp greenfly.

aphorism /ˈæfərɪzəm/ *n* short wise saying; maxim.

▷ **aphoristic** /ˌæfəˈrɪstɪk/ *adj.*

aphrodisiac /ˌæfrəˈdɪzɪæk/ *n* [C, U], *adj* (substance or drug) arousing sexual desire.

Aphrodite /ˌæfrəˈdaɪtɪ/ (in Greek mythology) goddess of beauty, fertility and sexual love. According to one legend, she was born from the foam of the sea. Her Roman equivalent was *Venus.

apiary /ˈeɪpɪərɪ; *US* -ɪerɪ/ *n* place with a number of hives where bees are kept.

▷ **apiarist** /ˈeɪpɪərɪst/ *n* person who keeps bees.

apiece /əˈpiːs/ *adv* to, for or by each one of a group: *three cakes apiece* ○ *costing 50p apiece* ○ *We wrote it together, a page apiece.*

apish /ˈeɪpɪʃ/ *adj* (*usu derog*) **1** of or like an ape; stupid. **2** imitating sb in a foolish way: *His apish devotion irritated her.*

aplasia /əˈpleɪzɪə; *US* ˌeɪˈpleɪʒə/ *n* [U] (*medical*) partial or complete failure of a bodily organ or area of tissue to develop.

aplomb /əˈplɒm/ *n* [U] confidence and self-control; poise: *She performs the duties of a princess with great aplomb.*

apnoea (*US* also **apnea**) /æpˈniːə, ˈæpnɪə/ *n* [U] (*medical*) temporary stopping of breathing.

apocalypse /əˈpɒkəlɪps/ *n* **1** [C] (usu *sing*) future event of great significance or violence, esp the end of the world. **2 the Apocalypse** [sing] = REVELATION (REVELATION 3).

▷ **apocalyptic** /əˌpɒkəˈlɪptɪk/ *adj* prophesying great and dramatic events, as at the end of the world. **apocalyptically** /-klɪ/ *adv.*

Apocrypha /əˈpɒkrɪfə/ *n* **the Apocrypha** [sing *v*] those books of the Old Testament that were not accepted by Jews as part of the Hebrew Scriptures and were not included in the Protestant Bible at the *Reformation. They are accepted by the Roman Catholic Church. They were written between about 300 BC and 100 AD and are valuable as showing beliefs of the period when Christianity was not fully separated from Judaism. ⇨ App 5.

▷ **apocryphal** /əˈpɒkrɪfl/ *adj* not likely to be genuine; untrue or invented: *Most of the stories about his private life are probably apocryphal.*

apogee /ˈæpədʒiː/ *n* **1** (*astronomy*) position in the orbit of the moon, a planet or a satellite when it is at its greatest distance from the earth. **2** (*fig*) highest or furthest point; climax.

apolitical /ˌeɪpəˈlɪtɪkl/ *adj* not interested or involved in politics.

Apollo /əˈpɒləʊ/ **1** (in Greek mythology) god of the sun, music, poetry, archery, prophecy, medicine and the care of animals. The son of *Zeus, Apollo is often shown in art as the ideal type of manly beauty. **2** US programme to land men on the moon. It was announced by President *Kennedy in 1961 and achieved its aim in the Apollo 11 mission on 20 July 1969.

apologetic /əˌpɒləˈdʒetɪk/ *adj* ~ (**about/for sth**) feeling or expressing regret; making an apology: *an apologetic letter, voice* ○ *He was deeply apologetic about his late arrival.*

▷ **apologetically** /-klɪ/ *adv.*

apologetics *n* [sing *v*] art or practice of defending ideas or beliefs (esp those of Christianity) by logical argument. Cf APOLOGY 2.

apologist /əˈpɒlədʒɪst/ *n* person who defends a doctrine by logical argument.

apologize, -ise /əˈpɒlədʒaɪz/ *v* [I, Ipr] ~ (**to sb**) (**for sth**) make an apology; say one is sorry: *I must apologize for not being able to meet you.* ○ *Apologize to your sister!*

apology /əˈpɒlədʒɪ/ *n* **1** ~ (**to sb**) (**for sth**) statement to say one is sorry for having done wrong or hurt sb's feelings: *offer/make/accept an apology* ○ *I made my apologies (to my host) and left early.* **2** (*fml*) explanation or defence (of beliefs, etc). Cf APOLOGETICS (APOLOGETIC). **3** (idm) **an apology for sth** inferior type of sth; poor replacement: *Please excuse this wretched apology for a meal.*

apophthegm (also **apothegm**) /ˈæpəθem/ *n* short forceful saying expressing a general principle; maxim.

apoplexy /ˈæpəpleksɪ/ *n* [U] sudden inability to feel or move, caused by the blockage or rupture of an artery in the brain. Cf STROKE[1] 7.

▷ **apoplectic** /ˌæpəˈplektɪk/ *adj* **1** of or suffering from apoplexy: *an apoplectic stroke/fit.* **2** (*infml*) red in the face; easily made angry; very angry: *apoplectic with fury.*

apostasy /əˈpɒstəsɪ/ *n* **(a)** [U] abandoning one's religious beliefs, principles, political party, etc. **(b)** [C] instance of this.

▷ **apostate** /əˈpɒsteɪt/ *n* person who renounces his former beliefs, etc.

a posteriori /ˌeɪ ˌpɒsterɪˈɔːraɪ/ (using reasoning that proceeds) from known facts to probable causes, eg saying *'The boys are very tired so they must have walked a long way.'* Cf A PRIORI.

apostle /əˈpɒsl/ *n* **1** (also **Apostle**) any of the twelve men sent out by Christ to spread his teaching: Saints Peter, Andrew, James, John, Philip, Bartholomew, Thomas, Matthew, James (the Less), Thaddaeus, Simon and Judas Iscariot. After the suicide of Judas, his place was taken by Matthias. Paul and Barnabas were also described as apostles. **2** leader or teacher of a new faith or movement.

▷ **apostolic** /ˌæpəˈstɒlɪk/ *adj* **1** of the Apostles or their teaching. **2** of the Pope. **the ˌApostolic ˈFathers** the Christian writers in the period immediately following the Apostles. **ˌapostolic sucˈcession** the passing of spiritual authority from the Apostles through successive popes and other bishops.

□ **the AˌpostlesˈˈCreed** statement of Christian belief used in the Western Church, dating from the 4th century AD, and believed, according to ancient tradition, to have been written by the Apostles. **aˈpostle spoon** spoon with a figure of an apostle on the handle.

apostrophe[1] /əˈpɒstrəfɪ/ *n* sign (') used to show that one or more letters or numbers have been omitted (as in *can't* for *cannot*, *I'm* for *I am*, *'76* for *1976*, etc), the possessive form of nouns (as in *the boy's*/*boys'* meaning *of the boy*/*boys*), and the plural of letters (as in *There are two l's in 'bell'*). ⇨ App 14.

apostrophe[2] /əˈpɒstrəfɪ/ *n* (*fml*) passage in a public speech, poem, etc addressed to a person (often dead or absent) or to a thing as if it were a person (eg Wordsworth's 'Milton! thou shouldst be living at this hour').

▷ **apostrophize, -ise** /əˈpɒstrəfaɪz/ *v* [Tn] (*fml*) make an apostrophe to (sb/sth).

apothecary /əˈpɒθəkərɪ; *US* -kerɪ/ *n* (*arch*) person who prepares and sells medicines and medical goods.

□ **apothecaries' weight** system of units formerly used in weighing drugs.

apothegm = APOPHTHEGM.

apotheosis /əˌpɒθɪˈəʊsɪs/ *n* (*pl* **-ses** /-siːz/) **1** (of a human being) making or becoming a god or a saint: *the apotheosis of a Roman Emperor.* **2** glorified ideal; highest development of sth: *The legends of King Arthur represent the apotheosis of chivalry.*

appal (*US* also **appall**) /əˈpɔːl/ *v* (**-ll-**) [Tn] fill (sb) with horror or dismay; shock deeply: *The newspaper reports of starving children appalled me.* ○ *We were appalled at the prospect of having to miss our holiday.*

▷ **appalling** *adj* (*infml*) shocking; extremely bad: *I've never seen such appalling behaviour.* ○ *I find much modern architecture quite appalling.* **appallingly** *adv*: *appallingly thin.*

Appalachian Mountains /ˌæpəˌleɪʃn ˈmaʊntɪnz/ **the Appalachian Mountains** (also **the Appalachians**) range of mountains in eastern N America, extending south-west from Quebec in Canada to Alabama in the USA. The highest peak is Mount Mitchell, 2 038 m (6 684 ft).

appanage (also **apanage**) /ˈæpənɪdʒ/ *n* land, money, etc granted by a king or queen to a member of the royal family: *The Duchy of Cornwall is one of the appanages of the British Crown.*

apparatchik /ˌæpəˈrɑːtʃɪk/ *n* (*pl* **~s** or **~i**) (*Russian*) **1** member of the administrative bureaucracy of the Communist Party in the USSR and other countries. **2** bureaucrat in any organization.

apparatus /ˌæpəˈreɪtəs; *US* -ˈrætəs/ *n* [U, C] (*rare pl* **~es**) **1** (**a**) set of instruments, etc used esp in scientific experiments: *laboratory apparatus.* (**b**) equipment used for doing sth, esp in gymnastics: *The vaulting horse is a difficult piece of apparatus to master.* ○ *Firemen needed breathing apparatus to enter the burning house.* ⇨ Usage at MACHINE. **2** complex structure of an organization: *the whole apparatus of government.* **3** system of bodily organs: *the respiratory apparatus.*

apparel /əˈpærəl/ *n* [U] (*dated or fml*) clothing; dress: *lords and ladies in rich apparel.*

apparent /əˈpærənt/ *adj* **1** [pred] clearly seen or understood; obvious: *Certain problems were apparent from the outset.* ○ *It became apparent that she was going to die.* ○ *Their motives, as will soon become apparent* (ie as you will soon see), *are completely selfish.* **2** seeming; unreal: *Her apparent indifference made him even more nervous.* ○ *Their affluence is more apparent than real,* ie They are not as rich as they seem to be.

▷ **apparently** *adv* according to appearances; as it seems: *He had apparently escaped by bribing a guard.* ○ *Apparently* (ie I have heard that) *they're getting divorced.*

□ **apˈparent time** (also **solar time**) time as shown on a sundial.

apparition /ˌæpəˈrɪʃn/ *n* **1** (**a**) appearance, esp of sth startling, strange or unexpected. (**b**) person or thing that appears thus: *a weird apparition in fancy dress.* **2** ghost or phantom: *You look as though you've seen an apparition.*

appeal /əˈpiːl/ *v* **1** [Ipr, Dpr·t] **~ to sb** (**for sth**); **~ for sth** make an earnest request: *I am appealing on behalf of the famine victims.* ○ *The police appealed to the crowd not to panic.* **2** [I, Ipr] **~** (**to sb**) be attractive or interesting (to sb): *The idea of camping has never appealed (to me).* ○ *Do these paintings appeal to you?* ○ *Her sense of humour appealed to him enormously.* **3** [I, Ipr] **~** (**to sth**) (**against sth**) (*law*) take a question to a higher court where it can be heard again and a new decision given: *I've decided not to appeal.* ○ *She appealed to the high court against her sentence.* **4** [I, Ipr] **~** (**to sb**) (**for**/**against sth**) (in cricket) ask (the umpire) to declare a batsman out or to give some other decision: *The whole side appealed for a catch.* ○ *The captain appealed against the light,* ie said that the light was not good enough for the game to continue.

▷ **appeal** *n* **1** (**a**) [C] **~** (**to sb**) (**for sth**) earnest request: *an appeal for help, food, extra staff* ○ *a charity appeal.* (**b**) [U] request for help or sympathy: *Her eyes held a look of silent appeal.* **2** [U] attractiveness; interest: *Does jazz hold any appeal for you?* ○ *The new fashion soon lost its appeal.* **3** [C] (*law*) act of appealing (APPEAL 3): *lodge an appeal* ○ *have the right of appeal* ○ [attrib] *an appeal court.* ⇨ article at LAW. **4** [C] (in cricket) act of asking the umpire for a decision.

appealing *adj* **1** attractive; charming: *I don't find small boys very appealing.* ○ *The idea of a holiday abroad is certainly appealing.* **2** causing sb to feel pity or sympathy: *an appealing glance.* **appealingly** *adv.*

appear /əˈpɪə(r)/ *v* **1** [I] (**a**) come into view; become visible: *A ship appeared on the horizon.* ○ *A light appeared at the end of the tunnel.* ○ *A rash has appeared on his body.* (**b**) arrive: *He promised to be here at four o'clock but didn't appear until six.* **2** [I] (**a**) present oneself publicly or formally: *The tenor soloist is unable to appear tonight because of illness.* ○ *I have to appear in court on a charge of drunken driving.* (**b**) act as a counsel in a lawcourt: *appear for the defendant*/*prosecution.* **3** [I] (of a book or an article) be published or printed: *His new book will be appearing in the spring.* ○ *The news appeared next day on the front page.* **4** [La, Ln, I, It] give the impression of being or doing sth; seem: *The streets appeared deserted.* ○ *Don't make him appear a fool.* ○ *She appears to have many friends.* ○ *There appears to have been*/*It appears that there has been a mistake.* ○ *You appear to have made*/*It appears that you have made a mistake.* ○ *'Has he been found guilty?' 'It appears so*/*not.'* **5** (idm) **it appears**/**appeared as if...**/**as though...** the impression is/was given that...: *It appears as if she's lost interest in her job.*

NOTE ON USAGE: The two pairs of synonyms **appear**/**seem** and **happen**/**chance** are intransitive verbs and are not generally used in the continuous tenses. They are commonly used in these two patterns: **1** *It appears*/*seems that he's resigned.* ○ *It happened*/*chanced that she spoke fluent Swahili.* **2** *He appears*/*seems to have resigned.* ○ *She happened*/*chanced to speak fluent Swahili.* **Chance** is more formal than **happen.** **Appear** and **seem** are used in a variety of other patterns: *She appeared*/*seemed very confident.* ○ *'Are they reliable?' 'It appears*/*seems not.'* ○ *'It's going to rain.' 'So it appears*/*seems.'* **So** is often used for emphasis with **happen**/**chance:** *It so happened*/*chanced that I'd met her a few years before.*

appearance /əˈpɪərəns/ *n* **1** [C] coming into view; arrival: *The sudden appearance of a policeman caused the thief to run away.* ○ *They finally made their appearance* (ie appeared, arrived) *at 11.30.* **2** [C] act of appearing in public as a performer, etc: *His first appearance on stage was at the age of three.* **3** [C, U] that which shows; what sb/sth appears to be: *Fine clothes added to his strikingly handsome appearance.* ○ *She gave every appearance of being extremely rich.* ○ *Don't judge by appearances — appearances can be misleading.* ○ *The building was like a prison in appearance.* **4** (idm) **ˌkeep up apˈpearances** maintain an outward show, esp of prosperity, in order to hide what one does not want others to see: *There's no point in keeping up appearances when everyone knows we're nearly bankrupt.* **ˌput in an apˈpearance** show oneself at or attend a meeting, party, etc, esp for a short time: *I don't want to go to the party but I'd better put in an appearance, I suppose.* **to all apˈpearances** so far as can be seen; outwardly: *He was to all outward appearances dead.*

appease /əˈpiːz/ *v* [Tn] make (sb/sth) quiet or calm, usu by making concessions or by satisfying demands: *appease sb's anger*/*hunger*/*curiosity.*

▷ **appeasement** *n* [U] **1** act or policy of appeasing. **2** (*derog*) British policy of making concessions to the demands of *Hitler and *Mussolini in 1937-39 in order to prevent their threatened aggression. The policy, strongly advocated by the prime minister Neville *Chamberlain, led to the *Munich Agreement (1938), which was shown to be worthless when Hitler occupied all of Czechoslovakia in the following year.

appellant /əˈpelənt/ *n* (*law*) person who appeals to a higher court.

appellation /ˌæpəˈleɪʃn/ *n* (*fml*) name or title; system of naming.

append /əˈpend/ *v* [Tn, Tn·pr] **~ sth** (**to sth**) (*fml*) attach or add sth (esp in writing): *append one's signature to a document* ○ *append an extra clause to the contract.*

appendage /əˈpendɪdʒ/ *n* thing that is added to, or that forms a natural part of, sth larger: *The elephant's trunk is a unique form of appendage.*

appendectomy /ˌæpenˈdektəmɪ/ (also **appendicectomy** /əˌpendɪˈsektəmɪ/) *n* (*medical*) surgical removal of the appendix(2).

appendicitis /əˌpendɪˈsaɪtɪs/ *n* [U] inflammation of the appendix(2).

appendix /əˈpendɪks/ *n* **1** (*pl* **-dices** /-dɪsiːz/) section that gives extra information at the end of a book or document: *This dictionary has several appendices, including one on irregular verbs.* **2** (*pl* **-dixes**) (also **ˌvermiform apˈpendix**) small tube-shaped bag of tissue attached to the intestine. ⇨ illus at DIGESTIVE SYSTEM.

apperception /ˌæpəˈsepʃn/ *n* [U] (*psychology*) process of perceiving sth and relating it to one's previous experience so that one understands it.

appertain /ˌæpəˈteɪn/ *v* [Ipr] **~ to sb**/**sth** (*fml*) belong or relate to sb/sth as a right; be appropriate to sb/sth: *the duties and privileges appertaining to one's high office.*

appetite /ˈæpɪtaɪt/ *n* **1** [U] physical desire, esp for food or pleasure: *When I was ill I completely lost my appetite.* ○ *Don't spoil your appetite by eating sweets before meals.* ○ (*fig*) *He had no appetite for the fight.* **2** [C] instance of a natural desire for sth: *The long walk has given me a good appetite.* ○ *He has an amazing appetite for hard work.* ○ *a person of gross sexual appetites.*

appetizer, -iser /ˈæpɪtaɪzə(r)/ *n* thing that is eaten or drunk before a meal to stimulate the appetite: *Small savoury biscuits provide a simple appetizer.*

appetizing, -ising /ˈæpɪtaɪzɪŋ/ *adj* (of food, etc) stimulating the appetite: *an appetizing smell from the kitchen* ○ *The list of ingredients sounds very appetizing.* ▷ **appetizingly, -isingly** *adv.*

Appian Way /ˌæpɪən ˈweɪ/ **the Appian Way** main road from Rome to S Italy in ancient times, named after the statesman Appius Claudius Caecus, who began the building of it in 312 BC.

applaud /əˈplɔːd/ *v* **1** [I, Tn] show approval of (sb/sth) by clapping the hands: *The crowd applauded (him/the performance) for five minutes.* **2** [Tn] praise (sb/sth); approve: *I applaud your decision.*

applause /əˈplɔːz/ *n* [U] **1** approval expressed by clapping the hands: *He sat down amid deafening applause.* **2** warm approval: *Her new novel was greeted by reviewers with rapturous applause.*

apple /ˈæpl/ *n* **1** (a) round fruit with firm juicy flesh and green, red or yellow skin when ripe: [attrib] *an apple pie* ○ *apple sauce.* ⇨ illus at FRUIT. (b) (also **ˈapple tree**) tree bearing this fruit: [attrib] *apple blossom.*

There are various significant references to the apple in Western culture. First, there is the apple in the *garden of Eden which, when eaten by *Adam and *Eve, caused the loss of man's innocence. In popular legend, we remember the apple that William *Tell, in punishment for his rebelliousness, was forced to shoot off his son's head. And the 17th-century physicist, Sir Isaac *Newton, is said to have discovered his law of gravity on seeing an apple fall from a tree.

2 (idm) **an/the ˌapple of ˈdiscord** (*fml*) cause of an argument or a quarrel. **the ˌapple of sb's ˈeye** person or thing that is loved more than any other: *She is the apple of her father's eye.* **in ˌapple-pie ˈorder** very neatly arranged.

□ **ˈapplecart** *n* (idm) **upset the/sb's applecart** ⇨ UPSET.

ˈapplejack *n* [U] (*US*) strong alcoholic drink distilled from fermented cider.

Appleton /ˈæpltn/ Sir Edward Victor (1892-1965), English physicist who showed that radio waves are reflected back to earth when they strike the ionized part of the upper atmosphere.

appliance /əˈplaɪəns/ *n* **1** instrument or device for a specific purpose: *a kitchen full of electrical appliances*, eg a washing-machine, dish washer, liquidizer, etc. ⇨ Usage at MACHINE. **2** = FIRE-ENGINE (FIRE).

applicable /ˈæplɪkəbl, *also* əˈplɪkəbl/ *adj* [pred] ~ **(to sb/sth)** that can be applied (APPLY 4); appropriate or suitable: *This part of the form is not applicable* (ie does not apply) *to foreign students.* ▷ **applicability** /ˌæplɪkəˈbɪləti/ *n* [U].

applicant /ˈæplɪkənt/ *n* ~ **(for sth)** person who applies, esp for a job, etc: *As the wages were low, there were few applicants for the job.*

application /ˌæplɪˈkeɪʃn/ *n* **1** (a) [U] ~ **(to sb) (for sth)** formal request: *Keys are available on application to the principal.* (b) [C] instance of this: *We received 400 applications for the job.* ○ [attrib] *an application form*, ie a form on which to make an application. **2** (a) [U, C] ~ **(of sth) (to sth)** act of applying one thing to another: *lotion for external application only*, ie to be put on the skin, not swallowed ○ *three applications per day.* (b) [C] substance applied: *an application to relieve muscle pain.* **3** [U] making a rule, etc take effect: *the strict application of the law.* **4** [U] concentrated effort; hard work: *Success as a writer demands great application.* **5** [U, C] ~ **(to sth)** act of putting a theory, discovery, etc to practical use: *a new invention that will have application/a variety of applications in industry.*

applicator /ˈæplɪkeɪtə(r)/ *n* thing used to apply (APPLY 2) sth: *Use the applicator provided to spread the glue.*

applied ⇨ APPLY.

appliqué /æˈpliːkeɪ; *US* ˌæplɪˈkeɪ/ *n* [U] decorative needlework in which pieces of one type of material are cut out and attached to another.

▷ **appliqué** *v* (*pt, pp* **appliquéd**) [Tn] decorate (sth) in this way.

apply /əˈplaɪ/ *v* (*pt, pp* **applied**) **1** [I, Ipr] ~ **(to sb) (for sth)** make a formal request: *You should apply immediately, in person or by letter.* ○ *apply to the publishers for permission to reprint an extract* ○ *apply for a job, post, passport, visa.* **2** [Tn, Tn·pr] ~ **sth (to sth)** put or spread sth (onto sth): *apply the ointment sparingly* ○ *apply the glue to both surfaces* ○ (*fig*) *I'd never apply the word 'readable' to any of his books.* **3** [Tn] make (a law, etc) operate or become effective: *apply a law/rule/precept* ○ *apply economic sanctions.* **4** [I, Ipr] ~ **(to sb/sth)** be relevant (to sb/sth); have an effect: *These rules don't always apply.* ○ *What I have said applies only to some of you.* **5** [Tn, Tn·pr] ~ **sth (to sth)** cause (a force, etc) to affect sth: *apply force, pressure, heat, etc* ○ *apply the brakes hard.* **6** [Tn, Tn·pr] ~ **oneself/sth (to sth/doing sth)** concentrate one's thought and energy (on a task): *You will only pass your exams if you really apply yourself (to your work).* ○ *We must apply our minds to finding a solution.* **7** [Tn, Tn·pr] ~ **sth (to sth)** make practical use of sth: *The results of this research can be applied to new developments in technology.*

▷ **applied** /əˈplaɪd/ *adj* [usu attrib] used in a practical way; not merely theoretical: *applied mathematics*, eg as used in engineering ○ *applied linguistics.* Cf PURE 5.

appoggiatura /əˌpɒdʒəˈtjʊərə; *US* -ˈtʊərə/ *n* (*music*) additional note played or sung just before a main note, esp in 18th-century music. Cf ACCIACCATURA, GRACE-NOTE (GRACE). ⇨ illus at GRACE-NOTE.

appoint /əˈpɔɪnt/ *v* **1** [Tn, Tn·pr, Cn·n, Cn·n/a, Cn·t] ~ **sb (to sth);** ~ **sb (as sth)** choose sb for a job or position of responsibility: *They have appointed Smith/a new manager.* ○ *He was appointed to the vacant post.* ○ *Who shall we appoint (as) chairperson?* ○ *We must appoint sb to act as secretary.* **2** [Tn] create (sth) by choosing members: *appoint a committee.* **3** [Tn, Tn·pr] ~ **sth (for sth)** (*fml*) fix or decide on sth: *appoint a date to meet/for a meeting* ○ *The time appointed for the meeting was 10.30.*

▷ **appointee** /əpɔɪnˈtiː/ *n* person appointed to a job or position.

appointment /əˈpɔɪntmənt/ *n* **1** (a) [C, U] ~ **(to sth)** (act of) appointing a person to a job: *His promotion to manager was a popular appointment.* (b) [C] job to which sb is appointed: *I'm looking for a permanent appointment.* **2** [C, U] ~ **(with sb)** arrangement to meet or visit sb at a particular time: *make/fix an appointment with sb* ○ *keep/break an appointment* ○ *I have a dental appointment at 3 pm.* ○ *Interviews are by appointment only.* **3 appointments** [pl] equipment; furniture.

apportion /əˈpɔːʃn/ *v* [Tn, Tn·pr, Dn·n] ~ **sth (among/to sb)** give sth as a share; allot sth: *I don't wish to apportion blame among you/to any of you.* ○ *He apportioned the members of the team their various tasks.* Cf PORTION *v.* ▷ **apportionment** *n* [U].

apposite /ˈæpəzɪt/ *adj* ~ **(to sth)** (of a remark, etc) very appropriate (for a purpose or an occasion): *an apposite comment, illustration, example, etc* ○ *I found his speech wholly apposite to the current debate.* ▷ **appositely** *adv.* **appositeness** *n* [U].

apposition /ˌæpəˈzɪʃn/ *n* [U] (*grammar*) addition of one word or phrase to another word or phrase as an explanation: *In 'Queen Elizabeth, the Queen Mother' 'the Queen Mother' is in apposition to 'Queen Elizabeth'.*

appraise /əˈpreɪz/ *v* [Tn] assess the value or quality of (sb/sth): *appraise a student's work* ○ *an appraising glance* ○ *It would be unwise to buy the house before having it appraised.*

▷ **appraisal** /əˈpreɪzl/ *n* [C, U] (act of) appraising sb/sth; valuation.

appreciable /əˈpriːʃəbl/ *adj* that can be seen or felt; considerable: *an appreciable drop in temperature* ○ *The increase in salary will be appreciable.* ▷ **appreciably** /-əblɪ/ *adv*: *He's looking appreciably thinner.*

appreciate /əˈpriːʃɪeɪt/ *v* **1** [Tn] understand and enjoy (sth); value highly: *You can't fully appreciate foreign literature in translation.* ○ *I really appreciate a good cup of tea.* ○ *Your help was greatly appreciated*, ie We were grateful for it. **2** [Tn, Tf, Tw] understand (sth) with sympathy: *I appreciate your problem, but I don't think I can help you.* ○ *I appreciate that you may have prior commitments.* ○ *You don't seem to appreciate how busy I am.* **3** [I] increase in value: *Local property has appreciated (in value) since they built the motorway nearby.*

▷ **appreciative** /əˈpriːʃətɪv/ *adj* ~ **(of sth)** feeling or showing understanding or gratitude: *an appreciative letter, audience, look* ○ *I'm most appreciative of your generosity.* **appreciatively** *adv.*

appreciation /əˌpriːʃɪˈeɪʃn/ *n* **1** [U] understanding and enjoyment: *She shows little or no appreciation of good music.* **2** [U] grateful recognition of an action: *Please accept this gift in appreciation of all you've done for us.* **3** [C] (*fml*) (esp written) statement of the qualities of a work of art, person's life, etc: *an appreciation of the poet's work.* **4** [U] increase in value: *The pound's rapid appreciation is creating problems for exporters.*

apprehend /ˌæprɪˈhend/ *v* **1** [Tn] (*fml*) seize (sb); arrest: *The thief was apprehended (by the police) in the act of stealing a car.* **2** [Tn, Tf] (*dated or rhet*) grasp the meaning of (sb/sth); understand: *Do I apprehend you aright*, ie Do you mean what I think you mean? Cf COMPREHEND.

apprehension /ˌæprɪˈhenʃn/ *n* **1** [U, C] anxiety about the future; fear: *filled with apprehension* ○ *I feel a certain apprehension about my interview tomorrow.* **2** [U] understanding. Cf COMPREHENSION. **3** [U] seizing; arrest: *the apprehension of the robbers, escaped prisoners, etc.*

apprehensive /ˌæprɪˈhensɪv/ *adj* ~ **(about/of sth);** ~ **(that.../for sb/sth)** feeling anxiety; fearful; uneasy: *apprehensive about the results of the exams* ○ *apprehensive that he would be beaten* ○ *apprehensive for sb's safety.* ▷ **apprehensively** *adv.*

apprentice /əˈprentɪs/ *n* **1** person who has agreed to work for a skilled employer for a fixed period in return for being taught his trade or craft: [attrib] *an apprentice plumber.* **2** beginner or novice.

▷ **apprentice** *v* [esp passive: Tn, Tn·pr] ~ **sb (to sb)** make sb work as an apprentice (for sb).

apprenticeship /-tɪʃɪp/ *n* (time of) being an apprentice: *serve an/one's apprenticeship with a carpenter.*

apprise /əˈpraɪz/ *v* [Tn·pr esp passive] ~ **sb of sth** (*fml*) inform sb of sth: *I was apprised of the committee's decision.*

appro /ˈæprəʊ/ *n* (idm) **on appro** (*Brit infml*) = ON APPROVAL (APPROVAL).

approach /əˈprəʊtʃ/ *v* **1** [I, Tn] come near or nearer to (sb/sth) in space or time: *The time is approaching when we must think about buying a new house.* ○ *As you approach the town the first building you see is the church.* **2** [Tn] be similar in quality or character to (sb/sth): *Few writers even begin to approach Shakespeare's greatness.* **3** [Tn] go to (sb) for help or support or in order to offer sth: *approach one's bank manager for a loan* ○ *approach a witness with a bribe* ○ *I find him difficult to approach*, ie not easy to talk to in a friendly way. **4** [Tn] begin to tackle (a task, problem, etc): *Before trying to solve the puzzle, let us consider the best way to approach it.*

▷ **approach** *n* **1** [sing] act of approaching: *Heavy footsteps signalled the teacher's approach.* ○ *At her approach the children ran off.* **2** [C] ~ **to sth** thing resembling sth in quality or character: *That's the nearest approach to a smile he ever makes.* **3** [C] way leading to sth; path; road: *All the approaches to the palace were guarded by troops.* ○ [attrib] *Police are patrolling the major approach roads to the stadium.* **4** [C] way of dealing with a person or thing: *a new approach to language teaching.* **5** [C] attempt to reach agreement or become friendly with sb: *The club has made an approach to a local business firm for sponsorship.* ○ *She resented his persistent approaches.* **6** [C] final part of an aircraft's flight before landing: *the approach to the runway.* **7** [C] (in golf) stroke from the fairway to the green. **8** (idm) **easy/difficult of approach** (*fml*) easy/difficult to talk to in a friendly way.

approachable *adj* **1** (of people or things) that can be approached: *The house is only approachable from the south.* **2** friendly and easy to talk to. **approachability** /əˌprəʊtʃəˈbɪləti/ *n* [U].

approbation /ˌæprəˈbeɪʃn/ *n* [U] (*fml*) approval;

consent: *awaiting the approbation of the court.*

appropriate[1] /əˈprəʊprɪət/ *adj* ~ **(for/to sth)** suitable; right and proper: *Sports clothes are not appropriate for a formal wedding.* ○ *His formal style of speaking was appropriate to the occasion.* ○ *You will be informed of the details at the appropriate time.* ▷ **appropriately** *adv.* **appropriateness** *n* [U].

appropriate[2] /əˈprəʊprɪeɪt/ *v* **1** [Tn] take (sth) for one's own use, esp without permission or illegally: *He was accused of appropriating club funds.* **2** [Tn·pr] ~ **sth for sth** put (esp money) on one side for a special purpose: *£5000 has been appropriated for a new training scheme.*

▷ **appropriation** /əˌprəʊprɪˈeɪʃn/ *n* **1** **(a)** [U] appropriating or being appropriated. **(b)** [C] instance of this. **2** [C] thing, esp a sum of money, that is appropriated: *make an appropriation of £20000 for payment of debts* ○ *the US Senate Appropriations Committee*, ie dealing with funds for defence, welfare, etc.

approval /əˈpru:vl/ *n* [U] **1** feeling or showing or saying that one thinks sth is good or acceptable or satisfactory: *give one's approval* ○ *Do the plans meet with your approval?* ○ *a nod of approval.* **2** (idm) **on apˈproval** (of goods) supplied to a customer on condition that they may be returned if they are not satisfactory. **seal of approval** ⇨ SEAL[2].

approve /əˈpru:v/ *v* **1** [I, Ipr] ~ **(of sb/sth)** say, show or feel that sb/sth is good or acceptable or satisfactory: *She doesn't want to take her new boy-friend home in case her parents don't approve (of him).* ○ *I approve of your trying to earn some money, but please don't neglect your studies.* **2** [Tn] confirm (sth); accept: *The minutes of the last meeting were approved.* ○ *The auditors approved the company's accounts.* ▷ **approving** *adj*: *She received many approving glances.* **approvingly** *adv.*

□ **apˈproved school** (formerly) place for housing, training and educating young offenders. Cf BORSTAL, REFORMATORY.

approx *abbr* approximate; approximately.

approximate[1] /əˈprɒksɪmət/ *adj* almost correct or exact but not completely so: *an approximate price, figure, amount, etc* ○ *What is the approximate size of this room?* ▷ **approximately** *adv*: *It cost approximately £300 — I can't remember exactly.*

approximate[2] /əˈprɒksɪmeɪt/ *v* [Ipr] ~ **to sth** be almost the same as sth: *Your story approximates to the facts we already know.*

▷ **approximation** /əˌprɒksɪˈmeɪʃn/ *n* **1** [C] amount or estimate that is not exactly right but nearly so: *3000 students each year would be an approximation.* **2** [U] process of being or getting near (in number, quality, etc).

appurtenance /əˈpɜ:tɪnəns/ *n* (usu *pl*) (*law*) **1** minor piece of property; accessory. **2** privilege or right that goes with the ownership of property: *He inherited the manor and all its appurtenances.*

Apr *abbr* April: *14 Apr 1986.*

après-ski /ˌæpreɪ ˈski:/ *n* (*French*) time of leisure after a day's skiing in a resort: *I enjoyed the après-ski more than the skiing itself.* ○ [attrib] *après-ski clothes, activities.*

apricot /ˈeɪprɪkɒt/ *n* **1** [C] **(a)** round stone-fruit with soft flesh, related to the plum and peach and orange-yellow when ripe: [attrib] *ˌapricot ˈjam.* **(b)** tree bearing this fruit. **2** [U] colour of a ripe apricot.

April /ˈeɪprəl/ *n* [U, C] (*abbr* **Apr**) the fourth month of the year, next after March: *She was born in April.* ○ *When were you born? The first of April/April the first/(US) April first.* ○ *We went to Japan last April/the April before last.* ○ [attrib] *April showers*, ie short periods of rain alternating with fine weather.

□ ˌ**April** ˈ**Fool** victim of a practical joke traditionally played on 1 April. ˌ**April** ˈ**Fool's Day** (also ˌ**All** ˈ**Fools' Day**) 1 April.

a priori /ˌeɪ praɪˈɔ:raɪ/ (using reasoning that proceeds) from known causes to imagined effects, eg saying '*They've been walking all day so they must be hungry.*' Cf A POSTERIORI.

apron /ˈeɪprən/ *n* **1** **(a)** garment worn over the front part of the body to keep the wearer's clothes clean while working. ⇨ illus. **(b)** any similar covering worn as part of ceremonial dress. **2** hard-surfaced area on an airfield, where aircraft are manoeuvred, loaded or unloaded. **3** (also ˌ**apron** ˈ**stage**) (in the theatre) part of the stage that extends into the auditorium in front of the curtain. **4** (idm) **(tied to) one's mother's, wife's, etc apron strings** (too much under) the influence and control of one's mother, etc.

apropos /ˌæprəˈpəʊ/ *adv, adj* [pred] (in a way that is) appropriate or relevant to what is being said or done: *You'll find the last paragraph extremely apropos.*

□ **apropos of** *prep* with reference to (sth); concerning: *Apropos of what you were just saying….*

apse /æps/ *n* semicircular or many-sided recess with an arched or domed roof, esp at the east end of a church.

apsis /ˈæpsɪs/ *n* (*pl* **apsides** /-sɪdi:z/) either of two points in the orbit of a planet or satellite that are furthest from and nearest to the planet or other object round which it moves.

apt /æpt/ *adj* **(-er, -est)** **1** suitable; appropriate: *an apt quotation.* **2** ~ **(at doing sth)** quick at learning: *She's one of my aptest students.* ○ *very apt at programming a computer.* **3** [pred] ~ **to do sth** likely or having a tendency to do sth: *apt to be forgetful, careless, quick-tempered, etc* ○ *My pen is rather apt to leak.*

▷ **aptly** *adv* suitably; appropriately: *aptly punished for one's misdeeds.*

aptness *n* [U].

APT /ˌeɪ pi: ˈti:/ *abbr* (*Brit*) Advanced Passenger Train.

apt *abbr* apartment.

aptitude /ˈæptɪtju:d; *US* -tu:d/ *n* [U, C] ~ **(for sth/doing sth)** natural ability or skill: *Does she show any aptitude for games?* ○ *He has an unfortunate aptitude for saying the wrong thing.*

□ ˈ**aptitude test** test to find if sb is suitable for a particular type of work or course of training. Cf INTELLIGENCE TEST (INTELLIGENCE).

Apuleius /ˌæpjʊˈli:əs/ (born c 123 AD), Roman writer, born in Africa. His best-known work is the *Metamorphoses* (usu called *The Golden Ass*), which is the only Latin novel that still exists in complete form. It tells the story of a man called Lucius who is transformed into a donkey.

Aqualung /ˈækwəlʌŋ/ *n* (*propr*) portable underwater breathing apparatus used by divers.

aquamarine /ˌækwəməˈri:n/ *n* **1** [C] bluish-green precious stone, a variety of beryl. **2** [U] its colour.

aquaplane /ˈækwəpleɪn/ *n* board on which a person stands while being towed across water by a speedboat.

▷ **aquaplane** *v* [I] **1** ride on an aquaplane. **2** (of a vehicle) skid or glide forward uncontrollably on the wet surface of a road.

aqua regia /ˌækwə ˈri:dʒɪə/ *n* [U] (*chemistry*) mixture of nitric acid and hydrochloric acid, used to dissolve gold, platinum and other metals.

aquarium /əˈkweərɪəm/ *n* (*pl* ~**s** or **-ria**) (building containing an) artificial pond or glass tank where live fish and other water creatures and plants are kept.

Aquarius /əˈkweərɪəs/ *n* **1** [U] the eleventh sign of the zodiac, the Water-carrier. **2** [C] person born under the influence of this sign. ▷ **Aquarian** *n, adj.* ⇨ Usage at ZODIAC. ⇨ illus at ZODIAC.

aquatic /əˈkwætɪk/ *adj* [usu attrib] **1** (of plants, animals, etc) growing or living in or near water: *Many forms of aquatic life inhabit ponds.* **2** (of sports) taking place on or in water: *Swimming and water-skiing are both aquatic sports.*

aquatint /ˈækwətɪnt/ *n* **1** [U] process of etching on copper using nitric acid. **2** [C] picture made in this way.

aqua vitae /ˌækwə ˈvaɪti:/ *n* [U] (*arch or rhet*) strong alcoholic drink, esp brandy.

aqueduct /ˈækwɪdʌkt/ *n* structure for carrying water across country, esp one built like a bridge over a valley or low ground.

aqueous /ˈeɪkwɪəs/ *adj* of or like water; produced by water: *chemicals dissolved in an aqueous solution.*

□ ˌ**aqueous** ˈ**humour** (*anatomy*) watery substance that fills the space between the cornea and the lens of the eye in vertebrates.

aquilegia /ˌækwɪˈli:dʒə/ *n* [C, U] = COLUMBINE.

aquiline /ˈækwɪlaɪn/ *adj* of or like an eagle: *an aquiline nose*, ie one curved like an eagle's beak.

Aquinas /əˈkwaɪnəs/ Saint Thomas (1225-74), Italian theologian and philosopher, known as 'the Angelic Doctor'. His many writings include commentaries on Aristotle and the Bible and philosophical and theological works. He made the work of Aristotle acceptable in Christian Western Europe, his own philosophy being a development of Aristotle's. He distinguished between what can be discovered by human reason and what can be known only by special revelation from God. His arguments for the existence of God have also been influential.

Arab /ˈærəb/ *n* **1** any of the Semitic people descended from the original inhabitants of the Arabian Peninsula, now inhabiting the Middle East and N Africa generally. **2** type of horse originally bred in Arabia.

▷ **Arab** *adj* of Arabia or the Arabs: *the Arab countries.*

□ **the** ˌ**Arab** ˈ**League** organization of independent Arab countries, formed in 1945 to develop Arab unity and co-operation.

arabesque /ˌærəˈbesk/ *n* **1** (in art) elaborate design of intertwined leaves, branches, scrolls, etc. **2** (in ballet) position of a dancer balanced on one leg with the other stretched horizontally backwards.

Arabia /əˈreɪbɪə/ (also **the Arabian Peninsula**) peninsula in SW Asia, situated between the Red Sea and the Persian Gulf, bounded on the north by Jordan and Iraq. ⇨ map.

Arabian /əˈreɪbɪən/ *adj* of Arabia or the Arabs: *the Arabian Sea.*

▷ **Arabian** *n* (*dated*) Arab(1).

□ **the A**ˌ**rabian** ˈ**Nights** (also **the** ˌ**Thousand and** ˌ**One** ˈ**Nights**) collection of folk stories (eg *Aladdin, Ali Baba* and *Sinbad*) written in Arabic, from Indian, Persian and Arabic sources, dating from the mid 9th century.

Arabic /ˈærəbɪk/ *adj* of the Arabs, esp their language or literature.

▷ **Arabic** *n* [U] Semitic language widely spoken in W Asia and N Africa.

□ ˌ**arabic** ˈ**numerals** (also ˌ**arabic** ˈ**figures**) the symbols 0, 1, 2, 3, 4, etc. ⇨ App 9, Cf ROMAN NUMERALS (ROMAN).

Arabist /ˈærəbɪst/ *n* student of or expert in Arabic culture, language, history, etc.

arable /ˈærəbl/ *n* [U], *adj* (land that is) suitable for ploughing and for growing crops.

arachnid /əˈræknɪd/ *n* any of the class of animals including spiders, scorpions, ticks and mites.

arachnoid membrane /əˌræknɔɪd ˈmembreɪn/ (*anatomy*) the middle one of the three membranes that surround the brain and spinal cord in vertebrates. Cf DURA MATER, PIA MATER.

Arafat /ˈærəfæt/ Yasser (1929-), Palestinian leader, one of the founders of the guerilla movement Al Fatah, and leader of the Palestine

the Arabian Peninsula

Liberation Organization since 1968.

Araldite /ˈærəldaɪt/ *n* [U] (*propr*) type of epoxy resin used as a strong cement for mending broken china, etc.

Aramaic /ˌærəˈmeɪɪk/ *n* [U] Semitic language that was the main language of SW Asia from about the 6th century BC to the 6th century AD. A modern form of Aramaic is spoken in small communities in Syria and Turkey.

Aran /ˈærən/ *adj* [attrib] made in the knitted patterns traditional in the Aran Islands: *an Aran sweater*.

□ **the ˈAran Islands** group of three islands off the west coast of Ireland.

arbiter /ˈɑːbɪtə(r)/ *n* **1** ~ **(of sth)** person who has power to decide what will be done, accepted, etc with regard to sth: *the arbiters of fashion*. **2** (*dated or Scot*) = ARBITRATOR.

arbitrage /ˌɑːbɪˈtrɑːʒ, ˈɑːbɪtrɪdʒ; *US* ˈɑːrbətrɑːʒ/ [U] buying stocks and shares, commodities, currencies, etc on one market and immediately selling them on another market in order to profit from the difference in price.

▷ **arbitrageur** /ˌɑːbɪtrɑːˈʒɜː(r)/ (also **arbitrager** /ˈɑːbɪtrɑːʒə(r)/) *n* person whose business is arbitrage.

arbitrary /ˈɑːbɪtrərɪ; *US* ˈɑːrbɪtrerɪ/ *adj* **1** based on personal opinion or impulse, not on reason: *The choice of players for the team seems completely arbitrary.* **2** using uncontrolled power without considering others; dictatorial: *an arbitrary ruler* ○ *arbitrary powers*. ▷ **arbitrarily** *adv*. **arbitrariness** *n* [U].

arbitrate /ˈɑːbɪtreɪt/ *v* [I, Ipr, Tn, Tn·pr] ~ **(sth) (between A and B)** make a judgement about or settle (a dispute) between two parties (usu when asked by them to do so): *He was asked to arbitrate (a serious dispute) between management and the unions.*

arbitration /ˌɑːbɪˈtreɪʃn/ *n* **1** [U] settling of a dispute by a person or people chosen to do this by both sides in the dispute: *take/refer the matter to arbitration*. **2** (idm) **ˌgo to arbiˈtration** ask sb to settle a dispute by arbitrating: *The union finally agreed to go to arbitration as a way of ending the strike.*

arbitrator /ˈɑːbɪtreɪtə(r)/ (also **arbiter**) *n* person chosen to settle a dispute between two parties.

arbor /ˈɑːbə(r)/ *n* axle or spindle on which a wheel, etc revolves in a machine.

arboreal /ɑːˈbɔːrɪəl/ *adj* (*fml*) of or living in trees: *Squirrels are arboreal creatures.*

arboretum /ˌɑːbəˈriːtəm/ *n* (*pl* **-tums** or **-ta**) place where trees are grown for scientific study or for display.

arboriculture /ˈɑːbərɪkʌltʃə(r), ɑːˈbɔːrəkʌltʃə(r)/ *n* [U] growing of trees and shrubs.

arbour (*US* **arbor**) /ˈɑːbə(r)/ *n* shady place among trees or climbing plants, esp one made in a garden for people to sit in.

arbutus /ɑːˈbjuːtəs/ *n* [C, U] any of various evergreen shrubs and trees with white or pink flowers and reddish berries, esp the strawberry-tree of S Europe.

arc /ɑːk/ *n* **1** part of the circumference of a circle or some other curved line. ⇨ illus at CIRCLE. **2** thing with this shape: *the arc of a rainbow*. **3** luminous electric current passing across a gap between two terminals.

▷ **arc** *v* (*pt, pp* **arced** /ɑːkt/, *pres p* **arcing** /ˈɑːkɪŋ/) [I] form an electric arc.

□ **ˈarc lamp** (also **ˈarc light**) lamp giving light produced by an electric arc.

ˌarc ˈwelding welding by means of an electric arc.

arcade /ɑːˈkeɪd/ *n* **1** covered passage or area, esp one with an arched roof and shops along one or both sides: *a shopping arcade*. **2** series of arches supported by columns. ⇨ illus.

arcade

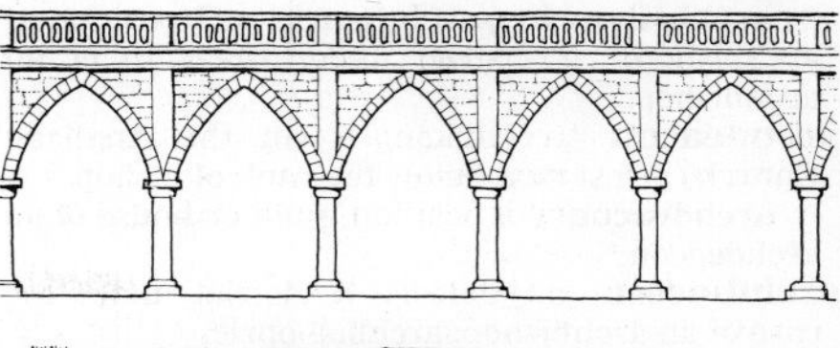

SHOPPING ARCADE

Arcadia /ɑːˈkeɪdɪə/ mountainous area of central Greece in ancient times, used as a symbol of a simple rural paradise in Greek, Roman and Renaissance literature.

▷ **Arcadian** *adj* **1** of Arcadia. **2** typical of a simple happy way of life in the country. — *n* **1** inhabitant of Arcadia. **2** person who lives a simple country life.

arcane /ɑːˈkeɪn/ *adj* secret; mysterious: *arcane rituals, ceremonies, customs, etc.*

arch[1] /ɑːtʃ/ *n* **1** curved structure supporting the weight of sth above it, eg a bridge or the upper storey of a building: *a bridge with three arches*. ⇨ illus at CHURCH, OGEE ARCH (OGEE). **2** (also **archway**) similar structure forming a passageway or an ornamental gateway: *Go through the arch and follow the path.* ○ *Marble Arch is a famous London landmark.* **3** thing shaped like an arch, esp the raised part of the foot between the sole and the heel. ⇨ illus at FOOT.

▷ **arch** *v* **1** [Tn] form (sth) into an arch: *The cat arched its back when it saw the dog.* **2** [Ipr] ~ **across/over sth** form an arch across sth; span sth: *Tall trees arched across the river.*

arch[2] /ɑːtʃ/ *adj* [attrib] playful in a deliberate or an affected way: *an arch smile, glance, look, etc.*

arch- *comb form* **1** chief; most important: *archangel* ○ *archbishop*. **2** extremely bad: *arch-enemy*.

archaeology /ˌɑːkɪˈɒlədʒɪ/ *n* [U] study of ancient civilizations by scientific analysis of physical remains found in the ground. Archaeology uses the basic principle that in a simple undisturbed series of layers, what is oldest is at the bottom and what is youngest is at the top. It also uses the comparative study of artefacts (eg pottery, tools and weapons) to link finds from one site with those of another. Material can be dated by scientific methods (eg the use of radioisotope carbon 14).

▷ **archaeological** /ˌɑːkɪəˈlɒdʒɪkl/ *adj* of or related to archaeology: *archaeological finds*.

archaeologist /ˌɑːkɪˈɒlədʒɪst/ *n* expert in archaeology.

archaic /ɑːˈkeɪɪk/ *adj* **1** of a much earlier or an ancient period in history. **2** (esp of words, etc in a language) no longer in current use: *'Thou art' is an archaic form of 'you are'.*

▷ **archaism** /ˈɑːkeɪɪzəm/ *n* **1** [C] archaic word or expression. **2** [U] use or imitation of what is archaic, esp in language and art.

archangel /ˈɑːkeɪndʒl/ *n* angel of the highest rank. *Michael is the only archangel mentioned in the New Testament of the Bible. In Christian tradition *Gabriel and *Raphael are also regarded as archangels.

archbishop /ˌɑːtʃˈbɪʃəp/ *n* bishop of the highest rank, responsible for a large church district: *the ˌArchbishop of ˈCanterbury*, ie the title of the religious head of the Church of England. ⇨

articles at ARISTOCRAT, CHURCH OF ENGLAND.
▷ **archbishopric** /ˌɑ:tʃˈbɪʃəprɪk/ *n* **1** position of archbishop. **2** district under the care of an archbishop.

archdeacon /ˌɑ:tʃˈdi:kən/ *n* (in the Anglican Church) priest next below the rank of bishop.
▷ **archdeaconry** *n* position, rank or house of an archdeacon.

archdiocese /ˌɑ:tʃˈdaɪəsɪs/ *n* district under the care of an archbishop; archbishopric.

archduke /ˌɑ:tʃˈdju:k; *US* -ˈdu:k/ *n* (*fem* **archduchess** /ˌɑ:tʃˈdʌtʃɪs/) duke of the highest rank, esp (formerly) the son of the Austrian Emperor.

arch-enemy /ˌɑ:tʃ ˈenəmɪ/ *n* **1** [C] chief enemy. **2 the Arch-enemy** [sing] the Devil.

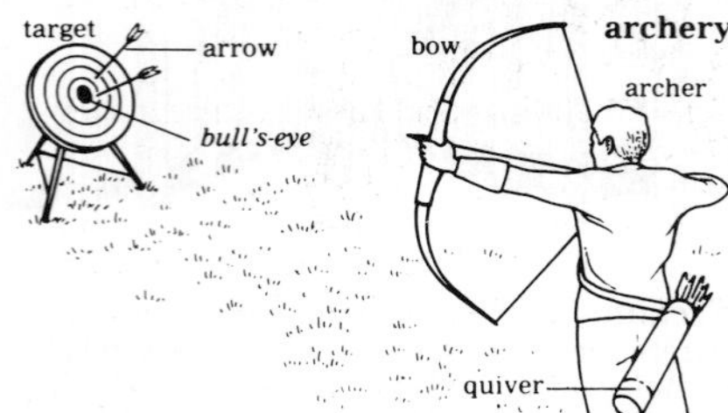

archer /ˈɑ:tʃə(r)/ *n* person who shoots with a bow and arrows, esp as a sport or (formerly) in battle. ⇨ illus.
▷ **archery** /ˈɑ:tʃərɪ/ *n* [U] skill or sport of shooting with a bow and arrows. ⇨ illus.

Archers /ˈɑ:tʃəz/ **the Archers** *n* [sing *v*] popular daily British radio programme about the everyday life of an imaginary farming family and community. It has been broadcast since 1950 and is the longest-running radio serial of its kind. Cf article at TOWN.

archetype /ˈɑ:kɪtaɪp/ *n* **1** original or ideal model from which others are copied; prototype. **2** typical example of sth. **3** (in the psychological theory of C G *Jung) inherited idea (eg the concept of the wise old man) that forms part of the collective unconscious (COLLECTIVE) of all human beings. ▷ **archetypal** /ˌɑ:kɪˈtaɪpl/ *adj*.

archimandrite /ˌɑ:kɪˈmændraɪt/ *n* **1** honorary title given to certain monastic priests. **2** head of a monastery or group of monasteries in the Orthodox Church.

Archimedes /ˌɑ:kɪˈmi:di:z/ (c 287-212 BC), Greek mathematician and inventor, famous for his work in geometry, mechanics and the behaviour of liquids that are not in motion. ▷ **Archimedean** /ˌɑ:kɪˈmi:dɪən/ *adj*.
□ ˌ**Archimedes**' ˈ**principle** principle that when an object is put into a liquid, the apparent loss in weight of the object equals the weight of the water that is displaced. According to legend, Archimedes made this discovery while having a bath, and ran through the streets shouting 'Eureka!' ('I have found it!').
ˌ**Archimedes**' ˈ**screw** (also **Archimedean screw**) device consisting of a large spiral screw in a tube which is rotated by a handle, used for drawing up water. It is said to have been invented by Archimedes.

archipelago /ˌɑ:kɪˈpeləgəʊ/ *n* (*pl* ~**s** or ~**es**) (sea surrounding a) group of many islands.

architect /ˈɑ:kɪtekt/ *n* person who designs buildings and supervises their construction: *the architect's plans for the new theatre* ○ (*fig*) *He was one of the principal architects of the revolution.*

architectonics /ˌɑ:kɪtekˈtɒnɪks/ *n* [sing *v*] **1** scientific study of architecture. **2** structural design of a thing. ▷ **architectonic** *adj*.

architecture /ˈɑ:kɪtektʃə(r)/ *n* [U] **1** art and science of designing and constructing buildings. **2** design or style of a building or buildings: *the architecture of the eighteenth century* ○ *Modern architecture depresses me.* ⇨ article.
▷ **architectural** /ˌɑ:kɪˈtektʃərəl/ *adj* of or related to architecture: *an architectural triumph.*
architecturally *adv*: *The house is of little interest architecturally.*

architrave /ˈɑ:kɪtreɪv/ *n* **1** moulded frame round a door or window. **2** horizontal piece resting on the columns of a classical building.

archives /ˈɑ:kaɪvz/ *n* **1** [pl] (collection of) historical documents or records of a government, town, etc: *I found this old map in the family archives.* **2** [C] place where such records are kept.
▷ **archivist** /ˈɑ:kɪvɪst/ *n* person who is trained to keep archives.

archon /ˈɑ:kən, ˈɑ:kɒn/ *n* any of the nine chief magistrates in ancient Athens.

archway /ˈɑ:tʃweɪ/ *n* = ARCH[1] 2.

Arctic /ˈɑ:ktɪk/ *adj* **1** [attrib] of the regions around the North Pole. ⇨ illus at GLOBE. **2 arctic** **(a)** very cold: *arctic weather* ○ *The conditions were arctic.* **(b)** [attrib] suitable for such conditions: *arctic clothing.*
▷ **the Arctic** *n* [sing] the regions around the North Pole, including parts of Greenland, Canada, the USA, the Soviet Union and Scandinavia, and the Arctic Ocean. The American explorer Robert E Peary was the first person to reach the North Pole (in 1909).
□ **the** ˌ**Arctic** ˈ**Circle** the line of latitude 66° 30′ N. This line marks the edge of the area where, for at least one day every year, the sun never sets. ⇨ illus at GLOBE.
the ˌ**Arctic** ˈ**Ocean** the ocean around the North Pole, largely covered by ice. Area 14 100 000 sq km (5 440 000 sq miles).

-ard *suff* (with *adjs* forming *ns*) having the specified (usu negative) quality: *drunkard* ○ *dullard.*

Ardennes /ɑ:ˈden/ **the Ardennes** forested hilly region in SE Belgium, W Luxemburg and NE France, where there was much heavy fighting in both World Wars. ⇨ map at BENELUX.

ardent /ˈɑ:dnt/ *adj* full of ardour; enthusiastic: *an ardent supporter of the local football team* ○ *ardent in her admiration of the artist.* ▷ **ardently** *adv*.

ardour (*US* **ardor**) /ˈɑ:də(r)/ *n* [U] ~ (**for sb/sth**) great warmth of feeling; enthusiasm; zeal: *His ardour for the cause inspired his followers.*

arduous /ˈɑ:djʊəs; *US* -dʒʊ-/ *adj* needing much effort or energy; laborious: *an arduous task* ○ *The work is arduous and the hours are long.* ▷ **arduously** *adv*.

are[1] ⇨ BE.

are[2] /ɑ:(r)/ *n* metric unit of area, equal to 100 square metres. ⇨ App 10.

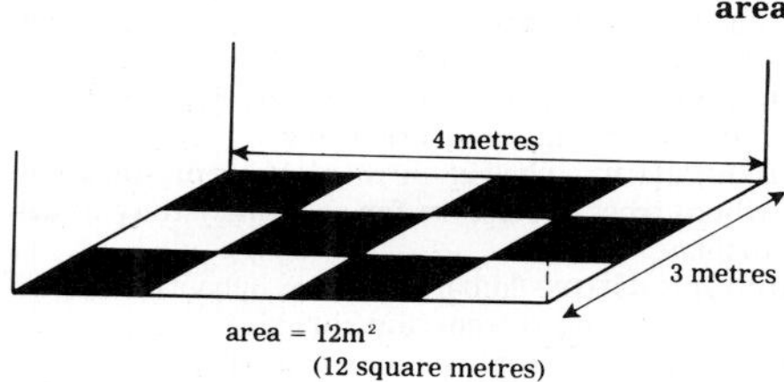

area /ˈeərɪə/ *n* **1** **(a)** [C, U] extent or measurement of a surface: *The area of the office is 35 square metres.* ○ *The kitchen is 12 square metres in area/has an area of 12 square metres.* ⇨ App 9. **(b)** [C] particular measured surface: *Compare the areas of these triangles.* ⇨ illus, Cf VOLUME 2. **2** [C] **(a)** part of a surface: *Clean the area round the cooker.* **(b)** region of the earth's surface; district of a city, etc: *mountainous, uninhabited, desert, etc areas of the world* ○ *Do you like the area* (ie neighbourhood) *where you're living?* ○ *an area of outstanding natural beauty*, ie a specially protected part of the countryside in England, Wales and Northern Ireland. **(c)** space reserved for a specific use: *a* ˈ*picnic area* ○ *the re*ˈ*ception area.* **3** [C] range of activity or interest: *the area of finance, training, development, etc* ○ *The meeting revealed certain areas of disagreement*, ie matters on which those present did not agree. **4** [C] small courtyard in front of the basement of a house, usu with access to the street: [attrib] *sitting on the area steps.*
□ ˈ**area code** (*US*) dialling code identifying an area or region, used before the local telephone number. ⇨ App 9.

areca /ˈærɪkə, əˈri:kə/ *n* tropical Asiatic palm-tree bearing white flowers and orange or red nuts.
□ **areca nut** (also **betel-nut**) seed of this tree.

arena /əˈri:nə/ *n* **1** level area in the centre of an amphitheatre or a sports stadium. **2** (*fig*) place or scene of activity or conflict: *the political arena.*

arenaceous /ˌærɪˈneɪʃəs/ *adj* **1** made of, like or containing sand: *arenaceous rocks.* **2** growing in sandy soil: *arenaceous plants.*

aren't /ɑ:nt/ *contracted form* (*infml*) **1** are not: *They aren't here.* **2** (in questions) am not: *Aren't I clever?* ⇨ BE.

areola /əˈrɪələ/ *n* (*pl* **-lae** /-li:/) **1** (*anatomy*) small coloured area, esp the one surrounding the nipple on the breast of humans. **2** (*biology*) small space, eg the area between the veins on a leaf.

Areopagus /ˌærɪˈɒpəgəs/ **(a)** hill in Athens, near the *Acropolis. **(b)** highest government council of Athens, which met on this hill in ancient times.

Ares /ˈeəri:z/ (in Greek mythology) god of war, son of Zeus and Hera. His Roman equivalent was *Mars.

arête /æˈret/ *n* sharp mountain ridge, esp in Switzerland.

Argentina

Argentina /ˌɑ:dʒənˈti:nə/ (also **the Argentine** /ˈɑ:dʒəntaɪn/) country in South America; pop approx 31 963 000; official language Spanish; capital Buenos Aires; unit of currency austral (= 100 cents). Argentina gained independence from Spain in 1816 and became a republic in 1852. In 1982 its claim to the Falkland Islands led to an unsuccessful war with Britain. The country's economy is based mainly on agriculture but there has been recent growth in textile, plastic and engineering industries. ⇨ map.
▷ **Argentinian** /ˌɑ:dʒənˈtɪnɪən/ (also **Argentine**) *adj* of Argentina or its people.

argillaceous /ˌɑ:dʒɪˈleɪʃəs/ *adj* of or containing clay: *argillaceous rocks.*

Argo /ˈɑ:gəʊ/ ship in which Jason and the *Argonauts sailed from Greece in search of the *Golden Fleece.

argon /ˈɑ:gɒn/ *n* [U] (*symb* **Ar**) colourless odourless element of the noble gas group. Argon constitutes nearly one per cent of the earth's atmosphere by volume. It is used in electric light bulbs. ⇨ App 11.

Argonauts /ˈɑ:gənɔ:ts/ *n* [pl] heroes who sailed with Jason on board the ship Argo in search of the

Architecture

The variety of architecture to be seen in Britain, from prehistoric monuments to the skyscrapers of modern London, provides a record of the nation's history. Buildings that are historically or architecturally important are recorded by the government as 'listed buildings' and are subject to conservation laws. These buildings may not be altered without 'planning permission' from the local authority, which is responsible to the Department of the Environment. If a listed building is demolished, a careful record of it is made by the Royal Commission on Historical Monuments.

The most important prehistoric monument in Britain is the stone circle at Stonehenge in Wiltshire, which was completed during the Bronze Age. Remains of the Roman occupation of Britain can be seen in many places, including Colchester, St Albans, Bath and Caerwent. The oldest surviving churches date from the 10th to the 12th centuries. Churches built before the Norman Conquest were formerly called Saxon and those built after 1066 Norman, but the style of this whole period is now usually called Romanesque. Romanesque cathedrals built after the Norman Conquest include those at Ely, Durham, Hereford and St Albans.

Apart from these early remains, it is the castles, churches, cathedrals and country houses of Britain that represent the architectural heritage of the country and attract tourists. The Normans built castles, most notably the Tower of London. Other famous castles include those at Windsor, Arundel, Dover and Norwich. In Wales there are famous castles at Caernarfon and Harlech, while Scotland has many medieval castles which, with their distinctive towers and turrets, are similar to the French châteaux on the River Loire. Edinburgh Castle is a fine example belonging to a later period, with its impressive ramparts built in the 18th century.

Many people regard Gothic as a particularly English style. It is usually classified into three stages of development: Early English (mainly 13th century), Decorated (14th century) and Perpendicular (15th and 16th centuries). The stages are distinguished by the development of the design of the windows and the introduction of vaulting and buttressing. The pointed arch of the windows is characteristic of the whole Gothic period and distinguishes it from the Romanesque style of rounded arches. Examples of the Early English period are the cathedrals at Salisbury, Peterborough, Ripon and Wells, while the Decorated style is found notably at Canterbury, Exeter, Lichfield and York. Cathedrals of the Perpendicular stage include Gloucester and Winchester, but the style is perhaps best seen in St George's Chapel, Windsor, King's College Chapel, Cambridge, and Henry VII's Chapel in Westminster Abbey.

Later architectural periods include the Tudor (first half of the 16th century), with its characterisic half-timbered houses, Elizabethan (second half of the 16th century), with its sculpted and moulded ornamentation, and Jacobean (early 17th century), a development of Elizabethan and not always easily distinguished from it. Hampton Court in London is a famous Tudor Palace and fine examples of Elizabethan mansions are Wollaton Hall, Nottinghamshire, Hardwick Hall, Derbyshire, and Burghley House in Cambridgeshire.

With the Tudor period, the influence of the Italian Renaissance was already beginning to make itself felt, and from about 1640 to 1830 almost all English architecture was inspired by the legacy of classical Rome. Important examples of the classical influence are the Baroque London churches of Christopher Wren (especially St Paul's Cathedral), the work of Vanbrugh, for example at Blenheim Palace and Castle Howard, the elegant Georgian houses in cities such as Bath, and the work of Inigo Jones in the 'Palladian' style, for example the Banqueting House at Whitehall and Somerset House on the bank of the Thames. Many large country houses such as Holkham Hall, Norfolk, and Chatsworth House in Derbyshire belong to this period. A particular development of the Georgian style, fashionable during the regency of the Prince of Wales (1810–20), was called Regency. Characterized by the use of stucco instead of the stone of Georgian buildings, it was used especially in Brighton, Cheltenham and the terraces in Regent's Park, London.

A more complex succession of styles is to be found in the buildings of the 19th century, including the Greek and Gothic Revivals. The Greek Revival influenced the style of many public buildings such as St George's Hall in Liverpool and Leeds Town Hall. The neo-Gothic style was used especially for the many Anglican churches built during the first half of the century and was also chosen for the Houses of Parliament, built in 1840, because of their proximity to Westminster Abbey.

In architecture the Victorian age was characterized by the recreation of styles from the past, the use of coloured brick as decoration and by the introduction of new methods of construction using iron, steel and glass. Crystal Palace, built for the Great Exhibition in 1851, and the main London railway terminals, were the spectacular products of the new building methods.

At the beginning of the 20th century, architects such as Philip Webb, Charles Voysey and Charles Rennie Mackintosh preferred a return to a simple, undecorated style, sometimes turning to medieval styles as a model. The development of the use of metal for the structure of buildings, together with the invention of reinforced concrete as a building material, had important implications for building design. Prefabricated building, which meant that sections of buildings could be made in factories where work does not depend on the weather, made construction quicker and cheaper. Popular opinion has on the whole favoured traditional methods of building and contemporary architecture has been a subject of public controversy throughout the 20th century. In recent years buildings such as Richard Rogers's Lloyds Building in London have aroused strong feelings for and against. The Prince of Wales entered the debate by publicly condemning certain modern trends, especially criticizing a lot of the new building in London. Much of the heated debate about modern versus traditional architecture has arisen when new development schemes involve the demolition of old buildings, as has happened on several occasions in the City of London. Criticisms of modern architecture is strengthened by the design problems of much of the rapidly constructed public housing of the 1960s.

In the USA the style of building of the early colonists can still be seen in New England and Virginia. In New England, where no brick was available, the houses were timber-framed with clapboards for weather protection, and the style is still popular today. Until the 20th century, English fashions in architecture were followed in the USA, but the invention of the skyscraper, made possible by the development of steel-framed buildings, created the essentially American skyline of New York and Chicago, a style which has been copied all over the world. Frank Lloyd Wright was one of the most influential American architects in the first half of the 20th century, but the emigration from Europe of architects such as Walter Gropius and Mies van der Rohe in the 1930s had an important effect on the development of modern architectural styles in the USA.

---

*Golden Fleece. Their story has various fairy-tale details and is one of the oldest Greek legends. It may be associated with early explorations in the Black Sea.

argosy /ˈɑːgəsɪ/ *n* (*arch*) **1** large merchant ship, esp one carrying valuable cargo. **2** fleet of such ships.

argot /ˈɑːgəʊ/ *n* [U] words and phrases used by a particular group, esp (formerly) thieves, and not intended to be understood by others; cant.

argue /ˈɑːgjuː/ *v* **1** [I, Ipr] ~ (**with sb**) (**about/over sth**) express an opposite opinion; exchange angry words; quarrel: *The couple next door are always arguing.* ○ *Don't argue with your mother.* ○ *We argued with the waiter about the price of the meal.* **2** [I, Ipr, Tf] ~ (**for/against sth**) give reasons for or against sth, esp with the aim of persuading sb: *He argues convincingly.* ○ *argue for the right to strike* ○ *I argued that we needed a larger office.* **3** [Tn] (*fml*) discuss (sth); debate: *The lawyers argued the case for hours.* **4** (idm) ˌ**argue the ˈtoss** say that one disagrees about a decision: *Let's not argue the toss — we have to accept his choice.* **5** (phr v) **argue sb into/out of doing sth** persuade sb to do/not to do sth by giving reasons: *They argued him into withdrawing his complaint.*

▷ **arguable** /ˈɑːgjʊəbl/ *adj* **1** that can be argued or asserted: *It is arguable that we would be just as efficient with fewer staff.* **2** not certain; questionable: *This account contains many arguable statements.* **arguably** /-əblɪ/ *adv* one can argue(2) that: *John sings very well though Peter is arguably the better actor.*

argument /ˈɑːgjʊmənt/ *n* **1** [C] ~ (**with sb**) (**about/over sth**) disagreement; quarrel: *get into/have an argument with the referee (about his decision).* **2** [U] discussion based on reasoning: *We agreed without much further argument.* **3** [C] ~ (**for/against sth**); ~ (**that...**) reason or reasons put forward: *There are strong arguments for and against capital punishment.* ○ *The Government's argument is that they must first aim to beat inflation.* **4** [C] summary of the subject matter of a book, etc; theme. **5** (idm) **for the sake of argument** ⇨ SAKE.

NOTE ON USAGE: **1** An **argument** (over/about sth) is a strong verbal disagreement between

Aristocratic Titles

Ordinary people in Britain are themselves often confused by the many titles and complicated hierarchy of the British aristocracy, but there are guiding rules for classifying the peerage by rank and title and the titles of members of the aristocracy are listed in Debrett's guides and Burke's Peerage.

There are five main grades of nobility, collectively known as peers or the peerage. In order, they are: dukes, marquesses, earls, viscounts and barons. All these are entitled to sit in the House of Lords, and all are called 'Lord'. There are also additional grades. The highest, ranking above dukes, are the royal dukes, that is, those dukes who are members of the royal family, at present five in number: the Duke of Edinburgh (Prince Philip), the Duke of Cornwall (Prince Charles), the Duke of York (Prince Andrew), the Duke of Gloucester and the Duke of Kent. Ranking between royal dukes and the dukes come the two archbishops, of Canterbury and York. Bishops, not all of whom have seats in the House of Lords, rank between viscounts and barons.

Some peers are life peers, that is they have not inherited their titles as hereditary peers do, but have been granted them by the monarch in either the New Year Honours List or the Birthday Honours List. Since 1958, all male life peers have been barons. Women who are made life peers are given the title countess or baroness.

Baronets, who rank below barons, hold the lowest British hereditary title of honour. They are not peers and are not called 'Lord' but 'Sir'. By definition they are therefore commoners, so do not sit in the House of Lords. Below baronet in rank is the non-hereditary title of 'knight'. Knights are also called 'Sir', and the wives of knights and baronets are called 'Lady'.

The sons and daughters of peers have courtesy titles, which have no legal significance, and do not entitle them to sit in the House of Lords. Younger sons of dukes and marquesses are called 'Lord', and the daughters of dukes, marquesses and earls are called 'Lady'. Sons and daughters of earls, viscounts and barons are called 'the Honourable' ('the Hon' for short).

Most peers have more than one title. Any secondary title is often adopted by a son or daughter as a courtesy title. Moreover, a peer's titles are usually different from the family surname. Thus, the Earl of Strafford, whose surname is Byng, has the secondary title of Viscount Enfield, and this is the courtesy title of his son and heir, the Hon William Byng.

people: *Most families have arguments over money.* ○ *I had an argument with my neighbour about a tree in his garden.* **2** A **quarrel** is a sharp, often angry, exchange of words between people: *The whole thing turned into a bitter quarrel.* **3** A **row** is angry and may involve shouting, usually for a short time: *She had a dreadful row with her parents and left home.* A **row** can also take place between public figures or organizations: *There was a huge row in Parliament and the minister resigned.* **4 Altercation** is a formal word and indicates a noisy argument. **5** A **fight** generally involves force or weapons rather than words: *The argument turned into a fight when knives were produced.*

argumentation /ˌɑːgjʊmenˈteɪʃn/ *n* [U] (*fml*) process of arguing; debate.

argumentative /ˌɑːgjʊˈmentətɪv/ *adj* fond of arguing (ARGUE 1). ▷ **argumentatively** *adj*.

Argus /ˈɑːgəs/ (in Greek mythology) monster with a hundred eyes, killed by *Hermes. After his death he turned into a peacock, or, according to a different version of the legend, *Hera took his eyes to form part of the peacock's tail.

argy-bargy /ˌɑːdʒɪ ˈbɑːdʒɪ/ *n* [U] (*Brit infml*) noisy but usu not serious quarrelling: *What's all this argy-bargy?*

Argyllshire /ɑːˈgaɪlʃə(r)/ *n* former county in W Scotland, now part of Strathclyde.

aria /ˈɑːrɪə/ *n* song for one voice and accompaniment, esp in an opera or oratorio.

Ariadne /ˌærɪˈædnɪ/ daughter of Minos and Pasiphae. She helped *Theseus to escape from the labyrinth of the *Minotaur. He abandoned her on the island of Naxos, where she was found by Dionysus who married her.

Arian /ˈeərɪən/ *adj* of Arianism.
▷ *n* supporter of Arianism.

-arian *suff* (forming *ns* and *adjs*) believing in; practising: *humanitarian* ○ *disciplinarian*.

Arianism /ˈeərɪənɪzəm/ *n* [U] heresy that denied that Christ was divine. Named after the Alexandrian priest Arius (c 250-c 336), Arianism stated that the Son of God was not eternal but was created by the Father out of nothing. This teaching was condemned by the Council of Nicaea in 325, and again by the Council of Constantinople (381).

arid /ˈærɪd/ *adj* **1** (of land or climate) having little or no rainfall; dry: *the arid deserts of Africa* ○ *Nothing grows in these arid conditions.* **2** dull; uninteresting: *have long, arid discussions about unimportant matters.* ▷ **aridity** /əˈrɪdətɪ/ *n* [U]. **aridly** *adv*. **aridness** *n* [U].

Aries /ˈeəriːz/ *n* **1** constellation in the northern hemisphere. **2** [U] the first sign of the zodiac, the Ram. **3** [C] (*pl* unchanged) person born under the influence of this sign. ⇨ Usage at ZODIAC. ⇨ illus at ZODIAC.

aright /əˈraɪt/ *adv* (*arch or rhet*) (never used in front of the *v*) rightly: *Do I hear you aright?*

Ariosto /ˌærɪˈɒstəʊ/ Ludovico (1474-1535), Italian poet, best known for his long romantic epic *Orlando Furioso* (final version 1532).

arise /əˈraɪz/ *v* (*pt* **arose** /əˈrəʊz/, *pp* **arisen** /əˈrɪzn/) **1** [I] become evident; appear; originate: *A new difficulty has arisen.* ○ *Use this money when the need arises.* ○ *A storm arose during the night.* **2** [Ipr] ~ **out of/from sth** follow as a result of sth: *problems arising out of the lack of communication* ○ *Are there any matters arising from the minutes of the last meeting?* **3** [I] (*arch*) get up or stand up.

Aristarchus /ˌærɪˈstɑːkəs/ of Samos (3rd century BC), Greek astronomer. He was the first to say that the earth spins on its axis and revolves around the sun.

Aristides /ˌærɪˈstaɪdiːz/ 'the Just' (5th century BC), Athenian statesman and general, famous for his honesty and the important part he played in the Greek victories over the Persians at Marathon (490), Salamis (480) and Plataea (479).

aristocracy /ˌærɪˈstɒkrəsɪ/ *n* **1** [CGp] highest social class; the nobility: *members of the aristocracy.* **2** (**a**) [U] (esp formerly) government by people of the highest social class. (**b**) [C] country or state with such a government. **3** [C] most able or gifted members of any class: *an aristocracy of talent.*

aristocrat /ˈærɪstəkræt; *US* əˈrɪst-/ *n* member of the aristocracy; nobleman or noblewoman. Cf COMMONER.
▷ **aristocratic** /ˌærɪstəˈkrætɪk; *US* əˌrɪstə-/ *adj* belonging to or typical of the aristocracy: *an aristocratic name, family, bearing, life-style.* ⇨ article. **aristocratically** /-klɪ/ *adv*.

Aristophanes /ˌærɪˈstɒfəniːz/ (c 450-385 BC), Greek comic dramatist. He wrote about 40 comedies, of which 11 survive, including *Birds, Clouds* and *Lysistrata*. In his plays, he used parody and satire to mock leading people of the time, eg *Socrates.

Aristotle /ˈærɪstɒtl/ (384-322 BC), Greek philosopher. A pupil of *Plato and tutor of *Alexander the Great, Aristotle founded a school and library (the Lyceum) in Athens in 335 BC. His surviving written works, in the form of lecture notes, constitute a vast system of analysis, covering biology, physics, zoology, psychology, logic, metaphysics, ethics, politics, poetics and rhetoric. From the 9th century his works influenced Islamic philosophy, theology and science, and in medieval times they became the basis of scholasticism.
▷ **Aristotelian** /ˌærɪstəˈtiːlɪən/ *adj* of Aristotle or his teachings. — *n* student or follower of Aristotle.

arithmetic /əˈrɪθmətɪk/ *n* [U] 1; branch of mathematics that deals with numbers and the operations of addition, subtraction, multiplication and division; calculation or calculations using numbers.
▷ **arithmetic** /ˌærɪθˈmetɪk/, **arithmetical** *adjs* of or concerning arithmetic. ˌ**arithmetic** ˈ**mean** average of two or more numbers obtained by dividing their total by the number of numbers in the set, eg the arithmetic mean of 4,9,12,17 and 23 is 13, ie $(4+9+12+17+23)\div5=13$. ˌ**arithmetic pro**ˈ**gression** (also ˌ**arith**ˌ**metical pro**ˈ**gression**) series of numbers that increase or decrease by the same amount each time, eg 1, 2, 3, etc or 8, 6, 4, etc. Cf GEOMETRIC PROGRESSION (GEOMETRY). **arithmetically** /-klɪ/ *adv*. **arithmetician** /əˌrɪθməˈtɪʃn/ *n* expert in arithmetic.

ark /ɑːk/ *n* **1** (in the Bible) ship in which *Noah, his family and animals were saved from the Flood. **2** (idm) **(come, etc) out of the** ˈ**ark** (*infml*) (be) extremely old: *This wardrobe looks as if it came straight out of the ark.*
□ **the** ˌ**Ark of the** ˈ**Covenant** the most sacred religious symbol of the Hebrew people, believed to represent the presence of God. It was in the form of a wooden chest in which the writings of Jewish law were originally kept.

Arkwright /ˈɑːkraɪt/ Sir Richard (1732-92), English cotton manufacturer who invented a water-powered machine (called a 'water frame') for spinning cotton.

arm[1] /ɑːm/ *n* **1** either of the two upper limbs of the human body, from the shoulder to the hand: *She held the baby in her arms.* ○ *He gave her his arm* (ie let her hold it for support) *as they crossed the road.* ○ *She was carrying a book under her arm*, ie between her arm and her body. ○ *He rushed into her arms*, ie to be embraced by her. ⇨ illus at HUMAN. **2** sleeve: *There's a tear in the arm of my jacket.* **3** thing that is shaped like or operates like an arm: *the arms of a chair*, ie parts on which the arms can rest ○ *an arm of the sea*, ie a long inlet ○ *an arm of a tree*, ie a large branch ○ *the (pick-up) arm of a record-player.* ⇨ illus at FURNITURE. **4** (idm) ˌ**arm in** ˈ**arm** (of two people) with the arm of one linked with the arm of the other: *strolling happily arm in arm.* ⇨ illus. **the (long) arm of the** ˈ**law** (extent of) the authority or power of the law: *He fled to Brazil trying to escape the long arm of the law.* **at arm's** ˈ**length** with the arm fully extended away from the body: *holding one's hand out at arm's length.* **a babe in arms** ⇨ BABE. **chance one's arm** ⇨ CHANCE[2]. **cost an arm and a leg** ⇨ COST[1]. **in the** ˌ**arms of** ˈ**Morpheus** (*rhet*) asleep. **fold one's arms** ⇨ FOLD[1]. **fold sb/sth in one's**

The Armed Forces

Both Britain and the USA have, like many other countries, three armed forces, the Navy, the Army and the Air Force.

In Britain, the Royal Navy (RN), sometimes called the 'senior service', dates from 1488, when Henry VII built the *Great Harry*. The Army (with no 'Royal' in its title) evolved in its present form from Oliver Cromwell's New Model Army of 1661, although some of the oldest regiments were formed before this. The Royal Air Force (RAF) was constituted by Act of Parliament in 1918. The Royal Marines (RM) were first formed in 1664, soon after the Army, and although the force is administered by the Navy, its ranks are the same as those in the Army. (Cf Appendix 4.)

In the USA, both the United States Navy and United States Army came into being in 1775. The United States Air Force (USAF) did not become a separate service, however, until after the Second World War. The United States Marine Corps (USMC), formed as part of the US Navy, was established in the same year as its parent force.

There was conscription (called 'the draft' in the USA) in both countries during the Second World War. In Britain it continued as 'National Service' until 1962, and was temporarily revived in the USA in the early 1970s at the time of the Vietnam War.

At the beginning of the 1990s the strength of the British armed forces was just over 300 000 with half this number in the Army, about a third in the RAF, and the remainder, less than a quarter, in the RN and the RM. Of the 16 700 women in the services, just over a third each were in the Women's Royal Air Force (WRAF, known as 'Wrafs', formerly 'Waafs') and the Women's Royal Army Corps (WRAC), and the rest in the Women's Royal Naval Service (WRNS, or 'Wrens').

The current military strength of the USA is just over 2 million. Of this total, just under a third are in the US Army, about a quarter in the USAF, and the remainder in the US Navy. In terms of manpower the US Navy is the largest in the world. US Marines comprise just under 10 per cent of the total. Unlike in Britain, the US Coast Guard is part of the country's military force, under the control of the Navy Department.

In both Britain and the USA female personnel are an integral part of the services, with women serving alongside men, mainly in support roles. American servicewomen are banned by law from combat roles in the front line, although they can be assigned to most other fields. Until recently, British servicewomen were barred from posts on board aircraft and ships.

In the British armed forces, engagements for non-commissioned ranks (below that of officer) are from 3 to 22 years. Personnel may leave the services at any time on giving 18 months' notice, but may also purchase their discharge or be granted it on compassionate grounds or for reasons of conscience. For officers, there are short, medium or long-term commissions.

Britain and the USA are members of NATO (the North Atlantic Treaty Organization). The RN is the largest European navy in NATO, and its prime allegiance is to the alliance. The Army and RAF are stationed in Germany as part of NATO and almost all the RAF's combat and support aircraft are assigned to NATO. In Northern Ireland, the army has ten units, in addition to the nine battalions of the Ulster Defence Regiment (UDR), which are responsible for fighting terrorism.

At home, the army has a role in ceremonial duties, especially those carried out at the Trooping the Colour and the Changing of the Guard at Buckingham Palace. The troops seen in their ceremonial uniforms on these royal occasions are the Household Cavalry and such well-known foot regiments as the Irish Guards, the Scots Guards and the Welsh Guards.

Auxiliary forces also have their part to play. In Britain, the Army is backed up by the Territorial Army (TA), which in turn is supported by a Home Defence Force. Other reserve forces include the Royal Naval Reserve (RNR), the Royal Naval Auxiliary Reserve (RNAS), the Royal Marines Reserve (RMR), and the Royal Auxiliary Air Force (RAAF). All these have grown in recent years to make a total of around 240 000 regular reserves and 90 000 volunteer and auxiliary reserves. Many doctors and nurses serve as medical reserves and were called up in 1991 during the Gulf War. The US auxiliary forces are the National Guard and the Army Reserve.

Recruiting to the services is carried out mainly through recruiting offices but also through cadet corps. Recruiting campaigns and publicity now emphasize the versatility and variety of professions and trades offered in the armed forces, rather than stressing a 'macho' image for the Army or luring volunteers to the Navy with the promise of travel to exotic places.

arms ⇨ FOLD[1]. **have a long arm** ⇨ LONG[1]. **keep sb at arm's length** not allow oneself to become too friendly with sb. **a shot in the arm** ⇨ SHOT[1]. **twist sb's arm** ⇨ TWIST. **with arms akimbo** with one's hands on one's hips and one's elbows pointed outwards. ⇨ illus. **with open ˈarms** ⇨ OPEN[1]. **would give one's right arm for sth/to do sth** ⇨ RIGHT[5].

arm

ARM IN ARM HAND IN HAND

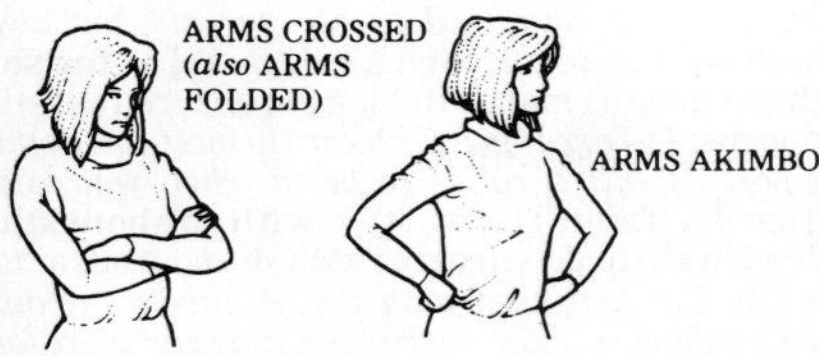

ARMS CROSSED (*also* ARMS FOLDED) ARMS AKIMBO

□ **ˈarm-band** (also **ˈarmlet**) *n* band of material worn round the arm or sleeve: *Many people at the funeral were wearing black arm-bands.*
ˈarmchair *n* chair with supports for the arms. ⇨ illus at FURNITURE. — *adj* [attrib] without having or providing practical experience of sth: *armchair critics* ○ *an armchair traveller*, ie sb who reads or hears about travel but does not travel himself ○ *armchair theatre*, eg plays on radio or TV.
ˈarmful /ˈɑːmfʊl/ *n* quantity that can be carried by one or both arms: *armfuls of flowers* ○ *carrying books by the armful.*
ˈarmhole *n* opening in a garment through which the arm is put.
armlet /ˈɑːmlɪt/ *n* = ARM-BAND.
ˈarmpit *n* hollow under the arm at the shoulder. ⇨ illus at HUMAN.

arm[2] /ɑːm/ *n* branch or division of a country's military forces: *troops supported by the air arm.*

arm[3] /ɑːm/ *v* **1** [I, Tn, Tn·pr] ~ **oneself/sb (with sth)** supply or equip oneself/sb with weapons; prepare for war or fighting: *The enemy is arming.* ○ *The mob armed themselves with sticks and stones.* ○ *Police say the man is armed and dangerous.* ○ *warships armed with nuclear weapons* ○ (*fig*) *She arrived at the interview armed with lists of statistics.* **2** [Tn] make (a bomb, etc) ready to explode. **3** (idm) **ˌarmed to the ˈteeth** having many weapons.
□ **the ˌarmed ˈforces, the ˌarmed ˈservices** a country's army, navy and air force. ⇨ article.
ˌarmed neuˈtrality policy of remaining neutral but prepared for defence against attack.

armada /ɑːˈmɑːdə/ *n* **1** [C] large fleet of ships. **2 the Armada** [sing] the fleet of 129 ships which was sent to attack England in 1588 by King Phillip II of Spain. It was defeated and destroyed in the English Channel by the much smaller English fleet.

armadillo /ˌɑːməˈdɪləʊ/ *n* (*pl* ~**s**) small burrowing mammal of S America with a shell of bony plates around its body which allow it to roll up into a ball when attacked.

Armageddon /ˌɑːməˈgedn/ *n* [sing] **1** (in the Bible) scene of the final conflict between good and evil at the end of the world. **2** (*fig*) any decisive conflict on a large scale.

Armagh /ɑːˈmɑː/ town and county of Northern Ireland.

armament /ˈɑːməmənt/ *n* **1** [C often *pl*] weapons, esp the guns on a tank, an aircraft, etc: [attrib] *the armaments industry.* **2** [C usu *pl*] military forces equipped for war. **3** [U] process of equipping military forces for war.

armature /ˈɑːmətʃə(r)/ *n* **1** part of a dynamo that rotates in a magnetic field to produce an electric current; rotating coil(s) in an electric motor. **2** (also **keeper**) bar of soft iron that is placed across the poles of a magnet to keep the magnet's strength. **3** framework around which a clay or plaster sculpture is modelled.

Armenia /ɑːˈmiːnɪə/ **1** country south of the Caucasus; pop approx 3 645 000; official language Armenian; capital Erevan; unit of currency rouble. A member of the former USSR, it became an independent republic in 1991. ⇨ map at UNION OF SOVIET SOCIALIST REPUBLICS. **2** former kingdom in western Asia, now divided between modern Armenia, Turkey and Iran.

Armenian /ɑːˈmiːnɪən/ *adj* of Armenia, its people or language.
▷ **Armenian** *n* **1** native or inhabitant of Armenia. **2** member of the Armenian Church. **3** language of Armenia.

Louis Armstrong

□ **the Armenian ˈChurch** independent Church of the Armenians founded in the early 4th century AD.

armistice /ˈɑːmɪstɪs/ *n* agreement during a war to stop fighting for a certain time; truce.

□ **ˈArmistice Day** (*US* **ˈVeterans' Day**) 11 November, the anniversary of the armistice that ended fighting in the First World War. Cf REMEMBRANCE SUNDAY (REMEMBRANCE).

armorial /ɑːˈmɔːrɪəl/ *adj* of heraldry or coats of arms (COAT): *armorial bearings.*

armour (*US* **armor**) /ˈɑːmə(r)/ *n* [U] **1** (formerly) protective, usu metal, covering for the body, worn when fighting: *a suit of armour.* **2** metal plates covering warships, tanks, etc to protect them from shells, missiles, etc. **3** group of vehicles protected in this way: *an attack by infantry and armour.* **4** (idm) **a chink in sb's armour** ⇨ CHINK[1]. **a knight in shining armour** ⇨ KNIGHT.

▷ **armoured** (*US* **armored**) *adj* **1** covered or protected with armour(2): *an armoured car* ○ *The cruiser was heavily armoured.* **2** equipped with armoured vehicles: *an armoured column, division, etc.*

armourer (*US* **armorer**) *n* **1** person who makes or repairs weapons and armour. **2** person in charge of firearms.

armoury (*US* **armory**) /ˈɑːmərɪ/ *n* place where arms and armour are kept; arsenal.

□ **ˈarmour-plate** (*US* **ˈarmor-**) *n* sheet of metal used as armour(2). **ˌarmour-ˈplated** (*US* **ˌarmor-**) *adj*: *ˌarmour-plated ˈvehicles, ˈwarships.*

arms /ɑːmz/ *n* [pl] **1** weapons, eg guns, rifles, explosives, etc: *arms and ammunition* ○ *Policemen on special duties may carry arms.* ○ [attrib] *an arms depot.* **2** = COAT OF ARMS (COAT). **3** (idm) **bear arms** ⇨ BEAR[2]. **brothers in arms** ⇨ BROTHER. **ground arms** ⇨ GROUND[2]. **ˌlay down one's ˈarms** (*dated*) stop fighting; surrender: *Tell your men to lay down their arms; the war is over.* **take up ˈarms (against sb)** (*fml*) (prepare to) go to war; begin to fight. **under ˈarms** equipped with weapons and ready to fight: *a force of 300 000 already under arms.* **(be) up in ˈarms (about/over sth)** protesting strongly about sth: *The whole village is up in arms about the proposal to build an airport nearby.*

□ **ˈarms race** competition among nations in which each tries to become militarily stronger than the others.

Armstrong[1] /ˈɑːmstrɒŋ/ Louis (1900-71), American jazz musician also known as 'Satchmo' (short for 'Satchelmouth'). One of the greatest performers of *Dixieland jazz, he was famous for his gravelly voice and his distinctive trumpet playing. ⇨ illus.

Armstrong[2] /ˈɑːmstrɒŋ/ Neil (1930-), American astronaut. As commander of the Apollo II space mission in 1969 he was the first person to step onto the moon.

army /ˈɑːmɪ/ *n* **1** (**a**) [CGp] part of a country's military forces that is organized and equipped for fighting on land: *The two armies fought for control of the bridge.* ⇨ article at ARMED FORCES. (**b**) **the army** [sing] profession of being a soldier: *go into, be in, join, leave, etc the army* ○ [attrib] *army life.* **2** [CGp] large number (of people, animals, etc): *an army of workmen, officials, ants.* **3** [CGp] organized group of people formed for a purpose: *an army of volunteers* ○ *the Salvation Army.*

Arne /ɑːn/ Thomas Augustine (1710-78), English composer, noted for his opera *Artaxerxes* and music for plays by Shakespeare. He also wrote the patriotic song 'Rule Britannia', originally for the masque *Alfred.*

Arnhem /ˈɑːnəm/ city in the Netherlands, on the River Rhine, and the site of a battle in the Second World War.

Arnold[1] /ˈɑːnəld/ Matthew (1822-88), English poet and critic. His first volume of poems was published in 1849 and was followed by several others, his most famous poems including 'The Scholar-Gipsy' and 'Dover Beach'. For 35 years he worked as an inspector of schools. His prose and essays on literary, cultural, educational and social themes established him as the leading social critic of his time.

Arnold[2] /ˈɑːnəld/ Thomas (1759-1842), headmaster of Rugby School (1828-42) and father of Matthew Arnold. He is famous for his reforms of British public school education. His pupils include Thomas Hughes, the author of *Tom Brown's Schooldays.*

aroma /əˈrəʊmə/ *n* (esp pleasant) distinctive smell; fragrance: *the aroma of coffee, cigars, hot chestnuts.*

▷ **aromatic** /ˌærəˈmætɪk/ *adj* **1** having a pleasant, distinctive smell; fragrant: *aromatic spices.* **2** (*chemistry*) (of an organic compound) containing one or more rings of six carbon atoms, as in benzene.

arose *pt* of ARISE.

around[1] /əˈraʊnd/ *adv* **1** on every side; in every direction: *hear laughter all around.* **2** (*infml esp US*) approximately; about[1](1): *around 100 people* ○ *at around five o'clock.* **3** (in measurements) following the circumference: *an old tree that was six feet around.*

around[2] /əˈraʊnd/ *adv part* (*esp US*) **1** (**a**) here and there; in many directions: *run, drive, walk, look, etc around* ○ *children playing around on the sand* ○ *travel around in Europe for six weeks.* (**b**) here and there within a particular area: *Several young girls were sitting around looking bored.* ○ *books left around on the floor.* **2** in circulation; available: *There was a lot of money around in those days.* ○ *There will be new potatoes around in the shops soon.* ○ *Cable television has been around for some time now.* **3** (**a**) in the surrounding area; near: *I can't see anyone around.* ○ *See you soon, I expect — I'll be around.* (**b**) throughout the surrounding area or building: *I'll send someone to show you around.* ○ *You have 15 minutes to look around.* **4** through an angle of 180°: *Turn around,* ie so as to face in the opposite direction. Cf ABOUT[2]. **5** (idm) **be around** be active and prominent in a particular field or profession: *a new tennis champion who could be around for the next few years* ○ *She's been around as a film director since the 1960's.* **have been around** have gained knowledge and experience of the world, esp in sexual matters: *He pretends he's been around but he's really very immature.* ○ *You won't fool her — she's been around, you know.*

around[3] /əˈraʊnd/ *prep* (*esp US*) **1** (**a**) here and there in; to many places (within a larger area): *running around the playground* ○ *travel around the world.* (**b**) here and there in; at many points within (a particular area): *Chairs were left untidily around the room.* ○ *Blobs of paint were dotted around the canvas.* **2** near (a place): *It's around here somewhere.* ○ *I saw him around the place this morning.* **3** (**a**) forming a circle round (sth); following such a route: *He put his arms around her shoulders.* ○ *run around the block* ○ *The earth moves around the sun.* (**b**) follow the curve of (sth): *going around the corner at 80 mph.* **4** (at) approximately (a time or date): *See you around 7.30.* ○ *It'll be finished around Christmas.* ○ *fashionable around the turn of the century* ○ *It happened around 10 years ago.* Cf ABOUT[3].

arouse /əˈraʊz/ *v* **1** [Tn, Tn·pr] ~ **sb (from sth)** wake sb from sleep: *He was aroused from his nap by the doorbell.* **2** [Tn] cause (sth) to appear; awaken: *Her strange behaviour aroused our suspicions.* ○ *He succeeded in arousing the nation's sympathy.* **3** (**a**) [Tn, Tn·pr] ~ **sb (from/out of sth)** cause sb to become active: *arouse sb from apathy, inactivity, etc.* (**b**) [Tn] stimulate (sb) sexually. Cf ROUSE. ▷ **arousal** /əˈraʊzl/ *n.*

arpeggio /ɑːˈpedʒɪəʊ/ *n* (*pl* ~**s**) (*music*) (**a**) notes of a chord[1] played quickly one after the other, not simultaneously. (**b**) playing or singing of a chord in this way: *practising arpeggios.*

arr *abbr* **1** (*music*) arranged (by): *English folk song, arr Percy Grainger.* **2** arrival; arrive(s); arrived; arriving: *arr London 06.00.* Cf DEP 1.

arrack /ˈæræk/ *n* [U] strong alcoholic drink made in Eastern countries.

arraign /əˈreɪn/ *v* **1** [Tn, Tn·pr] ~ **sb (for sth)** (*law*) bring a criminal charge against sb; bring sb to court for trial: *arraign sb on a charge of murder* ○ *He was arraigned for theft.* **2** [Tn] (*fml*) criticize (sth) strongly. ▷ **arraignment** *n* [U, C].

arrange /əˈreɪndʒ/ *v* **1** [Tn] put (sth) in order; make tidy, neat or attractive: *arrange the books on the shelves* ○ *arrange some flowers in a vase* ○ *She arranged all her business affairs before going on holiday.* **2** (**a**) [Tn] plan the details of (a future event); organize in advance: *arrange a dinner to celebrate their anniversary* ○ *arrange a programme, a timetable, an itinerary, etc* ○ *Her marriage was arranged by her parents,* ie They chose her future husband. (**b**) [Ipr, Tt] ~ **for sb/sth (to do sth)** make sth happen; ensure that sth happens: *I've arranged for a car (to meet you at the airport).* ○ *I'll arrange to be in when you call.* **3** [Ipr, Tn, Tn·pr, Tf, Tw, Tt] ~ **with sb about sth**; ~ **(with sb) to do sth** agree with sb about sth or to do sth: *I've arranged with the neighbours about feeding the cats.* ○ *Let's arrange a time and place for* *our next meeting.* ○ *I arranged with my parents that we could borrow their car.* ○ *They arranged to meet at 7 o'clock.* **4** [Tn, Tn·pr] ~ **sth (for sth)** adapt (a piece of music) for a particular instrument, voice, etc: *He arranged many traditional folk songs (for the piano).*

NOTE ON USAGE: The verbs **arrange**, **organize** and **plan** all have two main meanings. The first is connected with putting things in order, the second with making preparations in advance. **1 Arrange** is to put in a pleasing or correct order: *You must arrange these books in alphabetical order.* **Organize** is to put into a working system: *To write a good essay you must first organize your ideas logically.* **Plan** is to draw a diagram of a place, project, etc: *Before we buy anything, let's plan the kitchen on paper.* **2** When we **arrange** a meeting we invite all the necessary people: *Could you arrange a meeting with Mrs Wilson for Monday, please?* To **organize** a meeting we need to make all the necessary provisions, eg book a room, provide equipment and refreshments, etc: *Who's going to organize the sandwiches for Monday's meeting?* When we **plan** a meeting, we decide in detail on its length, on the agenda, etc: *If we don't plan this meeting properly, we'll get side-tracked into discussing unimportant issues.*

arrangement /əˈreɪndʒmənt/ *n* **1** (**a**) [U] putting in order; arranging: *Can I leave the arrangement of the tables to you?* (**b**) [C] result of this; thing arranged: *a plan of the seating arrangements* ○ *Her flower arrangement won first prize.* **2** [C usu *pl*] ~ (**about/for sth**) plan; preparation: *He's responsible for all the travel arrangements.* ○ *Please make your own arrangements for accommodation.* ○ *I'll make arrangements for you to be met at the airport.* **3** [U, C] ~ **(with sb) to do sth**; ~ **(with sb) (about/over sth)** agreement; settlement: *Appointments can be made by arrangement (with my secretary).* ○ *We can come to some arrangement over the price.* ○ *I have an arrangement with your bank to cash cheques here.* **4** [C] adaptation of a piece of music: *a new arrangement of a popular dance tune.*

arrant /ˈærənt/ *adj* [attrib] (of a bad person or thing) to the highest degree; utter: *an arrant fool, hypocrite, liar, rogue, etc* ○ *He's talking arrant nonsense.*

arras /ˈærəs/ *n* richly decorated tapestry or wall-hanging.

array /əˈreɪ/ *v* [Tn esp passive] (*fml*) **1** place (esp armed forces, troops, etc) in battle order: *His soldiers were arrayed along the river bank.* **2** dress or clothe (sb/oneself): *arrayed in ceremonial robes.*
▷ **array** *n* **1** [C] impressive display or series: *an array of facts, information, statistics, etc* ○ *an array of bottles of different shapes and sizes.* **2** [U] (*fml*) clothes; clothing: *The royal couple appeared in splendid array.* **3** [C] (*computing*) collection of data arranged so that it can be extracted by means of a special program.

arrears /əˈrɪəz/ *n* [pl] **1** money that is owed and should have been paid earlier: *arrears of salary* ○ *rent arrears.* **2** work that has not yet been done: *arrears of correspondence*, ie letters waiting to be answered. **3** (idm) **be in/fall into arrears (with sth)** (**a**) be late in paying money that is owed: *I have fallen into arrears with my rent.* ○ *Payment is made in arrears*, ie at the end of the period in which eg the work was done. (**b**) be late in doing work that is necessary: *I'm in arrears with the housework.*

arrest /əˈrest/ *v* [Tn] **1** seize (sb) with the authority of the law: *After the match three youths were arrested.* **2** (*fml*) stop or check (a process or movement): *Attempts are being made to arrest the spread of the disease.* **3** attract (sth): *An unusual painting arrested his attention.*
▷ **arrest** *n* **1** act of arresting (ARREST 1): *The police made several arrests.* **2** stoppage: *The patient died after suffering a cardiac arrest*, ie when his heart stopped functioning properly. **3** (idm) **be/place sb/put sb under arrest** be/be made a prisoner: *I am placing you under arrest for attempted burglary.* ○ *You are under arrest.*
arrester *n* **1** person who arrests people. **2** device for slowing an aircraft as it lands on an aircraft-carrier: [attrib] *the arrester gear.*
arresting *adj* attracting attention; striking: *an arresting smile.*

Arrhenius /əˈriːnɪəs/ Svante August (1859-1927), Swedish physicist and chemist. One of the founders of modern physical chemistry, Arrhenius was awarded the Nobel prize for chemistry in 1903 for his work on the physical chemistry of electrolytes.

arris /ˈærɪs/ *n* (*architecture*) sharp edge at which two surfaces meet to form an angle with each other.

arrival /əˈraɪvl/ *n* **1** [U] act of arriving: *Cheers greeted the arrival of the Queen.* ○ *On (your) arrival at the hotel please wait for further instructions.* ○ *to await arrival*, ie (on a letter, parcel, etc) to be kept until the person to whom it is addressed arrives. **2** [C] person or thing that arrives: *Late arrivals must wait in the foyer.* ○ *We're expecting a new arrival* (ie a new baby) *in the family soon.*

arrive /əˈraɪv/ *v* **1** [I, Ipr] ~ (**at/in...**) reach (a place), esp at the end of a journey: *arrive home* ○ *What time did you arrive?* ○ *We arrived at the station five minutes late.* ○ *They will arrive in New York at noon.* **2** [I] (of an event in time) come: *The great day has arrived.* ○ *The baby finally arrived* (ie was born) *just after midnight.* **3** [I] (*infml*) become well known or successful: *You know you've arrived when you're asked to appear on TV.* **4** (phr v) **arrive at sth** reach sth: *arrive at an agreement, a decision, a conclusion, etc.*

arriviste /ˌæriːˈviːst/ *n* (*French*) person who is ambitious and ruthless.

arrogant /ˈærəgənt/ *adj* behaving in a proud and superior manner; showing too much pride in oneself and too little consideration for others: *an arrogant tone of voice* ○ *It's arrogant of you to assume you'll win every time.* ▷ **arrogance** /ˈærəgəns/ *n* [U]. **arrogantly** *adv.*

arrogate /ˈærəgeɪt/ *v* [Tn·pr] (*fml*) **1** ~ **sth to oneself** claim or take sth to which one has no right: *arrogating all the credit to himself.* **2** ~ **sth to sb** say unjustly that sb thinks or acts wrongly: *arrogate evil motives to a rival.*

arrow /ˈærəʊ/ *n* **1** thin pointed stick designed to be shot from a bow[1](1). ⇨ illus at ARCHERY. **2** mark or sign resembling this (→), used to show direction or position: *Follow the arrows on the map.* **3** (idm) **straight as an arrow/die** ⇨ STRAIGHT[1].
□ ˈ**arrowhead** *n* pointed end of an arrow.

arrowroot /ˈærəʊruːt/ *n* (**a**) [U] edible starch prepared from the root of an American plant. (**b**) [U, C] this plant.

arroyo /əˈrɔɪəʊ/ *n* (*pl* ~**s**) (*US*) channel or gully cut by a stream, esp in arid country.

arse /ɑːs/ *n* (⚠ *sl*) **1** (*US* **ass** /æs/) buttocks; anus. **2** (usu following an *adj*) person: *You stupid arse!* **3** (idm) **lick sb's arse** ⇨ LICK. **not know one's arse from one's elbow** ⇨ KNOW.
▷ **arse** *v* (phr v) **arse about/around** (⚠ *Brit sl*) behave in a silly manner: *Stop arsing about and give me back my shoes.*
□ ˈ**arse-hole** (*US* ˈ**ass-hole**) *n* (⚠ *sl*) (often used as a term of abuse) anus.
ˈ**arse-licker** *n* (⚠ *sl*) person who tries to win favours by flattering people.

arsenal /ˈɑːsənl/ *n* **1** place where weapons and ammunition are made or stored. **2** store of weapons: (*fig*) *The speaker made full use of his arsenal of invective.*

arsenic /ˈɑːsnɪk/ *n* [U] (*symb* **As**) (*chemistry*) **1** poisonous brittle steel-grey chemical element. ⇨ App 11. **2** any of several poisonous compounds of this, used to poison vermin and in the manufacture of opalescent glass and enamel.

arson /ˈɑːsn/ *n* [U] criminal and deliberate act of setting fire to a house or other building, either from malice or in order to claim insurance money.
▷ **arsonist** /ˈɑːsənɪst/ *n* person who is guilty of arson.

art[1] /ɑːt/ *n* **1** [U] (**a**) creation or expression of sth beautiful, esp in a visual form, eg painting, sculpture, etc: *the art of the Renaissance* ○ *children's art* ○ [attrib] *an art critic, historian, lover, etc.* (**b**) skill in such creation: *Her performance displayed great art.* ○ *This tapestry is a work of art.* (**c**) instances of this: [attrib] *an* ˈ*art exhibition/gallery.* **2 the arts** [pl] = FINE ART (FINE). **3 arts** [pl] subjects of study (eg languages, literature, history) in which imaginative and creative skills are more important than the exact measurement and calculation needed in science: [attrib] *an arts degree with honours in sociology.* **4** [C, U] any skill or ability that can be learnt by practice, esp contrasted with scientific technique; knack: *the art of appearing confident at interviews* ○ *Threading a needle is an art in itself.* ○ *The art of letter-writing is fast disappearing.* **5** (**a**) [U] cunning; trickery. (**b**) [C] trick; wile: *well-practised in the arts of seduction.* **6** (idm) **get sth down to a fine art** ⇨ FINE[2].

art deco: the main entrance of the Hoover factory, West London

□ **art deco** /ˌɑːt ˈdekəʊ; *US* ˌɑː deɪˈkəʊ/ style of (esp interior) design of the 1920s and 1930s, marked by simple geometric shapes, bright colours, and the use of enamel, chrome and plastic. ⇨ illus.
ˈ**art-form** *n* type of artistic activity involving special materials or techniques: *Film-making is now accepted as an art-form.*
art nouveau /ˌɑː nuːˈvəʊ/ style of art, architecture and design from the 1890s to the early 1900s in W Europe and the USA, marked by long flowing lines and curving stylized natural forms, such as those of leaves and flowers. ⇨ illus.
ˌ**arts and** ˈ**crafts** decorative design and handicraft.
the ˌ**Arts and** ˈ**Crafts movement** English movement of the second half of the 19th century inspired by William *Morris, which tried to bring back the traditional ways of making objects by hand, in an age of industrial mass production.
the ˈ**Arts Council** organization established in 1946 to increase the understanding and practice of the arts, esp drama, music, the visual arts and literature, in Britain. The Arts Council is also responsible for making the arts more accessible to the British public, eg by subsidizing theatre companies. ⇨ article at PERFORMING ARTS.
ˈ**artwork** *n* photographs and illustrations in books, newspapers and magazines.

art nouveau: the staircase at Tassel House, Brussels, designed by Victor Horta

art[2] /ɑ:t/ *v* (*arch*) (*2nd pers sing pres t* form of *be*, used with *thou*): *'O rose, thou art sick.'*

Artaud /ɑ:ˈtəʊ/ Antonin (1896-1948), French actor, director and poet, noted for his influence on experimental theatre, esp his ideas on a non-verbal *Theatre of Cruelty.

artefact (also **artifact**) /ˈɑ:tɪfækt/ *n* thing made by man, esp a tool or weapon of archaeological interest: *prehistoric artefacts made of bone and pottery.*

Artemis /ˈɑ:tɪmɪs/ (in Greek mythology) daughter of Zeus, twin sister of Apollo and virgin goddess of hunting, who cared for women giving birth. Her Roman equivalent was *Diana.

arterial /ɑ:ˈtɪərɪəl/ *adj* of or like an artery: *the arterial system*, ie of the body ○ *arterial roads*, ie important main roads.

arteriosclerosis /ɑ:ˌtɪərɪəʊskləˈrəʊsɪs/ *n* [U] diseased condition in which the walls of the arteries become harder and hinder the circulation of the blood.

artery /ˈɑ:tərɪ/ *n* **1** any of the tubes carrying blood from the heart to all parts of the body. Cf VEIN. **2** important route for traffic or transport, eg a road, railway line or river.

artesian well

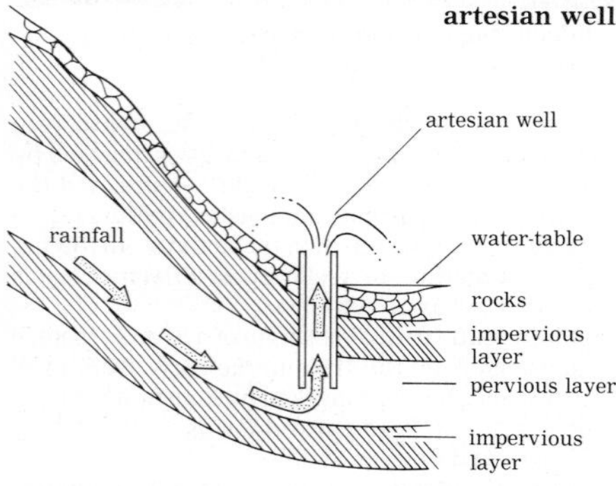

artesian well /ɑ:ˌti:zɪən ˈwel; *US* ɑ:rˈti:ʒn/ well sunk into a layer of rock that receives water from an area higher than the place where the well is. The pressure of water in this layer forces a steady supply of water up and out of the well. ⇨ illus.

artful /ˈɑ:tfl/ *adj* [usu attrib] **1** (of people) cunningly clever at getting what one wants; crafty: *He's an artful devil!* **2** (of things or actions) cleverly made or contrived: *an artful deception, trick, etc* ○ *an artful little gadget for opening tins.* ▷ **artfully** /ˈɑ:tfəlɪ/ *adv.* **artfulness** *n* [U]. Cf ARTLESS.

arthritis /ɑ:ˈθraɪtɪs/ *n* [U] inflammation of a joint or joints of the body, causing pain and stiffness. Cf FIBROSITIS, RHEUMATISM.

▷ **arthritic** /ɑ:ˈθrɪtɪk/ *adj* suffering from or caused by arthritis: *arthritic hands, pains.* — *n* person suffering from arthritis.

arthropod /ˈɑ:θrəpɒd/ *n* (*zoology*) animal with a hard outer body layer, a segmented body and jointed limbs. Over one million species of arthropods exist, including insects, spiders, crabs, centipedes and millipedes, making it the largest phylum in the animal kingdom.

Arthur /ˈɑ:θə(r)/ legendary king of Britain, historically perhaps a 5th-/6th-century Celtic chief or general who fought against the invading Saxons. There are numerous stories, including those told by Sir Thomas *Malory, which describe the exploits of Arthur, his knights of the Round Table, and the search for the *Holy Grail. These stories are still popular and King Arthur is regarded as a folk hero.

▷ **Arthurian** /ɑ:ˈθjuːrɪən/ *adj* [usu attrib] of or relating to King Arthur or his knights: *Arthurian legend, romances.*

artichoke /ˈɑ:tɪtʃəʊk/ *n* **1** (also **globe artichoke**) plant like a large thistle with a flowering head of thick leaf-like scales used as a vegetable. **2** (also **Jerusalem artichoke** /dʒəˌru:sələm ˈɑ:tɪtʃəʊk/) type of sunflower with tuberous roots used as a vegetable.

article /ˈɑ:tɪkl/ *n* **1** particular or separate thing, esp one of a set: *articles of clothing*, eg shirts, socks, hats, coats ○ *toilet articles*, eg soap, toothpaste, shaving-cream ○ *The articles found in the car helped the police identify the body.* **2** piece of writing, complete in itself, in a newspaper, magazine, etc: *an interesting article on/about education.* **3** (*law*) separate clause or item in an agreement or a contract: *articles of apprenticeship*, ie the formal agreement between an apprentice and his employer ○ *articles of association*, ie rules concerning the way in which the affairs of a company are managed. **4** (*grammar*) either of the determiners 'a/an' (*the indefinite article*) or 'the' (*the definite article*).

▷ **article** *v* [usu passive: Tn, Tn·pr] ~ **sb** (**to sb**) employ sb under contract as a trainee: *an articled clerk* ○ *articled to a solicitor.*

□ ˌ**article of ˈfaith** 1 basic point of sb's religious belief. **2** any firmly held belief.

articulate[1] /ɑ:ˈtɪkjʊlət/ *adj* **1** (of a person) able to express one's ideas clearly in words: *She's unusually articulate for a ten-year-old.* **2** (of speech) clearly pronounced. **3** having joints. ▷ **articulately** *adv.* **articulateness** *n* [U].

articulate[2] /ɑ:ˈtɪkjʊleɪt/ *v* **1** [I, Tn] speak (sth) clearly and distinctly: *I'm a little deaf — please articulate (your words) carefully.* **2** [Ipr, Tn·pr usu passive] ~ (**sth**) **with sth** form a joint or connect (sth) by joints with sth: *bones that articulate/are articulated with others.*

□ **arˌticulated ˈvehicle, arˌticulated ˈlorry** (*US* **tractor-trailer**) vehicle with sections connected by flexible joints so that it can turn more easily. ⇨ illus at LORRY.

articulation /ɑ:ˌtɪkjʊˈleɪʃn/ *n* **1** [U] making of speech sounds: *As he drank more wine his articulation became worse.* **2** [U, C] (connection by means of a) joint.

artifact = ARTEFACT.

artifice /ˈɑ:tɪfɪs/ *n* [C, U] (instance of) clever trickery; deception: *Pretending to faint was merely (an) artifice.*

artificer /ɑ:ˈtɪfɪsə(r)/ *n* skilled workman or mechanic, esp one in the army or navy.

artificial /ˌɑ:tɪˈfɪʃl/ *adj* **1** made or produced by man in imitation of sth natural; not real: *artificial flowers, light, limbs, pearls.* **2** affected; insincere; not genuine: *Her artificial gaiety disguised an inner sadness.* ▷ **artificiality** /ˌɑ:tɪfɪʃɪˈælətɪ/ *n* [U]. **artificially** /ˌɑ:tɪˈfɪʃəlɪ/ *adv.*

□ ˌ**artificial hoˈrizon** instrument similar to a gyroscope, used in an aircraft to show its position in relation to the horizon.

ˌ**artificial insemiˈnation** injection of semen into the womb (esp of animals) artificially, so that conception can occur without sexual intercourse.

ˌ**artificial inˈtelligence** (*abbr* **AI**) (study of) the capacity of machines to simulate intelligent human behaviour.

ˌ**artificial respiˈration** process of forcing air into and out of the lungs to stimulate natural breathing again when it has failed, eg in a person who has almost drowned.

artillery /ɑ:ˈtɪlərɪ/ *n* [U] **1** heavy guns (often mounted on wheels), eg cannon and mortars, with a calibre of more than 20mm, used in fighting on land: [attrib] *an artillery regiment.* **2** branch of an army that uses these: *a captain in the artillery.*

artisan /ˌɑ:tɪˈzæn; *US* ˈɑ:rtɪzn/ *n* (*fml*) skilled workman or craftsman: *an artisan in leatherwork.*

artist /ˈɑ:tɪst/ *n* **1** person who practises any of the fine arts, esp painting: *Constable was a great English artist.* **2** person who does sth with great skill: *The carpenter has made this cupboard beautifully — he's a real artist.* **3** = ARTISTE.

artiste /ɑ:ˈti:st/ *n* professional entertainer, eg a singer, a dancer, an actor, etc: *Among the artistes appearing on our show tonight we have....*

artistic /ɑ:ˈtɪstɪk/ *adj* **1** (**a**) having natural skill in any of the fine arts. (**b**) showing a sensitive appreciation of and liking for the fine arts: *She comes from a very artistic family.* **2** done with skill and good taste; beautiful: *The decor is so artistic.* **3** of art and artists: *an artistic temperament*, ie impulsive and eccentric behaviour thought to be typical of artists. ▷ **artistically** /ɑ:ˈtɪstɪklɪ/ *adv.*

artistry /ˈɑ:tɪstrɪ/ *n* [U] skill or work of an artist: *admire the artistry of the painter's use of colour.*

artless /ˈɑ:tlɪs/ *adj* simple and natural; without deceit: *as artless as a child of five* ○ *My artless comment was mistaken for rudeness.* Cf ARTFUL.

arty /ˈɑ:tɪ/ *adj* (*infml derog*) showing a pretentious artistic style or a false or exaggerated interest in art: *His arty clothes look out of place in the office.*

□ ˌ**arty-ˈcrafty** *adj* (*joc or derog infml*) (of furniture and household objects) appearing to be made by hand and designed for artistic effect rather than for usefulness or comfort.

arum lily /ˌeərəm ˈlɪlɪ/ type of tall cultivated lily with a long white funnel-shaped flower.

-ary *suff* (with *ns* forming *adjs* and *ns*) concerned with; of: *planetary* ○ *reactionary* ○ *budgetary* ○ *commentary.*

Aryan /ˈeərɪən/ *adj* **1** of the Indo-European group of languages. **2** of speakers of these languages.

▷ **Aryan** *n* **1** person who speaks an Indo-European language. **2** (formerly used in Germany under Nazi rule) person with non-Jewish Germanic ancestors.

as /əz, *strong form* æz/ *prep* **1** so as to appear to be (sb): *dressed as a policeman* ○ *They entered the building disguised as cleaners.* **2** having the function or character of (sb): *a job as a packer* ○ *work as a courier* ○ *I'm speaking as your employer.* ○ *Treat me as a friend.* ○ *accept sb as an equal* ○ *I respect him as a writer and as a man.* ⇨ Usage. **3** (**a**) since sb is (sth): *As her private secretary he has access to all her correspondence.* (**b**) when or while sb is (sth): *As a child she was sent to six different schools.*

▷ **as** *adv* **1 as...as** (used before *advs* and *adjs* in order to make a comparison) (**a**) (with the second *as* a *prep*) to the same extent...; equally...as: *as tall as his father* ○ *This dress is twice as expensive as that.* ○ *He doesn't play half as well as his sister.* ○ *I haven't known him as long as you.* ○ *As likely as not* (ie Very probably), *it will rain.* (**b**) (with the second *as* a *conj*) to the same extent...as; equally...as: *He looks as ill as he sounded on the phone.* ○ *His eyes aren't quite as blue as they look in the film.* ○ *Run as fast as you can.* ○ *He recited as much of the poem as he could remember.* ○ *She's as good an actress as she is a singer.* **2** not differently from; like: *As before he remained unmoved.* ○ *The 'h' is silent as in 'hour'.*

as *conj* **1** during the time when; while: *I watched her as she combed her hair.* ○ *As he grew older he lost interest in everything except gardening.* **2** (usu placed at the beginning of the sentence) since; because: *As you weren't there I left a message.* ○ *As she's been ill perhaps she'll need some help.* **3** (used after an *adj* or *adv* to introduce a clause of concession) although: *Young as I am, I already know what career I want to follow.* ○ *Talented as he is, he is not yet ready to turn professional.* ○ *Much as I like you, I couldn't live with you.* ○ *Try as he would/might, he couldn't open the door.* **4** in the way in which: *Do as I say and sit down.* ○ *Leave the table as it is,* ie Do not disturb the things on it. ○ *Why didn't you catch the last bus as I told you to?* **5** a fact which: *Cyprus, as you know, is an island in the Mediterranean.* ○ *The Beatles, as many of you are old enough to remember, came from Liverpool.* **6** (usu followed by *be* or *do* + subject) and so too: *She's unusually tall, as are both her parents.* ○ *He's a doctor, as was his wife before she had children.* ⇨ Usage. **7** (idm) **as against sth** in contrast with sth: *She gets Saturdays off in her new job as against working alternate weekends in her last one.* ○ *We had twelve hours of sunshine yesterday, as against a forecast of continuous rain.* **ˌas and ˈwhen** **(a)** (referring to an uncertain future event or action) when: *We'll decide on our team as and when we qualify for the competition.* Cf IF AND WHEN (IF). **(b)** (*infml*) when possible; eventually: *I'll tell you more as and when,* ie as soon as I can. **as for sb/sth** with regard to sb/sth: *As for the hotel, it was very uncomfortable and miles from the sea.* ○ *As for you, you ought to be ashamed of yourself.* **as from**; *esp US* **as of** (indicating the time or date from which sth starts): *As from next Monday you can use my office.* ○ *We shall have a new address as of 12 May.* **as if**; **as though** with the appearance of; apparently: *He behaved as if nothing had happened.* ○ *As if unsure of where she was, she hesitated and looked round.* ○ *He rubbed his eyes and yawned as though waking up after a long sleep.* **ˌas it ˈis** taking present circumstances into account; as things are: *We were hoping to have a holiday next week — as it is, we may not be able to get away.* ○ *I thought I might be transferred but as it is I shall have to look for a new job.* **ˌas it ˈwere** (used to comment on the speaker's own choice of words, which may give only an approximate meaning): *She seemed very relaxed — in her natural setting as it were.* ○ *He'd been watching the water rising for two hours — preparing to meet his destiny, as it were — before help arrived.* **as to sth**; **as regards sth** with regard to sth; regarding sth: *As to correcting our homework, the teacher always makes us do it ourselves.* ○ *There are no special rules as regards what clothes you should wear.* **as yet** ⇨ YET. **ˌas you ˈwere** (used as an order to soldiers, etc to return to their previous positions, activities, etc.)

NOTE ON USAGE: **1** When referring to the similarity between people, things and actions, both **as** and **like** are used. **Like** is a preposition and is used before nouns and pronouns: *Like me, she enjoys all kinds of music.* **As** is a conjunction and is used before a clause: *She enjoys all kinds of music, as I do.* In informal speech **like** is frequently used as a conjunction, replacing both **as** and **as if**: *Nobody understands him like/as I do.* ○ *It looks like/as if he won't arrive in time.* **2** Compare the use of **as** and **like** indicating occupations or functions: *She worked as a teacher* (ie was a teacher) *for many years. Our doctor always talks to me like a teacher talking to a child,* ie He is not a teacher but he has the manner of one.

ASA /ˌeɪ es ˈeɪ/ *abbr* **1** Advertising Standards Authority. **2** (also **ASA/BS**) (of a scale of film speeds) American Standards Association (/British Standard): *ASA/BS 100.* Cf BS, BSI, DIN, ISO.

asafoetida /ˌæsəˈfetɪdə, *Brit also* -ˈfi:t-/ *n* [U] resinous strong-smelling plant gum, formerly used in medicine.

asap /ˌeɪ es eɪ ˈpi:/ *abbr* as soon as possible.

asbestos /æsˈbestɒs, *also* əzˈbestəs/ *n* [U] soft fibrous grey mineral substance that can be made into fireproof material or used for heat insulation.
▷ **asbestosis** /ˌæsbesˈtəʊsɪs/ *n* [U] disease of the lungs caused by inhaling asbestos particles.

ascend /əˈsend/ *v* [I, Tn] (*fml*) go or come up (sth): *The path started to ascend more steeply at this point.* ○ *We watched the mists ascending from the valley below.* ○ *notes ascending and descending the scale* ○ (*fig*) *ascend the throne,* ie become king or queen.

ascendancy (also **ascendency**) /əˈsendənsɪ/ *n* [U] ~ **(over sb/sth)** (position of) having dominant power or control: *He has (gained) the ascendancy over all his main rivals.*

ascendant (also **ascendent**) /əˈsendənt/ *n* **1** (*astrology*) part of the zodiac that rises above the eastern horizon at a particular time, eg at the birth of a child. **2** (idm) **in the ascendant** rising in power and influence: *Though he is still a young man his political career is already in the ascendant.*

ascension /əˈsenʃn/ *n* **1** [U] act of ascending. **2 the Ascension** [sing] (in the Bible) departure of Jesus from the earth into heaven.
□ **Asˈcension Day** day on which the Ascension is commemorated in the Christian Church, ie the Thursday that is the fortieth day after Easter.

Ascension Island /əˈsenʃn aɪlənd/ small island in the S Atlantic, incorporated with St Helena; area 88 sq km (34 sq miles); pop approx 1 500.

ascent /əˈsent/ *n* **1** act of ascending: *the ascent of Mount Everest* ○ *Who was the first man to make an ascent in a balloon?* **2** upward path or slope: *The last part of the ascent is very steep.*

ascertain /ˌæsəˈteɪn/ *v* [Tn, Tf, Tw] (*fml*) discover (sth) so that one is certain; get to know: *ascertain the true facts* ○ *ascertain that the report is accurate* ○ *ascertain who is likely to come to the meeting* ○ *The police are trying to ascertain what really happened.* ▷ **ascertainable** *adj.* **ascertainment** *n* [U].

ascetic /əˈsetɪk/ *adj* [usu attrib] not allowing oneself pleasures and comforts; having or involving a very austere life: *the ascetic existence of monks and hermits.*
▷ **ascetic** *n* person who leads a very simple life without basic comforts, esp for religious reasons. **ascetically** /-klɪ/ *adv.* **asceticism** /əˈsetɪsɪzəm/ *n* [U].

ASCII /ˈæskɪ/ *abbr* (*computing*) American Standard Code for Information Interchange, a standard code for storing and transmitting information in computer systems.

Asclepius /əˈskli:pɪəs/ (in Greek mythology) son of Apollo and god of healing. Cf AESCULAPIUS.

ascorbic acid /əˌskɔ:bɪk ˈæsɪd/ vitamin found esp in citrus fruits and vegetables; vitamin C.

Ascot /ˈæskət/ racecourse near Windsor, Berkshire, England, where the four-day race-meeting called 'Royal Ascot' takes place every June. ⇨ article at SEASON.

ascribe /əˈskraɪb/ *v* [Tn·pr] ~ **sth to sb/sth** consider sth to be caused by, written by or belonging to sb/sth: *He ascribed his failure to bad luck.* ○ *This play is usually ascribed to Shakespeare.* ○ *You can't ascribe the same meaning to both words.*
▷ **ascribable** *adj* [pred] ~ **to sb/sth** that can be ascribed to sb/sth: *His success is ascribable simply to hard work.*

ascription /əˈskrɪpʃn/ *n* [C, U] ~ **(to sb/sth)** (*fml*) (act of) ascribing sth (to sb/sth).

asdic /ˈæzdɪk/ *n* [U] early form of sonar.

ASEAN /ˈæzɪæn/ *abbr* Association of South-East Asian Nations.

asepsis /ˌeɪˈsepsɪs; *US* əˈsep-/ *n* [U] state of being free from harmful bacteria.

aseptic /ˌeɪˈseptɪk; *US* əˈsep-/ *adj* (of wounds, dressings, etc) free from bacteria that cause a thing to become septic; surgically clean.

asexual /ˌeɪˈsekʃʊəl/ *adj* **1** without sex or sex organs: *asexual reproduction.* **2** having or showing no interest in sexual relations: *an asexual relationship.* ▷ **asexuality** /eɪˌsekʃʊˈælətɪ/ *n* [U].

ash[1] /æʃ/ *n* **(a)** [C] tree commonly found in forests, with silver-grey bark and hard close-grained wood. ⇨ illus at TREE. **(b)** [U] its wood, used for tool handles, etc.
□ **ˈash plant** *n* strong walking-stick made from the stem of a young ash tree.

ash[2] /æʃ/ *n* [U] powder that remains after sth (esp tobacco, coal, etc) has burnt: *cigarette ash* ○ *volcanic ash,* ie fine particles of rock and lava from a volcano ○ *Coke is an economical fuel but it leaves a lot of ash.* Cf ASHES.
□ **ˌash ˈblonde** **(a)** (of hair) very light greyish-blond in colour. **(b)** woman with hair of this colour.
ˈashpan *n* tray (placed underneath a fireplace, stove, etc) into which the ashes drop from a fire.
ˈashtray *n* small dish or container into which smokers put tobacco ash, cigarette ends, etc.
ˌAsh ˈWednesday first day of Lent. Cf SHROVE TUESDAY.

ashamed /əˈʃeɪmd/ *adj* [pred] **1** ~ **(of sth/sb/oneself)**; ~ **(that...)** feeling shame, embarrassment, etc about sth/sb or because of one's own actions: *ashamed of her behaviour at the party* ○ *You should be ashamed of yourself for telling such lies.* ○ *He felt ashamed of having done so little work.* ○ *I feel ashamed that I haven't written for so long.* **2** ~ **to do sth** reluctant to do sth because of shame or embarrassment: *I'm ashamed to say I haven't been to a dentist for three years.* ○ *He felt too ashamed to ask for help.* ○ *I'm ashamed to let you see my paintings.*

ashen /ˈæʃn/ *adj* like ashes in colour; very pale: *She listened to the tragic news ashen-faced.*

ashes /ˈæʃɪz/ *n* [pl] **1** powder that remains after sth has been destroyed by burning: *Ashes were all that remained of her books after the fire.* ○ *The house was burnt to ashes overnight.* Cf ASH. **2** remains of a human body after cremation: *His ashes were buried next to those of his wife.* **3 the Ashes** symbolic trophy won by the winning team after a series of cricket test matches between England and Australia. **4** (idm) **rake over old ashes** ⇨ RAKE[1]. **sackcloth and ashes** ⇨ SACKCLOTH (SACK[1]).

Ashkenazi /ˌæʃkəˈnɑ:zɪ/ *n* (*pl* **-nazim**) Jew of German or E European origin. Cf SEPHARDI.

ashlar /ˈæʃlə(r)/ *n* [U] **(a)** square-cut stones used for building. **(b)** thin slabs of these used for facing walls.

Ashmolean Museum /æʃˈməʊlɪən mju:ˈzi:əm/ **the Ashmolean Museum** museum of ancient history, art and archaeology in Oxford, England, founded in 1683 by Elias Ashmole. It is the oldest public museum in Britain. ⇨ article at MUSEUM.

ashore /əˈʃɔ:(r)/ *adv* to or on the shore or land: *We went ashore when the boat reached the port.* ○ *The ship was driven ashore* (ie forced onto the shore) *by the bad weather.*

ashram /ˈæʃrəm; *US* ˈɑ:ʃrəm/ *n* place of religious retreat, esp in India.

Ashton /ˈæʃtən/ Sir Frederick (1904-88), British ballet dancer and choreographer; one of the founders of the Royal Ballet and its director 1963-70. His ballets, which include *Façade, La Fille mal gardée,* and *A Month in the Country,* are softly lyrical and classical in style.

ashy /ˈæʃɪ/ *adj* of or like ashes; covered with ashes: *His face was ashy grey.*

Asia /ˈeɪʃə; *US* ˈeɪʒə/ largest of the world's continents, extending from Europe to the Pacific Ocean. It is connected to Africa by the isthmus of Suez, and generally regarded as being divided from Europe by a line formed by the Ural mountains and the Caspian Sea. The continent is currently dominated by the USSR, China and India.
▷ **Asian** /ˈeɪʃn; *US* ˈeɪʒn/ *n* (person descended from a) native or inhabitant of Asia. — *adj* of Asia: *of Asian blood/descent/origin.*
Asiatic /ˌeɪzɪ-/ *adj* of Asia: *the Asiatic plains.* — *n* (*offensive*) Asian person.
□ **ˌAsia ˈMinor** peninsula of W Asia between the Mediterranean and the Black Sea, including most of Turkey.

aside /əˈsaɪd/ *adv* **1** on or to one side of the main position, direction, etc: *pull the curtain aside* ○ *Stand aside and let these people pass.* ○ *He took me aside to tell me of his wife's illness.* ○ (*fig*) *You must put aside* (ie out of your thoughts) *any idea of a holiday this year.* **2** in reserve: *set aside some money for one's retirement* ○ *Please put this jumper aside* (ie reserve it) *for me.*

▷ **aside** *n* **1** (in the theatre) words spoken by an actor on stage that are intended to be heard by the audience but not by the other characters on stage. **2** incidental remark: *I mention it only as an aside.*
□ **aside from** *prep* (*esp US*) = APART FROM (APART).

Asimov /ˈæzɪmɒf/ Isaac (1920-), American writer, born in Russia, known particularly for his science-fiction stories and novels.

asinine /ˈæsɪnaɪn/ *adj* stupid or stubborn: *What an asinine thing to say!*

ask /ɑːsk/ *v* **1** [I, Ipr, Tn, Tn·pr, Tw, Dn·n, Dn·w] ~ **(sb) (about sb/sth)**; ~ **sth of sb** request information (about sb/sth) (from sb): *Ask (him) about the ring you lost — he may have found it.* ○ *Don't be afraid of asking questions.* ○ *Did you ask the price?* ○ (*fml*) *No questions were asked of us.* ○ *He asked if I could drive.* ○ *She asked them their names.* ○ *I had to ask the teacher what to do next.* **2** [Ipr, Tn, Tn·pr, Tw, Dn·w, Dn·t] ~ **(sb) for sth**; ~ **sth (of sb)** request that sb gives sth or does sth: *Did you ask (your boss) for a pay increase?* ○ *ask sb's advice, opinion, views, etc* ○ *If you want to camp in this field you must ask the farmer's permission.* ○ *May I ask a favour (of you)?* ○ *It's asking rather a lot of you to have my whole family to stay.* ○ *She asked (me) if I would drive her home.* ○ *I asked James to buy some bread.* **3** [Tw, Tt, Dn·w, Dn·t] request permission to do sth: *ask to use the car* ○ *ask to speak to sb*, eg on the phone ○ *I asked (the doctor) whether/if I could get up.* ○ *I must ask you to excuse me.* **4** [Tn·pr, Tn·p, Dn·t] ~ **sb (to sth)** invite sb: *ask them to dinner* ○ *He's asked me out several times already.* ○ *Shall we ask the neighbours in/round* (ie to our house)*?* ○ *She's asked him to come to the party.* **5** [Tn, Tn·pr] ~ **sth (for sth)** request sth as a price: *You're asking too much.* ○ *What are they asking for their house?* ○ *He's asking £80 a month rent for that flat.* **6** (idm) ˈ**ask for trouble/it** (*infml*) behave in a way that is likely to result in trouble: *Driving after drinking alcohol is asking for trouble.* **for the** ˈ**asking** if one merely asks: *The job is yours for the asking*, ie If you say you want it, it will be given to you. **I** ˈ**ask you** (*infml*) (expressing disbelief, surprise, annoyance, etc): *They're thinking of taxing textbooks — I ask you, we'll have to pay to go to bed next!* **if you ask** ˈ**me** if you would like to know my opinion: *If you ask me, he hasn't got long to live.* **7** (phr v) **ask after sb** request information about sb's health: *He always asks after you in his letters.* **ask for sb/sth** say that one wants to see or speak to sb or to be given or directed to sth: *ask for the manager, the tickets, the bar.*
□ ˈ**asking price** price at which sth is offered for sale: *Never offer more than the asking price for a house.*

NOTE ON USAGE: When making a request for somebody to do something, **ask** is the most usual and informal word: *I asked her to shut the window.* ○ *He asked me for a light.* The verb **request** is mainly used in formal speech and writing, often in public notices and commonly in the passive form: *Dear Sir, I have been requested to inform you that...* ○ *Passengers are kindly requested not to smoke at the buffet counter.* **Beg** suggests the asking of a great favour in a humble manner: *He knew he had hurt her and begged her to forgive him.* **Entreat**, **implore** and **beseech** are stronger and more formal than **beg:** *He entreated/implored/beseeched her not to desert him.*

askance /əˈskæns/ *adv* (idm) **look askance (at sb/sth)** look (usu sideways) at sb/sth with distrust or disapproval: *look askance at the price* ○ *She looked at me rather askance when I suggested a swim in the nude.*

askew /əˈskjuː/ *adj* [pred], *adv* not in a straight or level position; crooked(ly): *The picture is hanging askew.* ○ *He's got his hat on askew.* ○ *The line is drawn all askew.*

aslant /əˈslɑːnt; *US* əˈslænt/ *adv, prep* in a slanting direction or obliquely (across): *The evening sunlight shone aslant through the window.* ○ *The wrecked train lay aslant the track.*

asleep /əˈsliːp/ *adj* [pred] **1** not awake; sleeping: *Don't wake her up — she's fast/sound asleep.* ○ *He fell asleep during the sermon.* **2** (of limbs) having no feeling; numb: *I've been sitting on my leg and now it's asleep.*

ASLEF (also **Aslef**) /ˈæzlef/ *abbr* Associated Society of Locomotive Engineers and Firemen, a powerful British trade union. ⇨ article at TRADE UNION.

A/S level /eɪ ˈes levl/ (in Britain) GCE examination introduced in 1989 of a standard between GCSE and Advanced level, allowing students to study more subjects than at Advanced level.

asp /æsp/ *n* small poisonous snake found esp in N Africa, said to have been the type that killed *Cleopatra.

asparagus /əˈspærəgəs/ *n* [U] **(a)** plant with feathery leaves whose young shoots are cooked and eaten as a vegetable. **(b)** these shoots: *have (some) asparagus for lunch* ○ [attrib] *asparagus soup.*

aspect /ˈæspekt/ *n* **1** [C] particular part or feature of sth being considered: *look at every aspect of the problem.* **2** [sing] (*fml*) (esp of people) appearance or look: *a man of enormous size and terrifying aspect.* **3** [C usu *sing*] (*fml*) direction in which a building, room, window, etc faces: *The house has a southern aspect.* **4** [C] (in astrology) relative position of stars and planets, thought to influence events on earth. **5** [C] (*grammar*) range of meanings expressed by the verb forms *have* + past participle (eg *has worked*) or *be* + present participle (eg *is working*).
▷ **aspectual** /æˈspektʃʊəl/ *adj* (*grammar*) concerned with aspect(5): *There is an aspectual difference between 'He crossed the road' and 'He was crossing the road'.*

aspen /ˈæspən/ *n* any of several trees of the poplar family with leaves that flutter even in the slightest wind.

asperity /æˈsperətɪ/ *n* (*fml*) **1** [U] harshness or severity, esp of manner: *reply with asperity.* **2** [C usu *pl*, U] (instance of) very cold or severe weather: *suffer the asperities of winter near the North Pole.*

aspersions /əˈspɜːʃnz; *US* -ʒnz/ *n* [pl] (*fml or rhet*) **1** damaging or derogatory remarks: *I strongly resent such unwarranted aspersions.* **2** (idm) **cast aspersions** ⇨ CAST[1].

asphalt /ˈæsfælt; *US* -fɔːlt/ *n* [U] black sticky substance like coal tar, mixed with sand or gravel for making road surfaces, or used to make roofs, etc waterproof.
▷ **asphalt** *v* [Tn] cover (esp a road) with asphalt.

asphodel /ˈæsfədel/ *n* **1** plant of the lily family that grows esp in S Europe and has white or yellow flowers. **2** (in Greek mythology) immortal flower that grows in the Elysian fields.

asphyxia /əsˈfɪksɪə; *US* æsˈf-/ *n* [U] condition caused by lack of air in the lungs; suffocation.
▷ **asphyxiate** /əsˈfɪksɪeɪt/ *v* [Tn usu passive] cause (sb) to become ill or to die by preventing enough air from reaching the lungs; suffocate: *asphyxiated by the smoke and poisonous fumes.* **asphyxiation** /əsˌfɪksɪˈeɪʃn/ *n* [U].

aspic /ˈæspɪk/ *n* [U] clear meat jelly served with or around meat, fish, eggs, etc: *chicken in aspic.*

aspidistra /ˌæspɪˈdɪstrə/ *n* tall Asian plant with broad pointed leaves, usu grown indoors.

aspirant /əˈspaɪərənt/ *n* ~ **(to/after/for sth)** (*fml*) person who is ambitious (for fame, promotion, success, etc): *an aspirant to the presidency.*

aspirate /ˈæspərət/ *n* (*phonetics*) sound of 'h' or of a consonant containing it: *The word 'hour' is pronounced without an initial aspirate.*
▷ **aspirate** /ˈæspəreɪt/ *v* [Tn] pronounce (sth) with an 'h' sound: *The initial 'h' in 'hour' is not aspirated.*

aspiration /ˌæspəˈreɪʃn/ *n* **1** [U, C often *pl*] ~ **(for/after sth)**; ~ **(to do sth)** strong desire or ambition: *She was filled with the aspiration to succeed in life.* ○ *He has serious aspirations to a career in politics.* **2** [U] aspirating.

aspirator /ˈæspəreɪtə(r)/ *n* apparatus for removing liquid or air from a cavity in the body by means of suction.

aspire /əˈspaɪə(r)/ *v* [Ipr, It] ~ **after/to sth** desire strongly to achieve sth; have ambition for sth: *aspire after knowledge* ○ *aspire to become an author* ○ *Aspiring musicians must practise many hours a day.*

aspirin /ˈæsprɪn, ˈæspərɪn/ *n* **(a)** [U] white powder (acetylsalicylic acid) that is used to relieve pain and reduce fever: *Have you got any aspirin?* **(b)** [C] tablet(2) of this: *Take two aspirins for your headache.*

Asquith /ˈæskwɪθ/ Herbert Henry, 1st Earl of Oxford and Asquith (1852-1928), British statesman, Liberal prime minister (1908-16) and leader of the Liberal Party (1908-26). Asquith's government introduced the first provision for old-age pensions and also restricted the power of the House of Lords to veto legislation. Asquith led Britain into the First World War, forming a coalition with the Conservatives (1915-16). ⇨ App 2.

ass[1] /æs/ *n* **1** (also **donkey**) animal related to the horse, with long ears and a tuft at the end of its tail. **2** (*infml*) stupid person: *Don't be such an ass!* **3** (idm) **make an** ˈ**ass of oneself** behave stupidly so that one appears ridiculous: *I made a real ass of myself at the meeting — standing up and then forgetting the question.*

ass[2] /æs/ *n* (⚠ *US sl*) **1** [C] = ARSE. **2** [U] sexual intercourse.

assail /əˈseɪl/ *v* [Tn, Tn·pr] ~ **sb (with sth)** (*fml*) attack sb violently or repeatedly: *assailed with fierce blows to the head* ○ *assail sb with questions, insults, etc* ○ *assailed by worries, doubts, fears, etc.*
▷ **assailant** *n* (*fml*) person who attacks: *He was unable to recognize his assailant in the dark.*

Assam /æˈsæm/ state of NE India with very high rainfall, in which large quantities of tea are produced.

assassin /əˈsæsɪn; *US* -sn/ *n* killer, esp one who kills an important or famous person for money or for political reasons.

assassinate /əˈsæsɪneɪt; *US* -sən-/ *v* [Tn] kill (esp an important or famous person) for money or for political reasons.
▷ **assassination** /əˌsæsɪˈneɪʃn; *US* əˌsæsəˈneɪʃn/ *n* **(a)** [U] murder of this kind. **(b)** [C] instance of this.

assault /əˈsɔːlt/ *n* [C, U] ~ **(on sth)** sudden violent attack: *make an assault on the enemy lines* ○ *The roar of city traffic is a steady assault on one's nerves.* ○ *an alarming increase in cases of indecent assault*, eg rape.
▷ **assault** *v* [Tn] make an assault on (sb): *He got two years' imprisonment for assaulting a police officer.* ○ *Six women have been sexually assaulted in the area recently.*
□ **as**ˌ**sault and** ˈ**battery** (*law*) offence of threatening to attack sb and then actually attacking him.
asˈ**sault craft** portable boat with an outboard motor, used for making attacks across rivers, etc.

assay /əˈseɪ/ *n* testing of esp metals for quality: *make an assay of an ore.*
▷ **assay** *v* **1** [Tn] test the quality of (a metal); analyse (eg an ore). **2** [Tn, Tt] (*arch*) attempt (esp sth difficult).
□ **the As**ˈ**say Office** (in Britain) office that gives hallmarks to articles of gold and silver.

assegai /ˈæsəgaɪ/ *n* light iron-tipped throwing-spear used by S African tribes.

assemblage /əˈsemblɪdʒ/ *n* **1** [U] (*fml*) act of bringing or coming together; assembly. **2** [C] (*often joc*) collection of things or people: *an odd assemblage of broken bits of furniture.*

assemble /əˈsembl/ *v* **1** [I, Tn] (cause people or things to) come together; collect: *The whole school (was) assembled in the main hall.* ○ *assemble evidence, material, equipment, a collection of objects.* **2** [Tn] fit together (the parts of sth): *assemble the parts of a watch* ○ *The bookcase can easily be assembled with a screwdriver.*
▷ **assembler** /əˈsemblə(r)/ *n* computer program that translates instructions from a low-level language into a form that can be understood and

used by a computer.

assembly /əˈsemblɪ/ *n* **1** **(a)** [U] coming together of a group of people for a specific purpose: *Morning assembly is held in the school hall.* ○ *deny sb the right of assembly* ○ (*law*) *unlawful assembly* ○ [attrib] *assembly rooms.* **(b)** [CGp] group of people in such a meeting: *The motion was put to the assembly.* ○ *The national assembly has/have met to discuss the crisis.* ○ *the legislative assemblies of the USA.* **2** **(a)** [U] act or process of fitting together the parts of sth: *The assembly of cars is often done by machines.* ○ *Each component is carefully checked before assembly.* ○ [attrib] *an assembly plant*, eg in a factory. **(b)** [C] unit consisting of smaller manufactured parts that have been fitted together: *the tail assembly of an aircraft.* **3** [C] sound of a drum or bugle calling soldiers to assemble.

▷ **assemblyman** /əˈsemblɪmən/ *n* (*pl* **-men** /-mən/) (*US*) member of a legislative assembly.

□ **asˈsembly language** low-level computer programming language allowing the programmer to use a notation which he can easily read and remember.

asˈsembly line sequence of machines and workers along which a product moves as it is assembled in stages: *He works on the assembly line at the local car factory.*

assent /əˈsent/ *n* [U] ~ (**to sth**) (*fml*) agreement; approval: *give one's assent to a proposal* ○ *by common assent*, ie with everybody's agreement ○ *The new bill passed by Parliament has received the royal assent*, ie been approved by the monarch.

▷ **assent** *v* [I, Ipr] ~ (**to sth**) express agreement; consent: *I can never assent to such a request.*

assert /əˈsɜːt/ *v* **1** [Tn] **(a)** make others recognize (sth) by behaving firmly and confidently: *assert one's authority, independence, rights.* **(b)** ~ **oneself** behave in a confident manner that attracts attention and respect: *You're too timid — you must try to assert yourself more.* **2** [Tn, Tf] state (sth) clearly and forcefully as the truth: *She asserted her innocence/that she was innocent.*

assertion /əˈsɜːʃn/ *n* **1** [U] action of claiming or stating forcefully; insistence: *assertion of one's authority* ○ *an air of self-assertion* ○ *speak with assertion.* **2** [C] strong statement claiming the truth of sth: *I seriously question a number of your assertions.*

assertive /əˈsɜːtɪv/ *adj* showing a strong and confident personality; asserting oneself: *an assertive young man* ○ *state one's opinions in an assertive tone of voice.* ▷ **assertively** *adv.* **assertiveness** *n* [U].

assess /əˈses/ *v* **1** [Tn, Tn·pr] ~ **sth** (**at sth**) decide or fix the amount of sth: *assess sb's taxes/income* ○ *assess the damage at £350.* **2** [Tn] decide or fix the value of (sth); evaluate: *have a house assessed by a valuer.* **3** [Tn, Cn·n/a] ~ **sth** (**as sth**) estimate the quality of sth: *It's difficult to assess the impact of the President's speech.* ○ *I'd assess your chances as extremely low.*

▷ **assessment** *n* **1** **(a)** [U] action of assessing: *Continuous assessment is made of all students' work.* **(b)** [C] evaluation or opinion: *What is your assessment of the situation?* **2** [C] amount fixed for payment: *a tax assessment.*

assessor *n* **1** person who assesses taxes or the value of property, etc. **2** person who advises a judge in court on technical matters.

asset /ˈæset/ *n* **1** [C] ~ (**to sb/sth**) **(a)** valuable or useful quality or skill: *Good health is a great asset.* **(b)** valuable or useful person: *He's an enormous asset to the team.* **2 assets** [pl] all the resources (eg property, machinery, cash, etc) owned by a person, company, etc that have value. If necessary, assets can be used to pay debts: *His assets included shares in the company and a house in London.* Cf LIABILITY.

□ **ˈasset-stripping** *n* [U] (*commerce*) practice of buying at a cheap price a company with financial difficulties and then selling its assets individually to make a profit.

asseverate /əˈsevəreɪt/ *v* [Tn, Tf] (*fml*) state (sth) firmly and solemnly: *asseverate one's innocence/that one is innocent.* ▷ **asseveration** /əˌsevəˈreɪʃn/ *n* [U, C].

assiduity /ˌæsɪˈdjuːətɪ; *US* -duː-/ *n* [U] (*fml*) constant and careful attention to a task: *He shows great assiduity in all his work.*

assiduous /əˈsɪdjʊəs; *US* -dʒʊəs/ *adj* (*fml*) showing constant and careful attention: *be assiduous in one's duties* ○ *The book was the result of ten years' assiduous research.* ▷ **assiduously** *adv.*

assign /əˈsaɪn/ *v* **1** [Dn·n, Dn·pr] ~ **sth to sb** give sth to sb as a share of work to be done or of things to be used: *The teacher has assigned each of us a holiday task.* ○ *The two large classrooms have been assigned to us.* **2** [Tn·pr, Tnt] ~ **sb to sth** name sb for a task or position; appoint sb: *They've assigned their best man to the job.* ○ *One of the members was assigned to take the minutes.* **3** [Tn·pr, Cn·n/a] name or fix (a time, place, reason, etc for sth): *Shall we assign Thursdays for our weekly meetings?* ○ *It is impossible to assign an exact date to this building.* ○ *Can we assign jealousy as the motive for the crime?* **4** [Tn·pr] ~ **sth to sb** (*law*) transfer (property, rights, etc) to sb.

▷ **assignable** *adj* that can be assigned.

assignment *n* **1** [C] task or duty that is assigned to sb: *Your next assignment will be to find these missing persons.* ○ *She was sent abroad on a difficult assignment.* **2** [U] act of assigning (esp property, rights, etc): *a deed of assignment.*

assignation /ˌæsɪgˈneɪʃn/ *n* (*fml or rhet*) arrangement to meet sb, esp secretly or illicitly: *an assignation with a lover.*

assimilate /əˈsɪməleɪt/ *v* **1** [I, Tn] **(a)** (cause sth to) become absorbed into the body after digestion: *Some foods assimilate/are assimilated more easily than others.* **(b)** (allow sb/sth to) become part of another social group or state: *The USA has assimilated people from many different countries.* **2** [Tn] absorb (ideas, knowledge, etc) in the mind: *Children in school are expected to assimilate what they have been taught.* **3** [Tn·pr esp passive] ~ **sth to sth** make sth similar to sth.

▷ **assimilation** /əˌsɪməˈleɪʃn/ *n* [U] **1** process of assimilating or being assimilated. **2** (*phonetics*) change in a speech sound when it becomes similar to another speech sound next to it.

Assisi /əˈsiːsɪ/ town in central Italy, famous as the birthplace of St *Francis.

assist /əˈsɪst/ *v* **1** [I, Ipr, Tn, Tn·pr, Tnt] ~ (**sb**) **in/with sth**; ~ (**sb**) **in doing sth** (*fml*) help: *The head teacher's deputy assists with many of his duties.* ○ *Two men are assisting the police in their enquiries*, ie are answering questions which may lead to their arrest as suspected criminals or help the police find other suspects. ○ *You will be required to assist Mrs Smith in preparing a report.* ○ *an assisted area*, ie (in Britain) a region with high unemployment that receives special financial help from the government to encourage the development of industry. **2** [Ipr] ~ **at/in sth** (*fml*) be present at or take part in sth: *assist at the ceremony.*

▷ **assist** *n* (*US*) **1** act of helping. **2** (*sport*) player's action in helping to put out an opponent, score a goal, etc.

assistance *n* [U] (*fml*) help: *Please call if you require assistance.* ○ *Can I be of any assistance, sir?* ○ *Despite his cries no one came to his assistance.* ○ *I can't move this piano without assistance.*

assistant *n* **1** person who helps: *My assistant will operate the tape-recorder.* **2** person who serves customers in a shop. — *adj* [attrib] (*abbr* **asst**) helping, and ranking next below, a senior person: *the assistant manager* ○ *a senior assistant master*, ie in a school.

assize /əˈsaɪz/ *n* [C usu *pl*, U] (until 1972) lawcourt session held four times a year in each county of England and Wales for trying civil and criminal cases: *courts of assize.*

Assoc (also **assoc**) *abbr* associate(d); association.

associate[1] /əˈsəʊʃɪət/ *adj* [attrib] **1** joined or allied with a profession or organization: *an associate judge* ○ *the associate producer of a film.* **2** having a lower level of membership than full members: *Associate members do not have the right to vote.*

▷ **associate** *n* **1** partner; colleague; companion: *one's business associates* ○ *They are associates in crime.* **2** associate member.

associate[2] /əˈsəʊʃɪeɪt/ *v* **1** [Tn, Tn·pr] ~ **sb/sth** (**with sb/sth**) join (people or things) together; connect (ideas, etc) in one's mind: *You wouldn't normally associate these two writers — their styles are completely different.* ○ *Whisky is usually associated with Scotland.* ○ *I always associate him with fast cars.* **2** [Ipr] ~ **with sb** act together with or often deal with sb: *I don't like you associating with such people.* **3** [Tn·pr] ~ **oneself with sth** declare or show that one is in agreement with sth: *I have never associated myself with political extremism.*

association /əˌsəʊsɪˈeɪʃn/ *n* **1** [U] **(a)** ~ (**with sb/sth**) action of associating or being associated: *His English improved enormously because of his association with British people.* ○ *There has always been a close association between these two schools.* ○ *We are working in association with a number of local companies to raise money for the homeless.* **(b)** being in sb's company; friendship: *She became famous through her association with several poets.* **2** [C] mental connection between ideas: *What associations does the sea have for you?* **3** [C] group of people joined together for a common purpose; organization: *Do you belong to any professional associations?* **4** [C] plant community in which two or more dominant species occur in closer proximity to each other than would be expected on the basis of chance.

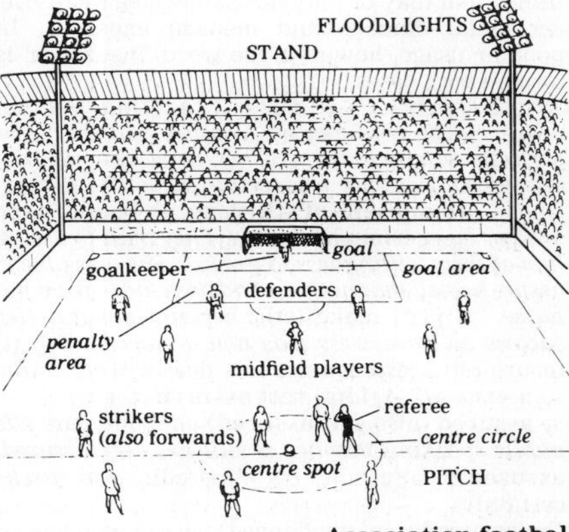

Association football

□ **Asˌsociation ˈfootball** (also **football**, **soccer**) form of football played by two teams of eleven players, using a round ball that must not be handled during play except by the goalkeeper.

assonance /ˈæsənəns/ *n* [U] (rhyme that depends on the) similarity between the vowel sounds only or the consonant sounds only of two words or syllables, as in *sharper* and *garter* or *killed* and *cold.*

assorted /əˈsɔːtɪd/ *adj* of different sorts; mixed: *a tin of assorted biscuits.*

▷ **assortment** /əˈsɔːtmənt/ *n* collection of different things or of different types of the same thing; mixture: *a wide assortment of gifts to choose from* ○ *wearing an odd assortment of clothes.*

Asst (also **asst**) *abbr* assistant: *Asst Sec.*

assuage /æˈsweɪdʒ/ *v* [Tn] (*fml*) make (sth) less severe; soothe: *assuage one's hunger, thirst, grief, longing, etc.*

assume /əˈsjuːm; *US* əˈsuːm/ *v* **1** [Tn, Tf, Tnt] accept (sth) as true before there is proof: *We cannot assume anything in this case.* ○ *I am assuming that the present situation is going to continue.* ○ *We must assume him to be innocent until he is proved guilty.* ○ *We can all leave together — assuming (that) the others aren't late.* **2** [Tn] put on or display (sth) falsely; pretend: *assume ignorance, indifference, an air of concern, etc* ○ *The look of innocence she assumed had us all fooled.*

3 [Tn] begin to act in or exercise (sth); undertake; take on: *assume office* ○ *He assumes his new responsibilities next month.* ○ *The problem is beginning to assume massive proportions,* ie become very great.

▷ **assumed** *adj* [attrib] pretended; false: *living under an assumed name.*

assumption /əˈsʌmpʃn/ *n* **1** [C] thing accepted as true or as sure to happen, but not proved: *The theory is based on a series of wrong assumptions.* ○ *We are working on the assumption that the rate of inflation will not increase next year.* **2** [U] ~ **of sth** act of displaying (insincere feelings, etc): *Their assumption of an air of confidence fooled nobody.* **3** [C] ~ **of sth** act of taking on (a position, etc): *her assumption of supreme power.* **4 the Assumption** [sing] (**a**) the taking of the Virgin Mary into Heaven in bodily form. (**b**) festival on 15 August celebrating this.

assurance /əˈʃɔːrəns; *US* əˈʃʊərəns/ *n* **1** (also **self-assurance**) [U] confident belief in one's own abilities and powers: *act with, display, possess assurance* ○ *She shows remarkable assurance on stage for one so young.* **2** [C] statement expressing certainty about sth; promise: *He gave me an assurance that it would be ready by Friday.* ○ *Despite repeated assurances he failed to repay the money he had borrowed.* **3** [U] (*esp Brit*) insurance, esp on sb's life. Insurance companies tend to use the word 'assurance' (as in 'a life assurance policy') of things that are certain to happen, esp death. The word 'insurance' is used in relation to things that may or may not happen, eg theft, fire, accidental damage and medical expenses. In popular usage, however, the word 'insurance' is used in both cases.

assure /əˈʃɔː(r); *US* əˈʃʊər/ *v* **1** (**a**) [Dn·f] tell (sb) positively or confidently: *I assure you they'll be perfectly safe with us.* ○ *They were assured that everything possible was being done.* (**b**) [Tn·pr, Dn·f] ~ **sb/oneself (of sth)** cause sb/oneself to be sure or feel certain about sth: *They tried to assure him of their willingness to work.* ○ *She was able to assure herself that nothing had been taken from her purse.* **2** [Tn] make (sth) certain; ensure: *Her success as an actress was now assured.* **3** [Tn] insure (sth), esp against sb's death: *What is the sum assured?* **4** (idm) **rest assured** ⇨ REST[1].

▷ **assured** (also **self-assured**) *adj* confident: *His public speaking manner is still not very assured.* **assuredly** /əˈʃɔːrɪdlɪ; *US* əˈʃʊərədlɪ/ *adv* (*arch*) certainly.

the assured *n* (*pl* unchanged) person who has an assurance policy on his life.

Assyria /əˈsɪrɪə/ ancient country in what is now northern Iraq, originally centred on the city of Ashur on the west bank of the Tigris. It first became prominent and expanded its borders in the 14th century BC. From the 8th to the 7th century BC Assyria created an empire that extended from Egypt to the Persian Gulf.

▷ **Assyrian** /əˈsɪrɪən/ *n, adj* (inhabitant or language) of Assyria.

AST /ˌeɪ es ˈtiː/ *abbr* (in Canada) Atlantic Standard Time.

Astaire /əˈsteə(r)/ Fred (1899-1987), American dancer and film star, whose best-known films are the 1930s musicals in which he starred with Ginger Rogers, including *Top Hat, Swing Time* and *Shall We Dance?*

Astarte /æˈstɑːtɪ/ Phoenician goddess of fertility and sexual love, identified with the Semitic Ashtaroth and the Egyptian Isis.

astatine /ˈæstətiːn/ *n* [U] (*symb* **At**) (*chemistry*) radioactive chemical element. It occurs naturally in tiny amounts but was first prepared artificially in 1940 by bombarding bismuth with alpha particles. ⇨ App 11.

aster /ˈæstə(r)/ *n* garden plant similar to the daisy with flowers that have a yellow centre and white, pink or purple petals.

asterisk /ˈæstərɪsk/ *n* star-shaped symbol (*) used in writing and printing to call attention to sth, eg a footnote, or to show that letters are omitted, as in *Mr J*n*s* for *Mr Jones.*

▷ **asterisk** *v* [Tn] mark (a word, phrase, etc) with an asterisk: *The asterisked questions may be omitted.*

astern /əˈstɜːn/ *adv* **1** in, at or towards the stern of a ship or the tail of an aircraft. **2** (of a ship) backwards: *Full speed astern!*

□ **astern of** *prep* behind (another ship): *They fell astern of us,* ie moved into position behind us.

asteroid /ˈæstərɔɪd/ *n* any of many small planets revolving round the sun, esp between the orbits of Mars and Jupiter.

asthenia /æsˈθiːnɪə/ *n* (*medical*) loss of strength; debility.

asthma /ˈæsmə; *US* ˈæzmə/ *n* [U] chronic chest illness causing wheezing and difficulty in breathing.

▷ **asthmatic** /æsˈmætɪk; *US* æz-/ *adj* of or suffering from asthma: *asthmatic pains* ○ *an asthmatic child.* — *n* person suffering from asthma.

astigmatism /əˈstɪgmətɪzəm/ *n* [U] defect in an eye or a lens that prevents correct focusing. ▷ **astigmatic** /ˌæstɪgˈmætɪk/ *adj.*

astir /əˈstɜː(r)/ *adv, adj* [pred] **1** in a state of excited movement: *News of the Queen's visit set the whole town astir.* **2** (*dated*) out of bed: *He's never astir before 10 o'clock.*

Aston /ˈæstən/ Francis William (1877-1945), English physicist and chemist who designed the first mass spectrograph. He also discovered many of the naturally occurring isotopes of non-radioactive elements. He was awarded the Nobel prize for chemistry in 1922.

astonish /əˈstɒnɪʃ/ *v* [Tn] surprise (sb) greatly: *The news astonished everyone.* ○ *It astonishes me that no one has thought of this before.* ○ *He was astonished to hear he had got the job.*

▷ **astonished** *adj* [usu pred] very surprised: *She looked astonished when she heard the news.*

astonishing *adj* very surprising: *I find it quite astonishing that none of you liked the play.* ○ *There were an astonishing number of applicants for the job.* **astonishingly** *adv.*

astonishment *n* [U] great surprise: *Imagine my astonishment when Peter walked in!* ○ *To my astonishment it had completely disappeared.* ○ *He looked at me in astonishment.*

Astor[1] /ˈæstə(r)/ John Jacob (1763-1848), German-born American businessman and millionaire. Astor gained a large fortune from his American Fur Company, investing the profits in property in New York. His son William (1792-1875) later became known as the city's 'landlord'.

Astor[2] /ˈæstə(r)/ Nancy Witcher, Viscountess (1879-1964), American-born British politician, a descendant of John Jacob Astor. She was the first woman Member of Parliament to sit in the House of Commons.

astound /əˈstaʊnd/ *v* [Tn usu passive] overcome (sb) with surprise or shock; amaze: *We were astounded to read your letter.*

▷ **astounding** *adj* amazing: *The figures revealed by the report are astounding.*

astragal /ˈæstrəgl/ *n* (*architecture*) small curved moulding round the top or bottom of a column.

astrakhan /ˌæstrəˈkæn; *US* ˈæstrəkən/ *n* [U] (**a**) skin of young lambs with tightly-curled wool. (**b**) material imitating this: [attrib] *an astrakhan hat.*

astral /ˈæstrəl/ *adj* [usu attrib] of or from the stars: *an astral body* ○ *astral beams.*

astray /əˈstreɪ/ *adv* **1** away from the right path or direction: *The misleading sign led me astray.* ○ (*fig*) *He had been led astray by undesirable friends.* **2** (idm) **go aˈstray** become mislaid: *Have you seen my book? It seems to have gone astray.*

astride /əˈstraɪd/ *adv* **1** with one leg on each side: *Ladies ride horses by sitting astride or side-saddle.* **2** with legs wide apart.

▷ **astride** *prep* with one leg on each side of (sth): *sitting astride a horse, a gate, sb's knee.*

astringent /əˈstrɪndʒənt/ *n* substance, used medically or in cosmetics, that makes skin or body tissue contract and so stops bleeding.

▷ **astringent** *adj* **1** of or having the effect of an astringent; styptic. **2** (*fig*) harsh; severe: *astringent criticism.* **astringency** /əˈstrɪndʒənsɪ/ *n* [U].

astro- *comb form* of the stars or outer space: *astronaut* ○ *astrology.*

astrodome /ˈæstrədəʊm/ *n* transparent dome fitted onto the top of an aircraft, through which stars, etc can be observed, eg to help in navigation.

astrolabe /ˈæstrəleɪb/ *n* instrument formerly used for measuring the altitude of the stars and planets. In its earliest form, which dates back to classical times, an astrolabe consisted of a disc with the degrees of the circle marked round its edge, and a pivoted pointer along which a star, etc could be sighted. From the 15th century, it was used by sailors to calculate latitude, until it was replaced by the sextant.

astrology /əˈstrɒlədʒɪ/ *n* [U] study of the positions of the stars and movements of the planets in the belief that they influence human affairs. Astrology was developed by the Babylonians and spread to Greece and Christian Europe via the Arabs. It played an important role in medieval and Renaissance Europe, court astrologers like *Nostradamus being employed to give guidance on politics and medical treatment. Despite the development of modern science, widespread interest in astrology has survived to the present. Personal horoscopes are a popular feature of many newspapers and magazines. Cf HOROSCOPE, ZODIAC.

▷ **astrologer** /-ədʒə(r)/ *n* person who is an expert in astrology.

astrological /ˌæstrəˈlɒdʒɪkl/ *adj.*

astronaut /ˈæstrənɔːt/ *n* person who travels in a spacecraft: *a rocket manned by trained astronauts.*

▷ **astronautics** /ˌæstrəˈnɔːtɪks/ *n* [sing *v*] science and technology of space travel.

astronomy /əˈstrɒnəmɪ/ *n* [U] scientific study of the sun, moon, stars, planets, etc. One of the oldest sciences in the world, astronomy flourished in Babylonia, China, Egypt and Greece. Results were originally gained from observation purely with the eye, but the invention of the telescope made it possible to study the sky in much greater detail. Nowadays, radio telescopes, rockets, satellites, space observatories, space probes, infra-red detectors, etc are all used in the study of the universe.

▷ **astronomer** /-nəmə(r)/ *n* person who studies or is an expert in astronomy. **Aˌstronomer ˈRoyal** honorary title awarded to an eminent British astronomer. Until 1972 it was the official title of the director of the Royal Greenwich Observatory.

astronomical /ˌæstrəˈnɒmɪkl/ *adj* **1** of astronomy. **2** (*infml*) very large in amount, size, etc: *He's been offered an astronomical salary.* **ˌastroˌnomical ˈunit** unit of distance equal to the mean distance between the earth and the sun, 149 597 870 km (about 93 000 000 miles).

astrophysics /ˌæstrəʊˈfɪzɪks/ *n* [sing *v*] branch of astronomy dealing with the physics and chemistry of the stars, planets, etc. It deals mainly with the energy of star systems and the relation between this energy and the evolution of the solar system.

astute /əˈstjuːt; *US* əˈstuːt/ *adj* clever and quick at seeing how to gain an advantage; shrewd: *an astute lawyer, businessman, judge of character, etc* ○ *It was an astute move to sell just before prices went down.* ▷ **astutely** *adv.* **astuteness** *n* [U].

asunder /əˈsʌndə(r)/ *adv* (*dated or fml*) into pieces; apart: *families torn asunder by the revolution* ○ *The house was ripped asunder by the explosion.*

ASV /ˌeɪ es ˈviː/ *abbr* American Standard Version (of the Bible).

Aswan /æsˈwɑːn/ city in SE Egypt on the River Nile. The Aswan High Dam (opened in 1971) dams the River Nile to form the reservoir Lake Nasser, which supplies water for irrigation and hydroelectric power.

asylum /əˈsaɪləm/ *n* **1** (**a**) [U] safety; refuge: *ask for/be granted political asylum,* ie protection given to a political refugee by a foreign country. (**b**) [C] place of safety or refuge. **2** [C] (*dated*) hospital for the care of mentally ill or destitute people.

asymmetric /ˌeɪsɪˈmetrɪk/ (also **asymmetrical**

/-ɪkl/) *adj* not having parts that correspond to each other in size, shape, etc; lacking symmetry: *Most people's faces are asymmetrical.*

asymptote /ˈæsɪmtəʊt/ *n* (*mathematics*) straight line that approaches nearer and nearer to a given curve, but does not meet it within a finite distance.

at /ət, *strong form* æt/ *prep* **1** (**a**) (indicating a point in space): *at the end of the runway* ○ *at the corner of the street* ○ *go in at the side door* ○ *change at Didcot* ○ *arrive at the airport* ○ *At the roundabout take the third exit.* ○ *I'll be at home* (ie not at work, school, church, etc) *all morning.* (**b**) (used with the name of a building, esp with reference to the activities going on inside): *She's at the theatre, cinema, etc,* ie watching a play, film, etc. ○ *She works at the hospital.* ○ *He's at* (ie staying at) *the Grand Hotel.* (**c**) among those who attend: *at a concert, conference, match, etc.* (**d**) (used with the name of a person + *'s* to refer to that person's home or place of work): *They're at Keith's.* ○ *I was at my father's.* ○ *They didn't have any bread at the baker's.* (**e**) (indicating place of employment or study): *He's been at the bank longer than anyone else.* ○ *I'm at the head office.* ○ *her three years at Oxford* (Cf *spend three days in Oxford as a tourist*). **2** (**a**) (indicating a point in time): *start, meet, leave, etc at 2 o'clock* ○ *at 3.15/a quarter past 3* ○ *He is to be shot at dawn.* ○ *I didn't know he was dead at the time of speaking,* ie when I spoke. ○ *At the moment you called I was in the garden shed.* ○ *at the end of the holiday.* (**b**) (indicating a period of time): *At night you can see the stars.* ○ *What are you doing at* (US *on*) *the weekend?* ○ *take a few days' holiday at Christmas, Easter, Whitsun, etc.* (**c**) (used to indicate the age at which sb does sth): *She got married at 55.* ○ *You can retire at 60.* ○ *He left school at (the age of) 16.* ⇨ Usage at TIME[1]. **3** (**a**) in the direction of or towards (sb/sth): *aim the ball at the hole* ○ *direct one's advertising at a wider audience* ○ *smile, grin, stare, wave, etc at sb* ○ *A man with a gun was shooting at the crowd.* ○ *The dog rushed at me, wagging its tail.* ○ *She shouted at me but I couldn't hear.* ○ *throw stones at the can in the water,* ie trying to hit it. (**b**) (used to show that sb tries to do sth but does not succeed or complete it): *clutch at a rope* ○ *guess at the meaning* ○ *She nibbled at a sandwich,* ie ate only tiny portions. **4** (indicating the distance away from sth): *Can you read a car number-plate at fifty metres?* ○ *hold sth at arm's length.* **5** (indicating a state, condition or continuous activity): *at war with their neighbours* ○ *stand at ease,* ie in a relaxed position ○ *put sb at risk* ○ *children at play* ○ *She's at work in the garden.* **6** (**a**) (indicating a rate, price, speed, etc): *House prices are rising at a higher rate than inflation.* ○ *I bought this coat at half-price/at 50% discount.* ○ *driving at 70 mph.* (**b**) (indicating order or frequency): *at the first attempt* ○ *at two-minute intervals,* ie once every two minutes. **7** in response to (sth): *attend the dinner at the chairman's invitation* ○ *at the king's command.* **8** (used with *his, her, our,* etc and a superlative *adj*): *This was Torvill and Dean at their best.* ○ *The garden's at its most beautiful in June.* ○ *an example of British craftsmanship at its finest.* **9** (used after many *adjs* and *ns*): *good, clever, skilled, etc at restoring furniture, etc* ○ *hopeless at (playing) chess* ○ *She's a genius at doing crossword puzzles.* ○ *busy at their homework* ○ *impatient at the delay* ○ *amused at the cartoons* ○ *delighted at the result* ○ *puzzled at her silence* ○ *his anger at being beaten.* **10** (idm) ˌ**where it's ˈat** (*infml*) place or activity that is very popular or fashionable: *Judging by the crowds waiting to get in this seems to be where it's at.* (For idioms such as **at hand**, **at once**, **at a low ebb**, etc see entries at **hand**[1], **once**, **low**[1], etc.)

Atalanta /ˌætəˈlæntə/ (in Greek mythology) huntress who agreed to marry any man who could run faster than her in a race. Melanion (or Hippomenes) won the race by throwing down three golden apples given to him by *Aphrodite, which were so beautiful that Atalanta stopped to pick them up.

Atatürk /ˈætətɜːk/ Kemal (1881-1938), Turkish general and statesman. The chief founder of modern Turkey and its first president (1923-38), Atatürk worked throughout his time in power to make Turkey a modern secular state. His real name was Mustapha Kemal; he took the name Atatürk (which means 'father-Turk') in 1934.

atavism /ˈætəvɪzəm/ *n* [U] reappearance in a person of a characteristic or quality that has not been seen in his family for many generations. Cf THROW-BACK (THROW[1]). ▷ **atavistic** /ˌætəˈvɪstɪk/ *adj*: *an atavistic urge.*

ataxia /ˌeɪtæksɪə, əˈtæksɪə/ *n* [U] lack of co-ordination between muscles, making one unable to control one's body movements properly.

ATC /ˌeɪ tiː ˈsiː/ *abbr* air traffic control.

ate *pt of* EAT.

-ate *suff* **1** (with *ns* forming *adjs*) full of or showing a specified quality: *affectionate* ○ *passionate* ○ *Italianate.* **2** (forming *ns*) (**a**) (group of people with a) status or function: *electorate* ○ *doctorate.* (**b**) (*chemistry*) salt formed by the action of a particular acid: *sulphate* ○ *nitrate.* **3** (with *ns* and *adjs* forming *vs*) give (to sth) the specified thing or quality: *hyphenate* ○ *chlorinate* ○ *activate.*
▷ **-ately** (forming *advs*): *affectionately.*

atelier /əˈtelɪeɪ; *US* ˌætlˈjeɪ/ *n* artist's studio or workshop.

Athanasius /ˌæθəˈneɪʃəs/ Saint (c 296–373 AD), bishop of Alexandria and defender of orthodox Christian beliefs, esp against *Arianism.
▷ **Athanasian** /ˌæθəˈneɪʃn/ *adj* **the** ˌ**Athanasian** ˈ**Creed** statement of Christian belief, esp about the *Trinity and the *Incarnation, once thought to have been written by Athanasius. It is now little used in the Western Church.

atheism /ˈeɪθɪɪzəm/ *n* [U] belief that there is no God. Cf AGNOSTICISM.
▷ **atheist** /ˈeɪθɪɪst/ *n* person who believes that there is no God. Cf HEATHEN, PAGAN.
atheistic /ˌeɪθɪˈɪstɪk/ *adj.*

Athenaeum /ˌæθɪˈniːəm/ **the Athenaeum** London club founded in 1824 for distinguished men of literature, art and science. Its name was taken from that of a temple in ancient Athens where learned men met.

Athene /əˈθiːnɪ/ (also **Athena** /əˈθiːnə/) (in Greek mythology) virgin goddess of wisdom and the arts, the equivalent of the Roman goddess *Minerva. She was born from the head of Zeus, fully grown, fully armed and uttering her war-cry. Athens is named after her.

Athens /ˈæθɪnz/ capital of Greece, dominated by the hill citadel of the *Acropolis, and 6 km (nearly 4 miles) from its port, Piraeus. Athens was a flourishing city-state from early times in ancient Greece, and by the mid-5th century BC it was the leading Greek city-state. Under *Pericles it became a major cultural and intellectual centre. Athens recovered only slowly from defeat by Sparta in the *Peloponnesian War (431-404 BC); in 146 BC it came under Roman rule. Its schools of philosophy were closed by the Roman emperor Justinian in 529 AD. The city was occupied by the Turks from 1456 to 1833, when it was chosen as the capital of the newly independent Greece.
▷ **Athenian** /əˈθiːnɪən/ *n, adj* (native or inhabitant) of Athens.

atherosclerosis /ˌæθərəʊskləˈrəʊsɪs/ *n* [U] (*medical*) disease in which fatty deposits form and harden on the inner walls of the arteries, hindering the flow of blood.

athlete /ˈæθliːt/ *n* **1** person who trains to compete in physical exercises and sports, esp running and jumping. **2** person who has the strength and skill to perform well at sports: *Most first-class footballers are natural athletes.*
□ ˌ**athlete's** ˈ**foot** (*infml*) fungous disease of the feet.

athletic /æθˈletɪk/ *adj* **1** [attrib] of athletes or athletics: *an athletic club* ○ *athletic sports.* **2** physically strong, healthy and active: *an athletic figure* ○ *She looks very athletic.*

athletics /æθˈletɪks/ *n* [sing *v*] physical exercises and competitive sports, esp running and jumping: [attrib] *an athletics meeting.* ⇨ App 9.

at-home /ət ˈhəʊm/ *n* (*dated*) informal party in sb's home, to which guests may come at any time within certain hours.

Athos /ˈæθɒs, *also* ˈeɪθɒs/ **Mount Athos** mountainous peninsula in NE Greece, projecting into the Aegean Sea; an autonomous district of Greece since 1927. It is inhabited by monks of the Eastern Orthodox Church in 20 monasteries.

athwart /əˈθwɔːt/ *adv, prep* (*esp nautical*) obliquely across (sth); from one side to the other side (of): *The ship was anchored athwart the harbour mouth.*

-ation ⇨ -ION.

atishoo /əˈtɪʃuː/ *interj* (indicating the sound made by sb sneezing).

-ative *suff* (with *vs* forming *adjs*) doing or tending to do (sth): *illustrative* ○ *imitative* ○ *talkative.*
▷ **-atively** (forming *advs*): *quantitatively.*

atlantes /ətˈlæntiːz/ *n* [pl] (*architecture*) male figures, representing Atlas, carved in stone, used as pillars to support an entablature or projecting roof. ⇨ illus at CARYATID. Cf CARYATID.

Atlantic /ətˈlæntɪk/ *n* **the Atlantic** [sing] the Atlantic Ocean.
▷ **Atlantic** *adj* of or bordering the Atlantic Ocean. **the At**ˌ**lantic** ˈ**Charter** the joint declaration made by Winston *Churchill and Franklin D *Roosevelt after their meeting in August 1941. It set out eight principles of international relations on behalf of Britain and her allies and of the USA. **the At**ˌ**lantic** ˈ**Ocean** the ocean between Europe and Africa in the east and North America and South America in the west; the world's second largest ocean. Area 106 500 000 sq km (41 100 000 sq miles).

Atlantis /ətˈlæntɪs/ (in ancient legend) large island continent that is said to have sunk below the Atlantic Ocean, west of the Straits of Gibraltar.

Atlas /ˈætləs/ (in Greek mythology) one of the *Titans who was punished for his part in the revolt against Zeus by being condemned to support the sky on his shoulders. A drawing of Atlas was commonly included in collections of maps in the 16th century, and so a book of maps came to be called an 'atlas'.

atlas /ˈætləs/ *n* **1** book of maps. **2** (*anatomy*) uppermost vertebra of the neck, supporting the skull.

Atlas Mountains /ˌætləs ˈmaʊntɪnz; *US* ˈmaʊntnz/ **the Atlas Mountains** mountain range in NW Africa, extending from Morocco to Tunisia. The highest peak is Mount Toubkal (4 165 m, 13 664 ft). ⇨ map at ALGERIA.

atm *abbr* atmosphere.

atman /ˈɑːtmən, *also* ˈɑːtmɑːn/ *n* (in Hinduism) personal soul or self; supreme principle of life in the universe.

atmosphere /ˈætməsfɪə(r)/ *n* **1** (**a**) **the atmosphere** [sing] the mixture of gases that surrounds the earth. The composition of dry air at sea-level is: nitrogen (78.8%), oxygen (20.95%), argon (0.93%), carbon dioxide (0.03%) and small proportions of other gases. The lowest level of the atmosphere, in which most of the weather occurs, is called the *troposphere.* The thickness of this layer varies from about 7 km (4.5 miles) at the North and South Poles to 28 km (17.5 miles) at the equator. In this layer, the temperature falls as the height increases. The next layer is the *stratosphere,* which goes up to about 50 km (31 miles). Here the temperature remains fairly constant. Above this is the *ionosphere,* which extends to about 1000 km (620 miles). The ionosphere contains ionized gases, by means of which radio waves are transmitted round the earth. From about 400 km (250 miles) the outermost region of the atmosphere is also called the *exosphere.* (**b**) [C] mixture of gases that surrounds any planet or star: *the moon's atmosphere* ○ *an atmosphere that supports life.* **2** [sing] air in or around a place: *The atmosphere is very stuffy in here — can we open a window?* **3** [sing] feeling in the mind that is created by a group of people or a place; mood: *An atmosphere of tension filled the room.* ○ *The atmosphere changed as soon as she walked in.* ○ *The atmosphere over dinner was warm and friendly.* **4** [C] (*abbr* **atm**) (*physics*) pressure of the atmosphere on the earth's surface, taken as a unit of pressure, about 10 newtons per sq cm.

atmospheric /ˌætməsˈferɪk/ *adj* **1** of or related to the atmosphere: *unusual atmospheric conditions* ○ *atmospheric pollution.* **2** creating an atmosphere(3): *atmospheric lighting.*

▷ **atmospherics** *n* [pl] (**a**) electrical disturbances in the atmosphere. (**b**) interference or crackling sounds on radios, etc caused by these.

□ ˌ**atmospheric** ˈ**pressure** pressure exerted by the weight of the air above it at any point on the earth's surface.

atoll /ˈætɒl/ *n* ring-shaped coral reef enclosing a lagoon.

atom /ˈætəm/ *n* **1** (**a**) [C] smallest part of an element that can exist chemically: *Two atoms of hydrogen combine with one atom of oxygen to form a molecule of water.* (**b**) [sing] this as a source of energy: *the power of the atom* ○ [attrib] *an atom scientist.* **2** [C] very small quantity or thing: *The tower was blown to atoms by the force of the explosion.* ○ *There isn't an atom of truth in the rumour.*

□ ˈ**atom bomb** = ATOMIC BOMB (ATOMIC).

atomic /əˈtɒmɪk/ *adj* [usu attrib] of an atom or atoms: *atomic physics* ○ *atomic warfare*, ie using atomic bombs.

□ **a**ˌ**tomic** ˈ**bomb** (also ˈ**A-bomb**, ˈ**atom bomb**) bomb whose explosive power comes from the rapid release of nuclear energy by fission of heavy atomic nuclei, with damaging effects caused by heat, blast and radioactivity. The first atomic bomb to be used in war was dropped on Hiroshima, Japan, on 6 August 1945 by the USA.

aˌ**tomic** ˈ**clock** very accurate clock that is controlled by the vibrations of an atomic system.

aˌ**tomic** ˈ**energy** energy obtained as the result of nuclear fission.

aˌ**tomic** ˈ**number** number of protons in the nucleus of an atom.

aˌ**tomic** ˈ**pile** early type of nuclear reactor.

aˌ**tomic** ˈ**theory** theory that all matter consists of atoms.

aˌ**tomic** ˈ**weight** (also ˌ**relative a**ˌ**tomic** ˈ**mass**) ratio between the mass of one atom of an element and one-twelfth of the mass of an atom of carbon 12.

atomicity /ˌætəˈmɪsɪtɪ/ *n* number of atoms in a particular molecule: *Oxygen(O_2) has an atomicity of 2.*

atomize, -ise /ˈætəmaɪz/ *v* [Tn] reduce (sth) to atoms or fine particles.

▷ **atomizer, -iser** *n* device for producing a fine spray from a liquid, eg perfume.

atonal /eɪˈtəʊnl/ *adj* (*music*) not written in any key or system of scales (SCALE[2] 6). ▷ **atonality** /ˌeɪtəʊˈnælətɪ/ *n* [U].

atone /əˈtəʊn/ *v* [I, Ipr] ~ (**for sth**) (*fml*) act in a way that compensates for a previous wrong, error, etc: *atone for a crime, a sin, one's mistakes, one's bad behaviour, etc* ○ *I have treated you unkindly — how can I atone (for it)?*

▷ **atonement** *n* **1** [C, U] (*fml*) act of atoning: *He sent her some flowers in atonement for his earlier rudeness.* **2 the Atonement** [sing] the suffering and death of Christ to atone for the sins of mankind.

atop /əˈtɒp/ *prep* (*dated or rhet*) at or on the top of: *a seagull perched atop the mast.*

-ator *suff* (with *vs* forming *ns*) person or thing that performs the specified action: *creator* ○ *percolator.*

ATP /ˌeɪ tiː ˈpiː/ *abbr* adenosine triphosphate, a chemical compound that is an important carrier of chemical energy in all living organisms.

Atreus /ˈeɪtrɪəs/ (in Greek mythology) king of Mycenae, son of Pelops, father of *Agamemnon and brother of Thyestes, with whom he was in conflict. According to one version of the story, Atreus served the flesh of Thyestes' children to their father at a banquet.

atrium /ˈeɪtrɪəm/ *n* (*pl* **-tria** /-trɪə/ or ~**s**) **1** central court of an ancient Roman house. **2** (*anatomy*) any of various cavities or chambers in the bodies of animals, esp one of the two upper chambers of the heart in higher vertebrates that receives blood from the veins and forces it into the lower chamber or a ventricle. ⇨ illus at HEART.

atrocious /əˈtrəʊʃəs/ *adj* **1** very wicked, cruel or shocking: *atrocious crimes, injuries, acts of brutality, etc.* **2** (*infml*) very bad or unpleasant: *speak English with an atrocious accent* ○ *Isn't the weather atrocious?* ▷ **atrociously** *adv.* **atrociousness** *n* [U].

atrocity /əˈtrɒsətɪ/ *n* (**a**) [U] great wickedness or cruelty: *I am shocked by the atrocity of this man's crimes.* (**b**) [C esp *pl*] very wicked or cruel act: *Many atrocities are committed on innocent people in wartime.*

atrophy /ˈætrəfɪ/ *n* [U] wasting away of the body or part of it through lack of nourishment or use: (*fig*) *The cultural life of the country will sink into atrophy unless more writers and artists emerge.*

▷ **atrophy** *v* (*pt, pp* **-ied**) [I, Tn] (cause sth to) suffer atrophy: *atrophied limbs, muscles.*

atropine /ˈætrəpiːn, *or, in British use*, -pɪn/ *n* poisonous chemical compound obtained from the deadly nightshade plant and used in medicine as a muscle relaxant, eg to increase the heart rate, to treat colic and to dilate the pupil of the eye.

attaboy /ˈætəbɔɪ/ *interj* (*sl esp US*) (used to express admiration or encouragement).

attach /əˈtætʃ/ *v* **1** [Tn, Tn·pr] ~ **sth** (**to sth**) fasten or join sth (to sth): *a house with a garage attached* ○ *attach a label to each piece of luggage* ○ *a document attached to a letter (with a pin)* ○ *Attached* (ie Attached to this letter) *you will find....* Cf DETACH 1. **2** [Tn·pr] (**a**) ~ **oneself to sb/sth** join sb/sth as a (sometimes unwelcome or uninvited) companion or member: *A young man attached himself to me at the party and I couldn't get rid of him.* ○ *I attached myself to a group of tourists entering the museum.* (**b**) ~ **sb to sb/sth** (esp passive) assign sb to (a person or group) for special duties: *You'll be attached to this department until the end of the year.* **3** (**a**) [Tn·pr] ~ **sth to sth** connect sth with sth; attribute sth to sth: *Do you attach any importance to what he said?* (**b**) [Ipr] ~ **to sb** (*fml*) be connected with or attributable to sb: *No blame attaches to you in this affair.* **4** [Tn] (*law*) take or seize (sb or sb's property) by legal authority. **5** (idm) **no strings attached/without strings** ⇨ STRING[1].

▷ **attached** *adj* [pred] ~ (**to sb/sth**) full of affection for sb/sth: *I've never seen two people so attached (to each other).* ○ *We've grown very attached to this house and would hate to move.*

attachment *n* **1** [U] action of attaching; being attached: *She's on attachment to* (ie temporarily working in) *the Ministry of Defence.* **2** [C] thing that is or can be attached: *an electric drill with a range of different attachments.* **3** [U] ~ (**to/for sb/sth**) affection; devotion: *feel a strong attachment to one's family.* **4** [U] (*law*) seizing sb's property, etc with legal authority.

attaché /əˈtæʃeɪ; *US* ˌætəˈʃeɪ/ *n* person attached to an ambassador's staff with a particular responsibility: *the naval/military/air/press attaché.*

□ **at**ˈ**taché case** small rectangular case for carrying documents, etc.

attack /əˈtæk/ *n* **1** [C, U] ~ (**on sb/sth**) violent attempt to hurt, overcome or defeat sb/sth: *make an attack on the enemy, bridge, town* ○ *the victim of a terrorist attack* ○ *Our troops are now on the attack.* ○ *The patrol came under attack from all sides.* ○ (*saying*) *Attack is the best form of defence.* **2** [C, U] ~ (**on sb/sth**) strong criticism in speech or writing: *an attack on the Government's policies.* **3** [C] ~ (**on sth**) vigorous attempt to deal with sth: *an all-out attack on poverty, unemployment, smoking.* **4** [C] sudden start of an illness, etc: *an attack of asthma, flu, malaria, hiccups, nerves, etc* ○ *a* ˈ*heart attack* ○ (*fig*) *an attack of the giggles.* **5** [U] (esp vigorous) way of beginning sth: *This piece of music needs to be played with more attack.* **6** [C usu *sing*] (*sport*) (players who are in the) position of trying to score in a game, eg of football or cricket: *England's attack has been weakened by the injury of certain key players.* ○ *We must move more players into the attack.*

▷ **attack** *v* **1** [I, Tn] make an attack on (sb/sth): *They decided to attack at night.* ○ *attack a neighbouring country* ○ *A woman was attacked and robbed by a gang of youths.* **2** [Tn] criticize (sb/sth) severely: *a newspaper article attacking the Prime Minister.* **3** [Tn] begin to deal with (sth) vigorously; tackle: *The Government is making no attempt to attack unemployment.* ○ *Shall we attack the washing-up?* ○ *They attacked their meal with gusto.* **4** [Tn] act harmfully on (sth/sb): *a disease that attacks the brain* ○ *Rust attacks metals.* **attacker** *n* person who attacks.

attain /əˈteɪn/ *v* **1** [Tn] succeed in getting (sth); achieve: *attain a position of power* ○ *attain one's goal, objective, ambition, etc* ○ *attain our target of £50 000.* **2** [Ipr, Tn] ~ (**to**) **sth** (*usu fml*) reach or arrive at sth, esp with effort: *He attained the age of 25 before marrying.*

▷ **attainable** *adj* that can be attained: *These objectives are certainly attainable.*

attainment *n* **1** [U] success in reaching: *The attainment of her ambitions was still a dream.* **2** [C usu *pl*] thing attained, esp skill or knowledge: *a scholar of the highest attainments.*

attar /ˈætə(r)/ *n* [U] fragrant oil obtained from flowers: *attar of roses.*

attempt /əˈtempt/ *v* [Tn, Tt] make an effort to accomplish (sth); try (to do sth): *The prisoners attempted an escape/to escape, but failed.* ○ *Don't attempt the impossible.* ○ *He was charged with attempted robbery.* ○ *All candidates must attempt Questions 1-5.* ○ *They are attempting (to climb) the steepest part of the mountain.* ○ *She will attempt to beat the world record.*

▷ **attempt** *n* **1** ~ (**to do sth/at doing sth**) act of attempting sth: *They made no attempt to escape/at escaping.* ○ *My early attempts at learning to drive were unsuccessful.* ○ *They failed in all their attempts to climb the mountain.* **2** ~ (**at sth**) thing produced by sb trying to do or make sth: *My first attempt at a chocolate cake tasted horrible.* **3** ~ (**on sth**) effort to improve on or end sth; attack: *the latest attempt on the world land speed record* ○ *An attempt was made on the Pope's life.*

Attenborough /ˈætənbrə/ Sir Richard (1923-), British actor and director. Many of his films have historical subjects and he achieved his greatest success with *Gandhi*, which won eight Oscars.

attend /əˈtend/ *v* **1** [I, Ipr] ~ (**to sb/sth**) apply one's mind steadily; give careful thought: *Why weren't you attending when I explained before?* ○ *Attend to your work and stop talking.* **2** [Ipr] ~ **to sb/sth** give practical consideration to sb/sth: *A nurse attends to his needs.* ○ *Are you being attended to* (eg said by an assistant to a customer in a shop)*?* ○ *Could you attend to* (ie deal with) *this matter immediately?* **3** [Tn] take care of (sb); look after: *Dr Smith attended her in hospital.* **4** [Tn] go regularly to (a place); be present at: *attend school, church, etc* ○ *They had a quiet wedding — only a few friends attended (it).* ○ *The meeting was well attended*, ie Many people were there. **5** [Tn] (*fml*) be with (sb/sth); accompany: *The Queen was attended by her ladies-in-waiting.* ○ (*fig*) *May good fortune attend you!*

▷ **attender** *n* person who attends (ATTEND 4): *She's a regular attender at evening classes.*

attendance /əˈtendəns/ *n* **1** [U, C] action or time of being present: *Attendance at evening prayers is not compulsory.* ○ *You have missed several attendances this term.* **2** [C] number of people present: *They're expecting a large attendance at the meeting.* ○ *Attendances have increased since we reduced the price of tickets.* **3** (idm) **dance attendance on sb** ⇨ DANCE[2]. **in attendance** (**on sb**) present in order to look after, protect or serve sb: *A nurse was in constant attendance.* ○ *The President always has six bodyguards in close attendance.*

□ **at**ˈ**tendance allowance** (*Brit*) money paid by the state to sb who cares for a severely disabled relative, etc.

atˈ**tendance centre** (*Brit*) place where young offenders must go regularly for supervision, as an alternative to being sent to prison.

attendant /əˈtendənt/ *n* **1** person whose job is to provide a service in a public place: *a cloakroom, swimming-pool, museum, etc attendant.* **2** (esp *pl*) servant or companion: *the queen's attendants.*
▷ **attendant** *adj* [attrib] accompanying: *an attendant nurse* ○ *attendant circumstances* ○ *famine and its attendant diseases.*

attention /əˈtenʃn/ *n* **1** [U] action of applying one's mind to sth/sb or noticing sth/sb: *call sb's attention to sth* ○ *Please pay attention* (ie listen carefully) *(to what I am saying).* ○ *She turned her attention to a new problem.* ○ *Our attention was held throughout his long talk.* ○ *You must give your full attention to what you are doing.* ○ *I keep trying to attract the waiter's attention.* ○ *It has been brought to my attention* (ie I have been informed) *that....* **2** [U] special care or action; practical consideration: *He gives all his attention to his car.* ○ *This letter is for the attention of the manager.* ○ *The roof needs attention,* ie is to be repaired. **3** [C usu *pl*] *(fml)* kind or thoughtful act: *He showed his concern for his sick mother by his many little attentions.* **4** [U] soldier's drill position, standing upright with feet together and arms stretched downwards (used esp in the expressions shown): *come to/stand at attention.* Cf EASE[1] 2. **5** (idm) **catch sb's attention/eye** ⇨ CATCH[1]. **draw attention to sth** ⇨ DRAW[2]. **give one's undivided attention; get/have sb's undivided attention** ⇨ UNDIVIDED. **snap to attention** ⇨ SNAP[1].
▷ **attention** *interj* **1** (calling people to listen to an announcement, etc): *Attention, please! The bus will leave in ten minutes.* ○ *Attention all shipping, motorists, housewives....* **2** (also *infml* **shun** /ʃʌn/) (ordering soldiers to come to attention(4)).

attentive /əˈtentɪv/ *adj* ~ **(to sb/sth)** giving attention (to sb/sth); alert and watchful: *an attentive audience* ○ *A good hostess is always attentive to the needs of her guests.* ▷ **attentively** *adv*: *listening attentively to the speaker.*

attenuate /əˈtenjʊeɪt/ *v* [Tn] *(fml)* **1** make (sth/sb) thin or slender: *attenuated limbs.* **2** *(esp law)* reduce the force, strength or value of (sth); weaken: *attenuating circumstances,* ie facts that weaken the strength of an argument. ▷ **attenuation** /əˌtenjʊˈeɪʃn/ *n* [U].

attest /əˈtest/ *v (fml)* **1** [Ipr, Tn] ~ **(to) sth** be or give clear proof of sth: *His handling of the crisis attested to his strength of character.* ○ *Her outstanding abilities were attested by her rapid promotion.* ○ *These papers attest the fact that....* **2** [Tn] declare (sth) to be true or genuine; be a witness to (sth): *attest a signature.*
▷ **attestation** /ˌæteˈsteɪʃn/ *n* [U, C].
attested *adj (Brit)* certified to be free from disease, esp tuberculosis: *attested cattle/milk.*

Attic /ˈætɪk/ *adj* of Athens or Attica.
▷ **Attic** *n* literary dialect of Greek used by the ancient Athenians. It later became the basis of the common language of the Greek-speaking world.
□ ˌ**Attic** ˈ**salt** (also ˌ**Attic** ˈ**wit**) *(dated)* wit that is delicate and refined.

attic /ˈætɪk/ *n* space or room immediately below the roof of a house: *furniture stored in the attic* ○ [attrib] *an attic bedroom.* Cf GARRET.

Attica /ˈætɪkə/ region in the eastern part of central Greece, whose chief city is Athens.

Attila /ˈætɪlə, *also* əˈtɪlə/ (406-453 AD), king of the Huns 434-453, known as the 'Scourge of God' because of his savage attacks. He inflicted great devastation on the eastern Roman Empire (445-450) and then invaded the Western Empire, but he was defeated at Châlons in 451 by the Romans and the Visigoths.

attire /əˈtaɪə(r)/ *n* [U] *(dated or fml)* clothes; dress: *wearing formal attire.*
▷ **attire** *v* [Tn usu passive] *(dated)* dress (sb): *attired in robes of silk and fur.*

attitude /ˈætɪtju:d; *US* -tu:d/ *n* **1** ~ **(to/towards sb/sth)** way of thinking or behaving: *What is your attitude to abortion?* ○ *She shows a very positive attitude to her work.* ○ *Don't take that attitude with me, young man!* **2** *(fml)* way of positioning the body: *The photographer has caught him in the attitude of prayer,* eg kneeling. **3** position of an aircraft or a spacecraft in relation to given points. **4** (idm) **strike an attitude/a pose** ⇨ STRIKE[2].
▷ **attitudinize, -ise** /ˌætɪˈtju:dɪnaɪz; *US* -ˈtu:dən-/ *v* [I] speak, write or behave in an affected way in order to impress others.

Attlee /ˈætlɪ/ Clement Richard, 1st Earl Attlee (1883-1967), British statesman and prime minister 1945-51. Having been leader of the Labour Party since 1935, Attlee became the first Labour prime minister to have an absolute majority in the House of Commons. His government was noted for its nationalization of major industries, eg coal, gas and electricity, the establishment of the Welfare State and the granting of independence to India. ⇨ App 2.

attn *abbr (commerce)* (for the) attention of: *Publicity Dept, attn Mr C Biggs.*

atto- *comb form* denoting a factor of 10^{18}, or one trillionth.

attorney /əˈtɜ:nɪ/ *n* **1** person appointed to act for another in business or legal matters: *power of attorney,* ie authority to act as attorney ○ *a letter of attorney,* ie one giving sb this authority. **2** *(US)* lawyer, esp one qualified to represent or act for sb in legal matters: *a district attorney,* ie the public prosecutor for a particular region.
□ **At**ˌ**torney-**ˈ**General** *n (abbr* **Atty-Gen***)* **1** *(Brit)* chief legal officer of the government and a member of the government and of the House of Commons. The Attorney-General represents the government in lawcourts and advises the government on legal matters. **2** *(US)* chief legal officer in a state government or in the federal government. In the federal government, the Attorney-General is appointed by the president and is head of the Department of Justice. Cf SOLICITOR-GENERAL (SOLICITOR).

attract /əˈtrækt/ *v* [Tn] **1** pull (sth) towards itself/oneself by unseen force: *A magnet attracts steel.* **2** (**a**) arouse interest or pleasure in (sb/sth): *The light attracted a lot of insects.* ○ *The dog was attracted by the smell of the meat.* ○ *Babies are attracted to bright colours.* ○ *Do any of these designs attract you?* ○ *I'm very attracted to her,* ie I feel I would like to become more friendly with her. (**b**) arouse (sth); prompt: *attract sb's attention, interest, etc* ○ *The new play has attracted a good deal of criticism.*

attractant /əˈtræktənt/ *n* substance that attracts things, esp a chemical substance that attracts insects, etc.

attraction /əˈtrækʃn/ *n* **1** [U] action or power of attracting: *I can't see the attraction of sitting on the beach all day.* ○ *She felt an immediate attraction to him.* ○ *The television has little attraction for me.* **2** [C] thing that attracts (ATTRACT 2a): *One of the main attractions of the job is the high salary.* ○ *City life holds few attractions for me.* Cf REPULSION.

attractive /əˈtræktɪv/ *adj* having the power to attract(2a); pleasing or interesting: *I don't find him at all attractive.* ○ *Your proposal sounds very attractive.* ○ *goods for sale at attractive prices.* ⇨ Usage at BEAUTIFUL. ▷ **attractively** *adv*: *attractively arranged, displayed, presented, etc.* **attractiveness** *n* [U].

attribute[1] /əˈtrɪbju:t/ *v* [Tn·pr] ~ **sth to sb/sth** regard sth as belonging to, caused by or produced by sb/sth: *This play is usually attributed to Shakespeare.* ○ *She attributes her success to hard work and a bit of luck.*
▷ **attributable** /əˈtrɪbjʊtəbl/ *adj* [pred] ~ **to sb/sth** that can be attributed to sb/sth: *Is this painting attributable to Michelangelo?*
attribution /ˌætrɪˈbju:ʃn/ *n* **1** [U] attributing sth to sb/sth. **2** [C] thing or quality attributed to sb/sth.

attribute[2] /ˈætrɪbju:t/ *n* **1** quality regarded as a natural or typical part of sb/sth: *Her greatest attribute was her kindness.* ○ *Patience is one of the most important attributes in a teacher.* **2** object recognized as a symbol of a person or his position: *The sceptre is an attribute of kingly power.*

attributive /əˈtrɪbjʊtɪv/ *adj (grammar)* (of adjectives or nouns) used directly before a noun, to describe it. Cf PREDICATIVE. ▷ **attributively** *adv.*

attrition /əˈtrɪʃn/ *n* [U] **1** process of gradually weakening sb's strength and confidence by continuous harassment (used esp in the expression shown): *a war of attrition.* **2** wearing sth away by rubbing; friction. **3** *(religion)* sorrow for one's sins that arises from a fear of punishment. Cf CONTRITION. **4** *(esp US)* = NATURAL WASTAGE (NATURAL).

attune /əˈtju:n; *US* əˈtu:n/ *v* [Tn·pr usu passive] ~ **sth/sb to sth** bring sth/sb into harmony or agreement with sth; make sth/sb familiar with sth: *We/Our ears are becoming attuned to the noise of the new factory near by.*

Atty-Gen *abbr (esp US)* Attorney-General.

atypical /ˌeɪˈtɪpɪkl/ *adj* not representative or characteristic of its type; not typical: *a creature that is atypical of its species.* ▷ **atypically** /-klɪ/ *adv.*

Au *symb* gold.

aubade /əʊˈbɑ:d/ *n* (esp romantic) poem or song associated with the dawn or morning.

aubergine /ˈəʊbəʒi:n/ (also *esp US* **egg-plant**) *n* [C, U] (**a**) large (almost egg-shaped) dark purple fruit, used as a vegetable. (**b**) plant producing this fruit.

Aubrey /ˈɔ:brɪ/ John (1626-97), English antiquary and writer, remembered mainly for his *Brief Lives,* a collection of vivid sketches of eminent people (published after his death). Aubrey was also a pioneer of field archaeology and one of the first Fellows of the *Royal Society.

aubrietia /ɔ:ˈbri:ʃə/ *n* small perennial plant that flowers in spring and is often grown on stone walls, rockeries, etc.

auburn /ˈɔ:bən/ *adj* (esp of hair) reddish-brown.

Auckland /ˈɔ:klənd/ largest city and chief port of New Zealand, at the northern end of North Island. It was also formerly the country's capital.

au courant /ˌəʊ kʊˈrɒn; *US* ˌəʊ kʊˈrɑ:n/ *adj* [pred] ~ **(with sth)** *(French)* fully informed (about sth); up to date: *I don't feel entirely au courant with the situation.*

auction /ˈɔ:kʃn, *also* ˈɒkʃn/ *n* **1** [U] method of selling things in which each item is sold to the person who offers the most money for it. The auctioneer, acting as the agent of the seller, completes the sale to the highest bidder, usu by striking his desk with a hammer. If the bids do not reach a certain sum agreed by the seller, then the auctioneer withdraws the goods from the auction: *The house is up for auction/will be sold by auction.* ○ *It should fetch* (ie be sold for) *£100 000 at auction.* **2** [C] (also ˈ**auction sale**) public event when this takes place: *attend all the local auctions.*
▷ **auction** *v* **1** [Tn] sell (sth) by auction. **2** (phr v) **auction sth off** sell (esp surplus or unwanted goods) by auction: *The Army is auctioning off a lot of old equipment.*
auctioneer /ˌɔ:kʃəˈnɪə(r)/ *n* person whose job is conducting auctions.
□ ˈ**auction bridge** form of bridge[2] in which players bid for the right to name trumps.

audacious /ɔ:ˈdeɪʃəs/ *adj* **1** showing a willingness to take risks; daring; fearless: *an audacious plan, scheme, etc.* **2** impudent; recklessly bold: *an audacious remark.* ▷ **audaciously** *adv.* **audacity** /ɔ:ˈdæsətɪ/ *n* [U]: *He had the audacity to tell me I was too fat.*

Auden /ˈɔ:dn/ Wystan Hugh (1907-73), English poet. At Oxford he was the leading figure in a left-wing near-Marxist group (including *Day-Lewis, *MacNeice and *Spender) which responded to the public chaos of the 1930s. In 1939, with Christopher Isherwood, Auden left Europe to settle in America, becoming a US citizen in 1946. *Another Time* (1940) contained many of his most famous poems. Later, his work became increasingly Christian in tone. He was elected Professor of Poetry at Oxford in 1956. Auden's influence on later poets has been immense. He was a master of verse form, accommodating traditional patterns to fresh contemporary language.

audible /ˈɔ:dəbl/ *adj* that can be heard clearly: *Her* *voice was scarcely audible above the noise of the wind.* ▷ **audibility** /ˌɔːdəˈbɪlətɪ/ *n* [U]. **audibly** /-əblɪ/ *adv.*

audience /ˈɔːdɪəns/ *n* **1** [CGp] group of people who have gathered together to hear or watch sb/sth: *The audience was/were enthusiastic on the opening night of the play.* ○ *She has addressed audiences all over the country.* **2** [C] number of people who watch, read or listen to the same thing: *An audience of millions watched the royal wedding on TV.* ○ *His book reached an even wider audience when it was filmed for television.* **3** [C] formal interview with a ruler or an important person: *request an audience with the Queen* ○ *grant a private audience to a foreign ambassador.*

audio- *comb form* of hearing or sound: *audio-visual.*

audio frequency /ˌɔːdɪəʊ ˈfriːkwənsɪ/ (radio) frequency that is audible to the human ear.

audiometer /ˌɔːdɪˈɒmɪtə/ *n* instrument for measuring a person's sensitivity to sounds of different frequencies and intensities.

audio typist /ˈɔːdɪəʊ taɪpɪst/ person who listens to a tape-recording and types what is heard.

audio-visual /ˌɔːdɪəʊ ˈvɪʒʊəl/ *adj* (*abbr* **AV**) using both sight and sound: *ˌaudio-visual ˈaids for the classroom,* eg cassette recorders, video recorders, pictures, etc.

audit /ˈɔːdɪt/ *n* official (usu yearly) examination of accounts to see that they are in order.
▷ **audit** *v* [Tn] examine (accounts, etc) officially.

audition /ɔːˈdɪʃn/ *n* trial hearing of a person who wants to perform as an actor, a singer, a musician, etc: *I'm going to the audition but I don't expect I'll get a part.*
▷ **audition** *v* **1** [I] take part in an audition: *Which part are you auditioning for?* **2** [Tn] give an audition to (sb): *None of the actresses we've auditioned is suitable.*

auditor /ˈɔːdɪtə(r)/ *n* person who audits accounts.

auditorium /ˌɔːdɪˈtɔːrɪəm/ *n* (*pl* ~**s**) part of a theatre, concert hall, etc in which an audience sits.

auditory /ˈɔːdɪtrɪ; *US* -tɔːrɪ/ *adj* of or concerned with hearing: *the auditory nerve.*

J J Audubon: The American Wild Turkey Cock

Audubon /ˈɔːdəbən/ John James (1785-1851), American naturalist and artist, famous for his lifelike paintings of birds in his book *The Birds of America.* ⇨ illus.

AUEW /ˌeɪ juː iː ˈdʌbljuː/ *abbr* Amalgamated Union of Engineering Workers (of Britain).

au fait /ˌəʊ ˈfeɪ/ *adj* [pred] (*French*) ~**(with sth)** fully acquainted (with sth): *It's my first week here so I'm not yet au fait with the system.*

au fond /ˌəʊ ˈfɒn/ *adv* (*French*) basically: *The problem is that, au fond, he's very lazy.*

Aug *abbr* August: *31 Aug 1908.*

Augean /ɔːˈdʒiːən/ *adj* **1** of the legendary King Augeas or his filthy stables, which *Hercules, as one of his Labours, cleaned in a day by making a river flow through them. **2** (*fig*) dirty or corrupt; filthy.

auger /ˈɔːgə(r)/ *n* tool for boring holes in wood, like a gimlet but larger.

aught /ɔːt/ *pron* (*arch*) **1** anything. **2** (idm) **for aught/all sb knows** ⇨ KNOW.

augment /ɔːgˈment/ *v* [Tn] (*fml*) make (sth) larger in number or size; increase: *augment one's income by writing reviews.*
▷ **augment** /ˈɔːgmənt/ *n* (in Greek and Sanskrit) vowel prefixed to a verb to form a past tense.
augmentation /ˌɔːgmenˈteɪʃn/ *n* (*fml*) **1** [U] action of augmenting or being augmented. **2** [C] thing that is added to sth.
augmented *adj* (of a musical interval) made a semitone greater than a major or perfect interval: *an augmented fifth.* Cf DIMINISHED (DIMINISH).

au gratin /ˌəʊ ˈgrætæn/ *adv* (*French*) cooked with a crisp coating of breadcrumbs or grated cheese: *cauliflower au gratin.*

augur /ˈɔːgə(r)/ *n* (in ancient Rome) religious official who foretold future events by watching the behaviour of birds, etc.
▷ **augur** *v* **1** [Tn] be a sign of (sth); foretell: *Does this augur disaster for our team?* **2** (idm) **augur well/ill for sb/sth** (*fml*) be a good/bad sign for sb/sth in the future: *The quality of your work augurs well for the examinations next month.*
augury /ˈɔːgjʊrɪ/ *n* omen; sign.

August /ˈɔːgəst/ *n* [U, C] (*abbr* **Aug**) the eighth month of the year, next after July.
For the uses of *August* see the examples at *April.*

august /ɔːˈgʌst/ *adj* [usu attrib] inspiring feelings of respect and awe; majestic and imposing: *an august body of elder statesmen.*

Augustan /ɔːˈgʌstən/ *adj* **1** of the reign of the Roman emperor Augustus, when Latin literature flourished. **2** (of any literature) classical(1); stylish: *The Augustan age of English literature includes the writers Dryden, Swift and Pope.*

Augustine[1] /ɔːˈgʌstɪn/ Saint (died c 604 AD), first Archbishop of Canterbury. Sent from Rome by Pope Gregory the Great to refound the Church in Britain, Augustine and his group of monks landed in Kent in 597. They were favourably received by King Ethelbert, who was afterwards converted to Christianity. Augustine founded the first church and a monastery at Canterbury and was consecrated as archbishop. ⇨ article at CHURCH OF ENGLAND.

Augustine[2] /ɔːˈgʌstɪn/ Saint, of Hippo (354-430 AD), a Doctor of the Christian Church. Born in North Africa, Augustine taught rhetoric in Rome and then in Milan, where he was attracted to Neoplatonism. In 386 he became a Christian, and from then on led a monastic life as a priest and later as Bishop of Hippo in North Africa. His most famous works are his spiritual autobiography, *Confessions,* and *The City of God,* a defence of the Church against paganism. Augustine's influence on all later Western theology has been immense, with his deep psychological insight and his sense of man's complete dependence on God's grace.
▷ **Augustinian** /ˌɔːgəˈstɪnɪən/ *adj* of or relating to St Augustine of Hippo or his teachings. — *n* member of an Augustinian religious order, esp the Augustinian Canons or the Augustinian (or Austin) Friars.

Augustus /ɔːˈgʌstəs/ (63 BC-14 AD), first Roman emperor. Born Gaius Octavius (later known as Octavian), he was the great-nephew of *Julius Caesar. After Caesar's murder in 44 BC, Augustus became one of the three rulers of Roman territories and then gained supreme power by defeating *Mark Antony at the battle of Actium (31 BC). His rule was marked abroad by a series of military campaigns that expanded the Roman Empire and at home by moral and religious reforms intended to restore old Roman values. He was given the title Augustus (which means 'venerable' in Latin) in 27 BC.

auk /ɔːk/ *n* any of several types of northern sea-bird, eg the puffin and the guillemot, with a heavy body and short narrow wings.

auld lang syne /ˌɔːld læŋ ˈsaɪn/ (*Scot*) (title of a popular song sung esp at the beginning of each new year and expressing feelings of friendship for the sake of) good times long ago.

Auld Reekie /ˌɔːld ˈriːkɪ/ (esp formerly) nickname for *Edinburgh. Meaning 'Old Smoky', it refers to the smoke rising from the city's chimneys.

au naturel /ˌəʊ ˌnætjəˈrel; *US* ˌəʊ ˌnætʊˈrel/ *adv, adj* [pred] (*French*) uncooked or cooked in the plainest way.

aunt /ɑːnt; *US* ænt/ *n* **1** (**a**) sister of one's father or mother; wife of one's uncle: *Aunt Mary is my mother's sister. She is the only aunt I have.* ⇨ App 8. (**b**) woman whose brother or sister has a child. **2** (*infml*) (used by children, usu in front of a first name) unrelated woman friend, esp of one's parents.
▷ **auntie** (also **aunty**) /ˈɑːntɪ; *US* ˈæntɪ/ *n* (*infml*) aunt.
□ ˌ**Aunt ˈSally 1** wooden figure used as a target in a throwing-game at fairs, etc. **2** (*fig*) person or thing that is subjected to general abuse and criticism, often undeserved: *Any public figure risks being made an Aunt Sally by the popular press.*

au pair /ˌəʊ ˈpeə(r)/ person (usu from overseas) who receives board and lodging with a family in return for helping with the housework, etc: *We've got a German au pair for six months.* ○ [attrib] *an au pair girl.*

aura /ˈɔːrə/ *n* **1** distinctive atmosphere that seems to surround and be caused by a person or thing: *She always seems to have an aura of happiness about her.* **2** sensation that immediately precedes an attack of an illness, eg epilepsy or migraine.

aural /ˈɔːrəl *or, rarely,* ˈaʊrəl/ *adj* of or concerning the ear or hearing: *an aural surgeon* ○ *aural comprehension tests.* ▷ **aurally** *adv.*

aureate /ˈɔːrɪət/ *adj* (*fml*) (esp of literary style) brilliant; splendid.

Aurelius /ɔːˈriːlɪəs/ Marcus (121-180 AD), Roman emperor 161-180. A great part of his reign was occupied with wars against Germanic tribes invading the Roman Empire from the north. Aurelius was by nature a philosopher: his *Meditations* are a collection of personal thoughts based on his stoic attitude towards life.

aureola /ɔːˈrɪələ/ (also **aureole** /ˈɔːrɪəʊl/) *n* **1** halo, esp round the head of a holy person in a painting, etc. **2** bright circle of light round the sun or moon; corona.

au revoir /ˌəʊ rəˈvwɑː(r)/ (*French*) goodbye until we meet again: *Au revoir, see you again next year!*

auricle /ˈɔːrɪkl/ *n* **1** external part of the ear. ⇨ illus at EAR[1]. **2** small pouch in each of the two upper parts of the heart; atrium. ⇨ illus at HEART. Cf VENTRICLE 1.

auricular /ɔːˈrɪkjʊlə(r)/ *adj* of or like the ear: *an auricular confession,* ie one spoken privately into the ear of a priest.

auriferous /ɔːˈrɪfərəs/ *adj* (of rock) yielding gold.

Auriga /ɔːˈraɪgə/ constellation (also called 'the Charioteer') in the northern hemisphere near Orion.

aurochs /ˈɔːrɒks/ *n* extinct large long-haired wild European ox.

aurora /ɔːˈrɔːrə/ *n* **1 auˌrora boreˈalis** /bɔːrɪˈeɪlɪs/ (also **the northern lights**) bands of coloured light, mainly red and green, seen in the sky at night near the North Pole and caused by electrical radiation. **2 auˌrora auˈstralis** /ɒˈstreɪlɪs/ (also **the southern lights**) similar lights seen in the southern hemisphere.

aurous /ˈɔːrəs/ *adj* of or containing gold.

Auschwitz /ˈaʊʃvɪts/ town in S Poland, site of a Nazi concentration camp in the Second World War; Polish name **Oświęcim.**

auscultation /ˌɔːskəlˈteɪʃn/ *n* [U] listening with the ear, a stethoscope, etc to sounds within the body as part of a medical diagnosis.

auspices /ˈɔːspɪsɪz/ *n* [pl] (idm) **under the auspices of sb/sth** helped and supported by sb/sth; having sb/sth as a patron: *set up a business under the auspices of a government aid scheme.* **under favourable, etc auspices** with favourable, etc prospects: *The committee began its work under unfavourable auspices.*

auspicious /ɔːˈspɪʃəs/ *adj* showing signs of future success; favourable; promising: *I'm pleased that you've made such an auspicious start to the new term.*

Aussie /ˈɒzɪ/ *n, adj* (*infml*) (native or inhabitant) of Australia.

portrait of Jane Austen by her sister Cassandra

Austen /ˈɒstɪn, *also* ˈɔːstɪn/ Jane (1775-1817), English novelist. The daughter of a clergyman, Austen led an uneventful life in a large lively family. She never married. Her major works describe the social life of the upper classes and all end in marriage, achieved after difficulties have been overcome. They include *Sense and Sensibility*, *Pride and Prejudice*, *Northanger Abbey*, *Mansfield Park*, *Emma* and *Persuasion*. ⇨ illus.

austere /ɒˈstɪə(r), *also* ɔːˈstɪə(r)/ *adj* **1** (of a person or his behaviour) severely and strictly moral; having no pleasures or comforts: *monks leading simple, austere lives.* **2** (of a building or place) very simple and plain; without ornament or comfort: *The room was furnished in austere style.*
▷ **austerely** *adv.*
austerity /ɒˈsterətɪ, *also* ɔːˈsterətɪ/ *n* **1** [U] quality of being austere: *the austerity of the Government's economic measures* ○ *War was followed by many years of austerity.* **2** [C usu *pl*] condition, activity or practice that is part of an austere way of life: *Wartime austerities included food rationing and shortage of fuel.*

Austerlitz /ˈaʊstəlɪts, *also* ˈɔːst-/ town in the Czech Republic, site of *Napoleon's victory over the Austrians and Russians in 1805.

austral /ˈɔːstrəl/ *adj* of the south; southern.

Australasia /ˌɒstrəˈleɪʒə; *US* ˌɔːs-/ Australia, New Zealand and neighbouring islands in the southern Pacific Ocean.
▷ **Australasian** /ˌɒstrəˈleɪʒn; *US* ˌɔːs-/ *n, adj* (native or inhabitant) of Australasia.

Australia /ɒˈstreɪlɪə; *US* ɔːˈs-/ island country and continent of the southern hemisphere in the SW Pacific Ocean, formerly a British colony and now an independent member of the Commonwealth; pop approx 16 532 000; official language English; capital Canberra; unit of currency dollar (= 100 cents). Livestock produce wool, meat and dairy

Australia

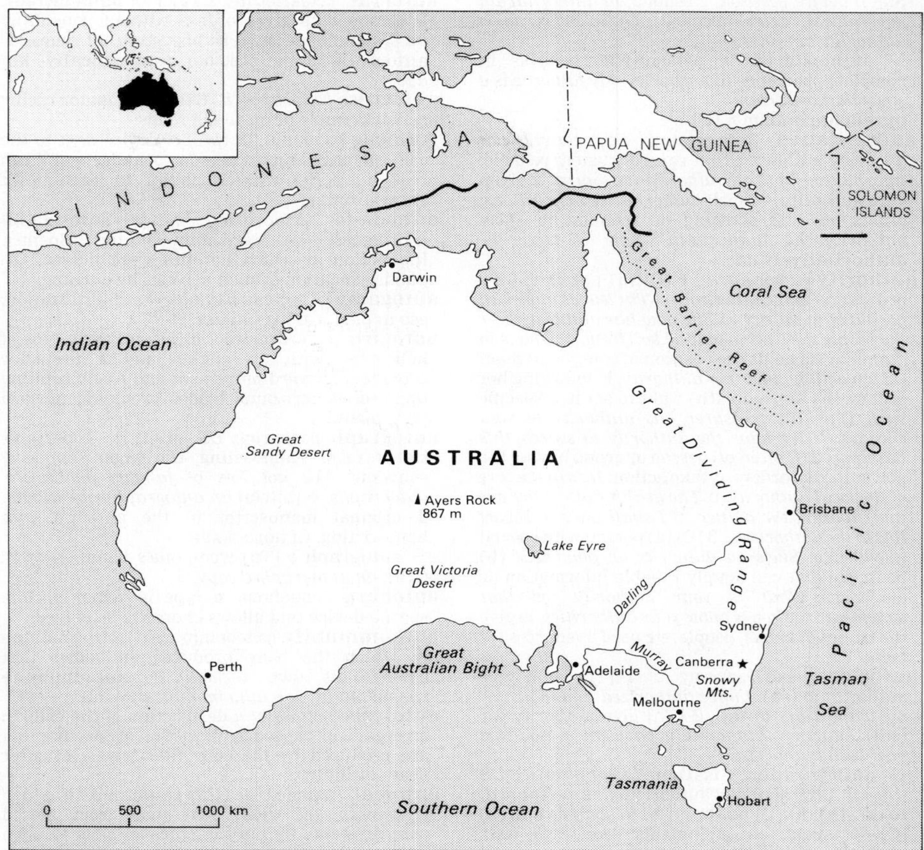

products for export. Cereal crops are also an important part of the economy and the country has significant mineral resources. ⇨ map.
▷ **Australian** /ɒˈstreɪlɪən; *US* ɔːˈs-/ *n, adj* (native or inhabitant) of Australia. **Ausˌtralian ˌCapital ˈTerritory** federal territory in New South Wales, SE Australia, containing the national capital Canberra. ⇨ map at App 1. **Ausˌtralian ˈRules** Australian game similar to Rugby, played by two teams of 18 players.

Australopithecus /ˌɒstrələʊˈpɪθɪkəs; *US* ɔːˌstreɪləʊˈpɪθəkəs/ *n* [U] type of extinct manlike primate of the late Pliocene and Pleistocene eras (about 5.5 million to 1 million years ago). Its fossil remains have been found in S and E Africa.

Austria /ˈɒstrɪə; *US* ˈɔːs-/ country in central Europe; pop approx 7 595 000; official language German; capital Vienna; unit of currency schilling (= 100 groschen). Much of Austria is mountainous, with the River Danube flowing through the north-east. Agriculture and forestry are important to the country's economy, and hydroelectric power has been developed for export. Since regaining her sovereignty after the Second World War (in 1955) Austria has emerged as a prosperous and stable democratic republic. ⇨ map. ▷ **Austrian** *adj, n.*

Austro- *comb form* Austrian; of Austria: *the Austro-Hungarian empire.*

autarchy /ˈɔːtɑːkɪ/ *n* [U] government of a country by a single ruler with unlimited power; despotism.

autarky /ˈɔːtɑːkɪ/ *n* [U] (esp economic) self-sufficiency.

authentic /ɔːˈθentɪk/ *adj* **1** known to be true or genuine: *an authentic document, signature, painting.* **2** trustworthy; reliable: *an authentic statement.*
▷ **authentically** /-klɪ/ *adv.*
authenticity /ˌɔːθenˈtɪsətɪ/ *n* [U] quality of being authentic: *The authenticity of the manuscript is*

Austria

beyond doubt.

authenticate /ɔːˈθentɪkeɪt/ *v* [Tn] prove (sth) to be valid or genuine or true: *authenticate a claim* ○ *Experts have authenticated the writing as that of Shakespeare himself.* ▷ **authentication** /ɔːˌθentɪˈkeɪʃn/ *n* [U].

author /ˈɔːθə(r)/ *n* **1** writer of a book, play, etc: *Dickens is my favourite author.* **2** person who creates or begins sth, esp a plan or an idea: *As the author of the scheme I can't really comment.*
▷ **authoress** /ˈɔːθərɪs/ *n* woman author.
authorship *n* [U] **1** origin of a book, etc: *The authorship of this poem is not known.* **2** state of being an author.

authoritarian /ɔːˌθɒrɪˈteərɪən/ *adj* favouring

complete obedience to authority (esp that of the State) before personal freedom: *an authoritarian government, regime, doctrine* ○ *The school is run on authoritarian lines.*

▷ **authoritarian** *n* person who believes in complete obedience to authority: *My father was a strict authoritarian.*

authoritarianism *n* [U].

authoritative /ɔːˈθɒrətətɪv; *US* -teɪtɪv/ *adj* **1** having authority; that can be trusted; reliable: *information from an authoritative source.* **2** given with authority; official: *authoritative instructions, orders, etc.* **3** showing or seeming to show authority: *an authoritative tone of voice.* ▷ **authoritatively** *adv.*

authority /ɔːˈθɒrətɪ/ *n* **1** [U] (**a**) power to give orders and make others obey: *The leader must be a person of authority.* ○ *She now has authority over the people she used to take orders from.* ○ *Who is in authority* (ie holds the position of command) *now?* ○ *I am acting under her authority*, ie following her orders. (**b**) ~ (**to do sth**) right to act in a specific way: *Only the treasurer has authority to sign cheques.* ○ *We have the authority to search this building.* **2** [C often *pl*] person or group having the power to give orders or take action: *He's in the care of the local authority.* ○ *The health authorities are investigating the matter.* ○ *I shall have to report this to the authorities.* **3** [C] (**a**) person with special knowledge: *She's an authority on phonetics.* (**b**) book, etc that can supply reliable information or evidence: *What is your authority for that statement?* ○ *Always quote your authorities*, ie give the names of books, people, etc used as sources for facts.

authorize, -ise /ˈɔːθəraɪz/ *v* **1** [Tn, Dn·t] give authority to (sb): *I have authorized him to act for me while I am away.* **2** [Tn] give authority for (sth); sanction: *authorize a payment* ○ *Has this visit been authorized?*

▷ **authorization, -isation** /ˌɔːθəraɪˈzeɪʃn; *US* -rɪˈz-/ *n* **1** [U] action of authorizing. **2** ~ (**for sth/to do sth**) (**a**) [U] power given to sb to do sth. (**b**) [C] document, etc giving this: *May I see your authorization for this?*

□ **the ˌAuthorized ˈVersion** (*abbr* **AV**) (also *esp US* **the King James Version**) English translation of the Bible made under James I for use in churches, published in 1611. The Authorized Version became the only familiar form of the Bible for generations of English-speaking people. It is still used in some churches today, although many favour the use of a more modern translation of the Bible.

autism /ˈɔːtɪzəm/ *n* [U] (*psychology*) serious mental illness, esp of children, in which one is unable to communicate or form relationships with others.

▷ **autistic** /ɔːˈtɪstɪk/ *adj* (*psychology*) suffering from autism.

auto /ˈɔːtəʊ/ *n* (*pl* ~**s**) (*infml esp US*) car.

aut(o)- *comb form* **1** of oneself: *autobiography* ○ *autograph.* **2** by oneself or itself; independent(ly): *autocracy* ○ *automobile.*

autobahn /ˈɔːtəbɑːn/ *n* motorway in Germany, Austria or Switzerland.

autobiography /ˌɔːtəbaɪˈɒgrəfɪ/ *n* **1** [C] story of a person's life written by that person: *She has just written her autobiography.* **2** [U] this type of writing.

▷ **autobiographic** /ˌɔːtəbaɪəˈgræfɪk/, **autobiographical** /-ɪkl/ *adjs* of or concerning autobiography: *His novels are largely autobiographical*, ie though fictional they describe many of his own experiences.

autochthon /ɔːˈtɒkθən/ *n* (*pl* ~**s** or ~**es** /-iːz/) original inhabitant of a region; aboriginal.

▷ **autochthonous** /ɔːˈtɒkθənəs/ *adj* (of plants, rocks, etc) originating in the place where they are found; native or indigenous.

autoclave /ˈɔːtəʊkleɪv/ *n* (**a**) strong vessel used for producing chemical reactions at high pressures or temperatures. (**b**) apparatus for sterilizing things using high-pressure steam.

autocracy /ɔːˈtɒkrəsɪ/ *n* (**a**) [U] government by one person with unlimited power; despotism. (**b**) [C] country governed in this way.

autocrat /ˈɔːtəkræt/ *n* **1** ruler of an autocracy. **2** person who gives orders without consulting others and expects to be obeyed at all times. ▷ **autocratic** /ˌɔːtəˈkrætɪk/ *adj.* **autocratically** /-klɪ/ *adv.*

autocross /ˈɔːtəʊkrɒs/ *n* [U] sport of motor racing across country or on rough roads.

Autocue /ˈɔːtəʊkjuː/ *n* (*propr*) device next to the camera from which a person speaking on TV can read the script without having to learn it. Cf TELEPROMPTER.

auto-da-fé /ˌɔːtəʊdɑːˈfeɪ/ *n* (*pl* **autos-da-fé**) (*Portuguese*) (**a**) ceremony of the *Spanish Inquisition at which heretics were judged. (**b**) public execution of such heretics by burning.

autogamy /ɔːˈtɒgəmɪ/ *n* (*biology*) self-fertilization, esp in plants. Cf ALLOGAMY.

autogiro /ˌɔːtəʊˈdʒaɪərəʊ/ *n* (*pl* ~**s**) early type of helicopter with an engine and a propeller providing forward movement and freely rotating unpowered horizontal blades providing upward movement.

autograph /ˈɔːtəgrɑːf; *US* -græf/ *n* **1** person's signature or handwriting, esp when kept as a souvenir: *I've got lots of famous footballers' autographs.* ○ [attrib] *an autograph book/album.* **2** original manuscript in the author's own handwriting. Cf HOLOGRAPH.

▷ **autograph** *v* [Tn] write one's name on or in (sth): *an autographed copy.*

autoharp /ˈɔːtəʊhɑːp/ *n* type of zither with a special device that allows chords to be played.

auto-immunity /ˌɔːtəʊɪˈmjuːnətɪ/ *n* [U] condition in which the body produces antibodies that damage its own tissues. ▷ **auto-immune** /ˌɔːtəʊɪˈmjuːn/ *adj*: *auto-immune diseases.*

autolysis /ɔːˈtɒləsɪs/ *n* destruction of the cells in an organism, caused by the action of enzymes that are produced by the cells themselves, eg after death or injury.

automat /ˈɔːtəmæt/ *n* (*US*) restaurant in which customers get their own food from closed compartments by putting coins in slots to open them.

automate /ˈɔːtəmeɪt/ *v* [Tn esp passive] cause (sth) to operate by automation: *This part of the assembly process is now fully automated.*

automatic /ˌɔːtəˈmætɪk/ *adj* **1** (of a machine) working by itself without direct human control: *an automatic washing-machine* ○ *automatic gears*, ie in a motor vehicle ○ *an automatic rifle*, ie one that continues firing as long as the trigger is pressed. **2** (of actions) done without thinking, esp from habit or routine; unconscious(2): *For most of us breathing is automatic.* **3** following necessarily: *A fine for this offence is automatic.*

▷ **automatic** *n* **1** automatic machine or gun or tool. **2** car with automatic transmission.

automatically /-klɪ/ *adv.*

□ **ˌautomatic ˈpilot** device in an aircraft or a ship to keep it on a set course without human control.

ˌautomatic transˈmission system in a motor vehicle that changes the gears automatically.

automation /ˌɔːtəˈmeɪʃn/ *n* [U] use of automatic equipment and machines to do work previously done by people: *Automation will mean the loss of many jobs in this factory.*

automatism /ɔːˈtɒmətɪzəm/ *n* action or behaviour without conscious thought or control.

automaton /ɔːˈtɒmətən; *US* -tɒn/ *n* (*pl* ~**s** or **-ta** /-tə/) **1** = ROBOT 1. **2** (*fig*) person who seems to act mechanically and without thinking. Cf ROBOT 2.

automobile /ˈɔːtəməbiːl, *also* ˌɔːtəməˈbiːl/ *n* (*esp US*) = CAR 1.

automotive /ˌɔːtəˈməʊtɪv/ *adj* concerned with motor vehicles.

autonomic /ˌɔːtəˈnɒmɪk/ *adj* occurring or functioning involuntarily: *the ˌautonomic ˈnervous system*, ie part of the nervous system in vertebrates which controls the involuntary muscles, the heart and the glands.

autonomous /ɔːˈtɒnəməs/ *adj* self-governing; acting independently: *an alliance of autonomous states.*

▷ **autonomy** /ɔːˈtɒnəmɪ/ *n* [U] self-government; independence: *Branch managers have full autonomy in their own areas.*

autopsy /ˈɔːtɒpsɪ/ *n* examination of a dead body to learn the cause of death; post-mortem: [attrib] *an autopsy report.* Cf BIOPSY.

autoradiography /ˌɔːtəʊˌreɪdɪˈɒgrəfɪ/ *n* [U] (*biology*) technique for examining the distribution of radioactivity in a specimen by placing it in contact with a photographic plate.

autoroute /ˈɔːtəʊruːt/ *n* (*French*) motorway in France.

autosome /ˈɔːtəsəʊm/ *n* (*biology*) any chromosome in a cell that is not one of the chromosomes which determine the sex of the organism.

autostrada /ˈɔːtəʊstrɑːdə/ *n* (*Italian*) motorway in Italy.

auto-suggestion /ˌɔːtəʊ səˈdʒestʃən/ *n* [U] (*psychology*) process by which a person under hypnosis or subconsciously suggests to himself a way of changing his own behaviour.

autotomy /ɔːˈtɒtəmɪ/ *n* [U] (*zoology*) way in which part of the body, eg the tail of a lizard, is discarded before growing again.

autotrophic /ˌɔːtəʊˈtrəʊfɪk/ *adj* (of organisms such as green plants) that can manufacture the organic materials required for nutrition from inorganic sources, eg carbon dioxide, water and nitrates, usu with sunlight as a source of energy. Cf HETEROTROPHIC.

autumn /ˈɔːtəm/ (*US* **fall**) *n* [U, C] the third season of the year, coming between summer and winter, ie from September to November in the northern hemisphere: *The leaves turn brown in autumn.* ○ *in the autumn of 1980* ○ *in (the) early/late autumn* ○ *It's been one of the coldest autumns for years.* ○ [attrib] *autumn colours, weather, fashions* ○ (*fig*) *in the autumn of* (ie the later part of) *one's life.*

▷ **autumnal** /ɔːˈtʌmnəl/ *adj* [usu pred] of or like autumn: *The weather in June was positively autumnal.*

auxanometer /ˌɔːksəˈnɒmɪtə(r)/ *n* instrument for measuring the growth or movement of plant organs.

auxiliary /ɔːgˈzɪlɪərɪ/ *adj* giving help or support; additional: *auxiliary troops* ○ *an auxiliary nurse* ○ *an auxiliary generator in case of power cuts.*

▷ **auxiliary** *n* **1** [C] person or thing that helps: *medical auxiliaries.* **2 auxiliaries** [pl] additional (esp foreign or allied) troops used by a country at war. **3** [C] (also **auˌxiliary ˈverb**) verb used with main verbs to show tense, mood, etc, and to form questions, eg *do* and *has* in *Do you know where he has gone?*

auxin /ˈɔːksɪn/ *n* any of a group of substances that control or modify the growth of plants.

AV /ˌeɪ ˈviː/ *abbr* **1** audio-visual. **2** Authorized Version (of the Bible).

avail /əˈveɪl/ *v* **1** [Tn·pr] ~ **oneself of sth** (*fml*) make use of sth; take advantage of sth: *You must avail yourself of every opportunity to speak English.* **2** [I, Ipr] (*dated*) be of value or help: *What can avail against the storm?* **3** (idm) **aˌvail sb ˈnothing** (*dated*) be of no use to sb.

▷ **avail** *n* (idm) **of little/no aˈvail** not very/not at all helpful or effective: *The advice we got was of no avail.* **to little/no aˈvail**; **without aˈvail** with little/no success: *The doctors tried everything to keep him alive but to no avail.*

available /əˈveɪləbl/ *adj* **1** (of things) that can be used or obtained: *Tickets are available at the box office.* ○ *You will be informed when the book becomes available.* ○ *This was the only available room.* **2** (of people) free to be seen, talked to, etc: *I'm available in the afternoon.* ○ *The Prime Minister was not available for comment.* ▷ **availability** /əˌveɪləˈbɪlətɪ/ *n* [U].

avalanche /ˈævəlɑːnʃ; *US* -læntʃ/ *n* mass of snow, ice and rock that slides rapidly down the side of a mountain: *Yesterday's avalanche killed a party of skiers and destroyed several trees.* ○ (*fig*) *We received an avalanche of letters in reply to our advertisement.*

Avalon /ˈævəlɒn/ island paradise of Celtic mythology. In Arthurian legend, Avalon was the place to which King *Arthur was taken after his death.

avant-garde /ˌævɒŋ ˈɡɑːd/ *adj* favouring new and progressive ideas, esp in art and literature: *avant-garde writers, artists, etc* ○ *the avant-garde movement.*

▷ **avant-garde** *n* [CGp] group of people introducing such ideas: *a member of the avant-garde.*

avarice /ˈævərɪs/ *n* [U] (*fml*) greed for wealth or gain: *Avarice makes rich people want to become even richer.* ▷ **avaricious** /ˌævəˈrɪʃəs/ *adj.* **avariciously** *adv.*

avatar /ˈævətɑː(r)/ *n* (in Hinduism) descent to earth of a god, esp Vishnu, in bodily form; incarnation.

avdp *abbr* avoirdupois.

Ave *abbr* Avenue: *5 St George's Ave.*

Avebury /ˈeɪvbrɪ/ village in Wiltshire in southern England, site of a large late neolithic monument of stone circles and ditches.

Ave Maria /ˌɑːveɪ məˈriːə/ (also **Hail Mary**) (in the Roman Catholic Church) prayer to the Virgin Mary. The Ave Maria (meaning 'Hail Mary', in Latin) is based on the greetings of the angel Gabriel and of Elizabeth to Mary in the Bible and has been the subject of many musical compositions.

avenge /əˈvendʒ/ *v* **1** [Tn] take or get revenge for (a wrong done to sb/oneself): *She avenged her father's murder.* **2** [Tn·pr] ~ **oneself on sb/sth** take or get revenge on sb/sth for such a wrong: *She avenged herself on her father's killers.* ▷ **avenger** *n.*

avenue /ˈævənjuː; *US* -nuː/ *n* **1** wide road or path, often lined with trees, esp one that leads to a large house. **2** (*abbr* **Ave**) wide street lined with trees or tall buildings. ⇨ Usage at ROAD. **3** way of approaching or making progress towards sth: *an avenue to success, fame, etc* ○ *Several avenues are open to us.* ○ *We have explored every avenue.*

aver /əˈvɜː(r)/ *v* (-rr-) [Tn, Tf] (*fml*) state (sth) firmly and positively; assert.

average /ˈævərɪdʒ/ *n* **1** [C] result of adding several amounts together and dividing the total by the number of amounts: *The average of 4, 5 and 9 is 6.* **2** [U] standard or level regarded as usual: *These marks are well above/below average.* **3** [U] damage to or loss of a ship or its cargo. **4** (idm) **the law of averages** ⇨ LAW. **on (the) ˈaverage** taking account of use, performance, etc over a period: *We fail one student per year on average.*

▷ **average** *adj* **1** [attrib] found by calculating the average: *The average age of the students is 19.* ○ *The average temperature in Oxford last month was 18°C.* **2** of the ordinary or usual standard: *children of average intelligence* ○ *Rainfall is about average for the time of year.*

average *v* **1** [I, Tn] find the average of (sth): *I've done some averaging to reach these figures.* **2** [Tn no passive] do or amount to (sth) as an average measure or rate: *This car averages 40 miles to the gallon.* ○ *The rainfall averages 36 inches a year.* **3** (phr v) **average ˈout (at sth)** result in an average (of sth): *Meals average out at £5 per head.* ○ *Sometimes I pay, sometimes he pays — it seems to average out* (ie result in a fair balance) *in the end.* **average sth out (at sth)** calculate the average of sth: *The tax authorities averaged his profit out at £3 000 a year over 5 years.*

Avernus /əˈvɜːnəs/ lake near Naples in Italy, filling the crater of an extinct volcano and believed by the ancient Romans to be the entrance to the underworld.

Averroës /əˈverəʊiːz, *also* æˌvəˈrəʊiːz/ (ibn-Rushd, 1126-98), Islamic philosopher, judge and physician born in Spain. Of his scientific, philosophical and religious writings the most famous are his commentaries on *Aristotle, which had a strong influence on medieval Western philosophy.

averse /əˈvɜːs/ *adj* [pred] ~ **to sth** (*fml or rhet*) not liking sth; opposed to sth: *He seems to be averse to hard work.* ○ *I'm not averse to a drop of whisky after dinner.*

aversion /əˈvɜːʃn; *US* əˈvɜːrʒn/ *n* **1** [C, U] ~ **(to sb/sth)** strong dislike: *I've always had an aversion to getting up early.* ○ *He took an immediate aversion to his new boss.* **2** [C] thing that is disliked: *Smoking is one of my pet* (ie particular, personal) *aversions.*

□ **aˈversion therapy** method of treating an undesirable habit, eg alcoholism, by associating it with sth unpleasant.

avert /əˈvɜːt/ *v* **1** [Tn, Tn·pr] ~ **sth (from sth)** turn sth away: *avert one's eyes/gaze/glance from the terrible sight.* **2** [Tn] prevent (sth); avoid: *avert an accident, a crisis, a disaster, etc by prompt action* ○ *He managed to avert suspicion.*

Avery /ˈeɪvərɪ/ Tex (1918-80), American cartoon maker. He created several famous cartoon characters, including Bugs Bunny and Droopy, whose adventures showed a new surreal form of humour.

Avesta /əˈvestə/ sacred writings of *Zoroastrianism. Cf ZEND-AVESTA.

avian /ˈeɪvɪən/ *adj* (*fml*) of or relating to birds.

aviary /ˈeɪvɪərɪ; *US* -vɪerɪ/ *n* large cage or building for keeping birds in, eg in a zoo.

aviation /ˌeɪvɪˈeɪʃn/ *n* [U] **1** science or practice of flying aircraft. **2** design and manufacture of aircraft: [attrib] *the aviation business/industry.*

▷ **aviator** /ˈeɪvɪeɪtə(r)/ *n* (*dated*) person who flies an aircraft as the pilot or one of the crew.

Avicenna /ˌævɪˈsenə/ (ibn-Sina, 980-1037 AD), Islamic philosopher and physician. His philosophical writings combined the teachings of *Aristotle with Neoplatonic ideas, and greatly influenced the development of medieval western philosophy. His *Canon of Medicine* was a standard work until the Renaissance.

avid /ˈævɪd/ *adj* ~ **(for sth)** eager; greedy: *an avid collector of old coins* ○ *avid for news of her son.*

▷ **avidity** /əˈvɪdətɪ/ *n* [U] (*fml*) eagerness. **avidly** *adv*: *She reads avidly.*

Avignon /ˈæviːnjɒn; *US* ˌæviːnˈjəʊn/ city on the River Rhône in SE France. As the residence of the popes in exile from 1309 to 1377, Avignon attracted many Italian artists, notably Simone Martini. The city remained the property of the Pope until the French Revolution.

avionics /ˌeɪvɪˈɒnɪks/ *n* **1** [sing *v*] science of electronics applied to aeronautics and astronautics. **2** [pl] electronic equipment in an aircraft or a spacecraft.

avitaminosis /ˌeɪˌvɪtəmɪˈnəʊsɪs; *US* ˌeɪˌvaɪtəməˈnəʊsəs/ *n* (*pl* **-noses** /-nəʊsiːz/) disease resulting from a lack of vitamins in the diet.

avocado /ˌævəˈkɑːdəʊ/ *n* (*pl* ~**s**) (also ˌ**avocado ˈpear**) **1** pear-shaped tropical fruit with rough dark-green skin and creamy flesh. **2** tropical American tree on which this fruit grows.

avocation /ˌævəˈkeɪʃn/ *n* **1** secondary activity undertaken in addition to one's main work. **2** (*infml*) one's occupation; calling. Cf VOCATION 3.

avocet /ˈævəset/ *n* wading bird with long legs and a slender upturned bill.

Avogadro /ˌævəˈɡɑːdrəʊ/ Amedeo (1776-1856), Italian chemist and physicist, noted for his work on gases.

□ ˌ**Avogadro's ˈconstant** (also ˌ**Avogadro's ˈnumber**) number of atoms or molecules in one mole[4] of a substance.

ˌ**Avogadro's ˈlaw** (also ˌ**Avogadro's hyˈpothesis**) supposition that equal volumes of all gases at the same temperature and pressure contain equal numbers of molecules.

avoid /əˈvɔɪd/ *v* **1** [Tn, Tg] **(a)** keep oneself away from (sb/sth): *avoid (driving in) the centre of town* ○ *I think he's avoiding me.* **(b)** stop (sth) happening; prevent: *Try to avoid accidents.* ○ *I just avoided running over the cat.* **2** [Tn] (*law*) make (a contract or deed) void; annul. **3** (idm) **avoid sb/sth like the ˈplague** (*infml*) try very hard not to meet sb/sth: *He's been avoiding me like the plague since our quarrel.*

▷ **avoidable** *adj* that can be avoided.

avoidance *n* [U] act of avoiding: *tax avoidance*, ie managing to pay the minimum amount of tax required by law.

avoirdupois /ˌævədəˈpɔɪz/ *n* [U] (*abbr* **avdp**) non-metric system of weights based on the pound, equal to 16 ounces or 7000 grains. ⇨ App 10.

Avon /ˈeɪvn/ county in SW England created in 1974 from areas formerly in Somerset and Gloucestershire, including Bath and Bristol. It takes its name from the River Avon. ⇨ map at App1.

avow /əˈvaʊ/ *v* [Tn, Cn·n, Cn·t] (*fml*) declare (sth) openly; admit: *avow one's belief, faith, conviction, etc* ○ *avow oneself (to be) a socialist* ○ *The avowed aim of this Government is to reduce taxation.*

▷ **avowal** *n* (*fml*) **(a)** [U] open declaration. **(b)** [C] instance of this: *make an avowal of his love.*

avowedly /əˈvaʊɪdlɪ/ *adv* (*fml*) admittedly; openly: *avowedly responsible for an error.*

avuncular /əˈvʌŋkjʊlə(r)/ *adj* (*fml*) of or like an uncle, esp in manner: *He adopts an avuncular tone of voice when giving advice to junior colleagues.*

AWACS /ˈeɪwæks/ *abbr* airborne warning and control system: *planes fitted with AWACS.*

await /əˈweɪt/ *v* [Tn] (*fml*) **1** (of a person) wait for (sb/sth): *awaiting instructions, results, a reply.* **2** be ready or waiting for (sb/sth): *A warm welcome awaits all our customers.* ○ *A surprise awaited us on our arrival.*

awake[1] /əˈweɪk/ *v* (*pt* **awoke** /əˈwəʊk/, *pp* **awoken** /əˈwəʊkən/) [I, Tn] **1** (cause a person or an animal to) stop sleeping; wake: *She awoke when the nurse entered the room.* ○ *He awoke the sleeping child.* **2** (*fig*) (cause sth to) become active: *The letter awoke old fears.* **3** (phr v) **awake to sth** become aware of sth; realize sth: *awake to the dangers, the opportunities, one's surroundings.*

awake[2] /əˈweɪk/ *adj* [pred] **1** not asleep, esp immediately before and after sleeping: *They aren't awake yet.* ○ *Are the children still awake?* ○ *They're wide* (ie fully) *awake.* **2** ~ **to sth** conscious or aware of sth: *Are you fully awake to the danger you're in?*

awaken /əˈweɪkən/ *v* **1** [I, Tn] (cause a person or an animal to) stop sleeping; waken: *We awakened to find the others had gone.* ○ *I was awakened by the sound of church bells.* ○ (*fig*) *They were making enough noise to awaken the dead.* **2** [Tn] cause (sth) to become active: *Her story awakened our interest.* **3** (phr v) **awaken sb to sth** cause sb to become aware of sth: *awaken society to the dangers of drugs.*

▷ **awakening** /əˈweɪknɪŋ/ *n* [sing] act of realizing: *The discovery that her husband was unfaithful to her was a rude* (ie shocking) *awakening.*

award /əˈwɔːd/ *v* [Tn, Dn·n, Dn·pr] ~ **sth (to sb)** make an official decision to give sth to sb as a prize, as payment or as a punishment: *The judges awarded both finalists equal points.* ○ *The court awarded (him) damages of £50000.* ○ *She was awarded a medal for bravery.*

▷ **award** *n* **1** [U] decision to give sth, made by a judge, etc: *the award of a scholarship.* **2** [C] thing or amount awarded: *She showed us the athletics awards she had won.* ○ [attrib] *an award presentation/ceremony.* **3** [C] (*Brit*) money paid to a student at university, etc to help meet living costs; grant: *Mary is not eligible for an award.*

aware /əˈweə(r)/ *adj* **1** [pred] ~ **of sb/sth**; ~ **that...** having knowledge or realization of sb/sth: *aware of the risk, danger, threat, etc* ○ *Are you aware of the time?* ○ *It happened without my being aware of it.* ○ *I'm (well) aware that very few jobs are available.* ○ *She became aware that something was burning.* ○ *I don't think you're aware (of) how much this means to me.* **2** well-informed; interested, esp in current events: *She's always been a politically aware person.* ▷ **awareness** *n* [U].

awash /əˈwɒʃ/ *adj* [pred] covered or flooded with sea water, being at or near the level of the waves: *These rocks are awash at high tide.* ○ *The ship's deck was awash in the storm.* ○ (*fig*) *The sink had overflowed and the kitchen floor was awash.*

away /əˈweɪ/ *adv part* (For special uses with *vs*, see the *v* entries.) **1** ~ **(from sb/sth)** to or at a distance in space or time (from sb/sth): *The sea is 2 miles away from the hotel.* ○ *The shops are a few minutes' walk away.* ○ *Christmas is only a week away.* ○

They're away on holiday for 2 weeks. ○ *Don't go away.* ○ *Have you cleared away your books from the table?* ○ *The bright light made her look away.* **2** continuously: *She was still writing away furiously when the bell went.* ○ *They worked away for two days to get it finished.* ○ *After five minutes they were talking away like old friends.* **3** until it disappears completely: *The water boiled away.* ○ *The picture faded away.* ○ *The hut was swept away by the flood.* ○ (*fig*) *They danced the night away*, ie all night. **4** (of a football, cricket, etc team) at the opponents' ground: *They're playing away tomorrow.* ○ [attrib] *We lost all our away matches.* Cf HOME[2] 3. **5** (idm) **away with sb/sth** (used in exclamations) remove sb/sth; make sb/sth leave: *Away with all these petty restrictions!* **right/straight away/off** ⇨ RIGHT[2].

awe /ɔː/ *n* [U] feeling of respect combined with fear or wonder: *Her first view of the pyramids filled her with awe.* ○ *I was/lived in awe of my father until I was at least fifteen.* ○ *My brother was much older and cleverer than me so I always held him in awe.*
▷ **awe** *v* [usu passive: Tn, Tn·pr] ~ **sb (into sth)** fill sb with awe: *awed by the solemnity of the occasion* ○ *They were awed into silence by the sternness of her voice.*
awesome /-səm/ *adj* causing awe: *His strength was awesome.*
□ ˈ**awe-inspiring** *adj* causing awe: *an awe-inspiring sight.*
ˈ**awestricken**, ˈ**awestruck** *adjs* suddenly filled with awe.

aweigh /əˈweɪ/ *adv* (*nautical*) (of an anchor) hanging just above the bottom of the sea: *Anchors aweigh!*

awful /ˈɔːfl/ *adj* **1** extremely bad or unpleasant; terrible: *an awful accident, experience, shock, etc* ○ *The plight of starving people is too awful to think about.* **2** (*infml*) very bad; dreadful: *What awful weather!* ○ *I feel awful.* ○ *It's an awful nuisance!* ○ *The film was awful.* **3** [attrib] (*infml*) very great: *That's an awful lot of money.* ○ *I'm in an awful hurry to get to the bank.*
▷ **awfully** /ˈɔːflɪ/ *adv* (*infml*) very; very much: *awfully hot* ○ *awfully sorry* ○ *It's awfully kind of you.* ○ *I'm afraid I'm awfully late.* ○ *Thanks awfully for the present.*

awhile /əˈwaɪl; *US* əˈhwaɪl/ *adv* for a short time: *Stay awhile.* ○ *We won't be leaving yet awhile*, ie not for a short time.

awkward /ˈɔːkwəd/ *adj* **1** badly designed; difficult to use: *The handle of this teapot has an awkward shape.* ○ *It's an awkward door — you have to bend down to go through it.* **2** causing difficulty, embarrassment or inconvenience: *an awkward series of bends in the road* ○ *You've put me in a very awkward position.* ○ *Please arrange the next meeting at a less awkward time.* ○ *It's very awkward of you not to play for the team tomorrow.* ○ *Stop being so awkward!* **3** lacking skill or grace; clumsy: *Swans are surprisingly awkward on land.* ○ *I was always an awkward dancer.* **4** embarrassed: *I realized they wanted to be alone together so I felt very awkward.* **5** (idm) **the** ˈ**awkward age** period of adolescence when young people lack confidence and have difficulty preparing for adult life. **an** ˌ**awkward** ˈ**customer** person or animal that is difficult or dangerous to deal with. ▷ **awkwardly** *adv.* **awkwardness** *n* [U].

awl /ɔːl/ *n* small pointed tool for making holes, esp in leather or wood.

awning /ˈɔːnɪŋ/ *n* canvas or plastic sheet fixed to a wall above a door or window and stretched out as a protection against rain or sun.

awoke *pt* of AWAKE[1].

AWOL /ˈeɪwɒl/ *abbr* absent without leave.

awry /əˈraɪ/ *adv* **1** crookedly; out of position; askew. **2** wrongly; amiss: *Our plans went awry.*
▷ **awry** *adj* [pred] crooked: *Her clothes were all awry.*

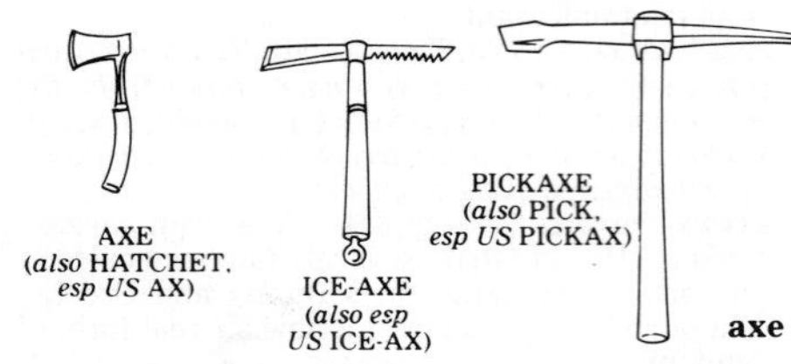

axe (also *esp US* **ax**) /æks/ *n* **1** tool with a handle and a heavy metal blade used for chopping wood, cutting down trees, etc: (*fig*) *apply the axe to* (ie drastically reduce) *local government spending.* ⇨ illus. **2** (idm) **get the** ˈ**axe** (*infml*) be removed or dismissed, esp from a job: *A lot of people in shipbuilding will get the axe.* ˌ**have an** ˈ**axe to grind** have private reasons for being involved in sth: *She's only doing it out of kindness — she's got no particular axe to grind.*
▷ **axe** (also *esp US* **ax**) *v* [Tn] **1** remove (sb/sth) or dismiss (sb): *He/His job has been axed.* **2** greatly reduce (costs, services, etc): *School grants are to be axed next year.*

axial /ˈæksɪəl/ *adj* of, forming or placed round an axis.
□ ˌ**axial** ˈ**skeleton** (in vertebrates) skeleton of the main part of the body and the head, not the arms or legs.

axil /ˈæksɪl/ *n* (*botany*) upper angle between a leaf and the main stem or between a branch and the trunk from which it grows.
▷ **axillary** /ækˈsɪlərɪ/ *adj* **1** (*anatomy*) of or relating to the armpit. **2** (*botany*) in or growing from the axil: *an axillary bud.*

axiom /ˈæksɪəm/ *n* statement that is accepted as true without further proof or argument.
▷ **axiomatic** /ˌæksɪəˈmætɪk/ *adj* of or like an axiom; clear and evident without needing to be proved: *It is axiomatic (to say) that a whole is greater than any of its parts.*

axis /ˈæksɪs/ *n* (*pl* **axes** /ˈæksiːz/) **1** [C] imaginary line through the centre of a rotating object: *The earth's axis is the line between the North and South Poles.* ⇨ illus at GLOBE. **2** [C] line that divides a regular figure into two symmetrical parts: *The axis of a circle is its diameter.* **3** [C] fixed reference line for measurement, eg on a graph: *the horizontal and vertical axes.* **4** [C] agreement or alliance between two or more countries. **5 the Axis** [sing] the alliance of Germany, Italy and Japan in the Second World War. **6** [C] (*anatomy*) second cervical vertebra, on which the first cervical vertebra and the skull turn. Cf ATLAS 2. **7** [C] (*botany*) stem of a plant.

axle /ˈæksl/ *n* **1** rod on which or with which a wheel turns. **2** rod that connects a pair of wheels on a vehicle: *The back axle is broken.* ⇨ illus at CAR.

Axminster /ˈæksmɪnstə(r)/ *n* (*Brit*) tufted carpet with a thick pile, named after a town in Devon in SW England where such carpets were originally made.

axolotl /ˌæksəˈlɒtl/ *n* type of newt-like amphibian found in Mexican lakes.

axon /ˈæksɒn/ *n* long thread-like extension of a nerve cell that conducts impulses away from the cell.

ayatollah /ˌaɪəˈtɒlə/ *n* senior Muslim religious leader in Iran.

Ayckbourn /ˈeɪkbɔːn/ Alan (1939-), British playwright and stage director based in Scarborough, North Yorkshire. He has written over 30 plays, depicting with humour, accuracy and sometimes cruelty the stresses of English middle-class life. They include *Absurd Person Singular*, the trilogy *The Norman Conquests*, and *A Small Family Business*.

aye[1] (also **ay**) /aɪ/ *interj* (*arch or dialect*) yes: ˌ*Aye,* ˈ*aye, sir!* eg in reply to an order by a naval officer.
▷ **aye** (also **ay**) *n* **1** (usu *pl*) vote in support of a motion at a meeting. **2** (idm) **the ayes** ˈ**have it** more people have voted for the motion than against it.

aye[2] /eɪ/ *adv* (*arch*) always.

Ayer /eə(r)/ Sir Alfred Jules (1910-89), English philosopher, noted chiefly for his contribution to logical positivism, esp in *Language, Truth and Logic* (1936).

Ayers Rock /ˌeəz ˈrɒk/ vast red mass of rock in Northern Territory, Australia. It is the largest monolith in the world, with a height of 348 m (1 143 ft) above sea-level and a circumference of about 9 km (6 miles). Its Aboriginal name is **Uluru**.

Ayrshire /ˈeəʃə/ **1** former county in SW Scotland, now part of Strathclyde. **2** hardy breed of brown and white dairy cattle that originated in Ayrshire.

Ayurvedic /ˌɑːjəˈveɪdɪk/ *adj* of the traditional Hindu science of medicine based on natural remedies and homoeopathic treatment.

azalea /əˈzeɪlɪə/ *n* flowering shrub of the rhododendron family.

azeotrope /əˈziːətrəʊp/ *n* (*chemistry*) mixture of liquids that boils without a change of composition, the composition of the vapour being the same as that of the liquid. ▷ **azeotropic** /ˌeɪzɪəˈtrɒpɪk/ *adj*: *an azeotropic mixture.*

Azerbaijan /ˌæzəbaɪˈdʒɑːn/ country bordering on the Caspian Sea; pop approx 7 136 000; official language Turkish in Latin script; capital Baku; unit of currency manat (= 100 gopik, or 10 roubles). Once part of Persia, and later of the USSR, it became an independent republic in 1991. The country has extensive oilfields. ⇨ map at UNION OF SOVIET SOCIALIST REPUBLICS.

azimuth /ˈæzɪməθ/ *n* **1** (*astronomy*) arc of the sky from the zenith to the horizon. **2** angular distance between a fixed point (eg north or south) and the vertical circle passing through the centre of an object. ▷ **azimuthal** /ˌæzɪˈmʌθl/ *adj.*

Azores /əˈzɔːz/ **the Azores** [pl] group of volcanic islands in the N Atlantic Ocean, about 1 200 km (745 miles) W of Portugal; pop approx 250 000; capital Ponta Delgada. The islands belong to Portugal but are partly autonomous. ⇨ map at PORTUGAL.

Azov /ˈɑːzɒv/ inland sea of the southern USSR, connecting, through a strait east of the *Crimea, with the Black Sea.

Azrael /ˈæzreɪəl/ (in Jewish and Islamic mythology) angel who separates the soul from the body at death.

Aztec /ˈæztek/ *n* **1** [C] member of a native Mexican people who ruled an empire in central Mexico until it was overthrown by *Cortés in the early 16th century. The Aztecs had an advanced and elaborate civilization, centred on the city of Tenochtitlán. **2** (also **Nahuatl**) [U] language of the Aztecs.
▷ **Aztec** *adj* of the Aztecs or their language.

azure /ˈæʒə(r), *also* ˈæzjʊə(r)/ *n* [U], *adj* bright blue, as of the sky: *a lake reflecting the azure of the sky* ○ *a dress of azure silk.*

B, b

B, b /bi:/ *n* (*pl* **B's, b's** /bi:z/) **1** the second letter of the English alphabet: *There are three b's in bubble.* **2** (*music*) the seventh note in the scale of C major. **3** academic mark of second highest standard: *get (a) B/'B' in English.*

□ **ˈB-film** (also *esp US* **ˈB-movie**) *n* film produced cheaply, using actors who are not famous.

ˈB-road *n* (in Britain) less important road than a motorway or an A-road, often narrow and winding: *stick to the B-roads to avoid the traffic.*

ˈB-side *n* (also **flip side**) side of a single-play gramophone record on which is recorded the song, etc that is expected to be less popular than the main one.

B /bi:/ *abbr* (of lead used in pencils) black, because soft: *a B/BB/2B pencil.* Cf H, HB.

B /bi:/ *symb* boron.

b *abbr* **1** book. **2** born: *Emily Jane Clifton b 1800.* Cf D 2.

BA /ˌbi: ˈeɪ/ *abbr* **1** (*US* **AB**) Bachelor of Arts: *have/be a BA in history* ○ *Jim Fox BA (Hons).* ⇨ article at POST-SCHOOL. **2** British Airways: *flight BA430 to Rome.*

Ba *symb* barium.

baa /bɑ:/ *n* cry of a sheep or lamb.

▷ **baa** *v* (*pres p* **baaing**, *pt* **baaed** or **baa'd** /bɑ:d/) [I] make this cry; bleat.

Baal /beɪl/ (in the Old Testament) pagan god worshipped by the enemies of the Hebrews.

baba /ˈbɑ:bɑ:/ *n* (also **rum baba**) sweet sponge-cake soaked in rum and eaten as a dessert.

Babbage /ˈbæbɪdʒ/ Charles (1791-1871), British mathematician and inventor, considered to be the founder of modern computing. In 1823 he began to make a 'difference engine' which could solve mathematical problems and print the answers, but because of lack of support he was unable to finish it. He also helped to prepare for the introduction of the British postal system.

Babbitt /ˈbæbɪt/ *n* (also **Babbitt metal**) [U] any of several alloys used for making bearings because it produces very little friction.

babble /ˈbæbl/ *v* **1** [I, Ipr, Ip] **(a)** talk in a way that is difficult or impossible to understand: *Stop babbling and speak more slowly.* ○ *tourists babbling (away) in a foreign language.* **(b)** chatter in a thoughtless or confused way: *What is he babbling (on) about?* **2** [Tn] reveal (information that should be kept secret): *Don't go babbling the date to anyone.* **3** [I] (of streams, etc) make a continuous murmuring sound: *a babbling brook.*

▷ **babble** *n* [U] **1 (a)** talk that is difficult or impossible to understand: *hear the babble of many voices.* **(b)** foolish talk. **2** gentle sound of water flowing over stones, etc.

babbler /ˈbæblə(r)/ *n* person who babbles.

babe /beɪb/ *n* **1** (*arch*) baby. **2** (*US sl*) young woman. **3** (idm) **a ˌbabe in ˈarms (a)** very young baby not able to walk or crawl. **(b)** innocent or helpless person. **ˌbabes in the ˈwood** people who are in a difficult situation but who do not have the experience they need to deal with it (from the title of a popular pantomime). **out of the mouths of babes and sucklings** ⇨ MOUTH[1].

babel /ˈbeɪbl/ *n* [sing] scene of noisy talking and confusion: *a babel of voices in the busy market.* Cf TOWER OF BABEL (TOWER).

baboon /bəˈbu:n; *US* bæ-/ *n* large African or Arabian monkey with a dog-like face. ⇨ illus at MONKEY.

baby /ˈbeɪbɪ/ *n* **1 (a)** very young child or animal: *Both mother and baby are doing well.* ○ *He was crying like a baby,* ie very loudly. ○ [attrib]: *a ˌbaby ˈboy/ˈgirl* ○ *a baby thrush, monkey, crocodile.* **(b)** (*infml*) youngest member of a family or group: *He's the baby of the team.* **(c)** childish or timid person: *Stop crying and don't be such a baby.* **2 (a)** (*sl esp US*) young woman, esp a man's girl-friend. **(b)** (*US sl*) person. **3** [attrib] very small of its kind: *a baby car.* **4** (idm) **be ˌone's ˈbaby** (*infml*) be sth that one has created or has in one's care: *It's your baby,* ie You must deal with it. **leave sb holding the baby** ⇨ LEAVE[1]. **smooth as a baby's bottom** ⇨ SMOOTH[1]. **start a baby** ⇨ START[2]. **throw the baby out with the bath water** foolishly discard a valuable idea, plan, etc at the same time as one is getting rid of sth unpleasant or undesirable. **wet the baby's head** ⇨ WET *v.*

▷ **baby** *v* (*pt, pp* **babied**) [Tn] treat (sb) like a baby; pamper: *Don't baby him.*

babyhood *n* [sing] **(a)** state of being a baby. **(b)** time when one is a baby.

babyish *adj* of, like or suitable for a baby: *Now that Ned can read he finds his early picture books too babyish.*

□ **ˈbaby buggy** (*US*) = PRAM.

ˈbaby carriage (*US*) = PRAM.

ˈbaby-faced *adj* having a smooth round babyish face.

ˌbaby ˈgrand small grand piano.

ˈbaby-minder *n* person paid to look after a baby for long periods (eg while the parents are working).

ˈbaby-sit *v* (**-tt-**; *pt, pp* **-sat**) [I] be a baby-sitter: *She regularly baby-sits for us.* **ˈbaby-sitter** *n* (*infml*) (also **sitter**) person who looks after a child for a short time while the parents are out. **ˈbaby-sitting** *n* [U].

ˈbaby-snatcher *n* woman who steals a baby, esp from its pram.

ˈbaby-talk *n* unnatural or simplified language used by or to babies before they can speak properly.

ˈbaby tooth (*esp US*) = MILK-TOOTH (MILK[1]).

Babylon /ˈbæbɪlən, -lɒn/ ancient city, now in ruins, situated in modern Iraq. It was the capital of Babylonia and the centre of a great civilization from around 1750 BC. Its famous 'Hanging Gardens', laid out in terraces and built in the 7th century BC, were one of the Seven Wonders of the World. The Bible tells how the Hebrews were enslaved by the King of Babylon. ▷ **Babylonian** /ˌbæbɪˈləʊnɪən/ *n, adj.*

baccalaureate /ˌbækəˈlɔ:rɪət/ *n* **1** last secondary school examination in France and in many international schools: *sit, take, pass, fail, etc one's baccalaureate.* **2** (*US*) sermon given at a commencement ceremony, when students graduate.

baccarat /ˈbækərɑ:/ *n* [U] card-game played by gamblers.

bacchanal /ˈbækənl/ *n* (*pl* **~s** or **~ia** /ˌbækəˈneɪlɪə/) (*dated or fml*) bout of noisy, drunken merry-making. ▷ **bacchanalian** /ˌbækəˈneɪlɪən/ *adj*: *bacchanalian revels.*

Bacchus /ˈbækəs/ another name for the Greek and Roman god *Dionysus.

baccy /ˈbækɪ/ *n* [U] (*Brit infml*) tobacco.

Bach /bɑ:k/ Johann Sebastian (1685-1750), German composer. His music is considered to be among the finest ever written. He is particularly famous for his sacred music, such as the *Saint Matthew Passion* and the *Christmas Oratorio* and for his music for orchestra, but he also excelled in every musical genre of his time. Several of his sons were also musicians.

Bacharach /ˈbækəræk/ Burt (1928-), American composer and pianist, famous for his film scores and popular songs.

bachelor /ˈbætʃələ(r)/ *n* **1 (a)** unmarried man: *He remained a bachelor all his life.* ○ *a confirmed bachelor,* ie one who has decided never to marry ○ [attrib] *a bachelor girl,* ie an unmarried woman who lives independently. Cf SPINSTER. **(b)** [attrib] of or suitable for an unmarried person: *a bachelor flat.* **2** person who holds a first university degree: *a bachelor's degree* ○ *Bachelor of Arts/Science.* ▷ **bachelorhood** *n* [U].

□ **ˌbachelor's ˈbuttons** any of various small plants with round button-like flowers, similar to the daisy.

bacillus /bəˈsɪləs/ *n* (*pl* **-cilli** /bəˈsɪlaɪ/) rod-like bacterium, esp one of the types that can spoil food or cause disease in the body.

back[1] /bæk/ *n* **1** [C] part or surface of an object that is furthest from the front; part that is less used, less visible or less important: *If you use mirrors you can see the back of your head.* ○ *The index is at the back (of the book).* ○ *The child sat in the back (of the car) behind the driver.* ○ *I was at the back (of the cinema) and couldn't see well.* ○ *Write your address on the back (of the cheque).* ○ *a room at the back of the house* ○ *a house with a garden at the back* ○ *You can't cut with the back of the knife.* ○ *the back of one's hand,* ie the side with the nails and the knuckles. Cf FRONT 1. **2** [C] **(a)** rear part of the human body from the neck to the buttocks; spine: *He lay on his back and looked up at the sky.* ○ *She broke her back in a climbing accident.* **(b)** part of an animal's body that corresponds to this: *Fasten the saddle on the horse's back.* ⇨ illus at HORSE. **3** [C] part of a garment covering the back. **4** [C] part of a chair against which a seated person's back rests. ⇨ illus at FURNITURE. **5** [C] (in football, etc) defensive player whose position is near the goal. **6 the Backs** [pl] (*Brit*) parts of the grounds behind certain *Cambridge colleges, next to the river Cam. **7** (idm) **at the ˌback of one's ˈmind** in one's thoughts, but without being of immediate or central concern: *At the back of his mind was the vague idea that he had met her before.* **the ˌback of beyˈond** an isolated place, far from a centre of social and cultural activity: *They live somewhere at the back of beyond.* **ˌback to ˈback** with back against back: *Stand back to back and let's see who's taller.*

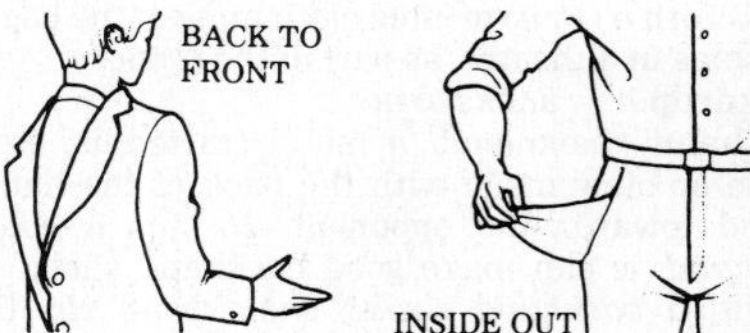

ˌback to ˈfront with the back placed where the front should be: *Your pullover is on back to front.* ⇨ illus. **be glad, etc to see the back of sb/sth** be pleased, etc that one will not see sb/sth again. **behind sb's ˈback** without sb's knowledge or consent: *They say nasty things about him behind his back.* Cf TO SB'S FACE (FACE[1]). **be on sb's ˈback** annoy, hinder or persecute sb. **break one's ˈback (to do sth)** work very hard (to achieve sth). **break the back of sth** finish the larger or more difficult part of (a task). **get/put sb's ˈback up** make sb angry: *His offhand manner put my back up.* **get off sb's ˈback** (*infml*) stop annoying, hindering or persecuting sb. **have one's ˌback to the ˈwall** be in a difficult position and forced to defend oneself. **have eyes in the back of one's head** ⇨ EYE[1]. **have a monkey on one's back** ⇨ MONKEY. **know sth like the back of one's hand** ⇨ KNOW. **make a rod for one's own back** ⇨ ROD. **on one's back** in bed because one is ill or injured: *He's still on his back with bronchitis.* **a pat on the back** ⇨ PAT[2] *n.* **pat sb/oneself on the back** ⇨ PAT[2] *v.* **put one's ˈback into sth** work at sth with all one's energy. **a stab in the back** ⇨ STAB *n.* **stab sb in the back** ⇨ STAB *v.* **turn one's back on sb/sth** avoid or reject sb/sth: *He turned his back on his family when he became famous.* **water off a duck's back** ⇨ WATER[1]. **you scratch my back and I'll scratch yours** ⇨ SCRATCH[1].

▷ **backless** *adj* (of dress) cut low at the back[1](2a).

□ **ˈbackache** *n* [U, C] ache or pain in the back[1](2a).

ˈbackbone *n* **1** [C] line of bones down the middle of the back from the skull to the hips; spine; spinal column. ⇨ illus at SKELETON. **2** [sing] (*fig*) chief support: *Such people are the backbone of the country.* **3** [U] (*fig*) strength; firmness: *He has no backbone,* ie lacks stamina, perseverance, strength of character, etc. **4** (idm) **to the ˈbackbone** thoroughly.

ˈback-breaking *adj* exhausting: *back-breaking work, effort, etc.*

ˈbackpack *n* (*esp US*) = RUCKSACK. **ˈbackpacker** *n.* **ˈbackpacking** *n* [U].

ˈbackrest *n* support for the back[1](2a).

ˈbackscratcher *n* device with claws on a long handle for scratching one's own back[1](2a).

ˈbackstroke *n* [U] swimming stroke done on one's back in the water.

back[2] /bæk/ *adj* (esp attrib and in compounds; no comparative or superlative) **1** situated behind: *a back garden* ○ *the back door* ○ *back teeth* ○ *ˈback streets,* ie usu narrow streets in a poor part of a town. **2** (**a**) of or for a past time: *back issues of a magazine.* (**b**) owed for a time in the past; overdue: *back pay/taxes/rent.* **3** (*phonetics*) (of a vowel) formed at the back of the mouth. **4** (idm) **by/through the back door** in an unfair illegal way: *He used his influential friends to help him get into the civil service by the back door.* **put sth on the back burner** (*infml*) put work, etc aside to be dealt with later.

□ **ˌback-ˈbench** *n* (usu *pl*) (*Brit*) seat in the House of Commons for a back-bencher: *sit on the back-benches* ○ [attrib] *ˌback-bench MˈPs* ○ *a ˌback-bench reˈvolt.* **ˌback-ˈbencher** *n* (*Brit*) member of Parliament who does not hold an important position in the government or opposition. ⇨ article at PARLIAMENT.

ˈbackblocks *n* [pl] (*Austral and NZ*) remote area in the interior of a country, where few people live.

ˌback ˈboiler boiler built into the back of a coal or gas fire, used for heating water.

ˈbackcloth *n* (*Brit*) printed cloth hung at the back of a stage in a theatre, as part of the scenery.

ˈbackdrop *n* = BACKCLOTH.

backhand /ˈbækhænd/ *n* [sing] (in tennis, etc) stroke or blow made with the back of the hand turned towards the opponent: *He has a good backhand,* ie can make good backhand shots. ○ [attrib] *a backhand stroke, shot, drive, etc.* Cf FOREHAND.

ˌbackˈhanded *adj* [usu attrib] **1** played as a backhand. **2** indirect: *a backhanded ˈcompliment,* ie one made in a sarcastic way so that it is not a compliment at all.

ˈbackhander *n* **1** (*sl*) bribe. **2** backhanded stroke; backhand.

ˈbacklist *n* publisher's list of books still in print.

ˈbacklog *n* (usu *sing*) accumulation of work or business not yet attended to: *a backlog of work, unanswered letters* ○ *After the postal strike there was a huge backlog of undelivered mail to be dealt with.*

ˌback ˈnumber 1 issue of a periodical of an earlier date, not now on sale. **2** person or thing that is considered out of date or useless: *As a force in politics he's now definitely a back number.*

ˌback proˈjection method of projecting a film onto a screen from behind, usu so that it can be used as a background for a scene being filmed in front of it.

ˈback road (*esp US*) = BY-ROAD.

ˌback ˈroom *n* **1** (esp unimportant) room at the back of a building. **2** (idm) **ˌback-room ˈboys** (*infml esp Brit*) scientists, engineers, research workers, etc who receive little public attention.

ˌback ˈseat 1 seat at the back of a car, etc. **2** (idm) **a ˌback-seat ˈdriver** (*derog*) passenger in a car who gives unwanted advice to the driver. **take a back seat** (*fig*) behave as if one were unimportant; take a less prominent part in sth.

ˈbackside *n* (*infml*) buttocks: *Get off your backside and do some work!*

ˈbackstage *adv* **1** behind the stage in a theatre: *I was taken backstage to meet the actors.* **2** (*fig*) unseen by the public: *I'd like to know what really goes on backstage in government.*

ˈbackstairs (also **ˈbackstair**) *adj* [attrib] kept secret from people outside a small group; clandestine: *backstairs gossip.*

ˈbackwater *n* (usu sing) **1** part of a river not reached by the current, where the water does not flow. **2** (*fig*) place that remains unaffected by events, progress, new ideas, etc: *I find this town too much of a backwater.*

ˈbackwoods *n* [pl] **1** uncleared forest land. **2** remote or sparsely inhabited region. **3** culturally backward area. **ˈbackwoodsman** /-mən/ *n* (*pl* **-men** /-mən/) person who lives in the backwoods.

ˌbackˈyard *n* (also **yard**) **1** (**a**) (*Brit*) (esp of terraced houses) usu paved area at the back of a house. (**b**) (*US*) whole area behind and belonging to a house, including the lawn, garden, etc. **2** (*fig*) area that is very close (used esp in the expression shown): *in one's own backyard,* ie within one's own organization. **3** (idm) **not in my, etc backyard** (*abbr* **NIMBY**) (*infml saying*) (representing the attitude of sb who favours a proposal, etc in theory provided that it does not cause him any inconvenience in practice): *Many people want to see more prisons being built, but not in their backyard,* ie not too close to their own homes.

back[3] /bæk/ *adv part* **1** (**a**) towards or at the rear; away from the front or centre: *Stand back to allow the procession to pass.* ○ *Sit well back in your chair.* ○ *You've combed your hair back.* ○ *The house stands back* (ie at some distance) *from the road.* ○ *We passed a garage, about a mile back.* Cf FORWARD[2] 1. (**b**) under control: *He could no longer hold back his tears.* ○ *The barriers failed to hold/keep the crowds back.* **2** (**a**) in(to) an earlier position, condition or stage: *Put the book back on the shelf.* ○ *Please give me my ball back.* ○ *My aunt is just back* (ie has just returned) *from Paris.* ○ *It takes me an hour to walk there and back.* ○ *We shall be back* (ie home again) *by six o'clock.* ○ *The party expects to be back in power after the election.* (**b**) (of time) ago; into the past: *(way) back in the Middle Ages* ○ *That was a few years back.* **3** in return: *If he kicks me, I'll kick him back.* ○ *Jane wrote him a long letter, but he never wrote back.* ○ *She smiled at him, and he smiled back.* **4** (idm) **ˌback and ˈforth** from one place to another and back again repeatedly: *ferries sailing back and forth between Dover and Calais.* (**in**) **back of sth** (*US infml*) behind sth: *the houses back of the church.*

□ **ˈbackbite** *v* (*pt, pp* **ˈbackbitten**) [I] (esp in the continuous tenses) slander the reputation of sb who is not present. **ˈbackbiter** *n* person who backbites. **ˈbackbiting** *n* [U].

ˈbackchat *n* [U] (*US* **back talk**) (*infml*) answering back cheekily: *I want none of your backchat!*

ˈbackcomb (also **tease**) *v* [Tn] comb (hair) from the ends back towards the scalp to give it a fuller appearance.

ˈbackdate *v* [Tn] declare that (sth) is to be regarded as valid from some date in the past: *a pay increase awarded in May and backdated to 1 January.*

ˈbackfire *v* **1** [I] ignite or explode too early, esp in an internal-combustion engine: *The car/engine backfired noisily.* **2** [I, Ipr] ~ (**on sb**) (*fig*) produce an unexpected and unwanted result esp for the people responsible for the action: *The plot backfired (on the terrorist) when the bomb exploded too soon.* Cf MISFIRE. — *n* early explosion, esp in an internal-combustion engine.

ˈback-formation *n* [U, C] (process of making a) word that appears to be the root of a longer word, eg *televise* from *television.*

ˈbacklash *n* **1** [sing] extreme (and usu violent) reaction to some event: *The fall of the fascist dictatorship was followed by a left-wing backlash.* **2** [U] effect that occurs when a piece of machinery moves backwards too strongly after moving forwards, caused by badly fitting parts.

back-ˈpedal *v* (**-ll-**; *US* **-l-**) **1** [I] pedal backwards on a bicycle, etc. **2** [I, Ipr] ~ (**on sth**) (*fig*) withdraw from an earlier statement or policy; reverse one's previous action: *The Government are back-pedalling on their election promises.*

ˈbackslide *v* (*pt, pp* **ˈbackslid**) [I] lapse from good ways into one's former bad ways of living: *He's a reformed criminal who may yet backslide.* **ˈbacksliding** *n* [U].

ˈbackspace *v* [I] move the carriage of a typewriter or the cursor on a computer monitor backwards one or more spaces by pressing the special key for this.

ˈbackspin *n* [U] spinning movement that makes an object (esp a ball in sport) slow down or move backwards when it hits the ground, etc: *The ball was hit with (a lot of) backspin.*

ˈback talk (*US*) = BACKCHAT.

ˈbacktrack *v* [I] **1** return by the way that one came. **2** (*fig*) withdraw from an earlier argument or policy.

ˈbackwash *n* **1** backward movement of water in waves, esp behind a moving ship. **2** (*fig*) (usu unpleasant) results of an action, a policy or an event: [attrib] *the backwash effect of the war years.*

back[4] /bæk/ *v* **1** [I, Ipr, Ip, Tn, Tn·pr, Tn·p] (cause sth to) move backwards: *back (a car) out of/into the garage, onto the road, into* (ie hitting) *a tree.* **2** [Ipr, Tn] ~ (**on/onto**) **sth** face sth at the back: *Our house backs on(to) the river.* **3** [Tn] (**a**) give help or support to (sb/sth): *She's the candidate who is backed by the Labour Party.* (**b**) give financial support to (sb/sth): *Who is backing the film?* **4** [Tn] bet money on (a horse, greyhound, etc): *I backed four horses but won nothing.* ○ *Did anyone back the winner?* ○ *The favourite was heavily backed,* ie Much money was bet on its winning the race. **5** [Tn, Tn·pr esp passive] ~ **sth** (**with sth**) cover the back of sth; be a lining to sth: *The photograph was backed with cardboard.* **6** [Tn] sign (sth) on the back as a promise to pay if necessary; endorse: *back a bill, note, etc.* **7** [I] (of wind) change gradually in an anticlockwise direction (eg from E to NE to N). Cf VEER 2. **8** (idm) **ˌback the wrong ˈhorse** support the loser (in a contest). **9** (phr v) **back away** (**from sb/sth**) move backwards in fear or dislike: *The child backed away from the big dog.* **back ˈdown**; *US* **back ˈoff** give up a claim to sth; yield: *He proved that he was right and his critics had to back down.* **back out** (**of sth**) withdraw from (an agreement, a promise, etc): *It's too late to back out (of the deal) now.* **back up** (*US*) = BACK[4] 1: *You can back up another two yards.* **back sb/sth up** give support or encouragement to sb/sth: *If I tell the police I was with you that day, will you back up my ˈstory/back me ˈup?* **back sth up** (*computing*) make a copy of (a file, program, etc) in case the original is lost or damaged.

▷ **backer** *n* **1** person who gives (esp financial) support to another person, an undertaking, etc. **2** person who bets money on a horse, etc.

backing *n* **1** (**a**) [U] help; support. (**b**) [sing] group of supporters: *The new leader has a large backing.*

2 [U] material used to form the back of sth or to support sth: *cloth, rubber, cardboard, etc backing.* 3 [U, C usu *sing*] (esp in pop music) musical accompaniment to a singer: *vocal/instrumental backing* ○ [attrib] *a backing group.*

□ ˈ**back-up** *n* 1 [U] support; reserve: *The police had military back-up.* ○ [attrib] *back-up services* ○ *the back-up team of a racing driver.* 2 [U, C] (*computing*) (making a) copy of a file, program, etc for use in case the original is lost or damaged: [attrib] *a back-up disc.*

backgammon /ˌbækˈgæmən, ˈbækgæmən/ *n* [U] game for two players played on a double board with draughts and dice.

background /ˈbækgraʊnd/ *n* 1 [sing] part of a view, scene or description that forms a setting for the chief objects, people, etc. Cf FOREGROUND. 2 [sing] (a) inconspicuous position (used esp in the expressions shown): *be/be kept/stay in the background,* ie not in the centre of public attention. (b) [attrib] unobtrusive: *background music.* Cf FOREGROUND. 3 (a) [sing] conditions and events surrounding and influencing sth: *These political developments should be seen against a background of increasing East-West tension.* ○ [attrib] *background information.* (b) [C] person's social class, education, training, etc: *He has a working-class background.* (c) [U] information that is needed to understand a problem, etc: *Can you give me more background on the company's financial position?*

backward /ˈbækwəd/ *adj* 1 directed towards the back or the starting-point: *a backward glance, somersault.* 2 having made or making less than normal progress: *a very backward part of the country, with no proper roads and no electricity* ○ *John was rather backward as a child; he was nearly three before he could walk.* 3 [pred] ~ (**in sth**) shy; reluctant; hesitant: *Sheila is very clever but rather backward in expressing her ideas.* 4 (idm) (**not be**) ˌ**backward in coming** ˈ**forward** (*usu joc*) (not be) unwilling to help or take part in some activity; reluctant: *The police have appealed for witnesses, but people are very backward in coming forward.* Cf FORWARD.

▷ ˌ**backwar**ˈ**dation** *n* (*Brit finance*) sum of money paid to a purchaser of stock[1](5a) by the seller when delivery of the stock is postponed for some reason.

backwards (also **backward**) *adv* 1 away from one's front; towards the back: *He looked backwards over his shoulder.* 2 with the back or the end first: *It's not easy to run backwards.* ○ *The word 'star' is 'rats' backwards.* 3 toward a worse or a previous state: *Let's take a journey backwards through time,* ie imagine we are going back to an earlier period in history. ○ *Instead of making progress, my work actually seems to be going backwards.* ⇨ Usage at FORWARD[2]. 4 (idm) ˌ**backward(s) and** ˈ**forward(s)** first in one direction and then in the other: *travelling backwards and forwards between London and the south coast* ○ [attrib] *a backward and forward movement.* **bend/lean over** ˈ**backwards (to do sth)** (*infml*) make a great effort: *Although we bent over backwards to please her, our new manager was still very critical of our work.* **know sth backwards** ⇨ KNOW.

backwardness *n* [U].

Bacon[1] /ˈbeɪkən/ Francis (1561-1626), Baron Verulam and Viscount St Albans, English lawyer and philosopher. He became Lord Chancellor, but was dismissed for corruption. His books show a scientific interest in the world which was new at that time, based primarily on inductive reasoning. Some people believe that Bacon wrote the plays of Shakespeare.

Bacon[2] /ˈbeɪkən/ Francis (1909-), Irish painter. His pictures, using gross distortion and lurid colours, often emphasize human fear and cruelty.

Bacon[3] /ˈbeɪkən/ Roger (c 1214–1294), English monk and scholar. He is considered to be the first great English philosopher, and was very interested in science and mathematics. He also made discoveries in optics and invented spectacles. His interest in science made some people think he was a heretic or sorcerer.

bacon /ˈbeɪkən/ *n* [U] 1 salted or smoked meat from the back or sides of a pig: *a rasher of bacon.* Cf GAMMON, HAM 1, PORK. 2 (idm) **bring home the bacon** ⇨ HOME[3]. **save one's bacon** ⇨ SAVE[1].

bacteria /bækˈtɪərɪə/ *n* [pl] (*sing* **-ium** /-ɪəm/) microscopic organisms that consist of a single cell but have no distinct nuclear membrane. They exist in large numbers in air, water and soil, and also in living and dead creatures and plants, and are often a cause of disease.

▷ **bacterial** /-rɪəl/ *adj* of or caused by bacteria: *bacterial contamination.*

bactericide /bækˈtɪərɪsaɪd/ *n* substance that is used to destroy bacteria.

bacteriology /bækˌtɪərɪˈblədʒɪ/ *n* [U] scientific study of bacteria. **bacteriologist** /-dʒɪst/ *n* person specializing in bacteriology.

Bactrian camel /ˌbæktrɪən ˈkæməl/ *n* camel from central Asia with two humps. Cf DROMEDARY. ⇨ illus at CAMEL.

bad[1] /bæd/ *adj* (**worse** /wɜːs/, **worst** /wɜːst/) 1 (a) of poor quality; below an acceptable standard; faulty: *a bad lecture, harvest* ○ *bad pronunciation, eyesight* ○ *You can't take photographs if the light is bad.* (b) (used with names of occupations or with *ns* derived from *vs*) not competent; not able to perform satisfactorily: *a bad teacher, hairdresser, poet, etc* ○ *a bad liar, listener, etc* ○ *a bad loser,* ie one who complains when he loses. 2 not morally acceptable; wicked: *It's bad to steal.* ○ *He led a bad life.* 3 unpleasant; disagreeable; unwelcome: *In the recession, our firm went through a bad time.* ○ *What bad weather we're having!* ○ *He's had some bad news: his father has died suddenly.* ○ *These rotting bananas are giving off a bad smell.* 4 [usu attrib] (of things that are in themselves undesirable) serious; noticeable: *a bad mistake, accident, fracture, headache.* 5 (of food) not fit to be eaten because of decay; rotting or rotten: *bad eggs, meat, etc* ○ *The fish will go bad if you don't put it in the fridge.* 6 [usu attrib] unhealthy or diseased: *bad teeth* ○ *a bad back,* ie one that causes pain. 7 [pred] ~ **for sb/sth** hurtful or injurious to sb/sth: *Smoking is bad for you/bad for your health.* ○ *Too much rain is bad for the crops.* 8 ~ (**for sth/to do sth**) unsuitable; difficult: *a bad time for buying a house/to buy a house* ○ *This beach is good for swimming but bad for surfing.* 9 (idm) **go from** ˌ**bad to** ˈ**worse** (of a bad condition, situation, etc) become even worse: *We were hoping for an improvement but things have gone from bad to worse.* (**be/get**) **in bad** (**with sb**) (*US infml*) (be/become) disapproved of or out of favour: *If you get in bad with the boss, you'll have problems.* **not** ˈ**bad** (*infml*) quite good; better than expected: *That was not bad for a first attempt.* ○ *'How are you feeling?' 'Not too bad!'* **too bad** (a) regrettable (used sympathetically): *It's too bad you can't come to the party.* (b) (*infml ironic*) unfortunate (used dismissively): *'My share's too small.' 'Too bad! It's all you're going to get.'* (For other idioms containing **bad**, see entries for other major words in each idiom, eg **turn up like a bad penny** ⇨ PENNY.)

▷ **bad** *adv* (*US infml*) badly(2): *That's what I want, and I want it bad.* ○ *Are you hurt bad?*

baddy *n* (*infml*) villain in a film, novel, etc: *In real life, it's not so easy to divide people into goodies and baddies.*

badly *adv* (**worse, worst**) 1 in an inadequate or unsatisfactory manner: *play, work, sing, etc badly* ○ *badly made, dressed, etc* ○ *I'm afraid our team's doing rather badly.* 2 (with expressions indicating a want, need, etc or undesirable conditions) very much; to a great extent: *badly in need of repair* ○ *badly wounded* ○ *badly beaten at football* ○ *They want to see her very badly.* 3 (idm) **badly** ˈ**off** in a poor position, esp financially: *We shouldn't complain about being poor — many families are much worse off (than we are).* **be badly** ˈ**off for sth** be in need (of sth); be inadequately supplied (with sth): *The refugees are badly off for blankets, and even worse off for food.*

badness *n* [U].

□ ˌ**bad** ˈ**debt** debt that is unlikely to be paid.

ˈ**bad lands** (also **badlands**) (*US*) barren regions, esp (**the Bad Lands**) parts of South Dakota and Nebraska in the USA, where the land has been deeply eroded, leaving sharp ridges of rock.

ˌ**bad** ˈ**language** obscene or profane words used insultingly or to add emphasis; swear-words.

ˈ**bad-mouth** *v* [Tn] (*US infml*) talk maliciously about (sb); slander.

ˌ**bad-**ˈ**tempered** *adj* usually cross.

bad[2] /bæd/ *n* **the bad** [U] 1 that which is wicked, unpleasant, etc. 2 (idm) **go to the** ˈ**bad** become completely immoral. **take the** ˌ**bad with the** ˈ**good** accept the unwelcome aspects (of life, a situation, etc) as well as the welcome ones. **to the** ˈ**bad** (used to describe a financial position) in debit: *I am £500 to the bad,* ie I have £500 less than I had.

bade ⇨ BID[1].

Baden-Powell /ˌbeɪdn ˈpəʊəl/ Robert Stephenson Smyth (1857-1941), British soldier and founder of the *Scout Movement. He became famous for defending the town of Mafeking during the *Boer War, but he left the army to found the Boy Scouts (in 1908), and, with his wife, the Girl Guides (in 1910). ⇨ article at YOUTH.

badge /bædʒ/ *n* (a) thing worn (usu a design on cloth or sth made of metal) to show a person's occupation, rank, membership of a society, etc: *a cap badge,* eg of a schoolboy or soldier. ⇨ illus at HAT. (b) (*fig*) thing that shows a quality or condition: *Chains are a badge of slavery.*

badger[1] /ˈbædʒə(r)/ *n* animal of the weasel family, grey with black and white stripes on its head, living in holes in the ground and moving about at night. ⇨ illus at ANIMAL.

badger[2] /ˈbædʒə(r)/ *v* [Tn, Tn·pr, Dn·t] ~ **sb** (**with/for sth**); ~ **sb** (**into doing sth**) pester sb; nag sb persistently: *Stop badgering your father with questions!* ○ *She badgered me into doing what she wanted.* ○ *Tom has been badgering his uncle to buy him a camera.*

badinage /ˈbædɪnɑːʒ; *US* ˌbædənˈɑːʒ/ *n* [U] (*French*) playful teasing; banter.

badminton /ˈbædmɪntən/ *n* [U] game for two or four people played with rackets and shuttlecocks on a court with a high net.

Baedeker /ˈbeɪdekə(r)/ Karl (1801-59), German publisher of guidebooks. These books covered Europe and the Middle East and were also known as 'Baedekers'. A modern series of Baedeker touring guides is now available.

Baffin Island /ˈbæfɪn aɪlənd/ the largest island in the Canadian Arctic. Its area is about 475 000 sq km (184 000 sq m).

baffle[1] /ˈbæfl/ *v* [Tn] 1 be too difficult for (sb) to understand; puzzle: *One of the exam questions baffled me completely.* ○ *Police are baffled as to the identity of the killer.* 2 prevent (sb) from doing sth; frustrate: *She baffled all our attempts to find her.* ▷ **bafflement** *n* [U]. **baffling** *adj*: *a baffling crime.*

baffle[2] /ˈbæfl/ *n* screen used to hinder or control the flow of sound, light or liquid.

BAFTA /ˈbæftə/ *abbr* British Academy of Film and Television Arts: *BAFTA awards.*

bag[1] /bæg/ *n* 1 (a) container made of flexible material (eg paper, cloth or leather) with an opening at the top, used for carrying things from place to place: *a* ˈ*shopping-bag* ○ *a* ˈ*handbag* ○ *a* ˈ*kitbag* ○ *a* ˈ*toolbag* ○ *a* ˈ*mailbag.* (b) such a container with its contents; the amount it contains: *two bags of coal.* 2 thing resembling a bag: *bags under the eyes,* ie loose folds of skin under the eyes, eg from lack of sleep. 3 all the birds, animals, etc shot or caught: *We got a good bag today.* 4 (*infml derog*) fussy, unattractive or bad-tempered (usu older) woman: *She's an awful*

old bag. **5** (idm) **ˌbag and ˈbaggage** with all one's belongings, often suddenly or secretly: *Her tenant left, bag and baggage, without paying the rent.* **a ˌbag of ˈbones** a very thin person or animal: *The cat had not been fed for weeks and was just a bag of bones.* **be in the ˈbag** (*infml*) (of a result, an outcome, etc) be as desired: *Her re-election is in the bag.* **let the cat out of the bag** ⇨ CAT[1]. **pack one's bags** ⇨ PACK[2]. **the whole bag of tricks** ⇨ WHOLE.
□ **ˈbag lady** (*esp US*) homeless woman who carries her belongings around the streets in (esp plastic) bags.

bag[2] /bæg/ *v* **(-gg-)** **1** [Tn, Tn·p] ~ **sth (up)** put into a bag or bags: *bag (up) wheat.* **2** [Tn] (of hunters) kill or catch (sth): *They bagged nothing except a couple of rabbits.* **3** [Tn] (*infml*) take (sth) without permission but without intending to steal: *Who's bagged my matches?* ○ *She bagged* (ie occupied, sat in) *the most comfortable chair.* ○ *try to bag an empty table*, ie to secure one, eg in a crowded restaurant. **4** [I, Ipr] sag or hang loosely, looking like a cloth bag: *trousers that bag at the knee.* **5** (idm) **bags (I)...** (*infml*) I claim...: *Bags I go first.*

bagatelle /ˌbægəˈtel/ *n* **1** [U] game played on a board with small balls that are hit into holes. **2** [C] something small and unimportant: *a mere bagatelle.* **3** [C] short piece of music.

Bagehot /ˈbædʒət/ Walter (1826-77), British economist and journalist. He is remembered in particular for his study *The English Constitution*, but he also wrote on historical, literary and philosophical subjects.

bagel /ˈbeɪgl/ *n* hard ring-shaped bread roll.

baggage /ˈbægɪdʒ/ *n* **1** [U] = LUGGAGE. **2** [U] equipment carried by an army. **3** [C] (*dated joc infml*) lively or mischievous girl: *Come here, you little baggage!* **4** (idm) **bag and baggage** ⇨ BAG[1].
□ **ˈbaggage car** (*US*) = LUGGAGE-VAN (LUGGAGE). **ˈbaggage room** (*US*) = LEFT-LUGGAGE OFFICE (LEFT[1]).

baggy /ˈbægɪ/ *adj* **(-ier, -iest)** hanging loosely: *baggy trousers.* ▷ **baggily** *adv.* **bagginess** *n* [U].

Baghdad /ˌbægˈdæd/ capital of Iraq, situated between the Tigris and the Euphrates rivers. In the early Middle Ages it was a major centre of Islam, and is now important for its trading and oil-refining activities.

bagpipes

bagpipes /ˈbægpaɪps/ (also **pipes**) *n* [pl] musical instrument, popular esp in Scotland, Ireland and Brittany, played by blowing air through a tube into a bag held under the arm, and then squeezing it out through pipes to produce a tune: *the Highland bagpipes.* ⇨ illus. ⇨ article at SCOTLAND.

bags[1] /bægz/ *n* [pl] (*infml*) trousers: *Oxford bags.*

bags[2] /bægz/ *n* [pl] ~ **(of sth)** (*infml*) plenty (of sth): *There's bags of room.* ○ *Don't worry about money: I've got bags.*

baguette /bæˈget/ *n* long narrow loaf of French bread.

bah /bɑː/ *interj* (expressing disgust or contempt).

Baha'i /bəˈhaɪ, bɑːˈhɑːiː/ *n* (member of a) religion founded in Persia in the 19th century, which seeks to bring about world peace and the unification of mankind: [attrib] *the Baha'i faith.* ▷ **Baha'ism** *n* [U].

Bahama Islands /bəˈhɑːmə aɪləndz/ (also **the Bahamas**) group of islands in the West Indies, an independent state since 1973; pop approx 245 000; official language English; capital Nassau; unit of currency dollar (= 100 cents). The sunny climate and many beaches make tourism the main industry. ⇨ map at WEST INDIES. ▷ **Bahamian** /bəˈheɪmɪən/ *n, adj*.

Bahrain /bɑːˈreɪn/ group of islands in the Persian Gulf, an independent state since 1971; pop approx 481 000; official language Arabic; capital Manama; unit of currency dinar (= 1 000 fils). The country has its own reserves of oil and refines oil brought from Saudi Arabia by pipeline. ⇨ map at ARABIAN PENINSULA.

Baikal /baɪˈkɑːl/ **Lake Baikal** the deepest lake in the world, in SE Siberia. It is frozen over for half of the year and many types of fish and other water animals live in it. Area approx 34 000 sq km (13 000 sq m).

bail[1] /beɪl/ *n* [U] **1** money paid by or for a person accused of a crime, as security that he will return for his trial if he is allowed to go free until then. **2** permission for a person to be released on such security: *The magistrate granted/refused him bail.* **3** (idm) **go/stand ˈbail (for sb)** give bail (to secure sb's freedom). **jump bail** ⇨ JUMP[2]. **(out) on ˈbail** free after payment of bail: *The accused was released on bail (of £1000) pending trial.*
▷ **bail** *v* (phr v) **bail sb out (a)** obtain or allow the release of sb on bail. **(b)** (*fig infml*) rescue sb from (esp financial) difficulties: *The club faced bankruptcy until a wealthy local businessman bailed them out.*

bail[2] (also **bale**) /beɪl/ *v* [I, Ip, Tn, Tn·p] ~ **(out)/sth (out)** throw (water) out of a boat with buckets, etc; clear (a boat) in this way: *bailing water (out)* ○ *bailing (out) the boat* ○ *The boat will sink unless we bail (out).*

bail[3] /beɪl/ *n* (in cricket) either of the two cross-pieces resting on each set of three stumps.

bailey /ˈbeɪlɪ/ *n* **1** outer wall of a castle. **2** courtyard enclosed by this wall.

Bailey bridge /ˈbeɪlɪ brɪdʒ/ portable military bridge made of prefabricated sections that can be fitted together quickly.

bailiff /ˈbeɪlɪf/ *n* **1** law officer who helps a sheriff in issuing writs and making arrests. **2** (*Brit*) landlord's agent or steward; manager of an estate or farm. **3** (*US*) official in a lawcourt, esp one who takes people to their seats and announces the arrival of the judge.

bain-marie /bænməˈriː/ *n* (*pl* **bains-marie** /bænmæˈriː/) device for cooking food slowly, consisting of a large container for hot water into which a pan containing the food is placed: *Make the sauce in a bain-marie.*

Baird /beəd/ John Logie (1888-1946), Scottish inventor. He is remembered for his work on early forms of television, though the systems he created did not become generally adopted.

bairn /beən/ *n* (*Scot*) child.

bait /beɪt/ *n* [U] **1** food or imitation food put on a hook to catch fish or placed in nets, traps, etc to attract prey: *The fish nibbled at/rose to/took/swallowed the bait.* ○ *live bait*, ie small fish used to catch larger fish. **2** (*fig*) thing that is used to attract or tempt. **3** (idm) **rise to the bait** ⇨ RISE[2]. **swallow the bait** ⇨ SWALLOW[1].
▷ **bait** *v* **1** [Tn, Tn·pr] ~ **sth (with sth)** put (real or imitation food) on or in sth to catch fish, animals, etc: *bait a trap* ○ *bait a hook with a worm.* **2** [Tn] **(a)** torment (a chained animal) by making dogs attack it, often as a form of entertainment: *ˈbear-baiting.* **(b)** torment (sb) by making cruel or insulting remarks.

baize /beɪz/ *n* [U] thick (usu green) woollen cloth used for covering billiard-tables, card-tables, doors, etc.

bake /beɪk/ *v* **1** [I, Tn, Dn·n, Dn·pr] ~ **sth (for sb)** (cause sth to) be cooked by dry heat in an oven: *bake bread, cakes, etc* ○ *The bread is baking/being baked.* ○ *I'm baking Alex a birthday cake/baking a birthday cake for Alex.* ○ *baked potatoes* ○ *baked beans*, ie haricot beans baked and tinned with tomato sauce. ⇨ Usage at COOK. **2** [I, Tn, Cn·a] (cause sth to) become hard by heating: *The sun baked the ground hard.* ○ *The bricks are baking in the kilns.* **3** [I] (*fig infml*) be or become very hot: *It's baking today!* ○ *We are baking in the sun.*
▷ **baker** *n* **1** person who bakes and sells bread, etc: *buy some rolls at the baker's.* **2** (idm) **a baker's ˈdozen** thirteen.
bakery /ˈbeɪkərɪ/ (*US* also **ˈbakehouse**, **ˈbakeshop**) *n* place where bread is baked for sale.
□ **ˌbaking-ˈhot** *adj* (*infml*) very hot: *a ˌbaking-hot ˈday.*
ˈbaking-powder *n* [U] mixture of powders used to make cakes, etc rise and become light during baking.
ˈbaking soda = SODIUM BICARBONATE (SODIUM).

Bakelite /ˈbeɪkəlaɪt/ *n* [U] (*propr*) type of plastic.

Bakewell /ˈbeɪkwel/ Robert (1725-95), English agriculturist. He introduced new methods of breeding cattle in order to increase productivity.

Bakewell tart /ˌbeɪkwel ˈtɑːt/ *n* (*Brit*) pastry tart containing almond-flavoured sponge-cake over a layer of jam. Bakewell is a town in Derbyshire.

baksheesh /bækˈʃiːʃ, also ˈbækʃiːʃ/ *n* [U] (in the Middle East) money given as a tip or to help the poor.

Balaclava /ˌbæləˈklɑːvə/ village in the Crimea where a battle of the Crimean war was fought in 1854. It is remembered for the Charge of the Light Brigade, when the British light cavalry made a hopeless charge against the enemy positions.

balaclava /ˌbæləˈklɑːvə/ *n* (also **ˌBalaclava ˈhelmet**) closely-fitting woollen hat that covers the head and neck, with an opening for the face.

balalaika /ˌbæləˈlaɪkə/ *n* musical instrument like a guitar with a triangular body and three strings, popular in Slav countries.

balance[1] /ˈbæləns/ *n* **1** [C] instrument used for weighing, with a central pivot, a beam and two scales or pans. ⇨ illus at SCALE[3]. **2** [U] **(a)** even distribution of weight; steadiness: *Riders need a good sense of balance.* **(b)** steadiness of mind; sanity: *His wife's sudden death upset the balance of his mind.* **3** [U, sing] **(a)** ~ **(in sth/between A and B)** condition that exists when two opposites are equal or in correct proportions: *Try to achieve a better balance between work and play.* ○ *This newspaper maintains a good balance in its presentation of different opinions.* **(b)** pleasing proportion of parts in a whole: *All the parts of the building are in perfect balance.* ○ *This painting has a pleasing balance of shapes and colours.* **4** (C usu *sing*) (*finance*) difference between two columns of an account, ie money received or owing and money spent or owed: *I must check my bank balance*, ie find out how much money I have in my account. **5 (a)** (C usu *sing*) amount (of money) still owed after some payment has been made: *The balance (of £500) will be paid within one week.* **(b)** **the balance** [sing] remainder of sth after part has already been used, taken, etc: *The balance of your order will be supplied when we receive fresh stock.* ○ *When will you take the balance of your annual leave?* ⇨ Usage at REST[3]. **6** (idm) **(be/hang) in the balance** (of a decision, result, sb's future, etc) (be) uncertain or undecided: *The future of this project is (hanging) in the balance.* **keep/lose one's ˈbalance** keep steady/become unsteady; remain upright/fall: *It is difficult to keep one's balance on an icy pavement.* ○ *She cycled too fast round the corner, lost her balance and fell off.* **(catch/throw sb) off balance** (find/cause sb to be) in danger of falling because his steadiness is disturbed: *I was caught off balance by the sudden wind and nearly fell.* **on ˈbalance** (*infml*) having considered every aspect, argument, etc: *Despite some failures, our firm has had quite a good year on balance.* **redress the balance** ⇨ REDRESS *v.* **strike a balance** ⇨ STRIKE[2]. **tip the balance** ⇨ TIP[2].
□ **ˌbalance of ˈnature** stable conditions maintained by the normal life cycles of living things: *Pollution has disturbed the balance of nature.*
ˌbalance of ˈpayments difference between the amount paid to foreign countries for imports and services and the amount received from them for exports, etc in a given period: [attrib] *a serious balance-of-payments deficit*, ie when the value of imports greatly exceeds that of exports.
ˌbalance of ˈpower 1 situation in which power is equally divided among rival states or groups of

states. **2** (*politics*) power held by a small group when rival larger groups are equal or almost equal in strength: *Since the two main parties each won the same number of seats, the minority party holds the balance of power.*

ˌ**balance of** ˈ**trade** difference in value between exports and imports: [attrib] *a balance-of-trade deficit*, ie when a country's exports are worth less than its imports.

ˈ**balance sheet** written record of money received and paid out, showing the difference between the two total amounts.

ˈ**balance wheel** (also **balance**) small wheel that regulates the speed of a clock or watch.

balance[2] /ˈbæləns/ *v* **1 (a)** [Tn, Tn·pr] keep or put (sth) in a state of balance[1](2a): *a clown balancing a stick on the end of his nose.* **(b)** [I, Ipr] be or put oneself in a state of balance: *He balanced precariously on the narrow window-ledge.* ○ *How long can you balance on one foot?* **2** (*finance*) **(a)** [Tn] compare the total debits and credits in (an account) and record the sum needed to make them equal: *balance an account/one's books* ○ *balance the budget*, ie arrange for income and expenditure to be equal. **(b)** [I] (of an account, a balance sheet, etc) show equal totals of debits and credits: *Do the firm's accounts balance?* **(c)** [Tn] be of the same value as (sth opposite); offset: *This year's profits will balance our previous losses.* ○ (*fig*) *His lack of experience was balanced by his willingness to learn.* **3** [Tn·pr] ~ **A against B** compare the value of one plan, argument, etc with that of another: *She balanced the attractions of a high salary against the prospect of working long hours.* **4** [Tn] give equal importance to (different parts of sth): *This school aims to balance the amount of time spent on arts and science subjects.* ○ *Try to balance your diet by eating more fruit and less protein.* **5** (idm) **a** ˈ**balancing act** attempt to do two or more things that are not easy to manage at the same time, such as pleasing people with different interests or finding time for various activities: *I have to do a balancing act between keeping my job and bringing up the children.*

▷ **balanced** *adj* [usu attrib] keeping or showing a balance: *a balanced state of mind*, ie a stable one, in which no single emotion is too strong ○ *a balanced decision*, ie one reached after comparing all the arguments ○ *a balanced diet*, ie one with the quantity and variety of food needed for good health.

Balanchine /ˈbæləntʃɪn, ˌbælənˈtʃi:n/ George (1904-83), American choreographer born in Russia. After working with Diaghilev, he went to America and founded the New York City Ballet.

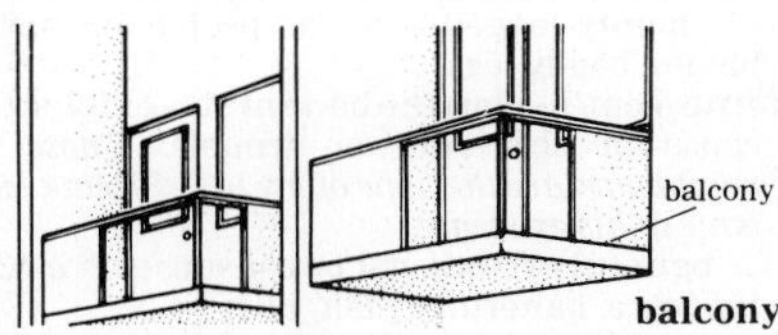

balcony

balcony /ˈbælkənɪ/ *n* **1** platform with a wall or rail built onto the outside wall of a building and reached from an upstairs room. ⇨ illus. **2** (*US*) = CIRCLE 3.

bald /bɔ:ld/ *adj* **1 (a)** (of people) having little or no hair on the scalp. **(b)** without the expected covering: *Our dog has a bald patch* (ie a patch with no hair) *on its leg.* ○ *bald* (ie badly worn) *tyres* ○ (*fig*) *a bald landscape*, ie one with no trees, bushes, etc. **2** without elaboration; plain or dull: *bald facts* ○ *a bald statement of the facts.* **3** (idm) **(as) bald as a coot** (*infml*) completely bald.

▷ **balding** *adj* becoming bald: *He was already balding at the age of 25.*

baldly *adv* in plain words; with no elaboration: *To put it baldly . . .*, ie If I may speak plainly, without trying to soften what I am saying . . . .

baldness *n* [U].

□ ˌ**bald** ˈ**eagle** (also **American eagle**) N American eagle with a white head and white tail feathers, used as an emblem of the USA. ⇨ article at NATIONAL.

baldachin /ˈbɔ:ldəkɪn/ *n* ornamental covering or structure fixed or held above an important place or person; canopy.

balderdash /ˈbɔ:ldədæʃ/ *n* [U] (*dated infml*) nonsense: *He's talking balderdash.*

Baldwin[1] /ˈbɔ:ldwɪn/ James (1924-), black American novelist and playwright. He achieved immediate success with his first novel, *Go, Tell it on the Mountain*, which, like much of his later work, deals with the condition of blacks in the USA.

Baldwin[2] /ˈbɔ:ldwɪn/ Stanley (1867-1947), British Conservative statesman and prime minister (1923-29 and 1935-37). He was responsible for an anti-union bill which defeated the *General Strike of 1926. In 1937 he resigned over the abdication of King *Edward VIII. ⇨ App 2.

bale[1] /beɪl/ *n* large bundle of paper, straw, goods, etc pressed together and tied with rope or wire ready to be moved, sold, etc: *bales of hay* ○ *The cloth was packed in bales.* ○ *How many bales of tobacco were sold?*

▷ **bale** *v* [Tn, Tn·p] ~ **sth (up)** make sth into or pack sth in bales: *baling hay.* **baler** *n* machine for packing straw into bales.

bale[2] /beɪl/ *v* **1** [I, Ip, Tn, Tn·p] = BAIL[2]. **2** (phr v) **bale out (of sth)** jump out using a parachute (from an aircraft that is damaged or out of control).

Balearic Islands /ˌbælɪˈærɪk aɪləndz/ (also **the Balearics**) group of islands in the Mediterranean, part of Spain; pop approx 560 000. The main islands are Majorca, Minorca and Ibiza. Tourism is the main industry.

baleen /bəˈli:n/ *n* whalebone.

baleful /ˈbeɪlfl/ *adj* threatening evil or harm; menacing: *a baleful look, influence, presence.* ▷ **balefully** /ˈbeɪlfəlɪ/ *adv.*

Bali /ˈbɑ:lɪ/ one of the islands of Indonesia, famous for its folk art. ▷ **Balinese** /ˌbɑ:lɪˈni:z/ *n, adj.*

balk[1] (also **baulk**) /bɔ:k/ *n* thick, roughly-squared wooden beam.

balk[2] (also **baulk**) /bɔ:k/ *v* **1** [I, Ipr] ~ **(at sth)** be reluctant to tackle sth because it is difficult, dangerous, unpleasant, etc: *The horse balked at* (ie refused to jump) *the high hedge.* ○ *His parents balked at the cost of the guitar he wanted.* **2** (*dated*) **(a)** [Tn] deliberately obstruct or prevent (sth): *balk sb's plans.* **(b)** [Tn·pr] ~ **sb of sth** prevent sb from getting sth: *They were balked of their prey.*

Balkans /ˈbɔ:lkənz/ **the Balkans** region forming a peninsula in SE Europe, surrounded by the Adriatic, Aegean and Black Seas. Since the Middle Ages the countries in it have often been at war with one another, and boundaries have often been changed. The modern Balkan states are Romania, Albania, Bulgaria, Greece, the republics of the former Yugoslavia, and the European part of Turkey. ▷ **Balkan** *adj.*

ball[1] /bɔ:l/ *n* **1 (a)** solid or hollow sphere used in games: *a* ˈ*football* ○ *a* ˈ*tennis-ball* ○ *a* ˈ*cricket ball.* ⇨ illus at BASKETBALL, HOCKEY. **(b)** any similar sphere: *Signs with three balls hang outside pawnbrokers' shops.* **2 (a)** (in cricket) single delivery of the ball by the bowler. **(b)** (in baseball) any strike or throw: *a foul ball.* **(c)** (in football, hockey, etc) movement of the ball by a player: *send over a high ball.* **3** round mass of material that has been pressed together, rolled or wound into shape: *a* ˈ*meat ball* ○ *a* ˈ*snowball* ○ *a ball of* ˈ*wool*/ˈ*string.* **4** rounded part: *the ball of the thumb*, ie the part near the palm. ⇨ illus at HAND[1]. ○ *the ball of the foot*, ie the part near the base of the big toe. **5** (usu *pl*) (*infml*) testicle. **6** (idm) **the ball is in one's/sb's** ˈ**court** one/sb must make the next move (in a negotiation, etc). **a ball of** ˈ**fire** (*infml*) person full of energy and enthusiasm. **have the ball at one's** ˈ**feet** have a good chance of succeeding. **keep/start the** ˈ**ball rolling** continue/start a conversation or an activity. **(be) on the** ˈ**ball** (*infml*) be alert and aware of new ideas, trends, etc: *The new publicity manager is really on the ball.* **play** ˈ**ball** (*infml*) co-operate: *They're refusing to play ball (with us).*

▷ **ball** *v* [Tn] form (sth) into a ball by winding, squeezing, etc: *ball one's fist.*

□ **ball-and-**ˈ**socket joint** (*anatomy*) joint in the body, eg the one at the shoulder, formed by the rounded end of one bone fitting into the cup-shaped hollow of another, allowing great freedom of movement.

ˌ**ball-**ˈ**bearing** *n* **(a)** type of bearing(5) in which small steel balls are used to reduce friction. **(b)** (usu *pl*) any of these balls.

ˈ**ballboy**, ˈ**ballgirl** *ns* young person who retrieves balls for the players in a tennis match.

ˈ**ballcock** *n* device with a floating ball that controls the water level in a cistern.

ˈ**ball game 1 (a)** any game played with a ball. **(b)** (*US*) game of baseball. **2** (*sl*) state of affairs: *We're into a whole new ball game.*

ˈ**ballpark** *n* **1** (*US*) place where baseball is played. **2** (*sl*) area; range: *a guess that's just not in the right ballpark*, ie one that is wildly inaccurate ○ [attrib] *a ballpark figure*, ie a rough estimate.

ˈ**ball-point** *n* (also **ball-point** ˈ**pen**) pen that writes with a tiny ball at its point which rolls ink onto the paper. Cf BIRO.

ˈ**ball-valve** *n* valve that is opened or closed by the rising or falling of a small ball.

ball[2] /bɔ:l/ *n* **1** formal social gathering for dancing. **2** (idm) **have (oneself) a** ˈ**ball** (*infml esp US*) have a very good time.

□ ˈ**ballroom** *n* large room used for dancing. Cf DANCE-HALL (DANCE[1]). **ballroom** ˈ**dancing** formal type of dancing to conventional rhythms.

ballad /ˈbæləd/ *n* **1** simple song or poem, esp one that tells a story: *a cowboy ballad.* **2** (usu slow) sentimental popular song.

ballade /bæˈlɑ:d/ *n* **1** poem with one or more verses, each having 7, 8 or 10 lines, and a short final verse. **2** romantic piece of music.

ballast /ˈbæləst/ *n* **1** [U] heavy material placed in a ship's hold to keep it steady. **2** [U] sand or other material carried in a balloon, that can be thrown out to make the balloon go higher. **3** [U] stones, etc used to make a foundation for a railway, road, etc. **4** [C] device used for stabilizing current in an electric circuit. **5** (idm) **in ballast** (of a ship) carrying only ballast.

▷ **ballast** *v* [Tn, Tn·pr] ~ **sth (with sth)** supply sth with ballast.

ballerina /ˌbæləˈri:nə/ *n* female ballet-dancer, esp one who takes leading parts.

ballet /ˈbæleɪ/ *n* **1 (a)** (sometimes **the ballet**) [U] style of dancing used to tell a story in a dramatic performance with music but without speech or singing: *enjoy (the) classical ballet* ○ [attrib] *ballet music.* **(b)** [C] story performed in this way: *Have you seen this ballet before?* **2** [CGp] group of dancers who regularly perform ballet together: *members of the Bolshoi Ballet.*

□ ˈ**ballet-dancer** *n* person who dances in ballets. The traditional 'classical' and 'romantic' styles of ballet developed in the 19th century, esp in France and Russia; *Swan Lake* and *The Sleeping Beauty* (with music by *Tchaikovsky) are famous examples. The 20th century brought newer styles, with choreographers like *Balanchine and dancers like Isadora Duncan, who moved away from ballet as a narrative art in favour of dance which responds directly to music.

ballistics /bəˈlɪstɪks/ *n* [sing *v*] study of things that are shot or fired through the air, eg bullets, missiles, etc: [attrib] *a ballistics expert.*

□ **bal**ˌ**listic** ˈ**missile** missile that is initially powered and guided and thereafter controlled by gravity.

ballocks (also **bollocks**) /ˈbɒləks/ *n* (⚠ *infml*) **1** [pl] testicles. **2** [U] nonsense: *What a load of ballocks!*

▷ **ballocks** *interj* (⚠ *infml*) nonsense.

balloon /bəˈlu:n/ *n* **1** brightly-coloured rubber bag that is filled with air, used as a child's toy or a decoration. **2** (also **hot-**ˈ**air balloon**) large flexible bag filled with hot air or gas to make it rise in the air, often carrying a basket, etc for passengers. **3** (in strip cartoons, etc) shape like a balloon (ie round with a narrow neck) in which speech is shown. **4** (idm) **when the bal**ˈ**loon goes up** (*infml*) when expected trouble begins: *I don't want to be around when the balloon goes up.*

▷ **balloon** *v* [I] **1** swell out like a balloon: *Her skirt ballooned in the wind.* **2** (usu **go ballooning**) travel in a balloon as a sport: *They like to go ballooning at weekends.*

balloonist *n* person who travels by balloon, esp as a sport.

ballot /ˈbælət/ *n* **1** (**a**) (also ˈ**ballot-paper**) [C] piece of paper used in secret voting. (**b**) [U] system of secret voting, usu by marking a piece of paper with a cross to show which person one wishes to elect or which policy one prefers: *elected by ballot.* (**c**) [C] instance of this: *hold a ballot of members* ○ *We should put it to a ballot.* **2** [C] number of votes recorded in a ballot.

▷ **ballot** *v* **1** [I, Ipr] ~ (**for sb/sth**) vote by ballot (for sb/sth). **2** [Tn, Tn·pr] ~ **sb** (**about/on sth**) cause sb to vote (on sth) secretly: *The union balloted its members on the proposed changes.*

□ ˈ**ballot-box** *n* box in which voters place their ballot-papers.

balls /bɔ:lz/ *n* (⚠ *infml*) **1** [sing *v*] mess: *What a balls you've made of it!* **2** [U] nonsense: *That's a load of balls!* ○ *What he said was all balls.*

▷ **balls** *interj* (⚠ *infml*) nonsense: *Absolute balls!*

balls *v* (phr v) **balls sth up**; (*US* also **ball sth up**) (⚠ *infml*) make a mess of sth: *He ballsed up all my plans by being so late.*

balls-up /ˈbɔ:lz ʌp/ (*US* also **ball-up** /ˈbɔ:l ʌp/) *n* (⚠ *infml*) mess; botched job: *I made a proper balls-up of that exam.*

bally /ˈbælɪ/ *adj, adv* (*dated Brit euph infml*) bloody[2](1): *It's a bally nuisance!*

ballyhoo /ˌbælɪˈhu:; *US* ˈbælɪhu:/ *n* [U] (*infml derog*) **1** noisy publicity or advertising. **2** unnecessary noise or fuss.

balm /bɑ:m/ *n* [U, C] **1** (also **balsam**) sweet-smelling oil or ointment obtained from certain types of tree, used for soothing pain or for healing. **2** any of several sweet-smelling garden herbs. **3** (*fig*) thing that soothes the mind: *The gentle music was (a) balm to his ears.*

▷ **balmy** *adj* (**-ier**, **-iest**) **1** (of air) gentle and pleasantly warm. **2** fragrant and soothing; like balm. **3** (*esp US*) = BARMY. **balmily** *adv.* **balminess** *n* [U].

Balmoral /bælˈmɒrəl/ castle in northern Scotland owned and used as a private home by the British royal family. ⇨ article at ROYAL FAMILY.

baloney = BOLONEY.

balsa /ˈbɔ:lsə/ *n* (**a**) [U] lightweight wood used for making models, rafts, etc. (**b**) [C] tropical American tree from which this comes.

balsam /ˈbɔ:lsəm/ *n* **1** [C] flowering plant grown in gardens. **2** (**a**) [C] tree yielding balm. (**b**) [U, C] = BALM 1.

Balthasar (also **Balthazar**) /ˈbælθəzɑ:(r)/ (in Christian tradition) one of the *Magi. ⇨ MAGUS.

Baltic Sea /ˌbɔ:ltɪk ˈsi:/ (also **the Baltic**) sea in northern Europe, connected with the North Sea by a channel and almost entirely surrounded by the coasts of Sweden, Finland, the Baltic republics, Poland, Germany and Denmark. The northern Baltic is ice-bound in the winter.

▷ **Baltic** *adj* of the Baltic Sea or the region surrounding it: *Baltic ports* ○ *Baltic republics*, ie the independent republics of Estonia, Latvia and Lithuania which were part of the USSR between 1940 and 1991 ○ *Baltic languages*, eg Latvian and Lithuanian.

baluster /ˈbæləstə(r)/ *n* any of the short pillars in a balustrade.

balustrade /ˌbæləˈstreɪd/ *n* row of upright posts or small pillars joined along the top by a rail or stonework, and placed round a balcony, terrace, flat roof, etc.

Balzac /ˈbælzæk/ Honoré de (1799-1850), French novelist. He wrote a great series of related novels, *La Comédie humaine*, giving a detailed and critical potrayal of contemporary French society.

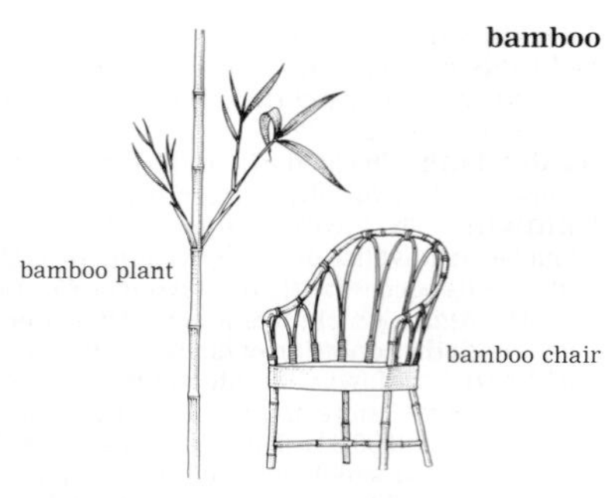

bamboo /bæmˈbu:/ *n* [C, U] tall plant of the grass family; its fibre can be used in making paper and medicines, and the hollow jointed stems are used for making canes, furniture, etc: *the bamboos growing by the river* ○ *a house of bamboo* ○ [attrib] *a bamboo chair.* ⇨ illus.

□ **the** ˌ**Bamboo** ˈ**Curtain** (*fig*) the political barriers that separate China from the rest of the world. Cf THE IRON CURTAIN (IRON[1]).

bamboozle /bæmˈbu:zl/ *v* (*infml*) **1** [Tn] mystify (sb); puzzle: *You've completely bamboozled me.* **2** (phr v) **bamboozle sb into (doing) sth** trick sb into (doing) sth: *He bamboozled me into believing that he'd lost all his money.* **bamboozle sb out of sth** cheat sb out of sth.

ban /bæn/ *v* (**-nn-**) **1** [Tn] officially forbid (sth): *The play was banned (by the censor).* ○ *The Government has banned the use of chemical weapons.* ○ *a ban-the-bomb demonstration*, ie one protesting against the use of nuclear weapons. **2** ~ **sb** (**from sth/from doing sth**) officially forbid sb (to do sth): *He was banned from (attending) the meeting.* ○ *She's been banned from driving for six months.*

▷ **ban** *n* ~ (**on sth/sb**) order that bans; prohibition: *put a ban on the import of alcohol.*

banal /bəˈnɑ:l; *US* ˈbeɪnl/ *adj* commonplace; uninteresting: *banal remarks, thoughts, sentiments, etc.*

▷ **banality** /bəˈnælətɪ/ *n* **1** [U] quality of being banal. **2** [C] banal remark: *a speech consisting mainly of banalities.*

banana /bəˈnɑ:nə; *US* bəˈnænə/ *n* **1** (**a**) long thick-skinned edible fruit that is yellow when ripe: *a hand* (ie bunch) *of bananas.* ⇨ illus at FRUIT. (**b**) tropical or semi-tropical tree bearing this fruit. **2** (idm) **go ba**ˈ**nanas** (*sl*) become mad or angry; act very foolishly.

□ **ba**ˈ**nana republic** (*derog*) small, often unstable, country whose economy depends on the export of fruit.

baˈ**nana skin** (*infml*) source of difficulty or embarrassment, esp to a public figure, an organization, etc: *The proposed tax changes are likely to prove a banana skin for the Government.*

baˌ**nana** ˈ**split** sweet dish made with a banana that is cut in half lengthwise and served with ice-cream, fruit, chopped nuts, etc.

band /bænd/ *n* **1** [C] (**a**) thin flat strip, hoop or loop used for fastening things together or for placing round an object to strengthen it: *iron bands round a barrel* ○ *papers kept together with a rubber band* ○ *the waistband of a dress.* (**b**) strip or line on sth, different in colour or design from the rest: *a white plate with a blue band round the edge.* **2** [CGp] organized group of people doing sth together with a common purpose: *a band of robbers, fugitives, revellers, etc.* **3** [CGp] (**a**) group of people playing esp wind instruments: *a brass* ˈ*band* ○ *a military* ˈ*band.* (**b**) group of people playing popular music, often for dancing: *a* ˈ*dance band* ○ *a* ˈ*jazz band.* Cf ORCHESTRA. **4** (also ˈ**waveband**) [C] (*radio*) range of wavelengths within specified limits: *the 19-metre band.*

▷ **band** *v* **1** [Tn] put a band(1a) on or round (sth). **2** [Ip] ~ **together** unite in a group: *band together to protest* ○ *band together against a common enemy.*

□ ˈ**bandmaster** *n* person who conducts a band(3a,b).

ˈ**band-saw** *n* machine-driven saw in the form of an endless belt.

ˈ**bandsman** /-mən/ *n* (*pl* **-men** /-mən/) person who plays in a band(3a).

bandstand /ˈbændstænd/ *n* covered platform for a band(3a) playing outdoors.

ˈ**bandwagon** *n* (idm) **climb/jump on the** ˈ**bandwagon** (*infml*) join others in doing sth fashionable or likely to be successful.

ˈ**bandwidth** *n* range of frequencies over which a radio signal can spread. Cf WAVEBAND.

Banda /ˈbændə/ Hastings Kamuzu (1906-), first president of Malawi after leading the country's struggle for independence. He was made president for life in 1966.

bandage /ˈbændɪdʒ/ *n* strip of material used for binding round a wound or an injury.

▷ **bandage** *v* [Tn, Tn·pr, Tn·p] ~ **sth/sb** (**up**) (**with sth**) wind a bandage round (a part of) sb: *bandage (up) a wound* ○ *a bandaged hand.*

Band-aid /ˈbændeɪd/ *n* [C, U] (*US propr*) type of sticking-plaster.

bandanna /bænˈdænə/ *n* large handkerchief with coloured spots, usu worn round the neck.

Bandaranaike /ˌbændərəˈnaɪkə/ Sirimavo (1916-), Sri Lankan prime minister (1960-65 and 1970-77). When her husband was killed she took over his post and became the world's first woman prime minister.

B and B (also **b and b**) /ˌbi: ən ˈbi:/ *abbr* (*Brit infml*) bed and breakfast.

bandbox /ˈbændbɒks/ *n* light cardboard box for hats, etc.

bandeau /ˈbændəʊ; *US* bænˈdəʊ/ *n* (*pl* **-deaux** /-dəʊz; *US* -ˈdəʊz/) narrow band worn round the head by a woman to keep her hair in place.

banderole /ˈbændərəʊl/ *n* long narrow flag with a forked end, often flown at the top of a ship's mast.

bandicoot /ˈbændɪku:t/ *n* **1** type of large rat found in India. **2** ratlike animal, found in Australia, which carries its young in a pouch.

bandit /ˈbændɪt/ *n* member of a gang of armed robbers: *Buses driving through the mountains have been attacked by bandits.*

▷ **banditry** *n* [U] activity of bandits.

bandoleer (also **bandolier**) /ˌbændəˈlɪə(r)/ *n* shoulder-belt with pockets for bullets or cartridges.

bandy[1] /ˈbændɪ/ *v* (*pt, pp* **bandied**) **1** (idm) **bandy** ˈ**words** (**with sb**) (*dated*) exchange words, etc, esp when quarrelling: *Don't bandy words with me, young man!* **2** (phr v) **bandy sth about** (usu passive) pass on (a rumour, information, etc), often in a thoughtless way: *The stories being bandied about are completely false.* ○ *Her name is being bandied about as the next chairperson.*

bandy[2] /ˈbændɪ/ *adj* (**-ier**, **-iest**) (*usu derog*) (of the legs) curving outwards at the knees.

□ ˈ**bandy-legged** *adj* (of people or animals) having bandy legs.

bane /beɪn/ *n* (idm) **the bane of sb's existence/life** cause of sb's ruin or trouble: *Those noisy neighbours are the bane of my life.* ○ *Drink was the bane of his existence.*

▷ **baneful** /-fl/ *adj* evil or causing evil: *a baneful influence.* **banefully** /-fəlɪ/ *adv.*

bang[1] /bæŋ/ *v* **1** (**a**) [Ipr, Tn, Tn·pr, Tn·p] strike (sth) deliberately and violently, often in order to make a loud noise: *He was banging on the door with his fist.* ○ *I banged the door.* ○ *She banged her fist on the table.* ○ *I banged the box down on the floor.* (**b**) [I, Ip, Tn, Tn·p] ~ (**sth**) (**down, to, etc**) close with a loud noise: *A door was banging somewhere*, ie opening and closing noisily. ○ *Don't bang the door!* ○ *He banged the lid down.* **2** (**a**) [Tn, Tn·pr] hit violently and often unintentionally: *She tripped and banged her knee on the desk.* (**b**) [Ipr] ~ **into sb/sth** collide with sb/sth violently: *He ran round the corner and banged straight into a lamp-post.* **3** [I, Ip] make a loud noise: *The fireworks banged impressively.* **4** (phr v) **bang about/around** move around noisily: *We could hear the children banging about upstairs.* **bang away** (**a**) (*infml*) work hard, esp using a typewriter. (**b**) (*sl*) have vigorous sexual intercourse. (**c**) (*infml*) fire continuously: *We were banging away at the enemy.* ○ *The guns banged away all day.*

NOTE ON USAGE: **1 Knock** means hitting something with a clear, sharp sound. One may knock to signal one's presence to others: *Can you go to the door? Someone's knocking.* ○ *He knocked at the window to be let in.* **Knock** can denote an accidental action which hurts or breaks something: *I knocked my hand against the table.* ○ *I knocked the plate off the table with my elbow.* **2 Bump** means hitting something by accident and with a dull sound: *The bus bumped into the back of the car.* ○ *He ran round the corner and bumped into an old lady.* ○ *I bumped my head on the low beam.* **3 Bang** suggests a harder blow and a louder sound. Banging may be intentional hitting, expressing anger or urgency: *He banged his fist on the table to emphasize his argument.* ○ *He banged on the door until it was opened.* Banging may also be accidental and painful: *I banged my elbow on the corner of the table.* **4 Bash** is informal and means breaking or injuring something or somebody by hitting hard: *The thieves bashed the woman over the head.* ○ *The car bashed into the tree.*

bang² /bæŋ/ *n* **1** violent blow: *He fell and got a nasty bang on the head.* **2** sudden loud noise: *She always shuts the door with a bang.* ○ *The firework exploded with a loud bang.* **3** (*sl*) act of sexual intercourse: *have a quick bang.* **4** (idm) **go (off) with a ˈbang; *US* go over with a ˈbang** (*infml*) (of a performance, etc) be successful.
▷ **bang** *interj* (used to imitate a loud noise): *'Bang! Bang! You're dead!' shouted the small boy.*

bang³ /bæŋ/ *adv* (*infml*) **1** suddenly, violently or noisily; abruptly: *I tripped and fell bang on the floor.* **2 (a)** exactly; precisely: *bang in the middle of the performance* ○ *Your guess was bang on target.* **(b)** completely: *This film is bang up to date.* **3** (idm) **bang goes sth** (*infml*) that is the (sudden) end of sth: *Bang went his hopes of promotion.* **be bang ˈon** (*sl*) be exactly right: *Her criticisms were bang on every time.* ○ *Your budget figures were bang on this year.* **go ˈbang** (*infml*) burst or explode with a loud noise.

bang⁴ /bæŋ/ *n* (usu *pl*) (*US*) = FRINGE 1.

banger /ˈbæŋə(r)/ *n* (*Brit infml*) **1** sausage: *bangers and mash*, ie served with mashed potato as a meal. **2** firework made to explode with a loud noise. **3** noisy old car.

Bangkok /ˌbæŋˈkɒk; *US* ˈbæŋkɒk/ capital of Thailand. Nearly all the country's industry is concentrated in the city and it is the only major port.

Bangladesh

Bangladesh /ˌbæŋgləˈdeʃ/ country in the Indian subcontinent and a member of the Commonwealth; pop approx 104 532 000; official language Bengali; capital Dhaka; unit of currency taka (= 100 paisas). Under the British Empire it was part of India, but in 1947 it became independent as East Pakistan, one of the two parts of the new Muslim state of Pakistan. Conflicts with West Pakistan led to it becoming a new state in its own right in 1971. It is the world's largest producer of jute, its main resource. Bangladesh often suffers from storms and flooding; much of the country is almost at sea-level. ➪ map. ▷ **Bangladeshi** *n, adj.*

bangle /ˈbæŋgl/ *n* large decorative ring worn round the arm or ankle.

banian (also **banyan**) /ˈbænɪən/ (also **ˈbanyan-tree**) *n* Indian fig-tree whose branches come down to the ground and take root.

banish /ˈbænɪʃ/ *v* [Tn, Tn·pr] **1** ~ **sb (from sth)** send sb away, esp out of the country, as a punishment: *He was banished (from his homeland) for life.* **2** ~ **sth (from sth)** drive (thoughts, etc) out (of the mind): *banish fear* ○ *She banished all thoughts of a restful holiday (from her mind).*
▷ **banishment** *n* [U] state or process of being banished: *lifelong banishment.*

banister /ˈbænɪstə(r)/ *n* (esp *pl*) handrail of a stair and the upright poles supporting it: *children sliding down the banister(s).* ➪ illus at STAIRCASE.

banjo /ˈbændʒəʊ/ *n* (*pl* ~**s**) stringed musical instrument like the guitar, but with a long neck and a round body, played by plucking with the fingers. It was a popular folk instrument among slaves in the southern USA and later in minstrel shows and jazz bands. ➪ illus. ▷ **banjoist** /ˈbændʒəʊɪst/ *n.*

bank¹ /bæŋk/ *n* **1** land sloping up along each side of a river or canal; ground near a river: *Can you jump over to the opposite bank?* ○ *My house is on the south bank (of the river).* ➪ Usage at COAST¹. **2** sloping ground, often forming a border or division: *low banks of earth between rice-fields* ○ *flowers growing on the banks on each side of the country lanes.* **3** = SANDBANK (SAND). **4** flat-topped mass of cloud, snow, etc, esp one formed by the wind: *The sun went behind a bank of clouds.*

bank² /bæŋk/ *v* **1** [I] (of an aircraft, etc) travel with one side higher than the other, usu when turning: *The plane banked steeply to the left.* **2** (phr v) **bank up** rise in the form of banks (BANK¹ 4): *The snow has banked up against the shed.* **bank sth up (a)** make sth into banks. **(b)** stop water of (a river, etc) from flowing by making a bank of earth, mud, etc: *bank up a stream.* **(c)** heap coal dust, etc on (the fire in a fireplace or furnace) so that the fire burns slowly for a long time.

bank³ /bæŋk/ *n* **1** establishment for keeping money, valuables, etc safely, the money being paid out on the customer's order (by means of cheques): *have money in the bank*, ie have savings ○ [attrib] *a ˈbank manager* ○ *a ˈbank account* ○ *a ˈbank loan*, ie money borrowed from a bank. ➪ article at FINANCE. **2** (in gambling) sum of money held by the keeper of a gaming table, from which he pays his losses. **3** store (of valuable things, information, etc): *build up a bank of useful addresses, references, information, etc* ○ *a ˈblood bank* ○ *a ˈdata bank.* **4** (idm) **ˌbreak the ˈbank (a)** (in gambling) win more money than is in the bank³(1). **(b)** (*infml*) cost more than one can afford: *Come on! One evening at the theatre won't break the bank.*
□ **ˈbank balance** amount of money credited to or owed by an individual bank account.
ˈbank-book (also **passbook**) *n* book containing a record of a customer's bank account.
ˈbank card = CHEQUE CARD (CHEQUE).
ˈbank draft (document used for) the transferring of money from one bank to another.
ˌbank ˈholiday 1 (*Brit*) day (not a Saturday or a Sunday) on which banks are officially closed, usu a public holiday (eg Easter Monday, Christmas Day, etc). ➪ article at HOLIDAY. **2** (*US*) any weekday on which banks are closed, usu on special instructions from the government.
ˈbanknote = NOTE¹ 4.
the ˌBank of ˈEngland national bank of the United Kingdom, in London, founded in 1694 and nationalized in 1946. It issues banknotes, advises the government on financial matters, and sets the bank rate. ➪ illus at SOANE. ➪ article at FINANCE.
ˈbank rate minimum rate of interest in a country as fixed by a central bank or banks.
ˈbankroll *n* (*US*) bundle of banknotes. — *v* [Tn] (*US infml*) provide money to pay for (sb/sth).
ˈbank statement printed record showing all the money paid into and out of a customer's bank account within a certain period.

bank⁴ /bæŋk/ *v* **1** [Tn] place (money) in a bank: *bank one's savings, takings, etc.* **2** [I, Ipr] ~ **(with sb/sth)** have an account (at a particular bank): *Who do you bank with?* ○ *Where do you bank?* **3** (phr v) **bank on sb/sth** base one's hopes on sb/sth: *I'm banking on your help/on you to help me.* ○ *He was banking on the train being on time.*
▷ **banker** *n* **1** owner, director or manager of a bank³(1). **2** (in gambling) person who holds the bank³(2). **ˌbanker's ˈorder** = STANDING ORDER (STANDING).
banking *n* [U] business of running a bank³(1): *choose banking as a career* ○ *She's in banking.*

bank⁵ /bæŋk/ *n* row or series of similar objects, eg in a machine: *a bank of lights, switches, etc* ○ *a bank of cylinders in an engine* ○ *a bank of oars.*

bankrupt /ˈbæŋkrʌpt/ *n* (*law*) person judged by a lawcourt to be unable to pay his debts in full, whose property is then taken by the court and used to repay his creditors.
▷ **bankrupt** *adj* **1 (a)** (*law*) declared by a court to be a bankrupt. **(b)** unable to pay one's debts: *go/be bankrupt.* **2** ~ **(of sth)** (*derog*) completely lacking (in sth that is good): *bankrupt of ideas, moral scruples* ○ *a society that is morally bankrupt.*
bankrupt *v* [Tn] make (sb) bankrupt.
bankruptcy /ˈbæŋkrəpsɪ/ *n* **(a)** [U] state of being bankrupt: [attrib] *in the bankruptcy court.* **(b)** [C] instance of this: *Ten bankruptcies were recorded in this town last year.*

Banks /bæŋks/ Sir Joseph (1743-1820), English naturalist who went with Captain *Cook on his first voyage round the world. He discovered and collected many new types of plants, esp from Australia, and helped to set up the botanic gardens at Kew near London, where there is a great collection of plants from all over the world. He was President of the *Royal Society for over 40 years.

banksia /ˈbæŋksɪə/ *n* flowering shrub, originally from Australia.

banner /ˈbænə(r)/ *n* **1** large strip of cloth showing an emblem or slogan, which is displayed or carried, usu on two poles, during eg political or religious processions: *The marchers carried banners with the words 'No Nuclear Weapons' in large letters.* ➪ illus at FLAG. **2** (*dated*) flag: *the banner of freedom.* **3** [attrib] (*US*) excellent: *a banner year for exports.* **4** (idm) **under the banner (of sth)** claiming to support (a particular set of ideas): *She fought the election under the banner of equal rights.*
□ **ˌbanner ˈheadline** (also **streamer**) large newspaper headline, often printed across a whole page.

Bannister /ˈbænɪstə(r)/ Sir Roger (1929-), British athlete and politician. In May 1954 he became the first man to run a mile race in less than four

Banks and Building Societies

In Britain, the central bank is the Bank of England. (Cf article at FINANCE.) There is a dense network of branches of the retail banks, with several banks represented in most towns, however small. The main banks, also known as the High Street banks, include the 'Big Four', National Westminster ('Natwest'), Barclays, Lloyds and the Midland, with the TSB (Trustee Savings Bank), the Royal Bank of Scotland and Abbey National (formerly a building society) also well represented. In all, there are more than 14 000 bank branches throughout Britain.

About eight adults out of ten in Britain have a bank account, using it chiefly for making and receiving payments by cheque, for withdrawing cash (now usually by automatic cash dispenser), or for receiving salary payments. Of the main kinds of account, the current account is the most widely used, although deposit accounts, which pay interest, are also available. The distinction between the two has recently been blurred, however, since many banks now pay interest on current accounts as a result of competition from the building societies. Standing orders and direct debits are payments made by the bank on behalf of the customer and are convenient ways of paying regular bills.

The cards issued by banks are widely used. They include cashcards (for the cash dispenser), cheque cards (to guarantee cheques), credit cards (the best-known being Access and Visa), and, most recently, direct debit cards (allowing a payment to be deducted directly from a customer's account). Both credit and debit cards now operate in shops that use the EFTPOS (electronic funds transfer at point of sale) system.

To enable customers to keep a check on their accounts, banks send them statements every month or every three months, while cash dispensers usually provide on request a printed record of the current balance of the account.

The High Street banks lend money to account holders, either as an overdraft on the account or a bank loan. They also provide finance for small businesses, especially for new businesses. The banks that deal with company finance on a larger scale, negotiating share issues, takeovers and mergers on behalf of companies, are called merchant banks.

In general, banks are open only on weekdays from 9.30 am to 3.30 pm, although the dispensers operate for 24 hours a day. The service they offer also includes a range of specialized financial services, such as life insurance, buying and selling stocks and shares, or making foreign transactions.

Building societies arose in Britain in the 19th century as a type of savings club. Their main purpose was to lend money to members for the purpose of buying (or, originally, building) a house. Even today, one of their prime functions is to lend money for a house-buyer's mortgage. But they are now usually regarded first and foremost as savings organizations, with most societies offering different types of savings schemes, depending on the amount saved. Overall, building societies today operate increasingly like banks, and offer most (if not all) the facilities that banks do, in competition with them.

About six out of ten adults have a building society account, with the three largest societies (Halifax, Nationwide Anglia and Woolwich) accounting for almost half of these, although there are over 100 societies altogether. Most towns have a selection of branches of different societies, competing with each other in terms of the interest offered to investors and charged to borrowers. Societies have an advantage over the banks in their opening hours which are usually 9.00 am to 5.00 pm, as well as Saturday mornings.

The state-run National Savings Bank, which has around 20 million accounts, is also popular with savers, while the Girobank offers both banking and savings facilities.

A recent development offered by both banks and building societies is the 'home banking' facility, whereby a customer or member can conduct financial transactions by telephone. For example, accounts can be checked and bills paid by this method. The facility is gradually being amalgamated with a similar one for 'teleshopping', in which a small computer unit is plugged into a telephone socket. (Cf article at TECHNOLOGY.)

The banking situation in the USA is quite different. There are over 14 000 commercial banks, this large number resulting from a law that prevents most banks from operating in more than one state. Most of the banks are small, so that American banking is dominated by the large 'money centre' banks such as Chase Manhattan and the Bank of America. Although US banks were originally based on the British banking system, they have developed their own distinctive features. One is that they are mainly banks of deposit and credit, and not banks that accumulate capital or 'stock and store' money, as they do in Britain. Another is that most of them are 'unit' organizations, ie they do not have branches. US banks issue cheque books and the various types of card facilities that British banks do.

The US equivalent of British building societies are the Savings and Loan associations, known as 'the thrifts'. Saver-members are not simply depositors but also owners of an association, so that it is run as a cooperative. Members buy shares of stock and receive dividends in proportion to the association's profits, rather than interest as with building societies. Moreover, investments in a thrift are long-term, meaning that they cannot easily be made 'liquid'. As a consequence, the associations arrange mortgages for longer terms than banks do. The thrifts were historically modelled on British building societies, however, and offer similar facilities (increasingly like banks). But although they arrange mortgages, they can also provide loans for other purposes than buying houses. This gives them a versatility that the British societies cannot quite match.

minutes. He later became a Conservative MP.

bannock /ˈbænək/ *n* (*esp Scot*) small round flat loaf, often made without yeast.

Bannockburn /ˈbænəkbɜːn/ village in central Scotland where the Scottish king Robert the Bruce defeated the army of the English king Edward II in 1314. This allowed Scotland to remain an independent kingdom. ⇨ article at SCOTLAND.

banns /bænz/ *n* [pl] public announcement in church, usu made on three Sundays in a row, that two people intend to marry each other unless there is a reason to prevent the marriage, eg the fact that a person is already married: *read/publish the banns* ○ *have one's banns called*, ie have one's forthcoming marriage announced. ⇨ article at WEDDING.

banquet /ˈbæŋkwɪt/ *n* elaborate formal meal, usu for a special event, at which speeches are often made: *a ˈwedding banquet.*
▷ **banquet** *v* **1** [Tn] give a banquet for (sb). **2** [I] take part in a banquet.

banquette /bæŋˈket/ *n* long seat with a padded back set against a wall, as in some railway carriages. Cf COUCHETTE.

banshee /bænˈʃiː; *US* ˈbænʃiː/ *n* (*esp Irish*) female spirit with a distinctive wail, thought by some to warn of death in a house.

bantam /ˈbæntəm/ *n* type of small domestic fowl: [attrib] *bantam cocks.*

bantamweight /ˈbæntəmweɪt/ *n* **1** boxer weighing between 51 and 53.5 kilograms, next above flyweight. **2** wrestler weighing between 52 and 57 kilograms.

banter /ˈbæntə(r)/ *n* [U] playful, good-humoured teasing: *players exchanging light-hearted banter with the crowd.*
▷ **banter** *v* [I] speak playfully or jokingly. **bantering** *adj* playfully teasing: *a bantering tone of voice.* **banteringly** *adv.*

Banting /ˈbæntɪŋ/ Sir Frederick Grant (1891-1941), Canadian physiologist and surgeon. He was awarded the Nobel prize for medicine in 1923 for the discovery of insulin to treat diabetes, made in collaboration with J J R Macleod.

Bantu /ˌbænˈtuː; *US also* ˈbɑːntuː/ *n* **the Bantu** (also **the Bantus**) [pl] large group of related Negroid peoples of central and S Africa.
▷ **Bantu** *adj* of these peoples or their languages.

Bantustan /ˌbæntuːˈstɑːn/ *n* any of the areas reserved for black Africans in the Republic of South Africa. Under apartheid, all black Africans were considered to be citizens of a Bantustan, although most lived elsewhere. Cf HOMELAND (HOME[1]).

banyan = BANIAN.

baobab /ˈbeɪəbæb; *US* ˈbaʊbæb/ *n* African tree with a very thick trunk and large fruit with edible pulp.

BAOR *abbr* British Army of the Rhine.

bap /bæp/ *n* (*Brit*) soft flat bread roll.

baptism /ˈbæptɪzəm/ *n* **1** (**a**) [U] ceremony marking a person's admission into the Christian Church either by dipping him in water or by sprinkling him with water, and often giving him a name or names. (**b**) [C] instance of this: *There were six baptisms at this church last week.* **2** (idm) **a ˌbaptism of ˈfire** (**a**) soldier's first experience of warfare. (**b**) introduction to an unpleasant experience: *a young teacher facing her baptism of fire.*
▷ **baptismal** /bæpˈtɪzməl/ *adj* [attrib] of or related to baptism: *a baptismal name, font* ○ *baptismal water.*

Baptist /ˈbæptɪst/ *n* **1** member of a Protestant Church that believes in baptism by immersion at an age when a person is old enough to understand what the ceremony means. Baptists form one of the largest Protestant groups, esp in the US: [attrib] *a ˌBaptist ˈminister.* ⇨ article at RELIGION. **2 the Baptist** *John the Baptist.

baptistery /ˈbæptɪstrɪ/ *n* part of a church, in some countries a separate building, where baptisms are held.

baptize, -ise /bæpˈtaɪz/ *v* [Tn, Cn·n esp passive] **1** give baptism to (sb); christen: *She was baptized Mary.* **2** admit into a specified church by baptism: *I was baptized a Catholic.* Cf CHRISTEN.

bar[1] /bɑː(r)/ *n* **1** [C] (**a**) piece of solid material: *a* *long iron bar* ○ *a bar of chocolate, soap.* (**b**) narrow piece of wood or metal placed (often parallel to others in a grid) as an obstacle in a doorway, window, etc, or to act as a grate in a fire, furnace, etc: *There's a strong bar on the door.* ○ *They fitted bars to their windows to stop burglars getting in.* **2** [C] narrow band (of colour, light, etc): *At sunset, there was a bar of red across the western sky.* **3** [C] strip of metal across the ribbon of a military medal to show service in a particular area or an additional award of that medal. **4** [C] (**a**) (also *esp US* **bar line**) vertical line dividing printed music into metrical units. (**b**) (*US* **measure**) ⇨ illus at MUSIC; one of these sections and the notes in it: *Hum the opening bars of your favourite tune.* **5** [C] (**a**) bank or ridge of sand, etc across the mouth of a river or the entrance to a bay: *The ship stuck fast on the bar.* (**b**) (usu *sing*) (*fig*) thing that hinders or stops progress; barrier: *Poor health may be a bar to success in life.* **6** [sing] barrier in a lawcourt separating the judge, prisoner, lawyers, etc from the spectators: *the prisoner at the bar* ○ (*fig*) *She will be judged at the bar of public opinion.* **7** [sing] (**a**) (*Brit*) railing where non-members of Parliament stand when answering or addressing members. (**b**) (*US*) similar place in the US Senate, House of Representatives, and State Legislatures. **8 the bar** [Gp, sing] (**a**) (*Brit*) (all those who belong to) the profession of barrister: *She's training for the bar.* ○ *be called to the bar*, ie be received into the profession of barrister. (**b**) (*US*) (all those who belong to) the legal profession. **9** [C] (**a**) counter where (esp alcoholic) drinks are served: *sitting on a stool by the bar* ○ [attrib] *bar snacks*, ie light food sometimes sold at a bar, esp in Britain. (**b**) room in a hotel, public house, etc in which such drinks are served: *They walked into the bar.* **10** [C] (esp in compounds) (**a**) place where certain types of food and drink are served across a counter: *a ˈsandwich bar* ○ *a ˈcoffee bar* ○ *a ˈwine bar.* (**b**) counter offering certain services: *a ˈheel bar*, ie where the heels, etc of shoes are repaired. **11** (idm) **beˌhind ˈbars** (*infml*) in prison: *The murderer is now safely behind bars.* **prop up the bar** ⇨ PROP[1].

□ ˌ**bar ˈbilliards** indoor game like billiards in which balls are aimed at holes in the table.

ˈ**bar chart** (also **histogram**) graph on which bars of equal width but varying height are used to represent quantities. ⇨ illus at CHART.

ˈ**bar code** pattern of thick and thin parallel lines printed on goods in shops, etc and containing coded information for a computer.

ˈ**barmaid** *n* woman who serves drinks, etc at a bar.

ˈ**barman** /-mən/ *n* (*pl* **-men** /-mən/) man who serves drinks, etc at a bar.

ˈ**bartender** *n* (*esp US*) = BARMAN.

bar[2] /bɑː(r)/ *v* (**-rr-**) **1** [Tn] fasten (a door, gate, etc) with a bar[1](1b) or bars. **2** [Tn] obstruct (sth) so as to prevent progress: *Soldiers barred the road so we had to turn back.* ○ (*fig*) *Poverty bars the way to progress.* **3** [Tn·pr] ~ **sb from sth/doing sth** prevent sb from using sth or from doing sth: *She was barred from (entering) the competition because of her age.* **4** [usu passive: Tn, Tn·pr] ~ **sth (with sth)** mark sth (with a stripe or stripes): *a sky barred with clouds.* **5** (phr v) **bar sb in (sth)/out (of sth)** keep sb from leaving or entering (a building, etc) by fastening the door, windows, etc with a bar or bars: *He barred himself in (the house).*

bar[3] /bɑː(r)/ *prep* **1** except; not counting: *The whole class is here bar two that are ill.* Cf BARRING. **2** (idm) **bar none** with no exception: *That's the best meal I've ever had, bar none.*

bar[4] /bɑː(r)/ *n* unit of atmospheric pressure used esp in meteorology, equal to 10^5 newtons per square metre: *Recommended tyre pressure: 1.7 bar(s).*

Barabbas /bəˈræbəs/ (*Bible*) robber set free instead of Jesus by Pontius Pilate.

barb /bɑːb/ *n* **1** point of an arrow, a fish-hook, etc curved backwards to make it difficult to pull out. ⇨ illus at HOOK. **2** (*fig*) hurtful remark: *cruel barbs of ridicule.*

▷ **barbed** *adj* having a barb or barbs: *a barbed hook* ○ (*fig*) *barbed comments.* **barbed wire** wire with short sharp points along it, used for fences, etc: *The barbed wire fence round the perimeter discouraged intruders.*

Barbados /bɑːˈbeɪdɒs/ island in the Caribbean, an independent state and member of the Commonwealth since 1966; pop approx 254 000; official language English; capital Bridgetown; unit of currency dollar (= 100 cents). The main industries are sugar production and tourism. ⇨ map at CARIBBEAN. ▷ **Barbadian** /bɑːˈbeɪdɪən/ *n, adj.*

barbarian /bɑːˈbeərɪən/ *n, adj* (*often derog*) (person who is) primitive, coarse or cruel: *barbarian tribes* ○ *football supporters acting like barbarians.*

barbaric /bɑːˈbærɪk/ *adj* (*often derog*) of or like barbarians; extremely wild, rough, cruel or rude: *barbaric splendour, cruelty, taste.* ▷ **barbarically** /-klɪ/ *adv.*

barbarism /ˈbɑːbərɪzəm/ *n* **1** [U] (*derog*) state of being uncivilized, ignorant, or rude. **2** [U, C] (use of a) word or expression that is unacceptable, usu because it is foreign or vulgar: *teaching students to rid their writing of barbarisms.*

barbarity /bɑːˈbærətɪ/ *n* (**a**) [U] savage cruelty. (**b**) [C] instance of this: *the barbarities of modern warfare.*

barbarize, -ise /ˈbɑːbəraɪz/ *v* [Tn] make (sb) barbarous.

Barbarossa /ˌbɑːbəˈrɒsə/ nickname (meaning 'red beard') of Frederick I (c 1123-90), Holy Roman Emperor (1152-90). He tried to gain control of Italy and the papacy, but was defeated at the Battle of Legnano (1176).

barbarous /ˈbɑːbərəs/ *adj* (*derog*) **1** unrefined in taste, habits, etc: *barbarous sounds.* **2** cruel or savage: *barbarous cruelty, treatment* ○ *barbarous soldiers.* ▷ **barbarously** *adv.* **barbarousness** *n* [U].

Barbary /ˈbɑːbərɪ/ old name for the western part of N Africa. From the 16th to the 19th centuries, the pirates who sailed along its coast were greatly feared.

□ ˌ**Barbary ˈape** type of small monkey with no tail, found in N Africa and Gibraltar.

barbecue /ˈbɑːbɪkjuː/ *n* **1** [C] metal frame for cooking meat, etc over an open fire. **2** [C] outdoor party at which food is cooked in this way and eaten. **3** [U] food cooked in this way: [attrib] *barbecue sauce*, ie a spicy sauce used for this type of food.

▷ **barbecue** *v* [Tn] cook (meat, etc) on a barbecue: *barbecued chicken.*

barbell /ˈbɑːbel/ *n* metal bar used in weight-lifting, with adjustable weights at each end. Cf DUMB-BELL 1.

Barber /ˈbɑːbə(r)/ Samuel (1910-81), American composer. His melodic and traditional style made him one of his country's most popular composers.

barber /ˈbɑːbə(r)/ *n* person whose trade is cutting men's hair and shaving them. Originally barbers also carried out surgical operations, and a red and white pole, a symbol of a bandage on a bleeding arm, may still be found outside their shops: *I'm going to the barber's (shop) to get my hair cut.* Cf HAIRDRESSER (HAIR).

□ ˈ**barber-shop** *n* (*US*) place where a barber works. — *adj* [attrib] (*US*) of a type of music for four unaccompanied male voices singing in close harmony: *a barber-shop quartet.*

Barbera /ˈbɑːbərə/ Joe (1910-), American cartoon maker, esp with Bill *Hanna.

barbican /ˈbɑːbɪkən/ *n* **1** [C] tower or similar building usu built over a bridge or gate in a medieval city to defend it. **2 the Barbican** [sing] arts centre and housing development in the City of London. It has a concert hall, theatres, an art gallery and a library.

barbiturate /bɑːˈbɪtjʊrət/ *n* any of a group of sedative drugs: *He died from an overdose of barbiturates.* ○ [attrib] *barbiturate poisoning.* ⇨ article at DRUG.

Barbuda ⇨ ANTIGUA AND BARBUDA.

barcarole /ˌbɑːkəˈrəʊl, -ˈrɒl/ *n* piece of music, esp for the piano, with a steady lilting rhythm.

barchan /bɑːˈkɑːn/ *n* sand-dune blown into a crescent shape by the wind.

bard /bɑːd/ *n* **1** Celtic minstrel, esp a Welsh poet who has been honoured at an eisteddfod. ⇨ article at WALES. **2** (*arch*) poet: *the Bard (of Avon)*, ie Shakespeare.

▷ **bardic** *adj.*

bardolatry /bɑːˈdɒlətrɪ/ *n* [U] (*derog*) excessive admiration for Shakespeare.

bare[1] /beə(r)/ *adj* (**-r, -st**) **1** (**a**) without clothing: *bare legs* ○ *bare to the waist*, ie wearing no clothes above the waist. (**b**) without the usual covering or protection: *bare floors*, ie without carpets, rugs, etc ○ *a bare hillside*, ie one without shrubs or trees ○ *trees that are already bare*, ie that have already lost their leaves ○ *with his head bare*, ie not wearing a hat ○ *with one's bare hands*, ie without tools or weapons. **2** ~ **(of sth)** empty or almost empty (of the expected contents): *a room bare of furniture* ○ *a larder bare of food* ○ *bare shelves.* **3** [attrib] only just sufficient; basic: *the bare necessities of life*, ie things needed merely to stay alive ○ *a bare majority*, ie a very small one ○ *the bare facts*, ie without any additional comment or detail. **4** (idm) **the bare ˈbones (of sth)** main or basic facts (of some matter or situation). **lay sth ˈbare** expose or make known sth secret or hidden: *lay bare the truth, sb's treachery, a plot.*

▷ **barely** *adv* **1** only just; scarcely: *We barely had time to catch the train.* ○ *He can barely read or write.* **2** in a bare way: *The room was barely furnished*, ie had little furniture in it.

bareness *n* [U].

□ ˈ**bareback** *adj, adv* on a horse without a saddle: *a bareback rider* ○ *ride bareback.*

ˈ**barefaced** *adj* [attrib] impudent; shameless: *a barefaced lie* ○ *It's barefaced robbery asking such a high price for that old bicycle!*

ˈ**barefoot** (also ˌ**bareˈfooted**) *adj, adv* without shoes or stockings: *children running barefoot in the sand.*

ˌ**bareˈheaded** *adj, adv* not wearing a hat.

ˌ**bareˈlegged** /-ˈlegd, -ˈlegɪd/ *adj, adv* wearing nothing on one's legs.

bare[2] /beə(r)/ *v* **1** [Tn] uncover (sth); reveal: *bare one's chest* ○ *He bared his head* (ie took off his hat to show respect) *as the funeral procession passed.* ○ *bare the end of a wire*, ie strip off the covering of rubber, etc before making an electrical connection. **2** (idm) **bare its ˈteeth** (of an animal) show its teeth when angry. **bare one's ˈheart/ˈsoul (to sb)** (*rhet or joc*) make known one's deepest feelings.

Barents Sea /ˌbærənts ˈsiː/ **the Barents Sea** shallow part of the Arctic Ocean, north of Russia, named after the Dutch explorer Willem Barents (d 1597) who discovered Spitsbergen.

barfly /ˈbɑːflaɪ/ *n* person who spends a lot of time drinking in bars.

bargain[1] /ˈbɑːgɪn/ *n* **1** agreement in which both or all sides promise to do sth for each other: *If you promote our goods, we will give you a good discount as our part of the bargain.* ○ *The bargain they reached with their employers was to reduce their wage claim in return for a shorter working week.* ○ *A bargain's a bargain*, ie When an agreement has been reached, it should be kept. **2** thing bought or sold for less than its usual price: *It's a bargain*, ie It is very good value for money. ○ [attrib] *a bargain price*, ie a low price. **3** (idm) **a bad ˈbargain** (**a**) agreement that is more beneficial to the other side(s) than to oneself. (**b**) thing bought because it was thought cheap but which one later regrets buying. **drive a hard bargain** ⇨ DRIVE[1]. **a good ˈbargain** (**a**) agreement that is more beneficial to oneself than to the other side(s): *You've got a good bargain there.* (**b**) thing, usu valuable, bought at a very low price. **into the ˈbargain**; *US* also **in the ˈbargain** (*infml*) in addition; moreover: *She was a distinguished scientist — and a gifted painter into the bargain.* **strike a bargain** ⇨ STRIKE[2].

□ ˌ**bargain ˈbasement** basement floor of a shop where goods are offered for sale at reduced prices.

ˈ**bargain counter** part of a shop where goods are

offered for sale at reduced prices.

ˈ**bargain-hunter** *n* person looking for goods at very low prices.

bargain[2] /ˈbɑːgɪn/ *v* **1** [I, Ipr] ~ (**with sb**) (**about**/**over**/**for sth**) discuss (with sb) prices, terms of trade, etc with the aim of buying or selling goods, or changing conditions, on terms that are favourable to oneself: *Never pay the advertised price for a car; always try to bargain.* ○ *Dealers bargain with growers over the price of coffee.* ○ *The unions bargained (with management) for a shorter working week.* **2** (phr v) **bargain sth away** give sth away (esp sth valuable in exchange for sth less so): *The leaders bargained away the freedom of their people.* **bargain for sth**; **bargain on sth** (*infml*) (often negative) expect; be prepared for: *The exam was more difficult than I had bargained for.* ○ *Tom didn't bargain on his wife returning so soon.* ○ *When the politician agreed to answer questions on television, he got more than he had bargained for,* ie was unpleasantly surprised at the consequences.

bargaining /ˈbɑːgɪnɪŋ/ *n* [U] discussion of prices, terms of trade, etc: *After much hard bargaining we reached an agreement.*

□ ˈ**bargaining counter** special advantage that can be used to outweigh an advantage possessed by an opponent: *Ownership of the land gives us a strong bargaining counter.*

ˈ**bargaining position** position, favourable or unfavourable, reached when bargaining: *We're now in a rather poor bargaining position.*

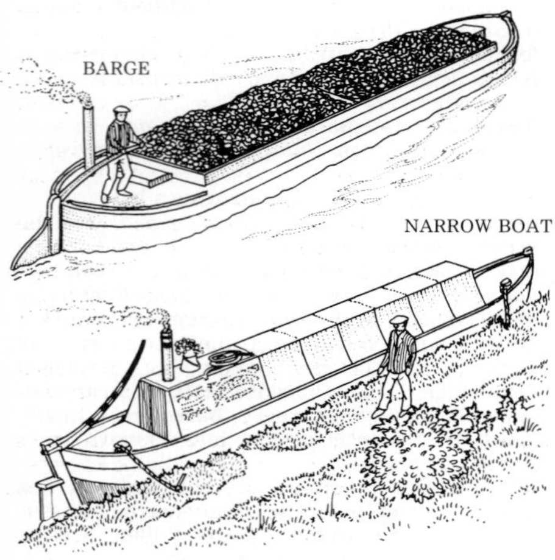

barge[1] /bɑːdʒ/ *n* **1** large flat-bottomed boat for carrying goods and people on rivers, canals, etc. ⇨ illus. Cf NARROW BOAT (NARROW). **2** large ornamental rowing-boat for ceremonial occasions.

▷ **bargee** /bɑːˈdʒiː/ *n* (*Brit*) (*US* **bargeman**) (**a**) person in charge of a barge. (**b**) member of a barge's crew.

□ ˈ**barge-pole** *n* **1** long pole used for guiding a barge. **2** (idm) **not touch sb/sth with a barge-pole** ⇨ TOUCH[1].

barge[2] /bɑːdʒ/ *v* (*infml*) **1** [I, Ipr, Ip] rush or bump heavily and clumsily: *Stop barging (into people)!* ○ *He barged past me in the queue.* **2** (phr v) **barge about** move about heavily and clumsily. **barge in**/**into sth** enter or interrupt sth rudely or clumsily: *I tried to stop him coming through the door but he just barged (his way) in.* ○ *Don't barge into the conversation.*

baritone /ˈbærɪtəʊn/ *n* (*music*) **1** male voice between tenor and bass. **2** singer with such a voice: [attrib] *a baritone aria.*

barium /ˈbeərɪəm/ *n* [U] (*symb* **Ba**) chemical element, a soft silvery-white metal, compounds of which are used in industry, eg for making glass and pigments. ⇨ App 11.

□ ˌ**barium** ˈ**meal** chemical substance, insoluble barium sulphate, opaque to X-rays, that is taken into a patient's digestive tract, usu by swallowing, before the tract is X-rayed.

bark[1] /bɑːk/ *n* [U, C] tough outer covering of tree trunks and branches. ⇨ illus at DENDROCHRONOLOGY.

▷ **bark** *v* [Tn] **1** remove the bark from (a tree). **2** accidentally scrape the skin off (one's knuckles, knees, etc): *He barked his shins (by falling) against some stone steps.*

bark[2] /bɑːk/ *n* **1** (**a**) sharp harsh sound made by dogs and foxes. (**b**) (*fig*) any similar sound, eg the sound of gunfire or of a cough. **2** (idm) **sb's bark is worse than his bite** (*infml*) though sb often sounds angry, fierce, etc, in fact he rarely carries out his threats.

▷ **bark** *v* **1** (**a**) [I, Ipr] ~ (**at sb/sth**) (of dogs, etc) give a bark or barks: *Our dog always barks at strangers.* (**b**) [I] (*fig*) (of people coughing, guns, etc) make a similar sound. **2** [I, Ipr, Tn, Tn·p] ~ (**at sb**); ~ **sth** (**out**) say (sth) in a sharp harsh voice: *When she's angry, she often barks at the children.* ○ *The sergeant barked (out) an order.* **3** (idm) **bark up the wrong** ˈ**tree** (esp in the continuous tenses) be mistaken about sth: *If you think that, you're barking up the wrong tree altogether.*

barker /ˈbɑːkə(r)/ *n* (*infml*) person who stands by a stall at a fair, a market, an auction, etc and shouts loudly to attract customers.

barley /ˈbɑːlɪ/ *n* [U] (grass-like plant producing) grain used for food and for making beer and whisky. Cf MALT. ⇨ illus at CEREAL.

□ ˈ**barleycorn** *n* [U] grain of barley.

ˈ**barley sugar** hard clear sweet[2](1) made from boiled sugar.

ˈ**barley water** (*Brit*) drink, sometimes flavoured, made by boiling barley in water and then straining it: *lemon barley water.*

bar mitzvah /ˌbɑː ˈmɪtsvə/ **1** Jewish boy who has reached the age of 13, when he assumes the religious responsibilities of an adult. **2** ceremony at which he does this.

barmy (also *esp US* **balmy**) /ˈbɑːmɪ/ *adj* (**-ier**, **-iest**) (*infml*) foolish; crazy.

barn /bɑːn/ *n* **1** simple building for storing hay, grain, etc on a farm. **2** (*fig derog*) any unattractive large building: *They live in that great barn of a house.* **3** (*US*) (**a**) building for sheltering farm animals, eg cows or horses. (**b**) building for a fleet of buses, vans, etc.

□ ˈ**barn dance** **1** type of traditional country dance. **2** informal social occasion at which such dances are performed.

barn-ˈ**owl** *n* type of owl that often nests in barns and other buildings. ⇨ illus at BIRD.

ˈ**barnyard** *n* area on a farm around a barn.

Barnabas /ˈbɑːnəbəs/ one of the earliest disciples of Jesus, who later went with St Paul on his missionary journeys to Cyprus and Asia Minor.

barnacle /ˈbɑːnəkl/ *n* small shellfish that attaches itself to objects under water, eg rocks or the bottoms of ships: (*fig*) *He clung to his mother like a barnacle,* ie followed her closely everywhere.

Barnard /ˈbɑːnɑːd/ Christiaan (1922-), South African surgeon who in 1967 performed the first transplant of a human heart.

Barnardo /bəˈnɑːdəʊ/ Thomas John (1845-1905), British doctor who set up Dr Barnardo's Homes for the care and education of orphans and homeless children. ⇨ articles at ACCOMMODATION, CHARITY.

barney /ˈbɑːnɪ/ *n* (*sl*) argument.

▷ **barney** *v* [I, Ipr] ~ (**about**/**over sth**) have an argument about sth: *They were barneying over the referee's decision.*

barnstorm /ˈbɑːnstɔːm/ *v* [I] (*US*) travel quickly through rural areas making political speeches, presenting plays, etc. ▷ **barnstormer** *n.*

Barnum /ˈbɑːnəm/ Phineas Taylor (1810-91), American showman. He owned a touring circus, which often showed unusual people or animals, some of them with physical deformities. With his great rival J A Bailey he later formed 'Barnum and Bailey's Circus'.

barograph /ˈbærəgrɑːf/ *n* type of barometer that makes a continuous record of changes in atmospheric pressure.

barometer /bəˈrɒmɪtə(r)/ *n* **1** instrument for measuring atmospheric pressure, used esp for forecasting the weather. The main types are the *mercury barometer* and the *aneroid barometer*: *The barometer is falling,* ie Wet weather is indicated. ⇨ article at WEATHER. **2** (*fig*) thing that indicates changes (in public opinion, market prices, sb's mood, etc): *a reliable barometer of public feeling.* ▷ **barometric** /ˌbærəˈmetrɪk/ *adj*: *barometric pressure.*

baron /ˈbærən/ *n* **1** member of the lowest rank of the British peerage (called *Lord X*) or of non-British nobility (called *Baron Y*). ⇨ article at ARISTOCRAT. **2** powerful and wealthy leader of industry: *a* ˈ*press baron* ○ ˈ*oil barons.*

▷ **baroness** /ˈbærənɪs, *also* ˌbærəˈnes/ *n* **1** woman holding the rank of baron in her own right. **2** wife of a baron.

baronial /bəˈrəʊnɪəl/ *adj* [usu attrib] of or suitable for a baron.

baronet /ˈbærənɪt/ *n* (*abbrs* **Bart**, **Bt**) member of the lowest hereditary titled order in Britain, below a baron but above a knight: *Sir John Williams, Bart.* ⇨ article at ARISTOCRAT.

▷ **baronetcy** /ˈbærənɪtsɪ/ *n* rank or title of a baronet.

baroque /bəˈrɒk; *US* bəˈrəʊk/ *adj, n* (of the) highly ornate style fashionable in the arts (esp architecture) in Europe in the 17th and 18th centuries. ⇨ article at ARCHITECTURE.

barque /bɑːk/ *n* sailing-ship with 3, 4 or 5 masts and sails.

barrack /ˈbærək/ *v* **1** [I, Tn] (*Brit*) shout protests or jeer at (players in a game, speakers, performers, etc): *The crowd started barracking (the slow rate of play).* **2** [Ipr, Tn] ~ (**for**) **sb** (*Austral*) cheer on (players, speakers, etc that one supports). ▷ **barracking** *n* [C, U]: *The crowd gave the visiting politician quite a barracking.*

barracks /ˈbærəks/ *n* **1** [sing or pl *v*] large building or group of buildings for soldiers to live in: *As punishment, the men were confined to barracks.* ○ *There used to be a barracks in this town.* **2** [sing *v*] (*fig infml*) any large ugly building: *Their house was a great barracks of a place.*

▷ **barrack-** (in compounds) of a barracks: *a barrack-square,* ie the ground near a barracks where soldiers are drilled.

□ ˌ**barrack-room** ˈ**lawyer** (*infml derog*) person who enjoys arguing in a pompous manner.

barracuda /ˌbærəˈkuːdə/ *n* large fierce Caribbean fish.

barrage /ˈbærɑːʒ; *US* bəˈrɑːʒ/ *n* **1** barrier built across a river to store water for irrigation, prevent flooding, etc. **2** (**a**) heavy continuous gunfire directed onto a particular area to restrict enemy movement: *lay down a barrage.* (**b**) (*fig*) large number (of questions, criticisms, etc) delivered quickly, one after the other: *face a barrage of angry complaints.*

□ ˈ**barrage balloon** large balloon that floats in the air while tied to the ground by wires, etc intended to hinder enemy aircraft.

barre /bɑː(r)/ *n* long rail, usu in front of a mirror, for ballet-dancers to hold on to while doing exercises.

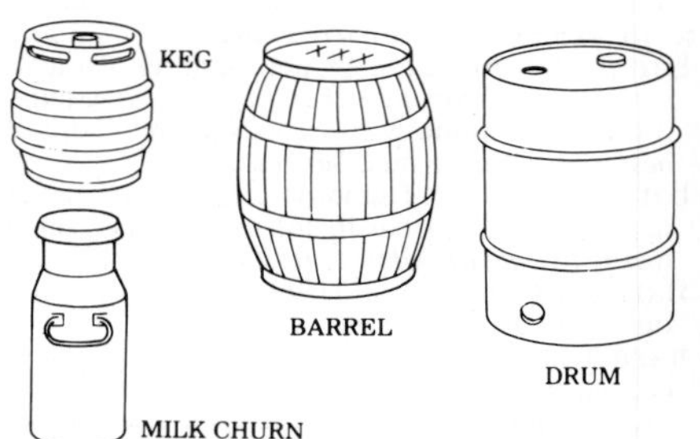

barrel /ˈbærəl/ *n* **1** (**a**) large round container with flat ends and bulging in the middle, made of wood,

metal or plastic. ⇨ illus. (**b**) amount that a barrel contains. (**c**) (*abbr* **bbl**) (as a measure of mineral oil) 35 imperial gallons or 42 American gallons. **2** long metal tube forming part of sth, esp a gun or a pen. ⇨ illus at GUN. **3** (idm) **lock, stock and barrel** ⇨ LOCK[2]. **(get/have sb) over a barrel** (*infml*) (have sb) at one's mercy; in a helpless position. **scrape the barrel** ⇨ SCRAPE[1].
▷ **barrel** *v* (-ll-; *US* -l-) [Tn] put (sth) in a barrel or barrels.
□ ˌ**barrel-ˈchested** *adj* (esp of a man) having a large chest curving outwards.
ˈ**barrel-organ** *n* mechanical instrument from which music is produced by turning a handle, usu played in the streets for money.

barrel vault

ˈ**barrel vault** plain vault with a curved roof like the upper half of a circular tube. ⇨ illus.

barren /ˈbærən/ *adj* **1** (of land) not good enough to produce crops. **2** (of plants or trees) not producing fruit or seeds. **3** (*dated or fml*) (of women or female animals) unable to bear young. **4** [usu attrib] (*fig*) without value, interest or result: *a barren discussion.* ▷ **barrenness** /ˈbærənnɪs/ *n* [U].

Barrett /ˈbærət/ Elizabeth ⇨ BROWNING[1].

barricade /ˌbærɪˈkeɪd, ˈbærəkeɪd/ *n* barrier hastily built as a defence or an obstacle. The building of barricades is commonly associated with popular unrest or rebellion: *The soldiers stormed the barricades erected by the rioting crowd.* ○ *a call to the barricades,* eg to join in a revolt or revolution.
▷ **barricade** *v* (phr v) **barricade sb in (sth)/out (of sth)** keep sb in/out by making a barricade: *They barricaded themselves in (their rooms).* **barricade sth off** block (eg a street) with a barricade: *The police barricaded off the entrance to the square.*

Barrie /ˈbærɪ/ Sir James Matthew (1860-1937), Scottish playwright and novelist. His novels, like *The Little Minister*, combine sentimentality and gentle humour. His most famous play is *Peter Pan*, the story of a boy who refuses to grow up, the copyright of which Barrie gave to the Great Ormond Street Children's Hospital in London.

barrier /ˈbærɪə(r)/ *n* **1** (**a**) thing that prevents or controls progress or movement: *The Sahara Desert is a natural barrier between North and Central Africa.* ○ *Show your ticket at the barrier.* (**b**) (*fig*) hindrance: *Poor health may be a barrier to success* ○ *trade barriers,* ie taxes or regulations that make it difficult to sell goods normally to another country. **2** thing that keeps people apart: *barriers of race and religion* ○ *the language barrier.*
□ ˈ**barrier cream** cream used for protecting skin from damage or infection.
ˌ**barrier ˈreef** coral reef separated from land by a channel: *the Great Barrier Reef,* ie off the coast of NE Australia.

barring /ˈbɑːrɪŋ/ *prep* not including or allowing for (sth); if there is/are not: *Barring accidents, we should arrive on time.* Cf BAR[3] 1.

barrio /ˈbærɪəʊ/ *n* (*pl* ~**s**) (*esp US*) part of a town or city where (usu poor) Spanish-speaking people live, esp as immigrants from Latin America.

barrister /ˈbærɪstə(r)/ *n* (in English law) lawyer who has the right to speak and argue as an advocate in higher lawcourts. Cf ADVOCATE *n* 2, SOLICITOR 1. ⇨ article at LAW.

barrow[1] /ˈbærəʊ/ *n* **1** = WHEELBARROW (WHEEL). **2** small cart with two wheels, pulled or pushed by hand.
□ ˈ**barrow boy** person who sells things from a barrow in the street.

barrow[2] /ˈbærəʊ/ *n* mound built over a burial place in prehistoric times. Cf TUMULUS.

the Houses of Parliament, designed by Sir Charles Barry

Barry /ˈbærɪ/ Sir Charles (1795-1860), English architect. He is famous for his design for the Houses of Parliament in London, built in Gothic style. ⇨ illus.

Barrymore /ˈbærɪmɔː(r)/ family of American actors, Lionel (1878-1954), Ethel (1879-1959) and John (1882-1942). Lionel began in the theatre, first appeared in films directed by D W *Griffith and later played habitually testy characters from his wheelchair. Ethel also appeared in films, but was most famous as a theatre actress. John was famous for his roles as a silent romantic hero, eg in *Don Juan* (1926).

Bart /bɑːt/ *abbr* Baronet.

barter /ˈbɑːtə(r)/ *v* **1** [Tn, Tn·pr, Tn·p] ~ **sth (for sth)**; ~ **sth (away)** exchange (goods, property, etc) for other goods, etc without using money: *barter wheat for machinery* ○ *He bartered his best possessions for a horse.* ○ (*fig*) *barter away one's rights, honour, freedom.* **2** [I, Ipr] ~ **(with sb) (for sth)** trade by exchanging sth for sth else without using money: *The prisoners tried to barter with the guards for their freedom.*
▷ **barter** *n* [U] exchange of goods for other goods without using money: *On these islands a system of barter is used.*

Barth /bɑːt; *US also* bɑːθ/ Karl (1886-1968), Swiss theologian. Regarded as one of the major Protestant thinkers of the 20th century, he emphasized the need for a return to the principles of the Reformation and the preaching of the Bible, and the dependence of humanity on the grace of God.

Bartholomew /bɑːˈθɒləmjuː/ Saint, one of the twelve apostles of Jesus and patron saint of tanners.

Bartók /ˈbɑːtɒk/ Béla (1881-1945), Hungarian pianist and composer. Although well-known as a collector of Hungarian folk music, his own style was more influenced by other composers of his time, such as *Debussy and Richard *Strauss. In 1940 he emigrated to the USA, where he died in poverty.

baryon /ˈbærɪɒn/ *n* (*physics*) elementary particle, either a hyperon or a nucleon.

barysphere /ˈbærɪsfɪə(r)/ *n* (*geology*) dense central part of the earth, below the crust.

basalt /ˈbæsɔːlt; *US* ˈbeɪsɔːlt, bəˈsɔːlt/ *n* [U] type of dark rock of volcanic origin, formed by the cooling of lava. The *Giant's Causeway is made of basaltic columns. ▷ **basaltic** /bəsɔːltɪk; *US* beɪ-/ *adj*.

bascule bridge /ˈbæskjuːl/ *n* type of bridge weighted so that one end is raised when the other end is lowered. ⇨ illus at BRIDGE.

base[1] /beɪs/ *n* **1** (**a**) lowest part of sth, esp the part on which it rests or is supported: *the base of a pillar, column, etc.* (**b**) (*geometry*) line or surface on which a figure stands: *the base of a triangle, pyramid, etc.* (**c**) (*fig*) starting-point; underlying principle: *She used her family's history as a base for her novel.* ○ *His arguments had a sound economic base.* **2** (*chemistry*) substance which is a proton acceptor (eg an alkali) capable of reacting with an acid to form a salt. **3** main part or ingredient to which other things are added: *a drink with a rum base* ○ *Some paints have an oil base.* ○ *Put some moisturizer on as a base before applying your make-up.* **4** place at which armed forces, expeditions, etc have their stores: *a ˈnaval base* ○ *an ˈair base* ○ [attrib] *a base camp,* eg for a mountaineering expedition ○ *establish, set up a base.* **5** (*mathematics*) number on which a numerical system is built up, eg 10 in the decimal system, 2 in the binary system. **6** (in baseball) each of the four positions to be reached by a runner. ⇨ illus at BASEBALL. **7** (idm) **not get to first base** ⇨ FIRST BASE (FIRST[1]). **off base** (*US infml*) (**a**) mistaken: *You're a bit off base there.* (**b**) unprepared: *Her reply caught him off base.*
▷ **baseless** *adj* without cause or foundation: *baseless fears, rumours, suspicions.*
□ ˈ**baseboard** *n* (*US*) = SKIRTING-BOARD (SKIRT).
ˈ**base hit** (also **single**) (in baseball) hit that enables a batter to reach first base.
ˈ**baseline** *n* (*sport*) line marking each end of the court in tennis or the boundary of the running track in baseball. ⇨ illus at TENNIS.
ˈ**base rate** (*finance*) interest rate used by individual banks as a basis for fixing their interest rates for borrowers and investors.
base ˈunit unit of measurement that is defined arbitrarily rather than in terms of other units: *The ampere is a base unit in the SI system.*

base[2] /beɪs/ *v* **1** [Tn·pr] ~ **sth on sth** use sth as grounds, evidence, etc for sth else: *I base my hopes on the good news we had yesterday.* ○ *This novel is based on historical facts.* ○ *Direct taxation is usually based on income,* ie A person's income is used to calculate the amount of tax he has to pay. **2** [esp passive: Tn·pr, Tn·p] ~ **sb in/at...** place sb in (a place from which to work and travel): *Where are you based now?* ○ *Most of our staff are based in Cairo.*

base[3] /beɪs/ *adj* (**-r, -st**) **1** (*fml derog*) dishonourable; despicable: *acting from base motives.* **2** not pure: *base coin.* **3** low in value: *base metal.* Cf PRECIOUS 1.
▷ **basely** *adv* in a base[3](1) manner.
baseness *n* [U] state of being base[3](1).

baseball
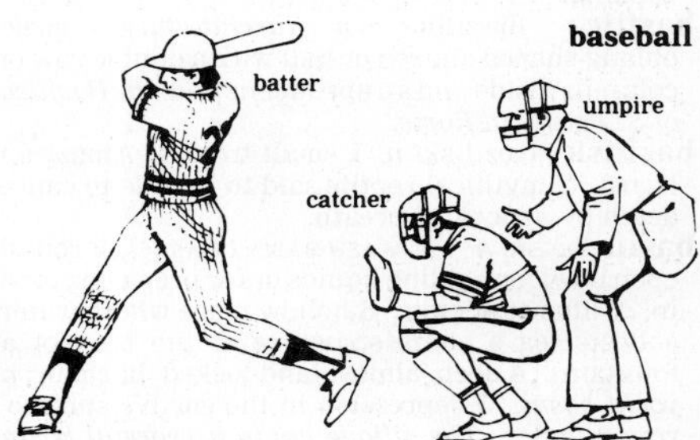

baseball /ˈbeɪsbɔːl/ *n* [U] game popular in the USA, played with a bat and ball by two teams of nine players each on a field with four bases (BASE[1] 6):

[attrib] *a baseball pitch.* ⇨ App 9. ⇨ illus. Cf ROUNDERS. ⇨ article at SPORT.

basement /ˈbeɪsmənt/ *n* lowest room or rooms in a building, partly or wholly below ground level.

basenji /bəˈsendʒɪ/ *n* breed of small dog, originally from Africa, which rarely barks.

bases **1** *pl* of BASIS. **2** *pl* of BASE[1].

bash /bæʃ/ *v* (*infml*) **1** [Tn, Tn·pr] strike (sb/sth) heavily so as to break or injure: *bash sb on the head with a club.* **2** [Ipr, Tn·pr] ~ **(sth) against/into sb/sth** (cause sth to) collide violently with sb/sth: *He tripped and bashed his head against the railing.* **3** (phr v) **bash ahead/away/on (with sth)** continue doing sth quickly and enthusiastically, but not carefully. **bash sth in/down** cause sth to collapse inwards by striking it violently: *bash in the lid of a box* ○ *They bashed the door down.* **bash sb up** (*Brit infml*) treat sb violently: *He was bashed up in the playground by some older boys.*

▷ **bash** *n* **1** (*infml*) violent blow: *give sb a bash on the nose.* **2** (idm) **have a bash (at sth)** (*infml*) attempt sth (usu sth previously untried): *I've never tried water-skiing before, but I'd love to have a bash at it.*

bashing *n* [U, C] (often in compounds) violent attack (often on members of specific groups): *union-bashing,* ie the practice of trying to discredit a trade union by fierce criticism, etc ○ *give sb a bashing.* ⇨ Usage at BANG[1].

bashful /ˈbæʃfl/ *adj* shy and self-conscious. ▷ **bashfully** /-fəlɪ/ *adv.* **bashfulness** *n* [U].

BASIC (also **Basic**) /ˈbeɪsɪk/ *abbr* (*computing*) beginners' all-purpose symbolic instruction code, a simple programming language.

basic /ˈbeɪsɪk/ *adj* **1** ~ **(to sth)** forming a base or starting-point; fundamental: *argue from basic principles* ○ *the basic vocabulary of a language,* ie those words that must be learnt ○ *These facts are basic to an understanding of the case.* **2** simplest or lowest in level; standard: *basic pay,* ie without extras such as overtime payments ○ *our basic requirements* ○ *My knowledge of physics is pretty basic,* ie is only at the elementary level. **3** (*chemistry*) (of a substance) having the properties of or containing a base[1](2): *a basic solution.*

▷ **basically** /-klɪ/ *adv* with reference to essential matters (which are often seen as different from what is superficially apparent); fundamentally: *Despite her criticisms, she is basically very fond of you.* ○ *Basically I agree with your proposals, although there are a few small points I'd like to discuss.*

basics *n* [pl] essential matters: *Let's stop chatting and get down to basics,* ie concentrate on important matters.

□ ˌ**Basic** ˈ**English** simplified form of English with a vocabulary of 850 words, devised to be used internationally for the teaching and learning of English.

ˌ**basic** ˈ**slag** fertilizer containing phosphates obtained during the manufacture of steel.

Basie /ˈbeɪsɪ/ William 'Count' (1904-84), American jazz musician. He formed his own orchestra in 1935, leading it from the piano. It became famous for its distinctive 'big band' sound.

basil /ˈbæzl/ *n* [U] sweet-smelling herb used in cooking.

basilica /bəˈzɪlɪkə/ *n* (*architecture*) large oblong-shaped church or hall with a double row of columns inside and an apse at one end: *the Basilica of St Peter's in Rome.*

basilisk /ˈbæzɪlɪsk/ *n* **1** small tropical American lizard. **2** mythical reptile said to be able to cause death by its look or breath.

basin /ˈbeɪsn/ *n* **1** = WASH-BASIN (WASH[2]). **2** round open bowl for holding liquids or for preparing food in. ⇨ illus at BUCKET. **3** hollow place where water collects (eg a stone structure at the base of a fountain). **4** deep, almost land-locked, harbour: *a yacht basin.* **5** depression in the earth's surface; round valley: *The village lay in a peaceful basin surrounded by hills.* **6** area of land drained by a river: *the Thames basin.*

▷ **basinful** /-fʊl/ *n* amount that a basin contains: *two basinfuls of water.*

basis /ˈbeɪsɪs/ *n* (*pl* **bases** /ˈbeɪsiːz/) **1** main principle that underlies sth; foundation: *the basis of morality, friendship, etc* ○ *arguments that have a firm basis,* ie that are founded on facts ○ *Rates of work are calculated on a weekly basis.* **2** starting-point for a discussion: *No basis for negotiations has been agreed upon.* ○ *This agenda will form the basis of our next meeting.*

bask /bɑːsk; *US* bæsk/ *v* [I, Ipr] ~ **(in sth)** sit or lie enjoying warmth: *basking in the sunshine, by the fire, on the beach* ○ (*fig*) *basking in sb's favour, approval, etc.*

□ ˈ**basking shark** large shark that often floats on or just below the surface of the water.

basket /ˈbɑːskɪt; *US* ˈbæskɪt/ *n* **1** (**a**) container, usu made of material that bends and twists easily (eg reed, cane, wire), with or without a handle: *a* ˈ*shopping basket* ○ *a* ˈ*clothes basket* ○ *a* ˌ*waste-*ˈ*paper basket.* (**b**) amount that a basket contains: *They picked three baskets of apples.* **2** (idm) **put all one's eggs in/into one basket** ⇨ EGG[1].

▷ **basketful** /-fʊl/ *n* = BASKET 1b.

basketball

□ **basketball** /ˈbɑːskɪtbɔːl; *US* ˈbæs-/ *n* [U] game played by two teams of five players in which goals are scored by throwing a large ball into an open-ended net fixed high on a hoop at the opponents' end of the court. ⇨ App 9. ⇨ article at SPORT.

ˈ**basket weave** style of weaving cloth in a pattern that looks like basketwork.

ˈ**basketwork** *n* [U] (**a**) art of weaving material in the style of a basket. (**b**) material woven in this way: *a fine piece of basketwork.*

Basque /bæsk, *Brit also* bɑːsk/ *n* **1** [C] member of a people living in the region on either side of the western Pyrenees, partly in France and partly in Spain. Since 1979 the Basque Provinces of Spain have had autonomous status. The main city is Bilbao. **2** [U] language of the Basques.

▷ **Basque** *adj* of the Basques or their language (which is unrelated to any other known language). Cf ETA 2.

bas-relief /ˌbæs rɪˈliːf, *also* ˈbɑː rɪliːf/ *n* (**a**) [U] form of sculpture or carving in which a figure or design projects only slightly from its background. (**b**) [C] example of this.

bass[1] /bæs/ *n* (*pl* unchanged or ~**es**) any of several freshwater or sea fish of the perch family used as food: *a shoal of bass* ○ *They caught three basses.*

bass[2] /beɪs/ *n* **1** (**a**) lowest male voice: *Is he a bass or a baritone?* (**b**) singer with such a voice: *He is a very fine bass.* **2** lowest part in music (for voice or instruments): *He sings bass.* **3** = DOUBLE-BASS (DOUBLE[1]). **4** (also **bass guitar**) electric guitar producing very low notes.

▷ **bass** *adj* [attrib] low in tone: *a bass* ˈ*voice* ○ *a bass clari*ˈ*net* ○ *the* ˌ*bass* ˈ*clef,* ie symbol in music showing that the notes following in it are low in pitch. Cf TREBLE[2].

basset /ˈbæsɪt/ (also ˈ**basset-hound**) *n* short-legged dog used in hunting.

bassinet /ˌbæsɪˈnet/ *n* baby's wicker cradle with a hood.

bassoon /bəˈsuːn/ *n* low-pitched woodwind instrument with a double reed. ⇨ illus at MUSIC.

basso-profundo /ˌbæsəʊ prəˈfʊndəʊ/ *n* (*pl* ~**s**) (*music*) (singer with an) unusually deep bass voice.

bast /bæst/ *n* fibre from the inner bark of (esp lime) trees, used for tying and weaving baskets, mats, etc.

bastard /ˈbɑːstəd; *US* ˈbæs-/ *n* **1** illegitimate child: [attrib] *a bastard child/daughter/son.* **2** (*sl derog*) (**a**) (usu male) person regarded with contempt; ruthless or cruel person: *You rotten bastard!* ○ *He's a real bastard, leaving his wife in that way.* (**b**) thing that causes difficulty, pain, etc: *It's a bastard of a problem, this one.* ○ *My headache's a real bastard.* **3** (*sl*) (**a**) (used to address sb, usu a male friend, informally): *Harry, you old bastard! Fancy meeting you here!* (**b**) (used for showing sympathy, usu about a man) unfortunate fellow: *The poor bastard! He's just lost his job.* **4** [usu attrib] not genuine or authentic; showing an odd mixture: *a bastard style, language.*

▷ **bastardize, -ise** *v* [Tn] (used esp in the past participle) make (sth) less pure or authentic: *a bastardized form of English.* **bastardization, -isation** *n* [U].

bastardy *n* [U] (*law*) state of being a bastard(1).

baste[1] /beɪst/ *v* [Tn] sew (pieces of material) together with long temporary stitches.

baste[2] /beɪst/ *v* [Tn] pour fat, juices, etc over (meat, etc) to keep it moist during cooking.

Bastille /bæˈstiːl/ **the Bastille** medieval fortress in Paris, used as a prison in the 18th century. Although almost empty it was attacked and captured by the local people on 14 July 1789 at the start of the French Revolution. It was later demolished.

bastinado /ˌbæstɪˈnɑːdəʊ, -ˈneɪd-/ *n* (*pl* ~**s**) beating with a stick on the soles of the feet.

▷ **bastinado** *v* [Tn] punish or torture (sb) by beating in this way.

bastion /ˈbæstɪən/ *n* **1** part of a fortification that projects from the rest. **2** military stronghold near enemy territory. **3** (*fig*) person or thing defending or protecting sth that is threatened: *a bastion of democracy, freedom, etc* ○ *'The last bastions of privilege are crumbling,' announced the speaker.*

bat[1] /bæt/ *n* **1** small mouse-like animal that flies at night and feeds on fruit and insects. ⇨ illus at ANIMAL. **2** (idm) **blind as a bat** ⇨ BLIND[1]. **have** ˌ**bats in the** ˈ**belfry** (*infml*) be crazy; have strange ideas. **like a** ˌ**bat out of** ˈ**hell** (*infml*) quickly; at top speed: *He dashed out of the door like a bat out of hell.*

bat[2] /bæt/ *n* **1** (usu wooden) implement of a specified size and shape, and with a handle, used for hitting the ball in games such as cricket, baseball and table tennis. ⇨ illus at CRICKET. **2** = BATSMAN (BAT[2]): *He's a useful bat.* **3** (idm) ˌ**off one's own** ˈ**bat** (*infml*) without help or encouragement from anyone else; unaided: *She made the suggestions off her own bat,* ie without being asked for them.

▷ **bat** *v* (**-tt-**) **1** [I] (**a**) use a bat: *He bats well.* (**b**) have a turn with a bat: *Green batted for two hours.* **2** [Tn, Tn·p] hit (sth) with a bat: *batting a ball about.* ˈ**batter** *n* (*US*) (esp in baseball) person who bats. ⇨ illus at BASEBALL.

□ ˈ**batsman** /-smən/ *n* (*pl* **-men**) player who bats in cricket: *He's a good batsman but a poor bowler.* ⇨ illus at CRICKET.

bat[3] /bæt/ *n* (idm) **at a rare, surprising, terrific, etc** ˈ**bat** (*infml*) at a fast, etc speed.

bat[4] /bæt/ *v* (**-tt-**) (idm) **not bat an** ˈ**eyelid** (*infml*) not show any surprise or feelings: *The condemned man listened to his sentence without batting an eyelid.*

batch /bætʃ/ *n* **1** number of loaves, cakes, etc baked together: *baked in batches of twenty.* **2** number of people or things dealt with as a group: *a new batch of recruits for the army* ○ *a batch of letters to be answered.* **3** (*computing*) set of jobs that are processed together by a computer with no input from individual terminals: [attrib] *a batch run.*

□ ˌ**batch** ˈ**processing** (*computing*) system of processing a batch of jobs as a group.

bated /ˈbeɪtɪd/ *adj* (idm) **with** ˌ**bated** ˈ**breath** holding one's breath anxiously or excitedly: *We waited with bated breath for the winner to be* *announced.*

Batesian mimicry /ˌbeɪtsɪən ˈmɪmɪkrɪ/ way in which certain animals and insects defend themselves by looking or behaving like other creatures, thus deterring possible attackers. The phenomenon is named after the English naturalist Henry Walter Bates (1825-92).

bath /bɑːθ; *US* bæθ/ *n* (*pl* ~**s** /bɑːðz; *US* bæðz/) **1** [C] washing of the whole body, esp when sitting or lying in water: *I shall have a hot bath and go to bed.* ○ *He takes a cold bath every morning.* **2** [C] **(a)** (also ˈ**bath-tub, tub**) large, usu oblong, container for water in which a person sits to have a bath. **(b)** water placed in this ready for use: *Please run a bath for me.* ○ *Your bath is ready.* **3** [C] (container for) liquid in which sth is washed or dipped in chemical and industrial processes: *an* ˈ*oil bath*, eg for parts of machinery ○ *a bath of red dye.* **4 baths** [pl] **(a)** (*Brit*) indoor public swimming-pool: *heated swimming-baths.* **(b)** building where baths may be taken: *Turkish* ˈ*baths.* **5** (idm) **throw the baby out with the bath water** ⇨ BABY.

▷ **bath** *v* (*Brit*) **1** [Tn] give a bath to (sb/sth): *bath the baby.* **2** [I] take a bath: *I bath every night.*

□ ˈ**bath cube** solid cube of bath salts which dissolves in hot water.

ˈ**bath mat** small absorbent mat for a person to stand on after getting out of a bath.

ˈ**bathrobe** (also **robe**) *n* **1** loose, usu towelling, garment worn before and after taking a bath. **2** (*US*) = DRESSING-GOWN (DRESSING).

ˈ**bathroom** *n* **1** (*Brit sometimes euph*) room in which there is a bath (and also usu a wash-basin and sometimes a toilet): *Go and wash your hands in the bathroom.* **2** (*US*) (room with a) toilet: *I need to go to the bathroom.* ⇨ Usage at TOILET.

ˈ**bath salts** pleasant-smelling powdery substance sprinkled in bath water to soften or perfume it.

ˈ**bath-tub** *n* = BATH 2.

Bath bun /ˌbɑθ ˈbʌn/ (*Brit*) round spiced bun made with currants, and with icing on top.

bath chair /ˌbɑːθ ˈtʃeə(r)/ type of wheelchair for an invalid.

bathe /beɪð/ *v* **1** [Tn] apply water to (sth); soak in water: *The doctor told him to bathe his eyes twice a day.* ○ *The nurse bathed the wound.* **2** [I] (*esp Brit*) go swimming in the sea, a river, a lake, etc for enjoyment: *On hot days we often bathe/go bathing in the river.*

▷ **bathe** *n* (esp *sing*) (*esp Brit*) action of swimming in the sea, etc: *It's a sunny day. Let's go for a bathe.*

bathed *adj* [pred] ~ **in/with sth** wet or bright all over with sth: *Her face was bathed in tears.* ○ *After the match, I was bathed with sweat.* ○ *The countryside was bathed in brilliant sunshine.*

bather /ˈbeɪðə(r)/ *n.*

bathing /ˈbeɪðɪŋ/ *n* [U] (*esp Brit*) action of going into the sea, etc to bathe: *She's fond of bathing.* ○ *Bathing prohibited!* ie Swimming, etc is not allowed here, eg because it would be unsafe.

□ ˈ**bathing-cap** *n* close-fitting rubber cap worn over the hair while swimming.

ˈ**bathing-costume** (also ˈ**bathing-suit**) *n* (*Brit becoming dated*) = SWIMMING-COSTUME (SWIM).

Bath Oliver /ˌbɑːθ ˈɒlɪvə(r)/ (*Brit*) type of thin dry unsweetened biscuit.

bathos /ˈbeɪθɒs/ *n* [U] sudden change (in writing or speech) from what is deeply moving or important to what is foolish or trivial; anticlimax.

bathy- *comb form* (also **batho-**) deep (esp in water).

bathyscaphe /ˈbæθɪskæf/ *n* type of small manned vessel used for deep-sea exploration.

bathysphere /ˈbæθɪsfɪə(r)/ *n* large, strongly built, hollow sphere that can be lowered deep into the sea (usu for observing marine life).

batik /bəˈtiːk, *also* ˈbætɪk/ *n* **1** [U] method of printing coloured designs on cloth by waxing the parts that are not to be dyed. **2** [C] material dyed in this way: [attrib] *a batik dress.*

batiste /bæˈtiːst, *also* bəˈt-/ *n* [U] fine thin linen or cotton cloth.

Batman /ˈbætmæn/ American comic strip character who wears a batlike costume and, with his companion Robin, is dedicated to fighting crime.

batman /ˈbætmən/ *n* (*pl* **-men** /-mən/) (*Brit*) soldier who acts as an army officer's personal servant.

baton /ˈbætn, ˈbætɒn; *US* bəˈtɒn/ *n* **1** = TRUNCHEON: [attrib] *a baton charge*, ie one made by police, etc armed with batons to drive a crowd back. **2** short thin stick used by the conductor of a band or orchestra. **3** short stick that indicates a certain rank: *a Field Marshal's baton.* **4** short stick carried and handed on in a relay race. **5** decorative stick held and twirled by drum majors, etc.

bats /bæts/ *adj* [pred] (*infml*) (esp of people) mad; eccentric. Cf BATTY.

battalion /bəˈtælɪən/ *n* (*abbr* **Bn**) army unit composed of several companies and forming part of a regiment or brigade.

batten[1] /ˈbætn/ *n* **1** long board, esp one used to keep other boards in place, or to which other boards are nailed. **2** (on a ship) strip of wood or metal used to fasten down covers or tarpaulins over a hatch. **3** strip of wood carrying a series of lights for a theatre stage.

▷ **batten** *v* [Tn, Tn·p] ~ **sth (down)** (esp on a ship) fasten sth securely with battens: *batten down the hatches*, eg when a storm is expected.

batten[2] /ˈbætn/ *v* (phr v) **batten on sb/sth** (*esp derog*) thrive or live well at the expense of sb/sth, or so as to injure sb/sth: *She avoided having to work by battening on her rich relatives.*

Battenberg /ˈbætnbɜːg/ *n* [C, U] (also **Battenberg cake**) (*Brit*) rectangular sponge-cake covered with marzipan. When cut, each slice shows four squares of alternating colours, two yellow and two pink.

batter[1] /ˈbætə(r)/ *v* **1** [Ipr, Ip, Tn] (~ **at/on**) **sth** hit (sb/sth) hard and often: *He kept battering (away) at the door.* ○ *battered babies/wives*, ie ones that suffer repeated violence from parents/husbands. **2** (phr v) **batter sth down** flatten sth by hitting it repeatedly: *Let's batter the door down.* **batter sth to sth** cause sth to become a specified shape by hitting it hard and often: *The huge waves battered the wrecked ship to pieces.* ○ *The victim's face was battered to a pulp.*

▷ **battered** *adj* out of shape because of age, regular use or frequent accidents: *a battered old hat* ○ *Your car looks rather battered.*

□ ˈ**battering-ram** *n* large heavy log with an iron head formerly used in war for breaking down walls, etc.

batter[2] /ˈbætə(r)/ *n* [U] beaten mixture of flour, eggs, milk, etc for cooking: *fish fried in batter* ○ *pancake batter.*

battery /ˈbætərɪ/ *n* **1** [C] portable container of a cell or cells for supplying electricity: *a* ˈ*car battery* ○ *a* ˈ*torch battery* ○ *This pocket calculator needs two batteries.* ⇨ illus at CAR. **2** [C] **(a)** group of big guns on a warship or on land. **(b)** army unit consisting of big guns, with men and vehicles. **3** [C] large and often confusing set of similar tools, instruments, etc used together: *a battery of lights* ○ (*fig*) *She faced a battery of questions.* **4** [C] series of cages in which hens, etc are kept (to make them lay more eggs or grow fatter): [attrib] *a battery hen* ○ *battery eggs.* Cf FREE-RANGE (FREE[1]). **5** [U] (*law*) unlawfully hitting sb or touching him or his clothes threateningly. **6** (idm) **recharge one's batteries** ⇨ RECHARGE.

□ ˌ**battery** ˈ**farm** farm where large numbers of hens are kept in batteries. ˌ**battery** ˈ**farming** ⇨ article at ANIMAL.

battle /ˈbætl/ *n* **1** [C, U] fight, esp between organized armed forces: *a fierce battle* ○ *the battle of Waterloo* ○ *go out to battle* ○ *die in battle* ○ *the noise of battle.* **2** [C] (*fig*) any contest or struggle: *a battle of words, wits* ○ *Their whole life was a constant battle against poverty.* **3** (idm) **do battle (with sb) (about sth)** fight or argue fiercely (with sb) (about sth). **fight a losing battle** ⇨ FIGHT[1]. **give** ˈ**battle** (*dated*) show that one is ready to fight. **half the battle** an important or the most important part of achieving sth: *When you're ill, wanting to get well again is often half the battle.* **join battle** ⇨ JOIN.

▷ **battle** *v* [I, Ipr, Ip] ~ **(with/against sb/sth) (for sth)**; ~ **(on)** struggle: *battling against ill health* ○ *They battled with the wind and the waves.* ○ *I'm battling with my employers for a pay-rise.* ○ *Progress is slow but we keep battling on.*

□ ˈ**battleaxe** *n* **1** (formerly) heavy axe with a long handle, used as a weapon. **2** (*infml derog*) unpleasantly domineering (usu older) woman.

ˈ**battle-cruiser** *n* large warship, faster and lighter than a battleship.

ˈ**battle-cry** *n* **(a)** (esp formerly) rallying cry used in battle. **(b)** (*fig*) slogan or rallying cry of a group of people fighting for the same cause.

ˈ**battledress** *n* [U] soldier's uniform of blouse and trousers.

ˈ**battlefield**, ˈ**battleground** *ns* place where a battle is or was fought.

the ˌ**Battle** ˌ**Hymn of the Re**ˈ**public** patriotic song written by Julia Ward Howe for the soldiers of the Union army during the *American Civil War.

the ˌ**Battle of** ˈ**Britain** series of battles between British and German aircraft over London and the south of England at the beginning of the Second World War, in 1940. The climax of the battle is commemorated each year on Battle of Britain day (15 September).

ˌ**battle** ˈ**royal** long and fierce argument, esp one involving several people: *There is likely to be a battle royal when Parliament debates the new bill.*

ˈ**battleship** *n* large warship with big guns and heavy armour.

battlements /ˈbætlmənts/ *n* [pl] (flat roof of a tower or castle surrounded by) low walls with openings at intervals made for shooting through. ⇨ illus at CASTLE.

batty /ˈbætɪ/ *adj* (**-ier, -iest**) (*infml*) (of people, ideas, etc) crazy; slightly mad. Cf BATS.

bauble /ˈbɔːbl/ *n* (*usu derog*) showy ornament of little value.

baud /bəʊd/ *n* unit used to measure speed of transmission in telecommunications, equal to one bit, digit or symbol per second: [attrib] *a 300 baud modem.*

Baudelaire /ˈbəʊdəleə(r); *US* ˌbəʊdˈleər/ Charles (1821-67), French poet, probably the most influential of the 19th century. *Les Fleurs du mal*, his most famous work, tries to express his almost mystic view of beauty and evil in the real world, but it was condemned as offensive when it appeared. He also wrote articles about other artistic figures of his day, such as *Delacroix, *Wagner and Flaubert.

Bauhaus /ˈbaʊhaʊs/ **the Bauhaus** school of design founded by *Gropius in Germany in 1919. Klee, Kandinsky and Mies van der Rohe were also involved in the movement. It advocated architecture as 'total' design and tried to arrive at an anonymous group style and to bring principles of artistic design to everyday objects, using a functional and geometric style. The school was closed by the Nazis in 1933.

baulk = BALK.

bauxite /ˈbɔːksaɪt/ *n* [U] clay-like substance from which aluminium is obtained.

Bavaria /bəˈveərɪə/ state in the south of Germany; German name **Bayern**. It is famous for its fine scenery and its beer. The capital is Munich.

bawdy /ˈbɔːdɪ/ *adj* (**-ier, -iest**) amusing in a coarse or indecent way: *bawdy jokes, stories, etc.*

▷ **bawdily** *adv.*

bawdiness *n* [U].

bawdy *n* [U] (*dated*) bawdy talk or stories.

bawl /bɔːl/ *v* **1** [I, Ipr, Ip, Tn, Tn·pr, Tn·p] ~ **(sth) (out)** shout or cry loudly: *That baby has been bawling for hours.* ○ *He bawled at me across the street.* ○ *We bawled for help but no one heard us.* ○ *The sergeant bawled (out) a command (to his men).* **2** (phr v) ˌ**bawl sb** ˈ**out** (*esp US infml*) scold sb severely.

Bax /bæks/ Sir Arnold (1883-1953), English composer. He is now most famous for his tone-poems, written in a romantic style. He was fascinated by Ireland, and wrote short stories under the name Dermot O'Byrne.

the Bayeux tapestry

bay[1] /beɪ/ (also ˈ**bay-tree**) *n* laurel with dark green leaves and purple berries. The ancient Greeks and Romans made crowns of bay-leaves to reward the winners at sporting contests or generals who won victories: *(fml) victors crowned with bays*, ie woven bay-leaves.

□ ˈ**bay-leaf** *n* (*pl* **-leaves**) dried leaf of the bay-tree, spicy when crushed, used as seasoning in cooking.

bay[2] /beɪ/ *n* part of the sea, or of a large lake, enclosed by a wide curve of the shore: *the Bay of Bengal* ○ *Hudson Bay.*

□ **the** ˌ**Bay of** ˈ**Pigs** bay on the south-west coast of Cuba where on 17 April 1961 about 1 500 Cuban exiles, with American support, made an unsuccessful attempt to invade the country from Guatemala and overthrow the Communist regime of Fidel *Castro.

bay[3] /beɪ/ *n* **1** (**a**) one of a series of compartments in a building, a structure or an area, esp one designed for storing things, parking vehicles, etc: *a* ˈ*parking bay* ○ *Put the equipment in No 3 bay.* (**b**) (esp in compounds) any special compartment or area: *the* ˈ*bomb-bay*, ie the compartment in the fuselage of an aircraft where bombs are carried ○ *the* ˈ*sick-bay*, ie part of a ship, building, school, etc set aside for the care of the sick or the injured. **2** recess in a room or building.

□ ˌ**bay** ˈ**window** window, usu with glass on three sides, projecting from an outside wall. ⇨ illus at HOME.

bay[4] /beɪ/ *n* **1** deep bark, esp of hounds while hunting. **2** (idm) **at** ˈ**bay** (esp of a hunted animal) forced to face its attackers and show defiance because unable to escape. **bring sb/sth to** ˈ**bay** force (a fleeing enemy, a hunted animal, etc) into a position from which escape is impossible. **hold/keep sb at** ˈ**bay** prevent (an enemy, pursuers, etc) from coming near: *I'm trying to keep my creditors at bay.*

▷ **bay** *v* [I] (esp of hounds, etc) bark with a deep note: *the baying cry of a wolf.*

bay[5] /beɪ/ *n, adj* (horse) of a reddish-brown colour: *riding a big bay (mare).*

Bayeux tapestry /baɪˌjɜː ˈtæpəstrɪ/ **the Bayeux tapestry** fine embroidered wall-covering, possibly finished in 1077 and now kept at Bayeux in northern France. It is 48 cm (19 inches) wide and 70 m (230 feet) long, and tells the story of the invasion of England by William the Conqueror in 1066 in a series of scenes like a strip cartoon. ⇨ illus.

Baylis /ˈbeɪlɪs/ Lilian Mary (1874-1937), English theatre manager. She ran the *Old Vic theatre, famous for its Shakespeare productions, and the *Sadler's Wells theatre, the home of the companies that were to become the Royal Ballet and English National Opera.

bayonet /ˈbeɪənɪt/ *n* dagger-like blade that can be fixed to the muzzle of a rifle and used in hand-to-hand fighting.

▷ **bayonet** /ˈbeɪənɪt, *also* ˌbeɪəˈnet/ *v* [Tn] stab (sb/sth) with a bayonet: *bayoneted to death.*

□ ˈ**bayonet fitting** socket, eg for a light bulb, with two L-shaped openings at the sides to receive the pins on the sides of the bulb, etc.

ˈ**bayonet plug** electric plug which is fixed into its socket by pushing and then twisting. ⇨ illus at PLUG.

bayou /ˈbaɪuː/ *n* (in the southern USA) slow-moving marshy part of a river away from the main stream.

Bayreuth /baɪˈrɔɪt/ German town where *Wagner lived and a special theatre for his operas was built in 1876. Bayreuth still holds regular festivals of Wagner's operas.

bay rum /ˌbeɪ ˈrʌm/ type of perfumed dressing for the hair, made by distilling rum and the berries of a West Indian tree.

bazaar /bəˈzɑː(r)/ *n* **1** (in eastern countries) group of shops or stalls or part of a town where these are. **2** (in Britain, USA, etc) (place where there is a) sale of goods to raise money for charitable purposes: *a church bazaar.*

bazooka /bəˈzuːkə/ *n* portable weapon used for launching anti-tank rockets.

BBC /ˌbiː biː ˈsiː/ *abbr* British Broadcasting Corporation: *listen to the BBC* ○ *BBC English*, ie a form of English with a high standard of correctness. Cf IBA, ITV. ⇨ articles at RADIO, TELEVISION.

BBFC /ˌbiː biː ef ˈsiː/ *abbr* British Board of Film Censors.

bbl *abbr* barrel (esp of oil).

BC /ˌbiː ˈsiː/ *abbr* **1** Before Christ: *in (the year) 2000 BC.* Cf AD. **2** British Columbia. **3** British Council (a government-sponsored organization for the promotion of English language and culture in other countries).

BD /ˌbiː ˈdiː/ *abbr* Bachelor of Divinity.

BDS /ˌbiː diː ˈes/ *abbr* Bachelor of Dental Surgery.

BE /ˌbiː ˈiː/ *abbr* Bachelor of Education.

Be *symb* beryllium.

be[1] /bɪ; *strong form* biː/ *v* ⇨ Usage at BE[2]. **1** (used after *there* and before *a/an, no, some,* etc + *n*) (**a**) exist; occur; live: *Is there a God?* ○ *For there to be life there must be air and water.* ○ *There are no easy answers.* ○ *There are many such people.* ○ *Once upon a time there was a princess.* ○ *There have been cows in that field since my grandfather's time.* (**b**) be present; stand: *There's a bus-stop (Cf The bus-stop is) down the road.* ○ *There were no books on the shelf.* ○ *There are some good photographs in this exhibition.* **2** (with an *adv* or a prepositional phrase indicating position in space or time) (**a**) be situated: *The lamp is on the table.* ○ *The stable is a mile away.* ○ *Mary's upstairs.* ○ *John's out in the garden.* ○ *They are on holiday in the Lake District.* (**b**) happen; occur; take place: *The party is after work.* ○ *The election was on Monday.* ○ *The concert will be in the school hall.* ○ *The meetings are on Tuesdays and Thursdays in the main hall.* (**c**) remain: *She has been in her room for hours.* ○ *They're here till Christmas.* (**d**) attend; be present: *Were you at church yesterday?* ○ *I'll be at the party.* **3** (with an *adv* or a prepositional phrase indicating direction, a starting-point, etc) leave; arrive: *I'll be on my way very soon.* ○ *She's from Italy*, ie Her native country is Italy. **4** (usu with an *adv* or a prepositional phrase indicating destination; in the perfect tenses only) visit or call: *I've never been to Spain.* ○ *She had been abroad many times.* ○ *Has the plumber been* (ie called) *yet?* **5** [La, Ln] (indicating a quality or a state): *Life is unfair.* ○ *The world is round.* ○ *He is ten years old.* ○ *I am of average height.* ○ *Be quick!* ○ *She's a great beauty.* ○ *'How are you?' 'I'm quite well, thanks.'* **6** [La, Ln] (in exclamations): *Were* ˈ*they surprised to see us!* ○ *Aren't you a great cook!* ○ *Wasn't that a good film!* **7** [Ln] (indicating the name, profession, pastime, etc of the subject): *Today is Monday.* ○ *You are the man I want.* ○ *'Who is that?' 'It's the postman.'* ○ *Susan is a doctor.* ○ *Peter is a keen footballer in his spare time.* ○ *He wants to be* (ie become) *a fireman when he grows up.* **8** [Ln] (indicating possession, actual or intended): *The money's not yours, it's John's*, ie It belongs to John and not to you. ○ *This parcel is for you.* **9** [Ln] (showing equivalence in value, number, etc) (**a**) cost: *'How much is that dress?' 'It's £50.'* (**b**) amount to; equal: *Twice two is four.* ○ *Three and three is six.* ○ *Four threes are twelve.* (**c**) constitute: *(saying) Two is company; three's a crowd.* ○ *London is not England*, ie Don't think that all of England is like London. (**d**) represent: *Let x be the sum of a and b.* (**e**) mean; signify: *It is nothing to me.* ○ *A thousand pounds is nothing to a rich man.* **10** (idm) **the** ˌ**be-all and** ˈ**end-all (of sth)** (*infml*) the most important part; all that matters: *Her boyfriend is the be-all and end-all of her existence.* **(he, etc has) been and** ˈ**done sth** (*infml*) (expressing protest and surprise): *Someone's been (and gone) and eaten my porridge!* **be one**ˈ**self** act naturally: *Don't act sophisticated — just be yourself.* ˌ**be that as it** ˈ**may** despite that; nevertheless: *I accept that he's old and frail; be that as it may, he's still a good politician.* **it is/was as if.../as though...** it seems/seemed that...: *It's as if he never listens to a word I say.* **...that was** ...as sb used to be called: *Miss Brown that was*, ie before her marriage. **-to-**ˈ**be** (in compounds) future: *his* ˌ*bride-to-*ˈ*be*, ie his future bride ○ ˌ*mothers-to-*ˈ*be*, ie pregnant women. (For other idioms containing **be**, see entries for *ns, adjs,* etc, eg **be the death of sb** ⇨ DEATH.)

be[2] /bɪ; *strong form* biː/ *aux v* ⇨ Usage. **1** (used with a past participle to form the passive): *He was killed in the war.* ○ *Where were they made?* ○ *The thief was caught.* ○ *The house is/was being built.* ○ *You will be severely punished if you do not obey.* **2** (used with present participles to form continuous tenses): *They are/were reading.* ○ *I am studying Chinese.* ○ *I shall be seeing him soon.* ○ *What have you been doing this week?* ○ *I'm always being criticized.* **3** (with *to* + infinitive) (**a**) (expressing duty, necessity, etc): *I am to* (ie I have been told to) *inform you that...* ○ *You are to* (ie must/should) *report to the police.* (**b**) (expressing arrangement, intention or purpose): *They are to be married*, ie will be married. ○ *Each participant was to pay his own expenses.* ○ *The telegram was to say that she'd be late.* (**c**) (expressing possibility): *The book was not to be* (ie could not be) *found.* (**d**) (expressing destiny): *He was never to see his wife again*, ie Although he did not know it at the time, he did not see her again. ○ *The celebrations were not to be*, ie They did not, in fact, take place. (**e**) (only in the form *were*, expressing supposition): *If I were to tell you/Were I to tell you that I killed him, would you believe me?* ○ *If it were to rain, we would have to cancel the match tomorrow.*

NOTE ON USAGE: **Be** is used as a main verb (**be**[1]) and as an auxiliary verb (**be**[2]). The various written and spoken forms are the same for both verbs: **am** (*pres t* with *I*) /əm, m/, *strong form* /æm/; written contraction **I'm** /aɪm/; negative question **aren't I?** /ˈɑːntaɪ; *US* ˈɑːrəntaɪ/. **is** (*pres t* with *he, she, it*) /s, z/, *strong form* /ɪz/; written contractions **it's** /ɪts/, **Jack's** /dʒæks/, **he's** /hiːz, hɪz/, **she's** /ʃiːz, ʃɪz/, **the cow's** /ðə kaʊz/; negative **isn't** /ˈɪznt/. **are** (*pres t* with *you, we, they*) /ə(r)/, *strong form* /ɑː(r)/; written contractions **we're** /wɪə(r)/, **you're** /jʊə(r), jɔː(r)/, **they're** /ðeə(r)/; negative **aren't** /ɑːnt; *US* ˈɑːrənt/. **was** (*pt* with *I, he, she, it*) /wəz/, *strong form* /wɒz; *US* wʌz/; negative **wasn't** /ˈwɒznt; *US* ˈwʌznt/. **were** (*pt* with *you, we, they*) /wə(r)/, *strong form* /wɜː(r)/; negative **weren't** /wɜːnt; *US* ˈwɜːrənt/. **being** (*pres p*) /ˈbiːɪŋ/. **been** (*pp*) /biːn; *US also* bɪn/.

be- *pref* **1** (with *vs* and *adjs* ending in *-ed*) all around; all over: *besmear* ○ *bedeck* ○ *bejewelled.* **2** (with *ns* and *adjs* forming transitive *vs*) make or treat as: *befriend* ○ *belittle.* **3** (with intransitive *vs* forming transitive *vs*): *bemoan* ○ *bewail.*

beach /biːtʃ/ *n* **1** stretch of sand or pebbles along the edge of the sea or a lake; shore between high- and low-water mark: *holiday-makers sunbathing on the beach.* ⇨ illus at COAST. **2** (idm) **not the only pebble on the beach** ⇨ PEBBLE. ⇨ Usage at COAST[1].

▷ **beach** *v* [Tn] bring (esp a boat or ship) on shore from out of the water.

□ **ˈbeach-ball** *n* large lightweight inflated ball for games on the beach.

ˈbeach buggy small motor vehicle used for racing on beaches, waste ground, etc.

ˈbeachcomber /-kəʊmə(r)/ *n* **1** person without a regular job who lives by selling whatever he can find on beaches. **2** long wave rolling in from the sea.

ˈbeach-head *n* strong position on a beach established by an army which has just landed and is preparing to advance and attack. Cf BRIDGEHEAD (BRIDGE[1]).

ˈbeachwear *n* [U] clothes for swimming, sunbathing, playing games, etc on the beach.

beacon /ˈbiːkən/ *n* **1** fire lit on a hilltop as a signal. **2** (a) light fixed on rocks or on the coast to warn or guide ships, or on a mountain, tall building, etc to warn aircraft. (b) flashing light on an airfield for the guidance of pilots. **3** signal station such as a lighthouse. **4** radio station or transmitter whose signal helps ships and aircraft to discover their position. **5** (*Brit*) = BELISHA BEACON.

bead /biːd/ *n* **1** (a) [C] small piece of (usu hard) material with a hole through it, for threading with others on a string, or for sewing onto material: *a string of glass beads.* (b) **beads** [pl] necklace made of beads. **2** [C] drop of liquid: *beads of sweat on his forehead.* **3** (idm) **draw a bead** ⇨ DRAW[2]. **count/say/tell one's ˈbeads** (*dated*) say one's prayers, counting them with the help of a rosary(2).

▷ **beading** *n* [U, C] strip of wood or stone, rounded or with a pattern of beads, used as decorative edging.

beadle /ˈbiːdl/ *n* (*Brit*) **1** officer helping in certain church or college ceremonies. **2** (formerly) parish officer who helped the priest by keeping order in church, giving money to the poor, etc.

beady /ˈbiːdɪ/ *adj* (of eyes) small, round and bright like beads: *Not much escapes our teacher's beady eye*, ie Our teacher sees almost everything.

beagle /ˈbiːgl/ *n* small short-legged dog with a black and white or brown and white coat, used for hunting hares.

▷ **beagling** /ˈbiːglɪŋ/ *n* [U] hunting on foot with beagles.

beak[1] /biːk/ *n* **1** hard horny part of a bird's mouth. ⇨ illus at BIRD. **2** anything shaped like this, esp a hooked nose.

▷ **beaked** /biːkt/ *adj* (usu in compounds) having a beak (of the specified type): *long-beaked.*

beak[2] /biːk/ *n* (*Brit sl*) **1** magistrate: *brought up before the beak.* **2** schoolmaster.

beaker /ˈbiːkə(r)/ *n* **1** open glass container with a lip for pouring, used in chemistry laboratories. **2** tall narrow cup for drinking, often without a handle: *a beaker of coffee from the drinks machine.*

□ **ˈBeaker Folk** prehistoric people who came to Britain from Europe in the early Bronze Age. They used a distinctive type of wide-mouthed drinking cup; many such cups have been found in their burial places.

beam /biːm/ *n* **1** long piece of wood, metal, concrete, etc, usu horizontal and supported at both ends, that carries the weight of part of a building or some other structure. **2** (a) any of the horizontal cross-timbers of a ship, joining the sides and supporting the deck. (b) breadth of a ship at its widest part. **3** horizontal bar of weighing-scales from which the pans hang. ⇨ illus at SCALE. **4** ray or stream of light or other radiation (eg from a lamp or a lighthouse, the sun or the moon): *the beam of the torch, searchlight, etc* ○ *The car's headlights were on full beam*, ie not dipped to avoid dazzling other drivers. **5** bright and happy look or smile: *a beam of pleasure.* **6** series of radio or radar signals used to guide ships or aircraft. **7** (idm) **broad in the beam** ⇨ BROAD[1]. **off (the) ˈbeam** (*infml*) mistaken; wrong: *Your calculation is way off beam.* **on the ˈbeam** (*infml*) on the right track; correct.

▷ **beam** *v* **1** (a) [I] (of the sun, etc) send out light and warmth. (b) [I, Ipr] ~ (**at sb**) smile happily and cheerfully: *The winner beamed with satisfaction.* **2** [Tn, Tn·pr] ~ **sth (to...) (from...)** broadcast (a message, television programme, etc): *The World Cup Final was beamed live from Britain to Japan.*

□ **beam-ˈends** *n* [pl] (idm) **on her beam-ends** (of a ship) lying over to one side; almost capsizing. **on one's beam-ends** (of a person) with very little money left; almost destitute.

ˈbeam hole hole in a nuclear reactor that allows beams of neutrons or other particles to escape during experiments.

bean /biːn/ *n* **1** (a) smooth, usu kidney-shaped, seed, used as a vegetable: *ˌbroad ˈbeans* ○ *ˈkidney beans* ○ *ˈsoya beans* ○ *ˌharicot ˈbeans.* (b) any of the various plants that bear these seeds in long pods. (c) pod containing such seeds, which is itself eaten as a vegetable: *ˌrunner ˈbeans.* **2** similar seed of other plants, eg cocoa or coffee. **3** (idm) **full of beans/life** ⇨ FULL. **a hill of beans** ⇨ HILL. **know how many beans make five** ⇨ KNOW. **not have a ˈbean** (*infml*) have no money. **spill the beans** ⇨ SPILL[1].

□ **ˈbean curd** (also **tofu**) thick jelly or paste made from mashed soya beans, eaten esp in eastern countries.

ˈbeanfeast (also **beano**) *n* (*dated Brit infml*) merry celebration or party.

ˈbeanpole *n* (*infml*) tall thin person.

ˈbean sprouts young sprouts of bean seeds often eaten uncooked, esp in Chinese dishes.

beanie /ˈbiːnɪ/ *n* (*esp US*) small close-fitting cap worn on the back of the head.

Beano /ˈbiːnəʊ/ popular British weekly comic for children, founded in 1938.

beano /ˈbiːnəʊ/ *n* (*pl* ~**s**) (*dated Brit infml*) = BEANFEAST (BEAN).

bear

bear[1] /beə(r)/ *n* **1** large heavy animal with thick fur: *polar bear* ○ *grizzly bear.* ⇨ illus. **2** rough or ill-mannered person. **3** (*finance*) person who sells stocks, shares, etc, hoping to buy them back at lower prices: [attrib] *a ˈbear market*, ie a situation in which share prices are falling rapidly. Cf BULL[1] 3. **4** (idm) **a bear garden** place or meeting at which there is much rough or noisy behaviour. **like a ˌbear with a sore ˈhead** (*infml*) irritable; bad-tempered: *When he's just woken up he's like a bear with a sore head.*

▷ **bearish** /ˈbeərɪʃ/ *adj* **1** rough or bad-tempered. **2** (*finance*) characterized by or causing a fall in the price of stocks: *a bearish market.* Cf BULLISH (BULL[1]).

□ **ˈbear-hug** *n* powerful tight embrace.

ˈbearskin *n* **1** fur of a bear: [attrib] *a bearskin rug.* **2** tall hat of black fur worn by British guardsmen.

bear[2] /beə(r)/ *v* (*pt* **bore** /bɔː(r)/, *pp* **borne** /bɔːn/) **1** [Tn] show (sth); carry visibly; display: *The document bore his signature.* ○ *The ring bears an inscription.* ○ *The coach bears the royal coat of arms.* ○ *I saw a tombstone bearing the date 1602.* ○ *He was badly wounded in the war and still bears the scars.* ○ *She bears little resemblance to* (ie is not much like) *her mother.* ○ *The title of the essay bore little relation to the contents*, ie was not much connected with them. **2** [Tn] be known by (sth); have: *a family that bore an ancient and honoured name* ○ *A married woman usually bears her husband's surname.* **3** [Tn, Tn·pr, Tn·p] (*dated or fml*) carry (sb/sth), esp while moving: *bear a heavy load* ○ *three kings bearing gifts* ○ *They bore his body to the tomb.* ○ *The canoe was borne along by the current.* ⇨ Usage at CARRY. **4** [Tn] (a) support (sb/sth); sustain: *The ice is too thin to bear your weight.* (b) take (responsibility, etc) on oneself; shoulder: *Do the bride's parents have to bear the cost of the wedding?* ○ *The President has to bear the blame.* ○ *He's a carefree fellow who bears his responsibilities lightly.* **5** (a) [Tn, Tt, Tg, Tsg] (more informal, with *can/could*, in negative sentences or questions) endure; tolerate; stand: *The pain was almost more than he could bear.* ○ *She bore her sorrow without complaint.* ○ *I can't bear (having) cats in the house.* ○ *How can you bear to eat that stuff?* ○ *He can't bear to be laughed at/bear being laughed at.* (b) [Tn, Tg] (in negative sentences, esp with the direct objects shown) be fit for (sth); allow: *Modern paintings don't bear comparison with those of the old masters*, ie because they are greatly inferior. ○ *The plan won't bear close inspection*, ie It will be found to be unsatisfactory when carefully examined. ○ *Her joke doesn't bear repeating*, ie because it is not funny or may offend. ○ *His sufferings don't bear thinking about*, ie because they are or were so terrible. **6** [Tn, Tn·pr, Dn·n] ~ **sth (against/towards sb)** keep (feelings, etc) in the mind (used esp as in the expressions shown): *bear a grudge against sb/bear sb a grudge* ○ *He bears no resentment towards them.* ○ *She bore him no ill will.* **7** [Tn, Tn·pr] ~ **oneself well, etc** move, behave or conduct oneself in a specified way: *He bears himself* (ie stands, walks, etc) *like a soldier.* ○ *He bore himself with dignity at a difficult time.* **8** [Tn, Dn·n] (*fml*) give birth to (sb): *bear a child* ○ *She has borne him six sons.* ⇨ Usage. **9** [Tn] produce (sth); yield: *trees bearing pink blossom* ○ *land which bears no crops* ○ (*fig*) *His efforts bore no result*, ie were unsuccessful. **10** [Ipr] ~ (**to the**) **north, left, etc** go or turn in the specified direction: *The road bears (to the) west.* ○ *When you get to the fork in the road, bear (to the) right.* **11** (idm) **bear ˈarms** (*arch*) serve as a soldier; fight. **bear the brunt of sth** receive the main force, shock or impact of sth: *bear the full brunt of the attack* ○ *His secretary has to bear the brunt of his temper.* **bear/stand comparison with sb/sth** ⇨ COMPARISON. **bear ˈfruit** have (usu the desired) results: *His efforts finally bore fruit and permission was granted.* **bear hard, heavily, severely, etc on sb** be a burden on sb; oppress sb: *Taxation bears heavily on us all.* **bear in mind (that)...** remember that...: *Stay in the foyer if you wish, but bear in mind (that) the performance begins in two minutes.* **bear/keep sb/sth in mind** ⇨ MIND[1]. **bear/have some/no reference to sth** ⇨ REFERENCE. **bear witness (to sth)** provide evidence of the truth (of sth); speak in support (of sth): *He/His evidence bore witness to my testimony.* ○ (*fig*) *The new housing bears witness to the energy of the Council.* **be borne ˈin on sb** come to be realized by sb: *The terrible truth was borne in* *on him*, ie He became fully aware of it. ○ *It was gradually borne in on us that defeat was inevitable.* **bring pressure to bear on sb** ⇨ PRESSURE. **bring sth to bear (on sb/sth)** apply sth (to sb/sth): *We must bring all our energies to bear upon the task.* ○ *Pressure was brought to bear on us to finish the work on time.* **grin and bear it** ⇨ GRIN. **12** (phr v) **bear sth/sb away/off** (*dated or fml*) seize and carry away: *They bore off several captives.* ○ *He bore away* (ie won) *the first prize.* **bear ˈdown** exert downward pressure, esp with the muscles of the uterus during childbirth. **bear down sb/sth** overcome or defeat sb/sth: *bear down the enemy, all resistance.* **bear down on sb/sth** move quickly and threateningly towards sb/sth: *The angry farmer was bearing down on us.* **ˈbear on sth** relate to sth; affect sth: *These are matters that bear on the welfare of the community.* **bear sb/sth ˈout** support (sb); confirm (sth): *The other witnesses will bear me out/bear out what I say.* **bear ˈup (against/under sth)** be strong enough not to despair; cope; manage: *He's bearing up well against all his misfortunes.* **ˈbear with sb/sth** tolerate sb/sth patiently: *We must bear with her* (ie treat her with sympathy) *during this difficult period.* ○ *If you will bear with me* (ie listen patiently to me) *a little longer….*

NOTE ON USAGE: The verb **bear** (past participle **borne**) in the sense of 'give birth to' is formal: *bear a child* ○ *She's borne him six children.* Less formal is: *She's had six children.* The past participle **borne** is not used in the passive in this sense. There is another past participle **born**, which is used only in the passive voice: *She was born in 1954.* ○ *Ten children are born in this hospital every day.* ○ *He was born to/of wealthy parents.*

bearable /ˈbeərəbl/ *adj* that can be endured; tolerable: *The climate is bearable.*

beard¹ /bɪəd/ *n* **(a)** [U, C] hair growing on the chin and the lower cheeks of a man's face: *a week's growth of beard* ○ *Who's that man with the beard?* ○ *He has (grown) a beard.* ⇨ illus at HEAD. Cf MOUSTACHE 1, WHISKER 1. **(b)** [C] similar hairy growth on an animal or plant: *a goat's beard.*
▷ **bearded** *adj* having a beard.
beardless *adj* having no beard: *a beardless youth*, ie an immature young man.

beard² /bɪəd/ *v* **1** [Tn] defy (sb/sth) openly; oppose bravely. **2** (idm) **beard the lion in his ˈden** visit sb important in order to challenge him, obtain a favour, etc.

Beardsley /ˈbɪədzlɪ/ Aubrey Vincent (1872-98), English artist. He is best known for his illustrations, mostly black and white, which were much influenced by the *Pre-Raphaelites and Japanese prints. His style, using sweeping lines and a strong sense of visual design, was often also frankly erotic and considered shocking by many. Beardsley was for a time editor of the quarterly periodical **The Yellow Book*. ⇨ illus.

bearer /ˈbeərə(r)/ *n* **1** person who brings a letter or message: *I'm the bearer of good news.* **2 (a)** person employed to carry things, eg equipment on an expedition; porter: *A team of African bearers came with us on safari.* **(b)** person who helps to carry a coffin, stretcher, etc. **3** person who has a cheque for payment on demand: *This cheque is payable to the bearer*, ie to the person who presents it at a bank.

bearing /ˈbeərɪŋ/ *n* **1** [sing] **(a)** way of standing, walking, etc; deportment: *a man of soldierly bearing.* **(b)** behaviour: *her dignified bearing throughout the trial.* **2** [U] ~ **on sth** relevance to sth: *What he said had not much bearing on the problem.* **3 bearings** [pl] aspects: *We must consider the question in all its bearings.* **4** [C] direction in degrees as measured from a known position: *take a (compass) bearing on the lighthouse.* **5** [C] device reducing friction in part of a machine where another part turns: *ball-ˈbearings.* **6** [C] heraldic emblem. **7** (idm) **get/take one's ˈbearings** find out where one is by recognizing landmarks, etc. **lose one's bearings**

book-plate designed by Aubrey Beardsley

⇨ LOSE. **past (all) ˈbearing** no longer to be tolerated.

bearish ⇨ BEAR¹.

Béarnaise sauce /ˌbeɪəˌneɪz ˈsɔːs/ *n* rich sauce made with butter, egg yolks, herbs and vinegar, usu served with red meat.

beast /biːst/ *n* **1** (*dated or fml*) animal, esp a large, four-footed one: *all the beasts of the earth* ○ *The lion is called the king of beasts.* **2 (a)** brutal or disgusting person: *When he's drunk he's a beast.* ○ *Drink brings out the beast in him*, ie emphasizes the brutal part of his nature. **(b)** (*infml*) (used playfully or reproachfully) unpleasant person: *Stop tickling me, you beast!* ○ *Don't be such a beast!*
▷ **beastly** *adj* **1** like a beast; brutal. **2** (*infml esp Brit*) unpleasant; nasty: *What beastly weather!* ○ *That's absolutely beastly of him.* — *adv* (*infml esp Brit*) very; extremely: *It's beastly cold outside!*
□ ˌ**beast of ˈburden** animal, such as a donkey, used for carrying heavy loads on its back.

beat¹ /biːt/ *v* (*pt* **beat**, *pp* **beaten** /ˈbiːtn/) **1** [Ipr, Tn, Tn·pr] hit (sb/sth) repeatedly, esp with a stick: *Somebody was beating at the door.* ○ *Who's beating the drum?* ○ *She was beating the carpet/beating the dust out of the carpet*, ie removing dust from the carpet by beating it. **2** [Cn·a] reduce (sb) to a specified state by hitting repeatedly: *They beat the prisoner unconscious.* ⇨ Usage at HIT¹. **3** [Tn, Tn·pr, Tn·p, Cn·a] change the shape of (esp metal) by blows; hammer: *beaten silver* ○ *The gold was beaten (out) into fine strips.* ○ *beat metal flat.* **4** [I, Tn] strike (bushes, undergrowth, etc) to raise game for shooting. **5** [Tn, Tn·pr] make (a path, etc) by pressing branches down and walking over them: *a well-beaten path*, ie one worn hard by much use ○ *The hunters beat a path through the undergrowth.* **6** [Ipr] ~ **against/on sth/sb** (of the rain, sun, wind, etc) strike sth/sb: *Hailstones beat against the window.* ○ *The waves were beating on the shore.* **7** [Tn, Tn·pr, Tn·p] ~ **sth (up)** mix sth vigorously using a fork, whisk, etc: *beat the eggs (up) (to a frothy consistency)* ○ *beat the flour and milk together.* **8 (a)** [I] (of the heart) expand and contract rhythmically: *He's alive — his heart is still beating.* **(b)** [I] give a rhythmical sound; pulsate: *We heard the drums beating.* **(c)** [I, Tn] (cause sth to) move up and down repeatedly; flap: *The bird's wings were beating frantically.* ○ *It was beating its wings.* **9 (a)** [Tn, Tn·pr] ~ **sb (at sth)** defeat sb; win against sb; do better than sb: *Our team was easily beaten.* ○ *He beat me (at chess, squash, etc).* **(b)** [Tn] be better than (sth); defeat: *Nothing beats home cooking.* ○ *You can't beat Italian clothes.* ○ *The Government's main aim is to beat inflation.* ○ *beat the speed record*, ie go faster than anyone before. **(c)** [Tn] (*infml*) be too difficult for (sb); puzzle: *a problem that beats even the experts* ○ *It beats me* (ie I don't know) *how/why he did it.* **10** (idm) ˌ**beat about the ˈbush** talk about sth without coming to the main point: *Stop beating about the bush and tell us who won.* **beat sb at his own game** defeat or do better than sb in an activity which he has chosen or in which he thinks that he is strong. ˌ**beat the ˈbounds** (*Brit*) perform the traditional ceremony of going round the boundaries of a parish and marking them by beating the ground with sticks. **beat one's ˈbreast** show that one knows one has done wrong and is sorry, often with an excessive display of grief, remorse, etc. **beat the ˈclock** finish a task, race, etc before a particular time. **beat/knock the daylights out of sb** ⇨ DAYLIGHTS. **beat the drum (for sb/sth)** speak enthusiastically in support of sb/sth. **beat/knock hell out of sb/sth** ⇨ HELL. **beat sb ˈhollow** beat sb decisively: *Our team was beaten hollow.* **ˈbeat it** (*sl*) go away: *This is private land, so beat it!* **beat the rap** (*US sl*) escape without being punished. **beat a (hasty) reˈtreat** go away or back hurriedly: *The poacher beat a hasty retreat when he saw the police coming.* **beat, etc sense into sb** ⇨ SENSE. **beat ˈtime (to sth)** mark or follow the rhythm (of music) by waving a stick or by tapping one's foot, etc: *He beat time (to the music) with his fingers.* ˌ**can you ˈbeat it!** (expressing surprise or shocked amusement). **if you can't beat them, join them** (*catchphrase*) if a rival group, firm, etc continues to be more successful than one's own, it is better to go over to their side and get any advantages one can by doing so. ˌ**off the** ˌ**beaten ˈtrack** in an isolated place where people rarely go: *They live miles off the beaten track.* **a rod/stick to beat sb with** fact, argument, event, etc that is used in order to blame or punish sb.

11 (phr v) **beat about (for sth)** try to find (esp an excuse).
beat sth down (a) force an entry by hitting (a door, etc) repeatedly: *The thieves had beaten the door down.* **(b)** flatten sth: *The wheat had been beaten down by the rain.* **beat down (on sb/sth)** (of the sun) shine with great heat: *The sun beat down (on the desert sand).* **beat sb/sth down (to sth)** persuade (the seller) to reduce (the price of sth): *He wanted £800 for the car but I beat him down (to £600).* ○ *I beat down the price (to £600).*
beat sb into/to sth bring sb to a specified state by hitting repeatedly: *The children were beaten into submission.* ○ *The dog was beaten to death.*
beat sb/sth off drive sb/sth away by fighting: *The attacker/attack was beaten off.*
beat sth out (a) produce (a rhythm, etc) by drumming: *He beat out a tune on a tin can.* **(b)** extinguish (a fire) by beating: *We beat the flames out.* **(c)** remove sth by striking with a hammer, etc: *beat out the dent in the car's wing.*
beat sb to… arrive at (a place) before sb: *I'll beat you to the top of the hill*, ie I'll race you and get there first. **beat sb to it** achieve, reach or take sth before sb else: *Scott aimed to get to the South Pole first, but Amundsen beat him to it.* ○ *I was about to take the last cake, but he beat me to it.*
beat sb up hit, kick or thrash sb severely: *He was badly beaten up by a gang of thugs.*
▷ **beat** *adj* [pred] tired out; exhausted: *I'm (dead) beat.*
beating *n* **1** hitting repeatedly with a stick, etc, usu as punishment: *give sb/get a good beating.* **2** (*infml*) defeat: *Our team got a sound beating.* **3** (idm) **take a lot of/some ˈbeating** be difficult to surpass: *She will take some beating*, ie It will be difficult to do better than her. ○ *His record will take a lot of beating.*
□ ˌ**beat-ˈup** *adj* (*infml esp US*) worn out; battered:

a ˌbeat-up old ˈcar.

beat[2] /biːt/ *n* **1** stroke (eg on a drum) or regular sequence of strokes; sound of this: *We heard the beat of a drum.* **2** emphasis repeated regularly, marking rhythm in music or poetry; strongly marked rhythm of pop or rock music: *The song has a good beat.* **3** route along which sb goes regularly; area allocated to a policeman, watchman, etc: *a policeman out on the/his beat.* **4** (idm) **out of/off one's ˈbeat** (*infml*) different from what one usually does; unfamiliar. **pound the beat** ⇨ POUND[3].

beater /ˈbiːtə(r)/ *n* **1** (often in compounds) utensil for beating things: *a ˈcarpet-beater* ○ *an ˈegg-beater.* **2** person employed to drive birds and animals out of the undergrowth towards huntsmen with guns.

beat generation /ˈbiːt dʒenəreɪʃn/ group of young people (esp writers and artists) in the 1950s and early 1960s who rejected the social values of their time. They tried to find a different way of life, experimenting with eastern religions and new forms of writing. The movement began in America and included writers like Jack *Kerouac and Allen *Ginsberg.

beatific /bɪəˈtɪfɪk/ *adj* (*fml*) showing or giving great joy and serenity; blissful: *a beatific smile* ○ *the beatific vision,* ie seeing God in heaven, esp for the first time. ▷ **beatifically** /-klɪ/ *adv.*

beatify /bɪˈætɪfaɪ/ *v* (*pt, pp* **-fied**) [Tn] (of the Pope) honour (a dead person) by stating officially that he or she is in heaven.

▷ **beatification** /bɪˌætɪfɪˈkeɪʃn/ *n* **(a)** [C] such an official statement. **(b)** [U] honouring or being honoured in this way.

beatitude /bɪˈætɪtjuːd; *US* -tuːd/ *n* **1** [U] (*fml*) great happiness; blessedness. **2 the Beatitudes** [pl] (in the Bible) series of eight statements by Christ on blessedness, each beginning 'Blessed are ...'.

Beatles /ˈbiːtlz/ **the Beatles** English pop group. Its members were George Harrison, John Lennon, Paul McCartney and Ringo Starr, all born in Liverpool. Their songs (mostly written by Lennon and McCartney) and their films were very popular in the 1960s, and although the group broke up in 1970, they have remained famous as the most gifted popular musicians of their time. John Lennon was murdered in New York in 1980.

beatnik /ˈbiːtnɪk/ *n* (*dated*) (in the 1950s and early 1960s) person behaving and dressing unconventionally as a defiant protest against Western morality and as a means of self-expression. Cf HIPPIE.

Beaton /ˈbiːtn/ Sir Cecil (1904-80), English photographer and dress designer. He is best known for his portraits of famous people and fashion models, as well as for his costumes for films and the theatre.

beau /bəʊ/ *n* (*pl* ~**x** /bəʊz/) **1** (*US*) boy-friend; lover. **2** (*dated*) dandy; fop.

□ **the beau monde** /ˌbəʊ ˈmɔːnd/ fashionable society.

Beaufort scale /ˈbəʊfət/ scale for measuring wind speed ranging from 0 (calm) to 12 (hurricane): *registering 6* (ie a strong breeze) *on the Beaufort scale.*

Beaujolais /ˈbəʊʒəleɪ; *US* ˌbəʊʒəˈleɪ/ *n* (*pl* unchanged) [C, U] (type of) light, usu red, wine from the Beaujolais district of France.

Beaumarchais /ˌbəʊmɑːˈʃeɪ/ Pierre Augustin Caron de (1732-99), French playwright. His most famous comedies, *The Barber of Seville* and *The Marriage of Figaro,* were later made into operas. ⇨ MOZART, ROSSINI.

Beaumont /ˈbəʊmɒnt/ Francis (1584-1616), English playwright. He wrote several plays with John *Fletcher, but *The Knight of the Burning Pestle,* for which he is best known, was probably written by him alone.

Beaune /bəʊn/ *n* [C, U] (type of) red Burgundy wine from the Beaune district of France.

beaut /bjuːt/ *n* (*US and Austral sl*) beautiful person or thing.

▷ **beaut** *adj, interj* (*sl esp Austral*) excellent; fine.

beauteous /ˈbjuːtɪəs/ *adj* (*arch*) beautiful.

beautician /bjuːˈtɪʃn/ *n* person whose job is to give beautifying treatments to the face or body.

beautiful /ˈbjuːtɪfl/ *adj* **1** having beauty; giving pleasure to the senses or the mind: *a beautiful face, baby, flower, view, voice, poem, smell, morning* ○ *beautiful weather, music, chocolate.* **2** very satisfactory: *The organization was beautiful.* ○ *What beautiful timing!*

▷ **beautifully** /-flɪ/ *adv* **1** in a lovely manner: *She sings beautifully.* **2** most satisfactorily: *That will do beautifully.* ○ *The car is running beautifully.*

□ ˌ**beautiful ˈpeople** (*US*) **1** rich and fashionable (esp young) people who are thought to have a very enjoyable way of life. **2** hippies.

NOTE ON USAGE: When describing people, **beautiful** and **pretty** are generally used of women and children, and **handsome** of men. They all relate to the pleasing appearance of the face. **Beautiful** is a serious and approving description, suggesting elegance and perfection. **Pretty** may suggest a delicate and feminine appearance and can be used disapprovingly of men. **Handsome** may be applied to women and suggest dignity and maturity. **Good-looking** and **attractive** are used of both men and women. **Fair** (meaning 'beautiful') is archaic. All these adjectives except **attractive** can be used of animals and all except **good-looking** with inanimate and abstract nouns: *a beautiful/an attractive voice* ○ *a handsome/good-looking horse* ○ *a beautiful/pretty village* ○ *a handsome/an attractive offer.*

beautify /ˈbjuːtɪfaɪ/ *v* (*pt, pp* **-fied**) [Tn] make (sb/sth) beautiful; adorn. Cf PRETTIFY. ▷ **beautification** /ˌbjuːtɪfɪˈkeɪʃn/ *n* [U].

beauty /ˈbjuːtɪ/ *n* **1** [U] combination of qualities that give pleasure to the senses (esp to the eye or ear) or to the mind: *the beauty of the sunset, of her singing, of poetry* ○ *She was a woman of great beauty.* ○ [attrib] *a beauty competition/contest,* ie one in which judges decide on the most beautiful competitor. **2** [C] **(a)** person or thing that is beautiful: *She was a famous beauty in her youth.* ○ *That new car is an absolute beauty.* **(b)** fine specimen; excellent example: *Look at these moths: here's a beauty.* ○ *That last goal was a beauty.* **(c)** pleasing or attractive feature: *I'm always finding new beauties in Shakespeare's poetry.* ○ *The beauty of living in California is that the weather is so good.* ○ *The machine needs very little attention — that's the beauty of it.* **3** (idm) **age before beauty** ⇨ AGE[1]. ˌ**beauty is in the ˌeye of the beˈholder** (*saying*) what one person thinks is beautiful may not seem so to sb else. **beauty is only skin ˈdeep** (*saying*) outward appearance is less important than hidden or inner qualities.

□ ˈ**beauty queen** woman judged to be the most beautiful in a beauty contest.

ˈ**beauty salon** (also ˈ**beauty parlour**) place where customers receive treatment (eg face-massage, hairdressing, manicuring) to increase their beauty.

ˈ**beauty sleep** (*joc*) sleep before midnight, light-heartedly regarded as important for a person's beauty: *Good night, I must get my beauty sleep.*

ˈ**beauty spot 1** place famous for its beautiful scenery. **2** mole or artificial spot on a woman's face, once thought to add to her beauty.

Beauty and the Beast /ˌbjuːtɪ ən ðə ˈbiːst/ traditional story about a young girl who manages to save a monster from a spell by her love. He turns into a handsome prince and they get married. The phrase 'beauty and the beast' is sometimes used to describe partners, one of whom is much more attractive than the other.

Beauvoir /ˈbəʊvwɑː(r)/ Simone de (1908-86), French writer and philosopher. Her most famous book is *The Second Sex,* an important work in the early days of the feminist movement. For many years she was the companion of Jean-Paul *Sartre.

beaux *pl* of BEAU.

beaux arts /bəʊz ˈɑː(r)/ (*French*) = FINE ART (FINE[2]).

beaver /ˈbiːvə(r)/ *n* **1** [C] fur-coated animal with strong teeth that lives both on land and in water and gnaws down trees to build dams: *work like a beaver,* ie very hard. **2** [U] its brown fur: [attrib] *a beaver hat.* ⇨ illus at DRESS. **3 Beaver** [C] member of a junior branch of the Scout Association. ⇨ article at YOUTH. **4** (idm) **an eager beaver** ⇨ EAGER.

▷ **beaver** *v* (phr v) **beaver away (at sth)** (*infml esp Brit*) work hard: *I've been beavering away at this job for hours.*

□ ˈ**beaver-board** *n* [U] lightweight board made from wood-fibre, used as a building material.

Beaverbrook /ˈbiːvəbrʊk/ William Maxwell Aitken, 1st Baron (1879-1964), British newspaper owner and politician (Lord Beaverbrook). Born in Canada, he settled in England and became a Member of Parliament in 1910. He was a Cabinet minister in both World Wars. He owned popular newspapers such as the *Daily Express* and the *Evening Standard,* where he strongly influenced style and editorial policy.

bebop /ˈbiːbɒp/ (also **bop**) *n* [U] type of jazz music with complex rhythms and harmonies. ⇨ article at MUSIC.

becalmed /bɪˈkɑːmd/ *adj* [usu pred] (of a sailing-ship) unable to move because there is no wind.

became *pt* of BECOME.

because /bɪˈkɒz; *US also* -kɔːz/ *conj* for the reason that: *I did it because he told me to.* ○ *Just because I don't complain, people think I'm satisfied.*

□ **because of** *prep* by reason of (sb/sth); on account of: *They are here because of us.* ○ *He walked slowly because of his bad leg.* ○ *Because of his wife('s) being there, I said nothing about it.*

béchamel sauce /ˌbeʃəmel ˈsɔːs/ *n* type of white sauce, thickened with cream.

Bechstein /ˈbekstaɪn/ *n* (*propr*) piano built by the company founded by the German Friedrich Bechstein in 1856: [attrib] *played on a Bechstein grand piano.*

beck[1] /bek/ *n* (*Brit dialect*) mountain stream; brook.

beck[2] /bek/ *n* (idm) **at one's/sb's ˌbeck and ˈcall** always ready to obey one's/sb's orders immediately: *The king has always had servants at his beck and call.* ○ *I'm not at your beck and call, you know.*

Becket /ˈbekɪt/ Saint Thomas (c1118-70), Archbishop of Canterbury. He was a close friend of King *Henry II, who made him chancellor and later archbishop (1162), hoping as a result to be able to control the English Church. Becket did not co-operate and they quarrelled. Acting (as they thought) on Henry's orders, four knights murdered Becket in Canterbury Cathedral, which became a centre of pilgrimage. His story has been made into plays by *Anouilh, *Eliot and *Tennyson.

Beckett /ˈbekɪt/ Samuel Barclay (1906-89), Irish novelist, poet and playwright. He is best known for his plays in the style of the *Theatre of the Absurd, eg *Waiting for Godot* and *Endgame.* Beckett settled in France early in his career and much of his work was first written in French. He was awarded the Nobel prize for literature in 1969. ⇨ article at PERFORMING ARTS.

beckon /ˈbekən/ *v* **1** [I, Ipr, Tn, Dn·t, Dpr·t] ~ **(to) sb (to do sth)** make a gesture to sb with the hand, arm or head, usu to make him come nearer or to follow: *She beckoned (to) me (to follow).* ○ (*fig*) *City life beckons* (ie attracts) *many a country boy.* **2** (phr v) **beckon sb in, on, over, etc** gesture to sb to move in a specified direction: *The policeman beckoned us over.* ○ *A girl standing at the mouth of the cave beckoned him in.* ○ *They beckoned me into the room.*

become /bɪˈkʌm/ *v* (*pt* **became** /bɪˈkeɪm/, *pp* **become**) **1** [La, Ln] **(a)** come to be; grow to be: *They soon became angry.* ○ *He has become accustomed to his new duties.* ○ *That child was to become a great leader.* ○ *They became great friends.* ○ *She became a doctor.* ○ *It has become a rule that we sing during our tea-break.* **(b)** begin to be: *It's becoming dangerous to go out alone at night.* ○ *The* *noise of traffic is becoming a cause for concern.* ○ *Those boys are becoming a nuisance.* ⇨ Usage. **2** [Tn] (*fml*) **(a)** be suitable for (sb); suit: *Her new hat certainly becomes her.* **(b)** be fitting or appropriate for (sb); befit: *Such language* (eg vulgar or insulting words) *does not become a lady like you.* ○ *It ill becomes you to complain.* **3** (idm) **what becomes of sb/sth** what is happening to sb/sth: *What will become of my child if I die?* ○ *I wonder what became of the people who lived next door?* ○ *What became of the dreams of our youth?* ie What we hoped for did not actually happen.

▷ **becoming** *adj* (*fml*) **1** (*approv*) (of dress, etc) well suited to the wearer: *a becoming hat, hair-style, etc* ○ *Your outfit is most becoming.* **2** suitable; appropriate; fitting: *He behaved with a becoming modesty/with a modesty becoming his junior position.* **becomingly** *adv.*

NOTE ON USAGE: When talking about a change in the state, appearance, etc of a person or thing, we often use **become**, **get**, **turn** and **go** followed by an adjective. In general, **become** and **turn** are more formal than **get** and **go. 1** When referring to temporary changes in a person's emotional or physical state or to permanent natural changes, we use **become** or **get** (less formal): *become/get angry, famous, fat, ill, old, etc.* **2 Become** and **get** are also used of changes in the weather and of social developments: *It's becoming/getting cold, dark, cloudy, etc* ○ *Divorce is becoming/getting more common.* **3** When indicating a worsening of someone's physical or mental powers, we use **go:** *go bald, deaf, insane, etc.* It is used similarly of things: *The meat's gone off/bad.* ○ *The radio's gone wrong.* **4 Go** and **turn** are used when people or things change colour: *She went/turned blue with cold.* ○ *The rotten meat went/turned green.*

Becquerel /ˌbekəˈrel/ Antoine-Henri (1852-1908), French physicist. He studied radiation and shared the Nobel prize for physics with the *Curies for the discovery of natural radioactivity in uranium.

becquerel /ˌbekəˈrel; *US* ˈbekərəl/ *n* (*abbr* **bq**) (*physics*) SI unit of radioactivity.

BEd /ˌbiː ˈed/ *abbr* Bachelor of Education: *have/get a BEd* ○ *Lisa Wood BEd.*

bed[1] /bed/ *n* **1 (a)** [C, U] thing to sleep or rest on, esp a piece of furniture with a mattress and coverings: *go to bed* ○ *be in bed* ○ *get out of/into bed* ○ *sit on the bed* ○ *a room with two single beds/a double bed* ○ *The tramp's bed was a park bench.* ○ *Can you give me a bed for the night? I've been on my bed of sickness* (ie ill in bed) *for a week.* ○ [attrib] *The doctor ordered bed rest,* ie that the patient should stay in bed and rest. ⇨ illus at FURNITURE. **(b)** [U] being in bed; use of a bed; sleep or rest: *I've put the children to bed.* ○ *He has a mug of cocoa before bed.* ○ *It's time for bed.* **(c)** [C] mattress: *a feather bed* ○ *a spring bed.* **(d)** [U] (*fig infml*) sexual intercourse: *They think of nothing but bed!* **2** [C] bottom of the sea, a river, a lake, etc: *explore the ocean bed.* **3** layer of clay, rock, etc below the surface soil; stratum: *a bed of clay, limestone, sand, etc.* **4** [C] **(a)** flat base on which sth rests; foundation: *The machine rests on a bed of concrete.* **(b)** layer of rock, stone, etc as a foundation for a road or railway. **5** garden plot; piece of ground for growing flowers, vegetables, etc: *a ˈseed-bed* ○ *ˈflower-beds* ○ *a bed of herbs.* **6** (idm) **as one ˌmakes one's bed, so one must ˈlie on it** (*saying*) one must accept the consequences of one's own actions. **ˌbed and ˈboard** overnight accommodation and meals. **ˌbed and ˈbreakfast** (*abbrs* **B and B**, **b and b**) sleeping accommodation and a meal the next morning, in hotels, etc: *Bed and breakfast costs £15 a night.* **a bed of ˈroses** pleasant carefree living: *Life isn't a bed of roses.* **die in one's bed** ⇨ DIE[2]. **early to bed and early to rise** ⇨ EARLY. **go to bed with sb** (*infml*) have sexual intercourse with sb. **have got out of bed on the wrong side** be bad-tempered for the whole day. **make the ˈbed** arrange the sheets, blankets, etc so that the bed is ready for somebody to sleep in. **reds under the bed** ⇨ RED[2]. **take to one's ˈbed** go to one's bed because of illness and stay there. **wet the/one's bed** ⇨ WET *v.*

□ **ˈbedbug** *n* wingless blood-sucking insect that lives in beds, etc.

ˈbedclothes *n* [pl] sheets, blankets, pillows, etc.

ˈbedfellow *n* **(a)** person with whom one shares a bed. **(b)** (*fig*) associate; companion: *The fortunes of war create strange bedfellows,* ie unexpected alliances.

ˈbed-linen *n* [U] sheets and pillowcases.

ˌbed of ˈnails (a) wooden board with sharp pointed nails sticking through it, on which eg fakirs lie. **(b)** (*fig*) situation that is hard to bear or deal with: *She thought her new job would be easy but it turned out to be a bed of nails.*

ˈbedpan *n* container for use as a lavatory by a person who is ill and in bed.

ˈbedpost *n* each of the upright supports at the corners of a bedstead (esp the old-fashioned type).

ˈbedridden *adj* confined to bed, esp permanently, because of illness or weakness.

ˈbedrock *n* [U] **(a)** solid rock beneath loose soil, sand, etc: *reach/get down to bedrock.* **(b)** (*fig*) basic facts or principles: *the bedrock of one's beliefs* ○ *Let's get down to bedrock,* ie deal with basic matters.

ˈbedroll *n* (*esp US and NZ*) portable bedding that can be rolled into a bundle (as used by campers).

ˈbedroom *n* room for sleeping in.

ˈbedside *n* [usu sing] **1** area beside a bed: [attrib] *a bedside table.* **2** (idm) **ˌbedside ˈmanner** doctor's way of dealing with a patient: *Dr Green has a good bedside manner,* ie He is tactful and pleasant.

ˌbed-ˈsitting-room (also *infml* **ˌbed-ˈsitter, ˈbed-sit**) *n* (*Brit*) room used for both living and sleeping in, usu rented by a person living alone. Cf STUDIO FLAT (STUDIO). ⇨ article at ACCOMMODATION.

ˈbedsore *n* sore on an invalid caused by lying in bed for a long time.

ˈbedspread *n* top cover spread over a bed.

ˈbedstead *n* framework of wood or metal supporting the springs and mattress of a bed.

ˈbedtime *n* [U] time for going to bed: *His bedtime is eight o'clock.* ○ *It's long past your bedtime.* ○ [attrib] *a bedtime story,* ie one read to a child at bedtime.

ˈbed-wetting *n* [U] urinating in bed while asleep.

bed[2] /bed/ *v* **(-dd-) 1** [Tn, Tn·pr] ~ **sth (in sth)** place or fix sth firmly; embed sth: *The bricks are bedded in concrete.* ○ *The bullet bedded itself in* (ie went deeply into) *the wall.* **2** [Tn, Tn·pr] plant (sth): *Bed the roots in the compost.* **3** [Tn, Tn·pr] accommodate (sb); provide with a bed: *The wounded were bedded in the farmhouse.* **4** [Tn] (*infml*) have casual sexual intercourse with (sb): *He's bedded more girls than he can remember.* **5** (phr v) **bed down** settle for the night: *The soldiers bedded down in a barn.* **bed sth down** provide (an animal) with straw, etc to rest on for the night. **bed sth out** transfer (young plants) from a greenhouse, etc to a garden bed: *bed out the seedlings, young cabbages, etc.*

▷ **-bedded** (forming compound *adjs*) having the specified type or number of beds: *a single-/double-/twin-bedded room.*

bedding *n* [U] **1** bedclothes and mattresses. **2** straw, etc for animals to sleep on. **ˈbedding plant** plant suitable for planting in a garden bed.

bedaub /bɪˈdɔːb/ *v* [esp passive: Tn, Tn·pr] ~ **sth/sb (with sth)** smear sth/sb (with sth dirty, sticky, etc): *faces bedaubed with grease-paint.*

bedazzle /bɪˈdæzl/ *v* [Tn] impress or confuse (sb) greatly, esp by splendour, ability, etc: *We were totally bedazzled by her performance.*

Bede /biːd/ the Venerable (c 673-735), English monk and historian. At his monastery in Jarrow he wrote many books, the most important of which, *The Ecclesiastical History of the English People,* was the first serious work of English history.

bedeck /bɪˈdek/ *v* [esp passive: Tn, Tn·pr] ~ **sth/sb (with sth)** adorn or decorate sth/sb: *streets bedecked with flags.*

bedevil /bɪˈdevl/ *v* (**-ll-**; *US* **-l-**) [Tn esp passive] trouble (sb/sth) greatly; torment; afflict: *an industry bedevilled with strikes* ○ *a family bedevilled by misfortune* ○ *Bad weather bedevilled our plans.*

Bedlam /ˈbedləm/ popular name for the Hospital of Saint Mary of Bethlehem in London (founded in 1247). It was originally a monastery, but later became a place for the mentally ill, then called 'lunatics'. People used to come to see the patients and be entertained by their disorganized living conditions.

bedlam /ˈbedləm/ *n* [U] scene of noisy confusion; uproar: *What's happening in that room? It's (like) bedlam in there.*

bedouin (also **Bedouin**) /ˈbedʊɪn/ *n* (*pl* unchanged) member of a nomadic Arab people living in tents in the desert: [attrib] *a bedouin tribe.*

bedraggled /bɪˈdrægld/ (also **draggled**) *adj* made wet or dirty by rain, mud, etc; untidy: *bedraggled appearance, clothes, hair* ○ *The tents looked very bedraggled after the storm.*

bee[1] /biː/ *n* **1** four-winged insect with a sting, that lives in a colony and collects nectar and pollen from flowers to produce wax and honey. Bees are often thought of as busy and hard-working: *lots of busy bees buzzing around.* ⇨ illus. **2** (idm) **the ˌbee's ˈknees** (*infml*) thing that is outstandingly good: *She thinks she's the bee's knees,* ie has a very high opinion of herself. **the birds and the bees** ⇨ BIRD. **busy as a bee** ⇨ BUSY. **have a ˈbee in one's bonnet (about sth)** (*infml*) have a particular idea which occupies one's thoughts continually: *Our teacher has a bee in his bonnet about punctuation.*

□ **ˈbeehive** *n* container made for bees to live in.

ˈbee-keeper person who keeps honey-bees.

ˈbee-keeping *n* [U].

bee[2] /biː/ *n* (*US*) meeting in a group, esp of neighbours and friends, for work or pleasure: *a ˈsewing bee* ○ *a ˈspelling bee.*

Beeb /biːb/ *n* **the Beeb** [sing] (*infml*) the British Broadcasting Corporation (BBC).

beech /biːtʃ/ *n* **1** (also **ˈbeech tree**) **(a)** type of tree with smooth bark, shiny leaves and small triangular nuts. ⇨ illus at TREE. **(b)** any of several similar (usu evergreen) trees that grow in the southern hemisphere. **2** [U] wood of any of these trees.

Beecham /ˈbiːtʃəm/ Sir Thomas (1879-1961), English conductor. A noted wit, he founded two of the great London orchestras, the London Philharmonic and the Royal Philharmonic, and helped to make English music of his time more popular, esp that of his friend *Delius.

Beeching /ˈbiːtʃɪŋ/ Dr Reginald (1913-), British industrialist and chairman of the British Railways Board. He is remembered as the man who drastically reduced the railway network in Britain, closing uneconomical services and many branch lines. ⇨ article at RAILWAY.

beef /biːf/ *n* **1 (a)** [U] flesh of an ox, a bull or a cow, used as meat: *roast beef and Yorkshire pudding,* ie the typical British Sunday lunch at one time; ⇨ article at FOOD: [attrib] *beef cattle,* ie those bred and reared for their meat. **(b)** [C] (*pl* **beeves** /biːvz/) ox, etc bred for meat. **2** [U] (*infml*) muscular strength: *He's got plenty of beef.* **3** [C] (*pl* **beefs**) (*sl*) grumble; complaint.

▷ **beef** *v* (*sl*) **1** [I, Ipr] ~ **(about sth/sb)** grumble; complain: *What are you beefing about now?* **2** (phr v) **beef sth up** (*infml esp US*) add force or weight to sth: *The new evidence beefed up their case.*

beefy *adj* (**-ier, -iest**) (*infml*) having a strong muscular body: *He's big and beefy.* **beefiness** *n* [U].

□ **beefburger** /ˈbi:fbɜ:gə(r)/ *n* hamburger.
ˈ**beefsteak** *n* thick piece of beef for grilling, etc.
beef ˈ**tea** drink, usu for people who are ill, made by boiling beef in water.

beefcake /ˈbi:fkeɪk/ *n* [U] (*sl esp US*) pictures of strong muscular men, esp as used in advertisements or sex magazines. Cf CHEESECAKE.

beefeater /ˈbi:fi:tə(r)/ *n* (*Brit*) guard at the Tower of London, who wears a uniform of the Tudor period; Yeoman of the Guard.

bee-line /ˈbi:laɪn/ *n* (idm) **make a** ˈ**bee-line for sth/sb** (*infml*) go directly towards sth/sb: *As soon as he arrived at the party he made a bee-line for the bar.*

Beelzebub /bi:ˈelzɪbʌb/ name for the Devil or an evil spirit.

been *pp* of BE.

NOTE ON USAGE: **Been** is used as the past participle of both 'be' and 'go': *I've never been seriously ill* (be). ○ *I've never been to London* (go). **Gone** is also a past participle of 'go'. *They've been to the cinema* means that they went and have returned. *They've gone to the cinema* means that they went and are not back yet.

beep /bi:p/ *n* short high-pitched sound, as made by a car horn or by electronic equipment.
▷ **beep** *v* [I] make this sound: *The computer beeps regularly.*

beer /bɪə(r)/ *n* **1 (a)** [U] alcoholic drink made from malt and flavoured with hops, etc: *a barrel, bottle, glass of beer* ○ [attrib] *a* ˈ*beer glass.* ○ *a* ˈ*beer belly*, ie a person's stomach that is very fat as a result of drinking a lot of beer. ⇨ article at DRINK. **(b)** [C] type of beer: *beers brewed in Germany.* **(c)** [C] glass of beer: *Two beers, please.* **2** [U, C] (esp in compounds) other fermented drink made from roots, etc: ˌ*ginger-*ˈ*beer.* **3** (idm) ˌ**beer and** ˈ**skittles** pleasure; amusement: *Marriage isn't all beer and skittles*, ie isn't always free of trouble. **small beer** ⇨ SMALL.
▷ **beery** /ˈbɪərɪ/ *adj* like or smelling of beer: *a beery taste, smell* ○ *beery men.*
□ ˈ**beer garden** (*Brit*) outdoor (usu grass-covered) part of a pub where people can sit and drink or eat when the weather is fine.
ˈ**beer-mat** *n* small, usu cardboard, table-mat for a beer glass.

Beerbohm /ˈbɪəbəʊm/ Sir Henry Maximilian ('Max') (1872-1956), English writer and critic. He is best remembered for his novel *Zuleika Dobson*, set in the Oxford of the 1890s. He also wrote witty theatre reviews and drew satirical caricatures.

beeswax /ˈbi:zwæks/ *n* [U] yellowish wax made by bees for building honeycombs, also used for making wood polish.

beet /bi:t/ *n* [U, C] **1** type of plant with a fleshy root which is used as a vegetable or for making sugar. **2** (*US*) = BEETROOT.

Beethoven /ˈbeɪthəʊvən/ Ludvig van (1770-1827), German composer. His music represents for many the supreme example of the late classical period and the beginning of romanticism. In works like the third symphony and the *Emperor* piano concerto, he gave new life to the traditional forms. He became very deaf from 1798 onwards, yet in his later years wrote some of his finest works, including the late piano sonatas and string quartets.

beetle[1] /ˈbi:tl/ *n* **1** any of several types of insect, often large and black, with hard wing-cases. **2** (also **Beetle**) (*infml*) popular name for the original Volkswagen small saloon car, with a rounded design.
▷ **beetle** *v* (phr v) **beetle along, about, away, off, etc** (*infml*) move along, etc quickly, either on foot or in a car; hurry: *The kids beetled off home.*

beetle[2] /ˈbi:tl/ *n* tool like a hammer, with a heavy head for beating, crushing, etc.

beetling /ˈbi:tlɪŋ/ *adj* [attrib] overhanging; jutting out: *beetling cliffs.*

Beeton /ˈbi:tn/ Mrs Isabella Mary (1836-65), English author of a classic book on cooking and running a household, which gives much information about middle-class home life in the 19th century.

beetroot /ˈbi:tru:t/ (*US* **beet**) *n* **1** [U, C] dark red fleshy root of the beet plant, eaten as a vegetable when cooked. **2** (idm) **red as a beetroot** ⇨ RED[1].

beeves *pl* of BEEF 1b.

BEF *abbr* British Expeditionary Force.

befall /bɪˈfɔ:l/ *v* (*pt* **befell** /bɪˈfel/, *pp* **befallen** /bɪˈfɔ:lən/) [I, Tn] (used only in the 3rd person) (*arch*) happen to (sb): *We shall never leave you, whatever befalls.* ○ *A great misfortune befell him.*

befit /bɪˈfɪt/ *v* (**-tt-**) [Tn] (used only in the 3rd person) (*fml*) be right and suitable for (sb); be appropriate for: *You should dress in a way that befits a woman of your position.* ○ *It ill befits a priest to act uncharitably.*
▷ **befitting** *adj* appropriate: *act with befitting modesty.* **befittingly** *adv.*

befog /bɪˈfɒg/ *v* (**-gg-**) [Tn] confuse (sb/sth); make unclear or obscure: *Old age had befogged his mind.*

before[1] /bɪˈfɔ:(r)/ *adv* at an earlier time; in the past; already: *You should have told me so before.* ○ *It had been fine the day/week before*, ie the previous day/week. ○ *That had happened long before*, ie a long time earlier. ○ *I've seen that film before.* ⇨ Usage at BEFORE[2]. Cf AFTER[1], AFTERWARDS.

before[2] /bɪˈfɔ:(r)/ *prep* **1** earlier than (sb/sth): *before lunch* ○ *the day before yesterday* ○ *two days before Christmas* ○ *The year before last he won a gold medal, and the year before that he won the silver.* ○ *She's lived there since before the war.* ○ *He arrived before me.* ○ *He taught English as his father had before him.* ○ *Something ought to have been done before now.* ○ *We'll know before long*, ie soon. ○ *Turn left just before* (ie before you reach) *the cinema.* Cf AFTER[2] 1. **2 (a)** (with reference to position) in front of (sb/sth): *We knelt before the throne.* ○ (*fig*) *The task before us is not an easy one.* Cf BEHIND[2] 1. **(b)** (with reference to order or arrangement) in front of (sb/sth); ahead of: *B comes before C in the alphabet.* ○ *Your name comes before mine on the list.* ○ *ladies before gentlemen* ○ *He puts his work before everything*, ie regards it as more important than anything else. Cf AFTER[2] 3. **3** in the presence of (sb): *He was brought before the judge.* ○ *She said it before witnesses.* ○ *He made a statement before the House of Commons.* **4** (*fml*) rather than (sth); in preference to: *death before dishonour.* **5** (*fml*) under pressure from (sb/sth): *Our troops recoiled before the attack.* ○ *They retreated before the enemy.* ○ *The ship sailed before the wind*, ie with the wind blowing from behind.

NOTE ON USAGE: **1 In front of** and **behind** are prepositions and opposite in meaning. They indicate the relative position of people or things: *Johnny is in front of me in the photo.* ○ *The garage is behind the house.* ○ *The dog ran in front of the bus.* ○ *The mouse ran behind the cupboard.* **2 In front** and **behind** are also adverbs: *I'd like to sit in front.* ○ *The taxi followed on behind.* **3 Before** and **after** relate to time and can be **(a)** adverbs: *the day after/before* ○ *I had met him before.* ○ *I'll see you after.* (Here **afterwards** is more common.) **(b)** prepositions: *the day after/before my birthday* ○ *I'll see you after the meeting.* **(c)** conjunctions: *We had dinner after/before they arrived.* **4 Before** and **after** can suggest place, especially when this is closely associated with time or order in a sequence. *I was before/after you in the queue.* ○ *C comes before E in the alphabet.*

before[3] /bɪˈfɔ:(r)/ *conj* **1** earlier than the time when: *Do it before you forget.* ○ *It may be many years before we meet again.* ○ *Before the week was out* (ie had ended), *they were dead.* ○ *It will be a long time before we finish this dictionary.* Cf AFTER[3]. **2** rather than: *I'd shoot myself before I apologized to him!*

beforehand /bɪˈfɔ:hænd/ *adv* **1** in advance; in readiness; earlier: *I had made preparations beforehand.* ○ *He warned me beforehand what to expect.* ○ *We were aware of the problem beforehand.* **2** ~ (**with sth**) early or too early: *She is always beforehand with the rent*, ie is ready to pay it before it is due. Cf BEHINDHAND.

befriend /bɪˈfrend/ *v* [Tn] act as a friend to (sb); be kind to (esp sb needing help): *They befriended the young girl, providing her with food and shelter.* ○ *We were befriended by a stray dog.*

befuddled /bɪˈfʌdld/ *adj* made stupid; confused: *his befuddled mind* ○ *be befuddled by drink, old age.*

beg /beg/ *v* (**-gg-**) **1** [I, Ipr, Tn, Tn·pr] ~ (**from sb**); ~ (**for**) **sth** (**from/of sb**) ask for (money, food, clothes, etc) as a gift or as charity; make a living in this way: *There are hundreds begging in the streets.* ○ *a begging letter*, ie one that asks for help, esp money ○ *He was so poor he had to beg (for) money from passers-by.* **2** [Ipr, Tn, Tn·pr, Tf, Tt, Cn·t] ~ **sth** (**of sb**)/~ (**sb**) **for sth** ask earnestly or humbly (for sth): *Set him free, I beg (of) you!* ○ *May I beg a favour (of you)?* ○ *He begged mercy (of the king).* ○ *He begged (her) for forgiveness.* ○ *The boy begged that he might be allowed/begged to be allowed to come with us.* ○ *I beg (of) you not to take any risks.* ⇨ Usage at ASK. **3** [I, Ipr] ~ (**for sth**) (of a dog) stand on the hind legs with the front paws raised expectantly: *teach one's dog to beg (for its food).* **4** (idm) **beg leave to do sth** (*fml*) ask for permission to do sth: *I beg leave to address the Council.* **beg sb's** ˈ**pardon** apologize to sb for sth one had done or said, or intends to do or say, that is inconvenient for others or is considered rude in polite society. **beg the** ˈ**question** not deal properly with the matter being discussed by assuming that a question needing an answer has been answered: *Your proposal begs the question whether a change is needed at all.* **go** ˈ**begging** (of things) be unwanted: *If that sandwich is going begging, I'll have it.* **I beg to differ** (used to express disagreement with sb): *'He's clearly the best candidate.' 'I beg to differ.'* **I beg your pardon (a)** I am sorry; please excuse me: *'You've taken my seat.' 'Oh I beg your pardon!'* **(b)** please repeat that: *I beg your pardon — I didn't hear what you said.* **(c)** (expressing anger) I must object; I am offended: *I beg your pardon but the woman you're insulting happens to be my wife.* **5** (phr v) **beg off** ask to be excused from doing sth: *He promised to attend but then begged off.* **beg sb off** ask that sb be excused or released, esp from a punishment.

began *pt* of BEGIN.

beget /bɪˈget/ *v* (**-tt-**; *pt* **begot** /bɪˈgɒt/ or, in archaic use, **begat** /bɪˈgæt/, *pp* **begotten** /bɪˈgɒtn/) [Tn] **1** (*arch*) be the father of (sb): *Abraham begat Isaac.* **2** (*fml or dated*) cause (sth); result in: *War begets misery and ruin.*

beggar /ˈbegə(r)/ *n* **1** person who lives by begging; very poor person. **2** (*infml*) person; fellow: *You lucky beggar!* ○ *The cheeky beggar!* **3** (idm) ˌ**beggars can't be** ˈ**choosers** (*infml saying*) when you have no choice, you must be satisfied with what is available: *I would have preferred a bed, but beggars can't be choosers so I slept on the sofa.*
▷ **beggar** *v* **1** [Tn] make (sb/sth) poor; impoverish; ruin: *a nation beggared by crippling taxes.* **2** (idm) **beggar de**ˈ**scription** be too extraordinary to describe adequately: *a sunset which beggared description* ○ *His conduct is so bad it beggars (all) description.*
beggarly *adj* **1** very poor. **2** mean; ungenerous: *a beggarly wage.*
beggary *n* [U] extreme poverty: *be reduced to beggary.*
□ ˌ**beggar-my-**ˈ**neighbour** *n* [U] card-game in which each player tries to win the cards of the other players: [attrib]. (*fig*) *a beggar-my-neighbour attitude*, ie helping oneself at the expense of other people.

begin /bɪˈgɪn/ *v* (**-nn-**; *pt* **began** /bɪˈgæn/, *pp* **begun** /bɪˈgʌn/) **1 (a)** [Tn] set (sth) in motion; start: *begin work, a meeting* ○ *The building hasn't even been begun.* ○ *I began school* (ie attended it for the first time) *when I was five.* ○ *He has begun* (ie started reading or writing) *a new book.* **(b)** [I] be set in motion; start: *When does the concert begin?* ○ *The meeting will begin at nine.* ○ *Building began last year.* **2 (a)** [Tt] (used to indicate states of mind, or mental activities, which are starting): *She began to feel dizzy.* ○ *I'm beginning to understand.* ○ *I was* *beginning to think you'd never come.* (**b**) [Tt, Tg] (used to indicate a process that is beginning, the subject being a thing, not a person): *The paper was beginning to peel off the walls.* ○ *The barometer began to fall.* ○ *The water is beginning to boil.* ⇨ Usage. **3** [I, Ipr] be the first to do sth or take the first step in doing sth: *Shall I begin* (ie take the first step or be the first to speak)*?* ○ *Let's begin at* (ie start from) *page 9.* ○ *She's begun on* (ie started writing or reading) *a new novel.* ○ *I have to begin with an apology.* **4** [I, Ipr] have its starting-point or first element; have its nearest boundary: *Where does Asia begin and Europe end?* ○ *The new fare will be £1, beginning (from) next month.* ○ *The English alphabet begins with 'A' and ends with 'Z'.* **5** [Tt] (*infml*) (usu in negative sentences) make an attempt to do sth; show some likelihood of doing sth: *The authorities couldn't even begin to assess the damage,* ie because it was so great. ○ *I can't begin to thank you,* ie I don't know what to say to thank you properly. ○ *He didn't even begin to understand.* ⇨ Usage. **6** (idm) **charity begins at home** ⇨ CHARITY. **to begin with** (**a**) in the first place; firstly: *I'm not going. To begin with I haven't a ticket, and secondly I don't like the play.* (**b**) at first: *To begin with he had no money, but later he became quite rich.* ⇨ Usage at HOPEFUL.

▷ **beginner** *n* **1** person who is just beginning to learn or do sth. **2** (idm) **beginner's ˈluck** good luck or accidental success at the start of learning to do sth.

beginning *n* **1** (**a**) first part: *I missed the beginning of the film.* ○ *You've made a good beginning.* (**b**) starting-point: *Recite the poem (right) from the (very) beginning.* ○ *I've read the book from beginning to end.* **2** (often *pl*) source; origin: *Did democracy have its beginnings in Athens?* ○ *Many big businesses start from small beginnings.* **3** (idm) **the ˌbeginning of the ˈend** first clear sign of the final (and usu unfavourable) outcome: *Defeat in this important battle was the beginning of the end for us.*

NOTE ON USAGE: **1** Very often **begin** and **start** can be used in the same way, though **start** is more common in informal speech: *What time do you begin/start work in the morning?* ○ *The concert begins/starts at 7.30 pm.* **2** After continuous tenses of **begin** and **start** we do not normally use the *-ing* form of a verb: *He began/started crying/to cry* but *It's starting/beginning to rain* (NOT *raining*). **3** In some senses only **start** can be used: *If we want to get there tonight, we should start* (ie set off) *now.* ○ *The car won't start/I can't start the car.*

begone /bɪˈɡɒn; *US* -ˈɡɔːn/ *interj* (*arch*) go away immediately.

begonia /bɪˈɡəʊnɪə/ *n* garden plant with brightly coloured leaves and flowers.

begorra /bɪˈɡɒrə/ *interj* (*Irish*) by God!

begot, begotten *pt, pp* of BEGET.

begrudge /bɪˈɡrʌdʒ/ *v* **1** [Tn, Tg, Tsg] resent or be dissatisfied with (sth): *I begrudge every penny I pay in tax.* **2** [Dn·n] envy (sb) the possession of (sth): *Nobody will begrudge you your success.* ▷ **begrudgingly** *adv.*

beguile /bɪˈɡaɪl/ (*dated or fml*) **1** (**a**) [Tn] charm (sb): *The travellers were beguiled by the beauty of the landscape.* (**b**) [Tn, Tn·pr] ~ **sb** (**with sth**) win the attention or interest of sb; amuse sb: *He beguiled us with many a tale of adventure.* (**c**) [Tn, Tn·pr] ~ **sth** (**with/by sth**) cause (time, etc) to pass pleasantly: *Our journey was beguiled with spirited talk.* **2** [Tn, Tn·pr] ~ **sb** (**into doing sth**) deceive sb: *They were beguiled into giving him large sums of money.* ▷ **beguilement** *n* [U]. **beguiling** *adj.* **beguilingly** *adv.*

beguine /bɪˈɡiːn/ *n* (**a**) West Indian dance. (**b**) its music or rhythm.

begum /ˈbeɪɡəm/ *n* (**a**) (in the Indian subcontinent) title of a married Muslim woman. (**b**) Muslim woman of high rank.

begun *pp* of BEGIN.

behalf /bɪˈhɑːf; *US* -ˈhæf/ *n* (idm) **on behalf of sb/on sb's behalf**; *US* **in behalf of sb/in sb's behalf** as the representative of or spokesman for sb; in the interest of sb: *On behalf of my colleagues and myself I thank you.* ○ *Ken is not present, so I shall accept the prize on his behalf.* ○ *The legal guardian must act on behalf of the child.* ○ *Don't be uneasy on my behalf,* ie about me.

behave /bɪˈheɪv/ *v* **1** [I, Ipr] ~ **well, badly, etc** (**towards sb**) act or conduct oneself in the specified way: *She behaves (towards me) more like a friend than a mother.* ○ *He has behaved shamefully towards his wife.* **2** [I, Tn] ~ (**oneself**) show good manners; conduct oneself well: *Children, please behave (yourselves)!* **3** [I] (of machines, etc) work or function well (or in another specified way): *How's your new car behaving?*

▷ **-behaved** (forming compound *adjs*) behaving in a specified way: *well-/ill-/badly-behaved children.*

behaviour (*US* **behavior**) /bɪˈheɪvjə(r)/ *n* **1** [U] way of treating others; manners: *She was ashamed of her children's (bad) behaviour.* ○ *Their behaviour towards me shows that they do not like me.* **2** [U] way of acting or functioning: *study the behaviour of infants, apes, bees.* **3** (idm) **be on one's best behaviour** ⇨ BEST[1].

▷ **behavioural** (*US* **-oral**) /-jərəl/ *adj* of behaviour. **behavioural ˈscience** study of human behaviour.

behaviourism (*US* **-orism**) /-jərɪzəm/ *n* [U] (*psychology*) doctrine that all human actions could, if full knowledge were available, be explained by stimulus and response. Such ideas were first set out in America by J B Watson, and are still controversial today. **behaviourist** (*US* **-orist**) /-jərɪst/ *n* believer in this doctrine.

□ **beˈhaviour therapy** way of treating neurotic disorders by using educational methods rather than psychoanalysis.

behead /bɪˈhed/ *v* [Tn] cut off the head of (sb), esp as a punishment: *Anne Boleyn was beheaded in 1536.*

beheld *pt, pp* of BEHOLD.

behemoth /bɪˈhiːmɒθ/ *n* enormous, or enormously powerful, animal or person or thing.

behest /bɪˈhest/ *n* (idm) **at sb's beˈhest** (*dated or fml*) on sb's orders: *at the king's behest/at the behest of the king.*

behind[1] /bɪˈhaɪnd/ *prep* **1** (**a**) in or to a position at the back of (sb/sth): *Who's the girl standing behind Richard?* ○ *Stay close behind me in the crowd.* ○ *The golf course is behind our house.* ○ *a small street behind the station* ○ *She glanced behind her.* ○ *work behind the counter,* eg as a sales assistant in a shop ○ *Don't forget to lock the door behind you,* ie when you leave. ○ (*fig*) *The accident is behind you now* (ie in the past)*, so forget about it.* (**b**) on the other side of (sb/sth): *hide behind a tree* ○ *Behind the curtain she found a door.* ○ *The sun disappeared behind the clouds.* Cf IN FRONT OF (FRONT). ⇨ Usage at BEFORE[2]. **2** making less progress than (sb/sth): *He's behind the rest of the class in reading.* ○ *Britain is behind Japan in developing modern technology.* ○ *be behind schedule,* ie late. **3** supportive of (sb/sth); in favour of: *My family is right behind me in my ambition to become a doctor.* ○ *He's trying to win the election with only 30% of voters behind him.* **4** responsible for starting or developing (sth): *the thought that was behind the suggestion* ○ *the man behind the scheme to build a new hospital.* **5** (idm) **be behind sth** be the reason for sth: *What's behind the smart suit and eager smile?*

behind[2] /bɪˈhaɪnd/ *adv part* **1** in or to a position at the back of sb/sth: *I cycled off down the road with the dog running behind.* ○ *The others are a long way behind.* ○ *What have we left behind* (ie after going away)*?* ○ *Don't look behind or you may fall.* ○ *He was shot from behind as he ran away.* ○ *We had fallen so far behind that it seemed pointless continuing.* ○ *I had to stay behind after school,* ie remain in school after lessons were over. Cf IN FRONT (FRONT). ⇨ Usage at BEFORE[2]. **2** ~ (**in/with sth**) failing to pay (money) or complete (work) by the date when it is due; in arrears (with sth): *I'm terribly behind (with the rent) this month.* ○ *He's behind in handing in homework.*

behind[3] /bɪˈhaɪnd/ *n* (*infml euph*) buttocks: *She fell and landed on her behind.* ○ *He kicked the boy's behind.*

behindhand /bɪˈhaɪndhænd/ *adj* [pred] ~ (**with/in sth**) in arrears or late (esp in paying a debt): *be behindhand with the rent* ○ *get behindhand in one's work* ○ *He is never behindhand in offering advice,* ie is always eager to advise. Cf BEFOREHAND.

behold /bɪˈhəʊld/ *v* (*pt, pp* **beheld** /bɪˈheld/) **1** [Tn] (*arch or rhet*) (often imperative) see (esp sth unusual): *The babe was a wonder to behold.* ○ *Behold the king!* **2** (idm) **lo and behold** ⇨ LO. ▷ **beholder** *n* (idm) **beauty is in the eye of the beholder** ⇨ BEAUTY.

beholden /bɪˈhəʊldən/ *adj* [pred] ~ **to sb** (**for sth**) (*dated or fml*) owing thanks or indebted to sb: *We were much beholden to him for his kindness.*

behove /bɪˈhəʊv/ (*US* **behoove** /bɪˈhuːv/) *v* [Tnt] (used with *it*; not in the continuous tenses) (*dated or fml*) be right or necessary for (sb): *It behoves you* (ie You ought) *to be courteous at all times.* ○ *It ill behoves Anne* (ie She ought not) *to speak thus of her benefactor.*

beige /beɪʒ/ *adj, n* [U] (of a) very light yellowish brown: *a beige carpet.*

Beijing /beɪˈdʒɪŋ/ (also **Peking** /piːˈkɪŋ/) capital of China. Kublai Khan chose it as his capital and it has been the capital for most of the time since then. It is the economic and cultural centre of the country. In the historic centre of Beijing is the Forbidden City, a walled area containing the palaces of the former emperors of China.

being /ˈbiːɪŋ/ *n* **1** [U] (**a**) existence: *the richest company in being today* ○ *What is the purpose of our being?* (**b**) one's essence or nature; self: *I detest violence with my whole being.* **2** [C] living creature: *human beings* ○ *a strange being from another planet.* **3** (idm) **bring sth into ˈbeing** cause sth to have reality or existence; create sth. **come into ˈbeing** begin to exist: *When did the world come into being?*

Beirut /beɪˈruːt/ capital and chief port of Lebanon. Formerly the cultural and financial centre of the Middle East, the city has been devastated by the long war inside the country, and divided along religious lines into mainly Muslim West Beirut and Christian East Beirut.

bejewelled (*US* **bejeweled**) /bɪˈdʒuːəld/ *adj* decorated or adorned with jewels.

bel /bel/ *n* unit used in measuring relative power levels in electrical communications and sound. Cf DECIBEL.

belabour (*US* **belabor**) /bɪˈleɪbə(r)/ *v* [Tn, Tn·pr] ~ **sb/sth** (**with sth**) (*arch*) beat sb/sth hard; attack sb/sth: *He belaboured the donkey mercilessly.* ○ (*fig*) *They belaboured us with insults.*

Belarus /ˈbelərʊs/ (also **Belorussia** /ˌbjeləˈrʌʃə/) country to the west of Russia; pop approx 10 260 000; official language Belorussian; capital Minsk; unit of currency zaichik. As part of the USSR and a founding member of the United Nations, it became an independent republic in 1991. ⇨ map at UNION OF SOVIET SOCIALIST REPUBLICS.

belated /bɪˈleɪtɪd/ *adj* coming very late or too late: *a belated apology, Christmas card.* ▷ **belatedly** *adv.*

belay /bɪˈleɪ/ *v* [Tn] (in mountaineering and sailing) fix (a rope) round a peg, rock, etc in order to secure it.

▷ **belay** /bɪˈleɪ, *also, in mountaineering,* ˈbiːleɪ/ *n* fixing a rope in this way.

bel canto /bel ˈkæntəʊ/ style of singing that is marked by beauty and richness of sound.

belch /beltʃ/ *v* **1** [I] send out gas from the stomach noisily through the mouth. **2** [Tn, Tn·pr, Tn·p] ~ **sth** (**out/forth**) send (sth) out from an opening or a funnel; gush sth: *factory chimneys belching smoke (into the sky)* ○ *The volcano belched out smoke and ashes.*

▷ **belch** *n* act or sound of belching: *He gave a loud belch.*

beleaguer /bɪˈliːɡə(r)/ *v* [Tn usu passive] **1** besiege (sb/sth): *a beleaguered garrison.* **2** harass (sb) continually: *beleaguered by naughty children.*

belemnite /ˈbeləmnaɪt/ *n* fossil of the *Jurassic era with a sharply pointed tapering shape.

Belfast /belˈfɑːst/ capital of Northern Ireland. Although it is an important industrial centre (the chief industries being shipbuilding and aircraft manufacture), there is relatively high unemployment. The city has suffered in recent years from the conflict in Northern Ireland. ⇨ map at App 1.

belfry /ˈbelfrɪ/ *n* **1** tower for bells; part of a church tower in which bells hang. ⇨ illus at CHURCH. **2** (idm) **have bats in the belfry** ⇨ BAT[1].

Belgium /ˈbeldʒəm/ country in western Europe; pop approx 9 925 000; official languages Flemish and French; capital Brussels; unit of currency franc (= 100 centimes). After the Second World War Belgium joined the *Benelux customs union, and was a founder member of the European Community. It is a highly industrialized country, and agriculture forms only a small sector of the economy. It is divided into French-speaking and Flemish-speaking regions, and there has been tension between the two communities. ⇨ map at BENELUX. ▷ **Belgian** *adj, n*.

Belgrade /belˈgreɪd/ capital of the former Yugoslavia, and a major industrial and commercial centre.

Belial /ˈbiːlɪəl/ (*Bible*) the Devil.

belie /bɪˈlaɪ/ *v* (*pres p* **belying**, *pp* **belied**) [Tn] **1** give a wrong or an untrue idea of (sth): *His cheerful manner belied his real feelings.* **2** fail to justify or fulfil (a hope, promise, etc): *Practical experience belies this theory.*

belief /bɪˈliːf/ *n* **1** [U] ~ **in sth/sb** feeling that sth/sb is real and true; trust or confidence in sth/sb: *I haven't much belief in his honesty*, ie cannot feel sure that he is honest. ○ *He has great belief in his doctor*, ie is confident that his doctor can cure him. ○ *She has lost her belief in God*, ie no longer thinks that God exists. **2** [C] **(a)** thing accepted as true or real; what one believes: *It is my belief that...*, ie It is my firm opinion that.... ○ *He acted in accordance with his beliefs.* **(b)** religion or sth taught as part of religion: *Christian beliefs.* **3** (idm) **beyond beˈlief** too great, difficult, dreadful, etc to be believed; incredible: *I find his behaviour (irresponsible) beyond belief.* **in the belief that...** feeling confident that...: *He came to me in the belief that I could help him.* **to the best of one's belief/knowledge** ⇨ BEST[3].

believe /bɪˈliːv/ *v* **1** [Tn, Tw] feel sure of the truth of (sth); accept the statement of (sb) as true: *I believe him/what he says.* ○ *I'm innocent, please believe me.* ○ *I'll believe it/that when I see it*, ie Until I have evidence, I remain sceptical. ○ *I'm told he's been in prison, and I can well believe it*, ie it doesn't surprise me. **2** [Tf, Tw, Tnt] think (perhaps mistakenly); suppose: *People used to believe (that) the world was flat.* ○ *Nobody will believe what difficulty we have had/believe how difficult it has been for us.* ○ *They believed him to be insane.* ○ *I believe it to have been a mistake.* ○ *Mr Smith, I believe*, ie I presume you are Mr Smith. ○ *'Is he coming?' 'I believe so/not.'* **3** [I] have religious faith: *He thinks that everyone who believes will go to heaven.* **4** (phr v) **believe in sb/sth** feel sure of the existence of sb/sth: *I believe in God.* ○ *Do you believe in ghosts?* **believe in sth/sb; believe in doing sth** trust sth/sb; feel sure of the worth or truth of sth: *I believe in his good character.* ○ *Do you believe in nuclear disarmament?* ○ *He believes in getting plenty of exercise.* **believe sth of sb** accept that sb is capable of a particular action, etc: *If I hadn't seen him doing it I would never have believed it of him.* **5** (idm) **believe it or ˈnot** it may sound surprising but it is true: *Believe it or not, we were left waiting in the rain for two hours.* **believe (you) ˈme** I assure you: *Believe you me, the government won't meddle with the tax system.* **give sb to believe/understand** ⇨ GIVE[1]. **lead sb to believe** ⇨ LEAD[3]. **make believe (that...)** pretend: *The boys made believe (that) they were astronauts.* Cf MAKE-BELIEVE (MAKE[1]). **not believe one's ˈears/ˈeyes** be unable to believe that what one hears or sees is real because one is so astonished. **seeing is ˈbelieving** (*saying*) one needs to see sth before one can believe it exists or happens. **would you beˈlieve (it)?** (expressing astonishment or dismay) although it is hard to believe: *Today, would you believe, she came to work in an evening dress!*

▷ **believable** *adj* that can be believed. **believably** /-əblɪ/ *adv*.

believer *n* **1** person who believes, esp sb with religious faith. **2** (idm) **be a (great/firm) believer in sth** feel sure of the worth of sth: *I'm not a great believer in (taking) regular physical exercise.*

Belisha beacon /bɪliːʃə ˈbiːkn/ (also **beacon**) (*Brit*) post with an orange flashing light on top, marking a pedestrian crossing. Belisha beacons are named after Leslie Hore-Belisha, the Minister of Transport when they were introduced.

belittle /bɪˈlɪtl/ *v* [Tn] make (a person or an action) seem unimportant or of little value: *Don't belittle yourself*, ie Don't be too modest about your abilities or achievements.

▷ **belittlement** *n* [U].

belittling *adj* making sb seem unimportant or worthless: *I find it belittling to be criticized by someone so much younger than me.*

Belize /beˈliːz/ country in Central America; pop approx 175 000; official language English; capital Belmopan; unit of currency dollar (= 100 cents). Formerly British Honduras, it became independent and a member of the Commonwealth in 1981. Its main industries are the production of sugar and wood. In the past there has been a border dispute with its neighbour, Guatemala. ⇨ map at CENTRAL AMERICA. ▷ **Belizian** *adj, n*.

Alexander Graham Bell

Bell[1] /bel/ Alexander Graham (1847-1922), Scottish scientist and inventor, best known for having invented the telephone and the gramophone. He emigrated to Canada and later America, where he founded the Bell Telephone Company, one of the largest corporations in the USA. ⇨ illus.

Bell[2] /bel/ Currer, Ellis and Acton, pen-names used by Charlotte, Emily and Anne *Brontë.

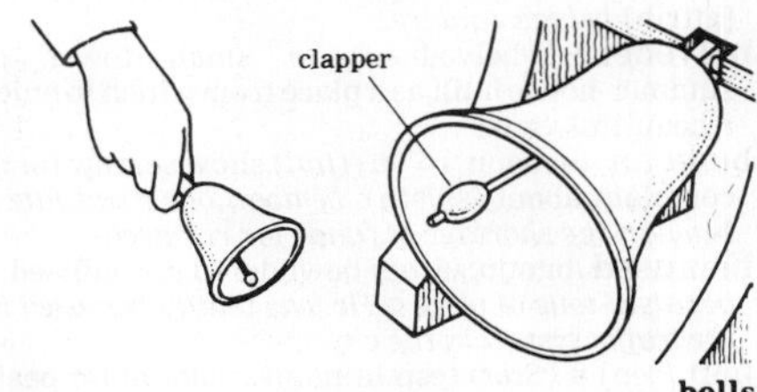

bells

bell /bel/ *n* **1** hollow metal object, usu shaped like a cup, that makes a ringing sound when struck: *church bells ringing out over the Sussex countryside* ○ *A bell was tolling*, eg to show that someone had died. ○ *a bicycle bell.* ⇨ illus at BICYCLE. ⇨ illus at CHURCH. **2** sound of this as a time-signal: *There's the bell for the end of the lesson.* ○ *The boxer was saved by the bell*, ie He escaped further severe treatment when the bell sounded. ○ *ship's bells*, ie the strokes on the ship's bell to mark the passage of time on board ship. **3** thing shaped like a bell. ⇨ illus at MUSIC. **4** (idm) **clear as a bell** ⇨ CLEAR[1]. **hell's bells** ⇨ HELL. **ring a bell** ⇨ RING[2]. **saved by the bell** ⇨ SAVE[1]. **sound as a bell** ⇨ SOUND[1].

Bells are used in churches to announce a service, so the sound of church bells is traditionally associated with Sunday mornings and with weddings. Before major services the bells are rung for up to half an hour, often by a team of bell-ringers. Each set (or *peal*) is rung in turn, the order in which they are rung varying each time according to an intricate pattern (called 'change-ringing'). Before minor services, and to announce funerals, a single bell is usually tolled for five or ten minutes. The consecration of the bread and wine in the Roman Catholic Mass is indicated by the sounding of a bell. And 'Great Tom', the big bell at Christ Church college in Oxford, is rung 101 times every evening, indicating the original number of scholars at the college.

□ **ˈbell-bottoms** *n* [pl] trousers made very wide below the knee. **ˈbell-bottomed** *adj* (of trousers) made in this way.

ˈbellboy *n* (*US*) = PAGE-BOY (PAGE[2]).

ˈbell-buoy *n* buoy with a warning bell that is made to ring by the movement of the waves.

ˈbell captain (*US*) person in charge of bellboys.

ˈbellhop, **ˈbellman** (*pl* **-men**) *ns* (*US*) = BELLBOY.

ˈbell-jar bell-shaped jar used in a laboratory for covering scientific experiments, or for containing gases.

ˈbell-pull *n* handle or cord pulled to make a bell ring.

ˈbell-push *n* button pressed to operate an electric bell.

ˈbell-ringer *n* [C], **ˈbell-ringing** *n* [U] (person) ringing church bells. Cf CAMPANOLOGY.

ˈbell-tent *n* tent supported by a central pole and shaped like a bell.

ˈbell-tower *n* tower (esp in a church) where bells are housed. Cf CAMPANILE.

ˈbell-wether *n* **1** sheep that wears a bell and leads a flock. **2** (*fig*) person that others tend to follow; ringleader.

belladonna /beləˈdɒnə/ *n* **1** [U, C] = DEADLY NIGHTSHADE (DEADLY). **2** [U] drug made from this plant.

belle /bel/ *n* beautiful woman or the most beautiful woman in a group, etc: *the belle of the ball*, ie the most beautiful woman present at a dance ○ *the belle of New York.*

Bellerophon /bəˈlerəfən/ (in Greek mythology) hero who killed the monster Chimaera with the help of *Pegasus.

belles-lettres /ˌbel ˈletrə/ *n* [sing or pl *v*] (*French*) literary studies and writings (contrasted with those on commercial, technical, scientific, etc subjects).

bellicose /ˈbelɪkəʊs/ *adj* (*fml*) eager to fight; warlike; aggressive: *a bellicose nation, nature.* ▷ **bellicosity** /ˌbelɪˈkɒsətɪ/ *n* [U].

-bellied ⇨ BELLY.

belligerent /bɪˈlɪdʒərənt/ *adj* **1** waging war; engaged in a conflict: *the belligerent powers*, ie those countries at war. **2** showing an eagerness to fight or argue; aggressive: *a belligerent person, manner, speech.*

▷ **belligerence** /-əns/, **belligerency** /-ənsɪ/ *ns* [U].

belligerent *n* country, group or person engaged in war.

Bellini[1] /beˈliːnɪ/ family of Venetian painters. Jacopo (c 1400-70) is known mainly through his drawings. His son Gentile painted portraits and dramatic scenes. His half-brother Giovanni (c 1430-1516) produced both religious and secular works in his long career. His enormously influential style continued to develop into his old age, and influenced that of his pupils *Giorgione and *Titian.

Bellini[2] /beˈli:nɪ/ Vincenzo (1801-35), Italian opera composer. His most famous work is *Norma*, a fine example of the bel canto style.

Belloc /ˈbelɒk/ Hilaire (1870-1953), British author born in France. A versatile writer (and for a time a Liberal Member of Parliament), he wrote a number of biographies and many travel books, but he is chiefly remembered for his popular light verse, eg *Cautionary Tales* and *A Bad Child's Book of Beasts*.

Bellow /ˈbeləʊ/ Saul (1915-), American novelist born in Canada. His novels often relate to his Jewish background. Some have great humour, others study the anxiety of modern intellectuals. He was awarded the Nobel prize for literature in 1976.

bellow /ˈbeləʊ/ *v* **1** [I] make a deep loud noise like a bull; roar, esp with pain: *The bull bellowed angrily.* **2** [I, Ipr, Tn, Tn·pr] ~ **(sth) (at sb)** say (sth) loudly or angrily; shout: *The music was so loud we had to bellow at each other to be heard.* ○ *The sergeant bellowed orders at the platoon.* ▷ **bellow** *n*.

bellows /ˈbeləʊz/ *n* [pl] apparatus for driving air into or through sth, eg through the pipes of a church organ: *a pair of bellows*, ie two-handled bellows for blowing air into a fire.

Bell's palsy /ˌbelz ˈpɔ:lzɪ/ (*medical*) condition in which the facial nerve becomes paralysed, causing the muscles on one side of the face to weaken and making it impossible to close the eye. Hearing and taste are also sometimes affected.

belly /ˈbelɪ/ *n* **1** (a) part of the body below the chest, containing the stomach, bowels and digestive organs; abdomen. ⇨ illus at HORSE. **(b)** (*infml*) front of the human body from the waist to the groin. **(c)** stomach: *with an empty belly*, ie hungry. **2** bulging or rounded part of sth: *in the belly of a ship.* **3** (idm) **fire in one's belly** ⇨ FIRE[1].

▷ **-bellied** /-belɪd/ (forming compound *adjs*) having a belly of the specified type: *ˌbig-ˈbellied* ○ *ˈpot-bellied*.

belly *v* (*pt, pp* **bellied**) (phr v) **belly (sth) out** swell out: *The sails bellied out.* ○ *The wind bellied out the sails.*

□ **ˈbellyache** *n* [C, U] (*infml*) stomach pain. — *v* [I] (*infml*) grumble repeatedly; complain, esp without good reason: *Do stop bellyaching all the time!*

ˈbelly-button *n* (*infml*) navel.

ˈbelly-dance *n* dance, originating in the Middle East, performed by a woman with erotic movements of the belly. **ˈbelly-dancer** *n*.

ˈbelly-flop *n* (*infml*) clumsy dive in which the body hits the water almost horizontally.

ˈbelly-landing *n* landing(1) in which an aircraft crashes onto the ground without lowering its wheels.

belly-laugh *n* (*infml*) deep loud unrestrained laugh.

bellyful /ˈbelɪfʊl/ *n* (idm) **have had a/one's ˈbellyful of sb/sth** (*infml*) have had as much as one can tolerate of sb/sth: *I've had a/my bellyful of your complaints.*

belong /bɪˈlɒŋ; *US* -lɔ:ŋ/ *v* **1** [Ipr] **(a)** ~ **to sb** be the property of sb: *These books belong to me*, ie are mine. ○ *Who(m) does this belong to?* **(b)** ~ **to sth** be connected with sth or a place; be correctly assigned to sth: *I belong to Glasgow.* ○ *That lid belongs to this jar.* **2** [Ipr] ~ **to sth** be a member of (a group, a family, an organization, etc): *He has never belonged to a trade union.* ○ *The daffodil belongs to the genus 'Narcissus'.* **3 (a)** [Ipr, Ip] ~ **(with sb/sth)** have a proper or usual place, as specified: *Where does this belong?* ie Where is it kept? ○ *The hammer belongs (in the shed) with the rest of the tools.* ○ *The vase belongs on this shelf.* ○ *A child belongs with* (ie should live with and be cared for by) *its mother.* ○ *These items don't belong under this heading*, ie are wrongly classified. **(b)** [I] fit a certain environment: *He doesn't feel he belongs/has no sense of belonging here*, ie He feels an outsider.

▷ **belongings** *n* [pl] person's movable possessions (ie not land, buildings, etc): *After his death his sister sorted through his (personal) belongings.* ○ *The tourists lost all their belongings in the hotel fire.*

beloved *adj* **(a)** /bɪˈlʌvd/ [pred] ~ **(by/of sb)** much loved: *This man was beloved by/of all who knew him.* **(b)** /bɪˈlʌvɪd/ [attrib] much loved; darling: *in memory of my beloved husband.*

▷ **beloved** /bɪˈlʌvɪd/ *n* dearly loved person; darling: *He wrote a sonnet to his beloved.*

below /bɪˈləʊ/ *prep* at or to a lower position, level, rank, etc than (sb/sth): *Please do not write below this line.* ○ *Skirts must be below* (ie long enough to cover) *the knee.* ○ *The body was visible below the surface of the lake.* ○ *The temperature remained below freezing all day.* ○ *A sergeant in the police force is below an inspector.* ○ *The standard of his work is well below the average of his class.* ○ *You can cross the river a short distance below* (ie downstream from) *the waterfall.* Cf ABOVE[2].

▷ **below** *adv part* **1** at or to a lower level, position or place: *the sky above and the sea below* ○ *live on the floor below* ○ *hear the music from below* ○ *See below* (eg at the foot of the page) *for references.* ○ *The passengers who felt seasick stayed below.* **2** (idm) **down below** ⇨ DOWN[1]. **here below** ⇨ HERE. Cf ABOVE[1].

Belshazzar /belˈʃæzə(r)/ last king of Babylon, son of Nebuchadnezzar. The Bible tells the story of a feast he held during which a mysterious message appeared on the walls of his palace, warning him of his death. It is the origin of the idiomatic expression 'the writing (is) on the wall'. Belshazzar was later killed by Cyrus. *Handel, *Byron and *Walton all used the story in their work.

belt /belt/ *n* **1** strip of leather, cloth, etc usu worn around the waist: *a coat with a belt attached* ○ *a ˈsword-belt* ○ *You don't need braces if you're wearing a belt!* **2** endless moving strap, used to connect wheels and so drive machinery or carry things along: *a ˈfan belt* ○ *a conˈveyor belt.* **3** area, region or extent that has some particular characteristic; zone: *a country's ˈcotton, ˈforest, inˈdustrial, etc belt* ○ *live in the comˈmuter belt* ○ *a belt of rain moving across the country.* Cf BIBLE BELT (BIBLE). **4** (*sl*) heavy blow. **5** (idm) **(hit sb) below the ˈbelt** (fight) unfairly. **tighten one's belt** ⇨ TIGHTEN (TIGHT). **under one's ˈbelt** (*infml*) achieved; obtained: *She already has good academic qualifications under her belt.*

▷ **belt** *v* **1 (a)** [Tn] put or fasten a belt round (sth): *Your mackintosh looks better belted.* **(b)** [Tn·pr, Tn·p] attach (sth) with a belt: *The officer belted his sword on.* **2** [Tn, Dn·n] (*sl*) thrash (sb); hit: *If you don't shut up, I'll belt you (one).* **3** (phr v) **belt along, up, down, etc** (*sl*) move very fast in the specified direction: *A car came belting along (the road).* ○ *He went belting up/down the motorway at 90 mph.* **belt sth out** (*sl*) sing or play sth loudly and forcefully: *a radio belting out pop music.* **belt ˈup (a)** (*infml*) fasten one's seat-belt (esp in a car). **(b)** (*sl*) be quiet: *Belt up, I can't hear what your mother is saying!*

belting *n* (*sl*) beating: *give the boy a good belting*, ie thrash him soundly.

□ **ˈbelt line** (*US*) bus or train service that operates around the edge of a city or city area.

ˈbeltway *n* (*US*) = RING ROAD (RING[1]).

beluga /bəˈlu:gə/ *n* (*pl* unchanged) large type of sturgeon found in the Black and Caspian Seas: [attrib] *beluga caviare.*

belvedere /ˈbelvədɪə(r)/ *n* small tower or summer-house built as a place from which to enjoy a beautiful view.

bemoan /bɪˈməʊn/ *v* [Tn] (*fml*) show sorrow for or complain about (sb/sth): *bemoan one's sad fate* ○ *bemoan the shortage of funds for research.*

bemused /bɪˈmju:zd/ *adj* bewildered or confused: *a bemused tone of voice* ○ *He was totally bemused by the traffic system in the city.*

ben /ben/ *n* (*Scot*) (esp in names) mountain peak: *Ben Nevis.*

Benares /bɪˈnɑ:rɪz/ sacred city, on the Ganges river in N India, famous for its temples.

bench /bentʃ/ *n* **1** [C] **(a)** long seat made of wood or stone: *a park bench.* **(b)** (*Brit*) (in the House of Commons) seat for a certain group of MPs: *the back-/cross-/front-benches* ○ *There was cheering from the Labour benches.* ○ *the Treasury bench*, ie where the Prime Minister and his or her colleagues sit. ⇨ article at PARLIAMENT. **2 the bench (a)** [sing] lawcourt: *the Queen's Bench*, ie a division of the British High Court of Justice. **(b)** [sing] judge's seat in court. **(c)** [Gp] judges or magistrates as a group. **(d)** [Gp] judge(s) or magistrate(s) hearing a case. **3** [C] long working-table for a carpenter, mechanic, scientist, etc. **4** (idm) **on the ˈbench** appointed as a judge or magistrate.

▷ **bencher** *n* (*Brit*) senior member of any of the *Inns of Court.

□ **ˈbench-mark** *n* **(a)** mark cut in a rock, concrete post, etc by surveyors for use in measuring comparative levels, etc. **(b)** (*fig*) standard example or point of reference for making comparisons.

ˈbench seat seat (for two or three people) across the whole width of a car.

ˈbench test thorough test, eg of a machine, in a workshop or laboratory. **bench-test** *v* [Tn] test (a machine, etc) thoroughly in a workshop or laboratory.

bend[1] /bend/ *v* (*pt, pp* **bent** /bent/) **1** [Tn, Tn·p] force (sth that was straight) into an angle; make crooked or curved: *It's hard to bend an iron bar.* ○ *The mast was bent during the storm.* ○ *The heat of the fire has bent these records.* ○ *Touch your toes without bending your knees.* ○ *Bend the wire up/down/forwards/back.* **2 (a)** [I, Ipr, Ip] (of an object) become curved or angular: *The road bends to the right after a few yards.* **(b)** [I, Ipr, Ip] (of an object) turn downwards in a curve: *The branch bent but didn't break when the boy climbed along it.* **(c)** [I, Ipr, Ip, Tn, Tn·pr, Tn·p] (cause sb/sth to) bow or stoop (in a specified direction): *She bent down and picked it up.* ○ *He bent forward to listen to the child.* ○ *The boy bent over to be caned.* ○ *They (were) bent double crouching under the table.* ○ *His head was bent over a book.* **3** [Tn·pr, Tn·p] turn (sth) in a new direction: *We bent our steps towards home.* **4** (idm) **bend one's mind to sth** direct one's thoughts to sth: *He couldn't bend his mind to his studies.* **bend/lean over backwards** ⇨ BACKWARDS (BACKWARD). **bend the ˈrules** change or interpret the rules, laws, etc in a way that suits oneself or the circumstances. **on bended ˈknee(s)** (as if) kneeling to pray or to beg humbly. **5** (phr v) **be bent on sth/on doing sth** be determined on (a course of action); have one's mind firmly set on (doing) sth: *be bent on pleasure, mischief, etc* ○ *He is bent on winning at all costs.* **bend (sb) to sth** (force sb to) submit to sth: *bend to sb's will* ○ *bend sb to one's will.*

▷ **bendy** *adj* (*infml*) **(a)** having many bends; winding: *a bendy road.* **(b)** that can be bent easily; flexible: *bendy material* ○ *a bendy twig.*

bend[2] /bend/ *n* **1** curve or turn, esp in a road, racecourse, river, etc: *a slight, gentle, sharp, sudden, etc bend.* **2** sailor's knot for tying rope. **3** (idm) **(drive sb/be/go) round the bend/twist** (*infml*) (make sb/be/become) crazy; mad: *His behaviour is driving me round the bend*, ie annoys me very much.

□ **ˌbend ˈsinister** bar from top right to bottom left on a coat of arms (COAT). It is a sign that the original owner of the coat of arms was illegitimate.

bender /ˈbendə(r)/ *n* (*sl*) period of wild drinking: *go on a drunken bender for three days.*

bends /bendz/ **the bends** *n* [pl] (*infml*) = DECOMPRESSION SICKNESS (DECOMPRESS).

beneath /bɪˈni:θ/ *prep* (*fml*) **1** in or to a lower position than (sb/sth); under: *They found the body buried beneath a pile of leaves.* ○ *The boat sank beneath the waves.* **2** not worthy of (sb): *He considers such jobs beneath him*, ie not suited to his rank or status. ○ *They thought she had married beneath her*, ie married a man of lower social status. Cf ABOVE[2].

▷ **beneath** *adv* (*fml*) in or to a lower position; underneath: *Her careful make-up hid the signs of age beneath.*

Benedict /ˈbenɪdɪkt/ Saint (c 480-c 550), Italian monk. His *Rule* lays down the way of life followed by monks in the Catholic Church, and especially by those of the Benedictine order, founded by him.

Benedictine *n* **1** /ˌbenɪˈdɪktɪn/ [C] monk or nun of the religious order founded by St Benedict. Benedictines traditionally devote themselves to a life that combines study, work and prayer: [attrib] *the Benedictine order.* **2** /ˌbenɪˈdɪkti:n/ [U, C] (*propr*) liqueur originally made by monks of this order.

benediction /ˌbenɪˈdɪkʃn/ *n* [C, U] blessing, esp one said before a meal or at the end of a church service: *pronounce/say the benediction* ○ *confer one's benediction on sb.*

benefaction /ˌbenɪˈfækʃn/ *n* (*fml*) **1** [U] action of giving or doing good. **2** [C] gift; donation: *She made many charitable benefactions.*

benefactor /ˈbenɪfæktə(r)/ *n* person who gives money or other help to a school, hospital, charity, etc.
▷ **benefactress** /ˈbenɪfæktrɪs/ *n* woman benefactor.

benefice /ˈbenɪfɪs/ *n* position (in charge of a parish) that provides a clergyman with his income.
▷ **beneficed** /ˈbenɪfɪst/ *adj* having a benefice: *a beneficed priest.*

beneficent /bɪˈnefɪsnt/ *adj* (*fml*) showing active kindness; generous; charitable: *a beneficent patron.* ▷ **beneficence** /bɪˈnefɪsns/ *n* [U].

beneficial /ˌbenɪˈfɪʃl/ *adj* ~ (**to sth/sb**) having a helpful or useful effect; advantageous: *a beneficial result, influence, etc* ○ *Fresh air is beneficial to one's health.* ▷ **beneficially** /-ʃəlɪ/ *adv.*

beneficiary /ˌbenɪˈfɪʃərɪ; *US* -ˈfɪʃɪerɪ/ *n* person who receives sth, esp one who receives money, property, etc when sb dies.

benefit /ˈbenɪfɪt/ *n* **1** (**a**) [U] profit; gain; future good (used esp with the *vs* and *preps* shown): *Because of illness she didn't get much benefit from her stay abroad.* ○ *I've had the benefit of a good education.* ○ *It was achieved with the benefit* (ie help, aid) *of modern technology.* ○ *The new regulations will be of great benefit to us all.* ○ *A change in the law would be to everyone's benefit.* (**b**) [C] thing from which one gains or profits; advantage: *the benefits of modern medicine, science, higher education.* **2** [U, C] allowance of money, etc to which sb is entitled from an insurance policy or from government funds: *medical, unemployment, sickness, etc benefit(s).* **3** [C, esp attrib] public performance or game held in order to raise money for a particular player, charity, etc: *a ˈbenefit match, performance, concert, etc.* **4** (idm) **for sb's benefit** in order to help, guide, instruct, etc sb: *The warning sign was put there for the benefit of the public.* ○ *Although she didn't mention me by name, I know her remarks were intended for my benefit.* **give sb the ˌbenefit of the ˈdoubt** accept that sb is innocent, right, etc because there is no clear evidence to support one's feeling that he may not be: *By allowing her to go free the judge gave the accused the benefit of the doubt.*
▷ **benefit** *v* (*pt, pp* **-fited**; *US also* **-fitted**) **1** [Tn] do good to (sb/sth): *These facilities have benefited the whole town.* **2** [I, Ipr] ~ (**from/by sth**) receive benefit or gain: *Who stands to* (ie is likely to) *benefit most by the new tax laws?* ○ *He hasn't benefited from* (ie become wiser with) *the experience.*
□ **ˌbenefit of ˈclergy** right formerly held by the clergy, which allowed them to be tried for crimes before special church courts rather than ordinary courts, and sometimes to avoid the normal punishment.
ˈbenefit society (*esp US*) = FRIENDLY SOCIETY (FRIENDLY).

Benelux /ˈbenɪlʌks/ collective name for Belgium, the Netherlands and Luxembourg, which formed a close economic union in 1948. ⇨ map.

benevolent /bɪˈnevələnt/ *adj* ~ (**to/towards sb**) **1** being, or wishing to be, kind, friendly and helpful: *a benevolent air, attitude, manner, etc* ○ *a benevolent dictator* ○ *benevolent despotism.* **2** doing good rather than making profit; charitable: *a benevolent institution/society/fund.*
▷ **benevolence** /bɪˈnevələns/ *n* [U] desire to do good; kindness and generosity.
benevolently *adv.*

Benelux

B Eng /ˌbi:ˈendʒ/ *abbr* Bachelor of Engineering: *have/be a B Eng* ○ *Greg James B Eng.*

Bengal /ˌbeŋˈgɔ:l/ region in the north-east part of the Indian subcontinent, now divided into the Indian state of West Bengal and *Bangladesh. The economy of the region is based on rice and jute.
▷ **Bengali** *n* (**a**) native or inhabitant of Bengal. (**b**) language of Bengal. — *adj* of Bengal, its people or its language.

benighted /bɪˈnaɪtɪd/ *adj* (*dated*) unenlightened morally or intellectually; ignorant; backward: *benighted savages.*

benign /bɪˈnaɪn/ *adj* **1** (of people or actions) kindly; gentle. **2** (of climate) mild; pleasant. **3** (of a tumour, etc) not likely to spread or recur after treatment; not dangerous. ▷ **benignly** *adv.* Cf MALIGNANT.

Benin /beˈnɪn, -ˈni:n/ country in W Africa; pop approx 4 446 000; official language French; capital Porto Novo; unit of currency franc. Formerly the French colony of Dahomey, it became independent in 1960, and adopted its present name in 1975. Benin was the name of an old African kingdom which was powerful from the 14th to the 17th centuries, and produced remarkable bronze and ivory sculptures. Its economy is mainly agricultural. ⇨ map at NIGERIA. ▷ **Beninese** /ˌbenɪˈni:z/ *adj.*

benison /ˈbenɪzn/ *n* (*arch*) blessing; benediction.

Bennett /ˈbenɪt/ Arnold (1867-1931), English novelist. His most famous works are his novels set in the *Potteries, eg *Anna of the Five Towns*, in which he describes the life of working people in great detail and creates some remarkable characters. He was also an influential book critic and wrote a number of plays.

Ben Nevis /ˌben ˈnevɪs/ mountain in western Scotland, the highest in Britain (1 343 m, 4 406 ft).

benny /ˈbenɪ/ *n* (*US sl*) amphetamine (esp Benzedrine) tablet, esp when taken by a drug addict.

bent[1] /bent/ *n* **1** (usu *sing*) ~ (**for sth/doing sth**) natural skill (at sth); liking or inclination (for sth/doing sth): *She has a (natural) bent for music.* ○ *He is of a studious bent.* **2** (idm) **follow one's bent** ⇨ FOLLOW.

bent[2] /bent/ *adj* (*sl esp Brit*) **1** dishonest; corrupt: *a bent copper*, ie a policeman who can be bribed. **2** [usu pred] (*derog*) homosexual.

bent[3] *pt, pp* of BEND[1].

Bentham /ˈbenθəm, *also* ˈbentəm/ Jeremy (1748-1832), English philosopher. According to his philosophy, known as 'utilitarianism', society should be organized so as to aim for 'the greatest happiness of the greatest number'. He wrote many short works that use this idea to explain the changes he thought should be made to society and the law. His ideas influenced many 19th-century thinkers. ▷ **Benthamism** *n* [U].

benthos /ˈbenθɒs/ *n* [U] plants and animals that live at the bottom of a sea or lake.

bentwood /ˈbentwʊd/ *n* [U] wood that has been artificially bent for use in making furniture: [attrib] *ˌbentwood ˈchairs.*

benumbed /bɪˈnʌmd/ *adj* (*fml*) made numb; with all feeling taken away: *fingers benumbed with cold.*

Benzedrine /ˈbenzədri:n/ *n* [U] (*propr*) type of amphetamine: [attrib] *a ˌBenzedrine inˈhaler*, eg for people with colds or hay fever.

benzene /ˈbenzi:n/ *n* [U] colourless liquid obtained from petroleum and coal tar, used in making plastics and many chemical products.

benzine /ˈbenzi:n/ *n* [U] colourless liquid mixture of hydrocarbons obtained from petroleum and used in dry-cleaning.

benzoin /ˈbenzəʊɪn/ *n* [U] strong-smelling resin of a Javanese tree, used in making perfumes and medicines.

benzol /ˈbenzɒl; *US* -zɔ:l/ *n* [U] (esp unrefined) benzene.

Beowulf /ˈbeɪəwʊlf/ epic poem in Old English, probably written in the 8th century, telling how the hero Beowulf kills two monsters. It was the first major European poem not written in Latin.

bequeath /bɪˈkwi:ð/ *v* [Tn, Dn·n, Dn·pr] ~ **sth** (**to sb**) (*fml*) **1** arrange, by making a will, to give (property, money, etc) (to sb) when one dies: *He bequeathed £1 000 (to charity).* ○ *She has bequeathed me her jewellery.* **2** (*fig*) pass on (knowledge, etc) (to those who come after): *discoveries bequeathed to us by scientists of the last century.*

bequest /bɪˈkwest/ *n* (*fml*) **1** act of bequeathing: *the bequest of one's paintings to a gallery.* **2** thing bequeathed; legacy: *leave a bequest of £2000 each to one's grandchildren.*

berate /bɪˈreɪt/ *v* [Tn] (*fml*) scold sharply.

Berber /ˈbɜ:bə(r)/ *n* member of a race of people that have lived in N Africa since very early times. ▷ **Berber** *adj*: *Berber languages.*

berceuse /beəˈsɜ:z/ *n* (*French*) (piece of music in the style of a) lullaby.

bereave /bɪˈri:v/ *v* [Tn, Tn·pr] ~ **sb** (**of sb**) (*fml*) deprive sb (esp of a relative) by death: *an accident which bereaved him of his wife and child* ○ *the bereaved husband*, ie the man whose wife had died.
▷ **the bereaved** *n* (*pl* unchanged) (*fml*) person who is bereaved: *The bereaved is/are still in mourning.*
bereavement *n* **1** [U] state of being bereaved: *We all sympathize with you in your bereavement.* **2** [C] instance of this: *She was absent because of a recent bereavement.*

bereft /bɪˈreft/ *adj* [pred] (*fml*) ~ (**of sth**) deprived of (a power or quality): *be bereft of speech*, ie be unable to speak ○ *bereft of hope*, ie without hope ○ *bereft of reason*, ie mad.

beret /ˈbereɪ; *US* bəˈreɪ/ *n* round flat cap with no peak, usu made of soft cloth or felt. ⇨ illus at HAT.

Berg /beəg/ Alban (1885-1935), Austrian composer, a pupil of *Schoenberg. His works, such as the operas *Wozzeck* and *Lulu*, are in a modern non-melodic style, but the emotion expressed in his music makes it easier to appreciate.

bergamot /ˈbɜːgəmɒt/ *n* [U] **1** perfume obtained from a type of citrus fruit. **2** type of sweet-smelling plant.

Bergman[1] /ˈbɜːgmən/ Ingmar (1918-), Swedish film and theatre director. Outside Sweden he is most famous for his films, such as *The Seventh Seal*, *Wild Strawberries* and *Fanny and Alexander*, which show his deep interest in childhood, relationships and faith.

Ingrid Bergman, Humphrey Bogart and Dooley Wilson in 'Casablanca'

Bergman[2] /ˈbɜːgmən/ Ingrid (1915-82), Swedish actor. She often portrayed the brave innocent, and her fame was founded on such classics as *Casablanca* and continued long after her ill-fated collaboration with *Rossellini. ⇨ illus.

Bergson /ˈbɜːgsn/ Henri (1859-1941), French philosopher. He saw the world as divided into life (or consciousness) and material things (or matter). According to him, we perceive matter through intellect but the 'life force' is perceived through intuition, which is stronger than intellect. Bergson also made a study of laughter and was awarded the Nobel prize for literature in 1927.

beriberi /ˌberɪˈberɪ/ *n* [U] mainly tropical disease affecting the nervous system, caused by lack of vitamin B.

Bering /ˈbeərɪŋ/ Vitus Jonassen (1681-1741), Danish explorer. He gave his name to the **Bering Sea**, the most northern part of the Pacific, and the **Bering Strait** between Alaska and far eastern Russia, which connects the Sea to the Arctic Ocean.

berk /bɜːk/ *n* (*Brit sl derog*) stupid person (esp a man).

Berkeley[1] /ˈbɜːklɪ/ Busby (1895-1976), American choreographer and director. He is chiefly famous for the lavish music and dance sequences he arranged for Hollywood films such as *42nd Street*.

Berkeley[2] /ˈbɑːklɪ/ George (1685-1753), Irish bishop and philosopher. He denied that matter exists, claiming instead that things only exist because the mind notices them, and that the real world is made up of ideas in the mind of God. Cf LOCKE[1].

Berkeley[3] /ˈbɑːklɪ/ Sir Lennox (1903-89), English composer. His lyrical style was particularly influenced by *Britten and *Poulenc. He wrote a wide variety of music, but is perhaps best known for his chamber works and some fine modern religious compositions.

berkelium /bɜːˈkiːlɪəm, ˈbɜːklɪəm/ *n* [U] (*symb* **Bk**) radioactive metallic element, artificially produced by bombarding americium with helium ions. ⇨ App 11.

Berlin[1] /bɜːˈlɪn/ city in Germany. Once the capital of the country, it was divided after the Second World War into East and West Berlin. West Berlin became a state of West Germany entirely surrounded by East Germany, with East Berlin the capital of East Germany. In 1961 a wall was built around West Berlin to prevent people leaving the eastern part, but in 1989 the wall was demolished and in 1990 the two parts of Germany reunited. In 1991 a decision was made to make Berlin once again the capital of Germany, although Bonn still remains the seat of government: [attrib] *the ˌBerlin ˈwall.*

Berlin[2] /bɜːˈlɪn/ Irving (1888-1989), American song-writer, born in Russia. Although he had little technical musical skill, he wrote over 1 000 popular songs. Many of his greatest successes, like 'White Christmas', were written for Hollywood films.

Berlioz /ˈbeəlɪəʊz/ Hector (1803-69), French composer. The force and brilliance of his music, as in the *Symphonie Fantastique*, makes him one of the great romantic composers. His own life was often as dramatic as his work.

Bermuda /bəˈmjuːdə/ group of islands off the east coast of America; pop approx 58 000; official language English; capital Hamilton. The islands are a British dependency. The main industry is tourism.

□ **Bermuda ˈshorts** shorts, usu with a colourful design, that reach down to the knees.

the Bermuda ˈTriangle area of the Atlantic Ocean between Bermuda and Florida which is thought to be dangerous, because of the number of ships and aircraft that have mysteriously disappeared there.

Bernadette /bɜːnəˈdet/ Saint (1844-79), born Marie Bernarde Soubirous. She was born in *Lourdes in France, where she claimed to have had visions of the Virgin Mary. As a result a shrine was built in the town. Bernadette later became a nun.

Bernard /ˈbɜːnəd/ Saint (1090-1153), French monk. He reformed the Cistercian order of monks and used his preaching to support the second Crusade. His writings show him to have been a man of deep faith, inspired by sublime mysticism.

Berne (also *German* **Bern**) /bɜːn, beən/ capital of Switzerland. It is in the German-speaking part of the country, and the federal government is based there, along with a number of international organizations.

□ **the ˌBerne Conˈvention** international agreement on questions of copyright. It has never been signed by the USA.

Bernhardt /ˈbɜːnhɑːt/ Sarah (1844-1923), French actress. Her talent brought her great international success, and she was famous for her roles as tragic heroines. Despite losing a leg after an accident late in life, she continued acting all over the world. There are many stories about her eccentric life-style.

Bernini /bɜːˈniːnɪ/ Gianlorenzo (1598-1680), Italian sculptor, painter and architect. A master of the baroque style, he was responsible for much of the completion of Saint Peter's Basilica in Rome, including the magnificent colonnaded piazza (1656-67).

Bernoulli /bɜːˈnuːlɪ/ family of Swiss mathematicians. The most important members were Jakob (1654-1705) and Johann (1667-1748), who both made important discoveries in calculus, and Daniel (1700-82), whose greatest contributions were to hydrodynamics and various branches of mathematical physics.

Bernstein /ˈbɜːnstaɪn/ Leonard (1918-91), American conductor and composer. He wrote a number of popular musicals, the most successful of which was *West Side Story*, but also composed several serious orchestral and choral works. As a conductor he was particularly associated with the New York Philharmonic, who made him 'conductor for life'. ⇨ article at MUSIC.

berry /ˈberɪ/ *n* **1** small juicy fruit without a stone: *blackberry* ○ *raspberry* ○ *holly berries.* **2** (*botany*) fruit with seeds enclosed in pulp (eg gooseberry, tomato, banana). **3** egg of a fish or lobster. **4** (idm) **brown as a berry** ⇨ BROWN.

berserk /bəˈsɜːk/ *adj* [usu pred] wild with rage: *send sb/go/be berserk.*

berth /bɜːθ/ *n* **1** sleeping-place on a ship, train, etc. **2** place for a ship to be tied up in a harbour, or to be at anchor: *find a safe berth*, eg one protected from bad weather. **3** (*infml*) job or position (esp an enjoyable one): *a snug/cosy berth.* **4** (idm) **give sb/sth a wide berth** ⇨ WIDE.

▷ **berth** *v* **1** [Tn usu passive] provide (sb) with a sleeping-place: *Six passengers can be berthed on the lower deck.* **2** (**a**) [Tn] tie up (a ship) in a harbour or at a suitable place; moor. (**b**) [I] (of a ship) come to a berth; moor: *The liner berthed at midday.*

beryl /ˈberəl/ *n* transparent precious stone, usu green.

beryllium /bəˈrɪlɪəm/ *n* [U] (*symb* **Be**) chemical element, a white metal that does not corrode and is used in alloys to make them harder. ⇨ App 11.

Besant /ˈbeznt/ Annie (1847-1933), English thinker and theosophist. She was active in many causes, esp the Indian independence movement.

beseech /bɪˈsiːtʃ/ *v* (*pt, pp* **besought** /bɪˈsɔːt/ or **beseeched**) (*fml*) **1** [Tn, Tn·pr, Dn·t] ~ **sb** (**for sth**) ask sb earnestly; implore sb; entreat sb: *Spare him, I beseech you.* ○ *The prisoner besought the judge for mercy/to be merciful.* **2** [Tn] ask earnestly for (sth); beg for: *She besought his forgiveness.* ⇨ Usage at ASK.

▷ **beseeching** *adj* [attrib] (of a look, tone of voice, etc) entreating or appealing for sth. **beseechingly** *adv.*

beset /bɪˈset/ *v* (**-tt-**; *pt, pp* **beset**) [Tn esp passive] (*fml*) surround (sb/sth) on all sides; trouble constantly; threaten: *beset by doubts* ○ *The voyage was beset with dangers.* ○ *the difficulties, pressures, temptations, etc that beset us all.*

▷ **besetting** *adj* [attrib] habitually affecting or troubling sb: *a besetting difficulty/fear/sin.*

beside /bɪˈsaɪd/ *prep* **1** at the side of (sb/sth); next to: *Sit beside your sister.* ○ *I keep a dictionary beside me when I'm doing crosswords.* **2** compared with (sb/sth): *Beside your earlier work this piece seems rather disappointing.* **3** (idm) **beˈside oneself** (**with sth**) having lost one's self-control because of the intensity of the emotion one is feeling: *He was beside himself with rage when I told him what I had done.*

besides /bɪˈsaɪdz/ *prep* **1** in addition to (sb/sth): *There will be five of us for dinner, besides John.* ○ *The play was badly acted, besides being far too long.* **2** (following a negative) except (sb/sth); apart from: *She has no relations besides an aged aunt.* ○ *No one writes to me besides you.*

▷ **besides** *adv* in addition; also: *I haven't time to see the film — besides, it's had dreadful reviews.* ○ *Peter is our youngest child, and we have three others besides.*

besiege /bɪˈsiːdʒ/ *v* **1** [Tn] surround (a place) with armed forces in order to make it surrender: *Troy was besieged by the Greeks.* **2** (*fig*) (**a**) [Tn] surround (sb/sth) closely; crowd round: *The Prime Minister was besieged by reporters.* (**b**) [Tn·pr esp passive] ~ **sb with sth** overwhelm sb with (questions, requests, etc): *The teacher was besieged with questions from his pupils.*

besmear /bɪˈsmɪə(r)/ *v* [Tn, Tn·pr] ~ **sth/sb** (**with sth**) (*fml*) make sth/sb dirty; smear sth/sb (with greasy or sticky stuff): *hands besmeared with oil.*

besmirch /bɪˈsmɜːtʃ/ (also **smirch**) *v* [Tn] (*fml*) dishonour (sb/sth); slander: *besmirch sb's reputation, name, honour, etc.*

besom /ˈbiːzəm/ *n* broom made by tying a bundle of twigs to a long stick.

besotted /bɪˈsɒtɪd/ *adj* [pred] ~ (**by/with sb/sth**) made silly or stupid, esp by love: *He is totally besotted with the girl*, ie deeply in love with her.

besought *pt, pp* of BESEECH.

bespangled /bɪˈspæŋgld/ *adj* [pred] ~ (**with sth**) decorated with (things that shine or sparkle): *a sky bespangled with stars.*

bespattered /bɪˈspætəd/ *adj* [pred] ~ (**with sth**) covered with (spots of dirt, etc): *Her clothes were bespattered with mud.*

bespeak /bɪˈspiːk/ *v* (*pt* **bespoke** /bɪˈspəʊk/, *pp* **bespoke** or **bespoken** /bɪˈspəʊkən/) [Tn] (*dated or fml*) be evidence of (sth); indicate: *His polite manners bespoke the gentleman.*

bespectacled /bɪˈspektəkld/ *adj* wearing spectacles.

bespoke /bɪˈspəʊk/ *adj* [usu attrib] **1** (of clothes) made according to the customer's specifications: *a bespoke suit.* **2** making such clothes: *a bespoke tailor.* **3** (*computing*) (of software) specially written to suit the needs of the individual user.

Bessemer /ˈbesɪmə(r)/ Sir Henry (1813-98),

English engineer and inventor. He is chiefly remembered for developing the **Bessemer process**, which was formerly much used for removing carbon, silicon, etc from molten pig-iron by means of a strong blast of air, thus producing a material suitable for steel-making. It was the first successful method of making large quantities of steel at low cost.

best[1] /best/ *adj* (*superlative of* GOOD[1]) **1** of the most excellent, desirable, suitable, etc kind: *my best friend* ○ *the best dinner I've ever had* ○ *The best thing to do would be to apologize.* ○ *The best thing about the party was the food.* ○ *He's the best man for the job.* ○ *What is the best* (ie the shortest, easiest, etc) *way to get there?* ○ *It's best to go by bus.* Cf GOOD[1], BETTER[1]. **2** (idm) **be on one's best beˈhaviour** behave as well as possible. **one's best bet** (*infml*) action most likely to bring success: *Your best bet would be to call again tomorrow.* **one's best bib and ˈtucker** (*dated or joc*) one's best clothes, worn only on special occasions. **one's best/strongest card** ⇨ CARD[1]. **the best/better part of sth** ⇨ PART[1]. **the best thing since sliced ˈbread** (*joc infml*) very good or popular thing, idea or event: *I think the programme's rubbish, but the children think it's the best thing since sliced bread.* **the devil has all the best tunes** ⇨ DEVIL. **make the best use of sth** use sth as profitably as possible: *She's certainly made the best use of her opportunities.* **put one's best ˈfoot forward** go as fast as one can. **with the ˌbest will in the ˈworld** even when one has made every effort to be fair, etc.

□ **ˌbest ˈman** male friend or relative of a bridegroom who supports him at his wedding. Cf BRIDESMAID. ⇨ article at WEDDING.

best[2] /best/ *adv* (*superlative of* WELL[2]) **1** (often in compounds) **(a)** in the most excellent manner: *the best-dressed politician* ○ *the best kept garden in the street* ○ *He works best in the mornings.* ○ *These insects are best seen through a microscope.* ○ *She's the person best able to cope.* ○ *Do as you think best*, ie as you think should be done. ○ *You know best*, ie You know better than anyone else what should be done, what is correct, etc. **(b)** to the greatest degree; most: *the best-known/best-loved politician* ○ *I enjoyed his first novel best (of all).* **2** (idm) **as ˌbest one ˈcan** not perfectly but as well as one is able to: *The facilities were not ideal but we managed as best we could.* **the ˌbest-laid ˌschemes/ˌplans of ˌmice and ˈmen (gang aft agley)** (*saying*) things often go wrong, even after careful preparations. **for reasons/some reason best known to oneself** ⇨ REASON[1]. **had better/best** ⇨ BETTER[2]. **know best** ⇨ KNOW.

□ **ˌbest ˈseller** product, esp a book, that sells in very large numbers: [attrib] *the best-seller list.* **ˌbest-ˈselling** *adj* having very large sales; very popular: *a ˌbest-selling ˈnovel, ˈauthor, ˈseries.*

best[3] /best/ *n* [sing] **1** that which is best; the outstanding thing or person among several: *She wants the best of everything*, ie wants her life, possessions, etc to be perfect. ○ *When you pay that much for a meal you expect the best.* ○ *He was acting from the best of motives.* ○ *She's the best of the lot/bunch.* ○ *He is among the best of our workers.* ○ *We're the best of friends*, ie very close friends. **2** most important advantage or aspect of sth: *That's the best of having a car.* ○ *The best we can hope for is that nobody gets killed.* **3** (idm) **all the ˈbest** (*infml*) (used esp when saying goodbye) I hope everything goes well for you: *Goodbye, and all the best!* ○ *Here's wishing you all the best in the coming year.* **at ˈbest** taking the most hopeful view: *We can't arrive before Friday at best.* **at its/one's best** in the best state or form: *modern architecture at its best* ○ *Chaplin was at his best playing the little tramp.* ○ *I wasn't feeling at my best at the party so I didn't enjoy it.* **(even) at the ˈbest of times** even when circumstances are most favourable: *He's difficult at the best of times — usually he's impossible.* **be (all) for the ˈbest** be good in the end, although not at first seeming to be good. **the best of both worlds** benefits of two widely differing activities that one can enjoy simultaneously: *She's a career woman and a mother, so she has the best of both worlds.* **the best of British (luck) (to sb)** (*Brit often ironic*) (used when wishing sb good luck in some activity, esp when he is thought unlikely to succeed). **(play) the best of ˈthree, etc** play(ing) up to three, five, etc games, the winner being the person who wins most of them: *We were playing the best of five but we stopped after three because John won them all.* **bring out the ˈbest/ˈworst in sb** reveal sb's best/worst qualities: *The family crisis really brought out the best in her.* **do, try, etc one's (level/very) ˈbest; do the best one ˈcan** do all that one can: *I did my best to stop her.* ○ *It doesn't matter if you don't win — just do your best.* **get/have the ˈbest of it, the deal, etc** win; gain the advantage. **look one's/its ˈbest** look as beautiful, attractive, etc as possible: *The garden looks its best in the spring.* **make the best of it/things/a bad deal/a bad job** do what one can and be as contented as possible in spite of misfortune, failure, etc. **make the ˈbest of oneself** make oneself as attractive as possible. **one's Sunday best** ⇨ SUNDAY. **to the best of one's aˈbility** using all one's ability. **to the best of one's beˈlief/ˈknowledge** so far as one knows (without being certain): *To the best of my knowledge she is still living there.* **to the best of one's memory** as far as one can remember: *To the best of my memory he always had a beard.* **with the ˈbest (of them)** as well as anyone: *At sixty he still plays tennis with the best of them.* **with the ˈbest of intentions** intending only to help or do good: *It was done with the best of intentions.*

best[4] /best/ *v* [Tn esp passive] defeat (sb); outwit.

bestial /ˈbestɪəl; *US* ˈbestʃəl/ *adj* (*derog*) of or like a beast; brutish; cruel: *a bestial person, act* ○ *bestial violence, lust, fury.*

▷ **bestiality** /ˌbestɪˈælətɪ; *US* ˌbestʃɪ-/ *n* **1** [U] **(a)** quality of being bestial: *an act of horrifying bestiality.* **(b)** sexual activity between a human and an animal. **2** [C] brutal act, esp of a sexually perverted kind.

bestially *adv.*

bestiary /ˈbestɪərɪ; *US* -tɪerɪ/ *n* medieval collection of stories about animals, including fables and legends.

bestir /bɪˈstɜː(r)/ *v* (-rr-) [Tn] ~ **oneself** (*fml or joc*) become active or busy: *He was too lazy to bestir himself even to answer the telephone.*

bestow /bɪˈstəʊ/ *v* [Tn, Tn·pr] ~ **sth (on sb)** (*fml*) present sth as a gift (to sb); confer: *an honour bestowed on her by the king.* ▷ **bestowal** /bɪˈstəʊəl/ *n* [U].

bestrew /bɪˈstruː/ *v* (*pt* **bestrewed**, *pp* **bestrewed** or **bestrewn**) (*fml or rhet*) **(a)** [Tn] lie scattered on or over (a surface): *petals bestrewed the lawn.* **(b)** [Tn·pr] ~ **sth with sth** cover (a surface) with scattered things: *a path bestrewn with petals* ○ *They bestrewed his path with petals.*

bestride /bɪˈstraɪd/ *v* (*pt* **bestrode** /bɪˈstrəʊd/, *pp* **bestridden** /bɪˈstrɪdn/) [Tn] (*fml*) sit or stand with one leg on each side of (sth): *bestride a horse, chair, ditch, fence.*

bet /bet/ *v* (-tt-; *pt, pp* **bet** or **betted**) **1** [I, Ipr, Tn·pr, Tf, Dn·n, Dn·f] ~ **(sth) (on sth)** risk (money) on a race or on some other event of which the result is doubtful: *I don't enjoy betting.* ○ *He spends all his money betting on horses.* ○ *She bet me £20 that I wouldn't be able to give up smoking.* ⇨ article at GAMBLING. **2** (idm) **bet one's bottom ˈdollar (on sth/that...); bet one's ˈboots that...; bet one's (sweet) ˈlife that...** (*infml*) be absolutely certain about sth: *You can bet your bottom dollar he won't have waited for us.* **I bet (that)...** (*infml*) I am certain: *I bet he arrives late — he always does.* **ˌyou ˈbet** (*infml*) you may be sure (of it): *'Are you going to the match?' 'You bet (I am)!'*

▷ **bet** *n* **1 (a)** arrangement to risk money, etc on an event of which the result is doubtful: *make a bet* ○ *have a bet on the Derby* ○ *win/lose a bet.* **(b)** money, etc risked in this way: *place/put a bet on a horse.* **2** (*infml*) opinion; prediction: *My bet is they've got held up in the traffic.* **3** (idm) **one's best bet** ⇨ BEST[1]. **hedge one's bets** ⇨ HEDGE.

beta /ˈbiːtə; *US* ˈbeɪtə/ *n* the second letter of the Greek alphabet (Β, β).

□ **ˈbeta-blocker** drug used to prevent unhealthy increases in the activity of the heart.

ˈbeta particle electron or positron emitted by a radioactive substance.

ˈbeta ray stream of beta particles.

betatron /ˈbiːtətrɒn; *US* ˈbeɪtətrɑːn/ *n* (*physics*) apparatus for accelerating electrons in a circular path.

betel /ˈbiːtl/ *n* [U] tropical Asian plant (*Piper betle*) whose leaf is chewed with the betel-nut.

□ **ˈbetel-nut** *n* [U, C] = ARECA NUT (ARECA).

Betelgeuse /ˈbiːtlʒɜːz; *US* ˈbiːtldʒuːs/ bright red star in the constellation of Orion.

bête noire /ˌbeɪt ˈnwɑː(r)/ (*pl* **bêtes noires** /ˌbeɪt ˈnwɑːz/) (*French*) person or thing that one particularly dislikes.

Bethlehem /ˈbeθlɪhem/ town near Jerusalem, where, according to the Bible, both King David and Jesus were born. ⇨ map at ISRAEL.

betide /bɪˈtaɪd/ *v* (idm) **woe betide sb** ⇨ WOE.

Betjeman /ˈbetʃəmən/ Sir John (1906-84), English poet. He produced some of the most popular poetry of the 20th century, writing about recognizable characters and social situations. His poems have wit and elegance, but there is also a note of sadness and religious questioning. He was made Poet Laureate in 1972. *Summoned by Bells* (1960) is a verse autobiography of his young days. Betjeman also produced books on architecture and campaigned against the destruction of Victorian buildings.

betoken /bɪˈtəʊkən/ *v* [Tn] (*fml*) be a sign of (sth); indicate: *milder weather betokening the arrival of spring.*

betray /bɪˈtreɪ/ *v* **1** [Tn, Tn·pr] ~ **sb/sth (to sb)** hand over or show sb/sth disloyally (to an enemy): *betraying state secrets* ○ *Judas betrayed Jesus (to the authorities).* **2** [Tn] be disloyal to (sth): *betray one's country, one's principles* ○ *In failing to return the money he betrayed our trust.* **3** [Tn] **(a)** show (sth) unintentionally; be a sign of: *She said she was sorry, but her eyes betrayed her secret delight.* ○ *His accent betrayed the fact that he was foreign.* **(b)** ~ **oneself** show what or who one really is: *He had a good disguise, but as soon as he spoke he betrayed himself*, ie he was recognized by his voice.

▷ **betrayal** /bɪˈtreɪəl/ *n* **(a)** [U] betraying or being betrayed: *an act of betrayal.* **(b)** [C] instance of this: *a betrayal of trust.*

betrayer *n.*

betroth /bɪˈtrəʊð/ *v* [usu passive: Tn, Tn·pr] ~ **sb (to sb)** (*arch or fml*) bind sb with a promise to marry; engage sb to marry: *She was betrothed (to the duke).* ○ *The pair were later betrothed.*

▷ **betrothal** /bɪˈtrəʊðl/ *n* [C, U] (*fml*) engagement to be married.

betrothed *n* [sing], *adj* (*fml*) (person) engaged to be married: *his betrothed* ○ *the betrothed couple.*

better[1] /ˈbetə(r)/ *adj* (*comparative of* GOOD[1]) **1 (a)** of a more excellent or desirable kind: *a better worker, job, car* ○ *You're a better man than I (am).* ○ *The weather couldn't have been better.* ○ *Life was difficult then but things have got better and better over the years.* ○ *He resolved to lead a better life* (ie be more virtuous) *in future.* **(b)** of a more precise or suitable kind: *Having talked to the witnesses I now have a better idea (of) what happened.* ○ *Can't you think of a better word than 'nice' to describe your holiday?* Cf BEST[1]. **2** partly or fully recovered from an illness: *The patient is much better today.* ○ *His ankle is getting better.* Cf WELL[2] 1, WORSE. **3** (idm) **against one's better ˈjudgement** even though one feels that it may be unwise: *He agreed, but very much against his better judgement.* **be better than one's ˈword** be more generous than one has promised to be. **be no better than she ˈshould be** (*dated euph*) (of a woman) have casual sexual relationships. **the best/better part of sth** ⇨ PART[1]. **one's better ˈfeelings/ˈnature** more honourable or virtuous part of one's character. **one's better ˈhalf** (*infml joc*) one's wife or husband. **ˌbetter luck ˈnext time** (*saying*) (used to encourage sb after a setback). **discretion is the better part of valour** ⇨ DISCRETION. **half a loaf is better than none/than no bread** ⇨ HALF[1]. **have**

seen/known better ˈdays be poorer or in a worse state now than formerly: *That coat has seen better days.* **(be) little/no better than** practically; almost the same as: *He's no better than a common thief.* **prevention is better than cure** ⇨ PREVENTION. **two heads are better than one** ⇨ TWO.

better[2] /ˈbetə(r)/ *adv* (*comparative of* WELL[3]) **1** in a more pleasant, efficient, desirable, etc way: *You would write better if you had a good pen.* ○ *She sings better than I (do).* **2** to a greater degree; more: *I like him better than her.* ○ *You'll like it better when you understand it more.* ○ *The better I know her, the more I admire her.* **3** more usefully: *His advice is better ignored*, ie it should be ignored. ○ *If the roads are icy, you'd be better advised* (ie it would be more prudent) *to delay your departure.* **4** (idm) **be better off (doing sth)** be wiser (to do sth specified): *He'd be better off going to the police about it.* **be better off without sb/sth** be happier or more at ease without sb/sth: *We'd be better off without them as neighbours.* **ˌbetter the ˌdevil you ˈknow (than the ˌdevil you ˈdon't)** (*saying*) it is easier to deal with an undesirable but familiar person, situation, etc than to risk a change which may make things worse. **ˌbetter ˈlate than ˈnever** (*saying*) **(a)** (used as an excuse or apology for one's lateness) **(b)** some success, however delayed or small it is, is better than none at all. **better ˌsafe than ˈsorry** (*saying*) it is wiser to be over-cautious and take proper care than to be rash and careless (and so do sth which one may regret). **better/worse still** ⇨ STILL[2]. **do better to do sth** be more sensible if one does sth: *Don't buy now — you'd do better to wait for the sales.* **go one ˈbetter (than sb/sth)** do better (than sb/sth); outdo sb/sth: *I bought a small boat, then he went one better and bought a yacht.* **had better/best** would be wise to: *You'd better not say that.* ○ *Hadn't we better take an umbrella?* ○ *I had better* (ie I think I should) *begin by introducing myself.* **know better** ⇨ KNOW. **not know any better** ⇨ KNOW. **old enough to know better** ⇨ OLD. **think better of sth** ⇨ THINK[1].

better[3] /ˈbetə(r)/ *n* **1** that which is better: *We had hoped for better.* ○ *I expected better of him*, ie I thought he would have behaved better. **2** (idm) **one's (elders and) ˈbetters** (older and) wiser, more experienced people: *You should show greater respect for your elders and betters.* **a change for the better/worse** ⇨ CHANGE[2]. **(feel) (all) the better for sth** benefiting physically or mentally from sth: *You'll feel all the better for (having had) a holiday.* **for ˌbetter (or) for ˈworse** in both good and bad fortune. **for ˌbetter or ˈworse** whether the result is good or bad: *It's been done, and, for better or worse, we can't change it now.* **get the better of sb/sth** defeat sb/sth: *You always get the better of me at chess.* ○ *His shyness got the better of him*, ie He was overcome by shyness. **get the better of sth** win in (an argument, etc): *She always gets the better of our quarrels.* **the less/least said (about sb/sth) the better** (*saying*) that person or thing is an unpleasant subject and it is better not to talk about him/it. **so much the ˈbetter/ˈworse (for sb/sth)** that is even better/worse: *The result is not very important to us, but if we do win, (then) so much the better.* **the sooner the better** ⇨ SOON. **think (all) the better of sb** ⇨ THINK[1].

better[4] /ˈbetə(r)/ *v* [Tn] **1 (a)** do better than (sth); surpass: *This achievement cannot be bettered.* **(b)** improve (sth): *The government hopes to better the conditions of the workers.* **2** ~ **oneself** get a better social position or status.

▷ **betterment** *n* [U] (*fml*) making or becoming better; improvement.

better[5] /ˈbetə(r)/ *n* person who bets; punter.

betting-shop /ˈbetɪŋ ʃɒp/ *n* bookmaker's office.

between /bɪˈtwiːn/ *prep* **1 (a)** in or into the space separating (two or more points, objects, people, etc): *Q comes between P and R in the English alphabet.* ○ *I lost my keys somewhere between the car and the house.* ○ *Peter sat between Mary and Jane.* ○ *Switzerland lies between France, Germany, Austria and Italy.* ○ *The baby crawled between her father's legs.* ○ (*fig*) *My job is somewhere between a typist and a personal assistant.* **(b)** in the period of time separating (two days, years, events, etc): *It's cheaper between 6 pm and 8 am.* ○ *I'm usually free between Tuesday and Thursday.* ○ *Children must attend school between 5 and 16.* ○ *Many changes took place between the two world wars.* **2** at some point along a scale from (one amount, weight, distance, etc) to (another): *cost between one and two pounds* ○ *weigh between nine and ten stones* ○ *London is between fifty and sixty miles from Oxford.* ○ *The temperature remained between 25°C and 30°C all week.* **3** (of a line) separating (one place) from another: *build a wall between my garden and my neighbour's* ○ *draw a line between sections A and B* ○ *the boundary between Sweden and Norway.* **4** from (one place) to (another): *fly between London and Paris twice daily* ○ *sail between Dover and Calais* ○ *a good road between London and Brighton.* **5** (indicating a connection or relationship): *an obvious link between unemployment and the crime rate* ○ *the bond between a boy and his dog* ○ *They have settled the dispute between them.* ○ *the affection, friendship, love, etc between people.* **6 (a)** shared by (two people or things): *We drank a bottle of wine between us.* ○ *This is just between you and me/between ourselves*, ie It is a secret. ○ *They carried only one rucksack between them.* **(b)** by the actions or contributions of (esp two people or things): *They wrote the book between them.* ○ *Between them they raised £500.* ○ *We can afford to buy a house between us.* ⇨ Usage at AMONG.

▷ **between** (also **in between**) *adv* **(a)** in or into the space separating two or more points, objects, people, etc: *One town ends where the next begins and there's a road that runs between.* ○ *You'd have a good view of the sea from here except for the block of flats in between.* **(b)** in the period of time separating two dates, events, etc: *We have two lessons this morning, but there's some free time in between.*

betwixt /bɪˈtwɪkst/ *adv, prep* (idm) **betwixt and between** in an intermediate position; neither one thing nor the other: *It's difficult buying clothes for ten-year-olds — at that age they're betwixt and between.*

Bevan /ˈbevn/ Aneurin (1897-1960), Welsh politician and noted orator. As Minister of Health in the Labour government after the Second World War, he was largely responsible for setting up the British *National Health Service. He was a pacifist, but at the end of his career he supported the idea of Britain having nuclear weapons.

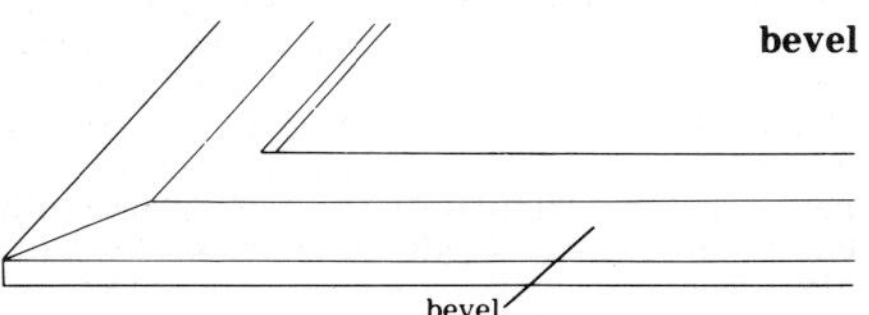

bevel /ˈbevl/ *n* **1** sloping edge or surface, eg at the side of a picture frame or a sheet of plate glass. ⇨ illus. **2** (in carpentry and stonework) tool for making such edges.

▷ **bevel** *v* (**-ll-**; *US* **-l-**) [Tn] give a sloping edge to (sth): *bevelled edges.*

□ **ˈbevel gear** either of a pair of gears with sloping toothed edges. ⇨ illus at GEAR.

beverage /ˈbevərɪdʒ/ *n* (*fml or joc*) any type of drink except water, eg milk, tea, wine, beer.

Beveridge /ˈbevərɪdʒ/ William Henry, first Baron (1879-1963), British economist (Lord Beveridge). He was for many years director of the London School of Economics, and was responsible for the report (in 1942) which led to the creation of the national insurance scheme in Britain.

Bevin /ˈbevɪn/ Ernest (1881-1951), English politician. He was a major figure in the Trade Union movement and was elected as a Labour Member of Parliament in 1940. He played an important role in the setting up of *NATO and the *Marshall Plan.

bevy /ˈbevɪ/ *n* **1** large group: *a bevy of beautiful girls.* **2** flock of birds, esp quails.

bewail /bɪˈweɪl/ *v* [Tn] (*fml*) express sorrow over (sth); mourn for: *bewailing one's lost youth, innocence, etc.*

beware /bɪˈweə(r)/ *v* [I, Ipr] (used only in the infinitive and imperative) ~ **(of sb/sth)** be cautious (of sb/sth); take care (about sb/sth): *He told us to beware (of pickpockets, the dog, icy roads).* ○ *Beware — wet paint!*

Thomas Bewick: Cattle

Bewick /ˈbjuːɪk/ Thomas (1753-1828), English artist. He worked mainly as a book illustrator and brought a new realistic style to the art of engraving. He is chiefly famous for his pictures of birds and other animals. ⇨ illus.

bewilder /bɪˈwɪldə(r)/ *v* [Tn] puzzle (sb); confuse: *The child was bewildered by the noise and the crowds.* ○ *I am totally bewildered by the clues to this crossword puzzle.*

▷ **bewildering** /bɪˈwɪldərɪŋ/ *adj* puzzling: *bewildering speed, complexity.*

bewilderment *n* [U] state of being bewildered: *watch, listen, gape in bewilderment.*

bewitch /bɪˈwɪtʃ/ *v* [Tn] **1** put a magic spell on (sb): *The wicked fairy bewitched the prince and turned him into a frog.* **2** delight (sb) very much; enchant: *He was bewitched by her beauty.*

▷ **bewitching** *adj* very delightful or attractive: *a bewitching smile.* **bewitchingly** *adv.*

beyond /bɪˈjɒnd/ *prep* **1** at or to a more distant point than (sth): *The new housing estate stretches beyond the playing-fields.* ○ *The road continues beyond the village up into the hills.* **2** later than (a specified time): *It won't go on beyond midnight.* ○ *I know what I shall be doing for the next three weeks but I haven't thought beyond that.* ○ *She carried on teaching well beyond retirement age*, ie when she was older than 60. **3** not within the range of (sth); surpassing: *The bicycle is beyond repair*, ie is too badly damaged to repair. ○ *After 25 years the town centre had changed beyond (all) recognition.* ○ *They're paying £75 000 for a small flat — it's beyond belief.* ○ *She's living beyond her means*, ie spending more than she earns. ○ *Her skill as a musician is beyond praise*, ie of extremely high quality. **4** except (sth); apart from: *He's got nothing beyond his state pension.* ○ *That's (going) beyond a joke.* ○ *I didn't notice anything beyond his rather strange accent.* **5** (idm) **be beyond sb** (*infml*) be impossible for sb to imagine, understand or calculate: *It's beyond me why she wants to marry Geoff.* ○ *How people design computer games is beyond me.*

▷ **beyond** *adv* at or to a distance: *Snowdon and the mountains beyond were covered in snow.* ○ *We must look beyond for signs of change.* ○ *The immediate future is clear, but it's hard to tell what lies beyond.*

bezel /ˈbezl/ *n* rim that holds sth in place, esp the glass cover of a watch or a jewel in a ring.

bezique /bɪˈziːk/ *n* [U] card-game for two players, using two packs of cards from which all cards from two to six have been removed.

bf *abbr* **1** (*euph*) bloody fool. **2** (*commerce*) brought forward.

BFPO /ˌbiː ef piː ˈəʊ/ *abbr* British Forces Post Office: *Capt John Jones, HMS Amazon, BFPO (ships)*, eg on a letter.

Bhagavadgita /ˌbɑːgəvɑːdˈgiːtə/ one of the most important Hindu sacred books. It is part of the Mahabharata and tells how Krishna, an incarnation of Vishnu, instructs the prince Arjuna before a battle.

bhang /bæŋ/ *n* [U] **(a)** Indian hemp. **(b)** its dried leaves, which can be chewed as a narcotic drug.

bhp *abbr* brake-horsepower.

Bhutan /buːˈtɑːn/ state lying between India and China; pop approx 1 451 000; official language Dzongkha; capital Thimphu; unit of currency ngultrum (= 100 chetrum) or Indian rupee. A remote mountainous country in the Himalayas, it is independent, but a protectorate of India. ⇨ map at INDIA.

Bi *symb* bismuth.

bi- *pref* two; twice: *biannual* ○ *bicentenary*. Cf DI-, TRI-.

NOTE ON USAGE: Note that **bi-** is used with certain expressions of time (eg *bimonthly*) to mean both 'every two' (months) and 'twice a' (month). There is a distinction between *biennial* (every two years) and *biannual* (twice a year).

biannual /baɪˈænjʊəl/ *adj* occurring twice a year: *a biannual meeting*. ▷ **biannually** *adv*.

bias /ˈbaɪəs/ *n* [U, C usu *sing*] **1** opinion or feeling that strongly favours one side in an argument or one item in a group or series; predisposition; prejudice: *The university has a bias towards/in favour of/against the sciences.* ○ *The committee is of a/has a conservative bias.* ○ *He is without bias*, ie is impartial. **2** slanting direction across threads of woven material: *The skirt is cut on the bias*, ie cut with the threads running diagonally across the weave. **3 (a)** (in bowls) tendency of the ball to swerve because of the way it is weighted. **(b)** weighting that causes this.

▷ **bias** *v* (-s-, -ss-) [Tn, Tn·pr] ~ **sb (towards/in favour of/against sb/sth)** give a bias to sb; prejudice sb; influence sb, esp unfairly: *a bias(s)ed account/jury*, ie one which is not impartial ○ *The newspaper/He is clearly bias(s)ed (in the government's favour).*

□ ˌ**bias** ˈ**binding** strip of fabric cut diagonally, used to bind edges.

biathlon /baɪˈæθlɒn/ *n* athletic contest in which participants compete at skiing and shooting. Cf DECATHLON, PENTATHLON.

bib /bɪb/ *n* **1** piece of cloth or plastic fixed under a child's chin to protect its clothes while it is eating. **2** front part of an apron, above the waist. **3** (idm) **one's best bib and tucker** ⇨ BEST[1].

bible /ˈbaɪbl/ *n* **(a)** (also **the Bible**) sacred writings of the Christian Church, comprising the *Old and *New Testaments. ⇨ App 5. **(b)** copy of these: *three bibles.* **(c)** (*fig*) any authoritative book: *the stamp-collector's bible.*

▷ **biblical** /ˈbɪblɪkl/ *adj* of or in the Bible: *a biblical theme, expression* ○ *biblical times, language.*

□ ˈ**bible-bashing**, ˈ**bible-punching** *ns* [U] (*infml derog*) evangelical preaching.

ˈ**Bible belt** (*US*) parts of southern and central USA, where many people have very strict religious views, including a fundamental belief in the truth of the Bible.

📖 One of the principles of the Reformation in Europe was that the Bible should be available in a vernacular translation instead of Latin. In England, the *Authorized Version* was published in 1611, and is still the best known and most popular version. It was produced by a panel of scholars, made up of translators and revisers of existing texts, on the order of King James I. For this reason, it is known as King James' Bible or the King James Version. The next important edition of the Bible to be published was the *Revised Version.* The New Testament of this, issued in 1881, was criticized for its modernization of many familiar passages, but the Old Testament section, issued in 1885, was generally regarded as an important improvement on the text of the *Authorized Version.* An American edition was published in 1901. There have been several new versions and translations in the 20th century. The most important of these are the *Revised Standard Version*, published between 1946 and 1952, the *New English Bible*, in modern English, published in 1961 (Old Testament) and 1970 (New Testament and Apocrypha), and the *Good News Bible*, published by the American Bible Society in 1966 (New Testament) and 1976 (complete text). This last Bible was simplified so that it could be easily understood by all readers, including those whose first language is not English.

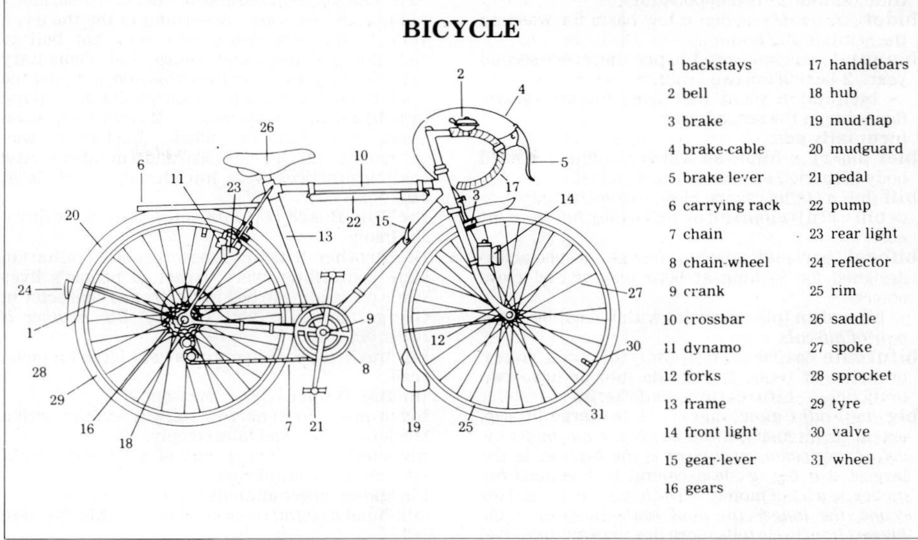

biblio- *comb form* (forming *ns* and *adjs*) of books: *bibliophile* ○ *bibliographical.*

bibliography /ˌbɪblɪˈɒgrəfɪ/ *n* **1** [C] list of books or articles about a particular subject or by a particular author: *There is a useful bibliography at the end of each chapter.* **2** [U] study of the history of books and their production. ▷ **bibliographer** /-ˈɒgrəfə(r)/ *n*. **bibliographical** /ˌbɪblɪəˈgræfɪkl/ *adj*.

bibliophile /ˈbɪblɪəfaɪl/ *n* person who loves or collects books.

bibulous /ˈbɪbjʊləs/ *adj* (*joc*) excessively fond of or addicted to alcoholic drink.

bicameral /ˌbaɪˈkæmərəl/ *adj* having two legislative chambers (eg in Britain the House of Commons and the House of Lords): *a bicameral system of government.*

bicarb *n* [U] (*infml*) = SODIUM BICARBONATE (SODIUM).

bicarbonate /ˌbaɪˈkɑːbənət/ (also ˌ**hydrogen** ˈ**carbonate**) *n* [U] (*chemistry*) salt of carbonic acid in which one hydrogen atom has been replaced.

□ **bi**ˌ**carbonate of** ˈ**soda** = SODIUM BICARBONATE (SODIUM).

bicentenary /ˌbaɪsenˈtiːnərɪ; *US* -ˈsentənerɪ/ *n* two-hundredth anniversary; celebration of this: *1949 was the bicentenary of Goethe's birth.* ○ [attrib] *bicentenary celebrations.*

bicentennial /ˌbaɪsenˈtenɪəl/ *adj* happening once in two hundred years; marking a bicentenary: *a bicentennial anniversary/celebration.*

▷ **bicentennial** *n* = BICENTENARY.

biceps /ˈbaɪseps/ *n* (*pl* unchanged) large muscle at the front of the upper arm, which bends the elbow: *His biceps is/are impressive.* Cf TRICEPS.

bicker /ˈbɪkə(r)/ *v* [I, Ipr] ~ **(with sb) (over/about sth)** quarrel about unimportant things: *The children are always bickering (with each other) (over their toys).*

bicuspid /ˌbaɪˈkʌspɪd/ *n* tooth with two points. There are four bicuspids on each side of the human mouth (between the molars and the canines).

bicycle /ˈbaɪsɪkl/ *n* two-wheeled vehicle on which a person rides, using pedals to drive it along: [attrib] *a* ˈ*bicycle pump*, ie one used for filling the tyres with air. Cf BIKE, CYCLE. ⇨ illus.

▷ **bicycle** *v* [I, Ipr, Ip] ride on a bicycle.

bicyclist *n*.

📖 After the Second World War the use of bicycles declined as more and more people owned cars. In recent years, because of the traffic congestion in cities and the damage that cars do to the environment, the bicycle has once again become popular both for journeys in towns and cities and for leisure.

□ ˈ**bicycle-clip** *n* each of a pair of clips for holding trousers at the ankles while cycling.

bid[1] /bɪd/ *v* (**-dd-**; *pt, pp* **bid** in sense 3, *pt* usu **bade** /bæd/, *pp* **bidden** /ˈbɪdn/) **1** [I, Ipr, Tn, Tn·pr] ~ **(sth) (for sth)**; *esp US* ~ **(sth) (on sth) (a)** offer (a price) in order to buy sth, esp at an auction: *What am I bid (for this painting)?* ○ *She bid £500 (for the painting).* ○ *We had hoped to get the house but another couple was bidding against us*, ie repeatedly offering a higher price than us. **(b)** offer (a price) for doing work, providing a service, etc: *Several firms have bid for the contract to build the new concert hall.* **2** [I, Tn] (in card-games, esp bridge) make a bid[2](4): *bid two hearts.* **3** (*arch or fml*) **(a)** [Dn·t] order (sb); tell: *Do as you are bidden.* ○ *She bade me (to) come in.* **(b)** [Dn·pr, Dn·t] invite (sb): *guests bidden to (attend) the feast.* **(c)** [no passive: Dn·n, Dn·pr] ~ **sth to sb** say sth as a greeting, etc: *bid sb good morning* ○ *He bade farewell* (ie said goodbye) *to his sweetheart.* **4** (idm) **bid fair to do sth** (*arch or rhet*) seem likely to do sth: *The plan for a new hospital bids fair to succeed.*

▷ **biddable** *adj* ready to obey; docile.

bidder *n* person or group that bids at an auction: *The house went to the highest bidder*, ie the person who offered the most money.

bidding *n* [U] **1** (*fml*) order; command: *do sb's bidding*, ie obey sb ○ *At his father's bidding he wrote to his lawyer.* **2** offering of prices at an auction: *Bidding was brisk*, ie Many offers were made one after the other. **3** (in card-games) process of bidding (BID[1] 2): *Can you remind me of the bidding* (ie who bid what)?

bid[2] /bɪd/ *n* **1** price offered in order to buy sth, esp at an auction: *make a bid of £50 for a painting* ○ *Any higher/further bids?* **2** (*esp US*) = TENDER[3]. **3** effort to do, obtain, achieve, etc sth; attempt: *He failed in his bid to reach the summit.* ○ *make a bid for power/popular support.* **4** statement of the number of tricks a player proposes to win in a card-game: *'It's your bid next.' 'No bid.'*

biddy /ˈbɪdɪ/ *n* (usu **old biddy**) (*infml usu derog*) old woman: *The café was full of old biddies gossiping over cups of tea.*

bide /baɪd/ *v* **1** (*arch*) = ABIDE. **2** (idm) **bide one's**

time wait for a good opportunity.

bidet /ˈbiːdeɪ; *US* biːˈdeɪ/ *n* low basin for washing the genitals and bottom.

biennial /baɪˈenɪəl/ *adj* **1** happening every second year. **2** lasting for two years.
▷ **biennial** *n* plant that lives for two years, flowering in the second year.
biennially *adv*.

bier /bɪə(r)/ *n* frame on which a coffin or a dead body is carried or placed before burial.

biff /bɪf/ *n* (*infml*) sharp blow, esp with the fist.
▷ **biff** *v* [Tn] (*infml*) hit or strike (sb): *biff sb on the nose.*

bifocal /ˌbaɪˈfəʊkl/ *adj* (esp of lenses in spectacles) designed for looking at both distant and close objects.
▷ **bifocals** *n* [pl] spectacles with bifocal lenses: *a pair of bifocals.*

bifurcate /ˈbaɪfəkeɪt/ *v* [I] (*fml*) (of roads, rivers, branches of trees, etc) divide into or have two branches. ▷ **bifurcation** /ˌbaɪfəˈkeɪʃn/ *n*.

big /bɪg/ *adj* (**-gger**, **-ggest**) **1** (**a**) large in size, extent or intensity: *a big garden, man, majority, defeat, explosion, argument* ○ *the big toe*, ie the largest ○ *a big 'g'*, ie a capital G ○ (*infml*) *big money*, ie a lot of money ○ *The bigger* (ie worse) *the crime, the longer the gaol sentence.* ○ *He's the biggest liar* (ie He tells more lies than anyone else) *I know.* ○ *She's a big eater/spender*, ie She eats/spends a lot. Cf SMALL. (**b**) (esp of animals) pregnant and near to giving birth. **2** (more) grown up: *my big sister*, ie my elder sister ○ *He's big enough to go out without his parents.* **3** [attrib] important: *the big match* ○ *a big decision* ○ *the biggest moment of my life* ○ *She's one of the biggest names* (ie one of the most famous and important people) *in the pop industry.* **4** (*infml*) ambitious; extravagant: *have big ideas/plans.* **5** (*infml esp US*) popular with the public: *Video games are big this year.* ⇨ Usage. **6** ~ **on sth** (*infml*) (*esp US*) keen on sth; enthusiastic about sth: *The firm is big on extravagant promotion drives.* **7** (*infml often ironic*) generous (used esp as in the expression shown): *He actually apologized. Big of him, wasn't it?* **8** (idm) **be/get too ˌbig for one's ˈboots** (*infml*) be/become very self-important or conceited. **a ˌbig ˈcheese** (*sl derog*) very important and powerful person. **big ˈdeal!** (*infml ironic*) I am not impressed: *We're getting a wage increase of £40 a year, before tax. Big deal!* **a big fish (in a little pond)** important and influential person (in a small community or restricted situation). **a big ˈgun** (also esp *US* **a big ˈwheel**) (*infml*) important or influential person: *She's got the support of the big guns in the party.* **a big ˈnoise/ˈshot** (*infml*) important person. **(carry, wave, etc) the big ˈstick** (threaten) the use of force, esp great military strength: *The army decided to use the big stick and fired on the protesters.* **the big ˈthree/ˈfour, etc** the three, four, etc most important nations, people, companies, things, etc: *a meeting of the big five.* **the ˈbig time** (*infml*) highest or most successful level in a profession, etc, esp in show business. **sb's eyes are bigger than his belly/stomach** ⇨ EYE[1]. **give sb/get a big ˈhand** applaud sb/be applauded loudly and generously: *Let's all give her a big hand.* **have bigger/other fish to fry** ⇨ FISH[1]. **in a big/small way** ⇨ WAY[1]. **think big** ⇨ THINK[1]. **what's the big iˈdea?** (*infml*) (used to protest about sth that is happening): *What's the big idea? Turn that television back on!*
▷ **big** *adv* (*sl*) **1** in a big manner; impressively; grandly: *Let's think big*, ie plan ambitiously. ○ *He likes to talk big*, ie is very boastful. **2** successfully: *a band which comes/goes over big with pop fans world-wide.* **3** (idm) **make it ˈbig** (*infml*) become successful: *She's a star in this country but she never made it big in the States.*
bigness *n* [U].
□ **the Big ˈApple** (*sl*) New York.
ˌbig bad ˈwolf wicked wolf in the traditional story of 'The Three Little Pigs'. He threatens each of them by saying 'I'll huff, and I'll puff, and I'll blow your house down,' but is finally defeated.
big ˈbang 1 explosion that is widely believed to have caused the creation of the universe many millions of years ago. According to the theory, a very small, very dense and very hot ball of radiation expanded and cooled, and elementary particles flew out from the explosion, forming the matter which eventually made up all the galaxies: [attrib] *the big ˈbang theory.* **2** (*infml*) occasion when the London Stock Exchange was deregulated (27 October 1986) and a number of new trading practices were introduced. ⇨ article at FINANCE.
the ˌBig ˈBoard (*US infml*) the New York Stock Exchange.
Big ˈBrother dictator or the forces of a totalitarian state controlling every aspect of people's lives while pretending to be kindly (from a character in George *Orwell's *1984*): (*saying*) *Big Brother is watching you.*
big ˈbusiness commerce on a very large financial scale.
the Big ˈDipper (*US*) = PLOUGH[2] 2.
big ˈdipper (*Brit*) narrow railway at fairs with a track that rises and falls steeply.
big ˈend (in an engine) end of a connecting rod encircling the crankshaft.
big ˈgame larger animals hunted for sport.
ˈbig-head *n* (*infml*) conceited person. **big-ˈheaded** *adj*.
big-ˈhearted *adj* very kind; generous.
ˈbighorn *n* type of sheep from the Rocky Mountains.
ˈbig mouth (*infml derog esp US*) boastful person: *OK, big mouth, let's see what you can really do.*
big ˈtop main tent at a circus.
big ˈwheel huge revolving vertical wheel with passenger cars, used at fairs.
ˈbigwig *n* (*infml*) important person.

NOTE ON USAGE: **1 Big** and **large** are used when talking about physical size, extent, capacity or number. **Big** is more informal. **Large** is not normally used to describe people: *They live in a big/large house in the country.* ○ *Which is the biggest/largest desert in the world?* ○ *Her husband is a very big man.* ○ *There was a big/large crowd at the football match.* **2 Great** is mostly used when talking (usually approvingly) about importance, quality, ability or extent. **Great** can be used with uncountable nouns: *He's a great painter, footballer, man, etc.* ○ *Peter the Great was a Russian ruler.* ○ *She lived to a great age.* ○ *with great enthusiasm, joy, pleasure, etc.* **3 Large** and **great** are very similar in meaning when used with *amount, quantity* and *number*: *They spent a large/great amount of money on their holidays.* Note also the phrase: *to a large/great extent.*

bigamy /ˈbɪgəmɪ/ *n* [U] (crime of) marrying a person when still legally married to someone else.
▷ **bigamist** *n* person guilty of bigamy.
bigamous /ˈbɪgəməs/ *adj* guilty of bigamy; involving bigamy: *a bigamous marriage.*
bigamously *adv*.

Big Ben /ˌbɪg ˈben/ (**a**) bell that strikes the hours inside the great clock of the Houses of Parliament in London. (**b**) the clock itself. ⇨ illus at BARRY. ⇨ article at NATIONAL.

bight /baɪt/ *n* **1** long inward curve in a coast: *The Great Australian Bight.* **2** loop made in a rope.

bigot /ˈbɪgət/ *n* person who holds strong (esp religious or political) beliefs and opinions, and is intolerant of anyone who disagrees: *religious bigots.*
▷ **bigoted** *adj* intolerant and narrow-minded: *bigoted views* ○ *He is so bigoted that it is impossible to argue with him.*
bigotry *n* [U] bigoted attitude or behaviour.

bijou /ˈbiːʒuː/ *n* (*pl* **bijoux** /ˈbiːʒuː/) (*French*) jewel.
▷ **bijou** *adj* [attrib] small and elegant: *a bijou residence.*

bike /baɪk/ *n* (*infml*) **1** bicycle. **2** motor cycle. Cf CYCLE.
▷ **bike** *v* [I] (*infml*) ride a bicycle or motor cycle: *Let's go biking.*

bikini /bɪˈkiːnɪ/ *n* scanty two-piece costume worn by women for swimming and sun-bathing: [attrib] *a bikini top*, ie the top half of a bikini.

bilabial /ˌbaɪˈleɪbɪəl/ *n* (*phonetics*) speech sound produced by using both lips: *In English, b, p, m and w are bilabials.* ▷ **bilabial** *adj*.

bilateral /ˌbaɪˈlætərəl/ *adj* having two sides; affecting or involving two parties, countries, etc: *a bilateral agreement/treaty.* Cf MULTILATERAL, UNILATERAL.
▷ **bilateralism** *n* [U] principle based on bilateral agreements between countries, esp in trade and finance.
bilaterally *adv*.

bilberry /ˈbɪlbrɪ; *US* -berɪ/ (also **blaeberry**, **whortleberry**) *n* (**a**) small N European shrub growing on moors and in mountain woods. (**b**) its edible dark blue berry. Cf BLUEBERRY.

bile /baɪl/ *n* [U] **1** bitter yellowish liquid produced by the liver to help the body to digest fats. **2** (*fig*) bad temper; irritability.
□ **ˈbile-duct** *n* (*anatomy*) tube taking bile to the duodenum. ⇨ illus at DIGESTIVE SYSTEM.

bilge /bɪldʒ/ *n* **1** [C] almost flat part of the bottom of a ship, inside or outside. **2** (also **ˈbilge-water**) [U] dirty water that collects in a ship's bilge. **3** [U] (*sl*) worthless ideas or talk; nonsense: *Don't give me that bilge!*

bilharzia /ˌbɪlˈhɑːtsɪə/ *n* [U] (*medical*) tropical disease caused by flatworms in the blood.

bilingual /ˌbaɪˈlɪŋgwəl/ *adj* **1** (**a**) able to speak two languages equally well: *He is bilingual (in French and Spanish).* (**b**) having or using two languages: *a bilingual community.* **2** expressed or written in two languages: *a bilingual dictionary.* Cf MONOLINGUAL, MULTILINGUAL.
▷ **bilingual** *n* bilingual person.
bilingually *adv*.

bilious /ˈbɪlɪəs/ *adj* **1** caused by or suffering from too much bile: *a bilious attack/headache* ○ *I feel a little bilious after last night's dinner.* **2** bad-tempered; irritable. **3** of a sickly yellowish colour (similar to bile): *a bilious (shade of) green.* ▷ **biliousness** *n* [U].

bilk /bɪlk/ *v* [Tn, Tn·pr] ~ **sb ((out) of sth)** avoid paying money to sb; cheat sb (out of sth): *He bilked us of all our money.*

bill[1] /bɪl/ *n* **1** (*esp Brit*) (*US* **check**) written statement of money owed for goods or services supplied: *telephone, gas, heating bills* ○ *a bill for £5* ○ *Have you paid the bill?* **2** written or printed advertisement; notice; poster, placard: *Stick no bills!* ie Sticking posters, etc here is forbidden. **3** programme of entertainment (at a cinema, theatre, etc): *a horror double bill* (ie programme consisting of two horror films) *on TV.* **4** draft of a proposed law, to be discussed by a parliament: *propose, pass, throw out, amend a bill* ○ *The Industrial Relations Bill.* ⇨ article at PARLIAMENT. **5** (*US*) = NOTE[1] 4: *a ten-dollar bill.* **6** (idm) **a clean bill of health** ⇨ CLEAN[1]. **fill/fit the ˈbill** be adequate or suitable (for a specific purpose): *If you're very hungry a double helping of spaghetti should fit the bill!* **foot the bill** ⇨ FOOT[2]. **head/top the ˈbill** be the most important item or person on a list or a programme of entertainments: *She topped the bill at the Palace Theatre.*
▷ **bill** *v* **1** [Tn, Tn·pr] ~ **sb (for sth)** send sb a bill (for sth): *I can't pay for the books now. Will you bill me (for them) later?* **2** [Tnt esp passive] announce or advertise; put in a programme: *He is billed to* (ie It is announced that he will) *appear as Othello.*
□ **ˈbillboard** *n* (*US*) large outdoor board for advertisements; hoarding.
ˈbillfold *n* (*US*) = WALLET.
bill of exˈchange written order to pay money to a named person on a given date.
bill of ˈfare list of dishes that can be ordered in a restaurant; menu.
bill of ˈlading list giving details of a ship's cargo.
bill of ˈrights statement of basic human rights. In British history, the Bill of Rights of 1689 was concerned with establishing Parliament as the most important power in government and making William and Mary constitutional monarchs. The American Bill of Rights, passed in 1791, forms the

first ten amendments of the Constitution of the USA. They are concerned with the rights of the citizen, the States and the federal government. ⇨ article at PARLIAMENT.
bill of ˈsale official document recording the sale of personal property.
ˈbillposter (also **ˈbillsticker**) *n* person who sticks posters or advertisements on walls, hoardings, etc.

bill[2] /bɪl/ *n* **1** bird's beak. ⇨ illus at BIRD. **2** (esp in geographical names) narrow promontory: *Portland Bill.*
▷ **bill** *v* **1** [I] (of doves) stroke each other with their beaks. **2** (idm) **bill and ˈcoo** (*infml*) (of lovers) exchange kisses and loving whispers.

billabong /ˈbɪləbɒŋ/ *n* (*Austral*) branch of a river that forms a backwater.

billet[1] /ˈbɪlɪt/ *n* **1** lodging for soldiers or evacuees, esp in a private house: *The troops are all in billets,* ie not in camp or barracks. **2** (*dated infml*) job; position: *a cushy billet,* ie an undemanding one.
▷ **billet** *v* [Tn, Tn·pr] ~ **sb** (**on/with sb**) place (soldiers) in lodgings: *The soldiers were billeted on an old lady.*

billet[2] /ˈbɪlɪt/ *n* **1** thick piece of firewood. **2** small metal bar.

billet-doux /ˌbɪleɪ ˈdu:/ *n* (*pl* **billets-doux** /ˌbɪleɪ ˈdu:z/) (*joc*) love-letter.

billhook /ˈbɪlhʊk/ *n* long-handled tool with a curved blade for pruning trees, etc.

billiards /ˈbɪlɪədz/ *n* [sing *v*] game for two people played with cues and three balls on an oblong cloth-covered table: *have a game of billiards* ○ *Billiards is played by women as well as men.*
▷ **billiard-** /ˈbɪlɪəd-/ (in compounds) of or used for billiards: *a billiard-cue/-room/-table.*

Billingsgate /ˈbɪlɪŋzgeɪt/ one of London's oldest markets, dealing mainly in fish. Its name is associated with bad language since people working in the market were traditionally regarded as abusive and foul-mouthed.

billion /ˈbɪlɪən/ *pron, det* **1** 1 000 000 000; one thousand million(s). ⇨ App 9. **2** (*Brit*) (formerly) 1 000 000 000 000; one million million(s). ⇨ App 9.
▷ **billion** *n* (*pl* unchanged or ~**s**) **1** (*Brit*) the number 1 000 000 000 000. **2** (*esp US*) the number 1 000 000 000. Cf MILLIARD.
For the uses of *billion* see the examples at *hundred.*
billionnaire /ˌbɪljəˈneə(r)/ *n* person who has a billion pounds, dollars, etc; very rich person.

billow /ˈbɪləʊ/ *n* **1** (*arch*) large wave. **2** swelling mass (eg of smoke or fog) like a wave.
▷ **billow** *v* [I, Ipr, Ip] rise or roll like waves: *sails billowing (out) in the wind* ○ *Smoke billowed from the burning houses.*
billowy *adj* rising or moving like waves.

billy /ˈbɪlɪ/ (also **ˈbillycan**) *n* tin can with a lid and handle used by campers for cooking.

billy-goat /ˈbɪlɪ gəʊt/ *n* male goat. ⇨ illus at GOAT. Cf NANNY-GOAT.

billy-oh (also **ˈbilly-o**) /ˈbɪlɪ əʊ/ *n* (idm) **like ˈbilly-oh** (*dated infml*) vigorously; fast: *go, work, run, etc like billy-oh.*

Billy the Kid /ˌbɪlɪ ðə ˈkɪd/ nickname of William H Bonney (1859-81), an American outlaw. Although he murdered several people before being himself killed by a sheriff, his life was later romanticized in popular novels and he has been variously portrayed in many films.

biltong /ˈbɪltɒŋ/ *n* [U] (in S Africa) strips of lean meat salted and dried in the sun.

bimbo /ˈbɪmbəʊ/ *n* (~**s**) (*sl*) **1** young attractive woman who likes to enjoy herself. **2** (*US*) prostitute or woman with low moral standards.

bimetallism /ˌbaɪˈmetəlɪzəm/ *n* [U] use of two metals, esp gold and silver, with a fixed ratio to each other as the monetary standard.
▷ **bimetallic** /ˌbaɪmɪˈtælɪk/ *adj* **1** made of or using two metals. **2** using the system of bimetallism.

bimonthly /ˌbaɪˈmʌnθlɪ/ *adj* produced or happening every second month or twice a month: *a bimonthly journal, event.*

bin /bɪn/ *n* **1** large container, usu with a lid, for storing bread, flour, coal, wine, etc: *a ˈbread bin.* **2** (*esp Brit*) = DUSTBIN (DUST).

binary /ˈbaɪnərɪ/ *adj* of or involving a pair or pairs.
□ **ˌbinary ˈcompound** compound containing two chemical elements or radicals, eg sodium chloride.
ˌbinary ˈdigit either the digit 0 or the digit 1, as used in binary notation.
ˌbinary noˈtation, ˌbinary ˈsystem system of numbers, common in computing, using only the two digits 0 and 1.
ˌbinary ˈstar two stars that revolve around a common centre.

binaural /ˌbaɪnˈɔ:rəl/ *adj* (**a**) of, or used with, both ears. (**b**) (of sound) recorded by two microphones and usu transmitted separately to the two ears.

bind /baɪnd/ *v* (*pt, pp* **bound** /baʊnd/) **1** [Tn, Tn·pr, Tn·p] ~ **A** (**to B**); ~ **A and B** (**together**) (**a**) tie or fasten, eg with rope: *The hostages were bound (with ropes) and gagged.* ○ *They bound his legs (together) so he couldn't escape.* ○ *He was bound to a chair and left.* (**b**) (*fig*) hold (people or things) together; unite: *the feelings that bind him to her.* **2** [Tn, Tn·p] ~ **sth** (**up**) tie a band or strip of material round sth: *bind (up)* (ie bandage) *a wound* ○ *hair bound up with ribbon.* **3** [Tn, Tn·pr] ~ **sth** (**in sth**) fasten (sheets of paper) between covers: *bind a book* ○ *a well-bound book* ○ *two volumes bound in leather.* **4** [Tn, Tn·pr] ~ **sth** (**with sth**) cover (the edge of sth) in order to strengthen it or as a decoration: *bind the cuffs of a jacket with leather* ○ *bind the edge of a carpet,* ie to prevent fraying. **5** [I, Tn, Tn·p] ~ **sth** (**up/together**) (cause sth to) stick together in a solid mass: *Add an egg yolk to the flour and fat to make it bind/to bind the mixture.* ○ *Frost binds the soil.* ○ *The earth is ˈfrost-bound,* ie frozen hard. ○ *Some foods bind the bowels/are binding,* ie cause constipation. **6** [Tn, Tn·pr, Cn·t] ~ **sb/oneself** (**to sth**) impose a duty or legal obligation on sb (to do sth): *bind sb to secrecy,* ie make him promise to keep sth secret ○ *bind sb to pay a debt.* **7** (idm) **bind/tie sb hand and foot** ⇨ HAND[1]. **8** (phr v) **bind sb over** (**to keep the peace**) (*law*) warn sb that he will appear in court again if he breaks the law: *The magistrate bound him over (to keep the peace) for a year.*
▷ **bind** *n* [sing] (*infml*) **1** nuisance: *It's a hell of a bind.* **2** (*esp US*) difficult situation: *The President is in a real bind over his foreign affairs policy.*
binder *n* **1** person who binds books; bookbinder. **2** machine that binds harvested corn into sheaves, or straw into bales. **3** cover for holding sheets of paper, magazines, etc together. **4** substance (eg bitumen, cement) that makes things stick together.
bindery *n* place where books are bound.
binding *n* **1** [C] strong covering holding the pages of a book together. **2** [U] fabric used for binding edges, eg braid. — *adj* ~ (**on/upon sb**) imposing a legal obligation (on sb): *The agreement is binding on both parties.*

bindweed /ˈbaɪndwi:d/ *n* [U, C] type of wild convolvulus.

bine /baɪn/ *n* twisting stem of a climbing plant, esp the hop.

binge /bɪndʒ/ *n* (*infml*) **1** time of wild or excessive eating and drinking: *He went on/had a three-day binge.* **2** excessive indulgence in anything; spree: *a ˈshopping binge.*

bingo /ˈbɪŋgəʊ/ *n* [U] gambling game in which players cover numbers on individual cards as the numbers are called at random: [attrib] *a ˈbingo hall.* ⇨ article at GAMBLING.
▷ **bingo** *interj* (used to express pleasure at suddenly finding the answer to a problem, winning sth, etc): *I was out of work for weeks, until bingo, this wonderful job came up!*

binnacle /ˈbɪnəkl/ *n* (*nautical*) non-magnetic case for a ship's compass.

binoculars /bɪˈnɒkjʊləz/ *n* [pl] instrument with a lens for each eye, making distant objects seem nearer: *watch from a distance through (a pair of) binoculars.*

binomial /baɪˈnəʊmɪəl/ *n* (*mathematics*) algebraic expression consisting of two terms joined by + or −. ▷ **binomial** *adj.*
□ **biˌnomial noˈmenclature** system for naming plants or animals, devised by *Linnaeus (LINNAEAN). A double name is used, the first one showing the genus and the second one the species. So the tiger is called *Panthera tigris,* while another member of the cat family, the lion, is called *Panthera leo.*
biˈnomial theorem formula for finding any power(8) of a binomial without lengthy multiplication.

bint /bɪnt/ *n* (*dated Brit sexist sl usu derog*) young woman.

bi(o)- *comb form* of living things; of (esp human) life: *biology* ○ *biodegradable* ○ *biography.*

biochemistry /ˌbaɪəʊˈkemɪstrɪ/ *n* [U] scientific study of the chemistry of living organisms.
▷ **biochemical** /ˌbaɪəʊˈkemɪkl/ *adj.*
biochemist /ˌbaɪəʊˈkemɪst/ *n* expert in biochemistry.

biodegradable /ˌbaɪəʊdɪˈgreɪdəbl/ *adj* (of substances) that can be made to rot by bacteria.

bioengineering /ˌbaɪəʊˌendʒɪˈnɪərɪŋ/ *n* [U] **1** use of artificial tissues, organs, etc to replace parts of the body that are damaged, lost or functioning badly, eg artificial limbs and heart valves. **2** application of engineering knowledge to medicine and zoology.

biofeedback /ˌbaɪəʊˈfi:dbæk/ *n* [U] use of equipment to monitor physical processes such as the heartbeat and rate of breathing, so that a patient may become aware of them and try to control them.

biography /baɪˈɒgrəfɪ/ *n* (**a**) [C] story of a person's life written by sb else: *Boswell's biography of Johnson.* (**b**) [U] such writing as a branch of literature: *I prefer biography to fiction.*
▷ **biographer** /baɪˈɒgrəfə(r)/ *n* person who writes a biography.
biographic, -ical /ˌbaɪəˈgræfɪk, -ɪkl/ *adjs.*

biological /ˌbaɪəˈlɒdʒɪkl/ *adj* of or relating to biology: *a biological experiment, reaction* ○ *biological soap-powders,* ie ones that clean by destroying the living organisms contained in dirt.
▷ **biologically** *adv.*
□ **bioˌlogical ˈclock** system in animals and plants which controls the regular pattern of certain activities, eg sleep.
bioˌlogical conˈtrol control of pests, esp insects, by the introduction of their natural enemy.
bioˌlogical ˈwarfare (also **ˌgerm ˈwarfare**) use of germs as a weapon in war.

biology /baɪˈɒlədʒɪ/ *n* [U] scientific study of the life and structure of plants and animals.
▷ **biologist** /-dʒɪst/ *n* expert in biology. Cf BOTANY, ZOOLOGY.

bionic /baɪˈɒnɪk/ *adj* (in science fiction) having parts of the body that are operated electronically; having superhuman strength as a result of this.

biophysics /ˌbaɪəʊˈfɪzɪks/ *n* [sing *v*] scientific study of the physical aspects of biology. ▷ **biophysical** *adj.* **biophysicist** *n.*

biopsy /ˈbaɪɒpsɪ/ *n* (*medical*) examination of fluids or tissue taken from a living body to diagnose a disease. Cf AUTOPSY.

biorhythm /ˈbaɪəʊrɪðəm/ *n* any of the recurring cycles of physical, emotional and intellectual activity said to affect human behaviour.

bioscope /ˈbaɪəskəʊp/ *n* (*S African*) cinema.

biosphere /ˈbaɪəsfɪə(r)/ *n* [sing] parts of the earth where living things are found, ie its surface, the parts just beneath the surface and the lower atmosphere.

biotechnology /ˌbaɪəʊtekˈnɒlədʒɪ/ *n* [U] branch of technology concerned with the forms of industrial production that use micro-organisms and their biological processes.

biotin /ˈbaɪətɪn/ *n* [U] vitamin in the vitamin B complex. It controls growth and is found esp in yeast and egg yolk.

bipartisan /ˌbaɪpɑ:tɪˈzæn; *US* ˌbaɪˈpɑ:rtɪzn/ *adj* of or involving two political parties: *a bipartisan policy* ○ *bipartisan talks.*

bipartite /ˈbaɪˈpɑ:taɪt/ *adj* **1** consisting of two parts. **2** shared by or involving two groups or parties: *a bipartite agreement, treaty, etc.*

biped /ˈbaɪped/ *n* animal with two feet.

BIRDS COMMON IN BRITAIN

All the drawings are to scale. With the exception of hen, males birds are shown throughout.

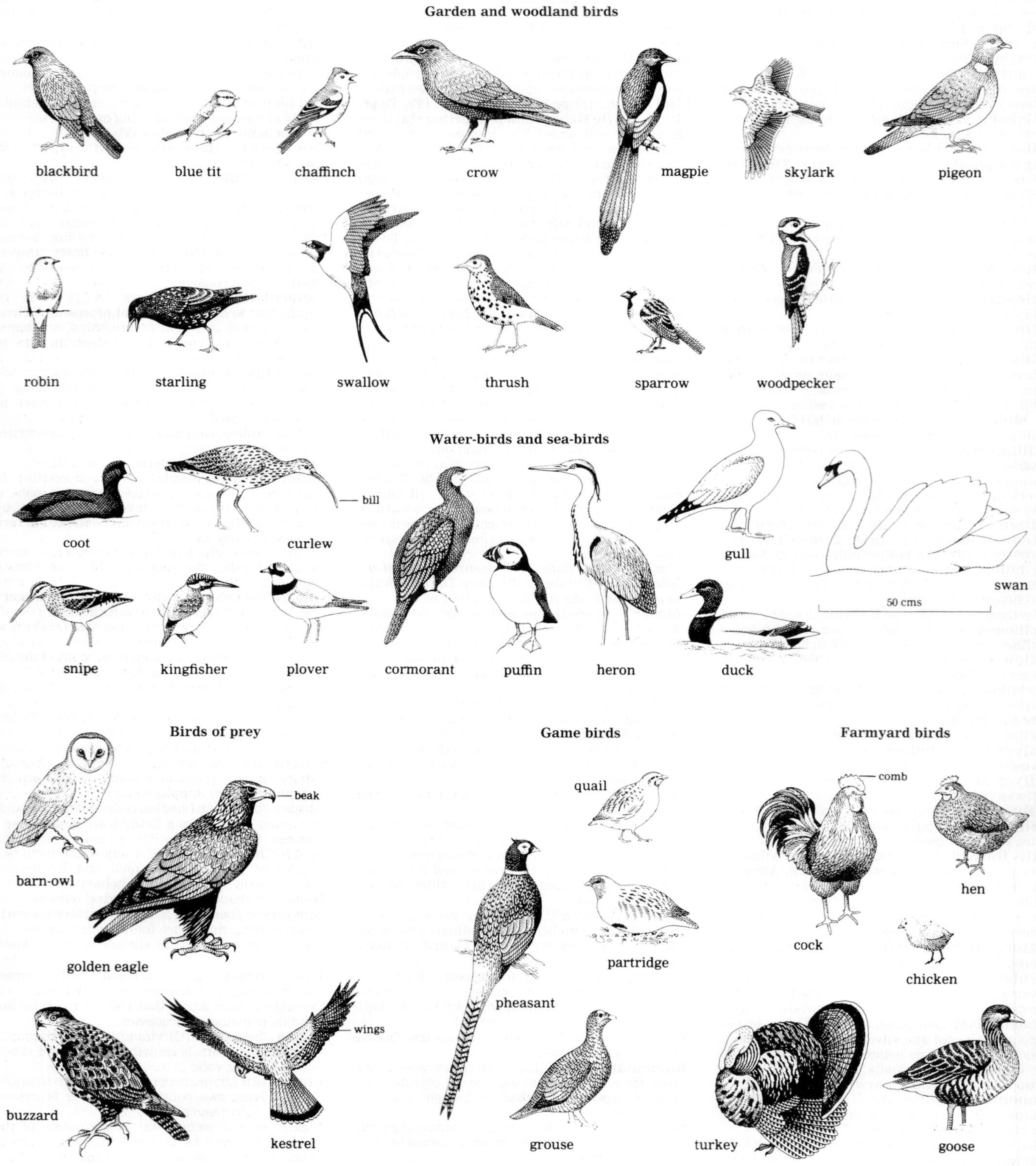

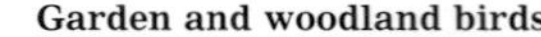

Garden and woodland birds
blackbird
blue tit
chaffinch
crow
magpie
skylark
pigeon
robin
starling
swallow
thrush
sparrow
woodpecker
Water-birds and sea-birds
coot
curlew
bill
gull
swan
50 cms
snipe
kingfisher
plover
cormorant
puffin
heron
duck
Birds of prey
barn-owl
beak
golden eagle
wings
buzzard
kestrel
Game birds
quail
partridge
pheasant
grouse
Farmyard birds
comb
cock
hen
chicken
turkey
goose

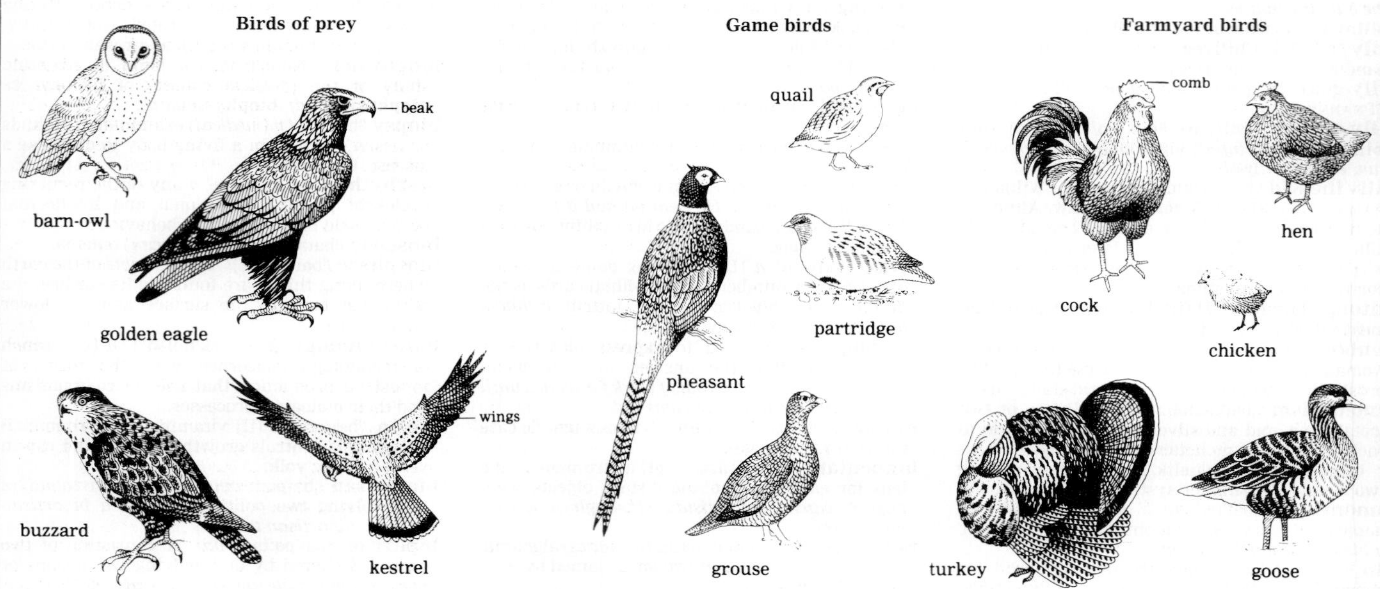

biplane /ˈbaɪpleɪn/ *n* early type of aeroplane with two sets of wings, one above the other. Cf MONOPLANE.

birch /bɜːtʃ/ *n* **1** [U, C] (wood of a) type of northern forest tree with smooth bark and thin branches. ⇨ illus at TREE. **2** [C] birch rod or a bundle of birch twigs, formerly used for flogging schoolboys and young offenders: *Should we bring back the birch as a punishment?*

▷ **birch** *v* [Tn] flog with a birch(2).

bird /bɜːd/ *n* **1** feathered animal with two wings and two legs, usu able to fly. ⇨ illus. **2** (*sl esp Brit*) young woman: *Terry's got a new bird*, ie girl-friend. **3** (*infml*) person: *a queer bird* ○ *a wise old bird* ○ *The professional footballer who also plays cricket is a rare bird nowadays*, ie There are very few of them. **4** (idm) **the bird has ˈflown** (*catchphrase*) the wanted person has escaped. **a bird in the ˈhand is worth two in the ˈbush** (*saying*) it is better to be content with what one has than to risk losing everything by being too greedy. **the birds and the ˈbees** (*euph*) basic facts about sex: *tell a child about the birds and the bees.* **a ˌbird's ˌeye ˈview (of sth)** (a) general view from a high position looking down: *From the plane we had a bird's eye view of London.* (b) general summary (of a subject). **birds of a ˈfeather (flock toˈgether)** (*saying*) people of the same sort (are found together). **an early bird** ⇨ EARLY. **the early bird catches the worm** ⇨ EARLY. **(strictly) for the birds** (*infml derog*) not important; worthless. **give sb/get the ˈbird** (*sl*) shout at sb/be shouted at rudely and disapprovingly: *The comedian got the bird*, ie was jeered at by the audience. **a home bird** ⇨ HOME[1]. **kill two birds with one stone** ⇨ KILL. **like a bird** (*infml*) without difficulty; smoothly: *My new car goes like a bird.* **a little bird told me** ⇨ LITTLE[1].

□ ˈ**bird-bath** *n* basin for birds to bathe in (usu in a garden).

ˈ**birdbrained** (*infml derog*) stupid; silly.

ˈ**birdcage** wire cage for a domestic bird or birds.

ˈ**bird dog** (*US*) **1** dog trained to fetch birds that have been shot by a hunter. **2** (*fig*) person hired to find special things or people.

ˈ**birdlime** (also **lime**) *n* [U] sticky substance spread on branches to catch small birds.

ˌ**bird of ˈparadise** New Guinea bird with very bright plumage.

ˌ**bird of ˈpassage 1** migratory bird. **2** (*fig*) person who passes through a place without staying there long.

ˌ**bird of ˈprey** bird that kills other animals for food. ⇨ illus at BIRD.

ˈ**bird sanctuary** area where birds are protected and helped to breed.

ˈ**birdseed** *n* [U] special seeds for feeding caged birds.

ˈ**bird-song** *n* [U] musical cry of birds.

ˈ**bird-table** *n* platform on which food for birds is placed.

ˈ**bird-watcher** *n* [C], ˈ**bird-watching** *n* [U] (person whose hobby is) studying birds in their natural surroundings.

birdie /ˈbɜːdɪ/ *n* **1** (*infml*) little bird. **2** score of one stroke under par for a hole at golf. Cf EAGLE 2, PAR 3.

biretta /bɪˈretə/ *n* square, usu black, cap worn by Roman Catholic priests.

biro /ˈbaɪərəʊ/ *n* (*pl* ~s) (*propr*) type of ball-point pen.

birth /bɜːθ/ *n* **1** (a) [U] emergence of young from the mother's body; being born or bearing young: *The father was present at the (moment of) birth.* ○ *The baby weighed seven pounds at birth.* ○ *He has been blind from birth*, ie all his life. (b) [C] instance of this: *There were three births at the hospital yesterday.* **2** [C] (*fig*) coming into existence; beginning: *the birth of capitalism, socialism, a political party, an idea.* **3** [U] family origin; descent: *of noble birth*, ie from an aristocratic family ○ *She is English by birth but French by marriage.* **4** (idm) **give birth (to sb/sth)** produce young: *She gave birth (to a healthy baby) last night.* ○ (*fig*) *Marx's ideas gave birth to communism.*

□ ˈ**birth certificate** official document giving the date and place of a person's birth.

ˈ**birth-control** *n* [U] controlling the number of children one has, esp by contraception: *The pill is one method of birth-control.*

ˈ**birthmark** *n* unusual coloured mark on a person's skin at birth.

ˈ**birthplace** *n* house or district where a person was born: *Mozart's birthplace is (in) Salzburg.*

ˈ**birth rate** ratio of births in one year to every thousand people.

ˈ**birthright** *n* privilege or property which a person may claim because of birth or status: *The estate is the birthright of the eldest son.* ○ (*fig*) *Freedom is our natural birthright.*

birthday /ˈbɜːθdeɪ/ *n* **1** (anniversary of the) day of a person's birth: *Happy birthday!* ○ [attrib] *a ˈbirthday card, party, present.*

2 (idm) **in one's ˈbirthday suit** (*infml joc*) naked.

□ ˌ**Birthday ˈHonours** titles, decorations, etc awarded in Britain by the Sovereign on his or her official birthday each year. Cf NEW YEAR HONOURS (NEW). ⇨ article at ARISTOCRAT.

📖 Birthdays, especially children's birthdays, are celebrated in a number of traditional ways in Britain. For a child's birthday, there is usually a party, held in the afternoon, to which family and friends come with cards and presents for the child. The birthday tea includes a big cake, iced and decorated with the same number of candles as the child's age. When everyone sings 'Happy birthday to you' the child tries to blow out all the candles in one breath, and then everyone claps and cheers. In adulthood, 'special' birthdays include the 'coming of age' at 18 or 21, the 80th, 90th and 100th. When a person reaches his or her 100th birthday he or she receives a congratulatory telegram from the monarch.

biscuit /ˈbɪskɪt/ *n* **1** [C] small flat thin piece of pastry baked crisp. **2** [C] (*US*) soft cake like a scone. **3** [U] light-brown colour. **4** (also **bisque** /bɪsk/) [U] pottery that has been fired (FIRE[2] 7) but not glazed. **5** (idm) **take the ˈbiscuit/ˈcake** (*Brit infml*) be extremely or specially amusing, annoying, surprising, etc: *He's done stupid things before, but this really takes the biscuit*, ie is the most stupid thing he's ever done.

bisect /baɪˈsekt/ *v* [Tn] divide into two (usu equal) parts. ▷ **bisection** /baɪˈsekʃn/ *n* [U, C].

bisexual /ˌbaɪˈsekʃʊəl/ *adj* **1** sexually attracted to both men and women. Cf HETEROSEXUAL, HOMOSEXUAL, EPICENE. **2** having both male and female sexual organs; hermaphrodite.

▷ **bisexual** *n* person who is bisexual.

bisexuality /ˌbaɪsekʃʊˈælətɪ/ *n* [U].

bishop /ˈbɪʃəp/ *n* **1** senior clergyman in charge of the work of the Church in a city or district: *the Bishop of Durham.* ⇨ article at ARISTOCRAT. **2** chess piece shaped like a bishop's hat. ⇨ illus at CHESS. **3** (idm) **as the actress said to the bishop** ⇨ ACTRESS.

▷ **bishopric** /ˈbɪʃəprɪk/ *n* **1** position of a bishop. **2** district under a bishop's control; diocese.

Bismarck /ˈbɪzmɑːk/ Otto Eduard Leopold, Prince von (1815-98), German statesman, known as the Iron Chancellor. He was largely responsible for the unification of Germany by his policy of 'blood and iron'.

bismuth /ˈbɪzməθ/ *n* [U] (*symb* **Bi**) (a) chemical element, a reddish-white metal which is a poor conductor of heat. It is used in alloys that have a low melting-point. ⇨ App 11. (b) compound of this used in medicine.

bison /ˈbaɪsn/ *n* (*pl* unchanged) **1** American buffalo. **2** European wild ox.

bisque[1] /bɪsk/ *n* **1** [C, U] thick soup usu made with shellfish: *lobster bisque.* **2** [C] extra turn given to a weaker player in some games, eg croquet and tennis.

bisque[2] /bɪsk/ *n* [U] unglazed white porcelain. Cf BISCUIT 4.

bistre /ˈbɪstə(r)/ *n* [U] (colour of) brown pigment made from the soot of burnt wood.

bistro /ˈbiːstrəʊ/ *n* (*pl* ~s) small restaurant.

bit[1] /bɪt/ *n* **1** (a) [C] small piece or amount (of sth): *bits of bread, cheese, paper* ○ *a bit of advice, help, luck, news* ○ *I've got a bit of* (ie some) *shopping to do.* (b) [sing] **a** ~ **(of sth)** (*infml ironic*) large amount: *'How much money has he got in the bank?' 'A fair bit.'* ○ *It takes quite a bit of time to get from London to Glasgow.* ○ *This novel will take a bit of reading*, ie a long time to read. **2** [C] (a) (*Brit*) small coin, esp an obsolete one worth three or six old pence: *a threepenny bit.* (b) (*US*) (usu *pl* and in phrases) 12½ cents: *two bits or a quarter (of a dollar).* **3** [sing] (*sl*) set of actions, attitudes, etc associated with a specific group, person or activity: *She couldn't accept the whole drug-culture bit.* **4** (idm) **a bit** (a) slightly; rather: *'Are you tired?' 'Yes, I am a bit (tired).'* ○ *This book costs a bit (too) much.* ○ *These trousers are a bit tight.* (b) short time or distance: *Wait a bit!* ○ *Move up a bit.* **bit by ˈbit** a piece at a time; gradually: *He assembled the model aircraft bit by bit.* ○ *He saved money bit by bit until he had enough to buy a car.* **a bit ˈmuch** (*infml*) unwelcome; excessive; unreasonable: *The noise from that party is getting a bit much.* ○ *It's a bit much ringing me up at three o'clock in the morning.* **a bit of a** (*infml*) rather a: *He's a bit of a bully, coward, fool, bore, etc.* ○ *This rail strike is a bit of a nuisance*, ie is rather inconvenient. **a bit of all ˈright** (*Brit sl*) very attractive or pleasing person or thing: *Dave's girl-friend is a bit of all right.* **a bit of ˈcrumpet/ˈfluff/ˈskirt/ˈstuff** (*Brit sl sexist*) pretty girl or woman. **a ˌbit on the ˈside** (*sl*) sexual relationship with sb who is not one's normal partner: *Their marriage broke up when he found out she was having a bit on the side.* **bits and ˈbobs; bits and ˈpieces** (*infml*) small objects or items of various kinds: *I always have a lot of bits and pieces in my coat pocket.* **a bit ˈthick** (*infml*) more than one can or wishes to tolerate; not fair or reasonable: *It's a bit thick expecting us to work on Sundays.* **do one's ˈbit** (*infml*) do one's share (of a task); make a useful contribution: *We can finish this job on time if everyone does his bit.* **every bit as good, bad, etc (as sb/sth)** just as; equally: *Rome is every bit as beautiful as Paris.* ○ *He's as clever as she is: every bit as.* **not a ˈbit; not one (little) ˈbit** not at all; not in any way: *'Are you cold?' 'Not a bit.'* ○ *It's not a bit of use* (ie There's no point in) *complaining.* ○ *I don't like that idea one little bit.* **not a ˈbit of it!** (*infml*) not at all; on the contrary: *You'd think she'd be tired after such a long journey, but not a bit of it!* **thrilled to bits** ⇨ THRILL. **to bits** into small pieces: *pull/tear sth to bits* ○ *The parchment came/fell to bits* (ie disintegrated) *in my hands.*

▷ **bitty** *adj* (*usu derog*) made up of bits; lacking unity: *a bitty conversation, interview, film* ○ *The play is rather bitty.*

□ ˈ**bit part** small part in a play or film.

bit[2] /bɪt/ *n* **1** metal part of a bridle put in a horse's mouth as a way of controlling it. ⇨ illus at HARNESS. **2** part of a tool that cuts or grips when twisted; tool for drilling holes. Cf DRILL[1], BRACE[1] 1. **3** (idm) **champ at the bit** ⇨ CHAMP[1]. **get/take the bit between one's/the ˈteeth** tackle a problem, task, etc in a determined, independent or headstrong way.

bit[3] /bɪt/ *n* (*computing*) unit of information, the smallest a computer can store or process, expressed as a choice between two possibilities; binary digit.

bit[4] *pt* of BITE[1].

bitch /bɪtʃ/ *n* **1** female dog, fox, otter or wolf: *a greyhound bitch.* Cf DOG[1] 1, VIXEN. **2** (a) (*sl derog*) spiteful woman: *Don't talk to me like that, you bitch!* (b) (*sl*) difficult problem or situation. **3** (idm) **son of a ˈbitch** ⇨ SON.

▷ **bitch** *v* [I, Ipr] ~ **(about sb/sth)** (*infml*) make spiteful comments; complain or grumble: *She's always bitching about the people at work.*

bitchy *adj* spiteful or bad-tempered: *a bitchy remark.* **bitchiness** *n* [U].

bite[1] /baɪt/ *v* (*pt* **bit** /bɪt/, *pp* **bitten** /ˈbɪtn/) **1** [I, Ipr, Tn] ~ **(into sth)** cut into or nip (sth) with the teeth: *Does your dog bite?* ie Is it in the habit of biting people? ○ *She bit into the apple.* ○ *That dog just bit me in the leg.* ○ *Stop biting your nails!*

2 [Tn] (of an insect) sting; (of a snake) pierce (sb's skin) with its teeth: *badly bitten by mosquitoes* ○ (*joc*) *We were bitten to death* (ie bitten a great deal) *by flies while camping.* **3** [I] (of fish) take or try to take the bait: *The fish won't bite today.* ○ (*fig*) *I tried to sell him my old car, but he wouldn't bite*, ie he didn't accept the offer. **4** [I, Tn] (cause sth to) smart or sting: *Her fingers were bitten by the frost/were ˈfrost-bitten.* **5** [I] take a strong hold; grip sth firmly: *Wheels won't bite on a slippery surface.* **6** [I] become effective, usu in an unpleasant way: *The miners' strike is really starting to bite.* **7** (idm) **be bitten by sth** have a strong interest in or enthusiasm for sth: *John's taken up stamp-collecting; he seems really bitten by it.* **bite the ˈbullet** accept sth unpleasant in a resigned way. **bite the ˈdust** (*infml*) (**a**) fall down dead. (**b**) be defeated or rejected: *Another of my great ideas bites the dust!* **bite the hand that ˈfeeds one** be unfriendly to or harm sb who has been kind to one. **bite sb's head off** (*infml*) criticize sb angrily (and often unfairly): *I was only five minutes late but she really bit my head off.* **bite one's ˈlip** grip one's lip or lips between the teeth to prevent oneself from saying sth, sobbing, showing emotion, etc. **bite off ˌmore than one can ˈchew** (*infml*) attempt to do too much or sth that is too demanding. **the biter ˈbit** the person that intended to cheat or harm sb was cheated or harmed himself. **bite one's tongue** try hard not to say what one thinks or feels; blame oneself for having said sth embarrassing, hurtful, etc. (**have**) **sth to bite on** (have) sth definite to do, examine, etc. **once bitten, twice shy** ⇨ ONCE. **what's biting him, you, etc?** (*infml*) what's worrying him, you, etc? **8** (phr v) **bite at sth** try to bite sth; snap at sth: *dogs biting at each other's tails.* **bite sth back** prevent oneself from saying sth, with an effort: *He was on the point of making a strong protest but managed to bite it back.* **bite sth off** cut sth off by biting: *bite off a large chunk of apple.*

▷ **biting** *adj* **1** causing a smarting pain: *a biting wind.* **2** (of remarks) sharply critical; cutting: *biting sarcasm.*
bitingly *adv.*

bite[2] /baɪt/ *n* **1** [C] (**a**) act of biting: *eat sth in one bite* ○ *The dog gave me a playful bite.* (**b**) piece cut off by biting: *A bite had been taken out of my sandwich.* **2** [sing] (*infml*) food: *I haven't had a bite (to eat) all morning.* **3** [C] wound made by a bite or a sting: *insect, mosquito, snake bites.* **4** [C] taking of bait by a fish: *anglers waiting for a bite.* **5** [sing, U] sharpness; sting: *There's a bite in the air*, ie It's cold. ○ *His words had no bite*, ie were harmless or ineffective. ○ *This cheese has a real bite*, ie a strong flavour. **6** [U] cutting power or firm grip: *This drill has no bite.* **7** (idm) **sb's bark is worse than his bite** ⇨ BARK[2]. **have/get two bites at the ˈcherry** have a second opportunity to do sth; make a second attempt at doing sth. **put the bite on sb** (*sl esp US*) try to borrow money from sb, esp by using threats.

bitten *pt* of BITE[1].

bitter /ˈbɪtə(r)/ *adj* **1** having a sharp taste like aspirin or unsweetened coffee; not sweet: *Black coffee leaves a bitter taste in the mouth.* **2** difficult to accept; causing sorrow; unwelcome: *learn from bitter experience* ○ *Failing the exam was a bitter disappointment to him.* **3** caused by, feeling or showing envy, hatred or disappointment: *bitter quarrels, enemies, words* ○ *shed bitter tears* ○ *She feels/is bitter about her divorce.* **4** piercingly cold: *a bitter wind.* **5** (idm) **a bitter ˈpill (for sb) (to swallow)** thing that is unpleasant or humiliating to accept: *Defeat in the election was a bitter pill for him to swallow.* **to the bitter ˈend** until all that is possible has been done: *fight, struggle, etc to the bitter end.*

▷ **bitter** *n* [U] (*Brit*) bitter beer strongly flavoured with hops: *A pint of bitter, please.* ⇨ article at DRINK.
bitterly *adv* in a bitter way: *be bitterly disappointed* ○ *She wept bitterly.* ○ *He is bitterly* (ie very deeply) *opposed to nuclear weapons.*
bitterness *n* [U].
bitters *n* [U] liquor flavoured with bitter herbs, used in cocktails: *gin and bitters* ○ *a dash of bitters.*

□ ˌ**bitter-ˈsweet** *adj* **1** sweet but with a bitter taste at the end. **2** (*fig*) pleasant but with a hint of sadness: *bitter-sweet experiences/memories.*

bittern /ˈbɪtən/ *n* marsh bird related to the heron, with a characteristic booming call.

bitumen /ˈbɪtjʊmən; *US* bəˈtu:mən/ *n* [U] black sticky substance obtained from petroleum, used for covering roads or roofs.

▷ **bituminous** /bɪˈtju:mɪnəs; *US* bəˈtu:-/ *adj* containing bitumen: *bituminous coal*, ie coal that burns with smoky yellow flames.

bivalent /ˈbaɪveɪlənt/ *adj* (*chemistry*) = DIVALENT.

bivalve /ˈbaɪvælv/ *n* (*zoology*) shellfish with a hinged double shell, eg a mussel or clam: [attrib] *a bivalve mollusc.*

bivouac /ˈbɪvʊæk/ *n* temporary camp without tents or any other cover, esp used by soldiers or mountaineers.

▷ **bivouac** *v* (**-ck-**) [I] make or camp in a bivouac: *We bivouacked on the open plain.*

bizarre /bɪˈzɑ:(r)/ *adj* strange in appearance or effect; grotesque; eccentric.

Bk *symb* berkelium.

bk *abbr* (*pl* **bks**) book: *Streamline Bk 2.*

blab /blæb/ *v* (**-bb-**) [I] (*infml*) **1** give away a secret by indiscreet talk; confess: *It'll remain a secret unless someone blabs.* **2** = BLABBER.

blabber /ˈblæbə(r)/ (also **blab**) *v* [I] (*infml*) talk foolishly or too much: *What's he blabbering (on) about?*

▷ **blabber** *n* [U] (*infml*) foolish or persistent talk.

□ ˈ**blabbermouth** *n* (*infml*) person who blabs.

black[1] /blæk/ *adj* **1** (**a**) of the very darkest colour, like coal or soot; opposite of white; of a colour very similar to this: *black shoes* ○ *a black suit* ○ *black coffee*, ie without cream or milk. Cf WHITE[1]. (**b**) (almost) without light; completely dark: *a black starless night.* (**c**) (of water, clouds, etc) dark; gloomy: *a deep, black pool* ○ *The sky looks black and threatening*, ie stormy. **2** (**a**) of a dark-skinned race: *Many black people emigrated to Britain in the 1950s.* ○ *Britain's black minority/population.* (**b**) of black people: *black culture.* **3** very dirty; covered with dirt: *hands black with grime.* **4** (*fig*) without hope; very sad or melancholy: *The future looks black.* ○ *black news* ○ *black* (ie very great) *despair* ○ *a black day, week, etc*, ie one full of sad or unwelcome events. **5** [usu attrib] very angry or resentful: *a black look/mood.* **6** evil or wicked; very harmful: *a black deed/lie.* **7** funny but in a cynical or macabre way: *black humour* ○ *a black joke.* **8** (of goods, etc) not to be handled by trade unionists while others are on strike: *The strikers declared the cargo black.* **9** (idm) (**beat sb**) **black and ˈblue** (hit sb until he is) covered with bruises. (**as**) **black as ˈink/ˈpitch/the ace of ˈspades** very dark; completely black. **not as black as it/one is ˈpainted** not as bad as it/one is said to be. **of the blackest/deepest dye** ⇨ DYE[2]. **the pot calling the kettle black** ⇨ POT[1].

▷ **blacken** /ˈblækən/ *v* [I, Tn] **1** make or become black or very dark. **2** [Tn] say unpleasant things about (sth): *blacken a person's character/name.*
blackness *n* [U].

The colour black is primarily associated with death and mourning in Britain. At funerals, mourners often wear black clothes and the hearse is black. Members of the armed forces also usually wear black on the occasion of a royal death. However, it is now very rare for people to wear black for long periods as a sign of mourning.

□ **black ˈart** = BLACK MAGIC.
ˌ**black-ˈbeetle** *n* type of cockroach.
ˌ**black ˈbelt** (person who has reached the) highest standard at judo.
blackberry /ˈblækbrɪ, -berɪ/ *n* **1** wild shrub with thorny stems. **2** its small dark edible fruit. — *v* [I] (*pt, pp* **-ried**) gather blackberries: *go blackberrying.*
ˈ**blackbird** *n* European songbird of the thrush family, the male of which is black. ⇨ illus at BIRD.
ˈ**blackboard** *n* (*US* ˈ**chalkboard**) dark-coloured board used for writing on with chalk, esp in a school classroom.
ˌ**black ˈbox** automatic device for recording details of the flight of a plane.
ˌ**black ˈbread** rough bread made from rye.
ˈ**blackcap** small songbird with a black patch on its head.
ˌ**black ˈcomedy** play, etc that presents the unpleasant or tragic realities of life in a comic way.
the ˈBlack Country smoky industrial area in the West Midlands of England.
ˌ**blackˈcurrant** *n* **1** common garden shrub. **2** its small dark edible berry.
the Black ˈDeath widespread epidemic of bubonic plague in the 14th century.
ˌ**black eˈconomy** unofficial system of employing and paying workers without observing legal requirements such as the payment of income tax: *The growing black economy is beginning to worry the Government.*
black ˈeye dark bruised skin around a person's eye, resulting from a blow: *give sb a black eye*, ie hit sb in the eye causing a bruise.
ˈ**blackfly** *n* (*pl* unchanged) any of various types of small black insects (*aphids*) that are harmful to plants.
ˈ**Black Friar** Dominican monk.
ˈ**blackhead** *n* small black pimple blocking a pore in the skin.
ˌ**black ˈhole** region in outer space from which no matter or radiation can escape.
the ˌBlack Hole of Calˈcutta name later given to the small cell in Calcutta where 146 British prisoners were confined on 20 June 1756. Only 23 remained alive next morning. The name is often used to describe any cramped and stuffy space.
ˌ**black ˈice** thin transparent layer of ice on a road surface: *The lorry skidded on a stretch of black ice.*
ˈ**blackjack** *n* **1** [C] (*esp US*) type of stick or club used as a weapon, esp a leather-covered metal pipe held by a strap or flexible handle. **2** [U] = PONTOON[2].
ˌ**blackˈlead** *n* [U] grey-black substance used in lead pencils and for polishing. — *v* [Tn] polish sth with blacklead.
ˌ**black ˈmagic** type of magic that involves calling on the powers of evil.
ˌ**Black Maˈria** /məˈraɪə/ (*infml*) police van for transporting prisoners.
ˌ**black ˈmark** sign of disapproval or discredit (placed against a person's name): (*fig*) *The public scandal left a black mark on his career.*
ˌ**black ˈmarket** illegal buying and selling of goods or currencies (esp where there is official rationing): *buy/sell sth on the black market* ○ [attrib] *black market goods.* ˌ**black ˌmarkeˈteer** person who trades on the black market.
ˌ**black ˈmass** travesty of the Mass, in which Satan is worshipped instead of God.
ˌ**Black ˈMuslim** member of a militant group of Blacks, esp in the USA, who follow Islam.
ˈ**black-out** *n* **1** (**a**) period when all lights must be put out or covered, esp as a precaution during an air attack: *Curtains must be drawn during the black-out.* (**b**) period of darkness caused by an electrical power failure. (**c**) (*theatre*) extinguishing of stage lights, eg at the end of a scene. **2** temporary loss of consciousness or sight or memory. **3** prevention of the release of information: *The government imposed a news black-out* (ie stopped the broadcasting and printing of news) *during the crisis.*
ˌ**Black ˈPanther** member of an American extremist group fighting for the rights of Black people, esp in the 1960s.
ˌ**black ˈpepper** hot seasoning made by grinding dried unripe berries of the pepper plant.
ˌ**Black ˈPower** movement supporting civil rights and political power for black people.
ˌ**black ˈpudding** type of large dark sausage made from cooked blood, pig fat and barley.
ˌ**Black ˈSash** women's anti-apartheid organization in S Africa.
ˌ**black ˈsheep** person regarded as a disgrace or a failure by other members of his family or group: *My brother is the black sheep of the family.*

ˈ**blackshirt** *n* member of a fascist organization.
ˈ**black spot** place where accidents often happen, esp on a road: *a notorious (accident) black spot.*
ˈ**blackthorn** *n* thorny European shrub with white blossom and purple fruit like a small plum.
black ˈ**tie** (**a**) black bow-tie worn with a dinner-jacket. (**b**) [esp attrib] requiring formal dress: *a black tie dinner/affair* ○ *It's black tie,* ie Dinner-jackets should be worn.
ˈ**blacktop** *n* [U] (*esp US*) black substance for surfacing roads.
ˌ**black** ˈ**velvet** drink made by mixing stout and champagne.
the ˌ**Black** ˈ**Watch** the Royal Highland Regiment of the British Army. Their uniform includes a kilt made of very dark-coloured tartan.
ˌ**black-water** ˈ**fever** very severe type of malaria with bloody urine.
ˌ**black** ˈ**widow** poisonous American spider, the female of which often eats its mate.

black[2] /blæk/ *n* **1** [U] black colour: *Black is not my favourite colour.* **2** [U] black clothes or material: *The mourners were dressed in black.* **3** (usu **Black**) [C] (*formerly derog, now the preferred word*) person of a dark-skinned race; negro: *Discrimination against Blacks is still common.* **4** [C] black piece or ball in a game: *She potted the black,* ie in snooker. **5 be in the** ˈ**black** have money in one's bank account. Cf BE IN THE RED (RED[2] 4). (idm) ˌ**black and** ˈ**white** (of television, photographs, etc) showing no colours except black, white and shades of grey: *I changed my black and white television for a colour set.* ○ *Most old films were made in black and white.* **in black and white** in writing or in print: *I want the contract in black and white.* (**in**) **black and white** (in) absolute terms, eg of good and bad, right and wrong: *see/view the issue in black and white.* **work like a black/Trojan** work very hard.
□ ˌ**Black and** ˈ**Tans** armed force sent by the British government to Ireland in 1921 to fight *Sinn Fein. They wore a mixture of the black uniform of the police and the khaki (tan) uniform of the army, and were hated in Ireland for their often brutal methods. ⇨ article at IRELAND.
Black is traditionally thought of as suggesting sadness or evil. People often wear black at funerals, and the black raven is associated with death. The Devil is often shown in pictures dressed in black. There are many expressions using the word 'black' to convey misfortune or cruelty. Black people sometimes object to this.

black[3] /blæk/ *v* **1** [Tn] make (sth) black; put polish on (shoes, etc). **2** [Tn] refuse to handle (goods, etc); boycott: *The lorry had been blacked by strikers and could not be unloaded.* **3** (phr v) **black** ˈ**out** lose consciousness or memory temporarily: *The plane dived suddenly, causing the pilot to black out.* **black sth out** (**a**) extinguish (lights, etc) completely or cover (windows, etc) so that light cannot be seen from outside: *houses blacked out during an air raid.* (**b**) cover (sth written or printed) with black ink, etc so that it cannot be read.

blackamoor /ˈblækəmɔː(r) *or, rarely,* -mʊə(r)/ *n* (*dated derog offensive*) negro or dark-skinned person.

blackball /ˈblækbɔːl/ *v* [Tn] prevent (sb) from joining a club or group by voting against him in a ballot: *blackball a candidate.*

blackguard /ˈblægɑːd/ *n* (*fml*) dishonourable man; scoundrel.
▷ **blackguardly** *adj* (*fml*) dishonest or immoral: *a blackguardly trick.*

blacking /ˈblækɪŋ/ *n* [U] (*dated*) black shoe polish.

blackleg /ˈblækleg/ *n* (*derog*) person who works when his fellow workers are on strike. Cf STRIKE-BREAKER (STRIKE[1]).
▷ **blackleg** *v* [I] (**-gg-**) (*derog*) act as a blackleg.

blacklist /ˈblæklɪst/ *n* list of people who are considered dangerous or who are to be punished: *The police drew up a blacklist of wanted terrorists.*
▷ **blacklist** *v* [Tn] put (sb) on a blacklist: *He was blacklisted because of his extremist views.*

blackmail /ˈblækmeɪl/ *n* [U] **1** demanding money (from sb) by threatening to reveal information which could harm him: *be found guilty of blackmail.* **2** use of threats to influence a person or group: *'Increase productivity or lose your jobs.' 'That's blackmail!'*
▷ **blackmail** *v* [Tn, Tn·pr] ~ **sb** (**into doing sth**) force sb to do sth by blackmail: *He was blackmailed by an enemy agent (into passing on state secrets).* ○ *The strikers refused to be blackmailed into returning to work.*
blackmailer *n* person who commits blackmail.

Black Prince /ˌblæk ˈprɪns/ **the Black Prince** nickname of Edward Plantagenet (1330-76), eldest son of Edward III of England. He won many battles in the *Hundred Years War, notably the one at Poitiers (1356).

Black Rod /ˌblæk ˈrɒd/ member of the British royal staff who is the official usher of the House of Lords. At the state opening of Parliament he uses his black gold-topped staff to knock at the door of the House of Commons and call Members of Parliament to the House of Lords.

Black Sea /ˌblæk ˈsiː/ **the Black Sea** sea in eastern Europe. It is almost entirely surrounded by land (USSR, Turkey, Bulgaria and Romania) and has no tides. It is connected to the Mediterranean by the Dardanelles.

blacksmith /ˈblæksmɪθ/ (also **smith**) *n* person whose job is to make and repair things made of iron, esp horseshoes.

bladder /ˈblædə(r)/ *n* **1** bag made of membrane in which urine collects in human and animal bodies. **2** similar bag that can be inflated for various uses (eg the rubber lining of a football).
□ ˈ**bladder-wrack** *n* [U] type of dark-coloured intertidal seaweed with air-filled swellings on its surface.

blade /bleɪd/ *n* **1** (**a**) flat cutting part of a knife, sword, chisel, etc: *a penknife with five blades.* ⇨ illus at KNIFE, SWORD. (**b**) = RAZOR-BLADE (RAZOR). **2** (*dated*) sword; swordsman. **3** flat wide part of an oar, a propeller, a spade, a cricket bat, etc. ⇨ illus at ROWING-BOAT. **4** (**a**) flat narrow leaf of certain plants, esp grasses and cereals: *a blade of grass/corn.* (**b**) flat part of a leaf or petal.

blaeberry /ˈbleɪbrɪ; *US* -berɪ/ *n* = BILBERRY.

blah /blɑː/ *n* [U] (*infml*) talk that sounds impressive but actually says very little: *That's just a lot of blah.* ○ *There he goes, blah blah blah, talking nonsense as usual.*

William Blake: Elohim creating Adam

Blake /bleɪk/ William (1757-1827), English artist and poet. Much of his work shows his mystical vision of the world. His poetry, in works like the *Songs of Innocence and Experience*, expresses a romantic idealism and a contempt for the hypocrisy of conventional morality. In other works he creates his own myths to convey his ideas, using images from the Bible. His vivid creative imagination is also evident in his highly original paintings and illustrations, such as those for the Book of Job. ⇨ illus.

blame /bleɪm/ *v* **1** [Tn, Tn·pr] ~ **sb** (**for sth**)/~ **sth on sb** consider or say that sb is responsible for sth done (badly or wrongly) or not done: *I don't blame you,* ie I think your action was justified. ○ (*saying*) *A bad workman blames his tools,* ie refuses to accept the responsibility for his own mistakes. ○ *If you fail the exam you'll only have yourself to blame,* ie it will be your own fault. ○ *She blamed him for the failure of their marriage/blamed the failure of their marriage on him.* **2** (idm) **be to blame** (**for sth**) be responsible for sth bad; deserve to be blamed: *Which driver was to blame for the accident?* ○ *She was in no way to blame.*
▷ **blame** *n* [U] ~ (**for sth**) **1** responsibility for sth done badly or wrongly: *bear/take/accept/get the blame (for sth)* ○ *Where does the blame for our failure lie?* ie Who or what is responsible? **2** criticism for doing sth wrong: *He incurred much blame for his stubborn attitude.* **3** (idm) **lay/put the blame** (**for sth**) **on sb** blame sb for sth.
blameless *adj* deserving no blame; innocent: *a blameless life* ○ *None of us is blameless in this matter.* **blamelessly** *adv.*
blameworthy *adj* deserving blame.

blanch /blɑːntʃ; *US* blæntʃ/ *v* **1** [Tn] prepare (food, esp vegetables) by putting briefly in boiling water; scald: *You blanch almonds to remove their skins.* **2** [I, Ipr] ~ (**with sth**) (**at sth**) become pale (with fear, cold, etc): *He blanched (with fear) at the sight of the snake.*

blancmange /bləˈmɒnʒ/ *n* [C, U] jelly-like pudding made with milk in a mould.

bland /blænd/ *adj* (**-er, -est**) **1** gentle or casual in manner; showing no strong emotions; suave. **2** (*sometimes derog*) (of food) not rich or stimulating; very mild in flavour; tasteless: *He eats only bland food because of his ulcer.* ○ *This cheese is rather bland.* **3** without striking features; uninteresting: *He has a bland appearance.* ▷ **blandly** *adv.* **blandness** *n* [U].

blandishment /ˈblændɪʃmənt/ *n* [usu *pl*] (*fml*) flattering or coaxing words and actions: *She resisted his blandishments.*

blank /blæŋk/ *adj* (**-er, -est**) **1** (**a**) without writing or print; unmarked: *a blank sheet of paper* ○ *a blank page* ○ *Write on one side of the page and leave the other side blank.* (**b**) (of a document, etc) with empty spaces for writing answers, a signature, etc: *a blank form.* (**c**) bare; empty: *a blank wall,* ie without doors, windows, pictures, etc. **2** without expression, understanding or interest; empty: *a blank expression/face/gaze* ○ *He looked blank,* ie puzzled. ○ *Her questions drew blank looks all round,* ie No one seemed to know how to answer them. ○ *Suddenly my mind went blank,* ie I was unable to remember anything or think properly. **3** [attrib] total; absolute: *a blank denial/refusal.*
▷ **blank** *n* **1** (**a**) empty space in a document, etc for writing answers, a signature, etc: *fill in the blanks on the question paper* ○ *If you can't answer the question, leave a blank.* (**b**) printed document with empty spaces: *I've filled in this form incorrectly. Can I have another blank?* **2** empty space; void: *My mind/memory was a (complete) blank — I couldn't think of a single answer.* **3** = BLANK CARTRIDGE. **4** dash[1](5) replacing letters in a word, eg in an obscene word that a writer does not wish to spell out. **5** (idm) **draw a blank** ⇨ DRAW[2].
blank *v* (phr v) **blank sth out** obscure or erase sth.
blankly *adv* with a blank expression: *look blankly at sb/sth.*
blankness *n* [U].
□ ˌ**blank** ˈ**cartridge** cartridge that contains powder but no bullet.
ˌ**blank** ˈ**cheque** (**a**) signed cheque with the amount to be paid left blank, for the payee to write in. (**b**) (*fig*) complete authority to do sth: *The architect was given/presented with a blank cheque to design a new city centre.*
ˌ**blank** ˈ**verse** verse written in lines of usu ten syllables, without rhyme: *Many Elizabethan plays are written in blank verse.*

blanket /ˈblæŋkɪt/ *n* **1** thick woollen covering used, esp on beds, for keeping people warm: *It's cold — I need another blanket.* **2** (*fig*) thick covering mass or layer: *a blanket of fog/cloud/smoke/snow.* **3** [attrib] covering all cases or classes; general; comprehensive: *a blanket* *agreement/term/rule.* **4** (idm) **be born on the wrong side of the blanket** ⇨ BORN. **a wet blanket** ⇨ WET.

▷ **blanket** *v* [Tn, Tn·pr] ~ **sth (in/with sth)** cover sth completely: *The countryside was blanketed with snow/fog.*

□ ˈ**blanket bath** washing of a patient who cannot get out of bed.

blare /bleə(r)/ *v* **1** [I, Ip] ~ **(out)** make a loud harsh sound like a trumpet: *Car horns blared.* ○ *The trumpets blared ˈout.* **2** [Tn, Tn·p] ~ **sth (out)** produce or utter (such sounds): *The radio blared out pop music.*

▷ **blare** *n* [U] blaring sound: *the blare of police sirens, a brass band.*

blarney /ˈblɑ:nɪ/ *n* [U] (*infml*) smooth talk that flatters and deceives people.

Blarney stone /ˈblɑ:nɪ stəʊn/ **the Blarney Stone** stone in Blarney Castle near Cork in Ireland. It is difficult to reach and is said to make those who kiss it charming and persuasive talkers, ie full of *blarney*. ⇨ article at IRELAND.

blasé /ˈblɑ:zeɪ; *US* blɑ:ˈzeɪ/ *adj* ~ **(about sth)** bored or not impressed by things because one has already experienced or seen them so often: *a blasé attitude/manner* ○ *She's very blasé about parties.*

blaspheme /blæsˈfi:m/ *v* [I, Ipr, Tn] ~ **(against sb/sth)** swear or curse using the name of God; speak in an irreverent way about (God or sacred things): *blaspheme (against) the name of God* ○ *He always swears and blasphemes when he's drunk.*

▷ **blasphemer** *n* person who blasphemes.

blasphemous /ˈblæsfəməs/ *adj* showing contempt or irreverence for God and sacred things: *blasphemous words/curses/language.* **blasphemously** *adv.*

blasphemy /ˈblæsfəmɪ/ *n* **(a)** [U] blasphemous behaviour or language: *the sin of blasphemy.* ⇨ article at TABOO. **(b)** [C] instance of this: *the blasphemies of the heretic.*

blast[1] /blɑ:st; *US* blæst/ *n* **1** [C, U] explosion; destructive wave of air from an explosion: *a bomb blast* ○ *Several passers-by were killed by (the) blast.* **2** [C] sudden strong gust of air: *the wind's icy blasts* ○ *a blast of hot air from the furnace.* **3** [C] loud sound made by a brass instrument, car horn, etc: *blow a blast on a bugle, trumpet, whistle, etc.* **4** [C] stream of hot air used to intensify the heat in a furnace. **5** (idm) **full blast** ⇨ FULL.

□ ˈ**blast-furnace** *n* furnace for melting iron ore using blasts of hot air forced into it.

blast[2] /blɑ:st; *US* blæst/ *v* **1** [I, Tn] destroy or break apart (esp rocks) using explosives: *Danger! Blasting in progress!* ○ *The village was blasted by enemy bombs.* **2** [Tn] damage or destroy (esp plants) by blight, cold, heat, etc; cause to wither: *buds/crops blasted by frost/wind.* **3** [I] make a loud harsh noise. **4** [Tn] (*infml*) criticize (sb/sth) severely: *The film was blasted by the critics.* **5** (phr v) **blast sth away, down, in, etc** break something in a specified way by blasting: *The explosion blasted the door open/down/in.* **blast ˈoff** (of spacecraft) be launched by the firing of rockets: *The space probe blasted off at noon.*

▷ **blast** *interj* (expressing annoyance) how infuriating!: *Blast! I've burnt the toast.*

blasted *adj* [attrib] (*infml*) very annoying: *What a blasted nuisance!*

blasting *n* (*infml*) harsh criticism: *give his work a terrific blasting.*

□ ˈ**blast-off** *n* (time of) launching of a spacecraft: *Blast-off is in 30 seconds.*

blatant /ˈbleɪtnt/ *adj* very obvious; unashamed; flagrant: *a blatant lie* ○ *blatant disobedience, disrespect, insolence, etc.*

▷ **blatancy** /ˈbleɪtnsɪ/ *n* [U] blatant quality: *the sheer blatancy of the crime.*

blatantly *adv.*

blather /ˈblæðə(r)/ (also **blether** /ˈbleðə(r)/) *v* [I, Ipr, Ip] ~ **(on) (about sb/sth)** (*esp Scot*) talk foolishly.

▷ **blather** (also **blether**) *n* [U] foolish talk.

blaze[1] /bleɪz/ *n* **1** [C] **(a)** bright flame or fire: *Dry wood makes a good blaze.* **(b)** very large (often dangerous) fire: *Five people died in the blaze.* **2** [sing] ~ **of sth (a)** very bright display (of light, colour, etc); brightness, brilliance: *The garden is a blaze of colour,* ie full of colourful flowers. ○ *The high street is a blaze of lights in the evening.* **(b)** (*fig*) striking display or show: *a blaze of glory/publicity.* **(c)** (*fig*) sudden outburst (of a violent feeling): *a blaze of anger/passion/temper.*

blaze[2] /bleɪz/ *v* **1** [I] burn brightly and fiercely: *A good fire was blazing in the grate.* ○ *When the firemen arrived the whole building was blazing.* **2** [I, Ipr, Ip] shine brightly: *Bright lights blazed all along the street.* ○ *The sun blazed down on the desert.* **3** [I, Ipr] ~ **(with sth)** (*fig*) show great feeling, esp anger: *She was blazing with indignation,* ie was extremely angry. ○ *a blazing row* ○ *His eyes blazed (with anger).* **4** (phr v) **blaze away** fire continuously with guns: *Our gunners/guns kept blazing away at the enemy.* **blaze up (a)** burst into flames: *The fire blazed up when he added paraffin.* **(b)** (*fig*) suddenly become angry: *He blazed up without warning.*

blaze[3] /bleɪz/ *n* **1** white mark on an animal's face. **2** mark cut in the bark of a tree to show sb which way to go.

▷ **blaze** *v* **1** [Tn] mark (a tree) by cutting off some bark. **2** (idm) **blaze a ˈtrail** do sth for the first time and show others how to do it; be a pioneer (in sth): *blazing a trail in the field of laser surgery.* Cf TRAIL-BLAZER (TRAIL).

blaze[4] /bleɪz/ (also **blazon**) *v* [Tn] make (sth) known; proclaim: *The news was blazed all over the daily papers.*

blazer /ˈbleɪzə(r)/ *n* jacket, without matching trousers, often showing the colours or badge of a club, school, team, etc. ⇨ article at CLOTHES.

blazes /ˈbleɪzɪz/ *n* [pl] (*sl*) **1** (esp in expressions of anger or surprise) hell: *Who/What the blazes is that?* ○ *What the blazes are you doing?* ○ *Go to blazes!* **2** (idm) **like blazes** vigorously, fast: *run/work like blazes.*

blazon /ˈbleɪzn/ *n* heraldic shield; coat of arms. ▷ **blazon** *v* [Tn] **1** = EMBLAZON. **2** = BLAZE[4].

bldg *abbr* building: *engineering bldg,* eg on a university campus.

bleach /bli:tʃ/ *v* [I, Tn] (cause sth to) become white or pale (by chemical action or sunlight): *bones of animals bleaching in the desert* ○ *bleach cotton, linen, etc* ○ *hair bleached by the sun.*

▷ **bleach** *n* [U, C] substance or process that bleaches or sterilizes: *soak shirts in bleach to remove the stains.*

□ ˈ**bleaching-powder** *n* substance used to remove colour from dyed materials, eg chloride of lime.

bleachers /ˈbli:tʃəz/ *n* [pl] (*US*) cheap seats at a sports ground that are not roofed over.

bleak /bli:k/ *adj* (**-er, -est**) **1 (a)** (of a landscape) bare; exposed; wind-swept: *bleak hills, mountains, moors, etc.* **(b)** (of the weather) cold and dreary: *a bleak winter day.* **2** (*fig*) not hopeful or encouraging; dismal; gloomy: *a bleak outlook/prospect* ○ *The future looks bleak.* ▷ **bleakly** *adv.* **bleakness** *n* [U].

bleary /ˈblɪərɪ/ *adj* (of eyes) blurred, esp because of tiredness; seeing dimly.

▷ **blearily** *adv* with bleary eyes: *look blearily at sb.*

□ ˌ**bleary-ˈeyed** *adj* having bleary eyes: *He's always bleary-eyed early in the morning.*

bleat /bli:t/ *n* cry of a sheep, goat or calf; any noise like this.

▷ **bleat** *v* **1** [I] make a bleat. **2** [I, Ip, Tn, Tn·p] ~ **(sth) (out)** (*fig*) say (sth) or speak feebly or plaintively: *What are you bleating about?* ○ *He bleated out a feeble excuse.*

bleed /bli:d/ *v* (*pt, pp* **bled** /bled/) **1 (a)** [I] lose or emit blood: *bleed to death.* **(b)** [I, Ipr] ~ **(for sth)** (*fig*) suffer wounds or die (for a cause, one's country): *those who bled for the revolution.* **2** [Tn] draw blood from (sb): *Doctors used to bleed people when they were ill.* **3** [Tn, Tn·pr] ~ **sb (for sth)** (*infml*) extort (money) from sb: *The blackmailers bled him for every penny he had.* **4** [I] (of a plant, tree, etc) lose sap or juice. **5** (idm) **bleed sb white** take away all sb's money. **one's heart bleeds for sb** ⇨ HEART.

bleeder /ˈbli:də(r)/ *n* (*Brit sl usu derog*) person: *You stupid bleeder!*

bleeding /ˈbli:dɪŋ/ *adj* [attrib] (*Brit sl*) = BLOODY[2].

bleep /bli:p/ *n* short high-pitched sound made by an electronic device to attract attention: *The computer gave a regular bleep.*

▷ **bleep** *v* **1** [I] emit bleeps. **2** [Tn] call (esp a doctor) with a bleeper: *Please bleep the doctor on duty immediately.* **bleeper** *n* device that emits bleeps.

blemish /ˈblemɪʃ/ *n* **1** mark or stain that spoils the beauty or perfection of sb/sth: *a blemish on a pear, carpet, table-cloth* ○ *She has a blemish above her right eye.* **2** (*fig*) defect, fault or flaw: *His character/reputation is without (a) blemish.*

▷ **blemish** *v* [Tn] spoil the beauty or perfection of (sb/sth); flaw; mar: *a blemished peach* ○ *The pianist's performance was blemished by several wrong notes.*

blench /blentʃ/ *v* [I] make a sudden movement because of fear; flinch.

blend /blend/ *v* **1** [Tn] mix (different types of sth) in order to get a certain quality: *blended whisky/tea/coffee/tobacco.* **2 (a)** [I, Ipr, Ip] ~ **(with sth)**/~ **(together)** form a mixture; mix: *Oil does not blend with water.* ○ *Oil and water do not blend.* **(b)** [Tn, Tn·pr, Tn·p] ~ **A with B**/~ **A and B (together)** mix one thing with another; mix things together: *Blend the eggs with the milk.* ○ *Blend the eggs and milk (together).* **3 (a)** [I, Ipr, Ip] ~ **(with sth)**/~ **(together)** combine with sth in a harmonious way; look or sound good together: *Those cottages blend perfectly with the landscape.* ○ *Their voices blend (together) well.* **(b)** [I, Ipr] ~ **(into sth)** (esp of colours) shade gradually into each other: *The sea and the sky seemed to blend into each another.* **4** (phr v) **blend in (with sth)** mix harmoniously (with sth): *The new office block doesn't blend in with its surroundings.* **blend sth in** (in cooking) add another ingredient to sth and mix the two: *Heat the butter gently and then blend in a little flour.*

▷ **blend** *n* **1** mixture of different sorts: *Which blend of coffee would you like?* ○ (*fig*) *His manner is a blend of charm and politeness.* **2** = PORTMANTEAU WORD (PORTMANTEAU).

blender *n* = LIQUIDIZER (LIQUIDIZE).

Blenheim /ˈblenɪm/ village in Bavaria where the first Duke of Marlborough beat the army of the French king Louis XIV in 1704. **Blenheim Palace** near Oxford is the home of the Dukes of Marlborough. It was built by *Vanbrugh and is a fine example of English baroque architecture. ⇨ illus at VANBRUGH. ⇨ article at ARCHITECTURE.

blenny /ˈblenɪ/ *n* small sea-fish with spiny fins and slimy scales.

bless /bles/ *v* (*pt, pp* **blessed** /blest/; in sense 5, *pp* **blest** /blest/) [Tn] **1** ask God's favour and protection for (sb/sth): *They brought the children to Jesus and he blessed them.* ○ *The Pope blessed the crowd.* ○ *The priest blessed the harvest.* **2** (esp in Christian ritual) make (sth) sacred or holy; consecrate: *The priest blessed the bread and wine,* ie before the celebration of the Eucharist. **3** (esp in Christian Church services) call (God) holy; praise; glorify: *'We bless Thy Holy Name.'* **4** (esp imperative in prayers) (*fml*) grant health, happiness and success to (sb/sth): *Bless* (ie We ask God to bless) *all those who are hungry, lonely or sick.* **5** (*pp* **blest**) (*dated infml*) (esp in exclamations expressing surprise): *Bless me!* ○ *Bless my soul!* ○ *Well, I'm blest!* ○ *I'm blest if I know!* ie I don't know at all. **6** (idm) **be blessed with sth/sb** be fortunate in having sth/sb: *He is blessed with excellent health.* ○ (*joc or ironic*) *Mrs Murphy is blessed with twelve children.* ˈ**bless you** (used as an *interj* to express thanks or affection, or said to sb who has sneezed): *You've bought me a present? Bless you!*

blessed /ˈblesɪd/ *adj* **1** holy; sacred: *the Blessed Virgin,* ie the mother of Jesus, the Virgin Mary. **2** (in religious language) fortunate: *Blessed are the meek.* **3** [attrib] giving pleasure; enjoyable: *a moment of blessed calm.* **4** (in the Roman Catholic

Church) (of a person) beatified by the Pope. **5** (*euph infml*) (used to express mild anger, surprise, etc) damned: *I can't see a blessed thing without my glasses.*
▷ **the Blessed** *n* [pl *v*] those who live with God in heaven.
blessedly *adv*: *It's so blessedly quiet here.*
blessedness /ˈblesɪdnɪs/ *n* [U].
□ **the ˌBlessed ˈSacrament** = SACRAMENT 2.
blessing /ˈblesɪŋ/ *n* **1** (usu *sing*) (**a**) God's favour and protection: *ask for God's blessing.* (**b**) prayer asking for this. (**c**) short prayer of thanks to God before or after a meal: *say a blessing.* **2** (usu *sing*) good wishes; approval: *I cannot give my blessing to such a proposal.* **3** thing that one is glad of; thing that brings happiness: *What a blessing you weren't hurt in the accident!* **4** (idm) **a blessing in disˈguise** thing that seems unfortunate, but is later seen to be fortunate: *Not getting into university may be a blessing in disguise; I don't think you'd have been happy there.* **count one's blessings** ⇨ COUNT[1].
blether = BLATHER.
blew *pt* of BLOW[1].
Bligh /blaɪ/ William (1754-1817), British naval officer. He is chiefly remembered as the commander of HMS *Bounty* whose crew mutinied and set him and a few officers adrift in a small boat in the Pacific. The mutiny, and Bligh's unyielding character, have made his name synonymous with harsh naval discipline.
blight /blaɪt/ *n* **1** [U] (**a**) disease that withers plants. (**b**) [sing] fungus or insect causing this. **2** [C] ~ (**on/upon sb/sth**) (*fig*) destructive or harmful force: *cast/put a blight on sb/sth* ○ *Unemployment is a blight on our community.* **3** [U] ugly or neglected part (esp of cities): *the blight of inner-city slums.*
▷ **blight** *v* [Tn] **1** affect (sth) with blight; wither: *The apple trees were blighted by frost.* **2** spoil (sth); mar: *a career blighted by ill health.*
blighter /ˈblaɪtə(r)/ *n* (*dated Brit infml*) **1** person; fellow: *You lucky blighter!* **2** contemptible or annoying person: *The blighter stole my purse!*
Blighty /ˈblaɪtɪ/ *n* (*dated Brit army sl*) (used by soldiers serving abroad) Britain; home.
blimey /ˈblaɪmɪ/ *interj* (*Brit sl*) (expressing surprise or annoyance): *Blimey, that's a funny hat!*
Blimp /blɪmp/ *n* (also ˌ**Colonel ˈBlimp**) (*Brit infml derog*) pompous and reactionary person (esp an old army officer). ▷ **blimpish** *adj.*
blimp /blɪmp/ *n* small airship without a rigid frame.
blind[1] /blaɪnd/ *adj* **1** unable to see: *a blind person* ○ *be blind from birth, in one eye.* **2** [attrib] of or for blind people: *a ˈblind school.* **3** [pred] ~ (**to sth**) unable or unwilling to understand or notice sth; oblivious (to sth); unaware (of sth): *I must have been blind not to realize the danger we were in.* ○ *He is completely blind to her faults.* **4** [usu attrib] (*fig*) (**a**) without reason or judgement: *blind hatred/obedience/prejudice* ○ *love/faith that is blind.* (**b**) not ruled by purpose; thoughtless; reckless: *the blind forces of nature/destiny* ○ *be in a blind fury/panic/rage* ○ *blind haste/speed.* **5** [usu attrib] concealed; hidden: *a blind driveway/entrance* ○ *a blind bend/corner/turning*, ie one that prevents the driver from seeing the road ahead ○ *a blind stitch*, ie one that can be seen on one side of the fabric only. **6** (of an aircraft manoeuvre in cloud, fog, etc) done with the aid of instruments only, without being able to see: *blind flying* ○ *a blind landing.* **7** (idm) (**as**) **blind as a ˈbat** unable to see clearly or easily; unable to see what is obvious to others: *He's as blind as a bat without his glasses.* **love is blind** ⇨ LOVE[1]. **rob sb blind** ⇨ ROB. **turn a blind ˈeye (to sth)** pretend not to notice: *The manager turned a blind eye when his staff were late.*
▷ **the blind** *n* [pl *v*] **1** blind people: *a school for the blind.* **2** (idm) **the blind leading the ˈblind** (*saying*) people without adequate experience or knowledge attempting to guide or advise others like them.
blind *adv* **1** without being able to see; with the aid of instruments only: *drive/fly blind.* **2** (idm) **blind ˈdrunk** (*infml*) very drunk. **swear blind** ⇨ SWEAR.
blindly *adv.*
blindness *n* [U].
□ ˌ**blind ˈalley 1** alley that is closed at one end; cul-de-sac. **2** (*fig*) course of action which may seem promising at first but which in the end has no satisfactory result.
ˌ**blind ˈdate** (*infml*) arrangement to meet socially made between a man and a woman who have not met each other before.
ˌ**blind-ˌman's ˈbuff** game in which a player who is blindfolded tries to catch and identify the other players.
ˈ**blind spot 1** part of the retina in the eye that is not sensitive to light. **2** area that a motorist cannot see: *I didn't see the car that was overtaking me — it was in my blind spot.* **3** subject about which a person is prejudiced or ignorant: *History is one of his blind spots.*
blind[2] /blaɪnd/ *v* **1** [Tn] make (sb) temporarily or permanently blind: *a blinding flash/light* ○ *He was blinded* (ie dazzled) *by the sunlight.* ○ *The soldier was blinded in the explosion.* **2** [Tn, Tn·pr] ~ **sb** (**to sth**) (*fig*) deprive sb of reason, judgement or good sense: *Her love for him blinded her (to his faults).* **3** (idm) **blind sb with science** confuse sb with a display of technical knowledge.
blind[3] /blaɪnd/ *n* **1** (*US* **shade**, **window shade**) screen for a window, esp one made of a roll of cloth fixed on a roller and pulled down: *draw/lower/raise the blinds.* **2** thing or person used in order to deceive or mislead: *His job as a diplomat was a blind for his spying.* **3** (*US*) = HIDE[1] *n.*
blinder /ˈblaɪndə(r)/ *n* (*Brit sl*) **1** time of excessive drinking: *be/go on a blinder.* **2** outstanding performance (in a game): *play a blinder (of a shot, game, etc)* ○ *The last goal was a blinder.*
blinders /ˈblaɪndəz/ *n* [pl] (*US*) = BLINKERS.
blindfold /ˈblaɪndfəʊld/ *v* [Tn] cover the eyes of (sb) with a bandage, cloth, etc so that he cannot see: *blindfold a hostage, prisoner, etc.*
▷ **blindfold** *n* such a cover for the eyes.
blindfold *adj, adv* with the eyes blindfolded: *I could do that blindfold*, ie easily, regardless of obstacles.
blindworm /ˈblaɪndwɜ:m/ *n* = SLOW-WORM.
blink /blɪŋk/ *v* **1** [I, Tn] shut and open the eyes quickly: *He blinked in the bright sunlight.* ○ *How long can you stare without blinking (your eyes)?* **2** [I] (of distant lights) shine unsteadily; flicker: *harbour lights blinking on the horizon.* **3** (idm) **blink the fact (that...)** refuse to consider; ignore: *You can't blink the fact that the country's economy is suffering.* **4** (phr v) **blink sth away/back** try to control or hide (esp tears) by blinking: *Though clearly upset, she bravely blinked back her tears.*
▷ **blink** *n* **1** act of blinking. **2** sudden quick gleam of light. **3** (idm) **on the blink** (*infml*) (of a machine) not working properly; out of order: *The washing machine's on the blink again.*
blinkered /ˈblɪŋkəd/ *adj* **1** (of a horse) wearing blinkers. **2** (*fig*) unable to understand or recognize sth; narrow-minded: *a blinkered attitude.*
blinkers /ˈblɪŋkəz/ (*US* **blinders**) *n* [pl] leather pieces fixed on a bridle to prevent a horse from seeing sideways. ⇨ illus at HARNESS.
blinking /ˈblɪŋkɪŋ/ *adj, adv* (*infml euph*) = BLOODY[2]: *It's a blinking nuisance.*
blip /blɪp/ *n* **1** spot of light on a radar screen. **2** quick popping sound.
Bliss /blɪs/ Sir Arthur (1891-1975), English composer. His early style was influenced by *Schoenberg and *Stravinsky, but he later followed in the English tradition of *Elgar and others. He was made Master of the Queen's Music in 1953.
bliss /blɪs/ *n* [U] perfect happiness; great joy: *a life of bliss* ○ *living in married/wedded bliss*, ie very happily married ○ *What bliss! I don't have to go to work today.*
▷ **blissful** /-fl/ *adj* extremely happy; joyful: (*ironic*) *blissful ignorance*, ie being unaware of sth unpleasant. **blissfully** /-fəlɪ/ *adv.*
blister /ˈblɪstə(r)/ *n* **1** bubble-like swelling under the skin, filled with watery liquid (caused by rubbing, burning, etc): *These tight shoes have given me blisters on my ankles.* **2** similar raised swelling on the surface of metal, painted wood, plants, etc.
▷ **blister** *v* [I, Tn] (cause sth to) form blisters: *My feet blister easily.* ○ *The hot sun blistered the paint.*
blistering /ˈblɪstərɪŋ/ *adj* **1** (of heat or speed) very great; extreme: *The runners set off at a blistering pace.* **2** (of criticism) severe; sharp: *blistering sarcasm, scorn, etc.* **blisteringly** *adv.*
□ ˈ**blister pack** package in which goods are sold, consisting of a transparent domed cover on a backing of cardboard, etc.
blithe /blaɪð/ *adj* [usu attrib] happy and carefree; casual: *a blithe lack of concern* ○ *a blithe spirit*, ie a happy person.
▷ **blithely** *adv* in a blithe manner: *He was blithely unaware of the trouble he had caused.*
blithering /ˈblɪðərɪŋ/ *adj* [attrib] (*infml*) absolute; contemptible: *You blithering idiot!*
B Litt /ˌbi: ˈlɪt/ *abbr* Bachelor of Letters: *have/be a B Litt in English* ○ *Sue Hill B Litt.*
blitz /blɪts/ *n* **1** [C] sudden intensive military attack, esp from the air: *carry out a blitz on enemy targets* ○ [attrib] *blitz bombing.* **2 the Blitz** [sing] intensive German air raids on Britain in 1940. **3** [C] ~ (**on sth**) (*fig infml*) any sudden or concentrated effort: *I had a blitz on the kitchen today, and now it's really clean.*
▷ **blitz** *v* [Tn] attack or damage (sth) in a blitz: *Many towns were badly blitzed during the war.*
□ **blitzkrieg** /ˈblɪtskri:g/ *n* sudden series of violent attacks intended to achieve a quick victory in a war.
blizzard /ˈblɪzəd/ *n* severe snowstorm.
bloated /ˈbləʊtɪd/ *adj* swollen with fat, gas or liquid: *a bloated face* ○ *I've had so much to eat I feel absolutely bloated.* ○ (*fig*) *bloated with pride.*
bloater /ˈbləʊtə(r)/ *n* salted smoked herring.
blob /blɒb/ *n* drop of (esp thick) liquid; small round mass or spot of colour: *a blob of paint, wax, cream.*
bloc /blɒk/ *n* group of countries or parties united by a common interest: *the Eastern/Western bloc.*
block[1] /blɒk/ *n* **1** (**a**) [C] large solid piece of wood, stone, metal, etc, usu with flat surfaces: *a block of concrete, granite, marble, etc.* (**b**) [C] piece of wood for chopping or hammering on: *a ˈchopping-block* ○ *a butcher's block.* (**c**) **the block** [sing] (formerly) large piece of wood on which a condemned person put his neck to have his head cut off: *go/be sent to the block.* **2** [C] child's wooden or plastic toy brick: *a set of (building) blocks.* **3** [C] large building divided into separate flats or offices: *blocks of ˈflats* ○ *an ˈoffice block* ○ *a ˈtower block*, ie a skyscraper. **4** [C] (**a**) group of buildings bounded by streets on four sides: *go for a walk round the block.* (**b**) (*esp US*) length of one side of such a group: *He lives three blocks away from here.* **5** [C] large quantity of things regarded as a single unit: *a block of theatre seats* ○ *a block of shares*, ie in a business ○ [attrib] *a block booking*, ie the booking at one time of a large number of seats. **6** [C] pad of paper for writing or drawing on. **7** [C] piece of wood or metal with designs engraved on it for printing. **8** [C usu *sing*] thing that makes movement or progress difficult or impossible; obstruction; obstacle: *a block in the pipe, gutter, drain, etc* ○ (*fig*) *The government's stubborn attitude was a block to further talks.* **9** [C] pulley enclosed in a wooden or metal casing. Cf BLOCK AND TACKLE. **10** (idm) **a chip off the old block** ⇨ CHIP[1]. **have a block (about sth)** fail to understand, feel, etc because of emotional tension: *He has a mental block about maths.* **knock sb's block/head off** ⇨ KNOCK[2].
□ ˌ**block and ˈtackle** lifting device consisting of ropes and pulleys.
ˌ**block ˈdiagram** diagram showing the general arrangement of parts of a system.
ˌ**block ˈletter** (also ˌ**block ˈcapital**) separate capital letter: *fill in a form in block letters.*
ˈ**block system** system used on railways to ensure that a train may only enter a section of track if it is clear.
ˌ**block ˈvote** (also ˈ**card vote**) voting system in

which each voter has influence in proportion to the number of people he represents.

block^{2} /blɒk/ *v* **1** (**a**) [Tn, Tn·p] ~ **sth** (**up**) make movement or flow difficult or impossible on or in sth; obstruct sth: *a drain blocked (up) by mud, dead leaves, etc* ○ *Heavy snow is blocking all roads into Scotland.* ○ *A large crowd blocked the corridors and exits.* ○ *My nose is blocked (up),* eg because of a heavy cold. (**b**) [Tn] prevent (sb/sth) from moving or progressing; hinder; obstruct: *block an opponent's move,* eg in a game of chess ○ *The accident blocked traffic in the town centre.* ○ *Progress in the talks was blocked by the Government's intransigence.* **2** [Tn] limit or prevent the use or expenditure of (currency, assets, etc): *blocked sterling.* **3** [Tn] (in cricket) stop (the ball) with the bat held defensively in front of the wicket. **4** (phr v) **block sth in/out** make a rough sketch or plan of sth: *block in the plan of a house.* **block sth off** separate (one place from another) using a solid barrier: *Police blocked off the street after the explosion.*

▷ **blockage** /ˈblɒkɪdʒ/ *n* (**a**) thing that blocks; obstruction: *a blockage in an artery, a drain-pipe, etc.* (**b**) state of being blocked.

blockade /blɒˈkeɪd/ *n* **1** surrounding or closing of a place (esp a port) by warships or soldiers to prevent people or goods getting in or out. **2** (idm) **break/run a blockade** (esp of a ship) get through a blockade. **lift/raise a blockade** end a blockade.

▷ **blockade** *v* [Tn] close (a town, port, etc) with a blockade: *The harbour was blockaded by enemy vessels.*

block-buster /ˈblɒkbʌste(r)/ *n* (*infml*) **1** very powerful bomb that can destroy many buildings. **2** book or film strongly promoted by its producers to increase sales. **3** (*US*) person who persuades people to sell their property quickly and cheaply out of fear of decreasing values.

▷ ˈ**block-busting** *n* [U] activity of block-busters (BLOCK-BUSTER 3).

blockhead /ˈblɒkhed/ *n* (*infml*) stupid person.

blockhouse /ˈblɒkhaʊs/ *n* **1** concrete structure strengthened to give shelter from gunfire, and with openings for defenders to shoot from. **2** (*US*) (formerly) wooden fort with openings in the walls for defenders to shoot from.

bloke /bləʊk/ *n* (*Brit infml*) man.

blond (also esp of a woman **blonde**) /blɒnd/ *n, adj* (person) having golden or pale-coloured hair: *Who was that blonde I saw you with last night?* Cf BRUNETTE, DUMB BLONDE (DUMB).

Blonde hair has often been associated with glamour. The novels by the American writer Anita Loos, *Gentlemen Prefer Blondes* and *But Gentlemen Marry Brunettes,* written in the 1920s, portrayed blonde-haired women as glamorous but shallow. Film actresses like Marilyn *Monroe reinforced the stereotype of the beautiful but helpless blonde. The traditional concept of the 'dumb blonde' is now generally considered offensive and revealing a sexist attitude towards women.

blood^{1} /blʌd/ *n* **1** [U] red liquid flowing through the bodies of humans and animals. Blood is pumped through the body by the heart. It carries many things needed by the body's tissues, including food, salts, oxygen and hormones. It also takes away waste products. In warm-blooded creatures it helps maintain an even temperature. Blood is made up of plasma, white and red cells, and platelets: *give blood,* eg so that it can be used in a blood transfusion ○ *He lost a lot of blood in the accident.* ○ *Much blood was shed* (ie Many people were killed) *in the war.* ○ [attrib] *blood sugar,* ie glucose contained in blood. **2** [U] (*fml*) family; descent; race: *of noble Scottish blood* ○ *They are of the same blood.* **3** [C] (*dated Brit*) rich and fashionable young man; dandy. **4** (idm) **bad blood** (**between A and B**) feelings of mutual hatred or strong dislike: *There's a lot of bad blood between those two families.* **be after/out for sb's** ˈ**blood** (*infml*) intend to hurt or humiliate sb, esp as a punishment or as revenge: (*joc*) *I was late for work again this morning — my boss is after my blood.* **be/run in one's/the** ˈ**blood** be part of one's nature or character because one has inherited it or become used to it: *Most of my family are musicians; it runs in the blood.* **blood and** ˈ**thunder** (*infml*) (in films, novels, etc) violent and melodramatic action: [attrib] *a blood-and-thunder story.* **blood is thicker than** ˈ**water** (*saying*) family relationships are the strongest ones. **sb's** ˈ**blood is up** sb is in a fighting mood: *After being insulted like that, my blood is really up!* (**have sb's**) ˈ**blood on one's hands** (carry) responsibility for the death of a person or people: *a dictator with much blood on his hands.* (**like getting/trying to get**) **blood out of/from a** ˈ**stone** (of money, sympathy, understanding, etc) almost impossible to obtain from sb: *Getting a pay rise in this firm is like getting blood from a stone.* **draw blood** ⇨ DRAW^{2}. **flesh and blood** ⇨ FLESH. **one's flesh and blood** ⇨ FLESH. **freeze one's blood; make one's blood freeze** ⇨ FREEZE. **in cold blood** ⇨ COLD^{1}. **make sb's** ˈ**blood boil** make sb very angry: *The way he treats his children makes my blood boil.* **make sb's blood run cold** fill sb with fear and horror: *The sight of the dead body made his blood run cold.* **new/fresh** ˈ**blood** (in a group, firm, club, etc) new members, esp young ones, with new ideas, skills or methods: *This company is badly in need of new blood.* **of the blood** (ˈ**royal**) related to the royal family: *a prince of the blood (royal).* **spill blood** ⇨ SPILL^{1}. **stir the/one's blood** ⇨ STIR^{1}. **sweat blood** ⇨ SWEAT.

□ ˈ**blood bank** place where blood is stored for use in hospitals, etc.

ˈ**blood-bath** *n* indiscriminate killing of many people; massacre: *The battle was a blood-bath.*

ˈ**blood-brother** *n* man who has sworn to treat another man as his brother, usu in a ceremony in which their blood is mixed together.

ˈ**blood count** (counting of the) number of red and white corpuscles in a sample of blood.

ˈ**blood-curdling** *adj* filling one with horror; terrifying: *a blood-curdling cry, scream, story.*

ˈ**blood-donor** *n* person who gives his blood for transfusions.

ˈ**blood feud** continuous quarrel between groups or families, with each murdering members of the other; vendetta.

ˈ**blood group** (also ˈ**blood type**) any of the several distinct classes of human blood: *His blood group is AO.*

ˈ**blood-heat** *n* [U] normal temperature of human blood (about 37°C, 98.4°F).

ˈ**blood-letting** *n* [U] **1** surgical removal of some of a patient's blood. **2** (*infml*) (**a**) bloodshed. (**b**) (*fig*) bitter quarrelling: *This blood-letting is damaging the reputation of the party.*

ˈ**blood-lust** *n* [U] strong desire to kill.

ˈ**blood-money** *n* [U] **1** money paid to a hired killer. **2** money paid to the family of a murdered person as compensation.

ˈ**blood orange** type of orange with red streaks in its pulp.

ˈ**blood-poisoning** (also **toxaemia**) *n* [U] infection of the blood with harmful bacteria, esp through a cut or wound.

ˈ**blood pressure** pressure of the blood on the walls of the arteries (varying with a person's age or health): *have high/low blood pressure* ○ (*fig*) *Politicians always raise his blood pressure,* ie make him extremely angry.

ˌ**blood-**ˈ**red** *adj* having the colour of blood; bright red: *Her finger-nails were blood-red.* ○ ˌ*blood-red* ˈ*nails.*

ˈ**blood-relation** *n* person related to sb by birth.

ˈ**bloodshed** *n* [U] killing or wounding of people: *The two sides called a truce to avoid further bloodshed.*

ˈ**bloodshot** *adj* (of eyes) red because of swollen or broken blood-vessels: *His eyes were bloodshot from lack of sleep.*

ˈ**blood sports** sports (eg fox-hunting) in which animals or birds are killed.

ˈ**blood-stained** *adj* **1** stained with blood: *a blood-stained shirt.* **2** (*fig*) characterized or disgraced by bloodshed: *a blood-stained reputation, regime, tyrant.*

ˈ**bloodstock** *n* [U] thoroughbred horses.

ˈ**bloodstream** *n* [sing] blood flowing through the body: *inject drugs into the bloodstream.*

ˈ**bloodsucker** *n* **1** animal that sucks blood, esp a leech. **2** (*fig infml*) person who tries to take as much money as possible from others.

ˈ**blood test** examination of a sample of blood, esp for medical diagnosis.

ˈ**blood transfusion** injection of blood into a blood-vessel of a person or an animal.

ˈ**blood-vessel** *n* any of the tubes (arteries, veins or capillaries) through which blood flows in the body: *burst a blood-vessel.*

blood^{2} /blʌd/ *v* [Tn] **1** (in hunting) allow (a young hound) to taste the blood of eg a fox for the first time. **2** (*fig*) give (sb) his first experience of an activity; initiate: *This will be her first match for her country; she hasn't yet been blooded.*

bloodhound /ˈblʌdhaʊnd/ *n* type of large dog with a good sense of smell, used for tracking.

bloodless /ˈblʌdlɪs/ *adj* **1** without blood or killing: *a bloodless coup/revolution/victory.* **2** pale; anaemic: *He has bloodless cheeks.* **3** (*fig*) (**a**) (of a person) lacking energy or enthusiasm; dull; lifeless. (**b**) lacking emotion; unfeeling.

bloodthirsty /ˈblʌdθɜːstɪ/ *adj* **1** (**a**) cruel and eager to kill; murderous: *a bloodthirsty killer, tribe, warrior.* (**b**) taking pleasure or showing interest in killing and violence: *bloodthirsty spectators.* **2** (of a book, film, etc) describing or showing killing and violence. ▷ **bloodthirstily** *adv.* **bloodthirstiness** *n* [U].

bloody^{1} /ˈblʌdɪ/ *adj* (**-ier, -iest**) **1** covered with blood; bleeding: *His clothes were torn and bloody.* ○ *give sb a bloody nose,* ie hit sb's nose so that it bleeds. **2** involving much bloodshed: *a bloody battle.* **3** cruel; bloodthirsty: *a bloody deed, murder, tyrant.*

▷ **bloodily** *adv.*

bloody *v* (*pt, pp* **bloodied**) [Tn] stain (sb/sth) with blood.

□ ˌ**Bloody** ˈ**Mary 1** (also **bloody mary**) drink made by mixing vodka and tomato juice. **2** nickname of Queen *Mary Tudor, because of the religious persecution and many executions during her reign.

bloody^{2} /ˈblʌdɪ/ *adj* [attrib], *adv* (⚠ *Brit infml*) **1** (used to emphasize a judgement or comment) utter(ly); absolute(ly); extreme(ly): *bloody nonsense, rubbish, etc* ○ *This rail strike is a bloody nuisance.* ○ *What a bloody waste of time!* ○ *That was a bloody good meal!* **2** (used to stress anger or annoyance): *What the bloody hell are you doing?* ○ *I don't bloody care.* **3** (idm) **bloody well** (*Brit infml*) (used to emphasize an angry statement, esp an order) certainly; definitely: *'I'm not coming with you.' 'Yes you bloody well are!'*

□ ˌ**bloody-**ˈ**minded** *adj* (*Brit infml*) deliberately unhelpful or obstructive: *Everybody else accepts the decision. Why must you be so bloody-minded?* **bloody-mindedness** *n* [U].

bloom /bluːm/ *n* **1** [C] flower, esp of plants admired chiefly for their flowers (eg roses, tulips, chrysanthemums): *These roses have beautiful blooms.* ⇨ illus at FLOWER. Cf BLOSSOM. **2** [U] (*fig*) freshness; perfection: *be in/have lost the bloom of youth.* **3** [U] covering of fine powder that forms on ripe plums, grapes, etc. **4** (idm) **in (full) bloom** (of plants, gardens, etc) flowering: *The garden looks lovely when the roses are in bloom.* ○ (*fig*) *Her genius was in full bloom,* ie at its best or highest point. **take the bloom off sth** cause sth to lose its freshness or perfection: *Their frequent rows took the bloom off their marriage.*

▷ **bloom** *v* **1** [I] (**a**) produce flowers; flower; blossom: *Daffodils and crocuses bloom in the spring.* (**b**) (*fig*) flourish; prosper: *Our friendship is blooming.* **2** [I, Ipr] ~ (**with sth**) (**a**) (of a garden, etc) be full of plants or flowers in bloom: *The garden is blooming with spring flowers.* (**b**) (*fig*) be in a healthy or flourishing condition (because of sth): *They were blooming with health and happiness.*

bloomer /ˈbluːmə(r)/ *n* (*Brit*) **1** (*infml*) serious mistake; blunder: *He made a tremendous bloomer.*

2 white loaf baked with slanting cuts across the top.

bloomers /ˈbluːməz/ *n* [pl] short loose trousers gathered at the knee, formerly worn by women for games, cycling, etc: *a pair of bloomers.*

blooming /ˈbluːmɪŋ/ *adj* [attrib], *adv* (*Brit infml euph*) = BLOODY[2].

Bloomsbury Group /ˈbluːmzbrɪ gruːp/ group of writers, artists and intellectuals who met regularly as friends in Bloomsbury (a district of London) at the beginning of the 20th century. They were noted for their radicalism and rejection of the attitudes of the Victorian era. They included many of the leading figures of the time, such as Virginia *Woolf, E M *Forster and Maynard *Keynes.

blooper /ˈbluːpə(r)/ *n* (*infml esp US*) embarrassing public blunder or mistake.

blossom /ˈblɒsəm/ *n* **1** [C] flower, esp of a fruit tree or flowering shrub. Cf BLOOM. **2** [U] mass of flowers on a tree or shrub: *apple, cherry, etc blossom.* **3** (idm) **in (full) blossom** (esp of trees and shrubs) bearing blossom: *The apple trees are in blossom.*

▷ **blossom** *v* **1** [I] (of a tree or shrub) produce blossom: *The cherry trees blossomed early this year.* **2** [I, Ipr, Ip] ~ **(out) (into sth)** (*fig*) **(a)** develop in a healthy or promising way; grow or develop (into sth); flourish: *a blossoming friendship, partnership, etc* ○ *Mozart blossomed (as a composer) very early in life.* ○ *She has blossomed (out) into a beautiful young woman.* **(b)** become more lively: *He used to be painfully shy, but now he's started to blossom (out).*

blot[1] /blɒt/ *n* **1** spot or stain made by ink, etc: *a page covered in (ink) blots.* **2** ~ **on sth** (*fig derog*) act or quality that spoils sb's good character or reputation: *His involvement in the scandal was a blot on his reputation.* **3** (idm) **a blot on sb's/the eˈscutcheon** (*joc*) act, event, etc that disgraces a family or some other group. **a blot on the ˈlandscape** object (esp an ugly building) that spoils the beauty of a place: *That new factory is a blot on the landscape.*

blot[2] /blɒt/ *v* (**-tt-**) **1** [Tn] make a blot or blots on (paper); stain (with ink): *an exercise book blotted with ink.* **2** [Tn] soak up or dry (sth) with blotting-paper: *blot spilt ink, one's writing-paper.* **3** (idm) **blot one's ˈcopy-book** (*infml*) spoil one's (previous) good record or reputation: *She blotted her copy-book by being an hour late for work.* **4** (phr v) **blot sth out (a)** cover or hide (writing, etc) with a blot: *Several words in the letter had been blotted out.* **(b)** (esp of mist, fog, etc) hide sth completely: *Thick cloud blotted out the view.* **(c)** (*fig*) remove or destroy (thoughts, memories, etc) completely.

▷ **blotter** *n* **(a)** pad or large piece of blotting-paper. **(b)** (*esp US*) book used for keeping a record of the events of each day: *a police blotter,* ie for noting arrests, enquiries, etc.

□ **ˈblotting-paper** *n* [U] absorbent paper for drying wet ink.

blotch /blɒtʃ/ *n* large discoloured mark, usu irregular in shape (on skin, paper, material, etc): *His face was covered in ugly red blotches.*

▷ **blotched, blotchy** *adjs* covered in blotches: *blotchy skin.*

blotto /ˈblɒtəʊ/ *adj* [pred] (*infml*) very drunk: *You were completely blotto last night.*

blouse /blaʊz; US blaʊs/ *n* **1** garment like a shirt, worn by women: *She was wearing a skirt and blouse.* **2** type of jacket worn by soldiers as part of their uniform.

blow[1] /bləʊ/ *v* (*pt* **blew** /bluː/, *pp* **blown** /bləʊn/ or, in sense 12, **blowed** /bləʊd/) **1** [I, Ipr] (often with *it* as the subject) (of the wind or a current of air) be moving: *It was blowing hard/blowing a gale,* ie There was a strong wind. ○ *A cold wind blew across the river.* **2** [I, Ipr, Tn·pr, Tn·p] send out (a current of air, etc) from the mouth: *You're not blowing hard enough!* ○ *blow on one's food,* ie to cool it ○ *blow on one's fingers,* ie to warm them ○ *The policeman asked me to blow into a plastic bag,* ie in order to breathalyse me. ○ *He drew on his cigarette*

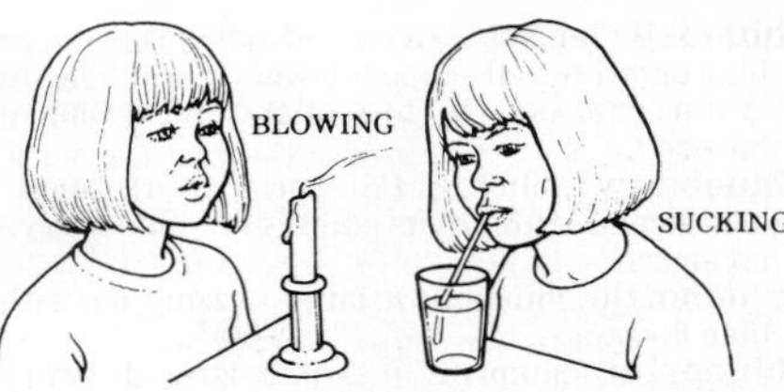

and blew out a stream of smoke. ⇨ illus. **3** [I, Ip] be moved by the wind: *hair blowing (about) in the wind.* **4** [Tn] make or shape (sth) by blowing: *blow smoke rings* ○ *blow bubbles,* eg by blowing onto a film of soapy water ○ *blow glass,* ie send a current of air into molten glass. **5** [Tn] use (sth) to make a current of air: *blow bellows.* **6 (a)** [Ipr, Tn] produce sound from (a brass instrument, whistle, etc) by blowing into it: *blow (on) a horn* ○ *The referee blew his whistle.* **(b)** [I] (of an instrument, etc) sound in this way: *the noise of trumpets blowing.* **7** [I, Tn] (cause sth to) melt with too strong an electric current: *A fuse has blown.* ○ *I've blown a fuse.* **8** [Tn] break (sth) with explosives: *The safe had been blown by the thieves.* **9** [Tn] (*sl*) reveal (sth): *The spy's cover was blown.* **10** [Tn, Tn·pr] ~ **sth (on sth)** (*infml*) spend a lot of money (on sth): *blow £50 on a meal.* **11** [Tn] spoil or fail to use (an opportunity): *He blew it/blew his chances by arriving late for the interview.* **12** (*pp* **blowed** /bləʊd/) [Tn] (*infml*) (used esp in the imperative in expressions of anger, surprise, etc) damn (sb/sth): *Blow it! We've missed the bus.* ○ *Well, blow me/I'm blowed! I never thought I'd see you again.* ○ *I'm blowed if I'm going to* (ie I certainly will not) *let him treat you like that.* **13** [Tn] (*US sl*) leave (a place) suddenly. **14** (idm) **blow one's/sb's ˈbrains out** kill oneself/sb by shooting in the head. **blow the ˈcobwebs away** (*infml*) make one's/sb's mind and spirits active and lively again: *You've been stuck indoors too long; a nice long walk should help to blow the cobwebs away.* **blow the ˈgaff** (*sl*) reveal a secret. **blow hot and ˈcold (about sth)** (*infml*) keep changing one's opinions (about sth); vacillate: *He blows hot and cold about getting married.* **blow (sb) a ˈkiss** kiss one's hand and then pretend to blow the kiss (towards sb). **blow one's/sb's ˈmind** (*sl*) produce a pleasant or shocking feeling in one/sb. **blow one's ˈnose** clear one's nose of mucus by breathing out strongly through it into a handkerchief. **blow off/let off steam** ⇨ STEAM. **blow one's own ˈtrumpet** (*infml*) praise one's own abilities and achievements; boast. **blow one's ˈtop**; *US* **blow one's ˈstack** (*infml*) lose one's temper. **blow the whistle on sb/sth** (*infml*) make sb suddenly stop doing sth, esp sth illegal, eg by informing the authorities. **puff and blow** ⇨ PUFF[2]. **see which way the wind is blowing** ⇨ WAY[1]. **15** (phr v) **blow (sb/sth) down, off, over, etc** move or be moved in the specified direction by the force of the wind, sb's breath, etc: *My hat blew off.* ○ *The door blew open.* ○ *Several chimneys blew down during the storm.* ○ *I was almost blown over by the wind.* ○ *The ship was blown onto the rocks.* ○ *The bomb blast blew two passers-by across the street.* ○ *He blew the dust off the book,* ie removed the dust by blowing.

blow in/blow into sth (*infml*) arrive or enter (a place) suddenly: *Look who's just blown in!*

blow out (a) (of a flame, etc) be extinguished by the wind, etc: *Somebody opened the door and the candle blew out.* **(b)** (of an oil or gas well) send out gas suddenly in an uncontrolled manner. **blow itself out** (of a storm, etc) lose its force; dwindle to nothing. **blow sth out** extinguish (a flame, etc) by blowing.

blow over pass away without having a serious effect: *The storm blew over in the night.* ○ *The scandal will soon blow over.*

blow up (a) explode; be destroyed by an explosion: *The bomb blew up.* ○ *A policeman was killed when his booby-trapped car blew up.* **(b)** start suddenly and with force: *A storm is blowing up.* ○ (*fig*) *A political crisis has blown up over the President's latest speech.* **(c)** (*infml*) lose one's temper: *I'm sorry I blew up at you.* **blow sb up** (*infml*) reprimand sb severely: *She got blown up by her boss for being late.* **blow sth up (a)** destroy sth by an explosion: *The police station was blown up by terrorists.* **(b)** inflate sth with air or gas: *This tyre's a bit flat; it needs blowing up.* **(c)** make (esp a photograph) bigger; enlarge sth: *What a lovely photo! Why don't you have it blown up?* **(d)** (*infml*) exaggerate or inflate sth: *His abilities as an actor have been greatly blown up by the popular press.* ○ *The whole affair was blown up out of all proportion.*

▷ **blowy** *adj* windy: *a blowy day.*

□ **ˈblow-dry** *v* (*pt, pp* **-dried**) [Tn] style (the hair) while drying it with a hand-held drier. — *n* act of drying and styling the hair in this way: *ask the hairdresser for a wash and blow-dry.*

ˈblow-hole *n* **1** vent for air, smoke, etc in a tunnel. **2** hole in the ice through which seals, etc breathe. **3** whale's nostril situated at the back of its skull.

ˌblowing-ˈup *n* scolding: *get a terrible blowing-up for sth.*

ˈblowlamp (*US* **torch**, **ˈblowtorch**) *n* burner for directing a very hot flame onto part of a surface, eg to remove old paint.

ˈblow-out *n* **1** bursting of a tyre on a motor vehicle: *have a blow-out on the motorway.* **2** melting of an electric fuse. **3** sudden uncontrolled escape of oil or gas from a well. **4** (*sl*) large meal.

ˈblowpipe *n* **1** tube used for blowing air into sth, esp to increase the heat of a flame, or by a glass-blower shaping molten glass. **2** tube from which (usu poisonous) darts may be shot by blowing through the tube.

ˈblow-up *n* enlargement (of a photograph): *Do a blow-up of this corner of the negative.*

blow[2] /bləʊ/ *n* **1** act of blowing: *give one's nose a good blow,* ie clear it thoroughly. **2** (idm) **go for/have a ˈblow** go for a short walk in the fresh air.

blow[3] /bləʊ/ *n* **1** hard stroke (given with the fist, a weapon, etc): *He received a severe blow on/to the head.* **2** ~ **(to sb/sth)** sudden shock, set-back or disaster (for sb/sth): *a blow to one's pride* ○ *His wife's death was a great blow (to him).* **3** (idm) **at one ˈblow; at a (single) ˈblow** with one stroke or effort: *He felled his three attackers at a single blow.* **a ˌblow-by-ˈblow account, description, etc (of sth)** account giving all the details (of an event) as they occur: *He gave us a blow-by-blow account of the evening's events.* **come to ˈblows (over sth)** start fighting (because of sth): *We almost came to blows over what colour our new carpet should be.* **deal sb/sth a blow** ⇨ DEAL[3]. **get a ˈblow/ˈpunch in** succeed in hitting sb. **strike a blow for/against sth** ⇨ STRIKE[2].

blower /ˈbləʊə(r)/ *n* **1** device that produces a current of air. **2** (*Brit infml*) telephone: *You can always get me on the blower.*

blowfly /ˈbləʊflaɪ/ *n* fly that lays its eggs on meat; bluebottle.

blown *pp* of BLOW[1].

blowzy /ˈblaʊzɪ/ *adj* (*derog*) (of a woman or her appearance) untidy and coarse-looking.

blub /blʌb/ *v* (**-bb-**) [I] (*Brit infml derog*) cry; blubber: *Don't start blubbing — you're not seriously hurt!*

blubber[1] /ˈblʌbə(r)/ *n* [U] fat of whales and other sea animals from which oil is obtained.

blubber[2] /ˈblʌbə(r)/ *v* [I] (*usu derog*) weep noisily: *Stop blubbering, you big baby!*

bludge /blʌdʒ/ *v* (*Austral and NZ sl derog*) **1** [I] avoid hard work; skive. **2** [Ipr] ~ **on sb** get things from sb without trying to give anything in return: *He's still bludging on his parents.* **3** [Tn, Tn·pr] ~ **sth (from sb)** try to get sth (from sb) by asking, usu unreasonably. ▷ **bludger** *n.*

bludgeon /ˈblʌdʒən/ *n* short thick stick with a heavy end, used as a weapon.

▷ **bludgeon** *v* **1** [Tn] hit (sb) repeatedly with a bludgeon, or with any heavy object: *He had been bludgeoned to death.* **2** [Tn, Tn·pr] ~ **sb (into doing sth)** (*fig*) force sb (to do sth): *They tried to* *bludgeon me into playing football again, but I refused.*

blue[1] /bluː/ *adj* **1** having the colour of a clear sky or the sea on a sunny day: *blue eyes* ○ *a blue dress, shirt, etc* ○ *a pair of faded blue jeans* ○ *He was blue in the face,* ie His face was a purplish colour because of cold or exertion. ○ *Her hands were blue with cold.* ⇨ illus at SPECTRUM. **2** [pred] (*infml*) sad; depressed: *Don't look so blue — smile!* **3** indecent; pornographic: *a blue film/movie/joke.* **4** (idm) **black and blue** ⇨ BLACK[1]. **sb's ˌblue-eyed ˈboy** (*infml esp Brit usu derog*) favourite of a person or group; darling; pet: *He's the manager's blue-eyed boy.* **once in a blue moon** ⇨ ONCE. **scream, etc blue ˈmurder** (*infml*) protest wildly and noisily: *The union yelled blue murder when one of its members was sacked.* **(do sth) till one is blue in the ˈface** (*infml*) (work, etc) as hard and as long as one possibly can (usu without success): *He can write me letters till he's blue in the face, I'm not going to reply.* ▷ **blueness** *n* [U].

□ **ˌblue ˈbaby** baby whose skin is blue at birth because of a heart defect.

ˌblue ˈblood aristocratic descent or birth. **ˌblue-ˈblooded** *adj*: *a ˌblue-blooded ˈfamily.*

ˈblue book **(a)** (*Brit*) parliamentary or Privy Council report. **(b)** (*US*) book that gives details of people who have an important position in society.

ˌblue ˈcheese cheese showing lines of blue mould.

ˌblue-ˈchip *n, adj* (*commerce*) (industrial share) considered to be a safe investment. ⇨ article at FINANCE.

ˌblue-ˈcollar *adj* [attrib] of or relating to manual workers: *blue-ˈcollar workers, jobs* ○ *a blue-ˈcollar union.* Cf WHITE-COLLAR (WHITE[1]). ⇨ article at CLASS.

ˌblue ˈensign (*Brit*) flag of government departments.

ˌblue ˈfunk = FUNK 1.

ˌblue ˈgiant very large bright star at the beginning of its life that burns a large amount of hydrogen at its centre, making its surface extremely hot.

blue grass 1 type of grass, blue when blossoming, found esp in the US states of Kentucky and Virginia. **2** type of jazz-like American folk-music.

ˈbluejacket *n* seaman in the navy.

ˌblue-ˈpencil *v* [Tn] alter or remove (parts of a book, film, play, etc); edit; censor.

ˌBlue ˈPeter blue flag with a central white square, used to show that a ship is about to sail.

ˌBlue ˈRiband trophy awarded to the ship that crosses the Atlantic in the fastest time.

ˌblue ˈribbon honour or prize awarded to the winner of a competition.

ˈblue tit type of small bird with a blue head, tail and wings and yellow underparts. ⇨ illus at BIRD.

ˌblue ˈwhale type of whale with a dorsal fin, the largest known living animal.

blue[2] /bluː/ *n* **1** **(a)** [C, U] blue colour: *light/dark blue* ○ *material with a lot of blue in it.* **(b)** [U] blue clothes: *dressed in blue.* **2** [C] **(a)** (*Brit*) distinction awarded to a sportsman who represents either Oxford or Cambridge University in a match between the two: *get a/one's blue for cricket, football, etc.* **(b)** person who has won a blue: *an Oxford/a Cambridge (hockey) blue.* **3 the blue** [sing] (*dated infml*) sea or sky: *The boat sailed off into the blue.* **4** [sing or pl *v*] **(a) the blues** slow melancholy jazz music originating among Blacks in the southern US: [attrib] *a blues singer, melody.* **(b) blues** song of this type: *sing a blues.* **5 the blues** [pl] (*infml*) feelings of deep sadness or depression: *have (an attack of) the blues.* **6** (idm) **a bolt from the blue** ⇨ BOLT[1]. **the boys in blue** ⇨ BOY[1]. **out of the ˈblue** unexpected(ly); without warning: *She arrived out of the blue.* ○ *His resignation came (right) out of the blue.*

blue[3] /bluː/ *v* [Tn] (*infml*) spend (money) recklessly: *He won £500 and then blued the lot in three days.*

Bluebeard /ˈbluːbɪəd/ character in a folk-tale who married many wives and killed each one in turn because they insisted on discovering the secret of a locked room in his castle. The room contained the bodies of his previous wives.

bluebell /ˈbluːbel/ *n* **(a)** (in S England) plant with blue or white bell-shaped flowers; wood hyacinth. ⇨ illus at PLANT. **(b)** (in Scotland and N England) harebell.

blueberry /ˈbluːbrɪ; *US* -berɪ/ *n* **(a)** small N American shrub. **(b)** its edible dark blue berry. Cf BILBERRY.

bluebottle /ˈbluːbɒtl/ *n* large buzzing fly with a blue body.

blueprint /ˈbluːprɪnt/ *n* **1** photographic print of building plans, with white lines on a blue background. **2** (*fig*) detailed plan or scheme: *a blueprint for success* ○ [attrib] *Plans have reached the blueprint stage.*

bluestocking /ˈbluːstɒkɪŋ/ *n* (*sometimes derog*) woman having, or pretending to have, literary tastes and learning.

bluff[1] /blʌf/ *v* **1** [I, Tn] try to deceive (sb) by pretending to be stronger, braver, cleverer, etc than one is: *I don't believe he'd really do what he threatens — he's only bluffing (us).* **2** (phr v) **bluff sb into doing sth** make sb believe or do sth by deceiving him: *They were bluffed into believing we were not ready for the attack.* **bluff it ˈout** survive a difficult situation by deceiving others. **bluff one's way out (of sth)** escape from a difficult situation by deceiving others.

▷ **bluff** *n* **1** [U, C] bluffing; threat intended to influence sb without being carried out: *The company's threat to sack anyone who went on strike was just (a) bluff.* **2** (idm) **call sb's bluff** ⇨ CALL[2].

bluff[2] /blʌf/ *n* cliff or headland with a broad and very steep face.

bluff[3] /blʌf/ *adj* **1** (esp of cliffs) with a broad, steep or vertical front. **2** (of a person, his manner, etc) frank and abrupt, but good-natured: *He is kind and friendly despite his rather bluff manner.* ▷ **bluffness** *n* [U].

bluish /ˈbluːɪʃ/ *adj* tending towards blue; fairly blue: *eyes of bluish green.*

Blunden /ˈblʌndən/ Edmund Charles (1896-1974), English poet. His best-known poems are about the English countryside and his experiences as a soldier in the First World War.

blunder /ˈblʌndə(r)/ *n* stupid or careless mistake: *I've made an awful blunder.* ⇨ Usage at MISTAKE.

▷ **blunder** *v* **1** [I] make a blunder: *The police blundered badly by arresting the wrong man.* **2** (phr v) **blunder about, around, etc** move about clumsily or uncertainly, as if blind: *He blundered about the room, feeling for the light switch.* **blunder into sth** walk into or strike sth through clumsiness or inability to see: *In the darkness, he blundered into the hall table.*

blunderer /ˈblʌndərə(r)/ *n* person who makes blunders.

blunderbuss /ˈblʌndəbʌs/ *n* old type of gun with a wide mouth, firing many bullets or small shot at short range.

blunt /blʌnt/ *adj* **(-er, -est) 1** without a sharp edge or a point: *a blunt knife, razor-blade, saw, pencil, etc.* **2** (*fig*) (of a person, remark, etc) frank and straightforward; not trying to be polite or tactful: *a blunt refusal* ○ *Let me be quite blunt (with you) — your work is appalling.*

▷ **blunt** *v* [Tn] make (sth) blunt or less sharp: *a knife blunted by years of use* ○ *a fine mind blunted by boredom.*

bluntly *adv* in a blunt(2) manner: *To put it bluntly, you're fired!*

bluntness *n* [U].

blur /blɜː(r)/ *n* thing that appears hazy and indistinct: *The town was just a blur on the horizon.* ○ *Everything is a blur when I take my glasses off.* ○ (*fig*) *My memories of childhood are only a blur.*

▷ **blur** *v* **(-rr-)** [I, Tn] (cause sth to) become unclear or indistinct: *Her eyes blurred with tears.* ○ *a blurred photograph* ○ *blurred writing* ○ *Mist blurred the view.* ○ (*fig*) *His memory is blurred by his illness.*

blurb /blɜːb/ *n* publisher's short description of the contents of a book, usu printed on the jacket or cover.

blurt /blɜːt/ *v* (phr v) **blurt sth out** say sth suddenly and tactlessly: *He blurted out the bad news before I could stop him.*

blush /blʌʃ/ *v* **1** [I, Ipr] ~ **(with sth) (at sth)** become red in the face (because of sth): *blush with shame, embarrassment, etc* ○ *the blushing bride* ○ *She blushed at (the thought of) her stupid mistake.* **2** [It] (*fig*) be ashamed: *I blush to admit/confess that....*

▷ **blush** *n* **1** reddening of the face (from shame, embarrassment, etc): *She turned away to hide her blushes.* **2** (idm) **spare sb's blushes** ⇨ SPARE[2].

blusher *n* [C, U] cosmetic used to give the cheeks a rosy colour.

blushingly *adv.*

bluster /ˈblʌstə(r)/ *v* **1** [I] (of the wind) blow fiercely or in strong gusts: *The gale blustered all night.* **2** [I] talk in an aggressive, boastful or threatening way (usu with little effect). **3** (phr v) **bluster one's way out of sth** try to escape from sth by talking aggressively, boastfully, etc: *He always tries to bluster his way out of difficult situations.*

▷ **bluster** *n* [U] **1** noise of a violent wind. **2** (*fig*) blustering talk or behaviour; noisy but empty threats: *I wasn't frightened by what he said — it was just bluster.*

blustery /ˈblʌstrɪ/ *adj* (of the weather) very windy; gusty: *a blustery day.*

Blyton /ˈblaɪtn/ Enid (1897-1968), English writer of over 600 children's books. Among her best-known works was the Noddy series, and although her writing has been criticized by educationalists as being of poor quality, her books have remained consistently popular with children.

BMA /ˌbiː em ˈeɪ/ *abbr* British Medical Association: *a member of the BMA.*

B Mus /ˌbiː ˈmʌs/ *abbr* Bachelor of Music: *have/be a B Mus* ○ *John Scott B Mus.*

BMX /ˌbiː em ˈeks/ *n* **1** [C] strong type of bicycle designed for trick riding or racing on a dirt-track. **2** [U] sport of riding or racing on these bicycles.

Bn *abbr* battalion: *1st Bn Coldstream Guards.*

BO (also **bo**) /ˌbiː ˈəʊ/ *abbr* (*infml esp Brit*) body odour: *have BO.*

boa /ˈbəʊə/ *n* **1** (also **ˈboa constrictor**) large non-poisonous S American snake that kills its prey by crushing it. ⇨ illus at SNAKE. **2** long thin type of scarf made of fur or feathers and worn by women: *a feather boa.*

Boadicea /ˌbəʊədɪˈsiːə/ = BOUDICCA.

boar /bɔː(r)/ *n* (*pl* unchanged or **~s**) **1** male wild pig. **2** uncastrated male domestic pig. Cf HOG 1, SOW[1].

board[1] /bɔːd/ *n* **1** [C] long thin flat piece of cut wood used for building walls, floors, boats, etc. **2** [U] (esp in compounds) material made of compressed wood fibres, etc and cut into thin stiff sheets: *ˈchipboard, ˈhardboard.* **3** [C usu *pl*] thick stiff paper (sometimes covered with cloth) used for book covers: *a book bound in cloth boards.* **4** [C] (esp in compounds) flat piece of wood or other stiff material used for a specific purpose: *a ˈnotice-board* ○ *an ˈironing-board* ○ *a ˈdiving-board* ○ *a ˈbreadboard,* ie for cutting bread on. **5** [C] flat surface marked with patterns, etc on which certain games are played: [attrib] *Chess, draughts and ludo are ˈboard games.* ⇨ illus at CHESS. **6 the boards** [pl] (*dated or joc*) the theatre; acting as a profession: *Are you still treading the boards?* **7** [CGp] group of people controlling a company or some other organization; committee; council: *the ˈcoal/ˈgas/elecˈtricity/ˈwater board* ○ *the board of governors (of a school)* ○ *a board of examiners* ○ *She has a seat on/is on the board (of directors) of a large company.* ○ *The board is/are unhappy about falling sales.* ○ [attrib] *a ˈboard meeting.* **8** [U] (cost of) daily meals (in rented accommodation): *He pays £40 a week (for) board and lodging.* **9** (idm) **(be) above ˈboard** (esp of a business transaction) honest and open: *The deal was completely above board.* ○ [attrib] *an aˌbove-board ˈdeal.* **aˌcross the ˈboard (a)** involving all members, groups or classes (of a company, an industry, a society, etc): *This firm needs radical changes across the board.* ○ [attrib] *an aˌcross-the-board ˌwage increase.* **(b)** (*US*) (of a bet) placed so that one wins if the horse, etc finishes the race in first, second or third place. **bed and board** ⇨ BED[1]. **free on board/rail** ⇨ FREE[1]. **ˌgo by the ˈboard** (of plans, etc) be abandoned or rejected; (of principles, etc) be ignored: *I'm afraid the new car will have to go by the board — we can't afford it.* **on ˈboard** on or in a ship or an aircraft: *Have the passengers gone on board yet?* **sweep the board** ⇨ SWEEP[1]. **take sth on ˈboard** (*infml*) accept (a responsibility, etc); recognize (a problem, etc): *I'm too busy to take this new job on board at the moment.*

▷ **boarding** *n* [U] (structure made of) boards (BOARD[1] 1).

□ **ˈboardroom** *n* room in which the meetings of the board of directors of a company are held.

ˈboardwalk *n* (*US*) promenade, usu made of planks, along a beach.

board[2] /bɔːd/ *v* **1** [Tn, Tn·p] ~ **sth** (**up**/**over**) cover sth with boards (BOARD[1] 1): *a boarded floor* ○ *All the windows were boarded up.* **2** (a) [I, Ipr] ~ (**at**.../**with sb**) take meals (and usu live) in sb's house: *He boarded at my house/with me until he found a flat.* (b) [Tn] provide (sb) with meals and accommodation: *She usually boards students during the college term.* **3** [Tn] get on or into (a ship, a train, an aircraft, a bus, etc): *Please board the plane immediately.* ○ *Flight BA193 for Paris is now boarding*, ie is ready for passengers to board. **4** (phr v) **board out** have meals away from the place where one lives. **board sb out** give sb food and lodging away from his place of work, school, etc: *Many students have to be boarded out in the town.*

▷ **boarder** *n* **1** person who boards at sb's house. **2** pupil who lives at a boarding-school during the term: *This school has 300 boarders and 150 day pupils.* **3** person who boards a ship, esp when attacking it.

□ **ˈboarding card** card allowing a person to board a ship or plane.

ˈboarding-house *n* house providing meals and accommodation. ⇨ article at ACCOMMODATION.

ˈboarding-school *n* school where some or all of the pupils live during the term: *Our son's at boarding-school — we only see him during the holidays.* Cf DAY-SCHOOL (DAY).

boast /bəʊst/ *v* **1** [I, Ipr, Tf] ~ (**about**/**of sth**) talk (about one's own achievements, abilities, etc) with too much pride and satisfaction: *He's always boasting about his children's success at school.* ○ *That's nothing to boast about.* ○ *He boasted of being/boasted that he was the best player in the team.* **2** [Tn] possess (sth to be proud of): *The town boasts a world-famous art gallery.*

▷ **boast** *n* **1** ~ (**that**...) (*derog*) boastful statement: *His boast that he could drink ten pints of beer impressed nobody.* **2** thing that one is proud of; cause for satisfaction: *It was his proud boast that he had never missed a day's work because of illness.*

boaster *n* person who boasts.

boastful /-fl/ *adj* (a) (of a person) often boasting. (b) (of a statement, etc) full of self-praise. **boastfully** /-fəlɪ/ *adv*.

boat /bəʊt/ *n* **1** small vessel for travelling in on water, moved by oars, sails or a motor: *a rowing-/sailing-boat* ○ *motor/fishing boats* ○ *We crossed the river in a boat/by boat.* ○ *Boats for hire — £5 an hour.* ○ *a ship's boats*, ie lifeboats carried on board a ship. **2** any ship: *'How are you going to France?' 'I'm going by/taking the boat* (eg the ferry).*'* **3** dish shaped like a boat for serving sauce or gravy. **4** (idm) **be in the same boat** ⇨ SAME[1]. **burn one's boats/bridges** ⇨ BURN[2]. **miss the boat/bus** ⇨ MISS[3]. **push the boat out** ⇨ PUSH[2]. **rock the boat** ⇨ ROCK[2].

▷ **boat** *v* [I] (usu **go boating**) travel or go in a boat for pleasure: *We go boating on the lake every weekend.*

□ **ˈboat-deck** deck on which a ship's lifeboats are kept ready for launching.

ˈboat-hook *n* long pole with a hook and a spike at one end, used for pulling or pushing boats.

ˈboat-house *n* shed beside a river or lake for keeping boats in.

ˈboatman /-mən/ *n* (*pl* **-men**) man who hires out small boats; man who transports people in small boats for payment.

ˈboat people refugees leaving a country in boats.

ˈboat race race between rowing-boats, esp (**the Boat Race**) the annual race between the rowing crews of Oxford and Cambridge Universities.

ˈboat-train *n* train that takes people to or from a passenger ship.

boater /ˈbəʊtə(r)/ *n* hard straw hat with a flat top and straight brim (originally worn for boating).

boatswain (also **bo'sn, bos'n, bo'sun**) /ˈbəʊsn/ *n* senior seaman on a ship who supervises the crew and is responsible for the ship's equipment.

□ **ˌboatswain's ˈchair** short piece of wood suspended by ropes and used as a seat by sailors working on the side of a ship.

bob[1] /bɒb/ *v* (**-bb-**) **1** [I, Ipr, Ip] ~ (**up and down**) move quickly up and down (esp on water): *toy boats bobbing (up and down) on the waves.* **2** (idm) **bob a curtsy** (**to sb**) curtsy quickly (to sb): *The ballerina bobbed a curtsy (to the audience) before leaving the stage.* **3** (phr v) **bob up** come to the surface quickly; (re)appear suddenly: *She dived below the surface, then bobbed up like a cork again a few seconds later.* ○ (*fig*) *He keeps bobbing up in the most unlikely places.*

▷ **bob** *n* **1** quick movement down and up; jerk: *a bob of the head.* **2** curtsy.

bob[2] /bɒb/ *v* (**-bb-**) [Tn] cut (a woman's hair) short so that it hangs loosely above the shoulders: *have/wear one's hair bobbed.*

▷ **bob** *n* **1** style of bobbed hair: *She wears her hair in a bob.* **2** weight on the end of a cord or rod, used esp to check that sth is straight, or as a pendulum: *a plumb bob.*

bob[3] /bɒb/ *n* (*pl* unchanged) (*infml*) former British coin, the shilling, replaced by the 5p coin.

bob[4] /bɒb/ *n* (idm) **bob's your ˈuncle** (*infml*) (used to express the ease with which a task can be completed successfully): *To switch the oven on, turn the knob, and bob's your uncle!*

bobbin /ˈbɒbɪn/ *n* small roller or spool for holding thread, yarn, wire, etc in a machine.

bobble /ˈbɒbl/ *n* small woolly ball used as a decoration (esp on a hat).

bobby /ˈbɒbɪ/ *n* (*Brit infml*) policeman.

bobby-dazzler /ˌbɒbɪˈdæzlə(r)/ *n* (*dated Brit infml*) person or thing that is remarkable or excellent: *a bobby-dazzler of a goal.*

bobby pin /ˈbɒbɪ pɪn/ (*US*) small metal hair-grip.

bobby socks (also **bobby sox**) /ˈbɒbɪ sɒks/ *n* (*dated esp US*) short socks covering the ankles, as worn esp by young girls: *She still wore bobby socks and a pony-tail.*

▷ **ˈbobby-soxer** *n* (*dated esp US*) teenage girl wearing bobby socks.

bobcat /ˈbɒbkæt/ *n* type of American lynx with a short tail.

bobolink /ˈbɒbəlɪŋk/ *n* N American songbird, the male having black, white and yellow feathers during the mating season.

bob-sleigh /ˈbɒbsleɪ/ (also **bob-sled** /-sled/) *n* large racing sledge for two or more people, with brakes, a steering-wheel and two sets of runners: *a two-/four-man bob-sleigh.*

▷ **bob-sleigh** *v* [I] ride in a bob-sleigh.

bobtail /ˈbɒbteɪl/ *n* **1** (horse or dog with a) tail cut short. **2** (idm) **ragtag and bobtail** ⇨ RAGTAG.

bob-white /ˈbɒbwaɪt/ *n* type of N American quail.

bocage /bɒˈkɑːʒ/ *n* **1** (area of) rural landscape in NW France, with small hedged or walled fields. **2** (in ceramics) representation of (an area of) woodland scenery.

Boccaccio /bɒˈkɑːtʃɪəʊ/ Giovanni (1313-75), Italian novelist and poet. His most famous work is the *Decameron*, a series of satirical stories, often with sexual themes, which influenced many writers, including *Chaucer.

bod /bɒd/ *n* (*Brit infml*) person (esp a man): *He's an odd bod.*

bode /bəʊd/ *v* **1** [Dn·n no passive] (*fml or dated*) be a sign of (sth coming): *This bodes us no good.* **2** (idm) **bode ˈwell/ˈill** (**for sb/sth**) be a good/bad sign (for sb/sth): *The bad trading figures do not bode well for the company's future.*

bodega /bəˈdiːgə/ *n* cellar or shop selling wine, esp in Spain.

bodice /ˈbɒdɪs/ *n* **1** upper part of a woman's dress, down to the waist. **2** woman's or child's close-fitting undergarment like a vest.

-bodied /-ˈbɒdɪd/ (forming compound *adjs*) having the specified type of body: *big-bodied* ○ *able-bodied* ○ *full-bodied.*

bodily /ˈbɒdɪlɪ/ *adj* [attrib] of the human body; physical: *bodily needs*, eg food, warmth ○ *bodily organs*, eg the heart, the liver ○ *bodily harm*, ie physical injury.

▷ **bodily** *adv* **1** as a whole or mass; completely: *The audience rose bodily to cheer the speaker.* ○ *The monument was moved bodily to a new site.* **2** by taking hold of the body; forcibly: *The prisoners were thrown bodily into the police van.*

bodkin /ˈbɒdkɪn/ *n* blunt thick needle with a large eye, used for pulling tape, etc through a hem.

Bodleian Library /ˌbɒdlɪən ˈlaɪbrərɪ/ **the Bodleian Library** main library of Oxford University. It was founded in the 14th century, has one of the finest collections of manuscripts in the world, and may claim a copy of every book published in the United Kingdom. ⇨ article at LIBRARY.

body /ˈbɒdɪ/ *n* **1** [C] whole physical structure of a human being or an animal: *Children's bodies grow steadily.* **2** [C] dead body; corpse or carcass: *The police found a body at the bottom of the lake.* ○ *His body was brought back to England for burial.* **3** [C] main part of a human body, apart from the head and limbs; trunk; torso: *He has a strong body, but rather thin legs.* ○ *She was badly burned on the face and body.* **4** [sing] **the** ~ **of sth** main part of sth, esp a vehicle or building: *the body of a plane, ship, car, etc* ○ *the body of a theatre, concert hall, etc*, ie the central part where the seats are ○ *The main body of the book deals with the author's political career.* **5** [CGp] group of people working or acting as a unit: *a body of troops, supporters, people, etc* ○ *a legislative, an elected body* ○ *A government body is investigating the problem.* ○ *The Governing Body of the school is/are concerned about discipline.* **6** [C] ~ **of sth** large amount of sth; mass or collection of sth: *a body of evidence, information, etc* ○ *large bodies of water*, eg lakes or seas ○ *There is a large body of support for nuclear disarmament.* **7** [C] distinct piece of matter; object: *heavenly bodies*, ie stars, planets, etc ○ *I've got a foreign body* (eg an insect or a speck of dirt) *in my eye.* **8** [U] full strong flavour, esp of wine: *a wine with plenty of body.* **9** [C] (*dated Brit infml*) person: *a cheerful old body.* **10** (idm) **body and ˈsoul** with all one's energies; completely: *love sb body and soul* ○ *He fought body and soul for his country.* **in a ˈbody** (of a group) all together: *The protesters marched in a body to the town hall.* **keep body and ˈsoul together** stay alive (though with some difficulty); survive: *He scarcely has enough money to keep body and soul together.* **over my dead body** ⇨ DEAD.

□ **ˈbody-blow** *n* **1** (in boxing) blow to the body(3). **2** (*fig*) severe disappointment or set-back: *The death of its leader was a body-blow to the party.*

ˈbody-building *n* [U] strengthening the muscles of the body through exercise.

ˈbody clock biological mechanism that automatically controls various recurring functions of the human body, eg the need to sleep: *I only arrived in London yesterday and my body clock is still on New York time.*

ˈbody language expressing how one feels by the way one sits, stands, moves, etc rather than by words.

ˈbodyline *n* [U] (in cricket) type of bowling in which the ball is aimed at the batsman's body rather than at the wicket.

ˈbody odour (*abbr* **BO**) smell of the human body, esp when unwashed, often regarded as unpleasant.

the ˌbody ˈpolitic the State as an organized group of citizens.

ˈbody-snatcher *n* (formerly) person stealing corpses from graves and selling them for dissection.

ˈ**body stocking** woman's undergarment covering the body(3) and legs.

ACTION	PART OF BODY	POSSIBLE EMOTION OR ATTITUDE EXPRESSED
clench	fist	anger, aggression
crease/furrow/knit	brow	concentration, puzzlement
drum	fingers	impatience
lick	lips	anticipation
purse	lips	disapproval, dislike
raise	eyebrows	inquiry, surprise
shrug	shoulders	doubt, indifference
stick out	tongue	disrespect
wrinkle	nose	dislike, distaste

bodyguard /ˈbɒdɪɡɑːd/ *n* [C, CGp] man or group of men whose job is to protect an important person: *The President's bodyguard is/are armed.*

bodywork /ˈbɒdɪwɜːk/ *n* [U] main outside structure of a motor vehicle: *paint, repair, damage the bodywork of a car.*

Boer /bɔː(r)/ *n* (formerly) African of Dutch descent; Afrikaner.

□ **the ˌBoer ˈWars** two wars between the Boers and Britain. The first (1880-81) led to an independent republic for the Boers. The second (1899-1902) was won by the British after a hard guerrilla struggle by the Boers.

boffin /ˈbɒfɪn/ *n* (*Brit infml*) scientist, esp one doing research.

bog /bɒɡ/ *n* **1** [C, U] (area of) wet spongy ground formed of decaying vegetation: *a peat bog* ○ *Keep to the path — parts of the moor are bog.* **2** [C] (*Brit sl*) lavatory.

▷ **bog** *v* (**-gg-**) (phr v) **bog (sth) down** (usu passive) (**a**) (cause sth to) sink into mud or wet ground: *The tank (got) bogged down in the mud.* (**b**) (*fig*) (cause sth to) become stuck and unable to make progress: *Our discussions got bogged down in irrelevant detail.*

boggy /ˈbɒɡɪ/ *adj* (of land) soft and wet: *boggy ground, moorland, etc.*

Bogart /ˈbəʊɡɑːt/ Humphrey (1899-1957), American film actor who often appeared as a tough but sympathetic hero (eg in *Casablanca* and *The African Queen*). ⇨ illus at BERGMAN.

bogey[1] = BOGY.

bogey[2] /ˈbəʊɡɪ/ *n* **1** (*esp Brit*) (in golf) standard score that a good player should make for a hole or course. Cf PAR 3. **2** (in golf) score of one over the standard for a hole.

boggle /ˈbɒɡl/ *v* **1** [I, Ipr] ~ (**at sth**) (*infml*) hesitate (at sth) in alarm or amazement: *He boggled at the thought of swimming in winter.* **2** (idm) **boggle sb's/the ˈmind** (*US infml*) amaze or shock sb: *It boggles my mind!* **the mind/imagination ˈboggles (at sth)** (*infml*) one can hardly accept or imagine (an idea, a suggestion, etc): *My neighbour wears his dressing-gown to work. The mind boggles!* Cf MIND-BOGGLING (MIND[1]).

bogie /ˈbəʊɡɪ/ *n* undercarriage with wheels fitted below the end of a railway vehicle and pivoted for going round curves.

bogus /ˈbəʊɡəs/ *adj* not genuine; false: *a bogus passport, doctor, claim.*

bogy (also **bogey**) /ˈbəʊɡɪ/ *n* **1** (**a**) (also ˈ**bogyman** /-mæn/) imaginary evil spirit (used to frighten children). (**b**) thing that causes fear, often without reason; bugbear: *Inflation is the bogy of many governments.* **2** (*children's sl*) small lump of mucus in the nose.

bohemian /bəʊˈhiːmɪən/ *n, adj* (person, esp an artist) having or displaying a very informal and unconventional way of life.

boil[1] /bɔɪl/ *n* (usu painful) infected swelling under the skin, producing pus.

boil[2] /bɔɪl/ *v* **1** (**a**) [I] (of a liquid) bubble up and change to vapour by being heated: *When water boils it turns into steam.* ○ *The kettle* (ie The water in the kettle) *is boiling.* ○ *Have the potatoes* (ie Has the water in which the potatoes are being cooked) *boiled yet?* ○ (*fig*) *The sea was boiling*, ie was rough and making bubbles like boiling water. ⇨ Usage at WATER[1]. (**b**) [I, Ip] ~ (**away**) continue to boil: *There's a saucepan boiling away on the stove.* **2** [Tn] cause (a liquid) to boil: *boil some water for the rice.* **3** [I, Tn, Dn·n, Dn·pr] ~ **sth** (**for sb**) cook or wash sth in boiling water: *boiled cabbage, carrots, potatoes, etc* ○ *Please boil me an egg/boil an egg for me.* ⇨ Usage at COOK. **4** [I, Ip] be very angry or agitated: *He was boiling (over) with rage.* **5** (idm) **boil ˈdry** (of a liquid) boil until there is none left: *Don't let the pan boil dry.* **keep the pot boiling** ⇨ POT[1]. **make sb's blood boil** ⇨ BLOOD[1]. **6** (phr v) **boil (sth) away** (cause sth to) boil until nothing remains; evaporate (sth): *The water in the kettle had all boiled away.* **boil (sth) down** reduce or be reduced by boiling. **boil sth down (to sth)** (*infml*) summarize sth; condense sth: *Could you boil that article down to 400 words?* **boil down to sth** (be able to) be summarized as sth: *The issue really boils down to a clash between left and right.* **boil over** (**a**) (of liquid in a pan, etc) boil and flow over the side of a pan, etc: *The milk is boiling over.* (**b**) (*infml*) be very angry. (**c**) (of a situation, quarrel, etc) reach a point of crisis; explode: *The crisis is in danger of boiling over into civil war.*

▷ **boil** *n* **1** act of boiling. **2** (idm) **be on the ˈboil** be boiling. **bring sth to the ˈboil** heat sth until it boils: *Bring the mixture to the boil, then let it simmer for ten minutes.* **come to the ˈboil** begin to boil. **off the ˈboil** having just stopped boiling: (*fig infml*) *He began by playing brilliantly but he's rather gone off the boil* (ie he has begun playing less well) *in the last few minutes.*

boiling *adj* = BOILING HOT: *You must be boiling in that thick sweater.* (idm) **the whole boiling** ⇨ WHOLE.

boiled ˈsweet sweet made of boiled sugar.

boiling ˈhot (*infml*) very hot: *a boiling hot day.*

ˈ**boiling-point** *n* **1** temperature at which a liquid begins to boil. ⇨ App 10. **2** (*infml*) condition or state of great excitement: *The match has reached boiling-point.*

boiler /ˈbɔɪlə(r)/ *n* **1** metal container in which water is heated, eg to produce steam in an engine. **2** tank in which hot water is stored, esp for central heating and other household needs. **3** large metal tub for boiling laundry. Cf COPPER[1] 3.

□ ˈ**boilermaker** *n* person who makes or repairs boilers, esp on ships.

ˈ**boiler suit** one-piece garment worn for rough work. Cf OVERALLS.

boisterous /ˈbɔɪstərəs/ *adj* **1** (of people or behaviour) noisy, lively and cheerful: *a boisterous party* ○ *The children are very boisterous today.* **2** (of the wind or sea), stormy; rough. ▷ **boisterously** *adv*. **boisterousness** *n* [U].

bolas /ˈbəʊləs/ *n* S American device used to trap animals, made from pieces of strong cord with weights at each end. When it hits the animal's legs it winds around them, making the animal trip and fall.

bold /bəʊld/ *adj* (*compar* **-er**, *superl* **-est**) **1** confident and brave; daring; enterprising: *a bold warrior* ○ *bold plans, tactics, etc* ○ *a bold scheme to rebuild the city centre.* **2** (*dated*) without feelings of shame; immodest: *She waited for him to invite her to dance, not wishing to seem bold.* **3** clearly visible; distinct; striking; vivid: *the bold outline of a mountain against the sky* ○ *bold, legible handwriting* ○ *She paints with bold strokes of the brush.* **4** printed in thick type: *The headwords in this dictionary are in bold type.* **5** (idm) **be/make so bold (as to do sth)** (*fml*) (esp in a social situation) dare (to do sth); presume or venture (to do sth): *One student made so bold as to argue with the professor.* **(as) bold as ˈbrass** very cheeky; impudent: *He walked in, bold as brass, and asked me to lend him £50.* **put on, show, etc a bold front** try to appear brave and cheerful in order to hide one's true feelings. ▷ **boldly** *adv*. **boldness** *n* [U].

bole /bəʊl/ *n* trunk of a tree.

bolero *n* (*pl* ~**s**) **1** /bəˈleərəʊ/ (music for a) type of Spanish dance. **2** /ˈbɒlərəʊ/ woman's short jacket with no front fastening. ⇨ illus at DRESS.

Boleyn /bəˈlɪn, bʊˈlɪn, ˈbʊlɪn/ Anne (1507-36), second wife of Henry VIII, who divorced Catherine of Aragon to marry her. However as she only produced a daughter (later *Elizabeth I) and no male heir, she lost his favour, was suspected of being unfaithful and was executed.

Bolivia

Bolivia /bəˈlɪvɪə/ country in South America; pop approx 6 993 000; official language Spanish; capital and seat of government La Paz; constitutional capital Sucre; unit of currency boliviano (= 1 000 000 pesos). It is crossed by the Andes and contains the Altiplano, a plateau 3 850 metres (12 500 feet) above sea-level. Exports include tin and other minerals. It is a politically unstable country where there have been many coups and changes of government. ⇨ map.

boll /bəʊl/ *n* seed-case of the cotton plant or flax.

□ ˌ**boll-ˈweevil** *n* destructive insect whose larvae eat cotton bolls.

bollard /ˈbɒlɑːd/ *n* **1** short thick post on a quay or ship's deck, to which a ship's mooring ropes are tied. **2** short post on a kerb or traffic island.

bollocks = BALLOCKS.

boloney (also **baloney**) /bəˈləʊnɪ/ *n* [U] (*infml*) nonsense; rubbish: *Don't talk boloney!*

Bolshevik /ˈbɒlʃəvɪk; *US also* ˈbəʊl-/ *n* **1** member of the majority socialist group supporting the Russian revolution in 1917. **2** (*infml derog*) any radical socialist. ▷ **Bolshevism** /ˈbɒlʃəvɪzəm/ *n* [U]. **Bolshevist** /ˈbɒlʃəvɪst/ *n*.

bolshie (also **bolshy**) /ˈbɒlʃɪ/ *adj* (**-ier**, **-iest**) (*Brit infml derog*) deliberately uncooperative; awkward; stubborn: *be in a bolshie mood* ○ *be bolshie about sth.*

bolster /ˈbəʊlstə(r)/ *n* long pillow, usu shaped like a roll, across the head of a bed.

▷ **bolster** *v* [Tn, Tn·p] ~ **sb/sth (up)** give support to sb/sth; strengthen or reinforce sth: *bolster sb's morale/courage* ○ *It bolstered my belief that...* ○ *The government borrowed money to bolster up the economy.*

bolt

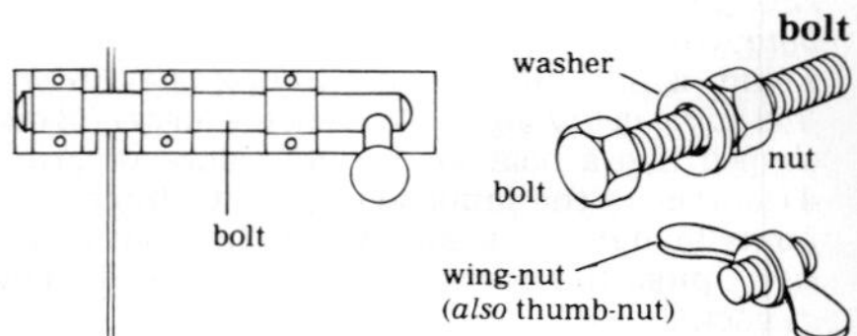

bolt[1] /bəʊlt/ *n* **1** metal bar that slides into a socket to lock a door, window, etc. **2** metal pin with a head at one end, and a thread (as on a screw), used with a nut for fastening things together. **3** short heavy arrow shot from a crossbow. **4** flash of lightning. **5** quantity of cloth, etc wound in a roll. **6** (idm) **a ˌbolt from the ˈblue** unexpected (and usu unwelcome) event; complete surprise: *The news of* *his death was (like) a bolt from the blue.* **the nuts and bolts** ⇨ NUT. **shoot one's bolt** ⇨ SHOOT[1].

▷ **bolt** *v* **1** (a) [I, Tn] fasten (sth) with a bolt[1](1): *The gate bolts on the inside.* ○ *Remember to bolt all the doors and windows.* (b) [Tn, Tn·pr, Tn·p] (phr v) ~ **A to B**; ~ **A and B (together)** fasten objects (together) with bolts (BOLT[1] 2): *The vice is bolted to the work-bench.* ○ *The various parts of the car are bolted together.* **2 bolt sb in/out** prevent sb from leaving/entering a room, house, etc by bolting the doors, etc.

bolt[2] /bəʊlt/ *v* **1** [I] (a) (esp of a horse) run away suddenly out of control: *The horse bolted in terror at the sound of the gun.* (b) (of a person) run away quickly: *When the police arrived the burglars bolted.* **2** [Tn, Tn·p] ~ **sth (down)** swallow (food) quickly: *Don't bolt your food — you'll get indigestion!* **3** [I] (of plants) grow quickly upwards and stop flowering when seeds are produced: *My lettuces have bolted.* **4** (idm) **lock, etc the stable door after the horse has bolted** ⇨ STABLE[2].

▷ **bolt** *n* **1** [sing] act of bolting (BOLT[2] 1b); sudden dash. **2** (idm) **make a bolt/dash/run for it** try to escape/to reach sth quickly: *When the police arrived he made a bolt for it/for the door.*

□ ˈ**bolt-hole** *n* place to which one can escape.

bolt[3] /bəʊlt/ *adv* (idm) **bolt** ˈ**upright** very straight; quite upright: *sit bolt upright.*

bomb /bɒm/ *n* **1** [C] container filled with explosive or incendiary material, made to explode when dropped or thrown, or by a timing device: *Enemy aircraft dropped bombs on the city.* ○ *Terrorists placed a 50-pound bomb in the railway station.* **2** [C] (in compounds) explosive device placed in or attached to a specified object: *a letter-bomb* ○ *a parcel/car bomb.* **3 the bomb** [sing] atomic or hydrogen bomb: *Anti-nuclear organizations want to ban the bomb.* **4 a bomb** [sing] (*infml*) a lot of money: *That dress must have cost (her) a bomb!* ○ *Some company directors make* (ie earn) *an absolute bomb.* **5** [C] (*US infml*) project, film, etc that turns out to be a failure. **6** (idm) **go like a** ˈ**bomb** (*infml*) (a) (of a vehicle) go very fast: *My new car goes like a bomb.* (b) be very successful: *Last night's party went like a bomb.* ○ *My new novel is going like a bomb.*

▷ **bomb** *v* **1** [Tn] attack (sb/sth) with bombs; drop bombs on: *London was heavily bombed during the last war.* ○ *Terrorists bombed several police stations.* **2** [I] (*US infml*) turn out to be a failure: *Her last play just bombed.* **3** (phr v) **bomb along, down, up, etc** (*Brit infml*) move very fast (usu in a vehicle) in the specified direction: *bombing down the motorway at ninety miles an hour.* **bomb sb out** (esp passive) make sb homeless by destroying his house with bombs: *Our parents were bombed out twice during the war.*

□ ˈ**bomb-bay** *n* compartment in an aircraft for carrying bombs.

ˈ**bomb-disposal** *n* [U] removal and detonation of unexploded bombs: [attrib] *a bomb-disposal squad/team/officer/unit.*

ˈ**bomb-proof** *adj* giving protection against bombs: *a bomb-proof shelter.*

ˈ**bomb-sight** *n* device in an aircraft for aiming bombs.

ˈ**bomb-site** *n* area in a town where all the buildings have been destroyed by bombs.

bombard /bɒmˈbɑːd/ *v* [Tn, Tn·pr] ~ **sb/sth (with sth) 1** (a) attack (a place) with bombs or shells (esp from big guns): *Enemy positions were bombarded before our infantry attacked.* (b) (*fig*) attack sb with persistent questions, abuse, etc: *Reporters bombarded the President with questions about his economic policy.* **2** (*physics*) direct a stream of high-speed particles at (an atom, etc). ▷ **bombardment** *n* [C, U].

bombardier /ˌbɒmbəˈdɪə(r)/ *n* **1** (*Brit*) non-commissioned officer in an artillery regiment below a sergeant. **2** (*US*) member of the crew of a bomber who aims and releases bombs.

bombast /ˈbɒmbæst/ *n* [U] pompous and meaningless words: *His speech was full of bombast.* ▷ **bombastic** /bɒmˈbæstɪk/ *adj* (of a person or his words) pompous and empty. **bombastically** /-klɪ/ *adv.*

Bombay /ˌbɒmˈbeɪ/ the largest city in India. It is a port and major commercial centre. Its industries include textiles, oil refining and the cinema.

□ ˌ**Bombay** ˈ**duck** small fish that is often dried and eaten with Indian food.

bomber /ˈbɒmə(r)/ *n* **1** aircraft that carries and drops bombs. **2** person (esp a terrorist) who throws or plants bombs.

□ ˈ**bomber jacket** short jacket, often made of leather, that fits tightly around the waist and cuffs, similar in style to jackets formerly worn by airmen.

bombshell /ˈbɒmʃel/ *n* (*infml*) shocking and usu unpleasant surprise: *The news of his death was a bombshell.*

bona fide /ˌbəʊnə ˈfaɪdɪ/ *adj* [esp attrib], *adv* genuine(ly); without fraud or deception; legal(ly): *a bona fide agreement/contract/deal.*

▷ **bona fides** /-dɪz/ *n* [U] (*law*) honest intention; sincerity: *establish one's bona fides.*

bonanza /bəˈnænzə/ *n* **1** source of sudden great wealth or luck; increase in profits: [attrib] *It's been a bonanza* (ie very profitable) *year for the tourist trade.* **2** (*US*) rich output from a gold mine, oil well, etc.

Bonaparte (also **Buonaparte**) /ˈbəʊnəpɑːt/ name of a Corsican family which included the two French rulers called *Napoleon.

bon-bon /ˈbɒnbɒn/ *n* sweet, esp one with a fancy shape.

Bond /bɒnd/ James, British secret agent, code-named '007' /ˌdʌbləʊˈsevn/, in the stories of Ian Fleming and the films based on them. He is famous for his charm, wit and resourcefulness.

bond /bɒnd/ *n* **1** [C] (a) written agreement or promise that has legal force; covenant: *We entered into a solemn bond.* (b) signed document containing such an agreement. **2** [C] certificate issued by a government or a company acknowledging that money has been lent to it and will be paid back with interest: *National Savings bonds* ○ *Government bonds.* **3** [C] thing that unites people or groups; link or tie: *the bonds of friendship/affection* ○ *The trade agreement helped to strengthen the bonds between the two countries.* **4** (a) [sing] state of being joined: *This glue makes a good firm bond.* (b) [C] (*chemistry*) force that holds atoms together in a chemical compound. (c) [C, U] method of making bricks overlap when building a wall, in order to make it strong: *English/Flemish bond.* **5 bonds** [pl] ropes or chains binding a prisoner: (*fig*) *the bonds of oppression, tyranny, injustice, etc.* **6** [U] (also ˈ**bond paper**) good-quality paper used for writing letters. **7** (idm) **in/out of** ˈ**bond** (*commerce*) (of imported goods) in/out of a bonded warehouse: *place goods in/take goods out of bond.* **sb's word is as good as his bond** ⇨ WORD.

▷ **bond** *v* **1** [Tn] put (goods) in a bonded warehouse: *bonded whisky, cigarettes, etc.* **2** [Tn, Tn·pr, Tn·p] ~ **A and B (together)**; ~ **A to B** join two things securely together; unite two things with a bond: *You need a strong adhesive to bond wood to metal.*

□ ˌ**bonded** ˈ**warehouse** warehouse where goods are stored until Customs duties are paid.

bondage /ˈbɒndɪdʒ/ *n* [U] (*dated or fml*) slavery; captivity: *keep sb in bondage.*

Bond Street /ˈbɒnd striːt/ street in the *West End of London where there are many expensive stores and art galleries.

bone /bəʊn/ *n* **1** [C] any of the hard parts that form the skeleton of an animal's body: *This fish has a lot of bones in it.* ○ *I've broken a bone in my arm.* ○ *Her bones were laid to rest,* ie Her body was buried. **2** [U] hard substance of which bones are made: *Buttons are sometimes made of bone.* **3** [C] thin strip of metal or plastic used to stiffen a brassière, shirt collar, etc. **4** (idm) **a bag of bones** ⇨ BAG[1]. **the bare bones** ⇨ BARE[1]. **a bone of con**ˈ**tention** subject about which there is disagreement: *The border has always been a bone of contention between these two countries.* **chill sb to the bone/marrow** ⇨ CHILL. **close to/near the** ˈ**bone** (*infml*) (a) (of a remark, question, etc) unkindly or tactlessly revealing the truth about sb/sth: *Some of his comments about her appearance were a bit close to the bone.* (b) (of a joke, story, etc) almost indecent; likely to offend some people: *Some scenes in the play are rather near the bone.* **cut, pare, etc sth to the** ˈ**bone** reduce sth considerably or drastically: *Train services have been cut to the bone.* ○ *Our budget has been pared to the bone.* **dry as a bone** ⇨ DRY[1]. **feel in one's bones** ⇨ FEEL[1]. **have a** ˈ**bone to pick with sb** have sth to argue or quarrel about with sb: *I've got a bone to pick with you. Where's the money I lent you last week?* **make no bones about (doing) sth** be frank about sth; admit sth readily; do not hesitate to do sth: *He made no bones about his extreme left-wing views.* ○ *She made no bones about telling her husband she wanted a divorce.* **skin and bone** ⇨ SKIN. **work one's fingers to the bone** ⇨ FINGER[1].

▷ **bone** *v* **1** [Tn] take bones out of (sth): *bone a fish, a chicken, a piece of beef, etc.* **2** (phr v) **bone up on (sth)** (*infml*) study hard (usu for a specific purpose): *I must bone up on my French before we go to Paris.* **-boned** (forming compound *adjs*) having the type of bones specified: *small-boned* ○ *large-boned.*

□ ˌ**bone** ˈ**china** thin china made of clay mixed with bone ash.

ˌ**bone-**ˈ**dry** *adj* [usu pred] completely dry.

ˌ**bone** ˈ**idle** (*derog*) very lazy.

ˈ**bone-meal** *n* [U] crushed animal bones used as fertilizer.

ˈ**bone-shaker** *n* (*infml joc*) rickety and uncomfortable old bicycle or car.

bonehead /ˈbəʊnhed/ *n* (*infml derog*) stupid person.

boner /ˈbəʊnə(r)/ *n* (*US infml*) stupid mistake; blunder.

bonfire /ˈbɒnfaɪə(r)/ *n* large fire made outdoors for burning rubbish or as a celebration: *We made a bonfire of dead leaves in the garden.*

📖 Every year British people celebrate 'Bonfire Night'. The occasion commemorates the Gunpowder Plot of 1605 in which Guy *Fawkes and his fellow Catholic conspirators attempted to blow up Parliament with gunpowder. For this night, a large bonfire is built and a dummy figure of Guy Fawkes is placed on top. There is usually a firework display too, and traditional things to eat and drink. Bonfires and firework displays are often organized by local councils in parks and people also hold private bonfire parties.

□ ˈ**Bonfire Night** (also **Guy Fawkes Night**) (in Britain) the night of 5 November.

bongo /ˈbɒŋgəʊ/ *n* (*pl* ~**s** or ~**es**) one of a pair of small drums played with the fingers.

bonhomie /ˈbɒnəmi; *US* ˌbɒnəˈmiː/ *n* [U] (*French*) hearty cheerfulness of manner.

bonkers /ˈbɒŋkəz/ *adj* [pred] (*Brit sl*) completely mad; crazy: *You're stark raving bonkers!*

bon mot /ˌbɒn ˈməʊ/ *n* (*pl* **bons mots** /ˌbɒn ˈməʊz/) (*French*) witty saying or remark.

bonnet /ˈbɒnɪt/ *n* **1** hat tied with strings under the chin, worn by babies and formerly by women. ⇨ illus at DRESS. **2** (in Scotland) man's round brimless cap. **3** (*US* **hood**) hinged cover over the engine of a motor vehicle. ⇨ illus at CAR. **4** (idm) **have a bee in one's bonnet** ⇨ BEE[1].

bonny /ˈbɒnɪ/ *adj* (**-ier, -iest**) (*approv esp Scot*) attractive or beautiful; healthy-looking: *a bonny lass/baby.* ▷ **bonnily** *adv.*

Bonny Prince Charlie /ˌbɒnɪ prɪns ˈtʃɑːlɪ/ nickname of Prince Charles Edward Stuart (1720-88), also known as the Young Pretender, grandson of *James II. In 1745 he led an army against the forces of *George II and tried to claim the British throne. His attempt failed and he fled to France. Cf JACOBITE. ⇨ article at SCOTLAND.

bonsai /ˈbɒnsaɪ/ *n* (a) [U] (originally Japanese) method of growing trees so that they remain very small. (b) [C] tree grown in this way. ⇨ illus.

bonus /ˈbəʊnəs/ *n* (*pl* ~**es**) **1** payment added to what is usual or expected, eg an extra dividend paid to shareholders in a company or to holders of an insurance policy: *a productivity bonus,* ie

bonsai

money added to wages when workers produce more goods, etc ○ *Company employees received a £25 Christmas bonus.* **2** anything pleasant in addition to what is expected: *The warm weather in winter has been a real bonus.*

bon voyage /bɒn vɔɪˈɑːʒ/ (*French*) (used to wish sb a pleasant journey).

bony /ˈbəʊnɪ/ *adj* (**-ier**, **-iest**) **1** of or like bone. **2** full of bones: *This fish is very bony.* **3** thin and having prominent bones: *bony fingers* ○ *a tall bony man.* ⇨ Usage at THIN.

bonze /bɒnz/ *n* Buddhist priest in Japan and other eastern countries.

boo /buː/ *interj, n* **1** sound made to show disapproval or contempt: *The Prime Minister's speech was greeted with boos and jeers.* **2** exclamation used to surprise or startle sb. **3** (idm) **not say boo to a goose** ⇨ SAY.
▷ **boo** *v* **1** [I, Tn] show disapproval or contempt for (sb/sth) by shouting 'boo': *You can hear the crowd booing.* **2** (phr v) **boo sb off (sth)** force sb to leave by booing: *The actors were booed off the stage.*

boob[1] /buːb/ (also **booboo** /ˈbuːbuː/) *n* (*infml*) stupid mistake.
▷ **boob** *v* [I] make a boob: *Oh dear, I've boobed again.*

boob[2] /buːb/ *n* (⚠ *sl*) (usu *pl*) woman's breast.

booby /ˈbuːbɪ/ *n* (*dated derog*) foolish person: *He's a great booby!*
□ ˈ**booby prize** (also **wooden spoon**) prize given as a joke to the person who is last in a race or competition.
booby trap 1 hidden trap designed to surprise sb, eg sth balanced on top of a door so that it will fall on the first person opening it. **2** hidden bomb designed to explode when an apparently harmless object is touched: *The police did not go near the abandoned car, fearing it was a booby trap.* ○ [attrib] *a booby-trap bomb.* ˈ**booby-trap** *v* (**-pp-**) [Tn] place a booby trap in or on (sth): *The car had been booby-trapped by terrorists.*

boodle /ˈbuːdl/ *n* [U] (*sl esp US*) money, esp money gained by stealing or bribery.

boogie /ˈbuːgɪ; *US* ˈbʊgɪ/ (also ˌ**boogie-ˈwoogie** /-ˈwuːgɪ; *US* -ˈwʊgɪ/) *n* [U] type of blues music, played on the piano, with a strong rhythmical beat: *play boogie* ○ [attrib] *a boogie beat.*

book[1] /bʊk/ *n* **1** [C] **(a)** number of printed or written sheets of paper bound together in a cover: *a leather-bound book.* **(b)** written work or composition, eg a novel, a dictionary, an encyclopedia, etc: *writing/reading a book about/on Shakespeare.* **2** [C] number of blank or lined sheets of paper fastened together in a cover and used for writing in: *Write the essay in your (exercise-)books, not on rough paper.* **3 books** [pl] written records of the finances of a business; accounts: *do the books*, ie check the accounts ○ *The company's books are audited every year.* **4** [C] number of similar items fastened together in the shape of a book: *a book of stamps/tickets/matches.* **5** [C] any of the main divisions of a large written work: *the books of the Bible.* **6** [sing] words of an opera or a musical; libretto. **7** [C] record of bets made, eg on a horse-race: *keep/make/open a book (on sth)*, ie take bets (on a match, race, etc). **8 the book** [sing] telephone directory: *Are you in the book?* **9** (idm) **be in sb's good/bad ˈbooks** (*infml*) have/not have sb's favour or approval: *You'll be in the boss's bad books if you don't work harder.* **bring sb to ˈbook (for sth)** require sb to give an explanation (of his behaviour): *bring a criminal to book.* **by the ˈbook** (*infml*) strictly according to the rules: *He's always careful to do things by the book.* **a closed book** ⇨ CLOSE[4]. **cook the books** ⇨ COOK. **every/any trick in the book** ⇨ TRICK. **the good book** the Bible. **in ˈone's book** in one's opinion: *In my book, such behaviour is inexcusable.* **(be) on the books of sth** (be) employed as a player by (a football club): *He's on Everton's books.* **an open book** ⇨ OPEN[1]. **read sb like a book** ⇨ READ. **suit one's/sb's books** ⇨ SUIT[2]. **take a leaf out of sb's book** ⇨ LEAF. **throw the book at sb** (*infml*) remind sb forcefully of the correct procedure to be followed in some task (and perhaps punish him for not following it).
□ ˈ**bookbinder** [C], ˈ**bookbinding** [U] *ns* (person whose job is) putting covers on books.
ˈ**bookcase** *n* piece of furniture with shelves for books.
ˈ**book club** club which sells books at a reduced price to members who agree to buy a minimum number.
ˈ**book-end** *n* (usu *pl*) either of a pair of supports to keep books upright.
ˈ**bookkeeper** [C], ˈ**bookkeeping** [U] *ns* (person whose job is) recording business transactions.
ˈ**bookmaker** (also *infml* **bookie**) [C], ˈ**bookmaking** [U] *ns* (person whose job is) taking bets on horse-races, etc.
ˈ**bookmark** (also ˈ**bookmarker**) *n* strip placed between the pages of a book to mark the reader's place.
ˈ**bookmobile** /-məʊbiːl/ *n* (*esp US*) vehicle used as a travelling library.
the ˌ**Book of** ˌ**Common** ˈ**Prayer** = THE PRAYER BOOK (PRAYER).
the ˌ**Book of** ˈ**Kells** famous illuminated manuscript of the gospels made by monks in the 8th or 9th century and now kept at Trinity College, Dublin, in Ireland.
ˈ**book-plate** *n* piece of paper, usu with a printed design, pasted in a book to show who owns it.
ˈ**book-rest** stand, cushion, etc used to hold up an open book.
ˈ**bookseller** *n* person whose job is selling books.
ˈ**bookshop** (*US* also ˈ**bookstore**) *n* shop which sells mainly books.
ˈ**bookstall** *n* (*US* ˈ**news-stand**) stall or stand at which books, newspapers and magazines are sold.
ˈ**book token** voucher that can be exchanged for books of a given value: *a £10 book token.*
ˈ**bookworm** *n* **1** grub that eats holes in books. **2** (*fig*) person who is very fond of reading books: *She's a bit of a bookworm.*

book[2] /bʊk/ *v* **1 (a)** [I, Tn, Tn·p] ~ **sth (up)** reserve (a place, accommodation, etc); buy (a ticket, etc) in advance: *Book early if you want to be sure of a seat.* ○ *book a hotel room, a seat on a plane* ○ *I'd like to book three seats for tonight's concert.* ○ *The hotel/performance is fully booked (up)*, ie There are no more rooms/tickets available. **(b)** [Tn·pr] ~ **sb on sth** reserve a place, ticket, etc for sb on (a plane, etc): *We're booked on the next flight.* **(c)** [Tn] engage or hire (sb) in advance: *We've booked a conjuror for our Christmas party.* **2** [Tn] (*infml*) enter the name of (sb) in a book or record, esp when bringing a charge: *The police booked me for speeding.* ○ *He was booked by the referee for foul play.* **3** (phr v) **book in** register at a hotel, an airport, etc. **book sb in** make a reservation for sb (at a hotel, etc): *We've booked you in at the Plaza for two nights.*
▷ **bookable** *adj* that can be reserved: *All seats are bookable in advance.*
booking *n* [C, U] (*esp Brit*) (instance of) reserving seats, etc in advance; reservation: *a block booking* ○ *We can't accept any more bookings.* ○ *She's in charge of booking(s).* ˈ**booking-clerk** *n* (*esp Brit*) person who sells tickets, eg at a railway station. ˈ**booking-office** *n* (*esp Brit*) office where tickets are sold.

bookie /ˈbʊkɪ/ *n* (*infml*) = BOOKMAKER (BOOK[1]).

bookish /ˈbʊkɪʃ/ *adj* **1** fond of reading; studious: *She was always a bookish child.* **2** having knowledge or ideas gained from reading rather than practical experience. ▷ **bookishness** *n* [U].

booklet /ˈbʊklɪt/ *n* thin book, usu in paper covers.

boom[1] /buːm/ *v* **1** [I, Ip] make a deep hollow resonant sound: *waves booming on the sea-shore* ○ *We could hear the enemy guns booming (away) in the distance.* ○ *The headmaster's voice boomed (out) across the playground.* **2** [I, Ip, Tn, Tn·p] ~ **(sth) (out)** utter (sth) in a booming voice: *'Get out of my sight!' he boomed.*
▷ **boom** *n* (usu *sing*) deep hollow sound: *the boom of the guns, the surf.*

boom[2] /buːm/ *n* sudden increase (in population, trade, etc); period of prosperity: *The oil market is enjoying a boom.* ○ [attrib] *a boom year (for trade, exports, etc).*
▷ **boom** *v* [I] have a period of rapid economic growth: *Business is booming.*
□ ˈ**boom town** town that grows or prospers during a boom.

boom[3] /buːm/ *n* **1** (on a sailing-boat) long pole used to keep the bottom of a sail stretched. ⇨ illus at YACHT. **2** (also **derrick boom**) pole attached to a derrick crane, used for loading and unloading a cargo. **3 (a)** barrier (usu of heavy chains) placed across a river or harbour entrance as a defence against enemy ships. **(b)** barrier (usu a mass of logs) placed across a river to prevent logs from floating away. **4** long movable arm for a microphone: [attrib] *a boom microphone.*

boomer /ˈbuːmə(r)/ *n* (*Austral*) large male kangaroo.

boomerang /ˈbuːməræŋ/ *n* **1** curved flat wooden missile (used by Australian Aborigines) which can be thrown so that it returns to the thrower if it fails to hit anything. **2** (*fig*) action or remark that causes unexpected harm to the person responsible for it: [attrib] *a boomerang effect.*
▷ **boomerang** *v* [I, Ipr] act as a boomerang: *The candidate's attempt to discredit his opponent boomeranged (on him) when he was charged with libel.*

boon[1] /buːn/ *n* **1** (*dated*) request or favour (used esp with the *vs* shown): *ask a boon of sb* ○ *grant a boon.* **2** thing that one is thankful for; benefit; advantage: *Parks are a great boon to people in big cities.* ○ *A warm coat is a real boon in cold weather.*

boon[2] /buːn/ *adj* (idm) **a boon companion** cheerful friend with whom one enjoys spending time: *Bill and Bob are boon companions.*

boondocks /ˈbuːndɒks/ *n* [pl] **the boondocks** (*US sl*) wild areas far away from any large town.

boondoggle /ˈbuːndɒgl/ *v* [I] (*US infml*) do work that is a waste of time.
▷ **boondoggle** *n* [C, U] (piece of) work that is a waste of time or money.

Boone /buːn/ Daniel (c1735-1820), American pioneer. He explored Kentucky and Missouri and set up the first settlements there, fighting against the resistance of the local Indians.

boor /bʊə(r), bɔː(r)/ *n* (*derog*) rough, rude or insensitive man: *Don't be such a boor!*
▷ **boorish** /ˈbʊərɪʃ, ˈbɔːrɪʃ/ *adj* of or like a boor: *boorish youths, behaviour, remarks.* **boorishly** *adv.* **boorishness** *n* [U].

Boorman /ˈbɔːmən/ John (1933-), British film director. Despite success with adventure films like *Deliverance* and *Excalibur*, his best work was the smaller-scale nostalgic account of his Second World War childhood, *Hope and Glory*.

boost /buːst/ *v* [Tn] increase the strength or value of (sth); help or encourage (sb/sth): *boost an electric current* ○ *boost imports, share prices, the dollar, etc* ○ *boost production* ○ *The unexpected win boosted the team's morale.*
▷ **boost** *n* increase; help; encouragement: *a boost in sales, exports, etc* ○ *give the economy, the pound, etc a boost* ○ *give sb's confidence a boost.*
booster *n* **1** thing that boosts: *a morale booster*, ie sth that makes one feel more confident. **2** device for increasing power or voltage. **3** (also ˈ**booster rocket**) rocket used to give initial speed to a missile or spacecraft. **4** dose or injection (of a medicine or drug) that increases the effect of an earlier one.

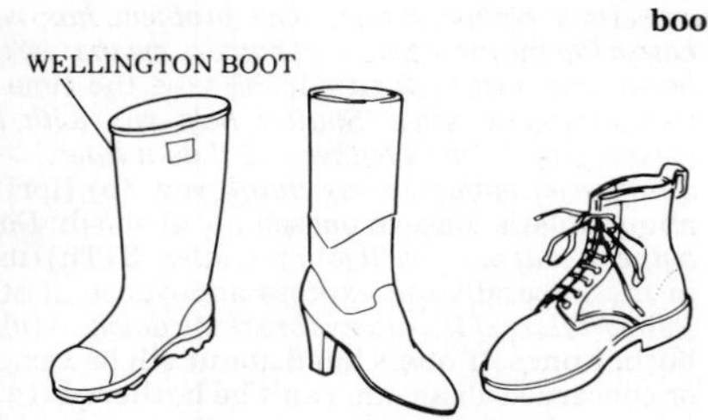

boot[1] /buːt/ *n* **1** outer covering for the foot and ankle, eg made of leather or rubber: *a pair of football boots* ○ *tough boots for walking.* ⇨ illus. Cf SANDAL, SHOE 1. **2** (usu *sing*) (*infml*) blow with the foot; kick: *He gave the ball a tremendous boot.* **3** (*Brit*) (*US* **trunk**) compartment for luggage, usu at the back of a motor car: *Put the luggage in the boot.* ⇨ illus at CAR. **4** (idm) **bet one's boots that...** ⇨ BET. **be/get too big for one's boots** ⇨ BIG. **the boot is on the other ˈfoot** the situation has been reversed. **die with one's boots on** ⇨ DIE[2]. **give sb/get the ˈboot** (*infml*) dismiss sb/be dismissed from a job: *If you're late once more you're getting the boot.* **have one's heart in one's boots** ⇨ HEART. **lick sb's boots** ⇨ LICK. **put the ˈboot in** (*infml esp Brit*) kick sb brutally; be ruthless. **tough as old boots** ⇨ TOUGH.

▷ **boot** *v* **1** [Tn, Tn·pr, Tn·p] kick (sth/sb): *boot a ball (about)* ○ *boot sb in the face.* **2** [I, Ip, Tn, Tn·p] ~ **(sth) (up)** (*computing*) load (an operating system, a program, etc) into a computer's memory, esp automatically; prepare (a computer) for operation in this way. **3** (phr v) **boot sb out (of sth)** (*infml*) (**a**) throw sb out by force: *His father booted him out of the house.* (**b**) dismiss sb from a job.

□ ˌ**Boot ˈHill** (*US joc infml*) cemetery, esp in a frontier town.

ˈ**bootlace** *n* string or leather strip for tying boots or shoes.

ˈ**bootlicker** *n* (*derog*) person who tries to flatter or please sb in order to get his approval or help.

ˈ**bootstrap** *n* (idm) **pull oneself up by one's bootstraps** ⇨ PULL[2].

boot[2] /buːt/ *n* (idm) **to boot** (*arch or joc*) in addition; as well: *She's an attractive woman, and wealthy to boot.*

bootee /buːˈtiː/ *n* **1** baby's woollen boot. **2** woman's short lined boot.

Booth /buːð/ William (1829-1912), English founder of the *Salvation Army. He had been a Methodist preacher and started the movement to bring Christianity to poor people while giving them food, clothes, etc.

booth /buːð; *US* buːθ/ *n* **1** small, usu temporary, stall where goods are sold or displayed at a market, a fair or an exhibition. **2** small enclosure or compartment for a specific purpose: *a telephone booth*, ie for a public telephone ○ *a polling booth*, ie for voting at elections.

bootleg /ˈbuːtleg/ *v* (**-gg-**) [Tn] **1** smuggle (alcohol). **2** make and sell (sth) illegally. ⇨ Usage at SMUGGLE.

▷ **bootleg** *adj* [attrib] (esp of alcohol) smuggled or made and sold illegally: *bootleg liquor* ○ *a bootleg record*, eg one recorded illegally at a concert.

bootlegger /-legə(r)/ *n*.

bootless /ˈbuːtlɪs/ *adj* (*arch*) that achieves nothing; unavailing; unsuccessful: *bootless pleading.*

booty /ˈbuːtɪ/ *n* [U] things taken by thieves or captured from an enemy in war; loot; plunder.

booze /buːz/ *v* (*infml*) [I] drink alcoholic liquor, esp in large quantities: *He likes to go out boozing with his mates.*

▷ **booze** *n* [U] (*infml*) **1** alcoholic drink. **2** (idm) **go/be on the booze** (*infml*) have a period of heavy drinking: *Her husband's been on the booze again.*

boozer *n* (*infml*) **1** person who boozes: *He's always been a bit of a boozer.* **2** (*Brit*) pub.

boozy *adj* (**-ier, -iest**) (*infml*) drinking or involving much alcoholic liquor; drunken: *a boozy old man* ○ *a boozy party.*

□ ˈ**booze-up** *n* (*Brit infml*) time of heavy drinking: *The party was a real booze-up.*

bop /bɒp/ *n* **1** [U] = BEBOP. **2** [C, U] (*infml*) dance or dancing to pop music: *Let's have a bop.*

▷ **bop** *v* (**-pp-**) [I] (*infml*) dance to pop music: *go bopping.* **bopper** *n* (*infml*) **1** person who dances to pop music. **2** = TEENY-BOPPER.

boracic /bəˈræsɪk/ *adj* = BORIC.

borage /ˈbɒrɪdʒ; *US* ˈbɔːrɪdʒ/ *n* [U] plant with blue flowers and hairy leaves which are used in salads and to flavour drinks.

borax /ˈbɔːræks/ *n* [U] white powder, a compound of boron, used in making glass, enamels and detergents.

Bordeaux /bɔːˈdəʊ/ *n* (*pl* unchanged) [U, C] type of red or white wine from the Bordeaux district of SW France. Cf CLARET.

bordello /bɔːˈdeləʊ/ *n* (*pl* ~**s**) (*esp US*) brothel.

Borden /ˈbɔːdn/ Lizzie (1860-1927). The trial in Massachusetts, at which she was accused of killing her father and stepmother with an axe, was a national sensation. She was acquitted for lack of evidence but became part of popular legend and the subject of many songs and books.

border /ˈbɔːdə(r)/ *n* **1** (**a**) [C] (land near the) line dividing two countries or areas; frontier: *The terrorists escaped across/over the border.* ○ [attrib] *a border town, guard, patrol* ○ *border incidents*, ie small fights between soldiers of two neighbouring countries. (**b**) **the Border** [sing] (area near) one particular border, esp that between England and Scotland, or the United States and Mexico. ⇨ Usage. **2** [C] band or strip, usu ornamental, around or along the edge of sth: *the border of a picture/photograph* ○ *a handkerchief, table-cloth, etc with an embroidered border.* **3** [C] strip of ground along the edge of a lawn or path for planting flowers or shrubs: *a herbaceous border* ○ *a border of tulips.* ⇨ illus at HOME.

▷ **border** *v* **1** [Tn] be a border to (sth); be on the border of (sth): *Our garden is bordered on one side by a stream.* ○ *How many countries border Switzerland?* **2** [Tn, Tn·pr] ~ **sth (with sth)** put a border(2) on sth: *a handkerchief bordered with lace.* **3** [Ipr] ~ **on sth** (**a**) be next to sth; adjoin sth: *The new housing estate borders on the motorway.* (**b**) (*fig*) be almost the same as sth; verge on sth: *The boy's reply to his teacher was bordering on rudeness.* ○ *Our task borders on the impossible.*

borderer *n* person who lives near a border, esp that between England and Scotland.

□ ˈ**borderland** /-lænd/ *n* **1** [C] district on either side of a border or boundary. **2** [sing] (*fig*) intermediate state or condition: *the borderland between sleeping and waking.*

ˈ**borderline** *n* line that marks a border: (*fig*) *The borderline between informal language and slang is hard to define.* — *adj* between two different groups or categories: *a borderline case* ○ *a borderline candidate*, ie sb who may or may not pass an examination, be suitable for a job, etc ○ *a borderline pass/failure (in an examination).*

ˌ**border ˈterrier** breed of small dog with rough hair.

NOTE ON USAGE: **Border** and **frontier** refer to the dividing line between two countries or states or the land near that line. **Border** is more often used when there is a natural division such as a river: *the border/frontier between Spain and Portugal* ○ *the Italian border/frontier* ○ *The Rio Grande marks the border between Mexico and the USA.* ○ *border/frontier villages.* **Frontier** is used of an inhabited region close to wild, unsettled territory, especially in North America in the early days of white settlement. **Frontier** is used figuratively, whereas **border** is not: *the frontiers of knowledge, science, etc.* A **boundary** is a precise line marking the outer limits of an area: *The lane is the boundary of our land.* **Boundary** is used with administrative areas smaller than a state or country: *the county, parish, etc boundary.*

bore[1] /bɔː(r)/ *v* **1** [I, Ipr, Tn, Tn·pr] make (a hole, well, tunnel, etc) with a revolving tool or by digging: *This drill can bore through rock.* ○ *bore a hole in wood* ○ *bore a tunnel through a mountain.* **2** [Ipr, Ip, Tn·pr, Tn·p] move by burrowing: *The mole bored (its way) underground.*

▷ **bore** *n* **1** (also ˈ**borehole**) deep hole made in the ground (esp to find water or oil). **2** (esp in compounds) (diameter of the) hollow part inside a gun barrel: *a twelve-bore shotgun* ○ *small-bore guns.*

bore[2] /bɔː(r)/ *v* **1** [Tn] make (sb) feel tired and uninterested by being dull or tedious: *I've heard all his stories before; they bore me/he bores me.* ○ *I'm bored: let's go to the cinema.* ○ *I hope you're not getting bored (by my conversation).* **2** (idm) **bore sb to ˈdeath/ˈtears** bore sb intensely: *Long novels bore me to tears.* **a crashing bore** ⇨ CRASH[2].

▷ **bore** *n* person or thing that bores; nuisance: *Don't be such a bore!* ○ *We've run out of petrol. What a bore!*

boredom /-dəm/ *n* [U] state of being bored.

boring /ˈbɔːrɪŋ/ *adj* uninteresting; dull; tedious: *a boring conversation, job, book, party.*

bore[3] /bɔː(r)/ *n* high tidal wave that moves along a narrow estuary from the sea.

bore[4] *pt* of BEAR[2].

Borgia /ˈbɔːdʒə/ name of a noble Italian Renaissance family, originally from Spain. The most famous members were Rodrigo (1431-1503), who became pope Alexander VI, and his children Cesare (1476-1507) and Lucrezia (1480-1519). Cesare was ruthless but a strong military commander. He was one of the earliest believers in the idea of a united Italy. Lucrezia married Alfonso d'Este, the future Duke of Ferrara, and her court became a great artistic centre. Despite this, the family as a whole have acquired a reputation for treachery, intrigue and cruelty.

boric /ˈbɔːrɪk/ *adj* of or containing boron.

□ ˌ**boric ˈacid** (also **boracic acid** /bəˌræsɪk ˈæsɪd/) substance derived from borax and used as an antiseptic.

born /bɔːn/ *v* (used only in the passive without *by*) **1 be born** come into the world by birth: *She was born in 1950.* ○ (*fig*) *The Trades Union movement was born* (ie founded) *in the early years of the century.* ○ *He was born* (ie destined from birth) *to be a great writer.* ⇨ Usage at BEAR[2]. **2** (idm) **(not) be born ˈyesterday** (not) be foolish or likely to be deceived because of lack of experience: *You can't fool me; I wasn't born yesterday, you know.* **be/be born/be made that way** ⇨ WAY[1]. ˌ**born and ˈbred** born, brought up and educated (in a specified place or manner): *He's London born and bred.* ○ *She was born and bred a Catholic.* **born in the purple** born in a royal or very aristocratic family. **born of sb/sth** owing one's existence to sb/sth; originating from sth: *He was born of German parents.* ○ *Her socialist beliefs were born of a hatred of injustice.* **born on the wrong side of the blanket** (*euph*) illegitimate. **born with a silver ˈspoon in one's mouth** (*saying*) having wealthy parents. **in all one's born ˈdays** (*infml*) in one's whole life: *I've never heard such nonsense in all my born days!* **there's one born every ˈminute** (*saying*) there are a lot of gullible people. **to the manner born** ⇨ MANNER.

▷ **born** *adj* [attrib] having a specific natural quality or ability: *be a born leader, loser, writer, athlete, etc.*

-born (forming compound *ns* and *adjs*) having a specific order, status or place of birth: *first-born* ○ *nobly-born* ○ *French-born.*

□ ˌ**born-aˈgain** *adj* [usu attrib] having been converted, esp to evangelical Christianity: *a* ˌ*born-again ˈChristian.*

borne *pp* of BEAR[2]. ⇨ Usage at BEAR[2].

Borneo /ˈbɔːnɪəʊ/ large island in the Malay archipelago. The state of *Brunei is in the north. The rest of the island belongs partly to *Indonesia (Kalimantan) and partly to *Malaysia (Sabah and Sarawak).

Borodin /ˈbɒrədɪn/ Alexander (1833-87), Russian composer, one of 'The Five'. He worked primarily as a scientist and composed relatively little, being best known for his opera *Prince Igor.*

boron /ˈbɔːrɒn/ *n* [U] (*symb* **B**) non-metallic chemical element used in metal-working and in nuclear reactors. ⇨ App 11.

borough /ˈbʌrə; *US* -rəʊ/ *n* **1** (*Brit*) (**a**) town or district with a corporation and certain rights of self-government granted by royal charter. (**b**) any of the administrative areas of Greater London. Cf PARISH 2. **2** (*US*) (**a**) any of the five administrative areas of New York City. (**b**) (in some states) town with a legal corporation.

Borromini /ˌbɒrəˈmiːnɪ/ Francesco (1599-1667), Italian architect. He designed some of the finest examples of the Roman baroque style, working on many of the churches of Rome, and had a great influence on the later rococo style.

borrow /ˈbɒrəʊ/ *v* [I, Ipr, Tn, Tn·pr] ~ (**sth**) (**from sb/sth**) **1** receive or obtain (sth) temporarily (from sb/sth), with the promise or intention of returning it: *borrow (money) from the bank, a friend* ○ *I've forgotten my pen. Could I borrow yours?* ○ *borrow a book from the library.* Cf LEND. **2** (**a**) take and use (sth) as one's own; copy (sth): *borrow freely from other writers* ○ *borrow sb's ideas, methods* ○ *Handel borrowed music from other composers.* (**b**) (of a language) adopt (a word or phrase) from another language: *The expression 'nouveau riche' is borrowed from French.* **3** (idm) **borrowed ˈplumage** display of eg learning or skill which one does not really have; pretentiousness. (**be living on**) **borrowed ˈtime** period of time for which one continues living after an illness or a crisis which might have caused one to die.

▷ **borrower** *n* person who borrows. Cf LENDER (LEND).

borrowing *n* thing borrowed, esp a word adopted by one language from another: *The company will soon be able to repay its borrowings from the bank.* ○ *English has many borrowings from French.*

Borstal /ˈbɔːstl/ *n* [C, U] institution for reforming young offenders: *be sent to Borstal.* Cf APPROVED SCHOOL (APPROVE), REFORMATORY.

bortsch (also **borsch**) /bɔːʃ/ *n* [U] Russian or Polish soup made with beetroot and cabbage and served hot or cold.

borzoi /ˈbɔːzɔɪ/ *n* type of large dog with long hair and a silky coat; Russian wolfhound.

Bosch /bɒʃ/ Hieronymus (c 1450-1516), Dutch painter. He is famous for paintings filled with fantastic creatures and demons as well as human figures in imaginary landscapes. They represent the dreadful consequences of human sin and stupidity.

bosh /bɒʃ/ *n* [U], *interj* (*infml*) nonsense: *You're talking bosh!*

bo'sn, bos'n = BOATSWAIN.

Bosnia-Herzegovina /ˌbɒznɪə ˌhɜːtsəˈgɒvɪnə/ country in south-eastern Europe; capital Sarajevo. Until 1992 it was one of the federal republics of Yugoslavia. ⇨ map at YUGOSLAVIA.

bosom /ˈbʊzəm/ *n* **1** [C] person's chest, esp a woman's breasts: *hold sb to one's bosom* ○ *She has a large bosom.* **2** [C] part of a dress covering the bosom. **3** [sing] **the ~ of sth** loving care and protection of sth: *live in the bosom of one's family* ○ *welcomed into the bosom of the Church.*

▷ **bosomy** *adj* (*infml*) (of a woman) having large breasts.

□ **bosom ˈfriend** very close friend.

Bosporus /ˈbɒspərəs/ **the Bosporus** strait connecting the Black Sea to the Sea of Marmara.

boss[1] /bɒs/ *n* (*infml*) person who controls or gives orders to workers; manager; employer: *ask one's boss for a pay rise* ○ *Who's (the) boss in this house?* ie Is the wife or the husband in control?

▷ **boss** *v* [Tn, Tn·p] ~ **sb** (**about/around**) (*infml derog*) give orders to sb in an overbearing way: *He's always bossing his wife about.*

bossy *adj* (**-ier, -iest**) (*derog*) fond of giving people orders; domineering. **bossily** *adv.* **bossiness** *n* [U]. **ˈbossy-boots** *n* (*pl* unchanged) (*Brit joc infml*) bossy person, esp a child: *Let her do it her own way, you little bossy-boots!*

boss[2] /bɒs/ *n* round projecting knob or stud, esp in the centre of a shield or as a decoration on a church ceiling.

bossa nova /ˌbɒsə ˈnəʊvə/ *n* [U, sing] (music for a) Brazilian dance like the samba: *dance/do the bossa nova.*

boss-eyed /ˈbɒsaɪd/ *adj* (*infml*) (**a**) blind in one eye. (**b**) cross-eyed.

boss-shot /ˈbɒsʃɒt/ *n* bad shot, guess or attempt: *make a boss-shot at/of sth.*

Boston /ˈbɒstən/ capital of the American state of Massachusetts. It is a major port and a commercial and cultural centre. ▷ **Bostonian** /bɒˈstəʊnɪən/ *n, adj.*

□ **the ˌBoston ˈTea Party** protest in 1773 which led to the American War of Independence. People in Boston objected to the British government's putting a tax on tea without giving them the right to be represented in Parliament. Some of them dressed as American Indians, boarded a ship in the harbour and threw its cargo of tea into the water.

bo'sun = BOATSWAIN.

Boswell /ˈbɒzwəl/ James (1740-95), Scottish writer. His ambition was to have a career in politics, but he became famous for his great biography of his friend Samuel *Johnson.

Bosworth Field /bɒzwəθ ˈfiːld/ site of one of the last battles of the *Wars of the Roses. Henry Tudor (Henry VII) defeated King Richard III of the House of York, who died there. Shakespeare dramatized the event in *Richard III.*

botany /ˈbɒtənɪ/ *n* [U] scientific study of plants and their structure. Cf BIOLOGY, ZOOLOGY.

▷ **botanical** /bəˈtænɪkl/ *adj* of or relating to botany. **botanical ˈgardens** park where plants and trees are grown for scientific study.

botanist /ˈbɒtənɪst/ *n* expert in botany.

botanize, -ise /ˈbɒtənaɪz/ *v* [I] study and collect wild plants.

Botany Bay /bɒtənɪ ˈbeɪ/ bay near Sydney, Australia. Captain *Cook landed there in 1770. During the 19th century it became notorious for the harsh conditions of the colony set up there for criminals sent from Britain.

botch /bɒtʃ/ *v* [Tn, Tn·p] ~ **sth** (**up**) spoil sth by poor or clumsy work; repair sth badly: *a botched job,* ie a piece of work that is done badly ○ *The actor botched* (ie forgot or stumbled over) *his lines.* ○ *The mechanic tried to repair my car, but he really botched it up.*

▷ **botch** (also **botch-up**) *n* piece of badly done work: *make a botch of sth.*

botcher *n* person who botches work.

both[1] /bəʊθ/ *adj* **1** (with *pl ns*; the *n* may be preceded by a *def art*, a *demons det* or a *possess det*) the two; the one as well as the other: *hold sth in both hands* ○ *Both books/Both the books/Both these books are expensive.* ○ *He is blind in both eyes.* ○ *There are shops on both sides of the street.* ○ *Both (her) children are at university.* **2** (idm) **have/want it/things ˈboth ways** (try to) combine two ways of thinking or behaving, satisfy two demands, obtain two results, etc which are, or might be thought to be, exclusive of each other: *You can't have it both ways,* ie You must decide on one thing or the other. ⇨ Usage at ALL[1].

both[2] /bəʊθ/ *pron* (**a**) ~ (**of sb/sth**) (referring back to a *pl n* or *pron*) the two; not only the one but also the other: *He has two brothers: both live in London.* ○ *His parents are both dead.* ○ *We both want to go to the party.* ○ *I like these shirts. I'll take both of them.* (**b**) ~ **of sb/sth** (referring forward to a *pl n* or *pron*) the two; not only the one but also the other: *Both of us want to go* (Cf *We both want to go*) *to the party.* ○ *Both of her children have* (Cf *Her children both have*) *blue eyes.* ⇨ Usage at ALL[1].

both[3] /bəʊθ/ *adv* ~... **and**... not only... but also...: *be both tired and hungry* ○ *She spoke both French and English.* ○ *Both his brother and sister are married.* ○ *She was a success both as a pianist and as a conductor.*

bother /ˈbɒðə(r)/ *v* **1** (**a**) [Tn, Tn·pr, Dn·t] ~ **sb** (**about/with sth**) cause trouble or annoyance to sb; pester sb: *I'm sorry to bother you, but could you tell me the way to the station?* ○ *Does the pain from your operation bother you much?* ○ *Does my smoking bother you?* ○ *Don't bother your father (about it) now; he's very tired.* ○ *He's always bothering me to lend him money.* (**b**) [Tn] worry (sb): *What's bothering you?* ○ *Don't let his criticisms bother you.* ○ *The problem has been bothering me for weeks.* ○ *It bothers me that he can be so insensitive.* **2** (**a**) [I, Tt] take the time or trouble (to do sth): *'Shall I help you with the washing-up?' 'Don't bother — I'll do it later.'* ○ *He didn't even bother to say thank you.* (**b**) [Ipr] ~ **about sb/sth** concern oneself about sb/sth: *Don't bother about us — we'll join you later.* **3** [Tn] (used in the imperative to express annoyance at sth): *Bother this car! It's always breaking down.* **4** (idm) **bother oneself/one's head about sth** be anxious or concerned about sth. **can't be bothered** (**to do sth**) not do sth because one considers it to be too much trouble: *The grass needs cutting but I can't be bothered to do it today.* ○ *He could produce excellent work but usually he can't be bothered.* **hot and bothered** ⇨ HOT.

▷ **bother** *n* **1** [U] trouble; inconvenience: *a spot of bother* ○ *Did you have much bother finding the house?* ○ *'Thanks for your help!' 'It was no bother.'* ○ *I'm sorry to have put you to all this bother,* ie to have caused you so much inconvenience. **2 a bother** [sing] annoying thing; nuisance: *What a bother! We've missed the bus.*

bother *interj* (used to express annoyance): *Oh bother! I've left my money at home.*

botheration /bɒðəˈreɪʃn/ *interj* (*infml*) = BOTHER *interj.*

bothersome /-səm/ *adj* causing bother; annoying.

Bothwell /ˈbɒθwel/ James Hepburn, fourth Earl of (c 1536-78), third husband of *Mary Queen of Scots. He was thought to be involved in the murder of her second husband, Darnley.

bo-tree /ˈbəʊtriː/ *n* type of Indian fig-tree, considered sacred by Buddhists. The Buddha is said to have reached nirvana under this tree.

Botswana /bɒˈtswɑːnə/ country in southern Africa, pop approx 1 212 000; official language English; capital Gaborone; unit of currency pula (= 100 thebe); an independent state since 1966 and a member of the Commonwealth. A large area of the country is occupied by the Kalahari desert. The economy is based on agriculture, but it does have some mineral resources. Many of its people live and work in the neighbouring state of South Africa. ⇨ map at NAMIBIA.

Botticelli /bɒtɪˈtʃelɪ/ Alessandro (1445-1510), Italian painter who worked mainly in Florence. His early works have mythological themes, such as *The Birth of Venus,* but he later turned to religious subjects. He is famous for his use of line, light and movement. In the 19th century the *Pre-Raphaelites were greatly influenced by his style.

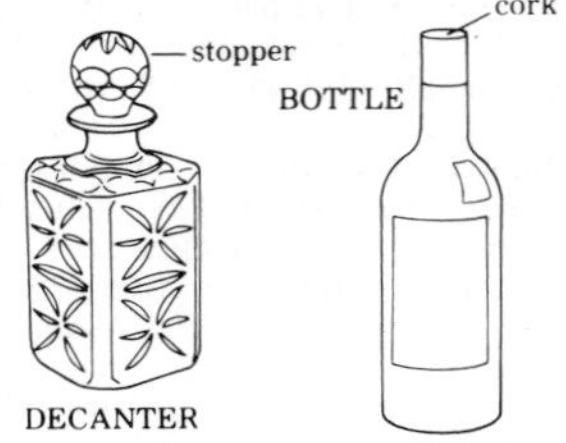

bottle /ˈbɒtl/ *n* **1** [C] (**a**) glass or plastic container, usu with a narrow neck, used for storing liquids: *a ˈwine bottle* ○ *a ˈmilk bottle* ○ *Come to my party on Saturday — and remember to bring a bottle,* ie of alcoholic drink. ⇨ illus. (**b**) amount contained in a bottle: *We drank a (whole) bottle of wine between us.* **2 the bottle** [sing] (*euph*) alcoholic drink: *She's a bit too fond of the bottle.* **3** [C usu *sing*] baby's feeding bottle or milk from this (used instead of mother's milk): *brought up on the bottle* ○ *give a baby its bottle.* **4** [U] (*Brit sl*) courage; impudence: *He's got (a lot of) bottle!* **5** (idm) **be on the ˈbottle** (*infml*) be an alcoholic: *He was on the bottle for five years.* **hit the bottle** ⇨ HIT[1].

▷ **bottle** *v* **1** [Tn] (**a**) put (sth) into bottles: *bottled beer.* (**b**) preserve (sth) by storing in glass jars: *Do you bottle your fruit or freeze it?* **2** (phr v) **bottle sth up** not allow (emotions) to be seen; restrain or suppress (feelings): *Instead of discussing their* *problems, they bottle up all their anger and resentment.*

□ ˈ**bottle bank** large container in which empty bottles are placed so that the glass can be reused.

ˈ**bottle-feed** *v* [Tn] feed (a baby) with a bottle: *Were you bottle-fed or breast-fed as a child?*

ˈ**bottle-green** *adj* dark green.

ˈ**bottle-neck** *n* **(a)** narrow or restricted stretch of road which causes traffic to slow down or stop. **(b)** anything that slows down production in a manufacturing process, etc.

ˈ**bottle-opener** *n* metal device for opening bottles of beer, etc.

ˈ**bottle-party** *n* party to which each guest brings a bottle of wine, etc.

ˈ**bottle-washer** *n* (*Brit joc infml*) person who has to do boring and unpleasant jobs (used esp as in the expression shown): *I'm the chief cook and bottle-washer round here.*

bottom /ˈbɒtəm/ *n* **1** [C usu *sing*] lowest part or point of sth: *the bottom of a hill, mountain, slope, valley, etc* ○ *The telephone is at the bottom of the stairs.* ○ *There are tea-leaves in the bottom of my cup.* ○ *The book I want is (right) at the bottom of the pile.* ○ *Sign your name at the bottom of the page, please.* **2** [C usu *sing*] part on which sth rests; underside: *The manufacturer's name is on the bottom of the plate.* **3** [C] part of the body on which one sits; buttocks: *fall on one's bottom* ○ *smack a child's bottom.* **4** [sing] farthest part or point (of sth); far end (of sth): *There's a pub at the bottom of the road.* ○ *The tool-shed is at the bottom of the garden,* ie at the end farthest from the house. **5** [sing] (person or group in the) lowest position in a class, list, etc: *He was always bottom of the class in maths.* ○ *Our team came/was bottom of the league last season.* ○ *She started at the bottom and worked her way up to become manager of the company.* **6** [sing] ground under a sea, lake or river: *The water is very deep here—I can't touch (the) bottom.* ○ *The 'Titanic' went to the bottom,* ie sank. **7** [C] ship's hull; keel. **8** [C usu *pl*] lower part of a two-piece garment: *pyjama bottoms* ○ *track suit bottoms.* **9** [U] lowest gear: *drive up a steep hill in bottom.* **10** (idm) **at bottom** in reality; really; basically: *He seems aggressive but at bottom he is kind and good-natured.* **be at the bottom of sth** be the basic cause or originator of sth: *Who is at the bottom of these rumours?* **the bottom (of sth) falls out** collapse occurs: *The bottom has fallen out of the market,* ie Trade has dropped to a very low level. ○ *The bottom fell out of his world* (ie His life lost its meaning) *when his wife died.* **bottoms** ˈ**up!** (*infml*) (said as a toast to tell people to finish their drinks). **from the bottom of one's** ˈ**heart** with deep feeling; truly; sincerely: *love sb, congratulate sb, regret sth from the bottom of one's heart.* **from top to bottom** ⇨ TOP[1]. **get to the bottom of sth** find out the real cause of sth or the truth about sth: *We must get to the bottom of this mystery.* **knock the bottom out of sth** ⇨ KNOCK[2]. **smooth as a baby's bottom** ⇨ SMOOTH[1]. **touch bottom** ⇨ TOUCH[1].

▷ **bottom** *adj* [attrib] **1** in the lowest or last position: *the bottom line (on a page)* ○ *the bottom rung (of a ladder)* ○ *the bottom step (of a flight of stairs)* ○ *Put your books on the bottom shelf.* ○ *go up a hill in bottom gear.* **2** (idm) **bet one's bottom dollar** ⇨ BET.

bottom *v* (phr v) **bottom out** (*commerce*) (of prices, shares, etc) reach the lowest level: *There is no sign that the recession has bottomed out yet.*

bottomless *adj* **1** very deep: *a bottomless pit, gorge, etc.* **2** (*fig*) unlimited; inexhaustible: *bottomless reserves of energy.*

bottommost /ˈbɒtəmməʊst/ *adj* [attrib] lowest: *the bottommost depths of the sea.*

□ ˌ**bottom** ˈ**drawer** (*US* ˈ**hope chest**) store of clothes, linen, cutlery, etc collected by a woman in preparation for marriage.

ˌ**bottom** ˈ**line** **(a)** last line of a set of accounts, showing the final profit or loss. **(b)** (*infml*) deciding or crucial factor; essential point (in an argument, etc): *If you don't make a profit you go out of business: that's the bottom line.*

botulism /ˈbɒtjʊlɪzəm/ *n* [U] type of severe food poisoning caused by bacteria in badly preserved food.

Boudicca /ˈbuːdɪkə, bəʊˈdɪkə/ (also **Boadicea**) (died AD 62) queen of the *Iceni at the time of the Roman invasion of Britain. She opposed the Roman armies and destroyed their camps at St Albans, Colchester and London before being defeated and committing suicide.

boudoir /ˈbuːdwɑː(r)/ *n* (esp formerly) woman's bedroom or private sitting-room.

bouffant /ˈbuːfɑːn/ *adj* (of a hair-style) made to appear puffed out by being combed back towards the roots: *a* ˌ*bouffant* ˈ*hair-do.*

bougainvillaea /ˌbuːgənˈvɪlɪə/ *n* tropical climbing shrub with large red or purple bracts.

bough /baʊ/ *n* any of the main branches of a tree.

bought *pt, pp* of BUY.

bouillabaisse /ˈbuːjəbes; *US* ˌbuːjəˈbeɪs/ *n* [U] type of French fish stew often made with white wine.

bouillon /ˈbuːjɒn/ *n* [U] thin clear soup or broth; stock[1](9).

boulder /ˈbəʊldə(r)/ *n* large rock worn and shaped by water or the weather.

□ ˈ**boulder clay** (also **till**) (*geology*) mixture of boulders, etc in clay deposited by the melting of a glacier.

boulevard /ˈbuːləvɑːd; *US* ˈbʊl-/ *n* **1** wide city street, often with trees on each side. **2** (*US*) broad main road.

Boulting /ˈbəʊltɪŋ/ John (1913-) and Roy (1913-), British film makers known as the Boulting Brothers. Roy produced and John directed a number of social comedies in the 1950s and 1960s, such as *I'm All Right, Jack*, which starred Peter *Sellers. The title became a popular catchphrase.

bounce /baʊns/ *v* **1** [I, Ipr, Tn, Tn·pr] (cause sth to) spring back when sent against sth hard: *A rubber ball bounces well.* ○ *The ball bounced over the wall.* ○ *The goalkeeper bounced the ball twice before kicking it.* ○ *She bounced the ball against the wall.* **2** [I, Ip, Tn] (cause sb to) move up and down in a lively manner (in the specified direction): *The child bounced (up and down) on the bed.* ○ *He bounced his baby on his knee.* ⇨ Usage at JUMP[2]. **3** [I] (*infml*) (of a cheque) be sent back by a bank as worthless (because there is no money in the account): *I hope this cheque doesn't bounce.* Cf DISHONOUR *v* 2. **4** (phr v) **bounce along, down, into, etc** move in the specified direction with an up and down motion: *He came bouncing into the room.* ○ *The car bounced along the bumpy mountain road.* **bounce back** (*infml*) recover well after a set-back: *Share prices bounced back this morning.* ○ *She's had many misfortunes in her life but she always bounces back.*

▷ **bounce** *n* **1** [C] act of bouncing: *catch a ball on the bounce/first bounce,* ie after it has bounced once. **2** [U] **(a)** ability to bounce. **(b)** (of a person) liveliness; vitality: *She's got a lot of bounce.*

bouncer *n* **1** (also **bumper**) (in cricket) bowled ball that bounces high and forcefully: *bowl sb a fast bouncer.* **2** (*infml*) person employed by a club, restaurant, etc to throw out trouble-makers.

bouncing *adj* ~ **(with sth)** strong and healthy: *a bouncing baby* ○ *He was bouncing with energy.*

bouncy *adj* **(-ier, -iest)** **1** (of a ball) able to bounce. **2** (of a person) lively.

bound[1] /baʊnd/ *v* [Tn usu passive] form the boundary of (sth); limit: *Germany is bounded on the west by France and on the south by Switzerland.* ○ *The airfield is bounded by woods on all sides.*

bound[2] /baʊnd/ *v* [Ipr, Ip] jump or spring; run with jumping movements (in a specified direction): *He bounded into the room and announced that he was getting married.* ○ *The dog came bounding up to its master.*

▷ **bound** *n* **1** bounding movement; leap; spring: *The dog cleared* (ie jumped over) *the gate in one bound.* **2** (idm) **by/in leaps and bounds** ⇨ LEAP.

bound[3] /baʊnd/ *adj* [pred] ~ **(for...)** going or ready to go in the direction of: *Where are you bound (for)?* ○ *We are bound for home.* ○ *This ship is outward bound/homeward bound,* ie sailing away from/towards its home port.

▷ **-bound** (forming compound *adjs*) heading for a specified place or in a specified direction: *We're London-bound.* ○ *Northbound traffic may be delayed because of an accident on the motorway.*

bound[4] *pt, pp* of BIND.

bound[5] /baʊnd/ *adj* [pred] ~ **to do sth** **1** certain to do sth: *The weather is bound to get better tomorrow.* ○ *You've done so much work that you're bound to pass the exam.* **2** obliged by law or duty to do sth: *I feel bound to tell you that you're drinking too much.* ○ *I am bound to say I disagree with you on this point.* **3** (idm) **bound** ˈ**up in sth** very busy with sth; very interested in sth: *He seems very bound up in his work.* **bound** ˈ**up with sth** closely connected with sth: *The welfare of the individual is bound up with the welfare of the community.* **honour bound** ⇨ HONOUR[1]. ˈ**I'll be bound** (*dated infml*) I feel sure: *The children are up to some mischief, I'll be bound!*

▷ **-bound** (forming compound *adjs*) **1** confined to a specified place: *I don't like being desk-bound* (eg in an office) *all day.* ○ *His illness has left him completely house-bound.* **2** obstructed or hindered by the specified conditions: *fogbound/snowbound airports* ○ *Strikebound travellers face long delays this weekend.*

boundary /ˈbaʊndrɪ/ *n* **1** line that marks a limit; dividing line: *The fence marks the boundary between my land and hers.* ○ *The ball was caught by a fielder standing just inside the boundary.* ○ (*fig*) *Scientists continue to push back the boundaries of knowledge.* ⇨ Usage at BORDER. **2** (in cricket) hit to or over the boundary, scoring 4 or 6 runs: *He scored 26 runs, all in boundaries.*

bounden /ˈbaʊndən/ *adj* (idm) **one's bounden** ˈ**duty** (*fml*) duty dictated by one's conscience.

bounder /ˈbaʊndə(r)/ *n* (*dated Brit infml derog*) man whose behaviour is morally unacceptable.

boundless /ˈbaʊndlɪs/ *adj* without limits: *boundless generosity, enthusiasm.* ▷ **boundlessly** *adv.*

bounds /baʊndz/ *n* [pl] **1** limits: *keep within/go beyond the bounds of reason, sanity, decency, propriety, etc* ○ *It is not beyond the bounds of possibility (that...).* ○ *Are there no bounds to his ambition?* ○ *Public spending must be kept within reasonable bounds.* **2** (idm) **beat the bounds** ⇨ BEAT[1]. **know no bounds** ⇨ KNOW. **out of** ˈ**bounds (to sb)** (*US* **off limits**) (of a place) not to be entered or visited (by sb): *The town's pubs and bars are out of bounds to troops.*

bounteous /ˈbaʊntɪəs/ *adj* (*dated or rhet*) **1** (of a person) generous. **2** freely given; plentiful: *God's bounteous blessings.* ▷ **bounteously** *adv.* **bounteousness** *n* [U].

bountiful /ˈbaʊntɪfl/ *adj* (*dated*) **1** giving generously. **2** abundant: *a bountiful supply of food.* ▷ **bountifully** /ˈbaʊntɪfəlɪ/ *adv.*

Bounty /ˈbaʊntɪ/ **HMS Bounty** ship on which a famous mutiny took place in 1789. According to the traditional story, the crew, led by Fletcher Christian, rebelled against their harsh commander William *Bligh. Bligh and some of his officers were set adrift in a lifeboat, which eventually took them all the way to Timor, a distance of 6400 km (4000 miles). The crew returned to Tahiti and some of them later went to live on *Pitcairn Island.

bounty /ˈbaʊntɪ/ *n* **1** [U] (*dated*) generosity in giving; liberality: *a monarch famous for his bounty.* **2** [C] (*dated*) generous gift. **3** [C] reward or payment offered (usu by a government) to encourage sb to do sth (eg to increase production of goods).

□ ˈ**bounty hunter** (*esp US*) **(a)** person who hunts wild animals in order to obtain a reward. **(b)** (esp formerly) person who tries to capture outlaws to obtain a reward.

bouquet /bʊˈkeɪ/ *n* **1** bunch of flowers for carrying in the hand (often presented as a gift): *a bride's bouquet* ○ *The soloist received a huge bouquet of roses.* **2** (*fig*) expression of praise; compliment. **3** characteristic aroma of a wine or liqueur: *This brandy has a fine bouquet.*

□ **bouquet garni** /ˌbuːkeɪ ˈgɑːniː/ bunch of herbs

used for flavouring soups, stews, etc.

Bourbon /ˈbʊəbən/ name of a European royal family. The House of Bourbon ruled France from 1589 to 1789, and came to the throne again when the monarchy was briefly restored (1814-30). Members of the family also became kings of Spain.

bourbon *n* **1** /ˈbɜːbən/ (**a**) [U] type of whisky distilled in the US chiefly from maize. (**b**) [C] glass of this. **2** /ˈbʊəbən/ (also **bourbon biscuit**) type of chocolate-flavoured biscuit with a chocolate cream filling.

bourgeois /ˈbɔːʒwɑː; *US* ˌbʊərˈʒwɑː/ *adj* **1** of or relating to the property-owning middle class. **2** (*derog*) (**a**) concerned with material possessions and social status: *They've become very bourgeois since they got married.* (**b**) conventionally respectable; conservative: *bourgeois tastes, attitudes, ideas, etc.* (**c**) unimaginative; philistine. **3** (in Marxist thought) of or relating to the bourgeoisie(2); capitalist.

▷ **bourgeois** *n* (*pl* unchanged) [C] (*usu derog*) bourgeois person.

bourgeoisie /ˌbɔːʒwɑːˈziː, ˌbʊəʒwɑːˈziː/ *n* [Gp] (*usu derog*) **1** middle classes, esp those owning property: *the rise of the bourgeoisie in the 19th century.* **2** (in Marxist thought) capitalist ruling class that exploits the working class. Cf PROLETARIAT.

bourse /bʊəs/ *n* European stock exchange, esp (**the Bourse**) the one in Paris.

bout /baʊt/ *n* **1** ~ (**of sth/doing sth**) (**a**) short period of a specified activity: *a ˈdrinking-bout* ○ *She has bouts of hard work followed by long periods of inactivity.* (**b**) attack (of an illness): *a bout of flu, bronchitis, rheumatism, etc* ○ *He suffers from frequent bouts of depression.* **2** boxing or wrestling contest.

boutique /buːˈtiːk/ *n* small shop selling clothes and other articles of the latest fashion.

bovine /ˈbəʊvaɪn/ *adj* **1** (*fml*) of or relating to cattle. **2** (*derog*) dull and stupid: *a bovine expression, character, mentality* ○ *bovine stupidity.*

bovver /ˈbɒvə(r)/ *n* [U] (*Brit sl*) trouble, esp violence or vandalism caused by young people.

□ ˈ**bovver boots** (*Brit sl*) heavy boots, esp those worn by young people in gangs.

ˈ**bovver boy** (*Brit sl*) boy belonging to a gang associated with violent behaviour, esp skinheads.

bow[1] /bəʊ/ *n* **1** piece of wood bent into a curve by a tight string joining its ends, used as a weapon for shooting arrows: *hunt with bows and arrows.* ⇨ illus at ARCHERY. **2** wooden rod with strands of horsehair stretched from end to end, used for playing stringed instruments. ⇨ illus at MUSIC. **3** knot made with loops; ribbon tied in this way: *tie shoelaces in a bow* ○ *a dress decorated with bows.* ⇨ illus. **4** (idm) **have two strings/a second, etc string to one's bow** have a second person, skill or resource available to one for a particular purpose, as a replacement for or an alternative to a first: *As both a novelist and a university lecturer, she has two strings to her bow.*

▷ **bow** *v* [I, Tn] use a bow on (a stringed instrument). **bowing** *n* [U] technique of using the bow to play a violin, etc: *The cellist's bowing was very sensitive.*

□ ˌ**bow-ˈlegs** *n* [pl] legs that curve outwards at the knees. ˌ**bow-ˈlegged** *adj*: *a ˌbow-ˈlegged gait.*

ˈ**bowman** /-mən/ *n* (*pl* **-men** /-mən/) archer.

bow

ˌ**bow-ˈtie** *n* man's necktie tied in a knot with a double loop, worn esp on formal occasions. ⇨ illus.

ˌ**bow-ˈwindow** *n* type of bay window with curved glass.

bow[2] /baʊ/ *v* **1** (**a**) [I, Ipr, Ip] ~ (**down**) (**to/before sb/sth**) bend the head or body as a sign of respect or as a greeting: *The cast bowed as the audience applauded.* ○ *We all bowed to the Queen.* ○ *The priest bowed down before the altar.* (**b**) [Tn] bend (the head or body) as a sign of respect: *The congregation bowed their heads in prayer.* **2** [usu passive: Tn, Tn·p] bend (sb/sth) under or as if under a weight: *His back was bowed with age.* ○ *branches bowed down by the snow on them.* **3** (idm) ˌ**bow and ˈscrape** (*usu derog*) behave in an obsequious or a servile manner: *The waiter showed us to our table with much bowing and scraping.* **4** (phr v) **bow sb in/out** bow to sb as he enters/leaves a room, etc. **bow out** (**of sth**) (**a**) withdraw from sth: *I'm bowing out of this scheme — I don't approve of it.* (**b**) retire from an important position: *After thirty years in politics, he is finally bowing out.* **bow to sth** submit to sth; accept sth: *bow to the inevitable* ○ *bow to sb's opinion, wishes, greater experience* ○ *We're tired of having to bow to authority.*

▷ **bow** *n* **1** bending of the head or body (as a greeting, etc): *acknowledge sb with a bow* ○ *He made a bow and left the room.* **2** (idm) **take a/one's ˈbow** (of an actor or actors) acknowledge applause by bowing (BOW[2] 1a).

bow[3] /baʊ/ *n* **1** (often *pl*) front or forward end of a boat or ship: *The yacht hit a rock and damaged her bows.* ⇨ illus at YACHT. **2** (in rowing) oarsman nearest the bow. Cf STROKE[1] 3. **3** (idm) **a shot across the bows** ⇨ SHOT[1].

Bow-bells /ˌbəʊˈbelz/ the bells of Bow Church (St Mary-le-Bow) in Cheapside, London. It is said that true cockneys are those born within the sound of Bow-bells.

bowdlerize, -ise /ˈbaʊdləraɪz/ *v* [Tn] (*sometimes derog*) remove words or scenes considered indecent from (a book, play, poem etc); expurgate; censor. ▷ **bowdlerization, -isation** /ˌbaʊdləraɪˈzeɪʃn; *US* -rɪˈz-/ *n* [C, U].

bowel /ˈbaʊəl/ *n* (usu *pl*, except in medical use and when used attributively) **1** part of the alimentary canal below the stomach; intestine: [attrib] *a bowel complaint/disorder* ○ *cancer of the bowel* ○ *move one's bowels*, ie defecate. **2** deepest or innermost part (of a place): *in the bowels of the earth*, ie deep underground.

□ ˈ**bowel movement** (**a**) discharge of waste matter from the bowels. (**b**) waste matter discharged; faeces.

bower /ˈbaʊə(r)/ *n* **1** (**a**) shady place under trees or climbing plants in a wood or garden; arbour. (**b**) summer-house. **2** (*dated*) lady's bedroom; boudoir.

□ ˈ**bower-bird** *n* type of Australian bird of paradise.

bowie knife

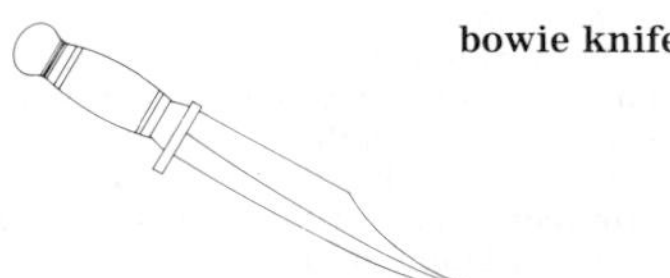

bowie /ˈbəʊɪ/ *n* (also ˈ**bowie knife**) long knife used by hunters. ⇨ illus.

bowl[1] /bəʊl/ *n* **1** (**a**) (esp in compounds) deep round dish, used esp for holding food or liquid: *a sugar bowl* ○ *a fruit bowl* ○ *a washing-up bowl.* (**b**) amount contained in a bowl: *a bowl of soup, cereal, porridge, etc.* ⇨ illus at BUCKET, PLATE. **2** hollow rounded part of certain objects: *the bowl of a spoon* ○ *a lavatory bowl* ○ *He filled the bowl of his pipe with tobacco.* **3** (*esp US*) amphitheatre (for open-air concerts, etc): *the Hollywood Bowl.*

bowl[2] /bəʊl/ *n* **1** [C] heavy plastic ball that is shaped so that it rolls in a curve, used in the game of bowls. **2** [C] heavy ball used in skittles and tenpin bowling. **3 bowls** [sing *v*] game played on a smooth lawn, in which two players take turns to roll bowls as near as possible to a small ball: *play bowls.*

bowl[3] /bəʊl/ *v* **1** [I] play a game of bowls or bowling. **2** [Tn] (in the games of bowls or bowling) roll (a ball). **3** [I, Tn] (in cricket) send (the ball) from one's hand towards the batsman by swinging the arm over the head without bending the elbow: *bowl fast/slow* ○ *Well bowled!* ○ *bowl a full toss* ○ *Who is going to bowl the first over?* **4** [Tn, Tn·p] ~ **sb** (**out**) dismiss (a batsman) by bowling a ball that hits the wicket behind him: *He was bowled for 120*, ie dismissed in this way after scoring 120 runs. **5** (phr v) **bowl along, down, etc** (of a car or its passengers) move fast and smoothly (in the specified direction): *We were bowling along (the motorway) at seventy miles per hour.* **bowl sb over** (**a**) knock sb down. (**b**) surprise sb greatly; astound sb: *We were bowled over by the news of her marriage.*

bowler[1] /ˈbəʊlə(r)/ *n* **1** person who bowls in cricket: *a fast, slow, etc bowler* ○ *a left-arm spin bowler.* ⇨ illus at CRICKET. **2** person who plays bowls.

bowler[2] /ˈbəʊlə(r)/ *n* (also ˌ**bowler ˈhat**, *US* **derby**) hard, usu black, felt hat with a curved brim and rounded top: *Some London businessmen wear bowlers.* ⇨ illus at HAT.

bowline /ˈbəʊlɪn/ *n* (also ˈ**bowline knot**) knot forming a secure loop at the end of a rope, used by sailors, climbers, etc.

bowling /ˈbəʊlɪŋ/ *n* [U] **1** any of various games (eg skittles, ten-pin bowling) in which heavy balls are rolled along a special track towards a group of wooden pins: *a bowling match.* **2** the game of bowls. **3** (in cricket) sending the ball from the hand towards the batsman: *a good piece of bowling.*

□ ˈ**bowling-alley** *n* (**a**) long narrow track along which balls are rolled in bowling or skittles. (**b**) building containing several of these.

ˈ**bowling-green** *n* area of grass cut short for playing bowls on.

bowls ⇨ BOWL[2] 3.

bowser /ˈbaʊzə(r)/ *n* (*propr*) **1** petrol tanker that supplies filling stations, aircraft, etc. **2** (*Austral and NZ*) petrol pump.

bowsprit /ˈbəʊsprɪt/ *n* long pole projecting from the front of a ship, to which the ropes supporting the sails are fastened.

Bow Street Runners /ˌbəʊ striːt ˈrʌnəz/ popular name for the police force in London in the early 19th century. It was organized by the writer Henry *Fielding who was a magistrate at Bow Street Court in London.

bow-wow /ˌbaʊ ˈwaʊ/ *interj* (imitating the bark of a dog).

▷ ˈ**bow-wow** *n* (used by or to young children) dog.

boxes

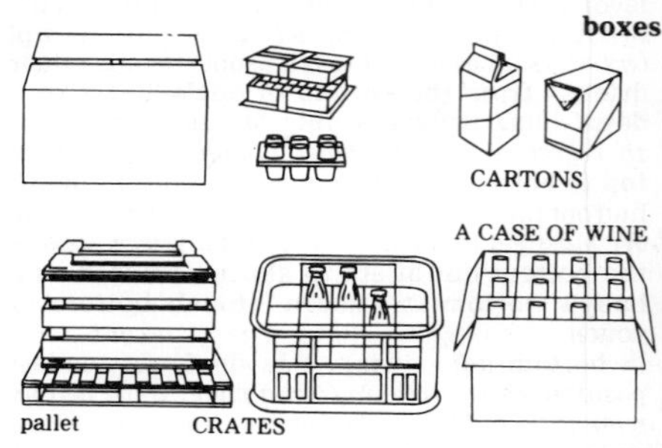

box[1] /bɒks/ *n* **1** [C] (**a**) (esp in compounds) container made of wood, cardboard, metal, etc with a flat base and usu a lid, for holding solids: *a tool-box* ○ *a money-box* ○ *a shoe box* ○ *a cigar box* ○ *She packed her books in cardboard boxes.* (**b**) box with its contents: *a box of chocolates, matches, cigars.* **2** [C] (**a**) separate compartment or enclosed area, eg for a group of people in a theatre, stadium, etc, for witnesses in a lawcourt, or for a horse in a stable: *reserve a box at the theatre* ○ *the witness box* ○ *a horse-box.* ⇨ illus at THEATRE. (**b**) small hut or shelter for a specific purpose: *a sentry-box* ○ *a signal-box* ○ *a telephone-box.* **3** [C] (**a**) area marked off by lines, eg on a form or on the ground: *Tick the appropriate box.* (**b**) penalty area on a football pitch. (**c**) (*US*) (in baseball) place where the pitcher or the batter stands. **4** (in cricket) rounded plastic shield worn by batsmen and wicket-keepers to protect the genitals. **5 the box** [sing] (*Brit infml*) television: *What's on the box tonight?* **6** [C] = BOX NUMBER.

▷ **box** *v* **1** [Tn] put (sth) into a box: *a boxed set of records.* **2** (phr v) **box sb/sth in** prevent (a runner, horse, car, etc) from moving freely (esp in a race): *One of the runners got boxed in on the final bend.* **box sb/sth in/up** shut sb/sth in a small space: *He feels boxed in, living in that tiny flat.* ○ *She hates being boxed up in an office all day.*

boxful *n* full box (of sth): *a boxful of books, clothes, toys.*

□ **ˈboxcar** *n* (*US*) enclosed railway goods van.

ˈbox junction (*Brit*) area of road where two roads cross, marked with a criss-cross pattern of yellow stripes on which vehicles must not stop, designed to help the flow of traffic.

ˈbox-kite *n* kite with an open box-like frame.

box ˈlunch (*US*) light meal, usu of sandwiches and fruit, provided in a cardboard box or similar container.

ˈbox number number given in newspaper advertisements to which replies may be sent.

ˈbox-office *n* office at a theatre, cinema, etc where tickets are bought or reserved: [attrib] *The film was a box-office success*, ie It was financially successful because many people went to see it.

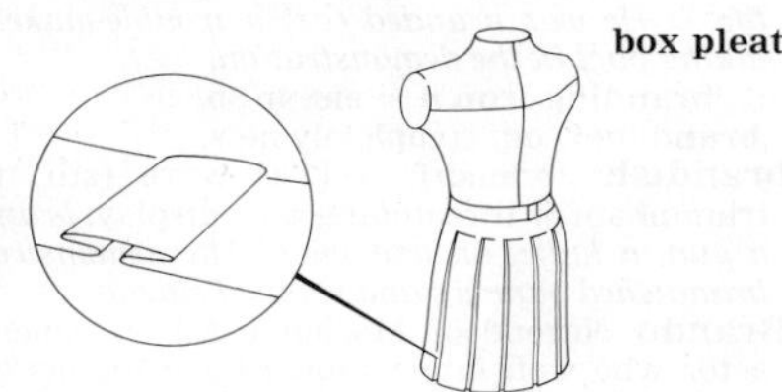

ˈbox pleat fold on a skirt, etc formed by two pleats made parallel to each other. ⇨ illus.

ˈbox-room *n* small room used for storing things.

ˈbox-spring any of a set of vertical springs inside a mattress, chair, etc.

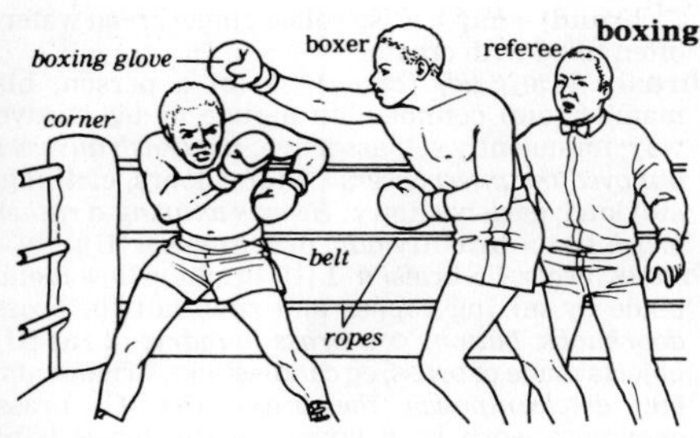

box² /bɒks/ *v* **1** [I, Ipr, Tn] ~ **(with/against sb)** fight (sb) with the fists, esp wearing padded gloves, as a sport: *Did you box at school?* **2** (idm) **box sb's ears** hit sb on the ear with the open hand or fist: *He boxed the boy's ears for being cheeky.*

▷ **box** *n* (usu *sing*) blow (usu on sb's ear) with the open hand or fist.

boxer *n* **1** person who boxes, esp as a sport: *a heavyweight boxer.* **2** breed of dog like a bulldog but with longer legs. **ˈboxer shorts** man's loose-fitting underpants.

boxing *n* [U] sport of fighting with the fists.

ˈboxing-glove *n* either of a pair of padded gloves worn for boxing. ⇨ illus. **ˈboxing-match** *n* fight between two boxers.

box³ /bɒks/ *n* **1** [C, U] small evergreen shrub with thick dark leaves, used esp for garden hedges. **2** (also **ˈboxwood**) [U] hard wood of this shrub.

Box and Cox (also **box and cox**) /ˌbɒks ənd ˈkɒks/ two people who take turns at living somewhere or doing or using sth, usu meeting only rarely: *I'm out all day and my wife's on night duty as a nurse — we're Box and Cox at the moment.*

Boxer /ˈbɒksə(r)/ *n* member of a secret society in China in the 19th century that took part in the **Boxer Rebellion** (1899). The aim of this uprising was to end the domination of China by other countries, and it was defeated by a European army helped by Japan and the USA.

Boxing Day /ˈbɒksɪŋ deɪ/ the first weekday after Christmas Day. ⇨ article at CHRISTMAS.

boy¹ /bɔɪ/ *n* **1** [C] male child; son: *The Joneses have two boys and a girl.* ○ *His eldest boy is at university.* **2** [C] young man; lad; youth: *He lived in Edinburgh as a boy.* ○ *A group of boys were playing football in the street.* ○ *How many boys are there in your class at school?* **3** [C] (esp in compounds) boy or young man who does a specified job: *the paper-boy.* **4 the boys** [pl] (*infml*) group of men who are friends and go out together: *a night out with the boys*, eg at a public house ○ *He plays football with the boys on Saturday afternoons.* ○ *He likes to feel that he's one of the boys.* **5** [C] (*derog offensive*) (in some countries) male servant or labourer. **6** (idm) **back-room boys** ⇨ BACK-ROOM (BACK²). **sb's blue-eyed boy** ⇨ BLUE¹. **the boys in ˈblue** (*Brit infml*) the police or a group of police officers. **ˌboys ˌwill be ˈboys** (*saying*) young boys, and also sometimes grown men, occasionally behave in a childish way, and this may be excused. **the golden boy/girl** ⇨ GOLDEN. **jobs for the boys** ⇨ JOB. **man and boy** ⇨ MAN¹. **sort out the men from the boys** ⇨ SORT².

▷ **boyhood** *n* [U, C usu *sing*] state or time of being a boy: *a happy, unhappy, lonely, etc boyhood* ○ [attrib] *boyhood friends.*

boyish *adj* (*often approv*) of or like a boy: *boyish ambitions, hopes, enthusiasm* ○ *He/She has boyish good looks.*

□ **ˈboy-friend** *n* regular male companion of a girl or woman, with whom she is romantically or sexually involved: *She had lots of boy-friends before she got married.*

Boy ˈScout = SCOUT 2.

boy² /bɔɪ/ *interj* (*infml esp US*) (expressing surprise, pleasure, relief or contempt): *Boy, am I glad to see you!*

Boyce /bɔɪs/ William (1711-79), English composer. He is best known for his church music, but his symphonies have gained new popularity. He also edited an important collection of music used in English cathedrals.

boycott /ˈbɔɪkɒt/ *v* [Tn] **(a)** (usu of a group of people) refuse to have social or commercial relations with (a person, company, country, etc). **(b)** refuse to handle or buy (goods); refuse to take part in (eg a meeting): *boycotting foreign imports* ○ *Athletes from several countries boycotted the Olympic Games.*

▷ **boycott** *n* refusal to deal or trade with (a person, country, etc); refusal to handle (goods): *place/put sth under a boycott.*

Boyle /bɔɪl/ Robert (1627-91), British scientist. In his writings he showed a new objective approach to science. Before chemical elements were discovered, he suggested the idea that matter is made up of 'corpuscles'. He was a founder member of the *Royal Society.

□ **ˈBoyle's law** (*chemistry*) law stating that the volume of a fixed quantity of gas at a constant temperature is inversely proportional to its pressure.

Boyne /bɔɪn/ river in the Republic of Ireland. At the Battle of the Boyne in 1690 the Protestant forces of William III defeated those of James II, the king he had replaced on the English throne.

boyo /ˈbɔɪəʊ/ *n* (*pl* ~**s**) (*Welsh and Irish infml*) (used esp as a cheerful term of address) boy or man: *Let's all go down to the pub, boyos!*

Boz /bɒz/ pen-name used by Charles *Dickens for some of his work.

bozo /ˈbəʊzəʊ/ *n* (*pl* ~**s**) (*US sl often derog*) man: *You mean the bozo with the glasses?*

BP /ˌbiː ˈpiː/ *abbr* **1** British Petroleum: *work for BP.* ⇨ article at OIL. **2** British Pharmacopoeia.

BPC /ˌbiː piː ˈsiː/ *abbr* (esp on labels of chemical products) British Pharmaceutical Codex.

B Phil /ˌbiː ˈfɪl/ *abbr* Bachelor of Philosophy: *have/be a B Phil* ○ *Jill Green B Phil.*

bq *abbr* becquerel.

BR /ˌbiː ˈɑː(r)/ *abbr* British Rail: *BR's Southern Region services.*

Br *abbr* **1** British. **2** (*religion*) Brother: *Br Peter.*

Br *symb* bromine.

bra /brɑː/ *n* = BRASSIÈRE.

brace¹ /breɪs/ *n* **1** [C] device that clamps things together or holds and supports them in position. Cf BIT² 2. **2** [C] wire device worn inside the mouth (esp by children) for straightening the teeth: *My daughter has to wear a brace on her teeth.* **3 braces** [pl] (*US* **suspenders**) straps for holding trousers up, fastened to the waistband at the front and the back and passing over the shoulders: *a pair of braces.* **4** [C] either of the two marks { and } used in printing or writing to show that words, etc between them are connected. Cf BRACKET.

□ **ˌbrace and ˈbit** hand tool for boring holes, with a revolving handle and a removable drill.

brace² /breɪs/ *n* (*pl* unchanged) pair (esp of game birds): *two brace of partridge(s).*

brace³ /breɪs/ *v* **1** [Tn] **(a)** support (sth) with a brace¹(1): *The struts are firmly braced.* **(b)** make (sth) stronger or firmer; reinforce. **2** [Tn, Tn·pr] place (one's hand or foot) firmly in order to resist an impact or balance oneself: *He braced his foot against the wall and jumped.* **3** [Tn, Tn·pr] ~ **oneself (for sth)** steady or prepare oneself for sth difficult or unpleasant: *We braced ourselves for a bumpy landing.* **4** (phr v) **brace up** (*esp US*) not become sad or dispirited, eg after a defeat or disappointment; take heart.

▷ **bracing** *adj* (esp of weather conditions) invigorating; stimulating: *bracing sea air* ○ *a bracing walk.*

bracelet /ˈbreɪslɪt/ *n* **1** [C] ornamental band worn on the wrist or arm. **2 bracelets** [pl] (*sl*) handcuffs.

bracken /ˈbrækən/ *n* [U] **(a)** large fern growing on hillsides and heathland. **(b)** mass of such ferns.

bracket /ˈbrækɪt/ *n* **1 (a)** wooden or metal angle-shaped support fixed to or built into a wall to hold a shelf, etc. **(b)** support on a wall for a lamp. **2** (usu *pl*) (in printing or writing) any one of the marks used in pairs for enclosing words, figures, etc to separate them from what precedes or follows, eg () (*round brackets* or *parentheses*), [] (*square brackets*), < > (*angle brackets*), {} (*braces*): *Put your name in brackets at the top of each page.* ⇨ App 14. **3** group or category within specified limits: *be in the lower/higher income bracket* ○ *the 20-30 age bracket*, ie those people between the ages of 20 and 30.

▷ **bracket** *v* **1** [Tn] support (sth) with a bracket. **2** [Tn] (in printing or writing) enclose (words, figures, etc) in brackets (BRACKET 2). **3** [Tn, Tn·pr, Tn·p] ~ **A and B (together)**; ~ **A with B** group things or people in the same category (to suggest that they are similar, equal or connected in some way): *It's wrong to bracket him with the extremists in his party — his views are very moderate.*

brackish /ˈbrækɪʃ/ *adj* (of water) slightly salty.

bract /brækt/ *n* leaf-like and often brightly coloured part of a plant, growing below the flower (eg in bougainvillaea and poinsettia).

brad /bræd/ *n* thin flat nail with no head or a very small head.

bradawl /ˈbrædɔːl/ *n* small hand-tool with a sharp point for boring holes.

Bradman /ˈbrædmən/ Sir Donald George (1908-), Australian cricketer, nicknamed 'The Don'. He set up a number of records in his sport and scored 117 centuries in first-class cricket.

Bradshaw /ˈbrædʃɔː/ informal name for *Bradshaw's Railway Guide*, a formerly published timetable of British passenger services.

brae /breɪ/ *n* (*Scot*) steep slope; hillside.

brag /bræg/ *v* (**-gg-**) [I, Ipr, Tf] ~ **(about/of sth)** talk with too much pride (about sth); boast: *Stop bragging!* ○ *He's been bragging about his new car.* ○ *She bragged that she could run faster than me.*

▷ **brag** *n* [U, C] boastful talk or statement.

braggart /ˈbrægət/ *n* person who brags.

Brahe /ˈbrɑːə/ Tycho (1546-1601), Danish astronomer. He made detailed observations of the stars and drew up tables of their movements. In 1572 he discovered a supernova, which was later named **Tycho's star**.

Brahma /ˈbrɑːmə/ supreme god of creation in early forms of Hinduism, who later formed a group of three with *Vishnu and *Siva.

Brahman /ˈbrɑːmən/ supreme being in Hindu philosophy, often identified with the inner core of the individual.

brahmin /ˈbrɑːmɪn/ **1** (also **brahman** /-ən/) *n* member of the highest or priestly Hindu caste. **2** (*US infml*) member of an upper class, usu of white Anglo-Saxon descent: *Boston Brahmins*.

Brahms /brɑːmz/ Johannes (1833-97), German composer. He did not complete his first symphony until he was over forty, complaining that it was hard to escape the influence of *Beethoven. He produced works in all the classical forms except opera, including many fine piano and chamber pieces. His style is expressive and romantic, esp in *A German Requiem*, in which he set his own choice of texts to music.

braid /breɪd/ *n* **1** [U] number of threads of silk, cotton, etc woven together in a narrow band for decorating clothes and material: *The general's uniform was trimmed with gold braid.* **2** [C] (*US*) = PLAIT: *She wears her hair in braids.* ⇨ illus at PLAIT.

▷ **braid** *v* [Tn] **1** decorate (clothes or material) with braid: *She braided the neckline, hem and cuffs of the dress.* **2** (*US*) = PLAIT: *She braids her hair every morning.*

Braille /breɪl/ *n* [U] system of reading and writing for blind people, using raised dots to represent letters which can be read by touching them.

the brain

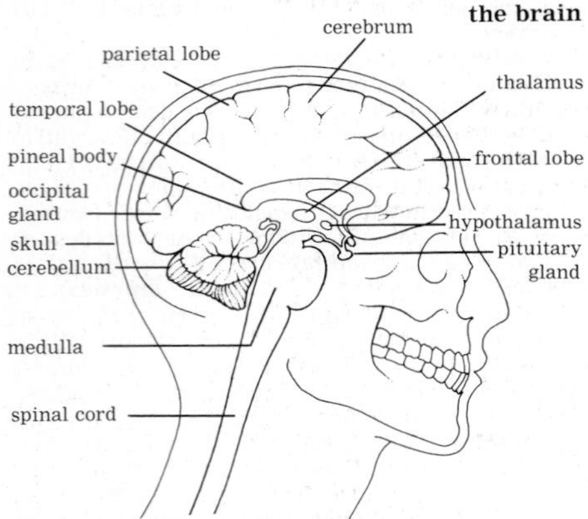

brain /breɪn/ *n* **1** [C] organ of the body that controls thought, memory and feeling, consisting of a mass of soft grey matter inside the head: *a disease of the brain* ○ *The brain is the centre of the nervous system.* ○ [attrib] *brain surgery.* ⇨ illus. **2** [U, C often *pl*] mind or intellect; intelligence: *He has very little brain.* ○ *She has an excellent brain.* ○ *You need brains to become a university professor.* ○ *He has one of the best brains in the university.* **3** (**a**) [C] (*infml*) clever person; intellectual: *He is one of the leading brains in the country.* (**b**) **the brains** [sing *v*] (*infml*) cleverest person in a group: *He's the brains of the family.* ○ *She was the brains behind the whole scheme.* **4** (idm) **beat, dash, knock, etc sb's/one's brains out** kill sb/oneself by hitting his/one's head violently. **blow one's brains out** ⇨ BLOW[1]. **cudgel one's brains** ⇨ CUDGEL. **have sth on the brain** (*infml*) think about sth constantly; be obsessed by sth: *I've had this tune on the brain all day but I can't remember what it's called.* **pick sb's brains** ⇨ PICK[3]. **rack one's brain(s)** ⇨ RACK[2]. **tax one's/sb's brains** ⇨ TAX.

▷ **brain** *v* [Tn] kill (a person or an animal) with a heavy blow on the head: (*fig infml*) *I nearly brained myself on that low beam.*

brainless *adj* stupid; foolish: *That was a pretty brainless thing to do.*

brainy *adj* (**-ier, -iest**) (*infml*) clever; intelligent: *Her children are all very brainy.*

□ ˈ**brain-child** *n* [sing] person's original plan, invention or idea: *The new arts centre is the brain-child of a wealthy local businessman.*

ˈ**brain-drain** *n* (usu *sing*) (*infml*) loss to a country when skilled and clever people emigrate from it to other countries.

ˈ**brain fever** inflammation of the brain.

ˈ**brainpower** *n* [U] mental ability or intelligence.

ˈ**brain-teaser** *n* difficult problem; puzzle.

ˈ**brains trust** (*US* **brain trust**) group of experts who answer questions and give advice, eg on a radio programme.

brainstorm /ˈbreɪnstɔːm/ *n* **1** sudden violent mental disturbance. **2** (*Brit infml*) moment of confusion or forgetfulness; sudden mental aberration: *I must have had a brainstorm — I couldn't remember my own telephone number for a moment.* **3** (*US infml*) = BRAINWAVE.

brainstorming /ˈbreɪnstɔːmɪŋ/ *n* [U] (*esp US*) method of solving problems in which all the members of a group suggest ideas which are then discussed: [attrib] *a brainstorming session.*

brainwash /ˈbreɪnwɒʃ/ *v* [Tn, Tn·pr] ~ **sb (into doing sth)** force sb to reject old beliefs or ideas and to accept new ones by the use of extreme mental pressure: (*fig*) *I refuse to be brainwashed by advertisers into buying something I don't need.* ▷ **brainwashing** *n* [U].

brainwave /ˈbreɪnweɪv/ (*US* **brainstorm**) *n* (*infml*) sudden clever idea: *Unless someone has a brainwave we'll never solve this problem.*

braise /breɪz/ *v* [Tn] cook (meat or vegetables) slowly with very little liquid in a closed container: *braised beef and onions* ○ *braising steak*, ie steak to be braised.

brake[1] /breɪk/ *n* (**a**) device for reducing the speed of or stopping a car, bicycle, train, etc: *put on/apply the brake(s)* ○ *His brakes failed on a steep hill.* ○ (*fig*) *The Government is determined to put a brake on public spending.* ○ *Ignorance acts as a brake to progress.* ⇨ illus at BICYCLE. (**b**) pedal, etc that operates such a device: *The brake (pedal) is between the clutch and the accelerator.* ⇨ illus at CAR.

▷ **brake** *v* [I, Tn] (cause sth to) slow down using a brake: *The driver braked hard as the child ran onto the road in front of him.*

□ ˈ**brake-drum** *n* metal cylinder attached to a wheel on which the brake-shoe presses in order to stop the movement of the wheel.

ˈ**brake fluid** liquid used in hydraulic brakes.

ˌ**brake-ˈhorsepower** *n* [U] power of an engine measured by the force needed to brake it.

ˈ**brake light** (*US* ˈ**stoplight**) red light at the back of a car, etc which lights up when the brakes are applied.

brakeman /ˈbreɪkmən/ *n* (*pl* **-men** /-mən/) (*esp US*) member of a train crew who checks the brakes.

ˈ**brake-shoe** *n* curved block or plate that presses against a wheel to brake it.

brake[2] /breɪk/ *n* area of brushwood, thick undergrowth or bracken; thicket.

brake[3] /breɪk/ *n* = ESTATE CAR (ESTATE).

bramble /ˈbræmbl/ *n* wild shrub with long prickly shoots; blackberry bush.

brambling /ˈbræmblɪŋ/ *n* small, brightly coloured finch.

bran /bræn/ *n* [U] outer covering of grain separated from the flour by sifting. Cf HUSK 1.

□ ˈ**bran-tub** *n* (*Brit*) tub containing bran or sawdust in which small gifts are hidden; lucky dip.

branch /brɑːntʃ; *US* bræntʃ/ *n* **1** arm-like division of a tree, growing from the trunk or from a bough: *He climbed up the tree and hid among the branches.* ⇨ illus at TREE. **2** similar division of a river, road, railway or mountain range: *a branch of the Rhine* ○ [attrib] *a branch line*, ie a division of a main railway line, serving country areas. **3** subdivision of a family, a subject of knowledge, or a group of languages: *His uncle's branch of the family emigrated to Australia.* ○ *Gynaecology is a branch of medicine.* **4** local office or shop belonging to a large firm or organization: *The bank has branches in all parts of the country.* ○ [attrib] *a branch post office.* **5** (idm) **root and branch** ⇨ ROOT[1].

▷ **branch** *v* [I] **1** (of a tree) send out or divide into branches. **2** (of a road) divide into branches: *The road branches after the level-crossing.* **3** (phr v) **branch** ˈ**off** (of a vehicle or road) turn from one road into a (usu) smaller one: *The car in front of us suddenly branched off to the left.* ○ *The road to the village branches off on the right.* **branch** ˈ**out (into sth)** extend or expand one's activities or interests in a new direction: *The company began by specializing in radios but has now decided to branch out into computers.* ○ *She's leaving the company to branch out on her own.*

brand /brænd/ *n* **1** (**a**) particular make of goods or their trade mark: *Which brand of toothpaste do you prefer?* ○ [attrib] *a* ˈ*brand name* ○ *brand loyalty*, ie tendency of customers to continue buying the same brand. (**b**) particular type or kind: *a strange brand of humour.* **2** piece of burning wood. **3** (**a**) mark of identification (esp on cattle and sheep) made with a hot iron. (**b**) (also ˈ**branding-iron**) iron used for this. ⇨ illus at IRON.

▷ **brand** *v* **1** [Tn, Tn·pr] ~ **sth (on sth)** mark sth with or as if with a brand(3a): *On big farms cattle are usually branded.* ○ (*fig*) *The experiences of his unhappy childhood are branded on his memory.* **2** [Tn, Cn·n, Cn·n/a] ~ **sb (as sth)** give a bad name to sb; denounce sb: *The scandal branded him for life.* ○ *He was branded (as) a trouble-maker for taking part in the demonstration.*

□ ˈ**branding-iron** *n* = BRAND 3b.

ˌ**brand-ˈnew** *adj* completely new.

brandish /ˈbrændɪʃ/ *v* [Tn] wave (sth) in a triumphant or threatening way; display: *brandish a gun, a knife, an axe, etc* ○ *The demonstrators brandished banners and shouted slogans.*

Brando /ˈbrændəʊ/ Marlon (1924-), American actor who won international fame for his early method performances (METHOD). More recently he has preferred cameo roles.

brandy /ˈbrændɪ/ *n* (**a**) [U] strong alcoholic drink distilled from wine or fermented fruit juice. (**b**) [C] type of brandy: *Cognac and Armagnac are fine brandies.* (**c**) [C] glass of brandy: *Two brandies and soda, please.*

□ ˈ**brandy-snap** *n* crisp rolled gingerbread wafer, often filled with cream.

brash /bræʃ/ *adj* (*derog*) **1** (of a person, his manner, etc) confident in a rude or aggressive way; impudently self-assertive: *His brash answers annoyed the interviewers.* **2** (of colours, clothing, etc) loud; garish; showy: *He was wearing a rather brash tie.* ▷ **brashly** *adv.* **brashness** *n* [U].

brass /brɑːs; *US* bræs/ *n* **1** [U] bright yellow metal made by mixing copper and zinc: [attrib] *brass doorknobs, buttons* ○ *a brass foundry.* **2** (**a**) [U] objects made of brass, eg candlesticks, ornaments, etc: *do/clean/polish the brass.* (**b**) [C] brass ornament worn by a horse. **3 the brass** [Gp] (group of people in an orchestra who play) wind instruments made of brass: *The brass is/are too loud.* ⇨ illus at MUSIC. **4** [C] (*esp Brit*) brass memorial tablet fixed to the floor or wall of a church. **5** [U] (*Brit sl*) money: *He's got plenty of brass.* **6** [U] (*infml*) impudence; cheek: *He had the brass to ask his boss for a 20% pay rise.* **7** (idm) **bold as brass** ⇨ BOLD. **get down to brass** ˈ**tacks** (*infml*) start to consider the basic facts or practical details of sth. **top brass** ⇨ TOP[1]. **where there's muck there's brass** ⇨ MUCK.

▷ **brassy** *adj* (**-ier, -iest**) **1** like brass in colour. **2** like a brass musical instrument in sound; harsh; blaring. **3** (esp of a woman, her manner, etc) vulgarly showy and impudent; loud and flashy. **brassily** *adv.* **brassiness** *n* [U].

□ ˌ**brass** ˈ**band** band playing brass and percussion instruments only.

ˌ**brass** ˈ**hat** (*infml esp Brit*) high-ranking officer in the army; any important person.

brass ˈ**knuckles** (*US*) = KNUCKLEDUSTER.

ˌ**brass** ˈ**plate** plate of brass displayed outside a house or office, giving the name and profession of the occupant.

ˈ**brass-rubbing** *n* **1** [U] making a copy of the design on a brass(4) by rubbing a piece of paper placed over it with chalk or wax. **2** [C] copy made in this way.

brasserie /ˈbræsərɪ/ *n* type of restaurant serving esp beer with food.

brassica /ˈbræsɪkə/ *n* any of the family of vegetables that includes the cabbage, turnip, Brussels sprout, etc.

brassière /ˈbræsɪə(r); *US* brəˈzɪər/ (also **bra** /brɑː/) *n* woman's undergarment worn to support the breasts.

brat /bræt/ *n* (*derog*) child, esp a badly-behaved one.

bravado /brəˈvɑːdəʊ/ *n* [U] (usu unnecessary or false) display of boldness: *Take no notice of his threats — they're sheer bravado.*

brave /breɪv/ *adj* (**-r**, **-st**) **1** (of a person) ready to face and endure danger, pain or suffering; having no fear; courageous: *brave men and women* ○ *Be brave!* ○ *It was brave of her to go into the burning building.* ○ *He was very brave about his operation.* **2** (of an action) requiring or showing courage: *a brave act, deed, speech* ○ *a brave fight against disease.* **3** (idm) **(a) brave new world** (*catchphrase often ironic*) new era resulting from revolutionary changes, reforms, etc in society. Aldous *Huxley described an advanced but inhumane scientific society in a novel with this title.

▷ **brave** *n* **1** [C] N American Indian warrior. **2 the brave** [pl *v*] brave people: *the brave who died in battle.*

brave *v* **1** [Tn] endure or face (sth/sb) without showing fear: *brave dangers* ○ *brave one's critics* ○ *We decided to brave* (ie go out in spite of) *the bad weather.* **2** (phr v) **brave it ˈout** face hostility, suspicion or blame defiantly: *He tried to brave it out when the police questioned him.*

bravely *adv.*

bravery /ˈbreɪvərɪ/ *n* [U] being brave; courage: *a medal for bravery in battle.*

bravo /ˌbrɑːˈvəʊ/ *interj, n* (*pl* **~s**) shout of approval, esp to an actor or a performer: *Bravo! Well played!*

bravura /brəˈvʊərə/ *n* [U] (in a musical performance) brilliant style or technique: [attrib] *a bravura performance.*

brawl /brɔːl/ *n* noisy quarrel or fight: *a drunken brawl in a bar.*

▷ **brawl** *v* [I] take part in a brawl: *gangs of youths brawling in the street.* **brawler** *n.*

brawn /brɔːn/ *n* [U] **1** strong muscles; muscular strength: *a job needing brains* (ie intelligence) *rather than brawn.* **2** (*Brit*) (*US* **head cheese**) meat, esp from a pig's or calf's head, boiled, chopped and pressed in a mould with jelly.

▷ **brawny** *adj* (**-ier**, **-iest**) strong and muscular: *brawny arms.*

bray /breɪ/ *n* **(a)** cry of a donkey. **(b)** sound like this.

▷ **bray** *v* [I] make this cry or sound: *a braying laugh.*

brazen /ˈbreɪzn/ *adj* **1** (*derog*) shameless; insolent: *brazen insolence, rudeness, etc* ○ *a brazen hussy.* **2 (a)** made of brass; like brass. **(b)** having a harsh brassy sound: *the brazen notes of a trumpet.*

▷ **brazen** *v* (phr v) **brazen it ˈout** behave, after doing wrong, as if one has nothing to be ashamed of.

brazenly *adv* shamelessly.

brazier /ˈbreɪzɪə(r)/ *n* open metal framework for holding a charcoal or coal fire.

Brazil /brəˈzɪl/ the largest country in South America; pop approx 144 428 000; official language Portuguese; capital Brasília; unit of currency new cruzado. It contains the vast Amazon river basin with its tropical forests, although large areas of these are being destroyed each year. The Brazilian economy is still largely based on agriculture (esp coffee-growing), but it has great mineral resources and modern industries are being developed. ⇨ map. ▷ **Brazilian** *n, adj.*

□ **Brazil** *n* (also **braˈzil nut**) large wedge-shaped nut from a Brazilian tree.

breach /briːtʃ/ *n* **1** [C, U] breaking or neglect (of a law, an agreement, a duty, etc): *a breach of loyalty,*

Brazil

trust, protocol, etc ○ *a breach of confidence*, ie giving away a secret ○ *sue sb for breach of contract* ○ *a breach of security*, ie failure to protect official secrets. **2** [C] break in usu friendly relations between people or groups: *a breach of diplomatic relations between two countries.* **3** [C] opening, eg one made in a wall by attacking forces or the sea: *The huge waves made a breach in the sea wall.* **4** (idm) **step into the breach** ⇨ STEP[1].

▷ **breach** *v* [Tn] make a gap in (a defensive wall, etc): *Our tanks have breached the enemy defences.*

□ **ˌbreach of ˈpromise** (*law*) (formerly) breaking of a promise to marry sb.

ˌbreach of the ˈpeace (*law*) crime of causing a public disturbance, eg by fighting in the street.

bread

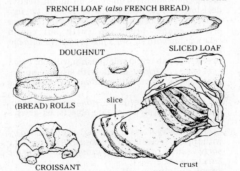

FRENCH LOAF (*also* FRENCH BREAD)

DOUGHNUT

SLICED LOAF

(BREAD) ROLLS

slice

CROISSANT

crust

bread /bred/ *n* [U] **1** food made of flour, water and usu yeast, kneaded then baked. Bread is traditionally considered to be the most basic of all foods, and many expressions given here reflect this. It sometimes suggests food in general, especially with the idea of a simple plain way of eating: *a loaf/slice/piece of bread* ○ *brown/white bread.* ⇨ illus. **2** (*sl*) money. **3** (idm) **the best thing since sliced bread** ⇨ BEST[1]. **ˌbread and ˈcircuses** food and entertainment provided (esp by the State) as a way of making ordinary people feel satisfied with the way they are governed. **ˌbread and ˈwater** plainest possible food: *I had to live on bread and water when I was a student.* **cast one's bread upon the water(s)** ⇨ CAST[1]. **one's daily bread** ⇨ DAILY. **half a loaf is better than none/than no bread** ⇨ HALF. **know which side one's bread is buttered** ⇨ KNOW. **take the bread out of sb's ˈmouth** take away sb's means of earning a living.

▷ **breaded** *adj* (of meat or fish) sprinkled with breadcrumbs for cooking.

□ **bread and butter** /ˌbred n ˈbʌtə(r)/ **1** slices of bread spread with butter. **2** (*infml*) (way of earning) one's living: *Acting is his bread and butter.* ○ *How does he earn his bread and butter?* ○ [attrib] *Jobs, pensions and housing are the bread-and-butter issues of politics*, ie the basic ones. **3** (idm) **a bread-and-ˈbutter letter** letter thanking a host or hostess for hospitality.

ˌbread-and-ˈbutter pudding (*Brit*) traditional pudding made from slices of bread and butter with raisins and sugar baked in an egg custard.

ˈbread-bin *n* container for keeping loaves of bread in.

ˈbreadboard *n* **1** board of wood, etc for cutting bread on. **2** (*infml*) board used for making a model of an electric circuit.

ˈbreadcrumbs *n* [pl] tiny pieces of bread, usu from the inner part of a loaf: *fish covered with breadcrumbs and then fried.*

ˌbread ˈsauce sauce made with milk and thickened with breadcrumbs, traditionally eaten hot with chicken or turkey.

bread-fruit /ˈbredfruːt/ *n* [C, U] round edible tropical fruit with white starchy pulp.

breadline /ˈbredlaɪn/ *n* **1** queue of people waiting for free food given as charity. **2** (idm) **on the breadline** very poor: *We've been living on the breadline for weeks.*

breadth /bretθ/ *n* **1** [U, C] distance or measurement from side to side; width: *a garden, room, river ten metres in breadth* ○ *pieces of material of different breadths.* ⇨ illus at DIMENSION. **2** [U] wide extent (eg of knowledge); range: *Her breadth of experience makes her ideal for the job.* **3** [U] freedom from narrow-mindedness or prejudice: *show breadth of mind, outlook, opinions, etc.* **4** (idm) **by a hair/a hair's breadth** ⇨ HAIR. **the length and breadth of sth** ⇨ LENGTH.

bread-winner /ˈbredwɪnə(r)/ *n* person whose earnings support his or her family: *Mum's the bread-winner in our family.*

break[1] /breɪk/ *v* (*pt* **broke** /brəʊk/, *pp* **broken** /ˈbrəʊkən/) **1 (a)** [I, Ipr] ~ **(in/into sth)** (of a whole object) separate into two or more parts as a result of force or strain (but not by cutting): *The string broke.* ○ *Glass breaks easily.* ○ *The bag broke under the weight of the shopping inside it.* ○ *She dropped the plate and it broke into pieces/in two.* **(b)** [Tn, Tn·pr] ~ **sth (in/into sth)** cause (a whole object) to do this: *break a cup, vase, window, etc* ○ *She fell off a ladder and broke her arm.* ○ *If you pull too hard you will break the rope.* ○ *He broke the bar of chocolate into two (pieces).* **2** [I, Tn] become unusable by being damaged; make (sth) unusable by damaging: *My watch is broken.* **3** [Tn] cut the surface of (the skin) so as to cause bleeding: *The dog bit me but didn't break the skin.* **4** [Tn] not follow or obey (sth); fail to observe (a law, promise, etc): *break the law, the rules, the conditions, etc* ○ *break an agreement, a contract, a promise, one's word, etc* ○ *break an appointment*, ie fail to come to it ○ *He was breaking the speed limit*, ie travelling faster than the law allows. **5** [I, Ip] ~ **(off)** stop doing sth for a while; pause: *Let's break for tea.* **6** [Tn] **(a)** destroy the continuity of (sth); interrupt: *break sb's concentration* ○ *We broke our journey (to London) at Oxford*, ie stopped in Oxford on the way to London. ○ *a broken night's sleep*, ie a night during which the sleeper keeps waking ○ *He failed to break (his opponent's) service*, ie to win a game (at tennis, etc) when his opponent was serving. **(b)** interrupt the flow of an electric current in (a circuit). **(c)** cause (sth) to be incomplete: *break a set of books, china, etc*, eg by giving away a part or parts of it. **(d)** cause (sth) to end: *She broke the silence by coughing.* **(e)** bring (sth) to an end by force: *break a blockade/siege* ○ *The employers have not broken the dockers' strike.* **7** [I] (of the weather) change suddenly after a settled period: *The fine weather/The heatwave broke at last.* **8** [I] show an opening; disperse: *The clouds broke and the sun came out.* **9** [I] **(a)** come into being: *Dawn/The day was breaking*, ie Daylight was beginning. Cf DAYBREAK (DAY). **(b)** begin suddenly and violently: *The storm broke.* **(c)** become known; be revealed: *There was a public outcry when the scandal broke.* **10 (a)** [Tn] weaken or destroy (sth): *break sb's morale, resistance, resolve, spirit, etc* ○ *The Government is determined to break the power of the trade unions.* ○ *The scandal broke him*, ie ruined his reputation and destroyed his self-confidence. **(b)** [I] become weak or be destroyed: *Throughout the ordeal his spirit never broke.* ○ *He broke under questioning* (ie was no longer able to endure it) *and confessed to everything.* **(c)** [Tn] overwhelm (sb) with a strong emotion, eg grief: *The death of his wife broke him completely.* **11** [I] **(a)** (of the voice) change its tone because of emotion: *Her voice broke as she told the dreadful news.* **(b)** (of a boy's voice) become deeper at puberty: *His voice broke when he was thirteen.* **12** [Tn] do better than or surpass (a record): *break the Commonwealth/World/Olympic 100 metres record.* **13** [I] (of the ball in cricket) change direction after hitting the ground; spin. **14** [I] (of two boxers) stop holding each other in a strong grip and continue fighting: *The referee ordered them to break and box on.* Cf CLINCH 3. **15** [I] (in snooker) begin the game by hitting the white ball so that it disturbs the red balls. **16** [I] (of the sea) curl and fall in waves: *the sound of waves breaking on the beach* ○ *The sea was breaking over the wrecked ship.* **17** [Tn] decipher (sth); solve: *break a code.* **18** (For idioms containing **break**, see entries for *ns, adjs*, etc, eg **break even** ⇨ EVEN[1]; **break sb's heart** ⇨ HEART.)

19 (phr v) **break away (from sb/sth)** **(a)** escape suddenly (from captivity): *The prisoner broke away from his guards.* **(b)** leave a political party, state, etc, esp to form a new one: *Several Labour MPs broke away to join the Social Democrats.* ○ *A province has broken away to form a new state.*

break down **(a)** cease to function because of a mechanical, electrical, etc fault: *The telephone system has broken down.* ○ *We* (ie Our car) *broke down on the motorway.* **(b)** fail; collapse: *Negotiations between the two sides have broken down.* ○ *If law and order break down, anarchy will result.* **(c)** (of sb's health) become very bad; collapse: *Her health broke down under the pressure of work.* **(d)** lose control of one's feelings: *He broke down and wept when he heard the news.* **break (sth) down** (esp of money spent) be divided or divide into parts by analysis: *Expenditure on the project breaks down as follows: wages £10m, plant £4m, raw materials £5m.* **break sth down (a)** make sth collapse by striking it hard: *Firemen had to break the door down to reach the people trapped inside.* **(b)** cause sth to collapse; overcome, conquer or destroy sth: *break down resistance, opposition, etc* ○ *break down sb's reserve, shyness, etc* ○ *How can we break down the barriers of fear and hostility which divide the two communities?* **(c)** change the chemical composition of sth: *Sugar and starch are broken down in the stomach.*

break sth from sth remove sth from sth larger by breaking: *He broke a piece of bread from the loaf.*

break in enter a building by force: *Burglars had broken in while we were away on holiday.* **break sb/sth in** train and discipline sb/sth: *break in new recruits, a young horse.* **break in (on sth)** interrupt or disturb (sth): *Please don't break in on our conversation.*

break into sth **(a)** enter sth by force: *His house was broken into* (eg by burglars) *last week.* **(b)** suddenly begin (to laugh, sing, cheer, etc): *As the President's car arrived, the crowd broke into loud applause.* **(c)** suddenly change (from a slower to a faster pace): *break into a trot/canter/gallop* ○ *The man broke into a run when he saw the police.* **(d)** (of an activity) use up (time that would normally be spent doing sth else): *All this extra work I'm doing is breaking into my leisure time.* **(e)** use (a banknote or coin of high value) to buy sth costing less: *I can't pay the 50p I owe you without breaking into a £5 note.* **(f)** open and use (sth kept for an emergency): *break into emergency supplies of food.* **(g)** start having some success in (a field of activity); establish oneself in sth: *Will this be the year we break into the Japanese market?* ○ *She'd broken into journalism even before leaving college.*

break off stop speaking: *He broke off in the middle of a sentence.* **break (sth) off** (cause sth to) become separated from sth as a result of force or strain: *The door handle has broken off.* ○ *She broke off a piece of chocolate and gave it to me.* **break sth off** end sth suddenly; discontinue sth: *break off diplomatic relations (with a country)* ○ *They've broken off their engagement/broken it off.*

break out (of violent events) start suddenly: *Fire broke out during the night.* ○ *Rioting broke out between rival groups of fans.* ○ *War broke out in 1939.* Cf OUTBREAK. **break out (of sth)** escape from a place by using force: *Several prisoners broke out of the jail.* Cf BREAK-OUT. **break out in sth** **(a)** suddenly become covered in sth: *His face broke out in a rash.* ○ *He broke out in a cold sweat*, eg through fear. **(b)** suddenly begin to show strong feelings: *She broke out in a rage.*

break through make new and important discoveries: *Scientists say they are beginning to break through in the fight against cancer.* **break through (sth)** **(a)** make a way through (sth) using force; penetrate (sth): *Demonstrators broke through the police cordon.* **(b)** (of the sun or moon) appear from behind (clouds): *The sun broke through at last in the afternoon.* **break through sth** overcome sth: *break through sb's reserve, shyness, etc.*

break up **(a)** (of members of a group) go away in different directions; disperse: *The meeting broke up at eleven o'clock.* **(b)** (*Brit*) (of a school, its staff or its pupils) begin the holidays when school closes at the end of term: *When do you break up for Christmas?* **(c)** become very weak; collapse: *He was breaking up under the strain.* **(d)** (esp of a period of fine weather) end: *The weather shows signs of breaking up.* **break (sth) up (a)** (cause sth to) separate into smaller pieces by cutting, striking, etc: *The ship broke up on the rocks.* ○ *The ship was broken up for scrap metal.* **(b)** (cause sth to) come to an end: *Their marriage is breaking up.* ○ *They decided to break up the partnership.* **break sth up** **(a)** disperse or scatter sth using force: *Police were called in to break up the meeting.* **(b)** divide sth by means of analysis, an administrative decision, etc: *Sentences can be broken up into clauses.* ○ *The Government has broken up the large private estates.* **break up (with sb)** end a relationship with sb: *She's just broken up with her boy-friend.*

break with sb end a relationship with sb: *break with one's girl-friend.* **break with sth** give up sth; abandon sth: *break with tradition, old habits, the past, etc.*

▷ **breakable** /ˈbreɪkəbl/ *adj* easily broken. **breakables** *n* [pl] breakable objects, eg glasses and cups.

□ ˈ**breakaway** *n* loss of members from a group by withdrawal; secession: *a breakaway from the Tory party* ○ [attrib] *a breakaway group on the left of the Labour party.*

ˈ**break-dancing** *n* [U] energetic and acrobatic style of dancing, often competitive or as a display, esp popular with young Black Americans.

ˈ**break-in** *n* forcible entry into a building: *Police are investigating a* ˈ*break-in at the bank.*

ˌ**breaking and** ˈ**entering** crime of entering a house, shop, etc by using force, eg by breaking down a door or breaking a window; housebreaking.

ˈ**breaking-point** *n* **(a)** point at which the strain on an object, eg a mechanical part, makes it break: *tested to breaking-point.* **(b)** (*fig*) stage at which psychological pressure becomes unbearable: *Their marriage was at/had reached breaking-point.*

ˈ**break-out** *n* escape from prison, esp one involving the use of force: *a mass break-out of prisoners.*

ˈ**breakthrough** *n* **1** act of breaking through an enemy's defences. **2** important development or discovery, esp in scientific knowledge: *a major breakthrough in cancer research* ○ *a breakthrough in negotiations.*

ˈ**breakup** *n* end (of a relationship or partnership): *The breakup of their marriage shocked their friends.*

break[2] /breɪk/ *n* **1** ~ **(in sth)** **(a)** opening made by breaking; broken place: *a break in a fence, wall, water-pipe.* **(b)** gap; space: *a break in the clouds*, ie where blue sky is visible ○ *Wait for a break in the traffic before crossing the road.* **2 (a)** interval, esp between periods of work; pause: *morning break*, eg between lessons at school ○ *lunch-break*, eg in an office, a school or a factory ○ *have/take an hour's break for lunch* ○ *work for five hours without a break* ○ *a break in a conversation.* **(b)** short holiday: *a weekend break in the country.* **3** ~ **(in sth)**; ~ **(with sb/sth)** **(a)** change or interruption in sth continuous: *a break in a child's education* ○ *a break in the weather*, ie a change from bad to good weather ○ *a break with tradition*, ie a significant change from what is accepted in art, behaviour, morals, etc. **(b)** discontinuation or end of a relationship: *a break in diplomatic relations* ○ *She's been depressed since the break with her boy-friend.* **4** (*infml*) piece of luck, esp one that leads to further success: *a big/lucky break* ○ *a bad break*, ie a piece of bad luck ○ *give sb a break*, ie a chance to show his ability. **5** (in cricket) change in direction of a bowled ball as it bounces: *an off/a leg break*, ie a ball that spins to the right/left on bouncing. **6** (also **break of service**, **service break**) (in tennis) instance of winning a game when one's opponent is serving: *Smith has had two breaks already in this set.* ○ [attrib] *break point*, eg when the score is 30-40. **7** (in billiards or snooker) series of successful shots by one player; score made by such a series: *a break of 52.* **8** (idm) **break of day** dawn: *at break of day.* **make a break (for it)** escape, esp from prison.

NOTE ON USAGE: **Break** applies especially to a rest during the working day or at school: *a lunch, coffee break* ○ *the mid-morning break* ○ *10 minutes' break.* It also covers the meanings of several other words. A **pause** is usually short and often applied to speech: *a pause for breath* ○ *a pause/break in the conversation.* **Recess** is the scheduled holiday of Parliament, and in US English it is also the break between school classes. An **interval** in British English is the break between the parts of a play, etc: *We had a quick drink in the interval.* This is also called an **intermission**, especially in US English. An **interlude** may be an interval or a short event during a longer activity, often contrasting with it: *Her time in Paris was a happy interlude in a difficult career.* A **rest** does not indicate a definite length of time, but suggests a necessary period of relaxation after an activity: *You look tired. You need a good rest.*

breakage /ˈbreɪkɪdʒ/ *n* **1** [C, U] act of or damage caused by breaking: *a parcel carefully packed to prevent breakage.* **2** [C] broken thing. **3** [C usu *pl*] broken objects: *The hotel allows £300 a year for breakages*, ie for the cost of replacing broken dishes, etc.

breakdown /ˈbreɪkdaʊn/ *n* **1** mechanical failure: *Our car/We had a breakdown on the motorway.* **2** collapse or failure: *a breakdown of negotiations on disarmament.* **3** weakening or collapse of sb's (esp mental) health: *The strain of his job led to the complete breakdown of his health.* ○ *She suffered a nervous breakdown.* **4** statistical analysis: *a breakdown of expenditure.*

breaker /ˈbreɪkə(r)/ *n* **1** large wave that breaks into foam as it moves towards the shore. **2** (esp in compounds) person or thing that breaks: *a ship-breaker* ○ *a law-breaker* ○ *a record-breaker.*

breakfast /ˈbrekfəst/ *n* [C, U] **1** first meal of the day: *a light/big/hearty breakfast* ○ *have bacon and eggs for breakfast* ○ *English or continental breakfast* ○ *They were having breakfast when I arrived.* ○ *She doesn't eat much breakfast.* **2** (idm) ˌ**bed and** ˈ**breakfast** ⇨ BED[1]. **a dog's breakfast**/

dinner ⇨ DOG[1]. eat sb for breakfast ⇨ EAT.
▷ **breakfast** *v* [I, Ipr] ~ (**on sth**) eat breakfast: *We breakfasted on toast and coffee.*
□ ˌ**breakfast** ˈ**television** television programmes shown early in the morning.

breakneck /ˈbreɪknek/ *adj* [attrib] dangerously fast: *drive, ride, travel, etc at breakneck speed.*

breakwater /ˈbreɪkwɔːtə(r)/ *n* wall built out into the sea to protect a coast or harbour from the force of the waves.

bream /briːm/ *n* (*pl* unchanged) **1** type of freshwater fish of the carp family. **2** (also ˈ**sea-bream**) type of salt-water fish similar to this.

breast /brest/ *n* **1** [C] either of the two parts of a woman's body that produce milk: *a baby at the breast* ○ *cancer of the breast* ○ *The breasts swell during pregnancy.* **2** [C] (**a**) (*rhet*) upper front part of the human body; chest: *clasp/hold sb to one's breast.* (**b**) part of a garment covering this: *a soldier with medals pinned to the breast of his coat.* **3** [C, U] part of an animal corresponding to the human breast, eaten as food: *chicken breasts* ○ *breast of lamb.* **4** (*dated*) source of feelings; heart: *a troubled breast.* **5** (idm) **beat one's breast** ⇨ BEAT[1]. **make a clean breast of sth** ⇨ CLEAN[1].
▷ **breast** *v* [Tn] **1** (**a**) touch (sth) with the breast(2a): *The runner breasted the tape*, ie to win a race. (**b**) face and move forward against (sth): *breasting the waves.* **2** reach the top of (sth): *breast a hill/rise.*
□ ˈ**breastbone** (also **sternum**) *n* thin flat vertical bone in the chest between the ribs. ⇨ illus at SKELETON.
ˈ**breast-feed** *v* (*pt, pp* ˈ**breast-fed**) [Tn] feed (a baby) with milk from the breast: *Were her children breast-fed or bottle-fed?*
ˌ**breast-**ˈ**high** *adj, adv* high as the breast: *The wheat was/stood breast-high.*
ˈ**breastplate** *n* piece of armour covering the breast.
ˌ**breast** ˈ**pocket** pocket on the breast of a jacket.
ˈ**breast-stroke** *n* [sing] swimming stroke, with chest downwards, in which the arms are extended in front of the head and then swept back, while the legs move in a corresponding way: *do (the) breast-stroke.*
ˈ**breastwork** *n* low wall of earth, etc put up as a temporary defence.

breath /breθ/ *n* **1** (**a**) [U] (also *infml* **puff**) air taken into and sent out of the lungs: *You can see people's breath on a cold day.* ○ *His breath smelt of garlic.* (**b**) [C] single act of taking air into the lungs: *take a deep breath*, ie fill the lungs with air. **2** ~ **of sth** [sing] slight movement of air; gently blowing: *There wasn't a breath of air/wind.* **3** ~ **of sth** [sing] (*fig*) slight suggestion or rumour of sth; hint of sth: *a breath of scandal* ○ *the first breath of spring.* **4** (idm) **a breath of fresh air** (**a**) opportunity to breathe clean air, esp out of doors. (**b**) person or thing that is a welcome and refreshing change: *Her smile is a breath of fresh air in this gloomy office.* **the breath of** ˈ**life** (**to/for sb**) thing that stimulates or inspires (sb); thing that is necessary (to sb): *Religion is the breath of life to/for her.* **catch one's breath** ⇨ CATCH[1]. **draw breath** ⇨ DRAW[2]. **draw one's first/last breath** ⇨ DRAW[2]. **get one's** ˈ**breath** (**again/back**) return to one's normal rate of breathing: *It took us a few minutes to get our breath back after the race.* **hold one's** ˈ**breath** stop breathing for a short time (eg during a medical examination or from fear or excitement): *How long can you hold your breath for?* ○ *The audience held its/their breath as the acrobat walked along the tightrope.* **in the same breath** ⇨ SAME[1]. **one's last/dying** ˈ**breath** last moment of one's life. **lose one's breath** ⇨ LOSE. (**be**) **out of/short of** ˈ**breath** breathing very quickly (eg after running fast); panting hard: *His heart condition makes him short of breath.* **save one's breath** ⇨ SAVE[1]. **say sth, speak, etc under one's** ˈ**breath** say sth, etc in a whisper. **take sb's** ˈ**breath away** startle or surprise sb. **waste one's breath** ⇨ WASTE[2]. **with bated breath** ⇨ BATED.
▷ **breathy** *adj* (**-ier, -iest**) (of the voice) with a noticeable sound of breathing.
□ ˈ**breath test** test of a driver's breath to measure how much alcohol he has drunk.

breathalyse /ˈbreθəlaɪz/ *v* [Tn] test (sb) with a breathalyser.
▷ **breathalyser** *n* (*Brit*) (*US* **breathalyzer, drunkometer**) device used by the police for measuring the amount of alcohol in a driver's breath.

breathe /briːð/ *v* **1** [I] take air into the lungs and send it out again: *People breathe more slowly when they are asleep.* ○ *She's still breathing*, ie still alive. ○ *He was breathing hard/heavily after racing for the train.* **2** [Ip, Tn, Tn·p] ~ **in/out**; ~ **sth** (**in/out**) take (air, etc) into or send (it) out of the lungs: *The doctor told me to breathe in and then breathe out (again) slowly.* ○ *It's good to breathe (in) fresh country air instead of city smoke.* **3** [Tn] say (sth) softly; whisper: *breathe loving words in sb's ear* ○ *breathe a threat.* **4** [Tn] show that one is full of (a feeling); exude: *The team breathed confidence before the match.* **5** (idm) (**be able to**) **breathe** (**easily/freely**) **again** feel calm or relieved after a period of tension, fear or exertion; relax: *Now my debts are paid I can breathe again.* **breathe down sb's** ˈ**neck** (*infml*) be close behind sb (eg in a race); watch sb (too) closely: *I can't concentrate with you breathing down my neck.* **breathe one's** ˈ**last** (*fml euph*) die. (**not**) **breathe a** ˈ**word** (**of/about sth**) (**to sb**) (not) tell sb sth (esp a secret); (not) reveal sth to sb: *Promise me you won't breathe a word of this to anyone.* **6** (phr v) **breathe sth into sb/sth** fill (a person or group) with (a feeling): *The new manager has breathed fresh life into* (ie revitalized) *the company.*
▷ **breathing** *n* [U] action of breathing: *heavy breathing* ○ [attrib] *breathing apparatus.*
ˈ**breathing-space** *n* [C, U] time to rest between periods of effort; pause: *The summer holidays gave us a welcome breathing-space.*

breather /ˈbriːðə(r)/ *n* (*infml*) **1** short pause for rest: *take/have a breather.* **2** short period to refresh oneself in the open air: *I must go out for a quick breather.*

breathless /ˈbreθlɪs/ *adj* **1** (**a**) breathing quickly or with difficulty; panting: *breathless after running up the stairs* ○ *Heavy smoking makes him breathless.* (**b**) causing one to be breathless; strenuous: *breathless haste/hurry/pace/speed.* **2** (**a**) [pred] holding one's breath (because of fear, excitement, etc): *breathless with terror, wonder, amazement, etc.* (**b**) [attrib] tense; making one hold one's breath: *a breathless hush in the concert hall.* **3** with no air or wind: *a breathless calm.* ▷ **breathlessly** *adv.* **breathlessness** *n* [U].

breathtaking /ˈbreθteɪkɪŋ/ *adj* very exciting; spectacular: *a breathtaking view, mountain range, waterfall* ○ *Her beauty was breathtaking.* ▷ **breathtakingly** *adv.*

Brecht /brekt/ Bertolt (1898-1956), German dramatist and poet. He wanted his plays to express his Marxist beliefs to a popular audience, and he often used songs to achieve this. His best-known play is *The Threepenny Opera*, with music by Kurt *Weill.

bred *pt, pp of* BREED.

breech /briːtʃ/ *n* back part of a gun barrel where the bullet or shell is placed: *a breech-loading gun.* Cf MUZZLE 2.
□ ˈ**breech birth** birth in which the baby's buttocks or feet appear first.
ˈ**breech-block** *n* steel block that closes the breech of a gun.

breeches /ˈbrɪtʃɪz/ *n* [pl] **1** short trousers fastened just below the knee, worn esp for horse-riding or as part of ceremonial dress: *a pair of* (ˈ*knee-*)*breeches* ○ ˈ*riding breeches.* **2** (*joc*) trousers. ⇨ illus at DRESS.
□ **breeches-buoy** *n* /ˈbriːtʃɪz bɔɪ/ apparatus for rescuing people at sea, consisting of canvas breeches attached to a lifebuoy that runs along a rope between a ship and the shore or between two ships.

breed /briːd/ *v* (*pt, pp* **bred** /bred/) **1** [I] (of animals) produce young: *How often do lions breed?* **2** [Tn] keep (animals) for the purpose of producing young, esp by selecting the best parents for mating: *breed cattle, dogs, horses, etc.* **3** [esp passive: Tn, Tn·pr, Cn·n/a, Cn·t] ~ **sb** (**as sth**) bring up; train; educate: *a well-bred child* ○ *Spartan youths were bred as warriors.* **4** [Tn] lead to (sth); cause: *Dirt breeds disease.* ○ *Unemployment breeds social unrest.* **5** (idm) **born and bred** ⇨ BORN. **breed like** ˈ**rabbits** (*often derog*) have many children or young: *If you don't get those cats seen to they'll breed like rabbits.* **familiarity breeds contempt** ⇨ FAMILIARITY.
▷ **breed** *n* **1** family or variety of animals, etc having a similar appearance and usu developed by deliberate selection: *a breed of cattle, sheep, etc* ○ *What breed is your dog?* **2** type; kind: *a new breed of politician.*
breeder *n* person who breeds animals: *a dog, horse, cattle, etc breeder* ○ *a breeder of racehorses.* ˈ**breeder reactor** type of nuclear reactor that produces more radioactive material than is put into it.
breeding *n* [U] **1** producing of young by animals: [attrib] *the breeding season.* **2** keeping of animals for breeding: *the breeding of horses.* **3** (good manners resulting from) training or family background: *a man of good breeding.* ˈ**breeding-ground** *n* **1** place where wild animals go to produce their young: *Some birds fly south to find good breeding-grounds.* **2** (*fig*) place where sth (usu harmful) can develop: *Damp, dirty houses are a breeding-ground for disease.*

breeze /briːz/ *n* **1** [C, U] light wind: *a sea breeze* ○ *A gentle breeze was blowing.* ○ *There's not much breeze today.* **2** [sing] (*infml esp US*) thing that is easy to do or enjoy: *Some people think learning to drive is a breeze.* **3** [C] (*Brit infml*) noisy quarrel. **4** (idm) **shoot the breeze** ⇨ SHOOT[1].
▷ **breeze** *v* (phr v) **breeze along, in, out, etc** (*infml*) move in a cheerful carefree way (in the specified direction): *Look who's just breezed in!* ○ *He breezes through life, never worrying about anything.*
breezy *adj* (**-ier, -iest**) **1** (**a**) slightly windy: *a breezy day* ○ *breezy weather.* (**b**) exposed to breezes: *a breezy corner, beach, hillside.* **2** (of a person, his manner, etc) cheerful; light-hearted: *You're very bright and breezy today!* **breezily** /ˈbriːzɪlɪ/ *adv.* **breeziness** /ˈbriːzɪnɪs/ *n* [U].
□ ˈ**breezeway** *n* (*US*) covered, often enclosed, passageway between two buildings.

breeze-block /ˈbriːz blɒk/ (*Brit*) *n* lightweight building block made of cinders, sand and cement.

Bren /bren/ *n* (also ˈ**Bren gun**) lightweight machine-gun that can fire quickly.

brent /brent/ *n* (*pl* unchanged or ~**s**) (also ˌ**brent-**ˈ**goose**) (*pl* **-geese**) smallest type of wild goose.

brethren /ˈbreðrən/ *n* [pl] (*arch* except when used of or by certain religious groups) brothers.

Breton /ˈbretn/ *n* **1** native or inhabitant of Brittany. **2** Celtic language spoken in Brittany. ▷ **Breton** *adj.*

breve /briːv/ *n* **1** (*music*) long note equal to two semibreves. **2** mark (˘) placed over a vowel to show that it is short or unstressed.

breviary /ˈbriːvɪərɪ; *US* -ɪerɪ/ *n* book of prayers to be said daily by Roman Catholic priests.

brevity /ˈbrevətɪ/ *n* [U] **1** shortness or briefness (of time): *the brevity of Mozart's life.* **2** conciseness (in speaking or writing): *He is famous for the brevity of his speeches.*

brew /bruː/ *v* **1** [Tn] make (beer) by mixing, boiling and fermenting malt, hops, etc and water: *He brews his own beer at home.* **2** (**a**) [Tn, Tn·p] ~ **sth** (**up**) prepare (a hot drink, esp tea) by mixing leaves, etc with boiling water: *We brewed (up) a nice pot of tea.* (**b**) [I] (esp of tea) become brewed: *There's (a pot of) tea brewing in the kitchen.* **3** (**a**) [Tn, Tn·p] ~ **sth** (**up**) prepare or plan (sth unpleasant): *Those boys are brewing mischief.* ○ *brew (up) a wicked plot.* (**b**) [I] (of sth unpleasant) grow in force; look likely to happen; develop: *A storm is brewing.* ○ *Trouble is brewing in the trade unions.* ○ *In 1938 war was brewing in Europe.* **4** (phr v) **brew up** (*infml*) prepare a drink of tea:

campers brewing up outside their tents.
▷ **brew** *n* **1** (**a**) (amount of) drink made by brewing (esp tea or beer): *home brew*, ie beer made at home ○ *What's your favourite brew (of beer)?* ○ *We'll need more than one brew* (eg of tea) *for twenty people.* (**b**) quality or nature of what is brewed: *I like a good strong brew.* **2** (*fig*) any mixture of circumstances, ideas, events, etc: *The film is a rich brew of adventure, sex and comedy.*
brewer *n* person whose job is brewing beer.
brewery /ˈbrʊərɪ/ *n* building in which beer is brewed. Cf DISTILLERY (DISTILLER).
□ ˈ**brew-up** *n* (*Brit infml*) act of making tea: *We always have a brew-up at 11 o'clock.*

briar = BRIER.

bribe /braɪb/ *n* thing given, offered or promised to sb to influence or persuade him to do sth (often dishonest) for the giver: *take/accept bribes* ○ *The policeman was offered/given a bribe of £500 to keep his mouth shut.*
▷ **bribe** *v* **1** (**a**) [Tn, Tn·pr, Tnt] ~ **sb** (**with sth**) give a bribe (of sth) to sb; try to persuade sb to do sth with a bribe: *attempt to bribe a jury with offers of money* ○ *One of the witnesses was bribed to give false evidence.* (**b**) [I] give bribes; practise bribery. **2** (idm) **bribe one's way into/out of sth, past sb, etc** get somewhere by using bribery: *He bribed his way past the guard and escaped.* **3** (phr v) **bribe sb into doing sth** make sb do sth with a bribe.
bribable /ˈbraɪbəbl/ *adj* able to be bribed. **bribery** /ˈbraɪbərɪ/ *n* [U] giving or taking of bribes: *accuse/convict sb of bribery.*

bric-à-brac /ˈbrɪkəbræk/ *n* [U] ornaments, trinkets and small items of furniture of little value: *She collects bric-à-brac.*

brick /brɪk/ *n* **1** [C, U] (usu rectangular block of) baked or dried clay used for building: *a pile of bricks* ○ *houses built/made of red brick* ○ [attrib] *a brick wall.* ⇨ illus at HOME. **2** [C] child's (usu wooden) toy building block. **3** [C] thing shaped like a brick, esp a block of ice-cream. **4** [C] (*Brit infml*) generous or loyal person: *She's been a real brick, looking after me while I've been ill.* **5** (idm) **bang, etc one's head against a brick wall** ⇨ HEAD[1]. **drop a brick/clanger** ⇨ DROP[2]. **like a cat on hot bricks** ⇨ CAT[1]. **like a ton of bricks** ⇨ TON. **make bricks without** ˈ**straw** try to work without adequate material, money, information, etc.
▷ **brick** *v* (phr v) **brick sth in/up** fill in, block or seal (an opening) with bricks: *brick up a window/doorway/fireplace to prevent draughts.*
□ ˈ**brickbat** *n* **1** piece of brick, esp one thrown as a weapon. **2** (*fig infml*) rude or derogatory remark; insult: *The Minister's speech was greeted with brickbats.*
ˈ**bricklayer** [C], ˈ**bricklaying** [U] *ns* (workman trained or skilled in) building with bricks.
ˈ**brickwork** *n* [U] **1** (part of a) structure built of bricks: *The brickwork in this house is in need of repair.* **2** building with bricks: *Are you any good at brickwork?*
ˈ**brickyard** *n* place where bricks are made.

bridal /ˈbraɪdl/ *adj* [attrib] of a bride or wedding: *the bridal party*, ie the bride and her attendants and close friends ○ *a bridal suite*, ie a suite of rooms in a hotel for a newly married couple.

bride /braɪd/ *n* woman on or just before her wedding-day; newly married woman. ⇨ article at WEDDING.

bridegroom /ˈbraɪdgrʊm, *also* -gru:m/ (also **groom**) *n* man on or just before his wedding-day; newly married man: *Let's drink (a toast) to the bride and bridegroom!*

bridesmaid /ˈbraɪdzmeɪd/ *n* young woman or girl (usu unmarried and often one of several) attending a bride at her wedding. Cf BEST MAN (BEST[1]). ⇨ article at WEDDING.

bridge[1] /brɪdʒ/ *n* **1** structure of wood, iron, concrete, etc providing a way across a river, road, railway, etc: *a bridge across the stream* ○ *a railway bridge*, ie one for a railway across a river, etc. ⇨ illus. **2** (*fig*) thing that provides a connection or contact between two or more things: *Cultural exchanges are a way of building bridges between nations.* **3** raised platform across the deck of a ship, from which it is controlled and navigated by the captain and officers. **4** (**a**) bony upper part of the nose. (**b**) part of a pair of glasses that rests on the nose. ⇨ illus at GLASS. **5** movable piece of wood, etc over which the strings of a violin, etc are stretched. ⇨ illus at MUSIC. **6** device for keeping false teeth in place, fastened to natural teeth on each side. **7** (idm) **burn one's boats/bridges** ⇨ BURN[2]. **cross one's bridges when one comes to them** ⇨ CROSS[2]. **a lot of/much water has flowed, etc under the bridge** ⇨ WATER[1]. **water under the bridge** ⇨ WATER[1].
▷ **bridge** *v* **1** [Tn] build or form a bridge over (sth): *bridge a river, canal, ravine, etc.* **2** (idm) **bridge a/the** ˈ**gap** (**a**) fill an awkward or empty space: *bridge a gap in the conversation* ○ *A snack in the afternoon bridges the gap between lunch and supper.* (**b**) reduce the distance (between widely contrasting groups): *How can we bridge the gap between rich and poor?*
□ ˈ**bridgehead** *n* area captured and fortified in enemy territory, esp on the enemy's side of a river. Cf BEACH-HEAD (BEACH).
ˈ**bridging loan** loan given (esp by a bank) for the period between two transactions, eg between buying a new house and selling the old one.

bridges

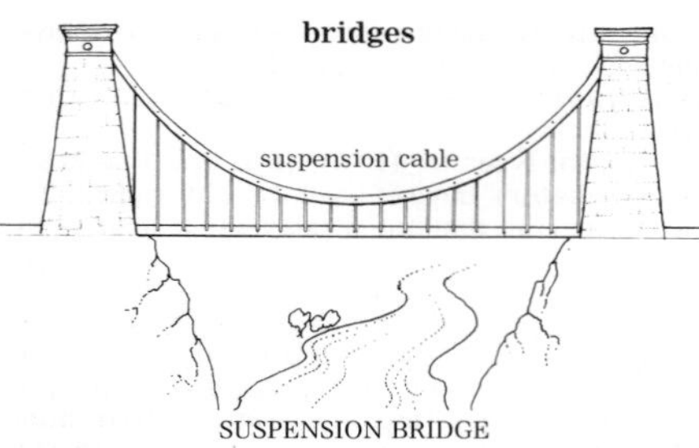

SUSPENSION BRIDGE

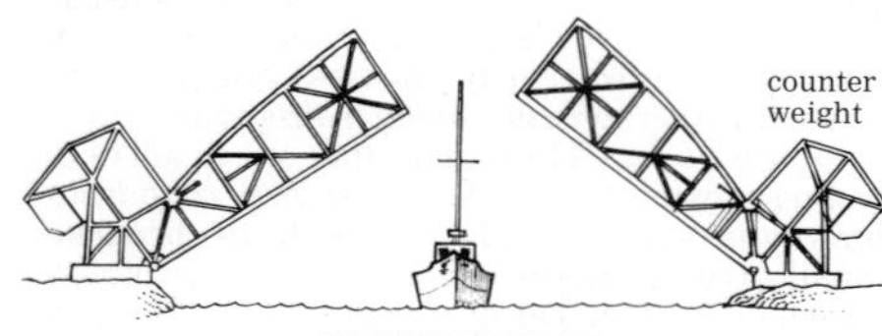

BASCULE BRIDGE

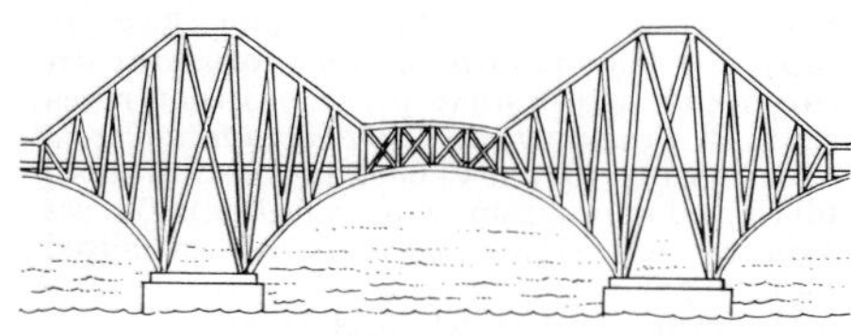
CANTILEVER BRIDGE

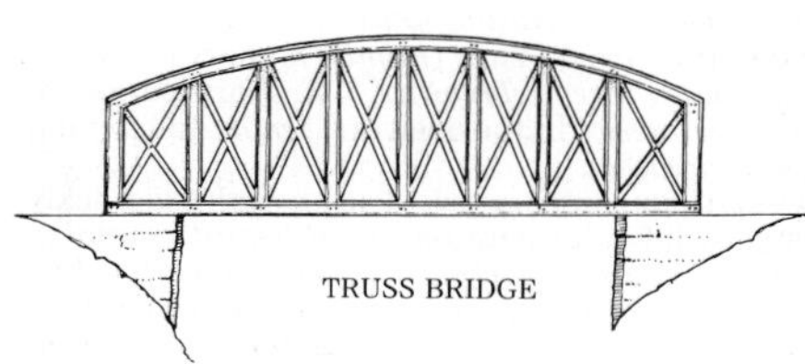
TRUSS BRIDGE

bridge[2] /brɪdʒ/ *n* [U] card-game for four players developed from whist, in which one player's cards are exposed on the table and played by his partner: *make up a four at bridge.*

Bridges /ˈbrɪdʒɪz/ Robert (1844-1930), English poet. His work is now less popular than in his lifetime, when he was for a time Poet Laureate. He was also responsible for publishing the poetry of his friend Gerald Manley *Hopkins.

bridle /ˈbraɪdl/ *n* part of a horse's harness that goes on its head, including the metal bit for the mouth, the straps and the reins.
▷ **bridle** *v* **1** [Tn] put a bridle on (a horse). **2** [Tn] (*fig*) keep (feelings, etc) under control; restrain: *bridle one's emotions/passions/temper/rage* ○ *bridle one's tongue*, ie be careful what one says. Cf UNBRIDLED. **3** [I, Ipr] ~ (**at sth**) show anger, resentment, etc (because of sth), esp by drawing one's head up or back: *He bridled (with anger) at her offensive remarks.*
□ ˈ**bridle-path** (also ˈ**bridle-way**) *n* path suitable for horse-riding, but not for cars, etc.

Brie /bri:/ *n* [U] type of soft French cheese.

brief[1] /bri:f/ *adj* (**-er, -est**) **1** (**a**) lasting only a short time; short: *a brief conversation, discussion, meeting, visit, delay* ○ *Mozart's life was brief.* (**b**) (of speech or writing) using few words; concise: *a brief account, report, description, etc of the accident* ○ *Please be brief*, ie say what you want to say quickly. **2** (of clothes) short; scanty: *a brief bikini.* **3** (idm) **in brief** in a few words: *In brief, your work is bad.*
▷ **briefly** *adv* **1** for a short time: *He paused briefly before continuing.* **2** in a few words: *Briefly, you're fired!*

brief[2] /bri:f/ *n* **1** (**a**) summary of the facts of a legal case prepared for a barrister. (**b**) case given to a barrister: *Will you accept this brief?* **2** instructions and information relating to a particular situation, job, or task: *stick to one's brief*, ie only do what one is required to do ○ *It's not part of my brief to train new employees.* **3** (idm) **hold no brief for (sb/sth)** not wish to support or be in favour of (sb/sth): *I hold no brief for those who say that violence can be justified.*
▷ **brief** *v* **1** [Tn, Tnt] give a brief[2](1a) to (sb): *The company has briefed a top lawyer to defend it.* **2** [Tn, Tn·pr] ~ **sb** (**on sth**) give sb detailed information or instructions in advance (about sth): *The Prime Minister was fully briefed before the meeting.* ○ *The Air Commodore briefed the bomber crew on their dangerous mission.* Cf DEBRIEF. **briefing** *n* [C, U] detailed instructions and information given at a meeting (esp before a military operation): *receive (a) thorough briefing* ○ [attrib] *a briefing session.*

briefcase /ˈbri:fkeɪs/ *n* flat leather or plastic case for carrying documents. ⇨ illus at LUGGAGE.

briefs /bri:fs/ *n* [pl] short close-fitting pants or knickers: *a new pair of briefs.*

brier (also **briar**) /ˈbraɪə(r)/ *n* **1** thorny bush; wild rose. **2** bush with a hard woody root used for making tobacco-pipes. **3** tobacco-pipe made from this.

brig /brɪg/ *n* **1** sailing-ship with two masts and square sails. **2** (*US*) prison, esp one on a warship for members of the Navy.

Brig *abbr* Brigadier: *Brig (John) West.*

brigade /brɪˈgeɪd/ *n* **1** army unit, usu of three battalions, forming part of a division. **2** group of people, esp one organized for a particular purpose: *the fire brigade* ○ (*joc*) *He's joined the bowler-hatted brigade working in the City.*
▷ **brigadier** /ˌbrɪgəˈdɪə(r)/ *n* officer in the British Army between the ranks of colonel and major general, commanding a brigade; staff officer having similar status. ⇨ App 4.

brigand /ˈbrɪgənd/ *n* (*dated*) member of a band of robbers, esp one attacking travellers in forests and mountains.

brigantine /ˈbrɪgənti:n/ *n* sailing-ship like a brig, but with fewer sails.

Bright /braɪt/ John (1811-89), English politician and reformer. With Richard *Cobden he was one of the leading campaigners for the repeal of the *Corn Laws. He was a minister several times in *Gladstone's governments.

bright /braɪt/ *adj* (**-er, -est**) **1** giving out or reflecting much light; shining: *bright sunshine* ○ *bright eyes* ○ *Tomorrow's weather will be cloudy with bright periods.* **2** (of a colour) intense; bold; vivid: *a bright blue dress* ○ *The leaves on the trees are bright green in spring.* **3** promising; hopeful: *a child with a bright future* ○ *Prospects for the coming year look bright.* **4** cheerful and lively: *She* has a bright personality. **5** clever; intelligent: *a bright idea/suggestion* ○ *He is the brightest (child) in the class.* **6** (idm) **(be/get up) bright and 'early** very early in the morning: *You're (up) bright and early today!* **(as) bright as a 'button** very clever; quick-witted. **ˌbright-ˌeyed and ˌbushy-'tailed** (*infml*) eager and alert: *She arrived, bright-eyed and bushy-tailed, for her first day at the office.* **the bright 'lights** (excitement of) city life: *He grew up in the country, but then found he preferred the bright lights.* **a bright 'spark** (*infml often ironic*) lively and intelligent person (esp one who is young and promising): *Some bright spark has left the tap running all night.* **look on the 'bright side** find sth to be cheerful or hopeful about in spite of difficulties.

▷ **bright** *adv* brightly: *The stars were shining bright.*

brighten /'braɪtn/ *v* [I, Ip, Tn, Tn·p] ~ **(sth) (up)** (cause sb/sth to) become brighter, more cheerful or more hopeful: *The sky/weather is brightening.* ○ *He brightened (up) when he heard the good news.* ○ *Flowers brighten (up) a room.*

brightly *adv*: *a brightly lit room* ○ *brightly coloured curtains.*

brightness *n* [U].

Bright's disease /'braɪts dɪzi:z/ acute inflammation of the kidney.

brill[1] /brɪl/ *n* flat-fish like a turbot.

brill[2] /brɪl/ *adj* [esp pred] (*Brit sl*) brilliant; very good: *The food was brill!* ▷ **brill** *interj*: *Brill! It's spaghetti tonight!*

brilliant /'brɪlɪənt/ *adj* **1** very bright; sparkling: *brilliant sunshine* ○ *a brilliant diamond* ○ *a sky of brilliant blue.* **2 (a)** very intelligent; highly skilled or talented: *a brilliant scientist, musician, footballer, etc* ○ *She has a brilliant mind.* **(b)** causing admiration; outstanding; exceptional: *a brilliant achievement, exploit, career, performance, etc* ○ *The play was a brilliant success.* ▷ **brilliance** /'brɪlɪəns/, **brilliancy** /'brɪlɪənsɪ/ *ns* [U]. **brilliantly** *adv.*

brilliantine /'brɪlɪənti:n/ *n* [U] oily substance used to make men's hair shiny and smooth.

brim /brɪm/ *n* **1** top edge of a cup, bowl, glass, etc: *full to the brim.* **2** projecting edge of a hat, that gives shade and protection against rain. ⇨ illus at HAT.

▷ **brim** *v* (**-mm-**) **1** [I, Ipr] ~ **(with sth)** be or become full to the brim: *a mug brimming with coffee* ○ *eyes brimming with tears* ○ (*fig*) *The team were brimming with confidence before the match.* **2** (phr v) **brim over (with sth)** overflow: *a glass brimming over with water* ○ (*fig*) *brim over with excitement, happiness, joy, etc.*

brimful (also **brim-full**) /ˌbrɪm'fʊl/ *adj* [pred] ~ **(of/with sth)** full to the brim (with sth): *The basin was brim-full (of water).* ○ (*fig*) *Our new manager is ˌbrimful of 'energy.*

-brimmed (forming compound *adjs*) (of a hat) having the type of brim specified: *a broad-/wide-/floppy-brimmed hat.*

brimstone /'brɪmstəʊn/ *n* [U] (*arch*) **1** sulphur. **2** (idm) **fire and brimstone** ⇨ FIRE[1].

brindled /'brɪndld/ *adj* (esp of cows, dogs and cats) brown with streaks of another colour.

brine /braɪn/ *n* [U] **1** very salty water used esp for pickling: *herrings pickled in brine.* **2** sea water.

▷ **briny** *adj* salty. **the briny** *n* [sing] (*dated joc*) the sea: *take a dip in the briny.*

bring /brɪŋ/ *v* (*pt, pp* **brought** /brɔ:t/) **1** [Tn, Tn·pr, Tn·p, Dn·n, Dn·pr] ~ **sb/sth (with one)**; ~ **sth (for sb)** come carrying sth or accompanying sb: *He always brings a bottle of wine (with him) when he comes to dinner.* ○ *She brought her boy-friend to the party.* ○ *The secretary brought him into the room/brought him in.* ○ (*fig*) *The team's new manager brings ten years' experience to the job.* ○ *Take this empty box away and bring me a full one.* ○ *Bring me a glass of water/Bring a glass of water for me.* **2 (a)** [Tn] result in (sth); cause; produce: *These pills bring relief from pain.* ○ *Spring brings warm weather and flowers.* ○ *The revolution brought many changes.* ○ *The sad news brought tears to his eyes,* ie made him cry. **(b)** [Tn, Dn·n] produce (sth) as profit or income: *His writing brings him £10000 a year.* ○ *Her great wealth brought her no happiness.* **3** [Tn·pr] ~ **sb/sth to sth** cause sb/sth to be in a certain state or position: *His incompetence has brought the company to the brink of bankruptcy.* **4** [Cn·g] cause (sb) to move in the way specified: *The full back brought him crashing to the ground,* ie caused him to fall heavily. ○ *Her cries brought the neighbours running,* ie caused them to come running to her. **5** [Tn, Tn·pr] ~ **sth (against sb)** put forward (charges, etc) in a lawcourt: *bring a charge/a legal action/an accusation against sb.* **6** [Cn·t] force or make (oneself) do sth: *She could not bring herself to tell him the tragic news.* **7** (used with *to* or *into* in many expressions to show that sb/sth is caused to reach the state or condition indicated by the *n*, eg *Her intervention brought the meeting to a close,* ie ended the meeting; *The mild weather will bring the trees into blossom,* ie cause the trees to blossom; for similar expressions, see entries for *ns*, eg *bring sth to an end* ⇨ END[1].) **8** (For idioms containing **bring**, see entries for *ns, adjs*, etc, eg **bring sb to book** ⇨ BOOK[1]; **bring sth to light** ⇨ LIGHT[1].)

9 (phr v) **bring sth about (a)** (*nautical*) cause (a sailing-boat) to change direction: *The helmsman brought us* (ie our boat) *about.* **(b)** cause sth to happen: *bring about reforms, a war, sb's ruin* ○ *The Liberals wish to bring about changes in the electoral system.* ⇨ Usage at CAUSE.

bring sb/sth back return sb/sth: *Please bring back the book tomorrow.* ○ *He brought me back* (ie gave me a lift home) *in his car.* **bring sth back (a)** restore or reintroduce sth: *MPs voted against bringing back the death penalty.* **(b)** call sth to mind: *The old photograph brought back many memories.* **bring sb back sth** return with sth for sb: *If you're going to the shops, could you bring me back some cigarettes?* **bring sb back to sth** restore sb to sth: *A week by the sea brought her back to health.*

bring sb/sth before sb present sb/sth for discussion, decision or judgement: *The matter will be brought before the committee.* ○ *He was brought before the court and found guilty.*

bring sb down (a) (in football) cause sb to fall over by fouling him: *He was brought down in the penalty area.* **(b)** (in Rugby) tackle sb. **(c)** cause the defeat of sb; overthrow sb: *The scandal may bring down the government.* **bring sth down (a)** cause (an aircraft) to fall out of the sky: *bring down an enemy fighter.* **(b)** land (an aircraft): *The pilot brought his crippled plane down in a field.* **(c)** cause (an animal or a bird) to fall over or fall out of the sky by killing or wounding it: *He aimed, fired and brought down the antelope.* **(d)** lower or reduce sth: *bring down prices, the rate of inflation, the cost of living, etc.* **(e)** (*mathematics*) transfer (a digit) from one part of a sum to another.

bring sth forth (*fml*) produce sth: *Trees bring forth fruit.*

bring sth forward (a) move sth to an earlier time; advance sth: *The meeting has been brought forward from 10 May to 3 May.* **(b)** (in bookkeeping) transfer (the total of a column of figures) to the next column: *A credit balance of £50 was brought forward from his September account.* **(c)** propose or present sth for discussion; raise sth: *Please bring the matter forward at the next meeting.*

bring sb in (a) (of the police) bring sb to a police station to be questioned or charged; arrest sb: *Two suspicious characters were brought in.* **(b)** introduce sb as an adviser, a helper, etc: *Experts were brought in to advise the Government.* **bring sth in (a)** pick and gather (crops, fruit, etc): *bring in a good harvest.* **(b)** introduce (legislation): *bring in a bill to improve road safety.* **(c)** pronounce (a verdict on an accused person): *The jury brought in a verdict of guilty.* **bring (sb) in sth** produce (an amount) as profit or income (for sb): *His freelance work brings (him) in £5000 a year.* ○ *He does odd jobs that bring him in about £30 a week.* **bring sb in (on sth)** allow sb to participate in sth: *Local residents were angry at not being brought in on* (ie not being consulted about) *the new housing scheme.*

bring sb off rescue sb from a ship: *The passengers and crew were brought off by the Dover lifeboat.* **bring sth off** (*infml*) manage to do (sth difficult) successfully: *The goalkeeper brought off a superb save.* ○ *It was a difficult task, but we brought it off.*

bring sb on help (a learner, etc) to develop or improve: *The coach is bringing on some promising youngsters in the reserve team.* **bring sth on (a)** lead to, result in or cause sth: *He was out in the rain all day and this brought on a bad cold.* ○ *nervous tension brought on by overwork.* **(b)** cause (crops, fruit, etc) to grow rapidly: *The hot weather is bringing the wheat on nicely.* **bring sth on oneself/sb** cause sth (usu unpleasant) to happen to oneself/sb else: *You have brought shame and disgrace on yourself and your family.*

bring sb out (a) cause sb to strike: *The shop-stewards brought out the miners.* **(b)** cause sb to lose his shyness: *She's nice — but needs a lot of bringing out.* **bring sth out (a)** cause sth to appear or open: *The sunshine will bring out the blossom.* **(b)** produce sth; publish sth: *The company is bringing out a new sports car.* ○ *bring out sb's latest novel* ○ *New personal computers are brought out almost daily.* **(c)** show sth clearly; reveal sth: *The enlargement brings out the details in the photograph.* **(d)** make sth clear or explicit: *bring out the meaning of a poem.* **(e)** cause (a quality) to be seen in sb; elicit sth: *A crisis brings out the best in her.* **bring sb out in sth** cause sb to be covered in sth: *The heat brought him out in a rash.*

bring sb over (to...) cause sb to come to a place from overseas: *Next summer he hopes to bring his family over from the States.* **bring sb over (to sth)** make sb change his way of thinking, loyalties, etc: *bring sb over to one's cause.*

bring sb round cause sb to regain consciousness after fainting: *Three women fainted in the heat but were quickly brought round with brandy.* **bring sth round** (*nautical*) make (a boat) face in the opposite direction. **bring sb round/around (to...)** cause sb to come to sb's house: *Do bring your wife round one evening; we'd love to meet her.* **bring sb round (to sth)** convert sb, esp to one's point of view: *He wasn't keen on the plan, but we managed to bring him round.* **bring sth round to sth** direct (a conversation) to a particular subject: *He brought the discussion round to football.*

bring sb through help sb to recover; save sb: *He was very ill, but the doctors brought him through.*

bring sb to = BRING SB ROUND. **bring sth to** (*nautical*) make (a boat) stop.

bring A and B together help (two people or groups) to end a quarrel; reconcile: *The loss of their son brought the parents together.*

bring sb under bring sb under control; subdue sb: *The rebels were quickly brought under.* **bring sth under sth** include sth within a category: *The points to be discussed can be brought under three main headings.*

bring sb up (a) (esp passive) raise, rear or educate sb: *She brought up five children.* ○ *Her parents died when she was a baby and she was brought up by her aunt.* ○ *a well-/badly-brought up child* ○ *He was brought up to* (ie taught as a child to) *respect authority.* Cf UPBRINGING. **(b)** (*law*) cause sb to appear for trial: *He was brought up on a charge of drunken driving.* **(c)** cause sb to stop moving or speaking suddenly: *His remark brought me up short/sharp/with a jerk.* **bring sb/sth up** move or call (soldiers, guns, etc) to the front line: *We need to bring up more tanks.* **bring sth up (a)** vomit sth: *bring up one's lunch.* **(b)** call attention to sth; raise sth: *These are matters that you can bring up in committee.* **bring sb up against sth** make sb face or confront sth: *Working in the slums brought her up against the realities of poverty.* **bring sb/sth up to sth** bring sb/sth to (an acceptable level or standard): *His work in maths needs to be brought up to the standard of the others.*

□ **ˌbring-and-'buy sale** (*Brit*) sale, often for charity, at which people bring items for sale and buy those brought by others.

brink /brɪŋk/ *n* **1** [C usu *sing*] **(a)** edge at the top of a steep high place, eg a cliff: *the brink of a precipice.* **(b)** edge of a stretch of (usu deep) water: *He stood shivering on the brink, waiting to dive in.* **2** [sing] **the ~ of sth** (*fig*) point or state very close to sth unknown, dangerous or exciting: *on the brink of death, war, disaster, success* ○ *Scientists are on the brink of (making) a breakthrough in the treatment of cancer.* ○ *His incompetence has brought us to the brink of ruin.*

brinkmanship /ˈbrɪŋkmənʃɪp/ *n* [U] art or practice of pursuing a dangerous policy to the limits of safety, eg to the brink of war.

briny ➪ BRINE.

brio /ˈbriːəʊ/ *n* [U] liveliness and enthusiasm; vivacity: *He danced with more brio than skill.*

brioche /ˈbriːɒʃ; *US* ˈbriːəʊʃ/ *n* small round sweetened bread roll.

briquette (also **briquet**) /brɪˈket/ *n* small block of compressed coal-dust used as fuel.

brisk /brɪsk/ *adj* (**-er**, **-est**) **1** quick; active; energetic: *a brisk walk, walker* ○ *at a brisk pace* ○ *a brisk and efficient manner* ○ *Business is brisk today.* **2** giving a healthy feeling; refreshing: *a brisk breeze.* ▷ **briskly** *adv.* **briskness** *n* [U].

brisket /ˈbrɪskɪt/ *n* [U] meat (usu beef) cut from the breast of an animal.

brisling /ˈbrɪzlɪŋ/ small herring or sprat.

bristle /ˈbrɪsl/ *n* **1** short stiff hair: *a face covered with bristles.* **2** one of the short stiff hairs in a brush: *My toothbrush is losing its bristles.*

▷ **bristle** *v* **1** [I, Ip] ~ **(up)** (of an animal's fur) stand up stiffly in fear or anger: *The dog's fur bristled as it sensed danger.* **2** [I, Ipr] ~ **(with sth)** show anger, indignation, etc: *bristle with defiance, pride, etc* ○ *She bristled (with rage) at his rude remarks.* **3** (phr v) **bristle with sth** be thickly covered with sth; have a large number of sth (usu unpleasant): *trenches bristling with machine-guns* ○ *The problem bristles with difficulties.*

bristly /ˈbrɪslɪ/ *adj* like or full of bristles; prickly; rough: *a bristly chin* ○ *She finds his beard too bristly.*

Bristol /ˈbrɪstl/ city in SW England. It is a port and an important industrial and commercial centre.

▷ **bristols** *n* [pl] (*Brit sl*) woman's breasts.

□ **the ˌBristol ˈChannel** inlet of the Atlantic separating the southern coast of Wales from England. The Avon and the Severn rivers flow into it.

ˌBristol ˈCream (*propr*) type of sweet sherry.

Brit /brɪt/ *n* (*esp joc or derog*) British person.

Britain /ˈbrɪtn/ *n* = GREAT BRITAIN (GREAT). ➪ Usage at GREAT.

Britannia, as seen on the 50 pence coin

Britannia /brɪˈtænjə/ **(a)** Britain represented (eg on certain coins, banknotes, etc) as a woman with a shield, a helmet and a three-pointed spear. More recently she has been shown also holding an olive-branch. ➪ illus. ➪ article at NATIONAL. **(b)** (*rhet*) Britain.

□ **Briˌtannia ˈmetal** silvery alloy of tin with antimony and copper.

Britannic /brɪˈtænɪk/ *adj* **Her/His Britannic Majesty** (*fml*) Queen/King of Britain.

Briticism /ˈbrɪtɪsɪzəm/ *n* English word or expression that is only used in Britain (and not in the US, etc): *Briticisms are labelled 'Brit' in this dictionary.*

British /ˈbrɪtɪʃ/ *adj* **1** of the United Kingdom (of Great Britain and Northern Ireland) or its inhabitants: *a British passport* ○ *the British Government* ○ *He was born in France but his parents are British.* **2** (idm) **the best of British** ➪ BEST[3].

▷ **the British** *n* [pl *v*] British people.

Britisher *n* (*US*) native or inhabitant of Britain, esp of England.

□ **the ˌBritish ˈCouncil** British organization set up in 1934 to develop a better understanding of Britain, British culture and the English language in other countries. Its activities include arranging overseas visits by British writers and student exchanges.

ˌBritish ˈEnglish English as spoken in the British Isles.

the ˌBritish ˈIsles Britain and Ireland with the islands near their coasts. ➪ illus at App 1. ➪ Usage at GREAT.

the British Legion ➪ THE ROYAL BRITISH LEGION (ROYAL).

the ˌBritish ˈLibrary the national library of Britain. It was originally the library of the British Museum, but there are now several departments which, from 1993, will be housed in a new building at St Pancras, London. It receives a copy of every book published in the UK. ➪ article at LIBRARY.

the ˌBritish Muˈseum the national museum of Britain, founded in 1753. The main building is in Bloomsbury in north London, but there are several other specialist departments. It has one of the world's finest collections of art and archaeological treasures. ➪ article at MUSEUM.

Briton /ˈbrɪtn/ *n* native or inhabitant of Britain. ➪ Usage at GREAT.

Brittany /ˈbrɪtənɪ/ region of NW France. It has its own language (Breton) and a rich Celtic cultural heritage.

Britten /ˈbrɪtn/ Benjamin (1913-76), English composer, pianist and conductor. He produced some of the best and most popular English classical music of the 20th century. His greatest achievements were in the field of vocal music, including *Peter Grimes*, *Noyes Fludde* (written for children to perform) and *Death in Venice*. Many of his pieces were written to be sung by his close friend, the tenor Peter Pears, including the song cycle *Les Illuminations*. ➪ article at MUSIC.

brittle /ˈbrɪtl/ *adj* **1** **(a)** hard but easily broken; fragile: *as brittle as thin glass.* **(b)** (*fig*) easily damaged; insecure: *He has a brittle temper*, ie loses his temper easily. ○ *Constant stress has made our nerves brittle.* **2** (of a sound) unpleasantly hard and sharp: *a brittle laugh* ○ *The orchestra was brittle in tone.* **3** (of a person) lacking in warmth; hard: *a cold, brittle woman.* ▷ **brittleness** *n* [U].

broach /brəʊtʃ/ *v* [Tn] **1** make a hole in (a barrel) to draw off the liquid inside; open (a bottle, etc) to use the contents: *Let's broach another bottle of wine.* **2** (*fig*) begin a discussion of (a topic): *He broached the subject of a loan with his bank manager.*

broad[1] /brɔːd/ *adj* (**-er**, **-est**) **1** large in size from one side to the other; wide: *a broad street, avenue, river, canal, etc* ○ *broad shoulders* ○ *He is tall, broad and muscular.* Cf NARROW 1, THIN 1. **2** (after a phrase expressing measurement) from side to side; in breadth: *a river twenty metres broad.* **3** (of land or sea) covering a wide area; extensive: *a broad expanse of water* ○ *the broad plains of the American West* ○ (*fig*) *There is broad support for the Government's policies.* **4** clear; obvious; unmistakable: *a broad grin/smile* ○ *The Minister gave a broad hint that she intends to raise taxes.* **5** [attrib] general; not detailed: *the broad outline of a plan, proposal, etc* ○ *The negotiators reached broad agreement on the main issues.* ○ *She's a feminist, in the broadest sense of the word.* **6** (of ideas, opinions, etc) tolerant; liberal: *a man of broad views.* **7** (of speech) having many of the sounds typical of a particular region: *a broad Yorkshire accent.* **8** indecent; coarse: *broad humour.* **9** (idm) **(in) broad ˈdaylight** (in) the full light of day: *The robbery occurred in broad daylight, in a crowded street.* **broad in the ˈbeam** (*infml*) (of a person) rather fat round the hips. **it's as broad as it's ˈlong** (*Brit infml*) it makes no real difference which of two alternatives one chooses.

▷ **broaden** /ˈbrɔːdn/ *v* [I, Ip, Tn] ~ **(out)** (cause sth to) become broader: *He* (ie His body) *broadened out in his twenties.* ○ *The road broadens (out) after this bend.* ○ *You should broaden your experience by travelling more.*

broadly *adv* **1** in a broad[1](4) way: *smile/grin broadly.* **2** generally: *Broadly speaking, I agree with you.*

broadness *n* [U] = BREADTH.

the Broads *n* [pl] group of shallow lakes in E Anglia, popular for boating holidays: *the Norfolk Broads.* ➪ map at UNITED KINGDOM. ➪ article at RIVER.

□ **broad ˈbean** **(a)** type of bean with large flat edible seeds. **(b)** one of these seeds.

Broad ˈChurch group within the Church of England favouring a liberal interpretation of doctrine.

ˈbroad jump (*US*) = LONG JUMP (LONG).

ˈbroad-leaved *adj* (of trees) having broad leaves (as distinct from the needles of coniferous trees): *the destruction of broad-leaved woodlands.*

broad-ˈminded *adj* willing to listen to opinions different from one's own; not easily shocked; tolerant. **broad-ˈmindedness** *n* [U].

ˈbroadsword *n* (formerly) large sword with a broad blade, used for cutting rather than stabbing.

broad[2] /brɔːd/ *n* (*US sl*) woman.

broadcast /ˈbrɔːdkɑːst; *US* ˈbrɔːdkæst/ *v* (*pt, pp* **broadcast**) **1** **(a)** [Tn] send out (programmes) by radio or television: *broadcast the news, a concert, a football match.* **(b)** [I] send out radio or television programmes: *The BBC broadcasts all over the world.* **2** [I] speak or appear on radio or television: *He broadcasts on current affairs.* **3** [Tn] make (sth) widely known: *broadcast one's views.* **4** [I, Tn] sow (seed) by scattering.

▷ **broadcast** *n* radio or television programme: *a party political broadcast*, eg before an election ○ *a broadcast of a football match.*

broadcaster *n* person who broadcasts: *a well-known broadcaster on political/religious affairs.*

broadcasting *n* [U] sending out programmes on radio and television: *work in broadcasting* ○ [attrib] *the British Broadcasting Corporation*, ie the BBC.

broadcloth /ˈbrɔːdklɒθ; *US* -klɔːθ/ *n* [U] fine cloth of cotton, wool or silk.

broadloom /ˈbrɔːdluːm/ *n, adj* (carpet) woven in broad widths.

Broadmoor /ˈbrɔːdmɔː(r)/ hospital in Berkshire, England, for the treatment of patients suffering from mental illness, esp mentally ill people who have committed serious crimes and cannot be sent to ordinary prisons.

broadsheet /ˈbrɔːdʃiːt/ *n* **1** large sheet of paper printed on one side only with information or an advertisement, etc. **2** newspaper printed on a large size of paper. Cf TABLOID.

broadside /ˈbrɔːdsaɪd/ *n* **1** **(a)** firing at the same time of all the guns on one side of a warship: *fire a broadside.* **(b)** (*fig*) fierce attack in words, either written or spoken: *The Prime Minister delivered a broadside at her critics.* **2** side of a ship above the water. **3** (idm) **broadside ˈon (to sth)** (of a ship) with one side facing (sth); sideways on: *The ship hit the harbour wall broadside on.*

Broadway /ˈbrɔːdweɪ/ longest street in the world, in Manhattan, New York, famous for its many theatres. Although still important as a theatrical centre, Broadway's true period of greatness was in the 1920s and 1930s, the era of the spectacular Broadway musical. Today, many plays are performed in other parts of New York and people talk of 'off-Broadway' plays. Experimental drama is sometimes described as 'off-off-Broadway'. ➪ article at PERFORMING ARTS.

brocade /brəˈkeɪd/ *n* [C, U] fabric woven with a raised pattern, esp of gold or silver threads: [attrib] *brocade curtains.*

▷ **brocade** *v* [Tn] decorate (cloth) with raised

patterns: *a dress brocaded with floral designs.*

broccoli /ˈbrɒkəlɪ/ *n* [U] type of cauliflower with many small greenish flower-heads, eaten as a vegetable. ⇨ illus at CABBAGE.

brochure /ˈbrəʊʃə(r); *US* brəʊˈʃʊər/ *n* booklet or pamphlet containing information about sth or advertising sth: *a travel/holiday brochure.*

broderie anglaise /ˌbrəʊdrɪ ɒːŋˈgleɪz/ *n* [U] open embroidery on white linen, etc; cloth embroidered in this way.

brogue[1] /brəʊg/ *n* (usu *pl*) strong outdoor shoe with thick soles and a pattern in the leather: *a pair of brogues.*

brogue[2] /brəʊg/ *n* (usu *sing*) strong regional accent, esp the Irish way of speaking English: *a soft Irish brogue.* Cf ACCENT 3, DIALECT.

broil /brɔɪl/ *v* **1** (*esp US*) (**a**) [Tn] cook (meat) on a fire or gridiron; grill: *broil a chicken.* (**b**) [I] be cooked in this way. **2** [I, Tn] (cause sb to) be or become very hot: *sit broiling in the sun* ○ *a broiling day.*

▷ **broiler** *n* young chicken reared for broiling or roasting: [attrib] *a broiler house,* ie a building in which such chickens are kept and reared. Cf ROASTER (ROAST).

broke[1] *pt* of BREAK[1].

broke[2] /brəʊk/ *adj* **1** [pred] (*infml*) having no money; penniless; bankrupt: *Could you lend me £10? I'm completely broke!* **2** (idm) **flat/stony broke** (*infml*) completely broke. **go for broke** (*infml esp US*) risk everything in one determined attempt at sth.

broken[1] *pp* of BREAK[1].

broken[2] /ˈbrəʊkən/ *adj* **1** [usu attrib] not continuous; disturbed or interrupted: *broken sleep* ○ *broken sunshine.* **2** [attrib] (of a foreign language) spoken imperfectly; not fluent: *speak in broken English.* **3** (of land) having an uneven surface; rough: *an area of broken, rocky ground.* **4** [attrib] (of a person) weakened and exhausted by illness or misfortune: *He was a broken man after the failure of his business.* **5** (idm) **a broken ˈreed** person who has become unreliable or ineffective.

□ **ˌbroken ˈchord** (*music*) chord in which the notes are played one after the other and not all together.

ˌbroken-ˈdown *adj* in a very bad condition; worn out or sick: *a ˌbroken-down old ˈcar, ˈman, ˈhorse.*

ˌbroken-ˈhearted *adj* overwhelmed by grief: *He was broken-hearted when his wife died.*

ˌbroken ˈhome family in which the parents have divorced or separated: *He comes from a broken home.*

broker /ˈbrəʊkə(r)/ *n* **1** person who buys and sells things (eg shares in a business) for others; middleman: *insurance broker.* **2** = STOCKBROKER (STOCK[1]). **3** official appointed to sell the goods of sb who cannot pay his debts.

▷ **brokerage** /ˈbrəʊkərɪdʒ/ *n* [U] broker's fee or commission.

brolly /ˈbrɒlɪ/ *n* (*infml esp Brit*) umbrella.

bromide /ˈbrəʊmaɪd/ *n* **1** [C, U] chemical compound of bromine, used in medicine to calm the nerves. **2** [C] (*infml*) old, stale idea or statement.

bromine /ˈbrəʊmiːn/ *n* [U] (*symb* **Br**) chemical element, a non-metallic liquid, compounds of which are used in medicine and photography. ⇨ App 11.

bronchial /ˈbrɒŋkɪəl/ *adj* [usu attrib] of or affecting the two main branches of the windpipe (**bronchial tubes** or **bronchi**) leading to the lungs: *bronchial asthma* ○ *bronchial pneumonia.* ⇨ illus at RESPIRE.

bronchitis /brɒŋˈkaɪtɪs/ *n* [U] inflammation of the mucous membrane inside the bronchial tubes.

▷ **bronchitic** /brɒŋˈkɪtɪk/ *adj* suffering from or prone to bronchitis.

bronco /ˈbrɒŋkəʊ/ *n* (*pl* ~**s**) wild or half-tamed horse of the western USA.

□ **ˈbronco-buster** *n* (*esp US*) cowboy who tames broncos.

portrait of the Brontë sisters by their brother Branwell

Brontë /ˈbrɒnteɪ/ Charlotte (1816-55), Emily (1818-48) and Anne (1820-49), English novelists. The Brontë sisters lived nearly all their lives in a small village in Yorkshire (N England). Their work was originally published under the pen-names of Currer, Ellis and Acton Bell. Charlotte was the only sister to achieve fame in her lifetime, with *Jane Eyre.* Emily's masterpiece *Wuthering Heights* did not appear until after her death. All three sisters died young. ⇨ illus.

brontosaurus /ˌbrɒntəˈsɔːrəs/ *n* (*pl* ~**es**) large plant-eating dinosaur.

Bronx cheer /ˌbrɒŋks ˈtʃɪə(r)/ (*US infml*) = RASPBERRY 2.

bronze /brɒnz/ *n* **1** [U] alloy of copper and tin: *a statue (cast) in bronze.* **2** [U] colour of bronze; reddish-brown: *tanned a deep shade of bronze.* **3** [C] (**a**) work of art, eg a statue, made of bronze: *a fine collection of bronzes.* (**b**) = BRONZE MEDAL.

▷ **bronze** *v* [Tn esp passive] make (sth) bronze in colour: *a face bronzed by the sun.*

bronze *adj* made of or having the colour of bronze: *a bronze vase, statue, bowl, axe, etc* ○ *the bronze tints of autumn leaves.*

□ **the ˈBronze Age** period when men used tools and weapons made of bronze (between the Stone Age and the Iron Age).

bronze ˈmedal medal awarded as third prize in a competition or race.

brooch /brəʊtʃ/ *n* ornament with a hinged pin and clasp, worn on women's clothes.

brood /bruːd/ *n* [C, Gp] **1** all the young birds or other animals produced at one hatching or birth: *a hen and her brood (of chicks).* **2** (*joc*) family of children: *There's Mrs O'Brien taking her brood for a walk.*

▷ **brood** *v* **1** [I] (of a bird) sit on eggs to hatch them. **2** [I, Ipr] ~ (**on/over sth**) think (about sth) for a long time in a troubled or resentful way: *When he's depressed he sits brooding for hours.* ○ *It doesn't help to brood on your mistakes.*

broody *adj* (**-ier, -iest**) **1** (**a**) (of a hen) wanting to brood. (**b**) (*fig*) (of a woman) badly wanting to have a baby. **2** (*fig*) moody; depressed: *Why are you so broody today?* **broodily** *adv.* **broodiness** *n* [U].

□ **ˈbrood-mare** *n* mare kept for breeding.

brook[1] /brʊk/ *n* small stream.

brook[2] /brʊk/ *v* [Tn, Tg, Tsg] (*fml*) (usu with a negative) tolerate (sth); allow: *a strict teacher who brooks no nonsense from her pupils* ○ *I will not brook anyone interfering with my affairs.*

Brooke /brʊk/ Rupert (1887-1915), English poet. He fought in and died during the First World War, and he became famous for his poems on war. Many readers prefer his earlier, lighter verse.

Brooks /brʊks/ Louise (1900-85), American film actor. Her role as Lulu in *Pabst's film *Pandora's Box* showed her to be a brilliantly natural actress. She was famous for her beauty and her boyish bobbed hair, but her career was hindered by clashes with the Hollywood studio moguls.

broom[1] /bruːm/ *n* [U] shrub with yellow or white flowers growing esp on sandy ground.

broom[2] /bruːm, also brʊm/ *n* **1** brush with a long handle for sweeping floors. **2** (idm) **a new broom** ⇨ NEW.

□ **ˈbroomstick** *n* handle of a broom (on which witches were said to ride through the air).

Bros *abbr* (*commerce*) Brothers: *Hanley Bros Ltd, Architects & Surveyors.*

broth /brɒθ; *US* brɔːθ/ *n* [U] **1** water in which meat, fish or vegetables have been boiled; stock. **2** soup made from this: *Scotch broth.* **3** (idm) **too many cooks spoil the broth** ⇨ COOK *n.*

brothel /ˈbrɒθl/ *n* house where men pay to have sex with prostitutes.

brother /ˈbrʌðə(r)/ *n* **1** man or boy having the same parents as another person: *my elder/younger brother* ○ *Does she have any brothers or sisters?* ○ *Have you invited the Smith brothers to the party?* ○ *He was like a brother to me,* ie very kind. ⇨ App 8. **2** person united with others by belonging to the same group, society, profession, etc, esp a trade union: *We are all brothers in the same fight against injustice.* ○ [attrib] *greatly respected by his brother doctors, officers, etc.* **3** (*pl* **brethren** /ˈbreðrən/) (**a**) (title of a) member of a religious order, esp a monk: *Brother Luke will say grace.* (**b**) member of certain evangelical Christian sects: *The Brethren hold a prayer meeting every Thursday.* **4** (idm) **brothers in ˈarms** soldiers serving together, esp in wartime.

▷ **brother** *interj* (*esp US*) (used to express irritation or surprise): *Oh, brother!*

brotherhood /-hʊd/ *n* **1** [U] (**a**) relationship of brothers: *the ties of brotherhood.* (**b**) comradeship; friendship between brothers: *live in peace and brotherhood.* **2** [C, Gp] members of an association formed for a particular purpose, eg a religious society or socialist organization.

brotherly *adj* of or like a brother: *brotherly love/affection/feelings.* **brotherliness** *n* [U].

□ **brother-in-law** /ˈbrʌðər ɪn lɔː/ (*pl* **-s-in-law** /ˈbrʌðəz ɪn lɔː/) **1** brother of one's husband or wife. **2** husband of one's sister. **3** husband of the sister of one's wife or husband. ⇨ App 8.

brougham /ˈbruːəm/ *n* (formerly) four-wheeled closed carriage drawn by one horse.

brought *pt, pp* of BRING.

brouhaha /ˈbruːhɑːhɑː; *US* bruːˈhɑːhɑː/ *n* [U] (*infml*) noisy excitement or commotion.

brow /braʊ/ *n* **1** [usu *pl*] = EYEBROW. **2** = FOREHEAD: *mop one's brow.* **3** slope leading to the top (of a hill); edge (of a cliff): *Our car stalled on the brow of a steep hill.* **4** (idm) **knit one's ˈbrow(s)** ⇨ KNIT.

browbeat /ˈbraʊbiːt/ *v* (*pt* **browbeat,** *pp* **browbeaten** /ˈbraʊbiːtn/) [Tn, Tn·pr] ~ **sb (into doing sth)** frighten sb with stern looks and words; bully; intimidate: *The judge browbeat the witness.* ○ *I won't be browbeaten into accepting your proposals.*

▷ **browbeaten** *adj* frightened through constant bullying: *a poor, browbeaten little clerk.*

Brown[1] /braʊn/ John (1800-59), American campaigner against slavery. He was executed after attempting to give weapons to Black slaves in Virginia, but his efforts inspired his followers. His name became famous through the marching-song 'John Brown's Body'.

Brown[2] /braʊn/ Lancelot (1716-83), English landscape architect. He is known as 'Capability Brown' because he is said to have told people that their gardens had 'great capabilities'. He designed gardens to look natural rather than formally laid out. Those at *Blenheim and Chatsworth are typical examples. ⇨ article at ARCHITECTURE.

brown /braʊn/ *adj* (**-er, -est**) **1** having the colour of toasted bread, or coffee mixed with milk: *brown eyes* ○ *dark brown shoes* ○ *leaves turning brown in the autumn.* **2** having skin of this colour;

sun-tanned: *He's very brown after his summer holiday.* **3** (idm) **(as) brown as a ˈberry** having skin tanned brown by the sun or the weather. **in a brown ˈstudy** in deep thought; in a reverie.

▷ **brown** *n* **1** [C, U] brown colour: *leaves of various shades of brown.* **2** [U] brown clothes: *Brown doesn't suit you.*

brown *v* [I, Tn] **1** become or make brown: *Heat the butter until it browns.* ○ *a face browned by the sun.* **2** (idm) **browned ˈoff** (*infml esp Brit*) bored; fed up; disheartened: *He's browned off with his job.*

browning *n* [U] substance for colouring gravy.

brownish, browny *adjs* tending towards brown; fairly brown.

□ **ˌbrown ˈbread** bread made with wholemeal flour.

ˌbrown ˈpaper strong coarse paper for wrapping parcels, etc.

ˈbrownstone *n* [U] reddish-brown sandstone used for building.

ˌbrown ˈsugar sugar that is only partly refined.

Browne /braʊn/ Sir Thomas (1605-82), English writer. He worked as a doctor, but wrote witty and learned books on a great range of subjects, often expressing his own humane religious faith.

Brownian motion /ˌbraʊnɪən ˈməʊʃn/ (also **Brownian movement**) random movement of tiny solid particles suspended in a fluid, caused by the molecules of the fluid continually hitting them.

brownie /ˈbraʊnɪ/ *n* **1** small good-natured fairy. **2 Brownie** (also **Brownie Guide**) member of the junior branch of the Guides (who wear brown uniforms). ⇨ article at YOUTH. **3** (*esp US*) small rich cake made with chocolate and nuts.

□ **ˈBrownie point** (*infml joc*) favour or credit that one gains with others as a result of doing sth helpful, behaving in a servile way, etc: *She's hoping to earn lots of Brownie points by cleaning the teacher's shoes.*

Browning[1] /ˈbraʊnɪŋ/ Elizabeth Barrett (1806-61), English poet. Her poetry was greatly admired in her own lifetime, but she is chiefly remembered as the wife of Robert Browning, with whom she eloped to Italy to escape from her harsh father.

Browning[2] /ˈbraʊnɪŋ/ Robert (1812-89), English poet. Many of his early works were meant for performance in the theatre, but they were not very successful. His greatest work has always been considered to be *The Ring and the Book.* In 1846 he secretly married Elizabeth Barrett and went to live in Italy. The couple were friendly with many other important writers, including *Carlyle and *Tennyson.

browse /braʊz/ *v* **1** (a) [I] examine books in a casual, leisurely way: *browse in a library/bookshop.* (b) [Ipr] ~ **through sth** look through (a book, etc) in this way: *browse through a magazine.* **2** [I] (of cows, goats, etc) feed by nibbling grass, leaves, etc: *cattle browsing in the fields.*

▷ **browse** *n* (usu *sing*) (act or period of) browsing: *have a browse in a bookshop.*

brucellosis /ˌbru:səˈləʊsɪs/ *n* [U] disease that affects domestic animals, esp cattle, and humans who drink infected milk, etc. It causes abortion in cattle and fever in humans.

Bruckner /ˈbrʊknə(r)/ Anton (1824-96), Austrian composer. He produced much music for the church, but his best known works are the large-scale, slow-moving symphonies.

Bruegel /ˈbrɔɪgəl/ Pieter (c 1525-69), Flemish artist. His most famous works are his peasant scenes and landscapes, remarkable for their detail and witty observation of people. His sons Pieter and Jan were also painters.

bruise /bru:z/ *n* injury caused by a blow to the body or to a fruit, discolouring the skin but not breaking it: *He was covered in bruises after falling off his bicycle.*

▷ **bruise** *v* **1** [Tn] cause a bruise or bruises on (sth/sb): *He fell and bruised himself/his leg.* ○ *Her face was badly bruised in the crash.* **2** [I] show the effects of a blow or knock: *Don't drop the peaches — they bruise easily.* ○ (*fig*) *Don't hurt her feelings — she bruises very easily.* **bruiser** *n* (*infml*) large strong tough man: *He looks a real bruiser.*

bruit /bru:t/ *v* (phr v) ~ **sth abroad/about** (*fml or joc*) spread (a rumour or report): *It's been bruited about that…* ○ *The news of the impending marriage was bruited abroad.*

Brum /brʌm/ (also **Brummagem** /ˈbrʌmədʒəm/) (*infml*) nickname for Birmingham in central England.

▷ **Brummie** *n* (*infml*) native or inhabitant of Birmingham.

Brummell /ˈbrʌməl/ George Bryan (1778-1840), known as 'Beau' Brummell, fashionable figure in Regency England. He was a friend of the Prince of Wales (later George IV) and greatly influenced style and dress during this period.

brunch /brʌntʃ/ *n* [C, U] (*infml esp US*) late morning meal eaten instead of breakfast and lunch.

Brunei /ˈbru:naɪ/ country in Borneo, an independent state since 1984 and a member of the Commonwealth; pop approx 241 000; official language Malay; capital Bandar Seri Begawan; unit of currency dollar (= 100 sen). It is divided into two parts, each surrounded by Malaysian territory, and its oil reserves make it very rich. ⇨ map at MALAYSIA.

Brunel /brʊˈnel/ Isambard Kingdom (1806-59), English engineer. He designed the Clifton suspension bridge, and made great advances in railway and ship design. The *Great Western*, built by Brunel, was the first steamship to cross the Atlantic. His father, Marc Isambard Brunel (1769-1849), also an engineer, constructed the first tunnel under the river Thames.

Brunelleschi /ˌbru:neˈleskɪ/ Filippo (1377-1446), Italian architect. He studied and applied the principles of classical Roman architecture, particularly in his use of perspective. His greatest work is considered to be the dome of the cathedral in Florence.

brunette /bru:ˈnet/ *n* white woman with dark-brown hair and (usu) darkish skin. Cf BLOND.

brunt /brʌnt/ *n* (idm) **bear the brunt of sth** ⇨ BEAR[2].

brush

HAIRBRUSH

SCRUBBING BRUSH

TOOTH-BRUSH

NAIL-BRUSH

PAINTBRUSH

brush[1] /brʌʃ/ *n* **1** [C] implement with bristles of hair, wire, nylon, etc set in a block of wood, etc and used for scrubbing, sweeping, cleaning, painting, tidying the hair, etc: *a ˈclothes-brush* ○ *a ˈtooth-brush* ○ *a ˈpaintbrush* ○ *a ˈhairbrush.* ⇨ illus. **2** [sing] act of brushing: *give one's clothes, shoes, teeth, hair a good brush.* **3** [sing] light touch (made in passing): *He knocked a glass off the table with a brush of his coat/arm.* **4** [C] fox's tail. ⇨ illus at ANIMAL. **5** [U] land covered by small trees and shrubs; undergrowth: [attrib] *a brush fire.* **6** [C] ~ **with sb** short unfriendly encounter with sb: quarrel: *a brush with the law/police* ○ *She had a nasty brush with her boss this morning.* **7** [C] brushlike piece of carbon or metal used to make an electrical contact, esp with a moving part. **8** (idm) **tarred with the same brush** ⇨ TAR[1].

□ **ˈbrushwood** *n* [U] **1** broken or cut branches or twigs. **2** = BRUSH[1] 5.

ˈbrushwork *n* [U] particular way in which an artist paints with a brush: *Picasso's brushwork is particularly fine.*

brush[2] /brʌʃ/ *v* **1** [Tn] use a brush on (sb/sth); clean, polish, make tidy or smooth with a brush: *brush your clothes, shoes, hair, teeth.* **2** [Cn·a] put (sth) into a particular state with a brush: *brush one's teeth clean.* **3** [Tn] touch (sb) lightly in passing: *leaves brushing one's cheek* ○ *His hand brushed hers.* **4** (phr v) **brush against/by/past sb/sth** touch sb/sth lightly while moving close to him/it: *She brushed past him without saying a word.* ○ *A cat brushed against her leg in the darkness.* **brush sb/sth aside** push sb/sth to one side; pay little or no attention to sb/sth: *The enemy brushed aside our defences.* ○ *He brushed aside my objections to his plan.* **brush sth away/off** remove sth (from sth) with or as if with a brush: *brush mud off (ones trouser's)* ○ *He brushed the fly away (from his face).* **brush oneself/sth down** clean oneself/sth by thorough brushing: *Your coat needs brushing down. It's covered in dust.* **brush off** be removed by brushing: *Mud brushes off easily when it's dry.* **brush sb ˈoff** (*infml*) refuse to listen to sb; ignore sb: *He's very keen on her but she's always brushing him ˈoff.* **brush sth up/brush up on sth** study or practise sth in order to get back a skill that was lost: *I must brush up (on) my Italian before I go to Rome.*

▷ **brushed** *adj* (of a fabric) that has a soft, slightly fluffy finish: *brushed denim, cotton, etc.*

□ **ˈbrush-off** *n* (*pl* **brush-offs**) (*infml*) rejection; snub: *She gave him the brush-off.*

ˈbrush-up *n* (*pl* **brush-ups**) **1** act of tidying one's appearance. **2** act of studying to get back former skill: *give one's Spanish a brush-up.*

brusque /bru:sk; *US* brʌsk/ *adj* (of a person, his manner, etc) rough and abrupt; curt: *a brusque attitude* ○ *His reply was brusque.* ▷ **brusquely** *adv.* **brusqueness** *n* [U].

Brussels /ˈbrʌslz/ *adj* [attrib] of or from Brussels in Belgium: *Brussels lace/carpets.*

□ **ˌBrussels ˈsprout** (also **sprout**) **1** type of cabbage with edible buds like tiny cabbages growing on its stem. **2** [esp pl] one of these buds, eaten as a vegetable. ⇨ illus at CABBAGE.

brutal /ˈbru:tl/ *adj* cruel; savage; merciless: *a brutal tyrant, dictator, murderer, etc* ○ *a brutal attack, murder, punishment.*

▷ **brutality** /bru:ˈtælətɪ/ *n* **1** [U] brutal behaviour; cruelty; savagery. **2** [C] brutal act: *the brutalities of war.*

brutalize, -ise *v* [Tn usu passive] make (sb) brutal or insensitive: *soldiers brutalized by a long war.*

brutally /ˈbru:təlɪ/ *adv.*

brute /bru:t/ *n* **1** animal, esp a large or fierce one: *That dog looks a real brute.* **2** (*sometimes joc*) brutal and insensitive person: *His father was a drunken brute.* ○ *You've forgotten my birthday again, you brute!* **3** unpleasant or difficult thing: *a brute of a problem* ○ *This lock's a brute — it just won't open.*

▷ **brute** *adj* [attrib] not involving thought or reason; unthinking: *brute force/strength.*

brutish *adj* of or like a brute: *brutish behaviour, manners, etc.* **brutishly** *adv.*

Brutus /ˈbru:təs/ Marcus Junius (c 85-42 BC), Roman senator. He was one of the leaders of the group of conspirators who killed *Julius Caesar. Caesar's supporters later defeated him in battle and he committed suicide.

bryony /ˈbraɪənɪ/ *n* [C, U] either of two types of climbing plant that form hedges (*white bryony* and *black bryony*).

BS /ˌbi: ˈes/ *abbr* **1** (*US*) Bachelor of Science. **2** (*Brit*) Bachelor of Surgery: *have/be a BS* ○ *Tom Hunt MB, BS.* **3** (on labels, etc) British Standard (showing the specification number of the British Standards Institution): *produced to BS4353.* Cf ASA 2.

BSC /ˌbi: es ˈsi:/ *abbr* British Steel Corporation.

BSc /ˌbi: es ˈsi:/ (*US* **BS**) *abbr* Bachelor of Science: *have/be a BSc in Botany* ○ *Jill Ayres BSc.* ⇨ article at POST-SCHOOL EDUCATION.

BSI /ˌbi: es ˈaɪ/ *abbr* British Standards Institution.

BST /ˌbi: es ˈti:/ *abbr* British Summer Time. Cf GMT.

Bt *abbr* Baronet: *James Hyde-Stanley Bt.*

BTA /ˌbi: ti: ˈeɪ/ *abbr* British Tourist Authority.

Bthu (also **Btu**) *abbr* British thermal unit(s).

bubble /ˈbʌbl/ *n* **1** floating ball formed of liquid and containing air or gas: *soap bubbles* ○ *Children love blowing bubbles.* **2** ball of air or gas in a liquid or a solidified liquid such as glass: *Champagne is full of bubbles.* ○ *This glass vase has a bubble in its*

base. 3 (idm) **prick the bubble** ⇨ PRICK².
▷ **bubble** *v* 1 [I] (of a liquid) rise in or form bubbles; boil: *stew bubbling in the pot.* 2 [I] make the sound of bubbles: *a bubbling stream/fountain.* 3 [I, Ipr, Ip] ~ **(over) (with sth)** (*fig*) be full of (usu happy) feelings: *be bubbling (over) with excitement, enthusiasm, high spirits, etc.* 4 (phr v) **bubble along, out, over, up, etc** move in the specified direction in bubbles or with a bubbling sound: *a spring bubbling out of the ground* ○ *Gases from deep in the earth bubble up through the lake.*
bubbly /ˈbʌblɪ/ *adj* **(-ier, -iest)** 1 full of bubbles: *bubbly lemonade.* 2 (*fig approv*) (usu of a woman) lively; vivacious; animated: *a bubbly personality.* — *n* [U] (*infml*) champagne: *Have some more bubbly!*
□ ˌ**bubble and ˈsqueak** cooked cabbage and potato mixed and fried.
ˈ**bubble bath** liquid, crystals or powder added to a bath to make it foam and smell pleasant.
ˈ**bubble car** type of small car, usu with three wheels, having a transparent rounded top.
ˈ**bubble gum** chewing-gum that can be blown into bubbles.
ˈ**bubble pack** type of packaging in which an article is sealed between a piece of card and a moulded top made of clear plastic.

bubonic plague /bjuːˌbɒnɪk ˈpleɪɡ/ (also **the plague**) contagious, usu fatal, disease spread by rats, causing swellings in the armpits and groin, fever and delirium.

buccaneer /ˌbʌkəˈnɪə(r)/ *n* 1 pirate. 2 unscrupulous and reckless person.
▷ **buccaneering** /ˌbʌkəˈnɪərɪŋ/ *adj* unscrupulous and reckless: *a buccaneering approach to business dealings.* — *n* [U].

Buchan /ˈbʌkn/ John (1875-1940), Scottish novelist and statesman. He combined writing with a political career, and became Lord Tweedsmuir and Governor-General of Canada. He is most famous for his adventure stories, which included *The Thirty-nine Steps* and *Greenmantle.*

Buchenwald /ˈbuːkənvælt/ village in eastern Germany, where there was a Nazi concentration camp in the Second World War.

buck¹ /bʌk/ *n* 1 (*pl* unchanged or ~s) male deer, hare or rabbit. Cf STAG 1. 2 (*US sl derog*) [esp attrib] young Indian or Negro man.
□ ˈ**buckskin** *n* [U] soft leather made from the skin of deer or goats, used for making gloves, bags, etc.
ˌ**buck-ˈtooth** *n* (*pl* **-teeth**) projecting upper front tooth.

buck² /bʌk/ *v* 1 (a) [I] (of a horse) jump with the four feet together and the back arched. (b) [Tn, Tn·p] ~ **sb (off)** throw (a rider) to the ground by doing this. 2 [Tn] (*US infml*) resist or oppose (sb/sth): *Don't try to buck the system.* 3 (idm) **buck one's iˈdeas up** (*infml*) become more alert; take a more serious and responsible attitude. 4 (phr v) **buck ˈup** (*infml*) hurry: *Buck up! We're going to be late.* **buck (sb) up** (*infml*) (cause sb to) become more cheerful: *The good news bucked us all up.* ○ *Buck up! Things aren't as bad as you think.*
▷ **bucked** *adj* [pred] (*infml esp Brit*) pleased and encouraged: *She felt really bucked after passing her driving test.*

buck³ /bʌk/ *n* 1 (*US infml*) US dollar. 2 (idm) **a fast buck** ⇨ FAST¹. ⇨ App 9.

buck⁴ /bʌk/ *n* 1 object formerly placed in front of a player whose turn it was to deal in poker. 2 (idm) **the buck stops ˈhere** (*catchphrase*) responsibility or blame is accepted here and cannot be passed on to sb else. **pass the buck** ⇨ PASS².

buckboard /ˈbʌkbɔːd/ *n* (*US*) light cart with a seat attached to a board laid between the axles.

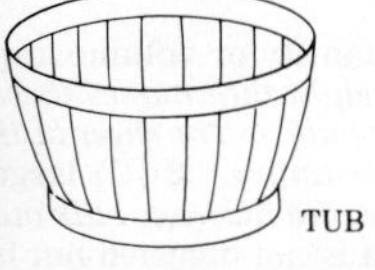

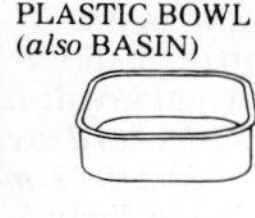

bucket /ˈbʌkɪt/ *n* 1 round open container with a handle for carrying or holding liquids, sand, etc: *build sandcastles with a bucket and spade.* ⇨ illus. 2 (also ˈ**bucketful**) amount a bucket contains: *two buckets/bucketfuls of water.* 3 scoop of a mechanical shovel, dredger, water-wheel, etc. 4 **buckets** [pl] large amounts (esp of rain or tears): *The rain came down/fell in buckets.* ○ *She wept buckets.* 5 (idm) **a drop in the bucket/ocean** ⇨ DROP¹. **kick the ˈbucket** ⇨ KICK¹.
▷ **bucket** *v* [I, Ip] ~ **(down)** (of rain) pour down heavily: *It/The rain bucketed down all afternoon.*
□ ˈ**bucket seat** (in a car or an aircraft) seat with a rounded back, for one person.
ˈ**bucket-shop** *n* (*infml derog*) unregistered business, esp one selling cheap airline tickets.

buckeye /ˈbʌkaɪ/ *n* (*US*) 1 horse-chestnut tree. 2 its shiny reddish-brown nut.

Buckingham Palace /ˌbʌkɪŋəm ˈpælɪs/ London home of the British sovereign, near St James's Park, Westminster. It was originally built for the Duke of Buckingham in the early 18th century. ⇨ articles at ROYAL FAMILY, LONDON.

buckle /ˈbʌkl/ *n* 1 metal or plastic clasp with a hinged spike for fastening a belt or straps. 2 ornamental clasp on a shoe.
▷ **buckle** *v* 1 [I, Ip, Tn, Tn·p] ~ **(sth) (up)** fasten (sth) or be fastened with a buckle: *My belt is loose; I didn't buckle it up tightly enough.* ○ *These shoes buckle at the side.* 2 [I, Tn] (cause sb/sth to) crumple or bend (usu because of pressure or heat): *The metal buckled in the heat.* ○ *The crash buckled the front of my car.* ○ (*fig*) *He's beginning to buckle under the pressure of work.* 3 (phr v) **buckle down to sth** (*infml*) start sth in a determined way: *She's really buckling down to her new job.* **buckle sb in/into sth** fasten sb in (a seat, etc) with a belt: *The parachutist was buckled into his harness.* **buckle (sth) on** (cause sth to) be attached with a buckle: *a sword that buckles on* ○ *buckle on one's belt.* **buckle ˈto** (*infml*) (esp of a group) make a special effort (usu in the face of difficulties): *The children had to buckle to while their mother was in hospital.*

buckler /ˈbʌklə(r)/ *n* small round shield held by a handle or worn on the arm.

buckram /ˈbʌkrəm/ *n* [U] stiff cloth used esp for binding books.

Buck's Fizz /ˌbʌks ˈfɪz/ (*Brit*) drink made from orange juice and champagne or sparkling white wine.

buckshee /ˌbʌkˈʃiː/ *adj, adv* (*Brit sl*) free of charge: *buckshee tickets* ○ *travel buckshee.*

buckshot /ˈbʌkʃɒt/ *n* [U] large size of lead shot¹(5) for firing from shotguns.

buckthorn /ˈbʌkθɔːn/ *n* [C, U] thorny shrub with black berries once used as a purgative.

buckwheat /ˈbʌkwiːt; *US* -hwiːt/ *n* [U] dark seeds of grain used for feeding horses and poultry.
□ ˈ**buckwheat flour** flour made from these seeds, used in US for breakfast pancakes.

bucolic /bjuːˈkɒlɪk/ *adj* of country life or the countryside; rustic.
▷ **bucolics** *n* [pl] poems about country life.

bud /bʌd/ *n* 1 small knob from which a flower, branch or cluster of leaves develops: *Buds appear on the trees in spring.* 2 flower or leaf not fully open. ⇨ illus at PLANT. 3 (idm) **(be) in bud** having or sending out buds: *The trees and hedgerows are in bud.* **nip sth in the bud** ⇨ NIP.
▷ **bud** *v* **(-dd-)** [I] produce buds: *The trees are budding early this year.* **budding** *adj* beginning to develop well: *a budding novelist, actor, sportsman, etc.*

Buddhism /ˈbʊdɪzəm/ *n* [U] Asian religion based on the teachings of the N Indian philosopher Gautama Siddartha or Buddha. ▷ **Buddhist** /ˈbʊdɪst/ *n, adj*: *a devout Buddhist* ○ *Buddhist monks* ○ *a Buddhist temple.*

buddleia /ˈbʌdlɪə/ *n* [C, U] any of several types of garden shrub with sweet-smelling flowers of various colours. The type that has light purple flowers is very attractive to butterflies.

buddy /ˈbʌdɪ/ *n* (*infml esp US*) friend: *Hi there, buddy!* ○ *He and I were buddies at school.*

budge /bʌdʒ/ *v* [I, Tn] (usu in negative sentences) 1 (cause sth to) move slightly: *My car's stuck in the mud, and it won't budge/I can't budge it.* 2 (cause sb to) change an attitude or opinion: *Once he's made up his mind, he never budges/you can never budge him (from his opinion).*

budgerigar /ˈbʌdʒərɪɡɑː(r)/ *n* type of Australian parakeet, often kept as a cage-bird.

budget /ˈbʌdʒɪt/ *n* 1 (a) estimate or plan of how money will be spent over a period of time, in relation to the amount of money available: *a weekly budget.* (b) annual government statement of a country's expenditure and how it will be financed: *The Chancellor of the Exchequer is expected to announce tax cuts in this year's budget.* ⇨ articles at TAXATION, PARLIAMENT. 2 amount of money needed or allotted for a specific purpose: *limit oneself to a daily budget of £10.* 3 (idm) **on a (tight) budget** having only a small amount of money: *A family on a budget can't afford meat every day.*
▷ **budget** *v* 1 [Tn, Tn·pr] ~ **sth (for sth)** plan the spending of or provide (money) in a budget: *The government has budgeted £10 000 000 for education spending.* 2 [I, Ipr] ~ **(for sth)** save or allocate money (for a particular purpose): *If we budget carefully, we'll be able to afford a new car.* ○ *budget for the coming year, for a holiday abroad, for a drop in sales, etc.*
budget *adj* [attrib] inexpensive; cheap: *a budget meal, holiday.*
budgetary /ˈbʌdʒɪtərɪ; *US* -terɪ/ *adj* of a budget: *budgetary provisions.*
□ ˈ**budget account** account at a shop, etc into which a customer makes regular payments, receiving credit in proportion to these; similar account at a bank, for paying regularly recurring bills.

budgie /ˈbʌdʒɪ/ *n* (*infml*) budgerigar.

buff¹ /bʌf/ *n* [U] 1 (a) strong soft dull-yellow leather. (b) colour of this. 2 (idm) **in the ˈbuff** (*infml esp Brit*) with no clothes on. **strip to the buff** ⇨ STRIP.
▷ **buff** *adj* made of or having the colour of buff: *a buff envelope, uniform.*
buff *v* [Tn, Tn·p] ~ **sth (up)** polish sth with a soft material: *buff (up) shoes with a cloth.*

buff² /bʌf/ *n* (preceded by a *n*) (*infml*) person who is enthusiastic and knowledgeable about a specified subject or activity: *a film, an opera, a tennis buff.*

buffalo /ˈbʌfələʊ/ *n* (*pl* unchanged or ~es) large ox of various kinds, including the wild S African buffalo, the tame (often domesticated) Asian buffalo and the N American bison: *fifty buffaloes* ○ *a herd of buffalo.*

Buffalo Bill /ˌbʌfələʊ ˈbɪl/ ⇨ CODY, WILLIAM.

buffer¹ /ˈbʌfə(r)/ *n* 1 device for lessening the effect of a blow or collision, esp on a railway vehicle or at the end of a railway track. 2 (*fig*) person or thing that lessens a shock or protects sb/sth against difficulties: *His sense of humour was a useful buffer when things were going badly for him.* 3 country or area between two powerful states, lessening the risk of war between them: [attrib] *a buffer state/zone.* 4 (*chemistry*) substance added to a solution in order to keep the degree of acidity constant. 5 part of a computer's memory in which data may be stored temporarily, eg before printing.
▷ **buffer** *v* [Tn] act as a buffer to (sb/sth).
□ ˈ**buffer stock** (*commerce*) stock¹(5a) of a commodity held in reserve so as to reduce fluctuation in prices when supplies are low.

buffer² /ˈbʌfə(r)/ *n* (usu **old buffer**) (*Brit infml*) foolish or incompetent old man: *a silly old buffer.*

buffet¹ /ˈbʊfeɪ; *US* bəˈfeɪ/ *n* 1 counter where food and drink may be bought and consumed, esp in a railway station or on a train. 2 meal at which guests serve themselves from a number of dishes; food provided for this: *Dinner will be a cold buffet, not a sit-down meal.* ○ [attrib] *a buffet lunch/supper.* 3 /*also* ˈbʌfɪt/ sideboard or cupboard in which plates, dishes, etc are kept.
□ ˈ**buffet car** railway carriage serving light meals.

buffet² /ˈbʌfɪt/ *n* blow (esp with the hand) or shock: (*fig*) *suffer the buffets of a cruel fate.*

▷ **buffet** *v* [Tn, Tn·p] ~ **sb/sth (about)** knock or push sb/sth roughly from side to side: *flowers buffeted by the rain and wind* ○ *(fig) be buffeted by misfortune* ○ *a boat buffeted (about) by the waves.* **buffeting** *n*: *The flowers took quite a buffeting in the storm.*

buffoon /bəˈfu:n/ *n* ridiculous but amusing person; clown: *play the buffoon.*

▷ **buffoonery** /-ərɪ/ *n* [U] ridiculous behaviour; clowning.

bug /bʌg/ *n* **1** [C] small flat foul-smelling insect infesting dirty houses and beds. **2** [C] (*esp US*) any small insect. **3** [C] (*infml*) (illness caused by a) germ or infectious virus: *I think I've caught a bug.* ○ *There are a lot of bugs about in winter.* **4** (usu **the bug**) [sing] (*infml*) obsessive interest (in sth specified): *He was never interested in cooking before, but now he's been bitten by/he's got the bug.* **5** [C] (*infml*) defect in a machine, esp a computer: *There's a bug in the system.* **6** [C] (*infml*) small hidden microphone placed (eg by intelligence services) so that conversations can be heard at a distance: *search a room for bugs* ○ *plant a bug in an embassy.* **7** (idm) **snug as a bug in a rug** ⇨ SNUG.

▷ **bug** *v* (**-gg-**) [Tn] **1** (**a**) fit (a room, telephone, etc) with a hidden microphone for listening to conversations: *This office is bugged.* (**b**) listen to (a conversation, etc) with a hidden microphone: *a bugging device* ○ *Be careful what you say; our conversation may be being bugged.* **2** (*infml esp US*) annoy (sb); irritate: *What's bugging you?* ○ *That man really bugs me.*

□ ˈ**bug-eyed** *adj* (*infml*) with bulging eyes.

ˈ**bughouse** *n* (*US sl offensive*) mental hospital. — *adj* (*sl esp US*) crazy; very eccentric: *He's gone completely bughouse.*

bugbear /ˈbʌgbeə(r)/ *n* thing that is feared or disliked or causes annoyance: *Inflation is the Government's main bugbear.*

bugger /ˈbʌgə(r)/ *n* (⚠ *esp Brit*) **1** (*law*) person who commits buggery; sodomite. **2** (*infml*) (**a**) annoying or contemptible person: *You stupid bugger! You could have run me over!* (**b**) (in expressions of sympathy or kind feeling) person or animal: *Poor bugger! His wife left him last week.* **3** (*infml*) thing that causes difficulties: *This door's a (real) bugger to open.* **4** (idm) **play silly buggers** ⇨ SILLY.

▷ **bugger** *v* (⚠) **1** [Tn] (*law*) have anal intercourse with (sb). **2** [Tn] (*infml*) (usu imperative, expressing anger or annoyance at sb/sth): *Bugger it! I've burnt the toast.* ○ *You're always late, bugger you.* **3** [Tn, Tn·p] ~ **sth (up)** (*infml*) spoil or ruin sth. **4** (idm) ˌ**bugger** ˈ**me** (*infml*) (expressing surprise or amazement): *Bugger me! Did you see that?* **5** (phr v) **bugger about/around** (*infml*) behave stupidly or irresponsibly: *Stop buggering about with those matches or you'll set the house on fire.* **bugger sb about/around** (*infml*) treat sb badly or in a casual way: *I'm sick of being buggered about by the company.* **bugger off** (*infml*) (esp imperative) go away: *Bugger off and leave me alone.* ○ *I was only two minutes late but they'd all buggered off.*

bugger *interj* (⚠ *infml*) (expressing anger or annoyance): *Oh bugger! I've left my keys at home.*

buggered *adj* (⚠ *infml*) [pred] very tired; exhausted: *I'm completely buggered after that game of tennis.* **buggery** /ˈbʌgərɪ/ *n* [U] (⚠ *law*) anal intercourse; sodomy.

□ ˌ**bugger-**ˈ**all** *n* [U] (⚠ *infml*) nothing: *There's bugger-all to do in this place.*

buggy /ˈbʌgɪ/ *n* **1** small strongly-built motor vehicle: *a beach buggy.* **2** (also ˈ**baby buggy**) (*US*) = PRAM. **3** (formerly) light carriage pulled by one horse, for one or two people.

bugle /ˈbju:gl/ *n* brass musical instrument like a small trumpet but without keys or valves, used for giving military signals. ⇨ illus.

▷ **bugler** /ˈbju:glə(r)/ *n* person who blows a bugle.

bugloss /ˈbju:glɒs/ *n* [C, U] plant with hairy stems and leaves, and blue flowers.

buhl /bu:l/ *n* [U] type of furniture decoration using inlaid brass, tortoiseshell or other materials: [attrib] *buhl work* ○ *a buhl table.*

build /bɪld/ *v* (*pt, pp* **built** /bɪlt/) **1** (**a**) [Tn, Tn·pr, Dn·n, Dn·pr] ~ **sth (of/from/out of sth)**; ~ **sth (for sb)** make or construct sth by putting parts or material together: *build a house, road, railway* ○ *a house built of stone, bricks, etc* ○ *Birds build their nests out of twigs.* ○ *His father built him a model aeroplane.* (**b**) [I] construct houses, etc: *The local council intends to build on this site.* **2** [Tn] develop (sth); establish: *build a business* ○ *build a better future, a new career, etc.* **3** (idm) ˌ**build (sth) on** ˈ**sand** work to achieve sth without having ensured the right conditions for success: *Without a good sales team you could find you're building on sand.* ˌ**Rome was not** ˌ**built in a** ˈ**day** (*saying*) time and hard work are necessary for a difficult or important task. **4** (phr v) **build sth in/build sth into sth** (esp passive) (**a**) make sth a fixed and permanent part of sth larger: *build a cupboard/bookcase into a wall* ○ *We're having new wardrobes built in.* (**b**) (*fig*) make sth a necessary part of sth: *build an extra clause into the contract.* **build sth into sth** put parts together to form sth: *build loose stones into a strong wall* ○ *build scraps of metal into a work of art.* **build sth on/build sth onto sth** add sth (eg an extra room) to an existing structure by building: *The new wing was built on(to the hospital) last year.* **build on sth** use sth as a foundation for further progress: *build on earlier achievements, success, results, etc.* **build sth on sth** base sth on sth: *build one's hopes on the economic strength of the country* ○ *an argument built on sound logic.* **build up** become greater, more numerous or more intense: *Traffic is building up on roads into the city.* ○ *Tension built up as the crisis approached.* **build oneself/sb up** make oneself/sb healthier or stronger: *You need more protein to build you up.* **build sb/sth up** (esp passive) speak with great (often undeserved or exaggerated) praise about sb/sth: *The film was built up to be a masterpiece, but I found it very disappointing.* **build sth up** (**a**) acquire, develop, increase or strengthen sth gradually: *build up a big library, a fine reputation, a thriving business* ○ *build up one's strength after an illness.* (**b**) (esp passive) cover (an area) with buildings: *The village has been built up since I lived here.*

▷ **build** *n* [U, C] shape and size (of the human body): *a man of athletic, powerful, slender, average, etc build* ○ *We are (of) the same build.* ○ *Our build is/builds are similar.*

builder *n* **1** person who builds, esp one whose job is building houses, etc. **2** (in compounds) person or thing that creates or develops sth: *an empire-builder* ○ *a confidence-builder.*

built (after *advs* and in compound *adjs*) having the specified build: *solidly built* ○ *a well-built man,* ie one who is broad and muscular.

□ ˈ**build-up** *n* **1** (**a**) gradual increase or accumulation: *a steady build-up of traffic* ○ *A build-up of enemy forces is reported.* (**b**) ~ (**to sth**) gradual approach (to a climax); gradual preparation (for sth): *the build-up to the President's visit.* **2** favourable description (esp of a performer or spectacle) in advance: *The press has given the show a tremendous build-up.*

ˌ**built-**ˈ**in** (also **in-built**) *adj* [attrib] constructed to form part of a structure: *a bedroom with* ˌ*built-in* ˈ*wardrobes* ○ (*fig*) *a pay deal with built-in guarantees of employment.*

ˌ**built-**ˈ**up** *adj* [usu attrib] covered with buildings: *a* ˌ*built-up* ˈ*area.*

building /ˈbɪldɪŋ/ *n* **1** [U] (art, business or profession of) constructing houses, etc: [attrib] *the building trade* ○ *building materials.* **2** [C] (*abbr* bldg) structure with a roof and walls: *Schools, churches, houses and factories are all buildings.*

□ ˈ**building block** (**a**) cube made of wood, plastic, etc for children to play with, esp when building toy houses, etc. (**b**) (*fig*) basic unit used to make sth: *Words are the building blocks of language.*

ˈ**building site** area of land on which a house, etc is being built.

ˈ**building society** (*Brit*) organization that accepts deposits and lends out money to people who wish to buy or build houses.

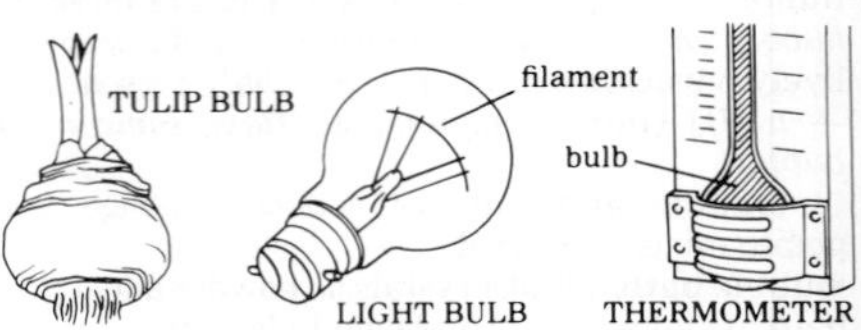

bulb /bʌlb/ *n* ⇨ illus. **1** thick rounded underground stem of certain plants (eg the lily, onion, tulip) sending roots downwards and leaves upwards. ⇨ illus at PLANT. **2** (also ˈ**light bulb**) pear-shaped glass container for the filament of an electric light: *change a bulb* ○ *a 60-watt light bulb.* **3** object shaped like a bulb, eg the bulging end of a thermometer.

▷ **bulbous** /ˈbʌlbəs/ *adj* **1** growing from a bulb. **2** shaped like a bulb; round and fat: *a bulbous nose.*

Bulgaria

Bulgaria /bʌlˈgeərɪə/ country in eastern Europe on the Black Sea; pop approx 8 995 000; official language Bulgarian; capital Sofia; unit of currency lev (= 100 stotinki). The economy is a mixture of agriculture and heavy industry. One of its most famous products is still the essence obtained from damask rose petals. Certain parts of the country have a large Turkish population. ⇨ map.

bulge /bʌldʒ/ *n* **1** rounded swelling; outward curve: *What's that bulge in your pocket?* **2** (*infml*) temporary increase in quantity: *a population bulge* ○ *After the war there was a bulge in the birth-rate.*

▷ **bulge** *v* [I, Ipr, Ip] ~ **(out) (with sth)** form a bulge: swell outwards: *I can't eat any more. My stomach's bulging.* ○ *His pockets were bulging with apples.*

bulgy /ˈbʌldʒɪ/ *adj.*

bulimia /bjʊˈlɪmɪə; *US* bu:-/ *n* [U] (also **bulimia nervosa** /nɜ:ˈvəʊsə/) (*medical*) mental illness that causes an abnormal desire to keep eating, followed by depression, vomiting, etc. Cf ANOREXIA.

bulk /bʌlk/ *n* **1** [U] size, quantity or volume, esp when great: *It's not their weight that makes these sacks hard to carry, it's their bulk.* ○ *The sheer bulk of Mozart's music is extraordinary.* **2** [C] large shape, body or person: *He heaved his huge bulk out of the chair.* **3** [U] food that is not digested but is eaten to stimulate the intestine; roughage: *You* *need more bulk in your diet.* **4** [sing] **the ~ (of sth)** main part (of sth): *The bulk of the work has already been done.* ○ *The eldest son inherited the bulk of the estate.* **5** (idm) **in 'bulk (a)** in large amounts: *buy (sth) in bulk.* **(b)** (of a cargo, etc) not packed in boxes; loose: *shipped in bulk.*

▷ **bulk** *v* **1** (idm) **bulk 'large** seem important; be prominent: *The war still bulks large in the memories of those who fought in it.* **2** (phr v) **bulk sth out** make sth bigger or thicker: *add extra pages to bulk a book out.*

bulky *adj* **(-ier, -iest)** taking up much space; awkward to move or carry: *the bulky figure of Inspector Jones* ○ *a bulky parcel, crate, load, etc.*

□ **ˌbulk 'buying** buying in large amounts, esp the buying of most of a producer's output by one purchaser.

bulkhead /ˈbʌlkhed/ *n* upright watertight partition or wall between compartments in a ship or aircraft.

bull[1] /bʊl/ *n* **1** uncastrated male of any animal in the ox family: [attrib] *a bull neck*, ie a short thick one, like a bull's. Cf BULLOCK, COW[1] 1, OX 1, STEER[2]. **2** male of the elephant, whale and other large animals. Cf COW[1] 2. **3** (in the Stock Exchange) person who buys shares hoping to sell them soon afterwards at a higher price: [attrib] *a bull market*, ie a situation in which share prices are rising. Cf BEAR[1] 3. **4** (*US sl*) policeman or detective. **5** = BULL'S-EYE. **6** (idm) **a bull in a 'china shop** person who is rough and clumsy when skill and care are needed. **a cock-and-bull story** ⇨ COCK. **like a ˌbull at a 'gate** with great energy but without proper thought: *She went at the stain (ie tried to remove it) like a bull at a gate, and only succeeded in making it worse.* **a red rag to a bull** ⇨ RED[1]. **take the bull by the 'horns** face a difficulty or danger boldly.

▷ **bullish** *adj* (in the Stock Exchange) characterized by or causing a rise in share prices. Cf BEARISH (BEAR[1]).

□ **'bullfight** *n* traditional public entertainment, esp in Spain and S America, in which bulls are baited and usu killed in the arena. **'bullfighter** *n*. **'bullfighting** *n* [U].

ˌbull-'headed *adj* obstinate or stubborn in a clumsy way.

ˌbull-'necked *adj* having a short thick neck.

'bullpen *n* (*US*) area where baseball pitchers can practise before joining the game.

'bullring *n* arena for bullfighting.

'bull session (*US*) informal discussion involving a group of people.

bull[2] /bʊl/ *n* official order or announcement from the Pope: *a papal bull.*

bull[3] /bʊl/ *n* [U] **1** (also **Irish bull**) foolish, amusing and illogical use of words (eg 'If you do not receive this letter, please write and tell me'). **2** (*sl*) = BULLSHIT: *That's a lot/a load of bull!* **3** (*Brit army sl*) tiresome routine tasks (esp the cleaning of boots, equipment, etc).

bulldog /ˈbʊldɒg/ *n* sturdy, powerful and courageous type of dog with a large head and a short thick neck. ⇨ illus at DOG. ⇨ article at NATIONAL.

□ **ˌbulldog 'clip** clip with a spring that closes tightly and is used for holding papers, etc together.

bulldozer

bulldoze /ˈbʊldəʊz/ *v* **1** [Tn] remove or flatten (sth) with a bulldozer: *The area was bulldozed to make way for a new road.* **2** [Tn, Tn·pr] **~ sb (into doing sth)** (*fig*) force sb to do sth, esp by frightening him: *They bulldozed me into signing the agreement.* **3** [Tn·pr] push sth with force in the specified direction: (*fig*) *He bulldozed his way into the room.* ○ *She bulldozed her plans past the committee.*

▷ **bulldozer** /ˈbʊldəʊzə(r)/ *n* powerful tractor with a broad steel blade in front, used for moving earth or clearing ground. ⇨ illus.

bullet /ˈbʊlɪt/ *n* **1** small missile, usu round or cylindrical with a pointed end, fired from a gun or rifle: *He was killed by a single bullet in the heart.* **2** (idm) **bite the bullet** ⇨ BITE[1].

□ **ˌbullet-'headed** /-ˈhedɪd/ *adj* having a small round head.

'bullet-proof *adj* that can stop bullets passing through it: *a bullet-proof shirt/vest/jacket.*

bulletin /ˈbʊlətɪn/ *n* **1** short official statement of news: *a news bulletin.* **2** printed newsletter produced by an association, a group or a society.

□ **'bulletin board** (*US*) = NOTICE-BOARD (NOTICE).

bullfinch /ˈbʊlfɪntʃ/ *n* songbird with a strong rounded beak and a pink breast.

bullfrog /ˈbʊlfrɒg/ *n* type of large American frog with a loud croak.

bullhorn /ˈbʊlhɔːn/ *n* (*US*) = LOUDHAILER (LOUD).

bullion /ˈbʊlɪən/ *n* [U] gold or silver in bulk or bars, before it is made into coins, etc: *The thieves stole £1 000 000 in gold bullion.*

bullock /ˈbʊlək/ *n* bull that has been castrated. Cf BULL[1] 1, OX 1, STEER[2].

bull's-eye /ˈbʊlzaɪ/ *n* **1 (a)** centre of a target, having the highest value in archery and darts. ⇨ illus at ARCHERY, DART. **(b)** shot that hits this: *scoring a bull's-eye.* **2** large hard round peppermint sweet. **3** small round window made of thick glass.

bullshit /ˈbʊlʃɪt/ (also **bull**) *n* [U], *interj* (⚠ *sl*) nonsense; rubbish: *a load/lot of bullshit* ○ *He's talking bullshit.*

▷ **bullshit** *v* **(-tt-)** [I, Tn] (⚠ *sl*) try to convince (sb) with false or unbelievable claims: *They're just bullshitting — take no notice.* ○ *Don't bullshit me.* **bullshitter** *n*.

bull-terrier /ˌbʊlˈterɪə(r)/ *n* dog of a breed produced by crossing (CROSS[2] 7) a bulldog and a terrier.

bully[1] /ˈbʊlɪ/ *n* person who uses his strength or power to frighten or hurt weaker people: *Leave that little girl alone, you big bully!* ○ *a playground bully.* Bullies are a traditional problem in schools. Various books in English literature have described the part they played in the life of English public schools. The most famous case is Flashman in *Tom Brown's Schooldays.*

▷ **bully** *v* (*pt, pp* **bullied**) **1** [Tn] frighten or hurt (a weaker person): *He was bullied by the older boys at school.* **2** (phr v) **bully sb into doing sth** (try to) force sb to do sth by frightening him: *The manager tried to bully his men into working harder by threatening them with dismissal.*

□ **'bully-boy** *n* rough violent man, esp one paid to frighten or injure others: [attrib] (*fig*) *bully-boy tactics.*

bully[2] /ˈbʊlɪ/ *n* [U] (also **'bully beef**) (*infml*) corned beef in tins.

bully[3] /ˈbʊlɪ/ *interj* (idm) **bully for sb** (*infml esp ironic*) well done: *You've solved the puzzle at last? Well, bully for 'you!*

bully[4] /ˈbʊlɪ/ *n* (in hockey) (formerly) way of starting a game in which two opposing players strike their sticks together three times before trying to hit the ball.

▷ **bully** *v* (*pt, pp* **bullied**) (phr v) **bully off** start play in this way.

bulrush /ˈbʊlrʌʃ/ *n* type of tall rush[3] with a thick velvety head.

bulwark /ˈbʊlwək/ *n* **1** wall, esp of earth, built as a defence. **2** (*fig*) person or thing that supports, defends or protects: *Democracy is a bulwark of freedom.* **3** (usu *pl*) ship's side above the level of the deck.

bum[1] /bʌm/ *n* (*infml esp Brit*) part of the body on which one sits; buttocks.

bum[2] /bʌm/ *n* (*infml esp US*) **1** wandering beggar; tramp; loafer: *bums sleeping rough in the streets.* **2** lazy irresponsible person: *You're just a no-good bum!* **3** (idm) **give sb/get the bum's 'rush** (*sl*) force sb/be forced to leave in a rough way: *If he makes another pass at you he's getting the bum's rush*, ie I shall get rid of him.

▷ **bum** *adj* [attrib] (*infml*) **(a)** of bad quality; useless: *a bum film, concert, party.* **(b)** (idm) **a bum 'rap** (*sl esp US*) prison sentence for a crime one did not commit: *I got two years on a bum rap.* **a bum 'steer** (*sl esp US*) false information or bad advice: *I shouldn't have listened to him — it was a bum steer he gave me.*

bum *v* **(-mm-)** (*infml*) **1** [Tn, Tn·pr] **~ sth (off sb)** get sth (from sb) by begging; cadge sth: *bum a lift* ○ *Can I bum a cigarette off you?* **2** (phr v) **bum a'round** travel around or spend one's time doing nothing in particular: *I bummed around (in) Europe for a year before university.*

bumble /ˈbʌmbl/ *v* **1** [I, Ipr, Ip] **~ (on) (about sth)** speak in a rambling and clumsy manner: *What are you bumbling (on) about?* **2** (phr v) **bumble about, along, etc** act or move in a specified direction in a clumsy disorganized manner: *The professor bumbled absent-mindedly along the road.*

▷ **bumbling** *adj* [attrib] behaving in a clumsy disorganized way: *You bumbling idiot!*

bumble-bee /ˈbʌmblbiː/ *n* large hairy bee with a loud hum.

bumf (also **bumph**) /bʌmf/ *n* (*Brit sl joc or derog*) paper, esp official forms and documents: *'What's in the post today?' 'Just a lot of bumf from the insurance people.'*

bummer /ˈbʌmə(r)/ *n* (*US sl*) **1** unpleasant experience, esp after taking a hallucinogenic drug. **2** lazy irresponsible person.

bump /bʌmp/ *v* **1** [Ipr] **~ against/into sb/sth** knock or strike sth with a dull-sounding blow; collide with sth: *In the dark I bumped into a chair.* ○ *The car bumped against the kerb.* **2** [Tn, Tn·pr] **~ sth (against/on sth)** hit or knock sth (esp a part of the body) (against sth): *bump one's head (on the ceiling)* ○ *The driver bumped the kerb while reversing.* ⇨ Usage at BANG[1]. **3** (idm) **ˌbump and 'grind** (*infml*) dance by moving the hips in a sexy way, as eg strip-tease artists do: *the old bump-and-grind routine.* **4** (phr v) **bump along, down, etc** move with a jolting action in the specified direction: *The old bus bumped along the mountain road.* **bump into sb** (*infml*) meet sb by chance: *Guess who I bumped into today?* **bump sb off** (*sl*) kill or murder sb. **bump sth up** (*infml*) increase or raise sth: *bump up prices, salaries, etc.*

▷ **bump** *n* **1** (dull sound of a) blow, knock or impact; collision: *The two children collided with a bump.* ○ *The passengers felt a violent bump as the plane landed.* **2** swelling on the body, esp one caused by a blow; lump or bulge: *covered in bumps and bruises* ○ *get a nasty bump on the head.* **3** uneven patch on a surface: *a road with a lot of bumps in it.*

bump *adv* **1** with a bump; suddenly: *He fell off the ladder and landed bump on the ground.* **2** (idm) **things that go bump in the night** ⇨ THING.

bumpy *adj* **(-ier, -iest) 1** with an uneven surface: *a bumpy road, track, etc.* **2** causing jolts: *a bumpy ride, flight, drive, etc.* **bumpily** *adv.* **bumpiness** *n* [U].

bumper[1] /ˈbʌmpə(r)/ *n* **1** bar fixed to the front and back of a motor vehicle to lessen the effect of a collision. ⇨ illus at CAR. **2** (*dated*) glass completely filled with wine.

□ **'bumper car** = DODGEM.

ˌbumper-to-'bumper *adj, adv* (of vehicles) in a line, each close behind the one in front: *We sat bumper-to-bumper in the traffic jam.* ○ *travel bumper-to-bumper.*

bumper[2] /ˈbʌmpə(r)/ *adj* [attrib] unusually large or plentiful: *a bumper crop/harvest* ○ *a bumper edition/issue/number*, eg of a magazine.

bumper[3] /ˈbʌmpə(r)/ *n* = BOUNCER 1.

bumph = BUMF.

bumpkin /ˈbʌmpkɪn/ *n* (*usu derog*) awkward or simple person from the country.

bumptious /ˈbʌmpʃəs/ *adj* (*derog*) (of a person, his manner, etc) self-important and conceited: *bumptious officials, behaviour.* ▷ **bumptiously** *adv.* **bumptiousness** *n* [U].

bun /bʌn/ *n* **1** small round sweet cake: *a currant bun.* Cf ROLL[1] 2. **2** (esp woman's) hair twisted into a tight knot at the back of the head: *put, wear one's hair in a bun.* **3** (idm) **have a ˈbun in the oven** (*infml joc*) be pregnant.
□ **ˈbun-fight** *n* (*infml*) tea-party.

bunch /bʌntʃ/ *n* **1** [C] number of things (usu of the same kind) growing, fastened or grouped together: *a bunch of bananas, grapes, etc* ○ *bunches of flowers* ○ *a bunch of keys.* ⇨ illus at GRAPE. **2** [CGp] (*infml*) group of people; gang; mob: *a bunch of thugs* ○ *I don't like any of them much, but he's the best of the bunch,* ie the least unpleasant.
▷ **bunch** *v* [I, Ip, Tn, Tn·p] ~ (**sth/sb**) (**up**) (cause sth/sb to) be formed into a bunch or bunches: *a blouse that bunches at the waist* ○ *runners all bunched together,* ie closely grouped ○ *Cross the road one at a time — don't bunch up.*

bundle /ˈbʌndl/ *n* **1** [C] collection of things fastened or wrapped together: *a bundle of sticks, clothes, newspapers* ○ *books tied up in bundles of twenty.* **2** [sing] **a ~ of sth** (*infml*) a lot of sth; a mass of sth: *That child is a bundle of mischief!* ○ *He's not exactly a bundle of fun,* ie an amusing person. **3** [sing] (*infml*) large amount of money: *That car must have cost a bundle.* **4** (idm) **a bundle of ˈnerves** in a very nervous state: *The poor chap was a bundle of nerves at the interview.* **go a bundle on sb/sth** (*infml*) be very fond of sb/sth: *I don't go a bundle on her new husband, do you?*
▷ **bundle** *v* **1** [Tn, Tn·p] ~ **sth** (**up**) make or tie sth into a bundle or bundles: *The firewood was cut and bundled (together).* ○ *We bundled up some old clothes for the jumble sale.* **2** (phr v) **bundle sth into sth** throw sth or put sth away quickly and untidily in the specified place: *She bundled her clothes into the drawer without folding them.* **bundle (sb) out, off, into, etc** go or send (sb) hastily or roughly in the specified direction: *We all bundled into the tiny car.* ○ *I was bundled into a police van.* ○ *She bundled her son off to school.* **bundle (sb) up** dress (sb) in warm clothes.

bung /bʌŋ/ *n* stopper for closing the hole in a barrel or jar.
▷ **bung** *v* **1** [esp passive: Tn, Tn·pr, Tn·p] ~ **sth** (**up**) (**with sth**) close or block sth with or as with a bung: *My nose is (all) bunged up. I must be getting a cold.* ○ *The drains are bunged up with dead leaves.* **2** [Tn·pr, Tn·p] (*Brit infml*) throw or toss (sth): *Bung the newspaper over here, will you?*
□ **ˈbung-hole** *n* hole for filling or emptying a barrel.

bungalow /ˈbʌŋgələʊ/ *n* small house with one storey. ⇨ illus at HOME.
Bungalows are generally popular as homes with elderly people, since all the rooms are on one floor and there are no stairs to climb. However, some people find them rather dull to look at, particularly when they make up a whole estate on the outskirts of a town, and they are sometimes associated with suburban monotony. ⇨ article at HOUSE.

bungle /ˈbʌŋgl/ *v* [I, Tn] do (sth) badly or clumsily; spoil (a task) through lack of skill: *It looks as though you've bungled again.* ○ *Don't let him mend your bike. He's sure to bungle the job.* ○ *The gang spent a year planning the robbery and then bungled it.*
▷ **bungle** *n* (usu *sing*) bungled piece of work: *The whole job was a gigantic bungle.*
bungler /ˈbʌŋglə(r)/ *n* person who bungles: *You incompetent bungler!*

bunion /ˈbʌnjən/ *n* painful swelling, esp on the first joint of the big toe.

bunk[1] /bʌŋk/ *n* **1** narrow bed built into a wall like a shelf, eg on a ship. **2** (also **ˈbunk bed**) one of a pair of single beds, fixed one above the other, esp for children. ⇨ illus at FURNITURE.

bunk[2] /bʌŋk/ *n* (idm) **do a ˈbunk** (*Brit infml*) run away: *The cashier has done a bunk with the day's takings.*

bunk[3] /bʌŋk/ *n* [U] (*infml*) = BUNKUM: *Don't talk bunk!*

bunker /ˈbʌŋkə(r)/ *n* **1** container for storing fuel, esp on a ship or outside a house. **2** (also *esp US* **ˈsand trap**) sandy hollow on a golf course, from which it is difficult to hit the ball. ⇨ illus at GOLF. **3** strongly built underground shelter for soldiers, guns, etc.
▷ **bunker** *v* **1** [Tn] fill (a ship's bunker) with fuel. **2** [Tn usu passive] (in golf) hit (the ball) into a bunker: *He/His ball is bunkered.*

Bunker Hill /ˌbʌŋkə ˈhɪl/ the first serious battle (1775) in the American War of Independence. The rebels were defeated by the British troops but fought bravely, and this gave them confidence to continue the war.

bunkum /ˈbʌŋkəm/ (also **bunk**) *n* [U] (*infml*) nonsense: *Don't believe what he's saying — it's pure bunkum.*

bunny /ˈbʌnɪ/ *n* **1** (used by and to small children) rabbit. **2** (also **ˈbunny girl**) (*often sexist*) night-club hostess, esp one wearing a costume that includes false rabbit's ears and a tail.

Bunsen burner /ˌbʌnsn ˈbɜːnə(r)/ *n* gas burner used in chemical laboratories, consisting of a vertical tube with an adjustable air valve.

bunt /bʌnt/ *v* [I, Tn] (*US*) (in baseball) hit (the ball) gently without swinging the bat.

bunting[1] /ˈbʌntɪŋ/ *n* any of various small songbirds related to the finch family, with short thick bills.

bunting[2] /ˈbʌntɪŋ/ *n* [U] (**a**) coloured flags and streamers used for decorating streets and buildings. (**b**) loosely-woven fabric used for making these.

Buñuel /ˈbuːnjʊel; *US* ˌbuːnˈwel/ Luis (1900-83), Spanish film director. Many of his films have been attacked for satirizing the Church, the State and bourgeois society. He often used the surrealist technique of showing action as if in a dream. On one of his most famous early films, *Un Chien Andalou,* he worked with Salvador *Dali.

Bunyan[1] /ˈbʌnjən/ John (1628-88), English writer. A Puritan who fought for the Parliamentary army in the Civil War, he later spent several years in prison for preaching illegally. There he began his most famous book, *The Pilgrim's Progress,* a story describing the Christian life in the form of a dream.

Bunyan[2] /ˈbʌnjən/ Paul, a giant hero of many legendary stories told by lumberjacks in northern US and Canada.

Buonaparte = BONAPARTE.

buoy /bɔɪ/ *n* **1** floating object anchored to the bottom of the sea, a river, etc to mark places that are dangerous for boats or to show where boats may go, etc. **2** = LIFEBUOY (LIFE).
▷ **buoy** *v* **1** [Tn, Tn·p] ~ **sth** (**out**) mark the position of sth with a buoy: *buoy submerged rocks.* **2** (phr v) **buoy sb/sth up** (esp passive) (**a**) keep sb/sth afloat: *The raft was buoyed up by empty petrol cans.* (**b**) (*fig*) keep (prices, etc) at a high or satisfactory level: *Share prices were buoyed up by hopes of an end to the recession.* (**c**) (*fig*) raise the hopes or spirits of sb; encourage sb: *We felt buoyed up by the good news.*

buoyant /ˈbɔɪənt/ *adj* **1** (**a**) (of an object) able to float: *The raft would be more buoyant if it was less heavy.* (**b**) (of a liquid) able to keep things floating: *Salt water is more buoyant than fresh water.* **2** (of stock-market prices, etc) tending to rise: *Share prices were buoyant today in active trading.* **3** (of a person, his manner, etc) able to recover quickly after a setback; cheerfully resilient: *a buoyant disposition, personality, etc.* ▷ **buoyancy** /-ənsɪ/ *n* [U]. **buoyantly** *adv.*

BUPA /ˈbuːpə/ *abbr* British United Provident Association, (an organization that provides private medical insurance).

bur (also **burr**) /bɜː(r)/ *n* (plant with a) prickly seed-case or flower-head that clings to hair or clothing: (*fig*) *She tried to get rid of him at the party but he stuck to her like a bur.*

Burbage /ˈbɜːbɪdʒ/ Richard (c 1567-1619), the first great English actor. He worked with Shakespeare and was the first to play such roles as Hamlet and Othello.

Burberry /ˈbɜːbərɪ/ *n* (*propr*) type of lightweight raincoat of good quality.

burble /ˈbɜːbl/ *v* **1** [I] make a gentle murmuring or bubbling sound. **2** [I, Ipr, Ip] ~ (**on**) (**about sth**) speak in a rambling manner: *What's he burbling (on) about?*

burden /ˈbɜːdn/ *n* **1** [C] thing or person that is carried; heavy load: *bear/carry/shoulder a heavy burden.* **2** [C] (*fig*) duty, obligation, responsibility, etc that is hard to bear: *the burden of heavy taxation on the tax-payer* ○ *the burden of grief, guilt, remorse, etc* ○ *His invalid father is becoming a burden (to him).* **3** [sing] **the ~ of sth** main theme of a speech, an article, etc: *The burden of his argument was that....* **4** [U] ship's carrying capacity; tonnage.
▷ **burden** *v* [Tn, Tn·pr] ~ **sb/oneself** (**with sth**) put a burden on sb/oneself; load sb/oneself: *refugees burdened with all their possessions* ○ (*fig*) *I don't want to burden you with my problems.* ○ *Industry is heavily burdened with taxation.*
burdensome /-səm/ *adj* hard to bear; troublesome: *burdensome duties, responsibilities, etc.*
□ **the ˌburden of ˈproof** (*law*) obligation to prove that what one says is true.

bureau /ˈbjʊərəʊ; *US* bjʊˈrəʊ/ *n* (*pl* **-reaux** or **-reaus** /-rəʊz/) **1** (*Brit*) writing-desk with drawers. ⇨ illus at FURNITURE. **2** (*US*) = CHEST OF DRAWERS (CHEST). **3** (*esp US*) government department: *Federal Bureau of Investigation.* **4** office; agency: *a travel bureau* ○ *an information bureau.*

bureaucracy /bjʊəˈrɒkrəsɪ/ *n* (*often derog*) **1** (**a**) [U] system of government through departments managed by State officials, not by elected representatives. (**b**) [C] country having such a system. (**c**) [CGp] officials appointed to manage such a system, as a group. **2** [U] excessive or complicated official routine, esp because of too many departments and offices.

bureaucrat /ˈbjʊərəkræt/ *n* (*often derog*) official working in a government department, esp one who follows administrative routine and the rules of the department very strictly: *insensitive, bungling, etc bureaucrats.*
▷ **bureaucratic** /ˌbjʊərəˈkrætɪk/ *adj* (*often derog*) of, like or relating to a bureaucracy or bureaucrats: *bureaucratic government* ○ *The report revealed a major bureaucratic muddle.* **bureaucratically** /-ɪklɪ/ *adv.*

burette (*US* **buret**) /bjʊəˈret/ *n* (*chemistry*) graduated glass tube with a tap, used for measuring small quantities of liquid let out of it.

burgeon /ˈbɜːdʒən/ *v* [I] **1** (*archaic*) (of a plant) put out leaves; sprout. **2** (*fml*) begin to grow rapidly; flourish: *a burgeoning population* ○ *a burgeoning talent.*

burger /ˈbɜːgə(r)/ *n* (*infml*) = HAMBURGER.
▷ **-burger** (forming compound *ns*) (*infml*) food prepared or cooked like or with a hamburger: *a ˈsteakburger* ○ *a ˈcheeseburger.*

Burgess /ˈbɜːdʒɪs/ Anthony (1917-) English writer. He is best known for his novels, including *A Clockwork Orange,* a disturbing study of violence and high technology in a future world, and *Earthly Powers,* in which the hero lives through some of the most dramatic real events of the 20th century. He has also written music and books of criticism.

burgh /ˈbʌrə/ *n* (*Scot*) borough.

burgher /ˈbɜːgə(r)/ *n* (*arch or joc*) (esp respectable) citizen of a particular town: *The pop festival has shocked the good burghers of Canterbury.*

burglar /ˈbɜːglə(r)/ *n* person who enters a building illegally, esp by force, in order to steal: *The burglar got into the house through the bedroom window.* Cf ROBBER (ROB), THIEF.
▷ **burglary** /ˈbɜːglərɪ/ *n* [C, U] (instance of the) crime of entering a building in order to steal: *A number of burglaries have been committed in this area recently.* ○ *be accused/convicted of burglary.*
□ **ˈburglar-alarm** *n* automatic device that rings an alarm bell when a burglar enters a building.
ˈburglar-proof *adj* (of a building) made so that burglars cannot break into it.

burgle /ˈbɜːgl/ (*US* **burglarize, -ise** /ˈbɜːgləraɪz/) *v* [Tn] steal from (a house or person) after entering a building illegally: *burgle a shop* ○ *We were burgled while we were on holiday.* ⇨ Usage at ROB.

burgomaster /ˈbɜːgəmɑːstə(r)/ *n* mayor of a Dutch or Flemish town.

Burgundy /ˈbɜːgəndɪ/ *n* **1** [U, C] any of various types of red or white wine from the Burgundy area of eastern France. **2** [U] dark purplish-red colour.

burial /ˈberɪəl/ *n* [U, C] burying, esp of a dead body; funeral: *Cremation is more common than burial in some countries.* ○ *The burial took place on Friday.* ○ [attrib] *the burial service.*

□ ˈ**burial-ground** *n* place where dead bodies are buried; cemetery: *a prehistoric burial-ground.*

Burke /bɜːk/ Edmund (1729-97), British writer and politician. He campaigned for American independence and the rights of Irish Catholics, but he was deeply opposed to the French Revolution.

Burke and Hare /ˌbɜːk ənd ˈheə(r)/ Irish criminals. They were hanged in 1829 for killing people and stealing bodies from graves so that doctors could carry out medical experiments on them.

Burke's Peerage /ˌbɜːks ˈpɪərɪdʒ/ short title of a book giving details about members of British noble families and other people with titles. It was first issued in 1826 by John Burke and has been published regularly ever since. Cf DEBRETT'S PEERAGE. ⇨ article at ARISTOCRAT.

Burkina /bɜːˈkiːnə/ country in western Africa, formerly called Upper Volta, an independent republic since 1960; pop approx 8 509 000; official language French; capital Ouagadougou; unit of currency franc. The northern part is semi-desert. The country is extremely poor and agricultural production is low, though some cotton is exported. ⇨ map at NIGERIA. ▷ **Burkinan** /bɜːˈkiːnən/ *n, adj.*

burlesque /bɜːˈlesk/ *n* **1** [C, U] (piece of writing that mocks sb/sth by) comic or exaggerated imitation; parody: *a burlesque of a novel, poem, etc.* **2** [U] (*US*) type of bawdy comedy show, often involving striptease.

▷ **burlesque** *adj* [usu attrib] of, relating to or using burlesque(1, 2): *a burlesque actor* ○ *burlesque acting.*

burlesque *v* [Tn] make a burlesque of (sb/sth); parody.

burly /ˈbɜːlɪ/ *adj* (**-ier, -iest**) with a strong heavy body; sturdy: *a burly policeman.* ▷ **burliness** *n* [U].

Burma (Myanmar)

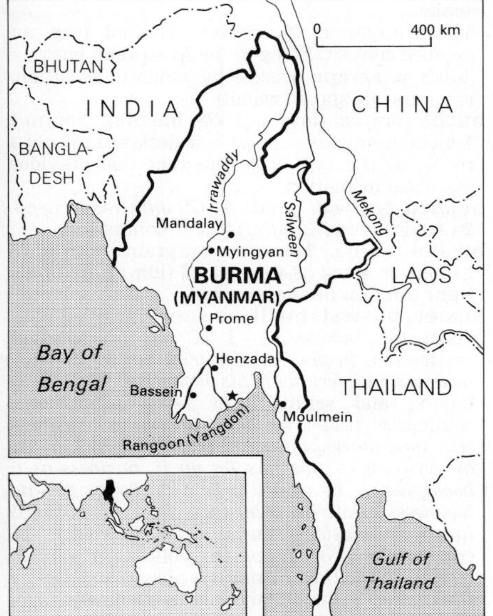

Burma /ˈbɜːmə/ (also **Myanmar** /ˈmɪənmɑː(r)/ country in SE Asia; pop approx 39 966 000; official language Burmese; capital Rangoon; unit of currency kyat (= 100 pyas). Agriculture is an important part of the economy, but the country also has some mineral resources. Previously part of British India, it became independent in 1948, but there has been continuing political unrest. ⇨ map.

▷ **Burmese** /ˌbɜːˈmiːz/ *n* **1** (*pl* unchanged) native or inhabitant of Burma. **2** official language of Burma, spoken by most of the population. — *adj.*

burn[1] /bɜːn/ *n* (*Scot*) small stream.

burn[2] /bɜːn/ *v* (*pt, pp* **burnt** /bɜːnt/ or **burned** /bɜːnd/). ⇨ Usage at DREAM[2]. **1** (**a**) [Tn] destroy, damage, injure or mark (sb/sth) by fire, heat or acid: *burn dead leaves, waste paper, rubbish, etc* ○ *The house was burnt to the ground*, ie completely destroyed by fire. ○ *All his belongings were burnt in the fire.* ○ *Sorry, I've burnt the toast.* ○ *His face was badly burnt by the hot sun.* ○ *The soup is very hot. Don't burn your mouth.* ○ *The child burnt its fingers/itself while playing with a match.* (**b**) [I] be marked, damaged or spoilt in this way: *Her skin burns easily.* ○ *I can smell something burning.* **2** [Tn, Tn·pr] make (a hole or mark) by burning: *The cigarette burnt a hole in the carpet.* **3** [Tn] use (sth) as fuel: *Do you burn coal as well as wood on this fire?* ○ *a central heating boiler that burns gas/oil/coke.* **4** [I, Tn] (cause a person or an animal to) be killed by fire: *Ten people burnt to death in the hotel fire.* ○ *Joan of Arc was burnt (alive) at the stake.* **5** (**a**) [La, I] be on fire or alight; produce heat or light: *a burning building* ○ *The house burned for hours before the blaze was put out.* ○ *A fire was burning merrily in the grate.* ○ *The fire had burnt low*, ie was nearly out. ○ *A single light burned in the empty house.* (**b**) [I] be able to catch fire: *Paper burns easily.* ○ *Damp wood doesn't burn well.* **6** [Tn] make (sth) by burning: *burn charcoal.* **7** [I, Tn] (cause sb/sth to) feel painfully hot: *Your forehead's burning. Have you got a fever?* **8** [Ipr] ~ **with sth** (usu in the continuous tenses) be full of strong emotion: *be burning with rage, desire, longing, etc.* **9** [Ipr, It] ~ **for sth** (usu in the continuous tenses) want to do sth very much: (*rhet*) *He was burning for vengeance/to avenge the death of his father.* **10** (idm) **burn one's ˈboats/ˈbridges** do sth that makes it impossible to go back to a previous situation: *Think carefully before you resign — if you do that you will have burnt your boats.* **burn the candle at both ˈends** exhaust oneself by trying to do too many things. **burn one's ˈfingers/get one's ˈfingers burnt** suffer (often financially) as a result of foolish behaviour or meddling: *He got his fingers badly burnt dabbling in the stock-market.* **burn the midnight ˈoil** study or work until late at night: *She takes her exams next week, so she's burning the midnight oil.* **burn sth to a crisp** cook sth too long, so that it becomes burnt: (*fig*) *I lay in the sun all day and got burnt to a crisp.* **sb's ears are burning** ⇨ EAR[1]. **feel one's ears burning** ⇨ FEEL[1]. **have money to burn** ⇨ MONEY. **money burns a hole in sb's pocket** ⇨ MONEY.

11 (phr v) **burn away** continue to burn: *a fire burning away in the grate.* **burn (sth) away** (**a**) (cause sth to) become less by burning: *Half the candle had burnt away.* (**b**) (cause sth to) be removed by burning: *Most of the skin on his face got burnt away in the fire.*

burn down (of a fire) burn less brightly or strongly: *The room grew colder as the fire burnt down.* **burn (sth) down** (cause sth to) be destroyed to the foundations by fire: *The house burnt down in half an hour.* ○ *Don't leave the gas on — you might burn the house down.*

burn sth off remove sth by burning: *Burn the old paint off before re-painting the door.*

burn (itself) out (**a**) (of a fire) stop burning because there is no more fuel: *The fire had burnt (itself) out before the fire brigade arrived.* (**b**) (of a rocket) finish its supply of fuel. **burn (sth) out** (cause sth to) stop working because of friction or excessive heat: *The clutch has burnt out.* ○ *burn out a fuse, motor, transformer.* **burn oneself out** exhaust oneself or ruin one's health, esp by working too hard: *If he doesn't stop working so hard, he'll burn himself out.* **burn sb out** (esp passive) force sb to leave his house by burning it: *The family was burnt out (of house and home) and forced to leave the area.* **burn sth out** (esp passive) completely destroy sth by burning; gut sth: *The hotel was completely burnt out.* ○ *the burnt-out wreck of a car.*

burn (sth) to sth (cause sth to) be reduced to the specified state by burning: *It burned to ashes.* ○ *You've burnt the toast to a cinder*, ie so that it is hard and black.

burn up (**a**) (of a fire) produce brighter and stronger flames: *put more wood on a fire to make it burn up.* (**b**) (of an object entering the earth's atmosphere) be destroyed by heat. **burn sb up** (*US infml*) make sb very angry. **burn sth up** get rid of sth by burning: *burn up all the garden rubbish.*

▷ **burn** *n* **1** injury or mark caused by fire, heat or acid: *He died of the burns he received in the fire.* **2** firing of the rockets in a spacecraft (to change its course).

burner *n* **1** part of a gas lamp, oven, etc from which the light or flame comes. **2** person who burns sth or makes sth by burning: *a charcoal-burner.* **3** (idm) **put sth on the back burner** ⇨ BACK[2].

burning *adj* [attrib] **1** intense; extreme: *a burning thirst* ○ *a burning desire for sth.* **2** very important; urgent; crucial: *one of the most burning issues of the day.*

burnt *adj* marked, damaged or hurt by burning: *rather burnt toast* ○ *Your hand looks badly burnt.*

burnt ˈoffering thing offered as a sacrifice by burning.

□ ˈ**burning-glass** *n* lens, eg of a magnifying glass, used to concentrate the sun's rays onto an object and set fire to it.

Sir Edward Burne-Jones: King Cophetua and the Beggar Maid

ˈ**burn-up** *n* (*Brit sl*) ride on a motor-cycle, etc at high speed.

Burne-Jones /ˌbɜːn ˈdʒəʊnz/ Sir Edward Coley (1833-98), English painter. He belonged to the *Pre-Raphaelite school, often taking his subjects from medieval legend. ⇨ illus.

Burney /ˈbɜːnɪ/ Fanny (1752-1840), English writer. She became famous through her novels, but is best remembered today for her diaries and letters, which record her experiences abroad and at the English court.

Burnham scale /ˈbɜːnəm skeɪl/ until 1987, the scale of salaries for teachers in most British schools and colleges.

burnish /ˈbɜːnɪʃ/ *v* [Tn] make (metal) smooth and shiny by rubbing; polish: *burnished copper*.

burnous /bɜːˈnuːs/ *n* type of cloak with a hood, worn by Arabs.

Burns /bɜːnz/ Robert (1759-96), Scottish poet. He wrote both in English and in the dialect of Lowland Scotland on love, the country, and the life of working people. The warmth and humanity of his verse has won it lasting popularity, even among people who normally read little poetry. He loved Scotland deeply and the Scots have long regarded him as their national poet. ⇨ article at SCOTLAND.

□ ˈ**Burns' night** 25 January, the birthday of Robert Burns, celebrated by the Scots and other lovers of the poet. Traditionally haggises and other Scottish dishes are eaten while bagpipe music is played and some of Burns's most popular poems are read aloud.

burp /bɜːp/ *n* (*infml*) belch.

▷ **burp** *v* (*infml*) **1** [I] belch. **2** [Tn] cause (a baby) to bring up wind from the stomach, esp by stroking or patting the back.

□ ˈ**burp gun** (*US infml*) automatic pistol.

burr[1] = BUR.

burr[2] /bɜː(r)/ *n* **1** (usu *sing*) whirring or humming sound made eg by parts of a machine turning quickly or by a telephone. **2** (usu *sing*) strong pronunciation of the 'r' sound, typical of certain English accents; accent using this: *speak with a soft West Country burr*. **3** rough edge of a metal object that has been made but not properly finished. **4** small drill used by a dentist.

▷ **burr** *v* [I] make a burr (1,2).

Burroughs[1] /ˈbʌrəʊz/ Edgar Rice (1875-1950), American novelist who created the jungle hero *Tarzan.

Burroughs[2] /ˈbʌrəʊz/ William Seward (1914-), American writer. He became a leading figure of the *beat generation with his novel *The Naked Lunch*. His writings reflect his background as a homosexual and a drug addict, and his fascination with the violent side of life.

burrow /ˈbʌrəʊ/ *n* hole made in the ground and used as a home or shelter by rabbits, foxes, etc.

▷ **burrow** *v* **1** (**a**) [Tn] make (sth) by digging: *Rabbits had burrowed holes in the grassy bank*. (**b**) [I] dig a hole; tunnel. **2** (phr v) **burrow (one's way) into, through, under, etc** move in the specified direction by or as if by digging: *The fox burrowed (its way) under the fence to reach the chickens.* ○ *The prisoners escaped by burrowing under the wall.* ○ *The child burrowed under the bedclothes.* ○ (*fig*) *We had to burrow through a mass of files to find the documents we wanted.*

bursar /ˈbɜːsə(r)/ *n* **1** person who manages the finances of a school or college. **2** person holding a scholarship at a university.

▷ **bursary** /ˈbɜːsərɪ/ *n* **1** college bursar's office. **2** scholarship or grant awarded to a student.

burst[1] /bɜːst/ *v* (*pt, pp* **burst**) **1** [I, Tn] (cause sth to) break violently open or apart, esp because of pressure from inside; explode: *If you blow that balloon up any more it will burst.* ○ *The dam burst under the weight of water.* ○ *Water-pipes often burst in cold weather.* ○ (*fig*) *I've eaten so much I feel ready to burst!* ○ *The river burst its banks and flooded the town.* ○ *Don't get so angry! You'll burst a blood-vessel!* **2** [I, Ipr] ~ (**with sth**) (only in the continuous tenses) be full to the point of breaking open: *'More pudding?' 'No thanks. I'm bursting!'* ○ *May I use your lavatory — I'm bursting!* ie I need to urinate urgently. ○ *a bag bursting with shopping* ○ (*fig*) *be bursting with happiness, pride, excitement, etc.* **3** (idm) **be bursting at the** ˈ**seams** (*infml*) be very full or tight: *I've eaten so much I'm bursting at the seams.* **be bursting to do sth** be very eager to do sth: *She was bursting to tell him the good news.* **burst (sth)** ˈ**open** (cause sth to) open suddenly or violently: *The police burst the door open.* **4** (phr v) **burst** ˈ**in** enter (a room, etc) suddenly: *The police burst in (through the door) and arrested the gang.* **burst in on sb/sth** interrupt sb/sth (by arriving suddenly): *burst in on a meeting* ○ *How dare you burst in on us without knocking!* **burst into sth** send out or produce sth suddenly and violently: *The aircraft crashed and burst into flames*, ie suddenly began to burn. ○ *burst into tears, song, angry speech*, ie suddenly begin to cry, sing, speak angrily ○ *trees bursting into leaf/bloom/blossom/flower.* **burst into, out of, through, etc sth** move suddenly and forcibly in the specified direction; appear suddenly from somewhere: *An angry crowd burst through the lines of police and into the street.* ○ *The oil burst out of the ground.* ○ *The sun burst through the clouds.* **burst on/upon sb/sth** come suddenly and unexpectedly to sb/sth: *The truth burst upon him*, ie He suddenly realized it. ○ *A major new talent has burst on the literary scene.* **burst out** (**a**) speak suddenly and with feeling; exclaim: *'I hate you!' she burst out.* (**b**) (with the *-ing* form) suddenly begin (doing sth): *burst out crying/laughing/singing.*

burst[2] /bɜːst/ *n* **1** (**a**) bursting; explosion: *the burst of a shell, bomb.* (**b**) split caused by this: *a burst in a water-pipe.* **2** brief violent effort; spurt: *a burst of energy, speed, etc* ○ *work in short bursts.* **3** sudden outbreak of sth: *a burst of anger, enthusiasm, etc* ○ *a burst of applause.* **4** short series of shots from a gun: *a burst of machine-gun fire.*

Burton /ˈbɜːtn/ Richard (1925-84), Welsh actor. He was noted for his stage performances in Shakespearean roles before achieving wider fame in films. He had a famous screen partnership with Elizabeth *Taylor (to whom he was twice married) in films such as *Who's Afraid of Virginia Woolf?* and *Cleopatra*.

burton /ˈbɜːtn/ *n* (idm) **go for a** ˈ**burton** (*Brit infml*) be lost, destroyed or killed: *It's pouring with rain, so I'm afraid our picnic's gone for a burton.*

Burundi /bʊˈrʊndɪ/ country in East Africa; pop approx 5 149 000; official languages French and Kirundi; capital Bujumbura; unit of currency franc. The country is very poor, with a basically agricultural economy. It gained independence in 1962, but has suffered since from ethnic conflict between the Hutu and Tutsi populations. ⇨ map at TANZANIA.

bury /ˈberɪ/ *v* (*pt, pp* **buried**) **1** [Tn] (**a**) place (a dead body) in a grave or in the sea: *He was buried with his wife.* ○ *Where is Shakespeare buried?* ○ *He's been dead and buried for years!* (**b**) (*euph*) lose (sb) by death: *She's eighty-five and has buried three husbands.* **2** [Tn, Tn·pr, Cn·a] hide (sb/sth) in the earth; cover with soil, rocks, leaves, etc: *buried treasure* ○ *Our dog buries its bones in the garden.* ○ *The house was buried under ten feet of snow.* ○ *The miners were buried alive when the tunnel collapsed.* **3** [Tn, Tn·pr] hide (sb/sth) from sight; cover up: *Your letter got buried under a pile of papers.* ○ *She buried her face in her hands and wept.* **4** [Tn] dismiss (sth) from one's mind; completely forget about: *It's time to bury our differences and be friends again.* **5** [Tn·pr] ~ **sth (in sth)** plunge sth (into sth): *The lion buried its teeth in the antelope's neck.* ○ *He walked slowly, his hands buried in his pockets.* ○ *Her head was buried in the book she was reading.* **6** (idm) ˌ**bury the** ˈ**hatchet** stop quarrelling and become friendly. **bury/hide one's head in the sand** ⇨ HEAD[1]. **7** (phr v) **bury oneself in sth** (**a**) go to (a place where one will meet few people): *He buried himself (away) in the country to write a book.* (**b**) involve oneself in or concentrate deeply on sth: *In the evenings he buries himself in his books.*

bus /bʌs/ *n* (*pl* **buses**; *US* also **busses**) **1** large vehicle carrying passengers between stopping-places along a fixed route: *Shall we walk or go by bus?* ○ [attrib] *a bus driver/conductor* ○ *a bus station.* **2** (idm) **miss the boat/bus** ⇨ MISS[3].

▷ **bus** *v* (*pres p* **busing**; also *esp US* **bussing**, *pt, pp* **bused**; also *esp US* **bussed**) **1** [I] (also **bus it**) travel by bus: *I usually bus (it) to work in the morning.* **2** [Tn] (**a**) transport (sb) by bus. (**b**) (*US*) transport (children) by bus from white areas to schools in black areas and vice versa, to create racially integrated schools. **3** (*US*) [I] work as a busboy.

□ ˈ**bus lane** strip of road for use by buses only.

ˈ**busman** /-mən/ *n* (idm) **a busman's** ˈ**holiday** holiday spent doing the same thing that one does at work.

ˈ**bus-shelter** *n* structure at a bus-stop providing shelter for people waiting for a bus.

ˈ**bus-stop** *n* regular stopping-place for a bus; sign marking this.

British buses are either single-deckers or double-deckers. The red double-deckers in London are particularly well known. Many buses no longer have conductors, in which case it is necessary to state your destination and pay the driver the correct fare when you get on the bus. Smoking is usually only allowed on the upper deck of double-deckers. Long-distance buses, usually called 'coaches', are generally cheaper than trains. Tickets normally need to be bought in advance, either from a travel agency or directly from the coach station.

busboy /ˈbʌsbɔɪ/ *n* (*US*) an assistant who helps a waiter or waitress by clearing tables, etc.

busby /ˈbʌzbɪ/ *n* tall fur cap worn by hussars, gunners, etc for ceremonial parades, etc.

bush[1] /bʊʃ/ *n* **1** [C] (**a**) low thickly-growing plant with several woody stems coming up from the root; shrub: *a rose bush* ○ *gooseberry bushes.* Cf TREE. (**b**) thing resembling this, esp a clump of hair or fur. **2** (often **the bush**) [U] wild uncultivated land, esp in Africa, Australia and (with forests) Canada. **3** (idm) **beat about the bush** ⇨ BEAT[1]. **a bird in the hand is worth two in the bush** ⇨ BIRD.

▷ **bushy** *adj* (**-ier, -iest**) **1** covered with bushes. **2** growing thickly; shaggy: *a bushy moustache* ○ *bushy eyebrows.* **3** (idm) **bright eyed and bushy-tailed** ⇨ BRIGHT. **bushiness** *n* [U].

□ ˈ**bush-baby** *n* small African lemur with large eyes and a long tail.

ˈ**Bushman** /-mən/ *n* (*pl* **-men**) member of various S W African tribes living and hunting in the bush.

ˈ**bushmaster** *n* largest American poisonous snake.

ˈ**bush-ranger** *n* (formerly) criminal (esp an escaped convict) living in the Australian bush.

ˌ**bush** ˈ**telegraph** process by which information, rumours, etc spread rapidly.

bush[2] /bʊʃ/ *n* (also *esp US* **bushing** /ˈbʊʃɪŋ/) **1** metal lining for a round hole designed to hold a revolving pin, etc. **2** flexible tube that provides electrical insulation.

bushed /bʊʃt/ *adj* [pred] **1** (*US infml*) very tired. **2** (*Austral and NZ infml*) lost or confused.

bushel /ˈbʊʃl/ *n* **1** measure for grain and fruit (8 gallons or about 36.4 litres). **2** (idm) **hide one's light under a bushel** ⇨ HIDE[1].

busier, busiest, busily ⇨ BUSY.

business /ˈbɪznɪs/ *n* **1** [C, U] one's usual occupation; profession: *He tries not to let (his) business interfere with his home life.* **2** [U] (**a**) buying and selling (esp as a profession); commerce; trade: *We don't do (much) business with foreign companies.* ○ *He's in* (ie works in) *the oil business.* ○ *She has set up in business as a bookseller.* ○ *He wants to be a doctor or go into business.* ○ [attrib] *a business trip* ○ *a business lunch* ○ *business sense*, ie knowledge of commercial procedures. (**b**) volume or rate of buying and selling: *Business is always brisk before Christmas.* **3** [C] commercial establishment; firm; shop: *have/own one's own business* ○ *She runs a thriving grocery business.* ○ *Many small businesses have gone bankrupt recently.* **4** [U] thing that one is rightly concerned with or interested in; duty;

task: *It is the business of the police to protect the community.* ○ *I shall make it my business to find out who is responsible.* ○ *My private life is none of your business/is no business of yours.* **5** [U] things that need to be dealt with; matters to be discussed: *The main business of this meeting is our wages claim.* ○ *Unless there is any other business, we can end the meeting.* **6** [sing] (*often derog*) matter; affair: *an odd, a strange, a disturbing, etc business* ○ *What a business it is moving house!* ○ *I'm sick of the whole business.* ○ *That plane crash was an awful business.* ○ *What's this business I hear about you losing your job?* **7** [U] gestures, facial expressions, etc made by actors on stage to give extra effect to what they are saying. **8** (idm) **be in 'business** have everything one needs to do what one wants to do: *Fetch me a corkscrew and we're in business!* **business as 'usual** (*catchphrase*) things will proceed normally despite difficulties or disturbances. **the 'business end (of sth)** (*infml*) part of a tool, an instrument, a weapon, etc that performs its particular function: *Never hold a gun by the business end.* **ˌbusiness is 'business** (*catchphrase*) in financial and commercial matters one must not be influenced by friendship, pity, etc. **funny business** ⇨ FUNNY. **get down to 'business** start the work that must be done. **go about one's 'business** occupy oneself with one's own affairs: *streets filled with people going about their daily business.* **go out of 'business** become bankrupt. **have no business to do sth/doing sth** have no right to do sth: *You've no business to be here — this is private property.* **like 'nobody's business** (*infml*) very much, fast or well: *My head hurts like nobody's business.* **mean business** ⇨ MEAN[1]. **mind one's own business** ⇨ MIND[2]. **on 'business** for the purpose of doing business: *I'll be away on business next week.* **send sb about his business** ⇨ SEND.

□ **'business address** address of one's place of work.

'business card small card printed with sb's name and details of his job and company.

'business hours hours during which a shop or an office is open for work.

'businesslike *adj* efficient; systematic: *Negotiations were conducted in a businesslike manner.*

'businessman /-mæn, -mən/, **'businesswoman** *ns* **1** person working in business, esp the manager of a company. **2** person who is skilful and alert in financial matters: *I ought to have got a better price for the car but I'm not a very good businessman.* ⇨ Usage at CHAIR.

'business studies study of economics and management.

busk /bʌsk/ *v* [I] (*infml*) entertain people in a public place, eg by playing music, for money. ▷ **busker** *n.* **busking** *n* [U].

bust[1] /bʌst/ *n* **1** sculpture of a person's head, shoulders and chest. **2 (a)** woman's breasts; bosom. **(b)** measurement round a woman's chest and back: [attrib] *What is your bust size, madam?* ▷ **busty** *adj* having large breasts.

bust[2] /bʌst/ *v* (*pt, pp* **bust** or **busted**) (*infml*) **1** [Tn] break (sth); smash: *I dropped my camera on the pavement and bust it.* **2** [Tn, Tn·pr] ~ **sth/sb (for sth)** (of the police) raid (a house) or arrest sb: *Mickey's been busted for drugs.* **3** [Tn] reduce (sb) to a lower military rank; demote: *He was busted (to corporal) for being absent without leave.* **4** (idm) **bust a 'gut (to do sth/doing sth)** (*Brit sl*) make a great effort: *I bust a gut to get my article written on time and now they don't want it after all.* **5** (phr v) **bust up** (*infml*) (esp of a married couple) quarrel and separate: *They bust up after five years of marriage.* **bust sth up** cause sth to end; disrupt sth: *bust up a meeting* ○ *It was his drinking that busted up their marriage.*

▷ **bust** *n* raid or arrest by the police.

bust *adj* [pred] (*infml*) **1** broken; not working: *My watch is bust.* **2** bankrupt. **3** (idm) **go 'bust** (of a person or a business) become bankrupt; fail financially.

-buster (forming compound *ns*) person who fights against sth specified (eg an illegal activity or those taking part in it): *a crime-buster.*

□ **'bust-up** *n* **1** violent quarrel. **2** breaking up of a relationship, esp marriage.

bustard /'bʌstəd/ *n* large land bird that can run very fast.

buster /'bʌstə(r)/ *n* (*US infml usu derog*) (used as a form of address to a man): *Get lost, buster!*

bustle[1] /'bʌsl/ *v* **1** [I, Ipr, Ip, Tn, Tn·pr, Tn·p] (cause to) move busily and energetically (in the specified direction): *bustling about in the kitchen* ○ *She bustled the children off to school.* **2** [I, Ipr] ~ **(with sth)** be full of (noise, activity, etc): *bustling streets* ○ *The city centre was bustling with life.*

▷ **bustle** *n* [U] excited and noisy activity: *the (hustle and) bustle of city life.*

bustle[2] /'bʌsl/ *n* (formerly) frame or padding used to puff out a woman's dress at the back. ⇨ illus at DRESS.

busy /'bɪzɪ/ *adj* (**-ier, -iest**) **1** ~ **(at/with sth)**; ~ **(doing sth)** having much to do; working (on sth); occupied (with sth): *Doctors are busy people.* ○ *Could I have a word with you, if you're not too busy?* ○ *She's busy at/with her homework.* ○ *Please go away — can't you see I'm busy?* ○ *She's busy writing letters.* **2** full of activity: *a busy day, life, time of year, etc* ○ *a busy office, street, town* ○ *Victoria is one of London's busiest stations.* ○ *The shops are very busy at Christmas.* **3 (a)** = ENGAGED (ENGAGE). **(b)** being used (and so not available): *The (telephone) line is busy.* ○ *The photocopier has been busy all morning.* **4** (of a picture or design) too full of detail: *This wallpaper is too busy for the bedroom.* **5** (idm) **(as) busy as a bee** very busy (and happy to be so): *The children are busy as bees, helping their mother in the garden.* **get busy** start working: *We've only got an hour to do the job — we'd better get busy.*

▷ **busily** *adv*: *busily engaged on a new project.*

busy *v* (*pt, pp* **busied**) [Tn, Tn·pr, Tng] ~ **oneself (with sth)**; ~ **oneself (in/with) doing sth** occupy oneself or keep oneself busy (with sth): *busy oneself in the garden, with the housework, etc* ○ *He busied himself cooking the dinner.*

busybody /'bɪzɪbɒdɪ/ *n* (*derog*) person who interferes in other people's affairs: *He's an interfering busybody!*

but[1] /bʌt, *also* bət/ *adv* **1** (*esp dated or fml*) only: *He's but a boy.* ○ *If I had but known she was ill, I would have visited her.* ○ *I don't think we'll succeed. Still, we can but try.* **2** (idm) **one cannot/could not but...** (*fml*) one can only...; one is obliged to...: *It was a rash thing to do, yet one cannot but admire her courage.* ○ *I could not but admit that he was right and I was wrong.*

but[2] /bət; *strong form* bʌt/ *conj* (often used to introduce a word or phrase contrasting with or qualifying what has gone before) **1** on the contrary: *You've bought the wrong shirt. It's not the red one I wanted but the blue one.* ○ *Tom went to the party, but his brother didn't.* ○ *He doesn't like music but his wife does.* **2 (a)** yet; however; in spite of this: *She cut her knee badly, but didn't cry.* ○ *I'd love to go to the theatre tonight, but I'm too busy.* ○ *This restaurant serves cheap but excellent food.* ○ *He's hard-working, but not very clever.* **(b)** yet also; at the same time: *He was tired but happy after the long walk.* **3** (*dated or fml*) (usu after a negative) without the result that...; without it also being the case that...: *I never pass my old house but I think of the happy years I spent there.* ○ *No man is so cruel but he may feel some pity.* **4** (showing disagreement, surprise or astonishment): *'I'll give you ten pounds to repair the damage.' 'But that's not nearly enough!'* ○ *'I'm getting married.' 'But that's wonderful!'* **5** (used to emphasize a word): *Nothing, but nothing will make me change my mind.* **6** (idm) **ˌbut me no 'buts** don't argue with me or make excuses. **ˌbut that...** (*dated or fml*) **(a)** were it not for the fact that...: *But that you had seen me in the water, I would have drowned.* ○ *He would have come with us but that he had no money.* **(b)** (after a negative) that...: *I don't deny/doubt/question but that you're telling the truth.* **(c)** other than: *Who knows but that what he says is true? We have no proof that he is lying.* **but then** on the other hand; moreover; nevertheless: *He speaks very good French — but then he did live in Paris for three years.* **not only...but also...** both...and...: *He is not only arrogant but also selfish.*

but[3] /bət; *strong form* bʌt/ *prep* **1** (used after the negatives *nobody, none, nowhere,* etc, the question words *who, where,* etc and also *all, everyone, anyone,* etc) except (sb/sth); apart from; other than: *The problem is anything but easy.* ○ *Everyone was there but him.* ○ *Nobody but you could be so selfish.* ○ *Nothing but trouble will come of this plan.* **2** (idm) **but for sb/sth** /'bʌt fə/ except for sb/sth; without sb/sth: *But for the rain we would have had a nice holiday.* ○ *But for the safety-belt I wouldn't be alive today.*

but[4] /bʌt, *also* bət/ *rel pron* (*dated or fml*) (after a negative) who/that do/does not: *There is no man but feels* (ie no man who does not feel) *pity for starving children.* ○ *There is not one of us but wishes* (ie not one of us that does not wish) *to help you.*

butane /'bju:teɪn/ *n* [U] inflammable gas produced from petroleum, used in liquid form as a fuel (for cooking, heating, lighting, etc).

butch /bʊtʃ/ *adj* (*infml*) **1** (*often derog*) (of a woman) having a masculine appearance and behaviour. **2** (*often approv*) (of a man) exaggeratedly or aggressively masculine.

butcher /'bʊtʃə(r)/ *n* **1** person whose job is killing animals for food or cutting up and selling meat: *buy meat at the butcher's (shop).* **2** (*derog*) person who kills people unnecessarily and brutally: *a mindless butcher of innocent people.* **3** (idm) **have/take a 'butcher's (at sth)** (*Brit sl*) have/take a look: *Have a 'butcher's at this picture in the paper.*

▷ **butcher** *v* [Tn] **1** kill and prepare (animals) for meat. **2** (*derog*) kill (people or animals) unnecessarily and brutally: *Woman and children were butchered by the rebels.* **3** (*fig*) make a mess of (sth); ruin: *None of the cast can act at all — they're butchering the play.*

butchery *n* [U] **1** butcher's trade. **2** unnecessary or brutal killing.

Butler[1] /'bʌtlə(r)/ Samuel (1612-80), English writer. His main work was the comic poem *Hudibras,* a satire on the society and politics of his time.

Butler[2] /'bʌtlə(r)/ Samuel (1835-1902), English writer. His two most famous works are the satire *Erewhon* and the partly autobiographical *The Way of All Flesh.* Both wittily attack the attitudes and prejudices of contemporary society.

butler /'bʌtlə(r)/ *n* chief male servant of a house, usu in charge of the wine-cellar.

Butlin's /'bʌtlɪnz/ British company that runs a group of holiday centres, the first of them opened in 1936. These 'holiday camps' were very popular in the 1950s (before travel abroad became cheap), providing a wide range of activities and entertainments for all ages. The centres have since changed in style but still attract many holiday-makers: *We always go to Butlin's for our summer holiday.* ⇨ article at HOLIDAY.

butt[1] /bʌt/ *n* **1** large cask or barrel for storing wine or beer. **2** large barrel for collecting rainwater, eg from a roof.

butt[2] /bʌt/ *n* **1** (also **butt-'end**) thicker end of a tool or weapon: *a rifle butt.* ⇨ illus at GUN. **2** (also **'butt-end**) short piece at the end of a cigar or cigarette that is left when it has been smoked; stub: *an ashtray full of butts.* **3** (*infml esp US*) buttocks; bottom: *Get off your butts and do some work!*

butt[3] /bʌt/ *n* **1 (a)** [C] mound of earth behind the targets on a shooting-range. **(b) the butts** [pl] shooting-range. **2** [C] person or thing that is often mocked or teased: *be the butt of everyone's jokes.*

butt[4] /bʌt/ *v* **1** [Tn, Tn·pr] hit or push (sb/sth) with the head (like a goat): *butt sb in the stomach.* **2** [Tn·pr] hit (one's head) on sth: *He butted his head against the shelf as he was getting up.* **3** (phr v) **butt in (on sb/sth)** (*infml*) interrupt (sb/sth) or interfere (in sth): *Don't butt in like that when I'm speaking.* ○ *May I butt in on your conversation?*

butte /bju:t/ *n* (*US*) hill that rises abruptly from the surrounding land, esp one with high steep sides and a flat top.

butter /ˈbʌtə(r)/ *n* **1** [U] fatty food substance, made from cream by churning, that is spread on bread, etc or used in cooking: *Would you like some more bread and butter?* ○ *Shall I use oil or butter for frying the onions?* **2** [U] (in compounds) similar food substance made from the specified material: *peanut butter.* **3** (idm) **(look as if/as though) ˌbutter would not ˌmelt in one's ˈmouth** appear innocent, although one is probably not. **like a knife through butter** ⇨ KNIFE.

▷ **butter** *v* **1** [Tn] spread or put butter on (esp bread): *(hot) buttered toast* ○ *buttered carrots.* **2** (idm) **know which side one's bread is buttered** ⇨ KNOW. **3** (phr v) **butter sb up** (*infml*) flatter sb: *I've seen you buttering up the boss!*

buttery *adj* like, containing or covered with butter.

□ **ˈbutter-knife** (*esp Brit*) *n* knife with a blunt edge used for serving oneself with butter during a meal.

ˈbuttermilk *n* [U] liquid that remains after butter has been separated from milk.

ˌbutter ˈmuslin thin, loosely woven cloth used originally for wrapping butter: *a ˌbutter ˌmuslin ˈblouse.* Cf CHEESECLOTH.

ˈbutterscotch *n* [U] hard toffee made by boiling butter and sugar together.

butter-bean /ˈbʌtə biːn/ *n* large white type of bean, often dried before being sold.

buttercup /ˈbʌtəkʌp/ *n* wild plant with bright yellow cup-shaped flowers. ⇨ illus at PLANT.

butter-fingers /ˈbʌtəfɪŋgəz/ *n* (*pl* unchanged) (*infml*) person who is likely to drop things.

the life cycle of a butterfly

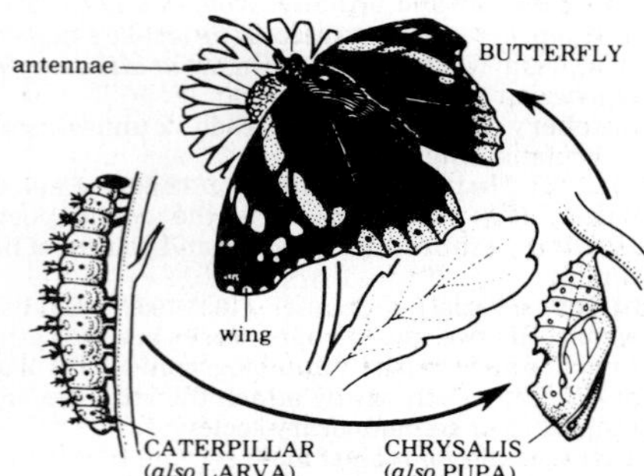

butterfly /ˈbʌtəflaɪ/ *n* **1** [C] insect with a long thin body and four (usu brightly coloured) wings. ⇨ illus. **2** [C] (*fig*) person who never settles down to one job or activity for long: *a social butterfly.* **3** [sing] (also **ˈbutterfly stroke**) stroke in swimming in which both arms are raised and lifted forwards at the same time while the legs move up and down together: *doing (the) butterfly.* **4** (idm) **have ˈbutterflies (in one's stomach)** (*infml*) have a nervous feeling in one's stomach before doing sth.

□ **ˈbutterfly-nut** *n* type of wing-nut. ⇨ illus at BOLT.

buttock /ˈbʌtək/ *n* (esp *pl*) either of the two fleshy rounded parts of the body on which a person sits: *the left/right buttock* ○ *a smack on the buttocks.* ⇨ illus at HUMAN.

button /ˈbʌtn/ *n* **1** knob or disc made of wood, metal, etc sewn onto a garment as a fastener or as an ornament: *a coat, jacket, shirt, trouser button* ○ *lose a button* ○ *sew on a new button* ○ *do one's buttons up.* ⇨ illus at JACKET. **2** small knob that is pressed to operate a doorbell, a switch on a machine, etc: *Which button do I press to turn the radio on?* **3** (idm) **bright as a button** ⇨ BRIGHT. **on the ˈbutton** (*US infml*) precisely: *You've got it on the button!*

▷ **button** *v* **1** (a) [Tn, Tn·p] ~ **sth (up)** fasten sth with buttons: *button (up) one's coat, jacket, shirt, etc.* (b) [I, Ip] ~ **(up)** be fastened with buttons: *This dress buttons at the back.* **2** (idm) **button (up) one's lip** (*US sl*) be silent. **3** (phr v) **button sth up** (*infml*) complete sth successfully: *The deal should be buttoned up by tomorrow.*

□ **ˌbutton-down ˈcollar** collar with ends that are fastened to the shirt with buttons.

ˌbuttoned ˈup silent and reserved; shy: *I've never met anyone so buttoned up.*

ˈbuttonhole *n* **1** slit through which a button is passed to fasten clothing. ⇨ illus at JACKET. **2** flower worn in the buttonhole of the lapel of a coat or jacket. — *v* [Tn] make (sb) stop and listen, often reluctantly, to what one wants to say.

ˈbuttonhook *n* hook for pulling a button into place through a buttonhole.

ˌbutton ˈmushroom small unopened mushroom.

buttress /ˈbʌtrɪs/ *n* **1** support built against a wall. ⇨ illus at CHURCH. **2** thing or person that supports or reinforces sth, or protects against sth: *a country admired as a buttress of democracy* ○ *He was a buttress against extremism in the party.*

▷ **buttress** *v* [Tn, Tn·p] ~ **sth (up)** support or strengthen sth: (*fig*) *More government spending is needed to buttress industry.* ○ *You need more facts to buttress up your argument.*

butty /ˈbʌtɪ, *usual regional pronunciation* ˈbʊtɪ/ *n* (*Brit dialect*) slice of bread and butter, esp one made into a sandwich: *a jam butty.*

buxom /ˈbʌksəm/ *adj* (*usu approv esp joc*) (of women) plump and healthy-looking; having a large bosom.

buy /baɪ/ *v* (*pt, pp* **bought** /bɔːt/) **1** [I, Tn, Tn·pr, Cn·a, Dn·n, Dn·pr] ~ **sth (for sb)** obtain (sth) by giving money; purchase: *House prices are low; it's a good time to buy.* ○ *Where did you buy that coat?* ○ *I bought this watch (from a friend) for £10.* ○ *Did you buy your car new or second-hand?* ○ *I must buy myself a new shirt.* ○ *She's buying a present for her boy-friend.* **2** [Tn] be the means of obtaining (sth): *He gave his children the best education that money could buy.* ○ *Money can't buy happiness.* ○ *A pound today buys much less than it did a year ago.* **3** [Tn usu passive] obtain (sth) by a sacrifice: *His fame was bought at the expense of health and happiness.* ○ *The victory was dearly bought,* ie Many people were killed to achieve it. **4** [Tn] (*infml*) accept (sth) as valid; believe: *No one will buy that excuse.* **5** [Tn] bribe (sb): *He can't be bought,* ie is too honest to accept a bribe. **6** (idm) **ˈbuy it** (*euph infml*) be killed, esp in war or an accident: *The passengers survived but the driver bought it.* **buy a pig in a ˈpoke** buy sth without seeing it or knowing if it is satisfactory. **buy ˈtime** delay sth that seems to be about to happen: *The union leaders are trying to buy time by prolonging the negotiations.* **7** (phr v) **buy sth in** (a) buy a stock of sth: *buy in coal for the winter.* (b) (at an auction) buy back (an item for which the bidding has not reached the agreed price) for the owner. **buy into sth** buy a share of sth; buy shares (SHARE¹3) in (a trading company): *The bank wouldn't help when I was starting the business but they want to buy into it now.* **buy sb off** pay sb not to act against one's interests: *Unless he drops the charge we'll have to buy him off.* **buy sb out** pay sb to give up a share in a business (usu in order to become the sole owner of it oneself): *Having bought out all his partners he now owns the whole company.* **buy sb over** bribe sb. **buy sth up** buy all or as much as possible of sth: *A New York business man has bought up the entire company.*

▷ **buy** *n* act of buying sth; thing bought: *a good buy,* ie a useful purchase or a bargain ○ *Best buys of the week are carrots and cabbages, which are plentiful and cheap.*

buyer *n* **1** person who buys: *Have you found a buyer for your house?* **2** person employed to choose and buy stock for a large shop. **buyer's market** state of affairs when goods are plentiful and prices are low.

buzz /bʌz/ *v* **1** [I] (a) make a humming sound: *bees, flies and wasps buzzing round a pot of jam.* (b) (of the ears) be filled with a humming sound: *My ears began buzzing.* **2** [I, Ipr] ~ **(with sth)** be full of excited talk, gossip or rumours: *The courtroom buzzed as the defendant was led in.* ○ *The village was buzzing with excitement at the news of the Queen's visit.* ○ *The office is buzzing with rumours.* **3** [Ipr, Tn] ~ **(for) sb** summon sb with a buzzer: *The doctor buzzed (for) the next patient.* **4** [Tn] (*infml*) telephone (sb): *I'll buzz you at work.* **5** [Tn] fly close to (sb/sth) as a warning: *Two fighters buzzed the convoy as it approached the coast.* **6** (phr v) **buzz about/around (sth)** move quickly and busily: *She buzzed around the kitchen making preparations for the party.* **buzz ˈoff** (*Brit infml*) (esp imperative) go away: *Just buzz off and leave me alone!*

▷ **buzz** *n* **1** [C] humming sound (esp one made by an insect): *the angry buzz of a bee/wasp.* **2** [sing] (a) low confused sound of people talking: *the buzz of voices in the crowded room.* (b) rumour: *There's a buzz going round that the boss has resigned.* **3** [C] sound of a buzzer. **4** [sing] (*infml esp US*) feeling of pleasure or excitement: *Flying gives me a real buzz.* **5** (idm) **give sb a ˈbuzz** (*infml*) make a telephone call to sb.

buzzer *n* electrical device that produces a buzzing sound as a signal.

□ **ˈbuzz-saw** *n* (*US*) = CIRCULAR SAW (CIRCULAR).

ˈbuzz-word *n* specialist or technical word or phrase that becomes fashionable and popular. Cf VOGUE-WORD (VOGUE).

buzzard /ˈbʌzəd/ *n* type of large hawk. ⇨ illus at BIRD.

BVM /ˌbiː viː ˈem/ *abbr* Blessed Virgin Mary.

by¹ /baɪ/ *adv part* **1** near: *He stole the money when no one was by.* ○ *He lives close/near by.* **2** past: *drive, go, run, walk, etc by* ○ *He hurried by without speaking to me.* ○ *Excuse me, I can't get by.* ○ *Time goes by so quickly.* **3** aside; in reserve: *lay/put/set sth by* ○ *I always keep a bottle of wine by in case friends call round.* **4** (idm) **by and ˈby** (*dated*) before long; soon: *They'll be arriving by and by.* **by the by/bye** = BY THE WAY (WAY¹). **by and large** ⇨ LARGE.

by² /baɪ/ *prep* **1** near (sb/sth); at the side of; beside: *a house by the church, river, railway* ○ *The telephone is by the window.* ○ *Come and sit by me.* ○ *We had a day by the sea.* **2** (showing the route taken) passing through (sth or a place); along; across: *He entered by the back door.* ○ *We travelled to Rome by Milan and Florence.* ○ *We came by country roads, not by the motorway.* **3** past (sb/sth): *He walked by me without speaking.* ○ *I go by the church every morning on my way to work.* **4** not later than (a time); before: *Can you finish the work by five o'clock/tomorrow/next Monday?* ○ *By this time next week we shall be in New York.* ○ *He ought to have arrived by now/by this time.* ○ *By the time (that) this letter reaches you I will have left the country.* **5** (usu without *the*) (emphasizing the circumstances of an action) during (a period of time) or in (sth): *travel by day/night* ○ *She sleeps by day and works by night.* ○ *The view is best seen by daylight/moonlight.* ○ *Reading by* (ie with the use of) *artificial light is bad for the eyes.* **6** (usu after a passive *v*) (a) through the action, power or work of (sb/sth): *a play (written) by Shakespeare* ○ *a church designed by Wren* ○ *He was arrested by the police.* ○ *He was shot by a terrorist with a machine-gun.* ○ *run over by a bus* ○ *struck by lightning.* (b) through the means of (sth/doing sth): *The room is heated by gas/oil.* ○ *May I pay by cheque?* ○ *I shall contact you by letter/telephone.* ○ *He earns his living by writing.* ○ *You switch the radio on by pressing this button.* ○ *By working hard he gained rapid promotion.* **7** (without *the*) as a result of (sth); because of; through: *meet by chance* ○ *achieve sth by skill, determination, etc* ○ *do sth by mistake/accident* ○ *The coroner's verdict was 'death by misadventure'.* **8** with the action of (doing sth): *Let me begin by saying ...* ○ *He shocked the whole company by resigning.* **9** (indicating a means of transport or a route taken): *travel by boat/bus/car/plane* ○ *travel by air/land/sea.* **10** (indicating a part of the body, or an item of clothing touched, held, etc): *take sb by the hand* ○ *seize sb by the hair, collar, lapel, etc* ○ *grab sb by the scruff of the neck.* **11** (with *the*) using (sth) as a standard or unit: *rent a car by the day/week/month* ○ *sell eggs by the* *dozen, material by the yard, coal by the ton* ○ *pay sb by the day/hour* ○ *We sell ice-creams by the thousand in the summer.* **12** in successive units, groups or degrees of: *improving day by day, little by little, bit by bit, etc* ○ *The children came in two by two.* **13 (a)** (showing the dimensions of a rectangle or a cube): *The room measures fifteen feet by twenty feet.* **(b)** (in multiplication or division): *6 (multiplied/divided) by 2 equals 12/3.* **14** to the extent of (sth): *The bullet missed him by two inches.* ○ *The carpet is too short by three feet.* ○ *It would be better by far* (ie much better) *to....* **15** according to (sth); from the evidence of: *By my watch it is two o'clock.* ○ *Judging by appearances can be misleading.* ○ *I could tell by the look on her face that something terrible had happened.* **16** in accordance with (sth); in agreement with: *play a game by the rules* ○ *by sb's leave*, ie with sb's permission. **17** with respect to (sb/sth); with regard to: *be German by birth, a solicitor by profession, a joiner by trade* ○ *do one's duty by sb.* **18** (in oaths) in the name of (sb/sth): *By God!* ○ *I swear by Almighty God..., by all that I hold dear..., etc.* **19** (idm) **have/keep sth by one** have sth close to one; have sth within easy reach: *I keep a dictionary by me when I'm doing crosswords.*

by- (also **bye-**) *pref* (with *ns* and *vs*) **1** of secondary importance; incidental: *by-product* ○ *bye-law.* **2** near: *bystander* ○ *bypass.*

bye[1] /baɪ/ *n* (*sport*) **1** (in cricket) run scored from a ball that passes the batsman without being hit by him. **2** situation in which a player having no opponent in one round of a tournament proceeds to the next round as if he had won.

bye[2] /baɪ/ (also **bye-bye** /ˌbaɪˈbaɪ, bəˈbaɪ/) *interj* (*infml*) goodbye: *Bye(-bye)! See you next week.*

bye-byes /ˈbaɪbaɪz/ *n* [U] (used esp when speaking to young children) sleep: *It's time to go to/time for bye-byes!*

by-election /ˈbaɪɪlekʃn/ *n* election of a new Member of Parliament in a single constituency whose member has died or resigned. Cf GENERAL ELECTION (GENERAL).

bygone /ˈbaɪgɒn/ *adj* [attrib] past: *a bygone age* ○ *in bygone days.*

▷ **bygones** *n* (idm) **let ˌbygones be ˈbygones** (*saying*) let us forgive and forget past quarrels.

by-law /ˈbaɪlɔː/ *n* **1** (also **ˈbye-law**) law or regulation made by a local, not a central, authority. ⇨ article at LAW. **2** (*US*) regulation of a club or company.

byline /ˈbaɪlaɪn/ *n* line at the beginning or end of an article in a newspaper, etc, giving the writer's name.

bypass /ˈbaɪpɑːs; *US* -pæs/ *n* **1** road by which traffic can go round a city, busy area, etc instead of through it: *If we take the bypass we'll avoid the town centre.* **2** (*medical*) alternative passage for blood to circulate through during a surgical operation, esp on the heart: [attrib] *bypass surgery.*

▷ **bypass** *v* [Tn] **1** provide (a town, etc) with a bypass: *a plan to bypass the town centre.* **2** go around or avoid (sth), using a bypass: *We managed to bypass the shopping centre by taking side-streets.* ○ (*fig*) *bypass a difficulty, problem, etc.* **3** ignore (a rule, procedure, etc) or fail to consult (sb) in order to act quickly: *He bypassed his colleagues on the board and went ahead with the deal.*

by-play /ˈbaɪpleɪ/ *n* [U] (*theatre*) action apart from and less important than that of the main story: (*fig*) *While the chairman was speaking, two committee members were engaged in heated by-play at the end of the table.*

by-product /ˈbaɪprɒdʌkt/ *n* **1** substance produced during the making of sth else: *Ammonia, coal tar and coke are all by-products obtained in the manufacture of coal gas.* **2** secondary result; side effect: *An increase in crime is one of the by-products of unemployment.*

Byrd /bɜːd/ William (1543-1623), English composer. He was a pupil of *Tallis and one of the greatest musicians of the Tudor period. He wrote many fine choral pieces for the Anglican Church, although his reputation and friends enabled him to remain a Catholic. His masses are perhaps his greatest works. He also wrote madrigals and some keyboard and instrumental music. ⇨ article at MUSIC.

byre /ˈbaɪə(r)/ *n* cowshed: *a wooden byre.*

by-road /ˈbaɪrəʊd/ *n* (*US* **back road**) minor road.

Byron /ˈbaɪərən/ George Gordon, 6th baron (1788-1824), English poet. His private life caused great controversy: he probably had a child by his half-sister, had many love affairs and was often in debt. He is one of the great figures of the romantic movement and his poetry has always been admired, esp outside Britain. He embodies the romantic hero, melancholy and rebellious, though his works display a subtle irony and wit. Rejected by English society, he spent much of his life abroad, and died helping the Greek struggle against Turkish rule. ⇨ illus.

▷ **Byronic** /baɪˈrɒnɪk/ *adj* of or typical of Byron, considered esp as a romantic figure.

bystander /ˈbaɪstændə(r)/ *n* person standing near, but not taking part, when sth happens; onlooker: *an innocent bystander* ○ *Police interviewed several bystanders after the accident.*

Lord Byron

byte /baɪt/ *n* (*computing*) fixed number of binary digits, often representing a single character.

byway /ˈbaɪweɪ/ *n* **1** [C] = BY-ROAD: *highways and byways.* **2 byways** [pl] (*fig*) less important or well-known areas (of a subject): *the byways of German literature.*

byword /ˈbaɪwɜːd/ *n* **1** ~ **for sth** person or thing considered to be a notable or typical example of a quality: *His name has become a byword for cruelty.* ○ *The firm is a byword for excellence.* **2** common saying or expression.

Byzantine /baɪˈzæntaɪn, ˈbɪzəntaɪn/ *adj* **1** of Byzantium or the E Roman Empire. **2** of or relating to the Byzantine style of architecture. **3** (*usu derog*) like Byzantine politics, ie complicated, secretive and difficult to change: *an organization of Byzantine complexity.*

Byzantium /baɪˈzæntɪəm/ **1** ancient Greek city on the site of the present city of Istanbul in Turkey. In the 4th century it became the capital of the Emperor Constantine who renamed it Constantinople. **2** Byzantine empire and culture.

C, c

C, c /siː/ *n* (*pl* **C's, c's** /siːz/) **1** the third letter of the English alphabet: *'Cat' starts with (a) C/'C'.* **2** (*music*) the first note in the scale of C major. **3** academic mark indicating the third highest standard: *get (a) C/'C' in physics.*

C *abbr* **1** Cape: *C Horn*, eg on a map. **2** (degree or degrees) Celsius; centigrade: *Water freezes at 0°C.* Cf F *abbr* 1. **3** (also **c**) Roman numeral for 100 (Latin *centum*). **4** (also *symb* ©) (*commerce*) copyright: *© Oxford University Press 1986.*

C *symb* carbon.

c *abbr* **1** cent(s). **2** century(1b): *in the 19th c* ○ *a c19 church.* Cf CENT *abbr.* **3** (also **ca**) (esp before dates) about; approximately (Latin *circa*): *c 1890.*

Ca *symb* calcium.

CAA /ˌsiː eɪ ˈeɪ/ *abbr* (*Brit*) Civil Aviation Authority.

cab /kæb/ *n* **1** = TAXI: *Shall we walk or take a cab/go by cab?* **2** driver's compartment in a train, lorry or crane. **3** (formerly) horse-drawn carriage for public hire.

□ ˈ**cab-driver** *n* driver of a cab.

ˈ**cabstand** *n* (*US*) = TAXI RANK (TAXI).

CAB /ˌsiː eɪ ˈbiː/ *abbr* (*Brit*) Citizens' Advice Bureau. ⇨ article at VOLUNTARY.

cabal /kəˈbæl/ *n* [CGp, C] (group of people involved in a) secret political plot.

cabaret /ˈkæbəreɪ; *US* ˌkæbəˈreɪ/ *n* **1** [U, C] entertainment (esp singing or dancing) provided in a restaurant or night-club while the customers are eating or drinking: *Have you done any cabaret?* **2** [C] such a restaurant or night-club: *a singer in a cabaret.*

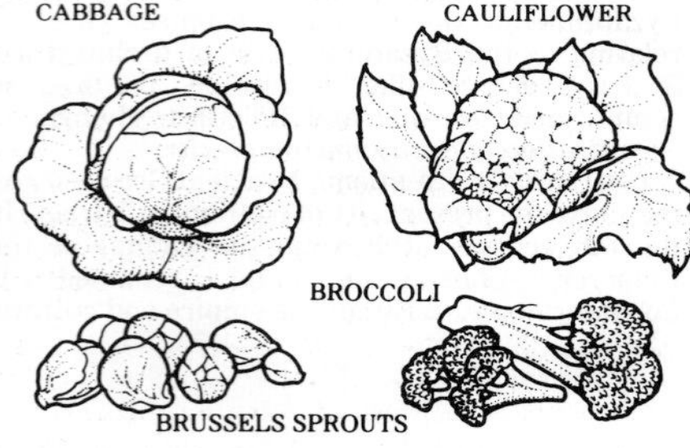

cabbage /ˈkæbɪdʒ/ *n* **1** (**a**) [C] any of various types of vegetable with green or purple leaves, usu forming a round head. ⇨ illus. (**b**) [U] these leaves (usu cooked and) eaten as food. **2** [C] (*Brit infml*) (**a**) dull inactive person without interests or ambition. (**b**) person who has lost his mental faculties, eg because of brain damage or illness, and is completely dependent on others.

□ ˌ**cabbage** ˈ**white** common type of white butterfly that feeds on cabbages or similar plants.

cabbala /kəˈbɑːlə; *US also* ˈkæbələ/ *n* (usu **the cabbala**) method of interpreting the Old Testament that was popular esp in the Middle Ages, claiming a special understanding through secret codes and mystical symbols.

▷ **cabbalistic** /ˌkæbəˈlɪstɪk/ *adj* (**a**) relating to the cabbala: *cabbalistic symbols.* (**b**) (*derog*) mysterious or difficult to understand; occult: *a cabbalistic mentality.*

cabby (also **cabbie**) /ˈkæbɪ/ *n* (*infml*) taxi-driver.

caber /ˈkeɪbə(r)/ *n* long heavy wooden pole thrown in the air as a trial of strength in the Scottish sport of tossing the caber.

cabin /ˈkæbɪn/ *n* **1** small room or compartment on a ship, an aircraft or a spacecraft: *book a cabin on a boat* ○ *the pilot's cabin.* **2** small hut or shelter, usu made of wood.

□ ˈ**cabin-boy** *n* boy who works as a waiter on a ship.

ˈ**cabin class** second highest standard of accommodation on a ship.

ˈ**cabin cruiser** = CRUISER (CRUISE).

cabinet /ˈkæbɪnɪt/ *n* **1** [C] piece of furniture with drawers or shelves for storing or displaying things: *a filing cabinet* ○ *a medicine cabinet* ○ *a china cabinet.* **2** [C] case or container for a radio, record-player or television. **3** (also **the Cabinet**) [CGp] group of the most important government ministers, responsible for government administration and policy: *Members of the Cabinet are chosen by the Prime Minister.* ○ [attrib] *a cabinet minister, meeting, reshuffle.* ⇨ articles at GOVERNMENT, PARLIAMENT.

□ ˈ**cabinet-maker** *n* craftsman who makes fine wooden furniture.

cable /ˈkeɪbl/ *n* **1** [C, U] (length of) thick strong rope made of fibre or wire, used esp for tying up ships. **2** [C] rope or chain of an anchor. **3** [C] (as a nautical measure) one tenth of a nautical mile, about 200 yards. ⇨ App 10. **4** [C] (**a**) set of insulated wires (esp one laid underground or on the bottom of the sea) for carrying messages by telegraph. (**b**) (also **cablegram**) message sent abroad in this way: *send sb/receive a cable.* Cf TELEGRAM. **5** [C] set of insulated wires for carrying electricity overhead. **6** [U, C] = CABLE STITCH. **7** [U] = CABLE TELEVISION. ⇨ articles at TECHNOLOGY, TELEVISION.

▷ **cable** *v* (**a**) [I, Ipr] ~ (**to sb**) (**from...**) send a cable(4b) to sb abroad: *Please write or cable.* (**b**) [Tn, Tn·pr, Tf] inform (sb) by cable: *Don't forget to cable us as soon as you arrive.* (**c**) [Tn, Dn·n, Dn·pr] send (money, a message, etc) by cable: *News of his death was cabled to his family.*

□ ˈ**cable-car** *n* car supported and drawn by a moving cable, usu carrying passengers up or down a mountain.

ˈ**cablegram** /ˈkeɪblɡræm/ *n* = CABLE *n* 4.

cable ˈ**railway** railway on a steep slope along which cars are drawn up and down by a moving cable with power from a stationary engine at the bottom or the top.

ˈ**cable stitch** stitch in knitting that resembles twisted rope.

cable ˈ**television** (also ˈ**cablevision**, **cable**) system of broadcasting television programmes by cable to subscribers.

caboodle /kəˈbuːdl/ *n* (idm) **the whole caboodle** ⇨ WHOLE.

caboose /kəˈbuːs/ *n* **1** kitchen on a ship's deck. **2** (*US*) guard's van, esp on a goods train.

Cabot /ˈkæbət/ John (died c 1498), Italian explorer. With his son Sebastian (died 1557) he sailed across the Atlantic and landed in N America before *Columbus, though it is not known exactly where on the coast he arrived.

cabriolet /ˈkæbrɪəleɪ; *US* ˌkæbrɪəˈleɪ/ *n* (formerly) light carriage with two wheels pulled by one horse.

cacao /kəˈkɑːəʊ, *also* kəˈkeɪəʊ/ *n* (*pl* ~**s**) (**a**) (also **ca**ˈ**cao-bean**) seed from which cocoa and chocolate are made. (**b**) (also **cac**ˈ**ao-tree**) tropical tree on which this grows.

cachalot /ˈkæʃəlɒt/ *n* = SPERM WHALE (SPERM).

cache /kæʃ/ *n* (**a**) place for hiding food, treasure or weapons. (**b**) hidden store of food, etc: *an arms cache.*

▷ **cache** *v* [Tn] place (sth) in a cache.

cachet /ˈkæʃeɪ; *US* kæˈʃeɪ/ *n* **1** [U] respect or admiration that sb gets because of his reputation or his achievements; prestige: *Her success in business had earned her a certain cachet in society.* **2** [C] distinguishing mark showing the excellence or authenticity of sth: *Rembrandt's paintings show the cachet of genius.*

cachou /ˈkæʃuː; *US* kəˈʃuː/ *n* scented sweet eaten (esp formerly) to make the breath smell pleasant.

cack-handed /ˌkækˈhændɪd/ *adj* (*infml*) showing a lack of skill; clumsy or awkward: *a cack-handed attempt to repair the damage.*

cackle /ˈkækl/ *n* **1** [U] loud clucking noise that a hen makes after laying an egg: *the cackle of hens/geese.* **2** [C] loud raucous or silly laugh: *The old woman gave a loud cackle.* **3** [U] noisy chatter. **4** (idm) **cut the** ˈ**cackle** (*infml*) stop talking about irrelevant or unimportant matters.

▷ **cackle** *v* [I, Ip] **1** (of a hen) make a cackle. **2** (of a person) laugh or chatter noisily: *cackling on for hours.*

cacophony /kəˈkɒfənɪ/ *n* [U, C usu *sing*] loud unpleasant mixture of discordant sounds. ▷ **cacophonous** /-nəs/ *adj.*

cactus

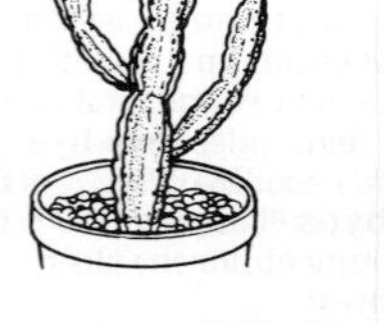

cactus /ˈkæktəs/ *n* (*pl* ~**es** or **cacti** /ˈkæktaɪ/) any of various types of plants growing in hot dry regions, with thick fleshy stems and usu prickles, but no leaves. ⇨ illus.

cad /kæd/ *n* (*dated derog*) man who behaves dishonourably: *He's no gentleman, he's a cad.*

▷ **caddish** /ˈkædɪʃ/ *adj* of or like a cad: *a caddish trick.*

cadaver /kəˈdɑːvə(r), *also* -ˈdeɪv-; *US* kəˈdævər/ *n* (*esp medical*) dead body of a person; corpse.

▷ **cadaverous** /kəˈdævərəs/ *adj* looking like a corpse; very pale and gaunt.

caddie (also **caddy**) /ˈkædɪ/ *n* person who carries a golfer's clubs for him during a game.

▷ **caddie** *v* [I, Ipr] ~ (**for sb**) act as a caddie: *Would you like me to caddie for you?*

caddis-fly /ˈkædɪs flaɪ/ *n* small fly living near water. Its larvae are used as bait by anglers.

caddy /ˈkædɪ/ *n* = TEA-CADDY (TEA).

cadence /ˈkeɪdns/ *n* **1** rhythm in sound. **2** rise and fall of the voice in speaking: *recite poetry with beautiful cadences.* **3** sequence of chords that is recognized as bringing a piece of music to an end.

cadenza /kəˈdenzə/ *n* (*music*) elaborate passage played by the soloist, usu near the end of a movement in a concerto.

cadet /kəˈdet/ *n* **1** young person training to become a police officer or an officer in the armed forces: *army/naval/air force cadets* ○ *a police cadet.* **2** (*fml*) younger son or brother: [attrib] *the cadet branch of the family*, ie the descendents of the younger son.

□ **ca**ˈ**det corps** (in some British schools) organization giving military training to older boys. ⇨ article at YOUTH.

cadge /kædʒ/ *v* [I, Ipr, Tn, Tn·pr] ~ (**sth**) (**from sb**) (*sometimes derog*) get or try to get (sth) (from sb) by asking, often unreasonably: *Could I cadge a lift with you?* ○ *He's always cadging meals from his friends.* ▷ **cadger** *n.*

cadmium /ˈkædmɪəm/ *n* [U] chemical element, a soft bluish-white metal that looks like tin. ⇨ App 11.

cadre /ˈkɑːdə(r); *US* ˈkædrɪ/ *n* **1** small permanent group of trained workers, soldiers, etc that can be enlarged when necessary. **2** /ˈkɑːdə(r), *also* ˈkeɪdə(r); *US* ˈkædrɪ/ group of workers actively supporting a revolutionary party.

caecum (*US* **cecum**) /ˈsiːkəm/ *n* (*pl* **-ca**) first part of the large intestine, resembling a large baggy tube.

Caedmon /ˈkædmən/ (7th century AD), English poet. *Bede says that he was a peasant looking after cattle when he had a vision and became able to put parts of the Bible into English verse. Only one fragment of his work survives.

Caenozoic = CAINOZOIC.

Caerphilly /keəˈfɪlɪ, kə-/ *n* [U] type of mild white crumbly cheese, originally made in Caerphilly, Wales.

Caesar /ˈsiːzə(r)/ *n* **1** title of the Roman Emperors from Augustus to Hadrian. Cf JULIUS CAESAR. **2** (idm) **Caesar's wife** person whom everyone expects to be guiltless.

Caesarean /sɪˈzeərɪən/ *n* (also **Cesarian**, **Caeˌsarean ˈsection**) surgical operation for delivering a baby by cutting the walls of the mother's abdomen and uterus: *It was a difficult birth: she had to have a Caesarean.*

caesium /ˈsiːzɪəm/ *n* [U] soft silvery-white metallic element, the heaviest alkali metal. It is used in photoelectric cells and a radioactive isotope is used in radiotherapy.

□ ˈ**caesium clock** highly accurate clock which uses changes in the state of caesium atoms to mark regular one-second periods.

caesura /sɪˈzjʊərə; *US* sɪˈʒʊərə/ *n* pause near the middle of a line of poetry, often marking a pause in the sense.

café /ˈkæfeɪ; *US* kæˈfeɪ/ *n* small inexpensive restaurant serving light meals and (in Britain usu non-alcoholic) drinks. ⇨ article at EAT.

cafeteria /ˌkæfəˈtɪərɪə/ *n* restaurant (esp in a factory or college) in which customers collect their meals on trays from a counter.

caffeine /ˈkæfiːn/ *n* [U] stimulant drug found in tea leaves and coffee beans.

caftan (also **kaftan**) /ˈkæftæn/ *n* **1** long loose garment, usu with a belt at the waist, worn by men in the Near East. **2** woman's long loose dress.

Cage /keɪdʒ/ John (1912-), American composer famous for his unconventional music. He has written works where chance decides the notes, and used everyday noises and 'prepared pianos', whose sound is changed by metal and wood placed on the strings.

cage /keɪdʒ/ *n* **1** structure made of bars or wires in which birds or animals are kept or carried. **2** enclosed platform used to raise and lower people and equipment in the shaft of a mine.

▷ **cage** *v* **1** [Tn] put or keep (sb/sth) in a cage. **2** (phr v) **cage sb in** make sb feel that he is in a cage: *I felt terribly caged in in that office.*

□ ˈ**cage-bird** bird kept as a pet, usu in a cage.

cagey /ˈkeɪdʒɪ/ *adj* (**cagier**, **cagiest**) ~ (**about sth**) (*infml*) cautious about giving information; wary; secretive: *He's very cagey about his family.* ▷ **cagily** *adv*. **caginess** (also **cageyness**) *n* [U].

Cagney /ˈkægnɪ/ James (1899-1986), American film actor. He became famous for his gangster roles, eg in *Public Enemy*, but he was also a skilled song and dance artist, as he showed in *Yankee Doodle Dandy*.

cagoule /kəˈguːl/ *n* light long waterproof jacket with a hood.

cahoots /kəˈhuːts/ *n* (idm) **be in cahoots (with sb)** (*infml esp US*) be planning sth (usu dishonest) with sb; be in league (with sb): *The two criminals were in cahoots (with each other).*

caiman = CAYMAN.

Cain /keɪn/ **(a)** (in the Old Testament) eldest son of *Adam and murderer of his brother *Abel. **(b)** (idm) **raise Cain** ⇨ RAISE.

Caine /keɪn/ Michael (1933-), British film actor. A versatile screen performer with an understated acting style, he has appeared in many popular successes, including *Alfie* and *Hannah and her Sisters*.

Cainozoic (also **Caenozoic**) /kaɪnəˈzəʊɪk/ (also *esp US* **Cenozoic** /kiːnə-/) *adj*, *n* (of the) most recent geological era (from about 65 million years ago to the present day), in which mammals, birds and plants evolved and developed.

cairn /keən/ *n* **1** mound of rough stones built as a landmark or as a memorial, eg on a mountain top. **2** (also ˌ**cairn** ˈ**terrier**) small rough-haired terrier with short legs.

cairngorm /ˈkeəngɔːm/ *n* [U] yellow to dark red semi-precious stone found in the Cairngorm mountains of Scotland.

Cairo /ˈkaɪrəʊ/ capital of Egypt. It is the largest city in Africa, a port on the river *Nile, and one of the most important centres in the Muslim world, with many mosques, including that of Al Azhar which contains an Islamic university. The Pyramids and the *Sphinx are nearby. ⇨ map at ALGERIA.

caisson /ˈkeɪsn/ *n* **1** large watertight box or chamber in which men can work under water (eg when building foundations). **2** large box (usu on wheels) in which ammunition is carried.

□ ˈ**caisson disease** = DECOMPRESSION SICKNESS (DECOMPRESS).

cajole /kəˈdʒəʊl/ *v* [Tn, Tn·pr] **(a)** ~ **sb (into/out of sth)**; ~ **sb (into/out of doing sth)** persuade sb (to do sth) by flattery or deceit; coax sb: *She was cajoled into (accepting) a new contract.* **(b)** ~ **sth out of sb** get (information, etc) from sb in this way: *The confession had to be cajoled out of him.* ▷ **cajolery** *n* [U].

Cajun /ˈkeɪdʒən/ *n* **1** [C] descendant of a group of French Canadians (*Acadians*) who went to live in Louisiana: *Cajun music, cooking.* **2** [U] their French dialect.

cake /keɪk/ *n* **1** [C, U] sweet food made from a mixture of flour, eggs, butter, sugar, etc baked in a certain shape or size and usu iced or decorated: *a sponge cake* ○ *a chocolate cake* ○ *a fruit cake* ○ *a piece/slice of (birthday) cake* ○ *an assortment of fancy cakes* ○ *Have some more cake.* **2** [C] other food mixture cooked in a round flat shape: ˈ*fish cakes* ○ *poˈtato cakes.* **3** [C] shaped or hardened mass of a substance: *a cake of soap.* **4** (idm) **cakes and** ˈ**ale** pleasurable things in life: *Life isn't all cakes and ale, you know.* **get, want, etc a slice/share of the** ˈ**cake** get, etc a share of the benefits or profits one is or feels entitled to, eg as an employee of a business or an industry or as a member of a profession: *As workers in a profit-making industry, miners are demanding a larger slice of the cake.* **have one's cake and** ˈ**eat it** (*infml*) enjoy the benefits from two alternative courses of action, etc when only one or the other is possible: *He wants a regular income but doesn't want to work. He can't have his cake and eat it!* **the icing on the cake** ⇨ ICING. **a piece of cake** ⇨ PIECE[1]. **sell like hot cakes** ⇨ SELL. **take the biscuit/cake** ⇨ BISCUIT.

▷ **cake** *v* **1** [esp passive: Tn, Tn·pr] ~ **sth (in/with sth)** cover sth thickly (with sth that becomes hard when dry): *His shoes were caked with mud.* **2** [I] harden into a compact mass: *Blood from the wound had caked on his face.*

CAL (also **Cal**) /kæl/ *abbr* computer-aided/-assisted learning.

cal *abbr* calorie(s).

calabash /ˈkæləbæʃ/ *n* **1** large fruit or gourd of which the hard outer skin is used as a container for liquids. **2** tropical American tree on which this grows.

calaboose /ˈkæləbuːs, ˌkæləˈbuːs/ *n* (*US infml*) prison.

calabrese /ˈkæləbriːs/ *n* [U] type of broccoli with large flower-heads, eaten as a vegetable.

Calabria /kəˈlæbrɪə/ mountainous region of SE Italy, the 'toe' of the country.

calamine /ˈkæləmaɪn/ *n* [U] (also **calamine lotion**) pink lotion used to soothe sore or burnt skin.

calamity /kəlˈæmətɪ/ *n* serious misfortune or disaster: *The earthquake was the worst calamity in the country's history.* ○ (*joc*) *There are worse calamities than failing your driving test.*

▷ **calamitous** /kəˈlæmɪtəs/ *adj* ~ **(to sb/sth)** involving or causing a calamity; disastrous.

Calamity Jane /kəˌlæmətɪ ˈdʒeɪn/ **1** nickname of Martha Jane Burke (c 1852-1903), a famous figure of the American West. She dressed as a man and was a skilful horse-rider and marksman. **2** (*infml*) person who habitually expects disasters to happen: *Don't be such a Calamity Jane — things aren't that bad!*

calcareous /kælˈkeərɪəs/ *adj* of or containing calcium carbonate.

calcify /ˈkælsɪfaɪ/ *v* (*pt*, *pp* **-fied**) [I, Tn] (cause sth to) harden by a deposit of calcium salts. ▷ **calcification** /ˌkælsɪfɪˈkeɪʃn/ *n* [U].

calcine /ˈkælsaɪn/ *v* [I, Tn] (cause sth to) be reduced to powder by burning; burn to ashes. ▷ **calcination** /ˌkælsɪˈneɪʃn/ *n* [U] conversion of a metal into an oxide by burning.

calcite /ˈkælsaɪt/ *n* [U] calcium carbonate in its crystal form.

calcium /ˈkælsɪəm/ *n* [U] chemical element, a greyish-white metal found as a compound in bones, teeth, limestone and chalk. ⇨ App 11.

□ ˌ**calcium** ˈ**carbide** compound of calcium and carbon used in making acetylene.

ˌ**calcium** ˈ**carbonate** compound of calcium that occurs naturally in several forms, including lime, chalk and marble.

ˌ**calcium hy**ˈ**droxide** white amorphous compound of calcium; slaked lime.

ˌ**calcium** ˈ**oxide** = LIME[1] 1.

calculable /ˈkælkjʊləbl/ *adj* that can be calculated.

calculate /ˈkælkjʊleɪt/ *v* **1** [Tn, Tf, Tw] work (sth) out by using numbers or one's judgement; estimate: *calculate the cost of sth/how much sth will cost* ○ *Scientists have calculated that the world's population will double by the end of the century.* ○ *I calculate that we will reach London at about 3 pm.* **2** [Tn, Tf, Tnt] (*US infml*) suppose (sth); believe. **3** (idm) **be calculated to do sth** be intended or designed to do sth: *This advertisement is calculated to appeal to children.* ○ *His speech was calculated to stir up the crowd.* **a calculated** ˈ**insult** deliberate or premeditated insult. **a calculated** ˈ**risk** risk taken deliberately with full knowledge of the dangers. **4** (phr v) **calculate on sth/doing sth** depend or rely on sth: *We can't calculate on (having) good weather for the barbecue.*

▷ **calculating** *adj* selfishly scheming; shrewd: *a cold and calculating killer* ○ *a calculating businessman.*

calculation /ˌkælkjʊˈleɪʃn/ *n* **1** [C, U] (result of) calculating: *Our calculations show that the firm made a profit of over £1 000 000 last year.* ○ *You're out* (ie You have made a mistake) *in your calculations.* ○ *After much calculation* (ie careful thought) *they offered him the job.* **2** [U] scheming.

calculator /ˈkælkjʊleɪtə(r)/ *n* **1** small electronic device for making mathematical calculations. **2** person who calculates.

calculus /ˈkælkjʊləs/ *n* (*pl* **-li** /-laɪ/ or in sense 1 **-luses** /-ləsɪz/) **1** [U, C] branch of mathematics, divided into two parts (*differential calculus* and *integral calculus*), that deals with problems involving rates of variation. **2** [C] stone-like mass of minerals that can form in certain parts of the body, eg a gall-stone.

Calcutta /kælˈkʌtə/ second largest city (and formerly the capital) of India, an important port and industrial centre; pop approx 9 200 000. Cf THE BLACK HOLE OF CALCUTTA (BLACK[1]).

caldron (*esp US*) = CAULDRON.

Caledonian /ˌkælɪˈdəʊnɪən/ *adj* (*rhet or joc*) Scottish.

▷ **Caledonian** *n* (*usu joc*) Scottish person.

□ **the** ˌ**Cale**ˌ**donian Ca**ˈ**nal** system of canals and lakes crossing Scotland from the Atlantic Ocean to the North Sea.

calendar /ˈkælɪndə(r)/ *n* **1 (a)** chart showing the days, weeks and months of a particular year: *Do you have next year's calendar?* **(b)** device that can be adjusted to show the date each day: *a desk calendar.* **2** (usu *sing*) list of dates or events of a particular kind: *The Cup Final is an important date in the sporting calendar.* **3** system by which time is divided into fixed periods, and of marking the beginning and end of a year: *the Gregorian/Julian/Muslim calendar.*

□ ˌ**calendar** ˈ**month 1** any one of the twelve months of the calendar. Cf LUNAR MONTH (LUNAR). **2** period of time from a certain date in one month

to the same date in the next one.
ˌcalendar ˈyear (also year) period of time from 1 January to 31 December in the same year.

calender /ˈkælɪndə(r)/ *n* machine for pressing and smoothing cloth or paper.
▷ **calender** *v* [Tn] press (sth) in a calender.

calf[1] /kɑːf; *US* kæf/ *n* (*pl* **calves** /kɑːvz; *US* kævz/) **1** [C] (**a**) young of cattle. ⇨ illus at cow. Cf BULL[1] 1, cow[1] 1. (**b**) young of the seal, the whale and certain other animals. Cf BULL[1] 2, cow[1] 2. **2** [U] (also **ˈcalf·skin**) leather made from the skin of a calf. **3** (idm) **the golden calf** ⇨ GOLDEN. **(be) in/with ˈcalf** (of a cow) pregnant. **kill the fatted calf** ⇨ KILL.
□ **ˈcalf-love** = PUPPY-LOVE (PUPPY).

calf[2] /kɑːf; *US* kæf/ *n* (*pl* **calves** /kɑːvz; *US* kævz/) fleshy back part of the leg below the knee. ⇨ illus at HUMAN.

Caliban /ˈkælɪbæn/ character in Shakespeare's *The Tempest*. He is a semi-human monster, supposed to represent the lowest form of human nature. The name is sometimes used to describe a person who is very ugly or uncouth.

calibrate /ˈkælɪbreɪt/ *v* [Tn] mark or correct the units of measurement on (the scale of a thermometer or some other measuring instrument).
▷ **calibration** /ˌkælɪˈbreɪʃn/ *n* **1** [U] action of calibrating. **2** [C] units of measurement marked on a thermometer, etc.

calibre (*US* **caliber**) /ˈkælɪbə(r)/ *n* **1** [C] diameter of the inside of a tube or gun-barrel. **2** [U] quality; ability; distinction: *His work is of the highest calibre.* ○ *The firm needs more people of your calibre.*

calico /ˈkælɪkəʊ/ *n* (*pl* ~**es**; *US* ~**s**) [U, C] **1** (*esp Brit*) type of cotton cloth, esp plain white or unbleached. **2** (*esp US*) printed cotton fabric.
▷ **calico** *adj* **1** made of calico. **2** (*US*) (esp of horses) having a mottled colour; piebald.

California /ˌkælɪˈfɔːnɪə/ state on the Pacific coast of the USA. In 1848 gold was discovered there and this led to the *Gold Rush. The richest of all the states, with the highest population, it has a varied landscape and a rich economy which includes micro-electronics in *Silicon Valley and the film industry in *Hollywood. ⇨ map at App 1. ▷ **Californian** *n, adj.*

californium /ˌkælɪˈfɔːnɪəm/ *n* artificially made radioactive element, used in industry and medicine.

Caligula /kəˈlɪgjʊlə/ nickname of the Roman emperor Gaius Julius Caesar Germanicus (12-41AD). He was a cruel and vicious tyrant, whose short reign ended when his own soldiers murdered him.

caliper = CALLIPER.

caliph /ˈkeɪlɪf/ *n* (**a**) title formerly used by Muslim rulers who were successors of Muhammad. (**b**) chief civil and religious ruler in certain Muslim countries.
▷ **caliphate** /ˈkælɪfeɪt/ *n* position, reign or territory of a caliph.

calisthenics = CALLISTHENICS.

calk (*US*) = CAULK.

call[1] /kɔːl/ *n* **1** [C] shout; cry: *a call for help* ○ *They came at my call*, ie when I shouted to them. **2** [C] characteristic cry of a bird. **3** [C] signal sounded on a horn, bugle, etc. **4** [C] short visit (to sb's house): *pay a call on a friend* ○ *The doctor has five calls to make this morning.* ○ *We must return her call*, ie visit her because she visited us. **5** [C] (also **ˈphone call, ring**) act of telephoning; conversation on the telephone: *give sb/make/receive/return a call* ○ *Were there any calls for me while I was out?* **6** (**a**) [C] order, signal or invitation, esp to come or meet; summons: *The Prime Minister is waiting for a call to the Palace.* ○ *An actor's call tells him when to go on stage.* ○ *This is the last call for passengers travelling on flight BA 199 to Rome.* ○ (*fig*) *He answered the call of duty and enlisted in the army.* (**b**) [sing] ~ **(of sth)** inner urge to follow a course of action or profession; vocation: *feel the call (of the priesthood).* (**c**) [sing] ~ **of sth** attraction or fascination of (a particular place or activity): *the call of the sea, of the wild, of faraway places, etc.* (**d**) [C] ~ **for sth** request or demand for sth: *The President made a call for national unity.* ○ *There were calls for the Prime Minister's resignation from the Opposition parties.* **7** [U] ~ **for sth** (esp in negative sentences and questions) need or occasion for sth: *There isn't much call for such things these days.* ○ *There was no call for such rudeness.* **8** [C] ~ **on sb/sth** demand on sb/sth: *He is a busy man with many calls on his time.* **9** [C] (in card-games) player's bid or turn to bid: *It's your call, partner.* **10** (*finance*) option to buy stock at a fixed price on a given date. **11** (idm) **at one's/sb's beck and call** ⇨ BECK[2]. **a call of ˈnature** (*euph*) need to urinate or defecate. **a close call** ⇨ CLOSE[1]. **(be) on ˈcall** (esp of a doctor) available for work if necessary: *Who's on call tonight?* **a port of call** ⇨ PORT[1]. **within ˈcall** near enough to hear sb shouting (for help, etc).
□ **ˈcall-box** *n* = TELEPHONE-BOX (TELEPHONE).
ˈcall-girl *n* prostitute who makes appointments by telephone.
ˈcall-in = PHONE-IN (PHONE[1]).
ˈcall sign (also **ˈcall signal**) sign, usu a combination of numbers and letters, used by a radio operator to identify himself.

call[2] /kɔːl/ *v* **1** [I, Ipr, Ip, Tn, Tn·p] ~ **(out) to sb (for sth)**; ~ **(sth) (out)** say (sth) loudly to attract sb's attention; shout; cry: *I thought I heard sb calling.* ○ *Why didn't you come when I called (out) (your name)?* ○ *She called to her father for help.* ○ *The injured soldiers called out in pain.* ○ *The teacher called out the children's names*, eg to check they were all present. **2** [I] (of a bird or an animal) make its characteristic cry. **3** [Tn, Tn·pr, Tn·p, Dn·n, Dn·pr] order or ask (sb/sth) to come (to a specified place) by shouting, telephoning, writing, etc; summon: *call the fire brigade, the police, a doctor, an ambulance, etc* ○ *Call the children (in): it's time for tea.* ○ *Several candidates were called for a second interview.* ○ *The doctor has been called (away) to an urgent case.* ○ *The ambassador was called back to London by the Prime Minister.* ○ *I have to be at the airport in 20 minutes — please call (me) a taxi.* ○ *call sb's attention to sth*, invite sb to examine or think carefully about sth. **4** (**a**) [I, Ipr, Ip] ~ **(in/round) (on sb/at...) (for sb/sth)** make a short visit; go to sb's house, etc (to get sth or to go somewhere with him): *Let's call (in) on John/at John's house.* ○ *He was out when I called (round) (to see him).* ○ *I'll call for* (ie collect) *you at 7 o'clock.* ○ *Will you call in at the supermarket for some eggs and milk?* ⇨ Usage at VISIT. (**b**) [Ipr] ~ **at...** (of a train, etc) stop at (a place): *The train on platform 3 is for London, calling at Didcot and Reading.* **5** [I, Tn] telephone (sb): *I'll call (you) again later.* ○ *My brother called me (from Leeds) last night.* **6** [Tn] order (sth) to take place; announce: *call a meeting, an election, a strike.* **7** [Tn] wake (sb): *Please call me at 7 o'clock tomorrow morning.* **8** [Cn·a, Cn·n] (**a**) describe or address (sb/sth) as; name: *How dare you call me fat!* ○ *His name is Richard but we call him Dick.* ○ *What's your dog called?* ○ (*ironic*) *He hasn't had anything published and he calls himself a writer!* (**b**) consider (sb/sth) to be; regard as: *I call his behaviour mean and selfish.* ○ *I would never call German an easy language.* ○ *How can you be so unkind and still call yourself my friend?* ○ *You owe me £5.04 — let's call it £5*, ie settle the sum at £5. **9** [I, Tn] (in card-games) declare (a trump suit, etc); bid: *Have you called yet?* ○ *Who called hearts?* **10** (idm) **be/feel called to (do) sth** be/feel summoned to a particular profession or vocation: *be called to the bar*, ie become a barrister ○ *feel called to the ministry/the priesthood.* **bring/call sb/sth to mind** ⇨ MIND[1]. **call sb's ˈbluff** challenge sb to do what he is threatening to do (believing that he will not dare to do it). **call a ˈhalt (to sth)** stop (work, a habit, etc): *Let's call a halt (to the meeting) and continue tomorrow.* **call sth into being** (*fml*) create sth. **call sth into play** bring sth into operation: *Chess is a game that calls into play all one's powers of concentration.* **call sth in/into ˈquestion** doubt sth or cause sth to be doubted: *His honesty has never been called in question.* **call it a ˈday** (*infml*) decide or agree to stop (doing sth) temporarily or permanently: *After forty years in politics he thinks it's time to call it a day*, ie to retire. **call it ˈquits** (*infml*) agree to stop a contest, quarrel, etc on even terms. **call sb ˈnames** jeer at or insult sb. **call sth one's ˈown** claim sth as one's property: *He has nothing he can call his own.* **call the ˈshots/the ˈtune** (*infml*) be in a position to control a situation. **call a spade a ˈspade** speak plainly and frankly. **call sb to account (for/over sth)** make sb explain (an error, a loss, etc): *His boss called him to account for failing to meet the deadline.* **call sb/sth to order** ask (people in a meeting) to be silent so that business may start or continue. ˌ**call sb to ˈwitness (that...)** (*fml*) ask sb to confirm that what one is saying is true. ˌ**don't call ˈus, ˌwe'll call ˈyou** (*joc catchphrase*) (used to indicate that the speaker is not really interested in or impressed by what another person has offered, eg sth recited as part of an audition). **he who pays the piper calls the tune** ⇨ PAY[2]. **the pot calling the kettle black** ⇨ POT[1].
11 (phr v) **call by** (*infml*) visit a place or a person briefly when passing: *Could you call by later?*
call sb down (*US infml*) reprimand or scold sb severely. **call sth down on sb** (*fml*) invoke (curses, etc) on sb.
call for sth require, demand or need sth: *The situation calls for prompt action.* ○ *'I've been promoted.' 'This calls for a celebration!'* ○ *That rude remark was not called for!* Cf UNCALLED-FOR.
call sth forth (*fml*) cause sth to appear or be shown; elicit sth: *His speech called forth an angry response.*
call sth in order or request the return of sth: *The library called in all overdue books.* ○ *Cars with serious faults have been called in by the manufacturers.*
call sb/sth off order (dogs, soldiers, etc) to stop attacking, searching, etc: *Please call your dog off — it's frightening the children.* **call sth off** cancel or abandon sth: *call off a deal, a journey, a picnic, a strike* ○ *They have called off their engagement*, ie decided not to get married. ○ *The match was called off because of bad weather.*
call on/upon sb (to do sth) (**a**) formally invite or request sb (to speak, etc): *I now call upon the chairman to address the meeting.* (**b**) appeal to or urge sb (to do sth): *We are calling upon you to help us.* ○ *I feel called upon* (ie feel that I ought) *to warn you that....*
call sb out (**a**) summon sb, esp to an emergency: *call out the fire brigade, troops, guard, etc.* (**b**) order or advise (workers) to go on strike: *Miners were called out (on strike) by union leaders.*
call sb/sth up (**a**) (*esp US*) telephone sb. (**b**) bring sth back to one's mind; recall sth: *The sound of happy laughter called up memories of his childhood.* (**c**) summon sb for military service; draft sb.
▷ **caller** *n* person who makes a brief visit or a telephone call.
□ **ˈcalling-card** *n* (*US*) = VISITING-CARD (VISIT).
ˈcall-up *n* (*US* **draft**) [U, C esp *sing*] summons for military service: *receive one's call-up* ○ [attrib] *young men of call-up age.*

Callas /ˈkæləs/ Maria (1923-77), American operatic soprano famous for her highly distinctive voice and great dramatic talent in a wide range of parts.

calligraphy /kəˈlɪgrəfɪ/ *n* [U] (art of producing) beautiful handwriting. ▷ **calligrapher** *n.*

calling /ˈkɔːlɪŋ/ *n* **1** profession; trade. **2** strong urge or feeling of duty to do a particular job; vocation: *He believes it is his calling to become a priest.*

calliope /kəˈlaɪəpɪ/ *n* (*US*) musical instrument similar to an organ, with a keyboard and a set of steam whistles producing musical sounds.

callipers

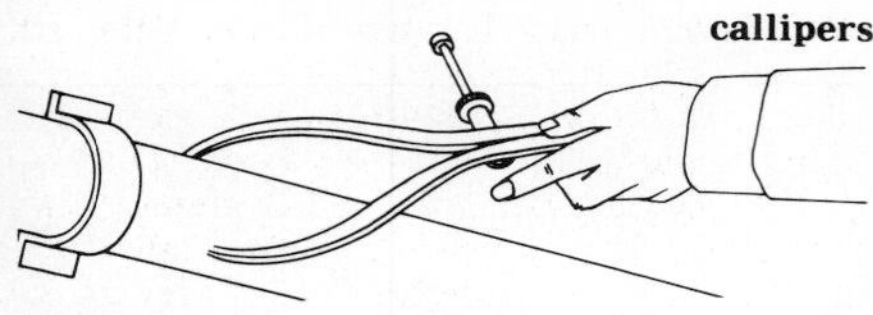

calliper (also **caliper**) /ˈkælɪpə(r)/ *n* **1** (C usu *pl*) metal support for weak or injured legs. **2 callipers** [pl] instrument for measuring the diameter of tubes or round objects: *a pair of callipers.* ⇨ illus.

callisthenics (also **calisthenics**) /ˌkælɪsˈθenɪks/ *n* [sing or pl *v*] exercises to develop strong and graceful bodies.

callosity /kæˈlɒsətɪ/ *n* (*fml*) area of hardened skin; callus.

callous /ˈkæləs/ *adj* **1** cruelly insensitive or unsympathetic: *a callous person, attitude, act.* **2** (of the skin) hardened, eg by rough work.
▷ **calloused** *adj* (of the skin) hardened; having calluses: *calloused hands.*
callously *adv* in a callous(1) way.
callousness *n* [U] callous(1) behaviour.

callow /ˈkæləʊ/ *adj* (*derog*) immature and inexperienced: *a callow youth* ○ *callow thinking.* ▷ **callowness** *n* [U].

callus /ˈkæləs/ *n* area of thick hardened skin: *calluses on one's palms.*

calm /kɑːm; *US also* kɑːlm/ *adj* (**-er, -est**) **1** (**a**) (of the sea) without large waves; still. (**b**) (of the weather) not windy: *a calm, cloudless day.* **2** not excited, nervous or agitated; quiet; untroubled: *It is important to keep/stay calm in an emergency.* ○ *The city is calm again after yesterday's riots.* ⇨ Usage at QUIET.
▷ **calm** *n* [C, U] **1** calm condition or period: *the calm of a summer evening* ○ *After the storm came a calm.* **2** (idm) **the calm before the storm** time of unnatural calm immediately before an expected outburst of violent activity, passion, etc.
calm *v* [I, Ip, Tn, Tn·p] ~ (**sb**) (**down**) (cause sb to) become calm: *Just calm down a bit!* ○ *Have a brandy — it'll help to calm you (down).*
calmly *adv*: *He walked into the shop and calmly* (ie impudently and self-confidently) *stole a pair of gloves.*
calmness *n* [U].

Calor gas /ˈkælə gæs/ *n* [U] (*propr*) liquid butane stored under pressure in containers for domestic use.

calorie /ˈkælərɪ/ *n* (*abbr* **cal**) **1** unit for measuring a quantity of heat. **2** unit for measuring the energy value of food: *An ounce of sugar has about 100 calories.* ○ *Her diet restricts her to 1500 calories a day.*
▷ **calorific** /ˌkæləˈrɪfɪk/ *adj* [usu attrib] of or producing heat: *calorific value*, ie the quantity of heat or energy produced by a given amount of fuel or food.
calorimeter /ˌkæləˈrɪmɪtə(r)/ *n* apparatus for measuring thermal energy.

calumny /ˈkæləmnɪ/ *n* (*fml*) **1** [C] false statement about sb, made to damage his character: *a victim of vicious calumnies.* **2** [U] slander: *accuse sb of calumny.*
▷ **calumniate** /kəˈlʌmnɪeɪt/ *v* [Tn] (*fml*) slander (sb).

calvados /ˈkælvədɒs/ *n* [U] type of apple brandy made in Normandy, France.

calve /kɑːv; *US* kæv/ *v* [I] give birth to a calf: *Our cows will be calving soon.*

calves *pl of* CALF[1], CALF[2].

Calvin /ˈkælvɪn/ John (1509-64), French Protestant theologian who spent most of his life in Geneva. He was one of the most important figures of the *Reformation. He taught that doctrine should come directly from the Bible, that Christians are saved by believing and not by doing good works, and that God chooses those who will be saved. He had a great influence on the Church of Scotland.
▷ **Calvinism** *n* [U] religious teaching of Calvin or his followers.
Calvinist *n, adj* (follower) of Calvin's teaching.

calypso /kəˈlɪpsəʊ/ *n* (*pl* ~**s**) West Indian song about a subject of current interest, having a variable rhythm and often improvised words.

calyx /ˈkeɪlɪks/ *n* (*pl* ~**es** or **calyces** /ˈkeɪlɪsiːz/) (*botany*) ring of leaves (called *sepals*) enclosing an unopened flower-bud. ⇨ illus at PLANT.

cam /kæm/ *n* projecting part on a wheel designed to change the circular motion of the wheel as it turns into up-and-down or backwards-and-forwards motion of another part.
□ **camshaft** /ˈkæmʃɑːft; *US* -ʃæft/ *n* shaft with a cam or cams on it, esp in a motor vehicle.

camaraderie /ˌkæməˈrɑːdərɪ; *US* -ˈræd-/ *n* [U] friendship and mutual trust; comradeship.

Camargue /kəˈmɑːg/ **the Camargue** marshy region of southern France known for its breed of white horses and as a nature reserve.

camber /ˈkæmbə(r)/ *n* slight upward curve on the surface of sth, esp a road.
▷ **camber** *v* [Tn] give a camber to (esp a road): *The street is quite steeply cambered at this point.*

Cambodia /kæmˈbəʊdɪə/ (also **the People's Republic of Kampuchea**) country in SE Asia, between Thailand and southern Vietnam; pop approx 7 280 000; official language Khmer; capital Phnom Penh. Formerly part of the *Khmer empire, it was ruled by France between 1863 and 1953. There was a civil war in the early 1970s and the *Khmer Rouge took over the country in 1975. In 1979 it was overthrown by a Vietnamese invasion. At the end of the 1980s the Vietnamese withdrew. The country's economy is mainly agricultural, rice being the main crop; there is little industry. ⇨ map at VIETNAM. ▷ **Cambodian** *adj, n.*

Cambrian /ˈkæmbrɪən/ *adj* **1** (*rhet*) Welsh. **2** of the earliest period of the *Palaeozoic era, lasting from about 590 to 505 million years ago, when much of the earth was covered by seas.

cambric /ˈkeɪmbrɪk/ *n* [U] fine thin linen or cotton cloth.

Cambridge[1] /ˈkeɪmbrɪdʒ/ city in Cambridgeshire in eastern England famous for its university which was founded in 1209 and made up of a number of colleges. From the 19th century onwards the city became a major centre of scientific research. ⇨ article at POST-SCHOOL.
□ ˌ**Cambridge** ˈ**blue** light blue.

Cambridge[2] /ˈkeɪmbrɪdʒ/ city in Massachusetts, USA, famous as the home of *Harvard University.

camcorder /ˈkæmkɔːdə(r)/ *n* portable video camera with a built-in video recorder.

came *pt of* COME.

camels

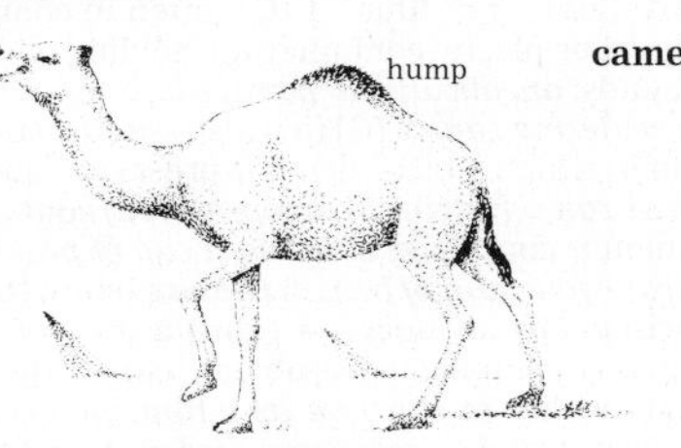

DROMEDARY

BACTRIAN CAMEL

camel /ˈkæml/ *n* **1** [C] animal with a long neck and one or two humps on its back, used in desert countries for riding and for carrying goods. ⇨ illus. Cf DROMEDARY. **2** [U] fawn colour.
□ ˈ**camel-hair** (also ˈ**camel's-hair**) *n* [U] **1** soft heavy yellowish cloth made of camel's hair or a mixture of camel's hair and wool: [attrib] *a camel-hair coat.* **2** fine soft hair used in artists' brushes.

camellia /kəˈmiːlɪə/ *n* (**a**) evergreen shrub from China and Japan with shiny leaves and white, red or pink flowers. (**b**) flower of this shrub.

Camelot /ˈkæməlɒt/ place where the legendary King *Arthur had his court.

Camembert /ˈkæməmbeə(r)/ *n* [U, C] type of soft creamy cheese from N France.

cameo /ˈkæmɪəʊ/ *n* (*pl* ~**s**) **1** small piece of hard stone with a raised design, esp one with two coloured layers so that the background is of a different colour from the design: [attrib] *a cameo brooch.* **2** (**a**) small but well-acted part in a film or play: [attrib] *a cameo performance/part/role.* (**b**) short piece of fine descriptive writing.

camera

camera /ˈkæmərə/ *n* **1** apparatus for taking photographs, moving pictures or television pictures. A camera is basically a box that lets no light in, containing a lens and a shutter mechanism. A light-sensitive film is fitted inside and when the shutter is opened this allows an image to form on the film. Television cameras convert visual images into electrical signals to produce television pictures ⇨ illus. **2** (idm) **in** ˈ**camera** in a judge's private room; not in public; privately: *The trial was held/The case was heard in camera.* **on** ˈ**camera** being filmed or televised at a particular moment: *You can relax, Prime Minister — we're not on camera for another two minutes.*
ˈ**cameraman** /-mæn/ *n* (*pl* **-men**) person whose job is operating a camera for film-making or television.
camera obscura /ɒbˈskjʊərə/ dark box or room containing a surface onto which it is possible to project an image of what is outside, using a special lens.
ˈ**camera-shy** *adj* (of a person) who does not like being photographed: *Since the reports appeared, he's become very camera-shy*, ie he does not want his picture in the newspapers.

Cameroon /ˌkæməˈruːn/ country on the west coast of Africa; pop approx 10 674 000; official languages French and English; capital Yaoundé; unit of currency franc. The former French and British colonies of Cameroon merged in 1961, a year after French Cameroon gained its independence. It has one of the most successful economies in Africa, and has oil reserves and well-organized agriculture. ⇨ map at NIGERIA.

camomile (also **chamomile**) /ˈkæməmaɪl/ *n* [U] (**a**) sweet-smelling plant with daisy-like flowers. (**b**) its dried leaves and flowers used in medicine as a tonic.

camouflage /ˈkæməflɑːʒ/ *n* **1** [U] way of hiding or disguising soldiers, military equipment, etc, eg with paint, netting or leaves, so that they look like part of their surroundings: *use the branches of trees as camouflage.* **2** [C] such a disguise: *The polar bear's white fur is a natural camouflage*, ie because the bear is hard to see in the snow.
▷ **camouflage** *v* [Tn] hide (sb/sth) by camouflage: *The soldiers camouflaged themselves with leaves and branches.*

camp[1] /kæmp/ *n* **1** (**a**) place where people (eg holiday-makers, Scouts or explorers) live temporarily in tents or huts: *a holiday camp* ○ *leave/return to camp* ○ *We pitched (our) camp* (ie put up our tents) *by a lake.* (**b**) place where prisoners or refugees are kept, often for long periods: *a prison camp* ○ *a concentration camp* ○ *a transit camp.* **2** place where soldiers are lodged or trained: *an army camp.* **3** group of people with the same (esp political or religious) ideas: *the socialist camp* ○ *They belong to different political camps.* **4** (idm) **carry the war into the enemy's camp** ⇨ CARRY. **have a foot in both camps** ⇨ FOOT[1]. **strike camp** ⇨ STRIKE[2].

▷ **camp** *v* **1** (**a**) [I] put up a tent or tents: *Where shall we camp tonight?* (**b**) [I, Ip] ~ (**out**) live in a tent: *They camped (out) in the woods for a week.* **2** [I] (usu **go camping**) spend a holiday living in tents: *The boys went camping in Greece last year.* **3** [I] live temporarily as if in a camp: *I'm camping on the floor in a friend's flat for two weeks.* **camper** *n* (**a**) person who camps. (**b**) large motor vehicle in which people can live while camping. Cf MOBILE HOME (MOBILE). **camping** *n* [U] holiday spent living in tents: *Do you like camping?* ○ [attrib] *camping equipment.*

□ ˌ**camp-ˈbed** (*US* ˈ**campcot**) *n* portable folding bed (not only for use in a camp).

ˈ**camp-fire** *n* outdoor fire made of logs, etc by campers.

ˈ**camp-follower** *n* **1** non-military person (eg a prostitute) following an army to sell goods or services. **2** (*often derog*) person who attaches himself to a particular group, party, etc although not a member of it; hanger-on.

ˈ**camp meeting** (*US*) religious meeting held outdoors or in a large tent.

ˈ**campsite** (also ˈ**camping-site**) *n* place for camping, usu specially equipped for holiday-makers.

camp[2] /kæmp/ *adj* (*infml*) **1** (of a man, his manner, etc) affected and effeminate; homosexual: *a camp walk, voice, gesture.* **2** exaggerated in style, esp for humorous effect; affectedly theatrical.

▷ **camp** *n* [U] camp behaviour: *Her performance was pure camp.*

camp *v* (phr v) **camp it up** (*infml*) (**a**) display one's homosexuality through effeminate behaviour. (**b**) overact grotesquely.

campaign /kæmˈpeɪn/ *n* **1** series of military operations with a particular aim, usu in one area: *He fought in the N African campaign during the last war.* **2** series of planned activities with a particular social, commercial or political aim: *a campaign against nuclear weapons* ○ *an advertising campaign*, ie to promote a particular product ○ *an election campaign* ○ *a campaign to raise money for the needy.*

▷ **campaign** *v* [I, Ipr, It] ~ (**for/against sb/sth**) take part in or lead a campaign: *She spent her life campaigning for women's rights.* ○ *campaign to have sanctions imposed.* **campaigner** *n* person who campaigns: *an old campaigner*, ie sb with much experience of a particular activity.

campanile /ˌkæmpəˈni:lɪ/ *n* bell-tower, esp one that is not part of another building.

campanology /ˌkæmpəˈnɒlədʒɪ/ *n* [U] (*fml*) study of bells and the art of bell-ringing. ▷ **campanologist** /-ədʒɪst/ *n.*

Camp David /ˌkæmp ˈdeɪvɪd/ country home used by the US President, in the Appalachian Mountains, Maryland.

camphor /ˈkæmfə(r)/ *n* [U] strong-smelling white substance used in medicine and mothballs and in making plastics.

▷ **camphorated** /ˈkæmfəreɪtɪd/ *adj* containing camphor: *camphorated oil.*

campus /ˈkæmpəs/ *n* (*pl* ~**es**) **1** grounds and buildings of a university or college: *He lives on (the) campus*, ie in a building within the university grounds. **2** (*US*) university or branch of a university: [attrib] *campus life.*

CAMRA (also **Camra**) /ˈkæmrə/ *abbr* (*Brit*) Campaign for Real Ale (ie beer brewed in the traditional way): *Camra pubs.* ⇨ article at DRINK.

Camus /ˈkæmju:, kæˈmu:/ Albert (1913-60), French writer born in Algeria. In his novels, plays and philosophical essays he expresses his view of the absurdity of life. He was awarded the Nobel prize for literature in 1957.

Canada and Greenland

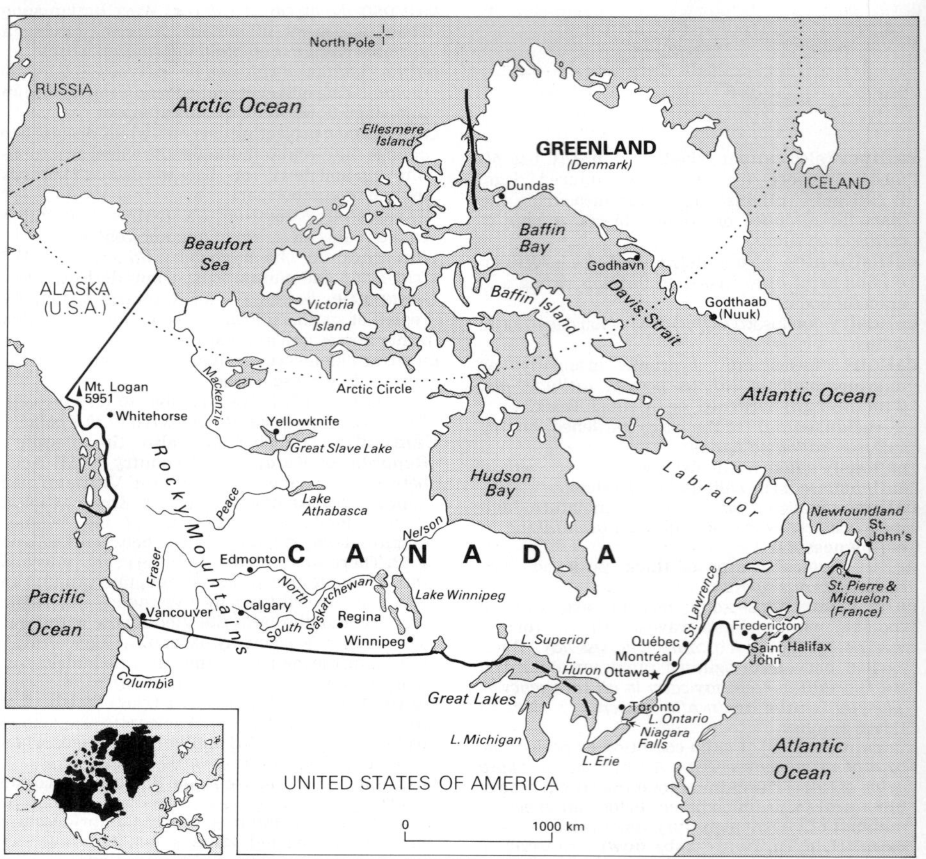

can

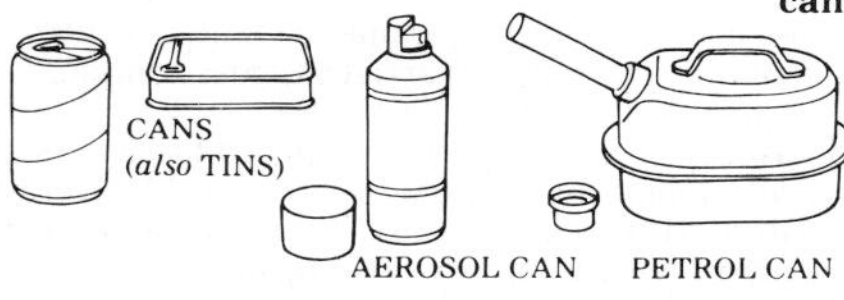

can[1] /kæn/ *n* ⇨ illus. **1** [C] (often in compounds) metal or plastic container for holding or carrying liquids: *an* ˈ*oilcan* ○ *a* ˈ*petrol can/a can of* ˈ*petrol* ○ *a* ˈ*watering-can.* **2** [C] (**a**) (also *esp Brit* **tin**) sealed tin in which food or drink is preserved and sold: *a* ˈ*beer can* ○ [attrib] *a can-opener.* (**b**) contents of or amount contained in a can: *a can of peaches* ○ *He drank four cans of beer.* **3 the can** [sing] (*US sl*) (**a**) prison. (**b**) lavatory. **4** (idm) **a** ˌ**can of** ˈ**worms** (*infml*) complicated problem. **carry the can** ⇨ CARRY. (**be**) **in the** ˈ**can** (of a film, video-tape, etc) recorded and edited; completed and ready for use.

▷ **can** *v* (**-nn-**) [Tn] **1** preserve (food) by putting it in a sealed can: *canned* ˈ*fruit* ○ *a* ˈ*canning factory.* **2** (*US sl*) dismiss (an employee) from a job: *He got canned for stealing.*

cannery /ˈkænərɪ/ *n* place where food is canned.

□ ˌ**canned** ˈ**music** (*infml usu derog*) music recorded for reproduction: *Restaurants often play canned music.*

can[2] /kən; *strong form* kæn/ *modal v* (*neg* **cannot** /ˈkænɒt/, *contracted form* **can't** /kɑ:nt; *US* kænt/; *pt* **could** /kəd; *strong form* kʊd/, *neg* **could not**, *contracted form* **couldn't** /ˈkʊdnt/) **1** (**a**) (indicating ability): *I can run fast.* ○ *Can you call back tomorrow?* ○ *He couldn't answer the question.* ○ *The stadium can be emptied in four minutes.* (**b**) (indicating acquired knowledge or skill): *They can speak French.* ○ *Can he cook?* ○ *I could drive a car before I left school.* (**c**) (used with verbs of perception): *I can hear music.* ○ *I thought I could smell something burning.* ○ *He could still taste the garlic they'd had for lunch.* **2** (indicating permission): *Can I read your newspaper?* ○ *Can I take you home?* ○ *You can take the car, if you want.* ○ *We can't wear jeans at work.* ○ *The boys could play football but the girls had to go to the library.* ⇨ Usage 1 at MAY[1]. **3** (indicating requests): *Can you help me with this box?* ○ *Can you feed the cat?* **4** (**a**) (indicating possibility): *That can't be Mary — she's in hospital.* ○ *He can't have slept through all that noise.* ○ *There's someone outside — who can it be?* ⇨ Usage 2 at MAY[1]. (**b**) (used to express bewilderment or incredulity): *What* ˈ*can they be doing?* ○ *Can he be serious?* ○ *Where* ˈ*can she have put it?* **5** (used to describe typical behaviour or state): *He can be very tactless sometimes.* ○ *She can be very forgetful.* ○ *Scotland can be very cold.* ○ *It can be quite windy on the hills.* **6** (used to make suggestions): *We can eat in a restaurant, if you like.* ○ *I can take the car if necessary.* ⇨ Usage 3 at SHALL.

Canaan /ˈkeɪnən/ region, later called Palestine, which was conquered and occupied by the Israelites in about the 11th century BC. In the Bible it is called 'the promised land'. ▷ **Canaanite** *adj, n.*

Canada /ˈkænədə/ second-largest country in the world, a member state of the Commonwealth, covering the northern half of North America with the exception of Alaska; pop approx 25 950 000; official languages English and French; capital Ottawa; unit of currency dollar (= 100 cents). Canada is a stable and prosperous country, despite tensions between francophones and anglophones. Both agriculture and industry are highly developed, and there are vast mineral resources. ⇨ map.

▷ **Canadian** /kəˈneɪdɪən/ *adj* of Canada or its people. — *n* native or inhabitant of Canada.

□ ˈ**Canada goose** wild goose with mainly brownish feathers, a black neck and white patches on the sides of the head.

canal /kə'næl/ *n* **1** channel cut through land for boats or ships to travel along, or to carry water for irrigation: *The Suez Canal joins the Mediterranean and the Red Sea.* Cf RIVER 1. ⇨ article at RIVER. **2** tube through which air or food passes in a plant or an animal's body: *the alimentary canal.*
▷ **canalize, -ise** /'kænəlaɪz/ *v* [Tn] **1** make a canal through (an area). **2** convert (a river) into a canal (by straightening it, building locks, etc). **3** direct (sth) to achieve a particular aim; channel: *canalize one's energies into voluntary work.* **canalization, -isation** /ˌkænəlaɪ'zeɪʃn; *US* -nəlɪ'z-/ *n* [U].
□ **ca'nal boat** long narrow boat used on canals.

Canaletto /ˌkænə'letəʊ/ usual name for Giovanni Antonio Canal (1697-1768), Italian painter. He is famous for his views of the canals of Venice and for scenes of the River Thames in London. His work has always been very popular in Britain.

canapé /'kænəpeɪ; *US* ˌkænə'peɪ/ *n* small biscuit or piece of bread, pastry, etc spread with cheese, meat, fish, etc and usu served with drinks at a party.

canard /kæ'nɑ:d, 'kænɑ:d/ *n* false report or rumour.

canary /kə'neərɪ/ *n* small yellow songbird, usu kept in a cage as a pet.
□ **caˌnary 'yellow** light yellow colour.

Canary Islands /kə'neərɪ aɪləndz/ **the Canary Islands** (also **the Canaries**) group of Spanish islands off the NW coast of Africa where there are popular holiday resorts. ⇨ map at SPAIN.

canasta /kə'næstə/ *n* [U] card-game similar to rummy and played with two packs of cards.

cancan /'kænkæn/ *n* [sing] lively dance with high kicking, performed by women in long skirts: *do/dance the cancan.*

cancel /'kænsl/ *v* (-ll-; *US* -l-) **1** [Tn] say that (sth already arranged and decided upon) will not be done or take place; call off: *cancel a holiday, concert, meeting,* eg because of illness ○ *The match had to be cancelled because of bad weather.* Cf POSTPONE. **2** [Tn] order (sth) to be stopped; make (sth) invalid: *cancel an agreement, a contract, a subscription, etc* ○ *He cancelled his order,* ie said he no longer wanted to receive the goods he had ordered. **3** [Tn] cross out (sth written): *Cancel that last sentence.* **4** [Tn] mark (a postage stamp or ticket) to prevent further use. **5** [Tn] (*mathematics*) remove (a common factor) from the numerator and denominator of a fraction, or from both sides of an equation, usu by crossing it out. **6** (phr v) **cancel (sth) out** be equal (to sth) in force and effect; counterbalance (sth): *These arguments cancel (each other) out.* ○ *Her kindness and generosity cancel out her occasional flashes of temper.*
▷ **cancellation** /ˌkænsə'leɪʃn/ *n* **1** [U] cancelling or being cancelled: *her cancellation of her trip to Paris* ○ *the cancellation of the match due to fog.* **2** [C] instance of this; thing that has been cancelled (CANCEL 1, 2), eg a theatre ticket: *Are there any cancellations for this evening's performance?* **3** [C] mark used to cancel a postage stamp, etc.

Cancer /'kænsə(r)/ *n* **1** the fourth sign of the zodiac, the Crab. **2** [C] person born under the influence of this sign. ⇨ Usage at ZODIAC. ⇨ illus at ZODIAC.

cancer /'kænsə(r)/ *n* **1** (**a**) [C, U] diseased growth in the body, often causing death; malignant tumour: *Doctors found a cancer on her breast.* ○ *The cancer has spread to his stomach.* (**b**) [U] disease in which such growths form: *lung cancer* ○ *cancer of the liver.* **2** [C] (*fig*) evil or dangerous thing that spreads quickly: *Violence is a cancer in our society.* Cf CANKER 3.
▷ **cancerous** /'kænsərəs/ *adj* of, like or affected with cancer: *Is the growth benign or cancerous?*

candela /kæn'delə/ *n* unit for measuring the intensity of light. ⇨ App 12.

candelabrum /ˌkændɪ'lɑ:brəm/ *n* (*pl* **-bra** /-brə/; also *sing* **candelabra**, *pl* **-bras** /-brəz/) large ornamental branched holder for candles or lights.

candid /'kændɪd/ *adj* not hiding one's thoughts; frank and honest: *a candid opinion, statement, person* ○ *Let me be quite candid with you: your work is not good enough.* ▷ **candidly**: *Candidly* (ie Speaking frankly), *David, I think you're being unreasonable. adv.* **candidness** *n* [U].

candidate /'kændɪdət; *US* -deɪt/ *n* **1** person who applies for a job or is nominated for election (esp to Parliament): *stand as Labour candidate in a parliamentary election* ○ *offer oneself as a candidate for a post.* **2** person taking an examination: *Most candidates passed in grammar.* **3** ~ (**for sth**) person considered to be suitable for a particular position or likely to get sth: *The company is being forced to reduce staff and I fear I'm a likely candidate (for redundancy).*
▷ **candidature** /'kændɪdətʃə(r)/ (also esp *Brit* **candidacy** /'kændɪdəsɪ/) *n* [U] being a candidate(1): *announce one's candidature.*

candied ⇨ CANDY.

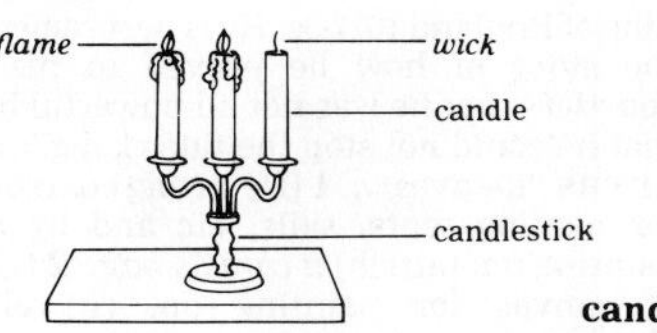

candle

candle /'kændl/ *n* **1** round stick of wax with a wick through it which is lit to give light as it burns. ⇨ illus. **2** (idm) **burn the candle at both ends** ⇨ BURN 2. **the game is not worth the candle** ⇨ GAME 1. **not hold a candle to sb/sth** (*infml*) be inferior to sb/sth: *She writes quite amusing stories but she can't hold a candle to the more serious novelists.*
□ **'candle-light** *n* [U] light produced by candles: *read, work, etc by candle-light.*
'candlepower *n* [U] unit of measurement of light, expressed in candelas: *a ten candlepower lamp.*
'candlestick *n* holder for one or more candles.

Candlemas /'kændlmæs/ Christian festival (2 February), involving the blessing of candles, which commemorates the Purification of the Virgin Mary and the presentation of Christ in the Temple.

candlewick /'kændlwɪk/ *n* [U] soft cotton fabric with a raised tufted pattern: [attrib] *a candlewick bedspread.*

candour (*US* **candor**) /'kændə(r)/ *n* [U] candid behaviour, speech or quality; frankness.

C and W *abbr* (*music*) country-and-western.

candy /'kændɪ/ *n* **1** [U] sugar hardened by repeated boiling. **2** (*esp US*) (**a**) [U] sweets or chocolate: [attrib] *a candy store.* (**b**) [C] a sweet or a chocolate.
▷ **candy** *v* (*pt, pp* **candied**) **1** [Tn esp passive] preserve (eg fruit) by boiling in sugar: *candied plums* ○ *candied peel,* eg of lemons or oranges. **2** [I, Tn] (cause sth to) form into sugar crystals.
□ **'candy-floss** *n* [U] (*US* also ˌ**cotton 'candy**) type of light fluffy sweet made by spinning melted sugar and eaten on a stick.
ˌ**candy 'stripes** alternating stripes of white and another colour (esp pink). **'candy-striped** *adj.*

candytuft /'kændɪtʌft/ *n* plant with clusters of white, pink or purple flowers.

cane /keɪn/ *n* **1** (**a**) [C] hollow jointed stem of certain plants, eg bamboo or sugar-cane. (**b**) [U] such stems used as a material for making furniture, etc: [attrib] *a cane chair.* **2** [C] thin woody stem of a raspberry plant. **3** (**a**) [C] length of cane, or a thin rod, used for supporting plants, as a walking-stick or for beating people as a punishment. (**b**) **the cane** [sing] (in some schools) the punishment in which children are beaten with a cane: *get/be given the cane* ○ *Many teachers wish to abolish the cane.*
▷ **cane** *v* [Tn] **1** punish (sb) by beating with a cane: *The headmaster caned the boys for disobedience.* **2** (*infml esp Brit*) defeat (sb) totally: *We really caned them in the last match.* **3** weave cane into (a chair, etc). **caning** *n* [U, C]: *give sb a good caning.*
□ **'cane-sugar** *n* [U] sugar obtained from the juice of sugar-cane.

canine /'keɪnaɪn/ *adj* of, like or relating to dogs.
▷ **canine** *n* **1** (*fml*) dog. **2** (also **canine tooth**) (in a human being) any of the four pointed teeth next to the incisors. ⇨ illus at TOOTH.

canister /'kænɪstə(r)/ *n* **1** small (usu metal) container for holding tea, coffee, etc. **2** cylinder, filled with shot or tear-gas, that bursts and releases its contents when fired from a gun or thrown.

canker /'kæŋkə(r)/ *n* **1** [U] disease that destroys the wood of plants and trees. **2** [U] disease causing ulcerous sores on the ears of animals, esp dogs and cats. **3** [C] (*fig*) evil or dangerous influence that spreads and corrupts people: *Drug addiction is a dangerous canker in society.* Cf CANCER 2.
▷ **canker** *v* [Tn] infect or corrupt (sb) with canker.
cankerous /'kæŋkərəs/ *adj* of, like or causing canker.

cannabis /'kænəbɪs/ *n* [U] **1** hemp plant. **2** any of various drugs made from the dried leaves and flowers of the hemp plant that are smoked or chewed for their intoxicating effect: *arrested for possessing cannabis.* Cf HASHISH, MARIJUANA.

cannelloni /ˌkænə'ləʊnɪ/ *n* [U] rolls of pasta filled with meat and seasoning.

cannery ⇨ CAN 1.

cannibal /'kænɪbl/ *n* (**a**) person who eats human flesh: [attrib] *a cannibal tribe.* (**b**) animal that eats its own kind.
▷ **cannibalism** /'kænɪbəlɪzəm/ *n* [U] practice of eating one's own kind. **cannibalistic** /ˌkænɪbə'lɪstɪk/ *adj* of or like cannibals.
cannibalize, -ise /'kænɪbəlaɪz/ *v* [Tn] use (a machine, vehicle, etc) to provide spare parts for others: *cannibalize an old radio to repair one's record-player.* **cannibalization, -isation** /ˌkænɪbəlaɪ'zeɪʃn; *US* -lɪ'z-/ *n* [U].

Canning /'kænɪŋ/ George (1770-1827), British politician. He had two periods as Foreign Secretary. During the second of these (1822-27) he gave British support to many of the nationalist independence movements in Europe and South America. He became Prime Minister shortly before his death. ⇨ App 2.

cannon /'kænən/ *n* [C] **1** (*pl* unchanged) old type of large heavy gun firing solid metal balls. **2** (*pl* unchanged) automatic gun firing shells (SHELL 3a) from an aircraft, a tank, etc: *two 20-millimetre cannon.* **3** (in billiards) shot in which the player's ball hits two other balls one after the other.
▷ **cannon** *v* (phr v) **cannon against/into sb/sth** collide heavily with sb/sth.
□ **'cannon-ball** *n* large metal ball fired from a cannon.
'cannon-fodder *n* [U] soldiers regarded only as material that is expendable in war.

cannonade /ˌkænə'neɪd/ *n* continuous firing of heavy guns.

cannot /'kænɒt/ = CAN NOT (CAN 2).

canny /'kænɪ/ *adj* (**-ier, -iest**) shrewd and careful, esp in business matters. ▷ **cannily** *adv.* **canniness** *n* [U]

canoe

canoe /kə'nu:/ *n* **1** light narrow boat moved by one or more paddles. ⇨ illus. **2** (idm) **paddle one's own canoe** ⇨ PADDLE 1.

▷ **canoe** *v* (*pt, pp* **canoed**, *pres p* **canoeing**) [I] (usu **go canoeing**) travel in a canoe. **canoeist** /kəˈnu:ɪst/ *n* person who paddles a canoe. ⇨ illus.

canon[1] /ˈkænən/ *n* **1** general rule, standard or principle by which sth is judged: *This film offends against all the canons of good taste.* **2** (**a**) list of sacred books accepted as genuine: *the canon of Holy Scripture.* (**b**) central part of the Roman Catholic Mass containing the words of consecration. (**c**) set of writings, etc accepted as genuinely by a particular author: *the Shakespeare canon.* **3** piece of music for several voices or instruments, in which each of the parts takes up the same theme one after the other.

▷ **canonical** /kəˈnɒnɪkl/ *adj* **1** according to canon law. **2** included in the canon[1](2a). **3** standard; accepted. **canonicals** *n* [pl] clothes worn by a priest during a church service. **caˌnonical ˈhours** times fixed for a formal set of prayers to be said, eg by monks.

□ ˌ**canon ˈlaw** rules established by the Christian Church for its members, dealing with matters of faith, morals and discipline.

canon[2] /ˈkænən/ *n* priest with special duties in a cathedral: *The Rev Canon Arthur Brown.*

canonize, -ise /ˈkænənaɪz/ *v* [Tn] officially declare (sb) to be a saint(1a).

▷ **canonization, -isation** /ˌkænənaɪˈzeɪʃn; *US* -nɪˈz-/ *n* [C, U] (instance of) canonizing or being canonized.

canoodle /kəˈnu:dl/ *v* [I, Ipr] ~ (**with sb**) (*esp Brit infml*) kiss and cuddle in a loving way.

canopy /ˈkænəpɪ/ *n* **1** hanging cover forming a shelter above a throne, bed, etc. **2** cover for the cockpit of an aircraft. **3** (*fig*) any overhanging covering: *the grey canopy of the sky* ○ *a canopy of leaves,* eg in a forest. **4** part of a parachute that opens out to slow down the rate of fall of the person using it.

Canova /kəˈnəʊvə/ Antonio (1757-1822), Italian neo-classical sculptor.

cant[1] /kænt/ *n* [U] **1** insincere talk, esp about religion or morality; hypocrisy. **2** specialized language of a particular group; jargon: *thieves' cant* ○ [attrib] *a cant expression.*

cant[2] /kænt/ *n* **1** sloping surface or position. **2** sudden movement that tilts or overturns sth.

▷ **cant** *v* [I, Ip, Tn, Tn·p] ~ (**sth**) (**over**) (cause sth to) tilt, overturn: *cant a boat to repair it.*

can't contracted form of CANNOT (CAN[2]).

Cantab /ˈkæntæb/ *abbr* (esp in degree titles) of Cambridge (University) (Latin *Cantabrigiensis*): *James Cox MA (Cantab).* Cf OXON 2.

cantabile /kænˈtɑ:bɪlɪ/ *adv* (*music*) (to be performed) in a smooth flowing way.

▷ **cantabile** *n* piece of music (to be) performed in this way.

cantaloup (also **cantaloupe**) /ˈkæntəlu:p/ *n* [C, U] type of melon: *a slice of cantaloup.*

cantankerous /kænˈtæŋkərəs/ *adj* bad-tempered; quarrelsome. ▷ **cantankerously** *adv.*

cantata /kænˈtɑ:tə/ *n* short musical work, often on a religious subject, sung by soloists and usu a choir, accompanied by an orchestra: *Bach's cantatas.* Cf ORATORIO.

canteen /kænˈti:n/ *n* **1** place serving food and drink in a factory, an office, a school, etc. **2** (*Brit*) case or box containing a set of knives, forks and spoons. **3** soldier's or camper's water-flask.

canter /ˈkæntə(r)/ *n* (usu *sing*) **1** (of a horse) movement that is faster than a trot but slower than a gallop. **2** ride on a horse moving at this speed: *go for a canter.* **3** (idm) **at a canter** without effort; easily: *win a race at a canter.*

▷ **canter** *v* [I, Tn] (cause a horse to) move at a canter: *We cantered our horses for several miles.*

Canterbury /ˈkæntəbərɪ/ city in Kent, England. St *Augustine used it as his base for converting England to Christianity. The Archbishop of Canterbury is the chief dignitary of the Church of England.

□ **the** ˌ**Canterbury ˈTales** ⇨ CHAUCER.

canticle /ˈkæntɪkl/ *n* hymn or chant with words taken from the Bible.

cantilever /ˈkæntɪli:və(r)/ *n* beam or bracket projecting from a wall to support eg a balcony.

□ ˈ**cantilever bridge** bridge made of two cantilevers projecting from piers and joined by girders. ⇨ illus at BRIDGE.

canto /ˈkæntəʊ/ *n* (*pl* ~**s**) any of the main divisions of a long poem.

canton /ˈkæntɒn/ *n* subdivision of a country, esp of Switzerland.

Cantonese /ˌkæntəˈni:z/ *n* [U] form of Chinese spoken in southern China and in Hong Kong.

cantonment /kænˈtu:nmənt; *US* -ˈtəʊn-/ *n* **1** place where soldiers live. **2** permanent military camp, esp in India.

cantor /ˈkæntɔ:(r)/ *n* leader of the singing in a church or synagogue.

Canuck /kəˈnʌk/ *n* (*US sl usu derog*) Canadian, esp a French Canadian.

Canute (also **Cnut**) /kəˈnju:t/ (c 994-1035), Danish king of England 1017-35. He is best remembered for the story of how he proved to his flattering courtiers that he was not all-powerful by showing that he could not stop the tide rising. ⇨ App 3.

canvas /ˈkænvəs/ *n* **1** [U] strong coarse cloth used for making tents, sails, etc and by artists for painting on: [attrib] *a canvas bag.* **2** [C] (**a**) piece of canvas for painting on. (**b**) oil-painting: *Turner's canvases.* **3** [C usu *sing*] floor of a boxing or wrestling ring: *put sb on the canvas,* ie with a punch or a wrestling throw. **4** (idm) **under canvas** (**a**) (of soldiers, campers, etc) living in tents: *sleep under canvas.* (**b**) (of a ship) with sails spread.

canvass /ˈkænvəs/ *v* **1** [I, Ipr, Tn, Tn·pr] ~ (**sb**) (**for sth**) go around an area asking (people) for (political support): *go out canvassing (for votes)* ○ *The Labour candidate will canvass the constituency next month.* **2** [Tn] find out the opinions of (eg voters before an election). **3** [Tn] suggest (an idea, etc) for discussion: *canvass the idea/notion/theory.* **4** [Tn] (*US*) check (votes cast in an election) to see that they are valid.

▷ **canvass** *n* act of canvassing. **canvasser** *n* person who canvasses.

canyon /ˈkænjən/ *n* deep gorge, usu with a river flowing through it: *the Grand Canyon, Arizona.*

caoutchouc /ˈkaʊtʃʊk/ *n* [U] rubber in its raw state.

CAP /ˌsi: eɪ ˈpi:/ *abbr* Common Agricultural Policy.

cap /kæp/ *n* **1** soft head-covering without a brim but often with a peak, worn by men and boys: *British schoolboys sometimes wear caps,* ie as part of their school uniform. ○ *a flat cap,* ie the type traditionally associated with working-class men in Britain, esp in northern England. ⇨ illus at HAT. **2** (esp in compounds) any close-fitting soft head-covering worn for various purposes: *a ˈbathing-cap* ○ *a ˈbaseball cap* ○ *a ˈnurse's cap* ○ *a ˈshower-cap.* **3** (*sport esp Brit*) (**a**) cap given to sb who is chosen to play for a school, county, country, etc, esp at cricket, football or Rugby: *He's won three caps* (ie been chosen to play three times) *for England.* (**b**) player chosen for such a team. **4** academic head-dress with a flat top and a tassel: *wear cap and gown on graduation day.* Cf MORTAR-BOARD (MORTAR[2]). **5** protective cover or top (for a pen, bottle, camera lens, etc). **6** natural covering shaped like a cap: *the polar ˈice-cap.* **7** (also **Dutch ˈcap**) = DIAPHRAGM 4. **8** (**a**) = PERCUSSION CAP (PERCUSSION). (**b**) small amount of explosive contained in a paper strip, for making a small explosion in a toy gun: [attrib] *a cap gun/pistol.* **9** (idm) **cap in ˈhand** humbly; in a servile manner: *go cap in hand to sb, asking for money.* **a feather in one's cap** ⇨ FEATHER[1]. **if the cap fits** (,**wear it**) if sb feels that a remark applies to him (he should act accordingly): *I have noticed some employees coming to work an hour late. I shall name no names, but if the cap fits ....* **set one's cap at sb** (*dated*) (of a girl or woman) try to attract a man as a husband or lover.

▷ **cap** *v* (**-pp-**) [Tn] **1** (**a**) put a cap(5) on (sth); cover the top or end of: *mountains capped with snow/mist.* (**b**) = CROWN[2] 4. **2** follow (sth) with sth better, bigger, funnier, etc: *cap a joke, story, etc.* **3** (*sport esp Brit*) award a cap to (a player); select (a player) for a national team: *He was capped 36 times for England.* **4** (in Scottish universities) award a degree to (sb). **5** (idm) **to cap it all** as a final piece of bad or good fortune: *Last week he crashed his car, then he lost his job and now to cap it all his wife has left him!*

□ ˌ**cap and ˈbells** long floppy pointed cap with bells sewn onto it, as worn by jesters in former times.

capability /ˌkeɪpəˈbɪlətɪ/ *n* **1** [U] (~ **to do sth/of doing sth**); ~ (**for sth**) quality of being able to do sth; ability: *You have the capability to do/of doing this job well.* ○ *nuclear capability,* ie power or capacity to fight a nuclear war. **2 capabilities** [pl] undeveloped gift or quality: *He has great capabilities as a writer.*

capable /ˈkeɪpəbl/ *adj* **1** having (esp practical) ability; able; competent: *a very capable woman.* **2** [pred] ~ **of** (**doing**) **sth** (**a**) having the ability or power necessary for sth: *You are capable of better work than this.* ○ *Show me what you are capable of,* ie how well you can work. ○ *He is capable of running a mile in four minutes.* (**b**) having the character or inclination to do sth: *He's quite capable of lying* (ie It wouldn't be surprising if he lied) *to get out of trouble.* **3** [pred] ~ **of sth** (*fml*) (of situations, remarks, etc) open to or allowing sth: *Our position is capable of improvement.*

▷ **capably** *adv* in a capable(1) way: *handle a situation, manage a business capably.*

capacious /kəˈpeɪʃəs/ *adj* (of things) that can hold much; roomy: *capacious pockets* ○ *a capacious memory.* ▷ **capaciousness** *n* [U].

capacitance /kəˈpæsɪtəns/ *n* [U] **1** ability (of a system, etc) to store electric charge. **2** ratio of the change in the electric charge of a body to the corresponding change in its electric potential.

capacitor /kəˈpæsɪtə(r)/ *n* device having capacitance, usu consisting of conductors separated by an insulator.

capacity /kəˈpæsətɪ/ *n* **1** [U] ability to hold or contain sth: *a hall with a seating capacity of 2 000* ○ *filled to capacity,* ie completely full ○ [attrib] *a capacity crowd,* ie one that fills a sports ground, etc. **2** [sing] power to produce sth: *factories working at full capacity.* **3** [sing] ~ (**for sth**) ability to produce, experience, understand or learn sth: *She has an enormous capacity for hard work.* ○ *Some people have a greater capacity for happiness than others.* ○ *This book is within the capacity of* (ie can be understood by) *younger readers.* **4** (idm) **in one's capacity as sth** in a certain function or position: *act in one's capacity as a poˈlice officer/in one's poˈlice capacity.*

caparison /kəˈpærɪsn/ *n* (usu *pl*) (formerly) decorated covering for a horse, or for a horse and knight.

▷ **caparison** *v* [Tn] put caparisons on (a horse).

cape[1] /keɪp/ *n* loose sleeveless garment like a cloak but usu shorter. ⇨ illus at DRESS.

cape[2] /keɪp/ *n* (*abbr* **C**) **1** [C] (often in geographical names) piece of high land sticking out into the sea: *Cape Horn.* **2 the Cape** [sing] (in S Africa) the Cape of Good Hope; Cape Province.

□ **Cape ˈColoured** (in S Africa) person of mixed race.

Cape Canaveral /ˌkeɪp kəˈnævərəl/ US rocket-launching base in Florida (renamed Cape Kennedy for a period).

Cape Horn /ˌkeɪp ˈhɔ:n/ southernmost tip of South America, known for its stormy weather. ⇨ map at ARGENTINA.

Cape of Good Hope /ˌkeɪp əv gʊd ˈhəʊp/ mountainous cape near the southernmost tip of South Africa.

Cape Province /ˌkeɪp ˈprɒvɪns/ southern province of the Republic of South Africa.

caper[1] /ˈkeɪpə(r)/ *v* [I, Ip] ~ (**about**) jump or run about playfully: *lambs capering (about) in the fields.*

▷ **caper** *n* **1** jump; leap. **2** (*infml*) (**a**) mischievous act; prank. (**b**) dishonest or criminal scheme: *What's your little caper?* **3** (idm) **cut a ˈcaper** jump about happily; act foolishly.

caper[2] /ˈkeɪpə(r)/ *n* **(a)** prickly shrub. **(b)** (usu *pl*) one of its buds pickled for use in sauces, etc.

capercaillie (also **capercailzie**) /ˌkæpəˈkeɪlɪ/ *n* type of large grouse.

Cape Verde Islands /ˌkeɪp ˈvɜːd aɪləndz/ country made up of a group of islands in the Atlantic Ocean west of Senegal; pop approx 358 000; official language Portuguese; capital Praia; unit of currency centavos (= 100 escudos). Portuguese settlers arrived there in the 15th century and Portuguese rule continued until the country gained independence in 1975. Prolonged droughts have seriously affected the economy, which is based largely on farming, and most of the country's food has to be imported. ▷ **Cape Verdean** /ˈvɜːdɪən/ *n, adj*. ⇨ map at ALGERIA.

capillary /kəˈpɪlərɪ; *US* ˈkæpɪlerɪ/ *n* **1** any of the very narrow blood vessels connecting arteries and veins in the body. **2** (also **capillarity** /ˌkæpɪˈlærətɪ/) [U], **caˌpillary ˈaction**) force by which a liquid is drawn along a very narrow tube.

capital[1] /ˈkæpɪtl/ *n* **1** town or city that is the centre of government of a country, state or province: *Cairo is the capital of Egypt.* ○ [attrib] *London, Paris and Rome are capital cities.* **2** (also **capital letter**) letter of the form and size used to begin a name or a sentence: *In this sentence, the word BIG is in capitals.* ○ *Write your name in block capitals, please.* **3** head or top part of a column. ⇨ illus at COLUMN.

▷ **capital** *adj* [usu attrib] **1** involving punishment by death: *a capital offence* ○ *capital punishment*, ie the death penalty. **2** (of letters) having the form and size used to begin a name or a sentence: *London is spelt with a capital 'L'.* **3** very serious: *a capital error.* **4** (*dated Brit*) excellent: *What a capital idea!* **5** (idm) **with a capital A, B, etc** (used to emphasize sth said or written about a person or thing): *She's a feminist with a capital F*, ie a very strong feminist.

capital[2] /ˈkæpɪtl/ *n* **1** [U] wealth or property that may be used to produce more wealth. **2** [sing] sum of money used to start a business: *set up a business with a starting capital of £100 000.* **3** [U] accumulated material wealth owned by a person or a business: [attrib] *capital assets.* **4** [U] capitalists or their interests: *capital and labour.* **5** (idm) **make capital (out) of sth** use (a situation, etc) to one's own advantage: *The Opposition parties made (political) capital out of the disagreements within the Cabinet.*

□ **capital exˈpenditure** money spent by a business on buildings, equipment, etc.

capital ˈgain profits made from the sale of investments or property. **capital ˈgains tax** tax on such profits.

capital ˈgoods goods (eg ships, railways, machinery, etc) used in producing other goods. Cf CONSUMER GOODS (CONSUMER).

capital-inˈtensive *adj* (of industrial processes) needing the investment of very large sums of money (as contrasted with a very large number of workers). Cf LABOUR-INTENSIVE (LABOUR[1]).

capital ˈlevy general tax on private wealth or property. Cf INCOME TAX (INCOME).

capital ˈsum single payment of money, eg to an insured person.

capital ˈtransfer transfer of money or property from one person to another, eg by inheritance.

capital ˈtransfer tax (formerly, in the UK) tax on such a transfer. Cf ESTATE TAX (ESTATE), INHERITANCE TAX (INHERIT).

capitalism /ˈkæpɪtəlɪzəm/ *n* [U] economic system in which a country's trade and industry are controlled by private owners for profit, rather than by the State.

▷ **capitalist** *n* **1** person who owns or controls much capital[2](1); rich person. **2** person who supports capitalism. — *adj* based on or supporting capitalism: *a capitalist economy.* **capitalistic** /ˌkæpɪtəˈlɪstɪk/ *adj*. Cf SOCIALISM.

capitalize, -ise /ˈkæpɪtəlaɪz/ *v* [Tn] **1** write or print (sth) with capital[1](2) letters. **2** convert (sth) into, use as or provide with capital[2](1). **3** (phr v) **capitalize on sth** use sth to one's own advantage; profit from sth: *capitalize on the mistakes made by a rival firm.* ▷ **capitalization, -isation** /ˌkæpɪtəlaɪˈzeɪʃn; *US* -lɪˈzeɪʃn/ *n* [U].

capitation /ˌkæpɪˈteɪʃn/ *n* tax, fee or grant of an equal amount for each person: [attrib] *a capiˈtation allowance.*

Capitol /ˈkæpɪtl/ **the Capitol 1** building in Washington in which the United States Congress meets. **2** temple of Jupiter in ancient Rome.

capitulate /kəˈpɪtʃʊleɪt/ *v* [I, Ipr] ~ (**to sb**) surrender (to sb), esp on agreed conditions.

▷ **capitulation** /kəˌpɪtʃʊˈleɪʃn/ *n* [C, U] (act of) capitulating.

capon /ˈkeɪpɒn, ˈkeɪpən/ *n* domestic cock[1](1) castrated and fattened for eating.

Capone /kəˈpəʊn/ Al (1899-1947), US gangster who controlled organized crime in Chicago in the 1920s.

cappuccino /kæpʊˈtʃiːnəʊ/ *n* (*pl* ~**s**) (*Italian*) espresso coffee with hot milk added.

Capra /ˈkæprə/ Frank (1897-1992), American film director. He is most famous for the good humour and optimism of the films he made in the 1930s and 40s, including *Mr Deeds Goes to Town* and *It's a Wonderful Life*.

Capri /ˈkæpriː, kəˈpriː/ island in the bay of Naples, off the west coast of Italy. It is a popular holiday resort.

caprice /kəˈpriːs/ *n* **1** **(a)** [C] sudden change in attitude or behaviour with no obvious cause; whim. **(b)** [U] tendency to such changes. **2** [C] short lively piece of music in an irregular style.

capricious /kəˈprɪʃəs/ *adj* characterized by sudden changes in attitude or behaviour; unpredictable; impulsive: *Romantic heroines are often capricious.* ○ (*fig*) *a capricious climate*, ie one that is always changing. ▷ **capriciously** *adv*. **capriciousness** *n* [U].

Capricorn /ˈkæprɪkɔːn/ *n* **1** the tenth sign of the zodiac, the Goat. **2** [C] person born under the influence of this sign. ⇨ Usage at ZODIAC. ⇨ illus at ZODIAC.

capriole /ˈkæprɪəʊl/ *n* high leap and kick, esp as done by a trained horse.

capsicum /ˈkæpsɪkəm/ *n* **(a)** tropical plant with seed-pods containing hot-tasting seeds. **(b)** one of these pods used as a vegetable. Cf PEPPER 2.

capsize /kæpˈsaɪz; *US* ˈkæpsaɪz/ *v* [I, Tn] (cause a boat to) overturn or be overturned: *The boat capsized in heavy seas.*

capstan /ˈkæpstən/ *n* **1** thick revolving post or cylinder round which a rope or cable is wound, eg to raise a ship's anchor. **2** revolving spindle that carries the spool on a tape recorder.

capsule /ˈkæpsjuːl; *US* ˈkæpsl/ *n* **1** seed-case of a plant that opens when the seeds are ripe. ⇨ illus at FRUIT. **2** small soluble case containing a dose of medicine and swallowed with it. **3** detachable compartment for men or instruments in a spacecraft.

Capt *abbr* Captain: *Capt (Terence) Jones.*

captain /ˈkæptɪn/ *n* **1** person in charge of a ship or civil aircraft. **2** **(a)** officer in the British Army between the ranks of lieutenant and major. ⇨ App 4. **(b)** officer in the British Navy between the ranks of commander and admiral. ⇨ App 4. **3** person given authority over a group or team; leader: *He was (the) captain of the football team for five years.* **4** (idm) **a captain of ˈindustry** person who manages a large industrial company.

▷ **captain** *v* [Tn] be captain of (a football team, etc): *Who is captaining the side today?*

captaincy /ˈkæptɪnsɪ/ *n* **(a)** [C, U] position of captain: *take over the captaincy* ○ *Captaincy suits him.* **(b)** [C] period of being captain: *during her captaincy.* **(c)** [U] quality of a captain's actions: *showing fine captaincy.*

caption /ˈkæpʃn/ *n* **1** short title or heading of an article in a magazine, etc. **2** words printed with an illustration or a photograph in order to describe or explain it. **3** words shown on a cinema or television screen, eg to establish the scene of a story (eg 'New York 1981').

▷ **caption** *v* [Tn esp passive] put a caption on (eg a cartoon or scene): *a blank white postcard captioned, as a joke, 'a polar bear in a snowstorm'.*

captious /ˈkæpʃəs/ *adj* (*fml*) fond of criticizing or raising objections about unimportant matters; quibbling. ▷ **captiously** *adv*. **captiousness** *n* [U].

captivate /ˈkæptɪveɪt/ *v* [Tn] fascinate (sb); charm; enchant: *He was captivated by her beauty.*

▷ **captivating** *adj* fascinating; charming: *a captivating woman* ○ *He found her captivating.* **captivation** /ˌkæptɪˈveɪʃn/ *n* [U].

captive /ˈkæptɪv/ *adj* **1** [esp attrib] held as a prisoner; unable to escape: *a captive bird.* **2** (idm) **hold/take sb ˈcaptive/ˈprisoner** keep or take sb as a prisoner: *They were held captive by masked gunmen.*

▷ **captive** *n* captive person or animal: *Three of the captives tried to escape.*

captivity /kæpˈtɪvətɪ/ *n* **(a)** [U] state of being captive: *He was held in captivity for three years.* ○ *Wild animals don't breed well in captivity.* **(b)** **the Captivity** [sing] (*Bible*) period in the 6th century BC when the Jewish people were kept as captives in Babylon.

□ **ˌcaptive ˈaudience** audience with little or no freedom to go away and therefore easily persuaded to listen or watch: *Television advertisers can exploit a captive audience.*

ˌcaptive balˈloon balloon held to the ground by a cable.

captor /ˈkæptə(r)/ *n* person who captures a person or an animal: *The hostages were well treated by their captors.*

capture /ˈkæptʃə(r)/ *v* [Tn] **1** take (sb/sth) as a prisoner: *capture an escaped convict* ○ (*fig*) *This advertisement will capture the attention of TV audiences.* **2** take or win (sth) by force or skill: *capture a town* ○ *capture one's opponent's queen*, ie in a game of chess. **3** succeed in representing (sb/sth) in a picture, on film, etc: *capture a baby's smile in a photograph.* **4** (*physics*) absorb (an atomic particle): *a captured neutron.* **5** [Tn] put (data, eg the text of a book) into a file on a computer: *All our patients' files have now been captured in a database.* **6** (of a river, stream, etc) bring the waters of (another river or its basin) into itself by washing away the ground in between. **7** (of a star or planet) bring (an object) into its field of gravity.

▷ **capture** *n* **1** [U] capturing or being captured: *the capture of a thief* ○ *He evaded capture for three days.* ○ *data capture*, ie on a computer. **2** [C] person or thing captured.

Capuchin /ˈkæpjʊtʃɪn/ *n* Franciscan friar in a branch of the order founded in 1528.

capybara /ˌkæpɪˈbɑːrə/ *n* large S American rodent resembling a guinea-pig.

cars

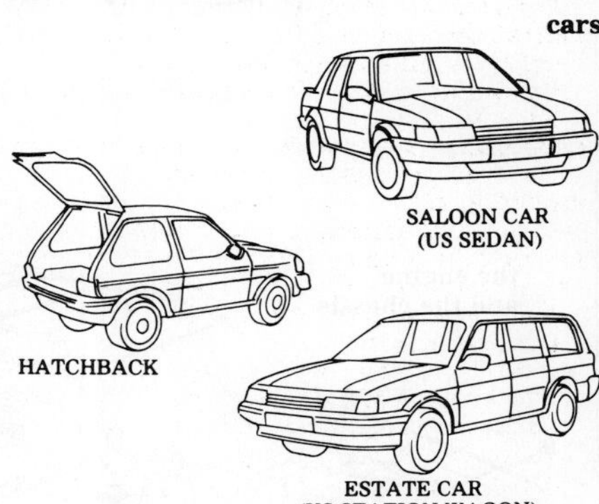

car /kɑː(r)/ *n* **1** (also **ˈmotor car**, *esp US* **automobile**) motor vehicle with (usu four) wheels for carrying passengers: *buy a new car* ○ *What kind of car do you have?* ○ *We're going (to London) by car.* ⇨ illus. **2** (in compound *ns*) **(a)** railway carriage of a specified type: *a dining-/sleeping-car.* **(b)** = CARRIAGE 2. **(c)** (*US*) any railway carriage or van: *a freight car.* **3** passenger compartment of an airship, a balloon, a cable railway or a lift.

□ **ˈcar-boot sale** (*esp Brit*) (*US* **garage sale**) outdoor sale at which people sell unwanted

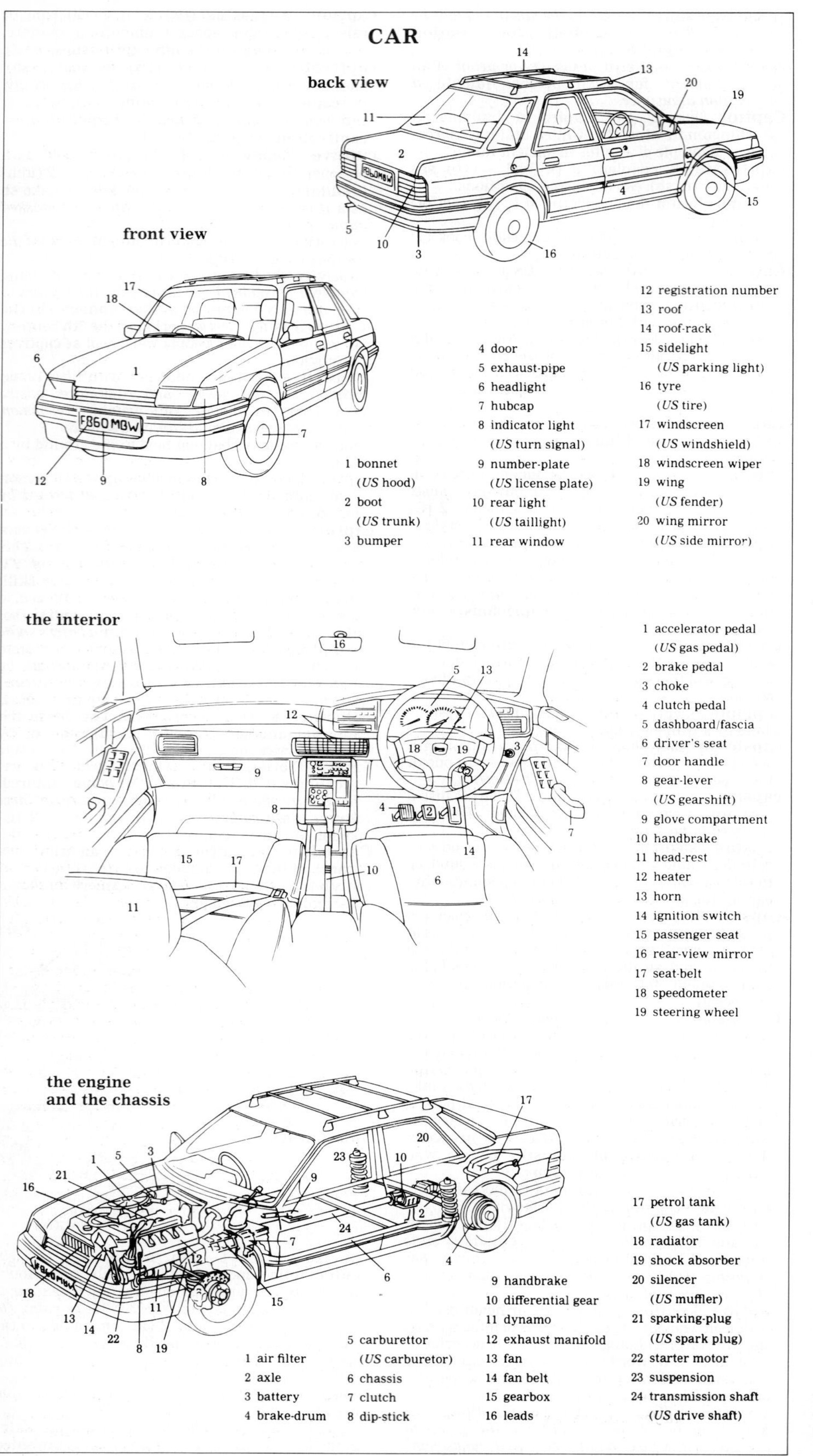

possessions, etc from the boots of their cars.

ˈ**car coat** short coat, designed esp for drivers, which reaches almost down to the knees.

ˈ**carfare** *n* (*US*) money that one must pay to travel on a bus or streetcar.

ˈ**car-ferry** *n* sea or air ferry for carrying cars (eg across the English Channel).

ˈ**car-park** (*US* **parking-lot**) *n* (usu outdoor) area for parking cars: *a multi-storey car-park.* ⇨ illus at MOTORWAY.

ˈ**car phone** special telephone that can be used in a car, etc.

ˈ**car-port** *n* shelter for a car, consisting of a roof supported by posts.

ˈ**carsick** *adj* [usu pred] affected with nausea caused by the movement of a car: *He's feeling car-sick.* ˈ**carsickness** *n* [U].

Caractacus /kəˈræktəkəs/ British king who led the resistance to the Romans. He was captured and died in Rome about 54 AD.

carafe /kəˈræf/ *n* **1** glass container in which wine or water are served at meals. ⇨ illus at BOTTLE. **2** amount contained in this: *I can't drink more than half a carafe.*

caramel /ˈkærəmel/ *n* **1** [U] burnt sugar used for colouring and flavouring food. **2** [U, C] type of toffee tasting like this: *a piece of caramel.* **3** [U] colour of caramel; light brown.

▷ **caramelize, -ise** /ˈkærəməlaɪz/ *v* [I, Tn] (cause sth to) turn into caramel.

carapace /ˈkærəpeɪs/ *n* shell on the back of a tortoise or crustacean.

carat /ˈkærət/ *n* (*abbr* **ct**) **1** unit of weight (200 milligrams) for precious stones. **2** (*US* **karat**) unit of measurement of the purity of gold (pure gold being 24 carats): *a 20-carat gold ring* ○ *a ring of 20 carats.*

Caravaggio /ˌkærəˈvædʒɪəʊ/ Michelangelo Merisi da (1573-1610), important and influential Italian painter, noted for his realistic treatment of traditional subjects and his dramatic use of light and shade.

caravan /ˈkærəvæn/ *n* **1** (*Brit*) (*US* **trailer**) large vehicle on wheels, equipped for living in and usu towed by a motor vehicle. **2** covered cart or wagon used for living in, and able to be pulled by a horse: *a gypsy caravan.* **3** group of people (eg merchants) travelling together across the desert.

▷ **caravan** *v* (**-nn-**) [I] (usu **go caravanning**) have a holiday in a caravan: *We're going caravanning in Spain this summer.*

caravanserai /ˌkærəˈvænsərɪ, -səraɪ/ *n* (in some Eastern countries) inn with a large central courtyard where caravans (CARAVAN 3) can stay for the night.

caraway /ˈkærəweɪ/ *n* (**a**) [C] plant with spicy seeds that are used for flavouring bread, cakes, etc. (**b**) [U] (also ˈ**caraway seed**) these seeds used in cooking.

carbide /ˈkɑ:baɪd/ *n* compound of carbon, esp calcium carbide.

carbine /ˈkɑ:baɪn/ *n* short light automatic rifle.

carbohydrate /ˌkɑ:bəʊˈhaɪdreɪt/ *n* **1** [C, U] any of various types of organic compound, such as sugar and starch, containing carbon, hydrogen and oxygen. **2 carbohydrates** [pl] foods containing carbohydrate, considered to be fattening: *You eat too many carbohydrates!*

carbolic acid /kɑ:ˌbɒlɪk ˈæsɪd/ (also **phenol**) strong-smelling and powerful liquid used as an antiseptic and disinfectant.

carbon /ˈkɑ:bən/ *n* **1** [U] non-metallic chemical element that is present in all living matter. It occurs in its pure form as diamond and graphite, and in less pure form in coal and charcoal. It can combine with many other elements to form molecules consisting of long chains or rings of atoms. The study of carbon and its compounds is known as *organic chemistry.* ⇨ App 11. **2** [C] stick of carbon used in an electric arc lamp. **3** [C] = CARBON PAPER. **4** [C] = CARBON COPY.

▷ **carbonaceous** /ˌkɑ:bəˈneɪʃəs/ *adj* (**a**) of or containing carbon. (**b**) of or like coal or charcoal.

carbonize, -ise *v* [Tn] convert (sth) into carbon by burning. **carbonization, -isation** /ˌkɑ:bənaɪˈzeɪʃn;

US -nɪˈz-/ *n* [U].
□ ˈ**carbon black** black powder made by partly burning oil, wood, etc, and used as a colouring or in the manufacture of rubber.
ˌ**carbon ˈcopy 1** copy made with carbon paper: *make a carbon copy of a document.* **2** (*fig*) exact copy or likeness: *She's a carbon copy of her sister.*
ˈ**carbon cycle 1** (*physics*) series of nuclear reactions involving hydrogen atoms. It creates a large amount of energy and it is thought that this is the major source of energy in large stars. **2** (*biology*) complex cycle that occurs in nature involving carbon and its compounds as they go through many different processes. For example, plants absorb carbon dioxide from the atmosphere and incorporate it into their tissues in photosynthesis. Human beings and animals may eat the plants and take in carbon. When they breathe they then release carbon dioxide into the atmosphere, completing the cycle.
ˌ**carbon ˈdating** method of calculating the age of very old objects by measuring the decay of radio-carbon (**carbon 14**) in them.
ˌ**carbon diˈoxide** colourless odourless gas formed by the burning of carbon, or given out by living things during respiration.
ˌ**carbon ˈfibre** very fine fibre made from carbon atoms that has great lightness and strength. It is now used in the manufacture of many things, from aircraft parts to tennis rackets, in combination with resins, ceramics, etc.
ˌ**carbon monˈoxide** poisonous gas formed when carbon burns incompletely, present eg in the exhaust fumes of petrol engines.
ˈ**carbon paper** (sheet of) thin paper coated with carbon or some other coloured substance and used between sheets of writing-paper for making copies.
ˌ**carbon ˌtetraˈchloride** toxic chemical once widely used in fire extinguishers and in dry-cleaning. Its main industrial use is now as a solvent.

carbonade /kɑːbəˈnɑːd, -ˈneɪd/ *n* rich beef stew containing beer.

carbonate /ˈkɑːbəneɪt/ *n* (*chemistry*) salt of carbonic acid in which all available hydrogen has been replaced. Cf HYDROGEN CARBONATE.

carbonated /ˈkɑːbəneɪtɪd/ *adj* containing carbon dioxide; fizzy: *carbonated drinks.*

carbonic acid /kɑːˌbɒnɪk ˈæsɪd/ weak acid made by dissolving carbon dioxide in water.

carboniferous /ˌkɑːbəˈnɪfərəs/ *adj* (*geology*) **1** producing coal: *carboniferous rocks.* **2 Carboniferous** of the geological period when coal deposits were formed, 350 to 270 million years ago.
▷ **Carboniferous** *n* the Carboniferous period.

carborundum /ˌkɑːbəˈrʌndəm/ *n* [U] hard compound of carbon and silicon, used for polishing and grinding things: [attrib] *a carborundum stone.*

carboy /ˈkɑːbɔɪ/ *n* large round glass or plastic bottle, usu enclosed in a protective framework, used for carrying dangerous liquids.

carbuncle /ˈkɑːbʌŋkl/ *n* **1** large inflamed swelling under the skin. **2** bright-red gem with a rounded shape.

carburation /ˌkɑːbjʊˈreɪʃn/ *n* [U] process of spraying air with hydrocarbon fuel to make an explosive mixture for an internal-combustion engine.

carburettor /ˌkɑːbəˈretə(r)/ (*US* **carburetor** /ˈkɑːrbəreɪtər/) *n* apparatus in a petrol engine for mixing fuel and air to make an explosive mixture. ⇨ illus at CAR.

carcass /ˈkɑːkəs/ *n* **1** dead body of an animal, esp one prepared for cutting up as meat: *vultures picking at a lion's carcass.* Cf CORPSE. **2** bones of a cooked bird: *You might find a bit of meat left on the chicken carcass.* **3** (*joc or derog*) person's body: *Shift your carcass!* **4** basic framework, eg of a ship or a house that is being built.

carcinogen /kɑːˈsɪnədʒen/ *n* (*medical*) substance that produces cancer.
▷ **carcinogenic** /ˌkɑːsɪnəˈdʒenɪk/ *adj* (*medical*) producing cancer.

carcinoma /ˌkɑːsɪˈnəʊmə/ *n* (*pl* ~**s** or ~**ta** /-tə/) (*medical*) cancerous growth.

card[1] /kɑːd/ *n* **1** [U] thick stiff paper or thin pasteboard. **2** [C] piece of this for writing or printing on, used to identify a person or to record information or as proof of membership: *an identity card* ○ *a record card* ○ *a membership card.* **3** [C] piece of this with a picture on it, for sending greetings, messages, etc: *a Christmas/birthday card* ○ *a get-well card,* ie one sent to sb who is unwell ○ *David sent us a card* (ie a postcard) *from Spain.* **4** [C] = PLAYING-CARD: *a pack of cards.* **5 cards** [pl] games played with a set of playing-cards; card-playing: *win/lose at cards* ○ *Let's play cards.* **6** [C] programme of events at a race-meeting, etc. **7** [C] (*dated infml*) odd or amusing person: *Bertie's quite a card.* **8** (idm) **one's best/strongest ˈcard** one's strongest or most effective argument. **(have) a card up one's sleeve** sth secret held in reserve until needed. **get one's ˈcards/give sb his ˈcards** (*infml*) be dismissed/dismiss sb from a job. **have the cards/odds stacked aˈgainst one** ⇨ STACK. **hold/keep one's cards ˌclose to one's ˈchest** be secretive about one's intentions. **a house of cards** ⇨ HOUSE. **lay/put one's ˈcards on the table** be honest and open about one's resources and intentions: *We can only reach agreement if we both put our cards on the table.* **make a ˈcard** (in card-games) win a trick with a particular card. **on the cards** (*infml*) likely or possible: *An early general election is certainly on the cards.* **play one's ˈcards well, right, etc** act in the most effective way to achieve sth: *You could end up running this company if you play your cards right.* **show one's hand/cards** ⇨ SHOW[2].
□ ˈ**card-carrying member** registered member of a political party, trade union, etc: *a card-carrying member of the Communist party.*
ˈ**card-game** *n* game using playing-cards: *Bridge, poker and whist are card-games.*
ˈ**card index** = INDEX 1b.
ˈ**cardphone** public telephone that can be used by inserting a magnetic card instead of money. ⇨ article at TELEPHONE.
ˈ**card-sharp** (also ˈ**card-sharper**) *n* person who earns a living by cheating at card-games.
ˈ**card-table** *n* (esp folding) table for playing cards on.
ˈ**card vote** = BLOCK VOTE (BLOCK[1]).

card[2] /kɑːd/ *n* wire brush or toothed instrument for cleaning or combing wool.
▷ **card** *v* [Tn] clean or comb (wool) with this.

cardamom /ˈkɑːdəməm/ *n* (**a**) [C] E Indian plant. (**b**) [U] its seeds used as a spice.

cardboard /ˈkɑːdbɔːd/ *n* [U] **1** thick stiff type of paper or pasteboard used for making boxes, binding books, etc: [attrib] *a cardboard box.* **2** [attrib] (*fig*) without real substance or worth: *a cardboard figure, character, dictator.*

cardiac /ˈkɑːdɪæk/ *adj* of or relating to the heart or heart disease: *cardiac muscles, disease, patients* ○ *cardiac arrest,* ie temporary or permanent stopping of the heartbeat ○ *cardiac massage,* ie process used to restart the heart of a person who has had a heart attack.

cardigan /ˈkɑːdɪgən/ *n* knitted woollen jacket, usu with no collar and with buttons at the front.

cardinal[1] /ˈkɑːdɪnl/ *adj* [usu attrib] most important; chief; fundamental: *cardinal sins, errors, etc* ○ *the cardinal virtues,* ie justice, prudence, temperance and fortitude.
▷ **cardinal** *n* (also ˌ**cardinal ˈnumber**) whole number representing quantity, eg 1, 2, 3, etc. Cf ORDINAL. ⇨ App 9.
□ ˌ**cardinal ˈpoints** the four main points of the compass, ie North, South, East and West.

cardinal[2] /ˈkɑːdɪnl/ *adj, n* [U] (of a) deep red colour.

cardinal[3] /ˈkɑːdɪnl/ *n* **1** any of a group of senior Roman Catholic priests who elect the Pope. **2** small red American songbird.

cardi(o)- *comb form* of the heart: *cardiogram* ○ *cardiologist.*

cardiogram /ˈkɑːdɪəʊgræm/ *n* chart showing the rhythm of muscles within the heart. Cf ELECTROCARDIOGRAM.

cardiograph /ˈkɑːdɪəʊgrɑːf; *US* -græf/ *n* recording device that represents the heartbeat in wave form. Cf ELECTROCARDIOGRAPH.

cardiology /ˌkɑːdɪˈɒlədʒɪ/ *n* [U] branch of medicine concerned with the heart and its diseases. ▷ **cardiologist** /-dʒɪst/ *n.*

cardio-vascular /ˌkɑːdɪəʊˈvæskjʊlə(r)/ *adj* of or involving the heart and blood vessels.

care[1] /keə(r)/ *n* **1** [U] ~ **(over sth/in doing sth)** (**a**) serious attention or thought: *She arranged the flowers with great care.* ○ *You should take more care over your work.* (**b**) caution to avoid damage or loss: *Care is needed when crossing the road.* ○ *Fragile — handle with care,* eg as a warning on a container holding glass. **2** [U] ~ **(for sb)** sympathetic concern: *a mother's care for her children* ○ *Old people need loving care and attention.* **3** (**a**) [U] worry; anxiety; troubled state of mind: *free from care.* (**b**) [C esp *pl*] cause of or reason for worry: *weighed down by the cares of a demanding job* ○ *not have a care in the world,* ie have no worries or responsibilities. **4** (idm) **care of sb** (*abbr* **c/o**) (esp written on envelopes) at the address of sb: *Write to him care of his solicitor.* **have a ˈcare** (*dated*) be more careful. **in the care of sb** in sb's charge; under sb's supervision: *in the care of a doctor* ○ *They left the child in a friend's care.* **take care (that.../to do sth)** be careful or cautious: *Take care (that) you don't drink too much/not to drink too much.* ○ *Good bye, and take care!* **take care of oneself/sb/sth** (**a**) make sure that one/sb is safe and well; look after oneself/sb: *My sister is taking care of the children while we're away.* ○ *He's old enough to take care of himself.* (**b**) be responsible for sb/sth; deal with sb/sth: *Mr Smith takes care of marketing and publicity.* ○ *Her secretary took care of all her appointments.* ⇨ Usage at CARE[2]. **take/put sb into/put sb in ˈcare** put (esp a child) in a home owned by a local authority (LOCAL) for special treatment: *The social worker advised them to put their handicapped child into care.*
□ ˈ**carefree** *adj* without responsibilities or worries or; cheerful: *young and carefree.*
ˈ**careworn** *adj* showing signs of much worry: *an old and careworn face.*

care[2] /keə(r)/ *v* **1** [I, Ipr, Tw] ~ **(about sth)** be worried, concerned or interested: *He failed the examination but he didn't seem to care.* ○ *Don't you care about this country's future?* ○ *I don't think she cares (about) what happens to her children.* ○ *All she cares about is her social life.* ⇨ Usage. **2** [Ipr, It] ~ **for sth** (in negative or interrogative sentences, esp with *would*) be willing or agree (to do sth); wish or like (to do sth): *Would you care for a drink?* ○ *Would you care to go for a walk?* ⇨ Usage at WANT[1]. **3** (idm) **for all one/sb cares** considering how little one/sb cares: *I might as well be dead for all he cares.* **not care ˈless** (*infml*) be completely uninterested or unmoved by sth: *I couldn't care less who wins the match.* **who ˈcares?** (*infml*) nobody cares; I don't care: *'Who do you think will be the next Prime Minister?' 'Who cares?'* **4** (phr v) **care for sb** (**a**) like or love sb: *He cares for her deeply.* (**b**) be responsible for sb; look after sb; take care of sb: *care for the sick* ○ *Who will care for him if his wife dies?* **care for sb/sth** (in negative or interrogative sentences) have a taste or liking for sb/sth: *I don't care much for opera.* ○ *I like him but I don't care for her.*
▷ **carer** *n* person who takes on the responsibility of caring for an old or sick person, esp in that person's own home and on a regular basis.
caring /ˈkeərɪŋ/ *adj* [esp attrib] showing or feeling care[1](2): *caring parents* ○ *Children need a caring environment.* ○ *the caring professions,* ie doctors, nurses, social workers and others who look after the sick and those needing help in society.

NOTE ON USAGE: **1** Both **take care of** (somebody or something) and **care for** (someone) can mean 'look after': *She takes great care of her children.* ○ *He's caring for his elderly parents.* **2**

Care for can also mean 'like' or 'love': *I'm fond of her but I don't care for her husband.* **3 Care for** something and **care to do** something mean 'wish' or 'like' and are rather formal. They are mostly used with *would* in negative sentences and in questions: *Would you care for a swim?* ○ *I wouldn't care to do her job.* **4 Care (about)** (somebody or something) means 'be interested' or 'be concerned'. It is also mostly used in negative sentences and in questions: *Don't you care about anybody?* ○ *I don't care (about) what happens to him.*

careen /kəˈriːn/ *v* **1** [Tn] turn (a ship) on its side (esp for cleaning or repairing). **2** [I] (of a ship) turn over or tilt. **3** [Ipr] (*US*) rush forward with a swaying or swerving motion: *The driver lost control and the car careened down the hill.*

career /kəˈrɪə(r)/ *n* **1** [C] profession or occupation with opportunities for advancement or promotion: *a career in accountancy, journalism, politics, etc* ○ *She chose an academic career.* ○ [attrib] *a career diplomat*, ie a professional one ○ *a careers teacher*, ie one who advises pupils on what career to choose. **2** [C] progress through life; development of a political party, etc: *look back on a successful career.* **3** [U] quick or violent forward movement: *in full career*, ie at full speed ○ *stop sb in mid career*, ie as he is rushing along.

▷ **career** *v* [Ipr, Ip] move about quickly and often dangerously: *careering down the road on a bicycle* ○ *The car careered off the road into a ditch.*

careerist /kəˈrɪərɪst/ *n* (*often derog*) person who is keen to advance his or her career by any possible means.

□ **caˈreer girl** (also **caˈreer woman**) (*esp sexist or derog*) woman who is more interested in a professional career than in eg getting married and having children.

careful /ˈkeəfl/ *adj* **1** [pred] ~ (**about/of/with sth**); ~ (**about/in**) **doing sth** taking care; cautious: *Be careful not to/that you don't hurt her feelings.* ○ *Be careful with the glasses*, ie Don't break them. ○ *Be careful of the dog; it sometimes bites people.* ○ *Be careful (about/of) what you say to him.* ○ *Be careful (about/in) crossing the road.* ○ *He's very careful with his money*, ie He doesn't spend it on unimportant things. **2** (**a**) giving serious attention and thought; painstaking: *a careful worker.* (**b**) done with care: *a careful piece of work* ○ *a careful examination of the facts.*

▷ **carefully** /ˈkeəfəlɪ/ *adv*: *Please listen carefully.* ○ *I always drive more carefully at night.* **carefulness** *n* [U].

careless /ˈkeəlɪs/ *adj* **1** ~ (**about/of sth**) not taking care; inattentive; thoughtless: *a careless driver, worker, etc* ○ *careless about spelling, money, one's appearance.* **2** resulting from lack of care: *a careless error, mistake, etc.* ▷ **carelessly** *adv.* **carelessness** *n* [U].

caress /kəˈres/ *n* loving touch or stroke.

▷ **caress** *v* [Tn] touch or stroke (sb/sth) lovingly: *She caressed his hand.*

caret /ˈkærət/ *n* symbol (ʌ) used to show where sth is to be inserted in written or printed material.

caretaker /ˈkeəteɪkə(r)/ *n* (*Brit*) (*US* **janitor**) person who is employed to look after a house, building, etc: *the school caretaker.*

▷ **caretaker** *adj* [attrib] holding power temporarily; interim: *a caretaker administration, government, prime minister.*

cargo /ˈkɑːgəʊ/ *n* [C, U] (*pl* ~**es**; *US* ~**s**) (load of) goods carried in a ship or aircraft: [attrib] *a cargo ship.*

NOTE ON USAGE: **1** Compare **cargo**, **freight** and **goods**. These words are used before the names of vehicles that transport things rather than passengers. They can also refer to the objects transported: *A cargo plane/ship/vessel carries cargo.* ○ *A goods/(US) freight train carries goods/freight.* ○ *A passenger train sometimes also has goods wagons/(US) freight cars.* **2 Cargo** [C] can also indicate a particular load that is being transported: *A cargo of steel was lost at sea.* **3** **Freight** [U] also indicates the action of transporting: *We can send it by air/sea freight.* ○ *What is the freight charge?* In this sense **freight** can also be a verb: *You can freight your belongings by air or sea.*

the Caribbean Islands

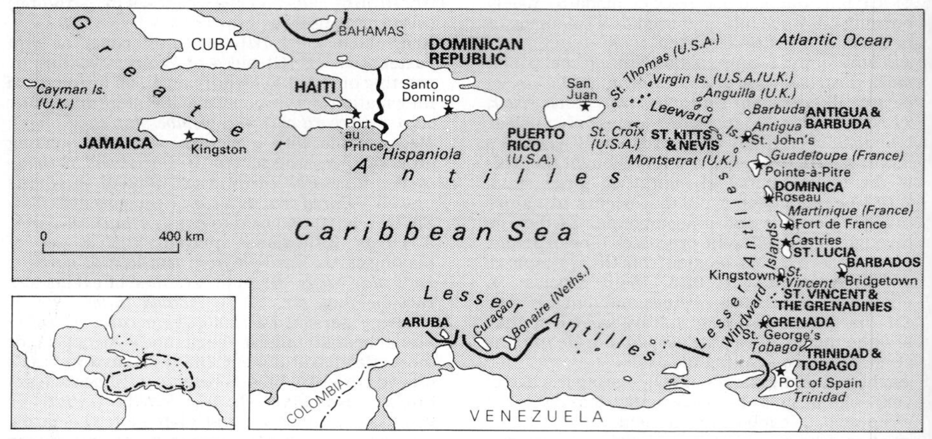

Carib /ˈkærɪb/ *n* **1** [C] member of a fierce American Indian tribe inhabiting the *Antilles, part of the S American coast and Brazil. 'Carib' is the root of the English word 'cannibal'. **2** [U] language of the Caribs.

Caribbean /ˌkærɪˈbiən/ **the Caribbean** **1** area in the Caribbean Sea where the Antilles and the Leeward and Windward Islands are situated. ⇨ map. **2** (also **Caribbean Sea**) sea to the east of Central America, enclosed by the Antilles, Central America and South America.

▷ *adj* of the Caribbean: *the Caribbean climate* ○ *Caribbean islands.*

caribou /ˈkærɪbuː/ *n* (*pl* unchanged or ~**s**) N American reindeer: *a herd of fifty caribou(s).*

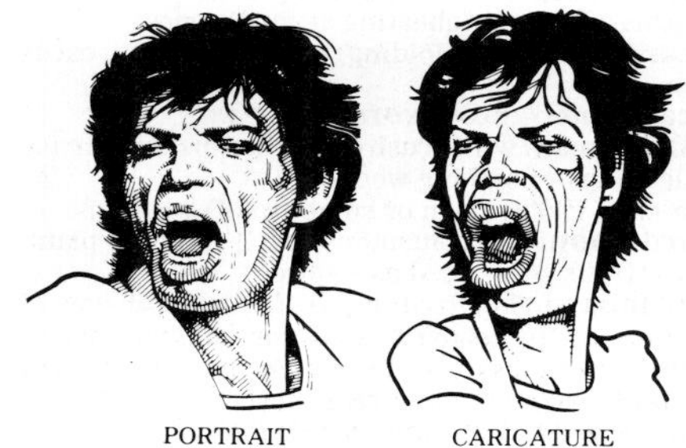

PORTRAIT CARICATURE

caricature /ˈkærɪkətjʊə(r)/ *n* (**a**) [C] picture, description or imitation of sb/sth that exaggerates certain characteristics in order to amuse or ridicule: *draw a caricature of a politician* ○ *He does very funny caricatures of all his friends.* ⇨ illus. (**b**) [U] art of doing this.

▷ **caricature** *v* [Tn] make or give a caricature of (sb/sth).

caricaturist *n.*

caries /ˈkeəriːz/ *n* [U] (*medical*) decay in bones or teeth: *dental caries.*

carillon /kəˈrɪljən; *US* ˈkærəlɒn/ *n* **1** set of bells sounded either from a keyboard or mechanically. **2** tune played on bells.

carious /ˈkeərɪəs/ *adj* (*medical*) (esp of bones or teeth) decayed; affected with caries.

Carlyle /kɑːˈlaɪl/ Thomas (1795-1881), Scottish historian and political philosopher who attacked social injustice and materialistic attitudes that resulted from the *Industrial Revolution. He was famous for his history of the French Revolution and for his popular public lectures.

Carmelite /ˈkɑːməlaɪt/ *n, adj* (friar or nun) belonging to a strict contemplative religious order founded in 1155. The great mystics Saint Teresa of Avila and Saint John of the Cross, who was also a poet, were Carmelites.

carminative /ˈkɑːmɪnətɪv/ *n, adj* (drug for) relieving flatulence.

carmine /ˈkɑːmaɪn/ *adj, n* [U] (of a) deep red colour.

Carnaby Street /ˈkɑːnəbɪ striːt/ small street in central London famous in the 1960s for its shops selling fashionable clothes, etc.

carnage /ˈkɑːnɪdʒ/ *n* [U] killing of many people: *a scene of carnage*, eg a battlefield.

carnal /ˈkɑːnl/ *adj* (*fml*) of the body; sexual or sensual: *carnal desires.* ▷ **carnally** /ˈkɑːnəlɪ/ *adv.*

carnation /kɑːˈneɪʃn/ *n* (**a**) garden plant with sweet-smelling usu white, pink or red flowers. (**b**) one of these flowers: *wear a carnation in one's buttonhole.* ⇨ illus at PLANT.

Carnegie /kɑːˈneɪgɪ/ Andrew (1835-1919), US industrialist and philanthropist born in Scotland. Having made a fortune in the steel industry he donated much of it to organizations for promoting education and culture. He also created the Carnegie Peace Fund to promote international peace.

carnet /ˈkɑːneɪ; *US* kɑːrˈneɪ/ *n* document of identification required to allow a vehicle to cross a frontier or use a camping-site.

carnival /ˈkɑːnɪvl/ *n* **1** (**a**) [C, U] (period of) public festivities and merry-making occurring at a regular time of year, eg in Roman Catholic countries during the week before Lent: [attrib] *a carnival atmosphere.* (**b**) [C] festival of this kind, usu with a procession: *a street carnival.* **2** (*US*) fun-fair or circus that travels from place to place.

carnivore /ˈkɑːnɪvɔː(r)/ *n* animal that eats the flesh of other animals, esp a mammal of the group that includes cats, dogs and bears. Cf HERBIVORE.

▷ **carnivorous** /kɑːˈnɪvərəs/ *adj* flesh-eating: *a carnivorous plant*, ie one that catches and digests insects.

Carnot /ˈkɑːnəʊ; *US* kɑːrˈnəʊ/ Nicholas Léonard Sadi (1796-1832), French scientist, noted for his contribution to thermodynamics.

carob /ˈkærəb/ *n* **1** [C] Mediterranean evergreen tree with edible horn-shaped seed pods. **2** [U] food made from its seed pods, sometimes used as a substitute for chocolate.

carol /ˈkærəl/ *n* joyful song, esp a Christmas hymn: *a Christmas carol* ○ *carol singers*, ie singers who visit people's houses at Christmas to sing carols and collect money, usu for charity.

▷ **carol** *v* (**-ll-**; *US* **-l-**) [I] **1** sing joyfully. **2** (usu **go carolling**) sing Christmas carols: *We often go carolling* (ie go from house to house, singing carols) *at Christmas.* **caroller** *n.*

Carolina ⇨ NORTH CAROLINA, SOUTH CAROLINA.

Caroline /ˈkærəlaɪn/ (also **Carolean** /ˌkærəˈliːən/) *adj* of the time of Charles I or Charles II of England.

Carolingian /ˌkærəˈlɪndʒɪən/ *n, adj* (member) of the Frankish dynasty founded by *Charlemagne.

carotene /ˈkærətiːn/ *n* [U] orange-red pigment that is found in carrots, tomatoes, etc and is a source of vitamin A.

carotid /kəˈrɒtɪd/ *adj, n* (relating to) either of the two large blood-vessels (**carotid arteries**) in the neck, carrying blood to the head.

carouse /kəˈraʊz/ *v* [I] (*dated*) drink and be merry with others (at a noisy meal, party, etc).
▷ **carousal** /kəˈraʊzl/ [C, U] (*dated*) (noisy party with) drinking and merry-making.

carousel (*US* **carrousel**) /ˌkærəˈsel/ *n* **1** (*US*) = ROUNDABOUT 1. **2** (esp at an airport) revolving apparatus or moving belt on which luggage is placed for collection by passengers. **3** circular holder that feeds slides (SLIDE[1] 4a) into a projector.

carp[1] /kɑːp/ *n* (*pl* unchanged) type of large edible freshwater fish that lives in lakes and ponds.

carp[2] /kɑːp/ *v* [I, Ipr] ~ (**at/about sb/sth**) (*derog*) complain continually about unimportant matters: *have a carping tongue* ○ *carping criticism* ○ *She's always carping at her children.*

carpal /ˈkɑːpl/ *adj* (*anatomy*) of the wrist.
▷ **carpal** *n* (*anatomy*) any of the bones in the wrist. ⇨ illus at SKELETON.

carpel /ˈkɑːpl/ *n* (*botany*) female reproductive organ of a flower, either a simple pistil in which seeds develop or part of a compound pistil.

carpenter /ˈkɑːpəntə(r)/ *n* person whose job is making or repairing wooden objects and structures. Cf JOINER.
▷ **carpentry** /-trɪ/ *n* [U] art or work of a carpenter: *learn carpentry* ○ *a fine piece of carpentry.*

carpet /ˈkɑːpɪt/ *n* **1** (**a**) [U] thick woollen or synthetic fabric for covering floors. (**b**) [C] piece of this shaped to fit a particular room: *lay a carpet*, ie fit it to a floor ○ *We have fitted carpets* (ie carpets from wall to wall) *in our house.* ○ *We need a new bedroom carpet.* Cf RED CARPET (RED[1]). **2** [C] thick layer of sth on the ground: *a carpet of leaves, moss, snow, etc.* **3** (idm) **on the ˈcarpet** (*infml*) summoned before sb in authority to be reprimanded: *The boss had me on the carpet over my expenses claim.* **pull the carpet/rug from under sb's feet** ⇨ PULL[2]. **sweep sth under the carpet** ⇨ SWEEP[1].
▷ **carpet** *v* **1** [Tn, Tn·pr] cover (sth) with or as if with a carpet: *carpet the stairs* ○ *a lawn carpeted with fallen leaves.* **2** [Tn esp passive] (*infml*) reprimand (sb): *be carpeted by one's boss.*
□ **ˈcarpet-bag** *n* (formerly) travelling bag made of carpet. **ˈcarpet-bagger** *n* (*derog*) political candidate, etc who hopes for success in an area where he is not known and is therefore resented.
ˈcarpet-slippers *n* [pl] soft slippers with woollen or cloth uppers, worn indoors.
ˈcarpet-sweeper *n* device with revolving brushes for sweeping carpets.

carpus /ˈkɑːpəs/ *n* (*pl* **-pi** /-paɪ/) set of small bones connecting the hand and the forearm, forming the wrist in man. Cf CARPAL.

carrel /ˈkærəl/ *n* small cubicle for a reader in a library.

carriage /ˈkærɪdʒ/ *n* **1** [C] (also **coach**) vehicle (usu with four wheels), pulled by a horse or horses, for carrying people. **2** [C] (*Brit* also **coach**) (*US* **car**) railway coach for carrying passengers: *a first-/second-class carriage.* **3** [U] (cost of) transporting goods from one place to another: *carriage forward*, ie The cost of carriage is to be paid by the receiver ○ *carriage free/paid*, ie The cost of carriage is paid by the sender. **4** [C] = GUN-CARRIAGE (GUN). **5** [C] moving part of a machine that supports or moves another part: *a typewriter carriage.* **6** [sing] (*dated*) way in which sb holds and moves his head and body: *have a very upright carriage.*
□ **ˈcarriage clock** small clock in a rectangular (usu metal) case with a handle on top.
ˈcarriage trade (*often joc*) (business done with) customers who spend a lot of money, esp in shops or restaurants: *The wine list is obviously aimed at the carriage trade*, ie The wines are very expensive.
ˈcarriageway *n* part of a road on which vehicles travel: *the northbound carriageway of a motorway.*

carrier /ˈkærɪə(r)/ *n* **1** person or thing that carries sth. **2** person or company that carries goods or people for payment: *Your carrier for this flight is British Airways.* **3** (usu metal) framework fixed to a bicycle, etc for carrying luggage or a small child: *strap a parcel to the carrier.* **4** person or animal that can transmit a disease to others without suffering from it: *Mosquitoes are carriers of malaria.* Cf VECTOR 2. **5** = AIRCRAFT-CARRIER (AIRCRAFT). **6** = CARRIER BAG.
□ **ˈcarrier bag** (*Brit*) paper or plastic bag for carrying shopping.
ˈcarrier pigeon pigeon trained to carry messages tied to its leg or neck.
ˈcarrier wave radio wave that can be modulated and used to send a radio, television or similar signal.

carrion /ˈkærɪən/ *n* [U] dead and decaying flesh.
□ **ˈcarrion crow** type of crow that eats carrion and small animals.

Carroll /ˈkærəl/ Lewis (pseudonym of Charles Dodgson 1832-98), English writer and lecturer in mathematics at Oxford University, famous as the author of the classic children's stories *Alice's Adventures in Wonderland* and *Through the Looking-Glass.* He also wrote nonsense verse. ⇨ illus at TENNIEL.

carrot /ˈkærət/ *n* **1** (**a**) [C] plant with a long pointed orange root. (**b**) [C, U] this root eaten as a vegetable: *boiled beef and carrots* ○ *Have some more carrots.* ○ *grated carrot.* **2** [C] (*fig*) reward or advantage promised to sb to persuade him to do sth: *hold out/offer a carrot to sb.* **3** (idm) **the carrot and the stick** the hope of reward and the threat of punishment as a means of making sb try harder: [attrib] *a carrot-and-stick approach.*
▷ **carroty** *adj* (of hair) having an orange-red colour.

carrousel (*US*) = CAROUSEL.

carry /ˈkærɪ/ *v* (*pt, pp* **carried**) **1** [Tn, Tn·pr, Tn·p] (**a**) support the weight of (sb/sth) and take (him/it) from place to place; take from one place to another: *carry shopping, a suitcase, a rucksack, etc* ○ *a train carrying commuters to and from work* ○ *The car had carried him 500 miles before it broke down.* ○ *She carried her baby in her arms.* ○ *He broke his leg during the match and had to be carried off.* ○ *Seeds can be carried for long distances by the wind.* ○ *The injured were carried away on stretchers.* (**b**) (of pipes, wires, etc) contain and direct the flow of (water, an electric current, etc); take; conduct: *a pipeline carrying oil* ○ *The veins carry blood to the heart.* ⇨ Usage. **2** [Tn] have (sth) with one: *Police in many countries carry guns.* ○ *I never carry much money (with me).* ○ (*fig*) *He'll carry the memory of the experience (with him) for the rest of his life.* ⇨ Usage at WEAR[2]. **3** [Tn] (*dated or fml*) (used esp in the continuous tenses) be pregnant with (sb): *She was carrying twins.* **4** [Tn] (esp of sth that does not move) support the weight of (sth): *These pillars carry the weight of the roof.* ○ *A road bridge has to carry a lot of traffic.* ○ (*fig*) *He is carrying the department (on his shoulders)*, ie It is only functioning because of his efforts and abilities. **5** [Tn] (**a**) have (sth) as an attribute; possess: *His voice carries the ring of authority.* (**b**) have (sth) as a result; involve; entail: *Power carries great responsibilty.* ○ *Crimes of violence carry heavy penalties.* **6** [Tn, Tn·pr, Tn·p] take (sth) to a specified point or in a specified direction: *The war was carried into enemy territory.* ○ *His ability carried him to the top of his profession.* ○ *He carries modesty to extremes*, ie is too modest. **7** [Tn] (in adding figures) transfer (a figure) to the next column. **8** [Tn esp passive] approve (sth) by a majority of votes: *The bill/motion/resolution was carried by 340 votes to 210.* **9** [Tn] win the support or sympathy of (sb): *His moving speech was enough to carry the audience.* **10** [Tn no passive] ~ **oneself** hold or move one's head or body in a specified way: *She carries herself well.* **11** (**a**) [In/pr] (of a missile, etc) cover a specified distance: *The full-back's kick carried 50 metres into the crowd.* (**b**) [I] (of a sound, voice, etc) be audible at a distance: *A public speaker needs a voice that carries (well).* **12** [Tn] (of a newspaper or broadcast) include (sth) in its content; contain: *Today's papers carry full reports of the President's visit.* **13** [Tn] (of a shop) have (sth) for sale; include in its regular stock: *I'm sorry, this shop doesn't carry cigarettes.* **14** (idm) **as fast as one's legs can carry one** ⇨ FAST[1]. **carry all/everything beˈfore one** be completely successful. **ˌcarry one's ˈbat** (of a batsman in cricket) reach the end of an innings without having been put out by the other team. **carry the can (for sth)** (*infml*) accept the responsibility or blame (for sth). **carry coals to ˈNewcastle** take goods to a place where they are already plentiful; supply sth unnecessarily. **carry the day** ⇨ DAY. **carry/gain one's ˈpoint** ⇨ POINT[1]. **carry/take sth too, etc far** ⇨ FAR[2]. **carry the war into the enemy's camp** attack (rather than being content to defend). **carry ˈweight** be influential or important: *Her opinion carries (great) weight (with the chairman).* **fetch and carry** ⇨ FETCH.
15 (phr v) **carry sb away** (usu passive) cause sb to lose self-control or be very excited: *He tends to get carried away when watching wrestling on TV.*
carry sb back (to sth) take sb back in memory: *The sound of seagulls carried her back to childhood holidays by the sea.*
carry sth forward (in bookkeeping) transfer (the total of figures in a column or on a page) to a new column or page.
carry sb off (*fml or joc*) (of a disease) kill sb who has been suffering from it: *Malaria carried off most of the expedition.* **carry sth off** win sth: *She carried off most of the prizes for swimming.* **carry it/sth off** handle a (difficult) situation successfully: *He carried the speech off well despite feeling very nervous.*
carry ˈon (*infml*) argue, quarrel or complain noisily; behave strangely: *He does carry on, doesn't he?* **carry on (with sth/doing sth); carry sth on** continue (doing sth): *Carry on (working/with your work) while I'm away.* ○ *They decided to carry on* (eg continue their walk) *in spite of the weather.* ○ *Carry on the good work!* **carry on (with sb)** (*infml*) (used esp in the continuous tenses) have an affair(5) with sb: *She's carrying on with her boss.* ○ *They've been carrying on for years.* **carry sth on** (**a**) take part in sth; conduct or hold sth: *carry on a conversation, discussion, dialogue, etc.* (**b**) conduct or transact sth: *carry on a business.*
carry sth out (**a**) do sth as required or specified; fulfil sth: *carry out a promise, a threat, a plan, an order.* (**b**) perform or conduct (an experiment, etc): *carry out an enquiry, an investigation, a survey, etc* ○ *Extensive tests have been carried out on the patient.*
carry sth over (**a**) postpone sth. (**b**) = CARRY STH FORWARD.
carry sb through (sth) help sb to survive a difficult period: *His determination carried him through (the ordeal).* **carry sth through** complete sth successfully: *It's a difficult job but she's the person to carry it through.*
▷ **carry** *n* **1** [U] (**a**) range of a gun. (**b**) distance that a golf ball travels before hitting the ground. **2** [sing] act of carrying sb/sth: *Would you like me to give the baby a carry?*
□ **ˈcarry-all** *n* (*US*) = HOLDALL.
ˈcarry-cot *n* portable cot for a baby.
carryings-ˈon *n* [pl] (*infml*) noisy or excited behaviour: *Did you hear the carryings-on next door last night?*
ˈcarry-on *n* [sing] (*infml esp Brit*) fuss: *I've never heard such a carry-on!*
ˈcarry-out *n* (*Scot or US*) = TAKE-AWAY (TAKE[1]).

NOTE ON USAGE: **Carry, bear, cart, hump** and **lug** share the meaning of 'take (somebody or something) from one place to another'. **Carry** is the most general term for the moving of loads of all weights. It can refer to passenger transport: *She came in carrying an important-looking piece of paper.* ○ *Could you carry this box to my car for me, please?* ○ *The plane was carrying 250 passengers when it crashed.* When **bear** indicates movement it is formal: *The ambassador arrived bearing gifts for the Queen.* ○ *The hero was borne aloft on the shoulders of the crowd.* **Cart** means 'carry (away) (as if) in a cart': *We've asked the Council to come and cart away all this rubbish.* Informally it suggests force or unwillingness: *The police carted the protesters off to jail.* ○ *I've been carting these books around for him all over the place.* **Hump** suggests that the load is heavy and difficult to move and is carried on one's back or shoulders: *We've spent all day humping furniture up and down stairs.* **Lug** indicates that what is carried is pulled or dragged behind unwillingly and/or with difficulty: *Do I have to lug those suitcases all the way to the station?*

cart /kɑ:t/ *n* **1** (a) vehicle with two or four wheels used for carrying loads and usu pulled by a horse: *a horse and cart.* Cf WAGON 1. (b) (also **ˈhandcart**) light vehicle with wheels that is pulled or pushed by hand. **2** (idm) **put the ˌcart before the ˈhorse** reverse the logical order of things, eg by saying that the result of sth is what caused it.
▷ **cart** *v* [Tn, Tn·pr, Tn·p] **1** carry (sth) in a cart: *carting hay* ○ *cart away the rubbish.* **2** (*infml*) carry (sth) in the hands: *I've been carting these cases around all day.* ⇨ Usage at CARRY.
carter *n* person whose job is driving carts or transporting goods.
□ **ˈcart-horse** *n* large strong horse used for heavy work.
ˈcart-load *n* amount that a cart holds.
ˈcart-track *n* rough track not suitable for motor vehicles.
ˈcart-wheel *n* **1** wheel of a cart, with thick wooden spokes and a metal rim. **2** sideways somersault: *do/turn cartwheels.* — *v* [I] perform a cart-wheel.

carte blanche /ˌkɑ:t ˈblɒnʃ/ (*French*) complete freedom to act as one thinks best: *give sb/have carte blanche.*

cartel /kɑ:ˈtel/ *n* [CGp] group of business firms which combine to control production and marketing, and to avoid competing with one another.

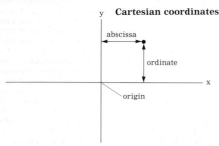

Cartesian coordinates

Cartesian /kɑ:ˈti:zɪən; *US* kɑ:rˈti:ʒn/ *adj* of *Descartes or his philosophy.
□ **Carˌtesian coˈordinates** system for locating a point by reference to its distance from two or three axes intersecting at right angles. ⇨ illus.

Carthage /ˈkɑ:θɪdʒ/ ancient city on the N African coast, founded by the Phoenicians in 814 BC. It became the capital of a powerful empire and this brought it into conflict with the Greeks and then with the Romans, who destroyed it in 146 AD. ▷ **Carthaginian** /ˌkɑ:θəˈdʒɪnɪən/ *adj, n.*

Carthusian /kɑ:ˈθju:zɪən/ *n, adj* (member) of a strict contemplative order of monks founded in 1084.

Cartier /ˈkɑ:tɪeɪ; *US* kɑ:rˈtjeɪ/ Jacques (1491-1557), French explorer who made three voyages to Canada between 1534 and 1541.

cartilage /ˈkɑ:tɪlɪdʒ/ *n* (a) [U] tough white flexible tissue attached to the bones and joints of adult animals; gristle: *I've damaged a cartilage in my knee.* (b) [C] structure made of this.
▷ **cartilaginous** /ˌkɑ:tɪˈlædʒɪnəs/ *adj* of or like cartilage.

cartographer /kɑ:ˈtɒgrəfə(r)/ *n* person who draws maps and charts.
▷ **cartography** /kɑ:ˈtɒgrəfɪ/ *n* [U] art of drawing maps and charts. **cartographic** /ˌkɑ:təˈgræfɪk/ *adj.*

carton /ˈkɑ:tn/ *n* light cardboard or plastic box for holding goods: *a carton of milk, cream, yoghurt, etc* ○ *a carton of 200 cigarettes,* ie with 10 packets of 20. ⇨ illus at BOX.

cartoon

cartoon /kɑ:ˈtu:n/ *n* **1** (a) amusing drawing in a newspaper or magazine, esp one that comments satirically on current events. ⇨ illus. (b) sequence of these telling a story. **2** (also **animated cartoon**) film made by photographing a series of gradually changing drawings, giving an illusion of movement: *a Walt Disney cartoon.* ⇨ article at HUMOUR. **3** drawing made by an artist as a preliminary sketch for a painting, tapestry, fresco, etc.
▷ **cartoonist** *n* person who draws cartoons (CARTOON 1a).

cartouche /kɑ:ˈtu:ʃ/ *n* **1** scroll-like ornament in architecture, etc. **2** oval emblem in ancient Egyptian art, inscriptions, etc, esp one enclosing the name and title of a king.

cartridge /ˈkɑ:trɪdʒ/ *n* **1** (*US* **shell**) tube or case containing explosive (for blasting), or explosive with a bullet or shot (for firing from a gun). ⇨ illus at GUN. Cf SHELL 3, SHOT[1] 4. **2** detachable end of a pick-up on a record player, holding the stylus. **3** sealed case containing recording tape, photographic film or ink, that is put into a tape-deck, camera, or pen.
□ **ˈcartridge-belt** *n* belt with loops for holding cartridges (CARTRIDGE 1).
ˈcartridge-clip *n* = CLIP[1] 2.
ˈcartridge paper thick strong paper for drawing on.

Caruso /kəˈru:səʊ/ Enrico (1873-1921), Italian operatic tenor who was extremely popular in his day.

carve /kɑ:v/ *v* **1** (a) [I, Ipr, Tn, Tn·pr] ~ (**in sth**); ~ **sth (out of/from/of/in sth)** form (sth) by cutting away material from wood or stone: *Michelangelo carved in marble.* ○ *The statue was carved (out of stone).* (b) [Tn, Tn·pr] ~ **sth (into sth)** cut or chip (solid material) in order to form sth: *carve wood.* **2** [Tn, Tn·pr] inscribe (sth) by cutting on a surface: *carve one's initials on a tree trunk.* **3** [I, Tn, Dn·n, Dn·pr] ~ **sth (for sb)** cut (cooked meat) into slices for eating: *Would you like to carve?* ○ *carve a joint, turkey, leg of mutton, etc* ○ *Please carve me another slice.* **4** (phr v) **carve sth out (for oneself)** build (one's career, reputation, etc) by hard work: *She carved out a name for herself as a reporter.* **carve sth up** (*infml*) divide sth into parts or slices: *The territory was carved up by the occupying powers.*
▷ **carver** *n* **1** person who carves. **2** = CARVING KNIFE.
carving *n* carved object or design.
□ **ˈcarving knife** knife used for carving meat. ⇨ illus at KNIFE.

carvel-built /ˈkɑ:vl bɪlt/ *adj* (of boats) made with planks which are flush and not overlapping. Cf CLINKER-BUILT.

Cary /ˈkeərɪ/ (Arthur) Joyce (Lunel) (1888-1957), English novelist, known for such works as *A House of Children* and *The Horse's Mouth.*

caryatid /ˌkærɪˈætɪd/ *n* (*architecture*) statue of a female figure used as a supporting pillar in a building. ⇨ illus. Cf ATLANTES.

Casanova /ˌkæzəˈnəʊvə, ˌkæs-/ **1** Giovanni Jacopo (1725-98), Italian adventurer whose memoirs describe his many sexual adventures in pursuit of women. **2** any man who is famous for his many love-affairs: *He was quite a Casanova in his youth.*

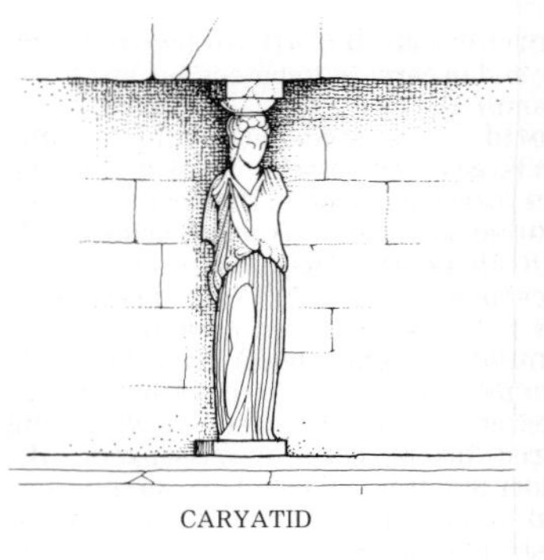

CARYATID

ATLAS

casbah = KASBAH.

cascade /kæˈskeɪd/ *n* **1** waterfall, esp one of a series forming a large waterfall. **2** (*fig*) thing that falls or hangs in a way that suggests a waterfall: *a cascade of blonde hair.*
▷ **cascade** *v* [I, Ipr, Ip] fall in or like a cascade: *Water cascaded down the mountainside.* ○ *Her golden hair cascaded down her back.*

cascara /kæˈskɑ:rə/ *n* [U] type of laxative made from the bark of a N American tree.

case[1] /keɪs/ *n* **1** [C] instance or example of the occurrence of sth: *The company only dismisses its employees in cases of gross misconduct.* ○ *It's a clear case of blackmail!* **2 the case** [sing] actual state of affairs; situation: *Is it the case* (ie Is it true) *that the company's sales have dropped?* ○ *If that is the case* (ie If the situation is as stated), *you will have to work much harder.* **3** [C usu *sing*] circumstances or special conditions relating to a person or thing: *In your case, we are prepared to be lenient.* ○ *I cannot make an exception in your case,* ie for you and not for others. **4** [C] instance of a disease or an injury; person suffering from this: *a case of typhoid* ○ *Cases of smallpox are becoming rare.* **5** [C] person having medical, psychiatric, etc treatment: *This boy is a sad case. His parents are divorced and he himself is severely handicapped.* **6** [C] matter that is being officially investigated, esp by the police: *a murder case/a case of murder.* **7** [C] (a) question to be decided in a court of law; lawsuit: *The case will be heard in court next week.* ○ *When does your case come before the court?* (b) (usu *sing*) set of facts or arguments supporting one side in a lawsuit, debate, etc: *the case for the defence/prosecution* ○ *the case for/against the abolition of the death penalty* ○ *You have a very strong case.* **8** [U, C] (*grammar*) (change in the) form of a noun, or pronoun, etc (esp in inflected languages) that shows its relationship to another word: *the nominative case* ○ *the accusative case* ○ *Latin nouns have case, number and gender.* Cf DECLENSION. **9** [sing] (*infml*) eccentric person: *He really is a case!* **10** (idm) **a case in ˈpoint** example that is relevant to the matter being discussed. **as the ˌcase may ˈbe** (used when describing two or more possible alternatives) as will be determined by the circumstances: *There may be an announcement about this tomorrow — or not, as the case may be.* **in ˈany case** whatever happens or may have happened. **(just) in case (...)** because of the possibility of sth happening: *It may rain — you'd better take an umbrella (just) in case (it does).* **in case of sth** if sth happens: *In case of fire, ring the alarm bell.* **in ˈno case** in no circumstances. **in ˈthat case** if that happens or has happened; if that is the state of affairs: *You don't like your job? In that case why don't you leave?* **make out a case (for sth)** give arguments in favour of sth: *The report makes out a strong case for increased spending on hospitals.* **meet the case** ⇨ MEET[1]. **prove one's/the case/point** ⇨ PROVE.

□ **ˈcase-book** *n* written record kept by doctors, lawyers, etc of cases they have dealt with.

ˈcase grammar (*linguistics*) type of transformational grammar in which the case relationships are used to describe the deep structure of sentences.

ˌcase ˈhistory record of a person's background, medical history, etc for use in professional treatment (eg by a doctor).

ˈcase-law *n* [U] law based on decisions made by judges in earlier cases. Cf COMMON LAW (COMMON[1]), STATUTE LAW (STATUTE).

ˈcase-load *n* all those people for whom a doctor, social worker, etc is responsible.

ˈcase-study *n* study of the development of a person or group of people over a period of time.

ˈcasework *n* [U] social work involving the study of individuals or families with problems. **ˈcaseworker** *n.*

case[2] /keɪs/ *n* **1** (**a**) (often in compounds) any of various types of container or protective covering: *a jewel case* ○ *a pencil case* ○ *a packing-case*, ie a large wooden box for packing goods in ○ *Exhibits in museums are often displayed in glass cases.* (**b**) this with its contents; amount that it contains: *a case* (ie 12 bottles) *of champagne.* ⇨ illus at BOX. **2** suitcase: *Could you carry my case for me?*

▷ **case** *v* **1** [Tn] enclose (sth) in a case; encase. **2** (idm) **case the joint** (*sl*) inspect a place carefully (esp before robbing it). **casing** *n* [U, C] protective covering: *wrapped in rubber casing.*

□ **ˈcase-bound** *adj* (of a book) bound in a hard cover: *It's available in case-bound and paperback editions.*

ˈcase-harden *v* [Tn] harden the surface of (a metal, esp iron) by a special process. **ˈcase-hardened** *adj* (*fig*) made callous by experience.

casein /ˈkeɪsiːn/ *n* [U] protein that is found in milk and that forms the basis of cheese.

casemate /ˈkeɪsmeɪt/ *n* part of a warship that is heavily protected by armour, enclosing the guns.

Casement /ˈkeɪsmənt/ Sir Roger David (1864-1916), British diplomat and Irish nationalist who was hanged by the British for trying to organize support for an Irish uprising.

casement /ˈkeɪsmənt/ *n* (also **casement window**) window that opens on hinges like a door. ⇨ illus at HOME.

cash /kæʃ/ *n* **1** [U] (**a**) money in coins or notes: *pay (in) cash* ○ *I have no cash on me — may I pay by cheque?* ○ *I never carry much cash with me.* (**b**) (*infml*) money in any form; wealth: *I'm short of cash at the moment.* **2** (idm) **cash ˈdown** with immediate payment of cash. **cash on deˈlivery** system of paying for goods when they are delivered.

▷ **cash** *v* **1** [Tn, Dn·n, Dn·pr] ~ **sth (for sb)** exchange sth for cash: *cash a cheque (for sb).* **2** (phr v) **cash in (on sth)** take advantage of or profit from sth: *The shops are cashing in on temporary shortages by raising prices.* **3** (idm) **ˌcash in one's ˈchips** (*US*) (**a**) exchange one's gambling chips for cash at a casino. (**b**) (*infml*) sell one's shares or other assets so as to make a cash profit. (**c**) (*sl*) die: *She gets the lot when her father cashes in his chips.* **cashable** *adj* that can be cashed.

□ **ˌcash and ˈcarry 1** system in which the buyer pays for goods in cash and takes them away himself. **2** shop operating this system: *buy food in bulk at the local cash and carry.*

ˈcashbook *n* book used to keep accounts of cash received and paid out.

ˈcashcard *n* plastic card issued by a bank to its customers for use in a cash dispenser.

ˈcash crop crop grown for selling, rather than for use by the grower. Cf SUBSISTENCE CROP (SUBSIST).

ˈcash desk desk or counter where payment is made in a shop.

ˈcash dispenser machine (in or outside a bank) from which cash can be obtained when a personal coded card is inserted and a special code-number keyed.

ˈcash flow movement of money into and out of a business as goods are bought and sold: [attrib] *a healthy cash flow situation*, eg having enough money to make payments when required to do so.

ˈcashpoint *n* = CASH DISPENSER.

ˈcash register machine used in shops, etc that has a drawer for keeping money in, and displays and records the amount of each purchase.

cashew /ˈkæʃuː/ *n* **1** tropical American tree. **2** (also **ˈcashew nut**) its small edible kidney-shaped nut. ⇨ illus at NUT.

cashier[1] /kæˈʃɪə(r)/ *n* person whose job is to receive and pay out money in a bank, shop, hotel, etc.

cashier[2] /kæˈʃɪə(r)/ *v* [Tn] dismiss (an army officer) from service, esp with dishonour.

cashmere /ˌkæʃˈmɪə(r)/ *n* [U] fine soft wool, esp that made from the hair of a type of Asian goat: [attrib] *a ˌcashmere ˈsweater.*

casino /kəˈsiːnəʊ/ *n* (*pl* ~**s**) public building or room for gambling and other amusements. ⇨ article at GAMBLING.

cask /kɑːsk; *US* kæsk/ *n* (**a**) barrel, esp for alcoholic drinks. (**b**) amount that it contains.

casket /ˈkɑːskɪt; *US* ˈkæskɪt/ *n* **1** small (usu decorated) box for holding letters, jewels or other valuable things. **2** (*US*) coffin.

Caspar /ˈkæspə(r)/ (in Christian tradition) one of the *Magi. ⇨ MAGUS.

Caspian Sea /ˌkæspɪən ˈsiː/ **the Caspian Sea** largest body of inland salt water in the world, enclosed by the USSR and Iran. Its surface is 28 m (92 ft) below sea-level.

Cassandra /kəˈsændrə/ **1** daughter of Priam, king of Troy. She was cursed by Apollo so that her prophecies, though true, were never believed. **2** any prophet of disaster.

cassata /kəˈsɑːtə/ *n* [C, U] type of ice-cream containing dried or candied fruit and nuts.

Mary Cassatt: Woman Bathing, c 1891

Cassatt /kəˈsæt/ Mary (1844-1926), American painter and print-maker. Much of her life was spent in France where she became a member of the *Impressionist group. She is known chiefly for her paintings of mothers and children, and for her pastels which show the influence of Japanese art. ⇨ illus.

cassava /kəˈsɑːvə/ *n* **1** [C] tropical plant with starchy roots. **2** [U] starch or flour obtained from these roots, used to make tapioca.

casserole /ˈkæsərəʊl/ *n* (**a**) [C] covered heat-proof dish in which meat, etc is cooked and then served at table. ⇨ illus at PAN. (**b**) [C, U] food cooked in a casserole: *a/some chicken casserole.*

▷ **casserole** *v* [Tn] cook (meat, etc) in a casserole.

cassette /kəˈset/ *n* small sealed case containing a reel of film or magnetic tape: [attrib] *a cassette recorder*, ie a tape-recorder with which cassettes are used.

Cassiopeia /ˌkæsɪəˈpiːə/ northern constellation recognizable by the 'W' shape of its five brightest stars.

cassiterite /kəˈsɪtəraɪt/ *n* [U] dark-coloured mineral from which tin is obtained.

Cassius /ˈkæsɪəs; *US* ˈkæʃəs/ (Gaius Cassius Longinus, died 42 BC), Roman general and joint leader with Marcus Brutus of the conspiracy to assassinate *Julius Caesar in 44 BC.

cassock /ˈkæsək/ *n* long (usu black or red) garment worn by certain clergymen and members of a church choir.

cassoulet /ˌkæsəˈleɪ, ˈkæsəleɪ/ *n* type of stew containing meat and beans.

cast[1] /kɑːst; *US* kæst/ *v* (*pt, pp* **cast**) **1** [Tn, Tn·pr, Tn·p] throw (sth), esp deliberately or with force: *cast a stone* ○ *The angler cast his line (into the water).* **2** [Tn] allow (sth) to fall or drop; shed: *Snakes cast their skins.* ○ *The horse cast a shoe*, ie One of its shoes came off. **3** [Tn, Tn·pr] turn or send (sth) in a particular direction; direct: *He cast a furtive glance at her.* ○ *The tree cast* (ie caused there to be) *a long shadow (on the grass).* ○ (*fig*) *The tragedy cast a shadow on/over their lives*, ie made them gloomy and depressed. ○ (*fig*) *His muddled evidence casts doubt on his reliability as a witness.* **4** (**a**) [Tn] shape (molten metal, etc) by pouring it into a mould: *cast bronze.* (**b**) [Tn, Tn·pr] ~ **sth (in sth)** make (an object) in this way: *a statue cast in bronze* ○ (*fig*) *The novel is cast in the form of a diary.* **5** (**a**) [I, Tn] choose actors to play parts in (a play, film, etc): *We're casting (the play) next week.* (**b**) [Tn, Tn·pr] ~ **sb (as sb)**; ~ **sb (in sth)** give sb a part in a play, etc: *He was cast as Othello/cast in the role of Othello.* **6** (idm) **cast ˈanchor** lower an anchor. **cast aspersions (on sb/sth)** make damaging or derogatory remarks (about sb/sth): *How dare you cast aspersions on my wife's character!* **cast one's bread upon the waters** (*fml or rhet*) do good deeds without expecting anything in return. **cast an eye/one's eye(s) over sb/sth** look or examine sb/sth quickly: *Would you cast your eye over these calculations to* **light on sth** ⇨ LIGHT[1]. **ˌcast ˈloose** stop being involved with a person, an organization, etc and live independently: *If I had the money I'd cast loose and start my own business.* **cast/draw lots** ⇨ LOT[3]. **cast one's mind back (to sth)** think about the past: *She cast her mind back to her wedding-day.* **cast one's net wide** cover a wide field of supply, activity, inquiry, etc: *The company is casting its net wide in its search for a new sales director.* **cast pearls before swine** (*saying*) offer beautiful or valuable things to people who cannot appreciate them. **cast a spell on sb/sth** put sb/sth under the influence of a magic spell. **cast a/one's ˈvote** give a vote. **the die is cast** ⇨ DIE[3]. **7** (phr v) **cast about/around for sth** try to find or think of sth hurriedly: *He cast about desperately for something to say.* **cast sb/sth aside** abandon sb/sth as useless or unwanted; discard sb/sth: *She has cast her old friends aside.* ○ *He cast aside all his inhibitions.* **cast sb away** (usu passive) leave sb somewhere as a result of a shipwreck: *be cast away on a desert island.* **cast sb down** (usu passive) cause sb to become depressed: *He is not easily cast down.* Cf DOWNCAST. **cast (sth) off** (**a**) untie the ropes holding a boat in position; release (a boat) in this way. (**b**) (in knitting) remove (stitches) from the needles. **cast sb/sth off** abandon or reject sb/sth: *She's cast off three boy-friends in a month.* **cast (sth) on** (in knitting) put (the first line of stitches) on a needle. **cast sb out** (*fml*) (esp passive) drive sb away; expel. Cf OUTCAST. **cast sth/sb up** (of the sea) leave sth/sb that has been in the sea on the shore: *beer cans cast up by the waves.*

▷ **casting** *n* **1** [C] object made by casting (CAST[1] 4a) molten metal, etc. **2** [U] process of choosing actors for a play, film, etc: *a strange bit of casting.*

□ **ˈcastaway** *n* person who has been shipwrecked and left in an isolated place.

ˌcasting ˈvote vote given (eg by a chairman) to decide an issue when votes on each side are equal.

ˌcast ˈiron hard alloy of iron made by casting in a mould. Cf WROUGHT IRON (WROUGHT). **ˌcast-ˈiron** *adj* **1** made of cast iron. **2** (*fig*) very strong; that cannot be broken: *He has a ˌcast-iron constiˈtution.* ○ *They won't find her guilty. She's got a ˌcast-iron deˈfence.*

ˈcast-off *adj* [attrib] (esp of clothes) no longer wanted; discarded: *cast-off shoes* ○ *a cast-off lover.* — *n* (usu *pl*) garment which the original owner will not wear again: *He wears his brother's cast-offs.*

cast[2] /kɑ:st; *US* kæst/ *n* **1** [C] act of throwing sth: *the cast of the dice* ○ *make a cast with a fishing-line/net.* **2** [C] **(a)** object made by pouring or pressing soft material into a mould. **(b)** mould used to make such an object. **(c)** = PLASTER CAST (PLASTER). **3** [CGp] all the actors in a play, etc: *a film with a distinguished cast*, ie with famous actors in it ○ *a cast of thousands*, eg for an epic film ○ [attrib] *a ˈcast list.* **4** [sing] type or kind (of sth): *He has an unusual cast of mind.* **5** [C] = WORM-CAST (WORM). **6** [C] (*dated*) slight squint: *She has a cast in one eye.*

castanets /ˌkæstəˈnets/ *n* [pl] pair of shell-shaped pieces of wood or ivory clicked together with the fingers, esp as a rhythmic accompaniment to a Spanish dance.

caste /kɑ:st/ *n* **1 (a)** [C] any of the hereditary Hindu social classes: *the lowest caste.* **(b)** [U] system based on these classes. The caste system, whose origins are unclear, ranks groups of individuals according to birth and occupation, and is governed by rules of marriage and social contact within the group. The system extends even to some non-Hindu sections of S Asian society. **2** [C] any exclusive social class. **3** [U] any social system based on rigid distinctions of birth, rank, wealth, etc. **4** [C] grouping among certain types of social insects, eg ants or bees, according to a function. Bees, for example, have three castes: queens, workers and drones. **5** (idm) **lose caste** ⇨ LOSE.

castellated /ˈkæstəleɪtɪd/ *adj* having turrets or battlements like a castle.

castigate /ˈkæstɪgeɪt/ *v* [Tn] (*fml*) scold, criticize or punish (sb) severely. ▷ **castigation** /ˌkæstɪˈgeɪʃn/ *n* [C, U]

Castile /kæˈsti:l/ area of central Spain, once a separate kingdom which, with Aragon, dominated Spain in the Middle Ages.

▷ **Castilian** /kæˈstɪlɪən/ *n* **1** [C] native of Castile. **2** [U] standard spoken and literary language of Spain. — *adj* of Castile.

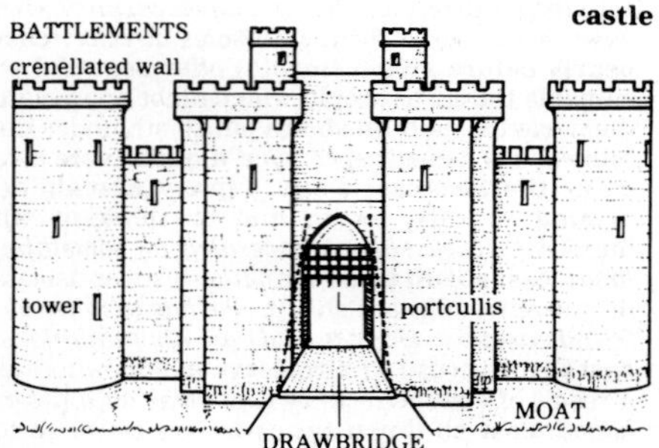

castle /ˈkɑ:sl/ *n* /*US* ˈkæsl/ **1** large fortified building or group of buildings with thick walls, towers, battlements and sometimes a moat: *a medieval castle* ○ *Windsor Castle.* ⇨ illus. **2** (also **rook**) (in chess) any of the four pieces placed in the corner squares of the board at the start of a game. ⇨ illus at CHESS. **3** (idm) **(build) castles in the ˈair/in ˈSpain** (have) plans or hopes that are unlikely to be realized; day-dreams. **an Englishman's home is his castle** ⇨ ENGLISHMAN (ENGLISH).

▷ **castle** *v* [I] (as a single move in chess) move either castle to the square next to the king and the king to the square on the other side of that castle.

Castlereagh /ˈkɑ:slreɪ/ Robert Stewart, Viscount Castlereagh (1769-1822), British statesman during and after the Napoleonic wars, who advocated a conservative system of relations between European states to preserve the balance of power.

Castor /ˈkɑ:stə(r)/ **1** (in Greek mythology) one of the twin sons of Leda. The other twin was Pollux. Pollux, whose father was *Zeus, was immortal, and Castor, whose father was the mortal Tyndareus, was mortal. **2** one of the two bright stars in the constellation Gemini, the other being Pollux. Cf POLLUX.

castor (also **caster**) /ˈkɑ:stə(r); *US* ˈkæs-/ *n* **1** any of the small swivelling wheels fixed to the bottom of a piece of furniture so that it can be moved easily. ⇨ illus at FURNITURE. **2** small container with holes in the top for sprinkling sugar, etc.

□ **ˌcastor ˈsugar** (also **ˌcaster ˈsugar**) white sugar in fine grains.

castor oil /ˌkɑ:stər ˈɔɪl; *US* ˈkæstər ɔɪl/ thick yellowish oil obtained from the seeds of a tropical plant and used as a laxative and a lubricant.

castrate /kæsˈtreɪt; *US* ˈkæstreɪt/ *v* [Tn] remove the testicles of (a male animal or person); geld: *A bullock is a castrated bull.* ▷ **castration** /kæˈstreɪʃn/ *n* [U].

castrato /kæˈstrɑ:təʊ/ *n* (*pl* **-ti** /-ti:/) (esp formerly) male singer castrated in boyhood to preserve his high-pitched voice.

Castro /ˈkæstrəʊ/ Fidel (1927-), Cuban statesman who led a successful revolution in 1959 and has been leader of Cuba ever since.

casual /ˈkæʒʊəl/ *adj* **1** [esp attrib] happening by chance: *a casual encounter, meeting, visit, etc.* **2 (a)** [esp attrib] made or done without much care or thought; offhand: *a casual remark.* **(b)** (*derog*) showing little concern; nonchalant; irresponsible: *His attitude to his job is rather casual.* **(c)** [esp attrib] not methodical or thorough; not serious: *a casual inspection* ○ *a casual glance at a book* ○ *a casual observer, reader, etc.* **3** (of clothes) for informal occasions; not formal: *casual wear.* **4** [attrib] not permanent; irregular; part-time: *earn one's living by casual labour* ○ *a casual labourer* ○ *casual sex*, ie not involving a lasting relationship. **5** [attrib] slight; superficial: *a casual acquaintance.*

▷ **casually** /ˈkæʒʊəlɪ/ *adv*: *meet sb casually* ○ *casually dressed* ○ *casually employed.*

casualness *n* [U].

casuals *n* [pl] informal clothes, esp men's slip-on shoes.

casualty /ˈkæʒʊəltɪ/ *n* **1** person who is killed or injured in war or in an accident: *Heavy casualties were reported* (ie It was reported that many people had been killed) *in the fighting.* ○ (*fig*) *Mr Jones was the first casualty of the firm's cut-backs*, ie the first to lose his job because of them. ○ [attrib] *a casualty list.* **2** thing that is lost, damaged or destroyed in an accident: *The cottage was a casualty of the forest fire.* **3** (also **ˈcasualty ward**, **ˈcasualty department**, *US* **emergency**) part of a hospital where people who have been hurt in accidents are taken for urgent treatment.

casuistry /ˈkæzjʊɪstrɪ/ *n* [U] (*fml usu derog*) resolving of moral problems, esp by the use of clever but false reasoning; sophistry.

▷ **casuist** *n* (*fml usu derog*) person who is skilled in casuistry.

casuistic /ˌkæzjʊˈɪstɪk/ (also **casuistical**) /-tɪkl/ *adj.* **casuistically** /-tɪklɪ/ *adv.*

casus belli /ˌkɑ:sʊs ˈbeli:, ˌkeɪsəs ˈbelaɪ/ (*Latin*) act or event which starts a war or is thought to justify starting a war.

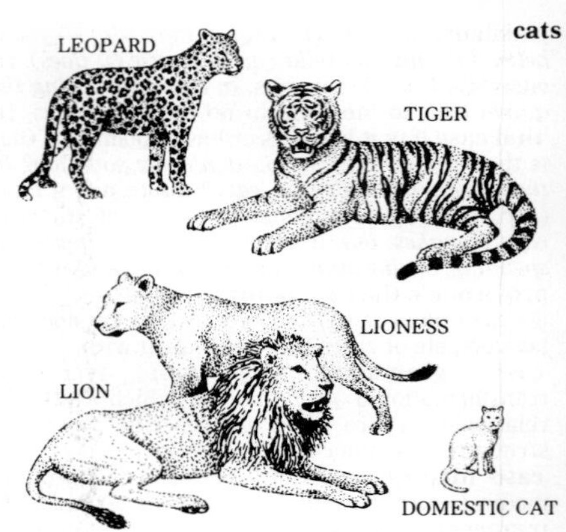

cat[1] /kæt/ *n* **1** [C] small furry domesticated animal often kept as a pet or for catching mice: *We've got three cats and a dog.* ○ [attrib] *ˈcat food.* ⇨ illus at MOUSE. **2** [C] wild animal related to this: *big ˈcats*, ie lions, tigers, leopards, etc ○ [attrib] *the cat family.* ⇨ illus. **3** [C] (*derog*) malicious woman. **4 the cat** [sing] = CAT-O'-NINE-TAILS. **5** (idm) **be the cat's ˈwhiskers/ˈpyjamas** (*infml*) be the best thing, person, idea, etc: *He thinks he's the cat's whiskers*, ie has a high opinion of himself. **a cat-and-dog life** a life in which partners are frequently or constantly quarrelling. **a cat in hell's chance (of doing sth)** (*infml*) no chance at all. **curiosity killed the cat** ⇨ CURIOSITY. **let the ˈcat out of the bag** reveal a secret carelessly or by mistake: *I wanted mother's present to be a secret, but my sister let the cat out of the bag.* **like a scalded cat** ⇨ SCALD. **(fight) like cat and ˈdog** in a quarrelsome way. **like a ˌcat on hot ˈbricks** (*infml*) very nervous: *He was like a cat on hot bricks before his driving test.* **like a Cheshire cat** ⇨ CHESHIRE. **no room to swing a cat** ⇨ ROOM. **play cat and mouse/play a cat-and-mouse game with sb** (*infml*) keep sb in a state of uncertain expectation, treating him alternately cruelly and kindly. **put/set the ˈcat among the pigeons** (*infml*) introduce sb/sth that is likely to cause trouble or disturbance: *The new vicar's a Marxist — that'll set the cat among the pigeons!* **rain cats and ˈdogs** ⇨ RAIN[2]. **wait for the cat to jump/to see which way the cat jumps** ⇨ WAIT[1].

▷ **cattery** *n* place were cats are bred, cared for, etc. Cf KENNELS (KENNEL).

□ **ˈcat burglar** (*Brit*) burglar who enters houses by climbing up walls, drain-pipes, etc.

ˌcat-o'-ˈnine-tails *n* [sing] whip with nine knotted lashes, formerly used for flogging prisoners.

ˌcat's-ˈcradle *n* game in which string is looped round and between the fingers to form patterns.

ˈCat's-eye *n* (*propr*) any one of a line of reflecting studs marking the centre or edge of a road as a guide to traffic when it is dark.

ˈcat's-paw *n* person who is used by sb else to do sth risky or unpleasant.

cat[2] /kæt/ *n* (*US infml*) = CATERPILLAR TRACTOR (CATERPILLAR).

CAT /ˌsi: eɪ ˈti:, a *or, in informal use*, kæt/ *abbr* (*Brit*) College of Advanced Technology.

cataclysm /ˈkætəklɪzəm/ *n* sudden violent change or disaster, eg a flood, an earthquake, a revolution or a war. ▷ **cataclysmic** /ˌkætəˈklɪzmɪk/ *adj*: *the cataclysmic events of 1939-45.*

catacombs /ˈkætəku:mz; *US* -kəʊmz/ *n* [pl] series of underground tunnels with openings along the sides for burying the dead (as in ancient Rome).

catafalque /ˈkætəfælk/ *n* decorated platform on which the coffin of a distinguished person lies before or during a funeral.

catalepsy /ˈkætəlepsɪ/ *n* [U] disease which causes a person to become temporarily unconscious and his body rigid.

▷ **cataleptic** /ˌkætəˈleptɪk/ *adj* of or suffering from catalepsy. — *n* person suffering from catalepsy.

catalogue (*US* also **catalog**) /ˈkætəlɒg; *US* -lɔ:g/ *n* 1 (book or booklet containing a) complete list of items, usu in a special order and with a description of each: *a library catalogue* ○ *an exhibition catalogue.* 2 (*fig*) series: *a catalogue of disasters.* ▷ **catalogue** *v* [Tn] list (sth) in a catalogue.

catalysis /kəˈtæləsɪs/ *n* [U] process of speeding up a chemical reaction with a catalyst.
▷ **catalytic** /ˌkætəˈlɪtɪk/ *adj* of or causing catalysis. ˌ**catalytic conˈverter** device fitted in the exhaust system of a motor vehicle for converting pollutant gases into harmless products.

catalyst /ˈkætəlɪst/ *n* 1 substance that speeds up a chemical reaction without itself changing. 2 (*fig*) person or thing that causes a change: *The offer of a new job provided just the catalyst she needed.*

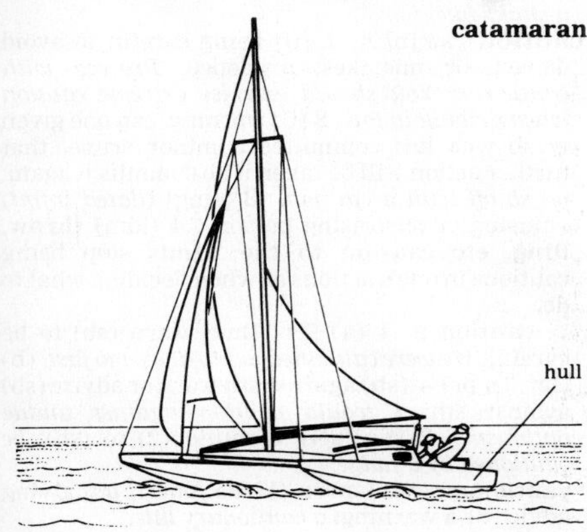

catamaran /ˌkætəməˈræn/ *n* 1 sailing-boat with two parallel hulls. ⇨ illus. 2 raft made of two boats or logs fastened side by side.

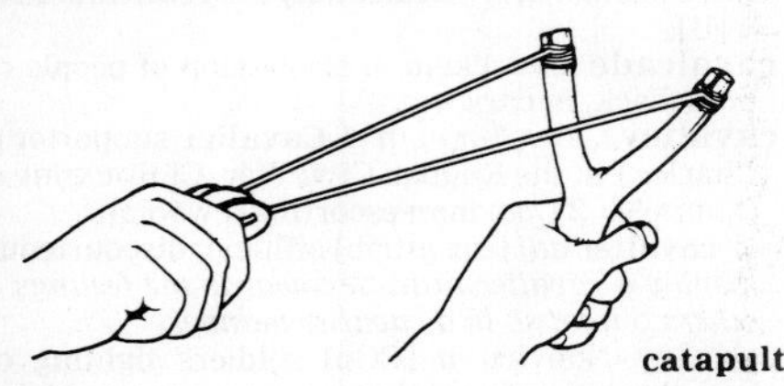

catapult /ˈkætəpʌlt/ *n* 1 (*US* **slingshot**) Y-shaped stick with a piece of elastic attached to it, used esp by children for shooting stones. ⇨ illus. 2 (in ancient times) machine for throwing heavy stones in war. 3 apparatus for launching gliders or for launching aircraft from the deck of a ship.
▷ **catapult** *v* 1 [Tn, Tn·pr] shoot or launch (sth) from a catapult. 2 [Ipr, Tn·pr] (cause sth to) be thrown suddenly and with force: *In the crash the driver (was) catapulted through the windscreen.*

cataract /ˈkætərækt/ *n* 1 large steep waterfall. 2 (*medical*) (a) disease in which the lens of the eye becomes cloudy, causing partial or total blindness. (b) area clouded in this way: *an operation to remove cataracts.*

catarrh /kəˈtɑ:(r)/ *n* [U] (a) inflammation of the mucous membrane of the nose and throat, causing an increased flow of mucus. (b) mucus forming in this way: *I've a bad cold and I'm full of catarrh.*

catastrophe /kəˈtæstrəfɪ/ *n* sudden great disaster or misfortune: *The earthquake was a terrible catastrophe.* ▷ **catastrophic** /ˌkætəˈstrɒfɪk/ *adj*: *a catastrophic failure.* **catastrophically** *adv.*

catcall /ˈkætkɔ:l/ *n* shrill whistle expressing disapproval: *The Minister's speech was greeted with jeers and catcalls.*
▷ **catcall** *v* [I] make catcalls.

catch[1] /kætʃ/ *v* (*pt, pp* **caught** /kɔ:t/) 1 (a) [Tn] stop and hold (a moving object) esp in the hands: *I threw a ball to her and she caught it.* ○ *Our dog likes catching biscuits in its mouth.* (b) [Tn, Tn·p] ~ **sb** (**out**) (in cricket) dismiss (a batsman) by catching the ball he has hit before it touches the ground. 2 [Tn, Tn·pr] capture (sb/sth) after a chase, in a trap, etc; seize and hold: *catch a thief* ○ *Cats catch mice.* ○ *How many fish did you catch?* ○ *I caught him* (ie met him and stopped him) *just as he was leaving the building.* ○ *catch sb by the arm, throat, scruff of the neck, etc.* 3 [Ipr, Cn·g] find or discover (sb doing sth); take by surprise: *I caught her with her fingers in the biscuit tin.* ○ *I caught a boy stealing apples from the garden.* ○ *You won't catch me working* (ie I would never work) *on a Sunday!* 4 [Tn] be in time for (and get on) (sth): *catch a bus, plane, train, etc* ○ *catch the post,* ie post letters before the box is emptied by the postman. 5 [Tn] (*US infml*) see or hear (sth); attend: *Let's eat now and maybe we could catch a movie later.* 6 [I, Ipr, Tn, Tn·pr] ~ (**sth**) (**in**/**on sth**) (cause sth to) become fixed, stuck or entangled in or on sth: *The lock won't catch,* ie cannot be fastened. ○ *Her dress caught on a nail.* ○ *He caught his thumb in the door.* ○ *He caught his foot on a tree root and stumbled.* 7 [Tn] become infected with (an illness): *catch (a) cold* ○ *catch flu, pneumonia, bronchitis, etc.* 8 [Tn] hear (sth); understand: *Sorry, I didn't quite catch what you said.* ○ *I don't catch your meaning.* 9 [Tn, Tn·pr, Dn·n] hit (sth): *The stone caught him on the side of the head.* ○ *She caught him a blow on the chin.* 10 [I] begin to burn: *These logs are wet: they won't catch.* 11 [Tn] reproduce (sth) accurately: *The artist has caught her smile perfectly.* 12 (idm) **be caught/taken short** ⇨ SHORT[2]. **catch sb ˈat it** = CATCH SB RED-HANDED. **catch sb's atˈtention/ˈeye** attract sb's attention: *Try to catch the waiter's eye.* ○ *A newspaper headline caught his attention.* **catch one's ˈbreath** stop breathing for a moment (because of fear, shock, etc): *He caught his breath in surprise.* **catch one's death (of cold)** (*infml*) catch a severe cold: *Don't go out without a coat: you'll catch your death.* **catch/take sb's fancy** ⇨ FANCY[1]. **catch ˈfire** begin to burn, esp accidentally: *She was standing too close to the fireplace and her dress caught fire.* **catch it** (*infml*) be punished or scolded: *If your father finds you here you'll really catch it!* **catch sb ˈnapping** find sb not paying attention: *Don't let the boss catch you napping!* **catch sb on the wrong ˈfoot** catch sb when he is not ready or expecting sth. **catch sb red-ˈhanded** discover sb in the act of doing sth wrong or committing a crime. **catch sight/a glimpse of sb/sth** see sb/sth for a moment: *She caught sight of a car in the distance.* ○ *He caught a glimpse of her before she vanished into the crowd.* **catch the ˈsun** become sun-burned: *Your back looks sore — you've really caught the sun today.* **catch/take sb unawares** ⇨ UNAWARES (UNAWARE). **catch sb with his pants/trousers down** (*infml*) catch or trap sb when he is unprepared or not being watchful. **the early bird catches the worm** ⇨ EARLY. **set a thief to catch a thief** ⇨ THIEF. **a sprat to catch a mackerel** ⇨ SPRAT. 13 (phr v) **catch at sth** ⇨ CLUTCH AT STH (CLUTCH). ˌ**catch ˈon (to sth)** (*infml*) understand (sth): *He is very quick/slow to catch ˈon.* ˌ**catch ˈon (with sb)** (*infml*) become popular or fashionable: *Mini-skirts first caught on in the 1960's.* ˌ**catch sb ˈout** show that sb is ignorant or doing sth wrong: *Ask me anything you like — you won't catch me out.* ˌ**catch ˈup (with sb)**; ˌ**catch sb ˈup** reach (and sometimes overtake) sb who is ahead (eg in a race); reach the same stage as sb: *Go on in front. I'll soon catch you up/catch up (with you).* ○ *After missing a term through illness he had to work hard to catch up (with the others).* ˌ**catch ˈup on sth** (a) spend extra time doing sth, in order to compensate for having neglected it: *I've got a lot of work to catch ˈup on.* (b) acquire information about sth belatedly: *Come over for a chat so we can catch up on each other's news.* **be/get** ˌ**caught ˈup in sth** be absorbed or involved in sth: *She was caught up in the anti-nuclear movement.*
▷ **catcher** *n* (in baseball) fielder who stands behind the batter. ⇨ illus at BASEBALL.
catching *adj* (of a disease) infectious.
catchy *adj* (**-ier**, **-iest**) (of a tune) pleasant and easy to remember.
□ ˈ**catch-all** *n* (*esp US*) 1 thing for holding many small objects. 2 word, phrase, etc that covers a range of possibilities without describing any of them precisely.
ˈ**catch crop** crop grown between rows of other crops.

catch[2] /kætʃ/ *n* 1 act of catching (esp a ball): *a difficult catch.* 2 (amount of) sth caught: *a huge catch of fish* ○ (*infml*) *He's a good catch,* ie worth getting as a husband. 3 device for fastening sth: *The catch on my handbag is broken.* 4 hidden difficulty or disadvantage: *The house is very cheap. There must be a catch somewhere.* ○ [attrib] *a ˈcatch question,* ie one intended to trick sb. 5 type of humorous song for three or more singers, each starting at a different time. 6 (idm) **catch-22** /ˌkætʃ twentɪˈtu:/ (*sl*) dilemma faced by sb who is bound to suffer, whichever course of action he takes: [attrib] *a catch-22 situation.*

catchment area /ˈkætʃmənt eərɪə/ 1 (also **catchment basin**) area from which rainfall flows into a river, reservoir, etc. 2 (also **catchment**) area from which people are sent to a particular school, hospital, etc: *a school with a large catchment area.*

catchpenny /ˈkætʃpenɪ/ *adj* [attrib] designed to make money: *a catchpenny novel, title, device, trick.*

catchphrase /ˈkætʃfreɪz/ *n* well-known phrase first used by, and later associated with, an entertainer, a political leader, etc.

catchword /ˈkætʃwɜ:d/ *n* 1 word or phrase placed where it will attract attention, eg above a paragraph in a newspaper article. 2 first or last word of a page in a dictionary, printed above the columns.

catechism /ˈkætəkɪzəm/ *n* (a) [U] summary of the principles of a religion in the form of questions and answers. (b) [C] series of such questions, used for religious instruction.

catechize, -ise /ˈkætəkaɪz/ *v* [Tn] teach (sb) (esp about religion) by means of questions and answers.

categorical /ˌkætəˈgɒrɪkl; *US* -ˈgɔ:r-/ *adj* (of a statement) unconditional; absolute; explicit: *a categorical denial, refusal, etc.* ▷ **categorically** /-klɪ/ *adv.*

category /ˈkætəgərɪ; *US* -gɔ:rɪ/ *n* class or group of things in a complete system of grouping: *place things in categories.*
▷ **categorize, -ise** /ˈkætəgəraɪz/ *v* [Tn] place (sth) in a category.

cater /ˈkeɪtə(r)/ *v* 1 (a) [I, Ipr] ~ (**for sth/sb**) provide food and services, esp at social functions: *cater for a party, banquet, etc* ○ *Fifty is a lot of people to cater for!* (b) [Tn] (*esp US*) provide food and services for (a party, banquet, etc). 2 [Ipr] (a) ~ **for sb/sth** provide what is needed or desired by sb/sth: *TV must cater for many different tastes.* (b) ~ **to sth** try to satisfy a particular need or demand: *newspapers catering to people's love of scandal.*
▷ **caterer** *n* 1 person whose job is providing food for large social events. 2 owner or manager of a hotel, restaurant, etc.
catering *n* [U] (trade of) providing food, etc for social events: *Who did the catering for your son's wedding?*

caterpillar /ˈkætəpɪlə(r)/ *n* 1 larva of a butterfly or moth. ⇨ illus at BUTTERFLY. 2 (a) (also **Caterpillar track**) (*propr*) endless belt passing round the wheels of a tractor or tank, enabling it to travel over rough ground. (b) (also **Caterpillar tractor**, *abbr* **cat**) tractor fitted with such a belt.

caterwaul /ˈkætəwɔ:l/ *v* [I] make a cat's shrill howling cry: *Do stop caterwauling, children!*
▷ **caterwaul** *n* [sing] shrill cry of or like a cat.

catfish /ˈkætfɪʃ/ *n* (*pl* unchanged) large (usu freshwater) fish with whisker-like feelers round its mouth.

catgut /ˈkætgʌt/ *n* [U] thin strong cord made from the dried intestines of animals and used for the strings of violins, tennis rackets, etc.

Cath *abbr* Catholic.

catharsis /kəˈθɑ:sɪs/ *n* (*pl* **-ses** /-si:z/) 1 [C, U] (instance of the) release of strong feelings through the effect of art, esp drama. 2 [U] (*medical*) emptying of the bowels.

▷ **cathartic** /kəˈθɑ:tɪk/ *adj* causing catharsis; purgative. — *n* (*medical*) purgative drug.
cathedral /kəˈθi:drəl/ *n* main church of a district under the care of a bishop: [attrib] *a cathedral city*.
Catherine wheel /ˈkæθrɪn wi:l/ *n* type of firework that spins when lit.
catheter /ˈkæθɪtə(r)/ *n* (*medical*) thin tube used to drain fluids from the body, esp one that is inserted into the bladder to extract urine.
▷ **catheterize, -ise** [Tn] insert a catheter into (sb/sth).
cathode /ˈkæθəʊd/ *n* negative electrode, by which an electric current leaves a device such as a battery. Cf ANODE.
□ ˌ**cathode** ˈ**ray** beam of electrons from the cathode in a vacuum tube. ˌ**cathode** ˈ**ray tube** vacuum tube, eg the picture tube of a TV set, in which cathode rays produce a luminous image on a fluorescent screen.
Catholic /ˈkæθəlɪk/ *adj* **1** = ROMAN CATHOLIC (ROMAN): *the Catholic Church* ○ *a Catholic priest, school*. Cf PROTESTANT. ⇨ article at RELIGION. **2** (also **catholic**) of or relating to all Christians or the whole Christian Church.
▷ **Catholic** *n* (*abbr* **Cath**) member of the Roman Catholic Church: *Is she a Catholic or a Protestant?*
Catholicism /kəˈθɒləsɪzəm/ *n* [U] = ROMAN CATHOLICISM (ROMAN).
catholic /ˈkæθəlɪk/ *adj* including many or most things; general; universal: *have catholic tastes, interests, views, etc.*
▷ **catholicity** /ˌkæθəˈlɪsətɪ/ *n* [U] universality or breadth (esp of interests).
Catiline /ˈkætɪlaɪn/ (Lucus Sergius Catalina, died 62 BC), Roman nobleman who conspired unsuccessfully to destroy Roman democracy.
cation /ˈkætaɪən/ *n* ion with a positive charge. Cf ANION.
catkin /ˈkætkɪn/ *n* tuft of soft downy flowers hanging from the twigs of such trees as willows or birches.
catmint /ˈkætmɪnt/ (also **catnip**) *n* [U] aromatic plant with blue flowers whose smell is attractive to cats.
catnap /ˈkætnæp/ *n* short sleep; doze.
▷ **catnap** *v* (**-pp-**) [I] have a catnap.
catnip /ˈkætnɪp/ *n* [U] = CATMINT.
Cato /ˈkætəʊ/ Marcius Porcus 'the Censor' (234-149 BC), Roman statesman, orator and writer, noted for his hostility to Carthage and his moral and social reforms.
catsuit /ˈkætsu:t/ *n* close-fitting garment that covers the body from the neck to the feet.
catsup /ˈkætsəp/ *n* [U] (*esp US*) = KETCHUP.
cattery /ˈkætərɪ/ *n* place where cats are bred, cared for, etc. Cf KENNELS (KENNEL).
cattle /ˈkætl/ *n* [pl *v*] animals with horns and cloven hoofs such as cows, bulls and bullocks, bred for their milk or meat; oxen: *a herd of cattle* ○ *twenty head of cattle*, eg twenty cows ○ *The prisoners were herded like cattle*. ○ [attrib] ˈ*cattle breeding* ○ ˈ*cattle sheds* ○ ˈ*cattle trucks*.
□ ˈ**cattle-cake** *n* [U] small blocks of concentrated food fed to cattle.
ˈ**cattle-grid** *n* (usu metal) grid covering a ditch in a road so that vehicles can pass but not cattle, sheep, etc.
ˈ**cattleman** *n* (*pl* **-men**) (*US*) person who breeds or looks after cattle.
catty /ˈkætɪ/ *adj* (**-ier, -iest**) (also **cattish**) malicious; spiteful: *catty remarks*. ▷ **cattily** *adv*. **cattiness** *n* [U].
Catullus /kəˈtʌləs/ Gaius Valerius (c 84 BC-c 54 BC), Roman poet famous for his love poems.
catwalk /ˈkætwɔ:k/ *n* raised narrow footway along a bridge, over a theatre stage, etc.
Caucasian /kɔ:ˈkeɪzɪən, kɔ:ˈkeɪʒn/ **1** (also **Caucasoid** /ˈkɔ:kəzɔɪd/) *adj* of or relating to the 'white' or light-skinned racial division of mankind. **2** of or relating to the Caucasus: *Caucasian languages*, ie those spoken in the Caucasus, eg Georgian.
▷ **Caucasian** *n* Caucasian person.
Caucasus /ˈkɔ:kəsəs/ **the Caucasus** mountain range in Georgia, between the Black Sea and the Caspian Sea. The highest mountain in the range is about 5 000 m (18 000 ft) high.
caucus /ˈkɔ:kəs/ *n* [CGp] (*sometimes derog*) **1** (meeting of the) parliamentary members of a particular political party or any other legislature. **2** (*US*) (meeting of the) members or leaders of a particular political party to choose candidates, decide policy, etc. **3** local organizing committee of a political party, which decides policy, etc.
caudal /ˈkɔ:dl/ *adj* of or like a tail.
caudate /ˈkɔ:deɪt/ *adj* having a tail.
caught *pt, pp* of CATCH[1].
caul /kɔ:l/ *n* (*anatomy*) (**a**) membrane enclosing a foetus in the womb. (**b**) part of this that is sometimes found on a child's head at birth.
cauldron (also **caldron**) /ˈkɔ:ldrən/ *n* large deep pot for boiling things in.
cauliflower /ˈkɒlɪflaʊə(r); *US* ˈkɔ:lɪ-/ *n* [C, U] type of cabbage with a large dense white head of flowers, eaten as a vegetable: *Have some more cauliflower*. ⇨ illus at CABBAGE.
□ **cauliflower** ˈ**cheese** (*Brit*) cauliflower cooked and served with a cheese sauce.
cauliflower ˈ**ear** (*Brit*) ear that has become swollen after repeated blows, eg in boxing.
caulk (also *esp US* **calk**) /kɔ:k/ *v* [Tn] (**a**) make (esp a boat) watertight by filling the seams or joints with waterproof material. (**b**) fill up (esp cracks in wood) with a sticky substance.
causal /kɔ:zl/ *adj* **1** of or forming a cause; relating to cause and effect. **2** (*grammar*) expressing or indicating a cause: *'Because' is a causal conjunction*.
▷ **causality** /kɔ:ˈzælətɪ/ (also **causation**) *n* [U] (**a**) relationship between cause and effect. (**b**) principle that nothing can happen without a cause.
causation /kɔ:ˈzeɪʃn/ *n* [U] **1** the causing or producing of an effect. **2** = CAUSALITY (CAUSAL).
causative /ˈkɔ:zətɪv/ *adj* **1** acting as a cause. **2** (*grammar*) (of words or forms of words) expressing a cause: *'Blacken' is a causative verb meaning 'cause to become black'*.
cause /kɔ:z/ *n* **1** [C] that which produces an effect; thing, event, person, etc that makes sth happen: *What was the cause of the fire?* ○ *Smoking is one of the causes of heart disease.* ○ *Police are investigating the causes of the explosion.* **2** [U] ~ (**for sth**) reason: *There is no cause for anxiety.* ○ *You have no cause for complaint/no cause to complain.* ○ *She is never absent from work without good cause.* ⇨ Usage at REASON[1]. **3** [C] aim, principle or movement that is strongly defended or supported: *a good cause*, ie one that deserves to be supported, eg a charity ○ *He fought for the republican cause in the civil war.* ○ *Her life was devoted to the cause of justice.* **4** [C] (*law*) question to be resolved in a court of law: *pleading one's cause.* **5** (idm) **a lost cause** ⇨ LOSE[2]. **make common cause with sb** ⇨ COMMON[1]. **the root cause** ⇨ ROOT[1].
▷ **cause** *v* [Tn, Tnt, Dn·n, Dn·pr] ~ **sth** (**for sb**) be the cause of (sth); make happen: *Smoking can cause lung cancer.* ○ *What caused the explosion?* ○ *The cold weather caused the plants to die.* ○ *He caused his parents much unhappiness.* ○ *She's always causing trouble for people.*

NOTE ON USAGE: The verbs **cause**, **bring about** and **make** indicate how a certain result, situation or event happens. These verbs are used in a variety of patterns. **Bring about** and **cause** can be used with a direct object indicating the result. **Bring about** is more formal and refers to a less direct cause: *Smoking can cause lung cancer.* ○ *The war brought about a reduction in the birth-rate.* **Cause** can connect the result with the person, etc affected: *My car has caused me a lot of trouble.* ○ *His parents were caused a lot of worry by his laziness.* **Cause** and **make** can be used with (*to* +) an infinitive, but not in the passive: *The pepper in the food caused me to/made me sneeze.* When **make** means 'compel', it can be used in the passive (with *to* + infinitive): *They made him pay for the damage he had done/He was made to pay for the damage he had done.*

cause célèbre /ˌkɔ:z seˈlebrə/ (*pl* **causes célèbres** /ˌkɔ:z seˈlebrə/) (*French*) lawsuit or other issue that arouses great interest.
causerie /ˈkəʊzərɪ/ *n* (*French*) informal article or talk, esp on a literary subject.
causeway /ˈkɔ:zweɪ/ *n* raised road or path, esp across low or wet ground.
caustic /ˈkɔ:stɪk/ *adj* **1** that can burn or destroy things by chemical action. **2** (*fig*) (of comments) sarcastic; cutting: *caustic remarks* ○ *a caustic wit.*
▷ **caustically** /-klɪ/ *adv* in a caustic(2) way.
□ ˌ**caustic** ˈ**soda** = SODIUM HYDROXIDE (SODIUM).
cauterize, -ise /ˈkɔ:təraɪz/ *v* [Tn] burn the surface of (body tissue) with a caustic substance or hot iron to destroy infection or stop bleeding: *cauterize a snake-bite*.
caution /ˈkɔ:ʃn/ *n* **1** [U] being careful to avoid danger or mistakes; prudence: *Proceed with caution.* ○ *You should exercise extreme caution when driving in fog.* **2** [C] warning, esp one given to sb who has committed a minor crime, that further action will be taken if he commits it again: *let sb off with a caution.* **3** [sing] (*dated infml*) amusing or surprising person. **4** (idm) **throw, fling, etc caution to the winds** stop being cautious in one's actions or when deciding what to do.
▷ **caution** *v* **1** (**a**) [Tn, Dn·t] warn (sb) to be careful: *We were cautioned not to drive too fast.* (**b**) [Ipr, Tn·pr] ~ (**sb**) **against sth** warn or advise (sb) against sth: *I would caution against undue optimism.* **2** [Tn] give a caution(2) to (sb): *be cautioned by a judge.*
cautionary /ˈkɔ:ʃənərɪ; *US* ˈkɔ:ʃənerɪ/ *adj* giving advice or a warning: *a cautionary tale.*
cautious /ˈkɔ:ʃəs/ *adj* ~ (**about/of sb/sth**) showing or having caution(1); careful: *a cautious driver* ○ *cautious of strangers* ○ *cautious about spending money.* ▷ **cautiously** *adv.* **cautiousness** *n* [U].
cavalcade /ˌkævlˈkeɪd/ *n* procession of people on horseback, in cars, etc.
cavalier /ˌkævəˈlɪə(r)/ *n* **1 Cavalier** supporter of Charles I in the English Civil War. Cf ROUNDHEAD (ROUND[2]). **2** (*joc*) man escorting a woman.
▷ **cavalier** *adj* [esp attrib] offhand; discourteous: *display a cavalier attitude towards the feelings of others* ○ *treat sb in a cavalier manner.*
cavalry /ˈkævlrɪ/ *n* [CGp] soldiers fighting on horseback (esp formerly) or in armoured vehicles: [attrib] *a cavalry officer/regiment.* Cf INFANTRY.
□ ˌ**cavalry** ˈ**twill** strong twill fabric used esp for making trousers.
cave /keɪv/ *n* **1** hollow place in the side of a cliff or hill, or underground. **2** (idm) **an Aladdin's cave** ⇨ ALADDIN.
▷ **cave** *v* **1** [I] (usu **go caving**) explore caves as a sport: *He likes caving.* **2** (phr v) **cave in** fall inwards; collapse: *The roof of the tunnel caved in (on the workmen).* ○ (*fig*) *All opposition to the scheme has caved in.*
□ ˈ**cave-dweller** *n* = CAVEMAN.
ˈ**cave-in** *n* sudden collapse of a roof, etc.
caveman /ˈkeɪvmæn/ *n* (*pl* **-men** /ˈkeɪvmen/) **1** person living in caves, esp in prehistoric times. **2** (*infml*) man of crude or violent feelings and behaviour.
caveat /ˈkævɪæt, *also* ˈkeɪvɪæt/ *n* **1** (*fml*) warning; proviso: *I recommend the deal, but with certain caveats.* **2** (*law*) procedure for requesting a court to suspend proceedings until the opposition has been heard.
caveat emptor /ˌkævɪæt ˈemptɔ:(r)/ (*Latin*) principle that a buyer buys goods at his own risk. It is Latin for 'let the buyer beware'.
Cavell /ˈkævl/ Edith (1865-1915), English nurse executed by the Germans in the First World War for helping Allied troops to escape from occupied Belgium.
cavern /ˈkævən/ *n* cave, esp a large or dark one.
▷ **cavernous** *adj* like a cavern; large and deep: *cavernous depths* ○ *cavernous eyes.*
caviare (also **caviar**) /ˈkævɪɑ:(r)/ *n* [U] **1** pickled

roe of sturgeon or other large fish, eaten as a delicacy. **2** (idm) **be ˌcaviare to the ˈgeneral** (*dated or joc*) be too refined or delicate to be appreciated by ordinary people.

cavil /ˈkævl/ *v* (**-ll-**; *US* **-l-**) [I, Ipr] ~ (**at sth**) (*fml*) make unnecessary complaints (about sth): *He cavilled at being asked to cook his own breakfast.*

cavity /ˈkævətɪ/ *n* empty space within sth solid, eg a hole in a tooth.

□ **ˌcavity ˈwall** wall consisting of two separate walls with a space between, designed to give extra insulation.

cavort /kəˈvɔːt/ *v* [I, Ip] ~ (**about/around**) jump about excitedly: *Stop cavorting around and sit still, just for five minutes!*

cavy /ˈkeɪvɪ/ *n* small S American rodent with a sturdy body and a very small tail.

caw /kɔː/ *n* harsh cry of a crow, rook or raven.

▷ **caw** *v* [I] make this cry.

Caxton /ˈkækstən/ William (c 1422-91), the first English printer. He printed his first English text in 1474, and produced about 80 more (many of them his own translations of French romances) before his death.

cay /kiː, keɪ/ small low island or reef.

cayenne /keɪˈen/ *n* [U] (also **ˌcayenne ˈpepper**) type of hot red powdered pepper(1), used for seasoning foods.

cayman (also **caiman**) /ˈkeɪmən/ *n* type of S American reptile like an alligator.

Cayman Islands /ˈkeɪmən aɪləndz/ group of three islands in the Caribbean Sea, a British dependency, south of Cuba; pop approx 21 000; official language English; capital George Town. ⇨ map at CARIBBEAN.

CB /ˌsiː ˈbiː/ *abbr* **1** citizens' band: *broadcast a message on CB radio.* **2** (*Brit*) Companion (of the Order) of the Bath.

CBC /ˌsiː biː ˈsiː/ *abbr* Canadian Broadcasting Corporation: *a CBC news programme* ○ *listen to (the) CBC.*

CBE /ˌsiː biː ˈiː/ *abbr* (*Brit*) Commander (of the Order) of the British Empire: *be (made) a CBE* ○ *John Adams CBE.* Cf DBE, KBE, MBE.

CBI /ˌsiː biː ˈaɪ/ *abbr* Confederation of British Industry, the employers' federation in the UK. ⇨ article at INDUSTRY.

CBS /ˌsiː biː ˈes/ *abbr* (*US*) Columbia Broadcasting System: *a CBS news broadcast* ○ *listen to CBS.* ⇨ article at TELEVISION.

cc /ˌsiː ˈsiː/ *abbr* **1** (*commerce*) carbon copy (to): *to Luke Petersen, cc Janet Gold, Marion Ryde.* **2** cubic centimetre(s): *an 850cc engine.*

CD /ˌsiː ˈdiː/ *abbr* **1** compact disc. **2** Corps Diplomatique.

Cd *symb* cadmium.

Cdr (also **Cmdr**) *abbr* Commander: *Cdr (John) Stone.*

Cdre (also **Cmdre**) *abbr* Commodore: *Cdre (James) Wingfield.*

CDT /ˌsiː diː ˈtiː/ *abbr* (*US*) Central Daylight Time.

CE *abbr* Church of England: *a CE junior school.* Cf C OF E.

Ce *symb* cerium.

cease /siːs/ *v* (*fml*) **1** [I, It, Tn, Tg] come or bring sth to an end; stop: *Hostilities* (ie Fighting) *between the two sides ceased at midnight.* ○ *The officer ordered his men to cease fire,* ie stop shooting. ○ *That department has ceased to exist.* ○ *The factory has ceased making bicycles.* **2** (idm) **wonders will never cease** ⇨ WONDER *n.*

▷ **cease** *n* (idm) **without ˈcease** (*fml*) without stopping; continuously.

ceaseless *adj* not stopping; without end; continuous: *His ceaseless chatter began to annoy me.* **ceaselessly** *adv.*

□ **ˌcease-ˈfire** *n* **1** signal to stop firing guns in war: *order a cease-fire.* **2** temporary period of truce: *negotiate a cease-fire.*

Cecilia /sɪˈsiːlɪə/ Saint (2nd or 3rd century AD), martyr and patron saint of music. She is the subject of an ode by *Dryden, set to music by *Handel.

cedar /ˈsiːdə(r)/ *n* (**a**) [C] tall evergreen coniferous tree. (**b**) (also **cedarwood** /ˈsiːdəwʊd/) [U] its hard, red, sweet-smelling wood, used for making boxes, furniture, pencils, etc: [attrib] *a ˌcedar ˈchest.*

cede /siːd/ *v* [Tn, Dn·pr] ~ **sth** (**to sb**) give up one's rights to or possession of sth: *cede territory to a neighbouring state.*

cedilla /sɪˈdɪlə/ *n* mark put under the c (¸) in certain languages (eg French and Portuguese) to show that it is pronounced /s/, as in *façade.*

Ceefax /ˈsiːfæks/ *n* [U] (*Brit propr*) television information service provided by the British Broadcasting Corporation.

CEGB /ˌsiː iː dʒiː ˈbiː/ *abbr* Central Electricity Generating Board (in the UK).

ceilidh /ˈkeɪlɪ/ *n* informal gathering for Scottish or Irish music, dancing, etc.

ceiling /ˈsiːlɪŋ/ *n* **1** top inner surface of a room: *Mind you don't bump your head on the low ceiling.* ○ [attrib] *a ceiling fan.* **2** cloud level. **3** maximum altitude at which a particular aircraft can normally fly: *an aircraft with a ceiling of 20 000 ft.* **4** upper limit: *The government has set a wages and prices ceiling of 10%.* **5** (idm) **hit the ceiling/roof** ⇨ HIT[1].

celandine /ˈseləndaɪn/ *n* small wild plant with yellow flowers.

celebrant /ˈselɪbrənt/ *n* priest leading a church service, esp the Eucharist.

celebrate /ˈselɪbreɪt/ *v* **1** (**a**) [Tn] mark (a happy or important day, event, etc) with festivities and rejoicing: *celebrate Christmas, sb's birthday, a wedding anniversary, etc* ○ *celebrate a victory, success, etc.* (**b**) [I] enjoy oneself in some way on such an occasion: *It's my birthday — let's celebrate!* eg with alcoholic drink. **2** [Tn] (of a priest) lead (a religious ceremony): *celebrate Mass/the Eucharist.* **3** [Tn] (*fml*) praise (sb/sth); honour: *Odysseus's heroic exploits are celebrated in 'The Odyssey'.*

▷ **celebrated** *adj* ~ (**for sth**) famous: *a celebrated actress, writer, pianist, etc* ○ *Burgundy is celebrated for its fine wines.*

celebration /ˌselɪˈbreɪʃn/ *n* [C, U] (act or occasion of) celebrating: *birthday celebrations* ○ *a day of celebration.*

celebrity /sɪˈlebrətɪ/ *n* **1** [C] famous person: *celebrities of stage and screen,* ie well-known actors and film stars. **2** [U] being famous; fame.

celeriac /sɪˈlerɪæk/ *n* [U] type of celery with a large edible root.

celerity /sɪˈlerətɪ/ *n* [U] (*arch*) quickness.

celery /ˈselərɪ/ *n* [U] garden plant with crisp stems that are used in salads or as a vegetable: *a bunch/stick/head of celery* ○ [attrib] *celery soup.*

celesta /sɪˈlestə/ *n* (*music*) small keyboard instrument with hammers that strike metal plates to produce a resonant sound.

celestial /sɪˈlestɪəl; *US* -tʃl/ *adj* **1** [attrib] of the sky: *celestial bodies,* eg the sun and the stars. **2** of heaven; divine: (*fig*) *the celestial beauty of her voice.* Cf TERRESTRIAL.

□ **ceˌlestial ˈsphere** imaginary sphere surrounding the earth, used by astronomers as a way of describing the positions of stars, planets, etc from the point of view of an observer on earth. The celestial sphere is divided into two equal hemispheres by the **celestial equator**.

celiac (*US*) = COELIAC.

celibate /ˈselɪbət/ *adj* **1** remaining unmarried, esp for religious reasons. **2** not having sexual relations.

▷ **celibacy** /ˈselɪbəsɪ/ *n* [U] (state of) living unmarried, esp for religious reasons: *Catholic priests take a vow of celibacy.*

celibate *n* unmarried person; person not having sexual relations.

cell /sel/ *n* **1** very small room, eg for a monk in a monastery or for one or more prisoners in a prison. **2** compartment in a honeycomb. **3** device for producing an electric current by chemical action, eg the metal plates in acid inside a battery. **4** microscopic unit of living matter. Nearly all organisms are made up of cells. The simplest, like bacteria, consist of a single cell, while in more complex plants and animals cells form colonies or tissues. Nearly all cells have a nucleus which contains the genetic information and this largely controls the activities of the cell: *cancer cells* ○ *white blood cells.* **5** small group of people forming a centre of (esp revolutionary) political activity: *a terrorist cell.*

□ **ˈcell division** formation of new cells from a single existing cell. The nucleus divides first and then a new membrane develops to separate off the two cells.

ˈcell membrane membrane that surrounds a cell, regulating the substances which pass into and out of the cell.

cellar /ˈselə(r)/ *n* **1** underground room for storing things: *a coal cellar.* **2** = WINE-CELLAR (WINE).

Cellini /tʃeˈliːnɪ/ Benvenuto (1500-71), Italian goldsmith and sculptor. His autobiography provides a vivid picture of the life of a Renaissance craftsman.

cello /ˈtʃeləʊ/ *n* (*pl* ~**s**) stringed musical instrument like a large violin, held between the knees by a seated player. ⇨ illus at MUSIC.

▷ **cellist** /ˈtʃelɪst/ *n* person who plays the cello.

Cellophane /ˈseləfeɪn/ *n* [U] (*propr*) thin transparent material made from viscose and used for wrapping things: [attrib] *cellophane wrapping.*

cellular /ˈseljʊlə(r)/ *adj* **1** of or consisting of cells (CELL 4): *cellular tissue.* **2** (of textile materials) loosely woven: *cellular blankets.*

celluloid /ˈseljʊlɔɪd/ *n* [U] **1** plastic made from cellulose nitrate and camphor, used for making many things, eg toys, toilet articles and (formerly) photographic film. **2** (*dated*) cinema films: [attrib] *the celluloid heroes of one's youth.*

cellulose /ˈseljʊləʊs/ *n* [U] **1** organic substance that forms the main part of all plants and trees and is used in making plastics, paper, etc. **2** any of various compounds of this used in making paint or lacquer.

Celsius /ˈselsɪəs/ *adj* = CENTIGRADE: *the Celsius scale* ○ *Boiling point is 100° Celsius.* ⇨ article at WEATHER.

Celt /kelt; *US* selt/ *n* (**a**) member of an ancient W European people some of whom settled in Britain before the coming of the Romans. At the height of their power the Celts were renowned as fierce fighters and fine horsemen. They were also skilful farmers, cultivating fields on a regular basis with ploughs pulled by oxen instead of manual tools. ⇨ article at WALES. (**b**) one of their descendants, esp in Ireland, Wales, Scotland, Cornwall or Brittany.

▷ **Celtic** *n, adj* (language) of the Celts. ⇨ article at LANGUAGE. **ˌCeltic ˈcross** cross with a circle around the central crossing point of the two arms. **the ˌCeltic ˈfringe** (*sometimes derog*) (people of) Scotland, Wales, Ireland and Cornwall, seen by the English as having a different way of life from their own. **the ˌCeltic ˈtwilight** (*sometimes derog*) atmosphere of mystery and romanticism associated with the Irish and their literature (from the name given by *Yeats to a collection of stories, etc based on Irish folk-tales).

cement /sɪˈment/ *n* [U] **1** grey powder, made by burning lime and clay, that sets hard after mixing with water and is used in building to stick bricks together or for making very hard surfaces: [attrib] *a cement-mixer,* ie a machine for mixing cement with water. **2** (**a**) any similar soft substance that sets firm and is used for sticking things together. Cf ADHESIVE *n,* GLUE. (**b**) substance for filling holes in teeth.

▷ **cement** *v* **1** [Tn] cover (sth) with cement(1). **2** [Tn, Tn·p] ~ **A and B** (**together**) join things together (as) with cement: *He cemented the bricks into place.* **3** [Tn] (*fig*) establish (sth) firmly; strengthen: *cement a friendship.*

cemetery /ˈsemətrɪ; *US* ˈsemәterɪ/ *n* area of land, not a churchyard, used for burying the dead.

CEng *abbr* Chartered Engineer.

cenotaph /ˈsenətɑːf; *US* -tæf/ *n* monument in memory of people buried elsewhere, esp soldiers killed in war. **The Cenotaph** in Whitehall in London honours those who died in the two World Wars.

Cenozoic (*US*) = CAINOZOIC.

censer /ˈsensə(r)/ *n* container in which incense is

burnt in churches.

censor /ˈsensə(r)/ *n* **1** person authorized to examine books, films, plays, letters, etc and remove parts which are considered indecent, offensive, politically unacceptable or (esp in war) a threat to security: *the British Board of Film Censors.* **2** (in ancient Rome) official who prepared a register of all citizens and supervised public morals.

▷ **censor** *v* [Tn] examine or remove parts from (sth), as a censor: *the censored version of a film.*

censorship *n* [U] act or policy of censoring books, etc: *Strict censorship is enforced in some countries.*

censorious /senˈsɔːrɪəs/ *adj* tending to find faults in people or things; severely critical. ▷ **censoriously** *adv.* **censoriousness** *n* [U].

censure /ˈsenʃə(r)/ *v* [Tn, Tn·pr] ~ **sb (for sth)** criticize sb severely; rebuke sb formally: *Two MPs were censured by the Speaker.*

▷ **censure** *n* [U] strong criticism or condemnation; reprimand: *pass a vote of censure (on sb)* ○ *lay oneself open to* (ie risk) *public censure.*

census /ˈsensəs/ *n* (*pl* ~**es**) official counting of a country's population or of other classes of things, eg traffic, for statistical purposes.

cent /sent/ *n* **1** (**a**) one 100th part of a US dollar or of certain other metric units of currency. (**b**) (*abbrs* **c**, **ct**) coin of this value. ⇨ App 9. **2** (idm) **not worth a red cent** ⇨ RED[1].

cent *abbr* century(1b): *in the 20th cent.* Cf c 2.

centaur /ˈsentɔː(r)/ *n* (in Greek mythology) one of a tribe of creatures with a man's head, arms and upper body on a horse's body and legs.

centenarian /ˌsentɪˈneərɪən/ *n, adj* (person who is) 100 years old or more.

centenary /senˈtiːnərɪ; *US* ˈsentənerɪ/ (*US* also **centennial**) *n* 100th anniversary of sth: *The club will celebrate its centenary next year.* ○ [attrib] *centenary year* ○ *centenary celebrations.*

centennial /senˈtenɪəl/ *n* (*US*) = CENTENARY.

▷ **centennial** *adj* **1** occurring every 100 years. **2** of a centenary. **centennially** *adv.*

center *n* (*US*) = CENTRE.

centesimal /senˈtesɪml/ *adj* reckoning or reckoned by hundredths.

cent(i)- *comb form* (forming *ns*) **1** hundred: *centigrade* ○ *centipede.* **2** (in the metric system) one hundredth part of: *centimetre.* ⇨ App 12.

centigrade /ˈsentɪgreɪd/ (also **Celsius**) *adj* (*abbr* **C**) of or using a temperature scale with the freezing-point of water at 0° and the boiling-point at 100°: *a centigrade thermometer* ○ *20°C means twenty degrees centigrade.* Cf FAHRENHEIT. ⇨ App 9,10.

centigram (also **centigramme**) /ˈsentɪgræm/ *n* one 100th part of a gram. ⇨ App 10.

centilitre (*US* **centiliter**) /ˈsentɪliːtə(r)/ *n* (*abbr* **cl**) one 100th part of a litre.

centime /ˈsɒntiːm/ *n* (**a**) one 100th part of a franc. (**b**) coin of this value.

centimetre /ˈsentɪmiːtə(r)/ *n* (*abbr* **cm**) one 100th part of a metre. ⇨ App 9,10.

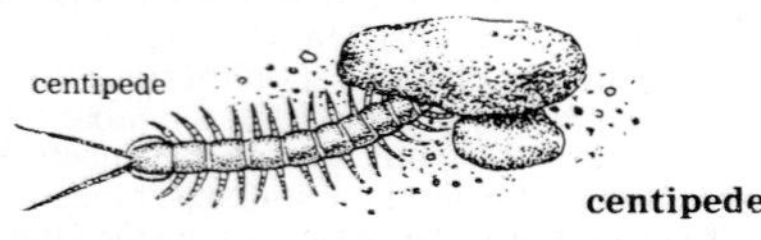

centipede

centipede /ˈsentɪpiːd/ *n* small crawling insect-like creature with a long thin body, numerous joints and a pair of legs at each joint. ⇨ illus.

central /ˈsentrəl/ *adj* **1** (**a**) of, at, near or forming the centre of sth: *We live in central London.* ○ *Our house is very central,* ie is in or close to the centre of the town. ○ *the central plains of N America.* (**b**) easily reached from surrounding areas; convenient: *a theatre with a very central location.* **2** most important; main; principal: *the central point of an argument* ○ *the central character in a novel* ○ *Reducing inflation is central to* (ie a major part of) *the government's economic policy.* **3** having overall power or control: *central government,* ie the government of a whole country, as contrasted with local government ○ *the central committee,* eg of a political party.

▷ **centralism** /ˈsentrəlɪzəm/ *n* [U] principle or system of centralizing.

centralist *n, adj.*

centralize, -ise /ˈsentrəlaɪz/ *v* [I, Tn] (cause sth to) come under the control of one central authority: *Is government becoming too centralized?* **centralization, -isation** /ˌsentrəlaɪˈzeɪʃn; *US* -lɪˈz-/ *n* [U]: *the centralization of power.*

centrally /ˈsentrəlɪ/ *adv.*

□ ˌ**central ˈbank** national bank that does business with the Government and other banks, and issues currency.

the ˌ**Central** ˌ**Criminal ˈCourt** ⇨ THE OLD BAILEY (OLD).

ˌ**central ˈheating** system for heating a building from one source by circulating hot water or hot air in pipes or by linked radiators.

the ˌ**Central Inˈtelligence Agency** (*abbr* **CIA**) federal US organization concerned with foreign affairs, esp spying and national security.

central ˈnervous system part of the nervous system consisting of the brain and spinal cord.

the ˌ**Central ˈPowers** Germany, Austria and Hungary before and during the First World War.

ˌ**central ˈprocessor** part of a computer that controls and co-ordinates the activities of other units and performs the actions specified in the program.

ˌ**central reserˈvation** grass or asphalt strip that separates the two sides of a motorway. ⇨ illus at MOTORWAY.

ˌ**Central ˈStandard Time** (*US*) (*abbr* **CST**) standard time used in a zone that includes the central states of the USA.

Central African Republic /ˌsentrəl ˌæfrɪkən rɪˈpʌblɪk/ **the Central African Republic** country in central Africa; pop approx 2 771 000; official language French; capital Bangui; unit of currency franc. Formerly a French colony it became fully independent in 1960. It is a very poor country, although it has good agriculture and exports diamonds. In 1976 the President, Jean Bédel Bokassa, declared himself emperor and changed the country's name to Central African Empire, until he was overthrown in 1979 following widespread unrest and allegations of atrocities. ⇨ map at ZAÏRE.

Central America /ˌsentrəl əˈmerɪkə/ countries forming the narrow region that joins the continents of North America and South America, ie between Mexico and Colombia. ⇨ map.

centre (*US* **center**) /ˈsentə(r)/ *n* **1** [C] point that is equally distant from all sides of sth; middle point or part of sth: *the centre of a circle* ○ *the centre of London* ○ *a town centre.* ⇨ illus at CIRCLE. **2** [C] point towards which people's interest is directed: *Children like to be the centre of attention.* ○ *The Prime Minister is at the centre of a political row over leaked Cabinet documents.* **3** [C] place from which administration is organized: *a centre of power* ○ *London is a centre of government.* **4** [C] place (eg a town or group of buildings) where certain activities or facilities are concentrated: *a centre of industry, commerce, the steel trade, etc* ○ *a shopping, sports, leisure, community centre.* **5** (esp **the centre**) [sing, Gp] moderate political position or party, ie one between the extremes of left and right: *This country lacks an effective party of the centre.* ○ *Are her views to the left or right of centre?* ○ [attrib] *a centre party.* **6** [C] (**a**) (in football, hockey, etc) centre-forward. (**b**) (in Rugby football) either of two players in the middle of the line of three-quarters. **7** [C] (in football, hockey, etc) kick or hit from the side towards the middle of the pitch. **8** [C] filling in a chocolate or similar sweet: *Do you prefer soft or hard centres?* **9** (idm) **left, right and centre** ⇨ LEFT[2].

▷ **centre** *v* **1** [Tn] place (sth) in or at the centre. **2** [I, Tn] (in football, hockey, etc) kick or hit (the ball) from the side towards the middle of the pitch. ⇨ illus at ASSOCIATION FOOTBALL. **3** (phr v) **centre (sth) on/upon/round sb/sth** have sb/sth as its centre or main concern or theme; be concentrated or concentrate on sb/sth: *The social life of the village centres round the local sports club.* ○ *Her research is centred on the social effects of unemployment.* ○ *Public interest centres on the outcome of next week's by-election.*

□ ˈ**centre-bit** *n* tool for boring holes in wood.

ˈ**centreboard** *n* movable board that can be raised or lowered through a slot in the keel of a sailing-boat to prevent drifting. ⇨ illus at DINGHY.

ˈ**centre-fold** *n* large coloured picture folded to form the middle pages of a newspaper or magazine.

ˌ**centre-ˈforward** (also **centre**) *n* (in football, hockey, etc) player or position in the middle of the forward line: *play (at) centre-forward.*

ˌ**centre-ˈhalf** *n* (in football, hockey, etc) player or position in the middle of the half-back line.

ˌ**centre of ˈgravity** point around which the weight of an object is evenly distributed.

ˈ**centre-piece** *n* (**a**) ornament for the centre of a table, etc. (**b**) most important item, eg in a display.

ˌ**centre ˈspread** two facing middle pages of a newspaper or magazine.

Central America

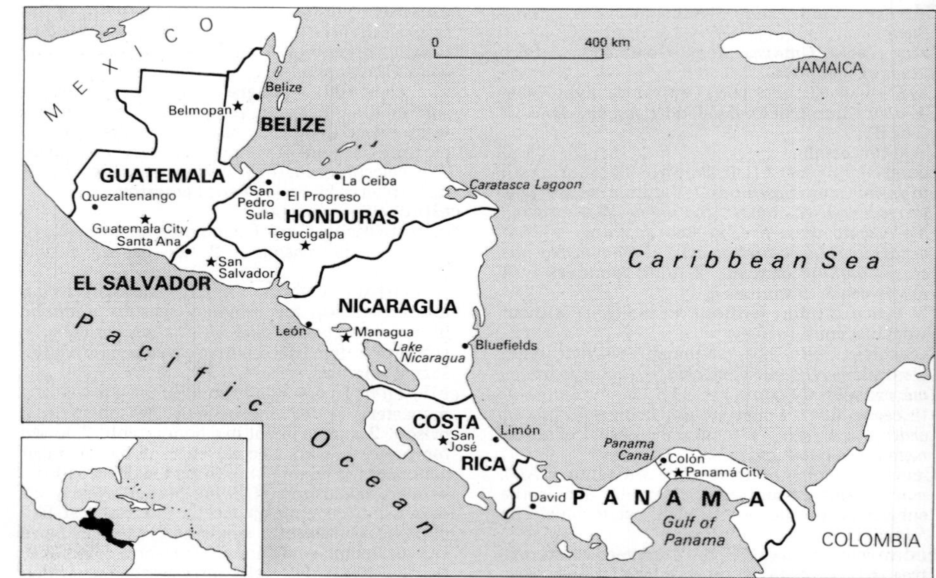

centrifugal /sen'trɪfjʊgl, *also* ˌsentrɪ'fju:gl/ *adj* (**a**) moving away from the centre or axis. (**b**) of or using centrifugal force.

□ **cenˌtrifugal 'force** force that appears to cause an object travelling round a centre to fly outwards and away from its circular path.

centrifuge /'sentrɪfju:dʒ/ *n* rotating machine using centrifugal force to separate substances, eg milk and cream.

centripetal /sen'trɪpɪtl, *also* ˌsentrɪ'pi:tl/ *adj* moving towards the centre or axis.

centrist /'sentrɪst/ *n* person who holds moderate political views. ▷ **centrism** /-ɪzəm/ *n* [U].

centurion /sen'tjʊərɪən; *US* -'tʊər-/ *n* (in ancient Rome) officer commanding a unit of 100 soldiers.

century /'sentʃərɪ/ *n* **1** (**a**) period of 100 years. (**b**) (*abbr* **c**, **cent**) any of the periods of 100 years before or after the birth of Jesus Christ: *the 20th century*, ie AD 1901-2000 or 1900-1999 ○ *at the turn of the century*, ie when one ends and the next begins. **2** (in cricket) score of 100 runs by one batsman in an innings: *make/score a century* ○ *a double century*, ie 200 runs in an innings.

cephalic /sɪ'fælɪk, *also* ke'fælɪk/ *adj* of or in the head: *the cephalic artery*.

cephalopod /'sefələpɒd/ *n* mollusc which has a distinct head with a ring of tentacles round the mouth, eg octopus, squid, etc.

ceramic /sɪ'ræmɪk/ *adj* of or relating to pottery: *ceramic tiles*, ie as used to cover walls or floors.

▷ **ceramics** *n* **1** [sing *v*] art of making and decorating pottery. **2** [pl] objects made of clay, porcelain, etc.

Cerberus /'sɜ:bərəs/ (in Greek mythology) monstrous watchdog with three heads guarding the entrance to *Hades.

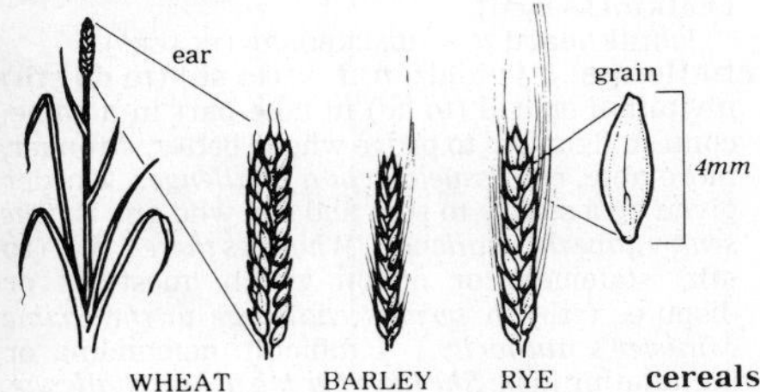

cereals

cereal /'sɪərɪəl/ *n* (**a**) [C] any of various types of grass producing edible grains, eg wheat, rye, oats, barley. ⇨ illus. (**b**) [U] grain produced by such a grass: [attrib] *cereal products*. (**c**) [C, U] (any of various types of) food made from the grain of cereals: *'breakfast cereals* ○ *a bowl of cereal*.

cerebellum /serɪ'beləm/ *n* (*pl* **-la** /-lə/ or **-lums** /-ləmz/) (*anatomy*) part of the brain that controls voluntary muscle movements. ⇨ illus at BRAIN.

cerebral /'serɪbrəl; *US* sə'ri:brəl/ *adj* **1** of the brain: *a cerebral haemorrhage*. **2** intellectual (rather than emotional): *His poetry is very cerebral*.

□ ˌ**cerebral 'cortex** outer layer of the brain in many vertebrates, controlling voluntary movement and the senses, as well as memory, language and thought.

ˌ**cerebral 'palsy** disease in which a person's movements become jerky and uncontrolled because of brain damage before or at birth. Cf SPASTIC.

cerebration /serɪ'breɪʃn/ *n* [U] (*fml or rhet or joc*) working of the brain; thinking.

cerebrospinal /ˌserɪbrəʊ'spaɪnl/ *adj* of the brain and the spine: *cerebro-spinal fluid*, ie the clear colourless fluid in the spaces inside and around the spinal cord and the brain.

cerebrum /'serɪbrəm, *also* sə'ri:brəm/ *n* (*pl* **-bra** /-brə/) principal part of the brain, located in the front of the skull. ⇨ illus at BRAIN.

ceremonial /ˌserɪ'məʊnɪəl/ *adj* of, used for or involving a ceremony; formal: *ceremonial dress* ○ *a ceremonial occasion*.

▷ **ceremonial** *n* [C, U] system of rules and procedures for ceremonies or formal occasions: *the ceremonials of religion* ○ *performed with due ceremonial*.

ceremonially /-nɪəlɪ/ *adv*.

ceremony /'serɪmənɪ; *US* -məʊnɪ/ *n* **1** [C] formal act or series of formal acts performed on a religious or public occasion: *a marriage/wedding ceremony*.

📖 There are different words for certain ceremonies, depending on whether the event is being referred to as a religious service or as a social occasion. For example, *baptism* is the religious term for the service in the Christian Church in which a child is named, but *christening* refers to the whole occasion. Similarly, when two people get married, the ceremony is a *marriage*, but the social event with all the celebration is a *wedding*. And a *burial* service is held for a dead person, but the whole occasion is called a *funeral*. We therefore talk about going to a christening, a wedding or a funeral.

2 [U] formal display or behaviour; formality: *There's no need for ceremony between friends.* ○ *The Queen was crowned with much ceremony.* **3** (idm) **stand on 'ceremony** behave formally: *Please don't stand on ceremony* (ie Please be natural and relaxed) *with me.*

▷ **ceremonious** /ˌserɪ'məʊnɪəs/ *adj* (**a**) full of ceremony; very formal. (**b**) elaborately performed: *He unveiled the picture with a ceremonious gesture.* **ceremoniously** *adv*.

cerise /sə'ri:z, sə'ri:s/ *adj*, *n* [U] (of a) light clear red colour.

CERN (also **Cern**) /sɜ:n/ *abbr* European Organization for Nuclear Research (French *Conseil Européen pour la Recherche Nucléaire*).

cert /sɜ:t/ *n* (*Brit infml*) thing that is sure to happen, be successful, etc; certainty: *Black Widow is a (dead) cert for* (ie is sure to win) *the next race*.

cert *abbr* certified.

certain /'sɜ:tn/ *adj* **1** [pred] ~ (**that...**); ~ (**to do sth**) sure beyond doubt; that can be relied on: *It is certain that he will agree/He is certain to agree.* ○ *One thing is certain: I'm not coming here again.* **2** [pred] ~ (**that...**); ~ (**of/about sth**) positive in one's mind; completely sure: *I'm certain (that) she saw me.* ○ *She saw me: I'm certain of that.* ○ *I'm not certain (of) what she wants.* **3** [attrib] sure to come, happen or be effective; assured: *There is no certain cure for this disease.* ○ *They face certain death unless they can be rescued today.* **4** [attrib] specific but not named or stated: *For certain reasons I will be unable to attend the meeting.* ○ *The terrorists will only release their hostages on certain conditions.* **5** [attrib] named but not known: *A certain Mr Brown telephoned while you were out.* **6** [attrib] slight; some: *There was a certain coldness in her attitude towards me.* ○ *I felt a certain reluctance to tell her the news.* **7** (idm) **for 'certain** without doubt: *I couldn't say for certain when he'll arrive.* ○ *I don't yet know for certain.* **make certain** (**that...**) inquire in order to be sure about sth: *I think there's a train at 8.20 but you ought to make certain.* **make certain of sth/of doing sth** do sth in order to be sure of (doing) sth else: *You'd better leave now if you want to make certain of getting there on time.*

▷ **certain** *pron* ~ **of...** some particular members of (a group of people or things): *Certain of those present had had too much to drink.*

certainly *adv* **1** without doubt; definitely: *He will certainly die if you don't call a doctor.* Cf SURELY. **2** (used in answer to questions) of course: *'May I borrow your pen for a moment?' 'Certainly.'* ○ *'Do you consider yourself a rude person?' 'Certainly not!'*

certainty /'sɜ:tntɪ/ *n* **1** [C] thing that is certain: *England will lose the match — that's a certainty!* ○ *That horse is a certainty*, ie is certain to win. **2** [U] state of being certain: *I can't say with any certainty where I shall be next week.* ○ *We can have no certainty of success.*

NOTE ON USAGE: **Sure** and **certain** are often used in the same way: *They're sure/certain to be late.* ○ *I'm sure/certain (that) they'll be late.* ○ *One thing was sure/certain: they'd be late.* ○ *They made sure/certain (that) they weren't late.* With 'it' as an indefinite subject or object only **certain** can be used: *It was certain/ I thought it certain that they would be late.* **Sure** can sound weaker than **certain**, especially in converstaion: *I'm sure he'll manage it*, ie I think/hope he will.

Cert Ed /ˌsɜ:t 'ed/ *abbr* Certificate in Education: *have/be a Cert Ed* ○ *Jim Smith BA Cert Ed*.

certifiable /ˌsɜ:tɪ'faɪəbl/ *adj* that can or should be certified, esp as insane: *He's certifiable*, ie mad.

certificate /sə'tɪfɪkət/ *n* official written or printed statement that may be used as proof or evidence of certain facts: *a 'birth/'marriage/'death certificate* ○ *an examination certificate*, ie proving that sb has passed an examination.

▷ **certificated** /-keɪtɪd/ *adj* having been awarded a certificate; qualified.

certification /ˌsɜ:tɪfɪ'keɪʃn/ *n* [U] action of certifying or state of being certified.

certify /'sɜ:tɪfaɪ/ *v* (*pt, pp* **-fied**) **1** [Tn, Tf, Cn·a, Cn·n/a, Cn·t] ~ **sb/sth as sth** formally declare (sth), esp in writing or on a printed document: *a document certifying sb's birth* ○ *He certified (that) it was his wife's handwriting.* ○ *The accused has been certified (as) insane/certified to be insane.* **2** [Tn esp passive] officially declare (sb) to be insane: *He was certified and sent to a mental hospital.*

□ ˌ**certified 'cheque** (*US*) cheque that is guaranteed by the bank.

ˌ**certified 'mail** (*US*) (mail sent by a) postal service in which delivery is confirmed by the receiver signing a form. Cf RECORDED DELIVERY (RECORD[2]).

ˌ**certified 'milk** milk produced in dairies that meet strict hygiene regulations.

certitude /'sɜ:tɪtju:d; *US* -tu:d/ *n* [U] (*fml*) feeling of certainty; lack of doubt.

Cervantes /sɜ:'vænti:z/ Miguel de (1547-1616), Spanish novelist and dramatist, famous for his satirical novel in two parts *Don Quixote* (1605,1615).

cervix /'sɜ:vɪks/ *n* (*pl* **cervices** /'sɜ:vɪsi:z/ or **~es** /-vɪksɪz/) (*anatomy*) narrow part of the womb where it joins the vagina. ⇨ illus at FEMALE.

▷ **cervical** /sɜ:'vaɪkl; *US* 'sɜ:vɪkl/ *adj* [esp attrib] **1** of or relating to the cervix: *cervical cancer* ○ *a cervical smear*, ie one taken from the cervix to test for cancer. **2** of or relating to the neck: *cervical vertebrae*.

Cesarian (also **Cesarean**) = CAESAREAN.

cessation /se'seɪʃn/ *n* [U, C] (*fml*) action or act of ceasing; pause: *The bombardment continued without cessation.* ○ *a temporary cessation of hostilities*.

cession /'seʃn/ *n* (*fml*) (**a**) [U] action of ceding sth, esp land or rights. (**b**) [C] thing that is ceded, esp land.

cesspit /'sespɪt/ (also **cesspool** /'sespu:l/) *n* **1** covered pit where liquid waste or sewage is stored temporarily. **2** (*fig*) dirty or corrupt place: *a cesspool of vice*.

CET /si: i: 'ti:/ *abbr* Central European Time.

cetacean /sɪ'teɪʃn/ *n*, *adj* (member) of the order of mammals that includes whales, dolphins and porpoises.

cetane /'si:teɪn/ *n* [U] hydrocarbon of the paraffin series, found in petroleum.

Ceylon /sɪ'lɒn/ former name of *Sri Lanka. ▷ **Ceylonese** /selə'ni:z/ *adj*.

Cézanne /seɪ'zæn/ Paul (1839-1906), French post-impressionist painter who greatly influenced modern art, esp cubism. His work, which is mostly landscape and still life, is dominated by his search for the cube, the cone and the cylinder in nature.

Cf *symb* californium.

cf /ˌsi: 'ef/ *abbr* compare (Latin *confer*). Cf CP.

CFC /ˌsi: ef 'si:/ *abbr* (*chemistry*) chloro-fluorocarbon (any of various gases used in refrigerators, aerosol containers, etc, and thought to be harmful to the earth's ozone layer).

CFE /ˌsiː ef ˈiː/ *abbr* (*Brit*) College of Further Education.

CH /ˌsiː ˈeɪtʃ/ *abbr* Companion of Honour.

ch (also **chap**) *abbr* chapter(1): *the Gospel of St John ch 9 v 4.*

Chablis /ˈʃæbliː/ *n* [U] dry white wine from E France.

cha-cha /ˈtʃɑː tʃɑː/ (also ˌ**cha-cha-ˈcha**) *n* (~**s**) ballroom dance performed with small steps and swaying hip movements: *dance/do the cha-cha.*

Chad /tʃæd/ country in north central Africa, a former French colony which became fully independent in 1960: pop approx 5 401 000; official language French; capital Ndjaména; unit of currency franc. Much of the country is desert but there are deposits of uranium and tungsten. Most of the population lives by agriculture, cotton being the chief crop. ⇨ map at ZAÏRE. ▷ **Chadian** /ˈtʃædɪən/ *n, adj.*

chafe /tʃeɪf/ *v* **1** [I, Ipr] ~ (**at/under sth**) become irritated or impatient (because of sth): *The passengers sat chafing at the long delay.* ○ *chafe under an illness.* **2** [I, Tn] (cause sth to) become sore by rubbing: *Her skin chafes easily.* ○ *His shirt collar chafed his neck.* ○ *chafed hands.* **3** [Tn] warm (sth) by rubbing, esp with the hands: *chafe a baby's feet.*

▷ **chafe** *n* sore place on the skin caused by rubbing.

chaff[1] /tʃɑːf; *US* tʃæf/ *n* [U] **1** outer covering of corn, etc, separated from the grain by threshing or winnowing. Cf HUSK. **2** hay or straw cut up as food for cattle. **3** (idm) **separate the wheat from the chaff** ⇨ SEPARATE[2].

chaff[2] /tʃɑːf; *US* tʃæf/ *v* [Tn, Tn·pr] ~ **sb** (**about sth**) (*dated or fml*) tease sb in a good-natured way: *They chaffed him about his love-life.*

▷ **chaff** *n* [U] good-natured teasing or joking.

chaffinch /ˈtʃæfɪntʃ/ *n* common type of European finch. ⇨ illus at BIRD.

chafing-dish /ˈtʃeɪfɪŋ dɪʃ/ *n* (*dated*) pan with a heater underneath it for cooking food or keeping it warm at table.

Chagall /ʃəˈgaːl/ Marc (1887-1985), Russian-born painter who spent most of his life in France. His use of fantastic images in bright colours was inspired by folk art and the *Fauve school.

chagrin /ˈʃægrɪn; *US* ʃəˈgriːn/ *n* [U] feeling of disappointment or annoyance (at having failed, made a mistake, etc): *Much to his chagrin, he came last in the race.*

▷ **chagrin** *v* [Tn usu passive] affect (sb) with chagrin: *be/feel chagrined at/by sth.*

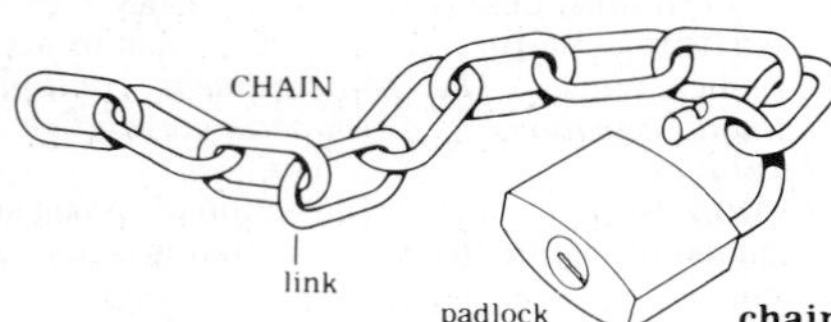

chain

chain /tʃeɪn/ *n* **1** (**a**) [C, U] (length of) connected metal links or rings, used for hauling or supporting weights or for fastening or restraining things: *keep a dog on a chain* ○ *pull the chain*, ie to flush the toilet ○ *Remember to put the chain on the door when you lock it.* ○ *a length of chain.* (**b**) [C] length or loop of chain used for a specific purpose: *a bicycle chain*, ie for transmitting power from the pedals to the wheels ○ *The mayor wore her chain of office round her neck.* ○ *She wore a locket hanging on a silver chain.* ⇨ illus at BICYCLE. ⇨ illus. **2** [C usu *pl*] (*fig*) thing that confines or restrains: *the chains of poverty.* **3** [C] series of connected things: *a chain of mountains/a mountain chain* ○ *a chain of circumstances, events, ideas.* **4** [C] group of shops or hotels owned by the same company: *a chain of supermarkets/a supermarket chain.* **5** [C] (formerly) unit of length (66 feet) for measuring land. ⇨ App 10. **6** (idm) **in chains** (**a**) (of a prisoner) bound with chains. (**b**) not free; kept as a prisoner.

▷ **chain** *v* [Tn esp passive, Tn·pr, Tn·p] ~ **sb/sth** (**to sb/sth**); ~ **sb/sth** (**up**) fasten or confine sb/sth with or as if with a chain: *prisoners chained to a wall, each other* ○ *chain (up) a dog for the night* ○ (*fig*) *Too many women feel chained to the kitchen sink*, ie feel that they spend all their time doing housework.

□ ˈ**chain-gang** *n* (*US*) group of prisoners chained together or forced to work in chains.

ˈ**chain-letter** *n* letter sent to several people each of whom is asked to make copies of it and send them to other people who will do the same.

ˈ**chain-mail** *n* [U] armour made of metal rings linked together.

ˌ**chain reˈaction** (**a**) chemical change forming products which themselves cause more changes so that new compounds are produced. (**b**) series of events each of which causes the next: *The Government fear the strike may produce a chain reaction in other industries.*

ˈ**chain-saw** *n* saw[2] with teeth set on an endless chain and driven by a motor.

ˈ**chain-smoke** *v* [I, Tn] smoke (cigarettes or cigars) continuously, esp by lighting each from the one just smoked. ˈ**chain-smoker** *n.*

ˈ**chain-stitch** *n* (**a**) [U] (in crochet or embroidery) type of sewing in which each stitch makes a loop through which the next stitch is taken. (**b**) [C] stitch made in this way.

ˈ**chain-store** *n* any of a series of similar shops owned by the same company. ⇨ article at SHOP.

chair /tʃeə(r)/ *n* **1** [C] movable seat with a back and sometimes with arms, for one person to sit on: *a table and chairs* ○ *Have/Take a chair*, ie Sit down. ⇨ illus at FURNITURE. **2 the chair** [sing] (position of the) person in charge of a meeting: *She takes the chair in all our meetings.* ○ *Who is in the chair today?* ○ *All remarks should be addressed to the chair.* **3** [C] position of a university professor; professorship: *He holds the chair of philosophy at Oxford.* **4 the chair** [sing] (*US infml*) = THE ELECTRIC CHAIR (ELECTRIC). **5** (idm) (**be/keep sb**) **on the edge of one's seat/chair** ⇨ EDGE[1].

▷ **chair** *v* **1** [Tn] act as chairman of (sth): *chair a meeting.* **2** [Tn, Tn·pr] (*Brit*) carry (sb who has won sth) in a sitting position on the shoulders of a group: *The winning team chaired their captain off the field.*

□ ˈ**chair-lift** *n* series of chairs suspended from an endless cable for carrying people up and down a mountain, etc.

ˈ**chairman** /-mən/ (*pl* **-men**, *fem* ˈ**chairwoman**) **1** person in charge of a meeting: *'Madam Chairman, ladies and gentlemen,' began the speaker.* **2** permanent president of a committee, board of directors of a company, etc: *chairman of the board of governors (of a school)* ○ *the chairman's report*, ie the annual report of a company, presented at its annual general meeting.

ˈ**chairperson** *n* chairman or chairwoman.

NOTE ON USAGE: The affix **-man** is used in a lot of words (eg **chairman**) to indicate positions and occupations which today are filled by both women and men. To avoid sexual bias and unnecessary repetition (*chairman or chairwoman*) **-person** can be used: *chairperson, spokesperson, business person, etc.* **Chair** is increasingly used to mean chairman or chairwoman: *She was the chair of the planning committee.*

chaise longue /ˌʃeɪz ˈlɒŋ; *US* ˈlɔːŋ/ (*pl* **chaises longues** /ˌʃeɪz ˈlɒŋ; *US* ˈlɔːŋ/) (*French*) low chair with a long seat on which the person sitting can stretch out his legs.

chalcedony /kælˈsedənɪ/ *n* [U] type of quartz including many varieties of precious stone.

chalet /ˈʃæleɪ/ *n* **1** (esp in Switzerland) type of mountain hut or cottage built of wood and with an overhanging roof. ⇨ illus. **2** house built in a similar style. **3** small hut in a holiday camp, etc.

chalice /ˈtʃælɪs/ *n* large cup for holding wine, esp one from which consecrated wine is drunk at the Eucharist. ⇨ illus at CHURCH.

chalet

chalk /tʃɔːk/ *n* **1** [U] type of soft white rock used for burning to make lime: [attrib] *a chalk-pit*, ie where chalk is dug ○ *the chalk downs of southern England.* **2** (**a**) [U] this or a similar substance made into white or coloured sticks for writing or drawing on blackboards: *a stick of chalk* ○ *a picture drawn in chalk* ○ *a teacher with chalk on his jacket* ○ [attrib] *chalk dust.* (**b**) [C] one of these sticks: *(a box of) coloured chalks.* **3** (idm) **different as chalk and/from cheese** ⇨ DIFFERENT. **not by a long chalk/shot** ⇨ LONG[1].

▷ **chalk** *v* **1** [I, Tn] write, draw or mark (sth) with chalk. **2** (phr v) **chalk sth out** draw (the outline of sth) with chalk: *The boys chalked out goalposts on the playground wall.* **chalk sth up** (*infml*) (**a**) write sth with chalk, esp on a blackboard: *chalk up one's score*, eg when playing darts. (**b**) achieve or register (a success): *The team has chalked up its fifth win in a row.* **chalk sth up** (**to sb/sth**) give credit (to sb or sb's account) for sth, esp drinks, etc bought in a pub: *Chalk this round up to me, please, barman.*

chalky *adj* (**-ier**, **-iest**) of or like chalk. **chalkiness** *n* [U].

□ ˈ**chalkboard** *n* = BLACKBOARD (BLACK[1]).

challenge[1] /ˈtʃælɪndʒ/ *n* **1** ~ (**to sb**) (**to do sth**) invitation or call (to sb) to take part in a game, contest, fight, etc to prove who is better, stronger, more able, etc: *issue/accept a challenge.* **2** order given by a sentry to stop and say who one is: *The sentry gave the challenge, 'Who goes there?'* **3** ~ (**to sth**) statement or action which questions or disputes (sth): *a serious challenge to the Prime Minister's authority.* **4** difficult, demanding or stimulating task: *She likes her job to be a challenge.* ○ *Reducing the gap between rich and poor is one of the main challenges facing the government.* **5** formal objection, eg to a member of a jury.

challenge[2] /ˈtʃælɪndʒ/ *v* **1** [Tn, Tn·pr, Dn·t] ~ **sb** (**to sth**) invite sb to do sth (esp to take part in a contest or to prove or justify sth): *challenge sb to a duel, a game of tennis* ○ *She challenged the newspaper to prove its story.* **2** [Tn] order (sb) to stop and say who he is: *The sentry challenged the stranger at the gates.* **3** [Tn] question the truth, rightness or validity of (sth); dispute: *challenge sb's authority/right to do sth* ○ *challenge a claim, an assertion, a verdict* ○ *This new discovery challenges traditional beliefs.* **4** [Tn] test the ability of (sb); stimulate: *The job doesn't really challenge him.* **5** [Tn] make a formal objection to (esp a member of a jury).

▷ **challenger** *n* person who challenges, esp in sport.

challenging *adj* offering problems that test sb's ability; stimulating: *a challenging job, test, assignment, etc.*

chalybeate /kəˈlɪbɪət/ *adj* (of mineral or spring water) containing iron salts.

chamber /ˈtʃeɪmbə(r)/ *n* **1** [C] (formerly) room, esp a bedroom. **2 chambers** [pl] (**a**) judge's room for hearing cases that do not need to be taken into court. (**b**) (*Brit*) set of rooms in a larger building, esp the offices in the Inns of Court used by barristers for interviewing clients, etc. **3** [C, CGp] (hall used by an) administrative or legislative assembly, eg one of the houses of a parliament: *The members left the council chamber.* ○ *the Upper/Lower Chamber*, eg (in Britain) the House of Lords/Commons. **4** [C] (**a**) enclosed space or cavity in the body of a animal, in a plant or in some

kinds of machinery: *the chambers of the heart*, ie the auricle and the ventricle ○ *a combustion chamber.* ⇨ illus at PISTON. **(b)** enclosed space under the ground: *The cavers discovered a vast underground chamber.* ○ *a burial chamber*, eg in a pyramid. **5** [C] part of a gun that holds the bullets.
□ ˈ**chamber concert** concert of chamber music.
ˈ**chambermaid** *n* woman whose job is cleaning and tidying bedrooms, usu in a hotel.
ˈ**chamber music** music written for a small group of players (eg a string quartet).
ˌ**chamber of** ˈ**commerce** group of businessmen organized to promote local commercial interests.
ˌ**chamber of** ˈ**horrors** place full of horrifying things, eg the room of criminals in Madame Tussaud's waxworks.
ˈ**chamber orchestra** small orchestra, esp one that performs baroque and early classical music.
ˈ**chamber-pot** *n* pottery vessel for urine, used in bedrooms.

Chamberlain /ˈtʃeɪmbəlɪn/ Arthur Neville (1869-1940), British statesman and Conservative Prime Minister 1937-40. He is chiefly remembered for his policy of appeasement towards Hitler and Germany. He was widely blamed for failing to prevent war and soon replaced as war leader by Winston *Churchill. ⇨ App 2.

chamberlain /ˈtʃeɪmbəlɪn/ *n* (formerly) official who managed the household of a monarch or nobleman.

chameleon /kəˈmiːlɪən/ *n* **1** any of various types of small lizard that can change colour according to its surroundings. **2** (*fig*) person who changes his behaviour or opinions to suit the situation.

chamfer /ˈtʃæmfə(r)/ *v* [Tn] (*architecture*) cut away the square edge of (a beam, post, etc) to give it a flat surface; bevel.
▷ **chamfer** *n* chamfered edge or corner.

chamois /ˈʃæmwɑː; *US* ˈʃæmɪ/ *n* (*pl* unchanged) type of small antelope living in the mountains of Europe and Asia.
□ ˈ**chamois-leather** (also **shammy-leather** /ˈʃæmɪ leðə(r)/, ˈ**shammy**) *n* **(a)** [U] soft leather made from the skin of goats, sheep, deer, etc. **(b)** [C] piece of this: *polish the car with a shammy.*

chamomile = CAMOMILE.

champ[1] /tʃæmp/ *v* **1** [I, Tn] (esp of horses) chew (food) noisily. **2** [Ipr, Tn] ~ **(at/on) sth** (of horses) bite at sth nervously or impatiently: *horses champing at the bit.* **3** [I, Ipr, It] ~ **(at sth)** (used esp in the continuous tenses) be eager or impatient, esp to begin sth: *He was champing with rage at the delay.* ○ *The boys were champing to start.* **4** (idm) ˌ**champ at the** ˈ**bit** (*infml*) be restlessly impatient to start doing sth.

champ[2] /tʃæmp/ *n* (*infml*) = CHAMPION 2.

champagne /ʃæmˈpeɪn/ *n* **1** [C, U] (any of various types of) sparkling white wine from E France: *a ˌglass of chamˈpagne* ○ [attrib] *ˌchampagne ˈcocktails.* **2** [U] colour of this; pale straw colour.

champers /ˈʃæmpəz/ *n* [U] (*sl*) = CHAMPAGNE: *a bottle of champers.*

champion /ˈtʃæmpɪən/ *n* **1** person, team, animal or plant that has defeated or excelled all others in a competition: *a chess champion* ○ *The English football team were world champions in 1966.* ○ *the heavyweight (boxing) champion of the world* ○ [attrib] *a champion swimmer, horse, marrow.* **2** person who fights, argues or speaks in support of another or of a cause(3): *a champion of the poor/of women's rights.*
▷ **champion** *v* [Tn] support the cause of (sb/sth); defend vigorously: *champion the cause of gay rights.*
championship *n* (often *pl*) **1** contest to decide who is the champion: *win the world championship* ○ *The European championships are being held in Rome.* ○ [attrib] *a championship medal.* **2** [C] position of being a champion: *The championship is ours.* ⇨ Usage at SPORT. **3** [U] vigorous support: *her championship of our cause.*
champion *adj* (*Brit or infml*) first-class; splendid: *She looks right champion in that dress!*

chance[1] /tʃɑːns; *US* tʃæns/ *n* **1** [U] way in which things happen without any cause that can be seen or understood; luck; fortune: *Chance plays a big part in many board games.* ○ *It was (pure) chance our meeting in Paris/that we met in Paris.* ○ *trust to chance* ○ *leave nothing to chance*, ie take great care in planning sth to reduce the chance of bad luck ○ *a game of chance*, ie one decided by luck, not skill ○ [attrib] *a chance meeting, encounter, occurrence, happening, etc.* **2** ~ **of (doing) sth/to do sth/that ...** [C, U] possibility; likelihood: *Is there any chance of getting tickets for tonight's performance?* ○ *What are the chances of his coming?* ○ *She has a good chance/no chance/not much chance/only a slim chance of winning.* ○ *What chance of success do we have?* ○ *There's a faint chance that you'll find him at home.* **3** [C] ~ **(of doing sth/to do sth)** occasion when success seems very probable; opportunity: *It was the chance she had been waiting for.* ○ *You won't get another chance of going there.* ○ *Please give me a chance to explain.* ○ *You'd be a fool to ignore a chance like that.* ○ *This is your big chance!* ie your best opportunity of success. ⇨ Usage at OCCASION. **4** [C] risk; gamble: *This road may not be the one we want — but that's a chance we're going to have to take.* **5** [C] unplanned event, esp a lucky one; accident: *By a happy chance a policeman was passing as I was attacked.* **6** (idm) **as ˌchance would ˈhave it** by coincidence; as it happens: *As chance would have it he was going to London as well and was able to give me a lift.* **by ˈany chance** perhaps; possibly: *Would you by any chance have change for £5?* **by ˈchance** by accident; accidentally; unintentionally: *I met her quite by chance.* **a cat in hell's chance** ⇨ CAT[1]. ˈ**chance would be a fine thing** (*infml*) I would like to do sth but will never have an opportunity to do it. **the chances are (that)...** (*infml*) it is likely that...: *The chances are that she'll be coming.* **an even chance** ⇨ EVEN[1]. **even chances/odds/money** ⇨ EVEN[1]. **a fat chance** ⇨ FAT[1]. **a fighting chance** ⇨ FIGHT[1]. **give sb/sth half a ˈchance** give sb/sth some opportunity of being or doing sth: *She's keen and I'm sure she'll succeed given half a chance.* **have an eye for/on/to the main chance** ⇨ EYE[1]. **no chance** (*infml*) there is no possibility of that. **not have a chance/hope in hell** ⇨ HELL. **on the (off) chance (of doing sth/that...)** in the hope of sth happening, although it is unlikely: *I didn't think you'd be at home, but I just called on the ˈoff chance.* **a sporting chance** ⇨ SPORTING. **stand a chance (of sth/of doing sth)** have a chance of (achieving) sth: *He stands a (good/fair) chance of passing the examination.* **take a ˈchance (on sth)** attempt to do sth, in spite of the possibility of failure; take a risk. **take ˈchances** behave riskily: *You should never take chances when driving a car.* **take one's ˈchance** profit as much as one can from one's opportunities.

chance[2] /tʃɑːns; *US* tʃæns/ *v* **1** (*fml*) happen by chance: *She chanced to be in/It chanced that she was in when he called.* ⇨ Usage at APPEAR. **2** [Tn, Tg] (*infml*) risk (sth): *'Take an umbrella.' 'No — I'll chance it (ie risk getting wet).'* ○ *We'll have to chance meeting an enemy patrol.* **3** (idm) ˌ**chance one's ˈarm** (*infml*) take a risk, although it is likely that one will fail. **4** (phr v) **chance on sb/sth** (*fml*) happen to meet sb or find sth.

chancel /ˈtʃɑːnsl; *US* ˈtʃænsl/ *n* part of a church near the altar, used by the priests and the choir. ⇨ illus at CHURCH.

chancellery /ˈtʃɑːnsələrɪ; *US* ˈtʃæns-/ *n* **1** [C] position, department or official residence of a chancellor. **2** [Gp] staff in a chancellor's department. **3** [C] office where business is done in an embassy or a consulate.

chancellor /ˈtʃɑːnsələ(r); *US* ˈtʃæns-/ *n* **1** head of government in Germany and Austria. **2** (*Brit*) honorary head of some universities: *chancellor of London University.* **3** State or law official of various kinds: *the Lord Chancellor*, ie the highest judge (and chairman of the House of Lords).
□ ˌ**Chancellor of the Exˈchequer** (in Britain) cabinet minister responsible for finance. The Chancellor decides the government's economic policy with the Prime Minister, and his department is known as the *Treasury. Cf BUDGET 1b. ⇨ article at PARLIAMENT.

chancery /ˈtʃɑːnsərɪ; *US* ˈtʃænsərɪ/ *n* **1** (*Brit*) Lord Chancellor's division of the High Court of Justice. ⇨ article at LAW. **2** (*US*) court that settles cases according to general principles of justice and fairness not covered by the law; court of equity. **3** office where public records are kept. **4** (idm) **ward in chancery** ⇨ WARD.

chancy /ˈtʃɑːnsɪ/ *adj* (**-ier, -iest**) risky; uncertain: *a chancy business.* ▷ **chancily** *adj.*

chandelier /ˌʃændəˈlɪə(r)/ *n* ornamental hanging light with branches for several bulbs or candles.

Chandler /ˈtʃɑːndlə(r); *US* ˈtʃæn-/ Raymond (Thornton) (1888-1959), American crime story writer who created the detective Philip Marlowe. His books include *The Big Sleep* and *Farewell My Lovely.*

chandler /ˈtʃɑːndlə(r); *US* ˈtʃænd-/ *n* (also **ship's chandler**) dealer in ropes, canvas and other supplies for ships.

change[1] /tʃeɪndʒ/ *v* **1** [I, Tn] (cause sb/sth to) become different; alter: *You've changed a lot since I last saw you.* ○ *Our plans have changed.* ○ *change one's attitude, ideas, opinion, etc* ○ *an event which changed the course of history.* ⇨ Usage. **2 (a)** [Ipr, Tn·pr] ~ **(sb/sth) (from sth) to/into sth** (cause sb/sth to) pass from one form to another: *Caterpillars change into butterflies or moths.* ○ *The witch changed the prince into a frog.* **(b)** [I, Ipr, Tn·pr] ~ **(sb/sth) (from A) (to/into B)** (cause to) pass from one stage to another: *The traffic lights have changed (from red to green).* ○ *Britain changed to a metric system of currency in 1971.* **3 (a)** [Tn, Tn·pr] ~ **sb/sth (for sb/sth)** take or use another instead of sb/sth; replace sb/sth with another: *change one's doctor* ○ *change one's job* ○ *change one's address*, ie move to a new home ○ *change a light bulb* ○ *change gear*, ie engage a different gear in a car, etc in order to travel at a higher or lower speed ○ *I must change these trousers* (ie put on a clean pair) — *they've got oil on them.* ○ *I'm thinking of changing my car for a bigger one.* **(b)** [Tn] move from one (thing, direction, etc) to another; switch: *change sides*, eg in a war, debate, etc ○ *The ship changed course*, ie began to travel in a different direction. ○ *The wind has changed direction.* **(c)** [Tn, Tn·pr] ~ **sth (with sb)** (used with a *pl* object) (of two people) exchange (positions, places, etc): *Can we change seats?/Can I change seats with you?* **(d)** [I, Ipr, Tn] ~ **(from sth to sth)** go from one (train, bus, etc) to another: *Change (trains) at Crewe for Stockport.* ○ *This is where we change from car to bus.* ○ *All change!* ie This train stops here; everyone must leave it. **(e)** [Tn] put different clothes or covering on (sb/sth): *change* (ie put a clean nappy on) *the baby* ○ *change* (ie put clean sheets on) *the beds.* **4** [I, Ipr] ~ **(out of sth) (into sth)** take off one's clothes and put others on: *go upstairs to change* ○ *change* (ie into more formal clothes) *for dinner* ○ *Go and change out of those damp clothes into something dry.* **5** [Tn, Tn·pr] ~ **sth (for/into sth)** give or receive (money) in exchange for the equivalent sum in coins or notes of smaller value or in a different currency: *Can you change a five-pound note?* ○ *I need to change my dollars into francs.* **6** (idm) **change ˈhands** pass into another person's possession: *The house has changed hands several times recently.* **change/swap horses in midstream** ⇨ HORSE. **change one's/sb's ˈmind** alter one's decision or opinion: *Nothing will make me change my mind.* **change ˈplaces (with sb)** (of two people, groups, etc) exchange positions, seats, etc: *Let me change places with you/Let's change places so you can be next to the window.* **change one's spots** (try to) be or do sth that is against one's nature. **change step** adjust one's step when marching so that one is marching in the correct rhythm. ˌ**change the ˈsubject** start talking about sth different. ˌ**change one's ˈtune** (*infml*) alter one's manner or attitude, eg becoming humble instead of insolent. **change one's ways** start to live one's life differently, esp in order to suit changed circumstances. **chop and change** ⇨

CHOP[3]. **a/the leopard can't change it/his spots** ⇨ LEOPARD. **7** (phr v) **change back (into sb/sth)** return to one's earlier form, character, etc: *Cats can never change back into kittens.* **change back (into sth)** take off one's clothes and put on others that one was wearing earlier: *Can I change back into my jeans now?* **change sth back (into sth)** give back (money) and receive the equivalent sum in the original currency: *change back francs into dollars.* **ˌchange ˈdown** engage a lower gear when driving a car, etc. **ˌchange ˈover (from sth) (to sth)** change from one system or position to another: *The country has changed over from military to democratic rule.* **ˌchange ˈup** engage a higher gear when driving a car, etc.

▷ **changeable** /ˈtʃeɪndʒəbl/ *adj* **1** tending to change; often changing: *a changeable person, mood* ○ *changeable weather.* **2** that can be changed.

□ **ˈchange-over** *n* change from one system to another: *a peaceful change-over to civilian rule.*

NOTE ON USAGE: **Change** has a general use and indicates any act of making something different: *Most English women change their names when they marry.* ○ *He changed the design of the house completely.* **Alter** indicates the making of a small difference in the appearance, character, use, etc of something: *I'll have to alter the diagram. I've made a mistake.* **Modify** is more formal. When applied to objects, especially machines, it suggests a partial change in structure or function: *The car has been modified for racing.* It can also indicate the softening of attitudes, opinions, etc: *He'll have to modify his views if he wants to be elected.* **Vary** describes the changing of something or its parts, often temporarily and repeatedly: *It's better to vary your diet rather than eat the same things all the time.* All these verbs (except **modify**) can also be used intransitively: *Her expression changed when she heard the news.* ○ *This place hasn't altered since I was a girl.* ○ *Political opinions vary according to wealth, age, etc.*

change[2] /tʃeɪndʒ/ *n* **1** [C, U] ~ **(in/to sth)** (act of) making or becoming different; alteration: *a change in the weather* ○ *There has been a change in the programme.* ○ *The Government plans to make important changes to the tax system.* ○ *Doctors say there is no change in the patient's condition.* ○ *Are you for or against change?* **2** [C] ~ **(of sth)** **(a)** act of changing one thing for another: *a change of job* ○ *Please note my change of address.* ○ *The party needs a change of leader.* ○ *This is the third change of government the country has seen in two years.* **(b)** thing used in place of another or others: *Don't forget to take a change of* (ie a second set of) *clothes.* **3** [C] ~ **(from sth) (to sth)** **(a)** act of going from one train or bus to another: *He had to make a quick change at Crewe.* **(b)** changed or different routine, occupation or surroundings: *a welcome change from town to country life* ○ *She badly needs a change.* **4** [U] **(a)** coins or notes of lower values equivalent to a single coin or note of a higher value: *Can you give me/Have you got change for a five-pound note?* **(b)** coins of low value: *I've no small change.* **(c)** money returned when the price of sth is less than the amount given in payment: *Don't forget your change!* ○ *25p change.* **5** [C esp *pl*] particular order in which church bells may be rung. **6** (idm) **a change for the ˈbetter/ˈworse** improvement/worsening of sth that already exists or that has gone before: *The situation is now so bad that any change is likely to be a change for the better.* **a ˌchange of ˈair/ˈclimate** different conditions or surroundings: *A change of air* (eg a holiday away from home) *will do you good.* **a ˌchange of ˈheart** great change in one's attitude or feelings, esp towards greater friendliness or co-operation. **the ˌchange of ˈlife** (*euph*) = MENOPAUSE. **for a ˈchange** to vary one's routine; for the sake of variety: *We usually go to France in the summer, but this year we're going to Spain for a change.* **get no change out of sb** (*infml*) receive no help, information, etc from sb. **ring the changes** ⇨ RING[2].

▷ **changeless** *adj* never changing.

□ **ˌchange of ˈphase** (also **ˌchange of ˈstate**) any of a series of changes occurring in matter, esp a solid becoming a liquid or a liquid becoming a vapour, always involving the release or absorption of energy.

ˈchange-ringing *n* [U] traditional ringing of church bells in different series of orders.

changeling /ˈtʃeɪndʒlɪŋ/ *n* child or thing believed to have been secretly substituted for another.

channel /ˈtʃænl/ *n* **1** [C] **(a)** sunken bed of a river, stream or canal. **(b)** passage along which a liquid may flow. **2** [C] navigable part of a stretch of water, deeper than the parts on either side of it: *The channel is marked by buoys.* **3** **(a)** [C] stretch of water joining two seas. **(b)** **the Channel** [sing] = THE ENGLISH CHANNEL (ENGLISH): [attrib] *The Channel crossing was very calm.* **4** [C] (*fig*) any way by which news, information, etc may travel: *Your complaint must be made through the proper channels.* ○ *He has secret channels of information.* **5** [C] **(a)** band of frequencies (FREQUENCY 2) used for broadcasting a particular set of radio or television programmes. **(b)** particular television station: *What's your favourite channel?* **6** [C] path along which electrical signals, esp data signals in a computer, flow.

▷ **channel** *v* (-ll-; *US* also -l-) **1** [Tn] form a channel or channels in (sth): *Deep grooves channelled the soft rock.* **2** [Tn, Tn·pr] carry (sth) in a channel; direct: *Water is channelled through a series of irrigation canals.* ○ (*fig*) *We must channel all our energies into the new scheme.*

Channel Islands /ˈtʃænl aɪləndz/ **the Channel Islands** group of islands in the English Channel off the NW coast of France, the largest of which are Jersey, Guernsey and Alderney. They are the only part of the former dukedom of Normandy still owing allegiance to Britain. The islands are popular with British tourists, having a mild sunny climate and favourable tax rates. ⇨ map at UNITED KINGDOM.

Channel Tunnel /ˌtʃænl ˈtʌnl/ **the Channel Tunnel** (also *infml* **the Chunnel**) tunnel linking Britain and France under the English Channel, now being constructed by a partnership of British and French companies. The tunnel was first proposed in the early 19th century, but political or practical problems prevented progress being made until recently. ⇨ article at RAILWAY.

chant /tʃɑːnt/ *n* **1** simple tune to which psalms or canticles are fitted by singing several syllables or words to the same note. **2** words sung or shouted rhythmically and repeatedly: *The team's supporters sang a victory chant.*

▷ **chant** *v* [I, Tn] **1** sing or recite (a psalm, etc) as a chant: *chant the liturgy.* **2** sing or shout (sth) rhythmically and repeatedly: *'We are the champions!' chanted the football fans.* **chanter** *n* **1** person who chants. **2** pipe with finger-holes that forms part of a set of bagpipes and on which the melody is played.

chanteuse /ʃɒnˈtɜːz; *US* ʃɑːnˈtuːz/ *n* (*French*) female singer of popular songs.

chanty, chantey (*US*) = SHANTY.

chaos /ˈkeɪɒs/ *n* [U] complete disorder or confusion: *The burglars left the house in (a state of) chaos.* ○ *The wintry weather has caused chaos on the roads.*

▷ **chaotic** /keɪˈɒtɪk/ *adj* in a state of chaos; completely disorganized: *With no one to keep order the situation in the classroom was chaotic.* **chaotically** /keɪˈɒtɪklɪ/ *adv.*

chap[1] /tʃæp/ *v* (-pp-) **(a)** [I] (of the skin) become cracked, rough or sore: *My skin soon chaps in cold weather.* **(b)** [Tn esp passive] cause (sth) to become cracked, rough or sore: *chapped lips* ○ *hands and face chapped by the cold.*

▷ **chap** *n* sore crack in the skin.

chap[2] /tʃæp/ *n* (*infml esp Brit*) man or boy; fellow: *Be a good chap and open the door for me, would you?*

chap[3] /tʃæp/ *n* lower jaw or half of the cheek, esp of a pig, as food.

chap *abbr* chapter(1).

chaparral /ˌʃæpəˈræl/ *n* [U] (*US*) dense tangled brushwood, esp in the south-western USA and Mexico.

chapatti (also **chapati**) /tʃəˈpɑːtɪ, *also* tʃəˈpætɪ/ *n* (in Indian cookery) flat thin cake of unleavened bread.

chapel /ˈtʃæpl/ *n* **1** [C] small building or room used for Christian worship, eg in a school, prison, large private house, etc: *a college chapel* ○ *Chapel is* (ie Services in chapel are) *at 8 o'clock.* **2** [C] separate part of a church or cathedral with its own altar, used for small services and private prayer: *a ˈLady chapel,* ie one dedicated to Mary, the mother of Jesus. ⇨ illus at CHURCH. **3** [C] (*Brit*) place used for Christian worship by Nonconformists: *a Methodist ˈchapel* ○ *She goes to/attends chapel regularly.* ○ (*dated*) *Are they church or chapel?* ie Do they belong to the Anglican Church or to a Nonconformist denomination? **4** [CGp] (members of a) branch of a trade union in a newspaper office or printing house: *The chapel voted against a strike.* **5** [C] (*esp US*) local branch of a club, society, etc.

□ **ˌchapel of ˈrest** room in an undertaker's establishment where the body of a dead person is kept before burial, etc so that friends and family may see it.

chaperon /ˈʃæpərəʊn/ *n* (esp formerly) older person, usu a woman, who looks after a girl or a young unmarried woman on social occasions.

▷ **chaperon** *v* [Tn] act as a chaperon for (sb). **chaperonage** *n* [U].

chaplain /ˈtʃæplɪn/ *n* clergyman attached to the chapel of a school, prison, etc, or serving in the armed forces: *an army chaplain.* Cf PADRE.

▷ **chaplaincy** *n* position, period of office or house of a chaplain.

chaplet /ˈtʃæplɪt/ *n* **1** wreath of leaves, flowers, jewels, etc for the head. **2** short string of beads for counting prayers.

Charlie Chaplin

Chaplin /ˈtʃæplɪn/ Sir Charles Spencer ('Charlie') (1889-1977), English film actor and director, who emigrated to the USA in 1910. He is generally regarded as one of the greatest comic actors of the silent cinema, famous for his portrayal of a tramp wearing baggy trousers and a bowler hat, and carrying a cane. He also directed, appeared in and wrote the music for a number of sound films.

chaps /tʃæps/ *n* [pl] thick leather trousers without seats worn by horsemen in the western states of the USA as protection against thorns, etc.

chapter /ˈtʃæptə(r)/ *n* **1** [C] (*abbrs* **ch, chap**) (usu numbered) division of a book: *I've just finished Chapter 3.* **2** [C] period of time: *the most glorious* *chapter in our country's history.* **3** [Gp] **(a)** all the canons of a cathedral or the members of a monastery or convent. **(b)** [C] meeting of these. **4** (idm) **ˌchapter and ˈverse** exact reference to a passage or an authority; exact details of sth: *I can't quote chapter and verse but I can give you the main points the author was making.* **a ˌchapter of ˈaccidents** series or sequence of unfortunate events.

□ **ˈchapter house 1** building or room in a cathedral or monastery where the chapter(3a) holds its meetings. **2** (*US*) building where a college fraternity or sorority holds its meetings.

char[1] /tʃɑː(r)/ *v* **(-rr-)** **(a)** [I, Tn] (cause sth to) become black by burning; scorch: *charred wood.* **(b)** [Tn] reduce (sth) to charcoal by burning: *the charred remains of the bonfire.*

char[2] /tʃɑː(r)/ *n* (*Brit*) = CHARWOMAN.

▷ **char** *v* **(-rr-)** [I] work as a charwoman.

char[3] /tʃɑː(r)/ *n* [U] (*dated Brit infml*) tea: *a cup of char.*

char[4] (also **charr**) /tʃɑː(r)/ *n* (*pl* unchanged) small freshwater fish like a trout.

charabanc /ˈʃærəbæŋ/ *n* (*dated Brit*) early type of bus with bench seats facing forward, used esp for pleasure trips.

character /ˈkærəktə(r)/ *n* **1** [C] **(a)** mental or moral qualities that make a person, group, nation, etc different from others: *What does her handwriting tell you about her character?* ○ *His character is very different from his wife's.* ○ *The British character is often said to be phlegmatic.* **(b)** all those features that make a thing, a place, an event, etc what it is and different from others: *the character of the desert landscape* ○ *The whole character of the village has changed since I was last here.* ○ *The wedding took on the character of* (ie became like) *a farce when the vicar fell flat on his face.* **2** [U] **(a)** striking individuality: *drab houses with no character.* **(b)** moral strength: *a woman of character* ○ *It takes character to say a thing like that.* ○ *Some people think military service is character-building.* **3** [C] **(a)** (*infml*) person, esp an odd or unpleasant one: *He looks a suspicious character.* **(b)** (*approv*) person who is not ordinary or typical; person with individuality: *She's a real/quite a character!* **4** [C] person in a novel, play, etc: *the characters in the novels of Charles Dickens.* **5** [C] reputation, esp a good one: *damage sb's character.* **6** [C] letter, sign or mark used in a system of writing or printing: *Chinese, Greek, Russian, etc characters.* **7** (idm) **in/out of character** typical/not typical of a person's character(1a): *Her behaviour last night was quite out of character.*

▷ **characterless** *adj* (*derog*) without character(2a); uninteresting; ordinary: *a characterless place.*

□ **ˈcharacter assassination** attempt to harm or destroy a person's reputation, eg by spreading rumours about him: *another example of character assassination by the gutter press.*

ˈcharacter actor, ˈcharacter actress actor who specializes in playing odd or eccentric characters.

ˈcharacter reference (*Brit*) written description of a person's qualities; testimonial.

characteristic /ˌkærəktəˈrɪstɪk/ *adj* ~ **(of sb/sth)** forming part of the character(1a) of a person or thing; typical: *He spoke with characteristic enthusiasm.* ○ *Such bluntness is characteristic of him.*

▷ **characteristic** *n* **1** distinguishing feature: *What characteristics distinguish the Americans from the Canadians?* ○ *Arrogance is one of his less attractive characteristics.* **2** part of a logarithm before the decimal point, eg 5 in 5.23. Cf MANTISSA.

characteristically /-klɪ/ *adv*: *Characteristically she took the joke very well.*

characterize, -ise /ˈkærəktəraɪz/ *v* **1** [Cn·n/a] ~ **sb/sth as sth** describe or portray the character of sb/sth as sth: *The novelist characterizes his heroine as capricious and passionate.* **2** [Tn esp passive] be typical of (sb/sth); be characteristic of: *the rolling downs that characterize this part of England* ○ *The giraffe is characterized by its very long neck.*

▷ **characterization, -isation** /ˌkærəktəraɪˈzeɪʃn/ *n* [U] action or process of characterizing(CHARACTERIZE 1), esp the portrayal of human character in novels, plays, etc: *Jane Austen's skill at characterization.*

charade /ʃəˈrɑːd; *US* ʃəˈreɪd/ *n* **1 charades** [sing *v*] game in which one team acts a series of little plays containing syllables of a word which the other team tries to guess. **2** [C] scene in a game of charades. **3** [C] (*fig*) absurd and obvious pretence.

charcoal /ˈtʃɑːkəʊl/ *n* **1** [U] black substance made by burning wood slowly in an oven with a little air, used as a filtering material or as fuel or for drawing: *a stick/piece/lump of charcoal* ○ [attrib] *a charcoal sketch.* **2** (also **charcoal ˈgrey**) [U] very dark grey colour.

□ **ˈcharcoal-burner** *n* (formerly) person making charcoal.

chard /tʃɑːd/ *n* [U] (also **Swiss chard**) type of beet whose leaves are eaten as a vegetable.

charge[1] /tʃɑːdʒ/ *n* **1** [C] claim that a person has done wrong, esp a formal claim that he has committed a crime; accusation: *arrested on a charge of murder/a murder charge* ○ *I resent the charges of incompetence made against me.* **2** [C] rushing violent attack (by soldiers, wild animals, footballers, etc): *lead a charge.* **3** [C] price asked for goods or services: *an admission/entry charge,* eg to visit a museum ○ *His charges are very reasonable.* ○ *All goods are delivered free of charge.* ⇨ Usage at PRICE. **4** **(a)** [U] responsible possession; care; custody: *leave a child in a friend's charge* ○ *He assumed full charge of the firm in his father's absence.* **(b)** [C] (*fml*) person or thing left in sb's care: *He became his uncle's charge after his parents died.* **5** [C] (*fml*) task; duty. **6** [C] amount of explosive needed to fire a gun or cause an explosion. **7** [C] **(a)** amount of electricity put into a battery or contained in a substance: *a positive/negative charge.* **(b)** energy stored chemically for conversion into electricity. **8** [C] (*fml*) instructions; directions: *the judge's charge to the jury,* ie his advice to them about their verdict. **9** [C] (in heraldry) design on a coat of arms; bearing(6). **10** (idm) **bring a charge (of sth) against sb** formally accuse sb (of a crime, etc). **a charge on sb/sth** person or thing that must be paid for as part of a particular area of expenditure: *They are a charge on the rates.* **face a charge/charges** ⇨ FACE[2]. **give sb in ˈcharge** (*esp Brit*) hand sb over to the police. **have charge of sth** have responsibility for sth. **in charge (of sb/sth)** in a position of control or command (over sb/sth): *Who's in charge here?* ○ *He was left in charge of the shop while the manager was away.* **in/under sb's charge** in the care of sb: *These patients are under the charge of Dr Wilson.* **lay sth to sb's charge** (*fml*) accuse sb of sth. **prefer a charge/charges** ⇨ PREFER. **put sb on a ˌcharge** charge sb with a specified offence, esp under military law. **reverse the charges** ⇨ REVERSE[3]. **take charge (of sth)** take control of sth; become responsible for sth: *The department was badly organized until she took charge (of it).*

□ **ˈcharge account** (*US*) = CREDIT ACCOUNT (CREDIT[1]).

ˈcharge card credit card that can be used in a particular store or group of stores, on condition that the account is paid in full when a statement is issued.

the ˌCharge of the ˈLight Brigade famous charge by British cavalry during the *Crimean War in 1854. The attack was pointless in military terms and made because an order had been misunderstood. 247 out of 637 men were killed. *Tennyson wrote a stirring poem about the event.

ˈcharge-sheet *n* (*Brit*) record kept in a police station of charges (CHARGE[1] 1) made.

charge[2] /tʃɑːdʒ/ *v* **1** **(a)** [Tn, Tn·pr] ~ **sb (with sth)** accuse sb of sth, esp formally in a court of law: *He was charged with murder.* ○ *She charged me with neglecting my duty.* **(b)** [Tf] (*fml*) claim; assert: *It is charged* (ie in a court of law) *that on 30 November, the accused….* **2** **(a)** [I, Ipr, Tn] ~ **((at) sb/sth)** rush forward and attack (sb/sth): *The troops charged (at) the enemy lines.* ○ *One of our strikers was violently charged by a defender,* ie in a game of football. **(b)** [Ipr, Ip] ~ **down, in, up, etc** rush in the specified direction: *The children charged down the stairs.* **3** [I, Ipr, Tn, Tn·pr, Dn·n] ~ **(sb/sth) for sth**; ~ **(sb) sth (for sth)** ask (an amount) as a price: *How much do you charge for mending shoes?* ○ *As long as you've paid in advance we won't charge you for delivery.* ○ *I'm not going there again — they charged (me) £1 for a cup of coffee!* **4** [Tn] **(a)** load (a gun). **(b)** (*fml*) fill (a glass): *Please charge your glasses and drink a toast to the bride and groom!* **5** **(a)** [Tn] put a charge[1](7a) into (sth): *charge a battery.* **(b)** [esp passive: Tn, Tn·pr] ~ **sth (with sth)** (*fig*) fill sth (with an emotion): *a voice charged with tension* ○ *The atmosphere was charged with excitement.* **6** [Tn, Cn·t] (*fml*) give (sb) a responsibility; command; instruct: *I charge you not to forget what I have said.* ○ *The judge charged the jury,* ie advised them about their verdict. **7** (phr v) **charge sth (up) to sb**; **charge sth up** record sth as a debt to be paid by sb: *Please charge these goods (up) to my account.* **charge sb/oneself with sth** (*fml*) give sb/oneself a duty or responsibility: *She was charged with an important mission.*

chargeable /ˈtʃɑːdʒəbl/ *adj* **1** **(a)** able or liable to be charged (CHARGE[2] 1a): *If you steal, you are chargeable with theft.* **(b)** liable to result in a legal charge: *a chargeable offence.* **2** ~ **to sb** (of a debt) to be paid by sb or put on sb's account: *Any expenses you may incur will be chargeable to the company.*

chargé d'affaires /ˌʃɑːʒeɪ dæˈfeə(r)/ *n* (*pl* **chargés d'affaires** /ˌʃɑːʒeɪ dæˈfeə(r)/) **1** diplomat who takes the place of an ambassador or a minister when the ambassador or minister is absent. **2** diplomat below the rank of ambassador or minister who heads a diplomatic mission in a minor country.

charger /ˈtʃɑːdʒə(r)/ *n* (*arch*) horse ridden by a soldier in battle; cavalry horse.

chariot /ˈtʃærɪət/ *n* horse-drawn open vehicle with two wheels, used in ancient times in battle and for racing.

▷ **charioteer** /ˌtʃærɪəˈtɪə(r)/ *n* person driving a chariot.

charisma /kəˈrɪzmə/ *n* (*pl* ~**s** or ~**ta**) **1** [U] power to inspire devotion and enthusiasm: *a politician with charisma.* **2** [C] (*religion*) power or talent given by God.

▷ **charismatic** /ˌkærɪzˈmætɪk/ *adj* **1** having charisma: *a charismatic figure, leader, politician, etc.* **2** (of a religious group) emphasizing the divine gifts, eg the power to heal the sick. **charismatically** /-klɪ/ *adv.*

charitable /ˈtʃærətəbl/ *adj* ~ **(to/towards sb) 1** generous in giving money, food, etc to poor people. **2** of, for or connected with a charity(4) or charities: *a charitable institution, organization, body, etc* ○ *a charitable venture,* ie one to raise money for charity. **3** kind in one's attitude to others: *That wasn't a very charitable remark.* ▷ **charitably** /-blɪ/ *adv.*

charity /ˈtʃærətɪ/ *n* **1** [U] loving kindness towards others. **2** [U] tolerance in judging others; kindness; leniency: *judge people with charity.* **3** [U] **(a)** (generosity in) giving money, food, help, etc to the needy: *do sth out of charity* ○ *raise money for charity* ○ [attrib] *a charity ball, concert, jumble sale, etc.* **(b)** help given in this way: *live on/off charity.* **4** [C] society or organization for helping the needy: *Many charities sent money to help the victims of the famine.* ⇨ article. **5** (idm) **charity begins at ˈhome** (*saying*) a person's first duty is to help and care for his own family.

□ **the ˈCharity Commission** organization responsible for controlling all the charities in Britain. **the ˌCharity Comˈmissioners** those who run this organization.

charlady /ˈtʃɑːleɪdɪ/ *n* = CHARWOMAN.

charlatan /ˈʃɑːlətən/ *n* person who falsely claims to have special knowledge or skill, esp in medicine.

▷ **charlatanism** *n* [U].

Charlemagne /ˈʃɑːləmeɪn/ (724-814), King of the

Charities

There are over 150 000 charities in Britain. They raise money for many different causes, from caring for the poor and disadvantaged to funding vital medical research. Among the best known, with the highest incomes, are the National Trust, the Royal Society for the Prevention of Cruelty to Animals (RSPCA), the Royal National Lifeboat Institution (RNLI), Oxfam, the Imperial Cancer Research Fund, the Cancer Research Campaign, the Salvation Army, Barnados, the Save the Children Fund, the Guide Dogs for the Blind Association, and the National Society for the Prevention of Cruelty to Children (NSPCC).

Charities raise money in many ways. Volunteers visit homes and ask for donations, or collect contributions on busy shopping streets on Saturdays. In both these cases the people who donate money are given a small paper sticker to wear. (Formerly, small paper 'flags' were pinned to clothing, so that such collection days were known as 'flag days', a term still sometimes used.) Some charities hold special national fund-raising weeks for this purpose.

At a local level, many kinds of events are held to raise money for national and local charities. They include coffee mornings, bring-and-buy sales, car-boot sales, fêtes, raffles, amateur sports contests or dramatic entertainments. Sponsored sporting events, in which people take part in an organized walk, run, swim, etc and are 'sponsored' by people who agree to give a certain sum to a particular charity if the event is successfully completed, are increasingly popular.

Charity appeals are regularly made on radio and television. One kind of fund-raising event on television is the 'telethon', in which famous people appear or perform for no fee. Such programmes can bring in millions of pounds from the public, and the 27-hour *Telethon* held by Independent Television in 1990 to raise money for old people, children, the disabled and regional charities raised over £26 million.

Many firms give to charity, with large companies like British Petroleum and Marks and Spencer donating millions of pounds annually. Some people, especially rich people who have no heirs, leave large sums to charity in their wills. Many charities obtain much of their income in this way.

Voluntary donations are also collected locally for 'good causes' other than registered charities. For example, a fête might be held to raise money for repairs to the roof of the parish church.

There is an established tradition of charity work among show business and sports personalities, and celebrities often 'sponsor' a favourite charity by becoming personally involved with its work and its fund-raising. Members of the royal family are involved with many charities, usually as president.

An official register of charities is kept by the Charity Commission, which is responsible for overseeing their activities, giving them advice and preventing fraud. One of the functions of the Commission is to receive the income from land and investments held by charities and to return it to them free of income tax. This tax relief helps charities considerably.

Franks and, from 800, Holy Roman Emperor. He conquered the Saxons, the Bavarians and the Lombards, reformed government and encouraged the development of learning at his court in Aachen.

Charles I /tʃɑ:lz/ (1600-49), son of James I and king of England, Scotland and Ireland 1625-49. He tried to rule without parliament from 1629 to 1640, until he became involved in war with Scotland. The *Long Parliament would not cooperate with him, and this led to the English Civil War in 1642. Royalist forces were finally defeated in 1648 and Charles was beheaded in 1649. ⇨ App 3.

Charles II /tʃɑ:lz/ (1630-85), son of Charles I and king of England, Scotland and Ireland, 1660-85. After nine years of exile, he was restored to the throne following the collapse of Cromwell's regime in 1660. ⇨ App 3.

Charles' Law /ˈtʃɑ:lz lɔ:/ (*chemistry*) law stating that the volume of an ideal gas at constant pressure is directly proportional to the absolute temperature.

Charleston /ˈtʃɑ:lstən/ *n* fast dance, popular in the 1920s, in which the knees are turned inwards and the legs kicked sideways.

charlie /ˈtʃɑ:lɪ/ *n* (*Brit infml*) foolish person: *You must have felt a proper charlie!* ○ *He looks a real charlie in that hat.*

charlotte /ˈʃɑ:lət/ *n* [C, U] pudding made of stewed apple or other fruit with a covering or layer of crumbs, biscuits, etc.

□ **charlotte russe** /ˌʃɑ:lət ˈru:s/ sweet dish consisting of a mould of custard or cream encased in sponge cake or sponge biscuits.

charm[1] /tʃɑ:m/ *n* **1** (**a**) [U] power of pleasing, fascinating or attracting people; attractiveness: *a woman of great charm* ○ *He has a lot of charm.* ○ *the charm of the countryside in spring*. (**b**) [C] pleasing or attractive feature or quality: *a woman's charms*, ie her beauty or attractive manner. **2** [C] (**a**) object worn because it is believed to protect the wearer and bring good luck. ⇨ article at SUPERSTITION. (**b**) small ornament worn on a chain or bracelet: [attrib] *a ˈcharm bracelet*. **3** [C] act or words believed to have magic power; magic spell. **4** (idm) **ˌwork like a ˈcharm** (*infml*) be immediately and completely successful: *Those new pills you gave me worked like a charm.*

charm[2] /tʃɑ:m/ *v* [Tn] **1** please, fascinate or attract (sb); delight: *He charms everyone he meets.* ○ *He was charmed by her vivacity and high spirits.* **2** influence or protect (sb/sth) by or as if by magic: *He has/leads a charmed life*, ie has escaped many dangers, as if protected by magic. **3** (phr v) **charm sth from/out of sb/sth** get sth from sb/sth by using charm: *She could charm the birds from the trees!*

▷ **charmer** *n* person who charms people of the opposite sex.

charming *adj* delightful: *a charming man, village, song*. **charmingly** *adv.*

charnel-house /ˈtʃɑ:nl haʊs/ *n* (formerly) place for keeping dead human bodies or bones.

Charolais (also **Charollais**) /ˈʃærəleɪ; *US* ˌʃærəˈleɪ/ *n* (*pl* unchanged) type of large white cow reared for its meat: [attrib] *a Charolais cow, herd.*

Charon /ˈkeərən/ (in Greek mythology) ferryman who took the souls of the dead across the rivers *Styx and *Acheron to *Hades.

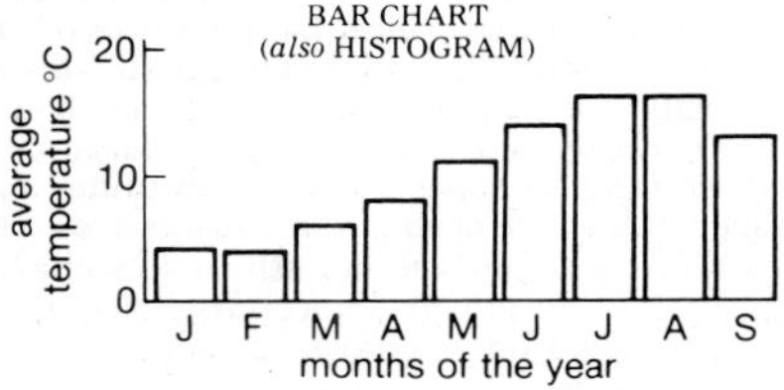

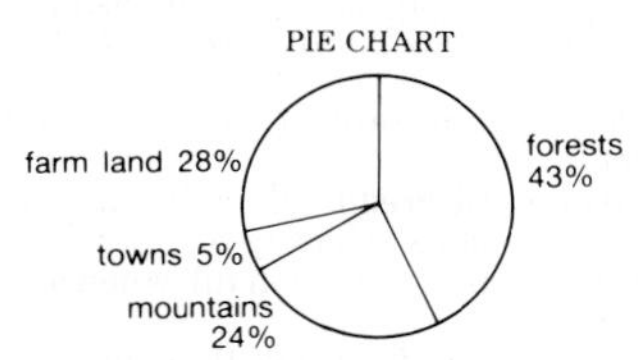

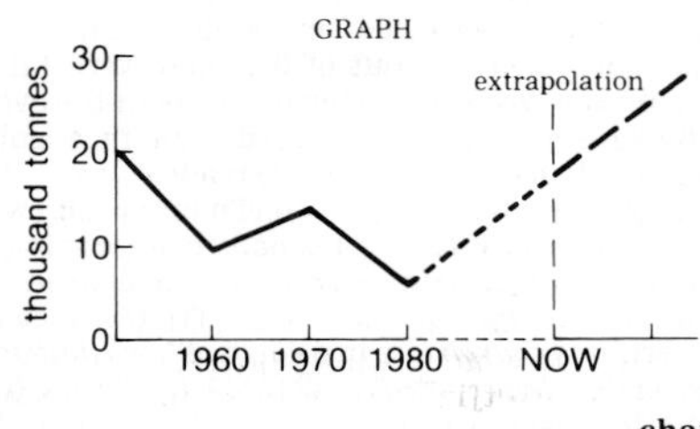

charts

chart /tʃɑ:t/ *n* **1** [C] (**a**) detailed map used to help navigation at sea, showing coasts, rocks, the depth of the sea, etc: *a naval chart*. (**b**) similar map for navigation by air. **2** [C] map, diagram, graph or table giving clear information, esp about sth that changes over a period of time: *a weather chart* ○ *a temperature chart*, ie one showing changes in a person's temperature ○ *a sales chart*, ie one showing the level of a company's sales. ⇨ illus. Cf MAP, PLAN 2. **3 the charts** [pl] weekly list of the best-selling pop music records.

▷ **chart** *v* **1** [Tn] make a chart of (sth); map. **2** [Tn] record or follow (sth) on or as if on a chart: *Scientists are carefully charting the progress of the spacecraft.*

charter /ˈtʃɑ:tə(r)/ *n* **1** (**a**) written statement by a ruler or a government granting certain rights and privileges to a town, company, university, etc: *privileges granted by royal charter*. (**b**) written statement of the main functions and principles of an organization or institution; constitution. **2** hiring of a ship, an aircraft or a vehicle for a particular purpose or group of people: [attrib] *a ˈcharter plane.*

▷ **charter** *v* [Tn] **1** grant a charter(1a) to (sb/sth). **2** hire (an aircraft, etc) for a particular purpose: *a chartered plane.*

chartered /ˈtʃɑ:təd/ *adj* [attrib] qualified according to the rules of a professional association which has a royal charter: *a chartered engineer, librarian, surveyor, etc.* **ˌchartered acˈcountant** (*Brit*) (*US* **ˌcertified ˌpublic acˈcountant**) fully trained and qualified accountant.

□ **ˈcharter flight** flight by a chartered aircraft.

ˈcharter-member *n* member who joins an organization when it is first formed.

ˈcharter-party *n* (*commerce*) agreement for the hire of a ship for a particular voyage or period of time.

Chartism /ˈtʃɑ:tɪzəm/ *n* [U] movement in Britain in the 1830s seeking electoral and social reform. ▷ **Chartist** /ˈtʃɑ:tɪst/ *n.*

chartreuse /ʃɑ:ˈtrɜ:z; *US* ʃɑ:ˈtru:z/ *n* [U] **1** green or yellow liqueur made with herbs. **2** yellowish-green colour.

charwoman /ˈtʃɑ:wʊmən/ (also **charlady**, **char**) *n* woman employed to clean a house, an office building, etc.

chary /ˈtʃeərɪ/ *adj* (**-ier**, **-iest**) ~ (**of sth**) **1** cautious; wary: *chary of lending money.* **2** sparing: *chary of giving praise*, ie seldom praising people. ▷ **charily** *adv.*

Charybdis /kəˈrɪbdɪs/ *n* (idm) **between Scylla and Charybdis** ⇨ SCYLLA.

chase[1] /tʃeɪs/ *v* **1** [Ipr, Tn] ~ **(after) sb/sth** run after in order to capture or overtake sb/sth: *My dog likes chasing rabbits.* ○ *He chased (after) the burglar but couldn't catch him.* **2** [Ipr, Tn] ~ **(after) sb** make sexual advances to sb in an unsubtle way: *He's always chasing (after) women.* **3** [Tn] (*infml*) try to win (sth): *Liverpool are chasing their third league title in four years.* **4** (phr v) **chase about, around, etc** rush or hurry in the specified direction: *I've been chasing around town all morning looking for a present for her.* **chase sb/sth away, off, out, etc** force sb/sth to run away, etc; drive sb/sth away, etc: *chase the cat out of the kitchen.* **chase sb up** (*Brit infml*) contact sb and try to obtain esp money or information: *chase up clients with outstanding debts.* **chase sth up** (*Brit infml*) try to investigate sth or make sth happen more quickly: *chase up a delayed order.*

chase[2] /tʃeɪs/ *n* **1** [C] act of chasing; pursuit: *The criminal was caught after a car chase.* **2 the chase** [sing] hunting, esp fox-hunting, considered as a sport. **3** [C] area of land that is not fenced in, where deer or other animals are bred and hunted. **4** (idm) **give ˈchase** begin to run after sb/sth: *After the robbery the police immediately gave chase.* **ˌgive up the ˈchase** stop chasing sb/sth. **a wild goose chase** ⇨ WILD.

chase[3] /tʃeɪs/ *v* [Tn] cut patterns or designs on (metal); engrave or emboss: *chased silver.*

chaser /ˈtʃeɪsə(r)/ *n* **1** horse for steeplechasing. **2** (*infml*) drink taken after another of a different kind, eg a weaker alcoholic drink after a strong one.

chasm /ˈkæzəm/ *n* **1** deep opening in the ground; abyss; gorge. **2** (*fig*) wide difference of feelings or interests between people, groups, etc: *the vast chasm separating rich and poor.*

chassé /ˈʃæseɪ; *US* ʃæˈseɪ/ *n* (*French*) gliding sideways step in dancing.

chassis /ˈʃæsɪ/ *n* (*pl* unchanged /ˈʃæsɪz/) framework on which the body and working parts of a vehicle, radio or television are built. ⇨ illus at CAR.

chaste /tʃeɪst/ *adj* **1** (*dated*) not having had sexual intercourse; virgin. **2** not having sexual intercourse except with the person to whom one is married. **3** pure; virtuous. **4** simple in style; not ornate. ▷ **chastely** *adv.*

chasten /ˈtʃeɪsn/ *v* [Tn] **1** punish (sb) in order to correct or improve; discipline. **2** subdue (sb); restrain: *a chastening experience* ○ *He was chastened by his failure.*

chastise /tʃæˈstaɪz/ *v* [Tn] (*fml*) punish (sb) severely, esp by beating.

▷ **chastisement** /tʃæˈstaɪzmənt, *also* ˈtʃæstɪzmənt/ *n* [C, U] (*fml*) severe punishment.

chastity /ˈtʃæstətɪ/ *n* [U] (state of) being chaste(1, 2, 3): *vows of chastity*, eg those taken by a nun or a monk.

chasuble /ˈtʃæzjʊbl/ *n* loose garment worn over all other vestments by a priest celebrating the Eucharist.

chat /tʃæt/ *n* [C, U] friendly informal conversation: *I had a long chat with her (about her job).* ○ *That's enough chat — get back to work.* ⇨ Usage at TALK.

▷ **chat** *v* (**-tt-**) **1** [I, Ipr, Ip] ~ **(away)**; ~ **(to/with sb) (about sth)** have a chat: *They were chatting (away) in the corner.* ○ *What were you chatting to him about?* **2** (phr v) **chat sb up** (*Brit infml*) talk to sb in a friendly or flirtatious manner in order to gain his or her confidence: *Who was that pretty girl you were chatting up last night?*

chatty *adj* (**-ier, -iest**) **1** fond of chatting. **2** resembling chat; informal: *a chatty description.* **chattily** *adv.* **chattiness** *n* [U].

□ **ˈchat show** television or radio programme in which (esp well-known) people are interviewed.

château /ˈʃætəʊ; *US* ʃæˈtəʊ/ *n* (*pl* ~**x** /-təʊz/) castle or large country house in France.

chatelaine /ˈʃætəleɪn/ *n* **1** woman who is head of a large household. **2** set of short chains attached to a woman's belt, for carrying keys, etc.

chattel /ˈtʃætl/ *n* (idm) **sb's goods and chattels** ⇨ GOODS.

chatter /ˈtʃætə(r)/ *v* **1** [I, Ipr, Ip] ~ **(away/on) (about sth)** talk quickly, continuously or foolishly about unimportant matters: *Do stop chattering on about the weather when I'm trying to read.* **2** [I, Ip] ~ **(away)** (of birds and monkeys) make short repeated high-pitched noises: *sparrows chattering in the trees.* **3** [I, Ip] ~ **(together)** (of the teeth) strike together with a clicking sound because of cold or fear.

▷ **chatter** *n* [U] **1** continuous rapid talk: *I've had enough of your constant chatter.* **2** chattering sound: *the chatter of monkeys.*

□ **ˈchatterbox** *n* talkative person, esp a child.

Chaucer /ˈtʃɔːsə(r)/ Geoffrey (c 1343-1400), English poet. His best-known work is *The Canterbury Tales*, a cycle of linked stories in narrative verse as told by a group of pilgrims travelling from London to Canterbury. He is often called 'the father of English poetry'.

chauffeur /ˈʃəʊfə(r); *US* ʃəʊˈfɜːr/ *n* person employed to drive a car, esp for sb rich or important.

▷ **chauffeur** *v* [Tn] drive (sb) as a chauffeur.

chauvinism /ˈʃəʊvɪnɪzəm/ *n* [U] **1** aggressive and irrational belief that one's own country is better than all others. **2** = MALE CHAUVINISM (MALE).

▷ **chauvinist** /ˈʃəʊvɪnɪst/ *n, adj* (person) displaying or feeling chauvinism. **chauvinistic** /ˌʃəʊvɪˈnɪstɪk/ *adj.* **chauvinistically** /-klɪ/ *adv.*

ChB /ˌsiː eɪtʃ ˈbiː/ *abbr* Bachelor of Surgery (Latin *Chirurgiae Baccalaureus*): *have/be a ChB* ○ *Philip Watt MB, ChB.*

cheap /tʃiːp/ *adj* (**-er, -est**) **1** (**a**) low in price; costing little money: *cheap tickets, fares* ○ *the cheap seats in a theatre* ○ *Cauliflowers are very cheap at the moment.* (**b**) worth more than the cost; offering good value: *£3 is very cheap for a hardback book.* **2** charging low prices: *a cheap hairdresser, restaurant.* **3** of poor quality; shoddy: *cheap furniture, jewellery, shoes.* **4** insincere; shallow(2): *cheap flattery.* **5** (of people, words or actions) not worthy of respect; despicable; contemptible: *a cheap gibe, joke, remark, retort, etc* ○ *That was a cheap trick to play on her.* ○ *He's just a cheap crook.* ○ *His treatment of her made her feel cheap.* **6** (*esp US*) excessively careful with one's money; mean; stingy. **7** (idm) **cheap/common as dirt** ⇨ DIRT. **ˌcheap and ˈcheerful** cheap but showing good taste and imagination: *walls covered in cheap and cheerful posters.* **ˌcheap and ˈnasty** costing little to buy and unattractive or of bad quality: *a rented flat full of cheap and nasty furniture.* **cheap at the price** so well worth having that the price, however high it is, does not seem too much: *The holiday will be very expensive but if it helps to make you fit and healthy again it will be cheap at the price.* **ˌhold sth ˈcheap** (*fml*) consider sth to be of little value or importance. **ˌmake oneself ˈcheap** do sth which causes other people to respect one less. **on the ˈcheap** (*infml*) without paying the usual, or a fair, price: *buy, sell, get sth on the cheap.*

▷ **cheap** *adv* (*infml*) **1** for a low price: *get sth cheap* ○ *sell sth off cheap.* **2** (idm) **ˌgo ˈcheap** (*infml*) be offered for sale at a low price: *The local shop has some radios going cheap.*

cheaply *adv* **1** for a low price: *buy, sell, get sth cheaply.* **2** in a cheap(1a) manner: *The room was cheaply furnished.* **3** (idm) **get off lightly/cheaply** ⇨ LIGHTLY (LIGHT[3]).

cheapness *n* [U].

cheapen /ˈtʃiːpən/ *v* **1** [I, Tn] (cause sth to) become cheap or cheaper: *cheapen the cost of sth.* **2** [Tn] make (oneself/sth) less worthy of respect; degrade: *It's only cheapening yourself to behave like that.*

cheapjack /ˈtʃiːpdʒæk/ *n* person who sells inferior goods at low prices.

▷ **cheapjack** *adj* inferior; shoddy.

cheapskate /ˈtʃiːpskeɪt/ *n* (*infml esp US*) mean or stingy person; miser.

cheat /tʃiːt/ *v* **1** [I, Ipr] ~ **(at sth)** act dishonestly or unfairly in order to win an advantage or profit: *accuse sb of cheating at cards.* **2** [Tn] trick or deceive (sb/sth): *cheat the taxman*, ie avoid one's taxes ○ (*fig*) *cheat death*, ie come close to dying but stay alive by luck or cunning. **3** [Ipr, Tn] ~ **(on) sb** (*esp US*) be unfaithful to one's wife, husband or lover. **4** (phr v) **cheat sb (out) of sth** prevent sb from having sth, esp in an unfair or a dishonest way: *He was cheated (out) of his rightful inheritance.*

▷ **cheat** *n* **1** person who cheats, esp in a game. **2** dishonest trick.

check[1] /tʃek/ *v* **1** (**a**) [I, Ip, Tf no passive, Tw no passive] ~ **(up)** make sure of sth by examining or investigating it: *I think I remembered to switch the oven off but you'd better check (up) (that I did).* ○ *Could you go and check if the baby's asleep?* (**b**) [Tn] examine (sth) in order to make sure that it is correct, safe, satisfactory or in good condition: *check the oil*, ie make sure there is enough oil in a car engine ○ *check the tyres*, ie make sure there is enough air in a car's tyres ○ *check the items against the list*, ie to see that it tallies ○ *He must check his work more carefully — it's full of mistakes.* (**c**) [I, Ipr] ~ **(with sth)** (*US*) agree or correspond (with sth) when compared; tally: *Ring his wife and see if his story checks (out).* ○ *His prints check with those on the gun.* **2** [Tn] (**a**) cause (sb/sth) to stop or go more slowly; slow down; control: *check the enemy's advance* ○ *check the flow of blood from a wound* ○ *The Government is determined to check the growth of public spending.* (**b**) hold (sth) back; restrain (sth/oneself): *unable to check one's laughter, tears, anger.* **3** [I] stop suddenly: *She went forward a few yards, checked and turned back.* **4** [I, Tn] (in chess) put (one's opponent) in a position in which he must move his king to prevent its capture. Cf CHECKMATE. **5** [Tn] (*US*) (**a**) leave (hats, coats, etc) to be stored for a short period. (**b**) leave (luggage, etc) ready to be despatched. **6** (phr v) **check in (at...)**; **check into...** register as a guest at a hotel or as a passenger at an airport, etc: *Passengers should check in for flight BA 125 to Berlin.* **check sth in** (**a**) leave or accept sth to be transported by train or by air: *check in one's luggage.* (**b**) (*esp US*) leave or accept sth for safe keeping in a cloakroom or left-luggage office: *Is there a place we can check in our coats?* **check sth off** mark (items on a list) as correct or as having been dealt with. **check (up) on sb** investigate sb's behaviour, background, etc: *The police are checking up on him.* **check (up) on sth** examine sth to discover if it is true, safe, correct, etc. **check out (of...)** pay one's bill and leave a hotel. **check sth out** (*esp US*) = CHECK (UP) ON STH.

▷ **check** *interj* (*US*) (used to show that one understands or agrees with sth): *Eight o'clock at your place? Check!*

checker *n* person who checks (esp stores, orders, etc).

□ **ˈcheck-in** *n* **1** act of checking in at an airport: [attrib] *the check-in desk* ○ *one's check-in time.* **2** place where one checks in at an airport before a flight.

ˈchecking account (*US*) = CURRENT ACCOUNT (CURRENT[1]).

ˈchecklist *n* list of items to be marked as present or having been dealt with: *a checklist of things to take on holiday.*

ˈcheck-out *n* **1** act of checking out (CHECK[1] 6). **2** place where customers pay for goods in a supermarket.

ˈcheck-point *n* place, eg on a frontier, where travellers are stopped and their vehicles and documents inspected.

ˈcheckroom *n* (*US*) (**a**) cloakroom in a hotel, theatre, etc. (**b**) left-luggage office.

ˈcheck-up *n* thorough examination, esp a medical one: *go for/have a check-up.*

check[2] /tʃek/ *n* **1** [C] ~ **(on sth)** (**a**) examination to make sure that sth is correct, safe, satisfactory or in good condition: *Could you give the tyres a check, please?* ○ *We conduct regular checks on the quality of our products.* **(b)** method of testing the accuracy or genuineness of sth. **2** [C] ~ **(on sb)** investigation: *The police made a check on all the victim's friends.* **3** [C] **(a)** slowing down or stopping; pause: *a check in the rate of production.* **(b)** ~ **(on sth)** thing that restrains or stops sth: *The presence of the army should act as a check on civil unrest.* **4** [sing] (in chess) situation in which a player must move his king in order to prevent its capture by his opponent: *You're in check!* Cf CHECKMATE. **5** [C] (*US*) = CHEQUE. **6** [C] (*US*) = BILL[1] 1: *I'll ask the waiter for the check.* **7** [C] (*US*) ticket or token used to identify and reclaim clothing or property left in a cloakroom or left-luggage office. **8** [C] (*US*) = TICK[1] 3. **9** (idm) **hold/keep sth in ˈcheck** prevent sth from advancing or increasing; control sth: *keep one's temper in check* ○ *The epidemic was held in check by widespread vaccination.* **take a rain check** ⇨ RAIN[1].

▷ **check** *interj* (in chess) call made to one's opponent to show that his king is in check.

□ **ˌchecks and ˈbalances** (*esp US*) system of procedures designed to ensure that no branch of government becomes too powerful or abuses the power it has.

ˈcheckbook *n* (*US*) = CHEQUE-BOOK (CHEQUE).

check[3] /tʃek/ *n* **(a)** [C] pattern of crossed lines (often in different colours) forming squares: *Which do you want for your new dress, a stripe or a check?* **(b)** [U] cloth with this pattern: [attrib] *a check skirt, jacket, table-cloth.*

▷ **checked** /tʃekt/ *adj* having a check pattern: *checked material.*

checker /ˈtʃekə(r)/ *v* (*US*) = CHEQUER.

checkers /ˈtʃekəz/ *n* [sing *v*] (*US*) = DRAUGHTS (DRAUGHT).

□ **ˈcheckerboard** *n* (*US*) = DRAUGHTBOARD (DRAUGHT).

checkmate /ˈtʃekmeɪt/ (also **mate**) *n* [sing] **1** (in chess) situation in which one player cannot prevent the capture of his king and the other player is therefore the winner. Cf CHECK[2] 4. **2** total defeat.

▷ **checkmate** *v* [Tn] **1** (in chess) put (one's opponent) in a position in which he cannot prevent the capture of his king. Cf CHECK[1] 4. **2** defeat (sb/sth) totally; frustrate. — *interj* (in chess) call made when checkmating one's opponent.

Cheddar /ˈtʃedə(r)/ *n* [U] type of firm yellowish cheese.

cheek /tʃi:k/ *n* **1** [C] either side of the face below the eye: *healthy pink cheeks* ○ *dancing cheek to cheek*, ie with the cheek of one partner touching that of the other. ⇨ illus at HEAD. **2** [C] (*infml*) either of the buttocks. **3** [U, sing] impertinent talk or behaviour; impudence: *That's enough of your cheek!* ○ *He had the cheek to ask me to do his work for him.* ○ *What (a) cheek!* ie How very cheeky! **4** (idm) **ˌcheek by ˈjowl (with sb/sth)** close together: *live/lie cheek by jowl.* **ˌturn the other ˈcheek** accept violent attack without being violent oneself. **with tongue in cheek** ⇨ TONGUE.

▷ **cheek** *v* [Tn] speak cheekily to (sb).

-cheeked (forming compound *adjs*) having the specified type of cheeks: *a rosy-cheeked boy.*

cheeky *adj* (**-ier**, **-iest**) (of a person, his manner, etc) lacking respect, esp in a bold or cheerful way; impertinent; impudent: *a cheeky boy, remark.* **cheekily** *adv.* **cheekiness** *n* [U].

□ **ˈcheek-bone** *n* bone below the eye.

cheep /tʃi:p/ *n* weak shrill cry of a young bird.

▷ **cheep** *v* [I] make this cry.

cheer[1] /tʃɪə(r)/ *v* **1** [I, Tn] give shouts of joy, praise, support or encouragement to (sb): *The crowd cheered loudly as the Queen appeared.* ○ *The winning team were cheered by their supporters.* **2** [Tn] give comfort, hope, support or encouragement to (sb); gladden: *He was greatly cheered by the news.* **3** (phr v) **cheer sb on** encourage sb to make greater efforts by cheering: *The crowd cheered the runners on as they started the last lap.* **cheer (sb) up** (cause sb to) become happier or more cheerful: *Try and cheer up a bit; life isn't that bad!* ○ *You look as though you need cheering up*, ie to be cheered up. ○ (*fig*) *Flowers always cheer a room up.* **4** (idm) **the cup that cheers** ⇨ CUP[1].

▷ **cheering** *adj* encouraging; gladdening: *cheering news.* — *n* [U]: *The cheering could be heard half a mile away.*

cheer[2] /tʃɪə(r)/ *n* **1** [C] shout of joy, praise, support or encouragement: *the cheers of the crowd* ○ *Three cheers for* (ie Shout 'hurray' three times to show admiration for) *the bride and groom!* **2** [U] (*arch*) happiness and hopefulness: *Christmas should be a time of great cheer.*

□ **ˈcheer-leader** *n* (*esp US*) person who leads the cheering by a crowd, esp at a sporting event.

cheerful /ˈtʃɪəfl/ *adj* **1** **(a)** in good spirits; happy: *a cheerful smile, disposition* ○ *You're very cheerful today.* **(b)** causing happiness; pleasant: *The news isn't very cheerful, I'm afraid.* **2** pleasantly bright: *cheerful colours* ○ *a cheerful room.* **3** not grudging; willing: *a cheerful worker.* **4** (idm) **cheap and cheerful** ⇨ CHEAP. ▷ **cheerfully** /-fəlɪ/ *adv*: *accept sth, smile, whistle, work cheerfully.* **cheerfulness** *n* [U].

cheerio /ˌtʃɪərɪˈəʊ/ *interj* (*Brit infml*) goodbye.

cheerless /ˈtʃɪəlɪs/ *adj* gloomy; dreary: *a cold, cheerless day* ○ *a damp, cheerless room.* ▷ **cheerlessly** *adv.* **cheerlessness** *n* [U].

cheers /tʃɪəz/ *interj* (*infml esp Brit*) **1** (used as a toast when drinking) good health! **2** goodbye; cheerio: *Cheers! See you tomorrow night.* **3** thank you.

cheery /ˈtʃɪərɪ/ *adj* (**-ier**, **-iest**) lively and cheerful; genial: *a cheery smile, greeting, wave.* ▷ **cheerily** *adv.* **cheeriness** *n* [U].

cheese /tʃi:z/ *n* **1** **(a)** [U] food made from milk curds: *Cheddar cheese* ○ *a lump/piece/slice of cheese* ○ [attrib] *a cheese sandwich.* **(b)** [C] particular type of this: *a selection of French cheeses.* **(c)** [C] shaped and wrapped portion or mass of this: *two cream cheeses.* **2** [U] type of thick jam: *lemon, damson cheese.* **3** (idm) **a big cheese** ⇨ BIG. **different as chalk and/from cheese** ⇨ DIFFERENT. **say cheese** ⇨ SAY.

▷ **cheese** *v* (phr v) **cheese sb off** (esp passive) (*infml*) make sb annoyed, bored or frustrated: *He's cheesed off with his job.*

cheesy *adj* (**-ier**, **-iest**) like cheese in taste or smell.

□ **ˈcheese-board** *n* board for cutting cheese on.

ˈcheeseburger *n* hamburger with a slice of cheese in it.

ˈcheese-cutter *n* thin wire, sometimes attached to a board, used for cutting through large pieces of cheese.

ˈcheese-paring *n* [U] (*derog*) excessive carefulness in the spending of money; stinginess. — *adj* (*derog*) stingy; mean.

ˌcheese ˈstraw thin strip of pastry flavoured with cheese, often served with drinks.

cheesecake /ˈtʃi:zkeɪk/ *n* **1** [C, U] type of tart made with cream cheese, eggs, sugar, etc on a base of pastry or crushed biscuits: *a cherry cheesecake* ○ *Have some more cheesecake.* **2** [U] (*infml*) pictures of women with shapely bodies, esp as used in advertisements. Cf BEEFCAKE.

cheesecloth /ˈtʃi:zklɒθ; *US* -klɔ:θ/ *n* [U] thin, loosely woven, cotton fabric: [attrib] *a cheesecloth shirt.*

cheetah /ˈtʃi:tə/ *n* African wild animal of the cat family with black spots and long legs, and able to run very fast.

chef /ʃef/ *n* professional cook, esp the chief cook in a restaurant.

chef-d'oeuvre /ʃeɪ ˈdɜ:vrə/ *n* (*pl* **chefs-d'oeuvre** /ʃeɪ ˈdɜ:vrə/) (*French*) masterpiece.

Chekhov /ˈtʃekɒf/ Anton Pavlovich (1860-1904), Russian dramatist and short-story writer, famous for such plays as *Uncle Vanya, Three Sisters* and *The Cherry Orchard*. His use of idiomatic dialogue was a major innovation in the theatre of his time and his work had a great influence on 20th-century drama.

Chelsea bun /ˌtʃelsɪ ˈbʌn/ type of rolled currant bun sprinkled with sugar.

Chelsea pensioner /ˌtʃelsɪ ˈpenʃənə(r)/ person living in the Chelsea Royal Hospital for old and disabled soldiers. Chelsea is a district of West London.

chemical /ˈkemɪkl/ *adj* **1** of or relating to chemistry: *the chemical industry.* **2** produced by or using chemistry or chemicals: *a chemical experiment* ○ *a chemical reaction*, ie one causing changes in the structure of atoms or molecules.

▷ **chemical** *n* substance obtained by or used in a chemical process: *fine chemicals*, ie those of high quality, usu used in small amounts, in experiments, etc ○ *heavy chemicals*, ie those used in large quantities in industry and agriculture.

chemically /-klɪ/ *adv.*

□ **ˌchemical ˈbond** force of attraction that holds atoms together in a molecule or crystal.

ˌchemical engiˈneering engineering that deals with processes involving chemical changes and with the equipment needed for these. **ˌchemical engiˈneer** *n.*

ˌchemical ˈwarfare use of poisonous gases and other harmful chemicals in war.

chemise /ʃəˈmi:z/ *n* **(a)** loose-fitting undergarment hanging straight from the shoulders, formerly worn by women. **(b)** dress similar to this.

chemist /ˈkemɪst/ *n* **1** (*US* **druggist**) person who prepares and sells medicines, and usu also sells cosmetics, toiletries, etc; pharmacist: *buy aspirin at the chemist's* (ie chemist's shop) *on the corner.* Cf PHARMACIST. **2** expert in chemistry.

chemistry /ˈkemɪstrɪ/ *n* [U] **1** scientific study of the structure of substances, how they react when combined or in contact with one another, and how they behave under different conditions: *Chemistry was her favourite subject at school.* ○ [attrib] *a chemistry lesson.* **2** chemical structure, properties (PROPERTY 4) and reactions of a particular substance: *the chemistry of copper.* **3** any mysterious or complex change or process: *the strange chemistry that causes two people to fall in love.*

chemotherapy /ˌki:məʊˈθerəpɪ/ *n* [U] treatment of disease by drugs and other chemical substances.

chenille /ʃəˈni:l/ *n* [U] **(a)** thick velvety cord used for trimming furniture. **(b)** fabric made of this.

cheque (*US* **check**) /tʃek/ *n* **1** (special printed form on which one writes an) order to a bank to pay a sum of money from one's account to another person: *write (sb)/sign a cheque for £50* ○ *Are you paying in cash or by cheque?* **2** (idm) **a blank cheque** ⇨ BLANK.

□ **ˈcheque-book** (*US* **ˈcheckbook**) *n* book of printed cheques. **ˌcheque-book ˈjournalism** (*usu derog*) payment of large sums of money by a newspaper to persuade a person involved in an important news event to tell his story in that newspaper and not in any other.

ˈcheque card card issued by a bank to sb who has an account with it, guaranteeing payment of his cheques up to a specified amount.

chequer (*US* **checker**) /ˈtʃekə(r)/ *n* pattern of squares, usu of alternate colours. ⇨ illus at PATTERN.

▷ **chequer** *v* [Tn esp passive] mark (sth) with a pattern of squares or patches of different colours or shades: *a lawn chequered with sunlight and shade.*

chequered (*US* **checkered**) *adj* [esp attrib] (*fig*) marked by periods of good and bad fortune: *a chequered career/history/past.*

Chequers /ˈtʃekəz/ large country house in Buckinghamshire, England, used as a country home by the British prime minister in office.

cherish /ˈtʃerɪʃ/ *v* [Tn] **1** protect or tend (sb/sth) lovingly; care for. **2** be fond of (sb/sth); love. **3** keep (a feeling or an idea) in one's mind or heart and think of it with pleasure: *cherish the memory of one's dead mother* ○ *cherish the hope of winning an Olympic medal* ○ *He cherishes the illusion that she's in love with him.*

chernozem /ˈtʃɜːnəʊzem/ *n* [U] very fertile black or dark brown soil, rich in humus and lime, found in the USSR , China and N America.

Cherokee /ˈtʃerəkiː, ˌtʃerəˈkiː/ *n* (*pl* unchanged) member of an American Indian tribe formerly inhabiting much of the southern USA.

cheroot /ʃəˈruːt/ *n* cigar with both ends open.

cherry /ˈtʃerɪ/ *n* **1** [C] small soft round fruit (red or black when ripe) containing a stone. ⇨ illus at FRUIT. **2** (also **ˈcherry-tree**) **(a)** [C] tree on which this fruit grows: *a flowering cherry* ○ [attrib] *cherry blossom.* **(b)** [U] wood of this tree. **3** [U] (also **ˌcherry ˈred**) bright red colour: [attrib] *cherry lips.* **4** (idm) **have/get two bites at the cherry** ⇨ BITE[2].

□ **ˌcherry ˈbrandy** type of brandy in which cherries have been left to soak.

ˈcherry-picker *n* (*infml*) crane used to raise and lower people working a long way above the ground, eg repairing street lamps.

cherub /ˈtʃerəb/ *n* **1** (*pl* ~**im** /ˈtʃerəbɪm/) (*Bible*) one of the second highest order of angels, usu represented in paintings as a plump child with wings. ⇨ illus at ANGEL. Cf SERAPH. **2** (*pl* ~**s**) **(a)** (in art) angelic plump child with wings. **(b)** sweet or innocent-looking child.

▷ **cherubic** /tʃɪˈruːbɪk/ *adj* (esp of a child) with a plump and innocent face.

Cherubini /ˌkeruˈbiːnɪ/ Luigi (1760-1842), Italian composer of operas and church music.

chervil /ˈtʃɜːvɪl/ *n* [U] **(a)** type of garden herb. **(b)** its leaves used to flavour soups and salads.

Cheshire /ˈtʃeʃə(r)/ **1** county in the northern midlands of England. ⇨ map at App 1. **2** (idm) **(grin, etc) like a Cheshire cat** with a broad fixed grin.

□ **ˌCheshire ˈcheese** type of firm crumbly cheese, originally made in Cheshire.

chess /tʃes/ *n* [U] game for two people, played on a board with 64 squares. Each player has 16 pieces (or *men*) that can be moved in particular ways. The most important pieces are the king and queen, and the object of the game is to get one's opponent's king into a position from which it cannot escape (*checkmate*).

□ **ˈchessboard** *n* chequered board with 64 black and white squares on which chess and draughts are played.

chess-man /ˈtʃesmæn/ *n* (*pl* **-men** /-men/) any of the pieces used in the game of chess. ⇨ illus.

chest /tʃest/ *n* **1** large strong box for storing or shipping things in: *a ˈtea chest* ○ *a ˈmedicine chest* ○ *a ˈtool chest.* **2** upper front part of the body from the neck to the stomach: *a hairy chest* ○ *What size are you round the chest?* ○ [attrib] *ˈchest pains* ○ *a ˈchest cold*, ie one that affects the lungs. ⇨ illus at HUMAN. **3** (idm) **ˌget sth off one's ˈchest** (*infml*) say sth that one has wanted to say for a long time: *You're obviously worried about something; why not get it off your chest?* **hold/keep one's cards close to one's chest** ⇨ CARD[1]. **put hairs on sb's chest** ⇨ HAIR.

▷ **-chested** (forming compound *adjs*) having the specified type of chest: *ˌbroad-ˈchested* ○ *ˌbare-ˈchested* ○ *She's ˌflat-ˈchested*, ie she has very small breasts.

chesty *adj* (*Brit infml*) tending to suffer from or showing the symptoms of bronchial disease: *She often gets chesty in wet weather.* ○ *a chesty cough.* **chestiness** *n* [U].

□ **ˌchest of ˈdrawers** (*US* also **bureau**) piece of furniture with drawers for storing clothes in. ⇨ illus at FURNITURE.

chesterfield /ˈtʃestəfiːld/ *n* sofa with a padded back, seat and ends.

Chesterton /ˈtʃestətən/ G(ilbert) K(eith) (1874-1936), English essayist, novelist and poet, widely remembered for his creation of the fictional detective, the Roman Catholic priest Father Brown.

chestnut /ˈtʃesnʌt/ *n* **1** **(a)** (also **ˈchestnut tree**) [C] any of various types of tree producing smooth reddish-brown nuts enclosed in prickly cases (those of some types being edible). **(b)** [C] one of these nuts: *roast chestnuts* ○ [attrib] *chestnut stuffing*, ie a mixture of chestnuts, herbs, etc used to stuff a chicken, turkey, etc. ⇨ illus at NUT. **(c)** wood of the chestnut tree: [attrib] *a chestnut table.* **2** [U] deep reddish-brown colour: [attrib] *chestnut hair* ○ *a chestnut mare.* **3** [C] horse of this colour. **4** [C] (*infml*) old joke or story that is no longer amusing: *an old chestnut.*

cheval-glass /ʃəˈvæl glɑːs/ *n* tall mirror fitted inside an upright frame so that it can be tilted.

Cheviot Hills /ˌtʃevɪət ˈhɪlz, ˌtʃiː-/ **the Cheviot Hills** (also **the Cheviots**) range of hills on the border between England and Scotland, famous for a hardy breed of sheep reared there for their wool.

chevron /ˈʃevrən/ *n* bent line or stripe in the shape of a normal or upside-down V, worn by a policeman or soldier to show his rank.

chew /tʃuː/ *v* **1** [I, Tn, Tn·p] ~ **sth (up)** work or grind (food) between the teeth: *Chew your food well before you swallow it.* **2** (idm) **bite off more than one can chew** ⇨ BITE[1]. **ˌchew the ˈcud (of sth)** reflect upon sth already said or done; ponder sth. **ˌchew the ˈfat/ˈrag** (*infml*) talk about sth, often in a grumbling or argumentative way. **3** (phr v) **chew sb ˈout** (*US sl*) express one's anger at sb for doing sth wrong; reprimand sb: *I got chewed out for leaving my room in a mess.* **chew sth ˈover** (*infml*) think about sth slowly and carefully: *ˌchew over a ˈproblem* ○ *I'll give you till tomorrow to ˌchew it ˈover.*

▷ **chew** *n* **1** act of chewing. **2** thing that can be chewed, eg a sweet or a piece of tobacco.

□ **ˈchewing-gum** (also **gum**) *n* [U] sticky substance flavoured and sweetened for prolonged chewing.

Cheyenne /ʃaɪˈæn, ʃaɪˈen/ *n* (*pl* unchanged) member of an American Indian tribe of the western plains of the USA, who were frequently at war with US troops, and fought the battle of Little Big Horn against General *Custer.

chez /ʃeɪ/ *prep* (*French joc or ironic*) at the house or home of: *a little dinner-party chez Elizabeth.*

Chiang Kai-shek /ˌtʃjæŋ kaɪˈʃek/ Chinese leader, a general in *Sun Yat-sen's army who later tried to unite China. He was defeated by the Communists after the Second World War and retreated to *Taiwan, where he set up a Nationalist Chinese state in 1949.

Chianti /kɪˈæntɪ/ *n* [C, U] (particular type of) dry red or white wine, from central Italy.

chiaroscuro /kɪˌɑːrəˈskʊərəʊ/ *n* [U] (*art*) **1** treatment of the light and dark parts in a painting. **2** use of contrast in literature, music, etc.

chic /ʃiːk/ *adj* elegant and stylish: *She always looks very chic.*

▷ **chic** *n* [U] stylishness and elegance: *She dresses with chic.*

Chicago /ʃɪˈkɑːgəʊ/ city in Illinois, on Lake Michigan, the third largest city of the USA. The world's first skyscrapers were built there.

chicane /ʃɪˈkeɪn/ *n* artificial barrier or obstacle on a motor-racing circuit.

chicanery /ʃɪˈkeɪnərɪ/ *n* **1** [U] use of clever but misleading talk in order to trick sb, esp in legal matters; dishonest practice: *accuse a politician of chicanery.* **2** [C] trick or deception.

chicano /tʃɪˈkɑːnəʊ/ *n* (*pl* ~**s**) (*US*) American person of Mexican origin.

chick /tʃɪk/ *n* **1** young bird, esp a young chicken, just before or after hatching: *a hen with her chicks.* **2** (*dated sexist*) young woman.

chickadee /ˈtʃɪkədiː/ *n* any of various N American birds of the tit family.

chicken /ˈtʃɪkɪn/ *n* **1** [C] young bird, esp of the domestic fowl. ⇨ illus at BIRD. **2** **(a)** [C] domestic fowl kept for its eggs or meat: *keep chickens.* Cf COCK[1], HEN. **(b)** [U] its flesh eaten as food: *slices of roast chicken.* **3** [C] (*sl*) coward. **4** [U] (*sl*) children's game that tests sb's courage in the face of danger. **5** (idm) **be ˌno (spring) ˈchicken** (*infml*) (esp of women) be no longer young. **count one's chickens** ⇨ COUNT[1].

▷ **chicken** *v* (phr v) **chicken out (of sth)** (*infml*) decide not to do sth because one is afraid: *He had an appointment to see the dentist but he chickened out (of it) at the last moment.*

chicken *adj* [pred] (*sl*) cowardly.

□ **ˈchicken-feed** *n* [U] **1** food for poultry. **2** (*fig infml*) small amount, esp of money: *Your salary is chicken-feed compared to what you could earn in America.*

ˌchicken-ˈhearted *adj* lacking courage; cowardly.

ˈchicken-pox *n* [U] disease, esp of children, with a mild fever and itchy red spots on the skin: *catch chicken-pox.*

ˈchicken-run *n* area surrounded by a fence where chickens are kept.

ˈchicken wire type of thin wire netting.

chick-pea /ˈtʃɪk piː/ *n* **(a)** Asian plant grown for its edible pea-like seeds. **(b)** one of these seeds.

chickweed /ˈtʃɪkwiːd/ *n* [U] common type of weed with small white flowers.

chicle /ˈtʃɪkl/ *n* [U] milky juice of a tropical American tree, the main ingredient of chewing-gum.

chicory /ˈtʃɪkərɪ/ *n* [U] **(a)** (also **endive**) blue-flowered plant, the leaves of which are eaten raw in salads. **(b)** these leaves. **(c)** root of this plant, roasted, ground and used with or instead of coffee.

chide /tʃaɪd/ *v* (*pt* **chided** /ˈtʃaɪdɪd/ or **chid** /tʃɪd/, *pp* **chided**, **chid** or **chidden** /ˈtʃɪdn/) [Tn, Tn·pr] ~ **sb (for sth)** (*dated or fml*) rebuke; scold: *She chided him for his laziness.*

chief /tʃiːf/ *n* **1** leader or ruler, esp of a tribe or clan. **2** person with the highest rank in an organization, a department, etc: *a chief of police.*

▷ **chief** *adj* **1** [esp attrib] most important; main; principal: *the chief rivers of India* ○ *The chief thing to remember is...* ○ *Smoking is one of the chief causes of lung cancer.* **2** [attrib] having the highest rank or authority: *the chief priest.* **chiefly** *adv* **(a)** above all; principally: *The Government is chiefly concerned with controlling inflation.* **(b)** mostly; mainly: *Air consists chiefly of nitrogen.*

□ **Chief ˈConstable** (*Brit*) head of the police force in a particular area.

ˌChief of ˈStaff (in the armed forces) highest ranking member of the group of officers serving under and advising a commander.

-in-ˈchief (forming compound *ns*): *editor-in-chief*, ie chief editor ○ *commander-in-chief.*

chieftain /ˈtʃiːftən/ *n* leader of a tribe or clan; chief: *a Highland chieftain.*

chiffchaff /ˈtʃɪftʃæf/ *n* small European songbird of the warbler family.

chiffon /ˈʃɪfɒn; *US* ʃɪˈfɒn/ *n* [U] thin, almost transparent fabric made of silk, nylon, etc: [attrib] *a chiffon scarf.*

chignon /ˈʃiːnjɒn/ *n* woman's hair twisted into a coil or thick knot at the back of the head.

chigoe /ˈtʃɪgəʊ/ (also **chigger** /ˈtʃɪgə(r)/) *n* tropical flea that burrows into the skin, causing painful sores.

chihuahua /tʃɪˈwɑːwə/ *n* type of very small smooth-haired dog, originally from Mexico.

chilblain /ˈtʃɪlbleɪn/ *n* (usu *pl*) painful swelling, esp on the hand or foot, caused by exposure to cold.

child /tʃaɪld/ *n* (*pl* **children** /ˈtʃɪldrən/) **1** (**a**) young human being below the age of puberty; boy or girl: *a child of six*, ie one who is six years old ○ [attrib] *a child actor*. (**b**) son or daughter (of any age): *an only child*, ie one with no brothers or sisters ○ *She is married with three children*. ⇨ App 8. (**c**) unborn or newly born human being; baby: *She is expecting* (ie is pregnant with) *her first child*. **2** (**a**) person who behaves like a child: *You wouldn't think a man of forty could be such a child*. (**b**) inexperienced person: *He's a child in financial matters*. **3** ~ **of sth** person or thing strongly influenced by a period, place or person: *She's a real child of the (19)60s*. **4** (idm) **be with child** (*arch*) be pregnant. **the child is father of the man** (*saying*) the experiences of childhood determine a person's character as an adult. ˈ**child's play** (*infml*) thing that is very easy to do: *It's not a difficult climb — it should be child's play for an experienced mountaineer*. **an only child** ⇨ ONLY[1]. **spare the rod and spoil the child** ⇨ SPARE[2].

▷ **childhood** /ˈtʃaɪldhʊd/ *n* **1** [U, C] condition or period of being a child: *the joys of childhood* ○ *She had an unhappy childhood*. ○ [attrib] *childhood memories*. **2** (idm) **a/one's second** ˈ**childhood** (*often joc*) period in later life when one acts as one did as a child: *He's in his second childhood, playing with his grandson's toy trains*.

childless *adj* having no children: *a childless couple/marriage*.

□ ˈ**child abuse** cruel or immoral treatment of children, by neglecting them, beating them or (esp) by involving them in sex acts.

ˈ**child-bearing** *n* [U] giving birth to children: [attrib] *She's past child-bearing age*.

child ˈ**benefit** (*Brit*) payment made by the Government to parents of children up to a certain age. ⇨ article at SOCIAL SECURITY.

ˈ**childbirth** *n* [U] process of giving birth to a child: *She died in childbirth*.

ˈ**childlike** *adj* (*esp approv*) like or characteristic of a child; innocent; not devious: *childlike enjoyment, trust, honesty, etc*. Cf CHILDISH.

ˈ**child-minder** *n* (*esp Brit*) person who is paid to look after children, esp those of parents who are both at work.

ˈ**child-proof** *adj* (of equipment, appliances, etc) which cannot be operated, opened, damaged, etc by a young child: *Most car doors are now fitted with child-proof locks*.

childish /ˈtʃaɪldɪʃ/ *adj* (**a**) (characteristic) of a child: *childish laughter*. (**b**) (*derog*) (of an adult) (behaving) like a child; immature; silly: *Don't be so childish!* ○ *a childish attitude, fear, remark*. Cf CHILDLIKE (CHILD). ▷ **childishly** *adv*: *behave childishly*. **childishness** *n* [U].

Chile /ˈtʃɪlɪ/ country on the west coast of South America between the Andes and the Pacific Ocean; pop approx 13 386 000; official language Spanish; capital Santiago; unit of currency peso (= 100 centavos). Since 1989 it has been returning to a democratic form of government. Chile is one of the world's major producers of copper and its mineral wealth also includes iron, nitrates, coal and oil. ⇨ map. ▷ **Chilean** /ˈtʃɪlɪən/ *adj, n*.

□ ˌ**Chile salt**ˈ**petre** (also ˌ**Chile** ˈ**nitre**) sodium nitrate as it occurs naturally, esp in Chile and Peru.

chili *n* (*US*) = CHILLI.

chill /tʃɪl/ *n* **1** [sing] unpleasant coldness in the air, in the body, in water, etc: *There's quite a chill in the air this morning*. ○ *The spell of sunny weather has taken the chill off the sea*, ie warmed the water slightly. **2** [C] illness caused by cold and damp, with shivering of the body; feverish cold: *catch a chill*. **3** [sing] (*fig*) feeling of gloom or depression: *The bad news cast a chill over the gathering*.

▷ **chill** *v* **1** [Tn] make (sb/sth) cold: *The March wind chilled us*. ○ (*fig*) *His sinister threat chilled* (ie frightened) *all who heard it*. **2** (**a**) [I, Tn] (cause food and drink to) become cool, eg in a refrigerator: *Let the pudding chill for an hour*. ○ *This wine is best served chilled*. (**b**) [Tn] preserve (food) at a low temperature without freezing it: *chilled beef*. **3** [Tn] lessen (sth); dampen: *The raw weather chilled our enthusiasm for a swim*. **4** [Tn] harden (molten metal, esp iron) by letting it touch cold material. **5** (idm) **chill sb to the** ˈ**bone**/ˈ**marrow** make sb very cold: *Come by the fire — you must be chilled to the marrow!*

chill *adj* = CHILLY: *a chill wind*.

chilling /ˈtʃɪlɪŋ/ *adj* frightening: *a chilling ghost story*.

chilly /ˈtʃɪlɪ/ *adj* (**-ier**, **-iest**) **1** rather cold; unpleasantly cold: *a chilly day, morning, room* ○ *feel chilly*. **2** (*fig*) unfriendly: *a chilly welcome, reception, stare* ○ *chilly politeness*. **chilliness** *n* [U].

Chile

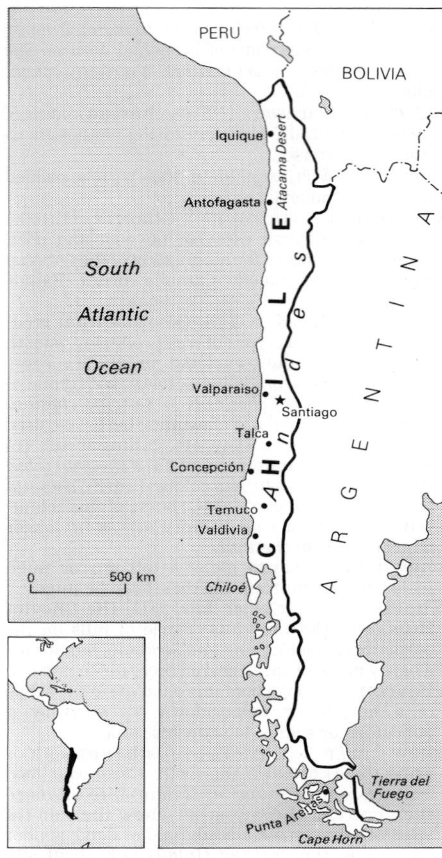

chilli (*US* **chili**) /ˈtʃɪlɪ/ *n* (*pl* **chillies**; *US* **chilies**) [C, U] small pod of a type of pepper plant, often dried or made into powder and used to give a hot taste to food: *How much chilli did you put in the curry?* ○ [attrib] *chilli peppers* ○ ˈ*chilli powder* ○ *chilli sauce*, ie with tomatoes and spices.

□ ˌ**chilli con** ˈ**carne** /kɒn ˈkɑːnɪ/ stew of minced beef and kidney beans, flavoured with chillies or chilli powder.

Chiltern Hundreds /ˌtʃɪltən ˈhʌndrədz/ **the Chiltern Hundreds** (*Brit*) former administrative district in Buckinghamshire, England, nowadays only used when a Member of Parliament (MP) wishes to resign. He 'applies for the stewardship of the Chiltern Hundreds', and since this is an office of the Crown, which he is not permitted to hold as an MP, he ceases to be an MP when granted it.

chime /tʃaɪm/ *n* **1** set of tuned bells: *a chime of bells*. **2** series of notes sounded by such a set: *ring the chimes* ○ *the chime of church bells/of the clock*.

▷ **chime** *v* **1** (**a**) [I] (of bells) sound a chime; ring: *cathedral bells chiming*. (**b**) [Tn] cause (bells) to ring. **2** [I, Tn] (of bells or a clock) show (the time) by ringing: *The church clock chimed (at) midnight*. **3** (phr v) **chime in** (**with sth**) (*infml*) interrupt a conversation: *He kept chiming in with his own opinions*. **chime** (**in**) **with sth** (*infml*) fit sth; suit sth: *It's good that your plans chime (in) with ours*.

chimera (also **chimaera**) /kaɪˈmɪərə/ *n* **1** imaginary monster made up of parts of several different animals. **2** (*fig*) wild or impossible idea.

▷ **chimerical** /kaɪˈmerɪkl/ *adj* unreal; fanciful: *chimerical ideas, schemes, etc*.

chimney /ˈtʃɪmnɪ/ *n* **1** structure through which smoke or steam is carried away from a fire, furnace, etc and through the roof or wall of a building: *a blocked chimney* ○ *factory chimneys*. ⇨ illus at HOME. **2** glass tube that protects the flame of an oil-lamp from draughts. **3** (in mountaineering) narrow opening in a rock or cliff up which a person may climb. ⇨ illus at MOUNTAIN.

□ ˈ**chimney-breast** *n* projecting part of the wall of a room which encloses the bottom of the chimney and the fireplace.

ˈ**chimney-piece** *n* = MANTELPIECE.

ˈ**chimney-pot** *n* short metal or earthenware pipe fitted to the top of a chimney. ⇨ illus at HOME.

ˈ**chimney-stack** *n* group of chimneys standing together, esp on a roof.

ˈ**chimney-sweep** (also **sweep**) *n* person whose job is removing soot, etc from inside chimneys.

chimp /tʃɪmp/ *n* (*infml*) chimpanzee.

chimpanzee /ˌtʃɪmpənˈziː, ˌtʃɪmpænˈziː/ *n* type of small African ape. ⇨ illus at APE.

chin /tʃɪn/ *n* **1** part of the face below the mouth; front part of the lower jaw: *a double chin*, ie a fold of fat under the chin. ⇨ illus at HEAD. **2** (idm) **chuck sb under the chin** ⇨ CHUCK[1]. **keep one's** ˈ**chin up** (*infml*) remain cheerful in difficult circumstances. **take sth on the** ˈ**chin** (*infml*) accept (eg criticism or bad luck) without complaining: *Most people would be upset at losing their job, but she just took it on the chin*.

▷ **chinless** *adj* **1** having a small chin, regarded as a sign of a weak character. **2** (idm) **a chinless** ˈ**wonder** (*Brit infml*) (esp young upper-class) person with a weak character.

□ ˈ**chin-strap** *n* strap on a helmet, etc, that fastens under the chin.

ˈ**chin-wag** *n* (*Brit infml*) chat: *have a chin-wag*.

China /ˈtʃaɪnə/ (also **People's Republic of China**) country in eastern Asia, the third-largest and most populous country in the world; pop approx 1 103 983 000; official language Chinese; capital Beijing (Peking); unit of currency yuan (= 10 jiao or 100 fen). It is primarily an agricultural country, with considerable mineral resources. From early times it was ruled by a series of dynasties until 1912, when the Manchu dynasty was overthrown by *Sun Yat-sen. Civil war and Japanese invasion followed and, after the Second World War, the Communists came to power. They have ruled since 1949. ⇨ map.

□ ˈ**Chinaman** *n* (*pl* **-men** /-mən/) (*usu derog*) native of China.

ˌ**China** ˈ**tea** type of tea made with the smoked leaves of a small-leaved tea plant grown esp in China: *Do you prefer China or Indian (tea)?*

ˈ**Chinatown** *n* part of a town or city, outside China and esp in Britain or the USA, where a large number of the inhabitants are Chinese.

china /ˈtʃaɪnə/ *n* [U] **1** (**a**) fine baked and glazed white clay; porcelain: *made of china* ○ [attrib] *a china vase*. (**b**) objects made of this, eg cups, saucers, plates: *household china* ○ *Shall we use the* (ie our) *best china?* **2** (idm) **a bull in a china shop** ⇨ BULL[1].

□ **china** ˈ**clay** = KAOLIN.

ˈ**china-cupboard** *n* cupboard in which china is kept or displayed.

ˈ**chinaware** *n* [U] = CHINA 1.

Chinagraph /ˈtʃaɪnəgrɑːf, -græf/ *n* (*propr*) type of waxy coloured pencil used for writing on china or glass.

China and its neighbours

chinchilla /tʃɪnˈtʃɪlə/ *n* **1** (a) [C] small squirrel-like S American animal. (b) [U] soft grey, highly valued fur of this animal. **2** breed of long-haired cat or rabbit.

chine /tʃaɪn/ *n* (a) animal's backbone. (b) joint of meat including part of this.

Chinese /tʃaɪˈni:z/ *adj* of China, its language or its people.

▷ **Chinese** *n* **1** [C] native or inhabitant of China. **2** [U] language of China.

□ ˌ**Chinese ˈcabbage** (also ˌ**Chinese ˈleaf**) type of cabbage with crisp lettuce-like leaves.

ˌ**Chinese ˈcheckers** game in which marbles or pegs are moved from hole to hole across a board.

ˌ**Chinese ˈlantern 1** collapsible paper lantern. **2** plant with an inflated orange calyx resembling a small lantern.

ˌ**Chinese ˈpuzzle** complicated puzzle or problem.

Ching /tʃɪŋ/ *Manchu dynasty which ruled in China from 1644 to 1912.

Chink /tʃɪŋk/ *n* (⚠ *sl derog offensive*) Chinese person.

chink¹ /tʃɪŋk/ *n* **1** narrow opening; crack; slit: *Sunlight entered the room through a chink in the curtains.* ○ *He peeped through a chink in the fence.* **2** (idm) **a chink in sb's ˈarmour** weak point or flaw in sb's argument, character, etc.

chink² /tʃɪŋk/ *n* ~ **(of sth)** light ringing sound (as) of coins, glasses, etc striking together: *the chink of crockery.*

▷ **chink** *v* [I, Ip, Tn, Tn·p] ~ **(A and B) (together)** (cause to) make this sound: *We chinked glasses and drank each other's health.*

chino /ˈtʃi:nəʊ/ *n* (*esp US*) **1** [U] (usu khaki-coloured) cotton twill cloth. **2 chinos** [pl] trousers made from this cloth.

chinoiserie /ʃi:nˈwɑ:zərɪ; *US* ˌʃi:nwɑ:zəˈri:/ *n* [U] imitation of Chinese designs in furniture or decoration; examples of this.

chinook /tʃɪˈnʊk *also*, ʃəˈnu:k/ *n* warm wind blowing in winter and spring down the eastern slopes of the *Rocky Mountains.

chintz /tʃɪnts/ *n* [U] type of (usu glazed) cotton cloth with a printed design, used for curtains, furniture covers, etc.

chip¹ /tʃɪp/ *n* **1** thin piece cut or broken off from wood, stone, china, glass, etc: *a chip of wood.* **2** place from which such a piece has been broken: *This mug has a chip in it.* ⇨ illus. **3** (*US* **French ˈfry**) (usu *pl*) thin strip of potato deep-fried in oil or fat: *a plate of chips* ○ ˌ*fish and ˈchips*, ie fish coated in batter, fried and served with chips, considered to be a British national dish ○ [attrib] *a ˈchip basket*, ie wire container in which chips are placed inside the pan of oil, etc for frying. ⇨ illus at POTATO. **4** (*US*) = CRISP *n*. **5** flat plastic counter²(1) used to represent money, esp in gambling. **6** = MICROCHIP. **7** (also ˈ**chip shot**) (esp in golf and football) shot or kick that travels steeply upwards and then lands within a short distance. **8** (idm) **cash in one's chips** ⇨ CASH. **a** ˌ**chip off the old ˈblock** (*infml*) person (esp a man or boy) who is like his father in character. **have a ˈchip on one's shoulder** (*infml*) be bitter, resentful or defiant because one feels that one's past, background, physical appearance, etc causes other people to be prejudiced against one: *She's got a chip on her shoulder about not having gone to university.* **have had one's ˈchips** (*Brit sl*) be dead, dying or defeated. **when the chips are down** (*infml*) when a crisis point is reached: *When the chips were down he found the courage to carry on.*

□ ˈ**chipboard** *n* [U] building material made of compressed wood chips and resin: *cheap chipboard desks and tables.*

ˈ**chip shop** (*Brit*) shop that sells meals of fish and chips, usu to be taken away. ⇨ article at EAT.

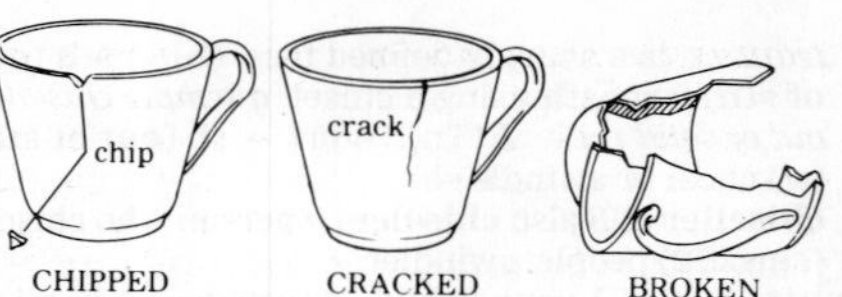

chip² /tʃɪp/ *v* (**-pp-**) **1** (a) [Tn] break or cut (sth) at the edge or surface: *a badly chipped saucer* ○ *chip a tooth* ○ *He chipped one of my best glasses.* ⇨ illus. (b) [I] (tend to) break at the edge or surface: *Be careful with these plates — they chip very easily.* ○ *The paint is chipping badly.* **2** (a) [Tn·pr, Tn·p] ~ **sth from/off sth;** ~ **sth off** break or cut (a small piece) from the edge or surface of sth: *A piece was chipped off the piano when we moved house.* ○ *We chipped the old plaster (away)* (ie removed it in small pieces) *from the wall.* (b) [Ipr, Ip] ~ **off (sth)** be broken off in small pieces: *The paint has chipped off where the table touches the wall.* **3** [Tn] shape or carve (sth) by cutting the edge or surface (with an axe, chisel, etc). **4** [Tn, esp passive] make (potatoes) into chips (CHIP¹ 3): *chipped potatoes.* **5** [I, Tn] (esp in golf and football, etc) strike or kick (the ball) so that it travels steeply upwards and then lands within a short distance. **6** (phr v) **chip away at sth** continuously break off small pieces from sth: *chipping away at a block of marble with a chisel* ○ (*fig*) *He kept chipping away at the problem until he had solved it.* **chip in (with sth)** (*infml*) (a) join in or interrupt a conversation: *She chipped in with some interesting remarks.* (b) contribute (money): *If everyone chips ˈin we'll be able to buy her a really nice leaving present.*

▷ **chippings** *n* [pl] chips of stone, etc used for making a road surface: *Danger! Loose chippings*, eg as a warning to motorists.

chipmunk /ˈtʃɪpmʌŋk/ *n* small striped squirrel-like N American animal.

chipolata /ˌtʃɪpəˈlɑ:tə/ *n* (*esp Brit*) small sausage.

Chippendale /ˈtʃɪpəndeɪl/ *n* [U] elegant style of 18th-century English furniture, named after its designer Thomas Chippendale: [attrib] *Chippendale chairs.*

chipper /ˈtʃɪpə(r)/ *adj* (*infml esp US*) cheerful; lively.

chippy /ˈtʃɪpɪ/ *n* (*Brit sl*) **1** shop selling fish and chips; chip shop. **2** carpenter.

chiromancy /ˈkaɪərəʊmænsɪ/ *n* [U] palmistry.

chiropodist /kɪˈrɒpədɪst/ (*US* **podiatrist**) *n* person whose job is treating or preventing minor disorders of people's feet.

▷ **chiropody** /kɪˈrɒpədɪ/ (*US* **podiatry**) *n* [U] such treatment.

chiropractor /ˈkaɪərəʊpræktə(r)/ *n* person whose job is treating diseases by manipulating people's joints, esp those of the spine.

▷ **chiropractic** /ˌkaɪərəʊˈpræktɪk/ *n* [U] such treatment.

chirp /tʃɜ:p/ *n* short sharp sound made by a small bird or a grasshopper: *the chirp of a sparrow.*

▷ **chirp** *v* [I, Ip] make this sound: *birds chirping (away) merrily in the trees.*

chirpy /ˈtʃɜ:pɪ/ *adj* (**-ier, -iest**) (*Brit infml*) lively and cheerful: *You seem very chirpy today!* ▷ **chirpily** *adv*: *whistle chirpily.* **chirpiness** *n* [U].

chirrup /ˈtʃɪrəp/ *n* series of chirps.

▷ **chirrup** *v* (**-p-**) [I] make a chirrup; twitter.

chisel

chisel /ˈtʃɪzl/ *n* tool with a sharp cutting edge at the end, for shaping wood, stone or metal. ⇨ illus.

▷ **chisel** *v* (**-ll-**; *US* also **-l-**) **1** [Tn, Tn·pr] (a) ~ **sth (into sth)** cut or shape sth with a chisel: *The sculptor chiselled the lump of marble into a fine statue.* ○ (*fig*) *a woman with (finely) chiselled*

features, ie a sharply defined face. **(b)** ~ **sth (out of sth)** form sth using a chisel: *a temple chiselled out of solid rock.* **2** [Tn, Tn·pr] ~ **sb (out of sth)** (*sl*) cheat or swindle sb.
chiseller (*US* also **chiseler**) *n* person who chisels (CHISEL 2) people; swindler.

chit[1] /tʃɪt/ *n* **1** young child. **2** (*usu derog*) small or thin young woman: *a mere chit of a girl.*

chit[2] /tʃɪt/ *n* **1** short written note or letter. **2** note showing an amount of money owed, eg for drinks at a hotel: *Can I sign a chit for the drinks I've ordered?*

chit-chat /ˈtʃɪt tʃæt/ *n* [U] (*infml*) chat; gossip.

chitin /ˈkaɪtɪn/ *n* [U] substance in the hard outer covering of certain insects, spiders and crustaceans (*arthropods*).

chivalry /ˈʃɪvəlrɪ/ *n* [U] **1 (a)** (in the Middle Ages) ideal qualities expected of a knight, such as courage, honour, courtesy and concern for the weak and helpless. **(b)** religious, moral and social system of the Middle Ages, based on these qualities: *the age of chivalry.* **2** courtesy and considerate behaviour, esp towards women.
▷ **chivalrous** /ˈʃɪvlrəs/ *adj* **1** (in the Middle Ages) showing the qualities of a perfect knight. **2** (of men) courteous and considerate towards women; gallant: *a chivalrous old gentleman.* **chivalrously** *adv.*

chive /tʃaɪv/ *n* [C] **(a)** small herb with purple flowers and slender onion-flavoured leaves. **(b)** (usu *pl*) these leaves chopped and used to flavour or decorate salads, etc.

chivvy (also **chivy**) /ˈtʃɪvɪ/ *v* (*pt, pp* **chivvied, chivied**) [Tn, Tn·pr, Tn·p, Cn·t] ~ **sb (into sth/along)** (*infml*) continuously urge sb to do sth, often in an annoying way: *His mother kept on chivvying him to get his hair cut.*

chloral /ˈklɔːrəl/ *n* [U] (also **chloral hydrate** /ˌklɔːrəl ˈhaɪdreɪt/) (*chemistry*) white crystalline compound used as a sedative.

chloride /ˈklɔːraɪd/ *n* [U] compound of chlorine and one other element: *sodium chloride.*

chlorine /ˈklɔːriːn/ *n* [U] chemical element, a poisonous greenish-yellow gas with a pungent smell, used to sterilize water and in industry. ⇨ App 11.
▷ **chlorinate** /ˈklɔːrɪneɪt/ *v* [Tn] treat or sterilize (esp water) with chlorine: *Is the swimming-pool chlorinated?* **chlorination** /ˌklɔːrɪˈneɪʃn/ *n* [U].

chloroform /ˈklɒrəfɔːm; *US* ˈklɔːr-/ *n* [U] colourless liquid, the vapour of which makes a person unconscious when it is breathed in.
▷ **chloroform** *v* [Tn] make (sb) unconscious with this.

chlorophyll /ˈklɒrəfɪl; *US* ˈklɔːr-/ *n* [U] green substance in plants that absorbs energy from sunlight to help them grow. Cf PHOTOSYNTHESIS.

ChM /ˌsiː eɪtʃ ˈem/ *abbr* Master of Surgery (Latin *Chirurgiae Magister*): *have/be a ChM* ○ *John Wall ChM.*

choc /tʃɒk/ *n* (*Brit infml*) chocolate: *a box of chocs.*
□ ˈ**choc-ice** (also ˈ**choc-bar**) *n* (*Brit*) small block of ice-cream thinly coated with chocolate.

chock /tʃɒk/ *n* block or wedge used to prevent a wheel, barrel, door, etc from moving.
▷ **chock** *v* [Tn] wedge (sth) with a chock or chocks.
□ ˌ**chock-a-**ˈ**block** *adj* [pred] ~ **(with sth/sb)** completely full; tightly packed: *The town centre was chock-a-block (with traffic).*
chock-ˈ**full** *adj* [pred] ~ **(of sth/sb)** completely full: *The dustbin is chock-full (of rubbish).*

chocolate /ˈtʃɒklət/ *n* **1** [U] brown edible substance in the form of powder or a block, made from roasted and crushed cacao seeds. **2** [U, C] sweet made of or coated with this: *a bar of (milk/plain) chocolate* ○ *a box of chocolates* ○ *Have another chocolate.* **3** [U] drink made by mixing powdered chocolate with hot water or milk: *a mug of hot chocolate.* **4** [sing] colour of chocolate; dark brown.
▷ **chocolate** *adj* **1** made or coated with chocolate: *chocolate sauce* ○ *a chocolate biscuit.* **2** having the colour of chocolate; dark brown: *a chocolate carpet.*
□ ˈ**chocolate-box** (also ˈ**chocolate-boxy**) *adj* [usu attrib] (*often derog*) pretty or attractive in a conventionally romantic way (like the pictures often printed on boxes of chocolates).

Choctaw /ˈtʃɒktɔː/ *n* **1** [C] member of a N American Indian tribe originally inhabiting Mississippi and Alabama. **2** [U] language of this tribe.

choice /tʃɔɪs/ *n* **1** [C] ~ **(between A and B)** act of choosing between two or more possibilities: *make a choice* ○ *We are faced with a difficult choice.* ○ *What influenced you most in your choice of career?* **2** [U] right or possibility of choosing: *He had no choice but to resign*, ie Resigning was the only thing he could do. ○ *If I had the choice, I would retire at thirty.* **3** [C] one of two or more possibilities from which sb may choose; alternative: *You have several choices open to you.* **4** [C] person or thing chosen: *She wouldn't be my choice as Prime Minister.* ○ *I don't like his choice of* (ie the people he chooses as his) *friends.* **5** [U] variety from which to choose; range: *There's not much choice in the shops.* **6** (idm) **be spoilt for choice** ⇨ SPOIL. **for choice** preferably. **of one's choice** that one chooses: *First prize in the competition will be a meal at the restaurant of your choice.* **out of/from choice** willingly: *do sth out of choice.* **you pays your money and you takes your choice** ⇨ PAY[2].
▷ **choice** *adj* (**-er, -est**) **1** [esp attrib] (esp of fruit and vegetables) of very good quality. **2** carefully chosen: *She summed up the situation in a few choice phrases.* ○ (*joc*) *He used some pretty choice* (ie rude or offensive) *language!*

choir /ˈkwaɪə(r)/ *n* **1** [CGp] organized group of singers, esp one that performs in church services: *She sings in the school choir.* **2** [C] part of a church where these singers sit: [attrib] *choir stalls.* ⇨ illus at CHURCH.
□ ˈ**choirboy** *n* boy who sings in a church choir.
ˈ**choirmaster** *n* person who trains and conducts a choir.
ˈ**choir school** school attached to or associated with a cathedral or college.

choke /tʃəʊk/ *v* **1** [I, Ipr] ~ **(on sth)** be unable to breathe because one's windpipe is blocked by sth: *She choked (to death) on a fish bone.* **2** [Tn] cause (sb) to stop breathing by squeezing or blocking the windpipe; (of smoke, etc) make (sb) unable to breathe easily: *choke the life out of sb* ○ *The fumes almost choked me.* **3** [I, Ipr, Tn] ~ **(with sth)** (cause sb to) become speechless: *She was choking with emotion.* ○ *Anger choked his words.* **4** [Tn, Tn·pr esp passive, Tn·p esp passive] ~ **sth (up) (with sth)** block or fill (a passage, space, etc); clog or smother sth: *The drains are choked (up) with dead leaves.* ○ *The garden is choked with weeds.* **5** (phr v) **choke sth back** restrain or suppress sth: *choke back one's tears, anger, indignation.* **choke sth down** swallow sth with difficulty. **choke sb off** (*infml*) **(a)** interrupt sb rudely or abruptly. **(b)** reprimand sb severely (for doing sth).
▷ **choke** *n* **1** act or sound of choking. **2** (knob which operates the) valve controlling the flow of air into a petrol engine: *Won't your car start? Try giving it a bit more choke*, ie letting more air into the engine by pulling out the choke. ⇨ illus at CAR. **3** coil of electric wire used in radio circuits to ensure an even electric current.
choked *adj* [pred] ~ **(about sth)** (*infml*) upset; angry: *He was pretty choked about being dropped from the team.*

choker /ˈtʃəʊkə(r)/ *n* close-fitting necklace or band of material worn round the throat by women: *a pearl choker.*

cholera /ˈkɒlərə/ *n* [U] infectious and often fatal disease causing severe diarrhoea and vomiting. It is transmitted by contaminated drinking water: *an outbreak of cholera* ○ [attrib] *a cholera epidemic.*

choleric /ˈkɒlərɪk/ *adj* easily angered; bad-tempered.

cholesterol /kəˈlestərɒl/ *n* [U] fatty substance found in animal fluids and tissue, thought to cause hardening of the arteries: [attrib] *A high cholesterol level in the blood can cause heart disease.*

chomp /tʃɒmp/ *v* [I, Ip, Ipr, Tn] ~ **(away)**; ~ **(on) sth** (*infml*) chew (food) noisily; munch: *chomping (on) a bar of chocolate.* Cf CHAMP[1].

Chomsky /ˈtʃɒmskɪ/ Avram Noam (1928-), American linguistics scholar and political theorist. In his theory of generative transformational grammar, he develops the view that language results from an innate ability, common to all people, and that linguistics is a part of psychology.

choose /tʃuːz/ *v* (*pt* **chose** /tʃəʊz/, *pp* **chosen** /ˈtʃəʊzn/) **1** [I, Ipr, Tn, Tn·pr, Cn·n/a, Cn·t] ~ **(between A and/or B)**; ~ **(A) (from B)**; ~ **sb/sth as sth** pick out or select (sb/sth that one prefers or considers the best, most suitable, etc) from a number of alternatives: *choose carefully* ○ *She had to choose between giving up her job or hiring a nanny.* ○ *We offer a wide range of holidays to choose from.* ○ *choose a carpet, career, chairman* ○ *We have to choose a new manager from a short-list of five candidates.* ○ *The Americans chose Mr Bush as president/to be president.* **2 (a)** [Tw no passive, Tt] decide (to do one thing rather than another): *Have you chosen what you want for your birthday?* ○ *We chose to go by train.* **(b)** [I, Tt] like; prefer: *You may do as you choose.* ○ *The author chooses to remain anonymous.* **3** (idm) **pick and choose** ⇨ PICK[3]. **there is nothing, not much, little, etc to choose between A and B** there is very little difference between two or more things or people.
□ **the** ˌ**chosen** ˈ**people** any of various peoples (esp the Jews) believing that they have a special purpose, given by God.

NOTE ON USAGE: **select** suggests a more carefully considered decision than **choose**: *Our shops select only the very best quality produce.* **Pick** is less formal than **select**: *Who are you going to pick for the team?* **Choose** suggests a freely made decision and can refer to a decision between only two items. (We usually **select** or **pick** from a number greater than two): *She chose the red sweater rather than the pink one.* **Opt (for)** refers to the choice of courses of action rather than of items and suggests the weighing up of advantages and disadvantages: *Most people opt for buying their own homes rather than renting them.*

choosy (also **choosey**) /ˈtʃuːzɪ/ *adj* (**-sier, -siest**) (*infml*) careful in choosing; fussy or hard to please: *She's very choosy about who she goes out with.* ▷ **choosiness** *n* [U].

chop[1] /tʃɒp/ *v* (**-pp-**) **1** [Tn, Tn·pr, Tn·p] ~ **sth (up) (into sth)** cut sth into pieces with an axe, a knife, etc: *chopping wood in the garden* ○ *He chopped the logs (up) into firewood*, ie into sticks. ○ *Chop the meat into cubes before frying it.* ○ *finely chopped onions, carrots, parsley, etc.* **2** [Tn] hit (sth) with a short downward stroke or blow. ⇨ Usage at CUT[1]. **3** [Tn esp passive] (*Brit infml*) stop or greatly reduce (sth): *Bus services in this area have been chopped.* **4** (phr v) **chop at sth** aim blows at sth with an axe, a knife, etc. **chop sth down** cause sth to fall down by cutting it at the base: *chop down a dead tree.* **chop sth off (sth)** remove sth (from sth) by cutting with an axe, etc: *He chopped a branch off the tree.* ○ (*infml*) *Charles I had his head chopped off.* **chop a/one's way through sth** make a path through sth by chopping branches, etc.

chop[2] /tʃɒp/ *n* **1** [C] **(a)** cutting stroke, esp one made with an axe: *She cut down the sapling with one chop.* **(b)** chopping blow, esp one made with the side of the hand: *a karate chop.* **2** [C] thick slice of meat, usu including a rib: *a pork/lamb/mutton chop.* **3 the chop** [sing] (*sl esp Brit*) act of dismissing or killing sb; act of discontinuing sth:

She got the chop after ten years with the company. ○ *The public spending cuts will mean the chop for several hospitals.*

□ ˈ**chop-house** *n* (*becoming dated*) (usu cheap) restaurant, esp one serving meals with chops or steaks.

chop[3] /tʃɒp/ *v* (**-pp-**) **1** (idm) ˌ**chop and** ˈ**change** keep changing one's plans, opinions, etc. **2** (phr v) **chop about/round** (of the wind) change direction suddenly. ⇨ Usage at CUT[1].

chop[4] /tʃɒp/ *n* (usu *pl*) **1** jaw, esp of an animal. **2** (idm) **lick/smack one's lips/chops** ⇨ LICK.

Chopin /ˈʃəʊpæn/ Fryderyk (Frédéric) (1810-49), Polish composer and pianist who spent much of his life in France. His music, most of it for the piano, is regarded by many as the finest ever written for that instrument and the perfect expression of poetry in music.

chopper /ˈtʃɒpə(r)/ *n* **1** chopping tool, esp a short axe or a butcher's heavy knife with a large blade. **2** (*infml*) helicopter.

choppy /ˈtʃɒpɪ/ *adj* (**-ier, -iest**) (of the sea) moving in short broken waves; slightly rough. ▷ **choppiness** *n* [U].

chopsticks /ˈtʃɒpstɪks/ *n* [pl] pair of thin sticks made of wood, ivory, etc, used in China, Japan, etc for lifting food to the mouth.

chop-suey /ˌtʃɒpˈsuːɪ/ *n* [U] Chinese dish of small pieces of meat fried with rice and vegetables.

choral /ˈkɔːrəl/ *adj* of, composed for or sung by a choir: *a choral society* ○ *choral evensong* ○ *Beethoven's choral symphony.*

chorale /kəˈrɑːl/ *n* **1** (music for a) hymn sung by a choir and congregation together, as part of a church service. **2** (*esp US*) group of singers; choir.

chord[1] /kɔːd/ *n* (in music) combination of notes usu sounded together in harmony.

chord[2] /kɔːd/ *n* **1** (*mathematics*) straight line that joins two points on the circumference of a circle or the ends of an arc. ⇨ illus at CIRCLE. **2** string of a harp, etc. **3** (idm) **strike a chord** ⇨ STRIKE[2]. **touch the right chord** ⇨ TOUCH[2].

chore /tʃɔː(r)/ *n* **1** small routine task: *do the chores,* eg the housework ○ *household/domestic chores,* ie dusting, ironing, making the beds, etc. **2** unpleasant or tiring task: *She finds shopping a chore.*

choreograph /ˈkɒrɪəgrɑːf, *also* -græf; *US* ˈkɔːrɪəgræf/ *v* [Tn] design and arrange steps and dances for (a ballet, etc).

choreography /ˌkɒrɪˈɒgrəfɪ; *US* ˌkɔːrɪ-/ *n* [U] (art of designing and arranging) steps for ballet and stage dancing. ▷ **choreographer** /ˌkɒrɪˈɒgrəfə(r)/ *n.* **choreographic** /ˌkɒrɪəˈgræfɪk/ *adj.*

chorister /ˈkɒrɪstə(r); *US* ˈkɔːr-/ *n* member of a choir, esp a choirboy.

chortle /ˈtʃɔːtl/ *n* loud chuckle of pleasure or amusement.

▷ **chortle** *v* [I] utter a chortle: *chortle with delight at a joke.*

NOTE ON USAGE: **Chuckle** and **chortle** both indicate laughing with pleasure and satisfaction. Chuckling is usually quiet and may be a response to private thoughts or reading: *He chuckled to himself when he remembered the trick he'd played on them.* Chortling is usually louder and more public: *When I told them what had happened to me, they all chortled with mirth.*

chorus /ˈkɔːrəs/ *n* **1** [CGp] (usu large) group of singers; choir: *the Bath Festival Chorus.* **2** [C] piece of music, usu part of a larger work, composed for such a group: *the Hallelujah Chorus.* **3** [C] part of a song that is sung after each verse, esp by a group of people: *Bill sang the verses and everyone joined in the chorus.* **4** [C] thing said or shouted by many people together: *a chorus of boos, cheers, laughter, etc* ○ *The proposal was greeted with a chorus of approval.* **5** [CGp] group of performers who sing and dance in a musical comedy: [attrib] *a chorus line.* **6** [CGp] (in ancient Greek drama) group of singers and dancers who comment on the events of the play. **7** [C] (esp in Elizabethan drama) actor who speaks the prologue and epilogue of a play. **8** (idm) **in chorus** all together; in unison: *act, speak, answer in chorus.*

▷ **chorus** *v* [Tn] sing or say (sth) all together: *The crowd chorused their approval (of the decision).*

□ ˈ**chorus-girl** *n* girl or young woman who sings or dances in a chorus(5).

chose, chosen *pt, pp* of CHOOSE.

Chou En-lai /ˌdʒəʊ enˈlaɪ/ (1898-1976), Chinese statesman. One of the founders of the Chinese Communist party, he became the first Premier of the People's Republic of China (1949-76).

chough /tʃʌf/ *n* type of crow with red legs and a red beak.

chow[1] /tʃaʊ/ *n* type of dog with a thick coat, originally from China.

chow[2] /tʃaʊ/ *n* [U] (*sl*) food.

chowder /ˈtʃaʊdə(r)/ *n* [U] (*US*) thick soup or stew made with vegetables and fish: *clam chowder.*

chow mein /ˌtʃaʊ ˈmeɪn/ *n* [U] Chinese dish of fried noodles with shredded meat and vegetables.

chrism /ˈkrɪzəm/ *n* [U] consecrated oil, used esp for anointing in the Catholic and Greek Orthodox Churches.

Christ /kraɪst/ *n* **(a)** title, also treated as a name, given to *Jesus as the one chosen by God to save the world. **(b)** image or picture of Christ.

▷ **Christ** *interj* (also **Jesus, Jesus Christ**) (⚠ *infml*) (expressing anger, annoyance, surprise, etc): *Christ! We're running out of petrol.*

□ ˈ**Christlike** *adj* like Christ in character or action: *showing Christlike humility.*

Christadelphian /ˌkrɪstəˈdelfɪən/ *n* member of a US religious sect claiming to return to the beliefs and practices of the earliest disciples of Jesus Christ. They believe that Christ will return to set up a world-wide theocracy beginning in Jerusalem.

christen /ˈkrɪsn/ *v* **1** [Tn] receive (sb) into the Christian Church by sprinkling water on his head and giving him a name. Cf BAPTIZE. **2** [esp passive: Tn, Cn·n] **(a)** give a name to (sb) at such a ceremony: *The child was christened Mary.* **(b)** give a name to (esp a ship when it is launched). **3** [Tn] (*fig infml*) use (sth) for the first time: *Let's have a drink to christen our new sherry glasses.*

▷ **christening** /ˈkrɪsnɪŋ/ *n* ceremony in which sb is christened; baptism: [attrib] *a christening service.*

Christendom /ˈkrɪsndəm/ *n* [sing] (*fml*) **(a)** all Christian people throughout the world. **(b)** (*dated*) the Christian countries of the world. ⇨ Usage at CHRISTIAN.

Christian /ˈkrɪstʃən/ *adj* **1** of or based on the teachings of Christ or the doctrines of Christianity: *the Christian Church, faith, religion* ○ *a Christian upbringing.* **2** of or believing in the Christian religion: *a Christian country.* **3** of Christians: *the Christian sector of the city.* **4** showing the qualities of a Christian; kind and humane: *That's not a very Christian way to behave.*

▷ **Christian** *n* **1** person who believes in the Christian religion. **2** (*infml*) person who has Christian qualities.

Christianity /ˌkrɪstɪˈænətɪ/ *n* [U] **1** the religion based on belief in Jesus Christ and on his teachings. Christians believe that Jesus was the son of God, and that he died and came back to life again in order to redeem the world from sin. Christianity originated in the Middle East but has spread to most parts of the world and exists in many forms: *She was converted to Christianity.* **2 (a)** being a Christian: *He derives strength from his Christianity.* **(b)** Christian character or qualities.

□ **the** ˌ**Christian** ˈ**Era** the period of history from the birth of Christ to the present day.

ˈ**Christian name** (*US* also ˈ**given name**) name given to sb when he is christened; first name. ⇨ Usage at NAME[1].

ˌ**Christian** ˈ**Science** Christian church and religious system whose teaching includes healing by prayer alone. ˌ**Christian** ˈ**Scientist** person who believes in this system.

NOTE ON USAGE: **Christianity**, **Islam** and **Judaism** are the names of religions or faiths followed by **Christians**, **Muslims** and **Jews** respectively. The word **Christendom**, which is now dated, refers to all Christian countries or all Christians in the world. Historically it has been used to mean the whole world from a European point of view: *Rome was the greatest city in all Christendom.* **Jewry** is the collective name for all Jews: *British Jewry.* **Muhammedanism** (now dated) is an alternative name for **Islam**, used particularly by non-Muslims.

Christie /ˈkrɪstɪ/ Dame Agatha (1890-1976), English writer of detective stories including *Murder on the Orient Express* and *Death on the Nile.* She is famous for creating the fictional detectives Hercule *Poirot and Miss Marple.

Christie's /ˈkrɪstɪz/ London firm of art auctioneers, founded in 1766. Cf SOTHEBY'S.

Christmas /ˈkrɪsməs/ *n* **1** (also ˌ**Christmas** ˈ**Day**) day (25 December) on which Christians annually celebrate the birth of Christ: [attrib] *Christmas dinner, carols, decorations.* **2** (also ˈ**Christmas-time**, ˈ**Christmas-tide**) period of several days before and after Christmas Day: *spend Christmas with one's family* ○ [attrib] *the Christmas holidays.* ⇨ article.

▷ **Christmassy** /ˈkrɪsməsɪ/ *adj* (*infml*) typical of Christmas; looking festive.

□ ˈ**Christmas box** *n* (*Brit*) small gift, usu of money, given at Christmas, esp to sb (eg a postman or a milkman) who provides a service throughout the year.

ˈ**Christmas cake** rich fruit cake, usu covered with marzipan and icing and eaten at Christmas.

ˈ**Christmas card** greetings card sent to friends at Christmas. ⇨ article at GREETING.

ˌ**Christmas** ˈ**cracker** = CRACKER 2b.

ˌ**Christmas** ˈ**Eve** (evening of the) day before Christmas Day; 24 December.

ˌ**Christmas** ˈ**pudding** rich steamed pudding made with dried fruit and eaten at Christmas.

ˌ**Christmas** ˈ**rose** type of plant (a hellebore, not a rose) that produces white flowers in winter.

ˌ**Christmas** ˈ**stocking** stocking traditionally hung up by children on Christmas Eve to be filled with presents, supposedly by Father Christmas.

ˈ**Christmas tree** evergreen or artificial tree decorated with lights, tinsel, etc at Christmas.

Christopher /ˈkrɪstəfə(r)/ Saint, legendary martyr and patron saint of travellers. He is traditionally depicted carrying the infant Christ on his shoulders.

chromatic /krəʊˈmætɪk/ *adj* **1 (a)** of colour. **(b)** in bright colours. **2** (*music*) using accidentals and moving freely from one key to another.

□ **chro**ˌ**matic** ˈ**scale** (*music*) series of notes rising or falling in semitones.

chromatin /ˈkrəʊmətɪn/ *n* [U] substance of which chromosomes are formed and that can be stained very easily.

chromatography /ˌkrəʊməˈtɒgrəfɪ/ *n* [U] (*chemistry*) separation of a mixture into its component substances by passing it over a material which adsorbs these at different rates, so that they appear as different layers, often of different colours.

chrome /krəʊm/ *n* [U] **1** chromium (esp when used as a protective coating on other metals). **2** yellow colouring matter obtained from a compound of chromium and used in paints.

□ ˌ**chrome** ˈ**steel** alloy of steel and chromium.

chromium /ˈkrəʊmɪəm/ *n* [U] metallic chemical element used in making alloys (such as stainless steel) and as a shiny protective coating on other metals: *chromium plating,* eg on a car bumper ○ *chromium-plated.* ⇨ App 11.

chromosome /ˈkrəʊməsəʊm/ *n* (*biology*) any of

Christmas

Christmas is the most important annual festival in both Britain and North America. In its origins, it combines the Christian celebration of the birth of Christ, on 25 December, with the ancient tradition of a winter feast during the darkest period of the year.

The religious preparation for Christmas begins four weeks earlier on Advent Sunday, and during Advent churches hold special carol services, such as the popular Festival of Nine Lessons and Carols. At this time, too, carol singers make door-to-door visits to people at home, collecting money for charity. In many towns, open-air carol services are held round a Christmas tree in the town centre. Children at school often perform nativity plays commemorating the birth of Christ. Church attendance on Christmas day is higher than at any other time of year. Some people like to go to midnight mass, a service held late on Christmas Eve. Churches are specially decorated and carols are sung.

Many weeks before Christmas, the first sign of its approach is usually the appearance of Christmas cards for sale. Millions of such cards are sent yearly both by individuals and firms. Many people use them as a way of keeping in touch with friends who live far away. The images used on the cards reflect the nostalgic mood of the season, with scenes of Victorian Christmas celebrations, or they use typical Christmas symbols such as stars, robins, holly, mistletoe, snow and snowmen. Biblical scenes, especially the Nativity, are also used.

Christmas is a time for giving presents, especially to children. Small children believe that Santa Claus, or Father Christmas, a white-bearded old man dressed in red, rides through the air on a sleigh pulled by reindeer and delivers presents to each child, coming into the house by the chimney. Children hang stockings up on Christmas Eve and find them filled with presents on Christmas morning.

The custom of having a decorated Christmas tree, usually a spruce or fir tree, was introduced to Britain from Germany in the 19th century. Trees are placed in town squares, outside churches and in many homes, decorated with coloured lights and with a large star or an angel at the top. In homes, presents are placed round the tree, or hung on it, and given out on Christmas day.

People decorate their houses with holly, mistletoe, candles and coloured paper chains and lanterns. 'Kissing under the mistletoe' is an old tradition that is still occasionally observed. Streets are often decorated with coloured lights and the Christmas lights in the main shopping streets in London's West End are a special attraction.

On Christmas day itself there is usually a celebration with family and friends, which includes a special Christmas meal of roast goose or turkey followed by Christmas pudding, which is soaked in brandy and set alight. The table is specially decorated, usually with Christmas crackers, containing paper hats, riddles and other novelties. Port and nuts are often served after the meal. Other Christmas foods are mince pies and a special Christmas cake, a fruit-cake covered in marzipan and icing. Many people listen to the message broadcast by the Queen to people in Britain and the Commonwealth on Christmas Day. The following day (26 December) is called Boxing Day. It was formerly the day when servants were given their 'Christmas box', a gift or money from their employer. Many households still give Christmas boxes to the people who deliver their post, milk, newspapers, etc.

the tiny threads or rods in animal and plant cells. In animals and humans they usually occur in identical pairs and carry the genes which decide their characteristics. Chromosomes with faults can lead to genetic diseases. Cf X CHROMOSOME (X), Y CHROMOSOME (Y).

chromosphere /ˈkrəʊməsfɪə(r)/ *n* region of the outer atmosphere of the sun, with temperatures of 10 000-20 000° Celsius.

chronic /ˈkrɒnɪk/ *adj* **1** (esp of a disease) lasting for a long time; continually recurring: *chronic bronchitis, arthritis, etc* ○ *the country's chronic unemployment problem.* Cf ACUTE. **2** having had a disease or a habit for a long time: *a chronic alcoholic, invalid, etc.* **3** (*Brit sl*) very bad: *The film was absolutely chronic.* ▷ **chronically** /ˈkrɒnɪklɪ/ *adv*: *the chronically ill.*

chronicle /ˈkrɒnɪkl/ *n* **1** (often *pl*) record of historical events in the order in which they happened: *He consulted the chronicles of the period.* ○ [attrib]: *chronicle plays,* ie ones which are based on historical subjects, eg Shakespeare's *Henry V.* **2 Chronicles** (*Bible*) either of two books in the Old Testament telling the history of Israel and Judah. ⇨ App 5.

▷ **chronicle** *v* [Tn] record (sth) in a chronicle: *chronicling the events of a war.* **chronicler** /ˈkrɒnɪklə(r)/ *n.*

chron(o)- *comb form* of or relating to time: *chronology* ○ *chronometer.*

chronological /ˌkrɒnəˈlɒdʒɪkl/ *adj* arranged in the order in which they occurred: *a chronological list of Shakespeare's plays,* ie in the order in which they were written. ▷ **chronologically** /-klɪ/ *adv.*

chronology /krəˈnɒlədʒɪ/ *n* **1** [U] science of fixing the dates of historical events. **2** [C] arrangement or list of events in the order in which they occurred: *a chronology of Mozart's life.*

chronometer /krəˈnɒmɪtə(r)/ *n* instrument that keeps very accurate time, used esp for navigating at sea.

chrysalis /ˈkrɪsəlɪs/ *n* (*pl* ~**es**) **1** form of an insect at the stage of its life when it changes from a grub to an adult insect, esp a butterfly or moth; pupa. ⇨ illus at BUTTERFLY. **2** hard case that encloses an insect during this stage.

chrysanthemum /krɪˈsænθəməm/ *n* (**a**) garden plant with brightly coloured flowers. (**b**) one of these flowers. ⇨ illus at PLANT.

chrysolite /ˈkrɪsəlaɪt/ *n* [C, U] yellowish-green precious stone.

Chrysostom /ˈkrɪsəstəm/ Saint John (c 347-407), bishop of Constantinople and one of the greatest early Christian preachers and scholars.

chub /tʃʌb/ *n* (*pl* unchanged) small freshwater fish with a thick body.

Chubb /tʃʌb/ *n* (also **Chubb lock**) (*propr*) type of lock containing a special device to prevent anyone picking it.

chubby /ˈtʃʌbɪ/ *adj* (**-ier, -iest**) round and plump; slightly fat: *chubby cheeks* ○ *a chubby child.* ⇨ Usage at FAT[1]. ▷ **chubbiness** *n* [U].

chuck[1] /tʃʌk/ *v* **1** [Tn, Tn·pr, Tn·p, Dn·n] (*infml*) throw (sth) carelessly or casually: *Chuck it in the bin!* ○ *chuck old clothes away/out* ○ *Chuck me (over) the newspaper if you've finished reading it.* **2** [Tn, Tn·p] ~ **sb/sth (in/up)** (*infml*) give up sb/sth; abandon: *She's just chucked her boy-friend,* ie ended her relationship with him. ○ *He chucked in his job last week.* **3** (idm) **chuck it** (*sl*) stop doing sth immediately: *I'm sick of your sarcastic remarks — just chuck it* (ie stop making them), *will you?* **chuck sb under the chin** touch or stroke sb lovingly or playfully under the chin. **4** (phr v) **chuck sb out (of sth)** (*infml*) force sb to leave (a place): *They were chucked out of the pub for being too rowdy.* ○ *He failed his exams and was chucked out of university.*

▷ **chuck** *n* **1** playful touch or stroke under the chin. **2** (idm) **give sb/get the chuck** (*infml*) dismiss or reject sb/be dismissed or rejected.

□ **chucker-out** /ˌtʃʌkər ˈaʊt/ *n* (*infml*) person whose job is to remove troublesome people from public-houses, meetings, etc.

chuck[2] /tʃʌk/ *n* (**a**) part of a lathe that grips the object to be worked on. (**b**) part of a drill that grips the bit. ⇨ illus at DRILL.

chuck[3] /tʃʌk/ *n* [U] (also ˈ**chuck steak**) cut[2](5) of beef taken from the neck to the ribs.

chuck[4] /tʃʌk/ *n* [U] (*US infml*) food.

□ ˈ**chuck-wagon** *n* cart carrying food and cooking equipment, esp for cowboys working on a ranch, etc.

chuckle /ˈtʃʌkl/ *v* [I, Ipr] laugh quietly or to oneself: *He chuckled (to himself) as he read the newspaper.* ○ *What are you chuckling about?* ⇨ Usage at CHORTLE.

▷ **chuckle** *n* quiet or partly suppressed laugh: *She gave a chuckle of delight.*

chuckle-head /ˈtʃʌklhed/ *n* (*infml*) stupid person. ▷ ˌ**chuckle-ˈheaded** *adj.*

chuff /tʃʌf/ *v* **1** [I] (of an engine, etc) work with a regular sharp puffing sound. **2** (phr v) **chuff along, past, etc** move while producing such sounds: *a steam locomotive chuffing down the line.*

chuffed /tʃʌft/ *adj* [pred] ~ **(about/at sth)** (*Brit infml*) very pleased: *look/feel chuffed* ○ *She was chuffed at/about getting a pay rise.*

chug /tʃʌg/ *v* (**-gg-**) **1** [I] make the short dull repeated sound of an engine running slowly. **2** (phr v) **chug along, down, up, etc** move steadily in the specified direction while making this sound: *The boat chugged along the canal.*

▷ **chug** *n* sound made by a chugging engine.

chukka /ˈtʃʌkə/ (also **chukker** /ˈtʃʌkə(r)/) *n* each of the periods of play in polo.

chum /tʃʌm/ *n* (*infml*) close friend: *an old school chum.*

▷ **chum** *v* (**-mm-**) (phr v) **chum up (with sb)** (*infml*) become very friendly (with sb).

chummy *adj* (*infml*) very friendly. **chummily** *adv.* **chumminess** *n* [U].

chump /tʃʌmp/ *n* **1** (*infml*) foolish person: *Don't be such a chump!* **2** short thick block of wood. **3** (*Brit* also ˌ**chump ˈchop**) thick end of a loin of lamb or mutton. **4** (idm) **off one's ˈchump** (*dated Brit sl*) crazy.

chunk /tʃʌŋk/ *n* **1** thick solid piece cut or broken off sth: *a chunk of bread, meat, ice, wood, etc.* **2** (*infml*) fairly large amount (of sth): *I've completed a fair chunk of my article.*

chunky /ˈtʃʌŋkɪ/ *adj* (**-ier, -iest**) **1** having a short thick body; stocky: *a chunky footballer.* **2** containing chunks of fruit, etc: *chunky marmalade.* **3** (of clothes) made of thick bulky (usu woollen) material: *a chunky sweater.* ▷ **chunkily** *adv*: *He's chunkily built.* **chunkiness** *n* [U].

Chunnel /ˈtʃʌnl/ *n* (*infml*) = CHANNEL TUNNEL.

chunter /ˈtʃʌntə(r)/ *v* [I, Ipr, Ip] (*Brit infml*) mutter; grumble; complain: *chuntering on about the price of food in the shops.*

church /tʃɜːtʃ/ *n* **1** [C] building used for public Christian worship: *The procession moved into the* church. ○ [attrib] *a church ˌsteeple* ○ *a church service.* ⇨ illus. **2** [U] service in such a building; public worship: *Church begins/is at 9 o'clock.* ○ *How often do you go to church?* ○ *They're in/at church*, ie attending a service. ⇨ Usage at SCHOOL[1]. **3 the Church** [sing] all Christians regarded as a group: *The Church has a duty to condemn violence.* **4 Church** [C] particular group of Christians; denomination: *the Anglican Church* ○ *the Catholic Church* ○ *the Free Churches.* **5 the Church** [sing] **(a)** (esp the Christian) religion regarded as an established institution: *the conflict between (the) Church and (the) State.* **(b)** the ministers of the Christian religion; the clergy or clerical profession: *go into/enter the Church*, ie become a Christian minister.

▷ **churchy** *adj* (*derog*) (esp of a person) excessively religious.

□ **ˈchurchgoer** *n* person who goes to church services regularly.

ˈchurchman (*fem* **ˈchurchwoman**) member of a church, esp a priest, minister, etc.

the ˌChurch of ˈEngland the Anglican Church in England, the established Church of the country. ⇨ article. ⇨ article at RELIGION.

the ˌChurch of ˈScotland the Presbyterian Church in Scotland, the established Church of the country. Unlike the Church of England it does not have bishops, and has *ministers* rather than priests. Local churches are run by a minister and a group of senior church members called *elders*.

churchˈwarden *n* (in a Church of England parish) one of usu two elected officials responsible for church money and property.

ˈchurchyard *n* enclosed area of land round a church, often used for burials.

Churchill /ˈtʃɜːtʃɪl/ Sir Winston Leonard Spencer (1874-1965), British statesman, who held several ministerial posts between 1911 and 1929. After warning of the threat of German military expansion in the 1930s, he became First Lord of the Admiralty, and then Conservative prime minister and war leader in May 1940. A powerful orator, he symbolized British resistance during the war, and served until 1945, when he was defeated in the general election. He served again as prime minister from 1951 to 1955. He also wrote several books of history, and was awarded the Nobel prize for literature in 1953. ⇨ App 2.

▷ **Churchillian** /tʃɜːˈtʃɪlɪən/ *adj* of or like Churchill, esp as a public speaker.

churl /tʃɜːl/ *n* (*dated*) bad-mannered or bad-tempered person. ▷ **churlish** *adj*: *It seems churlish to refuse such a generous offer.* **churlishly** *adv.* **churlishness** *n* [U].

churn /tʃɜːn/ *n* **1** machine in which milk or cream is beaten to make butter. **2** (*Brit*) large (usu metal) container in which milk is carried from a farm.

▷ **churn** *v* **1** [Tn] **(a)** beat (milk or cream) to make butter. **(b)** make (butter) in this way. **2 (a)** [Tn, Tn·p] ~ **sth (up)** cause sth to move violently; stir or disturb sth: *motor boats churning (up) the peaceful waters of the bay* ○ *The earth had been churned up by the wheels of the tractor.* ○ (*fig*) *The bitter argument left her feeling churned up* (ie agitated and upset) *inside.* **(b)** [I] (esp of liquids) move about violently: *the churning waters of a whirlpool* ○ *His stomach churned with nausea.* **3** (phr v) **churn sth out** (*infml*) produce sth (usu of bad quality) in large amounts: *She churns out romantic novels.*

chute /ʃuːt/ *n* **1** sloping or vertical passage down which things can slide or be dropped: *a rubbish chute*, eg from the upper storeys of a high building. **2** (*infml*) parachute.

chutney /ˈtʃʌtnɪ/ *n* [U] hot-tasting mixture of fruit, vinegar, sugar and spices, eaten with curries, cold meat, cheese, etc: *green tomato chutney.*

chutzpah /ˈhʊtspə/ *n* [U] (*infml usu approv*) shameless audacity; impudence: *It took chutzpah to say what she did in front of all those people.*

chyle /kaɪl/ *n* [U] milky fluid in the intestine, which contains absorbed food materials during the digestion of food.

chyme /kaɪm/ *n* [U] acid pulp consisting of partly digested food as it passes out of the stomach.

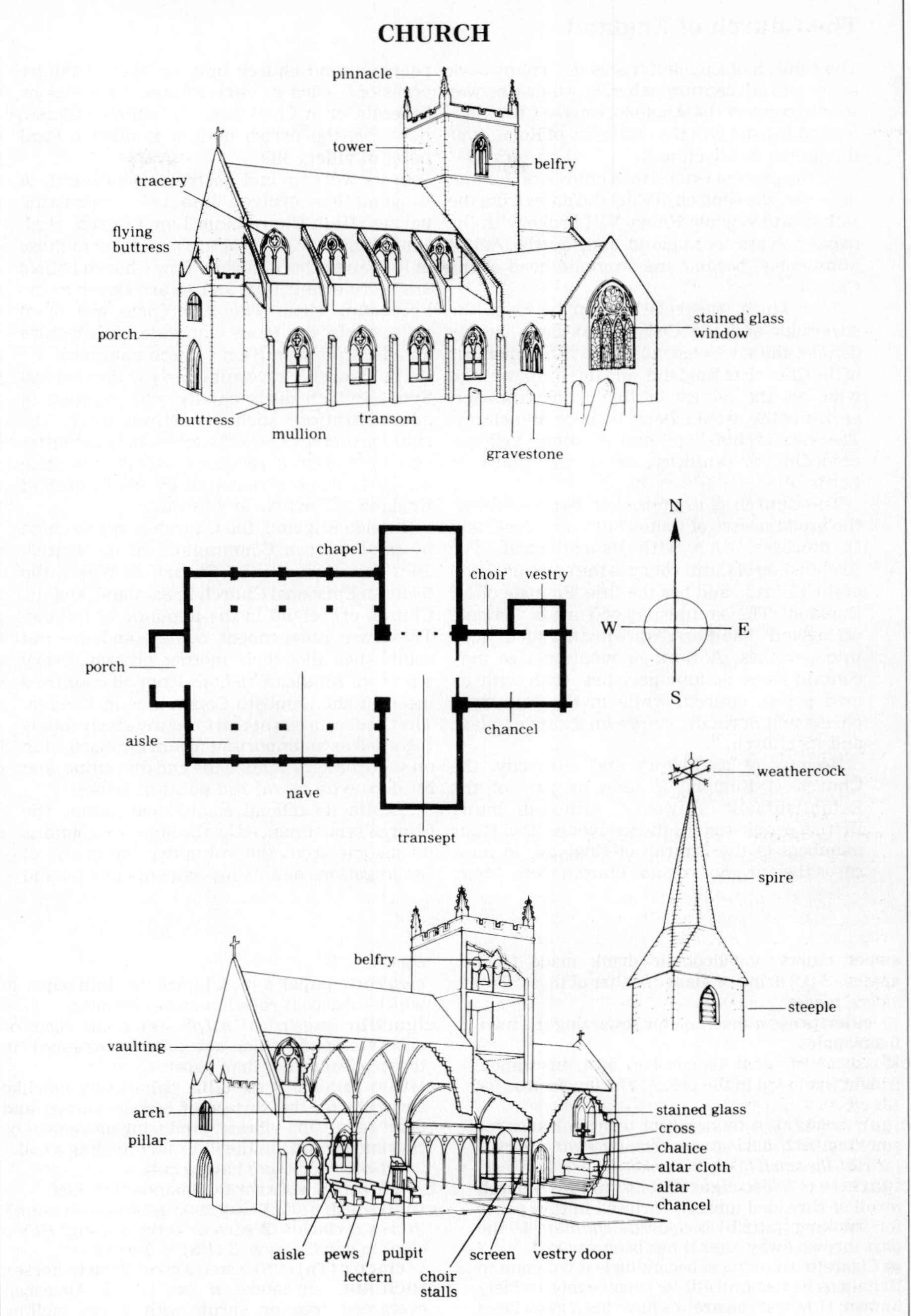

CI *abbr* (*Brit*) Channel Islands (Jersey, Guernsey, Alderney and Sark): *St Peter Port, Guernsey, CI*, eg in an address.

CIA /ˌsiː aɪ ˈeɪ/ *abbr* (*US*) Central Intelligence Agency: *working for the CIA.* Cf FBI.

cicada /sɪˈkɑːdə; *US* sɪˈkeɪdə/ *n* insect like a grasshopper, common in hot countries, the male of which makes a shrill chirping noise.

cicatrice /ˈsɪkətrɪs/ (also **cicatrix** /ˈsɪkətrɪks/) *n* (*pl* **-trices** /sɪkəˈtraɪsiːz/) scar left by a wound that has healed.

Cicero /ˈsɪsərəʊ/ Marcus Tullius (106-43 BC), Roman statesman, orator and writer. During his consulate, in 63 BC, he suppressed the Catiline conspiracy. His writings, which include many speeches, are considered a model of classical Latin prose.

cicerone /ˌtʃɪtʃəˈrəʊnɪ, ˌsɪsəˈrəʊnɪ/ *n* (*pl* **-eroni** /-ˈrəʊniː/) guide who shows antiquities, etc to visitors.

CID /ˌsiː aɪ ˈdiː/ *abbr* (*Brit*) Criminal Investigation Department: *an inspector from the CID.* ⇨ article at POLICE.

-cide *comb form* (forming *ns*) **1** act of killing sb: *genocide* ○ *patricide.* **2** person or thing that kills: *insecticide* ○ *fungicide.*

▷ **-cidal** *comb form* (forming *adjs*) of or related to killing: *homicidal.*

cider /ˈsaɪdə(r)/ *n* **1** (also **cyder**) [U] drink made from fermented apple-juice: *dry/sweet cider* ○ [attrib] *cider apples.* Cf PERRY. **2** [U] (*US* also

The Church of England

The Church of England traces its origins back to the late 6th century, when St Augustine was sent to convert the Anglo-Saxons to Christianity and to establish the authority of Rome over the native Celtic church.

As the present established church of Britain, however, the Church of England dates from the 16th century, when Henry VIII broke with the papal powers in England and, by the Act of Supremacy, became the supreme head of the Church.

Ever since, the relationship between the sovereign and the Church has been clearly defined: the sovereign must always be a member of the Church of England, and it is the sovereign who, on the advice of the prime minister, appoints the archbishops, bishops and clergy. The two archbishops and 21 other bishops, according to seniority, sit in the House of Lords.

The Church is organized in two provinces, the archdioceses of Canterbury and York, and 14 dioceses, each with its cathedral. The Archbishop of Canterbury is the spiritual head of the Church, and has the title 'Primate of All England'. The Archbishop of York is 'Primate of England'. The dioceses are further subdivided into parishes. A town of medium size may contain three or four parishes, each with its own parish church, while in the country a parish will normally centre on a single village and its church.

Because of its history and authority, the Church of England is seen as part of the Establishment. However, although many British people regard themselves as 'C of E', or members of the Church of England, in most cases they are not regular churchgoers. Many people attend church only on special family occasions, such as christenings, weddings or funerals, or at Christmas. In country villages, however, the parish church is often a focal point of village life.

In its worship and doctrine, the Church of England has evolved into two contrasting parties: High Church and Low Church. High Church beliefs and practice are closer to those of Roman Catholics, while Low Church beliefs are more evangelical and so are closer to the Protestant ideal. The differences are often reflected in the more elaborate architecture and decoration in High Church churches.

The Church's governing body is the General Synod, which deals chiefly with matters of administration, such as church work, the running of church schools, missionary activities and inter-church relations. About one state school in three is managed by the Church of England. (Cf article at SCHOOL.)

Outside England, the Church is represented by the Anglican Communion. In the British Isles this includes the Church of Wales, the Scottish Episcopal Church in Scotland, and the Church of Ireland in the Republic of Ireland. These are independent bodies, and are not established like their mother church. Every ten years Anglican bishops from all countries meet for the Lambeth Conference in London. The Conference is not an executive body, but is regarded as an important forum for discussion on such matters as doctrine and discipline, and for debate on moral and political issues.

Despite its official established status, the Church is not financed by the State, and obtains its income from the voluntary donations of congregations and its investments in land and property, which are managed by the Church Commissioners.

The main clergyman in a parish is known as either the vicar or the rector. (The names are historic and today there is little practical difference between the two.) The Church provides a house for the clergyman, called a vicarage or rectory, and pays a part of the cost of running it. It also pays his salary. The clergyman's wife frequently plays an active role in parish work, especially in its pastoral and social aspects.

An ordained clergyman is either a deacon or a priest. A deacon is junior to a priest, and is not authorized to conduct all church services. Although most of the clergy are men, it is now possible for women to be ordained as deacons, but not yet as priests. The issue of the ordination of women has been hotly debated in and outside the Church. In general, it is opposed by the High Church, but favoured by the Low.

Recent years have seen controversy in other areas of the Church. Many Anglicans were shocked when in 1984 the Rev David Jenkins, on his appointment as Bishop of Durham, publicly questioned the traditional doctrine on the Virgin Birth and the Resurrection. Later that year, after his consecration, he caused further controversy when he criticized the government's social and economic policies.

In general, the importance of the Church of England in British society is declining. Some people feel that the Church has become outdated, and others that it fails to give the moral and spiritual lead traditionally expected of it. (Cf article at RELIGION.)

sweet cider) non-alcoholic drink made from apples. **3** [C] drink or glass of either of these: *Two ciders, please.*

□ ˈ**cider-press** *n* machine for squeezing the juice from apples.

cif /ˌsi: aɪ ˈef/ *abbr* (*commerce*) cost, insurance, freight (included in the price): *The invoice was for £35 cif.*

cigar /sɪˈgɑ:(r)/ *n* tight roll of tobacco leaves for smoking: *rich businessmen smoking fat cigars* ○ [attrib] *the smell of cigar smoke.*

cigarette (*US* also **cigaret**) /ˌsɪgəˈret; *US* ˈsɪgərət/ *n* roll of shredded tobacco enclosed in thin paper for smoking: [attrib] *a cigarette end/butt*, ie the part thrown away after it has been smoked.

Cigarette smoking is becoming less common in Britain as its harmful effects become more widely known. However, cigarettes have been associated with various contrasting images. The flappers of the 1920s caused it to become a symbol of upper-class chic, especially when smoked in elegant cigarette holders. Later, in the period surrounding the Second World War, the majority of adults smoked and during that time a cigarette hanging from a person's lower lip came to symbolize the working class. The cigar, by contrast, is often associated with luxury and power, and the image of a rich man smoking a cigar has often been used in cartoons and in advertising.

□ **cigaˈrette-case** *n* small flat (usu metal) box for holding cigarettes.

cigaˈrette-holder *n* tube in one end of which a cigarette may be put for smoking.

cigaˈrette-lighter (also **lighter**) *n* device that produces a small flame for lighting cigarettes and cigars.

cigaˈrette-paper *n* [C, U] (piece of) thin paper in which tobacco is rolled to make cigarettes.

cigarillo /ˌsɪgəˈrɪləʊ/ *n* (*pl* ~**s**) small cigar or cigarette made from cut tobacco wrapped in tobacco leaf rather than paper.

cilium /ˈsɪlɪəm/ *n* (*pl* **cilia** /ˈsɪlɪə/) tiny hairlike structure on the surface of certain animal and plant cells. Cilia vibrate, producing movement or causing currents in the fluid surrounding a cell.

▷ **ciliate** /ˈsɪlɪət/ *adj* having cilia.

C-in-C /ˌsi: ɪn ˈsi:/ *abbr* Commander-in-Chief.

cinch /sɪntʃ/ *n* (*sl*) **1** easy task: *'How was the exam?' 'It was a cinch!'* **2** sure or certain thing: *He's a cinch to win the race.* **3** (*US*) = GIRTH 2.

▷ **cinch** *v* [Tn] (*US*) fasten a girth(2) on (a horse).

cinchona /sɪŋˈkəʊnə/ *n* (**a**) [C] S American evergreen tree or shrub with sweet-smelling flowers. (**b**) [U] its bark, from which quinine is obtained.

cincture /ˈsɪnktʃə(r)/ *n* (*fml*) belt or girdle.

cinder /ˈsɪndə(r)/ *n* **1** [C] small piece of partly burnt coal, wood, etc that is no longer burning but may still be hot. **2 cinders** [pl] ashes. **3** (idm) **burn, etc sth to a ˈcinder** cook (food) until it is hard and black: *The cakes were burnt to a cinder.*

□ ˈ**cinder-track** *n* running-track made with finely crushed cinders.

Cinderella /ˌsɪndəˈrelə/ *n* **1** character in a fairy story and pantomime who is badly treated by her family but with the help of her fairy godmother marries a prince. **2** girl or woman whose beauty or abilities have not been recognized, or who becomes rich and successful after a period of difficulty: [attrib] *a Cinderella story*, ie a case of this happening. **3** person or thing that has been persistently neglected: *This department has been the Cinderella of the company for far too long.*

cine- *comb form* of the cinema: *cine-projector.*

cinéaste (also **cineast**) /ˈsɪnɪæst/ *n* person who is very enthusiastic about cinema films.

cine-camera /ˈsɪnɪ kæmərə/ *n* camera used for taking moving pictures.

cine-film /ˈsɪnɪ fɪlm/ *n* [C, U] film used for taking moving pictures.

cinema /ˈsɪnəmɑ:, ˈsɪnəmə/ *n* **1** [C] (*US* **movie house**, **movie theatre**) building in which motion-picture films are shown: *go to the cinema*, ie to see a film. **2** (also **the cinema**) [sing] (*esp Brit*) (*US* **the movies**) films as an art-form or an industry: *She's interested in (the) cinema.* ○ *He works in the cinema.* ○ *cinema-goers, the cinema-going public*, ie people who go out to see films.

▷ **cinematic** /ˌsɪnəˈmætɪk/ *adj* of or relating to cinema.

cinematograph /ˌsɪnəˈmætəgrɑ:f; *US* -græf/ *n* early form of cinema projector.

cinematography /ˌsɪnəməˈtɒgrəfɪ/ *n* [U] art or science of making motion-picture films. **cinematographer** /ˌsɪnəməˈtɒgrəfə(r)/ *n.* **cinematographic** /ˌsɪnəmætəˈgræfɪk/ *adj.*

□ **CinemaScope** /ˈsɪnəməskəʊp/ *n* [U] (*propr*) process used in making films that can be projected onto a very wide screen: *filmed in CinemaScope.*

cinéma-vérité /ˌsɪnemɑ: ˈverɪteɪ/ *n* [U] (*French*) style of making esp documentary films popular in France and the USA in the 1960s. It involved filming events as they happened without a script or a director, to make them appear as realistic as possible on the screen.

cine-projector /ˈsɪnɪ prədʒektə(r)/ *n* machine for

showing moving pictures on a screen.

cinnabar /ˈsɪnəbɑ:(r)/ *n* **1** (a) [U] bright red mineral from which mercury is obtained. (b) red pigment obtained from this; vermilion. **2** [C] moth with reddish marks on its wings.

cinnamon /ˈsɪnəmən/ *n* **1** (a) [U] spice made from the inner bark of a SE Asian tree: [attrib] *cinnamon toast*, ie spread with a mixture of butter, sugar and cinnamon. (b) [C] this tree. **2** [U] yellowish-brown colour.

Cinque Ports /ˈsɪŋk pɔ:ts/ **the Cinque Ports** group of towns on the SE coast of England (the original 'five ports', Dover, Hastings, Hythe, Romney and Sandwich, and later Rye and Winchelsea). From the Middle Ages onwards they had the duty of protecting the coast and provided most of the English navy. In return they had certain trading privileges.

cipher (also **cypher**) /ˈsaɪfə(r)/ *n* **1** (a) [C, U] (method of) secret writing in which a set of letters or symbols is used to represent others; code: *a message in cipher*. (b) [C] message written in this way. (c) [C] key[1](5b) to a secret message. **2** [C] the symbol 0, representing nought or zero. **3** [C] any of the numbers from 1 to 9. **4** [C] (*fig derog*) person or thing of no importance: *a mere cipher*.

▷ **cipher** *v* [Tn] write (a message) in secret writing; encode.

circa /ˈsɜ:kə/ *prep* (*Latin*) (*abbrs* **c**, **ca**) (with dates) about: *born circa 150 BC*.

circadian /sɜ:ˈkeɪdɪən/ *adj* (*biology*) occurring regularly about once every 24 hours: *circadian rhythm*, eg the pattern of sleep in humans and animals, or of growth in plants. Cf BIORHYTHM.

Circe /ˈsɜ:sɪ/ in Homer's *Odyssey*, a goddess who turned Odysseus' men into pigs. A woman to whom men are strongly attracted is sometimes called a Circe.

circle

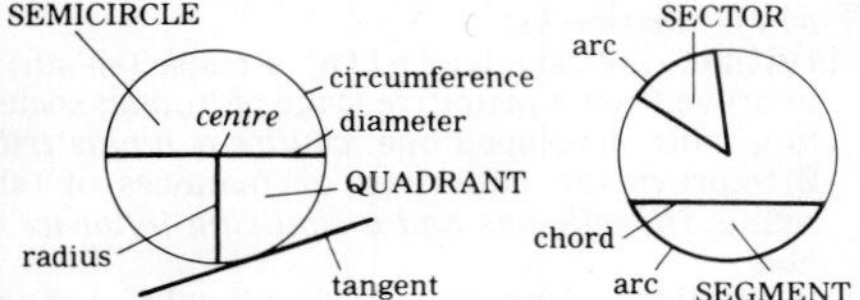

circle /ˈsɜ:kl/ *n* **1** (round space enclosed by a) curved line every point on which is the same distance from the centre: *Use your compasses to draw a circle.* ⇨ App 10. ⇨ illus. **2** thing shaped like this; ring: *a circle of trees, hills, spectators* ○ *standing in a circle*. **3** (*US* **balcony**) group of seats in curved and banked rows raised above the floor level of a theatre, cinema, concert-hall, etc: *We've booked seats in the circle.* ⇨ illus at THEATRE. **4** group of people who are connected by having the same interests, profession, etc: *be well known in business, political, theatrical, etc circles*, ie among people connected with business, politics, the theatre, etc ○ *move in fashionable circles* ○ *She has a large circle of friends.* **5** (idm) **come full circle** ⇨ FULL. **go round in ˈcircles** work busily at a task without making any progress. **square the circle** ⇨ SQUARE[3]. **a vicious circle** ⇨ VICIOUS.

▷ **circle** *v* **1** [I, Ipr, Ip] ~ (**about/around/round**) (**over sb/sth**) move in a circle, esp in the air: *vultures circling (round) over a dead animal.* **2** [Tn] (a) move in or form a circle round (sb/sth): *The plane circled the airport before landing.* ○ *The moon circles the earth every 28 days.* ○ *a town circled by hills.* (b) draw a circle round (sth): *spelling mistakes circled in red ink.*

circlet /ˈsɜ:klɪt/ *n* circular band, eg of precious metal, flowers, etc, worn round the head as an ornament.

circuit /ˈsɜ:kɪt/ *n* **1** line, route or journey round a place: *The circuit of the city walls is three miles.* ○ *The earth takes a year to make a circuit of* (ie go round) *the sun.* ○ *She ran four circuits of the track.* ○ *a motor-racing circuit*, ie the track itself. **2** (a) complete path along which an electric current flows: *There must be a break in the circuit.* (b) apparatus with a sequence of conductors, valves, etc through which an electric current flows: [attrib] *a circuit diagram*, ie one showing the connections in such an apparatus. **3** (a) regular journey made by a judge round a particular area to hear cases in court: *go on circuit*, ie make this journey ○ [attrib] *a circuit judge.* (b) area covered by such a journey. **4** (in sport) series of tournaments in which the same players regularly take part: *the American golf circuit.* **5** group of Methodist churches sharing the same preachers within a particular area.

□ ˈ**circuit-breaker** *n* automatic device for interrupting an electric current.

ˈ**circuit training** method of training using a series of different athletic exercises.

circuitous /səˈkju:ɪtəs/ *adj* (*fml*) long and indirect; roundabout: *a circuitous route.* ▷ **circuitously** *adv.*

circular /ˈsɜ:kjʊlə(r)/ *adj* **1** shaped like a circle; round. **2** moving round a circle: *a circular tour*, ie one taking a route that brings travellers back to the starting-point. **3** (of reasoning) using the point it is trying to prove as evidence for its conclusion: *a circular argument.* **4** [usu attrib] sent to a large number of people: *a circular letter.*

▷ **circular** *n* printed letter, notice or advertisement sent to a large number of people.

circularity /ˌsɜ:kjʊˈlærətɪ/ *n* [U].

circularize, -ise /ˈsɜ:kjʊləraɪz/ *v* [Tn] send a circular to (sb).

□ ˌ**circular ˈsaw** (*US* **buzz-saw**) rotating metal disc with a serrated edge used for cutting wood, etc.

circulate /ˈsɜ:kjʊleɪt/ *v* **1** (a) [I, Ipr, Tn, Tn·pr] (cause sth to) go round continuously: *Blood circulates through the body.* (b) [I] move about freely: *open a window to allow the air to circulate.* **2** [I, Ipr, Tn, Tn·pr] (cause sth to) pass from one place, person, etc to another: *The news of her death circulated* (ie spread) *quickly.* ○ *The host and hostess circulated (among their guests).* ○ *circulate a letter.* **3** [Tn] inform (sb) by means of a circular: *Have you been circulated with details of the conference?*

circulation /ˌsɜ:kjʊˈleɪʃn/ *n* **1** [C, U] movement of blood round the body from and back to the heart: *have (a) good/bad circulation.* **2** [U] (a) passing of sth from one person or place to another; spread: *the circulation of news, information, rumours, etc.* (b) state of circulating or being circulated: *Police say a number of forged banknotes are in circulation.* ○ *Pound notes have been withdrawn from circulation.* ○ (*fig*) *She's been ill but now she's back in circulation*, ie going out and meeting people again. **3** [C] number of copies of a newspaper, magazine, etc sold to the public: *a newspaper with a (daily) circulation of more than one million* ○ [attrib] *circulation figures.*

circulatory /ˌsɜ:kjʊˈleɪtərɪ; *US* ˈsɜ:kjələtɔ:rɪ/ *adj* of or relating to the circulation of blood: *circulatory disorders.*

circumcise /ˈsɜ:kəmsaɪz/ *v* [Tn] (a) cut off the foreskin of (a male person) as a religious rite or for medical reasons. (b) cut off the clitoris of (a female person).

▷ **circumcision** /ˌsɜ:kəmˈsɪʒn/ *n* [C, U] (action or ceremony of) circumcising.

circumference /səˈkʌmfərəns/ *n* (a) line that marks out a circle or other curved figure[1](2b). ⇨ App 10. (b) distance round this: *The circumference of the earth is almost 25 000 miles/The earth is almost 25 000 miles in circumference.* ⇨ illus at CIRCLE. Cf PERIMETER.

circumflex /ˈsɜ:kəmfleks/ *n* (also **circumflex accent**) mark put over a vowel in French and some other languages to show how it is pronounced, as in *rôle* or *fête*.

circumlocution /ˌsɜ:kəmləˈkju:ʃn/ *n* [C, U] (instance of the) use of many words to say sth that could be said in a few words. ▷ **circumlocutory** /ˌsɜ:kəmˈlɒkjʊtərɪ/ *adj.*

circumnavigate /ˌsɜ:kəmˈnævɪgeɪt/ *v* [Tn] (*fml*) sail round (esp the world): *Magellan was the first person to circumnavigate the globe.* ▷ **circumnavigation** /ˌsɜ:kəmˌnævɪˈgeɪʃn/ *n* [C, U].

circumpolar /ˌsɜ:kəmˈpəʊlə(r)/ *adj* (*astronomy*) circling the pole (and so above the horizon at all times): *a circumpolar star* ○ *circumpolar motion.*

circumscribe /ˈsɜ:kəmskraɪb/ *v* [Tn] **1** (*fml*) restrict (sth) within limits; confine: *a life circumscribed by poverty.* **2** draw a line round (a geometrical figure) so that it touches all the outside points: *circumscribe a square.*

▷ **circumscription** /ˌsɜ:kəmˈskrɪpʃn/ *n* [U] circumscribing or being circumscribed.

circumspect /ˈsɜ:kəmspekt/ *adj* [usu pred] considering everything carefully before acting; cautious; wary.

▷ **circumspection** /ˌsɜ:kəmˈspekʃn/ *n* [U] caution; prudence: *proceeding with great circumspection.*

circumspectly *adv.*

circumstance /ˈsɜ:kəmstəns/ *n* **1** [C usu *pl*] condition or fact connected with an event or action: *What were the circumstances of/surrounding her death?* ie Where, when and how did she die? ○ *She was found dead in suspicious circumstances*, ie She may have been murdered. ○ *He was a victim of circumstance(s)*, ie What happened to him was beyond his control. ○ *Circumstances forced us to change our plans.* **2 circumstances** [pl] financial position: *What are his circumstances?* ○ *in easy/poor circumstances*, ie having much/not enough money. **3** (idm) **in/under the ˈcircumstances** this being the case; such being the state of affairs: *Under the circumstances* (eg because the salary offered was too low) *he felt unable to accept the job.* ○ *She coped well in the circumstances*, eg even though she was feeling unwell. **in/under no circumstances** in no case; never: *Under no circumstances should you lend him any money.* **in straitened circumstances** ⇨ STRAITENED. **pomp and circumstance** ⇨ POMP.

circumstantial /ˌsɜ:kəmˈstænʃl/ *adj* **1** (of a description) giving full details. **2** (of evidence) consisting of details that strongly suggest sth but do not prove it: *You can't convict a man of a crime on circumstantial evidence alone.* ▷ **circumstantially** /-nʃəlɪ/ *adv.*

circumvent /ˌsɜ:kəmˈvent/ *v* [Tn] (*fml*) find a way of overcoming or avoiding (sth): *circumvent a law, rule, problem, difficulty.* ▷ **circumvention** /ˌsɜ:kəmˈvenʃn/ *n* [U].

circus /ˈsɜ:kəs/ *n* **1** (a) [CGp] travelling company of entertainers, including acrobats, riders, clowns and performing animals. The modern circus began in London in 1770 as a show of horse-riding by a former cavalry officer, who added acts by singers, dancers and clowns. The form was taken up in other countries and soon developed; the spectacular circuses of *Barnum and Bailey in America are perhaps the most famous. During the 20th century they have become less popular and more difficult to run, though State circuses still flourish in the USSR and China. (b) **the circus** [sing] public performance given by such a company, usu in a large tent: *go to the circus.* **2** [C] (*infml*) scene of lively action. **3** [C] (*Brit*) (in place-names) open space in a town where several streets meet: *Piccadilly Circus.* Cf ROUNDABOUT *n* 2. **4** [C] (in ancient Rome) round or oval arena for chariot racing and public games. **5** (idm) **bread and circuses** ⇨ BREAD.

cirque /sɜ:k/ (also **corrie, cwm**) steep-sided rock basin on the side of a mountain, originally formed by the action of a glacier.

cirrhosis /sɪˈrəʊsɪs/ *n* [U] chronic and often fatal disease of the liver, suffered esp by alcoholics: *cirrhosis of the liver.*

cirriped /ˈsɪrɪped/ *n* any of various small animals with shells, esp barnacles, that live in the sea and cling on to objects or other animals.

cirrocumulus /ˌsɪrəʊˈkju:mjʊləs/ *n* (*pl* **-li** /-laɪ/) [C, U] form of high cloud consisting of small roundish fleecy clouds in contact with each other.

cirrostratus /ˌsɪrəʊˈstrɑ:təs/ *n* (*pl* **-ti** /-taɪ/) [C, U] form of thin high cloud composed mainly of fine ice-crystals. A halo effect is sometimes produced when the sun shines through a cirrostratus layer.

cirrus /ˈsɪrəs/ *n* (*pl* **cirri** /ˈsɪraɪ/) [U] **1** type of light wispy cloud, high in the sky: [attrib] *cirrus clouds.* **2** stringlike part of a plant or simple animal used to hold on to things.

CIS /ˌsi: aɪ ˈes/ *abbr* Commonwealth of Independent States.

cisalpine /sɪsˈælpaɪn/ *adj* on the southern side of the Alps.

cislunar /sɪsˈlu:nə(r)/ *adj* between the earth and the moon: *cislunar space.* Cf TRANSLUNAR.

cissy *n* = SISSY.

Cistercian /sɪˈstɜ:ʃn/ *n, adj* (monk or nun) of a religious order founded as a stricter branch of the Benedictines. St *Bernard was responsible for reforms which led to the expansion of the order. The members of the order, also called *Trappists, are famous for their rule of silence.

cistern /ˈsɪstən/ *n* water tank, esp one connected to a lavatory or in the roof of a house with pipes to taps on lower storeys.

cistus /ˈsɪstəs/ *n* [C, U] shrub with large white or red flowers.

citadel /ˈsɪtədəl/ *n* **1** fortress on high ground overlooking and protecting a city. **2** hall where members of the *Salvation Army meet.

cite /saɪt/ *v* [Tn] **1** (**a**) speak or write (words taken from a passage, a book, an author, etc); quote: *She cited (a verse from) (a poem by) Keats.* (**b**) mention (sth) as an example or to support an argument; refer to: *She cited the high unemployment figures as evidence of the failure of government policy.* **2** (*US*) officially commend (esp a soldier) for bravery; mention: *He was cited in dispatches.* **3** (*law*) summon (sb) to appear in a court of law: *be cited in divorce proceedings.*

▷ **citation** /saɪˈteɪʃn/ **1** (**a**) [U] action of citing sth. (**b**) [C] passage cited; quotation: *Some dictionary writers use citations to show what words mean.* **2** [C] (*US*) (**a**) official commendation of a soldier for bravery. (**b**) written description of the reasons for this.

citizen /ˈsɪtɪzn/ *n* **1** person who has full rights as a member of a country, either by birth or by being granted such rights: *an American citizen* ○ *She is German by birth but is now a French citizen.* **2** person who lives in a town or city: *the citizens of Rome.* **3** (*esp US*) = CIVILIAN.

▷ **citizenship** *n* [U] (status of) being a citizen, esp of a particular country, with the rights and duties that involves: *apply for/be granted British citizenship.*

□ **Citizens' Adˈvice Bureau** (*abbr* **CAB**) office in many British towns where the public can go for free advice and information on civil matters.

citizen's aˈrrest arrest(1) made by a member of the public (allowable in certain cases under common law).

citizens' ˈband range of radio frequencies used by members of the public for local communication.

NOTE ON USAGE: **Citizen** and **subject** both indicate a person who has the rights given by a state to its members, eg the right to vote. **Subject** is used when the state is ruled by a monarch. **Citizen** is used in all types of state but especially republics: *a British subject/citizen* ○ *a French citizen.*

citrate /ˈsɪtreɪt/ *n* (*chemistry*) salt of citric acid.

citric acid /sɪtrɪk ˈæsɪd/ (*chemistry*) acid present in the juice of oranges, lemons, limes, etc.

citron /ˈsɪtrən/ *n* **1** pale yellow fruit like a lemon but larger, less sour and with a thicker skin. **2** small Asian tree bearing this fruit.

citronella /sɪtrəˈnelə/ *n* [U] sweet-smelling oil obtained from a grass of S Asia and used in insect repellent, perfume and soap.

citrus /ˈsɪtrəs/ *n* any of a group of related trees including the lemon, lime, orange and grapefruit: [attrib] *citrus fruit.*

▷ **citrous** *adj* of or relating to these trees or their fruit.

city /ˈsɪtɪ/ *n* **1** [C] large and important town: *Which is the world's largest city?* ○ [attrib] *the city ˈcentre,* ie the central area of a city. **2** [C] (**a**) (*Brit*) town with special rights given by royal charter and usu containing a cathedral: *the city of York.* (**b**) (*US*) town given special rights by State charter. **3** [CGp] all the people living in a city, as a group: *The city turned out to welcome back its victorious team.* **4 the City** [sing] the oldest part of London, now its commercial and financial centre: *She works in the City,* eg as a stockbroker. ○ *The City reacted sharply to the fall in oil prices.* ➪ articles at FINANCE, LONDON. **5** (idm) **the freedom of the city** ➪ FREEDOM.

□ **the ˌCity and ˈGuilds Institute** British organization that sets examinations and gives qualifications in technical and craft skills: *I've got my City and Guilds (diploma) in hairdressing.*

ˈ**city desk 1** (*Brit*) department of a newspaper dealing with financial news. **2** (*US*) department of a newspaper dealing with local news.

ˌ**city ˈeditor 1** (*Brit*) (on a newspaper) journalist responsible for financial news. **2** (*US*) (on a newspaper) journalist responsible for local news.

ˌ**city ˈfathers** people responsible for the administration of a city.

ˌ**city ˈhall** (*US*) (offices of the) officials in municipal government: *You can't fight city hall,* ie It is hard to oppose the people in charge of the city.

ˌ**city ˈslicker** (*esp US often derog*) smart and confident person living in a city, esp one regarded with suspicion by less sophisticated country people.

ˌ**city-ˈstate** *n* (formerly) independent state consisting of a city and the surrounding area (eg Athens in ancient times).

civet /ˈsɪvɪt/ *n* **1** (also ˈ**civet-cat**) [C] small spotted catlike animal living in central Africa and S Asia. **2** [U] strong-smelling substance obtained from its glands and used in making perfume.

civic /ˈsɪvɪk/ *adj* [usu attrib] **1** of a town or city; municipal: *a civic function,* eg the opening of a new hospital by the mayor of a town. **2** of citizens or citizenship: *civic pride,* ie citizens' pride in their town ○ *civic duties, responsibilities, etc.*

▷ **civics** /ˈsɪvɪks/ *n* [sing *v*] study of municipal government and the rights and responsibilities of citizens.

□ ˌ**civic ˈcentre** (*Brit*) area in which the public buildings of a town (eg the town hall, library, etc) are grouped together.

the ˌCivic ˈTrust British organization that seeks to preserve and improve the environment, eg by restoring old buildings or giving awards to good modern architecture. ➪ article at ARCHITECTURE.

civies = CIVVIES.

civil /ˈsɪvl/ *adj* **1** of or relating to the citizens of a country: *civil disorder,* eg rioting ○ *civil strife,* eg fighting between different political or religious groups within a country. **2** of or relating to ordinary citizens rather than the armed forces or the Church: *civil government* ○ *civil aviation,* ie flights by commercial and private aircraft, rather than by the air force. **3** polite and helpful: *How very civil of you!* ○ *Keep a civil tongue in your head!* ie Don't speak rudely! **4** involving civil law rather than criminal law: *civil cases* ○ *civil proceedings,* ie a court case to settle a dispute between individuals ○ *a civil court.* Cf CRIMINAL 2 (CRIME).

▷ **civility** /sɪˈvɪlətɪ/ *n* [C, U] (*fml*) (act of) politeness: *You should show more civility to your host.*

civilly /ˈsɪvəlɪ/ *adv* politely.

□ ˌ**civil deˈfence** organizing of civilians to protect people and property during air raids or other enemy attacks in wartime.

ˌ**civil disoˈbedience** refusal to obey certain laws, pay taxes, etc, as a peaceful means of (esp political) protest: *a campaign of civil disobedience.*

ˌ**civil engiˈneering** design and building of roads, railways, bridges, canals, etc. ˌ**civil engiˈneer**.

ˌ**civil ˈlaw** law dealing with the private rights of citizens, rather than with crime. ➪ article at LAW.

ˌ**civil ˈliberty** individual's freedom of action, limited only by laws designed to protect the community.

ˈ**civil list** (in Britain) allowance of money made by Parliament for the expenses of the monarch and the royal family in carrying out their duties. ➪ article at ROYAL.

ˌ**civil ˈmarriage** marriage which does not involve a religious ceremony but is recognized by law.

ˌ**civil ˈrights** rights of each citizen to freedom and equality (eg in voting and employment) regardless of sex, race or religion. ˌ**civil ˈrights movement** organized movement aiming to establish full civil rights for a particular group of citizens, eg for Blacks in the USA. ➪ article at ETHNIC.

ˌ**civil ˈservant** person employed by the Civil Service.

the ˌCivil ˈService (**a**) [sing] all government departments other than the armed forces. In Britain its members are responsible for carrying out the work of government at all levels. At the highest level there are those who advise and assist Cabinet ministers, while others are involved in scientific research or tax administration: *She works in the Civil Service in Whitehall,* ie in one of the ministries. (**b**) [Gp] all the people employed in these departments of government: *The Civil Service is/are threatening to strike.*

ˌ**civil ˈwar** war between groups of citizens of the same country: *the Spanish Civil War.*

civilian /sɪˈvɪlɪən/ *n* person not serving in the armed forces or the police force: *Two soldiers and one civilian were killed in the explosion.* ○ [attrib] *He left the army and returned to civilian life.*

civilization, -isation /ˌsɪvəlaɪˈzeɪʃn; *US* -əlɪˈz-/ *n* **1** [U] becoming or making sb civilized: *The civilization of mankind has taken thousands of years.* **2** (**a**) [U] (esp advanced) state of human social development. (**b**) [C] culture and way of life of a people, nation or period regarded as a stage in the development of organized society: *the civilizations of ancient Egypt and Babylon.* **3** [U] civilized conditions or society: *live far from civilization,* ie far from a large town or city ○ (*joc*) *It's good to get back to civilization after living in a tent for two weeks!*

civilize, -ise /ˈsɪvəlaɪz/ *v* [Tn] **1** cause (sb/sth) to improve from a primitive stage of human society to a more developed one: *civilize a jungle tribe.* **2** improve the behaviour or manners of (sb); refine: *His wife has had a civilizing influence on him.*

▷ **civilized, -ised** /ˈsɪvəlaɪzd/ *adj* polite; refined: *civilized society, behaviour.*

civvies (also **civies**) /ˈsɪvɪz/ *n* [pl] (*dated Brit sl*) clothes worn by civilians, ie not military uniform.

Civvy Street /ˈsɪvɪ stri:t/ (*dated Brit sl*) civilian life.

cl *abbr* **1** (*pl* unchanged or **cls**) centilitre: *75 cl.* **2** class: *two 2nd cl tickets.*

cl *symb* chlorine.

clack /klæk/ *n* short sharp sound (as) of hard objects being struck together: *the clack of high heels on a stone floor* ○ *the clack of knitting needles, a typewriter.*

▷ **clack** *v* [I, Tn] (cause sth to) make this sound: (*fig*) *Pay no attention to clacking tongues,* ie to people gossiping.

clad /klæd/ *adj* **1** (used after an *adv,* with *in* and a noun, or in compounds) (*dated or fml*) dressed; clothed: *warmly, scantily clad* ○ *motor-cyclists clad in leather/leather-clad motor-cyclists.* **2** (in compounds) (*fml*) covered: *an ivy-clad tower* ○ *iron-clad battleships.*

cladding /ˈklædɪŋ/ *n* [U] protective covering applied to the surface of sth. Different forms of cladding include the material used on the outside walls of a building, a thin layer of expensive metal over a cheaper one, and the covering of metal round a fuel element in a nuclear reactor.

clade /kleɪd/ *n* (*biology*) group of plants or animals that have developed from a common ancestor.

cladistics /kləˈdɪstɪks/ *n* [sing *v*] (*biology*) method of grouping plants and animals in classes (*clades*) according to shared characteristics, which are assumed to indicate common ancestry.

claim[1] /kleɪm/ *v* **1** (**a**) [Tn] demand or request (sth) because it is or one believes it is one's right or one's property: *claim diplomatic immunity, the* *protection of the law, etc* ○ *After the Duke's death, his eldest son claimed the title.* ○ *She claims ownership* (ie says she is the rightful owner) *of the land.* ○ *claim an item of lost property* ○ (*fig*) *Gardening claims* (ie takes up) *much of my time in the summer.* (**b**) [I, Ipr, Tn] ~ (**for sth**) demand (money) under an insurance policy, as compensation, etc: *Have you claimed (the insurance) yet?* ○ *You can always claim on the insurance.* ○ *claim for damages.* **2** [Tn, Tf, Tt] state or declare (sth) as a fact (without being able to prove it); assert: *claim knowledge* (ie to have knowledge) *of sth* ○ *After the battle both sides claimed victory.* ○ *She claims (that) she is related to the Queen/claims to be related to the Queen.* **3** [Tn] (of things) need (sth); deserve: *important matters claiming one's attention.* **4** [Tn] (of a disaster, an accident, etc) cause the loss or death of (sb): *The earthquake claimed thousands of lives/victims.* **5** (phr v) **claim sth back** ask for sth to be returned: *You can claim your money back if the goods are damaged.*

claim[2] /kleɪm/ *n* **1** [C] (**a**) ~ (**for sth**) demand for a sum of money (as insurance, compensation, a wage increase, etc): *put in/make a claim for damages, a pay rise, etc.* Cf NO-CLAIMS BONUS (NO). (**b**) sum of money demanded: *That's a very large claim!* **2** [C, U] ~ (**to sth**); ~ (**on sb/sth**) right to sth: *His claim to ownership is invalid.* ○ *a claim to the throne* ○ *You have no claim on* (ie no right to ask for) *my sympathy.* ○ *His only claim to fame* (ie The only remarkable thing about him) *is that he once met Stalin.* **3** [C] statement of sth as a fact; assertion: *Nobody believed his claim that he was innocent/to be innocent.* **4** [C] thing claimed, esp a piece of land for mining, etc. **5** (idm) **lay claim to sth** (**a**) state that one has a right to sth: *lay claim to an inheritance, an estate, a property, etc.* (**b**) (usu negative) state that one has knowledge, understanding, a skill, etc: *I lay no claim to being an expert economist.* **stake a/one's claim** ⇨ STAKE.

▷ **claimant** /ˈkleɪmənt/ *n* person who makes a claim[2](1a), esp in law.

clairvoyance /kleəˈvɔɪəns/ *n* [U] supposed power of seeing in the mind either future events or things that exist or are happening out of sight.

▷ **clairvoyant** /kleəˈvɔɪənt/ *n, adj* (person) having such power.

clam /klæm/ *n* large shellfish with a hinged shell.

▷ **clam** *v* (**-mm-**) **1** [I] (*US*) (usu **go clamming**) dig for clams (on a beach). **2** (phr v) **clam up** (*infml*) become silent; refuse to speak: *He always clammed up when we asked him about his family.*

□ ˈ**clambake** *n* (*US*) picnic on the sea-shore at which clams and other seafood are cooked and eaten.

clamber /ˈklæmbə(r)/ *v* [I, Ipr, Ip] climb, esp with difficulty or effort, using the hands and feet: *The children clambered over the rocks.*

▷ **clamber** *n* (esp *sing*) difficult or awkward climb.

clammy /ˈklæmɪ/ *adj* (**-ier, -iest**) unpleasantly moist and sticky; damp: *clammy hands* ○ *a face clammy with sweat* ○ *clammy* (ie close or humid) *weather.* ▷ **clammily** *adv.* **clamminess** *n* [U].

clamour (*US* **clamor**) /ˈklæmə(r)/ *n* [C, U] **1** loud confused noise, esp of shouting. **2** ~ (**for/against sth**) loud demand or protest: *a clamour for revenge.*

▷ **clamorous** /ˈklæmərəs/ *adj* (*fml*) making loud demands or protests.

clamour (*US* **clamor**) *v* **1** [I] make a clamour(1). **2** [Ipr, It] ~ **for/against sth** make a loud demand or protest: *The public are clamouring for a change of government.* ○ *The baby clamoured to be fed.*

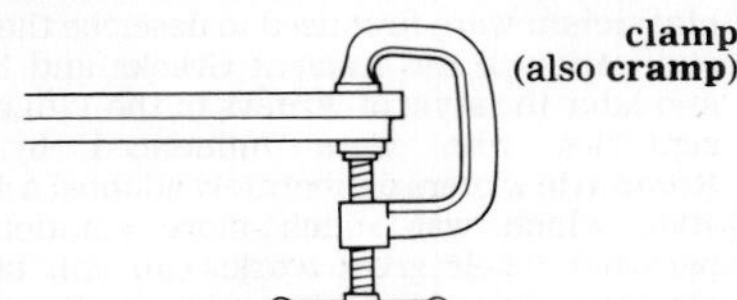
clamp (also **cramp**)

clamp /klæmp/ *n* **1** (also **cramp**) device for holding things tightly together, usu by means of a screw. **2** piece of wood, metal, etc used for strengthening other materials or fastening things together. ⇨ illus. **3** heavy metal device put on to the wheels of illegally parked cars to prevent them being moved before a fine is paid.

▷ **clamp** *v* **1** [Tn] grip or hold (sth) (as if) with a clamp: *He kept his pipe clamped between his teeth.* **2** [Tn, Tn·pr] ~ **A and B** (**together**); ~ **A to B** fasten (one thing to another) with a clamp: *clamp two boards together.* **3** [Tn] put a clamp on (a car or one of the wheels): *I've been* (ie My car has been) *clamped!* **4** (phr v) **clamp down on sb/sth** (*infml*) become stricter about sth; use one's authority against sb or to prevent or suppress sth: *The Government intends to clamp down on soccer hooliganism.*

□ ˈ**clamp-down** *n* sudden policy of increased strictness in preventing or suppressing sth.

clan /klæn/ *n* [CGp] **1** group of families, esp in Scotland, descended from a common ancestor: *the ˈCampbell clan/the clan ˈCampbell.* **2** (*infml*) large family forming a close group. **3** group of people closely connected by similar aims, interests, etc; coterie.

▷ **clannish** *adj* (*often derog*) (of members of a group) associating closely with each other and showing little interest in other people. **clannishly** *adv.* **clannishness** *n* [U].

□ ˈ**clansman** /-mən/ *n* (*pl* **-men**) /-mən/ (*fem* ˈ**clanswoman, -women**) member of a clan.

clandestine /klænˈdestɪn/ *adj* (*fml*) done secretly; kept secret; surreptitious: *a clanˌdestine ˈmarriage.*

clang /klæŋ/ *n* loud ringing sound (as) of metal being struck: *the clang of the school bell.*

▷ **clang** *v* [I, Tn] (cause sth to) make this sound: *The prison gates clanged shut.*

clanger /ˈklæŋə(r)/ *n* (*Brit infml*) **1** obvious and embarrassing mistake; gaffe. **2** (idm) **drop a brick/clanger** ⇨ DROP[2].

clangour (*US* **clangor**) /ˈklæŋə(r), ˈklæŋgə(r)/ *n* [U] continued clanging noise; series of clangs. ▷ **clangorous** /ˈklæŋərəs, ˈklæŋgərəs/ *adj.*

clank /klæŋk/ *n* dull metallic sound (as) of chains striking together.

▷ **clank** *v* [I, Tn] (cause sth to) make this sound: *The chains clanked as the drawbridge opened.*

clap[1] /klæp/ *v* (**-pp-**) **1** (**a**) [Tn, Tn·p] ~ **sth** (**together**) strike (the palms of one's hands) together: *She clapped her hands in delight.* ○ *They clapped their hands in time to the music.* (**b**) [I, Tn] do this continually to show approval of (sb/sth); applaud: *The audience clapped (her/her speech) enthusiastically.* **2** [Tn·pr] ~ **sb on sth** strike or slap sb lightly with an open hand, usu in a friendly way: *clap sb on the back.* **3** (idm) **clap/lay/set eyes on sb/sth** ⇨ EYE[1]. **clap hold of sb/sth** (*infml*) seize sb/sth suddenly or with force: *Here, clap hold of this!* **clap sb in/into jail, prison, etc** (*infml*) put sb in prison quickly (often without a trial). **4** (phr v) **clap sth on** (**sth**) (*infml*) add sth to the price of sth, esp in an unwelcome way: *The Government has clapped an extra ten pence on a packet of cigarettes.* (**be**) **clapped out** (*Brit infml*) (of people or things) completely worn out or exhausted: *a clapped-out old bicycle.*

▷ **clap** *n* **1** [sing] act or sound of clapping (CLAP[1] 1a): *Let's give her a big clap,* ie applaud her. **2** [C] ~ **on sth** friendly slap: *give sb a clap on the back.* **3** [C] sudden loud noise: *a clap of thunder.*

clap[2] /klæp/ (also **the clap**) *n* [U] (*sl*) venereal disease, esp gonorrhoea.

clapboard /ˈklæpbɔːd; *US* ˈklæbɔːrd/ *n* [U] (*US*) = WEATHER-BOARD (WEATHER[1]).

Clapham Junction /ˌklæpəm ˈdʒʌŋkʃn/ railway junction in south London, one of the busiest junctions in Britain: (*joc*) *We've got the builders in at the moment and the place is like Clapham Junction,* ie full of busy activity.

clapper /ˈklæpə(r)/ *n* **1** piece of metal, etc fixed loosely inside a bell and making it sound by striking the side. ⇨ illus at BELL. **2** (idm) **like the ˈclappers** (*Brit infml*) very fast or hard; vigorously: *go, run, work, etc like the clappers.*

□ ˈ**clapper-board** *n* (in film-making) pair of hinged boards brought together sharply to help in synchronizing the sound and the picture at the start of filming.

claptrap /ˈklæptræp/ *n* [U] worthless, insincere or pretentious talk; nonsense: *What a load of claptrap!*

claque /klæk/ *n* [CGp] group of people paid to go to a theatre, etc and applaud certain artists or disturb the performance of others.

Clare[1] /kleə(r)/ John (1793-1865), English poet. A farm worker, he wrote fine poems about the countryside and birds. He became mentally unbalanced and spent the last part of his life in an asylum, while continuing to write poetry.

Clare[2] /kleə(r)/ Saint (1194-1253), born in Italy, who founded the 'Poor Clares', an order of Franciscan nuns.

claret /ˈklærət/ *n* (**a**) [C, U] (any of various types of) dry red wine, esp from the Bordeaux area of France: *I prefer Burgundy to claret.* (**b**) [U] colour of this. Cf BORDEAUX.

▷ **claret** *adj* dark red.

clarify /ˈklærɪfaɪ/ *v* (*pt, pp* **-fied**) **1** [I, Tn] (cause sth to) become clear or easier to understand: *clarify a remark, statement* ○ *I hope that what I say will clarify the situation.* **2** [Tn] remove impurities from (fats), eg by heating: *clarified butter.*

▷ **clarification** /ˌklærɪfɪˈkeɪʃn/ *n* [U] clarifying or being clarified: *The whole issue needs clarification.*

clarinet /ˌklærəˈnet/ *n* musical instrument of the woodwind group with finger-holes and keys. ⇨ illus at MUSIC.

▷ **clarinettist** (also **clarinetist**) *n* person who plays the clarinet.

clarion /ˈklærɪən/ *adj* [attrib] loud, clear and rousing (suggesting the shrill sound of a *clarion*, a small military trumpet of former times): *a clarion call to action.*

clarity /ˈklærətɪ/ *n* [U] clearness; lucidity: *clarity of expression, thinking, vision.*

Clarke /klɑːk/ Arthur Charles (1917-), English author. He is famous for his science-fiction novels and for his writings on space travel.

clash[1] /klæʃ/ *v* **1** [I, Ip, Tn, Tn·p] ~ (**sth and sth**) (**together**) (cause things to) strike together with a loud harsh noise: *Their swords clashed.* ○ *She clashed the cymbals together.* **2** [I, Ipr] (**a**) ~ (**with sb**) come together and fight: *The two armies clashed.* ○ *Demonstrators clashed with police.* (**b**) ~ (**with sb**) (**on/over sth**) disagree seriously (about sth): *The Government clashed with the Opposition/The Government and the Opposition clashed on the question of unemployment.* **3** [I, Ipr] ~ (**with sth**) happen inconveniently at the same time (as sth else): *It's a pity the two concerts clash; I wanted to go to both of them.* ○ *Your party clashes with a wedding I'm going to.* **4** [I, Ipr] ~ (**with sth**) (of colours, designs, etc) not match or harmonize: *The (colour of the) wallpaper clashes with the (colour of the) carpet/The wallpaper and the carpet clash.*

clash[2] /klæʃ/ *n* **1** clashing noise: *a clash of cymbals, swords.* **2** (**a**) ~ (**with sb/sth**); ~ (**between A and B**) violent contact; fight: *clashes between police and demonstrators.* (**b**) ~ (**with sb/sth**) (**on/over sth**); ~ (**between sb and sb**) (**on/over sth**) serious disagreement; argument: *a clash between the Prime Minister and the leader of the Opposition on defence spending.* (**c**) serious difference; conflict: *a clash of interests, personalities, cultures, opinions.* **3** ~ (**between A and B**) coinciding of events or dates: *a clash between two classes.* **4** failure of colours, designs, etc to match or harmonize.

clasp[1] /klɑːsp; *US* klæsp/ *n* **1** device for fastening things (eg the ends of a belt or a necklace) together: *The clasp of my brooch is broken.* **2** (**a**) firm hold with the hand; grasp; grip: *He held her hand in a firm clasp.* (**b**) embrace. **3** silver bar on the ribbon of a medal, showing the name of the battle at which the wearer was present.

□ ˈ**clasp-knife** *n* folding knife with a catch for holding the blade open.

clasp[2] /klɑːsp; *US* klæsp/ *v* **1** (**a**) [Tn, Tn·p] hold

Class

Until the Second World War there were very distinct social groups in British society. There was an upper class that included the aristocracy and many people who lived on inherited wealth, a middle class that could be subdivided into upper middle class, middle class and lower middle class, and a working class that included both skilled craftsmen and unskilled industrial workers and agricultural labourers. The divisions between the classes were reflected in many aspects of life. Working-class children usually left school and went out to work at the age of 14. Upper-class children were educated in private schools and formed the majority of students at university. Pubs were divided into public bars and saloon (or lounge) bars which were more expensive and more comfortable. Trains had first, second and third class carriages. Theatres had a dress circle where theatre-goers wore evening dress, and a gallery where the seats were cheaper and evening dress was not worn.

Many aspects of this rigid structure have virtually disappeared in modern Britain, although the continued existence of a private education system that educates about seven per cent of children still reflects it. The policies of governments since the Second World War in areas such as health, education, housing and taxation have on the whole had the effect of reducing class differences in society. There has also been a decline in manufacturing or 'blue collar' jobs and an increase in 'white collar' jobs in service industries. Nevertheless, Britain is still far from being the classless society that many politicians have set out to achieve.

In modern Britain, the definitions of social class used by social scientists and market researchers are based on a division of society into six groups, according to occupation. Group A are professionals such as doctors, lawyers, senior civil servants and managers etc, group B are middle management, scientists, university lecturers etc, group C1 are other non-manual workers, eg nurses and sales and clerical staff, group C2 are skilled manual workers, group D are semi-skilled and unskilled manual workers and group E are the poorest in society, for example people living on the minimum state pension, the unemployed, single parents living on state benefits, etc. People move into and out of these groups as their occupation or circumstances change.

Class consciousness, however, is based not so much on economic differences as on class differences that reflect family background, education and accent rather than on differences based on occupation.

Class distinctions are popularly represented by stereotypes, especially in matters of clothing, speech and region of origin. This is best seen in caricatures of upper and lower class individuals, whether in literature or the contemporary media. Upper-class people are typically portrayed in country clothes, since they are primarily associated with land ownership and the three traditional aristocratic sports of hunting, shooting and fishing (sometimes written or pronounced as 'huntin', shootin' and fishin'' to represent their characteristic speech). Other typically upper-class sports are polo and riding. Distinctive items of upper-class wear are peaked caps for men, head-scarves for women, and green wellington boots ('green wellies') for either. Upper-class speech is portrayed as loud, drawling and affected, with much use of nicknames and slang. The typical upper-class person is usually thought of as a southerner, although it is perfectly possible to be Scottish and upper class.

The stock caricature of a working-class man shows him wearing a flat cap, braces (although these are now in fashion with some upper-class people) and boots. He is popularly thought of as living in the north of England. A working-class woman is often depicted as untidily dressed, wearing 'indoor' items such as hair curlers and bedroom slippers in the street. A popular portayal of a working-class husband and wife exists in the cartoons of the everyday life of Andy Capp and his wife Florrie in the *Daily Mirror*. Sports and pastimes such as football, dog-racing, betting (especially on horse-races and in football pools), snooker and card-playing, together with such pub games as darts, bar billiards, and shove-halfpenny, are considered to be typical working-class pastimes.

(sb/sth) tightly in the hand: *She was clasping a knife.* ○ *They clasped hands* (ie held each other's hands) *briefly before saying goodbye.* ○ *His hands were clasped (together) in prayer.* (**b**) [Tn, Tn·pr] hold (sb) tightly with the arms; embrace: *He clasped her to his chest.* ○ *They stood clasped in each other's arms.* **2** [I, Tn, Tn·pr] be fastened or fasten (sth) with a clasp[1](1): *clasp a bracelet round one's wrist.*

class /klɑ:s; *US* klæs/ *n* **1** (**a**) [CGp] group of people at the same social or economic level: *the working/middle/upper class* ○ *the professional class(es).* ⇨ article. (**b**) [U] system that divides people into such groups: [attrib] *class differences, distinctions, divisions, etc.* **2** (**a**) [CGp] group of students taught together: *We were in the same class at school.* ○ *Form 4 is/are a difficult class to teach.* (**b**) [C] occasion when this group meets to be taught; lesson: *I have a maths class at 9 o'clock.* (**c**) [CGp] (*US*) group of students who finish their studies at school or university in a particular year: *the class of '82.* **3** [C] set of people, animals or things grouped together, esp according to quality: *As an actress Jane is not in the same class as* (ie is not as good as) *Susan.* ○ [attrib] *a top-class athlete.* **4** [U] (*infml*) high quality; excellence; distinction: *She's got (a lot of) class.* ○ [attrib] *a class (tennis) player.* **5** [C] (esp in compounds) one of several different levels of comfort, etc available to travellers in a train, plane, bus, etc: *first class* ○ *tourist class* ○ [attrib] *a second-class compartment*, eg on a train. **6** [C] (*Brit*) (esp in compounds) one of several grades of achievement in a university degree examination: *a first-/second-/third-class (honours) degree.* **7** [C] (*biology*) second highest group into which animals and plants are divided, below a phylum and including several orders (ORDER[1] 9). Cf FAMILY 4, GENUS 1, SPECIES 1. **8** (idm) **in a class of one's/its ˈown; in a class by oneˈself/itˈself** better than everyone/anything else of his/its kind; unequalled: *Pele was in a class of his own as a footballer.*

▷ **class** *v* [Tn, Cn·n/a] ~ **sb/sth** (**as sth**) place sb/sth in a class(1b); classify sb/sth: *Immigrant workers were classed as resident aliens.*

classless *adj* **1** not clearly belonging to any particular social class: *a classless accent.* **2** without social classes: *a classless society.*

classy /ˈklɑ:sɪ; *US* ˈklæsɪ/ *adj* (**-ier**, **-iest**) (*infml*) of high quality; stylish; superior: *a classy hotel.* ○ *That's a very classy new car you're driving.*

□ **ˈclass-conscious** *adj* aware of belonging to a particular social class or of the differences between social classes. **ˈclass-consciousness** *n* [U].

ˈclass-feeling *n* [U] feelings of hostility between social classes.

ˈclass-list *n* (*Brit*) list showing the class of degree achieved by university students in their final examinations.

ˈclass-mate *n* person who was or is in the same class as oneself at school: *We were class-mates at primary school.*

ˈclass-room *n* room where a class of pupils or students is taught.

the ˈclass struggle (also **the ˈclass war**) (esp in Marxist thought) the continuing fight for economic and political power between the capitalist ruling class and the working class.

classic[1] /ˈklæsɪk/ *adj* [esp attrib] **1** having a high quality that is recognized and unquestioned; of lasting value and importance: *a classic novel, work of scholarship, game of football.* **2** very typical: *a classic example* ○ *classic symptoms of pneumonia* ○ *a classic case of malnutrition.* **3** (**a**) simple, harmonious and restrained; classical(3). (**b**) (of clothes, designs, etc) having a simple traditional style that is not affected by changes in fashion: *a classic dress.* **4** famous through being long established: *one of the classic events of the sporting calendar.*

□ **the ˈclassic races** (*Brit*) the five main flat races in the UK for three-year-old horses, ie the Derby, the Saint Leger, the Oaks, the Two Thousand Guineas and the One Thousand Guineas.

classic[2] /ˈklæsɪk/ *n* **1** [C] writer, artist or work of art recognized as being of high quality and lasting value: *This novel may well become a classic.* ○ *She enjoys reading the classics*, ie the great works of literature. **2** (**a**) [C] outstanding example of its kind: *The (football) match was a classic.* (**b**) **the classics** [pl] (*Brit*) the classic races (CLASSIC[1]). **3 Classics** [sing *v*] (study of) ancient Greek and Roman language and literature: *She studied Classics at university.* **4** [C] garment that is classic[1](3b) in style.

classical /ˈklæsɪkl/ *adj* [esp attrib] **1** of, relating to or influenced by the art and literature of ancient Greece and Rome: *classical studies* ○ *a classical scholar*, ie an expert in Latin and Greek ○ *a classical education*, ie one based on the study of Latin and Greek ○ *classical architecture.* ⇨ article at ARCHITECTURE. **2** (**a**) (of music) serious and traditional in style: *the classical music of India.* Cf POP[3]. (**b**) (of music) (characteristic) of the period 1750-1800: *classical composers such as Mozart and Haydn* ○ *the classical symphony.* **3** simple, restrained and harmonious in style: *a classical elegance.* **4** following or creating a standard that can be used as a point of reference: *the classical treatment for this disease* ○ *classical physics*, ie based on the ideas of Newton and others before the discovery of relativity ○ *classical economists*, ie those who first laid down the principles of economics in the 18th and 19th centuries, eg Hume, Smith, etc. ▷ **classically** /ˈklæsɪklɪ/ *adv*

NOTE ON USAGE: The terms **classical** and **classicism** were first used to describe the art and civilization of the Ancient Greeks and Romans, and later the style of writers in the 17th and 18th centuries who were influenced by them. **Romantic** writers deliberately adopted a different style which was much more emotional and personal. Their great works can still be called **classics**, however, like any work which is recognized as remarkable. Even modern works can be called **classical** if they pay great attention to traditional form and style.

classicism /ˈklæsɪsɪzəm/ *n* [U] **1** (following of the) style and principles of classical(1) art and literature. Cf IDEALISM 2, REALISM 2, ROMANTICISM (ROMANTIC). **2** simplicity and regularity of style or form.
▷ **classicist** /ˈklæsɪsɪst/ *n* **1** person who follows classicism in art or literature. **2** expert in or student of ancient Greek or Latin.

classification /ˌklæsɪfɪˈkeɪʃn/ *n* **1** [U] classifying or being classified. **2** [C] group or class into which sth is put. **3** [U] *(biology)* placing of animals and plants into groups according to similarities of structure, origin, etc. **4** [C] (in libraries, etc) system of grouping books, magazines, etc according to their subject.

classify /ˈklæsɪfaɪ/ *v* *(pt, pp* **-fied)** **1 (a)** [Tn] arrange (sth) systematically in classes (CLASS 3) or groups: *The books in the library are classified by/ according to subject.* **(b)** [Tn, Cn·n/a] ~ **sb/sth (as sth)** place sb/sth in a particular class(3): *Would you classify her novels as serious literature or as mere entertainment?* **2** [Tn] declare (information, documents, etc) to be officially secret and available only to certain people.
▷ **classifiable** /ˈklæsɪfaɪəbl/ *adj* that can be classified.
classified *adj* [usu attrib] **1** arranged in groups: *a classified directory*, ie one in which the names of firms, etc are entered under labelled headings, eg builders, electricians, plumbers. **2** declared officially secret (by a government) and available only to certain people: *classified information, documents.*
□ ˌ**classified adˈvertisements** (also ˌ**classified ˈads** /ædz/, *infml* **classifieds**, *esp US* ˈ**want ads**) small advertisements placed in a newspaper, etc by people wishing to buy or sell sth, employ sb, find a job, etc.

clastic /ˈklæstɪk/ *adj* (of rocks) formed from broken pieces of older rocks.

clatter /ˈklætə(r)/ *n* [sing] continuous noise (as) of hard objects falling or knocking against each other: *the clatter of cutlery, horses' hoofs, a typewriter.*
▷ **clatter** *v* **1** [I, Ipr, Tn] (cause sth to) make a clatter: *Don't clatter your knives and forks.* **2** (phr v) **clatter across, down, in, etc** move across, etc, making a clatter: *The children clattered* (ie ran noisily) *downstairs.* ○ *The cart clattered over the cobble-stones.*

Claude /kləʊd/ born Claude Gellée, also called Claude Le Lorrain and in Britain Claude Lorraine (1600-82), French landscape painter who spent most of his life in Rome. His paintings, evoking the serenity of ideal classical landscapes, are remarkable for their subtle treatment of light.

Claudius /ˈklɔːdɪəs/ (10 BC-54 AD), Roman emperor 41-54 AD. Although physically disabled, he was proclaimed emperor after the murder of *Caligula and proved a sensible and efficient ruler, continuing the expansion of the Empire and taking part in the invasion of Britain. His fourth wife, Agrippina, is said to have killed him with a dish of poisoned mushrooms.

clause /klɔːz/ *n* **1** *(grammar)* group of words that includes a subject[1](4a) and a verb, forming a sentence or part of a sentence: *The sentence 'He often visits Spain because he likes the climate' consists of a main clause and a subordinate clause.* **2** paragraph or section in a legal document (eg a will, contract or treaty) stating a particular obligation, condition, etc: *There is a clause in the contract forbidding tenants to sublet.*

Clausewitz /ˈklaʊzəvɪts/ Karl von (1780-1831), Prussian writer on military strategy. He stressed the need for all the people of a country to be involved in a war, but was misunderstood by some leaders who went on to see war as the best way of achieving political aims.

claustrophobia /ˌklɔːstrəˈfəʊbɪə/ *n* [U] abnormal fear of being in an enclosed space.
▷ **claustrophobic** /ˌklɔːstrəˈfəʊbɪk/ *adj* suffering from or causing claustrophobia: *feel claustrophobic* ○ *a claustrophobic little room.*

clavichord /ˈklævɪkɔːd/ *n* early type of keyboard instrument with a very soft tone.

clavicle /ˈklævɪkl/ *n* *(anatomy)* collar-bone. ⇨ illus at SKELETON.

clavier /kləˈvɪə(r), ˈklævɪə(r)/ *n* any musical instrument with a keyboard.

claw /klɔː/ *n* **1 (a)** any of the pointed nails (NAIL1) on the feet of some mammals, birds and reptiles: *Cats have sharp claws.* **(b)** (esp in birds) foot with claws: *The eagle held a mouse in its claws.* **2** pincers of a shellfish: *a lobster's claw.* ⇨ illus at SHELLFISH. **3** mechanical device like a claw, used for gripping and lifting things. **4** (idm) **get one's claws into sb** *(infml)* (esp of a woman) attach oneself to (a partner) in a determined way: *She's really got her claws into him!*
▷ **claw** *v* **1** [Ipr, Tn] ~ **(at) sb/sth** (try to) scratch or tear sb/sth with a claw or claws or with one's finger-nails: *The cats clawed at each other.* ○ *The prisoner clawed at the cell door in desperation.* ○ *His face was badly clawed.* **2** (idm) **claw one's way across, up, through, etc** move across, etc by using the claws or the hands: *They slowly clawed their way up the cliff.* **3** (phr v) **claw sth back** (of a government) recover, esp by taxation, money paid as an allowance to people who are not thought to need financial help.
□ ˈ**claw-back** *n* act of clawing sth back.
ˈ**claw-hammer** *n* hammer with one end of its head bent and divided for pulling out nails. ⇨ illus at HAMMER.

Clay /kleɪ/ Cassius ⇨ MUHAMMAD ALI.

clay /kleɪ/ *n* [U] **1** stiff sticky earth that becomes hard when baked, used for making bricks and pottery: [attrib] *clay soil* ○ *clay tiles.* **2** *(fig fml)* substance of which human bodies are made: *our mortal clay.* **3** (idm) **have feet of clay** ⇨ FOOT[1].
▷ **clayey** /kleɪɪ/ *adj* like, containing or covered with clay.
□ ˈ**clay pan** *(Austral)* hollow in clay soil, where water collects after rain.
clay ˈpigeon breakable disc thrown in the air as a target for shooting at: [attrib] *clay ˈpigeon shooting.*
clay ˈpipe tobacco pipe made of clay pottery.

claymore /ˈkleɪmɔː(r)/ *n* large two-edged sword, formerly used by Scottish Highlanders.

clean[1] /kliːn/ *adj* **(-er, -est)** **1 (a)** free from dirt or impurities: *clean hands* ○ *clean air*, ie free from smoke, etc ○ *a clean wound*, ie one that is not infected ○ *wash, wipe, scrub, brush, etc sth clean.* **(b)** that has been washed since it was last worn or used: *a clean dress, towel, knife* ○ *He wears clean socks every day.* ○ *put clean sheets on a bed.* **(c)** having clean habits; caring about cleanliness: *Cats are clean animals.* **2** not yet used; unmarked: *a clean sheet of paper.* **3 (a)** not obscene or indecent: *Keep it clean!* ie Don't tell dirty jokes! **(b)** *(dated)* good; innocent: *lead a clean life.* **(c)** showing or having no record of offences: *a clean driving-licence*, ie one with no endorsements ○ *She has a clean record.* **(d)** keeping to the rules; not unfair: *a hard-fought but clean match* ○ *a clean tackle*, eg in a game of football. **4** having a simple and pleasing shape; well-formed: *a car with clean lines.* **5** with a smooth edge or surface; regular; even: *A sharp knife makes a clean cut.* ○ *a clean break*, eg the breaking of a bone in one place. **6** (esp in sport) skilfully and accurately done: *a clean hit, stroke, blow, etc.* **7** *(infml)* (of a nuclear weapon) producing little radioactivity. **8** (of food, animals, etc) that can be eaten without breaking religious laws. **9** (idm) **(as) clean as a new ˈpin** *(infml)* very clean and tidy. **(as) clean as a ˈwhistle** *(infml)* **(a)** very clean. **(b)** skilfully; deftly: *The dog jumped through the hoop as clean as a whistle*, ie without touching it. **a clean bill of ˈhealth** report showing that one's health is good, esp after illness: *The doctor gave him a clean bill of health.* **a clean ˈsheet/ˈslate** record of work or behaviour that does not show any wrongdoing in the past: *He came out of prison hoping to start (life) again with a clean sheet*, ie with his previous offences forgotten. **(make) a clean sweep (of sth)** **(a)** the removing of things or people that are thought to be unnecessary: *The new manager made a clean sweep of the department.* **(b)** victory in all of a group of similar or related competitions, games, etc: *The Russians made a clean sweep of (the medals in) the gymnastics events.* **keep one's nose clean** ⇨ NOSE[1]. **make a clean break (with sth)** change one's previous manner of living entirely: *He's made a clean break with the past.* **make a clean breast of sth** make a full confession of sth: *He made a clean breast of his crime to the police.* **show a clean pair of heels** ⇨ SHOW[2]. **wipe the slate clean** ⇨ WIPE.
▷ **clean** *adv* **1** completely; entirely: *The bullet went clean through his shoulder.* ○ *The thief got clean away.* ○ *I clean forgot about it.* ○ *The batsman was clean bowled*, ie without the ball hitting the bat or the pads first. **2** (idm) **come clean (with sb) (about sth)** *(infml)* make a full and honest confession: *I've got to come ˈclean (with you) — I was the one who broke the window.*
□ **Clean ˈAir Acts** series of laws passed between 1956 and 1968 by the British Parliament to reduce air pollution, esp by banning the burning of coal in certain areas. ⇨ article at ENVIRONMENT.
ˌ**clean-ˈcut** *adj* **(a)** clearly outlined: ˌ*clean-cut ˈfeatures.* **(b)** *(approv)* looking neat and respectable: *a* ˌ*clean-cut ˈstudent.*
ˌ**clean-ˈlimbed** *adj* *(approv)* (esp of young people) having well-formed and slender limbs.
ˌ**clean-ˈliving** *adj* *(approv or joc)* (of a person) having a good character: *a* ˌ*decent,* ˌ*clean-living ˈboy.*
ˌ**clean-ˈshaven** *adj* (of men) not having a moustache or a beard.

clean[2] /kliːn/ *v* **1 (a)** [Tn] make (sth) clean or free of dirt, etc: *clean the windows, one's shoes, one's teeth* ○ *I must have this suit cleaned*, ie at the dry-cleaner's. ○ *The cat sat cleaning itself.* **(b)** [I] become clean: *This floor cleans easily*, ie is easy to clean. **2** [Tn] remove the internal organs of (eg a fish or chicken) before cooking. **3** (phr v) **clean sth down** clean sth thoroughly by wiping or brushing it: *clean down the walls.* **clean sth from/ off sth** remove sth from sth by brushing, scraping, wiping, etc: *She cleaned the dirt from her finger-nails.* **clean sth out** clean the inside of sth thoroughly: *clean out the stables.* **clean sb out (of sth)** *(infml)* use up or take all sb's money; take or buy all sb's stock: *I haven't a penny left; buying drinks for everyone has cleaned me out completely.* ○ *The burglars cleaned her out of all her jewellery.* **clean (oneself) up** *(infml)* wash oneself: *My hands are filthy; I'd better go and clean (myself) up.* **clean (sth) up (a)** remove (dirt, rubbish, etc) from a place to clean it; make (a place) clean by removing dirt, etc: *The workmen cleaned up (the mess) before they left.* ○ *clean up (a room) after a party.* **(b)** *(infml)* make or win (a lot of money): *He cleaned up a small fortune.* **clean sth up** remove criminals, harmful influences, etc from sth: *The mayor is determined to clean up the city.* ○ *a campaign to clean up* (ie reduce the amount of sex and violence shown on) *television.*
□ ˈ**cleaning woman** woman employed to clean offices, a private house, etc.
ˈ**clean-up** *n* **(a)** removal of dirt, etc from a person or place. **(b)** removal of criminals, harmful influences, etc.

cleaner /ˈkliːnə(r)/ *n* **1** (esp in compounds) person or thing that cleans: *an ˈoffice cleaner* ○ *a ˈfloor cleaner*, ie a substance that removes grease, stains, etc from floors. **2 cleaners** [pl] place where clothes and fabrics are cleaned, esp with chemicals: *send a suit to the cleaners.* **3** (idm) **take sb to the ˈcleaners** *(infml)* **(a)** rob or cheat sb of his money. **(b)** criticize sb harshly.

cleanly[1] /ˈkliːnlɪ/ *adv* easily; smoothly: *Blunt scissors don't cut cleanly.* ○ *catch a ball cleanly*, ie without fumbling.

cleanly[2] /ˈklenlɪ/ *adj* **(-ier, -iest)** habitually clean; having clean habits: *Cats are cleanly animals.*
▷ **cleanliness** *n* [U] **1** being clean. **2** (idm) ˌ**cleanliness is** ˌ**next to ˈgodliness** *(dated saying)*

keeping oneself clean is a sound religious thing to do (used esp to encourage children to wash properly).

cleanse /klenz/ *v* [Tn, Tn·pr] ~ **sb/sth (of sth)** make thoroughly clean: *a cleansing cream*, ie one that cleans the skin ○ (*fig fml*) *She felt cleansed of her sins after confession.*

▷ **cleanser** *n* substance that cleanses, eg a detergent or a lotion.

clear[1] /klɪə(r)/ *adj* (**-er** /ˈklɪərə(r)/, **-est** /ˈklɪərɪst/) **1** (**a**) easy to see through; transparent: *clear glass* ○ *the clear water of a mountain lake* ○ *clear soup*, eg consommé, in which there are no solid ingredients. (**b**) without cloud or mist: *a clear sky, day* ○ *clear weather.* (**c**) without spots or blemishes: *clear skin* ○ *a clear complexion.* **2** (**a**) easy to see or hear; distinct: *a clear photograph* ○ *a clear reflection in the water* ○ *a clear voice, speaker, sound.* (**b**) easy to understand: *a clear explanation, article, meaning* ○ *You'll do as you're told, is that clear?* **3** ~ (**about/on sth**) without doubt, confusion or difficulty; certain: *a clear thinker* ○ *a clear understanding of the problems* ○ *My memory is not clear on that point.* ○ *Are you quite clear about what the job involves?* **4** ~ (**to sb**) evident; obvious; definite: *a clear case of cheating* ○ *have a clear advantage/lead*, eg in a contest ○ *It is quite clear that she is not coming.* **5** ~ (**of sth**) (**a**) free from obstructions, obstacles, difficulties or dangers: *a clear view* ○ *Wait until the road is clear (of traffic) before crossing.* ○ *I want to keep next weekend clear so that I can do some gardening.* (**b**) free from guilt: *have a clear conscience.* (**c**) free from sth undesirable: *clear of debt* ○ *You are now clear of all suspicion.* **6** [pred] ~ (**of sb/sth**) not touching sth; away from sth: *The plane climbed until it was clear of the clouds.* ○ *Park (your car) about nine inches clear of the kerb.* **7** [attrib] complete: *Allow three clear days for the letter to arrive.* ○ *The bill was passed by a clear* (ie fairly large) *majority.* **8** [attrib] (of a sum of money) with nothing to be deducted; net: *a clear profit.* **9** (idm) (**as**) **clear as a ˈbell** clearly and easily heard. (**as**) **clear as ˈday** easy to see or understand; obvious. (**as**) **clear as ˈmud** (*infml*) very unclear; not apparent or well explained. **the coast is clear** ⇨ COAST[1]. **in the ˈclear** (*infml*) no longer in danger or suspected of sth: *She was very ill for a few days but doctors say she's now in the clear.* **make oneself ˈclear** express oneself clearly: *Do I make myself clear?* **make sth ˈclear (to sb)** make sth fully understood: *I made it clear to him that I rejected his proposal.*

▷ **clearly** *adv* **1** in a clear manner; distinctly: *speak clearly* ○ *It is too dark to see clearly.* **2** obviously; undoubtedly: *That clearly cannot be true.*

clearness *n* [U] state of being clear; clarity: *the clearness of the atmosphere* ○ *clearness of vision.*

□ ˌ**clear-ˈheaded** *adj* thinking or understanding clearly; sensible. ˌ**clear-ˈheadedly** *adv.* ˌ**clear-ˈheadedness** *n* [U].

ˌ**clear-ˈsighted** *adj* seeing, understanding or thinking clearly; discerning.

ˈ**clearway** *n* (*Brit*) road other than a motorway on which vehicles may not normally stop or park.

clear[2] /klɪə(r)/ *adv* **1** clearly; distinctly: *I can hear you loud and clear.* **2** ~ (**of sth**) out of the way of sth; no longer near or touching sth: *Stand clear of the doors.* ○ *He managed to leap clear of* (ie out of) *the burning car.* ○ *He jumped three inches clear of* (ie above) *the bar.* **3** completely: *The prisoner got clear away.* **4** (idm) **keep/stay/steer clear (of sb/sth)** avoid meeting sb or becoming involved with sth or going near a place or using sth: *Try to keep clear of trouble.* ○ *I prefer to keep clear of town during the rush-hour.* ○ (*infml*) *His doctor advised him to steer clear of alcohol.*

□ ˌ**clear-ˈcut** *adj* not vague; definite: ˌ*clear-cut* ˈ*plans, proˈposals, diˈstinctions.*

clear[3] /klɪə(r)/ *v* **1** (**a**) [I] become transparent: *The muddy water slowly cleared.* (**b**) [I] (of the sky or the weather) become free of cloud or rain: *The sky cleared after the storm.* (**c**) [I, Ip] ~ (**away**) (of fog, smoke, etc) disappear: *It was a fine day once the mist had cleared.* **2** (**a**) [Tn, Tn·pr] ~ **A (of B)**/~ **B (from A)** remove (sth that is unwanted or no longer needed) (from a place): *clear the table*, eg take away dirty plates, etc after a meal ○ *clear one's throat*, ie remove phlegm from one's throat by coughing slightly ○ *clear the court*, ie order all people not directly involved in a court case to leave the courtroom ○ *clear the streets of snow/clear snow from the streets* ○ *The land was cleared of trees.* ○ (*fig*) *clear one's mind of doubt.* (**b**) [Tn] remove (data that is no longer required) from the memory of a computer or calculator. **3** [Tn, Tn·pr] ~ **sb (of sth)** show or declare sb to be innocent: *clear one's name* ○ *She was cleared of all charges.* **4** [Tn] get past or over (sth) without touching it: *The horse cleared the fence easily.* ○ *The car only just cleared* (ie nearly hit) *the gatepost.* ○ *The winner cleared six feet*, ie jumped six feet without touching the bar. **5** (**a**) [Tn, Tn·pr] get permission for or allow (a ship, plane or cargo) to leave or enter a place or be unloaded: *clear goods through customs*, ie by paying the necessary duties ○ *clear a plane for take-off.* (**b**) [Tn] (of goods) pass through (sth) after satisfying official requirements: *Our baggage has cleared customs.* **6** [Tn esp passive] (**a**) officially approve (sb) before he is given special work or allowed to see or handle secret information: *She's been cleared by security.* (**b**) declare (sth) to be acceptable: *clear an article for publication.* **7** [Tn] pass (a cheque) through a clearing-house (CLEAR[3]). **8** [Tn] earn (money) as gain or profit: *clear £1 000 on a deal* ○ *clear* (ie make enough money to cover) *one's expenses.* **9** [Tn] repay (sth) fully: *clear one's debts, a loan, etc.* **10** [I, Tn] (in football, hockey, etc) kick or hit (the ball) away from the area near the goal. **11** (idm) **clear the ˈair** lessen or remove fears, worries or suspicions by talking about them openly: *A frank discussion can help to clear the air.* **clear the ˈdecks** (*infml*) prepare for a particular activity, event, etc by removing anything that is not essential to it. **12** (phr v) **clear (sth) away** remove (objects) in order to leave a clear space: *clear away the dishes.* **clear off** (*infml*) (esp imperative) go or run away: *You've no right to be here. Clear off!* ○ *He cleared off as soon as he saw the policeman coming.* **clear sth off** complete the payment of sth: *clear off a debt.* **clear out (of...)** (*infml*) leave (a place) quickly: *He cleared out before the police arrived.* **clear sth out** make sth empty or tidy by removing what is inside it: *clear out the attic.* **clear up** (**a**) (of the weather) become fine or bright: *I hope it clears up this afternoon.* (**b**) (of an illness, infection, etc) disappear as good health returns: *Has your rash cleared up yet?* **clear (sth) up** make (sth) tidy: *Please clear up (the mess in here) before you go.* **clear sth up** remove doubt about sth; solve sth: *clear up a mystery, difficulty, misunderstanding, etc.* **clear sb/sth with sb/sth** have sb/sth inspected or approved by sb in authority: *You'll have to clear it with management.*

□ ˈ**clearing bank** (*Brit*) any bank belonging to a clearing-house.

ˈ**clearing-house** *n* office at which banks exchange cheques and then pay in cash the amount they still owe each other.

clearance /ˈklɪərəns/ *n* **1** [C, U] (act of) clearing, removing or tidying sth: ˈ*slum clearance*, ie knocking down of slum houses ○ [attrib] *a* ˈ*clearance sale*, ie one in which all unwanted stock in a shop is sold at reduced prices. **2** [C] (in football, hockey, etc) act of kicking or striking the ball away from the goal: *a fine clearance by the full-back.* **3** [C, U] space left clear when one object moves past or under another: *a clearance of only two feet*, eg for a ship moving through a canal ○ *There is not much clearance for tall vehicles passing under this bridge.* **4** (**a**) [C, U] (document giving) authorization or permission, eg for a ship or plane to leave a place or for goods to pass through customs(2): *get clearance for take-off.* (**b**) [U] official permission for sb to work with secret information, etc: *give sb security clearance.* **5** [C, U] clearing of cheques at a clearing-house (CLEAR[3]).

clearing /ˈklɪərɪŋ/ *n* open space from which trees have been cleared in a forest.

cleat /kli:t/ *n* **1** small wooden or metal bar fastened to sth, on which ropes may be fastened by winding. **2** (usu *pl*) strip of rubber, wood, etc fastened to the sole of a boot or shoe, or to a gangway, to prevent slipping. **3** V-shaped wedge.

cleavage /ˈkli:vɪdʒ/ *n* **1** [C, U] (*infml*) hollow between a woman's breasts that can be seen above the low neckline of a dress: *That new gown shows a large amount of (her) cleavage!* **2** [C] (**a**) split or division: (*fig*) *a deep cleavage within the ruling party.* (**b**) line along which material such as rock or wood splits.

cleave[1] /kli:v/ *v* (*pt* **cleaved** /kli:vd/, **clove** /kləʊv/ or **cleft** /kleft/, *pp* **cleaved**, **cloven** /ˈkləʊvn/ or **cleft**) **1** [I] break or split, esp along a natural line: *This wood cleaves easily.* **2** [Tn, Tn·pr, Cn·a] divide (sth) by chopping (with a heavy axe, etc); split: *cleave a block of wood in two* ○ *cleave a man's head open with a sword.* **3** [Ipr, Tn, Tn·pr] ~ **through sth**/~ **sth (through sth)** make a way through (sth) (as if) by cutting: *The ship's bows cleaved (through) the waves.* ○ *cleave a path through the jungle* ○ (*fig*) *cleaving one's way/a path through the crowd.* **4** (idm) **be (caught) in a cleft ˈstick** be trapped in a situation where it is difficult to decide what to do.

□ ˌ**cleft ˈpalate** deformed condition in which the roof of a person's mouth is split at birth.

cleave[2] /kli:v/ *v* (*pt* **cleaved** /kli:vd/ or **clave** /kleɪv/, *pp* **cleaved**) [Ipr] ~ **to sb/sth** (*arch*) remain attached or faithful to sb/sth.

cleaver /ˈkli:və(r)/ *n* heavy knife with a broad blade used by a butcher for chopping meat.

cleavers /ˈkli:vəz/ *n* [sing or pl *v*] (also **goosegrass** [U]) plant that spreads very quickly and whose fruits have hooks that cling to skin, clothes, etc.

clef /klef/ *n* (*music*) symbol at the beginning of a stave showing the pitch of the notes: *treble/bass/alto clef.* ⇨ illus at MUSIC.

cleft[1] /kleft/ *n* crack or split occurring naturally (eg in the ground or in rock).

cleft[2] *pt, pp* of CLEAVE[1].

cleg /kleg/ *n* (*Brit dialect*) gadfly or horse-fly.

clematis /ˈklemətɪs, *also* kləˈmeɪtɪs/ *n* [U, C] climbing plant with white, purple or pink flowers.

Clemenceau /ˌklemənˈsəʊ/ Georges (1841-1929), French journalist and politician. He was noted for his strong opinions and opposition to corruption. He became prime minister in November 1917 and insisted on strict terms for the surrender of Germany at the end of the First World War.

Clemens /ˈklemənz/ Samuel Langhorne ⇨ TWAIN, MARK.

clement /ˈklemənt/ *adj* (*fml*) **1** (esp of weather) mild. **2** showing mercy.

▷ **clemency** /ˈklemənsɪ/ *n* [U] (*fml*) **1** mildness (esp of weather). **2** mercy (esp when punishing sb): *He appealed to the judge for clemency.*

clementine /ˈkleməntiːn/ *n* type of small orange.

clench /klentʃ/ *v* **1** [Tn] close (sth) tightly or press (two things) firmly together: *clench one's fist/jaws/teeth* ○ *a clenched-fist salute.* **2** [Tn, Tn·pr] ~ **sb/sth (in/with sth)** grasp or hold sb/sth firmly: *clench the railings (with both hands)* ○ *money clenched tightly in one's fist.*

Cleopatra /ˌklɪəˈpætrə/ (69-30 BC), ruler of Egypt, last of the line of the Ptolemies. She was the mistress of *Julius Caesar and later of *Mark Antony, and both helped her expand the Egyptian empire. This eventually angered Rome, and when Antony was defeated in the civil war she committed suicide.

□ ˌ**Cleopatra's ˈNeedle** nickname for a pink granite obelisk on the bank of the Thames in London. It is one of two that once stood in Heliopolis in Egypt. The other one is now in New York.

clerestory /ˈklɪəstɔ:rɪ/ *n* upper part of a wall in a large church, with a row of windows, above the roofs of the aisles.

clergy /ˈklɜ:dʒɪ/ *n* [pl *v*] people who have been ordained as priests or ministers of esp the

Christian Church: *All the local clergy attended the ceremony.* ○ *The new proposals affect both clergy and laity.* Cf LAITY 1.

□ **clergyman** /ˈklɜːdʒɪmən/ *n* (*pl* **-men** /-mən/) priest or minister of the Christian Church, esp the Church of England.

cleric /ˈklerɪk/ *n* (*dated*) clergyman.

clerical /ˈklerɪkl/ *adj* **1** of, for or made by a clerk(1) or clerks: ˈ*clerical work* ○ *a* ˌ*clerical* ˈ*error*, ie one made in copying or calculating sth. **2** of or for the clergy: *a* ˌ*clerical* ˈ*collar*, ie one that fastens at the back, worn by clergymen.

clerihew /ˈklerɪhjuː/ *n* short comic poem, usu about a famous person, consisting of two rhyming couplets with lines of varying length. The form was invented by Edmund Clerihew Bentley, who wrote many.

clerk /klɑːk; *US* klɜːrk/ *n* **1** person employed in an office, a shop, etc to keep records, accounts, etc: *a* ˈ*bank clerk* ○ *a* ˈ*filing clerk.* **2** official in charge of the records of a council, court, etc: *the Town* ˈ*Clerk* ○ *the Clerk to the* ˈ*Council* ○ *the Clerk of the* ˈ*Court* ○ *clerk of (the)* ˈ*works*, ie person responsible for materials, etc for building work done by contract. **3** (*US*) **(a)** (also ˈ**desk clerk**) assistant in a hotel. **(b)** assistant in a shop. **4** (*arch*) clergyman.

▷ **clerk** /klɜːrk/ *v* [I] (*US*) work as a clerk(1), esp in a shop.

□ ˌ**clerk of the** ˈ**course** official assisting the judges at horse-races or in motor racing.

clever /ˈklevə(r)/ *adj* (**-er** /ˈklevərə(r)/, **-est** /ˈklevərɪst/) **1 (a)** quick at learning and understanding things; intelligent: *clever at arithmetic* ○ *a clever student* ○ *Clever girl!* **(b)** skilful; nimble: *be clever with money, a needle, one's hands* ○ *be clever at making excuses* ○ *How clever of you to do that!* **2** (of things, ideas, actions, etc); showing intelligence or skill; ingenious: *a clever scheme* ○ *a clever little gadget.* **3** (*infml derog*) quick-witted or smart, often in a cheeky way: *Are you trying to be clever?* ○ *He was too clever for* (ie He outwitted) *us.* ▷ **cleverly** *adv.* **cleverness** *n* [U].

□ ˈ**clever-clever** *adj* [usu pred] (*infml derog*) trying to appear clever.

ˈ**clever Dick** (*infml derog*) person who thinks he is always right or knows everything: *She's such a clever Dick.*

clew /kluː/ *n* **1** (*nautical*) metal loop attached to the lower corner of a sail. **2** loop holding the strings of a hammock.

▷ **clew** *v* [Tn, Tn·p] ~ **sth (up/down)** (*nautical*) raise or lower (a sail).

cliché /ˈkliːʃeɪ; *US* kliːˈʃeɪ/ *n* **(a)** [C] phrase or idea which is used so often that it has become stale or meaningless: *a cliché-ridden style.* **(b)** [U] use of such phrases: *Cliché is a feature of bad journalism.*

click[1] /klɪk/ *n* **1** short sharp sound (like that of a key turning in a lock): *the click of a switch* ○ *He saluted with a click of his heels.* **2** sound like this made in certain African languages by tapping the top of the mouth with the tongue: [attrib] *click languages*, eg Xhosa.

click[2] /klɪk/ *v* **1** [I, Ipr, Tn] (cause sth to) make a slight sharp sound (as of a key turning in a lock): *The door clicked shut.* ○ *The new part clicked into place.* ○ *a clicking noise* ○ *click one's tongue/heels/fingers.* **2** [I, Ipr] ~ **(with sb)** (*Brit infml*) **(a)** become friendly at once: *We met on holiday and just clicked immediately.* **(b)** become popular (with sb): *The film has really clicked with young audiences.* **3** [I] (*infml*) suddenly become clear or understood: *I puzzled over it for hours before it finally clicked.*

client /ˈklaɪənt/ *n* **1** person who receives help or advice from a professional person (eg a lawyer, an accountant, a social worker, an architect, etc). **2** customer in a shop.

clientele /ˌkliːənˈtel; *US* ˌklaɪənˈtel/ *n* [Gp, U] **1** customers or clients as a group: *an international clientele.* **2** patrons of a theatre, restaurant, etc.

cliff /klɪf/ *n* steep, usu high, face of rock, esp at the edge of the sea. ⇨ illus at COAST.

□ ˈ**cliff-hanger** *n* story or contest whose outcome is uncertain till the end. ˈ**cliff-hanging** *adj.*

climacteric /klaɪˈmæktərɪk/ *n* period of life when physical powers begin to decline, eg (for women) the menopause.

climactic /klaɪˈmæktɪk/ *adj* forming a climax.

climate /ˈklaɪmɪt/ *n* **1 (a)** regular pattern of weather conditions (temperature, rainfall, winds, etc) of a particular region: *Britain has a temperate climate.* **(b)** area or region with certain weather conditions: *She moved to a warmer climate.* **2** general attitude or feeling; atmosphere: *a climate of suspicion* ○ *the present political climate* ○ *the current climate of opinion*, ie the general or fashionable attitude to an aspect of life, policy, etc. **3** (idm) **a change of air/climate** ⇨ CHANGE[2].

▷ **climatic** /klaɪˈmætɪk/ *adj* of climate: *climatic zones/regions*, ie those that have a particular type of climate, eg tropical, subtropical, temperate or polar. **climatically** /-klɪ/ *adv.*

climatology /ˌklaɪməˈtɒlədʒɪ/ *n* [U] science or study of climate.

□ ˈ**climate control** (*US*) (device that controls) air-conditioning.

climax /ˈklaɪmæks/ *n* **1 (a)** most interesting or significant event or point in time; culmination: *the climax of his political career* ○ *The climax of the celebration was a firework display.* **(b)** most intense part (esp of a play, piece of music, etc): *The music approached a climax.* ○ *His intervention brought their quarrel to a climax.* **2** peak of sexual pleasure; orgasm.

▷ **climax** *v* **1** [I, Ipr, Tn, Tn·pr] ~ **(sth) (in/with sth)** bring (sth) to or come to a climax(1a): *Her career climaxed in the award of an Oscar.* **2** [I] reach the peak of sexual pleasure.

climb /klaɪm/ *v* **1 (a)** [Tn] go up or over (sth) by effort, esp using one's hands and feet: *climb a wall, a mountain, a tree, a rope, the stairs* ○ *The car slowly climbed the hill.* **(b)** [I, Ipr, Ip] go or come in the specified direction, esp upwards, by effort: *climb up/down a ladder, along a ridge, into a car, out of bed, over a gate, through a hedge, etc* ○ *climb into/out of one's clothes*, ie get dressed/undressed ○ *This is where we start climbing*, ie upwards. ○ *Monkeys can climb well.* **2** [I] **(a)** go up mountains, etc as a sport: *He likes to go climbing at weekends.* **(b)** (of aircraft, the sun, etc) go higher in the sky: *The plane climbed to 20 000 feet.* **(c)** slope upwards: *The road climbs steeply for several miles.* **(d)** (of plants) grow up a wall or some other support by clinging or twining: *a climbing rose.* **3** [I] rise in social rank, etc by one's own effort. **4** [I] (of currency, temperature, etc) increase in value, etc: *The dollar has been climbing steadily all week.* **5** (idm) **climb/jump on the bandwagon** ⇨ BANDWAGON (BAND). **6** (phr v) **climb down (over sth)** (*infml*) admit a mistake or withdraw from a position in an argument, etc: *As new facts became known, the Government was forced to climb down over its handling of the spy scandal.*

▷ **climb** *n* **1** act or instance of climbing: *an exhausting climb* ○ *a rapid climb to stardom.* **2** place or distance (to be) climbed: *It's an hour's climb to the summit.*

climber *n* **1** person who climbs (esp mountains). **2** (*infml*) person who tries to improve his status in society: *a social climber.* **3** climbing plant. ⇨ illus at HOME.

□ ˈ**climb-down** *n* act of admitting one was mistaken, etc.

ˈ**climbing-frame** *n* structure of joined bars, etc for children to climb.

clime /klaɪm/ *n* (usu *pl*) (*arch or joc*) country; climate(1b): *seeking sunnier climes.*

clinch /klɪntʃ/ *v* **1** [Tn] fix (a nail or rivet) firmly in place by hammering sideways the end that sticks out. **2** [Tn] (*infml*) confirm or settle (sth) finally: *clinch a deal/an argument/a bargain.* **3** [I] (esp of boxers) hold each other tightly with the arms: *The boxers clinched and the referee had to separate them.* ○ (*infml*) *The scene ended as the lovers clinched.*

▷ **clinch** *n* **(a)** (in boxing) act or instance of clinching (CLINCH 3): *get into a clinch* ○ *break a clinch.* **(b)** (*infml*) embrace.

clincher *n* (*infml*) point or remark that settles an argument, etc.

cline /klaɪn/ *n* (*biology*) graded sequence of differences; continuum.

cling /klɪŋ/ *v* (*pt, pp* **clung** /klʌŋ/) **1** [Ipr, Ip] ~ **(on) to sb/sth;** ~ **on;** ~ **together** hold on tightly to sb/sth: *survivors clinging to a raft* ○ *They clung to each other/clung together as they said goodbye.* ○ *Cling on tight!* **2** [Ipr] ~ **(on) to sth** be unwilling to abandon sth; refuse to give sth up: *cling to a belief, an opinion, a theory, etc* ○ *cling to one's possessions* ○ *She clung to the hope that he was still alive.* **3** [I, Ipr] ~ **(to sth)** become attached to sth; stick to sth: *The smell of smoke clings (to one's clothes) for a long time.* ○ *a dress that clings to* (ie fits closely so as to show the shape of) *the body.* **4** [Ipr] ~ **to sb/sth** stay close to sb/sth: *The ship clung to the coastline.* ○ *Don't cling to the kerb when you're driving.* **5** [I, Ipr] ~ **(to sb)** (*esp derog*) be emotionally dependent on sb; stay too close to sb: *Small children cling to their mothers.* **6** (idm) **cling/stick to sb like a leech** ⇨ LEECH.

▷ **clinging** *adj* **1** (of clothes) sticking to the body and showing its shape. **2** emotionally dependent: *a clinging boyfriend.*

clingy *adj* (*infml*): *a shy, clingy child.*

□ ˈ**cling film** thin transparent plastic film used for wrapping food, etc. Cf SHRINK-WRAP (SHRINK).

clinic /ˈklɪnɪk/ *n* **1** private or specialized hospital: *He is being treated at a private clinic.* **2** place or session at which specialized medical treatment or advice is given to visiting patients: *a dental, diabetic, fracture, etc clinic* ○ *She is attending the antenatal clinic.* **3** occasion in a hospital when students learn by watching how a specialist examines and treats his patients.

clinical /ˈklɪnɪkl/ *adj* **1** [attrib] of or relating to the examination and treatment of patients and their illnesses: *clinical medicine* ○ *clinical training*, ie the part of a doctor's training done in a hospital. **2** coldly objective; unfeeling: *He watched her suffering with clinical detachment.* **3** (of a room, building, etc) very plain; undecorated: *the clinical style of some modern architecture.* ▷ **clinically** *adv*: *clinically dead*, ie judged to be dead from the condition of the body.

□ ˌ**clinical ther**ˈ**mometer** instrument for measuring the temperature of the human body.

clink[1] /klɪŋk/ *n* sharp ringing sound (as) of small pieces of metal or glass knocking together: *the clink of coins, keys, glasses.*

▷ **clink** *v* [I, Tn] (cause sth to) make this sound: *coins clinking in his pocket* ○ *They clinked glasses and drank each other's health.*

clink[2] /klɪŋk/ *n* [sing] (*sl*) prison: *be (put) in (the) clink.*

clinker /ˈklɪŋkə(r)/ *n* [U] rough stony material left in a furnace, etc after coal has burnt.

clinker-built /ˈklɪŋkə bɪlt/ *adj* (of a boat) made with the outside planks or metal plates overlapping downwards.

clinometer /klaɪˈnɒmɪtə(r)/ *n* instrument used by surveyors, etc for measuring the angle of a slope.

clip[1] /klɪp/ *n* [C] **1** (esp in compounds) any of various wire or metal devices used for holding things together: *a* ˈ*paper-clip* ○ *a* ˈ*hair-clip* ○ ˈ*bicycle-clips.* **2** (also ˈ**cartridge clip**) set of cartridges in a metal holder that is placed in a rifle, etc for firing. **3** piece of jewellery fastened to clothes by a clip: *a diamond* ˈ*clip.*

▷ **clip** *v* (**-pp-**) [Ipr, Ip, Tn·pr, Tn·p] ~ **(sth) (on) to sth;** ~ **(sth) on;** ~ **(A and B) together** be fastened or fasten (sth) to sth else with a clip: *Do you clip those ear-rings on/Do those ear-rings clip on?* ○ *There was a cheque clipped to the back of the letter.* ○ *clip documents together.*

□ ˈ**clipboard** *n* portable board with a clip at the top for holding papers.

ˈ**clip-on** *n* (usu *pl*), *adj* [attrib] (object) that is fastened to sth with a clip: *Are your ear-rings clip-ons?* ○ *a clip-on bow-tie.*

clip[2] /klɪp/ *v* **1** [Tn, Cn·a] cut (sth) with scissors or shears, esp in order to shorten it; trim: *clip a hedge, one's finger-nails* ○ *clip a sheep*, ie cut off its hair for wool ○ *The dog's fur was clipped short for the show.* **2** [Tn] make a hole in (a bus or train ticket) to show that it has been used. **3** [Tn] omit (parts of words) when speaking: *a clipped accent* ○ *He clipped his words when speaking.* **4** [Tn, Tn·pr] (*infml*) hit (sb/sth) sharply: *clip sb's ear/clip sb on the ear.* **5** (idm) **clip sb's ˈwings** prevent sb from being active or from doing what he is ambitious to do: *Having a new baby to look after has clipped her wings a bit.* **6** (phr v) **clip sth out of sth** remove sth from sth else with scissors, etc: *clip an article out of the newspaper.*

▷ **clip** *n* **1** act of clipping. **2** amount of wool cut from a (flock of) sheep at one time. **3** (*infml*) sharp blow: *She gave him a clip round the ear.* **4** short extract from a film. **5** (idm) **at a fair, good, etc ˈclip** (*infml*) at a fast speed: *The old car was travelling at quite a clip.*

clipping *n* **1** (usu *pl*) piece cut off: *hair, nail, hedge clippings.* **2** (*esp US*) = CUTTING[1] 1.

□ **ˈclip-joint** *n* (*sl*) place of entertainment, esp a night-club, that overcharges its customers.

NOTE ON USAGE: Compare **clip**, **pare**, **prune**, **trim** and **shave**. These verbs refer to cutting off an unwanted part to make an object smaller, tidier, etc. Note that with all except **pare** the direct object can be either (**a**) the main body that is made smaller, smoother, etc or (**b**) the part that is cut off. **Shave** is generally used of hair on the body: (**a**) *Monks shave their heads.* (**b**) *She shaved the hairs off her legs.* We **trim** something to make it tidy: (**a**) *trim one's beard, a hedge.* (**b**) *She trimmed the loose threads from her skirt.* **Clip** can relate to cutting off an unwanted part or to removing a part in order to keep it: (**a**) *Have you finished clipping the hedge?* (**b**) *I want to clip that picture from the magazine.* We **prune** plants to make them grow stronger: (**a**) *The roses need pruning.* (**b**) *I've pruned all the dead branches off the tree.* **Pare** indicates removing the outer layer or edge of something: *She pared the apple with a sharp knife.*

clip-clop /ˈklɪp klɒp/ *n* sound (like that) of horses' hoofs on a hard surface.

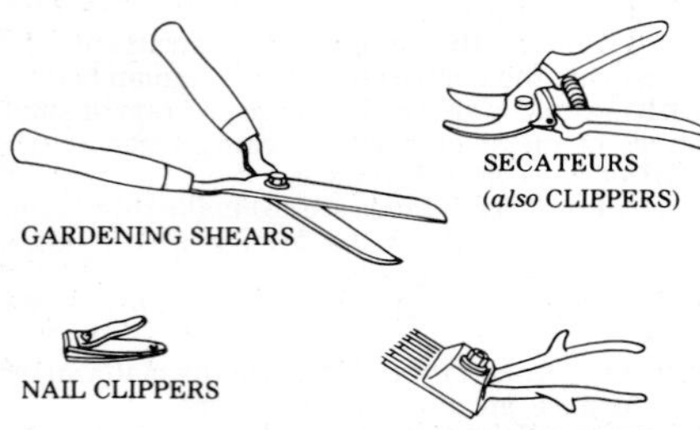

clipper /ˈklɪpə(r)/ *n* **1 clippers** [pl] instrument for clipping nails, hair, hedges, etc: *(a pair of) nail clippers.* ⇨ illus. **2** fast sailing-ship, esp one used in the 19th century for carrying tea. Their design enabled them to sail faster than ordinary ships, 'clipping' time off the voyage. The *Cutty Sark*, now moored at Greenwich in London, is a fine example.

clippie /ˈklɪpɪ/ *n* (*Brit infml*) woman bus conductor.

clique /kli:k/ *n* [CGp] (*sometimes derog*) small group of people, often with shared interests, who associate closely and exclude others from their group: *The club is dominated by a small clique of intellectuals.*

▷ **cliquy** (also **cliquey**, **cliquish**) *adj* (*derog*) (**a**) (of people) tending to form a clique. (**b**) dominated by a clique or cliques: *Our department is very cliquy.*

clitoris /ˈklɪtərɪs/ *n* small part of the female genitals which becomes larger when the female is sexually excited. ▷ **clitoral** /ˈklɪtərəl/ *adj.*

Clive /klaɪv/ Robert (1725-74), British soldier and colonial administrator. He earned the name 'Clive of India' from his success there in defeating the French and Indian forces. He was later made Governor of Bengal, but was wrongly accused of corruption and resigned.

Cllr *abbr* (*Brit*) Councillor: *Cllr Michael Booth.*

cloaca /kləʊˈeɪkə/ *n* (*pl* **-cae** /-ki:/) opening at the end of a bird's intestines, through which it excretes.

cloak /kləʊk/ *n* **1** [C] sleeveless outer garment hanging loosely from the shoulders, usu worn out of doors. ⇨ illus. **2** [sing] (*fig*) thing that hides or covers: *They left under (the) cloak of darkness.* ○ *The spy's activities were concealed by the cloak of diplomacy.*

▷ **cloak** *v* [Tn, Tn·pr] ~ **sth** (**in sth**) (*usu fig*) cover or hide (as if) with a cloak: *The negotiations were cloaked in secrecy.*

□ ˌ**cloak-and-ˈdagger** *adj* [attrib] (of a story, film, etc) involving intrigue and espionage.

cloakroom /ˈkləʊkrʊm/ *n* **1** room (usu in a public building) where coats, hats, etc may be left for a time. **2** (*Brit euph*) lavatory: *the ladies' cloakroom.*

clobber[1] /ˈklɒbə(r)/ *v* [Tn] (*infml*) **1** strike (sb) heavily and repeatedly: (*fig*) *The police intend to clobber drunk drivers*, ie punish them severely. ○ *The new tax laws will clobber small businesses*, ie harm them financially. **2** defeat (sb/sth) completely: *Our team got clobbered on Saturday.* **3** criticize (sb/sth) severely.

clobber[2] /ˈklɒbə(r)/ *n* [U] (*Brit infml*) clothing or equipment (esp for a specific activity): *You should see the clobber he takes when he goes climbing!*

cloche /klɒʃ/ *n* **1** portable glass or plastic cover used to protect outdoor plants. **2** woman's close-fitting bell-shaped hat. ⇨ illus at DRESS.

clock[1] /klɒk/ *n* **1** instrument for measuring and showing time (not carried or worn like a watch). **2** (*infml*) instrument (eg a taxi meter or a milometer) for measuring and recording things other than time: *a second-hand car with 20000 miles on the clock.* **3** round fluffy seed-head of a dandelion. There is a tradition that one can tell the time by counting the number of breaths it takes to blow the seeds away. **4** (idm) **around/round the ˈclock** all day and all night: *Surgeons are working round the clock to save his life.* ○ [attrib] *Doctors must provide a round-the-clock service.* **beat the clock** ⇨ BEAT[1]. **put the ˈclock back** return to a past age or to old-fashioned ideas, laws, customs, etc: *The new censorship law will put the clock back (by) 50 years.* **put the clock/clocks forward/back** (in countries which have official summer time) change the time, usu by one hour, at the beginning/end of summer: *Remember to put your clocks back (one hour) tonight.* **watch the clock** ⇨ WATCH[2]. ˌ**work against the ˈclock** work fast in order to finish a task before a certain time.

▷ **ˈclockwise** *adv, adj* moving in a curve in the same direction as the hands of a clock: *turn the key clockwise/in a clockwise direction.* Cf ANTICLOCKWISE.

□ **ˈclock-face** *n* part of a clock that shows the time, usu marked with numbers.

ˌ**clock ˈgolf** game in which players putt a golf-ball into a hole from points in a circle round it.

ˈclock tower tall structure, usu forming part of a building, with a clock at the top.

ˈclock-watcher *n* worker who is always checking the time to know when he may stop working. **ˈclock-watching** *n* [U].

clock[2] /klɒk/ *v* **1** [Tn] record the time of (sth) with a stop-watch; time. **2** [Tn, Tn·p] ~ **sth** (**up**) achieve or register (the stated time, distance or speed): *He clocked 9.6 seconds in the 100 metres.* ○ *My car has clocked up 50000 miles.* **3** (idm) **ˈclock sb one** (*Brit infml*) hit sb, esp in the face: *If you do that again, I'll clock you one.* **4** (phr v) **clock** (**sb**) **in/on**; **clock** (**sb**) **out/off** (*US* **punch** (**sb**) **in/out**) record the time that one (or sb else) arrives at or leaves work, esp by means of an automatic device: *Workers usually clock off at 5.30.* ○ *What is ˈclock-in/clocking-ˈin time at your office?*

clockwork /ˈklɒkwɜ:k/ *n* [U] **1** mechanism with wheels and springs, like that of a clock: [attrib] *a clockwork toy*, ie one driven by clockwork ○ *with clockwork* (ie absolute) *precision* ○ *as regular as clockwork*, ie very punctual. **2** (idm) **like ˈclockwork** with perfect regularity and precision; smoothly: *The operation went like clockwork.*

clod /klɒd/ *n* lump of earth or clay.

cloddish /ˈklɒdɪʃ/ *adj* (esp of a person or his manners) clumsy or foolish.

clodhopper /ˈklɒdhɒpə(r)/ *n* (*infml*) **1** (*derog*) clumsy person. **2** (usu *pl*); (*joc*) large heavy shoe.

clog[1] /klɒg/ *n* shoe made entirely of wood or with a wooden sole.

□ **ˈclog-dance** *n* dance performed by people wearing clogs.

clog[2] /klɒg/ *v* (**-gg-**) [I, Ipr, Ip, Tn, Tn·pr, Tn·p] ~ (**sth**) (**up**) (**with sth**) (cause sth to) become blocked with thick or sticky material: *The pipes are clogging up.* ○ *a drain clogged up with dead leaves* ○ *pores clogged with dirt* ○ *That heavy oil will clog up the machinery*, ie prevent it from working properly. ○ (*fig*) *Don't clog (up) your memory with useless facts.*

cloisonné /klwɑ:ˈzɒneɪ; *US* ˌklɔɪzəˈneɪ/ *n* [U] (*French*) technique of enamel decoration using thin strips of metal to separate areas of different colour: [attrib] *cloisonné work.*

cloister /ˈklɔɪstə(r)/ *n* **1** [C often *pl*] covered passage around an open court or quadrangle, with a wall on the outer side and columns or arches on the inner side, esp within a convent or college, or attached to a cathedral. **2** (**a**) [C] convent or monastery. (**b**) [sing] life in a convent or monastery: *the calm of the cloister.*

▷ **cloister** *v* [Tn, Tn·p] ~ **oneself/sb** (**away**) shut oneself/sb away (as if) in a cloister: *He cloistered himself away with his books.* **cloistered** *adj* secluded; sheltered: *a cloistered life.*

clone /kləʊn/ *n* **1** (*biology*) (any of a) group of plants or organisms produced asexually from one ancestor. **2** (*computing*) computer designed to copy the functions of another (usu more expensive) model: *an IBM clone.*

▷ **clone** *v* [I, Tn] (cause sth to) grow as a clone.

close[1] /kləʊs/ *adj* (**-r**, **-st**) **1** [pred] ~ (**to sb/sth**); ~ (**together**) near in space or time: *This station is our closest*, ie the nearest one to our home. ○ *The church is close to the school.* ○ *The two buildings are close together.* ○ *The children are close to each other in age.* ○ *Their birthdays are very close together.* **2** (**a**) near in relationship: *a close relative.* (**b**) ~ (**to sb**) intimate; dear: *a close friend* ○ *She is very close to her father/She and her father are very close.* **3** to a high degree: *in close proximity*, ie almost touching ○ *There's a close resemblance/similarity*, ie They are very alike. **4** with little or no space between; dense; compact: *material with a close texture* ○ *The soldiers advanced in close formation.* **5** (of a competition, game, etc) in which the competitors are almost equal: *a close contest, match, election, etc* ○ *a close finish* ○ *The game was closer than the score suggests.* **6** [attrib] careful; thorough; detailed: *On closer examination the painting proved to be a fake.* ○ *pay close attention to sth* ○ *close reasoning*, ie showing each step clearly ○ *a close* (ie exact) *translation.* **7** [attrib] strict; rigorous: *in close confinement* ○ *be (kept) under close arrest*, ie carefully guarded ○ *keep sth a close secret.* **8** (**a**) (of the weather) humid; oppressive; heavy: *It's very close and thundery today.* (**b**) (of a room) without fresh air; stuffy: *a close atmosphere* ○ *Open a window — it's very close in here.* **9** (*phonetics*) (of vowels) pronounced with the tongue raised close to the roof of the mouth: *The English vowels /i:/ and /u:/ are close.* **10** [pred] secretive; reticent: *be close about sth.* **11** [pred] mean; stingy: *He's very close with his money.* **12** near to the surface; very short: *A new razor gives a close shave.* **13** (idm) **at ˌclose ˈquarters** very near: *fighting at close quarters.* **a ˌclose ˈcall** (*infml*) almost an accident, a disaster or a failure: *We didn't actually hit the other car, but it was a close call.* **a ˌclose ˈshave** situation in which one only just manages to escape an accident, a disaster, etc. **a close/near thing** ➪ THING. **close to/near the bone** ➪ BONE. **close/dear/near to sb's heart** ➪ HEART. **close/near to home** ➪ HOME¹. **hold/keep one's cards close to one's chest** ➪ CARD¹. **keep a close ˈeye/ˈwatch on sb/sth** watch sb/sth carefully. **keep/lie ˈclose** stay hidden; not show oneself: *He decided to lie close for a while.* **ˌtoo close for ˈcomfort** worryingly near in space or time: *That lorry is much too close for comfort.* ○ *My exams are altogether too close for comfort,* ie I am worried because I am not ready for them.

▷ **closely** *adv* in a close manner: *listen closely,* ie carefully ○ *follow an argument closely* ○ *a closely contested election* ○ *She closely resembles her mother.* ○ *The two events are closely connected.*

closeness *n* [U].

□ **close ˈharmony** type of harmony used esp in singing where the notes of individual chords are very close together. Cf BARBER-SHOP (BARBER).

ˈclose season (also *esp US* **ˈclosed season**) time of the year when it is illegal to kill certain animals, birds and fish because they are breeding.

close² /kləʊs/ *adv* **1** leaving little space between; in a close position: *They live quite close.* ○ *hold sb close,* ie embrace sb tightly ○ *follow close behind sb* ○ *She stood close (up) against the wall.* **2** (idm) **close ˈby (sb/sth)** at a short distance (from sb/sth). **close on** almost; nearly: *She is ˌclose on ˈsixty.* ○ *It's ˌclose on ˈmidnight.* **close up (to sb/sth)** very near in space to sb/sth: *She snuggled close up to him.* **run sb/sth ˈclose** be nearly as good, fast, successful, etc as sb/sth else: *We run our competitors close for price and quality.* **sail close/near to the wind** ➪ SAIL.

ˌclose-ˈcropped (also **ˌclose-ˈcut**) *adj* (of hair, grass, etc) cut very short.

ˌclose-ˈfitting *adj* (of clothes) fitting close to the body.

ˌclose-ˈgrained *adj* (of wood) in which the lines formed by growth are close together.

ˌclose-ˈhauled *adj* (*nautical*) (of a sailing-ship) with the sails set for sailing as nearly as possible in the direction from which the wind is blowing.

ˌclose-ˈknit *adj* (of a group of people) bound together by shared beliefs, interests, etc: *the ˌclose-knit comˈmunity of a small village.*

ˌclose-ˈrun *adj* [usu attrib] (of a race, competition, etc) won by a very small margin: *The election was a ˌclose-run ˈthing.*

ˌclose-ˈset *adj* situated very close together: *ˌclose-set ˈeyes, ˈteeth.*

ˈclose-up *n* [C, U] photograph or film taken very close to sb/sth and giving a detailed view of him/it: *a close-up of a human eye* ○ *a television scene filmed in close-up.*

close³ /kləʊs/ *n* **1** (esp in street names) street closed off at one end; cul-de-sac: *Brookside Close.* **2** grounds and buildings surrounding and belonging to a cathedral, an abbey, etc.

close⁴ /kləʊz/ *v* **1** [I, Tn] (cause sth to) move so as to cover an opening; shut: *The door closed quietly.* ○ *This box/The lid of this box doesn't close properly,* ie The lid doesn't fit. ○ *close a door, a window, the curtains, etc* ○ *If you close your eyes, you can't see anything.* **2** [I, Tn, Tn·pr] ~ **sth (to sb/sth)** be or declare sth to be not open: *The shops close (ie stop trading) at 5.30.* ○ *Wednesday is early-ˈclosing day,* ie the day when the shops are not open in the afternoon. ○ *The theatres have closed for the summer.* ○ *The museum is closed (to visitors) on Sundays.* ○ *This road is closed to motor vehicles.* **3** [I, Ipr, Tn, Tn·pr] (cause sth to) come to an end: *The closing (ie last) day/date for applications is 1 May.* ○ *The speaker closed (the meeting) with a word of thanks to the chairman.* ○ *As far as I am concerned the matter is closed,* ie will not be discussed further. ○ *Steel shares closed at £15,* ie This was their value at the end of the day's business on the Stock Exchange. ➪ Usage. **4** [I, Tn] (cause sth to) become smaller or narrower: *The gap between the two runners is beginning to close,* ie One runner is catching the other up. **5** (idm) **a closed ˈbook (to sb)** subject about which one knows nothing: *Nuclear physics is a closed book to most of us.* **beˌhind closed ˈdoors** without the public being allowed to attend; in private: *The meeting was held behind closed doors.* **close a ˈdeal (with sb)** agree to the terms of a business agreement. **close one's ˈeyes to sth** ignore sth: *The Government seems to be closing its eyes to the plight of the unemployed.* **close one's ˈmind to sth** be unwilling to think about sth seriously. **close (the/one's) ˈranks (a)** (of soldiers) come closer together in a line or lines. **(b)** (of members of a group) forget disagreements and unite in order to protect or defend common interests: *In times of crisis party members should close ranks.* **shut/close one's eyes to sth** ➪ EYE¹. **with one's eyes shut/closed** ➪ EYE¹.

6 (phr v) **close around/round/over sb/sth** surround and enclose or grip sb/sth: *His hand closed over the money.* ○ *She felt his arms close tightly around her.*

close ˈdown (of a radio or television station) stop broadcasting: *It is midnight and we are now closing down.* **close (sth) down** (cause sth to) stop functioning or operating; shut (sth) down permanently: *Many businesses have closed down because of the recession.*

close ˈin (of days) gradually become shorter: *The days are closing in now that autumn is here.* **close in (on sb/sth) (a)** come nearer and attack from several directions: *The enemy is closing in (on us).* **(b)** surround or envelop sb/sth: *Darkness was gradually closing in.*

close ˈout (*US*) (of a storekeeper, etc) give up one's business; close down. **close sth out** (*US*) sell (unwanted goods or what is left of one's stock), usu at a reduced price: *a closing-out sale.*

close ˈup (of a wound) heal: *The cut took a long time to close up.* **close (sth) up (a)** come or bring (sth) closer together: *The sergeant-major ordered the men to close up.* **(b)** shut (sth), esp temporarily: *Sorry, madam, we're closing up for lunch.* ○ *He closes the shop up at 5.30.*

close with sb (a) accept an offer made by sb. **(b)** (*dated*) (of soldiers) come together and start fighting: *close with the enemy.* **close with sth** accept (an offer).

□ **ˈclose-down** *n* act of closing (sth) down.

ˈclosing price (usu *pl*) price of a share at the end of a day's business on the Stock Exchange.

ˈclosing-time *n* time when a shop, public house, etc ends business for the day.

NOTE ON USAGE: Generally, **close** means the same as **shut** and is more formal: *Shut/Close the door!* ○ *The box won't shut/close.* When referring to the opening hours of public places, both **shut** and **close** are used: *Shops/Offices shut/close at 5.30.* Note **closed** in the following example: *Museums are closed to the public on Mondays.* **Close** can mean 'terminate' and 'make smaller': *The meeting was closed after the demonstrators interrupted it.* ○ *Some politicians aim at closing the gap between rich and poor.* It is also used of roads, railways, etc: *They've closed the road because of an accident.* **Lock** means to close a door, box, suitcase, etc and fasten it with a lock and key.

close⁵ /kləʊz/ *n* [sing] **1** end of a period of time or an activity: *at the close of the day* ○ *towards the close of the 17th century* ○ *The day had reached its close.* ○ *at close of play,* ie at the end of the day's play in a cricket match. **2** (idm) **bring sth/come/draw to a ˈclose** end or conclude sth: *The ceremony was brought to a close by the singing of the national anthem.*

closed /kləʊzd/ *adj* **1 (a)** not communicating with or influenced by others; self-contained: *a closed society, economy.* **(b)** [esp attrib] limited to certain people; exclusive: *a closed membership* ○ *a closed scholarship.* **2** unwilling to accept new ideas: *He has a closed mind.*

□ **ˌclosed-ˌcircuit ˈtelevision** television system in which signals are transmitted by wires to a limited number of receivers.

ˈclosed season (*esp US*) = CLOSE SEASON (CLOSE¹).

ˌclosed ˈshop factory, business, etc whose employees must be members of a specified trade union: [attrib] *a closed-shop agreement.* ➪ article at TRADE UNION.

closet /ˈklɒzɪt/ *n* **1** (*esp US*) cupboard or small room for storing things. **2** (*arch*) small room for private meetings.

▷ **closet** *adj* [attrib] secret: *I never knew he was a closet queen,* ie homosexual. ○ *I suspect he's a closet fascist.*

closet *v* [usu passive: Tn, Tn·pr, Tn·p] ~ **A and B (together)**; ~ **A with B** shut sb away in a room for a private meeting: *He was closeted with the manager/He and the manager were closeted together for three hours.*

closure /ˈkləʊʒə(r)/ *n* [C, U] **1** closing or being closed: *pit closures,* eg closing of coal-mines because they are uneconomic ○ *The threat of closure affected the workers' morale.* **2** (*US* **cloture**) (in a parliament or other legislative body) method of ending a debate by taking a vote: *move the closure* ○ *apply the closure to a debate.* Cf GUILLOTINE 3.

clot /klɒt/ *n* **1** half-solid lump formed from a liquid, eg from blood when it is exposed to the air: *blood clots.* **2** (*Brit infml joc*) stupid person; fool: *You silly clot!*

▷ **clot** *v* (-tt-) [I, Tn] (cause sth to) form clots: *A haemophiliac's blood will not clot properly.*

□ **ˌclotted ˈcream** (*Brit*) thick cream made by scalding milk.

cloth /klɒθ; *US* klɔːθ/ *n* (*pl* ~**s** /klɒθs; *US* klɔːðz/) **1** [U] material made by weaving cotton, wool, silk, etc: *enough cloth to make a suit* ○ *good quality woollen cloth* ○ [attrib] *a cloth binding,* eg on a book. **2** [C] (esp in compounds) piece of cloth used for a special purpose: *a ˈdishcloth* ○ *a ˈfloorcloth* ○ *a ˈtable-cloth.* **3 the cloth** [sing] clothes worn by the clergy, seen as a symbol of their profession: *the respect due to his cloth* ○ *a man of the cloth,* ie a clergyman. **4** [C] sheet of painted canvas hung as scenery at the back of a theatre stage. **5** (idm) **cut one's coat according to one's cloth** ➪ COAT.

□ **ˌcloth ˈcap** (*Brit*) flat cap, made of (usu) woollen cloth with a peak, which is taken to symbolize working-class men: [attrib] *a ˌcloth-cap menˈtality.*

ˈcloth-eared *adj* (*Brit derog or joc infml*) unable to hear properly, slightly deaf: *I said come here, you cloth-eared fool!*

cloth of ˈgold silk or wool cloth with gold threads woven into it.

clothe /kləʊð/ *v* **(a)** [usu passive: Tn, Tn·pr] ~ **sb/oneself (in sth)** put clothes on sb/oneself; dress: *clothed from head to foot in white* ○ *warmly clothed.* **(b)** [Tn] provide clothes for (sb): *He can barely feed and clothe his family.* **(c)** [Tn·pr] ~ **sth in sth** cover sth as if with clothes: *a landscape clothed in mist.*

clothes /kləʊðz; *US* kləʊz/ *n* [pl] (not used with numerals) things worn to cover a person's body; garments: *warm, fashionable, expensive, etc clothes* ○ *put on/take off one's clothes.* ➪ article.

□ **ˈclothes-basket** *n* basket for clothes which need to be washed or have been washed.

ˈclothes-brush *n* brush for removing dust, mud, hair, etc from clothes.

ˈclothes-hanger *n* = HANGER 1.

ˈclothes-horse *n* frame on which clothes are hung to air after they have been washed and dried.

ˈclothes-line *n* rope stretched between posts on which washed clothes, etc are hung to dry. ➪ illus at HOME.

ˈclothes moth = MOTH 2.

ˈclothes-peg (*Brit*) (*US* **ˈclothes-pin**) *n* wooden or plastic clip for fastening clothes to a clothes-line. ➪ illus at PEG.

ˈclothes-prop *n* pole used for holding up the middle of a clothes-line.

Clothes

In Britain, there are traditional regional costumes and styles of dress associated with particular jobs or social groups. Wales and Scotland each have a national costume, although there is no English one. Welsh national dress is seen on such occasions as the annual Llangollen Eisteddfod. Women wear full skirts, laced bodices, colourful shawls and a distinctive tall crowned black hat, while men have bright waistcoats and flat black hats. The Scottish Highland dress, worn by both sexes and based on each clan's distinctive tartan, is considered the Scottish national dress. For men it includes a tweed jacket, a tartan kilt and tartan stockings, with a fur or leather sporran. Women's dress is similar, but with a tartan skirt in place of the kilt. Scottish costume is worn at many national events, such as the Highland Games, but also for everyday use by some Scots. A form of dress similar to the Scottish one is also worn by the Irish on ceremonial or formal occasions, showing the common Celtic and historical link between the two peoples.

As in most countries, members of particular professions and occupations often wear special dress. Among those regarded as distinctively British are the dark blue helmet and uniform of the policeman, the ceremonial red tunics and busbies of some army regiments, the 16th-century scarlet uniform of the Beefeaters (Yeomen of the Guard), the gown and 'mortar-board' of university students, and the wigs worn by judges. To this one could add the bowler hat, pin-striped trousers and rolled umbrella that were at one time almost a uniform for civil servants and City businessmen.

Many independent schools have distinctive uniforms, such as the Eton suit worn at Eton, or the boaters (straw hats) worn at Harrow and some girls' schools. Some state schools also have uniforms, with boys wearing a dark jacket or blazer, grey or black trousers, and white shirts, with a school tie. Girls usually wear a dark-coloured jumper and skirt with a white or pale-coloured blouse. The once familiar schoolgirl's gym tunic or gym slip is now rarely worn.

The blazer, whether dark blue or with bright stripes, is a distinctive garment still worn by many present and past members of schools, colleges and sporting clubs, with the institution's crest on the breast pocket. Blazers without a crest are worn as casual wear, as are tweed sports jackets.

As well as a blazer, many groups and clubs have a striped or crested tie to be worn by members. Some schools and colleges have more than one tie, for example for members of a particular team or club, or for former members ('old boys'). It is the 'old school tie' that traditionally serves as an identifying link between former members of a public school, and is sometimes regarded as a symbol of the upper-class outlook and attitudes of its wearer.

Items of clothing that are linked with particular social groups are the flat cap associated with working-class men and the more rounded cap worn by the 'country gentleman'. Although the British normally dress casually, there are still a few occasions when people like to dress up formally. Many weddings, for example, are very formal, with men wearing morning dress and women wearing extravagant hats. Women also usually wear hats at events where members of the royal family are present.

Allowing for national differences, there is much in common between British and American dress, although Americans of all ages have always been more colourful and adventurous than the British. Checked shirts and jeans are casual wear that the USA has exported to the rest of the world. The cowboy's broad-brimmed hat has become a symbol of the American West, and of the country as a whole.

Despite the constant changes of fashion and highly developed fashion industries. in both Britain and the USA, the majority of people wear casual and simple dress, with such garments as sweat shirts, jeans, denim jackets and training shoes (or 'trainers') worn by both sexes.

clothier /ˈkləʊðɪə(r)/ *n (dated)* person who makes or sells (esp men's) clothes.

clothing /ˈkləʊðɪŋ/ *n* [U] **1** clothes: *articles/items of clothing* ○ *waterproof clothing.* ⇨ App 9. **2** (idm) **a wolf in sheep's clothing** ⇨ WOLF.

cloture /ˈkləʊtʃə(r)/ *n (US)* = CLOSURE.

cloud[1] /klaʊd/ *n* **1** [C, U] (separate mass of) visible water vapour floating in the sky: *black clouds appearing from the west* ○ *There wasn't a cloud in the sky.* ○ *The top of the mountain was covered in cloud.* **2** [C] (**a**) mass of smoke, dust, sand, etc in the air. (**b**) mass of insects moving together in the sky: *a cloud of locusts.* **3** [C] blurred patch in a liquid or on a transparent object. **4** [C] *(fig)* thing that causes unhappiness, uncertainty, etc: *A cloud of suspicion is hanging over him.* ○ *Her arrival cast a cloud (of gloom) over the party.* **5** (idm) **every cloud has a silver ˈlining** *(saying)* there is always a comforting or more hopeful side to a sad or difficult situation. **have one's head in the clouds** ⇨ HEAD[1]. **on cloud ˈnine** *(infml)* extremely happy: *He was on cloud nine after winning the competition.* **under a ˈcloud** in disgrace or under suspicion.

▷ **cloudless** *adj* without clouds; clear: *a cloudless sky.*

cloudy *adj* (**-ier, -iest**) **1** covered with clouds: *a cloudy sky.* **2** (esp of liquids) not clear or transparent. **cloudiness** *n* [U].

□ **ˈcloud-bank** *n* thick mass of low cloud.

ˈcloudburst *n* sudden and violent rainstorm.

ˌcloud ˈchamber *(physics)* device containing vapour in which the paths of charged particles, X-rays and gamma rays can be observed by the trail of tiny drops of condensed vapour they produce.

cloud-ˈcuckoo-land *n* ideal place or state of affairs that exists only in the mind of an impractical or unrealistic person.

cloud[2] /klaʊd/ *v* **1** [I, Tn] (cause sth to) become dull, unclear or indistinct: *Her eyes clouded with tears.* ○ *Tears clouded her eyes.* ○ *Steam clouded the mirror,* ie covered it with condensation. ○ *(fig) Old age has clouded his judgement.* ○ *Don't cloud the issue,* ie Don't make it unnecessarily complicated. **2** [I, Ip] ~ (**over**) (of sb's face) show sadness or worry: *His face clouded (over) when he heard the news.* **3** [Tn] spoil (sth); threaten: *cloud sb's enjoyment, happiness, etc* ○ *I hope this disagreement won't cloud our friendship.* **4** (phr v) **cloud ˈover** (of the sky) become covered with clouds.

clout /klaʊt/ *n (infml)* **1** [C] heavy blow with the hand or a hard object: *get a clout across the back of the head.* **2** [U] power or influence: *This union hasn't much clout with the Government.*

▷ **clout** *v* [Tn] *(infml)* hit (sb/sth) heavily with the hand or a hard object.

clove[1] *pt* of CLEAVE[1].

clove[2] /kləʊv/ *n* dried unopened flower-bud of the tropical myrtle tree, used as a spice.

clove[3] /kləʊv/ *n* one of the small separate sections of a compound bulb: *a clove of garlic.* ⇨ illus at ONION.

clove hitch /ˈkləʊv hɪtʃ/ knot used to fasten a rope round a pole, bar, etc. ⇨ illus at KNOT.

cloven *pp* of CLEAVE[1].

clover /ˈkləʊvə(r)/ *n* **1** [U] small plant with (usu) three leaves on each stalk, and purple, pink or white flowers, grown as food for cattle, etc: *(a) four-leaf/-leaved ˈclover,* ie a rare type of clover with four leaves, thought to bring good luck to anyone who finds it. **2** (idm) **in clover** *(infml)* in comfort or luxury: *be/live in clover.*

□ **ˈclover-leaf** *n (pl* **-leafs** or **-leaves** /li:vz/) motorway intersection in a pattern resembling a four-leaf clover, allowing traffic to move in any of four directions.

clown /klaʊn/ *n* **1** comic entertainer (esp in a circus) who paints his face and dresses in a ridiculous way and performs funny or foolish tricks. **2** person who is always behaving comically.

▷ **clown** *v* [I, Ip] ~ (**about/around**) *(usu derog)* act in a foolish or comical way, like a clown: *Stop clowning around!*

clownish *adj* of or like a clown.

cloy /klɔɪ/ *v (dated fml)* **1** [I] (of sth sweet or pleasurable) become unpleasant by being tasted or experienced too often: *The pleasures of idleness soon cloy.* **2** [Tn esp passive] sicken (sb) with too much sweetness or pleasure: *cloyed with rich food.*

▷ **cloying** *adj* (of food, etc) sickeningly sweet: *(fig) a cloying smile, manner.*

cloze test /ˈkləʊz test/ comprehension test in which the person being tested tries to fill in words that have been left out of a text.

club[1] /klʌb/ *n* (esp in compounds) **1** (**a**) [C] group of people who meet together regularly to participate in a particular activity (esp a sport) or for relaxation: *a cricket, football, rugby, etc club* ○ *a working men's club* ○ *a youth club.* (**b**) [C] building or rooms used by a club: *have a drink at the golf club* ○ [attrib] *the club bar.* **2** [CGp, C] (organization owning a) building where elected (usu male) members may stay temporarily, have meals, read the newspapers, etc: *The club has/have decided to increase subscriptions.* ○ *He's a member of several London clubs.* ⇨ article. **3** [C] commercial organization offering benefits to members who agree to make regular payments of money: *a book club.* **4** [C] = NIGHT-CLUB (NIGHT). **5** (idm) **in the club** *(Brit sl)* pregnant. **join the club** ⇨ JOIN.

▷ **club** *v* (**-bb-**) (phr v) **club together (to do sth)** (of the members of a group) make contributions of money, etc so that the total can be used for a specific purpose: *They clubbed together to buy the chairman a present.*

clubbable /ˈklʌbəbl/ *adj* suitable to be a member of a club; sociable.

□ **ˈclub car** *(US)* first-class railway carriage offering comfortable seats and refreshments.

ˈclubhouse *n* building used by a sports club, esp a golf club.

clubland /ˈklʌblænd/ *n* [U] *(Brit)* area in London near Saint James's Park where there are many fashionable clubs (CLUB[1]2): *a well-known figure in London's clubland.*

clubman /ˈklʌbmən/ *n (pl* **-men**) man who is a member of several fashionable clubs (CLUB[1]2) or who spends a lot of time in his club.

ˌclub ˈsandwich *(esp US)* sandwich consisting of

Clubs

The London 'gentlemen's clubs' evolved from the coffee-houses and taverns that existed in the 17th and 18th centuries. They are characterized by their social exclusivity and their male-orientated organization and atmosphere. Even today there are a few clubs that do not admit women as members. In the past their role was to provide for upper-class men the all-male environment that they were used to at public school and in the army.

Membership is by election and normally involves both an admission fee and an annual subscription. Some clubs have thousands of members, many of whom live outside London and use their club as a place to stay when 'in town'. Most clubs have good restaurants and reading rooms, and provide comfortable surroundings where members can meet socially and invite their guests. The members of a particular club often share a professional interest or occupation. In some cases the interest is political, as in the Carlton, whose members are staunch Conservatives. Many members of the Garrick are actors or writers. Boodle's Club, one of the oldest, is used by high-ranking officers and bankers. Members of the Reform Club are predominantly Treasury officials, economists and judges. The Athenaeum, as its classical name implies, is known for its learned membership. A recently founded club, the Groucho, has a membership of people who work in the media. (The club was named after the American comic actor Groucho Marx, who once said that he would not want to belong to any club that would have him as a member.)

The oldest and most prestigious of London clubs is White's, founded in 1693, to which many members of royalty and the aristocracy have belonged. It was formerly a Tory political club, but is now purely social, with a reputation for extravagance and eccentricity.

Some clubs have names that indicate their specialization, such as the Army and Navy, the Cavalry and Guards, the Royal Automobile, the Traveller's and the United Oxford and Cambridge University Clubs. One of the best-known women's clubs is the University Women's Club, founded in 1886.

Most of the famous clubs are situated in and around Pall Mall and St James's Street, an area sometimes known as 'Clubland'. The club buildings themselves are often large and impressive, and as a sign of their exclusivity some do not even have their name outside.

There are also provincial clubs, mostly founded for a specific purpose. Many of them are attached to universities, such as the Amateur Dramatic Club, Cambridge, or the Oxford Union Society, Oxford (the university's debating club). The Leander Club, based at Henley-on-Thames, is Britain's oldest rowing club, with members drawn from the Oxford and Cambridge University crews.

Among the most exclusive types of sporting club are the yachting and sailing clubs, the best-known being the Royal Yacht Squadron, at Cowes Castle, Isle of Wight. Britain has numerous golf clubs, with membership of many of them being as socially exclusive as that of the London clubs. The country's leading golf club is the Royal and Ancient Golf Club ('R and A'), at St Andrews in Scotland.

At a more modest level, almost every town and community, from school to factory, has a club of some kind, even if its prime purpose is purely social. Working men's clubs were set up in the mid-19th century to provide educational and recreational facilities for their members, and still exist in many towns. They are not political, nor is membership of a trade union a condition for joining. On similar lines, the Royal British Legion has men's clubs throughout the country for ex-servicemen and women and their families. Local branches of the main political parties also have clubs which are a centre for political activity as well as fulfilling a social function.

There are many sports clubs and associations and youth clubs, the latter run by such organizations as the National Association of Youth Clubs or the National Association of Boys' Clubs. Rotary Clubs, associations of men and women who work in business or the professions, operate in many parts of the country.

Most towns also have what is in effect a club open to everybody, in the form of a community centre. This provides a wide range of facilities educational, recreational and social. There are also special clubs for retired people where they can go and chat to friends over a cup of tea.

In the USA, the equivalent of the London 'gentlemen's club' is the country club, usually located in an upper-class suburban area and providing social and sports facilities, notably golf. Country clubs are just as exclusive as London clubs, and often succeed in restricting membership in spite of the laws that prohibit racial or sexual discrimination. There is also a wide range of professional, political and social clubs of other types, including international ones, like the Rotary Club.

three slices of bread or toast and two layers of meat, lettuce, tomato, etc.

club[2] /klʌb/ *n* **1** heavy stick with one end thicker than the other, used as a weapon. **2** stick with a specially shaped end for hitting the ball in golf. ⇨ illus at GOLF.

▷ **club** *v* (**-bb-**) [Tn] hit or beat (sb/sth) with a club or heavy object: *The soldiers clubbed him (to death) with their rifles.*

□ ˌ**club-ˈfoot** *n* (**a**) [C] foot that is deformed from birth. (**b**) [U] condition of having such a foot. ˌ**club-ˈfooted** *adj.*

ˌ**club-ˈroot** *n* [U] disease affecting cabbages and similar plants, with swelling of the roots.

club[3] /klʌb/ *n* (**a**) **clubs** [sing or pl *v*] suit of playing-cards with a black three-leaf design on them: *Clubs is/are trumps.* ○ *the ace of clubs.* (**b**) [C] playing-card of this suit: *play a club.* ⇨ illus at PLAYING-CARD.

cluck /klʌk/ *n* noise that a hen makes, eg when calling her chicks.

▷ **cluck** *v* **1** [I] make a cluck. **2** [I, Tn] (of people) express (disapproval, etc) by making a similar noise.

clue /klu:/ *n* **1** ~ (**to sth**) fact or piece of evidence that helps to solve a problem or reveal the truth in an investigation: *The only clue to the identity of the murderer was a half-smoked cigarette.* ○ *We have no clue as to where she went after she left home.* **2** word or words indicating the answer to be inserted in a crossword puzzle. **3** (idm) **not have a ˈclue** (*infml*) (**a**) not know (anything about) sth; not know how to do sth: *'When does the train leave?' 'I haven't a clue.'* (**b**) (*derog*) be stupid or incompetent: *'Don't ask him to do it — he hasn't a clue.'*

▷ **clue** *v* (phr v) **clue sb in** (**about/on sth**) (*infml*) give information to sb: *You'll have to clue me in on what you've done so far.* **clue sb up** (**about/on sth**) (*infml*) (usu passive) make sb well-informed (about sth): *She's really clued up on politics.*

clueless /ˈklu:lɪs/ *adj* (*infml derog*) stupid or incompetent: *He's absolutely clueless.*

clump[1] /klʌmp/ *n* group or cluster (esp of trees, shrubs or plants): *a small clump of oak trees.*

▷ **clump** *v* [Tn, Tn·p esp passive] ~ **sth** (**together**) form a clump or arrange sth in a clump: *The children's shoes were all clumped together in a corner.*

clump[2] /klʌmp/ *v* [Ipr, Ip] ~ **about, around, etc** walk in the specified direction putting the feet down heavily: *clumping about (the room) in heavy boots.*

▷ **clump** *n* [sing] sound of heavy footsteps: *the clump of boots.*

clumsy /ˈklʌmzɪ/ *adj* (**-ier, -iest**) **1** awkward and ungraceful in movement or shape: *You clumsy oaf — that's the second glass you've broken today!* **2** (of tools, furniture, etc) difficult to use or move; not well designed: *a clumsy sideboard, pair of scissors* ○ *It's not easy walking in these clumsy shoes.* **3** done without tact or skill: *a clumsy apology, reply, speech, etc* ○ *a clumsy forgery*, ie one that is easy to detect. ▷ **clumsily** *adv.* **clumsiness** *n* [U].

clung *pt, pp* of CLING.

clunk /klʌŋk/ *n* dull sound (as) of heavy metal objects striking together.

▷ **clunk** *v* [I] make this sound.

Cluny /ˈklu:nɪ/ town in eastern France where a Benedictine monastery was founded in 910 AD. It played an important part in Church life in the Middle Ages. Its monks founded many other monasteries, and its architecture was widely copied. ▷ **Cluniac** /ˈklu:nɪæk/ *adj.*

cluster /ˈklʌstə(r)/ *n* **1** number of things of the same kind growing closely together: *a cluster of berries, flowers, curls* ○ *ivy growing in thick clusters.* **2** number of people, animals or things grouped closely together: *a cluster of houses, spectators, bees, islands, diamonds, stars* ○ *a consonant cluster*, eg *str* in *strong*.

▷ **cluster** *v* (phr v) **cluster/be clustered** (**together**) **round sb/sth** form a cluster round sb/sth; surround sb/sth closely: *roses clustering round the window* ○ *The village clusters round the church.* ○ *Reporters (were) clustered round the Prime Minister.*

□ ˈ**cluster bomb** type of bomb aimed at people, filled with small metal pellets which are sprayed over a wide area when it explodes.

clutch[1] /klʌtʃ/ *v* **1** (**a**) [Tn] seize (sb/sth) eagerly: *He clutched the rope we threw to him.* (**b**) [Tn, Tn·pr] hold (sb/sth) tightly in the hand(s): *clutch a baby in one's arms.* ○ *Mary was clutching her doll to her chest.* **2** (idm) **clutch at a straw/straws** try to grasp a slight opportunity to escape, rescue sb, etc in desperate circumstances. **3** (phr v) **clutch/catch at sth** try to seize sth: *He clutched at the branch but couldn't reach it.*

▷ **clutch** *n* **1** (**a**) [C] act of clutching or seizing: *make a clutch at sth.* (**b**) [sing] act of holding sth in the fingers or the hands; grip. **2 clutches** [pl] power or control (used esp as in the expressions shown): *be in sb's clutches* ○ *fall into the clutches of sb/sth* ○ *have sb in one's clutches* ○ *escape from sb's clutches.* **3** [C] (**a**) device that connects and disconnects working parts in a machine (esp the engine and gears in a motor vehicle): *let in/out the clutch*, ie when changing gear ○ *She released the clutch and the car began to move.* ⇨ illus at CAR. (**b**) pedal that operates this device: *take one's foot off* *the clutch.* ⇨ illus at CAR.

clutch² /klʌtʃ/ *n* (**a**) set of eggs that a hen sits on and that hatch together. (**b**) group of young chickens that hatch from these eggs.

clutter /ˈklʌtə(r)/ *n* (*derog*) (**a**) [U] (esp unnecessary or unwanted) things lying about untidily: *How can you work with so much clutter on your desk?* (**b**) [sing] untidy state: *His room is always in a clutter.*

▷ **clutter** *v* [esp passive: Tn, Tn·p] ~ **sth** (**up**) fill or cover sth in an untidy way: *a room cluttered (up) with unnecessary furniture* ○ *Don't clutter up my desk — I've just tidied it.* ○ (*fig*) *His head is cluttered (up) with useless facts.*

Clwyd /ˈkluːɪd/ county in NE Wales. ⇨ map at App 1.

Clyde /klaɪd/ river in SW Scotland, flowing through Glasgow and into the Irish Sea; length 170 km (106 miles). There were once a number of shipbuilding yards along its banks, but the industry has declined. ⇨ map at UNITED KINGDOM.

Clydesdale /ˈklaɪdzdeɪl/ *n* type of large horse used originally for pulling ploughs or carts.

Clytemnestra /ˌklaɪtɪmˈnestrə/ *n* (in Greek mythology) wife of *Agamemnon. She murdered him and was later killed in revenge by her son Orestes.

Cm *symb* curium.

cm *abbr* (*pl* unchanged or **cms**) centimetre: *600 cm × 140 cm*, ie as a measure of area.

Cmdr *abbr* = CDR.

Cmdre *abbr* = CDRE.

CND /ˌsiː en ˈdiː/ *abbr* (*Brit*) Campaign for Nuclear Disarmament. ⇨ article at PROTEST.

Cnut ⇨ CANUTE.

co- *pref* (used fairly widely with *adjs, advs, ns* and *vs*) together; jointly: *co-produced* ○ *co-operatively* ○ *co-driver* ○ *co-star*.

CO /ˌsiː ˈəʊ/ *abbr* Commanding Officer.

Co *abbr* **1** (*esp commerce*) company: *Pearce, Briggs & Co* ○ *the Stylewise Furniture Co* ○ (*infml*) *Were Jane and Mary and Co* /ˈmeərɪ ən kəʊ/ *at the party?* **2** county: *Co Down, Northern Ireland.*

Co *symb* cobalt.

c/o /ˌsiː ˈəʊ/ *abbr* (on letters, etc addressed to sb staying at sb else's house) care of: *Mr Peter Brown c/o Mme Marie Duval....*

coach¹ /kəʊtʃ/ *n* **1** bus (usu with a single deck) for carrying passengers over long distances: *travel by overnight coach to Scotland* ○ [attrib] *a coach station* ○ *a coach tour of Italy.* **2** = CARRIAGE 2. **3** large four-wheeled carriage pulled by horses and used (esp formerly) for carrying passengers: *a ˈstage-coach.* **4** (idm) **drive a coach and horses through sth** ⇨ DRIVE¹.

□ **coachman** /ˈkəʊtʃmən/ *n* (*pl* **-men** /-mən/) driver of a horse-drawn carriage.

ˈcoach screw large screw with a square head that is turned by a spanner.

ˈcoachwork *n* [U] main outside structure of a road or railway vehicle.

coach² /kəʊtʃ/ *n* **1** person who trains sportsmen and sportswomen, esp for contests: *a tennis, football, swimming, etc coach.* **2** teacher who gives private lessons to prepare students for examinations.

▷ **coach** *v* (**a**) [Tn, Tn·pr] ~ **sb** (**for/in sth**) teach or train sb, esp for an examination or a sporting contest: *coach a swimmer for the Olympics* ○ *coach sb in maths* ○ *She has talent but she will need coaching.* (**b**) [I] work or act as a coach: *She'll be coaching all summer.* ⇨ Usage at TEACH.

coagulate /kəʊˈægjʊleɪt/ *v* [I, Tn] (cause sth to) change from a liquid to a thick and semi-solid state; clot: *Blood coagulates in air.* ○ *Air coagulates blood.* ▷ **coagulation** /kəʊˌægjʊˈleɪʃn/ *n* [U].

coal /kəʊl/ *n* **1** (**a**) [U] black mineral found below the ground, used for burning to supply heat and to make coal gas and coal tar. The earth contains very large quantities of coal, produced over many thousands of years from the remains of dead plants and trees. There are many types of coal, from high-quality anthracite to the far less pure lignite. Coal is mined from under the surface of the earth, and although the mining industry now uses modern technology, it remains a dangerous activity which creates environmental problems. Burning coal often causes pollution and, like all fossil fuels, releases carbon dioxide which may lead to global warming. It is still the world's most plentiful form of fuel: *put more coal on the fire* ○ [attrib] *a coal ˈfire* ○ *a ˈcoal bunker* ○ *ˈcoal dust.* (**b**) [C] piece of this material, esp one that is burning: *A hot coal fell out of the fire and burnt the carpet.* **2** (idm) **carry coals to Newcastle** ⇨ CARRY. **haul sb over the coals** ⇨ HAUL. **heap coals of fire on sb's head** ⇨ HEAP.

▷ **coal** *v* **1** [Tn] load a supply of coal into (a ship). **2** [I] (of a ship) be loaded with a supply of coal.

□ **ˌcoal-ˈblack** *adj* very dark: *ˌcoal-black ˈeyes.*

ˈcoal-face (also **face**) *n* part of a coal-seam from which coal is being cut: *work at the coal-face.*

ˈcoalfield *n* district in which coal is mined.

ˈcoal gas [U] mixture of gases produced from coal, used for lighting and heating.

ˈcoal-hole *n* small cellar for storing coal.

ˈcoal measures series of layers of rock containing coal seams with other types of rock between them.

ˈcoal-mine (also **pit**) *n* place underground where coal is dug. **ˈcoal-miner** *n* person whose job is digging coal in a coal-mine.

ˈcoal oil *n* (*US*) = PARAFFIN.

ˈcoal-sack *n* part of the *Milky Way which appears as a very dark area, esp one near the Southern Cross.

ˈcoal-scuttle (also **scuttle**) *n* container for coal, usu kept by the fireside.

ˈcoal-seam *n* layer of coal under the ground.

ˌcoal ˈtar thick black sticky substance produced when gas is made from coal.

ˈcoal-tit *n* small greyish bird with a dark head.

coalesce /ˌkəʊəˈles/ *v* [I] (*fml*) combine and form one group, substance, mass, etc: *The views of party leaders coalesced to form a coherent policy.* ▷ **coalescence** /ˌkəʊəˈlesns/ *n* [U].

coalition /ˌkəʊəˈlɪʃn/ *n* **1** [U] action of uniting into one body or group. **2** [CGp] temporary alliance between political parties, usu in order to form a government: *form a coalition* ○ *a left-wing coalition* ○ [attrib] *a coalition government.*

coaming /ˈkəʊmɪŋ/ *n* raised rim round a ship's hatches to keep water out.

coarse /kɔːs/ *adj* (**-r**, **-st**) **1** (**a**) consisting of large particles; not fine: *coarse sand, salt, etc.* (**b**) rough or loose in texture: *bags made from coarse linen* ○ *a coarse complexion/skin.* **2** (of food, wine, etc) of low quality; inferior. **3** (**a**) not refined; vulgar: *coarse manners, laughter, tastes, etc.* (**b**) indecent or obscene: *coarse jokes, humour, language, etc.*

▷ **coarsely** *adv*: *chop onions coarsely*, ie into large pieces.

coarsen /ˈkɔːsn/ *v* [I, Tn] (cause sth to) become coarse: *The sea air coarsened her skin.*

coarseness *n* [U].

□ **ˌcoarse ˈfish** freshwater fish other than salmon and trout. **ˌcoarse ˈfishing** trying to catch coarse fish as a sport.

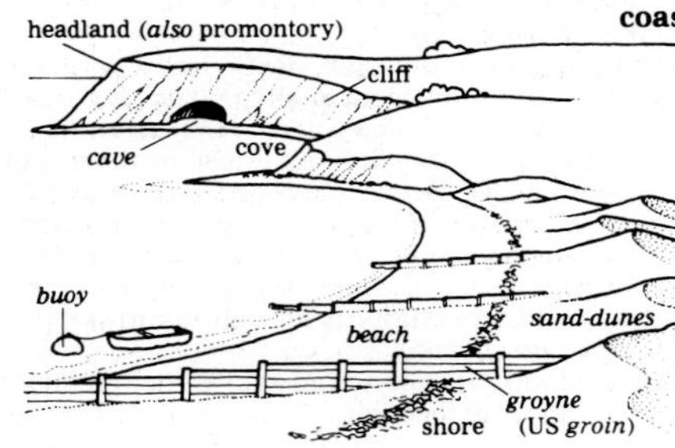

coast¹ /kəʊst/ *n* **1** land bordering the sea: *The ship was wrecked on the Kent coast.* ○ *islands off the Scottish coast* ○ *a village on the south coast*, eg of England ○ *spend a day by the coast*, ie the seaside ○ [attrib] *a coast road*, ie one that follows the line of the coast ○ *a ˌcoast-to-coast ˈjourney*, eg from the Pacific to the Atlantic coast of America. ⇨ illus. **2** (idm) **the ˌcoast is ˈclear** (*infml*) there is no danger of being seen or caught: *They waited until the coast was clear before loading the stolen goods into the van.*

▷ **coastal** *adj* [usu attrib] of or near a coast: *coastal waters* ○ *a coastal town, area, etc* ○ *a coastal plain*, ie between the coast and higher ground inland. Cf INLAND 1.

□ **ˈcoastguard** *n* [C, CGp] (one of a) group of people employed to watch the coast and report passing ships, prevent smuggling, etc.

ˈcoastline *n* shape or outline of a coast: *a rugged, rocky, indented, etc coastline.*

NOTE ON USAGE: **Coast** and **shore** both indicate land lying beside large areas of water. **Shore** suggests the limits of a lake or sea, or a narrow strip of land next to the water: *They camped on the shore of Lake Bala.* ○ *The survivors swam to the shore.* The land at the edge of a river or stream is a **bank. Coast** can refer to a wider area of land or a long stretch of land next to the sea or ocean: *We live at/on the coast.* ○ *the Atlantic coast of South America.* The **beach** is usually the sloping part of the shore often covered by the sea at high tide: *The beach was crowded with sunbathers.* **The seaside** is a coastal area where people go on holiday: *Brighton is a famous seaside resort.* ○ *We're spending August at the seaside.*

coast² /kəʊst/ *v* **1** [I, Ipr, Ip] (**a**) move, esp downhill (in a car, on a bicycle, etc), without using power: *coast down a hill* (ie in neutral gear) *to save petrol* ○ *coasting along on a bicycle*, ie without pedalling. (**b**) (*fig*) make progress without much effort: *The Socialists are coasting to victory* (ie winning easily) *in the election.* **2** [I] sail (from port to port) along a coast.

coaster /ˈkəʊstə(r)/ *n* **1** (**a**) small mat put under a drinking-glass to protect a polished table, etc from drips. (**b**) small tray for holding a decanter, wine bottle, etc. **2** ship that sails from port to port along a coast.

coat /kəʊt/ *n* **1** long outer garment with sleeves, usu fastened at the front with buttons: *a waterproof, fur, leather, etc coat.* **2** woman's jacket worn with a skirt: *a tweed coat and skirt.* **3** fur, hair or wool covering an animal's body: *a dog with a smooth, shaggy, etc coat* ○ *animals in their winter coats*, ie grown long for extra warmth. **4** layer of paint or some other substance put on a surface at one time: *give sth a second coat of paint.* **5** (idm) **ˌcut one's ˈcoat acˌcording to one's ˈcloth** (*saying*) spend money or produce sth within the limits of what one can afford: *We wanted to buy a bigger house than this but we had to cut our coat according to our cloth.* **turn one's coat** desert one side, party, etc and join another, esp because it is profitable or advantageous to do so.

▷ **coat** *v* [Tn, Tn·pr] ~ **sb/sth** (**in/with sth**) cover sb/sth with a layer of sth: *coat fish in batter* ○ *biscuits coated with chocolate* ○ *furniture coated with dust* ○ *a coated tongue.* **coating** *n* **1** [C] thin layer or covering: *a coating of wax, chocolate, paint.* **2** [U] material for making coats (COAT 1, 2).

□ **ˈcoat-hanger** *n* = HANGER.

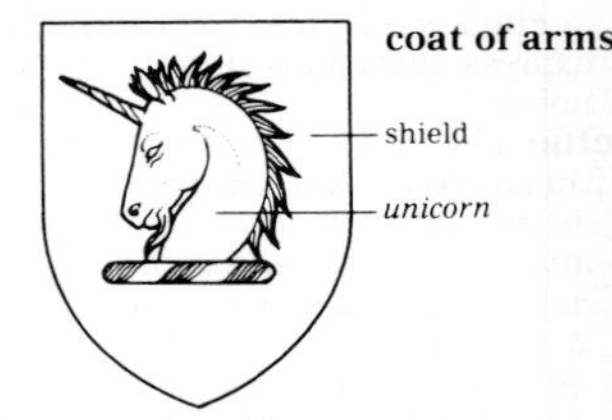

ˌcoat of ˈarms (also **arms**) design on a shield used as an emblem by a family, city, university, etc. ⇨ illus.

ˌcoat of ˈmail piece of armour made of interlocking metal rings or plates and worn on the

upper part of the body.
ˈ**coat-tails** *n* [pl] **1** divided tapering part at the back of a tailcoat (TAIL). **2** (idm) **on sb's ˈcoat-tails** using sb else's success, progress, etc to benefit oneself: *He only got where he is today (by riding) on the coat-tails of more able men.*

co-author /ˌkəʊˈɔːθə(r)/ *n* one of two or more people who write a book, an article, etc together.
▷ **co-author** *v* [Tn usu passive] be the co-author (of a book, etc): *co-authored by Dora and Edwin Wood.*

coax /kəʊks/ *v* [Tn, Tn·pr, Cn·t] **1** ~ **sb (into/out of (doing) sth)** persuade sb gently or gradually: *He coaxed her into letting him take her to the cinema.* ○ *She coaxed him out of his bad temper.* ○ *coax a child to take its medicine* ○ *(fig) coax a fire with* (ie make it burn by adding) *paraffin.* **2** (phr v) **coax sth out of/from sb** obtain sth from sb by gentle persuasion: *I had to coax the information out of him.* ○ *She coaxed a smile from the baby.*
▷ **coaxing** *n* [U] attempts to persuade sb: *It took a lot of coaxing before he agreed.* ○ *(fig) With a little coaxing* (ie After several attempts) *the engine started.* **coaxingly** *adv*: *speak coaxingly.*

coaxial /ˌkəʊˈæksɪəl/ *adj* having a common axis.
□ ˌ**coaxial ˈcable** electrical cable for transmitting high-frequency signals, consisting of a central conductor surrounded by an insulator which is in turn enclosed in an earthed sheath of another conductor.

cob /kɒb/ *n* **1** *(Brit)* small round loaf of bread. **2** strong short-legged horse for riding. **3** male swan. **4** (also ˈ**cob-nut**) large type of hazel-nut. **5** = CORN-COB (CORN[1]): *corn on the cob.*

cobalt /ˈkəʊbɔːlt/ *n* [U] **1** chemical element, a hard silvery-white metal. It is used esp in magnetic alloys and stainless steels, and one form of it (a radioisotope) is used in the treatment of cancer. A very small quantity of cobalt is essential in all living organisms. ⇨ App 11. **2** deep-blue colouring matter made from compounds of this element, used to colour glass and pottery: [attrib] *cobalt blue.*
□ ˈ**cobalt bomb** bomb that releases radioactive cobalt when it explodes.

cobber /ˈkɒbə(r)/ *n (Austral infml)* (esp used as a form of address between men) friend; mate.

Cobbett /ˈkɒbɪt/ William (1762-1835), English writer. In his books and articles, esp in *Rural Rides*, he attacked many aspects of the *Industrial Revolution and campaigned for political and social reform.

cobble[1] /ˈkɒbl/ (also ˈ**cobble-stone**) *n* rounded stone formerly used for covering the surfaces of roads, etc: *The cart clattered over the cobble-stones.*
▷ **cobble** *v* [Tn usu passive] cover the surface of (a road) with cobbles: *cobbled streets.*

cobble[2] /ˈkɒbl/ *v* **1** [Tn] repair (shoes). **2** [Tn, Tn·p] ~ **sth (together)** put sth together or make sth hastily or clumsily: *The student cobbled together an essay in half an hour.*

cobbler /ˈkɒblə(r)/ *n* **1** *(becoming dated)* person who repairs shoes. **2** *(esp US)* fruit pie with a thick cake-like crust. **3** *(esp US)* iced drink made with wine, lemon and sugar.

cobblers /ˈkɒbləz/ *n* [sing *v*] *(Brit sl)* nonsense; rubbish: *What a load of (old) cobblers!*

Cobden /ˈkɒbdən/ Richard (1804-65), English politician and reformer. With John *Bright he was a leading campaigner against the *Corn Laws and in favour of free trade.

COBOL (also **Cobol**) /ˈkəʊbɒl/ *abbr (computing)* common business-oriented language, a programming language designed for use in commerce.

cobra /ˈkəʊbrə/ *n* poisonous snake found in India and Africa. ⇨ illus at SNAKE.

cobweb /ˈkɒbweb/ *n* **1** (a) fine network of threads made by a spider. **(b)** single thread of this. Cf WEB 1. **2** (idm) **blow the cobwebs away** ⇨ BLOW[1].

coca /ˈkəʊkə/ *n* **(a)** [C] S American shrub. **(b)** [U] its dried leaves from which cocaine is obtained.

Coca-Cola /ˌkəʊkə ˈkəʊlə/ (also *infml* **Coke**) *n (propr)* **(a)** [U] popular non-alcoholic carbonated drink. **(b)** [C] bottle or glass of this.

cocaine /kəʊˈkeɪn/ *n* [U] drug used as a local anaesthetic by doctors, and as a stimulant by drug addicts. ⇨ article at DRUG.

coccyx /ˈkɒksɪks/ *n* (*pl* ~**es** or **coccyges** /ˈkɒksɪdʒiːz/) *(anatomy)* small bone at the bottom of the spine. ⇨ illus at SKELETON.

cochineal /ˌkɒtʃɪˈniːl/ *n* [U] bright red colouring-matter made from the dried bodies of certain tropical American insects.

cochlea /ˈkɒklɪə/ *n* (*pl* **-leae** /-lɪ-iː/) *(anatomy)* spiral-shaped part of the inner ear. ⇨ illus at EAR.

cock[1] /kɒk/ *n* **1** (*US* **rooster**) [C] adult male bird of the domestic fowl. ⇨ illus at BIRD. Cf HEN. **2** [C] (esp in compounds) male of any other bird, esp of a game bird: *a ˌcock ˈpheasant* ○ *a ˌcock ˈsparrow* ○ *a ˌcock ˈrobin.* **3** [sing] *(Brit sl)* (used as a form of address between men) friend; mate. **4** (idm) **a ˌcock-and-ˈbull story** absurd and improbable story, esp one used as an excuse or explanation: *He told us some cock-and-bull story about having lost all his money.* ˌ**cock of the ˈwalk** person who dominates others within a group. **live like fighting cocks** ⇨ LIVE[2].
□ **cock-a-doodle-doo** /ˌkɒk ə ˌduːdl ˈduː/ *n* **(a)** noise made by a cock[1](1). **(b)** (used by and to children) cock.
ˌ**cock-a-ˈhoop** *adj* [usu pred] very pleased, esp about being successful: *She's cock-a-hoop about getting the job.*
ˌ**cock-a-ˈleekie** /ˌkɒk ə ˈliːkɪ/ *n* [U] Scottish soup made of chicken boiled with vegetables.
ˈ**cock-crow** *n* [U] dawn: *wake at cock-crow.*
ˈ**cock-fight** *n* fight between (usu two) cocks fitted with sharp metal spurs on their feet, watched as a sport. ˈ**cock-fighting** *n* [U].

cock[2] /kɒk/ *n* **1** [C] tap or valve controlling the flow of a liquid or gas in a pipe. **2** [C] hammer of a gun. **3** [C] (⚠ *sl*) penis. **4** [U] *(sl)* nonsense; rubbish: *a load of cock.* **5** (idm) **at half/full ˈcock** (of a gun with a hammer that is raised before firing) half ready/ready to be fired. **go off at ˌhalf ˈcock** *(infml)* start before preparations are complete, so that the effect or result is not satisfactory.

cock[3] /kɒk/ *v* **1** [Tn, Tn·pr, Tn·p] ~ **sth (up)** cause sth to be upright or erect; raise sth: *The horse cocked (up) its ears when it heard the noise.* ○ *The dog cocked its leg (against the lamppost)*, ie in order to urinate. **2** [Tn, Tn·pr] cause (sth) to tilt or slant: *She cocked her hat at a jaunty angle.* ○ *The bird cocked its head to/on one side.* **3** [Tn] raise the cock[2](2) of (a gun) ready for firing. **4** (idm) **cock a snook at sb/sth (a)** make a rude gesture at sb by putting one's thumb to one's nose. **(b)** show cheeky contempt for or defiance of sb/sth: *cocking a snook at authority.* **5** (phr v) **cock sth up** *(Brit infml)* spoil or ruin sth by incompetence; bungle sth: *The travel agent completely cocked up the arrangements for our holiday.* ○ *Trust him to cock it/things up!*
□ ˌ**cocked ˈhat 1** hat with the brim turned up on three sides. **2** (idm) **knock sb/sth into a cocked hat** ⇨ KNOCK[2].
ˈ**cock-up** *n (Brit infml)* act of bungling sth; mess: *She made a complete cock-up of the arrangements.* ○ *What a cock-up!*

cock[4] /kɒk/ *n* small cone-shaped pile of straw or hay.
▷ **cock** *v* [Tn] pile (straw or hay) in cocks.

cockade /kɒˈkeɪd/ *n* piece of ribbon tied in a knot and worn on a hat as a badge.

Cockaigne /kɒˈkeɪn/ imaginary country where people live in luxury and idleness.

cockatoo /ˌkɒkəˈtuː/ *n* (*pl* ~**s**) type of parrot with a large crest.

cockchafer /ˈkɒktʃeɪfə(r)/ (also **ˈmay-bug**) *n* large beetle that flies at night with a loud whirring sound and feeds on leaves.

Cockcroft /ˈkɒkkrɒft/ Sir John Douglas (1897-1967), English physicist. With E T S Walton he succeeded in splitting the atom in 1932, paving the way for the development of nuclear and particle physics. The two shared the Nobel prize in 1951.

cocker /ˈkɒkə(r)/ *n* (also ˌ**cocker ˈspaniel**) small spaniel with golden-brown fur. ⇨ illus at DOG.

cockerel /ˈkɒkərəl/ *n* young cock[1](1) not more than one year old.

cock-eyed /ˈkɒk aɪd/ *adj (infml)* **1** not straight or level; crooked: *That picture on the wall looks cock-eyed to me.* **2** having a squint; squinting. **3** impractical; absurd: *a cock-eyed scheme.*

cockle /ˈkɒkl/ *n* **1 (a)** small edible shellfish. **(b)** its shell. **2** (also ˈ**cockle-shell**) small shallow boat. **3** wrinkle or small fold, eg in paper. **4** (idm) **warm the cockles** ⇨ WARM[2].
▷ **cockle** *v* [I, Tn] (cause sth to) become wrinkled; pucker.

cockney /ˈkɒknɪ/ *n* **1** [C] native of London, esp of the East End of the city. Traditionally, a true cockney was sb born within the sound of *Bow-bells, but the term is generally used of any Londoner with a local accent. One famous feature of cockney speech is its use of rhyming slang. ⇨ article at LONDON. **2** [U] dialect spoken by cockneys. ⇨ article at ACCENT.
▷ **cockney** *adj* [esp attrib] of cockneys or their dialect: *a cockney accent* ○ *cockney humour, slang, wit.*

cockpit /ˈkɒkpɪt/ *n* **1** compartment for the pilot and crew of an aircraft or a spaceship. ⇨ illus at AIRCRAFT. **2** driver's seat in a racing car. **3** enclosed part of a small yacht containing the wheel. ⇨ illus at YACHT. **4 (a)** (formerly) place used for cock-fights. **(b)** place where many battles have been fought: *Belgium has been called the cockpit of Europe.*

cockroach /ˈkɒkrəʊtʃ/ (also **roach**) *n* large dark-brown insect that infests kitchens and bathrooms.

cockscomb /ˈkɒkskəʊm/ *n* red fleshy crest on the head of a cock[1](1).

cock-shy /ˈkɒkʃaɪ/ *n* **1** (throw at a) target, esp at a fairground stall. **2** *(dated)* person or thing that people attack or mock with words.

cocksure /ˌkɒkˈʃɔː(r); *US* ˌkɒkˈʃʊər/ *adj* ~ **(about/of sth)** *(infml)* arrogantly or offensively confident: *He's so cocksure — I'd love to see him proved wrong.*

cocktail /ˈkɒkteɪl/ *n* **1** [C] alcoholic drink consisting of a spirit or spirits mixed with fruit juice, etc: [attrib] *a ˈcocktail party*, ie one held in the early evening, at which drinks and light refreshments are served ○ *a ˈcocktail shaker*, ie used for mixing cocktails. **2** [C, U] dish of seafood or fruit (used esp in the expressions shown): *(a) prawn ˈcocktail*, ie a mixture of prawns and mayonnaise eaten as a first course ○ *(a) fruit cocktail*, ie a mixture of small pieces of fruit, usu eaten as a dessert. **3** [C] *(infml)* any mixture of substances: *a lethal cocktail of drugs.*
□ ˈ**cocktail stick** small thin pointed stick for holding small pieces of food (eg small sausages or pieces of cheese) served at parties.

cocky /ˈkɒkɪ/ *adj* (**-ier, -iest**) *(infml)* conceited; arrogant. **cockily** *adv.* **cockiness** *n* [U]. **cocky** *n (Austral infml)* farmer who owns or works on a small farm.

coco /ˈkəʊkəʊ/ *n* (*pl* ~**s**) = COCONUT PALM (COCONUT).

cocoa /ˈkəʊkəʊ/ *n* **(a)** [U] dark brown powder made from crushed cacao seeds; powdered chocolate. **(b)** [C, U] (cup of a) hot drink made from this with milk or water: *a mug of cocoa.*
□ ˈ**cocoa butter** fatty substance obtained from cacao seeds, used in making chocolate, soap, etc.

coconut /ˈkəʊkənʌt/ *n* **(a)** [C] large hard-shelled seed of the coconut palm, with an edible white lining and filled with milky juice: [attrib] *coconut oil.* **(b)** [U] the edible lining of this, often shredded and used to flavour cakes, biscuits, etc: [attrib] *coconut icing.*
□ ˌ**coconut ˈice** *(Brit)* sweet made with sugar and dried flakes of coconut.
ˌ**coconut ˈmatting** floor covering made from the tough fibre of the coconut's outer husk.
ˈ**coconut palm** (also **coco**, ˈ**coco-palm**) tropical tree on which coconuts grow.
ˈ**coconut shy** fairground stall where people try to knock coconuts off stands by throwing balls at them.

cocoon /kəˈkuːn/ *n* **1** silky covering made by an

insect larva to protect itself while it is a chrysalis. **2** any soft protective covering: *wrapped in a cocoon of blankets*.

▷ **cocoon** *v* [esp passive: Tn, Tn·pr] cover or wrap (sb/sth) in a cocoon: *cocooned in luxury*.

cocotte /kəˈkɒt/ *n* small dish in which food (esp egg dishes) can be baked and then served.

Cocteau /ˈkɒktəʊ; *US* kɒkˈtəʊ/ Jean Maurice (1889-1963), French writer and film director. Throughout his life he experimented with new forms and fashions, from surrealism *Bunuel to trick photography. Outside France he is best known for his films, such as *La Belle et la Bête* and *Le Testament d'Orphée*.

cod[1] /kɒd/ *n* (*pl* unchanged) **1** (also ˈ**codfish**) [C] large sea-fish. **2** [U] its flesh eaten as food.

□ ˌ**cod-liver** ˈ**oil** *n* [U] oil obtained from cod livers, rich in vitamins A and D and used as a medicine.

the ˈ**cod war** (*Brit*) series of disputes in the 1970s between Iceland and Britain over fishing rights.

cod[2] /kɒd/ *adj* [attrib] imitating sth in a clever and amusing way; parodying: *a cod version of Hamlet's soliloquy*.

COD /ˌsi: əʊ ˈdi:/ (**a**) (*Brit*) cash on delivery. (**b**) (*US*) collect (payment) on delivery.

coda /ˈkəʊdə/ *n* (*music*) passage that brings a piece of music to a conclusion, often using new material.

coddle /ˈkɒdl/ *v* [Tn] **1** treat (sb) with great care and tenderness: *He'll need to be coddled after his illness*. **2** cook (eggs) in water just below boiling-point.

code /kəʊd/ *n* **1** [C, U] (often in compounds) (**a**) (system of) words, letters, symbols, etc that represent others, used for secret messages or for presenting or recording information briefly: *a letter in code* ○ *break/crack* (ie decipher) *a code* ○ [attrib] *a code book*, ie one that explains a particular code or codes ○ *a* ˈ*post-code*/ˈ*postal code*. (**b**) (system of) pre-arranged signals used to send messages by machine: ˌ*Morse* ˈ*code*. **2** [C] set of instructions for programming a computer. **3** [C] (**a**) set of laws or rules arranged in a system: *the penal* ˈ*code* ○ *the highway* ˈ*code*. (**b**) set of moral principles accepted by society or a group of people: *a code of be*ˈ*haviour*/ˈ*honour* ○ *a code of* ˈ*practice*, ie a set of professional standards agreed on by members of a particular profession.

▷ **code** *v* [Tn] put or write (sth) in code: *coded messages*.

□ ˈ**code-name** special name for sb/sth used for secrecy, eg by an army or a group of spies: *They referred to their informant by the code-name 'Rocky'*.—*v* [Tn esp passive]: *an operation code-named 'Magpie'*.

codeine /ˈkəʊdi:n/ *n* [U] drug made from opium, used to relieve pain or help people to sleep.

codex /ˈkəʊdeks/ *n* (*pl* **codices** /ˈkəʊdɪsɪ:z/) **1** handwritten book of ancient texts. **2** list of drugs with a description of each one: *the British Pharmaceutical Codex*, ie of drugs recognized by the British medical authorities.

codger /ˈkɒdʒə(r)/ *n* (*infml*) man, esp an old or peculiar one: *He's a funny old codger*.

codicil /ˈkəʊdɪsɪl; *US* ˈkɒdəsl/ *n* (*law*) later addition to a will, esp one that changes part of it: *She added a codicil to her will just before she died*.

codify /ˈkəʊdɪfaɪ; *US* ˈkɒdəfaɪ/ *v* (*pt, pp* **-fied**) [Tn] arrange (laws, rules, etc) systematically into a code(3a). ▷ **codification** /ˌkəʊdɪfɪˈkeɪʃn; *US* ˌkɒd-/ *n* [U].

codpiece /ˈkɒdpi:s/ *n* (in 15th- and 16th-century dress) bag or flap covering the opening at the front of a man's breeches.

codswallop *n* [U] (*Brit infml*) nonsense; rubbish: *He's talking (a load of) codswallop*.

Cody /ˈkəʊdɪ/ William Frederick, usu known as Buffalo Bill (1846-1917). Working as a frontier scout in the American West, he got his nickname as a hunter of buffalo (ie N American bison). He became famous with his 'Wild West Show', which claimed to show what life was like in America's pioneering days.

coed /ˌkəʊˈed/ *n* (*infml esp US*) female student at a coeducational school or college.

▷ **coed** *adj* (*infml*) coeducational: *Is your school coed?* ○ *a* ˌ*coed* ˈ*school*.

coeducation /ˌkəʊedʒʊˈkeɪʃn/ *n* [U] education of girls and boys together. ▷ **coeducational** /-ˈkeɪʃənl/ *adj*.

coefficient /ˌkəʊɪˈfɪʃnt/ *n* **1** (*mathematics*) quantity placed before and multiplying another quantity: *In 3xy, 3 is the coefficient of xy*. **2** (*physics*) measure of a particular property of a substance under specified conditions: *the coefficient of friction*.

coelacanth /ˈsi:ləkænθ/ *n* type of large bony fish. It was once thought to be extinct, but one species is now known to have survived.

coelenterate /si:ˈlentəreɪt/ *n* member of the family of sea animals that includes the jellyfish and sea anemone, having a simple body with one opening used for both eating and excreting.

coeliac (*US* **celiac**) /ˈsi:lɪæk/ *adj* (*fml*) of or relating to the abdomen.

□ ˈ**coeliac disease** disease that affects children, making them unable to digest fats properly.

coequal /ˌkəʊˈi:kwəl/ *adj* (*arch or rhet*) (esp of two or more people) equal.

coerce /kəʊˈɜ:s/ *v* [Tn, Tn·pr] ~ **sb (into sth/doing sth)** (*fml*) make sb do sth by using force or threats; compel sb to do sth: *coerce sb into submission* ○ *They were coerced into signing the contract*.

▷ **coercion** /kəʊˈɜ:ʃn; *US* -ʒn/ *n* [U] coercing or being coerced: *He paid the money under coercion*.

coercive /kəʊˈɜ:sɪv/ *adj* using force or threats: *coercive methods, measures, tactics, etc*.

coeval /ˌkəʊˈi:vl/ *adj* ~ (**with sb/sth**) (*fml*) existing at the same time or having the same age as sb/sth else; contemporary.

▷ **coeval** *n* (*fml*) coeval person or thing.

coexist /ˌkəʊɪgˈzɪst/ *v* [I, Ipr] ~ (**with sb/sth**) (**a**) exist together at the same time or in the same place. (**b**) (of opposing countries or groups) exist together without fighting.

▷ **coexistence** *n* [U] coexisting: *peaceful coexistence*, ie tolerance of each other by countries, groups, etc with different political systems, beliefs, etc.

coextensive /ˌkəʊɪkˈstensɪv/ *adj* ~ (**with sth**) (*fml*) that covers the same area or lasts the same time (as sth).

C of E /ˌsi: əv ˈi:/ *abbr* Church of England: *Are you C of E?* Cf CE.

coffee /ˈkɒfɪ; *US* ˈkɔ:fɪ/ *n* **1** [U] (powder obtained by grinding the roasted) seeds of the coffee tree: *half a pound of coffee* ○ *instant coffee*, ie coffee powder that dissolves in boiling water ○ [attrib] *a coffee cake*, ie one flavoured with coffee. **2** (**a**) [U] drink made by adding hot water to ground or powdered coffee: *a cup of coffee* ○ *make some coffee* ○ [attrib] *a* ˈ*coffee-pot*, ie for serving coffee from. (**b**) [C] cup of this drink: *Two black/white coffees, please*, ie without/with milk.

Coffee became very popular in Britain with the introduction of instant coffee in the 1950s. It was at this time too that many Italian espresso bars opened in British towns and cities and became popular meeting places for young people. Like tea, coffee is drunk throughout the day and is especially popular at breakfast time, during the day at work, and after dinner, when it is sometimes served black (without milk or cream) in small cups. Instant coffee is drunk more frequently than coffee freshly made from ground beans, since it is cheaper and quicker to prepare, and although 'real' coffee is gaining popularity, it is still not always easy to get a good cup of coffee in Britain. In recent years decaffeinated coffee has become increasingly popular, for health reasons.

3 [U] colour of coffee mixed with milk; light brown: [attrib] *a coffee carpet*.

□ ˈ**coffee bar** (*Brit*) place serving coffee, non-alcoholic drinks and snacks.

ˈ**coffee bean** seed of the coffee tree.

ˈ**coffee-break** *n* (at a meeting, in an office, etc) short period of time when work is stopped and coffee, etc may be taken.

ˈ**coffee grinder** (also ˈ**coffee-mill**) machine for grinding roasted coffee beans.

ˈ**coffee-house** *n* (formerly) place serving coffee and other refreshments, esp one that was a fashionable meeting-place in 18th century London.

ˈ**coffee morning** (*esp Brit*) gathering, often held in a private house, at which coffee, etc is served and money is sometimes raised for charity.

ˈ**coffee shop** (*US*) small restaurant serving coffee and simple meals.

ˈ**coffee-table** *n* small low table. ⇨ illus at FURNITURE. ˈ**coffee-table book** large expensive illustrated book, often placed where visitors may look at it.

ˈ**coffee tree** tropical shrub on which coffee beans grow.

coffer /ˈkɒfə(r)/ *n* **1** [C] large strong box for holding money or other valuables; chest. **2 coffers** [pl] (*fml*) store of money; treasury; funds: *The nation's coffers are empty*. **3** [C] (*architecture*) ornamental sunken panel in a ceiling, dome, etc. **4** (also ˈ**coffer-dam**) [C] watertight structure built or placed round an area of water which can then be pumped dry to allow building work (eg on a bridge) to be done inside it.

coffin /ˈkɒfɪn/ *n* **1** box in which a dead body is buried or cremated. **2** (idm) **a nail in sb's/sth's coffin** ⇨ NAIL.

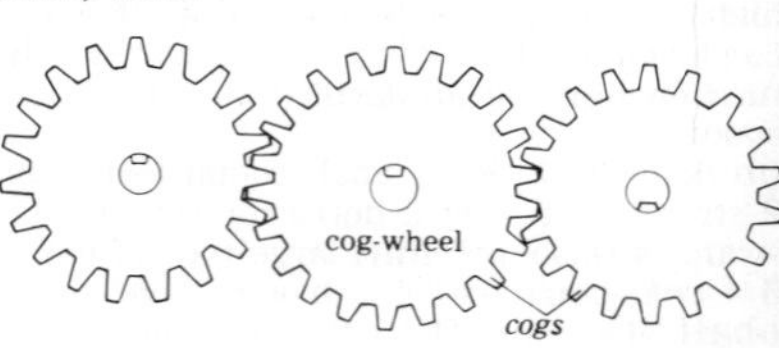

cog-wheel

cog /kɒg/ **1** each of a series of teeth on the edge of a wheel, that fit between those of a similar wheel, so that each wheel can cause the other one to move. ⇨ illus. **2** (idm) **a cog in the ma**ˈ**chine** (*infml*) person who plays a necessary but small part in a large organization or process.

□ ˈ**cog-railway** *n* (*esp US*) = RACK-RAILWAY (RACK[1]).

ˈ**cog-wheel** *n* wheel with teeth round the edge. ⇨ illus.

cogent /ˈkəʊdʒənt/ *adj* (of arguments, reasons, etc) convincing; strong: *He produced cogent reasons for the change of policy*.

▷ **cogency** /ˈkəʊdʒənsɪ/ *n* [U] (of arguments, reasons, etc) quality of being convincing; strength.

cogently *adv*: *Her case was cogently argued*.

cogitate /ˈkɒdʒɪteɪt/ *v* [I, Ipr, Tn] ~ (**about/on**) **sth** (*fml or joc*) think deeply about sth.

▷ **cogitation** /ˌkɒdʒɪˈteɪʃn/ *n* [C, U] (*fml*) (act of) thinking deeply: *After much cogitation I have decided to resign*.

cognac /ˈkɒnjæk/ *n* (**a**) [U] (type of) fine brandy made in W France. (**b**) [C] glass of this.

cognate /ˈkɒgneɪt/ *adj* ~ (**with sth**) **1** (*linguistics*) (of a word or language) having the same source or origin as another one: *The German word 'Haus' is cognate with the English word 'house'*. ○ *German and Dutch are cognate languages*. **2** having many things in common; related: *Physics and astronomy are cognate sciences*.

▷ **cognate** *n* (*linguistics*) word that is cognate with another: *'Haus' and 'house' are cognates*.

cognition /kɒgˈnɪʃn/ *n* [U] (*psychology*) action or process of acquiring knowledge, by reasoning or by intuition or through the senses.

▷ **cognitive** /ˈkɒgnɪtɪv/ *adj* of or relating to cognition: *a child's cognitive development*.

cognizance /ˈkɒgnɪzəns/ *n* [U] **1** (*fml*) knowledge; awareness: *have cognizance of sth*. **2** (*esp law*) scope or extent of sb's knowledge or concern: *These matters fall within/go beyond the cognizance of this court*. **3** (idm) **take cognizance of sth** (*esp law*) take notice of sth; acknowledge sth officially: *take cognizance of new evidence*.

▷ **cognizant** *adj* [pred] ~ **of sth** (*fml*) having knowledge of sth; aware of sth.

cognomen /kɒgˈnəʊmen/ *n* **1** (*fml*) nickname. **2** third name in the full name of an ancient Roman, as in Publius Vergilius *Maro*.

cognoscente /ˌkɒnjəˈʃentɪ/ *n* (*pl* **cognoscenti**) (*Italian*) (usu *pl*) connoisseur: *a restaurant favoured by the cognoscenti*.

cohabit /kəʊˈhæbɪt/ *v* [I, Ipr] ~ (**with sb**) (*fml*) (usu of an unmarried couple) live together: *They were cohabiting for three years before their marriage*. ▷ **cohabitation** /ˌkəʊhæbɪˈteɪʃn/ *n* [U].

cohere /kəʊˈhɪə(r)/ *v* [I] **1** stick together in a mass or group. Cf COHESION 1. **2** (of ideas, reasoning, etc) be connected logically; be consistent.

▷ **coherent** /ˌkəʊˈhɪərənt/ *adj* **1** (of ideas, thoughts, speech, reasoning, etc) connected logically or consistent; easy to understand; clear: *a coherent analysis, argument, description, etc* ○ *The Government lacks a coherent economic policy*. ○ *He's not very coherent on the telephone*. **2** (*physics*) (of radiation) in which two or more sets of waves are constantly in phase with each other. **coherence** /-rəns/ (also **coherency**) *n* [U] being coherent. **coherently** *adv*: *express one's ideas coherently*. Cf INCOHERENT.

cohesion /kəʊˈhi:ʒn/ *n* [U] **1** tendency to stick together; unity: *the cohesion of the family unit* ○ *a lack of cohesion*. Cf COHERE 1. **2** (*physics*) force that causes like[3] molecules to stick together.

▷ **cohesive** /kəʊˈhi:sɪv/ *adj* **(a)** tending to stick together: *a cohesive social unit*. **(b)** producing cohesion: *cohesive forces*. **cohesively** *adv*. **cohesiveness** *n* [U].

cohort /ˈkəʊhɔ:t/ *n* [CGp] **1** (in the army of ancient Rome) each of the ten units forming a legion. **2** number of people banded together.

COHSE /ˈkəʊzɪ/ *abbr* (*Brit*) Confederation of Health Service Employees, a British trade union to which many nurses and hospital workers belong. ⇨ article at TRADE UNION.

COI /ˌsi: əʊ ˈaɪ/ *abbr* (*Brit*) Central Office of Information.

coif /kɔɪf/ *n* (formerly) close-fitting cap covering the top, back and sides of the head.

coiffeur /kwɑ:ˈfɜ:(r)/ (*fem* **coiffeuse** /kwɑ:ˈfɜ:z/) *n* (*French*) hairdresser.

coiffure /kwɑ:ˈfjʊə(r)/ *n* (*French*) way in which (esp a woman's) hair is arranged; hairstyle.

coign /kɔɪn/ *n* (idm) **a ˌcoign of ˈvantage** (*dated or rhet*) place from which one has a good view of sth.

coil /kɔɪl/ *v* [Ipr, Ip, Tn, Tn·pr, Tn·p] ~ (**oneself/sth) round sth/up** wind or twist (oneself/sth) into a continuous circular or spiral shape: *The snake coiled (itself) round the branch*. ○ *coil (up) a length of rope, flex, wire, etc*.

▷ **coil** *n* **1** length of rope, etc wound into a series of loops: *a coil of flex*. **2** single ring or loop of rope, etc: *the thick coils of a python* ○ *a coil of hair*. **3** length of coated wire wound in a spiral to conduct an electric current. **4** = INTRA-UTERINE DEVICE (INTRA-UTERINE).

coin /kɔɪn/ *n* **1 (a)** [C] piece of metal used as money: *two gold coins* ○ *a handful of coins*. **(b)** [U] money made of metal: *£5 in coin*. **2** (idm) **the other side of the coin** ⇨ SIDE[1]. **pay sb in his own/the same coin** ⇨ PAY[2].

▷ **coin** *v* **1** [Tn] **(a)** make (coins) by stamping metal. **(b)** make (metal) into coins. **2** [Tn] invent (a new word or phrase): *coin words for new products*. **3** (idm) **ˈcoin it/money** (*infml*) earn a lot of money easily or quickly. **to coin a ˈphrase (a)** (used to introduce a new expression, or a well-known expression that one has changed slightly) **(b)** (*ironic*) (used to apologize for using a well-known expression rather than an original one).

coinage /ˈkɔɪnɪdʒ/ *n* **1** [U] **(a)** making coins. **(b)** coins made. **2** [U] system of coins in use: *decimal coinage*. **3 (a)** [U] inventing of a new word or phrase. **(b)** [C] newly invented word or phrase: *I haven't heard that expression before — is it a recent coinage?*

□ **ˈcoin-op** *n*, *adj* (*infml*) (launderette, etc) with automatic machines that are operated by putting in coins.

coincide /ˌkəʊɪnˈsaɪd/ *v* [I, Ipr] ~ (**with sth**) **1** (of events) occur at the same time or occupy the same period of time as sth else: *Her arrival coincided with our departure*. ○ *Our holidays don't coincide*. **2** (of two or more objects) occupy the same amount of space. **3** be identical or very similar to sth else: *Their stories coincided*. ○ *Her taste in music coincides with her husband's/Their tastes in music coincide*.

coincidence /kəʊˈɪnsɪdəns/ *n* **1** [C, U] (instance of the) occurrence of similar events or circumstances at the same time by chance: *'I'm going to Paris next week.' 'What a coincidence! So am I.'* ○ *By a strange coincidence we happened to be travelling on the same train*. ○ *The plot of the novel relies too much on coincidence to be realistic*. **2** [U] coinciding of events, tastes, stories, etc.

coincident /kəʊˈɪnsɪdənt/ *adj* (*fml*) happening at the same time by chance.

▷ **coincidental** /kəʊˌɪnsɪˈdentl/ *adj* [usu pred] resulting from coincidence: *The similarity between these two essays is too great to be coincidental*, ie One must have been copied from the other. **coincidentally** *adv*.

Cointreau /ˈkwɒntrəʊ; *US* kwɑ:nˈtrəʊ/ *n* [U] (*propr*) type of orange-flavoured liqueur.

coir /ˈkɔɪə(r)/ *n* [U] fibre from the outer husk of coconuts, used for making ropes, matting, etc.

coitus /ˈkəʊɪtəs/ (also **coition** /kəʊˈɪʃn/) *n* [U] (*medical or fml*) sexual intercourse. ▷ **coital** /ˈkəʊɪtl/ *adj*.

coke[1] /kəʊk/ *n* [U] black substance remaining after coal gas and coal tar have been removed from coal, used as a fuel: [attrib] *a coke furnace*.

▷ **coke** *v* [Tn] convert (coal) into coke.

coke[2] (also **Coke**) /kəʊk/ *n* [C, U] (*propr infml*) = COCA-COLA.

coke[3] /kəʊk/ *n* [U] (*sl*) cocaine.

Col *abbr* Colonel: *Col (Terence) Lloyd*.

col /kɒl/ *n* pass in a mountain range.

col *abbr* column(3).

cola (also **kola**) /ˈkəʊlə/ *n* **1** [C] W African tree. **2** [U] carbonated non-alcoholic drink flavoured with the seeds of this tree.

□ **ˈcola-nut** (also **kola-nut**) *n* seed of the cola tree, used as a flavouring or chewed.

colander (also **cullender**) /ˈkʌləndə(r)/ *n* metal or plastic bowl with many small holes in it, used to drain water from vegetables, etc, esp after cooking.

cold[1] /kəʊld/ *adj* (**-er, -est**) **1** of low temperature, esp when compared to the temperature of the human body: *feel cold* ○ *have cold hands, feet, ears, etc* ○ *a cold bath, climate, day, house, room, wind, winter* ○ *cold weather, water* ○ *It/The weather is getting colder*. Cf HOT, WARM[1]. **2** (of food or drink) not heated; having cooled after being heated or cooked: *Would you like tea or a cold drink?* ○ *have cold meat and salad for supper* ○ *Don't let your dinner get cold*, ie Eat it while it is still warm. **3 (a)** (of a person, his manner, etc) without friendliness, kindness or enthusiasm; without emotion: *a cold look, stare, welcome, reception, etc* ○ *cold fury*, ie violent anger kept under control. **(b)** sexually unresponsive; frigid. **4** suggesting coldness; creating an impression of coldness: *a cold grey colour* ○ *cold skies*. **5** (in children's games) not close to finding a hidden object, the correct answer, etc. **6** [pred] (*infml*) unconscious (used esp in the expression shown): *knock sb (out) cold*. **7** [pred] dead. **8** (of a trail left by a hunted animal) too old to be followed by dogs: (*fig*) *the police followed up a few clues about the murder, but then the trail went cold*. **9** (idm) **blow hot and cold** ⇨ BLOW[1]. **ˌcold ˈcomfort** thing that offers little or no consolation: *After losing my job it was cold comfort to be told I'd won the office raffle*. **a ˌcold ˈfish** (*derog*) person who shows no emotion or is very aloof. **ˌcold ˈsteel** (blades of) swords, bayonets, etc, esp when used in fighting: *There was hand-to-hand combat, where men fought with cold steel*. **ˌcold ˈturkey** (*sl esp US*) **(a)** way of treating a drug addict by suddenly stopping all his doses of the drug instead of gradually reducing them. **(b)** frank statement of the truth, often about sth unpleasant: *talk cold turkey to/with sb*. **come to sth ˈcold** (*infml esp US*) be faced with (eg a job or situation) for which one is not prepared: *She'd had experience of such negotiations before, but I was coming to it cold*. **get/have cold ˈfeet** (*infml*) become/be afraid or reluctant to do sth (esp sth risky or dangerous): *He got cold feet at the last minute*. **give sb/get the cold ˈshoulder** treat sb/be treated in a deliberately unfriendly way. **in cold ˈblood** without feeling pity or remorse; deliberately and callously: *kill, murder, shoot, etc sb in cold blood*. **in the ˌcold light of ˈday** when one's feelings of excitement, anger, etc are over and one is calm: *In the cold light of day, I regretted my hasty decision*. **leave sb ˈcold** ⇨ LEAVE[1]. **make sb's blood run cold** ⇨ BLOOD[1]. **pour/throw cold ˈwater on sth** be discouraging or unenthusiastic about sth: *pour cold water on sb's plans, ideas, hopes, etc*.

▷ **coldly** *adv* in an unfriendly or unenthusiastic way: *stare coldly at sb*.

coldness *n* [U] state of being cold: *his coldness* (ie unfriendly manner) *towards her*.

□ **ˌcold-ˈblooded** /-ˈblʌdɪd/ *adj* **1** (*biology*) having a blood temperature which varies with the temperature of the surroundings: *Reptiles are cold-blooded*. **2** (*derog*) (of people or actions) without pity; cruel: *a cold-blooded murderer, murder*.

ˈcold chisel chisel used to cut cold metal.

ˈcold cream ointment for cleansing and softening the skin.

ˈcold cuts (*esp US*) cooked meat, sliced and served cold.

ˈcold frame small glass-covered frame used to protect young plants.

ˌcold ˈfront leading part of a mass of cold air which is advancing and replacing a mass of warm air, usu associated with cloud and rain. Cf WARM FRONT (WARM).

ˌcold-ˈhearted /-ˈhɑ:tɪd/ *adj* without sympathy or kindness; unkind.

ˌcold-ˈshoulder *v* [Tn] be deliberately unfriendly to (sb); snub.

ˈcold snap (also *esp US* **ˈcold wave**) sudden short period of cold weather.

ˌcold ˈstorage storing of things in a refrigerated place to preserve them: (*fig*) *put a plan, an idea, etc into cold storage*, ie decide not to use it immediately but to reserve it for later.

ˌcold ˈsweat state in which sb sweats and feels cold at the same time, caused by fear or illness: *be in a cold sweat (about sth)*.

ˌcold ˈwar state of hostility between nations involving the use of propaganda, threats and economic pressure but no actual fighting: [attrib] *cold-war attitudes, diplomacy, rhetoric*.

cold[2] /kəʊld/ *n* **1** [U] lack of heat or warmth; low temperature (esp in the atmosphere): *shiver with cold* ○ *the heat of summer and the cold of winter* ○ *Don't stand outside in the cold*. ○ *She doesn't seem to feel the cold*. **2** [C, U] infectious illness of the nose or throat or both, with catarrh, sneezing, coughing, etc: *a bad, heavy, slight cold* ○ *have a cold in the head/on the chest* ○ *catch (a) cold*. **3** (idm) **(leave sb/be) ˌout in the ˈcold** excluded from a group or an activity; ignored: *When the coalition was formed, the Communists were left out in the cold*.

□ **ˈcold sore** (*infml*) cluster of painful blisters near or in the mouth, caused by a virus.

Coldstream Guards /ˌkəʊldstri:m ˈgɑ:dz/ **the Coldstream Guards** regiment of Guards, one of the oldest regiments in the British army (formed in 1650).

Coleoptera /ˌkɒlɪˈɒptərə/ *n* [pl] part of the insect family, the largest order(9) in the animal kingdom, including the beetles and weevils. ▷ **coleopterous** /-tərəs/ *adj*.

Coleridge /ˈkəʊlrɪdʒ/ Samuel Taylor (1772-1834), English poet. His joint collection with *Wordsworth, *Lyrical Ballads*, marked the beginning of the Romantic movement in Britain. His most famous poems are *Kubla Khan* and *The Ancient Mariner*. Much of his life was unhappy because of opium addiction and the failure of his marriage. His reputation grew in his last years, which he spent writing in support of moral and social reform.

coleslaw /ˈkəʊlslɔ:/ *n* [U] finely shredded raw

cabbage mixed with dressing(3) and eaten as a salad.

coleus /ˈkəʊlɪəs/ *n* [U, C] (*pl* unchanged) plant often grown indoors for its multicoloured leaves.

coley /ˈkəʊlɪ/ *n* [U, C] (*pl* unchanged or ~**s**) type of fish used as food, similar to cod.

colic /ˈkɒlɪk/ *n* [U] severe pain in the abdomen, suffered esp by babies.

▷ **colicky** *adj* of, like or suffering from colic.

colitis /kəˈlaɪtɪs/ *n* [U] (*medical*) inflammation of the lining of the colon[1].

collaborate /kəˈlæbəreɪt/ *v* [I, Ipr] **1** ~ **(with sb) (on sth)** work together (with sb), esp to create or produce sth: *She collaborated with her sister/She and her sister collaborated on a biography of their father.* **2** ~ **(with sb)** (*derog*) help enemy forces occupying one's country: *He was suspected of collaborating (with the enemy).*

▷ **collaboration** /kəˌlæbəˈreɪʃn/ *n* [U] **1** ~ **(with sb) (on sth)**; ~ **(between A and B)** collaborating (COLLABORATE 1): *She wrote the book in collaboration with her sister*, ie They wrote it together. **2** ~ **(with sb)** helping enemy forces occupying one's country.

collaborator /kəˈlæbəreɪtə(r)/ person who collaborates.

collage /ˈkɒlɑːʒ; *US* kəˈlɑːʒ/ *n* [C, U] (picture made by) fixing pieces of paper, cloth, photographs, etc to a surface.

collagen /ˈkɒlədʒən/ *n* [U] fibrous protein found in the connective tissues and bones of animals. It produces gelatin when boiled.

collapse /kəˈlæps/ *v* **1** [I] (break into pieces and) fall down or in suddenly: *The whole building collapsed.* ○ *The roof collapsed under the weight of snow.* ○ *The wind caused the tent to collapse.* **2** [I, Ipr] (of a person) fall down (and usu become unconscious) because of illness, tiredness, etc: *He collapsed in the street and died on the way to hospital.* ○ *collapse in a heap on the floor.* **3** [I] **(a)** fail suddenly or completely; break down: *His health collapsed under the pressure of work.* ○ *The enterprise collapsed through lack of support.* ○ *Talks between management and unions have collapsed.* **(b)** be defeated or destroyed: *All opposition to the scheme has collapsed.* **4** [I] (of prices, currencies, etc) suddenly decrease in value: *Share prices collapsed after news of poor trading figures.* **5** [I, Tn] (cause sth to) fold into a compact shape: *a chair that collapses for easy storage.* **6** [I, Tn] (cause a lung or blood-vessel to) become a flattened mass: *a collapsed lung.*

▷ **collapse** *n* [sing] **1** sudden fall; collapsing: *the collapse of the building, roof, bridge, etc.* **2** failure; breakdown: *the collapse of negotiations, sb's health, law and order* ○ *The economy is in a state of (total) collapse.* **3** sudden decrease in value: *the collapse of share prices, the dollar, the market.*

collapsible *adj* that can be folded into a compact shape: *a collapsible bicycle, boat, chair.*

collar /ˈkɒlə(r)/ *n* **1** band, upright or folded over, round the neck of a shirt, coat, dress, etc: *turn one's collar up against the wind*, ie to keep one's neck warm ○ *grab sb by the collar* ○ [attrib] *What is your collar size?* ○ *a stiff collar*, ie a starched detachable one, worn with a shirt. ⇨ illus at JACKET. **2** band of leather, metal, etc put round an animal's (esp a dog's) neck: *Our dog has its name on its collar.* **3** metal band or ring joining two pipes, rods or shafts, esp in a machine. **4** (idm) **hot under the collar** ⇨ HOT.

▷ **collar** *v* [Tn] **(a)** seize (sb) by the collar; capture: *The policeman collared the thief.* ○ (*infml*) *She collared me* (ie stopped me in order to talk to me) *as I was leaving the building.* **(b)** (*dated infml*) take (sth) without permission: *Who's collared my pen?*

□ ˈ**collar-beam** *n* horizontal beam connecting two rafters in a roof.

ˈ**collar-bone** *n* bone joining the breastbone and the shoulder-blade. ⇨ illus at SKELETON.

ˈ**collar-stud** *n* small piece of metal or plastic for fastening a detachable collar to a shirt.

collate /kəˈleɪt/ *v* **1** [Tn, Tn·pr] ~ **A and B**/~ **A with B** examine and compare (two books, manuscripts, etc) in order to find the differences between them: *collate a new edition with an earlier one.* **2** [Tn] collect together and arrange (information, pages of a book, etc) in the correct order.

▷ **collation** /kəˈleɪʃn/ *n* [U] action of collating.

collateral /kəˈlætərəl/ *adj* **1** side by side; parallel. **2** connected but less important; additional: *collateral evidence* ○ *a collateral aim.* **3** descended from the same ancestor, but by a different line: *a collateral branch of the family.*

▷ **collateral** *n* [U] (also **colˌlateral seˈcurity**) property pledged as a guarantee for the repayment of a loan: *The bank will insist on collateral for a loan of that size.*

collation /kəˈleɪʃn/ *n* (*fml*) light meal, esp at an unusual time: *a cold collation.*

colleague /ˈkɒliːg/ *n* person with whom one works, esp in a profession or business: *the Prime Minister's Cabinet colleagues* ○ *David is a colleague of mine/David and I are colleagues.*

collect[1] /kəˈlekt/ *v* **1** [Tn, Tn·p] ~ **sth (up/together)** bring or gather sth together: *collect (up) the empty glasses, dirty plates, waste paper* ○ *collect together one's belongings* ○ *the collected works of Dickens*, ie a series of books containing everything he wrote. **2** [I] come together; assemble or accumulate; gather: *A crowd soon collected at the scene of the accident.* ○ *Dust had collected on the window-sill.* **3** [I, Tn] obtain (money, contributions, etc) from a number of people or places: *He's collecting (money) for famine relief.* ○ *The Inland Revenue is responsible for collecting income tax.* **4** [Tn] obtain specimens of (sth) as a hobby or for study: *collect stamps, old coins, matchboxes, first editions.* **5** [Tn, Tn·pr] call for and take away (sb/sth); fetch: *The dustmen collect the rubbish once a week.* ○ *collect a child from school* ○ *collect a suit from the cleaners.* **6** [Tn] regain or recover control of (oneself, one's thoughts, etc): *collect oneself after a shock* ○ *collect one's thoughts before an interview.* **7** (idm) **collect/gather one's wits** ⇨ WIT.

▷ **collect** *adj, adv* (*US*) (of a telephone call) to be paid for by the receiver: *a collect call* ○ *call sb collect*, ie transfer the charge.

collected *adj* [pred] in control of oneself; calm (used esp as in the expression shown): *She always stays cool, calm and collected in a crisis.*

collectedly *adv.*

collect[2] /ˈkɒlekt/ *n* (in the Anglican or the Roman Catholic Church) short prayer, usu to be read on a particular day.

collection /kəˈlekʃn/ *n* **1** [C, U] (act of) collecting (COLLECT[1] 5) sth: *There are two collections a day from this letter-box*, ie The postman empties it twice a day. ○ *The council is responsible for refuse collection.* **2** [C] group of objects that have been collected (COLLECT[1] 4) systematically: *a fine collection of paintings*, eg in an art gallery ○ *a stamp, coin, record, etc collection* ○ *a collection of poems*, ie a group of poems published in one volume. **3** [C] range of new clothes, etc offered for sale by a designer or manufacturer: *You are invited to view our autumn collection.* **4** [C] **(a)** collecting (COLLECT[1] 3) of money during a church service or a meeting: *The collection will be taken (up)/made after the sermon.* ○ *a collection for famine relief.* **(b)** sum of money collected in this way: *a large collection.* **5** [C] heap or pile of objects; group of people: *a collection of junk, rubbish, etc* ○ *an odd collection of people.*

collective /kəˈlektɪv/ *adj* of, by or relating to a group or society as a whole; joint; shared: *collective action, effort, guilt, responsibility, wisdom* ○ *collective leadership*, ie government by a group rather than an individual. Cf INDIVIDUAL 2.

▷ **collective** *n* **1 (a)** [C] organization or enterprise (esp a farm) owned and controlled by the people who work in it: *a workers' collective.* **(b)** [CGp] these people as a group. **2** [C] = COLLECTIVE NOUN.

collectively *adv.*

collectivism /-ɪzəm/ *n* [U] theory advocating the ownership and control of land and the means of production by the whole community or by the State, for the benefit of everyone. **collectivist** *n, adj.*

collectivize, -ise /kəˈlektɪvaɪz/ *v* [Tn] change (farms, industries, land, etc) from private ownership to ownership by the State. **collectivization, -isation** /kəˌlektɪvaɪˈzeɪʃn; *US* -vɪˈz-/ *n* [U].

□ **colˌlective ˈbargaining** negotiation (about pay, working conditions, etc) between a trade union and an employer.

colˌlective ˈfarm (esp in Communist countries) farm or group of farms owned by the State and run by the workers.

colˌlective ˈnoun (*grammar*) noun that is singular in form but can refer to a number of people or things and agree with a plural verb: *'Flock' and 'committee' are collective nouns.*

colˌlective ˈownership ownership of land, the means of production, etc by all the members of a community for the benefit of everyone.

colˌlective unˈconscious (*psychology*) (in the theory of *Jung) part of the unconscious mind that is shared by all human beings and comes from the experiences of their ancestors.

collector /kəˈlektə(r)/ *n* (esp in compounds) person who collects (COLLECT[1] 4) things: *a ˈstamp-collector* ○ *a ˈtax-collector* ○ *a ˈticket-collector*, eg at a railway station.

□ **colˈlector's item** (also **colˈlector's piece**) thing worth putting in a collection because of its beauty, rarity, etc.

colleen /ˈkɒliːn/ *n* (*Irish*) young woman; girl.

college /ˈkɒlɪdʒ/ *n* **1** [C, U] institution for higher education or professional training: *a college of further education*, ie providing educational and vocational courses for adults ○ *the Royal College of Art* ○ *a secretarial college* ○ *Our daughter is going to college* (ie starting a course of study at a university or a college) *in the autumn.* ○ *She's at* (ie studying at) *college.* ⇨ Usage at SCHOOL[1]. **2 (a)** [C] (in Britain) any of a number of independent institutions within certain universities, each having its own teachers, students and buildings: *the Oxford and Cambridge colleges* ○ *New College, Oxford.* **(b)** (in the US) university, or part of one, offering undergraduate courses. **3** [C, U] building or buildings of a college(2): *Are you living in college?* ○ [attrib] *a college chapel.* **4** [CGp] staff and/or students of a college(1). **5** [C] (*Brit*) (in names) school: *Eton College.* **6** [C] organized group of professional people with particular aims, duties or privileges: *the Royal College of Surgeons* ○ *the College of Cardinals*, ie the whole group of them, esp as advisers and electors of the Pope.

▷ **collegian** /kəˈliːdʒɪən/ *n* (*fml*) member of a college.

□ **the ˌCollege of ˈArms** (also **the ˌCollege of ˈHeralds**) royal corporation in Britain set up to deal with matters relating to heraldry. It is responsible for granting coats of arms, eg to new life peers.

collegiate /kəˈliːdʒɪət/ *adj* [usu attrib] **1** of or relating to a college or its students. **2** consisting of or having colleges: *Oxford is a collegiate university.*

□ **colˌlegiate ˈchurch (a)** church that is not a cathedral but has a chapter of canons. **(b)** (in Scotland and the US) any of a group of churches served jointly by several ministers. Cf TEAM MINISTRY (TEAM).

collide /kəˈlaɪd/ *v* [I, Ipr] ~ **(with sb/sth)** **1** (of moving objects or people) strike violently against sth or each other: *As the bus turned the corner, it collided with a van.* ○ *The bus and the van collided.* ○ *The ships collided in the fog.* **2** (of people, aims, opinions, etc) be in disagreement or opposition; conflict: *The interests of the two countries collide.*

collie /ˈkɒlɪ/ *n* sheep-dog with shaggy hair and a long pointed muzzle. ⇨ illus at DOG.

collier /ˈkɒlɪə(r)/ *n* (*esp Brit*) **1** coal-miner. **2** ship that carries coal as its cargo.

colliery /ˈkɒlɪərɪ/ *n* (*esp Brit*) coal-mine with its buildings.

Collins /ˈkɒlɪnz/ (William) Wilkie (1824-89),

English novelist. His most famous works are *The Moonstone* and *The Woman in White*, the first real detective novels in English. He was a friend of *Dickens and influenced his later work.

collision /kəˈlɪʒn/ *n* [C, U] ~ **(with sb/sth)**; ~ **(between A and B)** 1 (instance of) one object or person striking against another; (instance of) colliding; crash: *a (head-on) collision between two cars* ○ *The liner was in collision* (ie collided) *with an oil-tanker.* ○ *The two ships were in/came into collision.* **2** strong disagreement; conflict or clash of opposing aims, ideas, opinions, etc: *Her political activities brought her into collision with the law.*
□ **colˈlision course** course or action that is certain to lead to a collision with sb/sth: *The Government and the unions are on a collision course.*

collocate /ˈkɒləkeɪt/ *v* [I, Ipr] ~ **(with sth)** (*linguistics*) (of words) be regularly used together in a language; combine: *'Weak' collocates with 'tea' but 'feeble' does not.* ○ *'Weak' and 'tea' collocate.*
▷ **collocation** /ˌkɒləˈkeɪʃn/ *n* **1** [U] collocating. **2** [C] regular combination of words: *'Strong tea' and 'by accident' are English collocations.*

colloid /ˈkɒlɔɪd/ *n* (*chemistry*) any of various substances in which fine particles are dispersed in a semi-fluid or gluelike state. Different types of colloid include gels and emulsions. ▷ **colloidal** /kəˈlɔɪdl/ *adj.*

colloquial /kəˈləʊkwɪəl/ *adj* (of words, phrases, etc) belonging to or suitable for normal conversation but not formal speech or writing. Cf INFORMAL, SLANG.
▷ **colloquialism** *n* colloquial word or phrase: *'The toaster's on the blink'* (ie not working properly) *is a colloquialism.*
colloquially /-kwɪəlɪ/ *adv.*

colloquium /kəˈləʊkwɪəm/ *n* (*pl* **-iums** or **-ia** /-kwɪə/) academic conference or seminar.

colloquy /ˈkɒləkwɪ/ *n* [C, U] (*fml*) conversation.

collude /kəˈlu:d/ *v* [I, Ipr] ~ **(with sb)** plot or conspire to deceive or cheat others.

collusion /kəˈlu:ʒn/ *n* [U] ~ **(with sb)**; ~ **(between sb and sb)** (*fml*) secret agreement or co-operation between two or more people with the aim of deceiving or cheating others: *There was collusion between the two witnesses*, eg They gave the same false evidence to protect the defendant. ○ *She acted in collusion with the other witness.* ▷ **collusive** /kəˈlu:sɪv/ *adj.*

collywobbles /ˈkɒlɪwɒblz/ *n* [pl] (*infml*) **1** pain or rumbling in the stomach. **2** feeling of fear or nervousness: *have an attack of (the) collywobbles.*

Cologne /kəˈləʊn/ city in Germany on the River Rhine; German name **Köln**. It has an ancient cathedral and university and is an important commercial and cultural centre. The city was badly damaged by bombing in the Second World War.

cologne /kəˈləʊn/ *n* [U] = EAU-DE-COLOGNE.

Colombia

Colombia /kəˈlɒmbɪə/ country in the north-western part of South America; pop approx 30 241 000; official language Spanish; capital Bogotá; unit of currency peso (= 100 centavos). Most of the population lives in the valleys of the Andes. The economy is basically agricultural, and coffee is a major export, but the country has considerable mineral and oil reserves. It is politically unstable, following the civil war of 1949-53. ⇨ map.

colon[1] /ˈkəʊlən/ *n* lower part of the large intestine. ⇨ illus at DIGESTIVE.

colon[2] /ˈkəʊlən/ *n* punctuation mark (:) used in writing and printing to show that what follows is an example, list or summary of what precedes it, or a contrasting idea. ⇨ App 14. Cf SEMICOLON.

colonel /ˈkɜ:nl/ *n* **(a)** army officer between the ranks of lieutenant-colonel and brigadier, commanding a regiment. **(b)** officer of similar rank in the US air force. ⇨ App 4.

colonial /kəˈləʊnɪəl/ *adj* [esp attrib] **1** of, relating to or possessing a colony(1a) or colonies: *France was once a colonial power.* ○ *Kenya was under (British) colonial rule for many years.* **2** (*esp US*) in a style of architecture typical of a colony, esp that used in the British colonies in N America in the 17th and 18th centuries: *colonial residences in New England* ○ *a colonial-style ranch.*
▷ **colonial** *n* person living in a colony who is not a member of the native population.
colonialism *n* [U] **1** policy of acquiring colonies and keeping them dependent. **2** (*derog*) tendency of a powerful country to use its colonies or countries that are economically dependent on it for its own economic or political benefit.
colonialist *n* supporter of colonialism.

colonist /ˈkɒlənɪst/ *n* person who settles in an area and colonizes it.

colonize, -ise /ˈkɑlənaɪz/ *v* [Tn] establish a colony in (an area); establish (an area) as a colony: *Britain colonized many parts of Africa.* ○ *Britain was colonized by the Romans.*
▷ **colonization, -isation** /ˌkɒlənaɪˈzeɪʃn; *US* -nɪˈz-/ *n* [U] colonizing or being colonized: *the colonization of N America by the British and French.*

colonnade /ˌkɒləˈneɪd/ *n* row of columns, usu with equal spaces between them and often supporting a roof, etc.
▷ **colonnaded** /ˌkɒləˈneɪdɪd/ *adj* having a colonnade.

colony /ˈkɒlənɪ/ *n* **1 (a)** [C] country or area settled or conquered by people from another country and controlled by that country: *a former British colony*, eg Australia. Cf PROTECTORATE 1. **(b)** [CGp] group of people who settle in a colony. **2** [CGp] **(a)** group of people from a foreign country living in a particular city or country: *the American colony in Paris.* **(b)** group of people with the same occupation, interest, etc living together in the same place: *an artists' colony* ○ *a nudist colony.* **3** [CGp] (*biology*) group of animals or plants living or growing in the same place: *a colony of ants* ○ *a seal colony.*

colophon /ˈkɒləfən; *US* -fɑ:n/ **1** publisher's symbol or logo that appears on the cover or title page of a book. **2** lines at the end of a book or manuscript, giving the name of the writer or printer and the date of publication, etc.

color (*US*) = COLOUR.

Colorado /ˌkɒləˈrɑ:dəʊ/ state in the centre of the USA. The great Colorado River (length 2 336 km; 1 450 miles) rises in the Rocky Mountains of Colorado and flows through the state into the Gulf of California. ⇨ map at App 1.
□ ˌ**Colorado ˈbeetle** beetle with yellow and black stripes, the larvae of which is very harmful to potato crops.

coloration /ˌkʌləˈreɪʃn/ *n* [U] colouring or arrangement of colours: *the distinctive coloration of the zebra.*

coloratura /ˌkɒlərəˈtʊərə/ *n* **1** [U] elaborate or ornamental passages in vocal music. **2** [C] (also **coloratura soprano**) female singer who specializes in singing such passages.

colossal /kəˈlɒsl/ *adj* very large; immense; huge: *a colossal building, man, price, amount.*

Colosseum /ˌkɒləˈsiəm/ *n* **1 the Colosseum** [sing] very large open-air theatre built in ancient Rome, where fights of various kinds were held to entertain the people. **2 colosseum** (also **coliseum**) [C] (*esp US*) large stadium for sports, etc.

colossus /kəˈlɒsəs/ *n* (*pl* **-lossi** /-ˈlɒsaɪ/ or ~**es** /-ˈlɒsəsɪz/) **1** statue much larger than life size. **2** person or thing of very great size, importance, ability, etc: *Mozart is a colossus among composers.*
□ **the Coˌlossus of ˈRhodes** huge bronze statue of the Greek god of the sun that stood at the entrance to the harbour in Rhodes. It was one of the *Seven Wonders of the World.

colostomy /kəˈlɒstəmɪ/ *n* surgical operation to make an opening through which the bowels can be emptied when they cannot excrete naturally.

colostrum /kəˈlɒstrəm/ *n* [U] liquid produced by female mammals before and immediately after giving birth, before they start producing proper milk. It is rich in vitamins, antibodies and protein.

colour[1] (*US* **color**) /ˈkʌlə(r)/ *n* **1 (a)** [U] visible quality that objects have, produced by rays of light of different wavelengths being reflected by them: *The garden was a mass of colour.* ○ *You need more colour in this room.* **(b)** [C] particular type of this; White light, ie ordinary light, is made up of various colours. Red has the longest wavelength and violet has the shortest. The retina of the human eye has cells which detect these wavelengths and recognize them as various hues of the colours of the spectrum: *Red, orange, green and purple are all colours.* ○ *'What colour is the sky?' 'It's blue.'* ○ *a sky the colour of lead*, ie a grey sky. **2 (a)** [C, U] substance (eg paint or dye) used to give colour to sth: *paint in ˈwater-colour(s)* ○ *use plenty of bright colour in a painting.* **(b)** [U] use of all colours, not only black and white: *Is the film in colour or black and white?* ○ [attrib] *colour photography, television, printing.* **3** [U] redness of the face, usu regarded as a sign of good health (used esp as the expressions shown): *He has very little colour*, ie is very pale. ○ *change colour*, ie become paler or redder than usual ○ *lose colour*, ie become paler ○ *She has a high colour*, ie a very red complexion. ○ *The fresh air brought colour to her cheeks.* **4** [U] colour of the skin as a racial characteristic: *be discriminated against on account of one's colour/on grounds of colour* ○ [attrib] *colour prejudice.* **5 colours** [pl] coloured badge, ribbon, clothes, etc worn to show one is a member of a particular team, school, political party, etc or worn by a racehorse to show who owns it. **6 colours** [pl] (*Brit*) award given to a regular or outstanding member of a sports team, esp in a school: *get/win one's (football) colours.* **7 colours** [pl] flag(s) of a ship or regiment: *salute the colours.* **8** [U] **(a)** interesting detail or qualities; vividness: *Her description of the area is full of colour.* **(b)** distinctive quality of sound in music; tone: *orchestral colour* ○ *His playing lacks colour.* **9** (idm) **give/lend ˈcolour to sth** make sth seem true or probable: *The scars on his body lent colour to his claim that he had been tortured.* **nail one's colours to the mast** ⇨ NAIL *v.* **off colour** (*infml*) **(a)** unwell; ill: *feel, look, seem a bit off colour.* **(b)** (esp of a joke) slightly indecent. **paint sth in glowing, etc colours** ⇨ PAINT[2]. **see the colour of sb's ˈmoney** make sure that sb has enough money to pay for sth: *Don't let him have the car until you've seen the colour of his money.* **trooping the colour** ⇨ TROOP. **one's true colours** ⇨ TRUE. **under false colours** ⇨ FALSE. **with flying colours** ⇨ FLYING.
▷ **colourable** (*US* **colorable**) *adj* that seems to be true but is actually false; specious: *colourable excuses, pretexts, etc.*
colourful (*US* **colorful**) /-fl/ *adj* **1** full of colour; bright: *a colourful dress, scene* ○ *colourful material.* **2** interesting or exciting; vivid: *a colourful character, life, story, period of history.*
colourless (*US* **colorless**) *adj* **1** without colour; pale: *a colourless liquid*, eg water ○ *colourless cheeks.* **2** dull and uninteresting: *a colourless*

character, existence, style.

□ ˈ**colour-bar** *n* (*US* ˈ**color line**) legal or social discrimination between people of different races, esp between whites and non-whites.

ˈ**colour-blind** *adj* unable to see the difference between certain colours, esp red and green. ˈ**colour-blindness** *n* [U].

ˈ**colour code** system of marking things (eg electrical wires, parts of a filing system, etc) with different colours to help people to distinguish between them. ˈ**colour-coded** *adj* marked in this way.

ˈ**colour-fast** *adj* (of a fabric) having a colour that will not change or fade when it is washed.

ˈ**colour scheme** arrangement of colours, esp in the decoration and furnishing of a room: *I don't like the colour scheme in their sitting-room.*

ˈ**colour-sergeant** *n* senior sergeant in a company of infantry in the British Army. ⇨ App 4.

ˈ**colour supplement** (*Brit*) magazine with colour photographs that forms part of a newspaper, esp a Sunday one: (*fig*) [attrib] *a* ˌ*colour-supplement* ˈ*kitchen,* ie one that is modern, fashionable and well-equipped.

colour[2] (*US* **color**) /ˈkʌlə(r)/ *v* **1** [Tn, Cn·a] put colour on (sth), eg by painting, dyeing or staining: *colour a picture* ○ *colour a wall green.* **2** (a) [I] become coloured; change colour: *It is autumn and the leaves are beginning to colour,* ie turn brown. (b) [I, Ipr, Ip] ~ (**up**) (**at sth**) become red in the face; blush: *She coloured (with embarrassment) at his remarks.* **3** [Tn esp passive] affect (sth), esp in a negative way; distort: *His attitude to sex is coloured by his strict upbringing.* ○ *Don't allow personal loyalty to colour your judgement.* ○ *She gave a highly coloured* (ie exaggerated) *account of her travels.* **4** (phr v) **colour sth in** fill (a particular area, shape, etc) with colour: *The child coloured in all the shapes on the page with a crayon.*

▷ **coloured** (*US* **colored**) *adj* **1** (often in compounds) having colour; having the specified colour: *coloured chalks* ○ ˈ*cream-coloured* ○ ˈ*flesh-coloured.* **2** (a) (*becoming dated*) (of people) of a race that does not have a white skin. (b) **Coloured** (in S Africa) person of mixed race.

colouring *n* [U] action of putting colour on sth: *Children enjoy colouring,* eg with crayons. ○ [attrib] *a colouring book.* **1** [U] (a) way or style in which sth is coloured. (b) way in which an artist uses colour in paintings. **2** [U] colour of a person's skin; complexion: *She has (a) very fair colouring.* **3** [C, U] (type of) substance used to give a particular colour to sth, esp to food: *This yoghurt contains no artificial flavouring or colouring.*

colt /kəʊlt/ *n* **1** young male horse up to the age of 4 or 5. Cf FILLY, GELDING (GELD), STALLION. **2** young inexperienced person, esp a member of a junior sports team: *He plays for the colts,* eg the junior team of a football club.

▷ **coltish** /ˈkəʊltɪʃ/ *adj* like a colt; frisky.

colter (*US*) = COULTER.

Coltrane /kɒlˈtreɪn; *US* kəʊlˈtreɪn/ John (1926-67), American jazz saxophone player. A leading figure in avant-garde jazz he played with Thelonius *Monk and Miles Davis before starting his own quartet in 1960.

Columba /kəˈlʌmbə/ Saint (c 521-97 AD), Irish missionary. He founded several monasteries and churches. The most famous was the monastery on the Scottish island of Iona, from which he brought Christianity to the surrounding parts of Scotland.

Columbine /ˈkɒləmbaɪn/ main female character of the *commedia dell'arte. She is the partner of *Harlequin. ⇨ illus at COMMEDIA DELL'ARTE.

columbine /ˈkɒləmbaɪn/ *n* garden plant with flowers that have thin pointed petals.

Columbus /kəˈlʌmbəs/ Christopher (1451-1506), Italian explorer. He persuaded King Ferdinand and Queen Isabella of Spain to pay for an expedition to find a new route to Asia by crossing the Atlantic. In 1492, thinking he had found the coast of Asia, he landed on one of the Caribbean islands. He made three further expeditions, but gradually fell from favour and died in poverty.

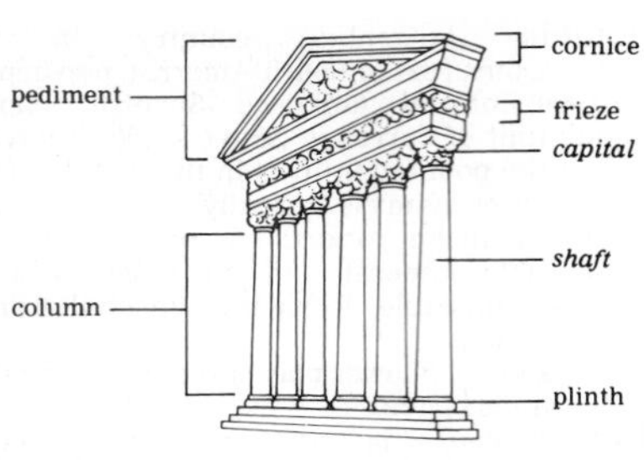

column /ˈkɒləm/ *n* **1** tall pillar, usu round and made of stone, either supporting part of the roof of a building or standing alone as a monument: *The temple is supported by massive columns.* ○ *Nelson's Column is a famous monument in London.* ⇨ illus. **2** thing shaped like a column: *a column of smoke,* ie smoke rising straight up ○ *the* ˌ*spinal* ˈ*column,* ie the backbone ○ *a column of mercury,* ie in a thermometer. **3** (*abbr* **col**) one of two or more vertical sections of printed material on a page: *Each page of this dictionary has three columns of text.* **4** part of a newspaper regularly dealing with a particular subject or written by the same journalist: *the* ˈ*fashion,* ˈ*motoring, fi*ˈ*nancial, etc column* ○ *the correspondence columns of 'The Times'* ○ *I always read her column in the local paper.* **5** (a) long line of vehicles, ships, etc following one behind the other. (b) large group of soldiers, tanks, etc moving forward in short rows. **6** series of numbers arranged one under the other: *add up a long column of figures.*

▷ **columnist** /ˈkɒləmnɪst/ *n* journalist who regularly writes an article commenting on politics, current events, etc for a newspaper or magazine: *a political columnist.*

□ ˌ**column-**ˈ**inch** *n* (usu *pl*) number of lines in a newspaper column that make up one inch, often used to show how important a story is or to measure advertising space: *Her resignation only rated two column inches.*

coma /ˈkəʊmə/ *n* state of deep unconsciousness, usu lasting a long time and caused by severe injury or illness: *go into a coma* ○ *He was in a coma for several weeks.*

▷ **comatose** /ˈkəʊmətəʊs/ *adj* **1** in a coma; deeply unconscious. **2** sleepy; drowsy; sluggish: *feeling comatose after a large meal.*

Comanche /kəˈmæntʃɪ/ *n* (*pl* unchanged or ~**s**) **1** [U] member of a North American Indian people from Texas and Oklahoma. **2** [U] their language.

comb /kəʊm/ *n* **1** [C] (a) piece of metal, plastic or bone with teeth, used for tidying and arranging the hair. (b) small piece of plastic or bone with teeth, worn by women to hold the hair in place or as an ornament. **2** [C usu *sing*] act of combing the hair: *Your hair needs a (good) comb.* **3** [C] thing shaped or used like a comb, esp a device for tidying and straightening wool, cotton, etc to prepare it for manufacture. **4** [C, U] = HONEYCOMB. **5** [C] red fleshy growth on the head of a domestic fowl, esp a cock. ⇨ illus at BIRD. **6** (idm) **with a fine-tooth comb** ⇨ FINE[2].

▷ **comb** *v* **1** [Tn] pass a comb through (the hair) in order to tidy or arrange it: *Don't forget to comb your hair before you go out!* **2** [Tn] prepare (wool, cotton, etc) for manufacture by tidying and straightening it with a comb(3). **3** [Ipr, Tn, Tn·pr] ~ (**through**) **sth** (**for sb/sth**) search sth thoroughly: *He combed through the files searching for evidence of fraud.* ○ *Police are combing the woods for the missing children.* **4** (phr v) **comb sth out** remove knots, tangles, etc from or shape (the hair) with a comb. **comb sth out** (**of sth**) (a) remove (dirt, tangles, etc) from the hair with a comb: *She combed the mud out of the dog's fur.* (b) remove (unwanted people or things) from a group.

combings /ˈkəʊmɪŋz/ *n* [pl] loose hair that comes out when combed.

combat /ˈkɒmbæt/ *n* [C, U] fight or fighting between two people, armies, etc: *armed/unarmed combat,* ie with/without weapons ○ *The troops were exhausted after months of fierce combat.* ○ [attrib] *a combat jacket, mission, zone.*

▷ **combat** *v* [Ipr, Tn] ~ (**against/with**) **sb/sth** (a) fight or struggle against sb/sth: *combat the enemy.* (b) try to reduce, weaken or destroy sth: *combating disease, inflation, terrorism.*

combatant /ˈkɒmbətənt/ *n, adj* (person) involved in fighting in a war: *In modern wars, both combatants and non-combatants* (ie civilians) *are killed.*

combative /ˈkɒmbətɪv/ *adj* eager or ready to fight or argue: *in a combative mood.* **combatively** *adv.*

□ ˈ**combat fatigue** mental disorder caused by the stress of combat. Cf SHELL-SHOCK (SHELL).

combe /ku:m/ *n* = COOMB.

comber /ˈkəʊmə(r)/ *n* long curling wave that breaks into foam as it gets near the shore; breaker.

combination /ˌkɒmbɪˈneɪʃn/ *n* **1** [U] joining or mixing together of two or more things or people; state of being joined or mixed together: *It is the combination of wit and political analysis that makes his articles so readable.* ○ *The firm is working on a new product in combination with several overseas partners.* **2** [C] number of things or people joined or mixed together; mixture; blend: *Pink is a combination of red and white.* ○ *A combination of factors led to her decision to resign.* ○ *The architecture in the town centre is a successful combination of old and new.* ○ *What an unusual combination of flavours!* **3** [C] sequence of numbers or letters used to open a combination lock. **4** [C] (*Brit*) motor-bike with a side-car attached to it. **5** **combinations** [pl] (formerly) one-piece undergarment covering the body and legs.

□ **combi**ˈ**nation lock** type of lock (eg on a safe) that can only be opened by turning a set of dials until they show a particular sequence of numbers or letters.

combine[1] /kəmˈbaɪn/ *v* **1** [I, Ipr, Tn, Tn·pr] ~ (**with sth**); ~ **A and B/A with B** (cause things to) join or mix together to form a whole: *Hydrogen and oxygen combine/Hydrogen combines with oxygen to form water.* ○ *Circumstances have combined to ruin our plans for a holiday.* ○ *Combine the eggs with a little flour and heat the mixture gently.* ○ *a kitchen and dining-room combined,* ie one room used as both ○ *Success was achieved by the combined efforts of the whole team.* **2** [Tn, Tn·pr] ~ **A and B/A with B** do (two or more things) at the same time or have (two or more different qualities) as a characteristic: *combine business with pleasure* ○ *He combines arrogance and incompetence in his dealings with the staff.*

□ **com**ˈ**bining form** (*linguistics*) form of a word which can combine with another word or another combining form to form a new word, eg *Anglo-, -philia.* ⇨ GUIDE TO ENTRIES 1.4.

combine[2] /ˈkɒmbaɪn/ *n* **1** group of people or firms acting together in business. **2** (also ˌ**combine** ˈ**harvester**) agricultural machine that both reaps and threshes grain. Cf HARVESTER (HARVEST).

combo /ˈkɒmbəʊ/ *n* (*pl* ~**s**) (*infml*) small band of (esp jazz) musicians.

combustible /kəmˈbʌstəbl/ *adj* **1** that can catch fire and burn easily: *Petrol is (highly) combustible.* **2** (*fig*) (of people) excitable: *a combustible temperament.*

▷ **combustible** *n* (usu *pl*) combustible substance or material.

combustion /kəmˈbʌstʃən/ *n* [U] **1** process of burning. **2** chemical process in which substances combine with oxygen in air, producing heat and light.

□ **com**ˈ**bustion chamber** enclosed space in which combustion(2) takes place, eg the space above the piston in an internal-combustion engine.

come /kʌm/ *v* (*pt* **came** /keɪm/, *pp* **come**) **1** (a) [I, Ipr, Ip] ~ (**to ...**) (**from ...**) move to, towards, into, etc a place where the speaker or writer is, or a place being referred to by him: *She came into the room and shut the door.* ○ *She came slowly down the stairs.* ○ *He has come all the way from Leeds to look for a job.* ○ *Come and visit us again soon!* ○ *She comes to work by bus.* ○ *Are you coming out for a* *walk?* ○ *Our son is coming home for Christmas.* ○ *Come here!* ⇨ Usage at AND. ⇨ Usage at VISIT. **(b)** [I, Ipr] ~ **(to ...)** arrive at a place where the speaker or writer is or at a place being referred to by him: *They came to a river.* ○ *They came* (eg arrived at my house) *at 8 o'clock.* ○ *What time will you be coming?* ○ *Have any letters come for me?* ○ *I've come to collect my book/come for my book.* ○ *Help has come at last.* ○ *There's a storm coming*, ie approaching. ○ *Spring came late this year.* ○ *The time has come* (ie Now is the moment) *to act.* **(c)** [I, Ipr] ~ **(to sth) (with sb)** move in order to be with sb at a particular place or be present at an event: *I've only come for an hour.* ○ *Are you coming (to the cinema) with us tonight?* ○ *'Would you like to come to dinner next Friday?' 'I'd love to.'* ○ *Are you coming to my party?* ○ *Who are you coming with?* ○ *I'll be coming with Keith.* **(d)** (used with the present participle) take part in the specified activity, esp a sport, usu with other people: *Why don't you come ice-skating (with us) tonight?* **2** [I] travel (a specified distance): *We've come fifty miles since lunch.* ○ (*fig*) *This company has come a long way* (ie made a lot of progress) *in the last five years.* **3** (used with a present participle to show that sb/sth moves in the way specified or that sb is doing sth while moving): *He came hurrying* (ie hurried) *to see her as soon as he heard she was ill.* ○ *The children came running* (ie ran) *to meet us.* ○ *She came sobbing* (ie was sobbing as she came) *into the room.* ○ *Sunlight came streaming through the window.* **4** [La, Ipr] (not in the continuous tenses) occupy a particular position in space or time; occur: *Easter comes early this year.* ○ *She came first* (ie received the highest mark) *in the examination.* ○ (*fig*) *His family comes first*, ie is the most important thing in his life. ○ *May comes between April and June.* ○ *'A' comes before 'B' in the alphabet.* ○ *Her death came as a terrible shock (to us).* ○ *Her resignation came as a surprise/It came as a surprise when she resigned.* **5** [I] (not in the continuous tenses) (of goods, products, etc) be available: *This dress comes in three sizes.* ○ *Do these shoes come in black?* ○ *New cars don't come cheap*, ie They are expensive. **6** [La] become; prove to be: *My shoe laces have come undone.* ○ *This envelope has come unstuck.* ○ *The handle has come loose.* ○ *It comes cheaper if you buy things in bulk.* ○ *Everything will come right in the end.* **7** [It] reach a point at which one realizes, understands, believes, etc sth: *She had come to see the problem in a new light.* ○ *In time he came to love her.* ○ *I have come to believe that the Government's economic policy is misguided.* **8** [It] (used in questions after *how* to ask for an explanation or a reason for sth): *How did he come to break his leg?* ○ *How do you come to be so late?* Cf HOW COME (COME 13). **9** [Ln] ~ **sth (with sb)** (*infml*) behave like or play the part of sth: *Don't come the bully with me!* ○ *She tried to come the innocent with me.* **10** (*infml*) (used before an expression of time) when the specified time comes: *We'll have been married for two years come Christmas.* ○ *Come* (ie By) *next week she'll have changed her mind.* **11** [I] (*infml*) have an orgasm. **12** (used with *to* or *into* + *n* in many expressions to show that the state or condition indicated by the *n* has been reached, eg *At last winter came to an end*, ie ended; *The trees are coming into leaf*, ie starting to grow leaves; for similar expressions, see entries for *ns*, eg **come to blows** ⇨ BLOW). **13** (idm) **be as ˌclever, ˌstupid, etc as they ˈcome** (*infml*) be very clever, stupid, etc. **come again?** (*infml*) (used to ask sb to repeat sth because one doesn't understand it or can hardly believe it): *'She's an entomologist.' 'Come again?' 'An entomologist — she studies insects.'* **ˌcome and ˈgo** exist or be present in a place for a short time and then stop or depart: *The pain in my leg comes and goes*, ie Sometimes my leg is painful and sometimes it is not. ○ *Governments come and go* (ie One government is replaced by another) *but does anything really change?* **come ˈeasily, ˈnaturally, etc to sb** (of an activity, skill, etc) be easy, natural, etc for sb to do: *Acting comes naturally to her.* **ˌcome over ˈdizzy, ˈfaint, ˈgiddy, etc** (*infml*) suddenly feel dizzy, faint, giddy, etc: *I suddenly came over (all) funny/queer and had to lie down.* **come to ˈnothing; not come to ˈanything** have no useful or successful result; be a complete failure: *All her plans have come to nothing.* ○ *How sad that his efforts should come to nothing.* **come to oneˈself** return to one's normal state: *The shock made her hesitate for a moment but she quickly came to herself again.* **come to ˈthat; if it comes to ˈthat** (*infml*) (used to introduce sth that is connected with and in addition to sth just mentioned): *He looks just like his dog — come to that, so does his wife!* **ˌcome what ˈmay** whatever happens; in spite of difficulties or problems that may arise: *He promised to support her come what may.* **have (got) sth ˈcoming (to one)** (*infml*) be likely to be punished (or possibly rewarded) in the future for sth one has done: *If I ever catch him he's really got it coming (to him).* **how come (...)?** (*infml*) how does/did it happen (that...)?; what is the explanation (of sth)?: *If she spent five years in Paris, how come she can't speak a word of French?* ○ *You were an hour late this morning, how ˈcome?* **not ˈcome to much** not be, become or do anything of importance: *He'll never come to much* (ie have a successful career)*, he's too lazy.* ○ *I don't think her idea of becoming a journalist ever came to much.* **to ˈcome** (used after a *n*) in the future: *In years to come...* ○ *for some time to come*, ie for a period of time in the future. **when it comes to sth/doing sth** when it is a case, matter or question of (doing) sth: *I'm as good a cook as she is except when it comes to (making) pastry.* (For other idioms containing **come**, see entries for *ns*, *adjs*, etc, eg **come a cropper** ⇨ CROPPER; **come clean** ⇨ CLEAN.).

14 (phr v) **come aˈbout** (of a sailing-boat) change direction. **come about (that...)** happen: *Can you tell me how the accident came aˈbout?* ○ *How did it come about that he knew where we were?*

come aˈcross (also **come ˈover**) **(a)** be understood or communicated: *He spoke for a long time but his meaning did not really come across.* **(b)** make an impression of the specified type: *She comes across well/badly in interviews.* ○ *He came across as sympathetic/a sympathetic person.* **come across sb/sth** meet or find sb/sth by chance: *I ˌcame across an old ˈschool friend in Oxford Street this morning.* ○ *She ˌcame across some old ˈphotographs in a drawer.* **come aˈcross (with sth)** (*dated infml*) give or hand over (money, information, etc): *He owes me five pounds but I doubt if he'll ever come across (with it).*

come after sb chase or pursue sb: *The farmer came after the intruders with a big stick.*

come aˈlong (a) arrive; appear: *When the right opportunity comes along, she'll take it.* ○ *'Is she married?' 'No. She says she's waiting for the right man* (ie the ideal husband) *to come along.'* **(b)** = COME ON d. **(c)** = COME ON e.

come aˈpart break or fall into pieces: *The teapot just came apart in my hands.*

come around (to sth) = COME ROUND (TO STH).

come at sb attack sb: *She came ˌat me with a ˈrolling-pin.* **come at sth** discover (facts, the truth, etc): *The truth is often difficult to ˈcome at.*

come aˈway (from sth) become detached (from sth): *The plaster had started to come away from the wall.* **come away with sth** leave a place with (a feeling, an impression, etc): *We came away with the distinct impression that all was not well with their marriage.*

come ˈback (a) return: *You came back* (ie came home) *very late last night.* ○ *The colour is coming back to her cheeks.* **(b)** become popular, successful or fashionable again: *Miniskirts are starting to come back.* **(c)** (of a rule, law or system) be restored or reintroduced: *Some people would like to see the death penalty come back.* **come ˈback at sb** reply to sb forcefully or angrily: *She came back at the speaker with some sharp questions.* **come ˈback (to sb)** return to the memory: *It's all coming back to me now*, ie I'm beginning to remember everything. ○ *Your French will soon come back.* **come ˈback to sb (on sth)** reply to sb about sth after a period of time: *Can I come back to you on that one* (ie on that subject) *later?*

come before sb/sth (a) be presented to sb/sth for discussion, decision or judgement: *The case ˌcomes before the ˈcourt next week.* **(b)** have greater importance than sb/sth else: *Fighting poverty and unemployment should come before all other political considerations.*

come between sb and sb interfere with or harm a relationship between two people: *It's not a good idea to come between a man and his wife.* ○ *I'd hate anything to come between us.* **come between sb and sth** prevent sb from doing or having sth: *He never lets anything come between him and his evening pint of beer.*

ˈcome by sth (a) obtain sth, usu by effort: *Jobs are hard to come by these days.* ○ *I hope that money was honestly come by.* **(b)** receive sth by chance: *How did you come by that scratch on your cheek?*

come ˈdown (a) collapse: *The ceiling came down.* **(b)** (of rain, snow, etc) fall: *The rain came down in torrents.* **(c)** (of an aircraft) land or fall from the sky: *We were forced to come down in a field.* ○ *Two of our fighters came down inside enemy lines.* **(d)** (of prices, the temperature, etc) become lower; fall: *The price of petrol is coming down/Petrol is coming down in price.* **come ˈdown (from...)** (*Brit*) leave a university (esp Oxford or Cambridge) after finishing one's studies: *When did you come down (from Oxford)?* **come down (from...) (to...)** come from one place to another, esp from the North of England to London, or from a city or large town to a smaller place: *We hope to come down to London next week.* ○ *They've recently come down from London to live in the village.* **come ˈdown on sb** (*infml*) **(a)** criticize sb severely; rebuke sb: *Don't come down too hard on her.* **(b)** punish sb: *The courts are coming down heavily on young offenders.* **come down on sb for sth** (*infml*) demand (payment or money) from sb: *His creditors came down on him for prompt payment of his bills.* **come down to sb** be passed from one generation to another: *stories that came down to us from our forefathers.* **come down to sth/doing sth** (*infml*) be forced by poverty, etc to do sth that one would never do normally; be reduced to sth: *He had come down to begging.* **come down to sth (a)** reach as far down as (a specified point): *Her hair comes down to her waist.* **(b)** be able to be summarized as sth; be a question of sth: *It comes down to two choices: you either improve your work, or you leave.* ○ *The whole dispute comes down to a power struggle between management and trade unions.* **come down with sth** become ill with (an illness): *I came down with flu and was unable to go to work.*

come ˈforward present oneself: *come forward with help, information, money* ○ *Police have asked witnesses of the accident to come forward.*

come from... (not used in the continuous tenses) have as one's birthplace or place of residence: *She comes from London.* ○ *Where do you come from?* **come from.../sth** be a product of (a place or a thing): *Much of the butter eaten in England comes from New Zealand.* ○ *Milk comes from cows and goats.* **come from sth** (also **come of sth**) be descended from sth: *She comes from a long line of actresses.* **come from doing sth** = COME OF STH/DOING STH.

come in (a) (of the tide) move towards the land; rise: *The tide was coming in fast.* **(b)** finish a race in a particular position: *Which horse came in first?* **(c)** (of a batsman in cricket) come to the wicket at the start of one's innings: *Who's coming in next?* **(d)** become fashionable: *Long hair for men came in in the sixties.* **(e)** become available (at a particular time of the year): *English strawberries usually come in in late June.* **(f)** be elected: *The socialists came in at the last election.* **(g)** be received as income: *She has a thousand pounds a month coming in from her investments.* **(h)** have a part to play in sth: *I understand the plan perfectly, but I can't see where I come in.* **(i)** (of news, a report, etc) be received by a television station, the offices of a newspaper, etc: *News is coming in of a serious train crash in Scotland.* **(j)** contribute to a discussion: *Would you like to come in at this point, Prime Minister?* **come in for sth** be the object of sth;

attract sth; receive sth: *The Government's economic policies have come in for much criticism in the newspapers.* **come in on sth** have a part or share in sth; join sth: *If you want to come in on the scheme, you must decide now.* **come in with sb** (*infml*) join sb in a scheme, venture, etc.

come into sth inherit sth: *She came into a fortune when her uncle died.*

ˈcome of sth = COME FROM STH. **come of sth/doing sth** (also **come from doing sth**) be the result of sth: *He promised to help, but I don't think anything will come of it.* ○ *This is what comes of being over-confident.* ○ *No harm can come of trying.*

come off (a) be able to be removed: *'Does this knob come off?' 'No, it's fixed on permanently.'* ○ *These stains won't come off, I'm afraid.* (**b**) (*infml*) take place; happen: *When's the wedding coming off?* ○ *Did your proposed trip to Rome ever come off?* (**c**) (*infml*) (of a plan, scheme, etc) be successful; have the intended effect or result: *Her attempt to break the world record nearly came off.* ○ *The film doesn't quite come off.* (**d**) (*infml*) (followed by an *adv*) fare; get on: *He always comes off badly in fights.* ○ *Who came off best in the debate?* **come off (sth) (a)** fall from sth: *come off one's bicycle, horse, etc.* (**b**) become detached or separated from sth: *When I tried to lift the jug, the handle came off (in my hand).* ○ *Lipstick often comes off on wine glasses.* ○ *A button has come off my coat.* **come ˈoff it** (*infml*) (used in the imperative to tell sb to stop saying things that one thinks or knows are untrue): *Come off it! England don't have a chance of winning the match.* **come off sth** (of an amount of money) be removed from (a price): *I've heard that ten pence a gallon is coming off the price of petrol.*

come on (**a**) (of an actor) walk onto the stage. (**b**) (of a sportsman) join a team as a substitute during a match: *Robson came on in place of Wilkins ten minutes before the end of the game.* (**c**) (of a bowler in cricket) begin to bowl: *Botham came on to bowl after lunch.* (**d**) (also **come along**) make progress; grow; improve: *The garden is coming on nicely.* ○ *Her baby is coming on well.* ○ *His French has come on a lot since he joined the conversation class.* (**e**) (also **come along**) (used in the imperative to encourage sb to do sth, esp to hurry, try harder or make an effort): *Come on, we'll be late for the theatre.* ○ *Come along now, someone must know the answer.* (**f**) begin: *I think I have a cold coming ˈon.* ○ *The rain came on/It ˌcame on to ˈrain.* ○ *It's getting colder: winter is coming ˈon.* (**g**) (of a film, play, etc) be shown or performed: *There's a new play coming on at the local theatre next week.* **come on/upon sb/sth** (*fml*) meet or find sb/sth by chance: *I came upon a group of children playing in the street.*

come ˈout (**a**) stop work; strike: *The miners have come out (on strike).* (**b**) (of a young girl) be formally introduced to high society: *Fiona came out last season.* ○ *a coming-out ball.* (**c**) (of the sun, moon or stars) become visible; appear: *The rain stopped and the sun came out.* (**d**) (of flowers, etc) begin to grow; appear; flower: *The crocuses came out late this year because of the cold weather.* (**e**) be produced or published: *When is her new novel coming out?* (**f**) (of news, the truth, etc) become known; be told or revealed: *The full story came out at the trial.* ○ *It came out that he'd been telling a pack of lies.* (**g**) (of photographs) be developed: *Our holiday photos didn't come out*, eg because the film was faulty. (**h**) be revealed or shown clearly: *The bride comes out well* (ie looks attractive) *in the photographs.* ○ *His arrogance comes out in every speech he makes.* ○ *Her best qualities come out in a crisis.* ○ *The meaning of the poem doesn't really come out in his interpretation.* (**i**) (of words, a speech, etc) be spoken: *My statement didn't come out quite as* (ie appeared to have a different meaning from the one) *I had intended.* (**j**) (of a sum, problem, etc) be solved: *I can't make this equation come out.* (**k**) declare openly that one is a homosexual: *She's been much happier since she came out.* (l) have a specified position in a test, examination, etc: *She came out first in the examination.* **come out (of sth)** (**a**) (of an object) be removed from a place where it is fixed: *The little girl's tooth came out when she bit into the apple.* ○ *I can't get this screw to come out of the wall.* (**b**) (of a mark, stain, etc) be removed from sth by washing, cleaning, etc: *These ink stains won't come out (of my dress).* ○ *Will the colour come out* (ie fade or disappear) *if the material is washed?* **come out against sth** say publicly that one is opposed to sth: *In her speech, the Minister came out against any change to the existing law.* **come out at sth** amount to a particular cost or sum: *The total cost comes out at £500.* **come out in sth** become partially covered in (spots, pimples, etc): *Hot weather makes her come out in a rash.* **come out with sth** say sth; utter sth: *He came out with a stream of abuse.* ○ *She sometimes comes out with the most extraordinary remarks.*

come over = COME ACROSS. **come over (to...)** = COME ROUND (TO...). **come over (to...) (from...)** move from one (usu distant) place to another: *Why don't you come over to England for a holiday?* ○ *Her grandparents came over* (eg to America) *from Ireland during the famine.* **come ˈover sb** (of a feeling) affect sb: *A fit of dizziness came over her.* ○ *I can't think what came over me*, ie I do not know what caused me to behave in that way. **come over (to sth)** change from one side, opinion, etc to another: *She will never come over to our side.*

come ˈround (a) come by a longer route than usual: *The road was blocked so we had to come round by the fields.* (**b**) (of a regular event) arrive; recur: *Christmas seems to come round quicker every year.* (**c**) (also **come ˈto**) regain consciousness, esp after fainting: *Pour some water on his face — he'll soon come round.* ○ *Your husband hasn't yet come round after the anaesthetic.* (**d**) (*infml*) become happy again after being in a bad mood: *Don't scold the boy; he'll come round in time.* **come round (to...)** (also **come over (to...)**) visit sb or a place (usu within the same town, city, etc): *Why don't you come round (to my flat) this evening?* ○ *Do come round and see us some time.* **come round (to sth)** (also **come around (to sth)**) be converted to sb else's opinion or view: *She will never come round (to our way of thinking).* **come round to sth/doing sth** (*infml*) do sth after a long delay: *It was several weeks before I eventually came round to answering her letter.*

come ˈthrough (of news, a message) arrive by telephone, radio, etc or through official channels: *A message is just coming through.* ○ *Your posting has just come through: you're going to Hong Kong.* **come through (sth)** recover from a serious illness or avoid serious injury; survive (sth): *He's very ill but doctors expect him to come ˈthrough.* ○ *With such a weak heart she was lucky to come through (the operation).* ○ *She came through without even a scratch*, eg was not even slightly injured in the accident. ○ *He has come through two world wars.*

come ˈto (a) = COME ROUND. (**b**) (of a boat) stop: *The police launch hailed to us to come to.* **ˈcome to sb (that...)** (of an idea) occur to sb: *The idea came to him in his bath.* ○ *It suddenly came to her that she had been wrong all along.* **ˌcome to ˈsth (a)** amount to sth; be equal to sth: *The bill came to £30.* ○ *I never expected those few items to come to so much.* (**b**) (used esp with *this, that* or *what* as object) reach a particular (usu bad) situation or state of affairs: *The doctors will operate if it proves necessary — but it may not come to that.* ○ *'There's been another terrorist bomb attack.' 'Really? I don't know what the world is coming to.'* ○ *Things have come to such a state in the company that he's thinking of resigning.* ○ *Who'd have thought things would come to this* (ie become so bad or unpleasant)? **come to sb (from sb)** (of money, property, etc) be given or left to sb as an inheritance: *The farm came to him on his father's death.* ○ *He has a lot of money coming to him when his uncle dies.*

come under sth (a) be included within a certain category: *What heading does this come under?* (**b**) be the target of sth: *We came under heavy enemy fire.*

come ˈup (a) (of plants) appear above the soil: *The snowdrops are just beginning to come up.* (**b**) (of the sun) rise: *We watched the sun come up.* (**c**) (of soldiers, supplies, etc) be moved to the front line. (**d**) occur; arise: *We'll let you know if any vacancies come up.* ○ *I'm afraid something urgent has come up; I won't be able to see you tonight.* (**e**) be mentioned or discussed; arise: *The subject came up in conversation.* ○ *The question is bound to come up at the meeting.* (**f**) be dealt with by a court: *Her divorce case comes up next month.* (**g**) (of a lottery ticket, number, etc) be drawn; win: *My number came up and I won £100.* **come ˈup (to...)** (*Brit*) begin one's studies at a university (esp at Oxford or Cambridge): *She came up (to Oxford) in 1982.*

come up (to...) (from...) come to one place from another, esp from a smaller place to London or from the South to the North of England: *She often comes up to London* (eg from Oxford) *at weekends.* ○ *Why don't you come up to Scotland for a few days?* **come up against sb/sth** be faced with or opposed by sb/sth: *We expect to come up against a lot of opposition to the scheme.* **come up for sth** be considered as an applicant or a candidate for sth: *She comes up for re-election next year.* **come up to sth (a)** reach up as far as (a specified point): *The water came up to my neck.* (**b**) reach (an acceptable level or standard): *His performance didn't really come up to his usual high standard.* ○ *Their holiday in France didn't come up to expectations.* **come ˈup with sth** find or produce (an answer, a solution, etc): *She came up with a new idea for increasing sales.*

come upon sb/sth = COME ON SB/STH.

▷ **come** *interj* (used to encourage sb to be sensible or reasonable, or to rebuke sb slightly): *Oh come (now), things aren't as bad as you say.* ○ *Come, come, Miss Jones, be careful what you say.*

□ **ˈcome-back** *n* **1** return to a former (successful) position: *an ageing pop star trying to make/stage a come-back.* **2** (*infml*) reply or retort to a critical or hostile remark. **3** way of obtaining compensation or redress: *If you're not insured and you get burgled, you have no come-back.*

ˈcome-down *n* (usu *sing*) (*infml*) loss of importance or social position: *Having to work as a clerk is a bit of a come-down after running his own business.*

ˌcome-ˈhither *adj* [attrib] (*dated infml*) flirtatious; inviting: *a ˌcome-hither ˈlook, ˈsmile, etc.*

ˈcome-on *n* (usu *sing*) (*infml*) gesture, remark, etc indicating that sb (esp a woman) is trying to attract sb sexually: *She gave him the come-on.*

Comecon /ˈkɒmɪkɒn/ association of Communist countries formed in 1949 to promote economic development.

comedian /kəˈmi:dɪən/ *n* **1** (*fem* **comedienne** /kəˌmi:dɪˈen/) (**a**) entertainer who tells jokes, performs sketches (SKETCH 3), etc to amuse an audience. (**b**) actor or actress who plays comic parts. **2** person who is always behaving comically.

Comédie française /ˌkɒmədɪ: frɑ:nˈsez/ **the Comédie française** France's first national theatre company, the oldest of its kind in the world, founded in 1680.

comedy /ˈkɒmədɪ/ *n* **1** (**a**) [C] light or amusing play or film, usu with a happy ending. (**b**) [U] plays or films of this type: *I prefer comedy to tragedy.* Cf TRAGEDY. **2** [U] amusing aspect of sth; humour: *He didn't appreciate the comedy of the situation.* ○ *the slapstick comedy of silent films.*

□ **comedy of manners** comedy that presents a satirical portrayal of social life.

comely /ˈkʌmlɪ/ *adj* (**-lier**, **-liest**) (*dated or fml*) (esp of a woman) good-looking; attractive. ▷ **comeliness** *n* [U].

comer /ˈkʌmə(r)/ *n* **1** person who comes (used esp as in the expressions shown): *The race is open to all comers*, ie anyone may take part in it. ○ *Late-comers will not be allowed in.* **2** (*infml esp US*) person who is likely to be successful; promising person.

comestibles /kəˈmestəblz/ *n* [pl] (*fml*) things to eat.

comet /ˈkɒmɪt/ *n* object that moves round the sun and looks like a bright star with a long, less bright tail.

come-uppance /kʌmˈʌpəns/ *n* (*infml*) deserved punishment; retribution (used esp as in the expression shown): *get one's come-uppance.*

comfit /ˈkʌmfɪt/ *n* (*arch*) type of sweet, esp a sugar-coated nut.

comfort /ˈkʌmfət/ *n* **1** [U] state of being free from suffering, pain or anxiety; state of physical or mental well-being: *live in comfort* ○ *They did everything for our comfort.* **2** [U] help or kindness to sb who is suffering; consolation: *a few words of comfort* ○ *The news brought comfort to all of us.* **3** [sing] person or thing that brings relief or consolation: *Her children are a great comfort to her.* ○ *It's a comfort to know that she is safe.* **4** [C esp *pl*] thing that creates physical ease or well-being: *The hotel has all modern comforts/every modern comfort,* eg central heating, hot and cold water, etc. ○ *He likes his comforts.* **5** (idm) **cold comfort** ⇨ COLD[1].

▷ **comfort** *v* [Tn] give comfort(2) to (sb): *comfort a dying man* ○ *The child ran to its mother to be comforted.*

comfortless *adj* without comforts (COMFORT 4): *a comfortless room.*

□ ˈ**comfort station** (*US euph*) public lavatory.

comfortable /ˈkʌmftəbl; *US* -fərt-/ *adj* **1** allowing, producing or having pleasant bodily relaxation: *a comfortable bed, position* ○ *She made herself comfortable in a big chair.* ○ *The patient is comfortable* (ie is not in pain) *after his operation.* **2** having or ensuring freedom from anxiety: *a comfortable life, job.* **3** [pred] (*infml*) quite wealthy: *They may not be millionaires but they're certainly very comfortable.* **4** more than adequate; reasonably large: *a comfortable income* ○ *She won by a comfortable margin.*

▷ **comfortably** /-təblɪ/ *adv* **1** in a comfortable way: *comfortably ensconced in a big armchair.* **2** by a clear margin: *The favourite won the race comfortably.* **3** (idm) ˌ**comfortably** ˈ**off** having enough money to live in comfort.

comforter /ˈkʌmfətə(r)/ *n* **1** person who comforts. **2** (*US*) quilt. **3** (*Brit*) (*US* **pacifier**) = DUMMY. **4** (*dated Brit*) woollen scarf worn round the neck.

comfrey /ˈkʌmfrɪ/ *n* [U] tall plant with rough leaves and bell-like flowers, commonly growing in ditches, etc.

comfy /ˈkʌmfɪ/ *adj* (**-ier**, **-iest**) (*infml*) comfortable.

comic /ˈkɒmɪk/ *adj* **1** [usu attrib] causing people to laugh; funny: *a comic song, performance, etc* ○ *His accident with the hose brought some welcome comic relief to a very dull party.* **2** [attrib] of, containing or using comedy: *comic opera* ○ *a comic actor.*

▷ **comic** *n* **1** [C] comedian: *a popular TV comic.* **2** [C] (*US* ˈ**comic book**) children's magazine containing stories told mainly through pictures.

📖 The oldest surviving British comics are *Dandy* and *Beano* which date from the 1930s. *Eagle*, a comic for boys and its companion publication for girls, *Girl*, were founded in the 1950s. *Eagle* is famous for its science-fiction adventure serial featuring Dan Dare, 'pilot of the future'. More recently, the most popular comics are *2000 AD* for children and *Viz* which is aimed at older teenagers and adults. Famous characters from American comics include Batman, Spiderman and Superman. ⇨ article at MAGAZINE.

3 comics [pl] (*esp US*) cartoon section of a newspaper.

comical /ˈkɒmɪkl/ *adj* (odd and) amusing: *He looked highly comical wearing that tiny hat.* **comically** /-klɪ/ *adv*: *clothes that were almost comically inappropriate.*

□ **comic** ˈ**strip** (also ˈ**strip cartoon**) sequence of drawings telling a humorous or adventure story, printed in newspapers, etc.

coming /ˈkʌmɪŋ/ *n* **1** arrival: *the coming of the space age.* **2** (idm) ˌ**comings and** ˈ**goings** (*infml*) arrivals and departures: *the constant comings and goings at a hotel* ○ *With all the comings and goings* (eg of visitors) *I haven't been able to do any work at all.*

▷ **coming** *adj* [usu attrib] **1** that follow(s) or come(s) next: *this coming Tuesday, this Tuesday coming* ○ *in the coming months* ○ *Coming generations will not forgive us.* **2** that is likely to be important or famous soon: *He is very much the coming man.*

Comintern /ˈkɒmɪntɜːn/ the third Communist *International (1919-43).

comity of nations /ˌkɒmɪtɪ əv ˈneɪʃnz/ (*fml*) respect shown by nations for each others' laws and institutions.

comma /ˈkɒmə/ *n* punctuation mark (,) to indicate a slight pause or break between parts of a sentence. ⇨ App 3.

command[1] /kəˈmɑːnd; *US* -ˈmænd/ *v* **1** [I, Tn, Tf, Dn·t] (of sb in authority) tell (sb) that he must do sth; order: *Do as I command (you).* ○ (*fml*) *The tribunal has commanded that all copies of the book (must) be destroyed.* ○ *The officer commanded his men to fire.* ⇨ Usage at ORDER[2]. **2** [I, Tn] have authority (over sb/sth); be in control (of): *Does seniority give one the right to command?* ○ *The ship's captain commands all the officers and men.* **3** [Tn no passive] be able to use (sth); have at one's disposal: *command funds, skill, resources, etc* ○ *She commands great wealth,* ie is very rich. ○ *A government minister commands the services of many officials.* ○ (*fig*) *The house commands a fine view,* ie A fine view can be seen from it. **4** [Tn no passive] deserve and get (sth): *Great men command our respect.* ○ *The plight of the famine victims commands everyone's sympathy.* **5** [Tn no passive] (of a place, fort, etc) be positioned so as to control (sth): *The castle commanded the entrance to the valley.*

▷ **commanding** *adj* **1** [attrib] having the authority to give formal orders: *one's commanding officer.* **2** [usu attrib] in a position to control or dominate: *The fort occupies a commanding position.* ○ *One team has already built up a commanding lead.* **3** [usu attrib] seeming to have authority; impressive: *a commanding voice, tone, look, etc.*

command[2] /kəˈmɑːnd; *US* -ˈmænd/ *n* **1** [C] **(a)** order: *Her commands were quickly obeyed.* ○ *Give your commands in a loud, confident voice.* **(b)** (*computing*) instruction to a computer. **2** [U] (*esp military*) control; authority (used esp with the *vs* and *preps* shown): *to have/take command of a regiment, etc* ○ *He should not be given command of troops.* ○ *Who is in command* (ie in charge) *here?* ○ *General Smith is in command of the army.* ○ *The army is under the command of General Smith.* ○ *He has twenty men under his command.* **3 Command** [C] part of an army, air force, etc organized and controlled separately: *Western Command* ○ *Bomber Command.* **4** [U, sing] ~ **(of sth)** ability to use or control sth; mastery: *He has (a) good command of the French language,* ie can speak it well. ○ *He has enormous funds at his command.* ○ *He has no command over himself,* ie cannot control his feelings, temper, etc. **5** (idm) **at/by sb's com**ˈ**mand** (*fml*) having been ordered by sb: *I am here at the King's command.* **at the word of command** ⇨ WORD. **be at sb's com**ˈ**mand** be ready to obey sb. **your wish is my command** ⇨ WISH.

□ **com**ˈ**mand module** part of a spacecraft carrying the crew and control equipment.

comˈ**mand paper** document presented for debate to the British Parliament by the monarch.

comˌ**mand per**ˈ**formance** performance (of a play, film, etc) given at the request of a head of state (who usu attends).

comˈ**mand post** headquarters of a military unit.

commandant /ˌkɒmənˈdænt/ *n* commanding officer, esp of a prisoner-of-war camp, military academy, etc.

commandeer /ˌkɒmənˈdɪə(r)/ *v* [Tn] take possession or control of (vehicles, buildings, etc) forcibly or for official (esp military) purposes.

commander /kəˈmɑːndə(r); *US* -ˈmæn-/ *n* **1** person who commands: *the commander of the expedition.* **2** (*Brit*) **(a)** officer in the British Navy immediately below the rank of captain. ⇨ App 4. **(b)** officer of high rank in London's Metropolitan Police. **3** (also ˌ**Knight Com**ˈ**mander**) member of the higher class in certain British orders of knighthood.

□ **com**ˌ**mander-in-**ˈ**chief** *n* (*pl* **commanders-in-chief**) commander of all the armed forces of a country.

commandment /kəˈmɑːndmənt; *US* -ˈmænd-/ *n* **(a)** (*fml*) command; order: *obeying God's commandments.* **(b) Commandment** (in the Bible) any of the ten laws given by God to Moses: *the Ten Commandments.*

commando /kəˈmɑːndəʊ; *US* -ˈmæn-/ *n* (*pl* ~**s** or ~**es**) (member of a) group of soldiers specially trained for carrying out quick raids in enemy areas.

commedia dell'arte

COLUMBINE HARLEQUIN PANTALOON

commedia dell'arte /kɒˌmeɪdɪə del ˈɑːteɪ/ *n* type of improvised drama, first developed in Italy in the 16th century, using a few standard characters (eg Harlequin, Columbine, Pantaloon) and a few basic plots adapted to suit each audience. It had considerable influence on later European drama. ⇨ illus.

comme il faut /ˌkɒm iːl ˈfəʊ/ (*French*) as it/one should be; proper(ly): *behaviour that is comme il faut,* ie that observes the rules of etiquette.

commemorate /kəˈmeməreɪt/ *v* [Tn] **(a)** keep (a great person, event, etc) in people's memories: *We commemorate the founding of our nation with a public holiday.* **(b)** (of a statue, monument, etc) be a reminder of (sb/sth): *This memorial commemorates those who died in the war.*

▷ **commemoration** /kəˌmeməˈreɪʃn/ *n* [C, U] (act of or ceremony for) commemorating: *a statue in commemoration of a national hero.*

commemorative /kəˈmemərətɪv; *US* -ˈmeməreɪt-/ *adj* helping to commemorate: *commemorative stamps, medals, etc.*

commence /kəˈmens/ *v* [I, Tn, Tg] (*fml*) begin (sth); start: *Shall we commence (the ceremony)?* ○ *After grace had been said, we commenced eating.*

▷ **commencement** *n* [U, C usu *sing*] **1** (*fml*) beginning. **2** (*esp US*) ceremony at which academic degrees are officially given.

commend /kəˈmend/ *v* **1** [Tn, Tn·pr] **(a)** ~ **sb (on/ for sth)**; ~ **sb/sth (to sb)** speak favourably to or of sb/sth; praise sb/sth: *She/Her entry was highly commended,* ie almost won a prize ○ *I commended the chef on the excellent meal. I later wrote to commend him to his employer, the restaurant owner.* **(b)** ~ **sb/sth (to sb)** (*fml*) recommend sb/sth: *That's excellent advice; I commend it to you,* ie suggest that you accept it. **2** [Tn·pr] ~ **oneself/ itself to sb** (*fml*) be acceptable to sb; be liked by sb: *Will this government proposal commend itself to the public?* **3** [Tn·pr] ~ **sth to sb** (*fml*) give sth to sb so that it will be kept safe; entrust sth to sb: *commend one's soul to God.*

▷ **commendable** /-əbl/ *adj* deserving praise (even if perhaps not completely successful): *a commendable effort.* **commendably** /-əblɪ/ *adv.*

commendation /ˌkɒmenˈdeɪʃn/ *n* **(a)** [U] praise; approval. **(b)** [C] ~ **(for sth)** (award involving the) giving of special praise: *a commendation for bravery* ○ *Her painting won a commendation from the teacher.*

commensal /kəˈmensl/ *adj* (of two plants or animals) living closely together in a way that benefits one and does not harm the other. ▷

commensalism /-səlɪzəm/ *n* [U]. Cf SYMBIOSIS.
commensurable /kəˈmenʃərəbl/ *adj* ~ **(to/with sth)** (*esp mathematics*) that can be measured by the same standard (as sth).
commensurate /kəˈmenʃərət/ *adj* ~ **(to/with sth)** (*fml*) in the right proportion (to sth); appropriate: *Her low salary is not commensurate with her abilities.*
comment /ˈkɒment/ *n* **1** [C, U] ~ **(on sth)** written or spoken remark giving an opinion on, explaining or criticizing (an event, a person, a situation, etc): *Have you any comment(s) to make on the recent developments?* ○ *The scandal caused a lot of comment*, ie of talk, gossip, etc. **2** (idm) **no ˈcomment** (said in reply to a question) I have nothing to say about that: *'Will you resign, Minister?' 'No comment!'*
▷ **comment** *v* [I, Ipr, Tf] ~ **(on sth)** make comments; give one's opinion: *Asked about the date of the election, the Prime Minister commented that no decision had yet been made.*
commentary /ˈkɒməntrɪ; *US* -terɪ/ *n* **1** [C, U] ~ **(on/of sth)** spoken description of an event as it happens: *a broadcast commentary of a football match.* **2** [C] ~ **(on sth)** set of explanatory notes on a book, etc: *a Bible commentary.*
commentate /ˈkɒmenteɪt/ *v* [I, Ipr] ~ **(on sth)** **(a)** describe, esp on TV or radio, an event as it happens: *commentate on an athletics meeting.* **(b)** (usu not in the continuous tenses) do this regularly, as a job.
▷ **commentator** /ˈkɒmənteɪtə(r)/ *n* ~ **(on sth)** **1** person who commentates. **2** person who comments: *an informed commentator on political events.* **3** writer of a commentary(2).
commerce /ˈkɒmɜːs/ *n* [U] trade (esp betweeen countries); buying and selling of goods: *We must promote commerce with neighbouring countries.*
commercial /kəˈmɜːʃl/ *adj* **1** **(a)** of or for commerce: *commercial law, activity, art.* **(b)** [usu attrib] of business practices and activities generally: *doing a commercial course at the local college.* **2** **(a)** [attrib] from the point of view of profit: *The play was a commercial success*, ie made money. **(b)** making or intended to make a profit: *commercial theatre, music, etc* ○ *Oil is present in commercial quantities*, ie There is enough to make extraction profitable. ○ *Her novels are well written and commercial as well.* **3** (of TV or radio) financed by broadcast advertisements: *I work for a commercial radio station.*
▷ **commercial** *n* advertisement on TV or radio.
commercialism /kəˈmɜːʃəlɪzəm/ *n* [U] (*often derog*) practices and attitudes concerned with the making of profit: *excessive commercialism in the theatre.* **commercialize, -ise** /kəˈmɜːʃəlaɪz/ *v* [Tn] (*often derog*) (try to) make money out of (sth): *Sport has become much more commercialized in recent years.*
commercially /-ʃəlɪ/ *adv*: *Commercially, the play was a failure, though the critics loved it.*
□ **commercial ˈart** style of art used in advertising. **commercial ˈartist**.
commercial ˈtraveller person who travels over a large area visiting shops, etc with samples of goods, trying to obtain orders.
commercial ˈvehicle van, lorry, etc for transporting goods.
commie /ˈkɒmɪ/ *n, adj* (also **Commie**) (*sl derog*) communist: *That's just commie propaganda!*
comminute /ˈkɒmɪnjuːt/ *v* [Tn] (*fml*) reduce (sth) to small fragments or to a powder; pulverize: *a comminuted fracture*, ie one in which the ends of the bone have been crushed. ▷ **comminution** /kɒmɪˈnjuːʃn/ *n* [U].
commiserate /kəˈmɪzəreɪt/ *v* [I, Ipr] ~ **(with sb)** **(on/over sth)** (*fml*) feel, or say that one feels, sympathy: *I commiserated with her on the loss of her job.*
▷ **commiseration** /kəmɪzəˈreɪʃn/ *n* [C usu *pl*, U] ~ **(on/over sth)** (*fml or joc*) (expression of) sympathy for sb: *I expressed my commiserations on his misfortune.* ○ *'I lost again.' 'Commiserations* (ie I am sorry)*!'*
commissar /ˈkɒmɪsɑː(r)/ *n* **1** (formerly) head of a government department in the USSR. **2** (formerly) officer in the army of the USSR giving political instruction.
commissariat /kɒmɪˈseərɪət/ *n* **1** department in the army responsible for supplying food, etc. **2** government department in the USSR.
commissary /ˈkɒmɪsərɪ; *US* ˈkɒməserɪ/ *n* (*US*) **1** store at a military base, where food and other goods are sold. **2** dining-room or restaurant in a film studio, factory, etc.
commission /kəˈmɪʃn/ *n* **1** [C] ~ **(to do sth)** action, task or piece of work given to sb to do: *She has received many commissions to design public buildings.* **2** (often **Commission**) [C] **(a)** group of people authorized to carry out a task: *the Civil Service Commission*, ie the body that selects staff for the Civil Service. **(b)** ~ **(on sth)** group of people officially set up to make an inquiry and write a report: *a Royal Commission on* (ie reporting on) *betting and gambling.* **3** [U] ~ **(of sth)** (*fml*) doing (sth wrong or illegal): *the commission of a crime* ○ *a sin of commission* (ie actually doing sth wrong) *rather than omission.* **4** [C, U] payment to sb for selling goods which increases with the quantity of goods sold: *You get (a) 10% commission on everything you sell.* ○ *earn £2000 (in) commission* ○ *She is working for us on commission*, ie is not paid a salary. **5** [C] (document signed by the monarch appointing sb to the) rank of an officer in the armed services: *He resigned his commission to take up a civilian job.* **6** (idm) **in/into comˈmission** (esp of a ship) in/into service: *Some wartime vessels are still in commission.* **out of comˈmission** **(a)** (esp of a ship) not in service: *With several of their planes temporarily out of commission, the airline is losing money.* **(b)** (*fig*) not available; not working: *I got flu and was out of commission for a week.*
▷ **commission** *v* **1** **(a)** [Tn, Dn·t] give a commission(1) to (sb): *commission an artist to paint a picture.* **(b)** [Tn] give sb the job of making (sth): *He commissioned a statue of his wife.* **2** [usu passive: Tn, Cn·n, Cn·n/a] ~ **sb as sth** appoint sb officially by means of a commission(5): *She was commissioned (as a) lieutenant in the Women's Army Corps.* **3** [Tn] bring (machinery, equipment, etc) into operation: *The nuclear plant now being built is expected to be commissioned in five years' time.*
□ **commissioned ˈofficer** officer in the armed forces who holds a commission(5).
commissionaire /kəmɪʃəˈneə(r)/ *n* (*esp Brit*) uniformed attendant at the entrance to a cinema, theatre, hotel, etc who opens the door for people, finds them taxis, etc.
commissioner /kəˈmɪʃənə(r)/ *n* **1** (usu **Commissioner**) member of a commission(2), esp one with particular duties: *the Commissioners of Inland Revenue*, ie those who are in charge of tax collection in Britain ○ *the Civil Service Commissioners*, ie those who conduct Civil Service examinations in Britain. **2** public official of high rank: *The London police force is headed by a commissioner.* ○ *In British India, district commissioners had judicial powers.*
□ **Commissioner for ˈOaths** (*Brit*) solicitor with special authority, to whom people can swear oaths relating to legal documents.
commissure /ˈkɒmɪʃʊə(r)/ *n* (*fml*) point at which two corresponding parts meet, eg the eyelids, two bones, or other parts of the body.
commit /kəˈmɪt/ *v* (**-tt-**) **1** [Tn] do (sth illegal, wrong or foolish): *commit murder, suicide, theft, a blunder, an unforgiveable error, etc.* **2** [Tn·pr] ~ **sb/sth to sth** give or transfer sb/sth to (a state or place) for safe keeping, treatment, etc: *commit a man to prison*, ie have him put in prison ○ *commit a patient to a mental hospital* ○ *commit sth to paper/to writing*, ie write sth down ○ *The body was committed to the flames*, ie was burnt. ○ *commit a list to memory*, ie memorize it. **3** [Tn, Tn·pr, Cn·t] ~ **sb/oneself (to sth/to doing sth)** make it impossible for sb/oneself not to do sth, or to do sth else, esp because of a promise; pledge sb/oneself: *I can't come on Sunday: I'm already committed*, ie I've arranged to do sth else. ○ *commit oneself to a course of action* ○ *Signing this form commits you to buying the goods.* ○ *The company has committed funds to an advertising campaign.* ○ *This regiment is already committed to* (ie It has been settled that it will fight on) *the eastern front.* ○ *He has committed himself to support his brother's children.* **4** [Tn, Tn·pr] ~ **oneself (on sth)** give one's opinion openly so that it is difficult to change it: *I asked her what she thought, but she refused to commit herself.* Cf NON-COMMITTAL. **5** [Tn, Tn·pr] ~ **sb (for sth)** send sb to a higher court to be tried: *The magistrates committed him for trial at the Old Bailey.*
▷ **committal** /kəˈmɪtl/ *n* [U] action of committing (COMMIT 2), esp to prison: [attrib] *At the committal proceedings the police withdrew their case.*
committed *adj* (*usu approv*) devoted (to a cause, one's job, etc): *a committed Christian, doctor, teacher, communist.* Cf UNCOMMITTED.
commitment *n* **1** [U] ~ **(to sth)** committing or being committed (COMMIT 3): *the commitment of a patient to a mental hospital* ○ *the commitment of funds to medicine.* **2** [C] ~ **(to sth/to do sth)** thing one has promised to do; pledge; undertaking: *I'm overworked at the moment — I've taken on too many commitments.* ○ *a commitment to pay £100 to charity.* **3** [U] (*approv*) state of being dedicated or devoted (to sth): *We're looking for someone with a real sense of commitment to the job.*
committee /kəˈmɪtɪ/ *n* [CGp] **1** group of people appointed (usu by a larger group) to deal with a particular matter: *be/sit on a committee* ○ *The committee has/have decided to dismiss him.* ○ *the transport committee* ○ *This was discussed in committee*, ie by the committee. ○ [attrib] *a committee meeting, member, decision.* **2 the Committee** (*Brit*) the House of Commons when it is sitting as a committee.
commode /kəˈməʊd/ *n* **1** piece of bedroom furniture to hold a chamber-pot. **2** chest of drawers. **3** (*esp US*) covered wash-stand.
commodious /kəˈməʊdɪəs/ *adj* (*fml*) having a lot of space available for use; roomy: *a commodious house, cupboard, suitcase.*
commodity /kəˈmɒdətɪ/ *n* **1** thing bought in a shop and put to use, esp in the home: *household commodities*, eg pots and pans, cleaning materials, etc ○ (*fig*) *I lead a very busy life, so spare time is a very precious commodity to me.* **2** (*finance*) article, product or material that is exchanged in (esp international) trade: *Trading in commodities was brisk.* ○ [attrib] *the commodity/commodities market.*
commodore /ˈkɒmədɔː(r)/ *n* **1** officer in the British Navy between the ranks of captain and rear-admiral. ⇨ App 4. **2** president of a yacht club. **3** senior captain of a shipping line: *the commodore of the Cunard Line.*
common[1] /ˈkɒmən/ *adj* **1** usual or familiar; happening or found often and in many places: *a common flower, sight, event* ○ *the common cold* ○ *Is this word in common use?* ie Is it commonly used? ○ *Robbery is not common in this area.* ○ *Pine trees are common throughout the world.* Cf UNCOMMON. **2** [attrib] ~ **(to sb/sth)** shared by, belonging to, done by or affecting two or more people, or most of a group or society: *common property, ownership* ○ *We share a common purpose.* ○ *He and I have a common interest: we both collect stamps.* ○ *He is French, she is German, but they have English as a common language*, ie they can both speak English. ○ *measures taken for the common good*, ie for the benefit of everyone ○ *A fruity quality is common to all wine made from this grape.* **3** [attrib] without special rank or quality; ordinary: *He's not an officer, but a common soldier.* ○ *the common people*, ie the average citizens of a country ○ *common salt.* **4** (*infml derog*) (of people, their behaviour and belongings) (typical) of the lower classes of society, showing a lack of taste and refinement; vulgar: *common manners, accents, clothes* ○ *She's so common, shouting like that so all the neighbours can hear!* **5** (*mathematics*) belonging to two or more quantities: *a common denominator/factor/multiple.* **6** (idm) **be common/public knowledge** ⇨ KNOWLEDGE. **(as) common as ˈdirt/ˈmuck** (*infml derog*) (of people) very common[1](4). **common or ˈgarden** ordinary; not unusual: *It isn't a rare bird, just a common or garden sparrow.* **the common ˈtouch** ability (esp of sb of high rank)

to deal with and talk to ordinary people in a friendly way and without condescension: *A politician needs the common touch.* **make common ˈcause (with sb)** (*fml*) unite to pursue a shared objective: *The rebel factions made common cause (with each other) to overthrow the regime.*

▷ **commonly** *adv* **1** usually; very often: *That very commonly happens.* ○ *Thomas, commonly known as Tom.* **2** (*infml derog*) in a common[1](4) manner.

□ **common ˈcarrier** (*esp law*) company or person that is allowed by law to charge money for transporting goods or people.

common ˈdecency polite behaviour to be expected from a reasonable person: *You'd think he'd have the common decency to apologize for what he said.*

common deˈnominator 1 (*mathematics*) number that is a multiple of each of the denominators of two or more fractions. **2** quality or thing that a group of people or things have in common: *We found that the only common denominator between us was a love of animals.*

Common ˈEntrance examination taken by children trying to get into British public schools (PUBLIC): *sit/take/pass/fail Common Entrance.* ⇨ article at SCHOOL.

common ˈfactor (*mathematics*) number by which two or more other numbers can be divided: *2 is a common factor of 6 and 10.*

common ˈground shared opinions, interests, aims, etc: *The two rival parties have no common ground between them.*

ˈcommon land land that belongs to or may be used by the community, esp in a village. Cf COMMON[2].

common ˈlaw (in England) law developed from old customs and from decisions made by judges, ie not created by Parliament. Cf CASE LAW (CASE[1]), STATUTE LAW (STATUTE). ⇨ article at LAW.

common-law ˈwife, common-law ˈhusband person with whom a man or woman has lived for some time and who is recognized as a wife or husband under common law, without a formal marriage ceremony.

the Common ˈMarket (also **the European Community**) economic association, established in 1958, and now including Belgium, Britain, Denmark, France, Greece, Ireland, Italy, Luxembourg, the Netherlands, Portugal, Spain and Germany, whose members give each other mutual trading advantages.

common ˈmultiple (*mathematics*) number into which two or more other numbers can be divided: *12 is a common multiple of 2, 3, 4 and 6.*

common ˈnoun (*grammar*) word that can refer to any member of a class of similar things (eg *book* or *knife*).

ˈcommon-room *n* room for use of the teachers or students of a school, college, etc when they are not in class.

common ˈsense practical good sense gained from experience of life, not by special study: [attrib] *I like her common-sense approach to everyday problems.*

common ˈtime (*music*) two or four beats (esp four crotchets) in a bar.

common[2] /ˈkɒmən/ *n* **1** area of unfenced grassland which anyone may use, usu in or near a village: *Saturday afternoon cricket on the village common.* Cf COMMON LAND (COMMON[1]). **2** (idm) **have sth in common (with sb/sth)** share interests, characteristics, etc: *Jane and I have nothing in common.* ○ *I have nothing in common with Jane.* **in common** for or by all of a group: *land owned in common by the residents.* **in common with sb/sth** together with sb/sth; like sb/sth: *In common with many others, she applied for a training place.*

commonality /kɒməˈnælətɪ/ *n* (*fml*) **1** [U] sharing of a feature, quality, etc. **2** [C] common occurrence.

commonalty /ˈkɒmənəltɪ/ *n* **the commonalty** [sing] (*fml*) ordinary people as a group.

commoner /ˈkɒmənə(r)/ *n* **1** one of the common people, not a member of the nobility. Cf ARISTOCRAT, NOBLEMAN (NOBLE). **2** student at some universities, esp Oxford and Cambridge, who does not have a scholarship or similar award.

commonplace /ˈkɒmənpleɪs/ *adj* (*often derog*) ordinary; not interesting: *He's not at all exciting; in fact he's really rather commonplace.*

▷ **commonplace** *n* **1** remark, etc that is ordinary or unoriginal; truism: *a conversation full of mere commonplaces* ○ *He uttered a few commonplaces about peace and democracy.* **2** event, topic, etc that is ordinary or usual: *Air travel is a commonplace nowadays.*

□ **ˈcommonplace-book** *n* book that sb keeps for writing interesting quotations, ideas, etc in.

commons /ˈkɒmənz/ *n* [pl] **1 the commons** (*arch*) the common people. **2 the Commons** (*Brit*) **(a)** = THE HOUSE OF COMMONS (HOUSE). **(b)** the members of the House of Commons: *the Lords and the Commons.* **3** (idm) **short commons** ⇨ SHORT[1].

commonwealth /ˈkɒmənwelθ/ *n* **1** [C] **(a)** independent State or community: *measures for the good of the commonwealth.* **(b)** group of States that have chosen to be politically linked: *the Commonwealth of Australia.* **2 the Commonwealth** [sing] (also **the ˌCommonwealth of ˈNations**) **(a)** association consisting of the UK and various independent States (previously subject to Britain) and dependencies. There are currently 49 members. The reigning British monarch is recognized as the head of the Commonwealth and its leaders meet for a conference every two years. **(b)** the government of Britain between 1649 and 1660, when the country was a republic, without a king. ⇨ App 3.

□ **Commonwealth of Independent States** (*abbr* **CIS**) multilateral grouping of sovereign states (not itself a sovereign state) formed after the break-up of the *USSR in late 1991. It comprises all the former Soviet republics except for Ukraine and the three Baltic republics. The aim is to work towards common economic and defence policies, but disagreements over the control of nuclear missiles, an all-rouble monetary system and ethnic minority issues point to deep-seated problems for the future. ⇨ map at UNION OF SOVIET SOCIALIST REPUBLICS.

commotion /kəˈməʊʃn/ *n* [U, C] (instance of) noisy confusion or excitement: *The children are making a lot of commotion.* ○ *Suddenly, there was a great commotion next door.*

communal /ˈkɒmjʊnl, kəˈmju:nl/ *adj* **1 (a)** for the use of all; shared: *communal land, facilities* ○ *The flat has four separate bedrooms and a communal kitchen.* **(b)** of or for a community: *communal life, work.* **2** between different groups in a community: *communal strife, disturbances, etc* ○ *communal riots between religious sects.* ▷ **communally** *adv.*

commune[1] /kəˈmju:n/ *v* [I, Ipr, Ip] ~ **(with sb/sth)**; ~ **(together)** talk to sb intimately; feel close to sb/sth: *commune with one's friends* ○ *commune with God in prayer* ○ *walking in the woods, communing with nature* ○ *friends communing together.*

commune[2] /ˈkɒmju:n/ *n* [CGp] **1** group of people, not all of one family, living together and sharing property and responsibilities. **2** (in France, Belgium, Italy and Spain) smallest unit of local government, with a mayor and council. **3 the Commune** local government set up in Paris and other French cities by citizens angry at France's surrender (1871) after its war with Prussia. Karl *Marx wrote in praise of the Commune and it helped to inspire the Russian Revolution.

communicable /kəˈmju:nɪkəbl/ *adj* that can be communicated or transmitted: *complex ideas not easily communicable to non-experts* ○ *a communicable disease.*

communicant /kəˈmju:nɪkənt/ *n* **1** person who receives Communion, esp regularly. **2** (*fml*) person who gives information; informer.

communicate /kəˈmju:nɪkeɪt/ *v* **1** [Tn, Tn·pr] ~ **sth (to sb/sth) (a)** make sth known; convey sth: *This poem communicates the author's despair.* ○ *The officer communicated his orders to the men by radio.* **(b)** pass on sth; transmit sth: *communicate a disease.* **2 (a)** [I, Ipr] ~ **(with sb)** exchange information, news, ideas, etc: *The police communicate (with each other) by radio.* **(b)** [I] convey one's ideas, feelings, etc clearly to others: *A politician must be able to communicate.* **3** [I, Ipr] ~ **(with sth)** be connected: *My garden communicates with the one next door by means of a gate.* ○ *communicating rooms,* ie rooms with a connecting door.

communication /kəmju:nɪˈkeɪʃn/ *n* **1** [U] act of communicating(1b, 2a, 2b): *the communication of disease* ○ *Being deaf and dumb makes communication very difficult.* **2** [C] (*usu fml*) thing that is communicated; message: *to receive a secret communication.* **3** [U] (also **communications** [pl]) means of communicating, eg roads, railways, telephone and telegraph lines between places, or radio and TV: *Telephone communications between the two cities have been restored.* ○ *The heavy snow has prevented all communication with the highlands.* ○ [attrib] *a communication satellite, link, etc* ○ *a world communications network.* **4** (idm) **be in communication with sb** exchange information regularly with sb, usu by letter or telephone.

□ **communiˈcation cord** cord that passes along the length of a train inside the coaches, and that passengers can pull to stop the train in an emergency.

communiˈcations satellite satellite used for transmitting (esp telephone, radio and television) signals worldwide.

communicative /kəˈmju:nɪkətɪv; *US* -keɪtɪv/ *adj* ready and willing to talk and give information: *I don't find Peter very communicative.* Cf RESERVED.

communion /kəˈmju:nɪən/ *n* **1 Communion** [U] (also **Holy Communion**) (in the Christian Church) celebration of the Lord's Supper: *go to Communion,* ie attend church for this celebration ○ [attrib] *Communion wine.* Cf EUCHARIST. **2** [C] group of people with the same religious beliefs: *We belong to the same communion.* **3** [U] ~ **(with sb/sth)** (*fml*) state of sharing or exchanging the same thoughts or feelings: *poets who are in communion with nature.*

communiqué /kəˈmju:nɪkeɪ; *US* kəˌmju:nəˈkeɪ/ *n* official announcement, esp to the press: *A government communiqué, issued this morning, states that....*

communism /ˈkɒmjʊnɪzəm/ *n* [U] **1** social and economic system in which there is no private ownership and the means of production belong to all members of society. **2 Communism (a)** political doctrine or movement that aims to establish such a society. **(b)** system of government by a ruling Communist Party, as in the Soviet Union.

▷ **communist** /ˈkɒmjʊnɪst/ *n* **1** supporter of communism. **2 Communist** member of a Communist party or movement. — *adj* characterized by, supporting or relating to communism: *have communist ideals* ○ *a Communist country, government, régime, etc* ○ *Communist leaders.* **communistic** /ˌkɒmjʊˈnɪstɪk/ *adj.*

□ **the ˈCommunist Party 1** political party supporting Communism. **2** (in Communist countries) single official ruling party of the State.

community /kəˈmju:nətɪ/ *n* **1 the community** [sing] the people living in one place, district or country, considered as a whole: *work for the good of the community* ○ [attrib] *community life.* **2** [CGp] group of people of the same religion, race, occupation, etc, or with shared interests: *the British community in Paris* ○ *a community of monks,* ie a group of the same order living together. **3** [U] condition of sharing, having things in common, being alike in some way: *community of interests* ○ [attrib] *a community spirit,* ie a feeling of sharing the same attitudes, interests, etc.

□ **comˈmunity centre** place where the people of a neighbourhood can meet for sporting activities, education classes, social occasions, etc.

comˈmunity chest (*US*) fund for helping local people in financial need.

comˌmunity ˈcollege (*US*) college offering post-school courses to local residents.

comˈmunity home (*Brit*) centre where young offenders are kept for training, before their release.

comˌmunity ˈservice unpaid work that benefits the local community. People convicted of an offence are sometimes ordered to do such work instead of paying a fine or going to prison.

com'munity singing organized singing in which all present may take part.

commutative /kəˈmjuːtətɪv; *US* ˈkɒmjəteɪtɪv/ *adj* (of an operation in mathematics) that produces the same result in whichever order the elements are taken, eg 3 x 4 = 12, 4 x 3 = 12.

commutator /ˈkɒmjuːteɪtə(r)/ *n* device for altering the direction of an electric current.

commute /kəˈmjuːt/ *v* **1** [I, Ipr, Ip] travel regularly by bus, train or car between one's place of work (usu in a city) and one's home (usu at a distance): *She commutes from Oxford to London every day.* ○ *She lives in Oxford and commutes (in).* **2** [Tn, Tn·pr] ~ **sth (to sth)** replace (one punishment) by another that is less severe: *commute a death sentence (to one of life imprisonment)* ○ *She was given a commuted sentence.* **3** [Tn, Tn·pr] ~ **sth (for/into sth)** change sth, esp one form of payment, for or into sth else: *commute one's pension* ○ *commute an annuity into a lump sum.*

▷ **commutable** /kəˈmjuːtəbl/ *adj* ~ **(for/into sth)** that can be made, paid, etc in a different form: *A pension is often commutable into a lump sum.*

commutation /ˌkɒmjuːˈteɪʃn/ *n* **1** [C, U] replacement of one punishment by another that is less severe: *He appealed for (a) commutation of the death sentence to life imprisonment.* **2** (a) [U] replacing one method of payment by another, eg a lump sum instead of a pension. (b) [C] payment made in this way. **commu'tation ticket** (*US*) bus or train ticket valid for a fixed number of trips during a given period of time. Cf SEASON TICKET (SEASON).

commuter *n* person who commutes (COMMUTE 1): *The five o'clock train is always packed with commuters.* ○ [attrib] *the commuter belt*, ie the area around a large city, from which people commute to work.

Comoros /ˈkɒmərəʊz/ **the Comoros** group of islands in the Indian ocean, an independent state since 1974; pop approx 488 000; official languages French and Arabic; capital Moroni; unit of currency franc. It is a former French colony and is still economically dependent on France. ⇨ map at TANZANIA.

compact[1] /kəmˈpækt/ *adj* **1** (a) closely packed together: *a compact mass of sand* ○ *Stamp the soil down so that it's compact.* (b) neatly fitted in a small space: *a compact flat, car, kit* ○ *The computer looks compact and functional.* **2** (of literary style) condensed; concise.

▷ **compact** *v* [Tn usu passive] press (sth) firmly together: *The compacted snow on the pavement turned to ice.*

compactly *adv.*

compactness *n* [U].

□ **comˌpact ˈdisc** (*abbr* **CD**) small disc for reproducing recorded sound by laser action.

compact[2] /ˈkɒmpækt/ *n* agreement or contract between two or more parties: *The two states made a compact to co-operate against terrorism.*

compact[3] /ˈkɒmpækt/ *n* **1** small flat portable case for face-powder, usu also containing a powder-puff and a mirror. **2** (*esp US*) small car.

companion /kəmˈpænɪən/ *n* **1** (a) person or animal that goes with, or spends much time with, another: *my companions on the journey* ○ *A dog is a faithful companion.* ○ (*fig*) *Fear was the hostage's constant companion.* (b) person who shares in the work, pleasures, misfortunes, etc of another: *companions in arms*, ie fellow soldiers ○ *companions in misfortune*, ie people suffering together. (c) person with similar tastes, interests, etc: *She's an excellent companion.* ○ *They're ˈdrinking companions.* ○ *His brother is not much of a companion for him.* **2** person employed to live with another (esp sb old or ill) as a friend: *to take a post as a ˌpaid comˈpanion.* **3** one of a matching pair or set of things: [attrib] *The companion volume will soon be published.* **4** (used in book titles) handbook; reference book: *the ˌGardener's Comˈpanion.* **5 Companion** member of certain distinguished orders (ORDER[1] 10a): *Comˌpanion of ˈHonour.* **6** (idm) **a boon companion** ⇨ BOON[2].

▷ **companionable** *adj* friendly; sociable.

companionship *n* [U] relationship between friends or companions: *the companionship of old friends* ○ *She turned to me for companionship.*

companion-way /kəmˈpænɪən weɪ/ (also **companion**) *n* staircase from a ship's deck to the saloon or cabins.

company /ˈkʌmpənɪ/ *n* **1** [U] being together with another or others: *I enjoy his company*, ie I like being with him. ○ *be good, bad, etc company*, ie be pleasant, unpleasant, etc to be with. **2** [U] group of people together; number of guests: *She told the assembled company what had happened.* ○ *We're expecting company* (ie guests, visitors) *next week.* **3** (often **Company**) [CGp] group of people united for business or commercial purposes: *a manufacturing company.* Cf FIRM[2]. **4** [CGp] group of people working together: *a company of players*, ie a number of actors regularly performing together ○ *a theatrical company* ○ *the ship's company*, ie the crew. **5** [CGp] subdivision of an infantry battalion, usu commanded by a captain or a major. **6** (idm) **the ˈcompany one keeps** the type of people with whom one spends one's time: (*saying*) *You may know a man by the company he keeps*, ie judge his character by his friends. **for company** as a companion: *I hate going out alone: I take my daughter for company.* **get into/keep bad ˈcompany** associate with undesirable people. **in company** in the presence of others: *It's bad manners to whisper in company.* **in company with sb** together with sb: *I, in company with many others, feel this decision was wrong.* **in good ˈcompany** doing the same as other, better people do: *'I'm late again!' 'Well, you're in good company. The boss isn't here yet.'* **keep sb company** remain with sb so that he is not alone: *I'll stay here and keep you company.* **part company** ⇨ PART[2]. **present company excepted** ⇨ PRESENT[1]. **two's company (, three's a crowd)** (*saying*) (used esp of people in love) it is better for two people to be alone with each other and without others present.

□ **ˈcompany union** (*esp US*) union for the workers within a particular company, often run by the company and not connected with a trade union.

comparable /ˈkɒmpərəbl/ *adj* ~ **(to/with sb/sth)** able or suitable to be compared: *The achievements of an athlete and a writer are not comparable.* ○ *His work is comparable with the very best.*

comparative /kəmˈpærətɪv/ *adj* **1** involving comparison or comparing: *comparative linguistics, religion, etc* ○ *a comparative study of the social systems of two countries*, ie one that analyses the similarities and differences between them. **2** measured or judged by comparing; relative: *living in comparative comfort*, eg compared with others, or with one's own life at an earlier period ○ *In a poor country, owning a bicycle is a sign of comparative wealth.* **3** (*grammar*) of adjectives and adverbs that express a greater degree or 'more', eg *better, worse, slower, more difficult.* Cf SUPERLATIVE 2.

▷ **comparative** *n* (*grammar*) form of adjectives and adverbs that expresses a greater degree: *'Better' is the comparative of 'good'.*

comparatively *adv* as compared to sth or sb else: *comparatively wealthy, small, good, old.*

compare /kəmˈpeə(r)/ *v* **1** [Tn, Tn·pr] ~ **A and B**; ~ **A with/to B** examine people or things to see how they are alike and how they are different: *Compare (the style of) the two poems.* ○ *If you compare her work with his/If you compare their work, you'll find hers is much better.* Cf CF, CP *abbrs.* **2** [Tn·pr] ~ **A to B** show the likeness between sb/sth and sb/sth else: *Poets have compared sleep to death.* ○ *A beginner's painting can't be compared to that of an expert*, ie is very different in quality. **3** [Ipr] ~ **with sb/sth** be compared with or be worthy to be compared with sb/sth: *This cannot compare with that*, ie No comparison is possible because they are so different. ○ *He cannot compare with* (ie is not nearly as great as) *Shakespeare as a writer of tragedies.* **4** [Tn] (*grammar*) form the comparative and superlative degrees of (an adjective or adverb). **5** (idm) **compare ˈnotes (with sb)** exchange ideas or opinions: *We saw the play separately and compared notes afterwards.*

▷ **compare** *n* (idm) **beyond comˈpare** (*fml*) to such an extent that no comparison can be made with anything or anyone else: *She is lovely beyond compare.*

comparison /kəmˈpærɪsn/ *n* **1** [U] comparing: *He showed us a good tyre for comparison (with the worn one).* **2** [C] ~ **(of A and/to/with B)**; ~ **(between A and B)** act of comparing: *the comparison of the heart to/with a pump* ○ *It is often useful to make a comparison between two things.* **3** (idm) **bear/stand comparison with sb/sth** be able to be compared favourably with sb/sth: *That's a good dictionary, but it doesn't bear comparison with this one.* **by/in comparison (with sb/sth)** when compared: *The tallest buildings in London are small in comparison with those in New York.* **comparisons are odious** (*saying*) people and things should be judged on their own merits and not measured against sb/sth else. **there's no comˈparison** (used to emphasize the difference between two people or things being compared): *'Is he as good as her at chess?' 'There's no comparison'*, ie She is much better.

compartment /kəmˈpɑːtmənt/ *n* any of the sections into which a larger area or enclosed space, esp a railway carriage, is divided: *The first-class compartments are in front.* ○ *a case with separate compartments for shoes, jewellery, etc.*

▷ **compartmentalize, -ise** /ˌkɒmpɑːtˈmentəlaɪz/ *v* [Tn, Tn·pr] ~ **sth (into sth)** divide sth into compartments or categories: *Life today is compartmentalized into work and leisure.*

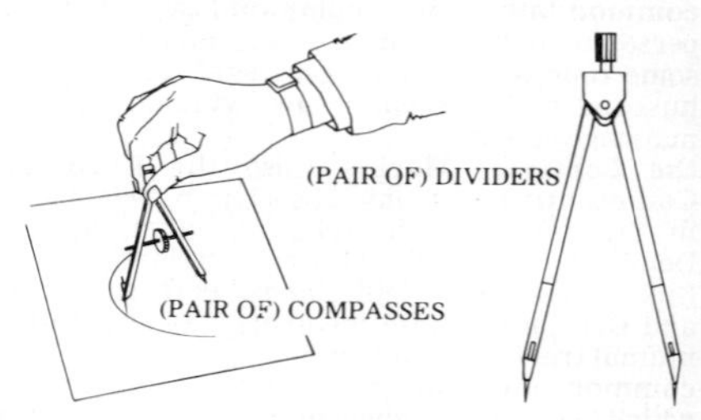

compass[1] /ˈkʌmpəs/ *n* **1** [C] (a) (also **magnetic compass**) device for finding direction, with a needle that points to magnetic north: *the points of the compass*, ie N, NE, E, SE, S, SW, W, NW, etc. (b) similar device for determining direction: *a radio compass.* **2** [C] (also **compasses** [pl]) V-shaped instrument with two legs joined by a hinge, used for drawing circles, measuring distances on a map or chart, etc: *a pair of compasses.* ⇨ illus. **3** [U] scope; range: *beyond the compass of the human mind* ○ *the compass of a singer's voice*, ie the range from the lowest to the highest note that he or she can reach.

compass card

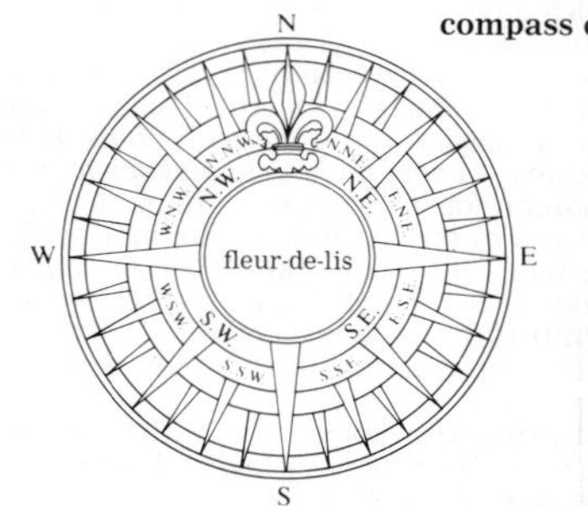

□ **ˈcompass card** card or disc marked with the 32 main points of the compass and attached to the compass needle. ⇨ illus.

ˌcompass ˈrose circular design marked with the 32 main points of the compass, often printed on maps.

compass² /ˈkʌmpəs/ *v* [Tn] (*arch*) = ENCOMPASS 2.

compassion /kəmˈpæʃn/ *n* [U] ~ (**for sb**) pity for the sufferings of others, making one want to help them: *be filled with compassion* ○ *a woman of great compassion* ○ *The plight of the refugees arouses our compassion.* ○ *Out of* (ie Because of) *compassion for her terrible suffering they allowed her to stay.* ○ *They took compassion on her children and offered them a home.*

▷ **compassionate** /kəmˈpæʃənət/ *adj* showing or feeling compassion. **compassionately** *adv.*

compassionate leave (*Brit*) leave²(1) granted (eg to a member of the armed forces) because of some special personal circumstance: *She was allowed compassionate leave from work to attend her father's funeral.*

compatible /kəmˈpætəbl/ *adj* ~ (**with sb/sth**) (**a**) (of people, ideas, arguments, principles, etc) suited; that can exist together: *The couple separated because they were not compatible.* ○ *driving a car at a speed compatible with safety*, ie at a safe speed. (**b**) (of equipment) that can be used together: *This printer is compatible with most microcomputers.*

▷ **compatibility** /kəmˌpætəˈbɪlətɪ/ *n* [U] ~ (**with sb/sth**); ~ (**between A and B**) state of being compatible.

compatibly /-əblɪ/ *adv.*

compatriot /kəmˈpætrɪət; *US* -ˈpeɪt-/ *n* person who was born in, or is a citizen of, the same country as another; fellow-countryman.

compeer /ˈkɒmpɪə(r)/ *n* (*fml*) person of equal status or ability: *be much respected by one's compeers.*

compel /kəmˈpel/ *v* (**-ll-**) **1** [Cn·t] (*fml*) make (sb) do sth; force: *We cannot compel you to (do it), but we think you should.* ○ *I was compelled to* (ie I had to) *acknowledge the force of his argument.* Cf IMPEL. **2** [Tn no passive] (*fml*) (**a**) get (sth) by force or pressure; make necessary: *You can compel obedience, but not affection.* ○ *Circumstances have compelled a change of plan.* (**b**) (not in the continuous tenses) (*fig*) inspire (sth) irresistibly: *His courage compels universal admiration.*

▷ **compelling** *adj* (**a**) extremely interesting and exciting, so that one has to pay attention: *a compelling novel, account, story, etc.* (**b**) that one must accept or agree with: *a compelling reason, argument, etc.* Cf COMPULSION.

compendious /kəmˈpendɪəs/ *adj* (*fml*) giving a lot of information briefly: *a compendious writer, handbook, catalogue.*

compendium /kəmˈpendɪəm/ *n* (*pl* **~s** or **-ia**) ~ (**of sth**) **1** brief but full account; summary: *This encyclopedia is truly a compendium of knowledge.* **2** (*Brit*) set of different board games sold in one box.

compensate /ˈkɒmpenseɪt/ *v* [Ipr, Tn, Tn·pr] ~ (**sb**) **for sth** give (sb) sth good to balance or lessen the bad effect of damage, loss, injury, etc; recompense: *Nothing can compensate for the loss of one's health.* ○ *The animal's good sense of smell compensates for its poor eyesight.* ○ *She was compensated by the insurance company for her injuries.*

▷ **compensatory** /ˌkɒmpenˈseɪtərɪ; *US* kəmˈpensətɔːrɪ/ *adj* compensating: *compensatory payments.*

compensation /ˌkɒmpenˈseɪʃn/ *n* ~ (**for sth**) (**a**) [U] compensating: *Compensation of injured workers has cost the company a lot.* (**b**) [U, C] thing given to compensate: *receive £5000 in compensation/by way of compensation/as a compensation for injury* ○ *My job is hard, but it has its compensations*, ie pleasant aspects that make it seem less bad.

compère /ˈkɒmpeə(r)/ *n* (*Brit*) person who introduces the performers in a variety programme or game show, esp on radio or television.

▷ **compère** *v* [Tn] (*Brit*) act as a compere for (a show).

compete /kəmˈpiːt/ *v* [I, Ipr, It] ~ (**against/with sb**) (**in sth**) (**for sth**) try to win sth by defeating others who are trying to do the same: *Several companies are competing (against/with each other) for the contract/to gain the contract.* ○ *a horse that has competed in the Grand National four times* ○ *We have limited funds and several competing claims, so it is hard to choose between them.*

competence /ˈkɒmpɪtəns/ *n* [U] **1** ~ (**for/as/in sth**); ~ (**in doing sth/to do sth**) being competent; ability: *No one doubts her competence as a teacher.* ○ *competence in solving problems.* **2** ~ (**to do sth**) (of a court, a judge, etc) legal authority: *matters within/beyond the competence of the court*, ie ones that it can/cannot legally deal with.

competent /ˈkɒmpɪtənt/ *adj* **1** ~ (**as/at/in sth**); ~ (**to do sth**) (of people) having the necessary ability, authority, skill, knowledge, etc: *a highly competent driver* ○ *competent at/in one's work* ○ *He's not competent to look after young children.* **2** quite good, but not excellent: *a competent piece of work* ○ *The novel may be a best seller, but it's no more than a competent piece of writing.* ▷ **competently** *adv.*

competition /ˌkɒmpəˈtɪʃn/ *n* **1** [C] event in which people compete; contest: *boxing, chess, beauty competitions* ○ *He came first in the poetry competition.* ⇨ Usage at SPORT. **2** [U] ~ (**between/with sb**) (**for sth**) competing; activity in which people compete: *Competition between bidders for this valuable painting has been keen.* ○ *We're in competition with* (ie competing against) *several other companies for the contract.* ○ *competition in nature*, eg between animals searching for food or between males wanting a mate. **3 the competition** [Gp] those competing against sb: *She had a chance to see the competition* (ie the other people who were trying to get the same job as she was) *before the interview.*

competitive /kəmˈpetətɪv/ *adj* **1** of or involving competition: *competitive examinations for government posts* ○ *competitive sports* ○ *the competitive spirit*, ie enjoying competition. **2** ~ (**with sb/sth**) able to do as well as or better than others: *Our firm is no longer competitive in world markets.* ○ *a shop offering competitive prices*, ie as low as in any other shop. **3** (of people) having a strong urge to win: *You have to be highly competitive to do well in sport nowadays.* ▷ **competitively** *adv*: *competitively priced goods.*

competitor /kəmˈpetɪtə(r)/ *n* person who competes: *The firm has better products than its competitors*, ie than rival firms. Cf CONTESTANT (CONTEST).

compile /kəmˈpaɪl/ *v* **1** [Tn, Tn·pr] (**a**) ~ **sth** (**for/from sth**) collect (information) and arrange it in a book, list, report, etc: *compiling statistics for a report on traffic accidents.* (**b**) ~ **sth** (**from sth**) produce (a book, list, report, etc) in this way: *The police have compiled a list of suspects.* ○ *a guidebook compiled from a variety of sources.* **2** [Tn] (*computing*) turn instructions in a high-level language into (information in a form that a particular computer can understand and act on).

▷ **compilation** /ˌkɒmpɪˈleɪʃn/ *n* (**a**) [U] compiling. (**b**) [C] thing that is compiled: *Her latest album is a compilation of all her best singles.*

compiler /kəmˈpaɪlə(r)/ *n* **1** person who compiles. **2** (*computing*) computer program that turns instructions in a high-level language into a form that the computer can understand and act on.

complacency /kəmˈpleɪsnsɪ/ (also **complacence** /-ˈpleɪsns/) *n* [U] ~ (**about sb/sth**) (*usu derog*) calm feeling of satisfaction with oneself, one's work, etc: *There's no room for complacency; we must continue to try to improve.*

complacent /kəmˈpleɪsnt/ *adj* ~ (**about sb/sth**) (*usu derog*) calmly satisfied with oneself, one's work, etc: *a complacent smile, manner, tone of voice* ○ *We must not be complacent about our achievements; there is still a lot to be done.* ▷ **complacently** *adv.*

complain /kəmˈpleɪn/ *v* **1** [I, Ipr, Tf, Dpr·f] ~ (**to sb**) (**about/at sth**) (*often derog*) say that one is dissatisfied, unhappy, etc: *You're always complaining!* ○ (*infml*) *'What was the weather like on your holiday?' 'Oh, I can't complain'*, ie It was as good as could be expected. ○ *She complained to me about his rudeness.* ○ *He complained (to the waiter) that his meal was cold.* **2** (phr v) **complain of sth** report (a pain, etc): *The patient is complaining of acute earache.* ▷ **complainingly** *adv*: *'Why me?' he asked complainingly.*

complainant /kəmˈpleɪnənt/ *n* (*law*) = PLAINTIFF.

complaint /kəmˈpleɪnt/ *n* **1** [U] complaining: *The road-works caused much complaint among local residents.* ○ *You have no cause/grounds for complaint.* **2** [C] ~ (**about/of sth**); ~ (**that...**) (**a**) reason for dissatisfaction: *I have a number of complaints about the hotel room you've given me.* (**b**) statement of dissatisfaction: *She lodged a complaint about the noise.* ○ *submit a formal complaint* ○ *We've received a lot of complaints of bad workmanship.* ○ *Management ignored our complaints that washing facilities were inadequate.* ○ [attrib] *follow the complaints procedure.* **3** [C] (*sometimes euph*) illness; disease: *a heart complaint* ○ *childhood complaints*, ie illnesses common among children.

complaisance /kəmˈpleɪzəns/ *n* [U] (*fml*) willingness to do what pleases others.

▷ **complaisant** /-zənt/ *adj* (*fml*) ready to please; obliging: *a complaisant husband.*

complement /ˈkɒmplɪmənt/ *n* **1** ~ (**to sth**) thing that goes well or suitably with sth else, or makes it complete: *Rice makes an excellent complement to a curry dish.* **2** the complete number or quantity needed or allowed: *We've taken on our full complement of new trainees for this year.* ○ *the ship's complement*, ie all the officers and other sailors. **3** (*grammar*) word(s), esp adjectives and nouns, used after linking verbs such as *be* and *become*, and describing the subject of the verb: *In the sentence 'I'm angry', 'angry' is the complement.*

▷ **complement** *v* [Tn] combine well (and often contrastingly) with (sth) to form a whole: *His business skill complements her flair for design.* Cf COMPLIMENT.

complementary /ˌkɒmplɪˈmentrɪ/ *adj* ~ (**to sth**) combining well to form a balanced whole: *They have complementary personalities*, ie Each has qualities which the other lacks. ○ *His personality is complementary to hers.* **complementarity** /ˌkɒmplɪmenˈtærətɪ/ *n* [U]. **ˌcomplementary ˈangle** either of two angles which together make 90°. **ˌcomplementary ˈcolour** colour of light which when combined with a given colour makes white light (eg blue with yellow).

complete¹ /kəmˈpliːt/ *adj* **1** having all its parts; whole: *a complete set, collection, etc* ○ *a complete edition of Shakespeare's works*, ie one that includes all of them ○ *a radio complete with a carrying case*, ie having it as an additional feature. **2** [pred] finished; ended: *When will the building work be complete?* **3** [usu attrib] thorough; in every way; total: *a complete stranger, idiot, nonentity* ○ *It was a complete surprise to me.*

▷ **completely** *adv* wholly; totally: *completely innocent, happy, successful.*

completeness *n* [U].

complete² /kəmˈpliːt/ *v* [Tn] **1** (**a**) make (sth) whole or perfect: *I only need one volume to complete my set of Dickens's novels.* ○ *A few words of praise from her would have completed his happiness.* (**b**) bring (sth) to an end; finish: *When will the railway be completed?* **2** fill in (a form, etc): *Complete your application in ink.*

completion /kəmˈpliːʃn/ *n* [U] **1** (**a**) action of completing: *Completion of the building work is taking longer than expected.* (**b**) state of being complete: *The film is nearing completion.* ○ [attrib] *its completion date.* **2** (*commerce*) formal completing of a contract of sale: *You may move into the house on completion.*

complex¹ /ˈkɒmpleks; *US* kəmˈpleks/ *adj* (**a**) made up of (usu several) closely connected parts: *a complex system, network, etc* ○ (*grammar*) *a complex sentence*, ie one containing subordinate clauses. (**b**) difficult to understand or explain because there are many different parts: *a complex argument, theory, subject, etc.* Cf COMPLICATED (COMPLICATE).

▷ **complexity** /kəmˈpleksətɪ/ *n* (**a**) [U] state of

being complex: *a problem of great complexity.* (**b**) [C] complex thing: *the complexities of higher mathematics.*

□ ˌ**complex ˈnumber** (*mathematics*) number that is made up of a real number and the product of a real and an imaginary number.

complex[2] /ˈkɒmpleks/ *n* **1** group of connected or similar things: *a big industrial complex*, ie a site with factories, etc ○ *a sports/leisure complex*, ie a set of buildings or facilities for sports/leisure. **2** (**a**) (*psychology*) abnormal mental state resulting from past experience or suppressed desires: *a persecution complex* ○ *an inferiority complex.* (**b**) (*infml*) obsessive concern or fear: *He has a complex about his weight/has a weight complex.*

complexion /kəmˈplekʃn/ *n* **1** natural colour and appearance of the skin of the face: *a good, dark, fair, sallow, etc complexion.* **2** (usu *sing*) general character or aspect of sth: *Her resignation puts a different complexion on things*, ie changes one's view of the affair. ○ *a victory that changed the complexion of the war*, ie made the probable result different, gave hope of an early end, etc.

compliance /kəmˈplaɪəns/ *n* [U] ~ (**with sth**) **1** action in accordance with a request or command; obedience: *Compliance (with the rules) is expected of all members.* ○ *In compliance with your wishes* (ie As you have requested) *we have withdrawn our suggestion.* **2** (*usu derog*) tendency to agree (too readily) to do what others want. Cf COMPLY.

compliant /kəmˈplaɪənt/ *adj* ~ (**with sb/sth**) (*usu derog*) (too) willing to comply (with other people, with rules, etc): *The Government, compliant as ever, gave in to their demands.*

complicate /ˈkɒmplɪkeɪt/ *v* [Tn] make (sth) more difficult to do, understand or deal with: *Her refusal to help complicates matters.*

▷ **complicated** *adj* (**a**) (*often derog*) made up of many interconnected parts: *complicated wiring, machinery* ○ *a complicated diagram.* (**b**) difficult to understand or explain because there are many different parts: *a complicated situation, process, relationship, plot* ○ *He's married to her, and she's in love with his brother-in-law, and...oh, it's too complicated to explain!* Cf COMPLEX[1].

complication /ˌkɒmplɪˈkeɪʃn/ *n* **1** [U] state of being complex, intricate or difficult; involved condition: *I have enough complication in my life without having to look after your sick pets!* **2** [C] thing that makes a situation more complex or difficult: *A further complication was Fred's refusal to travel by air.* **3 complications** [pl] (*medical*) new illness, or new development of an illness, that makes treatment more difficult: *Complications set in, and the patient died.*

complicity /kəmˈplɪsətɪ/ *n* [U] ~ (**in sth**) action of taking part with another person (in a crime or some other wrongdoing); shared responsibility: *He was suspected of complicity in her murder.*

compliment /ˈkɒmplɪmənt/ *n* **1** [C] ~ (**on sth**) expression of praise, admiration, approval, etc: *One likes to hear compliments on one's appearance.* ○ *She paid me a very charming compliment on my paintings*, ie praised them. ○ (*fig*) *These beautiful flowers are a compliment to the gardener's skill*, ie show how skilful he is. **2 compliments** [pl] (*fml*) greetings, usu as part of a message: *My compliments to your wife*, ie Please give her a greeting from me. ○ *Compliments of the season*, eg said at Christmas or the New Year. ○ *The flowers are with the compliments of* (ie are a gift from) *the management.* **3** (idm) **a left-handed compliment** ⇨ LEFT-HANDED (LEFT[2]).

▷ **compliment** /ˈkɒmplɪment/ *v* [Tn, Tn·pr] ~ **sb** (**on sth**) express praise or admiration of sb: *I complimented her on her skilful performance.* Cf COMPLEMENT.

□ ˈ**compliment slip** small piece of paper, usu with the words 'with compliments' on it, sent with a free sample, gift, etc.

complimentary /ˌkɒmplɪˈmentrɪ/ *adj* **1** expressing admiration, praise, etc: *a complimentary remark, review, pat on the back* ○ *She was highly complimentary about my paintings.* **2** given free of charge by the producer or owner: *a complimentary seat, ticket, copy of a book.*

compline /ˈkɒmplɪn/ *n* [U] (in the Roman Catholic and High Anglican church) last service of the day: *attend compline.*

comply /kəmˈplaɪ/ *v* (*pt, pp* **complied**) [I, Ipr] ~ (**with sth**) do as one is requested, commanded, etc; obey: *She was told to pay the fine, but refused to comply.* ○ *The rules must be complied with*, ie obeyed. Cf COMPLIANCE.

component /kəmˈpəʊnənt/ *n* (**a**) any of the parts of which sth is made: *the components of an engine, a camera, etc* ○ *a factory supplying components for the car industry* ○ (*fig*) *Surprise is an essential component of my plan.* (**b**) (*chemistry*) single type of chemical in a mixture: *A mixture of salt dissolved in water involves two components.*

▷ **component** *adj* [attrib] being one of the parts of a whole: *analysing the component parts of a sentence.*

comport /kəmˈpɔːt/ *v* [Tn·pr] ~ **oneself with sth** (*fml*) conduct oneself in the specified way; behave: *comport oneself with dignity/in a dignified manner.*

▷ **comportment** *n* [U] (*fml*) behaviour.

compose /kəmˈpəʊz/ *v* **1** (**a**) [I, Tn] write (music, opera, etc): *She began to compose (songs) at an early age.* (**b**) [Tn] (*fml*) write (a poem, speech, etc): *I'm composing a formal reply to the letter.* **2** [Tn no passive] (not in the continuous tenses) (*fml*) (of parts or elements of sth) form (a whole); constitute: *the short scenes that compose the play.* ⇨ Usage at COMPRISE. **3** [Tn no passive] bring (oneself/sth) under control; calm: *His mind was in such a whirl that he could hardly compose his thoughts.* ○ *Please compose yourself; there's no need to get excited!* Cf COMPOSURE. **4** [Tn] put (printing type) in order, to form words, paragraphs, pages, etc. Cf COMPOSITOR.

▷ **composed** *adj* **1** [pred] ~ **of sth** made up or formed from sth: *Water is composed of hydrogen and oxygen.* ○ *The committee was composed mainly of teachers and parents.* ⇨ Usage at COMPRISE. **2** with one's feelings under control; calm: *a composed person, manner, look.* **composedly** /kəmˈpəʊzɪdlɪ/ *adv*: *She talked composedly to reporters about her terrible ordeal.*

composer /kəmˈpəʊzə(r)/ *n* person who composes (esp music).

composite /ˈkɒmpəzɪt/ *n, adj* [attrib] (thing) made up of different parts or materials: *The play is a composite of reality and fiction.* ○ *a composite substance* ○ *a composite illustration*, ie one made by putting together two or more separate pictures.

composition /ˌkɒmpəˈzɪʃn/ *n* **1** [C] thing composed, eg a piece of music, a poem or a book: *'Swan Lake' is one of Tchaikovsky's best-known compositions.* **2** [U] (**a**) action of composing sth, eg a piece of music or writing, type for printing, etc: *He played a piano sonata of his own composition*, ie that he himself had composed. (**b**) art of composing music: *studying composition at music school.* **3** [C] short piece of non-fictional writing done as a school or college exercise; essay. **4** [U] the parts of which sth is made; make-up: *the composition of the soil* ○ (*fig*) *He has a touch of madness in his composition*, ie He is a little mad. **5** [U] arrangement of elements in a painting, photograph, etc: *Her drawing is competent, but her composition is poor.* **6** [C, U] substance, esp an artificial one, composed of more than one material: *a composition used as flooring material* ○ [attrib] *a composition floor.*

compositor /kəmˈpɒzɪtə(r)/ *n* skilled person who composes (COMPOSE 4) type for printing.

compos mentis /ˌkɒmpəs ˈmentɪs/ (also **compos**) *adj* [pred] (*Latin infml or joc*) having control of one's mind; sane: *He's not quite compos mentis*, ie He's a little mad.

compost /ˈkɒmpɒst/ *n* [U, C] mixture of decayed organic matter, manure, etc added to soil to improve the growth of plants: [attrib] *a* ˈ*compost heap*, eg in a garden, for producing compost quickly.

▷ **compost** *v* [Tn] (**a**) make (sth) into compost: *composting the kitchen waste.* (**b**) put compost on or in (sth): *compost the flower-beds.*

composure /kəmˈpəʊʒə(r)/ *n* [U] state of being calm in mind or behaviour: *keep/lose/regain one's composure* ○ *He showed great composure in a difficult situation.* Cf COMPOSE 3.

compote /ˈkɒmpɒt; *US* ˈkɒmpəʊt/ *n* [C, U] (**a**) dish of sweetened stewed fruit. (**b**) (*dated*) dish of fruit cooked in syrup.

compound[1] /ˈkɒmpaʊnd/ *n* **1** (**a**) thing made up of two or more separate things combined together. (**b**) substance consisting of two or more elements chemically combined: *Common salt is a compound of sodium and chlorine.* Cf ELEMENT 3, MIXTURE 3. **2** (*grammar*) noun, adjective, etc composed of two or more words or parts of words (written as one or more words, or joined by a hyphen): *'Bus conductor', 'dark-haired' and 'policeman' are compounds.* ▷ **compound** *adj* [attrib]: *compound nouns, adjectives, etc.*

□ ˌ**compound** ˈ**eye** eye (esp in insects) made up of a large number of separate cells that are sensitive to light.

ˌ**compound** ˈ**fracture** breaking of a bone in which part of the bone comes through the skin.

ˌ**compound** ˈ**interest** interest paid on both the original capital and the interest added to it. Cf SIMPLE INTEREST (SIMPLE).

ˌ**compound** ˈ**sentence** (*grammar*) sentence containing two or more co-ordinate clauses (linked by *and, but*, etc).

compound[2] /kəmˈpaʊnd/ *v* **1** (**a**) [Tn] mix (sth) together: *the vat in which the chemicals are compounded.* (**b**) [usu passive: Tn, Tn·pr] ~ **sth** (**of/from sth**) make sth by mixing: *a medicine compounded of* (ie made of) *herbs* ○ (*fig*) *Her character was compounded in equal parts of meanness and generosity.* **2** [Tn] make (sth bad) worse by causing further harm: *Initial planning errors were compounded by carelessness in carrying the plan out.* **3** [I, Ipr, Tn] ~ (**with sb**) (**for sth**) (*commerce*) reach an agreement (about sth); settle (a debt, etc): *He compounded with his creditors for a postponement of payment.* **4** [Tn] (*law*) agree not to reveal (a crime), esp in return for payment; condone: *guilty of compounding a felony.*

compound[3] /ˈkɒmpaʊnd/ *n* (**a**) area enclosed by buildings, esp in a military camp or a prison camp. (**b**) (in India, China, etc) area enclosed by a fence, etc, in which a house or factory stands.

comprehend /ˌkɒmprɪˈhend/ *v* **1** [Tn, Tf, Tw] understand (sth) fully: *failing to comprehend the full seriousness of the situation* ○ *I cannot comprehend how you could have been so stupid.* **2** [Tn] (*fml*) include (sth).

comprehensible /ˌkɒmprɪˈhensəbl/ *adj* ~ (**to sb**) that can be understood fully: *a book that is comprehensible only to specialists.* ▷ **comprehensibility** /ˌkɒmprɪˌhensəˈbɪlətɪ/ *n* [U].

comprehension /ˌkɒmprɪˈhenʃn/ *n* **1** [U] (power of) understanding: *a problem above/beyond sb's comprehension*, ie one that he cannot understand. **2** [U, C] exercise aimed at improving or testing one's understanding of a language (written or spoken): *a French comprehension* ○ [attrib] *a compreˈhension test.*

comprehensive /ˌkɒmprɪˈhensɪv/ *adj* **1** that includes (nearly) everything: *a comprehensive description, account, report, etc* ○ *She has a comprehensive grasp of the subject.* **2** (*Brit*) (of education) for pupils of all abilities in the same school.

▷ **comprehensive** *n* (*Brit infml*) comprehensive school.

comprehensively *adv*: *Our football team was comprehensively* (ie thoroughly) *defeated.*

comprehensiveness *n* [U].

□ ˌ**comprehensive in**ˈ**surance** insurance on motor vehicles that covers most risks, including fire, theft, damage and risks to the driver and others.

compreˈhensive school (*Brit*) large secondary school at which children of all abilities are taught.

compress[1] /kəmˈpres/ *v* [Tn, Tn·pr] ~ **sth** (**into sth**) **1** press sth together; force sth into a small(er) space: *compressed air*, ie at higher than atmospheric pressure ○ *compressing straw into blocks for burning.* **2** express (ideas, etc) in a shorter form; condense: *compress an argument into just a few sentences* ○ *The film compresses several years into half an hour.*

▷ **compression** /kəmˈpreʃn/ *n* [U] **1** compressing or being compressed: *the compression of gas.* **2** process of reducing the volume of the fuel mixture of an internal combustion engine, to increase its pressure before it is ignited.

compressor /kəmˈpresə(r)/ *n* (part of a) machine that compresses air or other gases.

compress² /ˈkɒmpres/ *n* pad or cloth pressed onto a part of the body to stop bleeding, reduce fever, etc: *a cold/hot compress.*

comprise /kəmˈpraɪz/ *v* [Tn] (not in the continuous tenses) **(a)** have as parts or members; be made up of: *a committee comprising people of widely differing views.* **(b)** be the parts or members of (sth); together form: *Two small boys and a dog comprised the street entertainer's only audience.*

NOTE ON USAGE: Note the use of **comprise.** It can mean: **1 consist of** or **be composed of** ie be formed of: *The British Parliament comprises/consists of/is composed of the House of Commons and the House of Lords.* **2 compose** or **constitute**, ie form: *The House of Commons and the House of Lords comprise/compose/constitute the British Parliament.* This use of **comprise** is less common and careful speakers avoid **be comprised of** in sense 1.

compromise /ˈkɒmprəmaɪz/ *n* **(a)** [U] giving up of certain demands by each side in a dispute, so that an agreement may be reached which satisfies both to some extent: *Most wage claims are settled by compromise.* ○ [attrib] *work out a compromise agreement.* **(b)** [C] ~ **(between/on sth)** settlement reached in this way: *Can the two sides reach a compromise?* ○ *The final proposals were a rather unsuccessful compromise between the need for profitability and the demands of local conservationists.*

▷ **compromise** *v* **1** [I, Ipr] ~ **(on sth)** settle a dispute, etc by making a compromise: *I wanted to go to Greece, and my wife wanted to go to Spain, so we compromised on* (ie agreed to go to) *Italy.* **2** [Tn] bring (sth/sb/oneself) into danger or under suspicion by foolish behaviour: *He has irretrievably compromised himself by accepting money from them.* ○ *He was photographed in compromising situations* (ie ones that showed him behaving immorally) *with a call-girl.* **3** [Tn] modify (sth); weaken: *She refused to compromise her principles*, ie insisted on keeping to them.

Compton-Burnett /ˌkʌmtən ˈbɜːnɪt/ Dame Ivy (1884-1969), English novelist. Although she wrote mainly between the two world wars, her novels are about repressed Victorian families with a domineering parent or grandparent, and the crimes that take place in them.

compulsion /kəmˈpʌlʃn/ *n* ~ **(to do sth) 1** [U] compelling or being compelled: *I refuse to act under compulsion*, ie because I am forced to. ○ *You need feel under no compulsion to accept*, ie do not have to accept. **2** [C] urge (esp to behave in an irrational way) that one cannot resist: *a compulsion to destroy things.*

compulsive /kəmˈpʌlsɪv/ *adj* **1** extremely interesting; fascinating: *a compulsive novel about politics.* **2 (a)** caused by an obsession: *compulsive gambling, eating, etc.* **(b)** (of people) forced to do sth by an obsession: *a compulsive eater, TV viewer, gambler* ○ *He's a compulsive liar*, ie He lies repeatedly. ▷ **compulsively** *adv*: *a compulsively readable book.*

compulsory /kəmˈpʌlsərɪ/ *adj* that must be done; required by the rules, etc; obligatory: *Is military service compulsory in your country?* ○ *Is English a compulsory subject?* ▷ **compulsorily** /kəmˈpʌlsərəlɪ/ *adv.*

□ **comˌpulsory ˈpurchase** (*Brit*) (*US* **eminent domain**) right of purchase by the government or a local authority of land which is needed for building, etc, and by which the owner is compelled to sell.

compunction /kəmˈpʌŋkʃn/ *n* [U] ~ **(about doing sth)** (*fml*) (usu in negative sentences) feeling of guilt or regret for one's action: *She kept us waiting without the slightest compunction.* ○ *If I could find the people responsible, I would have no compunction about telling the police.*

computation /ˌkɒmpjuːˈteɪʃn/ *n* **(a)** [C, U] (*fml*) (act of) computing; calculation: *A quick computation revealed that we would not make a profit.* ○ *Addition and division are forms of computation.* ○ *It will cost £5000 at the lowest computation.* **(b)** [U] use of a computer for calculation.

▷ **computational** *adj* [usu attrib] using computers: *computational linguistics.*

compute /kəmˈpjuːt/ *v* [Tn, Tn·pr] ~ **sth (at sth) 1** calculate sth with a computer: *Scientists have computed the probable course of the rocket.* **2** (*fml*) calculate sth; work sth out: *He computed his losses at £5000.*

▷ **computing** *n* [U] operation of computers: [attrib] *a computing course.*

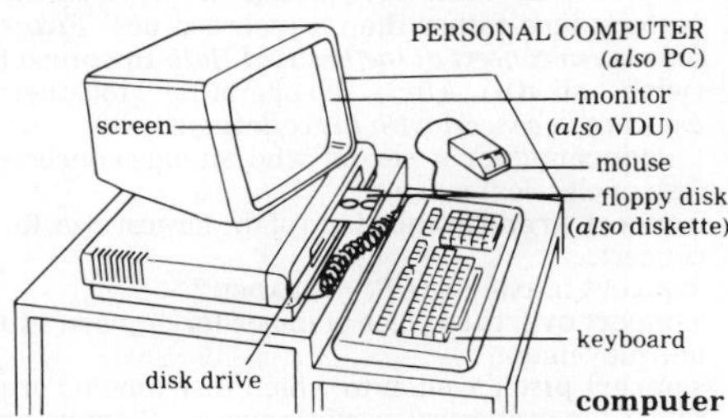

computer

computer /kəmˈpjuːtə(r)/ *n* electronic device for storing and analysing information fed into it, making calculations, or controlling machinery automatically. The principle of a computer is that it can carry out complex tasks very quickly once these are broken down into long series of simple instructions expressed in binary code. This is done partly by the central processing unit (part of the hardware) and partly by software designed to do particular tasks. When it is not being processed, data can be stored temporarily in the computer's memory or permanently on hard or floppy disks, tape, CD-ROM, etc. Data is inputted (ie put in) by typing at a keyboard, by putting in a disk, or by other input devices such as scanners or bar code readers. When a job has been done, other data can be output to a screen, a printer or another computer: *Is the information available on the computer?* ○ *The accounts are processed by computer.* ○ *a digital computer* ○ [attrib] *a computer programmer.* ⇨ illus.

▷ **computerize, -ise** /-təraɪz/ *v* [Tn] **(a)** provide a computer to do the work of or for (sth): *The accounts section has been completely computerized.* **(b)** store (information) in a computer: *The firm has computerized its records.* **computerization, -isation** /kəmˌpjuːtəraɪˈzeɪʃn; *US* -rɪˈz-/ *n* [U].

comrade /ˈkɒmreɪd; *US* -ræd/ *n* **1** fellow member of a trade union, or of a socialist or communist political party, etc: *We must fight for our rights, comrades!* **2** (*dated*) trusted companion who shares one's activities: *We were comrades in the war.* ○ [attrib] *an old comrades association*, ie of people who had been in the army, etc together. ▷ **comradely** /ˈkɒmreɪdlɪ/ *adj*: *some comradely advice.* **comradeship** /ˈkɒmreɪdʃɪp/ *n* [U].

□ **ˌcomrade-in-ˈarms** *n* (*pl* **ˌcomrades-in-ˈarms**) fellow soldier: (*fig*) *They'd long been comrades-in-arms in the Labour Party.*

comsat /ˈkɒmsæt/ *n* satellite(1b) used for communication.

Comus /ˈkəʊməs/ Roman god of revelry.

con¹ /kɒn/ *n* [sing] (*sl*) instance of cheating sb; confidence trick: *This so-called bargain is just a con!* ○ [attrib] *a con trick* ○ *He's a real con artist/merchant*, ie swindler.

▷ **con** *v* (-nn-) [Tn, Tn·pr] ~ **sb (into doing sth/out of sth)** (*infml*) swindle or persuade sb after gaining his trust: *You can't con me — you're not really ill!* ○ *I was conned into buying a useless car.* ○ *She conned me out of £100.*

□ **con man** /ˈkɒn mæn/ (*pl* **con men** /ˈkɒn men/) (*infml*) person who swindles others into giving him money, etc.

con² /kɒn/ *n* (*sl*) = CONVICT *n.*

con³ /kɒn/ *n* (idm) **the pros and cons** ⇨ PRO¹.

Conan Doyle /ˌkəʊnən ˈdɔɪl/ ⇨ DOYLE.

concatenation /kənˌkætɪˈneɪʃn/ *n* ~ **(of sth)** (*fml*) series of things or events linked together: *an unfortunate concatenation of mishaps.*

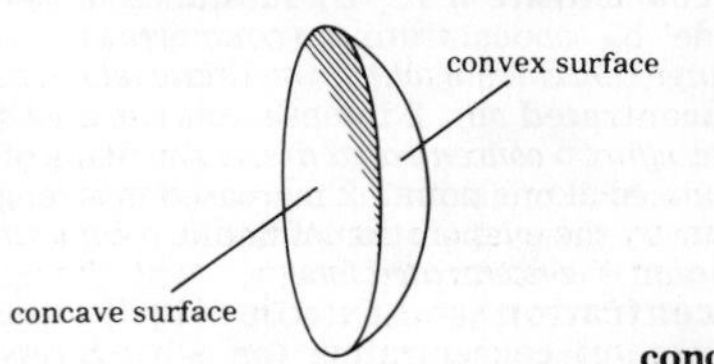

concave

concave /ˈkɒŋkeɪv/ *adj* (of an outline or a surface) curved inwards like the inner surface of a sphere or ball. ⇨ illus. Cf CONVEX.

▷ **concavity** /ˌkɒnˈkævətɪ/ *n* **(a)** [U] quality of being concave. **(b)** [C] concave surface.

conceal /kənˈsiːl/ *v* [Tn, Tn·pr] ~ **sth/sb (from sb/sth)** keep sth/sb from being seen or known about; hide sth/sb: *a tape recorder concealed in a drawer* ○ *He tried to conceal his heavy drinking from his family.* ○ *There's a concealed entrance just round the corner.* ○ *He spoke with ill-concealed contempt for his audience.*

▷ **concealment** *n* [U] action of concealing or state of being concealed: *Stay in concealment until the danger has passed.*

concede /kənˈsiːd/ *v* **1** [Tn, Tf, Dn·n, Dn·pr] ~ **sth (to sb)** admit that sth is true, valid, proper, etc: *concede a point (to sb) in an argument* ○ *concede defeat*, ie admit that one has lost ○ *I was forced to concede that she might be right.* ○ *It's certainly big, I'll concede you that.* **2** [Tn, Dn·pr] ~ **sth (to sb)** give sth away; allow (sb else) to have sth: *We cannot concede any of our territory*, ie allow another country to have it. ○ *England conceded a goal (to their opponents) in the first minute.* **3** [I, Tn] admit that one has lost (a game, an election, etc): *The chess-player conceded (the game) when he saw that his position was hopeless.* Cf CONCESSION 1.

conceit /kənˈsiːt/ *n* **1** [U] excessive pride in oneself or in one's powers, abilities, etc: *The conceit of the man — comparing his own work with Picasso's!* **2** [C] (*fml*) cleverly-phrased witty expression (esp in a work of literature).

▷ **conceited** *adj* full of conceit: *insufferably conceited.* **conceitedly** /-ɪdlɪ/ *adv.*

conceive /kənˈsiːv/ *v* **1** [I, Tn] become pregnant with (a child): *She was told she couldn't conceive.* ○ *The child was conceived on the night of their wedding.* **2** [Ipr, Tn, Tf, Tw, Cn·n/a] ~ **of sth**; ~ **sth (as sth)** form (an idea, a plan, etc) in the mind; imagine sth: *It was then that I conceived the notion of running away.* ○ *I cannot conceive* (ie do not believe) *that he would wish to harm us.* ○ *I cannot conceive why you allowed the child to go alone*, ie I think you were very foolish to allow it. ○ *The ancients conceived (of) the world as (being) flat*, ie They thought it was flat.

▷ **conceivable** /-əbl/ *adj* that can be conceived or believed; imaginable: *It is hardly conceivable (to me) that she should do such a thing.* ○ *We tried it in every conceivable combination.* **conceivably** /-əblɪ/ *adv*: *He couldn't conceivably have* (ie I don't believe he could have) *meant what he said.*

concentrate /ˈkɒnsntreɪt/ *v* **1 (a)** [I, Ipr, Tn, Tn·pr] ~ **(sth) (on sth/doing sth)** focus (one's attention, effort, etc) exclusively and intensely on sth, not thinking about other less important things: *I can't concentrate (on my studies) with all that noise going on.* ○ *We must concentrate our efforts on improving education.* **(b)** [Ipr] ~ **on sth** do one particular thing and no other: *Having failed* *my French exams, I decided to concentrate on science subjects.* ○ *a firm which concentrates on the European market.* **2** [Ipr, Tn·pr] come or bring together at one place: *Birds concentrate (in places) where food is abundant.* ○ *Troops are concentrating south of the river.* ○ *The Government's plan is to concentrate new industries in areas of high unemployment.* **3** [Tn] increase the strength of (a substance or solution) by reducing its volume (eg by boiling it). **4** (idm) **ˌconcentrate the/one's ˈmind** make sb consider sth urgently and seriously: *The threat of going bankrupt is very unpleasant but it certainly concentrates the mind.*

▷ **concentrate** *n* [C, U] substance or solution made by concentrating (CONCENTRATE 3): *an orange concentrate which you dilute with water.*

concentrated *adj* **1** intense: *concentrated study, hate, effort* ○ *concentrated fire,* ie the firing of guns all aimed at one point. **2** increased in strength or value by the evaporation of liquid: *a concentrated solution* ○ *concentrated food.*

concentration /ˌkɒnsnˈtreɪʃn/ *n* **1** [U] ~ **(on sth)** (power of) concentrating (on sth): *Stress and tiredness often result in a lack of concentration.* ○ *a book that requires great concentration* ○ *I found it hard to keep my concentration with such a noise going on.* **2** [C] ~ **(of sth)** grouping of people or things: *concentrations of enemy troops, industrial buildings.*

□ **concenˈtration camp** (esp in Nazi Germany) prison consisting usu of a set of buildings inside a fence, where political prisoners, prisoners of war, etc were kept in very bad conditions.

concentric /kənˈsentrɪk/ *adj* ~ **(with sth)** (of circles) having the same centre: *concentric rings.* Cf ECCENTRIC 2.

concept /ˈkɒnsept/ *n* ~ **(of sth/that...)** idea underlying sth; general notion: *the concept of freedom, meaning* ○ *He can't grasp the basic concepts of mathematics.* ○ *She seemed unfamiliar with the concept that everyone should have an equal opportunity.*

▷ **conceptual** /kənˈseptʃʊəl/ *adj* of or based on concepts. **conceptualism** /kənˈseptʃʊəlɪzəm/ *n* [U] (*philosophy*) belief that universals exist, but only as mental concepts. **conceptualize, -ise** /-tʃʊəlaɪz/ *v* [I, Tn] form a mental concept of (sth); imagine: *It is hard to conceptualize thought without language.*

conception /kənˈsepʃn/ *n* **1** [U, C] conceiving (CONCEIVE 1) or being conceived: *the moment of conception* ○ *an unplanned conception.* **2** (**a**) [U] thinking of (an idea or a plan): *The plan, brilliant in its conception, failed because of inadequate preparation.* (**b**) [C] ~ **(of sb/sth/that...)** idea, plan or intention: *The new play is a brilliant conception.* ○ *I have no conception of* (ie do not know) *what you mean.*

concern[1] /kənˈsɜːn/ *v* **1** [Tn] (**a**) be the business of (sb); be important to; affect: *Don't interfere in what doesn't concern you.* ○ *The loss was a tragedy for all concerned,* ie all those affected by it. ○ *Where the children are concerned...,* ie In matters where one must think of them... ○ *To whom it may concern...,* eg at the beginning of a public notice or a testimonial of sb's character, ability, etc. (**b**) be about (sth); have as a subject: *a report that concerns drug abuse.* **2** [Tn·pr] ~ **oneself with/in/about sth** be busy with sth; interest oneself in sth: *There's no need to concern yourself with this matter; we're dealing with it.* **3** [Tn] worry (sb); trouble; bother: *Our losses are beginning to concern me.* **4** (idm) **as/so far as sb/sth is concerned** ⇨ FAR[2]. **be concerned in sth** have some connection with or responsibility for sth: *He was concerned in the crime.* **be concerned to do sth** have it as one's business to do sth. **be concerned with sth** be about sth: *Her latest documentary is concerned with youth unemployment.*

▷ **concerned** *adj* ~ **(about/for sth/that...)** worried; troubled: *Concerned parents held a meeting.* ○ *We're all concerned for her safety.* ○ *I'm concerned that they may have got lost.* **concernedly** /-ˈsɜːnɪdlɪ/ *adv.*

concerning *prep* about (sb/sth): *a letter concerning your complaint.*

concern[2] /kənˈsɜːn/ *n* **1** (**a**) [U] ~ **(for/about/over sth/sb)**; ~ **(that...)** worry; anxiety: *There is no cause for concern.* ○ *There is now considerable concern for their safety.* ○ *public concern about corruption* ○ *There is growing concern that they may have been killed.* (**b**) [C] cause of anxiety: *Our main concern is that they are not receiving enough help.* **2** [C] thing that is important or interesting to sb: *What are your main concerns as a writer?* ○ *It's no concern of mine,* ie I am not involved in it or I have no responsibility for it. ○ *What concern is it of yours?* ie Why do you take an interest in it or interfere with it? **3** [C] company; business: *a huge industrial concern* ○ *Our little corner shop is no longer a paying concern,* ie is no longer profitable. **4** [C] ~ **(in sth)** share: *He has a concern in* (ie is a part-owner of) *the business.* **5** (idm) **a going concern** ⇨ GOING.

concert /ˈkɒnsət/ *n* **1** musical entertainment given in public by one or more performers: *an orchestral concert* ○ *give a concert for charity* ○ [attrib] *a concert pianist, hall, performance.* Cf RECITAL. **2** (idm) **in ˈconcert** giving a live public performance rather than a recorded one: *Frank Sinatra in concert at the Festival Hall.* **in concert (with sb/sth)** (*fml*) co-operating together: *working in concert with his colleagues.*

□ **ˈconcert-goer** *n* person who attends concerts (esp of classical music).

ˌconcert ˈgrand grand piano of the largest size, for concerts.

ˈconcert-master *n* (*US*) = LEADER 2.

ˈconcert overture piece of music for orchestra in one movement.

ˈconcert pitch 1 pitch to which instruments are tuned for orchestral performances. **2** (idm) **at concert pitch** in a state of full efficiency or readiness.

concerted /kənˈsɜːtɪd/ *adj* [usu attrib] arranged or done in co-operation: *a concerted effort, attack, campaign* ○ *concerted action by several police forces.*

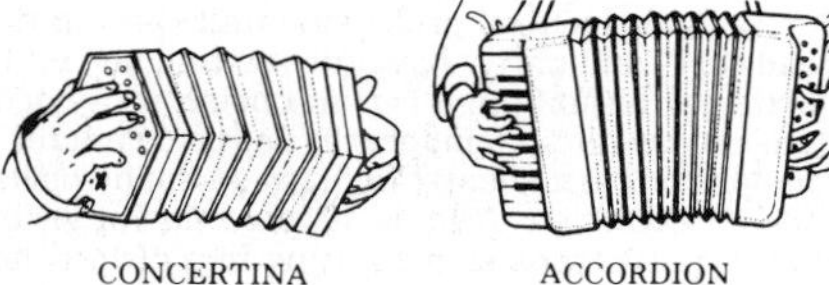

CONCERTINA ACCORDION

concertina /ˌkɒnsəˈtiːnə/ *n* musical instrument like a small accordion, consisting of a closed pleated tube, held in the hands and played by pressing the ends together to force air past reeds (REED 2). ⇨ illus.

▷ **concertina** *v* (*pt, pp* **concertinaed**, *pres p* **concertinaing**) [I] fold up (as if) by being pressed together from each end: *The lorry had concertinaed after crashing into the tree.*

concerto /kənˈtʃeətəʊ, -ˈtʃɜːt-/ *n* (*pl* ~**s**) musical composition for one or more solo instruments and an orchestra: *a ˈpiano concerto* ○ *a concerto for two violins.*

□ **conˌcerto ˈgrosso** /ˈgrɒsəʊ; *US* ˈgrəʊsəʊ/ type of concerto, popular esp in the 17th and 18th centuries, for a small group of soloists playing with the rest of the orchestra.

concession /kənˈseʃn/ *n* **1** ~ **(to sb/sth)** (**a**) [U] conceding: *There is a call for the concession of certain rights.* (**b**) [C] thing granted or yielded, esp after discussion, an argument, etc: *Employers made concessions to the workers in negotiations.* ○ *As a concession to her inexperience they allowed her to have some help.* Cf CONCEDE. **2** [C] price reduction for certain categories of people: *special concessions on all bus fares for old people.* **3** [C] ~ **(to do sth)** right given or sold to sb by the owner(s) of sth, allowing him to use or operate it: *oil/mining concessions,* ie allowing oil or minerals to be extracted from the ground ○ *a concession to drill for oil.*

▷ **concessionary** /kənˈseʃənərɪ; *US* -nerɪ/ *adj* involving a concession(2): *concessionary rates/prices.*

concessionaire /kənˌseʃəˈneə(r)/ *n* person who has been granted a concession(3), esp for the use of land or for trading.

concessive /kənˈsesɪv/ *adj* (*grammar*) expressing concession(1): *a concessive clause,* eg one introduced by *as, although* or *even if*, indicating a contrast with the main clause.

conch /kɒntʃ/ *n* (**a**) shellfish with a large spiral shell. (**b**) shell of this creature.

▷ **conchology** /kɒŋˈkɒlədʒɪ/ *n* [U] study of shells and shellfish.

concierge /ˌkɒnsɪˈeəʒ; *US* kəʊnˈsɪeərʒ/ *n* (in French-speaking countries) person whose job is to guard the entrance to a building (esp a block of flats); caretaker.

conciliate /kənˈsɪlɪeɪt/ *v* **1** [Tn] make (sb) less angry or more friendly (esp by being pleasant or making some concessions): *conciliate outraged customers.* **2** [I, Ipr, Tn] ~ **(between sb and sb)** bring (people who are disagreeing) into agreement: *conciliate (between) the parties in a dispute.*

▷ **conciliation** /kənˌsɪlɪˈeɪʃn/ *n* [U] conciliating or being conciliated: [attrib] *A conciliation service helps to settle disputes between employers and workers.*

conciliatory /kənˈsɪlɪətərɪ; *US* -tɔːrɪ/ *adj* intended or likely to conciliate: *a conciliatory gesture, smile, remark.*

concise /kənˈsaɪs/ *adj* (of speech or writing) giving a lot of information in few words; brief: *a concise summary, account, etc.* ▷ **concisely** *adv.* **conciseness, concision** /kənˈsɪʒn/ *ns* [U].

conclave /ˈkɒŋkleɪv/ *n* private meeting (eg of cardinals to elect a Pope): *sit/meet in conclave,* ie hold a private meeting.

conclude /kənˈkluːd/ *v* **1** [I, Ipr, Tn, Tn·pr] ~ **(sth) (with sth)** (*usu fml*) come or bring (sth) to an end: *The meeting concluded at 8 o'clock.* ○ *The story concludes with the hero's death.* ○ *He concluded by saying that...* ○ *She concluded her talk with a funny story.* ○ *a few concluding remarks.* **2** [Tn·pr, Tf] ~ **sth from sth** come to believe sth as a result of reasoning: *Those are the facts; what do you conclude from them?* ○ *The jury concluded, from the evidence, that she was guilty.* **3** [Tn, Tn·pr] ~ **sth (with sb)** arrange and settle (a treaty, etc) formally and finally: *Britain concluded a trade agreement with China.* ○ *Once the price had been agreed, a deal was quickly concluded.* **4** [Tf no passive, Tt] (*esp US*) decide, esp after discussion: *We concluded to go out/that we would go out.*

conclusion /kənˈkluːʒn/ *n* **1** [C usu *sing*] end: *at the conclusion of his speech* ○ *bring sth to a speedy conclusion.* **2** [C] ~ **(that...)** belief or opinion that is the result of reasoning: *I came to/reached the conclusion that he'd been lying.* ○ *What conclusions do you draw (from the evidence you've heard)?* **3** [U] formal and final arranging or settling of sth: *Hostilities ended with the conclusion of a peace treaty.* **4** (idm) **a foregone conclusion** ⇨ FOREGONE. **in conclusion** lastly: *In conclusion I'd like to say that....* **jump to conclusions** ⇨ JUMP[2].

conclusive /kənˈkluːsɪv/ *adj* (of facts, evidence, etc) convincing; ending doubt: *Her fingerprints on the gun were conclusive proof of her guilt.* ▷ **conclusively** *adv.*

concoct /kənˈkɒkt/ *v* [Tn] (*often derog*) **1** make (sth) by mixing ingredients (esp ones that do not usu go together): *concoct a drink out of sherry and lemon juice.* **2** (*derog*) invent (a story, an excuse, etc): *She'd concocted some unlikely tale about the train being cancelled.*

▷ **concoction** /kənˈkɒkʃn/ *n* (**a**) [U] concocting. (**b**) [C] thing that is concocted; (esp liquid) mixture: *Do you expect me to drink this vile concoction?*

concomitant /kənˈkɒmɪtənt/ *adj* ~ **(with sth)** (*fml*) accompanying; happening together: *concomitant circumstances, events, etc* ○ *travel and all its concomitant discomforts.*

▷ **concomitant** *n* ~ **(of sth)** (*fml*) thing that typically happens with sth else: *the infirmities that* *are the concomitants of old age.*

concord /ˈkɒŋkɔːd/ *n* **1** [U] (*fml*) harmony between people; lack of quarrelling and unfriendliness: *living in concord (with neighbouring states).* Cf DISCORD. **2** [U] (*grammar*) agreement between words in gender, number, etc, eg between a verb and a plural noun as its subject. **3** [C] (*music*) chord or interval that produces a satisfying sound; harmony(3b). Cf CONSONANCE, DISCORD.

concordance /kənˈkɔːdəns/ *n* **1** [C] alphabetical index of the words used by an author or in a book: *a ˈBible concordance ○ a concordance to Shakespeare.* **2** [U] (*fml*) agreement.

concordant /kənˈkɔːdənt/ *adj* ~ **(with sth)** (*fml*) in agreement; appropriate: *practice concordant with our principles.*

concordat /kənˈkɔːdæt/ *n* agreement, esp between a State and the Church on church affairs.

Concorde

Concorde /ˈkɒŋkɔːd/ name of the first commercial aircraft to fly faster than the speed of sound, developed jointly by the British and the French. It carried its first passengers in 1976. ⇨ illus.

concourse /ˈkɒŋkɔːs/ *n* **1** open area forming part of a building or large complex, where people may walk about: *The ticket office is at the rear of the station concourse,* ie its main hall. **2** (*fml*) gathering of people or things; crowd: *a vast concourse of pilgrims.*

concrete[1] /ˈkɒŋkriːt/ *adj* **1** existing in material form; that can be touched, felt, etc: *Physics deals with the forces acting on concrete objects.* Cf ABSTRACT. **2** definite; positive: *concrete proposals, evidence, facts ○ The police have nothing concrete to go on.* ▷ **concretely** *adv.*

□ ˌ**concrete** ˈ**music** music composed of natural sounds that are recorded and then rearranged.

ˌ**concrete** ˈ**poetry** poetry that uses its visual appearance on the page to achieve its effect.

concrete[2] /ˈkɒŋkriːt/ *n* [U] building material made by mixing cement with sand, gravel, etc and water: *a slab of concrete ○ modern buildings made of concrete ○* [attrib] *a concrete path, wall, etc.*

▷ **concrete** *v* [Tn, Tn·p] ~ **sth (over)** cover sth with concrete: *concrete a road (over).*

□ ˌ**concrete** ˈ**jungle** (*fig*) hard living conditions faced by (esp poor) people who live in big cities.

ˈ**concrete mixer** revolving container used to mix the ingredients of concrete.

concretion /kənˈkriːʃn/ *n* (*geology*) mass formed when sth soft or liquid becomes hard or solid, esp a mineral inside a surrounding rock.

concubine /ˈkɒŋkjʊbaɪn/ *n* (in countries where a man can legally have more than one wife) woman who lives with a man but is of lower status than a wife: *The sultan's wives and concubines live in the harem.*

concupiscence /kənˈkjuːpɪsns/ *n* [U] (*fml often derog*) strong sexual desire; lust.

concur /kənˈkɜː(r)/ *v* **(-rr-)** (*fml*) **1** [I, Ipr] ~ **(with sb/sth) (in sth)** agree; express agreement: *She has expressed her opposition to the plan, and I fully concur (with her) (in this matter).* **2** [I, It] (of events, etc) happen together; coincide: *Everything concurred to produce a successful result.*

▷ **concurrence** /kənˈkʌrəns/ *n* (*fml*) **1** [U, sing] agreement: *With your concurrence* (ie If you agree), *I will confirm the arrangement. ○ a concurrence* (ie similarity) *of ideas, views, etc.* **2** [sing] occurrence at the same time: *an unfortunate concurrence of events.*

concurrent /kənˈkʌrənt/ *adj* **1** ~ **(with sth)** existing, happening or done at the same time: *other developments concurrent with these.* **2** (*mathematics*) (of three or more lines) that meet or could meet at one point. **concurrently** *adv*: *He was given two prison sentences, to run concurrently.*

concuss /kənˈkʌs/ *v* [Tn esp passive] injure (sb's brain) by a blow or by violent shaking: *He was badly concussed in the collision.*

concussion /kənˈkʌʃn/ *n* [C, U] **(a)** injury to the brain caused by a blow, violent shaking, etc, resulting in temporary unconsciousness: *The patient is suffering from severe concussion following a blow to the head.* **(b)** violent shaking or shock (caused eg by a blow, an explosion, etc): *a mighty tremor followed by minor concussions.*

condemn /kənˈdem/ *v* **1** [Tn, Tn·pr, Cn·n/a] ~ **sb/sth (for/as sth)** say that one disapproves of sb/sth: *We all condemn cruelty to children. ○ The papers were quick to condemn him for his mistake. ○ She is often condemned as uncaring.* **2** [Tn, Cn·n/a] ~ **sth (as sth)** say officially that (sth) is faulty or not fit for use: *The meat was condemned as unfit for human consumption. ○ a condemned building.* **3 (a)** [Tn, Tn·pr, Cn·t] ~ **sb (to sth/to do sth)** (*law*) say what sb's punishment is to be; sentence sb (esp to death): *condemn sb to death/hard labour ○ He was found guilty and condemned to be shot.* **(b)** [Tn] make (sb) appear guilty: *His nervous looks condemned him.* **4** [esp passive: Tn·pr, Cn·t] ~ **sb to sth/to do sth** make sb take or accept sth unwelcome or unpleasant; doom sb: *an unhappy worker, condemned to a job he hates ○ As an old person, one is often condemned to live alone.*

▷ **condemnation** /ˌkɒndemˈneɪʃn/ *n* **(a)** [U] condemning or being condemned. **(b)** [C] instance of this: *many condemnations of her action.*

□ **conˌdemned** ˈ**cell** cell where a person who has been sentenced to death is kept.

condensation /ˌkɒndenˈseɪʃn/ *n* **1** [U, C] condensing or being condensed: *the condensation of steam to water ○ The report is a brilliant condensation of several years' work.* **2** [U] drops of liquid formed on a surface when vapour condenses: *His shaving mirror was covered with condensation.*

□ ˌ**condenˈsation trail** = VAPOUR TRAIL (VAPOUR).

condense /kənˈdens/ *v* **1** [I, Ipr, Tn, Tn·pr] ~ **(sth) (into/to sth) (a)** (cause sth to) become thicker or more concentrated: *Soup condenses when boiled,* ie by losing most of the water. *○ condensed milk,* ie concentrated and sweetened. **(b)** (cause sth to) change from gas or vapour to a liquid or (rarely) a solid: *Steam that condenses/is condensed into water when it touches a cold surface.* ⇨ Usage at WATER[1]. **2** [Tn, Tn·pr] ~ **sth (into sth)** put sth into fewer words: *condense a long report into a brief summary.*

condenser /kənˈdensə(r)/ *n* **1** device for cooling vapour and condensing it to liquid. **2** device for receiving and storing an electric charge (esp in a car engine). **3** mirror or lens that concentrates light, eg in a film projector.

condescend /ˌkɒndɪˈsend/ *v* **1** [It] (*often derog*) do sth that one regards as undignified or below one's level of importance: *She actually condescended to say hello to me in the street today. ○* (*ironic*) *Perhaps your father would condescend to help with the washing-up!* **2** [I, Ipr] ~ **(to sb)** (*derog*) behave kindly or graciously, but in a way that shows one feels that one is better than other people: *I do wish he wouldn't condescend to the junior staff in his department.*

▷ **condescending** *adj*: *a condescending person ○ condescending behaviour ○ She's so condescending!* **condescendingly** *adv.*

condescension /ˌkɒndɪˈsenʃn/ *n* [U] condescending (behaviour).

condign /kənˈdaɪn/ *adj* (*fml*) (of punishment, etc) severe and well deserved.

condiment /ˈkɒndɪmənt/ *n* [C esp *pl*, U] seasoning (eg salt or pepper) used to give flavour and relish to food.

condition[1] /kənˈdɪʃn/ *n* **1** [sing] particular state of existence: *the human condition ○ the condition of slavery,* ie being a slave. **2** [sing, U] **(a)** present state of a thing: *be in good, poor, excellent, etc condition ○ the rusty condition of the bicycle ○ The ship is not in a condition/is in no condition* (ie is unfit) *to make a long voyage.* **(b)** physical fitness; health: *He's in excellent condition for a man of his age. ○ I've had no exercise for ages; I'm really out of condition,* ie unfit. *○ She's in no condition* (ie is not well enough) *to travel.* **3** [C] **(a)** thing needed to make sth else possible; thing on which another thing depends: *One of the conditions of the job is that you should be able to drive,* ie In order to get the job you must be able to drive. *○ He was allowed to go out, but his parents made it a condition that he should get home before midnight. ○ I'll let you borrow it on one condition: (that) you lend me your bicycle in return.* **(b)** thing required as part of an agreement, a contract, etc; stipulation: *the terms and conditions of the lease.* **(c)** (*US*) subject in which a student has not reached the required standard and in which he must pass an examination in order to continue studying. **4 conditions** [pl] circumstances: *under existing conditions ○ poor working conditions ○ firemen having to operate in very difficult conditions.* **5** [C] illness; ailment: *a heart, liver, brain, etc condition ○ What is the treatment for this condition?* **6** [C] (*dated*) position in society; rank: *people of every condition/of all conditions.* **7** (idm) **in mint condition** ⇨ MINT[2]. **on condition (that)...** only if; provided (that): *You can go out on condition that you wear an overcoat.* **on no condition** (*fml*) not at all: *You must on no condition tell him what happened.*

condition[2] /ˌkənˈdɪʃn/ *v* **1** [Tn] have an important effect on (sb/sth); determine: *Environment conditions an animal's development.* **2** [Tn, Tn·pr, Cn·t] ~ **sb/sth (to sth/to do sth)** accustom sb/sth; train sb/sth: *We have all been conditioned by our upbringing. ○ It didn't take them long to become conditioned to the new environment. ○ Animals can be conditioned to expect food at certain times.* **3** [Tn] put (sth) into a proper or desired state for use: *leather conditioned by a special process ○ a lotion that conditions the skin,* ie keeps it healthy.

▷ **conditioner** /kənˈdɪʃənə(r)/ *n* [C, U] thing or substance that conditions, esp a liquid that keeps the hair healthy and shiny.

conditioning /-ʃənɪŋ/ *n* [U] (*psychology*) process by which people or animals can be trained to respond to a particular stimulus. Cf PAVLOV.

□ **conˌditioned** ˈ**reflex** response that a person or an animal is trained to make to a particular stimulus (even if it is not a normal or natural response).

conditional /kənˈdɪʃənl/ *adj* **(a)** ~ **(on/upon sth)** depending on sth: *conditional approval, acceptance, etc ○ Payment of the money is conditional upon delivery of the goods,* ie If the goods are not delivered, the money will not be paid. **(b)** (*esp grammar*) containing or implying a condition[1](3a) or qualification: *a conditional clause,* ie one beginning with *if* or *unless.* ▷ **conditionally** /-ʃənəlɪ/ *adv.*

condole /kənˈdəʊl/ *v* [Ipr] ~ **with sb (on sth)** (*fml*) express sympathy (for a misfortune, bereavement, etc).

▷ **condolence** /kənˈdəʊləns/ *n* [U, C often *pl*] (expression of) sympathy: *a letter of condolence ○ Please accept my condolences.*

condom /ˈkɒndəm/ (also *esp US* **prophylactic**) *n* contraceptive sheath worn on the penis during sexual intercourse.

condominium /ˌkɒndəˈmɪnɪəm/ *n* **1** country governed jointly by two or more other states. **2** (*US*) (also *infml* **condo** /ˈkɒndəʊ/) (apartment in a) block of apartments, each of which is owned by its occupier.

condone /kənˈdəʊn/ *v* [Tn, Tg, Tsg] treat or regard (an offence) as if it were not serious or wrong; overlook; forgive: *condone violence, adultery, fraud, etc ○ Not punishing them amounts to* *condoning their crime.* ▷ **condonation** /ˌkɒndəʊˈneɪʃn/ *n* [U] (*fml*).

condor /ˈkɒndɔ:(r)/ *n* type of large vulture found mainly in S America.

conduce /kənˈdju:s; *US* -ˈdu:s/ *v* [Ipr] ~ **to/towards sth** (*fml*) help to bring sth about: *A good diet conduces to good health.*

▷ **conducive** /kənˈdju:sɪv; *US* -ˈdu:s-/ *adj* [pred] ~ **to sth** allowing or helping sth to happen: *These noisy conditions aren't really conducive to concentrated work.*

conduct[1] /ˈkɒndʌkt/ *n* [U] **1** person's behaviour (esp its moral aspect): *the rules of conduct* ○ *The prisoner was released early because of good conduct.* **2** ~ **of sth** manner of directing or managing (a business, campaign, etc): *There was growing criticism of the Government's conduct of the war.*

conduct[2] /kənˈdʌkt/ *v* **1** [Tn·pr, Tn·p] lead or guide (sb/sth): *I asked the attendant to conduct him to the door/conduct him out.* ○ *A guide conducted the visitors round the museum.* ○ *We were given a conducted* (ie guided) *tour of the cathedral.* **2** (**a**) [Tn] direct (sth); control; manage: *conduct business, a meeting, negotiations, etc* ○ *She was appointed to conduct the advertising campaign.* (**b**) [I, Tn] direct the performance of (an orchestra, a choir, a piece of music, etc): *a concert by the Philharmonic Orchestra, conducted by Sir Colin Davis.* **3** [Tn·pr] ~ **oneself well, badly, etc** (*fml*) behave in the specified way: *conduct oneself honourably, with dignity, like a gentleman.* **4** [Tn] (of a substance) allow (heat, electric current, etc) to pass along or through it: *Copper conducts electricity better than other materials do.*

▷ **conductance** /kənˈdʌktəns/ *n* [U] degree to which a material is a good or bad conductor of electricity.

conduction /kənˈdʌkʃn/ *n* [U] conducting of electric current along wires or of heat by contact.

conductive /kənˈdʌktɪv/ *adj* that can conduct heat, electric current, etc. **conductivity** /ˌkɒndʌkˈtɪvətɪ/ *n* [U] property or power of conducting heat, electricity, etc: *a metal with high/low conductivity*, ie one that conducts heat, etc well/badly.

conductor /kənˈdʌktə(r)/ *n* **1** person who directs the performance of an orchestra, a choir, etc (esp by standing in front of them and gesturing with his arms). **2** (**a**) (*Brit*) person who collects fares on a bus. (**b**) (*US*) (*Brit* **guard**) person in charge of a train. **3** substance that conducts heat or electric current: *a ˈlightning conductor* ○ *Wood is a poor conductor.*

▷ **conductress** /kənˈdʌktrɪs/ *n* (*Brit*) woman conductor on a bus.

□ **conˈductor rail** rail (laid parallel to the tracks) from which a railway locomotive picks up electric current.

conduit /ˈkɒndɪt; *US* ˈkɒndju:ɪt, -dwɪt/ *n* (**a**) large pipe through which liquids flow. (**b**) tube enclosing insulated electric wires.

cone /kəʊn/ *n* **1** solid body that narrows to a point from a circular flat base. ⇨ illus at CUBE. **2** solid or hollow thing that has this shape, eg an edible container for ice-cream, a warning sign for road-works, etc. ⇨ illus at MOTORWAY. **3** fruit of certain evergreen trees (fir, pine, cedar) made of overlapping woody scales. ⇨ illus at TREE. **4** type of cell in the retina of the eye that is sensitive to bright light and colour. Cf ROD 6.

▷ **cone** *v* (phr v) **cone sth off** mark or separate sth with cones: *cone off a section of motorway during repairs* ○ *cone off parking spaces that must not be used.*

coney = CONY.

confab /ˈkɒnfæb/ *n* (*dated infml*) private friendly conversation; chat.

confection /kənˈfekʃn/ *n* (*fml*) thing made with sweet ingredients.

▷ **confectioner** *n* person who (makes and) sells sweets, cakes, etc: *I bought it at the confectioner's (shop).* **confectionery** /kənˈfekʃənərɪ; *US* -ʃənerɪ/ *n* (**a**) [U] sweets, chocolates, cakes, etc. (**b**) [C] confectioner's business or shop.

confederacy /kənˈfedərəsɪ/ *n* **1** [C] alliance or league, esp of states. **2 the** (**Southern**) **Confederacy** [sing] the Confederate States.

confederate[1] /kənˈfedərət/ *adj* joined together by an agreement or a treaty: *the Confederate States of America.*

▷ **confederate** *n* **1** person one works with (esp in sth illegal or secret); accomplice: *his confederates in the crime.* **2 Confederate** supporter of the Confederate States.

□ **the Conˌfederate ˈStates** the eleven states that separated from the US in 1860-61, thus causing the American Civil War.

confederate[2] /kənˈfedəreɪt/ *v* [I, Ipr] ~ (**with sb/sth**) join together in a larger organization for mutual benefit.

▷ **confederation** /kənˌfedəˈreɪʃn/ *n* (**a**) [U] confederating or being confederated. (**b**) [C] organization of smaller groups that have joined together for mutual benefit: *the Confederation of British Industry.*

confer /kənˈfɜ:(r)/ *v* (-**rr**-) **1** [I, Ipr] ~ (**with sb**) (**on/about sth**) have discussions (esp in order to exchange opinions or get advice): *She withdrew to confer with her advisers before announcing a decision.* **2** [Tn, Tn·pr] ~ **sth** (**on sb**) give or grant (a degree or title) to sb: *The Queen conferred knighthoods on several distinguished men.* ○ (*fig*) *He behaves as if high rank automatically confers the right to be obeyed.*

▷ **conferment** *n* [U, C] (*fml*) giving or granting (of degrees, honours, etc).

conference /ˈkɒnfərəns/ *n* [C, U] (meeting for) discussion or exchange of views: *Many international conferences are held in Geneva.* ○ *The Director is in conference now.*

confess /kənˈfes/ *v* **1** (**a**) [I, Ipr, Tn, Tf, Dn·pr] ~ (**to sth/doing sth**); ~ (**sth**) (**to sb**) say or admit, often formally (that one has done wrong, committed a crime, etc): *The prisoner refused to confess (his crime).* ○ *She finally confessed (to having stolen the money).* ○ *He confessed that he had murdered her.* (**b**) [Ipr, Tf, Cn·t, Cn·a] acknowledge, often reluctantly: *She confessed to (having) a dread of spiders*, ie admitted that she was afraid of them. ○ *I'm rather bored, I must confess.* ○ *He confessed himself (to be) totally ignorant of their plans.* **2** (**a**) [I, Ipr, Tn, Tn·pr, Tf, Dpr·f] ~ (**sth**) (**to sb**) (esp in the Roman Catholic Church) tell (one's sins) formally to a priest: *He confessed (to the priest) that he had sinned.* (**b**) [Tn] (of a priest) hear the sins of (sb) in this way: *The priest confessed the criminal.*

▷ **confessedly** /-ɪdlɪ/ *adv* by sb's own admission.

confession /kənˈfeʃn/ *n* **1** [C, U] statement of one's guilt; confessing: *to make a full confession of one's crimes.* **2** [C, U] (in the Roman Catholic Church) formal admission of one's sins to a priest: *The priest will hear confessions in English and French.* ○ *I always go to confession on Fridays.* **3** [C] declaration of one's religious beliefs, principles, etc: *a confession of faith.*

confessional /kənˈfeʃənl/ *n* private, usu enclosed, place in a church where a priest sits to hear confessions: *the secrets of the confessional.*

confessor /kənˈfesə(r)/ *n* priest who hears confessions.

confetti /kənˈfetɪ/ *n* [sing *v*] small pieces of coloured paper thrown over the bride and bridegroom at a wedding.

confidant (*fem* **-dante**) /ˌkɒnfɪˈdænt/ *n* trusted person to whom one speaks about one's private affairs or secrets.

confide /kənˈfaɪd/ **1** (**a**) [Tf, Dn·pr, Dpr·f] ~ **sth to sb** tell (a secret) to sb: *She confided her troubles to a friend.* ○ *He confided (to me) that he had applied for another job.* (**b**) [Tn·pr] ~ **sb/sth to sb/sth** (*fml*) give sb/sth to sb to be looked after; entrust: *Can I confide my children to your care?* **2** (phr v) **confide in sb** trust sb enough to tell a secret to him: *There's no one here I can confide in.*

▷ **confiding** *adj* [usu attrib] trusting; not suspicious: *have a confiding nature.* **confidingly** *adv.*

confidence /ˈkɒnfɪdəns/ *n* **1** [U] (**a**) ~ (**in sb/sth**) firm trust (in sb, in sb's ability, or in what is said, reported, etc): *to have/lose confidence in sb* ○ *I have little confidence in him.* ○ *Don't put too much confidence in what the papers say.* ○ *There is a lack of confidence in the Government*, ie People do not believe that its policies are wise. (**b**) feeling of certainty; trust in one's own ability: *He answered the questions with confidence.* ○ *You are too shy: you should have more confidence (in yourself).* **2** [C] secret which is told to sb: *The two girls sat in a corner exchanging confidences.* **3** (idm) **in (strict) confidence** as a secret: *I'm telling you this in (strict) confidence — so don't breathe a word of it.* **take sb into one's confidence** tell sb one's secrets, etc.

□ **the ˈconfidence game** activity of playing confidence tricks.

ˈconfidence trick act of swindling sb by first gaining his trust. **ˈconfidence trickster** (also *infml* **ˈcon man**) person who swindles people in this way.

confident /ˈkɒnfɪdənt/ *adj* ~ (**of sth/that...**) feeling or showing trust in oneself or one's ability: *a confident smile, manner, speech* ○ *feel confident of succeeding/that one will succeed* ○ *He is confident of victory.* ▷ **confidently** *adv.*

confidential /ˌkɒnfɪˈdenʃl/ *adj* **1** to be kept secret; not to be made known to others: *confidential information, files, letters.* **2** [attrib] trusted with secrets: *a confidential secretary.* **3** trusting: *speaking in a confidential tone.* ▷ **confidentiality** /ˌkɒnfɪˌdenʃɪˈælətɪ/ *n* [U]. **confidentially** /-ʃəlɪ/ *adv*: *He told me confidentially that he's thinking of resigning next year.*

configuration /kənˌfɪgəˈreɪʃn; *US* kənˌfɪgjəˈreɪʃn/ *n* arrangement of the parts of sth; shape or outline: *the configuration of the earth's surface, the vocal tract, the solar system.*

configure /kənˈfɪgə(r); *US* kənˈfɪgjər/ *v* [Tn] (*esp computing*) arrange (sth) for a particular purpose, usu so that it is compatible with other equipment.

confine /kənˈfaɪn/ *v* **1** [Tn, Tn·pr] ~ **sb/sth** (**in/to sth**) keep (a person or an animal) in a restricted space: *Is it cruel to confine a bird in a cage?* ○ *After her operation, she was confined to bed for a week.* ○ *I should hate to be confined in an office all day.* **2** [Tn·pr] ~ **sb/sth to sth** restrict or keep sb/sth within certain limits: *I wish the speaker would confine himself to the subject.* ○ *Confine your criticism to matters you understand.*

▷ **confined** *adj* (of space) limited; restricted: *It was difficult to work efficiently in such a confined space.*

confinement *n* **1** [U] being confined; imprisonment: *to be placed in confinement*, ie in a prison, mental hospital, etc ○ *The prisoner was sentenced to three months' solitary confinement*, ie kept apart from other prisoners. **2** (**a**) [U] time during which a baby is being born: *Her confinement was approaching.* (**b**) [C] instance of this; birth: *The doctor has been called to a home confinement*, ie a birth taking place at the mother's home rather than in hospital.

confines /ˈkɒnfaɪnz/ *n* [pl] (*fml*) limits; borders; boundaries: *beyond the confines of human knowledge* ○ *within the confines of family life.*

confirm /kənˈfɜ:m/ *v* **1** [Tn, Tf] provide evidence for the truth or correctness of (a report, an opinion, etc); establish the truth of: *The rumours of an attack were later confirmed.* ○ *The announcement confirmed my suspicions.* ○ *Please write to confirm your reservation*, ie send a letter to support a booking made by telephone. ○ *When asked, she confirmed that she was going to retire.* **2** [Tn, Tn·pr, Cn·n/a] ~ **sth;** ~ **sb** (**as/in sth**) ratify (a treaty, appointment, etc); make definite, or establish more firmly (power, a position, etc): *The new minister will be confirmed in office by the Queen.* ○ *After a six-month probationary period, she was confirmed in her post.* ○ *The incident confirmed him in* (ie established more firmly) *his dislike of dogs.* **3** [Tn] admit (sb) to full membership of the Christian Church: *She was baptized when she was a month old and confirmed when she was thirteen.*

▷ **confirmed** *adj* [attrib] settled in a particular

habit or state: *a confirmed bachelor*, ie a single man who is unlikely to marry ○ *a confirmed drunkard, gambler, etc.*

confirmation /ˌkɒnfəˈmeɪʃn/ *n* [U, C] confirming or being confirmed: *We are waiting for confirmation of our onward reservations*, ie waiting to be told that our further travel bookings are still valid. ○ *The bishop conducted a number of confirmations at the service.*

confiscate /ˈkɒnfɪskeɪt/ *v* [Tn] take possession of (sb's property) by authority, without payment or compensation: *The headmaster confiscated Tommy's pea-shooter.* ○ *If you are caught smuggling goods into the country, they will probably be confiscated.* ▷ **confiscation** /ˌkɒnfɪˈskeɪʃn/ *n* [C, U].

conflagration /ˌkɒnfləˈgreɪʃn/ *n* (*fml*) great and destructive fire.

conflate /kənˈfleɪt/ *v* [Tn usu passive] combine (two sets of information, texts, etc) into one: *The results of the two experiments were conflated.* ○ *Can these two definitions be conflated, or must they be kept separate?* ▷ **conflation** /kənˈfleɪʃn/ *n* [U, C].

conflict /ˈkɒnflɪkt/ *n* [C, U] **1** (**a**) struggle; fight: *soldiers involved in armed conflict.* (**b**) (*fig*) serious disagreement; argument; controversy: *a long and bitter conflict between employers and workers.* **2** (of opinions, desires, etc) opposition; difference; clash: *the conflict between one's duty and one's desires* ○ *a conflict of interests*, ie between the achievement of one aim and that of another ○ *Your statement is in conflict with the rest of the evidence.*
▷ **conflict** /kənˈflɪkt/ *v* [I, Ipr] ~ (**with sth**) be in opposition or disagreement; be incompatible; clash: *A and B conflict/A conflicts with B.* ○ *The statements of the two witnesses conflict.* ○ *Their account of events conflicts with ours.*

confluence /ˈkɒnfluəns/ *n* **1** place where two rivers flow together and become one: *the confluence of the Blue Nile and the White Nile.* **2** (*fml*) coming together, esp of large numbers of people.
▷ **confluent** /ˈkɒnfluənt/ *n* river or stream that joins another. — *adj* (*fml*) flowing or coming together; uniting.

conform /kənˈfɔːm/ *v* **1** [I, Ipr] ~ (**to sth**) keep to or comply with (generally accepted rules, standards, etc): *her refusal to conform (to the normal social conventions)* ○ *The building does not conform to safety regulations.* **2** [Ipr] ~ **with/to sth** agree or be consistent with sth: *His ideas do not conform with mine.*
▷ **conformable** /kənˈfɔːməbl/ *adj* ~ (**to/with sth**) (*fml*) that conforms (to or with sth): *results conformable with our intentions.*
conformist /kənˈfɔːmɪst/ *n* person who conforms to accepted behaviour, the established religion, etc: *She's too much of a conformist to wear silly clothes.*
conformity /kənˈfɔːmətɪ/ *n* **1** [U] ~ (**to/with sth**) (*fml*) (behaviour, etc) conforming to established rules, customs, etc. **2** (idm) **in conformity with sth** (*fml*) in accordance with sth; obeying sth: *act in conformity with the rules, law, etc* ○ *in conformity with your request, instructions, wishes, etc.*

conformation /ˌkɒnfɔːˈmeɪʃn/ *n* [U, C] (*fml*) way in which sth is formed; structure.

confound /kənˈfaʊnd/ *v* **1** [Tn] (*dated or fml*) puzzle and surprise (sb); perplex: *His behaviour amazed and confounded her.* ○ *I was confounded to hear that....* **2** [Tn, Tn·pr] ~ **sth** (**with sth**) (*dated*) confuse (ideas, etc). **3** [Tn] (*dated or fml*) (**a**) defeat (sb): *confound an enemy, a rival, a critic, etc.* (**b**) prevent (sth); thwart: *confound a plan, an attempt, etc.* **4** [Tn] (*infml*) (used as an *interj* to express anger): *Confound it!* ○ *Confound you!*
▷ **confounded** *adj* [attrib] (*infml*) (used to emphasize one's annoyance): *You're a confounded nuisance!* **confoundedly** *adv* (*infml*) very: *It's confoundedly hot.*

confrère /ˈkɒnfreə(r)/ *n* (*French fml*) fellow member of an organization, esp a professional or religious body: *our confrères in other branches of medicine.*

confront /kənˈfrʌnt/ *v* **1** [Tn·pr] ~ **sb with sb/sth** make sb face or consider sb/sth unpleasant, difficult, etc: *They confronted the prisoner with his accusers.* ○ *When confronted with the evidence of her guilt, she confessed.* **2** [Tn] (**a**) (of a difficulty, etc) face (sb) threateningly; oppose: *the problems confronting us* ○ *Confronted by an angry crowd the police retreated.* (**b**) face (sth) defiantly: *A soldier often has to confront danger.*
▷ **confrontation** /ˌkɒnfrʌnˈteɪʃn/ *n* [C, U] (instance of) angry opposition: *a confrontation between the Government and the unions.*

Confucius /kənˈfjuːʃəs/ (551-479 BC) Chinese philosopher, who taught the need for high moral standards, esp goodness, justice, loyalty and respect for parents and ancestor; Chinese name **Kong fu zi**.
▷ **Confucian** *adj, n.*
Confucianism *n* [U] Chinese philosophical and ethical system based on the teachings of Confucius. Cf TAOISM.

confuse /kənˈfjuːz/ *v* **1** [Tn usu passive] make (sb) unable to think clearly; puzzle; bewilder: *They confused me by asking so many questions.* **2** [Tn] put (sth) into disorder; upset: *Her unexpected arrival confused all our plans.* **3** [Tn, Tn·pr] ~ **A and/with B** mistake one person or thing for another: *I always confuse the sisters: they look so alike.* ○ *Don't confuse Austria and/with Australia.* ○ *This construction should not be confused with the regular passive.* **4** [Tn] make (sth) unclear; muddle: *a confused argument* ○ *Don't confuse the issue*, eg by introducing irrelevant topics.
▷ **confused** *adj* **1** unable to think clearly; bewildered: *All your changes of plan have made me totally confused.* ○ *The stroke left him confused and unable to recognize even his wife.* **2** mixed up; not clear: *a confused account of what happened.* **confusedly** /-ɪdlɪ/ *adv.*
confusing *adj* difficult to understand; puzzling: *a most confusing speech* ○ *The instructions on the box are very confusing.* **confusingly** *adv.*

confusion /kənˈfjuːʒn/ *n* [U] **1** bewilderment or embarrassment: *gazing in confusion at the strange sight.* **2** disorder: *Her unexpected arrival threw us into total confusion.* **3** mistaking of one person or thing for another: *There has been some confusion of names.* **4** state of uncertainty: *There is some confusion about what the correct procedure should be.*

confute /kənˈfjuːt/ *v* [Tn] (*fml*) prove (a person or an argument) to be wrong. ▷ **confutation** /ˌkɒnfjuːˈteɪʃn/ *n* [U, C].

conga /ˈkɒŋgə/ *n* (music for a) lively dance in which the dancers follow a leader linked together in a long winding line.

congeal /kənˈdʒiːl/ *v* [I, Tn] (of a liquid) (cause to) become thick or solid, esp by cooling: *The blood had congealed round the cut on her knee.* ○ *Use hot water to rinse the congealed fat off the dinner plates.*

congenial /kənˈdʒiːnɪəl/ *adj* **1** (of people) pleasing because of similarities in temperament, interests, etc: *a congenial companion.* **2** ~ (**to sb**) agreeable or pleasant because suited to one's nature or tastes: *a congenial climate, environment, hobby* ○ *I find this aspect of my job particularly congenial.* ▷ **congeniality** /kənˌdʒiːnɪˈælətɪ/ *n* [U]. **congenially** /-ɪəlɪ/ *adv.*

congenital /kənˈdʒenɪtl/ *adj* **1** (of diseases, etc) present from or before birth, caused either by defects in the chromosomes or by external influences in the womb (eg when the mother takes a drug or contracts rubella): *congenital defects, blindness* ○ *congenital herpes.* **2** [attrib] (of people) born with a certain illness or condition: *a congenital idiot, syphilitic, etc.*

conger /ˈkɒŋgə(r)/ *n* (also ˌ**conger** ˈ**eel**) large type of sea eel.

congeries /kənˈdʒɪəriːz/ *n* (*pl* unchanged) (*fml*) large number of things brought together in an untidy way; heap: *a congeries of old books.*

congested /kənˈdʒestɪd/ *adj* **1** ~ (**with sth**) too full; overcrowded: *streets congested with traffic.* **2** (**a**) (of parts of the body, eg the lungs) abnormally full of blood. (**b**) (of the nose) blocked with mucus: *He had a cold and was very congested.*

congestion /kənˈdʒestʃən/ *n* [U] state of being congested: *traffic congestion* ○ *congestion of the lungs.*

conglomerate /kənˈglɒmərət/ *n* **1** materials gathered together into a rounded mass. **2** rock made of small stones held together by cement, dried clay, etc. **3** (*commerce*) large corporation formed by merging several different firms: *a mining, chemical, etc conglomerate.*
▷ **conglomeration** /kənˌglɒməˈreɪʃn/ *n* **1** [C] (*infml*) assortment of different things gathered together or found in the same place: *a conglomeration of rusty old machinery.* **2** [U] process of becoming, or state of being, a conglomerate.

Congo /ˈkɒŋgəʊ/ **the Congo 1** country in Central Africa lying on the equator; pop approx 1 888 000; official language French; capital Brazzaville; unit of currency franc. Formerly a Belgian colony, it became fully independent in 1960. Although there are some oil and mineral resources, the economy is based mainly on forestry and agriculture. ⇨ map at ZAÏRE. **2** former name of the *Zaïre River.
▷ **Congolese** /ˌkɒŋgəˈliːz/ *adj* of the Congo. — *n* (*pl* unchanged) native or inhabitant of the Congo.

congratulate /kənˈgrætʃʊleɪt/ *v* [Tn, Tn·pr] **1** ~ **sb** (**on sth**) tell sb that one is pleased about his good fortune or achievements: *congratulate sb on his marriage, new job, good exam results, etc.* **2** ~ **oneself** (**on/upon** (**doing**) **sth**) consider oneself fortunate or successful; be proud (of sth): *You can congratulate yourself on having done a good job.*
▷ **congratulatory** /kənˈgrætʃʊlətərɪ; *US* -tɔːrɪ/ *adj* [usu attrib] intended to congratulate: *congratulatory words, letters, telegrams, etc.*

congratulation /kənˌgrætʃʊˈleɪʃn/ *n* **1** [U] congratulating or being congratulated: *a speech of congratulation for the winner.* **2 congratulations** [pl] (**a**) words of congratulation: *offer sb one's congratulations on his success.* (**b**) (used as an *interj*): *You've passed your driving test? Congratulations!* ○ *Congratulations on winning the prize!*

congregate /ˈkɒŋgrɪgeɪt/ *v* [I] come together in a crowd: *A crowd quickly congregated (round the speaker).*

congregation /ˌkɒŋgrɪˈgeɪʃn/ *n* [CGp] **1** group of people gathered together for religious worship (usu excluding the priest and choir). **2** group of people who regularly attend a particular church, etc.
▷ **congregational** *adj* [usu attrib] **1** of a congregation. **2 Congregational** of Congregationalism. **Congregationalism** *n* [U] beliefs and organizational system of a Protestant branch of the Christian Church (the **Congregational Church**) in which individual groups of believers organize themselves independently. The Church originated in the Puritan period in England and became a formal grouping there in 1832. It merged with the Presbyterian Church in 1972 to form the United Reformed Church. **Congregationalist** *n, adj* (member) of the Congregational Church.

congress /ˈkɒŋgres; *US* -grəs/ *n* [CGp] **1** formal meeting or series of meetings for discussion between representatives: *a medical, international, etc congress* ○ *the Church Congress.* **2 Congress** law-making body, eg of the USA. The American Congress is made up of two parts, the Senate or upper house and the House of Representatives. Each state has two senators who are elected for six years; elections for one-third of the seats are held every two years. All 435 members of the House of Representatives are elected every two years.: *the President's address to (the) Congress.* ⇨ article at POLITICS.
▷ **congressional** /kənˈgreʃənl/ *adj* of a congress or Congress: *a congressional investigation, committee.* **Conˌgressional Medal of ˈHonor** US medal awarded for great bravery in battle.
□ ˈ**Congressman** /-mən/ *n* (*pl* **-men** /-mən/), ˈ**Congresswoman** *n* (*pl* **-women**) member of the US Congress.

Congreve /ˈkɒŋgri:v/ William (1670-1729), English playwright. His plays, like *The Way of the World*, are fine examples of Restoration comedy, using witty but sometimes crude dialogue.

congruent /ˈkɒŋgrʊənt/ *adj* **1** (*geometry*) having the same size and shape: *congruent triangles.* **2** (also **congruous**) ~ (**with sth**) (*fml*) suitable; fitting: *measures congruent with the seriousness of the situation.*

congruous /ˈkɒŋgrʊəs/ *adj* ~ (**with sth**) (*fml*) = CONGRUENT 2. ▷ **congruity** /kɒŋˈgru:ətɪ/ *n* [U].

conic /ˈkɒnɪk/ *adj* (*geometry*) of a cone: *conic sections*, ie the shapes formed when a cone is intersected by a plane.
▷ **conical** /ˈkɒnɪkl/ *adj* cone-shaped: *a conical hat, shell, hill.*

conifer /ˈkɒnɪfə(r), *also* ˈkəʊn-/ *n* type of tree (eg pine, fir) that bears cones (CONE 3).
▷ **coniferous** /kəˈnɪfərəs; *US* kəʊˈn-/ *adj* (of trees) bearing cones.

conjecture /kənˈdʒektʃə(r)/ *v* [I, Ipr, Tn, Tf] ~ (**about sth**) (*fml*) form (and express) an opinion not based on firm evidence; guess: *It was just as I had conjectured.* ○ *Don't conjecture about the outcome.* ○ *What made you conjecture that?*
▷ **conjecture** *n* **1** [C] guess: *I was right in my conjectures.* **2** [U] guessing: *What the real cause was is open to conjecture.* ○ *Your theory is pure conjecture.* **conjectural** /kənˈdʒektʃərəl/ *adj* based on conjecture.

conjoin /kənˈdʒɔɪn/ *v* [I, Tn] (*fml*) (cause people or things to) join together; unite.
▷ **conjoint** /kənˈdʒɔɪnt, ˈkɒndʒɔɪnt/ *adj* (*fml*) united; associated. **conjointly** *adv.*

conjugal /ˈkɒndʒʊgl/ *adj* (*fml*) of marriage or the relationship between a husband and a wife: *conjugal life, bliss, rights.* ▷ **conjugally** /-gəlɪ/ *adv.*

conjugate /ˈkɒndʒʊgeɪt/ *v* **1** (*grammar*) (**a**) [Tn] give the different forms of (a verb), as they vary according to number, tense, etc. (**b**) [I] (of a verb) have different forms showing number, tense, etc: *How does this verb conjugate?* **2** [I] (*biology*) (of sexual cells) become united during reproduction.
▷ **conjugate** /ˈkɒndʒʊgət/ *adj* joined together, esp in pairs. ˌ**conjugate** ˈ**angles** two angles which together measure 360 degrees.
conjugation /ˌkɒndʒʊˈgeɪʃn/ *n* **1** (*grammar*) (**a**) [C, U] (method of) conjugating: *a verb with an irregular conjugation.* (**b**) [C] class of verbs that conjugate in the same way: *Latin verbs of the second conjugation.* **2** [U] (*biology*) process in which two cells unite via a tube in order to reproduce.

conjunct /kənˈdʒʌŋkt/ *adj* (*fml*) joined together or associated.

conjunction /kənˈdʒʌŋkʃn/ *n* **1** [C] (*grammar*) word that joins words, phrases or sentences, eg *and, but, or.* **2** (*fml*) (**a**) [C] combination (of events, etc): *an unusual conjunction of circumstances.* (**b**) [U] joining or being joined together; blend: *the conjunction of workmanship and artistry in making jewellery.* **3** [U] appearance of closeness to each other that stars, planets, etc sometimes have to an observer on earth: *I was born when Mars was in conjunction with Neptune.* **4** (idm) **in conjunction with sb/sth** together with sb/sth: *We are working in conjunction with the police.*

conjunctive /kənˈdʒʌŋktɪv/ *adj* (*esp grammar*) that joins or connects: *a conjunctive adverb.*
▷ **conjunctive** *n* conjunction(1).

conjunctivitis /kənˌdʒʌŋktɪˈvaɪtɪs/ *n* [U] inflammation of the thin transparent membrane which covers the eyeball.

conjuncture /kənˈdʒʌŋktʃə(r)/ *n* (*fml*) combination (of events or circumstances); conjunction(2a).

conjure[1] /ˈkʌndʒə(r)/ *v* **1** [I] do clever tricks which seem magical, esp with quick movements of the hands: *learn how to conjure.* **2** (idm) **a name to conjure with** ⇨ NAME. **3** (phr v) **conjure sth up** (**a**) make sth appear as a picture in the mind: *a tune which conjures up pleasant memories.* (**b**) ask (a spirit) to appear (esp by using a magic ceremony): *conjure up the spirits of the dead.* **conjure sth up**; **conjure sth (up) from/out of sth** make sth appear suddenly or unexpectedly, as if by magic: *I had lost my pen, but she conjured up another one for me from somewhere.* ○ *conjuring a delicious meal out of a few unpromising ingredients.*
▷ **conjurer** (also **conjuror**) /ˈkʌndʒərə(r)/ *n* person who performs conjuring tricks. Cf MAGICIAN (MAGIC).
conjuring /ˈkʌndʒərɪŋ/ *n* [U] performing of clever tricks which seem magical, esp involving quick movements of the hands: [attrib] *a* ˈ*conjuring trick.*

conjure[2] /kənˈdʒʊə(r)/ *v* [Tn, Dn·t] (*fml*) appeal solemnly to (sb): *Be on your guard, I conjure you.* ○ *I conjure you most earnestly to reconsider your position.* ▷ **conjuration** /ˌkɒndʒʊˈreɪʃn/ *n* [U].

conk[1] /kɒŋk/ *n* (*Brit sl*) nose.
▷ **conk** *v* [Tn] (*sl*) hit (sb), esp on the head.

conk[2] /kɒŋk/ *v* (phr v) **conk out** (*infml*) (**a**) (of a machine) stop working: *The car conked out at the crossroads.* (**b**) (of people) become exhausted and stop; fall asleep, faint or die: *Grandad usually conks out* (ie sleeps) *for an hour or so after lunch.*

conker /ˈkɒŋkə(r)/ *n* (*infml esp Brit*) **1** nut of the horse-chestnut tree. ⇨ illus at TREE. **2 conkers** [sing *v*] game played by children with horse-chestnuts. The conkers are hung on strings and each player takes turns in hitting the opponent's conker with his own until one is broken and its owner loses the game.

con man ⇨ CON.

connect /kəˈnekt/ *v* **1** [I, Ipr, Ip, Tn, Tn·pr, Tn·p] ~ (**sth**) (**up**) (**to/with sth**) come or bring together or into contact; join: *The wires connect (up) under the floor.* ○ *Where does the cooker connect with the gas-pipe?* ○ *The two towns are connected by a railway.* ○ *A railway connects Oxford and/with Reading.* ○ *Connect the fridge (up) to the electricity supply.* ○ *The thigh bone is connected to the hip bone.* ○ *The two rooms have a connecting door*, ie so that you can go straight from one room into the other. ○ *an ill-connected narrative.* **2** (**a**) [Tn, Tn·pr usu passive] ~ **sb** (**with sb/sth**) associate sb (with sb/sth); relate sb (to sb/sth): *a man connected with known criminals* ○ *The two men are connected by marriage.* ○ *She is connected with a noble family.* (**b**) [Tn, Tn·pr] ~ **sb/sth** (**with sb/sth**) think of (different things or people) as being related to each other: *I was surprised to hear them mentioned together: I've never connected them before.* ○ *People connect Vienna with waltzes and coffee-houses.* **3** [I, Ipr] ~ (**with sth**) (of a train, plane, etc) be timed to arrive so that passengers can transfer from or to another train, plane, etc: *These two planes connect.* ○ *The 9.00 am train from London connects with the 12.05 pm from Crewe.* ○ *There's a connecting flight at midday.* **4** [Tn, Tn·pr] ~ **sb** (**with sb**) (of a telephonist) put sb into contact by telephone: *Hold on, I'll just connect you (with Miss Jones).* **5** [I, Ipr] ~ (**with sb/sth**) (*infml*) (of a blow, etc) strike or touch: *a wild swing which failed to connect (with his chin).* Cf WELL-CONNECTED (WELL[3]).
□ **con**ˈ**necting rod** rod linking the piston and the crankshaft in an engine.

Connecticut /kəˈnetɪkət/ state on the east coast of the USA, one of the smallest in the country. It was one of the 13 original states. Although it has modern industry, much of it is still covered by forest.

connection (*Brit* also **connexion**) /kəˈnekʃn/ *n* **1** (**a**) [U] connecting or being connected: *How long will the connection of the telephone take?* ie How long will it take to install a telephone and connect it to the exchange? (**b**) [C] ~ **between sth and sth;** ~ **with/to sth** point where two things are connected; thing that connects: *There's a faulty connection in the fuse-box.* ○ *What is the connection between the two ideas*, ie How are they linked? ○ *Is there a connection between smoking and lung cancer?* ○ *His dismissal has no connection with* (ie is not due to) *the quality of his work.* **2** [C] train, plane, etc timed to leave a station, airport, etc soon after the arrival of another, enabling passengers to change from one to the other: *The train was late and I missed my connection.* **3** [C usu *pl*] person whom one knows socially or through business, esp one who has influence or high rank: *I heard about it through one of my business connections.* **4 connections** [pl] relatives: *She is British but also has German connections.* **5** [C] (*sl*) supplier of illegal drugs. **6** (idm) **in connection with sb/sth** with reference to sb/sth: *I am writing to you in connection with your job application.* **in this/that connection** (*fml*) with reference to this/that.

connective /kəˈnektɪv/ *adj* that connects things: *connective tissue.*
▷ **connective** *n* thing that connects, esp a linking word.

conning-tower /ˈkɒnɪŋ taʊə(r)/ *n* raised structure on a submarine containing the periscope.

conniption /kəˈnɪpʃn/ *n* (*US joc infml*) [usu pl] agitated state: *She went into conniptions at the idea.*

connive /kəˈnaɪv/ *v* [Ipr] ~ **at sth** (*derog*) disregard or seem to allow (a wrong action): *Not to protest is to connive at the destruction of the environment.*
▷ **connivance** /kəˈnaɪvəns/ *n* [U] ~ (**at/in sth**) conniving (at a wrong action): *a crime carried out with the connivance of/in connivance with the police.*
conniving *adj* acting slyly and unpleasantly so as to harm others: *You conniving bastard!*

connoisseur /ˌkɒnəˈsɜ:(r)/ *n* person with good judgement on matters in which appreciation of fineness or beauty is needed, esp the fine arts: *a connoisseur of painting, old porcelain, antiques, wine.*

connote /kəˈnəʊt/ *v* [Tn, Tf] (of words) suggest (sth) in addition to the main meaning: *a term connoting disapproval/that one disapproves of sth.*
▷ **connotation** /ˌkɒnəˈteɪʃn/ *n* idea which a word makes one think of in addition to the main meaning: *The word 'hack' means 'journalist' but has derogatory connotations.*

connubial /kəˈnju:bɪəl; *US* -ˈnu:-/ *adj* (*fml or joc*) of marriage; of husband and wife: *connubial life, bliss, etc.*

conquer /ˈkɒŋkə(r)/ *v* [Tn] **1** (**a**) take possession of (sth) by force: *The Normans conquered England in 1066.* (**b**) (*fig*) gain the admiration, love, etc of (sb/sth): *He set out to conquer the literary world of London.* ○ *She has conquered the hearts of many men*, ie they have fallen in love with her. **2** (**a**) defeat (an enemy, a rival, etc): *England conquered their main rivals in the first round of the competition.* (**b**) (*fig*) overcome (an obstacle, emotion, etc): *The mountain was not conquered* (ie successfully climbed) *until 1953.* ○ *Smallpox has finally been conquered.* ○ *You must conquer your fear of driving.*
▷ **conqueror** /ˈkɒŋkərə(r)/ *n* person who conquers: *William the Conqueror*, ie King William I of England.

conquest /ˈkɒŋkwest/ *n* **1** [U] conquering (eg of a country and its people); defeat: *the Norman Conquest*, ie of England by the Normans in 1066 ○ *the conquest of cancer.* **2** [C] (**a**) thing gained by conquering: *the Roman conquests in Africa.* (**b**) person whose admiration or (esp) love has been gained: *He is one of her many conquests.* ○ *You've made quite a conquest there*, ie He or she likes you!

conquistador /kɒnˈkwɪstədɔ:(r)/ *n* (*pl* ~**s** or ~**es**) one of the Spanish conquerors of Mexico and Peru in the 16th century.

Conrad /ˈkɒnræd/ Joseph (1857-1924), British novelist, born of Polish parents (original name Korzeniowski). He went to sea as a young man and used this as the background for many of his novels (eg *Lord Jim*), which explore the theme of human vulnerability and corruptibility. He was a leading modernist and is considered by many to be one of the greatest novelists in the English language.

Cons *abbr* (*Brit politics*) Conservative: *James Crofton (Cons).*

consanguineous /ˌkɒnsæŋˈgwɪnɪəs/ *adj* (*fml*) belonging to or descended from the same family: *a consanguineous relationship.* ▷ **consanguinity** *n* [U].

conscience /ˈkɒnʃəns/ *n* [C, U] **1** person's

awareness of right and wrong with regard to his own thoughts and actions: *have a clear/guilty conscience*, ie feel one has done right/wrong ○ *After she had committed the crime, her conscience was troubled*, ie she felt very guilty. ○ *She cheerfully cheats and lies; she's got no conscience at all.* ○ *I must go. It's a matter of conscience*, ie I think it would be morally wrong not to go. ○ *freedom/liberty of conscience*, ie to hold and express one's beliefs freely ○ *prisoners of conscience*, ie people imprisoned because they believe it is wrong to support a political system, etc. **2** (idm) **ease sb's conscience/mind** ⇨ EASE[2]. **have sth on one's conscience** feel troubled about sth one has done or failed to do: *He has several murders on his conscience.* **in all conscience** by any reasonable standard: *You cannot in all conscience regard that as fair pay.* **on one's ˈconscience** making one feel one has done wrong, or left sth undone: *It's still on my conscience that I didn't warn her in time.* **search one's heart/conscience** ⇨ SEARCH.

□ **ˈconscience clause** clause, esp in a law, which ensures that those whose conscience would not allow them to obey are not punished for their beliefs.

ˈconscience money money paid to make one feel less guilty, esp when one should have paid it before.

ˈconscience-stricken /-strɪkən/ *adj* filled with remorse.

conscientious /ˌkɒnʃɪˈenʃəs/ *adj* **1** (of people or conduct) careful to do what one ought to do, and do it as well as one can: *a conscientious worker, pupil, attitude.* **2** (of actions) done with great care and attention: *This essay is a most conscientious piece of work.* ▷ **conscientiously** *adv.* **conscientiousness** *n* [U].

□ **ˌconscientious obˈjector** person who refuses to serve in the armed forces because he thinks it is morally wrong. Cf PACIFIST (PACIFISM).

conscious /ˈkɒnʃəs/ *adj* **1** knowing what is going on around one because one is able to use bodily senses and mental powers; awake: *He was in a coma for days, but now he's (fully) conscious again.* ○ *She spoke to us in her conscious moments.* **2** ~ **of sth/that...** aware; noticing: *be conscious of being watched/that one is being watched* ○ *Are you conscious (of) how people will regard such behaviour?* **3** (of actions, feelings, etc) realized by oneself; intentional: *One's conscious motives are often different from one's subconscious ones.* ○ *I had to make a conscious effort not to be rude to him.* **4** being particularly aware of and interested in the thing mentioned: *trying to make the workers more politically conscious* ○ *Teenagers are very ˈfashion-conscious.* ▷ **consciously** *adv.*

consciousness /ˈkɒnʃəsnɪs/ *n* [U] **1** (a) state of being conscious(1): *The blow caused him to lose consciousness.* ○ *recover/regain consciousness after an accident.* **(b)** ~ **(of sth/that...)** state of being aware; awareness: *my consciousness of her needs* ○ *class consciousness*, ie awareness of the struggle between social classes and strong attachment to one's own class. **2** all the ideas, thoughts, feelings, etc of a person or people: *attitudes that are deeply ingrained in the English consciousness.*

conscript /kənˈskrɪpt/ *v* [Tn, Tn·pr] ~ **sb (into sth)** force sb by law to serve in the armed forces: *conscripted into the army* ○ (*fig*) *I got conscripted into the team when their top player was injured.* Cf DRAFT.

▷ **conscript** /ˈkɒnskrɪpt/ *n* person who has been conscripted: [attrib] *conscript soldiers* ○ *a conscript army.* Cf VOLUNTEER 2.

conscription /kənˈskrɪpʃn/ *n* [U] conscripting of people into the armed forces. ⇨ article at ARMED FORCES.

consecrate /ˈkɒnsɪkreɪt/ *v* **1** [Tn, Cn·n] bring (sth) into religious use or (sb) into a religious office by a special ceremony: *The new church was consecrated by the Bishop of Chester.* ○ *He was consecrated Archbishop last year.* **2** [Tn·pr] ~ **sth/sb to sth** reserve sth/sb for or devote sth/sb to a special (esp religious) purpose: *consecrate one's life to the service of God, to the relief of suffering.* Cf DEDICATE 3.

▷ **consecration** /ˌkɒnsɪˈkreɪʃn/ *n* [C, U] (instance of) consecrating or being consecrated: *the consecration of a bishop*, ie the ceremony at which a priest is made a bishop.

consecutive /kənˈsekjʊtɪv/ *adj* **1** coming one after the other without interruption; following continuously: *on three consecutive days, Monday, Tuesday and Wednesday.* **2** (of a grammatical clause) that expresses a consequence. ▷ **consecutively** *adv.*

consensus /kənˈsensəs/ *n* [C, U] ~ **(on sth/that...)** agreement in opinion; collective opinion: *The two parties have reached a consensus.* ○ *There is broad consensus (of opinion) in the country on this issue.* ○ [attrib] *consensus politics*, ie the practice of proposing policies which will be given support by (nearly) all parties.

consent /kənˈsent/ *v* [I, Ipr, It] ~ **(to sth)** give agreement or permission: *She made the proposal, and I readily consented (to it).* ○ *She won't consent to him staying out late/to his staying out late.* ○ *They finally consented* (ie agreed) *to go with us.* ○ *sex between consenting adults*, ie who both agree to it.

▷ **consent** *n* [U] **1** ~ **(to sth)** agreement; permission: *Her parents refused their consent to the marriage.* ○ *He gave his consent for the project to get under way.* ○ *She was chosen as leader by common consent*, ie Everyone agreed to the choice. ○ *Silence implies consent*, ie One is assumed to agree if one remains silent. **2** (idm) **with one consent** (*arch*) unanimously.

consequence /ˈkɒnsɪkwəns; *US* -kwens/ *n* **1** [C usu *pl*] thing that is a result or an effect of sth else: *Her investment had disastrous consequences: she lost everything she owned.* ○ *be ready to take/suffer/bear the consequences of one's actions*, ie accept the bad things which happen as a result. ○ *recent developments which could have far-reaching consequences for the country's economy.* **2** [U] (*fml*) importance: *It is of no consequence.* ○ *He may be a man of consequence* (ie an important man or man of high rank) *in his own country, but he's nobody here.* **3 consequences** [sing *v*] game in which a player writes down a line of a story and each player then takes it in turn to add further lines without knowing what other players have written. **4** (idm) **in consequence (of sth)** (*infml*) as a result (of sth): *She was found guilty, and lost her job in consequence (of it).*

consequent /ˈkɒnsɪkwənt/ *adj* **1** ~ **(on/upon sth)** (*fml*) following sth as a result or an effect: *his resignation and the consequent public uproar* ○ *the rise in prices consequent upon the failure of the crops.* **2** (*fml*) logically consistent.

▷ **consequent** *n* (*fml*) thing that is true as a consequence of another thing.

consequently *adv* as a result; therefore: *My car broke down and consequently I was late.*

consequential /ˌkɒnsɪˈkwenʃl/ *adj* (*fml*) **1** following as a result or an effect (esp indirect): *She was injured and suffered a consequential loss of earnings.* **2** (a) of far-reaching importance. **(b)** (*derog*) (of a person) self-important; pompous. ▷ **consequentially** /-ʃəlɪ/ *adv.*

conservancy /kənˈsɜːvənsɪ/ *n* (*Brit*) **1** (often **Conservancy**) [CGp] group of officials controlling a port, a river, an area of land, etc: *the Thames Conservancy* ○ *the Nature Conservancy.* **2** [U] official conservation (of forests, etc).

conservation /ˌkɒnsəˈveɪʃn/ *n* [U] **1** prevention of loss, waste, damage, destruction, etc: *the conservation of hedgerows, forests, water resources, old buildings, etc* ○ *wildlife conservation.* **2** preservation of the natural environment: *She is very interested in conservation.* ⇨ articles at COUNTRYSIDE, ENVIRONMENT.

▷ **conservationist** /-ʃənɪst/ *n* person who is interested in conservation(2).

□ **conserˈvation area** (*Brit*) area protected by law from changes that would damage its natural or architectural character.

conserˈvation law scientific law that says that the amount of energy, mass, electric charge or similar properties in a given amount of matter stays the same even if changes, such as chemical reactions, take place in it.

conserˌvation of ˈenergy the principle that the total quantity of energy in the universe never varies.

conserˌvation of ˈmass the principle that matter cannot be created or destroyed.

conservatism /kənˈsɜːvətɪzəm/ *n* [U] **1** tendency to resist great or sudden change (esp in politics): *people's innate conservatism.* **2** (usu **Conservatism**) the principles of the Conservative Party in British politics.

conservative /kənˈsɜːvətɪv/ *adj* **1** opposed to great or sudden change: *Old people are usually more conservative than young people.* **2** (usu **Conservative**) of the British Conservative Party: *Conservative principles, candidates, voters.* ⇨ article at POLITICS. **3** cautious; moderate; avoiding extremes: *There must have been a thousand people there, at a conservative estimate*, ie a low one. ○ *She is conservative in the way she dresses.*

▷ **conservative** *n* **1** conservative person. **2** (usu **Conservative**) member of the British Conservative Party.

conservatively *adv.*

□ **the Conˈservative Party** one of the main British political parties, which supports capitalism and free enterprise, and opposes socialism. It developed from the old *Tory party in the 1830s. Cf THE LABOUR PARTY (LABOUR[1]), THE LIBERAL DEMOCRATS (LIBERAL).

conservatoire /kənˈsɜːvətwɑː(r)/ (also **conservatory**) *n* school of music, drama, etc, esp in Europe.

conservatory /kənˈsɜːvətrɪ; *US* -tɔːrɪ/ *n* **1** room with glass walls and roof used to protect plants from cold, built against an outside wall of a house, and with a door into the house. ⇨ illus at HOME. **2** = CONSERVATOIRE.

conserve /kənˈsɜːv/ *v* [Tn] prevent (sth) from being changed, lost or destroyed: *conserve one's strength, health, resources, etc* ○ *new laws to conserve wildlife in the area.* Cf PRESERVE.

▷ **conserve** /ˈkɒnsɜːv/ *n* [C usu *pl*, U] jam, typically with quite large pieces of fruit in it. Cf PRESERVE *n*.

consider /kənˈsɪdə(r)/ *v* **1** [Tn, Tn·pr, Tw, Tg] ~ **sb/sth (for/as sth)** think about sb/sth, esp in order to make a decision; contemplate sb/sth: *We have considered your application carefully, but cannot offer you the job.* ○ *consider sb for a job/as a candidate* ○ *Have you considered how to get there?* ○ *We are considering going to Canada*, ie we may go there. **2** [Tf, Cn·a, Cn·n, Cn·n/a, Cn·t] ~ **sb/sth as sth** be of the opinion; regard sb/sth as sth: *We consider that you are not to blame.* ○ *We consider this (to be) very important.* ○ *Do you consider it wise to interfere?* ○ *He will be considered a weak leader.* ○ *a painting previously considered as worthless, but which now turns out to be very valuable* ○ *He's generally considered to have the finest tenor voice in the country.* ○ (*fml*) *He's very well considered* (ie people have a high opinion of him) *within the company.* ○ *Consider yourself* (ie You are) *under arrest.* **3** [Tn] take (sth) into account; make allowances for: *We must consider the feelings of other people.* ○ *In judging him you should consider his youth.* **4** [Tn] (*fml*) look at (sb/sth) carefully: *He stood considering the painting for some minutes.* **5** (idm) **all things considered** ⇨ THING. **one's conˌsidered oˈpinion** one's opinion arrived at after some thought: *It's my considered opinion that you should resign.*

considerable /kənˈsɪdərəbl/ *adj* great in amount or size: *a considerable quantity, sum, distance, etc* ○ *bought at considerable expense.*

▷ **considerably** /-əblɪ/ *adv* much; a great deal: *It's considerably colder this morning.*

considerate /kənˈsɪdərət/ *adj* ~ **(towards sb)**; ~ **(of sb) (to do sth)** careful not to hurt or inconvenience others; thoughtful: *a considerate person, act, attitude* ○ *considerate towards her employees* ○ *It was considerate of you not to play the piano while I was asleep.* ▷ **considerately** *adv.*

considerateness *n* [U].

consideration /kənˌsɪdəˈreɪʃn/ *n* **1** [U] action of considering (CONSIDER 1) or thinking about sth: *Please give the matter your careful consideration.* ○ *The proposals are still under consideration,* ie being considered. **2** [U] ~ (**for sb/sth**) quality of being sensitive or thoughtful towards others, their feelings, etc: *He has never shown much consideration for his wife's needs.* ○ *Out of consideration for the bereaved family's feelings the papers did not print the story.* **3** [C] thing that must be thought about or taken into account; reason: *Time is an important consideration in this case.* ○ *Several considerations have influenced my decision.* **4** [C] (*fml*) reward; payment: *I will do it for you for a small consideration (of £50).* **5** (idm) **in consideration of sth** (*fml*) in return for sth; on account of sth: *a small payment in consideration of sb's services.* **leave sth out of account/consideration** ⇨ LEAVE[1]. **take sth into consideration** take account of sth; make allowances for sth: *I always take fuel consumption into consideration when buying a car.*

considering /kənˈsɪdərɪŋ/ *prep, conj* in view of (the fact that); taking into consideration: *She's very active, considering her age.* ○ *Considering he's only just started, he knows quite a lot about it.* ○ *You've done very well, considering,* eg in view of the adverse circumstances.

consign /kənˈsaɪn/ *v* **1** [Tn·pr] (*fml*) (**a**) ~ **sb/sth to sb/sth** hand over sb/sth to sb/sth; give sb/sth up to sb/sth: *consign a child to/into its uncle's care* ○ *consign one's soul to God* ○ (*fig*) *The body was consigned to the flames,* ie burned. (**b**) ~ **sth to sth** put (sth unwanted) away: *an old chair that had been consigned to the attic.* **2** [Tn, Tn·pr] ~ **sth** (**to sb**) send (goods, etc) for delivery (esp to a buyer): *The goods have been consigned (to you) by rail.*

▷ **consignee** /ˌkɒnsaɪˈniː/ *n* person to whom sth is consigned (CONSIGN 2).

consigner, **consignor** /-nə(r)/ *ns* person who consigns goods.

consignment *n* **1** [U] consigning. **2** [C] goods consigned: *a consignment of wheat bound for Europe.* **3** (idm) **on consignment** with payment to be made after the goods have been sold by the receiver: *take/send/ship/supply goods on consignment.*

□ **conˈsignment note** note sent with a consignment of goods, giving details of the goods.

consist /kənˈsɪst/ *v* (not in the continuous tenses) (phr v) **consist of sth** (**a**) be composed or made up of sth: *The committee consists of ten members.* ○ *a mixture consisting of flour and water.* ⇨ Usage at COMPRISE. (**b**) **consist in sth** (*fml*) have sth as its chief or only element or feature: *The beauty of the plan consists in its simplicity.*

consistence /kənˈsɪstəns/ *n* [U] = CONSISTENCY 1.

consistency /kənˈsɪstənsɪ/ *n* **1** (also **consistence**) [U] (*approv*) quality of being consistent(1): *His views lack consistency: one day he's a conservative, the next he's a liberal.* **2** [C, U] degree of thickness, firmness or solidity, esp of thick liquids, or of sth made by mixing with a liquid: *Mix flour and liquid to the right consistency.* ○ *mixtures of various consistencies* ○ *It should have the consistency of thick soup.*

consistent /kənˈsɪstənt/ *adj* **1** (*approv*) (of a person, his behaviour, his views, etc) always keeping to the same pattern or style; unchanging: *You're not very consistent: first you condemn me, then you praise me.* **2** [pred] ~ (**with sth**) in agreement: *What you say now is not consistent with what you said last week.* ○ *The pattern of injuries is consistent with* (ie could have been caused by) *an attack with a knife.* ○ *I left as early as was consistent with politeness.* ▷ **consistently** *adv.*

consistory /kənˈsɪstərɪ/ *n* [CGp] formal council of the cardinals of the Roman Catholic Church, usu presided over by the Pope.

consolation /ˌkɒnsəˈleɪʃn/ *n* **1** [U] consoling or being consoled: *a few words of consolation* ○ *Money is no consolation when you don't like your work,* ie does not make up for not liking it. **2** [C] person or thing that consoles: *Your company has been a great consolation to me.* ○ *At least you weren't hurt — that's one consolation,* ie one good aspect of an otherwise bad situation.

□ **consoˈlation prize** prize given to sb who has just missed winning or has come last: (*fig*) *She missed out on the top job, but as a consolation prize was made deputy chairman.*

consolatory /kənˈsɒlətərɪ; *US* -tɔːrɪ/ *adj* tending or intended to console; comforting: *a consolatory letter, remark, etc.*

console[1] /kənˈsəʊl/ *v* [Tn, Tn·pr] ~ **sb** (**for/on sth**) give comfort or sympathy to (sb who is unhappy, disappointed, etc): *Nothing could console him when his pet dog died.* ○ *console sb for/on a loss* ○ *He consoled himself with the thought that it might have been worse.*

▷ **consolable** *adj* able to be consoled.

console[2] /ˈkɒnsəʊl/ *n* **1** panel for the controls of electronic or mechanical equipment. **2** radio or TV cabinet designed to stand on the floor. **3** frame containing the keyboard and other controls of an organ. **4** bracket to support a shelf.

consolidate /kənˈsɒlɪdeɪt/ *v* **1** [I, Tn] (cause sth to) become more solid, secure or strong: *The time has come for the firm to consolidate after several years of rapid expansion.* ○ *With his new play he has consolidated his position as the country's leading dramatist.* **2** [I, Ipr, Tn, Tn·pr] ~ (**sth**) (**into sth**) (*commerce*) (cause things to) unite or combine (into one): *All the debts have been consolidated.* ○ *The two companies consolidated for greater efficiency.*

▷ **consolidation** /kənˌsɒlɪˈdeɪʃn/ *n* [U] consolidating or being consolidated: *the consolidation of the party's position at the top of the opinion polls.*

□ **conˌsolidated anˈnuities** consols.

the ConˌsolidatedˈFund (in Britain) government fund into which money obtained by taxation is paid, used esp to pay interest on the national debt.

consols /ˈkɒnsɒlz/ *n* [pl] type of British government stock(5b) that pays a low rate of interest.

consommé /kənˈsɒmeɪ; *US* ˌkɒnsəˈmeɪ/ *n* [U] clear meat soup.

consonance /ˈkɒnsənəns/ *n* [U] (*fml*) **1** harmony. **2** (*fig*) ~ (**with sth**) agreement: *actions which were not in consonance with his words.*

consonant[1] /ˈkɒnsənənt/ *n* (*phonetics*) (**a**) speech sound produced by completely or partially obstructing the air being breathed out through the mouth. (**b**) letter of the alphabet or phonetic symbol for such a sound: *b, c, d, f,* etc. Cf VOWEL.

consonant[2] /ˈkɒnsənənt/ *adj* ~ **with sth** (*fml*) in agreement; suitable; consistent(2): *behaving with a dignity consonant with his rank.*

consort[1] /ˈkɒnsɔːt/ *n* **1** [C] husband or wife, esp of a ruler. Cf PRINCE CONSORT (PRINCE). **2** [CGp] group of musicians playing or singing early music, esp English music of the late 16th to early 18th centuries: *a consort of voices, viols.*

consort[2] /kənˈsɔːt/ *v* (*fml*) **1** [Ipr, Ip] ~ **with sb/together** (*esp derog*) spend time with sb/together; associate with sb: *He'd been consorting with known criminals.* **2** [Ipr] ~ **with sth** go well with sth; be in harmony with sth: *dubious practices which consort ill with* (ie contradict) *his public statements on morality.*

consortium /kənˈsɔːtɪəm; *US* -ˈsɔːrʃɪəm/ *n* (*pl* **-tia** /-tɪə; *US* -ʃə/) temporary association of a number of countries, companies, banks, etc for a common purpose: *A consortium of construction companies will build the power-station.*

conspectus /kənˈspektəs/ *n* (*pl* ~**es**) (*fml*) general view or survey of a subject, etc.

conspicuous /kənˈspɪkjʊəs/ *adj* **1** ~ (**for sth**) easily seen; noticeable; remarkable: *If you're walking along a badly-lit road at night you should wear conspicuous clothes.* ○ (*ironic*) *She wasn't exactly conspicuous for her helpfulness,* ie wasn't helpful. ○ *make oneself conspicuous,* ie attract attention by unusual behaviour, wearing unusual clothes, etc. **2** (idm) **conˌspicuous by one's ˈabsence** noticeably absent when one ought to be present: *When it came to cleaning up afterwards, the boys were conspicuous by their absence.* ▷ **conspicuously** *adv*: *conspicuously absent.* **conspicuousness** *n* [U].

conspiracy /kənˈspɪrəsɪ/ *n* ~ (**to sth/to do sth**) **1** [U] act of conspiring, esp joint planning of a crime: *accused of conspiracy to murder.* **2** [C] plan made by conspiring: *a conspiracy to overthrow the Government* ○ *a conspiracy of silence,* ie an agreement not to talk publicly about sth which should not remain secret. Cf PLOT[2] 2.

conspire /kənˈspaɪə(r)/ *v* **1** [I, Ipr, Ip, It] ~ (**with sb**) (**against sb**); ~ (**together**) (**against sb**) make secret plans (with others), esp to do wrong: *conspire with others against one's leader* ○ *They conspired to overthrow the Government.* **2** [Ipr, It] ~ **against sb/sth** (of events) seem to act together; combine disadvantageously for sb/sth: *circumstances conspiring against our success* ○ *events that conspired to bring about his downfall.*

▷ **conspirator** /kənˈspɪrətə(r)/ *n* person who conspires.

conspiratorial /kənˌspɪrəˈtɔːrɪəl/ *adj* of or like conspirators or conspiracy: *She handed the note to me with a conspiratorial air.*

Constable /ˈkʌnstəbl/ John (1776-1837), English painter. Along with *Turner, he is considered to be one of the greatest English landscape artists. He often took the countryside of East Anglia as his subject, esp the parts along the River Stour, known now as **Constable Country**. His paintings (eg *The Hay Wain*) show his detailed observation, and he is famous for his cloud studies. Towards the end of his career, he developed a more lyrical style, using thick layers of paint to create his effects. ⇨ illus.

constable /ˈkʌnstəbl; *US* ˈkɒn-/ *n* **1** = POLICE CONSTABLE (POLICE): [attrib] *Constable Johnson.* **2** title given to the governor of certain royal castles in Britain.

▷ **constabulary** /kənˈstæbjʊlərɪ; *US* -lerɪ/ *n* [Gp] police force of a particular area, town, etc: *the Royal Ulster Constabulary.*

constancy /ˈkɒnstənsɪ/ *n* [U] (*approv*) **1** quality of being firm and unchanging: *constancy of purpose.* **2** faithfulness: *a husband's constancy.*

constant /ˈkɒnstənt/ *adj* **1** [usu attrib] going on all the time; happening again and again: *constant chattering, complaints, interruptions* ○ *This entrance is in constant use; do not block it.* **2** unchanging; fixed: *a constant speed, value, etc* ○ *Pressure in the container remains constant.* **3** [usu attrib] (*approv*) firm; faithful: *a constant friend, companion, supporter, etc.*

▷ **constant** *n* (*mathematics or physics*) number or quantity that does not vary. Cf VARIABLE *n*.

constantly *adv* continuously; frequently: *He's constantly disturbing me.* ○ *She worries constantly.*

Constantine /ˈkɒnstəntaɪn/ (died 337AD), Roman emperor, known as Constantine the Great. He founded a new capital named after himself, Constantinople, formerly Byzantium. He took supreme power in the empire and under him Christianity gradually became its official religion.

constellation /ˌkɒnstəˈleɪʃn/ *n* **1** named group of stars (eg *the Great Bear*). **2** (*fig*) group of associated or similar people or things: *a constellation of Hollywood talent.*

consternation /ˌkɒnstəˈneɪʃn/ *n* [U] surprise and anxiety; great dismay: *filled with consternation* ○ *To her consternation, he asked her to make a speech.*

constipated /ˈkɒnstɪpeɪtɪd/ *adj* unable to empty the bowels: *If you're constipated you should eat more roughage.*

▷ **constipation** /ˌkɒnstɪˈpeɪʃn/ *n* [U] state of being constipated.

constituency /kənˈstɪtjʊənsɪ/ *n* [CGp] (**a**) (body of voters living in a) district having its own elected representative in parliament. ⇨ article at POLITICS. (**b**) group of people with the same interests that one can turn to for support: *Mr Jones has a natural constituency among steel workers.*

📖 There are 650 constituencies in Britain and most of these are named according to their geographical location. Since its entry into the

John Constable: The Hay Wain

European Community in 1973, Britain has also been divided into 81 larger constituencies, each represented by a member of the European Parliament (MEP), also known as a Euro-MP. MEPs are chosen in separate elections from members of the British Parliament (MPs).

constituent /kənˈstɪtjʊənt/ *adj* [attrib] forming or helping to make a whole: *Analyse the sentence into its constituent parts.*

▷ **constituent** *n* **1** member of a constituency. **2** component part: *the constituents of the mixture.*

□ **conˌstituent asˈsembly** one which has the power to make or alter a political constitution.

constitute /ˈkɒnstɪtju:t/ *v* **1** [Tn] (not in the continuous tenses); (*fml*) make up or form (a whole); be the components of: *Twelve months constitute a year.* ○ *The committee is constituted of members of all three parties.* ○ (*fig*) *He is so constituted* (ie His nature is such) *that he can accept criticism without resentment.* ⇨ Usage at COMPRISE. **2** [Ln] (not in the continuous tenses) be: *My decision does not constitute* (ie should not be regarded as) *a precedent.* ○ *The defeat constitutes a major set-back for our diplomacy.* **3** [Tn] give formal authority to (a group of people); establish: *The committee had been improperly constituted, and therefore had no legal power.* **4** [Cn·n] (*fml*) give (sb) formal authority to hold (a position, etc); appoint: *He seemed to have constituted himself our representative.*

constitution /ˌkɒnstɪˈtju:ʃn; *US* -ˈtu:ʃn/ *n* **1** [C] (system of) laws and principles according to which a state is governed: *Britain has an unwritten constitution, and the United States has a written constitution.* **2 (a)** [U] (*fml*) action or manner of constituting (CONSTITUTE 1, 3, 4): *the constitution of an advisory group.* **(b)** [C] (*fml*) general structure of a thing: *the constitution of the solar spectrum.* **3** [C] condition of a person's body with regard to health, strength, etc: *a robust/weak constitution* ○ *Only people with a strong constitution should go climbing.*

constitutional /ˌkɒnstɪˈtju:ʃənl; *US* -ˈtu:-/ *adj* **1** of a constitution(1): *constitutional government, reform, etc* ○ *a constitutional ruler,* ie one controlled or limited by a constitution ○ *They claimed that the new law was not constitutional,* ie not allowed by the constitution. **2** of a person's constitution(3): *constitutional weakness, robustness, etc.*

▷ **constitutional** *n* (*dated or joc*) short walk taken to improve or maintain one's health: *go for/take a constitutional.*

constitutionalism /-ʃənəlɪzəm/ *n* [U] (belief in) constitutional government or constitutional principles.

constitutionally /-ʃənəlɪ/ *adj.*

constitutive /ˈkɒnstɪtju:tɪv, kənˈstɪtjʊtɪv; *US also* -ˈstɪtʃʊ-/ *adj* (*fml*) having the power to take action, make appointments, etc: *a constitutive committee.*

constrain /kənˈstreɪn/ *v* [Tn, Cn·t] (*fml*) make (sb) do sth by strong (moral) persuasion or by force: *As an artist he didn't consider himself constrained* (ie restricted) *by the same rules of social conduct as other people.* ○ *I feel constrained to write* (ie I feel I must write) *and complain in the strongest possible terms.*

▷ **constrained** *adj* (of voice, manner, etc) forced; uneasy; unnatural.

constrainedly /-ɪdlɪ/ *adv.*

constraint /kənˈstreɪnt/ *n* **1** [U] constraining or being constrained: *act under constraint,* ie because one is forced to do so. **2** [C] ~ **(on sth)** thing that limits or restricts: *There are no constraints on your choice of subject for the essay,* ie You can choose whatever subject you like. **3** [U] (*fml*) strained manner; unwillingness to be friendly; uneasiness: *I was aware of a certain constraint on their part when they were in my presence.*

constrict /kənˈstrɪkt/ *v* [Tn] make (sth) tight, smaller or narrower: *a tight collar that constricts the neck* ○ *administering a drug that constricts the blood vessels* ○ (*fig*) *Our way of life is rather constricted* (ie We cannot do so many things) *now that our income is so reduced.*

▷ **constriction** /kənˈstrɪkʃn/ *n* **1** [U] constricting. **2** [C] **(a)** feeling of tightness: *a constriction in the chest.* **(b)** thing that constricts: *the constrictions of life on a low income.*

constrictor /kənˈstrɪktə(r)/ *n* **1** snake which kills by twisting itself very tightly round its victim and crushing it. Cf BOA. **2** muscle that tightens round an organ.

construct /kənˈstrʌkt/ *v* [Tn] **1** build (sth); put or fit together; form: *construct a factory, an aircraft, a model, a sentence, a theory* ○ *a hut constructed (out) of branches* ○ *a well-constructed novel.* **2** (*geometry*) draw (a line, figure, etc) in accordance with certain rules.

▷ **construct** /ˈkɒnstrʌkt/ *n* thing that is made by the mind, eg a system or theory: *the theoretical constructs of modern linguistics.*

constructor /kənˈstrʌktə(r)/ *n* person who constructs things: *oil-rig constructors.*

construction /kənˈstrʌkʃn/ *n* **1** [U] action or manner of constructing; being constructed: *the construction of new roads* ○ *The new railway is still under construction,* ie being constructed. ○ *The wall is of very solid construction,* ie is solidly constructed. ○ [attrib] *the construction industry,* ie the building of roads, bridges, buildings, etc. **2** [C] thing constructed; structure; building: *a complex construction of wood and glass* ○ *The shelter is a brick construction.* **3** [C] way in which words are put together to form a phrase, clause or sentence: *This dictionary gives the meanings of words and also illustrates the constructions they can be used in.* **4** [C] (*fml*) sense in which words, statements, etc are to be understood; meaning: *What construction do you put on his actions?* ie How do you understand their purpose? ○ *The sentence does not bear such a construction,* ie cannot be understood in that way. Cf CONSTRUE 1.

constructive /kənˈstrʌktɪv/ *adj* having a useful purpose; helpful: *constructive criticism, proposals, remarks, etc.* ▷ **constructively** *adv.*

construe /kənˈstru:/ *v* **1** [Tn, Tw, Cn·n/a] ~ **sth (as sth)** (*fml*) explain the meaning of (words, sentences, actions, etc); interpret sth: *How do you construe what he did?* ○ *Her remarks were wrongly construed,* ie were misunderstood. ○ *I construed his statement as a refusal.* Cf CONSTRUCTION 4. **2 (a)** [Tn] (*grammar*) analyse the syntax of (a sentence). **(b)** [I, Tn] (*dated*) translate (a piece of text, esp from Latin or Greek).

consubstantiation /ˌkɒnsəbˌstænʃɪˈeɪʃn/ *n* [U] doctrine that the bread and wine of the Eucharist continue to exist as bread and wine after the consecration as well as being the body and blood of Christ. Cf TRANSUBSTANTIATION.

consul /ˈkɒnsl/ *n* **1** official appointed by a state to live in a foreign city in order to help people from his own country who are travelling or living there, and protect their interests: *the British Consul in Marseilles.* Cf HIGH COMMISSIONER (HIGH[1]). **2** either of the two magistrates who ruled in ancient Rome before it became an Empire. **3** any one of the three chief magistrates of the French Republic, (1799-1804).

▷ **consular** /ˈkɒnsjʊlə(r); *US* -səl-/ *adj* of a consul.

consulship /-ʃɪp/ *n* **1** position of a consul: *appointed to the consulship.* **2** period of time during which a consul holds his position.

consulate /ˈkɒnsjʊlət; *US* -səl-/ *n* **1** offices of a consul(1): *the British consulate in Marseilles.* Cf EMBASSY 1, HIGH COMMISSION (HIGH[1]). **2 the Consulate** period of consular government in France.

consult /kənˈsʌlt/ *v* **1** [Tn, Tn·pr] ~ **sb/sth (about sth)** go to (a person, book, etc) for information, advice, etc: *consult one's lawyer, a map, a dictionary* ○ *a consulting engineer,* ie one who has specialized knowledge and gives advice ○ *I consulted a doctor about my pains.* **2** [Ipr] ~ **with sb** discuss matters with sb; confer with sb: *consult with one's partners.*

□ **conˈsulting room** room where a doctor talks to and examines patients.

consultant /kənˈsʌltənt/ *n* **1** ~ **(on sth)** person who gives expert advice (in business, law, etc): *a firm of management consultants* ○ *the president's consultant on economic affairs.* **2** ~ **(in sth)** (in Britain) hospital doctor of senior rank: *a consultant in obstetrics* ○ [attrib] *a consultant surgeon.* Cf REGISTRAR 2.

consultation /ˌkɒnslˈteɪʃn/ *n* **1** [U] consulting or being consulted: *acting in consultation with the director,* ie with his advice and agreement ○ *consultation of a dictionary.* **2** [C] **(a)** meeting for discussion: *top-level consultations between the US and Soviet delegations.* **(b)** meeting to discuss, or seek advice about, a sick person.

consultative /kənˈsʌltətɪv/ *adj* of or for consulting; advisory: *a consultative committee, document, etc.*

consume /kənˈsju:m; *US* -ˈsu:m/ *v* [Tn] **1 (a)** use (sth) up: *consume resources, time, stores, etc* ○ *The car consumes a lot of fuel.* ○ (*rhet*) *He soon consumed his fortune,* ie spent the money wastefully. (**b**) destroy (sb/sth) by fire, decay, etc: *The fire quickly consumed the wooden hut.* ○ (*fig*) *be consumed* (ie filled) *with envy, hatred, greed, etc.* **2** (*fml*) eat or drink (sth).

▷ **consuming** *adj* [attrib] that obsesses or dominates sb: *Building model trains is his consuming passion.*

consumer /kənˈsju:mə(r); *US* -su:-/ *n* person who buys goods or uses services: *Consumers are encouraged to complain about faulty goods.* ○ *electricity consumers* ○ [attrib] *consumer rights, protection, etc* ○ *consumer research*, ie to find out consumers' views. Cf PRODUCER.

▷ **consumerism** /-mərɪzəm/ *n* [U] (campaigning for the) protection of consumers' interests.

□ **conˌsumer ˈcredit** credit available to consumers to buy goods or services, eg through credit cards and loans.

conˌsumer ˈdurables = DURABLES (DURABLE).

conˈsumer goods goods bought and used by individual customers, eg food, clothing, domestic appliances. Cf CAPITAL GOODS (CAPITAL[2]).

consummate[1] /kənˈsʌmət/ *adj* [attrib] (*fml*) highly skilled; perfect: *a consummate artist, performance, piece of work* ○ *She dealt with the problem with consummate skill.* ○ (*derog*) *a consummate liar.*

consummate[2] /ˈkɒnsəmeɪt/ *v* [Tn] (*fml*) **1** make (sth) complete or perfect: *This award consummates my life's work.* **2** make (a marriage) legally complete by having sexual intercourse.

▷ **consummation** /ˌkɒnsəˈmeɪʃn/ *n* [C, U] action or point of completing, making perfect, or fulfilling: *the consummation of one's life's work, one's ambitions, a marriage.*

consumption /kənˈsʌmpʃn/ *n* [U] **1** (**a**) using up of food, energy, resources, etc: *The meat was declared unfit for human consumption.* ○ *conspicuous consumption which is an affront to people on low incomes.* (**b**) quantity used: *We have measured the car's fuel consumption.* **2** (*dated*) tuberculosis of the lungs.

consumptive /kənˈsʌmptɪv/ *adj* (*dated*) suffering or tending to suffer from consumption(2).

▷ **consumptive** *n* consumptive person.

cont *abbr* **1** contents. **2** (also **contd**) continued: *cont on p 74.*

contact /ˈkɒntækt/ *n* **1** [U] ~ (**with sb/sth**) (**a**) state of touching (used esp with the *vs* shown): *The two substances are now in contact (with each other), and a chemical reaction is occurring.* ○ *His hand came into contact with* (ie touched) *a hot surface.* ○ *The label sticks on contact*, ie when it touches a surface. ○ (*fig*) *The troops came into contact with* (ie met) *the enemy.* ○ (*fig*) *Pupils must be brought into contact with* (ie exposed to) *new ideas.* (**b**) communication: *in constant radio/telephone contact (with sb)* ○ *Beyond a certain distance we are out of contact with our headquarters.* ○ *She's lost contact with her son*, ie no longer hears from him, knows where he is, etc. ○ *two people avoiding eye contact*, ie avoiding looking directly at each other. **2** [C] instance of meeting or communicating: *extensive contacts with firms abroad.* **3** [C] person one has met or will meet, esp one who can be helpful: *I have a useful contact in New York.* **4** [C] (**a**) electrical connection: *A poor contact causes power to fail occasionally.* (**b**) device that makes an electrical connection: *The switches close the contacts and complete the circuit.* **5** [C] (*medical*) person who may be infectious because he has recently been near to sb who has a contagious disease. **6** (idm) **make contact (with sb/sth)** succeed in speaking to or meeting sb/sth: *They made contact with headquarters by radio.* ○ *I finally made contact with her in Paris.* **make/break ˈcontact** complete/interrupt an electric circuit.

▷ **contact** /kənˈtækt, ˈkɒntækt/ *v* [Tn] reach (sb/sth), by telephone, radio, letter, etc; communicate with: *Where can I contact you tomorrow?*

□ **contact lens** /ˌkɒntækt ˈlenz/ lens made of thin plastic placed on the surface of the eye to improve vision.

ˈcontact print photographic print made by placing a negative directly onto the printing paper and exposing it to light.

contagion /kənˈteɪdʒən/ *n* **1** [U] spreading of disease by being close to or touching other people. **2** [C] disease that can be spread by contact: *Fear spread through the crowd like a contagion*, ie quickly and harmfully. Cf INFECTION.

contagious /kənˈteɪdʒəs/ *adj* **1** (**a**) (of a disease) spreading by contact: *Scarlet fever is highly contagious.* (**b**) (of a person) having a disease that can be spread to others by contact. **2** (*fig*) spreading easily from one person to another: *contagious laughter, enthusiasm, etc* ○ *Yawning is contagious.* ▷ **contagiously** *adv.* Cf INFECTIOUS.

contain /kənˈteɪn/ *v* [Tn] (not in the continuous tenses) **1** (**a**) have or hold (sth) within itself: *The atlas contains forty maps.* ○ *Whisky contains a large percentage of alcohol.* ○ *What does that box contain?* ○ *Her statement contained several inaccuracies.* (**b**) be capable of holding (sth): *This barrel contains 50 litres.* **2** (**a**) keep (sth/oneself) under control; keep within limits; hold back: *I was so furious I couldn't contain myself*, ie had to express my feelings. ○ *Please contain your enthusiasm for a moment.* ○ *She could hardly contain her excitement.* (**b**) prevent (sth) from spreading harmfully or becoming more serious: *Has the revolt been contained?* **3** (*geometry*) form the boundary of (sth): *the angle contained by two sides of a triangle.* **4** (*mathematics*) be capable of being divided by (a number) exactly: *12 contains 1, 2, 3, 4, 6 and 12.*

▷ **containment** *n* [U] keeping sth within limits, so that it cannot spread harmfully: *Until we'd built up sufficient forces to drive the invaders back, we pursued a policy of containment.*

container /kənˈteɪnə(r)/ *n* **1** box, bottle, etc in which sth is kept, transported, etc: *The radioactive material is stored in a special radiation-proof container.* **2** large metal box of standard size for transporting goods by road, rail, sea or air: [attrib] *a conˈtainer train/ship/lorry*, ie one designed to transport such containers ○ *conˈtainer traffic, depots, ports, etc.*

▷ **containerize, -ise** /kənˈteɪnəraɪz/ *v* [Tn] **1** pack (goods) into a container(1, 2). **2** convert (a dock, ship, etc) so that it can use containers (CONTAINER 2). **containerization, -isation** /kənˌteɪnəraɪˈzeɪʃn; *US* -rɪˈz-/ *n* [U].

contaminate /kənˈtæmɪneɪt/ *v* [Tn, Tn·pr] ~ **sth/sb (with sth)** make sth/sb impure by adding dangerous or disease-carrying substances: *contaminated clothing*, eg by radioactive material ○ *a river contaminated by chemicals* ○ *Flies contaminate food.* ○ (*fig*) *They are contaminating the minds of our young people with these subversive ideas.*

▷ **contaminant** /kənˈtæmɪnənt/ *n* (*fml*) substance that contaminates things.

contamination /kənˌtæmɪˈneɪʃn/ *n* [U] contaminating or being contaminated: *the contamination of the water supply.*

contd *abbr* = CONT 2.

contemn /kənˈtem/ *v* (*arch*) [Tn] despise (sb or sth).

contemplate /ˈkɒntempleɪt/ *v* **1** (**a**) [Tn, Tw] look at or consider (sth) thoughtfully: *She stood contemplating the painting.* ○ *He contemplated what the future would be like without the children.* (**b**) [I, Tn, Tw] meditate (upon sth), esp as a religious practice: *a quiet time in the middle of the day to sit and contemplate* ○ *contemplating the death of Our Lord.* **2** [Tn, Tg, Tsg] consider the possibility of (sth): *She is contemplating a visit to* (ie may visit) *London.* ○ *I'm not contemplating retiring* (ie I do not intend to retire) *yet.* ○ *We don't contemplate him opposing our plan*, ie do not expect that he will oppose it.

▷ **contemplation** /ˌkɒntemˈpleɪʃn/ *n* **1** (**a**) [U] action of looking at sth/sb thoughtfully: *He returned to his contemplation of the fire.* (**b**) [U, C] deep thought; meditation: *He sat there deep in contemplation.* ○ *I'm sorry to interrupt your contemplations, but....* **2** [U] consideration; intention: *the Government's contemplation of new measures.*

contemplative /kənˈtemplətɪv, ˈkɒntempleɪtɪv/ *adj* **1** fond of contemplation; thoughtful: *a contemplative person, manner, look, etc.* **2** engaging in religious meditation: *a contemplative order of nuns.* — *n* contemplative(2) monk or nun. **contemplatively** *adv.*

contemporaneous /kənˌtempəˈreɪnɪəs/ *adj* ~ (**with sb/sth**) (*fml*) existing or happening at the same time: *contemporaneous events, developments, etc.* ▷ **contemporaneously** *adv.*

contemporary /kənˈtemprərɪ; *US* -pərerɪ/ *adj* **1** ~ (**with sb/sth**) of the time or period being referred to; belonging to the same time: *Many contemporary writers condemned the emperor's actions.* ○ *a contemporary record of events*, ie one made by people living at that time ○ *Dickens was contemporary with Thackeray.* **2** of the present time; modern: *contemporary events, fashions* ○ *furniture of contemporary style.* ⇨ Usage at NEW.

▷ **contemporary** *n* person who lives or lived at the same time as another: *She and I were contemporaries at college.*

contempt /kənˈtempt/ *n* [U] **1** (**a**) ~ (**for sb/sth**) feeling that sb/sth is completely worthless and cannot be respected: *I feel nothing but contempt for people who treat children so cruelly.* ○ *I shall treat that suggestion with the contempt it deserves.* (**b**) (*fml*) state of being regarded as worthless and shameful: *behaviour which is generally held in contempt*, ie despised. **2** ~ **of/for sth** disregard (of rules, danger, etc): *She rushed forward in complete contempt of danger.* ○ *remarks which betray a staggering contempt for the truth*, ie are completely untrue. **3** (idm) **beneath conˈtempt** completely unworthy of respect: *Such conduct is beneath contempt.* **familiarity breeds contempt** ⇨ FAMILIARITY.

▷ **contemptible** /kənˈtemptəbl/ *adj* deserving contempt; despicable: *contemptible cowardice.*

contemptuous /kənˈtemptʃʊəs/ *adj* ~ (**of sth/sb**) feeling or showing contempt: *a contemptuous person, attitude, etc* ○ *He threw it away with a contemptuous gesture.* ○ *be contemptuous of public opinion.*

contemptuously *adv.*

□ **conˌtempt of ˈcourt** (also **contempt**) disobedience to an order made by a court of law; disrespect for a court or judge: *She was jailed for contempt (of court).*

contend /kənˈtend/ *v* **1** [Ipr] ~ **with/against sb/sth;** ~ **for sth** struggle in order to overcome a rival, competitor or difficulty: *Several teams are contending for* (ie trying to win) *the prize.* ○ *She's had a lot of problems to contend with.* ○ *the captains of the contending* (ie rival) *teams.* **2** [Tf no passive] put forward (sth) as one's opinion; argue; assert: *I would contend that unemployment is our most serious social evil.*

▷ **contender** *n* person who tries to win sth in competition with others: *the two contenders for the heavyweight title.*

content[1] /kənˈtent/ *adj* [pred] ~ (**with sth**); ~ **to do sth** satisfied with what one has; not wanting more; happy: *Are you content with your present salary?* ○ *Now that she has apologized, I am content.* ○ *He is content to stay in his present job.* ○ *He is content to remain where he is now.* Cf CONTENTED.

▷ **content** *n* **1** [U] state of being content: *the quiet content of a well-fed child.* **2** (idm) **to one's heart's content** ⇨ HEART.

content *v* [Tn·pr] ~ **oneself with sth** accept sth, even though one would have liked more or better: *As there's no cream, we'll have to content ourselves with black coffee.*

contented *adj* showing or feeling content; satisfied: *a contented person, cat, smile, etc.*

contentedly *adv.*

contentment *n* [U] state of being content: *with a smile of contentment.*

content[2] /ˈkɒntent/ *n* **1 contents** [pl] that which is contained in sth: *the contents of a room, box, bottle, pocket* ○ *The drawer had been emptied of its contents.* ○ *She hadn't read the letter and so was* *unaware of its contents.* ○ *At the front of the book is a table of contents, giving details of what is in the book.* **2** [sing] that which is written or spoken about in a book, an article, a programme, a speech, etc: *The content of your essay is excellent, but it's not very well expressed.* **3** [sing] (preceded by a *n*) amount of sth contained in sth else: *the silver content of a coin* ○ *food with a high fat content.*

contention /kənˈtenʃn/ *n* **1** [U] ~ **(for sth/to do sth)** contending (CONTEND 1); competition: *two teams in contention for the title/to win the title,* ie competing for it. **2** [U] contending (CONTEND 2); angry disagreement: *This is not a time for contention.* **3** [C] ~ **(that...)** assertion made in an argument: *It is my contention that....* **4** (idm) **a bone of contention** ⇨ BONE.

contentious /kənˈtenʃəs/ *adj* **1** liking to argue; quarrelsome. **2** likely to cause disagreement: *a contentious book, law, speech* ○ *a contentious clause in a treaty.*

conterminous /kɒnˈtɜːmɪnəs/ *adj* = COTERMINOUS.

contest /kənˈtest/ *v* [Tn] **1** claim that (sth) is wrong or not proper; dispute: *contest a statement, point, etc* ○ *contest a will,* ie try to show it was not properly made in law. **2** (take part in and) try to win (sth): *As a protest, the party has decided not to contest this election.* ○ *contest a seat in Parliament* ○ *a hotly contested game,* ie one in which the participants play very hard and the result is close.

▷ **contest** /ˈkɒntest/ *n* **1** event in which people compete against each other for a prize; competition: *a boxing, archery, dancing, beauty, etc contest* ○ (*fig*) *The election was so one-sided that it was really no contest,* ie only one side was likely to win. ⇨ Usage at SPORT. **2** ~ **(for sth)** struggle to gain control: *a contest for the top job in the union.* **contestant** /kənˈtestənt/ *n* ~ **(for sth)** person who is in a contest; competitor.

context /ˈkɒntekst/ *n* [C, U] **1** words that come before and after a word, phrase, statement, etc, helping to show what its meaning is: *Can't you guess the meaning of the word from the context?* ○ *Don't quote my words out of context,* eg so as to mislead other people about what I mean. **2** circumstances in which sth happens or in which sth is to be considered: *In the context of the present economic crisis it seems unwise to lower taxes.* ○ *You have to see these changes in context: they're part of a larger plan.*

▷ **contextual** /kənˈtekstʃʊəl/ *adj* of or according to context: *Contextual clues can help one to find the meaning.*

contiguous /kənˈtɪgjʊəs/ *adj* ~ **(to/with sth)** (*fml*) touching; neighbouring; near: *the northern province and contiguous areas* ○ *The garden is contiguous to the field.*

▷ **contiguity** /ˌkɒntɪˈgjuːətɪ/ *n* [U] (*fml*) being contiguous.

continence /ˈkɒntɪnəns/ *n* [U] **1** (*fml*) control of one's feelings, esp in sexual matters. **2** (*medical*) ability to control one's bladder and bowels.

continent[1] /ˈkɒntɪnənt/ *n* **1** each of the main land masses of the Earth (Europe, Asia, Africa, etc). **2 the Continent** [sing] (*Brit*) the mainland of Europe: *holidaying on the Continent.*

▷ **continental** /ˌkɒntɪˈnentl/ *adj* **1** belonging to or typical of a continent: *a ˌcontinental ˈclimate,* ie with wide seasonal range of temperature. **2** (also **Continental**) (*Brit*) of the mainland of Europe: *ˌcontinental ˈwars, alˈliances, etc* ○ *a continental holiday.* — *n* (*Brit often derog*) inhabitant of the mainland of Europe. **ˌcontinental ˈbreakfast** light breakfast typically consisting only of coffee and rolls with jam. Cf ENGLISH BREAKFAST (ENGLISH). ⇨ articles at EAT, FOOD. **ˌcontinental diˈvide** line, often formed by a chain of mountains, that divides a continent and on either side of which rivers flow in opposite directions. **ˌcontinental ˈdrift** the slow movement of the continents towards and away from each other during the history of the Earth. **ˌcontinental ˈquilt** (*Brit*) = DUVET. **ˌcontinental ˈshelf** the part of a continent that continues below the sea before the sea bed drops away sharply.

continent[2] /ˈkɒntɪnənt/ *adj* **1** (*fml*) having control of one's feelings and (esp sexual) desires. **2** (*medical*) able to control one's bladder and bowels.

contingency /kənˈtɪndʒənsɪ/ *n* event that may or may not occur; event that happens by chance: *Be prepared for all possible contingencies,* ie for whatever may happen. ○ [attrib] *contingency plans/arrangements.*

contingent[1] /kənˈtɪndʒənt/ *adj* (*fml*) **1** ~ **on/upon sth** dependent on/upon sth that may or may not happen: *Our success is contingent upon your continued help.* **2** uncertain; accidental: *a contingent advantage, effect, etc.*

contingent[2] /kənˈtɪndʒənt/ *n* [CGp] **1** number of troops supplied to form part of a larger force: *a small British contingent in the UN peace-keeping force.* **2** group of people sharing particular characteristics (eg place of origin) attending a gathering: *A large contingent from Japan was present at the conference.* ○ *There were the usual protests from the anti-abortion contingent.*

continual /kənˈtɪnjʊəl/ *adj* (*esp derog*) going on all the time without stopping, or repeatedly: *continual rain, talking, interruptions* ○ *How do we prevent these continual breakdowns?*

▷ **continually** /-jʊəlɪ/ *adv* without stopping; repeatedly: *They're continually arguing.* ○ *I find I continually have to remind him of his responsibilities.*

NOTE ON USAGE: Compare **continual** and **continuous. Continual** usually describes an action which is repeated again and again: *Please stop your continual questions.* ○ *He was continually late for work.* **Continuous** indicates that the action or object carries on without stopping or interruption: *They chattered continuously for an hour* ○ *a continuous flow of traffic.*

continuance /kənˈtɪnjʊəns/ *n* [sing] (*fml*) continuing existence; remaining; staying: *Can we hope for a continuance of this fine weather?* ○ *We can no longer support the President's continuance in office.*

continuation /kənˌtɪnjʊˈeɪʃn/ *n* **1** [U, sing] **(a)** carrying sth on beyond a certain point without stopping; prolongation: *He argued for a continuation of the search.* **(b)** starting again after a stop; resumption: *Continuation of play after the tea interval was ruled out by rain.* **2** [C] thing that continues or extends sth else: *This road is a continuation of the motorway.* **3** [C] (*US law*) temporary stopping of a trial; adjournment.

continue /kənˈtɪnjuː/ *v* **1** [I, Ipr, Ip, Tn, Tn·pr, Tn·p] (cause sth to) go or move further: *How far does the road continue?* ○ *The desert continued as far as the eye could see.* ○ *We continued up the mountain on horseback.* ○ *They continued down until they came to some pockets of natural gas.* ○ *It's been decided to continue the motorway (to the coast),* ie build more of it until it reaches the coast. **2** [La, I, Ipr, Tn, Tt, Tg] ~ **(with sth)** (cause sth to) go on existing or happening; not stop: *Circumstances continue (to be) favourable.* ○ *Wet weather may continue for a few more days.* ○ *We will continue (with) the payments for another year.* ○ *In spite of my efforts to pacify it the baby continued to cry/continued crying.* ○ *How can you continue to work/continue working with all that noise going on?* **3** [Ipr] stay; remain: *He is to continue as manager.* ○ *continue at school, in one's job, etc.* **4 (a)** [I, Tn, Tt, Tg] start again after stopping; resume: *The story continues/is continued in the next issue of the magazine.* ○ *We continued to rehearse/continued rehearsing the chorus after the break.* **(b)** [I, Tn] speak or say (sth) again after stopping: *Please continue; I didn't mean to interrupt.* ○ *'And what's more,' he continued, 'they wouldn't even let me in!'*

▷ **continued** *adj* [attrib] going on without stopping: *continued opposition, resistance, etc.*

continuity /ˌkɒntɪˈnjuːətɪ; *US* -ˈnuː-/ *n* [U] **1** state of being continuous: *We must ensure continuity of fuel supplies.* **2** logical connection between parts of a sequence: *This article lacks continuity; the writer keeps jumping from one subject to another.* **3** (*cinema or TV*) correct sequence of action in a film, etc: *Continuity is ensured by using the same props in successive scenes.* ○ [attrib] *a contiˈnuity girl,* ie one who makes sure the correct sequence is kept. **4** (*broadcasting*) connecting comments, announcements, etc made between broadcasts: [attrib] *a continuity announcer.*

continuo /kənˈtɪnjʊəʊ/ *n* (*pl* ~**s**) bass part of a piece of baroque music from which a keyboard player extemporizes an accompaniment: *a harpsichord continuo* ○ [attrib] *continuo players.*

continuous /kənˈtɪnjʊəs/ *adj* going on without stopping or being interrupted: *Is this a continuous flight, or do we stop off anywhere?* ○ *Our political institutions are in continuous evolution.* ○ *A continuous belt feeds components into the machine.* ○ *continuous assessment,* ie evaluation of a student's progress throughout a course of study (instead of by examination alone). ⇨ Usage at CONTINUAL. ▷ **continuously** *adv.*

□ **conˈtinuous tense** (also **progressive tense**) (*grammar*) phrase consisting of part of *be* and a verb ending in *-ing* which expresses an action that continues over a period of time, as in 'I am/was writing', 'They are/were singing'.

continuum /kənˈtɪnjʊəm/ *n* (*pl* ~**s** or **-ua** /-ʊə/) graded sequence of things of a similar kind, so that the ones next to each other are almost identical, but the ones at either end are quite distinct; cline.

contort /kənˈtɔːt/ *v* [I, Ipr, Tn] ~ **(sth) (with sth)** (cause sth to) twist out of its natural shape: *Her face contorted/was contorted with pain.* ○ *contorted branches, limbs, etc* ○ (*fig*) *a contorted* (ie too complicated) *explanation, excuse, etc.*

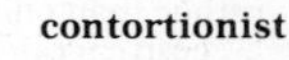

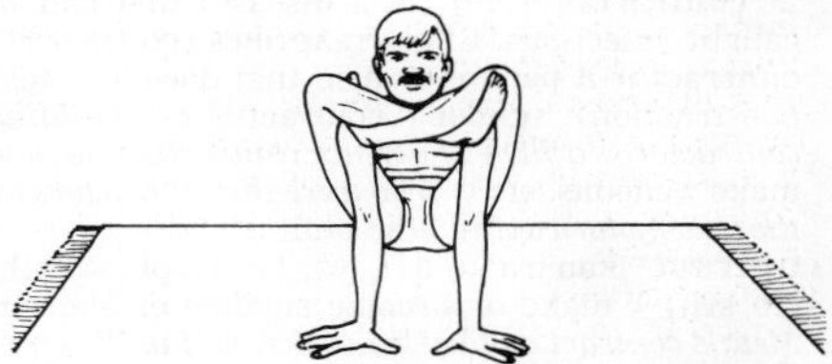

▷ **contortion** /kənˈtɔːʃn/ *n* **(a)** [U] contorting or being contorted (esp of the face or body). **(b)** [C] instance or result of this: *the contortions of a yoga expert.* **contortionist** /-ʃənɪst/ *n* person who is skilled in contorting his body.

contour /ˈkɒntʊə(r)/ *n* **1** outward curve of sth/sb (eg a coast, mountain range, body) thought of as defining its shape: *the smooth contours of a sculpture.* **2** (also **ˈcontour line**) line on a map joining points that are the same height above sea level. ⇨ illus at MAP.

▷ **contour** *v* [Tn] **1** mark (a map) with contour lines. **2** build (a road) so that it follows the contours of a hill.

□ **ˈcontour map** map with contour lines representing fixed intervals on the ground, eg of 25 metres.

contra-[1] *comb form* against: *contraflow.*

contra-[2] *pref* **1** (with *vs* and *ns*) opposite to; against: *contradistinction* ○ *contra-indication* ○ *ˈcontraflow.* **2** (with *ns*); (*music*) having a pitch an octave below: *contra-bassoon.*

contraband /ˈkɒntrəbænd/ *n* [U] goods brought into or taken out of a country illegally: [attrib] *contraband goods.*

contraception /ˌkɒntrəˈsepʃn/ *n* [U] preventing of conception(1).

▷ **contraceptive** /ˌkɒntrəˈseptɪv/ *n* device or drug for preventing conception(1). — *adj* preventing conception: *a contraceptive pill, device, drug, etc.*

contract[1] /ˈkɒntrækt/ *n* **1** ~ **(with sb) (for sth/to do sth)** (document setting out a) legally binding agreement: *You shouldn't enter into/make a contract until you have studied its provisions carefully.* ○ *We have a contract with the*

Government for the supply of vehicles/to supply vehicles. ○ *When the legal formalities have been settled, the buyer and seller of a house can exchange contracts*, ie to complete their agreement legally. ○ *He has agreed salary terms and is ready to sign a new contract*, ie of employment. ○ *I'm not a permanent employee; I'm working here on a fixed-term contract.* ○ [attrib] *the contract price, date, etc*, ie the price, date, etc agreed to ○ *a contract worker*, ie employed on a contract. **2** (idm) **be under contract (to sb)** have made a contract to work (for sb): *a pop group that is under contract to one of the big record companies.* **put sth out to 'contract** invite people to make a contract to do work, supply (goods, etc): *We haven't the resources to do the work ourselves, so we'll put it out to contract.*

▷ **contractual** /kən'træktʃʊəl/ *adj* of or contained in a contract: *contractual liability, obligations, etc.*

□ ˌ**contract 'bridge** type of bridge² in which a player can gain points only with tricks which he had undertaken to win before the game started.

contract² /kən'trækt/ *v* **1** (a) [Ipr, It] ~ **with sb for sth** make (a legal agreement) with sb for a purpose: *contract with a firm for the supply of fuel*, ie agree to buy fuel from it ○ *Having contracted (with them) to do the repairs, we cannot withdraw now.* (b) [Tn, Tn·pr] ~ **sth (with sb)** (*fml*) enter into or undertake sth formally: *She had contracted a most unsuitable marriage.* ○ *contract an alliance with a neighbouring state.* **2** [Tn] (a) catch or develop (an illness): *contract measles, a cold, etc.* (b) (*fml*) acquire (sth): *contract debts, bad habits.* **3** (phr v) **contract 'out (of sth)** (*Brit*) withdraw from, or not enter into, an agreement which applies to a large group: *You can contract out (of the pension scheme) if you wish.* **contract sth out (to sb)** arrange for (work) to be done by another firm rather than one's own.

▷ **contractable** *adj* (of a disease) that can be caught; infectious. Cf CONTRACTIBLE (CONTRACT³).

contractor *n* person or firm that does jobs (esp construction) under contract: *a building contractor* ○ *a firm of defence contractors*, ie who make weapons, etc ○ *Who were the contractors on the new motorway?* ie Who built it?

contract³ /kən'trækt/ *v* [I, Ipr, Tn, Tn·pr] ~ **(sth) (to sth) 1** make or become smaller or shorter: *Metals contract as they get cooler.* ○ *'I will' can be contracted to 'I'll'.* ○ (*fig*) *Our business has contracted a lot recently.* **2** (cause sth to) become tighter or narrower; constrict: *contract a muscle* ○ *The tunnel contracts to a narrow passageway as you go deeper.* Cf EXPAND.

▷ **contractible** *adj* that can be contracted. Cf CONTRACTABLE (CONTRACT²).

contractile /kən'træktaɪl; *US* -tl/ *adj* (*fml*) that can contract or be contracted: *contractile tissue.*

contraction /kən'trækʃn/ *n* **1** [U] contracting or being contracted: *the contraction of a muscle.* **2** [C] (*medical*) tightening of the womb that occurs at intervals in the hours preceding childbirth. **3** [C] shortened form of a word: *'Can't' is a contraction of 'cannot'.*

contradict /ˌkɒntrə'dɪkt/ *v* **1** [I, Tn] say sth that conflicts with (sth said or written) by (sb), suggesting that the person is mistaken or not telling the truth: *That is true, and don't you dare contradict (me).* ○ *The speaker had got confused, and started contradicting himself.* **2** [Tn] (of facts, evidence, etc) be contrary to sth; conflict with: *The two statements contradict each other.* ○ *The report contradicts what we heard yesterday.*

▷ **contradiction** /ˌkɒntrə'dɪkʃn/ *n* **1** (a) [U] contradicting: *She will permit no contradiction.* (b) [C] instance of this: *That's a flat contradiction of what you said before.* **2** ~ **(between sth and sth)** (a) [U] absence of agreement (between statements, facts, etc): *I find no contradiction between his publicly expressed opinions and his private actions.* ○ *His private actions are in direct contradiction to/with* (ie directly contradict) *his publicly expressed opinions.* (b) [C] instance of this: *It's a contradiction to love animals and yet wear furs.* **3** (idm) **a ˌcontradiction in 'terms** statement containing two words which contradict each other's meaning: *'A generous miser' is a contradiction in terms.*

contradictory /ˌkɒntrə'dɪktərɪ/ *adj* contradicting: *contradictory statements, reports, etc.*

contradistinction /ˌkɒntrədɪ'stɪŋkʃn/ *n* (idm) **in contradistinction to sth/sb** (*fml*) by contrast with sth/sb; as opposed to sth/sb: *I refer specifically to permanent residents, in contradistinction to temporary visitors.*

contraflow /'kɒntrəfləʊ/ *n* [U, C] transferring of traffic from its usual half of the road to the other half, so that it shares the lane with traffic coming in the other direction: [attrib] *While repairs are being carried out on this part of the motorway, a contraflow system is in operation.* ⇨ illus at MOTORWAY.

contra-indication /ˌkɒntrəɪndɪ'keɪʃn/ *n* (*medical*) sign that a particular drug may be harmful: *The contra-indications listed for the pills meant that she could not take them.*

contralto /kən'træltəʊ/ (also **alto**) *n* (*pl* ~**s**) **1** lowest female voice: *She sings contralto.* **2** woman with, or musical part to be sung by, such a voice: *A gifted young contralto.*

contraption /kən'træpʃn/ *n* (*infml*) apparatus or device, esp a strange or complicated one: *a peculiar contraption for removing pips from oranges.*

contrapuntal /ˌkɒntrə'pʌntl/ *adj* (*music*) of or in counterpoint.

contrariwise /'kɒntrərɪwaɪz; *US* -trerɪ-/ *adv* **1** on the contrary; on the other hand: *He always gives permission; she, contrariwise, always refuses it.* ○ *'Don't you find him very rude?' 'Contrariwise! I think he's most polite.'* **2** in the opposite way: *I work from left to right, he works contrariwise.* **3** /kən'treərɪwaɪz/ perversely; in a way that shows opposition: *They know they're not allowed to park there, but, contrariwise, they always do.*

contrary¹ /'kɒntrərɪ; *US* -trerɪ/ *adj* [usu attrib] opposite in nature, tendency or direction: *contrary beliefs* ○ *traffic moving in contrary directions* ○ *'Hot' and 'cold' are contrary terms.* ○ *The ship was delayed by contrary winds*, ie blowing against the direction of travel.

▷ **contrarily** /-rɪlɪ; *US* -rəlɪ/ *adv* in a contrary manner.

□ **contrary to** *prep* in opposition to (sth); against: *be contrary to the law, rules, etc* ○ *The results were contrary to expectation.* ○ *Contrary to the doctor's orders, he had gone back to work.*

contrary² /'kɒntrərɪ; *US* -trerɪ/ *n* **1 the contrary** [sing] the opposite: *The contrary of 'wet' is 'dry'.* ○ *I've never opposed it. The contrary is true: I've always supported it.* **2** (idm) **by contraries** in an opposite way to what is expected: *Many events in our lives go by contraries.* **on the 'contrary** the opposite is true; not at all: *It doesn't seem ugly to me; on the contrary, I think it's rather beautiful.* **to the 'contrary** indicating or proving the opposite: *I will come on Monday unless you write to the contrary*, ie telling me not to come. ○ *I will continue to believe it until I get proof to the contrary*, ie that it is not true.

contrary³ /kən'treərɪ/ *adj* obstinately refusing to help or obey: *He's an awkward, contrary child.* ▷ **contrarily** *adv.* **contrariness** *n* [U].

contrast¹ /kən'trɑ:st; *US* -'træst/ *v* **1** [Tn, Tn·pr] ~ **A and/with B** compare (two people or things) so that differences are made clear: *It is interesting to contrast the two writers.* ○ *contrast his work and/with hers.* **2** [I, Ipr] ~ **(with sb/sth)** show a difference when compared: *Her actions contrasted sharply with her promises.* ○ *Her actions and her promises contrasted sharply*, ie She did not do as she had promised.

contrast² /'kɒntrɑ:st; *US* -træst/ *n* ~ **(to/with sb/sth)**; ~ **(between A and B) 1** [U] action of contrasting: *Careful contrast of the two plans shows up some key differences.* ○ *His white hair was in sharp contrast to* (ie was very noticeably different from) *his dark skin.* ○ *She had almost failed the exam, but her sister, by contrast, had done very well.* ○ *In contrast with their system, ours seems very old-fashioned.* **2** [C, U] difference clearly seen when unlike things are compared or put together; thing showing such a difference: *The white walls make a contrast with the black carpet.* ○ *There is a remarkable contrast between the two brothers.* ○ *The work you did today is quite a contrast to* (eg noticeably better/worse than) *what you did last week.* ○ *The contrast of light and shade is important in photography.*

contravene /ˌkɒntrə'vi:n/ *v* [Tn] **1** act or be contrary to (a law, etc); break: *You are contravening the regulations.* ○ *Her actions contravene the rules.* **2** (of things) conflict with (sth); not agree with: *This evidence contravenes our theory.*

▷ **contravention** /ˌkɒntrə'venʃn/ *n* [C, U] (act of) contravening (a law, etc): *a blatant contravention of the treaty* ○ *acting in direct contravention of* (ie against) *my wishes.*

contretemps /'kɒntrətɒm/ *n* (*pl* unchanged) (*French fml or joc*) unfortunate event; mishap; set-back.

contribute /kən'trɪbju:t/ *v* **1** [I, Ipr, Tn, Tn·pr, Tw] ~ **(sth) (to/towards sth)** give one's share of (money, help, advice, etc) to help a joint cause: *contribute (ten pounds) to a charity collection* ○ *contribute aid for refugees* ○ *Everyone should contribute what he or she can afford.* ○ *The chairman encourages everyone to contribute to* (ie take part in) *the discussion.* **2** [Ipr] ~ **to sth** increase sth; add to sth: *Her work has contributed enormously to our understanding of this difficult subject.* **3** [Ipr] ~ **to sth** help to cause sth: *Does smoking contribute to lung cancer?* **4** [Ipr, Tn·pr] ~ **(sth) to sth** write (articles, etc) for a publication: *She has contributed (several poems) to literary magazines.*

▷ **contributor** *n* person who contributes (money to a fund, articles to a magazine, etc).

contribution /ˌkɒntrɪ'bju:ʃn/ *n* ~ **(to/towards sth)** (a) [U] action of contributing: *the contribution of money to charity.* (b) [C] thing contributed: *a small contribution* (ie of money) *to the collection* ○ *The editor is short of contributions* (ie articles) *for the May issue.* ○ (*fig*) *The signing of such a treaty would be a major contribution towards* (ie would help greatly to bring about) *world peace.*

contributory /kən'trɪbjʊtərɪ; *US* -tɔ:rɪ/ *adj* [usu attrib] **1** helping to cause sth: *a contributory factor, cause, etc* ○ *contributory negligence*, eg that helped to cause an accident. **2** paid for by contributions: *a conˌtributory 'pension scheme*, ie paid for by both employers and employees.

contrite /'kɒntraɪt/ *adj* filled with or showing deep regret for having done wrong; repentant: *a contrite apology, manner* ○ *She was contrite the morning after her angry outburst.* ▷ **contritely** *adv.*

contrition /kən'trɪʃn/ *n* [U] deep regret for having done wrong; repentance.

contrivance /kən'traɪvəns/ *n* **1** [C] ~ **(for doing sth/to do sth)** (a) device or tool, esp one made by an individual for a particular purpose: *a contrivance for cutting curved shapes* ○ *He erected some contrivance for storing rain-water.* (b) complicated or deceitful plan: *an ingenious contrivance to get her to sign the document without reading it.* **2** [U] capacity to do or accomplish sth: *Some things are beyond human contrivance.* **3** [U] action of contriving: *the contrivance of an effective method.*

contrive /kən'traɪv/ *v* (*fml*) **1** [Tn] plan (sth) cleverly or deceitfully; invent; design: *contrive a device, an experiment, a means of escape* ○ *contrive a way of avoiding paying tax* ○ *Their sudden outburst was obviously genuine; it couldn't have been contrived.* **2** [Tt] manage (to do sth) in spite of difficulties: *contrive to live on a small income* ○ (*ironic*) *He contrived to make matters worse*, ie unintentionally made them worse by what he did.

▷ **contrived** *adj* (*derog*) **1** planned in advance rather than being spontaneous or genuine: *a contrived incident intended to mislead the newspapers.* **2** obviously invented; not lifelike: *a novel with a very contrived plot.*

control¹ /kən'trəʊl/ *n* **1** [U] ~ **(of/over sb/sth)**

power or authority to direct, order or limit: *children who lack parental control*, ie are not kept in order by their parents ○ *He has no control over his emotions.* ○ *In the latest elections our party has got/gained control (of the council).* ○ *She managed to keep control of her car on the ice.* ○ *A military government took control (of the country).* ○ *The city is in/under the control of enemy forces.* ○ *The pilot lost control of the plane.* ○ *He got so angry he lost control (of himself)*, ie started to behave wildly. ○ *Due to circumstances beyond/outside our control, we cannot land here.* **2** [U] management; guidance; restriction: *control of traffic/traffic control* ○ *control of foreign exchange* ○ *She argued for import control*, ie the restricting of imports. ○ [attrib] *the power-station's control room*, ie from which its operations are controlled ○ *arms-control talks.* **3** [C] ~ **(on sth)** means of limiting or regulating: *government controls on trade and industry* ○ *The arms trade should be subject to rigorous controls.* **4** [C] standard of comparison for checking the results of an experiment: *One group was treated with the new drug, and a second group was treated with the old one as a control.* ○ [attrib] *a con'trol group.* **5** [C usu *pl*] switches, levers, etc by which a machine is operated or regulated: *the controls of an aircraft*, ie for direction, height, etc ○ *The pilot is at the controls.* ○ *the volume control of a radio*, ie the one which regulates loudness ○ *a studio with an array of electronic controls* ○ [attrib] *a control panel, board, lever, etc.* **6** [sing] place from which orders are issued or at which checks are made: *Mission control ordered the spacecraft to return to earth.* ○ *Our papers are checked as we go through passport control at the airport.* **7** (idm) **be in control (of sth)** direct, manage or rule (sth): *She may be old, but she's still in control (of all that is happening).* ○ *Who's in control of the project?* ○ *Enemy forces are in control of the city.* **be/get out of con'trol** be/become no longer manageable: *The children are out of control.* ○ *Inflation has got out of control.* **bring/get sth/be under con'trol** subdue or master sth/be subdued or mastered: *You must get your spending under control.* ○ *The fire has been brought under control.* ○ *Don't worry; everything's under control*, ie all difficulties are being dealt with.

□ **con'trol rod** any of a set of rods made of a material that absorbs neutrons, which are put into or taken out of the core of a nuclear reactor in order to vary the speed of the reaction.

con'trol tower building at an airport from which the taking off and landing of aircraft is controlled.

control² /kən'trəʊl/ *v* (**-ll-**) [Tn] **1** have power or authority over (sb/sth): *a dictator who controlled the country for over 50 years* ○ *Can't you control that child (ie make it behave properly)?* ○ *an aircraft which is hard to control at high speeds* ○ *I was so furious I couldn't control myself, and I hit him.* **2** regulate (sth): *control traffic, immigration, supplies, prices* ○ *This knob controls the radio's volume.* ○ *government efforts to control inflation*, ie stop it getting worse. **3** check (sth); verify: *regular inspections to control product quality.*

▷ **controllable** *adj* that can be controlled: *Drugs can make violent patients controllable.*

controller *n* person who controls or directs sth, esp a department or division of a large organization: *the controller of BBC Radio* ○ *an air-traffic controller.*

□ **con,trolling 'interest** (*finance*) possession of enough stock(5b) of a company to control decision-making: *have a controlling interest in a company.*

controversial /,kɒntrə'vɜːʃl/ *adj* causing or likely to cause controversy: *a controversial person, decision, organization, book.*

▷ **controversialist** /-ʃəlɪst/ *n* (*fml*) person who is good at or fond of controversy.

controversially /-ʃəlɪ/ *adv.*

controversy /'kɒntrəvɜːsɪ, kən'trɒvəsɪ/ *n* [U, C] ~ **(about/over sth)** public discussion or argument, often rather angry, about sth which many people disagree with: *The appointment of the new director aroused a lot of controversy*, ie Many people publicly disagreed with it. ○ *a bitter controversy about/over the siting of the new airport.*

controvert /,kɒntrə'vɜːt/ *v* [Tn] (*fml*) deny the truth of (sth); argue about: *a fact that cannot be controverted.*

contumacious /,kɒntjuː'meɪʃəs; *US* -tuː-/ *adj* (*fml*) obstinate and disobedient. ▷ **contumaciously** *adv.*

contumacy /'kɒntjʊməsɪ; *US* kən'tuːməsɪ/ *n* (*fml*) (**a**) [U] obstinate resistance or disobedience. (**b**) [C] instance of this.

contumely /'kɒntjuːmlɪ; *US* kən'tuːməlɪ/ *n* (*fml*) (**a**) [U] insulting language or treatment. (**b**) [C] instance of this; humiliating insult.

contuse /kən'tjuːz; *US* -'tuːz/ *v* [Tn esp passive] (*medical*) injure (a part of the body) without breaking the skin; bruise.

▷ **contusion** /kən'tjuːʒn; *US* -'tuː-/ *n* (*medical*) bruise.

conundrum /kə'nʌndrəm/ *n* **1** question, usu with a pun in its answer, that is asked for fun; riddle. **2** puzzling problem: *an issue that is a real conundrum for the experts.*

conurbation /,kɒnɜː'beɪʃn/ *n* large urban area formed by the expansion and joining together of several smaller towns.

convalesce /,kɒnvə'les/ *v* [I] regain one's health and strength after an illness: *She went to the seaside to convalesce after her stay in hospital.*

▷ **convalescence** /,kɒnvə'lesns/ *n* [sing, U] (period of) gradual recovery of health and strength.

convalescent /,kɒnvə'lesnt/ *n, adj* (person who is) recovering from illness: *a convalescent home*, ie a type of hospital where people convalesce.

convection /kən'vekʃn/ *n* [U] transmission of heat from one part of a liquid or gas to another by the movement of heated substances.

convector /kən'vektə(r)/ *n* (also **con,vector 'heater**) room heater that warms air by passing it over hot surfaces and then circulates it.

convene /kən'viːn/ *v* **1** [Tn] summon (people) to come together; arrange (a meeting, etc): *convene the members, a committee, etc.* **2** [I] come together (for a meeting, etc): *The tribunal will convene tomorrow.*

▷ **convener** (also **convenor**) *n* (**a**) person who convenes meetings. (**b**) (*Brit*) senior trade union official in a factory or some other place of work: *the works convenor.*

convenience /kən'viːnɪəns/ *n* **1** [U] quality of being convenient or suitable; freedom from trouble or difficulty: *a library planned for the users' convenience* ○ *I keep my reference books near my desk for convenience.* ○ *It was a marriage of convenience*, ie They married for material advantage, not for love. **2** [C] (**a**) arrangement, appliance or device that is useful, helpful or suitable: *It was a great convenience to have the doctor living near us.* ○ *The house has all the modern conveniences*, eg central heating, hot water supply, etc. (**b**) (*Brit euph*) lavatory for the use of the general public: *There is a public convenience on the corner of the street.* **3** (idm) **at one's con'venience** when and where it suits one: *With a caravan, you can stop at your own convenience; you're not dependent on hotels.* **at your earliest con'venience** ⇨ EARLY.

□ **con'venience food** food (eg in a tin, packet, etc) that needs very litttle preparation after being bought.

convenient /kən'viːnɪənt/ *adj* ~ **(for sb/sth) 1** fitting in well with people's needs or plans; giving no trouble or difficulty; suitable: *I can't see him now; it's not convenient.* ○ *Will it be convenient for you to start work tomorrow?* ○ *We must arrange a convenient time and place for the meeting.* ○ *A bicycle's often far more convenient than a car in busy cities.* **2** situated nearby; easily accessible: (*infml*) *a house that is convenient for* (ie is near) *the shops* ○ *It's useful to have a convenient supermarket.*

▷ **conveniently** *adv* in a convenient manner: *My house is conveniently near a bus-stop.*

convent /'kɒnvənt; *US* -vent/ *n* building(s) in which a community of nuns lives: *enter a convent*, ie become a nun ○ [attrib] *a convent school*, ie one run by nuns. Cf MONASTERY, NUNNERY (NUN).

conventicle /kən'ventɪkl/ *n* secret meeting of *Dissenters or *Nonconformists at the time when they were not allowed to practise their religion.

convention /kən'venʃn/ *n* **1** [C] conference of members of a profession, political party, etc: *a teachers', dentists', etc convention* ○ *hold a convention* ○ *the US Democratic Party Convention*, ie to elect a candidate for President. **2** (**a**) [U] general, usu unspoken, agreement about how people should act or behave in certain circumstances: *Convention dictates that a minister should resign in such a situation.* ○ *By convention the deputy leader is always a woman.* ○ *defy convention by wearing outrageous clothes* ○ *a slave to convention*, ie sb who always follows accepted ways of doing things. (**b**) [C] customary practice: *the conventions which govern stock-market dealing.* **3** [C] agreement between states, rulers, etc that is less formal than a treaty: *the Geneva Convention*, ie about the treatment of prisoners of war, etc.

conventional /kən'venʃənl/ *adj* **1** (**a**) (*often derog*) based on convention(2a): *conventional clothes, behaviour* ○ *She's so conventional in her views.* ○ *He made a few conventional remarks about the weather.* ○ *The conventional wisdom is that high wage rises increase inflation*, ie That is the generally accepted view. (**b**) following what is traditional or customary: *a conventional design, method.* **2** (esp of weapons) not nuclear: *conventional missiles, warfare, etc* ○ *a conventional power station*, ie fuelled by oil or coal, rather than being powered by a nuclear reactor.

▷ **conventionality** /kən,venʃən'ælətɪ/ *n* (**a**) [U] conventional quality or character: *the timid conventionality of his designs.* (**b**) [C] conventional remark, attitude, etc.

conventionalize, -ise /kən'venʃənəlaɪz/ *v* [Tn] make (sb/sth) conventional.

conventionally /-ʃənəlɪ/ *adv*: *conventionally dressed, designed, etc.*

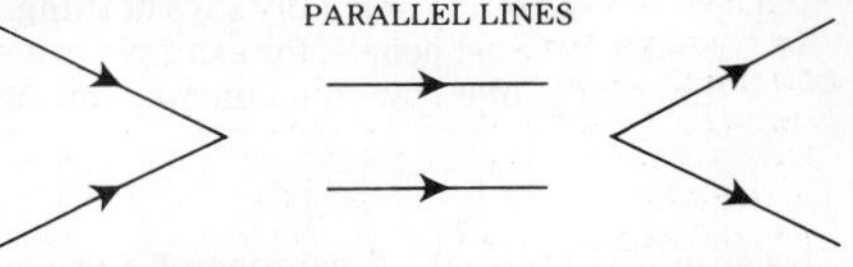

converge /kən'vɜːdʒ/ *v* **1** [I, Ipr] ~ **(on sb/sth);** ~ **(at sth)** (of lines, moving objects, etc) (come towards each other and) meet at a point: *armies converging on the capital city* ○ *Parallel lines converge at infinity.* ○ *Enthusiasts from around the world converge on* (ie come to) *Le Mans for the annual car race.* **2** [I] (*fig*) (tend to) become similar or identical: *Our previously opposed views are beginning to converge.* ○ *Some say that capitalism and socialism will eventually converge.* ▷ **convergence** /kən'vɜːdʒəns/ *n* [U]. **convergent** /kən'vɜːdʒənt/ *adj*: *convergent lines, opinions.* ⇨ illus. Cf DIVERGE.

conversant /kən'vɜːsnt/ *adj* [pred] ~ **with sth** (*fml*) having knowledge of sth; familiar with sth: *thoroughly conversant with all the rules.*

conversation /,kɒnvə'seɪʃn/ *n* ~ **(with sb) (about sth)** (**a**) [C] informal talk: *having a quiet conversation with a friend* ○ *She tended to monopolize the conversation.* (**b**) [U] informal talking: *He was deep in conversation with his accountant.* ○ *It can be very difficult, making conversation at a party*, ie trying to think of things to say. ⇨ Usage at TALK¹.

▷ **conversational** /-ʃənl/ *adj* (**a**) [attrib] of talking: *her limited conversational powers.* (**b**) appropriate to conversation; colloquial: *a conversational tone, manner, etc.*

conversationalist /-ʃənəlɪst/ *n* talker: *a fluent conversationalist.*

□ **conver'sation piece 1** thing, eg an ornament, that makes people comment on or talk about it

Social Conventions

The conventions of social behaviour have tended to be less formal in the USA that in Britain but the trend in both countries is towards less formality, especially among young people.

An almost universal way of greeting someone you know is 'Hello' or, even less formally, 'Hi'. 'Good Morning' or 'Morning' is more formal, and like 'Good Afternoon', 'Afternoon', 'Good Evening' and 'Evening' is mostly used to a person you have not met before, unless you wish to be very formal. An excess of formality can sometimes seem unfriendly. People often add a comment on the weather, such as 'Lovely morning', 'Nice day today, isn't it? or 'What terrible weather'.

When you are leaving someone, the most normal thing to say is 'Goodbye', but there are more informal alternatives like 'See you', 'Bye' and, most informal of all, 'Cheers'. In the USA, shop assistants often add 'Have a nice day', but this is not common in Britain.

'Please' is usually added at the end of a request, for example, 'Can you show me that pen, please?', but is not normally used in requests for information. It is thus usual to ask 'Can you tell me where the nearest bus stop is?' 'Excuse me' is used to attract someone's attention, or to begin a request, especially when you are interrupting them. For example, in a shop, a request for information from an assistant arranging goods on shelves might be 'Excuse me, do you sell toothpaste?' Some people say 'Er...' instead of 'Excuse me' ('Er... do you sell toothpaste?'). When slightly inconveniencing someone, for example by reaching in front of them to take something off a shelf, it is enough to say 'Excuse me'. The person spoken to normally says nothing. If you need to get past people, for example to a seat in the middle of a row in a cinema, you can say, 'I'm sorry to disturb you.'

'Thank you' (or 'Thank you very much', 'Thanks', 'Thanks a lot', or, more formally, 'Many thanks') is normally said when receiving something, whether it is goods or the answer to a question. An exchange might thus run: 'Excuse me, do you sell chewing gum?' 'Yes, over there by the checkout.' 'Thanks.' 'Cheers' is a very informal alternative to 'Thank you'. In Britain, it is generally acceptable to say nothing after being thanked for something, although some people do say 'It's a pleasure' or 'You're welcome'. The following exchange would thus be acceptable: 'Excuse me, can you tell me where the post office is?' 'Round the corner on the left.' 'Thank you.' In the USA it would be usual to add 'You're welcome'.

Certain acts of courtesy are regarded as normal, for example to hold a door open for someone, especially when passing through first oneself; to take the end place in a queue or line, and not 'jump' to the front; to move aside to pass someone on a pavement; to step aside to let someone pass when standing still in a restricted space, for example on a pavement or between counters in a shop; to put a handkerchief or hand over one's mouth when coughing, yawning or sneezing. It is considered impolite to speak with one's mouth full, even when eating a meal; to use a comb or a toothpick in public; to touch a person to attract their attention or when speaking to them, unless it is a matter of urgency; to stare at someone, however attractive or odd they are.

When you are introduced to someone, it is usual to shake hands and say 'How do you do?' or, less formally, 'Pleased to meet you' (or 'Nice to meet you'), or, least formally of all, 'Hello'. Some women also exchange a kiss. Men do not normally kiss a woman on being introduced to her, and to kiss a woman's hand is regarded as either very old-fashioned or merely amusing. It is possible to introduce yourself to a stranger by saying, 'I don't think we've met. I'm...' On saying 'Goodbye' to a person to whom one has been introduced, especially if the meeting was fairly formal or important, it is usual to shake hands a second time. Women often kiss each other on taking leave, and men and women occasionally do. It is not usual for men to kiss each other even within a family, nor do they normally kiss children.

Social conventions also apply to 'body language'. For example, it is considered impolite for a man to keep a hand in his pocket when he is being introduced to someone, or even to stand with arms folded when making polite conversation, as this suggests a 'repulsion' of the person spoken to. Some people regard it as impolite to cross one's legs when seated, especially on a formal occasion, such as an interview. At a social gathering, such as a drinks party, it is often regarded as impolite to sit down immediately, unless the party is in a place where this is usual, such as a restaurant. In general, when people are standing conversing at a social gathering, it is polite not to talk to any one person too long, but to 'circulate' and talk to other guests.

It is usual to apologize when disturbing or offending someone, however slightly. The usual apology is simply 'Sorry', although a more formal apology (or a more heartfelt one) is 'I beg your pardon'. The person apologized to normally says nothing, but may smile or nod. If a spoken acknowledgement of an apology is given, it will usually be 'That's all right' or, more casually, 'That's OK'. Americans often say 'Pardon me' or 'Excuse me' instead of 'Sorry' when apologizing.

because it is unusual. **2** painting of a group of people talking to each other.

converse[1] /kən'vɜːs/ *v* [I, Ipr, Ip] ~ **(with sb) (about sth)**; ~ **(together)** (*fml*) talk: *She sat conversing with the President.*

converse[2] /'kɒnvɜːs/ **the converse** *n* [sing] **1** the opposite: *He says she is satisfied, but I believe the converse to be true: she is very dissatisfied.* **2** (in logic) statement made by reversing two elements of another statement: *'He is happy but not rich' is the converse of 'He is rich but not happy'.*

▷ **converse** *adj* [usu attrib] opposite to sth: *They hold converse opinions.*

conversely *adv*: *You can add the fluid to the powder or, conversely, the powder to the fluid.*

conversion /kən'vɜːʃn; *US* kən'vɜːrʒn/ *n* ~ **(from sth) (into/to sth) 1** [U] converting or being converted: *the conversion of a barn into a house, of pounds into dollars* ○ *the conversion of the Anglo-Saxons by Christian missionaries* ○ *Conversion to gas central heating will save you a lot of money.* ○ [attrib] *a metric conversion table*, ie showing how to change metric amounts into or out of another system, by calculation. **2** [C] instance of this: *a building firm which specializes in house conversions*, eg converting large houses into several flats ○ *He kicked a penalty goal and two conversions*, ie in Rugby football. ○ *He used to support monetarist economics, but he underwent quite a conversion* (ie changed his opinion) *when he saw how it increased unemployment.*

convert[1] /kən'vɜːt/ *v* **1 (a)** [I, Ipr, Tn, Tn·pr] ~ **(sth) (from sth) (into/to sth)** change (sth) from one form or use to another: *Britain converted to a decimal currency system in 1971.* ○ *a ferry that was converted to carry troops during the war* ○ *a converted flat*, ie made by dividing up a large house ○ *convert rags into paper, a house into flats, pounds into francs* ○ *The room was converted from a kitchen to a lavatory.* **(b)** [Ipr] ~ **into/to sth** be able to be changed from one form or use to another: *a sofa that converts (in)to a bed.* **2** [I, Ipr, Tn, Tn·pr] ~ **(sb) (from sth) (to sth)** change one's beliefs, esp one's religion; persuade sb to change his beliefs: *He's converted to Catholicism.* ○ *convert sb from atheism to Christianity.* **3** [Tn] **(a)** (in Rugby football) gain extra points after scoring (a try) by kicking a goal. **(b)** (in American football) score a goal from (a pass). **4** (idm) **preach to the converted** ⇨ PREACH.

▷ **converter**, **convertor** *ns* **1** (*physics*) **(a)** device for converting alternating current to direct current or vice versa. **(b)** device that changes the wavelength of a radio signal. **2** vessel for refining molten metal.

convert[2] /'kɒnvɜːt/ *n* ~ **(to sth)** person converted to a different belief, esp a different religion: *a convert to socialism* ○ *Already the new newspaper is winning/gaining converts*, ie people who used to read other newspapers.

convertible /kən'vɜːtəbl/ *adj* ~ **(into/to sth)** that can be converted: *a sofa that is convertible (into a bed)* ○ *convertible currencies*, ie that can be exchanged for those of other countries.

▷ **convertibility** /kənˌvɜːtə'bɪlətɪ/ *n* [U].

convertible *n* car with a roof that can be folded down or removed.

convex /'kɒnveks/ *adj* with a curved surface like the outside of a ball: *a convex lens, mirror, etc.* ⇨ illus at CONCAVE. Cf CONCAVE.

▷ **convexity** /kɒn'veksətɪ/ *n* [U] state of being convex.

convey /kən'veɪ/ *v* **1** [Tn, Tn·pr] ~ **sb/sth (from ...) (to ...)** (*fml*) take sb/sth; carry sb/sth; transmit sb/sth: *Pipes convey hot water from the boiler to the radiators.* ○ *This train conveys both passengers and goods.* ○ *a message conveyed by radio.* **2** [Tn, Tf, Tw, Dn·pr, Dpr·f, Dpr·w] ~ **sth (to sb)** make (ideas, feelings, etc) known to another person: *a poem that perfectly conveys (to the reader) the poet's feelings/what the poet feels* ○ *Words cannot convey how delighted I was.* ○ *Please convey my good wishes to your mother.* ○ *Blenkinsop? No, the name doesn't convey anything to me*, ie I do not know or recognize it. **3** [Tn·pr] ~ **sth (to sb)** (*law*) transfer full legal rights to the ownership of (land, property, etc) to sb.

▷ **conveyor**, **conveyer** *ns* person or thing that conveys: *one of the largest conveyors of passenger traffic.* **con'veyor belt** (also **conveyor**) continuous belt or band that moves on rollers and is used for transporting loads (eg products in a factory, luggage at an airport).

conveyance /kən'veɪəns/ *n* **1** [U] (*fml*) conveying: *the conveyance of goods by rail.* **2** [C] (*fml*) thing that conveys; vehicle: *old-fashioned conveyances* ○ *a public conveyance.* **3** (*law*) **(a)** [U] conveying property: *an expert in conveyance.* **(b)** [C] document that conveys property: *draw up a conveyance.*

▷ **conveyancer** *n* person who prepares conveyances (CONVEYANCE 3b).

conveyancing *n* [U] conveying of property. ⇨ article at LAW.

convict /kən'vɪkt/ *v* [Tn, Tn·pr] ~ **sb (of sth)** (of a jury or judge) declare in a lawcourt that sb is guilty (of a crime): *She has twice been convicted (of fraud).* ○ *a convicted murderer.*

▷ **convict** /'kɒnvɪkt/ (also *infml* **con**) *n* person who has been convicted of crime and is being punished, esp by imprisonment: *an escaped convict.*

conviction /kən'vɪkʃn/ *n* **1** ~ **(for sth)** (**a**) [U] the convicting of a person for a crime: *an offence which carries, on conviction, a sentence of not more than five years' imprisonment.* (**b**) [C] instance of this: *She has six convictions for theft.* **2** [U, C] ~ **(that...)** firm opinion or belief: *It's my conviction* (ie I firmly believe) *that complacency is at the root of our troubles.* ○ *Do you always act in accordance with your convictions?* **3** [U] believable quality: *She'd made such promises before, and they lacked conviction/didn't carry much conviction.* **4** (idm) **have/lack the courage of one's convictions** ⇨ COURAGE.

convince /kən'vɪns/ *v* **1** [Tn, Tn·pr, Dn·f] ~ **sb (of sth)** make sb feel certain; cause sb to realize: *How can I convince you (of her honesty)?* ○ *What she said convinced me that I was mistaken.* ○ *I was convinced* (ie sure) *I saw you there, but it must have been someone else.* **2** [Cn·t] (*esp US*) persuade: *What convinced you to vote for them?*

▷ **convinced** *adj* [attrib] firm in one's belief: *a convinced Christian.*

convincible /kən'vɪnsəbl/ *adj* willing to be convinced.

convincing *adj* that convinces: *a convincing speech, argument, liar.*

convincingly *adv*: *a convincingly argued statement.*

convivial /kən'vɪvɪəl/ *adj* (*esp fml*) **1** cheerful and sociable; fond of being with others: *convivial companions.* **2** full of shared pleasure and friendliness: *a convivial evening, atmosphere.*

▷ **conviviality** /kənˌvɪvɪ'ælətɪ/ *n* [U] **1** cheerfulness; sociability. **2** shared pleasure, esp with drinking and eating.

convivially /-ɪəlɪ/ *adv.*

convocation /ˌkɒnvə'keɪʃn/ *n* **1** [CGp] formal assembly, esp the legislative body of the Church of England or of the graduates of some universities: *Convocation has/have ruled that....* **2** [U] (*fml*) convoking; calling together.

convoke /kən'vəʊk/ *v* [Tn] (*fml*) call together or summon (a meeting, etc): *convoke Parliament.*

convoluted /'kɒnvəlu:tɪd/ *adj* **1** coiled; twisted: *the convoluted folds of the brain.* **2** (*fig*) complicated and difficult to follow: *a convoluted argument, explanation, etc.*

convolution /ˌkɒnvə'lu:ʃn/ *n* (usu *pl*) coil; twist: *ornate carving with lots of curves and convolutions* ○ *the convolutions of the brain,* ie the folds on its surface ○ (*fig*) *the bizarre convolutions of the plot.*

convolvulus /kən'vɒlvjʊləs/ *n* (*pl* ~**es**) [C, U] type of twining plant with trumpet-shaped flowers.

convoy[1] /'kɒnvɔɪ/ *n* **1** (**a**) group of vehicles or ships travelling together: *a large convoy of coal lorries.* (**b**) group of vehicles or ships being escorted for protection while travelling: *The convoy was attacked by submarines.* **2** (idm) **in 'convoy** (of travelling vehicles) as a group; together: *The supply ships travelled in convoy.* **under 'convoy** escorted by a protecting force: *The missiles were moved under convoy.*

convoy[2] /'kɒnvɔɪ/ *v* [Tn·pr, Tn·p] (esp of a warship) travel with (other ships) in a group to protect them; escort: *The troop-ships were convoyed across the Atlantic.* ○ (*fig*) *parents taking it in turns to convoy children to and from school.*

convulse /kən'vʌls/ *v* [Tn usu passive] cause (sb/sth) to make sudden violent uncontrollable movements: *convulsed with laughter, anger, toothache* ○ *a country convulsed by earthquakes* ○ (*fig*) *Riots convulsed the cities,* ie caused violent disturbance.

convulsion /kən'vʌlʃn/ *n* **1** (usu *pl*) sudden violent uncontrollable body movement, caused by contraction of muscles: *The child reacted to the drug by going into convulsions.* **2** violent disturbance: *The leader's assassination led to political convulsions,* eg an attempt at revolution. **3 convulsions** [pl] uncontrollable laughter: *The story was so funny it had us in convulsions.*

convulsive /kən'vʌlsɪv/ *adj* **1** having, producing or consisting of convulsions: *a convulsive movement, spasm, etc.* **2** violently disturbing: *convulsive upheavals, such as urban riots.* ▷ **convulsively** *adv.*

cony (also **coney**) /'kəʊnɪ/ *n* (*pl* **conies**) **1** [U] fur of the rabbit used to make coats, etc. **2** [C] (*arch*) rabbit.

coo[1] /ku:/ *v* (*pt, pp* **cooed** /ku:d/, *pres p* **cooing**) **1** [I] (of a dove or pigeon) make its characteristic soft cry. **2** (*infml*) (**a**) [I] make a soft murmuring sound like that of a dove: *a baby cooing.* (**b**) [Tn] say (sth) in a soft murmur: *'It will be all right,' she cooed soothingly.* **3** (idm) **bill and coo** ⇨ BILL[2].

▷ **coo** *n* (*pl* **coos**) soft murmuring sound (like that) of a dove.

coo[2] /ku:/ *interj* (*Brit infml*) (used to express surprise).

cooee /ku:ɪ/ *interj* (*infml*) (used as a sound to attract attention): *Cooee! Is anybody there?*

▷ **cooee** *v* [I] (*infml*) shout 'Cooee!'

Cook[1] /kʊk/ James (1728-79), English explorer. He is best remembered for his voyages of discovery to the Pacific. During these he charted the coasts of Australia, New Zealand and New Guinea. He came close to discovering Antarctica, and on his final voyage he found Hawaii, where he was killed.

Cook[2] /kʊk/ Thomas (1808-92), English travel agent. He began his activities by organizing a chartered train excursion to a temperance meeting and developed them into a major travel company.

□ ˌ**Cook's 'tour** (*often joc*) tour that includes visits to many places in a very short time.

cook /kʊk/ *v* **1** (**a**) [I, Ipr, Tn, Dn·n, Dn·pr] ~ **sth (for sb)** prepare (food) by heating, eg boiling, baking, roasting, frying: *Where did you learn to cook?* ○ *These potatoes aren't (properly) cooked!* ○ *a cooked breakfast* ○ *He cooked me my dinner.* ○ *I like to cook (Chinese dishes) for my family.* (**b**) [I] be prepared in this way: *The vegetables are cooking.* ○ *The meat cooks slowly.* ○ *These apples cook well,* ie taste good when cooked. ⇨ Usage. **2** [Tn] (*infml derog*) alter (sth) secretly or dishonestly so as to deceive; falsify: *cook the accounts, statistics, figures.* **3** [I] (used in the continuous tenses) (*infml*) be planned; happen as a result of plotting: *What's cooking?* ○ *Everybody is being secretive: there's something cooking.* **4** (idm) ˌ**cook the 'books** (*infml*) falsify facts or figures in order to make one's financial position seem better than it really is. **cook sb's 'goose** (*infml*) ensure that sb fails: *When the police found his fingerprints he knew his goose was cooked,* ie knew that he would be caught. **5** (phr v) **cook sth up** (*infml*) invent sth, esp in order to deceive: *cook up an excuse, a story, a bizarre theory, etc.*

▷ **cook** *n* **1** person who cooks food: *employed as a cook in a hotel* ○ *I'm not much of a cook,* ie I don't cook well. ○ *Were you the cook?* ie Did you cook this food? Cf CHEF. **2** (idm) ˌ**too many ˌcooks ˌspoil the 'broth** (*saying*) if too many people are involved in sth, it will not be done properly: *I know they only meant to help, but it was a case of too many 'cooks, I'm afraid.*

cooking *n* [U] process of preparing food by heating: *She does all the cooking.* ○ *Chinese 'cooking* ○ [attrib] *'cooking apples, sherry, etc,* ie apples, sherry, etc suitable for cooking rather than eating raw or drinking.

□ '**cookbook** *n* = COOKERY BOOK (COOKERY).

'**cookhouse** *n* detached or outdoor kitchen, eg in a camp.

'**cook-out** *n* (*US*) party where food is cooked and served outdoors.

NOTE ON USAGE: When cooking we generally use **1** boiling water (in a saucepan) or **2** boiling fat/oil (in a frying-pan) or **3** dry heat (in an oven or under a grill). **1** We **boil** vegetables, eggs, rice, etc by covering them with water and heating it. We **steam** fish, puddings, etc by placing the food above boiling water. **2** Meat, fish, vegetables, etc can be **fried** in shallow oil or fat. Chips, chicken pieces, etc can be completely covered by oil and **deep-fried.** We **sauté** vegetables very quickly in a small amount of oil. **3** We **roast** large pieces of meat, potatoes, etc and we **bake** bread, cakes, etc in the oven. Small or flat pieces of meat, fish, etc are **grilled** (*US* **broiled**) by being placed under direct heat. **Boil, fry, roast** and **bake** can be used in two types of sentence: *We boil potatoes* and *The potatoes are boiling.* **Steam, sauté** and **grill** are generally only used in the first pattern. With **boil** we often use the container to refer to its contents: *The kettle's boiling.*

cooker /'kʊkə(r)/ *n* **1** kitchen appliance for cooking, consisting of an oven with a hob on top and often also a grill: *a 'gas cooker* ○ *an e'lectric cooker.* Cf STOVE 1. **2** type of fruit, esp an apple, grown for cooking: *These apples are good cookers.* Cf EATING APPLE (EAT). **3** (*US*) pot for cooking food in.

cookery /'kʊkərɪ/ *n* [U] art and practice of cooking: [attrib] *a cookery course, school, etc.*

□ '**cookery book** (also '**cookbook**) book giving recipes and instructions on cooking.

cookie (also **cooky**) /'kʊkɪ/ (*pl* **-kies**) *n* (*US*) **1** biscuit. **2** (*infml*) person: *He's a tough cookie.* **3** (idm) **that's the way the cookie crumbles** ⇨ WAY[1].

cool[1] /ku:l/ *adj* (**-er, -est**) **1** (**a**) fairly cold; not hot or warm: *a cool breeze, day, surface* ○ *cool autumn weather* ○ *Let's sit in the shade and keep cool.* ○ *The coffee's not cool enough to drink.* (**b**) giving a (usu pleasant) feeling of being not too warm: *a cool room, dress, etc* ○ *a cool cotton shirt.* (**c**) (of colours) suggesting coolness: *a room painted in cool greens and blues.* **2** calm; unexcited: *Keep cool!* ○ *She always remains cool, calm and collected in a crisis.* ○ *He has a cool head,* ie doesn't get agitated. **3** ~ **(about sth)**; ~ **(towards sb)** not showing interest, enthusiasm or friendliness: *She was decidedly cool about the proposal.* ○ *They gave the Prime Minister a cool reception.* **4** calmly bold or impudent: *You should have seen the cool way she took my radio without even asking.* **5** [attrib] (*infml*) (said esp of sums of money, distances, etc, emphasizing their largeness): *The car cost a cool twenty thousand.* **6** (*dated sl esp US*) pleasant; fine: *Her guy's real cool.* **7** (idm) **(as)** ˌ**cool as a 'cucumber** very calm and controlled, esp in difficult circumstances. **a cool 'customer** (*infml*) calmly bold or impudent person: *She just took out her purse and paid a thousand in cash: what a cool customer!* **play it 'cool** (*infml*) deal calmly with a situation; not get excited.

▷ **cool** *n* **1 the cool** [sing] cool air or place; coolness: *step out of the sun into the cool* ○ *the pleasant cool of the evening.* **2** (idm) **keep/lose one's cool** (*infml*) remain calm/get excited, angry, etc.

coolly /'ku:llɪ/ *adv* in a cool[1](3) way: *He received my suggestion coolly,* ie unenthusiastically.

coolness *n* [U] quality of being cool[1](3): *I noticed a certain coolness* (ie lack of friendliness) *between them.*

□ ˌ**cool-'headed** *adj* calm; not flustered or excitable.

cool[2] /ku:l/ *v* **1** [I, Ip, Tn, Tn·p] ~ **(sth/sb) (down/off)** become or make cool or cooler: *The hot metal contracts as it cools (down).* ○ *Let the hot pie cool (off) before serving.* ○ *A cooling drink is welcome on a hot day.* ○ (*fig*) *Her unresponsiveness failed to cool his ardour.* **2** (idm) '**cool it** (*sl*) calm down: *Cool it! Don't get so excited!* ˌ**cool one's 'heels** be kept waiting: *Let him cool his heels for a while: that'll teach him to be impolite.* **3** (phr v) **cool (sb) down/off** (cause sb to) become calm, less excited or less enthusiastic: *She's very angry; don't speak to her* *until she's cooled down a bit.* ○ *A day in jail cooled him off.*

□ ˌ**cooling-ˈoff period** (in industrial disputes) compulsory delay before a strike, to allow a compromise to be reached.

ˈ**cooling tower** large container used in industry to cool water before it is re-used.

coolant /ˈkuːlənt/ *n* [C, U] (type of) fluid used for cooling (eg in nuclear reactors).

cooler /ˈkuːlə(r)/ *n* **1** [C] container in which things are cooled: *a wine cooler.* **2** [C] (*US*) = REFRIGERATOR (REFRIGERATE). **3 the cooler** [sing] (*sl*) prison: *two years in the cooler.*

coolie /ˈkuːlɪ/ *n* (*dated* ⚠ *derog*) unskilled Asian labourer.

coomb (also **combe**) /kuːm/ *n* (*Brit*) **1** hollow or small valley on the side of a hill. **2** short valley near the coast.

coon /kuːn/ *n* **1** (*infml esp US*) raccoon: [attrib] *a coon-skin cap.* **2** (⚠ *sl derog*) black person.

coop /kuːp/ *n* cage for poultry.

▷ **coop** *v* (phr v) **coop sb/sth up (in sth)** (usu passive) restrict the freedom of sb/sth by keeping him/it inside; confine sb/sth: *I've been cooped up indoors all day.*

co-op /ˈkəʊ ɒp/ *n* (*infml*) **1** [C] co-operative: *a wine produced by the local growers' co-op.* **2 the Co-op** [sing] (in Britain) (shop or supermarket belonging to a) large retail chain founded originally to provide low-priced goods and share out its profits amongst purchasers: *He does all his shopping at the Co-op.*

Cooper[1] /ˈkuːpə(r)/ Gary (1901-61), American film actor. His acting style made him famous in characters showing dignity and calm bravery, like the sheriff in the classic western, *High Noon.*

Cooper[2] /ˈkuːpə(r)/ James Fenimore (1789-1851), American novelist. He is best remembered for works like *The Last of the Mohicans,* which describe the life of the American Indian peoples and the pioneers of the American West.

cooper /ˈkuːpə(r)/ *n* maker of barrels.

co-operate /kəʊˈɒpəreɪt/ *v* **1** [I, Ipr] ~ **(with sb) (in doing/to do sth)**; ~ **(with sb) (on sth)** work or act together with another or others: *co-operate with one's friends in raising/to raise money* ○ *The two schools are co-operating on the project.* **2** [I] be helpful and do as one is asked: *'If you co-operate we'll let you go,' said the policeman.* ▷ **co-operator** *n.*

co-operation /kəʊˌɒpəˈreɪʃn/ *n* [U] **1** ~ **(with sb) (in doing sth/on sth)**; ~ **(between A and B) (in doing sth/on sth)** acting or working together for a common purpose: *a report produced by the Government in co-operation with the chemical industry* ○ *co-operation between the police and the public in catching the criminal.* **2** willingness to be helpful and do as one is asked: *Please clear the gangways, ladies and gentlemen.Thank you for your co-operation.*

co-operative /kəʊˈɒpərətɪv/ *adj* **1** [usu attrib] marked by co-operation; joint: *a co-operative venture, attempt, etc.* **2** willing to be helpful: *The school was very co-operative when we made a film there.* **3** [usu attrib] (*commerce*) owned and run by those participating, with profits shared by them: *a co-operative farm.*

▷ **co-operative** *n* co-operative(3) business or other organization: *agricultural co-operatives in India and China* ○ *The bicycle factory is now a workers' co-operative.* ○ *a housing co-operative,* ie in which a house or group of houses is jointly owned by those who live there.

co-operatively *adv.*

□ **the Co-ˈoperative Movement** movement started in Britain in the 19th century by groups of working people, who each gave money in order to buy food, clothes, etc more cheaply. Some members worked for the Movement actually making these goods. It grew, and the **Co-operative Wholesale Society** (better known as **the Co-op**) now has supermarkets and department stores all over Britain. It also owns the Co-operative Bank and it is the largest undertaker in the country. Members still receive a dividend from its profits.

co-opt /kəʊˈɒpt/ *v* [Tn, Tn·pr] ~ **sb (onto sth)** (of the members of a committee) vote for the appointment of sb as an extra member of the committee: *co-opt a new member onto the committee.*

co-ordinate[1] /ˌkəʊˈɔːdɪnət/ *n* **1** (often **coordinate**) either of two numbers or letters used to fix the position of a point on a graph or map: *the x and y coordinates on a graph* ○ *coordinates of latitude and longitude* ○ [attrib] *co-ordinate geometry,* ie geometry using coordinates. ⇨ illus at MAP. **2 co-ordinates** [pl] matched items of women's clothing.

□ **co-ordinate ˈclause** (*grammar*) one of two or more clauses in a sentence that are equal in importance, have similar patterns and are often joined by *and, or, but,* etc. Cf SUBORDINATE CLAUSE (SUBORDINATE).

co-ordinate[2] /ˌkəʊˈɔːdɪneɪt/ *v* [Tn, Tn·pr] ~ **sth (with sth)** cause (different parts, limbs, etc) to function together efficiently: *co-ordinate one's movements when swimming* ○ *We must co-ordinate our efforts* (ie work together) *to help the flood victims.* ○ *The plan was not* (ie Its parts were not) *very well co-ordinated.*

▷ **co-ordination** /ˌkəʊˌɔːdɪˈneɪʃn/ *n* [U] **1** ~ **(with sb/sth)** action of co-ordinating: *the co-ordination of the work of several people* ○ *the perfect co-ordination of hand and eye* ○ *a pamphlet produced by the Government in co-ordination with* (ie working together with) *the Sports Council.* **2** ability to control one's movements properly: *have good/poor co-ordination* ○ *You need excellent co-ordination for ball games.*

co-ordinator *n* person who co-ordinates: *The campaign needs an effective co-ordinator.*

coot /kuːt/ *n* **1** type of water-bird with a white spot on the forehead. ⇨ illus at BIRD. **2** (*infml derog*) old man, esp one who is annoying: *a stubborn old coot.* **3** (idm) **bald as a coot** ⇨ BALD.

cop[1] /kɒp/ *n* (*sl*) policeman.

□ ˈ**cop-shop** (*Brit sl*) = POLICE STATION (POLICE).

cop[2] /kɒp/ *v* **(-pp-)** (*sl*) **1** [Tn] receive (sth); suffer: *He copped a nasty whack on the head.* ○ *The heavy rain missed the north of the country altogether, and the south copped the lot.* **2 (a)** [Tn, Tng] discover (sb) in the act of doing sth wrong; catch: *If I cop you cheating again you'll be in trouble.* **(b)** [Tn, Tn·pr] ~ **sb (for sth)** arrest sb: *He was copped for speeding.* **3** (idm) **cop hold of sth** take hold of sth; grasp sth: *Here, cop hold of the screwdriver while I try the hammer.* ˈ**cop it** be punished: *When he finds out who broke his radio, you'll really cop it!* **4** (phr v) **cop ˈout (of sth)** (*derog*) fail to do what one ought to do, esp through fear: *He was boasting about how brave he was at the start, but copped out (of it) at the finish.*

▷ **cop** *n* (idm) **a fair cop** ⇨ FAIR[1]. **not much ˈcop** (*sl*) not very good: *He's not much cop as a boxer.*

□ ˈ**cop-out** *n* (*sl derog*) act of or excuse for copping out: *The TV debate was a cop-out: it didn't tackle any of the real issues.*

copal /ˈkəʊpl/ *n* [U] resin of certain tropical trees, used as a varnish.

copartner /ˌkəʊˈpɑːtnə(r)/ *n* partner or associate in a business.

▷ **copartnership** *n* **1** [U] system of having copartners in business. **2** [C] pair or group of copartners.

cope[1] /kəʊp/ *v* [I, Ipr] ~ **(with sth)** manage successfully; be able to deal with sth difficult: *cope with problems, difficulties, misfortune, etc* ○ *Her husband's left her and the kids are running wild, so it's not surprising that she can't cope.* ○ *There was too much work for our computer to cope with.*

cope[2] /kəʊp/ *n* long loose cloak worn by priests on some special occasions.

copeck (also **kopeck**) /ˈkəʊpek, ˈkɒpek/ *n* unit of currency in the Soviet Union; 100th part of a rouble.

Copernicus /kəˈpɜːnɪkəs/ Nicolaus (1473-1543), Polish astronomer. He was the first European to suggest that the earth and other planets moved around the sun and that the earth was not the centre of the universe. ▷ **Copernican** /-kən/ *adj*: *the Copernican system.*

copier /ˈkɒpɪə(r)/ *n* ⇨ COPY[2].

co-pilot /ˌkəʊ ˈpaɪlət/ *n* assistant pilot in an aircraft.

coping /ˈkəʊpɪŋ/ *n* (*architecture*) top row of bricks or masonry, usu sloping, on a wall.

□ ˈ**coping saw** saw shaped like a capital D, used for cutting curves in wood.

ˈ**coping-stone** *n* (*esp Brit*) stone used in a coping: (*fig fml*) *The final scene is the coping-stone of the play,* ie the climax, which completes it appropriately.

copious /ˈkəʊpɪəs/ *adj* **1** plentiful; abundant: *copious flowers, tears, words* ○ *She supports her theory with copious evidence.* ○ *I took copious notes.* **2** (of a writer) writing or having written much; prolific: *a copious writer of detective stories.* ▷ **copiously** *adv.*

Copland /ˈkəʊplənd/ Aaron (1900-91), American composer. His work shows his interest in creating a distinctive American style of serious music. He borrowed from jazz and Mexican music and used traditional *Shaker and cowboy songs (eg in *Appalachian Spring*).

copper[1] /ˈkɒpə(r)/ *n* **1** [U] chemical element, a common reddish-brown metal: *the mining of copper in central Africa* ○ *Is the pipe copper or lead?* ○ [attrib] *a copper pipe, wire, alloy, etc* ○ *her copper-coloured hair.* ⇨ App 11. **2** [C] (*esp Brit*) coin made of copper or a copper alloy: *It only costs a few coppers,* ie is cheap. **3** [C] (*esp Brit*) large metal vessel, esp one in which clothes were formerly washed by boiling. Cf BOILER 3.

□ ˌ**copper ˈbeech** type of beech tree with copper-coloured leaves.

the ˈCopper Belt area in Central Africa, esp in Zambia, where there are many copper mines.

ˌ**copper-ˈbottomed** *adj* (*esp Brit*) safe in every way; certain not to fail: *a copper-bottomed guarantee, assurance, deal, etc.*

ˈ**copperhead** *n* poisonous snake found in the US.

ˌ**copperˈplate** *n* polished copper plate on which designs, etc are engraved. ˌ**copperplate ˈwriting, handwriting** (also **copperplate**) neat old-fashioned formal handwriting with looped sloping letters that are joined to each other.

copper[2] /ˈkɒpə(r)/ *n* (*infml*) policeman.

coppice /ˈkɒpɪs/ *n* small area of woodland from which branches are cut from time to time.

▷ **coppice** *v* [Tn] cut branches from (trees) so that new branches can grow.

Coppola /ˈkɒpələ/ Francis Ford (1939-), American film director. One of the new generation of university-trained directors, he is noted for large-scale productions, like *The Godfather* trilogy and *Apocalypse Now,* which handle important themes from recent American history.

copra /ˈkɒprə/ *n* [U] dried coconut, from which oil is extracted to make soap, etc.

copse /kɒps/ *n* small area of woodland with thick undergrowth and trees.

Copt /kɒpt/ *n* **1** member of the Coptic Church. **2** Egyptian who is descended from the ancient Egyptians.

▷ **Coptic** /ˈkɒptɪk/ *adj* of the Copts: *Coptic language, traditions.* — *n* [U] language used in the Coptic Church.

□ **the ˌCoptic ˈChurch** the ancient Christian Church of Egypt, now with members in Egypt and Ethiopia.

copula /ˈkɒpjʊlə/ *n* (*grammar*) type of verb that connects a subject with its complement: *In 'George became ill', the verb 'became' is a copula.*

copulate /ˈkɒpjʊleɪt/ *v* [I, Ipr] ~ **(with sb/sth)** (*fml*) (esp of animals) have sexual intercourse: *The male bird performs a sort of mating dance before copulating with the female.*

▷ **copulation** /ˌkɒpjʊˈleɪʃn/ *n* [U] act of copulating.

copulative /ˈkɒpjʊlətɪv; *US* -leɪtɪv/ *adj* (*fml*) having a connecting function. — *n* (*grammar*) word that connects (and implies that meanings are added together): *'And' is a copulative.*

copy[1] /ˈkɒpɪ/ *n* **1** [C] thing made to look like another, esp a reproduction of a letter, picture, etc:

Is this the original drawing or is it a copy? ○ *a perfect copy* ○ *Make three carbon copies of the letter.* ○ *Photocopies cost 6p per copy.* **2** [C] individual example of a book, newspaper, record, etc of which many have been made: *If you can't afford a new copy of the book, perhaps you can find a second-hand one.* ○ *You receive the top copy of the receipt, and we keep the carbon.* **3** [U] material that is to be printed: *The journalist has handed in her copy.* ○ *The government crisis will make good copy*, ie will make an interesting or exciting newspaper story. ○ *We can give you the text on computer disk, or as hard copy*, ie as writing or printing on paper.

□ **ˈcopy-cat** *n* (*infml derog*) person who always imitates others.

ˈcopy desk (*US*) desk in a newspaper office where copy[1](3) is edited and prepared for printing.

ˈcopy-typist *n* typist who types out written material.

ˈcopy-writer *n* person who writes advertising or publicity copy[1](3).

copy[2] /ˈkɒpɪ/ *v* (*pt, pp* **copied**) **1** (**a**) [Tn, Tn·pr, Tn·p] ~ **sth** (**down/out**) (**from sth**) (**in/into sth**) make a written copy[1](1) of sth: *copy out a letter*, ie write it out again completely ○ *The teacher wrote the sums on the board, and the children copied them down in their exercise books.* ○ *copy notes (from a book, etc) into a notebook.* (**b**) [Tn, Tn·pr] make a copy[1](1) of (sth): *copy documents on a photocopier.* **2** [Tn] (try to) do the same as (sb else); imitate: *She's a good writer: try to copy her style.* ○ *Don't always copy what the others do; use your own ideas.* **3** [I, Ipr] ~ (**from sb**) cheat by writing or doing the same thing as sb else: *She was punished for copying during the examination.*

▷ **copier** *n* machine that makes copies of documents on paper, esp by photographing them.

copyist *n* **1** person who makes copies of eg old documents. **2** imitator: *This painting is by a copyist.*

copy-book /ˈkɒpɪbʊk/ *n* **1** book of exercises containing models of handwriting for learners to imitate. **2** [attrib] perfect; textbook: *It was a copy-book operation by the police; all the criminals were arrested and all the stolen property quickly recovered.* **3** [attrib] (*dated*) unoriginal; commonplace: *copy-book maxims, sentiments, etc.* **4** (idm) **blot one's copy-book** ⇨ BLOT[2].

copyright /ˈkɒpɪraɪt/ *n* [U, C] ~ (**on sth**) exclusive legal right, held for a certain number of years, to print, publish, sell, broadcast, perform, film or record an original work or any part of it: *Copyright expires 50 years after the death of the author.* ○ *The poem is still under copyright, so you have to pay to quote it. in/out of copyright*, ie protected/no longer protected by these arrangements ○ *sued for breach of copyright/for infringing copyright* ○ *Who owns the copyright on this song?* ⇨ article at PUBLISHING.

▷ **copyright** *v* [Tn] obtain copyright for (a book, etc). — *adj* protected by copyright: *This material is copyright.*

□ **ˈcopyright library** any of the six libraries which are allowed by law to ask for a free copy of all printed works published in Britain, ie the British Library, the Bodleian Library, the Cambridge University Library, the National Libraries of Wales and Scotland, and Trinity College Library, Dublin. ⇨ article at LIBRARY.

coquetry /ˈkɒkɪtrɪ/ *n* (*fml*) (**a**) [U] flirting. (**b**) [C] instance of this; flirtatious act.

coquette /kɒˈket/ *n* (*fml often derog*) girl or woman who flirts.

▷ **coquettish** /kɒˈketɪʃ/ *adj* of or like a coquette: *a coquettish smile, manner.*

coquettishly *adv.*

coracle /ˈkɒrəkl/ *n* small light boat made of wickerwork and covered with watertight materials, used by fishermen on Welsh and Irish rivers and lakes.

coral /ˈkɒrəl; *US* ˈkɔːrəl/ *n* **1** [U] red, pink or white hard substance formed on the sea bed from the skeletons of tiny animals known as polyps: *a necklace made of coral.* **2** [C] coral-producing animal; polyp.

▷ **coral** *adj* like coral in colour; pink or red: *coral lipstick.*

coralline /ˈkɒrəlaɪn; *US* ˈkɔːr-/ *adj* of or like coral.

□ **ˌcoral ˈisland** island formed by the growth of coral.

ˌcoral ˈreef reef formed by the growth of coral.

the ˌCoral ˈSea part of the Pacific Ocean between Australia, New Guinea and Vanuatu. ⇨ map at AUSTRALIA.

ˈcoral snake poisonous snake of tropical America.

cor anglais /ˌkɔːr ˈɒŋgleɪ; *US* ɔːŋˈgleɪ/ (*pl* **cors anglais**) (*music*) woodwind instrument similar to the oboe, but larger and playing lower notes. ⇨ illus at MUSIC.

corbel /ˈkɔːbl/ *n* (*architecture*) stone or timber projection from a wall to support sth (eg an arch).

cord /kɔːd/ *n* **1** [C, U] (piece of) long thin flexible material made of twisted strands, thicker than string and thinner than rope: *parcels tied with cord.* **2** [C] part of the body like a cord in being long, thin and flexible: *the spinal cord* ○ *the vocal cords.* **3** [C, U] (*esp US*) = FLEX. **4** (*infml*) (**a**) [U] corduroy: [attrib] *cord trousers, skirts, etc.* (**b**) **cords** [pl] corduroy trousers: *a man wearing blue cords.*

▷ **cordless** *adj* (esp of a piece of household electrical equipment) that is not directly connected by an ordinary electric wire to an electric socket: *a cordless iron, kettle* ○ *a cordless phone*, ie one that uses a radio link between the base and the receiver instead of a wire.

cordage /ˈkɔːdɪdʒ/ *n* [U] cords, ropes, etc, esp the rigging of a ship.

cordial[1] /ˈkɔːdɪəl; *US* ˈkɔːrdʒəl/ *adj* **1** sincere and friendly: *a cordial smile, welcome, handshake, etc.* **2** [usu attrib] (of dislike) strongly felt: *cordial hatred, detestation, loathing, etc.*

▷ **cordiality** /ˌkɔːdɪˈælətɪ; *US* ˌkɔːrdʒɪ-/ *n* **1** [U] quality of being cordial[1](1). **2 cordialities** [pl] (*fml*) expressions of cordial[1](1) feelings: *After the cordialities, we sat down to talk.*

cordially /-dɪəlɪ; *US* -dʒəlɪ/ *adv.*

cordial[2] /ˈkɔːdɪəl; *US* ˈkɔːrdʒəl/ *n* [U, C] (*Brit*) sweetened non-alcoholic drink typically made from fruit juice: *lime juice cordial.*

cordillera /ˌkɔːdɪˈljeərə/ *n* any of a series of mountain ridges that are parallel to each other, esp in the Andes and Central America.

cordite /ˈkɔːdaɪt/ *n* [U] smokeless explosive substance used in bullets, shells, bombs, etc.

cordon /ˈkɔːdn/ *n* **1** line or ring of policemen, soldiers, etc, esp one which guards sth or prevents people entering or leaving an area: *Demonstrators tried to break through the police cordon.* **2** ornamental ribbon or braid of an order[1](10a), usu worn across the shoulder. **3** fruit-tree with all its side branches cut off so that it grows as a single stem, usu against a wall or along wires.

▷ **cordon** *v* (phr v) **cordon sth off** separate or enclose sth by means of a cordon(1): *Police cordoned off the area until the bomb was defused.*

cordon bleu /ˌkɔːdɒn ˈblɜː/ *adj* [usu attrib] (*French*) (of a cook, dish, etc) of the highest standard of skill in cooking, esp classical French cooking: *cordon bleu cuisine.*

corduroy /ˈkɔːdərɔɪ/ *n* **1** [U] strong cotton cloth covered with parallel soft raised ridges made up of short tufts: [attrib] *a corduroy jacket.* **2 corduroys** [pl] trousers made of this cloth: *a pair of corduroys.*

□ **ˌcorduroy ˈroad** (*esp US*) road made of tree trunks laid side-by-side across swampy land.

core /kɔː(r)/ *n* **1** (usu hard) centre of such fruits as the apple and pear, containing the seeds. **2** (**a**) central part of a magnet or an induction coil. (**b**) (*geology*) central part of the planet earth: *The earth has a core and a mantle around it.* ⇨ illus at EARTH. (**c**) (*physics*) central part of a nuclear reactor, where the fuel rods are kept and the nuclear reaction takes place. (**d**) (*computing*) very small magnetizable metal ring used formerly in a computer's memory for storing one bit[3] of data. (**e**) inner strand of an electric cable. **3** most important part of sth: *Let's get to the core of the argument.* ○ *This concept is at the very core of her theory.* ○ [attrib] *English is a subject on the core curriculum*, ie one which all the students have to do. **4** (idm) **to the ˈcore** right to the centre: *rotten to the core*, ie completely bad ○ *He is English to the core*, ie completely English in manner, speech, dress, etc. ○ *Her refusal shocked us to the core*, ie utterly.

▷ **core** *v* [Tn] take out the core of (sth): *core an apple.*

CORE (also **Core**) /kɔː(r)/ *abbr* (*US*) Congress of Racial Equality.

co-religionist /ˌkəʊ rɪˈlɪdʒənɪst/ *n* (*fml*) person who belongs to the same religion as sb else.

co-respondent /ˌkəʊ rɪˈspɒndənt/ *n* (*law*) (formerly) person accused of committing adultery with the respondent in a divorce case: *cite* (ie name) *sb as co-respondent.*

Corfu /kɔːˈfuː/ one of the largest of the *Ionian islands off the west coast of Greece. It is now a popular tourist resort.

corgi /ˈkɔːgɪ/ *n* breed of small Welsh dog.

coriander /ˌkɒrɪˈændə(r); *US* ˌkɔːr-/ *n* [U] plant whose leaves and dried seeds are used in cooking, to give a special taste.

Corinthian /kəˈrɪnθɪən/ *adj* **1** of Corinth /ˈkɒrɪnθ/ in (ancient) Greece. **2** (*architecture*) of the most highly decorated of the five classical orders (ORDER[1] 13) of Greek architecture, incorporating carvings of leaves: *a Corinthian column.* Cf DORIC, IONIC. ⇨ illus at ORDER.

▷ **Corinthian** *n* native of Corinth.

cork /kɔːk/ *n* **1** [U] light springy buoyant substance that is the thick bark of a type of oak tree growing around the Mediterranean: *Cork is often used for insulation.* ○ [attrib] *cork tiles, table mats, etc.* **2** [C] bottle-stopper made of this: *draw/pull out the cork.* ⇨ illus at BOTTLE.

▷ **cork** *v* **1** [Tn, Tn·p] ~ **sth** (**up**) close or seal (a bottle, barrel, etc) with a cork or sth similar: *cork a bottle.* **2** (phr v) **cork sth up** (*infml*) not express (feelings, etc): *Don't cork it all up: if you feel angry, show it.*

corked *adj* (of wine) made bad by a decayed cork.

□ **ˈcorkscrew** *n* **1** device for pulling corks from bottles. **2** (*fig*) thing with a spiral or winding shape: [attrib] *her corkscrew curls.* — *v* [I, Ip, Ipr] move downwards with a circling motion: *The glider continued to corkscrew down.*

corkage /ˈkɔːkɪdʒ/ *n* [U] charge made by a restaurant for opening wine a customer has bought elsewhere.

corker /ˈkɔːkə(r)/ *n* (*dated Brit sl*) very good or remarkable thing: *a real corker of a goal.*

▷ **corking** *adj* [usu attrib] (*dated Brit sl*) remarkably good or large: *He told me a corking joke!*

corm /kɔːm/ *n* (*botany*) underground reproductive part of certain plants (eg crocus and gladiolus), similar in appearance to a bulb(1), from which the new stalk grows each year. ⇨ illus at PLANT.

cormorant /ˈkɔːmərənt/ *n* large, long-necked, dark-coloured bird which lives near sea coasts and eats fish. ⇨ illus at BIRD.

corn

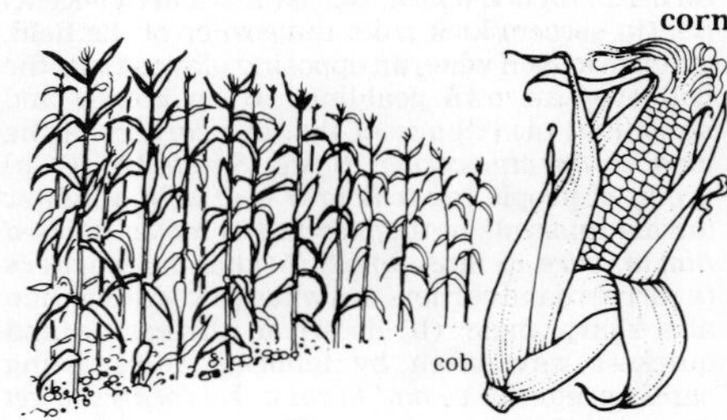

corn[1] /kɔːn/ *n* **1** [U] (**a**) (*esp Brit*) (seed of) any of various grain plants, chiefly wheat, oats, rye and maize; such plants while growing: *grinding corn to make flour* ○ *a field of corn* ○ *a ˈcorn-field* ○ *a sheaf of corn.* (**b**) (*esp US*) maize. ⇨ illus. **2** [U] (*infml derog*) music, verse, drama, etc that is banal, sentimental or hackneyed: *a romantic ballad that is pure corn.*

▷ **corny** /ˈkɔːnɪ/ *adj* (**-ier**, **-iest**) (*infml derog*) (**a**) too often heard or repeated; hackneyed: *a corny* *joke*. (**b**) banal; sentimental: *a corny song*.

□ ˈ**cornball** *n*, *adj* (*US infml*) (person who is) unsophisticated or too sentimental.

ˈ**corn-cob** *n* hard cylindrical part at the top of a maize stalk, on which the grains grow. ⇨ illus.

ˈ**corn dolly** doll made from corn stalks twisted together, usu as a decoration for sth.

ˈ**corn-exchange** *n* place where corn is bought and sold.

ˈ**cornflakes** *n* [pl] breakfast cereal made of maize that has been crushed and heated to make it crisp.

ˈ**cornflour** (*US* ˈ**cornstarch**) *n* [U] finely ground flour made esp from maize or rice.

ˈ**cornflower** *n* any of various plants growing wild in corn-fields, esp a blue-flowered kind that is also grown in gardens.

the ˈ**Corn Laws** (*history*) set of British laws, repealed in 1846, which restricted the import of corn to keep prices high.

ˌ**corn on the** ˈ**cob** maize cooked with all the grains still attached to the stalk.

ˈ**corn pone** (*US* also **pone**) /-pəʊn/ baked or fried maize bread.

ˈ**cornstarch** *n* [U] (*US*) = CORNFLOUR.

corn[2] /kɔːn/ *n* 1 small, often painful, area of hardened skin on the foot, esp on the toe. 2 (idm) **tread on sb's corns/toes** ⇨ TREAD.

cornea /ˈkɔːnɪə/ *n* (*anatomy*) transparent outer covering of the eye, which protects the pupil and iris. ⇨ illus at EYE.

▷ **corneal** /ˈkɔːnɪəl/ *adj* of the cornea: *a corneal graft*.

corned /kɔːnd/ *adj* (of meat) preserved in salt: *corned beef/pork*.

Corneille /kɔːˈneɪ/ Pierre (1606-84), French playwright. He and *Racine are considered the greatest writers of classical French tragedy. His most famous play is *Le Cid*, which like many of his works examines the conflict between love and duty.

cornelian /kɔːˈniːlɪən/ *n* semi-precious stone of a reddish, reddish-brown or white colour.

corner[1] /ˈkɔːnə(r)/ *n* 1 [C] place where two lines, sides, edges or surfaces meet; angle enclosed by two walls, sides, etc that meet: *A square has four corners; a cube has eight.* ○ *standing at a street corner* ○ *the pub on/at the corner* ○ *In the corner of the room stood a big old chair.* ○ *The address is in the top right-hand corner of the letter.* ○ *When I turned the corner (of the street) he had disappeared.* ○ *He hit his knee on the corner of the table.* 2 [C] (**a**) hidden, secret or remote place: *money hidden in odd corners*. (**b**) region; part; area: *She lives in a quiet corner of Yorkshire.* 3 [C] difficult or awkward situation: *Having lied that I still had the money, I was in rather a corner when they asked me to hand it over.* ○ *She'll need luck to get out of a tight corner like that.* ○ *The interviewer had driven her into a corner.* 4 [C usu *sing*] ~ (**in sth**) (*commerce*) complete ownership or control of supplies of sth, enabling one to decide its price: *a company with a corner in tin ore, wheat, etc.* 5 (also ˈ**corner-kick**) [C] (in soccer) kick from the corner of the field, given to a team when an opposing player kicks the ball over his own goal-line. 6 (in boxing and wrestling) (**a**) [C] any of the four corners of the ring: *In the blue corner, Buster Smith.* (**b**) [CGp] group of people (eg trainers) who help a fighter during intervals in the match: *His corner advised him to retire.* ⇨ illus at BOX. 7 (idm) **cut** ˈ**corners** (**a**) drive round corners in a wide curve rather than at a sharp angle. (**b**) do sth in the easiest and quickest way, often by ignoring rules, being careless, etc: *We've had to cut a few corners to get your visa ready in time.* **cut (off) a** ˈ**corner** (*esp Brit*) go across the corner of sth, not properly around it: *The lawn is damaged here because people cut (off) the corner.* **the four corners of the earth** the most distant parts of the earth: *Former students of this school are now working in the four corners of the earth.* **out of the corner of one's eye** by looking sharply sideways: *I caught sight of her out of the corner of my eye.* **(just) round the** ˈ**corner** very near: *Her house is (just) round the corner.* ○ *Good times are just round the corner*, ie will soon happen. **turn the** ˈ**corner** pass a critical point in an illness, a period of difficulty, etc and begin to improve.

▷ -ˈ**cornered** (in compound *adjs*) 1 with the specified number of corners: *a ˌthree-cornered ˈhat*. 2 with the specified number of participants: *The election was a three-cornered fight between Conservatives, Labour and SLD.*

□ ˈ**corner shop** (*Brit*) small shop near people's homes and away from large shopping centres, that sells groceries, household goods, etc, and is traditionally found at street corners: *The corner shop can't compete with supermarket prices.* ⇨ article at SHOP.

ˈ**corner-stone** *n* 1 stone that forms the base of a corner of a building, often laid in position at a ceremony. 2 (*fig*) thing on which sth is built; foundation: *Hard work was the corner-stone of his success.*

corner[2] /ˈkɔːnə(r)/ *v* 1 [Tn] (**a**) get (a person or an animal) into a position from which it is hard to escape: *The escaped prisoner was cornered at last.* ○ *The runaway horse was cornered in a field.* (**b**) put (sb) into a difficult situation: *The interviewer cornered the politician with a particularly tricky question.* 2 [I] (of a vehicle or driver) turn a corner: *The car corners well*, ie remains steady on curves. ○ *Don't corner so fast!* 3 [Tn] (*commerce*) gain monopoly control of (sth): *corner the market in silver*.

cornet /ˈkɔːnɪt/ *n* 1 brass instrument, like a trumpet but smaller, typically played in brass bands. 2 (*Brit*) cone-shaped container for ice-cream, made of thin crisp biscuit.

cornice /ˈkɔːnɪs/ *n* 1 (*architecture*) (**a**) ornamental moulding, eg in plaster, round the walls of a room, just below the ceiling. ⇨ illus at COLUMN. (**b**) horizontal strip of carved wood or stone along the top of an outside wall. 2 overhanging mass of snow or rock on the side of a mountain.

Cornish /ˈkɔːnɪʃ/ *adj* of Cornwall, its people or its language: *the Cornish coast* ○ *a Cornish cottage* ○ *Cornish grammar*.

▷ **Cornish** *n* [U] the Celtic language of Cornwall. ⇨ article at LANGUAGE.

□ ˌ**Cornish** ˈ**pasty** small pie consisting of pastry filled with meat and vegetables.

cornucopia /ˌkɔːnjʊˈkəʊpɪə/ *n* 1 (also **horn of** ˈ**plenty**) ornamental animal's horn shown in art as overflowing with flowers, fruit and corn, symbolizing abundance. 2 (*fml fig*) abundant source: *The book is a cornucopia of information.*

Cornwall /ˈkɔːnwəl/ county at the south-west tip of England. It was once a major producer of tin, but very few mines are left, and its scenery and mild climate now make it popular with tourists. ⇨ map at App1.

corolla /kəˈrɒlə/ *n* (*botany*) ring of petals forming the cup of a flower.

corollary /kəˈrɒlərɪ; *US* ˈkɒrəlerɪ/ *n* ~ (**of/to sth**) (*fml*) natural consequence or result; thing that logically must be so, once sth else has been established: *Neither of them knew about it, and the corollary of that is that someone else revealed the secret.*

corona /kəˈrəʊnə/ *n* (*pl* ~**s** /-nəz/ or ~**e** /-niː/) 1 (also **aureola, aureole, halo**) (*astronomy*) ring of light seen round the sun or moon, eg during an eclipse. 2 glow sometimes seen around an electrical conductor. 3 (*botany*) crownlike part of a flower. 4 type of thick cigar.

coronary /ˈkɒrənrɪ; *US* ˈkɔːrənerɪ/ *adj* (*anatomy*) of the arteries supplying blood to the heart: *coronary arteries*.

□ ˌ**coronary throm**ˈ**bosis** (also *infml* **coronary**) blocking of a coronary artery by a clot of blood, damaging the heart and possibly causing death; heart attack.

coronation /ˌkɒrəˈneɪʃn; *US* ˌkɔːr-/ *n* ceremony of crowning a king, a queen or some other sovereign ruler: *the coronation of Elizabeth II* ○ [attrib] *the coronation day, robes, coach*.

□ **Coro**ˈ**nation stone** = STONE OF SCONE (STONE).

coroner /ˈkɒrənə(r); *US* ˈkɔːr-/ *n* official who investigates any violent or suspicious death.

□ ˌ**coroner's** ˈ**inquest** proceedings held by a coroner, at which evidence about a death is presented and a jury gives a verdict on its cause.

coronet /ˈkɒrənet; *US* ˈkɔːr-/ *n* 1 small crown worn by a peer or peeress. 2 garland of flowers worn on the head.

Corot /ˈkɒrəʊ/ Jean-Baptiste (1796-1875), French painter. His paintings of the French and Italian landscape, often shown in a misty evening light, had some influence on the early *Impressionists.

Corp *abbr* 1 (also **Cpl**) Corporal: *Corp (Simon) Grey*. 2 (*US*) corporation: *West Coast Motor Corp.*

corporal[1] /ˈkɔːpərəl/ *adj* (*fml*) of the human body.

□ **corporal** ˈ**punishment** physical punishment, eg by whipping, beating.

corporal[2] /ˈkɔːpərəl/ *n* non-commissioned officer below the rank of sergeant in an army or air force. ⇨ App 4.

corporate /ˈkɔːpərət/ *adj* 1 of or shared by all the members of a group; collective: *corporate responsibility, action, etc.* 2 of or belonging to a corporation(2a, b): *corporate planning, policy, etc* ○ *Corporate executives usually have high salaries.* 3 united in a single group: *a corporate body*.

corporation /ˌkɔːpəˈreɪʃn/ *n* 1 [CGp] (*esp Brit*) group of people elected to govern a town; council: *the Lord Mayor and Corporation of the City of London* ○ *the municipal corporation* ○ [attrib] *corporation services, transport, refuse collection, etc.* 2 [CGp] (*abbr* **corp**) (**a**) group of people authorized to act as an individual, eg for business purposes: *Broadcasting authorities are often public corporations.* (**b**) (*esp US*) business company: *large multinational corporations.* 3 [C] (*joc esp Brit*) large fat stomach.

□ ˌ**corpo**ˈ**ration tax** tax paid by business companies on profits. ⇨ article at TAXATION.

corporeal /kɔːˈpɔːrɪəl/ *adj* (*fml*) 1 of or for the body; bodily: *corporeal needs*, eg food and drink. 2 material, rather than spiritual: *He is very religious and the corporeal world has little interest for him.*

corps /kɔː(r)/ *n* (*pl* unchanged /kɔːz/) [CGp] 1 (**a**) military force made up of two or more divisions: *the 6th Army Corps.* (**b**) one of the technical branches of an army: *the ˌRoyal ˌArmy ˈMedical Corps.* 2 group of people involved in a particular activity: *the Diploˈmatic Corps*, ie all the ambassadors, attachés, etc of foreign states in a particular country ○ *the ˈpress corps*, ie journalists.

□ **corps de ballet** /ˌkɔː də ˈbæleɪ/ (*French*) dancers in a ballet company who dance together as a group.

corpse /kɔːps/ *n* dead body (esp of a human being). Cf CARCASS.

corpulent /ˈkɔːpjʊlənt/ *adj* (*fml esp euph*) (of a person or his body) fat; bulky. ▷ **corpulence** /ˈkɔːpjʊləns/ *n* [U].

corpus /ˈkɔːpəs/ *n* (*pl* **corpora** /ˈkɔːpərə/) collection of written (or sometimes spoken) texts: *analyse a corpus of spoken dialect* ○ *the entire corpus of Milton's works.*

□ ˌ**Corpus** ˈ**Christi** /ˈkrɪstɪ/ name (Latin for 'the body of Christ') of a festival, esp in the Roman Catholic Church, which celebrates Christ's giving of the Eucharist to the Church. It is held on the Thursday after Trinity Sunday.

ˌ**corpus de**ˈ**licti** /dɪˈlɪktaɪ/, (*law*) (**a**) physical evidence, esp a dead body, which proves that a crime has been committed. (**b**) the various factors that make an act a crime.

corpuscle /ˈkɔːpʌsl/ *n* (*anatomy*) small mass in the body, esp any of the red or white cells in the blood.

corral /kəˈrɑːl; *US* -ˈræl/ *n* (*esp US*) 1 enclosure for horses, cattle, etc on a ranch or farm. 2 defensive circle of wagons, etc; laager.

▷ **corral** *v* (-**ll**-) [Tn] 1 drive (cattle, etc) into or shut up in a corral. 2 form (wagons, etc) into a corral.

correct[1] /kəˈrekt/ *adj* 1 true; right; accurate: *the correct answer* ○ *Do you have the correct time?* ○ *The description is correct in every detail.* ○ *Would I be correct in thinking that you are Jenkins?* ie Are you Jenkins? ○ *'Are you Jenkins?' 'That's correct.'* 2 (of behaviour, manners, dress, etc) in accordance with accepted standards or convention; proper: *Such casual dress would not be* *correct for a formal occasion.* ○ *a very correct young lady.* ▷ **correctly** *adv*: *answer correctly* ○ *behave very correctly.* **correctness** *n* [U].

correct[2] /kəˈrekt/ *v* [Tn] **1 (a)** make (sth) right or accurate; remove the mistakes from: *correct spelling, mistakes, misconceptions* ○ *I corrected my watch by the time signal.* ○ *Please correct my pronunciation if I go wrong.* ○ *Spectacles correct faulty eyesight.* ○ *'It was in April — no, May,' he said, correcting himself.* **(b)** (of a teacher, etc) mark the errors in (sth): *correct an essay, a test, etc.* **2** point out the mistakes or faults of (sb): *'Correct me if I'm wrong, but isn't that a llama?' 'No, it's not.' 'I stand corrected',* ie You have pointed out my mistake. **3** adjust (sth) so as to make it accurate: *Turn the wheel to the right to correct the steering.* ○ *Add salt to correct the seasoning.*

correction /kəˈrekʃn/ *n* **1** [U] correcting: *the correction of exam papers.* **2** [C] right mark, etc put in place of sth wrong: *a written exercise with corrections in red ink.* **3** [U] (*fml*) punishment: *the correction of young delinquents* ○ (*arch*) *a house of correction,* ie prison.

corrective /kəˈrektɪv/ *adj* having the effect of correcting sth: *corrective training,* eg for young offenders ○ *corrective surgery for a deformed leg.*
▷ **corrective** *n* ~ (**to sth**) thing that produces an opposing view which is more accurate, fairer, etc: *These artefacts are correctives to the usual view of these people as completely uncivilized.*

correlate /ˈkɒrəleɪt; *US* ˈkɔːr-/ *v* [I, Ipr, Tn, Tn·pr] ~ (**with sth**); ~ **A and/with B** have a mutual relation or connection, esp of affecting or depending on each other; (try to) show such a relation or connection between sth and sth else: *The results of this experiment do not correlate with the results of earlier ones.* ○ *Researchers cannot correlate the two sets of figures.* ○ *We can often correlate age with frequency of illness.*
▷ **correlation** /ˌkɒrəˈleɪʃn; *US* ˌkɔːr-/ *n* [sing, U] ~ (**with sth**); ~ (**between A and B**) mutual relationship: *the correlation between sb's height and weight.*
correlative /kɒˈrelətɪv/ *adj* having or showing a relation to sth else: *'Either' and 'or' are correlative conjunctions.*

correspond /ˌkɒrɪˈspɒnd; *US* ˌkɔːr-/ *v* [I, Ipr] **1** ~ (**with sth**) be in agreement; not contradict sth or each other: *Your account of events corresponds with hers.* ○ *Your account and hers correspond.* ○ *The written record of our conversation doesn't correspond with* (ie is different from) *what was actually said.* ○ *Does the name on the envelope correspond with the name on the letter inside?* **2** ~ (**to sth**) be equivalent or similar: *The American Congress corresponds to the British Parliament.* **3** ~ (**with sb**) exchange letters: *We've corresponded (with each other)* (ie written to each other) *for years but I've never actually met him.*
▷ **corresponding** *adj* that corresponds: *Imports in the first three months have increased by 10 per cent compared with the corresponding period last year.* **correspondingly** *adv*: *The new exam is longer and correspondingly more difficult to pass.*

correspondence /ˌkɒrɪˈspɒndəns; *US* ˌkɔːr-/ *n* **1** [C, U] ~ (**with sth/between sth and sth**) agreement; similarity: *a close/not much correspondence between the two accounts.* **2** [U] ~ (**with sb**) letter-writing; letters: *She has a lot of correspondence to deal with.* ○ *I refused to enter into any correspondence* (ie exchange letters) *with him about it.* ○ *Is commercial correspondence taught at the school?*
□ **correˈspondence course** course of study using books, exercises, etc sent by post.

correspondent /ˌkɒrɪˈspɒndənt; *US* ˌkɔːr-/ *n* **1** person who contributes news or comments regularly to a newspaper, radio station, etc, esp from abroad: *our Hong Kong, Middle East, etc correspondent* ○ *a foreign, war, cricket correspondent,* ie sb gathering news in a foreign country, in a war, about cricket. **2** person who writes letters to another: *He's a good/poor correspondent,* ie writes regularly/seldom.

corrida /kəˈriːdə/ *n* (*Spanish*) bullfight: *the corrida,* ie bullfighting as a sport.

corridor /ˈkɒrɪdɔː(r); *US* ˈkɔːr-/ *n* **1** long narrow passage, from which doors open into rooms or compartments. **2 (a)** long narrow strip of land belonging to one country that passes through the land of another country. **(b)** (also **air corridor**) route that must be followed by aircraft, esp over a foreign country. **3** (idm) **the corridors of ˈpower** the higher levels of the Government and administration, where important decisions are made: *an issue much discussed in the corridors of power.*
□ **ˈcorridor train** train with coaches which have compartments opening into a corridor.

corrie /ˈkɒri/ *n* = CWM.

corrigendum /ˌkɒrɪˈdʒendəm; *US* ˌkɔːr-/ *n* (*pl* **-da** /-də/) corrected error, esp one of a list printed at the beginning of a book. Cf ERRATUM.

corroborate /kəˈrɒbəreɪt/ *v* [Tn] confirm or give support to (a statement, belief, theory, etc): *Experiments have corroborated her predictions.*
▷ **corroboration** /kəˌrɒbəˈreɪʃn/ *n* [U] confirmation or support by further evidence, esp from a different source; additional evidence: *His possession of the gun is corroboration of his guilt.* ○ *In corroboration of his story* (ie to give support to it) *he produced a signed statement from his employer.*
corroborative /kəˈrɒbərətɪv; *US* -reɪtɪv/ *adj* tending to corroborate: *corroborative reports, evidence, etc.*

corroboree /kəˈrɒbərɪ/ *n* **1** celebration held at night by Australian Aborigines with traditonal dancing. **2** (*Austral infml*) noisy party.

corrode /kəˈrəʊd/ *v* [I, Ip, Tn, Tn·p] ~ (**sth**) (**away**) be destroyed or destroy (sth) slowly, esp by chemical action: *The metal has corroded (away) because of rust.* ○ *Acid has corroded the iron (away).* ○ (*fig*) *a bitter envy that had corroded their friendship.*
▷ **corrosion** /kəˈrəʊʒn/ *n* [U] corroding or being corroded; corroded area or part: *Clean off any corrosion before applying the paint.*

corrosive /kəˈrəʊsɪv/ *n, adj* (substance) that corrodes: *Rust and acids are corrosive.*

CORRUGATED IRON **corrugated**

corrugate /ˈkɒrəgeɪt; *US* ˈkɔːr-/ *v* [I, Tn usu passive] be shaped or shape (sth) into folds, wrinkles or furrows: *His brow corrugated with the effort of thinking.* ○ *muddy roads corrugated* (ie rutted and furrowed) *by cart-wheels.*
▷ **corrugated** /ˈkɒrəgeɪtɪd/ *adj* folded, wrinkled or furrowed: *corrugated cardboard,* ie used for packing fragile goods ○ *a corrugated roof,* ie made of corrugated iron. ⇨ illus.
corrugation /ˌkɒrəˈgeɪʃn; *US* ˌkɔːr-/ *n* fold; wrinkle.
□ **ˌcorrugated ˈiron** sheet iron pressed into curving folds, used for roofs, fences, etc.

corrupt[1] /kəˈrʌpt/ *adj* **1 (a)** immoral, esp sexually: *corrupt morals, behaviour, etc* ○ *a thoroughly corrupt novel which young people should not be allowed to read.* **(b)** dishonest, esp through accepting bribes: *corrupt officials who won't issue permits unless you bribe them* ○ *corrupt practices,* eg the offering and accepting of bribes. **2** (of languages, texts, etc) containing errors or changes: *a corrupt manuscript.* **3** (*arch*) impure: *corrupt air/blood.* ▷ **corruptly** *adv.* **corruptness** *n* [U].

corrupt[2] /kəˈrʌpt/ *v* [I, Tn] make (sb/sth) corrupt: *young people whose morals have been corrupted* ○ *corrupt an official,* ie gain his favour by offering bribes ○ *Pornography is defined by its 'tendency to deprave or corrupt'.*
▷ **corruptible** *adj* that can be corrupted: *corruptible young people, government officials, etc.*
corruptibility /kəˌrʌptəˈbɪlətɪ/ *n* [U].

corruption /kəˈrʌpʃn/ *n* [U] **1** corrupting or being corrupted: *officials who are open to corruption,* ie can be bribed ○ *claiming that sex and violence on TV led to the corruption of young people.* **2** (*fml*) decay: *the corruption of the body after death.*

corsage /kɔːˈsɑːʒ/ *n* small bouquet of flowers worn on the upper part of a woman's dress.

corsair /ˈkɔːseə(r)/ *n* (*history*) pirate or pirate ship attacking ships of European countries, esp off the coast of N Africa.

corselet (also **corslet**) /ˈkɔːslɪt/ *n* suit of armour, esp one covering the back, chest and stomach only.

corselette /ˈkɔːslɪt/ *n* piece of women's underwear combining a bra and corset.

corset /ˈkɔːsɪt/ *n* close-fitting undergarment worn to shape the body, or support it in case of injury.

Corsica /ˈkɔːsɪkə/ French island in the Mediterranean Sea. It is mountainous and has a less prosperous economy than the rest of France. It has its own language, similar to Italian, and there is a strong independence movement. *Napoleon was born there. ▷ **Corsican** *adj, n.*

cortege (also **cortège**) /kɔːˈteɪʒ/ *n* [CGp] (*French*) solemn procession, esp for a funeral.

Cortés /ˈkɔːtes/ Hernando (1485-1547), Spanish soldier. He led the Spanish forces that conquered Mexico and destroyed the Aztec empire.

cortex /ˈkɔːteks/ *n* (*pl* **cortices** /ˈkɔːtɪsiːz/) **1** (*medical*) outer layer of the brain or other organ: *the cerebral cortex* ○ *the renal cortex,* ie the outer layer of the kidney. **2** outer layer of a plant, eg the bark of a tree.
▷ **cortical** /ˈkɔːtɪkl/ *adj* of the cortex.

cortisone /ˈkɔːtɪzəʊn/ *n* [U] (*propr*) hormone from the adrenal gland, often made synthetically, used medically in the treatment of arthritis and some allergies.

corundum /kəˈrʌndəm/ *n* [U] hard crystallized mineral used chiefly in abrasives, or in powder form for polishing.

coruscate /ˈkɒrəskeɪt; *US* ˈkɔːr-/ *v* [I] (*fml*) flash; sparkle: (*fig*) *coruscating wit/humour.* ▷ **coruscation** /ˌkɒrəˈskeɪʃn; *US* ˌkɔːr-/ *n* [C, U].

corvette /kɔːˈvet/ *n* **1** small fast warship designed for escorting merchant ships. **2** (formerly) warship with sails and a single row of guns.

corymb /ˈkɒrɪmb/ *n* (*botany*) cluster of flowers on long stems, in which the flowers on the outside are on the longest stems, so that the cluster has a flat top.

cos[1] /kɒs/ *n* [C, U] (also ˌ**cos ˈlettuce**) (type of) long-leaved lettuce.

cos[2] (also **'cos**) /kɒz/ *conj* (*infml*) (esp in spoken English) because.

cos /kɒs/ *abbr* (*mathematics*) cosine. Cf SIN *abbr.*

Cosa Nostra /ˌkəʊzə ˈnɒstrə/ the American branch of the *Mafia.

cosec /ˈkəʊsek/ *abbr* cosecant.

cosecant /ˌkəʊˈsikənt/ *n* (*abbr* **cosec**) (*mathematics*) in a right-angled triangle, the ratio of the length of the hypotenuse to that of the opposite side.

cosh /kɒʃ/ *n* (*esp Brit*) length of lead pipe, rubber tubing filled with metal, etc, used for hitting people.
▷ **cosh** *v* [Tn] (*esp Brit*) hit (sb) with a cosh: *The train robbers coshed the guard.*

co-signatory /ˌkəʊˈsɪgnətərɪ; *US* -tɔːrɪ/ *n* ~ (**of/to sth**) person, state, etc signing jointly with others: *The USA and the Soviet Union were co-signatories of/to the treaty.*

cosine /ˈkəʊsaɪn/ *n* (*abbr* **cos**) (*mathematics*) in a right-angled triangle, the ratio of the length of a side adjacent to one of the acute angles to the length of the hypotenuse. Cf SINE, TANGENT 2.

cosmetic /kɒzˈmetɪk/ *n* (usu *pl*) substance for putting on the body, esp the face, to make it beautiful: *Lipstick and hair conditioner are cosmetics.*
▷ **cosmetic** *adj* **1** used as a cosmetic: *cosmetic preparations.* **2** (*usu derog*) intended to improve only the appearance of sth: *The reforms he claims to have made are in fact merely cosmetic.* **cosmetically** /-klɪ/ *adv.*

cosmetician /ˌkɒzmeˈtɪʃn/ *n* person who sells cosmetics or advises on their use.

□ **cosˌmetic ˈsurgery** surgery performed to restore or improve one's outward appearance (rather than restore health).

cosmic /ˈkɒzmɪk/ *adj* [usu attrib] of the whole universe or cosmos: *Physics is governed by cosmic laws.* ○ *(fig) a disaster of cosmic proportions*, ie very great.

□ **ˌcosmic ˈdust** fine particles of matter that gather into clouds in outer space.

ˌcosmic ˈrays radiation that reaches the earth from outer space.

cosmogony /kɒzˈmɒɡənɪ/ (also **cosmology**) *n* theory of the origin and development of the universe.

cosmology /kɒzˈmɒlədʒɪ/ *n* **1** [U] scientific study of the universe and its origin and development. **2** [C] = COSMOGONY. ▷ **cosmologist** /-ˈmɒlədʒɪst/ *n*.

cosmonaut /ˈkɒzmənɔ:t/ *n* Soviet astronaut.

cosmopolitan /ˌkɒzməˈpɒlɪtən/ *adj* **1** (**a**) containing people from all over the world: *a cosmopolitan city, club* ○ *the cosmopolitan gatherings at the United Nations Assembly.* (**b**) (*botany or zoology*) occurring in most parts of the world: *a cosmopolitan plant.* **2** (*approv*) (free from national prejudice because of) having wide experience of the world: *a cosmopolitan person, outlook.*

▷ **cosmopolitan** *n* cosmopolitan(2) person.

cosmos /ˈkɒzmɒs/ *n* **1 the cosmos** [sing] the universe, ie all space, seen as a well-ordered system. **2** [U] type of garden plant with pink, white or purple flowers.

Cossack /ˈkɒsæk/ *n* member of a people of S and SW Russia, famous for their skill with horses and their warlike character. Pioneers of Russian colonial expansion, in the time of the tsars they served in the Russian cavalry.

cosset /ˈkɒsɪt/ *v* [Tn] (*derog*) protect (sb/sth) too carefully; pamper: *industry cosseted by tariffs on foreign imports.*

cost[1] /kɒst; *US* kɔ:st/ *v* (*pt, pp* **cost**) (with the *n* phrase indicating price, etc often preceded by an indirect object) **1** [In/pr] (not usu in the continuous tenses) be obtainable at the price of; require the payment of: *These chairs cost £40 each.* ○ *How much/What does it cost?* ○ *It costs too much.* ○ *The meal cost us £30.* ○ *It costs (them) £1000 a year to run a car.* **2** [In/pr] (*fig*) (not usu in the continuous tenses) (**a**) result in the loss of (sth): *Dangerous driving could cost you your life.* ○ *The scandal cost her her career*, ie resulted in her having to resign, being dismissed, etc. (**b**) require a certain effort or sacrifice: *Her irresponsible behaviour cost her father many sleepless nights.* ○ *Compiling a dictionary costs much time and patience.* **3** [Tn] (*pt, pp* ~**ed**) (*commerce*) estimate the price to be charged for (an article or a service), based on the expense of producing or performing it: *Has this project been costed?* **4** [Tn] (*infml*) be expensive for (sb): *You can have the de luxe model if you like, but it'll cost you.* **5** (idm) **charge/cost/pay sb the earth** ⇨ EARTH. **cost an ˌarm and a ˈleg** (*Brit sl*) be very expensive: *The repairs are going to cost an arm and a leg.* **cost sb ˈdear** cause sb to suffer loss or injury: *That mistake cost him dear: he lost the game because of it.* **6** (phr v) **cost sth out** estimate the cost of sth: *I thought I could afford it, then I costed it out properly and found it was too expensive.*

▷ **costing** *n* [C, U] (*commerce*) estimation or fixing of prices or costs: *When we had done the costings on the project, it was clear it would not be economical to go ahead with it.* ○ [attrib] *the costing department, clerk.*

cost[2] /kɒst; *US* kɔ:st/ *n* **1** [U, C] price (to be) paid for a thing: *the high cost of car repairs* ○ *the costs involved in starting a business* ○ *She built the house without regard to cost*, ie not caring if it would be expensive. ○ *the cost of living/living costs*, ie the general level of prices ○ *the cost-of-living index.* ⇨ Usage at PRICE. **2** [U, sing] that which is used, needed or given to obtain sth; effort, loss or sacrifice: *the cost in time and labour* ○ *The battle was won at (a) great cost in human lives.* **3 costs** [pl] (*law*) expense of having sth settled in a lawcourt: *pay a £50 fine and £25 costs.* **4** (idm) **at ˈall costs** as the supremely important consideration: *We must at all costs prevent them from finding out about the plan.* **at ˈcost** at cost price: *goods sold at cost.* **at the cost of sth** involving the loss or sacrifice of sth: *She saved him from drowning, but only at the cost of her own life.* **count the cost** ⇨ COUNT[1]. **to one's ˈcost** to one's loss or disadvantage: *Wasp stings are serious, as I know to my cost*, ie as I know because I have suffered from them.

□ **ˈcost accountant, cost clerk** person who keeps a record of the expenses in a business, etc.

ˌcost ˈbenefit (*economics*) the relation of the cost of sth to the benefit it gives: [attrib] *cost-benefit analysis.*

ˌcost-efˈfective *adj* giving enough profit, benefit, etc compared to money spent: *It isn't cost-effective to build cars in such small quantities.* **ˌcost-efˈfectiveness** *n* [U].

ˈcost price (*commerce*) cost of producing sth or the price at which it may be bought wholesale. Cf SELLING PRICE (SELL).

costal /ˈkɒstl/ *adj* (*anatomy*) of or relating to the ribs.

co-star /ˈkəʊ stɑ:(r)/ *v* (**-rr-**) (*cinema or TV*) **1** [Tn no passive] (of a film, etc) have (a star(4)) with status equal to that of another or others: *The film co-starred Robert Redford (and Paul Newman).* **2** [I, Ipr] ~ (**with sb**) appear as a star with sb: *Laurence Olivier is in the film, and Maggie Smith co-stars (with him).*

▷ **co-star** /ˈkəʊstɑ:(r)/ *n* person who co-stars: *His co-star in the film was Maggie Smith.*

Costa Rica /ˌkɒstə ˈri:kə/ country in Central America; pop approx 2 851 000; official language Spanish; capital San José; unit of currency colone (= 100 céntimos). It has one of the highest standards of living in the region. The economy is mainly agricultural and coffee is a major export. It abolished its army in 1948. ⇨ map at CENTRAL AMERICA. ▷ **Costa Rican** *adj, n.*

costermonger /ˈkɒstəmʌŋɡə(r)/ *n* (*dated Brit*) person who sells fruit, vegetables, etc from a barrow in the street.

costive /ˈkɒstɪv/ *adj* (*dated*) constipated.

costly /ˈkɒstlɪ; *US* ˈkɔ:st-/ *adj* (**-ier, -iest**) costing much; expensive: *It would be too costly to repair the car.* ○ *a costly mistake*, ie one involving great loss. ▷ **costliness** *n* [U].

costume /ˈkɒstju:m; *US* -tu:m/ *n* **1** [C, U] garment or style of dress, esp of a particular period or group or for a particular activity: *People wore historical costumes for the parade.* ○ *The actor came on in full costume*, ie wearing all his stage clothes. ○ *Scotsmen in Highland costume*, ie wearing kilts, etc ○ *skiing costume* ○ [attrib] *a ˈcostume piece/play/drama*, ie one in which the actors wear historical costume. **2** [C] (*dated*) woman's suit (ie a skirt and short coat of the same material).

▷ **costumier** /kɒˈstju:mɪə(r); *US* -ˈstu:-/ *n* person who makes, deals in, or hires out costumes, esp for theatrical performances: *a theatrical costumier.*

□ **ˈcostume jewellery** jewellery made with artificial gems.

cosy (*US* **cozy**) /ˈkəʊzɪ/ *adj* (**-ier, -iest**) (*approv*) **1** (warm and) comfortable: *a cosy room, chair, feeling* ○ *a nice cosy little house* ○ *I felt all cosy tucked up in bed.* ○ *(fig derog) He's had it too cosy in that job; we ought to keep a stricter check on him.* **2** intimate and friendly: *a cosy chat by the fireside.* ▷ **cosily** *adv*: *sitting cosily in my armchair.* **cosiness** *n* [U].

cosy *n* cover to keep a teapot or boiled egg hot. — *v* (phr v) **cosy sb along** (*infml*) reassure sb in a dishonest way: *They cosied me along till I was ready to pay their price.*

cot /kɒt/ *n* **1** (*Brit*) (*US* **crib**) bed for a young child, usu with sides to prevent the child falling out. ⇨ illus at FURNITURE. **2** (*US*) simple narrow bed, eg a camp-bed, or a bunk bed on a ship.

□ **ˈcot-death** *n* [C, U] sudden unexplained death of a sleeping baby.

cotangent /kəʊˈtændʒənt/ *n* (*abbr* **cot**) (*mathematics*) (in a right-angled triangle) ratio of the length of a side adjacent to one of the acute angles to the length of the opposite side.

cote /kəʊt/ *n* (in compounds) shed, shelter or enclosure for domestic animals or birds: *a ˈdove-cote* ○ *a ˈsheep-cote.*

co-tenant /ˌkəʊ ˈtenənt/ *n* joint tenant.

coterie /ˈkəʊtərɪ/ *n* [CGp] (*often derog*) small group of people with shared activities, interests, tastes, etc, esp one that tends to be exclusive: *a literary coterie.*

coterminous /ˌkəʊˈtɜ:mɪnəs/ (also **conterminous**) *adj* [usu pred] ~ (**with sth**) (*fml*) having a shared boundary.

cotillion /kəˈtɪlɪən/ *n* **1** old dance with an elaborate pattern of steps. **2** (*US*) formal ball[2].

cotoneaster /kəˌtəʊnɪˈæstə(r)/ *n* shrub or tree that produces red or orange berries.

Cotswolds /ˈkɒtswəʊldz/ **the Cotswolds** (also **the ˌCotswold ˈhills**) range of hills in SW England, mostly in Gloucestershire. Sheep farming is common in the region, which was once a centre of the wool trade. It is now a popular tourist area. ⇨ map at UNITED KINGDOM. ⇨ article at COUNTRYSIDE. ▷ **Cotswold** *adj*: *a Cotswold village, cottage.* — *n* type of sheep first bred in the Cotswolds.

cottage /ˈkɒtɪdʒ/ *n* small simple house, esp in the country: *farm labourers' cottages.* ⇨ article at HOUSE.

▷ **cottager** /ˈkɒtɪdʒə(r)/ *n* person who lives in a cottage.

□ **ˌcottage ˈcheese** type of soft white cheese made from skimmed milk.

ˌcottage ˈhospital (*Brit*) small hospital in the country.

ˌcottage ˈindustry business that can be carried on at home, esp skilled manual work such as knitting, pottery, some kinds of weaving, etc.

ˌcottage ˈloaf (*Brit*) loaf consisting of a large round mass of bread with a smaller one on top.

ˌcottage ˈpie = SHEPHERD'S PIE (SHEPHERD).

cottar (also **cotter**) /ˈkɒtə(r)/ *n* (*arch or Scot*) person, esp a farm worker, living in a cottage provided by his employer.

cotter-pin /ˈkɒtə pɪn/ *n* (*engineering*) pin used to hold parts of machinery in place.

cotton[1] /ˈkɒtn/ *n* [U] **1** (**a**) soft white fibrous substance round the seeds of a tropical plant, used for making thread, cloth, etc: *bales of cotton.* (**b**) this plant when growing: [attrib] *working in the cotton fields.* **2** (**a**) thread spun from cotton yarn: *a needle and cotton.* (**b**) cloth made from this: [attrib] *a cotton dress.*

□ **ˌcotton ˈcandy** (*US*) = CANDY-FLOSS (CANDY).

ˈcotton-picking *adj* [attrib] (*US infml*) (used to express irritation about a person or thing): *I just hate this cotton-picking place!*

ˌcotton seed ˈoil oil obtained from cotton seed.

ˈcottontail *n* type of small N American rabbit.

ˌcotton ˈwool soft fluffy absorbent material, originally made from raw cotton, used for bandaging, cleaning, padding, etc: (*fig*) *You shouldn't wrap your children in cotton wool*, ie protect them too much from the world.

cotton[2] /ˈkɒtn/ *v* (phr v) **cotton on (to sth)** (*Brit infml*) come to understand or realize sth: *At last she's cottoned on to what they mean.* **cotton to sb** (*US infml*) take a liking to sb.

cotyledon /ˌkɒtɪˈli:dn/ *n* (*botany*) first leaf growing from a seed.

couch[1] /kaʊtʃ/ *n* long bedlike seat for sitting or lying on; sofa: *on the psychiatrist's couch.*

couch[2] /kaʊtʃ/ *v* **1** [Tn·pr usu passive] ~ **sth (in sth)** (*fml*) express (a thought, an idea, etc) (in words): *His letter was couched in conciliatory terms.* ○ *a carefully couched reply.* **2** [I] (*arch*) (of animals) lie flat, either in hiding or ready to jump forward.

couchant /ˈkaʊtʃənt/ *adj* (usu directly after a *n*) (*heraldry*) (of an animal on a coat of arms) lying with the body resting on the legs and the head raised: *a lion couchant.* Cf RAMPANT 3.

couchette /ku:ˈʃet/ *n* (*French*) bed in a railway

carriage which can be folded down to make the back of a seat during the day.

couch-grass /ˈkaʊtʃ grɑːs, ˈkuːtʃ-; *US* -ɡræs/ (also **couch**) *n* [U] type of grass with long creeping roots.

cougar /ˈkuːgə(r)/ *n* (*esp US*) = PUMA.

cough /kɒf; *US* kɔːf/ *v* **1** [I] send out air from the lungs violently and noisily, esp to clear one's throat or when one has a cold, etc: *She was coughing (away) all night.* ○ (*fig*) *The engine coughed and spluttered into life,* ie started noisily. **2** [Tn, Tn·p] ~ **sth (up)** get sth out of the throat or lungs by coughing: *He'd been coughing up blood.* **3** [I] (*sl*) confess to a crime: *The police have got him. Do you think he'll cough?* **4** (phr v) **cough (sth) up** (*Brit infml*) say or produce sth reluctantly: *He owes us money, but he won't cough (it) up.* ○ *Come on, cough up: who did it?*

▷ **cough** *n* **1** [C] act or sound of coughing: *She gave a quiet cough to attract my attention.* **2** [sing] illness, infection, etc that causes a person to cough often: *have a bad cough* ○ [attrib] ˈ*cough medicine, mixture, etc,* ie taken to relieve a cough.

could[1] /kəd; *strong form* kʊd/ *modal v* (*neg* **could not**, *contracted form* **couldn't** /ˈkʊdnt/) **1** (indicating permission): *Could I use your phone?* ○ *Could I borrow your bicycle?* ○ *Could I come round next week?* ⇨ Usage 1 at MAY[1]. **2** (indicating requests): *Could you baby-sit for us on Friday?* ○ *Could you type one more letter before you go?* ○ *Do you think I could have a cigarette?* **3** (indicating result): *I'm so unhappy I could weep.* ○ *What's for dinner? I could eat a horse.* **4** (indicating possibility): *You could be right, I suppose.* ○ *My wife's in hospital — our baby could arrive at any time.* ○ *Don't worry — they could have just forgotten to phone.* ○ *Somebody must have opened the cage — the lion couldn't have escaped on its own.* ○ *You could at least have sent a card,* ie It was possible but you didn't do it. ⇨ Usage 2 at MAY[1]. **5** (indicating suggestions): *We could write a letter to the headmaster.* ○ *You could always try his home number.* ⇨ Usage 3 at SHALL.

could[2] *pt of* CAN[2].

coulée /ˈkuːliː/ *n* (*US*) **1** stream of molten or solidified lava. **2** deep ravine that is dry in summer.

coulomb /ˈkuːlɒm/ *n* unit of electric charge, the amount of electricity from a current of one ampere in one second.

coulter (*US* **colter**) /ˈkəʊltə(r)/ *n* metal blade fixed vertically in front of a ploughshare, to cut the soil before it is lifted and turned by the share.

council /ˈkaʊnsl/ *n* [CGp] **1** group of people elected to manage affairs in a city, county, etc: *a city/county council* ○ *The local council is/are in charge of repairing roads.* ○ [attrib] *council services, elections.* **2** group of people appointed or elected to give advice, make rules, manage affairs, etc: *A council of elders governs the tribe.* ○ *In Britain, the Design Council gives awards for good industrial design.* ○ *a council of war,* ie a meeting of leaders, military commanders, etc to discuss tactics.

□ ˈ**council-chamber** *n* large room in which a council meets.

ˈ**council estate** (*Brit*) housing estate (HOUSING 1) built by a city, county, etc.

ˈ**council flat**, ˈ**council house** (*Brit*) flat/house built or provided by a city, county, etc. ⇨ article at HOUSE.

councillor (*US* also **councilor**) /ˈkaʊnsələ(r)/ *n* member of a council: *Councillor Jones.*

counsel[1] /ˈkaʊnsl/ *n* **1** [U] (*fml*) advice; suggestions: *Listen to the counsel of your elders.* ○ *wise counsel.* **2** [C] (*pl* unchanged) barrister conducting a law case: *counsel for the defence/prosecution* ○ *The court heard counsel for both sides.* Cf KING'S COUNSEL (KING). **3** (idm) **a ˌcounsel of deˈspair** advice to do sth one does not want to do, given because there seems to be no better alternative. **a ˌcounsel of perˈfection** advice that is very good but is difficult or impossible to follow. **hold/take counsel with sb** (*fml*) consult sb. **keep one's own ˈcounsel** keep one's opinions, plans, etc secret. **take ˈcounsel together** (*fml*) consult each other.

counsel[2] /ˈkaʊnsl/ *v* (**-ll-**; *US also* **-l-**) **1** [Tn] give professional advice to (sb with a problem): *a psychiatrist who counsels alcoholics.* **2** [Tn] give (the stated advice): *I would counsel caution in such a case.* **3** [Dn·t] (*fml*) advise: *He counselled them to give up the plan.*

▷ **counselling** /-səlɪŋ/ *n* [U] advice, esp from a professional person: *psychiatric/financial counselling* ○ [attrib] *a student counselling service.*

counsellor (*US* also **counselor**) /ˈkaʊnsələ(r)/ *n* **1** adviser: *a wise counsellor in time of need* ○ *a marriage guidance counsellor.* **2** (*US or Irish*) lawyer.

count[1] /kaʊnt/ *v* **1** [I, Ipr] ~ **(from sth) (to sth)** say or name numbers in order: *He can't count yet.* ○ *count from 1 to 20* ○ *I can count (up) to 100.* **2** [Tn, Tn·p] ~ **sth (up)** calculate the total of sth: *Don't forget to count your change.* ○ *Have the votes been counted up yet?* **3** [Tn] include (sb/sth) in a calculation: *fifty people, not counting the children.* **4** (a) [I, Ipr] ~ **(for sth)** be of value or importance: *Her opinion counts because of her experience.* ○ *Knowledge without common sense counts for little.* ○ *We've only a few bullets left, so make each one count,* ie use it effectively. **(b)** [I, Ipr] ~ **(as sth)** be accepted or valid: *You didn't shut your eyes before you made the wish, so it doesn't count!* ○ *A few lines of rhyming doggerel don't count as poetry.* **5** [Cn·a, Cn·n, Cn·n/a] ~ **sb/sth (as) sb/sth** consider sb/sth to be sb/sth: *I count myself lucky to have a job.* ○ *I count him a good judge of character.* ○ *We count her as one of our oldest friends.* **6** (idm) **count one's ˈblessings** be grateful for what one has: *Don't complain! Count your blessings!* **count one's ˈchickens (before they are ˈhatched)** be too confident that sth will be successful. **count the cost (of sth)** suffer the consequences of a careless or foolish action: *The town is now counting the cost of its failure to provide adequate flood protection.* **count ˈsheep** try to get to sleep, esp by imagining sheep jumping over a fence and counting them. **7** (phr v) **count against sb; count sth against sb** be considered/consider sth to be to the disadvantage of sb: *Your criminal record could count against you in finding a job.* ○ *He is young and inexperienced, but please do not count that against him.* **count among sb/sth; count sb/sth among sb/sth** be regarded/regard sb/sth as one of the stated group: *She counts among the most gifted of the current generation of composers.* ○ *I no longer count him among my friends.* **count down** signal the approach of a moment (eg for launching a space vehicle) by counting seconds backwards, eg 10, 9, 8, 7.... **count sb/sth in** include sb/sth: *See how many plates we have, but don't count in the cracked ones.* ○ *If you're all going to the party, you can count me in,* ie I will come with you. **count on sb/sth** rely on sb/sth with confidence: *count on sb's help/on sb to help* ○ *Don't count on a salary increase this year,* ie You may not get one. **count sb/sth out (a)** count (things) one by one, esp slowly: *The old lady counted out thirty pence and gave it to the shop assistant.* **(b)** count up to ten over (a boxer who has been knocked down), signifying his defeat: *The referee counted him out in the first round.* **(c)** (*infml*) not include sb/sth: *If it's going to be a rowdy party, you can count me out,* ie I shall certainly not attend. **count towards sth** be included as a qualification for sth: *These payments will count towards your pension.* **count up to sth** reach the specified total; add up to sth: *These small contributions soon count up to a sizeable amount.*

▷ **countable** *adj* that can be counted. ˈ**countable noun** = COUNT NOUN (COUNT[2]).

□ ˈ**counting-house** *n* (*dated*) building or room where accounts are kept, eg in a bank.

ˈ**countdown** *n* ~ **(to sth) (a)** [C] counting seconds backwards to zero before firing a rocket, etc. **(b)** [sing] (*fig*) period immediately before sth important happens: *the countdown to the local election.*

count[2] /kaʊnt/ *n* **1** [C] action of counting; number reached by counting: *a second count of the votes in an election* ○ *I want you to start on a count of 5,* ie after I have counted up to 5. ○ *By my count* (ie As I have counted them) *that's five cakes you've had already.* **2** [C usu *sing*] total number of things found in a sample tested: *a high pollen count.* **3** (usu **the count**) [sing] (in boxing) act of counting sb out (COUNT[1] 7): (*fig*) *Little Jimmy was really out for the count* (ie completely exhausted) *after that long tiring day.* **4** [C] **(a)** (*law*) any of a group of offences of which a person is accused: *two counts of forgery and one of fraud* ○ *She was found guilty on all counts.* **(b)** any of a set of points made in a discussion or an argument: *I disagree with you on both counts.* **5** (idm) **keep/lose ˈcount (of sth)** know/not know how many there are of sth: *So many arrived at once that I lost count (of them).*

□ ˈ**count noun** (also ˈ**countable noun**) (*grammar*) noun that can be used in the plural and with such words as *many* and *few*: *Count nouns are marked [C] in this dictionary.*

count[3] /kaʊnt/ *n* title of a nobleman in France, Italy, etc, equal in rank to a British earl. Cf COUNTESS.

countenance[1] /ˈkaʊntənəns/ *n* (*fml*) **1** [C] (expression on sb's) face: *a woman with a fierce countenance/of fierce countenance.* **2** [U] support; approval: *I would not give/lend countenance to such a plan.* **3** (idm) **keep one's ˈcountenance** (*fml*) maintain one's composure, esp by not laughing. **put/stare sb out of ˈcountenance** (*dated*) make sb feel embarrassed or at fault by staring at him.

countenance[2] /ˈkaʊntənəns/ *v* [Tn, Tg, Tsg] (*fml*) support or approve (sth): *countenance a fraud* ○ *How could you countenance such behaviour?* ○ *They would never countenance lying.*

counter[1] /ˈkaʊntə(r)/ *n* **1** long narrow flat surface over which goods are sold or served or business done in a shop, bank, etc. **2** (idm) **over the ˈcounter** (of medicines, etc) without a prescription(1a): *These tablets are available over the counter.* **under the ˈcounter** (of goods bought or sold in shops) secretly: *In Britain pornography was once sold under the counter.*

counter[2] /ˈkaʊntə(r)/ *n* **1** small disc used for playing or scoring in certain board games. **2** (used in compounds) device for counting repeated mechanical actions: *an engine's rev-counter.* **3** thing that can be exchanged for sth else: *Our missiles will be a useful bargaining counter in our negotiations with the Russians,* ie may be given up in exchange for concessions.

counter[3] /ˈkaʊntə(r)/ *adv* ~ **to sth** in the opposite direction to sth; in opposition to sth; contrary to sth: *act counter to sb's wishes* ○ *Economic trends are running counter to the forecasts.*

counter[4] /ˈkaʊntə(r)/ *v* [Ipr, Tn, Tn·pr, Tf] ~ **with sth**; ~ **sb/sth (with sth)** respond to (sb/sth) with an opposing view, a return attack, etc: *The champion countered with his right,* ie responded to a blow with a right-handed punch. ○ *They countered our proposal with one of their own.* ○ *The minister countered his critics with a strong speech defending his policies.* ○ *I pointed out the shortcomings of the scheme, but he countered that the plans were not yet finished.*

counter- *comb form* (forming *ns, vs, adjs* and *advs*) **1** opposite in direction or effect: *counter-attraction* ○ *counter-productive.* **2** made in response to, or so as to defeat: *counter-attack* ○ *counter-espionage.* **3** corresponding: *counterpart.* ⇨ Usage at ANTI-.

counteract /ˌkaʊntəˈrækt/ *v* [Tn] act against and reduce the force or effect of (sth): *counteract (the effects of) a poison, sb's bad influence, etc* ○ *We must counteract extremism in the party.*

▷ **counteraction** /ˌkaʊntəˈrækʃn/ *n* [U] counteracting.

counter-attack /ˈkaʊntər ətæk/ *n* attack made in response to an enemy's attack.

▷ **counter-attack** *v* [I, Tn] make a counter-attack on (sb/sth).

counter-attraction /ˌkaʊntər əˈtrækʃn/ *n* ~ **(to sth)** rival attraction: *There are so many counter-attractions these days that the live theatre is losing its audiences.*

counterbalance /ˈkaʊntəbæləns/ (also **counterpoise**) *n* ~ **(to sth)** weight or force that balances another.

▷ **counterbalance** /ˌkaʊntəˈbæləns/ *v* [Tn] act as a counterbalance to (sb/sth): *His level-headedness counterbalances her impetuousness.*

counterblast /ˈkaʊntəblɑːst; *US* -blæst/ *n* ~ **(to sth)** powerful reply: *Her article was a counterblast to her critics.*

countercheck /ˈkaʊntətʃek/ *v* [Tn] check (sth) a second time: *Our results have been checked and counterchecked.*

▷ **countercheck** *n* **1** extra check after a first check. **2** thing designed either to support or to oppose sth that hinders movement.

counterclaim /ˈkaʊntəkleɪm/ *n* claim made in opposition to another claim: *Amongst all the claims and counterclaims it was hard to say who was telling the truth.*

counter-clockwise /ˌkaʊntə ˈklɒkwaɪz/ *adv* (*US*) = ANTI-CLOCKWISE.

counterculture /ˈkaʊntəkʌltʃə(r)/ *n* way of life that rejects the usual values of society: *the counterculture of drugs.*

counter-espionage /ˌkaʊntər ˈespɪənɑːʒ/ *n* [U] action taken against an enemy's spying.

counterfeit /ˈkaʊntəfɪt/ *n, adj* (thing) made or done so that it is very similar to another thing, in order to deceive; fake: *counterfeit money, jewels, etc* ○ *This ten-dollar bill is a counterfeit.* Cf FORGERY (FORGE²).

▷ **counterfeit** *v* [Tn] copy or imitate (coins, handwriting, etc) in order to deceive: *a gang of criminals counterfeiting ten-pound notes.* Cf FORGE² 2. **counterfeiter** *n* person who counterfeits money, etc. Cf FORGER (FORGE²).

counterfoil /ˈkaʊntəfɔɪl/ *n* part of a cheque, ticket, etc which can be detached and kept as a record; stub.

counter-insurgency /ˌkaʊntər ɪnˈsɜːdʒənsɪ/ *n* [U] measures taken to prevent enemy troops from entering one's territory, esp in small groups.

counter-intelligence /ˌkaʊntər ɪnˈtelɪdʒəns/ *n* [U] measures taken to stop an enemy country from finding out one's secrets, to give them false information, etc.

counter-intuitive /ˌkaʊntər ɪnˈtjuːɪtɪv/ *adj* contrary to what one would naturally expect: *His solution to the problem is counter-intuitive.*

counter-irritant /ˌkaʊntər ˈɪrɪtənt/ *n* (*medical*) substance put on the skin to make it sore, and thus to relieve greater pain deeper in the body, eg rheumatism.

countermand /ˌkaʊntəˈmɑːnd; *US* -ˈmænd/ *v* [Tn] cancel (a command or an order already given), esp by giving a new and opposite one.

countermeasure /ˈkaʊntəmeʒə(r)/ *n* (often *pl*) course of action taken to remove, prevent, or protect against sth undesirable or dangerous: *countermeasures against a threatened strike.*

counteroffensive /ˈkaʊntərəfensɪv/ *n* attack made by a person or group against their attackers: *a counteroffensive led by the armoured division* ○ *The government is waiting to launch its counteroffensive.*

counter-offer /ˈkaʊntərɒfə(r)/ *n* offer made in response to, and esp to defeat, an offer made by sb else: *The first company made a very attractive counter-offer and won the order.*

counterpane /ˈkaʊntəpeɪn/ *n* (*dated*) covering for a bed; bedspread.

counterpart /ˈkaʊntəpɑːt/ *n* person or thing that corresponds to or has the same function as sb or sth else: *The sales director phoned her counterpart in a competing firm,* ie the other firm's sales director.

counterplot /ˈkaʊntəplɒt/ *n* plot made to defeat another plot.

▷ **counterplot** *v* (**-tt-**) [I, Ipr] ~ **(against sb/sth)** make a counterplot.

counterpoint /ˈkaʊntəpɔɪnt/ *n* (*music*) **1** [C] melody added as an accompaniment to another: (*fig*) *The dark curtains make an interesting counterpoint to* (ie contrast with) *the lighter walls.* **2** [U] art or practice of combining melodies according to fixed rules.

counterpoise /ˈkaʊntəpɔɪz/ *n* (*fml*) **1** [C] = COUNTERBALANCE. **2** [U] state of being in balance; equilibrium: *The two nations' nuclear forces are in perfect counterpoise,* ie are equal.

counter-productive /ˌkaʊntə prəˈdʌktɪv/ *adj* having the opposite effect to that intended: *It's counter-productive to be too tough: it just makes the staff resentful.* ▷ **counter-productively** *adv.* **counter-productiveness** *n* [U].

Counter-Reformation /ˈkaʊntə refəmeɪʃn/ **the Counter-Reformation** movement for reform within the Roman Catholic Church from the mid 16th to mid 17th centuries. The Council of Trent was set up to re-examine doctrine and Church organization. The movement checked the spread of Protestantism and some countries returned to Catholicism.

counter-revolution /ˌkaʊntə ˌrevəˈluːʃn/ *n* [C, U] revolution that overthrows the political regime introduced by a previous revolution; activity intended to bring this about: *stage a counter-revolution* ○ *the forces of counter-revolution.*

▷ **counter-revolutionary** /-ˈluːʃənərɪ; *US* -nerɪ/ *adj* of a counter-revolution: *counter-revolutionary movements, ideas, etc.* — *n* person who opposes or tries to overthrow a revolution.

countersign¹ /ˈkaʊntəsaɪn/ *v* [Tn] sign (a document, etc already signed by another person): *a cheque countersigned on the back.*

countersign² /ˈkaʊntəsaɪn/ *n* secret word which must be spoken to a guard, etc before one is allowed to pass; password: *give the countersign.*

countersink /ˈkaʊntəsɪŋk/ *v* (*pt* **-sank** /-sæŋk/, *pp* **-sunk** /-sʌŋk/) [Tn usu passive] **1** enlarge the top of (a hole) so that the head of a screw or bolt fits into it level with or below the surrounding surface. **2** insert (a screw or bolt) into such an enlarged hole.

counter-tenor /ˌkaʊntəˈtenə(r)/ *n* (*music*) (man with a) voice higher than tenor achieved by singing falsetto; male alto.

countervailing /ˈkaʊntəveɪlɪŋ/ *adj* [attrib] (*fml*) compensating: *all the disadvantages without any of the countervailing advantages.*

counterweight /ˈkaʊntəweɪt/ *n* weight designed to act as a balance to another. ⇨ illus at BRIDGE.

countess /ˈkaʊntɪs/ *n* **1** wife or widow of a count or earl. **2** woman with the rank of a count or earl.

countless /ˈkaʊntlɪs/ *adj* [esp attrib] numerous; too many to be counted: *I've told her countless times.*

countrified /ˈkʌntrɪfaɪd/ *adj* **1** having typical features of the countryside (eg open fields, trees, etc); rural: *quite a countrified area.* **2** (*derog*) having the unsophisticated ways, views, etc of country people; rustic.

country /ˈkʌntrɪ/ *n* **1** (**a**) [C] area of land that forms a politically independent unit; nation; state: *European countries* ○ *There will be rain in all parts of the country.* (**b**) **the country** [sing] the people of a country(1a); the nation as a whole: *The whole country resisted the invaders.* ⇨ Usage. **2 the country** [sing] land away from towns and cities, typically with fields, woods, etc and used for agriculture: *live in the country* ○ *a day in the country* ○ *We travelled across country,* ie across fields, etc or not by a main road. ○ [attrib] *country roads, life, areas.* **3** [U] (often with a preceding *adj*) area of land (esp with regard to its physical or geographical features): *rough, marshy, etc country* ○ *We passed through miles of wooded country.* ○ *This is unknown country to me,* ie I have not been here before, or (*fig*) This is an unfamiliar topic to me. **4** [U] (*esp US*) country-and-western music: [attrib] *a country singer* ○ *country music.* **5** (idm) **a country ˈcousin** (*infml esp derog*) person who is not used to town life and ways. **go to the ˈcountry** (*Brit*) dissolve Parliament and hold a general election.

□ ˌ**country-and-ˈwestern** *n* [U] (*abbr* **C and W**) type of music that derives from the folk music of the southern and western USA: [attrib] *a country-and-western singer.*

ˈ**country club** club in the country where members take part in outdoor sports, etc.

ˌ**country ˈdance** (*esp Brit*) traditional dance in which couples are arranged in two long lines or face inward from four sides.

ˌ**country-ˈhouse** *n* large house in the country surrounded by an estate, typically owned by a rich person.

ˌ**country ˈseat** = SEAT¹ 8.

ˌ**country-ˈwide** *adj, adv* all over a country: *country-wide protests against the new law.*

NOTE ON USAGE: **Country** is the most usual and neutral word for a geographical area identified by a name, such as France or China: *We passed through four countries on our way to Greece.* The word **state** emphasizes the political organization of the area under an independent government, and it can refer to the government itself: *the member states of the EEC* ○ *a one-party state* ○ *The State provides free education and health care.* A **state** may also be a constituent part of the larger unit: *There are 13 states in Malaysia.* **Nation** also indicates a political unit and is more formal than **state:** *the United Nations* ○ *the Association of South-East Asian Nations.* In addition, it can suggest a community of people who share a history and language but may not have their own country or state: *The Jewish nation is scattered around the world.* **Land** is more formal or poetic: *Exiles long to return to their native land.*

countryman /ˈkʌntrɪmən/ *n* (*pl* **-men** /-mən/, *fem* **countrywoman** /ˈkʌntrɪwʊmən/, *pl* **-women**) **1** person living in or born in the same country(1a) as sb else: *a hero much loved by his countrymen.* **2** person living in or born in the country(2).

countryside /ˈkʌntrɪsaɪd/ *n* (usu **the countryside**) [sing] fields, wooded areas, etc outside towns and cities: *The English countryside looks at its best in spring.* ○ *the preservation of the countryside.* ⇨ article.

□ **the ˈCountryside Commission** British organization responsible for the conservation of the countryside, esp the National Parks, and for improving facilities for those visiting it. ⇨ articles at ENVIRONMENT, TOWN.

county /ˈkaʊntɪ/ *n* **1** administrative division of Britain, the largest unit of local government: *the county of Kent* ○ [attrib] *a county boundary, councillor* ○ *county cricket.* Cf PROVINCE 1, STATE¹ 3. 📖 Many of Britain's counties changed when local government districts were reorganized in 1974. These changes were not welcomed by everybody. Some people, especially older people, objected because they felt no sense of belonging to their new county. Others felt sorry that the old boundaries, many of which had existed for centuries and been marked by rivers and mountains, were being replaced by artificial boundaries. Despite the changes, however, the names of some of the old counties are still in use today, for example in the names of county cricket teams such as Lancashire, Yorkshire and Middlesex.

2 (in USA and other countries) subdivision of a state.

▷ **county** *adj* (*Brit infml sometimes derog*) having the life-style and habits of English upper-class landowners (eg fond of fox-hunting): *She's awfully county.* ○ *He belongs to the county set,* ie people having this life-style.

□ ˌ**county ˈcouncil** body elected to govern a county. ⇨ article at GOVERNMENT.

ˌ**county ˈcourt** (in England) local lawcourt where non-criminal cases are dealt with. Cf CROWN COURT (CROWN¹).

ˌ**county ˈtown** (*esp Brit*), ˌ**county ˈseat** (*esp US*) main town of a county, the centre of its administration.

coup /kuː/ *n* (*pl* ~**s** /kuːz/) **1** surprising and successful action: *She pulled off a great coup in getting the president to agree to an interview.* **2** (also (*French*) **coup d'état** /kuː deɪˈtɑː/), (*pl* **coups d'état** /kuː deɪˈtɑː/) sudden unconstitutional, often violent, change of

The Countryside

The British countryside is very varied and in places very beautiful, especially in such regions as the West Country, the Lake District, the Yorkshire Dales, the mountains of Wales and Northern Ireland, and the Scottish Highlands. It comprises not just farmland but large areas of forest, moorland and upland. As well as mountainous country there are extensive areas of hills and downs, such as the Cotswolds, the Yorkshire Wolds, the Chilterns and the South Downs. There are also many attractive island groups including the Orkneys, the Shetlands, the Hebrides and the Scilly Isles. The overall charm of the countryside is enhanced by Britain's many rivers, streams and canals, and by the varied coastline, with its many bays and beaches. All this makes for a land where tourism is one of the major industries, and where a 'country walk' is regarded as one of the chief recreational pleasures.

Access to much of the countryside is free, even over privately owned fields and farmland, by a system of public footpaths and bridleways. The Country Code sets out rules for the public to observe in helping to protect farmland and the natural environment.

The government, mainly through the Countryside Commissions, has established areas where the countryside may be freely enjoyed. These range from national parks and 'areas of outstanding natural beauty' to long-distance footpaths like the 'National Trails', which are designed to take the walker through Britain's most attractive scenery, such as the fens of East Anglia or the mountains of Snowdonia. These paths are maintained by the local authorities. Large-scale Ordnance Survey maps, published for every part of the country, show footpaths and public rights of way.

Among special areas to be enjoyed are country parks, forest parks, 'national scenic parks' (in Scotland) and coastal tracts. Common land is also popular for walks. It is land that is open to the public, often the land that in medieval times was available to villagers for growing crops and grazing animals. The village green, a feature of many villages, is usually an area of common land and is a traditional setting for country fairs. Most country parks and forest parks provide such facilities as picnic sites for tourists, and many have special 'nature trails'.

Conservation of the environment is a major issue in Britain. Nature conservation is the responsibility of the Nature Conservancy Council. Forest land, unless it is privately owned, is under the care of the Forestry Commission. This body has also set up a number of 'sites of special scientific interest', whose most important aim is nature conservation. Many local authorities, too, have established nature reserves. Around the coast, undeveloped and ecologically valuable stretches of land are protected as 'heritage coast'.

Preservation of the coastline and of many other areas of scenic beauty is also the work of the National Trust. The Trust is a charity that raises money to preserve not only land but also historic buildings. It owns many famous country-houses, gardens and ancient monuments, as well as stretches of countryside.

'Green belts' have been established round many large cities, in order to control building development and to provide open land for the public to enjoy. (Cf article at TOWN.)

As a much larger country than Britain, the USA has an even greater variety and extent of scenic and historic regions to preserve. Many such regions are designated 'National', and include national parks, national battlefields, national memorials, national monuments, national preserves, national rivers and national recreation areas. Among the best-known and most popular national parks in the USA are the Great Smoky Mountains, extending across the frontier between Tennessee and North Carolina, the National Capital Parks, and, in the west, the Grand Canyon and Yellowstone Parks. National forests are major areas of conservation and recreation and are administered by the Forest Service in the Department of Agriculture.

The Federal Indian Reservations are special regions of conservation, established to provide lands for the various American Indian tribes. The largest single reservation is in Wyoming, while Arizona has the largest amount of land as reservation. Most reservations are owned either by the tribes or by individual Indians, and are held in trust by the federal government.

government: *The army staged a coup (d'état).* ○ *a bloodless coup.*

□ **coup de grâce** /ˌkuː də ˈgrɑːs; *US* ˈgræs/ (*pl* **coups de grâce** /ˌkuː də ˈgrɑːs; *US* -ˈgræs/) blow that kills a person or an animal, esp for reasons of mercy: (*fig*) *Poor exam results dealt the coup de grâce to* (ie ended) *his hopes of staying on at university.*

coupé /ˈkuːpeɪ/ *n* **1** (*US* **coupe** /kuːp/) two-door car with a sloping back. **2** closed horse-drawn carriage with an inside seat for two people and an outside seat for the driver.

couple[1] /ˈkʌpl/ *n* **1** two people or things that are seen together or associated, esp a man and woman together: *married couples* ○ *courting couples* ○ *Several couples were on the dance floor.* ○ *I won't have any more whiskies; I've had a couple already.* **2** (*physics*) two equal and parallel forces applied to the same body, which do not act in the same line and are able to cause rotation. **3** (idm) **a couple of people/things** (a) two people/things: *I saw a couple of men get out.* ○ *I'll stay for a couple more hours.* (b) a small number of people/things: *She jogs a couple of miles every morning.* **in two/a couple of shakes** ⇨ SHAKE[2].

couple[2] /ˈkʌpl/ *v* **1** [Tn, Tn·pr, Tn·p] ~ **A on (to B)**; ~ **A and B (together)** fasten or join (two things, esp two railway carriages) together: *The dining-car was coupled on (to the last coach).* **2** [Tn·pr] ~ **sb/sth with sb/sth** link or associate sb/sth with sb/sth: *The name of Mozart is coupled with the city of Salzburg.* ○ *The bad light, coupled with* (ie together with) *the wet ground, made play very difficult.* **3** [I] (*arch or rhet*) (of two people) have sexual intercourse.

▷ **coupling** /ˈkʌplɪŋ/ *n* **1** (a) [U] act of joining. (b) [C, U] (*arch or rhet*) (act of) sexual intercourse. **2** [C] link connecting two parts, esp two railway carriages or other vehicles. **3** [C] (choice of) an item to go with the main piece of music on a record, cassette, etc: *an unusual coupling of Bach and Bartok.*

couplet /ˈkʌplɪt/ *n* two successive lines of verse of equal length: *a rhyming couplet.*

coupon /ˈkuːpɒn/ *n* **1** small, usu detachable, piece of paper that gives the holder the right to do or receive sth (eg goods in exchange): *petrol coupons* ○ *10p off if you use this coupon.* **2** printed form, often cut out from a newspaper, etc, used to enter a competition, order goods, etc: *fill in a football coupon*, ie for a football pool competition.

courage /ˈkʌrɪdʒ/ *n* **1** [U] ability to control fear when facing danger, pain, etc; bravery: *He showed great courage in battle.* ○ *She didn't have the courage to refuse.* ○ *I plucked up/summoned up my courage* (ie controlled my fear) *and asked her to marry me.* **2** (idm) **Dutch courage** ⇨ DUTCH. **have/lack the courage of one's conˈvictions** be/not be brave enough to do what one feels to be right. **lose courage** ⇨ LOSE. **pluck up courage** ⇨ PLUCK. **screw up one's courage** ⇨ SCREW. **take one's ˌcourage in both ˈhands** make oneself do sth which one is afraid of.

▷ **courageous** /kəˈreɪdʒəs/ *adj* brave; fearless: *It was courageous of her to oppose her boss.* **courageously** *adv.*

Courbet /ˈkʊəbeɪ/ Gustave (1819-77), French painter. His socialist views led him to develop a 'realist' style which showed everyday scenes, esp of middle-class country life while continuing to use a classical technique.

courgette /kɔːˈʒet/ *n* (*Brit*) (*US* **zucchini**) small green marrow[2] eaten as a vegetable. ⇨ illus at MARROW.

courier /ˈkʊrɪə(r)/ *n* **1** person employed to guide and assist a group of tourists. **2** messenger carrying news or important papers.

course[1] /kɔːs/ *n* **1** [sing] forward movement in time: *In the course of* (ie During) *my long life I've known many changes.* ○ *the course of history* ○ *I didn't sleep once during the entire course of the journey.* **2** [C] (a) direction or route followed by a ship or an aircraft or by a river, boundary line, etc: *The plane was on/off course*, ie following/not following the right course. ○ *The course of the ship was due north.* ○ *The captain set a course for* (ie towards) *New York.* ○ *the course of the River Thames* ○ (*arch*) *the stars in their courses*, ie the way they appear to move ○ (*fig*) *The course of the argument suddenly changed*, ie It turned to a different subject. (b) way of acting or proceeding: *What courses are open to us?* ○ *The Government's present course will only lead to disaster.* ○ *The wisest course would be to ignore it.* **3** [C] (a) ~ **(in/on sth)** (*education*) series of lessons, lectures, etc: *a French, a chemistry, an art course* ○ *an elementary course in maths* ○ *taking a refresher course to improve my driving.* (b) ~ **(of sth)** (*medical*) series (of treatments, pills, etc): *prescribe a course of injections, X-ray treatment, etc.* **4** [C] (a) area for playing golf: *a ˈgolf-course.* ⇨ illus at GOLF. (b) stretch of land or water for races: *a ˈrace-course*, ie for horse-races ○ *a five-mile rowing course.* **5** [C] any of the separate parts of a meal, eg soup, dessert: *a five-course dinner* ○ *The main course was a vegetable stew.* **6** [C] continuous layer of brick, rock, etc in a wall: *a damp(-proof) course.* **7** (idm) **a course of action** activity planned to achieve sth; procedure followed to get sth done: *What is the best course of action we can take?* **be par for the course** ⇨ PAR[1]. **in course of sth** undergoing the specified process: *a house in course of construction*, ie being built. **in the course of sth** during sth: *in the course of our conversation*, ie while we were talking. **in (the) course of ˈtime** when (enough) time has passed; eventually: *Be patient: you will be promoted in the course of time.* **in due course** ⇨ DUE[1]. **in the ordinary, normal, etc course of events, things, etc** as things usually happen; normally: *In the ordinary course of events, I visit her once a week.* **a matter of course** ⇨ MATTER[1]. **a middle course** ⇨ MIDDLE. **of course** naturally; certainly: *'Do you study hard?' 'Of course I do.'* ○ *'Did she take it?' 'Of course not.'* ○ *That was 40 years ago, but of course you wouldn't remember it.* **run/take its ˈcourse** develop as is usual; proceed to the usual end: *We can't cure the disease; it must run its course.* ○ *The decision cannot be reversed; the law must take its course*, ie the punishment must be carried out. **stay the course** ⇨ STAY.

course[2] /kɔːs/ *v* [Ipr, Ip] (*esp rhet*) (esp of liquids) move or flow freely: *The blood coursed through his veins.* ○ *Tears coursed down her cheeks.*

▷ **coursing** /ˈkɔːsɪŋ/ *n* [U] sport of hunting hares with dogs which follow them using sight rather than scent.

courser /ˈkɔːsə(r)/ *n* **1** bird from Africa and Asia that runs very fast on land. **2** (*arch*) fast horse.

court[1] /kɔːt/ *n* **1** (**a**) [C, U] place where trials or other law cases are held: *a ˈcourt-room* ○ *a ˈmagistrate's court* ○ *a crown ˈcourt* ○ *a court of assize, a court of quarter-sessions*, ie courts in England and Wales before 1971 ○ *a (military or naval) court of inquiry*, ie one that deals with cases of indiscipline, etc ○ *The prisoner was brought to court for trial.* ○ *She had to appear in court to give evidence.* ○ [attrib] *a court usher, reporter* ○ *The case was settled out of court*, ie was settled without the need for it to be tried in court. ○ *an out-of-court settlement.* (**b**) **the court** [sing] people present in a court-room, esp those who administer justice: *The court rose* (ie stood up) *as the judge entered.* ○ *Please tell the court all you know.* Cf LAWCOURT (LAW). **2** (often **Court**) (**a**) [C, U] official residence of a sovereign: *the Court of St James*, ie the court of the British sovereign ○ *She had been received at all the courts of Europe.* ○ *be presented at court*, ie make one's first official appearance at the sovereign's court ○ [attrib] *the court jester*. (**b**) **the court** [sing] (institution consisting of the) sovereign and all his or her advisers, officials, family, etc: *The court moves to the country in the summer.* **3** [C] (*sport*) indoor or outdoor space marked out for tennis or similar ball games: *a ˈtennis/ˈsquash court* ○ *Do you prefer grass or hard courts?* ○ *Players must behave well on court.* ⇨ illus at TENNIS. **4** (also **ˈcourtyard**) [C] unroofed space partially or completely enclosed by walls or buildings, eg in a castle or an old inn; the buildings around such a space. **5** (idm) **the ball is in sb's/one's court** ⇨ BALL[1]. **go to court (over sth)** apply to have a case heard and decided by a court of law. **hold ˈcourt** entertain visitors, admirers, etc: *The film star held court in the hotel lobby.* **laugh sb/sth out of court** ⇨ LAUGH. **pay court to sb** ⇨ PAY[2]. **put sth out of ˈcourt** make sth not worthy of consideration: *The sheer cost of the scheme puts it right out of court.* **take sb to ˈcourt** make a charge against sb, to be settled in court; prosecute sb: *I took her to court for repayment of the debt.*

□ **ˈcourt-card** *n* (also **face-card**) playing-card that is a king, queen or jack.

ˌcourt ˈcircular notice in a British newspaper which gives details of events attended by members of the royal family.

ˈcourt-house *n* (**a**) building containing courts of law. (**b**) (*US*) administrative offices of a county.

ˌcourt of ˈlaw = LAWCOURT (LAW).

ˌcourt ˈorder legal order made by a judge in court, telling sb to do or not do sth.

ˈcourt shoe light woman's shoe which only covers the front part of the foot.

court[2] /kɔːt/ *v* **1** (**a**) [Tn] (*dated*) (of a man) try to win the affections of (a woman), with a view to marriage: *He had been courting Jane for six months.* (**b**) [I] (*esp dated*) spend time together, with a view to marriage: *The two have been courting for a year.* ○ *There were several courting couples in the park.* **2** [Tn] (**a**) try to gain the favour of (a rich or influential person): *He has been courting the director, hoping to get the leading role in the play.* (**b**) (*often derog*) try to win or obtain (sth): *court sb's approval, support, favour, etc* ○ *court applause.* **3** [Tn no passive] do sth that might lead to (sth unpleasant); risk: *court failure, defeat, death, etc* ○ *To go on such an expedition without enough supplies would be to court disaster.*

courteous /ˈkɜːtɪəs/ *adj* having or showing good manners; polite. ▷ **courteously** *adv.*

courtesan /ˌkɔːtɪˈzæn; *US* ˈkɔːtɪzn/ *n* (formerly) prostitute with wealthy or aristocratic clients.

courtesy /ˈkɜːtəsɪ/ *n* **1** [U] courteous behaviour; good manners: *They didn't even have the courtesy to apologize.* ○ *It would only have been common courtesy to say thank you.* **2** [C] courteous remark or act: *Do me the courtesy of listening* (ie Please listen) *to what I have to say.* **3** (idm) (**by**) **courtesy of sb** by the permission, kindness or favour of sb: *This programme comes by courtesy of* (ie is sponsored or paid for by) *a local company.*

□ **ˈcourtesy light** light inside a car that comes on when a door is opened and stays on until all the doors are closed.

ˈcourtesy title (*Brit*) title conventionally given to sb (eg the son or daughter of a lord) but with no legal validity. ⇨ article at ARISTOCRAT.

courtier /ˈkɔːtɪə(r)/ *n* companion or assistant of a sovereign at court: *the King and his courtiers.*

courtly /ˈkɔːtlɪ/ *adj* (**-ier**, **-iest**) polite and dignified: *the old gentleman's courtly manners.* ▷ **courtliness** *n* [U].

□ **ˌcourtly ˈlove** love as it was described in medieval poetry between a knight and his lady, involving complex social and psychological rules.

court martial /ˌkɔːtˈmɑːʃl/ *n* (*pl* **courts martial**) court for trying offences against military law; trial by such a court: *He faced a court martial for disobeying orders.*

▷ **court-martial** *v* (**-ll-**; *US* **-l-**) [Tn, Tn·pr] ~ **sb** (**for sth**) try sb in such a court: *be court-martialled for neglect of duty.*

courtship /ˈkɔːt-ʃɪp/ *n* **1** (**a**) [U] = COURTING (COURT[2] 1). (**b**) [C] period during which this lasts: *They married after a brief courtship.* **2** [U, C] special forms of behaviour between male and female animals at the time of mating: [attrib] *the courtship display of the male peacock*, ie to attract a female.

courtyard /ˈkɔːtjɑːd/ *n* = COURT[1] 4.

couscous /ˈkʊskʊs/ *n* (**a**) [U] crushed wheat that is cooked by steaming. (**b**) [U, C] N African dish made with this and served with a mixture of vegetables and often meat or fish.

cousin /ˈkʌzn/ *n* **1** (also **first cousin**) child of one's uncle or aunt: *She is my cousin.* ○ *We are cousins*, ie children of each other's aunts/uncles. Cf SECOND COUSIN (SECOND[1]). ⇨ App 8. **2** (idm) **a country cousin** ⇨ COUNTRY.

▷ **cousinly** *adj* of or suitable for cousins: *cousinly affection.*

couture /kuːˈtʊə(r)/ *n* [U] (*French*) = HAUTE COUTURE: [attrib] *couture clothes/dresses.*

▷ **couturier** /kuːˈtʊərɪeɪ/ *n* person who designs and makes high-fashion clothes for women.

covalent bond /ˌkəʊveɪlənt ˈbɒnd/ *n* chemical bond formed between two or more atoms by a pair of electrons which they share.

cove[1] /kəʊv/ *n* small bay[2]. ⇨ illus at COAST.

cove[2] /kəʊv/ *n* (*dated Brit infml*) man: *What a strange cove he is!*

coven /ˈkʌvn/ *n* meeting or group of witches.

covenant /ˈkʌvənənt/ *n* **1** [C] (*law*) formal agreement that is legally binding. **2** [C] formal promise to pay money regularly to a charity, trust(5), etc. **3 the Covenant** [sing] (*Bible*) the promises made by God and the Israelites to each other in the Old Testament (including eg the Israelites' promise that they would worship no other god but Him).

▷ **covenant** *v* [Ipr, Tn, Tn·pr, Tf, Tt] ~ **for sth;** ~ **sth** (**to/with sb**) promise or agree to (sth) under the terms of a covenant: *I've covenanted (for) £100/covenanted (with them) to pay/that I'll pay £100 a year.* **covenanter** *n* **1** person who covenants to pay money. **2 Covenanter** person who supported the Scottish National Covenant of 1638 and the Solemn League and Covenant of 1643, in which Scottish Presbyterians protested against the religious policies of *Charles I. Later Covenanters resisted attempts to restore an official church with bishops.

Covent Garden /ˌkɒvənt ˈgɑːdn/ district in London's *West End, famous for the Royal Opera House (also known as Covent Garden), the home of Britain's main opera and ballet companies. Until 1974 it was also the site of the Covent Garden market selling fruit and vegetables. The buildings are now used as a shopping precinct with open-air entertainment for tourists. ⇨ articles at LONDON, PERFORMING ARTS.

Coventry /ˈkɒvəntrɪ/ *n* (idm) **send sb to Coventry** ⇨ SEND.

cover[1] /ˈkʌvə(r)/ *v* **1** (**a**) [Tn, Tn·pr, Tn·p] ~ **sth** (**up/over**) (**with sth**) place sth over or in front of sth; hide or protect sth in this way: *Cover the table with a cloth.* ○ *He covered (up) the body with a sheet.* ○ *She covered her knees (up) with a blanket.* ○ *The hole was covered (over) with canvas.* ○ *He covered the cushion with new material.* ○ *He laughed to cover* (ie hide) *his nervousness.* ○ *She covered her face with her hands.* (**b**) [Tn] lie or extend over the surface of (sth): *Snow covered the ground.* ○ *Flood water covered the fields by the river.* ○ *Rubble covered the pavement.* **2** [Tn·pr] ~ **sb/sth in/with sth** sprinkle, splash or scatter a layer of liquid, dust, etc on sb/sth: *I was covered in/with mud by a passing car.* ○ *The wind blew from the desert and covered everything with sand.* **3** [Tn] include (sth); deal with: *research that covers a wide field* ○ *Her lectures covered the subject thoroughly.* ○ *Is that word covered in the dictionary?* ○ *Do the rules cover* (ie Can they be made to apply to) *a case like this?* ○ *the salesman covering the northern part of the country*, ie selling to people in that region. **4** [Tn] (of money) be enough for (sth): *£10 will cover our petrol for the journey.* ○ *The firm barely covers (its) costs; it hasn't made a profit for years.* **5** [Tn] travel (a certain distance): *By sunset we had covered thirty miles.* **6** [Tn] (of a journalist) report on (a major event such as a trial, an election, a riot, etc): *cover the Labour Party's annual conference.* **7** [I, Ipr] ~ (**for sb**) do sb's work, duties, etc during his absence: *I'll cover for Jane while she's on holiday.* **8** [Tn, Tn·pr] ~ **sb/sth** (**against/for sth**) insure sb/sth against loss, etc: *Are you fully covered against/for fire and theft?* **9** [Tn] (**a**) protect (sb) by shooting at a potential attacker: *Cover me while I move forward.* ○ *The artillery gave us covering fire*, ie shot to protect us. (**b**) (of guns, fortresses, etc) be in a position to shoot at and therefore control (an area, a road, etc); dominate: *Our guns covered every approach to the town.* (**c**) keep aiming a gun at sb (so that he cannot shoot or escape): *Cover her while I phone the police.* ○ *Keep them covered!* **10** [Tn] (of a male animal, esp a horse) copulate with (a female). **11** (idm) **cover/hide a multitude of sins** ⇨ MULTITUDE. **cover one's tracks** leave no evidence of where one has been or what one has been doing. **cover oneself with glory** (*rhet*) acquire fame and honour: *The regiment covered itself with glory in the invasion battle.* **12** (phr v) **cover sth in** put a protective covering over (an open space): *We're having the yard/passage/terrace covered in.* **cover (oneself) up** (**a**) dress warmly: *Do cover (yourself) up: it's freezing outside.* (**b**) put on (extra) clothes, esp to avoid embarrassment. **cover (sth) up** (*derog*) make efforts to conceal a mistake, sth illegal, etc: *The government is trying to cover up the scandal.* **cover up for sb** conceal sb's mistakes, crimes, etc in order to protect him.

▷ **covered** *adj* **1** ~ **in/with sth** [pred] having a great number or amount of sth: *trees covered in/with blossom/fruit* ○ (*fig*) *I was covered in/with confusion*, ie very confused and embarrassed. **2** having a cover, esp a roof: *a covered way.*

covering /ˈkʌvərɪŋ/ *n* thing that covers: *a light covering of snow on the ground.*

□ **ˌcovered ˈwagon** (*US*) large wagon with an arched canvas roof, used by pioneers for travel westward across the prairies.

ˌcovering ˈletter letter sent with a document, or with goods, etc, typically explaining the contents.

ˈcover-up *n* (*derog*) act of concealing a mistake, sth illegal, etc: *She said nothing was stolen, but that's just a cover-up.*

cover[2] /ˈkʌvə(r)/ *n* **1** [C] (**a**) thing that covers: *a plastic cover for a typewriter* ○ *Some chairs are fitted with loose covers.* (**b**) top; lid: *the cover of a saucepan.* **2** [U] place or area giving shelter or protection: *There was nowhere we could take cover* (ie go for protection) *from the storm.* ○ *The land was flat and treeless and gave no cover to the troops.* ○ *The bicycles are kept under cover*, eg in a shelter, shed, etc. **3** [C] either or both of the thick protective outer pages of a book, magazine, etc, esp the front cover: *a book with a leather cover* ○ *The magazine had a picture of a horse on the cover*, ie the front cover. ○ *read a book from cover to cover*, ie from beginning to end. **4 the covers** [pl] bedclothes: *push back the covers and get out of bed.* **5** [C usu *sing*] **(a)** ~ **(for sth)** means of concealing sth illegal, secret, etc: *His business was a cover for drug dealing.* **(b)** false identity: *The spy's cover was that she was a consultant engineer.* ○ *The agent's cover had been broken/blown* (ie revealed), *and he had to leave the country.* **6** [U] protection from attack: *Artillery gave cover* (ie fired at the enemy to stop them firing back) *while the infantry advanced.* ○ *For this operation we need plenty of air cover*, ie protection by military aircraft. **7** [U] ~ **(for sb)** performance of another person's work, duties, etc during his absence: *This doctor provides emergency cover (for sick colleagues).* **8** [U] ~ **(against sth)** insurance (against loss, injury, etc): *a policy that gives cover against fire.* **9** [C] envelope or wrapper: *a first-day cover*, ie an envelope with a newly issued stamp on it ○ *under plain cover*, ie in an envelope or a parcel that does not show the sender, contents, etc ○ *(commerce) under separate cover*, ie in a separate parcel or envelope. **10** [U] woods or undergrowth that can conceal animals, etc: *cover for game birds* ○ *The fox broke* (ie left) *cover and ran across the field.* Cf COVERT² 1. **11** [C] place laid at table for a meal: *Covers were laid for six.* **12 (a) the covers** [pl] (in cricket) area to the right of and in front of the batsman: *fielding in the covers.* **(b)** [C] player who fields in the covers: *The ball went past cover.* **13** (idm) **under cover of sth (a)** concealed by sth: *We travelled under cover of darkness.* **(b)** with pretence of sth: *under cover of friendship* ○ *crimes committed under cover of patriotism.*

□ ˈ**cover charge** (in a restaurant) charge to be paid in addition to the cost of food and drink.

ˈ**cover crop** crop that is grown mainly to protect or enrich a soil, esp soil which might be eroded by the wind.

ˈ**cover girl** girl whose photograph appears on the cover of a magazine.

ˈ**cover note** (*Brit*) document from an insurance company showing that one is insured, issued to cover the period before a policy is officially in force.

coverage /ˈkʌvərɪdʒ/ *n* [U] **1** reporting of events, etc: *TV coverage of the election campaign* ○ *There's little coverage of foreign news in the newspaper.* **2** extent to which sth is covered: *a thicker paint which gives good coverage* ○ *a dictionary with poor coverage of American words.*

coveralls /ˈkʌvərɔ:lz/ *n* [pl] (*US*) = OVERALL. (OVERALL²).

coverlet /ˈkʌvəlɪt/ *n* bedspread.

covert¹ /ˈkʌvət; *US* ˈkəʊvɜ:rt/ *adj* concealed; not open; secret: *covert glances, threats, payments* ○ *the covert activities of a spy.* ▷ **covertly** *adv.* Cf OVERT.

covert² /ˈkʌvə(r)/ *n* **1** area of thick low bushes, trees, etc in which animals, esp hunted animals, hide. Cf COVER² 10. **2** any of the feathers that cover the base of the wing or tail feathers on a bird.

covet /ˈkʌvɪt/ *v* [Tn] (*usu derog*) want very much to possess (esp sth that belongs to sb else): *covet sb's position, status, possessions, rewards* ○ *this year's winner of the coveted Nobel Prize*, ie which everyone would like to win.

▷ **covetous** *adj* ~ **(of sth)** (*derog*) having or showing a strong desire to possess esp sth that belongs to sb else: *covetous of his high salary* ○ *a covetous look, glance, etc.* **covetously** *adv.* **covetousness** *n* [U].

covey /ˈkʌvɪ/ *n* (*pl* ~**s**) [CGp] small flock of partridges: (*fig*) *a covey* (ie small group) *of reporters.*

cow suckling its calf

cow¹ /kaʊ/ *n* **1** fully-grown female of any animal of the ox family, esp the domestic kind kept by farmers to produce milk and beef: *milking the cows* ○ *a herd of cows.* ⇨ illus. Cf BULL¹ 1, CALF, HEIFER. **2** female elephant, rhinoceros, whale, etc. Cf BULL¹ 2. **3** (⚠ *derog sl*) woman: *You stupid cow!* **4** (idm) **a sacred cow** ⇨ SACRED. **till the ˈcows come home** (*infml*) for a very long time; for ever: *You can talk till the cows come home: you'll never make me change my mind.*

□ ˈ**cowbell** *n* bell hung round a cow's neck so that the cow can be found by the sound of its ringing.

ˈ**cowcatcher** *n* (*US*) metal frame fixed to the front of a railway engine to push obstacles off the track.

ˈ**cowgirl** *n* girl or woman who looks after cows.

ˈ**cowhand** *n* person who looks after cows.

ˈ**cowherd** *n* (*dated*) person who looks after grazing cows.

ˈ**cowhide** *n* **1** [U, C] leather made from the skin of a cow. **2** [C] strip of this leather used as whip.

ˈ**cowman** /-mən/ *n* (*pl* **-men**) man who looks after cows.

ˈ**cow-pat** *n* flat round mass of cow-dung on the ground.

ˈ**cowpoke** *n* (*US sl*) = COWBOY 1.

ˈ**cowshed** *n* farm building where cows are kept when not outside, or where they are milked.

cow² /kaʊ/ *v* [esp passive: Tn, Tn·pr] ~ **sb (into sth/into doing sth)** make sb do as one wants by frightening him; intimidate sb: *The men were cowed into total submission.* ○ *a cowed* (ie frightened and submissive) *look.*

Coward /ˈkaʊəd/ Sir Noël (1899-1973), English playwright, actor, composer and entertainer. He is famous for his witty plays set in the years between the two world wars, including *Hay Fever* and *Private Lives.* Among the works he wrote for the screen is the wartime film drama *In Which We Serve.* ⇨ article at MUSIC, PERFORMING ARTS.

coward /ˈkaʊəd/ *n* (*derog*) person who lacks courage; person who runs away from danger: *You miserable coward!* ○ *I'm a terrible coward when it comes to dealing with sick people*, ie It scares me and I avoid it.

▷ **cowardice** /ˈkaʊədɪs/ *n* [U] (*derog*) feelings or behaviour of a coward; fearfulness: *a battle lost owing to the troops' cowardice* ○ *abject cowardice.* **cowardly** *adj* (*derog*) lacking courage; of or like a coward: *cowardly lies, behaviour, actions* ○ *It was cowardly of you not to admit your mistake.*

cowboy /ˈkaʊbɔɪ/ *n* **1** man, usu on horseback, who looks after grazing cattle in the western parts of the USA: [attrib] *a cowboy movie*, ie one featuring adventures in the American West. **2** (*Brit infml derog*) tradesman or businessman whose work, business practices, etc are incompetent or dishonest: *The house has all these defects because it was built by cowboys.* ○ [attrib] *cowboy builders, stockbrokers, etc.*

cower /ˈkaʊə(r)/ *v* [I, Ipr, Ip] crouch down or move backwards in fear or distress: *He cowered away/back as she raised her hand to hit him.* ○ *The dog cowered (down) under the table.*

Cowes /kaʊz/ town on the *Isle of Wight where international yachting races are held each year during **Cowes week.** ⇨ article at SEASON.

cowl /kaʊl/ *n* **1** large hood on a monk's gown. **2** cap for a chimney, ventilating pipe, etc, usu of metal and often revolving with the wind, which is designed to improve the flow of air or smoke. ⇨ illus at HOME.

▷ **cowling** *n* removable metal covering for an engine, esp on an aircraft. ⇨ illus at AIRCRAFT.

cowlick /ˈkaʊlɪk/ *n* (*infml*) tuft of hair just above the forehead that will not lie flat.

Cowper /ˈku:pə(r)/ William (1731-1800), English poet. He suffered from severe depression for most of his life and much of his work has a pessimistic tone. He found some consolation in evangelical Christianity and wrote several well-known hymns.

cowpox /ˈkaʊpɒks/ *n* [U] mild contagious disease of cattle caused by a virus (which is also used in making smallpox vaccine).

cowrie /ˈkaʊrɪ/ *n* small shell formerly used as money in parts of Africa and Asia.

cowslip /ˈkaʊslɪp/ *n* small plant with yellow flowers, growing wild in temperate countries.

cox /kɒks/ *n* person who steers a rowing-boat, esp in races.

▷ **cox** *v* [I, Tn] act as cox of (a rowing-boat): *He coxed the Oxford boat.*

coxcomb /ˈkɒkskəʊm/ *n* (*arch*) foolish conceited man, esp one who pays too much attention to his clothes.

coxswain /ˈkɒksn/ *n* **1** man in charge of a ship's rowing-boat and its crew. **2** (*fml*) cox.

Coy /kɔɪ/ *abbr* (army) company.

coy /kɔɪ/ *adj* (**-er, -est**) (*usu derog*) **1** pretending to be shy or modest: *She gave a coy smile when he paid her a compliment.* **2** reluctant to give information, answer questions, etc; secretive: *He was a bit coy when asked about the source of his income.* ▷ **coyly** *adv.* **coyness** *n* [U].

coyote /kɔɪˈəʊtɪ; *US* ˈkaɪəʊt/ *n* small wolf of the plains of western N America.

coypu /ˈkɔɪpu:/ *n* beaver-like water-rodent from S America, bred for its fur.

cozy (*US*) = COSY.

CP /ˌsi: ˈpi:/ *abbr* Communist Party: *join the CP.*

cp *abbr* compare. Cf CF.

CPI /ˌsi: pi: ˈaɪ/ *abbr* Consumer Price Index.

Cpl *abbr* = CORP 1.

CPR /ˌsi: pi: ˈɑ:(r)/ *abbr* Canadian Pacific Railway.

CPRE /ˌsi: pi: ɑ:r ˈi:/ *abbr* Council for the Protection of Rural England.

cps /ˌsi: pi: ˈes/ *abbr* (also **c/s**) (*physics*) cycles per second.

Cr *symb* chromium.

crab¹ /kræb/ *n* **1 (a)** [C] ten-legged shellfish. ⇨ illus at SHELLFISH. **(b)** [U] its flesh as food: *dressed crab*, ie prepared for eating. **2 the Crab** [sing] the fourth sign of the zodiac; Cancer. **3** [C] (*infml*) = CRAB-LOUSE. **4** (idm) **catch a crab** ⇨ CATCH¹.

▷ **crabwise** /ˈkræbwaɪz/ *adv* sideways, often in a stiff or ungainly way: *shuffle crabwise across the floor.*

□ ˈ**crab-louse** *n* parasitic insect found in the hairy parts of the body.

ˌ**Crab ˈNebula** nebula in the constellation of *Taurus, which sends out strong radio waves. It has a pulsar at its centre.

crab² /kræb/ *v* (**-bb-**) [I, Ipr] ~ **(about sth)** (*infml derog*) complain; grumble; criticize: *The boss is always crabbing about my work.*

crab-apple /ˈkræbæpl/ (also **crab**) *n* **1** wild apple-tree. **2** its hard sour fruit.

Crabbe /kræb/ George (1754-1832), English poet. He is most famous for long narrative works like *The Village*, which give a harsh and realistic description of country life.

crabbed /ˈkræbɪd *or, rarely,* ˈkræbd/ *adj* **1** (of handwriting) small and difficult to read. **2** = CRABBY.

crabby /ˈkræbɪ/ *adj* (**-ier, -iest**) (*infml*) bad-tempered; irritable.

crack¹ /kræk/ *n* **1** [C] ~ **(in sth) (a)** line along which sth has broken, but not into separate parts: *a cup with bad cracks in it* ○ *Don't go skating today — there are dangerous cracks in the ice.* ○ (*fig*) *The cracks* (ie defects) *in the Government's economic policy are beginning to show.* ⇨ illus at CHIP. **(b)** narrow opening: *She looked through a crack in the curtains.* ○ *Open the door a crack*, ie Open it very slightly. **2** [C] sudden sharp noise: *the crack of a pistol shot* ○ *a crack of thunder.* **3** [C] ~ **(on sth)** sharp blow, usu one that can be heard: *give sb/get a crack on the head.* **4** [C] ~ **(about sth)** (*infml*) clever and amusing remark, often critical; joke: *She made a crack about his fatness.* **5** [C] ~ **at sth/doing sth** (*infml*) attempt at sth: *Have another crack at solving this puzzle.* **6** [U] highly addictive form of purified cocaine. **7** (idm) **the ˌcrack of ˈdawn** (*infml*) very early in the morning: *get up at the crack of dawn.* **the crack of ˈdoom** the end of the world: (*fig*) *To get a bus here you have to wait till the crack of doom,* ie an extremely long time. **a fair crack of the whip** ⇨ FAIR[1]. **paper over the cracks** ⇨ PAPER.

▷ **crack** *adj* [attrib] very clever or expert; excellent: *a crack regiment* ○ *He's a crack shot,* ie expert at shooting.

□ **ˈcrack-brained** *adj* (*infml*) crazy; foolish: *a crack-brained idea, scheme, etc.*

crack[2] /kræk/ *v* **1** [I, Tn] (cause to) develop a crack[1](1a) or cracks: *The ice cracked as I stepped onto it.* ○ *You can crack this toughened glass, but you can't break it.* ○ *She has cracked a bone in her arm.* ○ *a cracked mug.* **2** [Tn, Cn·a] break (sth) open or into pieces: *crack a nut* ○ *crack a safe,* ie open it to steal from it ○ *crack a casing open.* **3** [Tn, Tn·pr] ~ **sth (on/against sth)** hit sth sharply: *I cracked my head on the low door-frame.* **4** [I, Tn no passive] (cause sth to) make a sharp sound: *crack a whip, one's knuckles* ○ *The hunter's rifle cracked and the deer fell dead.* **5** [I, Tn] (cause sb to) cease to resist; (cause sth to) fail: *The suspect cracked under questioning.* ○ *They finally cracked the defence and scored a goal.* **6** [Tn] (*infml*) solve (a problem, etc): *The calculation was difficult, but we finally cracked it.* ○ *crack a code,* ie decipher it. **7** [I] (of the voice) change in depth, loudness, etc suddenly and uncontrollably: *In a voice cracking with emotion, he announced the death of his father.* ○ *A boy's voice cracks* (ie becomes deeper) *at puberty.* **8** [Tn] (*infml*) open (a bottle, esp of alcoholic drink) and drink its contents. **9** [Tn] (*infml*) tell (a joke). **10** [Tn] (*chemistry*) break down (heavy oils) by heat and pressure to produce lighter oils. **11** (idm) **cracked ˈup to be sth** (usu negative) (*infml*) reputed to be sth: *He's not such a good writer as he's cracked up to be.* **get ˈcracking** (*infml*) begin, esp energetically: *There's a lot to be done, so let's get cracking.* **12** (phr v) **crack down (on sb/sth)** impose more severe treatment or restrictions on sb/sth: *Police are cracking down on drug dealers.* **crack up** (*infml*) lose one's physical or mental health: *You'll crack up if you carry on working so hard.*

▷ **cracked** /krækt/ *adj* [usu pred] (*infml*) mad; crazy.

cracking /ˈkrækɪŋ/ *adv, adj* [usu attrib] (*Brit infml*) excellent: *That was a cracking (good) shot you played there.* — *n* [U] process of breaking down chemical compounds by heat and pressure, esp to produce lighter oils from heavy oils.

□ **ˈcrack-down** *n* ~ **(on sb/sth)** severe measures to restrict or discourage undesirable or criminal people or actions: *a crack-down on tax evasion.*

ˈcrack-up *n* (*infml*) loss of physical or mental health: *a crack-up due to overwork.*

cracker /ˈkrækə(r)/ *n* **1** thin flaky dry biscuit, typically eaten with cheese. **2** (**a**) small firework that explodes with a sharp sound. (**b**) (also **Christmas cracker**) party toy consisting of a cardboard tube wrapped in paper that makes a sharp explosive sound as its ends are pulled apart, with a small gift, paper hat, etc inside: *a box of crackers.* ⇨ article at CHRISTMAS. **3** (*Brit infml approv*) attractive girl or woman: *What a little cracker she is!* **4 crackers** [pl] = NUTCRACKERS (NUT).

crackers /ˈkrækəz/ *adj* [pred] (*Brit infml*) mad; crazy: *That noise is driving me crackers/making me go crackers.* ○ *You must be crackers!*

crackle /ˈkrækl/ *v* [I] make small cracking sounds, as when dry sticks burn: *a crackling camp-fire* ○ *The twigs crackled as we trod on them.* ○ (*fig*) *The atmosphere crackled with tension as the two boxers stepped into the ring.*

▷ **crackle** *n* [U] series of small cracking sounds: *the distant crackle of machine-gun fire* ○ *Can you get rid of the crackle on my radio?*

crackling /ˈkræklɪŋ/ *n* [U] **1** small cracking sounds. **2** crisp skin on roast pork.

□ **ˈcrackle-ware** *n* [U] china, etc covered with a network of what appear to be tiny cracks.

cracknel /ˈkræknəl/ *n* type of light crisp biscuit.

crackpot /ˈkrækpɒt/ *n* (*infml*) eccentric person with strange or impractical ideas: [attrib] *crackpot ideas, schemes, etc.*

cracksman /ˈkræksmən/ *n* (*pl* **-men**) (*dated*) burglar.

-cracy *comb form* (forming *ns*) government or rule of: *democracy* ○ *technocracy* ○ *bureaucracy.* Cf -CRAT.

cradle /ˈkreɪdl/ *n* **1** small bed for a baby, usu shaped like a box with curved parts underneath so that it can move from side to side: *The mother rocked the baby to sleep in its cradle.* ⇨ illus at FURNITURE. **2** ~ **of sth** (usu *sing*) (*fig*) place where sth begins: *Greece, the cradle of Western culture.* **3** (**a**) framework that looks like or is used like a cradle, eg the structure on which a ship rests while it is being repaired or built. (**b**) platform that can be moved up and down an outside wall by means of ropes and pulleys, used by window-cleaners, painters, etc. **4** part of a telephone on which the receiver rests. **5** (idm) **from the ˌcradle to the ˈgrave** from birth to death.

▷ **cradle** *v* [Tn, Tn·pr] ~ **sb/sth (in sth)** place or hold sb/sth (as if) in a cradle: *cradle a child in one's arms,* ie hold it gently, esp rocking it from side to side.

□ **ˈcradle-snatcher** *n* (*infml derog*) person, usu a man, who marries or has a sexual relationship with a much younger person.

ˈcradle song lullaby.

craft /krɑːft; *US* kræft/ *n* **1** [C] occupation, esp one that needs skill in the use of the hands; such a skill or technique: *the potter's craft* ○ *teach arts and crafts in a school* ○ *He's a master of the actor's craft.* **2** (*pl* unchanged) [C] (**a**) boat; ship: *Hundreds of small craft accompany the liner into harbour.* Cf VESSEL 1. (**b**) aircraft; spacecraft: *The astronauts piloted their craft down to the lunar surface.* **3** [U] (*fml derog*) skill in deceiving; cunning: *achieving by craft and guile what he could not manage by honest means.*

▷ **craft** *v* [Tn usu passive] make (sth) skilfully, esp by hand: *a beautiful hand-crafted silver goblet.*

-craft (forming compound *ns*): *handicraft* ○ *needlecraft* ○ *stagecraft.*

crafty *adj* (**-ier, -iest**) (*usu derog*) clever in using indirect or deceitful methods to get what one wants; cunning: *a crafty politician* ○ *He's a crafty old fox.* **craftily** *adv.* **craftiness** *n* [U].

craftsman /ˈkrɑːftsmən; *US* ˈkræfts-/ *n* (*pl* **-men**) **1** skilled workman, esp one who makes things by hand. **2** person who attends carefully to the details of a creative task: *In symphonic writing he is the master craftsman.*

▷ **craftsmanship** *n* [U] **1** skilled workmanship. **2** careful attention to details, etc.

crag /kræg/ *n* high, steep or rugged mass of rock.

▷ **craggy** *adj* (**-ier, -iest**) **1** having many crags. **2** (*usu approv*) (of the face) having strong-looking prominent features (cheek-bones, nose, etc) and deep lines: *his handsome craggy features.*

cram /kræm/ *v* (**-mm-**) **1** (**a**) [Tn·pr, Tn·p] ~ **sth into sth/in** push or force too much of sth into sth: *cram food into one's mouth, papers into a drawer* ○ *The room's full; we can't cram any more people in.* (**b**) [usu passive: Tn, Tn·pr] ~ **sth (with sth)** make sth (too) full: *cram one's mouth with food* ○ *an essay crammed with quotations* ○ *The restaurant was crammed (with people).* **2** ~ **(for sth)** (**a**) [I, Ipr] (*infml*) learn a lot of facts in a short time, esp for an examination: *cram for a chemistry test.* (**b**) [Tn] teach (sb) in this way: *cram pupils.*

▷ **crammer** *n* (*dated infml*) special school where students are crammed (CRAM 2b).

□ **ˌcram-ˈfull** *adj* [usu pred] (*infml*) very full: *cram-full of people.*

cramp[1] /kræmp/ *n* **1** [U] sudden and painful tightening of the muscles, usu caused by cold or too much exercise, making movement difficult: *The swimmer got cramp in his legs and had to be helped out of the water.* ○ *writer's cramp,* ie in the muscles of the hand. **2 cramps** [pl] (*esp US*) severe pain in the stomach.

cramp[2] /kræmp/ *v* **1** [Tn esp passive] give insufficient space or scope to (sb/sth); hinder or prevent the movement or development of (sb/sth): *All these difficulties cramped his progress.* ○ *I feel cramped by the limitations of my job.* **2** (idm) **be cramped for ˈroom/ˈspace** be without enough room, etc: *We're a bit cramped for space in this attic.* **cramp sb's ˈstyle** (*infml*) prevent sb from doing sth freely, or as well as he can: *It cramps my style to have you watching over me all the time.*

▷ **cramped** *adj* **1** (of handwriting) with small letters close together, and therefore difficult to read. **2** (of space) narrow and restricted: *Our accommodation is rather cramped.*

cramp[3] /kræmp/ *n* **1** (also **ˈcramp-iron**) metal bar with bent ends, used in building for holding together timbers or blocks of stone. **2** = CLAMP[1].

▷ **cramp** *v* [Tn] fasten (sth) with a cramp: *cramp a beam, wall, etc.*

crampon /ˈkræmpɒn/ *n* (usu *pl*) metal plate with spikes, worn on shoes for walking or climbing on ice and snow.

cranberry /ˈkrænbərɪ; *US* -berɪ/ *n* small red slightly sour berry of a small bush, used for making jelly and sauce.

crane[1] /kreɪn/ *n* **1** large bird with long legs, neck and beak. **2** machine or vehicle with a long movable arm from which heavy weights can be hung in order to lift or move them. ⇨ illus at OIL.

crane[2] /kreɪn/ *v* [I, Ipr, Tn, Tn·pr] stretch (one's neck): *crane (forward) in order to get a better view* ○ *crane one's neck to see sth.*

crane-fly /ˈkreɪn flaɪ/ (also *infml* **daddy-long-legs**) *n* type of fly with very long legs.

cranium /ˈkreɪnɪəm/ *n* (*pl* ~**s** or **crania** /ˈkreɪnɪə/) (*anatomy*) bony part of the head enclosing the brain; skull.

▷ **cranial** /ˈkreɪnɪəl/ *adj* (*anatomy*) of the skull. **ˌcranial ˈnerve** any of the pairs of nerves that come directly out of the brain, linking it to various parts of the body, esp in the head and neck (eg the eyes and ears).

crank[1] /kræŋk/ *n* L-shaped bar and handle for converting to-and-fro movement to circular movement: *The pedals of a cycle are attached to a crank.* ⇨ illus at BICYCLE.

▷ **crank** *v* **1** [Tn, Tn·p] ~ **sth (up)** cause sth to turn by means of a crank: *crank (up) an engine,* ie start it with a crank. (*fig infml*): *I cranked up the speed,* ie increased it. **2** (phr v) **crank sth out** (*infml*) produce sth with effort or without care: *She cranks out the same old lectures year after year.*

□ **ˈcrankcase** *n* case that encloses a crankshaft.

ˈcrankpin *n* pin that links a crank to connecting rods (CONNECT).

ˈcrankshaft *n* shaft that turns or is turned by a crank.

crank[2] /kræŋk/ *n* (*derog*) **1** person with strange fixed ideas, esp on a particular subject; eccentric person: *a health-food crank,* ie one who insists on eating unusual food for health reasons. **2** (*US infml*) bad-tempered person.

▷ **cranky** *adj* (**-ier, -iest**) (*infml derog*) **1** strange; eccentric: *a cranky person, ideas.* **2** (of machines, etc) unreliable; shaky; unsteady: *a rattling, cranky old engine.* **3** (*US*) bad-tempered.

Cranmer /ˈkrænmə(r)/ Thomas (1489-1556), first Anglican Archbishop of Canterbury. He supported *Henry VIII over his divorce with Catherine of Aragon and was a major figure of the English *Reformation. He was responsible for the new *Book of Common Prayer, still widely used today and famous for the beauty of its English. He was executed when the Catholic *Mary Tudor came to the throne. ⇨ article at CHURCH OF ENGLAND.

cranny /ˈkrænɪ/ *n* **1** small cavity or opening, eg in a wall. **2** (idm) **every nook and cranny** ⇨ NOOK.

▷ **crannied** *adj* full of crannies.

crap /kræp/ *v* (**-pp-**) [I] (⚠ *sl*) defecate: *a dog crapping on the lawn.*

▷ **crap** *n* (⚠ *sl*) **1** [U] excrement. **2** [sing] act of

defecating: *have a crap.* **3** [U] nonsense; rubbish: *You do talk a load of crap!*
crappy *adj* (*sl*) bad; worthless; unpleasant: *a crappy book, party, programme.*
crape /kreɪp/ *n* [U] black silk or cotton material with a wrinkled surface, formerly worn as a sign of mourning. Cf CREPE.
craps /kræps/ *n* [sing *v*] (also ˈ**crap-shooting** [U]) (*US*) gambling game played with two dice: *shoot craps*, ie play this game.
▷ **crap** *adj* [attrib] of or for craps: *a crap game.*
crapulent /ˈkræpjʊlənt/ *adj* (*fml*) feeling unwell as a result of eating or drinking too much. ▷ **crapulence** /-ləns/ *n* [U].
crash[1] /kræʃ/ *n* **1** (a) (usu *sing*) (loud noise made by a) violent fall, blow or breakage: *the crash of dishes being dropped* ○ *The tree fell with a great crash.* ○ *His words were drowned in a crash of thunder.* (b) accident involving a vehicle in a collision or some other impact: *a crash in which two cars collided* ○ *a* ˈ*car crash*/*an* ˈ*air crash.* **2** collapse, esp of a business or stock-market: *The great financial crash in 1929 ruined international trade.*
▷ **crash** *adj* [attrib] done intensively to achieve quick results: *a crash course in computer programming* ○ *a crash diet.*
crash *adv* with a crash: *The vase fell crash onto the tiles.*
□ ˈ**crash barrier** fence, rail, etc to restrain crowds, divide vehicles travelling in opposite directions on a motorway, etc. ⇨ illus at MOTORWAY.
ˈ**crash-dive** *n* sudden dive made by a submarine or an aircraft, eg to avoid being attacked. — *v* [I] dive in this way.
ˈ**crash helmet** hat made of very strong material (eg metal), worn by motor-cyclists, racing drivers, etc to protect the head.
ˌ**crash-**ˈ**land** *v* [I, Tn] land (an aircraft) or be landed roughly in an emergency, usu with resulting damage. ˌ**crash-**ˈ**landing** *n* landing of this kind: *make a crash-landing.*
crash[2] /kræʃ/ *v* **1** (a) [Ipr, Ip, Tn·pr, Tn·p] fall or strike (sth) suddenly and noisily: *The rocks crashed (down) onto the car.* ○ *The tree crashed through the window.* ○ *The dishes crashed to the floor.* ○ *She crashed the plates (down) on the table.* (b) [I, Ipr, Tn, Tn·pr] ~ (**sth**) (**into sth**) (cause sth to) have a collision: *The plane crashed (into the mountain).* ○ *He crashed his car (into a wall).* ○ *a crashed car, plane.* (c) [Ipr, Ip, Tn·pr, Tn·p] (cause sth to) move noisily or violently: *an enraged elephant crashing about in the undergrowth* ○ *He crashed the trolley through the doors.* **2** [I] make a loud noise: *The thunder crashed.* **3** (a) [I] (of a business company, government, etc) fail suddenly; collapse: *The company crashed with debts of £2 million.* (b) [I, Tn] (*computing*) (cause sth to) suddenly stop working: *The computer*/*disk*/*program*/*system crashed.* ○ *A single mistake could crash the system.* **4** [Tn] (*infml*) = GATECRASH (GATE). **5** [Ipr, Ip] ~ (**out**) (*sl esp US*) sleep in an improvised bed, esp when very tired: *Mind if I crash (out) on your floor tonight?* **6** [Tn] (*infml*) ignore (a red light or stop sign). **7** (idm) **a crashing** ˈ**bore** very boring person.
crass /kræs/ *adj* (**-ier**, **-iest**) (*fml derog*) **1** [attrib] complete; very great; utter: *crass stupidity, ignorance, etc.* **2** very stupid; insensitive: *Don't talk to him: he's so crass.* ▷ **crassly** *adv.* **crassness** *n* [U].
-crat *comb form* (forming *ns*) member or supporter of a type of government or rule: *democrat* ○ *technocrat* ○ *bureaucrat.*
▷ **-cratic** (forming *adjs*): *aristocratic.*
crate /kreɪt/ *n* **1** (a) large wooden container for transporting goods: *a crate of car components.* (b) container made of metal, plastic, etc divided into compartments for transporting or storing bottles: *a crate of milk.* ⇨ illus at BOX. **2** (a) (*sl joc*) worn-out car. (b) (*dated air force sl*) aircraft.
▷ **crate** *v* [Tn, Tn·p] ~ **sth** (**up**) put sth in a crate: *crating (up) a machine.*
crater /ˈkreɪtə(r)/ *n* **1** hole in the top of a volcano. ⇨ illus at VOLCANO. **2** hole in the ground made by the explosion of a bomb or shell, or by a meteorite landing, etc.
□ ˌ**crater** ˈ**lake** lake in the crater of an extinct volcano.
cravat /krəˈvæt/ *n* short strip of decorative material worn by men round the neck, folded inside the collar of a shirt.
crave /kreɪv/ *v* **1** [Ipr, Tn] ~ (**for**) **sth** have a strong desire for sth: *I was craving for a drink.* ○ *giving her the admiration she craves.* **2** [Tn] (*arch*) ask for (sth) earnestly; beg for: *crave sb's mercy*/*forgiveness*/*indulgence.*
▷ **craving** *n* ~ (**for sth**) strong desire: *a craving for food.*
craven /ˈkreɪvn/ *adj* (*fml derog*) cowardly: *craven behaviour, submission, etc* ○ *a craven deserter.*
craw /krɔː/ *n* **1** part of the stomach of a bird or an insect where digestion starts. **2** (idm) **stick in one's craw** ⇨ STICK[2].
crawfish /ˈkrɔːfɪʃ/ *n* (*pl* unchanged) = CRAYFISH.
Crawford /ˈkrɔːfəd/ Joan (1908-77), American film actor. One of the great Hollywood stars of the 1930s and 1940s, she had a long screen rivalry with Bette *Davis.
crawl /krɔːl/ *v* **1** [I, Ipr, Ip] (a) move slowly, with the body on or close to the ground, or on hands and knees: *a snake crawling along (the ground)* ○ *A baby crawls (around) before it can walk.* ○ *The wounded man crawled to the phone.* (b) (of traffic, vehicles, etc) move very slowly: *The traffic crawled over the bridge in the rush-hour.* **2** [Ipr] ~ **with sth** (esp in the continuous tenses) be covered with, or full of, things that crawl: *The ground was crawling with ants.* ○ (*fig*) *The area was crawling with* (ie was full of) *police.* **3** [I, Ipr] ~ (**to sb**) (*infml derog*) try to gain sb's favour by praising him, doing what will please him, etc: *She's always crawling (to the boss).* **4** (idm) **make one's/sb's flesh crawl/creep** ⇨ FLESH.
▷ **crawl** *n* **1** (a) [sing] (*derog*) very slow pace: *traffic moving at a crawl.* (b) [C] crawling movement: *the baby's laborious crawl.* **2** (often **the crawl**) [sing] fast swimming stroke using overarm movements of each arm in turn, accompanied by rapid kicks with the feet: *Can you do the crawl?*
crawler *n* **1** [C] (*infml derog*) person who crawls (CRAWL 3). **2 crawlers** [pl] overalls made for a baby to crawl about in.
crayfish /ˈkreɪfɪʃ/ (also **crawfish**) *n* (*pl* unchanged) freshwater shellfish like a small lobster.
crayon /ˈkreɪən/ *n* pencil or stick of soft coloured chalk, wax or charcoal, used for drawing: [attrib] *a crayon drawing.*
▷ **crayon** *v* [I, Tn] draw (sth) with crayons.
craze /kreɪz/ *n* (a) ~ (**for sth**) enthusiastic, usu brief, interest in sth: *a craze for collecting beer-mats* ○ *the current punk-hairstyle craze.* (b) object of such an interest: *Skateboards are the latest craze.*
crazed /kreɪzd/ *adj* (also **half-crazed**) ~ (**with sth**) wildly excited; insane: *a crazed look, expression, etc* ○ *She was crazed with grief.* ○ *drug-crazed fanatics.*
crazy /ˈkreɪzɪ/ *adj* (**-ier**, **-iest**) **1** (*infml*) (a) insane: *He's crazy; he ought to be locked up.* ○ *That noise is driving me crazy*/*making me go crazy*, ie annoying me very much. (b) very foolish; not sensible: *a crazy person, idea, suggestion* ○ *You must be crazy to go walking in such awful weather.* ○ *She's crazy to lend him the money.* **2** [pred] ~ (**about sth/sb**) (*infml*) wildly excited; enthusiastic: *The kids went crazy when the film star appeared.* ○ *I'm crazy about steam-engines.* ○ *She's crazy about him*, ie loves him a lot. **3** [attrib] (of pavements, quilts, etc) made up of irregularly shaped pieces fitted together: *crazy paving.* **4** (idm) **like** ˈ**crazy** (used as an *adv*) (*infml*) very intensely; very much: *work, talk, etc like crazy* ○ *run like crazy*, ie very fast. ▷ **crazily** *adv.* **craziness** *n* [U].
creak /kriːk/ *v* [I] make a harsh sound like that of an unoiled door-hinge, or badly-fitting floor-boards when trodden on: *The wooden cart creaked as it moved along.* ○ *the creaking joints of an old man.*
▷ **creak** *n* such a sound.
creaky *adj* (**-ier**, **-iest**) that creaks: *a creaky floor-board* ○ (*fig*) *The Government's policy is looking rather creaky*, ie as if about to fail. **creakily** *adv.*
cream[1] /kriːm/ *n* **1** [U] thick yellowish-white liquid that is the fatty part of milk: *peaches and cream* ○ *put cream in one's coffee* ○ *whipped cream* ○ [attrib] *cream buns, cake, etc*, ie containing cream. **2** [C, U] type of food containing or similar to cream: *ice-cream* ○ *chocolate creams*, ie soft chocolate sweets. **3** [U] smooth paste or thick liquid used as a cosmetic, in medicine, for polishing, etc: ˈ*face-cream* ○ ˈ*cold-cream* ○ *antiseptic cream.* **4 the cream** (also **the crème de la crème**) [sing] ~ (**of sth**) the best part of sth: *the cream of the crop* ○ *The cream of this year's graduates will get high-paid jobs.*
▷ **cream** *adj* yellowish-white: *a cream dress, jacket, etc* ○ *cream paper.*
creamery /ˈkriːmərɪ/ *n* **1** place where milk, cream, butter, etc are sold. **2** place where butter and cheese are made.
creamy *adj* (**-ier**, **-iest**) looking and feeling like cream; containing much cream: *creamy soup, yoghurt, etc.*
□ ˌ**cream** ˈ**cheese** soft white cheese containing a lot of cream.
ˌ**cream of** ˈ**tartar** purified form of tartaric acid, used for making baking powder.
ˌ**cream** ˈ**tea** (*Brit*) meal consisting of tea with scones, jam and whipped cream.
cream[2] /kriːm/ *v* [Tn] **1** mash (cooked vegetables, esp potatoes) with added milk or butter until they are soft and smooth. **2** mix (sth) together into a soft smooth paste: *cream butter and sugar.* **3** (*US infml*) defeat (a team, player, etc) heavily. **4** (phr v) **cream sb/sth off** take away (the best people or things): *The most able pupils are creamed off and put into special classes.* ○ *Our best scientists are being creamed off by other countries.*
▷ **creamer** *n* **1** [C] machine that separates cream from milk. **2** [C] (*esp US*) jug for serving cream. **3** [C, U] substance, usu a powder, that can be used like cream or milk in coffee, etc: *non-dairy creamer.*
crease /kriːs/ *n* **1** line made on cloth, paper, etc by crushing, folding or pressing: *iron a crease into one's trousers* ○ *crease-resistant cloth*, ie that does not easily get creases in it. **2** wrinkle in the skin, esp on the face: *creases round an old man's eyes.* **3** (in cricket) white line made at each end of the pitch to mark the positions of the bowler and batsman. ⇨ illus at CRICKET.
▷ **crease** *v* **1** [I, Tn] (cause sth to) get creases; make a crease or creases in (sth): *material that creases easily* ○ *Pack the clothes carefully so that you don't crease them.* **2** [Tn, Tn·p] ~ **sb** (**up**) (*Brit infml*) amuse sb greatly: *Her jokes really creased me (up).*
create /kriːˈeɪt/ *v* **1** [Tn] cause (sth) to exist; make (sth new or original): *God created the world.* ○ *A novelist creates characters and a plot.* ○ *create a role*, ie (of an actor) be the first to play it ○ *create more jobs.* **2** [Tn] have (sth) as a result; produce: *His shabby appearance creates a bad impression.* ○ *The outrageous book created a sensation.* ○ *create a fuss*, ie express anger, annoyance, etc. **3** [Tn, Cn·n esp passive] give (sb) a certain rank: *create eight new peers* ○ *He was created Baron of Banthorp.* **4** [I] (*Brit infml*) be angry, cause trouble, etc: *She really created because she wasn't served first.*
creation /kriːˈeɪʃn/ *n* **1** (a) [U] action of creating: *the creation of the world in seven days* ○ *the creation of a good impression* ○ *Economic conditions may be responsible for the creation of social unrest.* (b) (usu **the Creation**) [sing] making of the world, esp by God as told in the Bible. **2** (often **Creation**) [U] all created things: *all of God's creation* ○ *the biggest liar in Creation*, ie a very great liar. **3** [C] (a) thing made, esp by means of skill or intelligence: *the creations of poets and artists* ○ *The chef had produced one of his most spectacular creations, a*

whole roasted swan. (**b**) new type of garment or hat: *the latest creations from London's fashion houses.*

▷ **creationism** *n* [U] belief, held by certain Christians who reject evolutionary theory, that the world and all living things were created directly by God. They deny that the findings of modern geology and biology prove this to be untrue. **creationist** *n, adj.*

creative /kriːˈeɪtɪv/ *adj* **1** [attrib] of or involving creation: *The writer described the creative process.* ○ *He teaches creative writing,* ie teaches people to write fiction, plays, etc. **2** able to create: *She's very creative; she writes and paints.* ▷ **creatively** *adv.* **creativeness** *n* [U]. **creativity** /ˌkriːeɪˈtɪvətɪ/ *n* [U].

creator /kriːˈeɪtə(r)/ *n* **1** [C] person who creates: *Shakespeare, the creator of Hamlet.* **2 the Creator** [sing] God.

creature /ˈkriːtʃə(r)/ *n* **1** living being, esp an animal: *dumb creatures,* ie animals ○ *Your dog's a ferocious creature!* ○ *creatures from Mars.* **2** (with a preceding *adj*) person: *What a lovely creature!* ie a beautiful woman ○ *a poor creature,* ie a pitiable person. **3** (idm) **sb's creature/the creature of sb** (*fml derog*) person who is totally dependent on sb else, and does whatever he wants: *The king would appoint one of his creatures to the post.* **a creature of ˈhabit** person whose daily life tends to be governed by habit.

□ ˌ**creature ˈcomforts** things needed for bodily comfort, eg food, drink, warmth, etc.

crèche /kreɪʃ, kreʃ/ *n* **1** (*Brit*) nursery where babies are looked after while their parents work. **2** (*US*) = CRIB.

Crécy /ˈkresɪ/ village in N France, where the Battle of Crécy was fought in 1346. The English army of *Edward III defeated the much larger French forces, mainly because of its use of soldiers armed with longbows.

credence /ˈkriːdns/ *n* (idm) **attach/give credence to sth** (*fml*) believe (gossip, reports, etc): *I attach little credence to what she says.* **lend credence to sth/gain credence** (*fml*) make sth/become more believable.

□ ˈ**credence table** (also **credence**) table near the altar in a church, on which the wine, water and other things for the Eucharist are kept until they are needed.

credentials /krɪˈdenʃlz/ *n* [pl] **1** ~ **(for/as sth)**; ~ **(to do sth)** qualities, achievements, etc that make one suitable; qualifications: *She has the perfect credentials for the job.* **2** documents showing that a person is what he claims to be, is trustworthy, etc: *I examined his credentials.*

credible /ˈkredəbl/ *adj* that can be believed; believable: *a credible witness, statement, report* ○ *It seems barely credible,* ie seems almost impossible to believe. ○ *Is there a credible alternative to the nuclear deterrent?*

▷ **credibility** /ˌkredəˈbɪlətɪ/ *n* [U] **1** quality of being believable. **2** quality of being generally accepted and trusted: *After the recent scandal the Government has lost all credibility.* ˌ**crediˈbility gap** difference between what sb says and what is generally thought to be true: *the growing credibility gap that crippled Nixon's presidency.*

credibly /-əblɪ/ *adv*: *I am credibly informed that...,* ie I have been told by sb who can be believed.

credit[1] /ˈkredɪt/ *n* **1** (**a**) [U] permission to delay payment for goods and services until after they have been received; system of paying in this way: *refuse/grant sb credit* ○ *No credit is given at this shop,* ie Payment must be in cash. ○ *I bought it on credit,* ie did not have to pay for it until some time after I got it. ○ *High interest rates make credit expensive.* ○ *give sb six months' interest-free credit,* ie allow sb to pay within six months, without adding an extra charge for interest ○ [attrib] *a credit period, agreement.* (**b**) [U] sum of money in sb's bank account: *How much do I have to my credit?* ie How much money is in my account? ○ *Your account is in credit,* ie There is money in it. ○ [attrib] *I have a credit balance of £250.* (**c**) [C] sum of money lent by a bank, etc; loan: *The bank refused further credits to the company.* (**d**) [C] (in bookkeeping) (written record of a) payment received: *Is this item a debit or a credit?* Cf DEBIT. **2** [U] ~ **(for sth)** praise; approval; recognition (used esp with the *vs* shown): *He got all the credit for the discovery.* ○ *I can't take any credit; the others did all the work.* ○ *She was given the credit for what I had done.* ○ *At least give him credit for trying,* ie praise him, even though he did not succeed. ○ *Give credit where it's due.* ○ *There was little credit for those who had worked hardest.* ○ *His courage has brought great credit to/reflects credit on* (ie gives a good reputation to) *his regiment.* **3** [U] belief; trust; confidence: *The rumour is gaining credit,* ie More and more people believe it. ○ *Recent developments lend credit to* (ie strengthen belief in) *previous reports.* **4 credits** [pl] (also **credit titles**) list of actors, director, cameramen, etc who worked on a film, TV programme, etc, shown at the beginning or end. **5** [C] (*US education*) entry on a record showing that a student has completed a course: *gain credits in Math and English.* **6** [sing] addition to the reputation or good name of sb/sth: *This brilliant pupil is a credit to his teachers.* **7** (idm) **be to sb's credit; do sb credit; do credit to sb/sth** make sb worthy of praise: *Jack, to his credit, refused to get involved.* ○ *It is greatly to your credit that you gave back the money you found; your honesty does you great credit.* ○ *His improved performance does credit to his trainer.* ○ *It does her credit that she managed not to get angry.* **have sth to one's credit** have achieved sth: *He is only thirty, and already he has four films to his credit,* ie he has made four films.

□ ˈ**credit account** (*US* **charge account**) account with a shop, store, etc that allows one to pay for goods at fixed intervals (eg monthly) rather than immediately.

ˈ**credit card** card that allows its holder to buy goods and services on credit.

ˈ**credit limit** maximum amount of credit[1] (1a) that a bank, etc will allow to a customer.

ˈ**credit note** (*commerce*) note given to a customer who has returned goods to the seller, allowing him to have other goods with a value equal to those returned.

ˈ**credit rating** assessment of how reliable sb is in paying for goods bought on credit.

ˈ**credit-side** *n* right-hand side of an account, on which payments received are recorded: (*fig*) *We've lost some experienced players, but on the credit-side* (ie at least there is this favourable aspect) *there are some useful young ones coming into the team.*

ˈ**credit squeeze** government policy of controlling inflation by making it difficult to borrow money, eg by raising interest rates.

ˈ**credit transfer** transfer of money direct from one bank account to another, without using a cheque.

ˈ**credit union** (*esp US*) co-operative organization from which members can borrow money at a low rate of interest.

ˈ**credit-worthy** *adj* (of people, business firms, etc) accepted as safe to give credit to, because reliable in making repayment. ˈ**credit-worthiness** *n* [U].

credit[2] /ˈkredɪt/ *v* **1** [Tn·pr] ~ **sb/sth with sth**; ~ **sth to sb/sth** (**a**) believe that sb/sth has sth; attribute sth to sb/sth: *Until now I've always credited you with more sense.* ○ *The relics are credited with miraculous powers.* ○ *Miraculous powers are credited to the relics.* (**b**) record an amount as being paid into sb's bank account: *credit a customer with £8* ○ *credit £8 to a customer/an account.* **2** [Tn] (used mainly in questions and negative sentences) believe (sth): *Would you credit it?* ie It is incredible. ○ *I can barely credit what she said.*

creditable /ˈkredɪtəbl/ *adj* ~ **(to sb)** deserving praise (although perhaps not outstandingly good); bringing credit[1](2): *a creditable attempt, performance, etc* ○ *creditable work, progress, etc* ○ *conduct that is very creditable to him.* ▷ **creditably** /ˈkredɪtəblɪ/ *adv*: *She performed very creditably in the exam.*

creditor /ˈkredɪtə(r)/ *n* person to whom money is owed: *His creditors are demanding to be paid.*

credo /ˈkriːdəʊ, ˈkreɪdəʊ/ *n* (*pl* ~**s**) beliefs of a person or group, esp when they are deeply held or on a particular subject: *her extremist political credo.*

credulity /krɪˈdjuːlətɪ; *US* -ˈduː-/ *n* [U] too great a readiness to believe things: *a statement which stretches/strains one's credulity to the limit,* ie is almost impossible to believe.

credulous /ˈkredjʊləs; *US* -dʒə-/ *adj* too ready to believe things: *credulous people who believe what the advertisements say.* ▷ **credulously** *adv.*

creed /kriːd/ *n* **1** [C] system of beliefs or opinions, esp religious beliefs: *people of all colours and creeds,* ie of all sorts ○ *What is your political creed?* **2 the Creed** [sing] short summary of Christian belief, esp as said or sung as part of a church service.

creek /kriːk; *US also* krɪk/ *n* **1** (*Brit*) narrow stretch of water flowing inland from a coast; inlet. **2** (**a**) (*US*) small river or stream, esp a tributary. (**b**) (*Austral and NZ*) stream or brook. **3** (idm) **up shit creek** ⇨ SHIT. **up the ˈcreek** (*infml*) in difficulties: *I'm really up the creek without my car.*

creel /kriːl/ *n* angler's wicker basket for holding the fish he catches.

creep /kriːp/ *v* (*pt, pp* **crept**) **1** [Ipr, Ip] move slowly, quietly or stealthily, esp crouching low: *The cat crept silently towards the bird.* ○ *She crept up to him from behind.* ○ *The thief crept along the corridor.* ○ (*fig*) *A feeling of drowsiness crept over him.* ○ (*fig*) *Old age creeps up on you* (ie approaches you stealthily) *before you realize it.* ⇨ Usage at PROWL. **2** [I, Ipr, Ip] (of plants) grow along the ground, up walls, etc: *Ivy had crept up the castle walls.* ○ *a creeping vine.* **3** (idm) **make one's/sb's flesh crawl/creep** ⇨ FLESH.

▷ **creep** *n* **1** [C] (*infml derog*) person who tries to win sb's favour by always agreeing with him, doing things for him, etc. **2** [U] movement of soil and loose rock towards a lower level, caused esp by gravity and weather conditions. **3** [U] change in the shape of metals under stress, esp at high temperatures. **4** (idm) **give sb the ˈcreeps** (*infml*) (**a**) (of fear or horror) cause an unpleasant sensation in the skin, as if things are creeping over it. (**b**) make sb feel extreme dislike; repel sb: *I don't like him: he gives me the creeps.*

creeping *adj* [attrib] (of sth bad) gradual: *The disease results in creeping paralysis.* ○ *creeping inflation in the housing market.*

creeper /ˈkriːpə(r)/ *n* **1** plant that grows along the ground, up walls, etc, often winding itself round other plants. **2** (*dated sl*) shoe with a thick soft (usu crepe) sole. Cf BROTHEL-CREEPER (BROTHEL).

creepy /ˈkriːpɪ/ *adj* (**-ier, -iest**) (*infml*) **1** causing or having an unpleasant feeling of fear or horror: *a creepy ghost story* ○ *a sight that makes you feel creepy.* **2** disturbingly strange: *That was a really creepy coincidence.*

creepy-crawly /ˌkriːpɪˈkrɔːlɪ/ *n* (*infml esp joc*) insect, spider, etc thought of as unpleasant or frightening.

cremate /krɪˈmeɪt/ *v* [Tn] burn (a dead body) to ashes, esp ceremonially at a funeral: *He wants to be cremated, not buried.*

▷ **cremation** /krɪˈmeɪʃn/ *n* [C, U] (act of) cremating.

crematorium /ˌkreməˈtɔːrɪəm/ *n* (*pl* ~**s** or **-oria** /-ɔːrɪə/) (also *esp US* **crematory**) /ˈkremətərɪ; *US* -tɔːrɪ/ building in which bodies are cremated.

crème brûlée /ˌkrem ˈbruːleɪ/ *n* [U, C] (*French*) dessert made of cream, sweetened and baked, with a topping of slightly burnt caramel.

crème de la crème /ˌkrem də lɑː ˈkrem/ *n* **the crème de la crème** (*French*) = CREAM 4.

crème de menthe /ˌkrem də ˈmɒnθ/ *n* [U, C] (*French*) sweet thick green liqueur flavoured with peppermint.

crenellated (*US* **-elated**) /ˈkrenəleɪtɪd/ *adj* having battlements: *a crenellated castle/wall.* ⇨ illus at CASTLE.

creole /ˈkriːəʊl/ *n* **1** [C, U] language formed by a blending of two other languages, and used as the main language in the community in which it is spoken. Cf PIDGIN. **2** (usu **Creole**) [C] **(a)** descendant (either direct or of mixed European and African descent) of the original European settlers in the West Indies or Spanish America. **(b)** descendant of the original French or Spanish settlers in the southern states of the USA. ▷ **creole** *adj*: *Creole cuisine.*

creosote /ˈkrɪəsəʊt/ *n* [U] thick brown oily liquid obtained from coal tar, used to preserve wood.
▷ **creosote** *v* [Tn] paint (sth) with creosote.

crepe (also **crêpe**) /ˈkreɪp/ *n* **1** [U] light thin fabric with a wrinkled surface. Cf CRAPE. **2** (also ˌ**crepe** ˈ**rubber**) [U] tough rubber produced in sheets with a wrinkled surface, used for the soles of shoes: *crepe-soled shoes.* **3** [C] thin French-style pancake.
□ ˌ**crepe** ˈ**paper** thin paper with a wavy or wrinkled surface.
crepe suzette /ˌkreɪp suːˈzet; *US* ˌkreɪp-/ crepe(3) with an orange-flavoured liqueur poured on it, which is set alight when it is served.

crepitate /ˈkrepɪteɪt/ *v* [I] (*fml or medical*) make sharp crackling or grating sounds.
▷ **crepitation** /ˌkrepɪˈteɪʃn/ *n* [U, C] (*fml or medical*) crepitating (sound): *the tell-tale crepitation of a broken bone.*

crept *pt, pp* of CREEP.

crepuscular /krɪˈpʌskjʊlə(r)/ *adj* (*fml*) **1** of or like twilight; dim: *crepuscular shadows.* **2** (of animals) active at twilight or dawn: *Bats are crepuscular creatures.*

crescendo /krɪˈʃendəʊ/ *adj, adv* (*music*) of or with increasing loudness: *a crescendo passage.*
▷ **crescendo** *n* (*pl* ~**s**) **1** (*music*) gradual increase in loudness. **2** (*fig*) climax; high point: *The advertising campaign reached a crescendo at Christmas.* Cf DIMINUENDO.

crescent

crescent /ˈkresnt/ *n* **1** [C] **(a)** (thing with a) narrow curved shape that tapers to a point at each end, like the new moon. **(b)** (street consisting of a) semicircular row of houses or other buildings: *London's Regency squares and crescents* ○ *11, Park Crescent* ⇨ illus.
📖 'Crescent' as a street name derives from an architectural style developed in Britain in the 18th century, particularly associated with *Georgian architecture. One of the most famous crescents in Britain is the Royal Crescent in Bath, designed by Robert *Adam.
2 the Crescent [sing] (*fig*) the faith and religion of Islam: *the Cross* (ie Christianity) *and the Crescent.*

cress /kres/ *n* [U] any of various small plants with hot-tasting leaves used in salads and sandwiches.

crest /krest/ *n* **1** tuft of feathers on a bird's head. **2** **(a)** top of a slope or hill. **(b)** white top of a large wave. ⇨ illus at SURFING. **(c)** top part of a horse's neck, from which its mane grows. **3** design above the shield on a coat of arms, often represented on a seal or on notepaper: *the family crest*, ie one above the family's coat of arms. **4** **(a)** decorative tuft or plume formerly worn on top of a soldier's helmet. **(b)** (*fig rhet*) helmet. **5** (idm) **on the crest of a** ˈ**wave** at the point of greatest success, happiness, etc: *After its election victory, the party was on the crest of a wave.*
▷ **crest** *v* **1** [Tn] reach the crest of (a hill, etc): *As we crested the hill, we saw the castle.* **2** [I] (of a wave) form into a crest.
crested *adj* [attrib] **1** having a crest(3): *crested notepaper.* **2** (used in names of birds) having a crest(1): *the great crested grebe.*

crestfallen /ˈkrestfɔːlən/ *adj* sad because of unexpected failure, disappointment, etc.

cretaceous /krɪˈteɪʃəs/ *adj* (*geology*) **1** of or like chalk: *cretaceous rock.* **2** **Cretaceous** of the geological period lasting from about 144 to 65 million years ago, when the first flowering plants appeared and the dinosaurs became extinct. In Britain it was characterized by the formation of chalk, a pure white limestone: *Cretaceous fossils.*

Crete /kriːt/ Greek island in the eastern Mediterranean Sea. In the 16th and 15th centuries BC, Crete was the base of the highly developed *Minoan civilization, and there are important historical remains. ▷ **Cretan** /ˈkriːtn/ *n, adj.*

cretin /ˈkretɪn; *US* ˈkriːtn/ *n* **1** (*medical*) person who has arrested mental and physical development because of lack of thyroid secretion. **2** (⚠ *offensive*) very stupid person: *Why did you do that, you cretin?* ▷ **cretinous** /ˈkretɪnəs; *US* ˈkriːt-/ *adj.*

cretonne /ˈkretɒn/ *n* [U] thick cotton cloth with printed designs, used for curtains, furniture covers, etc.

crevasse /krɪˈvæs/ *n* deep open crack in the ice of a glacier.

crevice /ˈkrevɪs/ *n* narrow opening or crack in a rock, wall, etc.

crew[1] /kruː/ *n* [CGp] **1** **(a)** people working on a ship, an aircraft, an oil-rig, etc. **(b)** these people, except the officers: *the officers and crew of the SS London.* **(c)** rowing team: *the Cambridge crew.* **2** group of people working together; gang: *a track-repair crew* ○ *a camera crew.* **3** (*usu derog*) group of people: *The people she'd invited were a pretty motley crew.*
▷ **crew** *v* [I, Ipr, Tn] ~ (**for sb/on sth**) act as (a member of) the crew on (sth): *Will you crew for me on my yacht?* ○ *Men are needed to crew the lifeboat.*
□ ˈ**crew cut** very short hair-style for men.
ˈ**crew neck** type of round close-fitting collar, esp on a pullover. ⇨ illus at NECK.

crew[2] *pt* of CROW[2].

crewel /ˈkruːəl/ *n* [U] thin worsted thread used esp in embroidery.
□ ˈ**crewel-work** *n* [U] designs or embroideries made with crewel.

crib[1] /krɪb/ *n* **1** [C] wooden framework for holding animal food; manger. **2** [C] (*esp US*) = COT 1. **3** (*US* **crèche**) [C] model, eg in a church at Christmas, representing Christ's birth in Bethlehem. **4** [U] = CRIBBAGE.
▷ **crib** *v* (-**bb**-) [Tn, Tn·p] ~ **sb** (**up**) (*arch*) confine sb in a small space.

crib[2] /krɪb/ *n* **1** thing copied dishonestly from the work of another, eg in an examination: *This answer must be a crib: it's exactly the same as Jones's.* **2** thing used as an aid to understanding, eg an exact translation of a foreign text one is studying.
▷ **crib** *v* (-**bb**-) [I, Ipr, Tn, Tn·pr] ~ (**sth**) (**from/off sb**) copy (another student's written work) dishonestly: *In the exam, I cribbed (an answer) from the girl next to me.*

cribbage /ˈkrɪbɪdʒ/ (also **crib**) *n* [U] card-game for two, three or four players, in which the score is kept by putting small pegs in holes in a board.
□ ˈ**cribbage board** board for keeping the score in cribbage.

Crick /krɪk/ Francis Harry Compton (1916-), British biophysicist whose work with J D *Watson, M H F Wilkins and Rosalind Franklin led to the discovery of the structure of the DNA molecule. Watson, Crick and Wilkins were jointly awarded the Nobel prize in 1962.

crick /krɪk/ *n* [sing] painful stiffness, esp in the neck: *to have/get a crick in one's neck/back.*
▷ **crick** *v* [Tn] get a crick in (sth): *to crick one's neck/back.*

cricket[1] /ˈkrɪkɪt/ *n* small brown jumping insect that makes a shrill sound by rubbing its front wings together: *the chirping of crickets.*

cricket[2] /ˈkrɪkɪt/ *n* **1** [U] game played on grass by two teams of 11 players each, in which a ball is bowled at stumps and a batsman tries to hit it with a bat. The bowler's intention is to end the batsman's turn, which can be done in any of ten ways: the commonest are to hit his stumps with the ball, and for a member of the bowler's team to catch the ball after the batsman has hit it. The batsman's intention is to score runs, which he does by running from one end of the wicket to the other, typically after hitting the ball: [attrib] *a cricket match, ball, team* ⇨ illus. ⇨ App 9. ⇨ article at SPORTS AND GAMES. **2** (idm) **not** ˈ**cricket** (*dated Brit sl*) unfair; not honourable: *You can't do it without telling him; it just isn't cricket.*
▷ **cricketer** *n* cricket player.

cri de cœur /ˌkriː də ˈkɜː(r)/ *n* (*pl* **cris de cœur** /ˌkriː də ˈkɜː(r)/) (*French*) appeal or statement that shows a person's deep feelings: *How can you ignore the cri de cœur of a desperate father?*

cried *pt, pp* of CRY[1].

crier /ˈkraɪə(r)/ *n* = TOWN CRIER (TOWN).

cries /kraɪz/ **1** *3rd pers sing pres t of* CRY[1]. **2** *pl* of CRY[2].

crikey /ˈkraɪkɪ/ *interj* (*Brit infml*) (used to express surprise, fear, etc): *Crikey! What a big dog!*

crime /kraɪm/ *n* **1** **(a)** [C] offence for which one may be punished by law: *commit a serious crime* ○ *a minor crime like shoplifting* ○ *convicted of crimes against humanity.* **(b)** [U] such offences; law-breaking: *an increase in crime* ○ *The police prevent and detect crime.* ○ *He took to a life of crime*, ie became a criminal. ○ [attrib] *crime prevention, rates* ○ *crime fiction, writers, novels, etc*, ie dealing with crime, its detection, etc. ⇨article. **2** (usu **a crime**) [sing] foolish or immoral act: *It's a crime to waste money like that.* ○ *It's a crime the way he bullies his children.*
▷ **criminal** /ˈkrɪmɪnl/ *adj* **1** [usu attrib] of or being crime: *criminal offences, damage, negligence, etc.* **2** [attrib] concerned with crime: *criminal law*; ⇨ article at LAW: *a criminal lawyer.* Cf CIVIL 4. **3** disgraceful; immoral: *a criminal waste of public money* ○ *It's criminal the way she lies and cheats to get what she wants.* — *n* person who commits a crime or crimes. **criminally** /-nəlɪ/ *adv*: *criminally insane.*
□ ˌ**crime of** ˈ**passion** (also *French* **crime passionel** /ˌkriːm pæsjəˈnel/) crime, esp murder, committed out of sexual jealousy, towards which courts of law in some cultures are lenient.

Crimea /kraɪˈmɪə/ **the Crimea** peninsula in the *Ukraine. Its Black Sea coast has a number of spas and holiday resorts. ▷ **Crimean** /kraɪˈmɪən/ *adj.*
the ˌ**Crimean** ˈ**War** war between Russia and an alliance of Turkey, Britain, France and Sardinia, 1854-56. Russia had ambitions in Turkey, while the European powers wished to end Russian power in the Black Sea. The capture of Sebastopol marked Russia's defeat.

criminology /ˌkrɪmɪˈnɒlədʒɪ/ *n* [U] scientific study of crime. ▷ **criminologist** /-dʒɪst/ *n.*

crimp /krɪmp/ *v* [Tn] **(a)** press (cloth, paper, etc) into small folds or ridges. **(b)** make (hair) wavy by

Crime

Crime in both Britain and the USA is a cause of constant and serious concern, and increasing attention is being paid to methods of preventing it.

Over the past few years in Britain, there has been an increase in crimes of violence against people, in sexual offences, and in criminal damage. At the same time there has been a decrease in burglary and to a lesser extent in robbery, theft, and the handling of stolen goods.

Even so, the majority of crime is directed against property, with car theft accounting for a quarter of all crimes, and in Britain local crime prevention panels operate in conjunction with the police to discuss ways of tackling this type of crime. Methods include marking valuable goods and equipment and installing security devices such as burglar alarms. The setting-up of 'Neighbourhood Watch' schemes has been a practical move towards the prevention of break-ins and thefts from private houses, and in 1988 an independent crime prevention organization, Crime Concern, was established to encourage further schemes of this type. The risk of burglary is ten times higher in inner city areas than in rural areas.

The increase in sexual crimes has received much publicity, but some analysts maintain that the increase in such crime may be not so great as it appears, since people now report sexual crimes more readily. Special 'rape crisis' counselling groups have been set up and, in Britain, Childline, a confidential telephone service, is available for children who are being sexually abused.

In the USA, there has been a marked rise in violent crime among young people, with murder, rape and assault all on the increase. In both countries there have been incidents of mass shootings, which have resulted in a review of the regulations controlling the purchase of firearms. The import and sale of illegal drugs, in particular heroin and cocaine, is a growing area of crime, and has led to international co-operation between police forces in order to combat it.

The high level of crime in general has led to the coordination of efforts to fight it. Local authorities, private businesses and voluntary groups have collaborated with the police in some areas of Britain, notably in the inner cities.

In 1988 a Serious Fraud Office was set up in Britain to deal with complicated cases of fraud, especially within companies, and crimes like 'insider dealing', ie using confidential information when dealing in shares.

A different sort of offence, also increasingly frequent, is 'drinking and driving'. Government 'drink-drive' campaigns have been mounted, with some success, and police have introduced such measures as breath tests to combat the problem, which is especially acute during the Christmas holiday period.

In Britain, the police have not always effectively combated the problem of racial violence. There continue to be incidents of assault on members of ethnic minority groups, either by direct harassment in their homes or by acts of vandalism in shops run by them. A similar situation exists in the USA, where there have been cases of racial harassment on college campuses and of the mailing of letter bombs.

(Cf articles at LAW, POLICE and PUNISHMENT.)

pressing with a hot iron.

▷ **crimp** *n* (idm) **put a crimp in sth** (*infml esp US*) spoil or interfere with sth: *That put a crimp in the evening, didn't it?*

crimplene /ˈkrɪmpliːn/ *n* [U] (*propr*) cloth that does not crease easily, often used for dresses, shirts, etc.

crimson /ˈkrɪmzn/ *adj, n* [U] (of a) deep red.

▷ **crimson** *v* [I, Tn] (*fml*) (cause sb/sth to) become crimson: *crimson* (ie blush) *with embarrassment.*

□ ˌ**crimson** ˈ**lake** = LAKE².

cringe /krɪndʒ/ *v* **1** [I, Ipr] ~ (**at/from sth**) move back or lower one's body in fear; cower: *a child cringing in terror* ○ *The dog cringed at the sight of the whip.* ○ (*fig*) *I cringe with embarrassment* (ie feel very embarrassed) *when I reread those first stories I wrote.* **2** [I, Ipr] ~ (**to/before sb**) (*derog*) behave too humbly towards sb who is more powerful: *She's always cringing to the boss.*

crinkle /ˈkrɪŋkl/ *n* wrinkle or thin crease, esp in material such as tin foil or paper, or in skin.

▷ **crinkle** *v* [I, Ip, Tn, Tn·p] ~ (**sth**) (**up**) (cause sth to) have crinkles; produce crinkles in (sth): *crinkle the tin foil (up) by squeezing it* ○ *the dead plant's crinkled leaves.*

crinkly /ˈkrɪŋklɪ/ *adj* (**-ier, -iest**) (**a**) having crinkles. (**b**) (of hair) having tight curls.

crinoline /ˈkrɪnəlɪn/ *n* light framework covered with fabric, formerly worn under a long skirt to make it stand out.

cripes /kraɪps/ *interj* (*dated sl*) (used to express astonishment, etc): *Cripes! It just disappeared!*

cripple /ˈkrɪpl/ *n* person who is unable to walk or move properly because of disease or injury to the spine or legs.

▷ **cripple** *v* [Tn usu passive] **1** make (sb) a cripple: *crippled by polio* ○ *crippled with rheumatism* ○ *their crippled daughter.* **2** (*fig*) damage or weaken (sth) seriously: *a ship crippled by a storm* ○ *The business has been crippled by losses.* ○ *The country has crippling* (ie extremely large) *debts.*

crisis /ˈkraɪsɪs/ *n* (*pl* **crises** /ˈkraɪsiːz/) [C, U] time of great difficulty or danger; decisive moment in illness, life, history, etc: *a financial, political, domestic, etc crisis* ○ *come to/reach a crisis* ○ *In times of crisis it's good to have a friend to turn to.* ○ *a Government in crisis*, ie going through a difficult period ○ *The fever passed its crisis*, ie its most dangerous point. ○ [attrib] *The government is holding crisis talks with the unions.*

crisp /krɪsp/ *adj* (**-er, -est**) (*usu approv*) **1** (**a**) (esp of food) hard, dry and easily broken: *a crisp biscuit* ○ *crisp pastry, toast, etc* ○ *The snow was crisp underfoot.* (**b**) (esp of fruit or vegetables) firm and fresh: *a crisp apple, lettuce, etc.* (**c**) (esp of paper) slightly stiff: *a crisp new £5 note.* **2** (of the air or the weather) dry and cold: *a crisp winter morning* ○ *the crisp air of an autumn day.* **3** (of curls in hair) tight. **4** (of sb's manner, way of speaking, etc) brisk, precise and decisive: *a crisp order* ○ *crisp speech* ○ *a crisp and clear answer.*

▷ **crisp** *n* **1** (also poˌtato ˈ**crisp**, *US* **potato chip**, **chip**) thin slice of potato, fried and dried, often flavoured and sold in packets. ⇨ illus at POTATO. **2** (idm) **burn sth to a crisp** ⇨ BURN.

v [Tn, Tn·p] ~ **sth** (**up**) make sth crisp: *crisp the bread up in the oven.*

crisply *adv* in a crisp(4) manner.

crispness *n* [U].

crispy *adj* (**-ier, -iest**) (*infml*) = CRISP *adj* 1a, b: *crispy bacon.*

□ ˈ**crispbread** *n* [C, U] thin savoury biscuit, usu made with rye flour.

criss-cross /ˈkrɪskrɒs; *US* -krɔːs/ *adj* [attrib], *adv* with lines crossing each other: *a criss-cross pattern, design, etc* ○ *electricity cables erected criss-cross over the countryside.*

▷ **criss-cross** *v* **1** [I, Tn] form a criss-cross pattern (on sth): *Railway lines criss-cross in a dense network.* ○ *Rivers criss-cross the landscape.* **2** [Tn, Tn·pr usu passive] ~ **sth** (**with sth**) mark sth with lines that cross: *a sheet criss-crossed with pencil marks.*

criterion /kraɪˈtɪərɪən/ *n* (*pl* **-ria** /-rɪə/) standard by which sth is judged: *Success in making money is not always a good criterion of success in life.* ○ *What are the criteria for deciding* (ie How do we decide) *who gets the prize?*

critic /ˈkrɪtɪk/ *n* **1** person who expresses a low opinion of sb/sth, points out faults in sb/sth, etc: *I am my own severest critic.* ○ *She confounded her critics by breaking the record*, ie They said she would not be able to do so, but she did. **2** person who evaluates and describes the quality of sth, esp works of art, literature, music, etc: *a music, theatre, literary, etc critic* ○ *a play praised by the critics.*

critical /ˈkrɪtɪkl/ *adj* **1** ~ (**of sb/sth**) looking for faults; pointing out faults: *a critical remark, report, etc* ○ *The inquiry was critical of her work.* ○ (*derog*) *Why are you always so critical?* ○ (*approv*) *Try to develop a more critical attitude, instead of accepting everything at face value.* **2** [attrib] of the art of making judgements on literature, art, etc: *In the current critical climate her work is not popular.* ○ *The film has received critical acclaim*, ie praise from the critics. **3** of or at a crisis; decisive; crucial: *We are at a critical time in our history.* ○ *The patient's condition is critical*, ie He is very ill and may die. ○ *Her help was critical* (ie of great importance) *during the emergency.* **4** (idm) **go** ˈ**critical** (of a nuclear reactor) reach a state where a nuclear reaction sustains itself. ▷ **critically** /-ɪklɪ/ *adv*: *speak critically of sb* ○ *He is critically ill.*

□ ˌ**critical** ˈ**mass** minimum amount of uranium or similar material needed to keep a nuclear chain reaction going.

ˌ**critical** ˈ**path analysis** the study of a set of operations (eg in building a ship) to decide the quickest and most efficient order in which to do them.

ˌ**critical** ˈ**pressure** pressure at which a gas will become a liquid.

ˌ**critical** ˈ**temperature** temperature above which a gas cannot be liquefied.

criticism /ˈkrɪtɪsɪzəm/ *n* **1** (**a**) [U] looking for faults; pointing out faults: *a scheme that is open to criticism* ○ *He hates/can't take criticism*, ie being criticized. (**b**) [C] remark that points out a fault or faults: *I have two criticisms of your plan.* **2** (**a**) [U] art of making judgements on literature, art, etc: *literary criticism.* (**b**) [C] such a judgement.

criticize, -ise /ˈkrɪtɪsaɪz/ *v* **1** [I, Tn, Tn·pr, Tsg] ~ **sb/sth** (**for sth**) point out the faults of sb/sth: *Stop criticizing (my work)!* ○ *He was criticized by the committee for failing to report the accident.* ○ *He criticized my taking risks.* **2** [Tn] form and express a judgement on (a work of art, literature, etc): *teaching students how to criticize poetry.*

critique /krɪˈtiːk/ *n* critical analysis: *The book presents a critique of the Government's economic policies.*

croak /krəʊk/ *n* deep hoarse sound, like that made by a frog.

▷ **croak** *v* **1** [I] (of a frog, etc) utter a croak or croaks. **2** [I, Tn, Tn·p] ~ **sth** (**out**) (of a person) speak or say sth with a deep hoarse voice: *She could only croak because of her heavy cold.* ○ *He croaked (out) a few words.* **3** [I] (*sl*) die.

Croatia /krəʊˈeɪʃə/ country in south-eastern Europe; pop approx 4 760 000; majority language Croatian; capital Zagreb; unit of currency dinar. Until 1991 it was one of the federal republics of Yugoslavia. ⇨ map at YUGOSLAVIA.
▷ **Croat** /ˈkrəʊæt/ *n, adj* (native or inhabitant) of Croatia.
Croatian *n, adj* = CROAT. Cf SERBO-CROAT.

crochet /ˈkrəʊʃeɪ; *US* krəʊˈʃeɪ/ *n* [U] **(a)** method of making fabric by looping thread into a pattern of connected stitches, using a hooked needle (called a **crochet-hook**). **(b)** fabric made in this way.
▷ **crochet** *v* (*pt, pp* ~**ed** /-ʃeɪd/) [I, Tn] make (sth, eg a shawl) in this way: *a crocheted skirt.*

crock[1] /krɒk/ *n* (*dated*) **1** [C] large earthenware pot or jar, eg for containing water. **2 crocks** [pl] = CROCKERY. **3** [C usu *pl*] broken piece of earthenware.

crock[2] /krɒk/ *n* (*Brit infml*) **1** old useless vehicle. **2** old or worn-out person or animal: *What does a young girl like you want with an old crock like me?*
▷ **crocked** /krɒkt/ *adj* [usu pred] **1** (*Brit infml*) injured or broken: *My arm's crocked.* **2** (*US sl*) drunk: *They all got crocked.*

crockery /ˈkrɒkərɪ/ *n* [U] (also **crocks** [pl]) cups, plates, dishes, etc made of baked clay.

Crockett /ˈkrɒkɪt/ Davy or David (1786-1836), American folk hero. His adventures as a pioneer are recorded in his autobiography and have been the subject of many books and films. He was several times a member of the US Congress. He died as one of the defenders of the *Alamo.

Crockford's /ˈkrɒkfədz/ book containing names and other details of the clergy of the Church of England.

crocodile /ˈkrɒkədaɪl/ *n* **1 (a)** [C] large river reptile with a hard skin, a long body and tail, and very big tapering jaws, that lives in hot parts of the world. Cf ALLIGATOR. **(b)** [U] its skin used to make bags, shoes, etc: [attrib] *a crocodile wallet.* **2** [C] (*Brit infml*) long line of schoolchildren walking in pairs. **3** (idm) ˈ**crocodile tears** insincere sorrow: *She shed crocodile tears* (ie pretended to be sorry) *when she dismissed him from his job.*

crocus /ˈkrəʊkɪs/ *n* (*pl* ~**es** /-sɪz/) small plant that produces yellow, purple or white flowers early in spring. ⇨ illus at PLANT.

Croesus /ˈkri:səs/ *n* wealthy king in Asia Minor in the 6th century BC: (*saying*) *as rich as Croesus,* ie very rich.

croft /krɒft; *US* krɔ:ft/ *n* (*Brit*) **1** small farm, esp in Scotland. **2** (*arch*) small enclosed field.
▷ **crofter** *n* person who rents or ōwns a small farm, esp in Scotland.

croissant /ˈkrwʌsɒŋ; *US* krʌˈsɒŋ/ *n* (*French*) crescent-shaped bun made of light flaky pastry, eaten esp at breakfast. ⇨ illus at BREAD.

Cro-Magnon /krəʊˈmænjən; *US* krəʊˈmægnən/ hill in the Dordogne, SW France, in which there is a cave where human skeletons were found among remains of the palaeolithic period.
□ **Cro-Magnon** ˈ**man** type of human being that lived in western Europe around 34 000 to 29 000 years ago.

cromlech /ˈkrɒmlek/ (also **dolmen**) *n* prehistoric circle of large tall stones.

Cromwell[1] /ˈkrɒmwel/ Oliver (1599-1658), English general and leader. He was a Puritan and Member of Parliament and became the leader of the Parliamentary army in the English Civil War. After the trial and execution of *Charles I he continued to crush opposition in Ireland and from the Scottish supporters of *Charles II with considerable cruelty. In 1653 he dissolved Parliament, took the title of Lord Protector and ruled the country as a virtual dictator until his death. ⇨ App 3.

Cromwell[2] /ˈkrɒmwel/ Thomas (c 1485-1540), chief minister to *Henry VIII. After the fall of *Wolsey he arranged the king's divorce from Catherine of Aragon and later managed the *Dissolution of the Monasteries. He eventually lost the king's favour and was executed for treason.

crone /krəʊn/ *n* (*usu derog*) ugly withered old woman.

crony /ˈkrəʊnɪ/ *n* (*derog*) close friend or companion: *He spends every evening drinking in the pub with his cronies.*

crook /krʊk/ *n* **1** (*infml*) person who is habitually dishonest: *The crooks got away with* (ie The criminals stole) *most of the money.* ○ *That used-car salesman is a real crook.* **2** bend or curve, eg in a river or path: *carry sth in the crook of one's arm,* ie on one's arm, at the inside of the bent elbow. **3 (a)** long stick with a rounded hook at one end, as used in former times by shepherds for catching sheep. **(b)** long staff similar to this, carried ceremonially by a bishop; crosier. **4** (idm) **by hook or by crook** ⇨ HOOK[1].
▷ **crook** *v* [Tn] bend (esp one's finger or arm): *She crooked her little finger as she drank her tea.*
adj [usu pred] (*Austral infml*) ill: *I'm feeling a bit crook.*
□ ˈ**crook-back** *n, adj* (*arch*) hunch-back(ed).
ˈ**crook-backed** *adj.*

crooked /ˈkrʊkɪd/ *adj* (**-er, -est**) **1** not straight or level; twisted, bent or curved: *a crooked lane, branch, table* ○ *a crooked smile,* ie in which the mouth slopes down at one side ○ *You've got your hat on crooked.* **2** (*infml*) (of people or actions) dishonest; illegal: *a crooked businessman, deal.* ▷ **crookedly** *adv.* **crookedness** *n* [U].

Crookes /krʊks/ Sir William (1832-1919), British scientist. He discovered thallium and conducted experiments into radioactivity.
□ **Crookes** ˈ**tube** vacuum tube once used for observing electrical conduction in gases.
Crookes ˈ**glass** type of dark glass used for protecting the eyes from ultraviolet light.

croon /kru:n/ *v* [I, Ipr, Tn, Tn·pr] ~ **(sth) (to sb)** hum, sing or say (sth) softly and gently: *croon soothingly (to a child)* ○ *croon a sentimental tune* ○ *croon a baby to sleep* ○ *'What a beautiful little baby,' she crooned.*
▷ **crooner** *n* singer of the 1930s or 1940s who sang sentimental songs.

crop /krɒp/ *n* **1 (a)** [C] amount of grain, hay, fruit, etc grown in one year or season: *the potato crop* ○ *a good crop of rice* ○ *a bumper* (ie very large) *crop* ○ [attrib] *a crop failure.* **(b) crops** [pl] agricultural plants in the fields: *treat the crops with fertilizer.* **2** [sing] ~ **of sth** group of people or quantity of things appearing or produced at the same time: *this year's crop of students* ○ *The programme brought quite a crop of complaints from viewers.* **3** [C] very short hair-cut. **4** [C] bag-like part of a bird's throat where food is prepared for digestion before passing into the stomach. **5** [C] (also ˈ**hunting-crop**) whip with a short loop instead of a lash, used by riders. **6** (idm) **neck and crop** ⇨ NECK.
▷ **crop** *v* (**-pp-**) **1** [Tn, Cn·a] **(a)** cut short (sb's hair or an animal's ears, tail, etc): *with hair cropped (short).* **(b)** (of animals) bite the tops off and eat (grass, plants, etc): *Sheep had cropped the grass (short).* **2** [I] (of plants, fields, etc) bear a crop: *The beans cropped well this year.* **3** (phr v) **crop up** appear or happen, esp unexpectedly: *All sorts of difficulties cropped up.* ○ *The subject cropped up as we talked.*
□ ˈ**crop-dusting**, ˈ**crop-spraying** *ns* [U] dusting/spraying of crops with fertilizer or insecticide, eg from low-flying aircraft.
ˌ**crop-**ˈ**eared** *adj* **(a)** (esp of a horse) with cropped ears. **(b)** with the hair around the ears cut short.

cropper /ˈkrɒpə(r)/ *n* **1** (following *adjs*) plant that produces a crop of the specified kind: *a good, bad, heavy, light, etc cropper.* **2** (idm) **come a** ˈ**cropper** (*infml*) **(a)** fall over. **(b)** fail.

croquet /ˈkrəʊkeɪ; *US* krəʊˈkeɪ/ *n* [U] game played on a lawn, using wooden mallets to knock wooden balls through hoops. ⇨ article at SPORT.

croquette /krəʊˈket/ *n* ball of mashed potato, fish, etc coated with bread-crumbs and cooked in fat.

crore /krɔ:(r)/ *n* (*Indian*) ten million: *a crore of rupees.*

Crosby /ˈkrɒzbɪ/ Bing (1904-77), American actor and entertainer. He was famous as a crooner, his most successful song recording being *White Christmas.* He appeared in many comedy films with Bob *Hope.

crosier (also **crozier**) /ˈkrəʊzɪə(r); *US* ˈkrəʊʒər/ *n* bishop's long ceremonial staff, usu shaped like a shepherd's crook.

cross

SWASTIKA

MALTESE CROSS

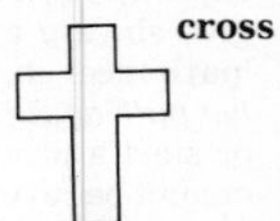
LATIN CROSS

cross[1] /krɒs; *US* krɔ:s/ *n* **1** [C] **(a)** mark made by drawing one line across another, eg x or +: *The place is marked on the map with a cross.* ○ *make one's cross,* ie put a cross on a document instead of one's signature, eg if one cannot write. **(b)** line or stroke forming part of a letter, eg the horizontal stroke on a 't' **2 (a) the Cross** [sing] the frame made of a long vertical piece of wood with a shorter horizontal piece joined to it near the top, on which Christ was crucified. **(b)** [C] thing representing this, as a Christian emblem: *She wore a small silver cross on a chain round her neck.* ⇨ illus at CHURCH. **(c)** [C] thing, esp a monument, in the form of a cross, eg a stone one in a village market-place. **(d)** [C usu *sing*] cross-shaped sign made with the right hand as a Christian religious act: *The priest made a cross over her head.* **(e) the Cross** [sing] (*fig*) the Christian religion: *the Cross and the Crescent,* ie Christianity and Islam. **3** (usu **Cross**) [C] small cross-shaped piece of metal awarded as a medal for courage, etc: *the Victoria Cross* ○ *the Distinguished Service Cross.* **4** [C usu *sing*] ~ **(between A and B) (a)** animal or plant that is the offspring of different breeds or varieties: *A mule is a cross between a horse and an ass.* **(b)** (*fig*) mixture of two different things: *a play that is a cross between farce and tragedy.* **5** [C] source of sorrow, worry, etc; problem: *We all have our crosses to bear.* **6** [C] movement across: *an actor's cross,* ie walk across the stage ○ *a goal scored from a cross by Wood,* ie after Wood had kicked the ball across the field. **7** (idm) **cut sth on the** ˈ**cross** cut cloth, etc diagonally.

cross[2] /krɒs; *US* krɔ:s/ *v* **1** [I, Ipr, Ip, Tn] ~ **(over) (from sth/to sth)** go across; pass or extend from one side to the other side of (sth): *The river is too deep; we can't cross (over).* ○ *cross from Dover to Calais* ○ *cross a road, a river, a bridge, a desert, the sea, the mountains* ○ *Electricity cables cross the valley.* **2 (a)** [I] pass across each other: *The roads cross just outside the village.* ○ (*fig*) *Our paths crossed* (ie We met by chance) *several times.* **(b)** [I, Tn no passive] (of people travelling, letters in the post) meet and pass (each other): *We crossed each other on the way.* ○ *Our letters crossed in the post.* **3** [Tn] put or place (sth) across or over sth else of the same type: *cross one's legs,* ie place one leg over the other, esp at the thighs ○ *cross one's arms on one's chest* ○ *a flag with a design of two crossed keys* ○ *a crossed line,* ie interruption of a telephone call because of a wrong connection. **4** [Tn] draw a line across (sth): *cross the t's* ○ *cross a cheque,* ie draw two lines across it so that it can only be paid through a bank ○ *a crossed cheque,* ie a cheque marked in this way. **5** [Tn no passive] ~ **oneself** make the sign of the cross[1](2a) on one's chest: *He* ˈ*crossed himself as he passed the church.* **6** [Tn] obstruct, oppose or contradict (sb, his plans or wishes); thwart: *She doesn't like to be crossed.* ○ *He crosses me in everything.* ○ *to be crossed in love,* ie fail to win the love of sb one loves. **7** [Tn, Tn·pr] ~ **(sth with sth)** cause (two different types of animal or plant) to produce offspring: *to cross a horse with an ass* ○ *Varieties of roses can be crossed to vary their colour.* **8** (idm) ˌ**cross one's** ˌ**bridges when one** ˈ**comes to them** not worry about a problem before it actually arrives: *We'll cross that bridge when we come to it.* **cross one's** ˈ**fingers** hope that one's plans will be successful: *I'm crossing my fingers that my proposal will be accepted.* ○ *Keep your fingers crossed!* **cross my** ˈ**heart (and hope to die)** (*infml saying*) (used to emphasize the honesty or sincerity of what one says or promises): *I saw him do it: cross my heart.* **cross one's** ˈ**mind** (of thoughts, etc) come into one's mind: *It never* *crossed my mind that she might lose*, ie I confidently expected her to win. ˌ**cross sb's** ˌ**palm with** ˈ**silver** give sb (esp a fortune-teller) a coin. ˌ**cross sb's** ˈ**path** meet sb, usu by chance: *I hope I never cross her path again.* ˌ**cross the** ˈ**Rubicon** take an action or start a process which is important and which cannot be reversed. **cross** ˈ**swords (with sb)** fight or argue (with sb): *The chairman and I have crossed swords before over this issue.* **dot one's i's and cross one's t's** ⇨ DOT. **get, have, etc one's lines crossed** ⇨ LINE[1]. **get one's wires crossed** ⇨ WIRE. **9** (phr v) **cross sth off (sth); cross sth out/through** remove sth by drawing a line through it: *We can cross his name off (the list), as he's not coming.* ○ *Two words have been crossed out.*

cross[3] /krɒs; *US* krɔ:s/ *adj* (**-er, -est**) **1** ~ (**with sb**) (**about sth**) (*infml*) rather angry: *I was cross with him for being late.* ○ *What are you so cross about?* ○ *She gave me a cross look.* **2** [attrib] (of winds) contrary; opposed: *Strong cross breezes make it difficult for boats to leave harbour.* Cf CROSS-WIND.
▷ **crossly** *adv.* **crossness** *n* [U].
□ ˈ**cross linkage** (*chemistry*) short crosswise chain of atoms linking two longer chains in a polymer.

cross- *comb form* (forming *ns, vs, adjs* and *advs*) movement or action from one thing to another or across: *cross-current* ○ *cross-fertilization* ○ *cross-cultural* ○ *cross-country* ○ *cross-Channel ferries.*

crossbar /ˈkrɒsbɑ:(r); *US* ˈkrɔ:s-/ *n* horizontal bar, eg one joining the two upright posts of a football goal, or the front and rear ends of a bicycle frame. ⇨ illus at BICYCLE.

crossbeam /ˈkrɒsbi:m; *US* ˈkrɔ:s-/ *n* horizontal beam between two supporting parts of a structure; girder.

cross-benches /ˈkrɒsbentʃɪz; *US* ˈkrɔ:s-/ *n* [pl] seats in the British parliament occupied by those members who do not regularly support a particular political party.
▷ **cross-bencher** *n* member of parliament who usu sits on these seats.

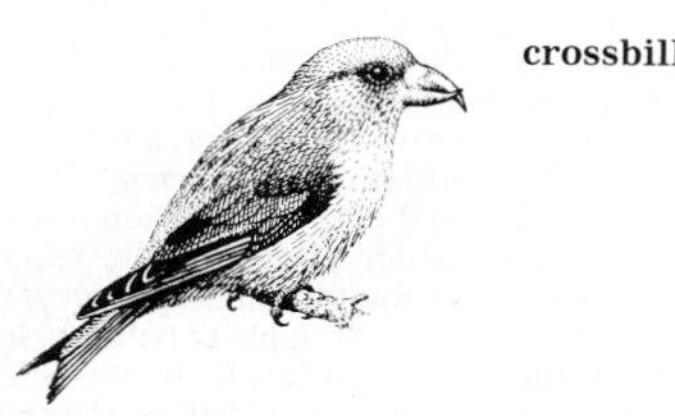
crossbill

crossbill /ˈkrɒsbɪl; *US* ˈkrɔ:sbɪl/ *n* bird with a beak whose upper and lower parts close in a crossed position. ⇨ illus.

cross-bones /ˈkrɒsbəʊnz; *US* ˈkrɔ:s-/ *n* [pl] ⇨ SKULL AND CROSS-BONES (SKULL).

crossbow /ˈkrɒsbəʊ; *US* ˈkrɔ:s-/ *n* small powerful bow mounted horizontally on a grooved support where the arrow is held and then released by pulling a trigger. Cf LONGBOW (LONG[1]).

cross-bred /ˈkrɒsbred; *US* ˈkrɔ:s-/ *adj* produced by different species or varieties breeding together: *a cross-bred sheep, dog, etc.*

cross-breed /ˈkrɒsbri:d; *US* ˈkrɔ:s-/ *n* animal, plant, etc produced by the breeding of different species or varieties.
▷ **cross-breed** *v* [I, Tn] breed (sth) in this way.

cross-check /ˌkrɒs ˈtʃek; *US* ˌkrɔ:s/ *v* [I, Tn, Tn·pr] ~ **sth (against sth)** make sure that information, a calculation, etc is correct by consulting a different source, using a different method, etc: *Cross-check your answer by using a calculator.*
▷ ˈ**cross-check** *n* check made in this way.

cross-country /ˌkrɒs ˈkʌntrɪ; *US* ˌkrɔ:s/ *adj* [usu attrib], *adv* across fields, etc rather than on main roads: *a* ˌ*cross-country* ˈ*run,* ˈ*race, etc* ○ *travel cross-country.*
▷ **cross-country** *n* cross-country race: *enter for the mile and the cross-country.*

cross-current /ˈkrɒs kʌrənt; *US* krɔ:s/ *n* **1** current that crosses another. **2** (*fig*) body of beliefs, views, etc contrary to those of the majority: *a cross-current of opinion against the prevailing view.*

cross-cut /ˈkrɒskʌt; *US* ˈkrɔ:s-/ *adj* [usu attrib] (of a saw, etc) with teeth designed for cutting across the grain of wood: *a cross-cut saw/blade.*

crosse /krɒs; *US* krɔ:s/ *n* curved stick with a net attached to it, used in the game of lacrosse.

cross-examine /ˌkrɒs ɪgˈzæmɪn; *US* ˌkrɔ:s/ *v* [Tn] **1** (*esp law*) question (sb) carefully to test the correctness of answers given to previous questions: *The prosecution lawyer cross-examined the defence witness.* **2** question (sb) aggressively or in great detail: *Whenever he comes in late his wife cross-examines him about where he's spent the evening.* Cf EXAMINE 3.
▷ **cross-examiner** *n.*
cross-examination /ˌkrɒs ɪgˌzæmɪˈneɪʃn; *US* ˌkrɔ:s/ *n* [U, C] (instance of) cross-examining: *He broke down under cross-examination* (ie while being cross-examined) *and admitted the truth.*

cross-eyed /ˈkrɒsaɪd; *US* ˈkrɔ:s-/ *adj* with one or both eyes turned inwards towards the nose.

cross-fertilize, -ise /ˌkrɒs ˈfɜ:təlaɪz; *US* ˌkrɔ:s/ *v* [Tn] **1** (**a**) (*botany*) fertilize (a plant) by using pollen from a different type of plant. (**b**) (*biology*) fertilize (an egg) with sperm from a different type of animal. **2** (*fig*) stimulate (sb/sth) usefully or positively with ideas from a different field, etc: *Literary studies have been cross-fertilized by new ideas in linguistics.* ▷ **cross-fertilization, -isation** /ˌkrɒs ˌfɜ:təlaɪˈzeɪʃn; *US* ˌkrɔ:s ˌfɜ:rtlɪˈzeɪʃn/ *n* [U, C].

cross-fire /ˈkrɒsfaɪə(r); *US* ˈkrɔ:s-/ *n* [U] **1** (*military*) firing of guns from two or more points so that the bullets, shells, etc cross each other. **2** (*fig*) situation in which two people or groups are arguing, competing, etc and another is unwillingly involved: *When two industrial giants clash, small companies can get caught in the cross-fire,* ie harmed incidentally.

cross-grained /ˌkrɒs ˈgreɪnd; *US* ˌkrɔ:s/ *adj* **1** (of wood) with the grain running diagonally or across rather than in a straight line. **2** difficult to please or get on with.

cross-hairs /ˈkrɒsheəz; *US* ˈkrɔ:s-/ (also **cross-wires**) *n* [pl] fine wires arranged in a cross shape used for focussing, eg in a camera or rifle sight.

cross-hatch /ˈkrɒs hætʃ; *US* ˌkrɔ:s/ *v* [Tn] mark or shade (sth) with sets of crossing parallel lines: *cross-hatch an area on a map.*
▷ **cross-hatching** *n* [U] pattern of such lines.

crossing /ˈkrɒsɪŋ; *US* ˈkrɔ:s-/ *n* **1** journey across a sea, wide river, etc: *a rough crossing from Dover to Calais.* **2** place where two roads, two railways, or a road and a railway, cross. Cf LEVEL CROSSING (LEVEL[1]). **3** (**a**) place, esp on a street, where pedestrians can cross safely. Cf PEDESTRIAN CROSSING (PEDESTRIAN), PELICAN CROSSING (PELICAN), ZEBRA CROSSING (ZEBRA). (**b**) place where one crosses from one country to another: *arrested by guards at the border crossing.*

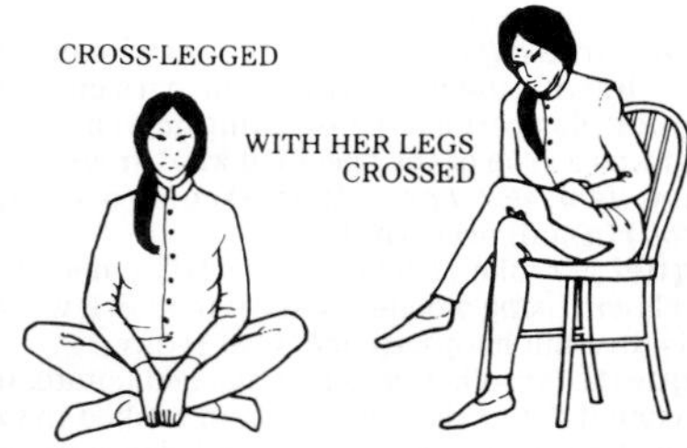

cross-legged /ˌkrɒs ˈlegd; *US* ˌkrɔ:s/ *adv* with one leg over the other, esp at the ankles: *sitting cross-legged on the floor.* ⇨ illus.

cross-over /ˈkrɒsəʊvə(r); *US* ˈkrɔ:s-/ *n* **1** (thing with an) arrangement of two parts, with one crossed over the other: [attrib] *a cross-over skirt.* **2** connection that allows a train or tram to be moved from one set of rails to another.

cross-patch /ˈkrɒspætʃ; *US* ˈkrɔ:s-/ *n* (*dated infml*) bad-tempered person.

cross-piece /ˈkrɒs pi:s; *US* ˈkrɔ:s/ *n* piece (of a structure, tool, etc) lying or fixed across another piece.

cross-ply /ˈkrɒsplaɪ; *US* ˈkrɔ:s-/ *adj* (of tyres) having layers of fabric with cords lying crosswise. Cf RADIAL.

cross-pollinate /ˌkrɒsˈpɒləneɪt; *US* ˌkrɔ:s-/ *v* [Tn] pollinate (a plant) from another.

cross-purposes /ˌkrɒs ˈpɜ:pəsɪz; *US* ˌkrɔ:s-/ *n* (idm) **at cross-**ˈ**purposes** (of people or groups) misunderstanding what the other side is talking about or concerned with: *We're at cross-purposes: I'm talking about astronomy, you're talking about astrology.*

cross-question /ˌkrɒs ˈkwestʃən; *US* ˌkrɔ:s/ *v* [Tn] question (sb) thoroughly and often aggressively; cross-examine(2).

cross-reference /ˌkrɒs ˈrefrəns; *US* ˌkrɔ:s/ *n* ~ (**to sth**) note directing a reader to another part of a book, file, etc for further information: *follow up all the cross-references.*
▷ **cross-reference** *v* [Tn usu passive] provide (a book, etc) with cross-references.

crossroads /ˈkrɒsrəʊdz; *US* ˈkrɔ:s-/ *n* **1** [sing *v*] place where two roads meet and cross: *We came to a crossroads.* **2** (idm) **at a/the** ˈ**crossroads** at a decisive point in one's life, career, etc: *Our business is at the crossroads: if this deal succeeds, our future is assured; if not, we shall be bankrupt.*

cross-section /ˌkrɒs ˈsekʃn; *US* ˌkrɔ:s/ *n* **1** (picture of the) surface formed by cutting through sth, esp at right angles: *examining a cross-section of the kidney under the microscope* ○ *The girder is square in cross-section.* **2** typical or representative sample: *a cross-section of the electors, population, etc* ○ *a broad cross-section of opinion.*

cross-stitch /ˈkrɒs stɪtʃ; *US* ˈkrɔ:s/ *n* **1** [C] stitch formed by two stitches crossing each other. **2** [U] needlework in which this stitch is used.

cross-talk /ˈkrɒs tɔ:k; *US* ˈkrɔ:s/ *n* [U] (*Brit*) rapid dialogue, eg between two comedians.

cross-town /ˈkrɒstaʊn; *US* ˈkrɔ:s-/ *adj* [attrib] (*US*) going across a town (rather than in and out of the centre): *a cross-town bus.*

cross-trees /ˈkrɒstri:z; *US* ˈkrɔ:s-/ *n* [pl] (*nautical*) two horizontal pieces of wood fastened to a lower mast to support the mast above and to support ropes, etc.

crosswalk /ˈkrɒswɔ:k; *US* ˈkrɔ:s-/ *n* (*US*) = PEDESTRIAN CROSSING (PEDESTRIAN).

cross-wind /ˈkrɒswɪnd; *US* ˈkrɔ:s-/ *n* wind blowing across the direction in which cars, aircraft, etc are travelling: *Strong cross-winds blew the aircraft off course.*

cross-wires /ˈkrɒswaɪəz; *US* ˈkrɔ:s-/ *n* [pl] = CROSS-HAIRS.

crosswise /ˈkrɒs waɪz; *US* ˈkrɔ:s/ *adj* [attrib], *adv* **1** across, esp diagonally: *a yellow flag with a red band going crosswise from top left to bottom right.* **2** in the form of a cross.

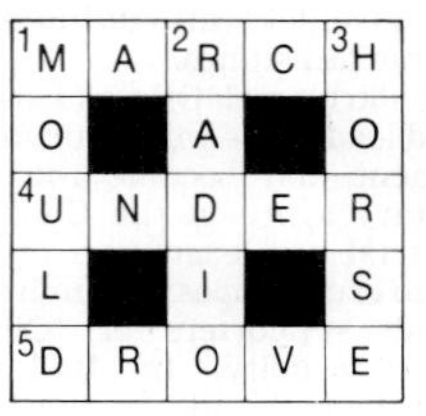

crossword

crossword /ˈkrɒswɜ:d; *US* ˈkrɔ:s-/ *n* (also ˈ**crossword puzzle**) puzzle in which words indicated by numbered clues have to be inserted vertically (clues *down*) and horizontally (clues *across*) in spaces on a chequered square. ⇨ illus.

crotch /krɒtʃ/ (also **crutch**) *n* place where a person's legs, or trouser legs, join at the top.

crotchet /ˈkrɒtʃɪt/ *n* (*US* ˈ**quarter note**) (*music*) note equal to half a minim. ⇨ illus at MUSIC.

crotchety /ˈkrɒtʃɪtɪ/ *adj* (*infml*) bad-tempered.

crouch /kraʊtʃ/ *v* [I, Ip] lower the body by bending

the knees, eg in fear or to hide: *The cat crouched, ready to leap.* ○ *I crouched behind the sofa.*

▷ **crouch** *n* [sing] crouching position: *drop down into a crouch.* ⇨ illus at KNEEL.

croup[1] /kru:p/ *n* [U] disease of children, in which there is coughing and difficulty in breathing.

croup[2] /kru:p/ *n* rump or buttocks of certain animals, esp the horse. ⇨ illus at HORSE.

croupier /ˈkru:pɪəɪ; *US* -pɪər/ *n* person in charge of a gambling table, who deals out the cards, throws the dice, etc and pays out money to the winner(s).

crouton /ˈkru:tɒn/ *n* (*French*) cube of toasted or fried bread, usu served with soup.

crow[1] /krəʊ/ *n* **1** any of various types of large black bird with a harsh cry. ⇨ illus at BIRD. **2** (idm) **as the ˈcrow flies** in a straight line. **eat crow** ⇨ EAT. **stone the crows** ⇨ STONE.

□ **ˈcrow's-feet** *n* [pl] wrinkles in the skin around the outer corner of the eye.

ˈcrow's-nest *n* platform fixed to the top of a ship's mast from which sb can see clearly a long way in all directions.

crow[2] /krəʊ/ *v* (*pt* **crowed** or, in archaic use, **crew** /kru:/, *pp* **crowed**) **1** [I] (of a cock) make a loud shrill cry, esp at dawn. **2** [I] (of a baby) make sounds showing pleasure. **3** [I, Ipr] ~ **(over sb/sth)** (*derog*) express gleeful triumph (about one's success, etc): *She won the competition and won't stop crowing (over her rivals/her rivals' failure).*

▷ **crow** *n* [sing] crowing sound.

crowbar /ˈkrəʊbɑ:(r)/ *n* straight iron bar, usu with a hooked end, used as a lever to open crates, move heavy objects, etc.

crowd[1] /kraʊd/ *n* **1** [CGp] **(a)** large number of people gathered together in the open: *A crowd had already collected outside the embassy gates.* ○ *He pushed his way through the crowd.* ○ *Police had to break up the crowd.* ○ [attrib] *crowd control.* **(b)** mass of spectators; audience: *The match attracted a large crowd.* ○ *The crowd cheered the winning hit.* **2 the crowd** [sing] (*derog*) people in general: *move with the crowd,* ie do as everybody else does. **3** [CGp] (*infml*) group; company: *I don't associate with that crowd.* **4** (idm) **crowds/a (whole) crowd (of)** very many (people): *There were crowds of people waiting to get in.* ○ *A whole crowd of us arrived at the party uninvited.* **follow the crowd** ⇨ FOLLOW. **rise above the crowds** ⇨ RISE[2].

□ **ˈcrowd-puller** *n* (*infml*) person or thing that attracts a large audience.

crowd[2] /kraʊd/ *v* **1** [Ipr, Ip] ~ **around/round (sb)** gather closely around (sb): *People crowded round to get a better view.* ○ *Pupils crowded round (their teacher) to ask questions.* **2** [Tn] fill (a space) so that there is little room to move: *Tourists crowded the pavement.* ○ *crowd a restaurant, theatre, beach, etc.* **3** [Tn] (*infml*) put pressure on (sb); harass: *Don't crowd me: give me time to think!* **4** (idm) **crowd on ˈsail** (*nautical*) raise many sails in order to increase speed. **5** (phr v) **crowd in on sb** (of thoughts, etc) come into the mind in large numbers: *Memories crowded in on me.* **crowd into sth; crowd in** move in large numbers into a small space: *Supporters crowded through the gates into the stadium.* ○ *We'd all crowded into Harriet's small sitting-room.* ○ (*fig*) *Disturbing thoughts crowded into my mind.* **crowd sb/sth into sth; crowd sb/sth in** put many people or things into a small space or period of time; cram (sb/sth) into sth: *They crowd people into the buses.* ○ *Guests were crowded into the few remaining rooms.* ○ *She crowds too much detail into her paintings.* **crowd sb/sth out (of sth)** **(a)** keep sb/sth out of a space by filling it oneself: *The restaurant's regular customers are being crowded out by tourists.* **(b)** prevent sb/sth from operating successfully: *Small shops are being crowded out by the big supermarkets.*

▷ **crowded** *adj* **1** having (too) many people: *crowded buses, roads, hotels.* **2** (*fig*) ~ **(with sth)** full (of sth): *days crowded with activity* ○ *We had a very crowded schedule on the trip.*

crown[1] /kraʊn/ *n* **1** **(a)** [C] ornamental head-dress made of gold, jewels, etc worn by a king or queen on official occasions. **(b)** **(the Crown** or **the crown)** [sing] the State as represented by a king or queen as its head: *land owned by the Crown* ○ *a minister of the Crown* ○ *Who appears for the Crown* (ie Who is prosecuting the accused person on behalf of the State) *in this case?* ○ [attrib] *Crown land, property, etc* ○ *a crown witness,* ie for the prosecution in a criminal case. **(c) the crown** [sing] the office or power of a king or queen: *She refused the crown,* ie refused to become queen. ○ *relinquish the crown,* ie abdicate. **2** [C] circle or wreath of flowers, leaves, etc worn on the head, esp as a sign of victory, or as a reward: *Christ's crown of thorns* ○ (*fig*) *two boxers fighting it out for the world heavyweight crown,* ie championship. **3** (usu **the crown**) [sing] **(a)** top of the head or of a hat. **(b)** top part of anything: *the crown of a hill, tree* ○ *the crown* (ie the highest part of the curved surface) *of a road* ○ *A motor cycle overtook us on the crown* (ie the middle or most curved part) *of the bend.* **4** [C] **(a)** part of the tooth that is visible outside the gum. **(b)** artificial replacement for this. **5** [C] crown-shaped emblem or ornament, eg a crest or badge: *A major has a crown on the shoulder of his uniform.* **6** [C] former British coin worth 5 shillings (25p).

□ ˌ**crown ˈcolony** colony ruled directly by the British government.

ˌ**crown ˈcourt** (in England and Wales) local court in which serious criminal cases are tried. Cf COUNTY COURT (COUNTY). ⇨ article at LAW.

ˌ**Crown ˈDerby** [U] type of fine china once made in Derby, marked with a crown over a letter D.

ˌ**crown ˈglass** [U] type of very clear glass often used in optical instruments.

ˌ**crown ˈgreen** type of bowling green found esp in N England with a slightly raised centre.

ˌ**crown ˈjewels** crown and other regalia worn or carried by a king or queen on formal occasions.

ˌ**crown ˈprince** prince who will become the next king.

ˌ**crown prinˈcess** wife of a crown prince.

ˈ**crown wheel** wheel in a piece of machinery that has teeth or cogs on its side.

crown[2] /kraʊn/ *v* **1** [Tn, Cn·n] put a crown on the head of (a new king or queen) as a sign of royal power: *She was crowned (queen) in 1952.* ○ *the crowned heads* (ie kings and queens) *of Europe.* **2** [Tn, Tn·pr usu passive] ~ **sth (with sth)** **(a)** (*rhet*) form or cover the top of sth: *The hill is crowned with a wood.* ○ *Beautiful fair hair crowns her head.* **(b)** complete or conclude sth in a worthy or perfect way: *The award of this prize crowned his career.* ○ *efforts that were finally crowned with success.* **3** [Tn] (*infml*) hit (sb) on the head: *Shut up or I'll crown you.* **4** [Tn] (also **cap**) put an artificial top on (a tooth). Cf CROWN[1] 4. (idm) **to crown it ˈall** as the final event in a series of fortunate or unfortunate events: *It was cold, raining, and, to crown it all, we had to walk home.*

▷ **crowning** *adj* [attrib] making perfect or complete: *The performance provided the crowning touch to the evening's entertainments.* ○ *the crowning success of her career* ○ *Her crowning glory is her hair.* ○ *The crowning* (ie most extreme) *irony was that I didn't even like her.*

crozier = CROSIER.

CRT /ˌsi: ɑ: ˈti:/ *abbr* cathode-ray tube.

crucial /ˈkru:ʃl/ *adj* ~ **(to/for sth)** very important; decisive: *a crucial decision, issue, factor* ○ *at the crucial moment* ○ *Getting this contract is crucial to the future of our company.* ▷ **crucially** /-ʃəlɪ/ *adv.*

crucible /ˈkru:sɪbl/ *n* **1** pot in which metals are melted. **2** (*fig rhet*) severe test or trial: *The alliance had been forged in the crucible of war.*

cruciferous /kru:ˈsɪfərəs/ *adj* (of a plant) belonging to the cabbage family, with flowers that have four petals of equal size and shape.

crucifix /ˈkru:sɪfɪks/ *n* model of the Cross with the figure of Jesus on it.

crucifixion /ˌkru:sɪˈfɪkʃn/ *n* [C, U] (instance of) crucifying or being crucified: *the Crucifixion,* ie of Jesus.

cruciform /ˈkru:sɪfɔ:m/ *adj* cross-shaped.

crucify /ˈkru:sɪfaɪ/ *v* (*pt, pp* **-fied**) [Tn] **1** kill (sb) by nailing or tying him to a cross[1](2a). **2** (*fig infml*) deal with (sb) very severely: *The minister was crucified* (ie very severely criticized) *in the press for his handling of the affair.*

crud /krʌd/ *n* (*infml esp US*) **1** [U] slimy or sticky substance; sth dirty or unwanted: *all the crud in the bottom of the saucepan.* **2** [C] (*offensive*) unpleasant person.

▷ **cruddy** *adj* (*infml esp US*) unpleasant.

crude /kru:d/ *adj* **(-r, -st)** **1** [usu attrib] in the natural state; unrefined: *crude oil, sugar, ore, etc.* **2** **(a)** not well finished; not completely worked out; rough: *a crude sketch, method, approximation* ○ *His paintings are rather crude,* ie not skilfully done. ○ *I made my own crude garden furniture.* ○ *You get a false impression from the crude statistics,* ie before they are properly adjusted. **(b)** not showing taste or refinement; coarse: *crude manners* ○ *He made some crude* (ie sexually offensive) *jokes.*

▷ **crudely** *adv*: *crudely assembled* ○ *express oneself crudely.*

crudity /ˈkru:dɪtɪ/ *n* [U] **1** state or quality of being crude(2a): *the crudity of his drawing.* **2** crude(2b) behaviour, remarks, etc: *I'd never met such crudity before.*

cruel /krʊəl/ *adj* **(-ller, -llest)** **1** (*derog*) ~ **(to sb/sth)** (of people) making others suffer, esp intentionally: *a cruel boss, master, dictator, etc* ○ *people oppressed by a cruel tyranny* ○ *Don't be cruel to animals.* **2** causing pain or suffering: *a cruel blow, punishment, disease* ○ *cruel* (ie bad) *luck* ○ *War is cruel.* **3** (idm) **be ˌcruel to be ˈkind** act severely so as to achieve a good result later: *You may resent the punishment now, but your father's only being cruel to be kind,* ie acting in the hope of making you a better person. ▷ **cruelly** /ˈkrʊəlɪ/ *adv*: *I was cruelly deceived.*

cruelty /ˈkrʊəltɪ/ *n* **1** [U] ~ **(to sb/sth)** readiness to cause pain or suffering to others; cruel actions: *his cruelty to his children* ○ *He saw a lot of cruelty in the prison camp.* **2** [C usu *pl*] cruel act: *the tyrant's infamous cruelties.*

cruet /ˈkru:ɪt/ *n* **1** small glass bottle containing oil or vinegar for use at meals. **2** (also ˈ**cruet-stand**) stand for holding cruets and containers for salt, pepper, mustard, etc.

Cruft's /krʌfts/ international dog show held each year in Britain. ⇨ article at ANIMAL.

George Cruickshank: illustration for Dickens's 'Oliver Twist'

Cruickshank /ˈkrʊkʃæŋk/ George (1792-1878), English artist. He is famous for his political cartoons, ridiculing figures like the Prince Regent (the future *George IV) and *Napoleon. He also illustrated the works of many famous novelists including *Dickens and *Scott. ⇨ illus.

cruise /kru:z/ *v* **1** [I, Ipr, Ip] sail about, either for pleasure or, in wartime, looking for enemy ships: *a destroyer cruising about (in) the Baltic Sea.* **2 (a)** [I, Ipr, Ip] (of a motor vehicle or an aircraft) travel at a moderate speed, using fuel efficiently: *cruising at 10 000 ft/350 miles per hour* ○ *a cruising speed of 50 miles per hour.* **(b)** [I, Ipr, Ip] drive a vehicle at a moderate speed: *Taxis cruised about, hoping to pick up late fares.* **3** [I] (*sl*) (esp of a homosexual) go about in public places looking for someone to have sex with.

▷ **cruise** *n* pleasure voyage: *go on/for a cruise* ○ *a round-the-world cruise* ○ [attrib] *a cruise ship.*

cruiser /ˈkruːzə(r)/ *n* **1** large warship. **2** (also **ˈcabin-cruiser**) motor boat with sleeping accommodation, etc, used for pleasure trips.

□ **ˈcruise missile** missile, usu with a nuclear warhead, that flies at low altitude and is guided by its own computer. ⇨ article at PROTEST.

cruller /ˈkrʌlə(r)/ *n* (*US*) small cake made of dough that is twisted and fried.

crumb /krʌm/ *n* **1** [C] very small piece, esp of bread, cake or biscuit, which has fallen off a larger piece: *sweep the crumbs off the table.* **2** [U] soft inner part of a loaf of bread. **3** [C] small piece or amount: *a few crumbs of information* ○ *I failed my exam, and my only crumb of comfort* (ie the only thing that consoles me) *is that I can take it again.* **4** [C] (*infml esp US*) contemptible person: *You little crumb!*

crumble /ˈkrʌmbl/ *v* **1** [I, Ipr, Ip, Tn, Tn·pr, Tn·p] ~ **(sth) (into/to sth)**; ~ **(sth) (up)** (cause sth to) be broken or rubbed into very small pieces: *crumble one's bread*, ie break it into crumbs ○ *The bricks slowly crumbled in the long frost.* ○ *crumbling walls*, ie that are breaking apart. **2** [I, Ipr] ~ **(into/to sth)** (*fig*) gradually deteriorate or come to an end: *The great empire began to crumble.* ○ *hopes that crumbled to dust* ○ *Their marriage is crumbling.* **3** (idm) **that's the way the cookie crumbles** ⇨ WAY[1].

▷ **crumble** *n* [U, C] pudding of stewed fruit with a crumbly topping of pastry, breadcrumbs, etc: *apple, rhubarb, etc crumble.*

crumbly /ˈkrʌmblɪ/ *adj* (**-ier, -iest**) that crumbles easily: *crumbly bread, soil, etc.*

crumbs /krʌmz/ *interj* (*Brit infml*) (used to express surprise, apprehension, etc).

crummy /ˈkrʌmɪ/ *adj* (**-ier, -iest**) (*infml*) bad; worthless; unpleasant: *a crummy little street in the worst part of town.*

crumpet /ˈkrʌmpɪt/ *n* **1** [C] (in Britain) flat round unsweetened cake, usu toasted and eaten hot with butter. **2** [U] (*Brit sl sexist*) women, regarded simply as sexually desirable objects: *There's not much crumpet around at this party.* **3** (idm) **a bit of crumpet/fluff/skirt/stuff** ⇨ BIT[1].

crumple /ˈkrʌmpl/ *v* **1** [I, Ipr, Ip, Tn, Tn·pr, Tn·p] ~ **(sth) (into sth)**; ~ **(sth) (up)** (cause sth to) be pressed or crushed into folds or creases: *material that crumples easily* ○ *a crumpled (up) suit* ○ *The front of the car crumpled on impact.* ○ *He crumpled the paper (up) into a ball.* ○ (*fig*) *The child's face crumpled up and he began to cry.* **2** [I, Ip] ~ **(up)** (*fig*) come suddenly to an end; collapse: *Her resistance to the proposal has crumpled.*

crunch /krʌntʃ/ (also **scrunch**) *v* **1** [Tn, Tn·p] ~ **sth (up)** crush sth noisily with the teeth when eating: *crunch peanuts, biscuits, etc* ○ *The dog was crunching a bone.* **2** [I, Tn] (cause sth to) make a harsh grating noise: *The frozen snow crunched under our feet.* ○ *The wheels crunched the gravel.*

▷ **crunch** *n* **1** (also **scrunch**) (usu *sing*) noise made by crunching; act of crunching: *There was a crunch as he bit the apple.* **2** (idm) **if/when it comes to the ˈcrunch; if/when the ˈcrunch comes** if/when the decisive moment comes: *He always says he'll help, but when it comes to the crunch, he does nothing.*

crunchy *adj* (**-ier, -iest**) (*often approv*) firm and crisp, and making a sharp sound when broken or crushed: *crunchy biscuits, snow.*

crupper /ˈkrʌpə(r)/ *n* **1** leather strap fixed to a saddle or harness and looped under a horse's tail. **2** rear part of a horse, above the back legs.

crusade /kruːˈseɪd/ *n* **1** any one of the military expeditions by the European Christian countries to recover the Holy Land from the Muslims in the Middle Ages. **2** ~ **(for/against sth)**; ~ **(to do sth)** any struggle or campaign for sth believed to be good, or against sth believed to be bad: *a crusade against corruption.*

▷ **crusade** *v* [I, Ipr] ~ **(for/against sth)** take part in a crusade: *crusading for fairer treatment of minorities.*

crusader *n* person taking part in a crusade.

cruse /kruːz/ *n* (*arch*) jar or pot made of earthenware.

crush[1] /krʌʃ/ *v* **1** [Tn, Tn·pr] press or squeeze (sth/sb) hard so that there is breakage or injury: *Don't crush the box; it has flowers in it.* ○ *Wine is made by crushing grapes.* ○ *Several people were crushed to death by the falling rocks.* **2** [Tn, Tn·p] ~ **sth (up)** break sth hard into small pieces or into powder by pressing: *Huge hammers crush (up) the rocks.* **3** [I, Tn] (cause sth to) become full of creases or irregular folds: *The clothes were badly crushed in the suitcase.* ○ *Some synthetic materials do not crush easily.* **4** [Tn] defeat (sb/sth) completely; subdue: *The rebellion was crushed by government forces.* ○ *Her refusal crushed all our hopes.* ○ *He felt completely crushed* (ie humiliated) *by her last remark.* **5** (phr v) **crush (sb/sth) into, past, through, etc sth** (cause sb/sth to) move into or through a narrow space by pressing or pushing: *A large crowd crushed past (the barrier).* ○ *You can't crush twenty people into such a tiny room.* ○ *The postman tried to crush the packet through the letter-box.* **crush sth out (of sth)** remove sth by pressing or squeezing: *crush the juice out of oranges* ○ (*fig*) *With his hands round her throat he crushed the life out of her.*

▷ **crushing** *adj* [usu attrib] **1** overwhelming: *a crushing defeat, blow, etc.* **2** intended to subdue or humiliate: *a crushing look, remark, etc.* **crushingly** *adv.*

crush[2] /krʌʃ/ *n* **1** [sing] crowd of people pressed close together: *a big crush in the theatre bar* ○ *I couldn't get through the crush.* **2** [C] ~ **(on sb)** (*infml*) strong but typically brief liking (for sb); infatuation: *Schoolchildren often have/get crushes on teachers.* **3** [U] (*Brit*) drink made from fruit juice: *lemon crush.*

□ **ˈcrush barrier** fence put up to control crowds.

crust /krʌst/ *n* **1 (a)** [C, U] hard outer surface of a loaf of bread; pastry covering of a pie, tart, etc: *a white loaf with a crisp brown crust* ○ *Cut the crusts off when you make sandwiches.* ⇨ illus at BREAD. **(b)** [C] (*esp rhet*) slice of bread, esp a thin dry one: (*fig*) *He'd share his last crust with you*, ie is very unselfish. **2** [C, U] hard surface: *a thin crust of ice, frozen snow, etc* ○ *the Earth's crust*, ie the part nearest its surface. **3** [C, U] hard deposit on the inside of a bottle of wine, esp old port. **4** (idm) **the upper crust** ⇨ UPPER.

▷ **crust** *v* (phr v) **crust over** become covered with a crust: *The surface of the liquid gradually crusted over.*

crusted *adj* **1** [usu pred] ~ **(with sth)** having a hardened covering; encrusted: *walls crusted with dirt.* **2** [usu attrib] (of port) blended from different vintages and matured in bottles.

crustacean /krʌˈsteɪʃn/ *n* any of various types of animal (eg crabs, lobsters, shrimps) that have a hard outer shell and live mostly in water; shellfish.

crusty /ˈkrʌstɪ/ *adj* (**-ier, -iest**) **1** having or resembling a crisp crust: *crusty French bread* ○ *a crusty pizza base.* **2** (*infml*) (esp of older people or their behaviour) easily angered; short-tempered: *a crusty old soldier.*

crutch /krʌtʃ/ *n* **1** support in the form of a pole, placed under the armpit to help a lame person to walk: *a pair of crutches* ○ *go about on crutches.* ⇨ illus. **2** (*fig*) person or thing that provides help or support: *He uses his wife as a kind of crutch because of his lack of confidence.* **3** = CROTCH: *These trousers are too tight in the crutch.*

crux /krʌks/ *n* [sing] most vital or difficult part of a matter, an issue, etc: *Now we come to the crux of the problem.*

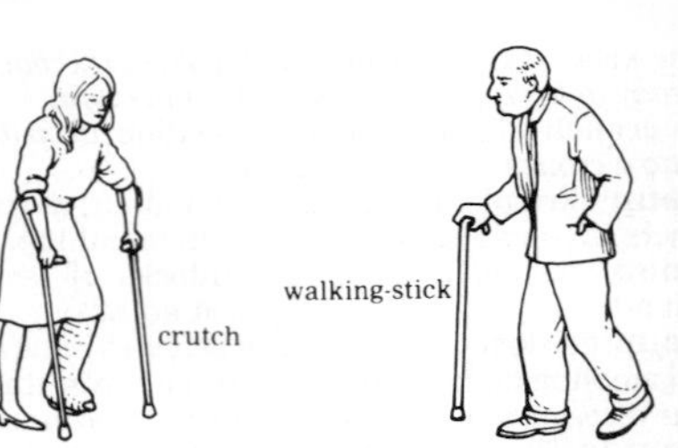

cry[1] /kraɪ/ *v* (*pt, pp* **cried**) **1** [I, Ipr, Tn no passive] ~ **(for/over sth/sb)**; ~ **(with sth)** weep; shed (tears): *He cried because he had hurt his knee.* ○ *cry for joy*, ie because one is happy ○ *The child was crying for* (ie because he wanted) *his mother.* ○ *cry with pain, hunger, etc* ○ *How many tears have I cried over* (ie because of) *you?* ⇨ Usage. **2 (a)** [I, Ip] ~ **(out)** (of people, animals, birds) make loud wordless sounds expressing fear, pain, etc: *The monkeys cry (out) shrilly when they see danger.* ○ *She cried (out) in pain when her tooth was pulled out.* ⇨ Usage at SHOUT. **(b)** [Ipr, Ip, Tn no passive] ~ **(out) (for sth)** call out loudly in words; exclaim: *He cried (out) for mercy.* ○ *'Help, help!' he cried.* ○ (*rhet*) *But what about the workers, I hear you cry*, ie say. **3** [Tn] (*dated*) announce (goods, etc) for sale by calling out: *cry one's wares.* **4** (idm) **cry one's ˈeyes/ˈheart out** weep bitterly. **cry over spilt ˈmilk** express regret for sth that has happened and cannot be remedied: *You've broken it now; it's no use crying over spilt milk!* **cry/sob oneself to sleep** ⇨ SLEEP[1]. **cry ˈwolf** say there is danger when there is none. **for ˌcrying out ˈloud** (used to express protest): *For crying out loud! Why did you do that?* **laugh till/until one cries** ⇨ LAUGH. **a shoulder to cry on** ⇨ SHOULDER. **5** (phr v) **cry sth down** say that sth is not very good, important, etc: *Don't cry down her real achievements.* **cry off** withdraw from sth one has promised to do: *I said I would go, but had to cry off at the last moment.* **cry out for sth** demand sth; require sth: *People are crying out for free elections.* ○ *This system is crying out for reform*, ie urgently needs to be reformed. **cry sb/sth up** (*infml sometimes derog*) praise or recommend sb/sth, esp exaggeratedly or undeservedly: *People are always crying up foreign cars.*

NOTE ON USAGE: Compare **cry**, **sob**, **weep**, **wail** and **whimper.** They all indicate people expressing emotions, often with tears. **Cry** has the widest use and may be the result of unhappiness, joy, etc or, especially with babies, of physical discomfort: *The little boy was crying because he was lost.* ○ *Babies cry when they are hungry.* **Weep** is more formal than cry and can suggest stronger emotions: *The hostages wept for joy on their release.* **Sob** indicates crying with irregular and noisy breathing. It is usually associated with misery: *He sobbed for hours when his cat died.* Children **whimper** with fear or in complaint. **Wail** indicates long noisy crying in grief or complaint: *The mourners were wailing loudly.* Note that all these verbs can be used instead of 'say' to indicate a way of speaking: *'I've lost my daddy,' the little boy cried/sobbed/wept/whimpered/wailed.*

cry[2] /kraɪ/ *n* **1** [C] **(a)** loud wordless sound expressing grief, pain, joy, etc: *a cry of terror* ○ *the cry of an animal in pain.* **(b)** loud utterance of words; call; shout: *angry cries from the mob.* **(c)** (usu *sing*) characteristic call of an animal or a bird: *the cry of the rook.* **2** [sing] act or period of weeping: *Have a good long cry: it will do you good.* **3** [C] (*dated*) words shouted to give information: *the cry of the night-watchman* ○ *the old street cries of London, eg 'Fresh herrings!'* **4** [C] (esp in compounds) slogan or phrase, used for a principle or cause: *a ˈbattle-cry* ○ *a ˈwar-cry* ○ *'Lower taxes' was their cry* (ie their public demand.). **5** (idm) **a far cry from sth/from doing sth** ⇨ FAR[1]. **hue and cry** ⇨ HUE[2]. **in full cry** ⇨ FULL.

□ **ˈcry-baby** *n* (*infml derog*) person who weeps too often or without good reason: *He's a dreadfu* *cry-baby*.

crying /ˈkraɪɪŋ/ *adj* [attrib] **1** (esp of sth bad, wrong, etc) extremely bad and shocking: *It's a crying shame, the way they treat their children.* **2** great and urgent (used esp in the expression shown): *a crying need.*

cryogenics /ˌkraɪəˈdʒenɪks/ *n* [sing *v*] scientific study or use of very low temperatures. Modern techniques can achieve extremely low temperatures at which the properties of many materials change. For example some lose all electrical resistance and are used as *superconductors, and some electronic devices become much more sensitive. ▷ **cryogenic** *adj.*

cryosurgery /ˌkraɪəʊˈsɜːdʒəri/ *n* [U] surgical treatment using extremely low temperatures, esp as a form of anaesthetic.

crypt /krɪpt/ *n* room beneath the floor of a church.

cryptic /ˈkrɪptɪk/ *adj* with a meaning that is hidden or not easily understood; mysterious: *a cryptic remark, message, smile, etc.* ▷ **cryptically** /-kli/ *adv*: *'Yes and no,' she replied cryptically.*

□ ˌ**cryptic coloˈration** colouring of certain animals that makes them less visible in their natural surroundings, and so protects them from their enemies.

crypt(o)- *comb form* (forming *ns*) hidden; secret: *cryptogram* ○ *a crypto-ˈfascist*, ie a person who has fascist sympathies but keeps them secret.

cryptogam /ˈkrɪptəgæm/ *n* any flowerless plant, such as a fern, moss or fungus.

cryptogram /ˈkrɪptəgræm/ *n* message written in code.

crystal /ˈkrɪstl/ *n* **1** (a) [U] transparent colourless mineral, such as quartz. (b) [C] piece of this, esp when used as an ornament: *a necklace of crystals* ○ [attrib] *a crystal bracelet, watch, etc.* **2** [U] high-quality glassware, made into bowls, vases, glasses, etc: *The dining-table shone with silver and crystal.* ○ [attrib] *a crystal vase, chandelier, etc.* **3** [C] (*chemistry*) regular many-sided shape which the atoms, ions or molecules of a substance can form when it is solid: *sugar and salt crystals* ○ *snow and ice crystals.* **4** [C] (*US*) glass or plastic cover of the face of a watch.

□ **crystal ˈball** clear glass sphere in which future events can supposedly be seen.

crystal ˈclear **1** (of glass, water, etc) entirely clear. **2** (*fig*) very easy to understand; completely understood: *I want to make my meaning crystal clear.*

ˈ**crystal-gazing** *n* [U] **1** looking into a crystal ball. **2** (*fig*) attempting to foretell future events.

ˈ**crystal set** early type of radio set.

crystalline /ˈkrɪstəlaɪn/ *adj* **1** made of or resembling crystals: *crystalline structure, minerals, etc.* **2** (*fml*) very clear; transparent: *water of crystalline purity.*

crystallize, -ise /ˈkrɪstəlaɪz/ *v* **1** [I, Tn] (cause sth to) form into crystals. **2** [I, Ipr, Tn, Tn·pr] ~ (**sth**) (**into sth**) (*fig*) (of ideas, plans, etc) become clear and definite; cause (ideas, plans, etc) to become clear and definite: *His vague ideas crystallized into a definite plan.* ○ *Reading your book helped crystallize my views.*

▷ **crystallization, -isation** /krɪstəlaɪˈzeɪʃn; *US* -lɪˈz-/ *n* [U].

crystallized, -ised *adj* (esp of fruit) preserved in sugar and covered with sugar-crystals: *a box of crystallized oranges.*

crystallography /krɪstəˈlɒgrəfi/ *n* [U] scientific study of the structure of crystals.

crystalloid /ˈkrɪstəlɔɪd/ *n* substance that has a crystal structure.

Crystal Palace /krɪstl ˈpælɪs/ large building of iron and glass, designed by Paxton for the British *Great Exhibition of 1851. It was later moved to south London where a fire destroyed it in 1936. ⇨ article at ARCHITECTURE.

Cs *symb* caesium.

c/s *abbr* = CPS.

CS gas /ˌsiːes ˈgæs/ type of gas used in riot control, causing severe irritation to the mouth, eyes, throat and respiratory system.

CSM /ˌsiː es ˈem/ *abbr* (*Brit*) Company Sergeant-Major.

CST /ˌsiː es ˈtiː/ *abbr* (*US*) Central Standard Time.

ct *abbr* (*pl* **cts**) **1** carat: *an 18 ct gold ring.* **2** cent: *50 cts.*

Cu *symb* copper.

cu *abbr* cubic: *a volume of 2 cu m*, ie 2 cubic metres.

cub /kʌb/ *n* **1** [C] young fox, bear, lion, tiger, etc. **2** (a) **the Cubs** [pl] junior branch of the Scout Association: *to join the Cubs.* (b) **Cub** [C] (also ˈ**Cub Scout**) member of this. **3** (*dated*) rude young man: *You cheeky young cub!*

□ ˈ**cub reporter** young and inexperienced newspaper reporter.

Cuba

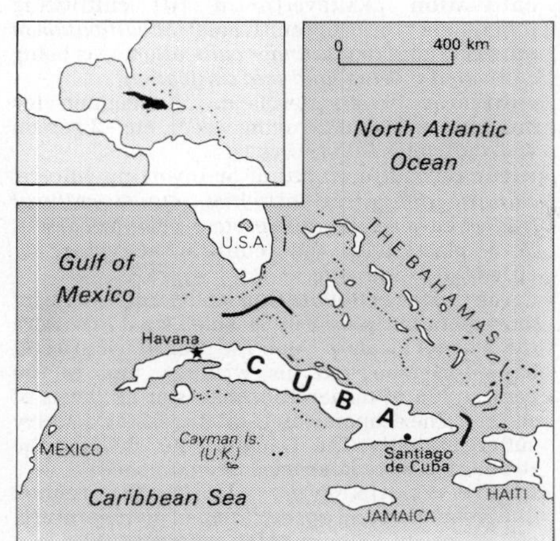

Cuba /ˈkjuːbə/ island and country in the Caribbean Sea; pop approx 10 410 000; official language Spanish; capital Havana; unit of currency peso (= 100 cents). Although there are mineral resources, the economy is based on sugar and tobacco. After the Communist revolution of 1959, Cuba traded mainly with the USSR, which gave it much economic aid until the late 1980s. Relations with the USA have improved slightly over recent years. ⇨ map. ▷ **Cuban** *adj, n.*

cubby-hole /ˈkʌbɪ həʊl/ *n* small enclosed space or room: *My office is a cubby-hole in the basement.*

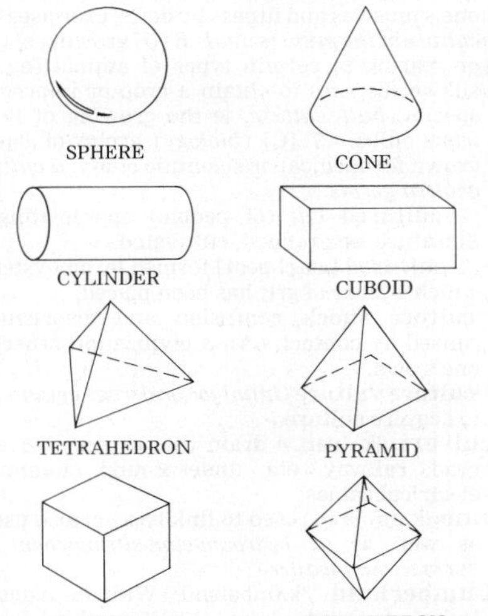

cube and other three-dimensional shapes

cube /kjuːb/ *n* **1** (a) (*geometry*) solid body with six equal square faces ⇨ illus. (b) six-sided piece of sth, esp food: *an ice cube* ○ *Cut the meat into cubes.* **2** (*mathematics*) result of multiplying a number by itself twice: *The cube of 5 (5^3) is 125 ($5 \times 5 \times 5 = 125$).* ⇨ App 10.

▷ **cube** *v* **1** [Tn usu passive] (*mathematics*) multiply (a number) by itself twice: *10 cubed is 1000.* **2** [Tn] cut (food) into cubes.

□ ˌ**cube ˈroot** number which, when cubed, produces the stated number: *The cube root of 64 ($\sqrt[3]{64}$) is 4 ($4 \times 4 \times 4 = 64$).*

cubic /ˈkjuːbɪk/ *adj* **1** [attrib] (a) having the volume of a cube with sides of the specified length: *a cubic metre of coal* ○ *a car with a 2000 cc capacity*, ie 2000 cubic centimetres. (b) measured or expressed in cubic units: *cubic content.* **2** (having the shape) of a cube: *a cubic figure.*

cubical /ˈkjuːbɪkl/ *adj* = CUBIC 2.

cubicle /ˈkjuːbɪkl/ *n* small compartment made by separating off part of a larger room, eg for dressing, undressing or sleeping in.

cubism /ˈkjuːbɪzəm/ *n* [U] modern style of art in which objects are represented as if they are made up of geometrical shapes.

▷ **cubist** /ˈkjuːbɪst/ *adj* (in the style) of cubism. — *n* cubist artist.

cubit /ˈkjuːbɪt/ *n* measure of length used in ancient times, roughly equal to the length of a man's forearm.

cuboid /ˈkjuːbɔɪd/ *n* (*mathematics*) solid with six rectangular faces. ⇨ illus at CUBE.

cuckold /ˈkʌkəʊld/ *n* (*arch usu derog*) man whose wife has committed adultery.

▷ **cuckold** *v* [Tn] (*arch*) (a) (of a man) make (another man) a cuckold by having sex with his wife. (b) (of a woman) make (her husband) a cuckold by having sex with another man.

cuckoo[1] /ˈkʊkuː/ *n* migratory bird with a call that sounds like its name, that leaves its eggs in the nests of other birds.

□ ˈ**cuckoo clock** clock which strikes the hours with sounds like a cuckoo's call.

ˈ**cuckoo spit** white froth often found on leaves in summer, produced by the larvae of certain insects.

cuckoo[2] /ˈkʊkuː/ *adj* [usu pred] (*infml*) foolish; mad: *He has gone absolutely cuckoo.*

cucumber /ˈkjuːkʌmbə(r)/ *n* **1** (a) [C, U] long, green-skinned fleshy vegetable used raw in sandwiches and salads, or pickled: *a huge cucumber* ○ *Have some cucumber.* ○ [attrib] *cucumber salad, sandwiches, etc.* ⇨ illus at SALAD. (b) [C] plant that produces this. **2** (idm) **cool as a cucumber** ⇨ COOL[1].

cud /kʌd/ *n* **1** [U] food that cattle, etc bring back from the stomach into the mouth to chew again. **2** (idm) **chew the cud** ⇨ CHEW.

cuddle /ˈkʌdl/ *v* **1** [I, Tn] hold (sb, sth, each other) close and lovingly in one's arms: *The lovers kissed and cuddled on the sofa.* ○ *The child cuddled her doll (to her chest).* **2** (phr v) **cuddle up (to/against sb/sth); cuddle up (together)** lie close and comfortably; nestle: *She cuddled up to her mother.* ○ *They cuddled up (together) under the blanket.*

▷ **cuddle** *n* [sing] act of cuddling; hug: *have a cuddle together.*

cuddlesome /-səm/, **cuddly** /ˈkʌdli/ (**-ier, -iest**) *adjs* (*infml*) pleasant to cuddle: *a cuddly teddy bear.*

cudgel /ˈkʌdʒəl/ *n* **1** short thick stick or club. **2** (idm) **take up the cudgels for/on behalf of sb/sth** (start to) defend or support sb/sth strongly.

▷ **cudgel** *v* (**-ll-**; *US* also **-l-**) **1** [Tn] hit (sb) with a cudgel. **2** (idm) **cudgel one's ˈbrains** think very hard: *Hard as I cudgelled my brains, I couldn't remember her name.*

cue[1] /kjuː/ *n* **1** ~ (**for sth/to do sth**) thing said or done to signal sb's turn to say or do sth, esp in a theatrical or other performance: *Actors have to learn their cues* (ie the last words of the speeches just before their own speeches) *as well as their own lines.* ○ *When I nod my head, that's your cue to interrupt the meeting.* ○ (*fig*) *And they all lived happily ever afterwards — which sounds like the cue* (ie an appropriate moment) *for a song.* **2** example of how to behave, what to do, etc: *take one's cue from sb*, ie be guided by the way sb does sth ○ *Follow her cue, and one day you'll be a great scholar.* **3** (idm) (**right**) **on cue** at exactly the appropriate or expected moment: *He said she would be back very soon and, right on cue, she walked in.*

▷ **cue** *v* (*pres p* **cueing**) [Tn, Tn·p] ~ **sb** (**in**) give a cue to sb (to do sth): *I'll cue you in* (ie give you a signal to start) *by nodding my head.*

cue[2] /kjuː/ *n* long tapering leather-tipped stick used for striking the ball in snooker, billiards, etc. ⇨ illus at SNOOKER.

cuesta /ˈkwestə/ *n* gentle slope, usu ending in a steep drop.

cuff[1] /kʌf/ *n* **1** [C] end of a coat or shirt sleeve at the wrist: *frayed cuffs.* ⇨ illus at JACKET. **2** (*US*) = TURN-UP (TURN[1]). **3 cuffs** [pl] (*sl*) handcuffs. **4** (idm) ˌ**off the** ˈ**cuff** without previous thought or preparation: *make a remark off the cuff* ○ [attrib] *an* ˌ*off-the-cuff* ˈ*joke,* ˈ*remark, etc.*

□ ˈ**cuff-link** *n* (usu *pl*) one of a pair of fasteners for shirt cuffs: *a pair of cuff-links.*

cuff[2] /kʌf/ *v* [Tn] give (sb) a light blow with the open hand, esp on the head.

▷ **cuff** *n* such a blow.

Cufic = KUFIC.

cuirass /kwɪˈræs/ *n* piece of armour protecting the upper body, consisting of a breastplate and back-plate fastened together.

cuisine /kwɪˈziːn/ *n* [U] (*French*) (style of) cooking: *French, Italian, etc cuisine* ○ *a restaurant where the cuisine is excellent.*

Cukor /ˈkjuːkɔː(r)/ George (1899-1983), American film director. He was noted for his sensitive direction of performers, esp the women. His work includes the classic comedy *The Philadelphia Story* and the show-business drama *A Star is Born.*

cul-de-sac /ˈkʌl də sæk/ *n* (*pl* **cul-de-sacs**) (*French*) street open at one end only; blind alley.

culinary /ˈkʌlɪnərɪ; *US* -nerɪ/ *adj* of or for cooking: *culinary skill, implements* ○ *a culinary triumph,* ie a very well cooked dish or meal.

cull /kʌl/ *v* **1** [Tn] (**a**) kill (a certain number of usu weaker animals) in a herd, in order to reduce its size: *Deer are culled by hunters.* (**b**) reduce (the herd) in this way: *The herd must be culled.* **2** [Tn, Tn·pr] ~ **sth** (**from sth**) select or obtain sth from various different sources: *information culled from various reference books.*

▷ **cull** *n* **1** [C] act of culling: *an annual seal cull.* **2** [sing] animal(s) culled: *sell the cull as meat.*

cullender = COLANDER.

Culloden /kəˈlɒdn/ moor near Inverness in Scotland, where in 1746 the army of the Duke of *Cumberland defeated the Highland supporters of Charles Edward *Stuart, the Young Pretender. The beaten forces were pursued and many were killed.

culminate /ˈkʌlmɪneɪt/ *v* [Ipr] ~ **in sth** (*fml*) have the specified final conclusion or result: *a long struggle that culminated in success* ○ *Her career culminated in her appointment as director.* ○ *a series of border clashes which culminated in full-scale war.*

▷ **culmination** /ˌkʌlmɪˈneɪʃn/ *n* [sing] eventual conclusion or result: *the successful culmination of a long campaign.*

culottes /kjuːˈlɒts/ *n* [pl] women's wide shorts that look like a skirt: *a pair of culottes.*

culpable /ˈkʌlpəbl/ *adj* ~ (**for sth**) deserving blame; blameworthy: *I cannot be held culpable (for their mistakes).* ○ *culpable negligence,* ie failure to do what one should do. ▷ **culpability** /ˌkʌlpəˈbɪlətɪ/ *n* [U]. **culpably** /ˈkʌlpəblɪ/ *adv.*

culprit /ˈkʌlprɪt/ *n* person who has done sth wrong; offender: *Someone broke a cup: who was the culprit?* ○ *Police are searching for the culprits.*

cult /kʌlt/ *n* **1** system of religious worship, esp one that is expressed in rituals: *the mysterious nature-worship cults of these ancient peoples.* **2** ~ (**of sb/sth**) (*often derog*) devotion to or admiration of sb/sth: *the cult of physical fitness* ○ *a personality cult,* ie admiration of a person rather than of what he does or the office he holds. **3** popular fashion or craze: *the current pop music cult* ○ [attrib] *a* ˈ*cult word,* ie one used because it is fashionable among members of a particular (usu small) group ○ *an artist with a cult following,* ie who is admired by such a group.

cultivable /ˈkʌltɪvəbl/ *adj* that can be cultivated: *cultivable soil, land, etc.*

cultivate /ˈkʌltɪveɪt/ *v* [Tn] **1** (**a**) prepare and use (land, soil, etc) for growing crops. (**b**) grow (crops). **2** (**a**) make (the mind, feelings, etc) more educated and refined: *reading the best authors in an attempt to cultivate her mind.* (**b**) (*sometimes derog*) (try to) acquire or develop (a relationship, an attitude, etc): *cultivating the friendship of influential people* ○ *cultivate an air of indifference.* (**c**) (*sometimes derog*) (try to) win the friendship or support of (sb): *You must cultivate people who can help you in business.*

▷ **cultivated** *adj* (of people, manners, etc) having or showing good taste and refinement.

cultivation /ˌkʌltɪˈveɪʃn/ *n* [U] cultivating (CULTIVATE 1) or being cultivated: *the cultivation of the soil* ○ *land that is under cultivation,* ie is being cultivated ○ *bring land into cultivation.*

cultivator /ˈkʌltɪveɪtə(r)/ *n* **1** machine for breaking up soil, destroying weeds, etc. **2** person who cultivates (CULTIVATE 1).

cultural /ˈkʌltʃərəl/ *adj* of or involving culture: *cultural differences, activities, etc* ○ *cultural studies,* eg of art, literature, etc ○ *a cultural desert,* ie a place with few cultural activities. ▷ **culturally** /-rəlɪ/ *adv.*

□ **the Cultural Revolution** /ˌkʌltʃərəl revəˈluːʃn/ movement in China 1966-68 which tried to restore the original ideals of *Mao Tse-tung. It led to a cult based on Mao and his writings, and to the persecution of moderate thinkers at all levels of society. The economy and stability of the country suffered greatly. The 'Gang of Four' who led the Revolution were later tried and punished.

culture /ˈkʌltʃə(r)/ *n* **1** [U] (**a**) refined understanding and appreciation of art, literature, etc: *a society without much culture* ○ *She is a woman of considerable culture.* ○ *Universities should be centres of culture.* (**b**) (*often derog*) art, literature, etc collectively: *tourists coming to Venice in search of culture.* **2** [U] state of intellectual development of a society: *twentieth-century mass culture* ○ *a period of high/low culture.* **3** [U, C] particular form of intellectual expression, eg in art and literature: *We owe much to Greek culture.* ○ *She has studied the cultures of Oriental countries.* **4** [U, C] customs, arts, social institutions, etc of a particular group or people: *the culture of the Eskimos* ○ *working-class culture.* **5** [U] development through training, exercise, treatment, etc: *physical culture,* ie developing one's muscles and fitness by doing exercises ○ *The culture of the mind is vital.* **6** [U] growing of plants or rearing of certain types of animal (eg bees, silkworms, etc) to obtain a crop or improve the species: *bulb culture,* ie the growing of flowers from bulbs. **7** [C] (*biology*) group of bacteria grown for medical or scientific study: *a culture of cholera germs.*

▷ **cultured** *adj* (of people) appreciating art, literature, etc; refined; cultivated.

□ ˈ**cultured pearl** pearl formed by an oyster into which a piece of grit has been placed.

ˈ**culture shock** confusion and disorientation caused by contact with a civilization other than one's own.

ˈ**culture vulture** (*infml joc or derog*) person eager to acquire culture.

culvert /ˈkʌlvət/ *n* drain that crosses beneath a road, railway, etc; underground channel for electrical cables.

cum /kʌm/ *prep* (used to link two *ns*) also used as; as well as: *a bedroom-cum-sitting-room* ○ *a barman-cum-waiter.*

Cumberland /ˈkʌmbələnd/ William Augustus, Duke of Cumberland (1721-65), third son of *George II. He led the English army against the Jacobite forces of Charles Edward *Stuart at the battle of *Culloden and showed extreme cruelty to the beaten survivors. He lost several other battles against the French.

cumbersome /ˈkʌmbəsəm/ *adj* **1** heavy and difficult to carry, wear, etc: *a cumbersome parcel, overcoat.* **2** slow and inefficient: *the university's cumbersome administrative procedures.*

Cumbria /ˈkʌmbrɪə/ **1** ancient British kingdom in N England. **2** county in NW England on the border with Scotland, consisting of the former counties of Cumberland, Westmorland and part of Lancashire. It contains the *Lake District and Scafell Pike, the highest mountain in England. ⇨ map at App 1. ▷ **Cumbrian** *adj, n.*

cumin /ˈkʌmɪn/ *n* [U] (plant with) pleasant-smelling seeds used for flavouring.

cummerbund /ˈkʌməbʌnd/ *n* sash worn around the waist, esp under a dinner-jacket.

Cummings /ˈkʌmɪŋz/ E(dward) E(stlin) (1894-1962), American poet. He did not use capital letters in his work, and his name is usually written e e cummings. His work was often satirical, but it also has great lyrical qualities.

cumquat = KUMQUAT.

cumulative /ˈkjuːmjʊlətɪv; *US* -leɪtɪv/ *adj* gradually increasing in amount, force, etc by one addition after another: *the cumulative effect of several illnesses.* ▷ **cumulatively** *adv.*

□ ˌ**cumulative** ˈ**voting** system of voting in which each voter has as many votes as there are candidates. These may all be given to one candidate or shared among several.

cumulonimbus /ˌkjuːmjʊləʊˈnɪmbəs/ *n* (*pl* **-bi** /-baɪ/ or ~**es**) type of cumulus cloud that develops into a towering dark mass and is associated with thunderstorms.

cumulus /ˈkjuːmjʊləs/ *n* (*pl* **-li** /-laɪ/) [U, C] cloud formed of rounded masses heaped on a flat base.

Cunard /ˈkjuːnɑːd/ Sir Samuel (1787-1865), Canadian ship-owner. He founded a passenger service across the Atlantic between Britain and N America. It became the Cunard shipping company, which now runs the liner Queen Elizabeth II.

cuneiform /ˈkjuːnɪfɔːm; *US* kjuːˈnɪəfɔːrm/ *adj* wedge-shaped: *cuneiform characters,* ie as used in old Persian or Assyrian writing.

cunnilingus /ˌkʌnɪˈlɪŋgəs/ *n* [U] stimulation of a woman's outer sexual organs with the mouth or tongue: *perform cunnilingus on sb.*

cunning /ˈkʌnɪŋ/ *adj* **1** (**a**) clever at deceiving people: *a cunning liar, spy, cheat, etc* ○ *He's a cunning old fox.* (**b**) showing this kind of cleverness: *a cunning smile, trick, plot, etc.* **2** ingenious: *a cunning device for cracking nuts.* **3** (*US*) attractive; cute: *a cunning baby, kitten, etc.*

▷ **cunning** *n* [U] cunning behaviour or quality: *When he couldn't get what he wanted openly and honestly, he resorted to low cunning.*

cunningly *adv*: *cunningly concealed.*

cunt /kʌnt/ *n* (⚠ *offensive*) **1** (*sl*) (**a**) vagina. (**b**) outer female sexual organs. **2** (*derog sl*) unpleasant person: *You stupid cunt!*

cup[1] /kʌp/ *n* **1** [C] small bowl-shaped container, usu with a handle, for drinking tea, coffee, etc from; its contents; the amount it will hold: *a* ˈ*teacup* ○ *a* ˌ*cup and* ˈ*saucer* ○ *a* ˌ*cup of* ˈ*coffee* ○ *a paper cup* ○ *She drank a whole cup of milk.* ○ *Use two cups of flour for the cake,* ie as a measure in cooking. ○ (*fig rhet*) *My cup (of joy) is full/overflowing,* ie I am extremely happy. ⇨ illus. **2** [C] (**a**) vessel, usu of gold or silver, awarded as a prize in a competition: *teams competing for the World Cup,* eg in football ○ *He's won several cups for shooting.* (**b**) such a competition: *We got knocked out of the Cup in the first round.* **3** [C] = CHALICE. **4** [C] thing shaped like a deep narrow bowl: *an* ˈ*egg-cup* ○ *the cup in which an acorn grows*

○ *the cups of a bra* ○ *She wears a ˈD cup*, ie size of bra. **5** [U] drink made from wine, cider, etc with other flavourings added: *ˈclaret-cup* ○ *ˈcider-cup*. **6** (idm) **(not) sb's cup of ˈtea** (*infml*) (not) what sb likes, is interested in, etc: *Skiing isn't really my cup of tea.* **the ˌcup that ˈcheers** (*Brit joc*) tea. **in one's ˈcups** (*dated fml*) drunk. **there's many a slip 'twixt cup and lip** ⇨ SLIP[1].
▷ **cupful** /ˈkʌpfʊl/ *n* amount that a cup will hold.
□ **ˈcup cake** small sponge-cake baked in a paper cup.
ˌcup ˈfinal (usu **Cup Final**) final match to decide the winner of a knock-out competition, esp in football. ⇨ article at SPORT.
ˈcup-tie *n* match between teams competing for a cup, esp in football.

cup[2] /kʌp/ *v* (**-pp-**) **1** [Tn] form (esp one's hands) into the shape of a cup: *She cupped her hands round her mouth and shouted.* **2** [Tn, Tn·pr] ~ **sth (in/with sth)** hold sth as if in cup: *cup one's chin in one's hands.*

cupboard /ˈkʌbəd/ *n* **1** set of shelves with a door or doors in front, either built into the wall of a room or as a separate piece of furniture, used for storing food, clothes, dishes, etc: *a ˌkitchen ˈcupboard* ○ *an ˈairing cupboard*, ie for airing clothes ○ (*fig*) *They ask for more funds, but the cupboard is bare*, ie there is no money to give them. ○ [attrib] *not enough cupboard space.* ⇨ illus at FURNITURE. **2** (idm) **ˈcupboard love** affection that is shown, esp by a child, in order to gain sth by it: *It's only cupboard love; he wants some sweets!* **a skeleton in the cupboard** ⇨ SKELETON.

Cupid /ˈkju:pɪd/ *n* **1** the Roman god of love. **2 cupid** [C] (picture or statue of a) beautiful boy with wings and a bow and arrow, representing love.

cupidity /kju:ˈpɪdətɪ/ *n* [U] (*fml*) greed, esp for money or possessions.

cupola /ˈkju:pələ/ *n* **1** (**a**) small dome forming (part of) a roof. (**b**) ceiling of this. **2** furnace for melting metals.

cuppa /ˈkʌpə/ *n* (*Brit infml*) cup of tea: *Shall we have a cuppa?* ⇨ article at DRINK.

cupreous /ˈkju:prɪəs/ *adj* (*chemistry*) of or like copper.

cupric /ˈkju:prɪk/ *adj* (*chemistry*) of copper.

cupro-nickel /ˌkju:prəʊˈnɪkl/ *n* [U] alloy of copper and nickel used for making coins.

cur /kɜ:(r)/ *n* (*dated*) **1** vicious or bad-tempered dog, esp a mongrel. **2** (*fig*) cowardly or worthless man: *You treacherous cur!*

curable /ˈkjʊərəbl/ *adj* that can be cured: *Some types of cancer are curable.* ▷ **curability** /ˌkjʊərəˈbɪlətɪ/ *n* [U].

curaçao (also **curaçoa**) /ˌkjʊərəˈsəʊ; *US* -ˈsaʊ/ *n* [U] liqueur flavoured with the peel of bitter oranges.

curacy /ˈkjʊərəsɪ/ *n* curate's job or position; holding of such a job or position: *a curacy at a church in Oxford* ○ *during his curacy.*

curare /kjʊˈrɑ:rɪ/ *n* [U] bitter substance obtained from various plants, used by S American Indians as a poison on their arrows.

curate /ˈkjʊərət/ *n* **1** (in the Church of England) clergyman who helps a parish priest. Cf VICAR. **2** (idm) **a curate's ˈegg** (*Brit usu derog*) thing with both good and bad aspects.

curative /ˈkjʊərətɪv/ *adj* helping to, able to or intended to cure illness, etc: *the curative properties of a herb.*

curator /kjʊəˈreɪtə(r); *US also* ˈkjʊərətər/ *n* person in charge of a museum, an art gallery, etc.

curb /kɜ:b/ *n* **1** ~ **(on sth)** thing that restrains or controls: *put/keep a curb on one's anger, feelings, etc* ○ *government curbs on spending.* **2** strap or chain passing under a horse's jaw, used to restrain the horse. **3** (*esp US*) = KERB. **4** border or frame built round eg a well.
▷ **curb** *v* [Tn] **1** prevent (sth) from getting out of control; restrain: *curb one's anger, feelings, etc* ○ *curb spending, waste, etc.* **2** control (a horse) by means of a curb.

curd /kɜ:d/ *n* **1** (usu **curds** [pl]) thick soft substance formed when milk turns sour, used to make cheese: *ˌcurds and ˈwhey* ○ [attrib] *curd ˈcheese.* **2** [U] (in compounds) substance made to look like curds: *ˌlemon-ˈcurd*, ie made from eggs, butter and sugar, flavoured with lemon, and used like jam ○ *soya-ˈbean curd.*

curdle /ˈkɜ:dl/ *v* [I, Tn] (cause sth to) form into curds: *The milk has curdled*, ie become sour. ○ *Lemon juice curdles milk.* ○ (*fig*) *a scream which was enough to curdle one's blood/make one's blood curdle*, ie fill one with horror.

cure[1] /kjʊə(r)/ *v* **1** (**a**) [Tn, Tn·pr] ~ **sb (of sth)** make sb healthy again: *The doctors cured her of cancer.* (**b**) [Tn] provide a successful remedy for (an illness, etc): *This illness cannot be cured easily.* **2** (**a**) [Tn] (*fig*) find a solution to (sth); put an end to: *Ministers hoped that import controls might cure the economy's serious inflation.* (**b**) [Tn·pr] ~ **sb of sth** (*fig*) stop sb from behaving unpleasantly, harmfully, etc: *That nasty shock cured him of his inquisitiveness for ever.* **3** [Tn] (**a**) treat (meat, fish, tobacco, etc) by salting it, smoking it, drying it, etc in order to keep it in good condition: *well-cured bacon.* (**b**) vulcanize (rubber). **4** (idm) **kill or cure** ⇨ KILL.

cure[2] /kjʊə(r)/ *n* **1** [C] act of curing or process of being cured: *The doctor cannot guarantee a cure.* ○ *Her cure took six weeks.* ○ *effect/work a cure.* **2** [C, U] ~ **(for sth)** substance or treatment that cures; remedy: *Is there a certain cure for cancer yet?* ○ *a disease with no known cure* ○ *He has tried all sorts of cures, but without success.* ○ (*fig*) *What is the cure for the plight of the homeless?* **3** [C, U] (*fml*) duties of a priest: *the cure of souls*, ie looking after people's spiritual welfare ○ *obtain/resign a cure*, ie a position as a priest. **4** (idm) **prevention is better than cure** ⇨ PREVENTION.

curé /ˈkjʊəreɪ; *US* kjʊəˈreɪ/ *n* (*French*) French priest, esp a parish priest.

curette /kjʊˈret/ *n* small instrument used by a surgeon for scraping.
▷ **curette** *v* [I, Tn] scrape (an internal part of the body, esp the lining of the womb) with this instrument. **curettage** /kjʊˈretɪdʒ; *US* ˌkjʊərəˈtɑ:ʒ/ *n* [U] use of this instrument. Cf D AND C.

curfew /ˈkɜ:fju:/ *n* signal or time after which people must stay indoors until the next day: *an 11 o'clock curfew* ○ *impose a curfew*, eg under martial law ○ *lift/end a curfew* ○ *You mustn't go out after curfew.*

Curia /ˈkjʊərɪə/ *n* **the Curia** [Gp] administrative offices of the Vatican which govern the Roman Catholic Church.

Curie /ˈkjʊərɪ/ Marie (1867-1934) and Pierre (1859-1906), French scientists. Marie was born in Poland and met her husband at university. Their research into radioactivity led to the discovery of radium and polonium. After Pierre's death Marie worked on medical uses of their discoveries in X-rays. They were jointly awarded the Nobel prize for physics in 1903 along with *Becquerel, and Marie won the prize again in 1911, this time for chemistry.

curie /ˈkjʊərɪ/ *n* unit of radioactivity.

curio /ˈkjʊərɪəʊ/ *n* (*pl* ~**s**) small object that is quite rare or unusual: *his valuable collection of curios.*

curiosity /ˌkjʊərɪˈɒsətɪ/ *n* **1** [U] ~ **(about sth/to do sth)** being curious(1a); inquisitiveness: *curiosity about distant lands* ○ *her burning curiosity to know what's going on* ○ *He gave in to curiosity and opened the letter addressed to his sister.* **2** [C] strange or unusual thing or person; strange or rare object: *She is so eccentric that she is regarded as a bit of a curiosity.* **3** (idm) **curiosity killed the ˈcat** (*saying*) (said to sb to stop him being too inquisitive).

curious /ˈkjʊərɪəs/ *adj* **1** ~ **(about sth/to do sth)** (**a**) (*approv*) eager to know or learn: *curious about the origin of mankind/the structure of atoms* ○ *I'm curious to know what she said.* ○ *He is a curious boy who is always asking questions.* (**b**) (*derog*) having or showing too much interest in the affairs of others: *curious neighbours* ○ *She's always so curious about my work.* ○ *Hide it where curious eyes won't see it.* ○ *Don't be so curious!* **2** strange; unusual: *She looks rather curious with green hair.* ○ *What a curious thing to say.* ○ *Isn't he a curious-looking little man?* ○ *It's curious that he didn't tell you.* ▷ **curiously** *adv*: *She was there all day but, curiously, I didn't see her.*

curium /ˈkjʊərɪəm/ *n* [U] (*symb* **Cm**) artificial radioactive element.

curl[1] /kɜ:l/ *n* **1** [C] thing, esp a small bunch of hair, that curves round and round like a spiral or the thread of a screw: *curls (of hair) falling over her shoulder* ○ *hair falling in curls over her shoulders* ○ *the little boy's golden curls*, ie curly hair ○ *a curl of smoke rising from a cigarette* ○ *'Of course not,' he said, with a curl of his lip*, ie expressing scorn. **2** [U] plant disease in which the leaves curl up.
▷ **curly** *adj* (**-ier, -iest**) curling; full of curls: *curly hair* ○ *a curly pattern* ○ *a ˌcurly-headed ˈgirl.* ⇨ illus at HAIR.

curl[2] /kɜ:l/ *v* **1** [I, Ip, Tn, Tn·p] ~ **(sth) (up)** (**a**) (cause sth to) form into a curl or curls; coil: *She has curled (up) her hair.* ○ *Does her hair curl naturally?* (**b**) (cause sth to) form into a curved shape, esp so that the edges are rolled up: *The frost made the leaves curl (up).* ○ *The heat curled the paper (up).* **2** [Ipr, Ip] move in a spiral; coil: *The smoke curled upwards.* ○ *The plant's tendrils curled up the stick.* **3** (idm) **curl one's lip** put on a sneering expression. **make sb's hair curl** ⇨ HAIR. **4** (phr v) **curl up** (**a**) lie or sit with curved back and one's legs drawn up close to the body: *curl up with a book* ○ *The dog curled up in front of the fire.* (**b**) bend at the waist: *A blow to the stomach made him curl up.* **curl (sb) up** (*infml*) (**a**) (cause sb to) feel very embarrassed: *My father's bad jokes always make me curl up.* (**b**) (cause sb to) laugh heartily: *I just curled up when I saw her dressed as a clown.*
▷ **ˈcurler** *n* small cylinder around which wet or warm hair is wound to curl it.
□ **ˈcurling-tongs**, **ˈcurling-irons** *ns* [pl] metal device for curling hair using heat.

curlew /ˈkɜ:lju:/ *n* water bird with a long thin beak that curves downwards. ⇨ illus at BIRD.

curlicue /ˈkɜ:lɪkju:/ *n* elaborate twist or curl, eg in a person's handwriting.

curling /ˈkɜ:lɪŋ/ *n* [U] game played on ice, esp in Scotland, with heavy flat round stones which are slid along the ice towards a mark.

curmudgeon /kɜ:ˈmʌdʒən/ *n* (*dated*) bad-tempered person. ▷ **curmudgeonly** *adj*: *a curmudgeonly person, act.*

currant /ˈkʌrənt/ *n* **1** small sweet dried seedless grape used in cookery: [attrib] *a currant bun.* **2** (usu in compounds) (cultivated bush with) small black, red or white fruit growing in clusters: *blackcurrants* ○ *redcurrants.*

currency /ˈkʌrənsɪ/ *n* **1** [C, U] money system in use in a country: *gold/paper currency* ○ *trading in foreign currencies* ○ *decimal currency* ○ *a strong currency* ○ [attrib] *a currency crisis, deal, etc.* **2** [U] (state of being in) common or general use (used esp with the *vs* shown): *ideas which had enjoyed a brief currency (ie were briefly popular) during the eighteenth century* ○ *The rumour soon gained currency*, ie became widespread. ○ *Newspaper stories gave currency to this scandal*, ie spread it.

current[1] /ˈkʌrənt/ *adj* **1** [usu attrib] of the present time; happening now: *current issues, problems, prices* ○ *the current issue of a magazine* ○ *the current year*, ie this year ○ *current events in India* ○ *her current boy-friend.* **2** in common or general use; generally accepted: *current opinions, beliefs, etc* ○ *words that are no longer current* ○ *a rumour that is current (ie widely known) in the city.* ⇨ Usage at NEW.
▷ **currently** *adv* at the present time: *our director, who is currently in London.*
□ **ˌcurrent acˈcount** (*esp Brit*) (*US* **checking account**) bank account from which money can be drawn without previous notice. Cf DEPOSIT ACCOUNT (DEPOSIT[2]), SAVINGS ACCOUNT (SAVING). ⇨ article at BANK.
ˌcurrent afˈfairs events of political importance happening in the world at the present time.
ˌcurrent ˈassets (*commerce*) assets which change in the course of business (eg money owed). Cf FIXED ASSETS (FIX[1]).

current² /ˈkʌrənt/ *n* **1** [C] movement of water, air, etc flowing in a certain direction through slower-moving or still water, air, etc: *The swimmer was swept away by the current.* ○ *She had to swim against the current.* ○ *Currents of warm air keep the hang-gliders aloft.* **2** [U, sing] flow of electricity through sth or along a wire or cable: *a 15-amp current* ○ *Turn on the current.* ○ *A sudden surge in the current made the lights fuse.* Cf ALTERNATING CURRENT (ALTERNATE²), DIRECT CURRENT (DIRECT¹). **3** [C] course or movement (of events, opinions, etc); trend: *Nothing disturbs the peaceful current of life in the village.* ○ *We must try to counteract the present current of anti-government feeling.*

curriculum /kəˈrɪkjʊləm/ *n* (*pl* ~**s** or **-la** /-lə/) subjects included in a course of study or taught at a particular school, college, etc: *Is German on your school's curriculum?* Cf SYLLABUS. ⇨ article at SCHOOL.

□ **curriculum vitae** /kəˌrɪkjʊləm ˈviːtaɪ/ (*abbr* **cv**) (*US* also **résumé**) brief account of sb's previous career, usu submitted with an application for a job.

curry¹ /ˈkʌrɪ/ *n* [C, U] dish of meat, fish, vegetables, etc cooked with certain hot-tasting spices, usu served with rice: *a chicken, beef, etc curry* ○ *eat too much curry.*

▷ **curried** *adj* [usu attrib] cooked with certain hot-tasting spices: *curried chicken, beef, etc.*

□ ˈ**curry powder** mixture of turmeric, cumin and other spices ground to a powder and used to make curry.

curry² /ˈkʌrɪ/ *v* (*pt, pp* **curried**) **1** [Tn] rub down and clean (a horse) with a curry-comb. **2** (idm) **curry favour (with sb)** (*derog*) try to gain sb's favour by flattery, etc.

□ ˈ**curry-comb** *n* pad with rubber or plastic teeth for rubbing down a horse.

curse¹ /kɜːs/ *n* **1** [C] impolite or obscene word or words used to express violent anger: *angrily muttering curses.* **2** [sing] word or words spoken with the aim of punishing, injuring or destroying sb/sth: *The witch put a curse on him*, ie used a curse against him. ○ *be under a curse*, ie suffer as a result of a curse ○ *lift a curse*, ie cancel it. **3** [C] cause of evil, harm, destruction, etc: *the curse of inflation* ○ *Gambling is often a curse.* ○ *His wealth proved a curse to him.* **4 the curse** [sing] (*dated infml*) menstruation: *I've got the curse today.*

curse² /kɜːs/ *v* **1** (a) [I, Ipr, Tn] ~ **(at sb/sth)** utter curses (CURSE¹ 2) (against sb/sth): *to curse and swear* ○ *He cursed (at) his bad luck* ○ *I cursed her for spoiling my plans.* (b) [Tn] use a curse (CURSE¹ 2) against (sb/sth): *The witch-doctor has cursed our cattle.* **2** (phr v) **be cursed with sth** be afflicted with sth, esp habitually; have the stated bad thing: *be cursed with bad health, a violent temper, bad luck, etc.*

▷ **cursed** /ˈkɜːsɪd/ *adj* [attrib] (used to show annoyance) hateful; unpleasant: *This work is a cursed nuisance.* **cursedly** *adv.*

cursive /ˈkɜːsɪv/ *adj* (of handwriting) with letters rounded and joined together.

cursor /ˈkɜːsə(r)/ *n* (*computing*) movable dot or other symbol on a computer screen that indicates a particular position.

cursory /ˈkɜːsərɪ/ *adj* (*often derog*) done quickly and not thoroughly; (too) hurried: *a cursory glance, look, inspection, etc* ○ *He put aside the papers after a cursory study.* ▷ **cursorily** /ˈkɜːsərəlɪ/ *adv.*

curt /kɜːt/ *adj* (*derog*) (of a speaker, his manner, what he says) rudely brief; abrupt: *a curt answer, rebuke, etc* ○ *He's rather curt when he's angry.* ○ *I was a little curt with him*, ie spoke sharply to him. ▷ **curtly** *adv.* **curtness** *n* [U].

curtail /kɜːˈteɪl/ *v* [Tn] make (sth) shorter or less; reduce: *curtail a speech, one's holidays* ○ *We must try to curtail our spending.* ○ *Illness has curtailed her sporting activities.*

▷ **curtailment** *n* [C, U] (act of) curtailing.

curtain /ˈkɜːtn/ *n* **1** [C] (a) (*US* **drape**) piece of material hung to cover a window, and usu movable sideways: *draw the curtains*, ie pull them across the window(s) ○ *lace curtains.* (b) similar piece of material hung up as a screen: *Pull the curtains round the patient's bed.* ○ *a shower curtain.* **2** [sing] (a) screen of heavy material that can be raised or lowered at the front of a stage: *The curtain rises/goes up*, ie The play/act begins. ○ *The curtain falls/comes down*, ie The play/act ends. ○ (*fig*) *The curtain has fallen on her long and distinguished career*, ie Her career has ended. (b) (*fig*) raising or lowering of such a curtain: *Tonight's curtain is at 7.30*, ie The play begins at 7.30. ○ *After the final curtain* (ie After the play had ended) *we went backstage.* **3** [C esp sing] (*fig*) thing that screens, covers, protects, etc: *a curtain of fog, mist, etc* ○ *A curtain of rain swept over the valley.* ○ *the curtain of secrecy that hides the Government's intentions.* **4 curtains** [pl] ~**s (for sb/sth)** (*infml*) hopeless situation; the end: *When I saw he had a gun, I knew it was curtains for me.* **5** (idm) **ring up/down the curtain** ⇨ RING².

▷ **curtain** *v* **1** [Tn] provide (a window, an alcove, etc) with a curtain or curtains: *curtained windows* ○ *enough material to curtain all the rooms.* **2** (phr v) **curtain sth off** separate or divide sth with a curtain or curtains: *curtain off part of a room.*

□ ˈ**curtain-call** *n* actor's appearance in front of the curtain at the end of a play to receive applause: *The performers took* (ie made) *their curtain-call.*

ˈ**curtain-raiser** *n* ~ **(to sth)** (a) short piece performed before the main play. (b) thing that precedes a similar but larger or more important event: *border incidents that were curtain-raisers to a full-scale war.*

ˌ**curtain** ˈ**wall 1** outer surface fixed to the wall of a modern building, that does not carry any of the weight of the roof or floors. **2** plain window-less outer wall, eg of a castle, usu between two towers.

Curtiz /ˈkɜːtɪs/ Michael (1888-1962), American film director. He made several films in his native Hungary before moving to the USA, where he made some of Hollywod's most popular pictures, including *Casablanca* with Humphrey *Bogart and Ingrid *Bergman.

curtsey (also **curtsy**) /ˈkɜːtsɪ/ *n* bend of the knees with one foot in front of the other, performed by women as a sign of respect, eg to a monarch: *make/drop/bob a curtsey (to sb).*

▷ **curtsey** (also **curtsy**) *v* (*pt, pp* **curtseyed, curtsied**) [I, Ipr] ~ **(to sb)** make a curtsey: *curtsey to the Queen.*

curvaceous /kɜːˈveɪʃəs/ *adj* (*esp sexist*) (of a woman) having an attractively rounded figure.

curvature /ˈkɜːvətʃə(r); *US* -tʃʊər/ *n* [U] curved form; curving: *the curvature of the earth's surface* ○ *to suffer from curvature of the spine.*

curve /kɜːv/ *n* **1** line of which no part is straight and which changes direction without angles: *a curve on a graph.* **2** thing shaped like this: *a curve in the road* ○ *a pattern full of curves and angles* ○ *her attractive curves*, ie pleasantly rounded figure.

▷ **curve** *v* **1** [I, Tn] (cause sth to) form a curve: *The road curved suddenly to the left.* ○ *a knife with a curved blade.* **2** [Ipr, Ip] move in a curve: *The spear curved through the air.*

curvy *adj* (**-ier, -iest**) (*infml*) **1** curving; curved: *curvy lines.* **2** curvaceous.

curvet /kɜːˈvet/ *n* playful leap by a horse.

▷ **curvet** *v* (**-tt-**) [I] (of a horse) leap in this way.

curvilinear /ˌkɜːvɪˈlɪnɪə(r)/ *adj* formed by or inside curved lines: *a curvilinear polygon.*

cushion /ˈkʊʃn/ *n* **1** small bag filled with soft material, feathers, etc, used to make a seat more comfortable, to kneel on, etc. **2** mass of sth soft: *a cushion of moss on the rock* ○ *A hovercraft rides on a cushion of air.* ○ *a* ˈ*pin-cushion* ○ (*fig*) *The three goals we scored in the first half give us a useful cushion* (ie protect us) *against defeat.* **3** soft bouncy lining of the inside edges of a snooker or billiard table, from which balls rebound. ⇨ illus at SNOOKER.

▷ **cushion** *v* **1** [Tn] soften (sth) by absorbing the effect of impact: *Powerful shock absorbers cushion our landing.* **2** [Tn, Tn·pr] ~ **sb/sth (against/from sth)** (*fig*) protect sb/sth (from sth harmful), sometimes excessively: *a child who has been cushioned from unpleasant experiences* ○ *Wage increases have cushioned us from the effects of higher prices.*

Cushitic /kʊˈʃɪtɪk/ *adj* of a group of E African languages spoken mainly in Ethiopia and Somalia.

cushy /ˈkʊʃɪ/ *adj* (**-ier, -iest**) (*infml often derog*) **1** (esp of a job) not requiring much effort: *Her job's so cushy: she does next to nothing and earns a fortune.* ○ *It's a cushy life for the rich.* **2** (idm) **a cushy** ˈ**number** (*infml*) job or situation in life that is pleasant, easy and undemanding: *He's got himself a very cushy little number.*

cusp /kʌsp/ *n* **1** pointed end where two curves meet: *the cusp of a crescent moon/a leaf.* **2** pointed part on the surface of the teeth at the side of the mouth (the *molars*).

cuss /kʌs/ *n* (*infml*) **1** curse. **2** (preceded by an *adj*) person: *He's an awkward/queer old cuss.* **3** (idm) **not give a** ˈ**cuss/**ˈ**damn (about sb/sth)** be completely unworried.

cussed /ˈkʌsɪd/ *adj* (*infml derog*) (of people) unwilling to agree or co-operate; obstinate; contrary(3): *She's so cussed she always does the opposite of what you ask.* ▷ **cussedly** *adv.* **cussedness** *n* [U] (*fig*): *It rained, with the usual cussedness of the English weather.*

custard /ˈkʌstəd/ *n* [U] sweet sauce, typically yellow, eaten with fruit, pastry, etc as a dessert, and made from flavoured cornflour mixed with sugar and milk: *apple pie and custard.*

□ ˈ**custard apple** round W Indian fruit with a pulp that tastes like custard.

ˌ**custard** ˈ**pie** flat round mass of soft wet or foamy matter, like a pie, which performers throw at each other in slapstick comedy.

Custer /ˈkʌstə(r)/ George Armstrong (1839-76), American general. He won a number of battles in the American Civil War, but he is remembered for 'Custer's Last Stand', the battle of Little Bighorn in which he and all his men were killed by Sioux Indians.

custodial /kʌˈstəʊdɪəl/ *adj* (*law*) involving imprisonment: *a custodial sentence.*

custodian /kʌˈstəʊdɪən/ *n* person who takes care of or looks after sth: *a self-appointed custodian of public morals* ○ (*US*) *the custodian of the block*, ie the caretaker.

custody /ˈkʌstədɪ/ *n* [U] **1** (right or duty of) taking care of sb/sth: *leave one's valuables in safe custody*, eg in a bank ○ *When his parents died, he was placed in the custody of his aunt.* ○ *The court gave the mother custody of the child*, eg after a divorce. ○ *parents involved in a battle over custody*, ie disputing who should have the right to look after the children. **2** imprisonment while awaiting trial: *The magistrate remanded him in custody for two weeks.* ○ *be held in custody* ○ *take sb into custody*, ie arrest him.

custom¹ /ˈkʌstəm/ *n* **1** (a) [C, U] usual, generally accepted and long-established way of behaving or doing things: *It is difficult to get used to another country's customs.* ○ *the customs of the Eskimos* ○ *a slave to custom*, ie sb who does what most people do and have always done ○ *procedures laid down by ancient custom.* (b) [C] thing that sb habitually does; practice: *It is my custom to rise early.* (c) [U] (*law*) traditions that are so generally accepted that they are considered part of the law. **2** [U] regular purchases from a tradesman, shop, etc: *We would like to have your custom*, ie would like you to buy our goods. ○ *We've lost a lot of custom since our prices went up*, ie Fewer goods have been bought from us. ○ *I shall withdraw my custom* (ie stop buying goods) *from that shop.*

custom² /ˈkʌstəm/ *adj* [attrib] made as the buyer specifies, rather than as a standard model: *a custom car.*

▷ **customize, -ise** *v* [Tn] make or alter (esp a car) according to the buyer's or owner's wishes.

□ ˌ**custom-**ˈ**built** (also ˌ**custom-**ˈ**made**) *adj* built or made as the buyer specifies: *a* ˌ*custom-built* ˈ*car* ○ ˌ*custom-made* ˈ*clothes,* ˈ*shoes, etc.*

customary /ˈkʌstəmərɪ; *US* -merɪ/ *adj* according to custom; usual: *Is it customary to tip waiters in your country?* ○ *She gave the customary speech of thanks to the chairman.* ▷ **customarily**

/ˈkʌstəmərəlɪ; *US* ˌkʌstəˈmerəlɪ/ *adv*.

customer /ˈkʌstəmə(r)/ *n* **1** person who buys sth from a tradesman, shop, etc: *one of the shop's best customers*. **2** (*infml*) (preceded by an *adj*) person that one has to deal with: *a queer, awkward, rum, tough, etc customer* ○ *an ugly customer* ○ *a cool customer*, eg one who remains calm in a crisis.

customs /ˈkʌstəmz/ *n* [pl] **1** taxes payable to the government on goods imported from other countries; import duties: *pay customs on sth*. **2** (also **the Customs**) Government department that collects these taxes: *The Customs have found heroin hidden in freight.* ○ *How long does it take to get through customs?* ie have one's baggage examined by customs officers at a port, airport, etc ○ [attrib] *a customs officer, search, check* ○ *customs duty, formalities, etc*. Cf EXCISE[1].

□ ˌ**Customs and** ˈ**Excise** British government department responsible for collecting indirect taxes such as VAT and duty on alcohol. ⇨ article at TAXATION.

ˈ**customs house** office, esp at a port, where customs duties are collected.

ˈ**customs union** agreement between states on what customs duties are to be paid on each other's goods.

cut[1] /kʌt/ *v* (**-tt-**; *pt, pp* **cut**) **1** [Ipr, Tn] make an opening, slit or wound in (sth) with a sharp-edged tool, (eg a knife or a pair of scissors): *You need a powerful saw to cut through metal.* ○ *He cut himself/his face shaving.* ○ *She cut her finger on a piece of broken glass.* ○ *cut sb's throat*, ie kill sb with a deep wound in the throat. **2** (**a**) [Tn, Tn·pr, Dn·n, Dn·pr] ~ **sth (from sth)**; ~ **sth (for sb)** remove sth (from sth larger) using a knife, etc: *cut some flowers* ○ *How many slices of bread shall I cut* (ie from the loaf) *?* ○ *She cut a slice of beef from the joint.* ○ *Please cut me a piece of cake/cut a piece of cake for me.* ○ *Cut yourself some pineapple.* ○ *Cut some pineapple for your sister.* (**b**) [Tn, Tn·pr, Tn·p] ~ **sth (in/into sth)** divide sth (into smaller pieces) with a knife, etc: *Will you cut the cake?* ○ *If you cut the bread* (ie into slices) *we'll make some toast.* ○ *She cut the meat into cubes.* ○ *cut apples into halves, thirds, quarters, etc* ○ *The bus was cut in half/in two by the train.* (**c**) [Tn] separate (sth) into two pieces; divide: *cut a rope, cable, thread, etc* ○ *Don't cut the string, untie the knots.* ○ *The Minister cut the tape to open a new section of the motorway.* (**d**) [Tn, Cn·a] shorten (sth) by cutting; trim: *cut one's hair, one's nails, a hedge* ○ *cut* (ie mow) *the grass* ○ *He has had his hair cut (short).* (**e**) [Tn, Tn·pr] make or form (sth) by removing material with a cutting tool: *cut a diamond* ○ *The climbers cut steps in the ice.* ○ *cut a hole in a piece of paper* ○ *cut one's initials on a tree.* ⇨ Usage. **3** [I] (**a**) be capable of being cut: *Sandstone cuts easily.* (**b**) be capable of cutting: *This knife won't cut.* **4** [Tn] cause physical or mental pain to (sb): *His cruel remarks cut her deeply.* **5** [Tn] harvest (a crop): *The wheat has been cut.* **6** [Tn] (of a line) cross (another line): *Let the point where AB cuts CD be called E.* ○ *The line cuts the circle at two points.* **7** [I, Tn] lift and turn up part of (a pack of playing-cards) in order to decide who is to deal, play first, etc: *Let's cut for dealer.* ○ *cut the cards/pack.* **8** (**a**) [Tn, Tn·pr] reduce (sth) by removing a part of it: *cut prices, taxes, spending, production* ○ *His salary has been cut (by ten per cent).* ○ *The new bus service cuts the travelling time by half.* ○ *Could you cut your essay from 10 000 to 5 000 words?* (**b**) [Tn, Tn·pr] ~ **sth (from sth)** remove sth (from sth); leave out or omit sth: *Two scenes were cut by the censor.* (**c**) [Tn] (*infml*) stop (sth): *Cut the chatter and get on with your work!* **9** (**a**) [Tn] prepare (a film or tape) by removing or rearranging parts of it; edit. (**b**) [I] (usu imperative) stop filming or recording: *The director shouted 'Cut!'* (**c**) [Ipr] ~ **(from sth) to sth** (in films, radio or television) move quickly from one scene to another: *The scene cuts from the shop to the street.* **10** [Tn] switch off (a light, car engine, etc). **11** [Tn] (*infml*) stay away from (sth) deliberately; not attend: *cut a class, lecture, tutorial, etc.* **12** [Tn] (*infml*) refuse to recognize (sb): *She cut me (dead) in the street the other day.* **13** [I, Tn] (in cricket) hit (the ball) in the direction one is facing with the bat held horizontally: *He cut the ball to the boundary.* **14** [Tn] have (a new tooth) beginning to appear through the gum[1]. **15** [Tn, Tn·pr] ~ **sth (with sth)** (*esp US*) make sth less pure; dilute or weaken sth: *cut whisky with water.* **16** [Tn] record music on (a gramophone record): *The Beatles cut their first disc in 1962.* **17** (idm) **cut and** ˈ**run** (*sl*) make a quick or sudden escape. (For other idioms containing **cut**, see entries for the *ns, adjs*, etc, eg **cut corners** ⇨ CORNER; **cut it/things fine** ⇨ FINE[3].).

18 (phr v) **cut across sth** not correspond to (the usual divisions between groups): *Opinion on this issue cuts across traditional political boundaries.*

cut across, along, through, etc (sth) go across, etc (sth), esp in order to shorten one's route: *I usually cut across/through the park on my way home.*

cut at sb/sth try to sever, open or wound sb/sth with a knife, etc: *His attacker cut at him with a razor.* ○ *She cut at the rope in an attempt to free herself.*

cut sth away (from sth) remove sth (from sth) by cutting: *They cut away all the dead branches from the tree.*

cut sth back shorten (a bush, shrub, etc) by cutting off shoots and branches close to the stem; prune sth: *cut back a rose bush.* **cut sth back; cut back (on sth)** reduce sth considerably: *If we don't sell more goods, we'll have to cut back (on) production.* Cf CUT-BACK.

cut sb ˈ**down** (*fml*) (**a**) kill or injure sb by striking him with a sword or some other sharp weapon. (**b**) (usu passive) kill sb: *He was cut down by pneumonia at an early age.* **cut sth down** (**a**) cause sth to fall down by cutting it at the base: *cut down a tree.* (**b**) reduce the length of sth; shorten sth: *cut down a pair of trousers* ○ *Your article's too long — please cut it down to 1000 words.* **cut sth down; cut down (on sth)** reduce the amount or quantity of sth; consume, use or buy less (of sth): *cut down one's expenses* ○ *The doctor told him to cut down his consumption of fat.* ○ *I won't have a cigarette, thanks — I'm trying to cut down (on them)*, ie smoke fewer. **cut sb down (to sth)** persuade sb to reduce a price: *He was asking £400 for the car, but we cut him down to £350.*

cut sb/sth from sth remove sb/sth from a larger object by cutting: *cut a branch from a tree* ○ *The injured driver had to be cut from the wreckage of his car.*

cut ˈ**in (on sb/sth)** (of a vehicle or driver) move suddenly in front of another vehicle, leaving little space between the two vehicles: *The lorry overtook me and then cut in (on me).* **cut in (on sb/sth); cut into sth** interrupt sb/sth: *She kept cutting in on/cutting into our conversation.* **cut sb in (on sth)** (*infml*) give sb a share of the profit (in a business or an activity): *cut sb in on a deal.*

cut sb ˈ**off** (**a**) (often passive) interrupt sb speaking on the telephone by breaking the connection: *We were cut off in the middle of our conversation.* ○ *'Operator, I've just been cut off.'* (**b**) leave sb nothing in one's will[4](4); disinherit sb: *He cut his son off without a penny.* (**c**) (usu passive) cause sb to die sooner than is normal: *a young man cut off in his prime.* **cut sb/sth off** (often passive) stop the supply of sth to sb: *If you don't pay your gas bill soon you may be cut off.* ○ *Our water supply has been cut off.* ○ *Her father cut off* (ie stopped paying) *her allowance.* **cut sth off** block or obstruct sth: *cut off the enemy's retreat* ○ *cut off an escape route* ○ *The fence cuts off our view of the sea.* **cut sth off (sth)** remove sth (from sth larger) by cutting: *Mind you don't cut your fingers off!* ○ *King Charles I had his head cut off.* ○ *He cut off a metre of cloth from the roll.* ○ *The winner cut ten seconds off* (eg ran the distance ten seconds quicker than) *the world record.* **cut sb/sth off (from sb/sth)** (often passive) prevent sb/sth from leaving or reaching a place or communicating with people outside a place: *an army cut off from its base* ○ *The children were cut off* (eg stranded on a rock) *by the incoming tide.* ○ *The village was cut off (from the outside world) by heavy snow for a month.* ○ *She feels very cut off* (ie isolated) *living in the country.*

cut sth open open sth by cutting: *She fell and cut her head open*, ie suffered a deep wound to the head.

cut ˈ**out** stop functioning: *One of the aircraft's engines cut out.* **cut sth out** (**a**) make sth by cutting: *cut out a path through the jungle* ○ (*fig*) *He's cut out a niche* (ie found a suitable job) *for himself in politics.* (**b**) cut the shapes of different parts of (a garment) from a piece of material: *cut out a dress.* (**c**) (*infml*) (esp imperative) stop doing or saying (sth annoying): *I'm sick of you two squabbling — just cut it out!* (**d**) (*infml*) leave sth out; omit sth: *You can cut out the unimportant details.* (**e**) (*infml*) stop doing, using or consuming sth: *cut out sweets in order to lose weight.* **cut sth out (of sth)** (**a**) remove sth (from sth larger) by cutting: *cut an article out of the newspaper.* **be cut out for sth; be cut out to be sth** (*infml*) have the qualities and abilities needed for sth; (of two people) be well matched: *He's not cut out for teaching/to be a teacher.* ○ *Sally and Michael seem to be cut out for each other.*

cut sth through sth make a path or passage through sth by cutting: *The prisoners cut their way through the barbed wire and escaped.*

cut sb up (**a**) (*infml*) injure sb with cuts and bruises: *He was badly cut up in the fight.* (**b**) destroy sb: *cut up the enemy's forces.* (**c**) (*infml*) (usu passive) cause sb to be emotionally upset: *He was badly cut up by the death of his son.* **cut sth up** divide sth into small pieces with a knife, etc: *cut up vegetables.*

□ ˈ**cutaway** *n* drawing or model of a house, machine, etc with the front part absent to show what is inside: [attrib] *a cutaway model/diagram.*

ˈ**cut-back** *n* reduction: *cut-backs in public spending.*

ˌ**cut** ˈ**glass** glass with patterns cut in it: [attrib] *a* ˌ*cut-glass* ˈ*vase.*

ˈ**cut-off** *n* **1** point at which sth is ended; limit: [attrib] *reach the cut-off point.* **2** device for stopping a flow of water, electricity, etc. **3** channel made across a loop in a river, either by digging or by a process of erosion.

ˈ**cut-out** *n* **1** shape (to be) cut out of paper or cardboard: *a cardboard cut-out.* **2** device that switches off or breaks an electric circuit.

ˌ**cut-**ˈ**price** (*US* ˌ**cut-**ˈ**rate**) *adj* [esp attrib] (**a**) sold at a reduced price: ˌ*cut-price* ˈ*goods* ○ *I bought it cut-price.* (**b**) selling goods at reduced prices: *a* ˌ*cut-price* ˈ*store.*

ˈ**cut-up** *n* (*US infml*) person who tells jokes or behaves in a funny way.

ˈ**cutwater** *n* **1** sharp edge of the front part of a ship. **2** part of a pillar on a pier or bridge which sticks out into the water.

NOTE ON USAGE: Compare **cut**, **saw**, **chop**, **hack**, **slash** and **tear.** Notice that they are used with a variety of prepositions and particles. **Cut** has the widest use and indicates making an opening in something or removing a part of something with a (usually) sharp instrument or object: *She cut her finger on some broken glass.* ○ *He cut the advertisement out of the newspaper.* We **saw** wood by cutting it with a saw and **chop** it by cutting it with an axe: *We can saw off any dead branches and chop them for firewood.* **Hack** suggests hitting something with violent cutting blows, usually in order to destroy or remove it completely: *The explorers hacked (away) at the undergrowth to make a path.* ○ *Developers have destroyed the landscape by hacking down all the trees.* **Slash** indicates damaging or injuring somebody or something with long swinging cuts of a knife or sword: *The football hooligans had slashed some of the seats in the train.* We **tear** things by pulling them apart with our hands: *Can I tear this article out of the newspaper?* ○ *She tore up his letter in anger.*

cut[2] /kʌt/ *n* **1** wound or opening made with a knife, pair of scissors, etc: *a deep cut in the leg* ○ *cuts on* *the face* ○ *make a cut in sth* ○ *a cut in the edge of the cloth.* **2** (**a**) act of cutting: *Your hair could do with a cut,* ie is too long. (**b**) stroke made with a knife, sword, whip, etc: *a cut across the hand.* **3** ~ (**in sth**) reduction in size, length, amount, etc: *a cut in expenditure, prices, production* ○ *He had to take a cut in (his) salary.* ○ *tax cuts* ○ *a power cut,* ie temporary reduction or stoppage of an electric current. **4** ~ (**in sth**) act of removing part of a play, film, book, etc: *There are several cuts in the film,* ie parts that have been cut out by the censor. ○ *Where can we make a cut in this long article?* **5** piece of meat cut from the carcass of an animal: *a lean cut of pork* ○ *a cut off the joint,* ie a slice from a cooked joint of meat. **6** style in which a garment is made by cutting: *I don't like the cut of his new suit.* **7** (in cricket) stroke played in the direction one is facing with the bat held horizontally: *a cut to the boundary.* **8** remark, etc that hurts sb's feelings: *What she said was a cut at* (ie was directed at) *me.* **9** (*infml*) share of the profits from sth: *Your cut will be £200.* **10** (idm) **a cut above sb/sth** (*infml*) rather better than sb/sth: *Her work is a cut above that of the others.* ○ *She's a cut above the rest (of her colleagues).* **cut and ˈthrust (of sth)** lively argument; attack and counter-attack: *the cut and thrust of parliamentary debate.* **the cut of sb's ˈjib** (*dated*) person's appearance, manner or style: *I must say I didn't like the cut of his jib.* **a short cut** ⇨ SHORT[1].

cutaneous /kju:ˈteɪnɪəs/ *adj* of the skin: *a cutaneous reaction.* Cf SUBCUTANEOUS.

cute /kju:t/ *adj* (**-r**, **-st**) (*sometimes derog*) **1** attractive; pretty and charming: *Isn't she a cute baby?* ○ *unbearably cute paintings of little furry animals.* **2** (*infml esp US*) sharp-witted; clever: *It was cute of you to spot that.* ○ *I have had enough of your cute remarks.* ○ *Don't be so cute!* ▷ **cutely** *adv.* **cuteness** *n* [U].

cuticle /ˈkju:tɪkl/ *n* skin at the base of a finger-nail or toe-nail. ⇨ illus at HAND.

cutie /ˈkju:tɪ/ *n* (*infml sexist*) attractive person, esp a woman or a baby: *Who's that little cutie he's with?*

cutis /ˈkju:tɪs/ *n* [sing] the thicker inside skin that is beneath the epidermis.

cutlass /ˈkʌtləs/ *n* short sword with a slightly curved blade, used formerly by sailors. ⇨ illus at SWORD.

cutler /ˈkʌtlə(r)/ *n* person who makes, sells or repairs knives and other cutting tools.

▷ **cutlery** /ˈkʌtlərɪ/ *n* [U] knives, forks and spoons used for eating and serving food: [attrib] *a cutlery box, set, etc.*

cutlet /ˈkʌtlɪt/ *n* **1** thick slice of meat or fish typically cooked by frying or grilling: *a lamb, veal, salmon, etc cutlet.* **2** minced meat or other food shaped to look like a cutlet: *a nut cutlet.*

cutpurse /ˈkʌtpɜ:s/ *n* (*arch*) pickpocket.

cutter /ˈkʌtə(r)/ *n* **1** (**a**) person or thing that cuts: *a tailor's ˈcutter,* ie who cuts out cloth ○ *a ciˈgar cutter,* ie a small tool for cutting the end off cigars. (**b**) **cutters** [pl] (esp in compounds) cutting tool: *ˈwire-cutters* ○ *ˈbolt-cutters.* **2** (**a**) sailing-boat with one mast. (**b**) ship's boat, used for trips between ship and shore.

cutthroat /ˈkʌtθrəʊt/ *adj* [usu attrib] ruthless; intense: *cutthroat competition, business practices, etc.*

□ ˌ**cutthroat ˈrazor** razor consisting of a long blade attached to a handle.

cutting[1] /ˈkʌtɪŋ/ *n* **1** (*US* **clipping**) article, story, etc cut from a newspaper, etc and kept for reference. **2** piece cut off a plant to be used to grow a new plant: *chrysanthemum cuttings* ○ *take a cutting (from a rose).* **3** (also **cut**) unroofed passage dug through high ground for a road, railway or canal.

□ ˈ**cutting-room** *n* room where film is edited.

cutting[2] /ˈkʌtɪŋ/ *adj* **1** [attrib] (of wind) sharply and unpleasantly cold. **2** hurtful; sarcastic: *cutting remarks, criticism, etc.*

▷ **cuttingly** *adv* in a cutting[2](2) way: *... she said cuttingly.*

cuttlefish /ˈkʌtlfɪʃ/ *n* sea animal with ten arms (tentacles), which sends out black fluid when threatened.

Cutty Sark /ˌkʌtɪ ˈsɑ:k/ British sailing-ship built in 1869 to bring tea from China. It is now moored on the Thames at Greenwich where it is a tourist attraction.

cutworm /ˈkʌtwɜ:m/ *n* any of various types of caterpillar that eat the stems of young plants near the ground.

cv /ˌsi: ˈvi:/ *abbr* record of a person's education and employment (Latin *curriculum vitae*).

cwm /ku:m, kʊm/ *n* rounded valley or hollow on a mountain.

CWO *abbr* cash with order.

cwt *abbr* (*pl* **cwts**) hundredweight (Latin *centum* + English *weight*): *a ½ cwt sack of potatoes.*

-cy (also **-acy**) *suff* **1** (with *adjs* and *ns* forming *ns*) state or quality of: *accuracy* ○ *supremacy* ○ *infancy.* **2** (with *ns* forming *ns*) status or position of: *baronetcy* ○ *chaplaincy.*

cyan /ˈsaɪən/ *n* [U] greenish-blue, esp as a colour in photography.

cyanide /ˈsaɪənaɪd/ *n* [U] highly poisonous chemical compound.

cyanosis /ˌsaɪəˈnəʊsɪs/ *n* [U] unhealthy blue colour of the skin caused by a lack of oxygen supply to the blood.

cybernetics /ˌsaɪbəˈnetɪks/ *n* [sing *v*] science of communication and control, esp concerned with comparing human and animal brains with machines and electronic devices. ▷ **cybernetic** *adj.*

cyclamate /ˈsaɪkləmeɪt, ˈsɪk-/ *n* chemical compound used as an artificial sweetener.

cyclamen /ˈsɪkləmən; *US* ˈsaɪk-/ *n* any of several types of plant with pink, purple or white flowers that have backward-turning petals.

cycle /ˈsaɪkl/ *n* **1** (**a**) series of events that are regularly repeated in the same order: *the cycle of the seasons* ○ *the cycle of economic booms and slumps.* (**b**) series of changes in the state of a thing, at the end of which the thing returns to its original state: *100 million cycles per second,* ie 100 megahertz. **2** complete set or series, eg of songs or poems: *a Schubert song cycle.* **3** (*infml*) bicycle, motor cycle: [attrib] *a cycle shop, race, etc.* Cf BIKE.

▷ **cycle** *v* [I, Ipr, Ip] ride a bicycle: *go cycling* ○ *He cycles to work every day.* ○ *She cycled along (the street).*

cyclic /ˈsaɪklɪk/ (also **cyclical** /ˈsaɪklɪkl/) *adj* recurring in cycles; regularly repeated: *the cyclical nature of economic activity.* ▷ **cyclically** *adv.*

□ ˌ**cyclic ˈcompound** (*chemistry*) compound that has a ring of atoms in its molecules.

cyclist /ˈsaɪklɪst/ *n* person who rides a bicycle.

cyclone /ˈsaɪkləʊn/ *n* **1** system of winds turning round a calm area of low pressure. **2** violent destructive wind-storm. Cf HURRICANE, TYPHOON.

▷ **cyclonic** /saɪˈklɒnɪk/ *adj* of or like a cyclone.

Cyclops /ˈsaɪklɒps/ *n* (*pl* **Cyclopes** /saɪˈkləʊpi:z/) (in Greek mythology) any of a race of one-eyed man-eating giants.

▷ **Cyclopean** /saɪˈkləʊpɪən/ *adj* **1** of or like a Cyclops. **2** (*rhet*) huge; immense.

cyclostyle /ˈsaɪkləstaɪl/ *n* machine for printing copies from a stencil, used esp before the introduction of photocopiers.

▷ **cyclostyle** *v* [Tn] produce (copies) with this: *some cyclostyled copies of his speech.*

cyclotron /ˈsaɪklətrɒn/ *n* device for making atomic particles move at a very high speed, used for experiments in nuclear research.

cyder = CIDER.

cygnet /ˈsɪgnɪt/ *n* young swan.

cylinder /ˈsɪlɪndə(r)/ *n* **1** (**a**) (*geometry*) solid or hollow curved body with circular ends and straight sides. ⇨ illus at CUBE. (**b**) thing shaped like this: *The string is wound round a cardboard cylinder.* ○ *the cylinder of a revolver,* ie the part in which the cartridges are placed. **2** cylinder-shaped hollow part inside which the piston moves in an engine: *a six-cylinder engine/car.* ⇨ illus. **3** (idm) **working/firing on all ˈcylinders** (*infml*) (operating) with full power or effort: *The office is working on all cylinders to get the job finished.*

▷ **cylindrical** /sɪˈlɪndrɪkl/ *adj* cylinder-shaped.

□ ˈ**cylinder block** part of an engine that contains the cylinders (CYLINDER 2).

ˈ**cylinder head** removable part that fits onto the top of a cylinder block.

cymbal /ˈsɪmbl/ *n* (usu *pl*) one of a pair of round brass plates struck together or hit with a stick to produce a clanging sound. ⇨ illus at MUSIC.

cyme /saɪm/ *n* type of flowering shoot in which the first flower to form develops at the top of the stalk and is followed by another flower on a stalk that comes out from just under it, and so on.

Cymric /ˈkʌmrɪk, *or, from non-Welsh speakers,* ˈkɪmrɪk/ *adj* (*rhet*) Welsh.

cynic /ˈsɪnɪk/ *n* **1** person who believes that people do not do things for good, sincere or noble reasons, but only for their own advantage. **2 Cynic** member of a school of ancient Greek philosophy that despised ease and comfort.

▷ **cynical** /ˈsɪnɪkl/ *adj* **1** of or like a cynic: *a cynical remark, attitude, smile* ○ *They've grown rather cynical about democracy,* ie no longer believe that it is an honest system. **2** contemptuously selfish and concerned only with one's own interests: *a cynical disregard for others' safety* ○ *The footballer brought down his opponent with a cynical foul.* **cynically** /-klɪ/ *adv.* **cynicism** /ˈsɪnɪsɪzəm/ *n* [U] cynical attitude.

cynosure /ˈsɪnəzjʊə(r); *US* ˈsaɪnəʃʊər/ *n* (*fml*) person or thing that attracts everybody's attention or admiration; centre of attraction: *She was the cynosure of all eyes,* ie Everyone was looking at her.

cypher = CIPHER.

cypress /ˈsaɪprəs/ *n* type of tall thin cone-bearing evergreen tree with dark leaves and hard wood. ⇨ illus at TREE.

Cyprus

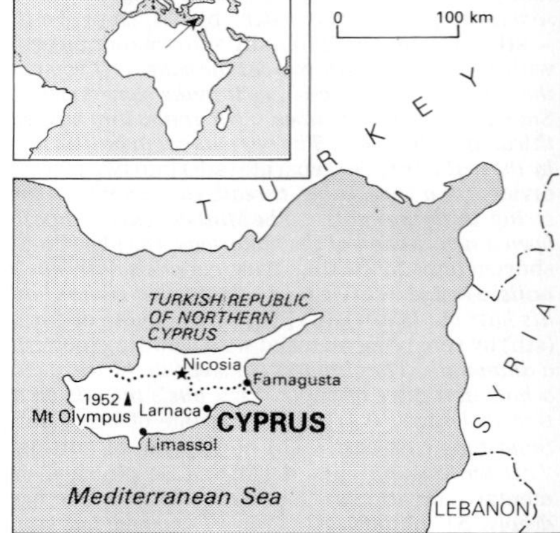

Cyprus /ˈsaɪprəs/ island and country in the eastern Mediterranean; pop approx 687 000; official languages Greek and Turkish; capital Nicosia; unit of currency pound (= 100 cents). The north and south of the island are mountainous and there is a plain in the centre. It was a British colony until its independence in 1960, but tensions between the Greek and Turkish populations continued. Turkey invaded the island in 1974 and a 'Turkish Federated State' was formed in the north, though this is not recognized by the United Nations. ⇨ map. ▷ **Cypriot** /ˈsɪprɪət/ *adj, n.*

Cyrano de Bergerac /ˌsɪrənəʊ də ˈbɜ:ʒəræk/ Savinien (1619-55), French soldier and man of letters. The image of him as a romantic hero with a huge nose, created by the French dramatist Rostand, has overshadowed his own witty plays and essays.

Cyrillic /sɪˈrɪlɪk/ *adj* of the alphabet used for Slavonic languages such as Russian and Bulgarian: *a Cyrillic letter, text, etc.* Cf THE ROMAN ALPHABET (ROMAN).

cyst /sɪst/ *n* hollow organ, bladder, etc in the body, containing liquid matter: *an ovarian cyst.*

▷ **cystic** *adj* (a) like a cyst. (b) of the bladder. **cystic fibrosis** /ˌsɪstɪk faɪˈbrəʊsɪs/ disease that usu affects children, weakening the pancreas and lungs.

cystitis /sɪˈstaɪtɪs/ *n* [U] (*medical*) inflammation of the bladder.

cytology /saɪˈtɒlədʒɪ/ *n* [U] scientific study of biological cells. ▷ **cytologist** *n.*

cytoplasm /ˈsaɪtəplæzəm/ *n* [U] jelly-like material surrounding the nucleus of a cell.

czar, czarina = TSAR, TSARINA.

Czech /tʃek/ *n* **1** [C] (a) native or inhabitant of the Czech Republic. (b) native or inhabitant of western former Czechoslovakia. (c) = CZECHOSLOVAK. **2** [U] language of the Czech Republic and of the former Czechoslovakia.

▷ **Czech** *adj* **1** of the Czech Republic and of the former western Czechoslovakia. **2** = CZECHOSLOVAK.

▷ **the Czech Republic** country in central Europe; pop approx 10 302 000; official language Czech; capital Prague; unit of currency koruna (= 100 heller). Created in 1993, formerly the western area (Bohemia, Moravia) of Czechoslovakia, it has an advanced industry and aims at maintaining an internationally competitive economy. It also has agricultural resources, esp timber. ⇨ map.

Czech Republic and Slovakia

Czechoslovakia /ˌtʃekəʊsləˈvækɪə/ former country in central Europe comprising the present Czech and Slovak Republics. It was formed in 1918 out of the old Czech western regions of Bohemia and Moravia, with Slovakia (and for a time Ruthenia) to the east. Communism took hold after 1945, the country remaining in the Soviet bloc until 1989 despite a liberal reform movement during 1968. Since 1993 the two present republics have been separated. ⇨ map.

▷ **Czechoslovak** /ˌtʃekəˈsləʊvæk/ (also **Czechoslovakian** /ˌtʃekəsləˈvækɪən/) *n, adj* (native or inhabitant) of the former Czechoslovakia.

D, d

D, d /di:/ *n* (*pl* **D's, d's** /di:z/) **1** the fourth letter of the English alphabet: *'David' begins and ends with a 'D'/D.* **2 D** (*music*) the second note in the scale of C major. **3 D** academic mark indicating a low standard of work.

D *abbr* (*US politics*) Democrat; Democratic. Cf R 3.

D *symb* **1** deuterium. **2** (also **d**) Roman numeral for 500. Cf D-DAY.

d *abbr* **1** (in former British currency) penny; pennies or pence (Latin *denarius; denarii*): *a 2d stamp* ○ *6d each.* Cf P 2. **2** died: *Emily Jane Clifton d 1865.* Cf B.

-d ⇨ -ED.

DA *abbr* **1** deposit account. **2** (*US*) District Attorney.

dab[1] /dæb/ *v* (**-bb-**) **1** [Tn] press (sth) lightly and gently: *She dabbed her eyes (with a tissue).* **2** [Ipr] ~ **at sth** lightly touch sth by pressing but not rubbing: *She dabbed at the cut with cotton wool.* **3** (phr v) **dab sth on/off (sth)** apply/remove (sth) with light quick strokes: *dab paint on a picture* ○ *dab off the excess water.*

▷ **dab** *n* **1** [C] (**a**) small quantity (of paint, etc) put on a surface. (**b**) act of lightly touching or pressing sth without rubbing: *One dab with blotting-paper and the ink was dry.* **2 dabs** [pl] (*Brit sl*) fingerprints.

dab[2] /dæb/ *n* type of flat-fish.

dab[3] /dæb/ *n* (idm) **(be) a dab (hand) (at sth)** (*Brit infml*) very skilled: *a dab hand at golf, at rolling cigarettes.*

dabble /ˈdæbl/ *v* **1** [Tn, Tn·pr] ~ **sth (in sth)** splash (hands, feet, etc) around in water: *She dabbled her fingers in the fountain.* **2** [I, Ipr] ~ **(in/at sth)** take part without serious intentions: *He just dabbles in politics.* ▷ **dabbler** /ˈdæblə(r)/ *n*: *He's not a dedicated musician, just a dabbler.*

dabchick /ˈdæbtʃɪk/ *n* small water-bird of the grebe family.

dace /deɪs/ *n* (*pl* unchanged) small freshwater fish.

dacha /ˈdætʃə/ *n* country house or villa in Russia.

dachshund /ˈdækshʊnd/ *n* type of small dog with a long body and short legs. ⇨ illus at DOG.

Dacron /ˈdækrɒn, ˈdeɪkrɒn/ *n* [U] (*US propr*) = TERYLENE.

dactyl /ˈdæktɪl/ *n* metrical foot consisting of one stressed syllable followed by two unstressed syllables, as in the line 'ˈunder the / ˈblossom that/ ˈhangs on the / ˈbough'. ▷ **dactylic** /dækˈtɪlɪk/ *adj*: *a dactylic line/verse.*

dad /dæd/ *n* (*infml*) father.

Dada /ˈdɑːdɑː/ *n* international movement in art and literature about 1915-22 which was opposed to the formal artistic conventions of the time. It set out to shock people with strange or disturbing images which challenged their ideas of what 'art' is. Among its leading members were the French painter Marcel Duchamp and the French sculptor Jean Arp. *Surrealism developed from it. ▷ **Dadaism** /-ɪzəm/ *n* [U].

daddy /ˈdædɪ/ *n* (used esp by and to children) father.

□ ˌ**daddy-ˈlong-legs** *n* (*infml*) = CRANE-FLY.

dado /ˈdeɪdəʊ/ *n* (*pl* ~**s**; *US* ~**es**) **1** lower part of the wall of a room, when it is different from the upper part in colour or material. **2** (*architecture*) central part or layer of the stone block on which a column, pillar, statue, etc is placed.

daemon /ˈdiːmən/ *n* **1** (esp in Greek mythology) supernatural being that is half god, half man. **2** spirit that inspires sb to action or creativity.

daffodil /ˈdæfədɪl/ *n* yellow flower with a tall stem and long narrow leaves that grows from a bulb. It blooms in Britain between February and April, and is identified with the coming of spring. ⇨ illus at PLANT. ⇨ article at NATIONAL.

daft /dɑːft; *US* dæft/ *adj* (**-er, -est**) (*infml*) foolish; silly: *Don't be so daft!* ○ *He's gone a bit daft (in the head),* ie He has become slightly insane. ▷ **daftness** *n* [U].

dagger /ˈdægə(r)/ *n* **1** short pointed two-edged knife used as a weapon. ⇨ illus at KNIFE. **2** printer's mark (†) used to refer the reader to a footnote, etc. **3** (idm) **at daggers drawn (with sb)** very hostile (towards sb): *She's at daggers drawn with her colleagues.* ○ *He and his partner are at daggers drawn.* **look daggers at sb** look very angrily at sb: *He looked daggers at me when I told him he was lazy.* Cf CLOAK-AND-DAGGER (CLOAK).

dago /ˈdeɪgəʊ/ *n* (*pl* ~**s**) (⚠ *sl offensive*) dark-skinned foreigner, esp an Italian, a Spaniard or a Portuguese.

daguerreotype /dəˈgerətaɪp/ *n* early type of photograph using a chemically treated plate.

dahlia /ˈdeɪlɪə; *US* ˈdælɪə/ *n* garden plant with brightly coloured flowers.

Dáil Éireann /ˌdɔɪl ˈeərən/ (also **the Dáil**) [Gp] the legislative assembly of the Republic of Ireland.

daily /ˈdeɪlɪ/ *adj* [attrib], *adv* **1** done, produced or happening every day: *a daily routine, visit, newspaper* ○ *The machines are inspected daily.* **2** (idm) **one's daily bread** (**a**) one's daily food. (**b**) (*infml*) one's livelihood: *That's how I earn my daily bread.* **one's daily dozen** (*infml*) a few routine exercises performed each day in order to keep oneself fit.

▷ **daily** *n* **1** newspaper published every weekday. **2** (also **daily help**) (*Brit infml*) = HELP[2] 3.

Daimler /ˈdaɪmlə(r)/ Gottlieb (1834-90), German engineer who contributed to the development of the internal-combustion engine and was a pioneer of car manufacture. The type of car named after him is pronounced /ˈdeɪmlə(r)/ in English.

dainty /ˈdeɪntɪ/ *adj* (**-ier, -iest**) **1** (of things) small and pretty: *dainty porcelain, lace, etc.* **2** (**a**) (of people) neat and delicate(2) in build or movement: *a dainty child.* (**b**) (of people) having refined taste[1](5) and manners; fastidious, esp about food: *a dainty eater.* **3** having a pleasant taste; delicious: *a dainty morsel.*

▷ **daintily** *adv* in a dainty way: *a daintily dressed doll.*

daintiness *n* [U].

dainty (usu *pl*) *n* small tasty piece of food, esp a small cake.

daiquiri /ˈdækərɪ, ˈdaɪ-/ *n* (*esp US*) iced drink made with rum, lime juice and sugar.

dairy /ˈdeərɪ/ *n* **1** place where milk is kept and milk products are made: [attrib] *dairy cream.* **2** shop where milk, butter, eggs, etc are sold.

□ ˈ**dairy cattle** cows kept to produce milk, not meat.

ˈ**dairy farm** farm that produces mainly milk and butter.

ˈ**dairymaid** *n* woman who works in a dairy(1).

ˈ**dairyman** /-mən/ *n* (*pl* **-men**) (**a**) dealer in milk, etc. (**b**) man who works in a dairy(1).

ˈ**dairy produce** food made from milk, eg butter, cheese, yoghurt.

dais /ˈdeɪɪs/ *n* (*pl* **-es** /-ɪz/) raised platform, esp at one end of a room, for a speaker, etc.

daisy /ˈdeɪzɪ/ *n* **1** (**a**) small white flower with a yellow centre, growing wild or commonly as a weed in garden lawns. ⇨ illus at PLANT. (**b**) any of many different types of plant with similar flowers, ie with petals that radiate from the centre like the spokes of a wheel. **2** (idm) **fresh as a daisy** ⇨ FRESH. **push up daisies** ⇨ PUSH[2].

□ ˈ**daisy wheel** small wheel used in a printer or an electric typewriter, with characters arranged around the circumference. Cf GOLF BALL (GOLF).

Dalai Lama /ˌdælaɪ ˈlɑːmə/ head of the Buddhist religion of Tibet. Until 1959, when China took over the country, the Dalai Lama was its ruler, and was worshipped almost as a god, but now he lives abroad. When each Dalai Lama dies he is replaced by a new one who is said to be a reincarnation of the previous one.

dale /deɪl/ *n* **1** valley, esp in Northern England: *the Yorkshire Dales.* **2** (idm) **up hill and down dale** ⇨ HILL.

Dalek /ˈdɑːlek/ *n* aggressive robot-like creature appearing in 'Dr Who', a British television science-fiction series which began in the 1960s.

Dali /ˈdɑːlɪ/ Salvador (1904-89), Spanish Surrealist painter. His pictures often show strangely distorted objects painted in a very accurate and realistic way, which gives them a disturbing quality. He was famous for his flamboyant behaviour and unconventional appearance.

dalliance /ˈdælɪəns/ *n* [U] (*fml*) frivolous behaviour, esp flirtation: *to spend time in idle dalliance.*

dally /ˈdælɪ/ *v* (*pt, pp* **dallied**) **1** [I, Ipr] ~ **(over sth)** waste time: *Come on. Don't dally!* ○ *She dallies over her work and rarely finishes it.* **2** (phr v) **dally with sb/sth** treat sb/sth frivolously: *She merely dallied with him/his affections,* ie flirted with him without really caring for him. **dally with sth** think about (an idea, etc) but not seriously: *dally with a proposal.*

Dalmatian /dælˈmeɪʃn/ *n* large short-haired dog, white with dark spots. ⇨ illus at DOG.

Dalton /ˈdɔːltən/ John (1766-1844), English chemist. Through experiments on gases he found that the atoms of various elements differ in weight. This discovery formed the basis of modern atomic theory. He was also the first person to publish a scientific description of colour-blindness.

Dalton plan /ˈdɔːltən plæn/ **the Dalton plan** educational system, originating in the USA, in which children learn by doing long projects.

dam[1] /dæm/ *n* **1** barrier (made of concrete, earth, etc) built across a river to hold back the water and form a reservoir, prevent flooding, etc. **2** reservoir formed by such a barrier.

▷ **dam** *v* **1** [Tn, Tn·p] ~ **sth (up)** build a dam across (a river, valley, etc). **2** (phr v) **dam sth up** (*fig*) hold back (emotions, etc): *to dam up one's feelings.*

dam[2] /dæm/ *n* mother of a four-footed animal.

damage /ˈdæmɪdʒ/ *n* **1** [U] ~ **(to sth)** loss of value, attractiveness or usefulness caused by an event, accident, etc: *The accident did a lot of damage to the car.* ○ *storm damage to crops* ○ *damage to her reputation.* **2 damages** [pl] money paid or claimed as compensation for damage(1), loss or injury: *The court awarded £5 000 (in) damages to the injured man.* **3** (idm) **what's the ˈdamage?** (*Brit infml*) what does/did sth cost?: *'I need a new coat.' 'Oh yes? What's the damage?'*

▷ **damage** *v* [Tn] cause damage to (sth): *damage a fence, a car, furniture, etc* ○ *damage sb's career* ○ *damage relations between two countries.*

damaging *adj* ~ **(to sth)** having a bad effect: *Smoking can be damaging to your health.* ○ *to make damaging allegations.*

damascene /ˈdæməsiːn/ *v* [Tn] decorate (metal) with a wavy pattern, esp by inserting other types of metal, eg gold or silver: *a damascened sword blade.*

damask /ˈdæməsk/ *n* [U] **1** silk or linen material, with designs made visible by the reflection of light: [attrib] *a damask table-cloth.* **2** steel with a pattern of wavy lines or with inlaid gold or silver.

□ ˌ**damask ˈrose** bright pink, sweet-scented type of rose.

dame /deɪm/ *n* **1** (*US sl*) woman: *Gee! What a dame!*

2 Dame (*Brit*) (title of a) woman, who has been awarded an order[1](10b) of knighthood. **3** (also **pantomime dame**) elderly female comic character in pantomime, usu played by a man.

damn[1] /dæm/ *v* **1** [Tn] (of God) condemn (sb) to suffer in hell. **2** [Tn] criticize (sth) severely: *The play was damned by the reviewers.* **3** [Tn] (also *euph* **darn**) (*infml*) (esp as an *interj*, used to express annoyance, anger, etc): *Damn! I've lost my pen.* ○ *Damn this useless typewriter!* **4** (idm) **as near as damn it/dammit** ⇨ NEAR[2]. **damn the consequences, expense, etc** never mind the difficulties: *Let's enjoy ourselves and damn the consequences.* **(I'm) damned if...** (*infml*) I certainly do, will, etc not...; I absolutely refuse to...: *I'm damned if I'm going to let her get away with that!* ○ *Damned if I know!* ie I certainly don't know. **damn sb/sth with faint ˈpraise** imply criticism by not praising enough. **I'll be damned!** (*infml*) (used as an expression of surprise): *Well I'll be damned: she won after all!* **publish and be damned** ⇨ PUBLISH.

▷ **damning** *adj* very unfavourable: *damning criticism, evidence* ○ *a damning remark, etc* ○ *She said some pretty damning things about him.*

damn[2] /dæm/ *n* (idm) **not be worth a damn, etc** ⇨ WORTH. **not care/give a ˈdamn (about sb/sth)** (*infml*) not care at all: *I don't give a damn what you say, I'm going.*

▷ **damn** *adj* [attrib] (*infml*) (expressing disapproval, anger, impatience, etc): *Where's that damn book?* ○ *My damn car has broken down!*

damn *adv* (*infml*) **1 (a)** (expressing disapproval, anger, etc) very: *Don't be so damn silly!* ○ *You know damn well what I mean!* **(b)** (expressing approval, etc) very: *damn good, clever, etc* ○ *We got out of there pretty damn fast.* **2** (idm) **damn ˈall** (*infml*) nothing at all: *I earned damn all last week.* ○ [attrib] *It's damn all use you telling me that now!*

damnable /ˈdæmnəbl/ *adj* **(a)** deserving disapproval; wicked; disgraceful: *damnable behaviour, crimes, etc.* **(b)** (*dated infml*) very bad: *damnable weather.* ▷ **damnably** /ˈdæmnəblɪ/ *adv.*

damnation /dæmˈneɪʃn/ *n* [U] **1** state of being damned: *to suffer eternal damnation.* **2** (*dated*) (used as an *interj* to express annoyance, anger, etc): *Damnation! I've lost my umbrella.*

damned /dæmd/ *adj, adv* = DAMN[2] *adj*, DAMN[2] *adv* 1.

▷ **the damned** *n* [pl *v*] people who suffer in hell: *the torments of the damned.*

damnedest /ˈdæmdɪst/ (idm) **do/try one's ˈdamnedest** do/try one's best: *She did her damnedest to get it done on time.*

damp[1] /dæmp/ *adj* (**-er, -est**) **1** not completely dry; slightly wet: *damp clothes* ○ *a damp surface* ○ *Don't sleep between damp sheets.* **2** (idm) **a damp ˈsquib** (*infml*) event, etc that is much less impressive than expected: *The party was a bit of a damp squib.*

▷ **damp** *n* [U] **1** state of being damp: *Air the clothes to get the damp out.* ○ *Don't stay outside in the damp*, ie in the damp atmosphere. **2** = FIRE-DAMP (FIRE[1]).

damply *adv.*

dampness *n* [U].

□ **ˈdamp-proof course** (also **ˈdamp course**) layer of material near the bottom of a wall to stop damp rising from the ground.

damp[2] /dæmp/ *v* **1** [Tn] = DAMPEN 1. **2** [Tn, Tn·p] ~ **sth (down) (a)** reduce (noise, etc): *Soft material damps down vibrations.* **(b)** make (sth) less strong; restrain: *damp (down) sb's spirits, energy, ardour, etc.* **3** (phr v) **damp sth down** cause sth to burn more slowly (by adding ash, etc or reducing the flow of air): *We damped the fire down before we went to bed.*

dampen /ˈdæmpən/ *v* **1** [Tn] make (sth) damp: *I always dampen shirts before ironing them.* **2** [Tn, Tn·p] ~ **sth (down)** make (sth) less strong; restrain: *dampen (down) sb's enthusiasm.*

damper /ˈdæmpə(r)/ *n* **1** movable metal plate that controls the flow of air into a fire in a stove, furnace, etc. **2** small pad that is pressed against a piano-string to stop it vibrating. **3** (idm) **put a damper on sth** (*infml*) cause (an event, atmosphere, etc) to be less cheerful, excited, etc: *Their argument put a bit of a damper on the party.*

damsel /ˈdæmzl/ *n* **1** (*arch*) girl; young unmarried woman. **2** (idm) **a damsel in distress** (*joc*) woman who needs help: *Most men will help a damsel in distress.*

damson /ˈdæmzn/ *n* **1 (a)** type of fruit tree that produces a small dark-purple plum. **(b)** its fruit: [attrib] *damson jam/jelly.* **2** dark-purple colour: [attrib] *a damson dress.*

dan /dæn/ *n* **(a)** level of skill in sports such as judo and karate. **(b)** person who has reached such a level: *She is a fourth dan at judo.*

dance[1] /dɑːns; *US* dæns/ *n* **1 (a)** [C] (series of) movements and steps in time to music: [attrib] *to learn new dance steps.* **(b)** [C] type of dance: *The rumba is a Latin-American dance.* **(c)** [C] one round or turn of a dance: *May I have the next dance?* **(d)** [C] music for a dance: *a gipsy dance played on the violin.* **(e)** (also **the dance**) [U] dancing as an art form: *She has written a book on (the) dance.* **2** [C] social gathering at which people dance: *to hold a dance in the village hall.* **3** (idm) **lead sb a dance** ⇨ LEAD[3]. **a song and dance** ⇨ SONG.

□ **ˈdance-band** *n* band that plays music for dancing.

ˈdance-hall *n* hall for public dances, which one pays to enter. Cf BALLROOM (BALL[2]).

dance[2] /dɑːns; *US* dæns/ *v* **1 (a)** [I, Ipr, Ip] move rhythmically in a series of steps, alone, with a partner or in a group, usu in time to music: *We danced to the disco music.* ○ *Would you like to dance?* ○ *I danced with her all night.* **(b)** [Tn] perform (a certain kind of dance, ballet, etc): *to dance a waltz, the cha-cha, etc.* **2** [I, Ipr, Ip] move in a lively way, usu up and down: *leaves dancing in the wind* ○ *a boat dancing on the waves* ○ *to dance for joy/with rage.* **3** [Tn·pr, Tn·p] cause (sb) to dance: *She danced the little child round the room.* ○ *He danced the baby* (ie bounced it up and down) *on his knee.* **4** (idm) **dance attendance (up)on sb** (*fml*) follow sb about, attending to his wishes: *She loves to have servants dance attendance (up)on her.* **dance to sb's tune** do as sb demands.

▷ **dancer** **(a)** person who dances: *He's a good dancer.* **(b)** person who dances for payment: *She's a (tap-/ballet-) dancer.*

dancing *n* [U] moving rhythmically in time to music: *ˈtap-dancing* ○ *ˈreggae dancing.* **ˈdancing-girl** *n* woman who dances professionally, often in a group. **ˈdancing shoes** light shoes worn for dancing.

dandelion /ˈdændɪlaɪən/ *n* small wild plant with a bright yellow flower and leaves with notched edges. ⇨ illus at FLOWER.

dander /ˈdændə(r)/ *n* (idm) **get sb's/one's ˈdander up** (*infml*) make sb/become angry: *It really got my dander up when she began accusing me of dishonesty.*

dandle /ˈdændl/ *v* [Tn] move (esp a child) up and down on one's knee(s) or in one's arms: *He dandled the baby to make it stop crying.*

dandruff /ˈdændrʌf/ *n* [U] small flakes of dead skin from the scalp, usu seen in the hair; scurf: *This shampoo will cure your dandruff.*

Dandy /ˈdændɪ/ popular British weekly comic for children, first published in 1937.

dandy[1] /ˈdændɪ/ *n* man who cares too much about the smartness of his clothes and his appearance.

▷ **dandified** /ˈdændɪfaɪd/ *adj* like or typical of a dandy: *dandified clothes.*

dandy[2] /ˈdændɪ/ *adj* (**-ier, -iest**) (*infml esp US*) very good; excellent: *all fine and dandy* ○ *That's just dandy!*

Dane /deɪn/ *n* **1** native of Denmark. **2** member of the Scandinavian peoples who invaded and settled in England from the 9th to the 11th centuries; Viking.

Danegeld /ˈdeɪngeld/ *n* [U] tax on the value of land levied in England from the 10th to the 12th centuries, originally as a bribe to stop the Vikings invading.

Danelaw /ˈdeɪnlɔː/ *n* [U] (from the 9th to the 11th centuries) the northern and eastern parts of England, occupied and ruled by the Danes.

danger /ˈdeɪndʒə(r)/ *n* **1** [U] ~ **(of sth)** chance of suffering damage, loss, injury, etc; risk: *There's a lot of danger in rock climbing.* ○ *Danger — thin ice!* ○ *In war, a soldier's life is full of danger.* ○ *Is there any danger of fire?* ○ *She was very ill, but is now out of danger*, ie not likely to die. ○ *Ships out in this storm are in great danger*, ie very liable to suffer damage, etc. ○ *His life was in danger.* **2** [C] ~ **(to sb/sth)** person or thing that may cause damage, injury, pain, etc; hazard: *be afraid of hidden dangers* ○ *Smoking is a danger to health.* ○ *That woman is a danger to society.* **3** (idm) **on the ˈdanger list** (*infml*) very ill and near to death: *She was on the danger list, but is much better now.*

□ **ˈdanger money** extra pay for dangerous work.

dangerous /ˈdeɪndʒərəs/ *adj* ~ **(for sb/sth)** likely to cause danger or be a danger: *a dangerous bridge, journey, illness* ○ *The river is dangerous for swimmers.* ○ *This machine is dangerous: the wiring is faulty.* ▷ **dangerously** *adv*: *driving dangerously* ○ *dangerously ill*, ie so ill that one might die.

dangle /ˈdæŋgl/ *v* **1 (a)** [I] hang or swing loosely: *a bunch of keys dangling at the end of a chain.* **(b)** [Tn] hold (sth) so that it swings loosely: *He dangled his watch in front of the baby.* **2** (phr v) **dangle sth before/in front of sb** offer sth temptingly to sb: *The prospect of promotion was dangled before him.*

□ **ˌdangling ˈparticiple** (also **misplaced modifier**) (*grammar*) participle that is formally linked to one word or phrase in a sentence but actually refers to another word or phrase, eg *being* in *Being a nervous person, loud noises frighten him* (where *being* formally modifies *noises* but actually refers to *him*). Such usage is generally regarded as incorrect English.

Daniel /ˈdænjəl/ **1** Hebrew prophet of the 6th century BC who, according to the Old Testament story, was thrown into a lions' den but was saved from death by God. **2** book of the Bible that tells the story of Daniel. ⇨ App 5.

Danish /ˈdeɪnɪʃ/ *n, adj* (language) of Denmark and the Danes.

□ **ˌDanish ˈblue** type of soft white cheese with blue veins.

ˌDanish ˈpastry pastry cake containing apple, almond paste, etc, with icing, nuts, etc on top.

dank /dæŋk/ *adj* (**-er, -est**) unpleasantly damp and cold: *a dank cellar, cave, etc.* ▷ **dankness** *n* [U].

Dante Alighieri /ˌdæntɪ ˌælɪˈgɪərɪ/ (1265-1321), Italian poet. His best-known work is the *Divine Comedy,* a long allegorical poem about the journey of the soul after death, which he began around 1307 and finished just before he died. It is in three parts. In the first, the *Inferno,* Dante is led through Hell by the Latin poet Virgil, who continues as his guide in the second part, the *Purgatorio.* In the final part, the *Paradiso,* he is taken into Heaven by Beatrice, a girl with whom he once fell in love. It was an extremely influential work, and some consider it to be the greatest poem of the Middle Ages.

Danton /ˈdɑːntɒn/ Georges Jacques (1759-94), French revolutionary leader who rallied French resistance against the Austrian invasion in 1792. He was at first an ally of *Robespierre, but gradually turned against his extreme policies, and eventually Robespierre had him executed.

Danube /ˈdænjuːb/ **the Danube** European river that flows through Germany, Austria, Slovakia, Hungary, and along the Romanian/Bulgarian border into the Black Sea. It is about 2 850 km (1 770 miles) long. The 'Blue Danube' is one of Johann *Strauss's most famous Viennese waltzes.

dapper /ˈdæpə(r)/ *adj* (*approv*) (usu of a small person) neat and smart in appearance; nimble in movement: *What a dapper little man!*

dapple /ˈdæpl/ *v* [Tn] mark (sth) with (often rounded) patches of different colour or shades of colour: *The sun shining through the leaves dappled the ground.*

▷ **dappled** *adj* having (often rounded) patches of different colour or shades of colour: *a dappled deer/horse* ○ *dappled shade*, eg when the sun shines through leaves.

□ ˌ**dapple-ˈgrey** *n, adj* (horse that is) grey with darker patches.

Darby and Joan /ˌdɑːbɪ ən ˈdʒəʊn/ old and loving married couple.

□ ˌ**Darby and ˈJoan club** (*Brit*) social club for old (esp married) people.

Dardanelles /ˌdɑːdəˈnelz/ **the Dardanelles** narrow stretch of water that joins the Aegean Sea with the Sea of Marmara, and separates Europe from Asia Minor. In ancient times it was known as the *Hellespont. In 1915 British, French, Australian and New Zealand troops attacked Turkey, landing in the Dardanelles. The attack was unsuccessful and many were killed. ⇨ map at TURKEY.

dare[1] /deə(r)/ *modal v* (*neg* **dare not**, *contracted form* **daren't** /deənt/; *rare or fml pt* **dared** /deəd/, *neg* **dared not**) **1** (used esp in negative sentences and questions, after *if*/*whether*, or with *hardly, never, no one, nobody*) have sufficient courage or impudence (to do sth): *I daren't ask her for a rise.* ○ *What's the matter — daren't you read what it says?* ○ *I wonder whether he dare stand up in public.* ○ *They hardly dared breathe as somebody walked past the door.* ○ *If you ever dare call me that name again, you'll be sorry.* ○ *Nobody dared lift their eyes from the ground.* **2** (idm) **how ˈdare you, he, she, etc** (used to express indignation at the actions of others): *How dare you suggest that I copied your notes!* ○ *How dare he take my bicycle without even asking!* **I dare say** I accept (sth) as a true or possible fact: *I ˈdare say you ˈare British but you still need a passport to prove it.* ○ *'I would imagine he's forgotten.' 'I ˌdare ˈsay!'*

dare[2] /deə(r)/ *v* **1** [Tt] have sufficient courage: *I don't know how she dares wear that dress.* ○ *I've never dared go back to look.* ○ *Privatize the national parks? They'd never dare, would they?* ○ *How did you dare to tell her?* ○ *Don't (you) dare leave the room!* **2** [Tn, Dn·t] suggest to (sb) that he tries to do sth beyond his courage or ability; challenge: *Throw it at him! I dare you!* ○ *I dare you to tell your mother!* ○ *Somebody dared me to jump off the bridge into the river.* **3** [Tn no passive] (*fml*) take the risk of having to face (sth): *He dared his grandfather's displeasure when he left the family business.*

▷ **dare** *n* (usu *sing*) **1** challenge to do sth dangerous or difficult: *'Why did you climb onto the roof?' 'It was a dare.'* **2** (idm) **for a ˈdare** because one has received a challenge: *He only entered the competition for a dare.*

□ **daredevil** /ˈdeədevl/ *n* person who is foolishly bold or reckless: *He's a daredevil on the racing-track.* ○ [attrib] *a ˌdaredevil ˈpilot* ○ *Don't try any of those daredevil stunts.*

daring /ˈdeərɪŋ/ *n* [U] adventurous courage; boldness: *the daring of the mountain climber* ○ *an ambitious plan of great daring*, ie that is bold and new.

▷ **daring** *adj* **1** courageous: *a daring person, exploit, attack.* **2** bold in a new or unusual way: *a daring plan, innovation, etc* ○ *a daring new art form* ○ *She said some daring* (ie bold and possibly shocking) *things.* **daringly** *adv.*

Darius /dəˈraɪəs/ 'the Great' (c 550-486 BC), king of ancient Persia who made great improvements in administration and communication in his country but whose invasion of Greece was halted by defeat at the battle of *Marathon in 490 BC.

Darjeeling /dɑːˈdʒiːlɪŋ/ *n* [U] type of tea grown around Darjeeling, a town in West Bengal, India.

dark[1] /dɑːk/ *n* **1 the dark** [sing] absence of light: *All the lights went out and we were left in the dark.* ○ *Are you afraid of the dark?* **2** (idm) **before**/**after dark** before/after the sun goes down: *Try to get home before dark.* ○ *I'm afraid to go out after dark in the city.* (**be**/**keep sb**) **in the ˈdark** (**about sth**) in a state of ignorance: *I was in the dark about it until she told me.* ○ *We were kept completely in the dark about his plan to sell the company.* **a leap**/**shot in the ˈdark** action, answer, etc that is risked in the hope that it is correct: *It's hard to know exactly what to do — we'll just have to take a shot in the dark.* **whistle in the dark** ⇨ WHISTLE.

dark[2] /dɑːk/ *adj* (**-er**, **-est**) **1** with no or very little light: *a dark room, street, corner, etc* ○ *It's awfully dark in here: put the light on.* ○ *It's too dark to play outside.* **2** (**a**) (of a colour) not reflecting much light; closer in shade(6) to black than to white: *dark green, red, grey, etc* ○ *a dark dress, suit, etc* ○ *dark-brown eyes.* (**b**) having brown(ish) or black skin or hair: *a dark youth, complexion* ○ *I have one fair and one dark child.* **3** (*fig*) (**a**) hidden; mysterious: *a dark secret*/*mystery.* (**b**) difficult to understand; obscure: *Your meaning is too dark for me.* **4** (*fig*) gloomy; sad: *dark predictions about the future* ○ *You always look on the dark side of things*, ie are always pessimistic. **5** evil: *dark powers*/*influence.* **6** (idm) **a dark ˈhorse** person who hides special personal qualities or abilities: *He's a bit of a dark horse: he was earning a fortune, but nobody knew.* **keep it**/**sth dark** (**from sb**) keep sth secret: *I'm getting married again, but keep it dark, will you?*

▷ **darkly** *adv* (*fig*) **1** mysteriously: *She hinted darkly at strange events.* **2** gloomily: *He spoke darkly of possible future disaster.*

darkness *n* [U] state of being dark: *The room was in complete darkness.*

□ **the ˈDark Ages** period of (European) history between the end of the Roman Empire and the tenth century AD, a time when, it was once thought, there was little cultural or social development.

the ˌDark ˈContinent (name given to) Africa before it was fully explored.

ˌ**dark ˈglasses** spectacles with tinted lenses.

ˈ**dark meat** flesh of a chicken, turkey, etc which appears dark when cooked. Cf RED MEAT (RED[1]), WHITE MEAT (WHITE[1]).

ˈ**dark-room** *n* room which can be made dark, used for processing photographs.

darken /ˈdɑːkən/ *v* [I, Tn] **1** (cause sth to) become dark: *We darkened the room to show the film.* ○ *The sky darkened as the storm approached.* **2** (idm) **darken sb's ˈdoor** (*joc or rhet*) come as an unwanted or reluctant visitor to sb's house: *Go! And never darken my door again!*

darky (also **darkie**) /ˈdɑːkɪ/ *n* (⚠ *infml offensive*) black or coloured person.

darling /ˈdɑːlɪŋ/ *n* (**a**) person or thing much liked or loved: *She's a little darling!* ○ *He's the darling* (ie favourite subject) *of the media just now.* (**b**) (as a form of address): *My darling! How sweet of you to come!*

▷ **darling** *adj* [attrib] **1** dearly loved. **2** (*infml*) charming; pleasing: *What a darling little room!*

darn[1] /dɑːn/ *v* [I, Tn] mend (a garment) by passing a thread through the material in two directions: *My socks have been darned again and again.* ○ *I must darn the hole in my pocket.*

▷ **darn** *n* place mended by darning.

darning *n* [U] task of darning; things needing to be darned: *I hate darning.* ○ *We sat doing the darning.*

ˈ**darning-needle** *n* large sewing needle used for darning.

darn[2] /dɑːn/ *v* [Tn] (*infml euph*) = DAMN[1] 3: *Well, I'll be darned!* ○ *Darn it! She beat me again!* ○ *Darn those blasted kids!*

▷ **darn** (also **darned**) *adj* (*infml euph*) (used to express annoyance, impatience, etc): *That darn(ed) cat has eaten my supper!*

darn *adv* (*infml euph approv or derog*) extremely; very: *a darn(ed) good try* ○ *What a darn(ed) stupid thing to say!*

darnel /ˈdɑːnl/ *n* [C, U] type of grass that grows as a weed among corn.

dart[1] /dɑːt/ *n* **1** [C] small pointed missile (often with feathers to aid flight) used as a weapon or in the game of darts. **2** [sing] sudden fast movement: *She made a dart for the exit.* **3** [C] (in dressmaking) stitched tapering fold. **4 darts** [sing *v*] game in which darts are thrown at a target marked with numbers for scoring: *Darts is often played in English pubs.* ⇨ illus.

□ ˈ**dartboard** *n* circular board used as the target in the game of darts.

dart[2] /dɑːt/ *v* [Ipr, Ip, Tn·pr, Tn·p] (cause sth to) move suddenly and quickly in the specified direction: *The mouse darted away when I approached.* ○ *Swallows are darting through the air.* ○ *She darted into the doorway to hide.* ○ *The snake darted out its tongue.* ○ *She darted an angry look* (ie suddenly glanced angrily) *at him.* ⇨ Usage at WHIZ.

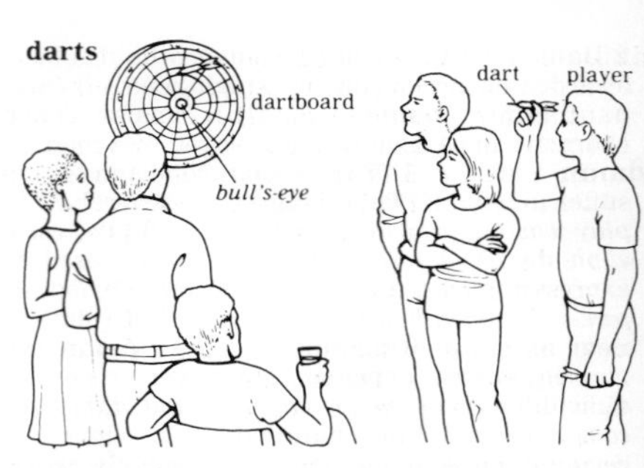

Dartmoor /ˈdɑːtmɔː(r)/ **1** area of high open treeless country in SW England, now a national park. Its area is 945 sq km (365 sq miles). **2** prison on Dartmoor for men serving long sentences.

□ ˌ**Dartmoor ˈpony** small strong long-haired type of pony.

Darwin /ˈdɑːwɪn/ Charles Robert (1809-82), British naturalist who developed the theory of evolution by natural selection. In 1831 he sailed to South America in HMS Beagle on a voyage of scientific discovery. The observations he made there led him in due course to put forward the idea that species of animals and plants change over time by retaining certain naturally occurring features which make them better able to survive. He published his theory in *On the Origin of Species* (1859). It appeared to conflict with the teachings of the Bible, and caused much controversy, but it has come to be accepted, with modifications, as a true account of the way species evolve. Cf WALLACE[1]. ▷ **Darwinian** /dɑːˈwɪnɪən/ *adj.* **Darwinism** /ˈdɑːwɪnɪzəm/ *n* [U].

dash[1] /dæʃ/ *n* **1** [sing] ~ (**for sth**) sudden forward movement: *to make a dash for freedom, shelter* ○ *We jumped into the car and made a dash for the ferry.* ○ *Mother said lunch was ready and there was a mad dash for the table.* **2** [C usu *sing*] (*esp US*) short race; sprint: *the 100-metres dash.* **3** [C esp *sing*] **a** ~ (**of sth**) small amount of sth added or mixed: *a dash of salt* ○ *red with a dash of blue* ○ *The flag adds a dash of colour to the grey building.* **4** [sing] ~ (**of sth**) (sound of) liquid striking or being thrown against sth: *the dash of waves on the rocks* ○ *A dash of water in his face will revive him.* **5** [C] horizontal stroke (—) used in writing, printing and Morse code. ⇨ App 14. **6** [U] ability to act vigorously; energy: *an officer famous for his skill and dash.* **7** [C] (*infml*) = DASHBOARD. **8** (idm) **cut a ˈdash** be exciting and stylish (in appearance or behaviour): *He really cuts a dash in his smart new uniform.* **make a bolt**/**dash**/**run for it** ⇨ BOLT[2].

□ ˈ**dashboard** (also **facia**, **fascia**) *n* board or panel below the windscreen of a motor vehicle, carrying various instruments and controls. ⇨ illus at CAR.

dash[2] /dæʃ/ *v* **1** [I, Ipr, Ip] move suddenly and quickly; rush: *I must dash* (ie leave quickly), *I'm late.* ○ *He dashed off with the money.* ○ *She dashed into the shop.* ○ *An ambulance dashed to the scene of the accident.* **2** [Ipr, Tn·pr, Tn·p] (cause sth to) strike forcefully: *Waves dashed against the harbour wall.* ○ *He dashed the glass to the ground.* ○ *The boat was dashed against the rocks.* ○ *A passing car dashed mud all over us.* **3** (idm) **dash** (**it**)**!** (*infml euph*) (used as a milder way of saying *damn*): *Dash it! I've broken my pen.* **dash**/**shatter sb's hopes** ⇨ HOPE. **4** (phr v) **dash sth off** write or draw sth quickly: *She dashed off a letter to her mother.*

▷ **dashing** *adj* (**a**) lively and exciting: *a dashing rider, officer, etc.* (**b**) (of clothes) smart and interesting: *a dashing uniform, hat, etc.* **dashingly** *adv.*

dastardly /ˈdæstədlɪ/ *adj* (*arch or rhet*) mean and cowardly.

data /ˈdeɪtə, *also* ˈdɑːtə; *US* ˈdætə/ *n* **(a)** [U or pl] facts or information used in deciding or discussing sth: *Very little data is available.* ○ *The data is/are still being analysed.* **(b)** [usu sing *v*] (*computing*) information prepared for or stored by a computer: [attrib] *data analysis, capture, retrieval* ○ *data protection*, ie legal restrictions on access to data stored in a computer. Cf DATUM.

□ ˈ**data bank** centre with a comprehensive file of computer data.

ˈ**database** *n* large store of computerized data, esp lists or abstracts of reports, etc.

ˌ**data** ˈ**capture** process of collecting data for use in a computer.

ˌ**data**-ˈ**processing** *n* [U] performing of computer operations on data to analyse it, solve problems, etc.

NOTE ON USAGE: There are a lot of nouns in English of Latin or Greek origin. They often end in **-us**, **-a**, **-um**, **-on**, etc. The plural forms of these nouns can cause difficulty. **1** Some, especially scientific terms, have kept their original singular and plural forms: *bacillus, bacilli* ○ *larva, larvae* ○ *criterion, criteria.* **2** Many, especially those in general use, now only have a regular English plural form: *arena, arenas* ○ *circus, circuses* ○ *electron, electrons.* **3** Some have alternative plural forms, which are both acceptable. The Latin form is more formal: *focus, focuses/foci* ○ *formula, formulas/formulae* ○ *spectrum, spectrums/spectra.* **4** There is uncertainty with some nouns as to whether they are singular or plural: *This data is correct* and *These data are correct* are both acceptable. **Paraphernalia** (a Greek plural) is used as a singular noun: *All my fishing paraphernalia is in the car.* **Media** (*sing* **medium**) is sometimes incorrectly used as a singular noun: *The media are* (NOT *is*) *often accused of being biased.*

date[1] /deɪt/ *n* **1** [C] **(a)** specific numbered day of the month, or specific year, usu given to show when sth happened or is to happen: *Today's date is the 23rd of June.* ○ *'What's the date?' 'The 10th.'* ○ *Has the date of the meeting been fixed?* ○ *'When was the date of the Battle of Waterloo?' 'June 1815.'* **(b)** indication written, printed or stamped (on a letter, coin, etc) of the time when it was written, made, etc: *There's no date on this cheque.* ○ *The manuscript bears the date 10 April 1937.* ⇨ App 9. **2** [U] period of time in history, eg one to which antiquities belong: *This vase is of an earlier date* (ie is older) *than that one.* **3** [C] (*infml*) **(a)** appointment to meet sb at a particular time: *We made a date to go to the opera.* **(b)** meeting with a person of the opposite sex: *I have a date (with my girl-friend) tonight.* **(c)** (*esp US*) person with whom one has a date[1](3b): *My date is meeting me at seven.* **4** (idm) **(be/go)** ˌ**out of** ˈ**date** **(a)** no longer fashionable: *Will denim jeans ever go out of date?* ○ [attrib] ˌ*out-of-date* ˈ*clothes,* iˈ*deas,* ˈ*slang.* **(b)** no longer valid: *My passport is out of date.* **to date** so far; up to now: *To date, we have not received any replies.* ○ *This is the biggest donation we've had to date.* **(be/bring sb/sth)** ˌ**up to** ˈ**date** **(a)** modern; fashionable: *She wears clothes that are right up to date.* **(b)** according to what is now known or required: *The list is up to date now that we've added the new members' names.* ○ [attrib] ˌ*up-to-date* ˈ*styles,* ˈ*methods,* ˈ*books.*

▷ **dateless** *adj* never becoming unfashionable or dated.

□ ˈ**date-line** *n* **(a)** (also **international date-line**) imaginary line running from north to south 180° from Greenwich, east and west of which the date differs by one day. **(b)** line in a newspaper above an article, etc, that shows the time and place of writing.

ˈ**date-stamp** *n* adjustable rubber stamp for printing the date on documents, etc.

date[2] /deɪt/ *v* **1** [Tn] write a date[1](1a) on (sth): *Don't forget to date your cheque.* ○ *His last letter was dated 24 May.* **2** [Tn] determine the age of (sth): *the method of dating rocks, fossils, tools, paintings.* **3** [I, Tn] seem or make (sb/sth) seem old-fashioned: *Young people's clothes date quickly nowadays.* ○ *Your taste in pop music really dates you.* **4** [Ipr] ~ **back to/from...** have existed since: *This castle dates from the 14th century*, ie was built then. ○ *Our partnership dates back to* (ie We have been partners since) *1960.* **5** [I, Tn] (*infml esp US*) go on a date[1](3b) with (sb), once or regularly: *They've been dating for a long time.* ○ *I only dated her once.*

▷ **datable** *adj.*

dated *adj* old-fashioned; no longer in use: *His clothes look so dated.* ○ *She uses rather dated words and phrases.*

date[3] /deɪt/ *n* **1** brown sweet edible fruit of a palm tree common in N Africa and SW Asia. **2** (usu ˈ**date-palm**) this tree.

dative /ˈdeɪtɪv/ *n* (*grammar*) special form of a noun, a pronoun or an adjective used (in some inflected languages) to indicate or describe esp the person who receives sth or benefits from an action.

▷ **dative** *adj* of or in the dative.

datum /ˈdeɪtəm, *also* ˈdɑːtəm; *US* ˈdætəm/ *n* (*pl* ~**s**) starting-point from which something is measured or calculated. Cf DATA.

daub /dɔːb/ *v* **1** [Tn, Tn·pr, Tn·p] ~ **A on (B)**; ~ **B (with A)** put (a soft substance) on (a surface) in a rough or careless way: *He daubed some red paint on (the canvas).* ○ *She daubed her face with thick make-up.* ○ *trousers daubed* (ie made dirty) *with mud.* **2** [I, Tn] (*infml*) paint (pictures) without skill or artistry.

▷ **daub** *n* **1** [C, U] (covering of) soft sticky material, eg clay, for walls. **2** [C] badly painted picture.

dauber *n* (*derog*) unskilful painter.

daughter /ˈdɔːtə(r)/ *n* **1** one's female child. ⇨ App 8. **2** female descendant: (*fig*) *Today's feminists are the spiritual daughters of Mrs Pankhurst.*

□ **daughter-in-law** /ˈdɔːtər ɪn lɔː/ *n* (*pl* ~**s-in-law** /ˈdɔːtəz ɪn lɔː/) wife of one's son. ⇨ App 8.

ˌ**Daughters of the A**ˌ**merican Revo**ˈ**lution** society whose members are female descendants of people who fought for American independence from Britain in 1775-83.

daunt /dɔːnt/ *v* **1** [Tn usu passive] discourage (sb); frighten: *I was rather daunted by the thought of addressing such an audience.* **2** (idm) **nothing** ˈ**daunted** (*fml or joc*) not at all discouraged: *Their guide deserted them, but, nothing daunted, they pressed on into the jungle.*

▷ **daunting** *adj* discouraging; frightening: *The prospect of meeting the President is quite daunting.*

dauntless /ˈdɔːntlɪs/ *adj* not easily discouraged or frightened: *dauntless bravery.* **dauntlessly** *adv.*

dauphin /ˈdɔːfɪn/ *n* (formerly) title of the king of France's eldest son.

davenport /ˈdævnpɔːt/ *n* **1** (*Brit*) writing desk with drawers and a hinged top. **2** (*US*) large sofa for two or three people, esp one that can be converted into a bed.

David[1] /ˈdeɪvɪd/ (died c 970 BC) king of Judah and later of all Israel. As a boy he killed the Philistine giant Goliath. When he became king, he made Jerusalem his capital. According to tradition he wrote the Psalms.

David[2] /ˈdeɪvɪd/ (Saint (c 520-600 AD), patron saint of Wales. ⇨ article at NATIONAL.

Davis /ˈdeɪvɪs/ Bette (1908-90), American film actress. She was one of Hollywood's most brilliant actresses and became famous for her portrayal of unpleasant characters, as in *The Little Foxes.*

Davis Cup /ˌdeɪvɪs ˈkʌp/ **the Davis Cup** cup presented annually to the country whose team wins an international tennis competition for men.

davit /ˈdævɪt/ *n* small crane[1](2) on a ship, usu one of a pair, used for supporting, lowering and raising a ship's boat.

Davy /ˈdeɪvɪ/ Sir Humphry (1778-1829), English chemist who pioneered the application of electricity to chemistry and discovered many new elements, including calcium, potassium and sodium.

□ ˈ**Davy lamp** early type of lamp used in mines, with a cover over the flame to prevent it from setting light to gas. It was invented by Sir Humphry Davy.

Davy Jones's locker (*infml often joc*) the bottom of the sea: *Their ship was sent to Davy Jones's locker*, ie was sunk.

dawdle /ˈdɔːdl/ *v* **1** [I] be slow; waste time: *Stop dawdling and hurry up: we're late.* ○ *She doesn't get her work done because she's always dawdling.* **2** (phr v) **dawdle sth away** waste (time): *He dawdles the hours away watching television.* ▷ **dawdler** /ˈdɔːdlə(r)/ *n.*

dawn[1] /dɔːn/ *n* [U, C] **1** time of day when light first appears; daybreak: *We must start at dawn.* ○ *He works from dawn till dusk.* ○ *It's almost dawn.* **2** (*fig*) beginning; first signs of sth: *the dawn of hope, love, intelligence, civilization* ○ *the dawn of a new age.* **3** (idm) **the crack of dawn** ⇨ CRACK[1].

□ ˌ**dawn** ˈ**chorus** sound of birds singing in the early morning.

dawn[2] /dɔːn/ *v* **1** [I] (often with *it* as subject) begin to grow light: *It was dawning as we left.* ○ *When day dawned, we could see the damage the storm had caused.* **2** [I, Ipr] ~ **(on sb)** gradually become clear to sb's mind; become evident (to sb): *It finally dawned (on me) that he had been lying.* ○ *The truth began to dawn on him.*

day /deɪ/ *n* **1** **(a)** [U] time between sunrise and sunset: *He has been working all day.* ○ *When I woke up, it was already day.* **(b)** [C] period of 24 hours: *There are seven days in a week.* ○ *I saw Tom three days ago.* ○ *I shall see Mary in a few days' time*, ie a few days from now. ○ *'What day of the week is it?' 'It's Monday.'* ⇨ App 10.

In Britain, almost every day of the week has its own characteristic. Monday, for example, is seen as the most unpopular, as it is the first day back at work after the weekend. It is also the day traditionally reserved for washing clothes, etc. Wednesday is often regarded as a half-way point in the week, and in many schools and colleges it is a half day when lessons finish at lunch-time and the afternoon is set aside for sports. Friday is a favourite day as it marks the start of the weekend, and on Friday nights many people go out to restaurants, theatres, pubs or discotheques. Saturday is normally associated with housework and going to town for shopping. Sunday, as a 'day of rest', is traditionally associated with Christian worship. It is still treated in Britain as a day of relaxation, and people often spend the day reading the Sunday newspapers, visiting friends, or eating a leisurely 'Sunday lunch' with family or friends, either at home or in a pub or restaurant. Although more services operate on Sundays than previously, most shops are closed, no letters are delivered and there is limited public transport.

(c) [C] hours of the day when one works: *I've done a good day's work.* ○ *Have you had a hard day at the office?* ○ *Her working day is seven hours.* ○ *The employees are demanding a six-hour day and a five-day week.* **2 days** [pl] specified time; period: *in his younger days* ○ *I was much happier in those days*, ie at that time ○ *in the days of Queen Victoria* ○ *in days of old/in the old days*, ie in former times. **3** (idm) **all in a day's** ˈ**work** part of the normal routine: *Injecting animals is all in a day's work for a vet.* ˈ**any day (of the week)** under any conditions: *I'd rather have butter any day*, ie I would much prefer to have butter. **at the end of the day** ⇨ END[1]. **break of day** ⇨ BREAK[2]. **by day/night** during daylight hours/after dark: *The fugitives travelled by night and rested by day.* **call it a day** ⇨ CALL[2]. **carry/win the** ˈ**day** (*infml*) be successful against sb/sth: *Despite strong opposition, the ruling party carried the day.* **clear as day** ⇨ CLEAR[1]. **day after** ˈ**day** for many days; continuously: *Day after day she waited in vain for him to telephone her.* **the day after to**ˈ**morrow**: *If today is Wednesday, the day after tomorrow will be Friday.* **the day before** ˈ**yesterday**: *If today is Wednesday, the day before yesterday was Monday.* **day by** ˈ**day** as time goes by: *Day by day she learnt more about her job.* **day** ˈ**in, day** ˈ**out** every day without exception: *Day in, day out, no matter what the weather is like, she walks ten miles.* **a day of**

ˈ**reckoning** (*fml*) time when wrongdoers will be punished: *You're enjoying yourself now, but a day of reckoning will come.* **sb's/sth's days are** ˈ**numbered** sb/sth is soon going to die, fail, lose favour, etc: *He has a serious illness, and his days are numbered.* ○ *This factory is no longer profitable, so its days are numbered*, ie it will soon close. **early days** ⇨ EARLY. **end one's days/life** ⇨ END[2]. **every dog has his/its day** ⇨ DOG[1]. **fall on evil days** ⇨ EVIL. **from day to** ˈ**day; from** ˌ**one day to the** ˈ**next** within a short period of time: *Things change from day to day.* ○ *You don't know what his mood will be from one day to the next.* **the good/bad old days** ⇨ OLD. **happy as the day is long** ⇨ HAPPY. **have had one's** ˈ**day** be no longer successful, prosperous, powerful, etc: *He was a great singer once but now he's had his day.* ○ *Colonialism has had its day*, ie is over. **have seen/known better days** ⇨ BETTER[1]. **high days and holidays** ⇨ HIGH[1]. **if he's, she's, etc a** ˈ**day** (in speaking of sb's age) at least: *He's eighty if he's a day!* **in all one's born days** ⇨ BORN. **in the cold light of day** ⇨ COLD[1]. **in one's** ˈ**day** in one's lifetime; in a period of success, prosperity, power, etc: *In his day, he was a very influential politician.* ○ *She was a great beauty in her day*, ie when she was young. **in** ˈ**this day and age** nowadays. **it's not sb's** ˈ**day** (*infml*) sb is especially unlucky: *My car broke down, then I locked myself out: it's just not my day!* **late in the day** ⇨ LATE[2]. **the livelong day/night** ⇨ LIVELONG. **make sb's** ˈ**day** (*infml*) make sb very happy: *If she wins, it'll make her day.* **name the day** ⇨ NAME[2]. **night and day** ⇨ NIGHT. **a** ˌ**nine days'** ˈ**wonder** person or thing that attracts attention for a short time but is soon forgotten: *As a pop star she was a nine days' wonder: she only made one successful record.* ˈ**one day** at a particular time in the future: *One day I'll get my revenge.* **one fine day** ⇨ FINE[2]. ˈ**one of these (fine) days** soon: *One of these days he'll realize what a fool he's been.* **one of those** ˈ**days** an especially unpleasant or unlucky day: *I've had one of those days: my train was late, and I lost my wallet.* **on one's** ˈ**day** when performing, etc as well as one can: *On his day he's the finest goalkeeper in the country.* **the order of the day** ⇨ ORDER[1]. **the other** ˈ**day** recently: *I saw her (only) the other day.* **pass the time of day** ⇨ PASS[2]. **peep of day** ⇨ PEEP[1]. **the present day** ⇨ PRESENT[1]. **a red-letter day** ⇨ RED[1]. **Rome was not built in a day** ⇨ BUILD. **salad days** ⇨ SALAD. **save, etc sth for a rainy day** ⇨ RAINY. **save the day** ⇨ SAVE[1]. ˈ**some day** at some time in the future: *Some day I'll come back and marry her.* ˈ**that'll be the day** (*ironic*) that's very unlikely: *'He says he'll do the washing-up.' 'That'll be the day!'* ˈ**these days** nowadays. ˌ**this day** ˈ**fortnight** a fortnight from today. ˌ**this day** ˈ**week** a week from today. ˈ**those were the days** that was a happier, better, etc time: *Do you remember when we first got married? Those were the days!* **to the** ˈ**day** exactly: *It's three years to the day since we met.* **to this** ˈ**day** even now: *To this day, I still don't know why she did it.* **turn night into day** ⇨ NIGHT.

□ ˈ**day-book** (*commerce*) *n* book for recording sales as they take place, before transferring them later to a ledger.

ˈ**day-boy**, ˈ**day-girl** *ns* pupil who attends a boarding-school daily but sleeps at home.

ˈ**daybreak** *n* dawn: *We will start our journey at daybreak.*

ˌ**day** ˈ**care** care for small children away from home, during the day: *Day care is provided by the company she works for.* ○ [attrib] *a* ˈ*day-care centre.*

ˈ**day-centre** *n* place where social facilities, such as food and entertainment, are provided during the daytime for the elderly, the handicapped, etc.

ˈ**day-dream** *n* idle and pleasant thoughts that distract one's attention from the present: *She stared out of the window, lost in day-dreams.* — *v* [I, Ipr] ~ (**about sth**) enjoy such thoughts: *He sat in the classroom, day-dreaming (about the holidays).*

ˈ**day-long** *adj* [attrib], *adv* (lasting) for the whole day.

ˈ**day nursery** place where small children are looked after while their parents are at work.

ˌ**day** ˈ**off** day on which one does not have to work: *I work from Tuesday to Saturday, and Sunday and Monday are my days off.*

ˌ**day re**ˈ**lease** system of allowing employees days off work for education.

ˌ**day-re**ˈ**turn** *n* return ticket (often at a reduced price) for passengers travelling both ways on the same day.

ˈ**day-room** *n* room (in a hospital, hostel, etc) where residents can sit, relax, watch TV, etc during the day.

ˈ**day-school** *n* school attended daily by pupils living at home. Cf BOARDING-SCHOOL (BOARD[2]).

ˈ**day shift** (group of workers who work for a) fixed period during the day. Cf NIGHT SHIFT (NIGHT).

ˈ**daytime** *n* [U] time between sunrise and sunset: *You hardly ever see owls in the daytime.*

ˌ**day-to-**ˈ**day** *adj* [attrib] (**a**) planning for only one day at a time: *I have organized the cleaning on a* ˌ*day-to-*ˈ*day basis, until the usual cleaner returns.* (**b**) involving daily routine: *She has been looking after the* ˌ*day-to-day admini*ˈ*stration.*

Day-Lewis /deɪ ˈlu:ɪs/ Cecil (1904-72), British poet and author. He was Poet Laureate from 1968. He also wrote detective stories under the name Nicholas Blake.

daylight /ˈdeɪlaɪt/ *n* [U] **1** light during daytime: *The colours look different when viewed in daylight.* ○ *I haven't seen your garden in daylight before.* ○ *before daylight*, ie before dawn. **2** visible distance between two competitors in a race: *Now there's daylight between the crews*, ie One is clearly ahead of the other. **3** (idm) **broad daylight** ⇨ BROAD[1]. ˌ**daylight** ˈ**robbery** (*infml*) charging too much: *Three pounds for two sandwiches? It's daylight robbery!* **see** ˈ**daylight** understand sth that was previously puzzling: *I struggled with the problem for hours before I saw daylight.*

□ ˌ**daylight** ˈ**saving** [U] way of making darkness fall later during summer by making clocks show a later time on a date in spring. ˌ**daylight** ˈ**saving time** (*US* also ˈ**daylight time**) period when this is in effect. Cf SUMMER TIME (SUMMER).

daylights /ˈdeɪlaɪts/ *n* [pl] (idm) **beat/knock the (living) daylights out of sb** (*infml*) beat sb very severely: *If I catch you stealing again, I'll beat the daylights out of you!* **frighten/scare the (living) daylights out of sb** (*infml*) frighten sb very much.

daze /deɪz/ *v* [Tn usu passive] (**a**) make (sb) confused and unable to react properly: *dazed with drugs* ○ *The blow on the head dazed him for a moment.* (**b**) surprise and bewilder (sb): *I was dazed by her sudden offer.*

▷ **daze** *n* (idm) **in a daze** in a confused state: *I've been in a complete daze since hearing the sad news.*

dazed /deɪzd/ *adj*: *a dazed look, manner, etc.*

dazzle /ˈdæzl/ *v* [Tn usu passive] (**a**) blind (sb) briefly with too much light, brilliance, etc: *I was dazzled by his headlights.* (**b**) (*fig*) impress (sb) greatly through splendour, ability, etc: *He was dazzled by her beauty and wit.*

▷ **dazzle** *n* [U] splendour; brilliance: *all the dazzle of the circus.*

dazzling *adj*: *a dazzling display of sporting skill.*

dB *abbr* decibel(s).

DBE /ˌdi: bi: ˈi:/ *abbr* (*Brit*) Dame Commander (of the Order) of the British Empire: *be made a DBE* ○ *Dame Susan Peters DBE.* Cf CBE, KBE, MBE.

DC /ˌdi: ˈsi:/ *abbr* **1** (*music*) repeat from the beginning (Italian *da capo*). **2** District of Columbia: *Washington, DC.* **3** (also **dc**) direct current (DIRECT[1]). Cf AC.

DCF /ˌdi: si: ˈef/ *abbr* discounted cash flow.

DD /ˌdi: ˈdi:/ *abbr* Doctor of Divinity: *have/be a DD* ○ *Colin Green DD.*

D-day /ˈdi: deɪ/ *n* **1** day (6 June 1944) on which the Allied forces landed in N France during the Second World War. **2** date on which something important is due to happen: *As D-day approached we still weren't ready to move house.*

DDT /ˌdi: di: ˈti:/ *abbr* dichlorodiphenyltrichloroethane (a colourless chemical that kills insects and is also harmful to animals).

de- *pref* (with *vs* and related *adjs, advs* and *ns*) **1** opposite or negative of: *defrost* ○ *decentralization.* **2** removal of: *defuse* ○ *derailment.*

deacon /ˈdi:kən/ *n* **1** (in Christian churches with ordained priests, eg the Church of England) minister ranking below a priest. ⇨ article at CHURCH OF ENGLAND. **2** (in nonconformist churches) lay person who deals with church business affairs.

▷ **deaconess** /ˌdi:kəˈnes, *also* ˈdi:kənɪs/ *n* woman with duties similar to those of a deacon.

deactivate /di:ˈæktɪveɪt/ *v* [Tn] make (sth dangerous, eg a bomb or a nuclear reactor) harmless by removing its source of power: *deactivate the fuse mechanism.*

dead /ded/ *adj* **1** (**a**) no longer alive: *a dead person, animal* ○ *dead flowers, cells* ○ *The tiger fell dead.* (**b**) never having been alive; inanimate: *dead matter*, eg rock. **2** (**a**) without movement or activity: *The town is dead now the mine has closed.* ○ *in the dead hours of the night*, ie when everything is quiet. (**b**) (*infml*) without interest and liveliness; dull: *What a dead place this is!* ○ *The acting was rather dead.* **3** no longer used, effective, valid, etc: *This debate is now dead.* ○ *My love for him is dead.* ○ *a dead language*, eg Latin. **4** (**a**) numb from cold, anaesthetic, etc: *My dead fingers could not untie the knot.* (**b**) [pred] ~ **to sth** not feeling (pity, guilt, etc): *He was dead to all feelings of shame.* **5** [attrib] complete; absolute: *dead calm, silence, etc* ○ *come to a dead stop*, ie stop suddenly ○ *dead centre*, ie exact centre ○ *a dead shot*, ie a person who shoots very accurately ○ *a dead sleep*, ie a very deep sleep ○ *He's a dead cert/certainty for* (ie He will certainly win) *the 100 metres.* **6** that does, can or will no longer function: *a dead match*, ie one that has been struck ○ *a dead battery*, ie one without power ○ *The telephone went dead*, ie produced no more sounds. **7** [usu attrib] (**a**) (of sounds) not resonant; dull: *It fell with a dead thud.* (**b**) (of colours) not brilliant: *The walls were a dead brown colour.* **8** (*sport*) (**a**) (of a ball) outside the playing area. (**b**) (of the ground) tending to make balls rolling on it stop quickly: *Rain had made the pitch rather dead.* **9** (idm) **be a dead ringer for sb** (*sl*) be very like sb in appearance: *She's a dead ringer for a girl I used to know.* **be the dead spit of sb** (*infml*) look exactly like sb else. **cut sb dead** pretend not to have seen sb; refuse to greet sb. (**as**) ˌ**dead as a/the** ˈ**dodo** (*infml*) no longer effective, valid, interesting, etc: *This organization is as dead as a dodo.* (**as**) ˌ**dead as a** ˈ**doornail/as** ˈ**mutton** (*infml*) quite dead: *It lay there with its eyes closed, dead as a doornail.* **a dead** ˈ**duck** (*infml*) scheme, etc which has been abandoned, or will fail: *The plan is a dead duck: there's no money.* **a dead** ˈ**end** (**a**) = CUL-DE-SAC. (**b**) point at which one can make no further progress in work, an enquiry, etc: *be at/come to a dead end* ○ *With the failure of the experiment, we had reached a dead end.* ○ [attrib] *a* ˌ*dead-end* ˈ*job/ca*ˈ*reer*, ie one that offers no prospect of promotion. ˌ**dead from the neck** ˈ**up** (*infml*) (of people) extremely stupid, lacking in interest or liveliness, etc. **the dead hand of sth** oppressive influence of sth: *The dead hand of bureaucracy is slowing our progress.* **a dead** ˈ**letter** (**a**) rule or law that is generally ignored. (**b**) outdated custom, issue or topic: *Many people say that détente is now a dead letter.* (**c**) letter kept by the post office because they cannot find either the person to whom it was sent or the person who sent it. **a dead** ˈ**loss** (*sl*) person or thing of no help or use to anyone: *This pen is a dead loss: it just won't write properly.* ˌ**dead men's** ˈ**shoes** job that one takes over from sb who has left unexpectedly or died: *She got early promotion by stepping into dead men's shoes.* ˌ**dead men** ˌ**tell no** ˈ**tales** (*saying*) if a person is killed he cannot cause difficulties by revealing sth that one does not wish to be known. ˌ**dead to the** ˈ**world** fast asleep. ˌ**dead** ˈ**wood** useless or unneeded people, material, papers, etc: *There is too much dead wood among the teaching staff.* ○ *The new manager wants to cut out the dead wood and streamline production.* **drop dead** ⇨ DROP[2]. **flog a dead horse** ⇨ FLOG. **in a dead** ˈ**faint**

completely unconscious. **over my dead ˈbody** (used to express one's strong opposition to sth): *They'll demolish this house over my dead body.* ○ *'I'm going out.' 'Over my dead body!'* **Queen Anne is dead** ⇨ ANNE[1]. **the quick and the dead** ⇨ QUICK. **wake the dead** ⇨ WAKE[1]. **wouldn't be seen ˈdead in, at, with, etc sth/doing sth** (*infml*) would refuse to be in, at, with, etc sth: *That dress is so ugly I wouldn't be seen dead in it.* ○ *She wouldn't be seen dead jogging; she hates exercise.*

▷ **dead** *adv* **1** completely; absolutely; thoroughly: *dead tired/drunk* ○ *dead sure/certain* ○ *dead level/straight* ○ *You're dead right!* ○ *dead slow*, ie as slowly as possible ○ *dead ahead*, ie directly ahead ○ *be dead against* (ie absolutely opposed to) *sth.* **2** (idm) **ˌdead ˈbeat** (*infml*) very tired; exhausted. **(be) ˌdead ˈset against sb/sth** (be) strongly opposed to sb/sth. **(be) dead set on sth** (be) determined to do sth: *He's dead set on getting a new job.* **stop dead** ⇨ STOP[1].

dead *n* **1 the dead** [pl *v*] those who have died: *We carried the dead and (the) wounded off the battlefield.* **2** (idm) **in the/at ˌdead of ˈnight** in the quietest part of the night: *We escaped at dead of night, when the guards were asleep.* **in the ˌdead of ˈwinter** in the coldest part of winter.

□ **ˌdead-and-aˈlive, ˌdead-aˈlive** *adjs* [usu attrib] (*Brit infml*) (of people or places or work) completely lacking in excitement or liveliness.

ˌdead-ˈbeat *n* (*infml*) **1** person who has no job and no money and has lost the will to live an active life. **2** (*US*) person who does not pay his debts.

ˈdead head dead flower that has become withered and faded. **ˈdead-head** *v* [Tn] remove the dead flowers from (a plant).

ˌdead ˈheat result in a race when two competitors finish at exactly the same time.

ˌdead man's ˈhandle handle on an electric train that cuts off the power if it is released.

ˈdead march slow solemn piece of music for marching to, played at funerals.

ˈdead nettle plant whose leaves are like those of the stinging nettle, but do not sting.

ˌdead-ˈpan *adj* expressionless: *a ˌdead-pan ˈface/ˈlook* ○ *ˌdead-pan ˈhumour*, ie when the speaker pretends to be very serious.

ˌdead ˈreckoning calculation of one's position by log[2] or compass (when visibility is bad).

ˌdead ˈweight heavy lifeless mass: *The drunken man was a dead weight in my arms.*

deaden /ˈdedn/ *v* **1** [Tn] lessen the force or intensity of (sth): *drugs to deaden the pain* ○ *My thick clothing deadened the blow.* ○ *Your constant criticism has deadened their enthusiasm.* **2** [Tn·pr] ~ **sb to sth** make sb insensitive to sth: *Unhappiness had deadened her to the lives of others.*

deadhead /ˈdedhed/ *n* (*infml*) **1** stupid or unenterprising person. **2** (*esp US*) person who goes to a theatre, concert, etc or rides on a bus, etc without paying for a ticket. Cf DEAD HEAD (DEAD).

deadline /ˈdedlaɪn/ *n* point in time by which sth must be done: *meet, miss a deadline* ○ *I have a March deadline for the novel*, ie It must be finished by March.

deadlock /ˈdedlɒk/ *n* **1** [C, U] complete failure to reach agreement or to settle a quarrel or grievance: *The negotiations have reached deadlock.* ○ *We can only make minor concessions, but it might break the deadlock*, ie allow a compromise. **2** [C] type of lock that can only be opened and closed with a key.

▷ **deadlock** *v* [Tn esp passive] bring (sth) to a state of deadlock(1): *The situation is deadlocked; a strike looks inevitable.*

deadly /ˈdedlɪ/ *adj* (**-ier, -iest**) **1** causing, or likely to cause, death: *deadly poison* ○ *deadly weapons.* **2** (*fig*) extremely effective, so that no defence is possible: *His aim is deadly*, ie is so accurate that he can kill easily. ○ *She uses wit with deadly effect.* **3** [attrib] filled with hate: *They are deadly enemies.* **4** [attrib] like that of death: *deadly paleness, coldness, silence.* **5** [attrib] extreme: *deadly seriousness* ○ *I'm in deadly earnest.* **6** (*infml*) very boring: *The concert was absolutely deadly.* **7** (idm) **the (seven) deadly ˈsins** serious sins that result in damnation.

▷ **deadly** *adv* (**a**) as if dead: *deadly pale/cold.* (**b**) (*infml*) extremely: *deadly serious, boring, dull, etc.*

deadliness *n* [U].

□ **ˌdeadly ˈnightshade** poisonous plant with red flowers and black berries.

Dead Sea /ˌded ˈsi:/ **the Dead Sea** large salt-water lake on the border between Israel and Jordan; area 1 049 sq km (405 sq miles). It is the lowest point on the earth's surface, nearly 400 m (1 300 ft) below sea-level. Its water is so salty that no creatures can live in it.

□ **the ˌDead Sea ˈScrolls** collection of Hebrew and Aramaic manuscripts discovered in caves near the Dead Sea between 1947 and 1956. They include texts of many of the books of the Old Testament, and also documents which reveal details of the way of life of the members of the ancient Jewish sect that wrote them.

deaf /def/ *adj* (**-er, -est**) **1** unable to hear at all or to hear well: *go deaf* ○ *be deaf in one ear* ○ *He's getting deafer in his old age.* **2** [pred] ~ **to sth** unwilling to listen to sth: *be deaf to all advice, requests, entreaties, etc.* **3** (idm) **(as) ˌdeaf as a ˈpost/ˈdoorpost** (*infml*) very deaf. **fall on deaf ˈears** be ignored or unnoticed by others: *All her appeals for help fell on deaf ears.* **turn a deaf ˈear (to sb/sth)** refuse to listen (to sb/sth): *She turned a deaf ear to our warnings and got lost.*

▷ **deaf** *n* **the deaf** [pl *v*] deaf people: *television subtitles for the deaf.*

deafness *n* [U].

□ **ˈdeaf-aid** *n* small (usu electronic) device that helps a person to hear; hearing-aid.

ˌdeaf-and-ˈdumb unable to hear or speak: [attrib] *a ˌdeaf-and-dumb ˈchild* ○ *the ˌdeaf-and-dumb ˈalphabet*, ie in which signs made with the hands are used for letters or words.

ˌdeaf ˈmute person who is deaf and dumb.

deafen /ˈdefn/ *v* [Tn] (**a**) make (sb) feel deaf or unable to hear sounds around him by making a very loud noise: *We're being deafened by next door's stereo.* (**b**) make (sb) deaf: *The head injury deafened her for life.*

▷ **deafening** *adj* very loud: *deafening thunder* ○ *Please turn the radio down — the noise is deafening.*

deafeningly *adv*: *deafeningly loud.*

deal[1] /di:l/ *n* [U] (*esp Brit*) (planks of) fir or pine wood: *made of white deal* ○ [attrib] *a deal table, floor, etc.*

deal[2] /di:l/ *n* (idm) **a good/great deal (of sth)** much; a lot: *spend a good deal of money* ○ *take a great deal of trouble* ○ *be a great deal better* ○ *see sb a great deal*, ie often.

deal[3] /di:l/ *v* (*pt, pp* **dealt** /delt/) **1** [I, Ipr, Tn, Tn·p, Dn·n, Dn·pr] ~ **sth (out)**; ~ **sth (to sb)** distribute (cards) in a game: *Whose turn is it to deal (the cards)?* ○ *She dealt me four cards.* **2** (idm) **deal sb/sth a ˈblow; deal a blow to sb/sth** (*fml*) (**a**) hit sb/sth: *She dealt him a tremendous blow with the poker.* (**b**) cause sb a set-back, shock, etc: *Her death dealt us a terrible blow.* **deal well, badly, etc by/with sb** (*dated or fml*) treat sb well, etc: *He has always dealt well by me.* ○ *You've been badly dealt with.* **wheel and deal** ⇨ WHEEL *v*. **3** (phr v) **deal in sth** (**a**) sell sth; trade in sth: *My bank deals in stocks and shares now.* ○ *We deal in hardware but not software.* (**b**) (*derog*) concern oneself with sth; indulge in sth: *deal in gossip and slander*, ie make a habit of gossiping about and slandering people. **deal sb in** give cards to (a new player in a game). **deal sth out** give sth out to a number of people; distribute sth: *The profits will be dealt out among the investors.* ○ *The judge dealt out harsh sentences to the rioters.* **deal with sb** tackle the problem or task set by sb; behave towards sb: *How would you deal with an armed burglar?* ○ *They try to deal politely with angry customers.* **deal with sb/sth** have social, business, etc relations with sb: *I hate dealing with large impersonal companies.* ○ *We don't deal with* (ie negotiate with) *terrorists.* **deal with sth** (**a**) attend to (a problem, task, etc); manage sth: *You dealt with an awkward situation very tactfully.* ○ *Haven't you dealt with* (ie replied to) *that letter yet?* (**b**) take or have sth as a subject; discuss sth: *The next chapter deals with verbs.* ○ *I'll deal with decimals in the next lesson.*

deal[4] /di:l/ *n* **1** agreement, esp in business, on certain terms for buying or doing sth: *to make/conclude/close/finalize a deal (with sb)* ○ *We did a deal with the management on overtime.* ○ *They both wanted to use the car, so they did a deal*, ie reached a compromise. ○ *It's a deal!* ie I agree to your terms. ○ *The deal fell through*, ie No agreement was reached. **2** (in games) distribution of playing-cards: *After the deal, play begins.* ○ *It's your deal*, ie your turn to deal the cards. **3** (idm) **big deal!** ⇨ BIG. **a fair/square ˈdeal** fair treatment in a bargain: *We offer you a fair deal on furniture*, ie We sell it at fair prices. **make the best of a bad deal** ⇨ BEST[3]. **a new deal** ⇨ NEW. **a raw/rough ˈdeal** (*infml*) unfair treatment: *If she lost her job for being late once, she got a pretty raw deal.*

dealer /ˈdi:lə(r)/ *n* **1** person who distributes playing-cards. **2** ~ **(in sth)** trader: *a used-car dealer* ○ *a furniture dealer* ○ *a dealer in* (ie sb who buys and sells) *stolen goods.*

NOTE ON USAGE: **Dealers, traders** and **merchants** are all people who earn money from selling goods. **1** A **trader** works informally and casually selling household goods, etc, especially in a market: *a market/street trader.* A **trader** can also be a company buying and selling internationally: *The company is an international trader in grain.* **2** A **merchant** sells particular (often imported) goods in large quantities: *He's a coal, wine, timber, tea, etc merchant.* **3** A **dealer** sells especially individual objects and has a specialized knowledge of these: *She's an antique, a used-car, etc dealer.* **Dealer** is also used of someone who buys and sells illegally: *He's a dealer in drugs/stolen goods.*

dealing /ˈdi:lɪŋ/ *n* **1** [U] way of behaving, esp in business: *Our company is proud of its reputation for fair dealing.* **2** (idm) **have dealings (with sb)** have relations (with sb), esp in business: *I'll have no further dealings with him.* ○ *We've had no previous dealings with this company.*

dealt *pt, pp* of DEAL[3].

Dean /di:n/ James (1931-55), American film actor. He studied method acting (METHOD) at the Actors' Studio and during his short career he embodied the image of youth in revolt in films like *East of Eden* and *Rebel Without a Cause*. He died in a car crash.

dean /di:n/ *n* **1** clergyman who is head of a cathedral chapter. **2** (also **ˌrural ˈdean**) (*esp Brit*) clergyman who is responsible for a number of parishes. **3** (**a**) (in some universities) person who is responsible for discipline. (**b**) head of a university department of studies: *dean of the faculty of law.* **4** (*US*) = DOYEN.

▷ **deanery** /ˈdi:nərɪ/ *n* (**a**) office or house of a dean(1, 2). (**b**) group of parishes under a rural dean.

dear /dɪə(r)/ *adj* (**-er, -est**) **1** ~ **(to sb)** loved (by sb); greatly valued: *my dear wife* ○ *his dearest possessions, friends* ○ *My daughter is very dear to me.* ○ *He lost everything that was dear to him.* **2** (used attributively with *little* and *old* to show fondness): *What a dear little child!* ○ *Dear old Paul!* **3** (used attributively as a form of address in letters, and politely or ironically in speech): *Dear Sir/Madam* ○ *Dear Mr Bond* ○ *My dear fellow, surely you don't mean that!* **4** [usu pred] (*Brit*) expensive: *Clothes are getting dearer.* ○ *dear money*, ie money on which a high rate of interest must be paid ○ *That shop is too dear for me*, ie Its prices are too high. **5** (idm) **close/dear/near to sb's heart** ⇨ HEART. **for dear life** vigorously or desperately (as if trying to save oneself from death): *run, swim, pull, shout, argue for dear life.* **hold sb/sth ˈdear** (*rhet*) cherish sb/sth; value sb/sth highly: *I said farewell to those I hold dear.* ○ *the ideals we hold dear.* **one's nearest and dearest** ⇨ NEAR[1].

▷ **dear** *adv* **1** at a high cost: *If you want to make money, buy cheap and sell dear.* **2** (idm) **cost sb dear** ⇨ COST[1].

dear *n* **1** lovable person: *Isn't that baby a dear?* ○ *Thank you, you are a dear.* ○ *Be a dear and* (ie Please) *give me that book.* **2** (used to address sb one knows very well): *Yes, dear, I'll write to mother.* ○ *Come here, my dear.*

dear *interj* (used in expressions of surprise, impatience, dismay, etc): *Oh dear! I think I've lost it!* ○ *Dear me! What a mess!*

dearest /ˈdɪərɪst/ *n* (used to address sb one likes very much): *Come, (my) dearest, let's go home.*

dearly *adv* **1** very much: *He loves his mother dearly.* ○ *She would dearly like to get that job.* **2** (*fig rhet*) with great loss, damage, etc: *She paid dearly for her mistake*, ie It caused her many problems. ○ *Victory was dearly bought*, eg because many soldiers died. **3** (idm) **sell one's life dearly** ⇨ SELL.

dearness *n* [U].

dearth /dɜ:θ/ *n* [sing] ~ **(of sth)** shortage; scarcity: *There seems to be a dearth of good young players at the moment.*

deary (also **dearie**) /ˈdɪərɪ/ *n* (*infml*) (used by an older person to a much younger one) dear(1); darling.

death /deθ/ *n* **1** [C] dying or being killed: *Her death was a shock to him.* ○ *There have been more deaths from drowning.* ○ *A bad driver was responsible for their deaths.* **2** [U] end of life; state of being dead: *Food poisoning can cause death.* ○ *burn, starve, stab, etc sb to death*, ie until he is dead ○ *You're drinking yourself to death.* ○ (*usu joc*) *Don't work yourself to death*, ie Don't work too hard. ○ *One mistake could mean death for him*, ie could result in his being killed. ○ *sentenced to death*, ie to be executed ○ *eyes closed in death* ○ *united in death*, eg of a husband and a wife in the same grave. **3** (also **Death**) [U] power that destroys life, pictured as a person: *Death is often shown in pictures as a human skeleton.* **4** [U] ~ **of sth** ending or destruction of sth: *the death of one's plans, hopes, etc* ○ *the death of capitalism.* **5** (idm) **(be) at death's ˈdoor** (*often ironic*) so ill that one may die: *Stop groaning! You're not at death's door!* **(be) at the point of death** ⇨ POINT[1]. **be the death of sb** (a) be the cause of sb's death: *That motor bike will be the death of you.* (b) (*often joc*) cause sb great worry: *Those kids will be the death of me, coming home so late every night.* **be ˌin at the ˈdeath** be present when sth fails, comes to an end, etc: *The TV cameras were in at the death and filmed the arrest.* **bore sb to death/tears** ⇨ BORE[2]. **catch one's death** ⇨ CATCH[1]. **dice with death** ⇨ DICE. **die the death** ⇨ DIE[2]. **ˌdo sth to ˈdeath** perform (a play, a piece of music, etc) so often that people become tired of seeing or hearing it: *That idea's been done to death.* **a fate worse than death** ⇨ FATE. **flog sth to death** ⇨ FLOG. **frighten/scare sb to death/out of his wits** ⇨ FRIGHTEN. **the kiss of death** ⇨ KISS. **(look/feel) like ˌdeath warmed ˈup** (*infml*) very tired or ill. **like grim death** ⇨ GRIM. **a matter of life and death** ⇨ MATTER[1]. **ˌput sb to ˈdeath** execute sb; kill sb: *The prisoner was put to death (by firing squad) at dawn.* **sick to death of sb/sth** ⇨ SICK. **sudden death** ⇨ SUDDEN. **tickled pink/to death** ⇨ TICKLE. **to the death** until sb is dead: *a fight to the death.*

□ **ˈdeathbed** *n* bed in which a person is dying or dies: *He forgave her on his deathbed*, ie as he lay dying. ○ [attrib] *a deathbed confession.*

ˈdeath-blow *n* (a) blow that kills. (b) event, act, etc that destroys or puts an end to sth: *Losing the contract was a death-blow to the company.*

ˈdeath camp camp to which political and other prisoners are taken in large numbers to be killed, esp such a camp used by the Nazis for killing Jews during the Second World War.

ˈdeath certificate official form that states the cause and time of sb's death.

ˈdeath duty (*Brit*) (formerly) tax paid on property after the owner's death, now called *inheritance tax.*

ˈdeath-mask *n* cast[2](2a) taken from the face of a person who has just died.

ˈdeath penalty punishment of being executed for a crime.

ˈdeath rate yearly number of deaths per 1000 people in a group.

ˈdeath-rattle *n* rattling sound in the throat of a dying person.

ˌdeath ˈrow (also **death house**) (*US*) group of prison cells for those condemned to death.

ˈdeath's head human skull as an emblem of death.

ˈdeath-toll *n* number of people killed (eg in a war or an earthquake).

ˈdeath-trap *n* (a) place where many people have died in accidents: *That sharp bend is a death-trap for motorists.* (b) place where many people could die (eg in a fire): *The cars blocking the exits could turn this place into a death-trap.*

ˈdeath-warrant *n* **1** (a) written order that sb should be executed. (b) act, decision, etc that causes the end of sth: *The tax is a death-warrant for small businesses.* **2** (idm) **sign sb's/one's own death-warrant** ⇨ SIGN[2].

ˌdeath-watch ˈbeetle small beetle whose larva bores into wood with a ticking sound.

ˈdeath-wish *n* (often subconscious) desire for one's own or sb else's death.

deathless /ˈdeθlɪs/ *adj* (*fml*) never to be forgotten; immortal: *deathless fame, glory, etc* ○ (*ironic*) *The letter was written in his usual deathless* (ie bad, unmemorable) *prose.*

deathlike /ˈdeθlaɪk/ *adj* like that of death: *a deathlike silence/paleness.*

deathly /ˈdeθlɪ/ *adj* (**-lier, -liest**) like or suggesting death: *a deathly stillness/hush/silence/pallor.* ▷ **deathly** *adv*: *deathly pale/cold.*

deb /deb/ *n* (*infml*) = DÉBUTANTE.

débâcle /deɪˈbɑ:kl/ *n* (a) sudden and complete failure; fiasco: *His first performance was a débâcle: the audience booed him off the stage.* (b) retreat by beaten troops who run away scared and in disorder: *Many men were shot or captured in the débâcle.*

debar /dɪˈbɑ:(r)/ *v* (**-rr-**) [esp passive: Tn, Tn·pr] ~ **sb (from sth)** (a) shut sb out (of a place): *People in jeans were debarred (from the club).* (b) prevent sb (from exercising a right, etc): *Convicted criminals are debarred from voting in elections.*

debark /dɪˈbɑ:k/ *v* [I, Ipr, Tn, Tn·pr] ~ **(sb/sth) (from sth)** = DISEMBARK. ▷ **debarkation** /ˌdi:bɑ:ˈkeɪʃn/ *n* [U] = DISEMBARKATION.

debase /dɪˈbeɪs/ *v* [Tn] **1** lower the quality, status or value of (sth): *Sport is being debased by commercialism.* ○ *You debase yourself by telling such lies.* **2** lower the value of (coins) by using less valuable metal in them. ▷ **debasement** *n* [U].

debatable /dɪˈbeɪtəbl/ *adj* not certain; open to question; arguable: *It's debatable whether or not the reforms have improved conditions.* ○ *a debatable point, claim, etc.* ▷ **debatably** /-blɪ/ *adv.*

debate /dɪˈbeɪt/ *n* [C, U] (a) formal argument or discussion of a question, eg at a public meeting or in Parliament, with two or more opposing speakers, and often ending in a vote: *After a long debate, the House of Commons approved the bill.* ○ *to open the debate*, ie be the first to speak ○ *the motion under debate*, ie being discussed. (b) argument or discussion in general: *After much debate, we decided to move to Oxford.* ○ *We had long debates at college about politics.* ○ *Her resignation caused much public debate.*

▷ **debate** *v* **1** [I, Ipr, Tn, Tw, Tg] ~ **(about sth)** have a debate(b) about (sth); discuss (sth): *What are they debating (about)?* ○ *We're just debating what to do next.* ○ *They debated closing the factory.* **2** [Tn, Tw, Tg] think (sth) over in order to decide: *I debated it for a while, then decided not to go.* ○ *I'm debating where to go on holiday.* ○ *He debated buying a new car, but didn't in the end.* **debater** *n* person who debates (DEBATE 1).

debauch /dɪˈbɔ:tʃ/ *v* [Tn] make (sb) act immorally by using bad influence: *He debauched* (ie seduced) *many innocent girls.*

▷ **debauch** *n* occasion of excessive drinking or immoral behaviour, usu involving several people: *go on a drunken debauch.*

debauched *adj* immoral, esp sexually: *to live a debauched life.*

debauchee /ˌdebɔ:ˈtʃi:/ *n* debauched person.

debauchery /dɪˈbɔ:tʃərɪ/ *n* (a) [U] immoral behaviour, esp in sexual matters: *a life of debauchery.* (b) [C] example or period of this: *His debaucheries ruined his health.*

debenture /dɪˈbentʃə(r)/ *n* certificate given by a business corporation, etc as a receipt for money lent at a fixed rate of interest until the loan is repaid: [attrib] *debenture shares.*

debilitate /dɪˈbɪlɪteɪt/ *v* [Tn] make (a person or his body) very weak: *a debilitating illness, climate* ○ *She has been debilitated by dysentery.* ○ (*fig*) *Huge debts are debilitating their economy.*

debility /dɪˈbɪlətɪ/ *n* [U] physical weakness: *After her operation she suffered from general debility.*

debit /ˈdebɪt/ *n* (a) (in bookkeeping) written note in an account of a sum owed or paid out. (b) sum withdrawn from an account: *My bank account shows two debits of £5 each.* Cf CREDIT, DIRECT DEBIT (DIRECT[1]).

▷ **debit** *v* [Tn, Tn·pr] ~ **sth (against/to sb/sth)**; ~ **sb/sth (with sth)** record (a sum of money) owed or withdrawn (by sb): *Debit £5 against my account.* ○ *Debit £50 to me.* ○ *She/Her account was debited with £50.*

□ **ˈdebit side** left-hand side of an account, on which debits are entered.

debonair /ˌdebəˈneə(r)/ *adj* (usu of men) cheerful and self-assured: *He strolled about, looking very debonair in his elegant new suit.*

debouch /dɪˈbaʊtʃ/ *v* [I, Ipr] ~ **(into sth)** (a) (*military*) (of troops) come out into open ground: *The army debouched from the mountains into a wide plain.* (b) (of a river, road, etc) merge into a larger body or area: *The stream debouches into the estuary.*

Debrett's Peerage /dəˌbrets ˈpɪərɪdʒ/ list of all the members of the British aristocracy, giving the history of each title and details of the present holder. It was first issued in 1803 by John Debrett, and until recently was published annually. Cf BURKE'S PEERAGE. ⇨ article at ARISTOCRAT.

debrief /ˌdi:ˈbri:f/ *v* [Tn, Tn·pr] (*esp military*) question (a soldier, an astronaut, a diplomat, etc) esp about a mission that he has just completed: *a debriefing session* ○ *While being debriefed the defector named two double agents.* ○ *Pilots were debriefed on the bombing raid.* Cf BRIEF[2].

debris /ˈdeɪbri:; *US* dəˈbri:/ *n* [U] scattered fragments; wreckage: *After the crash, debris from the plane was scattered over a large area.* ○ *searching among the debris after the explosion.*

debt /det/ *n* **1** (a) [C] sum of money owed to sb that has not yet been paid: *If I pay all my debts I'll have no money left.* (b) [U] owing money, esp when one cannot pay: *We were poor, but we avoided debt.* **2** [C usu *sing*] (*fig*) obligation to sb for their help, kindness, etc: *I'm happy to acknowledge my debt to my teachers.* ○ *owe sb a debt of gratitude.* **3** (idm) **be ˌin/ˌout of ˈdebt** owe/not owe a lot of money. **be in sb's ˈdebt** (*fml*) feel grateful to sb for his help, kindness, etc: *You saved my life: I am forever in your debt.* **a ˌdebt of ˈhonour** debt that one feels morally obliged to pay even though one is not required by law to do so. **ˌget/ˌrun into ˈdebt** reach a stage where one owes a lot of money. **ˌget out of ˈdebt** reach a stage where one no longer owes money.

▷ **debtor** /ˈdetə(r)/ *n* person who owes money to sb: *receive payment from one's debtors.*

debug /ˌdi:ˈbʌg/ *v* (**-gg-**) [Tn] (*infml*) **1** find and remove defects in (a computer program, machine, etc). **2** find and remove hidden microphones from (a room, house, etc): *The place has been completely debugged.*

debunk /ˌdi:ˈbʌŋk/ *v* [Tn] show that the reputation of (a person, an idea, an institution, etc) is undeserved or exaggerated: *debunk fashionable opinions.*

Debussy /dəˈbu:si:/ Claude (1862-1918), French composer who pioneered the use of the whole-tone scale. Among his best-known works are short piano pieces that suggest a particular scene or mood, such as *Clair de lune.* These have been compared with impressionist paintings of the same period, because of their dreamlike lyrical quality. Other major compositions by Debussy include the opera *Pelléas et Mélisande* and the orchestral pieces *La Mer* and *Prélude à l'après-midi d'un faune*.

début (also **debut**) /ˈdeɪbjuː; *US* dɪˈbjuː/ *n* first appearance in public as a performer (on stage, etc): *He marked his début by beating the champion.* ○ *She's making her New York début at Carnegie Hall.*

débutante /ˈdebjuːtɑːnt/ (also *infml* **deb**) *n* young woman making her first appearance in fashionable society.

Dec *abbr* December: *5 Dec 1909.*

dec (also **decd**) *abbr* deceased: *Simon Day dec.*

deca- *comb form* ten: *decathlon.* ⇨ App 12.

decade /ˈdekeɪd, *also esp US* dɪˈkeɪd/ *n* period of ten years: *the first decade of the 20th century,* ie 1901-1910 or 1900-1909.

Certain decades have acquired special associations. The 1890s, for example, are sometimes called the 'Naughty Nineties' in reference to the general atmosphere of relaxation which followed Victorian austerity. Music halls reached the height of their popularity during the 1890s. The end of the First World War and wartime deprivation brought about the 'Roaring Twenties' (the 1920s), which saw the emergence of flappers, and during which dances like the Charleston became very popular. The 1930s are known as the 'Hungry Thirties' because of the mass unemployment which characterized the decade. The 1960s, on the other hand, are looked back on as the 'Swinging Sixties', a decade which celebrated youth, energy and optimism. Youth cults such as hippies and flower power appeared and grew, the music of pop groups like the *Beatles and the *Rolling Stones became hugely popular, and fashion developed radically, notably with the invention of the miniskirt.

decadence /ˈdekədəns/ *n* [U] **(a)** (falling to a) lower level (in morals, art, literature, etc) esp after a period at a high level: *the decadence of late Victorian art.* **(b)** attitude or behaviour that shows this: *the decadence of the rich Western countries.* ▷ **decadent** /ˈdekədənt/ *adj*: *a decadent society, style* ○ *decadent behaviour.*

decaffeinated /ˌdiːˈkæfɪneɪtɪd/ *adj* with most or all of the caffeine removed: *decaffeinated coffee.*

Decalogue /ˈdekəlɒg; *US* -lɔːg/ *n* **the Decalogue** (in the Bible) the Ten Commandments given to Moses by God.

decamp /dɪˈkæmp/ *v* **1** [I, Ipr] ~ **(with sth)** go away suddenly and often secretly (taking sth with one): *She has decamped with all our money.* **2** [I] leave a camp or a place where one has camped: *The soldiers decamped at dawn.*

decanal /dɪˈkeɪnl, *also* ˈdekənl/ *adj* of a dean(1, 2).

decant /dɪˈkænt/ *v* [Tn, Tn·pr] ~ **sth (into sth)** pour (wine, etc) from a bottle into another container, esp slowly so that the sediment is left behind.

▷ **decanter** *n* (usu decorative) glass bottle with a stopper into which wine, etc may be decanted before serving. ⇨ illus at BOTTLE.

decapitate /dɪˈkæpɪteɪt/ *v* [Tn] cut the head off (esp a person or an animal). ▷ **decapitation** /dɪˌkæpɪˈteɪʃn/ *n* [U, C].

decapod /ˈdekəpɒd/ *n* crustacean with ten legs, eg a crab, lobster or shrimp.

decarbonize, -ise /ˌdiːˈkɑːbənaɪz/ (also (*infml*) **decoke**) *v* [Tn] remove carbon from (esp the cylinders of an internal-combustion engine).

decathlon /dɪˈkæθlɒn/ *n* athletic contest in which each participant must take part in all of ten events. Cf BIATHLON, PENTATHLON.

▷ **decathlete** /dɪˈkæθliːt/ *n* athlete who competes in a decathlon.

decay /dɪˈkeɪ/ *v* **1 (a)** [I, Tn] (cause sth to) become bad; rot; decompose: *decaying teeth, vegetables* ○ *Sugar decays your teeth.* **(b)** [I] (*physics*) (of a substance) change by the spontaneous disintegration of unstable (radioactive) nuclei. **2** [I] lose power, vigour, influence, etc: *a decaying culture, society, regime, etc* ○ *Our powers decay* (ie We become less strong, alert, etc) *in old age.*

▷ **decay** *n* [U] (state reached by the process of) decaying: ˈ*tooth decay* ○ *radioactive decay* ○ *The empire is in decay.* ○ *The feudal system slowly fell into decay,* ie stopped working.

decease /dɪˈsiːs/ *n* [U] (*law or fml*) death (of a person).

▷ **deceased** *adj* dead: *a deceased father, uncle, spouse, etc* ○ *Both her parents are deceased.* **the deceased** *n* (*pl* unchanged) (*law or fml*) person who has died, esp recently.

decedent /dɪˈsiːdnt/ *n* (*US law*) dead person.

deceit /dɪˈsiːt/ *n* **1** [U] deliberately leading sb to believe or accept sth that is false, usu so as to get sth for oneself; deceiving: *practice deceit on sb* ○ *She won her promotion by deceit.* **2** [C] dishonest act or statement: *She got them to hand over all their money by a wicked deceit.*

▷ **deceitful** /dɪˈsiːtfl/ *adj* **1** often deceiving people; dishonest: *You've been going there without telling me, you deceitful child!* **2** intended to mislead: *deceitful words, behaviour.* **deceitfully** /-fəli/ *adv.* **deceitfulness** *n* [U].

deceive /dɪˈsiːv/ *v* [Tn, Tn·pr] **1** ~ **sb/oneself (into doing sth)** make sb believe sth that is not true (so as to make him do sth); deliberately mislead sb: *You can't pass exams without working, so don't deceive yourself (into thinking you can).* ○ *We were deceived into believing that he could help us.* ○ *His friendly manner did not deceive us for long.* **2** ~ **sb (with sb)** be sexually unfaithful to (one's spouse, etc): *He's been deceiving his wife with another woman for months.*

▷ **deceiver** /-və(r)/ *n* person who deceives.

decelerate /ˌdiːˈseləreɪt/ *v* [I, Tn] (cause sth to) slow down. Cf ACCELERATE.

▷ **deceleration** /ˌdiːseləˈreɪʃn/ *n* [U] **(a)** slowing down or being caused to slow down. **(b)** rate of decrease of speed per unit of time.

December /dɪˈsembə(r)/ *n* [U, C] (*abbr* **Dec**) the twelfth month of the year, next after November. For the uses of *December* see the examples at *April.*

decency /ˈdiːsnsɪ/ *n* **1** [U] quality of being or appearing as respectable people would wish: *an offence against decency,* eg appearing naked in public ○ *Have the decency to* (ie Be polite and) *apologize for what you did!* **2 the decencies** [pl] standards of respectable behaviour in society: *We must observe the decencies and attend the funeral.*

decent /ˈdiːsnt/ *adj* **1 (a)** proper; acceptable: *We must provide decent housing for the poor.* ○ *The hospital has no decent equipment.* ○ *He's done the decent thing and resigned.* **(b)** not likely to shock or embarrass others; modest: *That dress isn't decent.* ○ (*infml*) *Are you decent?* ie Are you properly dressed? ○ *Never tell stories that are not decent,* ie that are obscene. Cf INDECENT. **2** satisfactory; quite good: *earn a decent wage, living, etc* ○ *That was quite a decent lunch.* ○ *They're a decent firm to work for,* ie They treat their employees well. ○ *He's a thoroughly decent* (ie honourable) *man.* **3** (in dated upper-class British speech) willing to help; kind: *It was jolly decent of him to lend us his car.*

▷ **decently** *adv* in a decent(1, 2) manner: *decently dressed* ○ *behave decently.*

decentralize, -ise /ˌdiːˈsentrəlaɪz/ *v* [I, Tn] **1** transfer (power, authority, etc) from central government to regional government: *If we decentralize, the provinces will have more autonomy.* **2** distribute (industry, workers, population, etc) over a wider area away from the centre. ▷ **decentralization, -isation** /ˌdiːsentrəlaɪˈzeɪʃn; *US* -lɪˈz-/ *n* [U].

deception /dɪˈsepʃn/ *n* **1** [U] deceiving or being deceived: *obtain sth by deception* ○ *practise deception on the public.* **2** [C] trick intended to deceive: *It was an innocent deception, meant as a joke.*

deceptive /dɪˈseptɪv/ *adj* likely to deceive; misleading: *Appearances are often deceptive,* ie Things are not always what they seem to be. ○ *Her simple style is deceptive: what she has to say is very profound.* ▷ **deceptively** *adv*: *The tank is deceptively small: it actually holds quite a lot.*

deci- *comb form* (in the metric system) one tenth part of: *decilitre* ○ *decimetre.* ⇨ App 12.

decibel /ˈdesɪbel/ *n* unit for measuring the relative loudness of sounds, or for measuring power levels in electrical communications.

decide /dɪˈsaɪd/ *v* **1** [I, Ipr, Tn, Tn·pr] settle (a dispute, an issue or a case); give a judgement on (sth): *The judge will decide (the case) tomorrow.* ○ *It's difficult to decide between the two.* ○ *The judge decided for/against the plaintiff.* ○ *Her argument decided the issue in his favour.* **2 (a)** [I, Ipr, Tn, Tf, Tw, Tt] ~ **(on/against sth/sb)** consider and come to a conclusion; make up one's mind; resolve: *With so many choices, it's hard to decide (what to buy).* ○ *After seeing all the candidates we've decided on* (ie chosen) *this one.* ○ *decide against changing one's job* ○ *I never thought she'd decide that!* ○ *It has been decided that the book should be revised.* ○ *She decided not to go alone.* **(b)** [Ipr, Tn, Tw] (of events, actions, etc) have an important, definite effect on (sth): *I wanted to be a painter, but circumstances decided otherwise,* ie forced me to be something else. ○ *A chance meeting decided my career.* ○ *This last game will decide who is to be champion.* **3** [Tn, Tn·pr, Tnt] cause (sb) to reach a decision: *What finally decided you against it?* ○ *That decided me to leave my job.*

▷ **decided** *adj* **1** [attrib] clear; definite: *There is a decided difference between the two sisters.* ○ *a person of decided views.* **2** ~ **(about sth)** determined: *a decided effort to improve sales* ○ *He won't go: he's quite decided about it.* **decidedly** *adv* definitely; undoubtedly: *I feel decidedly unwell this morning.*

decider *n* game, race, etc to settle a contest between competitors who have previously finished equal.

deciduous /dɪˈsɪdjʊəs, dɪˈsɪdʒʊəs/ *adj* (of a tree) that loses its leaves annually, usu in autumn: *deciduous forests.* Cf EVERGREEN. ⇨ illus at TREE.

decilitre /ˈdesɪliːtə(r)/ *n* unit of capacity in the metric system, equal to one tenth of a litre.

decimal /ˈdesɪml/ *adj* based on or reckoned in tens or tenths: *decimal coinage/currency.*

▷ **decimal** *n* (also ˌ**decimal** ˈ**fraction**) fraction expressed in tenths, hundredths, etc: *The decimal 0.61 stands for 61 hundredths.* ⇨ App 9.

decimalize, -ise /-məlaɪz/ *v* **1** [Tn] express a number as a decimal fraction: *$1\frac{1}{2}$ decimalized is 1.5.* **2** [I, Tn] change (currency) to a decimal system: *The country decided to decimalize (its coinage).* **decimalization, -isation** /ˌdesɪməlaɪˈzeɪʃn; *US* -lɪˈz-/ *n* [U].

□ ˌ**decimal** ˈ**point** dot or point placed after the unit figure in the writing of decimals, eg in 15.61. ˈ**decimal system** system of numbers, measures or currency based on the number ten.

decimate /ˈdesɪmeɪt/ *v* [Tn] **(a)** kill or destroy a large part of (sth): *Disease has decimated the population.* **(b)** (*infml*) reduce (sth) considerably: *Student numbers have been decimated by cuts in grants.* ▷ **decimation** /desɪˈmeɪʃn/ *n* [U].

decimetre /ˈdesɪmiːtə(r)/ *n* unit of length in the metric system, equal to one tenth of a metre.

decipher /dɪˈsaɪfə(r)/ *v* [Tn, Tw] succeed in understanding (a coded message, bad handwriting, etc): *I can't decipher what is inscribed on the pillar.* ○ (*infml*) *Can you decipher her scrawl?*

▷ **decipherable** /dɪˈsaɪfrəbl/ *adj* that can be deciphered.

decision /dɪˈsɪʒn/ *n* **1** ~ **(on/against sth)**; ~ **(to do sth)** **(a)** [U] deciding; making up one's mind: *It's a matter for personal decision,* ie Everybody must decide for themselves. **(b)** [C] conclusion reached; judgement: *arrive at/come to/make/reach a decision* ○ *his decision against going on holiday* ○ *We took the difficult decision to leave.* ○ *Her decision to retire surprised us all.* ○ *give a decision on an issue* ○ *The judge's decision was to award damages to the defendant.* ○ *Discussion should be part of the decision-making process.* **2** [U] ability to decide quickly: *Anyone who lacks decision* (ie who hesitates, can't decide questions) *shouldn't be a leader.*

decisive /dɪˈsaɪsɪv/ *adj* **1** having a particular, important or conclusive effect: *a decisive victory,* *battle, moment* ○ *The injury to their key player could be a decisive factor in the game.* **2** having or showing the ability to decide quickly: *a decisive person, answer, manner* ○ *Be decisive — tell them exactly what you think should be done!* ▷ **decisively** *adv*: *act, answer decisively.* **decisiveness** *n* [U].

deck[1] /dek/ *n* **1** [C] **(a)** any of the floors of a ship in or above the hull: *My cabin is on E deck.* ○ *below deck(s)*, ie in(to) the space under the main deck. ⇨ illus at YACHT. **(b)** any similar area, eg the floor of a bus: *the top deck of a double-decker bus.* **2** [C] (*esp US*) pack of playing-cards. **3** [C] **(a)** platform on which the turntable and pick-up arm of a record-player rest. **(b)** device for holding and playing magnetic tape, discs, etc in sound-recording equipment or a computer. **4 the deck** [sing] (*sl*) the ground or floor: *It was an easy catch, but he put it on the deck*, ie dropped it. **5** (idm) **clear the decks** ⇨ CLEAR[3]. **hit the deck** ⇨ HIT[1]. **on deck (a)** on the main deck of a ship. **(b)** (*esp US*) ready for action, duty, etc.

▷ **deck** *v* [Tn] (*US infml*) knock (sb) to the ground: *He decked him with his first punch.*

-decker (forming compound *ns* and *adjs*) having a specified number of decks or layers: *a ˌdouble-/ˌsingle-decker ˈbus* ○ *a ˌtriple-decker ˈsandwich*, ie one with three layers of bread.

□ **ˈdeck-chair** *n* portable folding chair with a (usu) canvas seat on a wood or metal frame, used out of doors, eg in parks and on the beach. ⇨ illus at HOME.

📖 Deck-chairs take their name from the fact that they were originally designed for use on the deck of a ship. Those once used in people's gardens have been largely replaced by more comfortable types of garden furniture. They are still often seen at British seaside resorts, however, where they are hired out for people to sit on by the sea.

ˈdeck-hand *n* member of a ship's crew who works on deck.

deck[2] /dek/ *v* [esp passive: Tn, Tn·pr, Tn·p] ~ **sb/sth (out) (in/with sth)** decorate sb/sth: *streets decked with flags* ○ *She was decked out in her finest clothes.*

declaim /dɪˈkleɪm/ *v* **1** [I, Tn] speak (sth) as if addressing an audience: *A preacher stood declaiming in the town centre.* ○ *He declaims his poetry*, ie recites it formally and with great feeling. **2** [Ipr] ~ **against sb/sth** attack sb/sth in words: *She wrote a book declaiming against our corrupt society.*

declamation /ˌdekləˈmeɪʃn/ *n* **(a)** [U] declaiming: *the declamation of poetry.* **(b)** [C] formal speech, esp one made with great feeling.

▷ **declamatory** /dɪˈklæmətərɪ; *US* -tɔːrɪ/ *adj* formal and rhetorical; (spoken) with great feeling: *her high-flown declamatory style.*

declaration /ˌdekləˈreɪʃn/ *n* **1 (a)** [U] declaring; formally announcing: *He was in favour of the declaration of a truce.* **(b)** [C] formal announcement: *a declaration of war* ○ *the Declaration of Human Rights*, ie by the United Nations, stating an individual's basic rights. **2** [C] written notification: *a declaration of income*, ie made to the tax authorities ○ *a customs declaration*, ie a form giving details of the contents of a parcel, consignment, etc on which duty may be payable.

declare /dɪˈkleə(r)/ *v* **1 (a)** [Tn, Tf, Tw, Cn·a, Cn·n, Cn·t, Dpr·f, Dpr·w] formally announce (sth); make known clearly: *'I'm not coming with you — and that's final!' declared Mary.* ○ *declare that the war is over* ○ *They then declared (to us all) what had been decided.* ○ *They declared him (to be) the winner.* ○ *I declare the meeting closed.* **(b)** [Tf, Cn·a, Cn·t] say (sth) solemnly: *He declared that he was innocent.* ○ *She was declared (to be) guilty.* **2** [Ipr] ~ **for/against sth/sb** say that one is/is not in favour of sth/sb: *The commission declared against the proposed scheme.* **3** [Tn] ~ **oneself** say openly who one is or what one's intentions or wishes are: *The party called upon all its supporters to declare themselves*, ie to show their support openly. **4** [Tn] tell the tax authorities about (one's income), or customs officers about (dutiable goods brought into a country): *You must declare all you have earned in the last year.* ○ *Have you anything to declare?* **5** [I, Cn·a] (in cricket) choose to end one's team's innings before all ten wickets have fallen: *The captain declared (the innings closed) at a score of 395 for 5 wickets.* **6** (idm) **declare an/one's ˈinterest** reveal to others any facts that might be thought to influence one's opinions or actions on a particular issue. **declare trumps** (in card-games) say which suit will be trumps. **declare ˈwar (on/against sb)** announce that one is at war (with sb): *War has been declared.*

▷ **declared** *adj* [attrib] that sb has openly admitted to be such: *He's a declared atheist.* ○ *Her declared ambition is to become a politician.*

declassify /ˌdiːˈklæsɪfaɪ/ *v* (*pt, pp* **-fied**) [Tn] declare (information) to be no longer secret: *Plans for nuclear plants have been declassified.* ▷ **declassification** /ˌdiːˌklæsɪfɪˈkeɪʃn/ *n* [U].

declension /dɪˈklenʃn/ *n* (*grammar*) **(a)** [U] varying the endings of nouns and pronouns according to their function in a sentence. Cf CASE[1] 8. **(b)** [C] class of words with the same range of endings for the different cases (CASE[1] 8): *In Latin, the nominative case of first declension nouns ends in 'a'.*

declination /ˌdeklɪˈneɪʃn/ *n* **1** [C] (*fml*) downward bend or turn. **2** [U] (*astronomy*) distance of a star from an imaginary line separating the northern heavens from the southern heavens, measured in degrees. **3** [U, C] (*physics*) deviation of the needle of a compass, east or west from true north.

decline[1] /dɪˈklaɪn/ *v* **1** [I, Tn, Tt] say 'no' to (sth); refuse (sth offered), usu politely: *I invited her to join us, but she declined.* ○ *decline an invitation to dinner* ○ *He declined to discuss his plans.* **2** [I] become smaller, weaker, fewer, etc; diminish: *Her influence declined after she lost the election.* ○ *a declining birth-rate* ○ *declining sales* ○ *He spent his declining years (ie those at the end of his life) in the country.* **3** (*grammar*) **(a)** [Tn] vary the endings of (nouns and pronouns) according to their function in a sentence. **(b)** [I] (of nouns and pronouns) vary in this way.

decline[2] /dɪˈklaɪn/ *n* **1** ~ **(in sth)** gradual and continuous loss of strength, power, numbers, etc; declining: *the decline of the Roman Empire* ○ *a decline in population, prices, popularity.* **2** (idm) **fall/go into a deˈcline** lose strength, influence, etc: *After his wife's death, he fell into a decline.* ○ *The company has gone into a decline because of falling demand.* **on the deˈcline** becoming weaker, fewer, etc: *She is on the decline, and may die soon.* ○ *The number of robberies in the area is on the decline.*

declivity /dɪˈklɪvətɪ/ *n* (*fml*) downward slope. Cf ACCLIVITY.

declutch /ˌdiːˈklʌtʃ/ *v* [I] disconnect the clutch (of a motor vehicle) before changing gear.

decoction /dɪˈkɒkʃn/ *n* **(a)** [U] boiling a liquid until most of the water disappears, to leave a very strong liquid. **(b)** [C] strong liquid produced by doing this; essence.

decode /ˌdiːˈkəʊd/ *v* [Tn] **(a)** find the meaning of (sth written in code). **(b)** analyse and interpret (an electronic signal). Cf ENCODE.

▷ **decoder** *n* **(a)** person or device that changes a code into understandable language. **(b)** device that decodes an electronic signal.

decoke /ˌdiːˈkəʊk/ *v* [Tn] (*infml*) = DECARBONIZE.

décolleté /deɪˈkɒlteɪ; *US* -kɒlˈteɪ/ *adj* (*French*) **(a)** (of a dress, etc) with a low neckline. **(b)** [pred] (of a woman) wearing a dress, etc with a low neckline: *She was daringly décolleté.*

▷ **décolletage** /ˌdeɪkɒlˈtɑːʒ/ *n* [U] (*French*) low neckline (on a dress, etc).

decolonize, -ise /ˌdiːˈkɒlənaɪz/ *v* [I, Tn] give independent status to (a colony). ▷ **decolonization, -isation** /ˌdiːˌkɒlənaɪˈzeɪʃn; *US* -nɪˈz-/ *n* [U].

decompose /ˌdiːkəmˈpəʊz/ *v* **1** [I, Tn] (cause sth to) become bad or rotten; decay: *a decomposing corpse.* **2** [Tn] separate (a substance, light, etc) into its parts: *A prism decomposes light.* ▷ **decomposition** /ˌdiːkɒmpəˈzɪʃn/ *n* [U].

decompress /ˌdiːkəmˈpres/ *v* [Tn] **(a)** gradually release the air pressure on (esp a deep-sea diver returning to the surface). **(b)** reduce compression in (a chamber, vessel, etc). ▷ **decompression** /ˌdiːkəmˈpreʃn/ *n* [U]: [attrib] *a decompression chamber*, ie one in which divers may return to normal pressure.

□ **ˌdecomˈpression sickness** (also **caisson disease**) pains in the joints and limbs (and in severe cases, paralysis and death) suffered by deep-sea divers who come to the surface too quickly; the bends.

decongestant /ˌdiːkənˈdʒestənt/ *n* [C, U] (*medicine*) substance that relieves congestion, esp in the nose. ▷ **decongestant** *adj*: *decongestant tablets.*

decontaminate /ˌdiːkənˈtæmɪneɪt/ *v* [Tn] remove (esp radioactive) contamination from (a building, clothes, an area, etc). ▷ **decontamination** /ˌdiːkənˌtæmɪˈneɪʃn/ *n* [U].

decontrol /ˌdiːkənˈtrəʊl/ *v* (**-ll-**) [Tn] remove controls (such as those imposed by a government during a war or an emergency) from (trade in certain goods).

décor /ˈdeɪkɔː(r); *US* deɪˈkɔːr/ *n* [U, sing] furnishing and decoration of a room, stage, etc: *a stylish, modern décor* ○ *Who designed the décor?*

decorate /ˈdekəreɪt/ *v* **1** [Tn, Tn·pr] ~ **sth (with sth)** make sth (more) beautiful by adding ornaments to it: *Bright posters decorate the streets.* ○ *The building was decorated with flags.* ○ *decorate a Christmas tree with coloured lights.* **2** [I, Tn] put paint, plaster, wallpaper, etc on (a room, house, etc): *We're decorating (the kitchen) again this summer.* **3** [Tn, Tn·pr] ~ **sb (for sth)** give a medal or some other award to sb: *Several soldiers were decorated for bravery.*

▷ **decorator** *n* person whose job is painting and wallpapering rooms, houses, etc: *Arthur Jones, painter and decorator.*

□ **ˈDecorated style** style of English Gothic architecture between about 1290 and 1350, featuring a lot of carved ornaments around windows, doors, etc.

decoration /ˌdekəˈreɪʃn/ *n* **1** [U] decorating or being decorated: *When will they finish the decoration of the bathroom?* **2** [U, C] thing used for decorating: *the carved decoration around the doorway* ○ *Christmas decorations.* **3** [C] medal, ribbon, etc given and worn as an honour or award.

decorative /ˈdekərətɪv; *US* ˈdekəreɪtɪv/ *adj* that makes sth look (more) beautiful: *decorative icing on the cake* ○ *The coloured lights are very decorative.*

decorous /ˈdekərəs/ *adj* dignified and socially acceptable: *decorous behaviour, speech.* ▷ **decorously** *adv.*

decorum /dɪˈkɔːrəm/ *n* [U] dignified and socially acceptable behaviour: *In the presence of elderly visitors our son was a model of decorum.*

decoy /ˈdiːkɔɪ/ *n* **(a)** (real or imitation) bird or animal used to attract others so that they can be shot or trapped. **(b)** (*fig*) person or thing used to lure sb into a position of danger.

▷ **decoy** /dɪˈkɔɪ/ *v* [Tn, Tn·pr] trick (a person or an animal) into a place of danger by using a decoy: *He was decoyed by a false message (into entering enemy territory).*

decrease /dɪˈkriːs/ *v* [I, Tn] (cause sth to) become smaller or fewer; diminish: *Student numbers have decreased by 500.* ○ *Interest in the sport is decreasing.*

▷ **decrease** /ˈdiːkriːs/ *n* **1** ~ **(in sth) (a)** [U] decreasing; reduction: *some decrease in the crime rate.* **(b)** [C] amount by which sth decreases: *a decrease of 3% in the rate of inflation* ○ *There has been a decrease in imports.* **2** (idm) **on the ˈdecrease** decreasing: *Is crime on the decrease?*

decree /dɪˈkriː/ *n* **1** order given by a ruler or an authority and having the force of a law: *issue a decree* ○ *rule by decree*, ie without seeking people's consent. **2** judgement or decision of certain lawcourts.

▷ **decree** *v* (*pt, pp* **decreed**) [Tn, Tf, Tw] order

(sth) (as if) by decree: *The governor decreed a day of mourning.* ○ *(fig) Fate decreed that they would not meet again.*

□ **deˌcree ˈabsolute** order of a lawcourt by which two people are finally divorced.

deˌcree ˈnisi /ˈnaɪsɪ, ˈnaɪsaɪ/ order of a lawcourt that two people will be divorced after a fixed period, unless good reasons are given why they should not.

NOTE ON USAGE: When talking about giving orders, **decree** and **dictate** can be used of individuals in positions of authority. **Decree** usually suggests the public announcement of a decision made by a ruler or government without consulting others: *The dictator decreed that his birthday would be a public holiday.* **Dictate** indicates people using their power over others: *Her skills were in such demand that she could dictate her own salary.* **Ordain** and **prescribe** suggest a more impersonal authority such as the law. **Ordain** is formal and can be used of God: *Is it ordained in heaven that women should work in the home?* **Prescribe** is used of the law: *Regulations prescribe certain standards for building materials.*

decrepit /dɪˈkrepɪt/ *adj* made weak by age or hard use: *a decrepit person, horse, bicycle.*

▷ **decrepitude** /dɪˈkrepɪtju:d; *US* -tu:d/ *n* [U] state of being decrepit.

decry /dɪˈkraɪ/ *v (pt, pp* **decried**) [Tn, Cn·n/a] ~ **sb/sth (as sth)** speak critically of sb/sth to make him/it seem less valuable, useful, etc; disparage sb/sth: *He decried her efforts (as a waste of time).*

dedicate /ˈdedɪkeɪt/ *v* **1** [Tn·pr] ~ **oneself/sth to sth** give or devote (oneself, time, effort, etc) to (a noble cause or purpose): *She dedicated her life to helping the poor.* ○ *dedicate oneself to one's work.* **2** [Tn·pr] ~ **sth to sb** address (one's book, a piece of one's music, etc) to sb as a way of showing respect, by putting his name at the beginning: *She dedicated her first book to her husband.* **3** [Tn, Tn·pr] ~ **sth (to sb/sth)** devote (a church, etc) with solemn ceremonies (to God, to a saint or to sacred use): *The chapel was dedicated in 1880.* Cf CONSECRATE.

▷ **dedicated** *adj* **1** devoted to sth; committed: *a dedicated worker, priest, teacher, etc.* **2** [esp attrib] (esp of computer equipment) designed for one particular purpose only: *a dedicated word processor.*

dedication /ˌdedɪˈkeɪʃn/ *n* ~ **(to sth) 1** [U] devotion to a cause or an aim: *I admire the priest's dedication.* **2 (a)** [U] action of dedicating a book, piece of music, etc to sb. **(b)** [C] words used in doing this. **3** [U] dedicating (of a church, etc).

deduce /dɪˈdju:s/ *v* [Tn, Tn·pr, Tf, Tw] ~ **sth (from sth)** arrive at (facts, a theory, etc) by reasoning; infer sth: *If a = b and b = c, we can deduce that a = c.* ○ *Detectives deduced from the clues who had committed the crime.*

▷ **deducible** /dɪˈdju:səbl; *US* dɪˈdu:səbl/ *adj* that may be deduced.

deduct /dɪˈdʌkt/ *v* [Tn, Tn·pr] ~ **sth (from sth)** take away (an amount or a part): *Tax is deducted from your salary.* Cf SUBTRACT.

▷ **deductible** /dɪˈdʌktəbl/ *adj* that may be deducted from one's taxable earnings: *Money spent on business expenses is deductible.*

deduction /dɪˈdʌkʃn/ *n* ~ **(from sth) 1 (a)** [U] reasoning from general principles to a particular case; deducing: *a philosopher skilled in deduction.* **(b)** [C] conclusion reached by reasoning: *It's an obvious deduction that she is guilty.* Cf INDUCTION 3. **2 (a)** [U] deducting: *the deduction of tax from earnings.* **(b)** [C] amount deducted: *deductions from pay for insurance and pension.*

▷ **deductive** /dɪˈdʌktɪv/ *adj* of, using or reasoning by deduction(1a). **deductively** *adv.*

deed /di:d/ *n* **1** *(fml)* **(a)** [C] thing done intentionally or consciously; act: *be rewarded for one's good deeds* ○ *deeds of heroism* ○ *Deeds are better than words when people need help.* ➪ Usage at ACT[1]. **(b)** [U] what one does; action: *loyal in word and deed.* **2** (often *pl*) *(law)* signed agreement, esp about the ownership of property or legal rights.

□ **ˈdeed-box** *n* strong box for keeping deeds and other documents.

ˌdeed of ˈcovenant signed promise to pay a regular amount of money annually to a person, society, etc enabling the receiver to reclaim in addition the tax paid on the amount by the giver.

ˈdeed poll legal deed made by one person only, esp to change his name.

deem /di:m/ *v* [Tf, Tnt esp passive, Cn·a esp passive, Cn·n] *(fml)* consider; regard: *He deemed that it was his duty to help.* ○ *She was deemed (to be) the winner.* ○ *It is deemed advisable.* ○ *I deem it a great honour to be invited to address you.*

deep[1] /di:p/ *adj* **(-er, -est) 1 (a)** extending a long way from top to bottom: *a deep well, river, trench, box.* Cf SHALLOW. **(b)** extending a long way from the surface or edge: *a deep wound, cleft, border, shelf* ○ *a big, deep-chested wrestler.* **(c)** (after *ns*, with words specifying how far) extending down, back or in: *water six feet deep* ○ *a plot of land 100 feet deep*, ie going back this distance from a road, fence, etc ○ *People stood twenty deep* (ie in lines of twenty people one behind the other) *to see her go past.* **(d)** (of a fielder in cricket) positioned far from the batsman: *deep square leg.* **2 (a)** [attrib] taking in or giving out a lot of air: *a deep sigh/breath.* **(b)** going a long way down or through sth: *a deep thrust/dive.* **3** (of sounds) low in pitch; not shrill: *a deep voice, note, rumbling, etc.* **4** (of sleep) from which one is not easily awakened. **5** (of colours) strong; vivid: *a deep red.* **6** [pred] ~ **in sth (a)** far down in sth: *with his hands deep in his pockets* ○ *rocks deep in the earth.* **(b)** absorbed in sth; concentrating on sth: *deep in thought, study, a book.* **(c)** very involved in sth; overwhelmed by sth: *deep in debt, difficulties.* **7** [usu attrib] *(fig)* **(a)** difficult to understand or find out: *a deep mystery, secret, etc.* **(b)** learned; profound: *a deep thinker* ○ *a person with deep insight* ○ *a deep discussion.* **(c)** concealing one's real feelings, motives, etc; devious: *He's a deep one.* **8 (a)** (of emotions) strongly felt; intense: *deep outrage, shame, sympathy, etc.* **(b)** extreme: *in deep disgrace, trouble.* **9** (idm) **beauty is only skin deep** ➪ BEAUTY. **between the devil and the deep blue sea** ➪ DEVIL[1]. **go off the ˈdeep end** *(infml)* become extremely angry or emotional: *When I said I'd broken it, she really went off the deep end.* **in deep ˈwater(s)** in trouble or difficulty: *Having lost her passport, she is now in deep water.* **of the blackest/deepest dye** ➪ DYE[2]. **throw sb in at the deep end** *(infml)* introduce sb to the most difficult part of an activity, esp one for which he is not prepared.

▷ **-deep** (forming compound *adjs*) as far as a specified point: *They stood knee-deep in the snow.* ○ *The grass was ankle-deep.*

deepen /ˈdi:pən/ *v* [I, Tn] (cause sth to) become deep or deeper: *The water deepened after the dam was built.* ○ *The mystery deepens*, ie becomes harder to understand. ○ *deepen a channel* ○ *the deepening colours of the evening sky.*

deeply *adv* **1** a long way down or through sth: *The dog bit deeply into his arm.* **2** greatly; intensely: *deeply interested, indebted, impressed* ○ *She felt her mother's death deeply.*

deepness *n* [U].

□ **ˈdeep-sea, ˈdeep-water** *adjs* [attrib] of or in the deeper parts of the sea, away from the coast: *ˌdeep-sea ˈfishing* ○ *a ˌdeep-sea ˈdiver.*

the ˌdeep ˈSouth southern states of the USA, esp Georgia, Alabama, Mississippi, Louisiana and South Carolina.

ˌdeep ˈspace far distant regions beyond the earth's atmosphere or the solar system.

deep[2] /di:p/ *adv* **(-er, -est) 1** far down or in: *We had to dig deeper to find water.* ○ *They dived deep into the ocean.* ○ *The gold lies deep in the earth.* ○ *He went on studying deep into the night.* **2** (idm) **deep ˈdown** *(infml)* in reality; in spite of appearances: *She seems indifferent, but deep down she's very pleased.* **go ˈdeep** (of attitudes, beliefs, etc) be strongly and naturally held or felt: *Her faith goes very deep.* ○ *Your maternal instincts go deeper than you think.* **still waters run deep** ➪ STILL[1].

□ **ˌdeep-ˈfreeze** *v (pt* **ˌdeep-ˈfroze**, *pp* **ˌdeep-ˈfrozen**) [Tn] freeze (food) quickly in order to preserve it for long periods: *ˌdeep-frozen ˈfish.* — *n* = FREEZER 1.

ˌdeep-ˈfry *v (pt, pp* **ˌdeep-ˈfried**) [Tn] fry (food) in hot fat that completely covers it. ➪ Usage at COOK.

ˌdeep-ˈlaid *adj* [usu attrib] (of schemes, etc) secretly and carefully planned.

ˌdeep-ˈmined *adj* (of coal) taken from far down in the earth. Cf OPEN-CAST (OPEN[1]).

ˌdeep-ˈrooted, ˌdeep-ˈseated *adjs* profound; not easily removed: *ˌdeep-rooted disˈlike, ˈprejudice, suˈspicion, etc* ○ *The causes of the trouble are deep-seated.*

deep[3] /di:p/ *n* **the deep** [sing] **1** *(dated or fml)* the sea. **2** area around the edge of a cricket field, far from the batsman: *fielding in the deep.*

deer

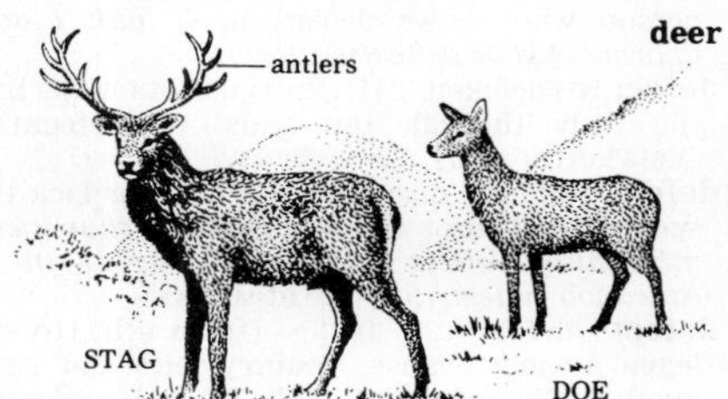

deer /dɪə(r)/ *n (pl* unchanged) any of several types of graceful, quick-running, ruminant animal, the male of which has antlers. ➪ illus.

📖 Deer were hunted in medieval times by royalty and the nobility, and today they are still hunted in parts of Britain, during a strictly defined period of the year. The sport has retained its aristocratic associations. Red deer are hunted on Exmoor and the Quantock Hills, and fallow deer are hunted in the New Forest. In Scotland, deer are hunted on foot (called 'stalking'). Deer are also kept for their beauty, and can sometimes be seen in the parks surrounding country houses. Magdalen College, Oxford, has kept deer since the 17th century, and they are a popular tourist attraction.

□ **ˈdeerskin** *n* [U] (leather made of) deer's skin: [attrib] *ˌdeerskin ˈsandals.*

deerstalker /ˈdɪəstɔ:kə(r)/ *n* cloth cap with two peaks, one in front and the other behind, and flaps for covering the ears. ➪ illus at HAT.

de-escalate /ˌdi:ˈeskəleɪt/ *v* [Tn] reduce the level or intensity of (a war, the arms race, etc). ▷ **de-escalation** /di:ˌeskəˈleɪʃn/ *n* [U].

deface /dɪˈfeɪs/ *v* [Tn] spoil the appearance or legibility of (sth) by marking or damaging the surface: *Don't deface library books.* ○ *The wall has been defaced with slogans.*

▷ **defacement** *n* [U] defacing or being defaced.

de facto /ˌdeɪ ˈfæktəʊ/ *(Latin)* existing in actual fact, whether rightly or not: *a de facto ruler, government, right* ○ *Though his kingship was challenged, he continued to rule de facto.* Cf DE JURE.

defame /dɪˈfeɪm/ *v* [Tn] attack the good reputation of (sb); say bad things about (sb): *The article is an attempt to defame an honest man.*

▷ **defamation** /ˌdefəˈmeɪʃn/ *n* [U] defaming or being defamed: *defamation of character.*

defamatory /dɪˈfæmətrɪ; *US* -tɔ:rɪ/ *adj* intended to defame: *a defamatory statement, book, etc.*

default[1] /dɪˈfɔ:lt/ *n* **1** [U] *(esp law)* failure to do sth, esp to pay a debt or appear in court. **2** (idm) **by deˈfault** because the other party, team, etc does not appear: *win a case/a game by default.* **in default of sth/sb** *(fml)* because or in case sth/sb is absent: *He was acquitted in default of strong evidence of his guilt.* ○ *The committee will not meet in default of a chairman.*

default[2] /dɪˈfɔ:lt/ *v* **(a)** [I] fail to do what one is supposed to do (eg to appear in a lawcourt): *A party to the contract defaulted.* **(b)** [I, Ipr] ~ **(on sth)** fail to pay (a debt, etc): *default on hire purchase payments.*

▷ **defaulter** *n* **1** person who defaults. **2** soldier guilty of a military offence.

defeat /dɪˈfi:t/ *v* **1** [Tn, Tn·pr] win a victory over (sb); overcome: *The enemy was defeated in a decisive battle.* ○ *He has been soundly defeated at chess.* **2** [Tn] (*infml*) be puzzling for (sb); baffle: *I've tried to solve the problem, but it defeats me!* ○ *Why you stay indoors on a beautiful day like this defeats me!* **3** [Tn] **(a)** stop (hopes, aims, etc) from becoming reality; thwart: *By not working hard enough you defeat your own purpose.* **(b)** prevent (an attempt, a proposal, etc) from succeeding: *We've defeated moves to build another office block.*
▷ **defeat** *n* **(a)** [U] defeating or being defeated: *suffer defeat* ○ *I never consider the possibility of defeat.* **(b)** [C] instance of this: *six wins and two defeats for the team.*
defeatism /-ɪzəm/ *n* [U] attitude or behaviour that shows one expects not to succeed: *Not bothering to vote is a sure sign of defeatism.* **defeatist** /-ɪst/ *n* person who shows defeatism. — *adj*: *I don't approve of your defeatist attitude.*

defecate /ˈdefəkeɪt/ *v* [I] (*fml*) push out waste from the body through the anus. ▷ **defecation** /ˌdefəˈkeɪʃn/ *n* [U].

defect[1] /ˈdi:fekt, *also* dɪˈfekt/ *n* fault or lack that spoils a person or thing: *a defect of character* ○ *mechanical defects in a car* ○ *defects in the education system.* ⇨ Usage at MISTAKE[1].

defect[2] /dɪˈfekt/ *v* [I, Ipr] ~ **(from sth) (to sth)** leave a party, cause, country, etc, and go to another: *She defected from the Liberals and joined the Socialists.* ○ *One of our spies has defected to the enemy.* ▷ **defector** *n*: *a high-ranking defector seeking political asylum.*

defection /dɪˈfekʃn/ *n* ~ **(from sth)** **1 (a)** [U] deserting a party, cause, religion, etc. **(b)** [C] instance of this: *Discontent in the party will lead to further defections.* **2 (a)** [U] leaving one's country permanently, usu because one disagrees with its political system. **(b)** [C] instance of this: *defections from a racist system.*

defective /dɪˈfektɪv/ *adj* ~ **(in sth)** having a defect or defects; imperfect or incomplete: *a defective machine, method, theory* ○ *defective in workmanship, character* ○ *Her hearing was found to be slightly defective.* ○ *a defective verb*, ie one without the full range of endings that other verbs have, eg *must*. ▷ **defectively** *adv.* **defectiveness** *n* [U].

defence (*US* **defense**) /dɪˈfens/ *n* **1** [U] ~ **(against sth)** **(a)** defending from attack; fighting against attack: *They planned the defence of the town.* ○ *to fight in defence of one's country* ○ *weapons of offence and defence.* **(b)** [C] weapon, barrier, etc used for defending or protecting: *The high wall was built as a defence against intruders.* ○ *The country's defences are weak.* ○ *coastal defences*, ie against attack from the sea ○ *Antibodies are the body's defences against infection.* **(c)** [U] military measures for protecting a country: *A lot of money is spent on defence.* **2 (a)** [C, U] ~ **(against sth)** (esp legal) argument used to answer an accusation or support an idea: *counsel for the defence* ○ *The lawyer produced a clever defence of his client.* ○ *The book is a brilliant defence of* (ie argues in favour of) *our policies.* ○ *She spoke in defence of her religious beliefs.* **(b) the defence** [Gp] lawyer(s) acting for an accused person: *The defence argue/argues that the evidence is weak.* Cf PROSECUTION 2. **3** (*sport*) **(a)** [U] protection of a goal or part of the playing area from opponents' attacks: *She plays in defence.* **(b)** (usu **the defence**) [Gp] members of a team involved in this: *He has been brought in to strengthen the defence.* Cf OFFENSE. **(c)** [C] sporting contest in which a champion is challenged: *his third successful defence of the title.*
▷ **defenceless** *adj* having no defence; unable to defend oneself: *a defenceless child, animal, city.* **defencelessly** *adv.* **defencelessness** *n* [U].
□ **deˈfence mechanism** **(a)** process by which the body produces substances to kill germs or other harmful organisms. **(b)** (*psychology*) mental process (eg repression) that develops to protect the mind from anxiety.

defend /dɪˈfend/ *v* **1** [Tn, Tn·pr] ~ **sb/sth (from/ against sb/sth)** **(a)** protect sb/sth from harm; guard sb/sth: *When the dog attacked me, I defended myself with a stick.* ○ *defend sb from attack, an attacker, injury* ○ *defend one's country against enemies.* **(b)** act, speak or write in support of sb/ sth: *defend one's actions, cause, ideas, leader* ○ *The newspaper defended her against the accusations.* ○ *defend a lawsuit*, ie fight against it in court ○ *You'll need stronger evidence to defend your claim to the inheritance.* **2 (a)** [I, Tn, Tn·pr] (*sport*) protect (the goal, etc) from one's opponents: *Some players are better at defending.* ○ *They had three players defending the goal (against attack).* **(b)** [Tn] (of a sports champion) take part in a contest to keep (one's position): *She's running to defend her 400 metres title.* ▷ **defender** *n*: *He had to beat several defenders to score.*

defendant /dɪˈfendənt/ *n* person accused or sued in a legal case. Cf PLAINTIFF.

defensible /dɪˈfensəbl/ *adj* that can be defended: *a defensible castle, position, theory.*

defensive /dɪˈfensɪv/ *adj* **1** used for or intended for defending: *defensive warfare, measures* ○ *a defensive weapon system to destroy missiles approaching the country.* **2** ~ **(about sb/sth)** showing anxiety to avoid criticism or attack; hiding faults: *When asked to explain her behaviour, she gave a very defensive answer.* ○ *She's very defensive about her part in the affair.* Cf OFFENSIVE 3.
▷ **defensive** *n* (idm) **on the defensive** expecting to be attacked or criticized: *The team was thrown on(to) the defensive as their opponents rallied.* ○ *Talk about boy-friends always puts her on the defensive.*
defensively *adv.*
defensiveness *n* [U].

defer[1] /dɪˈfɜ:(r)/ *v* (**-rr-**) **1** [Tn, Tn·pr, Tg] ~ **sth (to sth)** delay sth until a later time; postpone sth: *deferred payment*, ie made in instalments after purchase ○ *defer one's departure to a later date* ○ *defer making a decision.* **2** [Tn] (*US*) delay the compulsory taking of (sb) into the army, navy, etc.
▷ **deferment, deferral** /dɪˈfɜ:rəl/ *ns* [U, C].
□ **deˌferred ˈshares** shares (SHARE[1] 3) on which dividends are paid only after they have been paid on all other shares.

defer[2] /dɪˈfɜ:(r)/ *v* (**-rr-**) [Ipr] ~ **to sb/sth** give way to sb or sb's wishes, judgement, etc, usu out of respect: *On technical matters, I defer to the experts.* ○ *I defer to your greater experience in such things.*

deference /ˈdefərəns/ *n* [U] **1** giving way to the views, wishes, etc of others, usu out of respect; respect: *treat one's elders with due deference* ○ *show deference to a judge.* **2** (idm) **in deference to sb/ sth** out of respect for sb/sth: *In deference to our host I decided not to prolong the argument.*
▷ **deferential** /ˌdefəˈrenʃl/ *adj* showing deference. **deferentially** /-ʃəlɪ/ *adv.*

defiance /dɪˈfaɪəns/ *n* **1** [U] open disobedience or resistance; refusal to give way to authority or opposition; defying: *The protesters showed their defiance of the official ban on demonstrations.* **2** (idm) **glare defiance at sb/sth** ⇨ GLARE[2]. **in defiance of sb/sth** in spite of sb/sth; ignoring sb/ sth: *act in defiance of orders* ○ *She wanted him to stay, but he left in defiance of her wishes.*

defiant /dɪˈfaɪənt/ *adj* showing defiance; openly opposing or resisting sb/sth: *a defiant manner, look, speech.* ▷ **defiantly** *adv.*

deficiency /dɪˈfɪʃnsɪ/ *n* ~ **(in/of sth)** **1 (a)** [U] state of lacking sth essential: *Deficiency in vitamins/Vitamin deficiency can lead to illness.* ○ [attrib] *deficiency payments to farmers*, ie to make up the difference between the market price and the price guaranteed by the government. **(b)** [C] instance of this; shortage: *suffering from a deficiency of iron* ○ *deficiency diseases*, ie those caused by a deficiency of eg vitamins in diet. **2** [C] lack of a necessary quality; fault: *She can't hide her deficiencies as a writer.*

deficient /dɪˈfɪʃnt/ *adj* **(a)** [usu pred] ~ **in sth** lacking in sth: *be deficient in skill, experience, knowledge, etc* ○ *a diet deficient in iron.* **(b)** (*fml*) incomplete; inadequate: *deficient funds, supplies* ○ *Our knowledge of the matter is deficient.*

deficit /ˈdefɪsɪt/ *n* **(a)** amount by which sth, esp a sum of money, is too small: *We raised £100, and we need £250: that's a deficit of £150.* **(b)** excess of debts over income; amount of this excess: *Tax was low and state spending was high, resulting in a budget deficit.* Cf SURPLUS.
□ ˌ**deficit ˈspending** government spending of money obtained by borrowing rather than by taxation.

defied *pt, pp* of DEFY.

defile[1] /dɪˈfaɪl/ *v* [Tn] (*fml or rhet*) **1** make (sth) dirty or impure: *rivers defiled by pollution* ○ (*fig*) *a noble cause defiled by the greed of its supporters.* **2** make (sth) unfit for holy ceremonies; desecrate: *The altar had been defiled by vandals.*
▷ **defilement** *n* [U] defiling or being defiled.

defile[2] /ˈdi:faɪl/ *n* narrow pass through mountains
▷ **defile** *v* [I] (of troops) march in single file or a narrow column.

define /dɪˈfaɪn/ *v* **1** [Tn, Cn·n/a] ~ **sth (as sth)** state precisely the meaning of (eg words). **2** [Tn, Tw] state (sth) clearly; explain (sth): *The powers of a judge are defined by law.* ○ *It's hard to define exactly what has changed.* **3** [Tn] show (a line, shape, feature, etc) clearly; outline: *When boundaries between countries are not clearly defined, there is usually trouble.* ○ *The mountain was sharply defined against the eastern sky.* ○ *a well-defined profile.*
▷ **definable** /-əbl/ *adj* that can be defined.

definite /ˈdefɪnət/ *adj* **(a)** clear; not doubtful: *a definite decision, opinion, result, change* ○ *I have no definite plans for tomorrow.* ○ *I want a definite answer, 'yes' or 'no'.* **(b)** [pred] ~ **(about sth/ that...)** sure; certain: *He seemed definite about what had happened.* ○ *It's now definite that the plane crashed.*
▷ **definitely** /ˈdefɪnətlɪ/ *adv* **1** in a definite manner: *She states her views very definitely.* **2** certainly; undoubtedly: *That is definitely correct.* ○ *Definitely not*, ie No. **3** (*infml*) (in answer to questions) yes; certainly: *'Are you coming?' 'Definitely!'*
□ ˌ**definite ˈarticle** the word 'the'. Cf INDEFINITE ARTICLE (INDEFINITE).

definition /ˌdefɪˈnɪʃn/ *n* **1 (a)** [U] stating the exact meaning (of words, etc): *Dictionary writers must be skilled in the art of definition.* **(b)** [C] statement that gives the exact meaning (of words, etc): *Definitions should not be more difficult to understand than the words they define.* **2** [U] **(a)** clearness of outline; making or being distinct in outline: *The photograph has poor definition.* ○ *They concentrated on better definition of the optical image.* **(b)** power of a lens (in a camera or telescope) to show clear outlines. **3 (a)** [U] clear statement; outlining: *My duties require clearer definition.* **(b)** [C] instance of this; outline: *The book attempts a definition of his role in world politics.*

definitive /dɪˈfɪnətɪv/ *adj* clear and having final authority; that cannot or need not be changed: *a definitive answer, solution, verdict, etc* ○ *Her book is the definitive work on Milton.* ○ *a definitive edition* eg one revised by the author himself. ▷ **definitively** *adv.*

deflate *v* **1** /dɪˈfleɪt/ [Tn] **(a)** let air or gas out of (a balloon, tyre, etc); let down. **(b)** (*fig*) make (sb, esp sb proud or too confident) feel or appear embarrassed or discouraged: *I felt quite deflated by your nasty remark.* ○ *Nothing could deflate his ego, pomposity*, ie make him less self-assured or pompous. **2** /ˌdi:ˈfleɪt/ [I, Tn] reduce the amount of money in circulation in (an economy), in order to lower prices or keep them steady: *The Government decided to deflate.* Cf INFLATE, REFLATE.
▷ **deflation** /-eɪʃn/ *n* [U] action of deflating (DEFLATE 2) or state of being deflated. **deflationary** /ˌdi:ˈfleɪʃnərɪ; *US* -nerɪ/ *adj* causing or intended to cause monetary deflation: *a deflationary policy, measure, etc.*

deflect /dɪˈflekt/ *v* **1** [I, Ipr, Tn, Tn·pr] ~ **(sth) (from sth)** (cause sth to) turn from its direction of movement: *The missile deflected from its trajectory.* ○ *The ball hit one of the defenders and was deflected* *into the net.* ○ *The bullet hit a wall and was deflected from its course.* **2** [Tn, Tn·pr] ~ **sb (from sth)** (*fig*) turn sb away from his intended course of action: *not easily deflected from one's purpose/aim.*

▷ **deflection** /dɪˈflekʃn/ *n* **1** (**a**) [U] deflecting (DEFLECT 1) or being deflected. (**b**) [C] instance or amount of this: *The smallest deflection of the missile could bring disaster.* **2** [C, U] (amount of the) movement of a pointer or needle on a measuring device from its zero position.

deflower /ˌdiːˈflaʊə(r)/ *v* [Tn] (*arch or euph*) deprive (a woman) of her virginity, usu by sexual intercourse.

Defoe /dɪˈfəʊ/ Daniel (1660-1731), English writer who is widely regarded as the first true English novelist. For most of his life he worked as a political journalist, and he did not begin to write fiction until he was nearly sixty. His most famous novel, *Robinson Crusoe* (1719), tells the story of a man shipwrecked on a desert island. This was followed by *Moll Flanders, A Journal of the Plague Year* and *Roxana*.

defoliate /ˌdiːˈfəʊlieɪt/ *v* [Tn] destroy the leaves of (trees or plants): *forests defoliated by chemicals in the air.*

▷ **defoliant** /ˌdiːˈfəʊliənt/ *n* chemical used on trees and plants to destroy the leaves.

defoliation /ˌdiːfəʊlɪˈeɪʃn/ *n* [U].

deforest /ˌdiːˈfɒrɪst; *US* -ˈfɔːr-/ (also **disafforest**) *v* [Tn] remove forests from (a place). ▷ **deforestation** /diːˌfɒrɪˈsteɪʃn; *US* -ˌfɔːr-/ *n* [U].

deform /dɪˈfɔːm/ *v* [Tn] spoil the shape or appearance of (sth): *deform a structure, limb, spine.*

▷ **deformation** /ˌdiːfɔːˈmeɪʃn/ *n* (**a**) [U] process of deforming. (**b**) [C] result of this: *a deformation of the spine.*

deformed *adj* (of the body, or part of it) badly or unnaturally shaped: *She has a deformed foot and can't walk very easily.*

deformity /dɪˈfɔːmətɪ/ *n* (**a**) [U] being deformed. (**b**) [C] deformed part, esp of the body: *deformities caused by poor diet* ○ *He was born with a slight deformity of the foot which made him limp.*

defraud /dɪˈfrɔːd/ *v* [Tn, Tn·pr] ~ **sb (of sth)** get sth from sb by deception; cheat sb: *She was defrauded of her money by a dishonest accountant.*

defray /dɪˈfreɪ/ *v* [Tn] (*fml*) provide money for (sth); pay for (sth): *defray expenses, costs, etc* ○ *My father has to defray my education.* ▷ **defrayal** /dɪˈfreɪəl/ *n* [U].

defrock /ˌdiːˈfrɒk/ *v* [Tn] = UNFROCK.

defrost /ˌdiːˈfrɒst; *US* ˌdiːˈfrɔːst/ *v* **1** [Tn] remove ice or frost from (sth): *defrost the fridge, the car windscreen.* **2** [I, Tn] (cause sth to) become unfrozen: *A frozen chicken should be allowed to defrost completely before cooking.* ⇨ Usage at WATER[1]. Cf UNFREEZE 1.

deft /deft/ *adj* ~ **(at sth/doing sth)** skilful and quick, esp with the hands: *With deft fingers she untangled the wire.* ○ *She is deft at dealing with reporters.* ▷ **deftly** *adv.* **deftness** *n* [U].

defunct /dɪˈfʌŋkt/ *adj* (*fml or joc*) (**a**) (of people) dead. (**b**) (of practices, laws, etc) no longer in use. (**c**) no longer effective or treated with respect: *a defunct organization.*

defuse /ˌdiːˈfjuːz/ *v* [Tn] **1** remove or make useless the device that sets off (a bomb, etc). **2** (*fig*) reduce the dangerous tension in (a difficult situation): *defuse tension, anger, a crisis.*

defy /dɪˈfaɪ/ *v* (*pt, pp* **defied**) **1** [Tn] (**a**) disobey or refuse to respect (sb, an authority, etc): *They defied their parents and got married.* ○ *defy the Government, the law, etc.* (**b**) refuse to give in to (sb/sth); resist boldly: *The army defied the enemy's forces.* **2** [Tn] be so difficult as to make (sth) impossible: *The door defied all attempts to open it.* ○ *The problem defied solution*, ie could not be solved. **3** [Dn·t] challenge (sb) to do sth one believes he cannot or will not do: *I defy you to prove I have cheated.*

deg *abbr* (also *symb* °) degree (of temperature): *42 degs/42° Fahrenheit.*

Degas /ˈdeɪɡɑː; *US* dəˈɡɑː/ Edgar (1834-1917), French artist noted particularly for his treatment of people and animals in motion, eg in his paintings, pastels and sculptures of ballet-dancers and his paintings of racehorses. He is associated with the *Impressionist school.

de Gaulle ⇨ GAULLE.

degenerate /dɪˈdʒenəreɪt/ *v* [I, Ipr] ~ **(from sth) (into sth)** pass into a worse physical, mental or moral state than one which is considered normal or desirable: *His health is degenerating rapidly.* ○ *Her commitment to a great cause degenerated from a crusade into an obsession.*

▷ **degenerate** /dɪˈdʒenərət/ *adj* having lost the physical, mental or moral qualities that are considered normal or desirable: *a degenerate art, society, age.* **degeneracy** /dɪˈdʒenərəsɪ/ *n* [U] (**a**) state of being degenerate. (**b**) process of becoming degenerate.

degenerate *n* /dɪˈdʒenərət/ degenerate person or animal: *This degenerate seduced my daughter!*

degeneration /dɪˌdʒenəˈreɪʃn/ *n* [U] (**a**) process of degenerating: *the slow degeneration of his mental faculties with age.* (**b**) state of being degenerate.

degrade /dɪˈɡreɪd/ *v* **1** [Tn] cause (sb) to be less moral and less deserving of respect: *degrade oneself by cheating and telling lies* ○ *I felt degraded by having to ask for money.* **2** [I, Ipr, Tn, Tn·pr] (*chemistry or biology*) (cause sth to) become less complex in structure: *degrade molecules into atoms.*

▷ **degradation** /ˌdeɡrəˈdeɪʃn/ *n* [U] degrading or being degraded: *living in utter degradation*, eg extreme poverty ○ *Being sent to prison was the final degradation.*

degree /dɪˈɡriː/ *n* **1** [C] unit of measurement for angles: *an angle of ninety degrees (90°)*, ie a right angle ○ *one degree of latitude*, ie about 69 miles. ⇨ App 10. **2** [C] (*abbr* **deg**) unit of measurement for temperature: *Water freezes at 32 degrees Fahrenheit (32° F) or zero/nought degrees Celsius (0° C).* ⇨ App 10. **3** [C, U] step or stage in a scale or series: *She shows a high degree of skill in her work.* ○ *He was not in the slightest degree interested*, ie was completely uninterested. ○ *To what degree* (ie To what extent, How much) *was he involved in the crimes?* ○ *She has also been affected, but to a lesser degree.* ○ *I agree with you to some/a certain degree.* **4** [U] (*arch*) position in society: *people of high/low degree.* **5** [C] academic title; rank or grade given by a university or college to sb who has passed an examination, written a thesis, etc: *take* (ie be awarded) *a degree in law/a law degree* ○ *the degree of Master of Arts (MA).* ⇨ article at POST-SCHOOL. **6** [C] (esp in compounds with *first, second*, etc) step in a scale of seriousness: *murder in the ˌfirst deˈgree*, ie (in US) of the most serious kind ○ [attrib] *ˌfirst-degree ˈmurder* ○ *ˌthird-degree* (ie very serious) *ˈburns.* **7** [C] (*grammar*) each of the three forms of comparison of an adjective or adverb: *degrees of comparison* ○ *'Good', 'better' and 'best' are the positive, comparative and superlative degrees of 'good'.* **8** [C usu *pl*] (*esp law*) measure of the closeness with which one person is related to another within a family: *degrees of consanguinity.* **9** (idm) **by deˈgrees** gradually: *By degrees their friendship grew into love.* **to a deˈgree** (*infml*) very: *The film was boring to a degree.* **to the ˌnth deˈgree** ⇨ NTH.

dehumanize, -ise /ˌdiːˈhjuːmənaɪz/ *v* [Tn] take human qualities away from (sb): *Torture always dehumanizes both the torturer and his victim.* ▷ **dehumanization, -isation** /diːˌhjuːmənaɪˈzeɪʃn; *US* -nɪˈz-/ *n* [U].

dehydrate /ˌdiːˈhaɪdreɪt/ *v* **1** [Tn esp passive] remove water or moisture from (esp food, to preserve it): *dehydrated vegetables, eggs, milk*, eg in powdered form. **2** [I] (of the body, tissues, etc) lose water or moisture: *Her body had dehydrated dangerously with the heat.*

▷ **dehydration** /ˌdiːhaɪˈdreɪʃn/ *n* [U] (**a**) loss of water or moisture: *dying of dehydration.* (**b**) state of being dehydrated.

de-ice /ˌdiːˈaɪs/ *v* [Tn] remove ice from or prevent ice forming on (sth): *de-ice a windscreen.*

▷ **de-icer** *n* [C, U] substance put on a surface, esp by spraying, to remove ice or stop it forming.

deify /ˈdiːɪfaɪ/ *v* (*pt, pp* **-fied**) [Tn] make a god of (sb/sth); worship as a god: *Primitive peoples deified the sun.*

▷ **deification** /ˌdiːɪfɪˈkeɪʃn/ *n* [U] deifying or being deified: *the deification of a Roman emperor.*

deign /deɪn/ *v* [Tt] (*sometimes derog or ironic*) be kind or gracious enough (to do sth); condescend: *He walked past me without even deigning to look at me.*

deism /ˈdiːɪzəm/ *n* [U] belief in the existence of God that is based more on faith than on religious teaching. Cf THEISM.

▷ **deist** /ˈdiːɪst/ *n* person who holds such a belief.

deity /ˈdiːɪtɪ/ *n* **1** (**a**) [C] god or goddess: *Roman deities.* (**b**) **the Deity** [sing] God. **2** [U] divine quality or nature; state of being a god or goddess.

déjà vu /ˌdeɪʒɑː ˈvjuː/ (*French*) [U] **1** feeling that one remembers an event or scene that one has not experienced or seen before: *I had an odd sense of déjà vu just as you said that.* **2** (*infml*) feeling that one has experienced sth too often: *There was an awful feeling of déjà vu at the annual office party.*

dejected /dɪˈdʒektɪd/ *adj* depressed; sad: *dejected-looking campers in the rain* ○ *Repeated failure had left them feeling very dejected.* ▷ **dejectedly** *adv.*

dejection /dɪˈdʒekʃn/ *n* [U] sad or dejected state; depression: *The loser sat slumped in dejection.*

de jure /ˌdeɪ ˈdʒʊərɪ/ (*Latin*) by right; according to law: *the de jure king* ○ *be king de jure.* Cf DE FACTO.

Dekker /ˈdekə(r)/ Thomas (?1570-1632), English dramatist who wrote cheerful comedies vividly portraying London life. His best-known play is *The Shoemaker's Holiday*.

dekko /ˈdekəʊ/ *n* (idm) **have a dekko (at sth)** (*dated Brit sl*) have a look: *Have a dekko at this wheel: the tyre's flat.*

Delacroix /ˈdeləkrwɑː/ Ferdinand-Victor-Eugène (1798-1863), French painter. He specialized in large-scale dramatic paintings of classical and historical subjects, and is generally regarded as the greatest of the French romantic painters.

Delaware /ˈdeləweə(r)/ state of the USA on the Atlantic coast, one of the original 13 states. ⇨ map at App 1.

delay /dɪˈleɪ/ *v* **1** [I, In/pr, Tn] (cause sb to) be slow or late: *Don't delay! Book your holiday today!* ○ *She delayed (for) two hours and missed the train.* ○ *I was delayed by the traffic.* **2** [Tn, Tg] put (sth) off until later; postpone: *We must delay our journey until the weather improves.* ○ *Why have they delayed opening the school?*

▷ **delay** *n* **1** [U] delaying or being delayed: *We must leave without delay.* **2** [C] amount of time for which sb/sth is delayed: *There was a delay (of two hours) before the plane took off.*

□ **deˌlayed-ˈaction** *adj* [usu attrib] operating after an interval of time: *a deˌlayed-action ˈfuse, ˈbomb, ˈcamera.*

delectable /dɪˈlektəbl/ *adj* (*fml*) (esp of food) delightful; pleasant: *a delectable meal* ○ (*fig*) *What a delectable little girl!* ▷ **delectably** /-əblɪ/ *adv.*

delectation /ˌdiːlekˈteɪʃn/ *n* [U] (*fml or joc*) enjoyment; entertainment: *And now for your further delectation, we present a selection of popular melodies.*

delegate[1] /ˈdelɪɡət/ *n* person chosen or elected by others to express their views (eg at a meeting or conference).

delegate[2] /ˈdelɪɡeɪt/ *v* **1** [Tn, Tn·pr, Tnt] ~ **sb (to sth)** (**a**) choose or send sb as a representative: *delegate sb to a conference/to attend a conference.* (**b**) choose sb to carry out (duties, a task, etc): *The new manager was delegated to reorganize the department.* **2** [I, Tn, Tn·pr] ~ **(sth) (to sb)** entrust (duties, rights, etc) to sb in a lower position or grade: *A boss must know how to delegate (work).* ○ *The job had to be delegated to an assistant.*

delegation /ˌdelɪˈɡeɪʃn/ *n* **1** [U] delegating or being delegated. **2** [CGp] group of delegates: *She refused to meet the union delegation.*

delete /dɪˈliːt/ *v* [Tn, Tn·pr] ~ **sth (from sth)** cross out or deliberately omit (sth written or printed): *The editor deleted the last paragraph (from the article).*

▷ **deletion** /dɪˈli:ʃn/ *n* (**a**) [U] deleting or being deleted. (**b**) [C] word, passage, etc that has been deleted.

deleterious /ˌdelɪˈtɪərɪəs/ *adj* ~ **(to sb/sth)** *(fml)* harmful: *have a deleterious effect on a child's development.* ▷ **deleteriously** *adv.*

delft /delft/ (also **delftware** /ˈdelftweə(r)/) *n* [U] type of glazed earthenware, usu with blue decoration.

Delhi /ˈdelɪ/ city of India, situated on the river Jumna in the northern part of the country; pop approx 6 200 000. It consists of **Old Delhi**, the capital city of the former Mogul empire, and **New Delhi**, the modern city built by the British in the early 20th century, and the present capital of India.

deli /ˈdelɪ/ *n* *(infml)* delicatessen shop.

deliberate[1] /dɪˈlɪbərət/ *adj* **1** done on purpose; intentional: *a deliberate insult, lie, act.* **2** unhurried; careful: *She has a slow, deliberate way of talking.* ○ *making very deliberate gestures for emphasis.* ▷ **deliberately** *adv*: *a deliberately calm tone of voice* ○ *She said it deliberately to provoke me.*

deliberate[2] /dɪˈlɪbəreɪt/ *v* [I, Ipr, Tw] ~ **(about/on sth)** *(fml)* think or talk carefully: *We had no time to deliberate (on the problem).* ○ *deliberate what action to take* ○ *deliberate whether to leave or not.*
▷ **deliberative** /dɪˈlɪbərətɪv; *US* dəˈlɪbəreɪtɪv/ *adj* [esp attrib] of or for thorough discussion: *a deliberative assembly.*

deliberation /dɪˌlɪbəˈreɪʃn/ *n* **1** [U, C] careful consideration or discussion: *After long deliberation, they decided not to buy.* ○ *What was the result of your deliberation(s)?* **2** [U] slowness of movement; carefulness: *speak, take aim, walk with great deliberation.*

delicacy /ˈdelɪkəsɪ/ *n* **1** [U] softness or tenderness when touched: *the delicacy of the fabric, a child's skin.* **2** [U] delicate structure; fineness: *the delicacy of her features.* **3** (**a**) [U] skill or careful treatment: *the delicacy of her playing, workmanship, carving.* (**b**) [U] tact and restraint in human relations; sensitivity: *She spoke with delicacy of our recent loss.* ○ *Don't forget the delicacy of our position,* ie Remember the need for tact, etc. **4** [U] (of colours, food, smells) pleasantness that does not strongly affect the senses: *a shade, wine, scent of great delicacy.* **5** [C] type of food thought to be delicious, esp in a particular place: *The local people regard these crabs as a great delicacy.*

delicate /ˈdelɪkət/ *adj* **1** soft or tender when touched; made of sth fine or thin: *as delicate as silk* ○ *a baby's delicate skin.* **2** very carefully made or formed; fine; exquisite: *a delicate mechanism, structure, etc* ○ *the delicate beauty of a snowflake.* **3** (**a**) easily injured or damaged; fragile: *delicate china* ○ *a delicate plant.* (**b**) becoming ill easily; not strong: *a delicate child, constitution* ○ *She has been in delicate health for some time.* **4** (**a**) showing or needing much skill or careful treatment: *the delicate craftsmanship of a fine watch* ○ *a delicate surgical operation,* eg on sb's eyes ○ *her delicate playing of the sonata.* (**b**) showing or needing tact and good judgement in human relations; sensitive: *I admired your delicate handling of the situation.* ○ *We're conducting very delicate negotiations.* **5** (of the senses, or of instruments) able to detect or show very small changes or differences; sensitive: *a delicate sense of smell/touch* ○ *Only a very delicate thermometer can measure such tiny changes in temperature.* **6** (**a**) (of colours) not intense; soft: *a delicate shade of pink.* (**b**) (of food or its taste) pleasing and not strongly flavoured: *the gentle, delicate flavour of salmon* ○ *Veal is too delicate for a spicy sauce.* (**c**) (of smell) pleasing and not strong: *a delicate perfume, fragrance, aroma, etc.* ▷ **delicately** *adv*: *delicately carved statues* ○ *a delicately phrased compliment.*

delicatessen /ˌdelɪkəˈtesn/ *n* (**a**) [C] shop selling prepared foods, often unusual or imported, ready for serving (esp cooked meat, smoked fish, cheeses, etc). (**b**) [U] such food.

delicious /dɪˈlɪʃəs/ *adj* giving pleasure, esp to the senses of taste and smell: *a delicious meal, cake, flavour* ○ *It smells delicious!* ○ *(fig) What a delicious joke!* ▷ **deliciously** *adv*: *a deliciously creamy soup.*

delight[1] /dɪˈlaɪt/ *n* **1** [U] great pleasure; joy: *give delight to sb* ○ *To our great delight, the day turned out fine.* **2** [C] cause or source of pleasure: *Her singing is a delight.* ○ *the delights of living in the country.* **3** (idm) **take delight in sth/doing sth** find pleasure in sth/doing sth (esp sth cruel or wrong): *He takes great delight in proving others wrong.*
▷ **delightful** /-fl/ *adj* ~ **(to sb)** giving delight: *a delightful holiday, melody, conversation* ○ *No news could be more delightful to me.* **delightfully** /-fəlɪ/ *adv.*

delight[2] /dɪˈlaɪt/ *v* **1** [Tn] give great pleasure to (sb); please greatly: *Her singing delighted everyone.* **2** [Ipr no passive, It] ~ **in sth/doing sth** take great (and often cruel) pleasure in sth; enjoy sth: *He delights in teasing his younger sister.* ○ *(fml) She delights to be surrounded by admirers.*
▷ **delighted** *adj* ~ **(at sth/to do sth/that . . .)** very pleased; showing delight: *a delighted smile, look, child* ○ *I'm delighted at your success/to hear of your success/that you succeeded.* ○ *'Will you come to the party?' 'I'd be delighted (to)!'*

Delilah /dɪˈlaɪlə/ woman in the Bible who cut off *Samson's hair, robbing him of his strength, and betrayed him to the Philistines. Her name is sometimes used to mean any attractive but treacherous woman.

delimit /di:ˈlɪmɪt/ *v* [Tn] fix the limits or boundaries of (sth): *The first chapter delimits her area of research.* ▷ **delimitation** /di:ˌlɪmɪˈteɪʃn/ *n* [C, U].

delineate /dɪˈlɪnɪeɪt/ *v* [Tn] *(fml)* show (sth) by drawing or describing; portray: *delineate sb's features, character* ○ *delineate one's plans.* ▷ **delineation** /dɪˌlɪnɪˈeɪʃn/ *n* [C, U].

delinquency /dɪˈlɪŋkwənsɪ/ *n* (**a**) [U, C] minor crime such as vandalism, esp when committed by young people: *juvenile delinquency.* (**b**) [U] failure to perform one's duty: *The captain's delinquency led to the loss of the ship.*

delinquent /dɪˈlɪŋkwənt/ *n, adj* (person) doing wrong or failing to perform a duty: *a juvenile delinquent* ○ *delinquent behaviour* ○ *a delinquent soldier.*

deliquescent /ˌdelɪˈkwesnt/ *adj* *(chemistry)* (of a solid) becoming a solution by absorbing moisture from the air.

delirious /dɪˈlɪrɪəs/ *adj* **1** (**a**) suffering from delirium: *He's so delirious he doesn't know where he is.* (**b**) showing the effects of delirium: *a delirious condition, reply.* **2** *(fig)* very excited and happy: *The children were delirious (with joy) as they opened the parcels.* ▷ **deliriously** *adv*: *raving deliriously* ○ *deliriously happy.*

delirium /dɪˈlɪrɪəm/ *n* [U] **1** mental disturbance caused by (esp feverish) illness, resulting in restlessness and often wild talk: *exhausted by the fever and delirium.* **2** *(fig)* excited happiness.
□ **deˌlirium ˈtremens** /ˈtri:menz/ *(abbr* **DT(s)**) delirium caused by extreme alcoholism.

Delius /ˈdi:lɪəs/ Frederick (1862-1934), English composer who lived for the later part of his life in France. He is best known for his short lyrical orchestral pieces which suggest peaceful country scenes (eg *On Hearing the First Cuckoo in Spring*).

deliver /dɪˈlɪvə(r)/ *v* **1** [I, Ipr, Tn, Tn·pr] ~ **(sth) (to sb/sth)** take (letters, parcels, goods, etc) to the places or people they are addressed to: *We deliver (your order) to your door!* ○ *A courier delivered the parcels (to our office).* ○ *Did you deliver my message to my father?* **2** (**a**) [Tn·pr only passive] **be ~ed of sb** *(fml)* give birth to (a child): *She was delivered of a healthy boy.* (**b**) [Tn] help a mother to give birth to (a child): *Her baby was delivered by her own doctor.* (**c**) [Tn·pr] ~ **oneself of sth** *(fml)* state sth: *deliver oneself of an opinion, a judgement, etc.* **3** [Tn, Tn·pr, Tn·p] ~ **sth (up/over) (to sb)** *(fml)* give sth up; hand over sth; surrender sth: *deliver (up) a fortress to the enemy* ○ *deliver over one's property to one's children.* **4** [Tn, Tn·pr] give (a lecture, sermon, speech, etc): *She delivered a talk on philosophy to the society.* **5** [Tn, Tn·pr] ~ **s** **(from sth)** *(arch)* rescue sb (from sth); save sb free sb: *May God deliver us from evil.* **6** (**a**) [Tn throw or launch (sth) in flight; release: *In cricket the ball is delivered overarm.* ○ *The missile i delivered from underground.* (**b**) [Tn, Tn·pr] give (blow): *deliver a blow to the jaw* ○ *(fig) The teache delivered a sharp rebuke to the class.* **7** *(infml)* (**a** [I, Ipr] ~ **(on sth)** give what is expected o promised: *They promise to finish the job in June but can they deliver (on that)?* (**b**) [Tn] achieve (level of performance): *The new model deliver speed and fuel economy.* ○ *If you can't delive improved sales figures, you're fired!* **8** (idm) **com up with/deliver the goods** ⇨ GOODS.
▷ **deliverer** *n* **1** person who delivers (DELIVER 1, 2 3, 4). **2** rescuer; saviour.

deliverance /dɪˈlɪvərəns/ *n* [U] ~ **(from sth** being freed or rescued: *They prayed for an earl deliverance from captivity.*

delivery /dɪˈlɪvərɪ/ *n* **1** (**a**) [U] delivering (o letters, goods, etc): *Your order is ready for delivery* ○ *Please pay on* (ie at the time of) *delivery.* (**b**) [C goods, mail, etc delivered: *We had a big delivery o coal today.* (**c**) [C] instance of delivering (parcels goods, etc): *We have two postal deliveries each day* **2** [C, U] process of birth: *an easy/difficult delivery* ○ *the first stage of delivery.* **3** [sing] manner o speaking (in lectures, etc): *Her poor delivery spoil an otherwise good speech.* **4** (**a**) [U] throwing o launching in flight (of a ball, missile, etc). (**b**) [C ball thrown (esp one bowled in cricket or throw in baseball): *a fast, hostile delivery.* **5** (idm) **cash on delivery** ⇨ CASH. **take delivery (of sth** receive sth: *When can you take delivery of the car*
□ **deˈlivery note** *(esp Brit)* note, usu in duplicate sent with goods and signed by the person receivin them.
deˈlivery van (*US* **deˈlivery truck**) van used fo delivering goods.

dell /del/ *n* small valley, usu with trees on its sides

delouse /ˌdi:ˈlaʊs/ *v* [Tn] remove the lice from (sb sth).

Delphi /ˈdelfaɪ, *also* ˈdelfɪ/ religious site on the slopes of Mount Parnassus in Greece, where in ancient times there was an oracle of Apollo which answered questions put to it.

Delphic /ˈdelfɪk/ *adj* **1** of the ancient Greek oracle at Delphi. **2** mysterious or unclear because more than one meaning is possible: *a Delphic utterance*

delphinium /delˈfɪnɪəm/ *n* garden plant with tal spikes of (usu blue) flowers.

delta /ˈdeltə/ *n* **1** the fourth letter of the Greek alphabet (Δ, δ). **2** triangular area of alluvial land a a river's mouth, enclosed or crossed by branches of the river: *the Nile Delta.*
□ ˌ**delta wing ˈaircraft** aircraft with swept-back wings that give it a triangular appearance.

delude /dɪˈlu:d/ *v* [Tn, Tn·pr] ~ **sb (with sth/int doing sth)** deliberately mislead sb; deceive sb: *a poor deluded fool* ○ *delude sb with empty promises* ○ *delude oneself with false hopes* ○ *delude sb/onesel into believing that . . . .*

deluge /ˈdelju:dʒ/ *n* **1** (**a**) great flood or rush o water: *When the snow melts, the mountain strean becomes a deluge.* (**b**) heavy fall of rain: *I got caugh in the deluge on the way home.* **2** *(fig)* great quantity of sth that comes all at once: *a deluge o work, words, letters.*
▷ **deluge** *v* [esp passive: Tn, Tn·pr] **1** ~ **sth (with sth)** flood sth (with sth): *The town was delugec with thick slimy mud.* **2** ~ **sb/sth (with sth)** *(fig* send or give sb/sth a very large quantity of sth: *I was deluged with phone calls.* ○ *We advertised the job and were deluged with applications.*

delusion /dɪˈlu:ʒn/ *n* **1** [U] deluding or being deluded: *His arguments sound convincing bu they're based on delusion.* **2** [C] false opinion o belief, esp one that may be a symptom of madness *be under a delusion/under the delusion that . . .* ○ *suffer from delusions* ○ *Your hopes of promotion are a mere delusion.* **3** (idm) **delusions of ˈgrandeur** false belief in one's own importance: *She wants t travel first-class: she must have delusions o* grandeur.

delusive /dɪˈluːsɪv/ *adj* not real; misleading: *a delusive belief, impression, etc.* ▷ **delusively** *adv.*

de luxe /dəˈlʌks, *also* -ˈlʊks/ *adj* [esp attrib] of a very high quality, high standard of comfort, etc: *a de luxe hotel, car, bed* ○ *the de luxe edition of a book,* eg with a special leather binding.

delve /delv/ *v* **1** [Ipr] ~ **in/into sth** (**a**) search or rummage in sth: *She delved in her bag and pulled out a pen.* ○ *delve into a drawer, box, pocket, etc for sth.* (**b**) try to find information about sth; study sth: *a writer delving in medieval French literature* ○ *She delved into the origins of the custom.* **2** [I] (*arch*) dig.

Dem *abbr* (*US*) Democrat; Democratic. Cf REP 2.

demagnetize, -ise /ˌdiːˈmæɡnɪtaɪz/ *v* [Tn] remove the magnetic properties of (sth). ▷ **demagnetization, -isation** /ˌdiːmæɡnɪtaɪˈzeɪʃn; *US* -tɪˈz-/ *n.*

demagogue (*US* also **demagog**) /ˈdeməɡɒɡ/ *n* political leader who tries to win people's support by using emotional and often unreasonable arguments.

▷ **demagogic** /ˌdeməˈɡɒɡɪk/ *adj* of or like a demagogue.

demagogy /ˈdeməɡɒɡɪ/ *n* [U] principles and methods of a demagogue.

demand[1] /dɪˈmɑːnd; *US* dɪˈmænd/ *n* **1** [C] ~ (**for sb to do sth**); ~ (**for sth/that...**) command, or sth which is given as if it was a command: *receive a tax demand* ○ *It is impossible to satisfy all your demands.* ○ *The workers' demands for higher pay were refused by the employers.* ○ *There have been fresh demands for the Prime Minister to resign.* ○ *demands for reform/that there should be reform.* **2** [U] ~ (**for sth/sb**) desire of customers for goods or services which they wish to buy or use: *We blame poor overseas demand for the car's failure.* ○ *Demand for skilled workers is high; but there is no demand for unskilled ones.* ○ *Demand for fish this month exceeds supply.* **3** [C] (also **deˈmand note**) note that requires sb to pay money owed, eg income tax. **4** (idm) **in deˈmand** much wanted; popular: *Good secretaries are always in demand.* ○ *She is in great demand as a singer.* **make demands of/on sb** oblige sb to use a lot of skill, strength, etc: *This new aircraft makes tremendous demands of the pilot.* **on deˈmand** whenever asked for: *a cheque payable on demand* ○ *She's in favour of abortion on demand.*

□ **deˈmand bill, deˈmand loan** (*esp US*) bill or loan that must be paid when payment is demanded. Cf SUPPLY AND DEMAND (SUPPLY).

demand[2] /dɪˈmɑːnd; *US* dɪˈmænd/ *v* **1** [Tn, Tf, Tt] ask for (sth) as if one is commanding, or as if one has a right to do so: *demand an apology (from sb)* ○ *The workers are demanding better pay.* ○ *She demanded (to know) my business.* ○ *He demands that he be told/demands to be told everything.* **2** [Tn] require (sth); need: *This sort of work demands great patience.* ○ *Does the letter demand an immediate answer?* ie Must it be answered at once?

demanding /dɪˈmɑːndɪŋ; *US* dɪˈmændɪŋ/ *adj* (**a**) (of a task, etc) needing much patience, skill, effort, etc: *a demanding job, schedule, etc.* (**b**) (of a person) making others work hard, meet high standards, etc: *a demanding boss, father, etc* ○ *Children are so demanding: they need constant attention.*

demarcate /ˈdiːmɑːkeɪt/ *v* [Tn] mark or fix the limits of (sth): *The playing area is demarcated by a white line.*

demarcation /ˌdiːmɑːˈkeɪʃn/ *n* [U, C] (marking of a) limit or boundary, esp between types of work considered by trade unions to belong to workers in different trades: *a line of demarcation* ○ [attrib] *demarcation disputes in industry.*

démarche /ˈdeɪmɑːʃ/ *n* (*French*) political step or proceeding.

demean /dɪˈmiːn/ *v* [Tn, Tnt] ~ **oneself** lower oneself in dignity; deprive oneself of others' respect: *Don't demean yourself by telling such obvious lies.* ○ *I wouldn't demean myself to ask for favours from them.*

▷ **demeaning** *adj* lowering (sb's) dignity; degrading: *He found it very demeaning to have to work for his former employee.*

demeanour (*US* **-nor**) /dɪˈmiːnə(r)/ *n* [U] (*fml*) way of behaving; conduct: *I dislike his arrogant demeanour.*

demented /dɪˈmentɪd/ *adj* (**a**) mad: *a poor, demented creature.* (**b**) (*fig infml*) agitated because of worry, anger, etc: *When her child was two hours late, she became quite demented.* ▷ **dementedly** *adv.*

dementia /dɪˈmenʃə/ *n* [U] (*medical*) mental disorder due to degeneration of the brain.

□ **dementia praecox** /dɪˌmenʃə ˈpriːkɒks/ (*fml*) schizophrenia.

demerara /ˌdeməˈreərə/ *n* [U] (also ˌ**demerara** ˈ**sugar**) light-brown raw cane sugar.

demerit /diːˈmerɪt/ *n* **1** (*fml*) fault; defect: *consider the merits and demerits of a system.* **2** (*US*) mark recorded against a pupil for bad behaviour or performance at school.

demesne /dɪˈmeɪn/ *n* (*law*) (**a**) [U] possession and use of land as one's own property: *land held in demesne.* (**b**) [C] estate with land held in this way, ie without tenants living on it.

demi- *pref* (with *ns*) half; partly: *demigod.*

demigod /ˈdemɪɡɒd/ *n* (in classical mythology) being who is partly divine and partly human, esp the offspring of a god or goddess and a human.

demijohn /ˈdemɪdʒɒn/ *n* large bottle with a narrow neck, often in a wickerwork case.

demilitarize, -ise /ˌdiːˈmɪlɪtəraɪz/ *v* [Tn] remove military forces or installations from (an area) as a result of a treaty or an agreement: *a demilitarized zone.* ▷ **demilitarization, -isation** /ˌdiːˌmɪlɪtəraɪˈzeɪʃn; *US* -rɪˈz-/ *n* [U].

De Mille /də ˈmɪl/ C(ecil) B(lount) (1881-1959), American film producer and director who specialized in cinema epics with exciting action and large crowd scenes, often with stories taken from the Bible (eg *The Ten Commandments*).

demi-monde /ˈdemɪ mɒnd/ *n* [Gp] (*French*) **1** group of people whose actions are thought to be not entirely legal, respectable, etc: *the demi-monde of gambling clubs and sleazy bars.* **2** (formerly) women thought to be not entirely respectable and for this reason not acceptable to society.

demise /dɪˈmaɪz/ *n* [sing] **1** (*fml*) death. **2** (*fig*) end or failure (of an enterprise, etc): *This loss led to the demise of the business.*

demist /ˌdiːˈmɪst/ *v* [Tn] remove the mist from (eg the windscreen of a car).

▷ **demister** (*US* **defroster**) *n* device that warms (esp the windscreen of a vehicle) to stop mist forming.

dem(o)- *comb form* of people or population: *demagogue* ○ *democracy* ○ *demographic.*

demo /ˈdeməʊ/ *n* (*pl* ~**s**) (*infml esp Brit*) demonstration(3).

demob /ˌdiːˈmɒb/ *v* (**-bb-**) [Tn] (*Brit infml*) demobilize (sb).

▷ **demob** *n* [U] (*Brit infml*) demobilization.

demobilize, -ise /diːˈməʊbəlaɪz/ *v* [Tn] release (sb) from military service. ▷ **demobilization, -isation** /ˌdiːˌməʊbəlaɪˈzeɪʃn; *US* -lɪˈz-/ *n* [U].

democracy /dɪˈmɒkrəsɪ/ *n* **1** (**a**) [U] system of government by the whole people of a country, esp through representatives whom they elect: *parliamentary democracy.* (**b**) [C] country having such a system: *the Western democracies.* **2** [C, U] (country with a) government that allows freedom of speech, religion and political opinion, that upholds the rule of law and majority rule and that respects the rights of minorities: *the principles of democracy.* **3** (**a**) [U] treatment of each other by citizens as equals, without social class divisions: *Is there more democracy in Australia than in Britain?* (**b**) [C] society where such conditions exist. **4** [U] control of an organization by its members, who take part in the making of decisions: *industrial democracy.*

democrat /ˈdeməkræt/ *n* **1** person who believes in or supports democracy. **2 Democrat** (*abbr* **D**) member or supporter of the Democratic Party of the US. Cf REPUBLICAN 2. ⇨ article at POLITICS.

democratic /ˌdeməˈkrætɪk/ *adj* **1** based on the principles of democracy(1a): *democratic rights, elections* ○ *democratic government, rule, etc.* **2** of or supporting democracy(3); paying no or little attention to class divisions based on birth or wealth: *a democratic society, outlook.* **3** of or supporting control of an organization by its members: *democratic involvement, participation, etc.* ▷ **democratically** /-klɪ/ *adv*: *democratically elected, decided, etc.*

□ **the** ˌ**Demoˈcratic Party** one of the two main political parties in the US, which has liberal policies and favours social reform. Cf REPUBLICAN PARTY (REPUBLICAN).

democratize, -ise /dɪˈmɒkrətaɪz/ *v* [Tn] make (sth) democratic: *democratize the administration of an organization.* ▷ **democratization, -isation** /dɪˌmɒkrətaɪˈzeɪʃn; *US* -tɪˈz-/ *n* [U].

demography /dɪˈmɒɡrəfɪ/ *n* [U] study of statistics of births, deaths, diseases, etc in order to show the state of a community.

▷ **demographer** /dɪˈmɒɡrəfə(r)/ *n* expert in such studies.

demographic /ˌdeməˈɡræfɪk/ *adj.*

demolish /dɪˈmɒlɪʃ/ *v* [Tn] **1** (**a**) pull or knock down (a building, etc): *They've demolished the slum district.* (**b**) (*fig*) destroy (a theory, etc): *Her article brilliantly demolishes his argument.* **2** (*fig joc*) eat (sth) greedily: *She demolished two whole pies.* ▷ **demolition** /ˌdeməˈlɪʃn/ *n* [U, C]: *the demolition of the houses* ○ [attrib] *demolition contractors.*

demon /ˈdiːmən/ *n* **1** wicked or cruel spirit: *medieval carvings of demons.* **2** (*infml*) (**a**) person thought to be wicked, mischievous, etc: *Your son's a little demon.* (**b**) ~ (**for sth**) energetic person: *She's a demon for work,* ie works very hard. ○ [attrib] *a demon worker.* (**c**) fierce or aggressive player: [attrib] *a demon bowler,* ie in cricket. **3** (idm) **the demon ˈdrink** (*joc*) alcoholic drink, esp when it is the cause of wild noisy behaviour: *He's very violent: it's the demon drink, you know.* ▷ **demonic** /diːˈmɒnɪk/ *adj*: *demonic energy.*

demonetize, -ise /ˌdiːˈmʌnɪtaɪz/ *v* stop (a metal) being used as currency. ▷ **demonetization, -isation** /diːˌmʌnɪtaɪˈzeɪʃn; *US* -tɪˈz-/ *n* [U].

demoniac /dɪˈməʊnɪæk/ (also **demoniacal** /ˌdiːməˈnaɪəkl/) *adj* (**a**) very evil; devilish: *demoniac tortures, plans.* (**b**) frenzied; fiercely energetic: *demoniac energy, fury, etc.*

demonstrable /ˈdemənstrəbl; *US* dɪˈmɒnstrəbl/ *adj* that can be shown or proved: *a demonstrable lie, inaccuracy, etc.* ▷ **demonstrability** /ˌdemənstrəˈbɪlətɪ/ *n* [U]. **demonstrably** /-blɪ/ *adv.*

demonstrate /ˈdemənstreɪt/ *v* **1** (**a**) [Tn, Tn·pr, Tf, Tw] ~ **sth** (**to sb**) show sth clearly by giving proof or evidence: *demonstrate the truth of a statement (to sb)* ○ *How do you demonstrate that the pressure remains constant?* ○ *Can you demonstrate what you mean by that?* (**b**) [Tn, Tf, Tw] be an example of (sth); show: *The election demonstrates democracy in action.* ○ *His sudden departure demonstrates that he's unreliable/how unreliable he is.* **2** [Tn, Tn·pr, Tw] ~ **sth** (**to sb**) show and explain how sth works or a way of doing sth: *An assistant demonstrated the washing machine (to customers).* ○ *She demonstrated how best to defend oneself.* **3** [I, Ipr] ~ (**against/in favour of sb/sth**) take part in a public rally, etc, usu as a protest or to show support: *Thousands demonstrated against the price increases.* **4** [Tn] express (sth) by one's actions: *Workers have already demonstrated their opposition to the plans.* ○ *demonstrate strong feelings.*

demonstration /ˌdemənˈstreɪʃn/ *n* **1** [C, U] (instance of) showing sth by giving proof or evidence: *convinced by (a) scientific demonstration* ○ *a demonstration of a law of physics.* **2** [C, U] (instance of) showing and explaining how sth works: *a demonstration of the computer's functions.* ⇨ Usage. **3** [C] ~ (**against/in favour of sb/sth**) public, often organized, rally or march protesting against or supporting sb/sth: *a mass demonstration in support of the regime.* **4** [C] outward sign; example: *a demonstration of affection,* eg embracing sb ○ *a clear demonstration of their intentions.* **5** [C] show of military strength.

NOTE ON USAGE: **1** A **demonstration** and a **display** do not require a specific or permanent site. At a **demonstration** one sees how something works or is done: *a cookery demonstration* ○ *a demonstration of a new car.* **2** A **display** is often for public entertainment: *a flying, fireworks, fashion, etc display.* **3** A **trade exhibition/show/fair** is held in an **exhibition hall** or **centre** where commercial or industrial goods are advertised: *a book fair* ○ *the World Trade Fair* ○ *the Motor Show* ○ *the Great Exhibition.* **4** A **show** can also be of domestic animals or plants, often in competition for prizes. Paintings, drawings, etc are displayed in an **exhibition:** *the Chelsea Flower Show* ○ *a horse show* ○ *an art exhibition.* **5** A **fair** or **funfair** is also a collection of entertainments (roundabouts, stalls, etc) travelling from town to town.

demonstrative /dɪˈmɒnstrətɪv/ *adj* **1** (**a**) (of people) showing the feelings readily: *Some people are more demonstrative than others.* (**b**) expressing feelings, esp affection, openly: *He's very demonstrative: he kissed me on both cheeks.* **2** (*grammar*) (of a determiner or pronoun) indicating the person or thing referred to: *In 'This is my bike', 'this' is a demonstrative pronoun.* ▷ **demonstratively** *adv.* **demonstrativeness** *n* [U]: *embarrassed by demonstrativeness.*

demonstrator /ˈdemənstreɪtə(r)/ *n* **1** person who teaches or explains by demonstrating (DEMONSTRATE 2): *The demonstrators set up apparatus for the experiment.* **2** person who demonstrates (DEMONSTRATE 3): *The noisy demonstrators were dispersed by the police.*

demoralize, -ise /dɪˈmɒrəlaɪz; *US* -ˈmɔːr-/ *v* [Tn] weaken the courage or self-confidence of (sb); dishearten: *The troops were thoroughly demoralized by this set-back.* ○ *feel very demoralized* ○ *The news is very demoralizing.* Cf DISPIRIT. ▷ **demoralization, -isation** /dɪˌmɒrəlaɪˈzeɪʃn; *US* -ˌmɔːrəlɪˈz-/ *n* [U].

Demosthenes /dɪˈmɒsθəniːz/ (384-322 BC) Athenian statesman and orator who opposed the attempts by *Philip of Macedon to take over the independent Greek city-states. He is said to have been born with a stutter but to have overcome this by practising speaking with his mouth full of small stones.

demote /ˌdiːˈməʊt/ *v* [Tn, Tn·pr] ~ **sb (from sth) (to sth)** reduce sb to a lower rank or grade: *He was demoted from sergeant to corporal.* Cf PROMOTE. ▷ **demotion** /ˌdiːˈməʊʃn/ *n* [C, U].

demotic /dɪˈmɒtɪk/ *adj* of or used by ordinary people: *demotic Greek*, ie the informal, esp spoken, form of modern Greek.

demur /dɪˈmɜː(r)/ *v* (**-rr-**) [I, Ipr] ~ **(at sth)** (*fml*) express a doubt (about sth) or an objection (to sth): *I suggested putting the matter to a vote, but the chairman demurred.*

▷ **demur** *n* (idm) **without deˈmur** without objecting or hesitating.

demurrer /dɪˈmʌrə(r)/ *n* (*law*) claim made in a court that the other side's argument is not relevant.

demure /dɪˈmjʊə(r)/ *adj* (**a**) (pretending to be) quiet, serious and modest: *a very demure young lady.* (**b**) suggesting that one is demure: *a demure smile, reply, etc.* ▷ **demurely** *adv.* **demureness** *n* [U].

demystify /ˌdiːˈmɪstɪfaɪ/ *v* (*pt, pp* **-fied**) [Tn] make (sth) less mysterious; make clear: *We are trying to demystify the workings of government.*

▷ **demystification** /ˌdiːˌmɪstɪfɪˈkeɪʃn/ *n* [U] action of making sth less mysterious: *The demystification of the Resurrection upsets many Christians.*

demythologize, -ise /ˌdiːmɪˈθɒlədʒaɪz/ *v* [Tn] **1** remove mythical elements from (eg a legend). **2** remove the feeling of too great respect which people have for (sb/sth); debunk.

den /den/ *n* **1** animal's hidden home, eg a cave: *a bear's/lion's den.* **2** (*derog*) secret meeting-place: *an ˈopium den* ○ *a den of thieves.* **3** (*infml*) room in a home where a person can work or study without being disturbed: *retire to one's den.* **4** (idm) **beard the lion in his den** ⇨ BEARD². **a den of iˈniquity/ˈvice** (*often joc*) a place where evil or immoral activities go on: *He thought of New York as a den of iniquity.*

denarius /dɪˈneərɪəs/ *n* (*pl* **-rii** /-rɪaɪ/) ancient Roman silver coin of low value. Cf D *abbr.*

denationalize, -ise /ˌdiːˈnæʃənəlaɪz/ *v* [Tn] put (a nationalized industry) back into private ownership, usu by selling shares in it; privatize. Cf NATIONALIZE 1. ▷ **denationalization, -isation** /ˌdiːˌnæʃənəlaɪˈzeɪʃn; *US* -lɪˈz-/ *n* [U].

denatured /ˌdiːˈneɪtʃəd/ *adj* [esp attrib] (**a**) made unfit for eating and drinking (but possibly still usable for other purposes): *denatured alcohol.* (**b**) having lost its natural qualities: *denatured rubber*, ie no longer elastic.

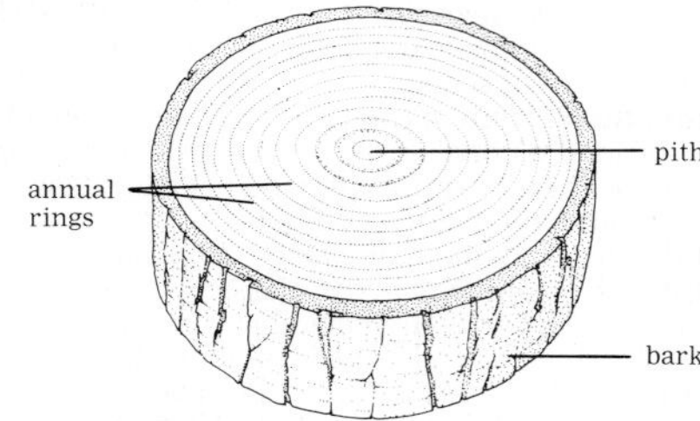

dendrochronology: cross-section of a tree trunk

dendrochronology /ˌdendrəʊkrəˈnɒlədʒɪ/ *n* [U] way of finding out how old trees are by studying growth rings in the wood. ⇨ illus.

dendrology /denˈdrɒlədʒɪ/ *n* [U] scientific study of trees.

dengue /ˈdeŋgɪ/ *n* [U] infectious fever involving severe pains in the joints.

deniable /dɪˈnaɪəbl/ *adj* that can be denied: *I suppose these charges are deniable?* ie We might convince others they are not true.

denial /dɪˈnaɪəl/ *n* **1** [C] ~ **(of sth/that...)** statement that sth is not true: *the prisoner's repeated denials of the charges against him* ○ *an official denial that there would be an election in May.* **2** [C, U] (**a**) ~ **of sth** refusal to grant (justice, rights, etc): *condemn the denial of basic human freedoms.* (**b**) ~ **(of sth)** refusal (of a request, etc): *the denial of his request for leave.*

denier /ˈdenɪə(r)/ *n* unit for measuring fineness of rayon, nylon and silk yarns: [attrib] *30 denier stockings.*

denigrate /ˈdenɪgreɪt/ *v* [Tn] claim (unfairly) that (sb/sth) is inferior, worthless, etc; belittle: *denigrate sb's character, achievements, etc.* ▷ **denigration** /ˌdenɪˈgreɪʃn/ *n* [U].

denim /ˈdenɪm/ *n* **1** [U] hard-wearing twilled cotton cloth (used for jeans, overalls, etc). **2 denims** [pl] (*infml*) jeans made from this cloth.

denizen /ˈdenɪzn/ *n* (*fml or joc*) person or type of animal or plant living or growing permanently in a place: *polar bears, denizens of the frozen north* ○ *Blenkinsop, a respected denizen of our school*, ie a teacher who has been there for a long time.

Denmark /ˈdenmɑːk/ Scandinavian country occupying most of the Jutland peninsula to the north of Germany and many adjacent islands; pop approx 5 130 000; official language Danish; capital Copenhagen; unit of currency krone (= 100 ore). A prosperous country with a successful dairy industry, it joined the European Community in 1973. ⇨ map. Cf DANISH.

denomination /dɪˌnɒmɪˈneɪʃn/ *n* **1** (*fml*) name, esp of a general class or type; classification: *agreed denominations for various species of fish.* **2** religious group or sect: *The Protestant denominations include the Methodists, the Presbyterians and the Baptists.* **3** class or unit of measurement or money: *The US coin of the lowest denomination is the cent.* ○ *We can reduce fractions to the same denomination, eg* $\frac{1}{2}$, $\frac{5}{8}$ = $\frac{8}{16}$, $\frac{10}{16}$.

▷ **denominational** /dɪˌnɒmɪˈneɪʃənl/ *adj* of denominations (DENOMINATION 2): *denominational schools.*

Denmark

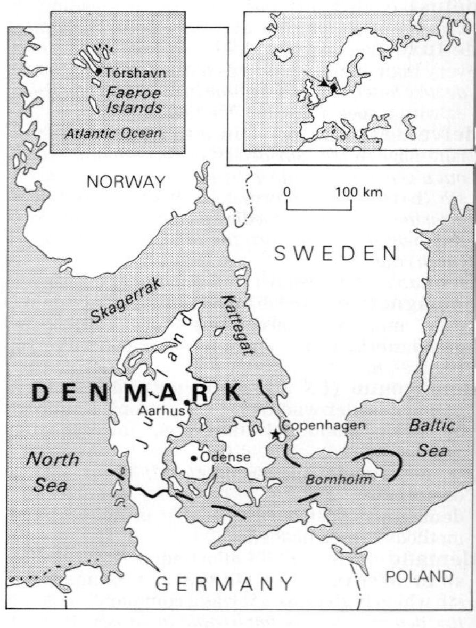

denominator /dɪˈnɒmɪneɪtə(r)/ *n* (*mathematics*) number below the line in a fraction, showing how many parts the whole is divided into, eg 4 in $\frac{3}{4}$. Cf NUMERATOR.

denote /dɪˈnəʊt/ *v* (**a**) [Tn] be the name, sign or symbol of (sth); refer to: *What does the term 'organic' denote?* ○ *In algebra, the sign x usually denotes an unknown quantity.* (**b**) [Tn, Tf] indicate (sth): *The mark ʌ denotes an omission.* ○ *This mark denotes that a word has been deleted.*

denouement /ˌdeɪˈnuːmɒŋ; *US* ˌdeɪnuːˈmɔːŋ/ *n* last part, esp of a novel, play, etc, in which everything is settled or made clear: *In a surprising denouement, she becomes a nun.*

denounce /dɪˈnaʊns/ *v* **1** (**a**) [Tn, Tn·pr, Cn·a] ~ **sb (to sb) (as sth)** give information (to the authorities) against sb: *An informer denounced him to the police (as a terrorist).* (**b**) [Tn, Cn·a] ~ **sb/sth (as sth)** say that sb/sth is wrong, unlawful, etc: *She strongly denounced the Government's hypocrisy.* ○ *Union officials denounced the action as a breach of the agreement.* **2** [Tn] announce one's withdrawal from (a treaty, etc).

dense /dens/ *adj* (**-r, -st**) **1** (**a**) very heavy in relation to each unit of volume: *a dense substance, rock, star.* (**b**) (of liquids or vapour) not easily seen through: *dense fog/smoke.* **2** (of people and things) crowded together in great numbers: *a dense crowd, forest.* **3** (*infml*) stupid: *How can you be so dense?* ▷ **densely** *adv*: *a densely populated country* ○ *densely wooded*, ie covered with trees growing close together. **denseness** *n* [U].

density /ˈdensətɪ/ *n* **1** [U] quality of being dense(1b, 2): *the density of a forest, the fog, etc.* **2** [C, U] (*physics*) relation of mass to volume.

dent /dent/ *n* **1** (also **dint**) hollow place in a hard even surface made by a blow or pressure: *a dent in the boot of my car.* **2** (idm) **(make) a dent in sth** (*infml*) (cause) a reduction in sth: *a dent in one's pride* ○ *The repairs made a dent in our funds*, ie cost us a lot.

▷ **dent** *v* (**a**) [Tn] make a dent or dents in (sth): *The back of the car was badly dented in a collision.* (**b**) [I] get a dent or dents: *a metal that dents easily.*

dental /ˈdentl/ *adj* **1** of or for the teeth: *dental care, treatment, etc.* **2** (*phonetics*) pronounced with the tip of the tongue near or touching the upper front teeth: *dental sounds*, eg /θ, ð/.

□ **ˈdental floss** soft thread used for cleaning the gaps between the teeth.

dental hyˈgienist /haɪˈdʒiːnɪst/ person who works, usu for a dentist, cleaning and polishing people's teeth.

ˈ**dental plate** = PLATE[1] 9.
ˈ**dental surgeon** dentist.

dentifrice /ˈdentɪfrɪs/ *n* [U] (*fml*) powder or paste used for cleaning the teeth.

dentine /ˈdentiːn; *US* denˈtiːn/ (*US* also **dentin** /ˈdentn/) *n* [U] hard inner substance of teeth, beneath the surface of enamel. ⇨ illus at TOOTH.

dentist /ˈdentɪst/ *n* person whose work is filling, cleaning and taking out teeth, and fitting artificial teeth.
▷ **dentistry** /ˈdentɪstrɪ/ *n* [U] work of a dentist.

denture /ˈdentʃə(r)/ *n* (usu *pl*): = PLATE[1] 9; *a set of dentures.*

denude /dɪˈnjuːd; *US* -ˈnuːd/ *v* [esp passive: Tn, Tn·pr] ~ **sth (of sth)** make sth bare; take the covering off sth: *trees denuded of leaves* ○ *hillsides denuded of trees.* ▷ **denudation** /ˌdiːnjuːˈdeɪʃn; *US* -nuː-/ *n* [U].

denunciation /dɪˌnʌnsɪˈeɪʃn/ *n* [C, U] (act of) denouncing: *her fierce denunciation(s) of her enemies.*

deny /dɪˈnaɪ/ *v* (*pt, pp* **denied**) **1** [Tn, Tf, Tnt, Tg] say that (sth) is not true: *deny a statement, a claim, an accusation, a charge, etc* ○ *deny that sth is true* ○ (*fml*) *She denied this to be the case.* ○ *He denied knowing anything about it.* ○ *He denied that he was involved.* ○ *There is no denying the fact that...*, ie Everyone must admit that.... Cf AFFIRM. **2** [Dn·n, Dn·pr] ~ **sth (to sb)** refuse to give sb, or prevent sb from having, (sth asked for or wanted): *He gave to his friends what he denied to his family.* ○ *She was angry at being denied the opportunity to see me.* ○ *He denies himself nothing.* **3** [Tn] say that one knows nothing about (sth); refuse to acknowledge; disown: *He denied any knowledge of their plans*, ie claimed to know nothing about them. ○ (*fml*) *He denied the signature*, ie said that it was not his.

deodorant /diːˈəʊdərənt/ *n* [U, C] substance that removes or disguises (esp bodily) odours.

deodorize, -ise /diːˈəʊdəraɪz/ *v* [Tn] remove (esp bad) smells from (sb/sth).

dep *abbr* **1** depart(s); departed; departing; departure: *dep Paris 23.05 hrs.* Cf ARR 2. **2** deputy.

depart /dɪˈpɑːt/ *v* (*fml*) **1** [I, Ipr] ~ **(for...)** **(from...)** go away; leave: *We departed for London at 10 am.* ○ *The 10.15 to Leeds departs from platform 4.* **2** (idm) **depart (from) this ˈlife** (*arch or rhet*) die. **3** (phr v) **depart from sth** behave in a way that differs from (what is usual or expected): *depart from routine, standard practice, old customs, etc* ○ *depart from the truth*, ie not be truthful.

departed /dɪˈpɑːtɪd/ *adj* [esp attrib] **1** (*fml or euph*) dead: *our departed heroes*, eg soldiers who died in battle ○ *your dear departed brother.* **2** (*fml*) past; bygone: *thinking of departed glories.*
▷ **the departed** *n* (*pl* unchanged) person who has died: *pray for the soul(s) of the departed.*

department /dɪˈpɑːtmənt/ *n* **1** (*abbr* **Dept**) each of several divisions of a government, business, shop, university, etc: *the Department of the Environment* ○ *the Education Department* ○ *the export sales department* ○ *the men's clothing department.* **2** area of activity or knowledge: *Don't ask me about our finances: that's my wife's department.* **3** administrative district, eg in France.
▷ **departmental** /ˌdiːpɑːtˈmentl/ *adj* of a department, rather than the whole organization: *a departmental manager, meeting.*
□ **deˈpartment store** large shop where many kinds of goods are sold in different departments. ⇨ article at SHOP.

departure /dɪˈpɑːtʃə(r)/ *n* **1** (a) [U] ~ **(from...)** departing; going away: *His departure was quite unexpected.* ○ [attrib] *the departure lounge*, ie in an airport. (b) [C] instance of this: *notices showing arrivals and departures of trains.* **2** (a) [C, U] ~ **from sth** action different from (what is usual or expected): *a departure from old customs, the standard procedure, etc.* (b) [C] course of action; venture: *Working on a farm is a new departure for him.* **3** (idm) **a point of departure** ⇨ POINT[1].

depend /dɪˈpend/ *v* **1** (idm) **that deˈpends; it (all) deˈpends** (used alone, or at the beginning of a sentence) the result will be decided by sth mentioned or implied: *'Can I come?' 'That depends: there might not be room in the car.'* ○ *It depends how you tackle the problem.* **2** (phr v) **depend on/upon sb/sth** (a) be sure, or confidently expect, that sth will happen: *I'm depending on you coming.* ○ *You can never depend on his arriving on time.* ○ (*ironic*) *You can depend on her to be* (ie She always is) *late.* ○ *Depend on it* (ie You can be sure)*: we won't give up.* (b) (be able to) believe that sb/sth will be reliable: *You can't depend on the train arriving on time.* ○ *She's a woman who can be depended on.* **depend on sb/sth (for sth)** (usu not in the continuous tenses) (a) need sb/sth for a particular purpose: *I haven't got a car, so I have to depend on the buses.* ○ *We depend on the radio for news.* (b) get money or other help from sb/sth: *This area depends on the mining industry.* ○ *Children depend on their parents for food and clothing.* **depend on sth** be decided by sth; follow from sth: *A lot will depend on how she responds to the challenge.* ○ *How much is produced depends on how hard we work.*
▷ **dependable** *adj* that may be depended on: *a dependable friend, car, service.* **dependability** /dɪˌpendəˈbɪlətɪ/ *n* [U]. **dependably** /-əblɪ/ *adv.*

dependant (also *esp US* **-ent**) /dɪˈpendənt/ *n* person who depends on others for a home, food, etc.

dependence /dɪˈpendəns/ *n* [U] ~ **on/upon sb/sth** **1** trust in sb/sth; reliance on sb/sth: *my complete dependence on her skill and experience.* **2** (a) state of having to be supported by others: *Find a job and end your dependence on your parents.* (b) state of being affected by or needing sb/sth: *the dependence of the crops on the weather* ○ *medical treatment for drug/alcohol dependence.*

dependency /dɪˈpendənsɪ/ *n* country governed or controlled by another: *The Hawaiian Islands are no longer a dependency of the USA.*

dependent /dɪˈpendənt/ *adj* **1** ~ **(on/upon sb/sth)** needing support from sb: *a woman with several dependent children* ○ *be dependent on one's parents, a grant.* **2** [pred] ~ **on/upon sth** affected or decided by sth: *Success is dependent on how hard you work.* **3** [pred] ~ **on/upon sth** needing sth physically: *be dependent on drugs/alcohol.*
▷ **dependent** *n* (*esp US*) = DEPENDANT.
□ **deˌpendent ˈclause** = SUBORDINATE CLAUSE (SUBORDINATE).

depersonalize, -ise /ˌdiːˈpɜːsənəlaɪz/ *v* [Tn] remove human or individual characteristics from (sb); make (sth) impersonal.
▷ **depersonalization, -isation** /ˌdiːˌpɜːsənəlaɪˈzeɪʃn; *US* -lɪˈz-/ *n* [U] (*psychology*) disturbed mental state in which one feels unreal and loses one's sense of being oneself.

depict /dɪˈpɪkt/ *v* [Tn, Cn·n/a, Cn·g] (a) show (sb/sth) as a picture; portray: *a picture depicting him as a clown* ○ *The drawing depicts her sitting on a sofa.* (b) describe (sth) in words: *Her novel depicts life in modern London (as an ordeal).* ▷ **depiction** /dɪˈpɪkʃn/ *n* [U, C].

depilatory /dɪˈpɪlətrɪ; *US* -tɔːrɪ/ *n, adj* (liquid, cream, etc) used for removing unwanted hair.

deplane /ˌdiːˈpleɪn/ *v* [I, Tn] (cause sb to) leave an aircraft: *The troops (were) deplaned an hour later.*

deplete /dɪˈpliːt/ *v* [Tn, Tn·pr] reduce greatly the quantity, size, power or value of (sth): *Our stock of food is greatly depleted.* ○ *This expense has depleted our funds.* ○ *a lake depleted of fish*, ie with many of the fish gone.
▷ **depletion** /dɪˈpliːʃn/ *n* [U] depleting or being depleted.

deplore /dɪˈplɔː(r)/ *v* [Tn] (a) be shocked or offended by (sth); condemn: *She deplored his scandalous actions.* (b) feel sorrow or regret about (sth).
▷ **deplorable** /dɪˈplɔːrəbl/ *adj* that is, or should be, condemned: *a deplorable attitude, speech* ○ *The acting was deplorable!* **deplorably** /-əblɪ/ *adv.*

deploy /dɪˈplɔɪ/ *v* (a) [I, Tn] (cause troops, etc to) move into the correct position for battle: *The infantry began to deploy at dawn.* ○ *Artillery was deployed in the west.* (b) [Tn] use (sth) effectively: *deploy one's arguments, resources, etc.* ▷ **deployment** *n* [U].

deponent /dɪˈpəʊnənt/ *n* (*law*) person who makes a written statement for use in a lawcourt.

depopulate /ˌdiːˈpɒpjʊleɪt/ *v* [Tn] reduce the number of people living in (a city, state, etc): *a country depopulated by war, famine, disease, etc.* ▷ **depopulation** /ˌdiːpɒpjʊˈleɪʃn/ *n* [U].

deport /dɪˈpɔːt/ *v* [Tn, Tn·pr] ~ **sb (from...)** legally force (a foreigner, criminal, etc) to leave a country: *He was convicted of drug offences and deported.*
▷ **deportation** /ˌdiːpɔːˈteɪʃn/ *n* [C, U] (instance of) deporting or being deported: *Years ago convicted criminals in England could face deportation to Australia.*
deportee /ˌdiːpɔːˈtiː/ *n* person who is or has been deported.

deportment /dɪˈpɔːtmənt/ *n* [U] (*fml*) (a) (*Brit*) way of standing and walking; bearing: *Young ladies used to have lessons in deportment.* (b) (*US*) behaviour.

depose /dɪˈpəʊz/ *v* **1** [Tn] remove (esp a ruler such as a king) from power. **2** [Ipr, Tf] ~ **to doing sth** (*law*) give (usu written) evidence, esp on oath in a lawcourt: *depose to having seen sth* ○ *depose that one saw sth.* Cf DEPOSITION.

deposit[1] /dɪˈpɒzɪt/ *v* [Tn, Tn·pr] **1** (a) put (money) into a bank, esp to earn interest, etc: *The cheque was only deposited yesterday, so it hasn't been cleared yet.* (b) ~ **sth (with sb)** give (sth valuable or important) to sb to be kept in a safe place: *deposit papers with one's lawyer.* **2** (a) pay (sth) as part of a larger sum, the rest of which is to be paid later: *I had to deposit 10% of the price of the house.* (b) pay (a sum) as a guarantee in case one damages or loses sth one is renting: *You must deposit £500 as well as the first month's rent.* **3** ~ **sth (on sth)** (*fml*) (a) lay or put sth down: *He deposited the books on the desk.* ○ *Some insects deposit their eggs on the ground.* (b) (esp of liquids or a river) cause (mud, silt, etc) to settle: *The Nile floods the fields and deposits mud on them.*

deposit[2] /dɪˈpɒzɪt/ *n* **1** [C] sum paid into an account, eg at a bank: *a £10 deposit* ○ *She made two deposits of £500 last month.* **2** [C] ~ **(on sth)** (a) payment of a part of a larger sum, the rest of which is to be paid later: *The shop promised to keep the goods for me if I paid a deposit.* (b) sum that sb pays in advance, in case he damages or loses sth he is renting: *I had to pay a £500 deposit to the landlord before I could move into the house.* **3** [C, U] (a) layer of matter laid down by a liquid, river, etc: *A thick deposit of mud lay on the fields when the flood went down.* (b) layer of matter (often deep in the earth) that has accumulated naturally: *Valuable deposits of oil have been found by drilling.* **4** (idm) **on deˈposit** in a deposit account: *have £2 000 on deposit.*
□ **deˈposit account** type of account, usu at a bank, in which money earns interest but cannot be taken out unless the bank is warned in advance. Cf CURRENT ACCOUNT (CURRENT[1]), SAVINGS ACCOUNT (SAVING). ⇨ article at BANK.

deposition /ˌdepəˈzɪʃn/ *n* **1** [U] removing (a ruler such as a king) from power; dethronement. **2** [U, C] (*law*) (action of making a) statement on oath: *The accused has made a deposition.* Cf DEPOSE.

depositor /dɪˈpɒzɪtə(r)/ *n* person who deposits (eg money in a bank).

depository /dɪˈpɒzɪtrɪ; *US* -tɔːrɪ/ *n* place where things, eg furniture, are stored; storehouse.

depot /ˈdepəʊ; *US* ˈdiːpəʊ/ *n* **1** (a) storehouse, esp for military supplies; warehouse. (b) place where vehicles, eg buses, are kept. **2** (*US*) railway or bus station.

deprave /dɪˈpreɪv/ *v* [Tn esp passive] (*fml*) make (sb) morally bad; corrupt: *a man depraved by bad company.*
▷ **depravation** /ˌdeprəˈveɪʃn/ *n* [U].
depraved /dɪˈpreɪvd/ *adj* morally bad; corrupt: *depraved thoughts, morals, companions* ○ *He was totally depraved.*

depravity /dɪˈprævətɪ/ *n* **1** [U] state of being depraved; corruption: *a life of depravity* ○ *sunk in depravity.* **2** [C] depraved act: *the depravities of a corrupt ruler.*

deprecate /ˈdeprəkeɪt/ *v* (*fml*) (**a**) [Tn, Tw, Tg, Tsg] feel and express disapproval of (sth): *Hasty action is to be deprecated.* ○ *He deprecates (her) changing the party's policy.* (**b**) [Tn, Tw] feel embarrassed or displeased by (sb's flattery, etc): *deprecate sb's compliments, charm, condescension, etc.* ▷ **deprecating** *adj*: *a deprecating smile.* **deprecatingly** *adv*. **deprecatory** /ˌdeprɪˈkeɪtərɪ; *US* -tɔːrɪ/ *adj*: *a deprecatory remark, view, etc.*

depreciate /dɪˈpriːʃɪeɪt/ *v* **1** [I] become less valuable: *Shares in the company have depreciated.* **2** [Tn] state that (sth) is not valuable, important, etc; disparage: *Don't depreciate my efforts to help/what I have done.* ▷ **depreciation** /dɪˌpriːʃɪˈeɪʃn/ *n* [C, U]: *suffer a sharp depreciation.* **depreciatory** /dɪˈpriːʃətərɪ; *US* -tɔːrɪ/ *adj*: *depreciatory remarks about a great achievement.*

depredations /ˌdeprəˈdeɪʃnz/ *n* [pl] (*fml*) damage caused by an attack, accident, etc: *The town survived the depredations of marauding gangs.* ○ *the depredations of the storm.*

depress /dɪˈpres/ *v* [Tn] **1** make (sb) sad and without enthusiasm: *Wet weather always depresses me.* **2** press, push or pull (sth) down: *depress a lever, a piano key, a button, etc.* **3** make (esp trade) less active: *depress a market* ○ *depress sales* ○ *A rise in oil prices depresses the car market.*

▷ **depressant** /-ənt/ *n, adj* (substance) that reduces mental or physical activity: *a depressant drug.*

depressed *adj* sad and without enthusiasm: *depressed about the election results.*

depressing *adj* making one feel depressed: *a depressing sight, prospect, film.* **depressingly** *adv*: *The crime rate is depressingly high.*

□ ˌ**depressed** ˈ**area** part of a country where there is little economic activity (resulting in poverty and unemployment).

depression /dɪˈpreʃn/ *n* **1** [U] (**a**) being depressed; low spirits. (**b**) (*psychology*) disturbed mental condition in which one feels extremely depressed, listless and inadequate. **2** [C] hollow sunken place in the surface of sth, esp the ground; dip: *depressions on the face of the moon* ○ *The soldiers hid from the enemy in a slight depression.* **3** (**a**) [C] period when there is little economic activity, and usu poverty and unemployment. (**b**) **the Depression** [sing] period of low economic activity in the Western world between 1929 and 1934, when many businesses failed and millions of people were out of work. **4** [C] (**a**) (winds caused by a) lowering of atmospheric pressure. (**b**) area where this happens: *a depression over Iceland.* Cf ANTICYCLONE.

depressive /dɪˈpresɪv/ *adj* **1** tending to depress; of depression: *a depressive drug, illness.* **2** intended to reduce trading activity: *a depressive financial policy.*

▷ **depressive** *n* person who often suffers from depression(1).

depressurize, -ise /ˌdiːˈpreʃəraɪz/ *v* [Tn] reduce the pressure of air or gas in (a vessel, cabin, etc). ▷ **depressurization, -isation** *n* [U].

deprive /dɪˈpraɪv/ *v* [Tn·pr] ~ **sb/sth of sth** take sth away from sb/sth; prevent sb/sth from enjoying or using sth: *deprived of one's civil rights* ○ *trees that deprive a house of light* ○ (*joc*) *Are you depriving us of your company* (ie leaving us)?

▷ **depri**ˌ**vation** /ˌdeprɪˈveɪʃn/ *n* **1** [U] (**a**) depriving or being deprived: *suffer deprivation of one's rights as a citizen.* (**b**) state of not having the normal benefits of adequate food, etc; poverty: *widespread deprivation caused by unemployment.* **2** [C] thing of which one is deprived: *Missing the holiday was a great deprivation.*

deprived *adj* without the normal benefits of adequate food, housing, health care, etc: *a deprived childhood, background, area* ○ *The poorest and most deprived people will receive special government help.*

Dept *abbr* Department(1): *Linguistics Dept*, eg of a university.

depth /depθ/ *n* **1** [C, U] (**a**) distance from the top down: *the depth of the well, mine, box, trunk* ○ *Water was found at a depth of 30 ft.* ○ *At what depth does the wreck lie?* ⇨ illus at DIMENSION. (**b**) distance from the front to the back: *shelves with a depth of 8 ins.* (**c**) distance from the surface inwards: *the depth of a wound, crack, etc.* **2** [C, U] (**a**) (of colours, darkness, etc) intensity. (**b**) (of sounds) lowness in pitch. **3** [U] (**a**) (of feelings, etc) sincerity; intensity: *the depth of her love.* (**b**) ability to understand or explain difficult ideas: *a writer of great depth and wisdom.* (**c**) having or showing this ability: *a novel that lacks depth.* **4** (idm) ˌ**in** ˈ**depth** thoroughly: *to study a subject in depth* ○ [attrib] *an* ˌ*in-depth* ˈ*study.* **in the** ~**(s) of sth** when or where sth is deepest, most severe, etc: *in the depth of winter* ○ *in the depths of despair* ○ *in the depth of the country*, ie a long way from a town. **(be/get) out of one's depth** (**a**) (be/go) in water too deep to stand in: *If you can't swim, don't get out of your depth.* (**b**) (be/become) unable to understand a subject or topic: *When they start talking about economics, I'm out of my depth.* **plumb the depths of sth** ⇨ PLUMB.

□ ˈ**depth charge** bomb used against submarines that explodes under water. Cf MINE[2] 2.

deputation /ˌdepjʊˈteɪʃn/ *n* [CGp] group of people given the right to act or speak for others.

depute /dɪˈpjuːt/ *v* (*fml*) **1** [Dn·pr] ~ **sth to sb** give (one's work, authority, etc) to sb else: *He deputed the running of the department to an assistant.* **2** [Dn·t] give (sb else) authority to act or speak on one's behalf: *They were deputed to put our views to the assembly.*

deputize, -ise /ˈdepjʊtaɪz/ *v* [I, Ipr] ~ **(for sb)** act or speak on sb's behalf: *Dr Mitchell's ill so I'm deputizing (for her).*

deputy /ˈdepjʊtɪ/ *n* **1** person who is given work, authority, etc (eg during sb's absence): *I'm acting as deputy till the headmaster returns.* **2** person who is immediately below the head of a business, school, etc: *the Director General and his deputy* ○ [attrib] *the deputy headmistress.* **3** (in some countries, eg France) member of a legislative assembly.

De Quincey /də ˈkwɪnsɪ/ Thomas (1785-1859), English writer of essays and criticism, a friend of *Wordsworth and *Coleridge. He was addicted to opium, and described its effects on him in his best-known book, *Confessions of an English Opium Eater*.

derail /dɪˈreɪl/ *v* [Tn] cause (a train, etc) to go off the rails: *The engine was derailed by a tree lying across the line.* ▷ **derailment** *n*.

deranged /dɪˈreɪndʒd/ *adj* unable to act and think normally, esp because of mental illness; seriously disturbed: *She's completely deranged.* ○ *a deranged attacker, mind, laugh.* **derangement** *n* [U].

derby[1] /ˈdɑːbɪ; *US* ˈdɜːrbɪ/ *n* **1 the Derby** [sing] annual horse race run at Epsom, England. ⇨ article at SEASON. **2** [C] (*US*) any of several annual horse races. **3** [C] any important sporting contest: *a local derby*, ie between local teams.

□ ˈ**Derby Day** day when the Derby is run (in June).

derby[2] /ˈdɜːrbɪ/ *n* (*US*) = BOWLER[2].

Derbyshire /ˈdɑːbɪʃə(r)/ north midland county of England. It contains the *Peak District national park. ⇨ map at App 1.

deregulate /ˌdiːˈregjʊleɪt/ *v* [Tn] remove the regulations from (sth): *deregulate the price of oil.* ▷ **deregulation** *n* [U].

derelict /ˈderəlɪkt/ *adj* deserted and allowed to fall into ruins; dilapidated: *a derelict house* ○ *derelict areas.*

▷ **derelict** *n* **1** poor (usu homeless) person who has been abandoned by society; vagrant. **2** item of property (esp a ship at sea) that has been left to fall into ruins.

dereliction /ˌderəˈlɪkʃn/ *n* **1** [U] being derelict: *a house in a state of dereliction.* **2** (idm) ˌ**dereliction of** ˈ**duty** (*fml*) (deliberate) failure to do what one ought to do: *be guilty of a serious dereliction of duty.*

derestrict /ˌdiːrɪˈstrɪkt/ *v* [Tn] remove a restriction, esp a speed limit, from (sth): *derestrict a road.*

deride /dɪˈraɪd/ *v* [Tn, Cn·n/a] ~ **sb/sth (as sth)** treat sb/sth as funny and not worthy of serious attention; mock sb/sth: *They derided his efforts (as childish).*

de rigueur /də rɪˈgɜː(r)/ (*French*) required by etiquette or custom: *Evening dress is de rigueur at the Casino.*

derision /dɪˈrɪʒn/ *n* [U] ridicule or mockery: *be an object of general derision*, ie be derided by everybody ○ *Her naive attitude provoked their derision.*

derisive /dɪˈraɪsɪv/ *adj* showing ridicule or mockery: *derisive laughter, booing, etc.* ▷ **derisively** *adv*.

derisory /dɪˈraɪsərɪ/ *adj* **1** not to be considered seriously: *a derisory offer*, eg £100 for a car that is worth £1 000. **2** = DERISIVE.

derivation /ˌderɪˈveɪʃn/ *n* **1** [U] development or origin (esp of words): *the derivation of words from Latin* ○ *a word of French derivation.* **2** [C] (**a**) first form and meaning of a word. (**b**) later change of form and meaning: *give the derivations of words.*

derivative /dɪˈrɪvətɪv/ *adj* (*usu derog*) derived from sth else; not original: *a derivative design, style, etc.*

▷ **derivative** *n* **1** derived word or thing: *'Assertion' and 'assertive' are derivatives of 'assert'.* **2** (*mathematics*) quantity measuring the rate of change of one quantity with respect to another quantity. **3** (*chemistry*) chemical compound formed from another closely related substance.

derive /dɪˈraɪv/ *v* **1** [Tn·pr] ~ **sth from sth** (*fml*) obtain sth from sth; get sth from sth: *derive great pleasure from one's studies* ○ *She derived no benefit from the course of drugs.* **2** (**a**) [Ipr] ~ **from sth** have sth as a starting-point, source or origin; originate from sth: *Thousands of English words derive from Latin.* (**b**) [Tn·pr] ~ **sth from sth** trace sth from (a source): *We can derive the word 'derelict' from the Latin 'derelictus'.*

derm(at)- *comb form* of skin: *dermatology* ○ *dermatitis.*

dermatitis /ˌdɜːməˈtaɪtɪs/ *n* [U] (*medical*) inflammation of the skin.

dermatology /ˌdɜːməˈtɒlədʒɪ/ *n* [U] medical study of the skin and its diseases, etc.

▷ **dermatologist** /ˌdɜːməˈtɒlədʒɪst/ *n* expert in dermatology.

dermis /ˈdɜːmɪs/ *n* (*anatomy*) layer of skin below the epidermis.

derogate /ˈderəgeɪt/ *v* [Ipr] ~ **from sth** (*fml*) cause sth to seem inferior; detract from sth: *remarks derogating from her merits, qualities, virtues, etc.*

derogatory /dɪˈrɒgətrɪ; *US* -tɔːrɪ/ *adj* (*abbr* **derog** in this dictionary) showing a hostile or critical attitude (to sb's reputation, etc); insulting: *The word 'pig' is a derogatory term for policeman.* ○ *remarks that were highly derogatory.*

derrick /ˈderɪk/ *n* **1** large crane for moving or lifting heavy weights, esp on a ship. **2** framework over an oil well or borehole, to hold the drilling machinery, etc. Cf OIL RIG (OIL).

derring-do /ˌderɪŋˈduː/ *n* [U] (*arch or joc*) heroic deeds: *stirring tales of derring-do.*

derringer /ˈderɪndʒə(r)/ *n* small pistol that can be carried in the pocket.

derris /ˈderɪs/ *n* [U] insecticide made from the powdered root of a tropical Asian plant.

derv /dɜːv/ *n* [U] (*Brit*) fuel oil for diesel engines (from *d*iesel-*e*ngined *r*oad *v*ehicle).

dervish /ˈdɜːvɪʃ/ *n* member of a Muslim religious order: *dancing dervishes*, ie those who take part in whirling dances.

DES /ˌdiː iː ˈes/ *abbr* (*Brit*) Department of Education and Science: *DES grants.*

desalinate /ˌdiːˈsælɪneɪt/ *v* [Tn] remove salt from (esp sea water). ▷ **desalination** /ˌdiːˌsælɪˈneɪʃn/ *n* [U].

descale /ˌdiːˈskeɪl/ *v* [Tn] remove scale[1](3) from (eg the inside of boilers and kettles).

descant /ˈdeskænt/ *n* (*music*) treble accompaniment (often improvised) which is sung or played to a melody.

▷ **descant** *v* /dɪˈskænt/ [Ipr] ~ **on/upon sth** **1** (*music*) sing or play a descant on sth. **2** (*fml*) talk for a long time about sth; comment on sth: *descant endlessly on the Government's failings.*

Descartes /ˈdeɪkɑːt; *US* deɪˈkɑːrt/ René (1596-1650), French philosopher and mathematician. In philosophy, he held that the only things any individual can be certain of are that he thinks, and that therefore he exists; and on this he based his theory that the world is composed of mind and matter. In mathematics he developed a system of co-ordinates for which he is regarded as the founder of analytic geometry. Cf CARTESIAN.

descend /dɪˈsend/ *v* **1** (*fml*) (**a**) [I, Tn] come or go down (sth): *The balloon descended gradually as the air came out.* ○ *She descended the stairs.* (**b**) [I] (of a hill, etc) lead downwards; slope: *We turned the corner and saw that the road descended steeply.* **2** [Ipr] ~ **from sb** (of properties, qualities, rights) pass from father to son; be inherited by sb from sb: *The title descends to me from my father.* **3** [I] (*fml*) (of night, darkness) fall: *Night descends quickly in the tropics.* **4** (idm) **be descended from sb** have sb as an ancestor: *She claims to be descended from royalty.* **5** (phr v) **descend on/upon sb/sth** (**a**) attack sb/sth suddenly: *The police descended on their hide-out.* (**b**) visit sb/sth unexpectedly or inconveniently: *My sister's family is descending on us this weekend.* **descend to sth** (no passive) do or say sth that is mean and unworthy of one; stoop to sth: *descend to fraud, abuse, bad language.*

▷ **descendant** /-ənt/ *n* person descended from another: *the descendants of Queen Victoria.* Cf ANCESTOR 1.

descent /dɪˈsent/ *n* **1** (**a**) [C *usu sing*] coming or going down: *The plane began its descent into Paris.* (**b**) [C] slope: *Here there is a gradual descent to the sea.* **2** [U] origins; ancestry: *of French descent*, ie having French ancestors ○ *He traces his descent from the Stuart kings.* **3** [C] ~ **(on/upon sb/sth)** (*fig*) (**a**) attack: *the invaders' descent on the town.* (**b**) unexpected or inconvenient visit: *a sudden descent by tax officials.* **4** [sing] change to behaviour that is low and unworthy: *a sharp descent to violent abuse.*

describe /dɪˈskraɪb/ *v* **1** [Tn, Tw, Cn·n/a, Dn·pr, Dpr·w] ~ **sb/sth (to/for sb)**; ~ **sth as sth** say what sb/sth is like; depict sth in words: *Words cannot describe the beauty of the scene.* ○ *Describe (to me) how you were received.* ○ *She described it as red with pink frills.* **2** [Cn·n/a] ~ **sb/sth as sth** state sb/sth to be sth; call: *I hesitate to describe him as really clever.* ○ *He describes himself as a doctor.* **3** [Tn] (**a**) draw (esp a geometrical figure): *describe a circle with a pair of compasses.* (**b**) move along (a line, curve, etc): *A bullet describes a curved path in the air.*

description /dɪˈskrɪpʃn/ *n* **1** (**a**) [U] saying in words what sb/sth is like: *He's not very good at description.* ○ *The scenery was beautiful beyond description.* (**b**) [C] picture in words: *Can you give me a description of the thief?* **2** (preceded by *of* and an *adj* or *some, every*, etc) (*infml*) type; sort: *boats of every description* ○ *a house of some description* ○ *wearing a dress of no particular description*, ie a very ordinary dress ○ *medals, coins and things of that description.* **3** (idm) **answer to a description** ⇨ ANSWER². **beggar description** ⇨ BEGGAR.

descriptive /dɪˈskrɪptɪv/ *adj* **1** (**a**) giving a picture in words: *a descriptive passage in a novel.* (**b**) describing sth with skill: *a very descriptive account of a journey* ○ *The report was so descriptive, I felt as if I were there.* **2** (*grammar*) describing how language is actually used, without giving rules for how it ought to be used. ▷ **descriptively** *adv.* **descriptiveness** *n* [U].

descry /dɪˈskraɪ/ *v* (*pt, pp* **descried**) [Tn] (*fml*) see (sth) esp a long way away; catch sight of: *I descry a sail on the horizon.*

desecrate /ˈdesɪkreɪt/ *v* [Tn] treat (a sacred thing or place) in an unworthy or evil way: *desecrate a grave, chapel, monument, etc.*

▷ **desecration** /ˌdesɪˈkreɪʃn/ *n* [U] desecrating or being desecrated.

desegregate /ˌdiːˈsegrɪgeɪt/ *v* [Tn] end racial segregation in (sth): *desegregate schools, buses.* ▷ **desegregation** /ˌdiːˌsegrɪˈgeɪʃn/ *n* [U].

deselect /ˌdiːsɪˈlekt/ *v* [Tn] (*Brit*) (of a local constituency party) reject (the existing Member of Parliament) as a candidate at a forthcoming election. ▷ **deselection** *n* [U].

desensitize, -ise /ˌdiːˈsensɪtaɪz/ *v* [Tn] make (a patient, nerve, etc) insensitive or less sensitive to light, pain, etc: *desensitize an area of skin.* ○ (*fig*) *people who are morally desensitized.* ▷ **desensitization, -isation** /ˌdiːˌsensɪtaɪˈzeɪʃn; *US* -tɪˈz-/ *n* [U].

desert¹ /dɪˈzɜːt/ *v* **1** [Tn] (**a**) go away from (a place) without intending ever to return: *desert a house, city, etc* ○ *The village had been hurriedly deserted, perhaps because terrorists were in the area.* (**b**) leave (sb) without help or support; abandon: *He deserted his wife and children and went abroad.* ○ *He has become so rude that his friends are deserting him.* **2** [I, Ipr, Tn] leave (esp service in the armed forces, or a ship) without authority or permission; run away: *A soldier who deserts (his post) in time of war is punished severely.* ○ *desert from the army.* **3** [Tn] fail (sb) when needed: *His courage/presence of mind deserted him.*

▷ **deserted** *adj* (**a**) with no one present: *a deserted street, area, etc* ○ *The office was quite deserted.* (**b**) abandoned: *a deserted hut, house, etc* ○ *a deserted wife*, ie one whose husband has left her.

deserter *n* person who deserts (DESERT¹ 2).

desertion /dɪˈzɜːʃn/ *n* [C, U] (instance of) deserting or being deserted: *Is desertion grounds for divorce?* ○ *Desertion from the army is punishable by death.*

desert² /ˈdezət/ *n* [C, U] (large area of) barren land, with very little water and vegetation, often sand-covered: *Vast areas of land have become desert.* ○ *the Sahara Desert* ○ [attrib] *desert wastes, sands, etc.*

□ ˌ**desert ˈisland** uninhabited island (esp in the tropics): *cast away* (ie stranded) *on a desert island.* 📖 Desert islands have captured people's imaginations since the days of Captain *Cook, who came home from his travels telling tales of the exotic, often uninhabited islands he had visited. Later on, people came to think of desert islands as places where wild men or strange creatures lived and where hidden treasure lay buried. This image was reinforced by classic tales, such as Daniel *Defoe's *Robinson Crusoe* (1719), and R L *Stevenson's *Treasure Island* (1881). The romantic image of the desert island still exists: *Desert Island Discs*, a popular BBC radio programme in which famous people are asked to choose eight records they would like to have with them on a desert island, has been broadcast regularly since the 1940s.

deserts /dɪˈzɜːts/ *n* [pl] what one deserves: *be rewarded/punished according to one's deserts* ○ *get/meet with one's just deserts.*

deserve /dɪˈzɜːv/ *v* (not used in the continuous tenses) **1** [Tn, Tt] be sth or have done sth for which one should receive (a reward, special treatment, etc); be entitled to; merit: *The article deserves careful study.* ○ *She deserves a reward for her efforts.* ○ *He richly deserved all that happened to him.* ○ *They deserve to be sent to prison.* ○ *much deserved praise.* **2** (idm) **deserve well/ill of sb** (*fml*) be worthy of good/bad treatment by sb: *She deserves well of her employers.* **one good turn deserves another** ⇨ TURN².

▷ **deservedly** /dɪˈzɜːvɪdlɪ/ *adv* according to what is deserved; justly; rightly: *She was deservedly praised.*

deserving /dɪˈzɜːvɪŋ/ *adj* ~ **(of sth)** worthy of help, praise, a reward, etc: *give money to a deserving cause* ○ *be deserving of sympathy* ○ *a very deserving case*, eg sb who used to be generous and now needs help.

déshabillé /ˌdeɪzæˈbiːeɪ/ *n* [U] (*French*) state of being only partly dressed: *appear in déshabillé.*

De Sica /də ˈsiːkə/ Vittorio (1901-74), Italian film actor and director. From the influential *Bicycle Thieves* of the post-war period to *The Garden of the Finzi Contini* at the end of his career he combined close observation of society with emotional sensitivity.

desiccant /ˈdesɪkənt/ *n* substance that absorbs moisture, and is often used to keep food in good condition.

desiccate /ˈdesɪkeɪt/ *v* [Tn] remove all the moisture from (esp solid food) to preserve it: *desiccated fruit/coconut.*

desideratum /dɪˌzɪdəˈrɑːtəm/ *n* (*pl* **-rata** /-ˈrɑːtə/) (*fml*) thing that is lacking and needed: *The report on the hospital mentions such desiderata as a supply of clean laundry.*

design /dɪˈzaɪn/ *n* **1** (**a**) [C] ~ **(for sth)** drawing or outline from which sth may be made: *designs for a dress, a garden, an aircraft.* (**b**) [U] art of making such drawings, etc: *study textile design* ○ *industrial design.* **2** [U] general arrangement or planning (of a building, book, machine, picture, etc): *The building seats 2 000 people, but is of poor design.* ○ *A machine of faulty design will not sell well.* **3** [C] arrangement of lines, shapes or figures as decoration on a carpet, vase, etc; pattern: *a bowl with a flower design.* **4** [U, C] purpose; intention: *We don't know if it was done by accident or by design*, ie deliberately. ○ *His evil designs were frustrated.* **5** (idm) **have designs on sb/sth** intend to harm sb/sth or take sb/sth for oneself: *She has designs on his money.* ○ *He has designs on her*, eg wants to seduce her.

▷ **design** *v* **1** (**a**) [I, Tn, Dn·n, Dn·pr] ~ **sth (for sb/sth)** decide how sth will look, work, etc, esp by making plans, drawings or models of it: *Do the Italians really design better than we do?* ○ *design a car, a dress, a tool, an office* ○ *They've designed us a superb studio.* ○ *We design kitchens for today's cooks.* (**b**) [Tn, Tn·pr] think of and plan (a system, procedure, etc); devise: *Can anyone design a better timetable?* ○ *We shall have to design a new curriculum for the third year.* **2** (idm) **be designed for sb/sth; be designed as sth; be designed to do sth** be made or planned for a particular purpose or use: *The gloves were designed for extremely cold climates.* ○ *This course is designed as an introduction to the subject.* ○ *The route was designed to relieve traffic congestion.* **designedly** /-ɪdlɪ/ *adv* intentionally; on purpose. **designing** *n* [U] art of making designs (for machinery, dresses, etc).

designate¹ /ˈdezɪgneɪt, -nət/ *adj* (following *ns*) appointed to a job (but not yet having officially started it): *the editor, director, archbishop, etc designate.*

designate² /ˈdezɪgneɪt/ *v* **1** [Tn] mark or point out (sth) clearly: *designate the boundaries of sth.* **2** [esp passive: Cn·n, Cn·n/a] ~ **sb/sth (as) sth** (*fml*) (**a**) choose sb/sth for a special purpose: *The town has been designated (as) a development area.* (**b**) give a particular name, title or position to sb: *She was designated (as) sportswoman of the year.* ○ *The chairman has designated Christina as his successor.*

designation /ˌdezɪgˈneɪʃn/ *n* (*fml*) **1** [U] ~ **(as sth)** appointing of sb to an office. **2** [C] name, title or description: *His official designation is Financial Controller.*

designer /dɪˈzaɪnə(r)/ *n* person whose job is designing (eg machinery, furniture, fashionable clothes): *an industrial designer* ○ *dressed by a leading New York designer* ○ [attrib] *designer jeans* ○ (*joc*) *designer stubble*, ie an unshaven look deliberately cultivated for effect.

designing /dɪˈzaɪnɪŋ/ *adj* [usu attrib] (*derog*) wanting to carry out one's own secret plans; cunning: *Designing colleagues stopped them from promoting me.*

desirable /dɪˈzaɪərəbl/ *adj* **1** ~ **(that...)** worth having; to be wished for: *a desirable residence, solution* ○ *It is most desirable that they should both come.* **2** (of a person) arousing sexual desire: *a very desirable woman.* ▷ **desirability** /dɪˌzaɪərəˈbɪlətɪ/ *n* [U]. **de·sir·ably** /-rəblɪ/ *adv.*

desire¹ /dɪˈzaɪə(r)/ *n* **1** (**a**) [U] ~ **(for sth/to do sth)** strong sexual longing: *my desire for her/to make love with her.* (**b**) [C] instance of this: *passionate, intense, strong, etc desires* ○ *satisfy one's desires.* **2** (**a**) [U] ~ **(for sth/to do sth)** longing; craving: *They had little desire for wealth/to get rich.* ○ *his country's desire for friendly relations/to establish friendly relations.* (**b**) [C] instance of this; wish: *enough to satisfy all your desires.* 3 [C] person or thing that is wished for: *She is my heart's desire.*

desire[2] /dɪˈzaɪə(r)/ *v* **1 (a)** [Tn, Tf, Tt, Tnt] (*fml*) wish for (sth); want: *We all desire happiness and health.* ○ *Our holiday was all that could be desired,* ie was entirely satisfactory. ○ *She desires you to come/that you come at once.* ○ *I have long desired to meet them.* **(b)** [Tn] be sexually attracted to (sb): *She desires his young, strong body.* **2** (idm) **leave a lot, etc to be desired** ⇨ LEAVE[1].

desirous /dɪˈzaɪərəs/ *adj* [pred] ~ **of sth/doing sth; ~ that...** (*fml or rhet*) having a wish for (sth); wanting: *desirous of peace* ○ *desirous of restoring relations between our two countries* ○ *desirous that these initiatives should lead to further exchanges.*

desist /dɪˈzɪst/ *v* [I, Ipr] ~ **(from sth/doing sth)** (*fml*) stop sth/doing sth; cease: *I wish he'd desist from entertaining his friends at all hours of the day and night.*

desk /desk/ *n* **1** piece of furniture with a flat or sloping top, often with drawers, at which one can read, write or do business: *an office desk* ○ *children seated at their desks* ○ [attrib] *a desk job.* ⇨ illus at FURNITURE. **2** table or counter in a public building behind which a receptionist, cashier, etc works: *an enquiry/information desk* ○ *leave a message at the desk of the hotel.* **3** office, eg in a newspaper or ministry, that handles a particular matter: *Jefferies is running the sports desk.*

□ **ˈdesk clerk** (*US*) = CLERK 3.

ˈdesk-top /-tɒp/ *n* top of a desk: [attrib] *a desk-top computer,* ie one that fits on a desk ○ [attrib] *desk-top publishing,* ie using a microcomputer and (esp a laser) printer to produce high-quality printed material.

desolate /ˈdesələt/ *adj* **1** (of a place) deserted and miserable: *a desolate industrial landscape* ○ *a desolate, windswept moorland area.* **2** miserable and without friends; lonely and sad: *a desolate person, life, existence* ○ *We all felt absolutely desolate when she left.*

▷ **desolate** /ˈdeseleɪt/ *v* [Tn esp passive] **1** leave (a place) ruined and deserted: *a city desolated by civil strife.* **2** make (sb) sad and hopeless: *a family desolated by the loss of a child.*

desolately *adv.*

desolation /ˌdesəˈleɪʃn/ *n* [U] **1** desolating or being desolated (DESOLATE *v* 1): *the desolation caused by war.* **2** misery; loneliness: *her utter desolation when she heard the bad news.*

despair /dɪˈspeə(r)/ *n* **1** [U] state of having lost all hope: *Your stupidity will drive me to* (ie make me feel) *despair.* ○ *He gave up the struggle in despair.* ○ *She was overcome by despair.* ○ *his despair of ever seeing his family again.* **2** (idm) **be the despair of sb** make sb give up hope: *Your son is the despair of all his teachers,* ie They no longer expect to be able to teach him anything. **a counsel of despair** ⇨ COUNSEL.

▷ **despair** *v* [I, Ipr] ~ **(of sb/sth)** (*fml*) have lost all hope (esp that sb/sth will improve): *despair of success/of ever succeeding* ○ *We've despaired of him; he can't keep a job for more than six months.*

despairing /dɪˈspeərɪŋ/ *adj* showing despair: *a despairing look/gesture.* **despairingly** *adv*: *look despairingly at the judge.*

despatch /dɪˈspætʃ/ *n, v* = DISPATCH.

desperado /ˌdespəˈrɑːdəʊ/ *n* (*pl* ~**es**; *US* also ~**s**) (*dated*) man who commits dangerous, esp criminal, acts without worrying about himself or other people: *the desperadoes who robbed the mail-train.*

desperate /ˈdespərət/ *adj* **1** feeling or showing great despair and ready to do anything regardless of danger: *The prisoners grew more desperate.* ○ *She wrote me a desperate letter.* **2** [attrib] violent and sometimes against the law: *a desperate criminal, act, robbery.* **3** [usu pred] ~ **(for sth/to do sth)** in great need (of sth/to do sth): *They're desperate for money.* ○ (*infml*) *Have you got some water? I'm desperate (for a drink).* ○ *I'm desperate to see her.* **4** extremely serious or dangerous: *a desperate situation, shortage, illness* ○ *The state of the country is desperate.* **5** [usu attrib] giving little hope of success; tried when all else has failed: *a desperate remedy, measure, etc.*

▷ **desperately** *adv.*

desperation /ˌdespəˈreɪʃn/ *n* [U] state of being desperate(1, 3): *driven to desperation* ○ *In desperation I pleaded with the attackers.*

despicable /dɪˈspɪkəbl, *rarely* ˈdespɪkəbl/ *adj* ~ **(of sb) (to do sth)** deserving to be despised; contemptible: *a despicable action, gesture* ○ *a despicable rogue.* ▷ **despicably** /-əblɪ/ *adv*: *behave despicably.*

despise /dɪˈspaɪz/ *v* [Tn, Tn·pr] ~ **sb/sth (for sth)** feel contempt for sb/sth; consider sb/sth as worthless: *despise his hypocrisy, meanness, conceit, etc* ○ *Strike-breakers are often despised by their workmates.*

despite /dɪˈspaɪt/ *prep* without being affected by (the factors mentioned): *They had a wonderful holiday, despite the bad weather.* ○ *Despite wanting to see him again, she refused to reply to his letters.* ○ *Despite what others say, I think he's a very nice chap.* Cf IN SPITE OF (SPITE).

despoil /dɪˈspɔɪl/ *v* [Tn, Tn·pr] ~ **sth (of sth)** (*fml*) rob (a place) of sth valuable; plunder sth: *Museums have despoiled India of many priceless treasures.*

despondent /dɪˈspɒndənt/ *adj* ~ **(about sth)** having or showing loss of hope; wretched: *a despondent loser, mood, look* ○ *Don't be so despondent.*

▷ **despondency** /dɪˈspɒndənsɪ/ *n* [U] loss of hope; misery: *her despondency about having no job.*

despondently *adv.*

despot /ˈdespɒt/ *n* ruler with unlimited powers, esp a cruel and oppressive one; tyrant: *an enlightened despot.*

▷ **despotic** /dɪˈspɒtɪk/ *adj* of or like a despot: *a despotic headmaster.* **despotically** /-klɪ/ *adv.*

despotism /ˈdespətɪzəm/ *n* [U] rule of a despot; tyranny.

dessert /dɪˈzɜːt/ (also **sweet**) *n* **(a)** [C] any sweet dish (eg pie, tart, ice-cream) eaten at the end of a meal: *a pineapple dessert.* Cf AFTERS, PUDDING 1. **(b)** [U] course in which this dish is served: *Shall we move on to dessert?* ○ [attrib] *a dessert apple, wine, etc,* ie served with or for dessert.

□ **deˈssert-spoon** *n* **(a)** medium-sized spoon. ⇨ illus at SPOON. **(b)** (also **deˈssert-spoonful**) /-fʊl/ amount held by this.

destination /ˌdestɪˈneɪʃn/ *n* place to which sb/sth is going or being sent: *Tokyo was our final destination.* ○ *arrive at/reach one's destination.*

destined /ˈdestɪnd/ *adj* [pred] (*fml*) **1** ~ **for sth/to do sth; be ~ that...** having a future which has been decided or planned beforehand: *Coming from a theatrical family, I was destined for a career on the stage,* ie I was expected to be an actor. ○ *They were destined never to meet again,* ie Fate had decided they should not meet again. ○ *It was destined that they would marry.* **2** ~ **for...** on the way to (a place): *a letter, a traveller, an aircraft destined for London.*

destiny /ˈdestɪnɪ/ *n* **1** [U] power believed to control events: *Destiny drew us together.* **2** [C] that which happens to sb/sth (thought to be decided beforehand by fate): *It was his destiny to die in a foreign country.* ○ *events which shaped his destiny.*

destitute /ˈdestɪtjuːt; *US* -tuːt/ *adj* **1** without money, food, etc and other things necessary for life; impoverished: *When he died, his family was left destitute.* **2** [pred] ~ **of sth** (*fml*) lacking sth: *officials who are destitute of ordinary human feelings.*

▷ **destitution** /ˌdestɪˈtjuːʃn; *US* -ˈtuːʃn/ *n* [U] being destitute: *live in complete destitution.*

destroy /dɪˈstrɔɪ/ *v* **1** [Tn] damage (sth) so badly that it no longer exists, works, etc; wreck: *a house destroyed by bombs, fire, explosion* ○ *Vandals destroyed the bus.* ○ *They've destroyed all the evidence.* ○ (*fig*) *destroy sb's hopes, career, reputation.* **2** [Tn esp passive] kill (a dog, horse, etc) deliberately, usu because it is sick or unwanted: *The injured dog had to be destroyed.*

▷ **destroyer** *n* **1** (*fml*) person or thing that destroys: *Death, the destroyer.* **2** small fast warship for protecting larger warships or convoys of merchant ships.

destruct /dɪˈstrʌkt/ *v* (*esp US*) **(a)** [Tn] destroy (esp a rocket one has launched) because it is not working properly. **(b)** [I] (esp of a rocket) be destroyed because it is not working properly.

▷ **destruct** *n* [U] (*esp US*) destruction of a faulty rocket.

destructible /dɪˈstrʌktəbl/ *adj* that can be destroyed. ▷ **destructibility** /dɪˌstrʌktəˈbɪlətɪ/ *n* [U].

destruction /dɪˈstrʌkʃn/ *n* [U] **(a)** destroying or being destroyed: *the total destruction of a town by an earthquake.* **(b)** person or thing that destroys or ruins: *Gambling was his destruction.*

destructive /dɪˈstrʌktɪv/ *adj* **(a)** causing destruction or serious damage: *the destructive force of the storm.* **(b)** wanting or tending to destroy: *destructive urges* ○ *Are all small children so destructive?* ○ *destructive criticism,* ie making no positive suggestions for improvement. ▷ **destructively** *adv.* **destructiveness** *n* [U].

desuetude /dɪˈsjuːɪtjuːd; *US* -tuːd/ *n* (idm) **fall into deˈsuetude** (*fml*) cease being used: *customs, fashions, words that have fallen into desuetude.*

desultory /ˈdesəltrɪ; *US* -tɔːrɪ/ *adj* going from one thing to another, without a definite plan or purpose; unmethodical: *desultory reading, work* ○ *desultory attempts to help.* ▷ **desultorily** *adv.* **desultoriness** *n* [U].

Det *abbr* Detective: *Det Supt* (ie Superintendent) *(John) Williams* ○ *Det Insp* (ie Inspector) *(Tim) Cox.*

detach /dɪˈtætʃ/ *v* **1** [Tn, Tn·pr] ~ **sth (from sth)** unfasten sth from sth; disconnect sth: *detach a link from a chain* ○ *a coach detached from a train.* Cf ATTACH 1. **2** [Tn, Tn·pr] ~ **sb/sth (from sth)** (*military*) send (a group of soldiers, ships, etc) away from the main force, esp to do special duties: *A number of men were detached to guard the right flank.*

▷ **detached** *adj* **1 (a)** not influenced by others; impartial: *a detached mind, assessment, judgement, etc* ○ *take a detached view of sth.* **(b)** not feeling emotional or involved: *her detached response to the crisis.* **2** (of a house) not joined to another on either side. ⇨ illus at HOME.

detachable /-əbl/ *adj* that can be detached: *a detachable lining in a coat.*

detachment /dɪˈtætʃmənt/ *n* **1** [U] detaching or being detached: *the detachment of units from the main force.* **2** [U] **(a)** state of being not influenced by others: *show detachment in one's judgements.* **(b)** lack of emotion; indifference: *He answered with an air of detachment.* **3** [C] group of soldiers, ships, etc sent away from a larger group, esp to do special duties: *a detachment of signallers.*

detail[1] /ˈdiːteɪl; *US* dɪˈteɪl/ *n* **1** [C] small, particular fact or item: *Please give me all the details.* ○ *I checked every detail of her research.* ○ *The details of the costume were totally authentic.* ○ *Spare me the details!* ie Don't provide any. **2** [U] **(a)** small, particular aspects of sth: *A good organizer pays attention to detail.* ○ *a novelist with an eye for detail,* eg who includes many small, realistic facts. **(b)** smaller or less important parts of a picture, pattern, etc: *The overall composition of the picture is good but some of the detail is distracting.* **3** [C] (*military*) group of soldiers given special duties: *the cookhouse detail.* **4** (idm) **go into ˈdetail(s)** speak or write about all aspects of sth: *He refused to go into details about his plans.* **in ˈdetail** discussing all facts or items fully: *to explain/describe sth in detail.*

detail[2] /ˈdiːteɪl; *US* dɪˈteɪl/ *v* **1** [Tn, Dn·pr] ~ **sth (to/for sb)** list sth fully, item by item; describe sth fully (to/for sb): *The computer's features are detailed in our brochure.* ○ *an inventory detailing all the goods in a shop* ○ *I detailed our plans to her.* **2** [Tn, Tn·pr, Dn·t] ~ **sb (for sth)** choose or appoint sb for special duties: *detail soldiers for guard duty/to guard a bridge.*

▷ **detailed** *adj* having many details or paying great attention to details; thorough: *a detailed description, account, analysis, etc.*

detain /dɪˈteɪn/ *v* [Tn] **1** prevent (sb) from leaving or doing sth; delay: *She was detained in the office by unexpected callers.* ○ *This question need not detain us long,* ie can be settled quickly. **2** keep (sb) in custody; lock up: *The police detained him for questioning.*

▷ **detainee** /ˌdiːteɪˈniː/ *n* person who is detained (by police, etc, eg sb suspected of a violent crime, terrorism, etc).

detect /dɪˈtekt/ *v* [Tn] **(a)** discover or recognize that (sth) is present: *The dentist could detect no decay in her teeth.* ○ *instruments that can detect minute amounts of radiation* ○ *Do I detect a note of irony in your voice?* **(b)** investigate and solve (crime, etc): *This police officer's job is to detect fraud.*

▷ **detector** *n* device for detecting changes in pressure or temperature, metals, explosives, etc.

detection /dɪˈtekʃn/ *n* [U] detecting; discovering: *the detection of radioactivity* ○ *the detection of crime* ○ *try to escape detection by disguising oneself.*

detective /dɪˈtektɪv/ *n* person, esp a police officer, whose job is to investigate and solve crimes: *employ a private detective.*

□ **deˈtective story, deˈtective novel** story in which the main interest is a puzzling crime and the process of solving it.

The detective has become familiar to the British through the stories of various writers. The best known detectives in British fiction are Sir Arthur Conan *Doyle's Sherlock *Holmes, and Agatha *Christie's Hercule *Poirot. The fictional detective evolved into a stereotype of a shrewd, rather eccentric person who, having searched for clues, often with the aid of a magnifying glass, discovers the identity of the culprit (usually a murderer) by a brilliant process of deduction. Familiar ingredients of the English detective story are a rural setting, a related or closed circle of suspects, the discovery of a corpse at the beginning, and a surprise solution at the end. Detective stories are known collectively as 'crime fiction' and informally as 'whodunits'.

détente /ˌdeɪˈtɑːnt/ *n* [U] *(French)* lessening of dangerous tension, esp between countries.

detention /dɪˈtenʃn/ *n* [U] **(a)** detaining or being detained, esp in prison: *detention without trial.* **(b)** punishment of being kept at school after it has closed: *be given two hours' detention.*

□ **deˈtention centre** place where young offenders are kept in detention for a short time.

deter /dɪˈtɜː(r)/ *v* **(-rr-)** [Tn, Tn·pr] ~ **sb (from doing sth)** make sb decide not to do sth: *Failure did not deter him (from making another attempt).* ○ *I was deterred from emigrating by the thought of leaving my family.*

detergent /dɪˈtɜːdʒənt/ *n* [U, C], *adj* (substance) that removes dirt, eg from the surface of clothes or dishes: *Most synthetic detergents are in the form of powder or liquid.*

deteriorate /dɪˈtɪərɪəreɪt/ *v* [I, Ipr] ~ **(into sth)** become worse in quality or condition: *Leather can deteriorate in damp conditions.* ○ *The discussion deteriorated into a bitter quarrel.* ▷ **deterioration** /dɪˌtɪərɪəˈreɪʃn/ *n* [U]: *a deterioration in superpower relations.*

determinant /dɪˈtɜːmɪnənt/ *n, adj (fml)* (thing) that determines or decides how or if sth happens: *The main determinant of economic success is our ability to control inflation.*

determinate /dɪˈtɜːmɪnət/ *adj (fml)* limited in range or scope; definite.

determination /dɪˌtɜːmɪˈneɪʃn/ *n* [U] **1** ~ **(to do sth)** quality of being firmly committed to doing sth; resoluteness: *a leader with courage and determination* ○ *with an air of determination,* ie showing this quality ○ *her dogged determination to learn English.* **2** precise fixing (of sth); deciding: *the determination of future policy.* **3** finding out (of an amount, a quality, etc); calculation: *the determination of a ship's position/the exact composition of a substance.*

determinative /dɪˈtɜːmɪnətɪv; *US* -neɪtɪv/ *adj (fml)* having the power to determine or limit sth: *a determinative factor in his psychological development.*

▷ **determinative** *n* thing having the power to determine or limit sth.

determine /dɪˈtɜːmɪn/ *v* **1** [Tn, Tw] *(fml)* fix (sth) precisely; decide: *determine a date for a meeting* ○ *His future has not been determined, but he may study medicine.* ○ *She will determine how it is to be done.* **2** [Tn, Tw] *(fml)* find out (sth that is not known); calculate: *determine the meaning of a word/what a word means* ○ *determine exactly what happened* ○ *determine the speed of light, how high a mountain is.* **3** [Ipr, Tf, Tw, Tt] ~ **on/upon sth** decide firmly that sth will be done; make up one's mind about sth; resolve: *We determined on an early start/(that) we'd make an early start.* ○ *determine on proving/to prove sb's innocence* ○ *They have determined where the new school will be built.* ○ *He determined to learn Greek.* **4** [Tn·pr] ~ **sb against sth** *(fml)* make sb decide not to do sth: *That determined her against leaving home.* **5** [Tn] decisively influence (sth); fix: *Do heredity and environment determine one's character?* ○ *The exam results could determine your career.*

▷ **determined** /dɪˈtɜːmɪnd/ *adj* ~ **(to do sth)** with one's mind firmly made up; resolute: *a determined fighter, look, attitude* ○ *I'm determined to succeed.*

determiner /dɪˈtɜːmɪnə(r)/ *n (grammar)* word, eg *the, some, my,* that comes before a noun to show how the noun is being used.

determinism /dɪˈtɜːmɪnɪzəm/ *n* [U] *(philosophy)* belief that one is not free to choose the sort of person one wants to be, or how one behaves, because these things are decided by one's background, surroundings, etc.

deterrent /dɪˈterənt; *US* -ˈtɜː-/ *n, adj* (thing) that deters or is meant to deter: *His punishment will be a deterrent to others.* ○ *deterrent weapons, measures.*

▷ **deterrence** /dɪˈterəns; *US* -ˈtɜː-/ *n* [U] action of deterring: *nuclear deterrence,* ie (a policy of) having nuclear weapons in order to make an enemy too frightened to attack.

detest /dɪˈtest/ *v* [Tn, Tg, Tsg] dislike (sb/sth) very much; hate: *detest dogs* ○ *detest having to get up early* ○ *I detest people complaining.*

▷ **detestable** /-əbl/ *adj* that one hates; hateful: *a detestable habit.* **detestably** /-əblɪ/ *adv.*

detestation /ˌdiːteˈsteɪʃn/ *n* [U] strong dislike; hatred.

dethrone /ˌdiːˈθrəʊn/ *v* [Tn] **(a)** remove (a ruler) from the throne; depose. **(b)** *(fig)* remove (sb) from a position of authority or influence: *a government adviser dethroned by a younger expert.* ▷ **dethronement** *n* [C, U].

detonate /ˈdetəneɪt/ *v* [I, Tn] (cause sth to) explode; (be) set off: *The bomb failed to detonate.* ○ *an explosive charge detonated by remote control.*

▷ **detonation** /ˌdetəˈneɪʃn/ *n* [C, U] explosion.

detonator /ˈdetəneɪtə(r)/ *n* part of a bomb, etc that explodes first, setting off the full explosion.

detour /ˈdiːtʊə(r); *US* dɪˈtʊər/ *n (esp US)* route that avoids a blocked road, etc; deviation: *We had to make a detour round the floods.* Cf DIVERSION.

▷ **detour** *v* [I, Tn] avoid (sth) by making a detour: *We had to detour a road-block.*

detoxify /ˌdiːˈtɒksɪfaɪ/ *v (pt, pp* **-fied)** [Tn] remove poison or harmful substances from (sb/sth): *detoxify the bloodstream.*

▷ **detoxification** /ˌdiːˌtɒksɪfɪˈkeɪʃn/ *n* [U] action of removing poison or harmful substances, eg addictive drugs: [attrib] *a detoxification centre,* ie where drug addicts or alcoholics are treated.

detract /dɪˈtrækt/ *v* [Ipr] ~ **from sth** make sth seem less valuable or important: *detract from the merit, value, worth, excellence, etc of sth* ○ *criticism that detracts from her achievements* ○ *This unpleasant incident detracted from our enjoyment of the evening.*

▷ **detraction** /dɪˈtrækʃn/ *n* [U] unfair criticism of sb/sth; belittling.

detractor *n* person who criticizes sb/sth unfairly: *The scheme is better than its detractors suggest.*

detrain /ˌdiːˈtreɪn/ *v* [I, Tn] *(fml)* leave or cause (sb) to leave a railway train: *The troops detrained near the battle zone.*

detribalize, -ise /ˌdiːˈtraɪbəlaɪz/ *v* [Tn] cause (sb) to abandon tribal customs; end tribal organization in (a society): *detribalized Indians in South America.* ▷ **detribalization, -isation** /ˌdiːˌtraɪbəlaɪˈzeɪʃn; *US* -lɪˈz-/ *n* [U].

detriment /ˈdetrɪmənt/ *n* (idm) **to the detriment of sb/sth; without detriment to sb/sth** harming/not harming sb/sth: *He works long hours, to the detriment of his health.* ○ *This tax cannot be introduced without detriment to the economy.*

▷ **detrimental** /ˌdetrɪˈmentl/ *adj* ~ **(to sb/sth)** harmful: *The measures had a detrimental effect.* ○ *activities detrimental to our interests.* **detrimentally** /-təlɪ/ *adv*: *detrimentally affected.*

detritus /dɪˈtraɪtəs/ *n* [U] matter such as sand, silt or gravel produced by the wearing away of rocks, etc.

de trop /dəˈtrəʊ/ *adj* [pred] *(French)* not wanted; unwelcome: *Their intimate conversation made me feel de trop.*

Deucalion /djuːˈkeɪlɪən/ (in Greek mythology) the only man on earth who survived a great flood sent by Zeus, chief of the Greek gods. He and his wife Pyrrha, the only female survivor, created a new race of men and women from stones which they threw over their shoulders. Cf NOAH.

deuce[1] /djuːs; *US* duːs/ *n* **1** two on playing-cards or dice (shown as pips and/or numbers). **2** (in tennis) score of 40-all, after which either side must gain two successive points to win the game.

deuce[2] /djuːs; *US* duːs/ *n (dated infml euph)* **1 the deuce** [sing] (used as an expression of annoyance): *The deuce! I've lost my keys!* ○ *Who/What/Where the deuce is that?* ○ *What the deuce is going on?* **2** (idm) **the deuce of a sth** a very bad case of sth: *I've got the deuce of a headache.*

▷ **deuced** /djuːst, ˈdjuːsɪd; *US* duːst/ *adj* (used as an expression of annoyance): *Where's that deuced boy?* — *adv* very: *What deuced bad luck!* **deucedly** /ˈdjuːsɪdlɪ; *US* ˈduː-/ *adv* very.

deus ex machina /ˌdeɪəs eks ˈmækɪnə/ *(Latin)* sudden unexpected arrival or event that solves a serious difficulty, esp in a play or story.

deuterium /djuːˈtɪərɪəm; *US* duːˈtɪrɪəm/ *n* [U] heavy form of hydrogen used in nuclear weapons and nuclear reactors.

Deuteronomy /ˌdjuːtəˈrɒnəmɪ/ fifth book of the Old Testament, in which the Mosaic Law is repeated, with additional comments. ⇨ App 5.

Deutschmark /ˈdɔɪtʃmɑːk/ *n (abbr* **DM)** unit of currency in Germany.

de Valera /də vəˈleərə/ Eamon (1882-1975), Irish statesman. One of the leaders of the 1916 uprising which led to independence from Britain, he later became president of the Irish Republic, having also served three times as prime minister.

devalue /ˌdiːˈvæljuː/ *v* [Tn] **(a)** reduce the value of (a currency) in relation to other currencies or gold: *devalue the dollar, pound, mark, etc.* **(b)** reduce the value or worth of (sth): *criticism that devalues our work.*

▷ **devaluation** /ˌdiːvæljʊˈeɪʃn/ *n* [C, U] (instance of) reducing a currency to a lower fixed value: *There's been a further devaluation of the dollar.*

Devanagari /ˌdeɪvəˈnɑːgərɪ/ *n* [U] writing system used for Sanskrit, Hindi and other Indian languages.

devastate /ˈdevəsteɪt/ *v* [Tn] **(a)** completely destroy (sth); ruin: *a house devastated by a bomb* ○ *War devastated the country.* **(b)** *(infml)* shock (sb); overwhelm: *She was devastated by his death.* ○ *I was devastated by the news of the crash.*

▷ **devastating** /ˈdevəsteɪtɪŋ/ *adj* **1** very destructive: *a devastating war, famine, storm, etc.* **2** causing severe shock: *devastating criticism, news.* **3** *(fig infml)* striking; impressive: *devastating wit* ○ *She looked devastating,* ie very beautiful. **devastatingly** *adv.*

devastation /ˌdevəˈsteɪʃn/ *n* [U] devastating or being devastated: *complete, utter devastation.*

develop /dɪˈveləp/ *v* **1** [I, Ipr, Tn, Tn·pr] ~ **(sb/sth) (from sth) (into sth)** (cause sb/sth to) grow gradually; become or make more mature, advanced or organized: *The child is developing well.* ○ *The plot for the novel gradually developed in my mind.* ○ *The argument developed into a bitter quarrel.* ○ *We've developed the project from an* *original idea by Stephen.* ○ *The place has developed from a fishing port into a thriving tourist centre.* **2** [I, Tn] (cause sth to) become noticeable, visible or active: *Symptoms of malaria developed,* ie appeared. ○ *The car has developed signs of rust,* ie is becoming rusty. **3** (*photography*) **(a)** [Tn] treat (an exposed film) with chemicals so that the picture can be seen: *take a film to be developed.* **(b)** [I] (of the image on an exposed film or plate) become visible. **4** [Tn] use (land) for the building of houses, etc and so increase its value: *The site is being developed by a London property company.*

▷ **developed** *adj* **1** advanced; mature: *a highly developed system of agriculture* ○ *She is well developed for her age.* **2** (*economics*) (of a country, an area, etc) with a highly organized economy: *one of the less developed countries.*

developer *n* **1** (*photography*) substance used to develop films. **2** person or company that develops land.

developing *adj* trying to become economically advanced: *a developing country* ○ *the developing world.*

development /dɪˈveləpmənt/ *n* **1** [U] developing or being developed (DEVELOP 1, 2, 3, 4): *the healthy development of children* ○ *encourage the development of small businesses* ○ *land that is ready for development,* ie ready to be built on. **2** [C] **(a)** new stage or event: *the latest development in the continuing crisis* ○ *We must await further developments.* **(b)** new product or invention: *Our electrically-powered car is an exciting new development.* **3** [C] piece of land with new buildings on it: *a commercial development on the outskirts of the town.*

□ **deˈvelopment area** (*Brit*) poor area where new industries are encouraged in order to create jobs.

deviant /ˈdiːvɪənt/ *n, adj* (*often derog*) (person who is) different in moral or social standards from what is considered normal: *a sexual deviant who assaults children* ○ *deviant behaviour.*

▷ **deviance** /-vɪəns/, **deviancy** *ns* [U] deviant tendencies or behaviour.

deviate /ˈdiːvɪeɪt/ *v* [Ipr] ~ **from sth** stop following (a course, standard, etc): *The plane deviated from its usual route.* ○ *I will never deviate from what I believe to be right.* ○ *deviate from one's plan, the norm, the accepted procedure, etc.*

deviation /ˌdiːvɪˈeɪʃn/ *n* ~ **(from sth) 1 (a)** [U] not following the normal or expected course, plan, etc; deviating: *There was little deviation from his usual routine.* ○ *sexual deviation.* **(b)** [C] instance of this: *a deviation from the rules.* **2** [U] (*politics*) moving away from the beliefs held by the group to which one belongs: *Party ideologists accused her of deviation.* **3** [C] difference between a numerical value and a norm or average: *a compass deviation of 5°,* ie from true north.

▷ **deviationism** /-ʃənɪzəm/ *n* [U] practice of political deviation.

deviationist /-ʃənɪst/ *n.*

device /dɪˈvaɪs/ *n* **1** thing made or adapted for a special purpose: *a device for measuring pressure* ○ *a labour-saving device* ○ *an explosive device* ○ *a nuclear device,* eg a nuclear bomb or missile. ⇨ Usage at MACHINE. **2** (*literature*) metaphor, combination of words, etc used by a writer to produce an effect on the reader: *a stylistic device.* **3** scheme; trick: *Her illness is merely a device to avoid seeing him.* **4** symbol or figure used as a sign by a noble family, eg on a crest or shield: *a heraldic device.* **5** (idm) **leave sb to his own devices** ⇨ LEAVE[1].

devil[1] /ˈdevl/ *n* **1 (a) the Devil** supreme evil being; Satan: *The Devil tempted Adam and Eve.* **(b)** wicked spirit: *He believes in devils and witches.* **2** (*infml*) **(a)** wicked or mischievous person: *My niece is a little devil.* ○ *He's a devil with* (ie flirts with) *the ladies.* **(b)** (used for emphasis) person: *The poor/lucky devil!* ○ *Which silly devil left the fire on all day?* **3** (idm) **be a ˈdevil** (*infml joc*) used to encourage sb to do sth he is hesitating to do: *Go on, be a devil — tell me what they said.* **better the devil you know** ⇨ BETTER[2]. **between the ˌdevil and the ˌdeep (blue) ˈsea** in a situation where there are two equally unacceptable alternatives. **bring out the ˈdevil in sb** (*infml*) make sb reckless or mischievous. **the devil** (used for emphasis in questions): *What/Who/Why/Where the devil is that?* **the (very) ˈdevil** (sth) difficult or unpleasant: *This job is the very devil.* ○ *These pans are the (very) devil to clean.* **the ˌdevil has all the best ˈtunes** (*saying*) wicked or forbidden pleasures are the most enjoyable (and this seems unfair). **the ˌdevil looks ˌafter his ˈown** (*saying*) success comes to those who deserve it least. **the ˌdevil makes ˌwork for ˌidle ˈhands** (*saying*) when people do not have enough work to do, they get into or make trouble. **a devil of a (sth)** (*dated infml*) (used for emphasis) very remarkable, difficult, awkward, etc thing or person: *a devil of a pretty woman.* **(a/the) devil's ˈadvocate** person who speaks against sb or sth simply to encourage discussion: *I don't really believe in capital punishment, I'm just playing the devil's advocate.* **the ˌdevil's ˌown ˈluck** (also **the ˌluck of the ˈdevil**) very good luck. **the devil take the ˈhindmost** everybody should look after himself and not care about others: *In this business you have to be tough, and the devil take the hindmost.* **the ˈdevil you will/won't, she can/can't, etc** (*infml*) (used to emphasize a statement of refusal, an expression of surprise, etc): *'I'm going to a party.' 'The devil you are!',* ie I forbid it. **give the devil his ˈdue** admit that sb whom one generally disapproves of has at least one good feature. **ˌgo to the ˈdevil!** (*dated*) damn you! **have a/the devil of a job/the devil's own job doing sth** (*infml*) find sth very difficult: *I'm having a devil of a job fixing my car.* **like the ˈdevil** (*infml*) very hard, intensively, etc: *run, work like the devil.* **needs must when the devil drives** ⇨ NEEDS (NEED[3]). **play the devil with sth** (*infml*) harm or make sth worse: *Cold weather plays the devil with my rheumatism.* **speak/talk of the ˈdevil** (*saying infml*) (said when sb one has been talking about appears). **there'll be the ˈdevil to pay** (*infml*) there will be trouble as the result of sth: *There'll be the devil to pay if you scratch my car!* **the world, the flesh and the devil** ⇨ WORLD.

□ **ˌdevil-may-ˈcare** *adj* [esp attrib] reckless.

devil[2] /ˈdevl/ *v* (-ll-; *US* -l-) **1** [Tn] grill (sth) with mustard, curry, etc: *devilled kidneys/ham/turkey.* **2** [I, Ipr] ~ **(for sb)** (*Brit*) work as an assistant to (a barrister). **3** [Tn] (*US*) annoy or tease (sb).

devilish /ˈdevəlɪʃ/ *adj* wicked; cruel: *a devilish plan* ○ *devilish cunning.*

▷ **devilish** *adv* (*dated infml*) very: *devilish hot.*

devilishly *adv*: *devilishly cruel, cunning, etc.*

devilishness *n* [U].

devilment /ˈdevlmənt/ (also **devilry** /ˈdevlrɪ/) *n* **1** [U] high spirits; mischief: *She played a trick on him out of sheer devilment.* **2** [C] mischievous act: *She's up to some devilry or other.*

devious /ˈdiːvɪəs/ *adj* **1** cunning; dishonest: *a devious lawyer, scheme, trick* ○ *get rich by devious means.* **2** (of a route, path, etc) winding; not straight: *The coach followed a rather devious course to its destination.* ▷ **deviously** *adv.* **deviousness** *n* [U].

devise /dɪˈvaɪz/ *v* [Tn] **1** think out (a plan, system, tool, etc); invent: *devise a scheme for redeveloping the city centre* ○ *devise a new type of transistor.* **2** (*law*) leave (property) to sb in one's will.

devitalize, -ise /ˌdiːˈvaɪtəlaɪz/ *n* [Tn] take strength and vigour away from (sb/sth): *a nation devitalized by a sustained war effort.* ▷ **devitalization, -isation** /ˌdiːˌvaɪtəlaɪˈzeɪʃn; *US* -lɪˈz-/ *n* [U].

devoid /dɪˈvɔɪd/ *adj* [pred] ~ **of sth** without sth; completely lacking in sth: *a criminal utterly devoid of conscience.*

devolution /ˌdiːvəˈluːʃn; *US* ˌdev-/ *n* [U] transfer of power or authority, esp from central government to regional authorities.

devolve /dɪˈvɒlv/ *v* (*fml*) **1** [Ipr] ~ **on/upon sb** (of work, duties) be transferred or passed to sb: *When the President is ill, his duties devolve upon the Vice-President.* **2** [Tn, Tn·pr] ~ **sth (to/upon sb)** transfer (work, duties, etc) to sb: *More power is to be devolved to regional government.*

Devon /ˈdevən/ (also **Devonshire** /ˈdevənʃə(r)/) county of SW England. Much of it is occupied by the high open treeless country of *Dartmoor and Exmoor. The coast has several holiday resorts. ⇨ map at App.

□ **ˌDevonshire ˈcream** = CLOTTED CREAM (CLOT): [attrib] *Devonshire cream teas,* ie afternoon meals, typically served in Devon, with scones, Devonshire cream and jam.

Devonian /dɪˈvəʊnɪən/ *adj* of the period in the earth's history between about 408 and 360 million years ago, in which fish became widespread and the first forests appeared.

devote /dɪˈvəʊt/ *v* [Tn·pr] ~ **oneself/sth to sb/sth** give (one's time, energy, etc) to sb/sth; dedicate: *devote oneself to a noble cause* ○ *devote all one's efforts to one's task.*

▷ **devoted** *adj* ~ **(to sb/sth)** very loving or loyal: *a devoted son, friend, supporter, etc* ○ *She is devoted to her children.* **devotedly** *adv.*

devotee /ˌdevəˈtiː/ *n* **(a)** person who is devoted to sth; enthusiast: *a devotee of sport, music, crime fiction, etc.* **(b)** zealous supporter (of a sect, etc).

devotion /dɪˈvəʊʃn/ *n* **1** [U] ~ **(to sb/sth) (a)** deep strong love: *a mother's devotion to her children.* **(b)** giving of oneself (to a person, cause, etc); loyalty: *devotion to duty* ○ *a teacher's devotion to her task* ○ *our devotion to our leader.* **2 (a)** [U] religious zeal; devoutness: *a life of great devotion.* **(b)** [C] prayer or religious practice: *a traditional devotion like the Way of the Cross* ○ *a priest at his devotions,* ie praying.

▷ **devotional** /-ʃənl/ *adj* of or used in religious worship: *devotional literature.*

devour /dɪˈvaʊə(r)/ *v* **1** [Tn] **(a)** eat (sth) hungrily or greedily: *devour the food ravenously.* **(b)** (*fig*) look at (sb/sth) avidly: *She devoured the new detective story.* ○ *He devoured her with his eyes,* ie looked at her lustfully. **(c)** (*fig*) destroy (sth): *Fire devoured a huge area of forest.* **2** (idm) **be devoured by sth** be filled with (curiosity, anxiety, etc).

devout /dɪˈvaʊt/ *adj* **1** sincerely religious; pious: *a devout Muslim, prayer.* **2** sincere; deeply felt: *a devout hope, wish, etc.* ▷ **devoutly** *adv*: *It is devoutly to be wished,* ie something I hope very much will happen. **devoutness** *n* [U].

dew /djuː; *US* duː/ *n* [U] tiny drops of moisture condensed on cool surfaces from water vapour in the air, esp at night: *The grass was wet with dew.*

▷ **dewy** *adj* wet with dew. **ˌdewy-ˈeyed** *adj* naive and trusting: *You can't be too dewy-eyed if you want to succeed.*

□ **ˈdew-claw** *n* small claw just above the foot in dogs and some other animals.

ˈdewdrop *n* drop of dew.

ˈdew-pond *n* (*Brit*) shallow pool of water, usu man-made, found esp in the chalk hills (downs) in S England and once thought to be fed by dew.

dewlap /ˈdjuːlæp; *US* ˈduː-/ *n* fold of loose skin hanging down from the throat of an animal such as a cow or an ox.

dexterity /dekˈsterətɪ/ *n* [U] skill, esp in using one's hands: *A juggler needs great dexterity.* ○ (*fig*) *The negotiations will call for considerable dexterity.*

dexterous (also **dextrous**) /ˈdekstrəs/ *adj* **(a)** skilful with one's hands: *She's very dexterous with the knitting needles.* **(b)** skilfully performed: *a dextrous movement.* ▷ **dexterously** (also **dextrously**) *adv.*

dextrose /ˈdekstrəʊs, -əʊz/ *n* [U] form of glucose.

DG /ˌdiː ˈdʒiː/ *abbr* **1** (on coins) by the grace of God (Latin *Dei Gratia*). **2** thanks be to God (Latin *Deo Gratias*). **3** director-general.

dharma /ˈdɑːmə/ *n* [U] (in Hinduism and Buddhism) the eternal law of the universe, which forms a guide for right conduct.

dhoti /ˈdəʊtɪ/ *n* loincloth worn by male Hindus.

dhow /daʊ/ *n* ship with one mast used along the coasts of Arab countries.

DHSS /ˌdiː eɪtʃ es ˈes/ *abbr* (*Brit*) Department of Health and Social Security.

di- *pref* **1** (with *ns*) two; double: *dicotyledon.*

2 (*chemistry*) (with *ns* in names of chemical compounds) containing two atoms or groups of the specified type: *dioxide* ○ *dichromate*. Cf BI-, TRI-.

diabetes /ˌdaɪəˈbi:ti:z/ *n* [U] disease of the pancreas which prevents sugar and starch being properly absorbed.

diabetic /ˌdaɪəˈbetɪk/ *adj* of diabetes.
▷ **diabetic** *n* person suffering from diabetes.

diabolic /ˌdaɪəˈbɒlɪk/ *adj* **(a)** of or like a devil. **(b)** clever and evil; wicked: *diabolic plan, trick, etc* ○ *diabolic cunning*.
▷ **diabolical** /-lɪkl/ *adj* **1** = DIABOLIC. **2** (*Brit infml*) very bad: *The film was diabolical.* ○ *a diabolical liberty*, ie an act that one resents very much. **diabolically** /-klɪ/ *adv*.

diachronic /ˌdaɪəˈkrɒnɪk/ *adj* of or describing the historical development of sth, esp language. Cf SYNCHRONIC.

diacritic /ˌdaɪəˈkrɪtɪk/ (also **diacritical** /-kl/) *adj* [attrib] of a mark (eg ´ ` ¨) placed above or below a written or printed letter to indicate different sounds.
▷ **diacritic** *n* diacritic mark (eg an accent, a diaeresis or a cedilla).

diadem /ˈdaɪədem/ *n* crown, worn as a sign of royal power.

diaeresis (also **dieresis**) /daɪˈerəsɪs/ *n* (*pl* **-eses** /-əsi:z/) mark (eg as in *naïve*) placed over a vowel to show that it is sounded separately from the vowel before it. Cf UMLAUT.

diagnose /ˈdaɪəgnəʊz; *US* ˌdaɪəgˈnəʊs/ *v* [Tn, Cn·n/a] ~ **sth (as sth)** find out the nature of (esp an illness) by observing its symptoms: *The doctor diagnosed measles.* ○ *diagnosed the tumour as benign* ○ *(fig) The book diagnoses our present economic ills*, ie shows what is wrong with the economy.

diagnosis /ˌdaɪəgˈnəʊsɪs/ *n* (*pl* **-noses** /-ˈnəʊsi:z/) **(a)** [U] diagnosing: *make one's diagnosis* ○ *a doctor skilled in diagnosis* ○ *accurate diagnosis of an electrical fault*. Cf PROGNOSIS. **(b)** [C] (statement of the) result of diagnosing.

diagnostic /ˌdaɪəgˈnɒstɪk/ *adj* [usu attrib] of diagnosis: *diagnostic skill, training, etc* ○ *symptoms that were of little diagnostic value*, ie that did not indicate the patient's disease.

diagonal /daɪˈægənl/ *adj* **(a)** crossing a straight-sided figure, eg a rectangle, from corner to corner. ⇨ illus at VERTICAL. **(b)** slanting; oblique: *diagonal stripes*. **(c)** crossed by slanting lines.
▷ **diagonal** *n* straight line crossing a straight-sided figure from corner to corner; slanting line.
diagonally /-nəlɪ/ *adv*.

diagram /ˈdaɪəgræm/ *n* drawing or plan that uses simple lines rather than realistic details to explain or illustrate a machine, structure, process, etc: *a diagram of a gear-box, a rail network.* ▷ **diagrammatic** /ˌdaɪəgrəˈmætɪk/ *adj*: *a diagrammatic map*. **diagrammatically** /-klɪ/ *adv*.

dial /ˈdaɪəl/ *n* **1** face of a clock or watch. **2** similar face or flat plate with a scale and a pointer for measuring weight, volume, pressure, the amount of gas used, etc: *the dial of an electricity meter*. **3** plate or disc, etc on a radio or television set showing the wavelengths or channels. **4 (a)** disc on a telephone that is turned when making a call. **(b)** set of keys on a telephone that are pressed when making a call.
▷ **dial** *v* (-ll-; *US* -l-) [I, Tn] use a telephone dial to call (a number or telephone service): *dial 071-230 1212* ○ *dial the operator*. ˈ**dialling code** numbers for an area or a country that are dialled before the number of the person one wants to speak to: *The dialling code for the central London area is 071.* ˈ**dialling tone** sound heard on the telephone showing that one can begin to dial the number wanted. ⇨ App 9.

dialect /ˈdaɪəlekt/ *n* [C, U] form of a language (grammar, vocabulary and pronunciation) used in a part of a country or by a class of people: *the Yorkshire dialect* ○ *a play written in dialect* ○ [attrib] *dialect words, pronunciations, etc.* Cf ACCENT 3, BROGUE. ▷ **dialectal** /ˌdaɪəˈlektl/ *adj*: *dialectal differences between two areas*.

dialectic /ˌdaɪəˈlektɪk/ *n* [U]) (also **dialectics** [sing *v*]) (*philosophy*) **1** art of discovering and testing truths by discussion and logical argument. **2** criticism that deals with metaphysical contradictions and how to solve them.
▷ **dialectical** /-kl/ *adj* of or relating to dialectic: *dialectical method*. **diaˌlectical maˈterialism** Marxist theory that political and historical events are due to the conflict of social forces caused by man's material needs. **dialectically** /-klɪ/ *adv*. **dialectician** /ˌdaɪəlekˈtɪʃn/ *n* person who is skilled in dialectic.

dialogue (*US* also **dialog**) /ˈdaɪəlɒg; *US* -lɔ:g/ *n* **1 (a)** [U, C] (writing in the form of a) conversation or talk: *Most plays are written in dialogue.* ○ *a novel with long descriptions and little dialogue.* **(b)** [C] conversation, esp in literature, plays and films: *a long dialogue in the opening scene.* **2** [C, U] discussion between people with different opinions: *a useful dialogue on common problems* ○ *More dialogue between world leaders is needed.*

dialysis /daɪˈælɪsɪs/ *n* (*pl* **-lyses** /-lɪsi:z/) [U, C] (*chemistry*) process of separating particles in a substance by means of a membrane which will not allow larger particles to pass through. It is used for artificially removing waste products from the blood of people whose kidneys are defective: *renal dialysis* ○ [attrib] *a dialysis machine*.

diamanté /daɪəˈmæntɪ, dɪəˈmɒnteɪ/ *adj* decorated with powdered crystal or some other sparkling substance: *diamanté ear-rings*.

diameter /daɪˈæmɪtə(r)/ *n* (length of a) straight line connecting the centre of a circle or sphere, or of the base of a cylinder, to two points on its sides: *the diameter of a tree-trunk* ○ *a lens that magnifies 20 diameters*, ie makes an object look 20 times longer, wider, etc than it is. ⇨ App 10. ⇨ illus at CIRCLE.
▷ **diametrical** /ˌdaɪəˈmetrɪkl/ *adj* of or along a diameter.

diametrically /ˌdaɪəˈmetrɪklɪ/ *adv* completely; entirely: *diametrically opposed/opposite*.

diamond /ˈdaɪəmənd/ *n* **1 (a)** [U, C] transparent precious stone of pure carbon in crystallized form, the hardest substance known: *a ring with a diamond in it* ○ [attrib] *a diamond ring, necklace, etc.* **(b)** [C] piece of this (often artificially made) used in industry, esp for cutting glass or as a stylus for playing records. **2** [C] figure with four equal sides and with angles that are not right angles. **3 (a) diamonds** [sing or pl *v*] suit of playing-cards marked with red diamond shapes: *the five of diamonds* ○ *Diamonds is/are trumps.* **(b)** [C] playing-card of this suit: *play a diamond.* ⇨ illus at PLAYING-CARD. **4** [C] (in baseball) space inside the lines connecting the bases. **5** (idm) **a rough diamond** ⇨ ROUGH¹.
□ ˌ**diamond ˈjubilee** (celebration of a) 60th anniversary. Cf GOLDEN JUBILEE (GOLDEN), SILVER JUBILEE (SILVER).
ˌ**diamond ˈwedding** 60th anniversary of a wedding. Cf GOLDEN WEDDING (GOLDEN), SILVER WEDDING (SILVER).

Diana /daɪˈænə/ Roman goddess of the moon, of hunting and of chastity. Her equivalent in Greek mythology was *Artemis.

dianthus /daɪˈænθəs/ *n* [U, C] garden plant with sweet-smelling flowers, typically pink. The carnation is a type of dianthus.

diapason /ˌdaɪəˈpeɪsn, -ˈpeɪzn/ *n* **1** complete range of notes produced by a voice or musical instrument. **2** either of two sets of pipes in an organ that produce notes of a particular quality.

diaper /ˈdaɪəpə(r); *US also* ˈdaɪpər/ *n* **1** [U] linen or cotton fabric with a pattern of small diamonds on it. **2** [C] (*US*) = NAPPY.

diaphanous /daɪˈæfənəs/ *adj* (of fabric) light, very fine and almost transparent: *a diaphanous veil* ○ *a dress of diaphanous silk*.

diaphragm /ˈdaɪəfræm/ *n* **1** wall of muscle, between the chest and the abdomen, that helps to control breathing. ⇨ illus at RESPIRE. **2** arrangement of thin plates in a camera that control how much light is let in through the lens. **3** vibrating disc or cone producing sound-waves, eg in telephone receivers, loudspeakers, etc. **4** (also **Dutch ˈcap, cap**) thin plastic or rubber membrane that is fitted over the neck of the womb before intercourse to prevent conception.

diarrhoea (*US* **diarrhea**) /ˌdaɪəˈrɪə/ *n* [U] condition that causes waste matter to be emptied from the bowels frequently and in a watery form: *have a bad attack of diarrhoea*.

diary /ˈdaɪərɪ/ *n* (book used for a) daily record of events, thoughts, appointments, etc. Most people regard their diaries as private, but some (eg politicians) write them with the intention that they will one day be published: *keep* (ie write regularly in) *a diary* ○ *Pepys's diary*.
▷ **diarist** /ˈdaɪərɪst/ *n* person who writes a diary, esp one that is later published.

Diaspora /daɪˈæspərə/ *n* **the Diaspora** [sing] **(a)** settling of the Jews among various non-Jewish communities after they had been exiled in 538 BC. **(b)** places where they settled: *People from every country of the Diaspora now live in Israel.*

diastase /ˈdaɪəsteɪs/ *n* [U] enzyme that converts starch to sugar, important in digestion.

diastole /daɪˈæstəlɪ/ *n* [C, U] regular expansion and relaxation of the heart when it fills with blood, which is then forced out by contraction (or *systole*), the two together making the heartbeat (or *pulse*). ▷ **diastolic** /ˌdaɪəˈstɒlɪk/ *adj*.

diatom /ˈdaɪətəm; *US* -tɒm/ *n* any of various types of microscopic one-cell plants living in water and forming fossil deposits.

diatonic /ˌdaɪəˈtɒnɪk/ *adj* (*music*) using the notes of the major or minor scale²(6) only, not of the chromatic scale.

diatribe /ˈdaɪətraɪb/ *n* ~ **(against sb/sth)** lengthy and bitter attack in words: *a diatribe against the police state*.

dibble /ˈdɪbl/ (also **dibber** /ˈdɪbə(r)/) *n* short wooden tool with a pointed end, used for making holes in the ground for seeds or young plants.
▷ **dibble** *v* (phr v) **dibble sth in** put (plants, etc) in the ground using a dibble.

dice

dice /daɪs/ *n* (*pl* unchanged) **1 (a)** [C] small cube of wood, bone, plastic, etc that has a different number of spots on each side, from one to six, used in games of chance: *a pair of dice* ○ *shake/roll/throw the dice.* ⇨ illus. **(b)** [U] game played with this: *play dice.* **2** (idm) **load the dice** ⇨ LOAD². **no ˈdice** (*sl esp US*) no agreement (to sth requested): *'Shall we change the plan?' 'No dice, we'll stick with the original one.'*
▷ **dice** *v* **1** [I] gamble using dice. **2** [Tn, Tn·p] cut (meat, vegetables, etc) into small cubes: *Dice the beetroot (up) neatly.* **3** (idm) **dice with death** (*infml*) risk one's life.

dicey /ˈdaɪsɪ/ *adj* (**dicier**, **diciest**) (*infml*) risky; dangerous: *The fog made driving a bit dicey.*

dichotomy /daɪˈkɒtəmɪ/ *n* ~ **(between A and B)** (*fml*) separation into or between two groups or things that are opposed, entirely different, etc: *the dichotomy between peace and war* ○ *They set up a false dichotomy between working and raising a family*, ie wrongly claim that one cannot do both.

dichromatic /ˌdaɪkrəʊˈmætɪk/ *adj* **1** two-coloured. **2** capable of seeing only two of the three primary colours: ˌ*dichromatic* ˈ*vision*.

dick /dɪk/ *n* **1** (⚠ *infml*) penis. **2** (*dated infml esp US*) detective: *The thief was caught by the hotel dick.*

Charles Dickens

Dickens /ˈdɪkɪnz/ Charles Huffham (1812-70), English novelist whose high reputation rests on his creation of a range of memorable and often odd characters (eg Scrooge and Mr Pickwick), on his descriptions of the bad conditions in which poor people lived in 19th-century Britain (which helped to bring about social reforms), and perhaps above all on his ability as a story-teller to make his readers laugh and cry. His novels (which were originally published in instalments) include *Pickwick Papers, David Copperfield, Oliver Twist* (based on Dickens's own harsh boyhood), *Bleak House, Great Expectations, Nicholas Nickleby, A Tale of Two Cities* and *A Christmas Carol*. Dickens was very popular during his lifetime, and frequently gave public readings from his books. ⇨ illus.

▷ **Dickensian** /dɪˈkenzɪən/ *adj* of or like the novels of Dickens, esp in their descriptions of bad social conditions or eccentric characters: *Dickensian slums.*

dickens /ˈdɪkɪnz/ *n* **the dickens** (*infml euph*) (used to give emphasis, esp in questions) the Devil: *Who/What/Where the dickens is that?* ○ *We had the dickens of a job finding the place.*

dicker /ˈdɪkə(r)/ *v* [I, Ipr] ~ **(with sb) (for sth)** argue (with the seller) about the price of sth; haggle: *She dickered (with the shopkeeper) for the best fruit.*

Dickinson /ˈdɪkɪnsn/ Emily Elizabeth (1830-86), American poet. The quality of her work, which uses difficult and sometimes violent imagery to describe the emotional struggles of her life, was not widely recognized until after her death.

dicky[1] (also **dickey**) /ˈdɪkɪ/ *n* (*infml*) **1** (also ˈ**dicky-seat**) (*Brit dated*) small extra folding seat at the back of some old-fashioned two-seater cars. **2** (*dated*) false shirt-front.

□ ˈ**dicky-bird** *n* **1** (used by or to young children) bird. **2** (idm) **not say a dicky-bird** ⇨ SAY.

dicky[2] /ˈdɪkɪ/ *adj* (**-ier, -iest**) (*dated Brit infml*) not healthy or strong: *That ladder looks a bit dicky.* ○ *have a dicky heart.*

dicotyledon /ˌdaɪkɒtəˈli:dən/ *n* flowering plant that has two leaves growing from the seed at the embryo stage.

Dictaphone /ˈdɪktəfəʊn/ *n* (*propr*) machine that records speech, esp dictated letters, and plays it back so that a secretary can type it out.

dictate /dɪkˈteɪt; *US* ˈdɪkteɪt/ *v* **1** [I, Ipr, Tn, Tn·pr] ~ **(sth) (to sb)** say or read aloud (words to be typed, written down or recorded on tape): *dictate a letter to one's secretary* ○ *The teacher dictated a passage to the class.* **2** [Tn, Tn·pr] ~ **sth (to sb)** state or order sth with the force of authority: *dictate terms to a defeated enemy.* **3** (phr v) **dictate to sb** (esp passive) give orders to sb, esp in an officious way: *I refuse to be dictated to by you.* ○ *You can't dictate to people how they should live.* ⇨ Usage at DECREE.

▷ **dictate** *n* /ˈdɪkteɪt/ (usu *pl*) command (esp one that reason, conscience, etc prompts one to obey): *Follow the dictates of common sense*, ie Do what common sense tells you to do.

dictation /dɪkˈteɪʃn/ *n* **1** [U] action of giving or taking sth dictated: *shorthand dictation.* **2** [C] passage, etc that is dictated: *three English dictations.*

dictator /dɪkˈteɪtə(r); *US* ˈdɪkteɪtər/ *n* **1** ruler who has total power over his country, esp one who has obtained it by force and uses it in a cruel way. **2** (*fig infml*) person who insists that people do what he wants: *Our boss is a bit of a dictator.*

▷ **dictatorial** /ˌdɪktəˈtɔ:rɪəl/ *adj* (**a**) of or like a dictator: *dictatorial government, powers, etc.* (**b**) fond of giving orders; domineering: *a dictatorial teacher, manner, tone.* **dictatorially** /-əlɪ/ *adv.*

dictatorship *n* **1** [C, U] (country with) government by a dictator. **2** [C] rank or office of a dictator.

diction /ˈdɪkʃn/ *n* [U] (**a**) style or manner of speaking or (sometimes) writing: *Clarity of diction is vital for a public speaker.* (**b**) choice and use of words.

dictionary /ˈdɪkʃənrɪ; *US* -nerɪ/ *n* (**a**) book that lists and explains the words of a language, or gives translations of them into one or more other languages, and is usu arranged in alphabetical order: *an English dictionary.* (**b**) similar book that explains the terms of a particular subject: *a dictionary of architecture.*

dictum /ˈdɪktəm/ *n* (*pl* ~**s** or **-ta** /-tə/) (**a**) saying; maxim: *the well-known dictum 'Knowledge is power'.* (**b**) formal expression of opinion.

did *pt* of DO[1, 2].

didactic /dɪˈdæktɪk, daɪ-/ *adj* (*fml*) **1** intended to teach: *didactic poetry, methods.* **2** (*usu derog*) that seems to treat the listener, reader, etc like a child in school: *I don't like her didactic way of explaining everything.* ▷ **didactically** /-klɪ/ *adv.*

diddle /ˈdɪdl/ *v* [Tn, Tn·pr] ~ **sb (out of sth)** (*infml*) cheat sb, esp in small matters: *I've been diddled! Half of these tomatoes are bad!* ○ *They've diddled me out of the rent!*

diddums /ˈdɪdəmz/ *interj* (*Brit*) (said to show sympathy or to comfort sb, esp a child).

didgeridoo /ˌdɪdʒərɪˈdu:/ *n* (*pl* ~**s**) musical instrument used by Australian aborigines, consisting of a long wooden tube that is blown to produce a single deep note.

didn't ⇨ DO[1].

Dido /ˈdaɪdəʊ/ queen of ancient *Carthage, who according to Virgil's *Aeneid* fell in love with *Aeneas and killed herself when he left her.

die[1] /daɪ/ *n* block of hard metal with a design, etc cut into it, used for shaping coins, printing-type, medals, etc or for stamping paper, leather, etc so that designs stand out from the surface.

□ ˈ**die-cast** *adj* made by casting metal in a mould: *die-cast toys*, eg small models of cars.

die[2] /daɪ/ *v* (*pt, pp* **died**, *pres p* **dying**) **1** (**a**) [I, Ipr] stop living; come to the end of one's life: *Flowers soon die without water.* ○ *die of an illness, hunger, grief* ○ *die from a wound* ○ *die by violence* ○ *die by one's own hand*, ie commit suicide ○ *die for one's country* ○ *die through neglect* ○ *die in battle* ○ *one's dying wish/words/breath*, ie uttered just before death ○ *I'll love you to my dying day*, ie until I die. (**b**) [La, Ln] be (sth) when one dies: *die happy, poor, young, etc* ○ *die a beggar, martyr, etc.* (**c**) [Tn] have (a particular kind of death): *die a lingering, natural, violent, etc death.* **2** [I] (*fig*) cease to exist; disappear: *love that will never die* ○ *dying traditions, customs, etc* ○ *His secret died with him*, ie He died without telling it to anyone. ○ *The flame died*, ie went out. **3** (idm) **be dying for sth/to do sth** have a strong desire for sth: *I'm dying for something to eat.* ○ *She's dying to know where you've been.* **die the** ˈ**death** (*joc*) end suddenly and completely: *After getting bad reviews the play quickly died the death.* **die** ˈ**hard** only be changed, disappear, etc with great difficulty: *Old habits die hard.* **die in one's** ˈ**bed** die of old age or illness. **die in** ˈ**harness** die while still working. **die laughing** (*infml*) laugh a lot: *It was so funny, I nearly died laughing.* **die/fall/drop like flies** ⇨ FLY[1]. **die with one's** ˈ**boots on/in one's** ˈ**boots** die while still vigorous and active. **one's last/dying breath** ⇨ BREATH. **never say die** ⇨ SAY. **4** (phr v) **die away** become so faint or weak that it is no longer noticeable: *The noise of the car died away in the distance.* ○ *The breeze has died away.* **die** ˈ**back** (of a plant) gradually wither and die, the process of decay starting from the tips of the leaves. **die** ˈ**down** gradually become less strong, loud, noticeable, etc: *flames, storms, pain dying down* ○ *These rumours will soon die down.* **die** ˈ**off** die one by one: *The members of the family had all died off.* **die** ˈ**out** (**a**) (of a family, species, etc) no longer have any members left alive: *The moth's habitat is being destroyed and it has nearly died out.* (**b**) (of a custom, practice, etc) no longer be common: *The old traditions are dying out.*

□ ˈ**die-hard** *n* person who is stubborn, esp in resisting change: *A few die-hards are trying to stop the reforms.* ○ [attrib] *a die-hard conservative, campaigner, sceptic.*

die[3] /daɪ/ *n* **1** (*dated*) = DICE. **2** (idm) **the die is cast** (*saying*) a decision has been made and cannot be changed. **straight as an arrow/a die** ⇨ STRAIGHT[1].

dielectric /ˌdaɪɪˈlektrɪk/ *adj* that does not conduct electricity; insulating.

▷ **dielectric** *n* dielectric substance, used as an insulator.

dieresis (*US*) = DIAERESIS.

diesel /ˈdi:zl/ *n* **1** [C] (also ˈ**diesel engine**) oil-burning engine (used eg for buses and locomotives) in which fuel is ignited by air that has been heated by sudden compression. It uses less fuel to produce the same amount of heat as an ordinary internal-combustion engine (in which the fuel is ignited by a spark). It was invented by the German engineer Dr Rudolf Diesel (1858-1913): [attrib] *a diesel lorry, train, etc.* **2** [U] (also ˈ**diesel fuel**, ˈ**diesel oil**) heavy fuel oil used in diesel engines. **3** [C] locomotive, motor vehicle or ship that uses diesel fuel.

□ ˌ**diesel-**ˈ**electric** *adj* driven by electric current from a generator driven by a diesel engine: *a diesel-electric train.*

diet[1] /ˈdaɪət/ *n* **1** [C] sort of food that is usually eaten (by a person, community, etc): *the Japanese diet of rice, vegetables and fish* ○ *Too rich a diet* (ie Too much rich food) *is not good for you.* ○ *illnesses caused by poor diet.* **2** [C] limited variety or amount of food that a person is allowed to eat, eg for medical reasons or in order to lose weight: *a salt-free diet* ○ [attrib] *diet aids.*

📖 The British have become increasingly aware in recent years of the benefits of a healthy diet. Since the 1980s, people have been concerned with eating more fibre, less fat and less salt, and with avoiding foods that contain non-nutritional additives. There has also been great interest in diets and exercises to aid slimming, and books on these subjects are continually among the top ten best-sellers. Fitness centres and health clubs are very popular too. Weight Watchers, founded in the United States in the 1960s, is one of the best-known organizations to help people lose weight. It now has many branches in Britain.

3 [sing] ~ **of sth** (*fig*) so much of sth that it becomes boring or unpleasant: *the constant diet of soap operas on TV.* **4** (idm) **(be/go/put sb) on a diet** allowed to eat only some foods or a little food, because of illness or to lose weight: *The doctor says I've got to go on a diet.*

▷ **diet** *v* [I] (be allowed to) eat only some foods or a little food, esp to lose weight: *You ought to diet and take more exercise.*

dietary /ˈdaɪətərɪ; *US* -erɪ/ *adj*: *dietary habits* ○ *dietary rules*, eg forbidding certain foods.

dietetic /ˌdaɪəˈtetɪk/ *adj* of diet and nutrition. **dietetics** *n* [sing *v*] science of diet and nutrition. **dietician** (also **dietitian**) /ˌdaɪəˈtɪʃn/ *n* expert in dietetics.

diet[2] /ˈdaɪət/ *n* **1** (esp formerly) series of meetings to discuss national, international or church affairs. **2** law-making assembly in certain countries, eg Japan.

Dietrich /ˈdiːtrɪk/ Marlene (1901-93), German-born actor famous for her attractively deep singing voice. Her role as a seductive cabaret singer in the film *The Blue Angel* established the style of her stage performances.

differ /ˈdɪfə(r)/ *v* [I, Ipr] **1** ~ (**from sb/sth**) not be the same (as sb/sth); be unlike: *The brothers differ widely in their tastes.* ○ *Tastes differ,* ie Different people like different things. ○ *have differing tastes, views, etc* ○ *In this respect, French differs from English/French and English differ.* **2** ~ (**with/from sb**) (**about/on sth**) disagree; not share the same opinion: *I'm sorry to differ with you on that.* ○ *We differ on many things.* **3** (idm) **agree to differ** ⇨ AGREE. **I beg to differ** ⇨ BEG.

difference /ˈdɪfrəns/ *n* **1** [C] ~ (**between A and B**); ~ (**in/of sth**) state or way in which two people or things are not the same, or in which sb/sth has changed: *the marked differences between the two children* ○ *Did you notice a difference (in her)?* ○ *It's easy to tell the difference* (ie distinguish) *between butter and margarine.* ○ *a difference of approach.* **2** [C, U] ~ (**in sth**) (**between A and B**) amount or degree in which two things are not the same or sth has changed: *There's an age difference of six years between them,* ie One of them is six years older than the other. ○ *I'll lend you 90% of the money and you'll have to find the difference,* ie the other 10%. ○ *We measured the difference(s) in temperature.* ○ *There's not much difference in price between the two computers.* **3** [C] ~ (**between A and B**) (**over sth**) disagreement, often involving a quarrel: *Settle your differences and be friends again.* ○ *We had a difference of opinion* (ie argued) *over who had won.* **4** (idm) **as near as makes no difference** ⇨ NEAR[2]. **for all the ˈdifference it/sth makes** considering how little difference it/sth makes. **make a, no, some, etc difference (to sb/sth)** (**a**) have an, no, some, etc effect (on sb/sth): *The rain didn't make much difference (to the game).* ○ *The sea air has made a difference to* (ie improved) *her health.* ○ *A hot bath makes all the difference* (ie makes you feel better) *in the morning.* (**b**) be important, unimportant, etc (to sb/sth); matter: *It makes no difference (to me) what you say: I'm not going.* ○ *It won't make much difference whether you go today or tomorrow.* ○ *Does that make any difference?* ie Is it important, need we consider it? ○ *Yes, it makes all the difference,* ie is very important. **make a difference between** treat differently: *She makes no difference between her two sons.* **sink one's differences** ⇨ SINK[1]. **split the difference** ⇨ SPLIT. **with a ˈdifference** (following *ns*) special; unusual: *She's an opera singer with a difference: she can act well!*

different /ˈdɪfrənt/ *adj* **1** ~ (**from/to sb/sth**); (*esp US*) ~ (**than sb/sth**) not the same (as sb/sth): *the same product with a different name* ○ *The room looks different with the furniture gone.* ○ *Their tastes are different from/to mine.* ○ *She is wearing a different dress every time I see her.* **2** separate; distinct: *I called on three different occasions, but he was out.* ○ *They are sold in different colours,* ie a variety of colours. **3** (idm) (**as**) ˌ**different as** ˌ**chalk and/from** ˈ**cheese** completely different. **a** (**very**) **different kettle of fish** (*infml*) a completely different person or thing from the one previously mentioned. **a horse of a different colour** ⇨ HORSE. **know different** ⇨ KNOW. **sing a different song/tune** ⇨ SING. ▷ **differently** *adv.*

NOTE ON USAGE: British and US English differ as regards the prepositions used after **different. 1** Before a noun or adverbial phrase, both **from** and **to** are acceptable in British English. Some speakers prefer **from. Different than** is not usual: *He's very different from/to his brother.* ○ *This visit is very different from/to last time.* In US English **than** is commonly used (not **to**): *Your trains are different from/than ours.* ○ *You look different than before.* **2** In both varieties, but especially in US English, **than** is an alternative to **from** before a clause: *His appearance was very different from what I'd expected/His appearance was very different than I'd expected.*

differential /ˌdɪfəˈrenʃl/ *adj* [attrib] of, showing or depending on a difference: *differential treatment of applicants for jobs,* eg varying according to their education, etc ○ *Non-EEC countries pay a higher differential tariff.*

▷ **differential** *n* **1** (also ˌ**differential** ˈ**wage**) (*esp Brit*) difference in rates of pay for different types of work or workers: *a dispute about the differential between men and women workers.* **2** (also ˌ**differential** ˈ**gear**) gear enabling a vehicle's back wheels to turn at different speeds when going round corners. ⇨ illus at CAR.

□ ˌ**differential** ˈ**calculus** (*mathematics*) branch of calculus concerned with calculating rates of change, maximum and minimum values, etc. Cf INTEGRAL CALCULUS (INTEGRAL).

differentiate /ˌdɪfəˈrenʃɪeɪt/ *v* **1** (**a**) [Ipr, Tn, Tn·pr] ~ **between A and B**; ~ **A** (**from B**) see or show (two things) to be different; show sth to be different (from sth else): *Can you differentiate between the two varieties?* ○ *Can you differentiate one variety from the other?* ○ *One character is not clearly differentiated from another.* (**b**) [Tn, Tn·pr] ~ **sth** (**from sth**) be a mark of difference between (people or things); distinguish: *The male's orange beak differentiates it from the female.* **2** [Ipr] ~ **between A and B** treat (people or things) in a different way, esp unfairly; discriminate: *It is wrong to differentiate between people according to their family background.* **3** [Tn] (*mathematics*) find the derivative of (a function) in differential calculus. **4** [I] (*biology*) (of a cell in an embryo) change during development from a simple to a more complex form with a specialized function. ▷ **differentiation** /ˌdɪfərenʃɪˈeɪʃn/ *n* [U].

difficult /ˈdɪfɪkəlt/ *adj* **1** ~ (**to do sth**) (of tasks) requiring effort or skill; not easy: *a difficult problem, language, translation* ○ *She finds it difficult to stop smoking.* ○ *This mountain is difficult to climb/It is difficult to climb this mountain.* ○ *Their refusal puts us in a difficult position.* ○ *They made it difficult for me to see her.* ○ *13 is a difficult age,* ie Children have problems then. **2** (of people) not easy to please or satisfy; unwilling to co-operate: *a difficult child, customer, boss, etc* ○ *Don't be difficult: just lend us the money.* **3** (idm) **easy/difficult of approach** ⇨ APPROACH.

difficulty /ˈdɪfɪkəltɪ/ *n* **1** [U] **in sth/in doing sth** state or quality of being difficult; trouble or effort that sth involves: *the sheer difficulty of the task* ○ *Bad planning will lead to difficulty later.* ○ *do sth with/without difficulty* ○ *She got the door open, but only with some difficulty.* ○ *I had the greatest difficulty in persuading her.* ○ *We had no difficulty (in) finding the house.* **2** [C usu *pl*] difficult thing to do, understand or deal with: *the difficulties of English syntax* ○ *be working under some difficulty,* ie in difficult circumstances ○ *She met with many difficulties when travelling.* ○ *financial difficulties,* ie problems about money ○ *We got into difficulty/difficulties with the rent,* ie found it hard to pay. ○ *I want to marry her, but my parents are making/creating difficulties,* ie making things hard for us.

diffident /ˈdɪfɪdənt/ *adj* ~ (**about sth**) not having or showing much belief in one's own abilities; lacking self-confidence: *an able but diffident young student* ○ *Don't be so diffident about your talents.* ▷ **diffidence** /-dəns/ *n* [U]. **diffidently** *adv.*

diffract /dɪˈfrækt/ *v* [Tn] (*physics*) break up (a beam of radiation, eg light) into separate parts (eg a series of dark and light bands or all the coloured bands of the spectrum). ▷ **diffraction** /dɪˈfrækʃn/ *n* [U].

diffuse[1] /dɪˈfjuːz/ *v* **1** [Tn] spread (sth) all around; send out in all directions: *diffuse a scent, an odour, light, heat, learning, knowledge* ○ *He diffuses enthusiasm all around him.* ○ *posters diffusing party propaganda* ○ *diffused lighting,* ie not coming directly from one source. **2** [I, Tn] (cause gases and liquids to) mix slowly: *A drop of milk diffused in the water, and it became cloudy.*

▷ **diffusion** /dɪˈfjuːʒn/ *n* [U] diffusing or being diffused: *the diffusion of knowledge through books and lectures* ○ *the diffusion of gases and liquids.*

diffuse[2] /dɪˈfjuːs/ *adj* **1** spread out; not concentrated: *diffuse light.* **2** using too many words; not concise: *a diffuse writer, style.* ▷ **diffusely** *adv.* **diffuseness** *n* [U].

dig[1] /dɪg/ *v* (-gg-; *pt, pp* **dug** /dʌg/) **1** (**a**) [I, Ipr, Ip, Tn, Tn·pr, Tn·p] use one's hands, a spade, a machine, etc to break up and move (earth, etc); advance by doing this: *I spent the morning digging.* ○ *They are digging through the hill to make a tunnel.* ○ *dig down into the soil* ○ *It is difficult to dig the ground when it is frozen.* ○ *dig the soil away from the bottom of the wall.* (**b**) [Tn] make (a hole, etc) by doing this: *dig a pit, tunnel, shaft, etc.* (**c**) [Ipr] ~ **for sth** search for (gold, etc) by doing this: *We are digging for mineral deposits.* **2** (*dated infml*) (**a**) [Tn] enjoy (sth); appreciate: *I don't dig modern jazz.* (**b**) [I, Tn] understand (sth): *I don't dig that crazy stuff.* ○ *You dig?* **3** (idm) ˌ**dig one's** ˈ**heels/**ˈ**toes in** be stubborn; refuse to give in. **dig sb in the ribs** nudge or prod sb hard in the side. **dig one's own grave** do sth which causes one's own downfall. **4** (phr v) **dig in; dig into sth** (*infml*) (begin to) eat hungrily or enthusiastically: *The food's ready, so dig in!* **dig sth in; dig sth into sth** (**a**) mix sth with soil by digging: *The manure should be well dug in.* (**b**) push or thrust sth into sth: *dig a fork into a pie* ○ *The rider dug his spurs into the horse's flank.* ○ *The dog dug its teeth in.* **dig oneself in** (**a**) (*military*) (of soldiers) protect oneself by digging a trench, etc. (**b**) (*infml*) establish oneself securely (in a place, job, etc): *He has dug himself in well at the college now.* **dig sb/sth out** (**of sth**) (**a**) get sb/sth out by digging: *They dug the potatoes out (of the ground).* ○ *He was buried by an avalanche and had to be dug out.* (**b**) get sth by searching or study: *dig information out of books and reports* ○ *dig out the truth.* (**c**) (*infml*) take out (sth not easy to get at): *dig out an old photo from the drawer.* **dig sth over** prepare (ground) thoroughly by digging: *dig the garden over.* **dig sth up** (**a**) break up (soil, etc) by digging: *dig up land for a new garden.* (**b**) remove (sth) from the ground by digging: *We dug up the tree by its roots.* (**c**) reveal and remove from the ground by digging (sth that has been buried or hidden): *An old Greek statue was dug up here last month.* (**d**) (*fig*) discover (information, etc); reveal sth: *Newspapers love to dig up scandal.*

dig[2] /dɪg/ *n* **1** (**a**) poke; prod: *give sb a dig in the ribs.* (**b**) ~ (**at sb**) (*fig*) remark that is meant to irritate or upset sb: *She makes mean little digs at him.* **2** (**a**) act of digging: *I gave the vegetable plot a quick dig.* (**b**) site being explored by archaeologists.

digest[1] /ˈdaɪdʒest/ *n* **1** short condensed account; summary: *a digest of the week's news.* **2** (*law*) summary of all the laws or legal decisions of a country.

digest[2] /dɪˈdʒest, daɪ-/ *v* **1** (**a**) [Tn] change (food) in the stomach and bowels so that it can be used by the body: *Fish is easy to digest when you're ill.* (**b**) [I] (of food) be changed in this way: *It takes hours for a meal to digest.* **2** [Tn] take (information) in mentally; fully understand: *Have you digested the report yet?* **3** [Tn] make a digest of (sth); summarize.

▷ **digestible** /dɪˈdʒestəbl, daɪ-/ *adj* that can be digested. **digestibility** /dɪˌdʒestəˈbɪlətɪ, daɪ-/ *n* [U].

digestion /dɪˈdʒestʃən, daɪ-/ *n* (**a**) [U] digesting: *foods which aid digestion.* (**b**) [C usu *sing*] power of digesting food: *have a good/poor digestion.*

digestive /dɪˈdʒestɪv, daɪ-/ *adj* [usu attrib] of digestion (of food): *the digestive process, juices* ○ *suffer from digestive trouble.*

□ **di**ˌ**gestive** ˈ**biscuit** (also **digestive**) (*Brit*) round, not very sweet, biscuit made from wholemeal flour.

diˈ**gestive system** organs of the body that digest food. ⇨ illus.

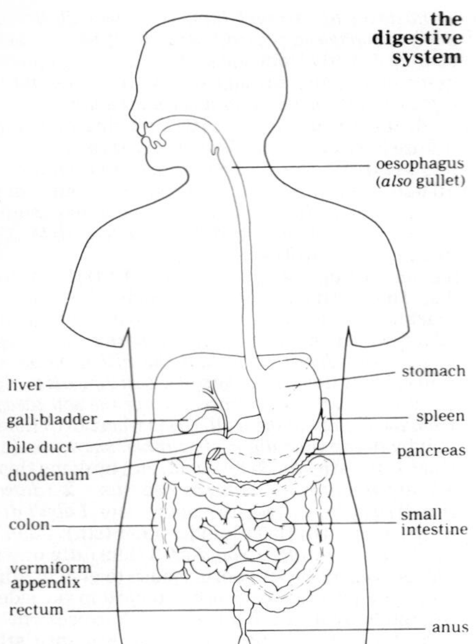

digger /ˈdɪgə(r)/ *n* **1** person who digs. **2** mechanical excavator. **3** (*sl*) Australian or New Zealander, esp a soldier.

digging /ˈdɪgɪŋ/ *n* **1** [U] action of digging. **2 diggings** [pl] place where people dig for tin, gold, etc.

digit /ˈdɪdʒɪt/ *n* **1** (*mathematics*) any of the ten Arabic numerals 0 to 9: *The number 57 306 contains five digits.* **2** (*anatomy*) finger or toe.
▷ **digital** /ˈdɪdʒɪtl/ *adj* **1** showing amounts by means of numbers. **2** of fingers or toes. ˌ**digital** ˈ**clock**, ˌ**digital** ˈ**watch** clock/watch that shows the time by digits rather than hands. ˌ**digital com**ˈ**puter** device that makes calculations, etc with data represented as a series of digits. Cf ANALOGUE COMPUTER (ANALOGUE). ˌ**digital re**ˈ**cording** [C, U] (recording made by a) process of converting sound into a series of electrical pulses (representing binary digits).

digitalis /ˌdɪdʒɪˈteɪlɪs/ *n* [U] drug obtained from the foxglove plant, used for making a weak heart beat more strongly.

dignify /ˈdɪgnɪfaɪ/ *v* (*pt, pp* **-fied**) (*fml*) **1** [Tn] make (sth) seem worthy or impressive; give dignity to: *a ceremony dignified by the presence of the ambassador.* **2** [Tn, Tn·pr] ~ **sb/sth (with sth)** give an important-sounding name to sb/sth: *dignify a small collection of books with the name of library* ○ *I wouldn't dignify this trash by calling it a novel.*
▷ **dignified** *adj* having or showing dignity: *a dignified person, walk, bow.*

dignitary /ˈdɪgnɪtərɪ; *US* -terɪ/ *n* (*fml*) person with a high rank or position: *civic dignitaries*, eg the mayor and councillors.

dignity /ˈdɪgnətɪ/ *n* **1** [U] quality that earns or deserves respect; true worth: *the dignity of labour* ○ *Only a truly free person has human dignity.* **2** [U] calm or serious manner or style: *She kept her dignity despite the booing.* **3** [C] (*fml*) high or honourable rank, post or title: *The Queen conferred the dignity of a peerage on him.* **4** (idm) **be**ˌ**neath one's** ˈ**dignity** (*often ironic*) below one's social, moral, etc standards: *Some husbands still think it beneath their dignity to do the shopping.* ˌ**stand on one's** ˈ**dignity** insist on behaving or being treated in a special way because one thinks oneself important: *She doesn't stand on her dignity and treat the rest of us as servants.*

digraph /ˈdaɪgrɑːf; *US* -græf/ *n* two letters that represent a single sound (eg *sh* /ʃ/, *ea* /iː/ in *sheaf*).

digress /daɪˈgres/ *v* [I, Ipr] ~ **(from sth)** turn or wander (from the main topic) in speech or writing: *Don't digress (from the subject) when lecturing.*
▷ **digression** /daɪˈgreʃn/ *n* (**a**) [U] digressing. (**b**) [C] passage, etc in which one digresses: *If you'll allow a slight digression, ...*

digs /dɪgz/ *n* [pl] (*Brit infml*) room(s) rented in sb else's house; lodgings: *the high cost of living in digs* ○ *take digs in London.*

dihedral /daɪˈhiːdrəl/ *n* (also **di**ˌ**hedral** ˈ**angle**) **1** (*geometry*) angle at which two flat surfaces meet. **2** (*aerospace*) angle between an aircraft's upward-pointing wing and the horizontal.

dike (also **dyke**) /daɪk/ *n* **1** ditch (for allowing water to flow away from land). **2** long wall of earth, etc (to keep back water and prevent flooding). **3** (⚠ *sl*) lesbian, esp a masculine one.
▷ **dike** *v* [I, Tn] make or provide (sth) with a dike(1, 2).

diktat /ˈdɪktæt; *US* dɪkˈtɑːt/ *n* [C, U] (**a**) set of harsh conditions which the loser of a war, dispute, etc is forced to accept by the winner. (**b**) (*derog*) order, esp an unreasonable one, that must be obeyed: *harsh new restrictions imposed by government diktat.*

dilapidated /dɪˈlæpɪdeɪtɪd/ *adj* (of furniture, buildings, etc) falling to pieces; in a bad state of repair: *a dilapidated chair, bed, etc* ○ *a dilapidated-looking car.* ▷ **dilapidation** /dɪˌlæpɪˈdeɪʃn/ *n* [U]: *in a dreadful state of dilapidation.*

dilate /daɪˈleɪt/ *v* **1** [I, Tn] (cause sth to) become wider, larger or further open: *The pupils of your eyes dilate when you enter a dark room.* ○ *The horse dilated its nostrils.* **2** (phr v) **dilate on sth** (*fml*) speak or write about sth for a long time: *a chapter in which she dilates on the benefits of vegetarianism.*
▷ **dilation** /daɪˈleɪʃn/ (also **dilatation** /ˌdaɪləˈteɪʃən/) *n* [U] dilating or being dilated.
□ **dila**ˌ**tation and** ˈ**curettage** (*abbr* **D and C**) (*medical*) operation in which the opening of the womb is widened and the inner lining of the womb removed (eg after a miscarriage).

dilatory /ˈdɪlətərɪ; *US* -tɔːrɪ/ *adj* (*fml*) (**a**) ~ **(in doing sth)** slow in acting: *The Government has been dilatory in condemning the outrage.* (**b**) causing delay: *dilatory behaviour, actions, etc.* ▷ **dilatorily** *adv.* **dilatoriness** *n* [U].

dilemma /dɪˈlemə, daɪ-/ *n* **1** situation in which one has to choose between two undesirable things or courses of action: *be in/place sb in a dilemma.* **2** (idm) **on the horns of a dilemma** ⇨ HORN.

dilettante /ˌdɪlɪˈtæntɪ/ *n* (*pl* ~**s** or **-ti** /-tiː/) (*often derog*) person who studies or does sth, but without serious interest or understanding: *a musical dilettante.* ▷ **dilettantish** /-ˈtæntɪʃ/ *adj*: *a dilettantish follower of the arts.*

diligence /ˈdɪlɪdʒəns/ *n* [U] ~ **(in sth/in doing sth)** steady effort; careful hard work: *She shows great diligence in her school work.* ○ *diligence in pursuing one's aims.*

diligent /ˈdɪlɪdʒənt/ *adj* ~ **(in sth/in doing sth)** showing care and effort (in what one does); hard-working: *a diligent worker, pupil, etc* ○ *They're very diligent in keeping records.* ▷ **diligently** *adv.*

dill /dɪl/ *n* [U] herb with scented leaves and seeds used for flavouring pickles.

dilly /ˈdɪlɪ/ *n* (*US infml*) person or thing considered excellent or remarkable: *She had a dilly of a bruise on her arm.*

dilly-dally /ˈdɪlɪ dælɪ/ (*pt, pp* **-dallied**) *v* [I] (*infml*) waste time; dawdle: *Don't dilly-dally! Make up your mind!*

dilute /daɪˈljuːt; *US* -ˈluːt/ *v* [Tn, Tn·pr] ~ **sth (with sth)** **1** make (a liquid or colour) thinner or weaker (by adding water or another liquid): *dilute wine with water.* **2** (*fig*) make (sth) weaker in force, effect, etc: *diluting standards in our schools.*
▷ **dilute** *adj* (of acids, etc) weakened by diluting: *dilute sulphuric acid.*
dilution /daɪˈljuːʃn; *US* -ˈluː-/ *n* (**a**) [U] diluting or being diluted. (**b**) [C] thing that is diluted.

dim /dɪm/ *adj* (**-mmer**, **-mmest**) **1** (**a**) where or which one cannot see well; not bright: *a dim corridor with no windows* ○ *the dim outline of buildings on a dark night* ○ *reading by dim candle-light.* (**b**) not clearly remembered; faint: *a dim memory/recollection.* **2** (*infml*) (of people) lacking intelligence. **3** (of the eyes, eyesight) not able to see well: *His sight is getting dim.* ○ *eyes dim with tears.* **4** (idm) **dim and distant** (*joc*) long past: *Once, in the dim and distant past, I was a student here.*
▷ **dim** *v* (**-mm-**) [I, Tn] (cause sth to) become dim: *The stage lights (were) dimmed, and the play's first act was over.* ○ *Old age hasn't dimmed her memory.*
dimly *adv* in a dim manner: *a dimly-lit room* ○ *I can dimly* (ie only just) *remember my fourth birthday.* ○ *react rather dimly to a question.*
dimness *n* [U].
□ ˈ**dim-wit** *n* (*infml*) stupid person. ˌ**dim-**ˈ**witted** *adj* (*infml*) stupid.

dime /daɪm/ *n* **1** coin of the US and Canada worth ten cents. ⇨ App 9. **2** (idm) **a** ˌ**dime a** ˈ**dozen** (*infml*) nearly worthless or very common: *Novels like this one are a dime a dozen: write something original!*

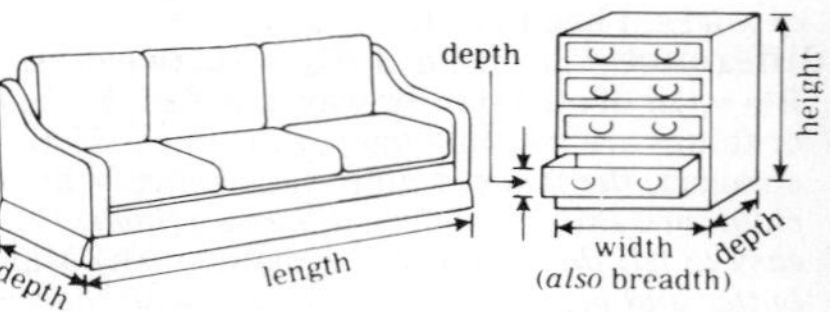

dimensions

dimension /dɪˈmenʃn, daɪ-/ *n* **1** [C, U] measurement of any sort (breadth, length, thickness, height, etc): *What are the dimensions of the room?* ⇨ App 9. ⇨ illus. **2 dimensions** [pl] size; extent: *a creature of huge dimensions* ○ (*fig*) *I hadn't realized the dimensions of the problem.* **3** [C] (*fig*) aspect: *There is a dimension to the problem that we have not discussed.*
▷ **-dimensional** /-ʃənəl/ (forming compound *adjs*) having the specified number of dimensions: *A square is two-dimensional and a cube is three-dimensional.*

NOTE ON USAGE: **1** It is sometimes difficult to decide whether **length** (*adj* **long**), **width** (*adj* **wide**) or **depth** (*adj* **deep**) is the correct term for a particular measurement. The measurements of a room or of a rectangular area or object are the **length** (measured along the longer sides) and the **width** (measured along the shorter sides): *The garage is 6 metres long and 3 metres wide.* When describing a piece of furniture that has a front and a back, both **length** and **width** can be used for the longer sides and **depth** is used for the measurement from front to back. **Length** is generally used when the measurement of the front is much greater than that of the depth. **Width** is used when the measurements of the front and of the depth are similar. (See illustration.) **2** Compare **wide** and **broad**. **Wide** is the more general word but **broad** is used of parts of the body: *a broad nose* ○ *broad shoulders.* Otherwise it is more formal than **wide** and is often used, especially in literary language, to describe features of the landscape: *a broad river* ○ *a broad expanse of unspoilt country.*

diminish /dɪˈmɪnɪʃ/ *v* [I, Tn] **1** (cause sth to) become smaller or less; decrease: *His strength has diminished over the years.* ○ *Nothing could diminish her enthusiasm for the project.* ○ *diminishing hopes, supplies, funds.* **2** (*fig*) make (sb/sth) seem less important than it really is; devalue: *The opposition are trying to diminish our achievements.* **3** (*music*) decrease (an interval) by a semitone: *a diminished fifth.*
□ **di**ˌ**minished responsi**ˈ**bility** (*law*) state of mind in which an accused person cannot be held fully responsible for a crime.

diminuendo /dɪˌmɪnjʊˈendəʊ/ *adj, adv* (*music*) of or with a gradual decrease in loudness: *a diminuendo passage.*
▷ **diminuendo** *n* (*pl* ~**s**) (*music*) gradual

decrease in loudness.

diminution /ˌdɪmɪˈnjuːʃn; US -ˈnuːʃn/ *n* **(a)** [U] diminishing or being diminished; reduction: *The diminution of one's resources.* **(b)** [C] amount of this; reduction: *hoping for a small diminution in taxes.*

diminutive /dɪˈmɪnjʊtɪv/ *adj* **1** unusually or remarkably small: *her diminutive figure.* **2** (*grammar*) (of a suffix) indicating smallness.
▷ **diminutive** *n* word formed by the use of a suffix of this kind, eg *eaglet* (= a young eagle), *kitchenette* (= a small kitchen).

dimity /ˈdɪmɪtɪ/ *n* [U] type of cotton cloth woven with raised strips or designs, used for bed covers, curtains, etc.

dimmer /ˈdɪmə(r)/ *n* (also ˈ**dimmer switch**) device with which one can vary the brightness of an electric light.

dimple /ˈdɪmpl/ *n* **(a)** small natural hollow in the chin or cheek (either permanent, or which appears eg when a person smiles). **(b)** slight hollow on a surface (esp of glass or water).
▷ **dimple** *v* [I, Tn] (cause sth to) form dimples: *Her cheeks dimpled as she smiled.* ○ *The surface of the water was dimpled by the breeze.*

DIN *abbr* (of a scale of film speeds) German Industry Standard (German *Deutsche Industrie-Norm*). Cf ASA 2, ISO.

din /dɪn/ *n* [U, sing] continuing loud confused noise: *They made so much din that I couldn't hear you.* ○ *Don't make such a din!* ○ *make/kick up a din.*
▷ **din** *v* (**-nn-**) **1** (idm) **din in sb's ears** sound or echo in one's ears: *They drove away from the city centre, the roar of the traffic still dinning in their ears.* **2** (phr v) **din sth into sb** tell sb sth again and again in a forceful way: *I dinned it into him that he had to manage things differently.*

dinar /ˈdiːnɑː(r)/ *n* unit of currency in Algeria, Bahrain, Iraq, Jordan, Kuwait, Libya, Yemen, Tunisia and Yugoslavia.

dine /daɪn/ *v* **1** [I, Ipr] ~ (**on sth**) (*fml*) eat dinner: *We dined on smoked salmon.* **2** [Tn] (*fml*) give a dinner for (sb): *We're dining the ambassador this week.* **3** (idm) **wine and dine** ⇨ WINE *v.* **4** (phr v) **dine out** dine away from one's home (eg at a restaurant or in the home of friends). **dine out on sth** be invited to dinner because one knows about a particular event, topic, etc, and can entertain the other guests by talking about it: *The prime minister actually gave me a lift when my car broke down — I should be able to dine out on this for weeks!*
□ ˈ**dining-car** *n* railway carriage in which meals are served.
ˈ**dining-room** *n* room in which meals are eaten.
ˈ**dining-table** *n* table used for eating on. ⇨ illus at FURNITURE.

diner /ˈdaɪnə(r)/ *n* **1** person eating dinner. **2** dining-car on a train. **3** (*US*) small restaurant, usu beside a highway.

dinette /daɪˈnet/ *n* (*esp US*) small room or part of a room, esp a kitchen, used for eating.

ding-dong /ˌdɪŋˈdɒŋ/ *n* **1** sound of bells striking again and again. **2** (*infml*) heated argument: *I had a bit of a ding-dong with him about his mistakes.* ○ [attrib] *a ˌding-dong ˈstruggle, ˈbattle, etc.*
▷ **ding-dong** *adv* with the sound of bells striking again and again: *a clock striking ding-dong.*

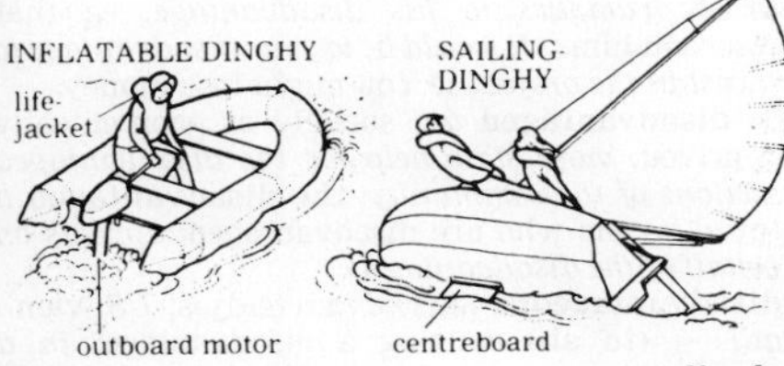

dinghy

dinghy /ˈdɪŋɡɪ/ *n* **(a)** any of various types of small open boat: *a sailing dinghy.* **(b)** inflatable rubber boat (used esp for rescuing passengers from ships and aircraft). ⇨ illus. Cf YACHT.

dingle /ˈdɪŋɡl/ *n* deep hollow in the landscape, usu with trees.

dingo /ˈdɪŋɡəʊ/ *n* (*pl* ~**es**) wild Australian dog.

dingy /ˈdɪndʒɪ/ *adj* (**-ier, -iest**) dirty-looking; not cheerful or bright; drab: *a dingy room in a cheap hotel* ○ *a dingy manufacturing town.* ▷ **dingily** *adv.* **dinginess** *n* [U].

dining ⇨ DINE.

dinkum /ˈdɪŋkəm/ *adj* (*Austral and NZ infml*) genuine; true; real: *D'you reckon his story's fair dinkum?* ie Is he telling the truth?
□ ˌ**dinkum** ˈ**oil** (*Austral and NZ infml*) the complete truth.

dinky /ˈdɪŋkɪ/ *adj* (**-ier, -iest**) (*infml*) **(a)** (*Brit*) small and attractively neat: *What a dinky little hat!* ○ *a dinky red car.* **(b)** (*US*) small and insignificant.

dinner /ˈdɪnə(r)/ *n* **1** [C, U] main meal of the day, whether eaten at midday or in the evening: *It's time for dinner.* ○ *Have you had dinner yet?* ○ (*US*) *Did you eat dinner yet?* ○ *She didn't eat much dinner.* ○ *I never eat a big dinner.* ○ *They're at* (ie eating) *dinner.* ○ *four dinners at £10 per person* ○ *Shall we ask him to dinner?* ⇨ Usage. **2** [C] **(a)** (usu large) formal social gathering at which this meal is eaten: *A dinner was given for the ambassador.* **(b)** (also ˈ**dinner-party**) private social gathering where this meal is eaten: *give a dinner for friends.* **3** (idm) **a dog's breakfast/dinner** ⇨ DOG[1].
□ ˈ**dinner-dance** *n* (*Brit*) (usu formal) dinner followed by dancing.
ˈ**dinner-jacket** *n* (*Brit*) (*US* **tuxedo**) jacket, usu black, worn with a bow-tie and (usu) matching trousers at formal occasions in the evening.
ˈ**dinner service**, ˈ**dinner set** set of plates, dishes, etc for dinner.

NOTE ON USAGE: The use of the terms **lunch**, **dinner**, **supper** and **tea** varies between social classes in Britain and to some extent between regions. If the midday meal is called **lunch**, the evening meal is **dinner** or **supper.** In this case **tea** consists of a drink and cake or biscuits in the afternoon. If the midday meal is called **dinner** then the evening meal is **tea** or **supper.** In this case **supper** may be a light snack before bedtime. At school, children have **school dinner/lunch** at midday or they may take a **packed/sandwich lunch** with them.

dinosaur

dinosaur /ˈdaɪnəsɔː(r)/ *n* large extinct reptile.

dint /dɪnt/ *n* **1** = DENT. **2** (idm) **by dint of sth** by means of sth: *He succeeded by dint of hard work.*

diocese /ˈdaɪəsɪs/ *n* district for which a bishop is responsible.
▷ **diocesan** /daɪˈɒsɪsn/ *adj* of a diocese.

Diocletian /ˌdaɪəˈkliːʃn/ (245-313 AD), Roman emperor 284-305. He divided the empire into two parts (east and west) so that it could be administered more easily, but he is chiefly remembered for his persecution of the early Christians.

diode /ˈdaɪəʊd/ *n* **1** electronic valve with two electrodes, between which current can pass in only one direction. **2** electronic device consisting of semiconducting material with two electrodes between which current can only pass in one direction, used for changing alternating current to direct current.

Dionysus /ˌdaɪəˈnaɪsəs/ (in Greek mythology) god of fertility and of wine, also known as Bacchus.
▷ **Dionysian** /ˌdaɪəˈnɪzɪən/ (also **Dionysiac** /-zɪæk/) *adj* **1** of Dionysus. **2** (often **dionysian**) full of wild unrestrained pleasure, esp of a sexual kind: *dionysian revelry.*

dioptre (*US* **diopter**) /daɪˈɒptə(r)/ *n* unit for measuring the power of a lens.

diorama /ˌdaɪəˈrɑːmə/ *n* **1** scene with model figures, a painted background, etc, viewed through an opening. Dioramas are used eg as museum exhibits. **2** painting of a scene in which particular effects (eg of sunrise) can be achieved by changing the light shone onto it. **3** small-scale model of a building, film-set, etc.

dioxide /daɪˈɒksaɪd/ *n* [U] (*chemistry*) oxide formed by combining two atoms of oxygen and one atom of another element: *carbon dioxide.*

dip[1] /dɪp/ *v* (**-pp-**) **1** [Tn, Tn·pr, Tn·p] ~ **sth (into sth)**; ~ **sth (in)** put or lower sth into a liquid: *Dip your pen (into the ink).* ○ *Dip your fingers in to see how hot the water is.* ○ *dip sheep,* ie immerse them in a liquid that disinfects them or kills vermin ○ *dip candles,* ie make them by dipping a wick into melted fat ○ *to dip a garment,* ie put it in a liquid dye to change its colour. **2** [I, Ipr, Ip] go below a surface or level: *The birds rose and dipped in flight.* ○ *The sun dipped (down) below the horizon.* **3** [I, Tn, Tn·pr] (cause sth to) go down and then up again: *The branches dipped in the wind.* ○ *dip the headlights of a car,* ie lower their beams (so as not to dazzle the driver of another car) ○ *Dip your head under the low arch.* **4** [I, Ip] slope downward: *The land dips (down) gently to the south.* **5** (phr v) **dip into sth** **(a)** take money from (eg one's savings): *dip into one's purse,* ie spend money. **(b)** make a brief study of (a book, an author, etc): *I've only had time to dip into the report.*
□ ˈ**dip-stick** *n* rod for dipping into a tank or some other container to measure the depth of the liquid in it (esp oil in the sump of an engine). ⇨ illus at CAR.
ˈ**dip-switch** *n* (*Brit*) switch for dipping a motor vehicle's headlights.

dip[2] /dɪp/ *n* **1** [C] act of dipping (DIP[1]). **2** [C] (*infml*) quick swim or bathe: *have/take/go for a dip.* **3** [U] cleansing liquid for dipping sheep. **4** [U, C] any of several types of thick sauce into which biscuits or pieces of vegetable are dipped before being eaten: *cheese dip.* **5** [C] downward slope: *a dip in the road* ○ *a dip among the hills.*

Dip *abbr* Diploma.

Dip Ed /ˌdɪp ˈed/ *abbr* Diploma in Education: *have/be a Dip Ed* ○ *Mary Hall BA Dip Ed.*

diphtheria /dɪfˈθɪərɪə/ *n* [U] serious contagious disease of the throat causing difficulty in breathing.

diphthong /ˈdɪfθɒŋ; US -θɔːŋ/ *n* union of two vowel sounds or vowel letters, eg the sounds /aɪ/ in *pipe* /paɪp/, the letters *ou* in *doubt.* Cf MONOPHTHONG.

diploid /ˈdɪplɔɪd/ *adj* having two sets of chromosomes in each cell, one from each parent.

diploma /dɪˈpləʊmə/ *n* (*abbr* **Dip**) certificate awarded for passing an examination, completing a course of study, etc: *a diploma in architecture.*

diplomacy /dɪˈpləʊməsɪ/ *n* [U] **1** management of relations between countries by each country's representatives abroad; skill in this: *International problems must be solved by diplomacy, not war.* **2** art of or skill in dealing with people; tact.

diplomat /ˈdɪpləmæt/ *n* **1** person in the diplomatic service, eg an ambassador. **2** person clever at dealing with people; tactful person.

diplomatic /ˌdɪpləˈmætɪk/ *adj* **1** of diplomacy(1): *settle disputes by diplomatic means.* **2** tactful; having or showing diplomacy(2): *a diplomatic answer, move, etc* ○ *be diplomatic in dealing with people.* ▷ **diplomatically** /-klɪ/ *adv.*
□ ˌ**diplomatic** ˈ**bag** any container for official letters, goods, etc sent to or from an embassy.
diploˈmatic corps all the ambassadors and embassy staff in a country.
diploˌmatic imˈmunity privilege granted to diplomatic staff working abroad, by which they may not be arrested, taxed, etc.
diploˈmatic service all the officials who conduct a country's diplomacy.

diplomatist /dɪˈpləʊmətɪst/ *n* (*fml*) = DIPLOMAT.

dipper /ˈdɪpə(r)/ *n* **1** cup-shaped container with a long handle, for ladling out liquids. **2** type of diving bird. Cf PLOUGH 2.

dippy /ˈdɪpɪ/ *adj* (**-ier, -iest**) (*infml*) slightly mad;

silly.

dipso /ˈdɪpsəʊ/ *n* (*pl* ~**s**) (*infml*) dipsomaniac person.

dipsomania /ˌdɪpsəˈmeɪnɪə/ *n* [U] extreme dependence on alcoholic drink.

▷ **dipsomaniac** /ˌdɪpsəˈmeɪnɪæk/ *n, adj* (person) suffering from dipsomania.

diptych /ˈdɪptɪk/ *n* painting or carving, esp on an altar, on two hinged panels that can be closed like a book.

dire /ˈdaɪə(r)/ *adj* **1** (*fml*) dreadful; terrible: *a dire situation, crisis, etc* ○ *The firm is in dire straits* (ie in a very difficult situation) *and may go bankrupt.* ○ (*joc*) *The film we saw was absolutely dire!* **2** (*infml*) extreme: *We're in dire need of your help.*

direct[1] /dɪˈrekt, daɪ-/ *adj* **1** [esp attrib] (going) straight; not curved or crooked; not turned aside: *follow a direct course, route, etc* ○ *a direct flight*, ie without stopping or changing planes ○ *a direct train*, ie that goes to a passenger's destination without stopping beforehand ○ *a direct hit/shot*, ie not turned aside by hitting sth else first ○ *the direct rays of the sun*, ie not reflected from or screened by sth. **2** (**a**) with nothing or no one in between; immediate: *a direct result, link, connection* ○ *I'm in direct contact with the hijackers.* (**b**) (of descent in a family) passing through sb's children, grandchildren, etc, rather than through his brothers, sisters, cousins, etc: *She descends in a direct line from the country's first President.* **3** straightforward; frank: *a direct person, manner, answer* ○ *She has a direct way of speaking.* ○ *He is very direct, so you always know what his real views are.* **4** [attrib] exact; complete: *the direct opposite* ○ *Your reply today is in direct contradiction to what you said last week.* Cf INDIRECT.

▷ **direct** *adv* **1** without interrupting a journey; using a straight route: *The train goes there direct.* **2** with no one in between; personally: *I prefer to deal with him direct.*

directness [U] *n*.

□ **diˌrect ˈaccess** (*computing*) = RANDOM ACCESS (RANDOM).

diˌrect ˈaction use of strikes, violence, etc instead of negotiation to achieve one's demands.

diˌrect ˈcurrent (*abbr* **DC**) electric current flowing in one direction. Cf ALTERNATING CURRENT (ALTERNATE[2]).

diˌrect ˈdebit order to a bank that allows sb else to withdraw agreed amounts of money from one's account on agreed dates, esp to pay bills. Cf STANDING ORDER (STANDING).

direct ˈmethod way of teaching a foreign language by using only the language being taught, and not allowing the learner to use his own language. Teaching of formal grammar rules is also avoided.

direct ˈobject (*grammar*) noun, noun phrase or noun clause which is directly affected by the action of a verb. Cf OBJECT[1] 5.

direct ˈspeech (use of a) speaker's actual words.

direct ˈtax tax that one pays direct to the Government (eg income tax) rather than eg sales tax which is paid to the seller before being passed on.

direct[2] /dɪˈrekt, daɪ-/ *v* **1** [Tn, Tn·pr] ~ **sb (to...)** tell or show sb how to get somewhere: *Can you direct me (to the station)?* **2** (**a**) [Tn, Tn·pr] ~ **sth (to...)** (*fml*) address (a letter, parcel, etc): *Shall I direct the letter to his business address or to his home address?* (**b**) [Tn·pr] ~ **sth to/at sb** (*fml*) intend that a particular person or group should notice (what one says or does): *Let me direct these remarks to the younger students.* ○ *advertising directed mainly at young consumers.* **3** (**a**) [Tn] manage (sth/sb); control: *She directed the planning of the festival.* ○ *direct a group of workers.* (**b**) [I, Tn] be in charge of (actors, a film, a play, etc): *I'd rather act than direct.* ○ *Who directed the play?* **4** [Tn·pr] ~ **sth to/towards...**; ~ **sth at sth** (*fml*) turn or aim sth in a particular direction: *The guide directed our attention to the other picture.* ○ *We directed our steps towards home.* ○ *direct a blow at sb's head* ○ *Our efforts should be directed towards greater efficiency.* **5** [Tf, Dn·t] (*fml*) order; command: *The owners directed that the factory be closed.* ○ *The officer directed them to advance.* ⇨ Usage at ORDER[2].

direction /dɪˈrekʃn, daɪ-/ *n* **1** (**a**) [C] course taken by a moving person or thing; way that a person or thing looks or faces: *Tom went off in one direction and Harry in another.* ○ *The aircraft was flying in a northerly direction.* ○ *The signpost points in a westerly direction.* ○ *When the police arrived, the crowd scattered in all directions.* (**b**) [C] (*fig*) way in which sb/sth develops or is developed: *new directions in current research* ○ *That is the present direction of government thinking.* ○ *We're making changes in various directions*, ie of various types. **2** [C usu *pl*] information or instructions about what to do, where to go, how to do sth, etc: *Simple directions for assembling the model are printed on the box.* ○ *I gave him full directions to enable him to find the house.* **3 directions** [pl] address on a letter, parcel, etc: *The parcel was returned to the sender because the directions were incorrect.* **4** [U] management; supervision; guidance: *He did the work under my direction.* ○ *She was entrusted with the direction of the project.* ○ *He feels the need for firm direction*, ie wants sb to guide and advise him.

▷ **directional** /-ʃənl/ *adj* of direction in space: *a directional aerial*, ie one that transmits or receives radio signals in one direction only.

□ **diˈrection-finder** *n* radio device that shows the direction from which radio signals are coming.

directive /dɪˈrektɪv, daɪ-/ *n* official instruction: *a directive from headquarters calling for increased output.*

directly /dɪˈrektlɪ, daɪ-/ *adv* **1** in a direct line or manner; straight: *He looked directly at us.* ○ *directly in front of me* ○ *She's directly responsible to the Minister.* ○ *She speaks very directly to people.* ○ *directly opposite.* **2** (**a**) at once; immediately: *Come in directly.* (**b**) in a short time: *I'll be there directly.*

▷ **directly** *conj* as soon as: *I went home directly I had finished work.*

director /dɪˈrektə(r), daɪ-/ *n* **1** (**a**) person who manages, esp as a member of a board[1](7), the affairs of a business company. (**b**) person who is in charge of an institution, a college, etc: *the orchestra's musical director.* **2** person in charge of a film, play, etc who supervises and instructs the actors, camera crew and other staff. Cf PRODUCER 2.

▷ **directorship** *n* (**a**) position of a director. (**b**) time during which a director holds his position.

□ **diˌrector-ˈgeneral** *n* main administrator of a large organization.

directorate /dɪˈrektərət, daɪ-/ *n* **1** position or office of a director. **2** board of directors.

directory /dɪˈrektərɪ, daɪ-/ *n* (book with a) list of telephone subscribers, business firms, etc of an area, or members of a profession, etc, usu arranged alphabetically.

dirge /dɜ:dʒ/ *n* (**a**) song sung at a burial or for a dead person. (**b**) (*infml derog*) mournful song.

dirigible /ˈdɪrɪdʒəbl/ *n* old-fashioned air balloon.

dirk /dɜ:k/ *n* (*Scot*) type of dagger.

dirndl /ˈdɜ:ndl/ *n* dress with a full wide skirt and a close-fitting bodice.

dirt /dɜ:t/ *n* [U] **1** matter that is not clean (eg dust, soil, mud), esp when it is where it is not wanted (eg on the skin, on clothes, in buildings): *His clothes were covered with dirt.* ○ *How can I get the dirt off the walls?* **2** loose earth or soil: *a pile of dirt beside a newly-dug trench.* **3** (*infml*) obscene thought or talk: *Be quiet! We don't want to hear that kind of dirt!* **4** (*infml*) excrement: *a pile of dog dirt on the road.* **5** (*infml*) malicious gossip: *He likes to hear all the dirt about his colleagues.* **6** (idm) (**as**) **cheap/common as ˈdirt** (*infml derog*) vulgar; low-class: *Don't invite her! She's as common as dirt.* **dish the dirt** ⇨ DISH[2]. **fling/throw dirt at sb** say slanderous things about sb. **treat sb like dirt/a dog** ⇨ TREAT.

□ **ˌdirt ˈcheap** (*infml*) very cheap(ly).

ˈdirt farmer (*US*) farmer who does all his own work, without hired help.

ˌdirt ˈroad (*US*) unpaved country road, made of earth or gravel that has been pressed down.

ˈdirt-track *n* track made of cinders, etc (eg for motor-cycle races).

dirty[1] /ˈdɜ:tɪ/ *adj* (**-ier, -iest**) **1** (**a**) not clean; covered with dirt: *dirty hands, clothes, floors.* (**b**) causing one to be dirty: *a dirty job* ○ *dirty work.* **2** (of the weather) rough; stormy: *I'm glad I don't have to go out on such a dirty night.* **3** [attrib] (of colours) not bright or clear: *a dirty brown sofa.* **4** (of a nuclear weapon) producing a lot of harmful radioactivity when it explodes. **5** obscene: *dirty book, joke, etc* ○ *You've got a dirty mind*, ie You have impure thoughts. **6** [usu attrib] (*infml*) unfair; underhand: *That's a dirty lie!* ○ *You dirty rat! How could you do a thing like that?* ○ *That was a mean and dirty thing to do!* **7** (idm) **a dirty old man** (*infml*) older man who takes an unhealthy interest in sex, or in young girls as sexually attractive. **a ˌdirty ˈtrick** mean or dishonourable action which harms sb else: *What a dirty trick to tell her she'd passed the exam when she'd failed!* **ˌdirty ˈtricks** (*esp US*) secret activities intended to harm the reputation of one's enemies, esp in politics. **a ˌdirty ˈweekend** (*esp joc*) weekend spent intimately (and often illicitly) with a sexual partner. (**be**) **a ˌdirty ˈword** thing or idea that is disliked or not respected: *My children think that work is a dirty word!* (**do sb's**) **ˈdirty work** (do) the tasks that sb else does not like or cannot face: *I had to tell them they'd lost their jobs: I always have to do the boss's dirty work (for him).* **do the dirty on sb** cheat or betray sb. **give sb/get a dirty ˈlook** look at sb disapprovingly or in disgust. **wash one's dirty linen in public** ⇨ WASH[2].

▷ **dirtily** *adv*.

dirty *adv* **1** (*infml*) very: *He was carrying a dirty great box.* **2** (idm) **talk dirty** ⇨ TALK[2].

dirty[2] /ˈdɜ:tɪ/ *v* (*pt, pp* **dirtied**) [I, Tn] become or make (sth) dirty: *White gloves dirty easily.* ○ *Don't dirty your new dress.*

dis- *pref* (with *adjs, advs, ns* and *vs*) negative, reverse or opposite of: *dishonest* ○ *disagreeably* ○ *disagreement* ○ *disengage.* ⇨ Usage at UN-.

disability /ˌdɪsəˈbɪlətɪ/ *n* **1** [U] state of being disabled; incapacity: *Physical disability causes mental anguish.* **2** [C] thing that disables; lack of sth necessary: *She swims well despite her disabilities.* ○ *Her lack of experience is a severe disability.* ○ [attrib] *a disability pension.*

disable /dɪsˈeɪbl/ *v* [Tn] make (sb) unable to do sth, esp by making a limb or limbs useless: *a soldier disabled by leg wounds.*

▷ **disabled** *adj* unable to use a limb or limbs: *a disabled child in a wheelchair.* **the disabled** *n* [pl *v*] people who are disabled: *walking aids for the disabled.*

disablement *n* [U].

disabuse /ˌdɪsəˈbju:z/ *v* [Tn·pr] ~ **sb of sth** (*fml*) free sb of (false ideas): *disabuse sb of mistaken notions, false assumptions, etc.*

disadvantage /ˌdɪsədˈvɑ:ntɪdʒ; *US* -ˈvæn-/ *n* **1** unfavourable condition; thing that tends to prevent sb succeeding, making progress, etc: *The other candidate's main disadvantage is her age.* ○ *The lack of decent public transport is a great disadvantage.* **2** (idm) **put sb/be at a disadvantage** put sb/be in an unfavourable position: *His inability to speak French puts him at a disadvantage.* **to sb's disadvantage** (*fml*) damaging sb or his reputation; causing some loss to sb: *rumours to his disadvantage*, eg that discredit him ○ *It would be to your disadvantage to invest in the project*, ie You might lose money.

▷ **disadvantaged** *adj* socially or economically deprived: *more state help for the disadvantaged sections of the community.* **the disadvantaged** *n* [pl *v*] people who are disadvantaged: *appeals on behalf of the disadvantaged.*

disadvantageous /ˌdɪsædvɑ:nˈteɪdʒəs; *US* -væn-/ *adj* ~ (**to sb**) causing a disadvantage: *in a disadvantageous position.* **disadvantageously** *adv*.

disaffected /ˌdɪsəˈfektɪd/ *adj* discontented; disloyal: *Disaffected members have left to form a new party.*

▷ **disaffection** /ˌdɪsəˈfekʃn/ *n* [U] discontent that

often leads to disloyalty.

disafforest /ˌdɪsəˈfɒrɪst; *US* -ˈfɔːr-/ *v* [Tn] = DEFOREST.

disagree /ˌdɪsəˈgriː/ *v* (*pt, pp* **-reed**) **1** [I, Ipr] **(a)** ~ **(with sb/sth) (about/on sth)** have a different opinion (from sb); not agree: *Even friends sometimes disagree.* ○ *disagree with sb/what sb says/sb's decision* ○ *We disagreed on future plans.* **(b)** ~ **(with sth)** not match; be different: *The reports from Rome disagree with those from Milan.* Cf AGREE. **2** (phr v) **disagree with sb** (of food, climate) have a bad effect on sb; cause sb to feel unwell: *I feel sick: that fish disagreed with me.*

disagreeable /ˌdɪsəˈgriːəbl/ *adj* unpleasant: *a disagreeable person, mood, experience.* ▷ **disagreeableness** *n* [U]. **disagreeably** /-əblɪ/ *adv.*

disagreement /ˌdɪsəˈgriːmənt/ *n* **1** [U] ~ **(about/on sth)** disagreeing; lack of agreement: *total disagreement on how to proceed.* **2** [C] instance of this; difference of opinion: *disagreements between colleagues.*

disallow /ˌdɪsəˈlaʊ/ *v* [Tn] refuse to accept (sth) as valid: *disallow a claim, goal.*

disappear /ˌdɪsəˈpɪə(r)/ *v* **1** [I] **(a)** no longer be visible; vanish: *The plane disappeared behind a cloud.* ○ *The rash soon disappeared.* **(b)** stop existing: *His anger soon disappeared.* ○ *The problem won't just disappear.* **(c)** be lost, esp without explanation: *My passport has just disappeared: it was in my pocket a moment ago.* ○ (*euph*) *Things tend to disappear when he's around,* ie He steals them. **2** (idm) **do a disappearing act** disappear, esp when needed or being looked for: *It's typical of Bob to do a disappearing act just when there's work to be done!*

▷ **disappearance** /-ˈpɪərəns/ *n* **(a)** [U] act or fact of disappearing: *At first nobody noticed the child's disappearance.* **(b)** [C] instance of sb disappearing, eg because he has been murdered or kidnapped: *Most disappearances are the result of terrorist activity.*

disappoint /ˌdɪsəˈpɔɪnt/ *v* [Tn] **1** fail to be or do sth as good, interesting etc as was hoped for or desired or expected by (sb): *The tenor disappointed us by singing flat.* ○ *I can't disappoint my public by retiring.* ○ *Don't disappoint me by being late again.* ○ *I've often been disappointed in love,* ie not been loved in return by sb I have loved. **2** prevent (a hope, plan, etc) from becoming reality: *disappoint sb's expectations, sb's calculations, etc.*

▷ **disappointed** *adj* ~ **(about/at sth)**; ~ **(in/with sb/sth)**; ~ **(to do sth/that...)** sad or dissatisfied because one/sb has failed, some desired event has not happened, etc: *be disappointed about/at sb's failure* ○ *I was disappointed with his performance.* ○ *I'm disappointed in you: I expected you to win.* ○ *He was disappointed to hear they were not coming.* ○ *I was disappointed not to be chosen.* **disappointedly** *adv.*

disappointing *adj* causing sb to be disappointed: *a disappointing novel* ○ *The weather this summer has been most disappointing.* **disappointingly** *adv*: *Disappointingly, he had nothing new to show us.*

disappointment /ˌdɪsəˈpɔɪntmənt/ *n* **1** [U] being disappointed: *To our great disappointment, it rained on the day of the picnic.* **2** [C] ~ **(to sb)** person or thing that disappoints: *Not getting the job was a terrible disappointment.* ○ *His children are a disappointment to him.*

disapprobation /ˌdɪsˌæprəˈbeɪʃn/ *n* [U] (*fml*) disapproval.

disapprove /ˌdɪsəˈpruːv/ *v* [I, Ipr] ~ **(of sb/sth)** consider (sb/sth) to be bad, immoral, foolish, etc: *She wants to be an actress, but her parents disapprove (of her intentions).*

▷ **disapproval** /-ˈpruːvl/ *n* [U] not approving (of sb/sth): *her disapproval of my methods* ○ *He shook his head in disapproval,* ie to show that he disapproved.

disapproving *adj* showing disapproval: *a disapproving look, frown, etc.* **disapprovingly** *adv*: *When I suggested a drink, she coughed disapprovingly.*

disarm /dɪsˈɑːm/ *v* **1** [Tn] take weapons away from (sb): *Five hundred rebels were captured and disarmed.* **2** [I] (of nations) reduce the size of or abolish one's armed forces; give up one's weapons: *The superpowers are unlikely to disarm completely.* **3** [Tn] make (sb) less suspicious, angry, hostile, etc: *By frankly admitting he wasn't a brilliant player, he disarmed us all.* ○ *I felt angry, but her smile disarmed me.*

▷ **disarmament** /dɪsˈɑːməmənt/ *n* [U] disarming or being disarmed (DISARM 2): *nuclear disarmament,* ie giving up nuclear weapons ○ [attrib] *a disarmament conference.*

disarming *adj* that disarms (DISARM 3): *her disarming smile, frankness, charm, etc.* **disarmingly** *adv*: *disarmingly frank, honest, etc.*

disarrange /ˌdɪsəˈreɪndʒ/ *v* [Tn] (*fml*) **(a)** make (sth) disorderly or untidy: *disarrange sb's papers, hair.* **(b)** upset (sth); disturb: *Her sudden departure has disarranged my plans.* ▷ **disarrangement** *n* [U].

disarray /ˌdɪsəˈreɪ/ *n* [U] state in which people or things are no longer properly organized: *The troops fled in disarray.* ○ *Changing offices has left my papers in complete disarray.*

disassociate = DISSOCIATE.

disaster /dɪˈzɑːstə(r); *US* -ˈzæs-/ *n* **1** [C] **(a)** event that causes great harm or damage, eg a fire, a serious defeat, the loss of a large sum of money: *Thousands died in the disaster.* ○ *Losing your job needn't be such a disaster.* ○ *a natural disaster,* ie an accident, such as an earthquake or a flood, that is not caused by human beings. **(b)** (*infml*) person or thing that is a complete failure: *As a teacher, he's a disaster.* ○ *The play's first night was a disaster.* **2** [U] failure: *His career is a story of utter disaster.*

▷ **disastrous** /dɪˈzɑːstrəs; *US* -ˈzæs-/ *adj* being or causing a disaster: *disastrous floods* ○ *a defeat that was disastrous to the country* ○ *Buying this house was a disastrous step: it's going to have a main road built behind it.* **disastrously** *adv.*

□ **diˈsaster area** area affected by a disaster, eg an earthquake, floods, etc: *declare a place a disaster area.*

disavow /ˌdɪsəˈvaʊ/ *v* [Tn] (*fml*) say one does not know of, is not responsible for, or does not approve of (sth): *She disavows any part* (ie says she was not involved) *in the plot.* ▷ **disavowal** /-ˈvaʊəl/ *n* [C, U].

disband /dɪsˈbænd/ *v* [I, Tn] (cause sth to) stop operating as an organization; break up: *The regiment disbanded when the war was over.* ○ *disband a club, society, etc.* ▷ **disbandment** *n* [U].

disbelieve /ˌdɪsbɪˈliːv/ *v* **1** [Tn] refuse to believe (sb/sth): *I disbelieve every word you say.* ○ *You have no reason to disbelieve their account of what happened.* **2** [Ipr] ~ **in sb/sth** not accept the existence of (sth): *disbelieve in ghosts.*

▷ **disbelief** /ˌdɪsbɪˈliːf/ *n* [U] lack of belief; failure to believe: *He listened in disbelief to this extraordinary story.* Cf UNBELIEF.

disburse /dɪsˈbɜːs/ *v* [Tn] (*fml*) pay out (money): *funds disbursed for travelling expenses.*

▷ **disbursement** *n* (*fml*) **(a)** [U] paying out money. **(b)** [C] sum of money paid out.

disc (also *esp US* **disk**) /dɪsk/ *n* **1** flat thin round plate, eg a coin: *He wears an identity disc round his neck.* **2** round surface that appears to be flat: *the moon's disc.* **3** = RECORD[1] 3: *recordings on disc and cassette.* **4** (*anatomy*) layer of cartilage between the bones of the spine: *a slipped disc,* ie one that is slightly dislocated.

□ **ˈdisc brake** brake which consists of a flat plate pressed against a rotating plate at the centre of a (car) wheel. Cf DRUM BRAKE (DRUM[1]).

ˈdisc harrow harrow with discs instead of teeth.

ˈdisc jockey (*abbr* **DJ**) person who plays and comments on recorded popular music, esp on radio or TV.

ˈdisc parking system for allowing a car, etc to be parked in a public street if the time of its arrival or departure is shown on a disc inside the vehicle.

discard /dɪˈskɑːd/ *v* [Tn] **(a)** throw (sth) out or away: *old, discarded clothes.* **(b)** stop using, wearing, etc (sth that is no longer useful): *discard one's winter clothes in spring* ○ (*fig*) *discard outdated beliefs.* **(c)** give up (unwanted playing-cards): *She discarded a four, and picked up a king.*

▷ **discard** /ˈdɪskɑːd/ *n* card or cards discarded in a card-game; discarded thing.

discern /dɪˈsɜːn/ *v* [Tn] see (sth) clearly (with the senses or the mind), esp with an effort: *In the gloom I could only just discern the outline of a building.* ○ *One can faintly discern the flavour of lemon.* ○ *discern sb's true intentions.*

▷ **discernible** *adj* that can just be discerned.

discerning *adj* (*approv*) showing careful judgement: *She is a very discerning art critic.*

discernment *n* [U] ability to judge well; insight.

discharge[1] /dɪsˈtʃɑːdʒ/ *v* **1** [Tn] unload (a ship); unload (cargo) from a ship. **2** [I, Tn] give or send out (liquid, gas, electric current, etc): *The Nile discharges* (ie flows) *into the Mediterranean.* ○ *The sewers discharge (their contents) into the sea.* ○ *Lightning is caused by clouds discharging electricity.* ○ *The wound is discharging (pus).* **3** [Tn] **(a)** fire (a gun, etc): *The rifle was discharged accidently.* **(b)** launch (eg a flying weapon): *arrows discharged at the enemy.* **4** [Tn] give official permission for (sb) to leave, eg after he has carried out a duty: *discharge a soldier, patient, etc* ○ *The accused man was found not guilty and discharged.* ○ *The members of the jury were discharged.* ○ *a discharged bankrupt,* ie sb who has been bankrupt, has done what the court requires, and has no further obligation to the court. **5** [Tn] (*fml*) **(a)** pay (a debt). **(b)** perform (a duty): *She undertook to discharge all the responsibilities of a Minister.*

discharge[2] /ˈdɪstʃɑːdʒ/ *n* **1** [U] discharging or being discharged: *the discharge of cargo* ○ *the discharge of water from the reservoir* ○ *the accidental discharge of a rifle* ○ *The soldier was found guilty of theft, and given a dishonourable discharge,* ie dismissed from the army for his bad behaviour. ○ *money accepted in full discharge of a debt* ○ *the conscientious discharge of one's duties.* **2** [U, C] that which is discharged (DISCHARGE[1] 2): *The wound hasn't healed — there's still some/a discharge.* ie it is still producing pus.

disciple /dɪˈsaɪpl/ *n* follower of a religious, political, artistic, etc leader or teacher.

disciplinarian /ˌdɪsəplɪˈneərɪən/ *n* person who believes in strict discipline: *a good/strict/poor disciplinarian* ○ *He's no disciplinarian,* ie He does not or cannot maintain discipline.

discipline[1] /ˈdɪsɪplɪn/ *n* **1** **(a)** [U] training, esp of the mind and character, aimed at producing self-control, obedience, etc: *school discipline* ○ *Strict discipline is imposed on army recruits.* ○ *monastic discipline.* **(b)** [U] result of such training; ordered behaviour, eg of schoolchildren, soldiers: *The soldiers showed perfect discipline under fire.* ○ *The children are happy at the school, but they lack discipline.* **2** [C] **(a)** method by which training may be given: *Yoga is a good discipline for learning to relax.* **(b)** set rules for conduct. **3** [U] punishment: *the teacher's cruel discipline.* **4** [C] branch of knowledge; subject of instruction: *scientific disciplines.*

▷ **disciplinary** /ˈdɪsɪplɪnərɪ; *US* -nerɪ/ *adj* concerning discipline: *disciplinary measures, problems, etc* ○ *a disciplinary hearing,* eg of a soldier accused of an offence.

discipline[2] /ˈdɪsɪplɪn/ *v* **1** [Tn, Cn·t] train (sb/sth) to be obedient, self-controlled, skilful, etc: *a well/badly disciplined orchestra, football team, etc* ○ *Parents have to discipline their children.* ○ *You must discipline yourself to finish your work on time.* **2** [Tn] punish (sb): *The teacher disciplined the class by giving them extra homework.*

disclaim /dɪsˈkleɪm/ *v* [Tn, Tg] say that one does not have (sth); renounce: *The gang disclaimed all responsibility for the explosion,* ie said they did not cause it. ○ *She disclaimed ownership of the vehicle.*

▷ **disclaimer** *n* statement that disclaims: *to issue/send a disclaimer.*

disclose /dɪsˈkləʊz/ *v* (*fml*) **(a)** [Tn, Dn·pr] ~ **sth (to sb)** allow sth to be seen: *He opened the box, disclosing the contents (to the audience).* **(b)** [Tn, Tf,

Tw, Dn·pr, Dpr·f, Dpr·w] ~ **sth (to sb)** make sth known: *refuse to disclose one's name and address* ○ *The Government disclosed that another diplomat has been arrested for spying.* ○ *She wouldn't disclose her friend's whereabouts to the police.*
▷ **disclosure** /dɪsˈkləʊʒə(r)/ *n* **(a)** [U] making sth known: *the magazine's disclosure of defence secrets.* **(b)** [C] thing, esp a secret, that is made known: *startling disclosures of police brutality.*

disco /ˈdɪskəʊ/ *n* (*pl* ~**s**) (also **discotheque** /ˈdɪskətek/) **1** club, party, etc, usu with flashing lights, where people dance to recorded pop music: *Is there a good disco round here?* **2** equipment that produces the sound and lighting effects of a disco: *We're hiring a disco for the party.*
□ **ˈdisco dancing** modern popular dancing with no fixed steps, with or without a partner.
ˈdisco music type of music played in discos.

discolour (*US* **discolor**) /dɪsˈkʌlə(r)/ *v* **1** [Tn] change or spoil the colour of (sth): *Smoking discolours the teeth.* **2** [I] (of colour) change or be spoilt.
▷ **discoloration** /ˌdɪskʌləˈreɪʃn/ *n* **(a)** [U] process of discolouring: *some discoloration of the paintwork.* **(b)** [C] discoloured spot; stain.

discomfit /dɪsˈkʌmfɪt/ *v* [Tn] (*fml*) confuse or embarrass (sb): *be discomfited by rude questions.* ▷ **discomfiture** /dɪsˈkʌmfɪtʃə(r)/ *n* [U]: *a look, air, expression, etc of discomfiture.*

discomfort /dɪsˈkʌmfət/ *n* **1** **(a)** [U] lack of comfort; slight pain: *He still suffers considerable discomfort from his injury.* **(b)** [C] thing that causes this: *the discomforts of travel.* **2** [U] mental unease; embarrassment.

discommode /ˌdɪskəˈməʊd/ *v* [Tn] (*fml*) cause (sb) inconvenience.

discompose /ˌdɪskəmˈpəʊz/ *v* [Tn] (*fml*) make (sb) feel uneasy or uncomfortable. ▷ **discomposure** /ˌdɪskəmˈpəʊʒə(r)/ *n* [U].

disconcert /ˌdɪskənˈsɜːt/ *v* [Tn usu passive] cause (sb) to feel confused, upset or embarrassed: *He was disconcerted to find the other guests formally dressed.* ▷ **disconcerted** *adj*: *a disconcerted look, glance, tone of voice, etc.* **disconcerting** *adj*: *a disconcerting reply, stare, silence, manner, etc.* **disconcertingly** *adv.*

disconnect /ˌdɪskəˈnekt/ *v* [Tn, Tn·pr] ~ **A (from B)** detach sth (from sth); undo a connection: *If you don't pay your bills they'll disconnect your electricity/gas.* ○ *disconnect a TV (from the power supply)*, ie unplug it ○ *Operator, I/we have been disconnected*, ie I have lost contact with the person I was telephoning.
▷ **disconnected** *adj* (of speech or writing) lacking in order; incoherent: *the disconnected ramblings of an old man.* **disconnectedly** *adv.*
disconnection *n* [U].

disconsolate /dɪsˈkɒnsələt/ *adj* unhappy, esp at the loss of sb/sth; refusing to be comforted: *The death of her father left Mary disconsolate.* ▷ **disconsolately** *adv.*

discontent /ˌdɪskənˈtent/ (also **discontentment** /ˌdɪskənˈtentmənt/) *n* [U] ~ **(with sth)** lack of satisfaction: *The strikes were a sign of discontent (with poor pay).*
▷ **discontented** *adj* dissatisfied: *discontented with one's job.* **discontentedly** *adv.*

discontinue /ˌdɪskənˈtɪnjuː/ *v* [I, Tn, Tg] (cause sth to) come to an end; stop (doing sth): *I'll have to discontinue these weekly visits.* ○ *The local rail service (was) discontinued in 1958.*
▷ **discontinuation** /ˌdɪskəntɪnjʊˈeɪʃn/ (also **discontinuance** /ˌdɪskənˈtɪnjʊəns/) *n* [U] ending the availability, production, etc of sth: *the discontinuation of our loss-making products.*
discontinuous /ˌdɪskənˈtɪnjʊəs/ *adj* not continuous; intermittent. **discontinuously** *adv.*

discord /ˈdɪskɔːd/ *n* (*fml*) **1** **(a)** [U] disagreement; quarrelling: *A note of discord crept into their relationship.* **(b)** [C] instance of this. **2** (*music*) **(a)** [U] lack of harmony between notes sounded together. **(b)** [C] instance of this; unpleasant sound. Cf CONCORD. **3** (idm) **an/the apple of discord** ⇨ APPLE.
▷ **discordance** /dɪˈskɔːdəns/ *n* [U].
discordant /dɪˈskɔːdənt/ *adj* **1** [usu attrib] not in agreement; conflicting: *discordant views, interests, etc.* **2** (of sounds) harsh. **discordantly** *adv.*

discotheque = DISCO.

discount[1] /ˈdɪskaʊnt/ *n* [U, C] **1** amount of money taken off the cost of sth: *We give (a) 10% discount for cash*, ie for immediate payment. **2** (*commerce*) amount deducted for paying a bill of exchange. Cf REBATE[1]. **3** (idm) **at a discount** **(a)** at a reduced price. **(b)** (*fig*) not highly valued; unfashionable: *Concern for others seems to be at (something of) a discount today.*
□ **ˈdiscount house** **1** (*Brit commerce*) establishment which deals in discounts (DISCOUNT[1] 2). **2** (*US*) = DISCOUNT SHOP.
ˈdiscount shop (also **ˈdiscount store**, **ˈdiscount warehouse**) shop which regularly sells goods at less than the usual price.

discount[2] /dɪsˈkaʊnt; *US* ˈdɪskaʊnt/ *v* [Tn] **1** regard (sth) as unimportant or untrue; ignore (sb/sth): *You can discount what Jack said: he's a dreadful liar.* **2** (*commerce*) buy or sell a bill of exchange for less than it will be worth when due.
□ **disˌcounted ˈcash flow** (*abbr* **DCF**) (*commerce*) way of calculating what the future value of income on an investment will be at the time when it is received.

discountenance /dɪsˈkaʊntɪnəns/ *v* [Tn] (*fml*) disapprove of (sb); discourage.

discourage /dɪˈskʌrɪdʒ/ *v* **1** [Tn, Tn·pr] ~ **sb (from doing sth)** take away sb's confidence or hope of doing sth: *Don't discourage her; she's doing her best.* **2** **(a)** [Tn] try to stop (sth): *Parents should discourage smoking.* **(b)** [Tn·pr] ~ **sb from doing sth** persuade sb not to do sth: *Parents should discourage their children from smoking.*
▷ **discouraged** *adj.*
discouragement *n* **(a)** [U] action of discouraging; state of feeling discouraged. **(b)** [C] thing that discourages: *Despite all these discouragements, she refused to give up.*
discouraging *adj*: *a discouraging result, reply.* **discouragingly** *adv.*

discourse /ˈdɪskɔːs/ *n* **1** [C] (*fml*) lengthy and serious treatment of a subject in speech or writing. **2** [U] (*linguistics*) continuous piece of spoken or written language: *analyse the structure of discourse* ○ [attrib] *discourse analysis.*
▷ **discourse** /dɪˈskɔːs/ *v* [Ipr] ~ **on/upon sth** (*fml*) talk, preach or lecture about sth (usu at length): *The speaker discoursed knowledgeably on a variety of subjects.*

discourteous /dɪsˈkɜːtɪəs/ *adj* (*fml*) bad-mannered; impolite: *It was discourteous of you to arrive late.*
▷ **discourteously** *adv.*
discourtesy /dɪsˈkɜːtəsɪ/ *n* [U, C] (*fml*) impoliteness; rude act or comment: *I must apologize for my discourtesy in arriving late.*

discover /dɪsˈkʌvə(r)/ *v* **1** [Tn, Tf, Tw] find or learn about (a place, fact, etc for the first time): *Columbus discovered America.* ○ *I've discovered a super restaurant near here!* ○ *I never discovered how to start the engine.* Cf INVENT 1. **2** [Tn, Tng] find (sb/sth) unexpectedly: *I discovered him kissing my wife.* **3** [Tn, Tf, Tw, Tnt esp passive] come to know or realize (sth): *Did you ever discover who did it?* ○ *We discovered that our luggage had been stolen.* ○ *He was later discovered to have been a spy.* ▷ **discoverer** *n.*

discovery /dɪˈskʌvərɪ/ *n* **1** **(a)** [U] discovering or being discovered: *a voyage of discovery* ○ *the discovery of Australia* ○ *the discovery by Franklin that lightning is electricity.* **(b)** [C] act of discovering: *Scientists have made many important discoveries.* ○ *He buried the treasure to prevent its discovery.* **2** [C] thing discovered: *Like many discoveries, atomic power can be used for good or evil.*

discredit[1] /dɪsˈkredɪt/ *v* [Tn] **1** damage the good reputation of (sb/sth): *The Government was discredited by the scandal.* **2** cause (sb/sth) to be disbelieved: *His theories were discredited by scientists.* **3** refuse to believe (sb/sth): *There is no reason to discredit what she says.*

discredit[2] /dɪsˈkredɪt/ *n* **1** [U] loss of reputation or respect; dishonour: *Violent fans bring discredit on their teams.* ○ *The police, to their discredit, arrived too late.* **2** [sing] ~ **to sb/sth** person or thing that causes loss of respect to sb/sth: *He is a discredit to his family.* **3** [U] disbelief; doubt: *The findings of the report threw discredit on the protesters' claims.*
▷ **discreditable** /-əbl/ *adj* causing a loss of reputation; dishonourable: *discreditable conduct, methods, tactics, etc.* **discreditably** /-əblɪ/ *adv.*

discreet /dɪˈskriːt/ *adj* careful or showing good judgement in what one says or does; not too obvious: *We must be extremely discreet; my husband suspects something.* ○ *I should make a few discreet enquiries about the firm before you sign anything.* ○ (*fig*) *a discreet perfume*, ie one that is not too obvious. ▷ **discreetly** *adv.*

discrepancy /dɪˈskrepənsɪ/ *n* ~ **(between A and B)** [C, U] difference; failure to agree: *There is (a) considerable discrepancy/There were many discrepancies between the two versions of the affair.*
▷ **discrepant** *adj.*

discrete /dɪˈskriːt/ *adj* separate; distinct: *discrete particles* ○ *a series of discrete events.* ▷ **discretely** *adv.* **discreteness** *n* [U].

discretion /dɪˈskreʃn/ *n* [U] **1** quality of being discreet; good judgement: *to act with discretion* ○ *This is a secret, but I know I can count on your discretion*, ie be sure you won't tell anyone. **2** freedom to decide for oneself what should be done: *Don't keep asking me what to do; use your own discretion.* **3** (idm) **the age/years of diˈscretion** maturity; age when one is considered able to judge and decide for oneself. **at sb's discretion** on the basis of sb's judgement: *A supplementary grant may be awarded at the discretion of the committee.* **diˌscretion is the ˌbetter part of ˈvalour** (*saying usu joc*) there is no point in taking unnecessary risks.
▷ **discretionary** /dɪˈskreʃənərɪ; *US* dɪˈskreʃənerɪ/ *adj* [esp attrib] used, adopted, etc when considered necessary: *discretionary powers, measures, etc* ○ *discretionary payments to old people.*

discriminate /dɪˈskrɪmɪneɪt/ *v* **1** [I, Ipr, Tn·pr] ~ **(between A and B)**; ~ **A from B** see or make a difference (between two things): *discriminate between two cases/one case from another* ○ *The law discriminates between accidental and intentional killing.* **2** [Ipr] ~ **against sb/in favour of sb** treat (one person or group) worse/better than others: *Society still discriminates against women/in favour of men.*
▷ **discriminating** *adj* **1** showing good judgement and perception: *discriminating taste, judgement, etc* ○ *a discriminating connoisseur, collector, customer, etc* ○ *She has an artist's discriminating eye.* **2** = DISCRIMINATORY.
discriminatory /dɪˈskrɪmɪnətərɪ; *US* dɪˈskrɪmɪnətɔːrɪ/ *adj* discriminating against sb/sth: *discriminatory measures, policies, actions, tariffs.*

discrimination /dɪˌskrɪmɪˈneɪʃn/ *n* [U] **1** good judgement and perception: *show discrimination in one's choice of friends, clothes, hobbies.* **2** ~ **(against/in favour of sb)** treating a person or group differently (usu worse) than others: *racial, sexual, religious, political, etc discrimination* ○ *This is a clear case of discrimination (against foreign imports).*

discursive /dɪˈskɜːsɪv/ *adj* (of the way a person speaks or writes) wandering from one point to another: *a rather discursive account of the events.*
▷ **discursively** *adv.* **discursiveness** *n* [U].

discus

discus /ˈdɪskəs/ *n* **(a)** [C] heavy disc thrown in athletic contests. **(b)** **the discus** [sing] discus-throwing event: *I see Britain did well in the discus.* ⇨ illus.

discuss /dɪˈskʌs/ *v* [Tn, Tn·pr, Tw, Tg, Tsg] ~ **sth (with sb)** talk or write about sth: *Jack was still discussing the game (with his friends) when I got there.* ○ *We discussed when to go/when we should go.* ○ *They discussed selling the house.* ○ *We're here to discuss Ann's joining the club.* ○ *Her latest book discusses the problems of the disabled.*

▷ **discussion** /dɪˈskʌʃn/ *n* **1** [C, U] (instance of) discussing sth: *After much discussion/several lengthy discussions they decided to accept our offer.* ⇨ Usage at TALK[1]. **2** (idm) **under discussion** being talked about: *The plans have been under discussion for a year now, but no decision has been reached.* ○ *the matter under discussion.*

disdain /dɪsˈdeɪn/ *n* [U] feeling that sb/sth is not good enough to deserve one's respect; contempt: *a look/tone/expression of disdain* ○ *treating other people's ideas with disdain.*

▷ **disdain** *v* **1** [Tn] treat (sth/sb) with disdain; despise: *disdain an invitation, an offer of help, a peace initiative.* **2** [Tg, Tt] (*fml*) refuse (doing/to do sth) because of one's disdain: *He disdains going to the cinema/to sit with people like us.*

disdainful /-fl/ *adj* ~ **(of sb/sth)** showing disdain: *a disdainful reply* ○ *He's disdainful of anyone from America.* **disdainfully** /-fəlɪ/ *adv.*

disease /dɪˈzi:z/ *n* [C, U] (case of) illness of the body, of the mind or of plants, caused by infection or internal disorder: *a serious, infectious, incurable disease* ○ *a disease of the nervous system* ○ *prevent/spread disease.*

▷ **diseased** *adj* suffering from a disease: *diseased kidneys, leaves* ○ (*fig*) *a diseased society, mentality, imagination.*

disembark /ˌdɪsɪmˈbɑ:k/ (also **debark**) *v* **(a)** [I, Ipr] ~ **(from sth)** (of people) leave a ship or an aircraft: *disembark from a ferry.* **(b)** [Tn, Tn·pr] ~ **sb/sth (from sth)** cause (people or goods) to leave a ship or an aircraft: *disembark passengers from the plane.* ▷ **disembarkation** /ˌdɪsembɑ:ˈkeɪʃn/ (also **debarkation**) *n* [U]: *After disembarkation, we went through passport control.*

disembarrass /ˌdɪsɪmˈbærəs/ *v* (*fml or rhet*) **1** [Tn, Tn·pr] ~ **sb/oneself (of sth)** take sth troublesome away from sb/oneself; relieve sb/oneself: *Allow me to disembarrass you of those heavy cases.* **2** [Tn] free (sb) from embarrassment.

disembodied /ˌdɪsɪmˈbɒdɪd/ *adj* [usu attrib] **1** (of a soul or spirit) separated from the body. **2** (*fig*) (of sounds) lacking any obvious source; eerie: *disembodied voices, screams, groans, etc.*

disembowel /ˌdɪsɪmˈbaʊəl/ *v* (**-ll-**; *US* also **-l-**) [Tn] remove the bowels of sb, usu as part of an execution.

disenchant /ˌdɪsɪnˈtʃɑ:nt; *US* ˌdɪsɪnˈtʃænt/ *v* [Tn] cause (sb) to lose his good opinion of sb/sth; disillusion: *Her arrogance has disenchanted many of her former admirers.* ▷ **disenchanted** *adj* ~ **(with sb/sth)**: *His disenchanted supporters abandoned him.* ○ *I'm becoming increasingly disenchanted with London.* **disenchantment** *n* [U].

disencumber /ˌdɪsɪnˈkʌmbə(r)/ *v* [Tn, Tn·pr] ~ **sb/sth (of sth)** (*fml*) free sb/sth from (a burden, an obstruction, etc): *disencumber oneself of financial responsibilities, social commitments.*

disenfranchise /ˌdɪsɪnˈfræntʃaɪz/ *v* [Tn] = DISFRANCHISE.

disengage /ˌdɪsɪnˈgeɪdʒ/ *v* **1** [Tn, Tn·pr] ~ **sth/sb (from sth/sb)** (*fml*) free or disconnect sth/sb from sth/sb that holds it/him firmly: *Disengage the clutch* (ie from the gear mechanism) *before changing gear.* ○ (*joc*) *He managed to disengage himself from Martha's embrace.* **2** [I, Ipr, Tn, Tn·pr] ~ **(sb/sth) (from sth)** (*military*) (cause sb/sth to) stop fighting and withdraw: *The fighter planes quickly disengaged (from the combat).* ○ *We must disengage our troops (from the conflict).*

▷ **disengaged** *adj* [usu pred] (*fml*) (of a person) free from social or professional obligations.

disengagement *n* [U].

disentangle /ˌdɪsɪnˈtæŋgl/ *v* **1** [Tn] make (rope, hair, etc) straight and free of knots. **2** [Tn, Tn·pr] ~ **sth/sb (from sth)** free sth/sb from sth that hooks into it/him: *He tried to disentangle himself (from the bushes into which he had fallen).* ○ (*fig*) *I wish I could disentangle myself from Jill,* ie from my relationship with her. ○ *disentangle the truth from a mass of lies.* ▷ **disentanglement** *n* [U].

disequilibrium /ˌdɪsi:kwɪˈlɪbrɪəm, *also* -ekw-/ *n* [U] (*fml usu fig*) loss or lack of balance: *a disequilibrium in the military forces of the two countries.*

disestablish /ˌdɪsɪˈstæblɪʃ/ *v* [Tn] end the official status of (a national Church): *those who want to disestablish the Church of England.* ▷ **disestablishment** *n* [U].

disfavour (*US* **disfavor**) /ˌdɪsˈfeɪvə(r)/ *n* [U] dislike; disapproval (used esp as in the expressions shown): *regard sb/sth with disfavour* ○ *incur sb's disfavour* ○ *be in/fall into disfavour.*

disfigure /dɪsˈfɪgə(r); *US* dɪsˈfɪgjər/ *v* [Tn] spoil the appearance of (sb/sth): *The accident disfigured him for life.* ○ *a landscape disfigured by a power station.* ▷ **disfigurement** *n* [U, C]: *the planners responsible for the disfigurement of the countryside.*

disfranchise /dɪsˈfræntʃaɪz/ (also **disenfranchise** /ˌdɪsɪnˈfræntʃaɪz/) *v* [Tn] take away the right to vote for a parliamentary representative from (a person or place). ▷ **disfranchisement** /dɪsˈfræntʃɪzmənt/ (also **disenfranchisement** /ˌdɪsɪnˈf-/) *n* [U].

disgorge /dɪsˈgɔ:dʒ/ *v* **1** [Tn, Tn·pr] ~ **sth (from sth)** throw out (food, etc) from the stomach or throat; vomit: *She was trying hard to disgorge a fish bone.* **2 (a)** [Ipr, Tn·pr] ~ **(itself) into sth** (of a river) let (its waters) flow out, esp into the sea or another river: *The Avon disgorges (itself) into the Severn.* **(b)** [Ipr, Tn, Tn·pr] ~ **(sth) (from sth) (into sth)** (*fig*) (let sth) pour out in a great mass: *Crowds disgorged from the theatre into the dark street.* ○ *The holed tanker was disgorging oil.* **3** [I, Tn] (*infml joc*) unwillingly hand (sth) over or back: *You owe me £5: come on, disgorge!*

disgrace[1] /dɪsˈgreɪs/ *n* **1** [U] state in which others think that one has behaved badly and no longer deserves respect: *bring disgrace on oneself, one's family, etc* ○ *There is no disgrace in being poor.* **2** [sing] **a** ~ **(to sb/sth)** thing or person that is so bad that one feels or should feel ashamed: *Your homework is a disgrace: rewrite it!* ○ *These slums are a disgrace to the city.* **3** (idm) **(be) in disgrace (with sb)** (be) regarded with deep disfavour: *He's in disgrace (with his father) because he told a lie.*

▷ **disgraceful** /-fl/ *adj* causing disgrace; very bad: *disgraceful manners, behaviour, etc* ○ *This cheating is disgraceful.* ○ *The bus is late again — it's absolutely disgraceful!* **disgracefully** /-fəlɪ/ *adv.*

disgrace[2] /dɪsˈgreɪs/ *v* [Tn] **1** bring disgrace on (sb/sth); be a disgrace to: *Your behaviour disgraces us all.* ○ *He got drunk and disgraced himself at the wedding.* **2** cause (sb) to lose a position of power, honour or favour: *After the defeat two generals were publicly disgraced.*

disgruntled /dɪsˈgrʌntld/ *adj* ~ **(at/about sth)**; ~ **(with sb)** resentful because sth has happened to displease one: *a disgruntled look, frown, scowl, etc* ○ *She's still disgruntled about missing the party.*

disguise[1] /dɪsˈgaɪz/ *v* **1** [Tn, Tn·pr, Cn·n/a] ~ **sb/sth (with sth)**; ~ **sb/sth (as sb/sth)** make sb/sth look or sound different from normal; give sb/sth a false appearance: *disguise one's voice* ○ *I disguised the spots on my face with make-up.* ○ *The raiders disguised themselves as security guards.* **2** [Tn] hide or cover up (eg one's real feelings or intentions): *I couldn't disguise my anger.* ○ *There's no disguising the fact* (ie It is clear) *that he's a liar.*

disguise[2] /dɪsˈgaɪz/ *n* **1** [C, U] thing worn or used for disguising: *put on (a) disguise* ○ *wear a beard as a disguise.* **2** [U] disguised condition; disguising: *a master of disguise.* **3** (idm) **a blessing in disguise** ⇨ BLESSING. **in disguise** disguised: *I didn't recognize him: he was in disguise.*

disgust[1] /dɪsˈgʌst/ *n* [U] ~ **(at sth) (for/with sb)** strong dislike for sth/sb that one feels is not right or good: *his disgust at the sight of the rotting food* ○ *The execution of political opponents aroused widespread disgust (with the regime).* ○ *She turned away in disgust.*

disgust[2] /dɪsˈgʌst/ *v* [Tn] cause disgust in (sb): *The use of torture must disgust any civilized person.*

▷ **disgusted** *adj* (~ **at/by/with sb/sth**): *We were (absolutely) disgusted at the size of the bill.*

disgustedly /dɪsˈgʌstɪdlɪ/ *adv* with disgust: *look disgustedly at sb.*

disgusting *adj* causing disgust: *disgusting personal habits* ○ *disgusting language.*

disgustingly *adv* **(a)** in a disgusting way. **(b)** (*joc*) extremely: *be disgustingly fit, well-read, successful.*

dish[1] /dɪʃ/ *n* **1 (a)** [C] container for holding or serving food (usu shallow and flat bottomed): *a glass, earthenware, ceramic, metal, etc dish.* ⇨ illus at PLATE. **(b)** [C] food, etc served in the container: *a big dish of curry.* **(c) the dishes** [pl] plates, bowls, cups, etc used for a meal; crockery: *wash, do, dry, put away, etc the dishes.* **2** [C] particular kind of food prepared for a meal: *a restaurant specializing in Indonesian dishes.* **3** [C] object shaped like a dish or bowl, esp the large concave reflector of a radio telescope. **4** [C esp *sing*] (*infml*) physically attractive person: *Mary's new boy-friend's quite a dish, isn't he?*

▷ **dished** /dɪʃt/ *adj* dish-shaped; concave.

dishful /ˈdɪʃfʊl/ *n* about as much as a dish will hold.

dishy /ˈdɪʃɪ/ *adj* (**dishier, dishiest**) (*infml*) (of a person) physically attractive.

□ **ˈdishcloth** *n* cloth for washing dishes, etc.

ˈdishwasher *n* machine or person that washes dishes.

ˈdish-water *n* [U] water used for washing dishes: (*joc*) *Her coffee tastes like dish-water,* ie It is weak and unpleasant.

dish[2] /dɪʃ/ *v* **1** [Tn] (*Brit infml*) ruin (sb's hope's or chances); prevent (sb) from succeeding: *The scandal dished his hopes of being elected.* ○ *dish one's opponents.* **2** (idm) **dish it ˈout** (*infml*) attack sb fiercely with words or blows: *Don't get into a fight with him: he can really dish it out.* **dish the ˈdirt** gossip in an unkind way; say scandalous things about sb: *journalists who dish the dirt about television stars.* **3** (phr v) **dish sth out** give away a lot of sth: *There were students dishing out leaflets to passers-by.* ○ *dish out compliments, insults, abuse, etc.* **dish sth up (a)** put (food) on plates; serve. **(b)** (*derog*) present or offer sth: *They're dishing up the usual arguments in a new form.*

disharmony /dɪsˈhɑ:mənɪ/ *n* [U] lack of harmony between people; disagreement: *He noted the disharmony between husband and wife.* ▷ **disharmonious** /ˌdɪshɑ:ˈməʊnɪəs/ *adj*: *a disharmonious relationship.*

dishearten /dɪsˈhɑ:tn/ *v* [Tn] cause (sb) to lose hope or confidence: *Don't let this set-back dishearten you.* ▷ **disheartening** /-hɑ:tnɪŋ/ *adj*: *disheartening news* ○ *a disheartening lack of interest.* **dishearteningly** *adv.*

dishevelled /dɪˈʃevld/ (*US* **disheveled**) *adj* (of the hair or clothes) untidy; ruffled.

dishonest /dɪsˈɒnɪst/ *adj* **1** (of a person) not honest: *a dishonest trader, partner, etc.* **2** [attrib] **(a)** intended to deceive or cheat: *dishonest behaviour, goings-on, competition.* **(b)** (of money) not honestly obtained: *dishonest earnings/gains.* ▷ **dishonestly** *adv.* **dishonesty** *n* [U].

dishonour /dɪsˈɒnə(r)/ (*US* **dishonor**) *n* [U, sing] (*fml or rhet*) loss of honour or respect: *bring dishonour on one's family, country, regiment, etc.*

▷ **dishonour** *v* [Tn] (*fml*) **1** bring dishonour on (sb/sth): *a cowardly act that dishonours his memory.* **2** (of a bank) refuse to cash (a cheque, etc). Cf BOUNCE.

dishonourable /-nərəbl/ *adj* not honourable: *a dishonourable record, reputation, etc.* **dishonourably** /-nərəblɪ/ *adv.*

disillusion /ˌdɪsɪˈlu:ʒn/ *v* [Tn] destroy the pleasant but mistaken beliefs or ideals of (sb): *She still believes in Santa Claus and it would be cruel to disillusion her.*

▷ **disillusioned** *adj* ~ **(with sb/sth)** disappointed in sb/sth that one had admired or believed in: *Disillusioned voters want an* *alternative to the two main parties.* ○ *She's disillusioned with life in general.*

disillusionment (also **disillusion**) *n* [U] state of being disillusioned: *the growing disillusionment with the government's policies.*

disincentive /ˌdɪsɪnˈsentɪv/ *n* [C] ~ **(to sth)** thing that discourages an action or effort: *Fixed wages and lack of promotion act as a disincentive to employees.*

disinclination /ˌdɪsɪnklɪˈneɪʃn/ *n* [sing] ~ **(for sth/to do sth)** *(fml)* unwillingness; reluctance: *a disinclination for work, exercise, politics* ○ *his disinclination to tackle the causes of inflation.*

disinclined /ˌdɪsɪnˈklaɪnd/ *adj* [pred] (~ **for sth/to do sth**) unwilling; reluctant: *feel disinclined for study, argument, discussion, etc* ○ *She was disinclined to believe him.*

disinfect /ˌdɪsɪnˈfekt/ *v* [Tn] clean (sth) by destroying germs that cause disease: *disinfect a wound, a surgical instrument, a hospital ward.* ▷ **disinfectant** /ˌdɪsɪnˈfektənt/ *n* [U, C] substance that disinfects: [attrib] *disinfectant liquid, cream, soap, etc.*
disinfection /ˌdɪsɪnˈfekʃn/ *n* [U].

disinfest /ˌdɪsɪnˈfest/ *v* [Tn] remove vermin or insects from (sb/sth). ▷ **disinfestation** /ˌdɪsɪnfeˈsteɪʃn/ *n* [U].

disinflation /ˌdɪsɪnˈfleɪʃn/ *n* [U] (process or policy of) reducing the general level of prices without at the same time causing a reduction in economic activity, employment, etc. Cf DEFLATION.

disinformation /dɪsˌɪnfəˈmeɪʃn/ *n* [U] deliberately false information, esp given out by governments or intelligence services. Cf MISINFORMATION (MISINFORM).

disingenuous /ˌdɪsɪnˈdʒenjʊəs/ *adj* *(fml)* insincere, esp in pretending that one knows less about sth than one really does: *It would be disingenuous to claim that we hadn't suspected them.* ▷ **disingenuously** *adv.* **disingenuousness** *n* [U].

disinherit /ˌdɪsɪnˈherɪt/ *v* [Tn] prevent (sb) from inheriting one's property (by making a new will naming another person as heir): *disinherit one's eldest son.* ▷ **disinheritance** /ˌdɪsɪnˈherɪtəns/ *n* [U].

disintegrate /dɪsˈɪntɪgreɪt/ *v* [I] **(a)** (cause to) break into small parts or pieces: *The plane flew into a mountain and disintegrated on impact.* **(b)** *(fig)* become less strong or united: *The family is starting to disintegrate.* ▷ **disintegration** /dɪsˌɪntɪˈgreɪʃn/ *n* [U]: *the gradual disintegration of traditional values.*

disinter /ˌdɪsɪnˈtɜː(r)/ *v* (-rr-) *(fml)* [Tn] dig up (sth buried): *permission to disinter the body* ○ *(fig) disinter an old scandal.* ▷ **disinterment** *n* [U, C].

disinterested /dɪsˈɪntrəstɪd/ *adj* not influenced by personal feelings or interests; unbiased: *a disinterested act of kindness* ○ *My advice is quite disinterested.* ⇨ Usage at INTEREST². ▷ **disinterestedly** *adv.* **disinterestedness** *n* [U].

disinvest /ˌdɪsɪnˈvest/ *v* [I, Ipr] *(finance)* reduce or dispose of one's investment (in a place, company, etc). ▷ **disinvestment** *n* [U].

disjointed /dɪsˈdʒɔɪntɪd/ *adj* (of talk, writing, etc) in which it is difficult to understand how the ideas, events, etc follow each other and develop: *The film was so disjointed that I couldn't tell you what the story was about.* ▷ **disjointedly** *adv.*

disjunctive /dɪsˈdʒʌŋktɪv/ *adj* *(grammar)* (of a conjunction) showing opposition or contrast between two ideas (eg *either ... or*).

disk /dɪsk/ *n* **1** *(esp US)* = DISC. **2** *(computing)* circular plate, coated with magnetic material, on which data can be recorded in a form that can be used by a computer. Cf FLOPPY DISK (FLOP), HARD DISK (HARD¹). ▷ **diskette** /dɪsˈket/ *n* = FLOPPY DISK (FLOP).
□ ˈ**disk drive** device which transfers data from a disk to the memory of a computer, or from the memory to the disk. ⇨ illus at COMPUTER.
ˈ**disk pack** set of computer disks mounted one above the other in a container.

dislike /dɪsˈlaɪk/ *v* [Tn, Tg, Tsg] not like (sb/sth): *My mother dislikes seeing you with me/dislikes our being together.* ○ *I like cats but dislike dogs.* ○ *I dislike it when you whistle.* ○ *If you go on like that you'll get yourself disliked,* ie become unpopular.
▷ **dislike** *n* **1 (a)** [U] ~ **(of sb/sth)** feeling of not liking: *a strong dislike of modern poetry.* **(b)** [C usu *pl*] thing that one dislikes: *have one's pet dislikes.* **2** (idm) **likes and dislikes** ⇨ LIKE². **take a dislike to sb/sth** start disliking sb/sth: *I don't know why, but I took a strong dislike to him as soon as I saw him.*

dislocate /ˈdɪsləkeɪt; *US* ˈdɪsləʊkeɪt/ *v* [Tn] **1** put (a bone) out of its proper position in a joint: *dislocate one's ankle, wrist, etc* ○ *a dislocated shoulder.* **2** stop (a system, plan, etc) from working as it should; disrupt: *Flights have been dislocated by the fog.* ▷ **dislocation** /ˌdɪsləˈkeɪʃn; *US* ˌdɪsləʊˈkeɪʃn/ *n* [C, U]: *treated her for a dislocation and muscle strain* ○ *The strike will cause some dislocation of rail traffic.*

dislodge /dɪsˈlɒdʒ/ *v* [Tn, Tn·pr] ~ **sb/sth (from sth)** move or force (sb/sth) from a previously fixed position: *The wind dislodged some tiles (from the roof).* ○ *There's something between my teeth and I can't dislodge it.* ○ *(fig) She became champion in 1982 and no one has been able to dislodge her.* ▷ **dislodgement** *n* [U].

disloyal /dɪsˈlɔɪəl/ *adj* ~ **(to sb/sth)** not loyal; unfaithful: *be disloyal to a cause, one's country, one's associates.* ▷ **disloyally** /-ˈlɔɪəlɪ/ *adv.* **disloyalty** /-ˈlɔɪəltɪ/ *n* [U, C].

dismal /ˈdɪzməl/ *adj* **1** causing or showing sadness; gloomy; miserable: *dismal weather, countryside* ○ *The news was as dismal as ever.* ○ *a dismal manner, tone of voice, look, etc.* **2** *(infml)* less good than expected; poor: *a dismal performance in the elections.* ▷ **dismally** /-məlɪ/ *adv.*

dismantle /dɪsˈmæntl/ *v* [Tn] **1** take (sth) to pieces: *dismantle a faulty motor, machine, etc (for repairs)* ○ *dismantle an exhibition, theatrical set, etc* ○ *(fig) We should dismantle our inefficient tax system.* **2** remove fittings and furnishings from (a building or ship).

dismay /dɪsˈmeɪ/ *n* [U] feeling of shock and discouragement: *be filled/struck with dismay (at the news, etc)* ○ *He learned to his dismay that he had lost his job.* ○ *We watched in blank dismay as she packed her bags.*
▷ **dismay** *v* [Tn usu passive] fill (sb) with dismay: *We were all dismayed at his refusal to co-operate.*

dismember /dɪsˈmembə(r)/ *v* [Tn] **1** cut or tear off the limbs of (a person or animal): *The victim's dismembered body was found in a trunk.* **2** divide (a country, etc) into parts; partition. ▷ **dismemberment** *n* [U].

dismiss /dɪsˈmɪs/ *v* **1** [Tn, Tn·pr] ~ **sb (from sth)** remove sb (esp an employee) from a position: *workers who have been unfairly dismissed.* **2** [Tn, Tn·pr] ~ **sb (from sth)** send sb away; allow sb to leave: *dismiss soldiers, a class* ○ *(fml) The duchess dismissed the servant (from her presence).* **3 (a)** [Tn, Tn·pr] ~ **sth (from sth)** put (thoughts, feelings, etc) out of one's mind: *He tried without success to dismiss her memory from his thoughts.* **(b)** [Tn, Cn·n/a] ~ **sb/sth (as sth)** consider sb/sth not worth thinking or talking about: *She was dismissed as a dreamer.* ○ *dismiss a suggestion, objection, idea, etc.* **4** [Tn] *(law)* reject (a case, appeal, etc). **5** [Tn] (in cricket) end the innings of (the other team or one of its batsmen).
▷ **dismissal** /dɪsˈmɪsl/ *n* **(a)** [U] act of dismissing: *a strike caused by the dismissal of two workers* ○ *his rash dismissal of the offer.* **(b)** [C] event of being dismissed: *The dismissals led to a strike.*
dismissive *adj* ~ **(of sb/sth)** dismissing in a rude, brief and casual way: *a dismissive gesture, tone of voice, shrug of the shoulders* ○ *Reviewers were dismissive, and the play closed within a week.* ○ *Don't be so dismissive of her talent.* **dismissively** *adv.*

dismount /ˌdɪsˈmaʊnt/ *v* **1** [I, Ipr] ~ **(from sth)** get off (a motor cycle, bicycle, horse, etc). Cf ALIGHT² 1. **2** [Tn] cause (sb) to fall, esp from a horse, etc.

Disney /ˈdɪznɪ/ Walter Elias ('Walt') (1901-66), American film producer who pioneered animated cartoons. Among his most famous creations are *Mickey Mouse and *Donald Duck, and his full-length cartoon films include *Snow White and the Seven Dwarfs* and *Pinocchio*. Disneyland in California and Walt Disney World in Florida are amusement parks based on elements of fantasy in Disney's films.

disobedient /ˌdɪsəˈbiːdɪənt/ *adj* not obedient: *a disobedient child* ○ *I was very disobedient towards my father.*
▷ **disobedience** /-ɪəns/ *n* [U] failure or refusal to obey: *an act of disobedience* ○ *He was punished for his disobedience.*
disobediently *adv.*

disobey /ˌdɪsəˈbeɪ/ *v* [I, Tn] not obey (a person, law, etc).

disoblige /ˌdɪsəˈblaɪdʒ/ *v* [Tn] *(fml)* refuse to help or co-operate with (sb). ▷ **disobliging** *adj*: *a disobliging manner, person, response* ○ *Sorry to be so disobliging, but I have no money to lend you.*
disobligingly *adv.*

disorder /dɪsˈɔːdə(r)/ *n* **1** [U] confused or untidy state; lack of order: *with one's papers, thoughts, financial affairs in (complete) disorder* ○ *Everyone began shouting at once and the meeting broke up in disorder.* **2 (a)** [U] disturbance of public order: *The capital is calm, but continuing disorder has been reported elsewhere.* **(b)** [C] riot: *The announcement led to violent civil disorders.* **3** [C, U] disturbance of the normal working of the body or mind: *He's suffering from severe mental disorder.* ○ *a disorder of the bowels.*
▷ **disorder** *v* [Tn] disturb the order of (sth): *disorder sb's papers, files, etc.*
disordered *adj* [usu attrib] suffering from lack of order or control: *a disordered imagination, flow of words, etc* ○ *He led a disordered life and died in poverty.*
disorderly *adj* [usu attrib] **1** untidy: *a disorderly heap of clothes.* **2** (of people or behaviour) showing a lack of self-control; disturbing public order: *a disorderly mob, demonstration, meeting, etc* ○ *(law) a disorderly house,* ie where prostitution or illegal gambling is carried on. **3** (idm) **drunk and disorderly** ⇨ DRUNK². **disorderliness** *n* [U].

disorganize, -ise /dɪsˈɔːgənaɪz/ *v* [Tn] spoil the organized way (sb/sth) is supposed to work: *disorganize a schedule, plan, etc.*
▷ **disorganization, -isation** /dɪsˌɔːgənaɪˈzeɪʃn; *US* -nɪˈz-/ *n* [U].
disorganized, -ised *adj* badly organized or planned: *She's so disorganized she never gets anything done.* ○ *a disorganized lesson, holiday, household.*

disorientate /dɪsˈɔːrɪənteɪt/ (also *esp US* **disorient** /dɪsˈɔːrɪənt/) *v* [Tn esp passive] **1** cause (sb) to lose all sense of direction: *We were quite disorientated by the maze of streets.* **2** confuse (sb): *I felt completely disorientated with the jet lag.* ▷ **disorientation** /dɪsˌɔːrɪənˈteɪʃn/ *n* [U].

disown /dɪsˈəʊn/ *v* [Tn] refuse to be connected with (sb/sth), esp because one is shocked by some action: *If you behave like that in front of my friends again, I'll disown you!*

disparage /dɪˈspærɪdʒ/ *v* [Tn] suggest, esp unfairly, that (sb/sth) is of little value or importance: *disparage sb's work, talents, achievements, character, etc.* ▷ **disparagement** *n* [U]. **disparaging** *adj*: *disparaging remarks/comments.* **disparagingly** *adv*: *speak disparagingly of sb/sb's efforts.*

disparate /ˈdɪspərət/ *adj* *(fml)* so different in kind or degree that they cannot be compared: *The five experiments gave quite disparate results.* ▷ **disparately** *adv.*

disparity /dɪˈspærətɪ/ *n* *(fml)* [U, C] difference or inequality: *disparity in age, rank, income, status, etc* ○ *Comparison of the two accounts revealed numerous disparities.*

dispassionate /dɪˈspæʃənət/ *adj* *(approv)* not influenced by emotion; impartial: *a dispassionate view, observer, judgement.* ▷ **dispassionately** *adv*: *She listened dispassionately but with great* *interest to both arguments.*

dispatch[1] (also **despatch**) /dɪˈspætʃ/ *v* **1** [Tn, Tn·pr] ~ **sb/sth (to...)** send sb/sth off to a destination or for a special purpose: *dispatch a letter, telegram, message, etc* ○ *American warships have been dispatched to the area.* **2** [Tn] finish (a job, meal, etc) quickly: *The chairman dispatched the meeting in 20 minutes.* **3** [Tn] give the death-blow to (sb/sth); kill: *A vet dispatched the injured horse.*

dispatch[2] (also **despatch**) /dɪˈspætʃ/ *n* **1** *(fml)* [U] dispatching; being dispatched: *We welcome the dispatch of the peace-keeping force.* **2** [C] **(a)** official message or report sent quickly. **(b)** report sent to a newspaper or news agency. **3** (idm) **mentioned in dispatches** ⇨ MENTION. **with diˈspatch** quickly and effectively: *act with dispatch.*

□ **diˈspatch-box** *n* **(a)** container for carrying official documents. **(b) the Diˈspatch Box** box in the British Parliament next to which Ministers stand when speaking.

diˈspatch-rider *n* (usu military) messenger who travels by motor cycle.

dispel /dɪˈspel/ *v* (-ll-) [Tn] drive (sth) away; cause to vanish: *dispel sb's doubts/fears/worries* ○ *The company is trying to dispel rumours about a take-over.*

dispensable /dɪˈspensəbl/ *adj* [usu pred] not necessary or essential: *A garage is useful but dispensable.*

dispensary /dɪˈspensərɪ/ *n* **(a)** place in a hospital, school, etc where medicines are given out. **(b)** place where patients are treated; clinic.

dispensation /ˌdɪspenˈseɪʃn/ *n* **1** [U] *(fml)* action of dispensing or distributing. **2** [U, C] *(fml)* apparent arrangement of events by Providence. **3** [C, U] *(religion)* (in the Roman Catholic Church) permission to break the normal rules of the church: *She needs a special dispensation to marry her cousin.* **4** [C] *(religion)* religious system prevalent at a certain period: *the Christian, Mosaic dispensation.*

dispense /dɪˈspens/ *v* **1** [Tn, Tn·pr] ~ **sth (to sb)** **(a)** give sth out; distribute sth: *On Saturday morning my father solemnly dispensed pocket money to each of the children.* ○ *a machine dispensing paper towels.* **(b)** *(law)* administer (justice) in court. **2** [Tn] prepare and give out (medicine, esp that prescribed by a doctor): *(Brit) a dispensing chemist* ○ *dispense a prescription*, ie medicine that has been prescribed. **3** (phr v) **dispense with sb/sth** manage without sb/sth; get rid of sb/sth: *He is not yet well enough to dispense with the pills.* ○ *Let's dispense with formalities!* ○ *Formalities were dispensed with*, ie People could speak frankly or naturally. ○ *Automation has largely dispensed with the need for manual checking*, ie made it unnecessary.

▷ **dispenser** *n* **1** device from which towels, liquid soap, paper cups, etc may be obtained: *a cash dispenser.* **2** person who dispenses medicine.

disperse /dɪˈspɜːs/ *v* [I, Ipr, Tn, Tn·pr] (cause sb/sth to) go in different directions; scatter; break up: *The crowd dispersed (in all directions).* ○ *The wind dispersed the clouds.*

▷ **dispersal** /dɪˈspɜːsl/ *n* [U] action or process of dispersing: *They called for the peaceful dispersal of the demonstrators.*

dispersion /dɪˈspɜːʃn; *US* dɪˈspɜːrʒn/ *n* [U] **(a)** dispersal, esp of light. **(b) the Dispersion** = THE DIASPORA.

dispirit /dɪˈspɪrɪt/ *v* [Tn] discourage (sb); depress: *She refused to be dispirited by her long illness.* Cf DEMORALIZE. ▷ **dispirited** *adj* [usu attrib]: *a dispirited air, look, expression, etc.* **dispiritedly** *adv.* **dispiriting** *adj*: *Our lack of progress is very dispiriting.*

displace /dɪsˈpleɪs/ *v* [Tn] **1** move (sb/sth) from the usual or correct place. **2** *(fml)* take the place of (sb/sth): *Moderates have displaced the extremists on the committee.* ○ *Weeds tend to displace other plants.*

□ **ˌdisplaced ˈperson** *(dated)* refugee.

displacement /dɪsˈpleɪsmənt/ *n* **1** [U] displacing or being displaced. **2** [C] *(nautical)* weight of water displaced by a ship floating in it, used as a measure of the ship's size: *a ship with a displacement of 10 000 tons.*

display[1] /dɪˈspleɪ/ *v* [Tn, Tn·pr] ~ **sth (to sb)** **1** put (sth) on show: *display a notice, goods for sale, one's wealth* ○ *It's the first time the painting has been displayed to the public.* **2** show signs of having (a quality or emotion, etc): *display one's ignorance, arrogance, fear, anger, etc* ○ *Her writing displays natural talent.*

display[2] /dɪˈspleɪ/ *n* **1** **(a)** [C, U] action of displaying: *a firework display* ○ *a display of karate, military might, courage, strength* ○ *an appalling display of incompetence, prejudice, greed.* **(b)** [C] goods, works of art, etc being displayed: *The displays in Harrods are one of the sights in London.* ⇨ Usage at DEMONSTRATION. **2** [C] *(computing)* words, pictures, etc shown on a visual display unit. **3** (idm) **on display** being displayed: *A collection of photographs was on display in the hall.* ○ *put sth on display*, ie display it.

displease /dɪsˈpliːz/ *v* [Tn] make (sb) feel upset or angry; annoy: *He'd do anything rather than displease his parents.* ○ *Her insolence greatly displeased the judge.* ▷ **displeased** *adj* ~ **(with sb/sth)**: *He was rather displeased with his friends (for not having phoned to say they were coming).* ○ *Many voters are displeased with the government's policies.* **displeasing** *adj* ~ **(to sb/sth)**: *Modern music can at first seem displeasing to the ear.* ○ *a displeasing habit (of talking too much).* **displeasingly** *adv.*

displeasure /dɪsˈpleʒə(r)/ *n* [U] displeased feeling; dissatisfaction: *His rash outburst incurred the displeasure of the judge.* ○ *express one's displeasure at sth.*

disport /dɪˈspɔːt/ *v* [Tn] ~ **oneself** *(fml or joc)* amuse oneself energetically: *children disporting themselves like puppies on the beach.*

disposable /dɪˈspəʊzəbl/ *adj* [esp attrib] **1** made to be thrown away after use: *disposable razors, nappies, syringes, plates.* **2** *(finance)* available for use: *disposable assets, capital, resources, etc* ○ *disposable income*, ie that one can spend oneself after paying one's income tax, social security contributions, etc.

disposal /dɪˈspəʊzl/ *n* **1** [U] action of getting rid of sth: *The safe disposal of nuclear waste is a major problem.* ○ *a bomb disposal squad.* **2** (idm) **at one's/sb's disposal** available for one to use as one wishes: *Students have a well-stocked library at their disposal.* ○ *The firm put a secretary at my disposal.*

dispose /dɪˈspəʊz/ *v* **1** [Tn] *(fml)* place (sb/sth) in a suitable way; arrange: *troops disposed in battle formation* ○ *dispose the chairs/singers in a semicircle.* **2** [Cn·t] *(fml)* make (sb) willing or ready to do sth: *His criminal record does not dispose me to trust him.* **3** (phr v) **dispose of sb/sth** **(a)** get rid of sb/sth that one does not want or cannot keep: *a better way of disposing of household waste* ○ *He was forced to dispose of* (ie sell) *his art treasures.* ○ *All the furniture has been disposed of.* **(b)** deal or finish with sb/sth that presents a problem: *She disposed of the champion in straight sets.* ○ *The president ruthlessly disposed of his rivals*, eg dismissed them, had them killed. ○ *Their objections were easily disposed of*, ie successfully argued against. **(c)** (no passive) *(fml)* have sb/sth available for use: *dispose of considerable wealth, power, influence, etc.*

disposed /dɪˈspəʊzd/ *adj* [pred] **1** ~ **(to do sth)** wanting or prepared to do sth: *I'm not disposed to meet them at the moment.* ○ *You're most welcome to join us if you feel so disposed.* **2** (following an *adv*) ~ **towards sb/sth** inclined to think that sb/sth is/is not good or worthwhile: *well/ill disposed towards sb/sth* ○ *She's favourably disposed towards new ideas.*

disposition /ˌdɪspəˈzɪʃn/ *n* (usu *sing*) **1** person's natural qualities of mind and character: *a calm, irritable, cheerful, boastful, etc disposition.* **2** ~ **to sth/to do sth** *(fml)* inclination; tendency: *a disposition to jealousy/to be jealous* ○ *There was a general disposition to ignore the problem.* **3** arrangement; placing: *A defector revealed the disposition of the enemy fleet.*

dispossess /ˌdɪspəˈzes/ *v* [Tn, Tn·pr] ~ **sb (of sth)** take away property, land, a house, etc from sb: *The nobles were dispossessed (of their estates) after the revolution.*

▷ **the dispossessed** *n* [pl *v*] people who have been dispossessed.

dispossession /ˌdɪspəˈzeʃn/ *n* [U].

disproof /dɪsˈpruːf/ *n (fml)* **1** [U] disproving. **2** [C] thing that disproves.

disproportion /ˌdɪsprəˈpɔːʃn/ *n* [C, U] ~ **(between sth and sth)** (instance of) being out of proportion: *disproportion in age, size, weight, importance* ○ *the disproportion between her salary and her responsibilities.*

▷ **disproportionate** /ˌdɪsprəˈpɔːʃənət/ *adj* relatively too large or small, etc; out of proportion: *You spend a disproportionate amount of your time on sport.* **disproportionately** *adv*: *Babies often seem to have disproportionately large heads.*

disprove /ˌdɪsˈpruːv/ *v* [Tn] show that (sth) is wrong or false: *The allegations have been completely disproved.*

disputable /dɪˈspjuːtəbl/ *adj* that may be questioned or argued about: *He made some very disputable claims about his record.* ▷ **disputably** /-əblɪ/ *adv.*

disputant /dɪˈspjuːtənt, *also* ˈdɪspjʊtənt/ *n (law or fml)* person who disputes.

disputation /ˌdɪspjuːˈteɪʃn/ *n (fml)* **1** [C, U] (instance of) disputing; controversy. **2** [C] *(arch)* formal academic debate.

disputatious /ˌdɪspjuːˈteɪʃəs/ *adj (fml)* fond of arguing; inclined to argue. ▷ **disputatiously** *adv.*

dispute[1] /dɪˈspjuːt/ *n* **1** [U] argument; debate: *There has been much dispute over the question of legalized abortion.* ○ *It is a matter of dispute (whether they did the right thing).* ○ *Their conclusions are open to dispute.* **2** [C] quarrel; controversy: *religious, political, industrial, etc disputes* ○ *a border dispute that could easily become a war.* **3** (idm) **beyond/past diˈspute** certain: *Her courage is beyond all dispute.* **in diˈspute** that can be or is being argued about: *The exact cause of the accident is still in dispute.* ○ *Your sincerity is not in dispute.* **in dispute (with sb)** involved in a (usu industrial) dispute: *We're in dispute (with the management) about overtime rates.* **without diˈspute** certainly: *He is without dispute the better player.*

dispute[2] /dɪˈspjuːt/ *v* **1** [I, Ipr] ~ **(with sb)** argue; debate: *Some people love to dispute (with everyone).* **2** **(a)** [Tn, Tw] argue about (sth): *They disputed at great length what they should do.* **(b)** [Tn] question the truth or validity of (sth): *dispute a statement, claim, decision, etc* ○ *The election result was disputed.* **3** [Tn] try to stop sb winning (sth) from one; fight for (sth): *Our soldiers disputed every inch of ground.*

disqualify /dɪsˈkwɒlɪfaɪ/ *v* (*pt, pp* **-fied**) [Tn, Tn·pr] ~ **sb (from sth/doing sth)** prevent sb from doing sth, usu because he has broken a rule or is not able enough: *Her criminal record disqualifies her from serving on a jury.* ○ *She was disqualified in the first round.* ○ *The team has been disqualified from next year's competition.* ▷ **disqualification** /dɪsˌkwɒlɪfɪˈkeɪʃn/ *n* [C, U]: *(a) disqualification for driving while drunk.*

disquiet /dɪsˈkwaɪət/ *n* [U] anxiety: *The strength of the dollar is causing considerable disquiet on the Stock Exchange.*

▷ **disquiet** *v* [Tn usu passive] make (sb) anxious; worry: *be greatly disquieted by the fall in public support.* **disquieting** *adj* causing disquiet: *disquieting news.* **disquietingly** *adv*: *a disquietingly large number of accidents.*

disquisition /ˌdɪskwɪˈzɪʃn/ *n* ~ **(on sth)** long elaborate spoken or written report or account.

Disraeli /dɪzˈreɪlɪ/ Benjamin, 1st Earl of Beaconsfield (1804-81), British statesman. After an early career as a novelist, he entered Parliament in 1837. He became leader of the Conservative Party, and created its modern centralized organization. He was briefly prime minister in 1868, and then again from 1874 to 1880. His foreign policy was to increase Britain's influence and prestige abroad, while at home he introduced several social reforms, including doubling the number of people entitled to vote in elections. His flamboyant style contrasted with that of his Liberal opponent, William *Gladstone. ⇨ App 2.

disregard /ˌdɪsrɪˈɡɑːd/ *v* [Tn] pay no attention to (eg a warning, an objection); treat (sth) as of no importance; ignore: *He completely disregarded my point of view.* ○ *You can't just disregard the security problem!*
▷ **disregard** *n* [U] ~ **(for/of sb/sth)** lack of attention or care: *She shows a total disregard for other people and their feelings.* ○ *fire-fighters working with a complete disregard of their own safety.*

disrepair /ˌdɪsrɪˈpeə(r)/ *n* [U] bad condition caused by lack of repairs: *be in/fall into (a state of) disrepair.*

disreputable /dɪsˈrepjʊtəbl/ *adj* **(a)** having a bad reputation: *Soho is one of London's more disreputable areas.* **(b)** not respectable or looking respectable: *a disreputable suit, manner, appearance* ○ *I've been accused of using disreputable methods to get what I want.* ▷ **disreputably** /-əblɪ/ *adv.*

disrepute /ˌdɪsrɪˈpjuːt/ *n* [U] state of having a bad reputation: *The use of drugs is bringing the sport into disrepute.* ○ *Since the scandal, the school has rather fallen into disrepute.*

disrespect /ˌdɪsrɪˈspekt/ *n* [U] ~ **(to/towards sb/sth)** lack of respect; rudeness: *He meant no disrespect by that remark,* ie did not mean to be rude. ○ *No disrespect (to you), but I think you are wrong.*
▷ **disrespectful** /-fl/ *adj* ~ **(to/towards sb/sth)** showing disrespect: *We often criticize the Government, but we're never disrespectful towards the Royal Family.* **disrespectfully** /-fəlɪ/ *adv.*

disrobe /dɪsˈrəʊb/ *v* [I] **(a)** *(fml or joc)* undress. **(b)** take official or ceremonial robes off: *The Queen disrobed after the ceremony.*

disrupt /dɪsˈrʌpt/ *v* [Tn] cause disorder in (sth): *Demonstrators succeeded in disrupting the meeting.* ○ *Fog disrupted traffic.*
▷ **disruption** /dɪsˈrʌpʃn/ *n* [C, U]: *violent disruption caused by rioters* ○ *disruptions of our production schedule.*
disruptive /dɪsˈrʌptɪv/ *adj* causing disruption: *A few disruptive students can easily ruin a class.* **disruptively** *adv*: *act, behave, etc disruptively.*

dissatisfaction /ˌdɪˌsætɪsˈfækʃn/ *n* [U] ~ **(with sb/sth)**; ~ **(at doing sth)** lack of satisfaction: *Letters from viewers express their dissatisfaction with current programmes.* ○ *MPs voice public dissatisfaction at having to pay higher taxes.*

dissatisfied /dɪˈsætɪsfaɪd/ *adj* ~ **(with sb/sth)**; ~ **(at doing sth)** not satisfied; discontented: *a dissatisfied customer* ○ *I'm thoroughly dissatisfied with your work.* ○ *She's very dissatisfied at not getting a bonus.*

dissect /dɪˈsekt/ *v* [Tn] **1** cut up (a dead body, a plant, etc) in order to study its structure. **2** *(fig)* examine (a theory, an event, etc) in great detail: *Commentators are still dissecting the election results.* ○ *The film has been minutely dissected by the critics.*
▷ **dissection** /dɪˈsekʃn/ *n* [C, U] (instance of) dissecting or being dissected: *Her first dissection made her change her mind about becoming a doctor.*

dissemble /dɪˈsembl/ *v* [I, Tn] *(fml)* hide or disguise (one's true thoughts and feelings); dissimulate: *dissemble one's intentions, meaning, motives, etc.*
▷ **dissembler** /dɪˈsemblə(r)/ *n* person who dissembles.

disseminate /dɪˈsemɪneɪt/ *v* [Tn] spread (ideas, beliefs, etc) widely: *They use the press to disseminate right-wing views.* ▷ **dissemination** /dɪˌsemɪˈneɪʃn/ *n* [U].

dissension /dɪˈsenʃn/ *n* [U, C] angry disagreement: *deal with dissension in the party* ○ *Father's will caused much dissension among his children.*

dissent[1] /dɪˈsent/ *n* [U] holding opinions which differ from common or officially held ones: *their public dissent from official party policy* ○ *In those days, religious dissent was not tolerated.*

dissent[2] /dɪˈsent/ *v* [I, Ipr] ~ **(from sth)** *(fml)* have or express opinions which are opposed to official views, religious teaching, etc: *I wish to dissent (from the motion).* ○ *Those who dissented from Anglican teachings could be heavily fined.*
▷ **dissenter** *n* **(a)** person who dissents. **(b)** **Dissenter** Protestant who refuses to accept the doctrines of the Church of England: *Presbyterians and other Dissenters.*
dissenting *adj* [attrib]: *a dissenting voice, opinion, vote, etc* ○ *a dissenting minister,* ie in a church that refuses to accept Anglican doctrine. Cf NONCONFORMIST.

dissertation /ˌdɪsəˈteɪʃn/ *n* [C] ~ **(on sth)** long essay on a particular subject, esp one written for a doctorate or similar degree; thesis: *a dissertation on Arabic dialects.*

disservice /dɪsˈsɜːvɪs/ *n* ~ **(to sb/sth)** [C, U] harmful or unhelpful action: *She did her cause (a) great disservice by concealing the truth.*

dissident /ˈdɪsɪdənt/ *n* person who strongly disagrees with or opposes official views and policies: *left-wing dissidents* ○ [attrib] *dissident groups, writings, opinions.* ▷ **dissidence** /ˈdɪsɪdəns/ *n* [U].

dissimilar /dɪˈsɪmɪlə(r)/ *adj* ~ **(from/to sb/sth)** not the same; unlike: *These wines are not dissimilar,* ie quite similar. ○ *Her latest book is quite dissimilar from her previous one.* ▷ **dissimilarity** /ˌdɪsɪmɪˈlærətɪ/ *n* [C, U]: *They correct any dissimilarity between batches of work.* **dissimilarly** *adv.*

dissimulate /dɪˈsɪmjʊleɪt/ *v* [I, Tn] *(fml)* hide or disguise (one's thoughts and feelings); dissemble.
▷ **dissimulation** /dɪˌsɪmjʊˈleɪʃn/ *n* [U, C].

dissipate /ˈdɪsɪpeɪt/ *v* **1** [I, Tn] (cause sth to) scatter or vanish: *The mist quickly dissipated as the sun rose.* ○ *Her son's letter dissipated all her fears and anxiety.* **2** [Tn] waste (time, money, etc) foolishly: *dissipate one's efforts, energies, fortune.*
▷ **dissipated** *adj* *(derog)* given to foolish and harmful pleasures: *lead a thoroughly dissipated life.*
dissipation /ˌdɪsɪˈpeɪʃn/ *n* [U] **1** dissipating or being dissipated. **2** dissipated living: *Years of dissipation had ruined his health.*

dissociate /dɪˈsəʊʃɪeɪt/ (also **disassociate**) *v* [Tn·pr] **1** ~ **sb/sth from sth** separate (people or things) in one's thoughts or feelings: *dissociate two ideas/one idea from another* ○ *You cannot dissociate the government's actions from the policies which underlie them.* **2** ~ **oneself from sb/sth** say that one does not agree with or support sb/sth: *I wish to dissociate myself from those views.*
▷ **dissociation** /dɪˌsəʊsɪˈeɪʃn/ *n* [U] **1** (also **disassociation**) /ˌdɪsəsəʊsɪˈeɪʃn/ dissociating or being dissociated. **2** *(chemistry)* process by which chemical compounds separate into their basic elements or into simpler components.

dissoluble /dɪˈsɒljʊbl/ *adj* that can be dissolved: *(fig) Is a marriage dissoluble?* ie Can it be ended?
▷ **dissolubility** /dɪˌsɒljʊˈbɪlətɪ/ *n* [U].

dissolute /ˈdɪsəluːt/ *adj* immoral; dissipated: *lead a dissolute life* ○ *a dissolute and worthless character.* ▷ **dissolutely** *adv.* **dissoluteness** *n* [U].

dissolution /ˌdɪsəˈluːʃn/ *n* [C, U] ~ **(of sth)** breaking up (of sth); dissolving: *the dissolution of a marriage, a business partnership, the Roman Empire* ○ *the dissolution of Parliament,* ie the ending of the current session by the monarch before a general election.
□ **the ˌDissolution of the ˈMonasteries** abolition of all English monasteries in the 1530s by *Henry VIII, carried out so that the king could increase his power over the Church and seize the monasteries' wealth for himself.

dissolve /dɪˈzɒlv/ *v* **1** **(a)** [Tn] (of a liquid) make (a solid) become liquid: *Water dissolves salt.* **(b)** [I, Ipr] ~ **(in sth)** (of a solid) become part of a liquid: *Salt dissolves in water.* **(c)** [Tn, Tn·pr] ~ **sth (in sth)** cause (a solid) to dissolve: *Dissolve the salt in water.* **2** [Tn, Tn·p] ~ **sth (away)** remove or destroy (sth solid, esp dirt): *The cream dissolves facial hair.* ○ *a powder that dissolves stains away.* **3** [I, Ipr] ~ **(in sth)** disappear; fade away: *All his hopes dissolved at the terrible news.* ○ *The view dissolved in mist.* **4** [I, Tn] (cause sth to) come to an end: *Parliament dissolves tomorrow.* ○ *dissolve a business partnership, marriage, society, etc.* **5** [Ipr] ~ **in sth** give way to emotion: *dissolve in tears/laughter/giggles.*

dissonance /ˈdɪsənəns/ *n* **1** [U] discord. **2** [C] *(music)* combination of notes that is discordant.

dissonant /ˈdɪsənənt/ *adj* not harmonious; discordant. ▷ **dissonantly** *adv.*

dissuade /dɪˈsweɪd/ *v* [Tn, Tn·pr] ~ **sb (from sth/doing sth)** (try to) stop sb by advice or persuasion: *The police managed to dissuade him from jumping off the building.*
▷ **dissuasion** /dɪˈsweɪʒn/ *n* [U].
dissuasive /dɪˈsweɪsɪv/ *adj* dissuading.

distaff /ˈdɪstɑːf; *US* ˈdɪstæf/ *n* **1** stick holding wool, flax, etc for spinning by hand. **2** (idm) **on the distaff side** on the mother's side of the family.

distance[1] /ˈdɪstəns/ *n* **1** [C, U] (amount of) space between two points or places: *A good cyclist can cover distances of over a hundred miles a day.* ○ *It's a great/some/no distance from here,* ie very/fairly/not far away. ○ *a short, long, great, etc distance* ○ *In the USA distance is measured in miles, not kilometres.* ○ *The beach is within walking distance of my house,* ie near enough to be reached easily on foot. ○ *(fig) at a distance of fifty years.* ⇨ App 9. **2** [C, U] distant place or point: *At a distance of six miles you can't see much.* ○ *He won't hit the target at that distance.* **3** [U] being separated in space or by time: *Distance is no problem with modern telecommunications.* **4** [U] coldness or remoteness in personal relationships: *Is his distance a result of snobbery or shyness?* **5** (idm) **go the ˈdistance** (esp in sports) continue to run, fight, etc until the end of a contest: *Nobody thought he'd last 15 rounds, but he went the full distance.* ○ *You need perseverance to win in politics and I doubt if he can go the distance.* **in the ˈdistance** far away. **keep sb at a ˈdistance** refuse to let sb become familiar or friendly. **keep one's ˈdistance (from sb/sth)** **(a)** not get too close (to sb/sth): *I would keep my distance from that dog, if I were you!* **(b)** not become friendly or familiar (with a person, cause, etc): *He was asked many times to join the party, but he always kept his distance.* Cf THE NEAR DISTANCE (NEAR[1]), THE MIDDLE DISTANCE (MIDDLE).

distance[2] /ˈdɪstəns/ *v* **1** [Tn, Tn·pr] ~ **sb (from sb/sth)** make sb less friendly or warm towards sb/sth: *That stupid quarrel has distanced us.* ○ *Voters have been distanced from the party by adverse publicity.* **2** [Tn·pr] ~ **oneself from sb/sth** not approve of or become involved with sb/sth: *She needs to distance herself from some of her more extreme supporters.*

distant /ˈdɪstənt/ *adj* **1** (sometimes used with measurements) far away in space or time: *a distant land, cry, flash of light* ○ *the distant horizon, past* ○ *The airport is about ten miles distant from the city.* **2** **(a)** [attrib] (of people) not closely related: *She is a distant cousin of mine.* **(b)** (of a connection, similarity, etc) not very strong or clear: *There is a distant connection between the two theories.* **3** not very friendly; reserved: *a distant nod, attitude, greeting, manner.* **4** (idm) **dim and distant** ⇨ DIM. ▷ **distantly** *adv*: *We're distantly related.* ○ *His style distantly resembles that of Wilde.* ○ *She smiled distantly at us.*

distaste /dɪsˈteɪst/ *n* [U] ~ **(for sb/sth)** dislike; aversion: *turn away in distaste* ○ *a distaste for violent sports.*
▷ **distasteful** /dɪsˈteɪstfl/ *adj* ~ **(to sb)** unpleasant; disagreeable: *distasteful behaviour,* ○ *a distasteful incident* ○ *Even the thought of her was distasteful to him.* **distastefully** /-fəlɪ/ *adv.* **distastefulness** /dɪsˈteɪstfəlnɪs/ *n* [U].

distemper[1] /dɪˈstempə(r)/ *n* [U] *(Brit)* (old method of painting with) colouring matter mixed with water and brushed on walls, etc.
▷ **distemper** *v* [Tn, Cn·a] paint (sth) with

distemper: *distemper the walls green.*

distemper[2] /dɪˈstempə(r)/ *n* [U] disease of dogs and some other animals, with coughing and weakness.

distend /dɪˈstend/ *v* [I, Tn] (*fml*) (cause sth to) swell by means of pressure from inside: *a distended intestine, stomach, vein, etc.*

▷ **distension** (*US* **distention**) /dɪˈstenʃn/ *n* [U] swelling or being swollen.

distich /ˈdɪstɪk/ *n* two lines of verse as a single unit; couplet.

distil /dɪˈstɪl/ (*US* **distill**) *v* (-ll-) **1** [Tn, Tn·pr] ~ **sth (from sth)** (**a**) turn (a liquid) to vapour by heating, then collect the drops of liquid that condense from the vapour when cooled: *distil fresh water from sea water.* (**b**) make (spirits or essences) in this way: *The Scots have distilled whisky for centuries.* **2** [Tn, Tn·pr] ~ **sth (from sth)** draw or derive sth (from sth): *useful advice distilled from a lifetime's experience.* **3** (phr v) **distil sth off/out** purify (a liquid) by turning it to vapour, etc: *Sea water can be made drinkable by distilling out the salt.*

▷ **distillate** /ˈdɪstɪlət/ *n* substance produced by distilling.

distillation /ˌdɪstɪˈleɪʃn/ *n* **1** [C, U] (substance made by) distilling. **2** [C, U] reduction; essence: *This book offers a distillation of Wittgenstein's thought in a mere fifty pages.*

distiller /dɪˈstɪlə(r)/ *n* person or company that distils (esp whisky, etc).

▷ **distillery** /dɪˈstɪlərɪ/ *n* place where gin, whisky, etc are distilled. Cf BREWERY (BREW).

distinct /dɪˈstɪŋkt/ *adj* **1** easily heard, seen, felt or understood; definite: *The footprints are quite distinct; they must be fresh.* ○ *I had the distinct impression that I was being watched.* ○ *There was a distinct sense of embarrassment in the air.* **2** ~ **(from sth)** different in kind; separate: *Although they look similar, these plants are actually quite distinct.* ○ *Mozart's style is quite distinct from Haydn's.* ○ *Astronomy, as distinct from astrology, is an exact science.*

▷ **distinctly** *adv* in a distinct manner; clearly: *But I distinctly remember you promising to phone me!* **distinctness** *n* [U].

distinction /dɪˈstɪŋkʃn/ *n* **1** [C, U] ~ **(between A and B)** difference or contrast between one person/ thing and another: *He drew a quite artificial distinction between men and women readers.* ○ *I don't understand your distinction: surely all painting is art?* **2** (*fml*) (**a**) [U] separation of things or people into different groups according to quality, grade, etc: *without distinction* (ie regardless) *of rank.* (**b**) [C] detail that separates in this way: *distinctions of birth and wealth.* **3** [C] mark of honour; title, decoration, etc: *an academic distinction,* eg a doctor's degree ○ *win a distinction for bravery.* **4** [U] quality of being excellent or distinguished: *a writer, novel, work of distinction* ○ *She had the distinction of being the first woman to swim the Channel.*

distinctive /dɪˈstɪŋktɪv/ *adj* ~ **(of sth)** that distinguishes sth by making it different from others: *a distinctive appearance, style, smell* ○ *Long complex sentences are distinctive of Henry James's later style.* ▷ **distinctively** *adv*: *distinctively coloured.* **distinctiveness** *n* [U].

distingué /dɪˈstæŋgeɪ; *US* ˌdiːstæŋˈgeɪ/ *adj* (*French*) having a distinguished(1) appearance or manner.

distinguish /dɪˈstɪŋgwɪʃ/ *v* **1** [Ipr, Tn·pr] ~ **(between) A and B**; ~ **A from B** recognize the difference between (people or things): *People who cannot distinguish between colours are said to be colour-blind.* ○ *The twins are so alike that no one can distinguish one from the other.* **2** [Tn, Tn·pr] ~ **A (from B)** (**a**) show the difference between (one person or thing and another): *The male is distinguished (from the female) by its red beak.* (**b**) be a characteristic mark or property of sb/sth; make sb/sth different: *Speech distinguishes human beings from the animals.* **3** [Tn] manage to see, hear, etc (sth): *distinguish distant objects, a shape in the mist, a whispered conversation.* **4** [Tn] ~ **oneself** deserve to be noticed by doing sth very well: *She distinguished herself by her coolness and bravery.*

▷ **distinguishable** /dɪˈstɪŋgwɪʃəbl/ *adj* [usu pred] ~ **(from sb/sth)**: *The coast was barely distinguishable in the mist.* ○ *Vipers are distinguishable from other snakes by their markings.*

distinguished *adj* **1** dignified in appearance or manner: *I think grey hair makes you look rather distinguished.* **2** showing remarkable qualities: *a distinguished career* ○ *She is a distinguished novelist and philosopher.*

distort /dɪˈstɔːt/ *v* [Tn] **1** pull or twist (sth) out of its usual shape: *a heap of distorted metal* ○ *a face distorted by pain.* **2** make (sth) look or sound unnatural: *a distorting mirror,* ie one which makes people look long and thin, short and fat, etc ○ *The announcement was so distorted that I couldn't understand what was said.* **3** give a false account of (sth); misrepresent: *distort sb's words, motives, point of view, etc* ○ *The government were accused of having systematically distorted the protesters' case.*

▷ **distortion** /dɪˈstɔːʃn/ *n* [C, U] (instance of) distorting or being distorted: *a distortion of the facts.*

distract /dɪˈstrækt/ *v* [Tn, Tn·pr] ~ **sb (from sth)** stop sb concentrating on sth: *Children are so easily distracted.* ○ *Don't distract my attention — I'm trying to study!* ○ *The film managed to distract me from these problems for a while.*

▷ **distracted** *adj* ~ **(with/by sth)** unable to concentrate properly, esp because of one's strong feelings: *distracted with joy, fear, sorrow, anxiety, etc.* **distractedly** *adv*: *He paced up and down distractedly.*

distracting *adj*: *a distracting noise.* **distractingly** *adv.*

distraction /dɪˈstrækʃn/ *n* **1** [U] distracting or being distracted. **2** [C] noise, sight, etc that distracts the attention and prevents concentration: *He found the noise of the photographers a distraction.* **3** [C] thing or event that amuses or entertains: *TV can be a welcome distraction after a hard day's work.* **4** [U] state of mental distress. **5** (idm) **to diˈstraction** almost to a state of madness: *He loves her to distraction.* ○ *You'll drive me to distraction with your silly questions!*

distrain /dɪˈstreɪn/ *v* [I, Ipr] ~ **(upon sb/sth)** (*law*) seize a person's property or belongings to force him to pay what he owes (esp rent).

▷ **distraint** *n* [U] act or process of distraining.

distrait /dɪˈstreɪt/ *adj* absent-minded; not paying attention.

distraught /dɪˈstrɔːt/ *adj* very troubled in mind with grief or worry.

distress[1] /dɪˈstres/ *n* **1** (**a**) [U, sing] (cause of) great pain, sorrow, suffering, etc: *Towards the end of the marathon several runners showed signs of distress.* ○ *Her death was a great distress to all the family.* (**b**) [U] (suffering caused by) lack of money, food, etc: *The government acted quickly to relieve the widespread distress caused by the earthquake.* **2** [U] state of being in danger or difficulty and requiring help: *a ship in diˈstress* ○ [attrib] *a diˈstress signal/call/flag.* **3** (idm) **a damsel in distress** ⇨ DAMSEL. ▷ **distressful** /dɪˈstresfl/ *adj* = DISTRESSING (DISTRESS[2]). **distressfully** *adv.*

distress[2] /dɪˈstres/ *v* [Tn usu passive] cause distress to (sb/sth): *I was most distressed to hear the sad news of your father's death.* ○ *Please don't distress yourself.* ie don't worry.

▷ **distressing** (also **distressful**) *adj* causing distress: *distressing news* ○ *a distressing sight.* **distressingly** (also **distressfully**) *adv.*

distribute /dɪˈstrɪbjuːt/ *v* [Tn, Tn·pr] **1** ~ **sth (to/ among sb/sth)** separate sth into parts and give a share to each person or thing: *In a co-operative profits are distributed among the work-force.* ○ *The demonstrators distributed leaflets to passers-by.* **2** spread sth; scatter; place at different parts: *Baggage loaded onto an aircraft must be evenly distributed.*

▷ **distribution** /ˌdɪstrɪˈbjuːʃn/ [C, U] **1** (instance of) giving or being given to each of several people, etc: *the distribution of catalogues, forms, prizes, etc.* **2** (instance of the) positioning or allocation of items, features, etc within an area: *the distribution of schools in this district* ○ *Pines have a very wide distribution.*

distributor /dɪˈstrɪbjʊtə(r)/ *n* **1** person or thing that distributes, esp an agent who supplies goods to shops in a certain area. **2** device that passes electric current to the sparking-plugs in an engine.

distributive /dɪˈstrɪbjʊtɪv/ *adj* [usu attrib] **1** concerned with distribution (DISTRIBUTE): *the distributive trades,* eg transport, retailing, etc. **2** (*grammar*) referring to each individual member of a class: *'Each', 'every', 'either' and 'neither' are distributive pronouns.* ▷ **distributively** *adv.*

district /ˈdɪstrɪkt/ *n* **1** part of a country or town having a particular quality: *mountainous, agricultural, outlying, poor, gloomy districts* ○ *the ˈLake District.* **2** area of a country or town treated as an administrative unit: *a ˈpostal district* ○ *rural and urban districts,* ie units of local government ○ [attrib] *district ˈcouncils.*

□ **district atˈtorney** (*US*) (*abbr* **DA**) public prosecutor representing a State or the Federal government in a judicial district.

district ˈnurse (*Brit dated*) nurse visiting patients in their homes.

District of Columbia /ˌdɪstrɪkt əv kəˈlʌmbɪə/ (*abbr* **DC**) district in the eastern USA, entirely occupied by the federal capital Washington.

distrust /dɪsˈtrʌst/ *n* [U, sing] lack of trust; suspicion: *Negotiations between unions and management are made more difficult by mutual distrust.* ○ *He has a distrust of strangers.*

▷ **distrust** *v* [Tn] have no confidence or belief in (sb/sth): *He's so suspicious he would distrust his own mother.*

distrustful /-fl/ *adj* having or showing distrust; suspicious. **distrustfully** /-fəlɪ/ *adv.*

disturb /dɪˈstɜːb/ *v* [Tn] **1** move (sth) from a settled or usual position or state: *Don't disturb the papers on my desk.* **2** break the rest, concentration or calm of (sb/sth): *She opened the door quietly so as not to disturb the sleeping child.* ○ *Exam in Progress — Do Not Disturb* ○ *No sound disturbed the silence of the evening.* **3** cause (sb) to worry: *disturbing developments, reports, symptoms.* **4** (idm) **disturb the ˈpeace** (*law*) break the law by making too much noise, quarrelling or fighting publicly, etc.

▷ **disturbed** *adj* (*psychology*) mentally ill: *He is emotionally disturbed.*

disturbance /dɪˈstɜːbəns/ *n* **1** (**a**) [U] disturbing or being disturbed. (**b**) [sing] person or thing that disturbs: *The teacher told him to leave as he was a disturbance to the other students.* **2** [C] instance of social unrest; riot: *violent disturbances in inner-city areas.* **3** [U] (*psychology*) mental illness: *suffer an emotional disturbance.*

disunion /dɪsˈjuːnɪən/ *n* [U] (*fml*) **1** separating or being separated. **2** disagreement.

disunite /ˌdɪsjuːˈnaɪt/ *v* [I, Tn] (cause sb/sth to) become separate.

disunity /dɪsˈjuːnətɪ/ *n* [U] lack of unity; disagreement: *There should be no disunity within our party.*

disuse /dɪsˈjuːs/ *n* [U] state of not being used: *rusty from disuse* ○ *words that have fallen into disuse.*

▷ **disused** /dɪsˈjuːzd/ *adj* no longer used: *a disused railway line.*

disyllable /dɪˈsɪləbl, daɪˈsɪləbl/ (*US* **dissyllable** /ˌdɪs-/) *n* disyllabic word or metrical foot. Cf MONOSYLLABLE.

▷ **disyllabic** /ˌdɪsɪˈlæbɪk, ˌdaɪsɪˈlæbɪk/ (*US* **dissyllabic** /ˌdɪs-/) *adj* consisting of two syllables.

ditch /dɪtʃ/ *n* **1** narrow channel dug at the edge of a field, road, etc, esp to hold or carry off water. **2** (idm) **dull as ditch-water** ⇨ DULL. **the last ditch** ⇨ LAST[1].

▷ **ditch** *v* **1** [I, Tn] land (an aircraft) in the sea in an emergency: *A sudden engine failure forced the pilot to ditch (in the Irish Sea).* **2** [Tn] (*infml*) abandon (sb/sth); get rid of: *I hear she's ditched her boy-friend,* ie stopped seeing him. ○ *When the road became impassable, we had to ditch the car and walk.* **3** [I] make or repair ditches: *hedging and ditching.*

dither /ˈdɪðə(r)/ *v* [I, Ipr] ~ (**about sth**) hesitate about what to do; be unable to decide: *Stop dithering about which film you want to see or you'll miss them both!*

▷ **dither** *n* **1** state of dithering: *in a dither.* **2** (idm) **all of a ˈdither** (*infml*) very confused and unable to decide. **have the ˈdithers** (*infml*) hesitate anxiously.

dithyramb /ˈdɪθɪræm/ *n* **1** song and dance performed in ancient Greece in honour of the god Dionysus. **2** speech, poem, etc full of wild passion. ▷ **dithyrambic** /ˌdɪθɪˈræmbɪk/ *adj.*

dittany /ˈdɪtənɪ/ *n* [U] plant of the mint family, formerly used in medicine.

ditto /ˈdɪtəʊ/ *n* (*abbr* **do**) (used in lists to avoid repetition) the same thing again: *1 doz bottles white wine £2.25 a bottle; ditto red £3.*

□ **ditto marks** marks (") representing *ditto* used in lists, tables, bills, etc.

ditty /ˈdɪtɪ/ *n* (*often joc*) short simple song.

diuretic /ˌdaɪjʊˈretɪk/ *n, adj* (*medical*) (substance) causing an increase in the flow of urine: *Coffee is a diuretic.* ○ *a diuretic drug.*

diurnal /daɪˈɜːnl/ *adj* **1** (*biology*) of the daytime; not nocturnal: *Unlike most other bats, this species is diurnal.* **2** (*astronomy*) occupying one day: *the diurnal movement of the planets.* ▷ **diurnally** *adv.*

Div *abbr* division(3b): *Manchester United, League Div 1.*

diva /ˈdiːvə/ *n* famous female opera singer; prima donna.

divalent /ˌdaɪˈveɪlənt/ (also **bivalent** /ˈbaɪveɪlənt/) *adj* (*chemistry*) (of an atom or a group of atoms) that can combine with two others which are themselves univalent.

divan /dɪˈvæn; *US* ˈdaɪvæn/ *n* **1** long low couch without a back or arms. **2** (also **diˌvan ˈbed**) low bed resembling this.

dive[1] /daɪv/ *v* (*pt, pp* **dived**; *US* also *pt* **dove** /dəʊv/) **1** [I, Ipr, Ip] ~ (**from/off sth**) (**into sth**); ~ (**off/in**) go head first into water: *He dived from the bridge to rescue the drowning child.* **2** [I, Ipr, Ip] ~ (**down**) (**for sth**) (of a submarine, diver, etc) go under water or to a deeper level under water: *The whale dived as the harpoon struck it.* ○ *dive for pearls.* **3** [I, Ipr, Ip] (of an aircraft) go steeply downwards. **4** [Ipr] ~ **into, under, etc sth** move quickly in a specified direction: *dive under the bed* ○ *When the rain started, we dived into a café.* **5** (phr v) **dive for sth** move quickly towards or in search of sth: *dive for the phone, the gun, etc* ○ *We dived for cover when the storm started.* **dive into sth/in** (*infml*) (**a**) move one's hand quickly into sth: *dive into one's pocket, briefcase, etc.* (**b**) involve oneself completely in sth: *dive into a new project.*

▷ **diver** *n* person who dives, esp one who works under water using a diving-suit.

□ **ˈdive-bomb** *v* [I, Tn] (of an aeroplane, a pilot, etc) drop bombs on (sth) after having dived steeply downwards. **ˈdive-bomber** *n* aircraft designed to do this.

ˈdiving-bell *n* bell-shaped device supplied with air in which people can work under water.

ˈdiving-board *n* board for diving from.

ˈdiving-suit *n* watertight suit worn by divers with a helmet into which air can be pumped.

dive[2] /daɪv/ *n* **1** act of diving: *The goalkeeper made a spectacular dive to save the goal.* **2** (*infml*) disreputable bar, gambling club, etc.

diverge /daɪˈvɜːdʒ/ *v* **1** [I, Ipr] ~ (**from sth**) (**a**) (of lines, roads, etc) separate and go in different directions, becoming further apart: *The M6 diverges from the M1 just north of Rugby.* ○ (*fig*) *Until their paths diverged Lennon and McCartney wrote many hits together.* ⇨ illus at CONVERGE. (**b**) (*fml*) (of opinions, etc) differ: *Our views diverged so greatly that it was impossible to agree.* **2** [Ipr] ~ **from sth** turn away from (a plan, standard, etc): *diverge from the truth, norm, usual procedure.* Cf CONVERGE. ▷ **divergence** /daɪˈvɜːdʒəns/ (also **divergency** /-dʒənsɪ/) *n* [C, U]. **divergent** /-dʒənt/ *adj*: *divergent paths, opinions.*

divers /ˈdaɪvəz/ *adj* (*arch*) various; several.

diverse /daɪˈvɜːs/ *adj* of different kinds; varied: *people from diverse cultures* ○ *Her interests are very diverse.*

diversify /daɪˈvɜːsɪfaɪ/ *v* (*pt, pp* **-fied**) **1** [Tn] give variety to (sth); vary: *diversify one's skills, interests, etc* ○ *We must try to diversify the syllabus to attract more students.* **2** [I, Ipr] ~ (**into sth**) (*commerce*) (esp of a business) vary the range of products, investments, etc in order to reduce risk or expand operations: *The choice facing the company is simple: diversify or go bankrupt.* ○ *Some publishers are now diversifying into software.* ▷ **diversification** /daɪˌvɜːsɪfɪˈkeɪʃn/ *n* [U, C].

diversion /daɪˈvɜːʃn; *US* daɪˈvɜːrʒn/ *n* **1** (**a**) [U] act of turning sth aside or changing its direction: *the diversion of a stream, one's thoughts* ○ *the diversion of flights because of fog.* (**b**) [C] instance of this. **2** [C] (*esp Brit*) (*US* **detour**) alternative route for use by traffic when the usual road is temporarily closed: *Sorry I'm late — there was a diversion.* **3** [C] entertaining activity, esp one that turns the attention from work, study, etc: *the diversions of city life* ○ *It's difficult to concentrate when there are so many diversions.* **4** [C] thing designed to draw attention away from sth one does not want to be noticed: *One of the gang created a diversion in the street while the others robbed the bank.* ▷ **diversionary** /daɪˈvɜːʃənərɪ; *US* daɪˈvɜːrʒənerɪ/ *adj*: *diversionary action, tactics, raids, etc.*

diversity /daɪˈvɜːsətɪ/ *n* [U, sing] state of being varied; variety: *a wide diversity of opinion.*

divert /daɪˈvɜːt/ *v* **1** [Tn, Tn·pr] ~ **sb/sth** (**from sth**) (**to sth**) turn sb/sth from one course to another: *divert traffic (from one road to another)* ○ *divert a ship (from its course)* ○ *divert sb's attention, thoughts, energies, etc.* **2** [Tn] entertain or amuse (sb): *Children are easily diverted.*

▷ **diverting** *adj* entertaining. **divertingly** *adv.*

divertissement /ˌdiːvəːˈtiːsmɒŋ/ *n* **1** short ballet between the acts of an opera or a play. **2** activity, etc that amuses or entertains; diversion(3).

divest /daɪˈvest/ *v* [Tn·pr] (*fml*) **1** ~ **sb of sth** take off (sb's clothes): *divest a queen of her robes.* **2** ~ **sb of sth** take away (sb's power, rights, responsibility, etc): *The disgraced official was divested of all authority.* **3** ~ **oneself of sth** rid oneself of (a feeling, idea, etc): *He could not divest himself of the suspicion that his wife was being unfaithful.*

divide[1] /dɪˈvaɪd/ *v* **1** [I, Ipr, Ip, Tn, Tn·pr, Tn·p] ~ (**sth**) (**up**) (**into sth**) (cause sth to) split or break into parts; separate: *The train divides at York.* ○ *divide a large house (up) into flats* ○ *divide a novel (up) into chapters* ○ *divide the class (up) into small groups.* **2** [Tn, Tn·pr, Tn·p] ~ **sth** (**out/up**) (**between/among sb**) break sth into parts and give a share to each of a number of individuals: *divide out/up the money, food, reward* ○ *We divided the work between us.* **3** [Tn, Tn·pr] ~ **sth** (**between A and B**) split sth up, esp one's time, and use parts of it for different activities, etc; apportion sth: *He divides his energies between politics and business.* **4** [Tn·pr] ~ **A from B** separate or be the boundary between (two people or things): *The English Channel divides England from France.* **5** [Tn] cause (two or more people) to disagree: *This issue has divided the government.* ○ *The government is divided (on this issue).* **6** (**a**) [Tn·pr] ~ **sth by sth** find out how many times one number is contained in another: *30 divided by 6 is 5.* (**b**) [Ip] ~ **into sth** be able to be multiplied to give another number: *5 divides into 30 6 times.* **7** [I, Tn] (*esp Brit*) (cause Parliament to) vote, by separating into groups for and against a motion: *After a long debate the House divided,* ie voted on the question. ○ *divide the House,* ie ask for a vote to be taken.

▷ **divider** *n* thing that divides sth: *a ˈroom divider,* ie screen, etc that divides a room into two parts.

divide[2] /dɪˈvaɪd/ *n* (*esp US*) line of high land separating two river systems; watershed: *the Continental/Great Diˈvide,* ie the watershed formed by the Rocky Mountains.

dividend /ˈdɪvɪdend/ *n* **1** (*commerce*) share of profits paid to shareholders in a company, or to winners in a football pool: *declare a dividend,* ie state what proportion of profits is to be divided among shareholders ○ *an annual dividend of 8%.* **2** (*mathematics*) number that is to be divided by another. Cf DIVISOR. **3** (idm) **pay dividends** ⇨ PAY[2].

dividers /dɪˈvaɪdəz/ *n* [pl] instrument used for measuring lines, angles, etc: *a pair of dividers.* ⇨ illus at COMPASS.

divination /ˌdɪvɪˈneɪʃn/ *n* [U] foretelling the future by supernatural means.

divine[1] /dɪˈvaɪn/ *adj* **1** [usu attrib] of, from or like God or a god: *Divine ˈService,* ie the public worship of God. **2** (*infml*) wonderful, lovely, etc: *You look simply divine, darling!* ▷ **divinely** *adv*: *You dance divinely.*

□ **Diˌvine ˈOffice** the prayers and bible readings that are used in the services held at set times throughout the day in the Roman Catholic Church.

diˌvine ˈright (**a**) (also **diˌvine right of ˈkings**) the idea that kings and queens are given their right to rule directly by God, and that therefore it is sinful to oppose them. The *Stuarts were the last in Britain to claim such a right. (**b**) complete right to do sth, which must not be denied or taken away: *He seems to think he has a divine right to run the company his own way.*

divine[2] /dɪˈvaɪn/ *v* [Tn, Tf] **1** (*fml*) sense (sth) by intuition; guess: *divine sb's thoughts, intentions, the truth.* **2** reveal (sth hidden, esp the future) by magical means: *Astrologers claim to be able to divine what the stars hold in store for us.*

▷ **diviner** (also **ˈwater-diviner**) *n* person who divines, esp one who searches for underground water using a divining-rod.

□ **diˈvining-rod** *n* Y-shaped stick used by a water-diviner.

divinity /dɪˈvɪnətɪ/ *n* **1** [U] quality of being divine[1](1): *the divinity of Christ.* **2** [C] god or goddess: *the Roman, Greek, Egyptian divinities.* **3** [U] theology: *a doctor of divinity.*

divisible /dɪˈvɪzəbl/ *adj* [usu pred] (*mathematics*) ~ (**by sth**) able to be divided, usu with no remainder: *8 is divisible by 2 and 4, but not by 3.*

division /dɪˈvɪʒn/ *n* **1** [U] (**a**) dividing or being divided: *the division of wealth.* (**b**) dividing one number by another: *Are you any good at division?* **2** [sing] (often preceded by an *adj*) result of dividing: *a fair/unfair division of money* ○ *an equal division of labour,* ie the sharing out of tasks to be done among different people or groups. **3** [C] (**a**) one of the parts into which sth is divided. (**b**) (*abbr* **Div**) major unit or section of an organization: *the ˈsales division of our company* ○ *Our team plays in the first diˈvision (of the football league).* ○ *the ˈparachute division.* **4** [C] dividing line: *A hedge forms the division between her land and mine.* **5** [C, U] (instance of) disagreement or difference in thought, way of life, etc: *the deep/widening divisions in society today.* **6** [C] (*esp Brit*) (in Parliament) act of voting: *The Bill was read without a division.* ○ *The opposition threatened to force a division on the motion.*

▷ **divisional** /dɪˈvɪʒənl/ *adj* [attrib] of a division(3): *divisional comˈmander, headˈquarters, etc.*

□ **diˈvision-bell** *n* (*Brit*) bell rung to warn Members of Parliament not present in the House that there is to be a division(6).

diˈvision lobby (also **lobby**) *n* (*Brit*) (in Parliament) one of two corridors where Members of Parliament go to vote.

diˈvision sign *n* sign (÷) placed between two numbers, showing that the first is to be divided by the second.

divisive /dɪˈvaɪsɪv/ *adj* causing disagreement or disunity among people: *a divisive influence, policy, effect.* ▷ **divisively** *adv.* **divisiveness** *n* [U].

divisor /dɪˈvaɪzə(r)/ *n* (*mathematics*) number by which another number is divided. Cf DIVIDEND.

divorce[1] /dɪˈvɔːs/ *n* **1** [C, U] ~ (**from sb**) (instance of the) legal ending of a marriage: *ask/sue for a divorce* ○ *get/obtain a divorce* ○ *grounds* (ie legal reasons) *for divorce* ○ *Divorce is on the increase.* ○ [attrib] *start di'vorce proceedings.* **2** [C] (*fig*) ending of a connection; separation: *the divorce between religion and science.*

divorce[2] /dɪˈvɔːs/ *v* **1** [Tn] legally end one's marriage to (sb): *They're divorcing each other/ getting divorced.* **2** [Tn·pr esp passive] ~ **sb/sth from sth** (*fig*) separate sb/sth from sth, esp in a false way: *You can't divorce science from ethical questions.* ○ *a politician totally divorced from* (ie unable to understand or deal with) *the real needs of the country.*

▷ **divorcee** /dɪˌvɔːˈsiː/ *n* divorced person.

divot /ˈdɪvət/ *n* piece of turf cut out by a golf-club when making a stroke.

divulge /daɪˈvʌldʒ/ *v* [Tn, Tn·pr, Tw] ~ **sth (to sb)** make known (sth secret): *divulge a confidential report, sb's identity, one's age* ○ *I cannot divulge how much it cost.* ▷ **divulgence** /daɪˈvʌldʒəns/ *n* [U].

divvy /ˈdɪvɪ/ *n* (*Brit infml*) (formerly) dividend(1), esp one paid by a co-operative society.

▷ **divvy** *v* (*pt, pp* **divvied**) (phr v) **divvy sth up** (*infml*) share sth out; distribute: *They divvied up the winnings between them.*

Dixie /ˈdɪksɪ/ *n* [sing] (*US infml*) southern states of the US, esp those that formed the Confederacy in 1860-61.

□ **ˈDixieland** /-lænd/ *n* **1** [sing] (*US*) Dixie. **2** (also **dixieland**) [U] style of jazz with strong two-beat rhythm, originating in New Orleans: *Do you like Dixieland?* ○ [attrib] *a dixieland band.*

DIY /ˌdiː aɪ ˈwaɪ/ *abbr* (*Brit infml*) do it yourself: *a DIY kit* ○ *DIY enthusiasts.* ⇨ article at HOBBY.

dizzy /ˈdɪzɪ/ *adj* (**-ier, -iest**) **1** (of a person) feeling as if everything is spinning around; unable to balance; confused: *After another glass of whisky I began to feel dizzy.* **2** of or causing this feeling: *a dizzy spell* ○ *a dizzy height, speed.*

▷ **dizzily** *adv.*

dizziness *n* [U].

dizzy *v* (*pt, pp* **dizzied**) [Tn] make (sb) dizzy.

DJ /ˌdiː ˈdʒeɪ/ *abbr* (*infml*) **1** (*Brit*) dinner-jacket. **2** disc jockey: *He's a radio DJ.*

Djibouti /dʒɪˈbuːtɪ/ country on the NE coast of Africa; pop approx 484 000; official languages French and Arabic; capital Djibouti; unit of currency Djibouti franc. Formerly known as French Somaliland and then as French Territory of the Afars and Issas, it gained independence in 1977. The land is largely stony desert and the chief occupation is nomadic animal-herding. The economy is based on the export of hides, cattle and coffee, and revenues derived from the port of Djibouti. ⇨ map at TANZANIA. ▷ **Djiboutian** *n, adj.*

dl *abbr* (*pl* unchanged or **dls**) decilitre: *10 dl.*

D layer /ˈdiː leɪə(r)/ lowest layer of the ionosphere, which can reflect low-frequency radio waves.

DLitt /ˌdiː ˈlɪt/ (also **Litt D**) *abbr* Doctor of Letters: *have/be a DLitt in English* ○ *Jane Pearce DLitt.*

DM (also **D-mark**) *abbr* unit of money in Germany (German *Deutsche Mark*): *DM 650.*

dm *abbr* (*pl* unchanged or **dms**) decimetre: *15 dm.*

DMus /ˌdiːˈmʌs/ *abbr* Doctor of Music: *have/be a DMus* ○ *Simon Potter DMus.*

DNA /ˌdiː en ˈeɪ/ *abbr* (*chemistry*) deoxyribonucleic acid (the main constituent of the gene).

DNB /ˌdiː en ˈbiː/ *abbr* Dictionary of National Biography (a reference book in many volumes giving the life stories of important British people).

D-notice /ˈdiː nəʊtɪs/ *n* official instruction sent by the British government to newspaper editors, telling them not to print items that may threaten national security.

do[1] /duː/ *aux v* (*neg* **do not**, *contracted form* **don't** /dəʊnt/; *3rd pers sing pres t* **does** /dəz; *strong form* dʌz/, *neg* **does not**, *contracted form* **doesn't** /ˈdʌznt/; *pt* **did** /dɪd/, *neg* **did not**, *contracted form* **didn't** /ˈdɪdnt/; *pp* **done** /dʌn/) **1** (**a**) (used in front of a full *v* to form negative sentences and questions): *I don't like fish.* ○ *They didn't go to Paris.* ○ *Don't forget to write.* ○ *Does she speak French?* ○ *Do you believe him?* ○ *Did they take you home?* (**b**) (used to make tag questions): *You live in London, don't you?* ○ *He married his boss's daughter, didn't he?* ○ *She doesn't work here, does she?* **2** (used when no other *aux v* is present to emphasize that a verb is positive): *He ˈdoes look tired.* ○ *She ˈdid write to say thank you.* ○ *Do shut up!* ○ *Do say you'll stay for supper!* **3** (used to reverse the order of the subject and *v* when an *adv* or adverbial phrase is moved to the front): *Not only does she speak Spanish, (but) she also knows how to type.* ○ (*fml*) *So much did they eat that they could not move for the next hour.* ○ *Rarely did she request help but this was a matter of urgency.* **4** (used to avoid repetition of a full *v*): *He drives faster than he did a year ago.* ○ *She works harder than he does.* ○ *'Who won?' 'I did.'*

do[2] /duː/ *v* (*3rd pers sing pres t* **does** /dʌz/, *pt* **did** /dɪd/, *pp* **done** /dʌn/)

►CARRYING OUT AN ACTIVITY **1** [Tn] (used esp with *what, anything, nothing* and *something*, to refer to actions which are unspecified or not yet known about): *'What are you doing this evening?' 'I'm going to the cinema.'* ○ *'Are you doing anything tomorrow evening?'* ○ *We will do what we can to help you.* ○ *The company ought to do something about the poor service.* ○ *What does she want to do* (ie What career does she want) *when she leaves school?* ○ *There's nothing to do in this place*, ie no means of passing one's leisure time enjoyably. ○ *He does nothing but complain/All he does is complain.* ○ *'It's so unfair that she's lost her job.' 'I know, but there's nothing we can do about it* (ie We can't change the situation).*'* ○ *'What can I do for you?' 'I'd like a pound of apples, please.'* **2** [I] act; behave: *Do as you wish/please.* ○ *Do as I do.* ○ *Why can't you do as you're told* (ie be obedient)*?* **3** [Tn] work at, or carry out, (an activity or a task): *do a university degree* ○ *do research into French history* ○ *He still has to do his military service.* ○ *I have a number of important things to do today.* ○ *She does aerobics once a week.* **4** [Tn] (used esp with *the* + *n* or *my, his*, etc + *n* to refer to everyday tasks such as cleaning, washing, arranging, mending, etc): *do* (ie brush) *one's teeth* ○ *do* (ie wash up) *the dishes* ○ *do* (ie polish) *the silver* ○ *do the flowers*, ie arrange them in vases ○ *I like the way you've done* (ie styled) *your hair.* ○ *We'll have to get someone to do* (ie mend) *the roof.* **5** [Tn] (used with *the, my, some, much*, etc + the *-ing* form of a *v* to refer to a wide range of actions): *do the ironing, cooking, washing, etc* ○ *We usually do our shopping at the weekend.* ○ *You do the painting and I'll do the papering.* ○ *She did a lot of acting* (ie acted in a lot of plays) *when she was at university.* ○ *He does some writing* (eg writes poems, novels, essays, etc) *in his spare time.*

►STUDYING OR SOLVING **6** [Tn] learn or study (sth): *Do you do science at school?* ○ *do accountancy, engineering, law, etc*, eg as a professional training ○ *She did economics at Sheffield University.* ○ *Have you done any* (ie studied any works by) *Shakespeare?* **7** [Tn] find the answer to (sth); solve: *I can't do this sum.* ○ *I could never do simultaneous equations.* ○ *Can you do crosswords?*

►MAKING OR PRODUCING **8** [Tn, Dn·n, Dn·pr] ~ **sth (for sb)** produce (sth); make: *do a drawing, painting, sketch, etc* ○ *She did five copies of the agenda.* ○ *Does this pub do* (ie provide) *lunches?* ○ *Who's doing* (ie organizing and preparing) *the food at the wedding reception?* ○ *I'll do a translation for you/do you a translation.* **9** [Tn] deal with or attend to (sb/sth): *The barber said he'd do me* (ie cut my hair) *next.* **10** [Tn] put on or produce (a play, opera, etc): *The Dramatic Society are doing ˈHamlet next year.* **11** [Tn] play the part of (sb); imitate (sb): *I thought he did Hamlet superbly.* ○ *She does Mrs Thatcher rather well.* **12** [I, Tn, Tg] (used in the perfect tense or the passive) finish (sth); complete: (*infml*) *Have you done* (ie finished what you were doing)*?* ○ *I've done talking — it's time to act.* ○ *The work won't take too long to do.* ○ *Did you get your article done in time?*

►COMPLETING AN ACTIVITY OR A JOURNEY **13** [Tn] (**a**) travel over (a distance): *How many miles did you do during your tour?* ○ *My car does 40 miles to the gallon*, ie uses one gallon of petrol to travel 40 miles. (**b**) complete (a journey): *We did the journey (from London to Oxford) in an hour.* (**c**) travel at or reach (a speed): *The car was doing 90 miles an hour.* **14** [Tn] (*infml*) visit (a place) as a sightseer; see the sights of: *We did Tokyo in three days.* **15** [Tn] spend (a period of time): *She did a year at university, but decided to give up the course.* ○ (*infml*) *He did six months (in prison) for burglary.*

►OTHER MEANINGS **16** [I, Ipr, Tn] ~ **(for sb/sth)**; ~ **(as sth)** be sufficient or satisfactory for (sb): *'Can you lend me some money?' 'Certainly — will £10 do?'* ○ *Will next Friday do for our meeting?* ○ *These shoes won't do* (ie are not strong enough) *for climbing.* ○ *This log will do fine as a table for our picnic.* ○ *This room will do (me) nicely, thank you*, ie It has all the comforts I need. **17** [I] (used with *advs*, or in questions after *how*) progress; perform: *She's doing very well at school*, ie Her work is good. ○ *How is the business doing?* ○ *Both mother and baby are doing well*, ie after the birth of the baby. ○ *Everything in the garden is doing* (ie growing) *splendidly.* ○ *She did well out of* (ie profited from) *the deal.* **18** [Tn] cook (sth): *Shall I do the casserole in the oven?* ○ *How would you like your steak done?* **19** (**a**) [Tn esp passive] (*infml*) cheat or swindle (sb): *This table isn't a genuine antique; I'm afraid you've been done!* ie you have paid a lot of money for an object of little value. (**b**) [Tn] (*sl*) rob or burgle (sth): *The gang did a warehouse and a supermarket.* **20** (*sl*) (**a**) [Tn] hurt or hit (sb): *Say that again and I'll do you!* (**b**) [esp passive: Tn, Tn·pr] ~ **sb (for sth)** arrest or convict sb (for a crime): *He got done for speeding.* **21** (idm) **be/have to do with sb/sth** be connected with or related to sb/sth: *'What do you want to see me about?' 'It's to do with that letter you sent me.'* **ˌdo as you would be ˈdone by** (*saying*) one should treat others as one would like to be treated. **have (got) something, nothing, a lot, etc to do with sb/sth** be connected or concerned to a specified extent with sb/sth: *Her job has something to do with computers.* ○ *Hard work has a lot to do with* (ie has contributed greatly towards) *her success.* ○ *'How much do you earn?' 'What's it got to do with you?'* ○ *We don't have very much to do with our neighbours*, ie don't meet them socially. **ˌhow do you ˈdo?** (used as a formal greeting when one meets sb for the first time). **it/that will never/won't ˈdo** (used to indicate that a state of affairs is unsatisfactory and should be changed or improved): *This is the third time you've been late for work this week; it simply won't do, I'm afraid.* **ˌnothing ˈdoing** (*sl*) (used to refuse a request): *'Could you lend me £10?' 'Nothing doing!'* **that ˈdoes it** (*infml*) (used to show that one will not tolerate sth any longer): *That does it! I've had enough of your sarcasm. I'm leaving.* **that's ˈdone it** (*infml*) (used to express dismay, anger, etc that a misfortune, accident or mistake has spoiled or ruined sth): *That's done it. We've run out of petrol. We'll never be in time for the train now.* **that will ˈdo** (used esp to order sb to stop doing or saying sth): *That'll do, you two; you're getting far too noisy.* (For other idioms containing **do**, see entries for *ns, adjs*, etc, eg **do a bunk** ⇨ BUNK[2]; **easier said than done** ⇨ EASY.) **22** (phr v) **do away with sth** (*infml*) get rid of sth; abolish sth: *She thinks it's time we did away with the monarchy.* ○ *The death penalty has been done away with in many European countries.* **do away with oneself/sb** (*infml*) kill oneself/sb: *She tried to do away with herself.*

do sb/sth down (*infml*) speak of sb/sth in a critical or unfavourable way; criticize or disparage sb/sth: *He's always doing his friends down.* ○ *It has become fashionable to do down traditional moral values.*

do for sb (*infml*) do housework for sb: *Old Mrs Green has done for us for over 20 years.* ○ *They can't afford a home help, so they have to do for themselves.*

do for sb/sth (usu passive) (*infml*) ruin, destroy

or kill sb/sth: *Unless the government provides more cash, the steel industry is done for.* **do for sth** (*infml*) (used in questions with *how* and *what*) manage to obtain: *How/What did you do for coal during the miners' strike?* **do sth for sb/sth** (*infml*) improve the appearance of sb/sth: *That new hair-style really does something/a lot for her.*

do sb ˈin (*infml*) (a) kill sb: *She was so depressed she felt like doing herself in.* (b) = DO SB OVER. (c) (usu passive) exhaust sb: *Come in and sit down — you look done in.* **do sth in** (*infml*) injure (a part of the body): *He did his back in lifting heavy furniture.*

do sth out (*infml*) clean or tidy (a room, cupboard, etc) by removing unwanted things from it: *Your desk drawer needs doing out.* **do sb out of sth** (*infml*) prevent sb from having sth, esp in an unfair or dishonest way: *She was done out of her promotion.*

do sb ˈover (*infml*) attack and beat sb severely: *He was done over by a gang of thugs after a football match.* **do sth over** clean or redecorate the surfaces of sth: *The paintwork is beginning to flake; it'll need doing over/to be done over soon.*

do sth to sb (*infml*) have an effect on sb; excite or stir sb: *Her voice really does something to me.* ○ *What have you done to your sister? She's very upset.* **do sth to sth** (esp in questions with *what*) cause sth to happen to sth: *What have you done to the television? It's not working properly.* ○ *What on earth have you done to your hair?* eg Why have you had it cut in that way?

do up be fastened; fasten: *This skirt does up at the back.* **do oneself ˈup** (*infml*) make oneself more attractive by putting on make-up, different clothes, etc. **do sth up** (a) fasten (a coat, skirt, etc) with buttons, a zip, etc: *He never bothers to do his jacket up.* ○ *She asked me to do up her dress for her at the back.* (b) make sth into a parcel or bundle; wrap or tie sth up: *She was carrying a parcel of books done up in brown paper.* (c) repair, redecorate or modernize (a house, room, etc): *If we decide to buy the cottage we'll have to do it up.* ○ *We're having the kitchen done up.*

do with sth (a) (used with *can* and *could* to express a need or desire for sth): *You look as if you could do with* (ie as if you need) *a good night's sleep.* ○ *I could do with a stiff drink!* (b) (used in the negative with *can* and *could*) tolerate sth: *I can't do with his insolence.* ○ *If there's one thing I can't do with, it's untidiness.* **do sth with sb/sth** (used in questions with *what*): *What have you done with* (ie Where have you put) *my umbrella?* ○ *Tell me what you did with yourselves* (ie how you passed the time) *on Sunday.* ○ *What are we going to do with* (ie How are we going to use) *the food left over from the party?* ○ *She doesn't know what to do with herself.*

do without (sb/sth) (used esp with *can* and *could*) manage without sb/sth: *He can't do without (the services of) a secretary.* ○ *If we can't afford a car, we'll just have to do without (one).* ○ *I could have done without being* (ie I wish I hadn't been) *woken up at 3 o'clock in the morning.*

□ **ˌdo-ˈgooder** *n* (*infml often derog*) person who performs or tries to perform good deeds, esp in an unrealistic, interfering or fussy way.

ˌdo it yourˈself (*abbr* **DIY**) activity of constructing, repairing or decorating things oneself (rather than employing professional workers to do it): *She's very keen on do it yourself.* ○ [attrib] *a do-it-yourself shop.*

do[3] /du:/ *n* (*pl* **dos** or **do's** /du:z/) **1** (*Brit infml*) party: *I hear the Newtons are having a big do tonight.* **2** (*Brit sl*) dishonest trick; swindle: *If you ask me, the whole thing's a do.* **3** (idm) **do's and don'ts** /ˌdu:z ən ˈdəʊnts/ rules: *If you want to lose weight, here are some do's and don'ts.* **fair do/dos/do's** ⇨ FAIR[1].

do[4] = DOH.

do *abbr* (also *symb* ״) ditto.

Dobermann pinscher /ˌdəʊbəmən ˈpɪnʃə(r)/ (also **Dobermann**) *n* type of large dog with smooth hair and a short tail, often used as a guard dog.

doc /dɒk/ *n* (*infml*) (used as a term of address) doctor.

docile /ˈdəʊsaɪl; *US* ˈdɒsl/ *adj* (of a person or animal) easy to control: *a docile child, dog, personality.* ▷ **docilely** /-saɪllɪ; *US* -səlɪ/ *adv.* **docility** /dəʊˈsɪlətɪ/ *n* [U].

dock[1] /dɒk/ *n* **1** [C] part of a port, etc where ships go for loading, unloading or repair, esp one fitted with gates to control the water level: *go into/be in dock* ○ [attrib] *dock workers.* **2 docks** [pl] grouping of docks with the wharves, sheds, etc round them: *work at the docks.* **3** [C] (*esp US*) ship's berth; wharf.

▷ **docker** *n* person who loads and unloads ships.

□ **ˈdockland** /-lænd/ *n* [U, C] district near a dockyard. ⇨ article at LONDON.

ˈdockyard *n* area with docks and equipment for building and repairing ships.

dock[2] /dɒk/ *v* **1** (a) [I] (of a ship) come into dock. (b) [Tn] bring (a ship) into dock. **2** (a) [I] (of spacecraft) join together: *docking manoeuvres/procedures.* (b) [Tn] join (two or more spacecraft) together in space.

dock[3] /dɒk/ *n* **1** part of a criminal court where the accused sits during his trial: *The judge looked over to the prisoner in the dock.* **2** (idm) **put sb/be in the dock** accuse sb/be accused of doing sth wrong: *This recent tragedy has put the manufacturers of the drug squarely in the dock.*

dock[4] /dɒk/ *v* **1** [Tn] cut short (an animal's tail). **2** [Tn, Tn·pr, Dn·n] ~ **sth (from/off sth)** take away (part of sb's wages, rations, etc): *They've docked my salary.* ○ *dock 15% from/off sb's earnings* ○ *They've docked me £20.*

dock[5] /dɒk/ *n* [U, C] common weed with large leaves. These are traditionally rubbed on the skin to soothe nettle stings.

docket /ˈdɒkɪt/ *n* **1** (*commerce*) document or label listing goods delivered, jobs done, contents of a package, etc. **2** (*US law*) list of cases awaiting trial.

▷ **docket** *v* [Tn] (a) write (sth) on a docket. (b) label (sth) with a docket.

doctor /ˈdɒktə(r)/ *n* (*abbr* **Dr**) **1** person who has been trained in medical science: *You'd better see a doctor about that cut.* ○ *Doctor Thompson.* **2** person who has received the highest university degree: *Doctor of Philosophy, Science, Letters, Law, etc.* **3** (idm) **(just) what the ˌdoctor ˈordered** (*infml*) exactly what is needed or wanted: *When you've been working outside on a hot day, a cold drink's just what the doctor ordered.*

▷ **doctor** *v* [Tn] **1** (*infml*) give medical treatment for (sth) or to (sb): *doctor a cold, a child.* **2** neuter (a cat, dog, etc). **3** (*infml*) add sth harmful to (food or drink): *They doctored her fruit juice with vodka for a joke.* **4** (*infml*) change (sth) in order to deceive: *doctor the evidence, the accounts, a report.*

doctoral /ˈdɒktərəl/ *adj* [attrib] of or relating to a doctorate: *a doctoral thesis.*

doctorate /ˈdɒktərət/ *n* highest university degree: *She's studying for her doctorate.*

doctrinaire /ˌdɒktrɪˈneə(r)/ *adj* (*derog*) rigidly applying a theory with no concern for practical problems: *doctrinaire attitudes, beliefs, criticisms.*

doctrine /ˈdɒktrɪn/ *n* [C, U] (any of a) set of beliefs held by a church, political party, group of scientists, etc: *Catholic doctrines* ○ *Marxist doctrine* ○ *This is a matter of doctrine,* ie must be accepted as true. ▷ **doctrinal** /dɒkˈtraɪnl; *US* ˈdɒktrɪnl/ *adj* [attrib]: *doctrinal controversy* ○ (*derog*) *a rigidly doctrinal approach, response, upbringing.*

document /ˈdɒkjʊmənt/ *n* paper, form, book, etc giving information about sth, evidence or proof of sth: *The spy stole secret government documents.* ○ *study all the documents in a case,* ie one being heard in court ○ *legal documents,* eg deeds of property, wills, etc.

▷ **document** /ˈdɒkjʊment/ *v* [Tn] prove or support (sth) with documents: *Can you document these claims?* ○ *a badly-/well-documented report,* ie (not) supporting its statements by referring to evidence.

documentation /ˌdɒkjʊmenˈteɪʃn/ *n* [U] **1** documenting or being documented. **2** documents provided as evidence or proof of sth: *We haven't enough documentation to process your claim.*

documentary /ˌdɒkjʊˈmentrɪ/ *adj* [attrib] **1** consisting of documents: *documentary evidence, proof, sources.* **2** giving a factual report of some subject or activity, esp by using pictures, recordings, etc of people involved: *a documentary account of the Vietnam war* ○ *documentary films showing the lives of working people.*

▷ **documentary** /ˌdɒkjʊˈmentrɪ/ *n* documentary film, or radio or TV programme: *a documentary on/about drug abuse.*

dodder /ˈdɒdə(r)/ *v* [I, Ipr, Ip] (*infml*) move or act in a shaky unsteady way, because of old age or weakness: *He doddered down the street.* ○ *dodder along, about, around, etc.*

▷ **dodderer** /ˈdɒdərə(r)/ *n* **1** (*infml*) person who dodders. **2** (*derog*) old person.

doddering /ˈdɒdərɪŋ/ (also **doddery** /ˈdɒdərɪ/) *adjs* weak and uncertain in movement.

doddle /ˌdɒdl/ *n* [sing] (*infml*) task or activity that is easily performed: *That hill's an absolute doddle (to climb).* ○ *It's no doddle being a teacher, you know.*

dodge[1] /dɒdʒ/ *v* **1** [I, Ipr, Ip, Tn] move quickly and suddenly to one side in order to avoid (sb/sth): *He dodged to left and right as the gunman opened fire.* ○ *She dodged round the corner.* ○ (*fig*) *I'll leave early so as to dodge the rush-hour.* **2** [Tn, Tg] (*infml*) avoid doing (sth) by cleverness or trickery: *dodge military service* ○ *dodge awkward questions* ○ *He always manages to dodge (doing) the housework.*

▷ **dodger** *n* (*infml*) person who avoids doing sth: *Make sure she pays her share — she's a bit of a dodger.*

dodge[2] /dɒdʒ/ *n* **1** (usu *sing*) quick movement to avoid sb/sth: *make a sudden dodge to the right.* **2** (*infml*) clever trick; way of avoiding sth: *a tax dodge* ○ *She's up to all the dodges,* ie knows and uses them all.

dodgems /ˈdɒdʒəmz/ [pl] *n* (also **ˈdodgem cars**) (*Brit*) (at fun-fairs) small electric cars whose drivers try to bump other cars while dodging those that try to bump them: *have a go on the dodgems.*

Dodgson /ˈdɒdʒsn/ Charles Lutwidge, real name of Lewis *Carroll, author of *Alice in Wonderland.*

dodgy /ˈdɒdʒɪ/ *adj* (**-ier, -iest**) (*infml esp Brit*) **1** (of a person) likely to be dishonest; cunning: *He's a dodgy bloke — I wouldn't trust him an inch.* **2** difficult or dangerous: *Cycle across America? Sounds a bit dodgy to me.*

dodo /ˈdəʊdəʊ/ *n* (*pl* ~**s**, ~**es**) **1** large bird, now extinct, that was unable to fly and that lived on Mauritius. **2** (idm) **dead as a/the dodo** ⇨ DEAD.

DOE /ˌdi: əʊ ˈi:/ *abbr* (*Brit*) Department of the Environment.

doe /dəʊ/ *n* female deer, reindeer, rabbit or hare. ⇨ illus at DEER. Cf FAWN[1] 1, HIND[2], STAG 1.

doer /ˈdu:ə(r)/ *n* (*approv*) person who does things rather than thinking or talking about them: *We need more doers and fewer organizers.*

does ⇨ DO[1,2].

doff /dɒf; *US* dɔ:f/ *v* [Tn] (*fml*) take off (one's hat). Cf DON[2].

dog[1] /dɒg; *US* dɔ:g/ *n* **1** [C] (a) common domestic animal kept by human beings for work, hunting, etc or as a pet. ⇨ illus. (b) male of this animal, or of the wolf or fox. Cf BITCH 1. (c) **the dogs** [pl] (*infml*) (betting on the result of) greyhound racing: *I won £10 on the dogs.* **2** [C] (a) (preceded by an *adj*) (*dated infml*) fellow: *a sly, lucky, gay dog* ○ *You dirty* (ie dishonourable) *dog!* (b) (*dated*) wicked or worthless man: *He's a vile dog!* **3** [C] mechanical device for gripping things. **4** [C] = ANDIRON. **5** (idm) **(a case of) ˌdog eat ˈdog** ruthless competition. **a ˌdog in the ˈmanger** person who stops others enjoying sth he cannot use or does not want: [attrib] *a ˌdog-in-the-manger ˈattitude.* **a dog's ˈbreakfast/ˈdinner** (*infml*) muddle or mess: *He's made a real dog's breakfast of these accounts.* **dressed like a dog's dinner** ⇨ DRESS[2]. **every dog has his/its ˈday** (*saying*) everyone enjoys good luck or success sooner or later. **(fight) like cat and dog** ⇨ CAT[1]. **give a dog a bad ˈname (and ˈhang him)** (*saying*) once a person has lost his reputation, it is difficult for him to regain it because others continue to condemn or suspect him. **go to the ˈdogs** (*infml*) (of an organization, institution, etc) change so that it is no longer as efficient, productive, etc as before: *This firm's gone to the dogs since you took over!* **a/the hair of the dog** ⇨ HAIR. **help a lame dog over a stile** ⇨ HELP[1]. **lead a dog's life; lead sb a dog's life** ⇨ LEAD[3]. **let sleeping dogs lie** ⇨ SLEEP[2]. **love me, love my dog** ⇨ LOVE[2]. **not have a ˈdog's chance** have no chance at all: *He hasn't a dog's chance of passing the exam.* **put on the dog** (*US sl*) show off. **rain cats and dogs** ⇨ RAIN[2]. **the tail wagging the dog** ⇨ TAIL. **teach an old dog new tricks** ⇨ TEACH. **top dog** ⇨ TOP[1]. **treat sb like dirt/a dog** ⇨ TREAT.

▷ **doggie** (also **doggy**) /ˈdɒgɪ; *US* ˈdɔ:gɪ/ *n* (*infml*) (used by and to children) dog. **ˈdoggie bag** bag for taking home uneaten food, esp one supplied by a restaurant to its customers.

□ **ˈdog-biscuit** *n* small hard biscuit fed to dogs. **ˈdogcart** *n* light two-wheeled horse-drawn vehicle. **ˈdog-collar** *n* **1** collar for a dog. **2** (*infml*) stiff white collar worn by a clergyman.

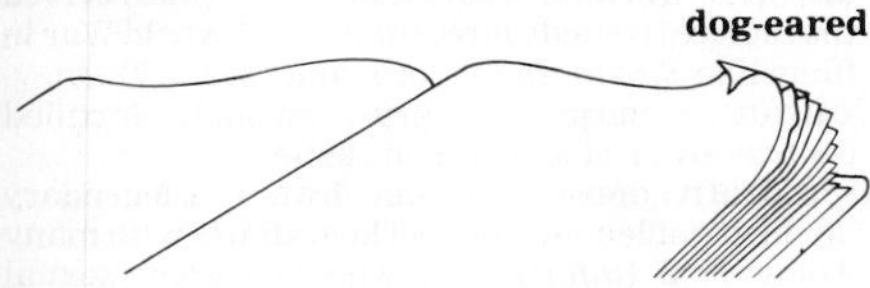
dog-eared

ˈdog-eared *adj* (of a book) having the corners of many pages turned down through use. ⇨ illus. **ˈdogfight** *n* **1** close combat between fighter aircraft. **2** rough uncontrolled fight. **ˈdoghouse** *n* **1** (*US*) kennel. **2** (idm) **in the doghouse** in disgrace; out of favour. **ˈdog-like** *adj* [usu attrib] of or like a dog: *dog-like devotion, fidelity, etc.* **ˈdog-leg** *n* sharp bend, esp on a golf-course. **ˈdog-paddle** (also **ˈdoggie-paddle**) *n* [U] simple swimming stroke, with short quick movements of the arms and legs. — *v* [I] swim in this way. **the ˈdog-star** *n* the star Sirius. **ˈdog-tag** *n* (*US*) small disc worn round the neck by a serviceman, giving his name, number, etc. **ˌdog-ˈtired** *adj* [usu pred] very tired. **ˈdog-tooth** *n* (*architecture*) small pyramid-shaped ornament carved into stonework. **ˈdog-trot** *n* gentle easy trot.

dog[2] /dɒg; *US* dɔ:g/ *v* (**-gg-**) [Tn] follow (sb) closely and persistently: *dog sb's footsteps* ○ (*fig*) *Her career was dogged by misfortune.*

dog days /ˈdɒgdeɪz; *US* ˈdɔ:g/ hottest period of the year (July and August).

doge /dəʊdʒ/ *n* (formerly) chief magistrate in the republics of Venice and Genoa.

dogfish /ˈdɒgfɪʃ; *US* ˈdɔ:g-/ *n* (*pl* unchanged) type of small shark.

dogged /ˈdɒgɪd; *US* ˈdɔ:gɪd/ *adj* [usu attrib] (*approv*) determined; not giving up easily: *a dogged defence of the city* ○ *Although he's less talented, he won by sheer dogged persistence.* ▷ **doggedly** *adv.* **doggedness** *n* [U].

doggerel /ˈdɒgərəl; *US* ˈdɔ:gərəl/ *n* [U] verse that (intentionally or not) produces a clumsy and ridiculous effect.

doggo /ˈdɒgəʊ; *US* ˈdɔ:g-/ *adv* (idm) **lie doggo** ⇨ LIE[2].

doggone /ˈdɒgɒn; *US* ˈdɔ:gɔ:n/ *v* [Tn] (*US infml*) (used to express annoyance or surprise): *Doggone it!* ○ *Well I'll be doggoned!*

▷ **doggone** (also **doggoned**) *adj* [attrib], *adv* (used to express annoyance or surprise): *I got another doggone traffic ticket.* ○ *Don't drive so doggoned fast!*

dogie /ˈdəʊgɪ/ *n* (*US*) motherless calf, esp on the range[1](7).

dogma /ˈdɒgmə; *US* ˈdɔ:gmə/ *n* [C, U] belief or set of beliefs put forward by some authority, esp a Church, to be accepted as a matter of faith: (*fig derog*) *political, social, economic, etc dogma*, ie ideas that are not expected to be questioned.

dogmatic /dɒgˈmætɪk; *US* dɔ:gˈmætɪk/ *adj* **1** of or based on dogma: *dogmatic theology.* **2** (*derog*) that claims or suggests that sth is true without taking account of evidence or other opinions: *a dogmatic attitude, approach, view, etc.* ○ *You can't be dogmatic in matters of taste.* ▷ **dogmatically** /-klɪ/ *adv*: *state sth dogmatically.*

BREEDS OF DOG

All the drawings are to scale and represent the average size reached.

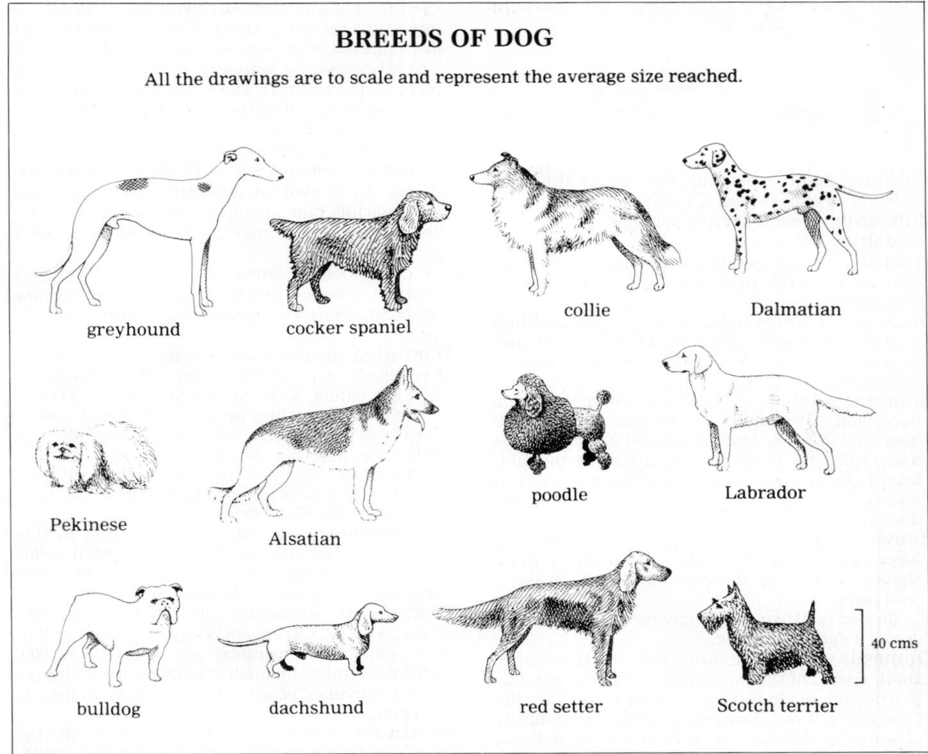

dogmatism /ˈdɒgmətɪzəm; *US* ˈdɔ:gmətɪzəm/ *n* [U] (*derog*) (quality of) being dogmatic: *the dogmatism of some music critics, popular preachers, etc.*

▷ **dogmatist** /-mətɪst/ *n* (*derog*) dogmatic person.

dogmatize, -ise /ˈdɒgmətaɪz; *US* ˈdɔ:gmətaɪz/ *v* [I, Ipr] ~ (**about sth**) (*derog*) make dogmatic statements: *You can't dogmatize about people's needs.*

dogrose /ˈdɒgrəʊz; *US* ˈdɔ:g-/ *n* wild rose, growing in hedges, etc.

dogsbody /ˈdɒgzbɒdɪ; *US* ˈdɔ:g-/ *n* (*Brit*) person who does boring or unpleasant jobs for others.

dog-watch /ˈdɒgwɒtʃ; *US* ˈdɔ:g-/ *n* (on ships) either of the two-hour watches (WATCH[1] 1a), 4 pm to 6 pm or 6 pm to 8 pm.

dogwood /ˈdɒgwʊd; *US* ˈdɔ:g-/ *n* [U, C] wild flowering shrub.

doh (also **do**) /dəʊ/ *n* (*music*) (in tonic sol-fa) the first and eighth notes of any major scale.

doily (also **doyley, doyly**) /ˈdɔɪlɪ/ *n* small ornamental mat of lace, paper, etc placed under a dish or under a cake, etc on a plate.

doings /ˈdu:ɪŋz/ *n* (*infml*) **1** [pl] things done or being done; activities: *I've been hearing a lot about your doings.* **2** [C] (*pl* unchanged) (*Brit*) thing(s) needed: *Where's the doings for mending punctures?* ie tools.

dol *abbr* (also *symb* $) dollar(s).

Dolby /ˈdɒlbɪ/ *n* [U] (*propr*) system of sound recording on tape that reduces unwanted noise.

doldrums /ˈdɒldrəmz/ *n* **1 the doldrums** [pl] parts of the ocean near the equator where there is little or no wind. **2** (idm) **in the ˈdoldrums** (**a**) feeling depressed; in low spirits: *He's been in the doldrums ever since she left him.* (**b**) not active or making progress: *Despite these measures, the economy remains in the doldrums.*

dole[1] /dəʊl/ *v* (phr v) **dole sth out** distribute (esp food, money, etc) in small amounts: *allowances grudgingly doled out to the elderly.*

dole[2] /dəʊl/ *n* **the dole** [sing] (*Brit infml*) weekly payment made by the state to unemployed people: *be/go on the dole*, ie register for/receive such payments.

doleful /ˈdəʊlfl/ *adj* sad; mournful: *a doleful face, manner, expression, etc.* ▷ **dolefully** /-fəlɪ/ *adv.* **dolefulness** *n* [U].

doll[1] /dɒl; *US* dɔ:l/ *n* **1** model of a baby or an adult, usu for a child to play with. **2** (*dated sl esp US*) attractive woman: *She's quite a doll!*

□ **ˈdoll's house 1** toy house used for playing with dolls. **2** (*fig*) very small house: *How do they all cram into that doll's house?*

doll[2] /dɒl; *US* dɔ:l/ *v* (*infml*) (phr v) **doll sb/oneself up** dress sb/oneself in a smart or showy way: *I'm going to get dolled up for the party.*

dollar /ˈdɒlə(r)/ *n* **1** [C] (*symb*) unit of money in the US, Canada, Australia, etc: *Oil from these fields is priced in dollars.* **2** [C] banknote or coin worth one dollar: *Have you got any dollars?* ⇨ App 9. **3 the dollar** [sing] (*finance*) value of the US dollar on international money markets: *The dollar closed two cents down.* **4** (idm) **bet one's bottom dollar** ⇨ BET. **(feel, look, etc) like a million dollars** (*infml*) very fit, healthy, beautiful, etc. **a/the sixty-four thousand dollar ˈquestion** important question that is very difficult to answer: *Will we all survive until the year 2000? That's the sixty-four thousand dollar question.*

dollop /ˈdɒləp/ *n* (*infml*) shapeless lump of sth soft, esp food: *a dollop of cream, jam, mashed potato, etc.*

dolly /ˈdɒlɪ; *US* ˈdɔ:lɪ/ *n* **1** (child's word for a) doll. **2** (*cinema*) movable support for a cine or television camera.

□ **ˈdolly-bird** (also **dolly**) *n* (*dated Brit infml sexist*) pretty, fashionably dressed girl who is not thought of as very intelligent. **ˈdolly mixture** (*Brit*) small, brightly coloured sweets.

dolman sleeve /ˈdɒlmən sli:v/ *n* sleeve that is wide and loose at the top and becomes narrower at the wrist.

dolmen /ˈdɒlmen/ *n* = CROMLECH.

dolorous /ˈdɒlərəs; *US* ˈdəʊlərəs/ *adj* [usu attrib] (*fml*) sorrowful.

dolour (*US* **dolor**) /ˈdɒlə(r); *US* ˈdəʊlər/ *n* [U, C] (*arch*) grief or sorrow.

dolphin

dolphin /ˈdɒlfɪn/ *n* mammal that looks like a large fish and lives in the sea. Cf PORPOISE.

dolt /dəʊlt/ *n* (*derog*) stupid person.
▷ **doltish** *adj* stupid.

Dom /dɒm/ *n* title used before the names of certain Roman Catholic high-ranking priests and of Benedictine monks.

-dom *suff* **1** (with *vs* and *adjs* forming *ns*) condition or state of: *boredom* ○ *freedom*. **2** (with *ns*) (**a**) rank or domain of: *dukedom* ○ *kingdom*. (**b**) group of: *officialdom*.

domain /dəʊˈmeɪn/ *n* **1** lands owned or ruled by a nobleman, government, etc: *trespass on the King's domain* ○ (*fig*) *The kitchen is my wife's domain; she doesn't like me going into it.* **2** field of thought, knowledge or activity: *(in) the domain of political science* ○ *Military history is really outside my domain.*

dome /dəʊm/ *n* **1** rounded roof with a circular base: *the dome of St Paul's Cathedral.* **2** thing shaped like this: *the dome of a hill, the night sky, a bald head.*
▷ **domed** *adj* [usu attrib] having or shaped like a dome: *a domed forehead.*

Domesday Book /ˈdu:mzdeɪ bʊk/ **the Domesday Book** record of the ownership, value, etc of lands in England, made in 1086 by order of William the Conqueror. It was the most comprehensive survey of property carried out in England in medieval times.

domestic /dəˈmestɪk/ *adj* [usu attrib] **1** of the home, household or family: *domestic water, gas, etc supplies* ○ *a domestic help*, ie a servant, esp a cleaner ○ *domestic bliss, unrest, upheavals, etc* ○ *She's very domestic*, ie prefers home life to going out, or is good at and likes cooking, housework, etc. **2** of or inside a particular country, not foreign or international: *domestic trade, imports, production, etc* ○ *domestic flights*, ie to and from places within a country. **3** (of animals) kept on farms or as pets; not wild.
▷ **domestic** *n* household servant, esp a cleaner. **domestically** /-klɪ/ *adv.*
□ **doˌmestic ˈscience** = HOME ECONOMICS (HOME[1]).

domesticate /dəˈmestɪkeɪt/ *v* [Tn esp passive] **1** make (sb) used to or fond of housework and home life: *He's become a lot more domesticated since he got married.* **2** tame (an animal). ▷ **domestication** /dəˌmestɪˈkeɪʃn/ *n* [U].

domesticity /ˌdəʊmeˈstɪsətɪ, ˌdɒm-/ *n* [U] home or family life: *a scene of cosy domesticity.*

domicile /ˈdɒmɪsaɪl/ *n* (*fml or law*) a person's place of residence, esp as officially established for purposes of taxation, etc.
▷ **domiciled** *adj* [pred] having one's domicile in a place: *be domiciled in Britain, London, etc.*

domiciliary /ˌdɒmɪˈsɪlɪərɪ; *US* ˌdɒmɪˈsɪlɪerɪ/ *adj* [pred] (*fml*) of, to or at sb's home: *a domiciliary visit*, eg by a doctor or a priest, etc.

dominant[1] /ˈdɒmɪnənt/ *adj* **1** ~ (**in sth**) most important or prominent; dominating: *She's the dominant child in the group.* ○ *the dominant flavour in a dish* ○ *The castle stands in a dominant position above the town.* **2** (*biology*) (of an inherited characteristic) appearing in offspring even when a genetically opposing characteristic is also inherited. Cf RECESSIVE. ▷ **dominance** /ˈdɒmɪnəns/ *n* [U]: *the absolute dominance of the governing party.*

dominant[2] /ˈdɒmɪnənt/ *n* **1** (*music*) fifth note of a scale; chord or key based on this. **2** (*biology*) dominant gene.

dominate /ˈdɒmɪneɪt/ *v* **1** [I, Tn] (**a**) have control of or a very strong influence on (people, events, etc): *He has authority, but he doesn't try to dominate (others).* ○ *She dominated the meeting by sheer force of character.* (**b**) be the most obvious or important person or thing in (sth): *Price tends to dominate all other considerations.* ○ *My weekend was dominated by housework.* **2** [Tn] (of a high place) overlook (sth): *The Acropolis dominates the city of Athens.* ▷ **domination** /ˌdɒmɪˈneɪʃn/ *n* [U]: *His defeat ended American domination of the sport.* ○ *under foreign domination.*

domineer /ˌdɒmɪˈnɪə(r)/ *v* [I, Ipr] ~ (**over sb**) (*derog*) try to make sb do exactly what one wants by ordering him about, regardless of what he wants to do: *He domineered, and the rest of us hated it.*
▷ **domineering** /ˌdɒmɪˈnɪərɪŋ/ *adj* wanting to control others; overbearing: *a domineering husband, manner, personality.* **domineeringly** *adv.*

Dominica /dɒmɪˈni:kə/ mountainous island in the Caribbean; pop approx 79 000; official language English; capital Roseau; unit of currency French franc, pound sterling or East Caribbean dollar. Once a British colony, it became independent in 1978. ⇨ map at CARIBBEAN.

Dominican /dəˈmɪnɪkən/ *adj* of the religious Order of Preachers founded by St Dominic in 1216, also called the Black Friars.
▷ **Dominican** *n* priest, brother or nun in this order. The Dominicans are an influential order and have always championed learning and orthodox religious beliefs and practices.

Dominican Republic /dəˌmɪnɪkən rɪˈpʌblɪk/ country in the Caribbean occupying about half of the island of Hispaniola; pop approx 6 867 000; official language Spanish; capital Santo Domingo; unit of currency peso (= 100 centavos). ⇨ map at CARIBBEAN.

dominion /dəˈmɪnɪən/ *n* **1** [U] ~ (**over sb/sth**) (*fml*) authority to rule; effective control: *under foreign dominion* ○ *have/be given dominion over peoples, lives, etc.* **2** [C] area controlled by one government or ruler: *the vast dominions of the Chinese Empire.* **3** (often **Dominion**) [C] (formerly) any of the self-governing territories of the British Commonwealth.
□ **DoˈMinion Day** 1 July, celebrated in Canada as the anniversary of the day in 1867 when the country became a self-governing dominion.

domino effect

domino /ˈdɒmɪnəʊ/ *n* (*pl* ~**es**) (**a**) [C] small flat oblong block marked on one side with two groups of dots, used in the game of dominoes. (**b**) **dominoes** [sing *v*] game played with a set of 28 dominoes.
□ **ˈdomino effect** effect of one (esp political) event in one place making similar events happen one after the other elsewhere: *Employers fear a domino effect if the strike is successful*, ie that there will be many other strikes as a result. ⇨ illus.

Domitian /dəˈmɪʃn/ (51-96 AD), Roman emperor (81-96) who ruled with great cruelty, having many of his enemies killed before he was himself assassinated.

don[1] /dɒn/ *n* **1** (*Brit*) teacher at a university, esp at an Oxford or a Cambridge college. **2** title used before a man's Christian name in Spanish-speaking countries: *Don Felipe.*
▷ **donnish** /ˈdɒnɪʃ/ *adj* (*esp Brit*) like (that of) a university don, who is usu considered to be clever, but unrealistic, forgetful, etc: *a donnish remark, manner, sense of humour.*

don[2] /dɒn/ *v* (**-nn-**) [Tn] (*fml*) put on (clothes, etc): (*fig*) *He quickly donned a welcoming smile as his guests arrived.*

Donald Duck /ˌdɒnəld ˈdʌk/ popular character in Walt *Disney's cartoons, a sometimes bad-tempered duck that talks with a distinctive quacking voice.

donate /dəʊˈneɪt; *US* ˈdəʊneɪt/ *v* [Tn, Dn·pr] ~ **sth** (**to sb/sth**) give (money, goods, etc), esp to a charity; contribute sth: *donate large sums to relief organizations.*
▷ **donation** /dəʊˈneɪʃn/ *n* (**a**) [C] thing donated: *a donation to/for Amnesty International.* (**b**) [U] donating or being donated.

done[1] *pp* of DO[1,2].

done[2] /dʌn/ *adj* [pred] **1** (of food) cooked enough: *The joint isn't quite done yet.* **2** (*infml*) socially acceptable: *Smoking between courses simply isn't done.* **3** (idm) **be the done thing** be conventional or acceptable behaviour: *For most people it is still the done thing to get married.* **be/have done with sb/sth** no longer work at sth or be involved with sb/sth: *Let's spend another half an hour painting and then have done with it.* **over and done with** completely finished: *Their relationship is over and done with.* **what is done cannot be undone** (*saying*) something that has already been done cannot be changed. ▷ **done** *interj* (used to show that one accepts an offer): *'I'll give you £500 for the car.' 'Done!'*

Donen /ˈdəʊnən/ Stanley (1924-), American film director. Working with Gene *Kelly, he revived the musical comedy after the Second World War in films like *Singin' in the Rain* and *On the Town.*

donjon /ˈdɒndʒən/ *n* large, strongly fortified central tower of a medieval castle.

Don Juan /ˌdɒn ˈdʒu:ən, ˌdɒn ˈhwɑ:n/ **1** legendary Spanish nobleman who had love affairs with many women. **2** (*infml*) man who has great sexual success with women: *Despite his looks he's said to be something of a Don Juan.*

donkey /ˈdɒŋkɪ/ *n* (*pl* ~**s**) **1** animal of the horse family, with short legs and long ears. ⇨ article at NATIONAL. **2** stupid or stubborn person: *He's an absolute donkey.* **3** (idm) **ˈdonkey's years** (*Brit infml*) a very long time: *It's donkey's years since we've seen each other.* ○ *The new motorway won't be ready for donkey's years.* **talk the hind legs off a donkey** ⇨ TALK[2].
□ **ˈdonkey engine** small extra engine, esp on a ship's deck.
ˈdonkey jacket workman's thick weatherproof jacket.
ˈdonkey-work *n* [U] hard dull part of a job; drudgery: *Typical — we do the donkey-work and he takes the credit!*

Donna /ˈdɒnə/ *n* title used before the names of Italian women to show respect.

Donne /dʌn/ John (1572-1631), English poet. He is generally regarded as the greatest of the *metaphysical poets, and his love poems, full of passion and wit, achieved great popularity in the 20th century. He was a clergyman, and from 1621 was Dean of St Paul's Cathedral.

donor /ˈdəʊnə(r)/ *n* **1** person who gives or donates sth. **2** (*medical*) person who provides blood for transfusion, organs for transplantation, etc: *a blood donor* ○ *The heart transplant will take place as soon as a suitable donor can be found.* ○ [attrib] *donor organs.*

Don Quixote /ˌdɒn ˈkwɪksət; ˌdɒn kɪˈhəʊtɪ/ **1** Spanish nobleman in *Cervantes's novel *Don Quixote* who spent his life searching unsuccessfully for romantic adventures. **2** person with high but completely unrealistic ideals; impractical dreamer. Cf QUIXOTIC.

don't ⇨ DO[1].

doodah /ˈdu:dɑ:/ *n* (*Brit infml*) (also *esp US* **doodad** /ˈdu:dæd/) small article whose name one does not know or cannot remember.

doodle /ˈdu:dl/ *v* [I, Ipr] make meaningless drawings, scribbles etc, while one is or should be thinking about sth else: *Stop doodling on my notebook!* ▷ **doodle** *n*: *a page covered in doodles.*

doohickey /ˈdu:hɪkɪ/ *n* (*US*) = DOODAH.

doom[1] /du:m/ *n* [U] **1** (*rhet*) death or ruin; any terrible and inevitable fate: *meet/go to one's doom* ○ *send a man to his doom.* **2** = DOOMSDAY. **3** (idm) **the crack of doom** ⇨ CRACK[1]. **a prophet of doom** ⇨ PROPHET.
□ **ˈdoomwatch** *n* [U] continuous observation of the natural environment to prevent its being

destroyed (eg by pollution).

doom[2] /du:m/ *v* [esp passive: Tn, Tn·pr, Cn·t] ~ **sb (to sth)** condemn sb (to death, destruction, failure, etc): *The plan was doomed from the start.* ○ *Are whales doomed to extinction?* ○ *We loathe each other, yet we seem doomed constantly to meet.*

doomsday /ˈdu:mzdeɪ/ *n* [U] **1** day of the Last Judgement; the end of the world. Cf DOMESDAY BOOK. **2** (idm) **till ˈdoomsday** for ever; a long time: *This work will take me till doomsday.*

door /dɔ:(r)/ *n* **1** (a) movable barrier that closes the entrance to a building, room, cupboard, car, etc: *hinged/sliding/revolving doors* ○ *hammer on the door* ○ *open, shut, close, lock, bolt the door* ○ *the front/back door*, ie main door at the front/back of a house ○ *a four-door saloon car.* ⇨ illus at HOME. ⇨ illus at CAR. (b) = DOORWAY. **2** (idm) **at death's door** ⇨ DEATH. **behind closed doors** ⇨ CLOSE[4]. **by/through the back door** ⇨ BACK[2]. **darken sb's door** ⇨ DARKEN. **(from) ˌdoor to ˈdoor** (from) house to house: *The journey takes about an hour, door to door.* ○ *He went from door to door, selling encyclopaedias.* ○ [attrib] *a ˌdoor-to-door ˈsalesman.* **the door to sth** the means of getting or reaching sth: *Our courses are the door to success in English.* **a foot in the door** ⇨ FOOT[1]. **keep the wolf from the door** ⇨ WOLF. **lay sth at sb's ˈdoor** say that sb is responsible for sth that has gone wrong: *The blame for the disaster has been laid firmly at the company's door.* **leave the door open** ⇨ LEAVE[1]. **lie at sb's door** ⇨ LIE[2]. **lock, etc the stable door after the horse has bolted** ⇨ STABLE[2]. **next ˈdoor (to sb/sth)** in the next building, room, etc: *go next door to borrow some milk* ○ *They live next door to the library.* **next door to** nearly; almost: *I'm afraid it's next door to impossible that we'll be there on time.* **(be) on the ˈdoor** (*infml*) (at a public meeting, concert, etc) (stand) at the door, eg to collect tickets, give directions, etc. **out of ˈdoors** in the open air: *eat, sleep, walk, etc out of doors.* **show sb the door; show sb to the door** ⇨ SHOW[2]. **shut/slam the door in sb's face** refuse to talk to or have any dealing with sb. **shut the door on sth** ⇨ SHUT. **two, three, etc doors aˈlong/aˈway/ˈdown** in the next house but one, two, etc: *Our other branch is just a few doors down the road.*

□ **ˈdoorbell** *n* bell inside a building that can be rung by visitors outside. ⇨ illus at HOME.

ˈdoor-frame *n* frame into which a door fits.

ˈdoor-handle *n* handle that opens and closes a door (by releasing a latch). ⇨ illus at CAR.

ˈdoor-keeper *n* = DOORMAN.

ˈdoorknob *n* round knob turned to open a door.

ˈdoor-knocker *n* = KNOCKER.

ˈdoorman /-mən/ *n* (*pl* **-men** /-mən/) (*US*) = PORTER[2]: *Leave a message with the doorman.*

ˈdoormat *n* **1** mat placed near a door, for wiping dirt from one's shoes. **2** (*fig infml*) person who allows others to treat him without respect: *Stand up for yourself a bit — don't be such a doormat!*

ˈdoornail *n* (idm) **dead as a doornail** ⇨ DEAD.

ˈdoor-plate *n* metal plate on a door showing the name of the person living or working in the room or building.

ˈdoorpost *n* (idm) **deaf as a post/doorpost** ⇨ DEAF.

ˈdoorstep *n* **1** step leading up to (usu) an outside door: *empty milk bottles on the doorstep.* ⇨ illus at HOME. **2** (*Brit infml*) very thick slice of bread. **3** (idm) **on one's ˈdoorstep** very near: *In our holiday villas you'll have both the beach and the mountains on your doorstep.*

ˈdoorstop *n* device to prevent a door from closing or from hitting a wall, etc when it is opened.

ˈdoorway *n* opening, filled by a door, into a building, room, car, etc: *standing in the doorway.*

ˈdooryard *n* (*US*) yard or garden outside the door of a house.

dope /dəʊp/ *n* **1** [U] (*sl*) (a) harmful drug (eg hashish); narcotic: [attrib] *a dope-addict.* (b) medicine, esp a sedative drug. **2** [C] (*infml*) stupid person: *You've got the picture upside-down, you dope!* **3** [U] ~ **(on sb/sth)** (*sl*) facts not generally known that are provided by a well-informed person: *I want the dope on his criminal connections.* **4** [U] thick liquid used as a lubricant, varnish, etc.

▷ **dope** *v* [Tn] (a) give a narcotic or stimulant drug to (esp a race-horse, an athlete, etc). (b) add a drug to (food, drink, etc).

dopey (also **dopy**) /ˈdəʊpɪ/ *adj* (**-ier, -iest**) **1** (*infml*) dazed or sleepy, as if drugged: *I'm feeling really dopey this morning.* **2** (*sl*) stupid.

dopester /ˈdəʊpstə(r)/ *n* (*US infml*) person who tries to predict the result of an election, sports event, etc.

doppelgänger /ˈdɒplgæŋə(r)/ *n* (*German*) **1** ghost of a living person. **2** person who looks exactly like another; double[4] (2a).

Doppler effect /ˈdɒplər ɪfekt/ change in the apparent frequency of sound waves and other waves as they approach and go away (as when the sound of a train whistle or ambulance siren gets lower as the vehicle passes and goes away from the hearer).

dorado /dəˈrɑ:dəʊ/ *n* (*pl* ~**s**) type of large, brightly coloured sea fish.

Doric /ˈdɒrɪk; *US* ˈdɔ:r-/ *adj* (*architecture*) of the oldest and simplest of the five orders (ORDER[1] 13) of classical Greek architecture. Cf CORINTHIAN 2, IONIC. ⇨ illus at ORDER.

dorm /dɔ:m/ *n* (*infml*) dormitory.

dormant /ˈdɔ:mənt/ *adj* temporarily inactive: *a dormant volcano*, ie neither extinct nor erupting ○ *Many plants lie dormant throughout the winter*, ie alive but not growing. ○ *As soon as they met again his dormant love for her was rekindled.*

dormer /ˈdɔ:mə(r)/ (also **ˌdormer-ˈwindow**) *n* upright window built in a sloping roof. ⇨ illus at HOME.

dormitory /ˈdɔ:mɪtrɪ; *US* -tɔ:rɪ/ *n* **1** sleeping-room with a number of beds, esp in a school or some other institution. **2** (*US*) building at a college, university, etc containing students' rooms for living and sleeping.

□ **ˈdormitory town** (*Brit*) town from which people travel to work elsewhere.

dormouse /ˈdɔ:maʊs/ *n* (*pl* **dormice** /ˈdɔ:maɪs/) small animal like a mouse with a furry tail.

dorsal /ˈdɔ:sl/ *adj* [attrib] (*anatomy*) of or on the back of an animal or a plant: *the dorsal fin*, eg of a shark. ⇨ illus at FISH. Cf VENTRAL.

Dorset /ˈdɔ:sɪt/ rural county of SW England. The novelist Thomas *Hardy set many of his stories there. ⇨ map at App 1.

dory[1] /ˈdɔ:rɪ/ *n* (*US*) light flat-bottomed rowing-boat used by fishermen off the Atlantic coast of the USA.

dory[2] *n* [C, U] (also **ˌJohn ˈDory**) type of edible sea fish.

dosage /ˈdəʊsɪdʒ/ *n* [U] (usu *sing*) amount of medicine to be taken at a time or over a period: *Do not exceed the recommended dosage.*

do's and don'ts ⇨ DO[3] 3.

dose /dəʊs/ *n* **1** amount of medicine to be taken at one time: *give/administer the correct dose.* **2** amount of radiation received by sb/sth at one time: *a lethal dose of radiation.* **3** (*fig infml*) (a) any experience of sth unpleasant: *a dose of flu, boring conversation, bad weather* ○ *I can only stand her in small doses*, ie for a short time. (b) any experience of sth enjoyable: *What you need is a good dose of laughter.* **4** (*sl*) venereal infection: *give sb/catch a dose.* **5** (idm) **like a dose of ˈsalts** (*sl*) very fast: *He gets through his pay like a dose of salts, and by Monday he's broke.*

▷ **dose** *v* [Tn, Tn·pr] ~ **sb/oneself (with sth)** give sb/oneself a dose (of sth): *heavily dosed with pain-killing drugs.*

doss /dɒs/ *v* (phr v) **doss down** (*Brit sl*) lie down to sleep, esp when one has not got a proper bed: *We dossed down on Tony's floor after the party.*

▷ **dosser** *n* (*Brit sl*) person without a home who sleeps in the streets or in cheap lodgings; vagrant.

□ **ˈdoss-house** *n* (*Brit sl*) cheap lodging-house, esp one used by vagrants.

dossier /ˈdɒsɪeɪ; *US also* ˈdɔ:sɪə(r)/ *n* set of documents containing information about a person, an event, etc; file.

Dostoevsky /ˌdɒstɔɪˈefskɪ/ Fedor Mikhailovich (1821-81), Russian novelist. Exiled in Siberia for four years for socialist activities, he later turned to writing, and produced a series of works (*Crime and Punishment, The Idiot, The Devils* and *The Brothers Karamazov*) whose psychological insights made them models for the development of the modern novel. There are strong religious and political elements in his work.

dot /dɒt/ *n* **1** small round mark: *Join the dots up to complete the drawing.* **2** such a mark used as a symbol in writing (eg above the letters i and j), mathematics (eg the decimal point), music, representing a short sound in Morse code, etc. ⇨ App 14. **3** anything resembling a dot; a small quantity: *The island was just a dot on the horizon.* ○ *I like just a dot of milk in my tea.* **4** (idm) **on the ˈdot** (*infml*) exactly on time, or at the time specified: *He's very punctual — always arrives on the dot.* ○ *leave at 5 o'clock on the dot/on the dot of 5 o'clock.* **the year dot** ⇨ YEAR.

▷ **dot** *v* (**-tt-**) **1** [Tn] mark (sth) with a dot. **2** [esp passive: Tn·pr, Tn·p] place (things or people) here and there; scatter: *The sky was dotted with stars.* ○ *We've dotted a few chairs about.* **3** [Tn, Tn·pr, Dn·n] (*infml*) hit (sb): *He dotted me in the eye.* ○ *Shut up or I'll dot you one!* **4** (idm) **dot one's/the ˌi's and cross one's/the ˈt's** complete the final details of a task.

□ **ˌdot ˈmatrix** (*computing*) grid of dots used to form letters, numbers, etc in printing: [attrib] *a ˌdot matrix ˈprinter.*

ˌdotted ˈline **1** line of dots showing where sth is to be written on a document, form, etc. **2** (idm) **sign on the dotted line** ⇨ SIGN[2].

dotage /ˈdəʊtɪdʒ/ *n* (idm) **in one's dotage** confused in one's mind because of old age.

dote /dəʊt/ *v* [Ipr] ~ **on sb/sth** show (too) much fondness for sb/sth: *She dotes on her grandchildren.* ○ *I just dote on hot buttered scones!*

▷ **doting** *adj* [attrib] very or excessively loving and devoted: *a doting husband, son, parent, etc.* **dotingly** *adv.*

dotterel /ˈdɒtərəl/ *n* type of small European and Asian bird of the plover family.

dottle /ˈdɒtl/ *n* [U] partly burnt tobacco left in a pipe after smoking.

dotty /ˈdɒtɪ/ *adj* (**-ier, -iest**) (*infml esp Brit*) **1** foolish; silly; eccentric: *She was getting a bit dotty and could never be left alone.* ○ *Not another of your dotty ideas for making money!* **2** [pred] ~ **about sb/sth** very fond of or enthusiastic about sb/sth: *She's dotty about this latest boy-friend.* ▷ **dottiness** *n* [U].

Douai /ˈdu:eɪ/ city in northern France where there were colleges for Roman Catholics exiled from England in the reign of Elizabeth I.

□ **ˈDouai version** English translation of the Bible used in the Roman Catholic Church. It was completed at Douai in the early 17th century.

double[1] /ˈdʌbl/ *adj* [usu attrib] **1** twice as much or as many (as usual): *a double helping* ○ *two double whiskies* ○ *the new bleach with double strength for killing germs.* **2** having or made of two things or parts that are equal or similar: *Look, double yellow lines — you mustn't park here.* ○ *'I didn't do nothing' is a double negative*, ie two negatives where only one is needed. ○ *a double-page advertisement* ○ *'Otter' is spelt with a double t.* **3** made for two people or things: *a double room, garage, etc* ○ *a double wedding*, ie of two couples. **4** combining two things or qualities: *a double meaning, purpose, aim, etc* ○ *the double advantage of being easy and cheap* ○ *She leads a double life*, ie Her life has two different (perhaps sharply contrasting) aspects, eg being a police officer and a drug dealer. **5** (of flowers) having more than the usual number of petals. **6** (idm) **in double ˈharness** with a partner, or with a husband or wife: *The brothers work in double harness.*

□ **ˌdouble ˈagent** person who spies for two rival countries at the same time.

ˌdouble-ˈbass (also **bass**) *n* largest and lowest-pitched instrument of the violin family. ⇨ illus at MUSIC.

ˌ**double** ˈ**bed** bed made for two people.
ˌ**double-**ˈ**bedded** *adj* [usu attrib] (of a hotel room) having a double bed (or two single ones).
ˌ**double** ˈ**bill** two films, plays, etc presented to an audience one after the other.
ˌ**double** ˈ**bind** dilemma.
ˌ**double** ˈ**bluff** clever deception, eg telling an enemy the truth while knowing that he will assume you are lying.
ˌ**double** ˈ**chin** fold of fat below the chin.
ˌ**double** ˈ**cream** (*Brit*) thick cream that contains a lot of milk fat.
ˌ**double** ˈ**date** (*esp US infml*) date involving two (separate) couples.
ˌ**double-**ˈ**dealer** *n* (*derog*) person who says one thing and means another; deceiver. ˌ**double-**ˈ**dealing** *n* [U].
ˌ**double-**ˈ**decker** *n* **1** (*esp Brit*) bus with two floors. **2** (*esp US*) sandwich with two layers of filling.
ˌ**double** ˈ**Dutch** (*Brit infml*) incomprehensible talk; written gibberish: *This article's so full of jargon it's just double Dutch to me.*
double entendre /ˌdu:bl ɑ:nˈtɑ:ndrə/ (*French*) word or phrase that can be understood in two ways, one of which contains a sexual allusion.
ˌ**double** ˈ**entry** (*commerce*) system of bookkeeping in which each transaction is entered as a debit in one account and a credit in another.
ˌ**double** ˈ**fault** (in tennis) failure twice in a row to serve the ball into the correct area, resulting in the loss of a point.
ˌ**double** ˈ**feature** cinema programme consisting of two full-length films.
ˌ**double** ˈ**figures** number that is 10 or over and 99 or less: *The inflation rate is into double figures*, ie above 10%.
ˌ**double** ˈ**first** (graduate who gains a) first-class degree in two subjects at the same time or in successive years.
double Gloucester /ˌdʌbl ˈglɒstə(r)/ type of orange-coloured cheese originally made in Gloucestershire, England.
ˌ**double** ˈ**header** (*US*) playing of two games (of baseball, hockey, etc) on the same day, usu by the same teams.
ˌ**double** ˈ**helix** two intertwined spirals, esp as in the structure of the molecules of DNA.
ˌ**double pneu**ˈ**monia** pneumonia affecting both lungs.
ˌ**double** ˈ**standard** set of (usu moral) principles that discriminates against one of two groups, individuals, etc: *He's got a double standard: it's all right for him to have affairs but not for her.*
ˌ**double** ˈ**star** two stars which are, or seem from the earth to be, close together.
ˌ**double** ˈ**take** delayed reaction to a situation, remark, etc, esp for comic effect: *He did a double take when I said I was getting married.*
ˈ**double-talk** *n* [U] way of talking that really means something very different from what it appears to mean, or nothing at all: *He gave us no real reasons, just the usual politician's double-talk.* — *v* [I, Tn·pr]: *double-talk one's way out of trouble.*
ˈ**double-think** *n* [U] (*derog*) accepting or advocating contradictory ideas, principles, etc.
ˌ**double** ˈ**time** twice the usual wage, paid for working on a public holiday, etc.
ˌ**double transitive** ˈ**verb** (*linguistics*) verb that takes an indirect object as well as a direct object, eg *offer* in *He offered me a job.*

double[2] /ˈdʌbl/ *det* twice as much or as many (as usual, than sb/sth, etc): *His income is double hers.* ○ *He earns double what she does.* ○ *We need double the amount we have.*

double[3] /ˈdʌbl/ *adv* in twos or in two parts: *When I saw her and her twin sister I thought I was seeing double.* ○ *sleep double*, ie two in a bed (for warmth, convenience, etc) ○ *fold a blanket double.*
□ ˌ**double-**ˈ**barrelled** *adj* **1** (of a gun) having two barrels. **2** (*Brit*) (of a surname) having two parts, usu joined by a hyphen (as in *Day-Lewis*).
ˌ**double-**ˈ**book** *v* [I, Tn] reserve (a particular hotel room, flight, ticket, etc) for more than one person at a time: *They'd double-booked our seats and we had to wait for the next plane.* ○ *They've double-booked me* (ie my seat, etc) *again!* ˌ**double-**ˈ**booking** *n* [U, C].
ˌ**double-**ˈ**breasted** *adj* (of a coat or jacket) made to overlap across the chest.
ˌ**double-**ˈ**check** *v* [I, Tn] check (sth) twice or with great care: *double-check figures, arrangements.* — *n: do a double-check on sth.*
ˌ**double-**ˈ**cross** *v* [Tn] (*derog*) cheat or betray (sb) after getting him to trust one. — *n: a double-cross that cost six lives.*
ˌ**double-**ˈ**dyed** *adj* [attrib] (*dated*) very evil: *a* ˌ*double-dyed* ˈ*rogue,* ˈ*scoundrel, etc.*
ˌ**double-**ˈ**edged** *adj* **1** (of a knife, etc) having two edges. **2** (*fig*) (of a remark) having two possible meanings; ambiguous: *a* ˌ*double-edged* ˈ*argument,* ˈ*compliment, re*ˈ*ply, etc.*
ˌ**double-**ˈ**faced** *adj* insincere.
ˌ**double-**ˈ**glaze** *v* [Tn] fit two layers of glass to (the windows of a room, etc) to reduce heat loss, noise, etc: *The house is double-glazed back and front.* ˌ**double-**ˈ**glazing** *n* [U]: *have double-glazing installed.*
ˌ**double-**ˈ**jointed** *adj* [usu pred] having very flexible joints that allow the fingers, arms or legs to bend backwards as well as forwards.
ˌ**double-**ˈ**park** *v* [I, Tn esp passive] park (a car, etc) beside one already parked in a street: *Hurry up! I'm double-parked and the warden's coming.*
ˌ**double-**ˈ**quick** *adj, adv* (*infml*) very quick(ly).
ˌ**double-**ˈ**stop** *v* [I, Tn] (*music*) play (two stopped notes) at the same time on a violin, etc.

double[4] /ˈdʌbl/ *n* **1** [U] twice the (usual) number or amount: *He's paid double for the same job.* **2** [C] (**a**) person or thing that looks very like another: *She's the double of her mother at the same age.* (**b**) (in a film) actor who replaces a star in the dangerous scenes. **3** [C] glass of spirits containing twice the usual amount: *Two Scotches, please — and make those doubles, will you?* **4** [C] bet on two horses in different races where any winnings from the first are staked again on the second. **5 doubles** [pl] game (esp of tennis) in which one pair plays another: *mixed doubles*, ie where each pair consists of a man and a woman. **6 the double** [sing] (*sport*) two prizes won in similar competitions: *She's going for the double this year, the Olympics and the World Championship.* **7** [C] (in bridge) act of doubling. **8** [C] (in the game of darts) hit on the outer ring of the board, scoring double. **9** (idm) **at the** ˈ**double** (*US* **on the** ˈ**double**) (*infml*) quickly; hurrying: *The boss wants you — you'd better get upstairs at the double.* ˌ**double or** ˈ**quits** paying twice what one owes or nothing at all, the decision being made by chance (eg throwing dice).

double[5] /ˈdʌbl/ *v* **1** [I, Tn] (cause sth to) become twice as much or as many: *The price of houses has virtually doubled over the past few years.* ○ *If you double all the quantities in the recipe it'll be enough for eight people.* **2** [Tn, Tn·p] ~ **sth (up/over/across/back)** bend or fold sth in two: *double a blanket (over) for extra warmth.* **3** [Tn] (*nautical*) sail round (a cape, headland, promontory, etc). **4** [Ipr] ~ **as sth** (**a**) have a secondary function or use as sth: *When we have guests, the sofa doubles as an extra bed.* (**b**) (of an actor) play (a second part) as well as another: *His main part is the ghost, but he doubles as Fortinbras.* **5** [Tn] (*music*) play or sing the same music as (another instrument or voice): *In this passage the violins double the sopranos.* **6** [I] (bridge) bid to cause the points lost or won by one's opponents to be twice as much as they would otherwise have been. **7** (phr v) **double back** turn back in the opposite direction, esp unexpectedly: *The road ahead was flooded so we had to double back.* **double (sb) up** (cause sb to) bend the body: *be doubled up with laughter, pain, anger, etc.* **double up (on sth/with sb)** (*infml*) form pairs in order to share sth: *We've only one room left: you'll have to double up with Peter.*

doublet /ˈdʌblɪt/ *n* **1** (formerly) short close-fitting jacket worn by men, with or without sleeves. ⇨ illus at DRESS. **2** either of a pair of similar things, esp one of two words with the same origin but a different form or meaning, eg *hospital/hostel.*

doubloon /dʌˈblu:n/ *n* former Spanish gold coin.

doubly /ˈdʌblɪ/ *adv* (used before *adjs*) **1** to twice the extent or amount: *Make doubly sure that all the doors are locked*, ie check twice. **2** in two ways: *She is doubly gifted: as a writer and as an artist.*

doubt[1] /daʊt/ *n* **1** [U, C] ~ **(about/as to sth)**; ~ **(as to) whether...** (feeling of) uncertainty or disbelief: *There's some doubt about his suitability for the job.* ○ *There is (no) room for doubt.* ○ *I have grave doubts about her honesty.* ○ *The latest scientific discoveries cast doubt on earlier theories.* ○ *She had her doubts (as to) whether he would come.* ○ *Although a very religious man, he is still troubled by occasional doubts.* **2** [U] ~ **about sth/that...** (used after negatives to emphasize conviction) reason for not believing sth: *There's not much doubt about it*, ie It is almost certain. ○ *I have no doubt that you will succeed.* **3** (idm) **beyond a/any** ˈ**doubt**; **beyond all (possible)** ˈ**doubt** certainly: *She was beyond all doubt the finest ballerina of her day.* **give sb the benefit of the** ˈ**doubt** ⇨ BENEFIT. **in** ˈ**doubt** uncertain; undecided: *Their acceptance of the contract is still in doubt.* ○ *If in doubt, don't*, ie Don't act unless you're certain. ˌ**no** ˈ**doubt** very probably: *No doubt he means to help, but in fact he just gets in the way.* **without (a)** ˈ**doubt** certainly: *He is without doubt the cleverest student I've ever taught.*

doubt[2] /daʊt/ *v* [I, Tn, Tf] feel uncertain (about sth); question the truth of (sth): *It is human to doubt.* ○ *Do you doubt my word* (ie think I am not telling the truth)? ○ *I don't doubt that he'll come*, ie I'm sure he will. ○ *I doubt whether he'll come.* ○ *I doubt if that was what he wanted.* ▷ **doubter** *n.*
□ ˌ**doubting** ˈ**Thomas** person who refuses to believe sth until he has clear proof: *She's a bit of a doubting Thomas — she won't believe you're back till she sees you.*

doubtful /ˈdaʊtfl/ *adj* **1** [usu pred] ~ **(about sth/doing sth)** (of a person) feeling doubt; unsure: *feel doubtful about (the wisdom of) going/about whether to go or not.* **2** causing doubt; uncertain: *The weather looks rather doubtful*, ie unsettled. ○ *a doubtful* (ie unreliable) *ally* ○ *It's a doubtful blessing*, ie It may or may not be one. **3** unlikely; improbable: *It is extremely doubtful that anyone survived the explosion.* **4** [attrib] possibly dishonest, disreputable, etc; causing suspicion; questionable: *a rather doubtful character, neighbourhood, past.* ▷ **doubtfully** /-fəlɪ/ *adv.*

doubtless /ˈdaʊtlɪs/ *adv* almost certainly; very probably: *Doubtless he'll be bringing his guitar, as usual.*

douche /du:ʃ/ *n* (device for directing a) stream of water into or onto a part of the body, esp the vagina, to clean it or for medical purposes.
▷ **douche** *v* [I, Tn] treat (sth) with a douche.

dough /dəʊ/ *n* [U] **1** thick mixture of flour, water, etc ready to be baked into bread, pastry, etc. **2** (*sl*) money.
▷ **doughy** *adj* of or like dough; soft, pale and flabby: *a doughy complexion.*
□ ˈ**doughnut** *n* small cake, usu in the shape of a ring or a ball, made from sweetened dough cooked in fat. ⇨ illus at BREAD.

doughboy /ˈdəʊbɔɪ/ *n* (*US infml*) soldier in a US infantry regiment.

doughty /ˈdaʊtɪ/ *adj* [usu attrib] (*arch or rhet*) brave and strong: *a doughty warrior.*

dour /dʊə(r)/ *adj* stern; severe; gloomy-looking; joyless: *dour looks* ○ *a dour silence.* ▷ **dourly** *adv.*

douse (also **dowse**) /daʊs/ *v* **1** [Tn, Tn·pr] ~ **sb/sth (in/with sth)** put sb/sth into (water); throw (water) over sb/sth: *douse the flames/a fire* ○ *As a joke, they doused him with a bucket of water.* **2** [Tn] put out or turn off (a light).

dove[1] /dʌv/ *n* **1** type of bird with short legs, a small head and a thick body, that makes a cooing sound and is often used as a symbol of peace. **2** (*fig*) person, esp a politician, who favours peace and negotiation rather than war or confrontation. Cf HAWK[1] 2.
□ **dovecote** /ˈdʌvkɒt, *also* ˈdʌvkəʊt/ *n* **1** building providing shelter and often nesting-boxes for pigeons and doves. **2** (idm) **flutter the dovecotes** ⇨ FLUTTER.

dove[2] (*US*) *pt* of DIVE[1].

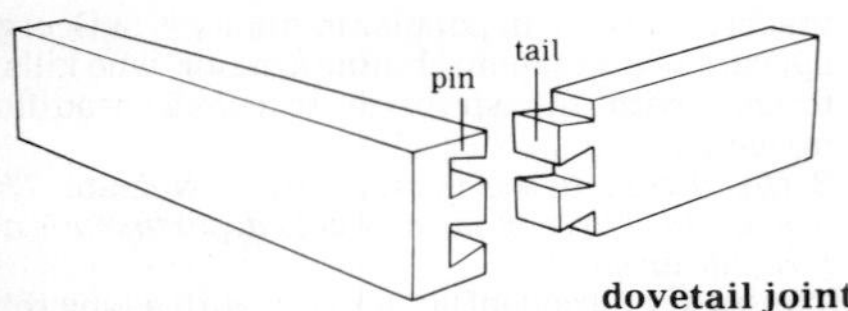

dovetail joint

dovetail /ˈdʌvteɪl/ *n* joint for fixing two pieces of wood together, with one piece cut in the shape of a wedge fitting into a groove of the same shape in the other. ⇨ illus.
▷ **dovetail** *v* **1** [Tn] join (two pieces of wood) in this way. **2** [I, Ipr, Tn, Tn·pr] ~ **(sth) (with sth)** (*fig*) fit together; combine neatly: *My plans dovetailed nicely with hers.*

dowager /ˈdaʊədʒə(r)/ *n* **1** woman who holds a title or property because of her dead husband's position: [attrib] *the dowager duchess.* **2** (*infml*) dignified, usu wealthy, elderly woman.

dowdy /ˈdaʊdɪ/ *adj* (**-ier, -iest**) (*derog*) **1** (of clothes, etc) dull; unfashionable; drab. **2** (of a person) dressed in dowdy clothes. ▷ **dowdily** *adv.* **dowdiness** *n* [U].

dowel /ˈdaʊəl/ *n* wooden or metal pin with no head for holding two pieces of wood, metal, stone, etc together.

dower house /ˈdaʊə haʊs/ small house near a larger house, as used originally by the widow of the owner of the large house.

Dow-Jones index /ˌdaʊ dʒəʊnz ˈɪndeks/ (also **Dow-Jones average**) figure indicating the average price of shares on the New York stock exchange on a particular day. ⇨ article at FINANCE.

Dowland /ˈdaʊlənd/ John (?1563-1626), English composer of songs and lute music.

down[1] /daʊn/ *adv part* (For special uses with many *vs*, see the *v* entries.) **1** (**a**) from a higher to a lower level: *pull down a blind* ○ *fall, climb, jump, etc down* ○ *The sun went down below the horizon.* ○ *The ice-cream slipped down easily — it was cold and delicious.* (**b**) (moving) from an upright position to a horizontal one: *knock sb down* ○ *go and lie down.* (**c**) with the body positioned at a lower level: *sit, kneel, crouch, etc down* ○ *He bent down to pick up his gloves.* Cf UP 1a. **2** (indicating place or state): *Mary is not down yet,* ie She is in bed or still in an upstairs room. ○ *The level of unemployment is down.* ○ *We're two goals down already,* ie The other team has scored two goals and we have scored none. Cf UP 2. **3** (**a**) away from an important place, esp a large city: *move down from London to the country.* (**b**) (*Brit*) away from a university, esp Oxford or Cambridge: *going down at the end of the year.* (**c**) to or in the south of the country: *living down south.* Cf UP 4. **4** (indicating a decrease in volume, activity or quality): *boil the liquid down* ○ *calm/quieten/settle down* ○ *The fire burnt down.* ○ *The noise was dying down.* ○ *The wine was watered down for the children.* ○ *The heels of these shoes are quite worn down.* **5** (**a**) (written) on paper: *write it down* ○ *copy/note/put/take sth down.* (**b**) added to a list: *Have you got me down for the team?* **6** ~ **(to sb/sth)** (indicating the upper (and lower) limits in a range): *Everyone played well, from the captain down.* ○ *Nobody was free from suspicion, from the head girl down to the youngest pupil.* **7** (**a**) (with a specified amount of money) spent or lost: *After paying all the bills, I found myself £5 down.* (**b**) as a deposit: *Pay me £50 down and the rest at the end of the month.* ○ [attrib] *Pay me £50 as a down payment.* **8** (used in measuring one's progress through a series of individual people, things, etc): *That's 10 down, another 5 candidates to see yet.* **9** (idm) **be down on sb** (*infml*) feel, show or express disapproval or hostility towards sb: *She's terribly down on people who don't do things her way.* **be down to sb** be dependent on sb: *It's down to you now to look after the family business.* **be down to sth** have only a little (money) left: *be down to one's last penny, pound, etc* ○ *I'm afraid I can't buy you a drink — I'm down to my last 50p.* **be/go down with sth** have or catch an illness: *Peter can't play tomorrow, he's (gone) down with flu.* **ˌdown and ˈout** having no home, money, etc; destitute: *He looked completely down and out.* ○ [attrib] *ˌdown-and-ˈout ˌhomeless ˈpeople.* **down below** in or to the basement of a building or to the hold of a ship, etc. **ˌdown ˈstage (of sb/sth)** at or to the part of the stage nearest the audience: *move down stage (of the other actors).* **down through sth** throughout (a considerable period of time): *Down through the years this town has seen many changes.* **down ˈunder** (*infml*) in Australia: *Down under they speak their own kind of English.* **down with sb/sth** (used to express a wish that a person, a group or an institution should be banned or abolished): *Down with the government!* ○ *Down with school uniforms!*
□ **ˈdown-and-out** *n* destitute person.
ˌdown-to-ˈearth *adj* practical; sensible: *He needs to marry a down-to-earth person who will organize his life for him.*

down[2] /daʊn/ *prep* **1** from a high or higher point on (sth) to a lower one: *The stone rolled down the hill.* ○ *Tears ran down her face.* ○ *Her hair hung down her back to her waist.* **2** at or to a lower part of (sth): *There's a bridge a mile down the river from here.* **3** (of flat surfaces or areas) along; towards the direction in which one is facing: *He lives just down the street.* ○ *Go down the road till you reach the traffic lights.* **4** (of periods of time) throughout: *an exhibition of costumes down the ages,* ie from all periods of history.

down[3] /daʊn/ *v* [Tn] **1** knock (sb) to the ground. **2** (*infml*) finish (a drink) quickly: *We downed our beer and left.* **3** (idm) **ˌdown ˈtools** (*Brit*) (**a**) (of workers) stop working, usu abruptly: *As soon as the clock strikes five, they down tools and off they go.* (**b**) refuse to continue working, as in a strike.

down[4] /daʊn/ *n* (idm) **have a down on sb/sth** (*infml*) disapprove of or feel hostile towards sb/sth: *She's got a ˈdown on me; I don't know why.* **ups and downs** ⇨ UP *n.*

down[5] *adj* [pred] depressed; gloomy: *I've been feeling rather down recently.*

down[6] /daʊn/ *n* [U] **1** very fine soft feathers: *pillows filled with down.* **2** fine soft hair: *The first down was beginning to appear on the young boy's face.*

downbeat /ˈdaʊnbi:t/ *n* (*music*) first beat of a bar (when the conductor's hand moves downwards). Cf UPBEAT.
▷ **downbeat** *adj* (*infml*) **1** gloomy; pessimistic. **2** relaxed; not showing strong feelings.

downcast /ˈdaʊnkɑ:st; *US* ˈdaʊnkæst/ *adj* **1** (of eyes) looking downwards. **2** (of a person, an expression, etc) depressed; sad: *He seemed very downcast at the news.*

down draught (*US* **down draft**) /ˈdaʊn drɑ:ft; *US* dræft/ downward current of air, esp one that moves down a chimney into a room.

downer /ˈdaʊnə(r)/ *n* (*sl*) **1** drug having a depressant effect, esp a barbiturate. Cf UPPER *n* 2. **2** depressing experience, person, etc: *What a downer that guy is!*

downfall /ˈdaʊnfɔ:l/ *n* [sing] **1** fall from a position of prosperity or power: *Greed led to his downfall.* **2** thing that causes this: *His vanity was his downfall.*

downgrade /ˈdaʊngreɪd/ *v* [Tn, Tn·pr] ~ **sb/sth (from sth) (to sth)** reduce sb/sth to a lower grade, rank or level of importance: *She's been downgraded (from principal) to deputy.* Cf UPGRADE.

down-hearted /ˌdaʊnˈhɑ:tɪd/ *adj* in low spirits; depressed: *Don't be too down-hearted; things will get better.*

downhill /ˌdaʊnˈhɪl/ *adv* **1** towards the bottom of a hill; in a downward direction. **2** (idm) **ˌgo downˈhill** get worse (in health, fortune, social status, etc); deteriorate: *This part of the town used to be fashionable, but it's starting to go downhill.*
▷ **downhill** *adj* **1** [attrib] going or sloping towards the bottom of a hill: *a ˌdownhill ˈrace.* **2** (*infml*) easy compared to what came before: *The difficult part is learning the new computer codes — after that it's all downhill.*

Downing Street /ˈdaʊnɪŋ stri:t/ (**a**) London street where the British Prime Minister's official residence is (at No 10). The official residence of the Chancellor of the Exchequer (No 11) and the Foreign and Commonwealth Office are also there. (**b**) (*fig*) the Prime Minister or the British Government: *Downing Street has so far refused to comment on these reports.*

download /ˌdaʊnˈləʊd/ *v* [Tn, Tn·pr] (*computing*) transfer (a program, data, etc) from (usu) a large computer system to a smaller one.

down-market /ˌdaʊn ˈmɑ:kɪt/ *adj* (of products, services, etc) designed to appeal to or satisfy people in the lower social classes. Cf UP-MARKET.

downpipe /ˈdaʊnpaɪp/ (*US* **downspout** /ˈdaʊnspaʊt/) *n* pipe for carrying rain-water from a roof to a drain.

downpour /ˈdaʊnpɔ:(r)/ *n* (usu *sing*) heavy, usu sudden, fall of rain: *be caught in a downpour.*

downright /ˈdaʊnraɪt/ *adj* [attrib] **1** (of sth undesirable) thorough; complete: *a downright lie* ○ *downright stupidity.* **2** frank; straightforward.
▷ **downright** *adv* thoroughly: *He wasn't just inconsiderate, he was downright rude.*

downs /daʊnz/ *n* [pl] **the downs** area of open rolling land, esp the chalk hills of S England: *the North, South, Sussex, etc Downs.*

Down's syndrome /ˈdaʊnz sɪndrəʊm/ (also **mongolism**) abnormal condition in which a person is born with a broad flattened skull, slanting eyes and mental deficiency.

downstairs /ˌdaʊnˈsteəz/ *adv* **1** down the stairs: *He fell downstairs and broke his wrist.* **2** on or to a lower floor: *They're waiting for us downstairs.* Cf UPSTAIRS.
▷ **downstairs** *adj* [attrib]: *the downstairs toilet.* **downstairs** *n* [sing *v*] lower floor of a building, esp the ground floor: *The whole downstairs needs repainting.*

downstream /ˌdaʊnˈstri:m/ *adv* in the direction in which a river flows: *drift, float, etc downstream.* Cf UPSTREAM.

downtown /ˌdaʊnˈtaʊn/ *adv* (*esp US*) to or in the centre of a city, esp the main business and commercial district: *go, move, live downtown* ○ [attrib] *downtown Manhattan.* Cf UPTOWN.

downtrodden /ˈdaʊntrɒdn/ *adj* kept down and badly treated; oppressed: *downtrodden workers.*

downturn /ˈdaʊntɜ:n/ *n* ~ **(in sth)** (usu temporary) reduction in the level of economic activity (eg the production of goods, buying and selling, etc); decline: *the expected economic downturn* ○ *a downturn in export sales.*

downward /ˈdaʊnwəd/ *adj* [usu attrib] moving, leading or pointing to what is lower or less important: *a downward movement, slope* ○ *a downward trend in prices* ○ (*fig*) *on the downward path,* ie getting worse.
▷ **downwards** (also **downward**) *adv* towards what is lower: *She laid the picture face downward on the table.* ○ *The garden sloped gently downwards towards the river.* ⇨ Usage at FORWARD[2].

downwind /ˌdaʊnˈwɪnd/ *adj, adv* ~ **(of sb/sth)** in the direction opposite to that from which the wind is blowing: *Get downwind of the deer; then it won't smell us.*

downy /ˈdaʊnɪ/ *adj* like or covered with down[6].

dowry /ˈdaʊərɪ/ *n* [C, U] property or money brought by a bride to her husband.

dowse[1] = DOUSE.

dowse[2] /daʊz/ *v* [I, Ipr] ~ **(for sth)** look for underground water or minerals by using a Y-shaped stick or rod that dips or shakes when it comes near water, etc.
▷ **dowser** *n* person who does this; diviner.

doxology /dɒkˈsɒlədʒɪ/ *n* hymn or other prayer praising God, esp one sung during a church service.

doyen /ˈdɔɪən/ (*US* usu **dean** /di:n/) (*fem* **doyenne** /dɔɪˈen/) *n* senior member of a group, profession, etc: *She founded the club and is now our doyenne.* ○ *the doyen of the French Department.*

Doyle /dɔɪl/ Sir Arthur Conan (1859-1930), British writer who created the fictional detective Sherlock *Holmes. He was originally a doctor, but began writing full-time after the success of his first

Holmes story, *A Study in Scarlet*, in 1887. He also wrote historical novels.

doyley, **doyly** = DOILY.

D'Oyly Carte /ˌdɔɪlɪ ˈkɑːt/ Richard (1844-1901), English theatrical producer who put on the first performances of the *Gilbert and *Sullivan operas. The D'Oyly Carte company continued performing the operas for many years after his death.

doz *abbr* dozen: *3 doz eggs.*

doze /dəʊz/ *v* [I, Ip] **1** sleep lightly. **2** (phr v) **doze off** fall into a light sleep: *I dozed off during the film.*
▷ **doze** *n* (usu *sing*) short light sleep: *I had a quick doze on the train.*

dozen /ˈdʌzn/ *n* (*pl* ~**s** or unchanged when counting sth) (*abbr* **doz**) **1** set of twelve: *Eggs are sold by the dozen.* ○ *They're 70p a dozen.* ○ *Pack them in dozens.* ○ [attrib] *Half a dozen* (ie 6) *eggs, please.* ○ *We need three dozen boxes.* ⇨ App 9. **2** (idm) **a baker's dozen** ⇨ BAKER. **one's daily dozen** ⇨ DAILY. **a dime a dozen** ⇨ DIME. **dozens of** (*infml*) lots of: *She's got dozens of boy-friends.* **talk, etc nineteen to the ˈdozen** talk, etc continually: *They were chatting away nineteen to the dozen.* **(it is) ˌsix of ˈone and ˌhalf a dozen of the ˈother** there is very little difference between the one and the other: *I can't tell whether he or she is to blame — it's six of one and half a dozen of the other.*

dozy /ˈdəʊzɪ/ *adj* (**-ier**, **-iest**) **1** sleepy: *I'm feeling a bit dozy this afternoon.* **2** (*Brit infml*) stupid: *Come on, you dozy lot — use your heads!*

DPhil /ˌdiː ˈfɪl/ *abbr* Doctor of Philosophy: *have/be a DPhil in History* ○ *Hugh Benson DPhil.* Cf PHD.

DPP /ˌdiː piː ˈpiː/ *abbr* (*Brit*) Director of Public Prosecutions.

Dr *abbr* **1** (academic or medical) Doctor: *Dr (James) Walker.* **2** (in street names) Drive: *21 Elm Dr.*

dr *abbr* **1** drachma(s): *dr 500.* **2** dram(s).

drab[1] /dræb/ *adj* (**-bber**, **-bbest**) dull; uninteresting: *a drab evening, existence, personality* ○ *dressed in drab colours.* ▷ **drably** *adv.* **drabness** *n* [U].

drab[2] ⇨ DRIBS.

drachma /ˈdrækmə/ *n* (*pl* **-mas** or **-mae** /-miː/) unit of money in Greece.

Draconian /drəˈkəʊnɪən/ *adj* (*fml*) very harsh: *Draconian measures, laws, policies, etc.*

Dracula /ˈdrækjʊlə/ fictional king of the vampires, creatures who supposedly suck the blood of living people. He was created by the Irish writer Bram Stoker in his novel *Dracula* (1897), and has been featured in many horror films.

draft[1] /drɑːft; *US* dræft/ *n* **1** [C] rough preliminary written version of sth: *This is only the draft of my speech, but what do you think of it?* ○ [attrib] *a draft amendment, copy, version.* **2** (*finance*) **(a)** [C] written order to a bank to pay money to sb: *a draft on an American bank.* **(b)** [U] payment of money by means of such an order. **3** [CGp] group of people chosen from a larger group for a special purpose: *We're sending a fresh draft of nurses to the worst hit area.* **4** (*US*) **the draft** [sing] = CALL-UP (CALL[2]). ⇨ article at ARMED FORCES. **5** [C] (*US*) = DRAUGHT.
□ **ˈdraft-card** *n* (*US*) card summoning a man to serve in the armed forces.
ˈdraft-dodger *n* (*US*) man illegally evading the draft[1](4).

draft[2] /drɑːft; *US* dræft/ *v* **1** [Tn] make a preliminary version of (a document): *draft a contract, parliamentary bill, treaty, etc* ○ *I'm still drafting the first chapter.* ○ *a badly drafted will.* **2** [Tn, Tn·pr, Tn·p] choose (people) and send them somewhere for a special task: *Extra police are being drafted in to control the crowds.* **3** [Tn, Tn·pr] ~ **sb (into sth)** (*US*) conscript sb: *be drafted into the Army, Navy, etc.*
▷ **draftee** /ˌdrɑːfˈtiː; *US* ˌdræfˈtiː/ *n* (*US*) conscript.

draftsman /ˈdrɑːftsmən; *US* ˈdræfts-/ *n* (*pl* **-men**) **1** person responsible for the careful and exact wording of a legal document or parliamentary bill. **2** (*US*) = DRAUGHTSMAN.

drafty (*US*) = DRAUGHTY.

drag[1] /dræg/ *n* **1** [C] thing made to be dragged, eg a drag-net, or heavy harrow (pulled over the ground to break up the soil). **2** [U] resistance of the air to the movement of an aircraft. Cf LIFT *n* 4. **3** [sing] (*sl*) boring person or thing: *Walking's a drag — let's take the car.* **4** [U] (*sl*) woman's clothes worn by a man: *in drag* ○ [attrib] *a drag artiste.* **5** [C] (*sl*) draw on a cigarette, etc. **6** [sing] ~ **on sb/sth** (*infml*) person or thing that makes progress difficult: *She loves her family, but they're a drag on her career.* **7** (*US infml*) street; road: *on the main drag.*
▷ **dragster** /ˈdrægstə(r)/ *n* car with a specially adapted motor for drag racing.
□ **ˈdrag-hunt** *n* hunt in which dogs follow the trail of a strong-smelling object dragged over the ground.
ˈdrag-net *n* **(a)** net pulled along the bottom of a river, etc, esp when searching for sth. **(b)** (*fig*) system of checks, raids, etc by the police for catching criminals.
ˈdrag race contest of acceleration between cars starting from a standstill. **ˈdrag racing**.

drag[2] /dræg/ *v* (**-gg-**) **1** [Tn, Tn·pr, Tn·p] pull (sb/sth) along with effort and difficulty: *The cat was dragging its broken leg.* ○ *We dragged the fallen tree clear of the road.* ○ *drag oneself along, home.* ⇨ illus at PULL. ⇨ Usage at PULL[2]. **2** [Ipr, Ip] move slowly and with effort: *She always drags behind.* **3** [Tn·pr, Tn·p] (*fig*) persuade (sb) to come or go somewhere unwillingly: *I could hardly drag the children away (from the party).* ○ *She dragged herself out of bed, still half asleep.* **4** [I, Ipr, Ip, Tn, Tn·pr] (cause sth to) trail on the ground: *Your coat's dragging in the mud.* ○ *The ship dragged her anchor during the storm,* ie The anchor did not stay in its place on the sea bottom. **5** [I, Ip] ~ **(on)** (of sth boring or irritating) go on too long: *The film dragged terribly.* ○ *How much longer is this going to drag on?* **6** [Tn] search (the bottom of a river, lake, etc) with nets, hooks, etc: *They dragged the canal for the missing child.* **7** (idm) **drag one's ˈfeet/ˈheels** be deliberately slow or ineffective: *I want to sell the house, but my husband is dragging his feet,* ie will not make a decision. **drag sb/sb's name through the mire/mud** bring disgrace to sb by behaving very badly. **8** (phr v) **drag sb down** make sb feel weak or depressed: *Hot weather always drags me down.* **drag sb down (to sth)** (*infml*) bring sb to a lower social level, standard of behaviour, etc: *I'm afraid the children will all be dragged down to his level.* **drag sth in/into sth** introduce (a subject which has nothing to do with what is being talked about) into the conversation: *Must you drag politics into everything?* **drag sb into doing sth** make sb take part in an activity against his will: *She had to be dragged into seeing the dentist.* **drag sth out** make sth longer than necessary: *Let's not drag out this discussion, we've got to reach a decision.* **drag sth out (of sb)** make sb reveal or give (information, etc) unwillingly: *drag a confession, fact, concession, etc out of sb.* **drag sb up** (*Brit*) raise (a child) badly and without proper care. **drag sth up** introduce unnecessarily into a conversation (a fact, story, etc that is considered unpleasant): *She dragged up that incident just to embarrass me.*

draggled /ˈdrægəld/ *adj* = BEDRAGGLED.

dragoman /ˈdrægəmən/ *n* (*pl* ~**s**) (esp formerly in some Middle Eastern countries) guide and interpreter.

dragon /ˈdrægən/ *n* **1** imaginary animal with wings and claws, able to breathe out fire. ⇨ illus. 📖 Dragons are often portrayed in art and literature as frightening creatures representing the forces of evil. In popular mythology, St George appears as a 'knight in shining armour' who kills a dragon with his spear to rescue a beautiful maiden.
2 (*fig derog*) fierce person, esp a woman: *The woman in charge of the accounts department is an absolute dragon!*

dragon-fly /ˈdrægənflaɪ/ *n* insect with a long thin body and two pairs of wings.

dragoon /drəˈguːn/ *n* heavily-armed cavalryman.
▷ **dragoon** *v* (phr v) **dragoon sb into doing sth** force sb to do sth; bully sb into doing sth: *We were dragooned into going to the opera.*

drain[1] /dreɪn/ *n* **1** pipe or channel that carries away sewage or other unwanted liquid: *We had to call a plumber to unblock the drains.* ⇨ illus at HOME. **2** (*US*) = PLUG-HOLE (PLUG). **3** (idm) **(go) down the ˈdrain/tubes** (*infml*) (be) wasted or spoilt: *A single mistake and all that time and money would go down the drain.* **a drain on sb/sth** anything that continuously uses up sb's strength, time, money, etc: *Military spending is a huge drain on the country's resources.* **laugh like a drain** ⇨ LAUGH.
□ **ˈdrain-pipe** *n* pipe used in a system of drains. ⇨ illus at HOME. **ˌdrain-pipe ˈtrousers** (*infml dated*) tight-fitting trousers with straight narrow legs.

drain[2] /dreɪn/ *v* **1** [I, Ipr, Ip, Tn, Tn·pr, Tn·p] ~ **(sth) (from sth)**; ~ **(sth) (away/off)** (cause liquid to) flow away: *All the blood drained from his face,* eg on hearing bad news. ○ *The bath-water slowly drained away.* ○ *The mechanic drained all the oil from the engine.* **2** [Tn, Cn·a] empty (a glass, etc): *drain one's glass dry.* **3** [I, Tn] (cause sth to) become dry as liquid flows away: *Leave the dishes to drain.* ○ *drain swamps/marshes* ○ *Land must be well drained for some crops.* **4** [Tn, Tn·pr] ~ **sb/sth (of sth)** (*fig*) make sb/sth weaker, poorer, etc by gradually using up his/its strength, money, etc: *feel drained of energy* ○ *a country drained of its manpower.* **5** (idm) **drink/drain sth to the dregs** ⇨ DREGS. **6** (phr v) **drain away** (*fig*) gradually disappear or fade: *Her life was slowly draining away,* ie She was dying.
□ **ˈdraining-board** (*US* **ˈdrainboard**) *n* sloping surface beside a sink, on which washed dishes, etc are put to drain.

drainage /ˈdreɪnɪdʒ/ *n* [U] **1** draining or being drained. **2** system of drains. **3** what is drained off; sewage.
□ **ˈdrainage-basin** *n* area from which water is drained away by a river.

Drake /dreɪk/ Sir Francis (c 1540-96), English sailor and explorer, born in Devon. After a successful career attacking and robbing Spanish ships in the Caribbean, he set off in 1577 with a fleet of five ships on a voyage round the world, which took just under three years. In 1587 he led a raid on Cadiz in Spain, setting fire to the Spanish fleet ('singeing the king of Spain's beard', as he termed it), and delaying the sailing of the *Armada by a year. When the Armada did arrive in the English Channel, he was vice-admiral of the English fleet that sailed against it.

drake /dreɪk/ *n* **1** male duck. Cf DUCK[1] 1. **2** (idm) **play ducks and drakes with sb** ⇨ DUCKS AND DRAKES (DUCK[1]).

dram /dræm/ *n* **1** (*abbr* **dr**) unit of weight, one-eighth of an ounce (apothecaries' weight) or one-sixteenth of an ounce (avoirdupois weight). **2** (*esp Scot*) small amount of alcoholic drink, esp whisky: *He's fond of his dram.*

drama /ˈdrɑːmə/ *n* **1** **(a)** [C] play for the theatre, radio or TV. **(b)** [U] plays as a branch of literature and as a performing art: *a masterpiece of Elizabethan drama* ○ (*dated or fml*) *lovers of the drama* ○ [attrib] *a drama critic, school, student.* **2** [C] series of exciting events: *a real-life hospital drama.* **3** [U, C] excitement: *Her life was full of drama.* **4** (idm) **make a drama out of sth** exaggerate a small problem or trivial incident: *He makes a drama out of a simple visit to the dentist.*

dramatic /drəˈmætɪk/ *adj* **1** [attrib] of drama: *a dramatic society* ○ *a dramatic representation of a real event.* **2** exciting or impressive: *dramatic* *changes, developments, news* ○ *Her opening words were dramatic.*

▷ **dramatically** /-klɪ/ *adv*: *Her attitude changed dramatically.*

dramatics *n* [usu sing *v*] **1** study or practice of acting and producing plays: *amateur dramatics.* **2** (*derog*) exaggerated or over-emotional behaviour: *I've had enough of your dramatics.*

□ **draˌmatic ˈirony** effect produced in a drama, etc when the audience understands the implications of words or actions better than the characters do themselves.

dramatis personae /ˌdræmətɪs pɜːˈsəʊnaɪ/ (*fml*) (list of the) characters in a play.

dramatist /ˈdræmətɪst/ *n* writer of plays.

dramatize, -ise /ˈdræmətaɪz/ *v* **1** [Tn] make (eg a novel or an event) into a play: *a dramatized documentary*, ie a play based on a report of real events. **2** [I, Tn] make (an incident, etc) seem more dramatic than it really is: *Don't believe everything she tells you; she tends to dramatize.* ○ *The affair was dramatized by the press.* ▷ **dramatization, -isation** /ˌdræmətaɪˈzeɪʃn, -tɪˈz-/ *n* [U, C]: *a TV dramatization of the trial.*

drank *pt* of DRINK².

drape /dreɪp/ *v* **1 (a)** [Tn·pr] ~ **sth round/over sth** hang (cloth, curtains, a cloak, etc) loosely on sth: *a fur coat draped round her shoulders* ○ *Dust-sheets were draped over the furniture.* **(b)** [Tn, Tn·pr] ~ **sb/sth (in/with sth)** cover or decorate sb/sth (with cloth, etc): *Dracula appeared, draped in a huge cloak.* ○ *walls draped with tapestries.* **2** [Tn·pr] ~ **sth round/over sth** allow sth to rest loosely on sth: *She draped her arms around his neck.*

▷ **drape** *n* **1** [sing] way in which a curtain, dress, etc hangs. **2** [C] (*US*) = CURTAIN.

draper /ˈdreɪpə(r)/ *n* (*Brit*) shopkeeper who sells cloth and clothing.

drapery /ˈdreɪpərɪ/ *n* **1** [U] (*Brit*) (*US* **dry goods**) draper's trade or goods: [attrib] *the drapery department.* **2** [C, U] cloth, etc hanging in loose folds.

drastic /ˈdræstɪk/ *adj* [usu attrib] **1** having a strong or violent effect: *Drastic measures will have to be taken to restore order.* **2** very serious: *a drastic shortage of food.* ▷ **drastically** /-klɪ/ *adv.*

drat /dræt/ *interj* (*infml*) (used to express one's annoyance with sb/sth): *Drat that child!* ▷ **dratted** *adj* [attrib] (*infml*): *This dratted pen won't work.*

draught /drɑːft/ (*US* **draft** /dræft/) *n* **1** [C] current of air in a room or some other enclosed space: *Can you close the door? There's an awful draught in here.* ○ *As the train began to move a pleasant draught cooled us all down.* **2** [U, sing] (*nautical*) depth of water needed to float a ship: *vessels of shallow draught.* **3** [C] one continuous process of swallowing liquid; the amount swallowed: *take a deep/long draught of beer* ○ *He emptied his glass at one draught.* ○ (*fig*) *He took a deep draught of air into his lungs.* **4 draughts** (*Brit*) (*US* **checkers**) [sing *v*] table game for two players using 24 round pieces on a chequered board. **5** [U] pulling of heavy loads: *animals employed for draught.* **6** [C] **(a)** act of pulling in a fishing-net. **(b)** fish caught by doing this. **7** (idm) **feel the draught** ⇨ FEEL¹. **on ˈdraught** drawn from a container, esp of beer from a barrel: *winter ale on draught.*

▷ **draught** *adj* [attrib] served on draught: *draught bitter, cider, lager, etc.*

□ **ˈdraught-board** (*Brit*) (*US* **ˈcheckerboard**) *n* board (identical to a chessboard) used for playing draughts.

ˈdraughthorse *n* horse used for pulling loads. Cf PACK-ANIMAL (PACK¹).

draughtsman /ˈdrɑːftsmən/ (*US* **draftsman** /ˈdræfts-/) *n* (*pl* **-men** /-mən/) **1** person whose job is to make plans and sketches of machinery, buildings, etc. **2** person who can draw well: *I'm no draughtsman, I'm afraid*, ie no good at drawing. **3** (*Brit*) (*US* **checker**) piece used in the game of draughts.

draughty /ˈdrɑːftɪ/ (*US* **drafty** /ˈdræftɪ/) *adj* (**-ier, -iest**) with draughts of air blowing through: *It's terribly draughty in here.* ▷ **draughtiness** *n* [U].

Dravidian /drəˈvɪdɪən/ *n* **1** [C] member of a dark-skinned people living in southern India and Sri Lanka. **2** [U] group of languages spoken by these people, including Tamil, Telugu and Malayalam.

▷ **Dravidian** *adj* of the Dravidian people or languages.

draw¹ /drɔː/ *n* **1 (a)** (usu *sing*) ~ **(for sth)** act of picking at random tickets in a lottery, matches in a tournament, etc: *The draw for the raffle takes place on Saturday.* ○ *the draw for the second round of the European Cup.* **(b)** lottery in which the winner is chosen this way. Cf RAFFLE. **2** result of a game in which neither player or side wins: *The match ended in a draw 2-2.* **3** (usu *sing*) person or thing that attracts people: *A live band is always a good draw at a party.* **4** act of drawing at a cigarette, pipe, etc. **5** (idm) **the luck of the draw** ⇨ LUCK. **(be) quick/slow on the ˈdraw (a)** quick/slow at pulling out one's gun, etc. **(b)** (*infml*) quick/slow to understand: *He's a nice lad, but a bit slow on the draw.*

draw² /drɔː/ *v* (*pt* **drew** /druː/, *pp* **drawn** /drɔːn/) **1** [I, Tn] make (pictures or a picture of sth) with a pencil, etc: *You draw beautifully.* ○ *She drew a house.* ○ *draw a diagram, plan, flow chart, etc* ○ (*fig*) *The report drew a grim picture of inefficiency and corruption.* **2** [Ipr, Ip] move in the specified direction: *The train drew in/into the station.* ○ *The car drew slowly away from the kerb.* ○ *One horse drew further and further ahead.* ○ *A pilot boat drew alongside*, ie next to a ship. ○ (*fig*) *Christmas is drawing near.* ○ *His life was drawing peacefully to its close.* **3 (a)** [Tn·pr, Tn·p] pull or guide (sb/sth) into a new position: *She drew a cover over the typewriter.* ○ *I drew my chair up (to the table).* ○ *She drew me onto the balcony.* ○ *I tried to draw him aside*, ie where I could talk to him privately. **(b)** [Tn, Tn·pr, Tn·p] (of horses, etc) pull or drag (eg a carriage, a plough): *The Queen's coach was drawn by six horses.* ⇨ Usage at PULL². **(c)** [Tn] open or close (curtains, etc). **4 (a)** [Tn·pr, Tn·p] ~ **sth out of/from sth;** ~ **sth out** pull sth smoothly out of its present position: *draw a file from a drawer* ○ *I drew the record out of its sleeve.* ○ *Can you draw the cork out?* **(b)** [Tn, Tn·pr] ~ **sth (from sth)** take out (a gun, knife, etc) from its holder, esp in order to attack sb: *She drew a revolver on me.* ○ *He came towards me with a drawn sword.* **5** [Tn, Tn·pr] ~ **sth (from sth)** gain or derive sth from study, experience, etc (used esp with the *ns* shown): *What conclusions did you draw (from your study)?* ○ *draw a moral from a story* ○ *We can draw some lessons for the future (from this accident).* **6** [Tn, Tn·pr] ~ **sb (about/on sth)** make sb say more (about sth): *She wouldn't be drawn about her private life.* ○ *I wanted to hear about possible changes, but I couldn't draw them (on that).* **7 (a)** [Tn·pr, Tn·p] make (eg a liquid or gas) go in a particular direction by pumping, sucking, etc: *The engine draws water along the pipe.* ○ *The diaphragm draws air into the lungs.* **(b)** [I] (of a chimney or fireplace) allow enough air to pass through a fire to make it burn properly: *The flue should draw better once it's been swept.* **(c)** [Ipr] ~ **at/on sth** breathe in smoke from (a cigarette, etc): *He drew thoughtfully on his pipe.* **8 (a)** [Tn, Tn·pr, Tn·p] ~ **sth (from sth)** take sth from a larger supply: *draw water (from a well)* ○ *He drew off a pint of beer from the barrel.* **(b)** [Tn·pr] ~ **sth from sb/sth** obtain (sth one needs) from sb/sth: *draw support, comfort, strength, etc from one's family* ○ *She drew inspiration from her childhood experiences.* ○ *We draw our readers from all classes of society.* **(c)** [Tn, Tn·pr] ~ **sth (from sth)** take (money) from a bank account: *Can I draw £50 from my account?* **(d)** [Tn] receive (wages, etc): *It's good to be drawing a monthly salary again.* **9** [Tn, Tn·pr] **(a)** ~ **sb (to sth)** attract or interest sb: *The film is drawing large audiences.* ○ *Her screams drew passers-by to the scene.* ○ *I felt drawn to this mysterious stranger.* ○ *What drew you to* (ie made you study) *medicine?* ○ *The course draws students from all over the country.* **(b)** ~ **sth (from sb)** produce (a reaction or response): *draw tears, applause, laughter, etc* ○ *The idea has drawn much criticism from both sides.* ○ *The competition has drawn a large post-bag.* **10** [Tn, Tn·pr] (*finance*) write out (a cheque, etc): *The bill was drawn on an American bank.* **11** [Ipr, Tn, Tn·pr] ~ **for sth;** ~ **sth (from sth)** get or take sth by chance: *Before playing cards we drew for partners*, ie decided who would partner whom by drawing cards. ○ *draw the winner/the winning ticket (in a raffle, etc)* ○ *draw cards from a pack* ○ *draw lots, names from a hat, etc* ○ *Italy have been drawn to play Spain in the World Cup.* **12** [I, Tn] finish (a game, etc) without either side winning: *The two teams drew.* ○ *draw three-all/for first place* ○ *The match was drawn.* **13** [I] (of tea) infuse; brew: *Let the tea draw (for three minutes).* **14** [Tn] (*nautical*) (of a ship) require (a certain depth of water) in which to float: *a ship drawing 20 feet.* **15** [Tn] (*dated*) pull out (a tooth). **16** [Tn] remove the inner organs of (a chicken, etc). **17** [Tn] pull back the string of (a bow) before firing an arrow. **18** [Tn] mould a thin string of (metal, plastic, etc) by passing it through a small hole. **19** (idm) **at daggers drawn** ⇨ DAGGER. **bring sth/come/draw to close** ⇨ CLOSE⁵. **cast/draw lots** ⇨ LOT⁴. **draw an aˈnalogy, a comˈparison, a ˈparallel, etc between sth and sth** show how one thing is like or contrasts with another. **draw (sb's) attention to sth** point sth out (to sb): *She drew my attention to an error in the report.* ○ *I'm embarrassed about my mistake; please don't draw attention to it*, eg by mentioning it to others. **draw a ˈbead (on sb/sth)** (*infml*) aim carefully at sb/sth with a gun, etc. **draw a ˈblank** get no response or result: *I tried looking him up in the directory but I drew a blank*, ie his name was not there. **draw ˈblood (a)** cause sb to bleed. **(b)** (*fig*) hurt sb's feelings: *His wounding remarks clearly drew blood.* **draw ˈbreath (a)** pause to breathe deeply after an effort. **(b)** live: *as kind a man as ever drew breath* ○ *You won't want for a friend as long as I draw breath.* **draw a distinction between sth and sth** show how two things differ. **draw sb's ˈfire (a)** make sb shoot at oneself rather than at another: *I'll draw his fire while you try to get round behind him.* **(b)** (*fig*) make sb direct his anger, criticism, etc at oneself, so that others do not have to face it. **draw one's first/last ˈbreath** be born/die. **draw in one's ˈhorns** become defensive or cautious, esp about one's finances: *You'll have to draw your horns in*, ie spend less money. **draw the line at sth/doing sth** refuse to do or to tolerate sth: *I don't mind helping, but I draw the line at doing everything myself.* ○ *A line has to be drawn somewhere — I can't go on lending you money.* **draw ˈstumps** (in cricket) mark the end of play (by removing the stumps). **draw sb's/sth's ˈteeth/ˈfangs** make sb/sth harmless: *Critics fear the bill will have its teeth drawn before it becomes law.* **draw ˈtrumps** (in various card-games) play the trump suit until one's opponents have none left. **draw oneself up to one's full ˈheight** stand as tall and straight as possible (esp as a sign of determination): *'Never!' she replied, drawing herself up to her full height.* **draw a veil over sth** tactfully not say anything about sth: *I propose to draw a veil over the appalling events that followed.* **20** (phr v) **draw back (from sth/doing sth)** not take action, esp because one feels unsure or nervous: *draw back from a declaration of/from declaring war.* **draw in** (of the hours of daylight) get shorter before winter: *The days are drawing in.* **draw sb into sth/doing sth; draw sb in** make sb take part in sth, esp against his will: *I found myself being drawn into another dreary argument.* ○ *We organize various social activities, but not all the members want to be drawn in.* **draw on** (of a time or season) approach: *Night was drawing on.* **draw on/upon sth** use sth: *We drew on her experience throughout the project.* ○ *I shall have to draw on my savings.* **draw sb on** attract or entice sb: *They drew investors on with visions of instant wealth.* **draw out** (of the hours of daylight) become longer in spring. **draw sb out (about sth)** encourage sb to talk, etc: *He's very shy* *and needs to be drawn out.* ○ *I drew the old man out about his war experiences.* **draw sth out** make (an event, etc) longer than usual: *She drew the interview out to over an hour.* ○ *a long-drawn-out discussion.* **draw up** (of a vehicle) come to a stop: *The taxi drew up outside the house.* **draw sb up** (usu passive) arrange (esp troops) in a special order: *troops drawn up in ranks.* **draw sth up** write out (eg a contract, a list).

□ **ˈdrawstring** *n* string that can be pulled so as to close a bag, purse, garment, etc.

drawback /ˈdrɔ:bæk/ *n* ~ (**of/to doing sth**) disadvantage; problem: *The great drawback to living on a main road is the constant noise.*

drawbridge /ˈdrɔ:brɪdʒ/ *n* bridge (esp formerly across the moat of a castle) that can be pulled up to stop people crossing: *lower/raise the drawbridge.* ⇨ illus at CASTLE.

drawer /drɔ:(r)/ *n* **1** box-like container, with one or more handles but no lid, that slides in and out of a piece of furniture, etc: *the middle drawer of my desk* ○ *clear out one's drawers.* ⇨ illus at FURNITURE. **2** /ˈdrɔ:ə(r)/ (**a**) (*finance*) person who draws a cheque, etc. (**b**) person who draws pictures: *I'm not a very good drawer.*

drawers /drɔ:z/ *n* [pl] (*dated*) knickers or underpants: *a pair of drawers.*

drawing /ˈdrɔ:ɪŋ/ *n* **1** [U] art of representing objects by lines, with a pencil, chalk, etc: *classes in figure drawing.* **2** [C] picture made in this way: *a collection of Italian drawings.*

□ **ˈdrawing-board** *n* **1** flat board to which paper is fixed while a drawing is made. **2** (idm) (**go**) **back to the drawing-board** prepare a new plan for sth because an earlier one has failed: *They've rejected our proposal, so it's back to the drawing-board, I'm afraid.*

ˈdrawing-pin (*US* **ˈthumb-tack**) *n* flat-headed pin for fastening paper, etc to a board, wall, etc.

drawing-room /ˈdrɔ:ɪŋ rʊm, ru:m/ *n* room, esp in a large private house, in which people relax and guests are received and entertained. Cf LIVING-ROOM (LIVING[2]).

drawl /drɔ:l/ *v* [I, Tn, Tn·p] speak or say (sth) in a slow lazy manner, with drawn-out vowels: *drawl (out) one's words.*

▷ **drawl** *n* [sing] drawling manner of speaking: *a broad Texan drawl.*

drawn[1] /drɔ:n/ *adj* (of a person or his face) looking very tired or worried: *She looked pale and drawn after weeks of sleepless nights.*

drawn[2] *pp* of DRAW[2].

dray /dreɪ/ *n* low flat cart for carrying heavy loads, esp barrels from a brewery.

□ **ˈdray-horse** *n* horse used for pulling a dray.

dread /dred/ *n* **1** [U, C] great fear; terror: *He has always stood in dread of his father.* ○ *She has a dread of hospitals.* **2** [C] thing that is greatly feared: *Poverty is many people's constant dread.*

▷ **dread** *v* [Tn, Tf, Tt, Tg, Tsg] fear (sth) greatly: *dread illness/being ill* ○ *I dread that I may never see you again.* ○ *We all dread to think what will happen if the factory closes.* ○ *The moment I had been dreading had arrived.* **dreaded** *adj* greatly feared: *the dreaded scourge of smallpox.*

dreadful /ˈdredfl/ *adj* **1** [esp attrib] causing great fear or suffering; shocking: *a dreadful accident, disease, nightmare* ○ *He has to live with the dreadful knowledge that he caused their deaths.* **2** (*infml*) bad, boring or annoying: *What dreadful weather!* ○ *a dreadful film, man, meal, country* ○ *The noise was dreadful.* **3** [attrib] (*infml*) (used intensively): *I'm afraid it's all a dreadful mistake.*

▷ **dreadfully** /-fəlɪ/ *adv* **1** in a serious or shocking manner: *dreadfully injured.* **2** (*infml*) badly: *This article is dreadfully written.* **3** (*infml*) very: *I'm afraid it's dreadfully late.*

dreadfulness *n* [U].

dreadlocks /ˈdredlɒks/ *n* [pl] hair worn in long curled strands, esp by *Rastafarians. ⇨ illus at PLAIT.

dreadnought /ˈdrednɔ:t/ *n* early 20th-century battleship.

dream[1] /dri:m/ *n* **1** [C] sequence of scenes and feelings occurring in the mind during sleep: *I have a recurrent dream that I've turned into an elephant.* ○ *Good night — sweet dreams!* **2** [sing] state of mind in which things happening around one seem unreal: *be/live/go around in a (complete) dream.* **3** [C] ambition or ideal, esp when it is unrealistic: *My son's dream is to be an astronaut.* ○ *the car, holiday, home of your dreams* ○ *If I win the tournament, it will be a dream come true,* ie something I wanted very much, but did not expect to happen. **4** [sing] (*infml*) beautiful or wonderful person or thing: *Her new dress is an absolute dream.* ○ [attrib] *a dream house, kitchen.* **5** (idm) **a bad ˈdream** situation that is so unpleasant one cannot believe it is real: *You can't be leaving me — this is a bad dream!* **beyond one's wildest dreams** ⇨ WILD. **go, etc like a ˈdream** (*infml*) work very well: *My new car goes like a dream.*

▷ **dreamless** *adj* [usu attrib] (of sleep) without dreams; deep and sound.

□ **ˈdream-land** /-lænd/ *n* [U] (*derog*) pleasant but unrealistic situation imagined by sb: *You must be in dream-land if you think he'll pay that much!*

ˈdreamlike *adj* like a dream.

ˈdream world state where sb imagines everything is the way he would like it to be.

dream[2] /dri:m/ *v* (*pt, pp* **dreamed** /dri:md/ or **dreamt** /dremt/) ⇨ Usage. **1** (**a**) [I] have a dream while asleep: *She claims she never dreams.* (**b**) [Ipr, Tn, Tf] ~ (**of sth/doing sth**); ~ **about sth/doing sth** experience sth in a dream: *I dreamt about flying last night.* ○ *Was it real or did I dream it?* ○ *I dreamt (that) I could fly.* **2** [I, Ipr, Tn, Tf] ~ (**of/about doing sth**) imagine sth: *I never promised to lend you my car: you must be dreaming!* ○ *He dreams of one day becoming a famous violinist.* ○ *Who'd have dreamt it? They're getting married!* ○ *I never dreamt (that) I'd see you again.* **3** (idm) **not dream of sth/doing sth** not do sth under any circumstances: *I should never have dreamt of saying such a thing.* ○ *I'd never dream of allowing my child to do that.* **4** (phr v) **dream sth away** spend (time) idly: *She dreamt her life away, never really achieving anything.* **dream on** (*infml ironic*) continue to hope for sth that will not happen: *So you want a rise? Dream on!* **dream sth up** (*infml*) think of (esp sth imaginative or foolish): *Trust you to dream up a crazy scheme like this!*

▷ **dreamer** *n* **1** person who is dreaming. **2** (*usu derog*) (**a**) person with (seemingly) impractical ideas, plans, etc: *People who said we would go to the moon used to be called dreamers.* (**b**) person who does not concentrate on what happens around him, but day-dreams instead: *Don't rely on his memory — he's a bit of a dreamer.*

NOTE ON USAGE: Several verbs have alternative regular and irregular past tense and past participle forms: **dream**, **dreamed/dreamt**; **spoil**, **spoiled/spoilt**. In British English the irregular form (**dreamt**, **spoilt**, etc) is preferred. The regular past tense is more often used when it describes an action that lasts some time: *He learnt his lesson.* ○ *She learned a lot about life from her mother.* ○ *He leant against the post and it broke.* ○ *He leaned out of the window watching the parade.* In US English there is a preference for the regular past tense and past participle forms (**dreamed**, **spoiled**, etc). In both British and US English the irregular form of the past participle is found in adjectival uses: *a spoilt child* ○ *spilt milk* ○ *a misspelt word.*

dreamy /ˈdri:mɪ/ *adj* (**-ier**, **-iest**) **1** (of a person) with thoughts far away from his present surroundings, work, etc. **2** vague or unclear: *a dreamy recollection of what happened.* **3** (*infml*) pleasantly gentle and relaxing: *dreamy music.* **4** (*infml*) wonderful: *What a dreamy little house!* ▷ **dreamily** /-ɪlɪ/ *adv.* **dreaminess** *n* [U].

dreary /ˈdrɪərɪ/ (also *arch* **drear** /drɪə(r)/) *adj* (**-ier**, **-iest**) **1** that makes one sad or depressed; dismal; gloomy: *a dreary winter day.* **2** (*infml*) boring; dull: *dreary people leading dreary lives.* ▷ **drearily** /ˈdrɪərəlɪ/ *adv.* **dreariness** *n* [U].

dredge[1] /dredʒ/ (also **dredger**) *n* machine for scooping or sucking mud, etc from the bottom of a river, canal, etc.

▷ **dredge** *v* **1** [Tn] deepen or clear (a river, etc) with a dredge: *They have to dredge the canal so that ships can use it.* **2** [I, Ipr, Tn, Tn·pr, Tn·p] ~ **sth** (**up**) (**from sth**) bring sth up using a dredge: *dredge for oysters* ○ *We're dredging (up) mud (from the river bed).* **3** (phr v) **dredge sth up** (*usu derog*) mention sth that has been forgotten, esp sth that is unpleasant or embarrassing: *dredge up details of that episode in Cairo.* **dredger** (also **dredge**) *n* boat or machine used for dredging.

dredge[2] /dredʒ/ *v* [Tn, Tn·pr] ~ **A** (**with B**); ~ **B over/on A** sprinkle (food) with (flour, sugar, etc): *dredge a cake with icing sugar* ○ *dredge icing sugar over a cake.*

▷ **dredger** *n* container with holes in the lid, used for dredging food.

dregs /dregz/ *n* [pl] **1** solid particles that sink to the bottom of certain liquids, esp wine and beer. **2** (*fig*) worst and most useless part (of sth): *the dregs of society.* **3** (idm) **drink/drain sth to the ˈdregs** drink all of sth.

drench /drentʃ/ *v* [esp passive: Tn, Tn·pr, Tn·p] **1** make (sb/sth) completely wet: *We were caught in the storm and got drenched (through/to the skin).* ○ *be drenched with rain.* **2** ~ **sb/sth** (**in/with sth**) apply (a liquid) freely to sb/sth: *drench oneself in perfume* ○ *The poster wouldn't stick even though I drenched it with glue.* **3** [Tn] give liquid medicine to (an animal).

▷ **drench** *n* dose of liquid medicine given to an animal.

drenching *n* thorough wetting.

Dresden /ˌdrezdən/ *n* [U] (also **Dresden China**) fine porcelain made at Meissen, near Dresden in Germany. The factory is famous for its small, delicately coloured china figures: [attrib] *With her golden curls and pink cheeks, she looked like a Dresden shepherdess.*

dress[1] /dres/ *n* **1** [C] garment for a woman or girl, consisting of a bodice and skirt in one piece; frock: *She makes all her own dresses.* **2** [U] clothes, esp outer garments, for either men or women: *casual/formal dress* ○ *evening dress.* ⇨ illus.

□ **ˈdress-circle** *n* (*Brit*) (*US* **first balcony**) first gallery in a theatre (where evening dress was formerly required). Cf MEZZANINE.

ˈdressmaker *n* person (esp a woman) who makes women's clothes. **ˈdressmaking** *n* [U].

ˈdress rehearsal **1** final rehearsal of a play, with the costumes, lighting, etc as they would be in a real performance. **2** (*fig*) practice: *The earlier revolts had just been dress rehearsals for full-scale revolution.*

ˈdress-shirt *n* shirt, sometimes with a frilly front, worn with a dinner jacket.

ˌdress ˈuniform elegant military dress worn by officers on ceremonial occasions.

dress[2] /dres/ *v* **1** [I, Tn] put clothes on (sb/oneself): *He takes ages to dress.* ○ *Hurry up and get dressed!* ○ *Is she old enough to dress herself yet?* ○ *He was dressed as a woman,* ie wearing a woman's clothes. ○ *a woman dressed in green.* **2** [I, Ipr] put on evening dress: *Do I need to dress for the theatre?* **3** [I, Tn] provide (sb/oneself) with clothes: *dress well, badly, fashionably, gaudily, etc* ○ *She can hardly dress her children on the allowance he gives her.* ○ *The princess is dressed by a rising young designer.* **4** [Tn] decorate (sth): *dress a shop window,* ie arrange a display of goods in it ○ *dress a street with flags* ○ *dress a Christmas tree with lights.* **5** [Tn] clean and bandage (a wound, etc). **6** [Tn] finish or treat the surface of (sth): *dress leather, stone, etc.* **7** [Tn] prepare (food) for cooking or eating: *dress a chicken,* ie clean it ready for cooking ○ *dress a salad,* ie add a dressing to it before serving. **8** [Tn] brush (a horse's coat); groom. **9** [I, Tn] draw up (troops) in line: *dress the ranks.* **10** [Tn] put fertilizer on (soil, land, etc) to improve it for growing crops. **11** (idm) (**be**) **dressed in sth** wearing sth: *The bride was dressed in white.* (**be**) **dressed like a ˌdog's ˈdinner** (*infml*) dressed very smartly or showily. (**be**) **dressed** (**up**) **to ˈkill** (*infml*) dressed so as to

DRESS

English costume through the ages

Tudor (early 16th century)

Elizabethan (late 16th century)

Stuart (mid-17th century)

Queen Anne (early 18th century)

Georgian (late 18th century)

Regency (early 19th century)

Early Victorian (mid-19th century)

Late Victorian (late 19th century)

Edwardian (early 20th century)

1920s and 1930s

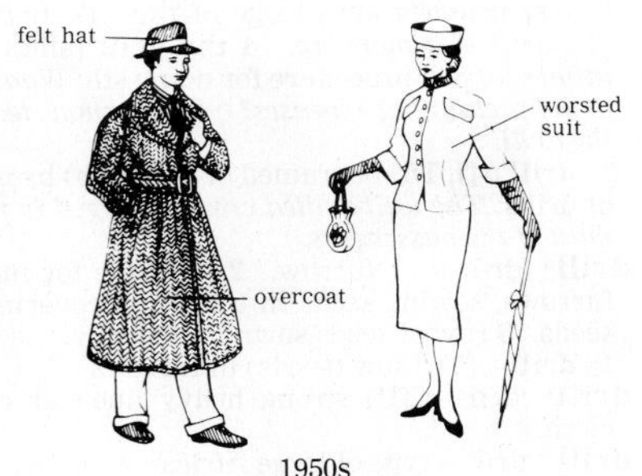

1950s

1960s

attract attention and admiration, esp from the opposite sex. (be) **dressed up to the nines** very elaborately dressed. **mutton dressed as lamb** ⇨ MUTTON. 12 (phr v) **dress sb down** scold sb; tell sb off. **dress up** wear one's best clothes: *Don't bother to dress up — come as you are.* **dress (sb) up (in sth/as sb/sth)** put on fancy dress, etc: *Children love dressing up.* ○ *dress (up) as a fairy, bandit, pirate, etc* ○ *They were dressed up in Victorian clothes.* **dress sth up** make sth seem better or different by careful presentation: *The facts are quite clear; it's no use trying to dress them up.* ○ *rumours dressed up as hard news.*

□ ˌ**dressing** ˈ**down** *n* severe scolding: *give sb/get a (good) dressing down.*

dressage /ˈdresɑːʒ/ *n* [U] (**a**) training a horse to perform various movements that show its obedience to its rider. (**b**) display of such actions in a competition.

dresser[1] /ˈdresə(r)/ *n* **1** (used with an *adj*) person who dresses in a specified way: *a smart, scruffy, snappy, etc dresser.* **2** (in a theatre) person who helps actors put on their costumes. **3** (*medical*) person who helps a surgeon during an operation.

dresser[2] /ˌdresə(r)/ *n* **1** (*esp Brit*) piece of kitchen furniture with shelves for dishes and cupboards below. ⇨ illus at FURNITURE. **2** (*US*) chest of drawers with a mirror on top.

dressing /ˈdresɪŋ/ *n* **1** [U] action of putting on clothes, bandaging wounds, etc: *Dressing always takes her such a long time.* **2** [C, U] bandage, ointment, etc for treating a wound: *apply, change a dressing.* **3** [C, U] sauce for food, esp a mixture of oil and vinegar for salads: *salad dressing.* **4** [U] (*US*) = STUFFING.

□ ˈ**dressing-gown** *n* (*US* usu **bathrobe**, **robe**) loose gown worn indoors, usu before dressing.

ˈ**dressing-room** *n* room for changing one's clothes, esp one where an actor puts on his costume. ⇨ illus at THEATRE.

ˈ**dressing-table** *n* piece of bedroom furniture with a mirror and drawers, used esp by women when they dress, make up, etc. ⇨ illus at FURNITURE.

dressy /ˈdresɪ/ *adj* (**-ier**, **-iest**) (*infml*) **1** (of a person) (fond of) wearing stylish or showy clothes: *They're a very dressy couple.* **2** (of clothes) elegant or elaborate, to be worn on special occasions: *You can't wear that to the reception — it's not dressy enough.*

drew *pt* of DRAW[2].

drey /dreɪ/ *n* squirrel's nest.

Dreyer /ˈdreɪə(r)/ Carl Theodor (1889-1968), Danish film director. His silent masterpiece, *The Passion of Joan of Arc*, is famous for the psychological intensity it brought to the early cinema.

Dreyfus /ˈdreɪfəs/ Alfred (1859-1935), French army officer who in 1894 was falsely accused of spying for Germany and imprisoned. After a long campaign his supporters, including the novelist Emile Zola, showed that he had been the victim of anti-Jewish feeling, and that the government had tried to cover up the mistakes it made in prosecuting him. He was then released.

dribble /ˈdrɪbl/ *v* **1** [I, Ipr] allow saliva to run from the mouth: *The baby's just dribbled down my tie.* **2** [I, Ipr, Ip, Tn, Tn·pr] (cause a liquid to) fall in drops or a thin stream: *water dribbling out (of a tap)* ○ *Dribble the oil into the beaten egg yolks.* **3** [I, Ipr, Tn, Tn·pr] (in football, hockey, etc) move (the ball) forward with repeated slight touches: *He dribbled (the ball) past the goalie to score.*

▷ **dribble** *n* (usu *sing*) **1** trickle: *a thin dribble of oil.* **2** act of dribbling a ball. **3** very small amount of a liquid: *There's only a dribble of coffee left, I'm afraid.*

driblet /ˈdrɪblɪt/ *n* small amount: *in driblets*, ie a little at a time.

dribs /drɪbz/ *n* [pl] (idm) **in** ˌ**dribs and** ˈ**drabs** (*infml*) in small amounts: *She paid me in dribs and drabs, not all at once.*

dried *pt, pp* of DRY[2].

drier[1] *compar* of DRY[1].

drier[2] ⇨ DRY[2].

drift[1] /drɪft/ *n* **1** [U] drifting movement: *the drift of the tide, current, wind, etc.* **2** [C] (*fig*) continuous uncontrolled movement or tendency towards sth bad: *a slow drift into debt, war, crisis, etc.* **3** [U] practice of being inactive and waiting for things to happen: *Is the Government's policy one of drift?* **4** [sing] (of speech, writing, etc) general meaning or sense; gist: *My German isn't very good, but I got the general drift of what she said.* **5** [C] (**a**) mass of sth, esp snow or sand, piled up by the wind: *deep snow-drifts.* (**b**) (*geology*) material deposited by the wind, the action of water, etc. **6** [U] deposits of earth, gravel, rock, etc left behind by a glacier. **7** [U] = DRIFTAGE. **8** [C] passage dug into the side of a mountain to allow minerals to be mined: [attrib] *a* ˈ*drift mine.* **9** (*S African*) shallow place where a river can be crossed; ford: *the battle of Rorke's Drift.*

▷ **driftage** /-ɪdʒ/ *n* [U] deviation by a ship from a set course, due to currents, winds, etc.

drift[2] /drɪft/ *v* **1** [I, Ipr, Ip] be carried along gently by a current of air or water: *We switched off the motor and started to drift (along).* ○ *The boat drifted down the river.* **2** [I, Ipr, Ip] (of snow, sand, etc) be piled into drifts by the wind: *Some roads are closed owing to drifting.* **3** [Tn, Tn·pr, Tn·p] cause (sth) to drift: *The logs are drifted downstream to the mill.* ○ *The wind drifted the snow into a high bank, blocking the road.* **4** [I, Ipr, Ip] (of people) move casually or aimlessly: *The crowds drifted away from the stadium.* ○ *She finally drifted in two hours after everyone else.* ○ (*fig*) *He doesn't want a career, he's just drifting.* ○ *I didn't mean to be a teacher — I sort of drifted into it.* ○ *They used to be friends, but now they've drifted apart.*

▷ **drifter** *n* **1** (*usu derog*) aimless or rootless person: *He's just a drifter — he can't settle down anywhere.* **2** boat used for fishing with a drift-net.

□ ˈ**drift-ice** *n* [U] masses of broken ice floating in the sea, a river, etc.

ˈ**drift-net** *n* large net into which fish move with the tide.

ˈ**drift-wood** *n* [U] wood floating on the sea or washed ashore by it.

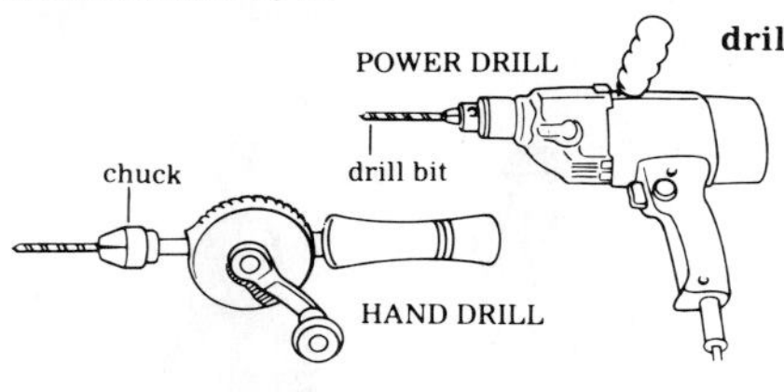

drill[1] /drɪl/ *n* tool or machine with a detachable pointed end for making holes: *a dentist's drill* ○ *a pneumatic drill.* Cf BIT[2] 2.

▷ **drill** *v* [I, Ipr, Tn, Tn·pr] make (a hole, etc) in some substance, esp with a drill: *drill for oil* ○ *They're drilling a new tunnel under the Thames.*

drill[2] /drɪl/ *n* **1** [U] training in military exercises: *New recruits have three hours of drill a day.* **2** (**a**) [U] thorough training by practical and usu repetitive exercises: *regular drill to establish good habits.* (**b**) [C] such an exercise: *pronunci*ˈ*ation drills.* **3** (**a**) [U] procedures to be followed in an emergency: ˈ*lifeboat drill.* (**b**) [C] practice session to test people's knowledge of this: *There'll be a* ˈ*fire-drill this morning.* **4 the drill** [sing] (*Brit infml*) correct procedure for doing sth: *What's the drill for claiming expenses?* ○ *learn, know, teach sb the drill.*

▷ **drill** *v* [I, Tn] be trained or train (sb) by means of drills: *The well-drilled crew managed to rescue most of the passengers.*

drill[3] /drɪl/ *n* **1** furrow. **2** machine for making furrows, sowing seeds in them and covering the seeds. **3** row of seeds sown in this way.

▷ **drill** *v* [Tn] sow (seeds) in furrows.

drill[4] /drɪl/ *n* [U] strong heavy linen or cotton cloth.

drill[5] /drɪl/ *n* type of large African monkey.

drily ⇨ DRY[1].

drink[1] /drɪŋk/ *n* **1** (**a**) [U, C] liquid for drinking: *food and drink* ○ *fizzy drinks.* ⇨ article. (**b**) [C] amount of liquid drunk or served: *a drink of water.* **2** (**a**) [U] alcoholic liquor: *Isn't there any drink in the house?* (**b**) [C] amount of this drunk or served: *How about a quick drink?* ○ *Drinks are on me*, ie I will pay for them. ○ *He's had one drink too many*, ie He is slightly drunk. **3** [U] habit of drinking too much alcohol: *Drink is a growing problem among the young.* ○ *take to drink because of domestic problems.* **4 the drink** [sing] (*sl*) the sea: *We crash-landed in the drink.* **5** (idm) **be the** ˌ**worse for** ˈ**drink** be very drunk. **the demon drink** ⇨ DEMON. **drive sb to drink** ⇨ DRIVE[1]. **meat and drink to sb** ⇨ MEAT.

drink[2] /drɪŋk/ *v* (*pt* **drank** /dræŋk/, *pp* **drunk** /drʌŋk/) **1** [I, Tn] take (liquid) into the mouth and swallow: *Some horses were drinking at a trough.* ○ *He drank a pint of milk in one go.* **2** [Tn, Tn·p] ~ **sth (in/up)** (of plants, the soil, etc) take in, absorb (usu water). **3** [I] take alcohol: *He never drinks.* ○ *They drink too much.* ○ *Don't drink and drive!* **4** [Tn·pr, Cn·a] bring (oneself) to a specified state by taking alcohol: *You're drinking yourself to death.* ○ (*infml*) *They drank themselves stupid.* **5** (idm) **drink sb's** ˈ**health/drink a health to sb** (*fml*) express one's respect or good wishes for sb, by drinking a toast. **drink like a** ˈ**fish** (*infml*) habitually drink large quantities of alcohol. **drink/drain sth to the dregs** ⇨ DREGS. **drink sb under the** ˈ**table** (*infml*) drink more alcohol than sb else without becoming as drunk. **eat, drink and be merry** ⇨ EAT. **you can take, etc a horse to water, but you can't make him drink** ⇨ HORSE. **6** (phr v) **drink sth down/up** drink the whole or the rest of sth, esp quickly: *I know the medicine tastes nasty, but drink it down.* ○ (*Brit*) *drinking-*ˈ*up time*, ie time allowed for finishing drinks before a public house closes. **drink sth in** watch or listen to sth with great pleasure or interest: *They stood drinking in the beauty of the landscape.* **drink (sth) to sb/sth** express good wishes to sb/sth by drinking (a toast): *drink to sb's health, happiness, prosperity, etc* ○ *Let's drink to the success of your plans.* ○ *I'll drink to that!* ie I agree.

▷ **drinkable** *adj* suitable or safe for drinking: *Is this water drinkable?* ○ (*fig*) *a drinkable* (ie pleasant but not particularly good) *wine.*

drinker *n* person who drinks (usu too much) alcohol: *a terrible/heavy/hardened/serious drinker.*

drinking *n* [U]: *Drinking is known to be harmful.* ○ [attrib] *a* ˈ*drinking-bout.*

□ ˈ**drinking-fountain** *n* device supplying drinking-water in a public place.

ˈ**drinking-song** *n* song, usu about the pleasures of drinking, to be sung at drinkers' parties.

ˈ**drinking-water** *n* [U] water safe for drinking.

drip[1] /drɪp/ *v* (**-pp-**) **1** (**a**) [Ipr, Ip] fall in drops: *Rain was dripping (down) from the trees.* (**b**) [Tn, Tn·pr] let (liquid) fall in drops: *Is that roof still dripping?* ○ *a dripping tap* ○ *He was dripping blood (onto the floor).* **2** (idm) **be dripping with sth** be full of or covered with sth: *His letter was dripping with compliments.* ○ *dripping with jewels.* **dripping/wringing wet** ⇨ WET.

□ ˌ**drip-**ˈ**dry** *adj* (of a garment) able to dry quickly when hung up to drip: *a* ˌ*drip-dry* ˈ*shirt,* ˈ*fabric.*

NOTE ON USAGE: **Drip, leak, ooze, run, seep** indicate the way in which a liquid escapes from a container or tap. Most (not **seep**) also indicate the way in which a container or tap allows a liquid to escape. **1 Drip** = (allow sth to) fall in regular drops: *Water is dripping from the pipe. The pipe is dripping (water).* **2 Leak** = (allow sth to) get out (through a hole in sth): *Wine is leaking from the barrel. The barrel is leaking (wine).* **3 Ooze** = (allow sth to) move slowly (out of sth) because thick: *Blood is oozing from the wound. The wound is oozing (blood).* **4 Run** = (allow sth to) flow continuously (from sth): *Water is running from the tap. The tap is running.* **5 Seep** = move slowly (through a small opening in sth): *Oil is seeping from the engine.*

drip[2] /drɪp/ *n* **1** (**a**) [sing] series of drops of falling liquid: *the steady drip of water from a leaky tap.* (**b**)

Drink

By tradition, the British national drink is tea. It is drunk not only on its own but with or after meals, from breakfast to supper and from early in the morning (often in bed) to last thing at night. It has given its name to the characteristically British meal, tea, either 'afternoon tea' or 'high tea', meaning the meal itself rather than just a cup of tea or 'cuppa'. The traditional way to make tea is in a teapot, which is first warmed with hot water. When the pot is warm, very hot water is poured onto the tea-leaves, and the tea is allowed to 'brew' for a few minutes before being poured out. Most people drink tea with milk and many add sugar.

In recent times coffee has become much more popular and for many people has replaced tea as the usual drink. It has always been served as an after-dinner drink, when it is often drunk black, ie without milk, and cafés and coffee shops serve 'morning coffee' in the middle of the morning. Other hot drinks are those made with milk, eg cocoa, hot chocolate and drinks sold under brand names such as Horlicks or Ovaltine. They are often drunk as a non-alcoholic 'nightcap', especially in winter.

Children often drink milk when adults drink tea or coffee. Milk used to be provided free in all schools as a mid-morning drink. It has been advertised with the slogan 'Drinka pinta milka day' (Drink a pint of milk a day) and a pint of milk is often called a 'pinta'. Fruit drinks of all kinds are also popular with children. They include fruit juice, squash and fizzy drinks, often sold in cans.

The trend towards healthier eating and drinking has brought an increase in the sales of mineral water, and water from many springs in Britain is now sold as well as imported brands. Sales of low-alcohol and alcohol-free beers and wines have also increased.

Among alcoholic drinks, beer is traditionally the most popular in Britain, especially with men. It is the main drink served in pubs, in pints or half-pints and is associated with leisure and conviviality. There are a number of different types, from the weakest, known as 'mild' to the strongest, called 'bitter'. 'A pint of best bitter' is a common order in a pub. Traditional draught beer is served from the barrel by means of a pump. The more modern type of beer is called keg beer. It is usually served colder than draught beer, using carbon dioxide so that it is also more fizzy. CAMRA, the Campaign for Real Ale, is an association that supports traditional draught beer, which is also being replaced by canned beer, especially lager. Stout, a dark type of beer, is also popular, especially in Ireland. Shandy, beer mixed with lemonade or ginger beer, is also served in pubs. Cider, made from apples, is another traditionally popular drink, especially in Devon, Somerset and Herefordshire, where it is made.

Wine has for centuries been imported to Britain from France, but it is only in recent years that wine drinking has become common. Wine is now imported from many other countries including Spain, Italy, Germany, the USA and Australia and is also produced in small but increasing quantities in southern England. Sherry, imported from Spain, is commonly drunk before a meal, and port, imported from Portugal, is often drunk at the end of a meal, especially a formal one, and at Christmas-time.

Whisky is not only a popular drink in Britain. It is one of the country's major exports. There are over a hundred distilleries in Scotland and more than 80 per cent of what they produce is exported. Whisky is often drunk diluted with water or soda water and is more often drunk by men than women. A glass of whisky and soda is a traditional 'nightcap'. Gin is often mixed with tonic water or with fruit drinks such as lime or orange. Less traditional but popular mixtures are rum and Coca Cola or vodka and orange juice. Brandy and fruit-flavoured liqueurs are sometimes drunk at the end of a meal with coffee.

There are high taxes on alcoholic drinks in Britain. People who make their own wine and beer can avoid paying these taxes, but it is illegal to sell home-made alcoholic drinks. Shops need a special licence to sell alcoholic drinks and there are laws that restrict the hours when alcohol may be sold. It is illegal to sell alcohol to anyone under the age of 18, either in a shop or in a bar or restaurant.

In the USA there are also legal restrictions on the sale of spirits, but not of wine or beer, which is by far the most popular alcoholic drink. In many states it is illegal to sell spirits to people under the age of 21. As in Britain, there are high taxes on alcohol. During the period of Prohibition (1920-33) it was illegal to make or sell alcoholic drinks in the USA, but the ban on alcohol led to the rise of organized crime as an illicit trade developed.

With the trend towards healthier living, cocktails, ie mixtures such as gin and dry vermouth (called a Martini) or whisky and dry vermouth (called a Manhattan) have become less fashionable, and long drinks like spritzers (a mixture of white wine and soda water) are becoming more popular. These are also called wine coolers.

Soft drinks are as popular in the USA as in Britain and Coca Cola is regarded throughout the world as a typically American drink. Drinks made with milk, especially milk shakes, are also popular.

The main wine-growing area in the USA is California but, as in Britain, wine is also imported from many countries in Europe and elsewhere.

[C] any one of these drops: *The roof is leaking — fetch a bucket to catch the drips.* **2** [C] (*medical*) device that lets (liquid food, medicine, etc) directly into a patient's vein: *put sb on a drip*, ie fit such a device to a patient. **3** [C] (*sl*) weak or boring person: *Don't be such a drip! Come and join in the fun.*

□ ˈ**drip-feed** *n* (use of) a drip²(2). — *v* (*pt, pp* **drip-fed**) [Tn] give, a person or an animal, liquid food, medicine, blood, etc using a drip-feed.

dripping /ˈdrɪpɪŋ/ (*US* also **drippings**) *n* [U] fat melted out of roast meat.

□ ˈ**dripping-pan** *n* pan in which dripping collects during roasting.

drive¹ /draɪv/ *v* (*pt* **drove** /drəʊv/, *pp* **driven** /ˈdrɪvn/) **1** (**a**) [I, Tn] (be able to) operate (a vehicle or locomotive) and direct its course: *Can you drive?* ○ *He drives a taxi*, ie That is his job. ○ *I drive* (ie own) *a Jaguar.* (**b**) [I, Ipr, Ip] come or go somewhere in a car, van, etc: *Did you drive*, ie come by car? ○ *I drive to work.* ○ *Don't stop — drive on!* ⇨ Usage at TRAVEL. (**c**) [Tn, Tn·pr, Tn·p] take (sb) somewhere in a car, taxi, etc: *Could you drive me to the station?* **2** [Tn, Tn·pr, Tn·p] cause (animals or people) to move in some direction by shouts, blows, threats, etc: *some cattle being driven by a man on a horse* ○ *drive sheep into a field* ○ *They drove the enemy back*, ie forced them to retreat. ○ (*fig*) *I was driven out of the club.* **3** [Tn, Tn·pr, Tn·p] (of wind or water) carry (sth) along: *Huge waves drove the yacht onto the rocks.* ○ *dead leaves driven along by the wind.* **4** [I, Ipr] move rapidly or violently: *driving rain, hail, snow, etc* ○ *The waves drove against the shore.* **5** [Tn·pr] (**a**) force (sth) to go in a specified direction or into a specified position: *drive a nail into wood, a stake into the ground, etc* ○ (*fig*) *drive a proposal through Parliament* ○ *She is the driving force behind* (ie Her energy and forcefulness are responsible for) *the company's success.* (**b**) construct (sth) with difficulty: *drive a new motorway across a mountain range* ○ *They drove a tunnel through the rock.* **6** (**a**) [Tn, Tn·p] force (sb) to act: *A man driven by jealousy is capable of anything.* ○ *The urge to survive drove them on.* (**b**) [Tn·pr, Cn·a, Cn·t] cause or compel (sb) to be in a specified state or do a specified thing: *drive sb crazy/to insanity/out of his mind* ○ *Hunger drove her to steal.* (**c**) [Tn] make (sb) work very hard, esp too hard: *Unless he stops driving himself like this he'll have a breakdown.* ○ *He drives the team relentlessly.* **7** [I, Ipr, Tn, Tn·pr] (*sport*) hit and send (a ball, etc) forward with force, esp in tennis, golf or cricket: *drive (the ball) into the rough* ○ *He drives beautifully*, ie plays this stroke well. **8** [Tn esp passive] (of electricity or some other power) keep (machinery) going: *a steam-driven engine.* **9** (idm) **be driving at** (always with *what* as the object) be trying to do or say: *What are you driving at?* ○ *I wish I knew what they were really driving at.* **drive a coach and horses through sth** disregard (eg a law or rule) in an obvious and a serious way without being punished, usu because of a loophole. **drive a hard ˈbargain** insist on the best possible price, arrangements, etc when negotiating with sb. **drive sth home (to sb)** make sb realize sth, esp by saying it often, loudly, angrily, etc: *drive one's point home* ○ *I drove home to him that he must be here by ten.* **drive sth into sb's ˈhead** make sb remember sth, esp with difficulty. **drive sb to ˈdrink** (*esp joc*) make sb so worried, frustrated, etc that he starts drinking too much alcohol: *Working here is enough to drive anyone to drink.* **drive a wedge between A and B** make (friends, colleagues, etc) quarrel or start disliking each other. **let drive (at sb)** hit or aim blows at sb. **needs must when the devil drives** ⇨ NEEDS (NEED³). **pure as the driven snow** ⇨ PURE. **10** (phr v) **drive sb back on sth** force sb to use (resources, methods, etc) he would prefer to avoid using. **drive off** (**a**) (of a driver, car, etc) leave. (**b**) (in golf) hit the ball to begin a game. **drive sb off** take sb away in a car, etc. **drive sb/sth off** defeat or chase away (an enemy or an attack).

□ ˈ**drive-in** *n* (*US*) place, esp a cinema or restaurant, where one is entertained, served, etc without leaving one's car: [attrib] *a drive-in bank.*

ˈ**driving-belt** *n* belt that is turned by an engine, etc and that then makes machinery turn.

ˈ**driving-licence** *n* (*US* **driver's license**) licence to drive a motor vehicle.

ˈ**driving school** school for teaching people to drive motor vehicles.

ˈ**driving-test** *n* test that must be passed to obtain a driving-licence.

ˈ**driving-wheel** *n* wheel that communicates power to other parts of a machine, or to which power is applied.

drive² /draɪv/ *n* **1** [C] journey in a car, van, etc:

Let's go for a drive in the country. ○ *He took her out for a drive.* ○ *a forty minute, an hour's, a fifteen mile, etc drive.* **2** [C] **(a)** (*US* usu ˈ**driveway**) private road, etc by which vehicles can approach a house from the road or street. ⇨ illus at HOME. **(b)** (*abbr* **Dr**) (esp in names) road in a town, with houses: *They live at 26 Manor Drive.* **3** [C] (*sport*) stroke made by driving in tennis, golf, cricket, etc. **4** [U] energy; ability to get things done: *Our sales people need determination and drive.* **5** [C, U] (*psychology*) desire to attain a goal or satisfy a need: *(a) strong sexual drive.* **6** [C] **(a)** organized effort or campaign to achieve sth: *a ˈsales, a reˈcruiting, an ˈexport, etc drive.* **(b)** series of military attacks. **7** [C] (*Brit*) social gathering to play card-games: *a ˈbridge/ˈwhist drive.* **8** [C, U] (apparatus for the) transmission of power to machinery: *electric, belt, fluid, etc drive* ○ *front-/rear-/four-wheel ˈdrive*, ie where the engine makes the front, rear, or all four wheels turn ○ *a car with left-hand drive*, ie with the steering-wheel and other controls on the left ○ [attrib] *the ˈdrive shaft.*

drivel /ˈdrɪvl/ *n* [U] silly nonsense: *Don't talk drivel!*

▷ **drivel** *v* (**-ll-**; *US* **-l-**) **1** [I, Ipr, Ip] ~ **(on) (about sth)** talk or write drivel: *He was drivelling on about the meaning of life.* **2** [I] have saliva running out of one's mouth; dribble.

driven *pp* of DRIVE[1].

driver /ˈdraɪvə(r)/ *n* **1** person who drives a vehicle: *a bus-, lorry-, taxi-driver* ○ *a learner driver*, ie sb who has not yet passed a driving-test. **2** (*golf*) club with a wooden head used for driving the ball from the tee. **3** person who drives animals. **4** (idm) **a back-seat driver** ⇨ BACK SEAT (BACK[2]). **(be) in the ˈdriver's seat** in control.

□ ˈ**driver's license** (*US*) = DRIVING-LICENCE (DRIVE[1]).

drizzle /ˈdrɪzl/ *v* [I] rain in many fine drops: *It had been drizzling all day.*

▷ **drizzle** *n* [U] fine misty rain. **drizzly** /ˈdrɪzlɪ/ *adj*: *a cold drizzly day.*

drogue /drəʊg/ *n* funnel-shaped piece of material used as a wind-sock, sea anchor, target, etc.

□ ˈ**drogue-parachute** *n* small parachute used to pull a larger one from its pack.

droll /drəʊl/ *adj* amusing in an odd or a quaint way: *a droll story* ○ (*ironic*) *So he thinks I'm going to apologize? How very droll!*

▷ **drollery** /-ərɪ/ *n* [C, U] (remark, etc showing) quaint humour.

dromedary /ˈdrɒmədərɪ; *US* -ədərɪ/ *n* animal of the camel family with only one hump. ⇨ illus at CAMEL.

drone[1] /drəʊn/ *n* **1** male honey-bee. Cf WORKER 3. **2** (*Brit derog*) person who does no useful work and lives on others.

drone[2] /drəʊn/ *v* **1** [I, Ip] make a low humming sound: *An aircraft droned overhead.* **2** [I, Ip, Tn, Tn·p] talk, sing or say (sth) in a flat monotonous tone of voice: *The chairman droned on for hours.* ○ *drone (out) a hymn.*

▷ **drone** *n* (usu *sing*) **1** low humming sound: *the drone of bees* ○ *the drone of a distant aircraft.* **2** monotonous talk: *a steady drone from the lecturer.* **3** (*music*) sustained bass note or chord, eg in bagpipe music.

drool /dru:l/ *v* **1** [I] let saliva flow from the mouth; dribble. **2** [I, Ipr] ~ **(over sb/sth)** (*derog*) show in a ridiculous way how much one enjoys or admires sb/sth: *drooling over a photo of a pop star.*

droop /dru:p/ *v* [I, Ipr, Ip] bend or hang downwards through tiredness or weakness: *flowers drooping for lack of water* ○ *Her head drooped sadly.* ○ (*fig*) *His spirits drooped at the news*, ie He became sad.

▷ **droopy** *adj* (**-ier, -iest**).

drop[1] /drɒp/ *n* **1** [C] small rounded or pear-shaped mass of liquid: *ˈrain-drops, ˈtear-drops, etc* ○ *drops of rain, dew, sweat, condensation, etc* ○ *Pour the oil in drops into the mixture.* **2** **drops** [pl] liquid medicine poured a drop at a time into the ears, eyes or nose: *comfort drops*, eg used to make contact lenses easier to wear. **3** [C esp *sing*] small quantity of liquid: *I like my tea with just a drop of milk.* ○ (*fig*) *He's had a drop too much*, ie He is drunk. **4** [C] thing shaped like a drop, esp a sweet or a hanging ornament. **5** [sing] steep or vertical distance: *There was a sheer drop of five hundred feet to the rocks below.* **6** [sing] (*fig*) decrease: *a drop in prices, temperatures, etc* ○ *a big drop in the number of people out of work.* **7** [C] act of dropping; thing that drops or is dropped: *Drops of supplies are being made to villages still cut off by the snow.* **8** [C] place where sth (eg stolen goods or a message for a spy) is hidden for sb else to collect. **9 the drop** [sing] (*sl*) execution by hanging: *He's for the drop!* ie He will be hanged. **10** [C usu *sing*] (*dated sl*) bribe. **11** (idm) **at the ˌdrop of a ˈhat** without delay, hesitation or good reason: *You can't expect me to move my home at the drop of a hat.* **(only) a ˌdrop in the ˈbucket/ˈocean** a quantity too small to make any improvement: *Aid to the Third World is at present little more than a drop in the ocean.* **get/have the drop on sb** (*infml*) get/have an advantage over sb.

▷ **droplet** /ˈdrɒplɪt/ *n* small drop.

□ ˈ**drop-goal** *n* (in Rugby football) goal scored with a drop-kick.

ˈ**drop-hammer**, ˈ**drop-forge**, ˈ**drop-press** *ns* machine for shaping or stamping metal, using the force of a dropped weight.

ˈ**drop-head** canvas roof on a car that can be folded back: [attrib] *a ˌdrop-head ˈcoupé.*

ˈ**drop-kick** *n* (in Rugby football) kick made as the ball bounces after being dropped to the ground. — *v* [I, Tn].

ˈ**drop scone** (*Brit*) small flat cake made by dropping a small amount of batter onto a hot cooking surface.

ˈ**drop shot (a)** (in tennis and badminton) shot hit so that the ball bounces close to the net after going over it. **(b)** (in squash and rackets) similar shot that drops close to the wall after hitting it.

drop[2] /drɒp/ *v* (**-pp-**) **1** [I, Ipr, Tn, Tn·pr] fall or allow (sth) to fall (by accident): *The bottle dropped and broke.* ○ *The climber slipped and dropped to his death.* ○ *Don't drop that or it'll break!* **2** [I, Ipr, Ip, Tn, Tn·pr, Tn·p] fall or cause (sth) to fall (on purpose): *She dropped to safety from the burning building.* ○ *Medical supplies are being dropped to the stricken area.* ○ *Drop the hammer down to me.* **3** [I, Ipr] (of people and animals) collapse from exhaustion: *I feel ready to drop*, ie very tired. ○ (*fig*) *She expects everyone to work till they drop*, ie very hard. **4** [I, Ipr, Tn, Tn·pr] (cause sth to) become weaker, lower or less: *The wind, temperature, water level, etc has dropped considerably.* ○ *His voice dropped to a whisper.* ○ *The cost of living seems set to drop for the third month in succession.* **5** [I, Ipr, Ip] form a steep or vertical descent: *The cliff drops sharply (away) (to the sea).* **6** [Tn, Tn·pr, Tn·p] ~ **sb/sth (off)** allow sb to get out of a car, etc; deliver sth on the way to somewhere else: *Could you drop me (off) near the post office?* **7** (*infml*) [Dn·n] send (a letter, etc) to sb: *drop sb a postcard.* **8** [Tn, Tn·pr] ~ **sb/sth (from sth)** omit sb/sth (by accident or on purpose): *She's been dropped from the team because of injury.* ○ *Many dated expressions are being dropped from the new dictionary.* **9** [Tn] **(a)** stop seeing (sb): *She's dropped most of her old friends — or they've dropped her!* **(b)** give up (a habit, custom, etc). **(c)** stop doing or discussing (sth): *Drop everything and come here!* ○ *Let's drop the formalities: call me Mike.* ○ *Look, can we just drop the subject?* **10** [Tn] (*infml*) lose (money), esp by gambling, etc: *I hear they've dropped over ten thousand on the deal.* **11** [I, Tn] (*sl*) take (illegal drugs) orally. **12** (idm) **die/drop/fall like flies** ⇨ FLY[1]. **ˌdrop one's ˈaitches** omit the 'h' sound from places in words where it is pronounced by educated speakers (often thought a sign of lower-class social origins). **drop a ˈbrick/ˈclanger** (*infml*) say or do sth that is insulting or embarrassing without realizing that it is. **drop ˈdead (a)** (*infml*) die suddenly and unexpectedly. **(b)** (*sl*) (used to tell sb forcefully and rudely to stop bothering one, interfering, etc). **drop a ˈhint (to sb)/drop (sb) a hint** make a suggestion indirectly or tactfully. **drop/dump sth in sb's lap** ⇨ LAP[1]. **drop sb a line** write a (usu short) letter to sb: *Drop me a line to say when you're coming.* **drop ˈnames** (*infml*) mention famous or powerful people one is supposed to know, so as to impress others. **drop a ˈstitch** (in knitting) let a stitch slip off the needle. **one's jaw drops** ⇨ JAW. **let sb/sth ˈdrop** do or say nothing more about sb/sth: *I suggest we let the matter drop.* **the penny drops** ⇨ PENNY. **13** (phr v) **drop back; drop behind (sb)** move or fall into position behind sb else: *The two lovers dropped back so as to be alone.* ○ (*fig*) *Britain is increasingly dropping behind her competitors in this field.* **drop by/in/over/round; drop in on sb; drop into sth** pay a casual visit (to a person or place): *Drop round some time.* ○ *I thought I'd drop in on you while I was passing.* ○ *Sorry we're late — we dropped into a pub on the way.* ⇨ Usage at VISIT. **drop off** (*infml*) **(a)** fall into a light sleep; doze: *I dropped off and missed the end of the film.* **(b)** become fewer or less: *Traffic has dropped off since the by-pass opened.* **drop on sb** scold or punish sb severely. **drop out (of sth) (a)** withdraw (from an activity, a contest, etc): *Since his defeat he's dropped out of politics.* **(b)** leave school, university, etc without finishing one's courses: *She got a scholarship to Cambridge but dropped out a year later.* **(c)** withdraw from conventional society.

▷ **dropper** *n* instrument consisting of a short glass tube with a rubber bulb at one end for measuring out drops of medicine or other liquids.

droppings *n* [pl] excrement of animals or birds.

□ ˈ**drop-out** *n* person who withdraws from conventional society.

dropsy /ˈdrɒpsɪ/ *n* [U] disease in which watery fluid collects in the body. ▷ **dropsical** /ˈdrɒpsɪkl/ *adj.*

dross /drɒs; *US* drɔ:s/ *n* [U] **(a)** scum of waste matter on melted metals. **(b)** (*fig*) least valuable, attractive, etc part of sth: *The best players go off to the big clubs, leaving us the dross.*

drought /draʊt/ *n* [C, U] (period of) continuous dry weather, esp when there is not enough water for people's needs: *areas of Africa affected by drought.*

drove[1] *pt* of DRIVE[1].

drove[2] /drəʊv/ *n* **1** herd of cattle, flock of sheep, etc being made to move from one place to another. **2** (usu *pl*) (*fig*) moving crowd of people or large number of things: *droves of sightseers* ○ *Letters of protest arrived in droves.*

▷ **drover** *n* person who moves cattle, sheep, etc to market or to new pastures.

drown /draʊn/ *v* **1 (a)** [I, Ipr] die in water (or other liquid) because one is unable to breathe: *a drowning man.* **(b)** [Tn, Tn·pr] kill (a person or animal) in this way: *drown a kitten.* **2** [Tn, Tn·pr] ~ **sth (in sth)** flood or drench sth: *a drowned valley* ○ *He drowned his meal in gravy.* **3** [Tn, Tn·p] ~ **sb/sth (out)** (of a sound) be louder than (another sound) and prevent it being heard: *She turned up the radio to drown (out) the noise of the traffic.* **4** (idm) **drown one's ˈsorrows (in drink)** (*esp joc*) get drunk in order to forget one's troubles. **(look) like a drowned ˈrat** soaking wet and miserable.

drowse /draʊz/ *v* **1** [I] be half asleep. **2** (phr v) **drowse sth away** spend (time) half asleep: *drowse away a hot afternoon.*

▷ **drowse** *n* [sing] state of being drowsy: *in a drowse.*

drowsy /ˈdraʊzɪ/ *adj* (**-ier, -iest**) **1** half asleep; feeling sleepy: *I'd just woken up and was still drowsy.* ○ *This drug can make you drowsy.* **2** making one feel sleepy: *drowsy summer weather.*

▷ **drowsily** /-əlɪ/ *adv*: *murmur sth drowsily.* **drowsiness** *n* [U].

drubbing /ˈdrʌbɪŋ/ *n* (idm) **give sb/get a good ˈdrubbing (a)** beat sb/be beaten soundly. **(b)** (*fig*) defeat sb/be defeated thoroughly.

drudge /drʌdʒ/ *n* person who has to do long hard boring jobs.

▷ **drudge** *v* [I, Ipr, Ip] ~ **(away) (at sth)** do jobs of that kind.

drudgery /-ərɪ/ *n* [U] hard boring work: *the endless drudgery of housework* ○ *soulless drudgery.*

drug /drʌg/ *n* **1** substance used as or in a medicine:

Drugs

In both Britain and North America the misuse of drugs, especially among the young, is a serious problem, because of the damage it causes both socially and physically. There is a high incidence of the use of both heroin and cocaine. Despite moves by the governments of both countries to reduce the illegal import of drugs, they continue to find their way onto the market, where they are sold to addicts for high prices. Customs officers regularly find large quantities of drugs worth millions of pounds when sold to users. Campaigns have been mounted on both sides of the Atlantic to warn people of the dangers of drug abuse.

In the second half of the 1980s the potential damage caused by drug abuse was increased because of AIDS. Many drug users risked contracting and transmitting the HIV virus by sharing needles and syringes. In Britain, government publicity campaigns about the dangers of drug abuse are aimed partly at reducing the spread of AIDS as well as informing young people of the dangers of injecting drugs, including amphetamines.

In sport, there have been cases of the misuse of anabolic steroids to increase physical performance and stamina. As a result of a campaign initiated by the Sports Council, random drug testing of athletes has been introduced and some athletes have been banned from competing as a result.

Drug addicts are treated at hospitals, often as out-patients, and many hospitals have special drug dependence units. Family doctors also treat cases of addiction, and are now conscious of the addictive nature of tranquillizers, which in the past have been very freely prescribed.

There are fashions in drug abuse as in most other things. In the 1960s the use of hallucinogenic drugs like marijuana (or 'pot') and LSD was associated with rebellion by young people against bourgeois society, and there was also a link that still exists today between rock music and the use of drugs. In the 1980s sniffing cocaine became fashionable among 'yuppies', successful young people working in the financial services industry in London and New York. Crack, an especially potent form of cocaine that can be smoked or inhaled, was also widely used in the late 1980s. Another recent fashion was the 'acid house party' in which sometimes thousands of young people met, often at a secluded country site, to listen to music and take 'ecstasy', a powerful amphetamine-based drug.

a pain-killing drug ○ *The doctor has put me on drugs*, ie prescribed them for me. **2** substance that affects the nervous system, esp one that is habit-forming, eg cocaine or heroin: *take/use/be on drugs* ○ *peddle/push drugs*. ⇨ article. **3** (idm) **a drug on the ˈmarket** thing that cannot be sold because no one wants it.

▷ **drug** *v* (**-gg-**) [Tn] **1** add a drug(2) to (food or drink). **2** give a drug(1, 2) to (sb), esp to make him unconscious: *in a drugged stupor*.

□ **ˈdrug addict** person who cannot stop taking harmful drugs (DRUG 2). **ˈdrug addiction**.

ˈdrug dealer, ˈdrug pusher person who sells drugs (DRUG 2) illegally.

drugget /ˈdrʌgɪt/ *n* [C, U] (floor-covering made of) coarse woven fabric.

druggist /ˈdrʌgɪst/ *n* (*esp US*) = CHEMIST[1].

drugstore /ˈdrʌgstɔ:(r)/ *n* (*US*) chemist's shop which also sells many kinds of goods and often serves light meals. ⇨ article at SHOP.

Druid /ˈdru:ɪd/ *n* priest of an ancient Celtic religion. ⇨ article at WALES.

drum[1] /drʌm/ *n* **1** (*music*) instrument consisting of a hollow round frame with plastic or skin stretched tightly across the open end(s) which is struck with sticks or the hands: *play the drum(s) in a band*. ⇨ illus at MUSIC. **2** thing shaped like this instrument, eg a barrel for oil, a hollow cylinder on which wire is wound, or the container for clothes in a washing-machine or clothes drier. ⇨ illus at BARREL. **3** = EAR-DRUM (EAR[1]). **4** (idm) **beat the drum** ⇨ BEAT[1].

□ **ˈdrumbeat** *n* (sound of a) stroke on a drum.

ˈdrum brake brake in which curved pads press against the inner cylindrical part of a vehicle's wheel. Cf DISC BRAKE (DISC).

ˈdrumhead part of the drum that is hit.

ˈdrumhead court-ˈmartial trial held during a military operation.

ˈdrum-kit *n* set of drums used in a band, etc.

ˌdrum ˈmajor 1 sergeant who leads a military band when it plays on parade. **2** (*US*) male leader of a marching band. **ˌdrum majoˈrette** /meɪdʒəˈret/ (*esp US*) girl wearing a fancy costume who leads a marching band.

ˈdrumstick *n* **1** stick for playing a drum. ⇨ illus at MUSIC. **2** lower part of the leg of a cooked chicken, turkey, etc.

drum[2] /drʌm/ *v* (**-mm-**) **1** [I] play a drum or drums. **2** [Ipr, Tn, Tn·pr] ~ (**sth**) **on sth** make a drum-like sound on sth; tap or beat (sth) continuously: *drum on the table with one's fingers* ○ *drum one's feet on the floor*. **3** (phr v) **drum sth into sb/into sb's head** make sb remember sth by repeating it often: *Our teacher used to drum our multiplication tables into us.* **drum sb out (of sth)** force sb to leave a group, an organization, etc, often in disgrace: *drummed out of the club, the regiment.* **drum sth up** try hard to get (support, customers, etc): *He's going round firms drumming up interest in the project.*

▷ **drummer** *n* **1** person who plays a drum or drums. **2** (*esp US infml*) commercial traveller.

drumming *n* [U, sing] continuous rhythmical sound: *the steady drumming of the rain on the tin roofs*.

drumlin /ˈdrʌmlɪn/ *n* smooth elongated hill formed by the action of a glacier.

drunk[1] *pp* of DRINK[2].

drunk[2] /drʌŋk/ *adj* **1** [usu pred] excited or confused by alcoholic drink: *be blind/dead* (ie completely) *drunk* ○ *They've put vodka in her fruit juice to get her drunk.* ○ *get drunk on cider*.

📖 Until modern times, the drunk was often presented in cartoons and plays, etc as a figure of fun. He would be typically shown walking unsteadily and slurring his speech, dressed untidily and having a bright red nose. In real life, many communities identified a local inhabitant who liked drinking as the 'town drunk'. Jokes are still made about drunk people but they are now generally thought to be in poor taste.

2 [pred] ~ **with sth** behaving in a strange, often unpleasant, way (because of the excitement of sth): *drunk with power, success, etc.* **3** (idm) **ˌdrunk and ˈdisorderly** (*law*); **ˌdrunk and inˈcapable** behaving in an unpleasant, uncontrolled way while drunk. (**as**) **ˌdrunk as a ˈlord** very drunk. **fighting drunk** ⇨ FIGHT[1].

▷ **drunk** *n* person who is drunk.

drunkard /-əd/ *n* (*fml*) person who often gets drunk; alcoholic.

□ **drunˈkometer** *n* (*US*) = BREATHALYSER.

drunken /ˈdrʌŋkən/ *adj* [attrib] **1** drunk: *a drunken reveller*. **2** who gets drunk regularly: *her drunken boss, husband, etc.* **3** caused by or showing the effects of drink: *a drunken argument, fury, stupor, sleep* ○ *drunken laughter, voices, singing*. ▷ **drunkenly** *adv*: *stagger about drunkenly*. **drunkenness** *n* [U].

drupe /dru:p/ *n* (*botany*) fruit with juicy flesh surrounding a hard stone with a seed, eg an olive or a peach.

Drury Lane /ˌdrʊərɪ ˈleɪn/ street in central London, near *Covent Garden, which contains the Theatre Royal. This dates back to the 17th century, and has associations with the actor David *Garrick and with Nell *Gwynn.

Druse /dru:z/ *n* member of a sect, living mainly in the Lebanon, which is of Muslim origin but also contains elements of Christianity.

dry[1] /draɪ/ *adj* (**drier, driest**) **1** not (or no longer) wet, damp or sticky; without moisture: *Is the washing dry yet?* ○ *Don't use this door until the paint is dry.* ○ *This pastry is too dry — add some water.* **2** with little rainfall: *a dry spell, climate, country* ○ *I hope it stays dry for our picnic.* **3** not supplying liquid: *The wells ran dry.* ○ *The cows are dry*, ie not producing milk. **4** without liquid: *a dry cough*, ie without phlegm ○ *My throat feels dry.* ○ *a dry shampoo*, ie in powder form. **5** (of a country or region) where it is illegal to buy or sell alcoholic drink: *Some parts of Wales are dry on Sundays.* **6** (*infml*) (making one) thirsty: *I'm a bit dry.* ○ *dry work.* **7** [attrib] without butter: *dry bread, toast, etc.* **8** (of wines, etc) not sweet or fruity: *a crisp dry white wine* ○ *a dry sherry*. **9** plain; without anything pleasant or interesting: *They offered no apology, just a dry explanation for the delay.* **10** (of humour) pretending to be serious: *a dry wit.* **11** unemotional; cold: *a dry manner, greeting, tone of voice.* **12** dull; boring: *Government reports tend to make rather dry reading.* **13** (idm) **boil dry** ⇨ BOIL[2]. (**as**) **ˌdry as a ˈbone** completely dry. (**as**) **ˌdry as ˈdust** very boring. **high and dry** ⇨ HIGH[1]. **home and dry** ⇨ HOME[3]. **keep one's powder dry** ⇨ POWDER. **milk/suck sb/sth dry** obtain from sb all the money, help, information, etc he has to give. **not a dry eye in the house** (*joc*) everybody in the audience was crying or deeply affected. ▷ **drily** (also **dryly**) /ˈdraɪlɪ/ *adv*: *'They're not likely to give you money,' he remarked dryly.* **dryness** *n* [U].

□ **ˌdry ˈbattery** electric battery with two or more dry cells.

ˌdry ˈcell cell in which the chemicals are in a firm paste which does not spill.

ˌdry-ˈclean *v* [Tn] clean (clothes, etc) without water, using a solvent which evaporates quickly. **ˌdry-ˈcleaner** *n*: *The blankets are at the dry-cleaner's.* **ˌdry-ˈcleaning** *n* [U].

ˌdry ˈdock dock from which water may be pumped out for work on a ship's bottom: *a ship in dry dock for repairs.*

ˌdry ˈgoods 1 grain, fruit, etc. **2** (*esp US*) clothing, textiles, etc (as opposed to groceries).

ˌdry ˈice solid carbon dioxide (used for refrigerating, theatrical effects, etc).

ˌdry ˈland land as distinct from sea, etc: *I'm no sailor and I couldn't wait to reach dry land.*

ˌdry ˈmeasure measure of capacity for dry goods.

ˈdry-nurse *n* nurse who does not suckle the baby she is caring for.

ˌdry ˈrot 1 decay of wood, causing it to turn to powder. **2** any fungus that causes this. **3** (*fig*) force that gradually spoils eg an organization or moral standards but which is not easily noticed at first.

ˌdry ˈrun (*infml*) rehearsal or practice, eg for a ceremony or procedure: *Let's do/have a dry run.*

ˈdry-shod *adj, adv* without getting one's feet or shoes wet: *go ashore dry-shod.*

ˈdrystone *adj* (of a stone wall) built without

mortar.
ˌ**dry-ˈwalling** *n* [U] building of drystone walls.

dry[2] /draɪ/ *v* (*pt, pp* **dried**) **1** [I, Ip, Tn, Tn·p] (cause sb/sth to) become dry: *Leave the dishes to dry (off).* ○ *Dry your hands on this towel.* **2** [I] (*infml*) (of an actor) forget one's lines. **3** (phr v) **dry (sb) out** (*infml*) treat (sb) or be treated for alcoholism. **dry (sth) out** (cause sth soaked in water, etc to) become completely dry: *Your clothes will take ages to dry out.* **dry up** (**a**) (of rivers, wells, etc) become completely dry. (**b**) (*fig*) (of any source or supply) no longer be available: *If foreign aid dries up the situation will be desperate.* (**c**) (*infml*) stop talking: *Dry up and listen to me.* (**d**) be unable to continue talking, esp because one has forgotten what one was going to say. **dry (sth) up** dry (dishes, cutlery, etc) with a towel after washing them.
▷ **drier** (also **dryer**) /ˈdraɪə(r)/ *n* **1** (esp in compounds) machine that dries: *a ˈclothes drier* ○ *a ˈhair-drier* ○ *a ˈtumble-drier.* **2** substance mixed with paint or varnish to make it dry more quickly.

dryad /ˈdraɪæd/ *n* (in Greek mythology) female spirit living in forests; wood-nymph.

Dryden /ˈdraɪdn/ John (1631-1700), English poet and dramatist who is generally regarded as the greatest English writer of classical tragedies (as perfected in French by *Racine). His best-remembered play is *All for Love*, about Antony and Cleopatra. His name is commonly linked with that of the other leading English literary figure of the period, Alexander *Pope. He was made Poet Laureate in 1688.

DSc /ˌdiː es ˈsiː/ *abbr* Doctor of Science: *have/be a DSc in Physics* ○ *Philip Jones DSc.*

DSO /ˌdiː es ˈəʊ/ *abbr* (*Brit*) (Companion of the) Distinguished Service Order: *be awarded the DSO for bravery* ○ *Robert Hill DSO.*

DSS /ˌdiː es ˈes/ *abbr* (in Britain) Department of Social Security. ⇨ articles at ACCOMMODATION, EMPLOYMENT, SOCIAL SECURITY.

DT /ˌdiː ˈtiː/ (also **DTs** /ˌdiː ˈtiːz/) *abbr* (*infml*) trembling delirium (Latin *delirium tremens*): *have (an attack of) the DTs.*

DTI /ˌdiː tiː ˈaɪ/ *abbr* (in Britain) Department of Trade and Industry.

dual /ˈdjuːəl; *US* ˈduːəl/ *adj* [attrib] having two parts or aspects; double: *his dual role as composer and conductor* ○ *She has dual nationality,* ie is a citizen of two different countries. ▷ **duality** /djuːˈælətɪ; *US* duː-/ *n* [U].
□ ˌ**dual ˈcarriageway** (*Brit*) (*US* **divided highway**) road with a central strip dividing streams of traffic moving in opposite directions.
ˌ**dual-conˈtrol** *adj* (having) two linked sets of controls, allowing operation by either of two people: [attrib] *a* ˌ*dual-control ˈcar,* ie one used for driving lessons, in which the instructor can operate the clutch and brakes.
ˌ**dual-ˈpurpose** *adj* serving two purposes.

dualism /ˈdjuːəlɪzəm/ *n* [U] **1** condition of being dual; duality. **2** religious or philosophical theory based on the existence of two opposite principles (eg good and evil or mind and matter).

dub /dʌb/ *v* (**-bb-**) **1** [Cn·n] make (a man) a knight by touching him on the shoulder with a sword. **2** [Cn·n] give (sb) a nickname: *The papers dubbed them 'The Fab Four'.* **3** [Tn, Tn·pr] ~ **sth (into sth)** create, add to or replace the soundtrack of (a film), esp in a different language: *a dubbed version* ○ *a German film dubbed into English.*

Dubai /duːˈbaɪ/ sheikhdom on the Persian Gulf, one of the *United Arab Emirates; pop approx 419 000; capital Dubai; official language Arabic. It contains an important international airport.

dubbin /ˈdʌbɪn/ *n* [U] thick grease for making leather soft and waterproof.
▷ **dubbin** *v* [Tn] treat (esp boots) with dubbin.

dubiety /djuːˈbaɪətɪ; *US* duː-/ *n* (*fml*) **1** [U] feeling of doubt. **2** [C] matter on which one is uncertain.

dubious /ˈdjuːbɪəs; *US* ˈduː-/ *adj* **1** [esp pred] ~ (**about sth/doing sth**) not certain and slightly suspicious about sth; doubtful: *I remain dubious about her motives.* **2** (*derog*) possibly or probably dishonest, disreputable or risky: *a rather dubious character* ○ *a dubious business venture* ○ *His background is a trifle dubious, to say the least.* **3** uncertain in result; in doubt: *The results of this policy will remain dubious for some time.* **4** (*esp ironic*) of which the value is doubtful; questionable: *a dubious compliment,* ie a disguised insult ○ *She had the dubious honour of being the last woman to be hanged in England.* ▷ **dubiously** *adv.* **dubiousness** *n* [U].

Dublin /ˈdʌblɪn/ capital city of the Republic of Ireland, situated at the mouth of the River Liffey.
▷ **Dubliner** /ˈdʌblɪnə(r)/ *n* native or inhabitant of Dublin.

ducal /ˈdjuːkl; *US* ˈduːkl/ *adj* [usu attrib] of or like a duke.

ducat /ˈdʌkət/ *n* gold coin used in former times in many European countries.

duchess /ˈdʌtʃɪs/ *n* (in titles **Duchess**) **1** wife or widow of a duke. **2** woman who holds ducal rank in her own right.

duchy /ˈdʌtʃɪ/ (also **dukedom** /ˈdjuːkdəm; *US* ˈduːk-/) *n* territory of a duke or duchess.

duck[1] /dʌk/ *n* (*pl* unchanged or ~**s**) **1** (**a**) [C] any of various types of common water-bird, domestic and wild: *ducks waddling about the yard.* ⇨ illus at BIRD. (**b**) [C] female of this. Cf DRAKE. (**c**) [U] its flesh as food: *roast duck.* **2** [C usu *sing*] (also **ducky, ducks**) (*Brit infml*) (as a form of address) dear. **3** [C] (in cricket) batsman's score of nought: *make a/be out for a duck* ○ *break one's duck,* ie score one's first run. **4** (idm) **a dead duck** ⇨ DEAD. **a lame duck** ⇨ LAME. **(take to sth) like a** ˌ**duck to** ˈ**water** without hesitation, fear or difficulty; naturally: *She's taken to teaching like a duck to water.* **a sitting duck** ⇨ SIT. **water off a duck's back** ⇨ WATER[1].
▷ **duckling** /-lɪŋ/ *n* **1** (**a**) [C] young duck. (**b**) [U] its flesh as food. **2** (idm) **an ugly duckling** ⇨ UGLY.
□ ˈ**duck-boards** *n* [pl] boards used to spread one's weight when moving over muddy ground, a weak roof, etc.
ˌ**ducks and** ˈ**drakes** **1** children's game in which flat stones are bounced across the surface of the water. **2** (idm) **play ducks and** ˈ**drakes with sth** spend (esp one's money) in a careless wasteful way.
ˈ**duckweed** *n* [U] plant that forms on the surface of ponds, etc.

duck[2] /dʌk/ *v* **1** [I, Ipr, Ip, Tn, Tn·pr, Tn·p] move (esp one's head) down quickly, to avoid being seen or hit: *I saw the gun and ducked under the window.* ○ *Duck your head down!* **2** [Tn, Tn·pr] push (sb) under water for a short time: *Her sisters ducked her in the river.* **3** [Ipr, Tn] ~ **(out of) sth** (*infml*) avoid or dodge (a duty, responsibility etc): *It's his turn to wash up but he'll try and duck out of it.*
▷ **ducking** *n* thorough soaking: *give sb a ducking,* ie push him into or under the water.

duck[3] /dʌk/ *n* **1** [U] strong linen or cotton cloth. **2 ducks** *n* trousers made of this.

duct /dʌkt/ *n* **1** tube or channel carrying liquid, gas, electric or telephone wires, etc; (esp in an air-conditioning system) tube through which air passes: *One of the air-ducts has become blocked.* **2** tube in the body or in plants through which fluid, etc passes: *ˈtear-ducts.*
□ ˌ**ductless** ˈ**gland** gland from which hormones, etc pass directly into the bloodstream, not through a duct.

ductile /ˈdʌktaɪl; *US* -tl/ *adj* **1** (of metals) that can be pressed, beaten or pulled into fine strands without being heated. **2** (*fig fml*) (of a person) easily led or influenced. ▷ **ductility** /dʌkˈtɪlətɪ/ *n* [U].

dud /dʌd/ *n* (*infml*) thing or person that fails to work properly: *Two of the fireworks in the box were duds.* ○ *The new manager is a complete dud.*
▷ **dud** *adj* defective; worthless: *These batteries are dud.* ○ *a dud cheque,* ie one that is forged or not backed by cash.

dude /djuːd; *US* duːd/ *n* (*US*) **1** city person, esp sb spending a holiday on a ranch: [attrib] *a dude ranch,* ie one used as a holiday centre. **2** dandy. **3** (*sl*) man: *Who's that dude over there?*

dudgeon /ˈdʌdʒən/ *n* (idm) **in** ˌ**high** ˈ**dudgeon** angry, offended or resentful: *He stormed out of the meeting in high dudgeon.*

duds /dʌdz/ *n* [pl] (*sl*) clothes.

due[1] /djuː; *US* duː/ *adj* **1** [pred] (**a**) ~ **(to sb)** owed as a debt or an obligation: *Have they been paid the money due to them?* ○ *I'm still due fifteen days' holiday.* (**b**) ~ **for sth** owed sth; deserving sth: *She's due for promotion soon.* **2** [pred] requiring immediate payment: *fall/become due* ○ *My rent isn't due till Wednesday.* **3** [pred] ~ **(to do sth)** scheduled; arranged; expected: *His book is due to be published in October.* ○ *The train is due (in)* (ie scheduled to arrive) *in five minutes.* **4** [attrib] suitable; right; proper: *after due consideration* ○ *With all due respect, I disagree completely.* **5** ~ **to sth/sb** caused by sb/sth; because of sb/sth: *The team's success was largely due to her efforts.* **6** (idm) **in** ˌ**due** ˈ**course** at the appropriate time; eventually: *Your request will be dealt with in due course.*

NOTE ON USAGE: **1** Some speakers are careful to use **due to** only after the verb *be*: *His lateness was due to the very heavy traffic on the motorway.* But it is also generally considered acceptable today as a synonym for **owing to**, which is used differently: *He was late owing to/due to the very heavy traffic.* ○ *Due to/Owing to the heavy traffic, he was late.* **2** **Due to** can be used immediately after a noun: *Accidents due to driving at high speed were very common that weekend.*

due[2] /djuː; *US* duː/ *n* **1** [sing] thing that should be given to sb by right: *He received a large reward, which was no more than his due,* ie at least what he deserved. **2 dues** [pl] charges or fees, eg for membership of a club: *I haven't paid my dues yet.* **3** (idm) **give sb his** ˈ**due** (*fml*) be fair to sb: *She's a slow worker but, to give her her due, she does try very hard.* **give the devil his due** ⇨ DEVIL[1].

due[3] /djuː; *US* duː/ *adv* (of points of the compass) exactly: *sail due east* ○ *walk three miles due north.*

duel /ˈdjuːəl; *US* ˈduːəl/ *n* **1** (formerly) formal fight between two men, using swords or pistols, esp to settle a point of honour: *challenge sb to a duel.* **2** (*fig*) contest or struggle between two people, groups, etc: *engage in a duel of words/wits.*
▷ **duel** *v* (**-ll-**; *US* also **-l-**) [I, Ipr] ~ **(with sb)** fight a duel: *duelling pistols,* ie pistols used in a duel. **duellist** /ˈdjuːəlɪst/ (*US* **duelist** /ˈduːəlɪst/) *n* person fighting a duel.

duenna /djuːˈenə; *US* duːˈenə/ *n* (esp in Spain and Portugal) elderly woman acting as governess and chaperon to the daughters of a family.

duet /djuːˈet; *US* duːˈet/ (also **duo**) *n* piece of music for two players or singers: *a duet for violin and piano* ○ *We sang a duet.*

duff /dʌf/ *adj* (*Brit sl*) worthless or useless.
▷ **duff** *v* (*Brit sl*) **1** [Tn] mishit (sth), esp in golf; bungle: *He duffed his drive off the first tee.* **2** (phr v) **duff sb up** punch or kick sb severely.

duffer /ˈdʌfə(r)/ *n* (*dated infml*) stupid or incompetent person: *I was always a bit of a duffer at maths.*

duffle (also **duffel**) /ˈdʌfl/ *n* [U] heavy woollen cloth with a soft surface.
□ ˈ**duffle bag** long tube-shaped canvas bag closed by a draw-string.
ˈ**duffle-coat** *n* coat made of duffle, usu with a hood, fastened with toggles.

dug[1] *pt, pp* of DIG[1].

dug[2] /dʌɡ/ *n* udder; teat.

dug-out /ˈdʌɡ aʊt/ *n* **1** (also ˌ**dug-out caˈnoe**) canoe made by hollowing out a tree trunk. **2** rough covered shelter, usu for soldiers, made by digging in the earth.

duke /djuːk; *US* duːk/ *n* (in titles **Duke**) (*fem* **duchess** /ˈdʌtʃɪs/) **1** (title of a) nobleman of the highest rank: *the Duke and Duchess of Gloucester.* ⇨ article at ARISTOCRAT. **2** (in some parts of Europe, esp formerly) male ruler of a small independent state.
▷ **dukedom** /-dəm/ *n* **1** position or rank of a duke. **2** = DUCHY.

dulcet /ˈdʌlsɪt/ *adj* [attrib] (*fml or joc*) sounding sweet; pleasing to the ear: (*ironic*) *I thought I recognized your dulcet tones*, ie the sound of your voice.

dulcimer /ˈdʌlsɪmə(r)/ *n* musical instrument played by striking metal strings with two hammers.

dull /dʌl/ *adj* (**-er, -est**) **1** not bright or clear: *a dull colour, glow, thud* ○ *dull* (ie cloudy) *weather* ○ *dull of hearing*, ie slightly deaf. **2** slow in understanding; stupid: *a dull pupil, class, mind.* **3** lacking interest or excitement; boring; monotonous: *The conference was deadly dull.* **4** not sharp: *a dull knife.* **5** (of pain) not felt sharply: *a dull ache.* **6** (of trade) not busy; slow: *There's always a dull period after the January sales.* **7** (idm) **(as) ˌdull as ˈditch-water** (*infml*) very boring.
▷ **dull** *v* [I, Tn] (cause sth to) become dull: *Watching television dulls one's wits.* ○ *She took drugs to dull the pain.* ○ (*fig*) *Time had dulled the edge of his grief.*
dullness *n* [U].
dully /ˈdʌl-lɪ/ *adj.*

dullard /ˈdʌləd/ *n* person who thinks slowly; stupid person.

duly /ˈdju:lɪ; *US* ˈdu:lɪ/ *adv* **1** in a due, correct or proper manner: *The president was duly elected.* **2** at the due and proper time; punctually: *I duly knocked on his door at three o'clock.*

dumb /dʌm/ *adj* (**-er, -est**) **1** unable to speak: *She's been dumb from birth.* ○ *our dumb friends*, ie animals ○ (*fig*) *be struck dumb* (ie left speechless) *with horror, fear, amazement, etc.* **2** [usu pred] temporarily silent; refusing to speak: *They begged him to explain, but he remained dumb.* **3** (*infml*) stupid: *That was a pretty dumb thing to do.* ○ *If the police question you, act dumb*, ie pretend you don't know anything. ▷ **dumbly** *adv.* **dumbness** *n* [U].
□ **ˌdumb ˈblonde** (*esp sexist*) blonde-haired woman who is beautiful but stupid.
ˈdumb show communication using gestures but no words; mime.
ˌdumb ˈwaiter **(a)** (*US* **ˌlazy ˈSusan**) revolving stand or one with shelves, for holding food ready to be served. **(b)** small lift for carrying food, etc from one floor to another, esp in a restaurant.

dumb-bell /ˈdʌmbel/ *n* **1** short bar with a weight at each end, used for exercising the muscles, esp those of the arms and shoulders. **2** (*US infml*) stupid person.

dumbfound (also **dumfound**) /dʌmˈfaʊnd/ *v* [Tn esp passive] make (sb) speechless with surprise; astonish: *We were completely dumbfounded by her rudeness.*

dumdum /ˈdʌmdʌm/ *n* (also **dumdum bullet**) soft-nosed bullet that expands on impact, causing a gaping wound.

dummy /ˈdʌmɪ/ *n* **1** [C] model of the human figure, used for displaying or fitting clothes, etc: *a tailor's dummy.* **2** [C] thing that appears to be real but is only an imitation: *The bottles of whisky on display are all dummies.* **3** [C] (*esp Brit*) (*Brit* also **comforter**, *US* **pacifier**) rubber teat, not attached to a bottle, for a baby to suck. **4** [sing] **(a)** (in card-games, esp bridge) player whose cards are placed facing upwards on the table and played by his partner. **(b)** these cards: *She played a jack from dummy.* **5** [C] act (eg a pretended pass or a sudden swerve) which deceives one's opponent in football: *He sold the full back* (ie deceived him with) *a dummy.* **6** [C] (*US infml*) stupid person.
▷ **dummy** *v* [Ipr, Tn] deceive (an opponent in football) with a dummy(5): *He dummied past three defenders.* ○ *He dummied the full back and scored.*
□ **ˌdummy ˈrun** trial or practice attack, performance, etc.

dump /dʌmp/ *v* [Tn, Tn·pr] **1** put (sth unwanted) in a place and leave as rubbish: *Some people just dump their rubbish in the river.* ○ *Sealed containers of nuclear waste have been dumped in the sea.* **2** put (sth) down carelessly, heavily or in a mass: *dump a load of gravel, a pile of newspapers, a bundle of dirty clothes* ○ *Just dump everything over there — I'll sort it out later.* **3** (*infml often derog*) leave or abandon (sb): *She dumped the kids at her mother's and went to the theatre.* ○ *He's dumped his wife and gone off with one of his students.* **4** (*derog commerce*) sell abroad at a very low price (goods that are not wanted in the home market). **5** (*computing*) transfer (data, etc) from one part of a system to another or from one storage system to another. **6** (idm) **drop/dump sth in sb's lap** ⇨ LAP[1].
▷ **dump** *n* **1** place where rubbish may be unloaded and left; rubbish-heap. Cf TIP[2] *n.* **2** temporary store of military supplies: *an ammuˈnition dump.* **3** (*infml derog*) dirty or unattractive place: *How can you live in this dump?*
dumper *n* (also **ˈdumper truck**, *US* **ˈdump truck**) small vehicle, used on building sites, etc, with a container that can be tilted to dump its contents.

dumpling /ˈdʌmplɪŋ/ *n* **1** small ball of dough steamed or boiled, eg in a stew. **2** baked pudding made of dough filled with fruit: *an apple dumpling.* **3** (*infml*) short plump person.

dumps /dʌmps/ *n* [pl] (idm) **(down) in the dumps** (*infml*) depressed; feeling gloomy.

dumpy /ˈdʌmpɪ/ *adj* (**-ier, -iest**) (esp of a person) short and fat. ▷ **dumpiness** *n* [U].

dun[1] /dʌn/ *adj, n* (of a) dull greyish-brown colour.

dun[2] /dʌn/ *v* (**-nn-**) [Tn] persistently demand payment of a debt from (sb).

dunce /dʌns/ *n* person, esp a pupil, who is stupid or slow to learn.
□ **ˈdunce's cap** pointed paper hat formerly given to dull pupils to wear in class as a punishment.

Dundee cake /dʌnˈdi: keɪk/ *n* [C, U] (*Brit*) large cake containing dried fruit and usu decorated on top with almonds.

dunderhead /ˈdʌndəhed/ *n* (*derog*) stupid person.

dune /dju:n; *US* du:n/ (also **ˈsand-dune**) *n* mound of loose dry sand formed by the wind.

dung /dʌŋ/ *n* [U] animal excrement, esp when used as manure.
□ **ˈdung-beetle** *n* type of beetle that eats and lays its eggs on dung.
ˈdunghill *n* heap of dung in a farmyard.

dungarees /ˌdʌŋgəˈri:z/ *n* [pl] overalls or trousers made of coarse cotton cloth: *a pair of dungarees.*

dungeon /ˈdʌndʒən/ *n* underground prison cell, esp in a castle.

dunk /dʌŋk/ *v* [Tn, Tn·pr] ~ **sth/sb (in/into sth) 1** dip (food) in liquid before eating: *dunk a biscuit in one's coffee.* **2** submerge (sb/sth) briefly in water: *They dunked her in the swimming-pool as a joke.*

Dunkirk /ˌdʌnˈkɜ:k/ port in northern France from which in 1940 the British army was evacuated by warships and many small private boats after it had been forced to retreat to the French coast by the German advance. French name **Dunkerque**.
□ **the ˌDunkirk ˈspirit** (*Brit approv*) refusal to surrender or give up when one is in severe difficulties: *displaying the Dunkirk spirit.*

Dunlop /ˈdʌnlɒp/ John Boyd (1840-1921), Scottish inventor of the air-filled rubber tyre, which was later made by a firm named after him. Cf PNEUMATIC.

dunno /ˈdʌnəʊ, dəˈnəʊ/ (*infml*) (I) do not know: *'Who's that?' 'Dunno.'*

Duns Scotus /ˌdʌnz ˈskəʊtəs/ John (c 1260-1308), Scottish philosopher and monk who considered that religious faith is a matter of will, and does not depend on logical proof. In later centuries his views became unpopular, and the word *dunce* is derived from his name.

duo /ˈdju:əʊ; *US* ˈdu:əʊ/ *n* (*pl* ~**s**) **1** pair of performers: *a comedy duo.* **2** = DUET.

duodecimal /ˌdju:əʊˈdesɪml; *US* ˌdu:əˈdesəml/ *adj* based on twelve or twelfths; proceeding by twelves: *a duodecimal system.*

duodenum /ˌdju:əˈdi:nəm; *US* ˌdu:əˈdi:nəm/ *n* (*anatomy*) first part of the small intestine, immediately below the stomach. ⇨ illus at DIGESTIVE. ▷ **duodenal** /ˌdju:əˈdi:nl; *US* ˌdu:əˈdi:nl/ *adj* [usu attrib]: *a duodenal ulcer.*

duologue /ˈdju:əlɒg; *US* ˈdu:əlɔ:g/ *n* conversation between two people.

dupe /dju:p; *US* du:p/ *v* [Tn, Tn·pr] ~ **sb (into doing sth)** deceive or trick sb (into doing sth).
▷ **dupe** *n* person who is duped; fool: *I won't be his dupe any longer.*

duple time /ˌdju:pl ˈtaɪm; *US* du:pl/ (*music*) rhythm with two beats in a bar.

duplex /ˈdju:pleks; *US* ˈdu:pleks/ *adj* having two parts.
▷ **duplex** *n* (*US*) **1 (a)** building divided into two dwellings. **(b)** either of these dwellings. **2** (also **duplex apartment**) apartment on two floors.

duplicate[1] /ˈdju:plɪkət; *US* ˈdu:pləkət/ *adj* [attrib] **1** exactly like sth else; identical: *a duplicate set of keys.* **2** having two identical parts; twofold; double: *a duplicate receipt, form, etc.*
▷ **duplicate** *n* **1** one of two or more things that are exactly alike; copy: *Is this a duplicate or the original?* **2** (idm) **in duplicate** (of documents, etc) as two identical copies: *complete a form, prepare a contract, etc in duplicate.*

duplicate[2] /ˈdju:plɪkeɪt; *US* ˈdu:pləkeɪt/ *v* **1** [Tn esp passive] make an exact copy of (sth). **2** [Tn] do (sth) again, esp unnecessarily; repeat: *This research merely duplicates work already done elsewhere.*
▷ **duplication** /ˌdju:plɪˈkeɪʃn; *US* ˌdu:pləˈkeɪʃn/ *n* [U] duplicating or being duplicated: *We must avoid wasteful duplication of effort.*
duplicator *n* machine for making copies of written or typed material.

duplicity /dju:ˈplɪsətɪ; *US* du:ˈplɪsətɪ/ *n* [U] (*fml*) deliberate deception.

durable /ˈdjʊərəbl; *US* ˈdʊərəbl/ *adj* lasting for a long time: *a durable peace, friendship, settlement* ○ *trousers made of durable material* ○ *This varnish provides a durable finish.*
▷ **durability** /ˌdjʊərəˌbɪlətɪ; *US* ˈdʊərəˈbɪlətɪ/ *n* [U].
durables *n* (also **conˌsumer ˈdurables**) [pl] goods expected to last for a long time after they have been bought, eg vacuum cleaners.

duration /djʊˈreɪʃn; *US* dʊˈreɪʃn/ *n* [U] **1** time during which sth lasts or continues: *of short, long, three years', etc duration* ○ *for the duration of this government.* **2** (idm) **for the duration** (*infml*) **(a)** until the end of the war. **(b)** (*fig*) for a very long time: *Well, I'm stuck here for the duration*, eg for the whole term.

Dürer /ˈdjʊərə(r)/ Albrecht (1471-1528), German painter and engraver famous for his highly detailed studies of animals, plants, etc, and for his engravings of religious and other subjects. He is generally regarded as the greatest German artist of the Renaissance period.

duress /djʊˈres; *US* dʊˈres/ *n* [U] threats or force used to make sb do sth; (usu illegal) compulsion: *sign a confession under duress.*

Durex /ˈdjʊəreks/ *n* (*propr*) **1** [U, C] (*pl* unchanged or ~**es**) (*Brit*) type of contraceptive sheath; condom: *a couple of Durex/Durexes* ○ *a packet of Durex.* **2** [U] (*Austral*) type of sticky tape (STICKY).

Durham /ˈdʌrəm/ **1** (also **ˌCounty ˈDurham**) county in NE England, formerly a major centre of coal-mining, steel-making and ship-building. ⇨ map at App 1. **2** (also **ˌDurham ˈCity**) city that is the administrative centre of County Durham, with a famous medieval cathedral and castle.

during /ˈdjʊərɪŋ; *US* ˈdʊər-/ *prep* **1** throughout (a period of time taken by an action or event): *There are extra trains to the seaside during the summer.* ○ *During his lifetime his work was never published.* ○ *He stopped for applause three times during his speech.* **2** within (a specified period of time): *They only met twice during the whole time they were neighbours.* ○ *There will be two intervals during the performance.* **3** at a particular time while (sth) progresses: *The phone rang during the meal.* ○ *There was a bomb scare during the procession.* ○ *Her husband was taken to hospital during the night.*

dusk /dʌsk/ *n* [U] time after twilight and before night: *The street lights come on at dusk and go off at dawn.*

dusky /ˈdʌskɪ/ *adj* (**-ier, -iest**) **1** shadowy; dim: *the dusky light inside the cave.* **2 (a)** dark-coloured: *dusky blue, red, etc.* **(b)** (*often offensive*) dark-skinned: *a dusky maiden* ○ *dusky tribes.* ▷ **duskiness** *n* [U].

dust[1] /dʌst/ *n* [U] **1** fine dry powder consisting of particles of earth, dirt, etc: *a speck of dust* ○ *The old furniture was covered in dust.* ○ *clouds of dust blowing in the wind* ○ *gold, chalk, etc dust*, ie fine particles of gold, chalk, etc ○ [attrib] *A dust-cloud* (ie A whirlwind carrying clouds of dust) *swept across the plain.* **2** (*rhet*) remains of a dead person. **3** (idm) **bite the dust** ⇨ BITE[1]. **dry as dust** ⇨ DRY[1]. **kick up/raise a ˈdust** (*infml*) make a fuss. **shake the dust off one's feet** ⇨ SHAKE[1]. **throw dust in sb's eyes** prevent sb from seeing the truth by misleading him. **when the dust has settled** when the present uncertainty, unpleasantness, etc is over.

□ **ˈdustbin** *n* (*Brit*) (*US* **garbage can, trash-can**) container for (esp household) rubbish.

ˈdust bowl area that has lost its vegetation through drought, over-cultivation, etc. The term is applied particularly to such an area in the western states of the USA whose vegetation was destroyed by cattle in the 1930s, leading to much poverty amongst the farming population (the theme of John *Steinbeck's novel *The Grapes of Wrath*).

ˈdust-cart *n* (*Brit*) (*US* **garbage truck**) vehicle for collecting rubbish from dustbins.

ˈdust-cover *n* **1** cover used for protecting a computer, gramophone turntable, etc from dust. **2** = DUST-JACKET. **3** = DUST-SHEET.

ˈdust-jacket *n* removable paper cover to protect the binding of a book.

ˈdustman /-mən/ *n* (*pl* **-men** /-mən/) (*Brit*) (*US* **garbage man**) man employed by a local authority to empty dustbins and remove rubbish.

ˈdustpan *n* pan into which dust is brushed from the floor.

ˈdust-sheet *n* sheet used for covering furniture that is not in use, to protect it from dust.

ˈdust-up *n* (*infml*) noisy quarrel or fight.

dust[2] /dʌst/ *v* **1** (a) [Tn] remove dust from (sth) by wiping, brushing or flicking: *dust the furniture, books, living-room.* (b) [Tn·p] ~ **sb down/off** remove dust from sb by brushing or flicking: *Dust yourself down — you're covered in chalk.* **2** (phr v) **dust sth off** begin to practise sth, esp a skill or a language that one knows but has not used for some time: *I'll have to dust off my French if we're going to move to Paris.* **dust sth onto, over, etc sth** sprinkle (sth powdery) over sth: *dust sugar onto a cake.* **dust sth with sth** sprinkle sth with (sth powdery): *dust a cake with icing sugar.*

▷ **duster** *n* cloth for dusting furniture, etc.

dusty /ˈdʌstɪ/ *adj* (**-ier, -iest**) **1** (a) full of dust; covered with dust: *This room's rather dusty, I'm afraid.* (b) like dust. **2** (idm) **a dusty answer** curt rejection of a request; unfriendly refusal. **not so dusty** (*dated Brit infml*) fairly good: *'How are you feeling?' 'Oh, not so dusty, thanks!'* ▷ **dustiness** *n* [U].

Dutch /dʌtʃ/ *adj* **1** of the Netherlands (Holland), its people or their language. **2** (idm) **Dutch courage** (*infml joc*) courage that comes from drinking alcohol. **a Dutch treat** a meal, an entertainment, etc at which each person pays for himself. **go Dutch (with sb)** share expenses. **talk (to sb) like a Dutch uncle** ⇨ TALK[2].

▷ **Dutch** *n* **1 the Dutch** [pl *v*] the people of the Netherlands. **2** [U] the language of the Dutch. Cf DOUBLE DUTCH (DOUBLE[1]).

□ ˌ**Dutch ˈauction** sale in which the price is gradually reduced until a buyer is found.

ˌ**Dutch ˈbarn** farm building consisting of a roof supported on poles, without walls, used as a shelter for hay, etc.

ˌ**Dutch ˈcap** = DIAPHRAGM 4.

ˌ**Dutch ˈelm disease** disease that kills elm trees, caused by a fungus.

ˈDutchman /-mən/ *n* (*pl* **-men**) **1** native of the Netherlands. **2** (idm) **I'm a Dutchman!** (used to express incredulity): *If he's only twenty-five, I'm a Dutchman!* ie I'm sure he's older than twenty-five.

ˌ**Dutch ˈoven** covered container used for cooking meat, etc slowly.

dutch /dʌtʃ/ *n* (usu *sing*) (usu **old dutch**) (*Brit sl*) wife: *my dear old dutch.*

duteous /ˈdju:tɪəs; *US* ˈdu:-/ *adj* (*fml*) = DUTIFUL.

dutiable /ˈdju:tɪəbl; *US* ˈdu:-/ *adj* on which customs or other duties (DUTY 3) must be paid: *dutiable goods.*

dutiful /ˈdju:tɪfl; *US* ˈdu:-/ (also **duteous**) *adj* (*fml*) showing respect and obedience; fulfilling all one's obligations: *a dutiful son, subject, servant, etc.* ▷ **dutifully** /-fəlɪ/ *adv*: *He dutifully followed his commander's instructions.* ○ *to serve one's country dutifully.*

duty /ˈdju:tɪ; *US* ˈdu:tɪ/ *n* **1** [C, U] moral or legal obligation: *It's your duty to go.* ○ *do one's duty* ○ *It's not something I enjoy. I do it purely out of a sense of duty.* ○ *I'll have to go, I'm afraid — duty calls.* **2** [C, U] task or action that sb must perform: *What are the duties of a traffic warden?* ○ *I'm doing night duty this week.* **3** [C, U] ~ **(on sth)** tax charged on certain goods, esp on imports: *customs/excise duties.* Cf TARIFF 2. **4** (idm) **one's bounden duty** ⇨ BOUNDEN. **dereliction of duty** ⇨ DERELICTION (DERELICT). **do duty for sth** serve as or act as a substitute for sth else: *An old wooden box did duty for a table.* **in the line of duty** ⇨ LINE[1]. **on/off duty** (of nurses, police officers, etc) engaged/not engaged in one's regular work: *I arrive at the hospital at eight o'clock, but I don't go on duty until nine.* ○ [attrib] *off-duty activities, hours.*

□ ˌ**duty-ˈbound** *adj* [pred] obliged by duty: *I'm duty-bound to help him.*

ˌ**duty-ˈfree** *adj, adv* (of goods) that can be imported without payment of customs duties: *You're allowed $1\frac{1}{2}$ litres of spirits duty-free.* ○ *There's a good duty-free shop* (ie one selling such goods) *on the ferry.* ○ *buy cigarettes duty-free.*

duvet /ˈdu:veɪ/ *n* quilt filled with soft feathers, etc, used on a bed instead of a top sheet and blankets. Cf EIDERDOWN.

DV /ˌdi: ˈvi:/ *abbr* God being willing (Latin *Deo volente*): *He should be back by Friday, DV,* ie if nothing prevents him.

DVLC /ˌdi: vi: el ˈsi:/ *abbr* Driver and Vehicle Licensing Centre (which issues British driving-licences and vehicle licences). ⇨ article at ROAD.

Dvořák /ˈdvɔ:ʒɑ:k, -ʒæk/ Antonín (1841-1904), Czech composer who incorporated traditional Czech folk-tunes into classical forms such as symphonies and quartets. His most famous piece, however, the 'New World' Symphony, uses American folk-tunes, which he discovered when he visited the USA in the 1890s.

dwarf /dwɔ:f/ *n* (*pl* ~**s**) **1** person, animal or plant that is much smaller than the normal size: [attrib] *a dwarf conifer.* **2** (in fairy stories) creature like a very small man with magic powers.

▷ **dwarf** *v* [Tn] **1** make (sb/sth) seem small by contrast or distance: *Our little dinghy was dwarfed by the big yacht.* **2** prevent the full growth of (sth); stunt.

dwarfism /ˈdwɔ:fɪzəm/ *n* [U] condition in which growth has stopped before full size is reached.

dwell /dwel/ *v* (*pt, pp* **dwelt** /dwelt/) **1** [Ipr] ~ **in, at, etc ...** (*arch or rhet*) live as an inhabitant of or reside at (a place). **2** (phr v) **dwell on/upon sth** think, speak or write at length about sth: *Let's not dwell on your past mistakes.*

▷ **dweller** *n* (esp in compound *ns*) person or animal living in the place specified: *ˈtown-dwellers* ○ *ˈflat-dwellers* ○ *ˈcave-dwellers.*

dwelling *n* (*fml*) place of residence; house, flat, etc: (*fml or joc*) *my humble dwelling.* **ˈdwelling-house** *n* (*esp law*) house used as a residence, not as a place of work.

dwindle /ˈdwɪndl/ *v* [I, Ipr, Ip] ~ **(away) (to nothing)** become gradually less or smaller: *dwindling hopes, popularity, profits* ○ *Their savings have dwindled (away) to nothing.*

Dy *symb* dysprosium.

dye[1] /daɪ/ *v* (*3rd pers sing pres t* **dyes**, *pt, pp* **dyed**, *pres p* **dyeing**) (a) [Tn, Cn·a] colour (sth), esp by dipping in a liquid: *dye one's hair* ○ *dye a white dress blue.* (b) [I] be able to be dyed: *a fabric that dyes well.* ▷ **dyer** *n.*

□ ˌ**dyed-in-the-ˈwool** *adj* [usu attrib] (*usu derog*) totally fixed in one's ideas, beliefs, etc: *a dyed-in-the-wool Marxist.*

dye[2] /daɪ/ *n* [C, U] **1** substance used for dyeing: *vegetable dyes* ○ *I bought some blue dye yesterday.* **2** colour given by dyeing. **3** (idm) **of the blackest/deepest dye** (*dated*) of the worst kind: *a villain, scoundrel, traitor, etc of the deepest dye.*

Dyfed /ˈdʌvɪd/ county in SW Wales formed in 1974 from Cardiganshire, Carmarthenshire and Pembrokeshire. ⇨ map at App 1.

dying ⇨ DIE[2].

dyke = DIKE.

Dylan /ˈdɪlən/ Bob (Robert Allen Zimmerman, 1941-), American singer and songwriter whose protest songs (eg 'The Times They Are A-Changin'' and 'Blowin' in the Wind'), sung to a guitar, were a major feature of the popular-music scene in the 1960s. His distinctive singing voice and often mysterious life-style have made him a cult figure, esp among young people.

dynamic /daɪˈnæmɪk/ *adj* **1** of power or forces that produce movement. Cf STATIC 2. **2** (of a person) energetic and forceful: *a dynamic personality.*

▷ **dynamic** *n* [sing] force that produces change, action, or effects: *the inner dynamic of a historical period, social movement, work of art.*

dynamically *adv.*

dynamics /daɪˈnæmɪks/ *n* **1** [sing *v*] branch of physics dealing with movement and force. **2** [pl] (*music*) amount of or variation in loudness.

dynamism /ˈdaɪnəmɪzəm/ *n* [U] **1** (in a person) quality of being dynamic. **2** (*philosophy*) theory that phenomena are the result of natural forces acting on each other.

dynamite /ˈdaɪnəmaɪt/ *n* [U] **1** powerful explosive used in mining, etc. **2** (*fig*) (a) thing likely to cause violent reactions: *The abortion issue is political dynamite.* (b) (*infml approv*) strikingly impressive person or thing: *Their new album is sheer dynamite.*

▷ **dynamite** *v* [Tn] blow (sb/sth) up with dynamite.

dynamo /ˈdaɪnəməʊ/ *n* (*pl* ~**s**) **1** device for converting steam-power, water-power, etc into electricity; generator. ⇨ illus at CAR. ⇨ illus at BICYCLE. **2** (*fig infml*) intensely energetic person: *a human dynamo.*

dynamometer /ˌdaɪnəˈmɒmɪtə(r)/ *n* instrument for measuring power or force.

dynasty /ˈdɪnəstɪ; *US* ˈdaɪ-/ *n* **1** series of rulers all belonging to the same family: *the Tudor dynasty.* **2** period during which a particular dynasty rules: *during the Ming dynasty.* ▷ **dynastic** /dɪˈnæstɪk; *US* daɪ-/ *adj* [usu attrib]: *dynastic succession.*

dysentery /ˈdɪsəntrɪ; *US* -terɪ/ *n* [U] inflammation of the bowels, causing severe diarrhoea, usu with a discharge of mucus and blood.

dyslexia /dɪsˈleksɪə; *US* dɪsˈlekʃə/ *n* [U] (*medical*) (also **word-blindness**) abnormal difficulty in reading and spelling, caused by a brain condition.

▷ **dyslexic** /dɪsˈleksɪk/ *n, adj* (person) suffering from dyslexia.

dyspepsia /dɪsˈpepsɪə; *US* dɪsˈpepʃə/ *n* [U] (*fml*) indigestion.

▷ **dyspeptic** /dɪsˈpeptɪk/ *adj, n* (typical of a) person suffering from dyspepsia or the irritability that it causes.

dysprosium /dɪsˈprəʊzɪəm/ *n* [U] (*symb* **Dy**) chemical element of the lanthanide series, a soft metal used, among other things, in the making of certain magnetic alloys.

dystrophy /ˈdɪstrəfɪ/ *n* [U] (*medical*) inherited condition that causes a progressive weakening of the body tissues, esp the muscles: *muscular dystrophy.*

E, e

E, e /iː/ *n* (*pl* **E's, e's** /iːz/) **1** the fifth letter of the English alphabet: *'Eric' begins with an 'E'/E.* **2 E** (*music*) the third note in the scale of C major.
□ **ˈE number** code number, beginning with the letter E, used for indicating the additives in food and drink.

E *abbr* **1** (esp on electric plugs) earth (connection). **2** east(ern): *E Asia* ○ *London E10 6RL*, ie as a postal code.

ea *abbr* each: *oranges 20p ea.*

each other

John and Paul are kicking the ball into the net.

John and Paul are kicking the ball to each other.

each /iːtʃ/ *indef det* (used with *sing* [C] *ns* and *sing vs*) **1** (of two or more) every (person, thing, group, etc) considered individually: *on each side of the road* ○ *a ring on each finger* ○ *Each day passed without any news.* **2** (idm) **ˌeach and ˈevery** every single (person or thing of a group or set): *Each and every one of you deserves* (ie All of you deserve) *a reward.*
▷ **each** *indef pron* every individual member (of a group): *each of the boys, books, buildings* ○ *Each of them phoned to thank me.* ○ *Each of us has a company car.* (Cf *We each have a company car.*) ○ *I'll see each of you separately.* (Cf *I'll see you each separately.*) ○ *He gave us £5 each.*
each *indef adv* every one separately: *The cakes are 20p each.*
□ **each ˈother** (used only as the object of a *v* or *prep*) the other one, reciprocally: *Paul and Linda helped each other*, ie Paul helped Linda and Linda helped Paul. ○ *We write to each other regularly.* Cf ONE ANOTHER (ONE[3]).

NOTE ON USAGE: **Each** and **every** are generally used as determiners before singular countable nouns. **Each** is used when the items in a group (of two or more) are considered individually: *Each child learns at his or her own pace.* **Every** indicates that all the items in a group (of three or more) are being regarded as members of that group. It can be modified by some adverbs: *Every/Nearly every child in the school passed the swimming test.* **Each (one) of** and **every one of** come before plural nouns or pronouns, but the verb is still singular: *Each of the houses is slightly different.* ○ *I bought a dozen eggs and every one of them was bad.* ○ *She gave each (one) of her grandchildren 50p.* **Each** can function as a pronoun on its own: *I asked all the children and each told a different story.* It can also follow a plural subject or an indirect object with a plural verb: *We each have a different point of view.*

eager /ˈiːgə(r)/ *adj* **1** ~ (**for sth/to do sth**) full of interest or desire; keen: *eager for success* ○ *eager to please.* **2** (idm) **an eager ˈbeaver** (*sometimes derog*) keen, hard-working and enthusiastic person. ▷ **eagerly** *adv.* **eagerness** *n* [U].

eagle /ˈiːgl/ *n* **1** large strong bird of prey of the falcon family with very good eyesight. The eagle is traditionally regarded as 'the king of birds' because of its size and power. The Roman and French empires used it as their symbol, and today it is the emblem of the USA. **2** (in golf) score of two strokes less than average. Cf BIRDIE 2, PAR[1] 3.
▷ **eaglet** /ˈiːglɪt/ *n* young eagle.
□ **ˌeagle ˈeye** (usu *sing*) **1** very good eyesight. **2** keen watchfulness: *The teacher's eagle eye was always on us*, ie She noticed everything. **ˌeagle-ˈeyed** *adj.*

Ealing comedies /ˌiːlɪŋ ˈkɒmədɪz/ series of British film comedies made at the Ealing studios near London during the late 1940s, including *The Lavender Hill Mob, Kind Hearts and Coronets* (in which Alec *Guinness played eight different roles), and *Passport to Pimlico.* They remain popular for their wit, invention and skilful acting.

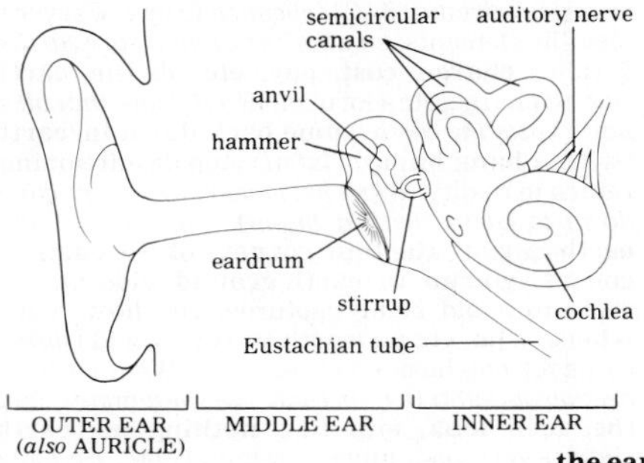

the ear

ear[1] /ɪə(r)/ *n* **1** [C] organ of hearing, esp either of the outer parts on each side of the head. The actual structures with which we hear are contained inside the head. The interior ear is also responsible for our sense of balance: *The doctor looked into my ears.* ○ *Rabbits have large ears.* ○ [attrib] *She's got an ˈear infection.* Cf INNER EAR (INNER), MIDDLE EAR (MIDDLE), ⇨ illus. **2** [sing] **an ~ (for sth)** sense of hearing; ability to discriminate sounds, esp in music and language: *She has a good ear for languages.* **3** (idm) **(be) all ˈears** (*infml*) listening attentively: *Tell me your news; I'm all ears.* **box sb's ears** ⇨ BOX[2]. **sth comes to/reaches sb's ˈears** sb finds out about sth, eg news or gossip: *If this news ever reaches her ears, she'll be furious.* **din in one's ears** ⇨ DIN *v.* **sb's ˈears are burning!** sb suspects that he is being talked about, esp in an unkind way: *All this gossip about Sarah — her ears must be burning!* **sb's ˈears are flapping** (*infml*) sb is listening carefully or inquisitively in case sth interesting is being said. **easy on the ear/eye** ⇨ EASY[1]. **fall on deaf ears** ⇨ DEAF. **feel one's ears burning** ⇨ FEEL[1]. **give sb/get a thick ear** ⇨ THICK. **go in (at) ˈone ear and out (at) the ˈother** be heard but either ignored or quickly forgotten: *You've forgotten to buy the eggs! It* (ie What I tell you) *goes in one ear and out the other.* **have, get, win, etc sb's ˈear** have or get sb's favourable attention. **have/keep an/one's ear to the ˈground** be aware of all that is happening and being said: *Peter'll know; he always keeps an ear to the ground.* **have a word in sb's ear** ⇨ WORD. **keep one's ears/eyes open** ⇨ OPEN[1]. **lend an ear** ⇨ LEND. **make a pig's ear of sth** ⇨ PIG. **meet the ear/eye** ⇨ MEET[1]. **music to one's ears** ⇨ MUSIC. **not believe one's ears/eyes** ⇨ BELIEVE. **(be) out on one's ˈear** suddenly expelled, dismissed, etc. **play (sth) by ˈear** play (music) by remembering how it sounds, ie without seeing a printed form. **play it by ˈear** (*infml*) act without preparation according to the demands of a situation; improvise: *I've had no time to prepare for this meeting, so I'll have to play it by ear.* **prick up one's ears** ⇨ PRICK[2]. **shut one's ears to sth/sb** ⇨ SHUT. **smile, etc from ear to ˈear** smile, etc broadly, showing that one is very pleased or happy. **turn a deaf ear** ⇨ DEAF. **(be) up to one's ears/eyes in sth** very busy with or overwhelmed by sth: *I'm up to my ears in work at the moment.* **walls have ears** ⇨ WALL. **with a flea in one's ear** ⇨ FLEA. **wet behind the ears** ⇨ WET. **with half an ˈear** not very attentively: *I was only listening to the radio with half an ear, while preparing some food.*
▷ **-eared** /ɪəd/ (usu in compound *adjs*) having ears of a specified kind: *the ˌlong-eared ˈowl.*
earful /ˈɪəfʊl/ *n* [sing] (*infml*) (idm) **give sb/get an ˈearful** give or receive a long angry or abusive speech: *If he bothers you again I'll give him an earful.*
□ **ˈearache** *n* [U, sing] pain in the ear-drum.
ˈear-drop *n* (usu *pl*) liquid medication dropped into the ears.
ˈear-drum (also **drum**) *n* thin membrane in the inner part of the ear which vibrates when sound waves strike it. ⇨ illus.
ˈear-flap *n* flap on a cap or hat (such as a deerstalker) that can be folded away or pulled down to cover the ears.
ˈear-muff *n* (usu *pl*) either of a pair of ear-coverings connected by a band across the top of the head, and worn to protect the ears, esp from the cold: *a pair of green ear-muffs.*
ˈearphone *n* (usu *pl*) **(a)** either of two receivers attached to each other so that they fit over the ears, used for listening to records, the radio, etc. **(b)** similar device with only one receiver that fits inside one ear.
ˈear-plug *n* (usu *pl*) either of two pieces of soft material put into the ears to keep out air, water or noise.
ˈear-ring *n* (often *pl*) piece of jewellery worn in or on the ear lobe.
ˈearshot *n* [U] (idm) **(be) out of/within ˈearshot** where one cannot/can be heard.
ˈear-splitting *adj* very loud; shrill: *an ear-splitting crash.*
ˈear-trumpet *n* trumpet-shaped tube formerly used by partially deaf people to magnify sound.

ear[2] /ɪə(r)/ *n* seed-bearing part of a cereal, eg wheat, barley, etc. ⇨ illus at CEREAL.

earl /ɜːl/ *n* (*fem* **countess**) (title of a) British nobleman ranking between a marquis and a viscount. ⇨ article at ARISTOCRAT.
▷ **earldom** *n* rank of an earl.

early /ˈɜːlɪ/ (**-ier, -iest**) *adj, adv* **1** near to the beginning of a period of time: *the early morning* ○ *in early spring* ○ *in his early twenties*, ie aged between 20 and 23 or 24 ○ *early works (of a composer, poet, writer, etc)*, ie those written at the beginning of a career ○ *early music, opera*, ie composed before the classical period ○ *Two players were injured early in the season.* Cf LATE[1] 2, LATE[2] 2. **2** before the usual or expected time: *early peaches*, ie peaches that ripen early in the season ○ *an early breakfast*, eg at 5 am ○ *I got up early today.* ○ *The bus arrived five minutes early.* Cf LATE[1] 1, LATE[2] 1. **3** (idm) **at your earliest conˈvenience** (*fml esp commerce*) as soon as possible: *Please deliver the goods at your earliest convenience.* **bright and ˈearly** ⇨ BRIGHT. **an ˈearly bird** (*joc*) person who arrives, gets up, etc early: *You're an early bird this morning!* **the ˌearly bird catches the ˈworm** (*saying*) the person who arrives, gets up, etc first will be successful. **early ˈdays (yet)** (*esp Brit*) too soon to be sure how a situation, etc will develop: *I'm not sure if our book will be a success — it's early days yet.* **the early ˈhours** very early in the morning, ie not long after midnight: *They were dancing till the early hours.* **an early/a late night** ⇨ NIGHT. **early ˈon** soon after the start of a past event: *I knew early on (in the film) that I wasn't going to enjoy it.* **an early/late riser** ⇨ RISER (RISE[1]). **ˌearly to ˈbed and ˌearly to ˈrise (makes a man healthy, wealthy and wise)** (*saying*) living sensibly and without excesses (will bring a person good health, money and wisdom). **keep early ˈhours** rise early or go to bed early. ▷ **earliness** *n* [U].

□ **early ˈclosing** (*Brit*) shutting of shops, etc on a particular afternoon every week: *It's early closing (day) today.* ⇨ article at SHOP.

ˌEarly ˈEnglish early style of Gothic architecture which developed in England in the 13th century. Its main characteristic is the lancet window without tracery. Cf PERPENDICULAR 4.

early ˈwarning early indication (eg by radar) of the approach of enemy aircraft, missiles, etc: [attrib] *early ˈwarning system.*

earmark /ˈɪəmɑːk/ *v* **1** [Tn, Tn·pr] ~ **sb/sth (for sth/sb)** assign or set aside sb/sth (to or for a special purpose): *earmark a sum of money for research* ○ *I've earmarked Peter for the job.* **2** [Tn] put a special mark on the ear of (an animal) to show who the owner is.

▷ **earmark** *n* owner's mark on the ear of an animal.

earn /ɜːn/ *v* **1** [Tn] (**a**) get (money) by working: *He earns £10000 a year.* ○ *She earned her living by singing in a nightclub.* ○ *earned/unearned income.* (**b**) get (money) as a return on a loan or investment: *Money earns more in a high interest account.* **2** [Tn, Dn·n] gain (sth deserved) in return for one's achievements, behaviour, etc: *You've certainly earned your retirement.* ○ *a well-earned rest* ○ *His honesty earned him great respect.* ○ *His bad manners earned him a sharp rebuke.* **3** (idm) **earn/turn an honest penny** ⇨ HONEST. **ˌearn one's ˈkeep** work hard enough to cover the costs of one's food, accommodation, etc.

▷ **earner** *n* (*Brit sl*) way of earning money easily, used esp as in the expression shown: *They breed pedigree Persian cats, which is a nice little earner.*

earnings *n* [pl] money earned: *I've spent all my earnings.* **ˌearnings-reˈlated** *adj* (of payments, etc) linked to and changing with one's earnings: *an ˌearnings-related ˈpension scheme.*

earnest[1] /ˈɜːnɪst/ *adj* (too) serious; determined; not light-hearted: *a terribly earnest young man.*

▷ **earnest** *n* (idm) **in (dead/deadly/real) ˈearnest** (**a**) with determination and energy: *It's beginning to snow in earnest,* ie heavily. (**b**) serious(ly); not joking(ly): *When she threatened to report us, she was in dead earnest.*

earnestly *adv*: *I earnestly beg you to reconsider your decision.*

earnestness *n* [U].

earnest[2] /ˈɜːnɪst/ *n* [sing] **1** sum of money paid as an instalment or a deposit to show that full payment will be made later. **2** thing meant as a sign or promise of what will follow: *As an earnest of my good intentions I will work overtime this week.*

the earth

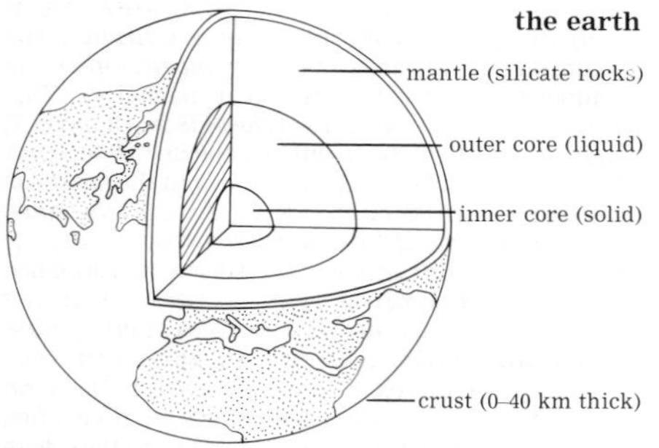

earth /ɜːθ/ *n* **1** (usu **the earth**) [sing] this world; the planet on which we live. The earth is the third closest planet to the sun, with an orbit between those of Venus and Mars, and is one of the smaller planets. It was probably formed about 4 600 million years ago. At its centre is a core of iron and nickel, whose outer layer is liquid; this is surrounded by the mantle, made of silicate rocks; and on the outside is the crust, only a few kilometres thick on land surfaces and even thinner beneath the seas which cover three quarters of the earth. It is the only one of the planets on which we know that life exists. In recent years science has started to see the earth not just as supporting life but as part of an overall ecosystem with a delicate balance which modern civilization is changing. The relation between human activity and its effect on the planet is being more carefully studied and the earth itself is viewed as an active, if not actually living environment: *The moon goes round the earth.* ○ *I must be the happiest woman on earth!* ⇨ illus. **2** [sing] land; the surface of the world as opposed to the sky or sea: *After a week at sea, it was good to feel the earth under our feet again.* ○ *The balloon burst and fell to earth.* **3** [U] soil: *a clod/lump of earth* ○ *fill a hole with earth* ○ *cover the roots of a plant with earth.* ⇨ Usage. **4** [C] hole of a wild animal, esp a fox or badger. **5** [C usu *sing*] (*esp Brit*) (*US* **ground**) (wire that provides a) connection with the ground completing an electrical circuit. **6** [C] (*chemistry*) any of several metallic elements: *an alkaline earth* ○ *rare earths.* **7** (idm) **charge, cost, pay, etc, sb the ˈearth** (*infml*) charge, etc a lot of money: *I'd love that bike, but it costs the earth.* **come back/down to ˈearth (with a bang/bump)** (*infml*) stop day-dreaming; return to reality: *When his money ran out, he came down to earth (with a bump).* **the ends of the earth** ⇨ END[1]. **the four corners of the earth** ⇨ CORNER. **go/run to earth/ground** hide oneself away to avoid being captured, etc. **how, why, where, who, etc on ˈearth/in the ˈworld** (*infml*) (used for emphasis) how, etc ever: *What on earth are you doing?* ○ *How on earth did she manage that?* **(be, feel, look, etc) like nothing on ˈearth** (*infml*) very bad, unwell, peculiar, etc: *He looks like nothing on earth in those weird clothes.* **move heaven and earth** ⇨ MOVE[2]. **promise the earth/moon** ⇨ PROMISE[2]. **run sb/sth to ˈearth** find sb/sth by searching hard: *The police eventually ran him to earth in Paris.* **the salt of the earth** ⇨ SALT. **wipe sth off the face of the earth/off the map** ⇨ WIPE.

▷ **earth** *v* **1** [Tn esp passive] (*esp Brit*) connect (an electrical appliance, etc) with the ground: *Is this plug earthed?* **2** (phr v) **earth sth up** cover (the roots of a plant, etc) with earth: *He earthed up the celery.*

earthy *adj* (**-ier, -iest**) **1** of or like earth or soil: *an earthy smell.* **2** (*fig*) (of people, jokes, etc) coarse; not refined or sensitive: *an earthy sense of humour.* **earthiness** *n* [U].

□ **ˈearthbound** *adj* **1** (moving) towards the earth. **2** (*derog*) lacking originality or inspiration: *an earthbound performance.*

earth science any of various sciences, such as geology or geography, concerned with the earth or part of it.

ˈearth-shaking, ˈearth-shattering *adjs* (*infml*) (eg of news or events) surprising and very important: *Nothing very earth-shattering's happened while you've been away.*

ˈearthwork *n* (formerly) large man-made bank of earth used as a fortification: *the remains of ancient earthworks.*

ˈearthworm *n* common type of worm that lives in the soil. ⇨ illus at WORM.

NOTE ON USAGE: Compare **earth**, **ground**, **floor** and **soil. The earth** (also **Earth**) is the name of the planet where we live and **earth** can also refer to the solid land in contrast to the sky above: *The parachutist floated gently down to earth.* **Ground** indicates an area or distance on the earth's surface: *The expedition covered a lot of ground.* In addition, **the ground** is the solid surface under our feet when we are in the open air: *You shouldn't sit on the ground when it's wet.* **The floor** is the solid surface under our feet inside a building: *He left his clothes lying all over the floor.* **Ground**, **earth** and especially **soil** refer to the natural material in which trees and plants grow. **Ground** is an area of soil and earth: *stony ground* ○ *black earth* ○ *sandy soil.*

earthen /ˈɜːθn/ *adj* [usu attrib] **1** made of earth: *earthen floors.* **2** made of baked clay: *earthen pots.* □ **ˈearthenware** *n* [U] pottery made of baked clay: [attrib] *an earthenware bowl.*

earthly /ˈɜːθlɪ/ *adj* **1** of this world; not spiritual: *earthly joys, possessions.* **2** (*infml*) (usu with negative) possible; conceivable: *You've no earthly hope of winning.* **3** (idm) **no earthly use** (*infml*) totally useless. **not have an ˈearthly** (*Brit infml*) not have the slightest chance or hope or idea: *'Why isn't it working?' 'I haven't an earthly* (ie I don't know at all.)'

earthquake /ˈɜːθkweɪk/ (also **quake**) *n* sudden violent movement of the earth's surface. Many earthquakes are relatively gentle, but the severe ones that cause great damage are caused by movements of the earth's crust. Geologists have discovered that under the continents and oceans the earth's crust is made up of a number of sheets of rock called 'plates' which can rub against each other or pull apart, creating the shock waves that form the earthquake. The strength of these waves is measured on the *Richter scale, and severe earthquakes usu register between 7 and 9 on the scale. ⇨ illus.

earwig /ˈɪəwɪg/ *n* small harmless insect with pincers at the rear end of its body.

ease[1] /iːz/ *n* [U] **1** freedom from work, discomfort, pain or anxiety: *a life of ease* ○ *ease of mind* ○ *The injection brought him immediate ease.* Cf EASY[1] 2. **2** (idm) **(stand) at ˈease** (as a military command) (stand) with feet apart and hands behind the back. Cf ATTENTION 4. **(be/feel) at (one's) ˈease** (be/feel) comfortable and unworried; (be/feel) completely relaxed: *I never feel at ease in his company.* ○ *Finish the work at your ease,* ie in your own time. **ill at ease** ⇨ ILL[1]. **put/set sb at (his, her, etc) ˈease** make sb feel comfortable, free from embarrassment, etc: *He had been dreading their meeting but her warm welcome soon put him at his ease.* **put/set sb's mind at ease/rest** ⇨ MIND[1]. **ˌtake one's ˈease** stop working or worrying; relax: *She sat down and took her ease by the fire.* **with ˈease** without difficulty: *He passed the test with ease.*

ease[2] /iːz/ *v* **1** (**a**) [Tn] relieve (the body or mind) from pain, anxiety, discomfort, etc: *The aspirins eased my headache.* ○ *Talking eased his anxiety.* (**b**) [Tn·pr] ~ **sb of sth** free sb from suffering, etc: *Walking helped to ease him of his pain.* **2** [I, Ip] (**a**) become less painful, severe, etc: *The pain eased.* (**b**) become less unpleasant or difficult: *The situation has eased (off).* **3** [Tn] make (sth) looser or less tight; slacken: *The coat needs to be eased under the armpits.* **4** (idm) **ease sb's ˈconscience/ˈmind** free sb from guilt, worry, etc: *It would ease my mind to know where he was.* **5** (phr v) **ease (sb/sth) across, along, away, etc** (cause to) move across, etc slowly and carefully: *He eased himself along the ledge to reach the terrified boy.* ○ *She eased her injured foot into her shoe.* **ˌease ˈdown** reduce speed: *Ease down: there's a sharp bend ahead.* **ˌease ˈoff/ˈup** become less severe, oppressive or urgent: *The tension between us has eased off a little.* ○ *The flow of traffic eased off.* ○ *I'm very busy just now; wait until things have eased up a little.* **ease up on sb/sth** be more moderate with sb/sth: *I should ease up on the cigarettes if I were you.*

easel /ˈiːzl/ *n* wooden frame for holding a blackboard or a picture (while it is being painted).

easement /ˈiːzmənt/ *n* [C, U] (*law*) right to use another person's land in some way, esp the right to cross it.

east /iːst/ *n* [sing] (*abbr* **E**) **1 the east** point of the horizon where the sun rises; one of the four main points of the compass. The sun rising in the east is a powerful symbol of hope and new life for many

earthquake

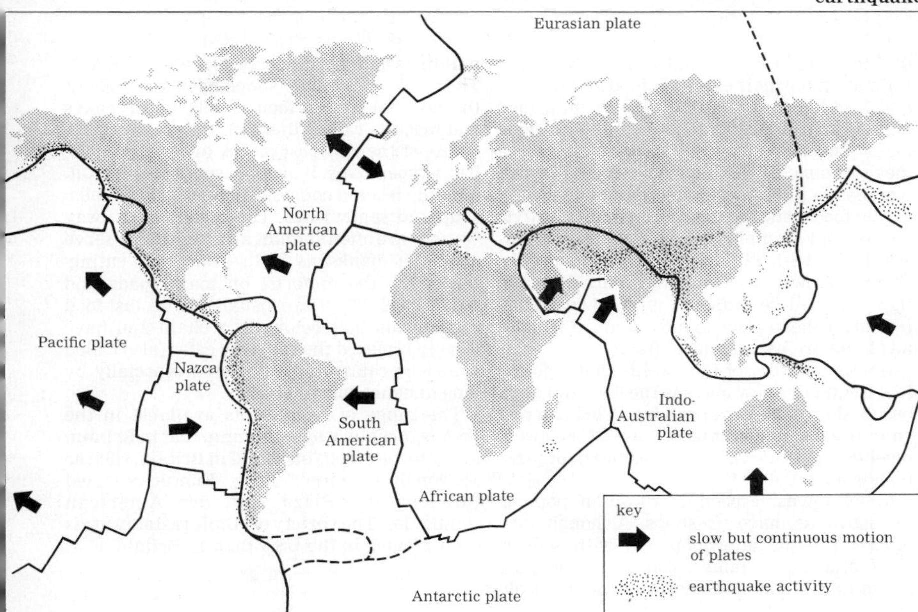

peoples. Early Christian churches were usu built with the main altar facing towards the east for this reason: *The wind is blowing from the east.* ○ *He lives to the east of* (ie further east than) *Exeter.* Cf NORTH, SOUTH, WEST. **2 the East** (a) countries of Asia, esp China and Japan: *philosophies of the East* ○ *Yoga originated in the East.* (b) any part of the world to the east of Europe: *the Middle East* ○ *the Near East* ○ *the Far East.* **3 the East** (*US*) eastern side of the USA: *I was born in the East, but now live in Los Angeles.*

▷ **east** *adj* [attrib] **1** in or towards the east: *He lives on the east coast.* **2** (of winds) from the east: *an east wind.* Cf EASTERLY.

east *adv* towards the east: *My window faces east.* ○ *We are travelling east.* ○ *a town east of the Danube.*

eastward /ˈiːstwəd/ *adj* towards the east: *in an eastward direction.*

eastward, eastwards *adv*: *to travel eastwards.* ➩ Usage at FORWARD².

□ **eastbound** /ˈiːstbaʊnd/ *adj* travelling towards the east: *Is this the eastbound train?* ○ *the eastbound section of the motorway.*

the ˌEast ˈEnd (*Brit*) thickly populated, mainly working-class part of East London. Cf THE WEST END (WEST). ➩ article at LONDON. **ˌEast-ˈEnder** *n* person living in the East End.

the ˈEast Side the eastern part of *Manhattan in *New York: *the Lower East Side*, ie its southern part, a poor area.

East Anglia /ˌiːst ˈæŋɡlɪə/ region of eastern England made up of Norfolk, Suffolk and parts of Cambridgeshire and Essex. It is an important agricultural area, famous in the Middle Ages for its wool and now producing large amounts of grain. It contains the *Fens.

Easter /ˈiːstə(r)/ *n* annual Christian festival, the most important in the Christian year, that occurs on a Sunday in March or April, and celebrates the resurrection of Christ after the crucifixion; period about this time: [attrib] *ˌEaster ˈDay* ○ *ˌEaster ˈSunday* ○ *ˈEaster week*, ie the week beginning on Easter Sunday ○ *the Easter holidays.*

□ **ˈEaster egg** egg made of chocolate or a hen's egg with a painted or dyed shell, eaten at Easter.

the ˌEaster ˈRising rebellion against British rule in Dublin and other Irish cities, which took place in 1916 at Easter. Those involved finally surrendered and some of the leaders were executed. ➩ article at IRELAND.

Easter Island /ˈiːstər aɪlənd/ island in the SE Pacific Ocean west of Chile, which administers the island. It is famous for the huge sculptures of human heads, up to 10 m high, found all over the island. Nothing is known of the civilization that produced them.

easterly /ˈiːstəlɪ/ *adj* [usu attrib], *adv* **1** in or towards the east: *in an easterly direction.* **2** (of winds) blowing from the east: *an easterly wind.*

▷ **easterly** *n* wind blowing from the east: *strong easterlies at sea.*

eastern /ˈiːstən/ (also **Eastern**) *adj* [attrib] of, from or living in the east part of the world or of a specified region: *Eastern customs, religions, etc* ○ *the eastern seaboard of the USA.*

▷ **ˈeasterner** *n* person from the east of a country, esp an American from the eastern states.

easternmost /ˈiːstənməʊst/ *adj* situated farthest east: *the easternmost city in Europe.*

□ **the ˌEastern ˈBloc** (between 1945 and 1989) communist countries of Eastern Europe considered as a group.

ˌEastern ˈStandard Time (also **ˈEastern Time**) standard time used in the eastern states of the USA and eastern Canada, five hours behind *Greenwich Mean Time.

East India Company /ˌiːst ˈɪndɪə kʌmpənɪ/ **the East India Company** company formed in 1600 to develop trade in the East Indies. By the 18th century it had its own army and political service, and was responsible for the administration of British India. In the 19th century the company was responsible for founding *Singapore, but in 1858 the British government took over its work following the *Indian Mutiny.

East Indies /ˌiːst ˈɪndɪz/ **the East Indies** islands off the south-east coast of Asia (eg Java, Borneo, the Philippines), now usu called the Malay Archipelago.

easting /ˈiːstɪŋ/ *n* (*nautical*) distance travelled or measured towards the east. Cf NORTHING.

East Sussex /ˌiːst ˈsʌsɪks/ county of SE England, formed in 1974 from the eastern part of Sussex. It is mainly agricultural, and its many coastal resorts (eg Brighton) are important tourist centres. ➩ map at App 1.

easy¹ /ˈiːzɪ/ *adj* **(-ier, -iest) 1** not difficult; done or obtained without great effort: *an easy exam* ○ *It is an easy place to reach.* ○ *The place is easy to reach.* **2** free from pain, discomfort, anxiety, trouble, etc: *lead an easy life* ○ *My mind is easier now.* Cf EASE¹ 1. **3** [attrib] not stiff or embarrassed: *have easy manners.* **4** [attrib] readily exploited, cheated, etc: *an easy victim* ○ *an easy prey.* **5** (idm) **as ˌeasy as ˈanything/as ˈpie/as ABˈC/as falling off a ˈlog/as ˈwinking** (*infml*) very easy or easily. **easy game** person or thing that can easily be attacked, exploited or made a victim. **easy/difficult of approach** ➩ APPROACH *n.* **ˌeasy ˈmoney** money obtained either dishonestly or for little work. **ˌeasy on the ˈear/ˈeye** (*infml*) pleasant to listen to or look at: *This music's easy on the ear late at night.* (*infml*) **an easy/a soft touch** ➩ TOUCH². **free and easy** ➩ FREE¹. **on easy ˈterms** (*commerce*) (of a loan) with a low rate of interest, or (of a purchase) allowing the buyer to pay gradually over a long period. **I'm ˈeasy** (*infml esp Brit*) (replying when a choice has been offered) I have no preference. **take the easy way out** escape from a difficult or an awkward situation by the least demanding (and possibly not the most honourable) course of action. **a woman of easy virtue** ➩ WOMAN.

▷ **easily** /ˈiːzəlɪ/ *adv* **1** without difficulty: *I can easily finish it tonight.* **2** without doubt: *It's easily the best film I've seen this year.* **3** possibly: *That could easily be the answer we're looking for.*

easiness *n* [U].

□ **ˌeasy ˈchair** large comfortable armchair.

ˌeasyˈgoing *adj* (of people) relaxed in manner; placid and tolerant: *My mother doesn't mind who comes to stay, she's very easygoing.*

ˈEasy Street (*infml*) situation in which one has plenty of money and can live comfortably: *living in/on Easy Street.*

easy² /ˈiːzɪ/ *adv* **(-ier, -iest) 1** (as a command) move sth gently and slowly: *Easy with that chair — one of its legs is loose.* **2** (idm) **ˌeasier ˌsaid than ˈdone** more difficult to do than to talk about: *'Why don't you get yourself a job?' 'That's easier said than done.'* **ˌeasy ˈcome, ˌeasy ˈgo** (*saying*) sth, esp money, obtained without difficulty is quickly lost or spent: *I often win money at cards but never save a penny — 'easy come, easy go' is my motto.* **ˈeasy/ˈgently ˌdoes it** (*infml*) this job, etc should be done slowly and carefully: *Take your time; easy does it.* **ˌgo ˈeasy** (*infml*) work less hard: *You should go easy, you're getting tired.* **go easy on/with sb/sth** (*infml*) be careful, gentle or moderate with sb/sth: *Go easy on the milk; we all want some.* ○ *You should go easy on* (ie be less strict with) *that boy; he's only young.* **ˌstand ˈeasy** (as a military command) stand with more freedom of movement than when at ease (EASE¹ 2). **take it/things ˈeasy** relax; not work too hard or do too much: *I like to take things easy when I'm on holiday.*

eat /iːt/ *v* (*pt* **ate** /et; *US* eɪt/, *pp* **eaten** /ˈiːtn/) **1** [I, Ip, Tn, Tn·p] ~ **(up)**/~ **sth (up)** take (solid food or soup) into the mouth and swallow it for nourishment: *He was too ill to eat.* ○ *Eat up* (ie finish eating) *now* ○ *Eat (up) your dinner.* ○ *Lions eat meat*, ie Meat is their diet. **2** [I] have a meal: *Where shall we eat tonight?* ➩ article. **3** (idm) **dog eat dog** ➩ DOG¹. **ˌeat sb aˈlive/ˌeat sb for ˈbreakfast** (*infml*) be able to dominate, or exploit sb: *She'll eat him for breakfast.* **ˌeat ˈcrow** (*US infml*) be forced to apologize, agree to sth, etc after refusing to do so. **eat, drink and be ˈmerry (for tomorrow we die)** (*saying*) one should enjoy life as much as possible without worrying about the future. **eat one's ˈheart out (for sb/sth)** endure envy, longing, frustration, etc in silence: *Since he left, she's been sitting at home eating her heart out.* **ˌeat humble ˈpie** be very apologetic: *When he realized his mistake, he had to eat humble pie.* **ˌeat like a ˈhorse** (*infml*) eat a lot. **eat out of sb's ˈhand** be submissive and compliant towards sb: *She soon had the class eating out of her hand.* **eat sb out of ˌhouse and ˈhome** (*infml often joc*) (of people) eat a lot of food which sb else has paid for: *I hope your brother won't stay much longer, he's eating us out of house and home!* **eat oneself ˈsick (on sth)** (*infml*) eat so much (of sth) that one feels or is sick: *The children would eat themselves sick on chocolate if I let them.* **ˌeat one's ˈwords** admit that what one said was wrong. **have one's cake and eat it** ➩ CAKE. **I'll ˌeat my ˈhat** (*infml*) (expression used by sb who believes that sth is so unlikely to

Eating Out

There is a wide variety of places to go when you want to eat out in Britain. In the most expensive restaurants and hotels, the style of cooking is often French and the menu is usually written in French, often with an English translation. Almost all hotels have a restaurant where non-residents can have lunch or dinner, and a lounge where they can have tea, coffee or a drink before their meal.

Most towns have a variety of restaurants offering the cuisine of several different countries, with Indian, Chinese and Italian restaurants the most popular. In London especially it is possible to eat the food of most countries in the world. Most of these ethnic restaurants are owned and run as small family businesses. Other restaurants are part of a chain, for example Berni or Harvester, and offer a standard menu throughout the country. Many of these are primarily steak bars with a choice of other dishes also available. They are often located in old or even historic buildings in town centres.

Almost all pubs now offer food, which may be snacks bought at the bar or meals in a separate dining area. Certain pubs have gained a reputation for their excellent food and service, and a guide to good pubs is now published annually in addition to the guides to good hotels and restaurants. Wine bars also serve meals or snacks with a wide selection of wine, whereas in pubs beer is the main drink.

Fast-food restaurants serving American-style pizzas and hamburgers are very popular, especially with children and young people. There are fewer cafés than there once were, but they can still be found in most towns. They provide a cheap place to have a cup of tea or a meal and are usually open all day.

Another feature of British life that is found less frequently nowadays is the 'fish and chip' bar or shop, where you can buy fried fish and chips to eat at home. Other kinds of 'take-away' meals are provided by Chinese, Indian or pizza restaurants.

Many towns, especially those in popular tourist areas, have tea-shops. Although they mainly provide afternoon tea, with scones, buns and cakes, many also serve morning coffee and lunch. Tea-shops are often in old buildings and the atmosphere is old-fashioned. There are also coffee shops open throughout the day, which serve food as well, mainly cakes and biscuits rather than full meals.

One of the cheapest places to eat is a snack bar, a type of café. It may not serve meals at all, but only tea and coffee, with food such as rolls, soup and sandwiches. The buffets at railway stations are often similar, although many serve alcoholic drinks as well. There are eating-places for the motorist on main roads and motorways. They are usually large fast-food restaurants that belong to a chain and have largely replaced the roadside cafés (also called transport cafés) that were used especially by long-distance lorry drivers.

The range of restaurants available in the USA is in many ways similar to that in Britain. Many fast-food chains found in Britain, such as McDonald's, Burger King, Kentucky Fried Chicken and Pizza Hut, are American companies. The variety of ethnic restaurants is even greater in the USA than in Britain.

happen that even to suggest it is absurd): *Rob's always late — if he gets here on time I'll eat my hat.* **the proof of the pudding is in the eating** ⇨ PROOF[1]. **what's eating you/him, etc?** (*infml*) why are you/is he upset, angry, etc? **4** (phr v) **eat sth away/eat away at sth** erode: *The river is eating away at the bank.* **eat into sth** (**a**) consume sth; destroy; dissolve; corrode: *Acids eat into metal.* (**b**) (*fig*) consume a part of sth: *Paying for that new carpet has eaten into my savings.* **eat out** have a meal in a restaurant, etc rather than at home: *I'm too tired to cook tonight; shall we eat out?* **eat sb up** (*fig*) (usu passive) consume; obsess; worry: *be eaten up with curiosity, anger, envy, etc* ○ *Jealousy was eating him up.*

▷ **eatable** fit to be eaten; good to eat: *Our school meals are hardly eatable.* Cf EDIBLE. — *n* (usu *pl*); (*infml*) food: *Have you brought the eatables?*

eater *n* **1** person who eats (in a particular way): *He's a big, greedy, etc eater,* ie He eats a lot, eats greedily, etc. **2** = EATING APPLE.

eats *n* [pl] (*infml*) food ready to be eaten: *There were plenty of eats, but not enough to drink.*

□ **ˈeating apple** type of apple that is suitable for eating uncooked. Cf COOKER 2.

ˈeating-house (also **ˈeating-place**) *n* restaurant.

eau-de-Cologne /ˌəʊ də kəˈləʊn/ (also **cologne**) *n* [U] perfume made originally at Cologne.

eaves /iːvz/ *n* [pl] overhanging lower edges of a roof: *birds nesting under the eaves.* ⇨ illus at HOME.

eavesdrop /ˈiːvzdrɒp/ *v* [I, Ipr] (**-pp-**) ~ (**on sb/sth**) listen secretly to a private conversation: *eavesdropping on the discussion, her parents.* ▷ **eavesdropper** *n*.

ebb /eb/ *v* [I, Ip] ~ (**away**) **1** (of the tide) go out; recede. Cf FLOW 5. **2** (*fig*) grow less; become slowly weak or faint: *Daylight was ebbing away.* ○ *Our enthusiasm soon began to ebb.*

▷ **ebb** [sing] **1** (usu **the ebb**) (of a tide) the flowing out: *The tide is on the ebb,* ie is going out. Cf FLOOD[2] 3. **2** (idm) **at a low ebb** ⇨ LOW[1]. **the ebb and flow (of sth)** (of noise, fashions, etc) regular increase and decrease in intensity; constant fluctuation: *the ebb and flow of conversation.* **on the ˈebb** diminishing; declining: *My luck is on the ebb.*

□ ˌ**ebb ˈtide** /ˌeb ˈtaɪd/ *n* = EBB *n* 1.

ebony /ˈebənɪ/ *n* [U] hard black wood of a tropical tree.

▷ **ebony** *adj* **1** made of ebony: *the ebony keys on a piano.* **2** black: *ebony skin.*

ebullient /ɪˈbʌlɪənt, *also* ɪˈbʊlɪənt/ *adj* full of energy and excitement; exuberant.

▷ **ebullience** /-əns/ *n* [U] state of being ebullient; exuberance: *She burst into the room with her usual ebullience, and immediately started talking to everyone.*

ebulliently *adv*.

EC /ˌiːˈsiː/ *abbr* **1** East Central: *London EC1 4PW*, ie as a postal code. **2** European Community (the Common Market).

eccentric /ɪkˈsentrɪk/ *adj* **1** (of people, behaviour) unusual; peculiar; not conventional or normal: *his eccentric habits* ○ *an eccentric old lady.* **2** (**a**) (of circles) not having the same centre. Cf CONCENTRIC. (**b**) (of orbits) not circular. (**c**) (of planets, etc) moving in an eccentric orbit.

▷ **eccentric** *n* **1** eccentric person: *The club seemed to be full of eccentrics.* **2** mechanical device consisting of a disc at the end of a shaft for changing circular movement into backward-and-forward movement.

eccentrically /-klɪ/ *adv*.

eccentricity /ˌeksenˈtrɪsətɪ/ *n* **1** [U] quality of being eccentric; strangeness of behaviour, etc: *eccentricity of style, clothing, manners, ideas.* **2** [C] instance of this; strange or unusual act or habit: *One of his eccentricities is sleeping under the bed instead of on it.*

Eccles cake /ˈeklz keɪk/ small round cake made of sugar-coated flaky pastry filled with currants.

Ecclesiastes /ɪˌkliːzɪˈæstiːz/ (*abbr* **Eccles**) book of the Old Testament traditionally but probably wrongly said to have been written by *Solomon. The author praises wisdom and the fear of God but refers to the vanity of human life. ⇨ App 5.

ecclesiastic /ɪˌkliːzɪˈæstɪk/ *n* clergyman (in the Christian Church).

▷ **ecclesiastical** /-kl/ *adj* [usu attrib] (**a**) of clergymen. (**b**) of the Christian Church.

ecclesiastically /-klɪ/ *adv*.

ECG /ˌiː siː ˈdʒiː/ *abbr* (*medical*) electrocardiogram: *have an ECG test.*

echelon /ˈeʃəlɒn/ *n* **1** level of authority or responsibility; rank in an organization: *the upper echelons of the Civil Service.* **2** step-like formation of troops, aircraft, ships, etc: *aircraft flying in echelon,* ie in a line stretching backwards to the left or right.

Echo /ˈekəʊ/ (in Greek mythology) nymph who, when her love was rejected by a young man called Narcissus, withered away until only her voice remained.

echo[1] /ˈekəʊ/ *n* (*pl* ~**es**) **1** (**a**) reflection and repetition of a sound, eg from a wall or inside an enclosed space: *This cave has a good echo.* (**b**) sound repeated in this way: *If you shout loudly, you'll hear the echo.* **2** (*fig*) person or thing that imitates another: *He has no original opinions; he's just his father's echo.* ○ *There are many echoes of Shakespeare in his work.* **3** (idm) **to the ˈecho** (*dated*) long and loudly: *Her performance was cheered to the echo.*

□ **ˈecho location** use of reflected sound waves to identify the position of objects, eg by bats and dolphins or by radar apparatus.

ˈecho-sounder *n* instrument used for determining the depth of sth underneath a ship by measuring the time taken for sound waves to be echoed back from it.

echo[2] /ˈekəʊ/ *v* **1** (**a**) [Tn, Tn·p] ~ **sth** (**back**) (of places) send back (an echo): *The valley echoed (back) his song.* (**b**) [Tn] (*fig*) (of people, places, etc) repeat (sth); imitate; recall: *They echoed their leader's every word.* **2** [I, Ipr] ~ (**to/with sth**) (of places) repeat a sound: *The hills echoed to the sound of their laughter.* **3** [I, Ipr, Ip] (of sounds) be repeated as an echo: *His footsteps echoed (in the empty hall).* ○ *Their shouts echoed through the forest.*

éclair /ɪˈkleə(r), eɪˈkleə(r)/ *n* (also ˌ**chocolate éˈclair**) small finger-shaped pastry cake, filled with cream and iced with chocolate.

éclat /ˈeɪklɑː; *US* eɪˈklɑː/ *n* [U] **1** brilliance; conspicuous success: *to perform with éclat.* **2** praise; applause: *Her latest novel was received with great éclat.*

eclectic /ɪˈklektɪk/ *adj* (*fml*) (of people, beliefs, etc) not restricted to one source of ideas, etc, but choosing from or using a wide range: *He has an eclectic taste in music.*

▷ **eclectic** *n* person who works, thinks, etc in an eclectic way.

eclectically /-tɪklɪ/ *adv*.

eclecticism /ɪˈklektɪsɪzəm/ *n* [U].

eclipse /ɪˈklɪps/ *n* [C] **1** blocking of the light of the sun (when the moon is between it and the earth) or of the moon (when the earth's shadow falls on it). *a total/partial eclipse of the sun.* **2** [C, U] (*fig*) loss of brilliance, fame, power, etc: *After suffering an eclipse, she is now famous again.* ○ *The writer's* *name remained in eclipse for many years after his death.*

▷ **eclipse** *v* [Tn] **1** (of the moon, the sun, a planet, etc) cause an eclipse of (sth); cut off the light from: *The sun is partly eclipsed (by the moon).* **2** *(fig)* make (sb/sth) appear dull by comparison; outshine: *He is eclipsed by his wife, who is much cleverer and more amusing than he is.*

eclogue /ˈeklɒg/ *n* short poem, esp one in the form of a dialogue between country people, like those written by *Virgil.

eco- *comb form* (usu forming *ns*) ecological or of ecology: *ecosystem* ○ *ecotype.*

ecoclimate /ˈi:kəʊklaɪmɪt/ *n* climatic conditions affecting a particular animal or plant habitat.

ecology /i:ˈkɒlədʒɪ/ *n* [U] (scientific study of) the relation of plants and living creatures to each other and to their surroundings. Ecology became one of the most important scientific studies in the late 20th century when the drastic effect of human activity on the earth was realized. The disappearance of many species of plants and animals showed how the delicate balance allowing organisms to live together can be affected by minor changes. Research is leading to new ways of conservation to preserve the earth's environment: *Chemicals in the factory's sewage system have changed the ecology of the whole area.*

▷ **ecological** /ˌi:kəˈlɒdʒɪkl/ *adj* of ecology: *the dangerous ecological effects of industry*, eg the pollution of the atmosphere, of rivers, etc. **ecologically** /-klɪ/ *adv.*

ecologist /i:ˈkɒlədʒɪst/ *n* student of or expert in ecology.

□ **the Eˈcology Party** (in Britain) former name of the Green Party.

Econ *abbr* Economics: *James Rigg MSc* (ie Master of Science)*(Econ).*

economic /ˌi:kəˈnɒmɪk, ˌekəˈnɒmɪk/ *adj* **1** [attrib] of economics(1), or of an economy: *the government's economic policy* ○ *economic development* ○ *economic sanctions*, ie punishment of another country by reducing or stopping trade with it. **2** [attrib] connected with trade and industry: *economic geography*, ie studied mainly in connection with industry. **3** designed to give a profit: *an economic rent*, ie one that brings the owner at least as much money as he has spent on the house ○ *It is not always economic for buses to run on Sundays.*

economical /ˌi:kəˈnɒmɪkl, ˌekəˈnɒmɪkl/ *adj* careful in the spending of money, time, etc and in the use of resources; not wasteful: *an economical car to run*, eg one with low petrol consumption ○ *She is economical with/in her use of salt when cooking.* ○ *an economical style of writing*, ie one that does not waste words. ▷ **economically** /-klɪ/ *adv*: *His scheme is not economically sound.*

economics /ˌi:kəˈnɒmɪks, ˌekəˈnɒmɪks/ *n* [sing *v*] **1** science or principles of the production, distribution and consumption of goods esp with reference to cost: *the economics of publishing.* **2** condition of a country as regards its wealth: *third world economics.*

economist /ɪˈkɒnəmɪst/ *n* student of or expert in economics.

economize, -ise /ɪˈkɒnəmaɪz/ *v* [I, Ipr] ~ **(on sth)** save (money, time, resources, etc); spend less than before; be economical: *Our electricity bills are higher than we can afford — we must start to economize.* ○ *economize on petrol.*

economy /ɪˈkɒnəmɪ/ *n* **1** [C, U] (instance of) avoidance of waste (of money, strength, time, resources, etc): *practise economy* ○ *It's an economy to buy good shoes; they cost more, but they last much longer than cheap ones.* ○ *economies of scale*, ie reductions in the average cost of producing goods and services as a result of producing them in large quantities ○ [attrib] *We're having an economy drive* (ie making a special effort to avoid waste or misuse of resources, etc) *at school.* ○ *an economy pack*, ie a large amount of a product offered for sale at a reduced price ○ *economy class*, ie the cheapest class of (air) travel. **2** [U] control and management of money, resources, etc of a community, society, household, etc: *political economy* ○ *domestic economy.* **3** [C] (often **the economy**) operation and management of a country's money supply, trade and industry; economic system: *The state of the economy is very worrying.* ○ *The economies of Japan and China.*

ecosystem /ˈi:kəʊsɪstəm/ *n* ecological unit consisting of a group of plants and living creatures interacting with each other and with their surroundings, esp in a self-sustaining way. An ecosystem may exist on a small scale, eg the branches of a tree, but the earth as a whole can also be viewed as an ecosystem.

ecstasy /ˈekstəsɪ/ *n* [U, C] (feeling or state of) great joy or happiness: *in an ecstasy of delight* ○ *religious ecstasy* ○ *be in/go into/be thrown into ecstasy/ecstasies (over sth).*

▷ **ecstatic** /ɪkˈstætɪk/ *adj* causing or showing ecstasy: *He was ecstatic at the news of his daughter's birth.* **ecstatically** /-klɪ/ *adv.*

ECT /ˌi: si: ˈti:/ *abbr* (*medical*) electroconvulsive therapy (used eg on psychiatric patients).

ectomorph /ˈektəmɔ:f/ *n* thin tall person, thought likely by some psychologists to have an introverted personality. Cf ENDOMORPH, MESOMORPH. ▷ **ectomorphic** *adj.*

-ectomy *comb form* (forming *ns*) indicating removal by surgical operation: *tonsillectomy* ○ *appendectomy.*

ectopic /ˌekˈtɒpɪk/ *adj* (of a pregnancy) in which the foetus develops outside the womb or in an abnormal position.

ectoplasm /ˈektəplæzəm/ *n* [U] substance that is thought by some to flow from a spiritualistic medium during a trance.

ECU (also **ecu**) /ˈeɪkju:/ *abbr* European Currency Unit (of the Common Market).

Ecuador

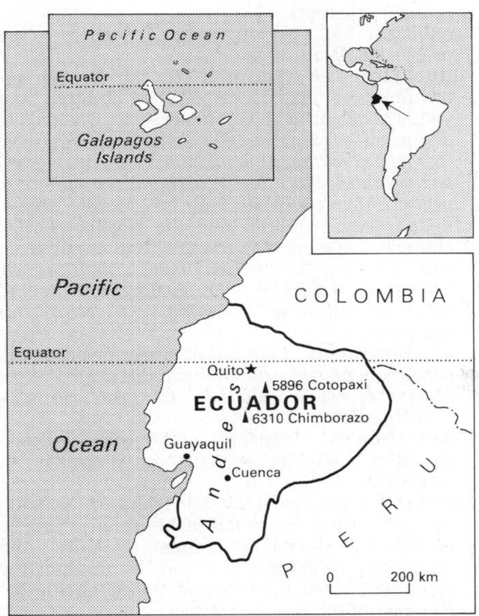

Ecuador /ˈekwədɔ:(r)/ country in NW South America lying on the equator; pop approx 10 204 000; official language Spanish; capital Quito; unit of currency Sucre (= 100 centavos). The country is divided into three parts: the coastal plain between the Pacific and the Andes; the mountains of the Andes, with a large part of the population; and the eastern region, largely covered in tropical forest. The coastal plain produces export crops of bananas, cacao and coffee, and livestock is reared on the Andean plateaus. The Pacific provides rich fishing grounds and there are important oil reserves. ⇨ map. ▷ **Ecuadorean** *n, adj.*

ecumenical (also **oecumenical**) /ˌi:kju:ˈmenɪkl, ˌekju:-/ *adj* **1** of or representing the whole Christian world or universal Church: *an Ecumenical Council*, eg of all the Roman Catholic Church as summoned by the Pope. **2** seeking the unity of the various Christian churches throughout the world: *the ecumenical movement.*

▷ **ecumenicalism** /-kəlɪzəm/ (also **ecumenism** /ɪˈkju:mənɪzəm/) *n* [U] belief in, or efforts towards, universal Christian unity.

ecumenically /-klɪ/ *adv.*

eczema /ˈeksɪmə; *US* ɪgˈzi:mə/ *n* [U] skin disease causing redness, severe itching and scaling of the skin.

ed *abbr* **1** edited (by); edition; editor. **2** educated: *Peter Jeffries, b 1932, ed Tonbridge Sch.*

-ed (also **-d**) *suff* (with *ns* forming *adjs*) having (the characteristics of); affected with: *talented* ○ *bigoted* ○ *diseased* ○ *quick-witted.*

Edam /ˈi:dæm; *US also* ˈi:dəm/ *n* [U, C] hard round Dutch cheese, usu yellow with a red rind.

Edda /ˈedə/ either of two collections of Scandinavian literature dating from the 13th century. The **Elder** or **Poetic Edda** contains poems on mythical or traditional subjects; the **Younger** or **Prose Edda**, attributed to the Icelandic historian Snorri Sturluson, is a guide to Icelandic poetry. Most of our knowledge of Scandinavian mythology comes from the Eddas.

eddy /ˈedɪ/ *n* circular or spiral movement of water, air, fog, dust, etc: *Eddies of mist rose from the valley.* ○ *Eddies of dust swirled in the road.*

▷ **eddy** *v* (*pt, pp* **eddied**) [I, Ip] move in or like an eddy; whirl: *(fig) groups of tourists eddying continually about the main square of the city.*

edelweiss /ˈeɪdlvaɪs/ *n* (*pl* unchanged) small Alpine plant with white flowers.

edema (*US*) = OEDEMA.

Eden /ˈi:dn/ (also **the garden of Eden**) (*Bible*) beautiful garden where Adam and Eve lived in great happiness before they disobeyed God by eating the fruit of the tree of knowledge. It has been claimed that its location was in *Mesopotamia, now part of Iraq: *(fig) Life is no garden of Eden* (ie is unpleasant) *at the moment.*

edentate /ɪˈdenteɪt/ *adj* (*fml*) having few or no teeth.

edge[1] /edʒ/ *n* **1** sharp cutting part of a blade, knife, sword, or some other tool or weapon: *a knife with a sharp edge* ○ *put an edge on an axe*, ie sharpen it. **2** (line marking the) outside limit or boundary of a solid (flat) object, surface or area: *the edge of a coin, plate, record* ○ *He fell off the edge of the cliff.* ○ *Don't put that glass on the edge of the table; it might fall off.* ○ *the water's edge* ○ *He lives at the edge of the forest.* **3** (idm) **(be/keep sb) on the edge of one's seat/chair** (be/make sb) very excited about what is happening: *The last reel of the film kept us on the edge of our seats, wondering what was going to happen.* **give sb/get the (rough) edge of one's/sb's tongue** (*infml*) speak to sb/be spoken to by sb angrily, rudely, critically, etc: *Her pupils often got the rough edge of her tongue when they disobeyed her.* **have, etc an ˈedge to one's voice** have or show a degree of anger, nervousness, annoyance, etc in the way in which one speaks: *She was trying to remain calm, but there was a distinct edge to her voice.* **have, etc an/the edge on/over sb/sth** (*infml*) have, etc a slight advantage over sb/sth: *The young tennis player definitely had the edge on his older opponent.* **(be) on ˈedge** (be) nervous, excited or irritable: *She was a bit on edge till she heard he was safe.* **on a razor's edge** ⇨ RAZOR. **set one's teeth on edge** ⇨ TOOTH. **take the edge off sth** reduce, dull or soften sth: *I need a sandwich to take the edge off my appetite.* ○ *His brother's failure took the edge off his own success.*

▷ **-edged** /edʒd/ (forming compound *adjs*) having an edge or edges of a specified type: *a ˌblunt-edged ˈknife* ○ *a ˌtwo-edged reˈmark.*

edge[2] /edʒ/ *v* **1** [Tn, Tn·pr usu passive] ~ **sth (with sth)** supply (sth) with a border: *The handkerchief is edged with white lace.* ○ *a road edged with grass.* **2** (phr v) **edge (sth/one's way) across, along, away, back, etc** move slowly and carefully across, etc: *The climber edged carefully along the narrow rock ledge.* ○ *I edged (my chair) towards the door.* ○ *The policeman slowly edged his way forward.* **edge**

sb/sth out (of sth) cause sb/sth gradually to lose a position or power: *He was edged out of his job by his ambitious assistant.* ○ *Their new product has edged all its competitors out of the market.*

Edgehill /edʒˈhɪl/ first important battle of the *English Civil War, in Warwickshire (1642). The Royalist troops won, but failed to take advantage of their victory.

edgeways /ˈedʒweɪz/ (also **edgewise** /ˈedʒwaɪz/) *adv* **1** with the edge outwards or forwards; sideways: *If you turn it edgeways you'll get the desk through the door.* **2** (idm) **(not) get a word in edgeways** ➪ WORD.

Edgeworth /ˈedʒwəθ/ Maria (1768-1849), Irish author. Her writings on women's education and her novels, often set in Ireland (eg *Castle Rackrent*), were widely admired in her day.

edging /ˈedʒɪŋ/ *n* [U, C] thing that forms the border or edge of sth: *a/some lace edging on a dress.*
□ ˈ**edging-shears** *n* tool for trimming grass on the edges of a lawn.

edgy /ˈedʒɪ/ *adj* (*infml*) nervous; easily upset or annoyed: *She's been very edgy recently, waiting for the examination results.* ○ *She's always been an edgy type of person.* ▷ **edgily** *adv.* **edginess** *n* [U].

edible /ˈedɪbl/ *adj* fit to be eaten: *This food is scarcely edible.* ○ *edible* (ie not poisonous) *wild berries.* Cf EATABLE (EAT).

edict /ˈiːdɪkt/ *n* order or proclamation issued by an authority: *by edict of the king* ○ *obey the edicts of parliament.*

edification /ˌedɪfɪˈkeɪʃn/ *n* [U] (*fml or joc*) improvement of mind or character: *I am telling you this simply for your edification.*

edifice /ˈedɪfɪs/ *n* (*fml or joc*) large or imposing building: *the ruined edifice on the hill* ○ (*fig*) *He had high ideals in his youth but gradually the whole edifice crumbled.*

edify /ˈedɪfaɪ/ *v* (*pt, pp* **-fied**) [Tn] (*fml or joc*) improve the mind or character of (sb).
▷ **edifying** *adj* morally improving: *edifying books* ○ *The President appearing on a TV chat show was not an edifying spectacle.*

Edinburgh /ˈedɪnbrə; *US* ˈedɪnbərəʊ/ capital of Scotland. It is the country's administrative centre and with Glasgow one of its two main cultural and intellectual centres, with two universities and many museums and art galleries. It is popular with tourists, esp during its annual international arts festival; besides the official programme presenting famous artists, the 'Fringe' accepts many thousands of performers, often specializing in avant-garde art-forms. ➪ map at UNITED KINGDOM.

Thomas Edison

Edison /ˈedɪsn/ Thomas Alva (1847-1931), American inventor. He had little formal education, but his interest in electricity led him to design many pieces of technology now in common everyday use, including the electric light, the phonograph (forerunner of the record-player) and an early form of thermionic valve. ➪ illus.

edit /ˈedɪt/ *v* [Tn] **1** prepare (a piece of writing, often another person's) for publication, eg in a book, newspaper, or magazine: *edit a Shakespeare play for use in schools* ○ *edit a book of poetry.* **2** be responsible for planning, directing and publishing (a newspaper, magazine, etc). **3** prepare (a film, tape recording, radio or television programme, book, etc) by putting together collected parts in a suitable sequence. **4** arrange (data) for processing by a computer. **5** (phr v) **edit sth out (of sth)** remove (unwanted words, phrases, etc from a book, script, etc) in the process of editing: *They must have edited bits of the interview out.*

edition /ɪˈdɪʃn/ *n* **1** (**a**) form in which a book is published: *a paperback, hard-cover, de luxe, etc edition.* (**b**) form in which a radio or television programme is broadcast. **2** total number of copies of a book, newspaper, etc issued at one time: *a first edition* ○ *a revised edition* ○ *in its sixth edition* ○ *the morning/evening/lunch-time edition of a newspaper.* Cf IMPRESSION 6, REPRINT *n.*

editor /ˈedɪtə(r)/ *n* person who edits (esp a book, newspaper, magazine, radio or television programme) or who is in charge of part of a newspaper: *the ˈsports, fiˈnancial, ˈfashion editor.*
▷ **editorship** *n* [U].

editorial /ˌedɪˈtɔːrɪəl/ *adj* [usu attrib] of an editor: *the editorial office* ○ *editorial work.*
▷ **editorial** *n* special article in a newspaper, etc, giving an opinion on some topical issue (usu written by the editor). ➪ article at NEWSPAPER.

EDP /ˌiː diː ˈpiː/ *abbr* electronic data processing.

EDT /ˌiː diː ˈtiː/ *abbr* (*US*) Eastern Daylight Time. Cf EST 1.

educate /ˈedʒʊkeɪt/ *v* [Tn, Tn·pr, Cn·t] ~ **sb (in sth)** train the mind and character of sb; teach sb; provide sb with an education: *The public should be educated in how to use energy more effectively.* ○ *Parents should educate their children to behave well.* ○ *Where were you educated?* ie Which school(s), etc did you go to? ➪ Usage at TEACH.
▷ **educated** /ˈedʒʊkeɪtɪd/ *adj* **1** having been educated: *a highly educated woman* ○ *self-educated* ○ *educated tastes in art.* **2** (idm) **an ˌeducated ˈguess** guess based on experience (and therefore probably correct).
educator *n* person who educates (esp professionally).

education /ˌedʒʊˈkeɪʃn/ *n* [U] **1** (system of) training and instruction (esp of children and young people in schools, colleges, etc) designed to give knowledge and develop skills: *A child receives its early education at home.* ○ *primary/secondary/tertiary/adult education* ○ *No country can afford to neglect the education of its young people.* **2** knowledge, abilities and the development of character and mental powers that result from such training: *intellectual, moral, physical, etc education.* **3** field of study dealing with how to teach: *a college of education* ○ *a lecturer in education.*
▷ **educational** /-ʃənl/ *adj* of, about or providing education: *an educational magazine* ○ *I found the experience most educational.* **educationally** /-ʃənəlɪ/ *adv.*
educationist /ˌedʒʊˈkeɪʃənɪst/ (also **educationalist** /ˌedʒʊˈkeɪʃənəlɪst/) *n* specialist in education.

Edward I /ˈedwəd/ (1239-1307) king of England 1272-1307. He spent much of his reign trying to extend his kingdom, annexing Wales and attempting to control Scotland. He brought the stone of *Scone to England and earned the title 'the Hammer of the Scots'. ➪ App 3.

Edward II /ˈedwəd/ (1284-1327), king of England 1307-27. He was the first Prince of Wales. He invaded Scotland but was defeated at *Bannockburn. He was deposed by his wife Isabella and her allies, and murdered. ➪ App 3.

Edward III /ˈedwəd/ (1312-77), king of England 1327-77. His claims to the French throne led to the *Hundred Years War. ➪ App 3.

Edward IV /ˈedwəd/ (1442-83), king of England 1461-70 and 1471-83. He temporarily lost his throne to *Henry VI during the *Wars of the Roses. ➪ App 3.

Edward V /ˈedwəd/ (1470-83), king of England 1483. After reigning for three months he was deposed by his uncle, *Richard III, and is said to have been murdered by him. Cf PRINCES IN THE TOWER (PRINCE). ➪ App 3.

Edward VI /ˈedwəd/ (1537-53), king of England 1547-53. He was the son of *Henry VIII. During his brief reign the government of the country was in the hands of his advisers. ➪ App 3.

Edward VII /ˈedwəd/ (1841-1910), king of Britain 1901-10. He spent most of his life as Prince of Wales during the reign of his mother Queen *Victoria. His own brief and popular reign was a period of peace and prosperity before the First World War. ➪ App 3.
▷ **Edwardian** /edˈwɔːdɪən, -ˈwɑːd-/ *adj* of or typical of the period of Edward VII's reign. ➪ illus at DRESS.

Edward VIII /ˈedwəd/ (1894-1972), king of Britain 1936 but never crowned. He abdicated because of opposition to his marriage to a divorced American, and spent most of the rest of his life in France. ➪ App 3.

Edward the Confessor /ˌedwəd ðə kənˈfesə(r)/ (c 1003-66), king of England 1042-66. He was famous for his piety, but took little interest in government at the end of his reign. He was succeeded by *Harold II, the son of his chief adviser. ➪ App 3.

-ee *suff* **1** (with *vs* forming *ns*) person affected by: *employee* ○ *payee.* Cf -ER, -OR. **2** (with *adjs, vs* and *ns* forming *ns*) person described as or concerned with: *absentee* ○ *refugee.*

EEC /ˌiː iː ˈsiː/ *abbr* European Economic Community (the Common Market), former name of the European Community (EC): *join the EEC* ○ *EEC members.*

EEG /ˌiː iː ˈdʒiː/ *abbr* (*medical*) electroencephalogram: *give sb an EEG.*

eel /iːl/ *n* long, snake-like fish that is difficult to catch hold of: *jellied eels,* ie cooked and eaten cold in a savoury jelly.

-eer *suff* **1** (with *ns* forming *ns*) person concerned with: *auctioneer* ○ *mountaineer.* **2** (with *ns* forming *vs*) (*often derog*) be concerned with: *electioneer* ○ *profiteer.*

eerie (also **eery**) /ˈɪərɪ/ *adj* (**-ier, -iest**) causing a feeling of mystery and fear: *an eerie scream* ○ *an eerie silence.* ▷ **eerily** /ˈɪərəlɪ/ *adv.* **eeriness** /ˈɪərɪnɪs/ *n* [U].

eff /ef/ *v* (⚠ *euph*) **1** (idm) **ˌeff and ˈblind** swear violently (using words like *fuck* and *bloody*). **2** (phr v) **eff off** go away; fuck off: *I told him to eff off.* ▷ **effing** *adj*: *It's an effing nuisance.*

efface /ɪˈfeɪs/ *v* [Tn] (*fml*) **1** rub or wipe (sth) out; cause to fade: *Time and weather had long ago effaced the inscription on the monument.* ○ *Time alone will efface those unpleasant memories.* **2** ~ **oneself** keep in the background in order to escape being noticed; make oneself appear unimportant.
▷ **effacement** *n* [U].

effect /ɪˈfekt/ *n* **1** [C, U] ~ **(on sb/sth)** change produced by an action or cause; result or outcome: *the effects of heat on metal* ○ *Did the medicine have any effect/a good effect?* ○ *The film had quite an effect on her.* ○ *I tried to persuade him, but with little or no effect.* **2** [C, U] impression produced on the mind of the spectator, listener, reader, etc (esp in plays, films, broadcasts, paintings, etc): *The general effect of the painting is overwhelming.* ○ *The stage lighting gives the effect of a moonlit scene.* ○ *She only dresses like that for the effect it creates/for effect.* ○ *The science fiction film had some marvellous special effects.* **3 effects** [pl] (*fml or law*) personal property; possessions: *personal effects* ○ *household effects.* **4** (idm) **bring/put sth into efˈfect** cause sth to come into use: *The new system will soon be put into effect.* **come into efˈfect** (esp of laws, rules, etc) reach the stage of being in use: *The new seat-belt regulations came into effect last week.* **give effect to sth** (*fml*) cause sth to become active or produce a result: *The new ruling gives effect to the recommendations of the special committee.* **in efˈfect** (**a**) for practical purposes; in fact: *The two systems are, in effect, identical.* (**b**) (of a rule, law, etc) in use: *Some ancient laws are still in effect.* **of/to no efˈfect** not having the result intended or hoped for: *My warning was of no effect.* ○ *We warned them, but to no effect.* **strain after effects/an effect** ➪ STRAIN[1]. **take efˈfect** (**a**)

produce the result intended or required: *The aspirins soon took effect.* (**b**) come into force or use; become active: *The new law takes effect from tomorrow.* **to good, etc ef'fect** producing a good, etc result or impression: *The room shows off her paintings to good effect.* **to this/that ef'fect** with this/that meaning or information: *He told me to get out, or words to that effect.* **to the effect that...** with the meaning, or giving the information, that...: *He left a note to the effect that he would not be returning.* **with effect from** (*abbr* **wef**) beginning at the stated time or date: *They have declared a state of emergency with effect from midnight tonight.*
▷ **effect** *v* [Tn] (*fml*) bring (sth) about; cause to occur: *effect a cure, a change, a sale.* ➪ Usage at AFFECT[1].

effective /ɪ'fektɪv/ *adj* **1** (**a**) having an effect; producing the intended result: *effective measures to reduce unemployment* ○ *The law is no longer effective.* (**b**) making a striking impression: *a very effective colour scheme* ○ *an effective speech.* **2** [attrib] (**a**) actual or existing: *the effective membership of a society.* (**b**) fit for service or work: *the effective strength of the army.*
▷ **effectively** *adv* **1** in an effective way. **2** for practical purposes; in effect: *This means that effectively we have no chance of finishing on time.* **effectiveness** *n* [U].

effectual /ɪ'fektʃʊəl/ *adj* (*fml*) (not used of people) producing the intended result: *take effectual action, measures, steps, etc.* ▷ **effectually** /-əlɪ/ *adv.*

effeminate /ɪ'femɪnət/ *adj* (*derog*) (of a man or his behaviour) like a woman; unmanly: *an effeminate manner, voice, walk.* ▷ **effeminacy** /ɪ'femɪnəsɪ/ *n* [U]. **effeminately** /-lɪ/ *adv.*

effervesce /ˌefə'ves/ *v* **1** [I] (of a liquid) release bubbles of gas; fizz. **2** [I, Ipr] ~ (**with sth**) (*fml*) (of people) be happy, lively and excited. ▷ **effervescence** /ˌefə'vesns/ *n* [U]. **effervescent** /-snt/ *adj.*

effete /ɪ'fi:t/ *adj* (**a**) weak, having lost power: *an effete civilization, empire, government, etc.* (**b**) lacking vitality and strength; feeble: *an effete young man.* ▷ **effeteness** *n* [U].

efficacious /ˌefɪ'keɪʃəs/ *adj* (*fml*) (not of people) producing the desired result; effective: *an efficacious treatment, medicine, etc.*
▷ **efficaciously** *adv.*
efficacy /'efɪkəsɪ/ *n* [U] state or quality of being efficacious: *test the efficacy of a new drug.*

efficient /ɪ'fɪʃnt/ *adj* **1** (of people) able to work well; capable: *an efficient secretary, teacher, administrator, etc* ○ *He's efficient at his job.* **2** (esp of tools, machines, systems, etc) producing a satisfactory result without wasting time or energy: *an efficient new filing system.*
▷ **efficiency** /ɪ'fɪʃnsɪ/ *n* [U] **1** state or quality of being efficient. **2** (*physics*) ratio of useful work performed to the total energy used or heat taken in.
efficiently /-lɪ/ *adv*: *get industry running more efficiently.*
□ **ef,ficient 'cause** (*philosophy*) the factors that make a thing what it is.

effigy /'efɪdʒɪ/ *n* **1** [C] carved figure or model representing a person or animal: *stone effigies of Buddha* ○ *On 5 November British children burn effigies of Guy Fawkes.* **2** (idm) **in effigy** as a model: *burn sb in effigy*, ie make a model of sb and burn it as a sign of hatred, etc.

efflorescence /ˌeflɔ:'resns/ *n* [U] (*fml esp fig*) action or time of bursting into flower: *a period of great efflorescence in the arts.* ▷ **efflorescent** /-snt/ *adj.*

effluent /'eflʊənt/ *n* **1** [U, C] (discharge of) liquid waste matter, sewage, etc, eg from a factory into a river: *The effluent from the factory makes the river unsafe for swimming.* **2** [C] stream flowing from a larger stream or from a lake.

effort /'efət/ *n* **1** [U] use of (much) strength and energy (to do sth): *a waste of time and effort* ○ *They lifted the heavy rock without effort.* ○ *He must put more effort into his work.* **2** [C] ~ (**to do sth**) energetic attempt; struggle: *His efforts were much appreciated.* ○ *It was a real effort to stay awake through the film.* ○ *I will make every effort* (ie do all I can) *to arrive on time.* **3** [C] result of an attempt: *That's a good effort*, ie That has been well done.
▷ **effortless** *adj* needing no or little effort: *She plays with seemingly effortless skill.* **effortlessly** *adv.* **effortlessness** *n* [U].

effrontery /ɪ'frʌntərɪ/ *n* (**a**) [U] boldness or rudeness without shame; impertinence: *He had the effrontery to say I was lying.* (**b**) [C esp *pl*] (*fml*) instance of this: *Everyone is tired of their blatant effronteries.*

effusion /ɪ'fju:ʒn/ *n* **1** (*fml*) (**a**) [U] pouring out, esp of liquid: *an effusion of blood.* (**b**) [C] quantity poured out. **2** [C] (*usu derog*) (esp unrestrained) pouring out of thoughts and feelings in words: *poetical effusions* ○ *effusions in love letters.*

effusive /ɪ'fju:sɪv/ *adj* (*often derog*) showing (too much) feeling; too emotional: *Her effusive thanks embarrassed everybody.* ▷ **effusively** *adv.* **effusiveness** *n* [U].

EFL /ˌi: ef 'el/ *abbr* (teaching, learning or studying) English as a Foreign Language. Cf ESL.

EFTA (also **Efta**) /'eftə/ *abbr* European Free Trade Association: *In 1972 Britain left EFTA and joined the EEC.*

eg /ˌi: 'dʒi:/ *abbr* for example; for instance (Latin *exempli gratia*): *popular pets, eg dogs, cats, rabbits, etc.* ➪ Usage at VIZ.

egalitarian /ɪˌgælɪ'teərɪən/ *n, adj* (person) showing or holding a belief in equal rights, benefits and opportunities for everybody: *an egalitarian attitude to voting.* ▷ **egalitarianism** /-ɪzəm/ *n* [U]

egg

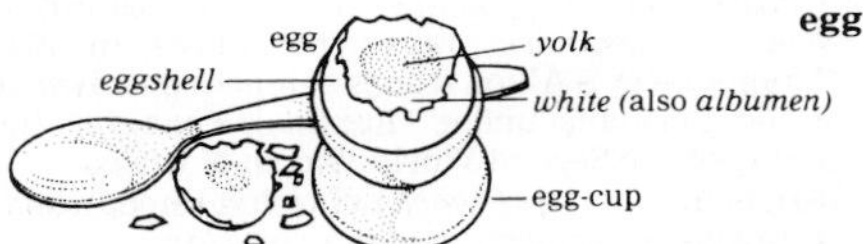

egg[1] /eg/ *n* **1** [C] in female mammals the cell from which the young is formed; ovum: *The male sperm fertilizes the female egg.* **2** (**a**) [C] oval object from which young are hatched, laid by birds, reptiles, insects, etc and usu covered by a thin hard shell: *The hen laid a large brown egg.* ○ *The blackbird's nest contained four eggs.* ○ *ants' eggs.* ➪ illus. (**b**) [U, C] (contents of) this, esp from a hen, used as food: *You've got some egg* (ie a bit of cooked egg) *on your shirt.* ○ *Do you want a boiled egg for breakfast?* ○ *ducks' eggs.* **3** (idm) **a bad 'egg/'lot** (*dated infml*) person considered to be dishonest and unreliable. **a curate's egg** ➪ CURATE. **get, have, be left with, etc 'egg on/all over one's face** (*infml*) appear foolish: *He was left with egg all over his face when his forecast was proved wrong.* **kill the goose that lays the golden eggs** ➪ KILL. **make an omelette without breaking eggs** ➪ OMELETTE. **ˌput all one's ˌeggs in/into one 'basket** risk everything one has on the success of one plan, eg by putting all one's money into one business. **teach one's grandmother to suck eggs** ➪ TEACH.
□ **ˌegg and 'spoon race** race in which each runner has to carry an egg on a spoon without dropping it.
'egg-beater *n* **1** = EGG-WHISK. **2** (*US sl*) helicopter.
'egg-cup *n* small cup for holding a boiled egg. ➪ illus.
ˌegg 'custard sweet food made from a mixture of eggs and milk baked together.
ˌegg 'flip (also **'egg nog**) drink made from rum, brandy, etc mixed with beaten egg, milk and various other ingredients.
'egghead *n* (*infml derog*) very intellectual person: *The eggheads at the university know nothing about business.*
'egg-plant *n* [C, U] (*esp US*) = AUBERGINE.
'eggshell *n* hard thin outer part of an egg. **eggshell 'china** very fine thin type of china. **eggshell 'paint** type of paint that is neither glossy nor matt.
'egg-timer *n* device for measuring time when boiling eggs.
'egg-whisk (also **'egg-beater**) *n* device for beating eggs.

egg[2] /eg/ *v* (phr v) **egg sb on (to do sth)** urge or strongly encourage sb to do sth: *I didn't want to do it but Peter kept egging me 'on.*

eglantine /'egləntaɪn/ (also **sweet-briar**) *n* [U] type of wild rose.

ego /'egəʊ; *US* 'i:gəʊ/ *n* **1** (*psychology*) individual's perception or experience of himself, esp in relation to other people or to the outside world; part of the mind that can think, feel and act. Cf ID, SUPER-EGO. **2** (*infml*) self-esteem: *Losing the match made quite a dent in his ego.*
□ **'ego-trip** *n* (*sl*) self-centred activity: (*derog*) *Her life is just one big ego-trip.*

egocentric /ˌegəʊ'sentrɪk; *US* ˌi:g-/ *adj* considering only oneself; self-centred. ▷ **egocentricity** /-sən'trɪsətɪ/ *n* [U].

egoism /'egəʊɪzəm; *US* 'i:g-/ *n* [U] **1** (*usu derog*) state of mind in which one is always thinking about oneself and what is best for oneself. **2** (*philosophy*) theory that our actions are always caused by a wish to benefit ourselves. Cf ALTRUISM.
▷ **egoist** /-ɪst/ *n* person who believes in or shows egoism. **egoistic** /ˌegəʊ'ɪstɪk; *US* ˌi:g-/, **egoistical** /-kl/ *adjs* of an egoist: *an egoistic act.* **egoistically** /-klɪ/ *adv.*

egotism /'egəʊtɪzəm; *US* 'i:g-/ *n* [U] (*usu derog*) practice of talking too often or too much about oneself; selfishness.
▷ **egotist** /-tɪst/ *n* person who practises or shows egotism; selfish person. **egotistic** /ˌegə'tɪstɪk; *US* ˌi:g-/, **egotistical** /-kl/ *adjs* of egotism; of or like an egotist. **egotistically** /-klɪ/ *adv.*

egregious /ɪ'gri:dʒɪəs/ *adj* [usu attrib] (*fml*) (usu of sb/sth bad) exceptional, outstanding: *egregious incompetence, cowardice, etc* ○ *an egregious fool.* ▷ **egregiously** *adv.*

egress /'i:gres/ *n* **1** [U] (*law*) (right of) going out. **2** [C] (*dated fml*) way out; exit. Cf INGRESS.

egret /'i:grɪt/ *n* type of heron with beautiful long white tail-feathers.

Egypt /'i:dʒɪpt/ country in NE Africa; pop approx 51 897 000; official language Arabic; capital Cairo; unit of currency pound (= 100 piastres). Most of the country is desert, and the majority of the population live along the fertile Nile valley. Agriculure, esp cotton growing, is the most important economic activity, but all crops are irrigated because of lack of rainfall. The country has important reserves of oil, and the Aswan High Dam makes it self-sufficient in energy. Egypt was the home of one of the world's most developed ancient civilizations and the pyramids of Giza are the only survivors of the *Seven Wonders of the World. ➪ map at ALGERIA.
▷ **Egyptian** /ɪ'dʒɪpʃən/ *n, adj.*
Egyptology /i:dʒɪp'tɒlədʒɪ/ *n* [U] study of the history and civilization of ancient Egypt. **Egyptologist** *n.*

eh /eɪ/ *interj* (*infml*) (used to express surprise or doubt, to invite agreement, or to ask for sth to be repeated): *'That was a good film, eh?'* ○ *'I want to go home!' 'Eh?' 'I said I want to go home!'*

eider /'aɪdə(r)/ *n* (also **'eider duck**) large duck whose soft feathers were formerly much used for filling pillows, eiderdowns, etc.
□ **'eiderdown** *n* **1** [U] feathers of an eider. **2** [C] quilt placed over blankets on a bed and filled with soft feathers or other soft material. Cf DUVET.

Eiffel Tower /ˌaɪfl 'taʊə(r)/ **the Eiffel Tower** tower on the left bank of the River Seine in Paris, built by Gustave Eiffel (1832-1923) for the Universal Exhibition of 1889. Its trellis of wrought-iron girders was a revolutionary architectural innovation. It has become a symbol of France.

eight /eɪt/ *pron, det* 8; one more than seven. ➪ App 9.
▷ **eight** *n* **1** the number 8. **2** crew of eight people in a rowing boat: *Is the Oxford eight winning?* **3** (idm) **have had ˌone over the 'eight** (*infml*) be slightly drunk.
eight- (in compounds) having eight of the thing specified.

eighth /eɪtθ/ *pron, det* 8th; next after seventh. — *n* one of eight equal parts of sth.

□ **eightsome** /ˈeɪtsəm/ *n* **1** group of eight people. **2** game played by eight people. **3** (also ˌ**eightsome** ˈ**reel**) lively Scottish dance for eight dancers.

For the uses of *eight* and *eighth* see the examples at *five* and *fifth*.

eighteen /eɪˈtiːn/ *pron, det* 18; one more than seventeen. ⇨ App 9.

▷ **eighteen** *n* the number 18.

eighteenth /ˌeɪˈtiːnθ/ *pron, det* 18th; next after seventeenth. — *n* one of eighteen equal parts of sth.

For the uses of *eighteen* and *eighteenth* see the examples at *five* and *fifth*.

eighty /ˈeɪtɪ/ *pron, det* 80; one more than seventy-nine. ⇨ App 9.

▷ **eightieth** /ˈeɪtɪəθ/ *pron, det* 80th; next after seventy-ninth. — *n* one of eighty equal parts of sth.

eighty *n* **1** [C] the number 80. **2 the eighties** [pl] numbers, years or temperature from 80 to 89. **3** (idm) **in one's eighties** between the ages of 80 and 90.

For the uses of *eighty* and *eightieth* see the examples at *fifty*, *five* and *fifth*.

Einstein /ˈaɪnstaɪn/ Albert (1879-1955), German-born physicist. Possibly the greatest scientist of the 20th century, he was awarded the Nobel prize in 1921. In 1905 he published his special theory of relativity, which led to the equation relating mass and energy, ($E = mc^2$), the basis of atomic energy. He pointed out its military applications, but after the Second World War he campaigned strongly against the use of nuclear weapons.

einsteinium /aɪnˈstaɪnɪəm/ *n* [U] (*symb* **Es**) artificial radioactive metallic element first discovered in the debris of the explosion of a hydrogen bomb.

Eire /ˈeərə/ former name of the Republic of *Ireland, sometimes still used outside Ireland to distinguish it from *Northern Ireland. ⇨ article at IRELAND.

Eisenhower /ˈaɪznhaʊə(r)/ Dwight D(avid) (1890-1969), American general and 34th president of the USA 1952-60. He was the Supreme Commander of the Allied Forces at the end of the Second World War. ⇨ App 2.

Eisenstein /ˈeɪznstaɪn/ Sergei (1896-1948), Soviet film-maker. His works, like *The Battleship Potemkin*, were made in the service of the new Soviet State and pioneered influential techniques of camera work and montage.

eisteddfod /ˌaɪˈsteðvɒd/ *n* any of several annual gatherings in Wales where competitions are held for poets and musicians. Eisteddfods are important celebrations of Welsh language and culture, and date back to the 12th century. ⇨ article at WALES.

either /ˈaɪðə(r), ˌiːðə(r)/ *indef det, indef pron* one or the other of two. **(a)** (*det*): *You can park on either side of the street.* ○ *Keep either one of the forms.* ○ *There's a staircase at either end* (ie both ends) *of the corridor.* **(b)** (*pron*) (used with a *sing v*): *I've bought two cakes — you can have either.* ○ *Take one of the books on the table — either of them will do.* ▷ **either** *indef adv* **1** (used after two negative *vs*): *I don't like the red shirt and I don't like the green one either*, ie I dislike both the red shirt and the green one. ○ *Mary won't go and Peter won't go either.* (Cf *. . .and neither will Peter.*) ○ *He can't hear and he can hardly speak either.* ⇨ Usage at ALSO. **2** (used to emphasize a negative phrase): *I know a good Italian restaurant. It's not far from here, either.* **3 either . . . or . . .** (used to show a choice of two alternatives): *either French or Spanish* ○ *I left it either on the table or in the drawer.* ○ *You can either write or phone to request a copy.*

ejaculate /ɪˈdʒækjʊleɪt/ *v* **1** [I] eject or rapidly discharge fluid, esp semen, from the body. **2** [I, Tn] (*fml*) say (sth) suddenly and briefly; exclaim.

▷ **ejaculation** /ɪˌdʒækjʊˈleɪʃn/ *n* **1** [C, U] sudden discharge or ejection of fluid, esp semen, from the body. **2** [C] (*fml*) thing said suddenly and briefly; exclamation: *an ejaculation of surprise.*

eject /ɪˈdʒekt/ *v* **1** [Tn, Tn·pr] ~ **sb/sth (from sth)** (*fml*) force sb/sth out; expel sb/sth: *The noisy youths were ejected from the cinema.* ○ *Cartridges are ejected from the gun after firing.* **2** [Tn] send (sth) out, usu violently or suddenly: *lava ejected from a volcano.* **3** [I, Ipr] ~ **(from sth)** be thrown quickly from an aircraft in an emergency, so that one can descend by parachute: *As the plane fell rapidly towards the ground, the pilot had to eject.*

▷ **ejection** /ɪˈdʒekʃn/ *n* [U].

ejector /ɪˈdʒektə(r)/ *n* device for ejecting people or things. **ejector seat** (*US* also **ejection seat**) seat in an aircraft that allows the pilot to eject(3).

eke /iːk/ *v* (phr v) **eke sth out (a)** make a small supply of sth last longer by adding sth else to it or by using it sparingly: *They eked out their coal by collecting firewood.* **(b)** manage to make (a living) laboriously by doing this: *eking out a meagre existence.*

el /el/ *n* **the el** [sing] (*US infml*) the elevated railway (ELEVATE) of New York.

elaborate /ɪˈlæbərət/ *adj* very detailed and complicated; carefully prepared and finished: *elaborate plans* ○ *an elaborate hairstyle* ○ *an elaborate five-course meal.*

▷ **elaborate** /ɪˈlæbəreɪt/ *v* **1** [Tn] (*fml*) work (sth) out in detail: *Please elaborate your plan.* **2** [I, Ipr] ~ **(on sth)** describe or explain sth in detail: *You understand the situation; I needn't elaborate any further.* **elaboration** /ɪˌlæbəˈreɪʃn/ *n* **1** [U] working sth out, or discussing sth, in detail: *the further elaboration of a theory.* **2** [C] additional, usu unnecessary, detail: *The elaborations of the plot made it a difficult book to read.*

elaborately *adv*: *an elaborately decorated room.*

elaborateness *n* [U] state of being elaborate.

El Alamein /el ˈæləmeɪn/ site 90 km (60 miles) west of Alexandria in Egypt, where in 1942 *Montgomery's Allied troops stopped the advance of the Germans under *Rommel, changing the course of the Second World War in N Africa.

élan /eɪˈlɑːn/ *n* [U] (*French*) vivacity; impetuosity; enthusiasm: *performing with great élan.*

eland /ˈiːlənd/ *n* large African antelope.

elapse /ɪˈlæps/ *v* [I] (*fml*) (of time) pass: *Three years have elapsed since we last met.*

elastic /ɪˈlæstɪk/ *adj* **1** returning to its normal or previous size or shape after being pulled or pressed: *a bra with elastic straps* ○ *Rubber is elastic.* **2** (*fig*) not fixed or unalterable; adaptable; flexible: *Our plans are fairly elastic.*

▷ **elastic** *n* [U] **1** elastic cord or material, usu made with rubber thread: *The elastic in my pants has gone*, ie has broken or perished. ○ [attrib] *an elastic bandage.* **2** (*US*) = RUBBER BAND (RUBBER).

elasticate /ɪˈlæstɪkeɪt/ *v* [Tn usu passive] insert elastic into (a fabric or garment): *a dress with an elasticated top* ○ *an elasticated belt.*

elasticity /ˌelæˈstɪsətɪ; *US* ɪˌlæ-/ *n* [U] quality of being elastic.

□ eˌ**lastic** ˈ**band** (*US*) = RUBBER BAND (RUBBER).

eˌ**lastic col**ˈ**lision** (*physics*) collision in which the bodies that collide (normally molecules) do not lose any of their kinetic energy.

elastomer /ɪˈlæstəmə(r)/ *n* natural or synthetic substance with elastic properties.

Elastoplast /ɪˈlæstəplɑːst, -plæst/ *n* [U] (*Brit propr*) adhesive dressing for cuts, etc.

elated /ɪˈleɪtɪd/ *adj* ~ **(at/by sth)** in high spirits; very happy or proud: *an elated smile* ○ *She was elated at/by the news.*

▷ **elatedly** /ɪˈleɪtɪdlɪ/ *adv.*

elation /ɪˈleɪʃn/ *n* [U] high spirits; joy: *She was filled with elation when her daughter was born.*

E layer /ˈiː leɪə(r)/ = HEAVISIDE LAYER (HEAVISIDE).

Elba /ˈelbə/ small island between Corsica and Italy. It is famous mainly as the place where *Napoleon was exiled in 1814-15.

elbow /ˈelbəʊ/ *n* **1** (outer part of the) joint where the arm bends: *He sat with his elbows on the table.* ⇨ illus at HUMAN. **2** part of the sleeve of a coat, jacket, etc which covers this: *a jacket patched at the elbows.* **3** sharp bend in a pipe, chimney, etc that is shaped like an elbow. **4** (idm) **at one's** ˈ**elbow** very near; within reach. **give sb/get the** ˈ**elbow** (*infml*) (cause sb to) be dismissed or rejected: *She gave me the elbow when she started going out with Roger.* **more power to sb's elbow** ⇨ POWER. **not know one's arse from one's elbow** ⇨ KNOW. **out at (the)** ˈ**elbows (a)** (of a garment) old and full of holes. **(b)** (of a person) in old shabby clothes; badly dressed.

▷ **elbow** *v* (phr v) **elbow sb out of the** ˈ**way/ a**ˈ**side** push sb to one side with the elbows: *He elbowed me out of the way.* **elbow one's way into, through, etc (sth)** force (one's way) in a specified direction by using one's elbows: *He elbowed his way through the crowd.* ○ *She elbowed her way forward.*

□ ˈ**elbow-grease** *n* [U] (*infml*) hard manual work, esp vigorous polishing or cleaning: *If you used a bit of elbow-grease you could get those boots clean.*

ˈ**elbow-room** *n* [U] space in which one can move freely: *I need (some) more elbow-room.*

elder[1] /ˈeldə(r)/ *adj* **1 (a)** [attrib] (of people, esp two closely related members of a family) older; senior: *my elder brother* ○ *her elder daughter*, ie the first-born of her two daughters. **(b) the elder** (used without an immediately following *n* to refer to an earlier or later *n*) the older person, etc (of two): *He is the elder of my two brothers.* ○ *There go my two sons. Can you guess which is the elder?* **2 the elder** (*fml*) (used before or after sb's name to distinguish him from another person with the same name): *Pitt the elder* ○ *the elder Pitt.* Cf YOUNG 3.

▷ **elder** *n* **1 my, etc elder** [sing] person older than me, etc: *He is her elder by several years.* **2 elders** [pl] people of greater age and authority: *the village elders*, ie the old and respected people of the village. ○ *Traditions were passed on by the elders of the tribe.* **3** [C] official in a Presbyterian church. **4** (idm) **one's (elders and) betters** ⇨ BETTER[3] 3.

□ ˌ**elder** ˈ**statesman** old and respected politician; person, usu retired, whose advice is still valued because of his long experience.

NOTE ON USAGE: The usual comparative and superlative forms of **old** are **older** and **oldest**: *My brother is older than me.* ○ *The cathedral is the oldest building in the city.* When comparing the ages of people, especially of members of a family, **elder** and **eldest** are often used, as adjectives and pronouns. They cannot be used with *than* and as adjectives they can only be used before the noun: *My elder sister lives in Canada.* ○ *He was the elder of her two sons.* ○ *I'm the eldest in the family.*

elder[2] /ˈeldə(r)/ *n* any of several types of small tree with scented white flowers and red or black berries.

□ **elderberry** /ˈeldəbrɪ; *US* ˈeldəberɪ/ *n* fruit of an elder. ˌ**elderberry** ˈ**wine** wine made from these berries.

elderly /ˈeldəlɪ/ *adj* (*often euph*) (of people) rather old; past middle age: *He's very active for an elderly man.* ⇨ Usage at OLD.

eldest /ˈeldɪst/ *adj* [attrib], *n* (of people, esp of three or more closely related members of a family) first-born; oldest: *Jill is my eldest daughter.* ○ *Jill is the eldest of my three children.* ○ *Jill is the eldest of three*, ie the oldest child in a family with three children. ○ *Jill is my eldest.* ⇨ Usage at ELDER[1].

El Dorado /ˌel dəˈrɑːdəʊ/ country or city once supposed to exist in South America, where huge quantities of gold could be found. Sir Walter *Raleigh set out to search for it on his last voyage.

eldorado /ˌeldəˈrɑːdəʊ/ *n* (*pl* ~**s**) imaginary place, situation, etc which might produce great wealth if it could be reached.

elect /ɪˈlekt/ *v* **1** [Tn, Tn·pr, Cn·n, Cn·t] ~ **sb (to sth)** choose sb by vote: *They elected a new president.* ○ *She was elected to parliament last year.* ○ *We elected James (to be) chairman.* **2** [Tt] (*fml*) choose or decide (to do sth): *She elected to become a lawyer.*

▷ **elect** *adj* (after the *n*) chosen for a position but not yet occupying it: *the president elect.*

the elect *n* [pl *v*] (*fml*) people specially selected as the best.

Electricity and Gas

Most homes in Britain, as well as virtually all businesses and manufacturing industries, are provided with a supply of electricity or gas, and in many cases both. In the home, electricity is used for lighting and for providing power for domestic appliances such as refrigerators, washing-machines, and radio and television sets, although many people have portable radios that use batteries. A large number of homes use electricity for cooking and heating, the domestic uses to which gas is also put.

The supply of both types of power to the home is measured by meters. The meters are read, usually quarterly, by an official from the appropriate company, which then sends a bill to the customer. Some homes, however, still have meters that operate only when a coin is inserted, but these are now generally regarded as old-fashioned and are being replaced. They exist mostly in temporary or rented accommodation such as hostels and 'bed-sits'.

Until recently, both the electricity and gas industries in Britain were public companies, operating through a number of regional boards. The main body of the electricity supply industry in England and Wales was the Central Electricity Generating Board (CEGB), which ran the power-stations and owned the 'national grid', the main transmission system of the country. In 1990 the electricity industry was privatized and the CEGB was split into four separate companies: PowerGen and National Power, both providing electricity from fossil-fuelled (non-nuclear) plants, Nuclear Electric, providing electricity from nuclear power stations, and the National Grid, owned by the country's 12 supply companies. PowerGen and the larger National Power carry out the same operations, and are in commercial competition with each other. Although a commercially independent company, Nuclear Electric remained in the public sector when the original plans to privatize the nuclear industry were shelved. (Cf article at NUCLEAR.)

The gas industry, formerly the business of the state-owned British Gas Corporation, was privatized in 1986 and operates as British Gas. Like the electricity industry, it organizes its domestic supply through 12 regional companies. Until the late 1960s, domestic and commercial gas was entirely produced as 'town gas' from coal gas. Then large supplies of natural gas were discovered under the North Sea, and this has now completely replaced town gas.

election /ɪˈlekʃn/ *n* [U, C] (instance of) choosing or selection by vote (of candidates for a position, esp a political office): *presidential elections* ○ *He's standing for election.* ○ [attrib] *the election results.* 📖 In Britain, **general elections** to choose a new parliament are held at least every five years, but the prime minister can call for such an election at any time. In each constituency, the candidate with the largest number of votes is elected, even if a minority of people have voted for him or her. **General elections** and **by-elections** in Britain are usually held on Thursdays and voting is according to the following procedure. Each ward of a constituency sets up a **polling-station**, often in a school or church hall. On entering the polling-station, the voter is given a **ballot-paper** on which the names of the candidates are written, goes into a booth and puts a cross against the name of the candidate chosen. The votes are counted and the result of the election is announced by the **returning officer**, either later the same day or on the following day. In the USA presidents are elected every four years; every two years there are elections for the House of Representatives and one third of the seats in the Senate.

▷ **electioneering** /ɪˌlekʃəˈnɪərɪŋ/ *n* [U] activity of trying to influence voters in an election by canvassing, making speeches, etc.

elective /ɪˈlektɪv/ *adj* **1** [usu attrib] having the power to elect: *an elective assembly.* **2** chosen or filled by election: *an elective office.* **3** (esp of an American university course, etc) not compulsory; optional: *elective subjects.* **4** not urgently necessary: *elective surgery.*

▷ **elective** *n* (*esp US*) optional course or subject studied at school or college: *She is taking French as an elective next year.*

elector /ɪˈlektə(r)/ *n* person who has the right to vote in an election: *Many electors didn't vote today because of the bad weather.*

▷ **electoral** /ɪˈlektərəl/ *adj* [attrib] of elections or electors: *the electoral register/roll,* ie list of the electors in an area. **eˌlectoral ˈcollege** body of people who elect a leader on behalf of others, esp the representatives of each of the US states who officially elect the president according to the votes cast by the people in their states.

electorate /ɪˈlektərət/ *n* [CGp] all the qualified electors considered as a group: *The electorate is/are disillusioned.*

Electra /ɪˈlektrə/ (in Greek mythology) daughter of *Agamemnon and *Clytemnestra. She urged her brother *Orestes to murder Clytemnestra and her lover Aegisthus who had killed Agamemnon.

□ **Eˈlectra complex** (in Freudian psychology) feeling of attraction of a young girl to her father and hostility to her mother.

electric /ɪˈlektrɪk/ *adj* **1** [attrib] (**a**) producing electricity: *an electric generator.* (**b**) produced by electricity: *an electric current.* ➪ App 12. (**c**) used in the conveying of electricity: *an electric plug, socket, flex, etc.* (**d**) using electrical power: *an electric cooker, iron, light, etc.* **2** (*fig*) causing sudden excitement, esp in a group of people: *an electric atmosphere* ○ *The news had an electric effect.*

▷ **electrics** *n* [pl] (*infml*) electrical equipment, esp the electric circuits in a motor vehicle: *something wrong with the electrics.*

□ **eˌlectric ˈblanket** blanket that is warmed electrically.

the eˌlectric ˈchair (in the US) chair in which criminals are executed by electrocution.

eˌlectric ˈeel eel-like fish that can give a strong electric shock to defend itself or stun its prey.

eˌlectric ˈeye (*infml*) = PHOTOELECTRIC CELL (PHOTOELECTRIC).

eˌlectric ˈfield (*physics*) area near an electric charge, in which a force is exerted on another charged particle.

eˌlectric ˈrazor = SHAVER (SHAVE).

eˌlectric ˈshock (also **shock**) effect of a sudden discharge of electricity through the body: *I got an electric shock from that faulty light switch.*

eˌlectric ˈstorm violent atmospheric disturbance that produces electricity.

electrical /ɪˈlektrɪkl/ *adj* of or concerned with electricity: *electrical engineering* ○ *This machine has an electrical fault.* ▷ **electrically** /-klɪ/ *adv*: *an electrically powered drill.*

electrician /ɪˌlekˈtrɪʃn/ *n* person whose job is to install, operate, repair, etc electrical equipment: *Our washing machine has broken; I'll ring the electrician.* ○ *We need an electrician to mend the iron.*

electricity /ɪˌlekˈtrɪsətɪ/ *n* [U] **1** form of energy occurring in certain particles (electrons and protons) and hence in larger bodies, since they contain these. Static electricity was observed in very early times. Benjamin *Franklin discovered positive and negative charges in the 18th century; in the late 19th century the electron and proton were identified. The electricity used in ordinary homes is simply a slow drift of electrons, flowing backwards and forwards if an alternating current is used. Electricity is usu produced using fossil fuels, hydraulic power or atomic reactions; in all cases energy is produced to drive a turbine, the turbine drives a generator and the power from the generator passes through a transformer to power lines. **2** supply of such energy in the form of electric current for lighting, heating, driving machines, etc: *Don't leave the lights on — it wastes electricity.* ○ *When did the village first get electricity?* **3** branch of science concerned with the study of this form of energy. ➪ article.

electrify /ɪˈlektrɪfaɪ/ *v* (*pt, pp* **-fied**) [Tn] **1** charge (sth) with electricity. **2** convert (a railway, etc) to the use of electric power. **3** (*fig*) stimulate (sb) as if by electricity; excite suddenly; startle: *the athlete's electrifying burst of speed.*

▷ **electrification** /ɪˌlektrɪfɪˈkeɪʃn/ *n* [U] conversion to electricity: *the electrification of the railways,* ie from steam to electricity.

electr(o)- *comb form* of electricity: *electrocardiogram* ○ *electrolysis.*

electrocardiogram /ɪˌlektrəʊˈkɑːdɪəʊgræm/ *n* (*abbr* **ECG**) (*medical*) record of sb's heartbeat traced by an electrocardiograph, used in the diagnosis of heart disease.

electrocardiograph /ˌɪlektrəʊˈkɑːdɪəʊgrɑːf; *US* -græf/ *n* (*medical*) instrument that detects and records the electric activity produced by the muscles of the heart.

electrochemistry /ɪˌlektrəʊˈkemɪstrɪ/ *n* [U] application of electricity to chemical processes.

electroconvulsive therapy /ɪˌlektrəʊkənˌvʌlsɪv ˈθerəpɪ/ (*abbr* **ECT**) controversial form of therapy using electric shocks, usu to treat psychiatric disorders.

electrocute /ɪˈlektrəkjuːt/ *v* [Tn usu passive] kill (a person or an animal) by means of an electric current. ▷ **electrocution** /ɪˌlektrəˈkjuːʃn/ *n* [U].

electrode /ɪˈlektrəʊd/ *n* (often *pl*) either of two solid conductors by which an electric current enters or leaves a battery, etc; terminal. Cf ANODE, CATHODE.

electroencephalograph /ɪˌlektrəʊenˈsefələgrɑːf; *US* -græf/ *n* instrument for detecting and recording the electric current produced by the activity of the brain.

▷ **electroencephalogram** /ɪˌlektrəʊenˈsefələgræm/ *n* (*abbr* **EEG**) pattern traced by an electroencephalograph.

electrolysis /ˌɪlekˈtrɒləsɪs/ *n* [U] **1** separation of a substance into its chemical parts by an electric current. **2** destruction of hair roots, tumours, etc by an electric current (for cosmetic or surgical reasons).

electrolyte /ɪˈlektrəlaɪt/ *n* [C, U] (substance that can dissolve to produce a) solution able to conduct electric current, esp in an electric cell or battery.

electromagnet /ɪˌlektrəʊˈmægnɪt/ *n* (*physics*) piece of soft iron that becomes magnetic when an electric current is passed through the coil surrounding it.

▷ **electromagnetic** /ɪˌlektrəʊmægˈnetɪk/ *adj* (*physics*) having both electrical and magnetic properties: *electromagnetic waves,* eg X-rays, radio-waves, light waves. **eˌlectromagˌnetic radiˈation** type of radiation that includes visible light, radio waves, etc, in which the electric and the magnetic fields vary simultaneously.

electromagnetism *n* [U] (study of the) magnetic

forces produced by electricity. Electromagnets have a very wide range of applications from electric motors, electric bells and automatic switches to loudspeakers, magnetic tape and television tubes.

electromotive /ɪˌlektrəˈməʊtɪv/ *adj* producing or tending to produce an electric current.

□ **electroˌmotive ˈforce** (*abbr* **EMF**) force set up by the difference of potential in an electric circuit.

electron /ɪˈlektrɒn/ *n* [C] (*physics*) minute particle of matter with a negative electric charge, found in all atoms. Electrons go round the nucleus of atoms. The flow of electrons constitutes an electron current. Electrons play an important part in the induction of heat through metals. Cf NEUTRON, POSITRON, PROTON.

▷ **electronic** /ɪlekˈtrɒnɪk/ *adj* [attrib] **1** (**a**) produced or operated by a flow of electrons: *an electronic calculator.* (**b**) concerned with electronic apparatus (eg computers): *This dictionary is available in electronic form.* ○ *electronic music,* ie produced by manipulating natural or artificial sounds with electronic equipment. **2** of or concerned with electrons or electronics: *an electronic engineer.* **electronically** /-klɪ/ *adv*: *process data electronically,* ie using a computer. **ˌelectronic ˈmail** (also **email, e-mail**) sending text, diagrams, etc by means of computers linked to a telecommunication network. **ˌelectronic ˈmailbox** device for receiving and storing electronic mail.

electronics *n* [sing *v*] **1** branch of science and technology that deals with the behaviour of electrons. **2** application of this, esp in developing equipment: *He's an expert in electronics.* ○ [attrib] *the electronics industry.*

□ **eˈlectron lens** device for focusing a beam of electrons using electric or magnetic fields.

eˌlectron ˈmicroscope very powerful microscope that uses beams of electrons instead of light rays. It is capable of magnifying things up to a million times.

eˈlectron-volt *n* unit of energy, ie the energy gained by an electron when it is accelerated through a potential difference of one volt.

electroplate /ɪˈlektrəpleɪt/ *v* [Tn usu passive] cover (sth) with a thin layer of metal, usu silver, by electrolysis: *electroplated spoons.*

elegant /ˈelɪgənt/ *adj* tasteful and stylish in appearance or manner: *an elegant woman, coat, style of writing* ○ *elegant manners.* ▷ **elegance** /ˈelɪgəns/ *n* [U]. **elegantly** *adv*: *He always dresses elegantly.*

elegiac /ˌelɪˈdʒaɪək/ *adj* **1** (of poetic metre) suitable for elegies: *elegiac couplets.* **2** (*fml*) mournful; expressing sorrow: *Her poetry has an elegiac quality.*

elegy /ˈelədʒɪ/ *n* poem or song expressing sorrow, esp for the dead; lament.

element /ˈelɪmənt/ *n* **1** [C] ~ (**in/of sth**) necessary or characteristic part of sth: *Justice is an important element of good government.* ○ *What a sensational story! It has all the elements of a soap opera.* **2** [C usu *sing*] ~ **of sth** small amount of sth; suggestion or trace of sth: *There's an element of truth in his story.* ○ *There's always an element of danger in mountain climbing.* **3** [C] (*chemistry*) any of about 100 substances which cannot be split by ordinary chemical methods into simpler substances. There are 92 elements that occur naturally; others have been formed synthetically by nuclear reactions. Each element has atoms with the same number of electrons or protons. The periodic table (PERIODIC) classifies elements according to their properties and the arrangement of their electrons: *Water is composed of the elements hydrogen and oxygen.* Cf COMPOUND[1] 1, MIXTURE 3. **4** [C] (according to ancient and medieval philosophers) any of the four substances, earth, air, fire and water, from which the universe was believed to be composed. **5 the elements** [pl] (*fml*) forces of nature, the weather, etc (esp bad weather): *exposed to (the fury of) the elements.* **6** [C usu *sing*] natural or suitable environment or habitat: *Water is a fish's natural element.* **7 elements** [pl] basic principles of a subject being studied; parts that must be learnt first: *You must understand the elements of mathematics before we can proceed further.* **8** [C] part of an electric kettle, etc that gives out heat: *This heater needs a new element.* **9** [C usu *pl*] (*fml*) the bread or wine used at the Eucharist. **10** (idm) **in/out of one's ˈelement** in/not in one's accustomed or preferred surroundings; doing/not doing what one is good at and enjoys: *I'm out of my element in political discussions.* ○ *The children are really in their element playing on the beach.*

▷ **elemental** /ˌelɪˈmentl/ *adj* [esp attrib] **1** (*fml*) powerful; uncontrolled; like the forces of nature: *the elemental fury of the storm.* **2** basic: *an elemental truth.*

elementary /ˌelɪˈmentrɪ/ *adj* **1** [attrib] (**a**) of or in the beginning stages (of a course of study): *an elementary class.* (**b**) dealing with the simplest facts (of a subject); basic: *elementary mathematics.* **2** easy to solve or answer: *The questions were so elementary that he easily passed the test.*

□ **eleˌmentary ˈparticle** (also **ˌfundamental ˈparticle**) (*physics*) any of the subatomic particles thought not to consist of smaller particles. Scientists discovered the existence of protons, electrons and neutrons in the structure of the atom in the early 20th century. Since 1930 they have discovered other particles that can exist outside the atom, eg the positron and the neutrino. Mesons are responsible for the strong interactions between the particles of the nucleus. Theoretical physicists have suggested that other particles may exist, such as the quark, and tried to describe their properties using terms like 'strangeness', 'charm' and 'colour'. Particles are classified into groups according to their properties. They include *hadrons, baryons, mesons, nucleons, hyperons, fermions* and *bosons.*

elephants

AFRICAN ELEPHANT

INDIAN ELEPHANT

elephant /ˈelɪfənt/ *n* **1** largest four-footed animal now living, with two curved ivory tusks, thick skin, and a long trunk. There are two distinct species, the African elephant and the smaller Indian elephant. The African elephant is now under threat because of the destruction of its habitat and the activities of poachers who kill animals to sell the ivory from their tusks. ⇨ illus article at NATIONAL. **2** (idm) **ˌelephants ˌnever ˈforget** (*saying*) elephants are noted for their good memories. **pink elephants** ⇨ PINK. **a white elephant** ⇨ WHITE.

▷ **elephantine** /ˌelɪˈfæntaɪn; *US* -tiːn/ *adj* (*derog or joc*) large and awkward like an elephant: *Their daughter is quite plump but their son is positively elephantine.*

elephantiasis /ˌelɪfənˈtaɪəsɪs/ *n* [U] disease, esp of tropical countries, in which limbs become abnormally enlarged and the skin thickens.

elevate /ˈelɪveɪt/ *v* [Tn, Tn·pr] ~ **sb/sth** (**to sth**) (*fml*) **1** lift sb/sth up; raise sb/sth to a higher place or rank: *He's been elevated to the peerage,* ie made a peer. **2** (*fig*) make (the mind, morals, etc) better or more educated: *The teacher hoped to elevate the minds of her young pupils by reading them religious stories.*

▷ **elevated** *adj* (*fml*) fine or noble: *elevated language, sentiments, thoughts.*

elevating *adj* (*fml or joc*) improving the mind or morals; uplifting: *an elevating book, sermon* ○ *The experience wasn't terribly elevating.*

□ **ˌelevated ˈrailway** (*US* **elevated railroad**) (*esp US*) railway built on piers (usu above the streets, etc of a town).

elevation /ˌelɪˈveɪʃn/ *n* **1** [C, U] (*fml*) elevating or being elevated: *elevation to the peerage.* **2** [U] (*fml*) nobility or dignity: *elevation of language, style, thought.* **3** [C] (**a**) height (of a place), esp above sea-level: *The city is at an elevation of 2 000 metres.* (**b**) (*fml*) hill or high place: *a small elevation of the ground.* **4** [C] (architect's plan or drawing of) one side of a building (drawn to scale): *the front/rear/side elevation of a house.* **5** [C] angle that the direction of sth (esp a gun or planet) makes with the horizontal: *The gun has an elevation of 45 degrees.*

elevator /ˈelɪveɪtə(r)/ *n* **1** (*US*) = LIFT. **2** one of two movable parts in the tail of an aircraft that are used to make it climb or dive. **3** tall storehouse for grain. **4** machine like a continuous belt with buckets at intervals, used for raising grain, goods, etc.

eleven /ɪˈlevn/ *pron, det* 11; one more than ten. ⇨ App 9.

▷ **eleven** *n* **1** the number 11. **2** team of eleven players for football, hockey or cricket.

eleven- (in compounds) having eleven of the thing specified: *an eleven-mile walk.*

eleventh /ɪˈlevnθ/ *pron, det* 11th; next after tenth. — *n* one of eleven equal parts of sth.

□ **eˌleven-ˈplus** *n* [sing] (*Brit*) (esp formerly) examination taken at the age of eleven, to decide which type of secondary school a child should go to. ⇨ article at SCHOOL.

For the uses of *eleven* and *eleventh* see the examples at *five* and *fifth.*

elevenses /ɪˈlevnzɪz/ *n* [usu sing *v*] (*Brit infml*) snack and/or drink taken at about eleven o'clock in the morning.

elf /elf/ *n* (*pl* **elves** /elvz/) type of small fairy; mischievous little creature.

▷ **elfin** /ˈelfɪn/ *adj* of or like an elf: *elfin music* ○ *She has elfin features.*

elfish /ˈelfɪʃ/ (also **elvish**) *adj* mischievous: *an elfish smile.*

Elgar /ˈelgɑː(r)/ Sir Edward (1857-1934), English composer. Although he is now regarded as one of the greatest composers England has produced, he had little success until 1899 when his *Enigma Variations* were first performed. Many of his earliest pieces were choral works (eg *The Dream of Gerontius*). His patriotic works, like the first *Pomp and Circumstance* march, which was turned into the song 'Land of Hope and Glory', are frequently performed, but his reputation is based on works like the two symphonies, the violin concerto and the cello concerto. ▷ **Elgarian** *adj.*

Elgin Marbles /ˌelgɪn ˈmɑːblz/ **the Elgin Marbles** set of marble sculptures now in the *British Museum taken from the outside of the *Parthenon in Athens. They date from the 5th century BC. They were bought by Lord Elgin in 1801-03 from the Turkish authorities then governing Greece, and the Greek government has frequently asked for them to be returned.

El Greco /el ˈgrekəʊ/ (1541-1614), Spanish painter born in Greece. He trained with *Titian and settled in Spain, where he specialized in religious scenes, noted for their elongated figures.

elicit /ɪˈlɪsɪt/ *v* [Tn, Tn·pr] ~ **sth** (**from sb**) (*fml*) draw (facts, a response, etc) from sb, sometimes with difficulty: *elicit a reply* ○ *At last we've elicited the truth from him.*

elide /ɪˈlaɪd/ *v* [Tn] leave out the sound of (part of a word) when pronouncing it: *The 't' in 'postman' may be elided.* Cf ELISION.

eligible /ˈelɪdʒəbl/ *adj* ~ **(for sth/to do sth)** suitable or fit to be chosen; having the right or proper qualifications: *eligible for a pension, a job, an award* ○ *eligible for promotion, membership* ○ *eligible to join a club* ○ *an eligible young man*, eg one who would be a satisfactory choice as a husband.
▷ **eligibility** /ˌelɪdʒəˈbɪlətɪ/ *n* [U] state of being eligible: *Her qualifications and experience confirm her eligibility for the job.*

Elijah /ɪˈlaɪdʒə/ prophet in the Old Testament who fought against the worship of *Baal, and whose story is told in the first and second book of *Kings.

eliminate /ɪˈlɪmɪneɪt/ *v* **1** [Tn, Tn·pr] ~ **sb/sth (from sth)** remove (esp sb/sth that is not wanted or needed): *eliminate mistakes from one's writing* ○ *The police have eliminated two suspects (from their enquiry).* ○ *eliminate waste matter from the body.* **2** [Tn] (*infml*) kill (sb) ruthlessly: *The dictator had eliminated all his political opponents.* **3** [esp passive: Tn, Tn·pr] ~ **sb (from sth)** exclude sb from further stages in a competition, through defeat, etc: *He was eliminated (from the contest) in the fourth round.* ▷ **elimination** /ɪˌlɪmɪˈneɪʃn/ *n* [U].

Eliot[1] /ˈelɪət/ George (1819-80), pen-name of Mary Ann Evans, English novelist. She rejected the Christian faith of her youth, but her writings show an almost religious attitude to love and duty. Works like *Scenes from Clerical Life* and *Middlemarch* show her as a remarkable observer of Victorian social and domestic life.

Eliot[2] /ˈelɪət/ T(homas) S(tearns) (1888-1965), American-born British poet. He was encouraged by *Pound to settle and write in England. Works like *The Waste Land* and *Four Quartets* express his disillusioned but deeply religious view of the world in a style that is moving and lyrical despite the plainness of his language. He also wrote several verse dramas (eg *Murder in the Cathedral*) and was an influential critic and publisher.

elision /ɪˈlɪʒn/ *n* **(a)** [U] leaving out of the sound of part of a word in pronunciation, as in *we'll, don't* and *let's*. **(b)** [C] instance of this. Cf ELIDE.

élite /eɪˈliːt/ *n* [CGp] (*often derog*) social group considered to be the best or most important because of their power, talent, wealth, etc: *the ruling, scientific élite* ○ [attrib] *an élite force, regiment.*
▷ **élitism** /eɪˈliːtɪzəm/ *n* [U] (*often derog*) (belief in a) system, leadership, etc that aims at developing an élite: *Many people believe that private education encourages élitism.*
élitist /-tɪst/ *n* (*often derog*) person who believes in élitism. — *adj* of the élite or élitism: *an élitist attitude to life.*

elixir /ɪˈlɪksə(r)/ *n* [U, C] **1** imaginary substance with which medieval scientists hoped to change metals into gold or make people live for ever: *the elixir of life.* **2** imaginary cure for all ills.

Elizabeth I /ɪˌlɪzəbəθ/ (1533-1603), queen of England and Ireland 1558-1603. She succeeded her Catholic half-sister, Mary Tudor, and restored the Protestant Church of England. She never married and came to be called 'the Virgin Queen'. Her more informal nickname was 'Good Queen Bess'. Her reign is considered one of the greatest periods of English history, with the voyages of *Raleigh and *Drake, the defeat of the *Armada, and the writings of *Shakespeare, *Marlowe and *Spenser. ⇨ App 3.
▷ **Elizabethan** /ɪˌlɪzəˈbiːθn/ *adj* [usu attrib] of the time of Elizabeth I: *Elizabethan drama* ○ *the Elizabethan age.* ⇨ illus at DRESS. ⇨ article at ARCHITECTURE. — *n* person who lived during the reign of Elizabeth I.

Elizabeth II /ɪˌlɪzəbəθ/ (1926-), queen of the United Kingdom 1952- . She has done much to preserve public affection for the monarchy, esp through her Christmas broadcasts, often showing the royal family's activities during the year. Her commitment to the Commonwealth has helped maintain its prestige and stability. The queen and her family undertake many overseas tours to Commonwealth and other countries. ⇨ App 3. ⇨ article at ROYAL FAMILY.

elk /elk/ *n* (~**s**) (*Brit*) (*US* **moose**) one of the largest types of living deer, found in N Europe, N Asia, and N America.

Ellington /ˈelɪŋtən/ Duke (1899-1974), American jazz composer, pianist and band-leader. He was one of the earliest stars of jazz and the first to give it an orchestral dimension. He composed over 900 pieces, many of which have become standard works of the jazz repertory.

ellipse /ɪˈlɪps/ *n* shape obtained when an upright cone is intersected by a plane making a smaller angle with the base than the side of the cone makes; regular oval. ⇨ illus at HYPERBOLA.
▷ **ellipsoid** /ɪˈlɪpsɔɪd/ *n* solid body formed when an ellipse is rotated about one of its axes.
elliptic /ɪˈlɪptɪk/, **elliptical** /ɪˈlɪptɪkl/ *adjs* shaped like an ellipse.

ellipsis /ɪˈlɪpsɪs/ *n* (*pl* **-pses** /-psiːz/) [C, U] (*grammar*) (instance of) leaving out a word or words from (the grammatical structure of) a sentence when the meaning can be understood without it/them: *The sentence 'He is dead and I alive' contains an ellipsis, ie of the word 'am'.* ⇨ App 14.
▷ **elliptical** /ɪˈlɪptɪkl/ *adj* containing ellipsis: *an elliptical style of writing*, ie one that implies more than is actually said. **elliptically** /-klɪ/ *adj.*

Ellis Island /ˈelɪs aɪlənd/ small island off Manhattan which was the official entrance and control point for immigrants to the USA from 1892 to 1943.

elm /elm/ *n* **1** [C] (also **ˈelm tree**) tall, deciduous tree with broad rough-edged leaves: [attrib] *an elm forest.* **2** [U] its hard heavy wood: *This bench is made of elm.*

elocution /ˌeləˈkjuːʃn/ *n* [U] art or style of speaking clearly and effectively, esp in public: [attrib] *elocution lessons.*
▷ **elocutionary** /-ənərɪ; *US* -enerɪ/ *adj* of elocution.
elocutionist /-ʃənɪst/ *n* person who teaches or is an expert in elocution.

elongate /ˈiːlɒŋgeɪt; *US* ɪˈlɔːŋ-/ *v* [Tn] make (sth) longer.
▷ **elongated** /ˈiːlɒŋgeɪtɪd; *US* ɪˈlɔːŋ-/ *adj* (made) long and thin; stretched out: *elongated figures in a painting.*
elongation /ˌiːlɒŋˈgeɪʃn; *US* -lɔːŋ-/ *n* **(a)** [U] making or becoming longer. **(b)** [C] thing that has been made longer (esp a line in a drawing, etc).

elope /ɪˈləʊp/ *v* [I, Ipr] ~ **(with sb)** run away with a lover, esp to get married: *The young couple eloped because their parents wouldn't let them marry.* ○ *He eloped with one of his students.* ▷ **elopement** *n* [C, U].

eloquence /ˈeləkwəns/ *n* [U] (skilful use of) expressive language, esp to impress or persuade an audience: *The crowd were swayed by his eloquence.*
▷ **eloquent** /-ənt/ *adj* (*fml*) having or showing eloquence: *an eloquent speaker, speech.* **eloquently** *adv.*

El Salvador /el ˈsælvədɔː(r)/ country on the Pacific coast of Central America; pop approx 5 376 000; official language Spanish; capital San Salvador; unit of currency colón (= 100 centavos). Much of the country is mountainous, with agriculture concentrated on the inland plateau. Coffee is the main export crop and maize the subsistence crop, but the country is not self-sufficient. Its economy was handicapped by internal guerrilla warfare until 1992; an earthquake in 1986 is still being paid for. ⇨ map at CENTRAL AMERICA.

else /els/ *adv* **1** (with indefinite, interrogative or negative *prons* and *advs*) in addition to or apart from (that already mentioned): *Did you see anybody else*, ie any other person(s)? ○ *Have you anything else to do?* ○ *Ask somebody else to help you.* ○ *That must be somebody else's* (ie some other person's) *coat; it isn't mine.* ○ *Nothing else* (ie I want nothing more), *thank you* ○ *We went to the cinema and nowhere else*, ie to no other place. ○ *I've tried to phone her six times today; what else can I do?* ○ *Who else was at the party?* ○ *How else* (ie In what other way) *would you do it?* ○ *We have a bit of bread and little/not much else*, ie not much more. **2** (idm) **or else (a)** otherwise; if not: *Run or else you'll be late.* ○ *He must be joking or else he's mad.* **(b)** (*infml*) (used to express a threat or warning): *Give me the money or else!*

elsewhere /ˌelsˈweə(r); *US* -ˈhweər/ *adv* in, at or to some other place: *Our favourite restaurant was full, so we had to go elsewhere.*

ELT /ˌiː el ˈtiː/ *abbr* (principles and practice of) English Language Teaching (to non-native speakers).

elucidate /ɪˈluːsɪdeɪt/ *v* [I, Tn] (*fml*) make (sth) clear; explain: *You have not understood; allow me to elucidate.* ○ *elucidate a problem, mystery* ○ *The notes helped to elucidate the most difficult parts of the text.* ▷ **elucidation** /ɪˌluːsɪˈdeɪʃn/ *n* [U] (*fml*): *This requires elucidation.*

elude /ɪˈluːd/ *v* [Tn] **1** escape (sb/sth), esp by a trick or cleverness; avoid: *elude one's enemies* ○ *He eluded capture for weeks by hiding underground.* **2** escape the memory or understanding of (sb): *I recognize her face, but her name eludes me*, ie I can't remember it.

elusive /ɪˈluːsɪv/ *adj* **(a)** tending to escape or disappear; difficult to capture: *a most elusive criminal.* **(b)** difficult to remember or understand: *an elusive perfume* ○ *an elusive word.*

elver /ˈelvə(r)/ *n* young eel.

elves *pl* of ELF.

Elysée Palace /eˌliːzeɪ ˈpælɪs/ **the Elysée Palace** (also **the Elysée**) official residence of the president of France, on the Champs Elysées in Paris. The term 'the Elysée' is often used to refer indirectly to the president.

Elysium /ɪˈlɪzɪəm/ **(a)** (in Greek mythology) home of the blessed after death, in the underworld. **(b)** (*fig*) place or state of perfect happiness. ▷ **Elysian** /ɪˈlɪzɪən/ *adj*: *the Elysian fields.*

em /em/ *n* unit of measurement used in printing, based on the width of a small letter 'm', approximately equal to one sixth of an inch.

'em /əm/ *pron* (*infml*) = THEM: *Don't let 'em get away!*

em- ⇨ EN-.

emaciated /ɪˈmeɪʃɪeɪtɪd/ *adj* made thin and weak: *very emaciated after a long illness* ○ *an emaciated child.* ⇨ Usage at THIN. ▷ **emaciation** /ɪˌmeɪsɪˈeɪʃn/ *n* [U].

email (also **e-mail**) /ˈiːmeɪl/ *n* [U] = ELECTRONIC MAIL (ELECTRON).

emanate /ˈeməneɪt/ *v* [Ipr] ~ **from sth/sb** (*fml or joc*) come or flow from sth/sb: *The idea originally emanated from his brother.* ○ *Delicious smells were emanating from the kitchen.* ▷ **emanation** /ˌeməˈneɪʃn/ *n* [C, U]: *The place gave off a strong emanation of evil.*

emancipate /ɪˈmænsɪpeɪt/ *v* [Tn, Tn·pr] ~ **sb (from sth)** set sb free, esp from political, legal or social restrictions: *emancipate slaves* ○ *Women are still struggling to be fully emancipated*, ie to be given the same rights, opportunities, etc as men.
▷ **emancipation** /ɪˌmænsɪˈpeɪʃn/ *n* [U] **(a)** action of emancipating: *the emancipation of women.* **(b)** state of being emancipated.

emasculate /ɪˈmæskjʊleɪt/ *v* [Tn] (*fml*) **1** remove the sexual organs of (a male animal); castrate. **2** deprive (sb/sth) of force or strength; weaken: *an emasculated regime, law.* ▷ **emasculation** /ɪˌmæskjʊˈleɪʃn/ *n.*

embalm /ɪmˈbɑːm; *US also* -bɑːlm/ *v* [Tn] **1** preserve (a dead body) from decay by using spices or chemicals: *The Egyptians used to embalm the bodies of their dead kings and queens.* **2** make (sth) fragrant. ▷ **embalmer** /ɪmˈbɑːmə(r)/ *n.* **embalmment** /ɪmˈbɑːmmənt; *US also* -bɑːlm-/ *n* [U].

embankment /ɪmˈbæŋkmənt/ *n* wall or ridge of earth, stone, etc made to keep water back or to carry a railway or road over low ground: *the Thames Embankment.*

embargo /ɪmˈbɑːgəʊ/ *n* (*pl* ~**es** /-gəʊz/) [C, U] ~ **(on sth)** official order that forbids sth, esp trade, the movement of ships, etc: *a gold embargo*, ie one that restricts or forbids the buying or selling of gold ○ *an embargo on trade with other islands* ○ *lift/raise/remove an embargo on sth*, ie start trading in sth again ○ *place sth under (an) embargo*, ie do no trade in sth.

▷ **embargo** *v* (*pt, pp* ~**ed** /-gəʊd/) [Tn] **1** put an embargo on (sth). **2** seize (ships, goods, etc) for use by the State.

embark /ɪmˈbɑːk/ *v* **1** [I, Ipr, Tn] ~ (**for...**) (cause sb/sth to) go or be taken on board a ship or an aircraft: *Passengers with cars must embark first.* ○ *We embarked for Calais at midday.* ○ *The ship embarked passengers and cargo at an Italian port.* **2** (phr v) **embark on sth** start or engage in (esp sth new or difficult): *embark on a long journey* ○ *He embarked on a new career.*

▷ **embarkation** /ˌembɑːˈkeɪʃn/ *n* [C, U] action or process of embarking: *the port of embarkation.*

embarrass /ɪmˈbærəs/ *v* [Tn esp passive] (**a**) cause (sb) to feel self-conscious, awkward or ashamed: *I was embarrassed by his comments about my clothes.* ○ *Are you trying to embarrass me?* (**b**) cause mental discomfort or anxiety to (sb): *embarrassed by lack of money* ○ *financially embarrassed.*

▷ **embarrassing** *adj*: *an embarrassing incident, question, mistake.* **embarrassingly** *adv*.

embarrassment *n* **1** (**a**) [U] embarrassing or being embarrassed: *He suffered much embarrassment in his youth.* (**b**) [C] person or thing that embarrasses: *He's an embarrassment to his family.* ○ *financial embarrassments.* **2** (idm) **an embarrassment of ˈriches** too many good things to do, choose from, etc.

embassy /ˈembəsɪ/ *n* **1** (official residence of an) ambassador and his staff: *the American embassy in London* ○ *He is with* (ie working at) *the French embassy.* ○ [attrib] *embassy officials.* Cf CONSULATE 1, HIGH COMMISSION (HIGH[1]). **2** (*dated*) deputation sent to a foreign government: *send sb/go/come on an embassy (to sb).*

embattled /ɪmˈbætld/ *adj* **1** (**a**) (of an army, etc) drawn up and prepared for battle: *embattled troops.* (**b**) in a condition of defence; fortified against attack: *the embattled city.* **2** (of a tower or building) having battlements.

embed /ɪmˈbed/ *v* (**-dd-**) [usu passive: Tn, Tn·pr] ~ **sth (in sth)** fix sth deeply and firmly (in a surrounding mass): *stones embedded in rock* ○ *The arrow embedded itself in the wall.* ○ (*fig*) *The idea became embedded in his mind.*

embellish /ɪmˈbelɪʃ/ *v* [Tn, Tn·pr] ~ **sth (with sth) 1** make sth beautiful by adding ornaments, etc: *a dress embellished with lace and ribbons.* **2** improve (a story, statement, etc) by adding often untrue details, eg to make it more interesting or amusing: *He often embellishes the tales of his travels.*

▷ **embellishment** *n* (**a**) [U] embellishing or being embellished: *the embellishment of a book, a building, a speech.* (**b**) [C] thing that embellishes; artistic addition: *a 16th-century church with 18th-century embellishments.*

ember /ˈembə(r)/ *n* (usu *pl*) small piece of burning or glowing wood or coal in a dying fire: *Only the embers of the bonfire remained.* ○ (*fig*) *the dying embers of a former passion.*

Ember days /ˈembə deɪz/ (in the Christian Church) three days in Lent once marked by fasting and special prayers.

embezzle /ɪmˈbezl/ *v* [Tn] use (money placed in one's care) in a wrong way to benefit oneself: *embezzle the pension fund* ○ *The treasurer embezzled £2 000 of the club's money.*

▷ **embezzlement** *n* [C, U] (instance of) embezzling: *petty embezzlements* ○ *He was found guilty of embezzlement.*

embezzler /ɪmˈbezlə(r)/ *n* person who embezzles.

embitter /ɪmˈbɪtə(r)/ *v* [Tn usu passive] fill (sb/sth) with bitter feelings: *embittered by repeated failures.* ▷ **embitterment** *n* [U] (*fml*).

emblazon /ɪmˈbleɪzən/ (also **blazon**) *v* [Tn] decorate (sth) with heraldic or other devices: *a shield emblazoned with red dragons.* ▷ **emblazonment** *n* [U].

emblem /ˈembləm/ *n* object that represents sth; symbol: *The dove is an emblem of peace.* ○ *The ring was important to her as an emblem of their love.* ○ *The thistle is the emblem of Scotland.*

▷ **emblematic** /ˌembləˈmætɪk/ *adj* [usu pred] ~ (**of sth**) (*fml*) serving as an emblem; symbolic.

embody /ɪmˈbɒdɪ/ *v* (*pt, pp* **-died**) [Tn, Tn·pr] ~ **sth (in sth)** (*fml*) **1** express or give visible form to (ideas, feelings, etc): *To me he embodies all the best qualities of a teacher.* **2** include or contain sth: *The latest computer model embodies many new features.*

▷ **embodiment** /ɪmˈbɒdɪmənt/ *n* person or thing that embodies sth or is embodied: *She's the embodiment of kindness.*

embolden /ɪmˈbəʊldən/ *v* [esp passive: Tn, Cn·t] (*dated or fml*) give courage or confidence to (sb): *emboldened by drink* ○ *His success emboldened him to expand his business.*

embolism /ˈembəlɪzəm/ *n* (*medical*) blockage of an artery or a vein caused by a clot of blood, an air-bubble, etc.

▷ **embolus** /ˈembələs/ *n* (*pl* **-li** /-laɪ/) clot, air-bubble, etc causing an embolism.

emboss /ɪmˈbɒs; *US* -ˈbɔːs/ *v* [esp passive: Tn, Tn·pr] ~ **A with B**/~ **B on A** decorate (the surface of sth) with a raised design; create (a raised design) on the surface of sth: *an address embossed on notepaper* ○ *embossed stationery* ○ *a leather briefcase embossed with one's initials.*

embrace /ɪmˈbreɪs/ *v* **1** [I, Tn] take (a person, etc) into one's arms as a sign of affection: *They embraced (each other) warmly.* ○ *She embraced her son before leaving.* **2** [Tn] (*fml*) accept or take (an idea, etc) willingly: *embrace Christianity* ○ *embrace an offer, opportunity.* **3** [Tn] (of things) include: *The term 'mankind' embraces men, women and children.*

▷ **embrace** *n* act of embracing: *He held her in a warm embrace.* ○ *She tried to avoid his embraces.*

embrasure /ɪmˈbreɪʒə(r)/ *n* (**a**) opening for a door or window, wider on the inside than the outside, in an interior wall, esp of an old castle. (**b**) similar opening in a castle, fort, etc for shooting through.

embrocation /ˌembrəˈkeɪʃn/ *n* [U] liquid for rubbing on the body to ease muscular aches, stiffness, etc; liniment: *A bit of embrocation will soothe your bruised knee.*

embroider /ɪmˈbrɔɪdə(r)/ *v* **1** [I, Tn, Tn·pr] ~ **A (on B)**/~ **B (with A)** decorate (cloth) with needlework: *She embroiders very well.* ○ *She embroidered flowers on the cushion (in gold thread).* ○ *She embroidered the cushion with flowers.* **2** [Tn] (*fig*) add untrue details to (a story, etc) to make it more interesting: *embroider the truth, the tale, the facts, etc.*

▷ **embroidery** /-dərɪ/ *n* [U] **1** decoration with needlework: *a beautiful piece of embroidery* ○ *He's good at embroidery.* **2** (*fig*) untrue details added for effect: *A little embroidery made the story quite entertaining.*

embroil /ɪmˈbrɔɪl/ *v* [esp passive: Tn, Tn·pr] ~ **sb/oneself (in sth)** get sb/oneself involved (in a quarrel or difficult situation): *I don't want to become embroiled in their arguments.* ○ *They are embroiled in a war against their will.*

embryo /ˈembrɪəʊ/ *n* (*pl* ~**s** /-əʊz/) **1** (**a**) young animal or plant in the early stages of its development before birth (or before coming out of its egg or seed): *an aborted embryo.* Cf FOETUS. (**b**) (*fig*) plan, scheme, etc in its very early stages: *an embryo of an idea* ○ [attrib] *The project is still at the embryo stage.* **2** (idm) **in embryo** existing but undeveloped: *My plans are still very much in embryo.*

▷ **embriology** /ˌembrɪˈɒlədʒɪ/ *n* [U] scientific study of the formation and development of embryos. **embryologist** *n* /ˌembrɪˈɒlədʒɪst/ expert in this.

embryonic /ˌembrɪˈɒnɪk/ *adj* [usu attrib] in an early stage of development: *an embryonic foetus* ○ (*fig*) *The scheme is still in its embryonic stage.*

□ **ˈembryo sac** large cell in flowering plants in which the egg nucleus is fertilized and becomes the embryo.

emcee /ˌemˈsiː/ *n* (*infml*) master of ceremonies; compère: *Who was (the) emcee of the show last night?* Cf MC 1.

▷ **emcee** *v* (*pt, pp* **emceed**) [I, Tn] act as master of ceremonies for (an event): *Who's emceeing (the show) tonight?*

emend /ɪˈmend/ *v* [Tn] remove errors from (eg a text before printing): *emend a passage in a book.*

▷ **emendation** /ˌiːmenˈdeɪʃn/ *n* (**a**) [U] action of emending. (**b**) [C] thing that is emended: *minor emendations to the official statement.*

emerald /ˈemərəld/ *n* bright green precious stone: *two diamonds and an emerald* ○ [attrib] *an emerald ring.*

▷ **emerald** *adj, n* [U] (also **emerald ˈgreen**) (of a) bright green colour: *an emerald hat.*

□ **the ˈEmerald Isle** (*often joc*) Ireland.

emerge /ɪˈmɜːdʒ/ *v* [I, Ipr] ~ (**from sth**) **1** (**a**) come out or up (from water, etc): *The swimmer emerged from the lake.* ○ *The moon emerged from behind the clouds.* (**b**) come into view or prominence: *He emerged as leader at the age of thirty.* **2** (of facts, ideas, etc) become known: *No new evidence emerged during the enquiry.*

▷ **emergence** /-dʒəns/ *n* [U] action of emerging: *her emergence as a well-known artist.*

emergent /-dʒənt/ *adj* [usu attrib] in the process of emerging: *the emergent countries of Africa*, ie those becoming politically independent and modernized, etc.

emergency /ɪˈmɜːdʒənsɪ/ *n* **1** [C, U] sudden serious event or situation requiring immediate action: *You should only use this door in an emergency.* ○ *The government has declared a state of emergency*, eg because of war, a natural disaster, etc. ○ [attrib] *the emergency exit.* ⇨ article. **2** [U] (*US*) = CASUALTY 3: [attrib] *the emergency ward.*

emeritus /ɪˈmerɪtəs/ *adj* (often placed after the *n*, and having a capital in titles) (of a university teacher, esp a professor) retired, but keeping his title as an honour: *the emeritus professor of biology* ○ *a professor emeritus* ○ *Emeritus Professor Johnson.*

Emerson /ˈeməsn/ Ralph Waldo (1803-82), American philosopher and poet. He developed the semi-religious concept of 'Transcendentalism', a form of mystic idealism and reverence for nature. He campaigned against the slave trade and was a friend of *Carlyle and *Thoreau.

emery /ˈemərɪ/ *n* [U] hard metallic substance used (esp in powdered form) for polishing, smoothing and grinding.

□ **ˈemery-board** *n* small strip of wood or cardboard covered in emery, used for filing the finger-nails.

ˈemery-paper *n* paper coated with emery, used for smoothing rough surfaces.

emetic /ɪˈmetɪk/ *n, adj* (medicine) causing vomiting: *He was given an emetic (medicine) after eating poisonous berries.*

EMF /ˌiː em ˈef/ *abbr* electromotive force.

emigrate /ˈemɪgreɪt/ *v* [I, Ipr] ~ (**from...**) (**to...**) leave one's own country to go and live in another: *emigrate from Britain to Australia to find work.* Cf IMMIGRATE.

▷ **emigrant** /ˈemɪgrənt/ *n* person who emigrates: *emigrants to Canada* ○ [attrib] *emigrant labourers.*

emigration /ˌemɪˈgreɪʃn/ *n* [U, C] emigrating. In the 19th and 20th centuries several important waves of emigration occurred, corresponding to periods of severe economic hardship in certain parts of the world. One striking example is the Potato Famine in Ireland in 1845-47, which led to massive emigration to the USA and the halving of Ireland's population by 1914. In the 20th century Nazi persecution of Jews led to further emigration from all over Europe, with the USA again often being the final destination. Several countries have been virtually built on the work of emigrants, notably the USA, Canada, Australia, Argentina and most recently Israel: *the mass emigration of refugees in wartime* ○ [attrib] *emigration officials.*

émigré /ˈemɪgreɪ; *US* ˌemɪˈgreɪ/ *n* (*French*) person who has left his own country, usu for political

Emergency Services

The main emergency telephone number in Britain is 999. In the USA it is 911. This calls the fire brigade, the police, the ambulance service, a coastguard rescue service (for sea and cliff rescue), or a mountain rescue party. The first three services are those most commonly used. The procedure is to dial the emergency number (the call is free), to tell the operator which service is needed, to give the number of the telephone being used to make the call, and to give the address or location where help is needed. The required service normally responds within minutes. The number 999 was chosen because, on the old dial phones, it was considered to be the easiest to dial in darkness or smoke.

The fire service usually deals with floods and with rescue work from a height, using an extendable ladder. The latter may be for a person trapped on a roof (or threatening suicide by jumping from a high place) or even for a pet animal trapped in a tree.

For emergencies involving gas, water or electricity, the usual procedure is to call the appropriate company. Gas companies usually have a special number for reporting escapes of gas (where a gas pipe or main is fractured). Water companies do not normally deal with emergencies inside the home, such as burst water pipes, but only with external incidents, such as a broken water main or sewage pipe. For water emergencies inside the home, the usual procedure is to call a plumber.

People who are in despair and feel suicidal can call the Samaritans, a voluntary organization that offers advice and friendship in such cases and operates on a regional basis. Children who feel that they are in danger from adults can now call the organization Childline, using the single national number 0800 1111. (Calls to numbers beginning 0800 are free in Britain.)

Where a specialized service is required, the call for help is often made to a branch of a national voluntary organization or charity. Their numbers are listed separately in the local telephone directory and include such bodies as Alcoholics Anonymous, the National Society for the Prevention of Cruelty to Children (NSPCC), Rape Crisis, and Relate (the former Marriage Guidance Council). The directory also lists the telephone numbers of local police stations and hospitals.

Britain's two main motoring organizations, the Automobile Association (AA), and the Royal Automobile Club (RAC), operate emergency services. Both organizations have emergency telephone points along many main roads for the use of their members. There are also emergency telephones on motorways for general use by motorists who break down. The location of the nearest such telephone is indicated by an arrow on a marker post by the side of the road.

Help for a medical emergency that happens at home is usually obtained by calling one's own family doctor (or any doctor), rather than the local hospital, although the ambulance service will respond to a 999 call in serious cases. People who try to obtain non-urgent medical help direct from a hospital casualty department are usually referred back to their own doctor, since it is the family doctor who arranges hospital treatment.

reasons: *He was one of the émigrés who left France after the French Revolution.*

eminence /ˈemɪnəns/ *n* **1** [U] state of being famous or distinguished: *reach eminence as a doctor* ○ *rise to eminence in one's profession.* **2** [C] (*dated or fml*) piece of rising ground; hill. **3 Eminence** [C] title used of or to a cardinal: *His/Your Eminence* ○ *Their/Your Eminences.*

éminence grise /ˌemɪnɑːns ˈɡriːz/ (*French*) person who has no official authority but has power or influence over a person in office.

eminent /ˈemɪnənt/ *adj* **1** (of a person) famous and distinguished: *an eminent architect* ○ *He is eminent both as a sculptor and as a portrait painter.* **2** [usu attrib] (of qualities) remarkable; outstanding: *a man of eminent goodness.*

▷ **eminently** *adv* obviously; outstandingly: *She seems eminently suitable for the job.*

□ ˌ**eminent doˈmain** (*US law*) = COMPULSORY PURCHASE (COMPULSORY).

emir /eˈmɪə(r)/ (also **amir**) *n* title of various Muslim rulers.

▷ **emirate** /eˈmɪəreɪt; *US* ˈemɪrɒt/ *n* position, reign or lands of an emir: *the United Arab Emirates.*

emissary /ˈemɪsərɪ/ *n* person sent to deliver a message (often an unpleasant or a secret one) or to conduct negotiations.

emission /ɪˈmɪʃn/ *n* **1** [U] (*fml*) sending out or giving off (of light, heat, fumes, matter, fluid from the body, etc): *the emission of light from the sun.* **2** [C] thing that is sent out or given off; discharge: *a nocturnal emission,* ie the discharge of semen during sleep.

▷ **emissivity** /emɪˈsɪvətɪ/ *n* [U] (*physics*) ratio of the power radiated by a surface to that radiated at the same temperature by a hypothetical body that absorbs all radiation.

emit /ɪˈmɪt/ *v* (**-tt-**) [Tn] give or send (sth) out; discharge: *A volcano emits smoke, lava and ashes.* ○ *She emitted a cry of pain.* ○ *The cheese was emitting a strong smell.*

emollient /ɪˈmɒlɪənt/ *n, adj* (substance) that soothes and softens the skin: *Use an emollient for dry skin.* ○ *an emollient cream.*

emolument /ɪˈmɒljʊmənt/ *n* (usu *pl*) (*fml or rhet*) profit made from being employed; fee or salary: *Her emoluments as a teacher amounted to £8500 a year.* ○ *He was paid a modest emolument.*

emotion /ɪˈməʊʃn/ *n* **1** [C] strong feeling of any kind: *Love, joy, hate, fear and jealousy are all emotions.* ○ *The speaker appealed to our emotions rather than to our minds.* **2** [U] excitement or disturbance of the mind or (more usu) the feelings: *overcome by/with emotion* ○ *He spoke of his dead wife with deep emotion.* ○ *She answered in a voice filled with emotion.*

▷ **emote** /ɪˈməʊt/ *v* [I] (*often derog*) show emotion, usu in a very dramatic way: *The tenor emoted wildly all through the opera.*

emotional /-ʃənl/ *adj* **1** [attrib] of the emotions: *emotional problems.* **2** causing or showing emotions: *an emotional response* ○ *emotional music, language.* **3** having emotions that are easily excited: *an emotional man, actor, character, nature* ○ *She is embarrassingly emotional in public.* **emotionally** /-ʃənəlɪ/ *adv*: *emotionally disturbed.*

emotionless *adj* without emotion.

emotive /ɪˈməʊtɪv/ *adj* (of words, etc) tending to affect the emotions: *an emotive speech* ○ *Capital punishment is an emotive issue.*

empanel (also **impanel**) /ɪmˈpænl/ *v* (**-ll-**; *US also* **-l-**) [Tn] (*fml*) list or select (sb) to serve on a jury.

empathy /ˈempəθɪ/ *n* [U] **1** ability to imagine and share another person's feelings, experience, etc: *There is a strange empathy between the old lady and her grandson.* **2** ability to identify oneself mentally with eg a work of art that one is looking at, and so to understand its meaning.

▷ **empathize, -ise** /ˈempəθaɪz/ *v* [I, Ipr] ~ (**with sb**) feel empathy: *try to empathize with one's students.*

emperor /ˈempərə(r)/ *n* (*fem* **empress** /ˈemprɪs/) ruler of an empire: *the Roman emperors* ○ *the Emperor Napoleon.*

□ ˌ**emperor ˈpenguin** largest species of penguin.

emphasis /ˈemfəsɪs/ *n* (*pl* **-ases** /-əsiːz/) [C, U] **1** force or stress given to a word or words when spoken, to make the meaning clear or to show importance: *give special emphasis to a phrase.* **2** ~ (**on sth**) (placing of) special meaning, value or importance (on sth): *Some schools put/lay/place great emphasis on language study.* ○ *The emphasis here is on hard work, not enjoyment.*

▷ **emphasize, -ise** /ˈemfəsaɪz/ *v* [Tn, Tf] put emphasis on (sth); give emphasis to (sth); stress: *Which word should I emphasize?* ○ *He emphasized the importance of careful driving/that careful driving was important.*

emphatic /ɪmˈfætɪk/ *adj* **1** having, showing or using emphasis: *an emphatic denial* ○ *He was most emphatic that I should go.* **2** definite and clear: *an emphatic victory.* **emphatically** /-klɪ/ *adv.*

emphysema /ˌemfɪˈsiːmə/ *n* [U] (*medical*) disease that affects the lungs and makes breathing difficult.

empire /ˈempaɪə(r)/ *n* **1** (**a**) [C] group of countries or states under a single ruler or ruling power: *the Roman Empire* ○ (*derog*) *the American/Soviet empire,* ie countries over which the USA/USSR has great influence. (**b**) **the Empire** [sing] any of the many empires that have existed throughout history, eg the British Empire, the Roman Empire, the Holy Roman Empire and those of Napoleon I and Napoleon III. **2** [U] (*fml*) supreme political power: *the responsibilities of empire.* **3** [C] (*fig*) large commercial organization controlled by one person or group: *a publishing empire.*

□ ˈ**empire-building** *n* [U] (*often derog*) process of deliberately acquiring extra territory, authority, etc.

ˈ**Empire style** style in dress and decoration during the Napoleonic period in France, which spread throughout Europe and corresponds to the Regency style in Britain. Dresses had high waists and elaborate embroidery; furniture and decoration were neo-classical with Egyptian influences. ⇨ illus at DRESS.

Empire State Building /ˌempaɪə ˈsteɪt bɪldɪŋ/ **the Empire State Building** skyscraper in Fifth Avenue, New York. It was for many years the tallest building in the world at 381m (1250ft). A radio mast was added later which further increased its height.

empirical /ɪmˈpɪrɪkl/ *adj* (of knowledge) based on observation or experiment, not on theory. Cf TRANSCENDENTAL.

▷ **empirically** /-klɪ/ *adv.*

empiricism /ɪmˈpɪrɪsɪzəm/ *n* [U] use of empirical methods.

empiricist /-sɪst/ *n* person who works in an empirical way.

□ **em**ˌ**pirical ˈformula** formula for a chemical compound which indicates the atoms in their simplest ratio. Cf MOLECULAR FORMULA (MOLECULE), STRUCTURAL FORMULA (STRUCTURE).

emplacement /ɪmˈpleɪsmənt/ *n* prepared position or platform for a heavy gun or guns.

employ /ɪmˈplɔɪ/ *v* [Tn, Tn·pr, Cn·n/a, Cn·t] **1** ~ **sb** (**in/on sth**); ~ **sb** (**as sth**) give work to sb, usu for payment: *She hasn't been employed* (ie has not had

Employment

People of working age can be divided into three groups: the employed, the self-employed, and the unemployed. At the end of the 1980s, Britain's total work-force was about 26 million, about two thirds of the adult population. Of this number, around 3 million people were self-employed, and there were about 2 million unemployed. About 40 per cent of the work-force are women, a proportion that is gradually growing.

As in many countries, there has been a gradual swing from employment in the manufacturing industries to jobs in service industries such as banking, retailing, hotels and catering, and public administration. About two thirds of the work-force are employed in service industries, compared with one quarter in manufacturing industry. During the 1980s, the largest rise was in the banking, insurance and finance sector, which increased by 50 per cent. The number of workers in transport, however, has declined.

During the 1980s there were years of high unemployment, with a peak of over 3 million unemployed in 1986. A number of government schemes, programmes and incentives were introduced to help unemployed people find work. These range from the Youth Training Scheme (YTS), giving young people the opportunity to obtain a vocational qualification while under training, to Employment Training (ET), an extensive adult training programme introduced in 1988 for people who had been out of work for more than six months.

Many unemployed people look for work in advertisements, such as those in local newspapers. Others make their first search through the government Jobcentres, where local jobs are advertised and where individual advice is given.

Instruction in practical skills is provided for the unemployed at Skillcentres. These were at first run by the Department of Employment but are now privately managed. Training of a more theoretical kind can also be obtained through the Open College, an independent body that provides courses by radio and television. Two further schemes are Business Growth Training, which offers financial help to employers training their own employees, and the Enterprise Allowance Scheme, which helps unemployed people start their own business.

Although many school-leavers obtain jobs after completing a one-year or two-year YTS course, some find the experience depressing and regard it as a waste of time.

If a person is unemployed for six months or longer, he or she may attend an interview with a 'Restart' counsellor, who will suggest alternative ways of finding work. One solution is for the person to attend a special five-day Restart course, with practical advice on the way to look for a job. Another is a place in a Jobclub, where the person is given similar advice followed by help in finding a job. A third possibility is self-employment under the Enterprise Allowance Scheme. People who remain unemployed for a year or more are recommended to see a Restart counsellor every six months.

Similar schemes operate in the USA where, as in Britain, an increasing number of workers are employed in service industries and where unemployment in 1990 was about 5 per cent. The Federal-State Employment Service refers employable applicants to job openings where they can make the best use of their skills. It also helps unemployed people to obtain advice or training.

The Job Training Partnership Act (JTPA), which came into force in 1983, provides job training and employment services for poor and disadvantaged people, with the aim of finding permanent jobs for as many people as possible. A special section of the Act caters for people who lose jobs in industries where they are unlikely to be able to find another job. Young unemployed people are given training by Job Corps residential training centres. In addition to these schemes, which are organized on a federal basis, individual states also provide employment training which is paid for from state taxes.

a job) *for six months now.* ○ *They've just employed five new waiters.* ○ *He's employed on the oil rigs.* ○ *She's employed as a taxi driver.* ○ *They employed him to look after the baby.* **2** ~ **sb/sth (in/on sth)**; ~ **sth (as sth)** (*fml*) make use of sb/sth; occupy (time, attention, etc): *You could employ your spare time better.* ○ *He was busily employed in cleaning his shoes.* ○ *He employed his knife as a lever.* ○ *The police employed force to open the door.*

▷ **employ** *n* [U] (*fml*) service or employment: *I left their employ after an argument.* ○ *How long has she been in your employ* (ie employed by you)*?*

employable /-əbl/ *adj* [usu pred] that can be employed.

employee /ˌemplɔɪˈiː, *also* ɪmˈplɔɪiː/ *n* person who works for sb or for a company in return for wages: *The manager sacked three employees.*

employer *n* person or company that employs others: *They're not good employers*, ie They treat their workers badly.

employment /ɪmˈplɔɪmənt/ *n* [U] **1** **(a)** act of employing: *The expansion of the factory will mean the employment of sixty extra workers.* **(b)** state of being employed: *be in/out of regular full-time employment.* **2** occupation (esp regular paid work): *give employment to sb* ○ *find employment* ○ [attrib] *government employment office.* ⇨ Usage at TRADE[1] ⇨ article.

□ **emˈployment agency** private business that helps people to find work and employers to find workers.

emporium /ɪmˈpɔːrɪəm/ *n* (*pl* **-riums** or **-ria** /rɪə/) (*joc or fml*) **(a)** centre of trade; market. **(b)** (*esp US*) large shop.

empower /ɪmˈpaʊə(r)/ *v* [Cn·t esp passive] (*fml*) give lawful power or authority (to sb) to act: *The new laws empower the police to stop anybody in the street.* ○ *The lawyer was empowered to pay all her bills.*

empress /ˈemprɪs/ *n* **(a)** female ruler of an empire. **(b)** wife or widow of an emperor.

Empson /ˈempsn/ Sir William (1906-84), English poet and critic. His complex language and mathematical imagery make his poetry difficult, but his book *Seven Types of Ambiguity* had a great influence on literary criticism.

empty[1] /ˈemptɪ/ *adj* **1** **(a)** having nothing inside: *an empty box* ○ *an empty lorry*, ie one without a load ○ *Your glass is empty.* **(b)** with nobody in it: *an empty house, room, chair, bus* ○ *empty streets* ○ *The cinema was half empty.* **2** **(a)** [pred] ~ **of sth** (*fml*) without or lacking in (a quality): *words empty of meaning.* **(b)** without sense or purpose: *empty threats, words, promises, dreams* ○ *My life feels empty now the children have left home.* **3** (*infml*) hungry: *I feel jolly empty!* **4** (idm) **on an empty ˈstomach** having eaten nothing: *It's not good to drink on an empty stomach.*

▷ **empties** *n* [pl] (*infml*) empty bottles, boxes, crates, etc: *Put your empties on the doorstep for the milkman.*

emptiness /ˈemptɪnɪs/ *n* [U].

□ ˌ**empty-ˈhanded** *adj* [pred] bringing back or taking away nothing: *They always arrive at parties empty-handed.* ○ *return empty-handed from an unsuccessful shopping trip.*

ˌ**empty-ˈheaded** *adj* (of people) foolish and without common sense: *an* ˌ*empty-headed young* ˈ*idiot.*

NOTE ON USAGE: **Empty** and **full** have wide uses. Any container or building can be **full** (of things or people) or **empty:** *The theatre was almost empty last night.* ○ *This bottle was full yesterday and now it's empty.* **Vacant** and **occupied** relate to the long-term use of a building, etc: *There are some vacant offices on the third floor.* ○ *All the flats are occupied now.* They can also refer to the short-term use of a room, etc: *The lavatory is vacant.* ○ *All the seats are occupied.*

empty[2] /ˈemptɪ/ *v* (*pt, pp* **emptied**) **1** **(a)** [Tn, Tn·pr, Tn·p] ~ **sth (out) (onto/into sth)**; ~ **sth (of sth)** make sth empty: *empty one's glass into the sink* ○ *empty (out) a drawer* ○ *He emptied his pockets of their contents.* ○ *This dreadful film soon emptied the cinema of people.* **(b)** [I, Ipr] ~ **(of sb/sth)** become empty: *The streets soon emptied (of people) when the rain started.* ○ *The cistern empties in five minutes.* **2** **(a)** [Tn, Tn·pr, Tn·p] ~ **sth (out) (into/onto sth)** remove (the contents of sth) and put them somewhere else: *Have you emptied (out) the rubbish?* ○ *She emptied the milk into the pan.* ○ *We emptied the waste paper onto the floor.* **(b)** [I, Ipr] ~ **(from/out of sth) (into/onto sth)** flow or pour out: *The water slowly emptied (from the cistern).* ○ *The River Rhone empties into the Mediterranean.* ○ *The rubbish from the cart emptied onto the street.*

empyrean /ˌempaɪˈriːən/ *n* **the empyrean** [sing] (*rhet*) the heavens; the sky.

EMS /ˌiː em ˈes/ *abbr* European Monetary System.

emu /ˈiːmjuː/ *n* large Australian bird that runs quickly but cannot fly.

emulate /ˈemjʊleɪt/ *v* [Tn, Tn·pr] ~ **sb (at sth)** (*fml*) try to do as well as or better than sb: *emulate her sister's sporting achievements* ○ *emulate her elder sister at the piano.*

▷ **emulation** /ˌemjʊˈleɪʃn/ *n* [U] (*fml*) action or state of emulating: *She worked hard in emulation of her elder sister.*

emulsify /ɪˈmʌlsɪfaɪ/ *v* (*pt, pp* **-fied**) [I, Tn] become an emulsion or make an emulsion of (sth): *The sauce has emulsified.* ○ *emulsify the oil.*

▷ **emulsifier** /-aɪə(r)/ *n* substance that allows an emulsion to remain stable.

emulsion /ɪˈmʌlʃn/ *n* [C, U] **1** creamy liquid in which particles of oil or fat are evenly distributed. Cf COLLOID. **2** medicine or paint in this form: [attrib] *emulsion paint*, ie paint that has a matt rather than a glossy finish when dry. **3** light-sensitive substance on the surface of photographic film.

en- (also **em-**) *pref* **1** (with *ns* and *vs* forming *vs*) put into or on: *encase* ○ *endanger* ○ *empanel.* **2** (with *adjs* or *ns* forming *vs*) make into; cause to be: *enlarge* ○ *enrich* ○ *empower.*

-en *suff* **1** (with *ns* forming *adjs*) made of: *golden* ○ *wooden.* **2** (with *adjs* forming *vs*) make or become: *blacken* ○ *sadden.*

enable /ɪˈneɪbl/ *v* **1** [Cn·t] make (sb) able to do sth by giving him the necessary authority or means:

This pass enables me to travel half-price on trains. ○ *A rabbit's large ears enable it to hear the slightest sound.* **2** [Tn] make (sth) possible: *The conference will enable greater international co-operation.*

□ **e'nabling act** law that makes it possible for a person or organization to take certain action.

enact /ɪ'nækt/ *v* **1** [Tn esp passive] *(fml)* perform (a part, play, etc) on, or as if on, the stage of a theatre: *a one-act drama enacted by children* ○ *A strange ritual was enacted before our eyes.* **2** [Tn esp passive, Tf] *(fml or law)* make or pass (a law): *enacted by Parliament* ○ *Be it further enacted that....*

▷ **enactment** *n* **1** [U] *(fml or law)* enacting: *the enactment of the drama* ○ *the enactment of the new bill.* **2** [C] law: *The enactment states that....*

enamel /ɪ'næml/ *n* [U] **1** glass-like substance used for coating metal, pottery, etc for decoration or as protection: *Some of the enamel on this pan is chipped off.* ○ [attrib] *enamel ware,* ie manufactured goods such as pots, pans, etc with hard enamel surfaces ○ *enamel paint,* ie paint that dries to make a hard glossy surface. **2** hard outer covering of teeth. ⇨ illus at TOOTH.

▷ **enamel** *v* (**-ll-**; *US also* **-l-**) [Tn] cover or decorate (sth) with enamel: *enamelled jewellery.*

enamoured (*US* **enamored**) /ɪ'næməd/ *adj* [pred] ~ **of/with sth** *(fml or joc)* fond of or delighted by sth: *enamoured of the sound of one's own voice* ○ *I'm not too enamoured with the idea of spending a whole day with him.*

en bloc /ˌɒn 'blɒk/ *(French)* all together; all at the same time: *They left the meeting en bloc.*

encamp /ɪn'kæmp/ *v* [I, Tn esp passive] settle in camp: *The soldiers are encamped in the forest.* ○ *(fig) The strikers have been encamping outside the factory for weeks.*

▷ **encampment** *n* place where troops, etc are encamped.

encapsulate /ɪn'kæpsjʊleɪt/ *v* [Tn, Tn·pr] ~ **sth (in sth)** *(fml)* **1** enclose sth (as if) in a capsule: *This story encapsulates scenes from his childhood.* **2** express sth briefly; summarize sth: *The chairman's short statement encapsulates the views of the committee.*

encase /ɪn'keɪs/ *v* [esp passive: Tn, Tn·pr] ~ **sth (in sth)** *(fml)* surround or cover sth (as) with a case: *His broken leg was encased in plaster.*

-ence ⇨ -ANCE.

encephalitis /ˌenkefə'laɪtɪs/ *n* [U] inflammation of the brain.

enchant /ɪn'tʃɑːnt; *US* -'tʃænt/ *v* [Tn] fill (sb) with great delight: *enchanted by/with the singing of the children.*

▷ **enchanted** /-ɪd/ *adj* placed under a magic spell: *an enchanted garden,* eg in a fairy story.

enchanter *n* person who enchants.

enchanting *adj* delightful: *What an enchanting little girl!* **enchantingly** *adv.*

enchantment *n* **1** [U] being enchanted. **2** [C] thing that enchants. **3** [U] delight: *Dancing has lost all its enchantment for her.*

enchantress *n* /-trɪs/ woman who enchants or is enchanting: *seduced by an enchantress.*

enchilada /ˌentʃɪ'lɑdə/ *n* tortilla served with a sauce seasoned with chilli.

encircle /ɪn'sɜːkl/ *v* [Tn esp passive] form a circle round; surround: *a lake encircled by trees* ○ *enemy troops encircling the town.* ▷ **encirclement** *n* [U].

encl *abbr* (*commerce*) enclosed; enclosure (used eg at the end of a letter sent with one).

enclave /'enkleɪv/ *n* small territory of one state surrounded by that of another: *British enclaves in Africa* ○ *(fig) Switzerland was an enclave of peace in war-torn Europe.*

enclose /ɪn'kləʊz/ *v* [Tn, Tn·pr] ~ **sth (with sth) 1** (also **inclose**) put a wall, fence, etc round sth: *enclose a garden with a wall* ○ *an enclosed order of monks,* ie one that lives in isolation from the outside world. **2** put sth in an envelope, letter, parcel, etc: *I'll enclose your letter with mine.* ○ *A cheque for ten pounds is enclosed.* ○ *(fml or commerce) Enclosed, please find...,* ie You will find, enclosed with this....

enclosure /ɪn'kləʊʒə(r)/ *n* **1 (a)** [U] enclosing of land: *opposed to the enclosure of common land.* **(b)** [C] (also **inclosure**) piece of land that is enclosed: *She keeps a horse in that enclosure.* ○ *the members' enclosure,* eg at a racecourse. **2** [C] thing that is enclosed (esp with a letter): *several enclosures in the envelope.*

encode /ɪn'kəʊd/ *v* [Tn esp passive] **(a)** put (a message, etc) into code. **(b)** *(computing)* put (data) into a coded form for processing by a computer. Cf DECODE.

encomium /ɪn'kəʊmɪəm/ *n* (*pl* **-miums** or **-mia** /-mɪə/) *(fml)* very high praise in speech or writing.

encompass /ɪn'kʌmpəs/ *v* [Tn] *(fml)* **1** include or comprise sth: *The general arts course at the university encompasses a wide range of subjects.* **2** (also **compass**) *(dated)* surround: *a lake encompassed by mountains.*

encore /'ɒŋkɔː(r)/ *interj* (called out by an audience) Again! Repeat!

▷ **encore** *n* (call for a) repetition (of a song, etc) or a further performance by the same person or people: *The violinist got an enthusiastic encore.* ○ *The group gave three encores.*

encounter /ɪn'kaʊntə(r)/ *v* [Tn] *(fml)* **1** meet or find oneself faced by (sth/sb unpleasant, dangerous, difficult, etc): *I encountered many difficulties when I first started this job.* ○ *We encountered four enemy aircraft.* **2** meet (a friend, etc) unexpectedly.

▷ **encounter** *n* ~ **(with sb/sth)** sudden or unexpected (esp hostile) meeting: *an encounter with an enemy* ○ *I had a brief encounter with an angry client.*

encourage /ɪn'kʌrɪdʒ/ *v* **1** [Tn, Tn·pr, Dn·t] ~ **sb (in sth)** give support, confidence or hope to sb: *Don't encourage bad habits in a child.* ○ *He felt encouraged by the progress he'd made.* ○ *Her parents encouraged her in her studies.* ○ *encourage sb to lose weight.* **2** [Tn] help (sth) to develop; stimulate: *encourage exports.*

▷ **encouragement** *n* ~ **(to sb) (to do sth) (a)** [U] action of encouraging: *shouts of encouragement.* **(b)** [C] thing that encourages: *The teacher's words were a great encouragement to him.*

encouraging *adj*: *encouraging words, news, signs* ○ *This year's sales figures are very encouraging.* **encouragingly** *adv.*

encroach /ɪn'krəʊtʃ/ *v* [I, Ipr] ~ **(on/upon sth)** *(fml)* go beyond what is right or natural or desirable; intrude: *encroach on sb's property* ○ *encroach on the liberty of the individual* ○ *The sea is gradually encroaching (on the land),* ie washing the land away.

▷ **encroachment** *n* ~ **(on/upon sth)** *(fml)* **(a)** [U] action of encroaching: *I resent the encroachment on my time.* **(b)** [C] thing gained by encroaching: *encroachments made by the sea upon the land.*

encrust /ɪn'krʌst/ *v* **1** [usu passive: Tn, Tn·pr] ~ **sth (with sth)** cover (a surface) with a crust or thin hard coating, sometimes for decoration: *a gold vase encrusted with diamonds* ○ *an encrusted wound.* **2** [I] form into a crust: *Salt from the sea had encrusted on the dry sand.*

encumber /ɪn'kʌmbə(r)/ *v* [usu passive: Tn, Tn·pr] ~ **sb/sth (with sth) 1** prevent sb/sth from moving or acting freely and easily: *Travelling is difficult when you're encumbered with two small children and a heavy suitcase.* ○ *encumbered with debts.* **2** *(derog)* crowd sth; fill up sth: *a room encumbered with old and useless furniture.*

▷ **encumbrance** /ɪn'kʌmbrəns/ *n* person or thing that encumbers.

encyclical /ɪn'sɪklɪkl/ *n* letter written by the Pope for wide circulation.

encyclopedia (also **-paedia**) /ɪnˌsaɪklə'piːdɪə/ *n* book or set of books giving information about every branch of knowledge, or about one particular subject, with articles in alphabetical order. The first important encyclopedias in Europe date from the *Renaissance, but it was during the 18th century that the first modern scientifically produced works appeared. Chambers' *Cyclopedia* was published in Edinburgh in 1728 and the first volumes of Diderot's *Encyclopédie* in 1751. The *Encyclopaedia Britannica*, the most famous in English, was begun by a 'society of Gentlemen in Scotland' in 1768 and still survives, although it is now a largely American publication: *an encyclopedia of music* ○ *a children's encyclopaedia.*

▷ **encyclopedic** (also **-paedic**) /ɪnˌsaɪklə'piːdɪk/ *adj* dealing with or having knowledge of a wide variety of subjects; comprehensive: *enˌcyclopedic 'knowledge.*

end[1] /end/ *n* **1** farthest or last part or point (of the length of sth); extreme limit: *the end of a road, stick, line* ○ *the house at the end of the street* ○ *join the end of the queue* ○ *the end of the tunnel* ○ *the west/east end* (ie the parts in the west/east) *of a town* ○ *We've travelled from one end of Britain to the other.* ○ [attrib] *the end house* ○ *the end carriage,* ie in a train. **2** final part of sth; finish; conclusion: *at the end of the day, month, year, century, etc* ○ *the end of a story* ○ *He said he'd love her till the end of time,* ie for ever. ○ *the end of an era.* **3** small piece left over after sth has been used: *a cigarette end* ○ *candle ends.* **4** *(often euph)* death: *He's nearing his end,* ie is dying. ○ *She came to an untimely end,* ie died young. **5** aim or purpose: *gain/win/achieve one's ends* ○ *with this end in view/to this end.* **6** half of a sports pitch, etc defended or occupied by one team or player: *At half-time the teams changed ends.* **7** part or share (esp of a business, etc) with which a person is concerned: *We need someone to handle the marketing end of the business.* ○ *Are there any problems at your end?* **8** (idm) **at a loose end** ⇨ LOOSE[1]. **(be) at an end** finished: *The war was at an end.* **at the ˌend of one's 'tether** having no power, patience, endurance, etc left: *I've been looking after four young children all day and I really am at the end of my tether!* **(be) at the end of sth** finishing sth; having no more of sth: *at the end of his patience.* **at the ˌend of the 'day** when everything is taken into consideration: *At the end of the day the new manager is no better than the previous one.* **(be) at the sharp end (of sth)** ⇨ SHARP. **at one's wits' end** ⇨ WIT. **be at/on the receiving end** ⇨ RECEIVE. **be the end** *(infml)* be the limit of what one can tolerate; be very bad, annoying, etc: *This is the end — I'm never coming to this hotel again.* ○ *They really are the end!* **the beginning of the end** ⇨ BEGINNING (BEGIN). **bring sth/come/draw to an end** (cause sth to) finish, usu after lasting some time: *The battle finally brought the war to an end.* ○ *At last the meeting came to an end.* **burn the candle at both ends** ⇨ BURN[2]. **the business end** ⇨ BUSINESS. **come to a bad/sticky 'end** be led by one's actions to ruin, disgrace, punishment, an unpleasant death, etc: *He'll come to a bad end one of these days.* ○ *I like films where the villain comes to a sticky end!* **a dead end** ⇨ DEAD. **an ˌend in it'self** thing that is considered important in its own right, though possibly originally having another purpose: *For the old lady buying the daily newspaper soon became an end in itself, since she really just wanted to chat with the shopkeeper.* **the ˌend ˌjustifies the 'means** *(saying)* even wrong or unfair methods may be allowed if the result or purpose of the action is good. **(reach) the ˌend of the 'line/'road** (reach) the point at which one does not wish, or cannot bear, to continue in the same way: *It's sad that they got divorced but they had reached the end of the line together.* **(not) the ˌend of the 'world** (not) completely disastrous for sb: *You must realize that failing one exam is not the end of the world.* **(go to) the ˌends of the 'earth** (go to) the most remote parts of the world: *(fig) I'd go to the ends of the earth to see her again.* **ˌend 'on** with the ends meeting: *The two ships collided end on,* ie The front (or back) of one struck the front (or back) of the other. **ˌend to 'end** in a line, with the ends touching: *arrange the tables end to end.* **get hold of the wrong end of the stick** ⇨ WRONG. **go off the deep end** ⇨ DEEP[1]. **in the 'end** at last; finally: *He tried many different jobs; in the end he became a postman.* **keep one's 'end up** *(Brit infml)* continue to be cheerful and play one's part despite difficulties. **light at the end of the tunnel** ⇨ LIGHT[1]. **make an end of sth** *(fml)* finish sth. **make**

(both) ends meet earn enough money to live without getting into debt; balance one's income and expenditure: *Being out of work and having two young children, they found it impossible to make ends meet.* **make one's hair stand on end** ⇨ HAIR. **a means to an end** ⇨ MEANS[1]. **no end of sth** (*infml*) very many or much; very great: *I've had no end of problems recently.* ○ *We had no end of trouble getting them to agree.* **not/never hear the end of sth** ⇨ HEAR. **odds and ends** ⇨ ODDS. **on ˈend (a)** upright: *He placed the box on (its) end and sat on it.* **(b)** continuously: *They argued for two hours on end.* **put an ˈend to one's life/oneself** kill oneself. **put an end/a stop to sth** stop sth from happening any more; abolish sth: *The government is determined to put an end to terrorism.* **the thin end of the wedge** ⇨ THIN. **throw sb in at the deep end** ⇨ DEEP[1]. **to the bitter end** ⇨ BITTER. **without ˈend** never reaching an end or finishing: *troubles without end* ○ *world without end.*

□ **ˈendpapers** *n* [pl] (usu blank) pages pasted to the inside covers of a book.

ˈend-product *n* final product of a manufacturing process.

ˈend zone (in American football) either of the areas 10 yards long next to the goals.

end[2] /end/ *v* **1** [I, Ipr, Tn, Tn·pr] (cause sth to) come to an end: *The road ends here,* ie goes no further. ○ *How does this story end?* ○ *They decided to end their relationship.* ○ *They ended the play with a song.* **2** (idm) **the be-all and end-all** ⇨ BE[1]. **ˌend it ˈall; ˌend one's ˈlife** commit suicide: *He was so miserable that he seriously thought about ending it all.* **ˌend one's ˈdays/ˈlife (in sth)** spend the last part of one's life (in a particular state or place): *The great singer ended his days in poverty.* **3** (phr v) **end in sth (a)** have sth as its tip or ending: *The word ends in -ous.* **(b)** have sth as a result or conclusion: *Their long struggle ended in failure.* ○ *The argument ended in tears.* ○ *The debate ended in uproar.* **end sth off (with sth/by doing sth)** finish sth (in a suitable or successful way): *We ended off the meal with coffee and brandy.* ○ *He ended off his speech by telling a very funny joke.* **end up** reach or come to a certain place, state or action, esp by a lengthy route or process: *If you continue to steal you'll end up in prison.* ○ *After much discussion about holidays abroad we ended up in Cornwall.* ○ *At first he refused to accept any responsibility but he ended up apologizing.* ○ *If he carries on driving like that, he'll end up dead.*

▷ **ending** *n* end, esp of a story, film, play or word: *a story with a happy ending.*

endanger /ɪnˈdeɪndʒə(r)/ *v* [Tn] cause danger to (sb/sth); put in danger: *Smoking endangers your health.* ○ *The giant panda is an endangered species,* ie is in danger of becoming extinct.

endear /ɪnˈdɪə(r)/ *v* [Tn·pr] ~ **sb/oneself to sb** (*fml*) make sb/oneself loved or liked by sb: *Her kindness to my children greatly endeared her to me.* ○ *He managed to endear himself to everybody.*

▷ **endearing** *adj* causing or resulting in affection: *an endearing remark, smile, habit.* **endearingly** *adv.*

endearment *n* [C, U] word or expression of affection: *He whispered endearments in her ear.* ○ *'Darling' is a term of endearment.*

endeavour (*US* **-vor**) /ɪnˈdevə(r)/ *n* (*fml*) attempt or effort: *Please make every endeavour to arrive punctually.*

▷ **endeavour** *v* [It] (*fml*) try: *They endeavoured to make her happy but in vain.*

endemic /enˈdemɪk/ *n, adj* [often pred] (disease) that is regularly found in a particular country or area, or among a particular group of people: *Malaria is endemic in/to many hot countries.* ○ (*fig*) *the violence endemic in the city.* Cf EPIDEMIC, PANDEMIC.

endive /ˈendɪv; *US* -daɪv/ *n* [C, U] **1** (*US* also **escarole**) type of plant with curly leaves used as salad. **2** (*US*) = CHICORY.

endless /ˈendlɪs/ *adj* **1** (seemingly) without end: *endless patience* ○ *an endless choice of things to do* ○ *The hours of waiting seemed endless.* **2** (of a belt, chain, cable, etc) with the ends joined; continuous: *wheels in a machine driven by an endless belt.* ▷ **endlessly** *adv.*

endo- *comb form* internal; internally.

endocrine gland /ˈendəʊkraɪn glænd/ (also **ductless gland**) gland that produces hormones and passes them directly into the blood.

endodermis /ˌendəʊˈdɜːmɪs/ *n* [U] innermost part of the outer layer of a plant, found in the roots and sometimes in the stem.

endogenous /ɪnˈdɒdʒənəs/ *adj* (*biology*) growing or originating from within: *endogenous spores.*

endomitosis /ˌendəʊmaɪˈtəʊsɪs/ *n* [U] division of chromosomes in a cell nucleus without division of the nucleus itself. Cf MITOSIS.

endomorph /ˈendəʊmɔːf/ *n* person with a large rounded soft body, thought likely by some psychologists to have an extrovert personality. Cf ECTOMORPH, MESOMORPH. ▷ **endomorphic** *adj.*

endorphin /enˈdɔːfɪn/ *n* substance produced naturally by the body and acting as a pain-killer.

endorse /ɪnˈdɔːs/ *v* [Tn] **1** write one's name on the back of (esp a cheque). **2 (a)** write comments, etc in or on the back of (a document). **(b)** (*Brit*) record details of a motoring offence in (a driving licence): *He's had his licence endorsed for dangerous driving.* **3** give one's (official) approval or support to (a claim, statement, etc): *I am afraid I can't endorse your opinion of the government's record.* **4** say in an advertisement that one uses and approves of (a product): *Well-known sportsmen can earn large sums of money from manufacturers by endorsing clothes and equipment.*

▷ **endorsement** *n* **(a)** [U] act of endorsing: *the endorsement of a cheque* ○ *official endorsement of the scheme.* **(b)** [C] instance of this; statement that endorses: *Her son has had two endorsements for speeding.*

endoscope /ˈendəʊskəʊp/ *n* instrument used for examining the internal parts of the body.

▷ **endoscopy** /enˈdɒskəpɪ/ *n* [U] use of such instruments in medical examinations.

endoskeleton /ˈendəʊskelɪtn/ *n* skeleton of the type found in vertebrates and other animals, which exists inside the body and supports it. Cf EXOSKELETON.

endosperm /ˈendəʊspɜːm/ *n* tissue that surrounds and feeds the developing embryo in the seed of a flowering plant.

endothermic /ˌendəʊˈθɜːmɪk/ *adj* (of a chemical reaction) that absorbs heat from its surroundings. Cf EXOTHERMIC.

endow /ɪnˈdaʊ/ *v* **1** [Tn, Tn·pr] ~ **sb/sth (with sth)** give money, property, etc to provide a regular income for (eg a school, a college): *endow a bed in a hospital.* **2** [Tn·pr usu passive] ~ **sb with sth** provide sb naturally with (any good quality or ability): *She's endowed with intelligence as well as beauty.*

▷ **endowment** *n* **1** [U] action of endowing: *the endowment of many schools by rich former pupils.* **2** [C usu *pl*] money, property, etc given to provide an income: *The Oxford and Cambridge colleges have numerous endowments.* **3** [C usu *pl*] natural talent, quality or ability: *Not everyone is born with such endowments as you.* **enˈdowment policy** form of life insurance where a certain sum is paid on a specified date to the insured person or is paid to that person's dependents if he dies before that date.

endue /ɪnˈdjuː; *US* -ˈduː/ *v* [Tn·pr usu passive] ~ **sb with sth** (*fml*) provide or supply sb with a good quality, ability etc: *endued with gentleness.*

endurance /ɪnˈdjʊərəns; *US* -ˈdʊə-/ *n* [U] state or power of enduring: *He showed remarkable endurance throughout his illness.* ○ *His treatment of her was beyond endurance,* ie impossible to endure any longer. ○ [attrib] *The soldiers eventually completed the endurance tests,* ie tests of how long they could endure harsh conditions. ○ (*fig*) *Jane's party was more of an endurance test than anything else.*

endure /ɪnˈdjʊə(r); *US* -ˈdʊər/ *v* **1** [I, Tn] suffer or undergo (sth painful or uncomfortable) patiently: *endure toothache* ○ *He endured three years in prison for his religious beliefs.* **2** [Tn, Tt, Tg] (esp in negative sentences) bear; tolerate: *I can't endure that woman.* ○ *I can't endure to see/seeing children suffer.* **3** [I] continue in existence; last: *fame that will endure for ever* ○ *as long as life endures* ○ *These traditions have endured throughout the ages.*

▷ **endurable** /-rəbl/ *adj* that can be endured; bearable: *He found the boredom scarcely endurable.*

enduring *adj* continuing in existence; lasting: *enduring memories* ○ *an enduring peace* ○ *Her influence was the most enduring of all.* **enduringly** *adv.*

endways /ˈendweɪz/ (also **endwise** /ˈendwaɪz/) *adv* **1** with the end facing forwards: *The table was pushed endways through the door.* **2** end to end: *The child put the toy cars together endways.*

Endymion /enˈdɪmɪən/ (in Greek mythology) beautiful youth who was loved by the moon goddess Selene. She put him to sleep for ever so that she could always enjoy his beauty.

enema /ˈenɪmə/ *n* **1** injection of liquid into the rectum by means of a syringe (eg to clean out the bowels before an operation): *give a patient an enema.* **2** liquid used for this.

enemy /ˈenəmɪ/ *n* **1** [C] person who strongly dislikes or wants to injure or attack sb/sth: *Jane and Sarah used to be friends but now they are bitter enemies,* ie of each other. ○ *His arrogance made him many enemies,* ie made many people hate him. **2 (a) the enemy** [Gp] (armed) forces of a nation, side, etc with which one's country, side, etc is at war: *an encounter with the enemy* ○ *The enemy was/were forced to retreat.* ○ [attrib] *enemy forces, aircraft, ships, etc* ○ *enemy propaganda.* **(b)** [C] member of such a hostile force. **3** [C] anything that harms or weakens: *Poverty and ignorance are the enemies of progress.* **4** (idm) **one's own worst enemy** ⇨ WORST. **carry the war into the enemy's camp** ⇨ CARRY.

energy /ˈenədʒɪ/ *n* **1** [U] ability to act or work with strength and eagerness: *She's full of energy.* ○ *His work seemed to lack energy.* ○ *It's a waste of time and energy.* **2 energies** [pl] person's powers available for working or other activities: *I must concentrate my energies on decorating today.* ○ *apply/devote all one's energies to a task.* **3** [U] (*physics*) ability of matter or radiation to do work because of its motion, its mass, its electric charge, etc. Energy can be neither created nor destroyed, but only changed from one form to another. *Einstein showed that in theory matter can be regarded as a form of energy. Its usual forms include kinetic energy, heat energy, potential energy and electrical energy. **4** [U] fuel and other resources used for operating machinery, etc: *It is important to conserve energy.* ○ [attrib] *an energy crisis,* eg when sources of energy are scarce or unavailable.

▷ **energetic** /ˌenəˈdʒetɪk/ full of or done with energy(1): *an energetic child* ○ *take some energetic exercise.* **energetically** /-klɪ/ *adv.*

energize, -ise /ˈenədʒaɪz/ *v* [Tn] **(a)** give energy to (sb/sth). **(b)** cause electricity to flow to (a device).

enervate /ˈenəveɪt/ *v* [Tn] cause (sb) to lose strength or energy: *an enervating climate* ○ *a long, enervating illness.*

en famille /ˌɒn fæˈmiː/ (*French*) at home; among one's family: *I always enjoy winter evenings spent en famille.*

enfant terrible /ˌɒnfɒn teˈriːbl/ (*pl* **enfants terribles** /ˌɒnfɒn teˈriːbl/) (*French often joc*) (esp young) person whose behaviour, ideas, etc annoy, shock or embarrass those with more conventional opinions: *Her advanced ideas have made her the enfant terrible of the art world.*

enfeeble /ɪnˈfiːbl/ *v* [Tn esp passive] (*fml*) make weak or feeble: *enfeebled by a long illness.*

enfilade /enfɪˈleɪd/ *n* [C, U] gunfire aimed along the entire length of a target (eg a column of soldiers or a trench).

enfold /ɪnˈfəʊld/ *v* [Tn, Tn·pr] ~ **sb/sth (in/with sth)** (*fml*) enclose sb/sth, esp in one's arms; clasp or embrace sb/sth: *He enfolded the child in an affectionate embrace.*

enforce /ɪnˈfɔːs/ *v* **1** [Tn, Tn·pr] ~ **sth (on sb)** force people to obey (a law, etc); make sth effective: *The*

England

Although 'England' is strictly speaking the name of the largest of the countries that make up the United Kingdom (the others being Scotland, Wales, and Northern Ireland), it is nevertheless frequently equated with 'Britain' as a whole. This is probably because English (not 'British') is the name of the language that is common to all parts of the United Kingdom as well as to the British Isles as a whole, including the Republic of Ireland.

Traditionally, the English have a reputation for being taciturn, unsociable and long-suffering. This last quality is popularly said to have produced the characteristic English 'stiff upper lip', or display of stoicism or extreme patience in adversity. (The phrase itself appears to have become popular only in the 19th century.)

A combination of these three qualities has resulted in a general picture of the English as both bold and brave, yet inflexible and stubborn, as proud and haughty, yet correct and courteous. To some extent this is true, and the coldness and aloofness associated with the English may be partly due to their insularity. Living on an island, the English have been unaccustomed to frequent and easy social contact with their neighbours in other countries.

This insularity is evident in the xenophobic attitude of some English people, who regard themselves as superior to foreigners. This attitude shows itself in different ways, as for example in the general reluctance of the English to learn foreign languages (subconsciously supported by the knowledge that English is widely spoken and understood in other countries), or in the violent behaviour and hooliganism of some British football supporters when abroad.

It is also true that the insularity of the English (and the British as a whole) is evident in their patriotism, which is sometimes taken to extremes. It is significant that the concept of 'jingoism' evolved (in the 19th century) on British soil. Expressions of national feeling range from displays of popular belligerence (seen during the Falklands War in 1982) to the annual enthusiastic participation of the audience in the singing of patriotic songs such as 'Rule, Britannia' and 'Land of Hope and Glory' at the Last Night of the Proms. (Cf article at MUSIC.)

The traditional love of the English for their home is another aspect of insularity. The sentiment is summed up in the old saying that 'an Englishman's home is his castle'.

Within England itself, however, there is a marked distinction between the North and South. This has less to do with the much-debated 'North/South Divide', relating to the higher unemployment and lower living standards of the industrial north by comparison with the more affluent south, as with a marked difference of character. Southerners in general seem to be more introspective, reserved and self-centred than northerners, who are by contrast more extrovert, friendly and convivial.

police are there to enforce the law. **2** [Tn] make (sth) happen or bring (sth) about by force: *enforced silence, discipline, idleness.* **3** [Tn] give greater force or strength to (an argument, a belief, etc): *Have you any statistics that would enforce your argument?*

▷ **enforceable** /-əbl/ *adj* that can be enforced: *Such a strict law is not easily enforceable.*

enforcement *n* [U] enforcing or being enforced: *strict enforcement of a new law.*

enfranchise /ɪnˈfræntʃaɪz/ *v* [Tn esp passive] *(fml)* **1** give (sb) political rights, esp the right to vote at parliamentary elections: *In Britain women were enfranchised in 1918.* **2** set free (slaves). ▷ **enfranchisement** /ɪnˈfræntʃɪzmənt/ *n* [U].

Eng *abbr* **1** engineer(ing): *Tim Dale BSc (Eng).* **2** England; English.

engage /ɪnˈgeɪdʒ/ *v* **1** [Tn, Cn·n/a] ~ **sb (as sth)** *(fml)* arrange to employ sb; hire sb: *engage a new secretary* ○ *He's been engaged to decorate the house.* ○ *She was engaged as an interpreter.* **2** [Tn] *(fml)* occupy or attract (sb's thoughts, time, etc): *Nothing engages his attention for long.* ○ *The woman's plight engaged our sympathy.* **3** [I, Tn] *(fml)* begin fighting with (sb): *Our orders are to engage (the enemy) immediately.* ○ *The two armies were fiercely engaged for several hours.* **4** (a) [I, Ipr] ~ **(with sth)** (of parts of a machine, etc) lock or fit together: *The two cog-wheels engaged and the machine started.* ○ *One cog-wheel engages with another.* (b) [Tn] cause (parts of a machine, etc) to lock together or fit into each other: *engage the clutch/first gear*, eg in a car, when driving. **5** [Tt] *(dated fml)* bind oneself by a promise; guarantee: *a lawyer engaged to undertake the sale of the house immediately.* **6** (phr v) **engage (sb) in sth** (cause sb to) take part in or be occupied in sth: *I have no time to engage in gossip.* ○ *be engaged in politics, business* ○ *I engaged him in conversation.*

▷ **engaged** *adj* [usu pred] **1** (of a person) busy; occupied: *I can't come to dinner on Tuesday; I'm otherwise engaged*, ie I've already arranged to do something else. **2** *(Brit)* (*US* **busy**) (of a telephone line) in use: *Sorry! That number's engaged.* ○ [attrib] *the engaged tone/signal*, ie sound that tells the caller that the telephone line is engaged. **3** ~ **(to sb)** (of a person or two people) having agreed to marry: *She's engaged to Peter.* ○ *They're engaged (to be married)*, ie to each other. ○ *We've just got engaged.* ○ [attrib] *an engaged couple.* **4** (a) (esp of a toilet) occupied; already in use. (b) (of seats, tables, etc) reserved for later use.

engaging *adj* likely to attract or occupy the attention; charming: *an engaging smile, manner, person.* **engagingly** *adv.*

engagement /ɪnˈgeɪdʒmənt/ *n* **1** [C] agreement to marry: *Their engagement was announced in the local paper.* ⇨ article at WEDDING. **2** [C] arrangement to go somewhere, meet sb or do sth at a fixed time; appointment: *I have several engagements for next week.* ○ *The orchestra has several concert engagements.* **3** [C] *(fml)* formal promise or guarantee, esp in writing: *He doesn't have enough money to meet all his engagements*, ie to make the payments he has promised to make. **4** [C] *(fml)* battle: *The general tried to avoid an engagement with the enemy.* **5** [U] arrangement to employ; action of engaging: *the engagement of three new assistants.* **6** [U] action or result of engaging (parts of a machine, etc): *after engagement of the clutch.*

□ **enˈgagement ring** ring (usu containing precious stones) that a man gives to a woman when they agree to marry.

Engels /ˈeŋglz/ Friedrich (1820-95), German socialist thinker. He worked with Karl *Marx on the *Communist Manifesto* and is considered with Marx to have been one of the founders of Communism.

engender /ɪnˈdʒendə(r)/ *v* [Tn] *(fml)* be the cause of (a situation or condition): *Some people believe poverty engenders crime.*

engine /ˈendʒɪn/ *n* **1** machine with moving parts that converts energy such as heat, electricity, etc into motion: *This car has a new engine.* ○ *a steam/diesel/petrol engine.* ⇨ illus at CAR. **2** (also **locomotive**) machine that pulls or pushes a railway train: *I prefer to sit* (ie in a railway carriage) *facing the engine.* **3** *(arch)* machine or instrument: *engines of war*, eg cannons ○ *siege engines.*

□ **ˈengine-driver** *n* *(Brit)* (*US* **engineer**) person who drives a railway engine.

ˈengine room 1 part of a ship where the engines are. **2** *(fig)* place where things are organized, decisions are taken, etc.

engineer /ˌendʒɪˈnɪə(r)/ *n* **1** person who designs, builds or maintains engines, machines, bridges, railways, mines, etc: *a civil/mining/electrical/mechanical engineer.* **2** skilled person who controls an engine or engines, esp on a ship or aircraft: *the chief engineer on a cruise liner.* **3** *(US)* = ENGINE-DRIVER (ENGINE). **4** soldier trained to design and build military works: *He's in the Royal Engineers*, ie a branch of the British Army.

▷ **engineer** *v* [Tn] **1** *(infml derog)* arrange or cause (sth), esp by cunning or secret means: *His enemies engineered his downfall.* ○ *engineer a plot, scheme, revolt, etc.* **2** build or control (sth) as an engineer.

engineering /ˌendʒɪˈnɪərɪŋ/ *n* [U] (a) practical application of scientific knowledge in the design, construction and control of machines, public services such as roads, bridges, etc, electrical apparatus, chemicals, etc: *civil/electrical/chemical/mechanical engineering* ○ *The new bridge is a triumph of engineering.* (b) work, science or profession of an engineer: *She's studying engineering at university.* ○ [attrib] *an engineering degree.*

England /ˈɪŋglənd/ largest country in the United Kingdom, east of Wales and south of Scotland; capital London. It is a mainly low-lying country with much picturesque countryside; the highest ground is along the *Pennines, and in the *Peak District, *Lake District and *Cheviot Hills. Much of the land is farmed and it has one of the most efficient agricultural industries in Europe. Most of the population, however, live in the towns and cities. Traditional heavy and manufacturing industries declined at the end of the 20th century, but the service sector, including banking, insurance and tourism expanded greatly. The term 'England' is often wrongly used, esp by the English themselves, to refer to the United Kingdom as a whole. ⇨ map at UNITED KINGDOM. ⇨ article. ⇨ App 1.

English /ˈɪŋglɪʃ/ *n* **1** [U] the language of England, used in Britain, most countries in the British Commonwealth, the USA and some other countries. The ancestor of modern English was Anglo-Saxon, or Old English. This developed into Middle English, which was influenced by French in the period after the Norman conquest. By the 16th century it was recognizable as essentially the language used today. English is now spoken by over 350 million people and used by many more as a second language for international communication: *He speaks excellent English.* ○ *I must work to improve my English.* **2 the English** [pl *v*] the people of England (sometimes wrongly used to mean the British, ie to include the Scots, the Welsh and the Irish). **3** (idm) **in plain English** ⇨ PLAIN. **the King's/Queen's ˈEnglish** good, correct standard English: *She speaks a dialect, not the Queen's English.*

▷ **English** *adj* **1** of England or its people: *the English countryside* ○ *English characteristics* ○ *He is very English in his attitudes.* **2** [attrib] of, written in, or spoken in the English language: *He's studying English literature.*

□ **ˌEnglish ˈbreakfast** breakfast usu consisting of

cereals, cooked bacon and eggs, toast and marmalade, and tea or coffee. Cf CONTINENTAL BREAKFAST (CONTINENT[1]).

the English ˈChannel (also **the Channel**) the area of the sea between England and France.

Englishman /-mən/ (*pl* **-men**), **Englishwoman** (*pl* **-women**) *ns* **1** person born in England or one whose parents are English or one who has become an English citizen. **2** (idm) **an ˌEnglishman's ˌhome is his ˈcastle** (*saying*) an English person's home is a place where he may be private and safe and do as he wishes.

the English Civil War war in England (and Scotland) between the supporters of *Charles I and those of Parliament (1642-49). The king's hostility to Parliament and his refusal of its demands for reform in 1642 led to the outbreak of the war. It was not until the battles of Marston Moor (1644) and Naseby (1645) that the Parliamentarians achieved military superiority under *Cromwell. Charles surrendered in Scotland in 1646. The war ended with the execution of the king, but Cromwell never succeeded in establishing a practical alternative government and the monarchy was restored in 1660. ⇨ article at PARLIAMENT.

engrave /ɪnˈɡreɪv/ *v* **1** [Tn, Tn·pr] ~ **B on A**/~ **A (with B)** cut or carve (words, designs, etc) on (a hard surface): *His initials were engraved on the cigarette case.* ○ *The cigarette case was engraved with his initials.* ○ *engraving a design on a metal plate*, eg for printing. **2** [Tn·pr esp passive] ~ **sth on sth** (*fig*) impress sth deeply on (the memory or mind): *Memories of that terrible day are forever engraved on my mind.*

▷ **engraver** *n* person who engraves designs, etc on stone, metal, etc.

engraving /ɪnˈɡreɪvɪŋ/ *n* **1** [U] art of cutting or carving designs on metal, stone, etc. **2** [C] picture printed from an engraved metal plate: *I bought an old engraving of the High Street.*

engross /ɪnˈɡrəʊs/ *v* [Tn] **1** (usu passive) occupy all the time or attention of sb: *be engrossed in one's work* ○ *an engrossing story.* **2** (*law*) write (eg a legal document) in large letters or in formal legal style.

engulf /ɪnˈɡʌlf/ *v* [Tn esp passive] (*fml*) (of the sea, flames, etc) surround (sth) or cause (sth) to disappear; envelop: *a boat engulfed in/by the waves* ○ (*fig*) *engulfed in silence, misery.*

enhance /ɪnˈhɑːns; *US* -ˈhæns/ *v* [Tn] increase (the good qualities of sb/sth); make (sb/sth) look better: *enhance the status, reputation, position, etc of sb* ○ *Those clothes do nothing to enhance her appearance.*

▷ **enhancement** *n* (**a**) [U] action of enhancing. (**b**) [C] thing that enhances.

enigma /ɪˈnɪɡmə/ *n* question, person, thing, circumstance, etc that is difficult to understand; mystery: *I've known him for many years, but he remains something of an enigma to me.*

▷ **enigmatic** /ˌenɪɡˈmætɪk/ *adj* difficult to understand; mysterious: *an enigmatic character, smile, statement.* **enigmatically** /-klɪ/ *adv.*

enjoin /ɪnˈdʒɔɪn/ *v* [Tn, Tn·pr, Tf, Dn·t] ~ **sth (on sb)** (*fml or law*) impose (an action or prohibition) on sb; order: *He enjoined obedience on his followers.* ○ *The leader enjoined that the rules should be obeyed.*

enjoy /ɪnˈdʒɔɪ/ *v* **1** [Tn, Tg] get pleasure from: *I enjoyed that meal.* ○ *She enjoys playing tennis.* **2** [Tn] have (sth) as an advantage or a benefit: *enjoy good health, a high standard of living, great prosperity, etc* ○ *Men and women should enjoy equal rights.* **3** (idm) **enˈjoy oneself** experience pleasure; be happy: *He enjoyed himself at the party.* ○ *The children enjoyed themselves playing in the water.* ○ *I hope you enjoy yourself this evening.*

▷ **enjoyable** /-əbl/ *adj* giving joy; pleasant: *an enjoyable weekend* ○ *The film was quite enjoyable.* **enjoyably** /-əblɪ/ *adv.*

enjoyment /ɪnˈdʒɔɪmənt/ *n* **1** [U] pleasure; satisfaction: *He spoiled my enjoyment of the film by talking all the time.* ○ *live only for enjoyment.* **2** [C] (*fml*) thing that gives pleasure or joy: *Gardening is one of her chief enjoyments.* **3** [U] (*fml*) possession and use: *the enjoyment of equal rights.*

enkindle /ɪnˈkɪndl/ *v* [Tn] (*dated or fml*) (**a**) cause (flames, passion, etc) to flare up. (**b**) inflame (sb) with passion, etc; arouse.

enlarge /ɪnˈlɑːdʒ/ *v* **1** (**a**) [I, Tn] (cause sth to) become larger: *I want to enlarge the lawn.* (**b**) [Tn] reproduce (esp a photograph) on a larger scale: *The police had the photograph of the missing girl enlarged.* **2** [I, Ipr] ~ **(on sth)** say or write more about sth; add detail: *Can you enlarge on what has already been said?*

▷ **enlargement** *n* **1** [U] action of enlarging or being enlarged: *He's working on the enlargement of the business.* **2** [C] thing that has been enlarged, esp a photograph: *enlargements of the wedding photographs.* Cf REDUCTION.

enlarger *n* apparatus for making photographic enlargements.

enlighten /ɪnˈlaɪtn/ *v* [Tn, Tn·pr] ~ **sb (as to sth)** give more knowledge or information to sb; free sb from false beliefs or ignorance: *Can you enlighten me as to* (ie help me to understand better) *the new procedure?*

▷ **enlightened** *adj* [esp attrib] free from prejudice, ignorance, superstition, etc: *in these enlightened days* ○ *enlightened opinions, attitudes, ideas, etc* ○ *an enlightened approach to teaching.*

enlightenment *n* [U] (*fml*) **1** act of enlightening or state of being enlightened: *The teacher's attempts at enlightenment failed; I remained as confused as before.* ○ *In an age of enlightenment such cruelty is unforgivable.* ○ *the Buddhist eightfold path to enlightenment*, ie release from earthly preoccupations. **2 the Enlightenment** period in the 18th century in Europe when some thinkers and writers believed that reason and science, not religion, would advance human progress. Its foundations were laid by the philosophy of *Locke and the science of *Newton. The great figures of the Enlightenment include writers like *Gibbon, *Voltaire, Lessing and *Rousseau. It accompanied great social and technological change and many see it as having led to the American and French Revolutions.

enlist /ɪnˈlɪst/ *v* **1** [I, Ipr, Tn, Tn·pr, Cn·n/a] ~ **(sb) (in/for sth)**; ~ **(sb) (as sth)** enter or cause (sb) to enter the armed forces: *Have you enlisted yet?* ○ *He enlisted as a soldier in the army as soon as he was old enough.* ○ *They enlisted four hundred recruits for the navy.* **2** (**a**) [Tn, Tn·pr] ~ **sb/sth (in/for sth)** obtain (help, support, etc): *I've enlisted the co-operation of most of my neighbours in my campaign.* ○ *Can I enlist your help in raising the money?* (**b**) [Tn, Cn·t] get the support or help of (sb): *We've enlisted a few volunteers to help clean the hall.* ○ *Sarah has been enlisted to organize the party.*

▷ **enlistment** *n* **1** [U] enlisting or being enlisted. **2** [C] instance of this.

□ **enˌlisted ˈman** (*esp US*) soldier, sailor or airman below a non-commissioned officer in rank.

enliven /ɪnˈlaɪvn/ *v* [Tn] make (sb/sth) more lively or cheerful: *How can we enliven this party?*

en masse /ˌɒn ˈmæs/ (*French*) in a mass or crowd; all together: *Individually the children are delightful; en masse they can be unbearable.* ○ *The Joneses are coming for lunch en masse — all twelve of them!*

enmesh /ɪnˈmeʃ/ *v* [Tn usu passive, Tn·pr] ~ **sb/sth (in sth)** (*usu fig*) entangle (as) in a net: *He was enmeshed in a web of deceit and lies.*

enmity /ˈenmətɪ/ *n* [U, C] condition or feeling of being an enemy; hostility: *I don't understand his enmity towards his parents.* ○ *Personal enmities must be forgotten at a time of national crisis.*

ennoble /ɪˈnəʊbl/ *v* [Tn] (*fml*) **1** make (sb) a member of the nobility. **2** (*fig*) make (sb) dignified or more honourable: *In a strange way she seemed ennobled by the grief she had experienced.* ▷ **ennoblement** *n* [U].

ennui /ɒnˈwiː/ *n* [U] weariness of mind caused by lack of anything interesting or exciting to do; feeling of boredom: *Since losing his job, he has often experienced a profound sense of ennui.*

enormity /ɪˈnɔːmətɪ/ *n* **1** [U] great wickedness: *The enormity of the crime has shocked even experienced policemen.* **2** [C usu *pl*] (*fml*) serious crime: *Such enormities would not be tolerated today.* **3** [U] (*infml*) immense size; enormousness: *the enormity of the task of feeding all the famine victims.*

enormous /ɪˈnɔːməs/ *adj* very large; immense: *an enormous amount of money* ○ *an enormous house.*

▷ **enormously** *adv* to a very great extent: *enormously rich* ○ *My tastes have changed enormously over the years.* ○ *I'm enormously grateful for your help.*

enormousness *n* [U].

enough[1] /ɪˈnʌf/ *indef det* (used in front of a plural *n* or a [U] *n*) ~ **sth (for sb/sth)**; ~ **sth (for sb) to do sth** as many or as much of sth as necessary; sufficient: *Have you made enough copies?* ○ *Have we got enough sandwiches for lunch?* ○ *Surely 15 minutes is enough time for you to have a coffee.* ○ *I've got enough money to pay for a taxi.* ○ *There isn't enough space for my address.* ○ (*dated*) *There's food enough on the table.* ○ *We have time enough to get to the airport.*

▷ **enough** *indef pron* **1** as many or as much as necessary: *Six bottles of wine will be enough.* ○ *Is £100 enough for all your expenses?* ○ *I hope enough of you are prepared to help with the show.* ○ *They were able to save enough of their furniture to fill a room.* **2** (idm) **eˌnough is eˈnough** (*saying*) it is unnecessary and possibly harmful to say or do more. **have had eˈnough (of sth/sb)** be unable or unwilling to tolerate sth/sb any more: *After three years without promotion he decided he'd had enough and resigned.* ○ *I've had enough of her continual chatter.* ○ *I'm surprised you haven't had enough of him yet — I found him very boring.*

enough[2] /ɪˈnʌf/ *adv* (used after *vs*, *adjs* and *advs*) **1** ~ **(for sb/sth)**; ~ **(to do sth/for doing sth)** to a satisfactory degree; sufficiently: *You don't practise enough at the piano.* ○ *Is the river deep enough for swimming/to swim in?* ○ *At 14 you aren't old enough to buy alcohol.* ○ *She isn't good enough for* (ie to pass) *the exam.* ○ *I wish you'd write clearly enough for us to read it.* **2** (used to suggest that sth only deserves slight praise) to a significant extent; fairly: *She plays well enough for a beginner.* **3** (idm) **curiously, oddly, strangely, etc enough** it is very curious, etc that...: *Strangely enough, I said the same thing to my wife only yesterday.* **fair enough** ⇨ FAIR[2]. **sure enough** ⇨ SURE.

en passant /ˌɒn ˈpæsɒn/ (*French*) in passing; by the way: *He mentioned en passant that he was going away.*

enquire, enquiry = INQUIRE, INQUIRY.

enrage /ɪnˈreɪdʒ/ *v* [Tn esp passive] make (sb) very angry: *enraged at/by sb's stupidity* ○ *His arrogance enraged her.*

enrapture /ɪnˈræptʃə(r)/ *v* [Tn esp passive] (*fml*) fill (sb) with great delight or joy: *We were enraptured by the view of the mountains.*

enrich /ɪnˈrɪtʃ/ *v* [Tn, Tn·pr] ~ **sb/sth (with sth) 1** make sb/sth rich or richer: *a nation enriched by the profits from tourism.* **2** improve the quality, flavour, etc of sth: *soil enriched with fertilizer* ○ *Reading enriches the mind.* ▷ **enrichment** *n* [U].

enrol (also *esp US* **enroll**) /ɪnˈrəʊl/ *v* (**-ll-**) [I, Ipr, Tn, Tn·pr, Cn·n/a] ~ **(sb) (in/as sth)** become or make (sb) a member (of sth): *enrol in evening classes* ○ *enrol new students* ○ *We enrolled him as a member of the society.*

▷ **enrolment** (also *esp US* **enrollment**) *n* (**a**) [U] enrolling or being enrolled: *the enrolment of five new members.* (**b**) [C] number of people enrolled: *This school has an enrolment of 800 pupils.*

en route /ˌɒn ˈruːt/ ~ **(from...) (to...)**; ~ **(for...)** (*French*) on the way: *We stopped at Paris en route from Rome to London.* ○ *They passed through Paris en route for Rome.*

Ens *abbr* Ensign: *Ens (Peter) Dwyer.*

ensconce /ɪnˈskɒns/ *v* [Tn·pr esp passive] ~ **oneself/sb in sth** (*fml or joc*) establish or settle oneself in a safe, secret, comfortable, etc place: *happily ensconced by the fire with a good book* ○ *We have ensconced ourselves in the most beautiful villa in the South of France.*

Entertaining

The most usual way to entertain friends at home is to invite them for a meal, either in the evening or at lunch-time on a Sunday. In smaller communities, for example a country village, people also invite each other for a drink before a meal, for morning coffee or afternoon tea.

When guests are invited for a meal, they often sit and chat while they have a drink before the meal, and coffee is usually served afterwards. Several friends are sometimes invited at once to make a small party. These parties are almost always informal. Formal occasions, when written invitations are sent out and people dress formally, rarely take place in people's homes, although they did in the past.

Larger parties are arranged to celebrate a particular event. Children's birthdays are often celebrated with a tea-party for the child's friends. The meal will often be followed by party games, or a children's entertainer such as a conjuror may perform. Parties are held to celebrate a person's coming of age (formerly at 21 but now at 18), a couple's silver wedding anniversary (after 25 years of marriage), a couple's engagement and New Year's Eve. In the USA a person's 40th birthday is often marked with a special celebration. A house-warming party is sometimes held to invite friends to one's new home.

In summer, if the weather is fine, people may hold a barbecue in the garden. A much grander, more formal occasion is a garden party, held in the afternoon, when tea is served.

ensemble /ɒnˈsɒmbl/ *n* **1** thing viewed as a whole; general effect: *The arrangement of the furniture formed a pleasing ensemble.* **2** complete matching set of (esp women's) clothes designed to be worn together: *A pair of white shoes completed the striking ensemble.* **3 (a)** passage of music in which all the performers play or sing together. **(b)** group of musicians (smaller than an orchestra) who play together regularly: *a woodwind ensemble.*

enshrine /ɪnˈʃraɪn/ *v (fml)* **(a)** [Tn, Tn·pr] ~ **sth (in sth)** place or keep sth (in, or as if in, a shrine or holy place): *relics enshrined in a casket* ○ *memories enshrined in the heart.* **(b)** [Tn] serve as a shrine for (sth): *The constitution enshrines the basic rights of all citizens.*

enshroud /ɪnˈʃraʊd/ *v* [Tn usu passive] *(fml)* cover completely; hide from view: *hills enshrouded in mist* ○ *His background is enshrouded in mystery.*

ensign /ˈensən/ *n* **1 (a)** (esp naval) flag or banner. **(b)** *(Brit)* special form of the national flag flown by ships: *the red/white/blue ensign.* **2** *(US)* officer of the lowest rank in the navy. ⇨ App 4. **3** /ˈensaɪn/ *(Brit)* (formerly) infantry officer who carried the regimental flag.

enslave /ɪnˈsleɪv/ *v* [Tn] *(often fig)* make a slave of sb: *Her beauty enslaved many young men.* ▷ **enslavement** *n* [U].

ensnare /ɪnˈsneə(r)/ *v* [Tn esp passive, Tn·pr] ~ **sb/sth (in sth)** *(often fig)* catch sb/sth in, or as if in, a trap or snare: *ensnared by love* ○ *ensnare a rich husband.*

ensue /ɪnˈsju:; *US* -ˈsu:/ *v* [I, Ipr] ~ **(from sth)** happen afterwards or as a result; follow: *Bitter arguments ensued from this misunderstanding.* ○ *in the ensuing* (ie following) *debate.*

en suite /ˌɒn ˈswi:t/ *(French)* (of rooms, etc) forming a single unit: *Each bedroom in the hotel has a bathroom en suite.* ○ [attrib] *en suite facilities.*

ensure (*US* **insure**) /ɪnˈʃɔ:(r); *US* ɪnˈʃʊər/ *v* **1** [Tn, Tf] make sure; guarantee: *The book ensured his success.* ○ *Please ensure that all the lights are switched off at night.* **2** [Dn·n] make (sb) certain to get (sth); assure: *These pills should ensure you a good night's sleep.*

ENT /ˌi: en ˈti:/ *abbr (medical)* ear, nose and throat: *an ENT specialist.*

-ent ⇨ -ANT.

entablature /ɪnˈtæblətʃə(r)/ *n (architecture)* (in classical architecture) the upper part of a building that is supported by columns and includes the architrave, frieze and cornice.

entail /ɪnˈteɪl/ *v* **1** [Tn] make (sth) necessary; involve: *This job entails a lot of hard work.* ○ *That will entail an early start tomorrow morning.* **2** [esp passive: Tn, Tn·pr] ~ **sth (on sb)** *(law)* leave (land) to a line of heirs in such a way that none of them can give it away or sell it: *The house and estate are entailed on the eldest daughter.* ○ *He would have sold the property long ago had it not been entailed.*

▷ **entail** *n (law)* **(a)** [U] practice of entailing (ENTAIL 2) land. **(b)** [C] entailed property.

entangle /ɪnˈtæŋgl/ *v* [Tn esp passive, Tn·pr] ~ **sb/sth/oneself (in/among/with sth)** **1** cause sb/sth/oneself to become twisted, tangled or caught (in sth): *The bird got entangled in the wire netting.* ○ *a fishing line entangled among the weeds* ○ *Her long hair entangled itself in the rose bush.* **2** *(fig)* involve sb/oneself (in difficulties or complicated circumstances): *become entangled in money problems.*

▷ **entanglement** *n* **1** [U] entangling or being entangled. **2** [C] (often *pl*) situation that entangles: *entanglements with the police* ○ *emotional entanglements.* **3 entanglements** [pl] *(military)* barrier of stakes and barbed wire to impede an enemy's advance.

entente /ɒnˈtɒnt/ *n* **(a)** [C, U] friendly understanding, esp between countries. **(b)** [CGp] group of two or more countries having such an understanding between them.

□ **ˌentente ˌcordiˈale** /ˌkɔ:dɪˈɑ:l/ entente between two governments, esp between those of Britain and France. The original entente cordiale was the improvement of relations between Britain and France during the reign of Louis Philippe (1830-48). However the term usu refers to the diplomatic agreements reached esp on colonial matters from 1904 onwards.

enter /ˈentə(r)/ *v* **1 (a)** [I, Tn] come or go in or into (sth): *Don't enter without knocking.* ○ *enter a room* ○ *The train entered the tunnel.* ○ *Where did the bullet enter the body?* **(b)** [I] come or go onto a stage: *Enter Hamlet/Hamlet enters,* eg stage directions in a printed play. **2** [Tn no passive] become a member of (sth); gain admission to (sth): *enter a school, college, university, etc* ○ *enter the Army/Navy/Air Force* ○ *enter a profession* ○ *enter the Church,* ie become a priest. **3** [Tn, Tn·pr, Tn·p] ~ **sth (up) (in sth)** record (names, details, etc) in a book, computer etc: register sth: *I haven't entered your name and occupation yet.* ○ *All expenditure must be entered (up) in the account book.* **4** [Tn] declare that one will take part in (a competition, etc): *enter a race, an examination.* **5** [Tn] *(fml)* present (sth) for consideration: *enter a plea of not guilty* ○ *enter a protest.* **6** (idm) **enter the lists (against sb)** challenge sb or accept a challenge from sb to a contest. **enter sb's ˈhead/ˈmind** (mainly in questions and negative sentences) (esp of an idea) be considered or thought of by sb: *The idea of doing the washing up would never enter his head,* ie He never does it. **7** (phr v) **enter into sth** **(a)** begin to deal with sth: *Let's not enter into details at this stage.* **(b)** be able to understand and appreciate sth: *enter into the spirit of an occasion,* ie begin to enjoy and feel part of it. **(c)** (not passive) form part of sth: *This possibility never entered into our calculations.* **enter into sth (with sb)** begin sth; open sth: *enter into negotiations with a business firm* ○ *(fml) I dared not enter into conversation with him.* **enter on/upon sth** *(fml)* **(a)** make a start on sth; begin sth: *enter upon a new career* ○ *The President has just entered upon another term of office.* **(b)** *(law)* take possession of sth; begin to enjoy sth: *He entered on his inheritance when he was 21.* **enter (sb) for sth** give the name of (oneself or sb else) for a competition, race, etc: *I've entered for the high jump.* ○ *The teacher entered him for the examination.* ○ *enter a horse for a race.*

enteric /enˈterɪk/ *adj* [usu attrib] of the intestines: *enteric fever,* ie typhoid.

▷ **enteritis** /ˌentəˈraɪtɪs/ *n* [U] inflammation of the intestines: *suffering from enteritis.*

enterprise /ˈentəpraɪz/ *n* **1** [C] project or undertaking, esp one that is difficult or needs courage: *his latest business enterprise* ○ *The music festival is a new enterprise which we hope will become an annual event.* Cf VENTURE 1. **2** [U] courage and willingness to be involved in such projects: *a woman of great enterprise* ○ *He got the job because he showed the spirit of enterprise.* **3 (a)** [U] participation in projects; business activity: *Conservative governments in Britain favour private enterprise rather than nationalization.* **(b)** [C] business company or firm: *one of the most successful enterprises of its kind.*

▷ **enterprising** *adj* having or showing enterprise(2): *an enterprising young man* ○ *She may not have been the cleverest candidate but she was certainly the most enterprising.* **enterprisingly** *adv.*

□ **ˈenterprise zone** (in Britain) area, usu an urban area with economic problems, to which the government encourages firms to come by giving grants and tax advantages and removing the normal planning controls.

entertain /ˌentəˈteɪn/ *v* **1** [I, Tn, Tn·pr] ~ **sb (to sth)** receive sb as a guest; provide food and drink for sb, esp in one's home: *I don't entertain very often.* ○ *They do a lot of entertaining,* ie often give dinner parties, etc. ○ *Bob and Liz entertained us to dinner last night.* ⇨ article. **2** [Tn, Tn·pr] ~ **sb (with sth)** amuse sb: *Could you entertain the children for an hour, while I make supper?* ○ *He entertained us for hours with his stories and jokes.* **3** [Tn] *(fml)* (not in the continuous tenses) **(a)** be ready and willing to consider (sth): *He refused to entertain our proposal.* **(b)** hold (sth) in the mind or feelings: *entertain ideas, doubts, etc.*

▷ **entertainer** *n* person who entertains (ENTERTAIN 2), esp professionally: *He's a popular television entertainer.*

entertaining *adj* amusing and pleasing: *a very entertaining film* ○ *a most entertaining guest.* **entertainingly** *adv.*

entertainment *n* **1** [U] entertaining or being entertained: *the entertainment of a group of foreign visitors* ○ *He fell in the water, much to the entertainment of the children.* ○ *a place of entertainment.* **2** [C] thing that entertains; public performance (at a theatre, cinema, circus, etc): *The local entertainments are listed in the newspaper.*

enthral (also *esp US* **enthrall**) /ɪnˈθrɔ:l/ *v* (-ll-) [Tn esp passive] capture the whole attention of (sb) as if by magic; please greatly; captivate: *enthralled by her beauty.* ▷ **enthralling** *adj*: *an enthralling performance.* **enthralment** (also *esp US* **enthrallment**) *n* [U].

enthrone /ɪnˈθrəʊn/ *v* [Tn esp passive] *(fml)* place (a king, queen or bishop) on a throne, esp with ceremony; exalt: *The queen was enthroned in an ancient abbey.* ▷ **enthronement** *n* [U, C].

enthuse /ɪnˈθjuːz; US -θuːz/ v [I, Ipr] ~ (**about/over sth/sb**) show great admiration or interest for: *He hasn't stopped enthusing about his holiday since he returned.* ○ *They all enthused over the new baby.*

enthusiasm /ɪnˈθjuːzɪæzəm; US -ˈθuː-/ n ~ (**for/about sth**) **1** [U] strong feeling of admiration or interest; great eagerness: *The proposal aroused little enthusiasm in the group.* ○ *feel no enthusiasm for/about an idea* ○ *an outburst of enthusiasm* ○ *His enthusiasm made everyone else interested.* **2** [C] object of this feeling: *One of my great enthusiasms is music.* ○ *Gardening is his latest enthusiasm.*

▷ **enthusiast** /-ˈθjuːzɪæst; US -ˈθuː-/ n ~ (**for/about sth**) person filled with enthusiasm: *a sports enthusiast* ○ *an enthusiast for/about all kinds of pop music.*

enthusiastic /ɪnˌθjuːzɪˈæstɪk; US -θuː-/ adj ~ (**about/over sth/sb**) full of enthusiasm: *He doesn't know much about the subject, but he's very enthusiastic.* ○ *She's very enthusiastic about singing.* **enthusiastically** /-klɪ/ adv: *She greeted him enthusiastically with a kiss.*

entice /ɪnˈtaɪs/ v [Tn, Tn·pr, Tn·p, Cn·t] ~ **sb (away) (from sth)**; ~ **sb (into sth/doing sth)** try to tempt or persuade sb, usu by offering sth pleasant or a reward: *Advertisements are designed to entice people into spending money/to spend money.* ○ *He enticed the young girl away from home.*

▷ **enticement** n **1** [U] enticing or being enticed: *the enticement of a child into a car.* **2** [C] thing that entices: *There were so many enticements offered that I could not refuse the job.*

enticing adj attractive or tempting: *quite an enticing offer* ○ *An enticing smell came from the bakery.* **enticingly** adv.

entire /ɪnˈtaɪə(r)/ adj [attrib] with no part left out; whole; complete: *The entire village was destroyed.* ○ *I've wasted an entire day on this.* ○ *We are in entire agreement with you.*

▷ **entirely** adv completely: *entirely unnecessary* ○ *Although they are twins, they look entirely different.* ○ *I'm not entirely happy with that idea.*

entirety /ɪnˈtaɪərətɪ/ n [U] state of being entire; completeness: *We must examine the problem in its entirety*, ie as a whole, not in parts only.

entitle /ɪnˈtaɪtl/ v **1** [Cn·n usu passive] give a title to (a book, play, etc): *He entitled the book 'Savage Love'.* ○ *She read a poem entitled 'The Apple Tree'.* **2** [Tn·pr esp passive, Tnt] ~ **sb to sth** give sb a right to have or do sth: *You are not entitled to unemployment benefit if you have never worked.* ○ *After a hard day's work she felt entitled to a rest.* ○ *This ticket doesn't entitle you to travel first class.*

▷ **entitlement** n **1** [U] entitling (ENTITLE 2) or being entitled: *We have no record of your entitlement to free travel.* **2** [C] thing to which one is entitled: *Have you all claimed your full holiday entitlements?*

entity /ˈentətɪ/ n **1** [C] thing with distinct and real existence: *a separate political entity.* **2** [U] (*fml*) thing's existence (contrasted with its qualities, relations with other things, etc).

entomb /ɪnˈtuːm/ v [Tn usu passive] (*fml*) (**a**) place (a person or an animal) in, or as if in, a tomb: *Many people were entombed in the rubble of the bombed buildings.* (**b**) serve as a tomb for (a person or an animal).

entomology /ˌentəˈmɒlədʒɪ/ n [U] scientific study of insects: *His hobby is entomology.*

▷ **entomological** /ˌentəməˈlɒdʒɪkl/ adj.

entomologist /-dʒɪst/ n student of or expert in entomology.

entourage /ˌɒntʊˈrɑːʒ/ n [CGp] all those who accompany and attend an important person: *the President and his entourage* ○ (*fig*) *She always has an entourage of admiring young men.*

entr'acte /ˈɒntrækt/ n (**a**) interval between the acts of a play. (**b**) piece of music or dance performed during such an interval.

entrails /ˈentreɪlz/ n [pl] internal organs of a person or animal, esp the intestines: *The dish was made from the entrails of a sheep.*

entrance[1] /ˈentrəns/ n **1** [C] ~ (**to sth**) opening, gate, door, passage, etc by which one enters sth: *Where's the entrance to the cave?* ○ *There is a front and a back entrance to the house.* ○ *I'll meet you at the entrance to the theatre.* **2** [U, C] ~ (**into/onto sth**) coming or going in; entering: *the Prime Minister's entrance into office* ○ *The hero makes his entrance (on stage) in Act 2.* ○ *An actress must learn her entrances and exits*, ie when to enter and leave the stage. **3** [U] ~ (**to sth**) right of entering; admission: *They were refused entrance to the club.* ○ [attrib] *a university entrance examination* ○ *an entrance fee*, ie money paid so that one may enter an exhibition, etc or join a club, society, etc.

entrance[2] /ɪnˈtrɑːns; US -ˈtræns/ v [usu passive: Tn, Tn·pr] ~ **sb (by/with sth)** fill sb with great emotion and delight as if by magic: *entranced at the beautiful sight* ○ *They were completely entranced by/with the music.* ○ *We sat entranced by her beauty.*

entrant /ˈentrənt/ n **1** ~ (**for sth**) person or animal that enters, esp for a race, a competition or an examination: *There are fifty entrants for the dog show.* ○ *university entrants.* **2** ~ (**to sth**) person who enters a profession: *an entrant to the diplomatic service* ○ *women entrants to the police force.*

entrap /ɪnˈtræp/ v (**-pp-**) [esp passive: Tn, Tn·pr] (*fml*) **1** ~ **sb/sth (by/in sth)** catch sb/sth (as) in a trap. **2** ~ **sb (into doing sth)** trick or deceive sb: *He felt he had been entrapped into marrying her.*

entreat /ɪnˈtriːt/ v [Tn, Tn·pr, Dn·t] ~ (**sth of**) **sb** (*fml*) ask sb (for sth) earnestly and feelingly; beg: *Please don't go, I entreat you.* ○ *May I entreat a favour of you?* ○ *I entreat you to show mercy.* ⇨ Usage at ASK. ▷ **entreatingly** adv.

entreaty /ɪnˈtriːtɪ/ n [C, U] earnest request or requesting: *deaf to all entreaties* ○ *with a look of entreaty.*

entrecôte /ˈɒntrəkəʊt/ n boneless steak cut from the sirloin: [attrib] *an entrecôte steak.*

entrée /ˈɒntreɪ/ n (*fml*) **1** [U, C] ~ (**into sth**) right or privilege of admission or entry: *Her wealth and reputation gave her (an) entrée into upper-class circles.* **2** [C] dish served between the fish and meat courses at a formal dinner: *What did you have as an entrée?* ○ [attrib] *an entrée dish.*

entrench (also **intrench**) /ɪnˈtrentʃ/ v [Tn usu passive] **1** surround or protect (sb/sth) with a trench or trenches: *The enemy were strongly entrenched on the other side of the river.* **2** (*fig sometimes derog*) establish (sb/sth) very firmly: *entrenched ideas*, ie ones that are firmly fixed in the mind ○ *entrenched rights*, ie those that are guaranteed by legislation ○ *She is entrenched in her right-wing views.*

▷ **entrenchment** n **1** [C] system of trenches made for defence. **2** [U] action of entrenching or being entrenched.

entrepôt /ˈɒntrəpəʊ/ n (**a**) warehouse where goods being sent from one place to another may be stored temporarily. (**b**) trading centre or port for the import, export, collection and distribution of goods.

entrepreneur /ˌɒntrəprəˈnɜː(r)/ n **1** person who starts or organizes a commercial enterprise, esp one involving financial risk: *He would not have succeeded in such a risky business if he had not been such a clever entrepreneur.* **2** person who works under contract as an intermediary in the business affairs of others. ▷ **entrepreneurial** /-ˈnɜːrɪəl/ adj: *entrepreneurial flair, skills, etc.*

entropy /ˈentrəpɪ/ n [U] (*physics*) measure of the disorder of the molecules in substances. Thermodynamic theory suggests that the entropy of the universe can increase but will never decrease, and that therefore the universe will reach a state where the temperature is the same throughout.

entrust /ɪnˈtrʌst/ v [Tn·pr] ~ **A with B**/~ **B to A** trust sb to take charge of sth/sb: *entrust an assistant with the task/entrust the task to an assistant* ○ *Can I entrust you with the secret plans?* ○ *He's entrusted his children to me/to my care for the day.*

entry /ˈentrɪ/ n **1** [C] ~ (**into sth**) act of coming or going in: *The children were surprised by the sudden entry of their teacher.* ○ *the entry of the USA into world politics* ○ *The thieves had forced an entry into the building.* **2** [U] ~ (**to sth**) right of entering: *We can't go along that road because the sign says 'No Entry'.* ○ *He finally gained entry to the hotel by giving some money to the doorman.* ○ [attrib] *an entry visa*, ie a stamp or signature on a passport allowing sb to enter a particular country. **3** [C] (**a**) (place of) entrance, esp a passage or small entrance hall: *You can leave your umbrella in the entry.* ○ *the entry to a block of flats.* (**b**) narrow passage between buildings. **4** (**a**) [C] ~ (**in sth**) item written in a list, a diary, an account book, etc: *There's no entry in his diary for that day.* ○ *I'll have to check the entries in the ledger.* ○ *entries in a dictionary.* (**b**) [U] recording of such an item: *The entry of all expenditure is necessary.* **5** ~ (**for sth**) (**a**) [C] person or thing that is entered for a competition: *fifty entries for the 800 metres* ○ *a last-minute entry for the pony race* ○ *This painting is my entry for the art competition.* (**b**) [sing] list or total number of persons, etc entered for a competition: *There's a large entry for the flower show this year.*

Entryphone /ˈentrɪfəʊn/ n (*propr*) type of telephone placed on the wall by the entrance to a building, esp a block of flats, to enable visitors to speak to individual occupants before being allowed to enter.

entwine /ɪnˈtwaɪn/ v [Tn, Tn·pr] ~ **sth (with/round sth)** (**a**) make sth by twisting one thing around another: *entwine a garland of flowers.* (**b**) wind one thing with or round another: *They walked along with (their) arms entwined.*

enumerate /ɪˈnjuːməreɪt; US ɪˈnuː-/ v [Tn] name (things on a list) one by one; count: *She enumerated the items we had to buy — sugar, tea, soap, etc.*

▷ **enumeration** /ɪˌnjuːməˈreɪʃn; US ɪˌnuː-/ n [U, C].

enumerator n (*Brit*) person who enumerates, esp sb employed to help with a census.

enunciate /ɪˈnʌnsɪeɪt/ v **1** [I, Tn] say or pronounce (words or sounds) clearly: *That actor enunciates very well.* ○ *She enunciated each word slowly for her students.* **2** [Tn] express (a theory, etc) clearly or distinctly: *He is always willing to enunciate his opinions on the subject of politics.* ▷ **enunciation** /ɪˌnʌnsɪˈeɪʃn/ n [C, U].

envelop /ɪnˈveləp/ v [Tn, Tn·pr] ~ **sth/sb (in sth)** wrap sth/sb up; cover or surround sth/sb completely (in sth): *mountains enveloped in cloud* ○ *a baby enveloped in a blanket* ○ *The coat was far too big — it completely enveloped him.* ○ (*fig*) *envelop a subject in mystery.* ▷ **envelopment** n [U].

envelope /ˈenvələʊp, *also* ˈɒn-/ n **1** wrapper or covering, esp one made of paper for a letter: *writing paper and envelopes* ○ *an airmail envelope.* **2** gas container of an air-ship or a balloon.

envenom /ɪnˈvenəm/ v [Tn esp passive] (*fml*) **1** put poison on or in (eg a weapon): *an envenomed dagger.* **2** (*fig*) fill (sth/sb) with bitter hatred: *arguments envenomed with spite.*

enviable /ˈenvɪəbl/ adj (of people or things) causing envy; desirable enough to cause envy: *an enviable achievement* ○ *an enviable examination result* ○ *an enviable woman*, eg one whose life is happy and successful. ▷ **enviably** /-blɪ/ adv: *enviably rich.*

envious /ˈenvɪəs/ adj ~ (**of sb/sth**) full of envy; feeling, showing or expressing envy: *I'm so envious of you getting an extra day's holiday.* ○ *She cast envious glances at her sister's dress.* ○ *He was envious of his brother's success.* ▷ **enviously** adv.

environment /ɪnˈvaɪərənmənt/ n **1** [C, U] conditions, circumstances, etc affecting people's lives: *An unhappy home environment can affect a child's behaviour.* ○ *A noisy smoke-filled room is not the best environment to work in.* **2 the environment** [sing] natural conditions, eg land, air and water, in which we live: *Many people are concerned about the pollution of the environment.* ○ *measures to protect the environment*, ie prevent spoiling it further ○ *the Department of the*

The Environment

Protecting the environment and the fight against pollution of all kinds is now a major concern in Britain, as in many other countries.

Conservation efforts are mainly directed towards the protection of the natural environment and to the preservation of old and historic buildings. (Cf article at ARCHITECTURE). The government body responsible for these matters is the Department of the Environment (DoE), which works with the support of a number of voluntary organizations.

Two Countryside Commissions, one for England and one for Scotland, are responsible for conserving the countryside, while the Nature Conservancy Council promotes nature conservation by setting up and managing nature reserves. All these are government bodies. There are also several voluntary nature conservation trusts, affiliated to the Royal Society for Nature Conservation, which is also supported by the Royal Society for the Protection of Birds (RSPB).

There have been many causes of environmental pollution in Britain. These include the dumping of chemical and other poisonous waste on the land, the emission into the air of smoke and other toxic substances from factories and industrial sites, the discharge of industrial effluents into rivers, and the dumping of oil and garbage into the sea. Many of Britain's bathing beaches have become health hazards through the discharge of untreated sewage into the sea. The Control of Pollution Act of 1974 set out powers enabling local authorities to deal with all kinds of pollution, but the seriousness of the problem has obliged the government to introduce new measures and set up specific national bodies to combat and control it. In 1987 it combined three existing organizations into a single body, Her Majesty's Inspectorate of Pollution (HMIP), and in 1989 it set up the National Rivers Authority specifically to control river pollution.

The British have earned the unsavoury reputation of being Europe's 'litter louts'. Although there are usually litter bins in most British towns and public places, many people do not use them, but simply drop unwanted wrappers, cans, etc on the ground. The government has attempted to tackle the nuisance by a public advertising campaign, using the slogan 'Keep Britain Tidy', by increasing fines for dropping litter, and by setting up a special 'Tidy Britain Group'. In addition, local authorities now provide public 'bottle banks', 'paper banks' and 'can banks' so that a proportion of waste material can be recycled.

'Smoke control areas' exist in many urban districts, and the emission of smoke from chimneys in such areas is a punishable offence. In general, the pollution of air and water is now more effectively controlled than it has been in the past. The air is now cleaner in many towns, and fish have reappeared in rivers, such as the Thames in London, where they had long been absent. London's infamous fogs and smogs have now been entirely eliminated, largely as a result of the Clean Air Act of 1955, when the whole of London was declared a 'smokeless zone'. However, specific problems of pollution such as acid rain and global warming, caused partly by damage to the ozone layer, have made special measures necessary. Serious air pollution is caused by carbon dioxide emissions from industrial plants such as coal-burning power-stations and from the ever-increasing number of vehicles on Britain's roads. Additional legislation has therefore been introduced to control industrial emissions, and to encourage the use of unleaded petrol in vehicles by making it cheaper than leaded.

Environmental issues in the USA are the concern of the Environmental Protection Agency (EPA), a government organization. Many of the problems of pollution are the same as in Britain. One spectacular problem that has existed for many years but has not yet been satisfactorily solved is the dense air pollution of Los Angeles, where a thick 'smog' is continually present as a result of the high level of vehicle emissions. Other cities have suffered similarly.

Many people, and particularly many young people, now regard such issues as of major social importance. This has made all the main political parties pay greater attention to their own 'green' policies, and has influenced the steps taken by the government to protect the country's environment.

Environment, ie the British Government department responsible for land planning, transport, preservation of public amenities, pollution control, protection of the coast and countryside, etc. ⇨ article. ⇨ article at PROTEST.

▷ **environmental** /ɪnˌvaɪərənˈmentl/ *adj* **1** of or caused by a person's environment: *disturbing environmental influences.* **2** of the environment: *environmental science.* **environmentalist** /ɪnˌvaɪərənˈmentəlɪst/ *n* person who is concerned about and wants to improve or protect the environment: [attrib] *an environmentalist protest.* **environmentally** /-təlɪ/ *adv*: *Building a new factory there would be environmentally disastrous.*

environs /ɪnˈvaɪərənz/ *n* [pl] (*fml*) districts surrounding a town, etc: *Berlin and its environs.*

envisage /ɪnˈvɪzɪdʒ/ *v* [Tn, Tf, Tw, Tg, Tsg] picture (an event, action, etc) in the mind as a future possibility; imagine: *Nobody can envisage the consequences of total nuclear war.* ○ *I can't envisage the plan('s) working.*

envoy /ˈenvɔɪ/ *n* **1** messenger or representative, esp one sent to deal with a foreign government: *the Archbishop of Canterbury's envoy.* **2** (also ˌ**envoy exˈtraordinary**) diplomatic agent next in rank below an ambassador.

envy[1] /ˈenvɪ/ *n* [U] **1** ~ (**of sb**); ~ (**at/of sth**) feeling of discontent caused by sb else's good fortune or success, esp when one wishes this for oneself: *He couldn't conceal his envy of me/envy at my success.* ○ *His new car excited their envy.* ○ *They only say such unkind things about you out of envy*, ie because they are full of envy. **2** (idm) **the envy of sb** thing that causes sb to feel envy: *Her many talents were the envy of all her friends.* ○ *He's the envy of the whole street.* Cf JEALOUSY.

envy[2] /ˈenvɪ/ *v* (*pt, pp* **envied**) [Tn, Dn·n] feel envy of (sb) or at (sth): *I envy you.* ○ *I have always envied your good luck.* ○ *I don't envy him his money problems*, ie I'm happy I don't have them.

enwrap /ɪnˈræp/ *v* (**-pp-**) [Tn, Tn·pr] ~ **sb/sth** (**in sth**) (*fml*) wrap or enfold sb/sth.

enzyme /ˈenzaɪm/ *n* (*chemistry*) **1** organic chemical substance, entirely or chiefly of protein, found in all cells and essential to life. Enzymes assist chemical processes (eg in digestion) without being changed themselves. The shape of each enzyme is such that it assists only a specific type of reaction. **2** similar substance produced artificially for use in detergents, etc: *Washing powders containing enzymes are said to remove stains more efficiently.*

eolian = AEOLIAN.

eolithic /ˌiːəˈlɪθɪk/ *adj* of the earliest part of the Stone Age, represented by the use of simple flint tools. Cf PALAEOLITHIC.

eon = AEON.

EP /ˌiː ˈpiː/ *abbr* extended-play (record): *a collection of EPs.* Cf SINGLE *n* 5, LP.

epaulette (also *esp US* **epaulet**) /ˈepəlet/ *n* shoulder ornament on a naval or military officer's uniform.

épée /ˈeɪpeɪ/ *n* thin sharp-pointed sword used (with the end blunted) in fencing (FENCE[2]). Cf FOIL[3], SABRE 2.

ephemera /ɪˈfemərə/ *n* **1** [pl] things that are used, enjoyed, etc for only a short time and then forgotten: *a collection of worthless ephemera.* **2** [C] (*pl* **-eras** or **-erae** /-əriː/) type of insect that lives for only a short time; mayfly.

ephemeral /ɪˈfemərəl/ *adj* living, lasting, etc for a very short time: *ephemeral pleasures* ○ *Slang words are often ephemeral.*

Ephesians /ɪˈfiːʒnz/ *n* **E**ˌ**pistle to the E**ˈ**phesians** book of the New Testament, thought to have been written by St Paul, in the form of a letter to the Christians at Ephesus on the coast of *Asia Minor. ⇨ App 5.

epic /ˈepɪk/ *n* **1** (**a**) long poem about the deeds of one or more great heroes, or a nation's past history: *Homer's Iliad is a famous epic.* (**b**) long film, story, etc dealing with heroic deeds and exciting adventures: *yet another epic about the Roman empire.* **2** (*infml or joc*) subject fit to be regarded as heroic: *Mending the car became something of an epic.*

▷ **epic** *adj* [usu attrib] of or like an epic; heroic; grand: *an epic encounter, struggle, achievement.*

epicene /ˈepɪsiːn/ *adj* having the characteristics of both sexes or of neither sex. Cf BISEXUAL, HERMAPHRODITE.

epicentre (*US* **epicenter**) /ˈepɪsentə(r)/ *n* (**a**) point at which an earthquake reaches the earth's surface. (**b**) (*fig*) central point of a difficult situation: *the epicentre of the riot.*

epicure /ˈepɪkjʊə(r)/ *n* person who takes a special interest in and gets great pleasure from food and drink: *This cookery book has been written by a real epicure.*

Epicurus /ˌepɪˈkjʊərəs/ (341-270 BC) Greek philosopher who proposed a materialist theory of the universe, and a moral theory which stressed avoidance of pain and calmness of mind. This theory was later misunderstood to mean that people should seek sensual pleasure. Cf EPICURE.

▷ **Epicurean** /ˌepɪkjʊˈriːən/ *n, adj* **1** (follower) of Epicurus. **2 epicurean** (person who is) fond of pleasure and luxury: *In his youth he was an extravagant epicurean.* ○ *an epicurean feast.* **Epicureanism** *n* [U].

epidemic /ˌepɪˈdemɪk/ *n, adj* (disease) spreading quickly among many people in the same place for a time: *an influenza epidemic* ○ (*fig*) *an epidemic of crime in our major cities* ○ *Football hooliganism is now reaching epidemic proportions*, ie is very widespread. Cf ENDEMIC, PANDEMIC.

epidemiology /ˌepɪˌdiːmɪˈɒlədʒɪ/ *n* [U] branch of medicine concerned with the study of the frequency and distribution of diseases and the use of this information to trace outbreaks of disease to their source. ▷ **epidemiologist** /-ˈɒlədʒɪst/ *n.*

epidermis /ˌepɪˈdɜːmɪs/ *n* [U, C] **1** (*anatomy*) outer layer of the skin: *a damaged epidermis.* **2** (*biology*) (**a**) outer layer of cells of an invertebrate. (**b**) outer layer of cells in a plant.

epidural /ˌepɪˈdjʊərəl/ *adj* (*medical*) (of an anaesthetic) injected round the nerves in the spine and having the effect of anaesthetizing the lower part of the body.
▷ **epidural** *n* epidural injection: *Epidurals are now often used during childbirth.*

epiglottis /ˌepɪˈglɒtɪs/ *n* (*anatomy*) thin flap of tissue at the back of the tongue that covers the windpipe during swallowing to prevent food or drink from entering the lungs. ▷ **epiglottal** /-ˈglɒtl/ *adj.*

epigram /ˈepɪgræm/ *n* short poem or saying expressing an idea in a clever and amusing way: *The playwright Oscar Wilde was famous for his epigrams.*
▷ **epigrammatic** /ˌepɪgrəˈmætɪk/ *adj* expressing things, or expressed, in a short and witty way: *an epigrammatic style.*

epigraph /ˈepɪgrɑːf; *US* -græf/ *n* inscription, esp one on a building or monument.

epilepsy /ˈepɪlepsɪ/ *n* [U] disease of the nervous system marked by changes in the rhythm of electrical currents in the brain. Two of the main forms are known as *grand mal,* in which the sufferer falls unconscious and has convulsions, and *petit mal,* which lasts for a few seconds and involves partial loss of consciousness.
▷ **epileptic** /ˌepɪˈleptɪk/ *adj* of epilepsy: *an epileptic fit.* — *n* person who suffers from epilepsy: *She's been an epileptic from birth.*

epilogue /ˈepɪlɒg/ (*US* **epilog** /-lɔːg/) *n* (**a**) part or section added at the end of a book, play, film, programme, etc, as a comment on the main action. (**b**) short speech or poem spoken by one of the characters at the end of a play: *Fortinbras speaks the epilogue in Shakespeare's 'Hamlet'.* Cf PROLOGUE.

Epiphany /ɪˈpɪfənɪ/ *n* Christian festival held on 6 January, in memory of the coming of the Magi to the baby Jesus at Bethlehem.

episcopal /ɪˈpɪskəpl/ *adj* (*fml*) of or governed by a bishop or bishops: *the Episcopal Church,* ie (esp) the Anglican Church in the US and Scotland. Cf PRESBYTERIAN.
▷ **episcopalian** /ɪˌpɪskəˈpeɪlɪən/ *n, adj* (member) of an episcopal church: *Are you a Roman Catholic or an Episcopalian?* **Episcopalianism** /ɪˌpɪskəˈpeɪlɪənɪzəm/ *n* [U].
episcopate /ɪˈpɪskəpət/ *n* **1** [C] office of a bishop. **2 the episcopate** [sing or pl *v*] the bishops as a group.

episiotomy /ɪˌpiːzɪˈɒtəmɪ/ *n* (*medical*) cut made at the opening of the vagina during childbirth to aid the delivery of the baby.

episode /ˈepɪsəʊd/ *n* [C] **1** (description of an) event occurring as part of a long series of events as in a novel, one's life, etc: *That's an episode in my life I'd rather forget!* ○ *One of the funniest episodes in the book occurs in Chapter 6.* **2** part of a TV or radio serial broadcast at one time: *the final episode* ○ *Listen to the next exciting episode tomorrow night.*
▷ **episodic** /ˌepɪˈsɒdɪk/ *adj* (**a**) occurring irregularly; sporadic: *episodic fits of depression.* (**b**) (of a story, novel, etc) containing or consisting of a series of events: *an episodic style.* **episodically** /-klɪ/ *adv.*

epistemology /ɪˌpɪstɪˈmɒlədʒɪ/ *n* [U] theory of knowledge, esp the analysis of its validity and limits. ▷ **epistemological** /ɪˌpɪstɪməˈlɒdʒɪkl/ *adj.*

epistle /ɪˈpɪsl/ *n* **1** (*usu joc*) letter: *Her mother sends her a long epistle every week.* **2 Epistle** (*Bible*) any of the letters included in the New Testament, written by the Apostles: *the Epistle of St Paul to the Romans* ⇨ App 5.
▷ **epistolary** /ɪˈpɪstələrɪ; *US* -lerɪ/ *adj* (*fml*) of, carried on by, or written in the form of letters: *an epistolary friendship* ○ *an epistolary novel.*

epitaph /ˈepɪtɑːf; *US* -tæf/ *n* words written or said about a dead person, esp words inscribed on a tombstone.

epithalamium /ˌepɪθəˈleɪmɪəm/ *n* (*pl* **-mia**) /-ˈleɪmɪə/ song or poem celebrating a wedding.

epithelium /ˌepɪˈθiːlɪəm/ *n* (*pl* **-lia** /-ˈθiːlɪə/) (*anatomy or biology*) tissue forming the outer layer of the body or lining a hollow structure. Cf EPIDERMIS.

epithet /ˈepɪθet/ *n* adjective or descriptive phrase that refers to the character or most important quality of a person or thing, eg Alfred *the Great,* Attila *the Hun.*

epitome /ɪˈpɪtəmɪ/ *n* **1** thing that shows on a small scale all the characteristics of sth much larger: *The divisions we see in this school are the epitome of those occurring throughout the whole country.* **2** person or thing that is a perfect example of a quality, type, etc: *the absolute epitome of a schoolteacher* ○ *She's the epitome of kindness.* **3** (*dated*) short summary of a book, speech, etc.
▷ **epitomize, -ise** /ɪˈpɪtəmaɪz/ *v* [Tn] be an epitome of (sth): *He epitomizes everything I dislike.* ○ *She epitomizes the loving mother.*

EPNS /ˌiː piː en ˈes/ *abbr* (on cutlery, tableware, etc) electroplated nickel silver.

epoch /ˈiːpɒk; *US* ˈepək/ *n* (beginning of a) period of time in history, life, the history of the earth, etc, esp one marked by notable events or characteristics: *Einstein's theory marked a new epoch in mathematics.*
□ ˈ**epoch-making** *adj* (*fml or joc*) important and remarkable enough to change the course of history and begin a new epoch: *the epoch-making discovery of America* ○ *I told him his idea was not exactly epoch-making.*

epode /ˈepəʊd/ *n* third part of a choral ode sung by the chorus in ancient Greek drama. Cf ANTISTROPHE, STROPHE.

eponym /ˈepənɪm/ *n* person (real or imaginary) after whom an invention, a discovery, a place, an institution, etc is named or thought to be named.
▷ **eponymous** /ɪˈpɒnɪməs/: *The eponymous hero of the novel 'Tom Jones' is Tom Jones himself.*

epoxy /ɪˈpɒksɪ; *US* ˈepɒksɪ/ *adj* of a compound in which an oxygen atom and two carbon atoms form a ring.
□ **eˌpoxy ˈresin** type of tough synthetic resin, often used as an adhesive.

Epsom /ˈepsəm/ town in Surrey famous for its racecourse, where the *Derby horse-race is run.

Epsom salts /ˌepsəm ˈsɔːlts/ magnesium sulphate, a bitter white powder used medically to empty the bowels.

Jacob Epstein: portrait of Esther

Epstein /ˈepstaɪn/ Sir Jacob (1880-1959), British sculptor. Born in New York, but living mainly in England from 1905, he introduced the modernist style into British sculpture. ⇨ illus.

equable /ˈekwəbl/ *adj* **1** free from extremes of heat or cold; moderate: *an equable climate.* **2** (of a person) not easily upset or annoyed; even-tempered: *an equable temperament* ○ *It's lucky that his parents are so equable.* ▷ **equably** /ˈekwəblɪ/ *adv.*

equal /ˈiːkwəl/ *adj* **1** the same in size, amount, value, number, degree, status, etc: *They are of equal height.* ○ *Divide the cake into equal parts.* ○ *Equal amounts of flour and sugar should be added to the mixture.* ○ *He speaks Arabic and English with equal ease.* ○ *Women are demanding equal pay for equal work,* ie equal to that of men. ○ *In intelligence, the children are about equal.* **2** [pred] ~ **to/doing sth** having the strength, courage, ability, etc for sth: *She feels equal to the task.* ○ *He'* *equal to* (ie able to deal with) *the occasion.* ○ *He doesn't seem equal to meeting our demands.* **3** (idm) **on equal terms (with sb)** (meeting or speaking) as equals, with no difference in status or rank: *Now that she has been promoted she is on equal terms with her ex-boss.* **other things being equal** ⇨ THING.
▷ **equal** *n* person or thing equal to oneself in some way: *He's my equal in strength.* ○ *She's the equal of her brother as far as intelligence is concerned.* ○ *We consider ourselves equals.*
equal *v* (-ll-) (*US* -l-) [Tn, Tn·pr] ~ **sb/sth (in sth)** be equal to sb/sth: *equalling the Olympic record* ○ *x plus y equals z,* ie x + y = z.
equality /ɪˈkwɒlətɪ/ *n* [U] state of being equal: *Women are still struggling for true equality with men.* ○ *equality of opportunity,* ie having an equal chance of being considered for jobs, promotion, etc.
equalize, -ise /ˈiːkwəlaɪz/ *v* [I, Tn] (cause sth to) become equal (in size, amount, etc): *West Germany were winning the match until just before the end when the other team equalized,* ie scored another goal to make the scores equal. **equalization, -isation** /ˌiːkwəlaɪˈzeɪʃn; *US* -lɪˈz-/ *n* [U].
equally /ˈiːkwəlɪ/ *adv* **1** in an equal manner or to an equal degree: *They are equally clever.* **2** in equal parts: *They share the housework equally between them.* **3** also; similarly; in addition: *We must try to think about what is best for him; equally we must consider what he wants to do.*
□ **the ˌEqual Opporˈtunities Commission** (in Britain) government body set up in 1975 to promote equal opportunities and rates of pay for men and women in employment, education, etc.

equanimity /ˌekwəˈnɪmətɪ/ *n* [U] calmness of mind or temper: *She maintained her equanimity throughout her long ordeal.* ○ *Nothing disturbs his equanimity.*

equate /ɪˈkweɪt/ *v* [Tn, Tn·pr] ~ **sth (to/with sth)** consider sth as equal or equivalent (to sth else): *You can't equate the education system of Britain to that of Germany.* ○ *He equates poverty with misery.*

equation /ɪˈkweɪʒn/ *n* **1** [C] (*mathematics*) statement that two expressions (connected by the sign =) are equal, eg *2x + 5 = 11.* **2** (*chemistry*) formula indicating a chemical reaction by means of symbols. **3** [U] action of making equal or regarding as equal: *The equation of wealth with happiness can be dangerous.*

equator /ɪˈkweɪtə(r)/ *n* imaginary line (or one drawn on a map) around the earth at an equal distance from the North and South Poles. The *celestial equator* is an imaginary circle in the sky the plane of which is parallel to the earth's axis. The *magnetic equator* is a line round the earth on which a magnetic needle in a compass remains horizontal: *It is very hot near the equator.* ⇨ illus at GLOBE.
📖 When a British ship sails across the equator, a joke 'crossing the line' ceremony is usually held for people who have not crossed the equator before. One of the crew dresses up as the sea-god Neptune and summons them to his court 'for trial'. They line up before him and are then ducked

'shaved' with mock lather, and sometimes made to swallow a 'soap-pill'. The custom is probably a remnant of an ancient rite to placate a sea-god.

▷ **equatorial** /ˌekwəˈtɔ:rɪəl/ *adj* of or near the equator: *an equatorial climate* ○ *equatorial jungles.*

Equatorial Guinea /ˌekwətɔ:rɪəl ˈgɪnɪ/ small W African country on the coast between Cameroon and Gabon; official language Spanish; capital Malabo; pop approx 420 000; unit of currency franc. It was formerly a Spanish colony. ⇨ map at NIGERIA.

equerry /ɪˈkwerɪ, *also* ˈekwərɪ/ *n* (in Britain) officer attending the king, the queen or a member of the royal family: *He is equerry to the Prince of Wales.*

equestrian /ɪˈkwestrɪən/ *adj* [usu attrib] of horse-riding: *equestrian skill* ○ *an equestrian statue*, ie of a person on a horse ○ *equestrian events at the Olympic Games.*

▷ **equestrian** *n* person who is skilled at horse-riding.

equi- *comb form* equal; equally: *equipoise* ○ *equidistant.*

equidistant /i:kwɪˈdɪstənt/ *adj* [pred] ~ **(from sth)** (*fml*) at an equal distance (from two or more places, etc): *Our house is equidistant from the two pubs in the village.*

equilateral /i:kwɪˈlætərəl/ *adj* (*geometry*) having all sides equal: *an equilateral triangle.*

equilibrium /ˌi:kwɪˈlɪbrɪəm, *also* ˌek-/ *n* [U] **1** state of being balanced: *This pair of scales is not in equilibrium.* ○ *He can't maintain enough equilibrium to ride a bike.* **2** (*fig*) balanced state of mind, feelings, etc: *She lost her usual equilibrium and shouted at him angrily.* **3** (*chemistry*) condition in which a chemical reaction and its reverse reaction take place at the same rate.

equine /ˈekwaɪn/ *adj* of or like a horse or horses: *the equine species* ○ (*fig*) *He has a long equine face.*

equinox /ˈi:kwɪnɒks, *also* ˈek-/ *n* either of the two times in a year when the sun crosses the equator and day and night are of equal length. In the northern hemisphere the *spring* (or *vernal*) *equinox* occurs around 21 March and the *autumnal equinox* around 22 September. In the southern hemisphere the dates are reversed. Cf SOLSTICE, PRECESSION.

▷ **equinoctial** /ˌi:kwɪˈnɒkʃl, *also* ˌek-/ *adj* [usu attrib] of, at or near the equinox: *equinoctial gales/tides.*

equip /ɪˈkwɪp/ *v* (**-pp-**) [Tn, Tn·pr] ~ **sb/sth (with sth)** supply sb/sth (with what is needed, for a particular purpose): *They equipped themselves for the expedition.* ○ *Please equip yourself with a sharp pencil and a rubber for the exam.* ○ *The soldiers were well equipped with weapons and ammunition.* ○ *A good education should equip you for life.*

▷ **equipment** *n* [U] **1** things needed for a particular purpose: *office equipment*, eg typewriters, photocopiers, stationery, etc ○ *sports equipment* ○ *a factory with modern equipment.* **2** action of equipping: *The equipment of the photographic studio was expensive.*

equipage /ˈekwɪpɪdʒ/ *n* (*fml*) horse-drawn carriage and attendants.

equipoise /ˈekwɪpɔɪz/ *n* (*fml*) **1** [U] balanced state, esp of the mind; equilibrium. **2** [C] thing that counterbalances.

equitable /ˈekwɪtəbl/ *adj* (*fml*) fair and just; reasonable: *the most equitable solution to the dispute* ○ *Each person must have an equitable share.* ▷ **equitably** /-blɪ/ *adv.*

equity /ˈekwətɪ/ *n* **1** [U] fairness; right judgement: *The equity of the referee's decision was accepted by everyone.* **2** [U] (*law esp Brit*) principles of justice used to correct laws when these would seem unfair in special circumstances. **3** [U] value of shares issued by a business company. **4** [U] value of a property remaining when any debts have been paid which were lent with the property as security. **5 equities** [pl] ordinary stocks and shares that carry no fixed interest. **6 Equity** trade union to which most actors in Britain belong: [attrib] *Equity members.*

equivalent /ɪˈkwɪvələnt/ *adj* ~ **(to sth)** equal in value, amount, meaning, importance, etc: *What is £5 equivalent to in French francs?* ○ *250 grams or an equivalent amount in ounces.*

▷ **equivalence** /-ləns/ *n* **1** [U] state or quality of being equivalent. **2** [C] thing that is equivalent.

equivalent *n* thing, amount or word that is equivalent: *the metric equivalent of two miles* ○ *Is there a French word that is the exact equivalent of the English word 'home'?*

equivocal /ɪˈkwɪvəkl/ *adj* **1** having a double or doubtful meaning; ambiguous: *The politician gave an equivocal answer.* **2** (of behaviour, circumstances, etc) questionable; suspicious.

▷ **equivocate** /ɪˈkwɪvəkeɪt/ *v* [I] speak in an ambiguous way to hide the truth or mislead people: *Don't equivocate with me — I want a straight answer to a straight question!* **equivocation** /ɪkwɪvəˈkeɪʃn/ *n* **1** [U] use of equivocal statements to mislead people. **2** [C] equivocal expression.

ER *abbr* (eg on post-boxes) Queen Elizabeth (Latin *Elizabetha Regina*). Cf GR.

Er *symb* erbium.

er /ɜ:(r)/ *interj* (expressing hesitation): *It's, er, five o'clock, I think.*

-er /-ə(r)/ *suff* **1** (with *vs* forming *ns*) person or thing that does: *lover* ○ *computer.* Cf -EE, -OR. **2** (with *ns* forming *ns*) **(a)** person concerned with: *astronomer* ○ *philosopher.* **(b)** person belonging to: *New Yorker* ○ *villager* ○ *sixth-former.* **(c)** thing that has: *three-wheeler* ○ *double-decker.*

era /ˈɪərə/ *n* [C] **1** period in history starting from a particular time or event: *the Elizabethan era.* **2** period in history marked by an important event or development: *the era of the miniskirt* ○ *We are living in the computer era.*

eradicate /ɪˈrædɪkeɪt/ *v* [Tn] destroy (sth) completely; put an end to (sth): *Smallpox has almost been eradicated.* ○ *attempts to eradicate crime.*

▷ **eradicable** /ɪˈrædɪkəbl/ *adj* that can be eradicated: *a disease that is not easily eradicable.* **eradication** /ɪrædɪˈkeɪʃn/ *n* [U].

eradicator /ɪˈrædɪkeɪtə(r)/ *n* [C, U] person or thing that eradicates, esp a chemical substance that removes ink marks: *a bottle of ink eradicator.*

erase /ɪˈreɪz; *US* ɪˈreɪs/ *v* **1** [Tn, Tn·pr] ~ **sth (from sth)** rub or scrape sth out; remove all traces of sth: *erase pencil marks* ○ (*fig*) *She couldn't erase the incident from her memory.* **2** [Tn] remove a recording from (magnetic tape).

▷ **eraser** /ɪˈreɪzə(r); *US* -sər/ *n* (*US*; *Brit fml*) (*Brit* also **rubber**) thing that erases, esp a piece of rubber, etc for removing pencil marks. **eraser head** device on a cassette or video player for erasing material recorded on magnetic tape.

erasure /ɪˈreɪʒə(r)/ *n* (*fml*) **1** [U] action of erasing. **2** [C] **(a)** word, etc that has been erased. **(b)** place or mark where sth has been erased: *erasures in a letter.*

Erasmus /ɪˈræzməs/ Desiderius (c 1469-1536), Dutch Christian humanist and the most famous scholar in Europe during his lifetime. He published the first Greek edition of the New Testament in 1516.

ere /eə(r)/ *conj, prep* (*arch or rhet*) before: *ere break of day* ○ *ere long*, ie soon.

erect[1] /ɪˈrekt/ *adj* **1** standing on end; upright; vertical: *stand erect* ○ *hold a banner erect.* **2** (of a part of the body, esp the penis) swollen and stiff from sexual excitement. ▷ **erectness** *n* [U].

erect[2] /ɪˈrekt/ *v* [Tn] (*fml*) **1** build; set up; establish: *erect a monument* ○ *A statue was erected to* (ie to honour the memory of) *Queen Victoria.* **2** set upright; put up: *erect a tent, a flagstaff.*

▷ **erection** /ɪˈrekʃn/ *n* **1** [U] (*fml*) action of erecting; state of being erected: *The erection of the building took several months.* **2** [C] (*fml sometimes derog*) thing that has been erected; building or structure: *She calls the new opera house 'that hideous erection'.* **3** [C] hardening and swelling (esp of the penis) in sexual excitement: *get/have an erection.*

erectile /ɪˈrektaɪl; *US* -tl/ *adj* (*anatomy*) (of parts of the body, esp the penis) that can become swollen and stiff from sexual excitement: *erectile tissue.*

erg /ɜ:g/ *n* (*physics*) former unit of energy in the c.g.s. system, defined as the work done by a force of one dyne when it acts through a distance of one centimetre.

ergo /ˈɜ:gəʊ/ *adv* (*usu joc*) therefore.

ergonomics /ɜ:gəˈnɒmɪks/ *n* [sing *v*] study of work and working conditions in order to improve people's efficiency.

ergot /ˈɜ:gət/ *n* [U] **1 (a)** disease of rye, etc caused by a fungus. **(b)** this fungus. **2** drug prepared from this fungus.

Erie /ˈɪərɪ/ **Lake Erie** one of the five *Great Lakes of N America.

Erin /ˈɪərɪn, ˈerɪn/ (*arch or fml*) Ireland.

Eritrea /ˌerɪˈtreɪə; *US* ˌerɪˈtri:ə/ country on the NE coast of Africa; pop approx 3 500 000; official languages English and Arabic; capital Asmara; unit of currency Ethiopian birr (= 100 cents). Formerly a province of Ethiopia, it gained independence in 1993. The new government is rebuilding an economy devastated by 30 years of guerrilla warfare. ⇨ map at TANZANIA. ▷ **Eritrean** *n, adj.*

erl-king /ˈɜ:lkɪŋ/ *n* (in Germanic mythology) bearded giant who carries children away to the land of death.

ermine /ˈɜ:mɪn/ *n* **1** [C] (*pl* unchanged or ~**s**) small animal of the weasel family whose fur is brown in summer and white in winter. Cf FERRET, STOAT, WEASEL. **2** [U] its white winter fur, esp as used to trim the robes of judges, etc: *a gown trimmed with ermine* ○ [attrib] *ermine robes.*

Ermine Street /ˈɜ:mɪn stri:t/ name given to one of the main Roman roads in Britain, from London to York.

Ernie /ˈɜ:nɪ/ (*Brit*) device used for drawing the prize-winning numbers of *Premium Bonds. Its name is formed from the initial letters of *electronic random number indicator equipment.* ⇨ article at GAMBLING.

erode /ɪˈrəʊd/ *v* [Tn esp passive] (of acids, rain, wind, etc) destroy or wear (sth) away gradually: *Metals are eroded by acids.* ○ *The sea has eroded the cliff face over the years.* ○ (*fig*) *The rights of the individual are being steadily eroded.*

▷ **erosion** /ɪˈrəʊʒn/ *n* [U] process of eroding or being eroded: *the erosion of the coastline by the sea* ○ *attempts to reduce soil erosion* ○ (*fig*) *the steady erosion of the President's credibility.*

erosive /ɪˈrəʊsɪv/ *adj.*

erogenous /ɪˈrɒdʒənəs/ *adj* (of areas of the body) particularly sensitive to sexual stimulation: *erogenous* ˈ*zones.*

Eros /ˈɪərɒs/ god of sexual love in Greek mythology. The name has been given to the popular statue of a winged figure over the fountain in *Piccadilly Circus in London.

erotic /ɪˈrɒtɪk/ *adj* of or arousing sexual desire: *erotic art, verse, photography, etc* ○ *an erotic painting* ○ *the erotic urge.*

▷ **erotica** /ɪˈrɒtɪkə/ *n* [pl] books, pictures, etc intended to arouse sexual desire: *a collection of erotica.*

erotically /-klɪ/ *adv.*

eroticism /ɪˈrɒtɪsɪzəm/ *n* [U] (quality of stimulating) sexual desire: *the film's blatant eroticism.*

err /ɜ:(r); *US* eər/ *v* (*fml*) **1** [I] **(a)** make mistakes; be wrong. **(b)** do wrong; sin. **2** (idm) **err on the side of sth** show too much of a (usu good) quality: *It's better to err on the side of tolerance* (ie be too tolerant rather than too severe) *when dealing with young offenders.* **to err is** ˈ**human (to forgive is di**ˈ**vine)** (*saying*) it is human nature to sin and make mistakes (and therefore one should be as forgiving as possible).

errand /ˈerənd/ *n* **1** short journey to take a message, get or deliver goods, etc: *He was tired of running errands for his sister.* **2** object or purpose of such a journey: *I've come on a special errand.* **3** (idm) **an errand of** ˈ**mercy** journey to bring help to sb who is in distress. **a fool's errand** ⇨ FOOL[1].

errant /ˈerənt/ *adj* (*arch or joc*) **1** [attrib] doing wrong; misbehaving: *an errant* (ie unfaithful) ˈ*husband/*ˈ*wife.* **2** wandering in search of adventure (esp in the expression shown): *a knight* ˈ*errant.*

erratic /ɪˈrætɪk/ *adj* (*usu derog*) irregular or uneven in movement, quality or behaviour;

unreliable: *Deliveries of goods are erratic.* ○ *The singer gave an erratic performance.* ○ *This clock is rather erratic.* ▷ **erratically** /-klɪ/ *adv*: *Being out of practice the team played very erratically.*

□ **erˌratic ˈblock** (*geology*) large block of rock carried by a glacier and deposited some distance away from where it was formed.

erratum /eˈrɑːtəm/ *n* (*pl* **-ta** /-tə/) (*fml*) error in printing or writing: *a list of errata* ○ *an erratum slip*, ie a piece of paper inserted into a book after printing, listing errors, misprints, etc.

erroneous /ɪˈrəʊnɪəs/ *adj* (*fml*) incorrect; mistaken: *erroneous ideas, conclusions, statements, etc.* ▷ **erroneously** *adv*: *a poem erroneously attributed to Shakespeare.*

error /ˈerə(r)/ *n* **1** [C] thing done wrongly; mistake: *spelling errors* ○ *a computer error* ○ *printer's errors*, ie misprints. **2** [U] state of being wrong in belief or behaviour: *The letter was sent to you in error*, ie by mistake. ○ *The accident was the result of human error.* **3** [C] (in calculations, etc) amount of inaccuracy: *an error of 2 per cent.* ⇨ Usage at MISTAKE[1]. **4** (idm) **an ˌerror of ˈjudgement** a mistake in one's assessment of a situation, etc. **the ˌerror of one's ˈways** aspects of one's way of life that are wrong and should be changed: *Jones used to be a thief, but now he's seen the error of his ways and is trying to rebuild his life.* **trial and error** ⇨ TRIAL.

ersatz /ˈeəzæts, ˈɜːsɑːts/ *adj* (*often derog*) imitation or substitute, usu inferior to the original: *ersatz coffee, whisky, silk.*

Erse /ɜːs/ *adj*, *n* [U] Irish Gaelic (language).

erstwhile /ˈɜːstwaɪl; *US* -hwaɪl/ *adj* [attrib] former; previous: *She had cut herself off from her erstwhile friends.*

erudite /ˈeruːdaɪt/ *adj* (*fml*) having or showing great learning; scholarly: *an erudite lecture.*
▷ **eruditely** *adv*.

erudition /ˌeruːˈdɪʃn/ *n* [U] learning: *display one's erudition* ○ *a man of immense erudition.*

erupt /ɪˈrʌpt/ *v* **1** [I] (of a volcano) suddenly throw out lava, etc: *It's many years since Mount Vesuvius last erupted.* **2** [I, Ipr] (*fig*) break out suddenly and violently: *Violence has erupted on the streets.* ○ *The demonstration erupted into violence.* ○ (*infml*) *When I saw the size of the bill I simply erupted*, ie became furiously angry. **3** [I] (of spots, etc) appear on the skin: *A rash has erupted all over my back.*
▷ **eruption** /ɪˈrʌpʃn/ *n* [C, U] **1** outbreak of a volcano. **2** (*fig*) outbreak of war, disease, etc: *the eruption of hostilities.* **3** sudden appearance of spots, etc on the skin.

-ery (also **-ry**) *suff* **1** (with *vs* and *ns* forming *ns*) **(a)** place where: *bakery* ○ *brewery*. **(b)** art or practice of: *cookery* ○ *pottery*. **2** (with *ns* and *adjs* forming usu uncountable *ns*) **(a)** state or character of: *snobbery* ○ *bravery* ○ *rivalry*. **(b)** group or collection of: *machinery* ○ *greenery* ○ *gadgetry*.

erysipelas /ˌerɪˈsɪpɪləs/ *n* [U] (*medical*) contagious disease that causes fever and deep red inflammation of the skin.

erythrocyte /ɪˈrɪθrəsaɪt/ *n* red blood cell that transports oxygen and carbon dioxide to and from the body's tissues.

Es *symb* einsteinium.

ESA /ˌiː es ˈeɪ/ *abbr* European Space Agency.

escalate /ˈeskəleɪt/ *v* [I, Tn] (cause sth to) increase or develop by successive stages; become or make (sth) more intense: *the steadily escalating level of unemployment* ○ *House prices have escalated rapidly.* ○ *The Government is deliberately escalating the war for political reasons.* ▷ **escalation** /ˌeskəˈleɪʃn/ *n*: *an escalation in food prices* ○ *try to prevent an escalation of the war.*

escalator /ˈeskəleɪtə(r)/ *n* moving staircase carrying people up or down between floors or different levels (in a shop, an underground railway, etc).

□ **ˈescalator clause** clause in a contract, etc providing for changes in prices, wages, etc under certain conditions.

escalope /eˈskælɒp/ *n* slice of boneless meat, usu coated in egg and breadcrumbs and fried: *escalopes of veal.*

escapade /ˌeskəˈpeɪd, ˈeskəpeɪd/ *n* daring, mischievous or adventurous act; prank: *a foolish, childish, boyish, etc escapade.*

escape[1] /ɪˈskeɪp/ *v* **1** [I, Ipr] ~ (**from sb/sth**) get free; get away (from imprisonment or control): *Two prisoners have escaped.* ○ *A lion has escaped from its cage.* ○ *She longed to escape from her mother's domination.* ○ (*fig*) *When life became too difficult, he escaped into a dream world of his own.* **2** [I, Ipr] ~ (**from sth**) (of gases, liquids, etc) find a way out (of a container, etc); leak; seep out: *There's gas escaping somewhere — can you smell it?* ○ *Make a hole to let the water escape.* ○ *heat escaping through a window.* **3** [I, Tn no passive, Tg] keep free or safe from (sth unpleasant); avoid: *Where can we go to escape the crowds?* ○ *escape punishment/being punished* ○ *You can't escape the fact that....* **4** [Tn no passive] be forgotten or unnoticed by (sb/sth): *Her name escapes me*, ie I can't remember it. ○ *The fault escaped observation* (ie was not spotted) *for months.* ○ *Nothing escapes you/your attention*, ie You notice everything. **5** (idm) **escape (sb's) ˈnotice** be missed or not noticed (by sb): *It won't have escaped your notice that I've been unusually busy recently.*

escape[2] /ɪˈskeɪp/ *n* **1** [C, U] ~ (**from sth**) (act or action of) escaping; instance of having escaped: *Escape from Dartmoor prison is difficult.* ○ *There have been few successful escapes from this prison.* ○ *When the guard's back was turned, she made her escape.* **2** [C] means of escaping: *The fire-escape is at the back of the building.* ○ [attrib] *The police have just found the escape vehicle.* ○ *He showed us our escape route on the map.* ○ *escape-pipe/-valve*, ie to release excess steam or water when the pressure is too great. **3** [sing] (thing that provides a) temporary distraction from reality or dull routine: *He listens to music as an escape from the pressures of work.* **4** [C] leak: *an escape of gas.* **5** (idm) **make ˌgood one's eˈscape** manage to escape completely and satisfactorily.

□ **eˈscape clause** (also **ˈget-out clause**) part of a contract that releases a person, etc from obligations under certain conditions.

eˈscape-hatch *n* emergency exit from a ship, an aircraft, etc.

eˈscape road road, often ending in a pit of sand, to be used by a vehicle when its brakes have failed or when it cannot make a turn on a race-track, hill, etc.

eˈscape velocity speed at which a spacecraft, etc must travel in order to leave the gravitational field of a planet, etc.

escapee /ɪˌskeɪˈpiː/ *n* person who has escaped (esp from prison).

escapement /ɪˈskeɪpmənt/ *n* part of a clock or watch that regulates the movement.

escapism /ɪˈskeɪpɪzəm/ *n* [U] (*often derog*) (habit of) trying to forget unpleasant realities by means of entertainment, fantasy, etc: *Drug-taking is a form of escapism for some people.*
▷ **escapist** /-pɪst/ *n* person whose behaviour is characterized by escapism: [attrib] *escapist literature*, eg romantic fiction.

escapology /ˌeskəˈpɒlədʒɪ/ *n* [U] practice or technique of escaping from confinement (esp chains, bags, etc) as a form of entertainment.
▷ **escapologist** /-lədʒɪst/ *n* entertainer who specializes in this.

escarole /ˈeskərəʊl/ *n* [C, U] = ENDIVE 1.

escarpment /ɪˈskɑːpmənt/ *n* long steep slope or cliff separating two areas at different levels, usu a plateau and a low-lying plain.

eschatology /ˌeskəˈtɒlədʒɪ/ *n* [U] (*religion*) branch of theology concerned with the end of the world and God's judgement of mankind after death.

escheat /ɪsˈtʃiːt/ *n* [U] (*law*) **(a)** (formerly) process by which property passed to the State when its owner died without heirs and without leaving a will. **(b)** property passing to the State in this way.

eschew /ɪsˈtʃuː/ *v* [Tn] (*fml*) keep away from (sth); abstain from; avoid: *eschew political discussion.*

escort[1] /ˈeskɔːt/ *n* **1** [CGp] person or group of people, ships, vehicles, etc accompanying sb/sth to give protection or as an honour; person, etc accompanying valuable goods to guard them: *The government provided an armed escort for the visiting head of State.* ○ *The Queen's yacht had an escort of ten destroyers.* ○ *The gold bullion was transported under police escort.* ○ [attrib] *soldiers on escort duty.* **2** [C] (*dated or fml*) person, esp a man and usu not a regular companion, who accompanies a member of the opposite sex on a particular social occasion.

escort[2] /ɪˈskɔːt/ *v* [Tn, Tn·pr, Tn·p] ~ **sb (to sth)** accompany sb as an escort: *a princess escorted by soldiers* ○ *May I escort you to the ball?* ○ *Her brother's friend escorted her home.*

escritoire /ˌeskrɪˈtwɑː(r)/ *n* writing-desk with drawers for paper, envelopes, etc.

escrow /ˈeskrəʊ, esˈkrəʊ/ *n* [U] (*law*) deed, bond, sum of money, etc held by a third party and only returned when a certain condition has been fulfilled: *in escrow*, ie held in trust as escrow.
▷ **escrow** *v* [Tn] place (sth) in escrow.

escutcheon /ɪˈskʌtʃən/ *n* **1** shield displaying a coat of arms. **2** (idm) **ˈa blot on sb's/the escutcheon** ⇨ BLOT[1].

-ese /-iːz/ *suff* **1** (with proper *ns* forming *adjs* and *ns*) (inhabitant or language) of: *(the) Milanese* ○ *(the) Japanese.* **2** (with *ns* forming *ns*) (*esp derog*) in the literary style of: *journalese* ○ *officialese.*

esker

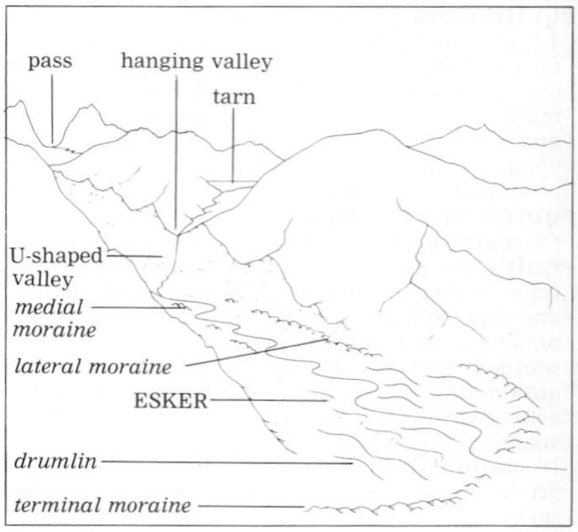

pass
hanging valley
tarn
U-shaped valley
medial moraine
lateral moraine
ESKER
drumlin
terminal moraine

esker /ˈeskə(r)/ *n* (*geology*) long ridge of gravel in a river valley, originally deposited by a stream that is formed by the melting of ice under a glacier. ⇨ illus.

Eskimo /ˈeskɪməʊ/ (*pl* unchanged or ~**s** /-məʊz/) (also **Innuit**, **Inuit**) *n* **1** [C] member of a people living in the Arctic regions of N America and E Siberia. The Eskimos used to inhabit the coasts and islands of the Arctic western hemisphere in large numbers. They generally live together in small family units rather than larger communities, and have adapted their way of life to the harsh environment and climate of the regions they inhabit: [attrib] *Eskimo art.* **2** [U] language of this people. Cf ALEUT.

ESL /ˌiː es ˈel/ *abbr* (teaching, learning or studying) English as a Second Language. Cf EFL.

ESN /ˌiː es ˈen/ *abbr* educationally subnormal (because mentally handicapped).

esophagus (*US*) = OESOPHAGUS.

esoteric /ˌesəʊˈterɪk, ˌiːsəʊ-/ *adj* (*fml*) likely to be understood by only those with a special knowledge or interest; mysterious; obscure: *esoteric poetry, imagery, language, etc.*

ESP /ˌiː es ˈpiː/ *abbr* **1** (teaching, learning or studying) English for Special/Specific (eg scientific, technical, etc) Purposes. **2** extra-sensory perception.

esp *abbr* especially.

espadrille /ˈespədrɪl/ *n* light canvas shoe with a plaited rope sole.

espalier /ɪˈspælɪeɪ; *US* ɪˈspæljər/ *n* (tree or shrub whose branches are trained on a) wooden or wire frame in a garden.

esparto /ɪˈspɑ:təʊ/ *n* [U] type of coarse grass found in Spain and N Africa, used in paper-making.

especial /ɪˈspeʃl/ *adj* (**a**) exceptional; outstanding; special: *a matter of especial interest.* (**b**) belonging mainly to one person or thing; particular: *for your especial benefit.*

▷ **especially** /ɪˈspeʃəlɪ/ *adv* in particular; specially: *This is especially for you.* ○ *I love the country, especially in spring.*

Esperanto /ˌespəˈræntəʊ/ *n* [U] language designed for world use by L L Zamenhof, a Polish physician, in 1887. Its words are based mainly on roots commonly found in Romance and other European languages.

espionage /ˈespɪənɑ:ʒ/ *n* [U] practice of spying or using spies to obtain secret information: *found guilty of espionage* ○ *engage in espionage* ○ *industrial espionage*, ie spying on the secret plans of rival companies.

esplanade /ˌespləˈneɪd/ *n* level area of open ground where people may walk, ride or drive for pleasure, esp by the sea.

espouse /ɪˈspaʊz/ *v* [Tn] (*fml*) give one's support to (a cause, theory, etc): *espousing feminism.*

▷ **espousal** /ɪˈspaʊzl/ *n* [U] (*fml*) ~ **of sth** espousing of (a cause, etc): *his recent espousal of communism.*

espresso /eˈspresəʊ/ *n* (*pl* ~**s**) [C, U] (cup of) coffee made by forcing boiling water under pressure through ground coffee: *'Two espressos, please.'*

esprit /eˈspri:/ *n* [U] (*French*) lively wit.

□ **esprit de corps** /eˌspri: də ˈkɔ:(r)/ (*French*) loyalty and devotion uniting the members of a group.

espy /ɪˈspaɪ/ *v* (*pt, pp* **espied**) [Tn] (*dated or joc*) catch sight of (sb/sth): *Was it you I espied jogging in the park this morning?*

Esq *abbr* (*fml esp Brit*) Esquire: *Edgar Broughton, Esq*, eg on a letter addressed to him.

-esque /-esk/ *suff* (used with *ns* to form *adjs*) in the style or manner of: *statuesque* ○ *Kiplingesque.*

Esquire /ɪˈskwaɪə(r); *US* ˈes-/ *n* (*Brit fml*) (*abbr* **Esq**) polite title added after a man's surname (instead of *Mr* before it), esp in addressing letters: *He wrote 'Peter Mitchell, Esq' on the envelope.*

-ess /-ɪs, -es/ *suff* (with *ns* forming *ns*) female: *lioness* ○ *actress.*

NOTE ON USAGE: The 'feminine' suffixes **-ess** and **-ette**, in such words as *poetess* and *usherette*, are frequently avoided today, because it is unnecessary to make a distinction between men and women doing the same job. The same word can often be used to apply to both sexes: *author, host, manager, usher*. The use of an alternative word is sometimes possible; for example, instead of *headmaster* or *headmistress* we can use *headteacher*.

essay[1] /ˈeseɪ/ *n* piece of writing, usu short and in prose, on any one subject. The word is also used in the titles of longer treatises, eg on philosophy, theology, etc, as in *Locke's *Essay concerning Human Understanding*, *Bacon's *Essays* and *Lamb's *Essays of Elia*: *We had to write three essays in the history exam.*

▷ **essayist** /-ɪst/ *n* writer of essays, esp for publication: *Bacon was a famous essayist.*

essay[2] /eˈseɪ/ *v* [Tn] (*dated fml*) try (sth); attempt: *essay a task.*

▷ **essay** /ˈeseɪ/ *n* (*dated fml*) ~ (**at/in sth**) attempt.

essence /ˈesns/ *n* **1** [U] that which makes a thing what it is; most important or indispensable quality of sth: *The essence of his argument is that capitalism cannot succeed.* ○ *She was the essence of kindness.* **2** [C, U] extract of a plant, drug, etc, containing all its important qualities in concentrated form: *vanilla essence* ○ *meat essences.* **3** (idm) **in** ˈ**essence** fundamentally; essentially: *The two arguments are in essence the same.* **of the** ˈ**essence** very important; indispensable: *Speed is of the essence in dealing with an emergency.*

essential /ɪˈsenʃl/ *adj* **1** [esp pred] ~ (**to/for sth**) necessary; indispensable; most important: *Is money essential to happiness?* ○ *It's essential that you attend all the meetings.* ○ *'Secretary wanted: previous experience essential.'* **2** [attrib] relating to sb's/sth's basic nature; fundamental: *His essential decency makes it impossible to dislike him.* ○ *What is the essential theme of the play?*

▷ **essential** *n* (usu *pl*) fundamentally necessary element or thing: *A knowledge of French is an absolute essential.* ○ *the essentials of English grammar* ○ *We only had time to pack a few essentials.*

essentially /ɪˈsenʃəlɪ/ *adv* in his/its true nature; basically: *He's essentially a very generous man.*

□ **es**ˌ**sential** ˈ**oil** oil extracted from a plant and used in making perfume, flavourings, etc.

Essex /ˈesɪks/ county of eastern England. ⇨ map at App 1.

EST /ˌi: es ˈti:/ *abbr* **1** (*US*) Eastern Standard Time. Cf EDT. **2** (*medical*) electro-shock treatment (used esp on psychiatric patients).

est (also **estd**) *abbr* **1** established: *Hyde, Jekyll and Co, est 1902.* **2** estimate(d).

establish /ɪˈstæblɪʃ/ *v* **1** [Tn] set (sth) up on a firm or permanent basis: *This business was established in 1860.* ○ *establish a close relationship with sb.* **2** [Tn only passive, Tn·pr only passive, Cn·n/a] ~ **sb/oneself (in sth) (as sth)** place sb/oneself in a position, office, etc, usu on a permanent basis: *We are now comfortably established in our new house.* ○ *He established himself as governor of the province.* ○ *She's now firmly established (in business) as an art dealer.* **3** [Tn, Tf, Tw] show (sth) to be true; prove: *We've established his innocence/(the fact) that he's innocent.* ○ *The police can't establish where he was at the time.* **4** [Tn, Cn·n/a] cause people to accept (a belief, custom, claim, etc): *Established practices are difficult to change.* ○ *His second novel established his fame as a writer.*

▷ **established** *adj* [attrib] (of a Church or religion) made official for a country: *Anglicanism is the established religion in England.* **Established** ˈ**Church** Church recognized as the national Church of a country.

establishment /ɪˈstæblɪʃmənt/ *n* **1** [U] action of creating or setting up: *the establishment of a new college.* **2** [C] (*fml or joc*) (premises of a) business organization or large institution: *an educational establishment*, eg a school ○ *What made you come and work in this establishment?* **3** [sing] group of people employed in an organization, a household, etc: *We have a large establishment*, ie many staff. **4 the Establishment** [sing] *n* (*esp Brit often derog*) group of powerful people who influence or control policies, ideas, taste, etc and usually support what has been traditionally accepted: *the musical, intellectual, artistic, etc Establishment* ○ [attrib] *an Establishment figure.*

estate /ɪˈsteɪt/ *n* **1** [C] area of land, esp in the country, with one owner: *He owns a large estate in Scotland.* **2** [C] (*esp Brit*) large area of land developed for a specific purpose, eg for houses or factories: *a housing/a trading/an industrial estate.* **3** [U, C] (*law*) all the money and property that a person owns, esp that which is left at death: *Her estate was divided between her four children.* **4** [C] (*dated fml*) political or social group or class: *the three Estates of the Realm*, ie (in Britain) the bishops, the lords and the common people. **5** [sing] (*dated fml*) condition; stage in life: *the holy estate of matrimony.*

□ **es**ˈ**tate agent** (*US* **realtor**, **real estate agent**) person whose job is to buy and sell houses for others. ⇨ article at HOUSE.

esˈ**tate car** (also **shooting-brake**, **brake**, *US* **station wagon**) car with a large area for luggage behind the rear folding seats and a door or doors at the back for easy loading. ⇨ illus at CAR.

esˈ**tate tax** (*US*) tax paid on property when it is inherited. Cf CAPITAL TRANSFER TAX (CAPITAL[2]).

estd *abbr* = EST.

esteem /ɪˈsti:m/ *v* (*fml*) (not used in the continuous tenses) **1** [Tn] have a high opinion of (sb/sth); respect greatly: *I esteem his work highly.* **2** [Cn·n] consider; regard: *I esteem it a privilege to address such a distinguished audience.*

▷ **esteem** *n* high regard; favourable opinion: *Since he behaved so badly he's gone down in my esteem*, ie I do not esteem him so highly. ○ *She is held in great/high/low esteem by those who know her well.*

ester /ˈestə(r)/ *n* chemical compound formed by the interaction between an organic acid and an alcohol.

esthete, esthetic (*US*) = AESTHETE, AESTHETIC (AESTHETE).

estimable /ˈestɪməbl/ *adj* (*dated or fml*) worthy of great respect.

estimate[1] /ˈestɪmət/ *n* **1** judgement or calculation of the approximate size, cost, value, etc of sth: *I can give you a rough estimate of the number of bricks you will need.* ○ *This is an outside estimate of the price*, ie an estimate of the highest probable price. **2** statement of the price a builder, etc will probably charge for doing specified work: *We got estimates from three different contractors before accepting the lowest.* Cf QUOTATION 4. **3** judgement of the character or qualities of sb/sth: *I don't know her well enough to form an estimate of her abilities.*

estimate[2] /ˈestɪmeɪt/ *v* **1** [Tn, Tn·pr, Tnt, Tf, Tw] ~ **sth (at sth)** form an approximate idea of sth; calculate roughly the cost, size, value, etc of sth: *We estimated his income at/to be about £8 000 a year.* ○ *She estimated that the work would take three months.* ○ *Can you estimate its length/how long it is?* **2** [Ipr] ~ **for sth** calculate the probable price of (a specified job): *We asked our builder to estimate for the repair of the ceiling.* Cf QUOTE 3.

estimation /ˌestɪˈmeɪʃn/ *n* **1** [U] judgement; opinion; regard: *In my estimation, he's the more suitable candidate.* **2** (idm) **go up/down in sb's estimation** be regarded more/less highly by sb: *She's certainly gone up in my estimation since she told the boss what she thought of him.*

Estonia /eˈstəʊnɪə/ country on the south coast of the Gulf of Finland; pop approx 1 575 000; official language Estonian; capital Tallinn; unit of currency kroon (= 100 sent). An independent republic from 1918, it became part of the USSR in 1940 and regained independence in 1991. ⇨ map at UNION OF SOVIET SOCIALIST REPUBLICS.

▷ **Estonian** *adj* of Estonia, its people or its language. — *n* **1** [C] native or inhabitant of Estonia. **2** [U] language of Estonia.

estrange /ɪˈstreɪndʒ/ *v* [esp passive: Tn, Tn·pr] ~ **sb (from sb)** cause (sb formerly loving or friendly) to become unfriendly to sb: *He's estranged from his wife*, ie no longer living with her. ○ *They are estranged.*

▷ **estrangement** *n* **1** [U] state of being estranged. **2** [C] instance of this: *cause an estrangement between two old friends.*

estuary /ˈestʃʊərɪ; *US* -ʊerɪ/ *n* [C] wide river mouth into which the tide flows: *the Thames estuary.*

ETA *abbr* **1** (also **eta**) /i: ti: ˈeɪ/ *abbr* estimated time of arrival (when travelling): *leave London 10.05, eta Paris 12.30.* **2** /ˈetə/ Basque separatist movement (Basque *Euzkadi ta Askatsuna*).

et al /ˌet ˈæl/ *abbr* (*infml*) and other people or things (Latin *et alii/alia*): *The concert included works by Mozart et al.*

et cetera /ɪt ˈsetərə, et-/ (*usu abbr* **etc**) and other similar things; and the rest; and so on.

etceteras /ɪtˈsetərəz, et-/ *n* [pl] (*infml*) the usual extra things: *It's not just the food for the guests I have to think about — there are all the etceteras as well.*

etch /etʃ/ *v* (**a**) [Tn, Tn·pr] ~ **sth (on/onto sth)** use a needle and acid to make (a picture, etc) on a metal plate from which copies may be printed: (*fig*) *The incident remained etched on her memory for years.* (**b**) [I] make pictures, etc in this way: *She enjoys etching.*

▷ **etcher** *n* person who etches.

etching *n* **1** [U] art of making etched prints. **2** [C] copy printed from an etched plate: *Hanging on the wall was a fine etching of the church.*

ETD /ˌi: ti: ˈdi:/ *abbr* estimated time of departure (when travelling): *arrive Paris 12.30, etd (for) Lyons 14.00.* Cf ETA 1.

eternal /ɪˈtɜ:nl/ *adj* **1** without beginning or end; lasting or existing for ever: *the Eternal God* ○ *eternal life*, ie life after death of the body ○ *eternal love.* **2** [attrib] (*infml*) seeming never to stop; (too)

Ethnic Minorities

The populations of Britain, and even more so the USA, include sizeable proportions of immigrant people. The integration of immigrants with the native majority has not always been easy. In both countries there have been many problems of an inter-racial nature.

Until the Second World War the main groups of immigrants into Britain were the Irish who came to find work and the Jews who came to escape persecution in Europe, especially towards the end of the 19th century and in the 1930s. During the 1950s and '60s many people came to settle in Britain from various parts of the Commonwealth, especially the West Indies, India, Pakistan and Bangladesh, as well as from Hong Kong. Since 1962 immigration from the Commonwealth as well as from other countries has been restricted by the introduction of quotas. There are sizeable groups of immigrants from outside the Commonwealth, notably North America, Greece, Turkey, Italy and Spain. At the end of the 1980s about five per cent of the British population was non-white, about half of them of Indian, Pakistani or Bangladeshi origin and one fifth of West Indian origin. About 45 per cent of the non-white population were born in Britain.

Many inner city areas are populated by a distinctive ethnic group. About 14 per cent of the population of London is black or Asian and other cities with sizeable populations from the ethnic minorities include Birmingham, Bradford, Leicester and Manchester. London's Notting Hill area has become famous for its annual carnival which was first organized in 1966 as a West Indian event and now a colourful pageant in which people of many races participate.

The Race Relations Act of 1976 made racial discrimination in areas like housing and employment illegal, and established the Commission for Racial Equality, which has the power to investigate instances of racial discrimination and to promote good practice in the area of race relations. Despite legislation, however, racial intolerance and harassment persist and many people from ethnic minorities experience discrimination, especially in the areas of employment and housing. There have been several incidents of riots in recent years where young black people have clashed with the police in inner city areas. Measures have been taken to increase recruitment of non-white people in the police force, where they are thinly represented. (Representation of ethnic minorities is also thin in the House of Commons, where, in 1990, out of 650 MPs three were black and one was Asian.)

At the time of the first census in 1790 the population of the USA included, in addition to the American Indians, English and Scottish people (almost 90 per cent of the total white population), German, Dutch, Irish and French groups as well as three quarters of a million black people who had been brought during the previous century from Africa to work as slaves on the plantations in the southern states. (Many Africans were also transported at the same time to the West Indies and it is their descendants who form the majority population group in these islands today.)

As well as the descendants of the early immigrants, the population of the USA today includes many Chinese, Japanese, Filipinos, Mexicans, Indians, Italians and Poles. As in Britain, immigration is now restricted.

Racial segregation existed in the southern states until the 1960s, when after campaigns by the Civil Rights movement, reforms were introduced to abolish it. Racial prejudice still exists today, however; unemployment is higher for black Americans than for white people, and the poor inner-city areas have high black populations especially in New York and Chicago. Nevertheless, black Americans today work in all the professions, and some progress towards racial equality has been made.

frequent: *Stop this eternal chatter!* ○ *I am tired of your eternal arguments.* **3** (idm) **the eˌternal ˈtriangle** situation in which two people are both in love with the same person of the opposite sex. **the eˌternal ˈverities** fundamental moral principles; laws of God. **hope springs eternal** ⇨ HOPE *n*.

▷ **eternally** /ɪˈtɜːnəlɪ/ *adv* **1** throughout all time; for ever. **2** (*infml*) (**a**) always: *I'll be eternally grateful to you.* (**b**) (too) frequently: *He's eternally telephoning me early in the morning.*

□ **the Eˌternal ˈCity** Rome.

eternity /ɪˈtɜːnətɪ/ *n* **1** [U] (*fml*) time without end; state or time of life after death. **2 an eternity** [sing] (*infml*) a very long time that seems endless: *It seemed an eternity before the police arrived.*

□ **eˈternity ring** finger-ring with gems set all round it symbolizing eternity: *He gave her an eternity ring when their son was born.*

ethane /ˈiːθeɪn; *US* ˈeθeɪn/ *n* [U] (*chemistry*) hydrocarbon gas of the paraffin series.

ethanol /ˈeθəˌnɒl/ (also **absolute alcohol**, **ethyl alcohol** /ˌeθɪl ˈælkəhɒl *or, rarely,* ˌiːθaɪl/) base of alcoholic drinks, also used as a fuel or solvent.

Ethelred /ˈeθəlred/ 'the Unready' (c 969-1016), king of England 978-1016. For much of his reign he was forced to pay tribute (*Danegeld*) to the Danes to prevent them attacking. ⇨ App 3.

ethene /ˈeθiːn/ *n* [C, U] carbon compound occuring in natural gas and used in making polythene, etc.

ether /ˈiːθə(r)/ *n* [U] **1** colourless liquid made from alcohol, used in industry as a solvent to dissolve fats, etc and (esp formerly) medically as an anaesthetic. **2** (also **aether**) (**a**) (*arch or joc*) the upper air: *Today's news goes into the ether and is soon forgotten.* (**b**) type of substance formerly believed to fill all space through which light waves were thought to travel.

ethereal (also **aetherial**) /ɪˈθɪərɪəl/ *adj* **1** of unearthly delicacy and lightness; seeming too spiritual or fairy-like for this world: *ethereal music, beauty.* **2** (*arch*) of the pure upper air above the clouds.

ethic /ˈeθɪk/ *n* **1** [sing] system of moral principles; rules of conduct: *the Puritan ethic* ○ *the Christian ethic.* **2 ethics** (**a**) [sing *v*] science that deals with morals: *Ethics is a branch of philosophy.* (**b**) [pl] moral correctness: *The ethics of his decision are doubtful.* ○ *Medical ethics* (ie those observed by the medical profession) *forbid a doctor to have a love affair with a patient.*

▷ **ethical** /-kl/ *adj* **1** of morals or moral questions: *largely an ethical problem* ○ *an ethical basis for education.* **2** morally correct: *His behaviour has not been strictly ethical.* **3** (of a drug, medicine, etc) available only with a doctor's prescription. **ethically** /-klɪ/ *adv.*

Ethiopia /ˌiːθɪˈəʊpɪə/ country in NE Africa bordering on the Red Sea; pop approx 47 882 000; official language Amharic; capital Addis Ababa; unit of currency birr (= 100 cents). One of the poorest countries in the world, in recent years it has suffered continuing civil war and widespread famine. ⇨ map at TANZANIA.

ethnic /ˈeθnɪk/ *adj* **1** of a national, racial or tribal group that has a common cultural tradition: *ethnic minorities, groups, communities, etc.* ⇨ article. **2** (typical) of a particular cultural group: *ethnic clothes, food, music* ○ *an ethnic restaurant.*

▷ **ethnic** *n* (*US*) member of an ethnic group, esp a minority one.

ethnically /-klɪ/ *adv.*

ethnography /eθˈnɒgrəfɪ/ *n* [U] scientific description of the different human races.

▷ **ethnographer** /eθˈnɒgrəfə(r)/ *n* student of or expert in ethnography.

ethnographic /ˌeθnəˈgræfɪk/ *adj.*

ethnology /eθˈnɒlədʒɪ/ *n* [U] science of the different human races, their characteristics, their relations to one another, etc. Cf ANTHROPOLOGY, SOCIOLOGY.

▷ **ethnological** /ˌeθnəˈlɒdʒɪkl/ *adj* of ethnology.

ethnologist /eθˈnɒlədʒɪst/ *n* student of or expert in ethnology.

ethology /iːˈθɒlədʒɪ/ *n* [U] scientific study of animal behaviour, esp with regard to the way it influences natural selection (NATURAL).

ethos /ˈiːθɒs/ *n* (*fml*) characteristic spirit, moral values, ideas or beliefs of a group, community or culture: *the revolutionary ethos* ○ *His book captures exactly the ethos of Elizabethan England.*

ethyl alcohol = ETHANOL.

etiolate /ˈiːtɪəʊleɪt/ *v* [Tn] **1** (*botany*) make (a plant) pale through lack of light: *an etiolated seedling.* **2** (*fml*) cause (sb) to become pale and weak, eg through malnutrition: *an etiolated adolescent* ○ (*fig*) *an etiolated society.* ▷ **etiolation** /ˌiːtɪəʊˈleɪʃn/ *n* [U].

etiology (*US*) = AETIOLOGY.

etiquette /ˈetɪket, -kət/ *n* [U] formal rules of correct and polite behaviour in society or among members of a profession: *Etiquette was considered very important in Victorian England.* ○ *medical, legal etiquette.*

Etna /ˈetnə/ (also **Mount Etna**) volcano in Sicily, the highest European volcano (3 323 m, 10 902 ft) and still active.

Eton College /ˌiːtn ˈkɒlɪdʒ/ English public school (PUBLIC) for boys near Windsor, Berkshire, founded in 1440 by Henry VI. Its pupils are mainly from wealthy families, and many of Britain's public figures were educated there. Former pupils are known as Old Etonians. The school is also famous for the **Eton Wall Game**, played with a ball against a red brick wall in the College. ⇨ article at SCHOOL.

□ **ˌEton ˈcollar** broad stiff white collar worn outside the jacket.

ˌEton ˈjacket short black jacket, as worn by boys at Eton College.

Etruscan /ɪˈtrʌskən/ *adj* of ancient Etruria, its people or its language. The Etruscans used to inhabit the area in Italy between the Arno and Tiber rivers. Their empire was at its height around 500 BC, and their civilization influenced the Romans, who completely subdued them by the end of the 3rd century BC.

▷ **Etruscan** *n* **1** [C] native of ancient Etruria. **2** [U] language of ancient Etruria.

et seq /ˌet ˈsek/ *abbr* (*pl* **et seqq**) and the following (page(s), item(s), etc) (Latin *et sequens/sequentia*): *for further information see pp 9 et seq.*

-ette /-et/ *suff* (with *ns* forming *ns*) **1** small: *cigarette* ○ *kitchenette.* **2** imitation: *flannelette* ○ *leatherette.* **3** female: *usherette.* ⇨ Usage at -ESS.

étude /eɪˈtjuːd; *US* ˈeɪtuːd/ *n* short musical composition, usu for one instrument: *playing a Chopin étude.*

etymology /ˌetɪˈmɒlədʒɪ/ *n* **1** [U] study of the

origin and history of words and their meanings. **2** [C] account of the origin and history of a particular word: *This dictionary does not give etymologies.*
▷ **etymological** /ˌetɪməˈlɒdʒɪkl/ *adj* of etymology. **etymologist** /ˌetɪˈmɒlədʒɪst/ *n* student of or expert in etymology.

EU /ˌiː ˈjuː/ *abbr* European Union.

Eu *symb* europium.

eucalyptus /ˌjuːkəˈlɪptəs/ *n* (*pl* ~**es** or **-lypti** /-ˈlɪptaɪ/) **1** (also **euca'lyptus tree**) any of several types of tall evergreen trees (including the Australian gum-tree), from which oil, timber and gum are obtained. **2** (also **euca'lyptus oil**) [U] oil obtained from its leaves, used as a treatment for colds.

eucharist /ˈjuːkərɪst/ *n* **the Eucharist** [sing] (the bread and wine taken at) the Christian ceremony based on Christ's last supper. Cf COMMUNION.

euchre /ˈjuːkə(r)/ *n* American card-game for two, three or four people.
▷ **euchre** *v* (*US*) **1** [Tn] gain an advantage over (sb) at euchre. **2** [Tn, Tn·pr] ~ **sb** (**into/out of sth**) (*fig*) deceive or outwit sb: *euchred out of all one's money.*

Euclid /ˈjuːklɪd/ Greek mathematician of the 3rd century BC, famous for his work on geometry.
□ **Euˌclidean geˈometry** /juːˌklɪdɪən/ geometry based on the postulates used by Euclid, eg that parallel lines never meet and that the sum of the angles of a triangle is 180°.

eugenics /juːˈdʒenɪks/ *n* [sing *v*] science of the production of healthy intelligent children with the aim of improving the human genetic stock[1](6), esp by selecting those who are allowed to breed. ▷ **eugenic** *adj.*

eulogize, -ise /ˈjuːlədʒaɪz/ *v* [I, Tn] (*fml or joc*) praise (sb/sth) highly in speech or writing: *eulogizing over the vintage wine.*
▷ **eulogist** /ˈjuːlədʒɪst/ *n* person who does this. **eulogistic** /ˌjuːləˈdʒɪstɪk/ *adj* (of a speech or piece of writing) full of high praise: *eulogistic articles about his latest book.*

eulogy /ˈjuːlədʒɪ/ *n* [C, U] (*esp fml*) (speech or piece of writing containing) high praise of a person or thing: *a poem of eulogy to the princess* ○ *Her latest film has brought eulogies from the critics.*

eunuch /ˈjuːnək/ *n* castrated man, esp one formerly employed in the women's quarters of some oriental courts: *the eunuchs of the harem.*

euphemism /ˈjuːfəmɪzəm/ *n* [C, U] (example of the) use of pleasant, mild or indirect words or phrases in place of more accurate or direct ones: *'Pass away' is a euphemism for 'die'.* ○ *'Pass water' is a euphemism for 'urinate'.*
▷ **euphemistic** /ˌjuːfəˈmɪstɪk/ *adj* (of speech or writing) consisting of or containing euphemisms: *euphemistic language, expressions, terms, words, etc.* **euphemistically** /-klɪ/ *adv.*

euphonium /juːˈfəʊnɪəm/ *n* large brass musical wind instrument, a type of tuba.

euphony /ˈjuːfənɪ/ *n* (*fml*) (**a**) [U] pleasantness of sound, esp in words. (**b**) [C, U] pleasing sound: *the euphony of a speaker's voice.*
▷ **euphonious** /juːˈfəʊnɪəs/ *adj* of a pleasing sound: *euphonious musical notes.*

euphoria /juːˈfɔːrɪə/ *n* [U] intense feeling of happiness and pleasant excitement: *She was still in a state of euphoria hours after her victory.* ▷ **euphoric** /juːˈfɒrɪk; *US* -ˈfɔːr-/ *adj*: *euphoric shouts of victory.*

Euphrates /juːˈfreɪtiːz/ river of SW Asia, about 2 430 km (1 510 miles) long. It rises in the mountains of eastern Turkey and flows through Syria and Iraq where it joins the Tigris and flows into the Persian Gulf.

Eurasia /jʊəˈreɪʒə/ *n* Europe and Asia.
▷ **Eurasian** /jʊəˈreɪʒn/ *n, adj* (person) of mixed European and Asian parentage; of Europe and Asia.

Euratom /jʊərˈætəm/ European Atomic Energy Community.

eureka /jʊəˈriːkə/ *interj* (*joc*) I have found it! (a cry of triumph at making a discovery): *Eureka — a job at last!*

eurhythmics (also **euryth-**) /juːˈrɪðmɪks/ *n* [sing *v*] (**a**) system of exercising the body through movement to music. (**b**) dancing in this style.

Euripides /jʊəˈrɪpɪdiːz/ (c 485-c 406 BC) Greek writer of tragedies. His most famous dramas include *Medea, Iphigenia in Tauris, Iphigenia in Aulis, Electra, Bacchae* and *Hippolytus.*

Eur(o)- *comb form* European; of Europe: *Eurasian* ○ *Euro-Communist.*

Eurocheque /ˈjʊərəʊtʃek/ *n* (cheque issued under an) arrangement between European banks allowing customers in one country to cash cheques, etc in another.

Eurocrat /ˈjʊərəkræt/ *n* person, esp one in a senior position, who works in the administration of the European Community: *the Brussels Eurocrats.*

Eurodollar /ˈjʊərəʊdɒlə(r)/ *n* US dollar put into European banks to act as an international currency and help the financing of trade and commerce.

Euro-MP /ˌjʊərəʊ emˈpiː/ *n* Member of the *European Parliament.

Europe /ˈjʊərəp/ **1** continent of the northern hemisphere consisting of the western part of the land mass of which Asia forms the eastern part, and including Scandinavia and the British Isles. It contains about 20 per cent of the world's population. It was the most powerful part of the world politically and economically in the 18th and 19th centuries, during which its modern nation states emerged. It has a high standard of living and great political stability compared with the developing countries of the world. **2** (*Brit*) (**a**) the European Economic Community: *going into Europe.* (**b**) Europe excluding the British Isles.
📖 As an island nation, British people have tended in the past to think of their country as separate from the rest of Europe, and people in Britain often talk about 'travelling to Europe' or 'taking a holiday in Europe'; or going 'on the Continent'. In fact, when Britain joined the European Community in 1973, people referred to it as 'going into Europe'.

European /ˌjʊərəˈpɪən/ **1** *n, adj* (native) of Europe: *ˌEuropean ˈlanguages.* **2** *adj* happening in or extending over Europe: *an author with European recognition.*
□ **the ˌEuropean Comˈmunity** (*abbr* **EC**) (also **the Common Market**) former names of an economic association of European countries giving each other mutual trading advantages, set up by the Treaty of Rome (1957). The original members were Belgium, France, the Federal Republic of Germany, Italy, Luxemburg and the Netherlands; Denmark, Ireland and the UK joined in 1973, Greece in 1981, and Spain and Portugal in 1986. The association has been renamed **the European Union** (*abbr* **EU**), but the former names are still often used.
the ˌEuropean ˌEconomic Comˈmunity (*abbr* **EEC**) former name of the European Community.
the ˌEuropean ˈParliament advisory assembly of the European Union.

europium /jʊəˈrəʊpɪəm/ *n* [U] (*symb* **Eu**) (*chemistry*) soft metallic element of the lanthanide series.

Eustachian tube /juːˌsteɪʃn ˈtjuːb; *US* ˈtuːb/ (*anatomy*) narrow passage extending from the middle ear to the throat: *The child has earache caused by blocked Eustachian tubes.* ⇨ illus at EAR.

eustasy /ˈjuːstəsɪ/ *n* [U] uniform change of sea-level throughout the world, caused eg by the melting of glaciers. ▷ **eustatic** /juːˈstætɪk/ *adj.*

euthanasia /ˌjuːθəˈneɪzɪə; *US* -ˈneɪʒə/ *n* [U] (bringing about of a) gentle and painless death for a person suffering from a painful incurable disease, extreme old age, etc: *It is against the law for doctors to practise euthanasia*, ie to kill patients to prevent suffering.

eutrophic /ˌjuːˈtrəʊfɪk/ *adj* (of lakes, ponds, etc) rich in nutrients and thus able to support large amounts of plankton and vegetation.

evacuate /ɪˈvækjʊeɪt/ *v* **1** [Tn, Tn·pr] ~ **sb** (**from...**) (**to...**) remove sb from a place of danger to a safer place, esp in time of war: *The children were evacuated to the country when the city was being bombed.* **2** [Tn] (*esp military*) leave or withdraw from (a place) esp because of danger: *The soldiers evacuated the area as the enemy advanced.* ○ *The region near the erupting volcano was evacuated rapidly.* **3** [Tn] (*fml*) ~ **sth** (**of sth**) empty (esp the bowels) of their contents.
▷ **evacuation** /ɪˌvækjʊˈeɪʃn/ *n* **1** [U] act of evacuating or state of being evacuated: *the evacuation of thousands of people after a flood* ○ *the evacuation of a town.* **2** [C] instance of this.
evacuee /ɪˌvækjʊˈiː/ *n* person who is evacuated (EVACUATE 1): *evacuees from the battle area.*

evade /ɪˈveɪd/ *v* [Tn] **1** get or keep out of the way of (sb/sth): *evade the police, an attack, an enemy.* **2** find a way of not doing (sth, esp sth that legally or morally ought to be done); avoid: *evade military service* ○ *evade capture by the police.* **3** avoid answering (a question) fully or honestly: *The policeman evaded all the difficult questions.*

evaluate /ɪˈvæljʊeɪt/ *v* [Tn] find out or form an idea of the amount or value of (sb/sth); assess: (*fml*) *evaluate her chances of success* ○ *I can't evaluate his ability without seeing his work.* ▷ **evaluation** /ɪˌvæljʊˈeɪʃn/ *n* [C, U]: *I don't accept that evaluation of the situation.*

evanescent /ˌiːvəˈnesnt; *US* ˌev-/ *adj* (*fml*) quickly fading; soon disappearing from memory: *as evanescent as snowflakes on a river* ○ *a pop singer's evanescent fame.* ▷ **evanescence** /-sns/ *n* [U].

evangelical /ˌiːvænˈdʒelɪkl/ *adj* **1** of or according to the teachings of the Christian Gospel, or the Christian religion. **2** of a Protestant group which believes that the soul can be saved only by faith in Christ.
▷ **evangelical** *n* member of this group. **evangelicalism** /-əlɪzəm/ *n* [U] evangelical(2) beliefs and teachings.

evangelist /ɪˈvændʒəlɪst/ *n* **1** any one of the four writers (Matthew, Mark, Luke, John) of the Gospels in the Bible. **2** preacher of the Gospel, esp one who travels around holding evangelical(2) religious meetings: *converted to Christianity by a fervent American evangelist.* ▷ **evangelism** *n* [U]. **evangelistic** /ɪˌvændʒəˈlɪstɪk/ *adj.*

evangelize, -ise /ɪˈvændʒəlaɪz/ *v* [I, Tn] (**a**) (*fml*) preach or spread the Christian gospel to (sb) with the aim of converting. (**b**) try to win support from (sb) for a cause: *Health food supporters are always evangelizing.*

evaporate /ɪˈvæpəreɪt/ *v* **1** [I, Tn] (cause sth to) change into vapour and disappear: *The water soon evaporated in the sunshine.* ○ *Heat evaporates water into steam.* ⇨ Usage at WATER[1]. **2** [I] (*fig*) be lost or cease to exist: *His hopes evaporated*, ie he no longer felt any hope.
▷ **evaporation** /ɪˌvæpəˈreɪʃn/ *n* [U] process by which a liquid changes into a vapour at a temperature below the boiling-point of the liquid.
□ **eˌvaporated ˈmilk** thick unsweetened milk, usu bought in tins, which has had some of the liquid removed by evaporation: *The pudding was made with evaporated milk.*

evasion /ɪˈveɪʒn/ *n* **1** [C, U] keeping out of the way of sb; avoidance: *the burglar's evasion of the police* ○ *evasion of responsibility* ○ *He's been accused of tax evasion.* **2** [C] statement, excuse, etc made to avoid fully answering a question: *His answers to my questions were nothing but clever evasions.*

evasive /ɪˈveɪsɪv/ *adj* **1** (**a**) having the aim or intention of avoiding capture, of not giving a direct answer, etc: *evasive tactics* ○ *Her manner was always very evasive; she would never look straight at me.* (**b**) not direct or straightforward: *an evasive answer to a question.* **2** (idm) **take evasive action** (esp of a plane, ship, etc in war) do sth in order to avoid danger, etc: *The pilot took evasive action to avoid a collision with the enemy aircraft.* ○ (*joc*) *Stephen didn't want to see his sister, so he quickly took evasive action and hid under the bed.* ▷ **evasively** *adv.* **evasiveness** *n* [U]: *Politicians are often accused of evasiveness.*

Eve /iːv/ *n* (in the Bible story of the Creation) the first woman on earth, created by God from the rib of Adam. The devil tempted Eve to eat the fruit of the tree of knowledge of good and evil, and then she tempted Adam to eat it, which led to their expulsion from the Garden of *Eden.

eve /iːv/ *n* **1** day or evening before a religious

festival or holiday: *Christmas Eve*, ie 24 December ○ *New Year's Eve*, ie 31 December. **2** time just before an important event: *the eve of the election.* **3** (*arch*) evening: *a perfect summer eve.*

Evelyn /ˈiːvlɪn/ John (1620-1706), English writer and traveller, best known for his diaries, which record in great detail the extraordinary variety of his life.

even[1] /ˈiːvn/ *adj* **1** level; smooth; flat: *the most even part of the golf course* ○ *A billiard-table must be perfectly even.* **2** unchanging in quality; regular; steady: *This wine cellar stays at an even temperature all year round.* ○ *an even colour* ○ *even breathing* ○ *The child's pulse is now even.* **3** (**a**) (of amounts, distances, values) equal: *Our scores are now even.* ○ *The two horses were even in the race.* (**b**) (of two people or things) equally balanced or matched: *I'd say the two players are pretty even.* ○ *an even game.* **4** (of numbers) divisible by two with no remainder: *4, 6, 8, 10, etc are even numbers.* Cf ODD. **5** (of temperament, etc) not easily upset; calm: *of an even disposition* ○ *She has a very even temper.* ○ *an even-tempered baby.* **6** (idm) **an even ˈchance (of doing sth)** an equally balanced probability (of sth happening or not): *I'd say he has an even chance of winning the match.* **be/get even (with sb)** have/get one's revenge on sb: *Bill swore he'd get even with his brother, who'd played a dirty trick on him.* **break ˈeven** make neither a loss nor a profit: *It will be a year before the firm makes a profit but at least it's breaking even.* **even ˈchances/ˈodds/ˈmoney** (also **evens**) (**a**) (in betting) equal probability of a horse, etc winning or losing: *It's even money whether the new horse comes first or last.* (**b**) equal probability of sth happening or not happening: *It's even odds/The odds are even that he'll be late.* **honours are even** ⇨ HONOUR[1]. **on an even ˈkeel** (**a**) (of a ship) without movement to one side or the other. (**b**) (*fig*) maintaining steady undisturbed progress (in life): *It took him a long time to get back on an even keel after his wife died.*

▷ **even** *v* (phr v) **even out** become level or regular: *The path ran steeply up the hill and then evened out.* ○ *House prices keep rising and falling but they will eventually even out.* **even sth out** spread sth evenly over a period of time or among a number of people: *Payments can be evened out on a monthly basis over the year.* ○ *The manager tried to even out the distribution of work among his employees.* **even (sth) up** (cause sth to) become even or equal: *That will even things up a bit*, ie make them more equal.

▷ **evenly** *adv* in an even manner: *evenly balanced/matched* ○ *evenly divided/distributed.*

evenness /ˈiːvənnɪs/ *n* [U].

□ ˌ**even-ˈhanded** *adj* fair and impartial: *ˌeven-handed ˈjustice.*

even[2] /ˈiːvn/ *adv* **1** (used to emphasize sth unexpected or surprising in what one is saying, or to invite a comparison with what might have happened, etc): *He never even ˈopened the letter*, ie so he certainly didn't read it. ○ *He didn't answer even ˈmy letter*, ie so he certainly didn't answer any others. ○ *It was cold there even in Juˈly*, ie so it must have been very cold in winter. ○ *Even a child can understand the book*, ie so adults certainly can. **2** (used to emphasize a comparative) still; yet: *You know even less about it than I do.* ○ *Sally drives fast, but Olive drives even faster.* ○ *She's even more intelligent than her sister.* **3** (used to add force to a more exact or precise version of a word, phrase, etc): *It's an unattractive building, even ugly/ugly even.* **4** (idm) **even a worm will turn** ⇨ WORM. **even as** (*fml*) (used as a compound *conj*) just at the same time when (sb does sth, sth else happens): *Even as he shouted the warning the car skidded.* **even if/though** (used as *conjs*) in spite of the fact or belief that; no matter whether: *Even if I have to walk all the way I'll get there.* ○ *I like her even though she can be annoying.* ˌ**even ˈnow/ˈthen** (**a**) in addition to previously; in spite of what has/had happened, etc: *I've shown him the photographs but even now he won't believe me.* ○ *Even then he would not admit his mistake.* (**b**) (*fml*) (with continuous tenses only, often between the *aux* and the main *v*) at this or that precise moment: *The troops are even now preparing to march into the city.* ˌ**even ˈso** (used as a *conj*) in spite of that; nevertheless: *There are many spelling mistakes; even so it's quite a good essay.*

evening /ˈiːvnɪŋ/ *n* **1** [C, U] part of the day between the afternoon and bedtime: *I'll come round tomorrow evening.* ○ *We were at home yesterday evening.* ○ *One warm summer evening.../ On a warm summer evening...* ○ *In the evening I usually read.* ○ *Let's meet on Sunday evening.* ○ [attrib] *the evening show.* **2** [C] outing or party of a specified type, happening in the evening: *A theatre evening* (ie an evening at the theatre) *has been arranged.* ○ *musical evenings*, ie evenings especially for listening to or playing music. **3** (*fig fml*) the last part (esp of one's life): *in the evening of his life.* ⇨ Usage at MORNING.

▷ **evenings** *adv* (*US*) in the evening; every evening: *I like to sit on the porch and read evenings.*

□ **ˈevening dress 1** [U] clothes worn for formal occasions in the evening: *Everyone was in evening dress.* **2** [C] woman's (long) formal dress: *All the evening dresses were beautiful.*

ˌ**evening ˈpaper** newspaper published after midday: *the local evening paper.*

ˌ**evening ˈprayer** = EVENSONG.

ˌ**evening ˈprimrose** plant with pale yellow flowers that open in the evenings: *Oil of evening primrose is used as a herbal medicine.*

the ˌ**evening ˈstar** planet (Venus or Mercury) seen in the western sky after sunset.

evensong /ˈiːvnsɒŋ/ (also ˌ**evening ˈprayer**) *n* service of evening prayer in the Church of England: *We attended evensong as well as morning service.*

event /ɪˈvent/ *n* **1** thing that happens, esp sth important; incident: *one of the chief events of 1964* ○ *the chain* (ie sequence) *of events that led to the Prime Minister's resignation* ○ *It was quite an event when a woman first became prime minister.* ⇨ Usage at OCCURRENCE. **2** any of the races, competitions, etc in a sports programme: *Which events have you entered for?* ○ *The 800m is the fourth event of the afternoon.* **3** (idm) **at ˈall events/in ˈany event** whatever happens; in any case: *In any event, the worst that she can do is say 'no'.* **be wise after the event** ⇨ WISE. **in ˈeither event** whichever (of two things) happens: *In either event, I'll be there to support you.* **a happy event** ⇨ HAPPY. **in ˈthat event** if that happens: *You could be right, and in that event they'll have to pay you back.* **in the eˈvent** as it in fact happened; as it turned out: *I was worried about the hotel bill, but in the event I had enough money to pay.* **in the event of sth** (*fml*) if sth happens: *in the event of an accident* ○ *In the event of his death Sheila will inherit the money.* **a/the turn of events** ⇨ TURN[2].

▷ **eventful** /-fl/ *adj* full of memorable or notable events: *He's had an eventful life.* ○ *an eventful year.*

eventide /ˈiːvntaɪd/ *n* (*arch*) evening.

□ ˌ**eventide ˈhome** home for elderly people.

eventing /ɪˈventɪŋ/ *n* [U] (*esp Brit*) sport of taking part in horse-riding competitions, esp three-day events involving cross-country riding, jumping and dressage.

eventual /ɪˈventʃʊəl/ *adj* [attrib] happening at last as a result; ultimate: *his foolish behaviour and eventual failure.*

▷ **eventuality** /ɪˌventʃʊˈælətɪ/ *n* [C] (*fml*) possible event or result: *We must consider every eventuality.*

eventually /-tʃʊəlɪ/ *adv* in the end; at last: *He fell ill and eventually died.* ○ *Eventually he tired of trying so hard.*

eventuate /ɪˈventʃʊeɪt/ *v* [I, Ipr] ~ (**from/in sth**) (*fml*) be the outcome; result: *disease eventuating from malnutrition/malnutrition eventuating in disease.*

ever /ˈevə(r)/ *adv* **1** (usu in negative sentences and questions, or sentences expressing doubt or condition; usu placed before the *v*) at any time: *Nothing ever happens in this village.* ○ *Do you ever wish you were rich?* ○ *She seldom, if ever, goes to the cinema.* ○ *If you ever visit London, you must come and stay with us.* **2** (with the perfect tenses in questions) at any time up to the present: *'Have you ever flown a helicopter?' 'No, never.'* ○ *'Have you ever seen an elephant?' 'Yes I have'.* ○ *I wondered if he'd ever stopped to think how I felt.* (*Ever* is rarely used in the answer: say either 'Yes I have' or 'No, never', etc). **3** (with comparatives after *than* or with superlatives) at any time (before/up till now): *It's raining harder than ever.* ○ *This is the best work you've ever done.* ○ *He hated her more than ever, when he got that letter.* **4 ever-** (in compounds) always, continuously: *the ever-growing problem* ○ *the ever-increasing cost of food.* **5** (*infml dated*) (after **as...as**, as an intensifier): *Work as hard as ever you can!* **6** (used after *when, where*, etc): *When/Where/How ever did you lose it?* ○ *What ever do you mean?* **7** (idm) **am I ever; is he/she ever, etc** (*infml esp US*) (used to emphasize an exclamation): *Boy, is he ever stupid!* ie He is very stupid indeed. **(as) bad, good, etc as ˈever; (as) badly, well, etc as ˈever** bad, badly, etc to the same degree as before (usu surprisingly so): *Despite the good weather forecast, the next morning was as wet as ever.* ○ *He broke his arm last year but he plays the piano as skilfully as ever.* **did you ever (...)!** (*infml*) (used as part of a rhetorical question or used alone to express surprise, indignation, disbelief, etc): *Did you ever hear such nonsense!* ○ *It cost 50p to go to the toilet; well, did you ˈever!* **ever and anon** (*dated or fml*) several times, at regular intervals. **ever more** (*fml*) increasingly; more and more: *She became ever more nervous as the interview continued.* **ever since (...)** continuously since (a specified time): *ever since I was at school.* **ever so/ever such** (**a**) (*infml esp Brit*) very; to a very great degree: *He's ever so rich.* ○ *ever such a handsome man.* **for ever and ˈever** (*rhet or joc*): *Once he gets a drink in his hand he's here for ever and ever.* **if** ˌ**ever there ˈwas one** of that there is no doubt; that is certainly true: *That was a fine meal if ever there was one!* **yours ˈever/ever ˈyours** (*infml*) (sometimes used at the end of a letter, before the signature).

Everest /ˈevərɪst/ (also **Mount Everest**) highest mountain in the world (8848 m, 29028 ft), in the Himalayas between Nepal and Tibet. It was first climbed in 1953 by the New Zealander Edmund *Hillary and the local mountain guide Tenzing Norgay. ⇨ map at INDIA.

everglade /ˈevəgleɪd/ *n* (usu *pl*) marshy region of land, esp (**the Everglades**) that in southern Florida, USA.

evergreen /ˈevəgriːn/ *n, adj* (tree or shrub) having green leaves throughout the year. The leaves of evergreens, eg the needles of conifers, are often specially adapted to reduce water loss. Each leaf is shed individually every two or three years.: *The pine, the cedar and the spruce are all evergreens.* Cf DECIDUOUS. ⇨ illus at TREE.

everlasting /ˌevəˈlɑːstɪŋ; *US* -ˈlæst-/ *adj* **1** going on or lasting for ever: *everlasting fame, glory* ○ *everlasting life.* **2** lasting a long time: *everlasting flowers*, ie flowers keeping shape and colour when dried. **3** (*derog*) repeated too often; lasting too long: *I'm tired of his everlasting complaints.* **4 the Everlasting** God.

▷ **everlastingly** *adv* (*infml*) in an everlasting(3) manner: *everlastingly complaining.*

evermore /ˌevəˈmɔː(r)/ *adv* for ever; always: *for evermore.*

every /ˈevrɪ/ *indef det* **1** (**a**) (used with *sing* [C] *ns* to refer to groups of three or more which are seen as wholes) each individual: *Every child in the class passed the examination.* ○ *I've got every record she has ever made.* ○ *I couldn't hear every word of his speech.* ○ *He examined every item in the set carefully.* (**b**) (used with *sing* [C] *ns* to emphasize the separate units) each individual: *He enjoyed every minute of his holiday.* ○ *I have had to work for every single penny I earned.* ○ *They were watching her every movement.* ○ *Every time he phones I always seem to be in the bath.* ⇨ Usage at EACH. **2** (used with abstract *ns*) all possible: *We have every reason to think he may still be alive.* ○ *You have every chance of success.* **3** (used to indicate regular occurrence at specified intervals) each:

The buses go every 10 minutes. 4 (idm) **each and every** ⇨ EACH. **every other** (a) all the other (people or things): *Every other girl except me is wearing jeans.* (b) alternate: *They visit us every other week.*

□ **everybody** /ˈevrɪbɒdɪ/ (also **everyone** /ˈevrɪwʌn/) *indef pron* every person; all people: *The police questioned everybody in the room.* ○ *It's impossible to remember everybody's name.* ⇨ Usage at SOMEBODY.

everyday /ˈevrɪdeɪ/ *adj* [attrib] used or happening daily; familiar: *an everyday occurrence* ○ *a compact dictionary for everyday use.*

everyplace /ˈevrɪpleɪs/ *indef adv* (*US infml*) = EVERYWHERE.

everything /ˈevrɪθɪŋ/ *indef pron* 1 all things: *Everything was destroyed.* ○ *I'll tell you everything I know.* 2 the most important thing: *Money isn't everything.*

everywhere /ˈevrɪweə(r); *US* -hweə(r)/ *indef adv* in or to every place: *I've looked everywhere.*

Everyman /ˈevrɪmæn/ 1 (hero of a) 15th-century morality play (MORALITY). 2 (*fig*) normal or average person: *specialized information not known by Everyman.*

evict /ɪˈvɪkt/ *v* [esp passive: Tn, Tn·pr] ~ **sb (from sth)** remove (a tenant) from a house or land, esp with the support of the law: *They were evicted from their flat for not paying the rent.*

▷ **eviction** /ɪˈvɪkʃn/ *n* ~ **(from sth)** 1 [U] evicting or being evicted: *He's had nowhere to live since his eviction.* ○ [attrib] *an eviction order*, ie an order to leave given by the courts. 2 [C] instance of this: *There have been four evictions from this street recently.*

evidence /ˈevɪdəns/ *n* 1 [U] ~ **(to do sth/that...)** (*esp law*) information that gives a reason for believing sth or proves sth: *There wasn't enough evidence to prove him guilty.* ○ *Have you any evidence to support this statement?* ○ *His statement to the police was used in evidence against him.* ○ *A scientist must produce evidence in support of a theory.* ○ *not a bit/piece/scrap/shred of evidence.* 2 [U, C] indication or trace: *The room bore evidence* (ie showed signs) *of a struggle.* ○ *evidences of glacial action on the rocks.* 3 (idm) **(be) in evidence** clearly or easily seen: *He's the sort of man who likes to be very much in evidence at important meetings*, ie who likes to be seen and noticed. **on the evidence of sth** using sth as evidence: *On the evidence of their recent matches it's unlikely the Spanish team will win the cup.* **turn King's/Queen's ˈevidence** (*Brit*) (*US* **turn State's ˈevidence**) (of a criminal) give evidence in court against one's partners in order to receive a less severe sentence oneself. **weigh the evidence** ⇨ WEIGH.

▷ **evidence** *v* [Tn] (*fml*) prove (sth) by evidence; be evidence of: *His answer evidenced a guilty conscience.*

evident /ˈevɪdənt/ *adj* ~ **(to sb) (that...)** obvious (to the eye or mind); clear: *It must be evident to all of you that he has made a mistake.* ○ *He looked at his children with evident pride.*

▷ **evidently** *adv* obviously; it appears that: *Evidently he has decided to leave.*

evidential /evɪˈdenʃl/ *adj* (*fml*) of, based on, or providing evidence: *evidential proof.*

evil /ˈiːvl/ *adj* 1 morally bad; wicked: *evil thoughts* ○ *an evil man.* 2 very unpleasant or harmful: *an evil smell* ○ *an evil temper* ○ *evil weather.* 3 (idm) **the evil ˈday, ˈhour, etc** time when sth unpleasant that one would like to avoid (but cannot) will happen: *I know I need to go to the dentist but I've been putting off the evil day as long as possible.* **(give sb) the evil ˈeye** supposed power to harm people by a look or glance. **the ˈEvil One** (*dated*) the Devil. **an evil ˈtongue** tendency to say malicious things about people: *She has an evil tongue.* **one's good/evil genius** ⇨ GENIUS. **fall on evil days** (*fml*) suffer hardship or misfortune.

▷ **evil** *n* (*fml*) 1 [U] wrongdoing or wickedness: *the spirit of evil in man* ○ *return good for evil* ○ *speak no evil* ○ *You cannot pretend there's no evil in the world.* 2 [C] evil thing; disaster: *War, famine, and flood are terrible evils.* ○ *the evils of drink.* 3 (idm) **the lesser of two evils** ⇨ LESSER. **a necessary evil** ⇨ NECESSARY.

evilly /ˈiːvəlɪ/ *adv* in an evil manner: *He eyed her evilly.*

□ **ˈevildoer** *n* [C] (*fml*) person who does evil: *thieves, murderers and other evildoers.*

ˌevil-ˈminded *adj* having evil thoughts and desires: *a wicked, ˌevil-minded old ˈman.*

evince /ɪˈvɪns/ *v* [Tn] (*fml*) show clearly that one has (a feeling, quality, etc); exhibit: *a child who evinces great intelligence* ○ *evincing powers of recovery.*

eviscerate /ɪˈvɪsəreɪt/ *v* [Tn] (*fml*) remove the internal organs of (a body); disembowel.

evocative /ɪˈvɒkətɪv/ *adj* ~ **(of sth)** that evokes or is able to evoke memories, feelings, etc (of sth): *That smell is evocative of school.* ○ *evocative words.*

evoke /ɪˈvəʊk/ *v* [Tn] 1 bring to mind (a feeling, memory, etc); summon up: *The music evoked memories of her youth.* 2 (*fml*) produce or cause (a response, reaction, etc): *evoke admiration, surprise, interest, sympathy, etc* ○ *Her speech evoked great anger.* ▷ **evocation** /ˌiːvəʊˈkeɪʃn/ *n* [C, U] (*fml*).

evolution /ˌiːvəˈluːʃn; *US* ˌev-/ *n* 1 [U] (*biology*) (theory of the) gradual development of the characteristics of plants and animals over many generations, esp the development of more complicated forms from earlier simpler forms. Charles *Darwin, in his book *On the Origin of Species*, proposed the theory that existing species produce new species by adapting differently to new surroundings. This theory remains one of the central basic concepts in modern biology. Cf NATURAL SELECTION (NATURAL). 2 [U] process of gradually developing; evolving: *the evolution of farming methods* ○ *In politics Britain has preferred evolution to revolution*, ie gradual development to sudden violent change. 3 [C] (*fml*) (of troops, warships, dancers, etc) movement according to plan.

▷ **evolutionary** /ˌiːvəˈluːʃənrɪ; *US* ˌevəˈluːʃənerɪ/ *adj* (*fml*) of or resulting from (the theory of) evolution; developing: *evolutionary processes.*

evolutionist *n* person who supports the theory of evolution.

evolve /ɪˈvɒlv/ *v* 1 [I, Tn] (*fml*) (cause to) develop naturally and (usu) gradually: *The American constitution was planned; the British constitution evolved.* ○ *He has evolved a new theory after many years of research.* 2 [I] (*biology*) (of plants, animals, etc) gradually develop from a simple form to a more complex one: *Many Victorians were shocked by the notion that Man had evolved from lower forms of life.*

ewe /juː/ *n* female sheep. ⇨ illus at SHEEP. Cf LAMB 1, RAM 1, TUP.

ewer /ˈjuːə(r)/ *n* large wide-mouthed jug for holding water, esp as formerly used with a basin in a bedroom without a piped water supply.

ex[1] /eks/ *n* (*infml*) (*pl* ~**es**, ~**'s**) former wife or husband; former boy-friend or girl-friend: *My ex shares custody of the children.* ○ *He is one of her many exes.*

ex[2] /eks/ *prep* 1 (*commerce*) (of goods, etc) as sold from (a ship, factory, etc) excluding cost of delivery to the buyer: *ex warehouse price.* 2 excluding (sth); not included: *ex dividend*, ie not including a dividend that is about to be paid ○ *an ex-directory number.*

ex- /eks/ *pref* (used widely with *ns*) former: *ex-wife* ○ *ex-President* ○ *ex-convict.*

exacerbate /ɪɡˈzæsəbeɪt/ *v* [Tn] (*fml*) make (pain, disease, a situation) worse; aggravate: *Scratching exacerbates a skin rash.* ○ *Her mother's interference exacerbated the difficulties in their marriage.* ▷ **exacerbation** /ɪɡˌzæsəˈbeɪʃn/ *n* [U].

exact[1] /ɪɡˈzækt/ *adj* 1 correct in every detail; precise: *What were his exact words?* ○ *I don't know the exact size of the room.* ○ *He's in his mid-fifties; well, fifty-six to be exact*, ie more accurately. 2 capable of being precise and accurate: *an exact scholar* ○ *She's a very exact person.* ○ *the exact sciences*, ie those in which absolute precision is possible, eg mathematics.

▷ **exactitude** /ɪɡˈzæktɪtjuːd; *US* -tuːd/ *n* [U] (*fml*) over-correctness: *He spoke with pompous exactitude.*

exactly *adv* 1 quite; just: *That's exactly what I expected.* ○ *You've arrived at exactly the right moment.* 2 in precise detail; correctly: *Your answer is exactly right.* ○ *Where exactly were you in France?* 3 (as a reply or confirmation) just so; you are quite right: *'So she wants to sell the house and move to London.' 'Exactly.'* 4 (idm) **not exactly** (*infml ironic*) by no means: *He wasn't exactly pleased to see us; in fact he refused to open the door.*

exactness *n* [U].

exact[2] /ɪɡˈzækt/ *v* 1 [Tn, Tn·pr] ~ **sth (from sb)** (a) demand and enforce the payment of sth: *exact payment (from a client)* ○ *The kidnappers exacted a ransom of £10 000 from the family.* (b) insist on and obtain sth: *exact obedience from one's staff.* 2 [Tn] (of work, circumstances, etc) make (sth) necessary; require: (*fml*) *Her work exacts great care and attention to detail.*

▷ **exacting** *adj* making great demands; requiring great effort: *an exacting teacher* ○ *an exacting piece of work.*

exaction /ɪɡˈzækʃn/ *n* (*fml*) 1 (a) [U] action of exacting money, etc: *the exaction of income tax.* (b) [C] something that is exacted, esp a tax that is considered to be too high: *unreasonable exactions.* 2 [C] great demand (on one's time, strength, etc): *the exactions of a senior post in government.*

exaggerate /ɪɡˈzædʒəreɪt/ *v* [I, Tn] make (sth) seem larger, better, worse, etc than it really is; stretch (a description) beyond the truth: *He always exaggerates to make his stories more amusing.* ○ *You are exaggerating the difficulties.* ○ *That dress exaggerates her height.*

▷ **exaggerated** *adj* (a) made to seem larger, better, worse, etc than it really is: *a highly exaggerated version of the incident* ○ *He has an exaggerated sense of his own importance.* (b) produced, stated, etc in a false or an unnatural way; distorted: *an exaggerated laugh* ○ *a clown's exaggerated make-up* ○ *with exaggerated politeness.* **exaggeratedly** *adv.*

exaggeration /ɪɡˌzædʒəˈreɪʃn/ *n* 1 [U] action of exaggerating. 2 [C] exaggerated description, statement, etc: *a story full of exaggerations.*

exalt /ɪɡˈzɔːlt/ *v* [Tn] (*fml*) 1 make (sb) higher in rank or greater in power. 2 praise (sb) highly. ▷ **exalted** *adj* (*fml or joc*): *a person of exalted rank* ○ *from his exalted position in the firm.*

exaltation /ˌeɡzɔːlˈteɪʃn/ *n* [U] state of spiritual delight; elation.

exam /ɪɡˈzæm/ *n* (*infml*) examination(2): *school exams.*

examination /ɪɡˌzæmɪˈneɪʃn/ *n* 1 [U] action of examining; being examined: *Careful examination of the ruins revealed new evidence.* ○ *On* (ie As a result of) *further examination it was found that the signature was not genuine.* 2 (also **exam**) [C] testing of knowledge or ability by means of questions, practical exercises, etc: *an examination in Physics* ○ *sit/take an examination*, ie have one's knowledge tested by a written examination ○ *pass/fail an examination*, ie be/not be successful in an examination ○ *an oral examination* ○ *an entrance examination*, eg to test an applicant wishing to enter a school, college, etc ○ [attrib] *an examination paper*, ie sheet(s) of paper with a list of questions set by an examiner. 3 [C] close inspection of sb/sth or inquiry into sth: *a medical examination by a doctor* ○ *an examination of business accounts.* 4 [C, U] (action of) questioning by a lawyer in a lawcourt: *a fresh examination of the witness* ○ *After further examination by the prosecution the witness was allowed to leave the court.* 5 (idm) **under examiˈnation** being examined: *The prisoner is still under examination.* ○ *The proposals are still under examination*, ie have not yet been approved.

examine /ɪɡˈzæmɪn/ *v* [Tn, Tn·pr] 1 ~ **sth/sb (for sth)** (a) look at carefully in order to learn about or from; inspect closely: *examine an old manuscript* ○ *examine facts, a theory, evidence, etc* ○ *The detective* *examined the window frame for fingerprints.* (**b**) inspect carefully (a patient or part of his body) to check for disease: *have one's teeth examined for decay* ○ *The doctor examined her patient carefully.* **2** ~ **sb (in/on sth)** (*fml*) test the knowledge or ability of (sb) by written or oral questions: *examine students in mathematics/on their knowledge of mathematics.* **3** (*law*) question (sb) formally in order to get information; interrogate: *examine a witness in a court of law.* Cf CROSS-EXAMINE. **4** (idm) **need, etc one's head examined** ⇨ HEAD[1].

▷ **examinee** /ɪgˌzæmɪˈniː/ *n* (*fml*) person being tested in an examination(2): *Ten of the examinees were failed.*

examiner /ɪgˈzæmɪnə(r)/ *n* **1** person who tests knowledge or ability: *He is one of the science examiners.* **2** (idm) **satisfy the examiners** ⇨ SATISFY.

example /ɪgˈzɑːmpl; *US* -ˈzæmpl/ *n* **1** [C] fact, event, etc that illustrates or represents a general rule: *This dictionary has many examples of how words are used.* ○ *That outburst was a typical example of his lack of self-control.* **2** [C] specimen showing the quality of others in the same group or of the same kind: *This church is a fine example of Norman architecture.* ○ *This is a good example of Shelley's lyric poetry.* ○ *It is a classic example of how not to design a new city centre.* **3** [C, U] thing, person or quality that is worthy of imitation: *She was an example to the rest of the class.* ○ *His bravery should be an example to all of us.* ○ *learn by example.* **4** [C] warning: *Let this be an example* (ie May this punishment serve as a warning) *to you.* **5** (idm) **follow sb's example/lead** ⇨ FOLLOW. **for example** (*abbr* **eg**) by way of illustration: *I know many women who have a career and a family — Alison for example.* **make an example of sb** punish (sb) as a warning to others: *The headmaster decided to make an example of the pupil and expel him from the school.* **set (sb) an example/set a good, bad, etc example (to sb)** behave in a way worthy/not worthy of imitation (by sb): *The headmistress likes to arrive early at school to set (the other teachers) an example.* ie a good example.

exasperate /ɪgˈzæspəreɪt/ *v* [Tn] irritate or annoy (sb) greatly: *That child exasperates me!* ○ *She was exasperated at/by his stupidity.*

▷ **exasperating** *adj* extremely annoying: *He's probably the most exasperating man I've ever met.* ○ *It's exasperating to run for a train and then miss it by half a minute.* **exasperatingly** *adv.*

exasperation /ɪgˌzæspəˈreɪʃn/ *n* [U] state of being exasperated: *'Stop that noise,' he cried out in exasperation.*

Excalibur /eksˈkælɪbə(r)/ magic sword of the legendary English King *Arthur.

ex cathedra /ˌeks kəˈθiːdrə/ *adv, adj* (*Latin fml*) with full authority: *an ex cathedra statement.*

excavate /ˈekskəveɪt/ *v* [Tn] **1** (*fml*) make (a hole or channel) by digging; remove (soil, etc) by digging: *excavate a trench.* **2** uncover or extract by digging (esp sth from earlier times): *excavate a buried city, a Greek vase.*

▷ **excavation** /ˌekskəˈveɪʃn/ *n* **1** [U] activity of excavating: *Excavation of the site will begin tomorrow.* **2 excavations** [pl] place that is being or has been excavated: *visit the excavations.*

excavator *n* person engaged in or machine used for excavating: *excavators on an archaeological site* ○ *mechanical excavators.*

exceed /ɪkˈsiːd/ *v* [Tn] (**a**) be greater or more numerous than (esp a quantity): *The price will not exceed £100.* ○ *The number admitted must not exceed 200.* ○ *Their success exceeded all expectations*, ie was greater than anyone expected. (**b**) go beyond what is allowed, necessary or advisable: *exceed the speed limit*, ie drive faster than is allowed ○ *exceed one's instructions/authority*, ie do more than one has permission to do.

▷ **exceedingly** *adv* extremely; to an unusual degree: *an exceedingly difficult problem.*

excel /ɪkˈsel/ *v* (**-ll-**) **1** [Ipr] ~ **in/at sth** be exceptionally good at sth: *excel in foreign languages* ○ *The firm excels at producing cheap transistor radios.* **2** (idm) **exˈcel oneself** do better than ever before: *His meals are always very good, but this time he's excelled himself.* ○ (*ironic*) *So you've broken three windows today — you've really excelled yourself.*

excellence /ˈeksələns/ *n* **1** [U] ~ **(in/at sth)** quality of being excellent; great merit: *a prize for excellence in furniture design* ○ *known for excellence in/at all forms of sport.* **2** [C] (*fml*) thing or quality in which a person excels: *They do not recognize her many excellences.*

Excellency /ˈeksələnsɪ/ *n* title given to ambassadors, governors, their husbands or wives, and some other officers and officials: *Your/His/Her Excellency* ○ *His Excellency the French Ambassador.*

excellent /ˈeksələnt/ *adj* **1** very good; of very high quality: *an excellent meal* ○ *She speaks excellent French.* **2** (used to indicate approval or pleasure): *They won't be coming then? Excellent!* ▷ **excellently** *adv.*

except[1] /ɪkˈsept/ *prep* ~ **(for sb/sth)**; ~ **(that...)** not including (sb/sth); but not: *The restaurant is open every day except Monday.* ○ *Everyone except me got an invitation.* ○ *I understand everything except why she killed him.* ○ *I can answer all the questions except for the last.* ○ *The meal was excellent except for* (ie with the exception of) *the first course.* ○ *She remembered nothing (about him) except that his hair was black.* ○ *The two books are the same except (for the fact) that this one has an answer key at the back.*

except[2] /ɪkˈsept/ *v* **1** [esp passive: Tn, Tn·pr] ~ **sb/sth (from sth)** (*fml*) (often with a negative) leave sb/sth out; exclude sb/sth: *Only children under five are excepted from this survey.* ○ *We all had to take part in the training run, with nobody excepted.* ○ *the whole staff, not excepting the headmaster.* **2** (idm) **present company excepted** ⇨ PRESENT[1].

exception /ɪkˈsepʃn/ *n* **1** [C, U] (an instance of) leaving out or excluding; person or thing that is not included: *Most of the buildings in this town are rather unattractive, but this church is an exception.* ○ *The children did well, the only exception being Jo, who failed.* ○ *All students without exception must take the English examination.* ○ *I enjoyed all his novels with the exception of his last.* **2** [C] thing that does not follow a rule: *an exception to a rule of grammar.* **3** (idm) **the exception proves the ˈrule** (*saying*) the excepting of some cases proves that the rule exists, or that it applies to all other cases: *All his family have red hair except him. He is the exception which proves the rule.* **make an exception (of sb/sth)** treat sb/sth as a special case: *You must all be here at 8 am; I can make no exceptions*, ie I cannot excuse any of you. **take exception to sth** object to sth; be offended by sth: *He took great exception to what I said.* ○ *She took exception to having to wait outside in the rain.*

▷ **exceptionable** /-ʃənəbl/ *adj* (*fml*) that sb can object to: *There are no exceptionable scenes in the play.*

exceptional /ɪkˈsepʃənl/ *adj* very unusual; outstanding: *This weather is exceptional for June.* ○ *show exceptional musical ability.*

▷ **exceptionally** /-ʃənəlɪ/ *adv* unusually; outstandingly: *an exceptionally beautiful child.*

excerpt /ˈeksɜːpt/ *n* [C] ~ **(from sth)** passage, extract, from a book, film, piece of music, etc: *excerpts from a novel* ○ *I've seen a short excerpt from the film on television.*

excess[1] /ɪkˈses/ *n* **1** [sing] **an** ~ **of sth** (*derog*) more than the reasonable, expected or moderate degree or amount of sth: *an excess of enthusiasm, anger, emotion, zeal, etc* ○ *An excess of fat in one's diet can lead to heart disease.* **2** [U] going beyond the normal or accepted limits; immoderation: *Don't carry your anger to excess.* ○ *Luggage in excess of 100 kg will be charged extra.* **3** [C] amount by which sth is larger than sth else: *She was charged an excess of £4 over the amount stated on the bill.* **4** [U] (*esp Brit*) agreed sum taken by an insurance company from the total amount to be paid to an insured person who makes a claim: *You will have to pay the first £50 of the cost of repairing your damaged car as there is an excess of £50 on your policy.* **5 excesses** [pl] (*fml*) personal acts which go beyond the limits of good behaviour, or humanity: *The excesses* (ie acts of cruelty) *committed by the occupying troops will never be forgotten.* ○ *His excesses at parties are well known.* **6** (idm) **to exˈcess** to an extreme degree: *He drinks to excess.*

▷ **excessive** /ɪkˈsesɪv/ *adj* greater than what is normal or necessary; extreme: *excessive prices* ○ *an excessive amount of alcohol* ○ *an excessive enthusiasm for sport.* **excessively** *adv.*

excess[2] /ˈekses/ *adj* [attrib] extra or additional (to the usual or permitted amount): *excess fare*, eg for travelling further than is allowed by one's ticket ○ *A company which makes high profits must pay excess profits duty to the government.*

□ ˌ**excess ˈbaggage** (also ˌ**excess ˈluggage**) amount of luggage that is over the weight that may be carried free on an aircraft.

ˌ**excess ˈpostage** amount charged to a person who receives a letter, etc which does not carry stamps of high enough value.

exchange[1] /ɪksˈtʃeɪndʒ/ *n* **1** [C, U] (action or process of) giving one thing or person in return for another: *Is five apples for five eggs a fair exchange?* ○ *The exchange of prisoners during a war is unusual.* ○ *the exchange of contracts*, ie the final stage of buying or selling a house ○ *an exchange of glances* ○ *an exchange of houses* ○ *an exchange of gun-fire* ○ *He's giving her French lessons in exchange for* (ie as an exchange for) *her teaching him English.* **2** [C] (angry) conversation or argument: *bitter exchanges between MP's in parliament.* **3** [U] relation in value between kinds of money used in different countries: *What is the rate of exchange between the dollar and the pound?* ○ *I want to change my dollars into pesetas — what is the exchange rate?* **4 Exchange** [C] place where business people or financiers meet for business: *the ˈCorn Exchange* ○ *the ˈStock Exchange*, ie for the buying and selling of stocks, shares, etc. **5** [C] = TELEPHONE EXCHANGE (TELEPHONE). **6** [C] reciprocal visit between two (often young) people or groups from different countries: *be on, do, organize an exchange* ○ *Sarah is going on an exchange to Paris to stay with Pierre, and he is coming to stay with her here in Scotland next year.* ○ [attrib] *exchange students* ○ *exchange visits* ○ *She is an exchange teacher.* **7** (idm) **fair exchange is no robbery** ⇨ FAIR[1].

exchange[2] /ɪksˈtʃeɪndʒ/ *v* **1** (**a**) [Tn, Tn·pr] ~ **A for B**; ~ **sth (with sb)** give or receive sth/sb (of the same kind or value) in place of another: *He exchanged the blue jumper for a red one.* ○ *Ali exchanged seats with Ben.* ○ *The enemy countries exchanged prisoners.* ○ *They exchanged hostages with each other.* (**b**) [Tn] give sth and receive sth (from another person) in return: *exchanging blows*, ie hitting each other ○ *They exchanged glances*, ie looked at each other. ○ *The two men exchanged greetings*, ie Each greeted the other. **2** (idm) **exchange (angry, etc) ˈwords** quarrel; argue: *They exchanged angry words before the meeting but were finally persuaded to agree.*

▷ **exchangeable** /-əbl/ *adj* that can be exchanged: *Sale goods in this shop are not exchangeable.*

exchequer /ɪksˈtʃekə(r)/ *n* **1 the Exchequer** [sing] (*Brit*) government department in charge of public money: *The Chancellor of the Exchequer is the minister in charge of finance in Britain.* **2** [C] (**a**) public or national supply of money; treasury. (**b**) (*often joc*) person's supply of money: *There's nothing left in the exchequer this month.*

excise[1] /ˈeksaɪz/ *n* [U] **1** government tax on certain goods manufactured, sold or used within a country: *the excise on beer/spirits/tobacco* ○ *customs and excise* ○ [attrib] *an excise officer*, ie an official employed in collecting excise. Cf CUSTOMS[1]. **2** any of various taxes paid in the form of licence fees for the right to certain privileges.

▷ **excise** *v* [Tn] impose excise on (goods, privileges, etc).

excise[2] /ɪk'saɪz/ *v* [Tn, Tn·pr] ~ **sth (from sth)** (*fml*) remove by, or as if by, cutting (esp a part of the body or a passage from a book): *The surgeon excised the lump from her breast.* ○ *The censor insisted on excising the passage from the film.*
▷ **excision** /ɪk'sɪʒn/ *n* (*fml*) **1** [U] action of excising: *the excision of a tumour.* **2** [C] thing that is excised: *The excisions have destroyed the literary value of the text.*

excitable /ɪk'saɪtəbl/ *adj* (of a person, animal or temperament) easily excited: *an excitable child* ○ *an excitable breed of dog* ○ *an excitable race of people.*
▷ **excitability** /ɪkˌsaɪtə'bɪlətɪ/ *n* [U] quality of being excitable.

excite /ɪk'saɪt/ *v* **1** [Tn esp passive, Tn·pr] cause strong feelings of eagerness, happiness, nervousness, etc in (a person or an animal): *The children were very excited by the pantomime.* ○ *Don't excite yourself,* ie Keep calm. **2** [Tn, Tn·pr, Cn·t] ~ **sb (to sth)** (*fml*) cause or bring about (sth) by arousing strong feelings in sb: *excite a riot* ○ *Agitators were exciting the people to rebel/to rebellion against their rulers.* **3** [Tn, Tn·pr] **(a)** ~ **sth (in sb)** arouse (an emotion) in sb; cause (a response or reaction) in sb: *excite public suspicion* ○ *The recent discoveries have excited great interest among doctors.* ○ *excite envy, admiration, greed, etc (in sb).* **(b)** arouse (sexual desire): *Some people are sexually excited by pornographic magazines.* **4** [Tn] (*fml*) cause (part of the body) to be active: *drugs that excite the nervous system.* **5** [Tn] (*physics*) **(a)** cause (a substance) to emit radiation. **(b)** put (an atom, a molecule, etc) into a state of higher energy.
▷ **excited** /ɪk'saɪtɪd/ *adj* feeling or showing excitement: *sexually excited* ○ *The excited children forgot to take the presents to the party.* ○ *It's nothing to get excited about.* **excitedly** *adv.*
exciting *adj* causing great interest or enthusiasm: *an exciting piece of work* ○ *an exciting story* ○ *an exciting discovery.* **excitingly** *adv.*

excitement /ɪk'saɪtmənt/ *n* **1** [U] state of strong emotion or feeling, esp one caused by sth pleasant: *The news caused great excitement.* ○ *jumping about in excitement at the discovery.* **2** [C] (*fml*) thing that excites; exciting incident, etc: *the excitements associated with a cruise around the world.*

exclaim /ɪk'skleɪm/ *v* [I, Ipr, Tf] cry out suddenly and loudly from pain, anger, surprise, etc: *'What,' he exclaimed, 'Are you leaving without me?'* ○ *He could not help exclaiming at how much his son had grown.* ○ *He exclaimed that it was untrue.*

exclamation /ˌekskləˈmeɪʃn/ *n* (short) sound(s) or word(s), expressing sudden surprise, pain, etc: *'Oh!', 'Look out!' and 'Ow!' are exclamations.*
□ **ˌexcla'mation mark** (*US* **ˌexcla'mation point**) mark (!) written after an exclamation. ⇨ App 14.

exclamatory /ɪk'sklæmətrɪ; *US* -tɔ:rɪ/ *adj* (*fml*) of, using or containing an exclamation: *an exclamatory sentence.*

exclude /ɪk'sklu:d/ *v* **1** [Tn, Tn·pr] ~ **sb/sth (from sth) (a)** prevent sb from entering somewhere, taking part in sth, etc; keep sb out: *exclude a person from membership of a society* ○ *Women are often excluded from positions of authority.* **(b)** prevent sth from getting in; keep sth out: *All air must be excluded (from the bottle) if the experiment is to work.* ○ *All draughts must be excluded from the room.* **2** [Tn] reject (sth) as a possibility; ignore as a consideration: *The police have excluded robbery as a motive for the murder.* ○ *We must not exclude the possibility that the child has run away.* **3** [Tn] leave (sth) out; not include: *lunch costs £5 per person, excluding drinks* ○ *That price excludes accommodation.*

exclusion /ɪk'sklu:ʒn/ *n* **1** [U] ~ **(of sb/sth) (from sth)** action of excluding; being excluded: *the exclusion of women from the temple* ○ [attrib]: *an exclusion zone,* ie an area into which sb/sth, esp enemy shipping, is not allowed to go. **2** (idm) **to the exclusion of sb/sth** so as to exclude (all other members of a group): *He spent his spare time gardening, to the exclusion of all other interests.*

exclusive /ɪk'sklu:sɪv/ *adj* **1 (a)** (of a group, society, etc) not readily admitting new members (esp if they are thought to be socially inferior); select: *He is part of an exclusive social circle and belongs to an exclusive club.* **(b)** (of a high-class shop, goods sold in it, etc) not found elsewhere; reserved for the wealthy: *exclusive styles, designs, articles* ○ *an exclusive restaurant, private school.* **2** reserved for or limited to the person(s) or group concerned: *exclusive privileges of the aristocracy* ○ *an exclusive agency for the sale of Ford cars in this town* ○ *The interview is exclusive to this magazine.* **3** excluding all but the thing specified: *Painting has not been her exclusive occupation.* **4** not admitting sth else; rejecting other considerations: *The two plans are mutually exclusive,* ie If you accept one you must reject the other. **5** ~ **of sb/sth** not including sb/sth; not counting sb/sth: *The ship has a crew of 57 exclusive of officers.* ○ *The price of the holiday is exclusive of accommodation.*
▷ **exclusive** *n* (also **exclusive story**) newspaper or magazine story given to and published by only one newspaper: *a Daily Mirror exclusive.*
exclusively *adv*: *This special offer has been exclusively designed for readers of this magazine.*
exclusiveness (also **exclusivity**) /ˌeksklu:'sɪvətɪ/ *n* [U] quality of being exclusive: *The shop was proud of its exclusiveness.*

excommunicate /ˌekskə'mju:nɪkeɪt/ *v* [Tn] exclude (sb) as a punishment from the rights and privileges of membership of the Christian Church.
▷ **excommunication** /ˌekskəˌmju:nɪ'keɪʃn/ *n* **1** [U] action of excommunicating or being excommunicated. **2** [C] example of this; official statement announcing this.

excoriate /eks'kɔ:rɪeɪt/ *v* [Tn] (*fml*) **1** remove some of the skin from (a person or an animal). **2** (*fig*) criticize (sb) angrily.

excrement /'ekskrɪmənt/ *n* [U] (*fml*) solid waste matter passed from the body through the bowels; faeces: *The pavement was covered in dogs' excrement.*

excrescence /ɪk'skresns/ *n* (*fml*) abnormal (ugly and useless) growth on an animal body or a plant: (*fig*) *The new office block is an excrescence on the landscape.*

excreta /ɪk'skri:tə/ *n* [U] (*fml*) liquid and solid waste (excrement, urine, sweat) passed from the body: *the smell of excreta in the hospital ward.*

excrete /ɪk'skri:t/ *v* [Tn] (*fml*) (of an animal or a plant) pass out (waste matter, sweat, etc) from the system.
▷ **excretion** /ɪk'skri:ʃn/ *n* **(a)** [U] action of excreting. **(b)** [C, U] that which is excreted.

excruciating /ɪk'skru:ʃɪeɪtɪŋ/ *adj* (of physical or mental pain) intense; acute: *He has excruciating backache.* ○ *excruciating misery* ○ (*joc*) *He's an excruciating bore.* ○ *an excruciating concert.* ▷ **excruciatingly** *adv*: *an excruciatingly painful experience.*

exculpate /'ekskʌlpeɪt/ *v* [Tn, Tn·pr] ~ **sb (from sth)** (*fml*) free sb from blame; say that sb is not guilty: *exculpate a person from a charge* ○ *exculpate oneself from blame.*

excursion /ɪk'skɜ:ʃn; *US* -ɜ:rʒn/ *n* **(a)** short journey, esp one made by a group of people together for pleasure: *go on/make a day excursion to the mountains,* ie there and back in one day ○ *Many excursions had been arranged by the holiday company.* ○ [attrib] *an excursion train* ○ *an excursion ticket,* ie one issued at a reduced fare. **(b)** short journey made for a particular purpose: *a shopping excursion.* ⇨ Usage at JOURNEY.

excuse[1] /ɪk'skju:s/ *n* ~ **(for sth/doing sth) 1** (true or invented) reason given to explain or defend one's behaviour; apology: *He's always making excuses for being late.* ○ *There's no excuse for such behaviour.* ○ *He made his excuses* (ie He apologized) *and left the meeting.* ○ *Please offer/give them my excuses.* ○ *I can't attend the meeting — would you make my excuses* (ie apologize and give my reasons for not attending), *please?* ○ (*fml*) *Those who are absent without (good) excuse* (ie without giving a (good) excuse) *will be dismissed.* **2** (idm) **an excuse for sth** poor specimen of sth specified: *Who made this excuse for a chair? It's already falling apart.*

excuse[2] /ɪk'skju:z/ *v* **1 (a)** [Tn, Tn·pr, Tsg] ~ **sb/sth (for sth/doing sth)** forgive or overlook (a fault, etc); pardon sb/sth: *Please excuse my late arrival.* ○ *Excuse me for being late.* ○ *Excuse my interrupting you.* **(b)** [Tn, Tn·pr] ~ **sb/sth (for sth/doing sth)** give reasons showing, or intended to show, that (a person or his actions) cannot be blamed: *Nothing can excuse such rudeness.* ○ *She stood up, excused herself* (ie apologized for leaving) *and walked out of the meeting.* ○ *He excused himself for being late by saying that his car had broken down.* **2** [esp passive: Tn, Tn·pr, Dn·n] ~ **sb (from sth)** set sb free from a duty, requirement, punishment, etc: *He was excused (from) piano practice.* ○ *They may be excused (from doing) this exercise.* **3** (idm) **excuse me (a)** (used as an apology when one interrupts, disagrees, disapproves or has to behave impolitely): *Excuse me, is anybody sitting here?* ○ *Excuse me, but I don't think that's quite true.* **(b) excuse me?** (*esp US*) Please repeat what you said. **excuse/pardon my French** ⇨ FRENCH. **may I be excused?** (*euph Brit*) (used esp by schoolchildren) may I go to the toilet?
▷ **excusable** /ɪk'skju:zəbl/ *adj* that may be excused: *an excusable mistake.* **excusably** /-əblɪ/ *adv.*

NOTE ON USAGE: **1** We say **Excuse me** to someone if we want to get his or her attention or before we do something that might disturb him or her, eg interrupt him/her, push him/her in a crowd, disagree with him/her: *Excuse me, can I get past, please?* **2** We say **Sorry** or (formally) **I beg your pardon** when we need to apologize for something: *Sorry, did I tread on your toe?* ○ *I beg your pardon. I think you were next in the queue.* In US English **Pardon me** and **Excuse me** are used for apologies. **3** We say **Pardon?** when we did not hear what someone said and want them to repeat it. In this case **Sorry?** is also used in British English and **Excuse me?** or **Pardon me?** in US English.

ex-directory /ˌeks dɪ'rektərɪ/ *adj* (*US* **unlisted**) (of a telephone number) not listed in the telephone directory at the wish of the phone-owner (for reasons of security, privacy, etc): *an ex-directory number* ○ *go ex-directory because of hoax telephone calls.*

exeat /'eksɪæt/ *n* (*Brit*) time when one has permission to be absent from a college, school, etc.

execrable /'eksɪkrəbl/ *adj* (*fml*) very bad; terrible: *execrable manners, weather.* ▷ **execrably** /-blɪ/ *adv.*

execrate /'eksɪkreɪt/ *v* [esp passive: Tn] (*fml*) express or feel hatred of (sb/sth); curse. ▷ **execration** /ˌeksɪ'kreɪʃn/ *n* [U, C].

execute /'eksɪkju:t/ *v* [Tn] **1** (*fml*) carry out, or perform (what one is asked or told to do): *execute sb's commands* ○ *execute a plan, a piece of work, a purpose.* **2** (*law*) **(a)** put (sth) into effect: *execute a will.* **(b)** make (sth) legally valid: *execute a legal document,* ie by having it signed, witnessed, sealed and delivered. **3** kill (sb) as a legal punishment: *He was executed for treason.* ○ *execute a murderer.* **4** (*fml*) perform (sth) on the stage, at a concert, etc: *execute a dance step* ○ *The piano sonata was badly executed.* **5** (*computing*) carry out (the instructions of a computer program).

execution /ˌeksɪ'kju:ʃn/ *n* **1** [U] carrying out or performance of a piece of work, plan, design, duty, etc: *His original idea was good, but his execution of the scheme was disastrous.* ○ *The plans were finally put into execution.* **2** [U] (*law*) action of carrying out the orders of a will: *The solicitor is proceeding with the execution of my mother's will.* **3** [C, U] (act of) killing sb as a legal punishment: *execution by hanging* ○ *five executions last year.* **4** [U] (*fml*) skill in performing eg music: *The pianist's execution of the concerto was marvellous.* **5** (idm) **a stay of execution** ⇨ STAY *n.*
▷ **executioner** /ˌeksɪ'kju:ʃənə(r)/ *n* public official who carries out a death sentence.

executive /ɪɡˈzekjʊtɪv/ *adj* [usu attrib] **1** (esp in business) concerned with the management and carrying out of plans, decisions, etc: *executive duties* ○ *possess executive ability.* **2** having power to carry out decisions, laws, decrees, etc: *executive authority* ○ *the executive branch of the Government* ○ *the executive committee of a political party* ○ *the executive head of State,* eg the President of the US.
▷ **executive** *n* **1** [CGp] person or group in a business organization, trade union, etc with administrative or managerial powers: *a sales executive* ○ *She's an executive in a computer company.* ○ *The executive has/have been making decisions about the future of the company.* ○ [attrib] *an executive briefcase.* **2** [C] (in the Civil Service) person who carries out what has been planned or decided: [attrib] *executive officer.* **3 the executive** [Gp] executive branch of a government.
□ **exˌecutive ˈsession** (*US*) session of a legislative body, usu closed to the public and held eg to consider appointments or ratify treaties.

executor /ɪɡˈzekjʊtə(r)/ *n* person who is appointed by the maker of a will to carry out the terms of the will.

exegesis /ˌeksɪˈdʒiːsɪs/ *n* (*pl* **-ses** /-siːz/) [U, C] (*fml*) explanation and interpretation of a written work, esp the Bible.

exemplar /ɪɡˈzemplə(r)/ *n* person or thing to be imitated or copied; model; example: *She is an exemplar of the dedicated writer.*

exemplary /ɪɡˈzemplərɪ/ *adj* **1** serving as an example; suitable for imitation: *exemplary behaviour* ○ *an exemplary student.* **2** (*fml*) serving as a warning: *exemplary punishment.*

exemplify /ɪɡˈzemplɪfaɪ/ *v* (*pt, pp* **-fied**) [Tn] **1** be a typical example of (sth): *This painting exemplifies the artist's early style.* **2** (*fml*) give an example of (sth); illustrate by example: *exemplify the problems involved.*
▷ **exemplification** /ɪɡˌzemplɪfɪˈkeɪʃn/ *n* **1** [U] exemplifying. **2** [C] (*fml*) example.

exempt /ɪɡˈzempt/ *adj* [pred] ~ (**from sth**) free from an obligation, duty or payment; not liable: *exempt from military service* ○ *exempt from working overtime* ○ *goods exempt from tax* ○ *Children under 16 are exempt from prescription charges.*
▷ **exempt** *v* [Tn, Tn·pr] ~ **sb/sth (from sth)** (*fml*) make sb/sth exempt: *His bad eyesight exempted him from military service.* **exemption** /ɪɡˈzempʃn/ *n* [U, C].

exercise[1] /ˈeksəsaɪz/ *n* **1** [U] use or practice (of the mind or esp the body) through effort or action: *The doctor advised him to take more exercise.* ○ *Jogging is a healthy form of exercise.* ○ *Doing crosswords gives the mind some exercise.* **2** [C] activity or task intended for physical or mental training: *vocal, gymnastic, keep-fit, deep-breathing, etc exercises* ○ *exercises for the piano, flute, harp, etc* ○ *The teacher set her class a mathematics exercise for homework.* ○ [attrib] *an exercise book,* ie a book for writing in with soft covers and lined pages. **3** [U] ~ **of sth** (effective) use or application: *The exercise of patience is essential in diplomatic negotiations.* ○ *the exercise of one's civil rights* ○ *His stories showed considerable exercise of the imagination.* **4** [C often *pl*] series of movements or operations for training troops, etc: *military exercises* ○ (*fig*) *an exercise in diplomatic relations.* **5 exercises** [pl] (*US*) ceremonies: *graduation exercises* ○ *opening exercises,* eg speeches at the start of a conference.

exercise[2] /ˈeksəsaɪz/ *v* **1** [I] perform some kind of physical exercise: *He exercises twice a day.* **2** [Tn, Tn·pr] ~ **sb/sth (in sth)** give exercise[1](1) to sb/sth; train sb/sth (by means of exercises): *Horses get fat and lazy if they are not exercised.* ○ *Swimming exercises the whole body.* **3** [Tn] make use of (sth); employ: *exercise patience, tolerance, power, control, etc* ○ *exercise one's rights as a citizen* ○ *Teachers exercise authority over their pupils.* **4** [Tn usu passive] (*fml*) worry or trouble (sb): *This problem is exercising our minds very much at the moment.* ○ *I am very much exercised about the education of my son.*

exert /ɪɡˈzɜːt/ *v* [Tn, Tn·pr] **1** ~ **sth (on sb/sth)** bring (a quality, skill, pressure, etc) into use; apply sth: *He exerted all his influence to make them accept his plan.* ○ *Her husband exerted a lot of pressure on her to succeed.* **2** [Tn no passive] ~ **oneself** make an effort: *You'll have to exert yourself more if you want to pass your exam.* ○ *He doesn't have to exert himself on my behalf.*

exertion /ɪɡˈzɜːʃn; *US* -ɜːrʒn/ *n* (**a**) [U] action of applying influence, etc: *Exertion of authority over others is not always wise; persuasion may be better.* (**b**) [C, U] (instance of) great effort: *incapable of physical exertion* ○ *He failed to lift the rock in spite of all his exertions.* ○ *Now that I'm 90, I find the exertions of travelling too great.*

exeunt /ˈeksɪʌnt/ (*Latin*) (as a stage direction) they leave the stage: *Exeunt Antony and Cleopatra.* Cf EXIT *v* 2.
□ **ˌexeunt ˈomnes** /ˈɒmneɪz/ (*Latin*) (as a stage direction) they all leave the stage.

ex gratia /ˌeks ˈɡreɪʃə/ *adv, adj* (*Latin*) done or given as a favour; not from (esp legal) obligation: *an ex gratia payment.*

exhale /eksˈheɪl/ *v* [I, Tn] (*fml*) **1** breathe (sth) out: *She exhaled slowly to show her annoyance.* ○ *exhale air from the lungs* ○ *exhale smoke.* **2** give off or expel (gas or vapour).
▷ **exhalation** /ˌekshəˈleɪʃn/ *n* (*fml*) **1** [C] act of exhaling. **2** [U, C] thing exhaled: *an exhalation of smoke.*

exhaust[1] /ɪɡˈzɔːst/ *n* **1** [U] waste fumes, gases, steam, etc expelled from an engine or a machine: *the smell of the exhaust* ○ [attrib] *exhaust fumes.* **2** (also **exhaust-pipe**) [C] outlet or pipe through which these gases are sent out: *My car needs a new exhaust.* ⇨ illus at CAR.

exhaust[2] /ɪɡˈzɔːst/ *v* [Tn] **1** [esp passive] make (a person or an animal) very tired: *The long cycle ride exhausted her.* ○ *He exhausted himself in the attempt.* **2** use (sth) up completely: *exhaust one's patience, strength* ○ *exhaust a money supply.* **3** make (sth) empty; take out the contents of: *exhaust a well.* **4** say, find out, all there is to say about (sth): *I think we've just about exhausted that subject.*
▷ **exhausted** /ɪɡˈzɔːstɪd/ *adj* very tired: *I'm exhausted!* ○ *The exhausted troops surrendered.*

exhaustion /ɪɡˈzɔːstʃən/ *n* [U] **1** total loss of strength; extreme tiredness: *They were in a state of exhaustion after climbing the mountain.* **2** (*fml*) action of using up completely: *the rapid exhaustion of the earth's natural resources.*

exhaustive /ɪɡˈzɔːstɪv/ *adj* very thorough; complete: *an exhaustive enquiry, search.* ▷ **exhaustively** *adv.*

exhibit[1] /ɪɡˈzɪbɪt/ *n* **1** object or collection of objects displayed for the public, eg in a museum: *a priceless exhibit* ○ *The museum has some interesting new exhibits from India.* ○ *Do not touch the exhibits.* **2** document, object, etc produced as evidence in a lawcourt: *The first exhibit was a knife which the prosecution claimed was the murder weapon.* **3** (idm) **exˌhibit ˈA** (*often joc*) person or thing regarded as an important piece of evidence.

exhibit[2] /ɪɡˈzɪbɪt/ *v* **1** (**a**) [Tn] show or display (sth) for the public (for pleasure, for sale, in a competition, in a lawcourt, etc): *exhibit flowers at a flower show* ○ *documents exhibited in a lawcourt.* (**b**) [I, Tn] (of an artist) present (works of art) for the public, esp in an art gallery: *The young painter has exhibited (his work) in several galleries.* **2** [Tn] (*fml*) show clearly that one possesses (a quality or feeling): *He exhibited total lack of concern for the child.* ○ *She exhibited great powers of endurance during the climb.*
▷ **exhibitor** *n* person who displays pictures, flowers, etc at a show: *Nearly fifty exhibitors have provided pictures for the display.*

exhibition /ˌeksɪˈbɪʃn/ *n* **1** [C] (**a**) collection of things shown publicly (eg works of art, industrial or commercial goods for advertisement): *Have you seen the Picasso exhibition?* ie exhibition of paintings by Picasso ○ [attrib] *one of the exhibition halls at the Frankfurt book fair.* (**b**) public display of animals, plants, flowers, etc (esp as shown in a competition for prizes). **2** (**a**) [sing] act of showing (a quality or feeling): *an exhibition of bad manners* ○ *The quiz was a good opportunity for the exhibition of his knowledge.* (**b**) [C] public demonstration of a skill: *There's an exhibition of pottery-making at the fair.* ○ *a dancing exhibition* ⇨ Usage at DEMONSTRATION. **3** [C] (*Brit*) money allowance to a student from school or college funds for a number of years to pay for the costs of study. **4** (idm) **make an exhiˈbition of oneself** (*derog*) behave foolishly or badly in public: *People at the party were embarrassed when Frank got drunk and made an exhibition of himself.*
▷ **exhibitioner** /-ʃənə(r)/ *n* (*Brit*) student who receives an exhibition(3).
exhibitionism /-ʃənɪzəm/ *n* [U] **1** tendency to behave in a way intended to attract attention to oneself: *She was embarrassed by his exhibitionism at the party.* **2** (*fml*) offence of indecently exposing one's sexual organs in public.
exhibitionist /-ʃənɪst/ *n* person who is given to exhibitionism: *Children are natural exhibitionists.*

exhilarate /ɪɡˈzɪləreɪt/ *v* [Tn usu passive] make (sb) feel very happy or lively: *exhilarated by the news* ○ *We felt exhilarated by our walk along the beach.*
▷ **exhilarating** *adj* very exciting; causing happiness: *Our first parachute jump was an exhilarating experience.*
exhilaration /ɪɡˌzɪləˈreɪʃn/ *n* [U].

exhort /ɪɡˈzɔːt/ *v* [Tn, Tn·pr, Dn·t] ~ **sb (to sth)** (*fml*) advise sb strongly or earnestly; urge sb: *The chairman exhorted the party workers to action.* ○ *The teacher exhorted him to work hard.*
▷ **exhortation** /ˌeɡzɔːˈteɪʃn/ *n* **1** [U] (*fml*) action of exhorting. **2** [C] earnest request; speech, etc that exhorts: *All his father's exhortations were in vain.*

exhume /eksˈhjuːm; *US* ɪɡˈzuːm/ *v* [Tn] take (a dead body) from the ground (for examination): *When the police exhumed the corpse they discovered traces of poison in it.*
▷ **exhumation** /ˌekshjuːˈmeɪʃn; *US* ˌeɡzuː-/ *n* (*fml*) **1** [U] exhuming or being exhumed. **2** [C] instance of this.

ex hypothesi /eks haɪˈpɒθəsɪ, -θəsaɪ/ *adv* (*Latin*, *fml*) according to the proposed hypothesis.

exigency /ˈeksɪdʒənsɪ/ *n* [C often *pl*, U] (*fml*) (condition of) urgent need or demand; emergency: *The people had to accept the harsh exigencies of war.*
▷ **exigent** /-dʒənt/ *adj* (*fml*) **1** requiring immediate action; urgent: *an exigent set of circumstances.* **2** requiring much; exacting: *an exigent employer.* **exigently** *adv.*

exiguous /eɡˈzɪɡjʊəs/ *adj* (*fml*) very small (in amount); scanty: *an exiguous diet* ○ *the last of the old man's exiguous savings.*

exile /ˈeksaɪl/ *n* **1** [U] being sent away from one's native country or home, esp for political reasons or as a punishment; forced absence: *be/live in exile* ○ *go/be sent into exile* ○ *a place of exile.* **2** [C] long stay away from one's country or home: *After an exile of ten years her uncle returned to Britain.* **3** [C] person who lives away from his own country from choice or because he is forced to: *a tax exile,* ie a rich person who moves to another country where the rate of income tax is lower ○ *There were many French exiles in England after the Revolution.* **4 the Exile** [sing] the captivity of the Jews in Babylon in the 6th century BC.
▷ **exile** *v* [esp passive: Tn, Tn·pr] ~ **sb (from...** send sb into exile: *exiled for life* ○ *She was exiled from her country because of her part in the plot against the government.*

exist /ɪɡˈzɪst/ *v* [I, Ipr] **1** ~ **(in/on sth)** (**a**) be real or actual; have being: *Do you believe fairies exist?* ie that there are really fairies? ○ *The idea exists only in the minds of poets.* ○ *laws that have existed for hundreds of years* ○ *Does life exist on Mars?* (**b**) be found; occur: *This plant exists only in Australia.* **2** ~ **(on sth)** continue living, esp with difficulty or with very little money; survive: *We cannot exist without food or water.* ○ *He exists on rice and water,* ie by eating rice and water. ○ *I can hardly exist on the wage I'm getting; there is no money for luxuries.*
▷ **existence** /-əns/ *n* **1** [U] state or fact of existing

Do you believe in the existence of ghosts? ○ *This is the oldest Hebrew manuscript in existence*, ie that exists. ○ *When did the world come into existence*, ie begin to exist? ○ *I was unaware of his existence until now.* **2** **(a)** [sing] manner of living, esp when this is difficult, boring, etc; way of living: *We led a happy enough existence as children.* ○ *living a miserable existence miles from the nearest town.* **(b)** [sing, U] continuance in life; survival: *The peasants depend on a good harvest for their very existence*, ie for existence itself. ○ *They eke out a bare existence* (ie They scarcely manage) *on his low salary.* **3** (idm) **the bane of sb's existence** ⇨ BANE.

existent /-ənt/ *adj* (*fml*) existing; actual.

existentialism /ˌegzɪˈstenʃəlɪzəm/ *n* [U] (*philosophy*) theory (deriving from Kierkegaard and made popular by *Sartre) that man is a unique and isolated individual in a meaningless or hostile world, responsible for his own actions and free to choose his destiny. Existentialism rejects the idea that external factors or general principles govern human behaviour, and regards behaviour as sincere and authentic if it results from an absolute inner conviction.

▷ **existential** /ˌegzɪˈstenʃl/ *adj* **1** (*fml*) of or relating to (esp human) existence. **2** of or relating to the theory of existentialism.

existentialist /-ʃəlɪst/ *n, adj*: *He's an existentialist.* ○ *He holds existentialist views.*

exit /ˈeksɪt; *US* ˈegzɪt/ *n* **1** action of leaving; departure, esp that of an actor from the stage: *The heroine makes her exit (from the stage).* ○ *When his ex-wife arrived at the party he made a swift exit*, ie he left quickly. ○ [attrib] *an exit visa*, ie a stamp or signature on a passport giving permission to leave a particular country. **2** way out (of a public building): *There are four emergency exits in the department store.* ○ [attrib] *The exit signs in cinemas are usually illuminated.* **3** point at which a road, etc turns off from a motorway or roundabout, allowing vehicles to leave: *At the roundabout, take the third exit.* ○ *Leave the motorway at the Stokenchurch exit.*

▷ **exit** *v* [I] **1** go out; (esp of an actor) leave (the stage): *At the end of the third scene the actress exits.* ○ (*joc*) *We exited from the party as soon as we could.* **2** (*3rd pers sing only*) (as a printed stage direction in plays) he or she leaves the stage: *Exit Macbeth.* Cf EXEUNT.

□ ˈ**exit poll** unofficial poll based on interviews with voters as they leave a polling station after voting.

Exmoor pony /ˌeksmɔː ˈpəʊnɪ/ small but strong breed of pony, originally from Exmoor, the high moorland area of *Somerset and *Devon, and often trained for children to ride.

exo- *comb form* external, outside or beyond: *exoskeleton*, ie external covering on an animal, eg the shell of a crab ○ *exogamous*, ie marrying outside one's religion, caste, etc.

exocrine gland /ˈeksəʊkraɪn glænd; *US* ˈeksəkrən/ gland that releases its secretion into a body cavity (such as the gut) or onto the body surface, eg the sweat glands or the mammary glands.

exodus /ˈeksədəs/ *n* **1** [sing] ~ **(from...)** **(to...)** (*fml or joc*) departure of many people at one time: *the mass exodus of people to the sea and mountains for the summer holidays* ○ *The play was so awful that there was a general exodus from the theatre at the interval.* **2** **the Exodus** [sing] the departure of the Israelites from Egypt, in about 1300 BC. **3** **Exodus** the second book of the Old Testament, telling the story of this departure. ⇨ App 5.

ex officio /ˌeks əˈfɪʃɪəʊ/ *adv, adj* (*Latin*) because of one's position, office or rank: *present at the meeting ex officio* ○ *an ex-officio member of the committee.*

exonerate /ɪgˈzɒnəreɪt/ *v* [esp passive: Tn, Tn·pr] ~ **sb (from sth)** declare sb free from blame: *He was exonerated from all responsibility for the accident.* ▷ **exoneration** /ɪgˌzɒnəˈreɪʃn/ *n* [U].

exorbitant /ɪgˈzɔːbɪtənt/ *adj* (*fml*) (of a price, charge, etc) much too high or great; unreasonable: *exorbitant rents* ○ *The price of food here is exorbitant.* ▷ **exorbitance** /-təns/ *n* [U] (*fml*). **exorbitantly** *adv*: *exorbitantly expensive.*

exorcize, -ise /ˈeksɔːsaɪz/ *v* [Tn, Tn·pr] ~ **sth (from sb/sth)** (*esp religion*) drive out or expel (an evil spirit) by prayers or magic: *A priest exorcized the ghost from the house.* ○ (*fig*) *We gradually exorcized her feelings of panic and terror.*

▷ **exorcism** /ˈeksɔːsɪzəm/ *n* [C, U] (instance of) exorcizing.

exorcist /ˈeksɔːsɪst/ *n* person who exorcizes.

exoskeleton /ˈeksəʊskelɪtn/ *n* hard external covering of the body in certain animals, eg the shell of a mollusc or the bony plates of a tortoise. Cf ENDOSKELETON.

exothermic /ˌeksəʊˈθɜːmɪk/ *adj* (of a chemical reaction) releasing heat into the surroundings. Cf ENDOTHERMIC.

exotic /ɪgˈzɒtɪk/ *adj* **1** introduced from another country; not native: *exotic houseplants* ○ *monkeys and other exotic animals* ○ *mangoes and other exotic fruits.* **2** striking or attractive because colourful or unusual: *exotic plumage* ○ *exotic clothes.*

exotica /ɪgˈzɒtɪkə/ *n* [pl] remarkably strange or rare objects.

expand /ɪkˈspænd/ *v* **1** [I, Ipr, Tn, Tn·pr] ~ **(sth) (into sth)** (cause sth to) become greater in size, number or importance: *Metals expand when they are heated.* ○ *A tyre expands when you pump air into it.* ○ *His modest business eventually expanded into a supermarket empire.* ○ *Our foreign trade has expanded greatly in recent years.* ○ *Why not try to expand your story into a novel?* **2** [I, Ipr] spread out; unfold: *The petals of the flowers expanded in the sunshine.* ○ *His face expanded in a smile of welcome.* Cf CONTRACT[3]. **3** [I] (of a person) become more friendly or talkative: *The guests expanded a little when they'd had a glass or two of wine.* **4** (phr v) **expand on sth** develop or give more of (a story, an argument, etc): *You mentioned the need for extra funding. Would you expand on that?*

□ **exˌpanded ˈmetal** sheet metal cut and stretched into a mesh used (esp) to reinforce concrete.

exˌpanded polyˈstyrene light packaging or insulation material made of air-filled plastic.

exˌpanding ˈuniverse the universe regarded as continually expanding so that the galaxies are moving further apart all the time.

expanse /ɪkˈspæns/ *n* ~ **(of sth)** wide and open area (of land, sea, etc): *the wide expanses of the Pacific* ○ *the blue expanses of the sky* ○ *a broad expanse of brow.*

expansion /ɪkˈspænʃn/ *n* [U] action of expanding (EXPAND 1); state of being expanded: *the expansion of gases when heated* ○ *the expansion of his business interests* ○ *the expansion of the school system.*

▷ **expansionism** /-ʃənɪzəm/ *n* [U] belief in, or practice of, expansion, esp of one's territory or business: *Expansionism was advocated by many British politicians in the late 19th century.* ○ *The owners of the firm feared the manager's vigorous expansionism.*

expansionist /-ʃənɪst/ *n* person who wishes esp a country or business to expand(1): [attrib] *Hitler's expansionist policies* ○ *expansionist business plans.*

expansive /ɪkˈspænsɪv/ *adj* **1** able or tending to expand: *He greeted us with an expansive gesture* (eg he stretched his arms wide) *and a wide smile.* **2** (of a person, his manner, etc) willing to talk a lot; unreserved: *an expansive after-dinner speaker* ○ *be in an expansive mood after a few drinks.* ▷ **expansively** *adv*. **expansiveness** *n* [U].

expatiate /ɪkˈspeɪʃɪeɪt/ *v* [Ipr] ~ **on/upon sth** (*fml*) write or speak at great length or in detail about a subject: *The chairman expatiated for two hours on his plans for the company.*

expatriate /ˌeksˈpætrɪət; *US* -ˈpeɪt-/ (also *Brit infml* **expat** /ˌeksˈpæt/) *n* person living outside his own country: *American expatriates in Paris* ○ [attrib] *expatriate Englishmen in Spain.*

▷ **expatriate** /-rɪeɪt/ *v* [Tn] cause (sb) to leave his native country; expel: *expatriated on suspicion of spying for the enemy.* **expatriation** /-ˈeɪʃn/ *n* [U].

expect /ɪkˈspekt/ *v* **1** **(a)** [Tn, Tn·pr, Tf, Tt, Tnt] ~ **sth (from sb/sth)** think or believe that sth will happen or that sb/sth will come: *This is the parcel which we have been expecting (from New York).* ○ *I expect (that) I will be back on Sunday.* ○ *You would expect that there would be/there to be strong disagreement about this.* ○ *You can't expect to learn a foreign language in a week.* ○ *We expected him to arrive yesterday.* **(b)** [Tn, Tn·pr] ~ **sth (from sb)** hope and feel confident that one will receive sth (from sb): *I was expecting a present from her, so I was disappointed I didn't receive one.* ○ *Don't expect any sympathy from me!* ⇨ Usage at WAIT[1]. **2** [Tn, Tn·pr, Tf, Tnt] ~ **sth (from sb)** require sth (from sb), esp as a right or duty: *The sergeant expects obedience from his men/that his men will obey him/his men to obey him.* ○ *I expect you to be punctual.* ○ *You will be expected to work on Saturdays.* **3** [Tn, Tf, Tt] (not in the continuous tenses) (*infml esp Brit*) suppose (sth); assume: *'Who has eaten all the cake?' 'Tom, I expect/I expect (that) it was Tom.'* ○ *'Will you need help?' 'I don't expect so.'* ○ *'Will he be late?' 'I expect so.'* **4** (idm) **be expecting (a baby/child)** (*infml euph*) be pregnant: *I hear Sally's expecting again.* **expect too ˈmuch (of sb)** believe or assume sb can do more than he can: *'I can't finish this job by Friday — you expect too much of me.'* **(only) to be exˈpected** likely to happen; quite normal: *A little tiredness after taking these drugs is to be expected.* ○ *It is only to be expected your son will leave home eventually.*

▷ **expectancy** /ɪkˈspektənsɪ/ *n* [U] state of expecting or hoping: *a look/feeling of expectancy* ○ *She went to meet him with an air of expectancy*, ie as if expecting him to bring sth. Cf LIFE EXPECTANCY (LIFE).

expectant /ɪkˈspektənt/ *adj* expecting (esp sth good); hopeful: (*fml*) *children with expectant faces waiting for the pantomime to start.* **expectantly** *adv*. **exˌpectant ˈmother** woman who is pregnant.

expected *adj* [usu attrib] that is expected: *expected objections to the plan.*

expectation /ˌekspekˈteɪʃn/ *n* **1** [U] ~ **(of sth)** firm belief that sth will happen; hope of gaining sth/that sth will happen: *There's no expectation of snow tonight.* ○ *The children waited patiently in expectation of* (ie expecting) *the magician* ○ *He has little expectation of winning a prize.* **2** [C usu *pl*] confident feelings (about sth): *His parents have great expectations for his future.* ○ *She had high expectations of what university had to offer.* ○ *The holiday was beyond all expectations*, ie better than was hoped for. **3** (idm) **aˌgainst/ˌcontrary to (all) expecˈtation(s)** quite different from what was expected: *a gold medal that was against all expectations.* ˌ**expectation of ˈlife** years a person is expected to live. **fall short of sb's/not come up to (sb's) expecˈtations** be less good than was expected: *Unfortunately the restaurant he recommended fell far short of our expectations.* ○ *His film performance didn't come up to expectations.*

expectorate /ɪkˈspektəreɪt/ *v* [I, Tn] (*fml or medical*) send out (phlegm from the throat, blood from the lungs) by coughing; spit: *In cases of tuberculosis blood is expectorated.*

▷ **expectorant** /-rənt/ *n* medicine that helps sb to expectorate: *The cough medicine contains an expectorant.*

expedient /ɪkˈspiːdɪənt/ *adj* [usu pred] (of an action) useful, helpful or advisable for a particular purpose, though not necessarily fair or moral: *Since there was soon to be a general election, the Prime Minister decided that a change of policy was politically expedient.* ○ *actions that were expedient rather than principled.*

▷ **expedience** /-əns/ (also **expediency** /-ənsɪ/) *n* [U] suitability or usefulness for a purpose, though not necessarily fair or moral: *He acted from expediency, not from principle.*

expedient *n* means of achieving an aim, which may not be fair or moral: *resort to various expedients to get the money together.*

expediently *adv*.

expedite /ˈekspɪdaɪt/ *v* [Tn] (*fml*) help the progress of (work, business, etc); hasten or speed up: *Please do what you can to expedite the building work.*

expedition /ˌekspɪˈdɪʃn/ *n* **1** (**a**) organized journey or voyage with a particular aim: *send a party of people on an expedition* ○ *go on an expedition to the North Pole* ○ *a hunting expedition* ○ (*joc*) *a shopping expedition*. (**b**) people, vehicles, ships, etc making this journey: *members of the Mount Everest expedition*. **2** (*fml*) speed; promptness: *We carried out the captain's orders with all possible expedition*.
▷ **expeditionary** /-ʃənərɪ; *US* -nerɪ/ *adj* [attrib] of or forming an expedition: *an expeditionary force*, eg an army sent to take part in a war abroad.

expeditious /ˌekspɪˈdɪʃəs/ *adj* (*fml*) done with speed and efficiency: *an expeditious response*. ▷ **expeditiously** *adv*: *We will carry out the enquiry as expeditiously as possible*.

expel /ɪkˈspel/ *v* (**-ll-**) [Tn, Tn·pr] ~ **sb** (**from sth**) **1** force (sb) to leave (esp a country, school or club): *Following reports of drug-taking at a boarding-school, several senior boys have been expelled*. ○ *Two attachés at the embassy were expelled from the country*. **2** send or drive (sth) out by force: *expel smoke from the lungs* ○ *a fan in the kitchen for expelling cooking smells*.

expend /ɪkˈspend/ *v* [Tn, Tn·pr] ~ **sth** (**on/upon sth/doing sth**) (*fml*) **1** spend, use (money, etc) in doing sth: *expend time, effort and money on a project*. **2** use (sth) up; exhaust: *expend all one's ammunition, stores, fuel*.
▷ **expendable** *adj* (*fml*) that may be consumed, destroyed, etc to achieve a purpose: *In the Great War soldiers were considered expendable*. ○ *In these conservation-conscious times, areas of grassland are no longer expendable*.

expenditure /ɪkˈspendɪtʃə(r)/ *n* **1** [U] action of spending or using: *the expenditure of money on weapons* ○ *expenditure of energy on a project*. **2** [C, U] amount (esp of money) spent: *an expenditure of £500 on new furniture* ○ *Limit your expenditure(s) to what is essential*. Cf RECEIPT 3.

expense /ɪkˈspens/ *n* **1** (**a**) [U] spending of money etc; cost: *an expense of time, energy and cash* ○ *He hired a plane, regardless of expense*. ○ *Most children in Britain are educated at public expense*. (**b**) [C] cause of spending: *An annual holiday is a big expense*. ○ *Running a car is a great expense*. **2 expenses** [pl] money spent in doing a specific job, or for a specific purpose: *travelling expenses* ○ *House repairs, holidays and other expenses reduced her bank balance to almost nothing*. ○ *Who's meeting the expenses of your trip?* **3** (idm) **at sb's expense** (**a**) with sb paying: *We were entertained at the editor's expense*. (**b**) at sb who has behaved foolishly, been tricked, etc: *They had a good laugh* (ie were very amused) *at Sam's expense*. **at great, little, no, etc exˈpense** (**to sb/oneself**) with a lot of, little, no, etc money being spent (by sb/oneself): *We can redecorate the room at little expense, if we use this old paint*. **at the expense of sth** with loss or damage to sth: *He built up a successful business but it was all done at the expense of his health*. (**all**) **expenses ˈpaid** with an employer, etc paying for everything: [attrib] *She's just returned from an all-expenses-paid trip to France*. **go to/put sb to the expense of sth/doing sth** spend/cause sb to spend money on sth: *It's stupid to go to the expense of taking music lessons if you never practise*. ○ *put sb to a lot of expense*. **no expense(s) ˈspared** with no regard for the cost: *I'm going to take you out to dinner, no expense spared*. **spare no expense** ⇨ SPARE.
□ **exˈpense account** record of money spent by an employee in the course of his work (and later paid by his employer): *Whenever he buys petrol, he puts it on his expense account*.

expensive /ɪkˈspensɪv/ *adj* costing a lot (of money): *an expensive car* ○ *Houses are very expensive in this area*. ○ *It's too expensive for me to buy*. ▷ **expensively** *adv*: *an expensively dressed lady*.

experience /ɪkˈspɪərɪəns/ *n* **1** [U] (process of gaining) knowledge or skill acquired from seeing and doing things: *We all learn by experience*. ○ *Does she have much experience of teaching?* ○ *He hasn't had enough work experience* (ie experience of work) *for the job*. ○ *I know from experience that he'll arrive late*. **2** [C] event or activity that affects one in some way; event or activity that has given one experience(1): *an unpleasant, a trying, an unusual, etc experience* ○ *You must try some of her home-made wine — it's quite an experience!* ie it's very unusual. ○ *He had many interesting experiences while travelling in Africa*.
▷ **experience** *v* [Tn] have experience of (sth); feel: *experience pleasure, pain, difficulty, great hardships, etc* ○ *The child had never experienced kindness*. ○ *I don't think I've ever experienced real depression*. **experienced** *adj* having experience; having knowledge or skill as a result of experience: *an experienced nurse* ○ *He's experienced in looking after children*.
experiential /ɪkˌspɪərɪˈenʃl/ *adj* (*fml*) of or based on experience: *experiential philosophy*, ie treating all knowledge as based on experience.

experiment /ɪkˈsperɪmənt/ *n* [C, U] (esp scientific) test or trial done carefully in order to study what happens and gain new knowledge: *perform/carry out/conduct an experiment* ○ *The researchers are repeating the experiment on rats*. ○ *prove a theory by experiment* ○ *learn by experiment* ○ (*fig*) *The play was staged as an experiment*.
▷ **experiment** *v* [I, Ipr] ~ (**on/upon sb/sth**); ~ (**with sth**) make an experiment: *We experimented until we succeeded in mixing the right colour*. ○ *experiment upon animals* ○ *experiment with new methods*.
experimentation /ɪkˌsperɪmenˈteɪʃn/ *n* [U] (*fml*) activity, process or practice of experimenting: *Many people object to experimentation on animals*. ○ [attrib] *experimentation methods*.

experimental /ɪkˌsperɪˈmentl/ *adj* of, used for, using or based on experiments: *experimental methods* ○ *an experimental farm* ○ *an experimental physicist* ○ *experimental theatre* ○ *The technique is still at the experimental stage. It hasn't been fully developed yet*. ▷ **experimentally** /-təlɪ/ *adv*: *We are using the substance experimentally at first*.

expert /ˈekspɜːt/ *n* ~ (**at/in/on sth/doing sth**) person with special knowledge, skill or training in a particular field: *an agricultural expert* ○ *an expert in psychology* ○ *get the advice of the experts* ○ *an expert at playing golf* ○ *an expert on ancient Greek vases*.
▷ **expert** *adj* ~(**at/in sth/doing sth**) done with, having, or involving great knowledge or skill: *according to expert advice* ○ *an expert rider* ○ *an expert job* ○ *He's expert at/in cooking good cheap meals*. **expertly** *adv*. **expertness** *n* [U]: *The expertness of her driving surprised him*.

expertise /ˌekspɜːˈtiːz/ *n* [U] expert knowledge or skill, esp in a particular field: *Customers will be impressed by the expertise of our highly trained employees*. ○ *We were amazed at his expertise on the ski slopes*.

expiate /ˈekspɪeɪt/ *v* [Tn] (*fml*) accept punishment for (wrong one has done) and do something to show one is sorry; make up for: *expiate one's sin/a crime/one's guilt*. ▷ **expiation** /ˌekspɪˈeɪʃn/ *n* [U] (*fml*): *large sums paid to the family in expiation of the wrongs done to them*.

expire /ɪkˈspaɪə(r)/ *v* [I] **1** (of sth that lasts a period of time) come to an end; become no longer in use: *Our present lease on the flat expires next month*. ○ *When does your driving licence expire?* **2** (*esp medical*) breathe out (air). **3** (*dated fml*) die.
▷ **expiration** /ˌekspɪˈreɪʃn/ *n* [U] (*fml*) **1** ending, esp of the period when a contract, etc is in force: *the expiration of the lease, tenancy, agreement, contract, etc*. **2** (*esp medical*) breathing out (of air).

expiry /ɪkˈspaɪərɪ/ *n* ~ (**of sth**) ending, esp of the period when a contract or agreement is in force: *the expiry of a driving licence, a lease, a credit card, a contract, an agreement, etc* ○ [attrib] *the expiry date*.

explain /ɪkˈspleɪn/ *v* **1** [Tn, Tw, Dn·pr] ~ **sth** (**to sth**) make sth plain or clear; give the meaning of sth: *A dictionary explains the meaning of words*. ○ *He explained his plan in some detail*. ○ *Could you explain why you left?* ○ *Please explain this problem to me*. **2** [Tn, Tf, Tw, Dn·pr, Dpr·f, Dpr·w] ~ **sth** (**to sb**) give or be a reason for sth; account for sth: *That explains his absence*. ○ *He explained that hi train had been delayed*. ○ *They explained what ha happened*. ○ *She explained her conduct to her boss* ○ *She explained to the children that the school ha been closed*. ○ *The manager has explained t customers why the goods were late*. **3** (idm **exˈplain oneself** (**a**) make one's meaning clear: *don't understand your argument. Could yo explain yourself a bit more?* (**b**) give reasons fo one's behaviour: *In recent weeks you've been lat every day. Please explain yourself*. **4** (phr v **explain sth away** give excuses why one shoul not be blamed for (a fault, mistake, etc) or why st is not important: *You will find it difficult to explai away your use of such offensive language*. ○ *H explained away his late arrival by blaming it on th crowded roads*.

explanation /ˌekspləˈneɪʃn/ *n* **1** [U] (process of explaining: *He left the room without explanation*. ○ *I should say a few words (by way) of explanation*. ○ *Had he anything to say in explanation of hi behaviour?* **2** [C] statement, fact, circumstance etc that explains sth: *That's not an adequat explanation*. ○ *a satisfactory explanation of th mystery* ○ *His explanations are always difficult t believe*.

explanatory /ɪkˈsplænətrɪ; *US* -tɔːrɪ/ *adj* [usu attrib] giving, serving or intended as ar explanation: *explanatory notes at the back of book*.

expletive /ɪkˈspliːtɪv; *US* ˈeksplətɪv/ *n* (*fml*) violen (often meaningless) exclamation said in anger pain, etc; swear-word: *'Damn!' is an expletive*. ○ *H uttered several vigorous expletives when he droppe the iron on his foot*.

explicable /ɪkˈsplɪkəbl, *also* ˈeksplɪkəbl/ *adj* (*fml* that can be explained: *His behaviour is explicabl in the light of his recent illness*. ○ *Scientists ha maintained that the crop failure was not explicable*

explicate /ˈeksplɪkeɪt/ *v* [Tn] (*fml*) explain an analyse (esp an idea, a statement or a work o literature) in detail: *explicate one's moral values*.

explicit /ɪkˈsplɪsɪt/ *adj* **1** (**a**) (of a statement, etc clearly and fully expressed: *He gave me explici directions on how to get there*. ○ *They gave explici reasons for leaving*. (**b**) (of a person) saying st clearly, exactly and openly: *She was quite explici about why she left*. **2** with nothing hidden o implied: *explicit sex scenes in the film*. ▷ **explicitl** *adv*: *She was explicitly forbidden to attend*. **explicitness** *n* [U].

explode /ɪkˈspləʊd/ *v* **1** [I, Tn] (cause sth to) burs with a loud noise; blow up: *When the boile exploded many people were injured*. ○ *The firewor exploded in his hand*. ○ *explode a bomb*. Cf IMPLODE **2** [I, Ipr] (**a**) (of feelings) burst out suddenly: *At las his anger exploded*. (**b**) ~ (**with/in/into sth**) (o people) show sudden violent emotion: *He explode with rage, fury, jealousy, etc*. ○ *She exploded int loud laughter*. **3** [I] (of a population, etc) increas suddenly or quickly: *the exploding worl population*. **4** [Tn] destroy (a theory, an idea, etc by showing it to be false: *explode a superstition* ○ *The myth that eating carrots improves you eyesight was exploded years ago*.
□ **exˌploded ˈdiagram** diagram showing the part of a structure in their relative positions bu slightly separated from each other.

exploit[1] /ˈeksplɔɪt/ *n* [C] brave or adventurou deed or action: *The daring exploits of th parachutists were much admired*. ○ (*joc*) *I'm no interested in hearing about Bill's amorous exploits* ⇨ Usage at ACT[1].

exploit[2] /ɪkˈsplɔɪt/ *v* [Tn] **1** use, work or develo fully (esp mines and other natural resources) *exploit oil reserves, water power, solar energy, etc* **2** use (sb/sth) selfishly and unfairly for one's ow advantage or profit: *child labour exploited i factories* ○ *exploit a situation for one's ow advantage* ○ *They exploited her generosit shamelessly*.
▷ **exploitable** *adj* that can be exploited: *feu exploitable coal-mines*.
exploitation /ˌeksplɔɪˈteɪʃn/ *n* [U] exploiting o being exploited: *full exploitation of oil wells* ○ *th*

exploitation of child labour.

explore /ɪkˈsplɔ:(r)/ *v* **1** [I, Tn] travel into or through (a place, esp a country) in order to learn about it: *explore the Arctic regions* ○ *Columbus discovered America but did not explore the new continent.* ○ *explore a castle* ○ *As soon as they arrived in the town they went out to explore.*

Historical explorations have always been linked with romance and adventure. Explorers in British history, such as Sir Francis *Drake, Captain James *Cook, David *Livingstone and Sir Henry Morton *Stanley have often been portrayed in rather heroic terms, as brave, strong men whose continuous quest for knowledge and strong spirit of adventure took them to remote and dangerous places.

2 [Tn] examine (sth) thoroughly in order to test or find out about it: *explore one's conscience* ○ *We explored several solutions to the problem.*

▷ **exploration** /ˌekspləˈreɪʃn/ *n* **1** [U] activity of exploring: *the exploration of space* ○ *a voyage of exploration* ○ *detailed exploration of a subject.* **2** [C] instance of this: *in the course of his explorations of the country* ○ *an exploration of the subconscious mind.*

exploratory /ɪkˈsplɒrətrɪ; *US* -tɔ:rɪ/ *adj* for the purpose of finding out sth: *exploratory medical tests* ○ *an exploratory expedition up the Amazon river.*

explorer /ɪkˈsplɔ:rə(r)/ *n* person who explores (EXPLORE 1): *Christopher Columbus was one of the great explorers.*

explosion /ɪkˈspləʊʒn/ *n* **1** (**a**) (loud noise caused by) sudden and violent bursting; exploding: *a bomb explosion* ○ *gas explosions* ○ *The explosion was heard a mile away.* (**b**) sudden outburst (of anger, laughter, etc): *an explosion of rage.* **2** great and sudden increase: *a population explosion* ○ *the explosion of oil prices.*

explosive /ɪkˈspləʊsɪv/ *adj* **1** likely or easily able to explode: *an explosive mixture of chemicals* ○ *explosive materials* ○ *Hydrogen is highly explosive.* **2** that arouses strong feelings or leads to violent outbursts: *an explosive situation, issue* ○ *Politics can be an explosive subject.* ○ *an explosive temper.*

▷ **explosive** *n* [C] substance that is likely or able to explode: *Dynamite is an explosive.* ○ *The bomb was packed with high explosive,* ie a substance that explodes with great force.

explosively *adv.*

exponent /ɪkˈspəʊnənt/ *n* **1** person or thing that explains and supports a theory, belief, cause, etc: *an exponent of free trade* ○ *Huxley was an exponent of Darwin's theory of evolution.* **2** person able to perform skilfully a particular activity: *the most famous exponent of mime* ○ *She's a practised exponent of the sport of water-skiing.* **3** (*mathematics*) figure or symbol that shows the power to which a quantity is raised: *In* $a^3 = a \times a \times a$, *the figure* ^{3} *is the exponent.* ○ *In* x^n, *the symbol* ^{n} *is the exponent.*

▷ **exponential** /ˌekspəʊˈnenʃl/ *adj* (*mathematics*) **1** of or indicated by an exponent(3): 2^4 *is an exponential expression.* **2** produced or indicated by multiplying a set of numbers by themselves: *an exponential increase* ○ *an exponential equation* ○ *an exponential curve,* eg on a graph indicating population increase. **exponentially** /-ʃəlɪ/ *adv*: *increase exponentially.*

□ ˌ**exponential** ˈ**function** (*mathematics*) function that varies as the power of another quantity.

ˌ**exponential** ˈ**growth** form of population growth in which the rate of growth is related to the number of individuals present.

export[1] /ˈekspɔ:t/ *n* **1** [U] (business or action of) exporting: *a ban on the export of gold* ○ [attrib] *an* ˈ*export licence* ○ *the* ˈ*export trade* ○ ˈ*export duties,* ie tax paid on exported goods. **2** [C usu *pl*] thing exported: *Last year's exports exceeded imports in value.* ○ *What are the chief exports of Botswana?* Cf IMPORT[2].

export[2] /ɪkˈspɔ:t/ *v* [I, Tn] send (goods) to another country for sale: *This company has a large home market* (ie many buyers within the country) *but doesn't export.* ○ *India exports tea and cotton to many different countries.* Cf IMPORT[1].

▷ **exportation** /ˌekspɔ:ˈteɪʃn/ *n* [U] exporting of goods: *articles for exportation abroad* ○ *He manufactures paper for exportation only.*

exporter *n* person, company or country that exports goods: *Argentina is a big exporter of beef products.* ○ *He is a successful exporter of diamonds.*

expose /ɪkˈspəʊz/ *v* **1** [Tn, Tn·pr] (**a**) uncover or make (sth) visible; display: *When he smiled he exposed a set of perfect white teeth.* (**b**) ~ **sth/sb/oneself** (**to sth**) uncover or leave sb/sth/oneself uncovered or unprotected: *The soil was washed away by the flood, exposing bare rock.* ○ *expose soldiers to unnecessary risks* ○ *expose one's skin to the sun* ○ *The baby was left exposed to the wind and rain.* ○ (*fig*) *expose oneself to criticism, ridicule, mockery, etc.* **2** [Tn] (**a**) make known (sth secret); reveal: *expose a plot, project, plan, etc* ○ *That unfortunate remark exposed his ignorance of the subject.* (**b**) make known (the guilt or wrongdoing) of (a secretly guilty person): *expose crime, scandal, injustice, fraud, etc* ○ *expose a criminal, an impostor, a culprit, etc.* **3** [Tn, Tn·pr] (in photography) allow light to reach (film, etc): *expose a reel of film.* **4** [Tn] ~ **oneself** indecently show one's sexual organs in public: *An old man was arrested for exposing himself to young children.*

▷ **exposed** *adj* (of a place) not sheltered (from wind, weather, etc): *The cottage is in a very exposed position at the top of the hill.*

exposé /ekˈspəʊzeɪ; *US* ˌekspəˈzeɪ/ *n* **1** short statement of a number of facts or beliefs. **2** account of the facts of a situation, esp when these are shocking or have been kept deliberately secret: *The newspaper published an exposé of the film star's past life.* ○ *an exposé of corruption within the government.*

exposition /ˌekspəˈzɪʃn/ *n* (*fml*) **1** (**a**) [U] explaining or making clear by giving details. (**b**) [C] instance of this; explanation of a theory, plan, etc: *an exposition of the advantages of nuclear power.* **2** [C] exhibition of goods, etc: *an industrial exposition.* **3** [C] (*music*) part of a composition in sonata form in which the main themes are first presented.

ex post facto /ˌeks pəʊst ˈfæktəʊ/ *adj, adv* (*Latin*) retrospective(ly): *an ex post facto law* ○ *The law applies ex post facto.*

expostulate /ɪkˈspɒstʃʊleɪt/ *v* [I, Ipr] ~ (**with sb**) (**on/about sth**) (*fml*) make a protest (to sb); reason or argue (with sb), esp to persuade him not to do sth: *They expostulated with him about the risks involved in his plan.*

▷ **expostulation** /ɪkˌspɒstʃʊˈleɪʃn/ *n* [U, C] (making a) protest; reasoned persuasion, etc: *My expostulation(s) had no effect.*

exposure /ɪkˈspəʊʒə(r)/ *n* **1** [U] action of exposing or state of being exposed: *Exposure of the body to strong sunlight can be harmful.* ○ *The baby died of exposure,* ie as a result of being exposed to the weather. ○ *the exposure of his ignorance* ○ *The exposure of the plot against the President probably saved his life.* ○ *The exposure of photographic film to light.* **2** [C] instance of exposing or being exposed (EXPOSE 2b, 3): *As a result of these exposures* (ie facts being made known to the public) *several ministers resigned from the government.* ○ *An exposure of one-hundredth of a second will be enough,* ie Exposing the film for that length of time will make a good picture. ○ *How many exposures have you got left?* ie How many pictures remain on the camera film? **3** [U] publicity (on television, in newspapers, etc): *Her new film has had a lot of exposure on television recently.*

□ **ex**ˈ**posure meter** (also **light meter**) device to measure illumination and to indicate how long a film should be exposed to light.

expound /ɪkˈspaʊnd/ *v* [Tn, Tn·pr] ~ **sth** (**to sb**) (*fml*) explain or make sth clear by giving details: *expound a theory* ○ *He expounded his views on education to me at great length.*

express[1] /ɪkˈspres/ *adj* **1** going, sent or delivered quickly: *express delivery* ○ *an express letter* ○ *an express messenger.* **2** clearly and definitely stated; explicit: *It was his express wish that you have his gold watch after he died.*

▷ **express** *adv* by express delivery; by express train: *The parcel was sent express.* ○ *travel express.*

expressly *adv* **1** clearly; definitely: *You were expressly told not to touch my papers.* **2** with a special purpose: *a dictionary expressly compiled for foreign students of English.*

□ **ex**ˈ**pressway** (also ˈ**throughway**) *n* (*US*) = MOTORWAY: *a major accident on the expressway.* ⇨ Usage at ROAD.

express[2] /ɪkˈspres/ *n* **1** [C] (also **ex**ˈ**press train**) fast train that stops at few stations: *the 8.00 am express to Edinburgh.* **2** [C] (*US*) company that delivers goods quickly. **3** [U] service provided by the post office, railways, road services, etc for carrying goods quickly: *send goods by express.*

express[3] /ɪkˈspres/ *v* **1** [Tn, Tw, Dn·pr, Dpr·w] ~ **sth** (**to sb**) show or make known (a feeling, an opinion, etc) by words, looks, actions, etc: *The guests expressed their thanks before leaving.* ○ *His actions express his love more than any words could do.* ○ *He could not express his feelings of sadness to his mother.* ○ *I can't express to you how grateful I am for your help.* **2** [Tn] ~ **oneself** speak or write (clearly) what one thinks, feels, etc: *Learning to express oneself well is an important part of education.* ○ *He is still unable to express himself in English.* **3** [Tn, Tn·pr] ~ **sth** (**from/out of sth**) (*fml*) press or squeeze out (esp juices or oil): *juice expressed from grapes* ○ *milk expressed from a mother's breast.* **4** [Tn] (*Brit*) send (a letter, parcel, etc) fast by special delivery.

▷ **expressible** /ɪkˈspresəbl/ *adj* that can be expressed: *feelings not expressible in words.*

expression /ɪkˈspreʃn/ *n* **1** (**a**) [U] action or process of expressing (EXPRESS[3] 1): *She gave expression to her sadness,* ie said or showed how sad she was. ○ *The school encourages free expression in art, drama and creative writing.* ○ *The scenery was beautiful beyond expression,* ie too beautiful to describe. ○ *The poet's anger finds expression* (ie a means of expressing itself) *in the last line of the poem.* (**b**) [C] (*fml*) instance or example of this: *expressions of welcome to the queen* ○ *They greeted the president with many expressions of pleasure.* **2** [C] look on a person's face that shows a mood or feeling: *a happy expression* ○ *'I don't understand,' he said, with an expression of complete surprise (on his face).* **3** [U] showing feeling for the meaning when playing music or speaking: *recite a poem with expression* ○ *She puts great expression into her violin playing.* **4** [C] word or phrase: *'Shut up' (meaning 'Stop talking') is not a polite expression.* ○ *slang expressions.* **5** [C] (*mathematics*) group of symbols expressing a quantity: $3xy^2$ *is a mathematical expression.*

▷ **expressionless** *adj* not showing feelings, thoughts, etc: *an expressionless face, voice, tone, etc* ○ *His recitation was almost expressionless.*

expressionism /ɪkˈspreʃənɪzəm/ *n* [U] style of painting, music, drama, film, etc which tries to express the artist's or writer's emotional experience rather than to show the physical world in a realistic way. The term ˈexpressionismˈ was first used in the early 20th century of painters who used violent colour and linear distortions. Its influence on poetry and the theatre was particularly noticeable in Germany in the years after 1910, and in the German cinema of that period. Its style was typically satirical, grotesque, visionary, exclamatory, violent, but always anti-naturalistic. ▷ **expressionist** /-ʃənɪst/ *adj, n*: *of the expressionist school* ○ *an expressionist film* ○ *He's an expressionist.*

expressive /ɪkˈspresɪv/ *adj* **1** showing one's feelings or thoughts: *an expressive face, gesture* ○ *an expressive piece of music.* **2** [pred] ~ **of sth** (*fml*) expressing sth: *a cry expressive of pain* ○ *a look expressive of despair.* ▷ **expressively** *adv*: *He reads his poems very expressively.* **expressiveness** *n* [U].

expropriate /eksˈprəʊprɪeɪt/ *v* [Tn, Tn·pr] (*fml or*

law) **1** ~ **sth (from sb)** (**a**) take away (property, etc) for public use without payment to the owner: *The new government expropriated his estate for military purposes.* (**b**) ~ **sb (of sth)** dispossess sb in this way: *She was expropriated (of her land).* **2** ~ **sth (from sb/sth)** take away (property, money, etc) illegally from the owners for one's own use: *He expropriated the jewels from the bank's safe.* ▷ **expropriation** /ˌeksˌprəʊprɪˈeɪʃn/ *n* [U, C].

expulsion /ɪkˈspʌlʃn/ *n* ~ (**from...**) **1** [U] action of expelling or being expelled: *Expulsion from school is a harsh form of punishment.* ○ [attrib] *an expulsion order*, ie an official order expelling a person from a country. **2** [C] instance of this: *There have been three expulsions from the school this year.*

expunge /ɪkˈspʌndʒ/ *v* [Tn, Tn·pr] ~ **sth (from sth)** (*fml*) remove or wipe out (words, names, etc) from a list, book, etc: *Her name was expunged from the list.* ○ (*fig*) *He could not expunge the incident from his memory.*

expurgate /ˈekspəgeɪt/ *v* [Tn] remove (what are considered to be) improper or objectionable parts from (a book, etc): *an expurgated edition of a novel.* ▷ **expurgation** /ˌekspəˈgeɪʃn/ *n* [C, U].

exquisite /ˈekskwɪzɪt, *also* ɪkˈskwɪzɪt/ *adj* **1** extremely beautiful or delicate; finely or skilfully made or done: *(an) exquisite painting* ○ *exquisite workmanship* ○ *an exquisite piece of lace.* **2** (*fml*) (**a**) (of emotion) strongly felt; acute: *exquisite joy, happiness, etc* ○ *exquisite pain, agony, etc.* (**b**) (of power to feel) delicate; sensitive: *exquisite taste* ○ *exquisite sensibility.* ▷ **exquisitely** *adv.* **exquisiteness** *n* [U].

ex-service /ˌeksˈsɜːvɪs/ *adj* formerly belonging to the armed forces.

□ **ex-serviceman** /-mən/ (*pl* **-men** /-mən/), **ex-servicewoman** /-wʊmən/ (*pl* **-women** /-wɪmɪn/) *n* (*esp Brit*) person who was formerly in one of the armed services: *an ex-servicemen's organization.*

ext *abbr* **1** extension (number) (eg of a telephone): *ext 4299.* **2** exterior; external. Cf INT 1.

extant /ekˈstænt; *US* ˈekstənt/ *adj* (esp of documents, etc) still in existence: *the earliest extant manuscript of this poem* ○ *an ancient but extant law.*

extemporaneous /ekˌstempəˈreɪnɪəs/ *adj* (*fml*) spoken or done without preparation; extempore. ▷ **extemporaneously** *adv.*

extempore /ekˈstempərɪ/ *adj, adv* (spoken or done) without previous thought or preparation; impromptu: *an extempore speech* ○ *speak extempore*, ie without notes.

▷ **extemporize, -ise** /ɪkˈstempəraɪz/ *v* [I] (*fml*) speak or perform extempore: *He had to extemporize because he had forgotten to bring his notes.* **extemporization, -isation** /ɪkˌstempəraɪˈzeɪʃn; *US* -rɪˈz-/ *n* [U, C].

extend /ɪkˈstend/ *v* **1** [Tn] make (sth) longer or larger (in space or time): *extend a fence, wall, railway, garden* ○ *extend credit*, ie prolong the time for payment of a debt ○ *Can you extend your visit a few days longer?* **2** [Tn, Tn·pr] lay or stretch out (the body or a limb) at full length: *The gymnast extended her arms horizontally.* ○ *The bird extended its wings in flight.* ○ *He extended his hand to* (ie offered to shake hands with) *the new employee.* **3** [Tn, Dn·n, Dn·pr] ~ **sth (to sb)** offer or give sth: *They extended the Queen a warm welcome.* ○ *extend hospitality, an invitation, a greeting to sb* ○ *They extended a warm welcome to her.* **4** [In/pr] (of space, land, time, etc) reach or stretch; be continuous: *The road extends for miles and miles.* ○ *My garden extends as far as the river.* **5** [Tn, Tn·pr] cause (sth) to reach or stretch: *extend the ladder* ○ *extend a cable between two posts.* **6** [Tn esp passive] use or stretch the abilities or powers of (oneself, a person or an animal) to the greatest possible degree: *Jim didn't really have to extend himself in the examination.* ○ *The horse was fully extended by the long ride up the mountain.*

□ **exˌtended ˈfamily** family structure (as in parts of Africa) where uncles, aunts and cousins are regarded as close relatives, with an obligation to help and support each other.

extension /ɪkˈstenʃn/ *n* **1** [U] process or action of extending (EXTEND 1,2,3); state of being extended: *The extension of the garden will take several weeks.* ○ *the extension of scientific knowledge* ○ *the extension of a warm welcome.* **2** [C] (**a**) ~ (**to sth**) added part; addition; enlargement: *build an extension to a hospital* ○ *Our extension is nearly finished.* (**b**) ~ (**of sth**) additional period of time: *an extension of one's summer holidays* ○ *get an extension (of time)*, eg for paying a debt ○ *He's got an extension to finish writing his thesis.* **3** [C] telephone line leading from the main phone or switchboard to another room or office in a (large) building; its number: *There are telephone extensions in every office.* ○ *She has an extension in the kitchen and in the bedroom.* ○ *'Extension 326, please.'* **4** [U] (*medical or fml*) (**a**) action of stretching out a limb or finger: *Extension of the injured arm was painful.* (**b**) its position when stretched out: *The leg is now at full extension.*

extensive /ɪkˈstensɪv/ *adj* **1** large in area; extending far: *an extensive view* ○ *extensive farming* ○ *the extensive grounds of a country house.* **2** large in amount; wide-ranging: *extensive alterations to a building* ○ *Her knowledge of the subject is extensive.* **3** (of agriculture) using large areas of land with relatively little cost or labour. Cf INTENSIVE. ▷ **extensively** *adv*: *He has travelled extensively in Europe.* **extensiveness** *n* [U] (*fml*): *The extensiveness of his knowledge surprised them.*

extent /ɪkˈstent/ *n* **1** [U] length; area; range: *From the roof we could see the full extent of the park.* ○ *I was amazed at the extent of his knowledge.* ○ *The new race-track is nearly six miles in extent.* **2** (idm) **to some, what, such an, a certain, etc extent** to the degree specified: *To some extent you are correct.* ○ *To what extent can he be believed?* ○ *The carpet was badly stained, to such an extent that* (ie so much that) *you couldn't tell its original colour.* ○ *I agree with you to a certain extent, but...* ○ *He's in debt to the extent of £200.*

extenuate /ɪkˈstenjʊeɪt/ *v* [Tn] (*fml esp law*) make (wrongdoing) less serious (by providing an excuse): *Nothing can extenuate such appalling behaviour.* ○ *Because of extenuating circumstances* (ie facts taken into consideration that might be regarded as an excuse), *the court acquitted him of the crime.*

▷ **extenuation** /ɪkˌstenjʊˈeɪʃn/ *n* (*fml*) [U] action of extenuating; being extenuated: *He pleaded poverty in extenuation of* (ie as an excuse for) *the theft.*

exterior /ɪkˈstɪərɪə(r)/ *adj* [usu attrib] on or coming from the outside; outer: *paint the exterior walls of a house* ○ *exterior features of a building.* Cf INTERIOR.

▷ **exterior** *n* **1** [sing] outward appearance or surface; outside: *The exterior of the building is very unattractive.* ○ *a gentle man with a rough exterior.* **2** [C] scene set outside in a painting or play.

exterminate /ɪkˈstɜːmɪneɪt/ *v* [Tn] destroy completely (a race or group of people or animals); wipe out: *exterminate all the inhabitants of the village* ○ *exterminate rats to prevent the spread of disease.* ▷ **extermination** /ɪkˌstɜːmɪˈneɪʃn/ *n* [U].

external /ɪkˈstɜːnl/ *adj* **1** (of or for the) outside; situated on the outside of sth (esp the body): *for external use only*, eg on a label on a skin cream ○ *All his injuries are external*, ie He hasn't been injured inside the body. **2** coming from outside (a place, sb's mind, etc): *a tribe hardly affected by external influences* ○ *This news programme only covers external events*, ie foreign news. Cf INTERNAL.

▷ **external** *n* **1** [C] (*infml*) = EXTERNAL EXAMINER. **2 externals** [pl] (*fml*) outward features or appearances: *Do not judge people by externals alone.* ○ *the externals of religion*, ie acts and ceremonies (contrasted with inner and spiritual aspects).

externalize, -ise /-nəlaɪz/ *v* [Tn] (*fml*) make (sth) external: *externalize one's thoughts, emotions, etc.*

externally /ɪkˈstɜːnəlɪ/ *adv.*

□ **exˌternal ˈevidence** evidence obtained from independent sources, not from what is being examined.

exˌternal examiˈnation examination arranged by authorities outside the school, college, etc of the person(s) taking the examination.

exˌternal eˈxaminer (also **external**) person who conducts an external examination.

extinct /ɪkˈstɪŋkt/ *adj* **1** (esp of a type of animal, etc) no longer in existence: *an extinct species* ○ *If we continue to destroy the countryside many more animals will become extinct.* **2** (**a**) (of a volcano) no longer active. (**b**) (*fig rhet*) (of feelings, beliefs, etc) dead: *Nothing could rekindle her extinct passion.*

extinction /ɪkˈstɪŋkʃn/ *n* [U] **1** action of making extinct; state of being extinct: *We may live to see the extinction of the whale.* ○ *a tribe threatened by/with extinction.* **2** (*fml*) act of extinguishing: *the extinction of a fire, a political movement, youthful hopes.*

extinguish /ɪkˈstɪŋgwɪʃ/ *v* [Tn] **1** (**a**) cause (sth) to stop burning; put out: *Please extinguish your cigarettes.* ○ *They tried to extinguish the flames.* (**b**) (*fig fml*) end the existence of (hope, love, passion, etc): *His behaviour extinguished the last traces of affection she had for him.* **2** clear or pay off (a debt). ▷ **extinguisher** *n* = FIRE EXTINGUISHER (FIRE).

extirpate /ˈekstəpeɪt/ *v* [Tn] (*fml*) remove or destroy (sth) completely: *extirpate social evils* ○ *extirpate dissent, opposition, etc.* ▷ **extirpation** /ˌekstəˈpeɪʃn/ *n* [U].

extol /ɪkˈstəʊl/ *v* (**-ll-**) [Tn, Tn·pr, Cn·n/a] (*fml*) praise (sb/sth) highly: *extol the merits of small businesses* ○ *extol sb's virtues to the skies*, ie greatly ○ *extol sb as a hero.*

extort /ɪkˈstɔːt/ *v* [Tn, Tn·pr] ~ **sth (from sb)** obtain sth by violence, threats, etc: *extort money from sb* ○ *The police used torture to extort a confession from him.*

▷ **extortion** /ɪkˈstɔːʃn/ *n* **1** [U] action of extorting: *obtain money by extortion.* **2** [C] instance of this. **extortioner** /-ʃənə(r)/, **extortionist** /-ʃənɪst/ *ns* person who extorts: [attrib] *extortionist methods.*

extortionate /ɪkˈstɔːʃənət/ *adj* (*derog*) (of demands, prices) much too great or high; excessive: *The prices in this shop are extortionate.* ○ *They are asking an extortionate amount of money for their house.* ▷ **extortionately** *adv*: *They charged me extortionately for a simple job.*

extra /ˈekstrə/ *adj* more than or beyond what is usual, expected or necessary; additional: *extra pay for extra work* ○ *buy an extra pint of milk* ○ *The bus company provided extra buses because there were so many people.* ○ *The football match went into extra time*, eg because of injury to players or a drawn score.

▷ **extra** *adv* **1** more than usually: *an extra strong box* ○ *extra fine quality.* **2** in addition: *20% extra* ○ *price £1.30, packing and postage extra.*

extra *n* **1** extra thing; thing that costs extra: *Her school fees are £440 a term; music and dancing are extras.* **2** (in cinema, TV, etc) person employed and paid (usu by the day) for a minor part, eg in a crowd scene: *We need hundreds of extras for the battle scenes.* **3** (in cricket) run scored otherwise than from a hit by the bat. **4** special edition of a newspaper containing special or later news: *a late night extra.*

extra- /ekstrə-/ *pref* (with *adjs*) **1** outside; beyond: *extramarital* ○ *extrasensory.* **2** very; to an exceptional degree: *extra-thin* ○ *extra-sensitive.*

extract /ɪkˈstrækt/ *v* [Tn, Tn·pr] ~ **sth (from sb/sth)** **1** (**a**) take or get sth out, usu with effort or by force: *extract a cork from a bottle* ○ *have a tooth extracted.* (**b**) obtain (money, information, etc) usu from a person unwilling to give it: *extract a contribution from everyone* ○ *The police finally extracted the information after hours of questioning.* ○ *It took me days to extract the truth from her.* **2** obtain (juices, etc) by crushing, pressing, etc: *extract juice from oranges* ○ *extract oil from olives, sunflower seeds, etc.* **3** select and present (passages, examples, words, etc) from a book, speech, etc: *poems extracted from a modern collection* ○ *She extracted passages for the students to translate.*

▷ **extract** /ˈekstrækt/ *n* **1** [U, C] substance that has been extracted (EXTRACT 2) and concentrated: *beef extract ○ extract of malt ○ yeast extract*, ie a savoury spread. **2** [C] passage selected (from a poem, book, film, piece of music, etc): *a short extract from a piano sonata ○ an extract from a long poem ○ She read out extracts from his letters.*
extraction /ɪkˈstrækʃn/ *n* **1** (**a**) [U] action of extracting (EXTRACT 1a): *the extraction of a tooth ○ the extraction of financial contributions ○ the extraction of information ○* [attrib] *an extraction process at a diamond mine.* (**b**) [C] instance of extracting a tooth: *He needs two extractions.* **2** [U] (*fml*) descent; parentage: *an American of Hungarian extraction.*
extractor /ɪkˈstræktə(r)/ *n* person or device that extracts (EXTRACT 2): *He makes fresh orange juice with an electric extractor.* **exˈtractor fan** ventilator fan (in a kitchen, etc) for removing bad smells, etc. ➪ illus at FAN.

extra-curricular /ˌekstrəkəˈrɪkjələ(r)/ *adj* [usu attrib] outside the regular course of work or studies at a school or college: *She's involved in many extra-curricular activities, such as music, sport and drama.*

extradite /ˈekstrədaɪt/ *v* [Tn] **1** give up or send back (sb accused or convicted of a crime) to the country where the crime was (said to be) committed: *The Spanish police have refused to extradite a man wanted for a bank robbery in France.* **2** obtain (such a person) for trial or punishment.
▷ **extraditable** /-əbl/ *adj* (**a**) (of an offender) liable to be extradited. (**b**) (of a crime, etc) for which sb may be extradited: *an extraditable offence.*
extradition /ˌekstrəˈdɪʃn/ *n* [C, U]: *the extradition of war criminals.*

extra-marital /ˌekstrəˈmærɪtl/ *adj* of (a married person's) sexual relationships outside marriage: *have extra-marital relations with sb ○ extra-marital affairs.*

extramural /ˌekstrəˈmjʊərəl/ *adj* [usu attrib] **1** (of university teaching, courses, etc) for people who are not full-time residential members of a university: *extramural studies, lectures, courses, students ○ the extramural department of a university.* **2** (of work, etc) not done as part of one's official (paid) duties: *on an extramural basis.*

extraneous /ɪkˈstreɪnɪəs/ *adj* ~ (**to sth**) **1** not belonging to or directly connected with the subject or matter being dealt with: *extraneous information ○ extraneous material in a book.* **2** coming from outside: *extraneous interference.*

extraordinary /ɪkˈstrɔːdnrɪ; *US* -dənerɪ/ *adj* **1** beyond what is ordinary; very unusual; remarkable: *Her talents are quite extraordinary. ○ extraordinary weather for the time of year ○ an extraordinary film about a highly gifted child.* **2** [attrib] (*fml*) (of arrangements, meetings, etc) additional to what is usual or ordinary: *an extraordinary general meeting.* **3** (used immediately after a *n*) (*fml*) (of an official) specially employed; additional to the usual one: *envoy/ambassador extraordinary.* ▷ **extraordinarily** /ɪkˈstrɔːdnrəlɪ; *US* -dənerəlɪ/ *adv*: *extraordinarily beautiful, thoughtful, rude.*

extrapolate /ɪkˈstræpəleɪt/ *v* [Tn, Tn·pr] ~ **sth** (**from sth**) (*fml*) **1** (*mathematics*) calculate (an unknown quantity) approximately from known values or measurements. **2** estimate (sth unknown) from facts that are already known: *One can extrapolate the size of the building from the measurements of an average room.* Cf INTERPOLATE.
▷ **extrapolation** /ɪkˌstræpəˈleɪʃn/ *n* [U] ~ (**from sth**) (*fml*): *He estimated his income tax bill by extrapolation from figures submitted in previous years.* ➪ illus at CHART.

extra-sensory perception /ˌekstrəˌsensərɪ pəˈsepʃn/ (*abbr* **ESP**) (supposed) ability to perceive outside, past or future events without the use of the known senses: *He seems to know when his wife is away from home by some kind of extra-sensory perception.*

extraterrestrial /ˌekstrətəˈrestrɪəl/ *adj* of or from outside the earth and its atmosphere: *extraterrestrial life, beings, forces.*

extraterritorial /ˌekstrəˌterɪˈtɔːrɪəl/ (also **exterritorial** /ˌeksˌterɪˈtɔːrɪəl/) *adj* (*fml*) (of an ambassador, etc) free from the laws of the country in which one lives: *extraterritorial rights and privileges.*

extravagant /ɪkˈstrævəgənt/ *adj* **1** (in the habit of) using or spending too much; (of actions) showing this tendency: *an extravagant man ○ extravagant tastes and habits ○ an extravagant use of natural resources.* **2** (of ideas, speech or behaviour) going beyond what is reasonable, usual or necessary: *extravagant praise, behaviour, claims ○ pay extravagant compliments.*
▷ **extravagance** /-gəns/ *n* **1** [U] being extravagant(1): *His extravagance explains why he is always in debt.* **2** [C] extravagant act, statement, etc: *I do not regard books as extravagances.*
extravagantly *adv*: *extravagantly dressed.*

extravaganza /ɪkˌstrævəˈgænzə/ *n* entertainment with elaborate and colourful costumes, scenery, etc: *a costly musical extravaganza on television.*

extreme /ɪkˈstriːm/ *adj* **1** [attrib] as far away as possible (esp from the centre or beginning); remote: *in the extreme north of a country ○ the extreme edge of the forest ○ in extreme old age.* **2** [usu attrib] of the highest degree or intensity; greatest possible: *show extreme patience, kindness, gentleness, etc ○ in extreme pain ○ an extreme climate*, ie one with hot summers, cold winters and little rainfall. (*fml*): *The extreme penalty of the law in some countries is the death penalty.* **3** (*often derog*) (of people and their opinions) far from moderate: *hold extreme views ○ a supporter of the extreme left/right*, ie a person who supports communism/fascism ○ *His ideas are too extreme for me.*
▷ **extreme** *n* [C usu *pl*] **1** feeling, condition, etc as far apart or as different from another as possible: *the extremes of misery and bliss ○ Love and hate are extremes of passion. ○ He was once terribly shy but now he's gone to the opposite extreme.* **2** greatest or highest degree; either end of anything: *He could not tolerate the extremes of heat in the desert.* **3** (idm) **go, etc to exˈtremes** act or be forced to act in a way that is far from moderate or normal: *In the jungle, they were driven to extremes in order to survive.* **in the exˈtreme** (*fml*) to the highest degree; extremely: *This is inconvenient in the extreme.*
extremely *adv* (with *adjs* and *advs*) to a very high degree: *That's extremely interesting. ○ I'm extremely sorry for the delay.*
extremist *n* (*usu derog*) person who holds extreme(3) views (esp in politics): *When it comes to talking about patriotism, he's an extremist. ○* [attrib] *extremist policies.* **extremism** *n* [U] holding of such views: *The council was often accused of extremism. ○ the extremism of some feminists.*
extremity /ɪkˈstremətɪ/ *n* **1** (**a**) [C] (*fml*) furthest point, end or limit of sth: *the extremities of the world.* (**b**) **extremities** [pl] furthest parts of the human body, eg hands and feet: *Cold affects the extremities first.* **2** [sing] (*fml*) extreme degree (esp of misery, suffering, etc); great misfortune or distress: *reach an extremity of despair ○ How can we help them in their extremity?* **3** [C usu *pl*] (*fml*) exceptionally cruel or violent behaviour: *Both armies were guilty of extremities.*
□ **exˌtreme ˈunction** last rites for a person about to die in the Roman Catholic and Orthodox Churches.

extricate /ˈekstrɪkeɪt/ *v* [Tn, Tn·pr] ~ **sb/sth** (**from sth**) (*fml*) set sb/sth free; release sb/sth: *The bird had to be extricated from the netting. ○ extricate oneself from an unhappy love affair.*

extrinsic /ekˈstrɪnsɪk/ *adj* ~ (**to sth**) (*fml*) (of qualities, values, etc) not belonging to or part of the real nature of a person or thing; coming from outside: *extrinsic facts ○ information extrinsic to the situation.* Cf INTRINSIC.

extrovert /ˈekstrəvɜːt/ *n* **1** person more interested in what is happening around him than in his own thoughts and emotions: *Extroverts prefer lively conversation to brooding on the meaning of life.* **2** (*infml*) lively, cheerful and sociable person: *She's a good person to invite to a party because she's such an extrovert.* Cf INTROVERT.
▷ **extroversion** /ˌekstrəˈvɜːʃn; *US* -ˈvɜːrʒn/ *n* [U] (*fml*) state of being an extrovert.
extrovert (also **extroverted**) *adj* being or characteristic of an extrovert.

extrude /ɪkˈstruːd/ *v* [Tn, Tn·pr] ~ **sth** (**from sth**) (*fml*) **1** force or squeeze out sth under pressure: *extrude glue from a tube.* **2** shape (metal, plastic, etc) by forcing it through a die: *nylon extruded as very thin fibres.* ▷ **extrusion** /ɪkˈstruːʒn/ *n* [C, U] (*fml*).

exuberant /ɪgˈzjuːbərənt; *US* -ˈzuː-/ *adj* **1** (esp of people and their behaviour) overflowing with happiness and excitement; very lively and cheerful: *exuberant children at a fair ○ She gave an exuberant account of the party.* **2** (of plants, etc) growing vigorously; luxuriant: *plants with exuberant foliage ○* (*fig*) *an exuberant imagination.*
▷ **exuberance** /-rəns/ *n* [U] state or quality of being exuberant: *the natural exuberance of young children ○ The speaker's exuberance enlivened a boring conference.*
exuberantly *adv.*

exude /ɪgˈzjuːd; *US* -ˈzuːd/ *v* **1** [I, Ipr, Tn, Tn·pr] (*fml*) ~ (**sth**) (**from/through sth**) (of drops of liquid, etc) come or pass out slowly; ooze out: *Sweat exudes through the pores. ○ The hot sun made him exude sweat.* **2** [Tn, Tn·pr] give out or radiate an air or feeling of (sth): *exude cheerfulness ○ He exudes confidence and energy.* ▷ **exudation** /ˌeksjuːˈdeɪʃn; *US* ˌeksuː-/ *n* [U] (*fml*).

exult /ɪgˈzʌlt/ *v* (*fml*) [I, Ipr, It] ~ (**at/in sth**) get great pleasure from sth; rejoice greatly: *exult at her sister's success ○ He obviously exulted in winning. ○ exulting to find that one has succeeded.*
▷ **exultant** /-ənt/ *adj* ~ (**at sth**) exulting; triumphant: *an exultant shout of victory ○ exultant at one's success.* **exultantly** *adv*: *exultantly proud.*
exultation /ˌegzʌlˈteɪʃn/ *n* [U] ~ (**at sth**) great happiness: *the exultation of the winner.*

-ey ➪ -Y[1].

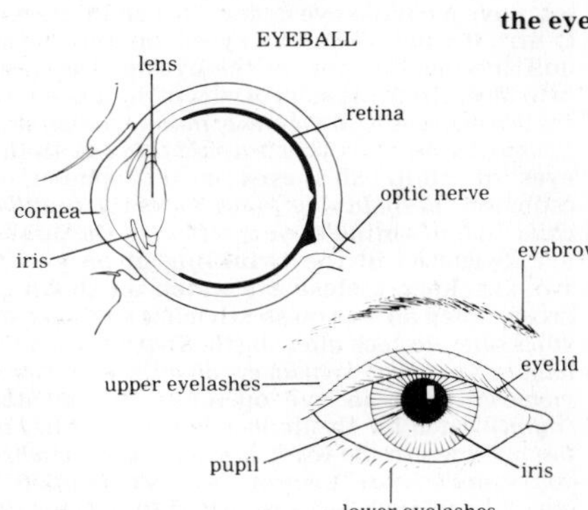

eye[1] /aɪ/ *n* **1** (**a**) organ of sight: *I can't see out of this eye. ○ She opened/closed her eyes. ○ He is blind in one eye. ○ He lost an eye in the war. ○* [attrib] *The surgeon is performing an eye operation.* ➪ illus. (**b**) visible coloured part of this; iris: *have blue eyes.* **2** power of seeing; observation: *She has sharp eyes*, ie very good eyesight. ○ *To her expert eye, the painting was terrible. ○ His eyes fell upon* (ie he saw) *an advertisement in the magazine.* **3** thing like an eye: *the eye of a needle*, ie the hole for the thread ○ *a hook and eye*, ie fastening with a hook and loop for a dress, etc ○ *the eye of a potato*, ie point from which a leaf bud will grow. **4** (idm) **a bird's eye view** ➪ BIRD. **the apple of sb's eye** ➪ APPLE. **as far as the eye can see** ➪ FAR[2]. **be all ˈeyes** be watching intently: *The children were all eyes as we opened the parcel.* **beauty is in the eye of the beholder** ➪ BEAUTY. **cast an eye/one's**

eye(s) over sb/sth ⇨ CAST[1]. **catch sb's attention/eye** ⇨ CATCH[1]. **clap/lay/set eyes on sb/sth** see sb/sth: *I disliked the place the moment I clapped eyes on it.* ○ *I hope I never set eyes on him again.* **close one's eyes to sth** ⇨ CLOSE[4]. **cry one's eyes/heart out** ⇨ CRY[1]. **do sb in the ˈeye** (*infml*) hurt or humiliate sb: *He certainly did his colleagues in the eye when he got the boss's approval.* **easy on the ear/eye** ⇨ EASY[1]. **the evil eye** ⇨ EVIL. **an ˌeye for an ˈeye** a punishment as severe as the injury that was suffered; retaliation: *The death penalty for murder works on the principle of an eye for an eye.* **the eye of the ˈstorm** a relatively calm spot in the centre of a storm, esp a hurricane. **the eye of the ˈwind** (also **the wind's ˈeye**) point from which the wind is blowing. **sb's eyes are bigger than his ˈstomach** (*saying*) someone is too greedy in asking for or taking more food than he can eat. **eyes ˈright/ˈleft/ˈfront** (as a military command) turn the head and look to the right, etc. **feast one's eyes** ⇨ FEAST. **find/lose favour with sb/in sb's eyes** ⇨ FAVOUR[1]. **for ˌsb's eyes ˈonly** only to be looked at, read, etc by the person specified: *The top secret file was marked 'For the President's eyes only'.* **get one's ˈeye/ˈhand in** (in ball games) become able, through practice, to follow with one's eyes the movement of the ball/to hit the ball accurately: *Now that she's got her eye in she plays an excellent game of tennis.* **give sb/get the (glad) ˈeye** (*infml*) give sb/get inviting or amorous looks: *The woman at the next table was giving him the glad eye.* **glance one's eye down/over/through sth** ⇨ GLANCE. **a gleam in sb's eye** ⇨ GLEAM. **have an eye for sth** be a good judge of or have a proper sense of sth: *He has an eye for a bargain.* **have eyes in the back of one's ˈhead** observe everything (without seeming to do so): *How did you know I was behind you? You must have eyes in the back of your head.* **have/with an eye to sth/doing sth** have/having sth as one's aim or purpose: *He always has an eye to business*, ie looks for a chance of doing business. ○ *He kept the customer talking with an eye to selling him something else.* **have/with an eye for/on/to the main ˈchance** look/looking for an opportunity for personal gain (esp to make money). **have, etc one's eyes on stalks** be looking at sth with fascination, astonishment, etc. **have a roving eye** ⇨ ROVE. **hit sb in the eye** ⇨ HIT[1]. **if you had half an eye** if you were not so dull and unobservant. **in the eyes of the ˈlaw, ˈworld, etc** from the point of view of the law, etc; as the law, etc sees it: *In the eyes of the law she is guilty though few ordinary people would think so.* **in the eyes of ˈsb/in ˈsb's eyes** in the opinion or estimation of sb: *In your father's eyes you're still a child.* **in one's mind's eye** ⇨ MIND[1]. **in the public eye** ⇨ PUBLIC. **in the twinkling of an eye** ⇨ TWINKLE. **keep a close eye/watch on sb/sth** ⇨ CLOSE[1]. **keep an ˈeye on sb/sth** make sure that sb/sth is safe, etc; look after sb/sth: *Keep an eye on the baby.* ○ *Could you keep an eye on my suitcase for a moment?* **keep an eye open/out (for sb/sth)** (*infml*) watch for sb/sth; look out for sb/sth: *I've lost my ring — could you keep an eye out for it when you clean the house?* **keep one's ears/eyes open** ⇨ OPEN[1]. **keep one's ˈeyes peeled/skinned (for sb/sth)** watch carefully; be observant: *The tramp always keeps his eyes peeled for coins lying on the ground.* ○ *Keep your eyes skinned for a campsite!* **keep a weather eye open** ⇨ WEATHER[1]. **lift one's eyes** ⇨ LIFT. **(be unable to) look sb in the ˈeye(s)/ˈface** (be unable to) look at sb steadily (because one feels ashamed, embarrassed, etc): *Can you look me in the eyes and say you didn't break the window?* **make (ˈsheep's) ˈeyes at sb** look amorously at sb: *The lovers were making sheep's eyes at each other over the table.* **meet sb's eye** ⇨ MEET[1]. **meet the ear/eye** ⇨ MEET[1]. **the mote in sb's eye** ⇨ MOTE. **(all) ˌmy ˈeye** (*infml*) (esp of sth said that is intended to deceive or mislead) completely untrue or nonsensical: *She said she was only twenty-two — twenty-two my eye!* **the naked eye** ⇨ NAKED. **never/not (be able to) take one's ˈeyes off sb/sth** never/not (be able to) stop watching sb/sth: *He couldn't take his eyes off the beautiful newcomer.* **not believe one's ears/eyes** ⇨ BELIEVE. **not a dry eye in the house** ⇨ DRY[1]. **one in the eye (for sb/sth)** (*infml*) hard or unkind rejection or defeat: *If she gets the job, that's one in the eye for Peter: he was desperate to get it.* **only have eyes for/have eyes only for sb** only be interested in or in love with (a specified person): *It's no use asking Kim to go out with you; she only has eyes for Mark.* **open one's/sb's eyes (to sth)** ⇨ OPEN[2]. **out of the corner of one's eye** ⇨ CORNER[1]. **pull the wool over sb's eyes** ⇨ PULL[2]. **the scales fall from sb's eyes** ⇨ SCALE. **(not) see eye to ˈeye with sb** (not) agree entirely; (not) have similar views: *Jim and I have never seen eye to eye on this matter.* **see, etc sth with ˈhalf an eye** see, etc sth at a glance. **shut/close one's eyes to sth** refuse to see or take notice of sth: *The government shuts its eyes to poverty.* ○ *She closed her eyes to her husband's infidelities.* **a sight for sore eyes** ⇨ SIGHT. **there is more in/to sb/sth than meets the eye** ⇨ MEET[1]. **throw dust in sb's eyes** ⇨ DUST[1]. **turn a blind eye** ⇨ BLIND[1]. **under/before one's very ˈeyes (a)** in one's presence; in front of one: *'Ladies and gentlemen! Before your very eyes I will cut this man in half,' said the magician.* **(b)** without attempting to hide what one is doing: *He stole the stuff from under my very eyes.* **(be) up to one's ears/eyes/eyebrows/neck in sth** ⇨ EAR. **the wind's eye** = THE EYE OF THE WIND. **with one's ˈeyes open** fully aware of what one is doing: *I moved to this country with my eyes open; so I'm not complaining.* ○ *He married her with his eyes wide open.* **with one's ˈeyes shut/closed** without much effort; easily: *He's cooked that meal so often he can do it with his eyes closed.*

▷ **-eyed** (forming compound *adjs*) having an eye or eyes of the specified kind: *a blue-eyed girl* ○ *a one-eyed man*, ie man with only one eye.

ˈeyeful /fʊl/ *n* **1** thing thrown or blown into one's eye: *get an eyeful of sand.* **2** (*infml*) interesting or attractive sight: *She's quite an eyeful!* **3** (idm) **have/get an eyeful (of sth)** (*infml*) have a good long look (at sth interesting, remarkable, unusual, etc): *'Come and get an eyeful of this — there's a giraffe in the garden!'*

□ **ˈeyeball** *n* **1** round part of the eye within the eyelids and socket. ⇨ illus. **2** (idm) **ˌeyeball to ˈeyeball (with sb)** (*infml*) confronting a person closely; face to face: *We must discuss the situation eyeball to eyeball.* — *v* [Tn] (*US sl*) look closely and fixedly at (sb/sth); stare at.

ˈeye-bath *n* small cup shaped to fit round the eye for holding lotion, etc in which to bathe the eye.

ˈeyebrow *n* **1** arch of hair above the human eye: *pluck one's eyebrows.* ⇨ illus. ⇨ Usage at BODY. **2** (idm) **raise one's eyebrows** ⇨ RAISE. **up to one's ears/eyes/eyebrows/neck in sth** ⇨ EAR. **ˈeyebrow pencil** make-up pencil used for darkening the eyebrows.

ˈeye-catching *adj* striking and noticeable, esp because pleasant to look at: *an eye-catching suit, hat, etc.*

ˈeye contact contact made when two people look at each other: *make eye contact with sb.*

ˈeyeglass *n* lens (for one eye) to help poor eyesight: *The old man wore an eyeglass attached to a piece of ribbon.*

ˈeyehole *n* **1** socket containing the eye. **2** hole to look through.

ˈeyelash (also **lash**) *n* hair, or one of the rows of hairs, on the edge of the eyelid: *She was wearing false eyelashes*, ie artificial eyelashes, stuck to the eyelids. ⇨ illus.

ˈeyeless *adj* (*fml*) without eyes; without sight.

ˈeye-level *adj* [usu attrib] level with a person's eyes when looking straight ahead: *an eye-level grill.*

ˈeyelid (also **lid**) *n* **1** upper or lower of two movable folds of skin that close to cover the eyeball: *His eyelid is swollen.* ⇨ illus. **2** (idm) **not bat an eyelid** ⇨ BAT[4].

ˈeye-liner (also **liner**) *n* cosmetic applied as a line round (part of) the eye.

ˈeye-opener *n* **1** event, etc that reveals an unexpected fact or causes surprise: *My trip to India was quite an eye-opener.* **2** (*US*) drink taken when one wakes up in order to make one fully awake.

ˈeyepiece *n* lens at the end of a telescope or microscope through which the observer looks. ⇨ illus at MICROSCOPE.

eye-rhyme *n* incomplete rhyming of words that correspond in spelling but not in pronunciation, eg *love* and *move*, *dear* and *pear*.

ˈeye-shade *n* device worn above the eyes to protect them from strong light: *The tennis umpire wore an eye-shade.*

ˈeye-shadow *n* [C, U] type of cosmetic applied to the eyelids.

ˈeyesight *n* [U] power of seeing; ability to see: *have good/bad/poor eyesight.*

ˈeyesore *n* ugly object; thing that is unpleasant to look at: *That old block of flats is a real eyesore!*

ˈeye-strain *n* [U] tired condition of the eyes (caused, eg by reading very small print, or in dim light).

ˈeye-tooth *n* (*pl* **ˈeye-teeth**) **1** canine tooth in the upper (human) jaw, under the eye. **2** (idm) **cut one's ˈeye-teeth** acquire experience in the ways of the world: *He'll have to cut his eye-teeth before he gets promoted.* **give one's eye-teeth for sth** wish to possess or obtain sth very much: *He'd give his eye-teeth to own a car like that.*

ˈeyewash *n* [U] **(a)** liquid for bathing the eyes. **(b)** (*infml*) thing said or done to deceive or create a false impression; nonsense: *He pretends to care so much about his children, but it's all eyewash: he never even takes them out.*

ˈeyewitness *n* = WITNESS: [attrib] *an eyewitness account of a crime.*

eye[2] /aɪ/ *v* **1** [Tn, Tn·pr] **(a)** observe or watch (sb/sth) in the specified way: *He eyed me with suspicion.* ○ *They were ey(e)ing us jealously.* **(b)** look at (sth) with longing: *The children were ey(e)ing the sweets.* **2** (phr v) **eye sb up (and down)** (*infml*) look at sb amorously (in order to try to attract): *Did you see that creep eyeing up every woman at the party?*

eyelet /ˈaɪlɪt/ *n* [C] small hole in cloth, in a sail, etc for a rope, etc to go through; metal ring round such a hole, to strengthen it.

eyrie (also **eyry, aery**) /ˈaɪərɪ, ˈeərɪ/ *n* eagle's nest; nest of other birds of prey built high up among rocks.

Ezekiel /ɪˈziːkɪəl/ **1** Hebrew prophet of the 6th century BC who prophesied the destruction of Jerusalem and the Jewish nation. **2** book of the Old Testament containing his prophecies. ⇨ App 5.

Ezra /ˈezrə/ **1** Jewish priest and scribe involved in the reform of Judaism in the 5th or 4th century BC. **2** book of the Old Testament dealing with the return of the Jews from Babylon and the rebuilding of the Temple. ⇨ App 5.

F, f

F, f /ef/ *n* (*pl* **F's, f's** /efs/) **1** the sixth letter of the English alphabet: *'Fabric' starts with an 'F'/F.* **2 F** (*music*) the fourth note in the scale of C major.

F *abbr* **1** (degree or degrees) Fahrenheit: *Water freezes at 32°F.* Cf C *abbr* 2. **2** (in academic degrees) Fellow of: *FRCM*, ie Fellow of the Royal College of Music. Cf A *abbr* 3. **3** (of lead used in pencils) fine.

F *symb* fluorine.

f *abbr* **1** (also **fem**) (esp on forms) female (sex). **2** (also **fem**) (*grammar*) feminine (gender). **3** (*music*) loudly (Italian *forte*). Cf P 3.

FA /ˌef ˈeɪ/ *abbr* (*Brit*) Football Association: *the FA Cup.* ⇨ article at SPORT.

fa (also **fah**) /fɑː/ *n* (*music*) the fourth note in the sol-fa scale.

fab /fæb/ *adj* (*dated Brit sl*) marvellous; fabulous(2).

Fabian /ˈfeɪbɪən/ *n, adj* **1** (person) patiently planning to defeat the enemy gradually: *Fabian tactics.* **2** (*Brit*) (person) aiming to build socialism by means of gradual reform: *the Fabian Society*, ie an organization with this policy supporting the British Labour Party, whose early members included the *Webbs and George Bernard *Shaw.

fable /ˈfeɪbl/ *n* **1** (a) [C] short story not based on fact, often with animals as characters, that conveys a moral. The most famous ones are by *Aesop and La Fontaine, and some moral satires, like *Orwell's *Animal Farm* can be considered as fables: *the fable of the tortoise and the hare*, ie telling how the slow but persevering tortoise beat the quick burt careless hare in a race. (b) [U] such stories and legends considered as a group: *a land famous in fable.* **2** [C, U] untrue statement(s) or account(s): *distinguish fact from fable.*
▷ **fabled** /ˈfeɪbld/ *adj* famous in fables; legendary.

fabric /ˈfæbrɪk/ *n* **1** [C, U] type of cloth, esp one that is woven: *woollen, silk, cotton, etc fabrics.* **2** [sing] **the ~ (of sth)** (a) walls, floors and roof (of a building, etc): *The entire fabric of the church needs renovation.* (b) (*fig*) structure (of sth): *the fabric of society.*

fabricate /ˈfæbrɪkeɪt/ *v* [Tn] **1** invent (a false story): *fabricate an excuse, an accusation, etc* ○ *The reason he gave for his absence was obviously fabricated.* **2** forge (a document): *a fabricated voting paper.*
▷ **fabrication** /ˌfæbrɪˈkeɪʃn/ *n* **1** [U] action or result of fabricating: *That's pure fabrication!* **2** [C] thing that has been fabricated, eg a forged document or a false account of events: *Her story was nothing but a series of fabrications.*

fabulous /ˈfæbjʊləs/ *adj* **1** incredibly great: *fabulous wealth.* **2** (*infml*) wonderful; marvellous: *a fabulous performance.* **3** [attrib] (*fml*) appearing in fables; legendary: *fabulous heroes, monsters, etc.*
▷ **fabulously** *adv* incredibly: *fabulously rich.*

façade /fəˈsɑːd/ *n* **1** (*fml*) front (of a building). **2** (*fig*) outward appearance, esp a deceptive one: *a façade of indifference* ○ *Squalor and poverty lay behind the city's glittering façade.*

FACE UP

FACE DOWN

face[1] /feɪs/ *n* **1** front part of the head from the forehead to the chin: *a pretty, handsome, etc face* ○ *Go and wash your face.* ○ *He was so ashamed that he hid his face in his hands.* ○ *I saw many familiar/strange faces*, ie people whom I recognized/did not recognize. **2** expression shown on a face: *a sad face* ○ *smiling faces* ○ *She had a face like thunder*, ie She looked very angry. ○ *You are a good judge of faces*, ie You can judge a person's character by (the expression on) his face. **3** (a) surface or side (of sth): *A cut diamond has many faces.* ○ *They disappeared from/off the face of the earth*, ie totally disappeared. ○ *The team climbed the north face of the mountain.* (b) front or main side (of sth): *the face of a clock* ○ *He put the cards face down/up on the table*, ie hiding/showing which ones they were. ⇨ illus. (c) = COAL-FACE (COAL). (d) surface that is used for hitting, working, etc esp the striking-surface of a bat or the working-surface of a tool. **4** = TYPEFACE (TYPE[2]). **5** (idm) **be staring sb in the face** ⇨ STARE. **cut off one's nose to spite one's face** ⇨ NOSE[1]. **one's face falls** one's expression shows disappointment, dismay, etc: *Her face fell when she heard the news.* **face to face (with sb/sth)** close to and looking at (sb/sth): *His ambition was to meet his favourite pop star face to face.* ○ *The burglar turned the corner and found himself face to face with a policeman.* ○ *The two rival politicians came/were brought face to face in a TV interview.* **fall flat on one's face** ⇨ FLAT[3]. **fly in the face of sth** ⇨ FLY[2]. **grind the faces of the poor** ⇨ GRIND. **have, etc egg on/all over one's face** ⇨ EGG[1]. **have the face (to do sth)** (*infml*) be bold or impudent enough: *How can you have the face to ask for more money when you do so little work?* **have one's face lifted** have a face-lift(1). **in the face of sth** (a) in spite of sth: *succeed in the face of danger* ○ *continue in the face of criticism.* (b) confronted by sth: *We are powerless in the face of such forces.* **keep a straight face** ⇨ STRAIGHT[1]. **laugh in sb's face** ⇨ LAUGH. **laugh on the other side of one's face** ⇨ LAUGH. **a long face** ⇨ LONG[1]. **look sb in the eye/face** ⇨ EYE[1]. **lose face** ⇨ LOSE. **make/pull ˈfaces/a ˈface (at sb)** grimace (at sb); pull the face into amusing, rude, disgusted, etc expressions: *The schoolboy made a face at his teacher's back.* ○ *The clowns pulled funny faces.* **not just a pretty face** ⇨ PRETTY. **on the ˈface of it** (*infml*) judging by appearances: *On the face of it, he seems to be telling the truth though I suspect he's hiding something.* **plain as the nose on one's face** ⇨ PLAIN[1]. **put a bold, brave, good, etc ˈface on sth** accept (bad news, etc) courageously, pretending that it is not as bad as it is: *Her exam results were disappointing but she tried to put a brave face on it.* **put one's ˈface on** (*infml joc*) apply make-up to one's face. **save face** ⇨ SAVE[1]. **set one's face against sb/sth** be determined to oppose sb/sth: *You shouldn't set your face against all forms of progress.* **show one's face** ⇨ SHOW[2]. **shut/slam the door in sb's face** ⇨ DOOR. **shut one's mouth/face** ⇨ SHUT. **a slap in the face** ⇨ SLAP *n.* **till one is blue in the face** ⇨ BLUE[1]. **to sb's ˈface** openly and directly so that sb can hear: *I am so angry that I'll tell him to his face what I think of him.* ○ *They called their teacher 'Fatty' but never to his face.* Cf BEHIND SB'S BACK (BACK[1]). **wipe sth off the face of the earth** ⇨ WIPE.
▷ **faceless** *adj* not known by name; with no clear character or identity: *faceless civil servants.*
□ **ˈface-card** *n* = COURT-CARD (COURT).
ˈface-cloth (*Brit* also **ˈface-flannel, flannel**; *US* also **wash-cloth**) *n* small square of towelling material used for washing the face, hands, etc.
ˈface-cream *n* [U] cosmetic cream for the skin of the face.
ˈface-lift *n* **1** (also **ˈface-lifting**) operation in which the skin is tightened to smooth out wrinkles and make the face look younger. **2** (*fig*) improvement in the appearance of sth; renovation (of a building, etc): *The town centre certainly needs a face-lift.*
ˈface-pack *n* cream or paste applied to clean or refresh the skin on the face.
ˈface-saver *n* thing that prevents sb from being embarrassed or losing dignity. **ˈface-saving** *adj* [usu attrib] acting as a face-saver: *a face-saving action, excuse, gesture.*
ˌface ˈvalue 1 value printed or stamped on money or postage stamps. **2** (idm) **take sth/sb at (its, his, etc) face value** assume that sth/sb is genuinely what it, he, etc appears to be: *She seems friendly enough but I shouldn't take her at (her) face value.*

face[2] /feɪs/ *v* **1** [Tn] have or turn the face towards (sb/sth); be opposite to: *Turn round and face me.* ○ *Who's the man facing me?* ○ *The window faces the street.* ○ *The picture faces page 10.* ○ *'Which way does your house face?' 'It faces south.'* **2** [Tn] meet (sb/sth) confidently or defiantly without trying to avoid sb/sth: *He turned to face his attackers.* ○ (*fig*) *face dangers* ○ *face one's responsibilities* ○ *face facts*, ie accept the situation that exists. **3** [Tn] require the attention of (sb/sth); confront: *the problems that face the Government.* **4** [Tn, Tn·pr] **~ sth (with sth)** cover sth with a layer of different material: *face a wall (with plaster).* **5 face a charge (of sth)/face ˈcharges** be forced to appear in court accused of sth: *face serious charges, a charge of shoplifting.* **face the ˈmusic** (*infml*) accept the criticisms, unpleasant consequences, etc that follow a decision or action of one's own: *You've been caught cheating — now you must face the music.* **let's ˈface it** (*infml*) we must acknowledge that...: *Let's face it, we won't win whatever we do.* **6** (phr v) **face off** (in ice hockey or lacrosse) start playing. **face sth out** deal with (an awkward or embarrassing situation) by not showing any sign of embarrassment, worry, etc: *I knew they suspected me of having lied to them but I decided to try and face it out.* **face up to sth** accept and deal with sth unpleasant or demanding honestly and bravely: *He must face up to the fact that he is no longer young.* ○ *She's finding it difficult to face up to the possibility of an early death.*
▷ **-faced** (forming compound *adjs*) with the specified type of face: *red-faced* ○ *baby-faced.*
□ **ˈface-off** *n* start of play in ice hockey or lacrosse.

facet

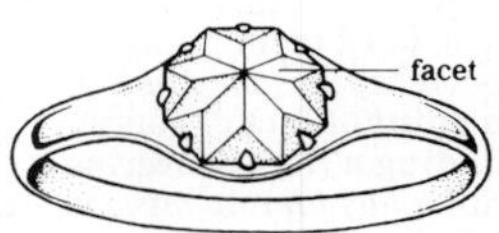

facet /ˈfæsɪt/ *n* **1** any of the many sides of a cut stone or jewel. **2** aspect of a situation or problem: *There are many facets to this question.*
▷ **-faceted** (forming compound *adjs*) with the specified number of sides or aspects: *many-faceted/multi-faceted.*

facetious /fəˈsiːʃəs/ *adj* (*usu derog*) intended to be amusing, often inappropriately: *a facetious young man* ○ *She kept interrupting our discussion with facetious remarks.* ▷ **facetiously** *adv.* **facetiousness** *n* [U].

facia (also **fascia**) /ˈfeɪʃə/ *n* **1** = DASHBOARD (DASH[1]), ⇨ illus at CAR. **2** board, etc with a name on it, put above the front entrance of a shop.

facial /ˈfeɪʃl/ *adj* of or for the face: *a facial expression* ○ *a facial massage.*
▷ **facial** *n* beauty treatment for the face: *I've made*

an appointment for a facial next week.
facially /ˈfeɪʃəlɪ/ *adv* as far as the face is concerned: *She may resemble her father facially, but in other respects she's not at all like him.*

facile /ˈfæsaɪl; *US* ˈfæsl/ *adj* **1** (*usu derog*) (**a**) [attrib] easily obtained or achieved (and so not highly valued): *a facile success, victory, etc.* (**b**) (of speech or writing) easily produced but superficial or of poor quality: *a facile remark.* **2** [attrib] (of a person) saying or doing things easily; fluent: *a facile speaker.*

facilitate /fəˈsɪlɪteɪt/ *v* [Tn] (*fml*) (of an object, a process, etc but not of a person) make (sth) easy or less difficult: *It would facilitate matters if you were more co-operative.* ▷ **facilitation** /fəˌsɪlɪˈteɪʃn/ *n* [U].

facility /fəˈsɪlətɪ/ *n* **1** [U, sing] ability to learn or do things easily: *have (a) great facility for (learning) languages* ○ *He plays the piano with surprising facility.* **2 facilities** [pl] circumstances, equipment, etc that make it possible, or easier, to do sth; aids: *ˈsports facilities,* eg running tracks, swimming pools ○ *ˈwashing, ˈpostal, ˈshopping, ˈbanking, etc facilities* ○ *facilities for study,* eg libraries.

facing /ˈfeɪsɪŋ/ *n* **1** outer layer covering a surface (eg of a wall). **2** layer of material covering part of a garment either to decorate it in a different colour or to strengthen it: *a blue jacket with black facings.*

facsimile /fækˈsɪməlɪ/ *n* [U, C] exact copy or reproduction of writing, printing, a picture, etc: *reproduced in facsimile,* ie exactly ○ [attrib] *a facsimile edition.*

fact /fækt/ *n* **1** [C] thing that is known to have happened or to be true or to exist: *No one can deny the fact that fire burns.* ○ *Poverty and crime are facts.* ○ *He's resigned: I know it for a fact,* ie I know that it is really true. ○ (*infml*) *He came here yesterday, and that's a fact!* Cf FICTION. **2** [C] thing that is believed or claimed to be true: *I disagree with the facts on which your argument is based.* **3** [U] what is true; reality: *The story is founded on fact.* ○ *It's important to distinguish fact from fiction.* **4** (idm) **accessory before/after the fact** ⇨ ACCESSORY. **an accomplished fact** ⇨ ACCOMPLISH. **blink the fact** ⇨ BLINK. **as a matter of fact** ⇨ MATTER 1. **a ˌfact of ˈlife** thing that cannot be ignored, however unpleasant: *We must all die some time: that's just a fact of life.* **the fact (of the matter) is (that)...; the fact remains (that)...** despite what has been said, the truth is...: *A holiday would be wonderful but the fact of the matter is (that) we can't afford one.* ○ *I agree that he tried hard but the fact remains that he has not finished the job in time.* **ˌfacts and ˈfigures** (*infml*) precise information: *Before we make detailed plans, we need some more facts and figures.* **the ˌfacts of ˈlife** (*euph*) details of human sexuality, esp as told to children. **the facts speak for themselves** the facts noted about a situation or an occurrence show what conclusions can be reached, without further interpretation or explanation. **hard facts** ⇨ HARD[1]. **in ˈfact** in truth; really: *For eight years she was in fact spying for the enemy.* **in point of fact** ⇨ POINT[1].
□ **ˈfact-finding** *n* [U] discovering the truth about sth: [attrib] *a fact-finding mission, expedition, etc.*

faction[1] /ˈfækʃn/ *n* [C] (*usu derog*) small united group within a larger one, esp in politics: *rival factions within the party.*
▷ **factious** /ˈfækʃəs/ *adj* **1** of or caused by faction. **2** fond of faction; quarrelsome: *a factious individual.*

faction[2] /ˈfækʃn/ *n* [U] films, plays, etc that have a story partly based on things that have actually happened (ie that are a mixture of *fact* and *fiction*).

factitious /fækˈtɪʃəs/ *adj* (*fml*) deliberately created or developed; unnatural; artificial: *factitious enthusiasm* ○ *a factitious demand for goods,* ie one created artificially by widespread advertising, etc.

factor /ˈfæktə(r)/ *n* **1** fact, circumstance, etc that helps to produce a result: *environmental factors* ○ *the factors that influenced my decision* ○ *an unknown factor,* ie sth unknown that is likely to influence a result. **2** (*mathematics*) number by which a number can be divided exactly: *1, 2, 3, 4, 6 and 12 are factors of 12.* **3** person or organization acting as a business agent. **4** (*Scot*) land-agent; steward.
▷ **factorize, -ise** /ˈfæktəraɪz/ *v* [Tn] (*mathematics*) find the factors of (a number). **factorization, -isation** /ˌfæktəraɪˈzeɪʃn; *US* -rɪˈz-/ *n* [U].
□ **ˌfactor of ˈsafety** (also **ˈsafety factor**) ratio between the load or stress which a structure or material can bear before breaking and the actual load or stress placed on it.

factorial /fækˈtɔ:rɪəl/ *adj, n* (*mathematics*) (of the) product of a whole number and all those whole numbers below it: *factorial 5 (represented as 5!),* ie the product of 5 x 4 x 3 x 2 x 1.

factory /ˈfæktərɪ/ *n* building(s) in which goods are manufactured: *They're closing the local factory and putting 300 out of work.* ○ [attrib] *ˈfactory workers* ○ *We met outside the factory gates after work.*
□ **ˈFactory Acts** British laws concerning the safety and conditions of people working in factories. The first ones were passed in the 19th century.
ˈfactory farm farm in which animals are kept and reared in a way designed to produce the maximum yield (of meat, young, milk, eggs, etc). **ˈfactory farming.**
ˈfactory ship ship to which ships in a fishing fleet bring their catch for processing, and often quick-freezing, while still at sea.

NOTE ON USAGE: **Factory**, **mill**, **plant** and **works** all refer to industrial buildings or places but they indicate different products or processes. **Factory** is the most common word for the buildings where products are manufactured or assembled: *a car, shoe, bottle, etc factory* ○ *factory workers.* **Works** suggests a larger group of buildings and machinery, generally not producing finished goods: *a gasworks, ironworks.* **Plant** is more common in US English and relates especially to industrial processes: *a power, chemical plant.* **Mill** has the most limited meaning, relating to the processing of certain raw materials: *a paper/cotton/woollen/steel mill.*

factotum /fækˈtəʊtəm/ *n* (*fml or joc*) person employed to do all kinds of work: *a general factotum.*

factual /ˈfæktʃʊəl/ *adj* based on or containing facts: *a factual account.* ▷ **factually** /-tʃʊəlɪ/ *adv*: *factually correct.*

faculty /ˈfækltɪ/ *n* **1** [C] any of the powers of the body or mind: *the faculty of sight* ○ *the mental faculties,* ie the power of reason ○ *be in possession of all one's faculties,* ie be able to see, hear, speak, understand, etc. **2** [sing] ~ **of/for doing sth** particular ability for doing sth: *have a great faculty for learning languages.* **3** (**a**) [C] department or group of related departments in a university, etc: *the Faculty of Law, Science, etc.* (**b**) [CGp] all the lecturers, etc in one of these: [attrib] *a faculty meeting.* (**c**) [CGp] (*US*) the whole teaching staff of a university, etc.

fad /fæd/ *n* fashion, interest, preference, enthusiasm, etc that is not likely to last: *Will Tom continue to collect stamps or is it only a passing fad?*
▷ **faddish** *adj* (*derog*) having peculiar likes and dislikes.
faddy *adj* (*infml derog*) faddish, esp about food. **faddiness** *n* [U].

fade /feɪd/ *v* **1** [I, Tn] (cause sth to) lose colour, freshness or vigour: *the fading light of evening* ○ *Will (the colour in) this material fade?* ○ *Flowers soon fade when cut.* ○ *She is fading fast,* ie rapidly losing strength. ○ *The strong sunlight had faded the curtains.* ○ *faded denims,* ie ones that have lost their original colour. **2** [I, Ipr, Ip] ~ (**away**) disappear gradually (from sight, hearing, memory, etc); become indistinct: *As evening came, the coastline faded into darkness.* ○ *The sound of the cheering faded (away) in the distance.* ○ *All memory of her childhood had faded from her mind.* ○ *His hopes faded.* **3** (phr v) **fade away** (of people) disperse; die: *The crowd just faded away.* ○ *She's fading away,* ie dying. **fade (sth) in/out** (*cinema or broadcasting*) (cause a picture to) increase/decrease gradually in sharpness; (causethe volume of sound to) become gradually audible/inaudible: *As the programme ended, their conversation was faded out.*
□ **ˈfade-in** *n* (*cinema or broadcasting*) gradual strengthening (of sounds, pictures, etc).
ˈfade-out *n* (*cinema or broadcasting*) gradual weakening (of sounds, pictures, etc).

faeces (*US* **feces**) /ˈfi:si:z/ *n* [pl] (*fml*) waste matter passed from the bowels.
▷ **faecal** (*US* **fecal**) /ˈfi:kl/ *adj* [usu attrib] (*fml*) of faeces.

Faeroe Islands /ˈfeərəʊ aɪlandz/ **the Faeroe Islands** (also **the Faroe Islands**, **the Faeroes**, **the Faroes**) group of islands in the N Atlantic. They belong to Denmark but are largely self-governing; pop approx 42000; capital Thorshaun.
▷ **Faeroese** (also **Faroese**) /ˌfeərəʊˈi:z/ *adj, n.*

faff /fæf/ *v* (phr v) **faff aˈbout/aˈround** (*Brit infml*) behave in a fussy and inefficient way; dither: *Stop faffing around and get to the point.*

fag /fæg/ *n* **1** [sing, U] (*infml*) tedious and tiring job: *I've got to tidy my room. What a fag!* ○ *It's too much (of a) fag.* **2** [C] (*Brit infml*) cigarette. **3** [C] (*Brit*) (formerly) junior boy at a public school performing certain duties for a senior boy. **4** [C] (*esp US*) = FAGGOT 3.
▷ **fag** /fæg/ *v* (**-gg-**) **1** [I, Ipr, Ip] ~ (**away**) (**at sth/at doing sth**) (*infml*) do very tiring work: *fagging (away) in the office, at her work.* **2** [I, Ipr] ~ (**for sb**) act as a fag(3) (for sb). **3** (phr v) **fag sb/sth out** (*infml*) make (a person or an animal) very tired: *Running soon fags me out.* ○ *He was completely fagged out,* ie exhausted.
□ **ˈfag-end** *n* (*Brit infml*) **1** end of a cigarette after it has been smoked. **2** (*fig*) inferior or useless remnant; worthless part of anything: *He only heard the fag-end of their conversation.*

faggot (*US* **fagot**) /ˈfægət/ *n* **1** bundle of sticks or twigs tied together for burning. **2** ball of chopped seasoned meat, etc cooked by baking or frying. **3** (also *esp US* **fag**) (*infml derog*) male homosexual.

Fagin /ˈfeɪgɪn/ character in Charles *Dickens's *Oliver Twist* who receives stolen goods and trains young boys to steal. The name is sometimes used of a person acting illegally in this way.

fah = FA.

Fahrenheit /ˈfærənhaɪt/ *adj* of a temperature scale with the freezing-point of water at 32° and the boiling-point at 212°: *The temperature today is seventy degrees Fahrenheit.* ⇨ App 9, 10. Cf CELSIUS, CENTIGRADE. ⇨ article at WEATHER.

faience /ˌfaɪˈɑ:ns/ *n* [U] decorated and glazed earthenware or porcelain.

fail /feɪl/ *v* **1** (**a**) [I, Ipr, Tn, Tt] ~ (**in sth**) be unsuccessful in (sth): *If you don't work hard, you may fail.* ○ *I passed in maths but failed in French.* ○ *He failed his driving-test.* ○ *She failed to reach the semi-finals.* (**b**) [Tn] decide that (a candidate) is unsuccessful: *The examiners failed half the candidates.* Cf SUCCEED 1. **2** [It] forget, neglect or be unable (to do sth): *He never fails to write* (ie always writes) *to his mother every week.* ○ *She did not fail to keep* (ie She did keep) *her word.* ○ *Your promises have failed to* (ie did not) *materialize.* **3** [I, Tn] not be enough for (sb); end or be lacking while still needed or expected by (sb): *The crops failed because of drought.* ○ *Our water supply has failed (us).* ○ *Words fail me,* ie I cannot find words (to describe my feelings, etc). **4** [I] (**a**) (of health, eyesight, etc) become weak: *His eyesight is failing.* ○ *He has suffered from failing health/has been failing in health for the last two years.* (**b**) stop working properly: *The brakes failed.* **5** [I] become bankrupt: *Several banks failed during the depression.*
▷ **fail** *n* **1** failure in an examination: *I had three passes and one fail.* **2** (idm) **without ˈfail** certainly, even though there may be difficulties; whatever happens; definitely: *I'll be there at two o'clock without fail.*

□ **ˈfail-safe** *adj* [attrib] (of equipment, machinery, etc) designed to compensate automatically for a breakdown or failure: *the fail-safe mechanism.*

failing[1] /ˈfeɪlɪŋ/ *n* weakness or fault (of character); shortcoming: *We all have our little failings.*

failing[2] /ˈfeɪlɪŋ/ *prep* **1** if (sth) does not happen; without (sth): *failing this*, ie if this does not happen ○ *failing an answer*, ie if no answer is received. **2** if (sb) is not available: *Failing Smith, try Jones.*

failure /ˈfeɪljə(r)/ *n* **1** (a) [U] lack of success: *Failure in one examination should not stop you trying again.* ○ *The enterprise was doomed to failure.* ○ *All my efforts ended in failure*, ie were unsuccessful. (b) [C] instance of this: *Success came after many failures.* (c) [C] person, attempt or thing that fails: *He was a failure as a teacher.* ○ *Our new radio is an utter failure.* **2** (a) [U] state of being inadequate; not functioning as is expected or required: *a case of heart failure* ○ *Failure of crops often results in famine.* (b) [C] instance of this: *ˈengine failures* ○ *another crop failure.* **3** (a) [U] ~ **to do sth** neglecting or forgetting to do sth: *failure to comply with the regulations.* (b) [C] ~ **to do sth** instance of this: *repeated failures to appear in court.*

fain /feɪn/ *adj* ~ **to do sth** (*arch*) willing or forced to do sth.

▷ **fain** *adv* (*arch*) willingly: *I would fain* (ie would prefer to) *decline.*

faint[1] /feɪnt/ *adj* (**-er, -est**) **1** that cannot be clearly perceived by the senses; indistinct; not intense in colour or sound or smell: *The sounds of music grew fainter in the distance.* ○ *Only faint traces of the tiger's tracks could be seen.* **2** (of ideas, etc) weak; vague: *There is a faint hope that she may be cured.* **3** (a) (of physical abilities) lacking strength: *in a faint voice* ○ *His breathing became faint.* (b) [pred] (of people) likely to lose consciousness; giddy: *She looks/feels faint.* (c) [pred] (of people) weak; exhausted: *The explorers were faint from hunger and cold.* **4** (of actions, etc) weak; unlikely to have much effect: *a faint show of resistance* ○ *make a faint attempt to do sth.* **5** (idm) **damn sb/sth with faint praise** ⇨ DAMN[1]. **not have the ˈfaintest/ˈfoggiest (idea)** (*infml*) not know at all: *'Do you know where she is?' 'Sorry, I haven't the faintest.'* ▷ **faintly** *adv.* **faintness** *n* [U].

□ **ˌfaint-ˈhearted** *adj* timid; not brave. **ˌfaint-ˈheartedly** *adv.* **ˌfaint-ˈheartedness** *n* [U].

faint[2] /feɪnt/ *v* [I, Ipr] lose consciousness (because of heat, shock, loss of blood, etc): *He fainted (from hunger).*

▷ **faint** *n* **1** [sing] act or state of fainting. **2** (idm) **in a (dead) faint** (completely) unconscious: *She fell to the ground in a dead faint.*

fair[1] /feə(r)/ *adj* **1** (a) ~ **(to/on sb)** treating each person, side, etc equally and according to the law, rules, etc; impartial: *Our teacher isn't fair: he always gives the highest marks to his favourites.* ○ *She deserves a fair trial.* ○ *The punishment was quite fair.* ○ *The ruling was not fair to everyone.* (b) in accordance with what is deserved or expected or with existing rules: *a fair share, wage, price* ○ *It was a fair fight*, ie The rules of boxing were observed. ○ *It's not fair to give him the prize/not fair that he should be given the prize.* **2** (a) average; moderately good: *There's a fair chance that we might win this time.* ○ *His knowledge of French is fair, but ought to be better.* (b) [attrib] (*infml*) quite large, long, etc: *A fair number of people came along.* **3** (a) (of the weather) good; dry and fine: *hoping for fair weather.* (b) (of winds) favourable: *They set sail with the first fair wind.* **4** (of the skin or the hair) pale; light in colour: *a fair complexion* ○ *fair hair.* **5** (*arch*) beautiful: *a fair maiden.* ⇨ Usage at BEAUTIFUL. **6** (idm) **by ˌfair means or ˈfoul** somehow or other, whether by good or evil methods: *She's determined to win, by fair means or foul.* **by one's ˌown fair ˈhand** (*joc*) by oneself: *I hope you'll appreciate this: it's all done by my/mine own fair hand.* **a fair ˈcop** (*sl*) legitimate arrest (usu made while the crime is being committed). **a fair crack of the ˈwhip** (*infml*) reasonable chance to share in sth, to be successful, etc: *give him a fair crack of the whip.* **a fair/square deal** ⇨ DEAL[4]. **fair ˈdo/ˈdos/ˈdo's** (*Brit infml*) (used esp as an *interj*) fair treatment; fair shares: *Come on, fair dos — you've had a long go on the computer and now it's my turn.* **ˌfair exˌchange is ˌno ˈrobbery** (*dated saying usu joc*) (said when two people agree to an exchange which suits them both, or by one person after exchanging sth with another who is not satisfied with the deal). **fair ˈgame** person or thing that it is considered reasonable to chase, ridicule, etc: *The younger teachers were fair game for playing tricks on.* **(give sb/get) a fair ˈhearing** opportunity of being listened to impartially, usu in a lawcourt. **fair ˈplay** equal treatment of both or all sides because of respect for the rules: *determined to see fair play*, ie to see that no injustice is done. **a fair ˈquestion** question that is reasonable to ask (but often difficult to answer): *'If the proposals are obviously sensible, why do you oppose them?' 'That's a fair question.'* **fair's ˈfair** (*infml*) (used as a protest or a reminder that) sb should be dealt with fairly: *'Come on, Sarah. Give me a bit more — fair's fair!'* **a fair ˈshake** (*US infml*) just or reasonable arrangement; fair chance. **have, etc (more than) one's fair share of sth** have, etc (more than) a usual or an expected amount of sth: *We got more than our fair share of rain on holiday.* **in a fair way to do sth** likely to do sth: *in a fair way to succeed.* **in a fair way of ˈbusiness** having quite a large, successful, etc business. **set ˈfair** (of the weather) fine and with no sign of change. ▷ **fairness** *n* [U].

□ **ˌfair ˈcopy** neat copy of a corrected document: *Please make a fair copy of this letter.*

ˌfair-ˈhaired *adj* with light-coloured or blond hair.

ˌfair-ˈminded *adj* fair in judgement; not prejudiced.

the ˈfair sex (*dated or joc*) women.

ˌfair-to-ˈmiddling (*infml*) *adj* slightly better than average.

ˌfair-weather ˈfriend person who stops being a friend when one is in trouble.

fair[2] /feə(r)/ *adv* **1** in a fair[1](1) manner. **2** (idm) **fair and ˈsquare** (a) exactly on target. (b) with no uncertainty or possibility of error, misunderstanding, etc: *The blame rests fair and square on my shoulders.* **fair eˈnough** (used esp as an *interj*) (*infml*) (sometimes showing unwilling agreement) all right; I accept. **play ˈfair** play or act fairly. following rules or accepted standards: *Come on, you're not playing fair.*

fair[3] /feə(r)/ *n* **1** (a) = FUN-FAIR (FUN): *Saint Giles fair in Oxford.* (b) market (esp for farm animals and farm products) held regularly in a particular place, often with entertainments: *the county fair.* (c) social event often held to raise money for charity, with stalls, raffles and other attractions; bazaar: *the Christmas fair at the parish church.* **2** large-scale exhibition of commercial and industrial goods: *a world fair* ○ *a trade fair.* ⇨ Usage at DEMONSTRATION.

□ **ˈfairground** *n* outdoor area where fun-fairs are held.

Fairbanks /ˈfeəbæŋks/ Douglas (1883-39), American film actor. A hero of the silent screen, he specialised in swashbuckling roles, as in *Robin Hood* and *The Thief of Bagdad.* His son, Douglas Fairbanks Junior (1909-) also played the leading man in many Hollywood films.

fairing /ˈfeərɪŋ/ *n* specially shaped part attached to a ship, an aircraft, etc to make it more streamlined.

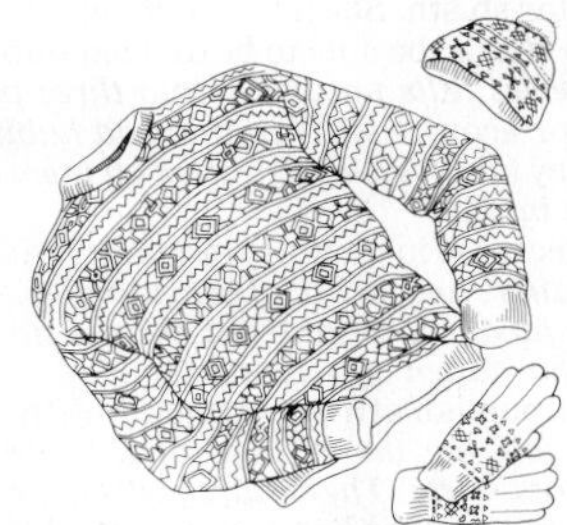

Fair Isle sweater, hat and gloves

Fair Isle /ˈfeər aɪl/ island in the *Shetlands famous for the intricate coloured knitting patterns of the woollen garments originally produced there: *a Fair Isle sweater.* ⇨ illus.

fairly /ˈfeəlɪ/ *adv* **1** in a fair manner; honestly: *You're not treating us fairly.* **2** (before *adjs* and *advs*) to a certain extent; moderately: *This is a fairly easy book.* ○ *We must leave fairly soon*, ie before very long. **3** completely; actually: *Her suggestion fairly took me by surprise.* ○ *I fairly jumped for joy.* ○ *The time fairly raced by.* **4** (idm) **fairly and squarely** = FAIR AND SQUARE (FAIR[2]).

NOTE ON USAGE: The adverbs **fairly**, **quite**, **rather** and **pretty** can all mean 'moderately', 'to some extent' or 'not very' and are used to alter the strength of adjectives and adverbs. **Fairly** is the weakest and **pretty** the strongest and most informal, but their effect is very much influenced by intonation. Generally, the more any of these adverbs is stressed, the more negative the sentence sounds. **1** When **rather** or **pretty** is used with a positive quality, it can sound enthusiastic: *a rather/pretty good play.* With a negative or variable quality they express disapproval: *rather/pretty poor work* ○ *I'm rather/pretty warm.* ○ *It's rather/pretty small/big.* **2 Fairly** is mostly used with positive qualities: *fairly tidy, spacious, friendly, etc* (compare: *rather untidy, cramped, unfriendly, etc*). **3** Only **rather** can be used with comparative expressions and **too:** *The house is rather bigger than we thought.* ○ *These shoes are rather too small.* **4 Rather** and **quite** can precede the indefinite article when followed by an adjective + noun: *rather/quite a nice day* ○ *a rather/quite/fairly/pretty nice day.* See also note on usage at QUITE.

fairway /ˈfeəweɪ/ *n* **1** part of a golf-course between the tee and the green, kept free of rough grass. ⇨ illus at GOLF. Cf ROUGH[3] 1. **2** channel that ships can sail through easily.

fairy /ˈfeərɪ/ *n* **1** small imaginary being with magical powers. For most people, fairies belong to children's stories. In some places however, eg Ireland and Cornwall, they are taken more seriously and there are many legends about them. Fairies are usually kind, but punish those who interfere in their affairs. The most popular fairy is probably the **tooth fairy**, who children are told leaves money in return for teeth they have lost: [attrib] *fairy voices, footsteps.* **2** (*sl derog*) male homosexual.

□ **ˌfairy ˈgodmother** person who provides unexpected help.

ˈfairyland /-lænd/ *n* **1** home of fairies. **2** (*fig*) beautiful or enchanted place: *The toy-shop is a fairyland for young children.*

ˈfairy lights small coloured electric lights used as decoration.

ˌfairy ˈring dark ring on grass caused by a fungus. Children are sometimes told that these rings are left when fairies have danced there.

ˈfairy story, ˈfairy-tale 1 story about fairies, magic, etc, usu for children. Giants, dwarfs, witches, etc often appear in fairy stories, as well as talking animals, though the heroes and heroines are usu ordinary human beings. In Britain, many pantomimes are based on traditional fairy stories, eg *Cinderella, Puss in Boots, Jack and the Beanstalk* and *The Sleeping Beauty.* **2** untrue or incredible story; falsehood: *'Now tell me the truth: I don't want any more of your fairy stories.'* **fairy-tale** *adj* [attrib] romantic, magical, etc, like the characters and situations in fairy stories: *a fairy-tale wedding* ○ *fairy-tale Alpine scenery.*

fait accompli /ˌfeɪt əˈkɒmpli:; *US* əkɒmˈpli:/ (*pl* **faits accomplis**) (*French*) thing already done, that cannot be undone and is therefore not worth arguing about: *She married the man her parents disapproved of and presented them with a fait accompli.*

faith /feɪθ/ *n* **1** [U] ~ **(in sb/sth)** trust; strong belief; unquestioning confidence: *put one's faith in God* ○ *Have you any faith in what he says?* ○ *I* *haven't much faith in this medicine.* ○ *I've lost faith in that fellow*, ie I can no longer trust him. **2** [U, sing] strong belief, without proof, in God or in an established religion: *a strong faith* ○ *lose one's faith* ○ *Faith is stronger than reason.* **3** [C] religion: *the Christian, Jewish and Muslim faiths.* **4** (idm) **break/keep faith with sb** break/keep one's promise to sb; be disloyal/loyal to sb. **in good ˈfaith** with honest intentions: *She signed the letter in good faith, not realizing its implications.* ○ *He bought the painting in good faith*, eg not realizing that it had been stolen.

□ **ˈfaith-cure** *n* [C], **ˈfaith-healing** *n* [U] cure, etc that depends on faith rather than on medicines or other treatment. **ˈfaith-healer** *n*.

faithful /ˈfeɪθfl/ *adj* **1** ~ (**to sb/sth**) loyal (to sb/sth): *a faithful friend* ○ *faithful to his beliefs* ○ *She was always faithful to her husband*, ie never had a sexual relationship with anyone else. **2** [attrib] able to be trusted; conscientious: *a faithful worker* ○ *a faithful correspondent*, ie one who writes regularly. **3** true to the facts; accurate: *a faithful copy, description, account, etc.*

▷ **the faithful** *n* [pl *v*] true believers (in a religion).

faithfully /-fəlɪ/ *adv* **1** in a faithful manner: *The old nurse had served the family faithfully for thirty years.* ○ *He followed the instructions faithfully.* **2** (idm) **yours faithfully** ⇨ YOURS (YOUR). ⇨ Usage at YOUR.

faithfulness *n* [U].

faithless /ˈfeɪθlɪs/ *adj* not trustworthy; not loyal: *a faithless friend, wife, ally, etc.* ▷ **faithlessly** *adv.* **faithlessness** *n* [U].

fake /feɪk/ *n* (**a**) object (eg a work of art) that seems genuine but is not: *That's not a real diamond necklace, it's just a fake!* Cf COUNTERFEIT, FORGERY (FORGE[2]). (**b**) person who tries to deceive by pretending to be what he is not: *He looked like a postman but he was really a fake.*

▷ **fake** *adj* not genuine: *fake furs, jewellery, etc* ○ *a fake policeman.*

fake *v* [Tn] **1** make (sth false) so that it seems genuine: *He faked his father's signature.* ○ *Her whole story had been faked*, ie was completely untrue. **2** pretend (sth); feign: *fake surprise, grief, illness.* **faker** *n*.

fakir /ˈfeɪkɪə(r); *US* fəˈk-/ *n* **1** Hindu religious beggar regarded as a holy man. **2** member of a Muslim holy sect who lives by begging.

falcon /ˈfɔːlkən; *US* ˈfælkən/ *n* small bird of prey.

▷ **falconer** *n* (**a**) person who trains falcons to hunt and kill other birds or animals for sport. (**b**) person who keeps trained falcons.

falconry /-rɪ/ *n* [U] (**a**) sport of hunting with falcons. (**b**) art of breeding and training falcons.

Falkland Islands /ˈfɔːklənd aɪləndz/ **the Falkland Islands** (also **the Falklands**) group of small islands in the southern Atlantic. They are a British colony, but claimed by Argentina, where they are called the Malvinas. The economy is based on sheep-farming. In 1982 Argentinian troops occupied the Falklands for three months before British forces recaptured them.

fall[1] /fɔːl/ *v* (*pt* **fell** /fel/, *pp* **fallen** /ˈfɔːlən/) **1** [I, Ipr, Ip] come or go down from force of weight, loss of balance, etc; descend or drop: *The rain was falling steadily.* ○ *The leaves fall in autumn.* ○ *He slipped and fell ten feet.* ○ *That parcel contains glass — don't let it fall.* ○ *The book fell off the table onto the floor.* ○ *He fell into the river.* ○ *I need a new bicycle lamp — my old one fell off and broke.* **2** [I, Ipr] ~ (**on/upon sb/sth**) come as if by dropping suddenly; descend: *A sudden silence fell.* ○ *Darkness falls quickly in the tropics.* ○ *Fear fell upon them.* **3** [I, Ipr, Ip] ~ (**down/over**) stop standing, esp suddenly; collapse: *Many trees fell in the storm.* ○ *He fell on his knees* (ie knelt down) *and begged for mercy.* ○ *The toddler tried to walk but kept falling down.* ○ *She fell over and broke her leg.* ○ (*fig*) *Six wickets fell* (ie Six batsmen in cricket were dismissed) *before lunch.* **4** [Ipr] hang down: *Her hair fell over her shoulders in a mass of curls.* ○ *His beard fell to his chest.* **5** [I] decrease in amount, number or intensity: *Prices fell on the stock market.* ○ *Her spirits fell* (ie She became sad) *at the bad news.* ○ *Her voice fell as they entered the room.* ○ *The temperature fell sharply in the night.* **6** [I, Ip] ~ (**away/off**) slope downwards: *Beyond the hill, the land falls (away) sharply towards the river.* **7** [I] (**a**) lose one's position, office or power; be defeated: *The government fell after the revolution.* (**b**) die in battle; be shot: *Half the regiment fell before the enemy onslaught.* ○ *Six tigers fell to his rifle.* (**c**) (of a fortress, city, etc) be captured: *Troy finally fell (to the Greeks).* **8** [I] (*dated*) sin; do wrong: *Eve tempted Adam and he fell.* **9** [Ipr] ~ **on/over sth** take the direction or position specified: *Which syllable does the stress of this word fall on?* ○ *My eye fell on* (ie I suddenly saw) *a curious object.* ○ *A shadow fell over the room.* **10** [La, Ln, Ipr] ~ (**into sth**) pass into a specified state; become: *fall asleep* ○ *The horse fell lame.* ○ *He fell silent.* ○ *Has she fallen ill again?* ○ *When does the rent fall due?* ie When must it be paid? ○ *She fell an easy prey to his charm.* ○ *He fell into a doze*, ie began to doze. ○ *The house fell into decay.* **11** [I, Ipr] happen or occur; have as a date: *Easter falls early this year.* ○ *Christmas Day falls on a Monday.* **12** [I, Ipr] be spoken: *I guessed what was happening from a few words she let fall*, ie from what she said. ○ *Not a word fell from his lips.* **13** (For idioms containing **fall**, see entries for *ns, adjs*, etc, eg **fall in love (with sb)** ⇨ LOVE[1]; **fall flat** ⇨ FLAT[2].)

14 (phr v) **fall about** (*infml*) laugh uncontrollably: *We all fell about (laughing/with laughter) when he did his imitation of the tea-lady.*

fall apart break; fall to pieces; disintegrate: *My car is falling apart.* ○ *Their marriage finally fell apart.*

fall away (**a**) desert; leave: *His supporters fell away as his popularity declined.* (**b**) disappear; vanish: *In a crisis, old prejudices fall away and everyone works together.*

fall back move or turn back; retreat: *The enemy fell back as our troops advanced.* **fall back on sb/sth** (be able to) go to sb for support or use sth when in difficulty: *At least we can fall back on candles if the electricity fails.* ○ *She's completely homeless — at least I have my parents to fall back on.*

fall behind (**sb/sth**) be overtaken (by sb/sth); fail to keep level (with sb/sth): *The major world powers are afraid of falling behind in the arms race.* ○ *France has fallen behind (Germany) in coal production.* **fall behind with sth** fail to pay for sth or to do sth for a period of time: *Don't fall behind with the rent, or you'll be evicted.* ○ *I've fallen behind with my correspondence.*

fall down be shown to be false or inadequate; collapse: *The plan fell down because it proved to be too expensive.* **fall down on sth** (*infml*) fail to do sth properly or successfully: *fall down on one's promises* ○ *He fell down on the job.*

fall for sb (*infml*) be attracted to sb; fall in love with sb: *They met, fell for each other and got married six weeks later.* **fall for sth** (*infml*) allow oneself to be persuaded by sth, esp unwisely: *The salesman said the car was in good condition, and I was foolish enough to fall for it.*

fall in collapse: *The roof of the tunnel fell in.* **fall (sb) in** (cause sb to) form a military formation; (cause sb to) go on parade: *The sergeant ordered his men to fall in.* **fall in with sb/sth** (**a**) meet sb by chance; join sb; become involved with sb/sth: *He fell in with bad company.* (**b**) agree to or show support for sb/sth: *She fell in with my idea at once.*

fall into sth (**a**) be able to be divided into sth: *The lecture series falls naturally into three parts.* (**b**) develop or acquire sth: *fall into bad habits.* (**c**) be trapped by sth: *We played a trick on them and they fell right into it.*

fall off decrease in quantity or quality: *Attendance at my lectures has fallen off considerably.* ○ *It used to be my favourite restaurant but the standard of cooking has fallen off recently.*

fall on/upon sb/sth (**a**) attack sb/sth fiercely: *Bandits fell on the village and robbed many inhabitants.* ○ (*fig*) *The children fell on the food and ate it greedily.* (**b**) be borne or incurred by sb: *The full cost of the wedding fell on me.*

fall out happen; occur: *We were pleased with the way things fell out.* **fall (sb) out** (cause sb to) leave military formation; go or send off parade: *The men fell out quickly after their march.* **fall out (with sb)** quarrel (with sb): *They fell out with each other just before their marriage.*

fall over sb/sth stumble or trip after hitting sb/sth with one's feet when walking, etc. **fall over oneself** be very clumsy: *He was an awkward child, always falling over himself and breaking things.* **fall over oneself to do sth** (*infml*) be specially eager to do or achieve sth: *People were falling over themselves to be introduced to the visiting film star.*

fall through fail to be completed; come to nothing: *Our holiday plans fell through because of transport strikes.*

fall to (**doing sth**) begin (to do sth): *They fell to (eating) with great gusto.* ○ *She fell to brooding about what had happened to her.* **fall to sb (to do sth)** become the duty or responsibility of sb: *It fell to me to inform her of her son's death.*

fall under sth be classified among sth: *What heading do these items fall under?*

▷ **the fallen** *n* [pl *v*] (*dated or fml*) those killed in war.

□ **ˈfall-out** *n* [U] radioactive waste carried in the air after a nuclear explosion.

falling star = SHOOTING STAR (SHOOT[1]).

fall[2] /fɔːl/ *n* **1** [C] act or instance of falling: *I had a fall (from a horse) and broke my arm.* ○ *That was a nasty fall.* **2** ~ (**of sth**) (**a**) [C] amount of sth that falls or has fallen: *a heavy fall of snow/rain* ○ *a fall of rock(s).* (**b**) [C esp *sing*] distance through which sb/sth falls or descends: *a fall of twenty feet* ○ *a twenty-foot fall.* **3** [C] decrease in value, quantity, intensity, etc: *a steep fall in prices* ○ *a fall in the numbers attending.* **4** [sing] ~ (**of sth**) (esp political) defeat; collapse: *the fall of the Roman Empire* ○ *The fall of the Government resulted in civil war.* **5** [C] (*US*) = AUTUMN: *in the fall of 1970* ○ *several falls ago* ○ [attrib] *fall fashions.* **6** (**a**) [C] ~ (**from sth**) loss of innocence or a state of goodness: *a fall from grace.* (**b**) **the Fall** [sing] (*Bible*) loss of mankind's innocence following the disobedience of Adam and Eve. **7** [C] (usu *pl*, esp in geographical names) large amount of water falling down from a height; waterfall: *The falls upstream are full of salmon.* ○ *Niagara Falls.* **8** [C] (in wrestling) act of forcing or throwing an opponent down onto his back. Cf SUBMISSION. **9** (idm) **pride comes/goes before a fall** ⇨ PRIDE. **ride for a fall** ⇨ RIDE[2].

□ **ˈfall line** line that marks a sudden change from high ground to low ground, eg between a plateau and a plain, where waterfalls occur in rivers.

fallacy /ˈfæləsɪ/ *n* **1** [C] false or mistaken belief: *It's a fallacy to suppose that wealth brings happiness.* **2** [U] false reasoning or argument: *a statement based on fallacy.*

▷ **fallacious** /fəˈleɪʃəs/ *adj* misleading; based on error: *fallacious reasoning.* **fallaciously** *adv.*

fallen *pp* of FALL[1].

fall guy /ˈfɔːl gaɪ/ (*esp US*) (**a**) = SCAPEGOAT. (**b**) person who is easily tricked or fooled.

fallible /ˈfæləbl/ *adj* liable to make mistakes: *We are fallible beings.* ▷ **fallibility** /ˌfæləˈbɪlətɪ/ *n* [U].

Fallopian tube /fəˌləʊpɪən ˈtjuːb; *US* ˈtuːb/ (*anatomy*) either of the two tubes along which egg-cells move from the ovaries to the womb. ⇨ illus at FEMALE.

fallow /ˈfæləʊ/ *adj* (of land) ploughed but left unplanted to restore its fertility: *allow land to lie fallow.*

▷ **fallow** *n* [U] fallow land.

fallow deer /ˈfæləʊ dɪə(r)/ (*pl* unchanged) small Eurasian deer with a brownish-yellow coat that has white spots in summer.

false /fɒls, fɔːls/ *adj* **1** wrong; incorrect: *sing a false note* ○ *'A whale is a fish. True or false?'* **2** (**a**) not genuine; artificial: *false hair, teeth, etc.* (**b**) sham, pretended: *false modesty* ○ *false tears.* (**c**) [usu attrib] misleading; not what it appears: *a false sense of security*, ie feeling safe when one is really in danger ○ *false economy* ○ *give a false impression of great wealth* ○ *hounds following a false scent.* (**d**)

Family

The traditional image of the family in both Britain and the USA is of a stable family unit consisting of a married couple and two or more children. As a result of the social changes and changes in legislation in recent years, the majority of families no longer conform to this image. Family size is decreasing and the average number of children per family is less than two. Many couples cohabit without being married, and the stigma that used to be associated with illegitimacy is disappearing. The trend towards early marriage that was evident in the 1960s has been reversed. In Britain the average age for people marrying for the first time is 26 for men and 24 for women. Changes in legislation have made it easier to obtain a divorce. About one in three marriages in Britain and one in two in the USA end in divorce. Many people marry again after divorce so that a high proportion of children live with a step-parent. The proportion of families led by a single parent, normally the mother, has also increased.

People often move to different parts of the country to work, so that many children have little contact with their grandparents, aunts, uncles and cousins except at family reunions, held traditionally at Christmas. Students often leave home when they go to university and people may leave home to find work from the age of 16. People may marry at 16 with their parents' consent and at 18 without it. It is usual for young people to move away from home once they are adult, and many young single people live alone, as do many retired people. (Cf article at RETIREMENT.)

Most parents encourage their children to become independent and the relationship between parents and children is more relaxed than in the past. Fathers often play a greater part in the care and upbringing of children, reflecting the changes in the respective roles of both parents as more mothers work outside the home.

deliberately made incorrect in order to deceive: *false weights, scales, dice, etc* ○ *a false passport* ○ *a false bottom*, ie the disguised bottom of a suitcase, etc concealing a secret compartment. **3** deliberately meant to deceive; lying: *false evidence* ○ *present false claims to an insurance company.* **4** ~ **(to sb)** unfaithful; disloyal: *a false friend/lover.* **5** [attrib] inaccurately named: *the false acacia*, ie not really an acacia tree, despite its name. **6** (idm) **a false aˈlarm** warning or panic about sth which does not happen: *The rumours of a petrol shortage turned out to be a false alarm.* **(make) a false ˈmove** unwise or forbidden action that may have unpleasant consequences: *'One false move and you're a dead man,' snarled the robber.* **(make) a false ˈstart (a)** (in athletics) start made before the signal (eg for a race) has been given. **(b)** unsuccessful beginning: *After several false starts, she became a successful journalist.* **(take) a false ˈstep** (make) a wrong move or action: *A false step could have cost the climbers their lives.* **in a false poˈsition** in circumstances which result in sb being misunderstood or acting against his principles. **on/under false preˈtences** pretending to be sb else or to have certain qualifications, etc in order to deceive: *obtaining money on false pretences.* **strike/sound a false ˈnote** say or do the wrong thing: *He struck a false note when he arrived for the wedding in old clothes.* **(sail) under false ˈcolours (a)** (of a ship) displaying a flag which it has no right to use. **(b)** pretending or appearing to be different from what one really is.

▷ **false** *adv* (idm) **play sb ˈfalse** deceive or cheat sb.

falsely *adv.*

falseness *n* [U].

falsehood /ˈfɔːlshʊd/ *n* (*fml*) **1** [C] untrue statement; lie: *How can you utter such falsehoods?* **2** [U] telling lies; lying: *guilty of falsehood.*

falsetto /fɔːlˈsetəʊ/ *n* (*pl* ~**s**) [C, U] (man with an) unusually high voice, esp when singing: *sing falsetto* ○ [attrib] *in a falsetto tone.*

falsify /ˈfɔːlsɪfaɪ/ *v* (*pt, pp* **-fied**) [Tn] **1** alter (eg a document) falsely: *falsify records, accounts, etc.* **2** present (sth) falsely: *falsify an issue, facts, etc.* **3** prove (sth) to be false: *falsify a theory.*

▷ **falsification** /ˌfɔːlsɪfɪˈkeɪʃn/ *n* **(a)** [U] falsifying or being falsified. **(b)** [C] change made in order to deceive.

falsity /ˈfɔːlsətɪ/ *n* **(a)** [U] falsehood; error. **(b)** [C] instance of this.

Falstaff /ˈfɔːlstɑːf; *US* -stæf/ Sir John, character in Shakespeare (*Henry IV, Parts I* and *II* and *The Merry Wives of Windsor*). He is fat, witty, boastful and often drunk. ▷ **Falstaffian** /ˌfɔːlˈstɑːfɪən/ *adj*: *a Falstaffian* (ie cheerfully dissolute) *character.*

falter /ˈfɔːltə(r)/ *v* [I] **1** move, walk or act hesitantly, usu because of weakness, fear or indecision: *Jane walked boldly up to the platform without faltering.* **2 (a)** (of the voice) waver: *His voice faltered as he tried to speak.* **(b)** speak hesitantly: *The lecturer faltered after dropping his notes.* ▷ **falteringly** /ˈfɔːltərɪŋlɪ/ *adv.*

fame /feɪm/ *n* [U] (condition of) being known or talked about by many people: *achieve fame and fortune* ○ *The young musician rose quickly to fame.*

▷ **famed** *adj* [pred] ~ **(for sth)**: *famed for their courage.*

familiar /fəˈmɪlɪə(r)/ *adj* **1** [pred] ~ **with sth** having a good knowledge of sth: *facts with which every schoolboy is familiar* ○ *I am not very familiar with botanical names.* **2** ~ **(to sb)** well known (to sb); often seen or heard: *facts that are familiar to every schoolboy* ○ *the familiar scenes of one's childhood* ○ *the familiar voices of one's friends.* **3** ~ **(with sb)** friendly and informal: *She greeted them by their first names in a familiar way.* ○ *I'm on familiar terms with my bank manager.* **4** ~ **(with sb)** too informal; more friendly and informal than is acceptable: *The children are too familiar with their teacher.*

▷ **familiar** *n* close friend or spirit: *a witch's familiar.*

familiarly *adv* in a familiar manner; informally: *William, familiarly known as Billy.*

familiarity /fəˌmɪlɪˈærətɪ/ *n* **1** [U] ~ **with sth** good knowledge of sth: *His familiarity with the local languages surprised me.* **2 (a)** [U] ~ **(to/towards sb)** (esp excessively) friendly informality: *You should not address your teacher with such familiarity.* **(b)** [C usu *pl*] instance of this; act that lacks formality: *Try to discourage such familiarities from your subordinates.* **3** (idm) **familiarity breeds conˈtempt** (*saying*) knowing sb/sth very well may lead to a loss of respect, fear, etc.

familiarize, -ise /fəˈmɪlɪəraɪz/ *v* [Tn·pr] ~ **sb/oneself with sth** give sb/acquire a thorough knowledge of sth: *familiarizing oneself with a foreign language, the use of a new tool, the rules of a game.* ▷ **familiarization, -isation** /fəˌmɪlɪəraɪˈzeɪʃn; *US* -rɪˈz-/ *n* [U].

family /ˈfæməlɪ/ *n* **1 (a)** [CGp] group consisting of parents and their children: *Almost every family in the village owns a television.* ○ *All my family enjoy skiing.* ○ *He's a friend of the family*, ie is known and liked by the parents and their children. **(b)** [CGp] group consisting of parents, their children and close relatives: *the Royal Family*, ie the children and close relatives of the Sovereign ○ *All our family came to our grandfather's eightieth birthday party.* ⇨ article. **(c)** [attrib] suitable for all members of this group to enjoy together, regardless of age: *a family film* ○ *family entertainment.* **2** [CGp, U] person's children or relatives: *Give my regards to Mr and Mrs Jones and family.* ○ *Do they have any family?* ○ *We have family over there.* ○ *They have a large family.* **3 (a)** [CGp] all the people descended from a common ancestor: *Some families have farmed in this area for hundreds of years.* ○ *She comes from a famous family.* ○ [attrib] *the family estate* ○ *the family jewels.* **(b)** [U] ancestry: *a man of good family.* **4** [C] **(a)** group of related genera of animals or plants: *Lions belong to the cat family.* Cf PHYLUM, CLASS 7, ORDER[1] 9, GENUS 1, SPECIES 1. **(b)** group of things (eg languages) with common features and a common source: *the Germanic family of languages.* **5** (idm) **(put sb/be) in the family way** (*infml*) (make sb/be) pregnant. **run in the ˈfamily** be a feature that keeps coming back in different generations of a family: *Red hair runs in his family.* **start a family** ⇨ START[2].

□ **ˌfamily ˈcircle** friendly group of close relatives.

ˌfamily ˈdoctor general practitioner normally consulted by a family.

ˌfamily ˈlikeness physical resemblance between members of a family: *This must be your brother: I can see a family likeness.*

ˈfamily man man who has a wife and children, and enjoys home life.

ˈfamily name surname. ⇨ Usage at NAME[1].

ˌfamily ˈplanning planning the number of children, intervals between births, etc in a family by using birth-control.

ˌfamily ˈtree diagram that shows the relationship between different members of a family. ⇨ App 8.

famine /ˈfæmɪn/ *n* [C, U] (instance of) extreme scarcity of food in a region: *a famine in Ethiopia* ○ *The long drought was followed by months of famine.*

famished /ˈfæmɪʃt/ *adj* [usu pred] (*infml*) very hungry: *When's lunch? I'm famished!*

famous /ˈfeɪməs/ *adj* **1** ~ **(for sth)** known to very many people; celebrated: *Paris is a famous city.* ○ *New York is famous for its skyscrapers.* ○ *She is famous as a writer.* **2** (*dated infml*) excellent: *We've won a famous victory.* **3** (idm) **famous last words** (*joc catchphrase*) (said when sb has made an important, optimistic, etc statement which may turn out to be untrue and which he may regret saying).

▷ **famously** *adv* (*infml*) extremely well: *The two children got on famously.*

fan

FAN

EXTRACTOR FAN

fan[1] /fæn/ *n* ⇨ illus. **1 (a)** object, often shaped like a semicircle, held in the hand and waved to create a current of cool air ⇨ illus at DRESS. **(b)** thing spread or shaped like a fan, eg the tail of a peacock. **2** device with rotating blades, operated mechanically to create a current of cool air: *It's so hot — please turn the fan on.* ⇨ illus at CAR. **3** (idm) **when the shit hits the fan** ⇨ SHIT.

□ ˈ**fan belt** belt driving the fan that cools the radiator of a car, etc. ⇨ illus at CAR.

ˈ**fan heater** device that blows hot air into a room.

fan[2] /fæn/ *v* (**-nn-**) **1** [Tn] make a current of air blow onto (sb/sth) with or as if with a fan: *cool one's face by fanning it with a newspaper* ○ *fan a fire*, ie to make it burn more strongly. **2** [Tn] blow gently on (sb/sth): *The breeze fanned our faces.* **3** [Tn, Tn·p] ~ **sth (out)** spread (esp playing-cards) in the form of a fan: *He fanned (out) the cards in his hand before playing.* **4** (idm) **fan the flames (of sth)** make (emotions, etc) stronger or (activity) more intense: *Her wild behaviour merely fanned the flames of his jealousy.* **5** (phr v) **fan out** (esp of soldiers) spread out from a central point: *The troops fanned out as they advanced.*

fan[3] /fæn/ *n* enthusiastic admirer or supporter of sth/sb: *football, jazz, cinema fans* ○ *The police arrested six fans outside the ground.* ○ *Fans had travelled from all over the country for the concert.*

□ ˈ**fan club** organized group of a person's admirers.

ˈ**fan mail** letters from fans to the person they admire.

fanatic /fəˈnætɪk/ *n* person who is too enthusiastic about sth, esp religion or politics: *a religious, political fanatic* ○ *model train fanatics.*

▷ **fanatic** (also **fanatical** /-kl/) *adj* ~ (**about sth**) obsessively enthusiastic: *a fanatic jogger* ○ *She's fanatical about keeping fit.* **fanatically** /-klɪ/ *adv.* **fanaticism** /-tɪsɪzəm/ *n* [U, C] great or obsessive enthusiasm.

fancier /ˈfænsɪə(r)/ *n* (esp in compounds) person with a special interest in and love for sth: *a* ˈ*dog-fancier* ○ *a* ˈ*pigeon-fancier*.

fanciful /ˈfænsɪfl/ *adj* **1** (of people) using the imagination rather than reason: *Children are very fanciful.* **2** (of things) designed or decorated in an odd but creative manner. ▷ **fancifully** /-fəlɪ/ *adv.*

fancy[1] /ˈfænsɪ/ *n* **1** [U] power of the mind to imagine (esp unreal things): *the novelist's fancy.* **2** [C] thing imagined: *Did I really hear someone come in, or was it only a fancy?* ○ *I have a fancy* (ie a vague idea) *that he will be late.* **3** [sing] ~ (**for sth**) desire; liking: *I have a fancy for some wine tonight.* **4** [C usu *pl*] small decorated cake: *fancies served with coffee.* **5** (idm) **catch/take sb's fancy** please or attract sb: *She saw a dress in the shop window and it caught her fancy immediately.* **a flight of fancy** ⇨ FLIGHT[1]. **take a fancy to sb/sth** become fond of sb/sth, often without an obvious reason: *I've suddenly taken a fancy to detective stories.*

□ ˌ**fancy-ˈfree** *adj* [usu pred] **1** not in love; not committed to anything. **2** (idm) **footloose and fancy-free** ⇨ FOOTLOOSE (FOOT[1]).

fancy[2] /ˈfænsɪ/ *adj* **1** [attrib] (esp of small things) brightly coloured; made to please the eye or taste: *fancy cakes/goods.* **2** not plain or ordinary; unusual: *That's a very fancy pair of shoes!* **3** extravagant or exaggerated: *fancy ideas, prices.* **4** (*esp US*) (of food, etc) above average quality: *fancy vegetables.* **5** [attrib] bred for particular points of beauty: *fancy dogs, pigeons, etc.*

□ ˌ**fancy** ˈ**dress** (wearing) clothes that are amusing because one would not normally wear them, eg a historical costume or a uniform: *Everybody turned up at the office wearing fancy dress* ○ [attrib] *a fancy dress ball/party.*

📖 People in Britain often like wearing unusual or even ridiculous clothes for parties and other social events. Fancy dress parties often have a theme, such as 'famous people in history' or 'bad taste', and prizes are sometimes awarded for the best or most outrageous costumes. Young children's birthday parties are often celebrated in this way too, and children may dress up as their favourite character from a book or television programme. Fancy dress also plays a part in fund-raising events such as a university or college rag week, when students, dressed in funny clothes and wearing a lot of make-up, go into town centres to raise money for charity.

ˈ**fancy man**, ˈ**fancy woman** (*derog or joc infml*) person's lover.

fancy[3] /ˈfænsɪ/ *v* (*pt, pp* **fancied**) **1** [Tf] think or believe (sth); imagine: *I fancy (that) it's going to rain today.* ○ *He fancies she likes him.* ○ *He fancied he heard footsteps behind him.* **2** [Tn] (*infml*) have a desire or wish for (sth); want: *I fancy a cup of tea.* ○ *What do you fancy for supper?* **3** [Tn] (*Brit infml*) find (sb) attractive: *He rather fancies her.* **4** [I, Tn, Tg, Tsg] (usu imperative, expressing surprise, disbelief, shock, etc): *Fancy that!* ○ *Just fancy!* ○ *Fancy her being so rude!* ○ *Fancy never having seen the sea!* **5** (idm) **fancy oneself (as sth)** (*infml*) have a very high opinion of oneself; be conceited: *She rather fancies herself as a singer.*

fandango /fænˈdæŋgəʊ/ *n* (*pl* ~**es**) **1** (music for a) lively Spanish or S American dance. **2** nonsense: *Politics before an election can be quite a fandango.*

fanfare /ˈfænfeə(r)/ *n* short ceremonial piece of music, usu played on trumpets: *A fanfare was played as the queen entered.*

fang /fæŋ/ *n* **1** long sharp tooth, esp of dogs and wolves: *The dog growled and showed its fangs.* **2** snake's tooth with which it injects poison. **3** (idm) **draw sb's/sth's teeth/fangs** ⇨ DRAW[2].

fanlight /ˈfænlaɪt/ *n* small window above a door or another window.

fanny /ˈfænɪ/ *n* **1** (*Brit* ⚠ *sl*) female sex organs. **2** (*sl esp US*) buttocks.

fantail /ˈfænteɪl/ *n* type of pigeon with a fan-shaped tail.

fantasia /fænˈteɪzɪə; *US* -ˈteɪʒə/ *n* (also **fantasy**) imaginative musical or other composition with no fixed form.

fantasize, -ise /ˈfæntəsaɪz/ *v* [I, Ipr, Tf] ~ (**about sth**) imagine or create a fantasy; daydream: *He liked to fantasize that he had won a gold medal.*

fantastic /fænˈtæstɪk/ *adj* **1** (**a**) wild and strange: *fantastic dreams, stories.* (**b**) impossible to carry out; not practical: *fantastic schemes, proposals, etc.* **2** (*infml*) marvellous; excellent: *She's a fantastic swimmer.* ○ *You passed your test? Fantastic!* **3** (*infml*) very large; extraordinary: *Their wedding cost a fantastic amount of money.* ▷ **fantastically** /-klɪ/ *adv*: *You did fantastically well in the exam.*

fantasy (also **phantasy**) /ˈfæntəsɪ/ *n* **1** [U] imagination or fancy[1](2), esp when completely unrelated to reality: [attrib] *live in a fantasy world.* **2** [C] product of the imagination; wild or unrealistic notion: *sexual fantasies* ○ *Stop looking for the perfect job — it's just a fantasy.* **3** [C] = FANTASIA.

FAO /ˌef eɪ ˈəʊ/ *abbr* Food and Agriculture Organization (of the United Nations).

far[1] /fɑː(r)/ *adj* (**farther** /ˈfɑːðə(r)/ or **further** /ˈfɜːðə(r)/, **farthest** /ˈfɑːðɪst/ or **furthest** /ˈfɜːðɪst/) [attrib] **1** (*dated or fml*) distant: *a far country* ○ *to journey into far regions.* **2** more remote: *at the far end of the street* ○ *on the far bank of the river* ○ *She's on the far right*, ie holds extreme right-wing views. **3** (idm) **a far cry from sth/doing sth** (*infml*) a very different experience from sth/doing sth: *Life on a farm is a far cry from what I've been used to.*

□ **the Far ˈEast** China, Japan and other countries of E and SE Asia.

the Far ˈWest (*US*) the part of the USA near the Pacific coast.

far[2] /fɑː(r)/ *adv* (**farther** /ˈfɑːðə(r)/ or **further** /ˈfɜːðə(r)/, **farthest** /ˈfɑːðɪst/ or **furthest** /ˈfɜːðɪst/) **1** (usu in questions and negative sentences) (of space) at or to a great distance: *How far is it to London from here?* (Cf *London's a long way from here.*) ○ *How far have we walked?* (Cf *We've walked only a short way.*) ○ *We didn't go far.* **2** (preceding particles and *preps*) (**a**) (of space) by a great distance: *far above the clouds* ○ *not far from here* ○ *far beyond the bridge* ○ *Call me if you need me; I won't be far away/off.* (**b**) (of time) a long way: *far back in history* ○ *as far back as 1902* ○ *events that will happen far in the future* ○ *We danced far into the night.* (**c**) (used within idioms) to a great extent: *to live far beyond one's means* ○ *He's fallen far behind in his work.* **3** (preceding comparative *adjs* and *advs*) considerably; very much: *a far better solution* ○ *He runs far faster than his brother.* **4** (idm) **as far as** to the place mentioned, but no further: *I've read as far as the third chapter.* ○ *I'll walk with you as far as the post office.* ○ *We'll go by train as far as London, and then take a coach.* **as/so far as** (**a**) the same distance as: *We didn't go so far as the others.* (**b**) to the extent that; as much as: *So far as I know/As far as I can see, that is highly unlikely.* ○ *His parents supported him as far as they could.* (**c**) (of progress) up to a specified point but not beyond: *We've got as far as collecting our data but we haven't analysed it yet.* **as/so far as in me** ˈ**lies** (*fml*) to the best of my ability; as much as I can. **as/so far as it, etc** ˈ**goes** to a limited extent, usu less than desirable: *Your plan is a good one as far as it goes, but there are several points you've forgotten to consider.* **as/so far as sb/sth is concerned** in the way, or to the extent, that sb/sth is involved or affected: *The rise in interest rates will be disastrous as far as small firms are concerned.* ○ *The car is fine as far as the engine is concerned but the bodywork needs a lot of attention.* ○ *As far as I'm concerned you can do what you like.* **as far as the eye can** ˈ**see** to the horizon: *The prairies stretch on all sides as far as the eye can see.* **by** ˈ**far** (following comparative or superlative *adjs* or *advs*, preceding or following comparative or superlative expressions with *the* or *a*) by a great amount: *It is quicker by far to go by train.* ○ *She is the best by far/She is by far the best.* **carry/take sth too, etc** ˈ**far** continue (doing) sth beyond reasonable limits: *Don't be such a prude — you can carry modesty too far!* ○ *It's time to be serious; you've carried this joke far enough.* **far/farther/further afield** ⇨ AFIELD. **far and a**ˈ**way** (preceding comparative or superlative *adjs*) by a very great amount; very much: *She's far and away the best actress I've seen.* **far and** ˈ**near**/ˈ**wide** everywhere; from or to a large area: *They searched far and wide for the missing child.* ○ *People came from far and near to hear the famous violinist.* **far be it from me to do sth (but...)** (*infml*) I certainly don't want you to think I would do sth (but...): *Far be it from me to interfere in your affairs but I would like to give you just one piece of advice.* **far from doing sth** instead of doing sth: *Far from enjoying dancing, he loathes it.* **far from sth/from doing sth** not at all sth; almost the opposite of sth: *The problem is far from easy*, ie is in fact very difficult. ○ *Your account is far from (being) true/is far from the truth.* **far** ˈ**from it** (*infml*) certainly not; almost the opposite: *'Are you happy here?' 'No, far from it; I've never been so miserable in my life.'* **few and far between** ⇨ FEW. **go as/so far as to do sth/as that, etc** be willing to go to extreme limits in dealing with sth: *I won't go so far as to say that he is dishonest*, ie I won't actually accuse him of dishonesty, even though I might suspect him of it. **go** ˈ**far** (**a**) (of money) buy many goods, etc: *A pound doesn't go very far* (ie You can't buy very much for a pound) *nowadays.* (**b**) (of food, supplies, etc) be enough for what is needed; last: *Four bottles of wine won't go far among twenty people.* **go** ˈ**far/a long** ˈ**way** (of people) be very successful: *Someone as intelligent as you should go far.* **go far/a long way towards sth/doing sth** help greatly in (achieving) sth: *Their promises don't go very far towards solving our present problems.* **go too** ˈ**far** behave in a way that is beyond reasonable limits: *He's always been rather rude but this time he's gone too far.* **in so far as** to the extent that: *This is the truth in so far as I know it.* **not far** ˈ**off**/ˈ**out**/ˈ**wrong** (*infml*) correct or almost correct: *Your guess wasn't far out.* ˈ**so far** until now; up to this/that point, time, etc: *So far the work has been easy but things may change.* ˌ**so** ˈ**far** (*infml*) only to a limited extent: *I trust you only so far (and no further).* ˌ**so far, so** ˈ**good** (*saying*) up to now everything has been successful.

□ ˈ**far-away** *adj* [attrib] **1** distant; remote: *far-away places.* **2** dreamy, as if thinking of sth else: *You have a far-away look in your eyes.*

ˌ**far-**ˈ**fetched** *adj* (*usu derog*) **1** (of a comparison) strained; unnatural. **2** (*infml*) (of a story, an account, etc) exaggerated; incredible: *It's an interesting book but rather far-fetched.*

ˌ**far-ˈflung** *adj* [usu attrib] **1** spread over a wide area; distributed widely: *a far-flung network of contacts.* **2** distant: *Her fame has reached the most far-flung corners of the globe.*

ˌ**far ˈgone** (*infml*) **1** very ill: *The injured man was fairly far gone by the time the ambulance arrived.* **2** very drunk: *You mustn't drive, you're too far gone!*

ˈ**far-off** *adj* [attrib] remote: *a far-off country.*

ˌ**far-ˈreaching** *adj* likely to have a wide influence or many results: *far-reaching proposals.*

ˌ**far-ˈseeing** *adj* (*approv*) seeing future problems and possibilities clearly and planning for them.

ˌ**far-ˈsighted** *adj* **1** (*approv*) **(a)** = FAR-SEEING. **(b)** (of ideas, etc) showing an awareness of future needs: *far-sighted changes in the organization.* **2** (*esp US*) = LONG-SIGHTED (LONG[1]).

farad /ˈfærəd/ *n* unit of capacitance such that one coulomb of charge causes a potential difference of one volt.

Faraday /ˈfærədeɪ/ Michael (1791-1867), English scientist. His family was poor and he was largely self-taught. As a laboratory assistant to Sir Humphrey *Davy, he concentrated initially on analytical chemistry. But his most famous discovery was electromagnetic induction, the condition under which a permanent magnet can generate electricity; this later led to the development of the electric dynamo and motor. He also set out **Faraday's laws** of electrolysis and studied electrical fields.

farce /fɑːs/ *n* **1 (a)** [C] funny play for the theatre based on unlikely situations and events. **(b)** [U] plays of this type: *I prefer farce to tragedy.* **2** [C] absurd and pointless proceedings: *The prisoner's trial was a farce.*

▷ **farcical** /ˈfɑːsɪkl/ *adj* absurd; ridiculous. **farcically** /-klɪ/ *adv.*

fare[1] /feə(r)/ *n* **1** money charged for a journey by bus, ship, taxi, etc: *What is the bus fare to London?* ○ *travel at half/full/reduced fare* ○ *economy fares.* **2** passenger who pays a fare, esp in a taxi.

□ ˈ**fare-stage** *n* part of a bus route regarded as a unit in calculating the fare.

fare[2] /feə(r)/ *n* [U] food, esp when offered at a meal: *fine/simple/wholesome/traditional fare.*

fare[3] /feə(r)/ *v* [I] (*fml*) progress; get on: *How did you fare* (ie What were your experiences) *while you were abroad?*

farewell /ˌfeəˈwel/ *interj* (*arch or fml*) **1** goodbye: *Farewell until we meet again!* **2** (idm) **(bid/say) farewell to sb/sth** (have) no more of sb/sth: *You can say farewell to seaside holidays as we once knew them.*

▷ **farewell** *n* saying goodbye: *make one's last farewells* ○ [attrib] *a farewell party, gift, speech.*

farinaceous /ˌfærɪˈneɪʃəs/ *adj* starchy or floury: *farinaceous foods,* eg bread, potatoes.

farm[1] /fɑːm/ *n* **1** area of land, and the buildings on it, used for growing crops or raising animals: *We've lived on this farm for twenty years.* ○ [attrib] *farm produce* ○ *farm machinery.* **2** farmhouse and the buildings near it: *get some eggs at the farm.* **3** place where certain fish or animals are raised: *a trout-/mink-/pig-farm.*

□ ˈ**farm-hand** *n* person who works as a labourer on a farm.

ˈ**farmhouse** *n* farmer's house.

ˈ**farmstead** /ˈfɑːmsted/ *n* farmhouse and the buildings near it.

ˈ**farmyard** *n* space enclosed by or next to farm buildings.

farm[2] /fɑːm/ *v* **1 (a)** [I] grow crops or rear animals: *He is farming in Africa.* **(b)** [Tn] use (land) for this: *She farms 200 acres.* **(c)** [Tn] breed (animals) on a farm: *farm beef cattle.* **2** (phr v) **farm sb out (to sb)** arrange for sb to be cared for by others: *The children were farmed out to nannies at an early age.* **farm sth out (to sb)** send out or delegate (work) to be done by others: *We're so busy we have to farm out a lot of work.*

▷ **farmer** *n* person who owns or manages a farm: *Farmer Giles,* ie the popular image of a British farmer as a cheerful character who loves country life.

farming *n* [U] profession of working on or managing a farm: *take up farming* ○ *pig farming* ○ [attrib] *farming subsidies, equipment.*

farrago /fəˈrɑːgəʊ/ *n* (*pl* ~**s**; *US* ~**es**) confused collection; mixture: *a farrago of useless bits of knowledge.*

farrier /ˈfærɪə(r)/ *n* blacksmith who makes and fits horseshoes.

farrow /ˈfærəʊ/ *v* [I] give birth to young pigs: *When will the sow farrow?*

▷ **farrow** *n* **1** number of young pigs born at the same time to one mother. **2** giving birth to young pigs: *Our sow had 15 at one farrow.*

fart /fɑːt/ *v* (⚠) **1** [I] send air from the bowels out through the anus. **2** (phr v) **fart about/around** (*sl*) be silly; play the fool: *Stop farting around and behave yourself!*

▷ **fart** *n* (⚠) **1** releasing of air through the anus. **2** (*sl derog*) person who is disliked or despised.

farther /ˈfɑːðə(r)/ *adj* (*comparative of* FAR[1]) more distant in space, direction or time: *on the farther bank of the river* ○ *The cinema was farther down the road than I thought.* ○ *Rome is farther from London than Paris is.*

▷ **farther** *adv* (*comparative of* FAR[2]) **1** at or to a greater distance in space or time; more remote: *We can't go any farther without resting.* ○ *Looking farther forward to the end of the century....* **2** (idm) **far/farther/further afield** ⇨ AFIELD.

NOTE ON USAGE: **Further** is now more common than **farther** in British English. They can both be used in relation to distance: *I can throw much further/farther than you.* ○ *Bristol is further/farther than Oxford.* In US English **farther** is usually used in relation to distance. In British and US English only **further** can be used to indicate addition: *Are there any further questions?* ○ *a College of Further Education.*

farthest /ˈfɑːðɪst/ *adj* (*superlative of* FAR[1]) **1** most distant in space, direction or time: *Go to the farthest house in the village and I'll meet you there.* **2** longest; most extended in space: *The farthest distance I've run is ten miles.*

▷ **farthest** *adv* (*superlative of* FAR[2]) **1** at or to the greatest distance in space or time; most remote: *Who ran (the) farthest?* ○ *It's ten miles away, at the farthest.* **2** to the highest degree or extent; most: *She is the farthest advanced of all my students.*

farthing /ˈfɑːðɪŋ/ *n* **1** former British coin worth one quarter of an old penny. **2** (idm) **not care/give a farthing** not care at all.

fascia = FACIA.

fascinate /ˈfæsɪneɪt/ *v* [Tn] **1** attract or interest (sb) greatly: *The children were fascinated by the toys in the shop window.* **2** take away power of movement from (eg an animal) by a strong light, etc: *The rabbit sat without moving, fascinated by the glare of our headlights.*

▷ **fascinating** *adj* having great attraction or charm: *a fascinating voice, story, glimpse.* **fascinatingly** *adv.*

fascination /ˌfæsɪˈneɪʃn/ *n* **1** [U, C] fascinating quality; process of fascinating: *Stamp collecting holds a certain fascination for me.* ○ *The fascinations of the circus are endless.* **2** [U, *sing*] state of being fascinated: *a fascination for Chinese pottery.*

fascism (also **Fascism**) /ˈfæʃɪzəm/ *n* [U] extreme right-wing dictatorial political system or views, esp (**Fascism**) as originally seen in Italy between 1922 and 1943. The Italian movement was imitated elsewhere, eg in Britain by Sir Oswald *Mosley, who founded the British Union of Fascists in 1932.

▷ **fascist** (also **Fascist**) /ˈfæʃɪst/ *n* (*usu derog*) person who supports fascism. — *adj* (*usu derog*) extremely right-wing; reactionary: *a fascist state* ○ *fascist opinions.*

fashion /ˈfæʃn/ *n* **1** [sing] manner or way of doing sth: *He walks in a peculiar fashion.* **2** [C, U] popular style (of clothes, behaviour, etc) at a given time or place: *dressed in the latest fashion* ○ *Fashions in art and literature are changing constantly.* ○ *New York and London may have their designers, but Paris and Milan are still regarded as the capitals of fashion.* ○ [attrib] *a fashion show* ○ *fashion magazines.* **3** (idm) **after a ˈfashion** to a certain extent, but not satisfactorily: *I can play the piano after a fashion.* **after/in the fashion of sb** (*fml*) like sb; imitating the style of sb: *She paints in the fashion of Picasso.* **(be) all the ˈfashion/ˈrage** (be) the latest style or trend: *Suddenly, collecting antiques is all the fashion.* **come into/be in ˈfashion** become/be popular: *Long skirts have come into fashion again. Faded jeans are still in fashion too.* **go/be out of fashion** become/be unpopular as a style.

▷ **fashion** *v* [Tn, Tn·pr] ~ **A from B/B into A** give form or shape to sth; design or make sth: *fashion a doll (from a piece of wood)* ○ *fashion a lump of clay into a bowl.*

fashionable /ˈfæʃnəbl/ *adj* **1** following a style that is currently popular: *fashionable clothes, furniture, ideas, ladies* ○ *It is fashionable to have short hair nowadays.* **2** used or visited by people following a current fashion: *a fashionable hotel, resort, etc.*

▷ **fashionably** /-əblɪ/ *adv* in a fashionable manner: *fashionably dressed.*

Fassbinder /ˈfæsbɪndə(r)/ Rainer Werner (1945-82), German film director. During his short career he made a large number of films, many of them allegories of the German past, including *Effi Briest* and *Lili Marlene.*

fast[1] /fɑːst; *US* fæst/ *adj* (**-er, -est**) **1 (a)** moving or done quickly; rapid: *a fast car, horse, runner,* ie one that can move at high speed. **(b)** happening quickly: *a fast journey, trip, etc.* **2** (of a surface) producing or allowing quick movement: *a fast road, pitch.* **3** (of a watch or clock) showing a time later than the true time: *I'm early — my watch must be fast.* ○ *That clock's ten minutes fast.* **4** (of photographic film) very sensitive to light, allowing a short exposure. **5** (*dated*) (of a person) spending too much time and energy on pleasure and excitement; reckless: *lead a fast life.* **6** (idm) **fast and ˈfurious** (of games, parties, shows, etc) lively and energetic. **a fast ˈbuck** (*derog sl*) money that is earned without effort, often illegally; easy money: *His reputation in the City is of being someone who's only interested in (making) a fast buck.* **pull a fast one** ⇨ PULL[2].

▷ **fast** *adv* **1** quickly: *Can't you run any faster than that?* ○ *Night was fast approaching.* **2** (idm) **run, etc as fast as one's legs can carry one** as fast as one is able.

□ **fast ˈfood** food such as hamburgers, chips, etc that can be cooked easily, and is sold by restaurants to be eaten quickly or taken away: [attrib] *a ˌfast food ˈcounter, ˈrestaurant.*

fast time (*US infml*) = SUMMER TIME (SUMMER).

fast[2] /fɑːst; *US* fæst/ *adj* **1 (a)** [pred] firmly fixed or attached; secure: *The post is fast in the ground.* ○ *make a boat fast,* ie moor it securely. **(b)** [attrib] (*dated*) loyal; close: *a fast friend/friendship.* **2** (of colours) not likely to fade or run. **3** (idm) **hard and fast** ⇨ HARD[1].

▷ **fast** *adv* **1** firmly; securely; tightly: *be fast asleep,* ie sleeping deeply ○ *The boat was stuck fast in the mud.* **2** (idm) **hold fast to sth** continue to believe in (an idea, a principle, etc) resolutely or stubbornly. **play fast and ˈloose (with sb/sth)** change one's attitude towards sb/sth repeatedly in an irresponsible way; trifle with sb/sth: *Stop playing fast and loose with that girl's feelings — can't you see you're upsetting her?* **stand ˈfast/ˈfirm** not retreat, change one's views, etc. **thick and fast** ⇨ THICK.

fast[3] /fɑːst; *US* fæst/ *v* [I] go without (certain kinds of) food, esp for religious reasons: *Muslims fast during Ramadan.*

▷ **fast** *n* (period of) going without food: *a fast of three days* ○ *break one's fast* ○ [attrib] *fast days.*

fasten /ˈfɑːsn; *US* ˈfæsn/ *v* **1** [Tn, Tn·p] **(a)** ~ **sth (down)** secure or fix sth firmly: *fasten (down) the lid of a box* ○ *Please fasten your seat-belts.* ○ *Have you fastened all the doors and windows?* **(b)** ~ **sth (up)** close or join sth: *Fasten (up) your coat.* ○ *The tent flaps should be tightly fastened.* **(c)** [Tn, Tn·pr,

Tn·p] ~ **sth (on/to sth)**; ~ **A and B (together)** firmly attach sth to sth or two things together: *fasten a lock on/to the door* ○ *fasten a brooch on a blouse* ○ *fasten two sheets of paper (together) with a pin* ○ (*fig*) *He fastened his eyes on me.* ○ *They're trying to fasten the blame on others.* **2** [I, Ip] become closed or attached: *The door fastens with a latch.* ○ *This dress fastens (up)* (ie has buttons, a zip, etc) *at the back.* **3** (phr v) **fasten on sb/sth** take and use sb/sth for a particular purpose; seize on sb/sth: *fasten on an idea* ○ *He was looking for someone to blame and fastened on me.*

▷ **fastener** /ˈfɑːsnə(r); *US* ˈfæs-/, **fastening** /ˈfɑːsnɪŋ; *US* ˈfæs-/ *ns* device that fastens sth: *a zip fastener*.

fastidious /fəˈstɪdɪəs, fæ-/ *adj* **1** selecting carefully; choosing only what is good. **2** (*sometimes derog*) hard to please; easily disgusted: *She is so fastidious about her food that I never invite her for dinner.* ▷ **fastidiously** *adv.* **fastidiousness** *n* [U].

fastness[1] /ˈfɑːstnɪs; *US* ˈfæs-/ *n* [U] quality of being fast[2](2): *We guarantee the fastness of these dyes.*

fastness[2] /ˈfɑːstnɪs; *US* ˈfæs-/ *n* fortified place that is easily defended; stronghold: *a mountain fastness*.

fat[1] /fæt/ *adj* (**-tter**, **-ttest**) **1** covered with or having a lot of fat: *fat meat.* **2** (of the body) large in size; containing too much fat: *If you eat too much chocolate you'll get fat.* ○ *Why are people so obsessed about being fat?* ⇨ Usage. Cf THIN 2. **3** large; round: *a big fat apple.* **4** thick; well filled: *a fat wallet*, ie one stuffed with banknotes. **5** rich; fertile: *fat lands.* **6** (*infml*) large in quantity: *a fat price, sum, profit, income, etc* ○ *He gave me a nice fat cheque*, ie one for a lot of money. **7** (idm) **a fat chance** (*sl ironic*) very little chance: *A fat chance I've got of getting time off!* **a fat lot (of good, etc)** (*sl ironic*) very little: *A fat lot you care*, ie You don't care at all. ○ *A fat lot of good that did me*, ie It didn't help me at all.

▷ **fatness** *n* [U].

fatted /ˈfætɪd/ *adj* (idm) **kill the fatted calf** ⇨ KILL.

fattish *adj* rather fat.

□ **fat cat** (*infml esp US*) person who is rich and powerful.

ˈ**fat-head** *n* (*infml*) stupid person.

ˈ**fatstock** *n* [U] animals that are reared and fattened to be killed for food.

NOTE ON USAGE: **Fat** is the most usual and direct adjective to describe people with excess flesh, but it is not polite: *That suit's too tight - it makes you look really fat.* More insulting are **flabby**, which suggests loose flesh, and **podgy**, used especially of fingers and hands. To be polite we can use **plump**, suggesting slight or attractive fatness, or **stout**, indicating overall heaviness of the body. **Tubby** is often used in a friendly way of people who are also short, and **chubby** indicates pleasant roundness in babies and cheeks. The most neutral term is **overweight**, while doctors use **obese** to describe people who are so overweight that they are unhealthy.

fat[2] /fæt/ *n* **1** [U] (**a**) white or yellow greasy substance found in animal bodies under the skin: *This ham has too much fat on it.* (**b**) oily substance found in certain seeds. **2** [C, U] fat from animals, plants or seeds, purified and used for cooking: *Vegetable fats are healthier than animal fats.* ○ *Fried potatoes are cooked in deep fat.* **3** (idm) **chew the fat/rag** ⇨ CHEW. **the fat is in the ˈfire** (*infml*) there will be a lot of trouble now. **live off/on the fat of the land** ⇨ LIVE[2]. **run to ˈfat** (of persons) tend to gain weight; become fat.

fatal /ˈfeɪtl/ *adj* ~ (**to sb/sth**) **1** causing or ending in death: *a fatal accident* ○ *fatal injuries.* **2** causing disaster: *His illness was fatal to our plans*, ie caused them to fail. ○ *a fatal mistake.* **3** (*fml*) fateful; decisive: *the fatal day/hour.*

▷ **fatally** *adv* in a fatal manner: *Many people were fatally wounded during the bomb attacks.*

fatalism /ˈfeɪtəlɪzəm/ *n* [U] belief that events are decided by fate(1); acceptance of all that happens as inevitable.

▷ **fatalist** /ˈfeɪtəlɪst/ *n* person who believes in fate(1) or accepts everything as inevitable.

fatalistic /ˌfeɪtəˈlɪstɪk/ *adj* showing a belief in fate: *a fatalistic person, attitude, outlook.*

fatality /fəˈtælətɪ/ *n* **1** [C] death caused by accident or in war, etc: *There have been ten swimming fatalities* (ie Ten people have lost their lives while swimming) *this summer.* **2** [U] sense of being controlled by fate(1): *There was a strange fatality about their both losing their jobs on the same day.* **3** [U] fatal influence; deadliness: *the fatality of certain diseases.*

fate /feɪt/ *n* **1** [U] power believed to control all events in a way that cannot be resisted; destiny: *I wanted to go to India in June, but fate decided otherwise.* **2** [C] (**a**) person's destiny or future: *The court met to decide our fate(s).* ○ *I am resigned to my fate.* (**b**) death or destruction: *He met his fate* (ie died) *bravely.* **3 the Fates** [pl] (in Greek mythology) three goddesses who decided the course of people's lives. Their names were Clotho, Lachesis and Atropos: (*fig*) *Who knows what the Fates have in store for us* (ie what may happen to us)*?* **4** (idm) **a ˌfate worse than ˈdeath** (*joc*) very unpleasant experience: *Having to watch their home movies all evening was a fate worse than death!* **tempt fate/providence** ⇨ TEMPT.

▷ **fate** *v* [only passive: Tf, Cn·t] destine: *It was fated* (ie Fate decided) *that we would fail.* ○ *He was fated to die in poverty.*

fateful /ˈfeɪtfl/ *adj* [usu attrib] **1** important and decisive: *fateful events, moments* ○ *a fateful decision.* **2** causing or leading to great and usu unpleasant events: *His heart sank as he listened to the judge uttering the fateful words.* ▷ **fatefully** /-fəlɪ/ *adv.*

father[1] /ˈfɑːðə(r)/ *n* **1** male parent: *That baby looks just like her father! They ask the father to cut the umbilical cord now* ○ *You've been (like) a father to me.* ⇨ App 8. **2** (usu *pl*) ancestor: *the land of our fathers.* **3** founder or first leader: *city fathers* ○ *the Pilgrim Fathers*, ie English Puritans among the first European settlers in the USA ○ *the Father of English poetry*, ie Chaucer. **4 Father** God: *Our (Heavenly) Father* ○ *God the Father.* **5** title of a priest, esp the Roman Catholic and Orthodox Churches. **6** (idm) **be gathered to one's fathers** ⇨ GATHER. **the child is father of the man** ⇨ CHILD. **from ˌfather to ˈson** from one generation of a family to the next: *The farm has been handed down from father to son since 1800.* **like ˌfather, like ˈson** (*saying*) a son's character, actions, etc resemble, or can be expected to resemble, his father's. **old enough to be sb's mother/father** ⇨ OLD. **the wish is father to the thought** ⇨ WISH *n.*

▷ ˈ**fatherhood** *n* [U] state of being a father: *The responsibilites of fatherhood are many.*

ˈ**fatherly** *adj* like or typical of a father: *fatherly advice.*

□ ˌ**Father** ˈ**Christmas** (also **Santa Claus**) (*esp Brit*) old man with a white beard and a red robe trimmed with fur, who, children are told, comes down chimneys at Christmas to bring presents. Cf KRISS KRINGLE. ⇨ article at CHRISTMAS.

ˈ**father-figure** *n* older man who is respected because he guides and protects others.

ˈ**father-in-law** *n* /ˈfɑːðər ɪn lɔː/ (*pl* **fathers-in-law**) father of one's husband or wife. ⇨ App 8.

ˈ**fatherland** *n* /-lænd/ country where one was born (used esp of Germany).

ˈ**Father's Day** day when fathers traditionally receive cards and gifts from their children, usu the third Sunday in June.

ˌ**Fathers of the** ˈ**Church** (also ˌ**Church** ˈ**Fathers**) theological writers of the first five centuries AD, whose works helped to express the doctrines of the Christian Church.

ˌ**Father** ˈ**Time** old man, carrying a scythe and an hourglass, who symbolizes time.

father[2] /ˈfɑːðə(r)/ *v* [Tn] **1** be the male parent of (sb); beget: *father a child.* **2** (*fig*) create (sth); originate: *father a plan, an idea, a project, etc.* **3** (phr v) **father sb/sth on sb** say that sb is the father or originator of sb/sth: *It's not my scheme; try fathering it on somebody else.*

fathom /ˈfæðəm/ *n* measure (6 feet or 1.8 metres) of the depth of water: *The harbour is four fathoms deep.* ○ *The ship sank in twenty fathoms.* ⇨ App 10.

▷ **fathom** *v* [Tn] **1** measure the depth of (water). **2** understand or comprehend (sb/sth) fully: *I cannot fathom his remarks.* **3** (phr v) **fathom sth out** find a reason or explanation for sth: *Can you fathom it out?*

fathomless *adj* (*rhet*) too deep to measure: *the fathomless ocean.*

fatigue /fəˈtiːɡ/ *n* **1** [U] great tiredness, usu resulting from hard work or exercise: *We were all suffering from fatigue at the end of our journey.* **2** [U] weakness in metals, etc caused by repeated stress: *The aeroplane wing showed signs of metal fatigue.* **3** [C] non-military duty of soldiers, such as cooking, cleaning, etc: *Instead of training the men were put on fatigues/fatigue duty.* **4 fatigues** [pl] (*US*) uniform worn for fatigue duty or when in battle.

▷ **fatigue** *v* [Tn] make (sb) very tired: *feeling fatigued* ○ *fatiguing work.*

fatted ⇨ FAT[1].

fatten /ˈfætn/ *v* (**a**) [Tn, Tn·p] ~ **sb/sth (up)** make sb/sth fat or fatter: *fatten cattle for (the) market.* (**b**) [I, Ip] ~ (**up**) become fat or fatter: *They're fattening up nicely.*

fatty /ˈfætɪ/ *adj* (**-ier**, **-iest**) (**a**) like fat. (**b**) containing a lot of fat: *fatty bacon.*

▷ **fatty** /ˈfætɪ/ *n* (*infml derog*) fat person.

□ ˌ**fatty** ˈ**acid** any of a series of acids that are either found in natural fats or made from them.

fatuous /ˈfætʃʊəs/ *adj* stupid and silly; foolish: *a fatuous person, smile, remark.*

▷ **fatuity** /fəˈtjuːətɪ; *US* -ˈtuːətɪ/ *n* **1** [U] state of being fatuous. **2** [C] fatuous remark, act, etc.

fatuously *adv.*

fatuousness *n* [U].

faucet /ˈfɔːsɪt/ *n* **1** tap for a barrel, etc. **2** (*esp US*) any kind of tap.

Faulkner /ˈfɔːknə(r)/ William (1879-1962), American novelist, many of whose novels describe life in small towns in the American South. The technical brilliance of his writing had a great influence on the modern novel, and he was admired by Arnold *Bennett and Jean-Paul *Sartre. He was awarded the Nobel prize for literature in 1949.

fault /fɔːlt/ *n* **1** [C] imperfection or flaw: *I like him despite his faults.* ○ *There is a fault in the electrical system.* ⇨ Usage at MISTAKE[1]. **2** [U] (responsibility for a) mistake or offence: *'Whose fault is this?' 'Mine, I'm afraid.'* **3** [C] incorrect serve in tennis, etc. **4** [C] (place where there is a) break in the continuity of layers of rock, caused by movement of the earth's crust. **5** (idm) **at fault** responsible for a mistake; in the wrong: *My memory was at fault.* **find fault** ⇨ FIND[1]. **to a ˈfault** excessively: *She is generous to a fault.*

▷ **fault** *v* [Tn] discover a fault in (sb/sth): *No one could fault his performance.*

faultless *adj.* **faultlessly** *adv.*

faulty *adj* (**-ier**, **-iest**) having a fault or faults; imperfect: *a faulty switch* ○ *a faulty argument.*

faultily *adv* in a faulty manner.

□ ˈ**faultfinding** *n* [U] (*usu derog*) looking for faults in other people's work or behaviour.

faun /fɔːn/ *n* (in Roman myths) god of the fields and woods, with goat's horns and legs but a human torso.

fauna /ˈfɔːnə/ *n* [U, C] (*pl* ~**s**) all the animals of an area or a period of time: *the fauna of East Africa.* Cf FLORA.

Fauntleroy /ˈfɔːntlərɔɪ/ hero of Frances Hodgson Burnett's novel *Little Lord Fauntleroy*, a child with a very gentle nature. The name is often used of weak or girlish young boys.

Fauré /ˈfɔːreɪ; *US* fəʊˈreɪ/ Gabriel (1845-1924), French composer. He developed a distinctly French melodic style in works such as the *Requiem* and his settings of Verlaine's poems in *la Bonne Chanson*. As a teacher he influenced many other composers, including *Ravel.

Faust /faʊst/ character based on a 16th-century German astronomer who is the subject of many plays and legends. According to the story, he sold his soul to the Devil in return for magic powers. In some versions he is saved from Hell, in others he is damned. Writers who have used the story include *Marlowe, *Goethe and *Mann. ▷ **Faustian** *adj*: *the Faustian dilemma of the human condition.*

faute de mieux /ˌfəʊt də ˈmjɜː/ (*French*) because there is nothing better: *Faute de mieux, I accepted their offer.*

fauve (also **Fauve**) /fəʊv/ *n* any of a group of artists led by *Matisse who produced work painted in very bright colours, mainly as a reaction against impressionism. The group were active between 1905 and 1910 and included Derain, Dufy and Vlaminck. ▷ **fauvism** (also **Fauvism**) *n* [U]. **fauvist** (also **Fauvist**) *adj, n.*

faux pas /ˌfəʊ ˈpɑː/ (*pl* **faux pas** /ˌfəʊpɑːz/) (*French*) embarrassing mistake; indiscreet remark, etc.

favour[1] (*US* **favor**) /ˈfeɪvə(r)/ *n* **1** [U] liking; goodwill; approval (used esp with the *vs* shown): *win sb's favour* ○ *look on a plan with favour*, ie approve of it. **2** [U] treating one person or group more generously or leniently than others; partiality: *He obtained his position more by favour than by merit or ability.* **3** [C] act of kindness beyond what is due or usual (used esp with the *vs* shown): *May I ask a favour of you* (ie ask you to do sth for me)*?* ○ *Do me a favour and turn the radio down while I'm on the phone, will you?* **4** [C] small token or badge worn to show that one supports sb/sth: *Everyone at the rally wore red ribbons as favours.* **5 favours** [pl] (used of a woman offering herself freely to a man) pleasure through sexual intercourse: *bestow one's favours on sb* ○ *be (too) free with one's favours.* **6** (idm) **be/stand high in sb's favour** ⇨ HIGH[3]. **be in/out of ˈfavour (with sb); be in/out of sb's ˈfavour** have/not have sb's regard, approval, etc. **curry favour** ⇨ CURRY[2]. **find, lose, etc favour with sb/in sb's eyes** win/lose sb's approval. **in favour of sb/sth (a)** in sympathy with sb/sth; in support of sb/sth: *Was he in favour of the death penalty?* **(b)** (of cheques) payable to (the account of) sb/sth: *Cheques should be written in favour of Oxfam.* **in sb's favour** to the advantage of sb: *The exchange rate is in our favour today*, ie will benefit us when we change money. ○ *The court decided in his favour.* ○ *The decision went in his favour.* **without fear or favour** ⇨ FEAR[1].

favour[2] (*US* **favor**) /ˈfeɪvə(r)/ *v* [Tn] **1** support (sb/sth); prefer: *Of the two possible plans I favour the first.* **2** show a preference for (sb); treat (sb) with partiality: *She always favours her youngest child (more than the others).* **3** (of events or circumstances) make (sth) possible or easy: *The wind favoured their sailing at dawn.* **4** (*dated*) look like (sb); resemble (sb) in features: *You can see that she favours her father.* **5** (phr v) **favour sb with sth** (*dated or fml*) do sth for sb; oblige(2) sb with sth: *I should be grateful if you would favour me with an early reply.*

favourable (*US* **favor-**) /ˈfeɪvərəbl/ *adj* **1 (a)** giving or showing approval: *It's encouraging to receive a favourable report on one's work.* **(b)** ~ **(to/toward) sb/sth)** tending to support sb/sth: *Is he favourable to the proposal?* **(c)** pleasing; positive: *You made a favourable impression on the examiners.* ○ *We formed a very favourable impression of her.* **2** ~ **(for sth)** helpful; suitable: *favourable winds* ○ *conditions favourable for skiing.*
▷ **favourably** (*US* **favor-**) /-əblɪ/ *adv* in a favourable manner: *speak favourably of a plan* ○ *look favourably on sb.*

favourite (*US* **favor-**) /ˈfeɪvərɪt/ *n* ~ **(of sb) 1** person or thing liked more than others: *These books are great favourites of mine.* ○ *He is a favourite with his uncle/a favourite of his uncle's/his uncle's favourite.* **2 the favourite** (in racing) the horse, competitor, etc expected to win: *The favourite came in third.*
▷ **favourite** (*US* **favor-**) *adj* [attrib] best liked: *my favourite occupation, hobby, restaurant, aunt* ○ *Who is your favourite writer?*

favouritism (*US* **-vor-**) /-ɪzəm/ *n* [U] (*derog*) practice of giving unfair advantages to the people that one likes best: *Our teacher is guilty of blatant favouritism.*
□ ˌ**favourite ˈson** (*esp US*) **1** candidate who has won the approval of a particular state in his campaign to be elected, esp as president. **2** famous person who is popular in his home town: *'Glasgow's favourite son wins Olympic gold'*, eg as a newspaper headline.

Fawkes /fɔːks/ Guy (1570-1606), one of the conspirators in the *Gunpowder Plot. He was captured with the gunpowder and tortured until he gave the names of the others involved.
□ **Guy ˈFawkes Night** = BONFIRE NIGHT (BONFIRE).

fawn[1] /fɔːn/ *n* **1** [C] deer less than one year old. Cf DOE, STAG 1. **2** [U] light yellowish brown: *a raincoat in fawn.*
▷ **fawn** *adj* fawn-coloured: *a fawn raincoat.*

fawn[2] /fɔːn/ *v* [I, Ipr] ~ **(on sb) 1** (of dogs) show affection by wagging the tail, pawing or licking sb, etc. **2** (*derog*) try to win sb's approval by flattery or by obsequious behaviour: *fawning behaviour, looks.*

fax /fæks/ *v* [Tn, Dn·n, Dn·pr] ~ **sth (to sb)** send the copy of (a document, an illustration, etc) by an electronic system using telephone lines: *Please fax me the layout for the new catalogue.* ○ *The plans were faxed to us by our New York office.*
▷ **fax** *n* **(a)** [U] system for sending such a copy: *sent by fax* ○ [attrib] *a fax machine.* **(b)** [C] copy sent in this way.

faze /feɪz/ *v* [Tn] (*infml esp US*) fluster (sb): *She's so calm; nothing seems to faze her.*

FBI /ˌef biː ˈaɪ/ *abbr* (*US*) Federal Bureau of Investigation: *head of the FBI* ○ *an FBI agent.* Cf CIA. ⇨ articles at LAW, POLICE.

FC *abbr* (*Brit*) Football Club: *Leeds United FC.*

FCO /ˌef siː ˈəʊ/ *abbr* (*Brit*) Foreign and Commonwealth Office (combined in 1968): *an official from the FCO.* Cf FO.

FD /ˌef ˈdiː/ (also **Fid Def**) *abbr* (on British coins) Defender of the Faith (Latin *Fidei Defensor*).

FDA /ˌef diː ˈeɪ/ *abbr* (in the USA) Food and Drugs Administration.

Fe *symb* iron.

fealty /ˈfiːəltɪ/ *n* [C, U] (*arch*) (oath of) loyalty owed by a feudal tenant, etc to his lord: *take an oath of fealty.*

fear[1] /fɪə(r)/ *n* **1 (a)** [U] emotion caused by the nearness or possibility of danger, pain, evil, etc: *unable to speak from fear* ○ *overcome by fear* ○ *feel, show no fear.* **(b)** [C] this emotion caused by sth specific: *a fear of heights* ○ *The doctor's report confirmed our worst fears.* ○ *overcome/dispel/allay, sb's fears.* **2** (idm) **for fear of sth/of doing sth; for fear (that/lest)...** in case; to avoid the danger of sth happening: *We spoke in whispers for fear of waking the baby/for fear (that) we might wake the baby.* **hold no fears/terrors for sb** not frighten sb: *Hang-gliding holds no fears for her.* **in fear and trembling** in a frightened or cowed manner: *They went to the teacher in fear and trembling to tell her that they'd broken a window.* **in fear of sb/sth** in a state of fear about sb/sth: *The thief went in constant fear of discovery.* **in ˌfear of one's ˈlife** anxious for one's own safety. ˌ**no ˈfear** (*infml*) (used when answering a suggestion) certainly not: *'Are you coming climbing?' 'No fear!'* **put the fear of God into sb** (*infml*) make sb very frightened. **there's not much fear of sth/that...** it is unlikely that sth will happen: *There's not much fear of an enemy attack (taking place).* **without ˌfear or ˈfavour** (*fml*) showing impartial justice.
▷ **fearful** /-fl/ *adj* **1** ~ **(of sth/of doing sth;** ~ **(that/lest...)** nervous and afraid: *fearful of waking the baby/fearful that we might wake the baby.* **2** terrible; horrifying: *a fearful railway accident.* **3** (*infml*) very great; very bad: *What a fearful mess!* **fearfully** /-fəlɪ/ *adv.* **fearfulness** *n* [U].
fearless *adj* ~ **(of sth)** not afraid (of sth): *a fearless mountaineer* ○ *fearless of the consequences.* **fearlessly** *adv.* **fearlessness** *n* [U].

fearsome /ˈfɪəsəm/ *adj* frightening in appearance: *The battlefield was a fearsome sight.* ○ (*fig*) *a fearsome task*, ie one that frightens by being difficult.

fear[2] /fɪə(r)/ *v* **1 (a)** [Tn] be afraid of (sb/sth): *fear death, illness* ○ *The plague was greatly feared in the Middle Ages.* **(b)** [I, Tt] feel fear (about doing sth): *Never fear* (ie Don't worry)*, everything will be all right.* ○ *She feared to speak in his presence.* **2** [Tn, Tf] have an uneasy feeling about or anticipation of (esp sth bad): *They feared the worst*, ie thought that the worst had happened or would happen. ○ *'Are we going to be late?' 'I fear so.'* ○ *I fear (that) he is going to die.* **3** [Tn] (*arch or fml*) have respect and awe for: *fear God.* **4** (phr v) **fear for sb/sth** be anxious or concerned about sb/sth: *I fear for her safety in this weather.*

feasible /ˈfiːzəbl/ *adj* that can be done; practicable; possible: *a feasible idea, suggestion, scheme, etc* ○ *It's not feasible to follow your proposals.* ▷ **feasibility** /ˌfiːzəˈbɪlətɪ/ *n* [U]: [attrib] *We should do a feasibility study before adopting the new proposals.* **feasibly** /-əblɪ/ *adv.*

feast /fiːst/ *n* **1 (a)** unusually large or elaborate meal. **(b)** (*fig*) thing that pleases the mind or the senses with its richness or variety: *a feast of colours, sounds, etc.* **2** religious festival celebrated with rejoicing: *the feast of Christmas.*
▷ **feast** *v* **1 (a)** [I, Ipr] ~ **(on sth)** enjoy a feast: *They celebrated by feasting all day.* **(b)** [Tn, Tn·pr] ~ **sb (with sth)** provide sb with a feast: *They feasted their guests with delicacies.* **2** (idm) **feast one's eyes (on sb/sth)** enjoy the beauty of sb/sth: *She feasted her eyes on the beauty of the valley.*

feat /fiːt/ *n* successful completion of sth needing skill, strength or courage: *brilliant feats of engineering* ○ *perform feats of daring.* ⇨ Usage at ACT[1].

feather

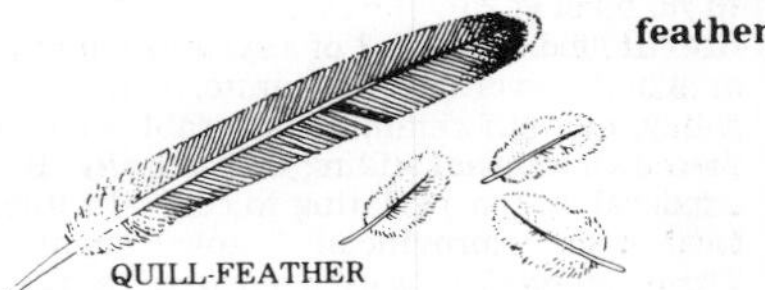

feather[1] /ˈfeðə(r)/ *n* **1** any of the many light fringed structures that grow from a bird's skin and cover its body. ⇨ illus. **2** (idm) **birds of a feather** ⇨ BIRD. **(be) a ˈfeather in one's cap** an achievement, etc that one can be proud of: *Winning the gold medal was yet another feather in her cap.* **light as air/as a feather** ⇨ LIGHT[3] 1. **ruffle sb's feathers** ⇨ RUFFLE. **show the white feather** ⇨ SHOW[2]. **smooth sb's ruffled feathers** ⇨ SMOOTH[2]. **you could have knocked me down with a feather** ⇨ KNOCK[2].
▷ **feathery** /ˈfeðərɪ/ *adj* **1** light and soft like feathers: *feathery snowflakes.* **2** covered or adorned with feathers: *a feathery hat.*
□ ˌ**feather ˈbed** mattress stuffed with feathers. ˌ**feather-ˈbed** *v* (-dd-) [Tn] make things easy for (sb), esp by helping financially; pamper: *They have been so feather-bedded in the past that they can't cope with hardship now.*
ˈ**feather-brained** *adj* (*derog*) foolish; silly.
ˌ**feather ˈduster** soft brush made from a bunch of feathers attached to a stick, used for dusting.
ˈ**featherweight** *n* **1** boxer weighing between 53.5 and 57 kilograms, next above bantamweight. **2 (a)** (*infml*) thing or person that is light in weight. **(b)** (*infml derog*) thing or person of little merit or importance.

feather[2] /ˈfeðə(r)/ *v* **1** [Tn] cover or fit (sth) with feathers: *feather an arrow.* **2** [I, Tn] (in rowing) turn (one's oar) so that it passes flat just above the surface of the water: *The crew feathered (their oars) for the last few yards of the race.* **3** (idm) **feather one's (own) ˈnest** (*usu derog*) make oneself richer, more comfortable, etc, usu at sb else's expense. **tar and feather sb** ⇨ TAR[1] *v.*

feature /ˈfiːtʃə(r)/ *n* **1 (a)** [C] one of the named parts of the face (eg nose, mouth, eyes) which together form its appearance: *His eyes are his most* *striking feature.* ⇨ illus at HEAD. (**b**) **features** [pl] face viewed as a whole: *a woman of handsome, striking, delicate, etc features.* **2** [C] distinctive characteristic; aspect: *an interesting feature of city life* ○ *memorable features of the Scottish landscape* ○ *Many examples and extra grammatical information are among the special features of this dictionary.* **3** [C] (**a**) ~ (**on sb/sth**) (in newspapers, television, etc) special or prominent article or programme (about sb/sth): *This magazine will be running a special feature on education next week.* (**b**) full-length film as part of a cinema programme: *the main feature following the cartoon* ○ [attrib] *a feature film.*

▷ **feature** *v* **1** [Tn] give a prominent part to (sb/sth): *a film that features a new French actress.* **2** [Ipr] ~ **in sth** have an important or prominent part in sth: *Does a new job feature in your future plans?*

featureless *adj* without distinct features(FEATURE 2); uninteresting.

Feb *abbr* /feb in informal use/ February: *18 Feb 1934.*

febrile /ˈfi:braɪl/ *adj* (*fml*) (**a**) caused by a fever: *a febrile cough.* (**b**) having a fever: *a febrile patient.*

February /ˈfebrʊərɪ; *US* -ʊerɪ/ *n* [U, C] (*abbr* **Feb**) the second month of the year, next after January. For the uses of *February* see the examples at *April.*

feces (*US*) = FAECES. ▷ **fecal** (*US*) = FAECAL (FAECES).

feckless /ˈfeklɪs/ *adj* (*derog*) inefficient; irresponsible. ▷ **fecklessly** *adv.* **fecklessness** *n* [U].

fecund /ˈfi:kənd, ˈfekənd/ *adj* (*fml*) fertile; productive: (*fig*) *a fecund imagination.* ▷ **fecundity** /fɪˈkʌndətɪ/ *n* [U].

Fed /fed/ *n* (*US infml*) member of the Federal Bureau of Investigation.

fed *pt, pp* of FEED¹.

federal /ˈfedərəl/ *adj* **1** of a system of government in which several states unite, usu for foreign policy, etc, but retain considerable control over their own internal affairs: *federal unity.* **2** (within a federal system) relating to central rather than local or provincial government: *The Trans-Canada highway is a federal responsibility.* **3 Federal** (*US*) supporting the union party in the US Civil War.

▷ **federalism** /-ɪzəm/ *n* [U].

federalist /ˈfedərəlɪst/ *n* supporter of federal union or power.

federally *adv* by the federal government: *This development is federally funded.*

□ **the ˌFederal ˌBureau of Investiˈgation** (*abbr* **FBI**) (in the USA) department responsible for investigating violations of federal law and protecting national security.

the ˌFederal Reˈserve System (in the USA) national banking system with central cash reserves available to a number of major regional banks.

federate /ˈfedəreɪt/ *v* [I] (of states, organizations, etc) unite into a federation.

▷ **federation** /ˌfedəˈreɪʃn/ *n* **1** [C] union of states in which individual states retain control of many internal matters but in which foreign affairs, defence, etc are the responsibility of the central (federal) government. **2** [C] similarly organized union of societies, trade unions, etc. **3** [U] action of forming a federation.

fedora /fɪˈdɔ:rə/ *n* type of low soft felt hat.

fed up /ˌfed ˈʌp/ *adj* [pred] ~ (**about/with sb/sth**) (*infml*) tired or bored; unhappy or depressed: *What's the matter? You look pretty fed up.* ○ *I'm fed up with waiting for her to telephone.*

fee /fi:/ *n* **1** [C] (**a**) (usu *pl*) amount paid for professional advice or service, eg to private teachers, doctors, etc: *pay the lawyer's fees* ○ *a bill for school fees.* ⇨ Usage at INCOME. (**b**) amount paid to sit an examination, join a club, etc: *If you want to join, there's an entrance fee of £20 and an annual membership fee of £10.* **2** [U] (*law*) (**a**) rights (esp the right to bequeath) in property that one has inherited. (**b**) such property.

feeble /ˈfi:bl/ *adj* (**-r, -st**) (**a**) weak; faint: *a feeble old man* ○ *a feeble cry.* (**b**) (*derog*) lacking force: *a feeble argument, attempt, gesture, excuse.* ▷ **feebleness** *n* [U]. **feebly** /ˈfi:blɪ/ *adv.*

□ ˌ**feeble-ˈminded** *adj* having less than usual intelligence; mentally subnormal.

feed¹ /fi:d/ *v* (*pt, pp* **fed** /fed/) **1** (**a**) [Tn, Tn·pr] ~ **sb/sth** (**on sth**) give food to (a person or an animal): *She has a large family to feed.* ○ *Have the pigs been fed yet?* ○ *Have you fed the chickens?* ○ *The baby needs feeding.* ○ *The baby can't feed itself yet,* ie can't put food into its own mouth. ○ *What do you feed your dog on?* (**b**) [Dn·n, Dn·pr] ~ **sth to sb/sth** give (a person or an animal) sth as food: *feed the baby some more stewed apple* ○ *feed oats to horses.* **2** (**a**) [I, Ipr] ~ (**on sth**) (of animals, or jokingly of humans) eat: *Have you fed yet?* ○ *The cows were feeding on hay in the barn.* (**b**) [Tn] serve as food for (a person or an animal): *There's enough here to feed us all.* **3** [Tn, Tn·pr] ~ **A** (**with B**)/~ **B into A** supply (sth) with material; supply (material) to sth: *The lake is fed by several small streams.* ○ *feed the fire (with wood)* ○ *The moving belt feeds the machine with raw material/feeds raw material into the machine.* **4** [Tn] (in football, etc) send passes to (a player). **5** (idm) **bite the hand that feeds one** ⇨ BITE¹. **6** (phr v) **feed on sth** be nourished or strengthened by sth: *Hatred feeds on envy.* **feed sb up** give extra food to sb to make him more healthy: *You look very pale; I think you need feeding up a bit.*

□ ˈ**feeding-bottle** *n* bottle with a rubber teat for feeding liquid foods to young babies or animals.

ˈ**feeding-time** *n* time at which animals in a zoo are fed: (*joc*) *The children's tea-party was like feeding-time at the zoo!*

feed² /fi:d/ *n* **1** [C] meal, usu for animals or babies: *When is the baby's next feed?* **2** [U] (**a**) food for animals: *There isn't enough feed left for the hens.* (**b**) material supplied to a machine. **3** [C] pipe, channel, etc along which material is carried to a machine: *The petrol feed is blocked.*

□ ˈ**feedbag** *n* (*US*) = NOSEBAG (NOSE¹).

feedback /ˈfi:dbæk/ *n* [U] **1** (**a**) information about a product, etc that a user gives back to its supplier, maker, etc: *We need more feedback from the consumer in order to improve our goods.* (**b**) reactions, eg to work that has been done or an idea that has been suggested, expressed to those responsible for it: *Initial feedback from the public has been hostile.* **2** return of part of the output of a system to its source, esp so as to modify the output: *The brain gets feedback from the muscles and increases the supply of hormones.* ○ *feedback from the loudspeakers,* ie the whistling noise produced when a microphone detects noise from a loudspeaker ○ *The feedback from the computer enables us to update the program.* Cf BIOFEEDBACK.

feeder /ˈfi:də(r)/ *n* **1** (preceded by an *adj*) thing, esp an animal or a plant, that feeds in a specified way: *a gross, dainty, greedy, etc feeder.* **2** (*Brit*) baby's bib or feeding-bottle. **3** subsidiary route or means of transport that links outside areas with the main route, service, etc: [attrib] *a new feeder road for the motorway.* **4** feeding apparatus in a machine.

feel¹ /fi:l/ *v* (*pt, pp* **felt** /felt/) **1** [Tn, Tw] explore or perceive (sth) by touching or by holding in the hands: *feel a rock, a piece of cloth, etc* ○ *Can you feel the bump on my head?* ○ *Can you tell what this is by feeling it?* ○ *Feel how rough this is.* **2** [Tn, Tng, Tni] (not usu in the continuous tenses) be aware of or experience (sth physical or emotional); have the sensation of; sense: *We all felt the earthquake tremors.* ○ *Can you feel the tension in this room?* ○ *After the accident, she couldn't feel anything in her left leg,* ie it was numb. ○ *I can feel a nail sticking into my shoe.* ○ *I felt something crawl(ing) up my arm.* **3** [La] be in the specified physical, emotional or moral state: *feel cold, hungry, comfortable, sad, happy, etc* ○ *How are you feeling today?* ○ *You'll feel better after a good night's sleep.* ○ *She felt betrayed.* ○ *I feel rotten about not taking the children out.* ○ *It makes me feel very bad* (ie sorry or ashamed) *about not going.* **4** [Ipr] ~ (**to sb**) (**like sth/sb**) (not in the continuous tenses) give a sensation or an impression of sth or of being sth/sb: *The water feels warm.* ○ *How does it feel to be alone all day?* ○ *Nothing feels right in our new house.* ○ *This wallet feels to me like leather.* ○ *It feels like rain,* ie seems likely to rain. ⇨ Usage. **5** ~ **as if.../as though...** (not in the continuous tenses) have or give the impression that...: *I feel as if I'm going to be sick.* ○ *My cold feels as though it's getting better.* ○ *It felt as though a great weight had been lifted from us.* **6** [Tn] be particularly conscious of (sth); be affected by: *He feels the cold a lot.* ○ *Of all the children, she felt her mother's death the most.* ○ *We all felt the force of her arguments.* ○ *Don't you feel the beauty of the countryside?* **7** [I] be capable of sensation: *The dead cannot feel.* **8** [Tf, Cn·a, Cn·t] have as an opinion; consider; think; believe: *We all felt (that) our luck was about to turn.* ○ *She felt in her bones that she would succeed.* ○ *I felt it advisable to do nothing.* ○ *He felt the plan to be unwise/felt that the plan was unwise.* **9** [I, Ipr, Ip] ~ (**about**) (**for sb/sth**) search with the hands, the feet, a stick, etc: *He felt in his pocket for some money.* ○ *I had to feel about in the dark for the light switch.* ○ *She felt along the wall for the door.* **10** (idm) **be/feel called to sth** ⇨ CALL². ˌ**feel the ˈdraught** be badly affected by a situation, esp a financial crisis: *As a recession becomes more likely many small businesses are already beginning to feel the draught.* ˌ**feel ˈfree** (*infml*) (said when giving permission): *'May I use your phone?' 'Feel free.'* ˌ**feel one's ˈage** realize that one is growing old, as one becomes less strong or one's ideas are thought to be old-fashioned: *My children's skill with computers really makes me feel my age!* **feel one's ˈears burning** think or imagine that others are talking about one. **feel ˈgood** feel happy, confident, etc: *It makes me feel good to know you like me.* **feel** (**it**) **in one's ˈbones** (**that...**) know or sense (sth) intuitively: *I know I'm going to fail this exam — I can feel it in my bones.* **feel like sth/doing sth** think that one would like (to do/have) sth; want (to do) sth: *I feel like (having) a drink.* ○ *We'll go for a walk if you feel like it.* **feel one's oats** (*infml*) be in an energetic and lively mood and act accordingly. **feel oneˈself** feel fit and healthy: *I don't quite feel myˈself today.* **feel the ˈpinch** (*infml*) (begin to) suffer from a lack of (esp) money: *The high rate of unemployment is making many families feel the pinch.* **feel/take sb's pulse** ⇨ PULSE¹. **feel one's ˈway** (**a**) move along carefully, eg in darkness, by touching walls, objects, etc. (**b**) (*fig*) proceed cautiously: *At this early stage of the negotiations both sides were still feeling their way.* **look/feel small** ⇨ SMALL. **make one's presence felt** ⇨ PRESENCE. **11** (phr v) **feel for sb** have sympathy for sb: *I really felt for her when her husband died.* **feel up to** (**doing**) **sth** consider oneself capable of (doing) sth: *If you feel up to it, we could walk into town after lunch.*

NOTE ON USAGE: There are several verbs relating to the five senses of sight, smell, hearing, taste and touch. They are often used with the verb **can.** Normally, only the simple tenses are used. **1 See**, **smell**, **hear**, **taste** and **feel** indicate the experiencing of something through one of the senses: *He saw a light in the window.* ○ *I heard an explosion last night.* ○ *I can smell gas.* **2** These verbs can also indicate somebody's physical ability to perceive with the senses: *He can't see, hear, etc very well.* **3 Look**, **smell**, **taste**, **sound** and **feel** are used to describe how somebody or something is experienced through one of the senses, usually in one of these patterns: (**a**) *She looks happy,* ie She's smiling. (**b**) *The wine tastes like water,* ie It's very weak. (**c**) *The singer sounds as though she's got a sore throat,* ie The sound of her voice suggests that she has a sore throat. **4 Look**, **smell**, **listen**, **taste**, **feel** can indicate that somebody is making a deliberate effort to perceive something: (**a**) *'I can't see the spot.' 'Well look harder.'* (**b**) *'I can't hear any music.' 'Listen carefully.'* (**c**) *'I can't taste anything.' 'Try tasting this.'* **5 Feel** and **look** can express the physical or emotional state of a person. Here, the continuous tenses can be used: *I feel sick, nervous,* *disappointed, etc.* ○ *He was feeling tired so he didn't come to the party.* ○ *You're looking happy. Have you had good news?*

feel[2] /fi:l/ *n* [sing] **1** act of feeling: *Let me have a feel.* **2 the feel** sense of touch: *rough, smooth, etc to the feel,* ie when touched or felt. **3 the feel (a)** sensation that sth gives when touching or being touched: *You can tell it's silk by the feel.* ○ *She loved the feel of the sun on her skin.* **(b)** sensation created by a situation, etc: *the feel of the place, the meeting, the occasion.* **4** (idm) **get the feel of sth/of doing sth** (*infml*) become familiar with (doing) sth: *You haven't got the feel of the gears in this car yet.* **have a feel for sth** (*infml*) have a sensitive appreciation or an easy understanding of sth: *He has a good feel for languages.*

feeler /ˈfi:lə(r)/ *n* **1** long slender part in certain animals, esp insects, for testing things by touch. **2** (idm) **put out feelers** (*infml*) cautiously check the views of others: *I'll try to put out some feelers to gauge people's reactions to our proposal.*

□ ˈ**feeler gauge** one of a set of metal blades used for measuring gaps, etc.

feeling /ˈfi:lɪŋ/ *n* **1** [U] ability to feel: *I've lost all feeling in my legs.* **2 (a)** [C] ~ **(of sth)** thing that is felt through the mind or the senses: *a feeling of hunger, well-being, discomfort, gratitude, joy, etc.* **(b)** [sing] ~ **(of sth/that...)** vague notion or belief not based wholly on reason: *a feeling of danger* ○ *I can't understand why, but suddenly I had this feeling that something terrible was going to happen.* **(c)** [sing] attitude; opinion: *The feeling of the meeting* (ie The opinion of the majority) *was against the proposal.* ○ *My own feeling is that we should buy it.* **3** [U] **(a)** sensitivity; appreciation: *He plays the piano with great feeling.* ○ *She hasn't much feeling for the beauty of nature.* **(b)** ~ **(for sb/sth)** sympathetic understanding (of sb/sth): *You have no feeling for the sufferings of others.* **4** [C, U] strong emotion, esp of discontent, resentment, etc: *The candidate's speech aroused strong feeling(s) on all sides.* ○ *She spoke with feeling about the high rate of unemployment.* ○ *Feeling over the dismissal ran high,* ie There was much resentment, anger, etc about it. **5 feelings** [pl] person's emotions rather than intellect: *The speaker appealed more to the feelings of her audience than to their reason.* ○ *You've hurt my feelings,* ie You've offended me. **6** (idm) **bad/ill ˈfeeling** resentment; dissatisfaction: *His rapid promotion caused much bad feeling among his colleagues.* **have mixed feelings about sb/sth** ⇨ MIXED. **no hard feelings** ⇨ HARD[1]. **one's better feelings/nature** ⇨ BETTER[1]. **relieve one's feelings** ⇨ RELIEVE. **a/that sinking feeling** ⇨ SINK[1]. **spare sb's feelings** ⇨ SPARE[2].

▷ **feeling** *adj* **1** sympathetic: *She is very feeling/is a very feeling person.* **2** [attrib] showing strong emotion; heartfelt: *a feeling remark.* **feelingly** *adv* with deep emotion: *He spoke feelingly about his dismissal.*

feet *pl* of FOOT[1].

feign /feɪn/ *v* [Tn] pretend (sth): *feign illness, madness, ignorance, etc* ○ *feigned innocence.*

feint[1] /feɪnt/ *n* (in war, boxing, fencing, etc) pretended attack to distract an opponent's attention from the main attack.

▷ **feint** /feɪnt/ *v* [I] make a feint.

feint[2] /feɪnt/ *adj* [usu attrib] (of paper, etc) having faintly printed lines: *a narrow feint pad,* ie one with narrowly-spaced faint lines.

feisty /ˈfaɪstɪ, ˈfi:stɪ/ *adj* (**-ier, -iest**) (*US infml*) **1** (*approv*) spirited; energetic; forceful. **2** (*derog*) irritable; quarrelsome: *a feisty old man.*

feldspar /ˈfeldspɑ:(r)/ (also **fel·spar** /ˈfelspɑ:(r)/) *n* [U] white or red mineral rock that contains aluminium and other silicates.

felicitate /fəˈlɪsɪteɪt/ *v* [Tn, Tn·pr] ~ **sb (on sth)** (*fml*) congratulate sb. ▷ **felicitation** /fəˌlɪsɪˈteɪʃn/ *n* [U, C usu *pl*].

felicitous /fəˈlɪsɪtəs/ *adj* (*fml*) (esp of words) well-chosen; apt: *felicitous remarks* ○ *Her choice of music is felicitous.* ▷ **felicitously** *adv.*

felicity /fəˈlɪsətɪ/ *n* (*fml*) **1** [U] great happiness. **2** [C, U] (instance of a) pleasing style of speaking or writing: *the many felicities of her language* ○ *He expressed himself with great felicity.*

feline /ˈfi:laɪn/ *adj, n* (of or like an) animal of the cat family: *walk with a feline grace.*

fell[1] *pt* of FALL[1].

fell[2] /fel/ *adj* **1** (*arch*) fierce; destructive. **2** (idm) **at one fell swoop** in a single deadly action.

fell[3] /fel/ *n* stretch of bare rocky moorland or hilly land in northern England: *the Lakeland Fells.*

fell[4] /fel/ *v* [Tn] **1** cut down (a tree). **2** knock down (sb) with a blow: *He felled his enemy with a single blow.*

fellatio /fəˈleɪʃɪəʊ/ *n* [U] (*fml*) stimulation of the penis by sucking or licking.

Fellini /feˈli:ni:/ Federico (1920-), Italian film director. In pictures like *La Dolce Vita* and *Amarcord* he has developed a distinctive visual style, often extravagant and visionary, and expressing a wry view of the world.

fellow /ˈfeləʊ/ *n* **1** (esp *pl,* often in compounds) companion; comrade: ˈ*playfellows* ○ ˈ*bedfellows* ○ *fellows in good fortune, misery* ○ *Her fellows share her interest in computers.* **2** [attrib] of the same class, kind, etc: *a fellow member* ○ *one's ˌfellow-ˈcountrymen.* **3** (*esp Brit*) member of a learned society: *Fellow of the Royal Academy.* **4** member of the governing body of some colleges or universities. **5** (*esp US*) graduate student holding a fellowship. **6** (*fml or rhet*) one of a pair: *Here's one of my shoes, but where's its fellow?* **7** (*infml*) man or boy; chap: *He's a nice fellow.* ○ *Poor fellow!* ○ (*joc*) *Where can a fellow* (ie Where can I) *get a bite to eat round here?* **8** (idm) **be hail-fellow-well-met (with sb)** ⇨ HAIL[2].

□ ˌ**fellow-ˈfeeling** *n* [U] sympathy with sb whose experience, etc one shares.

ˌ**fellow-ˈtraveller** *n* **1** person who sympathizes with the aims of a political party (esp the Communist Party) but is not a member. **2** person one is travelling with.

fellowship /ˈfeləʊʃɪp/ *n* **1** [U] friendly association with others; companionship: *enjoy fellowship with people* ○ *fellowship in misfortune.* **2 (a)** [C] group or society of people sharing a common interest or aim. **(b)** [U] membership in such a group or society: *admitted to fellowship.* **3** [C] (*esp Brit*) position of a (college) fellow. **4** [C] award of money to a graduate student in return for some teaching, research assistance, etc: *We give three research fellowships a year.*

felony /ˈfelənɪ/ *n* [C, U] (*law*) serious crime, eg murder, armed robbery or arson: *a series of felonies* ○ *be convicted of felony.*

▷ **felon** /ˈfelən/ *n* person guilty of felony.

felonious /fəˈləʊnɪəs/ *adj* of or involving felony; criminal.

felspar = FELDSPAR.

felt[1] *pt, pp* of FEEL[1].

felt[2] /felt/ *n* [U] wool, hair or fur, compressed and rolled flat into a thick cloth: [attrib] *felt hats, slippers, etc.*

□ ˌ**felt-ˈpen** *n* (also ˌ**felt-ˈtip**, ˌ**felt-tipped ˈpen**) pen with a tip made of felt.

felucca /fəˈlʌkə/ *n* narrow ship with oars or sails or both, used on Mediterranean coasts.

fem *abbr* female; feminine. Cf MASC.

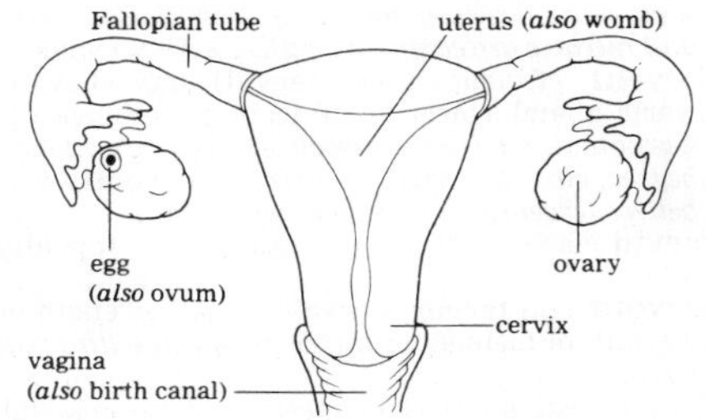

female /ˈfi:meɪl/ *adj* **1 (a)** of the sex that can give birth to children or produce eggs: *a female dog, cat, pig, etc.* **(b)** (of plants and flowers) producing fruit: *a female fig-tree.* **2** of or typical of women: *female suffrage* ○ *the female mentality.* **3** (of a plug, socket, etc) having a hollow part designed to receive an inserted part.

▷ **female** *n* **1** female animal or plant. **2** (*often derog*) woman: *Who on earth is that female he's with?*

NOTE ON USAGE: **1 (a) Male** and **female** are nouns and adjectives used to indicate the sex of living things: *a male/female giraffe, bird, sardine, child, flower, etc* ○ *The males in the herd protect the females and the young.* **(b)** When speaking of humans the adjectives **male/female** refer especially to the physical features of one sex or the other: *The male voice is deeper than the female.* ○ *the female figure.* **(c)** When speaking about occupations, we usually say: *a woman doctor/women doctors* (NOT *a female doctor/female doctors,* though we do say *a male doctor,* NOT *a man doctor*). **(d)** The nouns **male/female** should not be used to refer to people (as opposed to their qualities, etc). They can give offence, esp **female.** We use **man/woman** instead: *Men have more body hair than women.* **2 (a) Masculine** and **feminine** are adjectives used to describe the behaviour, appearance, etc considered normal or acceptable for humans of one sex or other. They can therefore be used of the 'opposite' sex: a man can be described as **feminine** but not ***female***:*She dresses in a very feminine way.* ○ *She has a deep masculine voice.* **(b)** As nouns and adjectives **masculine** and **feminine** (as well as **neuter**) indicate grammatical gender.

feminine /ˈfemənɪn/ *adj* **1** of or like women; having the qualities or appearance considered characteristic of women: *a feminine voice, figure, appearance.* **2** (*grammar*) belonging to a class of words in English referring to female persons, animals, etc and often having a special form.: *'Lioness' is the feminine form of 'lion'.* ○ *The feminine form of 'count' is 'countess'.*

▷ **feminine** *n* (*grammar*) feminine word or gender.

femininity /ˌfeməˈnɪnətɪ/ *n* [U] quality of being feminine. ⇨ Usage at FEMALE. Cf MASCULINE.

feminism /ˈfemɪnɪzəm/ *n* [U] **(a)** belief in the principle that women should have the same rights and opportunities (legal, political, social, economic, etc) as men. **(b)** movement in support of this.

▷ **feminist** /ˈfemɪnɪst/ *n* supporter of feminism: *Suffragettes were among the first feminists in Britain.* ○ [attrib] *He has strong feminist opinions.*

femme fatale /ˌfæm fəˈtɑ:l/ (*pl* **femmes fatales** /ˌfæm fəˈtɑ:l/) (*French*) woman to whom a man feels irresistibly attracted, with dangerous or unhappy results: *She was his femme fatale.*

femur /ˈfi:mə(r)/ *n* (*pl* ~**s** or **femora** /ˈfemərə/) (*anatomy*) thigh-bone. ⇨ illus at SKELETON. ▷ **femoral** /ˈfemərəl/ *adj.*

fen /fen/ *n* **1** [C] area of low marshy land. **2 the Fens** [pl] (also **the Fen District**) low marshy areas in parts of East Anglia, England. They contain many drains and sluices, built to make the land suitable for farming and to protect it from flooding. ⇨ map at UNITED KINGDOM.

fence[1] /fens/ *n* **1** structure of rails, stakes, wire, etc, esp one put round a field or garden to mark a boundary or keep animals from straying. ⇨ illus at HOUSE. **2** (idm) **come down on one side of the fence or the other** ⇨ SIDE[1]. **mend one's fences** ⇨ MEND. **sit on the fence** ⇨ SIT.

▷ **fence** *v* **1** [Tn] surround, divide, etc (sth) with a fence: *Farmers fence their fields.* ○ *His land was fenced with barbed wire.* **2** (phr v) **fence sb/sth in (a)** surround or enclose sb/sth with a fence: *The grounds are fenced in to prevent trespassing.* **(b)** restrict the freedom of sb: *She felt fenced in by domestic routine.* **fence sth off** separate (one area from another) with a fence: *One end of the garden was fenced off for chickens.*

fencing /ˈfensɪŋ/ [U] material used for making fences, eg wood, wire, etc.

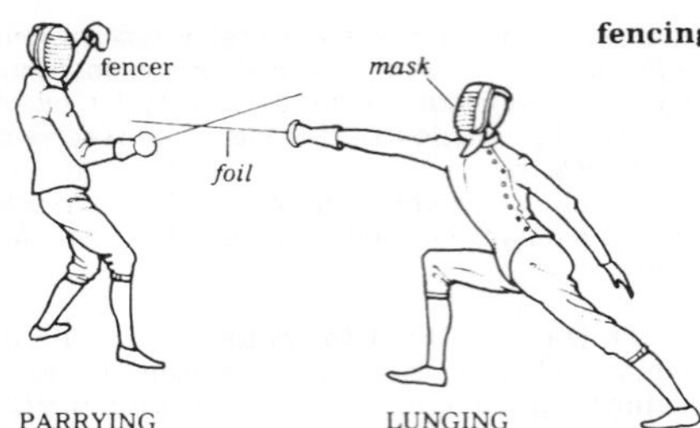

fence[2] /fens/ *v* **1** [I] (*sport*) fight with a long slender sword (foil, épée or sabre). **2** [I, Ipr] ~ (**with sb/ sth**) be evasive; avoid giving a direct answer to a question(er): *Stop fencing with me — answer my question!*

□ **fencer** *n* person who fences (FENCE[2] 1).

fencing *n* [U] art or sport of fighting with foils or other types of sword. ⇨ illus.

fence[3] /fens/ *n* person who knowingly buys and resells stolen goods.

fend /fend/ *v* (phr v) **fend for one'self** take care of or look after oneself; support oneself: *It is time you left home and learnt to fend for yourself.* **fend sth/ sb off** defend oneself from sth/sb; fight sth/sb off: *fend off a blow* ○ *The minister had to fend off some awkward questions from reporters.* ○ *He tried to kiss her but she fended him off.*

fender /ˈfendə(r)/ *n* **1** metal frame placed around a fireplace to prevent burning coal, etc from falling out or young children from falling in. **2** mass of rope, piece of wood, rubber tyre, etc, hung on the side of a boat to prevent damage, eg when it is alongside a wharf or another boat. **3** (*US*) (**a**) mudguard (MUD) of a bicycle, etc. (**b**) = WING 4.

Fenian /ˈfi:nɪən/ *n* **1** member of a 19th-century revolutionary organization (founded in the USA) that fought to end British rule in Ireland. **2** (*derog offensive*) Irish Roman Catholic. ▷ **Fenian** *adj*.

fennel /ˈfenl/ *n* [U] herb with yellow flowers, used for flavouring food.

fenugreek /ˈfenu:gri:k/ *n* [U] (**a**) strong-tasting seeds of a Mediterranean plant used in cookery and herbal medicine. (**b**) this plant.

feral /ˈfɪərəl; *US* ˈferəl/ *adj* (*fml*) (of animals) wild or savage, esp after escaping from captivity or from life as a pet: *feral cats.*

ferment[1] /fəˈment/ *v* [I, Tn] **1** (make sth) change chemically through the action of organic substances (esp yeast): *Fruit juices ferment if they are kept a long time.* ○ *When wine is fermented it gives off bubbles of gas.* **2** (*fig*) (cause sth to) become excited or agitated: *ferment trouble among the factory workers.*

▷ **fermentation** /ˌfɜ:menˈteɪʃn/ *n* [U] (action or process of) fermenting: *Sugar is converted into alcohol through the process of fermentation.* ○ *The fermentation of milk causes it to curdle.*

ferment[2] /ˈfɜ:ment/ *n* **1** [C] substance, eg yeast, that causes sth to ferment. **2** [U] (esp political or social) excitement or unrest: *The country was in a (state of) ferment.*

Fermi /ˈfɜ:mɪ/ Enrico (1901-54), American atomic physicist, born in Italy. He worked on artificial radioactivity, predicted the existence of the neutrino, and helped to develop the first atom bomb. In 1936 he was awarded the Nobel prize for physics.

fermium /ˈfɜ:mɪəm/ *n* [U] (*symb* **Fm**) chemical element, an artificially made radioactive metal.

fern /fɜ:n/ *n* [C, U] type of flowerless plant with feathery green leaves: *ferns growing in pots* ○ *hillsides covered in fern* ○ *a spray of ornamental fern.* ▷ **ferny** *adj*.

ferocious /fəˈrəʊʃəs/ *adj* fierce, violent or savage: *a ferocious beast* ○ *ferocious cruelty* ○ *a ferocious onslaught* ○ (*fig*) *a ferocious campaign against us in the press.* ▷ **ferociously** *adv*: *snarling ferociously.*

ferocity /fəˈrɒsətɪ/ *n* **1** [U] fierceness; violence: *The lion attacked its victim with great ferocity.* **2** [C] fierce or savage act.

ferret /ˈferɪt/ *n* small animal of the weasel family, kept for driving rabbits from their burrows, killing rats, etc. Cf ERMINE, WEASEL.

▷ **ferret** *v* **1** [I] (usu **go ferreting**) hunt (rabbits, rats, etc) with ferrets. **2** [I, Ipr, Ip] ~ (**about**) (**for sth**) (*infml*) search; rummage: *I spent the day ferreting (about) in the attic (for old photographs).* **3** (phr v) **ferret sth out** (*infml*) discover sth by searching or asking questions thoroughly: *ferret out a secret, the truth, the facts, etc.*

Ferris wheel /ˈferɪs wi:l; *US* hwi:l/ (in fairgrounds, etc) large upright wheel revolving on a fixed axle and having seats hanging from its rim.

ferroconcrete /ˌferəʊˈkɒŋkri:t/ *n* [U] = REINFORCED CONCRETE (REINFORCE).

ferromagnetism /ˌferəʊˈmægnətizəm/ *n* [U] type of magnetism found in iron and some other substances which remain magnetic even after the source that magnetized them has been removed. ▷ **ferromagnetic** /ˌferəʊmægˈnetɪk/ *adj*.

ferrous /ˈferəs/ *adj* [attrib] containing or relating to iron: *ferrous and non-ferrous metals.*

ferrule /ˈferu:l; *US* ˈferəl/ *n* metal ring or cap placed on the end of a stick, an umbrella, etc to stop it splitting or wearing down.

ferry /ˈferɪ/ *n* **1** boat, hovercraft, etc that carries people and goods across a stretch of water: *The ferry leaves for France at one o'clock.* ○ *travel by ferry* ○ [attrib] *the cross-channel ferry service.* **2** place where such a service operates: *We waited at the ferry for two hours.*

▷ **ferry** *v* (*pt, pp* **ferried**) [Tn, Tn·pr, Tn·p] transport (people or goods) by boat, aeroplane, etc, usu a short distance over a stretch of water, or regularly over a period of time: *ferry goods to the mainland* ○ *Can you ferry us across?* ○ *ferry the children to and from school* ○ *planes ferrying food to the refugees.*

□ **ˈferry-boat** *n* boat used as a ferry.

ˈferryman /-mən/ *n* (*pl* **-men** /-mən/) person in charge of a (usu small) ferry.

fertile /ˈfɜ:taɪl; *US* ˈfɜ:rtl/ *adj* **1** (of land or soil) able to produce much; rich in nutrients: *The plains of Alberta are extremely fertile.* **2** (of plants or animals) able to produce fruit or young. **3** (of seeds or eggs) capable of developing into a new plant or animal; fertilized. **4** (of a person's mind) full of new ideas; inventive: *have a fertile imagination.* Cf STERILE.

▷ **fertility** /fəˈtɪlətɪ/ *n* [U] state or condition of being fertile: *the fertility of the soil* ○ *great fertility of mind.*

□ **the ˌFertile ˈCrescent** crescent-shaped region of the Middle East where the rich agricultural land has been farmed since the neolithic period. It extends from present-day Israel and Lebanon up to southern Turkey, across to Iraq and down to eastern Iran.

fertilize, -ise /ˈfɜ:təlaɪz/ *v* [Tn] **1** introduce pollen or sperm into (a plant, an egg or a female animal) so that it develops seed or young: *Flowers are often fertilized by bees as they gather nectar.* **2** make (soil, etc) fertile or productive: *fertilize the garden with manure.*

▷ **fertilization, -isation** /ˌfɜ:təlaɪˈzeɪʃn; *US* -lɪˈz-/ *n* [U]: *successful fertilization by the male.*

fertilizer, -iser *n* [U, C] natural or artificial substance added to soil to make it more fertile: *Get some more fertilizer for the garden.* ○ *Bone-meal and nitrates are common fertilizers.* Cf MANURE.

fervent /ˈfɜ:vənt/ (also **fervid**) *adj* showing warmth and sincerity of feeling; enthusiastic; passionate: *a fervent farewell speech* ○ *fervent love, hatred, etc* ○ *a fervent admirer.* ▷ **fervently** *adv*: *believe fervently in eventual victory.*

fervid /ˈfɜ:vɪd/ *adj* (*fml*) = FERVENT. ▷ **fervidly** *adv*.

fervour (*US* **fervor**) /ˈfɜ:və(r)/ *n* [U] strength or warmth of feeling; enthusiasm: *speak with great fervour.*

festal /ˈfestl/ *adj* (*fml*) of a festival; gay and joyful. Cf FESTIVE.

fester /ˈfestə(r)/ *v* [I] **1** (of a cut or wound) become infected and filled with pus: *a festering sore.* **2** (*fig*) (of feelings or thoughts) become more bitter and angry: *The resentment festered in his mind.*

festival /ˈfestəvl/ *n* **1** (day or time of) religious or other celebration: *Christmas and Easter are Christian festivals.* ○ [attrib] *a festival atmosphere.* **2** series of performances of music, drama, films, etc given periodically: *the Edinburgh Festival* ○ *a jazz festival.*

festive /ˈfestɪv/ *adj* of or suitable for a feast or festival; joyous: *the festive season*, ie Christmas ○ *The whole town is in festive mood.* Cf FESTAL.

festivity /feˈstɪvətɪ/ *n* **1** [U] rejoicing; merry-making: *The royal wedding was an occasion of great festivity.* **2 festivities** [pl] festive, joyful events; celebrations: *wedding festivities.*

festoon /feˈstu:n/ *n* chain of flowers, leaves, ribbons, etc hung in a curve or loop as a decoration.

▷ **festoon** *v* [esp passive: Tn, Tn·pr] ~ **sb/sth** (**with sth**) decorate sb/sth with festoons: *a room festooned with paper streamers.*

Festschrift (also **festschrift**) /ˈfestʃrɪft/ *n* book that consists of a collection of articles written in honour of a distinguished scholar, esp by his colleagues: *I'm editing a festchrift for Wood's sixtieth birthday.*

feta (also **fetta**) /ˈfetə/ *n* [U] very soft white cheese made from goat's milk or ewe's milk, originally from Greece.

fetal ⇨ FOETUS.

fetch /fetʃ/ *v* **1** [Tn, Tn·pr, Tn·p, Dn·n, Dn·pr] ~ **sb/ sth** (**for sb**) go for and bring back sb/sth: *Fetch a doctor at once.* ○ *Please fetch the children from school.* ○ *The chair is in the garden; please fetch it in.* ○ *Should I fetch you your coat/fetch your coat for you from the next room?* **2** [Tn, Tn·pr] (*dated*) cause (sth) to come out: *fetched a deep sigh* ○ *fetch tears to the eyes.* **3** [Tn, Dn·n] (of goods) be sold for (a price): *The picture should fetch £2 000 at auction.* ○ *Those old books won't fetch (you) much.* **4** [Dn·n] (*infml*) give (a blow) to (sb): *She fetched him a terrific slap in the face.* **5** (idm) **fetch and ˈcarry** (**for sb**) act like a servant (for sb); be busy with small duties: *He expects his daughter to fetch and carry for him all day.* **6** (phr v) **fetch up** (*infml*) arrive at a certain place or in a certain position; land up: *Where on earth have we fetched up now?*

fetching /ˈfetʃɪŋ/ *adj* (*dated infml*) attractive: *a fetching smile* ○ *You look very fetching in that hat.* ▷ **fetchingly** *adv*.

fête /feɪt/ *n* outdoor entertainment or sale, usu to raise money for a special purpose: *the school/ village/church fête.*

▷ **fête** *v* [Tn esp passive] honour or entertain (sb) in a special way: *The queen was fêted wherever she went.*

fetid /ˈfetɪd, ˈfi:tɪd/ *adj* smelling foul or unpleasant; stinking: *fetid air.*

fetish /ˈfetɪʃ/ *n* **1** object that is worshipped, esp because a spirit is believed to live in it. **2** (**a**) thing to which more respect or attention is given than is normal or sensible: *He makes a fetish of his new car.* (**b**) object or activity that is necessary for or adds to an individual's sexual pleasure; fixation: *Women's underclothes are a common fetish.* ▷ **fetishism** *n* [U]: *magazines which cater to fetishism in men.* **fetishist** *n*.

fetlock /ˈfetlɒk/ *n* part of a horse's leg above and behind the hoof, where a tuft of hair grows. ⇨ illus at HORSE.

fetter /ˈfetə(r)/ *n* (usu *pl*) **1** chain put round the feet of a person or animal to limit movement: *The prisoner was kept in fetters.* **2** (*fig*) thing that restricts or hinders: *the fetters of poverty.*

▷ **fetter** *v* [Tn] **1** put (sb) in fetters. **2** restrict or hinder (sb) in any way: *I hate being fettered by petty rules and regulations.*

fettle /ˈfetl/ *n* (idm) **in fine, good, etc ˈfettle** fit and cheerful: *The team are all in excellent fettle.*

fetus = FOETUS.

feud /fju:d/ *n* long and bitter quarrel between two people, families or groups: *a long-standing feud* ○ *Because of a family feud, he never spoke to his wife's parents for years.*

▷ **feud** *v* [I, Ipr] ~ (**with sb/sth**) carry on a feud: *feuding neighbours* ○ *The two tribes are always* *feuding (with each other).*

feudal /ˈfju:dl/ *adj* of or according to the feudal system: *the feudal barons* ○ *(fig derog) The way they treat their casual workers is positively feudal.*

▷ **feudalism** /-dəlɪzəm/ *n* [U] (attitudes and structure of) the feudal system. **feudalistic** /ˌfju:dəˈlɪstɪk/ *adj.*

□ **the ˈfeudal system** system within which society was organized in Europe during the Middle Ages. It was based on a series of relationships between the lord and those subject to him (his vassals). A nobleman would be the king's vassal and would receive land from him in return for fighting for him when required. Ordinary people like peasants were the nobleman's vassals and worked on his land, while he was supposed to protect them.

fever /ˈfi:və(r)/ *n* **1** [C, U] abnormally high body temperature, esp as a sign of illness: *He has a high fever.* ○ *Aspirin can reduce fever.* **2** [U] specified disease in which (a) fever occurs: *yellow, typhoid, rheumatic, etc fever.* **3** [sing] (state of) nervous excitement or agitation: *He waited for her arrival in a fever of impatience.* **4** (idm) **at/to ˈfever pitch** at/to a high level of excitement: *The speaker brought the crowd to fever pitch.*

▷ **fevered** *adj* [attrib] **1** affected by or suffering from a fever: *She cooled her child's fevered brow.* **2** highly excited: *a fevered imagination.*

feverish /ˈfi:vərɪʃ/ *adj* **1** having a fever; caused or accompanied by a fever: *The child's body felt feverish.* ○ *During her illness she had feverish dreams.* **2** excited; restless: *with feverish haste.* **feverishly** *adv* very quickly or excitedly: *searching feverishly for her missing jewels.*

few[1] /fju:/ *indef det, adj* [usu attrib] (**-er, -est**) **1** (used with *pl* [C] *ns* and a *pl v*) not many: *Few people live to be 100.* ○ *a man/woman of few words,* ie one who speaks very little ○ *There are fewer cars parked outside than yesterday.* ○ *The police found very few clues to the murderer's identity.* ○ *There are very few opportunities for promotion.* ○ *The few houses we have seen are in terrible condition.* ○ *There were too few people at the meeting.* ○ *Accidents on site are few.* (Cf *There are few accidents on site.*) ⇨ Usage at LESS. ⇨ Usage at MUCH[1]. **2** (idm) **ˌfew and ˌfar beˈtween** infrequent, with long periods of waiting involved: *The buses to our village are few and far between.* ○ *The sunny intervals we were promised have been few and far between.*

▷ **few** *indef pron* not many people, things, places, etc. **(a)** (referring back): *Of the 150 passengers, few escaped injury.* ○ *Few can deny the impact of his leadership.* ○ *(saying) Many are called but few are chosen.* ○ *Hundreds of new records are produced each week but few (of them) get into the charts.* **(b)** (referring forward): *Few of us will still be alive in the year 2050.* ○ *The few who came to the concert enjoyed it.* ○ *We saw few of the sights as we were only there for two hours.*

the few *n* [pl *v*] the minority: *a voice for the few.*

few[2] /fju:/ **a few** *indef det* (used with *pl* [C] *ns* and *pl vs*) a small number of; some: *a few letters* ○ *a few days ago* ○ *He asked us a few questions.* ○ *A few people are coming for tea.* ○ *Only a few* (ie Not many) *students were awarded distinctions.* ⇨ Usage at MUCH[1].

▷ **a few** *indef pron* **1** a small number of people, things, places, etc; some. **(a)** (referring back): *I didn't get any cards yesterday but today there were a few.* ○ *She's written hundreds of books but I've only read a few (of them).* **(b)** (referring forward): *A few of the seats were empty.* ○ *I recognized a few of the other guests.* **2** (idm) **a good few; not a few** a considerable number; significantly many: *There were a good few copies sold on the first day.* ○ *Not a few of my friends are vegetarian.* **ˈhave a few** (usu in the present perfect) drink a sufficient amount of alcohol to make one drunk or almost drunk: *I've had a few* (ie a few glasses of beer, whisky, etc) *already, actually.* ○ *She looks as if she's had a few.* **a few** *adv* a small but significant number: *a few more/less/too many.*

fey /feɪ/ *adj* **1** (*Scot*) having a feeling of approaching death; able to foretell disaster. **2** having a strange whimsical charm. **3** (*derog*) (of a person and his behaviour) not serious; frivolous.

▷ **feyness** *n* [U].

fez /fez/ *n* (*pl* **fezzes**) red felt hat with a flat top and a tassle but no brim, worn by men in certain Muslim countries. ⇨ illus at HAT.

ff *abbr* **1** and the following (pages, lines, etc): *early childhood, p 10 ff,* eg in the index of a book. **2** (*music*) very loudly (Italian *fortissimo*). Cf PP 3.

fiancé (*fem* **fiancée**) /fɪˈɒnseɪ; *US* ˌfi:ɑ:nˈseɪ/ *n* man or woman to whom one is engaged to be married: *his fiancée* ○ *her fiancé.*

Fianna Fáil /ˌfi:ənə ˈfɔɪl/ Irish political party, formed by *De Valera in 1926 as a republican party.

fiasco /fɪˈæskəʊ/ *n* (*pl* ~**s**; *US* also ~**es**) complete and ridiculous failure: *The party was a total fiasco because the wrong date was given on the invitations.*

fiat /ˈfaɪæt; *US* ˈfi:ət/ *n* [C, U] (*fml*) formal authorization, order or decree: *The opening of a market stall is governed by municipal fiat.*

□ **ˈfiat money** (*US*) paper money that has been authorized as legal tender but cannot be exchanged for its value in ordinary coin.

fib /fɪb/ *n* (*infml*) untrue statement, esp about sth unimportant: *Stop telling such silly fibs.* Cf LIE 1 *n.*

▷ **fib** *v* (**-bb-**) [I] say untrue things; tell a fib or fibs: *Stop fibbing!* **fibber** *n* person who tells fibs: *You little fibber!*

fibre (*US* **fiber**) /ˈfaɪbə(r)/ *n* **1** [C] any of the slender threads of which many animal and plant tissues are formed: *a cotton, wood, nerve, muscle fibre.* **2** [U] material or substance formed from a mass of fibres: *cotton fibre for spinning* ○ *The muscle fibre of this animal is diseased.* ○ *Eating cereals and fruit will give you plenty of fibre in your diet.* **3** [U] **(a)** texture or structure: *material of coarse fibre.* **(b)** (*fig*) person's character: *a woman of strong moral fibre.*

▷ **fibrous** /ˈfaɪbrəs/ *adj* like or made of fibres.

□ **ˈfibreboard** (*US* **ˈfiber-**), **ˈfibreglass** (*US* **ˈfiber-**) *ns* [U] (also **glass fibre**) material made from glass fibres and resin and sometimes mixed with plastic, used for insulation and in making cars, boats, etc: [attrib] *a fibreglass racing yacht.*

fibre ˈoptics (*US* **fiber optics**) transmission of information by means of infra-red light signals along a thin glass fibre. It is used in surgical devices which allow doctors to see inside the body, and in telecommunications.

fibrosis /faɪˈbrəʊsɪs/ *n* [U] abnormal increase or development of fibrous tissue or muscle.

fibrositis /ˌfaɪbrəˈsaɪtɪs/ *n* [U] inflammation of the fibrous tissue of the body, esp the muscles of the back, causing severe pain and stiffness. Cf ARTHRITIS, RHEUMATISM.

fibula /ˈfɪbjʊlə/ *n* (*pl* **fibulae** /-li:/) (*anatomy*) outer of the two bones between the knee and the foot. ⇨ illus at SKELETON.

fiche /fi:ʃ/ *n* [C, U] = MICROFICHE.

fickle /ˈfɪkl/ *adj* often changing; not constant: *fickle weather, fortune* ○ *a fickle person, lover, etc,* ie not faithful or loyal. ▷ **fickleness** *n* [U]: *the fickleness of the English climate.*

fiction /ˈfɪkʃn/ *n* **1** [U] type of literature (eg novels, stories) describing imaginary events and people: *works of fiction* ○ *He writes fiction.* ○ *Truth is often stranger than fiction.* Cf NON-FICTION. **2** [C] thing that is invented or imagined and not strictly true: *a polite fiction,* ie sth assumed to be true (though it may not be) for social reasons. Cf FACT.

▷ **fictional** /-ʃənl/ *adj* of fiction; told as a story: *fictional characters* ○ *a fictional account of life on a farm.*

fictionalize, -ise /ˈfɪkʃənəlaɪz/ *v* [Tn] write about (a true event) as if it were fiction or in the style of a fictional story, inventing some of the details, characters, etc: *fictionalized history.*

fictitious /fɪkˈtɪʃəs/ *adj* imagined or invented; not real: *The account he gives of his childhood is quite fictitious.* ○ *All the places and characters in my novel are entirely fictitious.*

Fid Def /ˌfɪd ˈdef/ *abbr* = FD.

fiddle /ˈfɪdl/ *n* **1** (*infml*) violin. **2** (*sl*) thing done dishonestly; swindle; fraud: *It's all a fiddle!* **3** (idm) **be on the ˈfiddle** (*sl*) behave illegally, or dishonestly. **fit as a fiddle** ⇨ FIT[1]. **play second ˈfiddle (to sb/sth)** be treated as less important than another person, activity, etc: *I have no intention of playing second fiddle to the new director, so I've resigned.* ○ *His family has had to play second fiddle to his political career.*

▷ **fiddle** *v* **1** [I, Tn] (*infml*) play (a tune on) the violin: *He learned to fiddle as a young boy.* **2** [I, Ip] ~ **(about/around)** play aimlessly; fidget or delay: *Stop fiddling (about) and do some work.* **3** [Ipr] ~ **(about/around) with sth** play carelessly with sth in one's hands: *She fiddled with her watch so much that it broke.* **4** [Tn] (*infml*) falsify (accounts, etc); get (sth) by cheating: *fiddle one's expenses* ○ *He fiddled a free ticket for the match.* **fiddler** /ˈfɪdlə(r)/ *n* **1** person who plays the violin. **2** (*infml*) person who cheats; swindler. **3** (also **ˈfiddler crab**) type of small crab.The male has one claw longer than the rest, which it moves about like a violinist's arm. **fiddling** /ˈfɪdlɪŋ/ *adj* [usu attrib] (*infml*) trivial; unimportant; petty: *fiddling little details.* **fiddly** /ˈfɪdlɪ/ *adj* (*infml*) awkward to do or use: *Changing a fuse is one of those fiddly jobs I hate.* ○ *This tin-opener is awfully fiddly.*

□ **fiddle-faddle** /ˈfɪdlfædl/ *n* [U] matters of no importance. — *v* [I] make a fuss over unimportant matters. — *interj* nonsense!

ˈfiddlesticks /ˈfɪdlstɪks/ *interj* (*dated*) nonsense.

fidelity /fɪˈdelətɪ; *US* faɪ-/ *n* [U] **1** ~ **(to sb/sth)** **(a)** loyalty; faithfulness: *fidelity to one's principles, religion, leader.* **(b)** accuracy; truthfulness: *fidelity to the text of the play* ○ *translate sth with the greatest fidelity.* **2** quality or precision with which sound is reproduced: [attrib] *a high fidelity recording.*

fidget /ˈfɪdʒɪt/ *v* [I, Ipr, Ip] ~ **(about) (with sth)** make small restless movements, thus annoying other people: *Stop fidgeting!* ○ *Hurry up, your father is beginning to fidget,* ie show signs of impatience. ○ *It's bad manners to fidget about (with the cutlery) at the table.*

▷ **fidget** *n* **1** [C] person who fidgets: *You're such a fidget!* **2 the fidgets** [pl] restless movements: *I always get the fidgets during long meetings.*

fidgety *adj* restless or inclined to fidget: *a fidgety child* ○ *Travelling in planes makes me fidgety.*

fiduciary /fɪˈdju:ʃərɪ; *US* fəˈdu:ʃɪerɪ/ *adj* (*fml*) **1** (of sth that is) held or given in trust: *fiduciary estates.* **2** (of paper money) issued wihout the security of gold reserves and depending for its value on the confidence of the public: *a fiduciary issue.*

fief /fi:f/ *n* **1** land held by a vassal under the feudal system. **2** (*fig fml*) person's special area of control or responsibility; domain: *The timetables are her fief and she doesn't like anyone else interfering with them.*

field[1] /fi:ld/ *n* **1** area of land (usu enclosed by a fence, hedge, etc) used for pasturing animals or cultivating crops: *working in the fields* ○ *a fine field of wheat.* **2** (usu in compounds) **(a)** wide area or expanse: *an ˈice-field,* eg around the North Pole. **(b)** open space used for a specified purpose: *a ˈbaseball, ˈcricket, etc field.* **3** (usu in compounds) area from which minerals, etc are obtained: *ˈcoalfields* ○ *ˈgold-fields* ○ *a new ˈoilfield.* **4** range of a subject, an activity or an interest: *in the field of politics, art, science, music, etc* ○ *That is outside my field,* ie not among the subjects I have studied. **5 (a)** area or space within which a specified force can be felt: *a magnetic ˈfield* ○ *the earth's gravitational ˈfield,* ie the space in which the earth's gravity has an effect. **(b)** range over which sth can operate effectively: *the field of a telescope* ○ *one's field of vision,* ie the area that one can see ○ *a gun with a good field of fire.* **6** area or place where a battle is or was fought: *the field of battle/ˈbattlefield.* **7** (*sport*) **(a)** all those taking part or competing in an event: *The field includes three world record holders.* **(b)** (in cricket and baseball) team that is not batting, with regard to their positions on the field: *bowling to a defensive field.* **8** (*computing*) one section of a record, representing a unit of information: *The firm's payroll has one field for gross pay and one for net pay.* **9** (idm) **hold the field (against sb/sth)** not be replaced by (sb/sth); remain dominant: *Einstein's ideas on physics have held the field for years.* **play the ˈfield** (*infml esp US*) avoid committing oneself to one person, activity, etc. **take the ˈfield** (**a**) begin a war or battle. (**b**) (*sport*) go onto the playing area.

□ **ˈfield-day** *n* **1** day on which military operations are practised. **2** day or period of great excitement and activity: *Whenever there's a government scandal the newspapers have a field-day.* **3** (*esp US*) (**a**) sports day at a school, college, etc. (**b**) day of outdoor scientific study.

ˈfield events *n* [pl] athletic sports other than races, eg jumping and discus-throwing. Cf TRACK EVENTS (TRACK).

ˈfieldfare *n* type of thrush that spends the winter, rather than the summer, in Britain or nearby countries.

ˈfield-glasses *n* = GLASSES (GLASS 6).

ˈfield goal (in American football and basketball) goal scored when the ball is in normal play.

ˈfield hockey (*US*) = HOCKEY.

ˌField ˈMarshal officer of the highest rank in the British Army ⇨ App 4.

ˈfield officer major or colonel in the army.

ˈfield sports outdoor sports, eg hunting, fishing and shooting.

ˈfield-test *v* [Tn] test (sth) by using it in the conditions for which it is meant: *The equipment has all been field-tested.* — *n*: *undergo rigorous field-tests.*

ˈfield-work *n* **1** [U] practical academic or social work done outside the laboratory or classroom. **2** [C] temporary fortification made by troops.

ˈfield-worker *n* person who helps in practical field work.

field[2] /fi:ld/ *v* (**a**) [I, Tn] (in cricket and baseball) (stand ready to) catch and throw back (the ball): *He fields well.* ○ *She fielded the ball.* (**b**) [I] (in cricket and baseball) be (in) the team not batting: *We're fielding first.* (**c**) [Tn] select (sb) to play in a game (of football, hockey, cricket, etc): *They're fielding a very strong side this season.* (**d**) [Tn] (*fig*) deal successfully with (a series of questions, etc): *The minister easily fielded all the journalist's awkward questions.* ▷ **ˈfielder** *n* = FIELDSMAN. ⇨ illus at CRICKET.

□ **ˈfieldsman** /-mən/ *n* (*pl* **-men** /-mən/) (in cricket, etc) member of the team not batting.

Fielding /ˈfi:ldɪŋ/ Henry (1707-54), English novelist whose early satirical plays led to the introduction of censorship. His most famous work, *Tom Jones*, has a long and cleverly constructed plot which presents a vivid picture of English society at the time. It had an important influence on the development of the English novel. Fielding became a Justice of the Peace in 1748 and founded the Bow Street Runners, an early police force, in his efforts to fight crime in London.

fiend /fi:nd/ *n* **1** evil spirit; devil: *the fiends of hell.* **2** (**a**) very cruel or spiteful person. (**b**) person who causes mischief or annoyance: *Stop teasing her, you little fiend!* **3** (*infml*) person who is fond of or strongly drawn to sth specified: *a ˌfresh-ˈair fiend.*
▷ **fiendish** *adj* **1** fierce or cruel: *a fiendish temper.* **2** (*infml*) clever and complicated: *a fiendish plot, plan, idea, etc.* **3** (*infml*) extremely bad, unpleasant or difficult: *fiendish weather* ○ *a fiendish problem.* **fiendishly** *adv* (*infml*) very; extremely: *a fiendishly difficult puzzle* ○ *It's fiendishly cold outside.*

fierce /fɪəs/ *adj* (**-r**, **-st**) **1** violent and angry: *fierce dogs, winds, attacks* ○ *look fierce/have a fierce look.* **2** (**a**) intense: *fierce concentration, loyalty, hatred.* (**b**) unpleasantly or uncontrollably strong: *fierce heat* ○ *His plan met with fierce opposition.* ▷ **fiercely** *adv.* **fierceness** *n* [U].

fiery /ˈfaɪərɪ/ *adj* [usu attrib] **1** (**a**) like or consisting of fire; flaming: *fiery red hair* ○ *a fiery sky* ○ *fiery eyes*, ie angry and glaring. (**b**) very spicy; producing a burning sensation: *a fiery Mexican dish* ○ *fiery liquor.* **2** (**a**) (of a person, his character, etc) quickly or easily made angry: *a fiery temper.* (**b**) (of words, etc) intense; passionate: *a fiery speech.* (**c**) full of high spirits: *a fiery horse.* ▷ **fierily** /-rəlɪ/ *adv.* **fieriness** *n* [U].

fiesta /fɪˈestə/ *n* (**a**) religious festival in Spanish-speaking countries. (**b**) any holiday or festival.

FIFA /ˈfi:fə/ *abbr* International Association Football Federation (French *Fédération Internationale de Football Association*).

fife /faɪf/ *n* small high-pitched musical instrument like a flute, used with drums in military music: [attrib] *a fife and drum band.*

fifteen /ˌfɪfˈti:n/ *pron, det* 15; one more than fourteen. ⇨ App 9.
▷ **fifteen** *n* **1** the number 15. **2** team of Rugby Union players.
fifteenth /ˌfɪfˈti:nθ/ *pron, det* 15th; next after fourteenth. — *n* one of fifteen equal parts of sth.
For the uses of *fifteen* and *fifteenth* see the examples at *five* and *fifth*.

fifth /fɪfθ/ *pron, det* 5th; next after fourth: *the fifth in line* ○ *Today is the fifth (of March).* ○ *the fifth book on the list* ○ *This is the fifth day of the conference.* ○ *Edward V*, ie Edward the Fifth. ⇨ App 9.
▷ **fifth** *n* **1** one of five equal parts of sth: *He gave her a fifth of the total amount.* ○ *They divided the money into fifths and took one fifth each.* **2** (*US*) bottle of whisky, gin, etc containing one fifth of an American gallon (0.76 litre).
fifthly *adv* in the fifth position or place.
□ **the ˌFifth Aˈmendment** one of the amendments to the Constitution in the American *Bill of Rights, which states that no person can be forced to give evidence against himself. People *take* or *plead the Fifth (amendment)* when they refuse to answer questions in court because the answers would show them to be guilty of a crime.
ˌfifth ˈcolumn organized group of people working for the enemy within a country at war. **ˌfifth ˈcolumnist** (**a**) member of a fifth column. (**b**) person who is secretly not loyal to an organization; traitor or spy.

fifty /ˈfɪftɪ/ *pron, det* 50; one more than forty-nine. ⇨ App 9.
▷ **fiftieth** /ˈfɪftɪəθ/ *pron, det* 50th; next after forty-ninth. — *n* one of fifty equal parts of sth.
fifty *n* **1** the number 50. **2 the fifties** [pl] numbers, years or temperature from 50 to 59: *The total amount is in the fifties.* ○ *She was born in the fifties*, ie in the 1950s. ○ *How warm is it today? It's in the (high/low) fifties.* **3** (idm) **in one's fifties** between the ages of 50 and 60: *She's in her early/mid/late fifties.*
□ **ˌfifty-ˈfifty** *adj, adv* (*infml*) shared or sharing equally between two: *divide the profits on a fifty-fifty basis*, ie take equal shares ○ *a fifty-fifty chance of winning*, ie an equal chance of winning or losing ○ *We went fifty-fifty on dinner*, ie shared the cost equally.
ˌfifty ˈpence (also **ˌfifty ˈp**, **50p**) (*Brit*) (coin worth) fifty new pence.
For the uses of *fifty* and *fiftieth* see the examples at *five* and *fifth*.

fig /fɪg/ *n* **1** soft sweet fruit, full of small seeds and often eaten dried. **2** (also **ˈfig-tree**) tree with broad leaves on which this grows. **3** (idm) **not care/give a ˈfig (for sb/sth)** not care at all; consider (sb/sth) valueless or unimportant: *I don't care a fig what others think of me.*
□ **ˈfig-leaf** *n* **1** leaf of a fig-tree, traditionally used for covering the genital organs of nude bodies in drawings, statues, etc. **2** (*fig*) thing used to try to disguise a fact that one does not want to admit: *The grant is a fig-leaf for the government's lack of interest in the arts.*

fig *abbr* **1** figurative(ly). **2** figure; illustration: *see diagram at fig 3.*

fight[1] /faɪt/ *v* (*pt, pp* **fought** /fɔ:t/) **1** (**a**) [I, Ipr] ~ (**against/with sb/sth**) struggle against sb/sth using physical force, in a war, battle, etc: *soldiers training to fight* ○ *Do stop fighting, boys!* ○ *The two dogs were fighting over a bone.* ○ *Britain fought with* (ie as an ally of) *France against Germany in the last war.* ○ *Have you been fighting with* (ie against) *your brother again?* (**b**) [Tn] struggle thus against (sb): *We must fight the enemy.* ○ *The boxer has fought many opponents.* **2** [Tn] engage in, take part in or carry on (a battle, etc): *fight a war, duel, etc* ○ *The government has to fight several by-elections in the coming months.* **3** [Ipr, Tn] ~ (**against**) **sth** strive to overcome, destroy or prevent sth: *fight (against) poverty, oppression, ignorance* ○ *fight an eviction notice* ○ *fight a fire.* **4** [Ipr, Tn·pr] make (one's way) or achieve (sth) by fighting or effort: *We had to fight (our way) through the crowded streets.* ○ *They fought the bill through Parliament.* **5** [I, Ipr] ~ (**about/over sth**) quarrel or argue: *It's a trivial matter and not worth fighting about.* **6** (idm) **fight like a ˈtiger** attack sb or defend oneself fiercely: *She fought like a tiger to get what she wanted.* **fight a losing ˈbattle (against sth)** struggle without (hope of) success to achieve or prevent sth: *Anyone who tries to resist the spread of new technology is fighting a losing battle.* **fight shy of sth/sb** be unwilling to undertake (a task) or confront (sb); avoid sth/sb: *He was unhappy in his job for years but always fought shy of telling his boss.* **fight to the ˈfinish** fight until one side wins conclusively. **a ˌfighting ˈchance** small but distinct chance of success if a great effort is made. **fighting ˈdrunk** (*infml*) drunk and likely to become violent. **fighting ˈfit** fully fit and ready to do what needs to be done. **fighting ˈtalk/ˈwords** defiant statement or challenge showing that one is ready to fight for sth. **live like fighting cocks** ⇨ LIVE[2]. **7** (phr v) **fight back** fight with renewed force and strength; show resistance or retaliation: *After a disastrous first half the team fought back to level the match.* ○ *Don't let them bully you. Fight back!* **fight sth back/down** suppress (feelings, etc): *fighting back tears* ○ *fighting down a sense of disgust.* **fight for sth** strive to obtain or accomplish sth: *fight for freedom, independence, human rights, etc.* **fight sb/sth off** resist or repel sb/sth by fighting: *fighting off repeated enemy attacks* ○ *fight off a cold, a feeling of tiredness.* **fight sth out** settle (an argument, a dispute, etc) by fighting: *I can't help them to resolve their quarrel — they must fight it out between them.*
▷ **fighter** *n* **1** person who fights in war or in sport. **2** (*usu approv*) person who does not yield without a struggle: *She won't give up easily: she's a real fighter.* **3** fast military aircraft designed to attack other aircraft: *a ˌjet-ˈfighter* ○ [attrib] *fighter planes* ○ *a fighter pilot.*
fighting *n* [U]: *outbreaks of street fighting.*

fight[2] /faɪt/ *n* **1** [C] act of fighting or struggling: *a fight between two dogs* ○ *the fight against poverty, crime, disease* ○ *a prize fight*, eg in boxing. ⇨ Usage at ARGUMENT. **2** [U] desire or ability to fight or resist; determination: *In spite of many defeats, they still had plenty of fight left in them.* ○ *Losing their leader took all the fight out of them.* **3** (idm) **a fight to the ˈfinish** struggle, etc that continues until one side wins conclusively. **pick a fight/quarrel** ⇨ PICK[3]. **put up a good, poor, etc ˈfight** fight with/without courage and determination.

figment /ˈfɪgmənt/ *n* thing that is not real but only imagined (used esp in the expression shown): *a figment of sb's imagination.*

figurative /ˈfɪgərətɪv/ *adj* (*abbr* **fig**) (of words) used in an imaginative or a metaphorical way rather than literally: *'He exploded with rage' shows a figurative use of the verb 'to explode'.* ▷ **figuratively** *adv.*

figure[1] /ˈfɪgə(r); *US* ˈfɪgjər/ *n* **1** [C] (**a**) written symbol for a number, esp 0 to 9: *Write the figure '7' for me.* ○ *He has an income of six figures/a six-figure income*, ie £100 000 or more. (**b**) (*usu sing*) sum of money; price: *We bought the house at a high/low figure*, ie for a high/low price. **2** [C] (**a**) diagram or illustration: *The figure on page 22 shows a political map of Africa.* (**b**) geometrical shape enclosed by lines or surfaces. **3** [C] decorative pattern or series of movements: *The skater executed a perfect set of figures.* ○ [attrib] *figure-skating.* **4** [C] representation of a person or an animal in drawing, painting, etc: *The central figure in the painting is the artist's daughter.* **5** [C] human form, esp its appearance, what it suggests, and how it is seen by others: *have a good figure*, ie be slim, shapely, etc ○ *I'm dieting to keep my figure*, ie in order not to get fatter. ○ *I saw a figure approaching in the darkness.* ○ *He was once a leading figure in the community, but now he has become a figure of fun*, ie His influence was considerable but now he appears merely ridiculous. ○ *She's a fine figure of a woman*, ie pleasing in shape and appearance. **6 figures** [pl] arithmetic: *Are you good at figures?* **7** (idm) **cut a fine, poor, sorry, etc ˈfigure** have a fine, etc appearance. **facts and figures** ⇨ FACT. **in round figures/numbers** ⇨ ROUND¹. **put a figure on sth** quote a price or specify a number for sth: *It's impossible to put a figure on the number of homeless after the flood.* **single figures** ⇨ SINGLE.

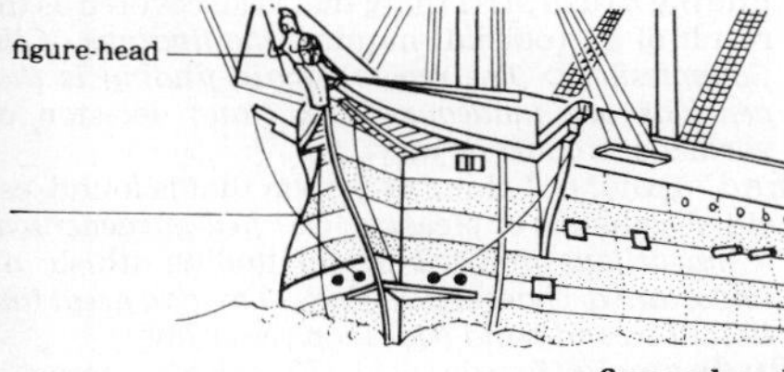

figure-head

□ **ˈfigure-head** *n* **1** (esp formerly) large wooden carving, usu representing a human figure, placed at the prow of a ship. ⇨ illus. **2** (*fig*) person in a high position but without any real authority.

ˌfigure of ˈeight (*US* also **figure eight**) thing that resembles the number 8 in shape: *skating figures of eight on the ice.*

figure of ˈspeech word or phrase used for vivid or dramatic effect and not literally: *I didn't really mean she was in outer space — it's just a figure of speech.*

figure² /ˈfɪgə(r); *US* ˈfɪgjər/ *v* **1** [I, Ipr] ~ **(in sth)** appear or be mentioned, esp prominently: *a character that figures in many of her novels* ○ *She figured conspicuously in the public debate on the issue.* **2 (a)** [Tn, Tf] (*esp US*) think (sth); calculate: *I figured (that) you wouldn't come.* ○ *It's what I figured.* **(b)** [I] (used with *it* or *that*) (*infml*) be likely or understandable: *'John isn't here today.' 'That figures, he looked very unwell yesterday.'* **3** (phr v) **figure sth in** (*US*) include sth in one's calculations: *Have you figured in the cost of food for our holiday?* **figure on sth** (*US*) include sth in one's plans; rely on sth: *I figure on being in New York in January.* **figure sb/sth out** (*esp US*) **(a)** come to understand sb/sth by thinking: *I've never been able to figure him out.* ○ *I can't figure out why he quit his job.* ○ *Have you figured out what's wrong with your car?* **(b)** discover sth by using arithmetic; calculate sth: *Have you figured out how much the holiday will cost?*

figurine /ˈfɪgəri:n; *US* ˌfɪgjəˈri:n/ *n* small ornamental statue, esp of a person.

Fiji /ˌfi:ˈdʒi:; *US* ˈfi:dʒi:/ country in the southern Pacific, consisting of about 840 islands; pop approx 727 000; official language English; capital Suva; unit of currency dollar (= 100 cents). The native Pacific islanders make up about half the population; the rest are descendants of Indians brought there by the British in the 19th century. The economy is based mainly on agriculture, fishing and tourism. In 1987 the election of an Indian-led government was followed by a military coup. Fiji became a republic shortly afterwards, and ceased to be a member of the Commonwealth. ⇨ map at MELANESIA. ▷ **Fijian** /ˌfi:ˈdʒi:ən; *US* ˈfi:dʒi:ən/ *adj, n.*

filament /ˈfɪləmənt/ *n* **1** very thin strand or fibre, like a thread. **2** thin wire in a light bulb that glows when electricity is passed through it. ⇨ illus at BULB.

filch /fɪltʃ/ *v* [Tn] (*infml*) steal (esp sth of small value): *Who's filched my pencil?*

file¹ /faɪl/ *n* metal tool with a rough surface for cutting, smoothing or shaping hard substances.

▷ **file** *v* **1** [Tn, Tn·pr, Cn·a] cut, smooth or shape (sth) with a file: *file one's fingernails* ○ *file sth smooth* ○ *file an iron bar in two.* **2** (phr v) **file sth down** make sth smooth and smaller in size by using a file. **filings** /ˈfaɪlɪŋz/ *n* [pl] particles removed by a file: *iron filings.*

file² /faɪl/ *n* **1 (a)** any of various types of drawer, shelf, holder, cover, box, etc, usu with a wire or metal rod for keeping loose papers together and in order, for reference purposes: *I need another file for my letters.* **(b)** file and its contents: *Where's the file of our recent correspondence?* ○ *have/open/keep a file on each member of staff.* **2** organized collection of related data or material in a computer: *I can't access the file on your company because I've forgotten the code.* **3** (idm) **on file** kept in a file: *We have all your particulars on file.*

▷ **file** /faɪl/ *v* **1** [Tn, Tn·pr, Tn·p] ~ **sth (away)** place sth in a file; store sth where it can be consulted: *file (away) letters in a drawer.* **2** [Tn] send (sth) so that it may be recorded: *file an application for divorce.* **3** [Tn] (of a journalist) send (a news story, etc) to a newspaper. **4** [I] (*US*) register formally as a candidate in a primary election.

□ **ˈfiling cabinet** piece of office furniture with drawers for holding files.

ˈfiling clerk (*US* **file clerk**) person who files correspondence, etc and does general office tasks.

file³ /faɪl/ *n* **1** line of people or things one behind the other. **2** (idm) **(in) Indian/single ˈfile** (in) one line, one behind the other. Cf THE RANK AND FILE (RANK¹).

▷ **file** *v* [I, Ipr, Ip] ~ **in, out, off, past, etc** march or walk in the specified direction in a single line: *The men filed onto the parade ground and past the general.*

filet /ˈfɪleɪ/ *n* (also **filet mignon** /ˌfɪleɪ ˈmi:njɒn/) (*US*) small tender piece of beef without bones, cut from a sirloin: *Two filets mignons, please.*

filial /ˈfɪlɪəl/ *adj* [usu attrib] of or expected from a son or daughter: *filial duty.*

filibuster /ˈfɪlɪbʌstə(r)/ *n* (*esp US*) **1** person who tries to delay or prevent the making of decisions in (esp parliamentary) meetings by making long speeches. **2** such a speech.

▷ **filibuster** *v* [I] (*esp US*) act as a filibuster: *filibustering tactics.*

filigree /ˈfɪlɪgri:/ *n* [U] fine ornamental work using gold, silver or copper wire: [attrib] *a filigree brooch* ○ *filigree ear-rings.*

filings ⇨ FILE¹.

Filipino /ˌfɪlɪˈpi:nəʊ/ *n* (*pl* ~**os**) native or inhabitant of the Philippines. ▷ **Filipino** *adj.*

fill¹ /fɪl/ *v* **1 (a)** [Tn, Tn·pr, Cn·a, Dn·n, Dn·pr] ~ **sth (with sth)**; ~ **sth (for sb)** make sth full (of sth); occupy all of the space in sth: *fill a hole with sand, a tank with petrol, a hall with people* ○ *Smoke filled the room.* ○ *The wind filled the sails*, ie made them swell out. ○ (*fig*) *I am filled with admiration for your bravery.* ○ *fill a bucket full of water* ○ *Please fill this glass for me/fill me this glass.* **(b)** [I, Ipr] ~ **(with sth)** become full: *The hall soon filled.* ○ *The sails filled with wind.* **2** [Tn, Tn·pr] ~ **sth (with sth)** block or plug (a hole, gap, etc): *A dentist often has to fill teeth.* ○ *I must fill that crack in the wall.* **3** [Tn] **(a)** hold (a position): *She fills the post satisfactorily*, ie performs her duties well. **(b)** appoint sb to (a position): *The vacancy has already been filled.* **4** (idm) **fill/fit the bill** ⇨ BILL¹. **fill sb's shoes** take over sb's function, duties, etc and perform them satisfactorily. **5** (phr v) **fill in (for sb)** take sb's place for a short time: *My partner is on holiday this week so I'm filling in (for him).* **fill sth in (a)** (*US* also **fill sth out**) add what is necessary to make sth complete: *fill in an application form*, ie write one's name and other details required. **(b)** fill sth completely: *The hole has been filled in.* **(c)** spend (time) while waiting for sth: *He filled in the rest of the day watching television.* **fill sb ˈin (on sth)** give sb full details (about sth): *Can you fill me in on what has been happening?* **fill ˈout** become larger, rounder or fatter: *Her cheeks began to fill out.* ○ *He used to be a very thin child but he's filled out a lot recently.* **fill sth out** ⇨ FILL STH IN /A. **fill (sth) up** become or make completely full: *The gutter has filled up with mud.* ○ *fill up the tank with petrol.*

▷ **filler** *n* object or material used to fill a hole in sth or to increase the size of sth.

□ **ˈfilling station** = PETROL STATION (PETROL), ⇨ illus at MOTORWAY.

fill² /fɪl/ *n* **1** [C] enough to fill sth: *a fill of tobacco/petrol/oil.* **2** [U] **one's** ~ **(of sth/sb)** (*fml*) **(a)** as much as one can eat or drink: *No more tea, thank you, I've had my fill.* **(b)** as much as one can tolerate: *She decided she had had her fill of his cruelty.*

fillet /ˈfɪlɪt/ *n* **1** [C, U] piece of meat or fish without bones: [attrib] *a/some fillet steak.* **2** [C] narrow band, ribbon, etc worn round the head to keep the hair in place or as an ornament.

▷ **fillet** *v* [Tn] cut (meat or fish) into fillets: *grilled filleted sole.*

filling /ˈfɪlɪŋ/ *n* **1** [C] (process of putting in) material used to fill a hole in a tooth: *I had to have two fillings at the dentist's today.* **2** [C, U] food put between slices of bread to make a sandwich, or between layers of cake, etc: *a cake with jam filling.*

fillip /ˈfɪlɪp/ *n* **1** stimulus or incentive; encouragement: *an advertising campaign to give a much-needed fillip to sales.* **2** quick flick made by pressing a finger against the thumb and then releasing it suddenly.

filly /ˈfɪlɪ/ *n* young female horse. Cf COLT¹, MARE¹ 1.

film¹ /fɪlm/ *n* **1** [C usu *sing*] ~ **(of sth)** thin coating or covering on or over sth: *a film of dust* ○ *a film of oil on water* ○ *a film of mist over the land.* **2** [C, U] roll or sheet of thin flexible light-sensitive material for use in photography: *put a new film in one's camera* ○ *expose/develop 50 feet of film.* **3** [C] motion picture: *What's your favourite film?* ○ *My cousin is in films*, ie works in the film industry. Cf MOVIE.

▷ **filmy** *adj* (**-ier, -iest**) [usu attrib] thin and almost transparent: *a filmy cotton blouse.*

□ **ˈfilm badge** badge containing photographic film which shows the amount of radiation to which the person wearing the badge has been exposed.

ˈfilm star well-known cinema actor or actress.

ˈfilm-strip *n* series of transparent still photographs that can be projected separately.

ˈfilm test photographic test to decide whether sb is suitable to act in films.

film² /fɪlm/ *v* **1 (a)** [Tn, Tng] make a film or motion picture of (a scene, story, etc): *They're filming a new comedy.* ○ *She filmed her children playing in the garden.* **(b)** [I] be engaged in doing this: *They've been filming for six months.* **2 (a)** [Tn] cover (sth) with a thin coating or covering layer: *Thin ice filmed the lake.* **(b)** [Ip] ~ **over** become covered in this way: *As she cried, her eyes filmed over.*

filter

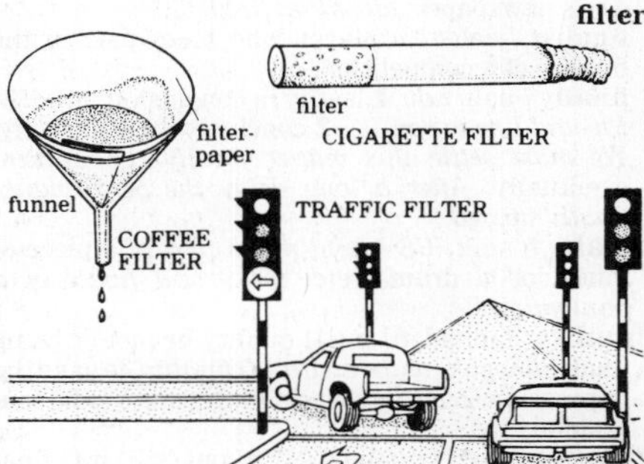

filter /ˈfɪltə(r)/ *n* **1** device containing paper, sand, cloth, etc used to hold back any solid material or impurities in a liquid or gas passed through it: *an oil filter* ○ *a coffee filter.* ⇨ illus. **2** screen (esp of coloured glass) that allows light only of certain wavelengths to pass through: *I took this picture with a red filter.* **3** device for suppressing certain electrical or sound waves. **4** (*Brit*) device that signals to show that traffic may turn left while other traffic waiting to go straight ahead or turn right is still stopped by a red traffic light. ⇨ illus.

▷ **filter** *v* **1** [Tn] (**a**) pass (liquid, light, etc) through a filter: *It won't take long to filter the coffee.* (**b**) purify (a liquid) by using a filter: *All drinking water must be filtered.* **2** [I, Ipr, Ip] ~ **in, out, through, etc** (*fig*) pass or flow slowly in a specified direction; become known gradually: *New ideas are slowly filtering into people's minds.* ○ *The news of the defeat started to filter through.* **3** [I] (*Brit*) (of traffic) turn left while other traffic waiting to go straight ahead or turn right is stopped by a red traffic light.

□ ˈ**filter-bed** *n* layer of gravel, sand, etc at the bottom of a reservoir used for filtering large quantities of water.

ˈ**filter feeding** process by which many aquatic vertebrates take in tiny food particles from the surrounding water.

ˈ**filter-paper** *n* [U] porous paper for filtering liquids.

ˈ**filter-tip** *n* (cigarette one end of which contains a) filter for smoke. ˈ**filter-tipped** *adj*.

filth /fɪlθ/ *n* [U] **1** disgusting dirt: *Look at the filth on your trousers!* **2** offensive and obscene words, literature, magazines, etc: *How can you read such filth?*

▷ **filthy** *adj* (**-ier, -iest**) **1** (**a**) disgustingly dirty: *a beggar dressed in filthy rags.* (**b**) obscene: *filthy language.* **2** (*infml*) (esp of weather) very unpleasant: *Isn't it a filthy day?* **filthily** *adv*. **filthiness** *n* [U].

filthy *adv* **1** in a filthy way: *filthy dirty.* **2** (*infml*) very: *filthy rich.* **3** (idm) **filthy lucre** (*derog or joc*) money or financial gain.

filtrate /ˈfɪltreɪt/ *n* filtered liquid.

▷ **filtration** /fɪlˈtreɪʃn/ *n* [U] process of filtering liquid, etc.

fin /fɪn/ *n* **1** thin flat projecting part of a fish, used for swimming and steering. ⇨ illus at FISH. **2** thing shaped like this on eg an aircraft or a rocket that helps to keep it stable. ⇨ illus at AIRCRAFT.

finable ⇨ FINE[1].

finagle /fɪˈneɪgl/ *v* (*infml derog*) (**a**) [I] cheat or deceive sb in a cunning way. (**b**) [Tn] obtain or arrange (sth) dishonestly or cunningly: *They finagled their way into the ground without tickets.*

final /ˈfaɪnl/ *adj* **1** [attrib] of the end; coming last: *the final chapter of a book.* **2** [usu pred] (of a decision, etc) conclusive; decisive; that cannot be changed: *The judge's ruling is final.* ○ *I'm not coming, and that's final!* **3** (idm) **in the last/final analysis** ⇨ ANALYSIS. **the last/final straw** ⇨ STRAW.

▷ **final** *n* **1** (**a**) last of a series of contests or competitions: *the tennis finals* ○ *the Cup Final*, ie the last in a series of esp football matches. (**b**) (usu *pl*) last set of university examinations: *sit/take one's finals* ○ *the law final(s).* **2** last edition of a day's newspaper: *late night final.*

finalist /-nəlɪst/ *n* player who takes part in the final(s) of a competition.

finally /-nəlɪ/ *adv* **1** lastly; in conclusion: *Finally, I would like to say....* **2** conclusively; decisively: *We must settle this matter finally.* **3** at last; eventually: *After a long delay the performance finally started.*

finale /fɪˈnɑːlɪ; *US* -ˈnælɪ/ *n* last part of a piece of music or a drama, etc: *the grand finale of a pantomime.*

finality /faɪˈnælətɪ/ *n* [U] quality or fact of being final: *She spoke with (an air of) finality*, ie gave the impression that there was nothing more to be said or done.

finalize, -ise /ˈfaɪnəlaɪz/ *v* [Tn] put (sth) into final form; complete: *finalize one's plans, arrangements, etc.* ▷ **finalization, -isation** /ˌfaɪnəlaɪˈzeɪʃn; *US* -lɪˈz-/ *n* [U].

finance /ˈfaɪnæns, fɪˈnæns/ *n* **1** [U] management of (esp public) money: *an expert in finance* ○ *the Minister of Finance.* ⇨ article. **2** [U] ~ (**for sth**) money used or needed to support an undertaking: *Finance for the National Health Service comes from taxpayers.* **3 finances** [pl] money available to a person, company or country: *Are the firm's finances sound?*

▷ **finance** *v* [Tn esp passive] provide money for (a project, etc); fund: *The scheme is partly financed by a government grant.*

□ ˈ**finance company** (also ˈ**finance house**) company that lends money for hire-purchase transactions.

financial /faɪˈnænʃl, fɪˈnæ-/ *adj* concerning money and finance: *in financial difficulties*, ie short of money ○ *Tokyo and New York are major financial centres.* ▷ **financially** /-ʃəlɪ/ *adv*.

□ **fiˌnancial ˈyear** (*US* **fiscal year**) period of 12 months over which annual accounts and taxes are calculated. In Britain it is traditionally from 6 April of one year to 5 April of the next.

financier /faɪˈnænsɪə(r); *US* ˌfɪnənˈsɪər/ *n* person engaged in financing businesses, etc on a large scale.

finch /fɪntʃ/ *n* (often in compounds) any of several types of small songbird with short, stubby bills: *a ˈchaffinch* ○ *a ˈgoldfinch* ○ *a ˈbullfinch.*

find[1] /faɪnd/ *v* (*pt, pp* **found** /faʊnd/) **1** [Tn, Tn·pr, Tn·p, Cn·a] discover (sth/sb) unexpectedly or by chance; come across: *Look what I've found.* ○ *I found a £5 note on the pavement.* ○ *He woke up and found himself in hospital.* ○ *I was disappointed to find you out* (ie that you were out) *when I called.* ○ *We came home and found her asleep on the sofa.* **2** [Tn, Tn·pr, Dn·n, Dn·pr] ~ **sth/sb** (**for sb**) discover sth/sb by searching, inquiry or effort: *After months of drilling, oil was found off the coast.* ○ *find a cure for cancer* ○ *find an answer to a question* ○ *I can find nothing new to say on this subject.* ○ *Can you find me a hotel/find a hotel for me?* **3** [Tn, Dn·n, Dn·pr] ~ **sth/sb** (**for sb**) obtain or get back (esp sth/sb that was lost): *Did you find the pen you lost?* ○ *The missing child has not been found yet.* ○ *I'll help you find your shoes/find your shoes for you.* **4** [Tn] succeed in obtaining (sth); provide or supply: *I keep meaning to write, but never seem to find (the) time.* ○ *Who will find the money to pay for this trip?* **5** [Tf, Cn·a] discover (sth/sb) by experience (to be or do sth); become aware of: *I find (that) it pays to be honest.* ○ *How do you find your new job?* ○ *She found it difficult to understand him/found him difficult to understand.* ○ *We found the beds very comfortable.* ○ *We found him (to be) dishonest.* **6** [Tn] arrive at (sth) naturally; reach: *Water will always find its own level.* ○ *The arrow found its mark.* **7** [Tn] (used in a statement of fact, indicating that sth exists): *You'll find* (ie There is) *a teapot in the cupboard.* ○ *These flowers are found* (ie exist, grow) *only in Africa.* **8** [Cn·a] (*law*) decide and declare as a verdict: *How do you find the accused?* ○ *The jury found him guilty (of manslaughter).* **9** (idm) **all ˈfound** (of wages) with free food and lodging included. **be found wanting** be shown to be not sufficiently reliable or capable of undertaking a task, etc. **find fault (with sb/sth)** look for and discover mistakes (in sb/sth); complain (about sb/sth): *I have no fault to find with your work.* ○ *She's always finding fault (with me).* **find/lose favour with sb/in sb's eyes** ⇨ FAVOUR[1]. **find one's ˈfeet** (**a**) become able to stand, walk, etc steadily: *After a six-week illness it took me some time to find my feet again.* (**b**) become able to act independently and confidently: *I only recently joined the firm so I'm still finding my feet.* (**not**) **find it in one's heart/oneself to do sth** (usu with *can/could*) (not) be able to do sth because of kindness or consideration: *I cannot find it in myself to condemn a mother who steals for a hungry child.* ○ *Can you find it in your heart to apologize?* ˈ**find oneself** discover one's true abilities, character and desires: *At twenty-two, he's just beginning to find himself.* **find/meet one's match** ⇨ MATCH[2]. **find one's own level** find and associate with the people with whom one is morally, socially or intellectually equal. **find/lose one's ˈvoice/ˈtongue** be able/unable to speak or express one's opinion: *Tell me what you think — or have you lost your tongue?* **find its way to...** reach a destination naturally: *Rivers find their way to the sea.* **find one's way (to...)** discover the right route (to a place): *I hope you can find your way home.* ○ *She couldn't find her way out of the building.* **take sb as one ˈfinds him** accept sb as he is without expecting him to behave in a special way: *We've only just returned from holiday so you must take us as you find us.* **10** (phr v) **find (sth) out** learn (sth) by study or inquiry: *Can you find out what time the train leaves?* **find sb out** discover sb who has done wrong, lied, etc: *He had been cheating the taxman but it was years before he was found out.* **find for/against sb** (*law*) give a verdict in favour of/against sb: *The jury found for the defendant.*

▷ **finder** *n* **1** person who finds sth: *Lost: one diamond ring. Finder will be rewarded.* **2** small telescope attached to a larger one used for locating an object for observation. **3** (idm) ˌ**finders ˈkeepers** (*saying*) whoever finds sth has the right to keep it.

finding *n* (usu *pl*) **1** thing that is discovered as the result of an (official) inquiry: *the findings of the Commission* ○ *The report's main finding is that pensions are inadequate.* **2** (*law*) decision or verdict of a court or jury.

find[2] /faɪnd/ *n* **1** thing or person that is found, esp sth/sb valuable or pleasing: *Our new gardener was a marvellous find.* **2** act of finding sth/sb: *an important archaeological find* ○ *I made a great find in that second-hand bookshop yesterday.*

fin de siècle /ˌfæn də ˈsjekl/ (*French often derog*) of or like the end of the 19th century, seen as a time when art, ideas, etc were changing rapidly. This was thought by many to be a sign of decadence: [attrib] *fin-de-siècle society.*

fine[1] /faɪn/ *n* **1** sum of money that must be paid as a punishment for breaking a law or rule: *Offenders may be liable to a heavy fine.* **2** (idm) **in ˈfine** (*fml*) (used to present a final point or to summarize an argument): *We should, in fine, make no further concessions.*

▷ **fine** *v* [Tn, Tn·pr, Dn·n] ~ **sb** (**for sth/doing sth**) punish sb by a fine: *fined for dangerous driving* ○ *The court fined him £500.*

finable /ˈfaɪnəbl/ *adj* (of an action) that is likely to be punished by a fine: *a finable offence.*

fine[2] /faɪn/ *adj* (**-r, -st**) **1** (**a**) of high quality: *a fine painting* ○ *a very fine performance* ○ *fine food, clothes, material.* (**b**) carefully and skilfully made; easily damaged; delicate: *fine workmanship* ○ *fine silk.* (**c**) good; beautiful; pleasing; enjoyable: *a fine view* ○ *We had a fine holiday in Switzerland.* (**d**) (*ironic*) bad: *This is a fine mess we're in!* ○ *You're a fine one to talk!* ie You have no right to say that, eg because you are as bad as those you are criticizing. **2** (of weather) bright; clear; not raining: *It poured all morning, but turned fine later.* **3** made of very small grains or particles: *fine powder, flour, dust, etc* ○ *Sand is finer than gravel.* **4** slender; thin: *fine thread* ○ *a pencil with a fine point.* **5** (of metals) refined; pure: *fine gold.* **6** (**a**) difficult to perceive; subtle: *You are making very fine distinctions.* (**b**) that can make delicate and careful distinctions: *a fine sense of humour* ○ *a fine taste in art.* **7** (of speech or writing) ornate; rhetorical; complimentary, esp in an insincere way: *His speech was full of fine words which meant nothing.* **8** in good health; well; comfortable: *'How are you?' 'Fine, thanks.'* **9** (*infml*) satisfactory: *I'm not very hungry — a small snack is fine for me.* **10** (idm) **chance would be a fine thing** ⇨ CHANCE[1]. **the finer points (of sth)** the details or aspects of sth which can be recognized and appreciated only by those who understand or know it well: *I don't understand the finer points of snooker but I enjoy watching it on TV.* **get sth down to a fine ˈart** (*infml*) learn to do sth perfectly: *She's got the business of buying birthday presents down to a fine art.* **not to put too fine a ˈpoint on it** to speak plainly: *I don't much like modern music — in fact, not to put too fine a point on it, I hate it.* **one fine ˈday** (in story-telling) on a certain day, in the past or in the future.

▷ **finely** *adv* **1** well; splendidly: *finely dressed.* **2** into small particles or pieces: *finely chopped herbs.* **3** with precision; in a subtle way: *a finely tuned engine* ○ *The match was finely balanced.*

Finance

The City of London was once considered the financial capital of the world and today it is still one of the world's most important financial centres. The area of the City called 'the Square Mile' contains banks that account for one fifth of total international bank lending, the world's largest insurance industry and one of the world's largest stock exchanges. In 1989 the financial sector was responsible for 14 per cent of Britain's total economic output.

Apart from the Stock Exchange, important institutions in the City include the Bank of England, Lloyd's, the Royal Exchange and the Baltic Exchange. The Bank of England, founded in 1694 and nationalized in 1946 is Britain's 'banker's bank', acting as banker both for the state and for the other banks. It is sometimes referred to as 'the old lady of Threadneedle Street', after the street where its building is situated. The Governor of the Bank of England is responsible for advising the government on banking matters, implementing Treasury policy, arranging government borrowing and managing the National Debt (the amount of money that the government owes). It is also responsible, together with the banks in Scotland and Northern Ireland, for issuing banknotes. (Coins are issued by the Royal Mint.)

The Stock Exchange, founded in 1773, is the main institution for the buying and selling of stocks and shares, of which more than 8 000 are listed. Many people in Britain own shares either directly or through the investments made by their pension funds. Share ownership has increased in recent years as a result of the Conservative government's programme of privatizing certain formerly state-owned companies and the introduction of employee share ownership schemes. About 20 per cent of the population now own shares directly, compared with less than 10 per cent in 1979. In 1986 the reorganization of the Stock Exchange (popularly known as 'Big Bang') introduced a screen-based dealing system to replace trading on the floor of the Exchange. The distinct roles of the stockbrokers, who dealt with clients, and the jobbers, who actually did the buying and selling, were merged into a single category of 'market maker'. (The term 'stockbroker belt' is still often used to describe the affluent parts of the Home Counties where many business-people live and commute daily to the City.)

The Royal Exchange is the home of the London International Financial Futures Exchange (LIFFE, pronounced like 'life'), a market set up in 1982 to provide facilities for dealing in futures (contracts for the sale or purchase of a financial commodity at an agreed price in the present to take effect at an agreed date in the future). The Baltic Exchange operates a market in freight as well as trading in commodities.

Lloyd's (which has no connection with Lloyds Bank, one of the High Street banks) began in the 17th century as a marine insurance company. It is now an association of underwriters for all kinds of insurance, although *Lloyd's List*, a daily bulletin of shipping information, is still published today.

Share prices are recorded daily in almost all newspapers and summarized in radio and television news broadcasts. The prices quoted are usually those of the Financial Times/Stock Exchange 100 Share Index (FT/SE 100, popularly called 'Footsie'). Introduced in 1984, this index is based on the prices of shares in 100 of the largest companies listed on the Stock Exchange. (The *Financial Times*, printed on distinctive pink paper, is the daily newspaper of the City.)

There are three different stock-markets. The main market is the London International Stock Exchange, the securities officially listed on the Stock Exchange. These include the so-called 'Blue Chip' shares, those of the largest companies, which can be readily bought and sold and are therefore considered to be the least risky for investors. The other markets are the Unlisted Securities Market, for smaller but well-established companies, and the Third Market, for new and very small companies.

Among other specialized financial institutions in the City are the finance houses, which lend money to companies; venture capital companies, which provide funds for new enterprises when money cannot be obtained from traditional sources like the stock-market or the banks; and the nine discount houses, which are unique to the City. They act as intermediaries between the Bank of England and other banks, and monitor the flow of funds between the government and the banks.

The London Stock Exchange is an independent organization, responsible for its own rules of conduct without government control. In this, it differs from the New York Stock Exchange (NYSE), which is subject to specific legislative regulation, even if the government does not directly participate in its operation. The New York Exchange dates from 1792 and is situated on Wall Street, the equivalent of Britain's City of London. It is usually referred to as Wall Street. Its share prices are quoted on the Dow Jones Index, named after the financial analysts Charles H Dow and Edward D Jones, who began to publish financial bulletins in the 1880s. (In 1889 they founded the *Wall Street Journal*, the New York equivalent of London's *Financial Times*.)

In the USA, the proportion of the population that owns shares is higher than in Britain. The number rose from some 30 million in 1970 to 47 million in 1985. An increasing number of Americans buy shares 'over the counter' through NASDAQ (the National Association of Securities Dealers Automated Quotations), and shares in 'high-tech' companies are especially popular. Shares in the smaller and lesser-known companies are traded through the American Stock Exchange.

Many American investors are not only shareholders but also bondholders. US Treasury Bonds are considered one of the safest of all investments. There are two kinds: some, like Savings Bonds, cannot be bought and sold after the original purchase. They are sold at 50 per cent of their face value and on maturing, five years later, will fetch 100 per cent of this value when cashed in. Others, like Treasury Bills (short-term bonds maturing in three, six or twelve months), Treasury Notes (from $500 in value, maturing in up to ten years) and Treasury Bonds (maturing in ten to 30 years, with a minimum investment of $1 000), can be bought and sold freely. (Cf article at BANK.)

fineness *n* [U].

□ **fine ˈart** (also **the fine ˈarts, art**) art or forms of art that appeal to the sense of beauty, eg painting, sculpture, etc: [attrib] *a fine-arts course.*

fine-ˈtooth comb (idm) **(go over, through, etc sth) with a fine-ˈtooth comb** (examine sth) closely and thoroughly: *Police experts are sifting all the evidence with a fine-tooth comb.*

the fine print = THE SMALL PRINT (SMALL).

fine[3] /faɪn/ *adv* **1** (*infml*) very well: *That suits me fine.* **2** (in compounds) in a fine[2](1, 6) way: *ˌfine-ˈdrawn* (ie subtle) *distinctions.* **3** (idm) **cut it/things ˈfine** leave oneself only the minimum amount, esp of time: *If we only allow five minutes for catching our train, we'll be cutting it too fine.*

□ **ˌfine-ˈspun** *adj* (of thread, fabric, etc) delicate: (*fig*) *a ˌfine-spun ˈargument*, ie one that is too elaborate to be convincing.

fine-ˈtune *v* [Tn] make small changes to a machine, etc so as to obtain the best possible results: (*fig*) *We're still fine-tuning our sales strategy.* **fine-ˈtuning** *n* [U].

finery /ˈfaɪnərɪ/ *n* [U] gay and elegant clothes or decoration: *court officials dressed in all their finery* ○ *The garden looks beautiful in its summer finery,* ie with its bright flowers, lawns, etc.

fines herbes /ˌfiːnz ˈeəb/ (*French*) mixed herbs used in cooking, esp for flavouring omelettes.

finesse /fɪˈnes/ *n* **1** [U] skill in dealing with people or situations cleverly or tactfully: *show finesse in averting a threatened strike* ○ *He wheedled money from his father with considerable finesse.* **2** [C] (in card-games) attempt to win a trick(5) by playing a card that is not the highest one held.

▷ **finesse** *v* [Tn] (in card-games) play (a card) as part of a finesse(2): *She succeeded in finessing her queen.*

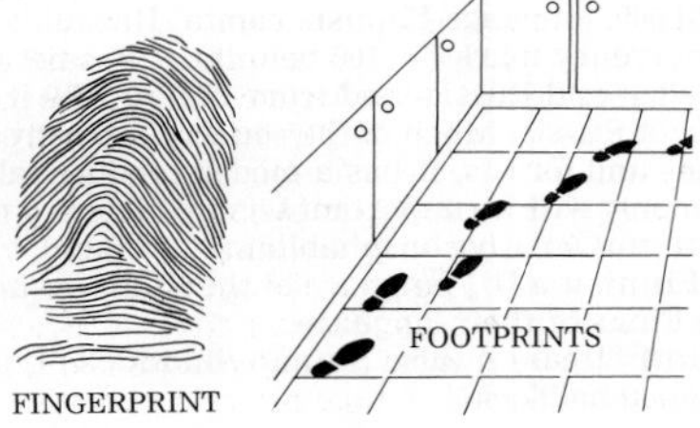

FINGERPRINT

finger[1] /ˈfɪŋgə(r)/ *n* **1** any of the five parts extending from each hand (*ˈlittle finger, ˈring finger, ˈmiddle finger, ˈforefinger/ˈindex finger, thumb*); any of these except the thumb: *There are five fingers (or four fingers and one thumb) on each hand.* ⇨ illus at HAND, ⇨ Usage at BODY. **2** part of a glove that fits over a finger. **3** (*infml*) measure of alcohol in a glass, roughly equal to the width of one finger: *He poured himself two fingers of whisky.* **4** (idm) **be all ˌfingers and ˈthumbs** be clumsy or awkward with one's hands: *Can you thread this needle for me? I'm all fingers and thumbs today.* **burn one's fingers/get one's fingers burnt** ⇨ BURN[2]. **cross one's fingers** ⇨ CROSS[2]. **get, pull, etc a/one's ˈfinger out** (*infml*) stop being lazy; work faster: *If you don't pull your finger out, you'll never get the job finished.* **have a finger in every ˈpie** (*infml*) be involved in everything that is happening. **have/keep one's ˈfinger on the pulse (of sth)** know all the latest news, developments, etc. **have, etc one's fingers in the till** (*infml*) steal money from one's place of work: *be caught with one's fingers in the till* ○ *He's had his fingers in the till for years.* **lay a ˈfinger on sb/sth** touch sb/sth, however slightly: *If you lay a finger on that boy* (ie harm him physically), *I'll never forgive you.* **lift/raise a finger/hand** ⇨ LIFT. **point the finger** ⇨ POINT[2]. **put one's finger on sth** identify precisely or point out (an error, the cause of a problem, etc): *I can't quite put my finger on the flaw in her argument.* **put the finger on sb** (*sl*) give information about (esp a criminal) to the police, etc. **slip through sb's fingers** ⇨ SLIP[2]. **snap one's fingers** ⇨ SNAP. **sticky fingers** ⇨ STICKY. **twist sb round one's little finger** ⇨ TWIST. **work one's fingers to the bone** work very hard.

□ ˈ**finger-board** *n* piece of wood (on a guitar, violin, etc) where the strings are pressed against the neck of the instrument with the fingers to vary the tone.

ˈ**finger-bowl** *n* small bowl for rinsing the fingers during meals.

ˈ**finger-mark** *n* mark, eg on a wall, made by a (dirty) finger: *leave finger-marks all over the shiny table.*

ˈ**finger-nail** *n* layer of nail(1) over the upper surface of the tip of a finger.

ˈ**finger-plate** *n* glass, metal or plastic plate fastened on a door near the handle or keyhole to prevent finger-marks.

ˈ**fingerprint** *n* mark made by the tip of a finger on a surface and used for identifying people, esp criminals. No two people make the same marks with their fingers and it is possible to classify the patterns scientifically: *take the prisoner's fingerprints.* ⇨ illus. — *v* [Tn] make a record of the fingerprints of (sb): *fingerprint the prisoner.*

ˈ**finger-stall** *n* protective cover for an injured finger.

ˈ**fingertip** *n* **1** extreme end of a finger. **2** (idm) **have sth at one's** ˈ**fingertips** be completely familiar with sth. **to one's** ˈ**fingertips** in every way; completely; through and through: *She's an artist to her fingertips.*

finger[2] /ˈfɪŋgə(r)/ *v* [Tn] **1** touch or feel (sth) with the fingers: *She fingered the silk to feel its quality.* ○ *I don't like eating food that's been fingered by someone else.* **2** play (a musical instrument) with the fingers. **3** (*sl*) give information about (esp a criminal) to the police, etc.

▷ **fingering** /ˈfɪŋgərɪŋ/ *n* [U] method of using the fingers in playing a musical instrument or in typing; numbers on a printed piece of music showing this: *a piano piece with tricky fingering.*

finial /ˈfɪnɪəl/ *n* decoration on the top of a gable, canopy, etc.

finicky /ˈfɪnɪkɪ/ (also **finical** /ˈfɪnɪkl/, **finicking** /ˈfɪnɪkɪŋ/) *adj* **1** (*derog*) too fussy about food, clothes, etc: *a finicky eater, dresser, etc.* **2** needing much attention to detail: *This job is too finicky for me.*

finish /ˈfɪnɪʃ/ *v* **1** (**a**) [I, Tn, Tg] come or bring (sth) to an end: *Term finishes next week.* ○ *finish one's work* ○ *finish (reading) a book.* (**b**) [I] reach the end of a task or an activity: *Wait — I haven't finished yet.* ○ *Two of the runners failed to finish.* ○ *She was leading for part of the race but finally finished fourth.* **2** [Tn, Tn·p] ~ **sth (off/up)** eat, drink or use what is left of sth: *We might as well finish (up) the cake; there isn't much left.* **3** [Tn, Tn·p] ~ **sth (off)** complete sth or make sth perfect: *a beautifully finished wooden bowl* ○ *put the finishing touches to a work of art* ○ *This blouse needs to be finished off before I can wear it.* **4** [Tn, Tn·p] ~ **sb (off)** (*infml*) exhaust sb completely: *That bike ride absolutely finished me (off).* **5** (phr v) **finish sb/sth off** (*infml*) destroy sb/sth: *That fever nearly finished him off.* ○ *The last bullet finished off the wounded animal.* ○ (*fig*) *It would finish me off to see her with him.* **finish with sb/sth** (**a**) no longer be busy with sb; no longer be using sth: *Can you wait a minute? I haven't finished with Ann yet.* ○ *You'll be sorry by the time I've finished with you,* eg finished punishing you. ○ *Please put the saucepan away if you've finished with it.* (**b**) end a relationship with sb or a connection with sth: *She should finish with him — he treats her very badly.* ○ *I've finished with gambling — it's a waste of money.* **finish (up) with sth** have sth at the end: *We had a quick lunch and finished up with a cup of coffee/and a cup of coffee to finish up with.* **finish up** (followed by an *adj* or *n*) be at the end; end up: *He could finish up dead or badly injured.*

▷ **finish** *n* **1** [C] last part or end of sth: *the finish of a race* ○ *There were several close finishes during the competition,* ie ones in which the leading competitors were close together at the end. **2** (**a**) [C, U] state of being finished or perfect: *furniture with a fine finish* ○ (*fig*) *His manners lack finish.* (**b**) [C] method, material or texture used for completing the surface of woodwork, etc: *varnishes available in a range of finishes.* **3** (idm) **be in at the** ˈ**finish** be present at the end of sth. **fight to the finish** ⇨ FIGHT[1]. **a fight to the finish** ⇨ FIGHT[2].

finisher *n* person or animal that finishes a race, etc.

□ ˈ**finishing school** private (usu expensive) school where girls are taught how to behave in fashionable society.

finished /ˈfɪnɪʃt/ *adj* **1** [pred] ~ **(with sb/sth)** (*infml*) in a state of having completed sth or no longer dealing with sb/sth: *I won't be finished for another hour.* ○ *I'm not finished with you yet.* ○ *She decided she was finished with working for others.* **2** [pred] no longer effective; ruined: *The scandal means he's finished in politics.* ○ *Everything is finished between her and him.* **3** [usu attrib] made; completed: *the finished product, article, etc.*

finite /ˈfaɪnaɪt/ *adj* **1** having bounds; limited; not infinite: *Human knowledge is finite,* ie There are things we do not know. **2** (*grammar*) of a verb form that agrees with its subject in person and number: *'Am', 'is', 'are', 'was' and 'were' are the finite forms of 'be'; 'be', 'being' and 'been' are the non-finite forms.*

fink /fɪŋk/ *n* (*US sl derog*) **1** person who gives information to the police about criminals. **2** person who continues to work while others are on strike. **3** unpleasant or contemptible person.

Finland

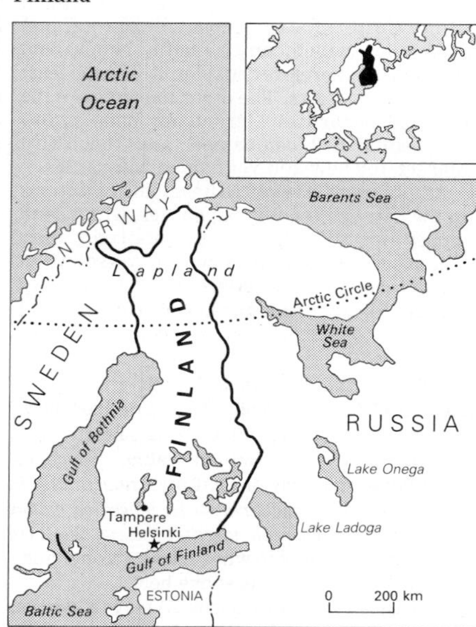

Finland /ˈfɪnlənd/ country in northern Europe with its coastline on the Baltic Sea; pop approx 4 951 000; language Finnish; capital Helsinki; unit of currency mark (= 100 pennis). It lies between Sweden and Russia, and from 1809 to 1919 it was part of Russia. Much of the country is covered by lakes and forests. It has a modern industrialized economy with an important service sector. ⇨ map.

Finn /fɪn/ *n* native or inhabitant of Finland.

▷ **Finnish** *n* [U] language of the Finns. — *adj* of the Finns or their language.

finnan /ˈfɪnən/ *n* (also ˌ**finnan** ˈ**haddock**) type of smoked haddock.

Finno-Ugric /ˌfɪnəʊ ˈjuːgrɪk/ *adj, n* (of a) group of languages that includes the *Finnic* languages (eg Finnish) and the *Ugric* languages (eg Hungarian). It is thought that they were originally spoken in central Russia.

fiord (also **fjord**) /fɪˈɔːd/ *n* long, narrow and often very deep inlet of the sea between high cliffs, as in Norway. Fiords are formed by the sea flowing into a valley created by a melted glacier.

fir /fɜː(r)/ *n* **1** [C] (also ˈ**fir-tree**) type of evergreen tree with leaves like needles on its shoots. **2** [U] wood of this tree.

□ ˈ**fir-cone** *n* fruit of the fir-tree.

fire[1] /ˈfaɪə(r)/ *n* **1** [U] burning that produces light and heat: *man's discovery of fire.* **2** (**a**) [U] destructive burning: *Have you insured your house against fire?* (**b**) [C] instance of this: *forest fires* ○ *a fire in the warehouse* ○ [attrib] *a fire hose.* **3** (**a**) [C] burning fuel in a grate, furnace, etc for cooking food or heating a room: *make/build a fire* ○ *lay a fire,* ie put paper, wood, etc together for a fire, usu in a grate ○ *a blazing/roaring fire.* (**b**) [C] apparatus for heating rooms, etc: *a gas/electric fire.* Cf HEATER (HEAT[2]), STOVE 2. **4** [U] shooting from guns: *The soldiers kept up a steady fire.* ○ *return sb's fire,* ie shoot back at sb. **5** [U] strong emotion; angry or excited feeling; enthusiasm: *His speech lacked fire,* ie was uninspiring. **6** (idm) **a ball of fire** ⇨ BALL[1]. **a baptism of fire** ⇨ BAPTISM. **between two** ˈ**fires** being shot at from two directions. **catch fire** ⇨ CATCH[1]. **draw sb's fire** ⇨ DRAW[2]. **the fat is in the fire** ⇨ FAT[2]. ˌ**fire and** ˈ**brimstone** torture suffered in Hell as a result of God's anger: (*fig*) *She was breathing fire and brimstone,* ie was furiously angry. ˌ**fire and** ˈ**sword** (*fml*) burning and killing, esp in war. **fire in one's** ˈ**belly** passionate enthusiasm, usu for a cause: *You need more fire in your belly if you want to make people believe you really care.* **get on like a house on fire** ⇨ HOUSE[1]. **go through** ˌ**fire and** ˈ**water (for sb/sth)** endure great hardship and danger (for sb/sth). **hang fire** ⇨ HANG[1]. **have, etc many irons in the fire** ⇨ IRON[1]. **heap coals of fire on sb's head** ⇨ HEAP *v.* **hold one's** ˈ**fire** stop shooting (for a period of time). **make up a** ˈ**fire** add wood, coal, etc to a fire to make it burn more strongly. **no smoke without fire** ⇨ SMOKE[1]. **on** ˈ**fire (a)** burning: *The house is on fire!* (**b**) (*fig*) burning with emotion, passion or sensation. **open fire** ⇨ OPEN[2]. **out of the frying-pan into the fire** ⇨ FRYING-PAN (FRY[1]). **play with** ˈ**fire** take foolish and dangerous risks. **set fire to sth/set sth on fire** cause sth to start burning. **(not/never) set the** ˈ**Thames** /temz/ **on fire** (not) do sth remarkable: *He's a good student, but he won't ever set the Thames on fire.* **set the world on fire** ⇨ WORLD. **under** ˈ**fire (a)** being shot at: *come under intense fire.* (**b**) (*fig*) being criticized severely: *The government is under fire from all sides on its economic policy.*

□ ˈ**fire-alarm** *n* bell or other device that gives warning of a fire; sound made by this.

ˈ**firearm** *n* (usu *pl*) portable gun of any sort, eg a rifle, revolver, etc: *carry firearms.*

ˈ**fire-ball** *n* **1** large bright meteor. **2** centre of an atomic explosion. **3** (*fig*) very energetic person.

ˈ**fire-bomb** *n* bomb that burns fiercely after it explodes, causing destruction by fire; incendiary.

ˈ**fire-box** *n* place where fuel is burned in a steam-engine or boiler.

ˈ**firebrand** *n* **1** piece of burning wood. **2** (*fig*) person who causes (esp social or political) trouble.

ˈ**fire-break** *n* strip of land cleared of trees to stop fire from spreading in a forest.

ˈ**fire-brick** *n* type of brick made to withstand great heat, used in building grates, furnaces, chimneys, etc.

ˈ**fire brigade** (*US* ˈ**fire department**) organized team of people trained and employed to extinguish fires: *call out the fire brigade.*

ˈ**fire-bug** *n* (*infml*) person with an uncontrollable desire to start fires; pyromaniac.

ˈ**fire-clay** *n* [U] type of clay used to make fire-bricks.

ˈ**firecracker** *n* (*esp US*) small firework that

explodes with a cracking noise.
ˈ**firedamp** (also **damp**) *n* [U] gas in coal-mines, explosive when mixed in certain proportions with air; methane.
ˈ**firedog** *n* = ANDIRON.
ˈ**fire-drill** *n* [C, U] (practice of) what people must do to escape safely from a burning building, ship, etc.
ˈ**fire-eater** *n* **1** person who appears to swallow fire as part of an entertainment act. **2** person who easily becomes angry or quarrelsome.
ˈ**fire-engine** (also **appliance**, *US* also ˈ**fire truck**) *n* special vehicle carrying equipment for fighting large fires.
ˈ**fire-escape** *n* special staircase or apparatus by which people may escape from a burning building, etc.
ˈ**fire extinguisher** (also **extinguisher**) portable metal container with water or a chemical mixture inside for putting out small fires.
ˈ**fire-fighter** *n* person who fights (esp forest) fires.
ˈ**firefly** *n* type of winged insect that glows in the dark.
ˈ**fire-guard** *n* protective metal frame or grating round a fire in a room.
ˈ**fire-irons** *n* [pl] tools used for tending a fire, usu kept near the fireplace, eg poker, tongs, shovel, etc.
ˈ**firelight** *n* [U] light from a fire in a fireplace: *sitting in the firelight.*
ˈ**fire-lighter** *n* [C, U] (piece of) inflammable material used to help start a fire in a grate.
ˈ**fireman** /-mən/ *n* (*pl* **-men** /-mən/) **1** member of a fire brigade. **2** person who tends the fire in a furnace, steam-engine, etc.
the ˌFire of ˈLondon = THE GREAT FIRE OF LONDON (GREAT).
ˈ**fireplace** *n* open space for a fire in a room, usu made of brick or stone and set into a wall.
ˈ**fire-plug** *n* (*esp US*) connection in a water-main for a fireman's hose; hydrant.
ˈ**fire-power** *n* [U] capacity to destroy, measured by the number and size of guns available.
ˈ**fireproof** *adj* that can resist great heat without burning, cracking or breaking: *a fireproof wall, door, etc.* — *v* [Tn] make (sth) fireproof.
ˈ**fire-raising** *n* [U] deliberately setting fire to property, etc; arson. ˈ**fire-raiser** *n.*
ˈ**fireside** *n* (usu *sing*) part of a room beside the fireplace: *sitting at/by the fireside* ○ [attrib] *a fireside chair.*
ˈ**fire station** (*US* also ˈ**firehouse**) building for a fire brigade and its equipment.
ˈ**fire-trap** place from which people would not be able to escape easily if a fire started.
ˈ**fire-walking** *n* [U] (usu religious) ceremony of walking barefoot over very hot stones, ashes, etc as an act of faith. ˈ**fire-walker** *n.*
ˈ**fire-watcher** *n* person who watches for fires, esp those caused by bombs during war.
ˈ**fire-water** *n* [U] (*infml*) strong alcoholic drink, eg whisky, gin, etc.
ˈ**firewood** *n* [U] wood used for lighting fires or as fuel.
ˈ**firework** *n* **1** [C] device containing chemicals that burn or explode spectacularly, used at celebrations or as a signal: *set off* (ie explode) *a few fireworks* ○ [attrib] *Firework Night*, ie Bonfire Night, 5 November, the main occasion in Britain for displays of fireworks. **2** ˈ**fireworks** [pl] (**a**) display of fireworks. (**b**) (*fig*) display of anger, wit, etc: *Just you watch the fireworks when your father catches those boys!*

fire² /ˈfaɪə(r)/ *v* **1** [I, Ipr, Tn, Tn·pr] ~ (**sth**) (**at sb/sth**); ~ (**sth**) **into sth** shoot with a gun (at sb/sth); shoot (a bullet) from a gun; shoot a bullet from (a gun): *'Fire!' ordered the captain.* ○ *The officer ordered his men to fire (at the enemy).* ○ *The police fired (several rubber bullets) into the crowd.* ○ *This weapon fires anti-aircraft missiles.* ○ *He fired several shots (at the target).* ○ *fire (a pistol) into the air* ○ *fire a 21-gun salute*, ie fire 21 shots from guns into the air as a sign of respect in a ceremony. **2** [Tn·pr] ~ **sth at sb** address (words) in quick succession at sb: *fire insults, questions, ideas, etc at sb.* **3** [Tn] (*infml*) dismiss (an employee) from a job: *He was fired for stealing money from the till.* **4** [Tn] ignite or set fire to (sth) with the aim of destroying it: *fire a haystack.* **5** [I] (of the explosive mixture in an engine) ignite: *The engine will not fire.* ○ *The engine is only firing on three cylinders.* **6** [Tn, Tn·pr] ~ **sb with sth**; ~ **sb into sth/doing sth** stimulate (the imagination); fill sb with (a strong emotion); inspire or excite sb to do sth: *Adventure stories fired his imagination.* ○ *fire sb with enthusiasm, longing, desire, etc* ○ *The party leader's rousing speech fired the members into action.* **7** [Tn] heat (an object made of clay) in an oven in order to harden and strengthen it: *fire pottery, bricks, etc in a kiln.* **8** (idm) **working/firing on all cylinders** ⇨ CYLINDER. **9** (phr v) **fire away** (usu as a command) (*infml*) begin asking questions; begin to speak: *'I've got a couple of questions I'd like to ask you.' 'Right, fire away.'* **fire sth off** shoot (a bullet) from a gun: *fire off a few rounds, all one's ammunition, etc.*
▷ **-fired** (forming compound *adjs*) supplied by or using the specified fuel: *gas-fired central heating* ○ *a coal-fired power station.*
firing /ˈfaɪərɪŋ/ *n* **1** [U] action of firing guns: *There was continuous firing to our left.* **2** [C, U] (act of) firing (FIRE² 7) a clay object: *It will take several firings to clear the shelves of all these pots.*
□ ˈ**firing-line** *n* **1** front line of battle, nearest the enemy. **2** (idm) **be in the ˈfiring line** be subject to criticism, blame, etc because of one's responsibilities or position: *She'll have to be careful now — she's directly in the firing-line of the new director.*
ˈ**firing-squad** *n* [CGp] group of soldiers ordered to shoot a condemned person: *He was sentenced to death by firing-squad.*

firm¹ /fɜːm/ *adj* (**-er**, **-est**) **1** (**a**) not yielding when pressed; fairly hard: *This wet ground is not firm enough to walk on.* ○ *firm soil* ○ *a firm cushion, mattress, sofa, etc* ○ *firm flesh/muscles.* (**b**) strongly fixed in place; secure or solid: *firm foundations* ○ *a firm foothold* ○ *firm concrete fencing.* **2** (of a movement) steady and strong; not weak or uncertain: *a firm handshake, grip, hold, etc.* **3** not subject to change; definite: *a firm belief/believer in socialism* ○ *a firm decision, date, arrangement, offer* ○ *firm opinions, convictions, principles, etc* ○ *firm news, evidence, information, etc* ○ *'Burnside' is the firm favourite to win the race*, ie the horse that is confidently expected to win. **4** ~ (**with sb**) strong and consistent in attitude and behaviour; not easily persuaded to change one's mind; decisive: *Parents must be firm with their children.* ○ *exercise firm leadership, control, discipline, etc* ○ *'I don't want to be unkind,' he said in a firm voice.* **5** [usu pred] ~ (**against sth**) not lower than another currency, etc and possibly about to rise in price: *The pound remained firm against the dollar, but fell against the yen.* **6** (idm) **be on firm ˈground** be sure of one's facts; be secure in one's position, esp in a discussion. **a firm ˈhand** strong discipline or control: *That boy needs a firm hand to help him grow up.* **have, etc a firm/tight hold on sth** ⇨ HOLD².
▷ **firm** *v* **1** [I, Ip, Tn, Tn·p] ~ (**sth**) (**up**) (cause sth to) become firm: *firm (up) soil.* **2** (phr v) **firm sth up** (**a**) put sth into a final fixed form: *firm up a contract, deal, agreement, etc.* (**b**) make (part of the body) firmer and less fatty: *Exercise will firm up your muscles.*
firm *adv* (idm) **hold firm to sth** not abandon a principle, theory, etc: *hold firm to one's beliefs, ideals, principles, etc.* **stand fast/firm** ⇨ FAST².
firmly *adv* in a firm way: *The fence posts were fixed firmly in the ground.* ○ *The business was soon firmly established in the town.* ○ *The suggestion was politely but firmly rejected by the chairman.*
firmness *n* [U].

firm² /fɜːm/ *n* **1** [CGp] (*esp infml*) business company: *a firm of accountants* ○ *Our firm has/have made 200 workers redundant.* **2** (idm) **the old firm** ⇨ OLD.

firmament /ˈfɜːməmənt/ *n* **the firmament** [sing] (*arch*) the sky.

first¹ /fɜːst/ *det* **1** (**a**) 1st; coming before all others in time, order, importance, etc: *the first public performance of the play* ○ *his first wife* ○ *their first baby* ○ *her first job* ○ *students in their first year at college* ○ *at first light*, ie dawn ○ *at the first* (ie earliest) *opportunity* ○ *the first signs that winter is approaching* ○ *one's first impression/reaction* ○ *She won first prize in the competition.* ○ *King Edward I* (ie said as 'King Edward the First') ○ *go back to first* (ie basic) *principles* ○ *of the first importance* ○ *the first violins*, ie in an orchestra ○ *Your first duty is to your family.* (**b**) never having happened or been experienced before: *It was the first time they had ever met.* ○ *his first real taste of success.* Cf LAST¹ 1. ⇨ App 9. **2** (idm) **first/last/next but one, two, three, etc**: *Take the first turning but one* (ie the second turning) *on your left.* ○ *I live in the last house but two* (ie the third house from the end) *in this street.* **first/last thing** ⇨ THING. ˌ**first things** ˈ**first** (*saying*) the most important or necessary duties or concerns must be dealt with before others. (For other idioms containing **first**, see the entries for the other major words in each idiom, eg **at first glance/sight** ⇨ GLANCE; **not have the first idea about sth** ⇨ IDEA.).
▷ **firstly** *adv* (in giving a list) to begin with: *The illness can develop in two ways: firstly, in cases of high blood pressure and secondly....*
□ ˌ**first** ˈ**aid** treatment given to an injured person before a doctor comes.
ˌ**first** ˈ**balcony** = DRESS CIRCLE (DRESS).
ˌ**first** ˈ**base 1** first of the bases (BASE¹ 6) that must be touched in a game of baseball. **2** (idm) **not get to first base** (**with sth**) (*infml esp US*) not make a successful start (in a project); not even achieve the first step.
ˌ**first** ˈ**class 1** most comfortable accommodation in a train, ship, etc: *Smoking is not allowed in first class.* ○ [attrib] *first-class seats, carriages, compartments, etc.* **2** class of mail most quickly delivered: *First class costs 5p more.* ○ [attrib] *A first-class letter should arrive the following day.* ○ *Ten first-class stamps, please.* ⇨ article at POST OFFICE. **3** in the best group or highest category; excellent: *The entertainment provided was first class.* ○ [attrib] *They can afford to eat at first-class restaurants.* ○ *She got first-class results in her exams.* ○ *They're first-class people — you'll like them.* — *adv* by the best or quickest form of transport or mail: *travel first class* ○ *I sent the letter first class on Monday.*
ˌ**first** ˈ**cousin** = COUSIN.
ˌ**first-day** ˈ**cover** envelope with a set of special stamps postmarked on the first day of issue. ⇨ article at POST OFFICE.
ˌ**first de**ˈ**gree**, **first-degree burn** burn of the least serious kind. **first-degree murder** (*US law*) murder that incurs the heaviest penalties.
ˌ**first e**ˈ**dition** (one of the) first set of copies of a book to be printed: *a collection of rare first editions.*
ˈ**first finger** finger next to the thumb; index finger.
ˌ**first** ˈ**floor** (usu **the first floor**) **1** (*Brit*) floor immediately above the floor on ground level: [attrib] *a* ˌ*first-floor* ˈ*flat.* **2** (*US*) floor on ground level. ⇨ Usage at FLOOR¹.
ˌ**first-**ˈ**footing** *n* [U] (esp Scottish) custom or practice of waiting for the first person to enter a house in the New Year before celebrations can begin.
ˈ**first-fruit** *n* (usu *pl*) **1** earliest agricultural produce, crops, etc of the season. **2** (*fig*) first results of sb's work or efforts.
ˌ**first** ˈ**gear** lowest gear on a car, bicycle, etc.
ˌ**first**ˈ**hand** *adj* [attrib], *adv* gained or coming directly from the original source: ˌ*firsthand infor*ˈ*mation* ○ *experience sth firsthand.*
ˌ**first** ˈ**lady 1 the First Lady** (*US*) wife of the President of the USA; wife of a state governor. **2** (usu *sing*) leading woman in a specified activity or profession: *recognized as the first lady of romantic fiction.*
ˌ**first** ˈ**light** dawn: *We set off at first light.*
ˈ**first name** personal name or names given to sb at his birth, usu coming before a surname or family name: *Mrs Thatcher's first name is Margaret.* ○ [attrib] *We are all on first-name terms with our*

boss, ie We call him by his first name (a sign of a friendly informal relationship). ⇨ Usage at NAME[1]. Cf FORENAME, GIVEN NAME (GIVEN), CHRISTIAN NAME (CHRISTIAN).

ˌfirst ˈnight first public performance of a play, film, etc; opening night: *the first night of 'The Sound of Music'* ○ [attrib] *suffer from ˌfirst-night ˈnerves.*

ˌfirst ofˈfender person who has been found guilty of a crime for the first time.

ˈfirst officer officer second in command to a captain on a merchant ship.

the ˌfirst ˈperson 1 (*grammar*) set of pronouns and verb forms used by a speaker to refer to himself: *'I am' is the first person singular of the present tense of the verb 'to be'.* ○ [attrib] *'I', 'me', 'we' and 'us' are first-person pronouns.* **2** style of story-telling in which the author writes or speaks as if telling the story personally: *Hemingway often writes in the first person.*

ˌfirst-rate *adj* excellent; of the best quality: *a ˌfirst-rate ˈmeal* ○ *The food here is first-rate.* — *adv* in very good health; very fit: *feel first-rate.*

first refusal right of deciding whether to accept or refuse sth before it is offered to others: *I hope you'll give me (the) first refusal on/of your house if you ever decide to sell it.*

ˈfirst school (in Britain) school for children between the ages of 5 and 8 or 9.

the ˌFirst World ˈWar (also **World War I** /ˌwɜːld wɔː ˈwʌn/) the major international war of 1914-18, fought mainly in Europe.

first[2] /fɜːst/ *adv* **1 (a)** before anyone or anything else; at the beginning: *Susan came into the room first.* ○ *Who came first in the race?* ie Who won? ○ *Ladies first,* ie said by a man, allowing a woman to enter a room, car, etc before he does. **(b)** before another event or time: *First I had to decide what to wear.* ○ *Think first, then act.* ○ *'Have some tea.' 'I'll finish my work first.'* Cf LAST[2]. **2** for the first time: *When did you first meet him?* ○ *The play was first performed in Paris.* ○ *When he first arrived in this country, he couldn't speak any English.* **3** (in giving a list) to begin with: *This method has two advantages: first it is cheaper and second(ly) it is quicker.* ⇨ Usage. **4** in preference to sth else: *He said he'd resign first,* eg rather than compromise his principles. **5** (idm) **at ˈfirst** at or in the beginning; initially: *At first I thought he was shy, but then I discovered he was just not interested in other people.* ○ (*saying*) *If at first you don't succeed, try, try again.* **come ˈfirst** be considered as more important than anything else: *You know that your wife and children come first.* **ˌfirst and ˈforemost** more than anything else; firstly and most importantly: *He does a bit of writing, but first and foremost he's a teacher.* **ˌfirst and ˈlast** (*fml*) taking everything into account; completely: *He was a real gentleman, first and last.* **ˌfirst ˈcome, ˌfirst ˈserved** (*saying*) people will be dealt with, seen, etc strictly in order of their arrival or application. **ˌfirst of ˈall** before (doing) anything else; initially; most importantly: *First of all she just smiled, then she started to laugh.* ○ *Well, first of all we can't possibly spare the time.* **first ˈoff** (*infml*) before anything else: *First off, let's see how much it'll cost.* **(be) first past the post** winning in an election because one has received the most votes though not necessarily an absolute majority. **head first** ⇨ HEAD[1]. **last in, first out** ⇨ LAST[2]. **put sb/sth ˈfirst** consider sb/sth to be more important than anyone/anything else: *put one's career, reputation, children first.* **see sb in hell first** ⇨ HELL.

□ **ˈfirst-born** *n, adj* [attrib] (*dated*) (child) born before other children; eldest: *their first-born son.*

NOTE ON USAGE: When ordering items in a list, **first(ly)**, **second(ly)**, **third(ly)**, etc are put at the beginning of the sentence or clause. They are usually followed by a comma. Some speakers prefer **first** to **firstly**: *There are three reasons for my resignation. First(ly), I am dissatisfied with my wages; secondly, the hours are too long; and thirdly, there is little chance of promotion.* Alternatively, **first**, **second**, **third**, etc could be used.

first[3] /fɜːst/ *n, pron* **1 the first** first person or thing mentioned or occurring: *Sheila was the first to arrive.* ○ *I'm the first in my family to go to university.* ○ *I'd be the first to admit* (ie I will most willingly admit) *I might be wrong.* ○ *The first I heard about the firm closing down* (ie The first time I became aware of it) *was when George told me.* **2** [C] (*infml*) notable achievement, event, etc never done or experienced before: *a real first for the German team.* **3** [C] ~ **(in sth)** (*Brit*) university degree of the highest class: *She got a first in maths at Exeter.* **4** [U] lowest gear on a car, bicycle, etc: *go up the hill in first.* **5** (idm) **from the (very) ˈfirst** from the beginning: *I found the idea attractive from the first, and now I'm convinced it's the only solution.* **from ˌfirst to ˈlast** from beginning to end; throughout.

firth /fɜːθ/ *n* (esp in Scotland) narrow inlet of the sea; part of a river when it flows into the sea: *the Firth of Forth.*

fiscal /ˈfɪskl/ *adj* of or related to government money or public money, usu taxes: *the government's fiscal policy,* ie on rates of tax, interest, government borrowing, etc. Cf PROCURATOR FISCAL.

□ **fiscal year** (*US*) = FINANCIAL YEAR (FINANCIAL).

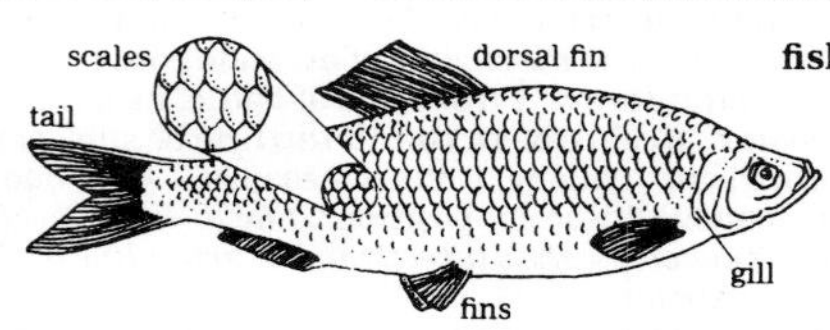

fish[1] /fɪʃ/ *n* (*pl* unchanged or ~**es**) ⇨ Usage. **1** [C] cold-blooded animal living in water and breathing through gills, with fins and a tail for swimming: *They caught several fish.* ○ *fishes, frogs and crabs* ⇨ illus. **2** [U] flesh of fish eaten as food: *frozen, smoked, fresh, etc fish* ○ *boiled, fried, grilled, etc fish* ○ *Fish was served after the first course.* **3** (idm) **a big fish** ⇨ BIG. **a cold fish** ⇨ COLD[1]. **a different kettle of fish** ⇨ DIFFERENT. **drink like a fish** ⇨ DRINK[2]. **a fine, etc kettle of fish** ⇨ KETTLE. **a ˌfish out of ˈwater** person who feels uncomfortable or awkward because he is in unfamiliar surroundings: *With my working-class background I feel like a fish out of water among these high-society people.* **have ˈbigger/ˈother fish to fry** have more important, interesting, etc things to do. **neither fish, flesh nor good red herring** (*saying*) difficult to identify or classify; vague; ambiguous. **an ˈodd/a ˈqueer fish** (*infml*) eccentric person; person whom others find hard to understand: *He's a bit of an odd fish — he's never been out of his house for years.* **play a ˈfish** (when fishing with a rod and line) allow a fish to exhaust itself by forcing it to pull against the line. **there are (plenty of) ˈother fish in the sea; there are (plenty) ˈmore (good) fish in the sea** there are many other people/things that are as good as the one that has proved unsuccessful.

▷ **fishy** *adj* (**-ier, -iest**) **1** of or like a fish, esp in smell or taste: *a fishy smell.* **2** (*infml*) causing a feeling of doubt or suspicion: *There's something rather fishy going on here.*

□ **ˌfish and ˈchips** fish fried in batter and eaten with fried potato chips: *Fish and chips is getting very expensive now.* ○ [attrib] *a ˌfish-and-ˈchip shop.*

ˈfish cake small flat cake of cooked fish and mashed potato, usu covered with breadcrumbs.

ˈfish eagle any of several types of eagle that catch and eat fish, esp the osprey.

ˌfish-eye ˈlens wide-angled lens with a distorting effect.

ˈfish-farm *n* area of water used to breed fish artificially.

ˌfish ˈfinger (*US* **ˌfish ˈstick**) small oblong piece of fish covered with breadcrumbs or batter.

ˈfish-hook *n* barbed metal hook for catching fish. ⇨ illus at HOOK.

ˈfish-kettle *n* oval pan used for boiling fish.

ˈfish-knife *n* blunt knife with a broad blade used for eating fish.

ˈfish-meal *n* [U] ground dried fish, often used by gardeners as a fertilizer.

ˈfishmonger /-mʌŋɡə(r)/ *n* (*Brit*) person whose job it is to sell fish in a shop: *buy fish at the fishmonger's/from the fishmonger.*

fish-net *n* **1** [C] net used for catching fish. **2** [U] fabric made with small holes: [attrib] *fish-net tights.*

ˈfish-slice *n* kitchen tool consisting of a broad flat blade that has slits in it and is attached to a long handle, used for turning or lifting food when cooking. ⇨ illus at KITCHEN.

ˈfishwife *n* **1** woman who sells fish. **2** (*derog*) nagging abusive person (usu a woman): *She was screaming like a fishwife!*

NOTE ON USAGE: **1 Fish** as a countable noun has two plural forms: **fish** and **fishes. 1 Fish** is the more usual form, used when referring to a mass of them in the water to be caught or seen: *The number of fish in coastal waters has decreased.* ○ *A lot of fish were caught during the competition.* **2 Fishes** is used to refer to different species of fish: *He studies in particular the fishes of the Indian Ocean.*

fish[2] /fɪʃ/ *v* **1 (a)** [I, Ipr] ~ **(for sth)** try to catch fish with hooks, nets, etc: *I often fish/go fishing at weekends.* ○ *fishing for salmon.* **(b)** [Tn] try to catch fish in (an area of water): *fish a river, lake, etc.* **2** [Ipr] ~ **for sth** search for sth, esp in an area of water or a hidden place: *fish for pearls* ○ *fishing (around) in the bag for the keys.* **3** (idm) **fish in troubled waters** try to gain advantages for oneself from a disturbed state of affairs. **4** (phr v) **fish for sth** try to gain sth by indirect methods: *fish for compliments, information, praise.* **fish sth out (of sth)** take or pull sth out (of sth), esp after searching for it: *Several old cars are fished out (of the canal) every month.* ○ *He fished a length of string out of his pocket.*

▷ **fishing** *n* [U] catching fish as a job, sport, or hobby: *deep-sea fishing* ○ *Fishing is still the main industry there.* ○ [attrib] *a fishing boat* ○ *a fishing ground.* **ˈfishing-line** *n* line[1](9a) with a hook attached for catching fish. **ˈfishing-rod** *n* (*US* **ˈfishing pole**) long wooden or (jointed) metal rod with a fishing-line attached to it. **ˈfishing-tackle** *n* [U] equipment used in fishing.

fisherman /ˈfɪʃəmən/ *n* (*pl* **-men**) person who catches fish, esp as a job but also as a sport or hobby. Cf ANGLER (ANGLE[2]).

fishery /ˈfɪʃərɪ/ *n* **1** (usu *pl*) part of the sea where fish are caught commercially: *offshore fisheries,* ie at some distance from the coast. **2** business or industry of fishing: *the Ministry of Agriculture, Fisheries and Food.*

fish-plate /ˈfɪʃpleɪt/ *n* flat piece of iron joining one length of railway line to the next.

fissile /ˈfɪsaɪl; *US* ˈfɪsl/ *adj* (*fml*) **1** capable of undergoing nuclear fission. **2** tending to split or divide: *fissile wood.*

fission /ˈfɪʃn/ *n* [U] **1** splitting of the nucleus of an atom with the release of a large amount of energy: *nuclear fission.* **2** (*biology*) splitting or division of biological cells as a method of reproduction.

▷ **fissionable** /-ʃənəbl/ *adj* (of material) with a nucleus that can be split.

fissiparous /fɪˈsɪpərəs/ *adj* reproducing by division of biological cells.

fissure /ˈfɪʃə(r)/ *n* long deep crack in rock or in the earth.

fist /fɪst/ *n* **1** hand when closed tightly with the fingers bent into the palm: *He struck me with his fist.* ○ *He clenched his fists.* ○ *She shook her fist at him,* ie as an angry threatening gesture. ⇨ Usage at BODY. **2** (idm) **an iron fist/hand in a velvet glove** ⇨ IRON[1]. **the mailed fist** ⇨ MAIL[2]. **make a good, poor, etc fist at/of sth** (*infml esp Brit*) make a good, poor, etc attempt at sth: *She'd never been skiing before but she made a pretty good fist at it.* **make money hand over fist** ⇨ MONEY.

▷ **fistful** /ˈfɪstfʊl/ *n* number or quantity that can be held in a fist: *a fistful of ten-pound notes.*

□ **fisticuffs** /ˈfɪstɪkʌfs/ *n* [pl] (*arch or joc*) fighting with the fists: *engage in fisticuffs.*

fistula /ˈfɪstjʊlə/ *n* **1** long pipelike ulcer with a narrow mouth. **2** abnormal or surgically made passage in the body.

fit[1] /fɪt/ *adj* (**-tter**, **-ttest**) **1** [usu pred] ~ **for sb/sth**; ~ **to do sth** suitable or suited for sb/sth; well adapted for sb/sth; good enough for sb/sth: *a land fit for heroes to live in* ○ *The food was not fit for human consumption/not fit to eat*, ie was too bad to be eaten. **2** [usu pred] ~ **to do sth** (*infml*) in such a condition as to be likely or ready to do or suffer sth specified: *They worked till they were fit to drop*, ie likely to collapse from exhaustion. ○ *He's so angry that he's in no fit state to see anyone.* ○ (used as an *adv* after a *v* and *to* + infinitive.) *He laughed fit to burst.* ○ *His shouting was fit* (ie loud enough) *to wake the dead.* **3** ~ (**for sth/to do sth**) in good health, esp because of regular physical exercise: *World-class athletes are extremely fit.* ○ *He's been ill and isn't fit for work yet.* ○ *He keeps himself fit by running 5 miles every day.* ○ *fighting fit*, ie in very good physical condition and ready for energetic action. ⇨ Usage at HEALTHY. **4** (*fml*) suitable and right, usu according to accepted social standards: *As George introduced Peter and Sarah it is only fit (and proper) that he should be best man at their wedding.* **5** (idm) **fighting fit** ⇨ FIGHT[1]. (**as**) ˌ**fit as a** ˈ**fiddle** in very good physical condition: *I felt as fit as a fiddle after my walking holiday.* **see/think** ˈ**fit** (**to do sth**) consider it correct, convenient or acceptable (to do sth); decide or choose: *The newspaper did not see fit to publish my letter.* ○ *Do as you think fit.*

▷ **fitness** *n* [U] **1** condition of being physically fit: *In many sports (physical) fitness is not as important as technique.* **2** ~ **for sth/to do sth** suitability for sth: *Her fitness for the job cannot be questioned.* **3** condition of an organism that is well adapted to its environment, measured by its ability to reproduce itself.

fit[2] /fɪt/ *v* (**-tt-**, *pt*, *pp* **fitted**; *US also* **fit**) **1** (**a**) [I, Tn] be the right shape and size for (sb): *These shoes don't fit (me).* ○ *Her coat fits (her) exactly.* ○ *I can never get clothes to fit me.* ○ *a close-fitting dress* ○ *The key doesn't fit the lock.* (**b**) [Tn·pr esp passive] ~ **sb for sth** try (clothing) on sb in order to adjust it to the right size and shape: *He went to the tailor's to be fitted for a coat.* **2** (**a**) [Ipr, Ip] be of the right size to go somewhere: *The cooker won't fit in/into your new kitchen.* ○ *The mask fitted tightly over his face.* ○ *a tightly-fitting mask* ○ *The lift was so small that only three people could fit in.* (**b**) [Tn·pr, Tn·p] ~ **sth into sth/in** find or have sufficient space or room for sth in a place: *We can't fit any more chairs into the room.* ○ *The envelope's too small – I can't fit the card in.* **3** [Tn, Tn·pr] ~ **A** (**on/to B**); ~ **B with A** supply sth and fix or put it into place: *fit handles on the cupboards/fit the cupboards with handles* ○ *The room was fitted with a new carpet.* **4** [Tn, Tn·pr, Tn·p] ~ **A** (**onto/to B**); ~ **A and B together** join one thing to another to make a whole: *fit the tail assembly to the fuselage* ○ *fit the pieces of a model kit together.* **5** [I, Tn] be in agreement with (sth); match or suit: *Something doesn't quite fit here.* ○ *All the facts certainly fit your theory.* ○ *The punishment ought to fit the crime.* **6** [Tn, Tn·pr, Cn·t] ~ **sb/oneself/sth for sth** make sb/oneself/sth suitable for a particular role or task: *Am I really fitted for the role of director?* ○ *His experience fitted him for the job/to do the job.* **7** (idm) **fill/fit the bill** ⇨ BILL[1]. **fit** (**sb**) **like a** ˈ**glove** (**a**) fit the wearer perfectly in size or shape: *My dress fits (me) like a glove.* (**b**) be very suitable and accurate: *'Cautious' is a description that certainly fits the new president like a glove.* **if the cap fits** ⇨ CAP. **8** (phr v) **fit sb/sth in**; **fit sb/sth in/into sth** succeed in finding time to see sb or to do sth: *I'll try and fit you in after lunch.* ○ *I had to fit ten appointments into one morning.* **fit in** (**with sb/sth**) be a smoothly fitting part (of sth); be in harmony (with sb/sth): *He's never done this type of work before; I'm not sure how he'll fit in (with the other employees).* ○ *Do these plans fit in with your arrangements?* **fit sb/sth out/up** (**with sth**) supply sb/sth with the necessary equipment, clothes, food, etc; equip: *fit out a ship before a long voyage* ○ *I'm getting the children fitted out with clothes for their new school.*

▷ **fitted** *adj* [attrib] **1** (of a carpet) cut so that it covers a floor completely and is fixed into place. **2** (**a**) (of furniture) built to be fixed into a particular space: *fitted cupboards.* (**b**) (of a room) having fitted furniture: *a fitted kitchen.* **3** (of a sheet) having sewn corners so that it fits tightly over a mattress.

fitter *n* **1** person whose job is to put together, adjust and repair machinery and equipment: *a gas fitter.* **2** person whose job is to cut out, fit and alter clothes.

fit[3] /fɪt/ *n* [sing] (usu with a preceding *adj*) way in which sth, esp a garment, fits: *The coat was a good, bad, tight, loose, etc fit.*

fit[4] /fɪt/ *n* **1** sudden attack of epilepsy or other disease with violent movements and loss of consciousness: *an epileptic* ˈ*fit.* **2** sudden (usu short) attack of a minor illness: *a fit of coughing* ○ *a* ˈ*fainting fit.* **3** sudden burst of (usu uncontrollable) laughter, activity, etc: *a fit of laughter/(the) giggles* ○ *We were all in fits (of laughter)* (ie laughing uncontrollably) *at his jokes.* ○ *a fit of energy, letter writing, spring-cleaning, etc.* **4** short period of an intense feeling: *a fit of anger, rage, frustration, etc.* **5** (idm) **by/in** ˌ**fits and** ˈ**starts** in irregular bursts of activity over a period of time: *Because of other commitments I can only write my book in fits and starts.* **have/throw a** ˈ**fit** (**a**) suffer a fit(1). (**b**) (*infml*) be greatly shocked, alarmed, outraged, etc: *Your mother would have a fit if she knew you were here.*

▷ **fitful** /-fl/ *adj* occurring in short periods, not regularly and steadily: *fitful bursts of energy* ○ *a fitful night's sleep.* **fitfully** /-fəlɪ/ *adv.*

fitment /ˈfɪtmənt/ *n* (usu *pl*) piece of furniture or equipment, esp one forming part of a unit or series: *kitchen fitments*, eg cupboards.

fitting[1] /ˈfɪtɪŋ/ *adj* suitable for the occasion; right or proper: *It was fitting that he should be here to receive the prize in person.*

fitting[2] /ˈfɪtɪŋ/ *n* **1** (usu *pl*) small standard part or component: *electrical fittings* ○ *stainless-steel light fittings.* **2** (usu *pl*) items, such as a cooker and shelves, that are fixed in a building but can be removed when the owner moves house. Cf FIXTURE 1, MOVABLES (MOVABLE). **3** process or occasion of having a garment fitted: *a fitting for a wedding dress* ○ *costume fittings.*

Fitzgerald /fɪtsˈdʒerəld/ (Francis) Scott (Key) (1896-1940), American novelist. In works like *The Great Gatsby* and *Tender is the Night* he describes the decadence of 'jazz-age' America in the 1920s and a life-style that closely resembled his own.

five /faɪv/ *pron*, *det* 5; one more than four: *Look at page five.* ○ *Everyone took the exam, but only five passed.* ○ *Five (of the students) passed.* ○ *There were five children at the party.* ○ *This shirt cost five pounds*, ie £5. ○ *He's five (years old) today.* ⇨ App 9.

▷ **five** *n* the number 5: *a birthday card with a big five on it* ○ *a row of fives on the blackboard* ○ *Five and five make ten.*

five- (in compounds) having five of the thing specified: *a five-day week*, ie working five days out of seven, usu Monday to Friday ○ *a five-year contract* ○ *a five-sided figure.*

fiver /ˈfaɪvə(r)/ *n* **1** (*Brit infml*) five pound note; £5: *Can I borrow a fiver?* **2** (*US infml*) five dollar note; $5.

□ ˌ**five o'clock** ˈ**shadow** dark appearance on a man's chin and face caused by the slight growth of hair that has occurred since he shaved in the morning.

ˌ**five** ˈ**pence** (also ˌ**five** ˈ**p**, **5p**) (*Brit*) (coin worth) five new pence.

ˈ**fivepenny** *adj* [attrib] (*Brit*) costing or worth five new pence.

ˌ**five-**ˈ**star** (of a hotel, restaurant, etc) of the highest class.

ˌ**five-year** ˈ**plan** plan for the economic development of a country (esp a centrally controlled economy) over five years.

fives /faɪvz/ *n* [sing *v*] (*Brit*) game in which a ball is hit with gloved hands or a bat against the walls of a court.

fix[1] /fɪks/ *v* **1** [Tn·pr] fasten (sth) firmly to sth: *fix a shelf to the wall* ○ *fix a post in the ground* ○ (*fig*) *fix the blame on sb* ○ *fix sb's name in one's mind*, ie make great efforts to remember it. **2** [Tn·pr] ~ **sth on sb/sth** direct (esp one's eyes) on sb/sth with steady attention: *Her eyes were fixed on the gun.* ○ *fix one's thoughts/attention on what one is doing.* **3** [Tn] decide (sth) definitely; set or determine: *The time for our meeting has been fixed already.* ○ *We will fix the rent at £100 a week.* **4** [Tn] repair or mend (sth): *My watch has stopped — it needs fixing.* **5** [Tn] put (sth) in order; adjust: *Let me fix my hair* (ie brush and comb it) *and I'll be ready.* **6** [Tn, Tn·p] ~ **sth** (**up**) arrange sth: *I'll fix (up) a meeting.* ○ *I could fix it up with Geoffrey.* **7** [Tn] find out (the exact nature, position, time, etc of sth). **8** [Tn, Dn·n, Dn·pr] ~ **sth** (**for sb**) (*esp US*) provide or prepare (esp food): *He's just fixing a snack.* ○ *Can I fix you a drink?* ○ *Let me fix supper for you.* **9** [Tn] treat (photographic film, dyed fabric, etc) with a chemical so that the colours do not change or fade. **10** [Tn] (of a plant) absorb (a gas, esp nitrogen) by forming an organic compound of it. **11** [Tn esp passive] (*infml*) influence the result or actions of (sth), by unfair or illegal means: *I knew the race was fixed.* ○ *The jury/judge had been fixed.* **12** [Tn] (*infml*) punish or kill (esp sb who has harmed one); get even with: *I'll fix him so that he never bothers you again.* **13** [I, Tn] (*sl*) inject oneself with (a narcotic drug). **14** (phr v) **fix on sb/sth** decide to have sb/sth; choose: *They've fixed on Ashby as the new chairman.* ○ *Have you fixed on a date for the wedding?* **fix sth up** repair, redecorate, or adapt sth: *He fixed up the cottage before they moved in.* **fix sb up** (**with sth**) (*infml*) arrange for sb to have sth; provide sb with sth: *I'll fix you up with a place to stay.* ○ *She's got herself fixed up with a cosy flat.* **fix sb with sth** (*fml*) direct one's gaze, attention, etc at sb: *He fixed her with an angry stare.*

▷ **fixed** /fɪkst/ *adj* **1** already arranged and decided; not changing; set: *fixed prices* ○ *a fixed rate of interest.* **2** (of ideas, wishes, etc) held firmly and sometimes obsessively: *He had the fixed idea that a woman's place was in the home.* **3** [attrib] (of an expression on sb's face) not changing; intent: *a fixed smile, glare, stare, etc.* **4** [pred] ~ **for sth** (*infml*) provided or supplied with sth: *How are you fixed for money, food, time, etc?* **5** (idm) (**of**) ˌ**no fixed a**ˈ**bode/ad**ˈ**dress** (*law*) (having) no permanent place to live in: *Lovejoy, of no fixed abode, was charged with murder.* **fixedly** /ˈfɪksɪdlɪ/ *adv* without altering one's gaze; intently: *stare fixedly at sb.* **fixed** ˈ**assets** permanent business assets, eg buildings and equipment. Cf CURRENT ASSETS (CURRENT[1]). **fixed** ˈ**costs** business costs that do not vary with the amount of work produced. ˌ**fixed** ˈ**income** income that does not vary over time, eg from a fixed pension or investments at a fixed rate of interest, rather than from a salary or wage: [attrib] *fixed-income groups.* ˌ**fixed** ˈ**star** star so far from the earth that it seems to have no movement.

fixer /ˈfɪksə(r)/ *n* **1** (*infml*) person who makes (usu illegal) arrangements. **2** (chemical) substance that fixes (FIX[1] 9) photographs or dyes.

fixity /ˈfɪksɪtɪ/ *n* [U] ~ **of sth** quality of being fixed; firmness: *She displayed great fixity of purpose.*

fix[2] /fɪks/ *n* **1** [C usu *sing*] (*infml*) awkward or difficult situation: *be in/get oneself into a fix.* **2** [C] (**a**) action of finding the position of a ship, an aircraft, etc by taking measurements with a compass, etc. (**b**) position found by these means. **3** [sing] (*infml*) thing arranged dishonestly: *Her promotion was a fix, I'm sure.* **4** [C] (*sl*) injection of a narcotic drug, eg heroin: *get oneself a fix.*

fixated /fɪkˈseɪtɪd/ *adj* [pred] ~ (**on sb/sth**) having an abnormal emotional attachment (to sb/sth): *He is fixated on things that remind him of his childhood.*

fixation /fɪkˈseɪʃn/ *n* ~ (**on sb/sth**) unhealthy emotional attachment (to sb/sth); obsession: *a mother fixation* ○ *fixations about marriage.*

fixative /ˈfɪksətɪv/ *n* [C, U] **1** substance used for fixing (FIX[1] 9) photographic film, dye, etc, or for preventing perfume from evaporating too quickly. **2** substance used for sticking things together or keeping things in position, esp false teeth or hair: *Dentures require a strong fixative.*

fixings /ˈfɪksɪŋz/ *n* [pl] (*US*) things that decorate or accompany sth, eg a dress or a dish; trimmings.

fixture /ˈfɪkstʃə(r)/ *n* **1** (usu *pl*) thing, such as a bath, water tank or toilet, that is fixed in a building and is not removed when the owner moves house: *plumbing fixtures* ○ *The price of the house included many existing fixtures and fittings that were not to our taste.* Cf FITTING² 2, MOVABLES (MOVABLE). **2** (day fixed or decided for a) sporting event. **3** (*infml*) person or thing that is firmly established and appears unlikely to leave a place or position: *Professor Gravity now seems to have become an unwanted fixture in the college.*

fizz /fɪz/ *v* [I] **1** (of a liquid) produce bubbles of gas; effervesce. **2** make a hissing or spluttering sound: *The match fizzed.*

▷ **fizz** *n* [U] **1** quality of having a lot of bubbles of gas in a liquid; effervescence: *This lemonade has lost its fizz.* **2** (**a**) fizzing sound: *the fizz of a firework.* (**b**) (*infml*) drink, eg champagne, that has a lot of bubbles of gas.

fizzle /ˈfɪzl/ *v* **1** [I] make a weak fizzing sound. **2** (phr v) **fizzle out** end or fail in a weak or disappointing way: *After a promising start, the project soon fizzled out.*

fizzy /ˈfɪzɪ/ *adj* (**-ier, -iest**) (of a drink) having a lot of bubbles of gas that make a hissing sound; effervescent or carbonated: *fizzy lemonade.* ▷ **fizziness** *n* [U].

fjord = FIORD.

fl *abbr* floor: *Accounts Office 3rd fl.*

flab /flæb/ *n* [U] (*infml derog*) soft loose fatty flesh on a person's body: *middle-age flab*, ie on people aged about 40-60 years.

▷ **flabby** /ˈflæbɪ/ *adj* (**-ier, -iest**) (*derog*) **1** (**a**) soft and loose; not strong or firm: *flabby muscles, thighs, flesh, etc.* (**b**) having soft loose fatty flesh: *He's getting fat and flabby because he doesn't have enough exercise.* ⇨ Usage at FAT¹. **2** feeble and weak; ineffective: *flabby excuses* ○ *a flabby argument, plot, speech, etc.* **flabbily** *adv.* **flabbiness** *n* [U].

flabbergast /ˈflæbəgɑːst; *US* -gæst/ *v* [Tn usu passive] (*infml*) overwhelm (sb) with shocked amazement: surprise very greatly: *He was flabbergasted when he heard that his friend had been accused of murder.*

flaccid /ˈflæksɪd/ *adj* (*fml*) soft and weak; loose and limp; not firm. ▷ **flaccidity** /flækˈsɪdətɪ/ *n* [U]

flag¹ /flæg/ *n* **1** (usu oblong or square) piece of cloth with a particular design, that can be attached by one edge to a rope, pole, etc and used as a symbol of a country, party, etc or as a signal: *The national flag of the United Kingdom is called the Union Jack.* ○ *The ship was sailing under the Dutch flag*, ie the Dutch flag was flying from its mast. ○ *All the flags were flying at half-mast*, ie in honour of a famous dead person. ○ *The guard waved his flag and the train left the station.* ○ *The white flag is a symbol of a truce or surrender.* ⇨ illus. **2** small piece of paper or cloth attached to a stick or pin, esp one given to sb who contributes to a charity appeal: *children selling flags for a cancer research appeal.* **3** sign displayed to show that a taxi is for hire. **4** (idm) **fly/show/wave the flag** make known one's support of or loyalty to one's country, party, movement, etc, esp in order to encourage others to do the same. **keep the ˈflag flying** continue to support one's country or a set of principles: *Our exporters proudly kept the flag flying at the international trade exhibition.* **put the ˈflags out** celebrate a success.

▷ **flag** *v* (**-gg-**) **1** [Tn esp passive] place a flag or flags on (sth); decorate with flags: *The streets were flagged to celebrate the royal wedding.* **2** [Tn] mark (sth) for particular attention with a special mark or label: *All the surnames in the list have been specially flagged so that the computer can print them out easily.* **3** (phr v) **flag sth down** signal to (a moving vehicle) to stop, usu by waving one's arm: *flag down a taxi.*

□ **ˈflag-day** *n* **1** (*US* **tag day**) day on which money is collected in public places for a charity, a small paper flag or sticker being given to those who contribute. ⇨ article at CHARITY. **2 Flag Day** (*US*) 14 June, anniversary of the day in 1777 when the Stars and Stripes became the national flag.

ˌ**flag of conˈvenience** ˈflag of a foreign country under which a ship registers to avoid the taxes and certain regulations of the owner's home country.

ˌ**flag of ˈtruce** white flag used by one side in a battle, etc to show they want a truce.

ˈ**flag officer 1** officer who is allowed to fly a flag, ie one above the rank of commodore in the British navy and above the rank of captain in the US navy and coastguard. **2** (*Brit*) commodore of a yacht club.

ˈ**flag-pole** *n* long pole on which a flag is flown.

ˈ**flagship** *n* **1** ship which has the commander of a fleet on board. **2** most important of a group of products, projects, services, etc: *This dictionary is the flagship of Oxford's range of learners' dictionaries.*

ˈ**flagstaff** *n* flag-pole.

ˈ**flag-waving** *n* [U] (esp excessive) expression of patriotic or group feeling(s): [attrib] *I didn't think much of that speech — it was just a flag-waving exercise*, ie one that did not deal with real issues.

flag² /flæg/ *v* (**-gg-**) [I] **1** become tired, less active, or less interesting; weaken: *My strength, interest, enthusiasm, etc is flagging.* **2** (esp of plants) become limp or feeble; hang down or droop: *Roses will flag in the summer heat.*

flag³ /flæg/ *n* = FLAGSTONE.

▷ **flagged** /flægd/ *adj* paved with flagstones: *a flagged terrace.*

flag⁴ /flæg/ *n* type of plant with blade-like leaves, usu growing in wet land. Cf IRIS 2.

flagellant /ˈflædʒələnt/ (*fml*) *n* person who whips himself or another person, either as a religious penance or to obtain or give sexual pleasure.

▷ **flagellate** /ˈflædʒəleɪt/ *v* [Tn] (*fml*) whip (sb or oneself), as a religious penance or for sexual gratification. **flagellation** /ˌflædʒəˈleɪʃn/ *n.*

flagellum /fləˈdʒeləm/ *n* (*pl* **-la** /-lə/) **1** (*biology*) thread-like part of certain cells, including those of some types of fungi and algae, which wave from side to side causing forward movement. **2** (*botany*) thin creeping shoot or runner on certain plants.

flagon /ˈflægən/ *n* **1** large rounded bottle in which wine, cider, etc is sold, usu holding about twice as much as an ordinary bottle. **2** container with a handle, lip and lid for serving wine at a table. **3** amount of liquid contained in a flagon: *drink a flagon of wine.*

flagrant /ˈfleɪgrənt/ *adj* (usu of an action) particularly bad, shocking and obvious: *a flagrant breach of justice* ○ *flagrant violations of human rights.* ▷ **flagrantly** *adv.*

flagstone /ˈflægstəʊn/ (also **flag**) *n* flat piece of stone (usu square or oblong) for a floor, path or pavement.

flail /fleɪl/ *n* tool consisting of a stick swinging from a long handle, used esp formerly to separate grain from chaff.

▷ **flail** *v* **1** [I, Tn] (cause sth to) wave or swing about wildly: *The dying lamb fell, its legs flailing (about) helplessly* ○ *flail one's arms/hands above one's head.* **2** [Tn] beat (sth) (as if) with a flail.

flair /fleə(r)/ *n* **1** [sing, U] ~ **for sth** natural ability to do sth well: *He doesn't show much flair for the piano.* ○ *She has a real flair for languages*, ie is quick at learning them. **2** [U] original and attractive quality; stylishness.

flak /flæk/ *n* [U] **1** guns shooting at enemy aircraft; fire from those guns: *run into heavy flak.* **2** (*infml*) severe criticism: *The plans for the new tax have come in for a lot of flak*, ie have been very strongly criticized.

□ **ˈflak jacket** heavy protective jacket reinforced with metal.

flake /fleɪk/ *n* small thin layer or piece, esp one that has broken off a surface or object; small loose bit: *Scrape off all the loose flakes of paint before redecorating.* ○ *snowflakes* ○ *soap-flakes.*

▷ **flake** *v* **1** [I, Ip] ~ (**off/away**) come or fall off in flakes: *The paint on the walls is beginning to flake (off).* **2** [I, Tn] separate (usu food) into flakes: *flaked fish.* **3** (phr v) **flake out** (*infml*) collapse or fall asleep from exhaustion: *When I got home from the airport, I flaked out in the nearest armchair.*

flaky *adj* (**-ier, -iest**) **1** made up of flakes; tending to break into flakes: *flaky pastry.* **2** (*sl esp US*) slightly mad; eccentric: *That's a pretty flaky idea.* **flakiness** *n* [U].

flambé /ˈflɒmbeɪ; *US* flɑːmˈbeɪ/ *adj* (*French*) (following *ns*) (of food) covered with brandy or other spirit, set alight and served: *pancakes flambé.*

flamboyant /flæmˈbɔɪənt/ *adj* **1** (of a person or his character, manner, etc) showy, very confident and extravagant: *rich flamboyant film stars* ○ *flamboyant gestures.* **2** brightly coloured or decorated: *flamboyant clothes.* ▷ **flamboyance** /-ˈbɔɪəns/ *n* [U]. **flamboyantly** *adv.*

flame¹ /fleɪm/ *n* **1** [C, U] hot glowing portion of burning gas that comes from something on fire: *The curtains were enveloped in a sheet of flame.* ○ *the tiny flame of a cigarette-lighter.* ○ *The house was in flames*, ie was on fire, burning. ○ *An oil heater was knocked over and burst instantly into flames*, ie suddenly began to burn strongly. ○ *The whole hotel went up in flames* (ie was destroyed by fire) *in minutes.* ⇨ illus at CANDLE. **2** [C] bright light or brilliant colour, usu red or orange: *The flowering shrubs were a scarlet flame.* **3** [C] (*rhet*) intense feeling, esp love: *the flame of passion* ○ *A flicker of interest soon turned into the burning flames of desire.* **4** [C] (*infml*) person with whom one was once in love; sweetheart or lover (used esp in the expression shown): *an old flame.* **5** (idm) **add fuel to the flames** ⇨ ADD. **fan the flames** ⇨ FAN². **pour oil on the flames** ⇨ POUR.

□ **ˈflame-thrower** *n* weapon that projects a stream of burning fuel.

flame² /fleɪm/ *v* **1** [La, I] burn with a brighter flame: *The burning coals started to flame yellow and orange.* **2** [La, I, Ipr] glow or shine like (the colour of) flames; blaze: *wooded hillsides that flame red in autumn* ○ *a flaming sunset* ○ *flaming red hair* ○ *His face flamed (with anger/embarrassment).*

▷ **flaming** *adj* [attrib] **1** passionate or violent: *a flaming row/argument/temper.* **2** (*infml*) (used to emphasize a judgement or comment) absolute; utter: *You flaming idiot!*

flamenco /fləˈmeŋkəʊ/ *n* [C, U] (*pl* ~**s**) (music for a) strongly rhythmical dance performed originally by Spanish gypsies.

flamingo /fləˈmɪŋgəʊ/ *n* (*pl* ~**s**) long-legged wading-bird with a long neck and pink feathers.

flammable /ˈflæməbl/ *adj* easily set on fire; that can burn easily: *Pyjamas made from flammable material have been removed from most shops.* Cf INFLAMMABLE, NON-FLAMMABLE. ⇨ Usage at INVALUABLE.

flan /flæn/ *n* open pastry or sponge pie case containing a fruit, jam or savoury filling: *an apple flan.* Cf PIE, TART².

Flanders /ˈflɑːndəz; *US* ˈflændərz/ area in NE France, N Belgium and the W Netherlands, on the North Sea. Many soldiers died there during the fighting in the First World War.

□ ˌFlanders ˈpoppy red corn poppy that grows wild in Flanders, used as a symbol of the soldiers of the Allies who died fighting in the First World War. Artificial poppies are still sold and worn around *Remembrance Sunday (sometimes called Poppy Day) in memory of the dead of both World Wars.

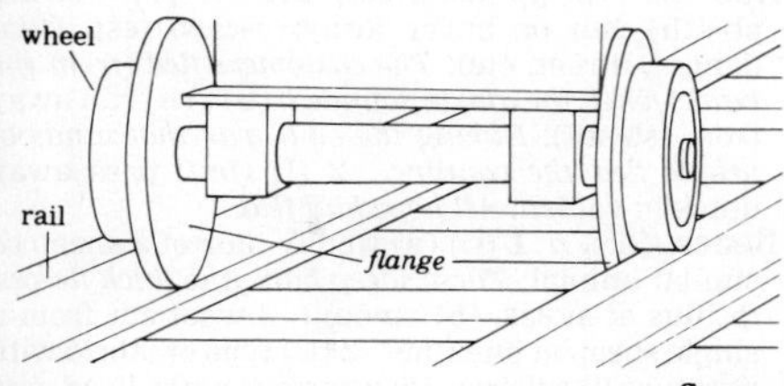

flange

flange /flændʒ/ *n* raised outside edge, eg of a railway wheel, to hold it in place.

flank /flæŋk/ *n* **1** fleshy part of the side of an animal or person between the ribs and the hip. ⇨ illus at HORSE. **2** side of sth, eg a building or mountain. **3** left or right side of an army or a body of troops: *Our orders are to attack their left flank.* ○ [attrib] *a flank attack.*

▷ **flank** *v* [Tn usu passive] place (sb/sth) on each side of or at the side of sb/sth: *The prisoner was flanked by the two detectives*, ie There was a detective on each side him. ○ *The garden is flanked to the north with large maple trees.* **flanker** *n* **(a)** (also **flank forward**, **wing forward**) (in Rugby football) forward[4] whose position is on the edge of the scrum. **(b)** (also **flanker back**) (in American football) player whose position is to one side of and slightly behind the scrimmage, to receive a pass.

flannel /ˈflænl/ *n* **1** [U] type of soft loosely woven woollen cloth: [attrib] *flannel trousers.* **2 flannels** [pl] men's trousers made of flannel: *a pair of cricket flannels.* **3** [C] = FACE-FLANNEL (FACE[1]). **4** [U] (*infml*) wordy language that avoids talking about sth directly and is often intended to flatter: *He gave me a lot of flannel but I still don't know the answer to my question.*

▷ **flannel** *v* (**-ll-**; *US* **-l-**) [I] (*infml*) speak or write flannel(4): *Stop flannelling and give a straight answer!*

flannelette /ˌflænəˈlet/ *n* [U] type of soft cotton material: [attrib] *flannelette night-gowns, sheets, pyjamas, etc.*

□ ˈ**flannel-mouth** *adj* (*US sl derog*) person who boasts or flatters to gain favour.

flap[1] /flæp/ *n* **1** ~ **(of sth)** flat piece of material that covers an opening or hangs down: *the flap of an envelope* ○ *the flap of a tent, pocket, etc* ○ *the flap of a table*, ie an extra hinged section that hangs down when not in use. **2** part of the wing on an aircraft that can be lifted in flight to change the aircraft's upward direction. ⇨ illus at AIRCRAFT. **3** action or sound of flapping; light blow, usu with something flat. **4** (idm) **be in/get into a flap** (*infml*) be in/get into a state of agitation, confusion, nervous excitement, etc: *I got into a real flap when I lost my keys.*

flap[2] /flæp/ *v* (**-pp-**) **1** [I, Tn] (cause sth to) move, swing, wave, etc up and down or from side to side, usu making a noise: *The sails were flapping gently in the wind.* ○ *The bird flapped its wings and flew away.* **2** [Ipr, Tn·pr] (attempt to) give a light blow at (sth) with a flat object: *flap at a fly with a cloth/flap a cloth at a fly.* **3** [I] (*infml*) become confused, excited or disturbed: *There's no need to flap!* **4** (idm) **sb's ears are flapping** ⇨ EAR[1]. **5** (phr v) **flap across, away, by, etc** (of a bird) fly in the specified direction by moving its wings: *The heron flapped slowly off across the lake.*

flapjack /ˈflæpdʒæk/ *n* **1** biscuit made from oats, butter and honey or syrup. **2** (*esp US*) thick pancake.

flapper /ˈflæpə(r)/ *n* **1** broad flat device used for killing flies, etc. **2** (*dated infml*) fashionable and unconventional young woman of the 1920s.

flare[1] /fleə(r)/ *v* **1** [I] burn brightly but briefly or unsteadily: *The match flared in the darkness.* ○ *flaring gas jets.* **2** [I] (*fig*) burst into sudden activity or anger: *Tempers flared at the conference.* **3** (phr v) **flare up (a)** burn suddenly more intensely: *The fire flared up as I put more logs on it.* **(b)** reach a more violent state; suddenly become angry: *Violence has flared up again.* ○ *He flares up at the slightest provocation.* **(c)** (of an illness) recur: *My back trouble has flared up again.*

▷ **flare** *n* **1** (usu *sing*) bright and unsteady or brief light or flame: *the sudden flare of a torch in the darkness.* **2** (device that produces a) flaring light used esp as a signal: *The captain of the sinking ship used flares to attract the attention of the coastguard.*

□ ˈ**flare-path** line of lights on a runway to guide aircraft landing or taking off.

ˈ**flare-up** *n* **1** sudden burst of light or flame. **2** sudden outburst of strong or violent activity or feeling.

flare[2] /fleə(r)/ *v* [I, Ip, Tn esp passive] (cause sth to) become wider at the bottom: *This skirt flares (out) at the hem.* ○ *Her nostrils flared angrily.* ○ *flared trousers.* Cf TAPER[2].

▷ **flare** *n* **1** gradual widening; flared shape: *a skirt with a slight flare.* **2 flares** [pl] (*infml*) flared trousers.

flash[1] /flæʃ/ *n* **1** [C] **(a)** sudden bright burst of light or flame: *a flash of lightning.* **(b)** (*fig*) sudden show of wit, understanding, etc: *a flash of inspiration, intuition, etc.* **2** [C] = NEWS FLASH (NEWS). **3** [C, U] device or system that produces a brief bright light for taking photographs indoors or in poor light: *This camera has a built-in flash.* ○ *I'll need flash for this shot; the light isn't good enough.* **4** [C] coloured stripe or patch of cloth worn as an emblem on a military uniform, eg on the shoulder. **5** [C usu *sing*] (*infml*) brief showing of the sexual organs, esp by men; indecent exposure. **6** [attrib] (*infml derog*) expensive-looking, showy and usu not in good taste: *a flash sports car.* **7** (idm) **a ˌflash in the ˈpan** sudden brilliant success that lasts only a short time and is not repeated: *His first novel was a flash in the pan, and he hasn't written anything decent since.* **in a/like a ˈflash** very quickly; at once; immediately: *I'll be back in a flash.* **quick as a flash** ⇨ QUICK.

□ ˈ**flashbulb** *n* bulb in a flash[1](3).

ˈ**flash-cube** *n* set of four flashbulbs arranged as a cube for taking photographs one after the other.

ˈ**flash-flood** *n* sudden destructive flood of water in a valley that is normally dry, caused by heavy rain, etc.

ˈ**flash-gun** *n* device that holds and operates the flashlight at the same time as the camera shutter opens.

ˈ**flashlight** *n* **1** (device that produces a) brief bright light for taking photographs indoors or in poor light. **2** (*esp US*) = TORCH. **3** (source of) light used for signalling, eg in a lighthouse.

ˈ**flash-point** *n* **1** temperature at which the vapour above a liquid such as oil gives a brief flash, but does not catch fire, when a flame is brought near it. **2** (*fig*) point at which violence or anger breaks out: *Community unrest is rapidly approaching the flashpoint.*

flash[2] /flæʃ/ *v* **1 (a)** [I] give or send out a brief bright light: *Lightning flashed during the storm.* ○ *A lighthouse was flashing in the distance.* ○ (*fig*) *His eyes flashed angrily.* **(b)** [Tn, Tn·pr] cause (sth) to shine briefly or suddenly: *flash a torch in sb's eyes/at sb.* **2** [Tn, Tn·pr] **(a)** communicate with a light: *flash a signal (to sb) with one's car headlights.* **(b)** send or reflect (sth) like a flash: *Her eyes flashed anger and defiance (at everyone).* **3** [Tn] send (sth) by radio, television, etc: *flash a message on the screen.* **4** [Tn, Tn·p] show or display (sth) briefly: *flash an identification card* ○ (*derog*) *He's flashing his money around*, ie to try to gain the admiration of others. **5** [I] (*infml*) (esp of a man) show one's sexual organs briefly and indecently. **6** (phr v) **flash along, by, past, through, etc** move very quickly in the specified direction: *The train flashed by at high speed.* ○ (*fig*) *An idea flashed into her mind.* **flash back** (of one's thoughts) return to an earlier time: *My mind flashed back to our previous meeting.*

▷ **flasher** /ˈflæʃə(r)/ *n* **1** (*infml*) person who flashes (FLASH[2] 5). **2** (device that controls esp a) flashing light on a vehicle used to indicate which way the vehicle is turning.

flashing *n* [C, U] (strip of) material, eg lead or bitumen, used to keep out water at roof joints.

□ ˈ**flashback** *n* part of a film, play, etc that shows a scene earlier in time than the main story: *The events that led up to the murder were shown in a series of flashbacks.*

ˈ**flash card** card on which a word or words are printed or written, used as a visual aid to learning.

flashy /ˈflæʃɪ/ *adj* (**-ier, -iest**) attractive but usu not in good taste; showy: *flashy clothes, jewellery, etc* ○ *a flashy car.* ▷ **flashily** *adv*: *flashily dressed.*

flask /flɑːsk; *US* flæsk/ *n* **1 (a)** bottle with a narrow neck, esp one used in scientific laboratories for mixing or storing chemicals. **(b)** similarly shaped container for storing oil, wine, etc. **2** (also ˈ**hip-flask**) small flat-sided bottle of metal or (often leather-covered) glass that is used for carrying alcoholic spirits in the pocket. **3** = VACUUM FLASK (VACUUM). **4** amount contained in a flask: *drink a flask of wine, whisky, tea, etc.*

flat[1] /flæt/ *n* (*esp Brit*) (also *esp US* **apartment**) set of rooms (living-room, bedroom, kitchen, etc) for living in, usu on one floor of a building: *a new block of flats* ○ *They're renting a furnished flat on the third floor.* ○ *Many large old houses have now been converted into flats.* ⇨ article at HOUSE.

▷ **flatlet** /-lɪt/ *n* very small flat.

flat[2] /flæt/ *adj* (**-tter, -ttest**) **1** smooth and level; even: *a flat surface for writing on* ○ *The countryside is very flat here*, ie has no hills. **2** spread out on a single plane; extending at full length: *People used to think that the world was flat; now we know it is round.* **3** with a broad level surface and little depth: *a flat cap* ○ *flat dishes, plates, etc* ○ *The cake was flat*, ie did not rise while cooking. **4** (of a tyre) not containing enough air, eg because of a puncture; deflated. **5** dull; uninteresting; monotonous: *speak in a flat voice* ○ *He felt a bit flat after his friends had gone.* **6** not having much trade or business: *The market has been flat today.* **7** having a single price for a variety of goods or services: *a flat fare of 70p* ○ *a flat rate* ○ *flat-rate* (ie standard and fixed) *contributions.* **8** (of a carbonated or gaseous liquid) having lost its gas or effervescence: *The lager tastes/has gone flat.* **9** (of a battery) unable to supply any more electric current; run down. **10** (*music*) lower than true or concert pitch: *B flat is a semitone below the note B.* ○ *Your piano is flat; it needs tuning.* Cf SHARP 12. **11 (a)** [usu pred] (of pictures, photographs or colours) without contrast or shading; with no sense of depth or contrast: *The colours used are flat and unvaried.* ○ *His paintings are deliberately flat, it's part of his style.* **(b)** (of paint) not glossy; matt. **12** absolute; unqualified: [attrib] *give sb a flat denial/refusal.* **13** (of feet) not having normal raised arches. **14** (idm) **and ˌthat's ˈflat** that's my final decision: *I'm not going out with you and that's flat!* **(as) flat as a pancake** completely flat: *The whole landscape looked as flat as a pancake.* ○ *The surprise party turned out as flat as a pancake*, ie was very disappointing.

▷ **flatly** *adv* **1** in a flat[2](5) manner: *'Maybe,' he said flatly, 'I'll see.'* **2** in an outright, direct manner; positively; absolutely: *The allegations were all flatly denied.* ○ *Our request was flatly rejected.*

flatness *n* [U].

□ ˌ**flat-ˈbottomed** *adj* (of a boat) having a flat bottom and used in shallow water.

ˈ**flatcar** *n* (*US*) railway carriage without a roof or raised sides, used for carrying freight.

ˈ**flat-fish** *n* type of fish with a flat body, eg plaice or sole.

ˌ**flat-ˈfooted** *adj* **1** having feet without normal raised arches. **2** (*infml*) clumsy or awkward: *His speed and skill makes other players look flat-footed.* **3** showing a lack of imagination; dull and pedestrian: *a very flat-footed performance from the tenor.*

ˈ**flat-iron** *n* heavy iron heated with coals or by the fire and used for pressing linen, etc.

ˈ**flat racing** horse-racing over level courses without jumps. Cf STEEPLECHASE 1.

ˌ**flat** ˈ**spin 1** fast, often uncontrollable, descent of an aircraft spinning nearly horizontally. **2** (idm) **be in/go into a flat** ˈ**spin** (*infml*) be/become very confused or agitated.

ˈ**flat-top** *n* (*US sl*) aircraft-carrier.

ˈ**flatware** [U] (**a**) plates, saucers, etc. Cf HOLLOWWARE (HOLLOW). (**b**) (*US*) cutlery.

ˈ**flatworm** *n* type of worm with a flattened body,eg the tapeworm.

flat[3] /flæt/ *adv* **1** lower than the true or correct pitch: *She sings flat all the time.* **2** stretched out on one level; lying at full length: *She lay flat on her back in the warm sunshine.* ○ *He knocked his opponent flat.* ○ *The earthquake laid the city flat*, ie demolished it, making all the buildings fall. **3** outright; positively; completely: *My boss told me flat that I could not leave early.* ○ *She went flat against my orders*, ie disobeyed or ignored them completely. ○ *I'm flat broke*, ie have absolutely no money. **4** (idm) **fall flat** (of a joke, story, performance, etc) fail completely to produce the effect intended or expected: *All my funny stories fell completely flat.* **fall flat on one's face** (*infml*) suffer a humiliating and undignified setback, esp after attempting sth that is too ambitious. **flat/ stony broke** ⇨ BROKE[2]. **flat** ˈ**out** (**a**) as fast as possible; using all one's strength or resources: *running, working, training, etc flat out.* (**b**) exhausted: *After running in the marathon, she was flat out for a week.* **in 10 seconds, 5 minutes, etc** ˈ**flat** in the period of time specified, but always implying an unexpectedly short period of time: *I can change a tyre in 2 minutes flat.* ○ *She was out of bed, dressed and at the breakfast table in 50 seconds flat.*

flat[4] /flæt/ *n* **1** [sing] **the** ~ (**of sth**) flat level part of sth: *the flat of the hand* ○ *the flat of a sword, a blade, an oar* ○ *on the flat*, ie level, not uphill or downhill. **2** [C usu *pl*] level ground; stretch of low flat land, esp near water: ˈ*mud flats* ○ ˈ*salt flats.* **3 the flat** [sing] season of flat racing for horses. **4** [C] (*music*) flat[2](10) note or sign (♭) indicating the lowering of a pitch by a semitone. ⇨ illus at MUSIC. Cf NATURAL 6, SHARP *n*. **5** [C] (*esp US infml*) flat[2](4) tyre. **6** [C] movable upright section of stage scenery mounted on a frame.

flatten /ˈflætn/ *v* **1** [I, Ip, Tn, Tn·p] ~ (**sth**) (**out**) become or make (sth) flat: *The land flattens out near the coast.* ○ *The graph flattens out gradually after a steep fall.* ○ *a field of wheat flattened by storms* ○ *flatten (out) a piece of metal by hammering it* ○ *flatten oneself against a wall to let people get by.* **2** [Tn] (*fig*) defeat (sb) completely; depress or humiliate: *He was totally flattened by her sarcasm.*

flatter /ˈflætə(r)/ *v* **1** [Tn] praise (sb) too much or insincerely, esp in order to gain favour for oneself: *If you flatter your mother a bit she might invite us all to dinner.* **2** [Tn usu passive] give a feeling of pleasure or honour to (sb): *I was very flattered by your invitation to talk at the conference.* **3** [Tn] represent (sb) in a way that makes him seem better-looking than he really is: (*ironic*) *This photograph certainly doesn't flatter you*, ie It makes you look rather ugly. **4** [no passive: Tn, Dn·f] ~ **oneself** (**that...**) believe, usu mistakenly, that one has achieved sth or has certain abilities or good qualities: *Do you really think he likes you? You flatter yourself!* ○ *He flatters himself that he speaks French well.*

▷ **flatterer** /ˈflætərə(r)/ *n* person who flatters: *Don't believe him — he's a real flatterer.*

flattering /ˈflætərɪŋ/ *adj* that flatters (FLATTER 3) a person: *That's a very flattering dress Ann's wearing.*

flattery /ˈflætərɪ/ *n* [U] insincere praise: *With a little flattery I might persuade him to do the job.* ○ (*saying*) *Flattery will get you nowhere*, ie I will not be influenced by your flattering remarks.

flatulent /ˈflætjʊlənt/ *adj* **1** causing or suffering from gas in the stomach or digestive tract. **2** (of a person's speech, behaviour, etc) pretentious or pompous.

▷ **flatulence** /ˈflætjʊləns/ *n* [U] **1** (**a**) gas in the stomach or digestive tract. (**b**) feeling of discomfort caused by this: *suffer from flatulence.* **2** pretentiousness or pomposity.

flaunt /flɔːnt/ *v* [Tn] (*usu derog*) **1** show (sth considered valuable) in order to gain the admiration of other people: *flaunt one's new clothes, car, etc* ○ *He's always flaunting his wealth.* **2** (*US*) disobey or ignore (eg a rule) openly and without respect: *The young have always flaunted convention.*

NOTE ON USAGE: The second sense of *flaunt* shown here ('to disobey or ignore sth openly and contemptuously') clearly arose from the similarity between *flaunt* and *flout*. Though it is now generally acceptable in American English, this usage is still regarded as incorrect in British English

flautist /ˈflɔːtɪst/ (*US* **flutist** /ˈfluːtɪst/) *n* person who plays the flute, esp as a profession.

flavour (*US* **flavor**) /ˈfleɪvə(r)/ *n* **1** [U] taste and smell, esp of food: *Adding salt to food improves the flavour.* **2** [C] distinctive or characteristic taste: *wines with a delicate flavour* ○ *six different flavours of ice-cream.* **3** [C, U] special quality, characteristic or atmosphere: *The film retains much of the book's exotic flavour.*

▷ **flavour** (*US* **flavor**) *v* [Tn, Tn·pr] ~ **sth** (**with sth**) give flavour to sth by adding herbs, spices, etc: *flavour a stew (with onions)* ○ *meat strongly flavoured with pepper.* **-flavouring** (*US* **-flavoring**) /ˈfleɪvərɪŋ/ *n* [C, U] thing added to food to give it flavour: *This orange drink contains no artificial flavourings.* ○ *The soup needs more flavouring.* **-flavoured** (*US* **-flavored**) (forming compound *adjs*) having a flavour of the specified kind: *lemon-flavoured sweets.*

flavourless (*US* **flavorless**) *adj* having no flavour.

flaw /flɔː/ *n* **1** crack or fault (in an object or in material); imperfection: *This vase would be perfect but for a few small flaws in its base.* **2** mistake that lessens the effectiveness or validity of sth: *an argument full of flaws* ○ *a flaw in a contract.* **3** weak part in sb's character: *Pride was the greatest flaw in his personality.*

▷ **flaw** *v* [Tn usu passive] cause (sth) to have a flaw: *His reasoning can't be flawed.* ○ *a flawed masterpiece*, ie a work of art that is very great despite its minor faults.

flawless *adj* perfect: *a flawless complexion* ○ *a flawless performance.* **flawlessly** *adv.*

flax /flæks/ *n* [U] **1** plant grown for its fibre and seeds. **2** fibre from the stem of this plant, used to make linen.

▷ **flaxen** /ˈflæksn/ *adj* (of hair) pale yellow: *a flaxen-haired child.*

flay /fleɪ/ *v* [Tn] **1** (**a**) remove the skin from (a dead animal). (**b**) whip violently and cruelly: *He was so angry he nearly flayed his horse alive*, ie He beat it so much that some of its skin came off and it almost died. **2** (*fig*) criticize (sb/sth) severely.

flea /fliː/ *n* **1** small jumping insect without wings that feeds on the blood of animals and humans: *I must have been bitten by a flea, my arms are itchy.* ○ *The cat's got fleas.* **2** (idm) **with a** ˈ**flea in one's ear** rebuked, reprimanded or humiliated after an attempt at sth: *He burst into our meeting and got sent away with a flea in his ear.*

□ ˈ**flea-bag** *n* (*sl*) **1** (*Brit*) dirty or unpleasant person or animal: *I hate the old lady next door — she's a real flea-bag.* **2** (*esp US*) cheap dirty hotel.

ˈ**flea-bite** *n* **1** bite of a flea. **2** small but annoying inconvenience.

ˈ**flea market** (*infml*) open-air market that sells old and used goods at low prices.

ˈ**flea-pit** *n* (*infml derog*) old and dirty cinema, theatre, etc.

fleck /ˈflek/ *n* ~ (**of sth**) **1** very small patch or spot of a colour: *flecks of brown and white on a bird's breast.* **2** small particle or grain of sth: *flecks of dust, soot, dandruff.*

▷ **fleck** *v* [Tn·pr usu passive] ~ **sth with sth** mark with flecks: *The sea was flecked with foam.*

fled *pt, pp* of FLEE.

fledged /fledʒd/ *adj* (of birds) having fully developed wing feathers for flying; able to fly.

fledgeling (also **fledgling**) /ˈfledʒlɪŋ/ *n* **1** young bird that is just able to fly. **2** inexperienced person.

flee /fliː/ *v* (*pt, pp* **fled** /fled/) **1** (**a**) [I, Ipr] ~ (**from sb/sth**) run or hurry away; escape (esp from danger, threat, etc): *The customers fled (from the bank) when the alarm sounded.* (**b**) [Tn] run away from (sb/sth): *During the civil war thousands of people fled the country.* **2** [I] (*fml*) pass away quickly; vanish: *All hope had fled.*

fleece /fliːs/ *n* **1** [C] (**a**) woolly hair of a sheep or similar animal: *These sheep have fine thick fleeces.* ⇨ illus at SHEEP. (**b**) amount of wool cut from a single sheep at one time. **2** [U] type of fabric with a texture like fleece: *My warmest coat is lined with fleece.*

▷ **fleece** *v* **1** [Tn, Tn·pr] ~ **sb** (**of sth**) (*infml*) take (a lot of money) from sb, esp by overcharging or tricking him: *Some local shops are really fleecing the holiday-makers (of their money).* **2** [Tn] cut or shear the fleece from (a sheep).

fleecy *adj* (**-ier**, **-iest**) (appearing) woolly and fluffy: *fleecy clouds.*

fleet[1] /fliːt/ *n* **1** (**a**) [C] group of warships, submarines, etc under one commander. (**b**) group of ships fishing together. (**c**) [CGp] (usu **the fleet**) all the warships, submarines, etc of a country; navy. **2** [C] group of aircraft, buses, taxis, etc owned and operated by one organization or travelling together: *the company's new fleet of vans.*

□ ˌ**fleet** ˈ**admiral** officer in the US navy of the highest rank. ⇨ App 4.

fleet[2] /fliːt/ *adj* (*dated*) fast; light and quick in running: *fleet of foot* ○ *fleet-footed.* ▷ **fleetness** *n* [U].

fleeting /ˈfliːtɪŋ/ *adj* passing quickly; lasting only a short time: *For a fleeting moment I thought the car was going to crash.* ○ *We paid her a fleeting visit before leaving the country.* ▷ **fleetingly** *adv.*

Fleet Street /ˈfliːt striːt/ **1** street in central London where several major newspapers formerly had their offices. During the 1980s new technology and economic circumstances made them move away to new sites. ⇨ articles at LONDON, NEWSPAPER. **2** the press in general; London journalism: *Fleet Street loves a good scandal.*

Fleming /ˈflemɪŋ/ Sir Alexander (1881-1955), Scottish bacteriologist. In 1928 he discovered the effects of penicillin on bacteria. With two colleagues, he was awarded the Nobel prize for medicine in 1945.

Flemish /ˈflemɪʃ/ *adj* of Flanders or its people or their language: *the Flemish school*, ie painters such as *Van Eyck, *Bruegel or *Rubens.

▷ **Flemish** *n* [U] one of the official languages of Belgium, similar to Dutch.

flesh /fleʃ/ *n* **1** [U] (**a**) soft substance between the skin and bones of animal bodies, consisting of muscle and fat: *The trap had cut deeply into the rabbit's flesh.* (**b**) this as food: *Tigers are flesh-eating animals.* **2** [U] soft pulpy part of fruits and vegetables, the part that is usu eaten. **3 the flesh** [sing] the (human) body contrasted with the mind or the soul: (*saying*) *The spirit is willing but the flesh is weak*, ie Although sb may want to do sth, he is too lazy, tired, weak, etc actually to do it. **4 the flesh** [sing] bodily or physical desire: *the pleasures/sins of the flesh.* **5** (idm) ˌ**flesh and** ˈ**blood** the human body or human nature with its emotions, weaknesses, etc: *It was more than flesh and blood could bear.* **go the way of all flesh** ⇨ WAY[1]. **in the** ˈ**flesh** in physical bodily form; in person: *His appearance in the flesh ended the rumours about his death.* ○ *I've got all her records but I've never seen her in the flesh.* **make one's/sb's** ˈ**flesh crawl/creep** make one/sb feel nervous, frightened or filled with loathing: *The mere sight of snakes makes my flesh creep.* **neither fish, flesh, nor good red herring** ⇨ FISH[1]. **one's** ˌ**own** ˌ**flesh and** ˈ**blood** close relatives in one's family: *I'll have* *to go to my aunt's funeral — she was my own flesh and blood after all.* **one's pound of flesh** ⇨ POUND[1]. **press the flesh** ⇨ PRESS[2]. **a thorn in sb's flesh/side** ⇨ THORN. **the world, the flesh and the devil** ⇨ WORLD.

▷ **flesh** *v* (phr v) **flesh sth out** add more details or information to sth: *Your summary will need fleshing out before you present it.*

fleshly *adj* (*fml*) of the body; sensual or sexual: *fleshly lusts.*

fleshy *adj* **1** of or like flesh; rather plump: *fleshy arms* ○ *a fleshy body.* **2** soft and pulpy: *fleshy peaches.*

□ **'flesh-pots** *n* [pl] **(a)** (places supplying) good food, wine, etc; luxurious living. **(b)** places, such as brothels, where sexual desires are satisfied.

'flesh-wound *n* wound that breaks the skin but does not reach the bones or internal organs of the body.

Fletcher /'fletʃə(r)/ John (1579-1625), English playwright. He was considered a great author in his own day, writing about 15 plays on his own as well as 16 with *Beaumont and others with *Jonson and *Shakespeare.

fleur-de-lis (also **fleur-de-lys**) /ˌflɜː də 'liː/ *n* (*pl* **fleurs-** /ˌflɜː də 'liː/) design representing a lily flower as used in heraldry, formerly the royal coat of arms of France. ⇨ illus at COMPASS CARD.

flew *pt* of FLY.

flex[1] /fleks/ *n* (*esp Brit*) (*US* **cord**) [C, U] (length of) flexible insulated wire used for carrying an electric current to an appliance.

flex[2] /fleks/ *v* **1** [Tn] bend or move (a limb, joint or muscle), esp in order to exercise one's body before an activity: *flex one's knee, toes, muscles, etc.* **2** (idm) **flex one's 'muscles** show one's strength and power, esp as a warning or to display pride in oneself.

▷ **flexion** /'flekʃn/ *n* **(a)** [C] act of bending sth, esp a limb or joint. **(b)** [U] condition of being bent.

flexible /'fleksəbl/ *adj* **1** that can bend easily without breaking: *flexible plastic tubing.* **2 (a)** easily changed to suit new conditions: *Our plans are quite flexible.* **(b)** (of people) willing and able to change according to different circumstances; adaptable. ▷ **flexibility** /ˌfleksə'bɪlətɪ/ *n* [U]. **flexibly** /'fleksəblɪ/ *adv.*

flexitime /'fleksɪtaɪm/ *n* [U] system in which employees can start and finish work at different times each day, provided that each of them works a certain number of hours in a week or month.

flibbertigibbet /ˌflɪbətɪ'dʒɪbɪt/ *n* irresponsible, silly and gossipy person.

flick /flɪk/ *n* **1** [C] quick light blow, eg with a whip or the tip of a finger. **2** [C] quick sharp movement; jerk: *He turned the pancake over with a strong flick of his wrist.* **3 (a)** [C] (*dated infml*) cinema film. **(b) the flicks** [pl] (*dated infml*) the cinema: *What's on at the flicks?*

▷ **flick** *v* **1** [Tn, Tn·pr] ~ **A (with B)**; ~ **B (at A)** strike (sb/sth) with a flick; give a flick with (sth): *He flicked the horse with his whip/flicked his whip at the horse.* **2** [Tn, Tn·p, Cn·a] ~ **sth (off, on, etc)** move sth with a flick: *flick the light switch (on)*, ie turn on the light ○ *He flicked the knife open.* **3** [Ipr, Ip] move quickly and lightly: *The cow's tail flicked from side to side.* **4** (phr v) **flick sth away; flick sth from/off sth** remove sth with a flick: *The waiter flicked the crumbs off the table.* **flick through (sth)** turn over the pages (of a book, etc) quickly, looking briefly at the contents: *Sam flicked through a magazine while he waited.*

□ **'flick-knife** *n* (*pl* **-knives**) (*US* **'switch-blade**) knife with a blade inside the handle that springs out quickly when a button is pressed.

flicker /'flɪkə(r)/ *v* **1 (a)** [I] (of a light or flame) burn or shine unsteadily: *All the lights flickered for a moment.* **(b)** [Ipr] (*fig*) (of an emotion) be felt or seen briefly: *A slender hope still flickered within him.* ○ *A faint smile flickered across her face.* **2** [I, Ipr] move back and forth lightly and quickly: *flickering eyelids* ○ *The leaves flickered gently in the breeze.*

▷ **flicker** *n* (usu *sing*) **(a)** flickering movement or light: *the flicker of pictures on the cinema screen.* **(b)** (*fig*) faint and brief experience, esp of an emotion: *a flicker of hope, despair, interest, etc.*

flier (also **flyer**) /'flaɪə(r)/ *n* **1** pilot of an aircraft; airman. **2** person, animal, vehicle, etc that moves very quickly. **3** small advertising leaflet that is widely distributed. **4** = HIGH-FLYER (HIGH).

flies /flaɪz/ *n* **the flies** [pl] space above the stage of a theatre, used for lights and storing scenery.

flight[1] /flaɪt/ *n* **1** [U] **(a)** action or process of flying through the air; ability to fly: *the age of supersonic flight* ○ *The bird had been shot down in flight*, ie while flying. **(b)** movement or path of a thing through the air: *the flight of an arrow, a dart, a missile, etc.* **2** [C] **(a)** journey made by air, esp in an aircraft on a particular route: *a smooth, comfortable, bumpy, etc flight* ○ *All flights have been cancelled because of fog.* **(b)** aircraft making such a journey: *We travelled aboard the same flight.* ○ *Flight number BA 4793 will arrive in London at 16.50.* **3** [U, C] passage or journey through space: *the history of manned space flight.* **4** [C] group of aeroplanes working as a unit: *an aircraft of the Queen's flight.* **5** [C] ~ **(of sth)** number of birds, insects, etc flying together or of arrows released together: *a flight of geese* ○ *a flight of arrows.* **6** [C] series of stairs between two floors or landings: *There was no lift and we had to climb six flights of stairs.* **7** [U] swift passage, esp of time. **8** [C] ~ **of sth** instance of sth very imaginative but usu not practical: *wild flights of imagination.* **9** [C] tail part of a dart. **10** (idm) **a flight of 'fancy** unrealistic idea, etc that exists only in sb's mind: *Her latest flight of fancy is to go camping in the Sahara desert!* **in the first/top 'flight** taking a leading place; excellent of his/its kind: *She's in the top flight of journalists.*

▷ **flight** *v* [Tn] (in cricket) give (the ball) a certain path through the air when bowling so as to deceive the batsman: *a well-flighted delivery.*

flightless *adj* (of birds) not able to fly.

□ **'flight attendant** member of an aircraft's crew who looks after the passengers; steward or air hostess.

'flight-deck *n* **1** (on a ship that carries aircraft) deck for the take-off and landing of aircraft. **2** control room of a large aircraft, from which the pilot and crew fly the plane.

ˌflight lieu'tenant officer in the Royal Air Force between the ranks of flying officer and squadron leader. ⇨ App 4.

'flight path direction or course of an aircraft through the air: *The flight paths of the aeroplanes crossed, with fatal results.*

'flight-recorder *n* (also **ˌblack 'box**) electronic device in an aeroplane that records details of the flight.

'flight sergeant non-commissioned officer in the Royal Air Force next above sergeant. ⇨ App 4.

'flight simulator device on the ground for training pilots by reproducing accurately all the conditions of flying.

flight[2] /flaɪt/ *n* **1** [C, U] act or instance of fleeing or running away: *Many soldiers fell wounded in their flight from the defeat.* ○ (*fig*) *the flight of capital*, ie the sending of money out of a country during a financial crisis. **2** (idm) **put sb to 'flight** force sb to flee: *The enemy was put to flight by the advancing army.* **take (to) 'flight** flee; run away: *The gang took (to) flight when they heard the police car.*

flighty /'flaɪtɪ/ *adj* (**-ier, -iest**) (esp of a woman or her behaviour) changeable and unreliable; not serious.

flimsy /'flɪmzɪ/ *adj* (**-ier, -iest**) **1 (a)** (of cloth or material) light and thin: *a flimsy dress.* **(b)** not strong or solid enough for the purpose for which it is used: *a flimsy cardboard box.* **2** (*fig*) weak or feeble; unconvincing: *a flimsy excuse* ○ *The evidence against him is rather flimsy.*

▷ **flimsily** /-ɪlɪ/ *adv.*

flimsiness *n.*

flimsy *n* [C, U] (sheet of) very thin paper on which a copy of the typing is produced when it is put under carbon paper.

flinch /flɪntʃ/ *v* **1** [I] move or draw back suddenly, from shock, fear or pain: *He listened to the jeers of the crowd without flinching.* **2** [Ipr] ~ **from sth/from doing sth** avoid thinking about or doing sth unpleasant: *We shall never flinch from (the task of) telling the people the whole truth.*

fling /flɪŋ/ *v* (*pt, pp* **flung** /flʌŋ/) **1** [Tn, Tn·pr, Tn·p] throw (sth) violently, angrily or hurriedly: *fling a stone (at a window)* ○ *He flung the paper away in disgust.* **2** [Tn·pr, Tn·p, Cn·a] put or push (sb/sth) somewhere quickly or roughly and forcefully: *She flung the papers on the desk and left angrily.* ○ *He flung her to the ground.* ○ *He was flung into prison*, ie put into prison roughly and perhaps without trial. ○ *He flung open the door.* **3** [Tn·pr, Tn·p] move (oneself or part of one's body) suddenly or forcefully: *She flung herself in front of a car.* ○ *He flung his arm out just in time to stop her falling.* **4** [Tn, Tn·pr, Tn·p] ~ **sth (at sb)** say or express sth (to sb) in a violent way: *You must be certain of your facts before you start flinging accusations (around) (at people).* **5** (phr v) **fling oneself at sb** = THROW ONESELF AT SB (THROW). **fling oneself into sth** start or do sth with a lot of energy and enthusiasm: *She flung herself into her new job.* **fling off, out, etc** move angrily or violently in the specified direction: *He flung out of the room.* **fling sth on** get dressed hurriedly and carelessly: *She flung on her coat and ran to the bus-stop.*

▷ **fling** *n* **1** act or movement of flinging; throw. **2** (*infml*) short period of enjoyment in some (often irresponsible) activity (used esp in the expressions shown): *a last/final fling* ○ *have a/one's fling* ○ *I had a few flings* (ie casual love affairs) *in my younger days.* **3** type of energetic (esp Scottish) dance: *the Highland fling.*

flint /flɪnt/ *n* **1** [U] very hard grey stone that can produce sparks when struck against steel: *This layer of rock contains a lot of flint.* ○ [attrib] *flint axes* ○ (*fig*) *He has a heart like flint*, ie He is unfeeling and stubborn. **2** [C] piece of this or of hard alloy used to produce sparks, eg in a cigarette lighter.

▷ **flinty** *adj* (**-ier, -iest**) **1** made of flint; very hard, like flint. **2** cruel; unyielding: *a flinty heart.*

□ **'flintlock** *n* old-fashioned gun, in which the gunpowder is lit by a spark struck from a flint.

flip /flɪp/ *v* (**-pp-**) **1** [Tn, Tn·pr] toss (sth) with a sharp movement of the thumb and forefinger so that it turns over in the air: *flip a coin (in the air).* **2** [Tn, Tn·p] ~ **sth (over)** turn sth over quickly: *flip the pages over.* **3** [Tn, Tn·p] move (sth) with a quick sharp movement; flick(2): *He flipped the light on.* **4** [I] (*sl*) become very angry, excited or enthusiastic: *My mother really flipped when I told her I was getting married.* **5** (idm) **ˌflip one's 'lid** (*infml*) lose one's self-control; go crazy. **6** (phr v) **flip through sth** = FLICK THROUGH STH (FLICK).

▷ **flip** *n* **1** [C] quick light blow or movement, esp one that tosses sth: *give a coin a flip.* **2** [U, C] type of alcoholic drink, usu containing beaten egg: *an egg-flip.* **3** [C] (*infml*) short trip, esp in an aircraft: *a quick flip over to France.*

flip *adj* (*infml*) glib; flippant: *a flip comment.*

flip *interj* (expressing annoyance or great surprise).

flipping *adj, adv* (*Brit infml*) (used as a mild alternative to a swear-word): *I hate this flipping hotel!* ○ *What flipping awful weather!*

□ **'flip-flop** *n* **1** (*US* **thong**) type of open sandal with a strap that goes between the big toe and the next toe: *a pair of flip-flops.* ⇨ illus at SANDAL. **2** (*US*) backward somersault. **3** electronic circuit, often used in computers, which can be changed from one stable state to another by a pulse.

'flip side = B-SIDE (B).

flippant /'flɪpənt/ *adj* not showing sufficient respect or seriousness: *a flippant answer, remark, attitude, etc.*

▷ **flippancy** /-ənsɪ/ *n* [U] (quality of) being flippant: *His flippancy makes it difficult to have a decent conversation with him.*

flippantly *adv.*

flipper /'flɪpə(r)/ *n* **1** broad flat limb of certain sea animals (not fish) used for swimming: *Seals, turtles and penguins have flippers.* **2** either of a pair of flat rubber attachments worn on the feet and used to help in underwater diving and swimming.

flirt /flɜːt/ *v* **1** [I, Ipr] ~ **(with sb)** behave (towards sb) in a romantic or suggestive way but without serious intentions: *It's embarrassing when they flirt like that in public,* ie with each other. ○ *He enjoys flirting (with the girls in the office).* **2** [Ipr] ~ **with sth (a)** pretend to be interested in sth; think about sth but not seriously: *I'm flirting with the idea of getting a job in China.* **(b)** behave so casually that one's life is put in danger: *flirt with danger/death/disaster.*

▷ **flirt** *n* person who flirts with many people: *They say he's a terrible flirt.*

flirtation /flɜːˈteɪʃn/ *n* **1** [U] flirting. **2** [C] **(a)** ~ **with sb** brief and frivolous romantic involvement: *carry on/have a flirtation with sb.* **(b)** ~ **with sth** superficial interest in sth: *a brief flirtation with the idea of starting his own business.*

flirtatious /flɜːˈteɪʃəs/ *adj* **(a)** fond of flirting: *an attractive flirtatious young woman.* **(b)** of or related to flirting: *flirtatious behaviour.*

flit /flɪt/ *v* (-tt-) **1** [Ipr, Ip] fly or move lightly and quickly from one place to another: *bees flitting (about) from flower to flower* ○ *He flits from one thing to another,* ie does not deal with anything seriously. ○ *(fig) A thought flitted through my mind,* ie came suddenly but then quickly disappeared. **2** [I] *(Brit infml)* move about from one house to another; move from one's home secretly, esp in order to avoid paying debts, etc.

▷ **flit** *n (Brit infml)* act of flitting (FLIT 2) (used esp in the expression shown): *do a (moonlight) flit.*

flitch /flɪtʃ/ *n* side[1](7) of bacon.

flitter /ˈflɪtə(r)/ *v* [Ip, Ipr] move about quickly and lightly; flit(1): *birds flittering (about) in the bushes.*

□ **ˈflittermouse** *n (dialect)* bat[1].

float[1] /fləʊt/ *v* **1 (a)** [I, Ipr] stay on or at the surface of a liquid and not sink; be held up in air or gas: *Wood floats (in water).* ○ *Try and float on your back.* **(b)** [Ipr] move without resistance in air, water or gas; drift slowly: *A balloon floated across the sky.* ○ *The raft was floating gently down the river.* ○ *(fig) Thoughts of lazy summer afternoons floated through his mind.* **2** [Tn, Tn·pr] bring (sth) to the surface of a liquid; cause (sth) to move on liquid or in air: *There wasn't enough water to float the ship.* ○ *float a raft of logs down the river* ○ *We waited for the tide to float the boat off the sandbank.* **3** [Tn] suggest (a plan or project); present for acceptance or rejection: *Let me float a couple of ideas.* **4** [I, Ipr, Ip] ~ **(about/around (sth))** *(infml)* (of a person) move vaguely or aimlessly from place to place; do nothing in particular: *My weekend was boring — I just floated about (the house) or watched TV.* **5** [Tn] start (a new business company) by selling shares in it to the public. **6 (a)** [Tn] allow the foreign exchange values of (a currency) to vary freely according to the value of other international currencies: *float the pound, dollar, yen, etc.* **(b)** [I] (of a currency) find its own value in this way. **7** (phr v) **float about/around** (esp in the continuous tenses) **(a)** (of a rumour) be heard or talked about a lot: *There's a rumour floating around of a new job in the unit.* **(b)** (of an object) be in an unspecified place: *Have you seen my keys floating about (anywhere)?*

▷ **floater** *n* **1** person or thing that floats. **2** = FLOATING VOTER. **3** *(sl)* mistake; blunder.

□ ˌ**floating** ˈ**capital** money that is not invested or otherwise committed.

ˌ**floating** ˈ**dock** large box-like structure that can be put under the water to allow a ship to enter it, and then floated to lift the ship out of the water.

ˌ**floating** ˈ**kidney** kidney that is out of its normal position.

ˈ**floating popu**ˈ**lation** population in which people are constantly moving from one place to another.

floating ˈ**rib** *(anatomy)* rib that is not joined to the breastbone.

ˌ**floating** ˈ**voter** (also **floater**) person who does not always support the same political party.

float[2] /fləʊt/ *n* **1 (a)** light object made of cork, etc that stays on the surface of a liquid, esp one attached to a fishing-line (to indicate when the bait has been taken) or to a net (to support it in water). **(b)** light buoyant object that non-swimmers can hold on to while learning to swim. **2** floating hollow ball or other air-filled container, used to control the flow of water, petrol, etc into a tank. **3** structure that enables an aircraft to float on water. **4 (a)** lorry, cart or low platform on wheels, used for showing things in a procession: *The club display was mounted on a huge float and paraded through the main street.* **(b)** vehicle with a low flat base, used for transporting the thing specified: *a milk float.* **5** sum of money used for everyday business expenses or for giving change. **6** tool with a flat rectangular surface used for smoothing plaster. **7** (also **floats** [pl]) footlights in a theatre.

flocculent /ˈflɒkjʊlənt/ *adj* (of particles produced in a liquid by a chemical reaction) grouped together in small masses with a woolly appearance.

▷ **flocculation** /ˌflɒkjʊˈleɪʃn/ *n* [U] process by which very small particles (eg of soil) join together in larger masses with a crumb-like or fluffy texture.

flock[1] /flɒk/ *n* [CGp] **1** ~ **(of sth)** group of sheep, goats or birds of the same kind, either kept together or feeding and travelling together: *a flock of wild geese* ○ *flocks (of sheep) and herds (of cattle).* **2** large crowd of people: *People came in flocks to see the royal procession.* **3** number of people in sb's care, esp Christian churchgoers under a priest: *a priest and his flock.*

▷ **flock** *v* [Ipr, Ip] gather, move, come or go together in great numbers: *In the summer, tourists flock to the museums and art galleries.* ○ *Huge numbers of birds had flocked together by the lake.*

flock[2] /flɒk/ *n* **1** [C usu *pl*] tuft of wool, cotton, hair, etc. **2** [U] soft material for stuffing cushions, mattresses, etc: [attrib] *a flock mattress* ○ *flock(ed) wallpaper,* ie with a raised pattern made of short tufts of material.

Flodden /ˈflɒdn/ hill in Northumberland where a battle was fought in 1513 between the armies of England and Scotland. It was a victory for the English, and the Scottish king James IV was killed along with many of his men.

floe /fləʊ/ *n* sheet of floating ice, usu on the sea: *Ice-floes are a threat to shipping in the area.*

flog /flɒg/ *v* (-gg-) **1** [Tn] beat (sb) severely, esp with a rod or whip, as a punishment: *The boy was cruelly flogged for stealing.* **2** [Tn, Dn·n, Dn·pr] ~ **sth (to sb)** *(Brit infml)* sell sth (to sb): *We should be able to flog the car (to someone) for a good price.* ⇨ Usage at SELL. **3** (idm) ˌ**flog a dead** ˈ**horse** waste one's efforts on an activity or a belief that is already widely rejected or has long been accepted. ˌ**flog sth to** ˈ**death** *(infml)* be so persistent or repetitive about sth that people lose interest in it: *I hope he won't tell that joke again; he's flogged it to death already.*

▷ **flogging** *n* [C, U] (instance of) beating or whipping.

flood[1] /flʌd/ *v* **1 (a)** [I, Tn] (cause a place that is usu dry to) be filled or overflow with water; inundate: *The cellar floods whenever it rains heavily.* ○ *The river had burst its banks and flooded the valley.* **(b)** [Tn] (of rain) fill (a river, etc) so that it overflows: *streams flooded by violent storms.* **2** [Ipr, Tn, Tn·pr] ~ **(sth) (with sth)** cover or fill (sth) completely; spread into (sth): *A powerful light flooded (into) the grounds.* ○ *The place was flooded with light.* **3** [Tn, Tn·pr] ~ **sth (with sth)** fill (the carburettor of a motor engine) with too much petrol so that the engine will not start. **4** [Ipr, Ip, Tn] *(fig)* (of a thought or feeling) flow powerfully over (sb); surge over (sb): *A great sense of relief flooded over him.* ○ *Memories of his childhood came flooding back.* **5** (idm) ˌ**flood the** ˈ**market** (cause sth to) be offered for sale in large quantities, often at a low price: *Japanese cars have flooded the American market.* **6** (phr v) **flood in; flood into sth** come to or arrive at (a place) in great quantities or numbers: *Applications flooded into the office.* **flood sb out** force sb to leave home because of a flood: *Half the village were flooded out by a burst water main.* **flood sb/sth with sth** arrive in great quantities for sb/at sth: *The office was flooded with complaints.*

▷ **flooding** *n* [U] covering of an area of land that is usu dry with a lot of water, eg when a river overflows: *Widespread flooding is affecting large areas of Devon.*

flood[2] /flʌd/ *n* **1 (a)** (coming of a) great quantity of water, esp over a place that is usu dry: *The heavy rain caused floods in the houses by the river.* ○ *There's a flood in the next valley.* ○ [attrib]: *flood water.* **(b) the Flood** *(Bible)* flood that was sent by God to punish humanity, as described in the Old Testament book of Genesis. Only *Noah and his family were saved, along with the animals in his ark. Similar stories of a great flood occur in a number of early legends. **2** ~ **(of sth)** great quantity or volume: *a flood of anger, abuse, indignation, etc* ○ *a flood of letters, refugees* ○ *The child was in floods of tears,* ie was crying uncontrollably. **3** flowing in of the tide from the sea to the land; rising tide: *The tide is at the flood.* Cf EBB *n* 1. **4** (idm) **in** ˈ**flood** (of a river) overflowing: *We can't cross the meadow there because the river is in flood.*

□ ˈ**floodgate** *n* **1** gate that can be opened or closed to control the flow of water. **2** (idm) **open the floodgates** ⇨ OPEN[2].

ˈ**flood plain** level area beside a river which is occasionally flooded. Flood plains are usu very fertile because of the sediment left by the flood waters.

ˈ**flood-tide** *n* rising tide.

floodlight /ˈflʌdlaɪt/ *n* (esp *pl*) large powerful light that produces a wide beam, used to light sports grounds, theatre stages, etc: *a match played under floodlights.* ⇨ illus at ASSOCIATION FOOTBALL.

▷ **floodlight** *v* (*pt, pp* **floodlighted** or **floodlit** /-lɪt/) [Tn usu passive] light (sth) using floodlights: *The Acropolis is floodlit in the evenings.*

floor[1] /flɔː(r)/ *n* **1** [C usu *sing*] surface of a room on which one stands, walks, etc: *There weren't enough chairs so I had to sit on the floor.* ○ *The bare concrete floor was cold on my feet.* ○ [attrib] *5000 square metres of floor space.* **2** [C usu *sing*] bottom of the sea or ground surface of a cave, etc: *the ocean, forest, valley, cave floor.* ⇨ Usage at EARTH. **3** [C] number of rooms, etc on the same level in a building; level or storey of a building: *Her office is on the second floor.* ⇨ Usage. **4 the floor** [sing] **(a)** part of an assembly hall where members sit, eg in the Houses of Parliament, US Congress, etc: *speak from the floor.* **(b)** right to speak in such an assembly or meeting: *The floor is yours — you may present your argument.* **5** [C usu *sing*] area where a particular activity is undertaken: *the dance floor,* ie part of the floor of a night-club, etc where guests dance ○ *the factory/shop floor,* ie part of a factory where the ordinary workers (ie not the managers) work. **6** [C] minimum level for wages or prices. **7** (idm) **be/get in on the ground floor** ⇨ GROUND FLOOR (GROUND[1]). ˌ**hold the** ˈ**floor** speak to an audience, esp at great length or with determination, so that no one else has a chance to say anything: *She held the floor for over an hour.* ˌ**take the** ˈ**floor (a)** get up to speak or address an audience: *I now invite the President to take the floor.* **(b)** get up and start to dance: *She took the floor with her husband.* **wipe the floor with sb** ⇨ WIPE.

▷ **flooring** *n* [U] material, eg boards or tiles, used for making floors.

□ ˈ**floor-board** *n* any of the long (wooden) planks or boards laid down to make a floor.

ˈ**floor-lamp** *n (US)* = STANDARD LAMP (STANDARD).

ˈ**floor-leader** *n (US)* leader of a political party in a law-making assembly, eg Congress.

ˈ**floor manager** person in a television studio who is responsible for the technical organization of a programme. Cf STAGE-MANAGER (STAGE).

ˈ**floor plan** plan showing the layout of rooms, corridors, etc on a floor of a building.

ˈ**floor show** series of performances, eg of singing and dancing, presented in a night-club, bar, etc.

NOTE ON USAGE: In British English the floor of a building at street level is the **ground floor** and the floor above that is the **first floor.** In US English the street-level floor is the **first floor** and the one above is the **second floor.**

floor[2] /flɔ:(r)/ *v* [Tn] **1** provide (a building or room) with a floor. **2** knock down (sb) in a fight: *He floored his opponent with a fine punch in the first round.* **3** (*infml*) defeat or confuse (sb) in an argument, discussion, etc: *Tom was completely floored by two of the questions in the exam.*

floozie (also **floosie**) /ˈflu:zɪ/ *n* (*infml derog*) woman of low morals; prostitute.

flop /flɒp/ *v* (**-pp-**) **1** [Ipr, Ip] move or fall clumsily, helplessly or loosely: *The pile of books flopped noisily onto the floor.* ○ *The fish we'd caught flopped around in the bottom of the boat.* **2** [I, Ipr, Ip] hang or sway heavily and loosely: *flopping stirrups* ○ *Her hair flopped (about) over her shoulders.* **3** [I, Ipr, Ip] sit or lie down heavily and clumsily, because of tiredness: *I'm ready to flop.* ○ *Exhausted, he flopped (down) into the nearest chair.* **4** [I] (*infml*) (of a book, play, etc) fail totally; be unsuccessful.

▷ **flop** *n* **1** (usu *sing*) flopping movement or sound. **2** (*infml*) total failure (of a book, play, etc): *Despite all the publicity, her latest novel was a complete flop.*

flop *adv* with a flop: *fall flop into the water.*

floppy *adj* (**-ier**, **-iest**) tending to flop; soft and flexible; falling loosely: *a floppy hat.* — *n* (*infml*) = FLOPPY DISK. **floppy disk** (also **floppy**, **diskette**) (*computing*) flexible disk for recording and storing data in a form that a computer can read. ⇨ illus at COMPUTER. Cf HARD DISK (HARD[1]).

flop-house /ˈflɒphaʊs/ *n* (*US infml*) cheap lodging house or hotel; doss-house.

flora /ˈflɔ:rə/ *n* [pl] all the plants of a particular area or period of time: *the flora of the Himalayas, the Palaeozoic era.* Cf FAUNA.

floral /ˈflɔ:rəl/ *adj* [usu attrib] (**a**) made of flowers: *floral arrangements, tributes.* (**b**) decorated with flowers: *floral wallpaper.*

Florence /ˈflɒrəns/ city in Tuscany, N Italy; Italian name **Firenze**. Esp under the Medici family, it was the most important centre of the Italian Renaissance, and great figures like *Dante, *Leonardo da Vinci and *Michelangelo all spent time there. Today it is still a major cultural centre.

▷ **Florentine** /ˈflɒrəntaɪn/ *n, adj* (native or citizen) of Florence: *Florentine art, artists.*

floret /ˈflɒrɪt; *US* ˈflɔ:rət/ *n* small flower that is part of a composite flower, esp in certain vegetables: *cauliflower florets.*

floribunda /ˌflɒrɪˈbʌndə; *US* ˈflɔ:rə-/ *n* plant (esp a rose) whose flowers grow in clusters rather than singly.

florid /ˈflɒrɪd; *US* ˈflɔ:r-/ *adj* **1** (*usu derog*) elaborate and ornate; excessively decorated or colourful: *florid music, poetry, art, etc* ○ *a florid room, painting.* **2** (of a person's face) red in colour; ruddy: *a florid complexion.*

Florida /ˈflɒrɪdə; *US* ˈflɔ:rədə/ state in the south-eastern USA, a peninsula between the Atlantic and the Gulf of Mexico. It has a varied economy based on agriculture, aerospace, electronics and tourism. ⇨ map at App 1.

florin /ˈflɒrɪn; *US* ˈflɔ:rɪn/ *n* former British coin worth two shillings or one tenth of £1 (now ten pence).

florist /ˈflɒrɪst; *US* ˈflɔ:r-/ *n* person who has a shop that sells flowers: *order a wreath from the florist* ○ *buy a bouquet at the florist's,* ie shop where flowers are sold.

floss /flɒs; *US* flɔ:s/ *n* [U] **1** rough silk threads from the outside of a silkworm's cocoon. **2** (also ˈ**floss silk**) spun (but not twisted) silk thread used for embroidery. **3** = DENTAL FLOSS (DENTAL).

flotation /fləʊˈteɪʃn/ *n* [C, U] starting of a new company by selling shares in it to the public.

flotilla /fləˈtɪlə/ *n* (**a**) fleet of boats or small ships. (**b**) small fleet of warships: *a destroyer flotilla.*

flotsam /ˈflɒtsəm/ *n* [U] **1** parts of a wrecked ship or its cargo found floating in the sea. Cf JETSAM. **2** (idm) ˌ**flotsam and** ˈ**jetsam** (**a**) people without homes or work or those who have had to leave their houses; vagrants and tramps or refugees. (**b**) various unimportant objects; bits and pieces; odds and ends.

flounce[1] /flaʊns/ *v* [Ipr, Ip] move about in an exaggerated, and usu impatient and angry manner: *She flounced out of the room, swearing loudly.* ○ *children flouncing around in their party clothes.*

▷ **flounce** *n* (usu *sing*) sudden impatient movement of the body; jerk: *with a flounce of the head.*

flounce[2] /flaʊns/ *n* wide strip of cloth or lace sewn by its upper edge to a garment, eg a skirt.

▷ **flounced** *adj* trimmed or decorated with flounces: *a flounced frock.*

flounder[1] /ˈflaʊndə(r)/ *v* [I, Ipr, Ip] **1** move or struggle helplessly or clumsily; move with difficulty, as through mud or deep snow: *Ann couldn't swim and was left floundering (about/around) in the deep end of the swimming-pool.* **2** hesitate or make mistakes when talking or when coming to a decision: *I wasn't expecting the interviewer to ask about my private life and was left floundering for a while.* ○ *flounder (on) through a badly prepared speech.*

flounder[2] /ˈflaʊndə(r)/ *n* small flat-fish that lives in the ocean and is eaten as food.

flour /ˈflaʊə(r)/ *n* [U] fine powder obtained by grinding grain, esp wheat or rye, and used for making bread, cakes, etc.

▷ **flour** *v* [Tn] cover or sprinkle (sth) with flour: *flour the pastry board.*

floury /ˈflaʊərɪ/ *adj* of or like flour; covered with flour: *floury potatoes,* ie ones that are soft and fluffy ○ *She wiped her floury hands with a damp cloth.*

flourish /ˈflʌrɪʃ/ *v* **1** [I] be successful, very active, or widespread; prosper: *No new business can flourish in the present economic climate.* ○ *a flourishing squash club.* **2** [I] grow healthily; be well and active: *This species of flower flourishes in a warm climate.* ○ *All the family are flourishing.* **3** [I, Ipr] (of ideas or people) be very active and influential (during the specified period): *In Germany the baroque style of art flourished in the 17th and 18th centuries.* **4** [Tn] wave sth about in order to attract attention to it: *He stormed into the office, flourishing a letter of complaint.*

▷ **flourish** *n* (usu *sing*) **1** bold sweeping movement or gesture, used esp to attract attention: *He opened the door for her with a flourish.* **2** flowing curve, esp in handwriting or decoration. **3** loud and elaborate piece of music; fanfare: *A flourish of trumpets marked the Queen's arrival.*

flout /flaʊt/ *v* [Tn] disobey (sb/sth) openly and scornfully: *flout the law, (a) convention, the rules* ○ *flout sb's advice.* ⇨ Usage at FLAUNT.

flow /fləʊ/ *v* **1** [I, Ipr, Ip] (**a**) (of a liquid) move freely and continuously: *Her tears flowed freely (down her cheeks).* ○ *Most rivers flow into the sea.* ○ *Blood suddenly started flowing out.* (**b**) move freely and continuously, esp within a closed system; circulate: *keep the traffic flowing* ○ *Electricity is flowing (in the circuit/wires).* ○ *Blood flows round the body.* ○ *In convection, hot currents flow upwards.* **2** [I] (of speech or writing) proceed evenly and continuously: *Conversation flowed freely when the speaker invited discussion.* **3** [I, Ipr, Ip] fall or hang (down) loosely and freely: *long flowing robes* ○ *Her hair flowed (down) over her shoulders.* **4** [I, Ipr] ~ (**with sth**) be available plentifully; be distributed freely: *The party became lively when the drink began to flow.* ○ *a land flowing with milk and honey,* ie place with rich natural resources. **5** [I] (of the sea tide) come in; rise: *The tide began to flow and our footprints were covered.* Cf EBB 1. **6** (phr v) **flow in/into sth** arrive in a steady stream: *The election results flowed in throughout the night.* ○ *Offers of help flowed into the office.* **flow from sth** come or derive from sth; result from sth: *Many benefits will flow from this discovery.* **flow out (of sth)** leave in a steady stream: *Profits are flowing out of the country.* **flow over sb** take place without affecting sb: *Office politics just seem to flow over him.*

▷ **flow** *n* (usu *sing*) **1** ~ (**of sth/sb**) (rate of a) flowing movement of sth/sb: *a steady flow of traffic* ○ *The government is trying to stop the increasing flow of refugees entering the country.* **2** ~ (**of sth**) (rate of a) continuous stream or supply of sth: *cut off the flow of oil* ○ *the constant flow of information.* **3** even and continuous outpouring of words: *I interrupted him while he was in full flow,* ie talking away strongly. **4** incoming tide: *the ebb and flow of the sea.* **5** (idm) **the ebb and flow (of sth)** ⇨ EBB *n.*

□ ˈ**flow chart** (also ˈ**flow diagram**) diagram showing the development of sth through the different stages or processes in a series.

flower /ˈflaʊə(r)/ *n* **1** part of a plant from which the seed or fruit develops, often brightly coloured and lasting only a short time: *The plant has a brilliant purple flower.* ⇨ illus at PLANT. **2** plant grown for the beauty of its flowers; flower and its stem: *arrange some flowers in a vase.*

📖 The rose, the national flower of England, is usually thought to be the most typically British flower. It has frequently been used in poetry as a symbol of romantic love. The violet is often seen as symbolizing modesty, and a shy, retiring person can be called 'a shrinking violet'. The daisy is one of the most common British wild flowers and carries the association of summer picnics and making daisy chains, by threading the stalk of one daisy through a slit made in the stalk of the next, and so on. Dandelions and buttercups have bright yellow petals and are also associated with the summer. Snowdrops, bluebells, daffodils and primroses are popular spring flowers, often found growing wild in woods. (The daffodil is also the national flower of Wales). Honeysuckle is associated with typical country cottages, and wisteria with stately homes. Popular garden flowers include roses, pansies, lupins, dahlias, gladioli, chrysanthemums, asters, carnations, irises and wallflowers. Flowers are used at weddings and funerals and have certain connotations. For example, carnations, especially white ones, are often worn by men at weddings in the buttonholes of their jackets, and chrysanthemums and white lilies are associated with funerals. Rose, Daisy, Iris, Violet and Lily were popular as girl's names in Victorian times, but are less common nowadays.

3 [sing] **the** ~ **of sth** (*rhet*) finest or best part of sth; prime or peak of sth: *the flower of the nation's youth* ○ *in the flower of one's maturity/strength/youth.* **4** (idm) **in/into** ˈ**flower** in/into the state of having the flowers open: *The roses have been in flower for a week.* ○ *The crocuses are late coming into flower.*

▷ **flower** *v* **1** [I] produce flowers; bloom: *These plants will flower in the spring.* ○ *a late-flowering chrysanthemum.* **2** [I] develop fully; mature or blossom: *Their friendship flowered while they were at college.* **flowered** /ˈflaʊəd/ *adj* [usu attrib] decorated with patterns of flowers: *flowered wallpaper, cloth, curtains, etc.* **flowering** /ˈflaʊərɪŋ/ *n* (usu *sing*) ~ (**of sth**) full development of (an idea, literary or political movement, etc): *the gradual flowering of modern democracy.*

flowery /ˈflaʊərɪ/ *adj* (**-ier**, **-iest**) **1** covered with or having a lot of flowers: *flowery fields.* **2** (of language, gestures or decoration) too elaborate or ornate: *a flowery speech.*

flowerless *adj* not having or not producing flowers: *flowerless plants.*

□ ˈ**flower-bed** *n* piece of ground in a garden or park, specially prepared for growing flowers.

ˈ**flower children** (also ˈ**flower people**) (esp in the 1960s) (usu young) people supporting universal love and peace, and carrying flowers as a symbol of their beliefs.

ˈ**flower-girl** *n* girl or woman who sells flowers in a market, etc.

ˈ**flowerpot** *n* container of plastic or earthenware, in which a plant is grown. ⇨ illus at POT.

ˈ**flower power** beliefs or cult of the flower

children.
ˈ**flower-show** *n* exhibition at which flowers are displayed.
flown *pp* of FLY[2].
fl oz *abbr* (*pl* unchanged or **fl ozs**) fluid ounce: *5 fl oz.*
Flt Lt *abbr* Flight Lieutenant: *Flt Lt (Robert) Bell.*
flu /fluː/ *n* (*infml*) = INFLUENZA.
flub /flʌb/ *v* (**-bb-**) [I, Tn] (*US infml*) handle (sth) badly; make a mess of (sth).
fluctuate /ˈflʌktʃʊeɪt/ *v* [I, Ipr] ~ (**between A and B**) **1** (of a price, number, rate, etc) rise and fall; change irregularly: *The price fluctuates between £5 and £6.* **2** (of an attitude or a state) change continually and irregularly; waver: *fluctuating opinions.* ▷ **fluctuation** /ˌflʌktʃʊˈeɪʃn/ *n* [C, U] ~ (**of/in sth**): *wide fluctuations of temperature* ○ *fluctuations in the state of his health.*
flue /fluː/ *n* channel, pipe, etc through which smoke, fumes or hot air pass from a boiler or oven, usu to a chimney.
fluent /ˈfluːənt/ *adj* **1** (of a person) able to speak or write a language or perform an action smoothly, accurately and with ease: *a fluent speaker (of Spanish)* ○ *be fluent in speech.* **2** (of speech, a language or an action) expressed in a smooth and accurate way: *speak/write fluent Russian* ○ *fluent movements*, ie ones that are flowing and graceful.
▷ **fluency** /ˈfluːənsɪ/ *n* [U] quality or condition of being fluent: *She speaks Swahili with great fluency.*
fluently *adv.*
fluff /flʌf/ *n* **1** [U] (**a**) soft feathery pieces of material shed by blankets, etc: *My best sweater is covered with fluff.* (**b**) soft fur or down of animals or birds. **2** [C] (*infml*) unsuccessful attempt at sth; mistake or blunder. **3** (idm) **a bit of fluff** ⇨ BIT[1].
▷ **fluff** *v* **1** [Tn, Tn·p] ~ **sth** (**out/up**) shake sth into a soft full mass; puff or spread sth out lightly: *fluff up the pillows* ○ *The bird fluffed (out) its feathers.* **2** [Tn] (*infml*) be unsuccessful at doing (sth); perform (sth) badly; bungle: *fluff a stroke*, eg in golf ○ *fluff one's lines in a play* ○ *He really fluffed his exams.*
fluffy *adj* (**-ier, -iest**) **1** like fluff; covered with fluff: *Most animals are soft and fluffy when first born.* **2** soft, light and airy: *light and fluffy mashed potatoes.* **fluffiness** *n* [U].
flugelhorn /ˈfluːglhɔːn/ *n* brass instrument, similar to a bugle but with valves.
fluid /ˈfluːɪd/ *adj* **1** able to flow freely, as gases and liquids do; not solid or rigid: *a fluid substance.* **2** not fixed; able to be changed: *fluid arrangements, ideas, opinions* ○ *The situation is still fluid.* **3** smooth and graceful in movement.
▷ **fluid** *n* [C, U] **1** any liquid substance: *Drink plenty of fluids.* ○ *There's some sort of sticky fluid on the kitchen floor.* **2** (*chemistry*) fluid substance.
fluidics /fluːˈɪdɪks/ *n* [sing *v*] use of jets of fluid to control mechanisms, esp where electronic devices might be affected by heat, magnetic fields, etc.
fluidity /fluːˈɪdətɪ/ *n* [U] quality or state of being fluid.
fluidize, -ise /ˈfluːɪdaɪz/ *v* [Tn] cause (eg grains of sand) to behave like a liquid by suspending it in a stream of gas. The process is used in industry, eg in transporting powdery substances like coal dust. **fluidization** /ˌfluːɪdaɪˈzeɪʃn; *US* -dɪˈz-/, **-isation** *n* [U].
□ ˈ**fluid mechanics** study of the mechanical properties of fluids.
fluid ounce (*abbr* **fl oz**) liquid measure equal to one twentieth of an Imperial pint or one sixteenth of an American pint. ⇨ App 9, 10.
fluke[1] /fluːk/ *n* (*usu sing*) (*infml*) thing that is accidentally successful; lucky stroke in a game: *Passing the exam was a real fluke — he didn't work for it at all.* ○ *That shot was a sheer fluke.* ▷ **fluky** (also **flukey**) *adj.*
fluke[2] /fluːk/ *n* **1** either of the two flat triangular ends of an anchor. **2** either of the two lobes of a whale's tail.
fluke[3] /fluːk/ *n* **1** flat-fish or flounder. **2** parasitic worm found in the liver of a sheep.
flummery /ˈflʌmərɪ/ *n* [U] foolish or meaningless talk; empty flattery; nonsense.
flummox /ˈflʌməks/ *v* [Tn esp passive] (*infml*) bewilder, confuse or disconcert (sb): *The politician was completely flummoxed by the questions put to her.*
flung *pt, pp* of FLING.
flunk /flʌŋk/ *v* (*infml esp US*) **1** [I, Tn] fail (an examination, academic course, etc): *flunk biology.* **2** [Tn] give a failing mark to (sb): *be flunked in chemistry.* **3** (phr v) **flunk out** be dismissed from a school or college for failure.
flunkey (also **flunky**) /ˈflʌŋkɪ/ *n* (*pl* ~**s** or **-kies**) (*infml derog*) **1** servant in uniform. **2** (*esp US*) person who does small unimportant tasks.
fluorescence /flɔːˈresns; *US* flʊəˈr-/ *n* [U] property that a substance has of emitting light while being exposed to light or some other radiation of a shorter wavelength. Cf PHOSPHORESCENCE.
▷ **fluoresce** *v* [I] send out light in this manner.
fluorescent /-snt/ *adj* **1** of, having or showing fluorescence: *fluorescent lighting* ○ *a fluorescent screen*, eg used for viewing X-rays. **2** having a very bright glowing appearance because of fluorescence: *wearing orange fluorescent clothing.*
□ **fluorˌescent ˈlamp** electric light, usu in the form of a long strip, that gives off a fluorescent light.
fluoride /ˈflɔːraɪd; *US* ˈflʊər-/ *n* chemical compound of fluorine.
▷ **fluoridate** /ˈflɔːrɪdeɪt; *US* ˈflʊər-/ *v* [Tn] add traces of fluoride to (the water supply), esp to prevent tooth decay. **fluoridation** /ˌflɔːrɪˈdeɪʃn; *US* ˌflʊər-/ *n* [U].
fluoridize, -ise /ˈflɔːrɪdaɪz; *US* ˈflʊər-/ *v* [Tn] = FLUORIDATE (FLUORIDE). **fluoridization, -isation** /ˌflɔːrɪdaɪˈzeɪʃn; *US* ˌflʊərɪdɪˈz-/ *n* [U] = FLUORIDATION.
fluorine /ˈflɔːriːn; *US* ˈflʊər-/ *n* [U] (*symb* **F**) chemical element, a pale yellow gas that is both poisonous and corrosive. It has many compounds, including the fluorides and fluorocarbons. ⇨ App 11.
fluorocarbon /ˌflɔːrəʊˈkɑːbən; *US* ˌflʊər-/ *n* compound obtained by replacing hydrogen atoms in a hydrocarbon by fluorine atoms. Such compounds are used eg for making oils and polymers.
fluorspar /ˈflʊəspɑː(r)/ *n* [U] calcium fluoride in mineral form.
flurry /ˈflʌrɪ/ *n* **1** short sudden rush of wind or fall of rain, snow, etc: *light snow flurries/flurries of snow.* **2** ~ (**of sth**) sudden burst of intense activity; commotion: *a flurry of activity/excitement* ○ *I'm always in a flurry* (ie confused and disorganized) *as deadlines get nearer.*
▷ **flurry** *v* (*pt, pp* **flurried**) [Tn usu passive] confuse and disturb; fluster: *Keep calm! Don't get flurried.*
flush[1] /flʌʃ/ *n* **1** [C usu *sing*] (**a**) flow of blood to the face that causes a red colouring; blush. (**b**) sudden rush of emotions, excitement, etc: *a flush of enthusiasm, anger, joy, etc.* **2** [sing] rush of water, esp for cleaning a toilet: *Give the toilet a flush.* **3** [C] new fresh growth, esp of plants. **4** (idm) (**in**) **the first/full flush of ˈyouth, etc** (in) the freshness or vigour of youth, etc; at its beginning/most fully developed stage: *the first flush of manhood* ○ *In the full flush of success, nothing was an obstacle.*
flush[2] /flʌʃ/ *v* **1** (**a**) [La, I] (of a person's face) become red because of a rush of blood to the skin; blush: *Mary flushed crimson with embarrassment.* (**b**) [Tn] (of illness, feelings, etc) cause (the face) to become red: *Fever flushed his cheeks.* **2** (**a**) [Tn] clean (esp a toilet or drain) with a rush of water: *Please flush the toilet after you've used it.* (**b**) [I] (of a toilet) be cleaned in this way: *The toilet won't flush properly*, ie it is blocked. **3** (phr v) **flush sth away, down, through, etc** dispose of sth with a rush of water: *flush waste down a sink.*
▷ **flushed** *adj* ~ (**with sth**) very excited (by sth); filled with emotion: *flushed with success, pride, joy, etc.*
flush[3] /flʌʃ/ *v* **1** (**a**) [Tn, Tn·pr] cause (birds) to fly suddenly, esp from undergrowth: *flush a pheasant (from cover).* (**b**) [I] (of birds) fly suddenly, esp from undergrowth. **2** (phr v) **flush sb out** (**of sth**) force sb to leave a hiding-place; drive sb out: *flush out spies, criminals, snipers, etc.*
flush[4] /flʌʃ/ *n* (in card-games) set of cards held by a player, all of which belong to the same suit: *She won with a royal flush*, ie the five highest cards of a suit.
flush[5] /flʌʃ/ *adj* ~ (**with sth**) **1** completely level or even with another surface: *flush fittings* ○ *The door should be flush with the wall.* **2** [pred] (*infml*) having a lot of sth, esp money; well supplied: *flush with funds.*
fluster /ˈflʌstə(r)/ *v* [Tn esp passive] make (sb) nervous and confused: *Don't get flustered!*
▷ **fluster** *n* [sing] nervous agitated state: *all in a fluster.*
flute[1] /fluːt/ *n* wind instrument in the form of a pipe, with holes stopped by fingers or keys and a mouth-hole at the side: [attrib] *a flute solo.* ⇨ illus at MUSIC. ▷ **flutist** /ˈfluːtɪst/ *n* (*US*) = FLAUTIST.
flute[2] /fluːt/ *v* [Tn usu passive] shape or carve long vertical grooves in (sth), as a decoration: *fluted columns/pillars.*
▷ **fluting** *n* [U] series of such grooves cut in a surface for decoration.
flutter /ˈflʌtə(r)/ *v* **1** (**a**) [I, Ipr] (of the wings of birds, butterflies, etc) move lightly and quickly: *The wings of the bird still fluttered after it had been shot down.* (**b**) [Tn] move (the wings) in this way: *The bird fluttered its wings in the cage.* **2** (**a**) [I, Ipr] move about in a quick irregular way: *a flag fluttering from the mast-head* ○ *curtains fluttering in the breeze.* (**b**) [Tn] move (sth) in this way: *She fluttered her eyelashes (at me).* **3** [I] (of the heart) beat weakly and irregularly, esp because of nervous excitement. **4** (idm) ˌ**flutter the ˈdovecotes** astonish, upset or alarm people who are used to a calm or conventional life. **5** (phr v) **flutter about, around, across, etc** (**a**) fly in the specified direction with quick light movements of the wings: *The wounded bird fluttered to the ground.* ○ *A moth was fluttering round the lamp.* (**b**) move in the specified direction in a quick irregular way: *autumn leaves fluttering to the ground* ○ *She fluttered nervously about, going from room to room.*
▷ **flutter** *n* **1** (usu *sing*) quick irregular movement: *the flutter of wings* ○ *with a flutter of her long dark eyelashes.* **2** [sing] state of nervous or confused excitement: *in a flutter* ○ *all of a flutter* ○ *The arrival of the first customer caused a flutter (of activity) in the shop.* **3** [U] (**a**) dangerous vibration in part of an aircraft, esp the wings. (**b**) rapid variation in the pitch or loudness of recorded sound. Cf WOW[2]. **4** [C] (*Brit infml*) ~ (**on sth**) small bet or gamble: *have a flutter (on a horse) at the races.*
fluvial /ˈfluːvɪəl/ *adj* of or found in rivers: *fluvial deposits of mud.*
□ **fluvioglacial** /ˌfluːvɪəʊˈgleɪsɪəl; *US* -ˈgleɪʃl/ *adj* of or formed by melting ice, esp from glaciers: *fluvioglacial deposits.*
flux /flʌks/ *n* **1** [U] continuous change or succession of changes; unsettled state: *Organization of the company was then in a state of flux.* **2** [sing] ~ (**of sth**) (rate of) flow or flowing (out); discharge: *a flux of neutrons* ○ *magnetic flux.* **3** [C, U] substance used to help metals fuse together.
fly[1] /flaɪ/ *n* **1** type of insect with two wings, esp the house-fly. **2** (usu in compounds) any of several types of flying insect: *a ˈdragonfly* ○ *a ˈbutterfly* ○ *a ˈtsetse-fly.* **3** natural or artificial fly used as bait in fishing. **4** (idm) **die/fall/drop like ˈflies** die or collapse in very large numbers: *Men were dropping like flies in the intense heat.* **a/the ˈfly in the ointment** person or thing that spoils an otherwise satisfactory situation or occasion. **a ˈfly on the wall** hidden or unnoticed observer: *I wish I could be a fly on the wall when they discuss my future.* (**there are**) **no flies on sb** (*infml*) sb is clever and not easily tricked. **not harm/hurt a ˈfly** be kind and gentle and unwilling to cause unhappiness: *Our dog may look fierce but he wouldn't hurt a fly.*
□ ˈ**fly-blown** *adj* **1** (of meat, etc) bad or unfit to eat, because contaminated by flies' eggs. **2** (*fig*) in

a bad condition; dirty or spoiled.

ˈ**flycatcher** *n* type of bird that catches insects in the air.

ˈ**fly-fish** *v* [I] fish using artificial flies as bait.

ˈ**fly-fishing** *n* [U].

ˈ**fly-paper** *n* [U, C] strip of sticky paper for catching flies.

ˈ**fly-spray** *n* poisonous liquid sprayed from a container to kill flies.

ˈ**fly-swatter** *n* = SWATTER (SWAT).

ˈ**fly-trap** any of various plants that catch flies, esp the *Venus fly-trap.

ˈ**flyweight** *n* **1** boxer of the lightest class, weighing between 48 and 51 kg. **2** wrestler weighing between 48 and 52 kg.

fly[2] /flaɪ/ *v* (*pt* **flew** /flu:/, *pp* **flown** /fləʊn/) **1** [I, Ipr, Ip] (of a bird or an insect) move through the air, using wings: *watch the birds learn to fly* ○ *A large bird flew past us.* **2** [I, Ipr, Ip] **(a)** (of an aircraft or a spacecraft) move through air or space: *I can hear a plane flying overhead.* **(b)** travel in an aircraft or a spacecraft: *I'm flying (out) to Hong Kong tomorrow.* ⇨ Usage at TRAVEL. **3 (a)** [I, Tn] direct or control the flight of (an aircraft, etc): *Only experienced pilots fly large passenger aircraft.* **(b)** [Tn, Tn·pr, Tn·p] transport (goods or passengers) in an aircraft: *Five thousand people were flown to Paris during the Easter weekend.* ○ *He had flowers specially flown in for the ceremony.* **(c)** [Tn] travel over (an ocean or area of land) in an aircraft: *fly the Atlantic.* **4 (a)** [I, Ipr, Ip] go or move quickly; rush along: *The children flew to meet their mother.* ○ *It's late — I must fly.* ○ *The train flew by.* ○ *The dog flew down the road after the cat.* **(b)** [La, Ipr, Ip] move suddenly and with force: *A large stone came flying through the window.* ○ *David gave the door a kick and it flew open.* **(c)** [I, Ip] (of time) pass very quickly: *Doesn't time fly?* ○ *Summer has just flown (by).* **5 (a)** [Tn] make (a kite) rise and stay high in the air. **(b)** [Tn] raise (a flag) so that it waves in the air: *fly the Union Jack.* **(c)** [Ipr, Ip] move about freely; be carried about in the air: *Her hair was flying about (in the wind).* **6** [I, Tn] (*rhet*) flee from (sb/sth): *The robbers have flown (the country).* **7** (idm) **as the crow flies** ⇨ CROW[1]. **the bird has flown** ⇨ BIRD. **fly/show/wave the flag** ⇨ FLAG[1]. **fly** ˈ**high** be ambitious. **fly in the face of sth** be contrary to sth; oppose sth: *His version of events flies in the face of all the evidence.* **fly into a** ˈ**passion,** ˈ**rage,** ˈ**temper, etc** become suddenly very angry. **fly a kite** (*Brit infml*) do or say sth in order to see how people will react, express their opinions, etc. **(go) fly a/one's kite** (*US infml*) (esp imperative) go away and stop interfering or annoying sb. **fly/go off at a tangent** ⇨ TANGENT. **fly off the** ˈ**handle** (*infml*) become wildly angry. **fly/go out of the window** ⇨ WINDOW. **keep the flag flying** ⇨ FLAG[1]. **let fly (at sb/sth) (with sth) (a)** shoot, throw sth (at sb/sth) violently: *He aimed carefully and then let fly,* ie fired. **(b)** reproach or criticize (sb) angrily: *Furious at his deceit, she let fly at him with a stream of abuse.* **make the** ˈ**fur/**ˈ**sparks fly** cause quarrelling or fighting: *The promotion of Russell instead of Sarah really made the sparks fly.* **pigs might fly** ⇨ PIG. **send sb/sth flying** ⇨ SEND. **send things flying** ⇨ SEND. **8** (phr v) **fly at sb** rush to attack sb.

□ **fly-away** /ˈflaɪəweɪ/ *adj* **1** (esp of hair) loose and wispy; difficult to control. **2** (*fig*) not sensible; frivolous or flighty.

fly-by /ˈflaɪbaɪ/ *n* (*pl* ˈ**fly-bys**) flight, esp by a spacecraft, past a point or target: *a fly-by of Jupiter.*

fly-by-night /ˈflaɪbaɪnaɪt/ *n* (*pl* **fly-by-nights**) person who evades financial responsibility, esp debts, by (secretly) leaving; unreliable person. — *adj* unreliable or dishonest, esp in financial and business matters: *a fly-by-night company.*

fly-half *n* (*pl* **fly-halves**) = STAND-OFF HALF (STAND[2]).

ˈ**fly-past** /-pɑ:st; *US* -pæst/ *n* (*Brit*) (*US* ˈ**flyover**) ceremonial flight of aircraft, usu at low altitude, as part of a military display.

fly[3] /flaɪ/ *n* **1** [C esp *pl*] (piece of material on a garment that contains or covers a) zip or buttoned opening, eg down the front of a pair of trousers: *John, your flies are/fly is undone!* **2** [C] flap of material, eg canvas, at the entrance to a tent.

fly[4] /flaɪ/ *adj* (*infml esp Brit*) not easily deceived; clever and sly: *He's a very fly character.*

flyer = FLIER.

flying /ˈflaɪɪŋ/ *adj* moving by flight; able to fly: *flying insects.*

▷ **flying** *n* [U] going in an aircraft for travel or sport: *I'm terrified of flying — I'd rather go by sea.*

□ ˌ**flying** ˈ**buttress** (*architecture*) arched structure that supports the outside wall of a large building, esp a church. ⇨ illus at CHURCH and at GOTHIC.

ˌ**flying** ˈ**colours 1** flags on display as a sign of victory or during a ceremony. **2** (idm) **with flying colours** with great and obvious success: *She came through/passed her exams with flying colours.*

ˌ**flying** ˈ**column** troops able to move rapidly and act independently.

ˌ**flying** ˈ**doctor** (esp in Australia) doctor who travels in an aircraft to visit patients who live in distant or isolated places.

ˈ**flying fish** type of tropical fish that can rise and move forward above the surface of the water using its wing-like fins.

ˌ**flying** ˈ**fox** type of large fruit-eating bat.

ˌ**flying** ˈ**jump** (also ˌ**flying** ˈ**leap**) forward jump/leap made while running quickly.

ˈ**flying officer** officer in the Royal Air Force between the ranks of pilot officer and flight lieutenant. ⇨ App 4.

ˌ**flying** ˈ**picket** worker or group of workers on strike who are ready to travel quickly to different factories, etc to persuade other workers to join the strike.

ˌ**flying** ˈ**saucer** (also **unidentified flying object**) spacecraft, shaped like a saucer or disc, that some people claim to have seen and that is believed to have come from another planet.

ˈ**flying squad** group of police officers who are always ready to move quickly, eg when a crime has occurred. ⇨ article at POLICE.

ˌ**flying** ˈ**squirrel** type of squirrel with folds of skin between its front and back legs, allowing it to glide long distances through the air.

ˌ**flying** ˈ**start 1** start to a race in which the competitors are already running as they cross the starting line. **2** (idm) **get off to a flying start** begin sth well; have an initial advantage: *Our holiday got off to a flying start because the weather was good and the trains were on time.*

ˌ**flying** ˈ**tackle** (in Rugby football, etc) tackle made while running or jumping.

ˌ**flying** ˈ**visit** very brief or hasty visit.

Flying Dutchman /ˌflaɪɪŋ ˈdʌtʃmən/ **the Flying Dutchman** ghostly ship that sailors say can be seen around the Cape of Good Hope when a disaster is about to occur. The legend was used by *Wagner in one of his operas.

flyleaf /ˈflaɪli:f/ *n* (*pl* **-leaves** /-li:vz/) blank page at the beginning or end of a book.

Flynn /flɪn/ Errol (1909-59), Australian film actor. He became famous as the handsome swashbuckling hero of Hollywood adventure films, esp those of Michael *Curtiz, such as *The Adventures of Robin Hood.*

flyover /ˈflaɪəʊvə(r)/ *n* **1** (*Brit*) (*US* **overpass**) bridge which carries one road or railway above another. ⇨ illus at MOTORWAY. **2** (*US*) = FLY-PAST (FLY[2]).

fly-post /ˈflaɪpəʊst/ *v* **(a)** [I] put up posters, etc in places where this is not allowed. **(b)** [Tn] cover (walls, etc) with posters in this way.

flysheet /ˈflaɪʃi:t/ *n* **1** additional outer cover for a tent to give protection from rain. **2** small pamphlet of two or four pages.

flywheel /ˈflaɪwi:l; *US* -hwi:l/ *n* heavy wheel revolving on a shaft to keep a machine operating at an even speed.

Fm *symb* fermium.

FM *abbr* **1** Field Marshal. **2** /ˌef ˈem/ (*radio*) frequency modulation. Cf AM 1.

fm *abbr* fathom(s).

f-number /ˈefnʌmbə(r)/ *n* (*photography*) number showing the ratio of focal length to the diameter of a camera lens. The lower the f-number is, the wider the aperture will be, causing the film to be more exposed.

FO /ˌef ˈəʊ/ *abbr* (*Brit*) (formerly) Foreign Office: *He used to work at the FO.* Cf FCO.

foal /fəʊl/ *n* **1** young of a horse or of a related animal, eg a donkey. **2** (idm) **in/with foal** (of a female horse, etc) pregnant.

▷ **foal** *v* [I] give birth to a foal.

foam /fəʊm/ *n* [U] **1 (a)** mass of small, usu white, air bubbles formed in or on a liquid: *The breaking waves left the beach covered with foam.* **(b)** frothy bubbles of saliva or perspiration. **2** any of various chemical substances forming a thick bubbly mass and used for different purposes: ˈ*shaving foam.* **3** rubber or plastic in a spongy form, used to fill seats, cushions, etc: [attrib] ˌ*foam* ˈ*rubber.*

▷ **foam** *v* [I, Ipr] form or send out foam; froth: *a glass of foaming beer* ○ *The sick dog foamed at the mouth.* ○ (*fig*) *After having to wait an hour the customer was foaming (at the mouth) with rage,* ie obviously very angry.

foamy *adj* full of or like foam.

fob[1] /fɒb/ *n* **1** chain or ribbon to which a pocket-watch is attached. **2** ornament, esp a watch, hung from such a chain. **3** ornament attached to a key-ring.

fob[2] /fɒb/ *v* (**-bb-**) (phr v) **fob sb off (with sth)** trick sb into being satisfied (with sth inferior, an excuse, etc): *I won't be fobbed off this time — I'm determined to say what I think.* ○ *You can't fob an expert off with cheap imitations.* **fob sth off on/onto sb** trick or deceive sb into buying or accepting sth inferior: *Don't try fobbing off last year's goods on me!*

fob /ˌef əʊ ˈbi:/ *abbr* (*commerce*) (of cargo) free on board (ie transported to the ship and loaded without the buyer paying extra).

focal /ˈfəʊkl/ *adj* [attrib] of or at a focus.

□ **focal** ˈ**length** (also **focal** ˈ**distance**) distance between the centre of a mirror or a lens and its focus.

ˈ**focal point** something that is the centre of interest or activity: *Reducing unemployment is the focal point of the government's plans.*

fo'c's'le = FORECASTLE.

focus /ˈfəʊkəs/ *n* (*pl* ~**es** or **foci** /ˈfəʊsaɪ/) ⇨ Usage at DATA. **1** [C] point at which rays (of light, sound, etc) meet or from which they appear to come. **2** [C] point or distance at which (the outline of) an object is most clearly seen by the eye or through a lens. **3** [C] adjustment or device on a lens to produce a clear image: *The focus on my camera isn't working properly.* **4** [C usu *sing*] centre of activity, interest, etc: *Her beauty makes her the focus of attention.* ○ *In tonight's programme our focus is on Germany.* **5** (idm) **be in** ˈ**focus; bring sth/come into focus** (cause sth to) be or become clearly seen or sharply defined: *Bring the object into focus if you want a sharp photograph.* **be/go out of** ˈ**focus** not be or no longer be clearly seen, etc: *The children's faces were badly out of focus* (ie were very blurred) *in the photograph.*

▷ **focus** *v* (**-s-** or **-ss-**) **1 (a)** [I] become able to see clearly: *His eyes focused slowly in the dark room.* **(b)** [Tn, Tn·pr] ~ **sth (on sth)** cause sth to be concentrated (at a point): *If you focus the sun's rays through a magnifying glass on a dry leaf, it will start to burn.* **(c)** [Tn, Tn·pr] ~ **sth (on sth)** adjust the focus(2) of (a lens or the eye): *Focus your camera (on those trees).* **2 (a)** [I, Ipr] ~ **(on sth)** concentrate (on sth): *I'm so tired I can't focus (on anything) today.* **(b)** [Tn, Tn·pr] ~ **sth (on sth)** concentrate (one's attention, etc) on (sth): *Please focus your minds on the following problem.*

fodder /ˈfɒdə(r)/ *n* [U] dried food, hay, etc for horses and farm animals.

foe /fəʊ/ *n* (*fml or dated*) enemy.

foetus (*US* **fetus**) /ˈfi:təs/ *n* young human, animal, bird, etc that has developed within the womb or egg but has not yet been born or hatched. Cf EMBRYO 1.

▷ **foetal** (*US* **fetal**) /ˈfi:tl/ *adj* of or like a foetus: *She curled up her legs and arms into a foetal position,* ie like that of a foetus in the womb.

fog /fɒg; *US* fɔ:g/ *n* **1 (a)** [U] thick cloud of tiny drops of water close to or just above land or sea; thick mist: *Dense fog is covering roads in the north and visibility is very poor.* ○ *Patches of fog will clear by mid-morning.* **(b)** [C] instance or period of this: *We get heavy fogs on this coast in winter.* ⇨ Usage. **2** [C, U] (area of) cloudiness on a photographic negative, etc, making the image unclear. **3** (idm) **in a fog** puzzled and confused: *I'm in a complete fog about computer technology — I don't understand it at all.*

▷ **fog** *v* (**-gg-**) **1** [I, Ip, Tn, Tn·p] cover (sth) or become covered with fog: *The windscreen has fogged (over/up).* ○ *Steam has fogged the bathroom mirror.* **2 (a)** [Tn] cause cloudiness on (a photographic negative, etc): *Shut the door or the light will fog the film.* **(b)** [I] (of a photographic negative, etc) become cloudy. **3** [Tn] puzzle or confuse (sb): *I'm a bit fogged by these instructions.* **4** [Tn] obscure or confuse (sth being discussed): *complicated language that just fogs the real issues.* **foggy** *adj* (**-ier, -iest**) **1** not clear because of fog; very misty: *foggy weather* ○ *a foggy day.* **2** obscure; confused; vague: *His ideas on this subject are a bit foggy.* **3** (idm) **not have the faintest/foggiest** ⇨ FAINT[1].

□ ˈ**fog-bank** *n* mass of dense fog on the sea.

ˈ**fog-bound** *adj* unable to travel or operate normally because of fog; trapped by fog: *fog-bound planes, passengers* ○ *a fog-bound airport, harbour.*

ˈ**fog-horn** *n* instrument that makes a loud blaring noise to warn ships of danger when it is foggy: (*joc or derog*) *He's got a voice like a fog-horn*, ie a loud, harsh voice.

ˈ**fog-lamp** *n* powerful light on the front of a car, etc for use in fog.

NOTE ON USAGE: **Fog**, **mist** and **haze** are all clouds of water vapour at ground level and above. They indicate different degrees of thickness: **fog** is the thickest and **haze** the least thick. **Haze** also occurs when it is very hot: *a heat-haze.* **Smog** is an unhealthy mixture of smoke and fog in the air of some industrial cities. Since the *Clean Air Acts smog has become quite rare in Britain, but air pollution makes it still common in certain cities in Europe and America

fogy (also **fogey**) /ˈfəʊgɪ/ *n* (*pl* **-ies** *or* ∼**s**) person with old-fashioned ideas which he is unwilling to change: *Come to the disco and stop being such an old fogey!*

foible /ˈfɔɪbl/ *n* small, usu harmless, peculiarity or weakness in a person's character: *We all have our little foibles.*

foil[1] /fɔɪl/ *n* **1** [U] metal rolled or hammered into a very thin flexible sheet: *tin, aluminium foil*, ie such as is wrapped round bars of chocolate. **2** [C] person or thing that contrasts with, and so emphasizes, the qualities of another: *Her sparkling jewellery served as the perfect foil for her fine complexion.*

foil[2] /fɔɪl/ *v* [Tn] prevent (sb) from carrying out a plan; prevent (a plan, etc) from succeeding; thwart; frustrate: *He was foiled in his attempt to deceive us/His attempt to deceive us was foiled.*

foil[3] /fɔɪl/ *n* long thin light sword with a protective button on the point, used in fencing (FENCE[2]). ⇨ illus at FENCING. Cf ÉPÉE, SABRE.

foist /fɔɪst/ *v* (phr v) **foist sth on sb** force sb into accepting sth not wanted: *He's religious but he doesn't try to foist his beliefs on everyone.*

fold

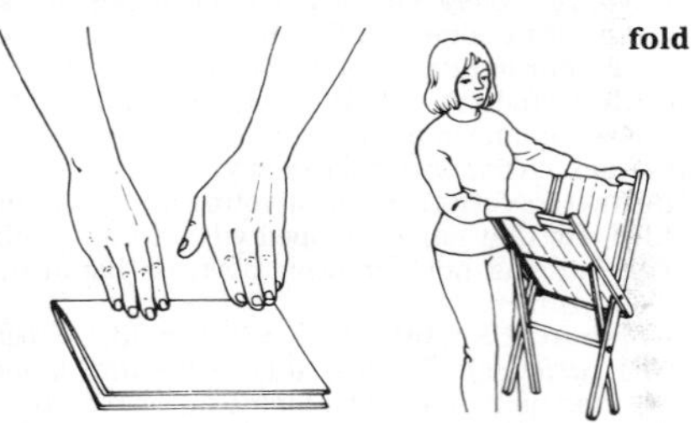

FOLD FOLD (UP)

fold[1] /fəʊld/ *v* **1 (a)** [Tn, Tn·pr, Tn·p] ∼ **sth (up)** bend or turn sth so that one part of it lies on another; close or flatten sth by pressing two parts of it together: *fold clothes (up) neatly* ○ *a folded newspaper* ○ *The bird folded its wings.* ○ *Fold the letter (in two) before putting it in the envelope.* **(b)** [I, Ip] ∼ **(up)** be able to be bent for storage, easy carrying, etc: *This garden table folds (up) flat.* ○ *a folding chair, bed, bicycle, etc.* ⇨ illus. **2** [Tn·pr] ∼ **A in B**/∼ **B around A** cover or wrap sth in sth: *Fold this glass bowl in newspaper/Fold newspaper round this glass bowl.* **3** [I, Ip] ∼ **(up)** (*infml*) **(a)** cease to function; stop trading: *The company folded (up) last week.* **(b)** cease to be performed: *The play folded within a fortnight.* **4** (idm) **fold one's** ˈ**arms** bring one's arms together and cross them over one's chest. **fold sb/sth in one's arms** hold sb/sth closely: *Father folded the tiny child in his arms.* **fold one's** ˈ**hands** bring or clasp one's hands together, eg when praying. **5** (phr v) **fold (sth) away** (cause sth to) become more compact for storage by folding: *The bed folds away (into the wall).* **fold sth in; fold sth into sth** (in cooking) mix one ingredient gently with another, usu with a spoon: *Fold in the beaten whites of two eggs.* **fold up** collapse because of pain or great laughter: *The boxer folded up in agony.* ○ *The comedian had the audience folding up.*

▷ **fold** *n* **1** part of sth, esp fabric, that is folded or hangs as if folded: *a dress hanging in loose folds.* **2** mark or line made by folding; crease. **3** hollow among hills or mountains. **4** bend in the line of rocks below the earth's surface that has been caused by movements in the earth's crust.

□ ˈ**foldaway** *adj* that can be folded up or away for storage; collapsible: *a foldaway bed.*

fold[2] /fəʊld/ *n* **1** [C] area in a field surrounded by a fence or wall where sheep are kept for safety. **2 the fold** [sing] group of people with the same (usu religious) beliefs. **3** (idm) **return to the fold** ⇨ RETURN[1].

-fold *suff* (with numbers forming *adjs* and *advs*) multiplied by; having the specified number of parts: *tenfold* ○ *twofold.*

folder /ˈfəʊldə(r)/ *n* cover for holding loose papers, etc, made of stiff material, esp cardboard, folded together.

foliage /ˈfəʊlɪɪdʒ/ *n* [U] (all the) leaves of a tree or plant; leaves with their stems and branches: *a mass of green foliage* ○ *My flower arrangement needs more foliage.*

foliate /ˈfəʊlɪət/ *adj* (*botany*) having leaves.

▷ **foliate** /ˈfəʊlɪeɪt/ *v* [I] (of metals) split into thin sheets or layers. **foliation** *n* [U].

folic acid /ˌfəʊlɪk ˈæsɪd, ˌfɒlɪk/ vitamin of the B complex found in leafy green vegetables, liver and kidney. A lack of it leads to anaemia.

folio /ˈfəʊlɪəʊ/ *n* (*pl* ∼**s**) **1 (a)** [C] large sheet of paper folded once, making two leaves or four pages of a book. **(b)** [C] book made of sheets folded in this way: *We have several early folios for sale.* **(c)** [U] largest size and format for a book: *drawings published in folio* ○ [attrib] *a folio volume.* **2** [C] **(a)** sheet of paper numbered on one side only. **(b)** page number of a book.

folk /fəʊk/ *n* **1** (also *esp US* **folks**) [pl *v*] **(a)** people in general: *Some old folk(s) have peculiar tastes.* ○ (sometimes used when talking to people in a friendly way) *Well, folks, what are we going to do today?* **(b)** people from a particular (part of a) country, or associated with a particular way of life: *country folk* ○ *townsfolk* ○ *farming folk.* **2 folks** [pl] (*infml*) **(a)** members of one's own family; relatives: *How are your folks?* **(b)** (*esp US*) parents: *Have you ever met my folks?* **3** = FOLK-MUSIC: [attrib] *a folk concert.*

□ ˈ**folk-dance** *n* (music for a) traditional dance of a community or country.

ˈ**folklore** *n* [U] (study of the) traditions, stories, customs, etc of a community. **folklorist** /ˈfəʊklɔːrɪst/ *n* person who studies folklore, esp as an academic subject.

ˈ**folk memory** the way in which the past is remembered by ordinary people, rather than recorded by historians.

ˈ**folk-music** (also **folk**), ˈ**folk-song** *ns* music or song in the traditional style of a country.

The study of folk-music was particularly popular in Britain and Europe in the early 20th century, and many folk-songs have been collected and used in classical music by composers like *Bartok, *Vaughan Williams and *Britten. Folk-music remains a popular form, and in the second half of the 20th century new songs, many of them protesting about social injustice, have been written, eg by Bob *Dylan. Folk songs did not actually evolve through oral tradition, as the name perhaps suggests, but are the work of individual composers (often unknown). Most British folk music is regional, the best known being English morris dancing, Scottish Highland dancing and the hornpipe, traditionally associated with English sailors. The English Folk Dance and Song Society, founded in the 1930s, records and preserves folk music.

ˈ**folk-tale** *n* popular story passed on in spoken form from one generation to the next.

folksy /ˈfəʊksɪ/ *adj* (*infml*) simple in manners and customs; friendly and sociable; typical of ordinary people.

foll *abbr* following.

follicle /ˈfɒlɪkl/ *n* very small cavity in the body that protects or nourishes a cell, esp one containing the root of a hair. ▷ **follicular** /fəˈlɪkjʊlə(r)/ *adj*: *follicular cells.*

follow /ˈfɒləʊ/ *v* **1 (a)** [I, Ip, Tn, Tn·pr] ∼ **sth (by/with sth)** (cause sth to) come, go or take place after (sb/sth else) (in space, time or order): *The duckling followed its mother everywhere.* ○ *You go first and I'll follow (on) later.* ○ *Monday follows Sunday.* ○ *One misfortune followed another.* ○ *The lightning was quickly followed by/with heavy thunder.* ○ *You should follow your treatment with plenty of rest in bed.* **(b)** [Tn] go after (sb) in order to catch him; chase: *The police were following him.* **2** [Tn] go along (a road, path, etc): *Follow this road until you get to the corner, then turn left.* **3** [Tn] **(a)** act according to (sth): *follow the instructions* ○ *follow sb's advice.* **(b)** accept (sb/sth) as a guide, leader or example; copy: *follow the latest fashions* ○ *follow the teachings of Muhammad.* **4** [Tn] carry on (sth) as one's particular job or trade; pursue: *follow a legal career.* **5** [I, Tn] understand (the explanation or meaning of sth); understand (the plot of a story): *I don't follow.* ○ *I couldn't follow his argument at all.* **6** [Tn] pay close attention to (sth); watch or listen very closely: *The President's wife follows his every word.* ○ *The cat followed the mouse's movements carefully.* **7** [Tn] take an active interest in (sth): *Have you been following the basketball tournament?* ○ *Millions of fans follow the TV soap operas devotedly.* **8** [Tn] read (a text) while listening to the same text being spoken by sb else; read (a musical score) while listening to the music being performed: *Follow the text while I read it out to you.* **9 (a)** [I, Ipr, Ip, Tn] ∼ **(on) (from sth)** result from sth; happen as a consequence: *Inevitably, a quarrel followed between the two sides.* ○ *Disease often follows (on from) starvation because the body is weakened.* **(b)** [I, Ipr] ∼ **(from sth)** happen as a necessary and logical consequence: *I don't see how that follows (from what you've said).* ○ *If a = b and b = c it follows that a = c.* ○ *She's not in the office but it doesn't necessarily follow that she's ill.* **10** [Tn] develop or happen in (a particular way): *His speech followed the usual pattern.* **11** (idm) **as follows** (used to introduce a list): *The main events were as follows: first, the president's speech, secondly the secretary's reply and thirdly, the chairman's summing-up.* **follow one's (own)** ˈ**bent** do what one is interested in and enjoys doing. **follow the** ˈ**crowd** be content to do what most people do: *Not wanting to make my controversial views known yet, I preferred to follow the crowd for a while.* **follow sb's example/lead** do as sb else has done; accept and follow sb else's decision: *I don't want you follow my example and rush into marriage.* **follow (the) hounds** hunt foxes with a pack of hounds. **follow in sb's** ˈ**footsteps** do as sb else does; follow a similar occupation or life-style as sb else: *She works in theatre, following in her father's footsteps.* **follow one's (own) ˈnose** (a) go straight forward: *The police station is a mile ahead up the hill - just follow your nose.* (b) act instinctively: *Since you don't know the language I can only suggest that you follow your nose.* **follow ˈsuit** act or behave in the way that sb else has just done: *One of the major banks has lowered its interest rates and the other banks are expected to follow suit.* **to follow** (in a restaurant, etc) as the next course of a meal: *To follow, we'll have peaches and cream, please.* **12** (phr v) **follow on** (of a side in cricket) bat again immediately after failing to get the necessary number of runs in the first innings. **follow through** (in tennis, golf, etc) complete a stroke by continuing to move the racket, club, etc after hitting the ball. **follow sth through** carry out or continue sth to the end; complete sth: *Starting projects is one thing, following them through is another.* **follow sth up** (a) take further action on sth; develop or exploit sth: *You should follow up your letter with a phone call.* (b) investigate sth closely: *follow up a lead, clue, rumour.*

▷ **follower** *n* person who follows; supporter of a particular person, cause or belief: *He's a follower, not a leader.* ○ *the followers of Mahatma Gandhi.*

□ **ˌfollow-my-ˈleader** (*US* **ˌfollow-the-ˈleader**) *n* [U] children's game in which the other players have to do exactly what the leader does, eg hop, hold out a hand, etc.

ˌfollow-ˈon *n* (in cricket) second innings of a team immediately following its first innings.

ˈfollow-through *n* (in tennis, golf, etc) final part of a stroke after the ball has been hit.

ˈfollow-up *n* something done to continue or exploit what has already been started or done: *As a follow-up to the television series the BBC is publishing a book.*

following /ˈfɒləʊɪŋ/ *adj* **1** next in time: *It rained on the day we arrived, but the following day was sunny.* **2** about to be mentioned: *Answer the following question(s).*

▷ **following** *n* **1** [sing] group of supporters: *Our party has a large following in the south.* **2 the following** [sing or pl *v*] what follows or comes next: *The following is of the greatest importance.* ○ *The following are extracts from the original article.*

following *prep* after (sth); as a result of: *demonstrations following the murder of the union leader.*

folly /ˈfɒlɪ/ *n* **1** [U] ~ (**to do sth**) foolishness; lack of wisdom: *an act of folly* ○ *It's utter folly to go swimming in this cold weather.* **2** [C] foolish or unwise act, idea or practice: *You'll pay later for your follies.* **3** [C] very expensive ornamental building that serves no practical purpose.

foment /fəʊˈment/ *v* [Tn] **1** arouse or increase (trouble or discontent): *foment discord, ill feeling, civil disorder, etc.* **2** apply warmth and moisture to (a part of the body) to lessen pain or discomfort.

▷ **fomentation** /ˌfəʊmenˈteɪʃn/ *n* **1** [U] act of fomenting. **2** [C] thing used for fomenting.

fond /fɒnd/ *adj* (**-er**, **-est**) **1** [attrib] (a) kind and loving; affectionate: *a fond look, gesture, embrace, etc* ○ *fond eyes.* (b) foolishly loving; indulgent or doting: *spoilt by fond parents.* **2** [pred] ~ **of sb/(doing) sth** having a great liking for sb/(doing) sth: *I've always been very fond of you.* ○ *fond of music, cooking, going to parties* ○ *John's extremely fond of pointing out other people's mistakes*, ie He enjoys doing this constantly. **3** [attrib] (of wishes or ambitions) hoped for, but not likely to be met or to come true; foolishly held: *fond hopes of success.*

▷ **fondly** *adv* **1** lovingly; gently: *He held her hand fondly.* **2** in a foolishly optimistic way; navely: *I fondly imagined that you cared.*

fondness *n* [U] ~ (**for sb/sth**) liking and affection: *his fondness for his eldest grandchild.*

Fonda /ˈfɒndə/ Henry (1905-82), American actor. His dignified acting style produced moving performances, esp in *The Grapes of Wrath* and *Twelve Angry Men*, as a figure fighting against fate or injustice.

fondant /ˈfɒndənt/ *n* [U, C] soft sweet made of flavoured sugar that melts in the mouth.

fondle /ˈfɒndl/ *v* [Tn] touch or stroke (sb/sth) gently and lovingly; caress: *fondle a baby, doll, kitten.*

fondue /ˈfɒndjuː/ *n* [C, U] **1** dish of melted cheese, mixed with wine and flavourings, into which pieces of bread are dipped. **2** dish of hot oil or sauce into which pieces of meat, seafood, etc are dipped: *fish fondue.*

font /fɒnt/ *n* **1** basin or vessel in a church, usu carved from stone, to hold water for baptisms; basin for holy water. **2** = FOUNT.

fontanelle /ˌfɒntəˈnel/ *n* gap, covered by a membrane, between the bones of a baby's skull before they grow together.

Fonteyn /ˈfɒnteɪn/ Dame Margot (1919-91), British ballet dancer. Her brilliant and expressive dancing won her international fame. She is particularly remembered for her performances with Rudolf *Nureyev and in the ballets of Sir Frederick *Ashton.

food /fuːd/ *n* **1** (a) [U] any substance that people or animals eat or drink or plants take in to maintain life and growth: *a shortage of food in some countries.* (b) [U] solid substance of this sort: *We cannot survive for long without food and drink.* ⇨ article. **2** [C, U] specific type of food: *breakfast food* ○ *baby, health foods* ○ *frozen, processed foods.* **3** (idm) **food for ˈthought** something to think about seriously.

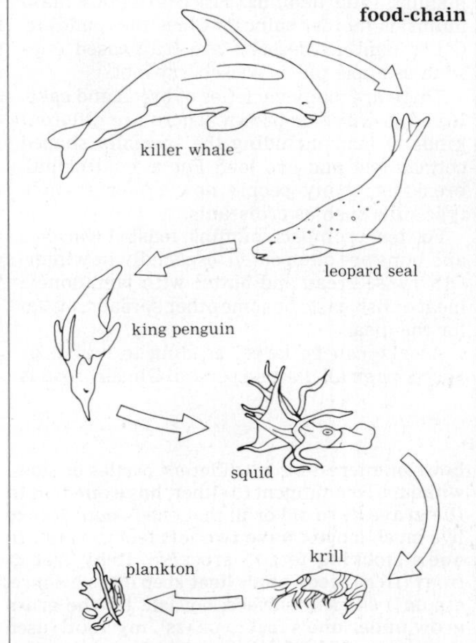

□ **ˈfood-chain** *n* series of living beings arranged so that each being feeds on the one below it in the series. A simple example of such a chain is: grass (eaten by sheep), sheep (eaten by humans), humans. As many animals feed on different types of food, more complex relationships, called **food-webs**, are created. ⇨ illus.

ˈfood-gatherer *n* member of an early civilization who collected food or obtained it through farming rather than by hunting. **ˈfood-gathering** *n* [U], *adj.*

ˈfood poisoning (also *dated* **ˈptomaine poisoning**) illness of the stomach caused by eating food that contains harmful bacteria.

ˈfood processor electrical appliance that mixes, slices or chops food.

ˈfoodstuff *n* any substance used as food: *essential foodstuffs.*

ˈfood value nutritional power of food, usu measured in vitamins, minerals, etc: *Most sweet things don't have much food value.*

fool[1] /fuːl/ *n* **1** (*derog*) person who acts unwisely; person lacking in good sense or judgement; idiot: *What fools we were not to see the trap!* ○ *And I was fool enough* (ie so stupid as) *to believe him.* **2** (formerly) man employed by a king, noble, etc to amuse others with jokes and tricks; clown or jester. **3** (idm) **act/play the fool** behave irresponsibly or so as to amuse (and perhaps annoy) others. **be a fool for one's ˈpains** do sth for which one gets no reward or thanks. **be ˌno ˈfool; be ˌnobody's ˈfool** be a wise and clever person; not be easily deceived. **a ˌfool and his ˌmoney are ˌsoon ˈparted** (*saying*) a foolish person spends, or can be tricked into spending, all his money. (**be sent/go on**) **a ˈfool's errand** (be sent/go on) a senseless or an unprofitable mission. (**be/live in**) **a fool's ˈparadise** (be/live in) a state of (false) happiness that cannot last. **make a ˈfool of oneself/sb** behave foolishly/trick sb into behaving foolishly. (**the**) **ˌmore fool ˈsb** (used as an exclamation) the person specified is especially unwise for behaving in the way he does. (**there is**) **ˌno fool like an ˈold fool** (*saying*) the foolish behaviour of an older person seems even more foolish because he is expected to act more sensibly than a younger person. **not/never suffer fools gladly** ⇨ SUFFER.

▷ **fool** *v* **1** (a) [I, Ip] ~ (**about/around**) behave stupidly or foolishly: *Stop fooling about with that knife or someone will get hurt.* (b) [I] tease or joke; pretend: *I was only fooling when I said I'd lost your keys.* **2** [Tn] trick or deceive (sb): *You can't/don't fool me!* **3** (phr v) **fool about/around** waste time; be idle: *I was meant to be working on Sunday, but I just fooled around all day.*

□ **ˌApril ˈFool** person tricked on April Fool's Day. **April ˈFool's Day** 1 April.

ˈfool's gold yellowish mineral, a sulphide of iron, that is sometimes mistaken for gold.

fool[2] /fuːl/ *n* [C, U] (usu in compounds) cold light pudding of crushed cooked fruit mixed with cream or custard: *rhubarb fool.*

foolery /ˈfuːlərɪ/ *n* [U, C] foolish behaviour.

foolhardy /ˈfuːlhɑːdɪ/ *adj* (**-ier**, **-iest**) foolishly bold or rash; reckless: *It was foolhardy (of him) to go swimming alone.* ▷ **foolhardiness** *n* [U].

foolish /ˈfuːlɪʃ/ *adj* **1** (a) (of people) lacking good sense or judgement; silly: *She's a foolish interfering old woman!* ○ *And I was foolish enough to believe him!* ○ *It would be foolish (of us) to pretend that the accident never happened.* (b) (of actions, statements, etc) showing a lack of good sense or judgement; unwise or stupid: *a foolish decision, comment, reply, etc.* **2** [usu pred] made to feel or look ridiculous and embarrassed; stupid: *I felt very foolish having to stand up and give a speech.* ○ *He's afraid of looking foolish in front of all his friends.* **3** (idm) **penny wise pound foolish** ⇨ PENNY. ▷ **foolishly** *adv.* **foolishness** *n* [U].

foolproof /ˈfuːlpruːf/ *adj* **1** not capable of going wrong or of being misunderstood; very plain and simple: *a foolproof method, plan, scheme, etc.* **2** not capable of going wrong or of being used wrongly; reliable and easy to operate: *a foolproof security system.*

foolscap /ˈfuːlskæp/ *n* [U] large size of writing or printing paper, about 330 x 200 (or 400) mm.

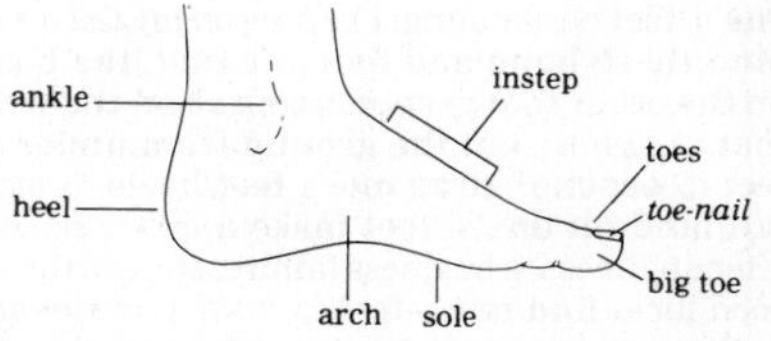

foot[1] /fʊt/ *n* (*pl* **feet** /fiːt/) **1** [C] lowest part of the leg, below the ankle, on which a person or animal stands: *He rose to his feet*, ie stood up. ○ *walking round the house in bare feet*, ie not wearing socks, shoes, etc ○ [attrib] *a foot switch, brake, pump, etc*, ie operated by one's foot, not one's hand. ⇨ illus. **2** [C *usu sing*] part of a sock, stocking, etc that

Food

Traditional British food, with its emphasis on puddings, pies, cakes, meat dishes and fried food, no longer forms a main part of most people's diet because of the trend towards lighter, more easily prepared food. Traditional methods of preserving meat and fish, such as salting and smoking, are no longer necessary and food such as kippers (smoked herrings), salt pork and beef, and bacon are eaten less frequently than before. Nevertheless, many traditional dishes survive, especially those associated with special occasions.

There are many regional dishes, usually named after a county, such as Lancashire hotpot, roast beef and Yorkshire pudding, and Cornish pasties, which are popular all over the country. There are many different kinds of regional cheese, including the best-known, Cheddar, as well as Cheshire, Leicestershire, Double Gloucester, Caerphilly, Wensleydale and Stilton, each with its own distinctive colour, flavour and consistency. Welsh rarebit is a popular dish of toasted cheese.

The British have always liked meat dishes, from the traditional roast beef to popular favourites such as 'bangers and mash' (sausages and potatoes), shepherd's pie (also called cottage pie), toad in the hole (sausages baked in batter), steak and kidney pudding, mixed grill, steak, and bacon and eggs. Scotland has its traditional haggis. Beef, lamb, mutton, pork and chicken are the most common kinds of meat. Sauces that traditionally accompany meat are mint sauce for lamb, horseradish sauce for beef, apple sauce for pork and cranberry sauce for turkey.

Fish and chips is a favourite fish dish, although fish fingers and fish cakes are also popular, especially with children. Kippers are eaten either for breakfast or supper. Plaice, cod, herrings and mackerel are the most common kinds of fish. Trout and salmon are usually considered a luxury, especially when they have been smoked.

Eggs are eaten boiled, fried, poached or scrambled, with boiled eggs usually preferred soft, and traditionally cooked for three minutes.

Potatoes ('spuds') are one of the most common vegetables, served either as chips, roast or mashed potatoes, or baked in their skins (jacket potatoes).

Breakfast often begins with fruit juice, followed by cereal to which milk and sugar are added. Some people, especially in Scotland, still prefer porridge to cereal, and eat it with milk and sugar or salt. A traditional English breakfast also includes a cooked dish such as bacon and eggs, but few people eat this nowadays, preferring a lighter 'continental' breakfast. Toast and marmalade, and tea or coffee, complete the meal.

Puddings of all kinds are typically British, and the word itself can describe both savoury and sweet dishes, or mean simply 'dessert' in general. Among the best-known sweet dishes are rice pudding, bread-and-butter pudding, steamed pudding, suet pudding and Christmas pudding. Plum pudding (which does not contain plums) is another name for Christmas pudding. Other familiar desserts are fruit-based ones such as apple pie or gooseberry fool.

There are many varieties of bread and cake. Bread is white or brown. There are different kinds of loaf, including the specially shaped cottage loaf and cob loaf. For a 'continental' breakfast, many people now prefer French-type rolls such as croissants.

For tea, crumpets, muffins, toasted teacakes and buns are often eaten, especially in winter. Otherwise bread and butter with jam, honey, meat or fish paste or some other spread is usual for the meal.

A cake can be large, needing to be cut or sliced, or small, for one person. Gingerbread is not bread but a ginger-flavoured cake. Bath buns, Chelsea buns and doughnuts are all made from bread dough. The many different kinds of biscuit include chocolate digestive biscuits, ginger nuts and custard creams. Water biscuits or cream crackers are usually eaten with cheese.

Some foods are traditionally prepared for a particular festival or celebration. Christmas pudding is eaten at Christmas, pancakes are often served (as a sweet course, with lemon and sugar) on Shrove Tuesday, and hot cross buns are eaten on Good Friday. Special big cakes are prepared for weddings and birthdays. Wedding cakes are usually elaborately iced and decorated, with two or more tiers; birthday cakes are also normally iced, with the person's age shown by the number of small candles stuck in the icing.

The British enjoy eating sweets, especially chocolate, and the many popular types of confectionery include toffee, marshmallows, mints and boiled sweets. Sticks of rock are traditionally popular in holiday resorts, as are ice cream, candy floss and other 'fun foods'.

In recent years there has been an increase in the consumption of 'convenience' and unhealthy 'junk' foods, but also a growing interest in healthy, natural or 'organic' foods. At the same time, the British diet now includes many dishes that would formerly have been regarded as exotic or unusual. Among the most popular are Chinese, Indian and Italian, which have largely been popularized by ethnic restaurants.

In the USA too the food of many different nationalities has become part of the national diet. Particularly American dishes, though, are clam chowder (a thick soup containing clams), southern fried chicken, pecan pie, pumpkin pie, hot dogs, burgers, apple pie and hash browns (potato pancakes, often served at breakfast).

covers the foot. 3 [C] (*pl* **feet** or, in informal use and attributively, **foot**) (*abbr* **ft**) measure of length: 12 inches: *We're flying at 35 000 feet.* ○ *'How tall are you?' 'Five foot nine'*, ie five feet and nine inches. ○ [attrib] *a 6-foot high wall.* ⇨ App 9, 10. 4 [sing] **the ~ of sth** (a) the lowest part of sth; base or bottom of sth: *at the foot of the stairs* ○ *They camped at the foot of the mountain.* ○ *at the foot of the page.* (b) the lower end of a bed or grave: *Spare blankets lay at the foot of each bed.* 5 [U] (*arch*) manner of walking or moving: *light/swift/fleet of foot.* 6 [C] unit of rhythm in a line of poetry containing one stressed syllable and one or more unstressed syllables, as in the four divisions of *For ˈmen / may ˈcome / and ˈmen / may ˈgo.* 7 (idm) **be on one's ˈfeet** be standing: *I've been on my feet all day.* **bind/tie sb hand and foot** ⇨ HAND[1]. **the boot is on the other foot** ⇨ BOOT. **catch sb on the wrong foot** ⇨ CATCH[1]. **cut the ground from under sb's feet** ⇨ GROUND[1]. **drag one's feet/heels** ⇨ DRAG[2]. **fall/land on one's ˈfeet** make a quick recovery after an illness, a business failure, etc, esp through good luck. **find one's feet** ⇨ FIND. **from head to foot/toe** ⇨ HEAD[1]. **get/have a foot in the door** gain/have a first introduction to a profession, an organization, etc: *It's difficult to get a foot in the door of publishing.* **get/have cold feet** ⇨ COLD[1]. **have feet of ˈclay** have some basic weakness or fault. **have the ball at one's feet** ⇨ BALL[1]. **have, etc one's/both feet on the ˈground** be sensible, realistic and practical. **have a foot in both ˈcamps** have an interest in two different parties or sides, without a commitment to either. **have one foot in the grave** be so old or ill that one is not likely to live much longer. **have two left feet** ⇨ LEFT[2]. **in one's stocking feet** ⇨ STOCKING. **itchy feet** ⇨ ITCHY (ITCH). **keep one's ˈfeet** keep one's balance, esp on a slippery surface; not fall. **let the grass grow under one's feet** ⇨ GRASS[1]. **my ˈfoot!** (used to express scornful rejection of what sb has just said) nonsense! rubbish! **on one's ˈfeet** completely recovered from an illness or a set-back: *After his wife's death it took him two years to get back on his feet.* ○ *Only our party's policies will put the country on its feet again.* **on foot** walking, rather than using any form of transport: *We're going on foot, not by car.* **the patter of tiny feet** ⇨ PATTER[2]. **pull the carpet/rug from under sb's feet** ⇨ PULL[2]. **put one's best foot forward** ⇨ BEST[1]. **put one's ˈfeet up** rest or relax in a chair or on a bed (esp, though not necessarily, with one's feet supported). **put one's ˈfoot down** be very firm in opposing sth which sb wishes to do: *Mother let us go to the party, but when it came to staying overnight, she put her foot down firmly.* **put one's ˈfoot in it** say or do sth that upsets, offends or embarrasses sb. **put a foot wrong** (esp in negative sentences) make a mistake: *I've never known him to put a foot wrong, no matter how delicate the issue.* **rush/run sb (clean) off his ˈfeet** make sb work very hard or move about a lot, so making him exhausted: *Before Christmas the shop assistants are rushed off their feet.* **set foot in/on sth** enter or visit (a place); arrive: *the first man to set foot on the moon* ○ *Don't ever set foot in this house again!* **set sb/sth on his/its ˈfeet** make sb/sth independent. **shake the dust off one's feet** ⇨ SHAKE[1]. **sit at sb's feet** ⇨ SIT. **stand on one's own (two) feet** be independent and able to take care of oneself: *Now that you're growing up you must learn to stand on your own two feet.* **start off on the right/wrong foot** ⇨ START[2]. **sweep sb off his feet** ⇨ SWEEP[1]. **take the weight off one's feet** ⇨ WEIGHT. **ten feet tall** pleased with and proud of onself: *be/feel/look/seem ten feet tall.* **under one's ˈfeet** disturbing one and being a nuisance: *The children are under my feet all day.* **wait on sb hand and foot** ⇨ WAIT[1]. **walk sb off his feet** ⇨ WALK[1].

▷ **-footer** /fʊtə(r)/ (forming compounds) person or thing of the specified length, height or width: *a six-footer*, ie a person who is six feet tall or thing that is six feet wide or long.

□ **ˌfoot-and-ˈmouth** *n* [U] (also **foot-and-mouth disease**) disease of cattle, etc which causes blisters on the mouth and feet.

ˈfoot-bridge *n* narrow bridge for the use of people who are walking.

ˈfootfall *n* sound of sb walking; sound of a footstep.

ˈfoot-fault *n* (in tennis) act of breaking the rules by placing one's feet inside the back line when serving.

ˈfoothill *n* [C usu *pl*] hill or low mountain at the base of a higher mountain or range of mountains.

ˈ**foothold** *n* 1 place where one's foot can be supported securely when climbing. 2 secure position in a business, profession, etc from which further progress may be made: *gain a firm foothold in the industry*.

ˈ**footlights** *n* [pl] row of lights along the front of the stage in a theatre. ⇨ illus at THEATRE.

ˈ**footloose** *adj* (idm) **footloose and fancy-ˈfree** without personal responsibilities or commitments; free to act as one pleases.

ˈ**footman** /-mən/ *n* (*pl* **-men**) male servant, usu in uniform, who admits visitors, serves food at table, etc.

ˈ**footmark** *n* = FOOTPRINT.

ˈ**footnote** *n* additional piece of information at the bottom of a page in a book. ⇨ App 14.

ˈ**footpath** *n* way or track along which people walk, esp in country areas. In England and Wales, footpaths are marked on *Ordnance Survey maps and are legal rights of way. They are often very old and people have the right to use them even if they cross private land. They allow people to discover the countryside, and organizations like the Ramblers' Association campaign to keep footpaths open and well maintained.

ˈ**footplate** *n* metal platform on which the driver and fireman stand in a locomotive.

ˈ**footprint** *n* [C usu *pl*] impression of a human or an animal foot on a surface; mark left by a foot: *leave footprints in the snow.* ⇨ illus: *muddy footprints on the kitchen floor*.

ˈ**foot-rot** *n* [U] 1 disease affecting the feet of cattle and sheep. 2 (*infml*) athlete's foot.

ˈ**foot-slog** *v* (**-gg-**) [I] (*infml*) walk for a long distance and so become very tired.

ˈ**footsore** *adj* having sore or tired feet, esp from walking a long way: *footsore travellers*.

ˈ**footstep** *n* [C] 1 (a) sound or mark of a step taken when walking: *I heard his footsteps in the hall.* (b) (distance covered by a) step taken when walking. 2 (idm) **follow in one's/sb's footsteps** ⇨ FOLLOW.

ˈ**footstool** (also **stool**) *n* low stool for resting the feet on when sitting in a chair.

ˈ**footway** *n* = FOOTPATH.

ˈ**footwear** *n* [U] anything worn on the feet, eg shoes and boots.

ˈ**footwork** *n* [U] (a) manner of moving or using the feet in sports such as boxing or dancing. (b) (*fig*) ability to react quickly to sudden danger, new opportunities, etc: *Thanks to agile footwork he always managed to escape his pursuers.*

foot[2] /fʊt/ *v* (idm) **foot the ˈbill (for sth)** be responsible for paying the cost of sth: *Who's going to foot the bill for all the repairs?* ˈ**foot it** (*infml*) walk; not travel by bus, etc.

▷ **-footed** (forming compound *adjs*) having feet of the specified kind or number: *bare-footed* ○ *flat-footed* ○ *four-footed*.

footage /ˈfʊtɪdʒ/ *n* [U] 1 length or distance measured in feet. 2 length of film made for the cinema or TV: *The film contained some old newsreel footage.*

football /ˈfʊtbɔːl/ *n* 1 [C] large round or oval inflated ball, usu of leather. 2 [U] any of several outdoor games between two teams, played with such a ball, esp *association football, Rugby football*, or *American football*. In Britain 'football' usu means association football, and this is the most popular form of the game in most parts of the world, though not in the USA: [attrib] (*Brit*) *a football match* ○ (*US*) *a football game*. ⇨ App 9. ⇨ article at SPORT.

▷ **footballer** *n* person who plays football, esp as a profession.

□ ˈ**football pools** (also **the pools**) form of gambling in which sb tries to forecast the results of football matches. ⇨ article at GAMBLING.

footing /ˈfʊtɪŋ/ *n* [sing] 1 secure grip with the feet; balance: *He lost his footing on the wet floor and fell.* 2 basis on which sth is established: *This enterprise is now on a firm footing and should soon show profits.* ○ *The army were put on a war footing*, ie were prepared for war. 3 position or status of sb/sth in relation to others; relationship: *The workers want to be on an equal footing with/on the same footing as the managers.*

footle /ˈfuːtl/ *v* [I, Ip] ~ (**about/around**) (*infml*) spend time aimlessly; do nothing in particular: *footle about all day.*

▷ **footling** /ˈfuːtlɪŋ/ *adj* unimportant; trivial: *footling little jobs.*

footsie /ˈfʊtsɪ/ *n* (idm) **play footsie with sb** (*infml*) touch sb's feet lightly with one's own feet, esp under a table, as a playful expression of affection or to arouse sexual interest.

fop /fɒp/ *n* (*derog*) man who is too concerned with his clothes and appearance; dandy.

▷ **foppish** *adj* of or like a fop.

for[1] /fə(r); *rare strong form* fɔː(r)/ *prep* 1 (indicating the person intended to receive or benefit from sth): *a letter for you* ○ *Are all these presents for me?* ○ *Save a piece for Mary.* ○ *Have you made a cup of tea for Mrs Watson?* 2 (indicating purpose or function): *go for a walk* ○ *It's a machine for slicing bread.* ○ *Are you learning English for pleasure or for your work?* ○ (*infml*) *What did you shout at him for?* ie Why did you shout at him? ○ *For sales to* (ie In order that sales may) *increase, we must lower our prices.* 3 (indicating destination, aim or reason): *depart for home* ○ *head for the shore* ○ *Is this the train for Glasgow?* ○ *Passengers for Oxford must change at Didcot.* ○ *She knew she was destined for a great future.* ○ *It's a book for* (ie intended to be read by or to) *children.* ○ *a chair for visitors* ○ *bicycles for sale or for hire.* 4 in order to help or benefit (sb/sth): *Would you please translate this letter for me?* ○ *What can I do for you?* ○ *fighting for their country* ○ *Take some aspirin for* (ie to lessen the pain caused by) *your headache.* ○ *The deputy manager ran the firm for* (ie instead of) *him while he was ill.* 5 as the price, reward or penalty of sth: *I bought a book for £3.* ○ *She gave me their old TV for nothing.* ○ *He got a medal for bravery.* ○ *You can go to prison for dangerous driving.* 6 as the replacement of (sth else): *exchange one's car for a new one* ○ *Don't translate word for word.* 7 in defence or support of (sb/sth): *Are you for or against the new road scheme?* ○ *Three cheers for the winner!* ○ *We're petitioning for our right to keep a school in our village.* ○ *I'm all for pubs being open all day.* 8 (a) as a representative of (sb/sth): *I am speaking for all the workers in this firm.* ○ *Who's the MP for Bradford?* (b) meaning (sth): *What's the 'S' for in A S Hornby?* ○ *Shaking your head for 'No' is not universal.* 9 (after a *v*) in order to obtain (sth): *search for treasure* ○ *hope for a settlement* ○ *pray for peace* ○ *fish for trout* ○ *ask the policeman for directions* ○ *go to a friend for advice* ○ *There were 50 applicants for the post.* 10 (after an *adj*) considering what can be expected from (sb/sth): *It's quite warm for January.* ○ *She's tall for her age.* ○ *He's not bad for a beginner.* 11 (after a comparative *adj*) following (sth): *You'll feel all the better for a good night's sleep.* ○ *This room would look all the better for a spot of paint.* 12 as the equivalent of (sth); in return for (sth): *There's one bad apple for every three good ones.* ○ *You get a coupon for every 3 gallons of petrol.* 13 with regard to (sb/sth); concerning (sb/sth): *anxious for sb's safety* ○ *ready for a holiday* ○ *eager for them to start* ○ *Fortunately for us, the weather changed.* 14 because of (sth); on account of (sth): *famous for its cathedral* ○ *for the following reasons* ○ *Please take care of her for my sake.* ○ *I couldn't speak for laughing.* ○ *He didn't answer for fear of hurting her.* ○ *He gave me roses for my birthday.* 15 (a) (indicating a length of time): *I'm going away for a few days.* ○ *He was in prison for twenty years.* ○ *You said you would love me for ever.* (b) (indicating that sth is intended to happen at the specified time): *a reservation for the first week in June* ○ *The appointment is for 12 May.* ○ *We're invited for 7.30.* (c) (indicating the occasion when sth happens): *I'm warning you for the last time — stop talking!* ○ *I'm meeting him for the first time today.* 16 (indicating a distance): *He crawled on his hands and knees for 100 metres.* ○ *The road went on for miles and miles.* 17 (a) (used after an *adj* and before a *n/pron* + infinitive): *It's impossible for me to leave my family.* ○ *It's useless for us to continue.* ○ (*fml*) *For her to have survived such an ordeal was remarkable.* ○ *It's customary for the women to sit apart.* (b) (used after a *n* and before a *n/pron* + infinitive): *no need for you to go* ○ *time for us to leave* ○ *a rush for them to finish* ○ *His greatest wish was for his daughter to take over the business.* (c) (used after *too* + *adj* or *adj* + *enough*): *The box is too heavy for me to lift.* ○ *Is it clear enough for you to read?* ○ *The coffee was too hot for her (to drink).* (d) (used before a *n/pron* + infinitive to show purpose or design): *letters for the manager to sign* ○ *money for you to invest wisely* ○ *I would give anything for this not to have happened.* ○ *It's not for me* (ie It is not my responsibility) *to say.* (e) (used after *more* with *than*): *Nothing could be more desirable than for them both to get jobs in Leeds.* ○ *Nothing would please me more than for her to win the next election.* 18 (idm) **be ˈfor it** (*infml*) expect to be punished or to get into trouble: *The headmaster saw me draw the picture on the blackboard — I'm for it now.* **for ˈall** despite; in spite of: *For all his talk about sports cars and swimming-pools he's just an ordinary bank-clerk.* ○ *For all you say, I think she's the best teacher we've got.* ○ *For all his wealth and fame, he's a very lonely man.* ○ *He has great power and wealth, but is still unhappy for all that.*

for[2] /fə(r); *strong form* fɔː(r)/ *conj* (*dated or fml*) (not used at the beginning of a sentence) because: *We listened eagerly, for he brought news of our families.* ○ *Prepare to alight, for we are almost there.*

for /ˌef əʊ ˈɑː(r)/ *abbr* (*commerce*) (of freight) free on rail (ie transported to the train and loaded without the buyer paying extra).

forage /ˈfɒrɪdʒ; *US* ˈfɔːr-/ *n* 1 [U] food for horses and cattle. 2 [C usu *sing*] a search or hunt, esp for food.

▷ **forage** *v* [I, Ipr, Ip] ~ (**for sth**); ~ (**about**) search or hunt for sth, esp food and supplies: *One group left the camp to forage for firewood.* ○ *She foraged* (ie rummaged) *about in her handbag, but couldn't find her keys.*

□ ˈ**forage crops** crops grown as food for horses and cattle.

forasmuch as /ˌfɔːrəzˈmʌtʃ əz/ *conj* (*arch or law*) because; since; seeing that.

foray /ˈfɒreɪ; *US* ˈfɔːreɪ/ *n* 1 sudden attack, esp to obtain sth; raid: *go on/make a foray into enemy territory.* 2 brief but vigorous attempt to be involved in a different activity, profession, etc: *the company's first foray into the computer market.*

▷ **foray** *v* [I] make a foray.

forbade (also **forbad**) *pt* of FORBID.

forbear[1] /fɔːˈbeə(r)/ *v* (*pt* **forbore** /fɔːˈbɔː(r)/, *pp* **forborne** /fɔːˈbɔːn/) [I, Ipr, Tt, Tg] ~ (**from sth/doing sth**) (*fml*) refrain from doing or saying sth in a patient or self-controlled way: *her mother's gentle and forbearing character* ○ *He could not forbear from expressing his disagreement.* ○ *He forbore to mention/mentioning the matter again.*

▷ **forbearance** /fɔːˈbeərəns/ *n* [U] (*fml*) patient self-control; tolerance: *show forbearance towards sb* ○ *exercise forbearance in dealing with people.*

forbear[2] = FOREBEAR.

forbid /fəˈbɪd/ *v* (*pt* **forbade** /fəˈbæd; *US* fəˈbeɪd/ or **forbad** /fəˈbæd/, *pp* **forbidden** /fəˈbɪdn/) 1 (a) [Tsg, Dn·n, Dn·t] order (sb) not to do sth: *I can't forbid you/your seeing that man again.* ○ *She was forbidden access to the club.* ○ *If you want to go, I can't forbid you.* ○ *He was forbidden to talk to her.* ○ *It is forbidden (for anyone) to smoke in this room.* (b) [Tn, Tg] order that (sth) shall not be done; not allow: *Her father forbade their marriage.* ○ *Photography is strictly forbidden in the cathedral.* ○ *forbidden subjects such as sex and politics* ○ *The law forbids building on this land.* 2 [Tn] make (sth) difficult or impossible; prevent or not allow: *Lack of space forbids further treatment of the topic here.* 3 (idm) **forˌbidden ˈfruit** thing that is desired because it is disapproved of or not allowed. **forˌbidden ˈground** (a) area that one is not allowed to enter. (b) subject, activity, etc that is not allowed or approved of. **God/Heaven forˈbid (that...)** (expressing a wish that sth may not happen): *Heaven forbid that anything awful should have happened to her.*

▷ **forbidding** *adj* looking unfriendly; stern; threatening: *a forbidding appearance, look, manner, etc* ○ *a forbidding coastline*, ie one that looks dangerous. **forbiddingly** *adv*.

□ **the For,bidden 'City 1** former palace of the emperors of China in *Beijing, which ordinary people were not allowed to enter. **2** Lhasa, in Tibet, which the Buddhist monks formerly refused to let foreigners enter.

forbore *pt* of FORBEAR[1].

forborne *pp* of FORBEAR[1].

force[1] /fɔːs/ *n* **1** [U] (**a**) physical strength or power: *the force of the blow, explosion, collision, etc* ○ *They used brute force to break open the door.* (**b**) violent physical action: *The soldiers took the prisoners away by force.* ○ *renounce the use of force.* **2** (**a**) [U] (intensity of) strength or power; influence: *the full force of her argument* ○ *He overcame his bad habits by sheer force of will.* ○ *Through force of circumstances the plans had to be changed.* (**b**) [C] person, thing, belief, etc with such strength or power; influence: *She's a force to be reckoned with*, ie someone to be treated seriously. ○ *the two main political forces of left and right* ○ *powerful economic forces* ○ *Is religion a force for good?* ○ *the forces of evil still at work today.* **3** [C, U] (in scientific use) measurable influence or intensity tending to cause acceleration or deformation. Force is defined in terms of the rate of change of momentum which it causes. The unit of force is the newton. Physicists recognize four basic forces which govern the way particles of matter interact in the everyday world: the strong nuclear force binding atomic particles together, the weaker nuclear force responsible for some forms of radioactivity, the electromagnetic force acting between charged particles, and the force of gravity: *The force of gravity pulls things towards the earth's centre.* **4** [C] (power of the) wind, rain or another of the natural elements: *fighting against the forces of nature.* ⇨ Usage at STRENGTH. **5** [C usu *sing*] measure of wind strength: *a force 9 gale.* **6** [CGp] group of people organized for a specified purpose: *a sales/labour force* ○ *Our work-force are completely dependable.* **7** [CGp] organized body of armed and specially trained people: *the police force* ○ *peace-keeping forces* ○ *the armed forces of a country*, ie the army, navy and air force. **8** [U] (legal) authority: *This decree has the force of law behind it.* **9** (idm) **break the force of sth** reduce or weaken the impact of sth such as a fall or blow: *The force of his fall was broken by the straw mats.* **bring sth/come into 'force** (cause a law, rule, etc to) become effective or come into operation: *When do the new safety rules come into force?* **(from/out of) force of 'habit** (because of) the tendency to do (some) things in a certain way from always having done so in the past: *It's force of habit that gets me out of bed at 7.15 each morning.* **in 'force** (**a**) (of people) in large numbers: *The police were present at the demonstration in (full) force.* (**b**) (of a law, rule, etc) effective or in operation: *The new safety regulations are now in force.* **join forces** ⇨ JOIN.

force[2] /fɔːs/ *v* **1** [Tn·pr, Cn·t] make (sb/oneself) do sth he/one does not want to do; compel; oblige: *force a confession out of sb* ○ *The thief forced her to hand over the money.* ○ *He forced himself to speak to her.* ○ *The president was forced into resigning/to resign.* **2** [Tn·pr, Tn·p] use physical strength to move (oneself) against resistance; use physical strength to move (sth): *force one's way through a crowd* ○ *force a way in/out/through* ○ *(fig) The government forced the bill through Parliament.* ○ *force clothes into a bag.* **3** [Tn, Cn·a] break (sth) open using physical strength: *force (open) a door, lock, window, safe.* **4** [Tn] cause or produce (sth) by effort, esp when under stress: *a forced smile/laugh*, ie not the natural result of amusement. **5** [Tn] cause (fruit, plants, etc) to reach maturity earlier than is normal by keeping them under special conditions. **6** (idm) **force sb's 'hand** make sb do sth unwillingly or sooner than he intended. **'force the issue** act so as to make an immediate decision necessary. **force the 'pace** go very fast in a race, etc in order to tire the other competitors.

Henry Ford I

7 (phr v) **force sth back** try very hard not to show (an emotion): *force back one's tears.* **force sth down** (**a**) compel sb/oneself to swallow (food and drink) when he/one does not want to: *After being ill I didn't feel like eating but I managed to force something down.* (**b**) compel (an aircraft) to land, eg because a bomb is found on board. **force sth on sb** make sb accept sth against his will: *force one's ideas, company, attention on sb* ○ *Higher taxes were forced on the people.*

□ **,forced 'labour** compulsory hard work, usu under harsh conditions.

,forced 'landing emergency landing that an aircraft has to make.

,forced 'march long emergency march made by troops.

force-feed /ˈfɔːsfiːd/ *v* (*pp*, *pt* **force-fed** /ˈfɔːsfed/) [Tn] compel (a person or an animal) to take food and drink: *All the prisoners on hunger strike had to be force-fed.*

forceful /ˈfɔːsfl/ *adj* strong and assertive: (*approv*) *a forceful speaker* ○ *a forceful argument, speech, style of writing, etc.* ▷ **forcefully** /-fəlɪ/ *adv*. **forcefulness** *n* [U].

force majeure /ˌfɔːs mæˈʒɜː(r)/ (*French law*) unforeseen circumstances, such as war, that excuses sb from keeping a promise, fulfilling a bargain, etc.

forcemeat /ˈfɔːsmiːt/ *n* [U] finely chopped meat mixed with herbs, etc and used as stuffing, eg in a roast chicken.

forceps /ˈfɔːseps/ *n* [pl] pincers or tongs used by dentists, surgeons, etc for gripping things: *a pair of forceps* ○ [attrib] *a forceps delivery*, ie one in which the baby is delivered with the aid of forceps.

forcible /ˈfɔːsəbl/ *adj* [attrib] **1** done by or involving the use of physical force: *make a forcible entry into a building.* **2** convincing and effective; forceful: *a forcible argument/reminder.* ▷ **forcibly** /-əblɪ/ *adv*.

Ford[1] /fɔːd/ Henry (1863-1947), American industrialist. He designed and built the famous Model T car, of which he sold 15 million by using new techniques of mass production to keep prices low. He also founded the charitable Ford Foundation. ⇨ illus.

Ford[2] /fɔːd/ John (1895-1973), American film director. Often working as an independent director, he specialized in westerns (eg *Stagecoach, The Searchers*), bringing a new epic and human quality to the form.

ford /fɔːd/ *n* shallow place in a river where one can walk or drive across.

▷ **ford** *v* [Tn] cross (a river) by walking or driving across a shallow part. **fordable** /-əbl/ *adj* that can be forded.

fore[1] /fɔː(r)/ *adj* **1** [attrib] situated in the front part of a vehicle: *in the fore part of the ship/plane/train.* Cf HIND[1]. **2** (idm) **be/come to the fore** be/become prominent or important: *She's always to the fore at moments of crisis.* ○ *After the election several new Members of Parliament came to the fore.* **fore and 'aft** (**a**) at the bow (front) and stern (back) of a ship. (**b**) (of sails) set lengthwise on a ship or boat.

▷ **fore** *adv* in, at or towards the front of a ship or aircraft.

fore *n* [U] front part (of a ship).

fore[2] /fɔː(r)/ *interj* (in golf) shout given to warn people that a player is about to hit the ball.

fore- *pref* (with *ns* and *vs*) **1** (of time or rank) before; in advance of: *forefather* ○ *foreman* ○ *foretell.* **2** (of position) in front of: *foreground* ○ *foreshorten.*

forearm[1] /ˈfɔːrɑːm/ *n* part of the arm from the elbow to the wrist or fingertips. ⇨ illus at HUMAN.

forearm[2] /ˌfɔːrˈɑːm/ *v* **1** [Tn usu passive] prepare (oneself/sb) in advance for possible danger, attack, etc; arm beforehand. **2** (idm) **forewarned is forearmed** ⇨ FOREWARN.

forebear (also **forbear**) /ˈfɔːbeə(r)/ *n* [C usu *pl*] person from whom one is descended; ancestor.

forebode /fɔːˈbəʊd/ *v* [Tn] (*fml*) be a sign or a warning of (esp trouble): *Her angry face forbode a confrontation.* ○ *These developments forebode disaster.*

▷ **foreboding** *n* [C, U] ~ (**that...**) strong feeling that danger or trouble is coming: *She had a sinister foreboding that the plane would crash.* ○ *Thoughts about the future filled him with foreboding.*

forecast /ˈfɔːkɑːst; *US* -kæst/ *v* (*pt, pp* **forecast** or **forecasted**) [Tn, Tf, Tw] tell in advance (what is expected to happen); predict with the help of information: *forecast a fall in unemployment* ○ *forecast that it will rain tomorrow* ○ *forecast what the outcome of the election will be.*

▷ **forecast** *n* statement that predicts sth with the help of information: *forecasts of higher profits* ○ *According to the (weather) forecast it will be sunny tomorrow.* ○ *The forecast said there would be sunny intervals and showers.* ⇨ article at WEATHER.

forecaster *n* person who forecasts sth, esp sb whose job is to forecast the weather.

forecastle (also **fo'c's'le**) /ˈfəʊksl/ *n* part of the front of certain ships where the crew live and sleep.

foreclose /fɔːˈkləʊz/ *v* [I, Ipr, Tn] ~ (**on sb/sth**) (of

a bank, etc that has lent money for a mortgage) take possession of the property of (sb), usu because repayments have not been made: *The bank foreclosed (on the mortgage).*
▷ **foreclosure** /fɔːˈkləʊʒə(r)/ *n* [C, U] (act of) foreclosing a mortgage.

forecourt /ˈfɔːkɔːt/ *n* **1** large open area or courtyard in front of a building, esp the front of a filling station where petrol is sold. **2** (in tennis, badminton, etc) part of the court between the service-line and the net.

foredoomed /fɔːˈduːmd/ *adj* ~ **(to sth)** intended (as if) by fate to be unsuccessful: *All attempts to revive the fishing industry were foredoomed to failure.*

forefather /ˈfɔːfɑːðə(r)/ *n* [C usu *pl*] person from whom one is descended; ancestor, esp a male: *the religion of his forefathers.*

forefinger /ˈfɔːfɪŋgə(r)/ *n* finger next to the thumb; index finger. ➪ illus at HAND.

forefoot /ˈfɔːfʊt/ *n* (*pl* **-feet** /-fiːt/) either of the two front feet of a four-legged animal.

forefront /ˈfɔːfrʌnt/ *n* [sing] **the** ~ **(of sth)** the most forward or important position or place: *in the forefront of my mind* ○ *The new product took the company to the forefront of the computer software field.*

foregoing /ˈfɔːgəʊɪŋ/ *adj* [attrib] (*fml*) preceding; just mentioned: *the foregoing analysis, description, discussion, etc.*
▷ **the foregoing** *n* [sing or pl *v*] (*fml*) what has just been mentioned: *The foregoing have all been included in the proposals.*

foregone /ˈfɔːgɒn; *US* -gɔːn/ *adj* (idm) **a** ˌ**foregone conˈclusion** result that can be predicted with certainty: *The outcome of the election is a foregone conclusion.*

foreground /ˈfɔːgraʊnd/ *n* **the foreground** [sing] (**a**) front part of a view, scene, picture, etc; part nearest the observer: *The red figure in the foreground is the artist's mother.* (**b**) (*fig*) position of greatest importance or prominence: *These teachers are keeping education in the foreground of public attention.* Cf BACKGROUND 1,2.

forehand /ˈfɔːhænd/ *adj* [attrib] (of a stroke in tennis, squash, etc) made with the palm of the hand turned towards one's opponent or towards the front of the court: *a forehand volley.*
▷ **forehand** *n* **1** forehand stroke. **2** (usu *sing*) (in tennis, squash, etc) the same side of a player as the hand in which he is holding the racket: *Hit the ball to her forehand.* Cf BACKHAND (BACK[2]).

forehead /ˈfɒrɪd, *also* ˈfɔːhed; *US* ˈfɔːrɪd/ (also **brow**) *n* part of the face above the eyebrows and below the hair. ➪ illus at HEAD.

foreign /ˈfɒrən; *US* ˈfɔːr-/ *adj* **1** (**a**) of, in or from a country or an area other than one's own: *foreign languages, goods, students.* (**b**) dealing with or involving other countries: *foreign affairs* ○ *foreign policy* ○ *foreign trade* ○ *foreign aid*, ie money, etc given by one country to another in need ○ *a foreign correspondent*, ie a news reporter working in a foreign country. **2** ~ **to sb/sth** (*fml*) not belonging naturally to sb/sth; alien to sb/sth; uncharacteristic of sb/sth: *Dishonesty is foreign to his nature.* **3** (*fml*) coming or introduced from outside, usu by accident: *a foreign body* (eg a hair or speck of dirt) *in the eye.*
▷ **foreigner** *n* **1** person from a country other than one's own. **2** person who is regarded as not belonging to a particular community; outsider or stranger.
□ **the** ˌ**Foreign and** ˈ**Commonwealth Office** (*abbr* **FCO**) (*Brit*) the government department that deals with foreign affairs. Cf THE HOME OFFICE (HOME[1]).
foreign exˈchange (system of buying and selling) foreign money: [attrib] *the foreign exchange markets.*
ˌ**Foreign** ˈ**Legion** group of soldiers forming an army of volunteers from foreign countries. The best known is the French Foreign Legion, which once had the reputation of accepting men who wished to forget their past lives, eg because of former crimes.
ˌ**Foreign** ˈ**Secretary** government minister in charge of the Foreign and Commonwealth Office.

foreknowledge /ˌfɔːˈnɒlɪdʒ/ *n* [U] knowledge of sth before it happens or exists.

foreland /ˈfɔːlənd/ *n* piece of land that extends into the sea; cape or promontory.

foreleg /ˈfɔːleg/ *n* either of the two front legs of a four-footed animal.

forelimb /ˈfɔːlɪm/ *n* front limb of an animal.

forelock /ˈfɔːlɒk/ *n* **1** piece of hair growing (and falling) over the forehead. **2** (idm) **touch, tug, etc one's** ˈ**forelock** (formerly) raise a hand to one's forehead when meeting sb of higher social rank, usu as a sign of respect.

foreman /ˈfɔːmən/ *n* (*pl* **-men** /-mən/, *fem* **forewoman** /-wʊmən/, *pl* **-women** /-wɪmɪn/) **1** experienced worker who supervises and directs other workers. **2** person who acts as the leader and spokesperson of a jury.

foremast /ˈfɔːmɑːst/ *n* mast nearest the bow or front of a ship.

foremost /ˈfɔːməʊst/ *adj* **1** [attrib] most famous or important; best or chief: *the foremost painter of his time.* **2** (idm) **first and foremost** ➪ FIRST[2].
▷ **foremost** *adv* in the first position: *She ranks foremost among the country's leading conductors.*

forename /ˈfɔːneɪm/ *n* (*fml*) name preceding the family name; person's first or Christian name. ➪ App 7. ➪ Usage at NAME[1].

forenoon /ˈfɔːnuːn/ *n* (*Scot* and in official, eg electoral, notices) part of the day between sunrise and noon; morning.

forensic /fəˈrensɪk; *US* -zɪk/ *adj* [attrib] of, related to or used in (courts of) law: *forensic medicine*, ie medical skill used to help with legal problems or police investigations.

foreordain /ˌfɔːrɔːˈdeɪn/ *v* [usu passive: Tn, Tf] (*fml*) (of God or fate) arrange or determine (sth) before it actually happens: *It was foreordained that the company would suffer a spectacular collapse.*

foreplay /ˈfɔːpleɪ/ *n* [U] sexual activity such as caressing the sexual organs and kissing before sexual intercourse.

forerunner /ˈfɔːrʌnə(r)/ *n* person or thing that prepares the way for the coming of sb or sth else more important; sign of what is to follow: *the forerunners of the modern diesel engine.*

foresail /ˈfɔːseɪl, *also* ˈfɔːsl/ *n* main sail on the front mast of a ship.

foresee /fɔːˈsiː/ *v* (*pt* **foresaw** /fɔːˈsɔː/, *pp* **foreseen** /fɔːˈsiːn/) [Tn, Tf, Tw] see or know that sth is going to happen in the future; predict: *The difficulties could not have been foreseen.* ○ *He foresaw that the job would take a long time.* ○ *They could not have foreseen how things would turn out.*
▷ **forseeable** /-əbl/ *adj* that can be foreseen: *(in) the forseeable future*, ie (during) the period of time (usu short) when one knows what is going to happen.

foreshadow /fɔːˈʃædəʊ/ *v* [Tn] be a sign or warning of (sth to come or about to happen): *The increase in taxes had been foreshadowed in the minister's speech.*

foreshore /ˈfɔːʃɔː(r)/ *n* (usu **the foreshore**) [sing] part of the shore between the limits of high and low tides, or between the sea and land that is cultivated or built on.

foreshorten /fɔːˈʃɔːtn/ *v* [Tn] (in drawing) represent (an object) by shortening certain lines to give an effect of distance and perspective.

foresight /ˈfɔːsaɪt/ *n* [U] ability to see what one's future needs are likely to be; careful planning: *The couple had the foresight to plan their retirement wisely.* Cf HINDSIGHT.

foreskin /ˈfɔːskɪn/ *n* loose fold of skin covering the end of the penis. ➪ illus at MALE.

forest /ˈfɒrɪst; *US* ˈfɔːr-/ *n* **1** [C, U] (large area of land thickly covered with) trees, bushes, etc: *the dense tropical forests of the Amazon basin* ○ *Very little forest is left unexplored nowadays.* ○ [attrib] *forest animals, fires.* **2** [C] (*fig*) dense mass of tall or narrow objects that looks like a forest: *a forest of television aerials.*
▷ **forested** *adj* covered in forest.
forester *n* **1** person who looks after a forest, eg by protecting the animals, planting new trees and guarding against fire. **2** person who lives and works in a forest.
forestry *n* [U] science and practice of planting, caring for, and managing forests. **the** ˈ**Forestry Commission** official organization responsible for forestry in Britain. It runs and maintains the forests owned by the State, and gives help and advice to private owners of forest land. ➪ article at COUNTRYSIDE.

forestall /fɔːˈstɔːl/ *v* [Tn] act before (sb else) so as to prevent him from doing sth: *forestall a competitor, a rival, etc* ○ *I had my objection all prepared, but Stephens forestalled me.*

foretaste /ˈfɔːteɪst/ *n* ~ **(of sth)** small experience of sth before it actually happens; sample: *a foretaste of the fierce conflict to come.*

foretell /fɔːˈtel/ *v* (*pt, pp* **foretold** /fɔːˈtəʊld/) [Tn, Tf, Tw] (*fml*) tell (what will happen in the future); predict: *No one could have foretold such strange events.* ○ *The gypsy had foretold that the boy would die.* ○ *You can't foretell how the war will end.*

forethought /ˈfɔːθɔːt/ *n* [U] careful thought or planning for the future: *With a little more forethought we could have bought the house we really wanted.*

foretold *pt, pp* of FORETELL.

forever /fəˈrevə(r)/ *adv* **1** (also **for ever**) for all time; always: *I'll love you forever!* ○ *You'll never get that ball back — it's lost forever.* ○ (*infml*) *It takes her forever* (ie an extremely long time) *to get dressed.* **2** (usu with *vs* in the continuous tenses) at all times; constantly or persistently: *They are forever arguing.* ○ *Why are you forever asking questions?*

forewarn /fɔːˈwɔːn/ *v* **1** [Tn, Tn·pr, Dn·f] ~ **sb (of sth)** warn sb before sth happens; advise sb (of possible dangers, problems, etc): *We had been forewarned of the risk of fire/that fire could break out.* **2** (idm) **fore**ˌ**warned is fore**ˈ**armed** (*saying*) knowledge of possible dangers, problems, etc allows one to prepare for them.

foreword /ˈfɔːwɜːd/ *n* short introduction to a book, printed at the beginning and usu written by a person other than the author. Cf PREFACE.

forfeit /ˈfɔːfɪt/ *v* [Tn] (have to) lose or give up (sth) as a consequence of or punishment for having done sth wrong, or in order to achieve sth: *Passengers who cancel their reservations will forfeit their deposit.* ○ *He has forfeited the right to represent the people.* ○ *The couple forfeited their independence in order to help those less fortunate.*
▷ **forfeit** *n* **1** [C usu *sing*] thing (to be) paid or given up as a penalty or punishment. **2** (**a**) **forfeits** [sing *v*] game in which a player gives up various articles if he makes a mistake and can have them back by doing sth ridiculous. (**b**) [C] article given up in this game: *Give me your watch as a forfeit.*
forfeit *adj* [pred] ~ **(to sb/sth)** (*fml*) (liable to be) lost, paid or given up as a forfeit: *All goods may be forfeit to the State in time of war.*
forfeiture /ˈfɔːfɪtʃə(r)/ *n* [U] ~ **(of sth)** (action of) forfeiting sth: *(the) forfeiture of one's property.*

forgather (also **foregather**) /fɔːˈgæðə(r)/ *v* [I] (*fml or rhet*) come together; meet socially.

forgave *pt* of FORGIVE.

forge[1] /fɔːdʒ/ *n* **1** workshop with a fire and an anvil where metals are heated and shaped, esp one used by a smith for making horseshoes. **2** (workshop, factory, etc with a) furnace for melting or refining metals.

forge[2] /fɔːdʒ/ *v* [Tn] **1** (**a**) shape (sth) by heating it in a fire and hammering: *forge a sword, a chain, an anchor, etc.* (**b**) (*fig*) create (usu a lasting relationship) by means of much hard work: *forge a bond, a link, an alliance, etc* ○ *a friendship forged by adversity.* Cf WELD. **2** make an imitation or copy of (sth) in order to deceive people: *forge a banknote, will, signature, etc.* Cf COUNTERFEIT *v.*
▷ **forger** *n* person who forges (FORGE[2] 2) money, a document, etc. Cf COUNTERFEITER (COUNTERFEIT).
forgery /ˈfɔːdʒərɪ/ *n* **1** [U] (crime or act of) forging (FORGE[2] 2) a document, picture, signature, etc: *He spent 5 years in prison for forgery.* **2** [C] document,

signature, etc that has been forged: *This famous painting was thought to be by Van Gogh, but it is in fact a forgery.* Cf COUNTERFEIT.

forging *n* [C] piece of metal that has been forged (FORGE[2] 1a) or shaped under a press.

forge[3] /fɔːdʒ/ *v* **1** [Ipr, Ip, Tn·pr] move forward steadily or gradually: *forge constantly onwards* ○ *forge into the lead*, ie gradually overtake sb. **2** (phr v) **forge ahead** advance or progress quickly; take the leading position in a race, etc: *One horse forged ahead, leaving the others behind.*

forget /fəˈget/ *v* (*pt* **forgot** /fəˈgɒt/, *pp* **forgotten** /fəˈgɒtn/) **1** [Ipr, Tn, Tf, Tw, Tg] ~ **about sth** (not used in the continuous tenses) fail to remember or recall (sth); lose the memory of: *He forgot (about) her birthday*, ie did not remember it at the proper time. ○ *I've forgotten her name.* ○ *Did you forget (that) I was coming?* ○ *She forgot how the puzzle fitted together.* ○ *I'll never forget seeing my daughter dance in public for the first time.* **2** (**a**) [I, Tt] fail to remember to do sth; neglect: *'Why didn't you buy any bread?' 'Sorry, I forgot.'* ○ *Don't forget to feed the cat.* ○ *He forgot to pay me.* (**b**) [Tn] fail to remember to bring, buy, etc (sth) or take care of (sth): *I forgot my umbrella.* ○ *Don't forget the waiter*, ie give him a tip. **3** [Ipr, Tn, Tf] ~ (**about sb/sth**) stop thinking about sb/sth; not think about sb/sth; put sb/sth out of one's mind: *Let's forget (about) our differences.* ○ *Try to forget (all) about him.* ○ *You can forget about a holiday this year — I've lost my job.* ○ *'How much do I owe you?' 'Forget it!'*, ie Don't bother to pay me back. ○ *The shop will accept cheques and credit cards, not forgetting* (ie and also) *cash, of course.* ○ *I was forgetting (that) David used to teach you.* ○ *After a dazzling start to his career he is now the forgotten man of British politics.* **4** [Tn] ~ **oneself** (**a**) behave without proper dignity: *I'm afraid I forgot myself and kissed him wildly.* (**b**) act unselfishly: *Forget yourself and think of someone else for a change.* **5** (idm) **elephants never forget** ⇨ ELEPHANT. **forgive and forget** ⇨ FORGIVE.

▷ **forgetful** /-fl/ *adj* **1** in the habit of forgetting; likely to forget: *Old people are sometimes forgetful.* **2** [pred] ~ **of sb/sth** not thinking about sb/sth; neglectful: *be forgetful of one's duties.* **forgetfully** /-fəlɪ/ *adv.* **forgetfulness** *n* [U].

forget-me-not /fəˈget mɪ nɒt/ *n* small plant with tiny blue flowers.

forgive /fəˈgɪv/ *v* (*pt* **forgave** /fəˈgeɪv/, *pp* **forgiven** /fəˈgɪvn/) **1** [Tn, Tn·pr, Dn·n] ~ **sth;** ~ **sb** (**for sth/doing sth**) stop being angry or bitter towards sb or about sth; stop blaming or wanting to punish sb: *I forgave her a long time ago.* ○ *I cannot forgive myself for not seeing my mother before she died.* ○ *She forgave him his thoughtless remark.* ○ (*religion*) *Forgive us our trespasses*, ie our sins. **2** [Tn, Tn·pr, Tsg] ~ **sb** (**for doing sth**) (used in polite expressions to lessen the force of what the speaker says and in mild apologies): *Forgive my ignorance, but what exactly are you talking about?* ○ *Please forgive me for interrupting/my interrupting.* **3** [Dn·n] say that sb need not repay (the money owed); not demand repayment from (sb): *Won't you forgive me such a small debt?* **4** (idm) **forˌgive and forˈget** dismiss from one's mind all unkind feelings and the desire to blame and punish sb.

▷ **forgivable** /-əbl/ *adj* that can be forgiven: *His harshness is forgivable.*

forgiveness *n* [U] forgiving or state of being forgiven; willingness to forgive: *He asked forgiveness for what he had done wrong.* ○ (*religion*) *the forgiveness of sins* ○ *She is sympathetic and full of forgiveness.*

forgiving *adj* ready and willing to forgive: *kind and forgiving parents* ○ *a forgiving nature.* **forgivingly** *adv.*

forgo /fɔːˈgəʊ/ *v* (*pt* **forwent** /fɔːˈwent/, *pp* **forgone** /fɔːˈgɒn; *US* -ˈgɔːn/) [Tn] give up or do without (esp sth pleasant): *The workers agreed to forgo a pay increase for the sake of greater job security.*

forgot *pt* of FORGET.

forgotten *pp* of FORGET.

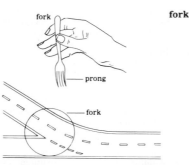

fork

fork /fɔːk/ *n* **1** small implement with a handle and two or more points or prongs, used for lifting food to the mouth or holding things (esp meat) firmly while they are cut: *eat with a knife and fork.* ⇨ illus. **2** farm or gardening tool with a handle and prongs, used for digging the ground, lifting hay, etc. ⇨ illus. **3** (**a**) place where a road, river, tree branch, etc divides into two parts: *Go up to the fork and turn left.* (**b**) either of the two parts divided in this way: *Take the right fork.* **4** (usu *pl*) two metal supporting pieces into which a wheel on a bicycle or motor cycle is fitted. ⇨ illus at BICYCLE. **5** thing shaped like a fork: *a ˈtuning-fork.*

▷ **fork** *v* **1** [Tn, Tn·pr, Tn·p] lift, dig, move, etc (sth) with a fork: *fork (over) the ground* ○ *fork in manure*, ie dig it into the soil with a fork. **2** [I] (**a**) (of a road, river, etc) divide into two parts: *The road forks just beyond the village.* (**b**) (of a person) turn (left or right) at a fork: *Fork left at the church.* **3** (phr v) **fork out** (**sth**) (*infml*) pay (money), usu reluctantly: *Why am I always forking out (money) on/for your school trips?*

forked *adj* divided into two (or more) parts; branched: *the forked tongue of a snake* ○ *a bird with a forked tail* ○ *forked lightning.*

□ **ˌfork-lift ˈtruck** truck with a fork-like mechanical device on the front for lifting and moving heavy objects.

forlorn /fəˈlɔːn/ *adj* **1** lonely and unhappy; uncared for: *a forlorn child sitting on the street corner.* **2** (of places) looking uncared for; wretched or forsaken: *deserted forlorn farmhouses.* **3** (idm) **a forlorn ˈhope** plan or undertaking that is almost certain not to succeed: *Going to their rescue in a rowing-boat is a bit of a forlorn hope.* ▷ **forlornly** *adv.* **forlornness** *n* [U].

form[1] /fɔːm/ *n* **1** [C, U] outward physical appearance of sb/sth; shape: *a jelly mould in the form of a motor car* ○ *We could just manage to see the form of an aircraft taking off in the fog.* ○ *her slender graceful form.* **2** [C] ~ (**of sth**) specific type of arrangement or structure of sth; manner in which sth exists or appears; kind or variety: *water in the form of ice* ○ *different forms of government* ○ *The training took the form of* (ie consisted of) *seminars and lectures.* ○ *the form* (ie set order of words) *of the marriage service.* **3** [U] general structure and arrangement of sth created such as a musical composition or piece of writing, in contrast to its content: *music in sonata form* ○ *literary form* ○ *This painting shows a good sense of form.* **4** [C, U] (*grammar*) (particular) spelling or pronunciation of a word: *The plural form of 'goose' is 'geese'.* ○ *The words 'elevator' and 'lift' are different in form but identical in meaning.* **5** [U] particular manner of behaving, speaking, or writing that is normally required or expected: *Although she is not entitled to attend the dinner, I think she should be invited as a matter of form*, ie because it is correct or polite. ○ *What is the form* (ie the correct thing to do)*?* **6** [U] (**a**) strength, fitness to compete with others, etc of an athlete, a horse, etc: *After six months training, the whole team is in superb form.* (**b**) record of the actions, behaviour, progress, etc of a person, team, etc: *On present/current form, Spain will win tonight's match.* ○ *Judging by recent form, he should easily pass the exam.* ○ *I've got no record of this horse's form.* **7** [U] person's feelings, humour or spirits: *They were both in fine/good form at dinner.* **8** (*Brit sl*) record of having been found guilty of crimes and (usu) of having received a prison sentence: *He's got no form!* **9** [C] class, esp in British private schools and some American private schools: *The youngest children are in the first form, the oldest in the sixth form.* **10** [C] long wooden bench, usu without a back. **11** [C] printed or typed piece of paper with questions, and spaces for answers: *fill in an application form.* **12** [C] place where a hare lives; lair. **13** (idm) **bad/good ˈform** (*dated*) incorrect/correct social behaviour according to accepted standards: *It is sometimes considered bad form to smoke between courses at a meal.* **a ˌform of adˈdress** style of addressing sb in speech or writing: *What form of address should one use when writing to a bishop?* **in any shape or form** ⇨ SHAPE[1]. **on/off ˈform; in/out of ˈform** in a good/bad state of fitness, ability, etc; performing as well as/not as well as usual: *The team were on excellent form throughout the whole competition.* **on present form** ⇨ PRESENT[1]. **true to form** ⇨ TRUE.

▷ **-former** (forming compound *ns*) child or young person in the specified form[1](9) at school: *a sixth-former.*

formless *adj* without a clear or definite shape or structure: *formless shadows, ideas, dreams.* **formlessly** *adv.*

□ **ˈform letter** standardized letter on a particular subject that can be used often and sent out to different people as necessary: *I got a form letter from the bank reminding me that I was overdrawn.*

form[2] /fɔːm/ *v* **1** (**a**) [Tn, Tn·pr] ~ **sth** (**from sth**) give shape or structure to sth; fashion sth; produce sth: *form a bowl from clay* ○ *form sentences and paragraphs* ○ *The reservoir was formed by flooding the valley.* ○ *The substances are formed from a mixture of liquids solidifying under pressure.* (**b**) [Ln] take a particular shape or structure; develop. **2** [Ipr, Tn, Tn·pr] ~ (**sb/sth**) **into sth** arrange (sb/sth) or be arranged in a certain order: *The children formed (into) a line/The teacher formed the children into a line.* ○ *The volunteers formed (themselves into) three groups.* **3** (**a**) [Tn, Tn·pr] ~ **sth** (**from sth**) bring sth into existence; develop or organize sth: *form a committee, society, company, etc* ○ *The Labour leader was asked to form a government.* ○ (*fig*) *form an idea, impression, opinion, etc (of sb/sth)* ○ *form a relationship.* (**b**) [Ipr] come into existence; take shape or develop: *thunder clouds forming in the distance* ○ *Ice forms* (ie Water becomes solid) *at 0°C.* ○ *A scab formed on his leg.* **4** [Ln] be the material of (sth); be an essential part of (sth); constitute: *His research formed the basis of his new book.* ○ *Should the new department form part of the Faculty of Arts?* ○ *The historical aspect formed the main theme of her essay.* **5** [Tn] instruct or train (sb/sth): *a character formed by strict discipline.* **6** [Tn] produce (sth) as the particular spelling or pronunciation of a word: *form the plural of a noun by adding 's'* **7** (phr v) **form** (**sb**) **up** move (sb) into position in lines, as on parade: *The battalion formed up by companies on the barrack square.*

-form (also **-iform**) *suff* (forming *adjs*) having the form of: *cruciform* ○ *cuneiform.*

formal /ˈfɔːml/ *adj* **1** following accepted rules of behaviour; showing or expecting careful, serious behaviour, as eg on official occasions or in distant, not close, relationships: *She has a very formal manner.* ○ *a formal dinner, luncheon, dance, etc* ○ *formal dress* ○ *'Request' is a more formal way of saying 'ask for'.* **2** regular or geometric in shape; symmetrical: *formal gardens.* **3** of the outward shape or appearance (in contrast to the content or substance): *There is only a formal resemblance between the two systems; they are in fact radically different.* **4** publicly declared and recognized as official: *a formal denial* ○ *a formal declaration of war.* **5** [attrib] (of education) officially given at a school, college, etc: *The job does not require any formal training.*

▷ **formalism** /-məlɪzəm/ *n* [U] **1** strict observance of external form, ceremony, technique, etc, often without concern for feeling or meaning, eg in art:

creativity reduced to an empty formalism. **2** approach to mathematics which treats it as the use of symbols with no real meaning.
formally /-məlɪ/ *adv*: *The new rates of pay have not been formally agreed.*

formaldehyde /fɔːˈmældɪhaɪd/ *n* [U] (*chemistry*) strong-smelling colourless gas used in the manufacture of resins and formerly as a preservative and disinfectant when dissolved in water.
▷ **formalin** /ˈfɔːməlɪn/ *n* (*chemistry*) solution of formaldehyde in water.

formality /fɔːˈmælətɪ/ *n* **1** [U] careful observance of rules, conventions, etc of language or behaviour: *At board meetings you have to get used to the formality of the language.* ○ *I found the formality of the occasion irritating.* **2** [C] (**a**) action required by convention or law: *comply with all the necessary formalities* ○ *go through the legal formalities.* (**b**) such an action which no longer has much real importance or meaning: *They said the interview was just a formality/a mere formality, as they've already given me the job.*

formalize, -ise /ˈfɔːməlaɪz/ *v* [Tn] make (a plan, etc) official, esp by writing it down: *formalize the arrangements for the conference.* ▷ **formalization, -isation** /ˌfɔːməlaɪˈzeɪʃn/ *n* [U].

Forman /ˈfɔːmən/ Miloš (1932-), Czech film director. Having offended the authorities in his own country with such studies of human absurdities as *The Fireman's Ball*, Forman moved to the USA where he made the Oscar-winning *One Flew Over the Cuckoo's Nest* and *Amadeus*.

format /ˈfɔːmæt/ *n* **1** shape, size, binding, etc of a book: *It's the same book, but a new format.* **2** general arrangement, plan, design, etc of sth: *The format of the meeting was such that everyone could ask a question.* **3** arrangement or organization of data for processing or storage by a computer.
▷ **format** *v* (-tt-) [Tn] arrange (sth) in a particular format, usu for a computer.

formation /fɔːˈmeɪʃn/ *n* **1** [U] organizing and developing (of sth): *the formation of a new government* ○ *the formation of national character.* **2** [C] thing that is formed, esp in a particular or characteristic way: *cloud, rock formations* ○ *new word formations.* **3** [U] particular arrangement or pattern: *aircraft flying in formation* ○ [attrib] *forˈmation flying.*

formative /ˈfɔːmətɪv/ *adj* [attrib] having an important and lasting influence on the development of sb's character: *a child's formative years* ○ *formative influences in one's life.*

former /ˈfɔːmə(r)/ *adj* [attrib] **1** of an earlier period or time: *the former world champion* ○ *my former landlady* ○ *in former times* ○ *She's back to her former self again*, eg after an illness. **2** being the first mentioned of two things or people: *The former option favours the married man.* **3** (idm) **a shadow of one's/its former self** ➪ SHADOW.
▷ **the former** *pron* the first mentioned of two things or people: *If I had to choose between fish and chicken I'd prefer the former*, ie fish.
formerly *adv* in earlier times; previously: *The company formerly belonged to an international banking group.* ○ *Namibia, formerly South West Africa.* Cf LATTER.

Formica /fɔːˈmaɪkə/ *n* [U] (*propr*) hard heat-resistant plastic made into sheets for covering surfaces.

formic acid /ˌfɔːmɪk ˈæsɪd/ colourless acid used in textile finishing, etc originally obtained from ants but now produced synthetically.

formidable /ˈfɔːmɪdəbl/ *adj* **1** causing fear or great anxiety; frightening; awesome: *a formidable appearance, look, prospect.* **2** difficult to deal with or overcome: *formidable obstacles, opposition, debts* ○ *a formidable task.* **3** inspiring awe and respect because of excellence and strength; very impressive: *a formidable athlete, competitor, list of qualifications.* ▷ **formidably** /-əblɪ/ *adv.*

formula /ˈfɔːmjʊlə/ *n* (*pl* ~**s** *or, in scientific use,* **-mulae** /-mjʊliː/) ➪ Usage at DATA. **1** [C] (**a**) (*chemistry*) set of symbols showing the elements that a substance is made of: *The formula for water is* H_2O. (**b**) (*mathematics or physics*) expression of a rule or relationship in algebraic symbols: *the formula for converting gallons into litres.* **2** [C] fixed arrangement of words, esp as used on social, legal or ceremonial occasions: *'How d'you do' and 'Excuse me' are social formulae.* ○ *know the formula for addressing bishops.* **3** [C] list of ingredients or set of instructions for making sth, esp medicines and fuels: *a formula for a new drug.* **4** [C] set of statements or plans that can be agreed on by two or more persons or groups: *Managers and workers are still working out a peace formula.* **5** [C] ~ (**for sth**) method, plan, or set of principles worked out to achieve a desired result: *There is no sure formula for success.* ○ *a formula for a happy marriage.* **6** [U] classification of racing cars of a particular size, engine capacity, etc: [attrib] *Formula 1 racing cars.* **7** [U] (*US*) artificial powdered milk for babies.
▷ **formulaic** /ˌfɔːmjʊˈleɪɪk/ *adj* made up of set patterns of words: *Anglo-Saxon poetry is formulaic.*

formulate /ˈfɔːmjʊleɪt/ *v* [Tn] **1** create (sth) in a precise form: *formulate a rule, policy, theory, etc.* **2** express (sth) clearly and exactly using particular words: *formulate one's thoughts carefully* ○ *The contract was formulated in difficult legal language.*
▷ **formulation** /ˌfɔːmjʊˈleɪʃn/ *n* (**a**) [U] action of formulating. (**b**) [C] result of this: *choose another formulation.*

fornicate /ˈfɔːnɪkeɪt/ *v* [I] (*fml esp derog*) (of people not married to each other) have sexual intercourse. ▷ **fornication** /ˌfɔːnɪˈkeɪʃn/ *n* [U]. **fornicator** *n.*

forsake /fəˈseɪk/ *v* (*pt* **forsook** /fəˈsʊk/, *pp* **forsaken** /fəˈseɪkən/) [Tn] **1** (*fml*) give (sth) up; renounce: *forsake one's former habits.* **2** leave (sb), esp when one should be helping him; abandon or desert: *forsake one's family and friends* ○ *a dreary forsaken beach in winter.*

forsooth /fəˈsuːθ/ *interj* (*arch or joc or ironic*) indeed; truly: *An honest fellow, forsooth!* ie I don't believe it.

Forster /ˈfɔːstə(r)/ E(dward) M(organ) (1879-1970), English novelist. His novels, like *A Room with a View* and *A Passage to India*, stress the importance of sensitivity and understanding in human relationships.

forswear /fɔːˈsweə(r)/ *v* (*pt* **forswore** /fɔːˈswɔː(r)/, *pp* **forsworn** /fɔːˈswɔːn/) (*fml*) **1** [Tn, Tg] (promise to) give up (sth); renounce: *He had forsworn smoking.* **2** [Tn] ~ **oneself** = PERJURE ONESELF (PERJURE).

Forsyth /ˈfɔːsaɪθ/ Bill (1947-), Scottish film director. He made a series of comedies including *Gregory's Girl* and *Local Hero* which make clever use of the background of modern Scotland.

forsythia /fɔːˈsaɪθɪə; *US* fərˈsɪθɪə/ *n* [U] bush with bright yellow flowers, blooming in the spring.

fort /fɔːt/ *n* **1** building(s) specially made or strengthened for the military defence of an area. **2** (idm) **hold the ˈfort** have the responsibility or care of sth/sb in the absence of others.

forte[1] /ˈfɔːteɪ; *US* fɔːrt/ *n* (usu *sing*) thing that sb does particularly well; strong point: *Mathematics was never my forte.*

forte[2] /ˈfɔːteɪ/ *adj, adv* (*abbr* **f**) (*music*) loud; (to be) played loudly. Cf PIANO[1].

fortepiano /ˈfɔːtɪpɪænəʊ/ *n* (*pl* ~**os**) pianoforte, esp of the type built in the late 18th and early 19th centuries.

forth /fɔːθ/ *adv part* **1** (*arch*) out from home, etc: *explorers who ventured forth to discover new lands.* **2** (*fml*) onwards; forwards: *from that day forth.* **3** (idm) **and** (**ˌso on and**) **ˈso forth** and other things of the kind that have already been mentioned: *They discussed investments, the state of the economy and so forth.* **back and forth** ➪ BACK[3].

forthcoming /ˌfɔːθˈkʌmɪŋ/ *adj* **1** [attrib] about to happen or appear in the near future: *the ˌforthcoming eˈlections* ○ *a list of ˌforthcoming ˈbooks*, ie those about to be published. **2** [pred] (often with a negative) ready or made available when needed: *The money we asked for was not forthcoming.* **3** [pred] ready to help, give information, etc: *The secretary at the reception desk was not very forthcoming.*

forthright /ˈfɔːθraɪt/ *adj* clear and honest in manner and speech; straightforward: *He has a reputation for being a forthright critic.* ○ *condemnation in the most forthright language.*

forthwith /ˌfɔːθˈwɪθ; *US* -ˈwɪð/ *adv* (*fml*) immediately; at once: *Mr Jones will be dismissed forthwith.*

fortieth ➪ FORTY.

fortify /ˈfɔːtɪfaɪ/ *v* (*pt, pp* **-fied**) **1** [Tn, Tn·pr] ~ **sth** (**against sth**) (**a**) strengthen (a place) against attack, by building walls, etc: *fortify a town against invasion* ○ *a fortified city.* (**b**) support or strengthen (sb) physically or morally: *Fortified against the cold by a heavy coat, he went out into the snow.* ○ *fortify oneself by prayer and meditation.* **2** [Tn usu passive] increase the nutritional value of (a variety of food) by adding vitamins: *cereal fortified with extra vitamins.*
▷ **fortification** /ˌfɔːtɪfɪˈkeɪʃn/ *n* **1** [U] fortifying; strengthening: *plans for the fortification of the city.* **2** [C usu *pl*] tower, wall, ditch, etc built to defend a place against attack: *These fortifications were all built during the last war.*
□ **fortified ˈwine** wine strengthened by adding strong alcohol: *Port and madeira are fortified wines.*

fortissimo /fɔːˈtɪsɪməʊ/ *adj, adv* (*abbr* **ff**) (*music*) very loud; (to be) played very loudly.

fortitude /ˈfɔːtɪtjuːd; *US* -tuːd/ *n* [U] courage, endurance and self-control in facing pain, danger or difficulty: *He bore the pain with great fortitude.*

Fort Knox /ˌfɔːt ˈnɒks/ US military establishment in Kentucky, where most of the country's gold reserves are kept in very secure vaults: (*fig*) *They've put so many locks on the doors of their house that it's like (trying to get into) Fort Knox!*

fortnight /ˈfɔːtnaɪt/ *n* (usu *sing*) (*esp Brit*) **1** (period of) two weeks: *a fortnight's holiday* ○ *a fortnight ago* ○ *a fortnight today/tomorrow/on Tuesday*, ie two weeks after the day specified. **2** (idm) **this day fortnight** ➪ DAY.
▷ **fortnightly** *adj, adv* (*esp Brit*) (happening) once a fortnight: *a fortnightly flight to Brazil* ○ *go home fortnightly.*

FORTRAN (also **Fortran**) /ˈfɔːtræn/ *abbr* (*computing*) formula translation, a programming language used esp for scientific calculations.

fortress /ˈfɔːtrɪs/ *n* castle or large fort; town strengthened against attack: *attempts to capture this well-protected fortress.*

fortuitous /fɔːˈtjuːɪtəs; *US* -ˈtuː-/ *adj* (*fml*) happening by chance or coincidence: *a fortuitous meeting.*

fortunate /ˈfɔːtʃənət/ *adj* having, bringing or brought by good fortune; lucky: *I was fortunate to have/in having a good teacher.* ○ *She's fortunate enough to enjoy good health.* ○ *Remember those less fortunate than yourselves.* ○ *It was very fortunate for him that I arrived on time.* ○ *I made a fortunate choice and won!*
▷ **fortunately** *adv* by good luck; luckily: *I was late, but fortunately the meeting hadn't started.* ○ *Fortunately (for him) Mark quickly found another job.*

fortune /ˈfɔːtʃuːn/ *n* **1** [U] chance, esp regarded as a power affecting people's lives; (good or bad) luck: *By a stroke* (ie instance) *of (good) fortune, he won the competition.* ○ *be a victim of ill* (ie bad) *fortune* ○ *I had the good fortune* (ie was lucky enough) *to be chosen for a trip abroad.* **2** [C usu *pl*] event or change in the life of a person or in the progress of a country, business, etc: *The party's fortunes were at their lowest level after the election defeat.* **3** [C] person's destiny or future; fate: *At the fair a gypsy told (me) my fortune*, eg by looking at playing-cards or the lines on my hand. **4** [C] large amount of money: *That ring is worth/must have cost a fortune.* ○ *She inherited a large fortune.* ○ *He made a considerable fortune selling waste materials.* **5** (idm) **the fortune(s) of ˈwar** the good or bad luck one meets with in war: *made homeless by the* *fortunes of war*. **a hostage to fortune** ⇨ HOSTAGE. **seek one's fortune** ⇨ SEEK. **a small fortune** ⇨ SMALL. **a soldier of fortune** ⇨ SOLDIER.

□ **ˈfortune cookie** (*US*) thin biscuit, folded to hold a printed message (eg a proverb, prophecy or joke), served in Chinese restaurants.

ˈfortune-hunter *n* (*derog*) person who wants to marry sb for money.

ˈfortune-teller *n* person who tells people's fortunes. ⇨ article at SUPERSTITION.

forty /ˈfɔːtɪ/ *pron, det, n* 40; one more than thirty-nine. ⇨ App 9.

▷ **fortieth** /ˈfɔːtɪəθ/ *pron, det* 40th; next after thirty-ninth. — *n* one of forty equal parts of sth.

forty *n* **1** [C] the number 40. **2 the forties** [pl] numbers, years or temperature from 40 to 49. **3** (idm) **in one's forties** between the ages of 40 and 50.

For the uses of *forty* and *fortieth* see the examples at *fifty, five* and *fifth*.

□ **forty-ˈfive** (also **45**) *n* small record that is designed to be played on a record-player at 45 revolutions a minute.

ˌ**forty-ˈniner** *n* miner who took part in the gold-rush to California in 1849.

forum /ˈfɔːrəm/ *n* **1** (usu sing) place where important public issues can be discussed: *The letters page serves as a useful forum for the exchange of readers' views.* **2** (in ancient Rome) public place where meetings were held.

forward[1] /ˈfɔːwəd/ *adj* **1** [attrib] **(a)** directed or moving towards the front: *forward movement.* **(b)** situated in front; near or at the front: *forward ranks of troops* ○ *The forward part of the train is for first-class passengers only.* **2** (of plants, crops, etc) having progressed more than is normal or expected; (of children) having developed certain abilities earlier than normal; well advanced: *The summer crops were forward this year.* ○ *a forward child.* **3** [attrib] of or relating to the future: *forward planning* ○ (*commerce*) *forward buying*, ie buying goods at present prices for delivery later. ⇨ Usage at FORWARD[2]. **4 (a)** ready and willing to be involved; eager: *be forward in helping others.* **(b)** too eager; too bold in one's manner; presumptuous: *a forward young girl* ○ *I hope you'll apologize — that was a very forward thing to do.* Cf BACKWARD.

▷ **forwardness** *n* [U] state of being forward[1](4b): *Such forwardness is deplorable.*

forward[2] /ˈfɔːwəd/ *adv* **1** (also **forwards**) towards the front or end, into a prominent position: *Move forward carefully or you'll slip.* ○ *play a tape-recording forwards, not backwards* ○ *push one's way forward.* Cf BACK[3] 1. **2** onward so as to make progress: *an important step forward* ○ *We are not getting any further forward with the project.* ○ *The project will go forward as planned.* **3** towards the future; onwards in time: *from this time forward* ○ *Look forward and consider the advantages of a larger house.* **4** (idm) **backward(s) and forward(s)** ⇨ BACKWARDS (BACKWARD). ˌ**backward in** ˌ**coming** ˈ**forward** ⇨ BACKWARD. **put one's best foot forward** ⇨ BEST[1]. **put the clock/clocks forward/back** ⇨ CLOCK[1].

□ **ˈforward-looking** *adj* (*approv*) concerned with the future; having modern ideas; progressive: *a young* ˌ*forward-looking* ˈ*company.*

NOTE ON USAGE: The suffix **-ward** means 'in the direction of' and forms adverbs and adjectives: *forward, backward, westward, homeward, etc.* The suffix **-wards** has the same meaning but only forms adverbs: *forwards, backwards, westwards, homewards, etc.* Compare: *They turned westward/westwards after crossing the river. They travelled in a westward direction.* ○ *He leant forward/forwards to see better. To move house requires forward planning.*

forward[3] /ˈfɔːwəd/ *v* **1 (a)** [I, Tn, Dn·n, Dn·pr] ~ **sth (to sb)** send (a letter, etc) to a new address: *please forward*, ie a note written on an envelope, a parcel, etc ○ *Please forward our post (to our new home) when we move.* **(b)** [Tn, Dn·n, Dn·pr] ~ **sth (to sb)** send or dispatch (esp goods or information) to a customer: *forward a shipment of gloves* ○ *We have today forwarded you our new catalogue.* **2** [Tn] help to advance or develop (sth); further: *forward sb's plans, career, interests, etc.*

□ **ˈforwarding address** new address to which post is to be forwarded: *He moved house without leaving a forwarding address.*

ˈforwarding agent person or company that forwards (FORWARD[3] 1a) goods.

forward[4] /ˈfɔːwəd/ *n* attacking player near the front in football, hockey, etc. Cf STRIKER 2.

forwent *pt* of FORGO.

Fosse Way /ˌfɒs ˈweɪ/ **the Fosse Way** name given to one of the main Roman roads in Britain, from Axminster to Lincoln (about 300 km, 200 miles). It was so called because of the 'fosse' or ditch on each side of it.

fossick /ˈfɒsɪk/ *v* [I, Ipr, Ip, Tn·p] (*Austral and NZ sl*) ~ **(about) (for sth)**; ~ **sth out/up (a)** search for (gold, etc), esp in abandoned mines. **(b)** hunt around for sth; rummage for sth. ▷ **fossicker** *n.*

fossil /ˈfɒsl/ *n* **1** remains of a prehistoric animal or plant preserved by being buried in earth and now hardened like rock. Most fossils are what is left of the hard parts of the animal or plant (eg the bones or wood) after they have turned into stone. Sometimes an entire animal survives preserved in ice or amber. Other forms are traces left by animals, such as their footprints or trails. Fossils provide important information about the dates of different geological periods: *This fossil may be over 2 million years old.* ○ [attrib] *fossil bones, shells, etc.* **2** (*infml derog*) person, esp an old one, who is unable to accept new ideas or adapt to new conditions: *Our literature teacher is an old fossil.*

▷ **fossilize, -ise** /ˈfɒsəlaɪz/ *v* [I, Tn usu passive] **1** (cause sth to) become a fossil: *fossilized leaves.* **2** (*fig*) make (sth) or become out of date or fixed: *old-fashioned fossilized attitudes.* **fossilization, -isation** /ˌfɒsəlaɪˈzeɪʃn; *US* -lɪˈz-/ *n* [U].

□ **ˈfossil fuel** fuel, eg coal or oil, formed from the decayed remains of prehistoric animals or plants.

foster /ˈfɒstə(r); *US* ˈfɔː-/ *v* **1** [Tn] help the growth or development of (sth); encourage or promote: *foster an interest, attitude, impression, etc* ○ *foster the growth of local industries.* **2** [I, Tn] take care of and bring up (a child that is not legally one's own): *People who cannot have a baby of their own sometimes foster (a child).* Cf ADOPT 1.

▷ **foster-** (forming compound *ns*) with a family connection through fostering rather than of birth: *a* ˈ*foster-parent, -mother, -child, -son, -sister, etc* ○ *a* ˈ*foster-home.*

fought *pt, pp* of FIGHT.

foul[1] /faʊl/ *adj* **1** having a bad smell or taste; dirty and disgusting: *foul stagnant ponds* ○ *a foul rubbish dump* ○ *This medicine tastes foul!* **2 (a)** unpleasant; dreadful: *'Go away! I've had a foul day at work.'* ○ *His boss has a foul temper.* **(b)** evil or wicked: *a foul crime.* **3** (of language) obscene and offensive; full of swear-words. **4** (of weather) very rainy and windy; stormy or rough: *The spring was foul this year — it was cold and wet for weeks.* **5** (*sport*) (of an action) against the rules; unfair: *a foul stroke.* **6** (of a chimney, pipe, etc) blocked with waste, etc so that nothing can pass through. **7** (idm) **by fair means or foul** ⇨ FAIR[1]. **fall foul of sb/sth** have a confrontation or disagreement with sb/sth, esp the government or the authorities: *The police never caught him in any criminal activity but he eventually fell foul of the tax authorities.*

▷ **foul** *n* (*sport*) action that is against the rules of a game: *That last foul (against/on Smith) lost us the match.*

foully /ˈfaʊllɪ/ *adv.*

foulness *n* [U].

□ ˌ**foul-ˈmouthed** *adj* using obscene and offensive language: *a* ˌ*foul-mouthed* ˈ*child.*

ˌ**foul** ˈ**play 1** action that is against the rules of a sport; unfair or illegal dealings: *fresh evidence of foul play in financial dealings.* **2** criminal violence that leads to murder: *The police suspect foul play rather than suicide.*

foul[2] /faʊl/ *v* **1** [Tn, Tn·p] ~ **sth (up)** make sth dirty: *Dogs are not permitted to foul* (ie excrete on) *the pavement.* ○ *The factories are responsible for fouling up the air for miles around.* **2** [I, Ip, Tn, Tn·p] ~ **(sth) (up)** (cause sth to) become caught or twisted (in sth): *The ropes have fouled (up).* ○ *My fishing-line got fouled (up) in an old net.* **3** [I, Tn] (*sport*) commit a foul[1] against (another player): *He fouled the same player again in the second half.* **4** (idm) **foul one's (own) nest** bring disgrace, etc to one's home, family, profession, country, etc. **5** (phr v) **foul sth up** (*infml*) spoil sth, usu by behaving in a thoughtless or foolish way; mess sth up: *Everything was just fine until Fred came along and fouled things up.* ○ *The weather has really fouled up my holiday plans.*

▷ **ˈfoul-up** *n* (*infml*) spoiling or upsetting of arrangements, relationships, etc: *We'll finish the project on time if there are no more foul-ups.*

foulard /ˈfuːlɑː(r); *US* fuːˈlɑːrd/ *n* [U] thin soft material of silk or silk mixed with cotton: [attrib] *a foulard silk scarf.*

found[1] **1** *pt, pp* of FIND. **2** (idm) **all found** ⇨ FIND.

found[2] /faʊnd/ *v* **1** [Tn] (begin to) build (sth); establish: *This settlement was founded in 1592.* ○ *The ancient Romans founded colonies throughout Europe.* **2** [Tn] start or establish (an organization, institution, etc), esp by providing money: *found a research institute, company, hospital, etc.* **3** [Tn·pr usu passive] ~ **sth on sth** base or construct sth on sth: *a novel founded on fact* ○ *a morality founded on religious principles.*

□ **founding ˈfather 1** person who establishes an institution, a popular movement, etc: *the founding fathers of modern linguistics.* **2 Founding Father** member of the body that in 1787 drew up the Constitution of the USA.

found[3] /faʊnd/ *v* [Tn] **1** melt (metal) and pour it into a mould. **2** make (an object) from metal in this way.

foundation /faʊnˈdeɪʃn/ *n* **1** [U] act of founding (an institution, organization, etc): *the foundation of the university.* **2** [C] **(a)** (organization set up to provide) sums of money for research, charity, etc: *the Ford Foundation* ○ *You may be able to get support from an arts foundation.* **(b)** institution, eg a college or hospital, that is established by means of such a fund. **3** [C usu *pl*] layer of bricks, concrete, etc forming the solid base of a building underground: *lay the foundations of a building* ○ *The huge lorries shook the foundations of the house.* **4** [C, U] principle, idea or fact on which sth is based; basis: *lay the foundations of one's career* ○ *The political scandal shook the nation to its very foundations.* ○ *The conclusions must have some solid foundation in reality.* ○ *That rumour has no foundation /is without foundation in fact.* **5** [U] (also **foundation cream**) cream put on the face before other make-up is applied.

□ **founˈdation course** course taken at a college, etc that usu covers a wide range of subjects and prepares students for more advanced studies.

founˈdation-stone *n* large block of stone laid at a special ceremony to mark the founding of a public building.

founder[1] /ˈfaʊndə(r)/ *n* person who founds or establishes sth: *founder of a city, institution, company, etc.*

□ **founder-ˈmember** *n* one of the first and founding members of a society, an organization, etc.

founder[2] /ˈfaʊndə(r)/ *v* **1** [I] (of a plan, etc) fail; break down: *The project foundered as a result of lack of finance.* **2** [I] (of a ship) fill with water and sink: *The boat foundered on rocks near the harbour.* **3** [I] (esp of a horse) fall or stumble: *The mare foundered under the heavy load and collapsed in the road.*

foundling /ˈfaʊndlɪŋ/ *n* (*arch*) abandoned child of unknown parents who is found by sb.

foundry /ˈfaʊndrɪ/ *n* place where metal or glass is melted and moulded into articles of particular shapes.

fount[1] /faʊnt/ *n* ~ **(of sth)** (*rhet or arch*) source or origin (of sth); fountain: *the fount of all wisdom.*

fount[2] /faʊnt/ (also **font** /fɒnt/) *n* set of printing type of one style and size.

fountain /ˈfaʊntɪn; *US* -tn/ *n* **1** jet of water, esp one forced up into the air artificially as an ornament: *The fountains of Rome are famed for their architectural beauty.* ○ *A fountain of water gushed from the broken fire hydrant.* **2** = DRINKING FOUNTAIN (DRINK[2]). **3** ~ **(of sth)** (*rhet or arch*) source or origin (of sth); fount: *the fountain of justice.*
□ **ˈfountain-head** *n* origin or source: *the fountain-head of power.*
ˈfountain-pen *n* pen with a container from which ink flows continuously to the nib.

four /fɔː(r)/ *pron, det* **1** 4; one more than three. ⇨ App 9. **2** (idm) **on all ˈfours** (of a person) with one's hands and knees (and usu also toes) on the ground: *The baby was crawling about on all fours.* ⇨ illus at KNEEL. **(be) on all fours (with sb/sth)** (be) the same in importance, function, etc (as sb/sth else).
▷ **four** *n* **1** the number 4. **2** group of four people or things. **3** (crew of a) rowing-boat for four people. **4** (in cricket) shot, scoring four runs, in which the ball crosses the boundary after having hit the ground.
four- (in compounds) having four of the thing specified: *a ˌfour-sided ˈfigure* ○ *a ˌfour-leaf ˈclover*, ie one that is rarely found and is therefore thought to bring good luck to anyone who finds it.
fourth /fɔːθ/ *pron, det* 4th; next after third. ⇨ App 9. **fourthly** *adv* in the fourth position or place. **the ˌfourth diˈmension** the dimension of time. **the ˌfourth eˈstate** (*usu joc*) the press (ie journalism and journalists in general) esp considered as influencing politics, public opinion, etc. **the ˌFourth of Juˈly** anniversary of the Declaration of Independence (1776) of the USA from Britain. — *n* one of four equal parts of sth.
For the uses of *four* and *fourth* see the examples at *five* and *fifth.*
□ **ˈfour-flush** *n* (*US*) **1** (in poker) almost worthless hand of five cards, in which four are of the same suit but not the fifth. **2** (*sl*) attempt to deceive sb by bluffing. **ˌfour-ˈflusher** *n* (*sl*) person who pretends to be what he is not; bluffer.
fourfold /ˈfɔːfəʊld/ *adj, adv* **1** four times as much or as many: *The population in this area has increased fourfold.* **2** having four parts.
the ˌFour ˌHorsemen of the Aˈpocalypse (*Bible*) four figures riding horses, mentioned in the Book of *Revelation. They represent the major disasters for humanity: war, destruction, famine and plague.
ˌfour-in-ˈhand *n* coach or carriage pulled by four horses and driven by one person.
ˌfour-letter ˈword any of various short words, usu referring to sexual or other bodily functions, that are considered obscene or offensive. ⇨ article at TABOO.
ˈfour-ply *adj* (of wool, wood, etc) having four strands or thicknesses.
ˌfour-ˈposter *n* (also **ˌfour-poster ˈbed**) (esp formerly) large bed with a tall post at each of the four corners to support curtains.
foursome /ˈfɔːsəm/ *n* **1** four people joining together to play a game, esp golf. **2** two couples undertaking a leisure activity together: *Let's make (up) a foursome and go out to a restaurant.*
ˌfour-ˈsquare *adj* **(a)** square-shaped. **(b)** solidly based; steady or resolute: *a ˌfour-square apˈproach to the problem.*
ˈfour-stroke *adj* (of an engine) having a cycle of combustion in which a piston makes four movements or strokes for each firing of a cylinder. Cf TWO-STROKE (TWO).
ˌfour-wheel ˈdrive (of a vehicle in which) power is applied to all four wheels.

fourteen /ˌfɔːˈtiːn/ *pron, det* 14; one more than thirteen. ⇨ App 9.
▷ **fourteen** *n* the number 14.
fourteenth /ˌfɔːˈtiːnθ/ *pron, det* 14th; next after thirteenth. — *n* one of fourteen equal parts of sth.
For the uses of *fourteen* and *fourteenth* see the examples at *five* and *fifth.*

fowl /faʊl/ *n* **1** [C] (*pl* unchanged or ~**s**) domestic cock or hen: *We keep a few fowls and some goats.* **2** [U] flesh of certain types of birds, eaten for food: *We had fish for the first course, followed by roast fowl and fresh vegetables.* **3** [C] (*arch*) any bird: *the fowls of the air.* **4** (in compounds) bird of the type specified: *ˈwaterfowl* ○ *barnyard fowl* ○ *ˈwildfowl.*
▷ **fowl** *v* [I] (usu **go ˈfowling**) hunt or snare wildfowl.
□ **ˈfowl pest** type of infectious disease among chickens, etc.

Fowler /ˈfaʊlə(r)/ Henry Watson (1858-1933), British lexicographer. With his brother Francis George Fowler he compiled the first *Concise Oxford Dictionary*, but he is best remembered for *Modern English Usage*, often simply called 'Fowler', a guide to the rules of good written English.

Fox /fɒks/ George (1624-91), founder of the Society of Friends, or *Quakers. He came to believe in the 'inner light of Christ', rather than traditional church doctrines, and was often put in prison for his beliefs.

fox /fɒks/ *n* **1 (a)** [C] (*fem* **vixen** /ˈvɪksn/) wild animal of the dog family, with reddish brown fur, a pointed face and a bushy tail. The fox is traditionally and in literature seen as a clever and cunning animal, able to flatter and trick others so as to obtain what it wants: *Hunting foxes is a peculiarly English sport.* ⇨ illus at ANIMAL. **(b)** [U] its skin and fur used to make coats, etc. **2** [C] (*infml esp derog*) person who is clever and able to get what he wants by deceiving or manipulating others: *a crafty/sly old fox.*
▷ **fox** *v* **1** [Tn] **(a)** be too difficult for (sb) to understand; baffle or confuse: *He was completely foxed by her behaviour.* **(b)** trick (sb) by cunning; deceive. **2** [Tn usu passive] discolour (the pages of a book) with brown marks: *This volume is foxed on the flyleaf.*
foxy /ˈfɒksɪ/ *adj* (**-ier, -iest**) **1** crafty or deceitful; cunning. **2** like a fox in appearance, ie reddish brown in colour or having a fox-like face. **3** (*sl approv esp US*) (of a woman) physically attractive; sexy: *a foxy lady.*
□ **ˈfoxhole** *n* hole in the ground dug by soldiers as a shelter against enemy fire and as a firing-point.
ˈfoxhound *n* type of dog trained to hunt foxes.
ˈfox-hunting *n* [U] sport in which a fox is hunted by foxhounds and people on horses. ⇨ articles at ANIMAL, PROTEST.
ˌfox-ˈterrier *n* type of short-haired dog, formerly used to drive foxes out of their holes.

foxglove /ˈfɒksglʌv/ *n* tall plant with purple or white bell-shaped flowers growing up its stem. ⇨ illus at PLANT.

foxtrot /ˈfɒkstrɒt/ *n* (music for a) formal dance with both slow and quick steps.
▷ **foxtrot** *v* (**-tt-**) [I] dance the foxtrot.

foyer /ˈfɔɪeɪ; *US* ˈfɔɪər/ *n* entrance hall or large open space in a theatre, hotel, etc where people can meet or wait: *I'll meet you in the foyer at 7 o'clock.*

FPA /ˌef piː ˈeɪ/ *abbr* (*Brit*) Family Planning Association.

Fr[1] *abbr* **1** (*religion*) Father: *Fr (Paul) Black.* **2** French.

Fr[2] *symb* francium.

fr *abbr* franc(s): *fr18.50.*

fracas /ˈfrækɑː; *US* ˈfreɪkəs/ *n* (*pl* unchanged /-kɑːz/; *US* ~**es** /-kəsəz/) (usu *sing*) noisy quarrel, fight, or disturbance: *The police were called in to break up* (ie stop) *the fracas.*

fraction /ˈfrækʃn/ *n* **1** small part, bit, amount, or proportion (of sth): *The car stopped within a fraction of an inch of the wall.* ○ *Could you move a fraction closer?* **2** precise division of a number, eg $\frac{1}{3}$, $\frac{5}{8}$, 0.76.
▷ **fractional** /-ʃənl/ *adj* **1** of or in fractions: *a fractional equation.* **2** very small; trivial or unimportant: *a fractional difference in prices.*
fractionally /-ʃənəlɪ/ *adv* to a very small degree; marginally: *One dancer was fractionally out of step.* **ˌfractional distilˈlation** process of distilling a mixture of liquids so as to separate them. As the vapours cool, the different liquids condense at different temperatures and can be removed at the appropriate stage. The process is widely used in oil refining.

fractious /ˈfrækʃəs/ *adj* (esp of children) irritable; bad-tempered. ▷ **fractiously** *adv.* **fractiousness** *n* [U].

fracture /ˈfræktʃə(r)/ *n* **(a)** [C] instance of breaking (esp a bone): *a fracture of the leg* ○ *He had several injuries, including three fractures.* ○ *a compound/simple fracture*, ie one in which the skin is/is not pierced by the broken bone ○ *a slight fracture in a pipe.* **(b)** [U] breaking or breakage, esp of a bone: *the site of fracture.*
▷ **fracture** *v* [I, Tn] (cause sth to) break or crack: *Her leg fractured in two places.* ○ *suffer from a fractured pelvis.*

fragile /ˈfrædʒaɪl; *US* -dʒl/ *adj* **1** easily damaged or broken; delicate: *fragile china/glass* ○ *a fragile plant* ○ (*fig*) *Human happiness is so fragile.* ○ *a fragile economy.* **2** (*infml*) not strong and healthy; weak, eg because one has drunk too much alcohol: *He's feeling a bit fragile after last night's party.* Cf FRAIL. ▷ **fragility** /frəˈdʒɪlətɪ/ *n* [U].

fragment /ˈfrægmənt/ *n* **1** small part or piece broken off (sth): *find several fragments of a Roman vase.* **2** separate or incomplete part (of sth): *I heard only a fragment of their conversation.*
▷ **fragment** /frægˈment/ *v* [I, Tn] (cause sth to) break into small pieces or parts; split up: *These bullets fragment on impact.* ○ (*fig*) *Ownership of the large estates is increasingly fragmented*, ie divided among several people.
fragmentary /ˈfrægməntrɪ; *US* -terɪ/ *adj* made up of small incomplete or unconnected parts: *fragmentary evidence.*
fragmentation /ˌfrægmenˈteɪʃn/ *n* [U]. **ˌfragmenˈtation bomb** bomb designed to break up into many small pieces.

fragrance /ˈfreɪgrəns/ *n* **(a)** [C usu *sing*] pleasant or sweet smell; scent or perfume: *Lavender has a delicate fragrance.* **(b)** [U] quality of having a pleasant or sweet smell.

fragrant /ˈfreɪgrənt/ *adj* having a pleasant or sweet smell: *fragrant herbs, flowers, etc.* ▷ **fragrantly** *adv.*

frail /freɪl/ *adj* **1** (of a person) physically weak or delicate: *a frail child* ○ *At 90, she's getting very old and frail.* **2** easily broken; fragile: *Careful: that chair's rather frail!* **3** morally weak: *frail human nature.*
▷ **frailty** /ˈfreɪltɪ/ *n* **1** [U] physical weakness. **2** [C, U] (instance of) weakness in character or morals; fault or imperfection: *She continued to love him despite his many frailties.* ○ *human frailty.*

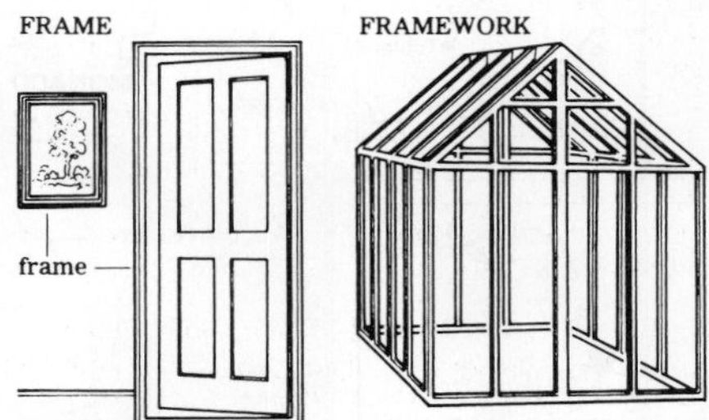

frame[1] /freɪm/ *n* **1** border of wood, metal, etc in which a picture, door, pane of glass, etc is enclosed or set: *a picture frame* ○ *a window frame.* **2** rigid structure of a piece of furniture, building, vehicle, etc which makes its shape and forms a support for its parts: *the frame of a cupboard, bed, rucksack* ○ *the frame of an aircraft, a car, etc.* ⇨ illus at BICYCLE, ⇨ illus. **3** (usu *pl*) structure of plastic, metal, etc that holds the lenses of a pair of glasses in place: *glasses with heavy black frames.* ⇨ illus at GLASS. **4** (usu *sing*) human or animal body; its form or structure: *Sobs shook her slender frame.* **5** general order or system that forms the background to sth: *the frame of contemporary society.* **6** (**a**) any of the single photographs that make up a cinema film. (**b**) single picture in a comic strip. **7** = COLD FRAME (COLD[1]). **8** (**a**) (in snooker, etc) triangular structure for positioning balls. (**b**) (in snooker, bowling, etc) single round of play. **9** (*US*) = FRAME-UP (FRAME[2]). **10** (idm) **a ˌframe of ˈmind** particular state of one's mind or feelings; mood: *I'm not in the right frame of mind to start discussing money.* **a ˌframe of ˈreference** set of principles, standards or observations used as a basis for one's judgement, behaviour, etc: *sociological studies conducted within a Marxist frame of reference.*

□ **ˈframe-house** *n* house with a wooden frame covered with boards.

ˈframework *n* **1** structure giving shape and support: *a bridge with a steel framework.* ⇨ illus. **2** social order or system: *civil unrest which shook the framework of the old system.* **3** set of principles or ideas used as a basis for one's judgement, decisions, etc: *All the cases can be considered within the framework of the existing rules.*

frame[2] /freɪm/ *v* **1** (**a**) [Tn] put or build a frame[1](1) round (sth): *frame a photograph, painting, etc.* (**b**) [Tn esp passive] serve or act as a frame[1](1) for (sb/sth): *He stood framed in the doorway to the hall.* ○ *A dense mass of black hair framed his face.* **2** [Tn] express (sth) in words; compose or formulate: *frame a question, argument, response, etc* ○ *frame a theory, plan, set of rules, etc.* **3** [Tn esp passive] (*infml*) produce false evidence against (an innocent person) so that he appears guilty: *The accused man said he had been framed.*

□ **ˈframe-up** (*US* **frame**) *n* (*infml*) situation in which false evidence is produced against an innocent person so that he appears guilty: *Don't you see — it was all a frame-up!*

franc /fræŋk/ *n* unit of currency in eg France, Belgium and Switzerland.

France

France /frɑːns/ country in western Europe; pop approx 55 873 000; language French; capital Paris; unit of currency franc (= 100 centimes). It has coastlines on the Atlantic, the Mediterranean and the English Channel. There are three main mountain regions, the Alps, the Pyrenees and the Massif Central. The temperate climate makes it an agricultural country, famous esp for its wine. The economy is however based mainly on the industrial and service sectors, and France is one of the world's six main economic powers. It is a close neighbour of Britain, and the two countries have often been at war, from the Norman invasion of 1066 to the *Napoleonic Wars. It is now one of Britain's partners in the European Community, of which it was a founder-member. ⇨ map.

franchise /ˈfræntʃaɪz/ *n* **1** [U] right to vote at public elections: *system of universal adult franchise* ○ *Women were not given the franchise in Britain until the twentieth century.* **2** [C] formal permission to sell a company's goods or services in a particular area: *buy a fast-food, printing, etc franchise* ○ *grant, withdraw a franchise.*

▷ **franchise** *v* [Tn] grant a franchise(2) to (sb).

Francis /ˈfrɑːnsɪs; *US* ˈfrænsɪs/ Saint, of Assisi (1181/2-1226), founder of the Franciscan order. He belonged to a rich family, but decided to live a life of poverty based on the teachings of Jesus. He stressed the value of a simple faith, generosity and humility, and is remembered for his love of nature. Pope John Paul II made him the patron saint of ecology.

Franciscan /frænˈsɪskən/ *n, adj* (friar or nun) of the Christian religious order founded by St Francis of Assisi.

francium /ˈfrænsɪəm/ *n* [U] (*symb* **Fr**) (*chemistry*) radio-active metallic element, found in uranium and thorium ores.

Franck /frɒŋk; *US* frɑːŋk/ César (1822-90), Belgian composer. He was a remarkable organist and this greatly influenced his style. Apart from his organ pieces, his most popular works are a string quartet, a piano quintet, a violin sonata and a symphony.

Franco /ˈfræŋkəʊ; *US* ˈfrɑːŋkəʊ/ Francisco (1892-1975), Spanish dictator. He was one of the leaders of the military uprising against the republican government which led to the Spanish Civil War (1936-39). After the war he set up a fascist regime which he led until his death.

Franco- *comb form* French; of France: *Franco-German history* ○ *Francophile*, ie (person who is) friendly towards France.

francophone /ˈfræŋkəʊfəʊn/ *adj, n* French-speaking (person): *the francophone countries of West Africa.*

franglais /ˈfrɒŋgleɪ/ *n* [U] (*French*) (**a**) humorous use of language mixing French words with English. ⇨ article at HUMOUR. (**b**) (*often derog*) English words (or words thought to come from English) used in French.

Frank /fræŋk/ *n* member of a Germanic people that conquered Gaul in the 6th century AD. ▷ **Frankish** *adj.*

frank[1] /fræŋk/ *adj* (**-er, -est**) ~ (**with sb**) (**about sth**) showing thoughts and feelings openly; honest and direct in speech; plain and blunt: *a frank reply, discussion, exchange of views, etc* ○ *To be (perfectly) frank with you, I think your son has little chance of passing the exam.*

▷ **frankly** *adv* **1** in a frank manner: *Tell me frankly what's wrong.* **2** speaking honestly; to be truthful: *Frankly, I couldn't care less.* ○ *Quite frankly, I'm not surprised.* ⇨ Usage at HOPEFUL.

frankness *n* [U]: *She spoke about her fears with complete frankness.*

frank[2] /fræŋk/ *v* [Tn] put a mark or a stamp on (a letter, etc) to show that postage has been paid or does not need to be paid.

□ **ˈfranking-machine** *n* device that automatically franks letters, etc and counts up the total postal charges.

Frankenstein /ˈfræŋkənstaɪn/ character in Mary *Shelley's book *Frankenstein* who makes a living creature from the bodies of other humans and is eventually killed by it. The story, and variations of it, have been the subject of many films.

□ **ˌFrankenstein's ˈmonster** thing that cannot be controlled by the person who creates it, and causes great trouble or damage.

frankfurter /ˈfræŋkfɜːtə(r)/ (*US* **frankfurt, frankfort, frankforter, wiener**) *n* type of small smoked sausage.

frankincense /ˈfræŋkɪnsens/ *n* [U] type of sweet-smelling gum from a tree, burnt as incense.

Franklin /ˈfræŋklɪn/ Benjamin (1706-90), American statesman and scientist. He founded the first public library in America and the American Philosophical Society (which became the University of Pennsylvania). He helped to bring about peace between Britain and the USA after the American War of Independence, and as an ambassador to France negotiated a treaty with that country. His scientific interests led to the invention of the lightning conductor and bifocal spectacles.

frantic /ˈfræntɪk/ *adj* **1** in an extreme state of emotion, esp fear or anxiety: *The child's parents were frantic when she did not return home on time.* ○ *frantic with worry, anger, grief, etc.* **2** hurried and excited but disorganized; frenzied; desperate: *a frantic dash, rush, search, etc* ○ *frantic activity.* ▷ **frantically** /-klɪ/ *adv*: *shouting frantically for help.*

frappé /ˈfræpeɪ; *US* fræˈpeɪ/ *n* **1** alcoholic drink served on chips of ice. **2** water-ice similar to a sorbet.

▷ **frappé** *adj* (esp of wine) chilled.

fraternal /frəˈtɜːnl/ *adj* (*esp rhet*) of a brother or brothers; brotherly or friendly: *fraternal love* ○ *fraternal greetings from fellow trade-unionists.* ▷ **fraternally** /-nəlɪ/ *adv.*

□ **fraˌternal ˈtwins** twins (of either sex) that develop from separate eggs and are therefore not identical.

fraternity /frəˈtɜːnətɪ/ *n* **1** [U] brotherly feeling; brotherhood: *There is a strong spirit of fraternity among these isolated people.* **2** [CGp] group of people sharing the same profession or common interests or beliefs: *the medical, banking, teaching, etc fraternity* ○ *the racing fraternity* ○ *the religious fraternity of St Benedict.* **3** [C] (*US*) organization formed by male students at a university as a social club, usu with a name made up of Greek letters. Cf SORORITY. ⇨ article at POST-SCHOOL.

fraternize, -ise /ˈfrætənaɪz/ *v* [I, Ipr] ~ (**with sb**) become friendly with enemy soldiers, or with civilians of a former enemy country: *Soldiers who fraternize with the enemy will be punished.* ○ *Army personnel are often forbidden to fraternize with the civilian population.* ▷ **fraternization, -isation** /ˌfrætənaɪˈzeɪʃn; *US* -nɪˈz-/ *n* [U].

fratricide /ˈfrætrɪsaɪd/ *n* (**a**) [U] crime of killing one's brother or sister. (**b**) [C] person who has done this. ▷ **fratricidal** /ˌfrætrɪˈsaɪdl/ *adj.*

fraud /frɔːd/ *n* **1** [C, U] (act of) deceiving sb illegally in order to make money or obtain goods: *found guilty of fraud* ○ *Thousands of frauds are committed every year.* **2** [C] person who deceives others by pretending to have abilities, skills, etc that he does not really have; impostor: *This woman is a fraud — she has no medical qualifications at all.*

▷ **fraudulent** /ˈfrɔːdjʊlənt; *US* -dʒʊ-/ *adj* **1** deceitful or dishonest: *a fraudulent display of sympathy.* **2** obtained or done by fraud; involving fraud: *fraudulent applications for shares* (ie type of investment) *in the new company.* **fraudulence** /ˈfrɔːdjʊləns; *US* -dʒʊ-/ *n* [U]. **fraudulently** /ˈfrɔːdjʊləntlɪ; *US* -dʒʊ-/ *adv.*

fraught /frɔːt/ *adj* **1** [pred] ~ **with sth** filled with sth; charged with sth: *a situation fraught with danger* ○ *a silence fraught with meaning.* **2** worried or anxious; worrying: *There's no need to look so fraught!* ○ *Next week will be particularly fraught as we've just lost our secretary.*

fray[1] /freɪ/ *n* **the fray** [sing] (*rhet or joc*) fight, contest or argument; lively or challenging action: *ready/eager for the fray* ○ *enter/join the fray*, ie take part in a fight, quarrel, etc.

fray[2] /freɪ/ *v* [I, Tn] **1** (cause sth to) become worn, so that there are loose threads, fibres or wires:

This cloth frays easily. ○ *Constant rubbing will fray even the thickest rope.* ○ *frayed shirt cuffs.* **2** (cause sth to) become strained and irritated: *Nerves/Tempers began to fray in the heat.* ○ *Relations between us have become frayed through a series of misunderstandings.*

Frazer /ˈfreɪzə(r)/ Sir James (1854-1941), Scottish scholar, regarded as the founder of social anthropology in Britain. In *The Golden Bough* he explains his theory of how mankind progresses from a belief in magic to religion and finally to scientific thought.

frazzle /ˈfræzl/ *n* (idm) **beaten, burnt, worn, etc to a ˈfrazzle** completely beaten, burnt, exhausted, etc.

freak[1] /fri:k/ *n* **1** (*infml derog*) person considered abnormal because of his behaviour, appearance, ideas, etc: *People think she's a freak just because she's religious.* ○ [attrib]: *a ˈfreak show*, ie one presenting people with physical deformities as entertainment, formerly popular in circuses. **2** (*infml*) person with a specified interest or obsession; fan: *ˈhealth/ˈhealth-food freaks* ○ *a ˈjazz freak* ○ *an ˈacid freak*, ie sb addicted to the drug LSD. **3** very unusual event or action: *By some freak (of chance) I was overpaid this month.* ○ [attrib] *a freak accident, storm, etc.* **4** (also **ˌfreak of ˈnature**) person, animal or plant that is abnormal in form.

▷ **freakish** *adj* unusual or abnormal; strange: *freakish weather* ○ *freakish behaviour.* **freakishly** *adv.* **freakishness** *n* [U].

freaky *adj* unusual; weird; freakish.

freak[2] /fri:k/ *v* (*infml*) **1** [I, Ip] ~ **(out)** have an extreme reaction to sth: *My parents (really) freaked (out) when they saw my purple hair*, ie were shocked and angry. ○ *When they told me I'd won a car, I absolutely freaked*, ie was extremely happy. **2** (phr v) **freak out** (a) temporarily lose control of oneself; go crazy; act abnormally, usu under the influence of drugs: *This ordinary quiet guy just freaked out and shot ten people.* ○ *John's party was really wild — everyone freaked out (on drugs)*, ie hallucinated. (b) adopt an unconventional style of life. **freak sb out** make sb feel extreme pleasure or unease: *Listening to a good stereo system always freaks me out.*

□ **ˈfreak-out** *n* wild and extreme experience, esp one produced by drugs.

freckle /ˈfrekl/ *n* (usu *pl*) any of the small light-brown spots on the human skin, esp of young people with a fair complexion: *Ann's face and back are covered with freckles.* Cf MOLE[1].

▷ **freckle** *v* [I, Tn] (cause skin to) become covered with freckles: *Do you freckle easily?* ○ *the boy's freckled arms.*

free[1] /fri:/ *adj* (**freer** /fri:ə(r)/, **freest** /fri:ɪst/) **1** (a) (of a person) not a slave or prisoner; allowed to move where one wants; having physical freedom: *After ten years in prison, he was a free man again.* ○ *The convicts were pardoned and set free.* ○ *The driver had to be cut free from the wreckage of his car.* (b) (of an animal) not kept in a cage or tied up; able to move at will: *In nature, all animals are wild and free.* ○ *The dog was chained, so how did it get free?* ○ *An escaped tiger is roaming free in the town.* **2** not fixed or held down; loose: *the free end of the rope* ○ *Let the rope run free.* ○ *One of the wheels of the cart has worked (itself) free.* **3** clear; not blocked; unrestricted: *Is the way/passage free?* ○ *A free flow of water came from the pipe.* ○ *The streets have been swept free of leaves.* **4** (of a country, its citizens and institutions) not controlled by a foreign government or the state itself: *This is a free country — I can say what I like.* ○ *We might have a free press, but that doesn't mean all reporting is true and accurate.* **5** ~ **(to do sth)** not controlled or restricted (by rules or conventions); permitted to do sth: *free movement of workers within the European Community* ○ *free access to secret information* ○ *You are free to come and go as you please.* ○ *She's a free spirit*, ie a person not hampered by convention. **6** [pred] ~ **from/of sth** (a) not harmed by sth dangerous; not spoilt by sth unpleasant: *free from harm, prejudice, pain* ○ *free of weeds, contamination, pollution, etc.* (b) not subject to certain rules, etc; unrestricted by sth: *a holiday free from all responsibilities.* **7** (a) costing nothing: *free tickets for the theatre* ○ *Admission is free.* ○ *a free sample* ○ *There's no such thing as a free lunch*, ie Nobody does favours without expecting sth in return. (b) [pred] ~ **(of sth)** not including, or not requiring, a specified payment, usu of tax or duty: *a payment of £30 000 free of tax* ○ *Delivery is free (of charge) if goods are paid for in advance.* **8** (a) (of a place) not occupied or being used; (of a time) not engaged or booked: *Is that seat free?* ○ *The bathroom's free now.* ○ *Is there a time when the conference room is free?* ○ *Friday afternoons are left free for revision.* (b) (of a person) without engagements or things to do; not busy: *I'm usually free in the afternoon.* ○ *Are you free for lunch?* **9** [pred] ~ **with sth** giving sth easily and readily; generous with sth: *He is very free with his time*, ie gives it willingly. ○ *He's a bit too free with his compliments.* **10** (*derog*) uncontrolled, often to the point of rudeness; too familiar: *I don't like him — he is too free in his language and manner.* **11** (of a translation) expressing the meaning of the original loosely, not exactly. Cf LITERAL 1a. **12** (a) (*chemistry*) not combined with another element: *free hydrogen.* (b) (*physics*) (of an electron) not bound in an atom or a molecule. **13** (idm) **feel free** ⇨ FEEL[1]. **(get sth) for ˈfree** without payment being required; for nothing: *I got this ticket for free from sb who didn't want it.* **ˌfree and ˈeasy** informal; relaxed: *The atmosphere in the office is quite free and easy.* **ˌfree on ˈboard/ˈrail** (of goods) without charge for delivery to a ship/train. **get, have, etc a free ˈhand** get, have, etc permission or an opportunity to do what one chooses and make one's own decisions, esp in a job: *My boss has given me a free hand in deciding which outside contractor to use.* **give, allow, etc free ˈplay/ˈrein to sb/sth** give, etc complete freedom of movement or expression to sb/sth: *In this picture the artist certainly allowed his imagination free rein.* **have one's hands free/tied** ⇨ HAND[1]. **make sb free of sth** allow sb full use or enjoyment of sth: *He kindly made me free of his library for my research.* **of one's own free will** without being ordered or forced: *I came here of my own free will.*

▷ **free** *adv* **1** without cost or payment; freely: *Children under five usually travel free on trains.* **2** (idm) **make free with sb/sth** treat sb/sth casually and without proper respect; use sth as if it belongs to oneself: *He made free with all his girl-friend's money.*

freely /ˈfri:lɪ/ *adv* **1** without any obstruction; in an unrestricted or uncontrolled manner: *Water flowed freely from the pipe.* ○ *drugs that are freely available.* **2** in an open and honest manner: *It may require courage to speak freely.* **3** willingly; readily: *I freely admit that I made a mistake.* **4** in a generous and willing manner: *Millions of people gave freely in response to the famine appeal.*

□ **free ˈagent** someone able to act as he pleases, because he is not responsible to anyone: *I wish I were a free agent, but my contract binds me for three more years.*

ˌfree associˈation (*psychology*) method of analysis in which a person says the first word that comes to his mind in response to one spoken by the analyst.

ˈfreeboard *n* part of the side of a ship between the level of the water and the deck.

ˈfree-born *adj* born as a free citizen.

ˌFree ˈChurch Church that does not follow the teaching or practices of established Churches such as the Roman Catholic or Anglican Church.

ˌfree ˈenterprise operation of business and trade without government control.

ˌfree ˈfall 1 movement through air or space under the force of gravity alone. **2** part of a parachute jump before the parachute opens.

ˈFreefone *n* [U] (*Brit*) system in which the person making a telephone call does not pay for the cost of the call: *Ring the operator and ask for Freefone 8921.* ⇨ article at TELEPHONE.

ˈfree-for-all *n* noisy fight or argument in which anyone present may join.

ˈfree-hand *adj, adv* (done) by hand, without the use of an instrument, eg a ruler or compass: *a free-hand sketch* ○ *sketched free-hand.*

ˌfree-ˈhanded *adj* generous, esp in spending or giving money.

ˈfreehold *n, adj* (*law*) (having) complete ownership of property for an unlimited period of time. Cf LEASEHOLD (LEASE). **ˈfreeholder** *n* person who owns land freehold.

ˈfree house (*Brit*) public house or inn not controlled by a brewery and therefore able to sell more than one brand of beer, etc. Cf TIED HOUSE (TIE[2]).

ˌfree ˈkick (in football) kick taken without interference, as a penalty against the opposing team.

ˈfreelance /lɑ:ns; *US* læns/ (also **freelancer**) *n* independent artist, writer, etc who earns his living by selling work to several employers: [attrib] *freelance journalism.* — *v* [I] work as a freelance: *I've freelanced for several years.*

free-ˈliving *adj* living for the pleasures of (esp) food and drink. **free-ˈliver** *n.*

free-ˈload *v* [I] (*infml esp US*) take advantage of free food and lodging, etc without giving anything in return; sponge. **free-ˈloader** *n* person who free-loads; sponger.

ˌfree ˈlove (*dated*) agreed sexual relations without marriage.

freeman *n* **1** /-mæn/ person who is not a slave. **2** /-mən/ person who has been given the freedom(5) of a city: *made a freeman of the City of London.*

ˌfree ˈmarket trading area in which prices are determined by the forces of supply and demand rather than by the government: [attrib] *a ˌfree-market eˈconomy.*

ˈfree port port open to all traders, with no restrictions, taxes or import duties.

ˈFreepost *n* [U] (*Brit*) system in which postage costs are paid by the receiver (usu a business company): *Reply to Publicity Department, FREEPOST, Oxford University Press, Oxford.*

ˌfree-ˈrange *adj* [attrib] produced by hens that are kept in natural conditions rather than in a battery(4): *ˌfree-range ˈeggs.*

ˌfree ˈspeech right to express (in public) opinions of any kind.

ˌfree-ˈspoken *adj* expressing one's views openly.

ˌfree-ˈstanding *adj* not supported by or fixed to anything: *a ˌfree-standing ˈsculpture.*

free ˈstate any US State in which slavery did not exist before the Civil War.

ˈfree-style *n* [U] **1** (a) swimming race in which any stroke may be used. (b) type of swimming stroke, usu the crawl(*n* 2). **2** type of wrestling with few restrictions on the holds permitted.

ˌfree-ˈthinker *n* person who forms ideas independently of generally accepted religious teachings. **ˌfree-ˈthinking** *adj.*

ˌfree ˈtrade (system in which) trade is carried on between countries without import restrictions, eg tax and duty.

ˌfree ˈverse poetry without a regular rhythm or rhyme.

ˌfree ˈvote vote in parliament in which members do not have to follow party policy.

ˈfreeway *n* (*US*) = MOTORWAY (MOTOR). ⇨ Usage at ROAD.

ˌfree ˈwheel (rear) wheel on a bicycle that continues to revolve when the pedals are not in use. **ˌfree-ˈwheel** *v* [I] **1** travel, usu downhill, by riding a bicycle without pedalling or driving a car without using engine power. **2** move or act freely or irresponsibly: *I think I'll just free-wheel this summer and see what happens.*

ˌfree ˈwill 1 ability to decide one's own course of action: *I did it of my own free will*, ie acting voluntarily. **2** (belief in the) power to decide a course of action independently of God or fate. **ˌfree-ˈwill** *adj* voluntary: *a ˌfree-will ˈoffering.*

the ˌfree ˈworld (used esp formerly by non-Communists) countries of the world that were not Communist or opposed Communism.

free[2] /fri:/ *v* (*pt, pp* **freed** /fri:d/) **1** [Tn, Tn·pr] ~ **sb/sth (from sth)** make (sb/sth) free; release or liberate: *free the prisoner* ○ *free an animal from a trap.* **2** [Tn·pr] ~ **sb/sth of/from sth** take away sth unpleasant, unwanted, etc from sb/sth; rid sb/sth of sth: *Relaxation exercises can free your body of tension.* ○ *Try to free yourself from all prejudices.* **3** [Tn, Tn·pr] ~ **sb/sth (from sth)** loosen sb/sth from sth that is preventing movement; disentangle or extricate sb/sth: *It took hours to free the victims (from the collapsed building).* ○ *Can you free the propeller from the weeds?* **4** [Tn·pr, Cn·t] ~ **sb/sth for sth** make sb/sth available for (a purpose or an activity): *The government intends to free more resources for educational purposes.* ○ *Retiring early from his job freed him to join several local clubs.*

-free *comb form* (forming *adjs* and *adv*) without; free from: *carefree* ○ *duty-free* ○ *trouble-free.*

freebie /ˈfri:bi:/ *n* (*infml esp US*) thing given away free: *I got these mugs as freebies at the supermarket.*

freedom /ˈfri:dəm/ *n* **1** [U] condition of being free; state of not being a prisoner or slave: *After 10 years in prison, he was given his freedom.* **2** (**a**) [U, C] ~ (**of sth**) right (esp political) to act, speak, etc as one pleases without interference: *freedom of speech, thought, worship, etc* ○ *press freedom* ○ *preserve the freedoms of the trade-union movement.* (**b**) [U] ~ (**of sth**); ~ (**to do sth**) state of being unrestricted in one's actions; liberty: *freedom of action, choice, decision, etc* ○ *He enjoyed complete freedom to do as he wished.* **3** [U] ~ **from sth** state of being without or not affected by the thing specified: *freedom from fear, pain, hunger, etc.* **4** [sing] **the** ~ **of sth** unrestricted use of sth: *I gave him the freedom of my house and belongings.* **5** (idm) **give, etc sb his ˈfreedom** agree to a divorce; allow one's husband/wife to leave without opposing him/her legally: *It seems foolish not to give Ann her freedom, if that's what she really wants.* **give sb, receive, etc the freedom of the ˈcity** give, etc special rights of citizenship, esp as an honour for public services.

□ **ˈfreedom fighter** person belonging to a group that use violent means to overthrow the government and achieve the independence of their country.

Freemason /ˈfri:meɪsn/ (also **Mason**) *n* member of an international secret society with the aims of offering mutual help and developing friendly relations among its members. They are organized into 'lodges' with elaborate rituals, and are sometimes accused of unfairly favouring their fellow members in business and other matters. The organization was originally a medieval association of qualified stonemasons, who later admitted honorary members known as 'accepted masons'.

▷ **Freemasonry** *n* [U] **1** system, practices and rites of the Freemasons. **2 freemasonry** natural sympathy and unspoken understanding between people sharing similar interests: *the freemasonry of TV reporters, professional photographers, etc.*

freesia /ˈfri:zɪə; *US* ˈfri:ʒə/ *n* plant with fragrant yellow, pink or white flowers.

freeze /fri:z/ *v* (*pt* **froze** /frəʊz/, *pp* **frozen** /ˈfrəʊzn/) **1** [I, Tn] (esp of water) change or be changed from liquid to solid by extreme cold: *Water freezes at 0°C.* ○ *The severe cold froze the pond.* Cf THAW. ⇨ Usage at WATER[1]. **2** [I, Ip, Tn, Tn·p] ~ (**sth**) (**up**) (cause sth to) become full of ice or hardened with ice: *The land itself freezes (up) in such low temperatures.* ○ *Our (water) pipes froze (up)* (ie were blocked with ice) *last winter.* ○ *The clothes were frozen on the washing-line.* **3** [I] (used with *it*) (of weather) be so cold that water turns to ice; be extremely cold: *It's freezing outside!* ○ *It may freeze tonight, so make sure the plants are covered.* **4** [I, Tn only passive] (cause a person or an animal to) be or feel very cold; (cause to) die from cold: *Shut the window — I'm freezing!* ○ *Two men froze to death/were frozen to death on the mountain.* **5** [I, Tn] (of food, etc) be able to be preserved by being stored at a temperature below freezing-point; preserve (food, etc), in this way: *Some fruits don't freeze well at all.* ○ *I'll buy extra meat and just freeze it.* ○ *Strawberries don't taste nice if they've been frozen.* ○ *a packet of frozen peas.* **6** [I, Tn] (cause a person or an animal to) stop suddenly; make or become unable to move, speak, or act, because of fear, shock, etc: *Ann froze with terror as the door opened silently.* ○ *The sudden bang froze us in our tracks.* **7** [Tn] hold (wages, prices, etc) at a fixed level officially for a period of time: *freeze wages, prices, fares, etc.* **8** [Tn] not allow (money or assets) to be used or exchanged, usu by government order: *freeze a society's funds* ○ *frozen assets.* **9** [Tn] stop (cine-film or videotape) at a particular point: *freeze the action,* ie stop the film so as to show a still picture. **10** (idm) **freeze one's ˈblood/make one's ˈblood freeze** fill one with feelings of fear and horror: *The sight of the masked gunman made my blood freeze.* **11** (phr v) **freeze on to sth** (*infml*) take hold of sth and not let go of it; cling to sth: *She had frozen on to my arm.* ○ (*fig*) *They froze on to this one idea,* ie would not consider anything else. **freeze sb ˈout** (*infml*) exclude sb from business or from society by harsh competition or unfriendly behaviour: *Small shops are being frozen out by the big supermarkets.* **freeze (sth) ˈover** (usu passive) (cause sth to) become covered by ice: *The lake was frozen over until late spring.* **freeze (sth) ˈup** (usu passive) freeze (sth) so as to prevent normal use: *The window has frozen up and I can't open it.*

▷ **freeze** *n* **1** (also **ˈfreeze-up**) period of weather during which temperatures are below freezing-point: *last year's big freeze* ○ *After the last freeze-up we put insulation round the pipes.* **2** official fixing of wages, prices, etc for a period of time: *a wage/price freeze.*

□ **ˈfreeze-dry** *v* (*pt, pp* **-dried**) [Tn] preserve (esp food) by freezing and then drying it in a vacuum.

ˈfreeze-frame *n* single picture that is part of a cine-film or videotape, created by stopping the film or repeating the same frame[1](6a).

ˈfreezing-point (also **freezing**) *n* [U] temperature at which a liquid, esp water, freezes: *The freezing-point of water is 0°C.* ○ *Tonight the temperature will fall to 3 degrees below freezing.* ⇨ App 10.

freezer /ˈfri:zə(r)/ *n* **1** (also **ˌdeep ˈfreeze**) large refrigerator or room in which food is stored for a long time at a temperature below freezing point. **2** small compartment in a refrigerator for freezing ice and storing frozen food.

freight /freɪt/ *n* [U] goods transported by ships, aircraft or trains: *send goods by air freight.* ⇨ Usage at CARGO.

▷ **freight** *v* **1** [Tn] transport (merchandise) as freight. **2** [Tn·pr] ~ **sth with sth** load (a ship, etc) with freight: *a barge freighted with bananas.*

freighter *n* ship or aircraft that carries mainly freight.

□ **freight car** (*US*) = WAGON 2.

ˈfreightliner *n* (also **liner train, liner**) fast train carrying goods in special large containers that can be loaded and unloaded quickly and easily.

ˈfreight train (*US*) (*Brit* **goods train**) train that carries goods only.

French /frentʃ/ *n* **1 the French** [pl *v*] the people who live in France: *The French are renowned for their cooking.* **2** [U] language spoken in France and parts of Belgium, Switzerland, and Canada: *French is a Romance language.* **3** (idm) **excuse/pardon my ˈFrench** (*infml euph*) excuse the swear-words I shall use: *Excuse my French, but he's a bloody nuisance!* **take French ˈleave** leave one's work, duty, etc without permission.

▷ **French** *adj* of France, its people or its language: *the French countryside.*

□ **ˌFrench ˈbean** kidney or haricot bean, the pod and seeds of which are eaten as a vegetable.

ˌFrench Caˈnadian Canadian whose native language is French.

ˌFrench ˈchalk finely powdered talc, used as a marker, dry lubricant, etc.

ˌFrench ˈcricket simple form of cricket played by children, using a soft ball with which the other players try to hit the batsman's legs.

ˌFrench ˈdressing salad dressing of seasoned oil and vinegar.

ˌFrench ˈfry (*esp US*) = CHIP[1] 3.

ˌFrench ˈhorn brass wind instrument with a long tube coiled in a circle and a wide bell. ⇨ illus at MUSIC.

ˌFrench ˈkiss kiss during which one partner's tongue is put into the other's mouth. **French-kiss** *v* [I, Tn] kiss (sb) in this way.

ˌFrench ˈletter (*infml esp Brit*) contraceptive sheath; condom.

ˌFrench ˈloaf (also **ˌFrench ˈbread**) long thin loaf of crusty white bread. ⇨ illus at BREAD.

ˈFrenchman /-mən/ *n* (*pl* **-men**) man of French birth or nationality.

ˌFrench ˈpolish varnish consisting of shellac and alcohol, painted onto wood to give a hard shiny surface. **French-polish** *v* [Tn] treat (wood) with French polish.

ˌFrench ˈseam seam on a garment, etc with the raw edges turned and sewn under.

ˌFrench ˈtoast (**a**) (*Brit*) bread toasted on one side and buttered on the other. (**b**) bread dipped into a mixture of egg and milk and lightly fried, often served at breakfast with bacon, sausages, etc.

ˌFrench ˈwindow (*US* also **ˌFrench ˈdoor**) one of a pair of doors with long glass panes, usu opening onto a garden or balcony. ⇨ illus at HOME.

ˈFrenchwoman *n* (*pl* **-women** /-wɪmɪn/) woman of French birth or nationality.

French Guiana /gɪˈɑ:nə, gɪˈænɑ/ region in NE South America on the Atlantic Coast, administered by France; capital Cayenne. ⇨ map at GUYANA.

Frenchified (also **frenchified**) /ˈfrentʃɪfaɪd/ *adj* (*often derog*) made to seem French, esp in style or appearance: *a restaurant with a pretentious frenchified menu.*

French Revolution /ˌfrentʃ revəˈlu:ʃn/ **the French Revolution** rebellion (1789-99) by the people of France because of complex grievances among the aristocracy, the middle class, urban workers and the peasants. A dramatic early event was the capture by Parisians of the *Bastille, the prison they saw as the symbol of oppression. At first the movement had high ideals, shown in the Declaration of the Rights of Man. Attempts at a constitutional monarchy failed when the king tried to escape to Austria. He was eventually executed and many people later died in the Reign of Terror. The Revolution failed to produce a stable form of republican government, and ended when *Napoleon came to power.

frenetic *adj* (also **phrenetic**) /frəˈnetɪk/ very excited; frenzied; frantic: *frenetic activity.* ▷ **frenetically** /-klɪ/ *adv.*

frenzy /ˈfrenzɪ/ *n* [sing, U] state of extreme excitement; extreme and wild activity or behaviour: *in a frenzy of zeal, enthusiasm, hate, etc* ○ *The speaker worked the crowd up into a (state of) frenzy.*

▷ **frenzied** /ˈfrenzɪd/ *adj* [usu attrib] wildly excited or agitated; frantic: *The dog jumped at the intruder with frenzied barks.* ○ *the mob's frenzied attack.* **frenziedly** *adv.*

frequency /ˈfri:kwənsɪ/ *n* **1** [U] (**a**) rate of occurrence or repetition of sth, usu measured over a particular period of time: *Fatal accidents have decreased in frequency over recent years.* ○ *the alarming frequency of computer errors.* (**b**) fact of being frequent or happening often: *the frequency of premature births in this region.* **2** [C, U] rate at which a sound wave or radio wave vibrates; band or group of similar frequencies: *high-/low-frequency sounds* ○ *a musical note with a frequency of 256 vibrations per second* ○ *In the evening this station changes frequency and broadcasts on another band.*

□ **ˌfrequency moduˈlation** (abbr **FM**) (in radio signals) modulation in which the frequency of the carrier wave is varied. Cf AMPLITUDE MODULATION (AMPLITUDE).

frequent[1] /ˈfri:kwənt/ *adj* happening often; habitual: *the car manufacturer's frequent changes of models* ○ *His visits became less frequent as time passed.*

▷ **frequentative** /frɪˈkwentətɪv/ *n, adj* (*grammar*) (verb) expressing frequent repetition of an action, like *ripple* or *shiver.*

frequently *adv* often: *Buses run frequently from*

the city to the airport.

frequent[2] /frɪˈkwent/ *v* [Tn] (*fml*) often go to or visit (a place): *He used to frequent the town's bars and night-clubs.*

fresco /ˈfreskəʊ/ *n* (*pl* ~**s** or ~**es** /-kəʊz/) picture painted in water-colour on a wall or ceiling before the plaster is dry. The technique requires great skill as the plaster dries quickly and makes the colours and design permanent. Famous examples are those in the Sistine Chapel by *Michelangelo and *Leonardo da Vinci's *Last Supper*.

fresh /freʃ/ *adj* (**-er**, **-est**) **1** (a) [usu attrib] new or different: *fresh evidence* ○ *a fresh piece of paper* ○ *make a fresh start* ○ *fresh problems* ○ *a fresh approach* (ie one that is original in a lively and attractive way) *to the difficulty.* (b) made, obtained or experienced recently and not changed: *fresh tracks in the snow* ○ *Their memories of the wedding are still fresh in their minds.* **2** (a) (usu of food) newly made, produced, gathered, etc; not stale: *fresh bread*, ie just baked ○ *fresh flowers, eggs, milk, etc.* (b) (of food) not preserved in tins, with salt or by freezing: *fresh vegetables, fruit, meat, etc.* **3** (of clothes) not already used or worn; clean: *put on some fresh clothes.* **4** (of water) not salty, stale or bitter; not sea water. **5** (a) (of the air) clean and refreshing; pure: *Open the window and let in some fresh air.* ○ *play in the fresh air*, ie outside. (b) (of weather) rather cold and windy; (of the wind) cool and fairly strong: *It's a bit fresh this morning, isn't it?* **6** [usu attrib] (a) (of colours) clear and bright; unfaded: *fresh colours in these old prints.* (b) (of skin) clear and healthy: *a fresh complexion.* **7** (of paint) just applied: *Fresh paint — please do not touch.* **8** [usu pred] having renewed strength; refreshed and ready to tackle work, etc: *I feel really fresh after my holiday.* **9** [pred] ~ **from/out of sth** having just come from (a place) or having just had (a particular experience); straight from sth: *students fresh from college.* [pred] **10** ~ **(with sb)** (*infml*) too forward in behaviour or speech, esp in a sexual manner, with a person of the opposite sex: *He then started to get fresh with me.* **11** (idm) **break fresh/new ground** ⇨ GROUND[1]. **a breath of fresh air** ⇨ BREATH. **(as) fresh as a ˈdaisy** vigorous and lively or attractive, esp in a clean fresh way. **new/fresh blood** ⇨ BLOOD[1].

▷ **fresh** *adv* (idm) **fresh out of sth** (*infml esp US*) having just used all one's supplies of sth: *We're fresh out of eggs.*

fresh- (forming compound *adjs*) newly; just: *fresh-baked bread* ○ *fresh-cut flowers.*

fresher *n* (*Brit infml*) student in his/her first year at university or college.

freshly *adv* (usu followed by past participles) recently; newly: *freshly picked strawberries* ○ *freshly laid eggs.*

freshness *n* [U].

□ **ˈfreshman** /-mən/ *n* (*pl* **-men** /-mən/) (*US*) student in his/her first year at college, high school or university. ⇨ article at POST-SCHOOL.

ˈfreshwater *adj* [attrib] from, of, living in or containing fresh (not salty or sea) water: *freshwater fish* ○ *freshwater lakes.* Cf SALT-WATER (SALT).

freshen /ˈfreʃn/ *v* **1** [Tn, Tn·p] ~ **sth (up)** make sth fresh: *A good clean will really freshen (up) the house.* **2** [I] (of the wind) become strong and cool. **3** [Tn] (*US*) add (more liquid, esp alcohol) to a drink: *Can I freshen your drink?* **4** (phr v) **freshen (oneself) up** wash and make (oneself) look clean and tidy after a journey, before a meeting, etc: *I'll just go and freshen (myself) up before the interview.*

▷ **freshener** /ˈfreʃnə(r)/ *n* thing that freshens sth: *an ˈair-freshener.*

fret[1] /fret/ *v* (**-tt-**) **1** [I, Ipr, Tn] ~ **(about/at/over sth)** (cause sb to) become unhappy, bad-tempered, or anxious about sth; worry: *Don't fret, we'll get there on time.* ○ *Fretting about it won't help.* ○ *Babies often fret (themselves) when their mothers are not near.* **2** [Tn] wear (sth) away by rubbing or biting: *a horse fretting its bit* ○ *a fretted rope.*

▷ **fret** *n* [sing] state of irritation, worry: *be in a fret.*

fretful /-fl/ *adj* irritable or complaining, esp because unhappy or worried: *a fretful child.* **fretfully** *adv.*

fret[2] /fret/ *v* (**-tt-**) [Tn esp passive] decorate (wood, etc) with patterns made by cutting or sawing: *an elaborately fretted border.*

□ **ˈfretsaw** *n* narrow saw fixed in a frame, used for cutting designs in thin sheets of wood.

ˈfretwork *n* [U] ornamental work in a decorative pattern, esp wood cut into patterns with a fretsaw.

fret[3] /fret/ *n* each of the bars or ridges on the finger-board of a guitar, etc, used as a guide for the fingers to press the strings at the correct place. ⇨ illus at MUSIC.

Freud /frɔɪd/ Sigmund (1856-1939), Austrian founder of psychoanalysis. His study of neurological disorders led him to develop his theories about the subconscious human mind, and the importance of sexuality in human behaviour. Cf JUNG. ▷ **Freudian** *adj* of or related to the theories of Freud, esp his theories about subconscious sexual ideas or feelings. **ˌFreudian ˈslip** unintentional error made by a speaker which is thought to reveal his true feelings, even though he may not realize them.

Fri *abbr* Friday: *Fri 7 March.*

friable /ˈfraɪəbl/ *adj* (*fml*) easily broken up or crumbled: *friable soil.* ▷ **friability** /ˌfraɪəˈbɪlətɪ/ *n* [U].

friar /ˈfraɪə(r)/ *n* man who is a member of one of certain Roman Catholic religious orders, and who works with people in the outside world rather than living in retreat. Cf MONK.

▷ **friary** /ˈfraɪərɪ/ *n* building in which friars live.

□ **ˌfriar's ˈbalsam** tincture of benzoin, used esp in inhalations for relief of colds, etc.

ˌFriar ˈTuck (in English legend) jovial friar who joined *Robin Hood's band of outlaws.

fricassee /ˈfrɪkəsi:/ *n* [C, U] dish of pieces of cooked meat or poultry served in a thick white sauce: *chicken fricassee.*

▷ **fricassee** *v* (*pp, pt* ~**d**) [Tn esp passive] cook (meat) in this way.

fricative /ˈfrɪkətɪv/ *n, adj* (consonant) made by forcing air through an opening made narrow by bringing the tongue or lips near to another part of the mouth: */f, v, θ/ are fricatives.*

friction /ˈfrɪkʃn/ *n* **1** [U] (a) rubbing of one surface or thing against another: *Friction between two sticks can create a fire.* (b) resistance of one surface to another surface or substance that moves over it: *The force of friction affects the speed at which spacecraft can re-enter the earth's atmosphere.* **2** [U, C] disagreement or conflict between people or parties with different views: *There is a great deal of friction between the management and the work force.* ○ *conflicts and frictions that have still to be resolved.* ▷ **frictional** /-ʃənl/ *adj*: *frictional resistance.*

Friday /ˈfraɪdɪ/ *n* [U, C] (*abbr* **Fri**) the sixth day of the week, next after Thursday.

For the uses of *Friday* see the examples at *Monday.*

fridge /frɪdʒ/ *n* (*infml*) refrigerator.

□ **ˌfridge-ˈfreezer** *n* upright unit containing separate refrigerator and freezer compartments.

fried *pt, pp* of FRY.

friend /frend/ *n* **1** person one knows and likes, but who is not a relation: *He's my friend.* ○ *We are all good friends.* ○ *I've known her for years, but she was never a friend.* **2** ~ **of/to sth** helper, supporter, or patron of sth: *a friend of the arts/the poor* ○ *a friend of justice, peace, etc* ○ *You are invited to become a Friend of the Bristol Hospice*, ie to contribute money regularly. **3** person who is of the same country, group, etc as oneself; ally: *Who goes there — friend or foe?* ○ *At last, among friends, he was free to speak his mind.* **4** thing that is very helpful or familiar: *Honesty has always been his best friend.* ○ *Let's look it up in our old friend, the dictionary.* **5 Friend** member of the Society of Friends; Quaker. **6** (*fml*) person being addressed in public: *Our friend from China will now tell us about her research.* ○ *Friends, it is with great pleasure that I introduce...* ○ *My learned friend*, ie used by a lawyer of another lawyer in a lawcourt ○ *My honourable friend*, ie used by a Member of Parliament to another Member of Parliament in the House of Commons. **7** (idm) **be/make ˈfriends (with sb)** be/become a friend (of sb): *They soon forgot their differences and were friends again*, ie after a quarrel. ○ *David finds it hard to make friends (with other children).* **a ˌfriend in ˈneed (is a ˌfriend inˈdeed)** (*saying*) a friend who helps one when one needs help (is a true friend).

▷ **friendless** *adj* without any friends.

friendly /ˈfrendlɪ/ *adj* (**-ier**, **-iest**) **1** (a) behaving in a kind and pleasant way; acting like a friend: *a friendly person* ○ *The children here are quite friendly with one another.* ○ *It wasn't very friendly of you to slam the door in his face.* ○ *friendly nations*, ie not hostile. (b) showing or expressing kindness and helpfulness: *a friendly smile, welcome, gesture, manner, etc* ○ *friendly co-operation.* (c) of a relationship in which people treat each other as friends: *friendly relations* ○ *on friendly terms with the boss.* **2** not seriously competitive: *a friendly game of football* ○ *a friendly argument* ○ *friendly rivalry.*

▷ **friendliness** *n* [U]

-friendly (in compound *adjs*) that is, or is intended to be, easy for the specified person to use: *a user-friendly computer system.*

□ **ˈfriendly match** (also **friendly**) game of football, etc that is not part of a serious competitive series: *There's a friendly between Leeds United and Manchester City next week.*

ˈFriendly Society (also **ˈProvident Society**) association formed to support its members when they are ill or old.

friendship /ˈfrendʃɪp/ *n* (a) [U] feeling or relationship between friends; state of being friends: *There were strong ties of friendship between the members of the society.* ○ *The aim of the conference is to promote international friendship.* (b) [C] instance of this: *At school she formed a close friendship with several other girls.* ○ *I've had many friendships, but never such an intimate one.*

Friesian /ˈfri:zɪən; *US* ˈfri:ʒn/ *n* type of black and white cow reared for its milk: [attrib] *a Friesian cow, herd.*

frieze /fri:z/ *n* **1** band of sculpture or decoration round the top of a wall or building. ⇨ illus at COLUMN. **2** series of pictures or designs running along a wall: *an alphabet frieze*, ie one that helps to teach the alphabet, each letter having pictures next to it of things whose names begin with that letter.

frig /frɪg/ *v* (**-gg-**) (phr v) **frig about/around** (⚠ *infml*) waste time; mess about: *I've been frigging about all day.*

frigate /ˈfrɪgət/ *n* small fast naval escort-vessel.

frigging /ˈfrɪgɪŋ/ *adj* [attrib] (⚠ *sl*) (used to emphasize a judgement or comment) utter; absolute; bloody: *You frigging idiot!*

fright /fraɪt/ *n* **1** (a) [U] feeling of sudden unpleasant fear: *trembling with fright.* (b) [C usu *sing*] instance of this: *You gave me (quite) a fright suddenly coming in here like that.* ○ *I got the fright of my life*, ie I was extremely frightened. **2** [C usu *sing*] (*infml*) person or thing that looks ridiculous or unattractive: *She thinks that dress is pretty — I think she looks a fright in it.* **3** (idm) **take fright (at sth)** be extremely frightened (by sth): *The animals took fright at the sound of the gun.*

frighten /ˈfraɪtn/ *v* **1** [Tn] fill (sb) with fear; make afraid; scare: *Sorry, I didn't mean to frighten you.* ○ *Loud traffic frightens horses.* **2** (idm) **frighten/scare sb to ˈdeath/out of his ˈwits; frighten the ˈlife out of sb** frighten sb very much; terrify or startle sb: *The child was frightened to death by the violent thunderstorm.* ○ *You frightened the life out of me/frightened me out of my wits suddenly knocking on the window like that!* **frighten/scare the daylights out of sb** ⇨ DAYLIGHTS. **3** (phr v) **frighten sb/sth away/off** force or drive (a person or an animal) to run away by frightening him/it: *The alarm frightened the burglars away.* ○ *The children's shouts frightened off the birds.* **frighten sb into/out of doing sth** cause sb to do/not to do sth by frightening him: *News of the robberies frightened many people into fitting new locks to*

their doors.
▷ **frightened** *adj* in a state of fear; afraid; scared: *Frightened children were calling for their mothers.* ○ *He looked very frightened as he spoke.* ○ *They're frightened of losing power.*
frightening /ˈfraɪtnɪŋ/ *adj* causing fear; alarming: *a frightening possibility, situation, development, etc* ○ *It is frightening even to think of the horrors of nuclear war.* **frighteningly** *adv*: *The film was frighteningly realistic.*

frightful /ˈfraɪtfl/ *adj* **1** very unpleasant; dreadful: *a frightful accident.* **2** [attrib] (*infml*) (used to emphasize a statement) extreme; extremely bad: *in a frightful rush* ○ *They left the house in a frightful mess.*
▷ **frightfully** /-fəlɪ/ *adv* (*infml*) very; awfully: *I'm frightfully sorry, but I can't see you today.*

frigid /ˈfrɪdʒɪd/ *adj* **1** very cold: *a frigid climate/zone.* **2** (esp of a woman) not responsive sexually. **3** formal and unfriendly, esp in relationships with other people: *a frigid glance, look, etc.* ▷ **frigidity** /frɪˈdʒɪdətɪ/ *n* [U]. **frigidly** *adv.*

frill

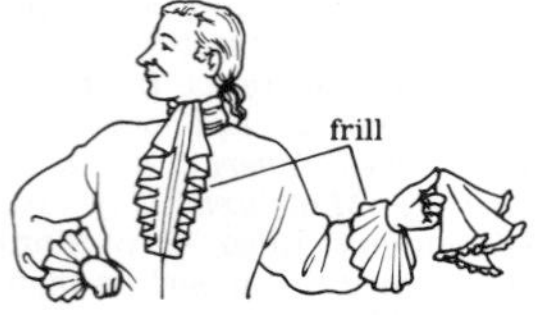

frill /frɪl/ *n* **1** ornamental border on a garment or curtain, gathered or pleated at one edge. ⇨ illus. **2** (usu *pl*) (*fig*) additional item that is not essential for something but makes it more decorative: *a straightforward presentation with no frills.*
▷ **frilled** *adj* decorated with frills (FRILL 1): *a frilled blouse.*
frilly /ˈfrɪlɪ/ *adj* having many frills (FRILL 1): *a frilly petticoat.*

fringe /frɪndʒ/ *n* **1** (*esp Brit*) (*US* **bang**) front hair cut so that it hangs over the forehead: *She has a fringe and glasses.* ⇨ illus at HAIR. **2** decorative edge on a garment, rug, etc consisting of loose or hanging threads or cords. **3** outer edge of an area, group or activity: *the fringe of a forest* ○ *on the fringes of society* ○ *on the radical fringe of the party* (ie the part having views not held by most people) ○ [attrib] *fringe theatre*, ie that stages unconventional and experimental productions; ⇨ article at PERFORMING ARTS: *a fringe meeting*, ie one which is not part of the main programme at a political conference. **4** (idm) **the lunatic fringe** ⇨ LUNATIC.
▷ **fringe** *v* **1** [Tn] make a fringe(2) for (sth); decorate with a fringe: *fringe a shawl.* **2** (idm) **be fringed by/with sth** have sth as a border: *The estate was fringed with stately elms.*
□ ˈ**fringe benefit** extra benefit, esp given to an employee in addition to salary or wages: *The fringe benefits of this job include a car and free health insurance.*

Frink /frɪŋk/ Dame Elizabeth (1930-). British sculptor and graphic artist, noted especially for her figures of horses and riders.

frippery /ˈfrɪpərɪ/ *n* **1** [U] unnecessary showy ornamentation, esp in clothing. **2** [C usu *pl*] cheap useless ornament.

Frisbee /ˈfrɪzbi:/ *n* (*propr*) light plastic disc, shaped like a plate, thrown between players in a game.

Frisco /ˈfrɪskəʊ/ (*infml*) San Francisco.

frisk /frɪsk/ *v* **1** [Tn] (*infml*) pass one's hands over (sb) in a search for hidden weapons, drugs, etc: *Everyone was frisked before getting on the plane.* **2** [I, Ip] (of animals) run and jump playfully: *lambs frisking (about) in the meadow.*
▷ **frisk** *n* [sing] **1** (*infml*) act of frisking (FRISK 1) a person. **2** act of playfully jumping and running.
frisky *adj* lively and energetic, wanting to enjoy oneself: *a frisky lamb* ○ *I feel quite frisky this morning.* **friskily** /-ɪlɪ/ *adv.*

frisson /ˈfri:sɒn; *US* fri:ˈsəʊn/ *n* (*French*) sudden feeling or thrill, esp of excitement or fear: *a frisson of delight, horror, fear, etc.*

fritter[1] /ˈfrɪtə(r)/ *v* (phr v) **fritter sth away (on sth)** waste (esp one's time or money) foolishly (on small useless things): *fritter away time/energy* ○ *fritter away one's money on gambling.*

fritter[2] /ˈfrɪtə(r)/ *n* (usu in compounds) piece of fried batter, usu containing sliced fruit, meat, etc: *banana fritters.*

Fritz /frɪts/ *n* (*dated sl offensive*) (used to refer to or address a German man, esp a soldier).

frivolous /ˈfrɪvələs/ *adj* **1** (of people, their character, etc) not sensible or serious; foolish and light-hearted: *At 18, he's still rather frivolous and needs to grow up.* ○ *frivolous comments, objections, criticisms, etc.* **2** (of activities) silly or wasteful: *She thought that reading romantic novels was a frivolous way of spending her time.*
▷ **frivolity** /frɪˈvɒlətɪ/ *n* **1** [U] frivolous behaviour: *youthful frivolity.* **2** [C usu *pl*] frivolous activity or comment: *I can't waste time on such frivolities.*
frivolously *adv.*

frizz /frɪz/ *v* [Tn] form (esp hair) into small tight curls: *You've had your hair frizzed.*
▷ **frizz** *n* hair that has been frizzed.
frizzy *adj* (of hair) tightly curled; frizzed.

frizzle[1] /ˈfrɪzl/ *v* [I, Ip, Tn, Tn·p] ~ (**sth**) (**up**) twist (hair) into small tight curls.

frizzle[2] /ˈfrɪzl/ *v* **1** [I, Tn] cook (food) with a sizzling noise: *bacon frizzling in the pan.* **2** [I, Ip, Tn, Tn·p] ~ (**sth**) (**up**) burn or shrivel (food) by frying it over a very strong heat; scorch: *The bacon is all frizzled up!*

fro /frəʊ/ *adv* (idm) **to and fro** ⇨ TO[3].

Frobisher /ˈfrəʊbɪʃə(r)/ Sir Martin (c1535-94), English sailor and explorer. He led an expedition in 1576 to find the Northwest Passage (NORTH) to China, reaching Labrador and discovering what became called **Frobisher Bay** in Canada.

frock /frɒk/ *n* **1** dress worn by women or girls: *All my frocks are for the summer.* **2** long loose gown with sleeves, worn by monks.
□ ˈ**frock-coat** *n* long coat worn (formerly) by men, now worn only on ceremonial occasions ⇨ illus at DRESS.

FROG

TOAD

frog /frɒg; *US* frɔ:g/ *n* **1** type of small cold-blooded smooth-skinned animal that lives in water or on land and has very long back legs for jumping, and no tail: *the croaking of frogs.* ⇨ illus. **2** ornamental fastener on a garment, consisting of a button and a looped cord that fits over it. **3 Frog** (*sl derog offensive*) French person. **4** (idm) **have, etc a ˈfrog in one's throat** have a (usu temporary) loss or hoarseness of the voice.
□ ˈ**frogman** /-mən/ *n* (*pl* **-men** /-mən/) swimmer with a rubber suit, flippers and an oxygen supply that enables him to work underwater for periods of time.
frog-spawn /ˈfrɒgspɔ:n/ *n* [U] soft almost transparent jelly-like mass of the eggs of a frog.

frog-march /ˈfrɒgmɑ:tʃ/ *v* [Tn, Tn·pr, Tn·p] **1** force (sb) to move forward with the arms held tightly together behind the back: *All prisoners were frogmarched (out) into the compound.* **2** carry (sb) face downwards with four people each holding an arm or a leg.

frolic /ˈfrɒlɪk/ *v* (*pt, pp* **frolicked**) [I, Ip] ~ (**about**) play about in a lively happy way: *children frolicking about in the swimming-pool.*
▷ **frolic** *n* [sing] lively and enjoyable activity: *having a frolic in the garden.*
frolicsome /-səm/ *adj* merry; playful: *a frolicsome kitten.*

from /frəm; *strong form* frɒm/ *prep* **1** (indicating the place or direction from which sb/sth starts): *go from Manchester to Leeds* ○ *a wind from the north* ○ *Has the train from London arrived?* ○ *She comes home from work at 7 pm.* ○ *A child fell from the seventh floor of a block of flats.* ○ *carpets stretching from wall to wall*, ie from one wall to the opposite one. **2** (indicating the time at which sth starts): *I'm on holiday from 30 June.* ○ *It's due to arrive an hour from now.* ○ *We lived in Scotland from 1960 to 1973.* ○ *There's traffic in the streets from dawn till dusk.* ○ *We're open from 8 am till 7 pm every day.* ○ *He was blind from birth.* **3** (indicating who sent, gave or communicated sth): *a letter from my brother* ○ *a present from a friend* ○ *I had a phone call from Mary.* ○ *the man from* (ie representing) *the Inland Revenue.* **4** (indicating where sb/sth originates or is stored): *I'm from New Zealand.* ○ *They come from the north.* ○ *the boy from the baker's* ○ *documents from the 16th century* ○ *famous quotations from Shakespeare* ○ *music from an opera* ○ *draw water from a well* ○ *powered by heat from the sun.* **5** (indicating distance between two places): *10 miles from the coast* ○ *100 yards from the scene of the accident* ○ (*fig*) *Far from agreeing with him, I was shocked by his remarks.* **6** (indicating the lower limit of a range of numbers, prices, etc): *write from 10 to 15 letters daily* ○ *Tickets cost from £3 to £11.* ○ *Our prices start from £2.50 a bottle.* ○ *Salaries are from 10% to 50% higher than in Britain.* **7** (indicating the state or form of sth/sb before a change): *Things have gone from bad to worse.* ○ *You need a break from routine.* ○ *translate from English to Spanish* ○ *The bus fare has gone up from 35p to 40p.* ○ *From being a librarian she is now an MP.* **8** (indicating the material from which sth is made, the material being changed in the process): *Wine is made from grapes.* ○ *Steel is made from iron.* Cf OF 5, OUT OF 5. **9** (**a**) (indicating separation, removal, etc): *separated from his mother for long periods* ○ *take the money from my purse* ○ *borrow a book from the library* ○ *release sb from prison* ○ *6 from 14 leaves 8.* (**b**) (indicating protection or prevention): *protect children from violence* ○ *save a boy from drowning* ○ *Wild fruit kept us from dying of starvation.* ○ *prevent sb from sleeping.* **10** (indicating the reason, cause or motive): *She felt sick from tiredness.* ○ *suffer from cold and hunger* ○ *She accompanied him from a sense of loyalty.* **11** considering (sth): *From the evidence we have heard so far...* ○ *From her looks I'd say she was Swedish.* ○ *From what I heard last night we're going to need a new chairman.* ○ *You can tell quite a lot from the handwriting.* **12** (used to make a distinction between two people, places or things): *Is Portuguese very different from Spanish?* ○ *I can't tell one twin from the other.* ○ *How do you know a fake from the original?* **13** (indicating a standpoint): *Seen from above the town covers a wide area.* ○ *From this angle it looks crooked.* ○ *From a teacher's point of view this dictionary will be very useful.* **14** (idm) **from...on** starting at the specified time and continuing for an indefinite period: *From now on you can work on your own.* ○ *From then on she knew she would win.* ○ *She never spoke to him again from that day on.*

frond /frɒnd/ *n* leaf-like part of a fern or palm.

front /frʌnt/ *n* **1** (esp **the front**) [sing] (**a**) most important part or side of sth; part or side that faces forward; most forward part of sth: *The front of the building was covered with ivy.* ○ *Put the statue so that the front faces the light.* ○ *The front of the car has a dent in it.* ○ *The young boy spilt some juice down his front*, ie the clothes covering his chest. (**b**) position directly before or ahead; most forward position or place: *All eyes to the front as we pass the other competitors!* ○ *The teacher made me move my seat to the front of the classroom.* ○ *At the front of the house, someone had planted a beautiful garden.* ○ *I prefer to travel in the front of the car*, ie next to the driver. Cf BACK[1] 1. **2 the front** [sing] the land along the edge of the sea or a lake; promenade: *walk along the (sea) front.* **3 the front** [sing] (in war) area where fighting takes place; foremost line of an army: *be sent to the front* ○ *serve at the front.* **4** [sing] outward appearance or show, esp of the specified type: *Her rudeness is just a front for her shyness.* ○ *put on/show/present a bold front* ○

We might argue among ourselves, but against the management we must present a united front, ie act and speak as a group. **5** [sing] **a ~ for sth** (*infml*) something that serves to hide an illegal or a secret activity: *The jewellery firm is just a front for their illegal trade in diamonds.* **6** [C] (of weather) forward edge of an advancing mass of warm or cold air: *A cold front is moving in from the north.* **7** [C] (usu with an *adj* or a *n*) specified area of activity: *on the domestic, financial, education, etc front.* **8** [sing] (esp in names) organized and often aggressively active political group: *the National Front.* **9** (idm) **back to front** ⇨ BACK[1]. **eyes right/left/front** ⇨ EYE[1]. **in front** *adv* in a position further forward than but close to sb/sth: *a small house with a garden in front* ○ *The children walked in twos with one teacher in front and one behind.* ○ *The British car has been in front now for several minutes.* Cf BEHIND[2]. **in front of** *prep* **(a)** in a position further forward than but close to (sb/sth): *The car in front of me stopped suddenly and I had to brake.* ○ *The bus stops right in front of our house.* ○ *I keep the children's photographs in front of me on the desk.* ○ *If you're phoning from outside central London, dial 071 in front of the number.* Cf BEHIND[1]. ⇨ Usage at BEFORE[2]. **(b)** in the presence of (sb): *The cheques must be signed in front of the cashier at the bank.* ○ *Please don't talk about it in front of the children.* **out ˈfront** in the part of a theatre where the audience sits. **up ˈfront** (*infml*) as payment in advance:. *We'll pay you half up front and the other half when you've finished the job.*

▷ **front** *adj* [attrib] of or at (the) front(1): *on the front page of the newspaper* ○ *front teeth* ○ *They keep the front room for visitors.* ○ *the front door*, ie the door that serves as the main entrance to a house ○ *the front seats of a bus.*

front *v* **1** [Ipr, Tn] **~ (onto) sth** have the front facing or directed towards sth; face: *hotels that front onto the sea* ○ *Attractive gardens fronted the houses.* **2** [Tn usu passive] provide (sth) with a front: *The monument was fronted with stone.* **3** [Tn] (*infml*) **(a)** serve as a leader or representative of (an organization). **(b)** present (a television or radio programme): *Dan Davies has been chosen to front a new discussion programme.*

□ **the ˌfront ˈbench** (either of the two rows of seats in the British Parliament occupied by the) leading members of the government and opposition: *members on the front bench(es) opposite* ○ [attrib] *the ˌfront-bench ˈspokesman on defence.* **front-ˈbencher** *n* Member of Parliament entitled to sit on the front bench. ⇨ article at PARLIAMENT.

ˈfront end (*computing*) **(a)** electronic device or computer system that provides access to another device: [attrib] *a ˌfront-end ˈsystem.* **(b)** part of a computer system that a user deals with directly.

the ˌfront ˈline 1 line of fighting which is closest to the enemy: [attrib] *front-line troops, units, etc.* **2** the most important, advanced or responsible position: *in the front line of research* ○ [attrib] *front-line states*, eg countries in southern Africa bordering on (and opposed to) South Africa.

ˈfront man (*infml*) **1** (person who acts as the) leader or representative of an organization. **2** presenter of a television or radio programme.

ˌfront-ˈpage *adj* [attrib] interesting or important enough to be printed on the front page of a newspaper: *ˌfront-page ˈnews.*

ˌfront ˈrunner person who seems most likely to succeed or win, eg in a race or contest: *Who are the front runners in the Presidential contest?*

frontage /ˈfrʌntɪdʒ/ *n* [C, U] extent of a piece of land or a building along its front, esp bordering a road or river: *For sale, shop premises with frontages on two streets.* ○ *a warehouse with good river frontage.*

□ **ˈfrontage road** (*US*) = SERVICE ROAD (SERVICE).

frontal /ˈfrʌntl/ *adj* [attrib] **1** at, from, in, or of the front: *a frontal view* ○ *a frontal attack*, ie one directed at the front or the main point ○ *full frontal nudity*, ie complete nudity, showing the whole of the front of the body. **2** (*medical*) of a person's forehead: *frontal lobes.* **3** concerning a weather front(6): *a frontal system.*

frontier /ˈfrʌntɪə(r); *US* frʌnˈtɪər/ *n* **1** [C] **(a)** ~ **(between sth and sth)**; ~ **(with sth)** border between two countries: *the frontier between Austria and Hungary.* **(b)** land on either side of such a border: [attrib] *a frontier zone* ○ *a frontier town* ○ *frontier disputes.* **2 the frontier** [sing] (*esp US*) extreme limit of settled land, beyond which the country is wild and undeveloped: *Beyond the frontier lay very real dangers.* **3 the frontiers** [pl] extreme limit, esp of knowledge about sth: *advance the frontiers of science* ○ *teach near the frontiers of one's subject*, ie give recently discovered information. ⇨ Usage at BORDER.

▷ **frontiersman** /-zmən/ *n* (*pl* **-men** /-mən/) man living on the frontier; one of the first settlers of an area.

frontispiece /ˈfrʌntɪspiːs/ *n* (usu *sing*) illustration at the beginning of a book, on the page opposite the title-page.

Frost /frɒst; *US* frɔːst/ Robert Lee (1874-1963), American poet. He grew up on a farm in *New England and much of his poetry expresses his love of nature and the countryside.

frost /frɒst; *US* frɔːst/ *n* **1 (a)** [U] weather condition in which the temperature falls below freezing-point, usu accompanied by the formation of frost(2): *Young plants are often killed by frost.* ○ *a temperature of 10 degrees of frost*, ie 10 degrees Celsius below freezing-point. **(b)** [C] instance or period of this: *There was a heavy* (ie severe) *frost last night.* ○ *early frosts*, ie in autumn ○ *late frosts*, ie in spring. **2** [U] dew or water vapour frozen into tiny white ice crystals that cover the ground, etc when the temperature falls below freezing-point: *The windscreen was covered with frost.*

▷ **frost** *v* **1** [Tn] cover (sth) with frost: *frosted pavements.* **2** [Tn usu passive] kill or damage (plants, etc) with frost(1). **3** [Tn] (*esp US*) decorate (a cake, etc) with icing or frosting. **4** [Tn] make (glass) opaque by giving it a rough frostlike surface: *frosted window panes.* **5** (phr v) **frost over/up** become covered with frost: *The car windscreen frosted over during the night.*

□ **ˈfrost-bite** *n* [U] injury to the body, esp fingers, toes, ears, etc, caused by extreme cold: *Two of the mountain climbers were suffering from frost-bite.*

ˈfrost-bitten *adj* suffering from or affected by frost-bite: *frost-bitten ears.*

ˈfrostbound *adj* (of the ground) made hard by frost.

frosting /ˈfrɒstɪŋ; *US* ˈfrɔːstɪŋ/ *n* [U] (*esp US*) = ICING.

frosty /ˈfrɒstɪ; *US* ˈfrɔːstɪ/ *adj* (**-ier, -iest**) **1 (a)** very cold; cold with frost: *frosty weather* ○ *It's sunny, but the air is frosty.* **(b)** covered with frost: *frosty fields.* **2** (*fig*) cold and unwelcoming in manner; not friendly: *a frosty look, response, welcome, etc.* ▷ **frostily** /-ɪlɪ/ *adv.* **frostiness** *n* [U]: *a certain frostiness in her greeting.*

froth /frɒθ; *US* frɔːθ/ *n* [U] **1** mass of small bubbles, esp on the surface of a liquid; foam: *I don't like beer with too much froth.* **2** (*derog*) light but worthless conversation, ideas, etc: *Their chatter was nothing but froth!*

▷ **froth** *v* **1** [Tn, Tn·p] **~ sth (up)** cause (a liquid) to foam: *froth (up) a milk shake.* **2** [I, Ipr] have or produce froth: *The water frothed as it tumbled down the rocks.* ○ *Animals with rabies often froth at the mouth.* ○ (*fig*) *He was so angry he was almost frothing at the mouth.*

frothy *adj* (**-ier, -iest**) **1** full of or covered with froth: *frothy beer* ○ *a frothy mixture of eggs and milk.* **2** light and trivial: *a novel written in a frothy style.* **frothily** *adv.* **frothiness** *n* [U].

frown /fraʊn/ *v* **1** [I, Ipr] **~ (at sb/sth)** bring the eyebrows together, so wrinkling the skin on one's forehead (to express anger, thought, worry, etc): *What's wrong? Why are you frowning?* ○ *Peter frowned at the noise coming from the boys' bedroom.* ○ *She read through the letter, frowning at its contents.* **2** (phr v) **frown on/upon sth** disapprove of sth: *My parents always frown on late nights out.* ○ *Gambling is frowned upon by some church authorities.* ⇨ Usage at SMIRK.

▷ **frown** *n* serious, angry, worried, etc look on the face causing lines on the forehead; expression of displeasure: *She looked up from her exam paper with a worried frown.* ○ *I noticed a slight frown of disapproval on his face.*

frowsty /ˈfraʊstɪ/ *adj* (*derog esp Brit*) (of the air conditions in a room) stale and stuffy.

frowzy /ˈfraʊzɪ/ *adj* (*esp Brit*) **1** untidy or unclean in appearance; shabby. **2** ill-smelling; stale and stuffy; musty.

froze *pt* of FREEZE.

frozen *pp* of FREEZE.

FRS /ˌef ɑːr ˈes/ *abbr* (*Brit*) Fellow of the Royal Society: *Charles May FRS.*

fructify /ˈfrʌktɪfaɪ/ *v* (*pt, pp* **-fied**) [I, Tn] (*fml*) (cause sth to) bear fruit or be fruitful. ▷ **fructification** /ˌfrʌktɪfɪˈkeɪʃn/ *n* [U].

fructose /ˈfrʌktəʊs, -əʊz/ *n* type of sugar found in fruit juice, honey, etc.

frugal /ˈfruːgl/ *adj* **(a)** careful and thrifty, esp with money and food: *a frugal housekeeper.* **(b)** of life in which such care is shown: *They lived a very frugal existence, avoiding all luxuries.* **(c)** costing little; small in quantity: *a frugal meal of bread and cheese.* ▷ **frugality** /fruˈgælətɪ/ *n* [U]. **frugally** /-gəlɪ/ *adv*

DRY FRUITS: POPPY HEAD

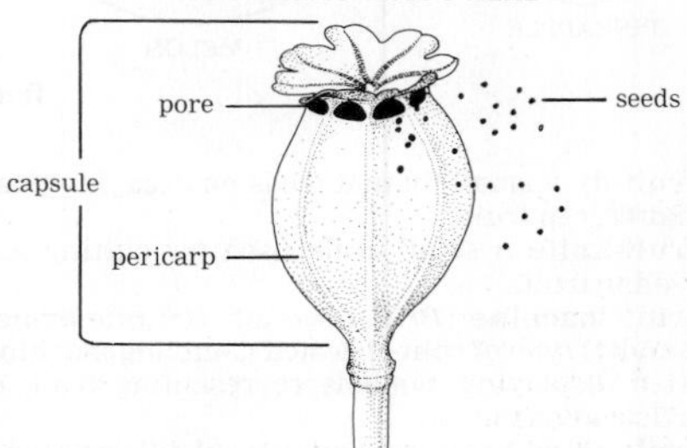

SUCCULENT FRUITS: RASPBERRY

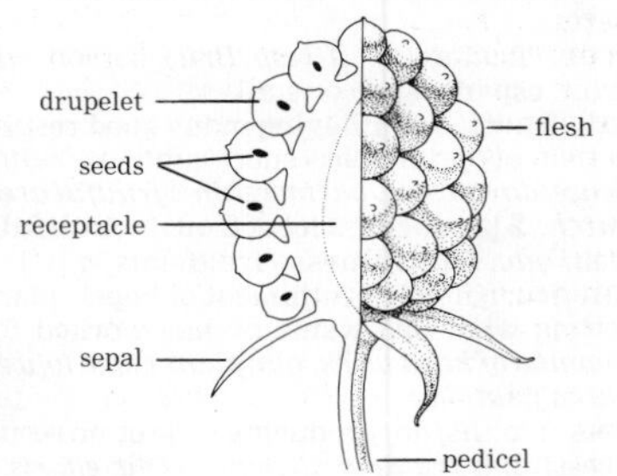

fruit /fruːt/ *n* **1** [C, U] fleshy seed-bearing part of a plant used as food; quantity of these: *The country exports tropical fruit(s).* ○ *Is a tomato a fruit or a vegetable?* ○ *Bananas, apples and oranges are all fruit.* ○ *This pudding has two pounds of fresh fruit in it.* ○ [attrib] *ˈfruit juice* ○ *ˈfruit trees.* ⇨ illus. **2** [C] (*botany*) part of a plant, tree or bush in which the seed is formed. Fruits are divided into two main groups. *Dry fruits* (eg poppy heads) enclose the seeds in a dry wall before they are carried away by wind or water, while *succulent fruits* (eg berries) have a fleshy, edible part around the seeds, which is usu eaten by animals or birds. ⇨ illus. **3** [C usu *pl*] any plant product used as food: *the fruits of the earth*, ie vegetables, cereals, etc. **4** (esp **the fruits** [pl]) result or reward of an action, hard work, etc: *enjoy the fruit(s) of one's labours.* **5** [U] (also **ˌdried ˈfruit**) currants, raisins, or sultanas, used as food or in baking. **6** (idm) **bear fruit** ⇨ BEAR[2]. **forbidden fruit** ⇨ FORBID.

▷ **fruit** *v* [I] produce fruit: *These apple trees have always fruited well.*

□ **ˈfruit-cake** *n* **1** [C, U] cake containing dried fruit. **2** (idm) **nutty as a fruit-cake** ⇨ NUTTY (NUT).

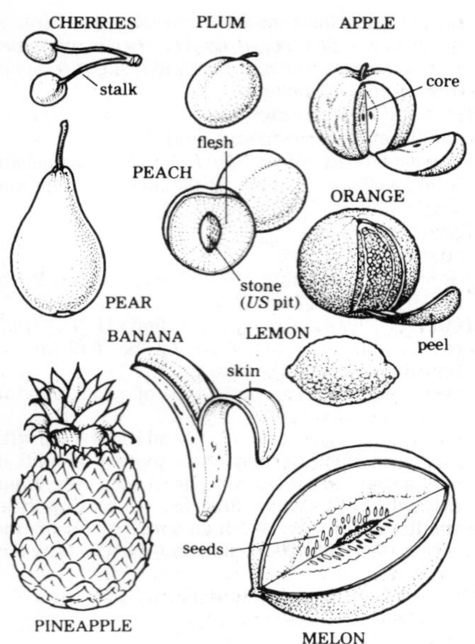

fruit

ˈfruit-fly *n* small fly that feeds on decaying plant matter, esp fruit.
ˈfruit-knife *n* small knife used for cutting and peeling fruit.
ˈfruit machine (*Brit*) (also *esp US* **ˌone-armed ˈbandit**) type of coin-operated gambling machine, often displaying symbols representing fruit. ⇨ article at GAMBLING.
ˌfruit ˈsalad 1 (*esp Brit*) mixture of different types of fruit, cut up and served as a dessert. **2** (*US*) dish of small pieces of fruit set in jelly(1a) and served as a dessert.

fruiterer /ˈfru:tərə(r)/ *n* (*esp Brit*) person who sells fruit, esp in a shop or stall.

fruitful /ˈfru:tfl/ *adj* **1** having many good results; productive or profitable; successful: *a fruitful experience, day's work, partnership* ○ *fruitful areas of research.* **2** producing a lot of fruit. ▷ **fruitfully** /ˈfru:tfəlɪ/ *adv.* **fruitfulness** /ˈfru:tfəlnɪs/ *n* [U].

fruition /fru:ˈɪʃn/ *n* [U] fulfilment of hopes, plans, etc; getting what one wants or has worked for: *After months of hard work, our plans came to/were brought to fruition.*

fruitless /ˈfru:tlɪs/ *adj* producing little or no result; unsuccessful: *a fruitless attempt* ○ *Our efforts to persuade her were fruitless — she didn't even listen.* ▷ **fruitlessly** *adv.* **fruitlessness** *n* [U].

fruity /ˈfru:tɪ/ *adj* (**-ier, -iest**) **1** like fruit in smell or taste; containing a lot of fruit: *a fruity wine* ○ *a fruity dessert.* **2** (*infml*) funny in a crude and often sexually suggestive way: *a fruity joke, remark, story, etc.* **3** (*infml*) (of a voice, etc) rich and deep in tone or quality: *a fruity chuckle.*

frump /frʌmp/ *n* (*derog*) person (usu a woman) who wears dull old-fashioned clothes. ▷ **frumpish** *adj*: *a frumpish outfit.*

frustrate /frʌˈstreɪt; *US* ˈfrʌstreɪt/ *v* [Tn] **1** (**a**) prevent (sb) from doing or achieving sth: *He had hoped to set a new world record, but was frustrated by bad weather.* (**b**) make (efforts, etc) useless; defeat: *Bad weather has frustrated plans to launch the spacecraft today.* **2** upset or discourage (sb): *Mary was frustrated by the lack of appreciation shown of her work.*
▷ **frustrated** *adj* **1** (**a**) [pred] discouraged; not satisfied: *As a nurse she got very frustrated, but being an administrator seems to suit her.* (**b**) [attrib] unable to be successful in one's chosen career: *Film directors are sometimes frustrated actors.* **2** not satisfied sexually.
frustrating *adj* annoying; discouraging: *I find it frustrating that I can't speak other languages.*
frustration /frʌˈstreɪʃn/ *n* **1** [U] (state of) being frustrated. **2** [C] instance of this; disappointment: *Every job has its frustrations.*

Fry[1] /fraɪ/ Christopher (1907-), English playwright. He became known through his poetic religious dramas, but his popularity is based on comedies, eg *The Lady's not for Burning*, and his translations of *Anouilh.

Fry[2] /fraɪ/ Elizabeth (1780-1845), English penal reformer. A strong Quaker, she campaigned for the improvement of conditions in British prisons and on behalf of convicts deported to Australia.

fry[1] /fraɪ/ *v* (*pt, pp* **fried** /fraɪd/) **1** [I, Tn] cook or be cooked (sth) in boiling fat or oil: *fried chicken* ○ *bacon frying in the pan.* ⇨ Usage at COOK. **2** (idm) **have bigger/other fish to fry** ⇨ FISH[1].
▷ **fry** *n* (*US*) party or social occasion at which people cook and eat fried food.
□ **ˈfrying-pan** (*US* **ˈfry-pan**) *n* **1** flat shallow pan with a long handle, used for frying food. ⇨ illus at PAN. **2** (idm) **out of the ˈfrying-pan into the ˈfire** from a bad situation to one that is worse.
ˈfry-up *n* (*Brit*) (dish of) fried food, esp bacon, eggs, sausages, etc: *We always have a fry-up for Saturday lunch.*

fry[2] /fraɪ/ *n* [pl *v*] **1** young or newly hatched fishes. **2** (idm) **ˈsmall fry** ⇨ SMALL.

fryer (also **frier**) /ˈfraɪə(r)/ *n* **1** large deep pan for frying food, esp fish. **2** (*esp US*) small young chicken suitable for frying.

FT /ˌef ˈti:/ *abbr* (*Brit*) Financial Times (newspaper): *the FT (share) index.*

Ft *abbr* (in names) Fort: *Ft William*, eg on a map.

ft *abbr* (also *symb* ′) feet; foot: *11 ft* × (ie by) *6 ft* (11′ × 6′) ○ *She was only 5 ft (tall).* Cf IN, YD.

fuchsia /ˈfju:ʃə/ *n* shrub with red, purple or white drooping flowers.

fuck /fʌk/ *v* (⚠ *sl*) **1** [I, Tn] have sexual intercourse with (sb). **2** [I, Tn] (esp imperative or as an *interj* in exclamations expressing extreme anger, annoyance or disgust): *Fuck (it)!* ○ *Fuck you — I don't care if I never see you again.* ○ *Fuck the bloody thing — it won't work.* **3** (idm) **ˈfucking well** (used to emphasize an angry statement, esp an order) certainly; definitely: *You're fucking well coming whether you want to or not.* **4** (phr v) **fuck aˈbout/aˈround** behave foolishly or unhelpfully: *Stop fucking around and come and give me a hand.* **fuck sb about/around** treat sb badly or inconsiderately: *This bloody company keeps fucking me about.* **fuck ˈoff** (esp imperative) go away. **fuck sth up** spoil or ruin sth.
▷ **fuck** *n* (usu *sing*) (⚠ *sl*) **1** act of sexual intercourse. **2** (*sexist*) person, esp a woman, considered as a sexual partner: *She's a good fuck.* **3** (idm) **not care/give a fuck (about sb/sth)** not care at all: *He doesn't give a fuck about anyone else.*
fucker *n* (⚠ *sl*) (as a general term of abuse) fool; idiot.
fucking (⚠ *sl*) *adj, adv* (used to add emphasis in expressions of anger, annoyance, etc): *I'm fucking sick of the whole fucking lot of you.*
□ **ˌfuck-ˈall** *n* [U] (⚠ *sl*) nothing at all: *You've done ˌfuck-ˈall today.* ○ [attrib] *He's ˌfuck-all ˌuse as a ˈgoalkeeper.*
fuck-up /ˈfʌkʌp/ *n* (⚠ *sl*) complete mess; disaster: *What a fuck-up!* ⇨ article at TABOO.

fuddle /ˈfʌdl/ *v* [Tn esp passive] confuse (sb/sth), esp with alcoholic drink: *in a fuddled state* ○ *one's mind fuddled with gin.*
▷ **fuddle** *n* (usu *sing*) confused state: *My brain's in a fuddle.*

fuddy-duddy /ˈfʌdɪdʌdɪ/ *n* (*infml derog or joc*) person who has old-fashioned ideas and habits: *You're such an old fuddy-duddy!* ○ [attrib] *You and your fuddy-duddy ideas!*

fudge[1] /fʌdʒ/ *n* [U] soft sweet made of sugar, butter and milk, often with added flavourings: *chocolate/walnut fudge.*

fudge[2] /fʌdʒ/ *v* [Tn] (*infml*) **1** do (sth) clumsily or inadequately: *He had to fudge a reply because he didn't know the right answer.* **2** misrepresent or falsify (sth); evade (sth): *Our manager has been fudging the issue of bonus payments for months.*

fuel /ˈfju:əl/ *n* **1** [U] (**a**) material burned to produce heat or power, eg wood, coal, oil, etc: *What sort of fuel do these machines need?* (**b**) material that produces nuclear energy. **2** [C] any particular type of fuel. **3** [C] (*fig*) thing that increases anger or other strong feelings: *His indifference was a fuel to her hatred.* **4** (idm) **add fuel to the flames** ⇨ ADD.
▷ **fuel** *v* (**-ll-**; *US* **-l-**) **1** [I] take in fuel: *All aircraft must fuel before a long flight.* **2** [Tn] supply (sth) with fuel: *fuelling a car with petrol* ○ *(fig) inflation fuelled by big wage increases.*
□ **ˈfuel cell** cell(3) that produces electricity directly from a chemical reaction.
ˈfuel injection (system in an internal-combustion engine allowing the) direct introduction of fuel under pressure into the combustion chamber so as to improve performance.

fug /fʌg/ *n* (usu *sing*); (*infml*) warm stuffy atmosphere, eg in a small or crowded room: *Open the window — there's quite a fug in here.* ▷ **fuggy** *adj.*

Fugard /ˈfju:gɑ:d/ Athol (1932-), South African playwright. Many of his works explore the racial tension and inequality created by the system of apartheid.

fugitive /ˈfju:dʒətɪv/ *n* ~ (**from sb/sth**) person who is running away or escaping: *fugitives from a country ravaged by war* ○ *a fugitive from justice.*
▷ **fugitive** *adj* **1** escaping; running away: *a fugitive criminal.* **2** [usu attrib] (*fml*) lasting only a short time; fleeting: *fugitive thoughts, impressions, sensations.*

fugue /fju:g/ *n* **1** piece of music in which three or more parts (ie singers, instruments, etc) develop a series of related themes, each part interweaving with the others. **2** (*psychology*) mental condition that causes a person to forget who he is and often to travel away from home for no apparent reason.

-ful *suff* **1** with *ns* and *vs* forming *adjs*; full of; having qualities of; liable to: *beautiful* ○ *masterful* ○ *forgetful.* **2** (with *ns* forming *ns*) amount that fills: *handful* ○ *mouthful.*

fulcrum /ˈfʊlkrəm/ *n* (*pl* ~**s** or **fulcra** /ˈfʊlkrə/) point on which a lever is supported. ⇨ illus at LEVER.

fulfil (*US* **fulfill**) /fʊlˈfɪl/ *v* (**-ll-**) [Tn] **1** perform (sth) or bring (sth) to completion: *fulfil a promise, prophecy.* **2** satisfy (sth); answer: *fulfil a desire, prayer, hope, need, dream, etc* ○ *Does your job fulfil your expectations?* **3** satisfy the specific requirements of (sth): *fulfil the terms of a contract* ○ *fulfil the conditions of entry to a university.* **4** perform (sth); do; obey fully: *fulfil a duty, a command, an obligation, etc.* **5** ~ **oneself** fully develop one's abilities and character: *He was able to fulfil himself through music.*
▷ **fulfilled** *adj* satisfied; completely happy: *He doesn't feel really fulfilled in his present job.*
fulfilment *n* [U] fulfilling or being fulfilled.

full /fʊl/ *adj* (**-er, -est**) **1** ~ (**of sth/sb**) (**a**) holding or containing as much or as many as possible; completely filled: *drawers full to overflowing* ○ *My cup is full.* ○ *The bin needs emptying; it's full of rubbish.* ○ *The theatre is full, I'm afraid you'll have to wait for the next show.* ⇨ Usage at EMPTY[1]. (**b**) having or containing much or many; crowded: *a lake full of fish* ○ *a room full of people* ○ *She's full of vitality.* **2** ~ **of sth** completely occupied in thinking about sth: *She was full of the news*, ie could not stop herself talking about it. **3** ~ (**up**) having had enough to eat and drink: *No more thank you, I'm full up.* **4** [attrib] (**a**) complete; plentiful: *give full information, details, instructions, etc.* (**b**) complete; reaching specified or usual limits: *The roses are in full bloom.* ○ *I had to wait a full hour for the bus.* ○ *He got full marks* (ie the highest marks possible) *for his essay.* ○ *full employment*, ie a situation in which the level of employment in an economy can only be increased further by changing the structure of that economy ○ *Her dress was a full three inches above the knee.* **5** [usu attrib] plump; rounded: *a full figure* ○ *rather full in the face.* **6** (of clothes) fitting loosely or made with plenty of material: *a full skirt* ○ *Please make this coat a little fuller across the back.* **7** (of a tone or voice) deep and mellow. **8** (idm) **at**

full ˈ**stretch** to the limit of one's ability: *working at full stretch.* **at half/full cock** ➪ COCK². **come full ˈcircle** return to the starting point after a series of events, experiences, etc. **come to a full ˈstop** stop completely: *The car came to a full stop at the traffic lights.* **draw oneself up to one's full height** ➪ DRAW². **the first/full flush of youth, etc** ➪ FLUSH¹. **(at) full ˈblast** at maximum power, activity, etc: *going, talking, shouting full blast* ○ *An orchestra playing at full blast is a tremendous sound.* **full of ˈbeans/ˈlife** having a lot of energy and vitality. ˌ**full of the ˌjoys of ˈspring** lively and light-hearted. **(at) full ˈlength** with the body stretched out and flat: *lying full length on the sofa.* ˈ**full of oneself** (*derog*) selfish and conceited: *You're very full of yourself today, I must say.* **full of one's own imˈportance** (*derog*) thinking that one is very important. **(at) full ˈpelt/ˈtilt/ˈspeed** with great speed or force: *He drove full tilt into the lamppost.* **full speed/steam ahead** (proceeding) with as much speed and vigour as possible. **give full/short measure** ➪ MEASURE. **give sb/sth full play** give sb/sth complete freedom of action or expression. **have one's hands full** ➪ HAND¹. **in full** completely; with nothing omitted: *publish a report in full* ○ *write one's name in full*, eg John Henry Smith, *not* J H Smith. **in full ˈcry** (of a pack of hunting hounds) barking together noisily as they chase their prey: (*fig*) *The pop group raced for their car, pursued by fans in full cry.* **in full play** fully operating or active. **in full sail** (of a ship) with all the sails spread or set. **in full ˈswing** fully active: *The party was in full swing when we arrived.* **in full ˈview (of sb/sth)** completely visible: *He performed the trick in full view of the whole audience.* **to the ˈfull** to the greatest possible extent: *enjoy life to the full.*

▷ **full** *adv* **1** exactly; directly: *John hit him full in the face.* **2** very: *as you know full well.*

fullness (also **fulness**) *n* [U] **1** completeness; being full(4b). **2** (idm) **in the fullness of time** at the appropriate or right time; eventually: *In the fullness of time they married and had children.*

fully *adv* **1** completely; entirely: *fully satisfied* ○ *She was fully dressed in five minutes.* ○ *I was fully expecting to lose my job, so this promotion has come as a complete surprise.* **2** at least; the whole of: *The journey will take fully two hours.* **3** (idm) **fully stretched** made to work, etc at the limits of one's capacities or talents. ˌ**fully-ˈfashioned** *adj* (of women's clothing) designed to fit the body closely. ˌ**fully-ˈfledged** *adj* **1** (of a young bird) having grown all its feathers. **2** (*fig*) mature and well established: *Computer science is now a fully-fledged academic subject.*

□ ˈ**full back** (in hockey, football, etc) defensive player near the goal.

ˌ**full-ˈblooded** *adj* **1** not of mixed race or breed: *a ˌfull-blooded ˈmare.* **2** vigorous and hearty: *a ˌfull-blooded and ˌpassionate ˈperson* ○ (*fig*) *a ˌfull-blooded ˈargument.*

ˌ**full-ˈblown** *adj* (esp of flowers) fully developed; quite open: *ˌfull-blown ˈroses.*

ˌ**full ˈboard** the providing of bed and all meals, in a hotel, etc: *The price is £20 for bed and breakfast, £25 full board.* Cf HALF BOARD (HALF³).

ˌ**full-ˈbodied** *adj* rich in quality, tone, etc: *a ˌfull-bodied red ˈwine.*

ˌ**full ˈface** so that the whole face can be seen (eg by a photographer): *Don't take her full face like a passport photo.*

ˌ**full ˈhouse 1** theatre, cinema, etc with all its seats occupied: *We have a full house tonight.* **2** (in poker) set of cards held by a player that consists of three cards of one value and two of another. **3** (in bingo, etc) set of numbers needed to win.

ˌ**full-ˈlength** *adj* **(a)** (of a picture, mirror, etc) showing the whole (human) figure. **(b)** not shortened; of the expected length: *a ˌfull-length ˈnovel* ○ *a ˌfull-length ˈskirt*, ie one that reaches the ankles.

ˌ**full ˈmarks** maximum marks possible in an examination, etc: (*fig*) *I must say I give you full marks for your tactful handling of a difficult situation.*

ˌ**full ˈmoon** the moon in its fullest phase, with its whole disc illuminated; time when this occurs. Cf NEW MOON (NEW).

ˌ**full ˈpage** *adj* filling a complete page: *a ˌfull page adˈvertisement.*

ˌ**full ˈpitch** = FULL TOSS.

ˌ**full-ˈscale** *adj* not reduced in size; the same size as the object itself; complete: *a ˌfull-scale ˈdrawing, ˈplan, ˈdesign, etc* ○ (*fig*) *a ˌfull-scale reorganiˈzation of the department.*

ˌ**full ˈstop** (also **full point**, *US* **period**) **1** punctuation mark (.) used at the end of a sentence or an abbreviation. ➪ App 14. **2** (used to indicate finality) without further qualification: *I just think he is very unpleasant, full stop.*

ˌ**full ˈtime** end of a game of football, etc.

ˌ**full-ˈtime** *adj* for or during the whole of the working day or week: *a ˌfull-time ˈjob.* — *adv* on a full-time basis: *ˌwork full-ˈtime.* Cf PART-TIME (PART¹).

ˌ**full ˈtoss** (also **full pitch**) (in cricket) bowled ball that reaches the batsman without touching the ground.

Fuller /ˈfʊlə(r)/ (Richard) Buckminster (1895-1983), American architect and engineer who had great insight into the nature of natural resources and the need to control them. His interest in functional buildings led him to design the geodesic dome and other ergonomic structures. ➪ illus at GEODESIC DOME.

fuller /ˈfʊlə(r)/ *n* person who cleans and thickens freshly woven cloth.

□ ˌ**fuller's ˈearth** type of clay used for this process.

fulminate /ˈfʌlmɪneɪt; *US* ˈfʊl-/ *v* [I, Ipr] ~ **(against sb/sth)** protest strongly and loudly.

▷ **fulmination** /ˌfʌlmɪˈneɪʃn; *US* ˌfʊl-/ *n* **(a)** [U] fulminating. **(b)** [C] instance of this; bitter protest or criticism.

fulsome /ˈfʊlsəm/ *adj* excessive and insincere: *fulsome words, compliments, etc* ○ *be fulsome in one's praise.* ▷ **fulsomely** *adv.* **fulsomeness** *n* [U].

fumble /ˈfʌmbl/ *v* **1** [I, Tn] touch or handle (sth) awkwardly or nervously: *He fumbled the ball and then dropped it.* **2** [Ipr] ~ **at/for/with sth** use the hands awkwardly in doing sth or in search of sth: *fumble in one's pocket for some coins* ○ *She fumbled with her notes and began to speak.* ○ *fumble for the light switch* ○ (*fig*) *fumble for the right thing to say.* **3** [Ip] ~ **about/around** move about clumsily in doing sth or in search of sth: *fumbling around in the dark.*

▷ **fumble** *n* [sing] act of fumbling.

fume /fjuːm/ *n* (usu *pl*) smoke, gas or vapour that smells strongly: *petrol fumes* ○ *The air was thick with cigar fumes.*

▷ **fume** *v* **1** [I, Ipr] ~ **(at sb/sth)** be very angry; show this anger: *fume at the delay* ○ *By the time we arrived an hour late she was fuming (with rage).* **2** [I] emit or give off fumes: *The smouldering wreck fumed for days.* **3** [Tn] treat (esp wood) with chemical fumes to darken it: *fumed oak.*

fumigate /ˈfjuːmɪgeɪt/ *v* [Tn] destroy infectious germs, insects, etc in (sth) with the fumes of certain chemicals: *The hospital wards were fumigated after the outbreak of typhus.* ▷ **fumigation** /ˌfjuːmɪˈgeɪʃn/ *n* [U].

fun /fʌn/ *n* [U] **1** enjoyment; pleasure: *We had lots of fun at the fair today.* ○ *It took all the fun out of the occasion when we heard that you were ill.* ○ *What fun it will be when we all go on holiday together.* ○ *Have fun!* ie Enjoy yourself! **2** source of this: *Sailing is (good/great) fun.* ○ *It's not much fun going to a party alone.* **3** playfulness; good humour: *She's very lively and full of fun.* **4** [attrib] (*esp US*) amusing; providing pleasure: *a fun hat.* **5** (idm) **(just) for ˈfun/for the ˈfun of it; (just) in ˈfun** for amusement; not seriously; as a joke: *I'm learning to cook, just for the fun of it.* ○ *He only said it in fun — he didn't really mean it.* **fun and ˈgames** (*infml*) light-hearted and playful activities: *That's enough fun and games! Let's get down to work.* **make fun of sb/sth** (cause people to) laugh at sb/sth, usu unkindly; ridicule sb/sth: *It's cruel to make fun of people who stammer.* **poke fun at sb/sth** ➪ POKE¹.

□ ˈ**fun-fair** (also **fair**) *n* collection of outdoor amusements, stalls and side shows, usu in a park.

📖 Fun-fairs visit many towns in Britain for a few days each year. Amusements include rides on the big wheel, the big dipper, dodgem cars and roundabouts, and stalls such as shooting-galleries, skittle alleys and amusement arcades. Other stalls sell things to eat and drink. Some towns and cities have traditional annual fairs. Amongst the best known of these are the Hampstead Heath Fair in London at Easter, the St Giles Fair in Oxford in September, and the Goose Fair in Nottingham and the Ilkeston Charter Fair in Derbyshire, both in October.

ˈ**fun run** race run for pleasure and often to raise money for charity, usu over a fairly long distance, with many people taking part.

function /ˈfʌŋkʃn/ *n* **1** special activity or purpose of a person or thing: *to fulfil a useful function* ○ *The function of the heart is to pump blood through the body.* ○ *It is not the function of this committee to deal with dismissals.* **2** important social event or official ceremony: *Heads of state have to attend numerous formal functions every year.* **3 (a)** (*mathematics*) variable quantity regarded in relation to another or others in terms of which it may be expressed or on which its value depends: *X is a function of Y and Z.* **(b)** (*fig*) thing whose size, importance, etc depends on something else: *Success is a function of determination.* **4** any of the basic operations of a computer: *What functions can this program perform?*

▷ **function** *v* **1** [I] work; operate: *His brain seems to be functioning normally.* ○ *This machine has stopped functioning*, ie is out of order. **2** [Ipr] ~ **as sth** work as sth; operate or perform the function(1) of the thing specified: *The sofa can also function as a bed.* ○ *Some English adverbs function as adjectives.*

functional /-ʃənl/ *adj* **1** of or having a function(1) or functions: *a functional duty, title, office* ○ *a functional disorder*, ie illness caused when an organ of the body fails to perform its function. **2** practical and useful; not decorative: *functional furniture, clothing, architecture.* **3** [pred] working; able to work: *Is this machine functional?* ○ *I'm hardly functional if I don't get eight hours' sleep!* **functionally** /-ʃənəlɪ/ *adv.*

□ ˈ**function key** (*computing*) key that causes an operation or sequence of operations to be performed: *a special function key that displays the help menu.*

functionalism /ˈfʌŋkʃənəlɪzəm/ *n* [U] principle in architecture, design, etc that the purpose and use of an object should determine its shape and construction. This view was held by several important architects in the early 20th century, including Frank Lloyd *Wright and *Le Corbusier.

▷ **functionalist** /-ʃənəlɪst/ *n, adj* (believer in the principle) of functionalism.

functionary /ˈfʌŋkʃənərɪ; *US* -nerɪ/ *n* (*often derog*) person with official duties: *a minor functionary.*

fund /fʌnd/ *n* **1** [C] sum of money saved or made available for a particular purpose: *a disaster/relief fund* ○ *the church restoration fund* ○ [attrib]: *a fund-raising event*, eg a concert from which the profits go to charity ○ *professional fund-raisers.* ➪ article at CHARITY. **2** [sing] stock or supply of sth: *a fund of jokes, knowledge, experience, etc.* **3 funds** [pl] financial resources; money: *government funds* ○ *I'm short of funds so I'll pay you next week.* **4** (idm) **in funds** having money to spend.

▷ **fund** *v* [Tn] **1** provide (an institution, a project, etc) with money: *The government is funding another unemployment scheme.* **2** make (a debt) long-term at a fixed rate of interest.

fundamental /ˌfʌndəˈmentl/ *adj* **1 (a)** of or forming the basis or foundation of sth; essential: *There are fundamental differences between your religious beliefs and mine.* **(b)** serving as a starting-point; basic: *the fundamental rules of mathematics.* **2** most important; central or primary: *His fundamental concern was for her welfare.* ○ *The fundamental question is a political one.* 3 ~ (**to sth**) essential or necessary: *Hard work is fundamental to success.*

▷ **fundamental** *n* 1 (usu *pl*) basic rule or principle; essential part: *the fundamentals of religion, philosophy, art, etc.* 2 (also **fundamental note**) (*music*) lowest note in a chord.

fundamentally /-təlɪ/ *adv* basically: *Her ideas are fundamentally sound, even if she says silly things sometimes.*

□ ˌ**fundamental** ˈ**particle** (*physics*) = ELEMENTARY PARTICLE (ELEMENTARY).

fundamentalism /ˌfʌndəˈmentəlɪzəm/ *n* [U] 1 (in Christian thought) belief that the Bible is literally true. Such a view is held by many Christians in the southern USA, and is often associated with right-wing political opinions and strict moral values. Cf CREATIONISM (CREATION). 2 total acceptance of the teachings of any religion in a literal way, esp when this leads to extreme political action.

▷ **fundamentalist** /-ɪst/ *n* supporter of fundamentalism: [attrib] *fundamentalist ideas.*

funeral /ˈfju:nərəl/ *n* 1 (usu religious) ceremony of burying or burning dead people: *When is his funeral?* ○ [attrib] *funeral rites* ○ *a funeral procession* ○ *a funeral march*, ie a sad and solemn piece of music suitable for funerals. 2 procession of people at a funeral. 3 (idm) **it's/that's my, etc funeral** (*infml*) it's/that's my, etc particular and unpleasant responsibility: *'You're going to fail your exams if you don't work hard.' 'That's my funeral, not yours.'*

▷ **funereal** /fju:ˈnɪərɪəl/ *adj* suitable for a funeral; gloomy; dismal: *a funereal expression, atmosphere.*

□ ˈ**funeral director** (*esp US*) = UNDERTAKER. ˈ**funeral parlour** (*US* ˈ**funeral home**) place where dead people are prepared for burial or cremation.

fungicide /ˈfʌndʒɪsaɪd/ *n* [C, U] substance that kills fungus.

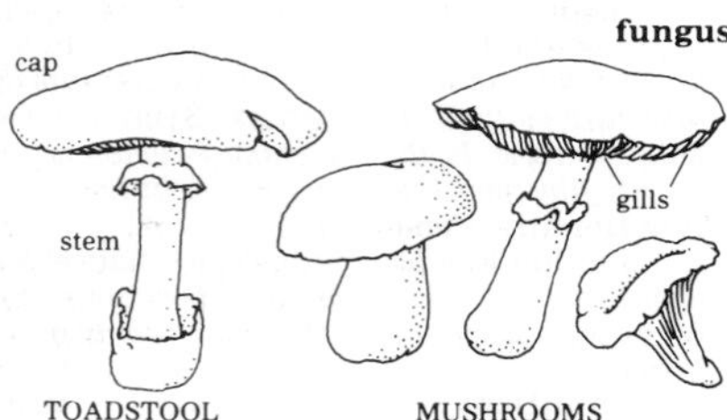

fungus /ˈfʌŋgəs/ *n* (*pl* **-gi** /-gaɪ, *also* -dʒaɪ/ or ~**es** /-gəsɪz/) 1 (a) [C] any of various simple organisms, existing either as single cells (eg yeast) or filaments (eg bread mould) which lack chlorophyll. Because of this they usu grow on other plants as parasites or break down decaying matter. Some, like certain mushrooms, can be eaten, some cause disease (eg athlete's foot, or mildew on plants), and others can be used as a source of antibiotics (eg the penicillin mould). Cf LICHEN, ⇨ illus. (b) [U] such plants as a group: *The lawn was covered with fungus.* 2 [U] types of fungus harmful to plants, etc: *The roses have fungus.* ○ [attrib] *fungus infections.*

▷ **fungoid** /ˈfʌŋgɔɪd/ *adj* of or like a fungus: *fungoid growths.*

fungous /ˈfʌŋgəs/ *adj* of, like or caused by fungus: *fungous diseases.*

funicular /fju:ˈnɪkjʊlə(r)/ *n* (also **funicular railway**) railway on a steep slope, with some cars being pulled up by a cable at the same time as others are lowered by it.

funk /fʌŋk/ *n* (*infml*) 1 [sing] (also **blue funk**) (state of) fear or anxiety: *She was in a funk about changing jobs.* 2 [C] (*derog*) coward.

▷ **funk** *v* [Tn, Tg] avoid (sth/doing sth) because of fear: *He funked telling her he had lost his job.*

funky /fʌŋkɪ/ *adj* (**-ier, -iest**) 1 (*sl*) (of music, esp jazz) having a characteristic rhythm and expressiveness, like early blues music. 2 (*infml approv*) very modern; fashionable: *a funky car, party, hairstyle.* 3 (*US sl*) having a strong unpleasant smell.

funnel /ˈfʌnl/ *n* 1 tube or pipe that is wide at the top and narrow at the bottom, used for pouring liquids, powders, etc into a small opening: *I need a funnel to pour petrol into the tank.* ⇨ illus at FILTER. 2 metal chimney on a steam-engine, ship, etc, through which smoke escapes.

▷ **funnel** *v* (**-ll-**; *US* **-l-**) [Ipr, Ip, Tn, Tn·pr, Tn·p] (cause sth to) move through a funnel or a narrow space: *funnel petrol into a can* ○ *The water funnelled through the gorge and out onto the plain.*

funny /ˈfʌnɪ/ *adj* (**-ier, -iest**) 1 causing amusement, laughter, etc: *funny stories* ○ *a funny man* ○ *That's the funniest thing I've ever heard.* 2 difficult to explain or understand; strange: *A funny thing happened to me today.* ○ *That's funny — he was here a moment ago and now he's gone.* ○ *The engine's making a very funny noise.* 3 (*infml*) (a) slightly unwell: *I feel a bit funny today — I don't think I'll go to work.* ○ *That drink has made me feel quite funny.* (b) slightly insane; eccentric: *a funny old lady* ○ *She went a bit funny after her husband died.* 4 (idm) ˈ**funny business** (*infml*) sth that is illegal, suspicious or not approved of: *I want none of your funny business.* **funny ha-**ˈ**ha** (*infml*) = FUNNY 1. **funny pe**ˈ**culiar** (*infml*) = FUNNY 2: *'He's a funny chap.' 'Do you mean funny ha-ha or funny peculiar?'*

▷ **funnily** /-ɪlɪ/ *adv* in a strange or odd way (expressing surprise at a coincidence, etc): *Funnily enough* (ie It so happened that) *I met her just yesterday.*

funniness *n* [U].

□ ˈ**funny-bone** *n* part of the elbow which has a very sensitive nerve, and which tingles unpleasantly when it is knocked.

ˈ**funny farm** (*sl offensive*) mental hospital.

fur /fɜ:(r)/ *n* 1 [U] soft thick hair covering the bodies of certain animals: *The puppies haven't got much fur yet.* 2 [U, C] animal skin(s) with fur on, esp as used for making clothes, etc: *a coat made of fur* ○ *fine fox furs* ○ *a rich woman covered in diamonds and furs* ○ (*joc*) *Furs look better on their original owners*, ie the live animals they came from. ○ [attrib]: *a fur coat.* 3 [C] garment made of fur: *He gave her an expensive fur for her birthday.* 4 [U] fabric made to look and feel like fur. 5 [U] coating on a person's tongue during illness. 6 [U] (*Brit*) (*US* **scale**) grey crusty coating that forms on the inside of a kettle, pipes, etc from water that contains lime. 7 (idm) **make the fur/sparks fly** ⇨ FLY[2].

▷ **fur** *v* (**-rr-**) [usu passive: I, Ip, Tn, Tn·p] ~ (**sth**) (**up**) (cause sth to) become covered with fur(5,6): *a furred tongue/kettle.*

furry /ˈfɜ:rɪ/ *adj* (**-ier, -iest**) 1 of or like fur. 2 covered with fur: *a furry toy.*

fur *abbr* furlong(s).

furbelow /ˈfɜ:bɪləʊ/ *n* (usu *pl*) showy or unnecessary ornament (on a dress, etc): *frills and furbelows.*

furbish /ˈfɜ:bɪʃ/ *v* [Tn, Tn·p] ~ **sth** (**up**) polish, clean or renovate (esp sth that has not been used for a long time): *furbish up an antique sword.*

furious /ˈfjʊərɪəs/ *adj* 1 ~ (**with sb**)/(**at sth**) full of violent anger: *She was absolutely furious (at his behaviour).* 2 violent; intense; unrestrained: *a furious struggle, storm, debate* ○ *She drove off at a furious speed.* 3 (idm) **fast and furious** ⇨ FAST[1].

▷ **furiously** *adv.*

furl /fɜ:l/ *v* 1 [Tn] roll up and fasten (a sail, a flag, an umbrella, etc). 2 [I] become furled: *This fan doesn't furl neatly.*

furlong /ˈfɜ:lɒŋ; *US* -lɔ:ŋ/ *n* distance of 220 yards or 201 metres; one eighth of a mile. ⇨ App 10.

furlough /ˈfɜ:ləʊ/ *n* [C, U] (permission for) absence from duty, esp that granted to civil servants, soldiers, etc working abroad: *six months' furlough* ○ *going home on furlough.*

▷ **furlough** *v* (*esp US*) (a) [Tn] give a furlough to (sb). (b) [I] spend a furlough.

furnace /ˈfɜ:nɪs/ *n* 1 enclosed fireplace for heating the water used to warm a building by means of pipes. 2 enclosed space or chamber for heating metal, glass, etc to a very high temperature: *It's like a furnace in here — can we open a window?*

furnish /ˈfɜ:nɪʃ/ *v* 1 [Tn, Tn·pr] ~ **sth** (**with sth**) provide sth with furniture; put furniture in (a place): *furnish a house, a room, an office, etc* ○ *a furnished flat*, ie one rented complete with its furniture ○ *The room was furnished with antiques.* 2 [Tn, Tn·pr, Dn·pr] ~ **sb/sth with sth**; ~ **sth** (**to sb/sth**) supply or provide sb/sth with sth: *furnish a village with supplies/furnish supplies to a village* ○ *furnish all the equipment for a major expedition* ○ *This scandal will furnish the town with plenty of gossip.*

▷ **furnishings** *n* [pl] furniture, equipment, fittings, etc in a room or house.

furniture /ˈfɜ:nɪtʃə(r)/ *n* 1 [U] movable articles, eg tables, chairs, beds, etc put into a house or an office to make it suitable for living or working in. 2 (idm) **a part of the furniture** ⇨ PART[1].

furore /fjʊˈrɔ:rɪ/ (*US* **furor** /ˈfju:rɔ:r/) *n* [sing] general uproar of admiration or anger: *His last novel created a furore among the critics.*

furrier /ˈfʌrɪə(r)/ *n* person who prepares or sells fur or fur clothing.

furrow /ˈfʌrəʊ/ *n* 1 long narrow trench cut in the earth, esp by a plough: *furrows ready for planting.* Cf RIDGE 1. ⇨ illus at PLOUGH. 2 groove resembling this, eg a deep wrinkle in the skin: *Deep furrows lined his brow.* 3 (idm) **plough a lonely furrow** ⇨ PLOUGH *v.*

▷ **furrow** *v* [Tn esp passive] make furrows in (sth): *newly furrowed fields* ○ *a forehead furrowed by old age and anxiety.*

furry ⇨ FUR.

further /ˈfɜ:ðə(r)/ *adj* 1 more distant in space, direction or time; farther: *The hospital is further down the road.* 2 additional; more: *further volumes* ○ *Have you any further questions?* ○ *There is nothing further to be said.* ○ *The museum is closed until further notice*, ie until another announcement about it is made.

▷ **further** *adv* 1 at or to a greater distance in space or time; more remote; farther: *It's not safe to go any further.* ○ *Africa is further from England than France.* ○ *Think further back into your childhood.* 2 in addition; also: *Further, it has come to my attention....* 3 to a greater degree or extent: *I must enquire further into this matter.* ○ *I can offer you £50, but I can't go any further than that.* 4 (idm) **far/farther/further afield** ⇨ AFIELD. ⇨ Usage at FARTHER.

further *v* [Tn] help the progress or development of (sth); promote: *further sb's interests* ○ *further the cause of peace.*

furtherance /ˈfɜ:ðərəns/ *n* [U] advancement of sb's interests, a cause, etc.

furthermore /ˌfɜ:ðəˈmɔ:(r)/ *adv* in addition; moreover.

furthermost /-məʊst/ *adj* most distant in space or time; furthest (FURTHER 1).

□ ˌ**further edu**ˈ**cation** formal (but not university) education provided for people older than school age.

furthest /fɜ:ðɪst/ *adj, adv* = FARTHEST.

furtive /ˈfɜ:tɪv/ *adj* (a) done secretly and quietly so as not to be noticed: *a furtive glance* ○ *furtive movements.* (b) (of a person or his behaviour) sly or secretive, suggesting that one is guilty of sth or does not want to be noticed. ▷ **furtively** *adv.* **furtiveness** *n* [U].

fury /ˈfjʊərɪ/ *n* 1 [U] wild and violent anger: *speechless with fury.* 2 [C] state or condition of extreme emotion, esp anger or excitement: *He was in one of his uncontrollable furies.* ○ *She flew into a fury when I wouldn't lend her any money.* 3 [U] strength or violence of activity, weather, etc: *The fury of the storm abated.* 4 [C] fiercely angry person, esp a woman or girl. 5 **the Furies** [pl] (in Greek mythology) goddesses with snakes instead of hair, sent from the underworld to punish crime. 6 (idm) **like fury** (*infml*) with great effort, speed, concentration, etc: *He ran like fury to catch the bus.*

furze /fɜ:z/ *n* [U] = GORSE.

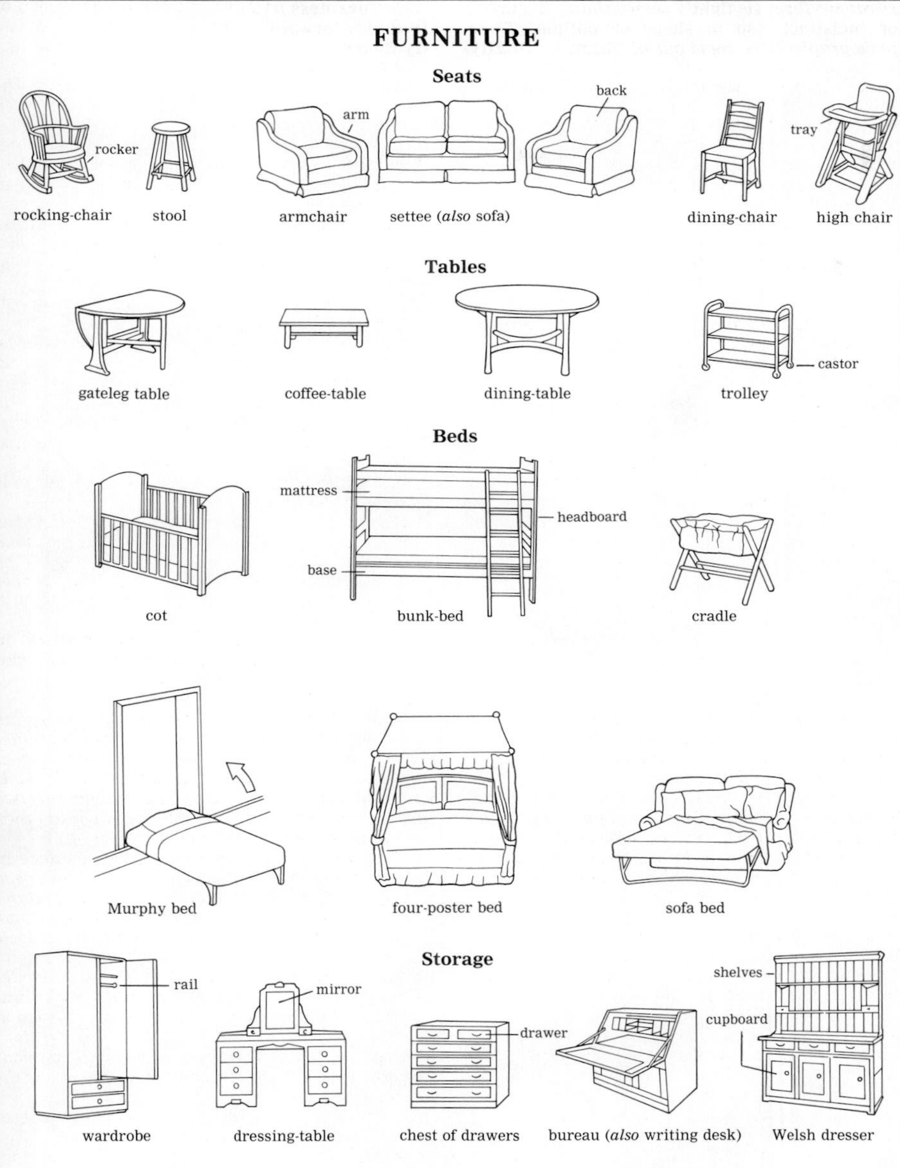

fuse[1] /fju:z/ *n* **1** piece of easily burnt material (eg rope, paper) along which a spark moves to ignite a firework, bomb, etc so that it explodes. **2** (*US* also **fuze** /fju:z/) device that makes a bomb, shell, etc explode either on impact or at a particular time: *The bomb had been set with a four-hour fuse.* **3** (idm) **on a short fuse** ⇨ SHORT[1].

fuse[2] /fju:z/ *v* [I, Ipr, Ip, Tn, Tn·pr, Tn·p] **1** (cause sth to) become liquid by means of heat: *fuse metals (into a solid mass).* **2** join (sth) or become joined by means of heat: *fuse two pieces of wire together* ○ (*fig*) *The two companies are fused by their common interests.*
▷ **fusible** /ˈfju:zəbl/ *adj* that can to be melted or joined together.

fuse[3] /fju:z/ *n* (in an electric circuit) short piece of wire that melts and breaks the circuit if the current exceeds a safe level: *It looks as though you've blown a fuse*, ie caused it to melt.
▷ **fuse** *v* **1** [I, Tn] (of an electric circuit) stop or cause to stop working because a fuse melts: *The lights have all fused.* ○ *I've fused all the lights.* **2** [Tn] put a fuse in (a circuit or an appliance).
□ ˈ**fuse-box** *n* small cupboard or box containing the fuses of an electrical system.
ˈ**fuse wire** wire used in electrical fuses.

fuselage /ˈfju:zəlɑ:ʒ; *US* ˈfju:səlɑ:ʒ/ *n* body of an aeroplane, ie the part to which the engine(s), wings and tail are fitted. ⇨ illus at AIRCRAFT.

fusilier /ˌfju:zəˈlɪə(r)/ *n* **1** [C] (formerly) soldier armed with a light gun called a *fusil.* **2** (**a**) (also *esp US* **fusileer**) [C] soldier in certain infantry regiments. (**b**) **Fusiliers** [pl] any of several infantry regiments formerly armed with light guns: *the Royal Welsh Fusiliers.*

fusillade /ˌfju:zəˈleɪd; *US* -sə-/ *n* **1** continuous or simultaneous shooting of guns. **2** (*fig*) great outburst of questions, criticism, etc.

fusion /ˈfju:ʒn/ *n* [C, U] **1** the blending or uniting of different things into one, by melting, etc: *the fusion of copper and zinc to produce brass* ○ (*fig*) *a fusion of ideas.* **2** union of atomic nuclei to form a heavier nucleus, usu with energy being released: *nuclear fusion.*

fuss /fʌs/ *n* **1** (**a**) [U] (esp unnecessary) nervous excitement or activity: *Stop all this fuss and get on with your work.* (**b**) [sing] display of excitement, worry, etc, esp over sth unimportant: *Don't get into a fuss about nothing.* **2** [sing] angry scene: *There will be a real fuss if you're caught stealing.* **3** (idm) **make, kick up, etc a fuss (about/over sth)** complain strongly: *She's kicking up an awful fuss about the high rent.* **make a fuss of/over sb/sth** pay particular and often excessive attention to sb/sth: *Don't make so much fuss over the children.* ○ *A lot of fuss was made of the play, but it wasn't a success.*
▷ **fuss** *v* **1** [I, Ip] ~ (**about**) be worried or excited, esp over small things: *Stop fussing and eat your food!* ○ *If you keep fussing about, we're sure to be late.* **2** [Tn] annoy or disturb (sb): *Don't fuss me while I'm driving.* **3** [Ipr] ~ **over sb** pay excessive attention to sb: *He's always fussing over his grandchildren.* **4** (idm) **not be fussed (about sb/sth)** (*infml*) not care very much: *'Where do you want to go for lunch?' 'I'm not fussed.'*
□ ˈ**fusspot** *n* (*infml*) very fussy(1,2) person.

fussy /ˈfʌsɪ/ *adj* (**-ier**, **-iest**) (*usu derog*) **1** nervously active or excited about small things: *fussy parents* ○ *a fussy manner.* **2** ~ (**about sth**) giving too much close attention to detail, etc and therefore difficult to please: *Our teacher is very fussy about punctuation.* ○ *Don't be so fussy (about your food).* **3** (of clothes, design, etc) too full of detail or decoration: *a fussy pattern.* ▷ **fussily** *adv.* **fussiness** *n* [U].

fustian /ˈfʌstɪən; *US* -tʃən/ *n* [U] **1** thick strong coarse cotton cloth: *a jacket (made) of fustian* ○ [attrib] *a fustian jacket.* **2** (*dated derog*) talk that sounds impressive but is in fact empty and worthless; bombast.

fusty /ˈfʌstɪ/ *adj* (**-ier**, **-iest**) (*derog*) **1** smelling old, stale or damp: *a fusty room* ○ *This blanket smells a bit fusty.* **2** old-fashioned; not up-to-date: *a fusty old professor*, ie one who has learned much from books, etc but does not know about modern ideas.
▷ **fustiness** *n* [U].

futile /ˈfju:taɪl; *US* -tl/ *adj* producing no result; useless; pointless: *a futile attempt/exercise* ○ *Their efforts to revive him were futile.* ○ *What a futile* (ie unnecessarily silly) *remark!*
▷ **futility** /fju:ˈtɪlətɪ/ *n* [U] uselessness; pointlessness: *the futility of war.*

future /ˈfju:tʃə(r)/ *n* **1** (**a**) [U] time that will come after the present: *in the near/distant future*, ie soon/not soon ○ *Who knows what will happen in the future?* (**b**) [U] events that will happen then: *History influences both the present and the future.* (**c**) [C] condition or state of sb/sth then: *Her future is uncertain.* ○ *The future of this project will be decided by the government.* **2** [U] possibility of success, happiness, etc coming later; prospects: *I gave up my job because there was no future in it.* **3 futures** [pl] (*commerce*) goods or shares (SHARE[1] 3) bought at agreed prices but delivered and paid for later. **4** (idm) **in future** from this time onwards: *Please be punctual in future.*
▷ **future** *adj* [attrib] of or taking place in the future: *her future husband, job, prospects* ○ *future events* ○ *a future life*, ie after death.
futureless *adj* without hope for a (successful) future: *a futureless career.*
futurology /ˌfju:tʃəˈrɒlədʒɪ/ *n* [U] forecasting the future, esp on the basis of present trends in society. **futurologist** /-lədʒɪst/ *n.*

futurism /ˈfju:tʃərɪzəm/ *n* [U] movement in art and literature that abandoned tradition and sought to express the energy and growth of a modern mechanized life-style. It was active esp in Italy before the First World War, and in Russia after the Revolution. It also had a great influence on *Dadaism and similar artistic movements.
▷ **futurist** *n, adj* (supporter) of futurism.
futuristic /ˌfju:tʃəˈrɪstɪk/ *adj* **1** looking suitable for the future or extremely modern; not traditional: *futuristic design, furniture, housing, etc.* **2** of or relating to futurism.

futurity /fju:ˈtjʊərətɪ; *US* -ˈtʊər-/ *n* (**a**) [U] future time; the future: *gazing into futurity.* (**b**) [C often *pl*, often pl] future events.

fuzz[1] /fʌz/ *n* [U] **1** mass of soft light particles; fluff: *A peach skin is covered with fuzz.* **2** short fine hair that sticks up.

fuzz[2] /fʌz/ *n* [Gp] **the fuzz** (*sl*) the police.

fuzzy /ˈfʌzɪ/ *adj* (**-ier**, **-iest**) **1** like fuzz; having a soft and fluffy texture: *a fuzzy teddy bear, blanket, sweater* ○ *fuzzy* (ie tightly curled) *hair*. **2** blurred or indistinct, esp in shape or outline: *These photographs have come out all fuzzy.* ▷ **fuzzily** *adv*. **fuzziness** *n* [U].

fwd *abbr* forward.

-fy ⇨ -IFY.

G, g

G, g /dʒiː/ *n* (*pl* **G's, g's** /dʒiːz/) **1** the seventh letter of the English alphabet: *'God' begins with (a) G/ 'G'.* **2 G** (*music*) the fifth note in the scale of C major.

g *abbr* **1** gram(s): *300g.* **2** /dʒiː/ (acceleration due to) gravity: *Spacecraft re-entering the earth's atmosphere are affected by g forces.*

Ga *symb* gallium.

gab /gæb/ *n* [U] (*infml*) **1** continuous, esp trivial, chatter: *Stop your gab!* **2** (idm) **the gift of the gab** ⇨ GIFT.
▷ **gab** *v* (-bb-) [I, Ip] ~ **(on/away)** (*infml*) chatter about unimportant things: *They've been gabbing (away) on the phone for nearly an hour.*

gabardine (also **gaberdine**) /ˈgæbədiːn, ˌgæbəˈdiːn/ *n* **(a)** [U] strong cloth woven in a twill pattern: [attrib] *a gabardine coat.* **(b)** [C] garment (esp a strong raincoat) made of this material.

gabble /ˈgæbl/ *v* **(a)** [I, Ip] ~ **(on/away)** talk quickly and indistinctly: *Take your time and don't gabble!* **(b)** [Tn, Tn·p] ~ **sth (out)** say sth too quickly to be clearly understood.
▷ **gabble** *n* [U] fast unintelligible speech: *He speaks at such a gabble!*

Gable /ˈgeɪbl/ Clark (1901-60), American film actor. His good looks and casual acting style made him a romantic screen idol in films like *Gone with the Wind*, after which he became known as the King of Hollywood.

gable /ˈgeɪbl/ *n* triangular upper part of the side or end of a building, under a sloping roof. ⇨ illus at HOME.
▷ **gabled** /ˈgeɪbld/ *adj* having one or more gables: *a gabled house/roof.*

Gabon /gæˈbɒn/ country on the west coast of Central Africa; pop approx 1 095 000; official language French; capital Libreville; unit of currency franc. The country gained independence from France in 1960. It has an equatorial climate, large areas of dense forest, and subsistence agriculture. Timber and mineral resources (including manganese and oil) are the country's main exports. ⇨ map at ZAÏRE. ▷ **Gabonese** /ˌgæbəˈniːz/ *adj, n* (*pl* unchanged).

Gabriel /ˈgeɪbrɪəl/ one of the chief angels mentioned in both the Bible and the Koran as a messenger from God. In the New Testament he appears to Mary, telling her that she will be the mother of Jesus.

gad /gæd/ *v* (-dd-) (phr v) **gad about/around** (*infml derog*) go around from one place to another (usu in search of pleasure and excitement): *While they gad about the world, their children are neglected at home.*
□ **ˈgadabout** *n* person who habitually gads about.

gadfly /ˈgædflaɪ/ *n* **1** fly that stings horses and cattle. **2** (*derog*) annoying person, esp one who provokes others into action by criticism, etc.

gadget /ˈgædʒɪt/ *n* small mechanical device or tool: *a complicated new gadget for opening tins.* ⇨ Usage at MACHINE.
▷ **gadgetry** *n* [U] gadgets collectively: *lots of modern gadgetry.*

gadolinium /ˌgædəˈlɪnɪəm/ *n* [U] (*symb* **Gd**) chemical element, a soft silvery metal used in magnetic alloys and in colour television sets.

Gaelic *n* [U], *adj* **1** /ˈgeɪlɪk/ (language) of the Celtic people of Ireland. **2** /ˈgælɪk, *also* ˈgeɪlɪk/ (language) of the Celtic people of Scotland. Both languages have the problem of competing with English, but while Irish Gaelic (or **Erse**) is taught in Irish schools, Scots Gaelic is spoken by only about 75 000 people in the far west of Scotland. Cf MANX. ⇨ article at LANGUAGE.

gaff[1] /gæf/ *n* stick with an iron hook for pulling large fish out of the water.
▷ **gaff** *v* [Tn] seize (fish) with a gaff.

gaff[2] /gæf/ *n* (idm) **blow the gaff** ⇨ BLOW[1].

gaffe /gæf/ *n* social blunder; indiscreet act or remark: *He didn't realize what a gaffe he'd made.*

gaffer /ˈgæfə(r)/ *n* (*infml*) **1** (*joc or derog*) old fellow: *That (old) gaffer going into the pub is 90 years old.* **2** (*Brit sl*) foreman (of a gang of workmen).

gag /gæg/ *n* **1** **(a)** thing, esp a piece of cloth, put in or over a person's mouth to prevent him from speaking or shouting. **(b)** thing placed in a patient's mouth by a dentist, doctor, etc to keep it open. **(c)** (*fig*) anything that restricts freedom of speech. **2** joke or funny story, esp as part of a comedian's act: *a few rather feeble gags.*
▷ **gag** *v* (-gg-) **1** [Tn] **(a)** put a gag(1a) into or over the mouth of (sb); silence. **(b)** (*fig*) deprive (sb/sth) of free speech: *The new censorship laws are an attempt to gag the press.* **2** [I, Ipr] ~ **(on sth)** (*infml*) choke or retch: *gagging on a piece of raw fish.* **3** [I] make jokes.

gaga /ˈgɑːgɑː/ *adj* [usu pred] (*infml*) senile; slightly crazy: *He has gone quite gaga.*

gage (*US*) = GAUGE.

gaggle /ˈgægl/ *n* **1** flock (of geese). **2** (*fig*) group of noisy or talkative people: *a gaggle of tourists, schoolchildren, etc.*

gaiety /ˈgeɪətɪ/ *n* [U] merriment; cheerfulness; being gay(2): *The colourful flags added to the gaiety of the occasion.* Cf GAYNESS (GAY).

gaily ⇨ GAY.

gain[1] /geɪn/ *n* **1** [U] increase in wealth; profit; advantage: *One man's loss is another man's gain.* ○ *We hope for some gain from our investment.* **2** [C] increase in amount or power; improvement: *a gain in weight of two pounds* ○ *Heavy gains were recorded on the Stock Exchange today.*
▷ **gainful** /-fl/ *adj* [usu attrib] profitable; bringing wealth: *gainful employment.* **gainfully** /-fəlɪ/ *adv* profitably; usefully.

gain[2] /geɪn/ *v* **1** **(a)** [Tn, Dn·n, Dn·pr] ~ **sth (for sb)** obtain or win (esp sth wanted or needed): *gain possession* ○ *gain access to secret information* ○ *gain sb's affections* ○ *I gained the impression that the matter had been settled.* ○ *His persistence gained him victory.* **(b)** [Tn] get more of (esp sth wanted or needed): *gain experience, power, strength, weight* ○ *Our campaign is gaining momentum.* ○ *The plane rapidly gained height.* **2** [Ipr] ~ **by/from (doing) sth** benefit or profit from sth/doing sth: *You can gain by watching how she works.* **3** [Tn] reach (sth) (usu with effort): *After swimming for an hour, he finally gained the shore.* **4** [I, Tn] (of a watch or clock) go fast; become ahead of the correct time: *My watch gains (by) several minutes a day.* **5** (idm) **carry/gain one's point** ⇨ POINT[1]. **gain credence** ⇨ CREDENCE. **gain ˈground** make progress; begin to succeed: *Your campaign is gaining ground.* **gain/make up ground** ⇨ GROUND[1]. **gain/win sb's hand** ⇨ HAND[1]. **gain/win one's laurels** ⇨ LAUREL. **gain time** obtain extra time by making excuses, deliberately using slow methods, etc: *try to gain time on the football pitch by feigning injury.* **gain, get, etc the upper hand** ⇨ UPPER. **nothing venture, nothing gain/win** ⇨ VENTURE. **6** (phr v) **gain in sth** obtain more of (a physical or an abstract quality): *gain in beauty, height, strength, weight, etc* ○ *gain in confidence, influence, knowledge, understanding, etc.* **gain on sb/sth** come closer to sb/sth, esp a rival or sth pursued: *gain on the leader in a race* ○ *The Socialists are gaining on the Conservatives in the opinion polls.*

gainsay /ˌgeɪnˈseɪ/ *v* (*pt, pp* **gainsaid** /-ˈsed/) [Tn] (*arch*) (usu in negative sentences or questions) contradict (sb/sth); deny (sth): *There's no gainsaying his honesty*, ie We cannot deny that he is honest.

Gainsborough /ˈgeɪnzbrə/ Thomas (1727-88), English artist. He became a fashionable portrait painter with the English gentry and aristocracy, but also painted many fine landscapes, which show the influence of *Rubens and other Dutch artists. Combining both skills, he often placed the subjects of his portraits in outdoor country settings, capturing the subtle effects of light with rapid yet delicate brushwork. Cf REYNOLDS. ⇨ illus.

Thomas Gainsborough: Mrs Siddons

gait /geɪt/ *n* [sing] manner of walking or running: *with an unsteady gait.*

gaiter /ˈgeɪtə(r)/ *n* covering of cloth, leather, etc for the leg from the ankle to below the knee: *a pair of gaiters.*

gal /gæl/ *n* (*dated infml*) girl.

gala /ˈgɑːlə; *US* ˈgeɪlə/ *n* social, sporting or theatrical occasion with special features: *a swimming gala* ○ [attrib] *a gala dinner, night, performance.*

galactic /gəˈlæktɪk/ *adj* of a galaxy or the Galaxy.

Galahad /ˈgæləhæd/ knight of King *Arthur's Round Table. Because of his purity he succeeded in finding the *Holy Grail: (*fig*) *I'm impressed by your son's behaviour — he's a real little Galahad*, ie a model of honesty, politeness, etc.

galantine /ˈgælənti:n/ *n* [U] white meat, boned, spiced, cooked in the form of a roll and served cold.

Galapagos Islands /gəˈlæpəgəs aɪləndz/ **the Galapagos Islands** group of islands in the Pacific Ocean, on the Equator, west of *Ecuador (to which they belong). Many varieties of wildlife live on the islands, some of them not found anywhere else, including cormorants that cannot fly and the giant tortoises that give the islands their Spanish name. A visit to the islands in 1835 influenced *Darwin's ideas about evolution. ⇨ map at ECUADOR.

galaxy /ˈgæləksɪ/ *n* **1** [C] any of the large systems of stars in outer space, held together by the force of gravity between them. They can appear as discs with spiral 'arms', or elliptical, or spherical; others are irregular in form. **2 the Galaxy** [sing] (also **the Milky Way**) system of stars that contains our solar system, seen as a luminous band in the sky. It is a spiral galaxy, containing about 100 000 million stars, and is about 100 000 light years across. **3** [C] (*fig*) group of brilliantly talented people: *a galaxy of talent, beautiful women, film stars.*

gale /geɪl/ *n* **1** very strong wind (force 8 on the Beaufort Scale); storm (at sea): *It's blowing a gale outside.* ○ *The ship lost its masts in the gale.* ○ [attrib] *a gale warning* ○ *gale-force winds.* **2** (*fig*) noisy outburst: *gales of laughter.*

Galilean[1] /ˌgælɪˈliːən/ *adj* **1** of (ancient) Galilee. **2** Christian.

▷ **Galilean** *n* **1** [C] native or inhabitant of Galilee. **2** (**a**) [C usu *pl*] Christian person. (**b**) **the Galilean** [sing] (*often derog*) Jesus Christ.

Galilean[2] /ˌgælɪˈleɪən/ *adj* of Galileo Galilei or his work.

Galilee /ˈgælɪliː/ northern part of ancient Palestine, west of the River Jordan, now in Israel. It is the area in which Jesus spent most of his life. The **Sea of Galilee** is a lake in NE Israel. The River Jordan flows through it from north to south.

Galileo Galilei /gælɪˌleɪəʊ gælɪˈleɪɪ/ usu called Galileo (1564-1642), Italian astronomer and physicist and one of the founders of modern science. He was condemned by the Catholic Church for his acceptance and confirmation of the theory of *Copernicus that the earth and planets moved round the sun. He developed a new type of telescope with which he observed the mountains of the moon, the moons of Jupiter and the phases of Venus. He also discovered the principle of inertia.

gall[1] /gɔːl/ *n* [U] **1** bitter liquid secreted by the liver; bile. **2** (*fig*) bitter feeling; hatred or resentment: *words full of venom and gall.* **3** (*infml fig*) impudence; impertinence: *Of all the gall!* ie What impudence!

□ **ˈgall-bladder** *n* (*anatomy*) organ attached to the liver that stores and releases bile. ⇨ illus at DIGESTIVE.

ˈgallstone *n* hard mass forming in the gall-bladder and sometimes causing pain. Cf STONE 6.

gall[2] /gɔːl/ *n* sore place on an animal, esp a horse, caused by rubbing (of a harness, etc).

▷ **gall** *v* [Tn] **1** cause pain to (an animal, part of the body, etc) by rubbing; chafe. **2** annoy (sb); humiliate: *It galled him to have to ask for a loan.* **galling** *adj* [usu pred] annoying; humiliating: *It was galling to have to apologize to a man she detested.*

gall[3] /gɔːl/ *n* unnatural growth on a tree produced by insects. Cf OAK-APPLE (OAK).

gall *abbr* (*pl* unchanged or **galls**) gallon(s): *petrol at 175p* (ie pence) *per gall.*

gallant /ˈgælənt/ *adj* **1** (*fml or rhet*) brave: *a gallant knight, soldier, etc* ○ *a gallant deed, effort, struggle.* **2** fine; grand; stately: *a gallant ship.* **3** /*also* gəˈlænt/ (of a man) giving special attention and respect to women.

▷ **gallant** /ˈgælənt, *also* gəˈlænt/ *n* fashionable young man, esp one who is attentive to women.

gallantly *adv.*

gallantry /ˈgæləntrɪ/ *n* **1** [U] bravery: *a medal for gallantry.* **2** [U, C] special attentiveness (of a man) to women: *He won many hearts by his gallantry.*

galleon /ˈgælɪən/ *n* large Spanish sailing-ship used from the 15th to the 17th century.

gallery /ˈgælərɪ/ *n* **1** [C] room or building for showing works of art: *a ˈpicture-gallery.* **2** (**a**) [C] highest and cheapest seats in a theatre: *Four tickets for the gallery, please.* (**b**) [Gp] people occupying these. **3** [C] raised covered platform or passage along an inner wall of a hall, church, etc. **4** [C] covered walk or corridor partly open at one side; colonnade. **5** [C] long narrow room, esp one used for a particular purpose: *a ˈshooting-gallery.* **6** [C] horizontal underground passage in a mine. Cf SHAFT 7. **7** (idm) **play to the ˈgallery** behave in an exaggerated way to attract the attention of onlookers.

galley /ˈgælɪ/ *n* **1** (formerly) long flat ship, usu rowed by slaves or criminals; ancient Greek or Roman warship. **2** kitchen in a ship or an aircraft. **3** long tray used by printers for arranging type.

□ **ˈgalley proof** (also **galley**) printed proof[1](4a) on a long slip of paper before it is divided into pages.

ˈgalley-slave *n* **1** person forced to row in a galley. **2** (*fig*) person made to work like a slave.

galley-west /ˌgælɪˈwest/ (idm) **knock sb/sth galley-west** (*US infml*) cause sb/sth to become confused, out of action, etc: *That's knocked all our arrangements galley-west.*

Gallic /ˈgælɪk/ *adj* (**a**) of *Gaul or the Gauls. (**b**) of the French people and their character: *Gallic charm, sophistication, wit, etc.*

▷ **Gallicism** /ˈgælɪsɪzəm/ *n* French word or expression used in another language: *'Déjà vu' is a Gallicism often used in English.*

Gallipoli /gəˈlɪpəlɪ/ peninsula on the European side of the *Dardanelles. In 1915-16 it was the scene of heavy fighting during an unsuccessful attack by the Allies against the Turks, with huge loss of life on both sides.

gallium /ˈgælɪəm/ *n* [U] (*symb* **Ga**) chemical element, a soft bluish-white metal used eg in high-temperature thermometers and semiconductors.

gallivant /ˌgælɪˈvænt, ˈgælɪvænt/ *v* (phr v) **gallivant about** (*infml derog*) (usu in the continuous tenses) go about from one place to another (usu in search of pleasure): *They should spend less time gallivanting about and more with their children.*

gallon /ˈgælən/ *n* **1** [C] (**a**) (*Brit*) measure of capacity, used for liquids and corn, etc, equal to eight pints and equivalent to 4 546 cc. (**b**) (*US*) measure of capacity, used for measuring liquids, equivalent to 3785 cc. **2 gallons** [pl] **~s (of sth)** (*infml*) a large amount: *We ate gallons of ice-cream.*

gallop /ˈgæləp/ *n* **1** (**a**) [sing] fastest pace (of a horse, etc) with all four feet off the ground at each stride: *He rode off at a gallop.* ○ *at full gallop.* Cf WALK[1] 1d. (**b**) [C] period of riding at this pace: *to go for a gallop.* **2** [sing] (*fig*) unusually fast speed: *to work at a gallop.*

▷ **gallop** *v* **1** (**a**) [I, Ipr, Ip] (of a horse, etc or a rider) go at a gallop: *The frightened horse galloped away.* ○ *I enjoy galloping over the fields.* ⇨ Usage at RUN[1]. (**b**) [Tn, Tn·pr, Tn·p] (of a rider) cause (a horse, etc) to go at a gallop: *He galloped the horse along the track.* **2** (phr v) **gallop ahead (of sb)** progress rapidly: *Japan is galloping ahead in the race to develop new technologies.* **gallop through sth** complete sth rapidly: *gallop through one's work, a lecture, a performance.*

galloway /ˈgæləweɪ/ *n* **1** cow or bull of a type originally bred in Galloway, SW Scotland. **2** type of small strong horse originally bred in Galloway.

gallows /ˈgæləʊz/ (also **the gallows**) *n* (pl unchanged; usu *sing* with *sing v*) wooden framework on which criminals are put to death by hanging: *to send a man to the gallows,* ie condemn him to death.

□ **gallows ˈhumour** jokes about unpleasant things like death, disease, etc.

Gallup poll /ˈgæləp pəʊl/ assessment of public opinion by questioning a representative sample of people, esp in order to forecast voting at an election.

galop /ˈgæləp, gæˈlɒp; *US also* gæˈləʊ/ *n* (piece of music originally for a) lively dance in duple time.

galore /gəˈlɔː(r)/ *adv* (*usu approv*) (following *ns*) in plenty: *to have books, food, friends, money galore.*

galoshes /gəˈlɒʃɪz/ *n* [pl] rubber overshoes worn in wet weather: *a pair of galoshes.*

Galsworthy /ˈgɔːlzwɜːðɪ/ John (1867-1933), English writer. Though he wrote several plays on social and moral themes, he is best remembered as the author of *The Forsyte Saga,* a series of novels about the declining fortunes of a wealthy Victorian middle-class family. He was awarded the Nobel prize for literature in 1932. ⇨ article at PERFORMING ARTS.

galumph /gəˈlʌmf/ *v* (phr v) **~ up, down, etc** (*infml joc*) walk, run, etc noisily or clumsily: *The children came galumphing into the house like a herd of elephants.*

galvanic /gælˈvænɪk/ *adj* **1** producing an electric current by chemical action: *a galvanic battery* ○ *galvanic electricity.* **2** (*fig*) sudden, jerky and dramatic (as if produced by an electric shock): *a galvanic effect, movement, smile.*

galvanize, -ise /ˈgælvənaɪz/ *v* **1** [Tn] coat (iron) with zinc to protect it from rust: *a galvanized bucket, nail, hinge, etc* ○ *galvanized wire.* **2** [Tn, Tn·pr] **~ sb (into sth/ doing sth)** shock sb into action: *The manager's arrival galvanized the workers into activity.* ▷ **galvanization, -isation** /ˌgælvənaɪˈzeɪʃən; *US* -nɪˈzeɪ-/ *n* [U].

galvanometer /ˌgælvəˈnɒmɪtə(r)/ *n* instrument for measuring small electric currents.

Gambia /ˈgæmbɪə/ **the Gambia** country in W Africa; pop approx 812 000; official language English; capital Banjul; unit of currency dalasi (= 100 bututs). The country lies on either side of the River Gambia and, except on the coast, is entirely surrounded by Senegal. Its economy is agricultural, the main crops being ground-nuts, rice and cotton. There is also a growing tourist industry. ⇨ map at NIGERIA. ▷ **Gambian** *n, adj.*

gambit /ˈgæmbɪt/ *n* **1** opening move(s) in chess in which a player sacrifices a piece in order to win an advantage later. **2** (*fig*) opening move in any situation that is calculated to win an advantage: *His opening gambit at the debate was a direct attack on Government policy.*

gamble /ˈgæmbl/ *v* **1** (**a**) [I, Ipr] play games of chance, etc for money: *gamble at cards, on the horses, etc* ○ *He spends all his time gambling in the casino.* (**b**) [Tn, Tn·pr] **~ sth (on sth)** spend (money) by playing such games, etc: *He gambled all his winnings on the last race.* **2** (phr v) **~ sth away** lose sth by gambling: *gamble away all one's money.* **gamble in sth** risk money by investing in (a specified commodity): *gamble in oil (shares).* **gamble on sth/doing sth** act in the hope of sth being successful, true, etc despite the risk of loss: *gamble on (having) sb's support* ○ *I wouldn't gamble on the weather being fine.*

▷ **gamble** *n* **1** act of gambling; undertaking with a risk of loss and a chance of profit: *Setting up this business was a bit of a gamble.* **2** (idm) **take a gamble (on sth)** gamble: *The company took a gamble by cutting the price of their products, and it paid off,* ie was financially successful.

gambler /ˈgæmblə(r)/ *n* person who gambles: *a habitual gambler.*

gambling /ˈgæmblɪŋ/ *n* [U] (**a**) playing games, etc for money: [attrib] *heavy gambling debts.* ⇨ article. (**b**) taking risks for possible advantage: *to have a taste for gambling.*

gamboge /gæmˈbuːʒ; *US* -ˈbəʊʒ/ *n* [U] (**a**) deep yellow resin used as colouring matter by artists. (**b**) colour of this.

gambol /ˈgæmbl/ *v* (**-ll-**) (*US* also **-l-**) [I, Ip] jump or skip about playfully: *children/lambs gambolling (about/around).*

▷ **gambol** *n* act of gambolling.

game[1] /geɪm/ *n* **1** [C] (**a**) form of play or sport with rules: *popular children's games* ○ *a game of chance/skill.* (**b**) instance of this: *to play a game of chess, football, hide-and-seek, etc* ○ *Let's have a game of snooker.* ⇨ Usage at SPORT. **2 games** [pl] (**a**) athletics or sport as part of a school curriculum: *Mary never played games at school.* (**b**) (also **the Games**) (international) athletic contests: *the Olympic/Commonwealth/Highland ˈGames.* **3** [C] part of a game (eg tennis or bridge) that forms a scoring unit: *We need another twenty points to make game,* ie in bridge. ○ *They lost the first game of the second set,* ie in tennis. ○ *(one) game all, two games all, etc,* ie each player or team has won one game, two games, etc ○ *Game, set and match (to...),* ie The tennis match has been won (by...). ○ [attrib] *game ˈpoint,* ie stage in a competition when one point is needed to win the game. **4** [C] set of equipment for playing a game: *My uncle always gives us a ˈboard game for Christmas.* **5** [C] (usu *sing*) (*infml*) (**a**) secret and cunning plan; trick: *So that's his (little) game!* ie Now I know what he has been planning. ○ *I wish I knew what her game is,* ie what she is planning to do. (**b**) type of activity or business: *the ˈpublishing game* ○ *the game of ˈpolitics* ○ *How long have you been in ˈthis game?*

Gambling

Gambling is popular in Britain, and takes many forms. There is no national lottery as such, but as part of the National Savings scheme, people can buy Premium Bonds, with the chance of winning large cash prizes. Interest on investors' money is paid into a prize fund instead of to investors, and a computer called 'Ernie' selects prizewinners from the bond-holders. Payments are made both weekly and monthly, with a maximum prize of £250 000, payable to one winner each month.

Football pools are one of the most popular forms of gambling. You pay a small amount of money and try to forecast weekly (Saturday) football match scores. It is possible to win a million pounds or more for a very small stake, and 'winning the pools' is a popular image of good luck.

Almost as popular is betting on the results of horse-races or greyhound races ('the dogs'). Racing bets can be made at the actual racecourse or track, but are mostly made in licensed betting-shops. At horse-races, the betting agents are known as bookmakers ('bookies') or turf accountants. An additional form of pooled betting on horse races is organized by the Horserace Totalisator Board (HTB, or 'the Tote').

Casinos and gaming clubs exist in the large cities but are used mostly by wealthy or experienced gamblers rather than the general public. Some people play for money when playing cards with friends, but the stakes are usually quite small.

Many pubs, railway buffets, etc, have a gaming machine ('fruit machine' or 'one-armed bandit'), and these machines can also be found in special amusement arcades and leisure centres. They almost always take more money than they pay out, although practised players can make modest gains.

Another popular form of gambling, especially among elderly people, is bingo, played in weekly sessions in special bingo halls (often converted cinemas) by an estimated 3 million people. Bingo is a game of chance, in which numbers printed on a card are covered or crossed through as they are called out. The player who first covers all his numbers wins a cash prize or a gift. In recent years the game has been adopted by popular newspapers with the aim of increasing their circulation. Cards are issued with the paper, and random numbers printed daily. A reader holding all the numbers telephones the newspaper to claim the prize. (A variant of this is also run by some quality papers—one in *The Times*, for example, has random numbers based on share price movements.) Popular newspapers also run other gambling games, such as 'spot the ball', in which the reader has to mark the point where the ball should be on the photograph of a football match.

Many local charities and appeals hold raffles to raise money. You buy a ticket for a sum of money and this gives you a chance of winning a cash prize or gift. Even people who object to gambling on principle often take part in raffles, arguing that their money is going to a good cause.

More generally, there are several ways in which cash prizes or gifts can be competed for, ranging from stalls at fêtes to competitions in magazines. A popular type of contest is a commercial one in which participants have to complete a simple quiz or test, then write a sentence (called a 'tie-breaker') saying why they like the particular product or service. The winning prize in such contests is usually a large cash sum or a gift such as a car or a free holiday.

All legal gambling in Britain is strictly regulated, although winnings from gaming and betting are not taxed.

Gambling of many types is very popular in the USA, but carries a greater stigma of social disapproval than it does in Britain. It is regulated by individual states, with the result that some states have a reputation for their high level of gambling. This is particularly true of Nevada, and especially the town of Las Vegas, whose many casinos are legalized by the state.

Another widespread type of gambling in the USA is the 'numbers game', a form of lottery. A small sum is bet on a three-figure number selected at random from an outside source, such as a bank's financial figures. The odds against winning are 998 to 1, and the holder of the winning number usually receives a payment of 540 times the original stake, with the 'runner' who accepted the bet getting 60 units. The overall profit of the promoters is about 40 per cent of the total staked. A 10-cent bet can thus win $54. The numbers game is, however, illegal, and the general level of unlawful and criminal gambling in the USA is considerably higher than in Britain.

6 [U] (flesh of) wild animals or birds hunted for sport or food: [attrib] *game ˈpie.* **7** (idm) **beat sb at his own game** ⇨ BEAT[1]. **easy game** ⇨ EASY[1]. **fair game** ⇨ FAIR[1]. **fun and games** ⇨ FUN. **the ˌgame is ˌnot worth the ˈcandle** (*saying*) the advantages to be gained from doing sth do not justify the trouble, expense, etc involved. **the game is ˈup** (usu said to or by a wrongdoer when he is caught) your/our crime, trickery, etc has been discovered. **a game that ˈtwo can play; ˈtwo can play at ˈthat game** (that is a) wrongdoing or trick that a victim can copy in return. **give the ˈgame away** carelessly reveal a secret. **the luck of the game** ⇨ LUCK. **a mug's game** ⇨ MUG[2]. **the name of the game** ⇨ NAME[1]. **(be) ˌoff one's ˈgame** unable to play as well as usual. **(be) on the ˈgame** (*sl*) involved in prostitution or thieving. **play a cat-and-mouse game with sb** ⇨ CAT[1]. **play ˈgames (with sb)** (*usu derog*) behave in a foolish and annoying way, eg by being secretive: *Stop playing games with me and come out of there!* **play the ˈgame** (a) play according to the rules. (b) (*fig*) act in a fair or honourable way: *John only pretends to do his share of the work; he's just not playing the game.* **play sb's game** act so as to further sb's plans intentionally or unintentionally: *She didn't realize that by complaining she was only playing Peter's game.* **a waiting game** ⇨ WAIT[1].

□ **ˈgame bird** bird that is hunted and killed for food or sport. ⇨ illus at BIRD.

ˈgamecock *n* cock bred for cock-fighting.

ˈgamekeeper *n* man employed to breed and protect game birds on an estate.

ˈgame plan detailed plan for achieving sth, eg in sport, business or politics; strategy: *Let me explain our game plan for this campaign.*

ˈgame reserve area of land reserved for the breeding and protection of game[1](6).

ˈgamesmanship *n* [U] art of winning games by upsetting the confidence of one's opponent.

ˈgame theory (also **ˈgames theory**) system that attempts to calculate mathematically the best strategy for each side in situations of conflict, eg in war, business or games of skill.

ˈgame-warden *n* person employed to manage a game reserve.

game[2] /geɪm/ *adj* ~ **(for sth/to do sth)** eager and willing to undertake sth risky; brave: *'Who'll climb up to get it?' 'I'm game (to try).'* ○ *He's always game for an adventure.* ▷ **gamely** *adv*: *fight, struggle, etc gamely,* ie bravely but perhaps unsuccessfully.

game[3] /geɪm/ *adj* (*dated infml*) lame; crippled (esp in the leg): *He is game in the leg/has a game leg.* Cf GAMMY.

gamete /ˈgæmi:t/ *n* (*biology*) sexual cell able to unite with another in reproduction. ▷ **gametic** /gəˈmetɪk/ *adj.*

gaming /ˈgeɪmɪŋ/ *n* [U] (*dated or law*) gambling: [attrib] *the Betting and Gaming Act* ○ *spending all night at the gaming tables.*

gamma /ˈgæmə/ *n* the third letter of the Greek alphabet.

□ **ˌgamma ˈglobulin** /ˈglɒbjʊlɪn/ (*medical*) form of protein, found in blood plasma, which gives protection against certain illnesses.

ˌgamma radiˈation radioactivity consisting of gamma rays.

ˈgamma ray (usu *pl*) ray of very short wavelength from radioactive materials.

gammon /ˈgæmən/ *n* [U] (*esp Brit*) bacon from the hind leg or side of a pig: [attrib] *gammon rashers.* Cf BACON, HAM 1, PORK.

gammy /ˈgæmɪ/ *adj* [usu attrib] (*infml*) (of a limb or joint) unable to function normally through pain or stiffness: *a gammy leg/knee.* Cf GAME[3].

gamut /ˈgæmət/ *n* **1 the gamut** [sing] complete range or scale (of sth): *the whole gamut of human emotions from joy to despair.* **2** (*music*) (in medieval or modern music) whole scale of notes used; major diatonic scale. **3** (idm) **run the gamut (of sth)** experience or perform the complete range of sth: *In his short life he had run the entire gamut of crime, from petty theft to murder.*

gamy /ˈgeɪmɪ/ *adj* **1** (of meat) having the strong flavour or smell of game[1](6) that has been kept for a long time. **2** (*esp US*) scandalous, esp in a sexual way: *gamy stories in the press.*

-gamy *comb form* (forming *ns*) marriage or sexual union: *monogamy* ○ *polygamy.* ▷ **-gamous, -gamously** (forming *adjs* and *advs*).

gander /ˈgændə(r)/ *n* **1** [C] male goose. **2** [sing] (*infml*) look, glance: *have/take a gander at sth.* **3** (idm) **what's sauce for the goose is sauce for the gander** ⇨ SAUCE.

Gandhi /ˈgɑ:ndi:/ Mohandas Karamchand (1869-1948), Indian statesman. He led the Indian struggle for independence from British rule, using campaigns of civil disobedience and spending several periods in prison. His philosophy of non-violence influenced people all over the world and won him the title Mahatma ('great soul'). He was assassinated shortly after independence was achieved.

gang /gæŋ/ *n* [CGp] **1** organized group of criminals: *The gang are being hunted by the police.* Cf GANGSTER. **2** group of young people, usu males in their teens and early twenties, who are typically troublesome: *The phone box was vandalized by a gang of youths.* ○ [attrib] *gang warfare,* ie fighting between rival gangs. **3** organized group of workers: *a gang of builders, roadmenders, etc.* **4** (*infml*) group of people who regularly associate together: *The whole gang's here tonight.* ○ *Don't go* *around with that gang or you'll come to no good!* ○ (*esp US*) *Hi, gang!* **5** [C] set of tools, pieces of equipment, etc arranged to work together.

▷ **gang** *v* **1** [Tn] arrange (tools, pieces of equipment, etc) to work together. **2** (phr v) **gang together**; **gang up (with sb) (against sb)** (*derog*) act together (with sb) (against sb). **gang up on sb** (*derog*) join together to hurt or frighten sb: *bigger/older boys ganging up on smaller/younger ones.* **ganger** /ˈgæŋə(r)/ *n* (*Brit*) foreman of a gang of workers.

□ ˈ**gang bang** (⚠ *sl*) occasion when several men in turn have sexual intercourse with one woman.

ˈ**gangland** *n* [sing] world of criminal gangs: [attrib] *gangland killings.*

ˌ**gang** ˈ**rape** raping of one woman by several men in turn.

Ganges /ˈgændʒiːz/ **the Ganges** river in N India, flowing 2 700 km (1 678 miles) from the *Himalayas to the Bay of Bengal. In the Hindu religion it is a sacred river which washes away sins.

gangling /ˈgæŋglɪŋ/ (also **gangly** /ˈgæŋglɪ/) *adj* (of a person) tall, thin and awkward-looking: *a gangling youth.*

ganglion /ˈgæŋglɪən/ *n* (*pl* ~**s** or **-lia** /-lɪə/) **1** group of nerve cells from which nerve fibres radiate. **2** (*fig*) centre of interest, activity or power.

gangplank /ˈgæŋplæŋk/ *n* movable plank for walking into or out of a boat; (small) gangway.

gangrene /ˈgæŋgriːn/ *n* [U] decay and death of body tissue when the blood supply has been stopped: *When gangrene set in, his foot had to be amputated.* ▷ **gangrenous** /ˈgæŋgrɪnəs/ *adj.*

gangster /ˈgæŋstə(r)/ *n* member of a gang of armed criminals: [attrib] *gangster films.*

gangue /gæŋ/ *n* [U] earthy or stony material of no value (eg quartz) that occurs in an ore with the valuable mineral.

gangway /ˈgæŋweɪ/ *n* **1** movable bridge for entering or leaving a ship. **2** (*Brit*) passage between two rows of seats in a theatre, concert-hall, etc. ▷ **gangway** *interj* (used for telling people to get out of one's way).

ganja /ˈgændʒə/ *n* [U] = CANNABIS.

gannet /ˈgænɪt/ *n* **1** large sea-bird that catches fish by diving. **2** (*fig infml*) person who is greedy for food: *It looks as though the gannets have been at the biscuits!*

gantry /ˈgæntrɪ/ *n* tall metal frame supporting a crane, signals on a railway or motorway, rocket-launching equipment, etc.

gaol (*US* usu **jail**) /dʒeɪl/ *n* [C, U] prison: *The castle had been used as a gaol.* ○ *be sent to gaol*, ie be imprisoned ○ *spend a year in gaol.*

📖 Three of the best-known gaols in British history are *Newgate gaol, the *Tower of London and the Marshalsea prison. Newgate gaol, built during the reign of King *John (1199-1216), housed many famous criminals. The public hangings which took place outside its gates and the dreadful conditions inside the prison made Newgate so notorious that the name came to be a common term for all prisons. The Tower of London, begun by *William the Conqueror, served as a state prison until the 19th century. Amongst its most famous royal and aristocratic inmates were the *Princes in the Tower, Sir Thomas *More, Anne *Boleyn, and Sir Walter *Raleigh. The Marshalsea prison was mainly for debtors. Charles *Dickens's father was imprisoned there in 1824, and the gaol is the setting of Dickens's novel *Little Dorrit*, written in 1856.

▷ **gaol** (*US* usu **jail**) *v* [Tn, Tn·pr] ~ **sb (for sth)** put sb in gaol: *He was gaoled for six months for his part in the robbery.*

gaoler (*US* usu **jailer, jailor**) /ˈdʒeɪlə(r)/ *n* person in charge of a gaol and the prisoners in it.

□ ˈ**gaolbird** (*US* usu ˈ**jailbird**) *n* (*dated infml*) person (habitually) sent to prison.

ˈ**gaolbreak** (*US* usu ˈ**jail-break**) *n* escape from prison.

gap /gæp/ *n* ~ **(in/between sth)** **1** opening or break in sth or between two things: *a gap in a fence, hedge, wall, etc* ○ *The road goes through a gap in/between the hills.* **2** unfilled interval of space: *a gap of five miles between towns* ○ (*fig*) *There were some unaccountable gaps in* (ie parts missing from) *his story.* **3** unfilled interval of time; lapse: *a gap in the conversation* ○ *After a gap of 30 years the custom was reintroduced.* ○ *a temporary job to fill the gap between school and university.* **4** (*fig*) separation: *a wide gap between the opinions of two people.* **5** (*fig*) deficiency which needs to be filled: *a gap in one's education* ○ *There was a terrible gap in her life after her husband died.* ○ *a gap in the market*, ie absence of a type of article which people might wish to buy. **6** (idm) **bridge a/the gap** ⇨ BRIDGE[1] *v.* **the generation gap** ⇨ GENERATION.

□ ˈ**gap-toothed** *adj* having teeth which are wide apart.

gape /geɪp/ *v* **1** [I, Ipr] ~ **(at sb/sth)** (*often derog*) stare with an open mouth, usu in surprise: *Don't gape : it's rude!* ○ *What are you gaping at?* **2** [La, I] be or become open wide: *A huge chasm gaped before them.* ○ *a gaping hole, wound, chasm* ○ *a shirt gaping open with a button missing.*

▷ **gape** *n* open-mouthed stare: *gapes of astonishment on the faces of the spectators.*

garage /ˈgærɑːʒ, ˈgærɪdʒ; *US* gəˈrɑːʒ/ *n* **1** building in which to keep one or more cars, vans, etc: *a house with a separate/built-in garage* ○ *a bus garage.* ⇨ illus at HOME. **2** (*Brit*) (*US* ˈ**service station**) roadside petrol station where vehicles can be serviced and repaired: [attrib] *a garage mechanic.*

▷ **garage** *v* [Tn] put (a motor vehicle) in a garage.

□ **garage sale** (*US*) = CAR-BOOT SALE (CAR).

garb /gɑːb/ *n* [U] (style of) clothing (esp as worn by a particular type of person): *military garb* ○ *a man in priest's garb/in the garb of a priest* ○ *in strange, unusual, odd, etc garb.*

▷ **garb** *v* [Tn usu passive] dress (sb) in the stated way: *a strangely garbed man* ○ *women garbed in black.*

garbage /ˈgɑːbɪdʒ/ *n* **1** [U] (*esp US*) **(a)** waste material, esp domestic refuse: [attrib] *garbage collection/disposal* ○ *a garbage truck.* **(b)** place or receptacle for disposing of this: *Throw any left-over food in the garbage.* **2** [U] (*fig infml*) nonsense; rubbish: *You do talk a load of garbage!* **3** [U] (*fig computing*) meaningless, corrupted or irrelevant data. **4** (idm) **garbage** ˈ**in, garbage** ˈ**out** (*infml*) (in computing) if you input wrong data, the output will also be wrong.

□ ˈ**garbage can** (*US*) = DUSTBIN (DUST[1]).

garbled /ˈgɑːbld/ *adj* (of a message) confused or misleading: *The injured man was still groggy and could only give a rather garbled account of the accident.*

Garbo /ˈgɑːbəʊ/ Greta (1905-90), Swedish film actor. Her beauty and screen presence made her one of the most remarkable performers in both silent and talking pictures. Her films include *Anna Karenina, Ninotchka* and *Queen Christina.* She retired suddenly in 1941, living the rest of her life in seclusion.

garden /ˈgɑːdn/ *n* **1** [C, U] (piece of) private ground used for growing flowers, fruit, vegetables, etc, typically with a lawn or other open space for recreation: *We've only a small garden.* ○ *a big house with a lot of garden* ○ *a formal garden* ○ *weeding the garden* ○ [attrib] *a garden wall* ○ *garden flowers/plants*, ie cultivated, not wild ones. ⇨ article. **2 gardens** [pl] public park: *botanical/zoological gardens.* **3** [C] **(a)** place where refreshments are served out of doors: *a beer/tea garden.* **(b)** (esp in place-names) large hall for public entertainment: *New York's Madison Square* ˈ*Garden.* **4** [sing] (*fig*) fertile region: *Kent is the garden of England.* **5** (idm) **a bear garden** ⇨ BEAR[1]. **common or garden** ⇨ COMMON[1]. **everything in the garden is** ˈ**lovely** (*saying*) everything is very satisfactory. **lead sb up the garden path** ⇨ LEAD[3].

▷ **garden** *v* [I] cultivate a garden: *She's outdoors gardening every afternoon.* **gardener** /ˈgɑːdnə(r)/ *n* person who works in a garden, either for pay or as a hobby. **gardening** /ˈgɑːdnɪŋ/ *n* [U] cultivating of gardens: *fond of gardening* ○ [attrib] *gardening gloves, tools.*

□ ˈ**garden centre** place where plants, seeds, gardening equipment, etc are sold.

garden ˈ**city**, ˈ**garden suburb** city or suburb designed with many open spaces and planted with many trees.

ˈ**garden flat** (*US* ˌ**garden a**ˈ**partment**) flat at ground level, with a garden for the use of the person living in it.

ˈ**garden party** formal social gathering on a lawn or in a garden, usu in the afternoon.

gardenia /gɑːˈdiːnɪə/ *n* **1** tree or shrub with large white or yellow flowers, usu sweet-smelling. **2** its flower.

gargantuan /gɑːˈgæntjʊən/ *adj* enormous; gigantic: *a gargantuan appetite, meal, person.*

gargle /ˈgɑːgl/ *v* [I, Ipr] ~ **(with sth)** wash the throat with liquid kept moving about by a stream of breath: *He always gargles (with salt water) before going to bed.*

▷ **gargle** *n* **1** [C] liquid used for gargling: *use a gargle of salt water.* **2** [sing] act of gargling: *have a gargle with salt water.*

gargoyle /ˈgɑːgɔɪl/ *n* stone or metal spout in the form of a grotesque human or animal figure, for carrying rain-water away from the roof of a church, etc.

Garibaldi /ˌgærɪˈbɔːldɪ/ Giuseppe (1807-82), Italian military leader. He played an important part in the struggle for a united and independent Italy, leading his 'Red Shirts' to victory in Sicily and southern Italy in 1860-61.

garibaldi /ˌgærɪˈbɔːldɪ/ *n* (*Brit*) type of biscuit with a layer of currants in the middle.

garish /ˈgeərɪʃ/ *adj* unpleasantly bright; over-coloured or over-decorated, esp in a vulgar way: *garish clothes, colours, lights.* ▷ **garishly** *adv*: *garishly coloured, dressed, illuminated.* **garishness** *n* [U].

garland /ˈgɑːlənd/ *n* circle of flowers, leaves or ribbons, worn (esp on the head or round the neck) or hung as a decoration: *a garland of victory.*

▷ **garland** *v* [usu passive: Tn, Tn·pr] ~ **sb (with sth)** put a garland or garlands on sb: *garlanded with roses.*

garlic /ˈgɑːlɪk/ *n* [U] onion-like plant with strong taste and smell, used in cooking: *a clove of garlic* ○ [attrib] *garlic butter, bread, sauce, etc*, ie flavoured with garlic. ⇨ illus at ONION.

▷ **garlicky** *adj* (*infml*) smelling or tasting of garlic: *garlicky breath, food.*

garment /ˈgɑːmənt/ *n* **1** (*fml or joc*) article of clothing: *a strange shapeless garment that had once been a jacket* ○ *his nether garments*, ie shorts, trousers, etc. **2** (*fig rhet*) covering: *In spring nature wears a new garment.*

garner /ˈgɑːnə(r)/ *v* [Tn, Tn·pr, Tn·p] ~ **sth (from sth)**; ~ **sth (in/up)** (*fml*) collect sth in and (usu) store it: *garner (in/up) the grain for the winter* ○ (*fig*) *garner knowledge, information, etc.* ○ *facts garnered from various sources.*

garnet /ˈgɑːnɪt/ *n* semi-precious gem of deep transparent red.

garnish /ˈgɑːnɪʃ/ *v* [Tn, Tn·pr] ~ **sth (with sth)** decorate (food for the table) with small additional amounts of food: *fish garnished with slices of lemon* ○ *meat garnished with parsley, fresh vegetables, etc.*

▷ **garnish** *n* vegetable, herb, etc used to decorate a dish of food or add to its flavour: *a garnish of mixed herbs.*

garniture /ˈgɑːnɪtʃə(r)/ *n* [U] (*fml*) things added to food, clothes, etc as decoration; trimmings.

garret /ˈgærət/ *n* room (often small, dark and unpleasant) on the top floor of a house (esp in the roof): *a poor man living in a garret.* Cf ATTIC.

Garrick /ˈgærɪk/ David (1717-79), English actor. He introduced a new, more natural style of acting, and made the plays of *Shakespeare popular again. He also wrote plays and ran his own theatre.

garrison /ˈgærɪsn/ *n* [CGp] troops stationed in a town or fort: *Half the garrison is/are on duty.* ○ [attrib] *garrison duty* ○ *a garrison town.*

▷ **garrison** *v* **1** [Tn, Tn·pr] ~ **sth (with sb)** defend (a place) with or as a garrison: *The town*

Gardens

Britain's temperate climate, with rainfall throughout the year, makes it possible to grow a great variety of plants and shrubs, and for many people gardening is a creative and satisfying pastime. Even for those living in towns and cities it is an opportunity to create a small piece of countryside beside their homes.

The private and public gardens of today developed from the great formal flower gardens of the late 16th and early 17th centuries and the informal 'landscape' gardens of the 18th century, especially those laid out in the parks of country-houses by people like William Kent and 'Capability' Brown.

Most British houses, even in towns, have a garden. Often there is a small flower garden at the front of the house and a larger garden at the rear, where flowers or vegetables are grown. Both front and back gardens often have a lawn.

Not all gardens are purely decorative: some are cultivated to provide home-grown vegetables and fruit, especially in summer. For families with young children or pets, a garden is considered almost a necessity. Many houses have a patio at the rear, a paved area between house and garden where people can sit and have meals in the summer. The edge of a garden is usually marked by a fence, hedge or wall, and neighbours often chat to each other 'over the garden fence'. Flowers grown in the garden are often used to decorate the house.

Many home-owners spend a large part of their spare time gardening. Most gardens are laid out fairly formally, with flower beds arranged round a lawn, or vegetable beds running at right angles from a central path.

Herbaceous borders, shrubberies and rockeries planted with alpine plants often form special features. Apple, plum and other fruit trees are frequently found in back gardens and there may also be decorative trees such as firs, beeches or willows. Owners of large gardens sometimes have a tennis court or swimming-pool. Ornamental features may include a fish pond or a bird bath. Brightly coloured models of gnomes are sometimes used as a rather eccentric way of decorating front gardens.

People often specialize in growing particular types of plants or vegetable. Many enter these in competitions at local shows, where prizes are awarded for the finest flowers and the largest vegetables. Keen gardeners usually have a greenhouse for their plants. Town-dwellers who only have a small garden may grow vegetables in an allotment, one of the small plots of land let to individuals by local authorities. Most towns have a garden centre, selling both plants and gardening equipment and furniture.

The popularity of gardening is reflected in the number of books published on the subject and radio and television programmes devoted to it. The Chelsea Flower Show is an enormously popular annual event held in London at which ideas for gardens and new varieties of plants are displayed.

Many country-houses and historic buildings have large gardens that are as much a tourist attraction as the house itself. Sometimes the gardens include exotic or tropical plants, or have special ornamental features such as mazes or topiary work. Some of the college gardens at Oxford and Cambridge are particularly fine, and many universities have botanical gardens.

Most towns in Britain have a park or some other kind of public garden, usually with lawns, flower-beds, seats and other facilities such as tennis courts. Many also have a play area for children, with swings, slides and roundabouts. In London, the Royal Parks, including Hyde Park, Regent's Park and St James's Park, provide welcome areas of greenery in the middle of the city. Another Royal Park, Kew Gardens to the west of London, is the headquarters of the Royal Horticultural Society, the national body responsible for research on plants.

Gardens in the USA, both private and public, are mostly more ornamental than in Britain, with an emphasis on sport and relaxation. Public gardens are laid out in the more formal English style. Nearly half the population take an active interest in gardening, with an increasing number of young gardeners. As in Britain, the care of the lawn is one of the highest priorities, although there is a trend towards 'meadow lawns', where wild flowers are planted and the grass is not mown.

was garrisoned with two regiments. **2** [Tn·pr] ~ **sb in/on sth** place (troops) as a garrison: *A hundred soldiers were garrisoned in the town.*

garrotte (also **garotte**, *US* also **garote**) /gəˈrɒt/ *v* [Tn] **1** execute (a condemned person) by strangling or throttling with a metal collar. **2** strangle (sb) with wire or rope.

▷ **garrotte** (also **garotte**, *US* also **garote**) *n* device used for garrotting (GARROTTE 1).

garrulous /ˈgærələs/ *adj* talking too much, esp about unimportant things: *becoming garrulous after a few glasses of wine* ○ *My garrulous neighbour had given away the secret.*

▷ **garrulity** /gəˈru:lətɪ/, **garrulousness** *ns* [U] talkativeness.

garrulously *adv.*

garter /ˈgɑ:tə(r)/ *n* **1** [C] (usu elastic) band worn round the leg to keep up a sock or stocking. **2 the Garter** [sing] badge or membership of the highest order of English knighthood: *be awarded the Garter.*

□ ˈ**garter-belt** *n* (*US*) = SUSPENDER BELT.

ˈ**garter stitch** plain stitch in knitting, forming ridges in alternate rows.

gas /gæs/ *n* (*pl* **gases**; *US* also **gasses**) **1** [C, U] air-like substance (ie not a solid or liquid). A gas occupies all the space available for it in its container, can be compressed, and consists of molecules or atoms which are not bound together and move freely. Air itself is a mixture of gases, esp nitrogen and oxygen: *a ventilation system to remove waste gases* ○ [attrib] *a gas balloon*, ie filled with gas, eg helium or hydrogen. **2** [U] **(a)** inflammable gas or mixture of gases used as fuel for heating, lighting or cooking: *Is your central heating gas or electricity?* ○ *Light the gas/Turn the gas on and we'll have a cup of tea.* ○ *butane/calor/coal/natural gas* ○ *cook on a low/medium/high gas*, ie on a gas cooker ○ [attrib] *a gas cooker, lighter* (ie cigarette lighter), *oven, ring, stove*, ie using gas as fuel. Cf METHANE. **(b)** gas (eg nitrous oxide) or mixture of gases used as an anaesthetic in surgery and dentistry: *I was given gas when they pulled my tooth out.* ○ *Did you have gas or an injection?* **(c)** poisonous gas (eg mustard gas) used in warfare: [attrib] *a gas attack.* **3** [U] (*US infml*) = PETROL. **4** [U] (*fig derog*) empty talk; boasting: *His long speech was nothing but gas and hot air.* **5 a gas** [sing] (*US sl*) amusing, exciting, etc thing or person: *The show was a real gas.* **6** (idm) ˌ**step on the** ˈ**gas** ⇨ STEP[1].

▷ **gas** *v* (**-ss-**) **1** [Tn] cause (sb) to breathe poisonous gas: *He was badly gassed in the war.* ○ *She couldn't face the future, and gassed herself*, ie killed herself with gas. **2** [I, Ipr] ~ **(about sth)** (*infml derog*) talk for a long time without saying much that is useful. **3** (phr v) **gas up** (*US infml*) fill a motor vehicle's tank with petrol.

□ ˈ**gasbag** *n* (*infml derog*) talkative person.

ˈ**gas board** (*dated*) (esp in Britain before the privatization of the gas supply) public body controlling the supply of gas for domestic and industrial use.

gas bracket pipe with one or more gas burners attached to a wall.

ˈ**gas chamber** room filled with gas for killing animals or people.

ˌ**gas chromaˈtography** (*chemistry*) technique for analysing the chemical composition of a substance by passing the sample in vapour form through a column. The different components move at different speeds and separate, so that they can be detected as they leave the column.

ˈ**gas cylinder** cylindrical metal container for storing gas.

ˌ**gas-ˈfired** *adj* using gas as fuel: ˌ*gas-fired* ˌ*central* ˈ*heating.*

gas-fitter *n* worker who installs gas-fittings.

ˈ**gas-fitting** *n* (usu *pl*) pipe, burner or other piece of apparatus for heating or lighting with gas.

ˈ**gasholder** *n* = GASOMETER.

ˈ**gas-lit** *adj* illuminated by light from burning gas.

ˈ**gas main** large pipe carrying gas from supplier to consumer.

ˈ**gasman** /-mæn/ *n* (*pl* **-men** /-men/) (*infml*) employee of a gas supply organization who checks gas meters and domestic gas apparatus.

ˈ**gas mask** breathing apparatus worn as protection against poison gas. ⇨ illus at MASK.

ˈ**gas meter** meter for measuring the amount of gas used.

ˈ**gas poker** hollow metal rod connected to a gas supply, for lighting a coal fire.

ˈ**gas ring** circular hollow device with holes for burning gas, either on a cooker or as a separate cooking unit.

ˈ**gas station** (*US*) = PETROL STATION (PETROL).

ˈ**gas tap** device for controlling the flow of gas from a pipe.

ˌ**gas** ˈ**turbine** turbine driven by gas, sometimes produced by combustion.

ˈ**gasworks** *n* (*pl* unchanged) [sing or pl *v*] place where gas for lighting and heating is manufactured.

gaseous /ˈgæsɪəs, ˈgeɪsɪəs/ *adj* like, containing or being gas: *a gaseous mixture.*

gash *n* ~ **(in sth)** long deep cut or wound: *a nasty gash in the arm, leg, etc* ○ *make a gash in the bark of a tree with a knife.*

▷ **gash** *v* [Tn, Tn·pr] ~ **sth (on/with sth)** make a gash in sth: *gash one's arm on a piece of broken glass.*

gasify /ˈgæsɪfaɪ/ *v* (*pt, pp* **-fied**) [I, Tn] (cause sth to) change into gas.

Gaskell /ˈgæskl/ Mrs Elizabeth (1810-65), English novelist. Her novels are usu set in the north of England and show her strong social concern, as in *North and South.* She wrote a biography of her friend Charlotte *Brontë.

gasket /ˈgæskɪt/ *n* soft flat sheet or ring of rubber, card, etc used to seal a joint between metal surfaces to prevent steam, gas, etc from escaping: *The engine had blown a gasket*, ie the gasket had suddenly let steam, etc escape.

gasoline (also **gasolene**) /ˈgæsəli:n/ *n* [U] (*US*) = PETROL.

gasometer /gæˈsɒmɪtə(r)/ *n* (also **gasholder**) very large round tank in which fuel gas is stored and from which it is distributed through pipes.

gasp /gɑːsp/ *v* **1** [I, Ipr] ~ (**at sth**); ~ (**for sth**) take one or more quick deep breaths with open mouth, because of surprise or exhaustion: *gasp like a fish out of water* ○ *I gasped in/with astonishment at the magician's skill.* ○ *The exhausted runner was gasping for air/breath.* **2** [Tn, Tn·p] ~ **sth** (**out**) utter sth in a breathless way: *She managed to gasp (out) a few words.* **3** [I, Ipr] ~ (**for sth**) (used in the continuous tenses) (*infml*) want sth very much, esp sth to drink or smoke: *'Do you need a drink?' 'Yes, I'm gasping!'* ○ *I was gasping for a cigarette.*
▷ **gasp** *n* **1** quick deep breath of pain, surprise, etc: *give a sudden audible gasp* ○ *There were gasps of horror from the spectators as he fell off the tightrope.* **2** (idm) **at one's last gasp** ⇨ LAST[1].

gassy /ˈgæsɪ/ *adj* (**-ier, -iest**) **1** of, like or full of gas, esp in the form of bubbles in liquid: *Fizzy lemonade can be very gassy.* **2** (*infml derog*) talkative, esp in a gossipy or boastful way: *a gassy old man, woman, etc.* ▷ **gassiness** *n* [U].

gastric /ˈgæstrɪk/ *adj* [attrib] (*medical*) of the stomach: *gastric ulcers* ○ *gastric juices.*
▷ **gastritis** /gæˈstraɪtɪs/ *n* [U] (*medical*) inflammation of the stomach.

gastro-enteritis /ˌgæstrəʊˌentəˈraɪtɪs/ *n* [U] (*medical*) inflammation of the stomach and intestines.

gastronomy /gæˈstrɒnəmɪ/ *n* [U] art and science of choosing, cooking and eating good food.
▷ **gastronome** /ˈgæstrənəʊm/ *n* person who enjoys good food; gourmet.
gastronomic /ˌgæstrəˈnɒmɪk/ *adj* of gastronomy: *Lyons, the gastronomic capital of France.*
gastronomically /-klɪ/ *adv*: *a gastronomically outstanding meal.*

gat /gæt/ *n* (*dated sl esp US*) gun, esp a revolver.

gate /geɪt/ *n* **1** (**a**) movable barrier, usu on hinges, which closes an opening in a wall, fence or hedge: *a wooden, iron gate* ○ *the garden gate* ○ *the gates of the city.* ⇨ illus at HOUSE. (**b**) opening closed by this; gateway: *The carriage passed through the palace gates.* (**c**) similar movable barrier which controls a stream of water: *a lock/sluice gate.* **2** means of entrance or exit (for passengers at an airport or spectators at a sports ground): *The flight is now boarding at gate 16.* **3** number of spectators at a sports event, esp a football match: *a gate of ten thousand* ○ *a good/poor/large/small gate.* **4** frame behind the lens in a cine-camera, through which the film passes. **5** slot in the floor of a car, etc in which the gear-lever is moved. **6** (also ˈ**gate money**) amount of money taken from tickets sold at a sports event, esp a football match: *Today's gate will be given to charity.* **7** (idm) **like a bull at a gate** ⇨ BULL[1].
▷ **gate** *v* [Tn, Tn·pr] ~ **sb** (**for sth**) (*Brit*) confine (a student) to college or school as a punishment.
□ ˈ**gatecrash** (also **crash**) *v* [I, Tn] enter (a private social occasion) without paying or being invited: *gatecrash a party.* ˈ**gatecrasher** *n* person who gatecrashes.
ˈ**gatehouse** *n* house built at or over a gate (eg at the entrance to a park or castle).
ˈ**gatekeeper** *n* keeper of a gatehouse.
ˌ**gatelegged** (also ˌ**gatelegged** ˈ**table**) table with legs that can be moved out to support a folding top. ⇨ illus at FURNITURE.
ˈ**gate money** = GATE 6.
ˈ**gatepost** *n* **1** post on which a gate is hung or against which it is closed. **2** (idm) **between you and me and the** ˈ**gatepost** (*infml*) in strict confidence.
ˈ**gateway** *n* **1** way in and out that can be closed by a gate or gates: *Don't stand there blocking the gateway!* **2** (usu *sing*) ~ **to sth** (*fig*) (**a**) place through which one must go to reach somewhere else: *The port of Dover is England's gateway to Europe.* (**b**) means of gaining sth desired: *A good education can be the gateway to success.*

gâteau /ˈgætəʊ; *US* gæˈtəʊ/ *n* (*pl* ~**x** or ~**s**) [C, U] large rich cream-cake, often decorated with fruit, nuts, chocolate, etc: *a (slice of) fresh cream gâteau.*

gather /ˈgæðə(r)/ *v* **1** (**a**) [I, Ipr, Ip, Tn, Tn·pr, Tn·p] ~ **round** (**sb/sth**); ~ **sb/sth round** (**sb/sth**) come or bring sb/sth together in one place: *A crowd soon gathered.* ○ *Gather round* (ie Form a group round me) *and listen, children!* ○ *a musical evening with the whole family gathered round the piano.* (**b**) [Tn, Tn·p] ~ **sth** (**together/up**) bring together (objects) that have been spread about: *Give me a moment to gather my notes together.* ○ *She gathered up her scattered belongings and left.* **2** (**a**) [Tn, Tn·pr] ~ **sth** (**from sth**) collect (plants, fruit, etc) from a wide area: *gather flowers, berries, nuts, etc* ○ *gathering mushrooms in the fields* ○ (*fig*) *information gathered* (ie obtained) *from various sources.* (**b**) [Tn, Tn·p] ~ **sth** (**in**) pick or cut and collect (crops) for storage: *The harvest has been safely gathered in.* **3** [Tn, Tn·pr, Tf] ~ **sth** (**from sb/sth**) understand sth; conclude: *'Smith's resigned.' 'I gathered as much from the newspapers.'* ○ *I gather you want to see the director.* ○ *'She won't be coming.' 'So I gather.'* ○ *I gathered from the way she replied that she wasn't very enthusiastic.* **4** [Tn·pr, Tn·p] ~ **sth round sb/sth;** ~ **sth up** pull (a garment) tighter to one's body: *She gathered the shawl round her/round her shoulders.* ○ *She gathered up her skirts and ran.* **5** [Tn, Tn·p] ~ **sth** (**in**) draw (a garment) together in folds or pleats: *a skirt gathered (in) at the waist.* **6** [I, Tn] increase (sth): *The darkness is gathering.* ○ *in the gathering gloom of a winter's afternoon* ○ *The car gathered speed.* **7** [Tn] (*fig*) bring (sth) together in order to make an effort; summon up: *He gathered all his strength and swung the axe.* ○ *She sat trying to gather her thoughts before making her speech.* **8** (idm) **be gathered to one's** ˈ**fathers** (*dated or rhet*) die. **collect/gather one's wits** ⇨ WIT. **gather** ˈ**dust** be neglected or unused for a long time. **a rolling stone gathers no moss** ⇨ ROLL[2].
▷ **gather** *n* fold or pleat in a garment.
gathering /ˈgæðərɪŋ/ *n* meeting or coming together of people: *a small family gathering* ○ *a gathering of friends.*

GATT /gæt/ *abbr* General Agreement on Tariffs and Trade (signed in 1947).

gauche /gəʊʃ/ *adj* **1** socially awkward or clumsy: *I find him terribly gauche.* ○ *a gauche manner, person, remark.* **2** (*fig*) (of literary or artistic work) clumsy: *a rather gauche style, technique, etc.*
▷ **gaucheness** /ˈgəʊʃnɪs/, **gaucherie** /ˈgəʊʃərɪ; *US* ˌgəʊʃəˈriː/ *ns* [U] gauche behaviour.

gaucho /ˈgaʊtʃəʊ/ *n* (*pl* ~**s**) South American cowboy, esp one of Spanish and Indian descent.

gaudy /ˈgɔːdɪ/ *adj* (**-ier, -iest**) (*derog*) too bright and showy, esp in a vulgar way: *gaudy decorations* ○ *cheap and gaudy jewellery.* ▷ **gaudily** /ˈgɔːdɪlɪ/ *adv.* **gaudiness** /ˈgɔːdɪnɪs/ *n* [U].

gauge (*US* also **gage**) /geɪdʒ/ *n* **1** [U, C] standard measure, esp of width or thickness: *the gauge of a sheet of metal* ○ *What gauge of wire should we use for this job?* **2** [C] distance between rails on a railway or tramway: *standard gauge*, ie 4ft $8\frac{1}{2}$ ins ○ *narrow/broad gauge*, ie narrower/wider than standard ○ [attrib] *a narrow-gauge railway.* **3** [C] instrument for measuring the amount or level of sth: *a petrol, pressure, rain, speed, etc gauge.* **4** [C] fact or circumstance which one can use in estimating or judging; measure: *Is a person's behaviour under stress a reliable gauge of his character?*
▷ **gauge** *v* **1** [Tn] (**a**) measure (sth) esp accurately: *precision instruments which can gauge the diameter to a fraction of a millimetre.* (**b**) make an estimate of (sth): *gauging the strength of the wind from the movement of the trees.* **2** [Tn, Tf, Tw] make a judgement about (sth): *trying to gauge reactions, sympathies, sentiments, etc* ○ *It was difficult to gauge how people would respond.* ○ *I gauged that it was not a good moment to speak to her.*

Gauguin /ˈgəʊgæn/ Paul (1848-1903), French painter. He left his family and career to become a full-time artist, at first following the *Impressionists. He settled in *Tahiti and produced works in a new style, using flat outlines and vivid colours for their decorative or emotional effect.

Gaul /gɔːl/ ancient region of Europe corresponding roughly to modern France and Belgium.
▷ **Gaul** *n* native or inhabitant of Gaul.

gaunt /gɔːnt/ *adj* **1** (of a person) made exceptionally thin by hunger or illness; haggard: *the gaunt face of a starving man.* **2** (of a place) bare; desolate: *the gaunt landscape of the moon.* ▷ **gauntness** *n* [U].

gauntlet[1] /ˈgɔːntlɪt/ *n* **1** metal glove forming part of a suit of armour, worn by soldiers in the Middle Ages. **2** strong glove with a wide covering for the wrist, used for driving, fencing, etc: *motor-cyclists with leather gauntlets.* ⇨ illus at GLOVE. **3** (idm) **pick up/take up the** ˈ**gauntlet** accept a challenge: *He was quick to take up the gauntlet thrown down by the opposition.* **throw down the** ˈ**gauntlet** challenge sb to do sth.

gauntlet[2] /ˈgɔːntlɪt/ *n* (idm) **run the** ˈ**gauntlet** be exposed to danger, anger, or criticism: *Before getting the proposals accepted, the government had to run the gauntlet of hostility from its own supporters.*

gauss /gaʊs/ *n* (*pl* unchanged or ~**es**) unit for measuring magnetic induction.

gauze /gɔːz/ *n* [U] **1** thin, often transparent, fabric of cotton, silk, etc: *a piece of (cotton, etc) gauze* ○ [attrib] *a gauze curtain* ○ *a gauze patch applied to his wound.* **2** netting made of very thin wire.
▷ **gauzy** *adj* of or like gauze.

gave *pt* of GIVE[1].

gavel /ˈgævl/ *n* small hammer used by an auctioneer or chairman as a signal for order or attention: *bang, rap, etc one's gavel on the table.*

gavotte /gəˈvɒt/ *n* (music for an) old French dance.

gawk /gɔːk/ *v* [I, Ipr] ~ (**at sb/sth**) (*infml*) stare impolitely or stupidly; gawp: *I hate being gawked at!*

gawky /ˈgɔːkɪ/ *adj* (**-ier, -iest**) (esp of a tall young person) awkward and clumsy: *a shy gawky teenager.* ▷ **gawkily** /ˈgɔːkɪlɪ/ *adv.* **gawkiness** /ˈgɔːkɪnɪs/ *n* [U]: *Despite her gawkiness she was clearly going to be a beautiful woman one day.*

gawp /gɔːp/ *v* [I, Ipr] ~ (**at sb/sth**) (*infml*) stare impolitely or stupidly; gawk: *crowds of onlookers coming to gawp at the wreckage of the aircraft.* ⇨ Usage at LOOK[1].

Gay /geɪ/ John (1685-1732), English poet and playwright. His writings were usu satirical, and his greatest success, *The Beggar's Opera*, was banned from the stage. He was a friend of *Pope and wrote the words for *Handel's *Acis and Galatea.*

gay /geɪ/ *adj* **1** homosexual: *a gay person, club, bar* ○ *I didn't know he/she was gay.* **2** [attrib] careless; thoughtless: *spending money with gay abandon.* **3** happy and full of fun; light-hearted; cheerful: *gay laughter, music* ○ *The streets look gay with bright flags and coloured lights.*
▷ **gaily** /ˈgeɪlɪ/ *adv*: *the gaily decorated buildings* ○ *She gaily announced that she was leaving the next day*, ie without having considered the trouble this would cause.
gay *n* homosexual person.
gayness /ˈgeɪnɪs/ *n* [U] homosexuality. Cf GAIETY.

gaze /geɪz/ *v* **1** [I, Ipr] look long and steadily (at sb/sth), usu in surprise or admiration: *She gazed at me in disbelief when I told her the news.* ○ *He just sat gazing into space/gazing through the window.* ⇨ Usage at LOOK[1]. **2** [Ipr] ~ **on/upon sb/sth** (*fml*) look at sb/sth: *She was the most beautiful woman he had ever gazed upon.*
▷ **gaze** *n* [sing] long steady look: *Under his intense gaze she felt uncomfortable.*

gazebo /gəˈziːbəʊ/ *n* (*pl* ~**s**) small, usu hutlike, building designed to give a wide view of the surrounding country.

gazelle /gəˈzel/ *n* (*pl* unchanged or ~**s**) small, graceful antelope: *a herd of gazelle.*

gazette /gəˈzet/ *n* **1** official journal with public notices and lists of government, military, legal and university appointments. **2** (used in the titles of newspapers): *the Evening Gazette, London Gazette, etc.*
▷ **gazette** *v* (*esp Brit*) **1** [Tn usu passive] publish

or announce (sth) in an official gazette: *His appointment was gazetted last week.* **2** [usu passive: Tn·pr, Cn·n] ~ **sb to sth** appoint sb, esp to a military post: *He was gazetted to a new regiment.* ○ *He was gazetted captain.*

gazetteer /ˌgæzəˈtɪə(r)/ *n* index of geographical names: *a world gazetteer.*

gazpacho /gæˈspætʃəʊ/ *n* (*pl* ~**s**) [C, U] type of Spanish soup made with tomatoes, peppers, garlic, etc and served cold.

gazump /gəˈzʌmp/ *v* [Tn usu passive] (*Brit infml derog*) raise the price of property, esp a house, after accepting an offer from (a buyer): *We shan't be buying the house: we've been gazumped (by the owner).*

▷ **gazumper** /gəˈzʌmpə(r)/ *n.*

gazumping /gəˈzʌmpɪŋ/ *n* [U] (*Brit infml derog*) practice of gazumping buyers.

GB /ˌdʒi: ˈbi:/ *abbr* Great Britain. ⇨ Usage at GREAT.

GC /ˌdʒi: ˈsi:/ *abbr* (*Brit*) George Cross (award to civilians for bravery): *be awarded the GC* ○ *William Lawson GC.* Cf VC 4.

GCSE /ˌdʒi: si: es ˈi:/ *abbr* (*Brit*) General Certificate of Secondary Education.

Gd *symb* gadolinium.

Gdn *abbr* (*pl* **Gdns**) (in street names) Gardens: *7 Windsor Gdns.*

GDP /ˌdʒi: di: ˈpi:/ *abbr* gross domestic product. Cf GNP.

GDR /ˌdʒi: di: ˈɑ:(r)/ *abbr* German Democratic Republic (East Germany before the reunification of Germany).

Ge *symb* germanium.

gear

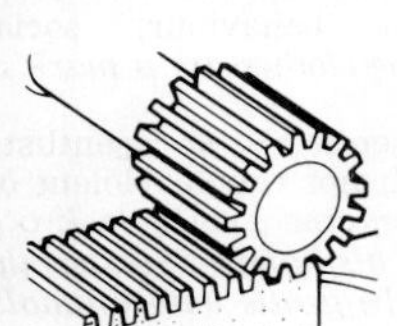

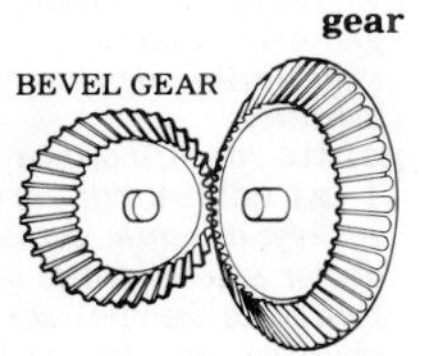

gear /gɪə(r)/ *n* **1** [U] equipment, clothing, etc needed for an expedition, a sport, etc: *All his camping gear was packed in the rucksack.* ○ *We're only going for two days; you don't need to bring so much gear!* ○ *wearing her party gear.* **2** [sing] (esp in compounds) piece or set of apparatus or machinery for a particular purpose: *The landing-gear has jammed.* ○ *winding gear for lifting heavy loads.* **3 (a)** [C often *pl*] set of toothed wheels which fit into another set to transmit power from a vehicle's engine to its road wheels: *Careless use of the clutch may damage the gears.* ○ *The car has four forward gears and one reverse gear.* ○ *The car started with a crashing of gears,* ie noise made by operating them badly. ⇨ illus at BICYCLE. ⇨ illus. **(b)** [U] particular position or setting of the gear mechanism: *The car is in/out of gear,* ie has the gears engaged/disengaged. ○ *low/bottom/first gear,* ie used for starting a vehicle or climbing a slope ○ *high/top gear,* ie used for high speeds ○ *change gear.* **4** [U] (*fig*) degree of speed or efficiency: *The party organization is moving into top gear as the election approaches.* ○ *The athlete changed gear* (ie suddenly accelerated) *and shot ahead of the others.*

▷ **gear** *v* (phr v) **gear down** (of a driver) change to a lower gear so as to have better control. **gear sth down (to sth)** reduce sth in force or intensity: *The period of exercise was geared down to ten minutes a day for men over 60.* **gear sth to/towards sth** adapt sth to a particular need or to an appropriate level or standard: *Industry must be geared to wartime needs.* ○ *Our effort is geared to a higher level of production.* **gear up (for/to sth)**; **gear sb/sth up (for/to sth)** become or make sb/sth ready (for sth): *The company's gearing up for the big export drive.* ○ *I was all geared up* (ie excitedly ready) *to go on holiday, and now it's been cancelled.* **gearing** /ˈgɪərɪŋ/ *n* [U] set or arrangement of gears: *The gearing of this machine is unusual.*

□ ˈ**gearbox** *n* case that encloses a vehicle's gear mechanism. ⇨ illus at CAR.

ˈ**gear-change** *n* movement from one position of the gear mechanism to another: *a smooth gear-change.*

ˈ**gear-lever**, ˈ**gear-stick** (*US* usu ˈ**gearshift**) *ns* lever used to engage, disengage or change gear. ⇨ illus at CAR, ⇨ illus at BICYCLE.

ˈ**gearwheel** *n* toothed wheel in a set of gears.

gecko /ˈgekəʊ/ *n* (*pl* ~**s** or ~**es**) small house lizard, found in warm countries.

gee[1] /dʒi:/ *interj* (also **gee-up**) /dʒi:ˈʌp/ (used for telling a horse, etc to start, go on or go faster).

▷ **gee** *v* (phr v) **gee sb/sth up** (*infml*) make sb/sth work or perform more quickly or efficiently.

gee-gee /ˈdʒi:dʒi:/ *n* (used by and to small children) horse.

gee[2] /dʒi:/ *interj* (also **gee whiz**) /dʒi: ˈwɪz/ (*esp US*) (used to express surprise, admiration, etc): *Gee, I like your new hat!*

geese *pl* of GOOSE.

geezer /ˈgi:zə(r)/ *n* (*infml*) man, esp an old one: *that old geezer over there.*

Geiger counter /ˈgaɪgə kaʊntə(r)/ device for detecting and measuring radioactivity.

geisha /ˈgeɪʃə/ *n* Japanese girl trained to entertain men with conversation, dancing or singing.

gel /dʒel/ *n* [C, U] (esp in compounds) semi-solid jelly-like substance: *bath-gel, hair-gel,* ie jelly-like soap or shampoo.

▷ **gel** *v* (**-ll-**) [I] **1** set into a jelly: *This liquid gels faster in cold weather.* **2** (*fig*) take definite form: *My ideas are beginning to gel.*

gelatine /ˈdʒeləti:n, -tɪn/ (also *esp US* **gelatin** /ˈdʒelətɪn/) *n* [U] clear tasteless substance used for making jelly as food, manufacturing photographic film, etc.

▷ **gelatinous** /dʒəˈlætɪnəs/ *adj* like jelly: *a gelatinous substance.*

geld /geld/ *v* [Tn] castrate (an animal).

▷ **gelding** /ˈgeldɪŋ/ *n* castrated animal, esp a horse. Cf STALLION.

gelid /ˈdʒelɪd/ *adj* (*fml*) very cold.

gelignite /ˈdʒelɪgnaɪt/ *n* [U] powerful explosive made from nitric acid and glycerine.

gem /dʒem/ *n* **1** precious stone or jewel, esp when cut and polished: *a crown studded with gems.* **2** (*fig*) thing highly valued for beauty or some other special quality: *This picture is the gem* (ie the best) *of the collection.* ○ *a gem of a place,* ie an excellent place ○ *That restaurant is a little gem.* ○ *She's a real gem!*

□ ˈ**gemstone** *n* precious or semi-precious stone, esp before cutting into shape.

Gemini /ˈdʒemɪnaɪ, -nɪ/ *n* **1** [U] the third sign of the zodiac, the Twins. **2** [C] person born under the influence of this sign. ▷ **Geminean** *n, adj.* ⇨ Usage at ZODIAC. ⇨ illus at ZODIAC.

gen /dʒen/ *n* [U] ~ **(on sth)** (*dated Brit infml*) information: *Give me the gen on this new project.*

▷ **gen** *v* (**-nn-**) (phr v) **gen (sb) up (on sth)** (*dated Brit infml*) obtain information, or provide sb with information (about sth): *He is fully genned up on the new project.*

Gen *abbr* General: *Gen (Stanley) Armstrong.*

gendarme /ˈʒɒndɑ:m/ *n* member of a military force employed on police duties, esp in France and French-speaking countries.

▷ **gendarmerie** /ʒɒnˈdɑ:mərɪ/ *n* **1** [pl *v*] whole body of gendarmes. **2** [C] headquarters of a body of gendarmes.

gender /ˈdʒendə(r)/ *n* [C, U] **1** (*grammar*) (in certain languages) classification of a noun or pronoun as masculine or feminine: *There are three genders in German: masculine, feminine and neuter.* ○ *In French the adjective must agree with the noun in number and gender.* **2** (*fml*) sexual classification; sex: *the male and female genders.*

gene /dʒi:n/ *n* (*biology*) unit in a chromosome which controls heredity: *a dominant/recessive gene* ○ *have sth in one's genes,* ie have an inherited quality.

genealogy /ˌdʒi:nɪˈælədʒɪ/ *n* **1** [U] study of family history, showing who the ancestors of particular people were and how they were related to each other. **2** [C] (diagram showing a) particular person's ancestry.

▷ **genealogical** /ˌdʒi:nɪəˈlɒdʒɪkl/ *adj* concerned with tracing family descent: *a genealogical expert* ○ *genealogical evidence, proof, records, etc* ○ *a genealogical table/tree,* ie a diagram with branches showing a family's ancestry. **genealogically** /-klɪ/ *adv.*

genealogist /ˌdʒi:nɪˈælədʒɪst/ *n* student of or expert in genealogy.

genera *pl* of GENUS.

general /ˈdʒenrəl/ *adj* **1 (a)** affecting all or most people, places or things: *a general lowering of standards* ○ *The announcement was met with general rejoicing.* ○ *a matter of general interest, concern, etc* ○ *Once quite rare, they are now in general use,* ie used by most people. ○ *That man's a general nuisance,* ie to most people at most times. ○ *the general public,* ie the majority of (ordinary) people ○ *a general meeting, strike, etc* ○ *The bad weather has been fairly general,* ie has affected most areas. ○ *The general impression was* (ie Most people thought) *that it had improved.* **(b)** [attrib] not limited to one part or aspect of a person or thing or to a particular time; overall: *There is still some weakness in the legs, but her general condition is good.* ○ *The opening chapter gives a general overview of the subject.* ○ *The old building was in a general state of decay/disrepair.* **2 (a)** not specialized in subject-matter: *a general degree* ○ *general knowledge, sciences, studies, etc* ○ *We kept the conversation/discussion fairly general.* **(b)** [attrib] not specialized or limited in range of work, use, activity, etc: *a general hospital* ○ *the general reader* ○ *a general factotum,* ie servant or assistant able to do all kinds of work. **3** [usu attrib] normal; usual: *The general practice in such cases is to apply for a court order.* ○ *a general principle* (ie one true of most cases) *to which there may be several exceptions* ○ *In the general way of things* (ie Usually) *not much happens here.* **4** showing the chief aspects of sth; not detailed; vague: *His description was too general to be of much use.* ○ *My general impression was that it was quite good.* ○ *bear a general resemblance to sb/sth* ○ *speak/write in general terms.* **5** [attrib] (often in titles with a capital letter and following the *n*) chief; head: *the general manager* ○ *the Attorney, Inspector, Governor, Secretary, etc General.* **6** (idm) **as a general ˈrule** in most cases. **be caviare to the general** ⇨ CAVIARE. **in ˈgeneral** mainly; mostly; usually: *In general her work has been good, but this essay is dreadful.*

▷ **general** *n* **1** army officer of very high rank, esp an officer in the British Army below the rank of field marshal: *a four-star general,* ie in the US army ○ [attrib] *General Roberts.* ⇨ App 4. **2** head of certain religious orders, eg the Jesuits. **generalship** /ˈdʒenrəlʃɪp/ *n* [U] skill and leadership (as) of a general, esp in battle.

□ ˌ**General Aˈssembly** main meeting of representatives (of the United Nations, etc).

ˌ**General Cerˌtificate of ˌSecondary Eduˈcation** (*abbr* **GCSE**) (certificate for passing) any of a range of examinations introduced in Britain from 1988 and usu taken after five years at secondary school.

ˈ**general ˈdealer** person who trades in all kinds of goods.

ˌ**general deˈlivery** (*US*) department of a post office that delivers letters, etc to people when they call to collect them.

ˌ**general eˈlection** national parliamentary election. Cf BY-ELECTION. ⇨ article at PARLIAMENT.

ˌ**general headˈquarters** (*abbr* **GHQ**) main centre of military organization and supplies.

ˌ**General of the ˈArmy**, ˌ**General of the ˈAir Force** officer holding the highest rank in the US

Army or Air Force. ⇨ App 4.

ˌ**General ˈPost Office** (*abbr* **GPO**) (**a**) (formerly in Britain) national organization of postal services (now called the Post Office). (**b**) (*Brit*) main post office in a town.

ˌ**general ˈpractice** (*Brit*) medical treatment of all types of illness within the community (as opposed to hospital work or specialization in treating a particular sort of disease). ˌ**general pracˈtitioner** (*abbr* **GP**) (*Brit*) doctor who is in general practice. ⇨ article at HEALTH.

ˌ**general-ˈpurpose** *adj* [attrib] that has a variety of uses: *a* ˌ*general-purpose* ˈ*farm vehicle*.

ˌ**general ˈstaff** officers assisting a military commander at headquarters.

ˌ**general ˈstrike** strike by workers in all parts of industry, esp (**the General Strike**) the one in Britain in 1926 in support of mining workers. ⇨ article at TRADE UNION.

generalissimo /ˌdʒenrəˈlɪsɪməʊ/ *n* (*pl* ~**s**) commander of combined military and naval and air forces, or of combined armies.

generality /ˌdʒenəˈrælətɪ/ *n* **1** [C] general statement, esp one that is vague or indefinite: *speak in generalities* ○ *Unfortunately the treaty is full of generalities, and fails to get down to specifics.* **2 the generality** [pl *v*] (*fml*) majority or greater part; most: *The generality of Swedes are blond.* **3** [U] quality of being general: *a rule of great generality*, ie one with few exceptions.

generalize, -ise /ˈdʒenrəlaɪz/ *v* **1** [I, Ipr, Tn, Tn·pr] ~ (**about sth**); ~ (**sth**) (**from sth**) draw (a general conclusion) from particular examples or evidence: *You cannot generalize about the effects of the drug from one or two cases.* ○ *generalize a conclusion from a set of facts.* **2** [I, Ipr] ~ (**about sth**) make general statements for which there is little evidence: *Europeans, if I may generalize, are all...* ○ *Perhaps you oughtn't to generalize about that.*

▷ **generalized, -ised** *adj* **1** widespread; general(1a): *Use of this drug is now fairly generalized.* **2** not specific; general(1b): *a sort of generalized malaise.*

generalization, -isation /ˌdʒenrəlaɪˈzeɪʃn; *US* -lɪˈz-/ *n* [C, U] (statement based on) generalizing: *a speech full of sweeping generalizations.*

generally /ˈdʒenrəlɪ/ *adv* **1** by most people; widely: *He is generally popular.* ○ *The plan was generally welcomed.* **2** in a general sense; without regard to details: *Generally speaking, it's quite a fair settlement.* **3** usually: *I generally get up early.* ⇨ Usage at HOPEFUL.

generate /ˈdʒenəreɪt/ *v* [Tn] cause (sth) to exist or occur; produce: *generate heat, electricity, power, etc* ○ *hatred generated by racial prejudice* ○ *grammatical rules for generating sentences.*

generation /ˌdʒenəˈreɪʃn/ *n* **1** [U] (**a**) production: *the generation of electricity by steam or water-power* ○ *the generation of heat by friction.* (**b**) (*biology*) production of living beings, esp offspring; procreation. **2** [C] single stage in a family history: *a family party at which all three generations were present*, ie children, parents and grandparents ○ *experience handed down from generation to generation.* **3** [C, Gp] all people born at about the same time: *My generation behaves differently from my father's and grandfather's.* ○ [attrib] *a first-, second-, third-, etc generation American*, ie sb who himself or whose parents or grandparents, etc emigrated to America. **4** [C] average period, usu considered to be 25-30 years, in which children grow up to become full adults: *a generation ago* ○ *within one generation.* **5** [C] single stage in the development of a type of product: *the new generation of supersonic airliners* ○ [attrib] *third-generation robots.*

□ **the geneˈration gap** difference in attitude, or lack of understanding, between young people and older people.

generative /ˈdʒenərətɪv/ *adj* **1** able to produce; productive: *generative processes* ○ *a generative grammar*, ie one which gives rules for accounting for all possible sentences in a language. **2** (*biology*) concerned with reproduction: *generative organs.*

generator /ˈdʒenəreɪtə(r)/ *n* **1** (*Brit*) (*US* **dynamo**) machine for producing electrical energy: *The generator has started up/broken down.* **2** machine or apparatus that produces steam, gas, vapour, etc. **3** person who generates or originates: *a generator of new ideas.*

generic /dʒɪˈnerɪk/ *adj* shared by or including a whole group or class; not specific: *The generic term for wine, spirits and beer is 'alcoholic beverages'.* ▷ **generically** /dʒɪˈnerɪklɪ/ *adv.*

generosity /ˌdʒenəˈrɒsətɪ/ *n* **1** [U] quality of being generous. **2** [C] generous act.

generous /ˈdʒenərəs/ *adj* (*approv*) **1** giving or ready to give freely: *generous with one's money/in giving help* ○ *It was generous of you to share your food with me.* **2** given freely; plentiful: *a generous gift, offer, increase* ○ *a generous helping of potatoes.* **3** free from meanness or prejudice; magnanimous: *a generous mind, spirit, etc* ○ *A wise ruler is generous in victory.* ▷ **generously** *adv*: *Please give generously.* ○ *a dress cut generously*, ie using plenty of material.

genesis /ˈdʒenəsɪs/ *n* (*pl* **geneses** /ˈdʒenəsi:z/) **1** (*fml*) beginning; starting-point; origin: *the genesis of civilization.* **2 Genesis** (*Bible*) the first book of the Old Testament, describing the creation of the world. ⇨ App 5.

genetic /dʒɪˈnetɪk/ *adj* of genes; of genetics: *genetic information, material, etc.*

▷ **genetically** /-klɪ/ *adv*: *genetically determined, linked, etc.*

geneticist /dʒɪˈnetɪsɪst/ *n* specialist in genetics.

genetics /dʒɪˈnetɪks/ *n* [sing *v*] scientific study of the ways in which characteristics are passed from parents (or, in plants, from parent stock) to their offspring.

□ **geˌnetic ˈcode** system of storage of genetic information in chromosomes.

geˌnetic ˌengiˈneering deliberate changes made to hereditary features by altering the structure or position of individual genes.

Geneva Convention /dʒəˌni:və kənˈvenʃn/ **the Geneva Convention** international agreement signed at Geneva in Switzerland in 1864 and later revised, which aims to limit the harmful effects of war and protect civilians, hospitals, prisoners of war, etc.

genial /ˈdʒi:nɪəl/ *adj* **1** kindly; pleasant; sociable: *a genial person, manner, smile.* **2** (of climate) mild; warm; favourable to growth: *the genial air of the Pacific Islands.*

▷ **geniality** /ˌdʒi:nɪˈælətɪ/ *n* **1** [U] quality of being genial. **2** [C] genial act, look or remark.

genially /ˈdʒi:nɪəlɪ/ *adv.*

-genic *suff* (esp with *ns* forming *adjs*) **1** producing: *carcinogenic.* **2** suited to: *photogenic.* **3** produced by: *cryogenic*, ie of or produced by extremely low temperatures.

genie /ˈdʒi:nɪ/ *n* (*pl* ~**s** or **genii** /ˈdʒi:nɪaɪ/) (in Arabian stories) spirit or goblin with strange powers.

genital /ˈdʒenɪtl/ *adj* [attrib] (*medical or fml*) of animal reproduction or reproductive organs: *the genital area* ○ *genital stimulation.*

▷ **genitals** /ˈdʒenɪtlz/ (also **genitalia** /ˌdʒenɪˈteɪlɪə/) *n* [pl] (*fml*) external sex organs.

genitive /ˈdʒenətɪv/ *n* (*grammar*) special form of a noun, a pronoun or an adjective used (in certain inflected languages) to indicate or describe esp possession. Cf POSSESSIVE *n* 2.

▷ **genitive** *adj* of or in the genitive: *The genitive forms of the pronouns 'I', 'we' and 'she' are 'my/mine', 'our/ours' and 'her/hers'.*

genius /ˈdʒi:nɪəs/ *n* (*pl* **geniuses**) **1** (**a**) [U] exceptionally great mental or creative ability: *a man of genius* ○ *It is rare to find such genius nowadays.* (**b**) [C] person who has this ability: *Einstein was a mathematical genius.* ○ *He is hard-working and able, but no genius.* **2** [sing] **a** ~ **for sth** exceptional natural ability for (doing) sth: *have a genius for languages, making friends, saying the wrong thing.* **3** [sing] **the** ~ (**of sth**) (**a**) guardian spirit (of a person, a place or an institution). (**b**) (*fml*) special character, spirit or principles of a language, a period of time, an institution, a nation, etc: *the genius of the English language, of the age.* **4** (idm) **one's good/evil ˈgenius** person or spirit supposed to have a strong influence on one for good or for evil: *Blame it on my evil genius!*

genocide /ˈdʒenəsaɪd/ *n* [U] deliberate extermination of a nation or race of people.

genotype /ˈdʒenətaɪp/ *n* (*biology*) genetic constitution of an individual living being.

-genous *suff* (forming *adjs*) producing or produced by: *erogenous.*

genre /ˈʒɑ:nrə/ *n* particular style or kind, esp of works of art or literature grouped according to their form or subject-matter: *The novel and short story are different genres.*

□ ˈ**genre-painting** *n* [U] style of painting that shows scenes, etc from ordinary life.

gent /dʒent/ *n* **1** [C] (*infml or joc*) gentleman: *This way, please, gents!* **2 gents** [pl] (esp in shops) men: *a gents' hairdresser, outfitter, etc.* **3 a/the Gents** [usu sing *v*] (*Brit infml*) public lavatory for men: *Where's the Gents?*

genteel /dʒenˈti:l/ *adj* **1** (*derog*) polite or refined in an affected or exaggerated way: *She is too genteel for words!* **2** (*dated*) of the upper social classes: *living in genteel poverty*, ie trying to maintain the style of upper-class living, though too poor to do so.

▷ **genteelly** /dʒenˈti:llɪ/ *adv.*

gentian /ˈdʒenʃn/ *n* [C, U] plant with blue flowers that grows in mountainous districts.

□ ˌ**gentian ˈviolet** dye used as an antiseptic, esp in the treatment of burns.

gentile /ˈdʒentaɪl/ *n, adj* (person who is) not Jewish.

gentility /dʒenˈtɪlətɪ/ *n* [U] (*approv or ironic*) genteel manners and behaviour; social superiority: *He thinks fine clothes are a mark of gentility.*

gentle /ˈdʒentl/ *adj* (**-r** /ˈdʒentlə(r)/, **-st** /ˈdʒentlɪst/) **1** (**a**) mild; kind; careful; not rough, violent or severe: *a gentle person, manner, voice, look* ○ *a doctor who is gentle with his hands* ○ (*sexist*) *the gentle* (ie female) *sex* ○ *be gentle with animals, children, etc* ○ *Be gentle with my best china!* (**b**) (of weather, temperature, etc) mild; temperate: *a gentle breeze* ○ *gentle rainfall* ○ *a gentle heat.* **2** not steep or abrupt: *a gentle slope.* **3** (*dated*) (of a family) with good social position: *of gentle birth.*

▷ **gentleness** /ˈdʒentlnɪs/ *n* [U].

gently /ˈdʒentlɪ/ *adv* **1** in a gentle(1a) manner: *handle sth gently* ○ *speak to sb gently* ○ *The beach slopes gently to the sea.* **2** (idm) **easy/gently does it** ⇨ EASY[2].

□ ˈ**gentlefolk** *n* [pl *v*] (*dated*) people belonging to respected upper-class families.

gentleman /ˈdʒentlmən/ *n* (*pl* **-men** /-mən/) **1** [C] (*approv or ironic*) man who is polite and shows consideration for the feelings of other people; man who always acts in an honourable way: *Thank you. You're a real gentleman.* ○ *He's no gentleman!* Cf LADY. **2** (**a**) **gentlemen** [pl] (*fml*) (as a polite form of address to men): *Gentlemen of the jury!* ○ *Ladies and gentlemen!* eg when beginning a speech. (**b**) [C] (as a polite way of referring to a man): *There's a gentleman at the door.* ⇨ Usage at LADY. **3** [C] (*dated*) man of wealth and social position, esp one who does not work for a living: *a country gentleman* ○ [attrib] *a gentleman farmer*, ie one who owns a farm, but does no manual work himself.

▷ **gentlemanly** *adj* (*approv*) of or like a gentleman(1): *of gentlemanly appearance* ○ *gentlemanly behaviour.*

□ **a** ˌ**gentleman's aˈgreement** agreement that cannot be enforced by law but depends on the mutual trust and good faith of those involved.

ˌ**gentleman-at-ˈarms** *n* (*Brit*) one of the sovereign's bodyguard.

gentlewoman /ˈdʒentlwʊmən/ *n* (*pl* **-women** /-wɪmɪn/) (*arch*) lady.

gentry /ˈdʒentrɪ/ *n* [pl *v*] (usu **the gentry**) people of good social position next below the nobility.

▷ **gentrify** /ˈdʒentrɪfaɪ/ *v* (*pt, pp* **-fied**) [Tn] (*infml*) restore and smarten (a house, an area, etc) to make it suitable for middle-class residents.

genuflect /ˈdʒenju:flekt/ *v* [I] (*fml*) bend the knee, esp in worship. ▷ **genuflexion** /ˌdʒenju:ˈflekʃn/ *n* [C, U].

genuine /ˈdʒenjʊɪn/ *adj* **1** real; truly what it is said to be; not fake or artificial: *a genuine Rubens*, ie a painting definitely by Rubens himself, not by an imitator ○ *a genuine pearl.* **2** (*fig*) sincere; honest: *She seems genuine but can I trust her?* ▷ **genuinely** *adv*. **genuineness** *n* [U].

genus /ˈdʒi:nəs/ *n* (*pl* **genera** /ˈdʒenərə/) **1** (*biology*) group of animals or plants within a family(4), often itself subdivided into several species(1). Cf PHYLUM, CLASS 7, ORDER[1] 9. **2** (*infml*) kind; type.

geo- *comb form* of the earth: ˌ*geo*ˈ*centric* ○ *ge*ˈ*ography* ○ *ge*ˈ*ology*.

geocentric /ˌdʒi:əʊˈsentrɪk/ *adj* **1** having the earth as its centre: *a geocentric view of the universe.* **2** measured from the centre of the earth.

geodesy /dʒi:ˈɒdɪsɪ/ *n* [U] scientific study of the shape and surface of the Earth.

geodesic dome

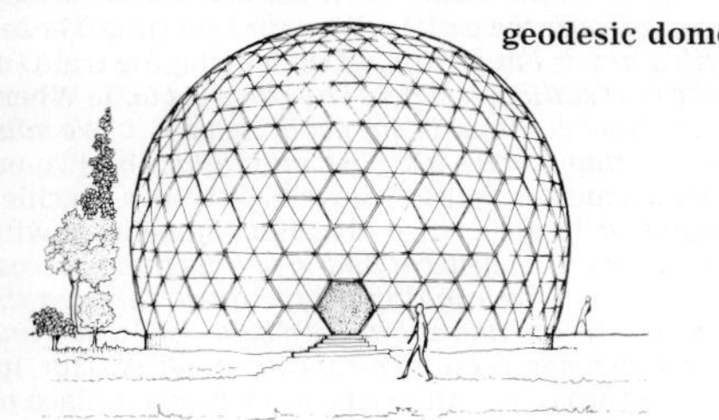

▷ **geodesic** /ˌdʒi:əʊˈdesɪk; *US* -ˈdi:sɪk/ (also **geodetic** /-ˈdetɪk/) *adj* of geodesy. ˌ**geodesic** ˈ**dome** dome formed from a light frame of straight bars or struts fitted with straight-sided panels. ⇨ illus. ˌ**geodesic** ˈ**line** shortest possible line between two points on a curved surface.

geography /dʒɪˈɒgrəfɪ/ *n* **1** [U] scientific study of the earth's surface, physical features, divisions, climate, products, population, etc: *physical/political/social geography* ○ [attrib] *a geography book, student, lecture.* **2** [sing] **the ~ (of sth)** (*infml*) arrangement of the features of a place: *getting to know the geography of a neighbourhood, house, kitchen, etc*, ie where things are in relation to each other.

▷ **geographer** /dʒɪˈɒgrəfə(r)/ *n* student of or expert in geography.

geographical /ˌdʒɪəˈgræfɪkl/ *adj* of or relating to geography: *geographical features, research.* **geographically** /-klɪ/ *adv*.

geology /dʒɪˈɒlədʒɪ/ *n* [U] scientific study of the earth's crust, rocks, strata, etc and of the history of its development: [attrib] *a geology course, department, field-trip.*

▷ **geological** /dʒɪəˈlɒdʒɪkl/ *adj* of or relating to geology: *a geological age, formation.* **geologically** /-klɪ/ *adv*.

geologist /dʒɪˈɒlədʒɪst/ *n* student of or expert in geology.

geometry /dʒɪˈɒmətrɪ/ *n* [U] branch of mathematics dealing with the properties and relations of lines, angles, surfaces and solids: [attrib] *a geometry set*, ie a collection of the instruments needed for drawing geometric figures.

▷ **geometric** /dʒɪəˈmetrɪk/ (also **geometrical** /-ɪkl/) *adj* of geometry; of or like the lines, figures, etc used in geometry: *a geometric design.* **geometrically** /-klɪ/ *adv*. **geometric progression** ordered set of numbers in which each is multiplied or divided by a fixed number to produce the next, as 1, 3, 9, 27, 81. Cf ARITHMETIC PROGRESSION (ARITHMETIC).

geomorphology /ˌdʒi:əʊmɔ:ˈfɒlədʒɪ/ *n* [U] scientific study of the origins and development of land-forms such as hills, valleys, coastlines, etc.

geophysics /ˌdʒɪəʊˈfɪzɪks/ *n* [sing *v*] scientific study of the physics of the earth, eg its magnetism, meteorology. ▷ **geophysical** /ˌdʒɪəʊˈfɪzɪkl/ *adj*. **geophysicist** /ˌdʒɪəʊˈfɪzəsɪst/ *n*.

geopolitics /ˌdʒɪəʊˈpɒlətɪks/ *n* [sing *v*] study of how politics is affected by geographical factors. ▷ **geopolitical** /ˌdʒɪəʊpəˈlɪtɪkl/ *adj* of geopolitics.

Geordie /ˈdʒɔ:dɪ/ *n* (*Brit infml*) person from the area of the River Tyne in NE England, esp from the city of Newcastle-upon-Tyne: [attrib] *a Geordie accent.* ⇨ article at ACCENT.

George[1] /dʒɔ:dʒ/ *n* **1** (*Brit sl*) name used to refer to the automatic pilot of an aeroplane: *George is flying the plane at the moment.* **2** (idm) ˌ**by** ˈ**George!** (*dated Brit*) (used as an exclamation of surprise or approval).

George[2] /dʒɔ:dʒ/ Saint, patron saint of England. He may have been a Christian martyr in the third century AD, but little is known about his life. According to legend he killed a fierce dragon, and he is often shown doing this in paintings, etc. Later he came to be regarded as a model of chivalry. ⇨ article at NATIONAL.

George I /dʒɔ:dʒ/ (1660-1727), king of Great Britain and Ireland 1714-27. The first of the Hanoverian kings, he came to Britain from Germany on the death of Queen *Anne. He was not popular, partly because he never learnt English, and left affairs of state to the ministers in the Cabinet, whose importance dates from this time. ⇨ App 3.

George II /dʒɔ:dʒ/ (1683-1760), king of Great Britain and Ireland 1727-60. Like his father George I, he took little interest in the government of Britain, allowing the development of the constitutional monarchy. He did, however, lead the country into war against France, and was the last British king to lead an army in battle. ⇨ App 3.

George III /dʒɔ:dʒ/ (1738-1820), king of Great Britain and Ireland 1760-1820. Unlike his grandfather George II, he was greatly interested in government affairs and actively opposed the *American Revolution. At the end of his life he suffered from an illness that affected his mind and his son was made Regent. ⇨ App 3.

George IV /dʒɔ:dʒ/ (1762-1830), king of Great Britain and Ireland 1820-30. As Prince of Wales and Regent he caused scandal by his lavish and immoral life-style. His reputation was further damaged when, as king, he tried to divorce his estranged wife. ⇨ App 3.

George V /dʒɔ:dʒ/ (1865-1936), king of Great Britain and Northern Ireland 1910-36. He was one of Britain's most popular kings, gaining respect through his patriotism during the First World War and his attention to the Empire and Commonwealth. ⇨ App 3.

George VI /dʒɔ:dʒ/ (1894-1952), king of Great Britain and Northern Ireland 1936-52. He became king after the abdication of his brother Edward VIII, and despite his stammer and shyness won the respect of the country, esp through his leadership in the Second World War. ⇨ App 3.

□ ˌ**George** ˈ**Cross**, ˌ**George** ˈ**Medal** British decorations for bravery, awarded esp to civilians and instituted by George VI in 1940.

georgette /dʒɔ:ˈdʒet/ *n* [U] thin silky dress-material.

Georgia[1] /ˈdʒɔ:dʒə/ country south of Russia, bordering on the Black Sea; pop approx 5 456 000; official language Georgian; capital Tbilisi; unit of currency Georgian coupon. An independent Christian republic in medieval times, it became part of the Russian empire in the 19th century and subsequently of the USSR. In 1991 Georgia regained its independence. ⇨ map at UNION OF SOVIET SOCIALIST REPUBLICS.

Georgia[2] /ˈdʒɔ:dʒə/ state in the south-eastern USA, on the Atlantic coast. One of the thirteen original states, Georgia suffered badly in the American Civil War, and in the 1960s it was the scene of many civil rights demonstrations. ⇨ map at App 1.

Georgian /ˈdʒɔ:dʒən/ *adj* (*Brit*) of the time of the British kings George I-IV (1714-1830): *a Georgian house* ○ *Georgian furniture.* ⇨ illus at DRESS.

geostationary /ˌdʒi:əʊˈsteɪʃənrɪ/ *adj* (of an artificial satellite of the earth) moving in orbit so that it always remains above the same point on the earth's surface.

geranium /dʒəˈreɪnɪəm/ *n* garden plant with red, pink or white flowers.

gerbil /ˈdʒɜ:bɪl, ˈdʒɜ:bl/ mouselike rodent with long back legs, often kept as a pet.

geriatrics /ˌdʒerɪˈætrɪks/ *n* [sing *v*] branch of medicine dealing with the diseases and care of old people.

▷ **geriatric** /ˌdʒerɪˈætrɪk/ *adj* of or relating to geriatrics: *the geriatric ward of a hospital.*

geriatrician /ˌdʒerɪəˈtrɪʃn/ *n* doctor specializing in geriatrics.

germ /dʒɜ:m/ *n* **1** [C] (*symb* **GE**) portion of a living organism capable of becoming a new organism; embryo of a seed. **2** [C] micro-organism, esp one capable of causing disease: *Disinfectant kills germs.* **3** [sing] **the ~ of sth** (*fig*) beginning from which sth may develop: *the germ of an idea.*

□ ˌ**germ** ˈ**warfare** = BIOLOGICAL WARFARE (BIOLOGICAL).

germane /dʒəˈmeɪn/ *adj* [pred] **~ (to sth)** (*fml*) relevant: *remarks that are germane to the discussion.*

germanium /dʒɜ:ˈmeɪnɪəm/ *n* [U] (*symb* **Ge**) hard greyish-white semi-metallic element used in semiconductors.

Germany

Germany /ˈdʒɜ:mənɪ/ country in central Europe; pop approx 77 865 000; official language German; unit of currency Deutschmark (= 100 pfennig). After the Second World War the country was occupied by the forces of the Western Allies and the Soviet Union. The areas occupied by the former became the Federal Republic of Germany with its capital in Bonn and the Soviet zone became the German Democratic Republic. Berlin was divided, with its eastern half the capital of the GDR. The GDR remained under the economic and political influence of the Soviet Union, while the Federal Republic was incorporated into the western defence and economic community as one of the most important industrial economies in the EC. In 1989 the changes that took place throughout eastern Europe led to the dismantling of the wall that divided Berlin and subsequently, in 1990, to the reunification of Germany as a federal republic with 16 states. The capital of the new Germany is Berlin, but Bonn, the former capital of the Federal Republic, remains the seat of government. ⇨ map.

▷ **German** /ˈdʒɜ:mən/ *adj* of Germany, its culture, its language or its people: *German industry, traditions, grammar.* — *n* **1** [C] native or inhabitant of Germany. **2** [U] language spoken in Germany, Austria and part of Switzerland.

Germanic /dʒəˈmænɪk/ *adj* having German

characteristics: *Germanic features, attitudes* ○ *the Germanic peoples*, ie early peoples who included the Scandinavians, Anglo-Saxons and Germans. — *n* [U] early language of the Germanic peoples, from which developed the group of languages that includes English, German, Dutch and the Scandinavian languages.

□ ˌ**German ˈmeasles** (*infml*) (also **rubella**) mild contagious disease causing red spots all over the body.

ˌ**German ˈshepherd** (*US*) = ALSATIAN.

germicide /ˈdʒɜːmɪsaɪd/ *n* [C, U] substance used for killing germs. ▷ **germicidal** /ˌdʒɜːmɪˈsaɪdl/ *adj*.

germinal /ˈdʒɜːmɪnl/ *adj* in the earliest stage of development: *in a germinal form*.

germinate /ˈdʒɜːmɪneɪt/ *v* [I, Tn] (cause sth to) start growing: *The cabbages germinated within a week.* ○ *to germinate cabbages, beans, etc.*

▷ **germination** /ˌdʒɜːmɪˈneɪʃn/ *n* [U] germinating; sprouting.

gerontology /ˌdʒerɒnˈtɒlədʒɪ/ *n* [U] scientific study of old age and the process of growing old.

gerrymander /ˌdʒerɪˈmændə(r)/ *v* [Tn] (*derog politics*) arrange the boundaries of or divide (an area) for voting in order to give unfair advantages to one party in an election.

▷ **gerrymander** *n* [C] such a rearrangement.

gerrymandering *n* [U] making such a rearrangement: *There has been some gerrymandering.*

Gershwin /ˈgɜːʃwɪn/ George (1898-1937), American composer and pianist. He had little musical training but wrote many successful songs, often for the musicals of the 1920s. He also wrote the opera *Porgy and Bess* and works for piano and orchestra, including *Rhapsody in Blue*. His elder brother Ira wrote the words for many of his songs. ⇨ article at MUSIC.

gerund /ˈdʒerənd/ *n* = VERBAL NOUN (VERBAL).

gesso /ˈdʒesəʊ/ *n* [U] plaster of Paris specially prepared for use in painting or sculpture: [attrib] *gesso work*.

gestalt /gəˈʃtælt; *US* gəˈstɑːlt/ *n* whole thing that is seen as more than the total of its various parts, eg a melody as distinct from its individual notes.

□ **ge**ˌ**stalt psy**ˈ**chology** approach to psychology that treats reactions, feelings, etc as gestalts. The psychologist must then analyse the conditions in which they are experienced and understood.

Gestapo /geˈstɑːpəʊ/ *n* **the Gestapo** [Gp] German secret police of the Nazi regime.

gestation /dʒeˈsteɪʃn/ *n* **1** (**a**) [U] carrying or being carried in the womb between conception and birth: [attrib] *Elephants have a gestation period of about 624 days.* (**b**) [sing] period of time taken by this. **2** [U] (*fig*) development of an idea, a work of art, etc.

gesticulate /dʒeˈstɪkjʊleɪt/ *v* [I] move the hands or arms (usu rapidly) instead of speaking or to emphasize one's words: *He was gesticulating wildly at me, but I could not understand what he was trying to tell me.*

▷ **gesticulation** /dʒeˌstɪkjʊˈleɪʃn/ *n* **1** [U] gesticulating. **2** [C] movement used in this: *wild gesticulations.*

gesture /ˈdʒestʃə(r)/ *n* **1** [C, U] expressive movement of a part of the body, esp the hand or head: *make a rude gesture* ○ *with a gesture of despair* ○ *communicating by gesture.* **2** [C] (*fig*) action showing one's (usu friendly) intentions or attitude: *a gesture of sympathy* ○ *The invitation was meant as a friendly gesture.*

▷ **gesture** *v* **1** [I] make expressive movements: *to gesture with one's hands.* **2** [Tn, Tn·pr, Tf, Dpr·f, Dpr·t] ~ **sth (to sb)** convey sth by making gestures: *She gestured her disapproval.* ○ *He gestured (to me) that it was time to go.* ○ *He gestured to them to keep quiet*, ie told them to do so by making gestures.

get /get/ *v* (**-tt-**, *pt* **got** /gɒt/, *pp* **got**; *US* **gotten** /ˈgɒtn/)

► RECEIVING OR OBTAINING **1** [Tn no passive] receive (sth): *I got a letter from my sister this morning.* ○ *Did you get my postcard?* ○ *What did you get for Christmas?* ○ *He gets* (ie earns) *£25 000 a year.* ○ *This room gets very little sunshine.* ○ *Schoolteachers get long holidays.* ○ *He got* (ie was hit by) *a bullet in the thigh.* ○ *She got a shock when she saw the telephone bill.* ○ *I got the impression that he was bored with his job.* **2** [no passive: Tn, Dn·n, Dn·pr] (**a**) ~ **sth (for oneself/sb)** obtain sth: *Where did you get* (ie buy) *that skirt?* ○ *Did you manage to get tickets for the concert?* ○ *She opened the door wider to get a better look.* ○ *Try to get some sleep.* ○ *He doesn't look as though he gets enough exercise.* ○ *Johnson got* (ie won) *the gold medal in the 100 metres.* ○ *She's just got* (ie been appointed to) *a job with a publishing company.* ○ *Why don't you get (yourself) a flat of your own?* ○ *Have you remembered to get your mother a birthday present/to get a birthday present for your mother?* (**b**) ~ **sb/sth (for oneself/sb)** fetch sb/sth: *Go and get a dictionary and we'll look the word up.* ○ *Somebody get a doctor! I think this woman's had a heart attack.* ○ *I have to go and get my mother* (ie collect her in a car) *from the station.* ○ *Could you get me that book (down) from the top shelf?* ○ *Can I get you a drink/get a drink for you?* **3** [no passive: Tn, Tn·pr] ~ **sth (for sth)** obtain or receive (an amount of money) by selling sth: *'How much did you get for your old car?' 'I got £800 (for it).'* **4** [Tn no passive] receive (sth) as a punishment: *He got ten years* (ie was sentenced to ten years in prison) *for armed robbery.* **5** [Tn no passive] (**a**) be able to receive broadcasts from (a particular television or radio station): *We can't get Channel 4 on our television.* (**b**) be connected with (sb) by telephone: *I wanted to speak to the manager but I got his secretary instead.* **6** [Tn no passive] regularly buy (a newspaper): *Do you get 'The Times' or the 'Guardian'?* **7** [Tn no passive] become infected with (an illness); suffer from or be affected by (a pain, etc): *get bronchitis, flu, measles, etc* ○ *She gets* (ie regularly suffers from) *bad headaches.* **8** [Tn no passive] achieve or be awarded (the specified examination grade, class of degree, etc): *She got a first in English at Oxford.*

► REACHING OR BRINGING TO A PARTICULAR STATE OR CONDITION **9** (**a**) [La] reach the specified state or condition; become: *get angry, bored, hungry, worried, etc* ○ *get fat, fit, thinner, etc* ○ *It/The weather is getting colder.* ○ *She's getting better*, eg after her illness. ○ *You'll get wet if you go out in the rain without an umbrella.* ○ *You'll soon get used to the climate here.* ○ *We ought to go; it's getting late.* ⇨ Usage at BECOME. (**b**) [La, Cn·a] cause oneself to be in the specified state or condition: *get dressed/undressed*, ie put one's clothes on/take one's clothes off ○ *They plan to get married in the summer.* ○ *She's upstairs getting (herself) ready (to go out).* (**c**) (used in place of *be* with a past participle to form passive constructions): *Do you think the Tories will get* (ie be) *re-elected?* ○ *I wouldn't go there after dark; you might get* (ie be) *mugged.* **10** [Cn·a] cause (sb/sth) to be or become: *She soon got the children ready for school.* ○ *I must get the dinner ready*, ie prepare it. ○ *Don't get your new trousers dirty!* ○ *Don't let the incident get you upset.* ○ *Do you think you'll get the work finished on time?* ○ *He got his wrist broken*, ie broke it accidentally. ○ *I couldn't get the car started this morning.* ○ *Go and get your hair cut!* ○ *She got her fingers caught in the door.*

► MAKING SOMETHING HAPPEN **11** [Cn·g] bring (sb/sth) to the point at which he/it is doing sth: *Can you really get that old car going again?* ○ *It's not hard to get him talking; the problem is stopping him!* **12** [Cn·t] cause, persuade, etc (sb/sth) to do sth: *I couldn't get the car to start* (ie make it start) *this morning.* ○ *He got* (ie persuaded) *his sister to help him with his homework.* ○ *You'll never get him to understand.* ○ *I can't get her to talk at all.*

► REACHING THE POINT WHERE ONE DOES SOMETHING **13** (**a**) [Tg] reach the stage at which one is doing sth; start doing sth: *I got talking to her/We got talking.* ○ *We got chatting and discovered we'd been at college together.* ○ *get working on a problem* ○ *You have an hour to clean the whole house — so get scrubbing!* (**b**) [It] reach the point at which one feels, knows, is, etc sth: *You'll like her once you get to know her.* ○ *How did you get to know* (ie discover or learn) *that I was here?* ○ *One soon gets to like it here.* ○ *She's getting to be an old lady now.* ○ *After a time you get to realize that these things don't matter.* ○ *His drinking is getting to be a problem.* ○ *Your mother will be furious if she gets to hear of this.* **14** [It] (*esp US*) have the chance or opportunity to do sth; manage to do sth: *Did you get to see the Louvre while you were in Paris?* ○ *One day we'll both get to see New York.* ○ *When do I get to go to a movie?*

► MOVING OR CAUSING TO MOVE **15** (**a**) [Ipr, Ip] move to or from a specified point or in a specified direction, sometimes with difficulty: *The bridge was destroyed so we couldn't get across* (ie cross) *the river.* ○ *She got back into bed.* ○ *She got down from the ladder.* ○ *He got into the car.* ○ *Can you get over the wall?* ○ *We didn't get* (ie go) *to bed till 3 am.* ○ *I'm getting off* (ie leaving the train) *at the next station.* ○ *Where have they got to?* ie Where are they? ○ *Please let me get by*, ie pass. ○ *We must be getting home; it's past midnight.* (**b**) [Tn·pr, Tn·p] cause (sb/sth) to move to or from a specified point or in a specified direction, sometimes with difficulty: *The general had to get his troops across the river.* ○ *We couldn't get the piano through the door.* ○ *He's drunk again; we'd better call a taxi and get him home.* ○ *I can't get the lid on/off.* (**c**) [Ipr, Ip] ~ **to/into ...**; ~ **in** arrive at or reach a place or point: *We got to London at 7 o'clock.* ○ *The train gets into Glasgow at 6 o'clock in the morning.* ○ *You got in/home very late last night.* ○ *What time did you get here?* ○ *I haven't got very far with the book I'm reading.* **16** [Tn no passive] travel by (bus, taxi, plane, etc); take (a bus, etc): *We're going to be late; let's get a taxi.* ○ *'How do you come to work?' 'I usually get the bus.'*

► OTHER MEANINGS **17** [Tn, Dn·n, Dn·pr] ~ **sth (for oneself/sb)** prepare (a meal): *Don't disturb your mother while she's getting (the) dinner.* ○ *I have to go home and get the children their supper/get supper for the children.* **18** [Tn, Tn·pr] (**a**) catch or seize (sb/sth): *He was on the run for a week before the police got him.* ○ *get sb by the arm, scruff of the neck, throat, wrist, etc.* (**b**) catch and harm, injure or kill (sb), often in revenge for sth: *She fell overboard and the sharks got her.* ○ *He thinks the Mafia are out to get him.* ○ *I'll get you for that, you bastard!* (**c**) hit or wound (sb): *Where did the stone get you?* ○ *The bullet got him in the neck.* ○ *I got him on the back of the head with a crowbar.* **19** [Tn no passive] (*infml*) (**a**) understand (sb/sth): *I don't get you/your meaning.* ○ *She didn't get the joke.* ○ *I don't get it; why would she do a thing like that?* (**b**) hear (sth): *I didn't quite get what you said.* **20** [Tn no passive] (*infml*) confuse or puzzle sb: *'What's the capital of Luxembourg?' 'I don't know; you've got me there!'* **21** [Tn no passive] annoy or irritate (sb): *It really gets me when she starts bossing people around.*

22 (idm) **be getting ˈon** (**a**) (of a person) be becoming old: *Grandma's getting on a bit and doesn't go out as much as she used to.* (**b**) (of time) be becoming late: *The time's getting on; we ought to be going.* **be getting on for...** be near to or approaching (the specified time, age or number): *It must be getting on for midnight.* ○ *He must be getting on for eighty!* **sb can't/couldn't get over sth** (*infml*) sb is/was shocked, surprised, amused, etc by sth: *I can't get over that shirt he was wearing.* ○ *I can't get over how rude she was.* **get aˈlong/ aˈway/ˈon (with you)** (*infml*) (used to express disbelief or to rebuke sb gently): *'How old are you?' 'I'm forty.' 'Get along with you! You don't look a day over thirty-five!'* **get (sb) anywhere/somewhere/ nowhere** (*infml*) (cause sb to) achieve something/ nothing or to make progress/no progress: *After six months' work on the project, at last I feel I'm getting somewhere.* ○ *Are you getting anywhere with your* *investigations?* **get aˈway from it all** (*infml*) have a short holiday in a place that is totally different from where one usu lives. **ˈget there** achieve one's aim or complete a task by patience and hard work: *I'm sure you'll get there in the end.* ○ *Writing a dictionary is a long and difficult business but we're getting there.* **how selfish, stupid, ungrateful, etc can you ˈget?** (*infml*) (used to express surprise, disbelief or disapproval that sb has been so selfish, etc): *He wouldn't even lend me ten pence; how mean can you get?* **there's no getting away from sth; one can't get away from sth** one has to admit the truth of (sth unpleasant): *There's no getting away from the fact that the country's economy is suffering.* (For other idioms containing **get**, see entries for *ns, adjs*, etc, eg **get sb's goat** ⇨ GOAT; **get even (with sb)** ⇨ EVEN[1].)

23 (phr v) **get aˈbout** (also **get aˈround**) (be able to) move from place to place: *He's getting about again after his accident.* ○ *She doesn't get around much these days.* **get aˈbout/aˈround/ˈround** (of news, a rumour, etc) spread from person to person; circulate: *The news of her resignation soon got about.*

get aˈbove oneself have too high an opinion of oneself: *She's been getting a bit above herself since winning her award.*

get (sth) aˈcross (to sb) (cause sth to) be communicated or understood: *Your meaning didn't really get across.* ○ *He's not very good at getting his ideas across.*

get aˈhead (of sb) progress (beyond sb): *She's keen to get ahead in her career.* ○ *By doing extra homework, he soon got ahead of his class-mates.*

get aˈlong (a) (usu in the continuous tenses) leave a place: *It's time we were getting along.* **(b)** = GET ON (A). **(c)** = GET ON (C). **get along with sb; get aˈlong (together)** have a harmonious or friendly relationship with sb; get on with sb: *Do you get along with your boss?/Do you and your boss get along?* ○ *We get along just fine.* **get along with sth** = GET ON WITH STH (A).

get around (a) = GET ABOUT. **(b)** ⇨ GET ABOUT/AROUND/ROUND. **get around sb** = GET ROUND SB. **get around sth** = GET ROUND STH. **get around to sth/doing sth** = GET ROUND TO STH/DOING STH.

ˈget at sb (*infml*) **(a)** (usu in the continuous tenses) criticize sb repeatedly; nag sb: *He's always getting at his wife.* ○ *She feels she's being got at.* **(b)** influence sb, esp unfairly or illegally: *One of the witnesses had been got at*, eg bribed. **get at sb/sth** gain access to sb/sth; reach sb/sth: *The files are locked up and I can't get at them.* **get at sth (a)** learn, discover or find out sth: *The truth is sometimes difficult to get at.* **(b)** (*infml*) (no passive; used only in the continuous tenses and usu in questions) suggest sth indirectly; imply sth: *What exactly are you getting at?*

get aˈway have a holiday: *We're hoping to get away for a few days at Easter.* **get away (from...)** succeed in leaving a place: *I won't be able to get away (from the office) before 7.* **get away (from sb/...)** escape from sb or a place: *Two of the prisoners got away (from their captors).* **get away with sth (a)** steal sth and escape with it: *Thieves raided the bank and got away with a lot of money.* **(b)** receive (a relatively light punishment): *For such a serious offence he was lucky to get away with a fine.* **(c)** (also **get away with doing sth**) (*infml*) not be punished for sth: *If you cheat in the exam you'll never get away with it.* ○ *Nobody gets away with insulting me like that.*

get ˈback return, esp to one's home: *What time did you get back last night?* ○ *We only got back from our holidays yesterday.* **get sth back** obtain sth again after having lost it; recover sth: *She's got her old job back.* ○ *I never lend books; you never get them back.* **get back (in)** (of a political party) return to power after having lost it: *The Democrats hope to get back (in) at the next election.* **get back at sb** (*infml*) take revenge on sb; retaliate against sb: *I'll find a way of getting back at him!* **get back to sb** speak or write to sb again later, esp in order to give a reply: *I hope to get back to you on the question of costs by next week.* **get back to sth** return to sth: *Could we get back to the original question of funding?*

get ˈbehind (with sth) not proceed at the necessary rate; not produce sth at the right time: *I'm getting behind (with my work).* ○ *He got behind with his payments for the car.*

get ˈby be considered good, smart, etc enough; be accepted: *I have no formal clothes for the occasion. Perhaps I can get by in a dark suit?* ○ *He should just about get by in the exam.* **get by (on sth)** manage to live, survive, etc (using the specified resources); manage; cope: *How does she get by on such a small salary?* ○ *He gets by on very little money.*

get ˈdown (of children) leave the table after a meal. **get sb ˈdown** (*infml*) make sb depressed or demoralized: *This wet weather is getting me down.* ○ *Don't let the incident get you down too much.* **get sth down (a)** swallow sth, usu with difficulty: *The medicine was so horrible I could hardly get it down.* **(b)** note or record sth; write sth down: *Did you get his telephone number down?* **get down to sth/doing sth** begin to do sth; give serious attention to sth; tackle sth: *get down to business* ○ *It's time I got down to some serious work.*

get in (a) (of a train, etc or a passenger) arrive at its destination: *The train got in late.* ○ *What time does your flight get in?* ○ *When do you normally get in from work?* **get ˈin; get into sth** be elected to a political position: *The Tory candidate stands a good chance of getting in.* ○ *Labour got in* (ie won the election) *with a small majority.* ○ *She first got into Parliament* (ie became an MP) *in 1959.* **get (sb) in; get (sb) into sth** (cause sb to) be admitted to a school, university, etc, esp after taking an examination: *He took the entrance exam but didn't get in.* ○ *She's got into Durham to read law.* ○ *She usually gets her best pupils into university.* **get sb in** call sb to one's house to perform a service: *We'll have to get a plumber in to mend that burst pipe.* **get sth in (a)** collect or gather sth: *get the crops, harvest, etc in.* **(b)** buy a supply of sth: *get coal in for the winter* ○ *Remember to get in some beers for this evening!* **(c)** manage to do or say sth: *I got in an hour's gardening between the showers.* ○ *She talks so much that it's impossible to get a word in.* **get in on sth** (*infml*) take part in (an activity): *She's keen to get in on any discussions about the new project.* **get in with sb** (*infml*) (try to) become friendly with sb, esp in order to gain an advantage: *Have you noticed how he's trying to get in with the boss?* ○ *He got in with a bad crowd at university.*

get into sb (*infml*) (of a feeling) affect, influence or take control of sb: *I don't know what's got into him recently; he's become very bad-tempered.* **get into sth (a)** put on (a garment), esp with difficulty: *I can't get into these shoes; they're too small.* **(b)** start a career in (the specified profession): *get into accountancy, journalism, publishing, etc.* **(c)** become involved in sth; start sth: *get into an argument, a conversation, a fight (with sb).* **(d)** acquire or develop sth: *get into bad habits.* **(e)** become familiar with sth; learn sth: *I haven't really got into my new job yet.* **(f)** (*infml*) develop a taste or liking for or an interest in sth: *I'm really getting into jazz these days.* ○ *How did she get into* (ie start taking) *drugs?* **get (oneself/sb) into sth** (cause oneself/sb to) pass into or reach (the specified state or condition): *get into a fury, rage, temper, etc* ○ *He got into trouble with the police while he was still at school.* ○ *She got herself into a real state* (ie became very anxious) *before the interview.*

get (sb) ˈoff (a) (cause sb to) leave a place or start a journey: *We got off immediately after breakfast.* ○ *get the children off to school.* **(b)** (cause sb to) fall asleep: *I had great difficulty getting off to sleep last night.* ○ *She got the baby off (to sleep) by rocking it.* **get off (sth)** leave (work) with permission: *I normally get off (work) at 5.30.* ○ *Could you get off (work) early tomorrow?* **get off sth** stop discussing (a particular subject): *Please can we get off the subject of dieting?* **get sth off** send sth by post: *I must get these letters off by the first post tomorrow.* **get sth off (sth)** remove sth from sth: *Her finger was so swollen that she couldn't get her ring off.* **get off (with sth)** escape or nearly escape injury in an accident: *She was lucky to get off with just a few bruises.* **get (sb) off (with sth)** (*infml*) (cause sb to) escape or nearly escape punishment: *A good lawyer might be able to get you off.* ○ *He got off with a small fine.* ○ *She was lucky to get off with a suspended sentence.* **get off with sb; get ˈoff (together)** (*Brit infml*) have a sexual or romantic experience with sb: *Steve got off with Tracey/Steve and Tracey got off (together) at Denise's party.*

get ˈon (a) (also **get aˈlong**) (esp followed by an *adv* or used in questions after *how*) perform or fare in a particular situation; make progress: *Our youngest son is getting on well at school.* ○ *How did you get along in your driving test?* ○ *How are you getting along these days?* ie Is your life enjoyable, successful, etc at the moment? **(b)** be successful in one's life or career: *Parents are always keen for their children to get on.* ○ *She's ambitious and eager to get on (in the world).* **(c)** (also **get along**) manage or cope: *I simply can't get along without a secretary.* ○ *We can get on perfectly well without her.* **get ˈon to sb (a)** contact sb by telephone or letter: *If you wish to lodge a complaint you'd better get on to the manager.* **(b)** become aware of sb's presence or activities; detect or trace sb: *He had been stealing money from the company for years before the police got on to him.* **(c)** begin to discuss (a new subject): *It's time we got on to the question of costs.* **get on with sb; get ˈon (together)** have a friendly relationship with sb; get along with sb: *She's never really got on with her sister/She and her sister have never really got on.* ○ *They don't get on at all well together/with one another.* ○ *Our new manager is very easy to get on with.* **get on with sth (a)** (also **get along with sth**) (esp followed by an *adv* or used in questions after *how*) make progress with a task: *How's your son getting on with his French?* ○ *I'm not getting on very fast with this job.* **(b)** continue doing sth, esp after an interruption: *Be quiet and get on with your work.*

get ˈout become known: *The secret got out.* ○ *If the news gets out there'll be trouble.* **get (sb) out** (in cricket) be dismissed or dismiss sb: *How did Gatting get out?* ○ *If England can get Richards out they might win the match.* **get sth out (a)** produce or publish sth: *Will we get the new dictionary out by the end of the year?* **(b)** say or utter sth with difficulty: *She managed to get out a few words of thanks.* **get out (of sth)** leave a place, esp in order to visit places, meet people, etc: *You ought to get out (of the house) more.* ○ *We love to get out into the countryside at weekends.* **get out of sth/doing sth (a)** avoid (a responsibility or duty); not do sth that one ought to do: *I wish I could get out of (going to) that meeting.* ○ *Don't you dare try and get out of the washing-up!* **(b)** (cause sb to) abandon, lose or give up (a habit, routine, etc): *I can't get out of the habit of waking at six in the morning.* ○ *Smoking is a habit she can't get out of.* **get sth out of sb** extract or obtain sth from sb, esp by force: *The police have got a confession out of her,* ie have made her confess. ○ *Just try getting money out of him!* ie He is very mean. **get sth out of sb/sth** gain or obtain sth from sb/sth: *She seems to get a lot out of life.* ○ *I never get much out of his lectures.* ○ *She always gets the best out of people.*

get over sth overcome, surmount or master sth: *She can't get over her shyness.* ○ *I can't get over* (ie I'm still amazed by) *how much your children have grown.* ○ *I think the problem can be got over without too much difficulty.* **get over sth/sb** return to one's usual state of health, happiness, etc after an illness, a shock, the end of a relationship with sb, etc: *He was disappointed at not getting the job, but he'll get over it.* ○ *He never got over the shock of losing his wife.* ○ *I was still getting over Peter when I met and fell in love with Harry.* **get sth over (to sb)** make sth clear to sb; communicate sth to sb: *She didn't really get her meaning over to her audience.* **get sth over (with)** (*infml*) complete sth unpleasant but necessary: *She'll be glad to get the exam over (and done) with.*

get round ⇨ GET ABOUT/AROUND/ROUND. **get round sb** (also **get around sb**) (*infml*) persuade sb to agree to sth or to do sth which he first opposed: *She knows how to get round her father.* **get round sth** (also **get around sth**) (**a**) tackle sth successfully; overcome sth: *Do you see a way of getting round the problem?* (**b**) evade or avoid (a law, regulation, etc) without acting illegally; circumvent sth: *A clever lawyer might find ways of getting round that clause.* **get round to sth/doing sth** (also **get around to sth/doing sth**) finally do sth after dealing with other matters; find the necessary time to do sth: *I'm very busy at the moment but I hope to get round to answering your letter next week.*

get through sth (**a**) use up or consume (the specified quantity or amount of sth): *She gets through forty cigarettes a day.* ○ *We got through a fortune while we were on holiday!* (**b**) (manage to) do or complete sth: *I've got through a lot of correspondence today.* ○ *Let's start; there's a lot of work to get through/to be got through.* **get (sb) ˈthrough (sth)** (help sb to) be successful in or pass (an examination, a test, etc): *Tom failed but his sister got through.* ○ *She got all her pupils through French 'A' Level.* **get (sth) ˈthrough (sth)** (cause sth to) be officially approved or accepted: *Do you think the Bill will get through (Parliament)?* ○ *get a proposal through a committee.* **get ˈthrough (to sb)** (**a**) reach (sb): *Thousands of refugees will die if these supplies don't get through (to them).* (**b**) make contact (with sb), esp by telephone: *I tried ringing you several times yesterday but I couldn't get through (to you).* **get ˈthrough (to sth)** (of a player or team) reach the next stage of a competition: *Everton have got through to the final.* **get ˈthrough to sb** make sb understand the meaning of what one is saying; communicate with sb: *I find her impossible to get through to.* ○ *Try to get through to him that he's wasting his life in that job.* **get through with sth** finish or complete (a job, task, etc): *As soon as I get through with my work I'll join you.*

get to doing sth reach the point where one does sth; begin to do sth: *He got to thinking that she perhaps wouldn't come after all.* **ˈget to sb** (*infml*) annoy, anger, or affect sb: *Her constant nagging is beginning to get to him.*

get sb/sth together assemble or collect (people or things): *Rebel leaders hastily tried to get an army together.* ○ *Could you get your things together? We're leaving in five minutes!* **get together with sb; get toˈgether** meet with sb for social purposes or to discuss sth: *The management should get together with the union/The management and the union should get together to discuss their differences.* ○ *We must get together for a drink some time.*

get up (**a**) stand after sitting, kneeling, etc; rise: *The class got up when the teacher came in.* ○ *He got up slowly from the armchair.* (**b**) (of the sea or wind) increase in force or strength; become violent: *The wind is getting ˈup.* **get (sb) up** (cause sb to) get out of bed: *What time do you get up (in the morning)?* ○ *She always gets up early.* ○ *Could you get me up* (ie wake me) *at 6.30 tomorrow?* **get oneself/sb up** (often passive) arrange the appearance of oneself/sb in the specified way: *She was got up* (ie dressed) *as an Indian princess.* **get sth up** (**a**) arrange or organize sth: *We're getting up a party for her birthday.* (**b**) acquire a knowledge of sth; study sth: *She's busy getting up the American constitution for tomorrow's exam.* **get up to sth** (**a**) reach (the specified point): *We got up to page 72 last lesson.* (**b**) be occupied or busy with (esp sth surprising or undesirable): *What on earth will he get up to next?* ○ *He's been getting up to his old tricks again!*

□ **get-at-able** /getˈætəbl/ *adj* [usu pred] (*infml*) that can be reached; accessible: *We've got a spare suitcase but it's not very get-at-able.*

ˈgetaway *n* escape, esp after committing a crime: *make one's getaway* ○ [attrib] *a getaway car*, ie one used to escape in.

ˈget-together *n* (*infml*) social gathering: *We're having a little get-together to celebrate David's promotion.*

ˈget-up *n* (*infml*) set of clothes, esp an unusual one; costume: *She wears the most extraordinary get-ups.* ○ *He looked absurd in that get-up.*

ˌget-up-and-ˈgo *n* [U] (*infml*) quality of being energetic and forceful: *She's got lots of get-up-and-go.*

Gettysburg /ˈgetɪzbɜːg/ small town in Pennsylvania, USA. The battle of Gettysburg (1863) in the American Civil War forced General Lee, the leader of the Southern forces, to abandon his invasion of the North, after his army was heavily defeated.

□ **the ˌGettysburg adˈdress** speech made by Abraham *Lincoln when America's national cemetery was created on the site of the battle of Gettysburg.

geum /ˈdʒiːəm/ *n* kind of small garden plant with red or yellow flowers.

gewgaw /ˈgjuːgɔː/ *n* (*derog*) showy but worthless ornament or plaything: [attrib] *gewgaw trifles.*

geyser /ˈgiːzə(r); *US* ˈgaɪzər/ *n* **1** column of hot water or steam sent up from the ground at intervals, caused by the heating of water deep in the Earth. **2** (*Brit*) apparatus formerly used for heating large amounts of water (usu by gas) in a kitchen or bathroom.

Ghana /ˈgɑːnə/ country in W Africa, with a southern coastline on the Atlantic; pop approx 14 131 000; official language English; capital Accra; unit of currency cedi (= 100 pesewas). It became independent in 1957 and is a member of the Commonwealth. It is a major producer of cocoa and has important mineral reserves, including the gold mines that gave it its former name of the Gold Coast. It one of the most industrially developed countries of Africa. ⇨ map at NIGERIA. ▷ **Ghanaian** /gɑːˈneɪən/ *n, adj.*

ghastly /ˈgɑːstlɪ; *US* ˈgæstlɪ/ *adj* (**-ier**, **-iest**) **1** [usu attrib] causing horror or fear: *a ghastly accident, experience, fright, murder.* **2** (*infml*) very bad; distasteful: *a ghastly error, mess, mistake, etc* ○ *Her hair-do and make-up look positively ghastly!* ○ *What a ghastly man!* **3** [usu pred] ill; upset: *I feel ghastly; I shouldn't have drunk so much!* ○ *I felt ghastly about refusing, but I had no alternative.* **4** (*fml*) very pale and death-like in appearance: *You look ghastly; are you all right?* ○ *She had a ghastly pallor.* ○ *His face was a ghastly white.* ▷ **ghastliness** *n* [U].

ghat (also **ghaut**) /gɑːt/ *n* **1** (in India) flight of steps leading down to a landing-place on a river bank or lakeside. **2** (also **burning ˈghat**) (usu *pl*) level area at the top of a river ghat on which Hindus cremate their dead. **3** mountain pass in India.

ghee /giː/ *n* [U] purified semi-liquid butter used in Indian cooking.

gherkin /ˈgɜːkɪn/ *n* small green cucumber for pickling.

ghetto /ˈgetəʊ/ *n* (*pl* ~**s**) **1** (formerly in some countries) Jewish quarter of a town. **2** (*often derog*) area of a town lived in by any minority national or social group, typically crowded and with poor housing conditions: *the clearance of slum ghettos to make way for new housing developments* ○ *a rich people's ghetto*, ie an area in a town where rich people live, surrounded by poorer people.

▷ **ghettoize, -ise** *v* [Tn] (*derog*) put (sb/sth) into a separate limited category, artificially cut off from others. **ghettoization, -isation** /ˌgetəʊaɪˈzeɪʃn; *US* -əʊɪˈz-/ *n* [U].

□ **ˈghetto blaster** (*infml*) large and powerful portable radio and cassette player.

ghost /gəʊst/ *n* **1** spirit of a dead person appearing to sb who is still living: *The ghost of Lady Margaret is supposed to haunt this chapel.* ○ *I don't believe in ghosts*, ie don't believe that they exist. ○ *He looked as if he had seen a ghost*, ie looked very frightened. **2** [sing] ~ **of sth** (*fig*) very faint, slight amount or trace of sth: *The ghost of a smile* (ie A very faint smile) *played round her lips.* ○ *You haven't a ghost of a chance*, ie You have no chance. **3** faint secondary image on a television screen. **4** (idm) **give up the ˈghost** (**a**) die. (**b**) (*joc*) fail to work or to make an effort: *The car seems to have given up the ghost.* **lay a ˈghost** (**a**) exorcise an evil spirit: *The ghost has been laid and will not return to haunt you again.* (**b**) (*infml*) finally overcome a previous failure which seemed impossible to recover from: *Her gold-medal victory laid the ghost of her shock defeat in the European Championships.*

▷ **ghost** *v* [Ipr, Tn] ~ (**for**) **sb** act as a ghost-writer for sb: *He ghosts for a number of sports personalities who 'write' newspaper columns.* ○ *her ghosted memoirs*, ie written by someone else.

ghostly /ˈgəʊstlɪ/ *adj* (**-ier**, **-iest**) of or being a ghost; like a ghost in appearance or sound: *a ghostly voice whispering in sb's ear* ○ *ghostly shapes of bats flitting about in the dark.*

ghostliness *n* [U]: *the ghostliness of the ship's outline.*

□ **ˈghost story** story about ghosts, intended to frighten the reader.

ˈghost town town whose former inhabitants have all left.

ˈghost-write *v* [I, Ipr, Tn esp passive] ~ **sth** (**for sb**) write (material) for sb else and allow him/her to publish it under his own name: *a ghost-written newspaper column.* **ˈghost-writer** *n* person who does this.

ghoul /guːl/ *n* **1** (in stories) spirit that robs graves and feeds on the corpses in them. **2** (*derog*) person with an unnaturally strong interest in death, disaster and other unpleasant things: *these ghouls who come and stare at road accidents.*

▷ **ghoulish** /ˈguːlɪʃ/ *adj* of or like a ghoul; very unpleasant; gruesome: *ghoulish behaviour, laughter, stories.*

GHQ /ˌdʒiː eɪtʃ ˈkjuː/ *abbr* General Headquarters: *orders received from GHQ.*

GI /ˌdʒiː ˈaɪ/ *n* enlisted soldier of the US army.

□ **ˌGI ˈbride** foreign woman who marries a US soldier on duty abroad.

the Cerne Giant

giant /ˈdʒaɪənt/ *n* **1** (in fairy-tales and myths) person of human shape but enormous size and strength.

In children's stories, like *Jack and the Beanstalk*, giants are often cruel, stupid and fond of eating children. Various places in the British Isles are associated with giants in folklore. St Michael's Mount in Cornwall is said to be the home of the Cornish giant, and the Cerne Giant is a well-known figure cut in a Dorset hillside. There are also many natural formations in other parts of the British Isles which have names like *Giant's Causeway, Giant's Grave, Giant's Chair and Giant's Hill. ⇨ illus.

2 unusually large person, animal, plant, business organization, etc: *His son is a giant of 6 feet already.* ○ *He's the giant of* (ie the tallest person in) *the family.* ○ *What a giant of a tree!* ○ *the multinational oil giants* ○ [attrib] *a giant cabbage* ○ *a cabbage of giant size.* **3** (*fig*) person of unusually great ability or genius: *Shakespeare is a giant among poets/the giant of poets.*

▷ **giantess** /ˈdʒaɪəntes/ *n* female giant.

□ **ˈgiant-killer** *n* person who defeats an apparently much stronger opponent: *The local giant-killers are hoping to play another first division team in the next round.*

ˌgiant ˈpanda = PANDA.

the ˌ**Giant's ˈCauseway** formation of six-sided basalt columns, reaching out into the sea from the coast of Antrim in Northern Ireland. According to legend, this was one end of a road built by a giant that led across to the Hebridean island of Staffa, where there is a similar formation.

ˈ**giant-size** (also ˈ**giant-sized**) *adj* very large; larger than usual: *a giant-sized packet of detergent.*

gibber /ˈdʒɪbə(r)/ *v* [I, Ipr, Ip] ~ (**away/on**) (**about sth/at sb**) (**a**) (of a monkey or a frightened person) talk quickly or make meaningless sounds: *monkeys gibbering at one another in the tree-tops* ○ *He cowered in the corner, gibbering with terror.* (**b**) (*derog*) talk a lot without seeming to say anything important: *What's he gibbering away about?* ○ *a gibbering idiot.*

▷ **gibberish** /ˈdʒɪbərɪʃ/ *n* [U] meaningless sounds; unintelligible talk; nonsense: *Don't talk gibberish!*

gibbet /ˈdʒɪbɪt/ *n* **1** (*arch*) gallows. **2** upright post with a projecting arm from which in former times the bodies of executed criminals were hung.

Gibbon /ˈɡɪbən/ Edward (1737-94), English historian. His *The History of the Decline and Fall of the Roman Empire*, the most famous work of history in English, links the fall of the empire to the rise of Christianity. His style and rationalism make him one of the great figures of the English *Enlightenment.

gibbon /ˈɡɪbən/ *n* long-armed ape of south-east Asia. ⇨ illus at APE.

Gibbons[1] /ˈɡɪbənz/ Grinling (1648-1721), English sculptor. He is famous for his realistic decorative carvings, mostly in wood, eg in Saint Paul's Cathedral in London. ⇨ illus.

Gibbons[2] /ˈɡɪbənz/ Orlando (1583-1625), English composer. Most of his work was for the Anglican Church; his services and anthems are still widely used. He also produced some fine keyboard pieces and madrigals. ⇨ article at MUSIC.

gibe (also **jibe**) /dʒaɪb/ *v* [I, Ipr] ~ (**at sb/sth**) jeer at or mock sb/sth; make fun of sb/sth: *It's easy enough for you to gibe at them, but could you do any better?*

▷ **gibe** (*US* **jibe**) *n* ~ (**about/at sb/sth**) taunt; mocking remark; cruel joke: *a cruel, malicious, nasty, etc gibe* ○ *cheap gibes about her fatness.*

giblets /ˈdʒɪblɪts/ *n* [pl] edible organs (heart, liver, etc) of a bird, taken out and usu cooked separately.

Gibraltar /dʒɪˈbrɔːltə(r)/ small town at the southern tip of Spain, a British dependency, claimed by Spain; pop approx 30 000; official languages English and Spanish. It is built on a large rock on the Strait of Gibraltar, where the Mediterranean Sea flows into the Atlantic, and is an important British naval and air base. ⇨ map at SPAIN. ▷ **Gibraltarian** /ˌdʒɪbrɔːlˈteərɪən/ *n, adj.*

giddy /ˈɡɪdɪ/ *adj* (**-ier, -iest**) **1** (**a**) [usu pred] having the feeling that everything is turning round and that one is going to fall: *I feel giddy; I must sit down.* ○ *have a giddy feeling* ○ (*fig*) *giddy with their first business success.* (**b**) [usu attrib] causing such a feeling: *travel at a giddy speed* ○ *look down from a giddy height* ○ (*fig*) *Life then was a succession of giddy triumphs*, ie exciting but not stable or lasting. **2** [usu attrib] (*dated derog*) too fond of excitement and pleasure; not serious: *a giddy girl, who will never settle down to anything serious.* **3** [attrib] (*dated*) (used to add emphasis to certain exclamations): *Oh my giddy aunt!* ○ *That really is the giddy limit!*

▷ **giddily** /ˈɡɪdɪlɪ/ *adv*: *stagger giddily round the room.*

giddiness /ˈɡɪdɪnɪs/ *n* [U] giddy feeling.

Gideon Bible /ˌɡɪdɪən ˈbaɪbl/ bible placed in a hotel room, hospital ward, etc by the **Gideons**, an originally American Christian organization.

Gielgud /ˈɡiːlɡʊd/ Sir John (1904-), English actor. He became famous in his early career for his performances of Shakespeare at the *Old Vic with Laurence *Olivier, but his many film and television roles, often in comedies, have brought him wider popularity.

gift /ɡɪft/ *n* **1** thing given willingly without payment; present: *a kind, generous, small, etc gift* ○ *a birthday, Christmas, wedding, etc gift* ○ *a gift to charity* ○ *a gift of chocolates, flowers, etc.* **2** ~ (**for sth/doing sth**) natural talent or ability: *I've always been able to learn languages easily; it's a gift.* ○ *He has many outstanding gifts.* ○ *have a gift for music* ○ *the gift of making friends easily* ○ (*ironic*) *a gift for doing/saying the wrong thing.* **3** (usu *sing*) (*infml*) (**a**) unusually cheap purchase; bargain: *At that price it's an absolute gift!* (**b**) (*fig*) thing that is very easy or too easy to do: *Their second goal was a real gift.* ○ *That exam question was an absolute gift!* ○ *It was a gift of a question.* ○ [attrib] *a gift question.* **4** (idm) **a gift from the ˈgods** advantageous thing that is unearned and unexpected: *To have such an easy examination paper was a gift from the gods.* **the gift of the ˈgab** (*sometimes derog*) the ability to speak fluently and eloquently. **God's gift to sb/sth** ⇨ GOD. **in the gift of sb** which sb has the right or power to give or grant: *a post in the sovereign's gift*, ie one which the sovereign has the right to appoint a person to. **look a gift horse in the ˈmouth** (usu with negatives) refuse or criticize sth that is given to one for nothing.

▷ **gifted** /ˈɡɪftɪd/ *adj* **1** ~ (**at/in sth**) having a great deal of natural ability or talent: *a gifted artist, pianist, etc* ○ *gifted at singing, writing, etc* ○ *gifted in art, music, etc.* **2** very intelligent or talented: *gifted children.*

□ ˈ**gift box**, ˈ**gift pack** box or pack specially designed to contain a gift.

ˈ**gift shop** shop that specializes in selling articles suitable as gifts.

ˈ**gift token**, ˈ**gift voucher** token or voucher that can be exchanged in a shop for goods of a certain value.

ˈ**gift-wrap** *v* [Tn usu passive] wrap (an article) in a shop ready for presentation as a gift. ˈ**gift-wrapping** *n* [U] special paper, etc used for wrapping a gift.

gig /ɡɪɡ/ *n* **1** small light two-wheeled carriage pulled by one horse. **2** (*infml*) engagement to play jazz or pop music, esp for a single night.

gigantic /dʒaɪˈɡæntɪk/ *adj* of very great size or extent; immense: *a gigantic person, with a gigantic appetite* ○ *a problem of gigantic proportions* ○ *a gigantic effort, improvement, success, etc.* ▷ **gigantically** /dʒaɪˈɡæntɪklɪ/ *adv*: *gigantically successful.*

gigantism /dʒaɪˈɡæntɪzəm/ *n* [U] medical condition in which an imbalance of hormones causes excessive growth.

giggle /ˈɡɪɡl/ *v* [I, Ipr] ~ (**at sb/sth**) laugh lightly in a nervous or silly way: *Stop giggling, children; this is a serious matter.* ○ *giggling at one of her silly jokes.*

▷ **giggle** *n* **1** [C] laugh of this kind: *There was a giggle from the back of the class.* **2** [sing] (thing which provides) amusement: *What a giggle!* ○ *Today's lesson was a bit of a giggle.* ○ *I only did it for a giggle.* **3 the giggles** [pl] continuous uncontrolled laughter of this kind (esp by young girls): *get the giggles* ○ *She had a fit of the giggles.* **giggly** /ˈɡɪɡlɪ/ *adj* (*often derog*) **1** inclined to giggle: *a giggly schoolgirl.* **2** having the sound or quality of giggling: *giggly laughter.*

NOTE ON USAGE: **1 Snigger** (*US* **snicker**) indicates childish and disrespectful laughing at something regarded as unusual or improper: *What are you sniggering at? Haven't you seen people kissing before?* **2 Giggle** is also childish. It is often uncontrolled (a **fit of giggling/(the) giggles**) and is either in response to something silly or a nervous reaction: *The children couldn't stop giggling at the teacher's high-pitched voice.* ○ *She giggled nervously when the judges congratulated her on her costume.*

gigolo /ˈʒɪɡələʊ/ *n* (*pl* ~**s**) **1** professional male dancing partner who may be hired by wealthy women. **2** (*derog*) paid male companion or lover of a wealthy older woman.

Gila /ˈhiːlə/ *n* (also ˈ**Gila monster**) large poisonous lizard found in the south-western USA.

Gilbert /ˈɡilbət/ Sir William Schwenk (1836-1911), English comic dramatist. He is most famous for the 14 comic operas he wrote with the composer Sir Arthur *Sullivan (including *The Mikado*, *The Gondoliers* and *HMS Pinafore*). They show his gift for absurd humour combined with gentle satire of British social conventions. 'Gilbert and Sullivan' is still popular and regularly performed in Britain, often by amateurs. ⇨ article at MUSIC.

▷ **Gilbertian** /ɡɪlˈbɜːtɪən/ *adj* absurd and complicated, like a situation in one of Gilbert's comedies.

gild /ɡɪld/ *v* [Tn] **1** cover (sth) with gold-leaf(3) or gold-coloured paint: *gild a picture-frame.* **2** (*fig rhet*) make (sth) bright as if with gold: *white walls of houses gilded by the morning sun.* **3** (idm) **gild the ˈlily** try to improve what is already satisfactory. **gild the ˈpill** make (sth) unpleasant but necessary seem attractive.

▷ **gilded** *adj* [attrib] wealthy and of the upper-classes: *the gilded youth* (ie young people) *of the Edwardian era.*

gilder /ˈɡɪldə(r)/ *n* person who gilds things.

gilding /ˈɡɪldɪŋ/ *n* [U] **1** applying of gilt to sth. **2** material with which things are gilded; surface made by such material.

gill[1] /ɡɪl/ *n* (usu *pl*) **1** opening on the side of a fish's head through which it breathes. ⇨ illus at FISH. **2** any of the thin vertical sheets on the underside of a mushroom. ⇨ illus at FUNGUS. **3** (*infml joc*) area of skin under a person's ears and jaw: *be/go green/white about the gills*, ie look pale with fear or sickness.

gill[2] /dʒɪl/ *n* one quarter of a pint (liquid measure). ⇨ App 10.

gillie /ˈɡɪlɪ/ *n* man or boy attending sb shooting or fishing for sport in Scotland.

gillyflower /ˈdʒɪlɪflaʊə(r)/ *n* any of various flowers with a fragrant smell, esp the wallflower or stock[1](16).

gilt /ɡɪlt/ *n* **1** [U] gold (or sth resembling gold) applied to a surface in a thin layer: [attrib] *a gilt brooch.* **2 gilts** [pl] (*finance*) gilt-edged securities. **3** (idm) **take the gilt off the ˈgingerbread** do or be sth which makes a situation or achievement less attractive or worthwhile.

□ ˌ**gilt-ˈedged** *adj* (*finance*) not risky; secure: *ˌgilt-edged seˈcurities/ˈshares/ˈstock*, ie investments that are considered safe and sure to produce interest.

gimbals /ˈdʒɪmblz/ *n* [pl] pivoting device for keeping instruments (eg a compass) horizontal in a moving ship, etc.

gimcrack /ˈdʒɪmkræk/ *adj* [attrib] worthless; flimsy; badly made: *gimcrack ornaments.*

gimlet /ˈɡɪmlɪt/ *n* small T-shaped tool for boring a screw hole in a piece of wood: (*fig*) *eyes like gimlets*, ie sharp eyes which seem to penetrate with their look.

gimmick /ˈɡɪmɪk/ *n* (*often derog*) unusual, amusing, etc thing whose only purpose is to attract attention, and which has little or no value or importance of its own: *a promotional/publicity/sales gimmick* ○ *a flashy expensive car with all sorts of gimmicks like self-winding windows.*

▷ **gimmickry** /ˈɡɪmɪkrɪ/ *n* [U] (*derog*) (use of) gimmicks: *There is too much advertising gimmickry.*

gimmicky /ˈɡɪmɪkɪ/ *adj.*

gin[1] /dʒɪn/ *n* **1** trap or snare for catching animals. **2** (also **cotton gin**) machine for separating raw cotton from its seeds.

gin[2] /dʒɪn/ *n* [U, C] colourless alcoholic drink distilled from grain or malt and flavoured with juniper berries, often used in cocktails: *pink gin*, ie with angostura ○ *I'll have a gin and tonic*, ie with tonic water. ⇨ article at DRINK.

□ ˈ**gin palace** (*infml derog*) showily decorated place serving alcohol, esp a pub: (*fig*) *floating gin palaces*, ie cabin-cruisers used by rich people for parties, etc.

gin ˈ**rummy** type of rummy (a card-game) for two players.

ginger /ˈdʒɪndʒə(r)/ *n* [U] **1** (plant with a) hot-tasting spicy root used as a flavouring: *crystallized ginger* ○ *ground, root, stem ginger.*

2 liveliness; spirit; energy: *The football team needs a bit more ginger in it.* 3 light reddish-yellow colour: *His hair was a bright shade of ginger.*
▷ **ginger** *adj* 1 [attrib] flavoured with ginger: *ginger cake.* 2 of the colour ginger: *ginger hair, whiskers, eyebrows, etc* ○ *a ginger cat.*
ginger *v* (phr v) **ginger sb/sth up** make sb/sth more vigorous or lively: *Some dancing would ginger up the party.* ○ *The Prime Minister appointed some new ministers to ginger up her administration.*
gingery /ˈdʒɪndʒərɪ/ *adj* (somewhat) like ginger: *a gingery flavour* ○ *a gingery colour.*
□ **ginger-ˈale, ginger-ˈbeer** *ns* [U] types of non-alcoholic fizzy drink flavoured with ginger.
ˈ**gingerbread** *n* [U] 1 ginger-flavoured treacle cake or biscuit. 2 (idm) **take the gilt off the gingerbread** ⇨ GILT.
ˈ**ginger group** group within a larger group (esp in a political party) urging a more active or livelier policy.
ˈ**ginger-nut**, ˈ**ginger-snap** *ns* types of ginger-flavoured biscuit.

gingerly /ˈdʒɪndʒəlɪ/ *adv* with great care and caution to avoid causing harm or making a noise: *Gingerly he opened the door of the rat's cage.*
▷ **gingerly** *adj* cautious: *She sat down in a gingerly manner.*

gingham /ˈgɪŋəm/ *n* [U] cotton or linen cloth with a striped or check pattern: [attrib] *a gingham dress.*

gingivitis /ˌdʒɪndʒɪˈvaɪtɪs/ *n* [U] (*medical*) inflammation of the gums.

Ginsberg /ˈgɪnzbɜːg/ Allen (1926-), American poet, one of the most important figures of the *Beat generation. In his poems he rejects conventional American life and culture, and appeals for individual freedom.

ginseng /ˈdʒɪnseŋ/ *n* [U] (plant with a) sweet-smelling root used esp in alternative medicine.

Giorgione /ˌdʒɔːˈdʒəʊnɪ/ (c 1478-1510), Italian painter. A major figure in the *Renaissance in Venice, he is said to have introduced a new method of painting, without first making drawings of his subjects. Many pictures copying his style were produced by lesser artists after his death, but few of his own have survived. *Titian was one of his pupils.

Giotto /ˈdʒɒtəʊ/ *n* (c 1267-1337), Italian painter. Working chiefly in Florence, he moved away from stylized stereotypes towards a new realism in painting, using a three-dimensional technique for the first time. Among his most famous works are the frescos in the Arena chapel in Padua.

gippy tummy /ˌdʒɪpɪ ˈtʌmɪ/ (*infml*) diarrhoea suffered by tourists, etc visiting hot countries.

gipsy *n* = GYPSY.

giraffe /dʒɪˈrɑːf; *US* dʒəˈræf/ *n* (*pl* unchanged or ∼**s**) African animal with a very long neck and legs and dark patches on its coat.

gird /gɜːd/ *v* (*pt, pp* **girded** or **girt** /gɜːt/) 1 [Tn, Tn·pr] ∼ **sth (with sth)** (*arch*) surround sth: *Trees girded the dark lake.* ○ *a sea-girt island.* 2 [Tn·pr] ∼ **sb (with sth)** (*arch*) clothe sb: *He girded himself with armour for the battle.* 3 (idm) **gird (up) one's ˈloins** (*rhet or joc*) prepare for action. 4 (phr v) **gird sth on** (*arch*) fasten sth on, esp with a belt: *He girded on his sword.*

girder /ˈgɜːdə(r)/ *n* long strong iron or steel beam used for building bridges and the framework of large buildings.

girdle[1] /ˈgɜːdl/ *n* 1 cord or belt fastened round the waist to keep clothes in position. 2 (*rhet*) thing that surrounds sth else: *a girdle of green fields round a town.* 3 (*anatomy*) connected ring of bones in the body: *the pelvic girdle.* 4 (*dated*) corset.
▷ **girdle** *v* [Tn, Tn·pr, Tn·p] ∼ **sth (about/around) (with sth)** (*rhet*) surround sth: *a village girdled with green fields* ○ *an island girdled about by deep blue water.*

girdle[2] /ˈgɜːdl/ *n* (*Scot*) = GRIDDLE.

girl /gɜːl/ *n* 1 [C] (a) female child: *a baby girl* ○ *a little girl of six (years old)* ○ *Good morning, girls and boys!* (b) daughter: *Their eldest girl's getting married.* 2 [C] (a) young, usu unmarried, woman: *a girl in her teens or early twenties* ○ *He was eighteen before he started going out with girls.* (b) woman of the specified type: *She's the new girl in the office, so give her any help she needs.* ○ *the old girl who owns the sweet shop* ○ *I'm a career girl*, ie I concentrate on my career rather than getting married, etc. 3 [C] (usu in compounds) female worker: *an office-girl, a shop-girl, a telephone-girl, etc.* 4 (man's) girl-friend: *taking his girl home to meet his parents.* 5 **girls** [pl] (*infml often joc*) (used for addressing a group of women of any age, by market-salesman, popular entertainers, etc). 6 **the girls** [pl] female friends of any age: *a night out with the girls.* 7 (idm) **the golden boy/girl of sth** ⇨ GOLDEN.
▷ **girlhood** /ˈgɜːlhʊd/ *n* [U] state or time of being a girl: *She spent her girlhood in Africa.* ○ [attrib] *my girlhood ambitions.*
girlie (also **girly**) /ˈgɜːlɪ/ *adj* [attrib] (*often derog*) containing erotic pictures of young women: *girlie magazines, calendars, etc.*
girlish /ˈgɜːlɪʃ/ *adj* of, for or like a young girl: *girlish games, behaviour, laughter.* **girlishly** /ˈgɜːlɪʃlɪ/ *adv.*
□ **girl ˈFriday** young woman with a wide range of office duties.
ˈ**girl-friend** *n* female companion, esp a man's regular (and possibly sexual) partner.
Girl ˈGuide (*Brit* also **Guide**, *US* **Girl ˈScout**) member of an organization for girls (equivalent to the Boy Scouts) which aims to develop practical skills, self-reliance and helpfulness. Cf SCOUT 2. ⇨ article at YOUTH.

giro /ˈdʒaɪrəʊ/ *n* (*pl* ∼**s**) (*commerce*) 1 [U, C] system for transferring money directly from one bank account or post-office account to another: *Money has been credited to your account by bank giro.* ○ *I'll pay by giro*, ie using the giro system. ○ *The British Post Office giro system is called the National Giro/Girobank.* ○ [attrib] *a (bank) giro credit, payment, transfer, etc* ○ *a giro account*, ie a special account for paying through the giro system ○ *a giro cheque*, ie for use with a giro account. 2 [C] (*Brit*) giro cheque, esp one issued by the government to pay social security benefit: *My giro hasn't arrived this week.*

girt *pt, pp* of GIRD.

girth /gɜːθ/ *n* 1 [U, C] (a) distance round sth of approximately cylindrical shape: *a tree 1 metre in girth/with a girth of* $1\frac{1}{2}$ *metres.* (b) waist measurement of a person: *His girth is* $1\frac{1}{2}$ *metres.* ○ *a man of enormous girth.* 2 [C] (*US* **cinch**) leather or cloth band or strap fastened tightly round the body of a horse, etc to keep the saddle in place.

gismo (also **gizmo**) /ˈgɪzməʊ/ *n* (*pl* ∼**s**) (*sl esp US*) (a) gadget: *an electronic gizmo that switches on the lights.* (b) thing whose name one does not know or has forgotten; thingummy: *Pass me that gizmo, will you?*

gist /dʒɪst/ *n* **the gist** [sing] main point or general meaning (of sth spoken or written): *get* (ie understand) *the gist of an argument, a conversation, a book.*

give[1] /gɪv/ *v* (*pt* **gave** /geɪv/, *pp* **given** /ˈgɪvn/)
► CAUSING SOMEBODY OR SOMETHING TO HAVE OR RECEIVE 1 [Dn·n, Dn·pr] ∼ **sth to sb** cause sb to receive, hold, have or own sth: *I gave each of the boys an apple.* ○ *I gave an apple to each of the boys.* ○ *Each of the boys was given an apple.* ○ *An apple was given to each of the boys.* ○ *She gave her mother the tickets/gave the tickets to her mother to look after.* ○ *Can I give you* (ie Would you like) *another slice of cake?* ○ *She was given a new heart* (ie had a heart transplant) *in an eight-hour operation.* ○ *He gave the old lady his arm* (ie allowed the old lady to lean on his arm) *as they crossed the road.* ○ *I've just been given a £2000 pay rise.* 2 (a) [Dn·n, Dn·pr] ∼ **sth to sb** cause sb to have sth as a present: *What are you giving (to) your brother for his birthday?* ○ *I'm giving all my friends books for Christmas.* ○ *Have you given the waiter a tip?* (b) [I, Ipr, Tn, Tn·pr] ∼ **(sth) to sth** contribute (money) to sth, esp a charity: *Handicapped children need your help — please give generously.* ○ *Please give generously to famine relief.* ○ *Many people regularly give money to charity.* 3 [Dn·n] allow (sb/sth) to have sth: *They gave me a week to make up my mind.* ○ (*infml*) *I give their marriage six months at the very most.* ie I think that it will last only six months. ○ *She wishes that she'd been given the chance to go to university.* ○ *She wants a job that gives her more responsibility.* ○ *What gives you the right to tell me what to do?* 4 [Tn·pr, Dn·n] ∼ **(sb) sth for sth** pay (the specified amount of money) to (sb) in order to have sth: *Do you mean to tell me you gave £1500 for that pile of scrap metal!* ○ *How much will you give me for my old car?* 5 [Tn, Dn·n, Dn·pr] ∼ **sth (to sb)** cause (sb) to have sth; provide or supply (sb) with sth: *The sun gives (us) warmth and light.* ○ *You may be called to give evidence at the trial.* ○ *She gives private lessons to supplement her income.* ○ *She gave me a lift as far as the station.* ○ *He gives the impression of not caring a damn.* ○ *Could you give me your honest opinion of the book?* ○ *What gave you the idea that I didn't like you?* ○ *They gave the name Roland to their first child.* 6 [Tn, Dn·n, Dn·pr] ∼ **sth to sb/sth** devote (time, thought, etc) to sb/sth: *I've given the matter a lot of thought/given a lot of thought to the matter.* ○ *The government should give top priority to rebuilding the inner cities.*

► CAUSING SOMEBODY TO SUFFER 7 [Dn·n, Dn·pr] ∼ **sth to sb** cause sb to undergo (the specified punishment, esp a period of time in prison): *The judge gave him a nine-month suspended sentence.* ○ *The headmaster gave the boys a scolding.* 8 [Dn·n, Dn·pr] ∼ **sth to sb** infect sb with (an illness): *You've given me your cold/given your cold to me.*

► COMMUNICATING 9 [Dn·n] (used in the imperative) offer (sth) to sb as an excuse or explanation: *Don't give me that rubbish about having a headache; I know you don't want to go to the party.* 10 [Dn·n] make (a telephone call) to sb: *I'll give you a ring tomorrow.* 11 [Dn·n] admit the truth of (sth) to sb; grant: *This government has a good record on inflation, I give you that, but what is it doing about unemployment?*

► PERFORMING OR PROVIDING 12 [Tn] perform or present (a play, concert, etc) in public: *give a poetry reading, a song recital, etc* ○ *How many performances of the play are you giving?* ○ *The play was given its first performance in June 1923.* ○ *The Prime Minister will be giving a press conference tomorrow morning.* 13 [Tn] provide (a meal, party, etc) as a host: *I'm giving a dinner party next Friday evening; would you like to come?* 14 [Tn] carry out or perform (an action): *She gave a shrug of her shoulders.* ○ *He gave a start and woke up suddenly.* 15 [Dn·n] perform (the specified action) on (sb/sth): *give sb a kick, push, shove, etc* ○ *give sb a punch on the nose* ○ *She gave him a kiss.* ○ *Do give your shoes a polish before you go out.*

► UTTERING OR DECLARING 16 [Tn] utter (the specified sound): *give a groan, laugh, sigh, yell, etc* ○ *He gave a strangled cry and fell to the floor.* 17 [Dn·n] (used in the imperative) ask (people) to drink a toast to (sb): *Ladies and gentlemen, I give you his Royal Highness, the Prince of Wales.* 18 [Cn·a] (esp of a referee, an umpire, etc in sport) declare that (sb/sth) is in the specified condition or position: *The umpire gave the batsman out (leg before wicket).*

► OTHER MEANINGS 19 [Dn·n] produce (the specified feeling) in (sb): *All that heavy lifting has given me a pain in the back.* ○ *Why don't you go for a walk? It'll give you an appetite for your lunch.* 20 [I] bend or stretch under pressure: *The branch began to give under his weight.* ○ (*fig*) *Unless one side gives, the strike could go on until Christmas.* 21 (combines with a *n* in many fixed expressions where *give* and the *n* together have the same meaning as a *v* related in form to the *n*, eg *give sb a surprise = surprise sb) Let me give you a piece of advice*, ie advise you. ○ *Her acting has given pleasure to* (ie pleased) *millions (of people).* ○ *The news gave us rather a shock*, ie rather shocked us. ○ *I trust that you can give an explanation for* (ie explain) *your extraordinary behaviour?* ○ *We will give you all the help* (ie help you in every way) *we can.* (For other similar expressions, see entries for the *ns*, eg *give one's approval to sth* ⇨ APPROVAL; *give one's permission* ⇨ PERMISSION.)

22 (idm) **sb doesn't/couldn't give a damn, a hoot, etc (about sb/sth)** (*infml*) sb does not care at all (about sb/sth): *He couldn't give a damn whether he passes the exam or not.* **ˌgive and ˈtake** be mutually tolerant and forgiving within a relationship: *For a marriage to succeed, both partners must learn to give and take.* **ˈgive it to sb** (*infml*) attack, criticize or rebuke sb severely: *The boss will really give it to you if you miss the deadline for the job.* **give me sth/sb** (*infml*) (used to show that one prefers the thing or person specified to sth/sb mentioned previously): *I can't stand modern music; give me Bach and Mozart every time!* ie I shall always prefer Bach and Mozart. **give or take sth** the specified amount, time, etc more or less: *'How long will it take us to get to Oxford?' 'About an hour and a half, give or take a few minutes.'* **give sb to believe/understand (that)...** (often passive); (*fml*) cause sb to believe/understand sth: *I was given to understand that she was ill.* **What ˈgives?** (*infml*) What is happening? (For other idioms containing **give**, see entries for *ns*, *adjs*, etc, eg **give ground** ⇨ GROUND[1]; **give rise to sth** ⇨ RISE[1].)

23 (phr v) **give sb away** (in a marriage ceremony) lead the bride to the bridegroom and 'give' her to him: *The bride was given away by her father.* **give sth away** (a) give sth free of charge: *He gave away most of his money to charity.* ○ (*infml*) *These watches are only a pound each; we're almost giving them away!* (b) distribute or present sth: *The mayor gave away the prizes at the school sports day.* (c) not use or take (a chance, an opportunity, etc) through carelessness: *They gave away their last chance of winning the match.* **give sth/sb away** reveal sth/sb intentionally or unintentionally; betray sth/sb: *She gave away state secrets to the enemy.* ○ *His broad Liverpool accent gave him away*, ie revealed who he really was.

give sb back sth; give sth back (to sb) (a) return sth to its owner: *Could you give me back my pen/give me my pen back?* (b) allow sb to have or enjoy sth again: *The operation gave him back the use of his legs.*

give sth for sth exchange or sacrifice (much) for sth: *I'd give a lot for the chance to go to India.*

give sth forth (*fml or joc*) produce or emit sth: *The engine gave forth a grinding noise, then stopped.*

give sth in hand over sth to sb who is authorized to receive it: *Please give your examination papers in (to the teacher) when you've finished.* **give ˈin (to sb/sth)** allow oneself to be defeated or overcome (by sb/sth): *The rebels were forced to give in.* ○ *She's a gutsy player, she never gives in.* ○ *The authorities showed no signs of giving in to the kidnapper's demands.*

give sth off send out or emit sth: *The cooker is giving off a funny smell.* ○ *This fire doesn't seem to be giving off much heat.*

give on to/onto sth have a view of sth; lead directly to sth: *The bedroom windows give onto the street.* ○ *This door gives on to the hall.*

give ˈout (a) come to an end; be exhausted: *After a month their food supplies gave out.* ○ *Her patience finally gave out.* (b) (of an engine, a motor, etc) stop working; break down: *One of the plane's engines gave out in mid-Atlantic.* **give sth out** (a) distribute or hand out sth: *The teacher gave out the examination papers.* (b) send out or emit sth: *The radiator is giving out a lot of heat.* (c) (often passive) announce or broadcast sth: *The news of the President's death was given out in a radio broadcast.* ○ *It was given out that the President had been shot.*

give over (doing sth) (*infml*) (used esp in the imperative or with a verb in the *-ing* form) stop doing sth: *Give over, can't you? I can't work with you chattering away like that.* ○ *Give over complaining!* **give oneself over to sth** sink into (the specified state); devote oneself completely to sth: *After his wife's death, he seemed to give himself over to despair.* ○ *In her later years she gave herself over to writing full-time.* **give sth over to sth** (usu passive) use sth specifically for sth: *The village hall is given over to civic functions and meetings.* ○ *The period after supper was given over to games.*

give ˈup abandon an attempt to do sth: *They gave up without a fight.* ○ *She doesn't give up easily.* ○ *I give up; tell me what the answer is.* **give sb up** (a) no longer hope for or expect the arrival or recovery of sb: *There you are at last! We'd given you up.* ○ *The doctors had given her up but she made a remarkable recovery.* (b) stop having a relationship with sb: *Why don't you give him up?* **give sth up** stop doing or having sth; renounce sth: *You ought to give up smoking; I gave it up last year.* ○ *She didn't give up her job when she got married.* **give oneself/sb up (to sb)** no longer avoid or protect oneself/sb from being captured; surrender: *After a week on the run he gave himself up (to the police).* **give sth up (to sb)** hand sth over to sb else: *He had to give his passport up to the authorities.* ○ *He gave up his seat to a pregnant woman*, ie stood up to allow her to sit down. **give up on sb** (*infml*) no longer believe that sb is going to be successful; lose hope in sb.

□ **ˈgive-away** *n* (*infml*) **1** thing that is given to sb without charge. **2** look, remark, etc that unintentionally reveals a secret: *The expression on her face was a (dead) give-away.*

give[2] /gɪv/ *n* **1** [U] quality of bending or stretching under pressure; elasticity: *This rope has too much give in it.* ○ *Don't worry if the shoes seem a bit tight at first; the leather has plenty of give in it.* **2** (idm) **ˌgive and ˈtake** (a) willingness to be mutually tolerant and forgiving within a relationship: *If the dispute is to be resolved there must be some give and take.* ○ [attrib] *Marriage is a give-and-take affair.* (b) exchange: *the lively give and take of ideas*, ie willingness to make concessions or compromises.

given /ˈgɪvn/ *adj* **1** [esp attrib] specified or stated: *all the people in a given area* ○ *They were to meet at a given time and place.* **2** (idm) **be given to sth/doing sth** be in the habit of doing sth: *She's much given to outbursts of temper.* ○ *He's given to going for long walks on his own.*

▷ **given** *prep* taking (sth) into account: *Given the government's record on unemployment, their chances of winning the election look poor.* ○ *Given her interest in children/Given that she is interested in children, I am sure teaching is the right career for her.*

□ **ˈgiven name** (*esp US*) = CHRISTIAN NAME (CHRISTIAN). ⇨ Usage at NAME[1].

giver /ˈgɪvə(r)/ *n* one who gives: *a cheerful, generous, regular giver.*

gizzard /ˈgɪzəd/ *n* pouchlike part in which a bird grinds up food before digesting it in its stomach.

glacé /ˈglæseɪ; US glæˈseɪ/ *adj* [attrib] (of fruits) preserved in sugar.

□ **ˌglacé ˈicing** icing made from icing sugar mixed with water, often coloured and used on cakes. Cf ROYAL ICING (ROYAL).

glacial /ˈgleɪsɪəl; US ˈgleɪʃl/ *adj* **1** (*geology*) (a) of the Ice Age: *glacial phases*, ie between which the earth's climate became slightly warmer. (b) caused by glaciers: *glacial deposits*, ie rocks deposited by a moving glacier ○ *glacial flow*, ie movement of a glacier. **2** very cold; like ice: *glacial winds, temperatures, etc* ○ *the glacial waters of the Arctic.* **3** (*fig*) icy in manner; showing no sign of human emotion: *a glacial smile, manner, silence* ○ *glacial indifference, politeness.* ▷ **glacially** *adv.*

□ **ˈglacial period** (also **glacial epoch**) time in the earth's history when the polar ice-caps and the sheets of ice on mountains extended to cover large parts of the earth's surface. The last glacial period was about 18 000 years ago when there was ice over much of Europe, N America and Asia, and the seas were up to 200 metres lower than they are today. The causes of such periods are not properly understood. One theory is that they were brought on by slight variations in the brightness of the sun.

glaciation /ˌgleɪsɪˈeɪʃn/ *n* [U] (*geology*) covering with glaciers or sheets of ice: *the effects of glaciation.*

glacier /ˈglæsɪə(r)/ *n* mass of ice, formed by snow on mountains, moving slowly down a valley.

glaciology /ˌgleɪsɪˈɒlədʒɪ; US ˌgleɪʃiːˈɒlədʒɪ/ *n* [U] scientific study of ice, esp of the effects of glaciers on the earth's surface.

glad /glæd/ *adj* (**-dder, -ddest**) **1** [pred] (a) ~ (**about sth/to do sth/that...**) pleased; delighted: *'I passed the test.' 'I'm so glad!'* ○ *I'm glad about your passing the test.* ○ *I'm glad to hear he's feeling better.* ○ *I'm glad he's feeling better.* (b) ~ (**about/of sth**); ~ (**to do sth/that...**) relieved: *I'm so glad I didn't agree to do it; it would have got me into serious trouble.* (c) ~ **of sth** grateful for sth: *I'd be glad of* (ie I'd like) *your help/a cup of tea.* (d) ~ **to do sth** willing and eager to do sth: *I'd be glad to lend you the money.* ○ *If you'd like me to help you, I'd be only too glad to.* **2** [attrib] (a) causing or bringing joy: *glad news/tidings* ○ *a glad day, moment, etc.* (b) (*rhet*) expressing joy: *the children's glad laughter.* **3** (idm) **give sb/get the glad ˈhand** (*infml often derog*) treat sb/be treated warmly and enthusiastically, but often insincerely: *I get the glad hand now she wants my support.* **ˈglad rags** (*infml*) clothes for a festive occasion: *put on one's glad rags.* **I would be glad if...** (*ironic*) (used instead of a direct command): *I'd be glad if you would go away!* ie Go away!

▷ **gladden** /ˈglædn/ *v* [Tn] make (sb) glad or happy: *gladden sb's heart*, ie make sb feel happy.

gladly *adv* **1** happily; gratefully: *She suggested it, and I gladly accepted.* **2** willingly: *I wouldn't gladly go through that unpleasant experience again.* **3** (idm) **not/never suffer fools gladly** ⇨ SUFFER.

gladness *n* [U] joy; happiness.

gladsome /-səm/ *adj* (*arch*) joyful.

□ **ˌglad-ˈhand** *v* [Tn] (*infml often derog*) greet (sb) enthusiastically but often insincerely.

glade /gleɪd/ *n* open space in a forest; clearing.

gladiator /ˈglædɪeɪtə(r)/ *n* (in ancient Rome) man trained to fight with weapons at public shows in an arena.

▷ **gladiatorial** /ˌglædɪəˈtɔːrɪəl/ *adj* of gladiators: *a gladiatorial combat, show, etc.*

gladiolus /ˌglædɪˈəʊləs/ *n* (*pl* **-li** /-laɪ/ or ~**es**) plant with long thin pointed leaves and spikes of brightly-coloured flowers.

Gladstone /ˈglædstən/ William Ewart (1809-98), British statesman. After leaving the Conservatives, he helped to form the Liberal Party, becoming its leader in 1867. With his great rival *Disraeli he dominated politics for over thirty years, serving four times as prime minister. He was responsible for many historic reforms: he made voting secret, gave the vote to nearly all men and made children's education compulsory. He tried hard but failed to give Home Rule (independence) to Ireland. ⇨ App 3.

□ **ˌGladstone ˈbag** type of suitcase with hinges that allow it to be opened out into two compartments.

glamour (*US* also **glamor**) /ˈglæmə(r)/ *n* [U] **1** attractive or exciting quality which sb/sth has, and which seems out of reach to others: *Now that she's an air hostess, foreign travel has lost its glamour for her.* ○ *hopeful young actors and actresses dazzled by the glamour of Hollywood.* **2** attractive beauty, usu with sex appeal: *a girl with lots of glamour* ○ [attrib] (*dated*) *a glamour girl/boy.*

▷ **glamorize, -ise** /-məraɪz/ *v* [Tn] make (sth) seem more attractive or exciting than it really is: *Television tends to glamorize acts of violence.*

glamorization, -isation /ˌglæməraɪˈzeɪʃn; US -rɪˈz-/ *n* [U].

glamorous /-mərəs/ *adj* full of glamour: *glamorous film stars.*

glamorously *adv*: *glamorously dressed.*

glance /glɑːns; US glæns/ *v* **1** [Ipr, Ip] take a quick look: *She glanced shyly at him and then lowered her eyes.* ○ *glance at one's watch* ○ *glance round a room*

○ *I glanced up to see who had come in.* **2** [Ipr] ~ **at/down/over/through sth** read sth quickly or superficially: *glance at the newspapers* ○ *glance down a list of names* ○ *glance over/through a letter.* **3** [Ipr] ~ **at sth** (*fig*) deal with sth in a superficial way; refer briefly to sth: *a book, an article, etc that only glances at a problem, question, topic, etc.* **4** [Tn, Tn·pr] (in cricket) deflect (the ball) with the bat: *glance the ball down to fine leg.* **5** [I] (used esp in the continuous tenses) (of bright objects) flash: *glancing lights* ○ *water glancing in the sunlight.* **6** (idm) **glance one's eye down/over/through sth** (*infml*) take a very quick, superficial look at sth: *glance one's eye over the newspaper.* **7** (phr v) **glance off (sth)** (of sth that strikes) be deflected off (sth): *The ball glanced off the goal-post into the net.* ○ *The tree was so hard that the blows of the axe simply glanced off.*

▷ **glance** *n* **1** ~ **(at sb/sth)** quick look: *take/have/cast a glance at the newspaper headlines* ○ *We exchanged glances,* ie looked quickly at each other. ○ *a brief, casual, fleeting, furtive, timid glance* ○ *She walked off without a glance in my direction.* ○ (*fig*) *Before the end of the programme, let's take a glance at* (ie refer briefly to) *the sports news.* **2** (idm) **at a (single) ˈglance** with one look: *He could tell at a glance what was wrong with the car.* **at first glance/sight** when seen or examined (often quickly) for the first time: *At first glance the problem seemed easy.* ○ *They fell in love at first sight.*

glancing /ˈglɑːnsɪŋ/ *adj* [attrib] that is deflected rather than striking with full force: *strike sb a glancing blow.*

gland /glænd/ *n* (*anatomy*) organ that separates from the blood those substances that are to be used by or removed from the body: *a snake's poison glands* ○ *sweat glands* ○ *suffer from swollen glands,* eg the salivary glands in the oral cavity ○ *have an overactive/underactive adrenal, pituitary, thyroid, etc gland.*

▷ **glandular** /ˈglændjʊlə(r); *US* -dʒʊ-/ *adj* of, like or involving a gland or glands. **glandular fever** infectious disease causing swelling of the lymph glands.

glanders /ˈglændəz/ *n* [sing *v*] contagious disease affecting horses and certain other animals.

glans /glænz/ *n* (*pl* **glandes** /ˈglændiːz/) rounded part forming the end of the penis or clitoris.

glare¹ /gleə(r)/ *n* **1** [U] strong unpleasant dazzling light: *avoid the glare of the sun, of car headlights, etc.* **2** [C] angry or fierce look; fixed look: *give sb a hostile glare.* **3** (idm) **the ˌglare of puˈblicity** constant attention from newspapers, television, etc: *The hearings were conducted in the full glare of publicity.*

glare² /gleə(r)/ *v* **1** [I, Ipr, Ip] ~ **(down)** shine with a dazzling, unpleasant light: *The searchlights glared, illuminating the prison yard.* ○ *the sun glaring (down) mercilessly from a clear sky.* **2** [I, Ipr] ~ **(at sb/sth)** stare angrily or fiercely: *He didn't shout or swear, but just glared silently at me.* **3** (idm) **glare defiance at sb/sth** stare at sb/sth with angry defiance.

▷ **glaring** /ˈgleərɪŋ/ *adj* **1** dazzling: *glaring lights.* **2** angry; fierce: *glaring eyes.* **3** [usu attrib] (*fig*) that cannot or should not be ignored; gross: *a glaring abuse, error, injustice, omission.* **glaringly** *adv.*

glasnost /ˈglæznɒst/ *n* [U] (*Russian*) (in the Soviet Union) greater openness and frankness in public affairs.

glass

glass /glɑːs; *US* glæs/ *n* **1** [U] hard brittle, usu transparent, substance (as used in windows). Glass is produced by mixing sand with soda or other substances. It was originally moulded into shape; then in the first century BC the technique of glass-blowing was developed. Plate glass was originally moulded between plates, then rolled and ground smooth. It is now produced by making it float on a large sheet of molten metal until it hardens and is perfectly flat: *cut oneself on broken glass* ○ *reinforced, toughened, frosted glass* ○ *a sheet/pane of glass* ○ *as smooth as glass* ○ [attrib] *glass jars,* ie made of glass ○ *a glass factory,* ie where glass is made. **2** [C] **(a)** (often in compounds) drinking-vessel made of glass: *a beer, brandy, sherry, whisky, etc glass* ○ *a wineglass.* ⇨ illus. **(b)** contents of this: *Could I have a glass of water, please?* **3** [U] vessels and articles made of glass: *All our glass and china is kept in the cupboard.* ○ *several areas under glass,* ie covered with glasshouses or glass-filled frames for growing plants. **4** [sing] protecting cover made of glass in a watch-case, picture or photo frame, fire alarm, etc: *In case of emergency, break the glass and press the button.* **5 glasses** (also **spectacles**, *infml* **specs**) [pl] pair of lenses in a frame that rests on the nose and ears (used to help a person's eyesight

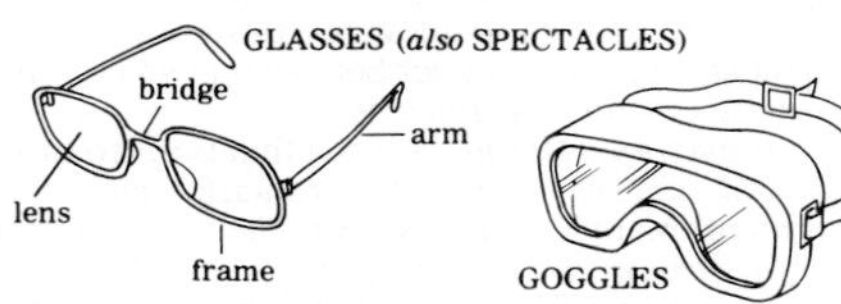

or protect the eyes from bright sunlight): *She wears glasses.* ○ *a new pair of glasses* ○ *dark, strong, reading, long-distance, etc glasses* ○ [attrib] *Where's my glasses case?* ⇨ illus. **6 glasses** (also **ˈfield-glasses**) [pl] binoculars for outdoor use. **7** [C usu *sing*] mirror; looking-glass: *He looked in the glass to check that his tie was straight.* **8 the glass** [sing] barometer: *The glass* (ie atmospheric pressure) *is falling.* **9** (idm) **raise one's glass to sb** ⇨ RAISE.

▷ **glass** *v* (phr v) **glass sth in/over** cover sth with (a roof or wall of) glass: *a glassed-in veranda.*

glassful /-fʊl/ *n* as much as a drinking-glass will hold.

□ **ˈglass-blower** *n* worker who blows molten glass to shape it into bottles, etc. **ˈglass-blowing** *n* [U]. **ˌglass ˈcase** case, usu with glass sides and a glass top, used for displaying objects, eg in a museum. **ˌglass ˈfibre** = FIBREGLASS. **ˈglasshouse** *n* **1 (a)** building with glass sides and roof, for growing plants; greenhouse. **(b)** (*Brit infml*) military prison. **2** (idm) **people in glasshouses shouldn't throw stones** ⇨ PEOPLE. **ˈglass-paper** *n* [U] paper covered with very fine particles of glass, used like sandpaper for smoothing rough surfaces. **ˈglassware** /-weə(r)/ *n* [U] articles made of glass. **ˈglassworks** *n* (*pl* unchanged) [sing or pl *v*] factory where glass is manufactured.

glassy /glɑːsɪ/ *adj* (**-ier, -iest**) **1** like glass: *a glassy sea,* ie smooth and shiny ○ *Be careful of the icy pavement; it's really glassy,* ie slippery. **2** (*fig*) with no expression; lifeless: *glassy eyes* ○ *a glassy look/stare.* ▷ **glassily** *adv.* **glassiness** *n* [U].

□ **ˌglassy-ˈeyed** *adj*: *a ˌglassy-eyed ˈlook, ˈstare, etc.*

Glastonbury /ˈglæstənbrɪ/ small town in Somerset, England. According to legend, its abbey, now in ruins, was founded by Joseph of Arimathea, the rich Israelite merchant who provided a tomb for *Jesus. King *Arthur and *Guinevere are also said to be buried here.

Glaswegian /glæzˈwiːdʒn/ *n, adj* (native) of Glasgow in Scotland: *a Glaswegian accent.*

Glauber's salt /ˌglaʊbəz ˈsɔːlt/ form of sodium sulphate, used as a laxative and in glass-making.

glaucoma /glɔːˈkəʊmə/ *n* [U] eye disease causing gradual loss of sight.

glaze /gleɪz/ *v* **1** [Tn] fit sheets or panes of glass into (sth): *glaze a window, house, etc.* **2** [Tn, Tn·pr, Tn·p] ~ **sth (with sth)**; ~ **sth (over)** cover sth with a thin shiny transparent surface: *glazed pottery, porcelain, bricks, etc,* ie covered with a liquid which when baked gives a hard glass-like surface ○ *Glaze the pie with beaten egg.* **3** (phr v) **glaze over** (of the eyes) become dull and lifeless: *After six glasses of vodka his eyes glazed over and he remembered nothing more.*

▷ **glaze** *n* **(a)** [C, U] (substances used to give a) thin shiny transparent surface to pottery, porcelain, etc: *The vase was sold cheaply because of a fault in the glaze.* **(b)** [C, U] (beaten egg, sugar, etc used to give a) shiny attractive surface to a pie, flan, etc. **(c)** (*US*) thin transparent layer of ice, esp on a road surface. Cf BLACK ICE (BLACK¹).

glazed *adj* dull and lifeless, esp with expressionless eyes: *the glazed faces/expressions of the survivors* ○ *eyes glazed with boredom.*

glazier /ˈgleɪzɪə(r); *US* -ʒər/ *n* person who fits glass into the frames of windows, etc.

GLC /ˌdʒiː el ˈsiː/ *abbr* (*Brit*) (formerly) Greater London Council. ⇨ article at LONDON.

gleam /gliːm/ *n* **1 (a)** [C] brief appearance of light: *A few faint gleams of sunshine lit up the gloomy afternoon.* ○ *the sudden gleam of a match in the darkness.* **(b)** [sing] soft diffused light, usu reflected: *the gleam of moonlight on the water* ○ *the gleam of polished brassware in the firelight.* **2** [sing] (*fig*) brief show of some quality or emotion: *a serious book with an occasional gleam of humour* ○ *a gleam of hope in an apparently hopeless situation* ○ *a man with a dangerous gleam in his eye,* ie with a threatening look. **3** (idm) **a gleam in sb's eye** (*infml*) person or thing that is expected at some time in the future but is thought about with pleasure or desire: *The plans for the new town hall were then still only a gleam in the architect's eye.*

▷ **gleam** *v* **1** [I, Ipr] shine softly: *He had polished the table-top until it gleamed.* ○ *moonlight gleaming on the water* ○ *water gleaming in the moonlight* ○ *a cat's eyes gleaming in the dark* ○ (*fig*) *anticipation, excitement, etc gleaming in their eyes.* **2** [Ipr] ~ **with sth** (*fig*) (of the face or eyes) show the specified emotion: *eyes gleaming with anticipation, excitement, etc.* **gleaming** /gliːmɪŋ/ *adj*: *gleaming white teeth.*

glean /gliːn/ *v* **1** [I, Tn] gather (grain left in a field by harvest workers). **2** [Tn, Tn·pr, Tf] ~ **sth (from sb/sth)** (*fig*) obtain (news, facts, information, etc), usu from various sources, in small quantities and with effort: *glean a few bits of information from overhearing various conversations* ○ *From what people said, I managed to glean that he wasn't coming.*

▷ **gleaner** *n* person who gleans.

gleanings *n* [pl] (*usu fig*) gleaned items: *a gossip column put together with a few gleanings from cocktail-party conversations.*

glebe /gliːb/ *n* (formerly) piece of land that was given to a clergyman taking charge of a parish, and from which he could get money, eg by renting it to farmers.

glee /gliː/ *n* **1** [U] ~ **(at sth)** feeling of great delight which makes one (want to) laugh, caused by sth good experienced by oneself, or sth bad that happens to sb else: *The children laughed with glee at the clown's antics.* ○ *He rubbed his hands with glee at the prospect of their defeat.* ○ *She couldn't disguise her glee at their discomfiture.* **2** [C] song for three or four voices singing different parts in harmony: [attrib] *a glee club,* ie a group of people who sing such songs.

▷ **gleeful** /-fl/ *adj* full of glee; joyous: *gleeful faces, laughter.* **gleefully** /-fəlɪ/ *adv.*

glen /glen/ *n* narrow valley, esp in Scotland or Ireland.

Glencoe /glenˈkəʊ/ glen in the Highlands of Scotland, remembered as the scene of a massacre in 1692, when a number of men from the clan Macdonald (probably about 40) were murdered by members of the clan Campbell. The Campbells were helped by the forces of William III, who wished to defeat the *Jacobite cause supported by the Macdonalds.

Glendower /glenˈdaʊə(r)/ Owen (c 1355-c 1417), Welsh chieftain who led resistance in Wales to the English king Henry IV, and was successful enough to hold his own parliament in 1404. His rebellion failed, but he was never captured. He was the last Welshman to hold the title of Prince of Wales and is seen as a symbol of Welsh nationalism. ⇨ article at WALES.

glengarry /glenˈgærɪ/ *n* type of tartan cap with a pointed front.

gley /gleɪ/ *n* [U] blue-grey soil that occurs in waterlogged conditions.

glib /glɪb/ *adj* (**-bber**, **-bbest**) (*derog*) speaking or spoken fluently and without hesitation, but not sincerely or trustworthily: *a glib talker, salesman, etc* ○ *a glib remark, speech, etc* ○ *glib arguments, excuses, etc* ○ *have a glib tongue*. ▷ **glibly** *adv*. **glibness** *n* [U].

glide /glaɪd/ *v* [I, Ipr, Ip] **1** move along smoothly and continuously: *So graceful was the ballerina that she just seemed to glide.* ○ *skiers gliding across the snow* ○ *a snake gliding along the ground* ○ *Silently the boat glided past.* ○ *She glided by unnoticed.* ○ (*fig*) *The days just glided by.* **2** fly without engine power (either in a glider or in an aeroplane with engine failure): *The pilot managed to glide down to a safe landing.*

▷ **glide** *n* (**a**) [sing] gliding movement: *the graceful glide of a skater*. (**b**) [C] (*phonetics*) gradual change of a speech sound made by moving (esp) the tongue from one position to another: *a palatal glide*.

glider /ˈglaɪdə(r)/ *n* light aircraft that is used for gliding.

gliding *n* [U] sport of flying in gliders. Cf HANG-GLIDING (HANG[1]).

□ ˈ**glide path** line followed by an aircraft as it comes in to land, esp one indicated to the pilot by radar.

glimmer /ˈglɪmə(r)/ *v* [I] send out a weak unsteady light: *lights (faintly) glimmering in the distance.*

▷ **glimmer** *n* **1** weak faint unsteady light: *a glimmer of light through the mist.* **2** (*fig*) small sign (of sth): *a glimmer of hope* ○ *not the least glimmer of intelligence.*

glimmering /ˈglɪmərɪŋ/ *n* glimmer: *We begin to see the glimmerings of a solution to the problem.*

glimpse /glɪmps/ *n* **1** (*usu sing*) ~ (**at sth**) short look: *a quick glimpse at the newspaper headlines* ○ *One glimpse at himself in the mirror was enough.* **2** (idm) **catch sight**/**a glimpse of sb**/**sth** ⇨ CATCH[1].

▷ **glimpse** *v* [Tn] get a quick look at (sb/sth): *glimpse someone between the half-drawn curtains.*

glint /glɪnt/ *v* [I] **1** give out small bright flashes of light: *She thought the diamond was lost until she saw something glinting on the carpet.* **2** (of sb's eyes) sparkle and indicate a particular emotion: *eyes glinting with mischief.*

▷ **glint** *n* **1** flash of light, esp as reflected from a hard shiny surface: *His eye caught the glint of a revolver among the bushes.* **2** sparkle in sb's eye indicating a particular emotion: *a glint of anger* ○ *He had a wicked glint in his eye*, ie suggesting mischievousness. ○ *before you were a glint in your father's eye*, ie before you were conceived.

glissade /glɪˈseɪd; *US* -ˈsɑːd/ *v* [I, Ipr, Ip] **1** (in mountaineering) slide on the feet down a steep slope of ice or snow (usu with the support of an ice-axe). **2** (in ballet) make a sliding step.

▷ **glissade** *n* such a slide or step.

glissando /glɪˈsændəʊ/ *n* (*pl* **-di** /-diː/ or ~**s**) (*music*) (in playing an instrument or singing) effect of sliding quickly up or down a scale, without separating the notes: *a series of glittering glissandi on the piano.*

glisten /ˈglɪsn/ *v* [I, Ipr] ~ (**with sth**) (esp of wet or polished surfaces) shine brightly; sparkle: *dew-drops glistening in the grass* ○ *grass glistening with dew-drops* ○ *eyes, faces, bodies, etc glistening with tears, sweat, oil.*

glitch /glɪtʃ/ *n* (*infml*) sudden irregularity in the working of machinery, electronic equipment, etc: *The space launch has been delayed by an unidentified glitch.*

glitter /ˈglɪtə(r)/ *v* **1** [I, Ipr] ~ (**with sth**) shine brightly with little sharp flashes of light; sparkle: *stars glittering in the frosty sky* ○ *a necklace glittering with diamonds.* **2** (idm) ˌ**all that** ˌ**glitters is not** ˈ**gold** (*saying*) what looks good on the outside may not really be so.

▷ **glitter** *n* [U] **1** brilliant, sparkling light: *the glitter of decorations on a Christmas tree.* **2** (*fig*) (superficial) attractiveness: *the glitter of a show-business career.*

glitterati /ˌglɪtəˈrɑːtɪ/ *n* [pl] (*sl*) fashionable people.

glittering /ˈglɪtərɪŋ/ *adj* (**a**) sparkling. (**b**) (*fig*) spectacularly excellent, opulent or successful: *a glittering occasion attended by the whole of high society* ○ *the glittering prizes*, ie things most desired in life ○ *A glittering career had been predicted for her in the Civil Service.*

glittery /ˈglɪtərɪ/ *adj* glittering: *little glittery eyes* ○ *a glittery occasion.*

glitz /glɪts/ *n* [U] (*sl*) showy glamour; glitter(2). ▷ **glitzy** *adj*: *The film star's wedding was a glitzy affair.*

gloaming /ˈgləʊmɪŋ/ *n* **the gloaming** [sing] (*arch*) twilight.

gloat /gləʊt/ *v* [I, Ipr] ~ (**about**/**over sth**) express or feel selfish delight at one's own success or good fortune or sb else's failure: *Stop gloating — just because you won the game!* ○ *It's nothing to gloat about.* ○ *a miser gloating over his gold.* ▷ **gloatingly** *adv*.

global /ˈgləʊbl/ *adj* **1** covering or affecting the whole world; world-wide: *a global tour* ○ *global warfare.* **2** covering the whole of a group of items, etc: *a global definition, rule.* ▷ **globally** /-bəlɪ/ *adv*.

□ ˌ**global** ˈ**warming** increase in the temperature of the earth's atmosphere, caused by the greenhouse effect (GREEN[1]).

the globe

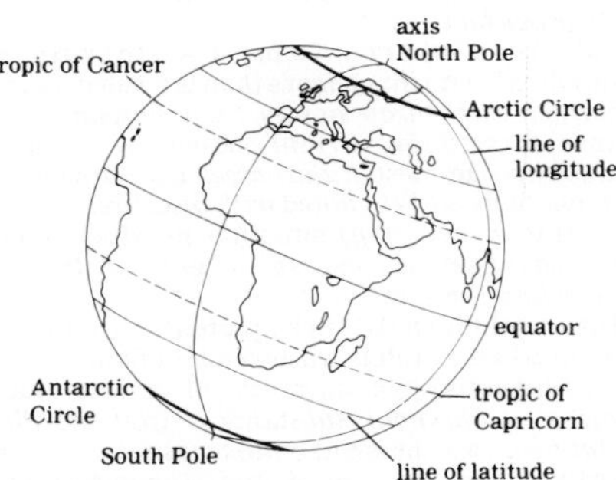

globe /gləʊb/ *n* **1** [C] small spherical model of the earth showing the continents and usu also countries, rivers, cities, etc. **2 the globe** [sing] the earth: *travel (all) round the globe.* **3** [C] thing shaped like a sphere: *The oil-lamp needs a new globe*, ie spherical lampshade. ○ *The silvery globe of the moon sank towards the horizon.*

□ **globe** ˈ**artichoke** = ARTICHOKE 1.

ˈ**globe-fish** *n* fish able to inflate itself into the shape of a globe.

ˈ**globe-trot** *v* [I] (**-tt-**) (*infml*) travel through many countries seeing as many different things as possible. ˈ**globe-trotter** *n* (*infml*) person who does this.

Globe Theatre /ˌgləʊb ˈθɪətə(r)/ **the Globe Theatre** open-air theatre built by Richard *Burbage in Southwark, London, in 1599. Many of *Shakespeare's plays were first performed there. It burned down in 1613, but was rebuilt a year later. It was closed along with all London's theatres when the English Civil War began in 1642. An exact copy of the original Globe Theatre is being built on the same site.

globule /ˈglɒbjuːl/ *n* tiny drop or ball, esp of liquid or a melted solid: *globules of wax from a candle.*

▷ **globular** /ˈglɒbjʊlə(r)/ *adj* shaped like a globe or ball; spherical.

glockenspiel /ˈglɒkənʃpiːl/ *n* musical instrument consisting of metal bars of varying length on a frame, which produce bell-like notes when struck with two light hammers.

glomerulus /glɒˈmerʊləs/ *n* (*pl* **-li** /-laɪ/) mass of blood capillaries inside one of the small tubes leaving the kidney, involved in the removal of waste products from the body.

gloom /gluːm/ *n* [U] **1** near darkness: *In the gathering gloom it was hard to see anything distinctly.* **2** feeling of sadness and hopelessness: *The news cast a deep gloom over the village.*

▷ **gloomy** /ˈgluːmɪ/ *adj* (**-ier**, **-iest**) **1** dark or unlighted, esp in a way that is depressing or frightening: *a gloomy corner, passage, room, house* ○ *a gloomy day*, ie with dark clouds and dull light. **2** (that makes people feel) sad and depressed: *a gloomy outlook, prospect, etc* ○ *What are you so gloomy about? Cheer up!* ○ *a gloomy face, expression, voice, person.* **gloomily** /-ɪlɪ/ *adv*. **gloominess** *n* [U].

gloria /ˈglɔːrɪə/ *n* (**a**) prayer or hymn praising God and beginning with the word *Gloria* (Latin for 'glory'). (**b**) musical setting of such a prayer or hymn. Cf DOXOLOGY.

glorify /ˈglɔːrɪfaɪ/ *v* (*pt*, *pp* **-fied**) [Tn] **1** (*derog*) make (sth/sb ordinary or bad) appear better or more noble than it/he really is: *a book which glorifies the horrors of war.* **2** (**a**) (*arch*) praise (sb/sth) highly; make glorious: *an ancient epic glorifying the hero's deeds in battle.* (**b**) (*Bible*) worship (sb): *glorify God.*

▷ **glorification** /ˌglɔːrɪfɪˈkeɪʃn/ *n* [U] glorifying or being glorified.

glorified *adj* [attrib] (*derog*) ordinary but described in a way that makes it seem very desirable: *a 'holiday cottage' which is only a glorified barn.*

glorious /ˈglɔːrɪəs/ *adj* **1** having, worthy of or bringing great fame or glory: *a glorious deed, victory, etc* ○ *the glorious days, years, reign, etc of Elizabeth I* ○ *die a glorious death*, ie esp in battle for one's country. **2** beautiful; splendid; magnificent: *a glorious day, sunset, view, prospect* ○ *glorious colours* ○ *It's been really glorious today*, ie warm and sunny. **3** (*infml*) very pleasant; enjoyable: *have a glorious time* ○ *What glorious fun!* **4** [attrib] (*ironic*) dreadful: *a glorious mess, muddle, etc.* ▷ **gloriously** *adv*.

□ **the** ˌ**Glorious Revo**ˈ**lution** the events that led to *James II being removed as king of Britain and replaced by his daughter Mary and her husband *William of Orange in 1688 and the subsequent constitutional changes.

the ˌ**Glorious** ˈ**Twelfth 1** (*Brit infml*) 12 August, when the season for shooting grouse begins. **2** (*sometimes offensive*) anniversary of the Battle of the *Boyne on 12 July 1690, as celebrated by Protestants in N Ireland.

glory /ˈglɔːrɪ/ *n* **1** [U] high fame and honour won by great achievements: *glory won on the field of battle* ○ *a proud father basking in his son's reflected glory*, ie sharing the fame achieved by his son ○ *Our team didn't exactly cover itself with glory today*, eg was heavily defeated. ○ *The regiment's motto was 'Death or Glory'.* **2** [U] (*Bible*) worship, adoration and thanksgiving: *'Glory to God in the highest.'* **3** [U] beauty; splendour: *the glory of a sunset, a summer's day, etc* ○ *the countryside in all its glory.* **4** [C, U] special cause for pride, respect or honour: *One of the glories of the British heritage is the right to a fair trial.* **5** (idm) **cover oneself with glory** ⇨COVER[1]. **go to** ˈ**glory** (*dated euph*) die.

▷ **glory** *v* (*pt*, *pp* **-ied**) [Ipr] ~ **in sth** (*approv or derog*) take (too much) pleasure or pride in sth: *glory in one's freedom, success, etc* ○ *military leaders who seem to glory in slaughter.*

□ ˈ**glory-hole** *n* (*Brit infml*) room, cupboard or drawer where belongings can be thrown untidily until needed.

Glos /glɒs/ *abbr* Gloucestershire.

gloss[1] /glɒs/ *n* [U, sing] **1** (**a**) brightness or shine on a smooth surface: *With this polish you can give a good high gloss to the wood.* ○ *the gloss on sb's hair.* **(b)** (often in compounds) substance (eg make-up) designed to give such a shine: ˈ*lip-gloss* ○ [attrib] *gloss paint*, ie paint which, when dry, has a hard shiny surface ○ *gloss photographs* ○ *a gloss finish*, ie a shiny surface (after painting, processing, etc). **(c)** gloss paint: *a tin of gloss.* Cf MATT. **2** *(fig)* deceptively good appearance: *acquire a pleasing social gloss*, ie attractive manners, etc ○ *the gloss and glitter of Hollywood* ○ *a gloss of respectability*, ie cover for a life of secret wrongdoing. Cf VENEER 2.

▷ **gloss** *v* (phr v) **gloss over sth** treat sth briefly, or in a superficial or an incomplete way, so as to avoid embarrassing details: *gloss over the awkward facts.*

glossy *adj* **(-ier, -iest)** smooth and shiny: *glossy hair, photographs* ○ *glossy magazines/periodicals*, ie printed on high-quality glossy paper, with many photographs, coloured illustrations, etc (esp fashion magazines). **glossily** /-ɪlɪ/ *adv.* **glossiness** *n* [U].

gloss[2] /glɒs/ *n* ~ **(on sth) 1** explanatory comment added to a text; brief definition: *a gloss on a word, phrase, etc.* **2** explanation; interpretation: *The minister has put a different gloss on recent developments in the Middle East.*

▷ **gloss** *v* [Tn] give an explanation or a brief definition of (a word); add a gloss to (a text): *a difficult word that needs to be glossed.*

glossary /ˈglɒsərɪ/ *n* list of technical or special words (esp those occurring in a particular text) explaining their meanings. Cf VOCABULARY 3.

glottis /ˈglɒtɪs/ *n (anatomy)* opening between the vocal cords in the upper part of the windpipe.

▷ **glottal** /ˈglɒtl/ *adj* of the glottis. ˌ**glottal ˈstop** speech sound produced by a complete closure of the glottis, followed by an explosive release of breath.

Gloucester /ˈglɒstə(r)/ *n* [U] type of hard cheese formerly made in the city of Gloucester, England. Cf DOUBLE GLOUCESTER (DOUBLE[1]).

Gloucestershire /ˈglɒstəʃə(r)/ *(abbr* **Glos)** county of SW England. It contains part of the *Cotswolds and extends across the river Severn to the border with Wales. ⇨ map at App 1.

gloves

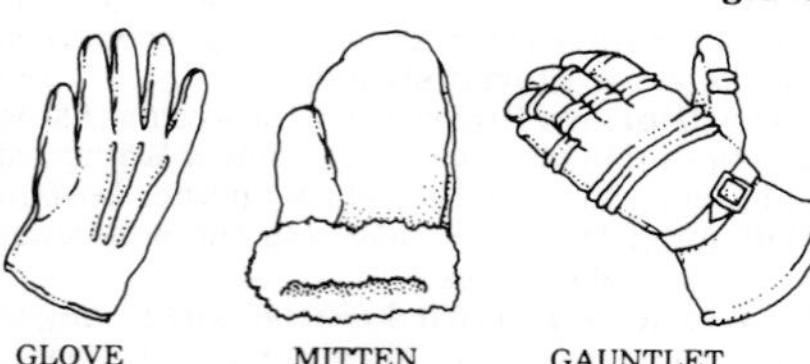

glove /glʌv/ *n* **1** covering of leather, knitted wool, etc for the hand, usu with separated fingers: *a pair of gloves* ○ *rubber gloves for washing up* ○ *strong leather gardening gloves* ○ *batting gloves.* ⇨ illus. **2** (idm) **fit like a glove** ⇨ FIT[2]. **the gloves are off** sb is ready for a fight. **hand in glove** ⇨ HAND[1]. **handle, etc sb with kid gloves** ⇨ KID[1]. **an iron fist/hand in a velvet glove** ⇨ IRON[1]. ▷ **gloved** *adj* [usu attrib]: *a gloved hand.*

□ ˈ**glove box** tightly sealed box in which there are two holes with thick gloves fixed to them, used eg for handling materials that are dangerous or that must not be contaminated by germs.

ˈ**glove compartment** compartment in a car in front of the passenger's or driver's seat for holding small articles. ⇨ illus at CAR.

ˈ**glove puppet** *(US* **hand puppet)** type of puppet worn on the hand and worked by the fingers. ⇨ illus at PUPPET.

glow /gləʊ/ *v* **1** [I] send out light and heat without flame: *glowing embers, charcoal, etc* ○ *glowing metal in a furnace* ○ *A cigarette glowed in the dark.* **2** [I, Ipr] ~ **(with sth)** be, look or feel warm or red (eg after exercise or because excited): *her glowing cheeks* ○ *glowing with health, pride, etc.* **3** [I, Ipr] ~ **(with sth)** be strongly or warmly colourful: *The countryside glowed with autumn colours.*

▷ **glow** *n* [sing] **1** dull light: *The fire cast a warm glow on the walls.* **2** warm look or feeling: *cheeks with a rosy/healthy glow.* **3** feeling of satisfaction: *the special glow you get from a truly unselfish act.*

glowing *adj* [usu attrib] giving enthusiastic praise: *a glowing account, report, etc* ○ *describe sth in glowing colours, terms, phrases, etc*, ie praise sth strongly. (idm) **paint (sth) in glowing, etc colours** ⇨ COLOUR[1]. **glowingly** *adv.*

□ ˈ**glow-worm** *n* insect of which the wingless female gives out a green light at its tail.

glower /ˈglaʊə(r)/ *v* [I, Ipr] ~ **(at sb/sth)** look in an angry or a threatening way: *He sat glowering at his opponent.* ○ *(fig) the glowering sky*, ie with dark clouds. ▷ **gloweringly** /ˈglaʊərɪŋlɪ/ *adv.*

gloxinia /glɒkˈsɪnɪə/ *n* tropical house plant with bell-shaped flowers, originally from South America.

glucose /ˈglu:kəʊs/ *n* [U] form of sugar (eg dextrose) found in fruit-juice, easily turned into energy by the human body.

glue /glu:/ *n* [U, C] thick sticky liquid used for joining things: *mend a broken cup with glue* ○ *He sticks to her like glue*, ie never leaves her. Cf ADHESIVE *n*, CEMENT 2.

▷ **glue** *v* **1** [Tn, Tn·pr, Tn·p] ~ **A (to/onto B)**; ~ **A and B (together)** stick or join a thing or things with glue: *glue wood (on)to metal* ○ *glue two pieces of wood together.* **2** (idm) **glued to sth** *(infml)* continually close to sth; unwilling to leave sth: *He's glued to the television*, ie watching it with close interest. ○ *with his ear glued to the keyhole*, ie listening hard to a conversation in another room.

gluey /ˈglu:ɪ/ *adj* sticky; like glue.

□ ˈ**glue-sniffing** *n* [U] practice of breathing in the fumes of certain types of glue for their intoxicating effect.

glum /glʌm/ *adj* **(-mmer, -mmest)** *(infml)* gloomy; sad: *glum expressions, faces, features.* ▷ **glumly** *adv*: *'Another rainy day,' he remarked glumly.* **glumness** *n* [U].

glut /glʌt/ *v* **(-tt-)** [Tn, Tn·pr] **1** ~ **sth (with sth)** supply sth with much more than is needed: *glut the market with cheap apples from abroad.* **2** ~ **oneself (with/on sth)** fill oneself (by eating too much); gorge oneself: *glut oneself with rich food, on cream buns* ○ *(fig) glutted with pleasure.*

▷ **glut** *n* (usu *sing*) situation in which supply exceeds demand; excess: *a glut of fruit, of American films, of talent.*

gluten /ˈglu:tn/ *n* [U] sticky protein substance that is left when starch is washed out of flour.

▷ **glutinous** /ˈglu:tənəs/ *adj* of or like gluten; sticky: *a glutinous substance* ○ *(fig) the film's glutinous* (ie excessive) *sentimentality.*

gluteus /ˈglu:tɪəs/ *n (pl* **-ei** /-tɪaɪ/) *(anatomy)* any of the three muscles in each buttock. ▷ **gluteal** /ˈglu:tɪəl/ *adj.*

glutton /ˈglʌtn/ *n* **1** person who eats too much: *You've eaten the whole pie, you glutton!* **2** ~ **for sth** *(infml)* person always ready for more (of sth difficult or unpleasant): *a glutton for punishment, (hard) work, etc.*

▷ **gluttonous** /ˈglʌtənəs/ *adj* very greedy for food. **gluttonously** *adv.*

gluttony /-tənɪ/ *n* [U] habit or practice of eating (and drinking) too much.

glycerine /ˈglɪsəri:n/ *(US* **glycerin** /-rɪn/) *n* [U] thick sweet colourless liquid made from fats and oils, used in medicines, toilet products and explosives.

glycogen /ˈglaɪkədʒən/ *n* molecule consisting of glucose units, occurring esp in the liver and muscles, which serves as a store of energy from carbohydrates.

Glyndebourne /ˈglaɪndbɔ:n/ estate near Lewes in Sussex, SE England, where an opera festival is held each summer. The setting is very beautiful and audiences often picnic in the grounds. ⇨ article at SEASON.

GM /ˌdʒi: ˈem/ *abbr (Brit)* George Medal: *be awarded the GM* ○ *John Green GM.*

gm (also **gr**) *abbr (pl* unchanged or **gms, grs)** gram(s); gramme(s): *10 gm.*

G-man /ˈdʒi: mæn/ *n (pl* **G-men** /ˈdʒi: men/) *(US infml)* agent of the *Federal Bureau of Investigation.

GMT /ˌdʒi: em ˈti:/ *abbr* Greenwich Mean Time. Cf BST.

gnarled /nɑ:ld/ *adj* **1** (of trees) twisted and rough; covered with knobs: *a gnarled oak, branch, trunk.* **2** (of hands or fingers) twisted, with swollen joints and rough skin; deformed: *hands gnarled with age.*

gnash /næʃ/ *v* [Tn] *(usu fig)* grind (one's teeth) together as a sign of great emotion: *I was gnashing my teeth with/in rage*, ie was extremely angry.

▷ **gnashers** *n* [pl] *(joc sl)* teeth.

gnat /næt/ *n* small two-winged fly that stings; small mosquito.

gnaw /nɔ:/ *v* **1** [Ipr, Tn] ~ **(at) sth** bite sth hard continually until it is worn away: *a dog gnawing (at) a bone* ○ *a boy gnawing his fingernails.* **2** [Ipr, Ip, Tn] ~ **(at) sb/sth** *(fig)* cause sb/sth continual distress and torment: *fear and anxiety gnawing (at) one's heart* ○ *the gnawing pains of hunger* ○ *guilt gnawing away at one's conscience.* **3** (phr v) **gnaw sth away/off** destroy sth gradually by gnawing: *Rats gnawed off the lid of the box.*

gneiss /naɪs/ *n* [U] *(geology)* coarse-grained igneous rock of quartz, feldspar and mica.

gnome /nəʊm/ *n* **1** (in stories) creature like a small human being living under the ground (often guarding treasure). **2** model of such a creature used as an ornament in a garden. **3** *(usu derog)* powerful international banker: *the gnomes of Zürich.*

gnomic /ˈnəʊmɪk/ *adj (fml)* (of a remark, etc) sounding like a proverb or saying: *gnomic utterances*, ie ones that are mysteriously brief and obscure. ▷ **gnomically** /-klɪ/ *adv.*

Gnosticism /ˈnɒstɪsɪzəm/ *n* [U] religious movement of partly pagan origin that flourished in the Christian Church in the second century AD. It attached great importance to acquiring knowledge of God and of the origin and destiny of humanity as a way of achieving spiritual grace.

▷ **Gnostic** /ˈnɒstɪk/ *n, adj* (person believing in the philosophy) of Gnosticism.

GNP /ˌdʒi: en ˈpi:/ *abbr* gross national product: *The country's GNP has risen by 10% this year.* Cf GDP.

gnu /nu:/ *n (pl* unchanged or **~s)** (also **wildebeest)** large thickset African antelope.

go[1] /gəʊ/ *v (3rd pers sing pres t* **goes** /gəʊz/, *pt* **went** /went/, *pp* **gone** /gɒn; *US* gɔ:n/). ⇨ Usage at BEEN.

► MOVEMENT (Senses 1, 2, 3, 4, 5 and 6 refer esp to movement *away from* the place where the speaker or writer is or a place where he imagines himself to be.) **1 (a)** [I, Ipr, Ip] move or travel from one place to another: *Are you going (there) by train or by plane?* ○ *She went into her room and shut the door behind her.* ○ *I have to go to London on business tomorrow.* ○ *I think you ought to go to/to go and see* (ie consult) *the doctor.* ○ *Would you go and get me a glass of water?* ○ *She has gone to see her sister this weekend.* ○ *We're going to France for our holidays this year.* ○ *She has gone to China*, ie is now in China or is on her way there. ○ *He goes to work by bus.* ○ *Go away and leave me alone!* ○ *Are you going home for Christmas?* ⇨ Usage at AND. **(b)** [I] leave one place in order to reach another; depart: *I must go/be going now.* ○ *They came at six and went at nine.* ○ *Has she gone yet?* ○ *When does the train go?* ○ *She's been gone an hour*, ie She left an hour ago. **(c)** [I, Ipr] ~ **(to sth) (with sb)** move or travel with sb to a particular place or in order to be present at an event: *I went to the cinema with Denise last night.* ○ *Dave's having a party tonight; are you going (to it)?* ○ *Who are you going with?* ○ *I'll be going with Keith.* ○ *His dog goes everywhere with him.* **2** [Ipr] ~ **to sth (a)** (usu without *a* or *the*) move or travel to (the place specified) for the purpose esp associated with it: *go to hospital*, ie for medical treatment ○ *go to prison*, ie be sent there for having committed a crime ○ *go to market*, ie to sell one's produce. **(b)** (usu without *a* or *the*) attend (a place), esp regularly: *go to church, chapel, school, college* ○ *Did you go to* (ie study at) *university?* **3** [Ipr] **(a)** ~ **for sth** (also used with the *-ing* form of a *v*) leave a place or travel to a place to take part in an activity or carry out an action: *go for a walk, swim, run, etc* ○ *Annie's not in; she's gone for a walk.* ○ *Shall we go for a drink* (ie at a pub or bar) *this evening?* ○ *go fishing, hiking, jogging, sailing, pot-holing, etc* ○ *I have to go shopping this afternoon.* **(b)** ~ **on sth** leave a place with the purpose of undertaking sth: *go on a journey, an outing, a trip, a cruise, (a) safari* ○ *Richard isn't at work this week; he's gone on holiday.* ○ *After leaving college she went on a secretarial course.* **4** [I] move or travel in the specified way or over a specified distance: *That car is going too fast.* ○ *We had gone about fifty miles when the car broke down.* ○ *We still have five miles to go*, ie until we reach our destination. **5** (used with the *-ing* form of a *v* to show that sb/sth moves in the specified way or that sb/sth is doing sth while moving): *The car went careering off* (ie careered off) *the road into a ditch.* ○ *The train went chugging* (ie chugged) *up the hill.* ○ *She went sobbing* (ie was sobbing as she went) *up the stairs.* **6** [I, Ipr] be sent or passed on: *Will this letter go by tonight's post?* ○ *Such complaints must go through the proper channels.* ○ *I want this memo to go to all departmental managers.* **7** [La, I, Ipr, Ip] ~ **(from ...) to ...** extend or lead from one place to another: *The roots of this plant go deep.* ○ (*fig*) *Differences between employers and workers go deep.* ○ *Does this road go to London?* ○ *I want a rope that will go from the top window to the ground.* ○ *Our garden goes down as far as the river.*

► POSITION **8 (a)** [I, Ipr] have as a usual or proper position; be placed: *This dictionary goes on the top shelf.* ○ *Where do you want the piano to go?* ie Where shall we put it? ○ *'Where does this teapot go?' 'In that cupboard.'* **(b)** [I, Ipr, Ip] be contained (in sth); fit (in sth): *This key won't go in (the lock).* ○ *My clothes won't all go into that tiny suitcase.* **(c)** [I, Ipr] (of a number) be contained in another number, esp without a remainder: *3 into 12 goes 4*, ie is contained in 12 four times. ○ *7 into 15 won't go/7 won't go into 15.*

► ACTIVITY **9** [I] (used with *advs*, or in questions after *how*) take place or happen in the way specified; turn out; progress: *'How did your holiday go?' 'It went (very) well.'* ○ *The election went badly for the Conservatives.* ○ *Did everything go smoothly?* ○ *The meeting went better than we had expected.* ○ *How's it going?/How are things going?* ie Is your life pleasant, enjoyable, etc at the moment? ○ *The way things are going the company will be bankrupt by the end of the year.* **10** [I] (esp in commands) start an activity: *I'll say 'One, two, three, go!' as a signal for you to start.* **11** [I] (of a machine, etc) function; work; operate: *This clock doesn't go.* ○ *Is your watch going?* ○ *This machine goes by electricity.*

► STATE **12** [La, Ln] pass into the specified condition; become: *go bald, blind, mad, pale, bankrupt* ○ *Her hair is going grey.* ○ *This milk has gone sour.* ○ *Fish soon goes bad* (ie rotten) *in hot weather.* ○ *The children went wild with excitement.* ○ *Britain went Labour* (ie changed politically by electing a Labour government) *in 1945.* ⇨ Usage at BECOME. **13** [La] be or live habitually in the specified state or manner: *She cannot bear the thought of children going hungry.* ○ *You'd better go armed*, ie carry a weapon. **14** (used with a negative past participle to show that an action does not take place): *Her absence went unnoticed*, ie was not noticed. ○ *Police are worried that many crimes go unreported*, ie are not reported to them.

► SOUND **15** [I, Ipr] ~ **like sth** (used esp in questions after *how*) (of a piece of music or writing) have a certain tune or wording: *How does that song go?* ○ *The national anthem goes like this ...* ○ *I forget how the next line goes.* ○ *The story goes that she poisoned her husband/She poisoned her husband, or so the story goes*, ie It is said that she poisoned him. **16 (a)** [Ln] make the specified sound: *The clock went 'tick-tock, tick-tock'.* ○ *The gun went 'bang'.* ○ *Cats go 'miaow.'* **(b)** [Ipr] make the specified movement: *She went like this with her hand.* **17** [I] be sounded as a signal or warning: *The whistle goes at the end of the match.* ○ *No one may leave the classroom until the bell goes.* ○ *If the fire-alarm goes, staff should assemble outside the building.*

► COMING TO AN END **18** [I] cease to exist; disappear; vanish: *Has your headache gone yet?* ○ *I rubbed hard but the stain just wouldn't go.* ○ *I left my bike outside the shop and when I came out again it had gone*, ie somebody had taken it. **19** [I] (used after *must*, *have to* or *can*) be thrown away, rejected or dismissed: *The old settee will have to go.* ○ *He's incompetent; he'll have to go.* **20** [I] get worse; be lost: *His sight is going.* ○ *Her hearing went* (ie She became deaf) *in her seventies.* ○ *His mind is going*, ie He is becoming senile. **21** [I] become damaged or stop functioning properly: *My jumper has gone* (ie has worn into holes) *at the elbows.* ○ *I was driving into town when my brakes went*, ie failed. ○ *This light bulb has gone.* ○ *Her voice has gone*, ie She cannot speak properly, eg because she has a sore throat. **22** [I] (*euph*) die: *Old Mrs Davis has gone.* **23** [I, Ipr, It] ~ **(on sth)** (of money) be spent or used up: *I don't know where the money goes!* ○ *All her earnings go on clothes.* ○ *Most of my salary goes on/in (paying) rent.* ○ *The money will go to finance a new community centre.* **24** [I, Ipr] ~ **(to sb) (for sth)** be sold: *These socks are going at £1 a pair.* ○ *The new dictionary is going well*, ie A lot of copies of it are being sold. ○ *We shan't let our house go for less than £50 000.* ○ *The antique table went to the lady in the pink hat.*

► COMMANDS **25** (used in negative commands with a *v* in the *-ing* form to tell sb not to do sth): *Don't go getting yourself into trouble!* **26** (*infml esp US*) (used in commands with a *v* in the infinitive without *to* to send sb away angrily): *Go jump in a lake!*

► OTHER MEANINGS **27** [It] contribute; help: *This all goes to prove my theory.* ○ *The latest unemployment figures go to show that government policy isn't working.* ○ *What qualities go to make a successful businessman?* **28** [I] (*infml*) (only in the continuous tenses) be available: *There simply aren't any jobs going in this area.* ○ *Is there any tea going?* ie Can I have some tea? **29** [I] (of time) pass; elapse: *Hasn't the time gone quickly?* ○ *There are only two days to go before the election*, ie It takes place in two days' time. **30** [Ipr, Ip] be willing to pay a certain amount of money for sth: *He's prepared to pay £2 500 for the car but I don't think he'll go any higher.* ○ *I'll go to £2 500 but no higher.* **31** [Tn no passive] (in the game of bridge) declare or bid: *go two spades, three no trumps, etc.* **32 (a)** (used with *to* or *into* + a *n* in many expressions to show that sb/sth has reached the state indicated by the *n*, eg *She went to sleep*, ie began to sleep; *The company has gone into liquidation*, ie become bankrupt; for similar expressions see entries for *ns*, eg **go to pot** ⇨ POT[1]). **(b)** (used with *out of* + a *n* in many expressions to show that sb/sth is no longer in the state indicated by the *n*, eg *Flared trousers have gone out of fashion*, ie are no longer fashionable; for similar expressions see entries for *ns*, eg **go out of use** ⇨ USE[2].)

33 (idm) **ˈanything goes** (*infml*) anything that sb says or does is accepted or allowed, however shocking or unconventional it may be: *Almost anything goes these days.* **as people, things, etc go** in comparison with the average person, thing, etc: *Twenty pounds for a pair of shoes isn't bad as things go nowadays*, ie considering how much shoes usually cost. **be going on (for) sth** be near to or approaching (the specified time, age or number); be getting on for sth: *It must be going on (for) midnight.* ○ *There were going on for* (ie nearly) *fifty people at the party.* ○ *He must be going on for ninety.* ○ *She's sixteen, going on seventeen.* **be going to do sth (a)** (used to show what sb is intending or planning to do in the future): *We're going to spend our holidays in Wales this year.* ○ *We're going to buy a house when we've saved enough money.* **(b)** (used to indicate sth that is about to happen or is likely to happen in the future): *I'm going to be sick.* ○ *I'm going to be twenty next month.* ○ *I'm going to tell you a story.* ○ *Look at those black clouds; there's going to be a storm.* **enough/something/sth to be going ˈon with** something that is sufficient or adequate for the time being: *'How much money do you need?' '£50 should be enough to be going on with.'* ○ *I can't lend you the whole amount now, but I can give you something to be going on with.* ○ *Here's a cup of tea to be going on with; we'll have something to eat later.* **go all ˈout for sth; go all out to ˈdo sth** make a very great effort to obtain sth or do sth: *The Labour Party are going all out for victory in/going all out to win the election.* **go and do sth** (used esp to express anger that sb has done sth foolish): *Trust him to go and mess things up!* ○ *Why did you (have to) go and upset your mother like that?* **go for ˈnothing** be wasted or in vain: *All her hard work has gone for nothing.* (phr v) **go ˈon (with you)** (used to rebuke sb gently or to express disbelief): *'How old are you?' 'I'm forty.' 'Go on with you — you don't look a day over thirty.'* **go ˈto it** (used esp in the imperative to encourage sb to do sth) give energy and time to doing sth; make a special effort to do sth: *Go to it, John! You know you can beat him.* ○ *We went to it and got the job done quickly.* **here ˈgoes/here we ˈgo** (*infml*) (used to show that one is about to do sth, esp sth new, exciting or risky): *Well, here goes — wish me luck!* **ˌhere we ˌgo aˈgain** (*infml catchphrase*) used when commenting on sth that has already been done or said too often: *Here we go again, the same old story about falling standards and lack of discipline.* **(have) a lot, plenty, not much, nothing, etc ˈgoing for one** (have) many, not many, etc advantages: *You're young, intelligent, attractive: you've got a lot going for you!* **ˌno ˈgo** (*infml*) not possible, permissible or desirable: *I tried to get him to increase my salary but it was clearly no go.* **there goes sth** (*infml*) (used to show regret that sth has been lost): *They've scored again — there go our chances of winning* (ie we are now certain to lose) *the match.* **there sb ˈgoes (again)** (*infml*) (used to show annoyance, exasperation or resignation that sth said or done before has been, or is about to be, repeated): *There you go again, prying into other people's affairs!* **to ˈgo** (*US infml*) (of cooked food sold in a restaurant or shop) to take away and eat elsewhere: *Two pizzas to go!* **what/whatever ˌsb says, ˈgoes** (*infml*) the specified person has total authority and must be obeyed: *My wife wanted the kitchen painted white, and what she says, goes.* **ˌwhere does sb ˌgo from ˈhere?** (esp of sb who is in a difficult situation) what action should sb take next (esp in order to improve the situation he is in)?: *Sales are down; redundancies are inevitable: where does the company go from here?* **ˌwho goes ˈthere?** (used by a sentry to order sb to say who he is): *Halt, who goes there?* (For other idioms containing **go**, see entries for *ns*, *adjs*, etc, eg **go bananas** ⇨ BANANA; **go haywire** ⇨ HAYWIRE.)

34 go aˈbout (a) ⇨ GO ROUND/AROUND/ABOUT. **(b)** (of a boat) change direction; tack. **go about sth** continue to do sth; keep busy with sth: *go about one's daily routine* ○ *Despite the threat of war, people went about their work as usual.* **go about sth/doing sth** start to work at sth; approach or tackle sth; set about sth: *You're not going about the job in the right way.* ○ *How should I go about finding a job?* **go about with sb** ⇨ GO ROUND/AROUND/ABOUT WITH SB.

go after sb chase or pursue sb: *He went after the burglars.* **go after sb/sth** try to get or obtain sb/sth: *He goes after* (ie tries to attract sexually) *every woman he meets.* ○ *We're both going after the same job.*

go against sb be unfavourable to sb: *The jury's verdict went against him.* ○ *The war is going against us.* **go against sb/sth** resist or oppose sb/

sth: *Don't go against your parents/your parents' wishes.* ○ *He went against the advice of his colleagues and resigned.* **go against sth** be opposed or contrary to sth; conflict with sth: *Paying for hospital treatment goes against her socialist principles.* ○ *His thinking goes against all logic.*

go aˈhead be carried out; take place: *Despite the bad weather the fête will go ahead.* ○ *The building of the new bridge will go ahead as planned.* **go aˈhead (with sth)** begin to do sth without hesitation: *'May I start now?' 'Yes, go ahead.'* ○ *The government intends to go ahead with its privatization plans.*

go aˈlong (**a**) (used esp after *as*) proceed with an activity; continue: *You may have some difficulty at first but you'll find it easier as you go along.* ○ *He made the story up as he went along.* (**b**) progress; develop: *Things are going along nicely.* **go aˈlong with sb/sth** agree with sb/sth; accept sth: *I can't go along with you on that point.* ○ *I don't go along with her views on nuclear disarmament.*

go around ⇨ GO ROUND/AROUND/ABOUT. **go around with sb** ⇨ GO ROUND/AROUND/ABOUT WITH SB.

go at sb attack sb: *They went at each other furiously.* **go at sth** make great efforts to do sth; work hard at sth: *They went at the job as if their lives depended on it.*

go aˈway (**a**) leave a place: *We're going away for a few days*, eg for a holiday. (**b**) disappear; fade: *The smell still hasn't gone away.*

go ˈback (to...) return: *The children have to go back to school next week.* ○ *This toaster is going back* (ie must be taken back) *to the shop — it doesn't work properly.* **go ˈback (to sth)** (**a**) return to an earlier point in space or time: *How far does your memory go back?* ○ *Once you have taken this decision, there will be no going back*, ie you will not be able to change your mind. ○ *Can I go back to what you said at the beginning of the meeting?* ○ *To trace the origins of the Irish problem, we have to go back over three hundred years.* **go back on sth** fail to keep (a promise); change one's mind about sth: *He never goes back on his word.* **go back to sth/doing sth** (**a**) start doing sth that one had stopped doing: *She's decided to go back to teaching.* (**b**) have existed since (a specified time) or for (a specified period): *His family goes back to the time of Queen Elizabeth I.* ○ *How far does the tradition go back?*

go beˈfore exist or happen in an earlier time: *The present crisis is more than any that have gone before.* **go before sb/sth** be presented to sb/sth for discussion, decision or judgement: *My application goes before the planning committee next week.*

go beyond sth exceed sth: *This year's sales figures go beyond all our expectations*, ie are much better than we thought they would be. ○ *The matter has gone beyond a joke*, ie has become too serious to be amusing.

go ˈby (of time) pass; elapse: *As time goes by my memory seems to get worse.* ○ *The weeks went slowly by.* **ˈgo by sth** (**a**) be guided or directed by sth: *I shall go entirely by what my solicitor says*, ie I shall follow his advice. ○ *That's a good rule to go by.* (**b**) form an opinion or a judgement from sth: *Have we enough evidence to go by?* ○ *It's not always wise to go by appearances.* ○ *If past experience is anything to go by, the plane will be late.*

go ˈdown (**a**) fall to the ground: *She tripped and went down with a bump.* (**b**) (of a ship, etc) sink: *Hundreds died when the liner went down.* (**c**) (of the sun and moon) disappear beneath the horizon; set: *We sat and watched the sun go down.* (**d**) (of food and drink) be swallowed: *This pill just won't go down*, ie I can't swallow it. ○ *A glass of wine would go down very nicely*, ie I would very much like one. (**e**) be reduced in size, level, etc: *The swelling has gone down a little.* ○ *The flood waters are going down.* (**f**) (of prices, the temperature, etc) become lower; fall: *The price of petrol is going down/Petrol is going down (in price).* (**g**) (of the wind) become less strong or violent: *We waited for the wind to go down.* (**h**) (*infml*) decrease in quality; deteriorate: *This neighbourhood has gone down a lot recently.* (**i**) (of a computer system) stop working properly; break down. **go ˈdown (from...)** leave a university (esp Oxford or Cambridge) at the end of a term or after finishing one's studies: *She went down (from Cambridge) in 1984.* **go ˈdown (in sth)** be written (in sth); be recorded or remembered (in sth): *It all goes down* (ie She writes it all) *in her notebook.* ○ *He will go down in history as a great statesman.* **go ˈdown (to sb)** be defeated by sb, esp in a match or contest: *Connors went down (to Becker) by three sets to one.* **go down (to...) (from...)** go from one place to another, esp from the north of Britain to London, or from a city or large town to a smaller place: *We're going down to London next week.* ○ *They've gone down to Brighton for a couple of days.* **go down (with sb)** (used with *advs* or in questions after *how*) (of a remark, performance, etc) be received by sb in the specified way: *Her speech went down well (with the conference).* ○ *His plays have gone down badly in America.* ○ *Rude jokes don't go down too well with* (ie are disapproved of by) *the vicar.* **go down to sth** reach or extend as far as (the specified time or period): *This volume only goes down to* (ie only deals with the period up to) *1945.* **go down with sth** become ill with (an illness): *Our youngest boy has gone down with mumps.*

go for sb attack sb: *She went for him with a carving knife.* ○ (*fig*) *The newspapers really went for him over his defence of terrorism.* **go for sb/sth** (**a**) apply to sb/sth: *What I said about Smith goes for you, too.* ○ *Britain has a high level of unemployment — but the same goes for many other countries.* (**b**) go to fetch sb/sth: *Shall I go for a doctor?* ○ *She's gone for some milk.* (**c**) be attracted by sb/sth; like or prefer sb/sth: *She goes for tall slim men.* ○ *I don't go much for modern art.* **go for sth** (**a**) choose sth: *I think I'll go for the fruit salad.* (**b**) attempt to have or achieve sth: *She's going for the world record in the high jump.*

go ˈin (**a**) (of the sun or moon) disappear behind a cloud: *The sun went in and it grew colder.* (**b**) (of a batsman in cricket) go to the wicket at the start of one's innings: *Who's going in next?* **go in for sth** (**a**) take (an examination) or take part in (a competition): *She's going in for the Cambridge First Certificate.* ○ *Which events is he going in for at the Olympics?* (**b**) choose sth as one's career: *Have you ever thought of going in for teaching?* **go in for sth/doing sth** have sth as an interest or a hobby: *go in for golf, stamp-collecting, growing orchids* ○ *She goes in for a lot of sport.*

go into sth (**a**) (of a vehicle) make (violent) contact with sth; hit sth: *The car skidded and went into a tree.* (**b**) join (an organization), esp in order to have a career in it; enter sth: *go into the Army, the Church, Parliament* ○ *go into banking, publishing, teaching, etc* ○ *When did Britain go into Europe* (ie join the EEC) *?* (**c**) (of a vehicle or driver) start the specified movement: *The lorry went into a spin on a patch of ice.* ○ *The plane went into a nosedive.* (**d**) begin to act or behave in the way specified: *He went into a long explanation of the affair.* ○ *She went into hysterics.* ○ *She went into fits/peals of laughter.* (**e**) examine or investigate sth carefully: *We need to go into the question of costs.* ○ *I don't want to go into the minor details now.* ○ *The problem will need a lot of going into.* ○ *The matter is being gone into.* (**f**) (of resources, time, etc) be spent or used to do sth: *More government money needs to go into rebuilding the inner cities.* ○ *Years of work have gone into the preparation of this dictionary.*

go ˈoff (**a**) (of an actor) leave the stage: *Hamlet goes off stage left.* (**b**) be fired; explode: *The gun went off by accident.* ○ *The bomb went off in a crowded street.* (**c**) make a sudden loud noise; be sounded: *The thieves ran away when the burglar alarm went off.* (**d**) (of electric power, a light, etc) stop functioning or operating: *Suddenly the lights went off.* ○ *The heating goes off at night.* (**e**) (*infml*) fall asleep: *Hasn't the baby gone off yet?* (**f**) become unfit to eat or drink; go bad: *This milk has gone off*, ie has turned sour. (**g**) become worse in quality; deteriorate: *Her books have gone off in recent years.* (**h**) (used with *advs* or in questions after *how*) take place or happen in the way specified; go: *The performance went off well.* ○ *How did the concert go off?* **go off sb/sth** lose interest in sb; lose one's taste for sth: *Jane seems to be going off Peter.* ○ *I've gone off beer.* **go off with sb** leave one's husband, wife, lover, etc in order to have a relationship with sb else: *He went off with his best friend's wife.* ○ *She went off with the milkman.* **go off with sth** leave a place with sth that does not belong to one: *He went off with £10 000 of the company's money.* ○ *Who's gone off with my pen?*

go ˈon (**a**) (of an actor) walk onto the stage: *She doesn't go on till Act 2.* (**b**) (of a sportsman) join a team as a substitute during a match: *Allen went on (in place of Lineker) just before half-time.* (**c**) (of a bowler in cricket) begin to bowl: *Dilley went on (to bowl) after tea.* (**d**) start to function; be lit: *Why won't the heating go on?* ○ *Suddenly all the lights went on.* (**e**) (of time) pass; elapse; go by: *She became more and more talkative as the evening went on.* ○ *Things will improve as time goes on.* (**f**) (esp in the continuous tenses) take place; happen: *What's going on here?* ○ *There must be a party going on next door.* (**g**) (of a situation or state of affairs) continue without changing: *The present state of affairs cannot be allowed to go on.* ○ *How much longer will this hot weather go on (for)?* ○ *We* (ie Our relationship) *can't go on like this — we seem to be always arguing.* (**h**) continue speaking, after a short pause: *She hesitated for a moment, and then went on.* (**i**) used to encourage or dare sb to do sth: *Go on! Have another drink.* **go on sth** (**a**) begin to receive (payments from the State because one is unemployed) or to take (a medicine): *go on social seˈcurity/the ˈdole* ○ *go on the ˈpill*, ie start using contraceptive pills. (**b**) (used with the negative or in questions) base an opinion or a judgement on sth: *The police don't have much evidence to go on.* **go ˈon (about sb/sth)** talk about sb/sth for a long time (esp in a boring or complaining way): *She does go on sometimes!* ○ *I know you don't like my smoking, but there's no need to go on about it.* **go ˈon (at sb)** complain to sb about his behaviour, work, etc; criticize sb; nag sb: *She goes on at her husband continually.* **go ˈon (with sth)** continue an activity, esp after a pause or break: *He paused to take a sip of water, and then went on (with his story).* ○ *If we don't finish painting the kitchen today, we can go on with it tomorrow.* **go on doing sth** continue an activity without stopping: *go on coughing, crying, laughing, talking, etc* ○ *You can't go on working without a break.* ○ *If you go on drinking like this you'll make yourself ill.* **go on to sth** pass from one item to the next: *Let's go on to the next item on the agenda.* **go on to do sth** do sth after completing sth else: *After attacking the Government's economic policy, he went on to describe how the Labour Party would reduce unemployment.*

go ˈout (**a**) leave one's house to go to social events: *She goes out a lot.* ○ *He goes out drinking most evenings.* (**b**) (of the tide) move away from the land; ebb. (**c**) stop work; strike: *Are we likely to gain anything by going out (on strike)?* (**d**) be sent: *Have the invitations gone out yet?* (**e**) (of a programme) be broadcast on radio or television: *The first episode goes out next Friday evening at 8.00 pm.* (**f**) (of news, information, etc) be announced or published: *Word went out that the Prime Minister had resigned.* (**g**) become unfashionable or cease to be used: *Flared trousers went out years ago.* (**h**) stop burning or shining; be extinguished: *The fire has gone out.* ○ *There was a power cut and all the lights went out.* (**i**) end; finish: *The year went out with blizzards and gales.* **go ˈout (of sth)** be eliminated from a competition, contest, etc: *She went out in the first round of the tournament/went out of the tournament in the first round.* **go ˈout (to...)** leave one's native country and go to a distant one: *Our daughter went out to Australia ten years ago.* **go out of sb/sth** (of a quality or feeling) no longer be present in sb/sth; disappear from sb/sth: *All the fight seemed to go out of him.* ○ *The heat has gone out of the argument.* **go**

out to sb (of feelings) be offered or extended to sb: *Our hearts/sympathies go out to relatives of the victims.* **go out with sb; go ˈout (together)** (*infml*) (esp of a young person) spend time with sb and have a romantic or sexual relationship with him: *Terry has been going out with Sharon for six weeks.* ○ *Sharon and Terry have been going out (together) for six weeks.*

go ˈover (used with *advs* or in questions after *how*) be received in the specified way: *How did her speech go over?* **go over sth (a)** look at sth carefully; inspect sth: *The surveyor went over the house thoroughly and advised us not to buy it.* **(b)** examine the details of sth; check sth: *You'll have to go over these figures again, they don't add up.* ○ *Go over your work carefully before you hand it in.* **(c)** study or review sth carefully; rehearse or revise sth: *He went over the events of the day in his mind,* ie thought about them carefully. ○ *She went over her lines before the first night of the play.* **(d)** clean sth, esp thoroughly: *She went over the room with a duster.* **go over (to...)** move from one (usu distant) place to another: *Many of the Irish went over to America during the famine.* **go over to sb/sth** (*broadcasting*) transfer to (a different reporter, studio, etc): *We are now going over to the news desk for an important announcement.* **go over to sth** change from one side, opinion, habit, system, etc to another: *Two Conservative MPs went over to the Liberals.* ○ *She's gone over to a milder brand of cigarettes.*

go ˈround (a) go by a longer route than usual: *The main road was flooded so we had to go round by narrow country lanes.* **(b)** (of a number or quantity of sth) be enough for everyone to have a share: *There aren't enough chairs to go round.* ○ *Is there enough food to go round?* **go round/around/about (a)** (used with an *adj*, or a *v* in the *-ing* form) move from place to place; move in society: *She goes about barefoot.* ○ *It's unprofessional to go round criticizing your colleagues.* **(b)** (of a rumour, story, etc) pass from person to person; circulate: *There's a rumour going round that Sue and David are having an affair.* **(c)** (of an illness) spread from person to person in a group or community: *There's a lot of flu going round at the moment.* **go round (to...)** visit sb or a place (usu within the same town, city, etc): *I'm going round to my parents' (house) later.* **go round/around/about with sb** be often in the company of sb: *He goes round with a bunch of thugs.*

go ˈthrough (a) (of a law, bill, etc) be officially approved or accepted: *The bill went through,* ie was passed by Parliament. ○ *As soon as my divorce goes through, we'll get married.* **(b)** be successfully completed: *The deal did not go through.* **go through sth (a)** wear a hole in sth: *I've gone through the elbows of my sweater.* **(b)** study or examine sth closely or systematically, esp in order to find sth: *I always start the day by going through my mail.* ○ *I've gone through all my pockets but I can't find my keys.* ○ *She went through the company's accounts, looking for evidence of fraud.* **(c)** discuss, study or review sth in detail: *Let's go through the arguments again.* ○ *Could we go through* (ie rehearse) *Act 2 once more?* **(d)** take part in sth; perform sth: *Certain formalities have to be gone through before one can emigrate.* **(e)** experience, endure or suffer sth: *She's been going through a bad patch* (ie a difficult or an unhappy time) *recently.* ○ *He's amazingly cheerful considering all that he's been through.* **(f)** (of a book) be published in (the specified number of editions): *The dictionary has gone through ten editions.* **(g)** use up or consume sth; get through sth: *I seem to be going through a lot of money at the moment.* **go through with sth** do what is necessary to complete or take (a course of action): *She decided not to go through with* (ie not to have) *the abortion.* ○ *He's determined to go through with the marriage despite his parents' opposition.*

go to sb be given to, awarded to or inherited by sb: *Proceeds from the concert will go to charity.* ○ *The first prize went to the youngest child in the class.* ○ *The estate went to the eldest son.*

go together ⇨ GO WITH SB, GO WITH STH.

go towards sth be used as part of the payment for sth; contribute to sth: *This money can go towards the new camera you're saving up for.*

go ˈunder (a) sink below the surface of the sea. **(b)** (*infml*) become bankrupt; fail: *The firm will go under unless business improves.*

go ˈup (a) (of the curtain on the stage of a theatre) be raised: *The curtain goes up on* (ie is raised to show) *a suburban living-room.* **(b)** be built: *New office blocks are going up everywhere.* **(c)** be destroyed by fire or an explosion; be blown up: *The whole building went up in flames.* **(d)** become higher in price, level, etc; rise: *The price of cigarettes is going up/Cigarettes are going up (in price).* ○ *Unemployment has gone up again.* **go ˈup (to...)** begin one's studies at a university (esp at Oxford or Cambridge): *She went up (to Cambridge) in 1977.* **go up (to...) (from...)** go from one place to another, esp from a smaller place to London or from the south to the north of Britain: *We're going up to London next weekend.* ○ *When are you next going up to Scotland?*

go with sb; ˈgo together (*sl*) have sb as a boy-friend or girl-friend; have sex with sb: *He goes with a different woman every week.* ○ *Are Kevin and Tracey going together?* **go with sth** be included with or as a part of sth: *A new car goes with the job.* ○ *Do the carpets and curtains go with* (ie Are they included in the price of) *the house?* **go with sth; go together (a)** combine well with sth; harmonize with sth: *Her blouse doesn't go with her skirt/Her blouse and skirt don't go (together).* ○ *I need some new shoes to go with these trousers.* ○ *White wine goes well* (ie is suitable to drink) *with fish.* **(b)** exist at the same time or in the same place as sth; be commonly found together: *Disease often goes with poverty/Disease and poverty often go together.*

go without (sth) (used esp after *can, could* and *have to*) endure the lack of sth; manage without sth: *I had to go without breakfast this morning as I was in a hurry.* ○ *How long can a human being go* (ie survive) *without food?* ○ *She went without sleep for three days.*

□ **ˈgo-ahead** *n* **the go-ahead** [sing] permission to do sth: *We've got the go-ahead from the council/The council have given (us) the go-ahead to start building.* — *adj* willing to try new methods; enterprising; progressive: *a go-ahead company, school, person.*

ˈgo-between *n* person who acts as a messenger or negotiator between two people; intermediary: *act as a go-between.*

ˈgo-by *n* (idm) **give sb the ˈgo-by** (*infml*) ignore sb; snub sb: *She gave me the go-by in the street yesterday.*

ˈgo-getter *n* (*infml*) person who is successful by being energetic and ambitious: *He's a real go-getter!*

ˌgo-ˈslow *n* type of industrial protest in which employees deliberately work more slowly than usual.

go² /gəʊ/ *n* (*pl* **goes** /gəʊz/) **1** [C] person's turn to play in a game: *Whose go is it?* ○ *It's your go.* **2** [U] (*infml esp Brit*) energy; vitality: *She's full of/She's got a lot of go!* **3** [C] (*infml*) attack of an illness: *He's had a bad go of flu.* **4** (idm) **at one ˈgo** in one single attempt: *He blew out all the candles on his birthday cake at one go.* **be all ˈgo** (*Brit infml*) be very busy; be full of activity: *It's all go in the office today.* **be on the ˈgo** (*infml*) be very active or busy: *I've been on the go all week.* **have a ˈgo (at sth/doing sth)** (*infml*) make an attempt to do sth: *He had several goes at the high jump before he succeeded in clearing it.* ○ *I'll have a go at mending your bike today.* **make a go of sth** (*infml*) make a success of sth: *She's determined to make a go of her new career.*

goad /gəʊd/ *n* **1** pointed stick for making cattle, etc move on. **2** (*fig*) thing urging a person to action: *motivated by the twin goads of punishment and reward.*

▷ **goad** *v* **1** [Tn, Tn·pr] ~ **sb/sth (into sth/doing sth)** (*fig*) continually provoke or annoy (a person or an animal): *Stop goading the poor beast!* ○ *His persistent questions finally goaded me into an angry reply/into replying angrily.* ○ *trying to goad these lazy fellows into action.* **2** (phr v) **goad sb on** continually urge and encourage sb to do sth: *goaded on by fierce ambition.*

goal /gəʊl/ *n* **1 (a)** (in football, hockey, etc) pair of posts with a crossbar, between which the ball has to be kicked, hit, etc in order to score: *He headed the ball into an open goal,* ie one temporarily unprotected by the goalkeeper. ○ *Who is keeping goal/is in goal* (ie is goalkeeper) *for Arsenal?* ⇨ illus at ASSOCIATION FOOTBALL (ASSOCIATION). **(b)** point scored when the ball goes into the goal: *score/kick a goal* ○ *win by three goals to one* ○ *score an own goal,* ie knock the ball into one's own goal (by accident), thus giving a point to the other team, or (*fig*) do sth that harms oneself. **2** (*fig*) object of one's efforts; target: *pursue, reach, attain, etc one's goal in life* ○ *The company has set itself some stiff* (ie high) *production goals for this year.* ○ *Their goal was to eradicate smallpox.*

▷ **goalless** /ˈgəʊllɪs/ *adj* [usu attrib] with no goal scored: *a goalless draw.*

□ **ˈgoal-area** *n* (in soccer) marked rectangular area in front of a goal. ⇨ illus at ASSOCIATION FOOTBALL (ASSOCIATION).

ˈgoalkeeper (also *infml* **goalie**) *n* player who stands in goal and tries to prevent the other team from scoring. ⇨ illus at HOCKEY.

ˈgoal-kick *n* (in soccer) kick by the defending side to put the ball back into play after the attacking side has sent it over the goal-line.

ˈgoal-line *n* either of the pair of lines marking the two ends of a pitch.

ˈgoal minder (also **ˈgoal tender**) (*US*) (in ice hockey) player who stands in goal and tries to prevent the other team from scoring; goalkeeper.

ˈgoal-mouth *n* area immediately in front of a goal: [attrib] *an exciting match with a lot of goal-mouth incidents.*

ˈgoal-post *n* **1** either of the two upright posts which together with the crossbar form a goal: *a cracking shot which hits the goal-post.* ⇨ illus at RUGBY. **2** (idm) **move the goal-posts** ⇨ MOVE².

goalie /ˈgəʊlɪ/ *n* (*infml*) = GOALKEEPER (GOAL).

goat

goat /gəʊt/ *n* **1** small lively horned animal with long hair: *goat's milk* ○ *climb like a mountain goat,* ie very nimbly ○ *eat like a goat,* ie indiscriminately. Cf BILLY-GOAT, NANNY-GOAT. ⇨ illus. **2** (*sl*) unpleasant old man, esp one who is sexually active: *Let go, you randy old goat!* **3** (idm) **act/play the (giddy) ˈgoat** (*infml*) behave frivolously or irresponsibly. **get sb's ˈgoat** (*infml*) greatly irritate or annoy sb. **separate the sheep from the goats** ⇨ SEPARATE².

▷ **goatee** /gəʊˈti:/ *n* man's small pointed beard like the tuft of hair on a goat's chin.

□ **ˈgoatherd** *n* person who looks after a flock of goats.

ˈgoatskin *n* **(a)** [U] leather made from the skin of a goat: [attrib] *a goatskin bag, purse, etc.* **(b)** [C] bottle made of this: *a goatskin filled with wine.*

ˈgoat's cheese cheese made from goat's milk.

gob¹ /gɒb/ *n* (*infml*) lump or drop of slimy substance (esp saliva, etc from the mouth): *Gobs of grease/spittle ran down his chin.*

▷ **gob** *v* (**-bb-**) [I] (*infml*) spit.

gob² /gɒb/ *n* (*Brit sl offensive*) mouth: *Shut your gob!* ie Be quiet.

□ **ˈgob-stopper** *n* (*Brit*) large ball-shaped sweet.

gobbet /ˈgɒbɪt/ *n* (*infml*) **1** lump or chunk, esp of food. **2** (*fig*) short extract from a text: *learn and quote gobbets of poetry.*

gobble[1] /ˈgɒbl/ *v* **1** [I, Tn, Tn·p] ~ **sth (up/down)** eat sth fast, noisily and greedily (leaving nothing behind): *Eat slowly and don't gobble!* ○ *gobble one's food (down) in a hurry* ○ *gobble up all the cakes.* **2** (phr v) **gobble sth up** (*infml*) use sth up quickly; swallow: *The rent gobbles up half his earnings.* ○ *Small family businesses are being gobbled up by larger firms.*

gobble[2] /ˈgɒbl/ *v* [I] **(a)** (of a male turkey) make its characteristic sound. **(b)** (of a person) make such a sound when speaking quickly, angrily, etc.
▷ **gobble** *n* sound made by a male turkey.
gobbler /ˈgɒblə(r)/ *n* (*US*) male turkey.

gobbledegook (also **gobbledygook**) /ˈgɒbldɪgu:k/ *n* [U] (*infml*) difficult or pompous language use by specialists; jargon: *Civil Service documents are often written in gobbledegook that ordinary people cannot understand.*

go-between /ˈgəʊ bɪtwi:n/ *n* ⇨ GO[1].

goblet /ˈgɒblɪt/ *n* glass, metal, etc drinking-vessel (for wine) with a stem and base, but no handle. ⇨ illus at GLASS.

goblin /ˈgɒblɪn/ *n* (in fairy stories) small ugly mischievous manlike creature.

goby /ˈgəʊbɪ/ *n* small fish with a set of fins on the abdomen that are joined to form a sucker.

go-cart /ˈgəʊkɑ:t/ *n* (*esp US*) light handcart. Cf GO-KART.

god /gɒd/ *n* **1** [C] being or spirit that is believed to have power over nature and control over human affairs: *Mars was the Roman god of war.* ○ *a feast/sight (fit) for the gods*, ie which is exceptionally fine. **2 God** [sing] (in various religions, esp Christianity, Judaism and Islam) the Supreme Being, creator and ruler of the universe: *God the Father, God the Son and God the Holy Ghost*, ie the Holy Trinity in the Christian religion ○ *I swear by Almighty God* (ie very solemnly) *that the evidence I shall give...* ○ *As God is my witness* (ie I solemnly swear), *that's the truth!* ○ *He likes to play God*, ie behave as if he could control people and events. ○ *a naive idea of God as an old man with a long white beard.*

📖 Many people retain in adulthood a rather childish vision of God as an old man with a white beard who listens to people's prayers and sometimes answers them. While the majority of people in Britain say they believe in God, relatively few pray regularly in a place of worship. Although the name of God is popularly associated with 'good', the two words are unrelated in origin.

3 [C] **(a)** person greatly admired or adored: *To people of our generation Kennedy was a god.* **(b)** thing to which too much attention is given: *Money is his god.* **4 the gods** [pl] gallery seats high up in a theatre: *sitting in the gods.* **5** (idm) **an act of God** ⇨ ACT[1]. **for God's, etc sake** ⇨ SAKE. **for the love of ˈGod, etc** ⇨ LOVE[1]. **God alˈmighty/God in ˈheaven/good ˈGod/(oh) (my) God** (used to express surprise, horror, etc): *God, what a stupid thing to do!* **God/goodness/Heaven knows** ⇨ KNOW. **God/Heaven forbid** ⇨ FORBID. **God/Heaven help sb** ⇨ HELP[1]. **God's gift to sb/sth** (*often ironic*) sb/sth that seems specially created to be useful to or enjoyed by a group of people, an industry, etc: *He seems to think he's God's gift to women.* **God ˈwilling** (used to express the wish that one will be able to do as one intends or plans): *I'll be back next week, God willing.* Cf DV. **honest to God/goodness** ⇨ HONEST. **in ˈGod's name** (used when asking angry or surprised questions): *What in God's name was that huge bang?* **in the lap of the gods** ⇨ LAP[1]. **a man of God** ⇨ MAN[1]. **please God** ⇨ PLEASE. **put the fear of God into sb** ⇨ FEAR[1]. **thank God, etc** ⇨ THANK. **a tin god** ⇨ TIN. **to God/goodness/Heaven** (used after a *v* to express a strong hope, wish, etc): *I wish to God he'd turn that radio down!* **ˌye ˈgods** (*dated or joc*) (used to express surprise).
□ **ˈgodchild**, **ˈgod-daughter**, **ˈgodson** *ns* person for whom sb takes responsibility as a godparent.
ˈgod-damn(ed) (*US* **goddam** /ˈgɒdæm/) *adj, adv* (⚠ *infml*) (used for adding force to an expression): *Where's that god-damned pen?* ○ *There's no need to be so goddam rude!*
ˈgodfather, **ˈgodmother**, **ˈgodparent** *ns* **1** person who promises, when a child is baptized, to see that it is brought up as a Christian. **2 godfather** head of a unit in the Mafia or a similar criminal organization.
ˈgod-fearing *adj* living a good life; sincerely religious.
ˈgod-forsaken *adj* (of places) dismal; wretched: *a god-forsaken little town in the middle of nowhere.*
ˈgodlike *adj* like God or a god in some quality: *his godlike beauty.*
God's ˈacre (*arch*) churchyard.
ˌGod ˈSave the ˈKing/ˈQueen the British national anthem.

Godard /ˈgɔ:dɑ:(r)/ Jean-Luc (1930-), French film director. His work, including *Pierrot le Fou* and *A Bout de Souffle*, challenges traditional forms of film-making, often ignoring narrative sequence and having a strong political and philosophical content.

god-awful /ˈgɒdɔ:fl/ *adj* (*infml*) extremely bad; terrible: *What a god-awful day I've had!*

goddess /ˈgɒdɪs/ *n* **1** female god, eg in Greek and Latin mythology: *Diana, the goddess of hunting.* **2** female person greatly adored or admired: *screen goddesses*, ie female film stars.

Gödel /ˈgɜ:dl; *US* ˈgəʊdəl/ Kurt (1906-78), American mathematician, born in Austria. He claimed that mathematics is essentially incomplete, since some true formulae must exist which cannot be proved or disproved.

godetia /gəˈdi:ʃə/ *n* garden plant with bright reddish or purple flowers.

godhead /ˈgɒdhed/ *n* **the Godhead** [sing] (*fml*) God: *worshipping the Godhead.*

Godiva /gəˈdaɪvə/ Lady, wife of an earl of Mercia in the 11th century. According to legend, she rode naked on a horse through Coventry when her husband said that he would only lower the taxes on the people there if she did this.

godless /ˈgɒdlɪs/ *adj* not respecting or believing in God; wicked. ▷ **ˈgodlessness** *n* [U].

godly /ˈgɒdlɪ/ *adj* (**-lier, -liest**) loving and obeying God; deeply religious. ▷ **godliness** *n* [U] (idm) **cleanliness is next to godliness** ⇨ CLEANLINESS (CLEANLY[2]).

godown /ˈgəʊdaʊn/ *n* (in Asia) warehouse.

godsend /ˈgɒdsend/ *n* unexpected piece of good luck; sth welcome because it gives great help in time of need: *The rent was due, so your cheque came as an absolute godsend!*

godspeed /ˌgɒdˈspi:d/ *interj, n* (*arch*) (used when wishing sb success on a journey, etc): *We bade/wished her godspeed*, ie said farewell to her.

godwit /ˈgɒdwɪt/ *n* wading bird similar to the curlew, with a long straight or slightly upcurved beak.

goer /ˈgəʊə(r)/ *n* **1** (*infml*) lively or enterprising person. **2** (*sexist*) woman or girl who enjoys having sex frequently with different men: *She's a real goer — she'll do anything with anyone!*
▷ **-goer** (only in compounds) person who regularly goes to or attends the specified place or event: *ˈcinema-/ˈconcert-/ˈtheatre-goers* ○ *He's a regular church-goer.*

Goethe /ˈgɜ:tə/ Johann Wolfgang von (1749-1832), German writer. He spent most of his life at the court of Weimar, where he served as prime minister. He is most famous, however, as a founder of German national literature through poems, plays and novels, esp his version of the *Faust legend.

gofer /ˈgəʊfə(r)/ *n* (*sl esp US*) person whose job involves taking messages and fetching things, esp on a film set or in an office.

Gog and Magog /ˌgɒg ən ˈmeɪgɒg/ figures from the Bible and legend. Gog, the prince of Magog, is mentioned in *Ezekiel; in the Apocalypse Gog and Magog rebel against God. Gogmagog is a giant in a medieval English history of Britain, and the Gogmagog Hills near Cambridge are named after him. Two huge wooden statues called Gog and Magog, dating originally from the 15th century, stand in London's *Guildhall.

go-getter ⇨ GO[1].

goggle /ˈgɒgl/ *v* [I, Ipr] ~ **(at sb/sth)** look (at sb/sth) with wide round bulging eyes: *He goggled at her in surprise.* ○ *a frog with goggling eyes.*
□ **ˈgoggle-box** *n* (*Brit infml*) TV set.
ˈgoggle-eyed *adj* with staring, prominent or wide-open eyes.

goggles /ˈgɒglz/ *n* [pl] large round spectacles with flaps at the sides to protect the eyes from wind, dust, water, etc (worn by racing motorists, frogmen, skiers, etc): *a pair of goggles.* ⇨ illus at GLASSES (GLASS).

Gogol /ˈgəʊgɒl; *US* ˈgɔ:gl/ Nikolai (1809-52), Russian writer. His early stories make use of the folklore of the Ukraine, where he was born. His later works, esp *Dead Souls*, are brilliant, often absurd, satires of Russian society.

going /ˈgəʊɪŋ/ *n* **1** [sing] act of leaving a place; departure: *We were all sad at her going.* **2** [U] condition or state of the ground, a road, a race-track, etc for walking, riding on, etc: *The path was rough going.* ○ *The going* (ie The surface of the race-track) *at Newmarket is soft today.* **3** [U] rate of progress, travel, etc: *It was good going to reach London by midday.* ○ *She was a company director before she was 25; that's not bad going!* **4** (idm) **comings and goings** ⇨ COMING. **get out, go, leave, etc while the ˌgoing is ˈgood** leave a place or stop doing sth while conditions are still favourable or while it is still easy to do so: *Life here is getting more difficult all the time — let's go while the going's good.* **heavy going** ⇨ HEAVY.
▷ **going** *adj* (idm) **a ˌgoing conˈcern** an active and prosperous business, institution, etc. **the ˌgoing ˈrate (for sth)** the usual amount of money paid for goods or services at a particular time: *The going rate for free-lance work is £5 an hour.*
□ **ˌgoing-ˈover** *n* (*pl* **goings-over**) **1** (*infml*) act of examining, cleaning or repairing sth thoroughly: *The document will need a careful going-over before we make a decision.* ○ *I gave the car a thorough going-over.* **2** (*sl*) beating or thrashing: *The thugs gave him a real going-over.*
ˌgoings-ˈon *n* [pl] (*infml*) unusual or surprising happenings or events: *There were some strange goings-on next door last night.*

goitre (*US* **goiter**) /ˈgɔɪtə(r)/ *n* [U] large swelling of the throat caused by disease of the thyroid gland.

go-kart /ˈgəʊkɑ:t/ *n* small low racing car with an open framework. Cf GO-CART.

gold /gəʊld/ *n* **1** [U] (*symb* **Au**) precious yellow metal used for making coins, ornaments, jewellery, etc. Gold has always been valued for its colour, brightness and durability. It does not normally rust or corrode. People refer to it as a symbol of excellence (*a gold medal, silence is golden*) and of riches. It is found in many types of rock, but only a few countries, eg S Africa and the USSR, have large quantities that can be mined economically. It usu occurs alloyed with silver, platinum or certain other elements, and its purity is measured in carats, the purest gold being 24 carats. *prospecting for gold* ○ *coins made of solid gold* ○ *pure gold* ○ *5-, 18-, 22-carat gold* ○ *payment in gold* ○ [attrib] *gold bars, bullion, etc* ○ *a gold bracelet, ring, watch, etc* ○ *a gold medal*, ie one given usu as first prize. ⇨ App 11. **2** [U] (*rhet*) money in large sums; wealth: *a miser and his gold.* **3** [U, C] colour of gold: *hair of shining gold* ○ *the reds and golds of the autumn trees* ○ [attrib] *gold lettering.* **4** [C] (*sport*) gold medal: *win a/the gold.* **5** (*sport*) spot at the centre of an archery target; bull's-eye. **6** (idm) **all that glitters is not gold** ⇨ GLITTER. **(as) ˌgood as ˈgold** very well-behaved: *The children were as good as gold while you were out.* **a heart of gold** ⇨ HEART. **strike gold/oil** ⇨ STRIKE[2]. **worth one's/its weight in gold** ⇨ WORTH.
□ **ˌgold ˈbrick** (*sl*) **1** thing that has no real value despite its appearance: *The deal sounds like a gold brick to me.* **2** (also **ˌgold-ˈbricker**) (*US*) lazy person; shirker.
ˈgold-digger *n* (*derog*) girl or woman who uses her

sexual attractions to get money from men.

ˈ**gold-dust** *n* [U] gold in the form of powder: *Good electricians are like gold-dust round here,* ie are very rare and sought-after.

ˈ**gold-field** *n* district in which gold is found in the ground.

ˌ**gold** ˈ**foil** (also ˌ**gold**-ˈ**leaf**) = LEAF 3.

ˌ**gold** ˈ**medallist** winner of a gold medal.

ˈ**gold-mine** *n* **1** place where gold is mined. **2** (*fig*) any source of wealth; prosperous business: *This shop is a regular gold-mine.*

ˌ**gold**-ˈ**plate** *n* [U] articles (spoons, dishes and other vessels) made of gold. — *v* [Tn esp passive] plate (a metal object) with gold: *a* ˌ*gold-plated* ˈ*watch.*

ˈ**gold reserve** gold kept by a central bank to guarantee and support the value of the country's currency.

ˈ**gold-rush** *n* rush to a newly discovered gold-field, esp the one in northern California in 1849.

ˈ**goldsmith** *n* person who makes articles of gold.

ˈ**gold standard** economic system in which the value of money is based on that of gold.

goldcrest /ˈgəʊldkrest/ *n* very small bird with a golden crest.

golden /ˈgəʊldən/ *adj* **1** of gold or like gold in value or colour: *a golden crown, ring, etc* ○ *golden hair, sand, light.* **2** [usu attrib] precious; fortunate: *golden days*, ie a specially happy period in sb's life ○ *a golden opportunity*, ie an excellent one which should not be missed. **3** (idm) **the** ˌ**golden** ˈ**boy**/ ˈ**girl of sth** man/woman who is very popular or successful in a specified field or activity: *the golden boy of British boxing* ○ *Only last year she was Hollywood's golden girl,* eg as the leading film star or film director. **the** ˌ**golden** ˈ**calf** money when it is considered the most important thing in life: *a society that worships the golden calf,* ie that is obsessed with money. **a** ˌ**golden** ˈ**handshake** (usu large) sum of money given to a senior member of a company, etc when he leaves. **kill the goose that lays the golden eggs** ⇨ KILL. **silence is golden** ⇨ SILENCE.

□ ˌ**golden** ˈ**age** period in the past when commerce, the arts, etc flourished: *The Elizabethan period was the golden age of English drama.* ○ *looking back to a past golden age.*

ˌ**golden** ˈ**eagle** large golden-brown eagle of northern parts of the world. ⇨ illus at BIRD.

the ˌ**Golden** ˈ**Fleece** (in Greek mythology) magic ram's fleece of gold guarded by a dragon that never slept. It was taken from the dragon by *Jason with the help of Medea.

the ˌ**Golden** ˈ**Gate** entrance to San Francisco Bay from the Pacific Ocean. The Golden Gate Bridge is one of the longest suspension bridges in the world.

ˌ**golden** ˈ**jubilee** (celebration of a) 50th anniversary. Cf DIAMOND JUBILEE (DIAMOND), SILVER JUBILEE (SILVER).

the ˌ**Golden** ˈ**Hind** ship in which Sir Francis *Drake made his voyage around the world in 1577-80.

the ˌ**golden** ˈ**mean** principle of moderation; balance between too much and too little of sth: *find the golden mean between drunkenness and total abstinence.*

ˌ**golden** ˈ**oldie** (*infml*) old record, film, etc that is still well known and popular.

ˌ**golden** ˈ**rule** very important principle which should be followed when performing a particular task: *The golden rule in playing tennis is to watch the ball closely.*

the ˌ**golden** ˈ**section** geometric proportion commonly used in painting, photography, etc to achieve a balanced effect, with the ratio 1:1.62 approximately.

ˌ**Golden** ˈ**Syrup** (*propr*) type of pale yellow refined treacle.

ˌ**golden** ˈ**wedding** 50th anniversary of a wedding. Cf DIAMOND WEDDING (DIAMOND), SILVER WEDDING (SILVER).

goldfinch /ˈgəʊldfɪntʃ/ *n* bright-coloured songbird with yellow feathers on its wings.

goldfish /ˈgəʊldfɪʃ/ *n* small (usu orange or red) fish (a type of carp) kept in ponds or in bowls as pets.

□ ˈ**goldfish bowl 1** bowl used for keeping goldfish. **2** (*fig joc*) room, office, etc with large glass windows so that the people inside can be easily seen from outside: *There's no privacy in this goldfish bowl!*

Golding /ˈgəʊldɪŋ/ William Gerald (1911-), English novelist. Many of his novels (like his first, *The Lord of the Flies*) explore the theme of human cruelty. He was awarded the Nobel prize for literature in 1983.

Goldsmith /ˈgəʊldsmɪθ/ Oliver (?1730-74), Irish author. His is most famous today for his witty play *She Stoops to Conquer*, and the novel *The Vicar of Wakefield*. Although his works brought him little success, he was widely admired by his contemporaries, esp Samuel *Johnson. ⇨ article at PERFORMING ARTS.

Goldwyn /ˈgəʊldwɪn/ Samuel (1882-1974), American film producer, born in Poland. He was a founder of the Metro-Goldwyn-Mayer company which produced many of Hollywood's greatest films. His colourful use of English included many phrases that are often quoted, eg 'You can include me out'.

golf

golf /gɒlf/ *n* [U] outdoor game in which the player tries to hit a small hard ball into a series of 9 or 18 holes using as few strokes as possible. Golf is traditionally said to have been invented in Scotland and the Scottish king James VI made it fashionable in England when he came to London. For many amateur players a game of golf and the activities of the golf club are an important part of middle-class social life: *play a round of golf.* ⇨ App 9. ⇨ illus.

▷ **golfer** *n* person who plays golf.

□ ˈ**golf ball 1** ball used in golf. **2** small metal sphere with raised letters on it, used in some electric typewriters. Cf DAISY WHEEL (DAISY).

ˈ**golf cart** small electric vehicle used by golf players to ride in or to carry their clubs around the course.

ˈ**golf-club** *n* stick used for striking the ball in golf.

ˈ**golf club (a)** association whose members play golf. **(b)** grounds and club-house where they meet and play.

ˈ**golf-course** (also ˈ**golf-links**) *n* area of land where golf is played.

ˌ**golf**-ˈ**widow** *n* (*joc*) woman whose husband often leaves her at home while he plays golf.

Golgi apparatus /ˈgɒldʒɪ æpəreɪtəs; *US* -rætəs/ (also **Golgi body**) complex structure in the cytoplasm of living cells, involved esp in the secretion of enzymes and hormones.

Golgotha /ˈgɒlgəθə/ (*Bible*) hill of Calvary where Jesus was crucified, meaning 'place of a skull' in Aramaic.

Goliath /gəˈlaɪəθ/ *n* **1** (in the Old Testament) giant Philistine soldier who was killed by the young *David using only a sling and a stone. **2** (*fig*) any very large and powerful person, organization, etc: *small businesses competing for orders against industrial Goliaths.*

golliwog /ˈgɒlɪwɒg/ (also **golly** /ˈgɒlɪ/) *n* black-faced doll with thick stiff hair.

golly /ˈgɒlɪ/ *interj* (*infml*) (used to express surprise).

goloshes = GALOSHES.

-gon *comb form* (forming *ns*) figure with a specified number of angles: *octagon, polygon, etc.*

▷ **-gonal** /-gənəl/ *comb form* (forming *adjs*) of or in the shape of such a figure: *octagonal, polygonal, etc.*

gonad /ˈgəʊnæd/ *n* male or female organ (eg testis or ovary) in which reproductive cells are produced.

gondola

gondola /ˈgɒndələ/ *n* **1** long flat-bottomed boat with high peaks at each end, used on canals in Venice. **2** cabin suspended from an airship or a balloon or from a cable-railway. **3** set of shelves (in a self-service shop) for displaying goods.

▷ **gondolier** /ˌgɒndəˈlɪə(r)/ *n* man who propels a gondola(1).

Gondwanaland /gɒndˈwɑːnəlænd/ (also **Gondwana** /gɒndˈwɑːnə/) vast continent that geologists believe once existed in the southern hemisphere. About 200 million years ago it began to separate and form Arabia, Africa, South America, Antarctica, Australia and India.

gone[1] *pp* of GO[1].

gone[2] /gɒn; *US* gɔːn/ *adj* **1** [pred] past; departed: *Gone are the days when you could buy a three-course meal for under £1.* **2** (used after a phrase expressing time in weeks or months) having been pregnant for the specified period of time: *She's seven months gone.* **3** (idm) **be gone on sb** (*infml*) be very much in love with sb; be infatuated with sb: *It's a pity Peter's so gone on Jane.* ˌ**going**, ˌ**going**, ˈ**gone** (said by an auctioneer to show that bidding must stop because an item has been sold).

▷ **gone** *prep* later than; past (in time): *It's gone six o'clock already.*

gong /gɒŋ/ *n* **1** metal disc that gives a resonant note when struck with a stick, used esp as a musical instrument or as a signal for meals (in a hotel, etc): *beat/sound a gong* ○ *Do I hear the dinner gong?* **2** (*Brit infml*) (esp military) medal.

gonna /ˈgɒnə/ (*infml esp US*) going to: *We're gonna win.*

gonorrhoea (also **gonorrhea**) /ˌgɒnəˈrɪə/ *n* [U] venereal disease which causes a painful discharge from the sexual organs.

goo /guː/ *n* [U] (*infml*) **1** sticky wet substance: *a baby's face covered in goo.* **2** (*fig derog*) sentimentality.

▷ **gooey** /ˈguːɪ/ (**gooier**, **gooiest**) *adj* (*infml*) **1** sticky: *a gooey face.* **2** (*fig derog*) sentimental: *gooey words, music.*

good[1] /gʊd/ *adj* (**better** /ˈbetə(r)/, **best** /best/) **1** of high quality; of an acceptable standard; satisfactory: *a good lecture, performance, harvest* ○ *good pronunciation, behaviour, eyesight* ○ *a good* (eg sharp) *knife* ○ *Is the light good enough to take photographs?* ○ *The car has very good brakes.* ○ *Her English is very good.* **2 (a)** ~ (**at sth**) (often used with names of occupations or with *ns* derived from *vs*) able to perform satisfactorily; competent: *a* *good teacher, hairdresser, poet, etc* ○ *good at mathematics, languages, describing things* ○ *a good loser*, ie one who doesn't complain when he loses. (**b**) [pred] ~ **with sth/sb** capable when using, dealing with, etc sth/sb: *good with one's hands*, eg able to draw, make things, etc ○ *He's very good with children*, ie can look after them well, amuse them, etc. **3** (**a**) morally acceptable; virtuous: *a good deed* ○ *try to lead a good life.* (**b**) (esp of a child) well-behaved: *Try to be a good girl.* **4** ~ (**to sb**) willing to help others; kind: *You were a good girl to help in the shop.* ○ *He was very good to me when I was ill.* ○ *Would you be good enough to carry this for me?* **5** pleasant; agreeable; welcome: *The firm has had good times and bad times.* ○ *What good weather we're having!* ○ *Have you heard the good news about my award?* ○ *It's good to be home again.* **6** (of food) fit to be eaten; not yet rotting or rotten: *good eggs, fruit, etc* ○ *Separate the good meat from the bad.* **7** [usu attrib] not diseased; healthy; strong: *good teeth and bones* ○ *Would you speak into my good ear, I can't hear in the other one.* **8** (of money) not fake or false; genuine: *This note is counterfeit, but that one's good.* ○ (*fig*) *I gave good money for that camera, and it turned out to be worthless.* **9** [attrib] (of clothes, etc) used only for more formal or important occasions: *My one good suit is at the cleaner's.* ○ *Wear your good clothes to go to church.* **10** [attrib] thorough; complete; sound: *give sb a good beating, scolding, telling-off, etc* ○ *go for a good long walk* ○ *We had a good laugh at that.* **11** [usu attrib] amusing: *a good story, joke, etc* ○ *'That's a good one!' she said, laughing loudly.* **12** ~ (**for sb/sth**) beneficial; wholesome: *the good* (ie clean, refreshing) *mountain air* ○ *Is this kind of food good for me?* ○ *Sunshine is good for your plants.* ○ *This cream is good for* (ie soothes and heals) *burns.* **13** ~ (**for sth/to do sth**) suitable; appropriate: *a good time for buying a house/to buy a house* ○ *This beach is good for swimming but bad for surfing.* ○ *She would be good for the job.* **14** ~ **for sth** (**a**) (of a person or his credit) such that he will be able to repay (a sum lent): *He/His credit is good for £5 000.* (**b**) having the necessary energy, fitness, durability, etc: *You're good for* (ie will live) *a few years yet.* ○ *This car's good for many more miles.* (**c**) valid for sth: *The return half of the ticket is good for three months.* **15** (used in greetings): *Good morning/afternoon/evening!* **16** (*fml*) (used as a polite, but more often patronizing, form of address or description): *my good sir, man, friend, etc* ○ *How is your good lady* (ie your wife)*?* **17** [attrib] (used as a form of praise): *Good old Fred!* ○ *Good man! That's just what I wanted.* **18** [attrib] (used in exclamations): *Good Heavens!* ○ *Good God!* **19** (with *a*) [attrib] (**a**) great in number, quantity, etc: *a good many people* ○ *We've come a good* (ie long) *way/distance.* (**b**) (used with expressions of measurement, quantity, etc) not less than; rather more than: *We waited for a good hour.* ○ *It's a good three miles to the station.* ○ *She ate a good half of the cake.* **20** (idm) **as good as** almost; practically: *He as good as said I'm a liar*, ie suggested that I was a liar without actually using the word 'liar'. ○ *The matter is as good as settled.* **good and ...** (*infml*) completely: *I won't go until I'm good and ready.* **the good book** the Bible. **a ˌgood ˈfew** a considerable number (of); several: *'How many came?' 'A good few.'* ○ *There are still a good few empty seats.* **ˌgood for ˈsb, ˈyou, ˈthem, etc** (*infml*) (used when congratulating sb) sb, etc did well: *She passed the exam? Good for her!* (For other idioms containing **good**, see entries for other major words in each idiom, eg (**as**) **good as gold** ⇨ GOLD; **in good time** ⇨ TIME[1].)

▷ **good** *adv* (*US infml*) well: *Now, you listen to me good!*

□ **good ˈfaith** honest or sincere intention: *I don't doubt your good faith.*

ˈgood-for-nothing *n, adj* [attrib] (person who is) worthless, lazy, etc: *Where's that good-for-nothing son of yours?*

ˌGood ˈFriday the Friday before Easter, commemorating the Crucifixion of Christ.

ˌgood-ˈhearted *adj* kind.

ˌgood ˈhumour cheerful mood or state of mind: *a meeting marked by good humour and friendliness* ○ *a man of great good humour.* **ˌgood-ˈhumoured** *adj* cheerful; amiable.

ˌgood ˈlooks pleasing appearance (of a person).

ˌgood-ˈlooking *adj* (esp of people) having a pleasing appearance: *She's terribly good-looking.* ○ *a ˌgood-looking ˈhorse.* ⇨ Usage at BEAUTIFUL.

ˌgood ˈnature kindness and friendliness of character. **ˌgood-ˈnatured** *adj* having or showing good nature: *a ˌgood-natured ˈperson, disˈcussion.*

ˌgood-ˈneighbourliness *n* [U] friendly relations with or a friendly attitude towards one's neighbours.

ˌgood ˈsense soundness in judgement; practical wisdom.

ˌgood-ˈtempered *adj* not easily irritated or made angry.

good[2] /gʊd/ *n* **1** [U] that which is morally right or acceptable: *the difference between good and evil* ○ *Is religion always a force for good?* **2** [U] that which gives benefit, profit, advantage, etc: *work for the good of one's country* ○ *I'm giving you this advice for your own good.* ○ *Do social workers do a lot of good?* Cf DO-GOODER (DO[2]). **3 the good** [pl *v*] virtuous people: *a gathering of the good and the great.* **4** (idm) **be no/not much/any/some ˈgood (doing sth)** be of no, not much, etc value: *It's no good (my) talking to him.* ○ *Was his advice ever any good?* ○ *This gadget isn't much good.* ○ *What good is it asking her?* **do (sb) ˈgood** benefit sb: *Eat more fruit: it will do you good.* ○ *This cough medicine tastes nice but it doesn't do much good*, ie isn't very effective. ○ (*usu ironic*) *Much good may it do you*, ie You won't get much benefit from it. **for ˈgood (and ˈall)** permanently; finally: *She says that she's leaving the country for good*, ie intending never to return to it. **to the ˈgood** (used to describe sb's financial state) in credit: *We are £500 to the good*, ie We have £500 more than we had. **up to no ˈgood** (*infml*) doing sth wrong, mischievous, etc: *Where's that naughty child now? I'm sure he'll be up to no good wherever he is.*

goodbye /ˌgʊdˈbaɪ, *also* ˌgʊˈbaɪ/ *interj, n* **1** (used when leaving or being left by sb): *say 'Goodbye!' to sb* ○ *We said our goodbyes* (ie said 'Goodbye!' to each other) *and left.* **2** (idm) **kiss sth goodbye/kiss goodbye to sth** ⇨ KISS.

goodish /ˈgʊdɪʃ/ *adj* [attrib] **1** quite good; not the best: *a goodish pair of shoes.* **2** fairly/quite large or great: *walk a goodish distance, eat a goodish amount.*

goodly /ˈgʊdlɪ/ *adj* (**-ier, -iest**) **1** (*arch*) handsome; pleasant to look at: *a goodly man* ○ *a goodly sight.* **2** [attrib] (*fml*) large (in amount): *a goodly sum of money.*

Goodman /ˈgʊdmən/ Benjamin David ('Benny') (1909-86), American jazz clarinet player. He was nicknamed 'the King of Swing' because of his new style of jazz playing. He also gave performances of classical works, including pieces written for him by *Bartók and others.

goodness /ˈgʊdnɪs/ *n* **1** [U] quality of being good; virtue; kindness (to sb): *praise God for his goodness and mercy* ○ *In spite of the bad things he's done I still believe in his essential goodness.* ○ *her goodness to her old parents.* **2** [U] quality that nourishes sb/sth or helps growth: *Much of the goodness in food may be lost in cooking.* ○ *Brown bread is full of goodness.* ○ *soil with a lot of goodness in it.* **3** [sing] (*euph*) (used in exclamations instead of 'God'): *Goodness, what a big toy!* ○ *Thank goodness!* ie expressing relief ○ *For goodness' sake!* ie expressing protest ○ *My goodness!/Goodness me!/Goodness gracious (me)!* ie expressing surprise. **4** (idm) **God/goodness/Heaven knows** ⇨ KNOW. **have the goodness to do sth** (*fml*) (used when requesting sb to do sth): *Have the goodness to step this way, please.* **honest to God/goodness** ⇨ HONEST. **to God/goodness/Heaven** ⇨ GOD.

goods /gʊdz/ *n* [pl] **1** movable property: *stolen goods.* **2** things for sale; merchandise: *cheap, expensive, low-quality, high-quality, etc goods* ○ *cotton, leather, woollen, etc goods* ○ *electrical goods.* **3** (*Brit*) (*US* **freight**) things carried by rail (contrasted with passengers): [attrib] *a goods train, wagon, etc*, ie not for passengers. ⇨ Usage at CARGO. **4** (idm) **come up with/deliver the ˈgoods** (*infml*) carry out or complete a task as expected, or fulfil a promise: *Under the terms of the agreement the union undertook to get the men back to work, but it was unable to deliver the goods*, ie the men stayed on strike. **sb's ˌgoods and ˈchattels** (*law*) sb's personal belongings. **the ˈgoods/a (nice) piece of ˈgoods** (*dated infml*) excellent or sexually desirable person. **price oneself/one's goods out of the market** ⇨ PRICE *v*.

□ **goods train** = FREIGHT TRAIN (FREIGHT).

goodwill /ˌgʊdˈwɪl/ *n* [U] **1** friendly, co-operative or helpful feeling: *a policy, spirit, etc of goodwill in international relations* ○ *show goodwill to/towards sb* ○ *Given goodwill on both sides I'm sure we can reach agreement.* **2** (financial value attached to the) good reputation of an established business: *The goodwill is being sold together with the shop.*

Goodwood /ˈgʊdwʊd/ racecourse in West Sussex, England, sometimes called 'Glorious Goodwood' because of its attractive setting. ⇨ article at SEASON.

goody /ˈgʊdɪ/ *n* (*infml*) **1** (usu *pl*) (**a**) pleasant thing to eat; sweet, cake, etc: *Too many goodies will make you sick.* (**b**) desirable thing: *I can now afford a new car, holidays abroad and lots of other goodies.* **2** hero (of a book, film etc); good person: *Is he one of the goodies or one of the baddies?*

▷ **goody** (also **goody ˈgumdrops**) *interj* (*infml*) (used esp by children, for expressing pleasure and excitement).

goody-goody /ˈgʊdɪ gʊdɪ/ *n, adj* (*pl* **goody-goodies**) (*derog*) (person) behaving so as to appear very virtuous and respectable.

gooey ⇨ GOO.

goof /gu:f/ *n* (*infml*) **1** silly or stupid person. **2** stupid error: *Sorry, that was a bit of a goof on my part!*

▷ **goof** *v* (*infml esp US*) **1** [I, Tn] fail to do (sth) properly; make a mess (of): *She had a great chance, but she goofed again*, ie failed to take the opportunity. ○ *The actor goofed his lines.* **2** (phr v) **goof about/around/off** behave stupidly or irresponsibly; mess around.

goofy *adj* (**-ier, -iest**) (*infml*) silly; stupid; crazy.

□ **ˈgoof ball** (*US sl*) **1** drug in tablet form, esp a barbiturate. **2** stupid person.

googly /ˈgu:glɪ/ *n* (in cricket) ball bowled as if to turn in a particular direction after bouncing, that actually turns the opposite way.

gook /gu:k/ *n* (*US sl offensive*) foreigner, esp from E Asia.

goon /gu:n/ *n* (*infml*) (**a**) stupid or crazy person. (**b**) (*US*) person employed to threaten or attack people.

goosander /gu:ˈsændə(r)/ *n* duck with a narrow, sharply serrated bill.

goose /gu:s/ *n* (*pl*, except in sense 3, **geese** /gi:s/) **1** (**a**) [C] web-footed water bird larger than a duck. ⇨ illus at BIRD. (**b**) (*masc* **gander** /ˈgændə(r)/) [C] female of this bird. (**c**) [U] the flesh of the goose served as food: [attrib] *goose-liver pâté.* **2** (*dated*) foolish or gullible person, esp female: *You silly goose!* **3** (*pl* ~**s**) traditional iron[1](2) with a long handle, used by tailors. **4** (idm) **ˌall sb's ˌgeese are ˈswans** (used when describing sb who overestimates or exaggerates the good qualities of other people). **cook sb's goose** ⇨ COOK *v*. **kill the goose that lays the golden eggs** ⇨ KILL. **not say 'boo' to a goose** ⇨ SAY. **what's sauce for the goose is sauce for the gander** ⇨ SAUCE.

□ **ˈgoose-egg** *n* (*US*) score of nought in a game.

ˈgoose-flesh *n* [U] (also **ˈgoose-pimples** [pl], *US* **ˈgoose bumps**) condition in which the skin is temporarily raised into little lumps, caused by cold or fear.

ˈgoose-step *n* [sing] way of marching in which the legs are raised high without bending the knees. It is used by many armies, but is commonly associated with the German and Italian armies before and during the Second World War.

gooseberry /ˈgʊzbərɪ; *US* ˈgu:sberɪ/ (also *Brit*

infml **goosegog** /ˈgʊzgɒg/) *n* **1** (bush with a) green, smooth, sour but edible berry (used for jam, tarts, etc): [attrib] *gooseberry jam.* **2** (*infml*) unwanted third person present when two people (esp lovers) wish to be alone together: *I didn't wish to play gooseberry*, ie be the unwanted person.
□ **gooseberry ˈfool** dessert made from crushed gooseberries and cream.

GOP /ˌdʒiː əʊ ˈpiː/ *abbr* (*US*) Grand Old Party (the Republican Party).

gopher /ˈgəʊfə(r)/ *n* **1** burrowing rat-like N American animal. **2** N American ground squirrel. **3** tortoise of the southern USA that digs burrows in which to shelter from the sun.

Gordian knot /ˈgɔːdɪən/ *n* **1** difficult or seemingly impossible problem or task. **2** (idm) **cut the Gordian ˈknot** solve a problem by forcefully direct but unorthodox methods.

Gordon /ˈgɔːdn/ Charles George (1833-85), British general. He was known as 'Chinese Gordon' after defeating rebels in China. Sent to help Egyptian troops fighting the *Mahdi, he was trapped in the garrison at Khartoum and killed there after a ten-month siege.

Gordonstoun /ˈgɔːdnstən/ school in NE Scotland, founded in 1934. It is renowned for the importance it gives to developing students' physical as well as academic abilities. Several members of the British royal family have attended the school.

gore[1] /gɔː(r)/ *n* [U] (*esp rhet*) (mainly in descriptions of fighting) thickened blood from a cut or wound: *a film with too much gore*, ie scenes of bloodshed. Cf GORY.

gore[2] /gɔː(r)/ *v* [Tn] pierce or wound (a person or an animal) with a horn or tusk: *gored to death by an angry bull.*

gore[3] /gɔː(r)/ *n* wedge-shaped section of a garment, an umbrella or a sail.
▷ **gored** /gɔːd/ *adj* made with gores: *a gored skirt.*

gorge[1] /gɔːdʒ/ *n* **1** narrow steep-sided valley, usu with a stream or river: *the Rhine gorge.* **2** (*US*) mass of ice, etc blocking a narrow passage. **3** (*dated*) throat; gullet: *a fish bone stuck in his gorge.* **4** (idm) **make sb's ˈgorge rise** fill sb with anger or disgust; sicken sb: *The sight of so many starving children made his gorge rise.*

gorge[2] /gɔːdʒ/ *v* [I, Ipr, Tn, Tn·pr] ~ (**oneself**) (**on/with sth**) eat greedily; fill (oneself): *gorging (herself) on cream-cakes.*

gorgeous /ˈgɔːdʒəs/ *adj* **1** (*infml*) giving pleasure and satisfaction; wonderful: *a gorgeous meal* ○ *gorgeous weather.* **2** (*infml*) very beautiful: *gorgeous hair.* **3** [usu attrib] (*esp rhet*) richly coloured; magnificent: *walls hung with gorgeous tapestries.* ▷ **gorgeously** *adv*: *gorgeously dressed, decorated, etc.*

Gorgon /ˈgɔːgən/ *n* **1** (in Greek mythology) any of three snake-haired sisters whose looks turned to stone anyone who saw them. Cf MEDUSA. **2 gorgon** (*fig*) domineering, frightening or repulsive woman: *Her step-mother, who hated her, was an absolute gorgon.*

Gorgonzola /ˌgɔːgənˈzəʊlə/ *n* [U] rich creamy blue-veined Italian cheese.

gorilla /gəˈrɪlə/ *n* very large powerful African ape. Although sometimes portrayed as fierce and aggressive, gorillas are normally shy and gentle animals, and are completely vegetarian. ⇨ illus at APE.

gormandize, -ise /ˈgɔːməndaɪz/ *v* [I] (*fml derog*) eat greedily for pleasure. Cf GOURMAND.
▷ **gormandizer, -iser** *n* person who does this.

gormless /ˈgɔːmlɪs/ *adj* (*Brit infml*) stupid; foolish: *What a gormless thing to do!* ○ *a gormless fellow.* ▷ **gormlessly** *adv.* **gormlessness** *n* [U].

gorse /gɔːs/ *n* (also **furze, whin**) [U] yellow-flowered evergreen shrub with sharp thorns, growing on heaths and wasteland.

Gorsedd /ˈgɔːseð/ *n* (*Welsh*) meeting of druids and bards, esp before a session of an eisteddfod. ⇨ article at WALES.

gory /ˈgɔːrɪ/ *adj* (**-ier, -iest**) **1** (*esp rhet*) covered with gore[1]. **2** full of violence and bloodshed: *a gory battle, fight, film, spectacle, etc* ○ (*fig*) *'Have you heard about their divorce?' 'Spare us the gory* (ie sensational) *details.'*

gosh /gɒʃ/ *interj* (*infml euph*) (used as a mild alternative to 'God' to express surprise or strong feeling): *Gosh, I'm hungry!* ○ *I said I'd do it and, by gosh, I did!*

goshawk /ˈgɒshɔːk/ *n* large hawk with short wings.

gosling /ˈgɒzlɪŋ/ *n* young goose.

gospel /ˈgɒspl/ *n* **1** (*Bible*) **(a) the Gospel** [sing] (the life and teaching of Jesus as recorded in) the first four books of the New Testament: *preach the Gospel.* **(b)** [C] any one of these books: *the Gospel according to St John* ○ *St John's Gospel* ○ [attrib] *the gospel message, story, etc.* ⇨ App 5. **2** [C usu sing] set of principles: *spreading the gospel of hard work* ○ *the gospel according to which one lives* ○ *Health of body and mind is my gospel.* **3** [U] (*infml*) the truth (esp of an unlikely story or a rumour): *Is that gospel?* ○ *You can take this as absolute gospel*, ie should believe it. ○ [attrib] *gospel truth*, ie completely reliable. **4** [U] religious music of black American origin in a popular or folk style: [attrib] *gospel singers.*

gossamer /ˈgɒsəmə(r)/ *n* [U] **1** fine silky substance of webs made by small spiders, floating in calm air or spread over grass, etc. **2** (*fig esp rhet*) soft light delicate material: *a veil spun of the finest gossamer* ○ [attrib] *the gossamer wings of a fly.*

gossip /ˈgɒsɪp/ *n* **1** [U] (*derog*) casual talk about the affairs of other people, typically including rumour and critical comments: *Don't believe all the gossip you hear.* ○ *She's too fond of idle gossip.* ○ *It's common gossip that they're having an affair*, ie Everyone is saying so. **2** [U] (*often derog*) informal writing about people and social events, eg in letters or newspapers: [attrib] *the gossip column*, ie of a newspaper ○ *a gossip columnist/writer*, ie a writer of such material. **3** [C] conversation including gossip: *have a good gossip with a friend, neighbour, etc.* **4** [C] (*derog or joc*) person fond of gossip: *You're nothing but an old gossip!*
▷ **gossip** *v* [I, Ipr] ~ (**with sb**) (**about sth**) talk gossip: *I can't stand here gossiping all day.* ⇨ Usage at TALK[1].
gossipy /ˈgɒsɪpɪ/ *adj*: *a gossipy letter.*

got *pt, pp* of GET.

Goth /gɒθ/ *n* member of a Germanic people that invaded the Roman Empire between the third and fifth centuries AD. The Ostrogoths from the east settled in Italy and the Visigoths from the west in Spain.

Gothic architecture: Westminster Abbey

Gothic /ˈgɒθɪk/ *adj* **1** of the Goths or their language. **2** (*architecture*) of or in a style common in W Europe from the 12th to the 16th centuries and characterized by pointed arches, arched roofs, tall thin pillars, etc: *a Gothic church, cathedral, arch, window.* ○ *Victorian Gothic designs*, ie which imitated the medieval style ⇨ illus. ⇨ article at ARCHITECTURE. **3** of or in an 18th-century style of literature which described romantic adventures in mysterious or frightening settings: *Gothic novels, horror.* **4** (of printing type) with pointed letters made up of thick lines and sharp angles, as formerly used for German: *Gothic lettering, type, etc.* ⇨ illus.

Gothic lettering

Gothic

▷ **Gothic** *n* [U] **1 (a)** Gothic language. **(b)** Gothic type: *printed in Gothic.* **2** the Gothic architectural style.
□ **the ˌGothic reˈvival** reintroduction of the Gothic style in the Victorian period, by architects like *Barry and *Pugin. ⇨ illus at SCOTT.

gotta /ˈgɒtə/ (*infml esp US*) (have) got to: *I gotta/I've gotta go.*

gotten (*US*) *pp* of GET.

gouache /ˈgʊɑːʃ/ *n* [U] type of thick water-colour paint; method of painting pictures using this material.

Gouda /ˈgaʊdə; *US also* ˈguːdə/ *n* [U] type of mild-flavoured Dutch cheese.

gouge /gaʊdʒ/ *n* tool with a sharp semicircular edge for cutting grooves in wood.
▷ **gouge** *v* **1** [Tn, Tn·pr] ~ **sth** (**in sth**) make (a hole) in sth roughly or destructively: *A maniac had gouged several holes in the priceless painting.* **2** [Tn] (*US infml*) trick (sb) out of money, eg by overcharging. **3** (phr v) **gouge sth out** remove sth by digging into a surface with a sharp tool, one's fingers, etc: *gouge out a narrow groove* ○ *gouge out a stone from a horseshoe* ○ *gouge sb's eyes out.*

goulash /ˈguːlæʃ/ *n* [C, U] dish of Hungarian origin consisting of stewed beef seasoned with paprika.

gourd /gʊəd/ *n* **1** (large hard-skinned fleshy fruit of a) type of climbing or trailing plant. **2** bottle or bowl consisting of the dried skin of this fruit: *a wine gourd.*

gourmand /ˈgʊəmənd/ *n* (*often derog*) lover of food; glutton.
▷ **gourmandize, -ise** /ˈgʊəməndiːz/ *n* [U] (excessive) love of eating; gluttony.

gourmet /ˈgʊəmeɪ/ *n* person who enjoys and is expert in the choice of fine food, wines, etc: [attrib] *gourmet restaurants*, ie serving fine food.

gout /gaʊt/ *n* [U] disease causing painful swellings in joints, esp toes, knees and fingers.
▷ **gouty** *adj* suffering from gout.

Gov *abbr* **1** Governor: *Gov (Stephen) King.* **2** (also **Govt**) Government.

govern /ˈgʌvn/ *v* **1** [I, Tn] rule (a country, etc); control or direct the public affairs of (a city, country, etc): *In Britain the Queen reigns, but elected representatives of the people govern the country.* **2** [Tn] prevent the expression of (a strong emotion); control: *govern one's feelings, passion, temper, etc.* **3** [Tn] influence (sth/sb) decisively; determine: *Self-interest governs all his actions.* ○ *The law of supply and demand governs the prices of goods.* ○ *I will be governed by you*, ie will do as you suggest. **4** [Tn] (*grammar*) (esp of a *v* or *prep*) require the object to be in (a particular grammatical case): *In Latin, several verbs govern the dative.*
▷ **governing** /ˈgʌvənɪŋ/ *adj* [attrib] having the power or right to govern: *the governing body of a school, college, etc.*

governance /ˈgʌvənəns/ *n* [U] (*fml or rhet*) governing; government(1): *the governance of Britain.*

governess /ˈgʌvənɪs/ *n* (esp formerly) woman employed to teach young children in their home (usu living as a member of the household): *act, serve as (a) governess to a family.*

government /ˈgʌvənmənt/ *n* **1** [U] governing; power to govern: *If we do not have strong government, there will be rioting and anarchy.* ○ *weak, ineffectual, corrupt, etc government.* **2** [U] method or system of governing: *Democratic government gradually took the place of an all-powerful monarchy.* ○ *liberal, totalitarian,*

Government

The British government operates at both national (central) and local levels. Nationally, it is represented by the body of ministers who administer the country's affairs under the Prime Minister. The Sovereign appoints as prime minister the leader of the party that has a majority in the House of Commons.

The Prime Minister not only presides over the ministers but by tradition holds the post of First Lord of the Treasury and Minister for the Civil Service. The Prime Minister also appoints an advisory council of about 20 ministers. This is the Cabinet, which meets once or twice a week, whether Parliament is sitting or not.

Most but not all the Cabinet ministers are in charge of a government department and have the title 'Secretary of State' or simply 'Minister'. The head of the finance department, called the Treasury, has the title 'Chancellor of the Exchequer'. There are Secretaries of State for the Home Office, Foreign and Commonwealth Affairs, Wales, Employment, Defence, Trade and Industry, Health, Education and Science, Scotland, Transport, Energy, Social Security, the Environment, and Northern Ireland. All these are in the Cabinet, as are holders of other traditional offices, such as the Lord President of the Council, who do not have responsibility for a government department.

After the Cabinet ministers come the four Law officers, under the Lord Chancellor, and the Ministers of State, who work with the heads of department and who often have specific functions. They in turn are followed by the junior ministers, who are usually known as 'Under-Secretaries of State'. Like the Ministers of State, they work with specific departments.

Until the system of Cabinet government developed in the 18th century, the chief executive body was the Privy Council. This still exists, but is now the private council of the Queen, as head of state. It comprises all Cabinet ministers, as 'Privy Councillors', together with a number of other distinguished people from both Britain and the Commonwealth. There are about 390 Privy Councillors. A full session of the Privy Council is held only on the death of the sovereign or when he or she announces an intention to marry.

Apart from the government departments, there are other bodies that play a part in the process of government. Examples of these are the Arts Council of Great Britain, the British Council, and the Commission for Racial Equality.

Local government is carried out by local authorities led by elected councils, which may not necessarily represent the political party of the central government in Parliament. Their link with central government is through the Department of the Environment. Other departments also concerned with local government functions are the Department of Education and Science, the Department of Social Security, and the Home Office. In Scotland local government is the overall responsibility of the Scottish Office, in Wales of the Welsh Office, and in Northern Ireland of the Department of the Environment for Northern Ireland.

Elected councils operate at several levels. There are town councils, borough councils, district councils and county councils. There are also parish councils in rural areas. There are 53 counties in Britain, within which are 369 districts. In London, the local authorities are the councils of the 32 boroughs and the Corporation of the City of London. Until recently Greater London had its own council, the Greater London Council (GLC), but this was abolished in 1986.

County councils, which are responsible for the widest areas, deal with the general planning and administration in a county, while district councils operate more locally. This means that county councils are responsible for such aspects as transport, education, police, the fire service and social services, while district councils oversee such matters as housing, environmental health and refuse collection.

State schools are the responsibility of the local education authority (LEA), answerable to the Department of Education and Science (DES). Until recently, education in Inner London was run by a single body, the Inner London Education Authority (ILEA), but in 1990 the government abolished the ILEA and transferred its powers to individual borough councils.

In the USA, the Constitution, drawn up in 1787, established the structure of government. Power is divided between the federal government and the governments of the individual states. There are three branches of the federal government, the executive, the legislative and the judicial. The executive branch is led by the President who chooses a cabinet made up of the heads of the administrative departments. The legislative branch is the Congress, made up of the Senate and the House of Representatives. The federal courts, including the Supreme Court, make up the judicial branch.

At the state level, each of the states has its own system of local government, which can take different forms. The most common administrative areas are counties and cities, with some cities also incorporating towns or boroughs. In US usage, 'local government' usually means the governing body of the district, that is, it is similar to the British 'local authority'. (Cf articles at PARLIAMENT and POLITICS.)

parliamentary, etc government. **3** (often **the Government**) [CGp] body of persons governing a state: *lead, form a government* ○ *Foreign governments have been consulted about this decision.* ○ *She has resigned from the Government,* ie from her job as a minister. ○ *The Government* (ie its members) *are discussing the proposal.* ○ *The Government* (ie collectively) *welcomes the proposal.* ○ [attrib] *a government department, grant, publication* ○ *government policies, money, ministers* ○ *government-controlled industries,* ie those controlled by the government. ⇨ article. **4** (idm) **in government** being the government; governing: *The Labour Party was in government from 1964 to 1970.*

▷ **governmental** /ˌgʌvnˈmentl/ *adj* of or connected with government: *governmental institutions.*

□ ˌ**Government** ˈ**House** official residence of the Governor (of a province, etc).

governor /ˈgʌvənə(r)/ *n* **1** (**a**) person appointed to govern a province or state (esp a colony abroad): *a provincial governor.* (**b**) elected head of each state in the USA: *the Governor of New York State.* **2** (**a**) head of an institution: *a prison governor* ○ *the governor of the Bank of England.* (**b**) member of a governing body: *the board of governors of a school, college, hospital, etc.* **3** (*Brit infml*) (**a**) (also **guvnor** /ˈgʌvnə(r)/) person having power or authority over the speaker, eg an employer or a father: *I shall have to ask permission from the/my governor.* (**b**) (also **guv** /gʌv/, **guvnor**) (used by a man when addressing another man, esp one of higher social status): *Can I see your ticket, guvnor?* **4** (*engineering*) mechanism that controls automatically the speed, temperature, etc of a machine.

□ ˌ**Governor-**ˈ**General** *n* official representative of the Crown, in a Commonwealth country.

Govt *abbr* = Gov 2.

gown /gaʊn/ *n* **1** woman's dress, esp a long one for special occasions: *a* ˈ*ball-gown* ○ [attrib] *a gown shop.* **2** loose flowing robe worn to indicate profession or status (eg a judge, lawyer, teacher, member of a university): *a BA gown.* **3** garment worn over other clothes to protect them, eg by a surgeon.

▷ **gowned** /gaʊnd/ *adj* wearing a (legal or academic) gown.

goy /gɔɪ/ *n* (*pl* **goyim** /ˈgɔɪɪm/ or **goys**) (used esp by Jews) person who is not a Jew.

GP /ˌdʒiː ˈpiː/ *abbr* general practitioner: *consult your local GP.*

Gp Capt *abbr* Group Captain: *Gp Capt (Tom) Fletcher.*

GPMU /ˌdʒiː piː em ˈjuː/ *abbr* (*Brit*) Graphical, Paper and Media Union (a trade union for employees in the printing and related trades, formed in 1991 by a merger of SOGAT and NGA).

GPO /ˌdʒiː piː ˈəʊ/ *abbr* (*Brit*) General Post Office.

GR *abbr* (eg on coins) King George (Latin *Georgius Rex*). Cf ER.

gr *abbr* **1** = GM. **2** gross: *gr income £15 000.*

Graafian follicle /ˌgrɑːfɪən ˈfɒlɪkl/ (also **Graafian vesicle** /ˈvesɪkl/) fluid-filled cavity that surrounds and protects the developing egg inside a mammal's ovary.

grab /græb/ *v* (**-bb-**) **1** (**a**) [I, Tn, Tn·pr] ~ **sth** (**from sb/sth**) grasp sth suddenly or roughly; snatch sth selfishly or rudely: *Don't grab!* ○ *He grabbed my collar and pulled me towards him.* ○ *He just grabbed the bag from my hand and ran off.* (**b**) [Tn] (*fig*) take (an opportunity, etc) eagerly: *When I gave him the chance, he grabbed it at once.* **2** [Ipr] ~ **at sb/sth** (attempt to) seize sb/sth eagerly or desperately: *He grabbed at the boy, but could not save him from falling.* ○ (*fig*) *grabbing at any excuse to avoid an unpleasant task.* **3** [Tn] (*infml joc*) have or take (sth) esp in a casual or hasty manner: *Grab a seat and make yourself at home.* ○ *Let's grab a quick sandwich and watch TV.* **4** [Tn] (*sl*) impress (sb); excite: *'How does this music grab you?' 'It doesn't grab me at all.'*

▷ **grab** *n* **1** [sing] sudden (attempt to) snatch: *make a grab at sth.* **2** [C] (*engineering*) mechanical device for picking up and holding sth to be lifted or moved. **3** (idm) **up for** ˈ**grabs** (*US infml*) available for anyone to take: *His old job is up for grabs.*

grabber *n* selfish person always trying to get things for himself.

□ ˈ**grab-bag** *n* (*US*) = LUCKY DIP (LUCKY).

Grace /greɪs/ Dr William Gilbert (1848-1915), English cricketer. Nicknamed 'WG', he is generally regarded as one of the greatest cricketers of all time, and set many records for the game.

grace /greɪs/ *n* **1** [U] quality of simple elegant beauty (esp in smoothly controlled movement): *the grace with which a ballerina leaps into the air.*

2 [U] God's mercy and favour towards mankind; influence and result of this: *By the grace of God their lives were spared.* ○ *Did he die in a state of grace?* ie strengthened and inspired by God, esp after having been pardoned and given the Sacraments. ○ (*saying*) *There, but for the grace of God, go I/we*, ie sth equally bad might have happened to me/us. **3** [U] extra time allowed to renew a licence, pay an insurance premium, etc after the day when it is due: *have a couple of days' grace* ○ *Payment is due today, but I gave her a week's grace*, ie an extra week to pay. **4** [U] favour; goodwill: *He had been the king's favourite, and his sudden fall from grace surprised everyone.* ○ *an act of grace*, ie freely given, not taken as a right. **5** [C usu *pl*] pleasing accomplishment: *well-versed in the social graces.* **6** [U, C] short prayer of thanks before or after a meal: *Father said (a) grace.* **7 His/Her/Your Grace** [C] (used as a title when speaking to or of an archbishop, a duke or a duchess): *Good morning, Your Grace!* ○ *Their Graces, the Duke and Duchess of Kent.* **8 the Graces** [pl] (in Greek myth) three beautiful sister goddesses who gave beauty, charm and happiness to humans. **9** (idm) **airs and graces** ⇨ AIR[1]. **have the grace to do sth** be polite enough to do sth: *He might have had the grace to say he was sorry!* **in sb's good 'graces** approved of and favoured by sb: *I'm not in her good graces at the moment.* **a saving grace** ⇨ SAVE[1]. **with (a) bad/good 'grace** reluctantly and rudely/willingly and cheerfully: *She apologized with (a) bad grace.* ○ *They withdrew their objections with as good a grace as they could manage.* **year of grace** ⇨ YEAR.

▷ **grace** *v* **1** [Tn] decorate or adorn (sth): *Fine paintings graced the walls of the room.* **2** [Tn, Tn·pr] ~ **sb/sth (with sth)** give honour or dignity to sb/sth: *The Queen is gracing us with her presence.* ○ *The occasion was graced by the presence of the Queen.*

□ **ˌgrace-and-'favour** *adj* [usu attrib] (*Brit*) (esp of a house) owned by the king or queen, who allows sb to live in it without paying rent.

'grace-note *n* (*music*) extra note that is sung or played to ornament a melody. In printed music grace-notes are shown in a smaller size than other notes. ⇨ illus.

graceful /ˈgreɪsfl/ *adj* **1** showing a pleasing beauty of form, movement or manner: *a graceful dancer* ○ *a graceful leap* ○ *the graceful curves of the new bridge.* **2** pleasing in both style and attitude; polite and considerate: *His refusal was worded in such a graceful way that we could not be offended.* ▷ **gracefully** /-fəlɪ/ *adv.*

graceless /ˈgreɪslɪs/ *adj* **1** without grace or elegance: *a room cluttered with ugly graceless furniture.* **2** ungracious; rude: *graceless behaviour* ○ *a graceless remark, refusal, etc.* ▷ **gracelessly** *adv.* **gracelessness** *n* [U].

gracious /ˈgreɪʃəs/ *adj* **1** ~ **(to sb)** (of persons and behaviour) kind, polite and generous (esp to sb who is socially inferior): *a gracious lady, hostess, etc* ○ *a gracious manner, reply, invitation, smile* ○ *He was most gracious to everyone, smiling and thanking them.* ○ *It was gracious of the Queen to speak to the elderly patients.* **2** [attrib] (*fml*) (used as a polite term for royal people or their acts): *her gracious Majesty the Queen* ○ *by gracious permission of Her Majesty.* **3** ~ **(to sb)** (of God) merciful: *He is kind and gracious to all sinners who repent.* **4** [usu attrib] marked by luxury, elegance and leisure: *gracious living.* **5** (*dated*) (used in exclamations expressing surprise): *Good(ness) gracious!* ○ *Gracious me!* ▷ **graciously** *adv.* **graciousness** *n* [U].

gradation /grəˈdeɪʃn/ *n* **1** [U, C] gradual change from one thing to another: *Note the subtle gradation of/in colour in this painting.* **2** [C] any of the stages or steps into which sth is divided: *It was hard to understand all the minute gradations of their bureaucracy.* **3** [C] mark showing a division on a scale: *the gradations on a thermometer.*

grade[1] /greɪd/ *n* **1** step, stage or degree of rank, quality, etc; level of classification: *a person's salary grade*, ie level of pay ○ [attrib] *high-/low-grade civil servants, milk, pigs, materials* ○ *Grade A potatoes are the best in quality.* **2** (**a**) mark given in an examination or for school work: *Pupils with 90% or more are awarded Grade A.* ○ *She got excellent grades in her exams.* (**b**) level of (esp musical) skill at which a pupil is tested: *He's got Violin Grade 6*, ie has passed a test at that level of skill. **3** (*US*) division of a school based on the age of the pupils; pupils in such a division: *My son's in the third grade.* **4** (*US*) = GRADIENT. **5** (idm) **make the 'grade** (*infml*) reach the required or expected standard; succeed. **on the 'up/'down grade** getting better/worse: *Business is on the up grade.*

□ **'grade crossing** (*US*) = LEVEL-CROSSING (LEVEL[1]).

'grade school (*US*) = PRIMARY SCHOOL (PRIMARY).

'grade teacher (*US*) teacher in a grade school.

grade[2] /greɪd/ *v* **1** [esp passive: Tn, Tn·pr, Cn·n] ~ **sth/sb by/according to sth**; ~ **sth/sb from sth to sth** arrange sth/sb in order by grades or classes, ie assessed and marked with the standard or grade(1) obtained: *The potatoes are graded by/according to size.* ○ *Eggs are graded from small to extra-large.* **2** [Tn, Cn·n] (*esp US*) mark (written work); give (a student) a mark: *The term papers have been graded.* ○ *A student who gets 90% is graded A.* **3** [Tn] make (land, esp for roads) more nearly level by reducing the slope.

gradient /ˈgreɪdɪənt/ *n* degree of slope, as on a road, railway, etc: *a steep gradient* ○ *a hill with a gradient of 1 in 4 (or 25%).*

gradual /ˈgrædʒʊəl/ *adj* (**a**) taking place by a series of small changes over a long period; not sudden: *gradual decline, progress, etc* ○ *a gradual increase, decrease, recovery.* (**b**) (of a slope) not steep: *a gradual rise, fall, incline, etc.*

▷ **gradually** /-dʒʊlɪ/ *adv* in a gradual way; by degrees: *Things gradually improved.*

gradualness *n* [U].

graduate[1] /ˈgrædʒʊət/ *n* **1** ~ **(in sth)** person who holds a degree (esp the first or bachelor's) from a university or polytechnic: *a graduate in law, history, etc* ○ *a law graduate* ○ *a graduate of Oxford/an Oxford graduate* ○ [attrib] *a graduate student*, ie one studying for a master's or a doctor's degree. Cf POSTGRADUATE, UNDERGRADUATE. **2** (*US*) person who has completed a course at an educational institution: *a high-school graduate* ○ [attrib] *a graduate nurse*, ie one from a college of nursing.

graduate[2] /ˈgrædʒʊeɪt/ *v* **1** [I, Ipr] ~ **(in sth) (at/from sth)** (**a**) complete a course for a degree: *graduate in law, history, etc at Oxford.* ○ *She graduated from Cambridge with a degree in law.* (**b**) (*US*) complete an educational course: *She's just graduated from the School of Cookery.* **2** [Tn, Tn·pr] ~ **sb (from sth)** (*esp US*) give a degree, diploma, etc to sb: *The college graduated 50 students from the science department last year.* **3** [Tn esp passive] divide (sth) into graded sections: *In a graduated tax scheme the more one earns, the more one pays.* **4** [esp passive: Tn, Tn·pr] ~ **sth (in/into sth)** mark sth into regular divisions or units of measurement: *a ruler graduated in both inches and centimetres.* **5** [Ipr] ~ **(from sth) to sth** (*fig approv*) make progress; move on (from sth easy or basic) to sth more difficult or important: *Our son has just graduated from a tricycle to a proper bicycle.*

▷ **graduation** /ˌgrædʒʊˈeɪʃn/ *n* **1** [U] (**a**) graduating at a university, etc: *students without jobs to go to after graduation.* (**b**) ceremony at which degrees, etc are conferred: [attrib] *graduˈation ceremony, day, etc.* **2** [C] gradation(3): *The graduations are marked on the side of the flask.*

□ **ˌgraduated 'pension** pension in which the contributions paid (while working) and the size of pension (after retirement) are related to the amount of salary earned: [attrib] *a graduated pension scheme.*

Graeco- (also *esp US* **Greco-**) *comb form* Greek; of Greece: *Graeco-Roman.*

graffiti /grəˈfiːtɪ/ *n* [pl] drawings or writing on a public wall, etc, usu humorous, obscene or political.

graft[1] /grɑːft; *US* græft/ *n* **1** piece cut from a living plant and fixed in a cut made in another plant, to form a new growth; process or result of doing this: *A healthy shoot should form a strong graft.* **2** (*medical*) piece of skin, bone, etc removed from a living body and attached to another body or another part of the same body, usu to replace unhealthy or damaged tissue; process or result of doing this: *a 'skin graft.*

▷ **graft** *v* [Tn, Tn·pr, Tn·p] ~ **sth onto**; ~ **sth in/on** attach sth as a graft: *graft one variety of apple onto another* ○ *New skin had to be grafted on.* ○ (*fig*) *trying to graft some innovations onto an outdated system.*

graft[2] /grɑːft; *US* græft/ *n* [U] **1** (*esp US*) (**a**) use of illegal or unfair means (esp bribery) to gain an advantage in business, politics, etc: *graft and corruption.* (**b**) profit obtained in this way. **2** (*Brit*) hard work: *Hard graft is the only way to succeed in business.*

▷ **graft** *v* **1** [I] (*esp US*) practice graft[2](1a). **2** [I, Ip] ~ **(away)** (*Brit*) work hard: *grafting (away) all day.* **grafter** *n* hard worker.

Grahame /ˈgreɪəm/ Kenneth (1859-1932), Scottish author. His most famous children's book, *The Wind in the Willows*, was based on bedtime stories for his son. It was later adapted as a musical stage play, *Toad of Toad Hall*, by A A *Milne.

grail /greɪl/ *n* (usu **the Holy Grail**) plate or cup used by Jesus at the Last Supper, in which one of his followers is said to have received drops of his blood at the Crucifixion. In the legends of King *Arthur, the knights of his Round Table go on a quest for the Grail, and it is eventually found by *Galahad and his companions: (*fig*) *a cure for cancer, the Holy Grail of medical researchers*, ie what they are trying to find.

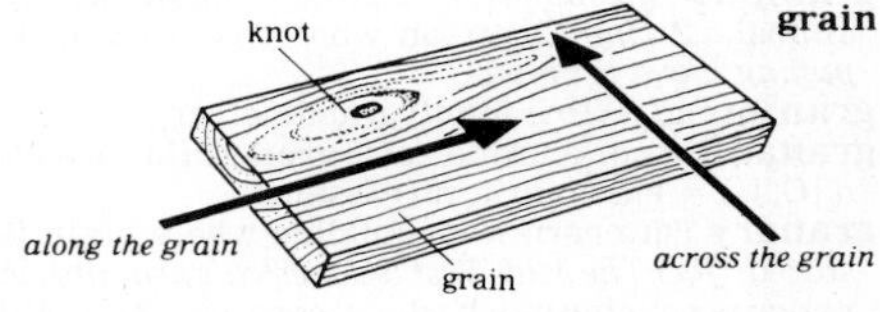

grain /greɪn/ *n* **1** [U] (*esp commerce*) small hard seeds of food plants such as wheat, rice, etc: [attrib] *America's grain exports.* **2** [C] single seed of such a plant: *a few grains of rice in a bowl.* ⇨ illus at CEREAL. **3** [C] tiny hard bit: *a grain of sand, gold, etc.* **4** [C] smallest unit of weight in various measuring systems, $\frac{1}{7000}$ lb or 0.065 gm: *The analysis showed a few grains of arsenic in the solution.* ⇨ App 10. **5** [C] (*fig*) very small amount: *There isn't a grain of* (ie any) *truth in it.* **6** [U] (**a**) (surface) texture produced by particles: *a stone of fine/medium/coarse grain*, ie containing small/medium/large particles. (**b**) pattern made by the lines of fibres in wood, or of layers in rock, coal, etc: *cut a piece of wood along/across the grain.* ⇨ illus. (**c**) rough appearance of a photographic print, as if made up of small particles of light and dark. **7** (idm) **(be/go) against the 'grain** (be) contrary to one's nature or inclination: *It really goes against the grain to have to go into the office at weekends*, ie I do not like it.

▷ **-grained** (forming compound *adjs*) having a grain(3, 6) of the specified kind: *coarse-grained* ○ *fine-grained.*

grainy *adj* (esp of a photograph) having a

noticeable grain(6).
Grainger /ˈgreɪndʒə(r)/ Percy Aldridge (1882-1961), Australian composer and pianist. He settled in England in 1901 and is famous for his collection and arrangements of English folk-songs.
gram (also **gramme**) /græm/ *n* (*abbr* **g**) metric unit of weight. ⇨ App 10.
-gram *comb form* (forming *ns*) **1** metric unit of weight: *milligram, kilogram.* **2** thing written or drawn: *telegram.*
graminaceous /ˌgræmɪˈneɪʃəs/ *adj* of or like grass.
graminivorous /ˌgræmɪˈnɪvərəs/ *adj* (of an animal) that feeds on grass, cereals, etc.
grammar /ˈgræmə(r)/ *n* **1** [U] (study or science of) rules for forming words and combining them into sentences: *a good understanding of grammar* ○ *the rules of English grammar* ○ *transformational grammar.* Cf MORPHOLOGY, SYNTAX. **2** [C] book containing a description of such rules for a particular language: *I'm writing a grammar of modern English.* ○ *I want to buy a French grammar.* **3** [U] person's knowledge and use of a language: *I'm trying to improve my grammar.* ○ *use bad grammar* ○ (*infml*) *Is that grammar* (ie correct usage)*?*
▷ **grammarian** /grəˈmeərɪən/ *n* expert in grammar.
□ ˈ**grammar school 1** (*Brit*) (esp formerly) type of secondary school providing academic (contrasted with technical) courses. ⇨ article at SCHOOL. **2** (*US*) **(a)** = PRIMARY SCHOOL (PRIMARY). **(b)** school attended after a primary school and before a high school.
grammatical /grəˈmætɪkl/ *adj* of, about or in accordance with the rules of grammar: *a grammatical treatise* ○ *a grammatical error* ○ *That sentence is not grammatical.* ▷ **grammatically** /-klɪ/ *adv*: *grammatically irregular* ○ *write grammatically.*
gramme /græm/ *n* = GRAM.
gramophone /ˈgræməfəʊn/ *n* (*dated*) = RECORD-PLAYER (RECORD[1]): [attrib] *a gramophone record.*
Grampians /ˈgræmpɪənz/ (also **the Grampians, the Grampian Mountains**) range of mountains of central Scotland that includes the *Cairngorms, popular with climbers and hill walkers. The highest peak is *Ben Nevis.
□ **Grampian** (also ˈ**Grampian Region**) local government region in NE Scotland. ⇨ map at UNITED KINGDOM.
grampus /ˈgræmpəs/ *n* **1** large dolphin-like sea animal. **2** (*infml*) person who breathes noisily: *puffing like a grampus.*
gran /græn/ *n* (*Brit infml*) grandmother.
granadilla /ˌgrænəˈdɪlə/ (also **grenadilla** /ˌgren-/) *n* [C, U] = PASSION-FRUIT (PASSION).
granary /ˈgrænərɪ/ *n* **1** building where grain is stored: (*fig*) *The Mid-West is America's granary,* ie region producing much wheat, corn, etc. **2** [attrib] (*Brit*) (of bread) containing whole grains of wheat: *a granary loaf.*
grand /grænd/ *adj* (**-er, -est**) **1** magnificent; splendid; big; of great importance (also in names of places, buildings, etc): *We dined in grand style.* ○ *It's not a very grand house, just a little cottage.* ○ *a grand occasion, procession* ○ *make a grand entry/exit,* eg on the stage, in a way that attracts the attention of everyone ○ *the Grand Canyon* ○ *The Grand Hotel.* **2** (*usu derog*) dignified; imposing; proud; self-important: *put on a grand air/manner,* ie pretend to be important ○ *make a grand gesture,* ie a generous act intended to make a great impression ○ *She loves to play the grand lady.* **3** (*dated infml or Irish*) very fine; excellent: *It's grand weather!* ○ *It's a grand day today!* ○ *I feel grand,* ie very well. ○ *have a grand* (ie very enjoyable) *time* ○ *You've done a grand job.* **4 Grand** [attrib] (used in the title of very high-ranking people): *The Grand Vizier.* **5** (idm) **a/the** ˌ**grand old** ˈ**man (of sth)** man long and highly respected in a particular field: *the grand old man of the English theatre.*
▷ **grand** *n* **1** (*pl* unchanged) (*sl*) $1 000; £1 000: *It'll cost you 50 grand!* **2** grand piano: *a concert grand.* ⇨ illus at PIANO.
grandly *adv*: *live rather grandly* ○ *gesture grandly.*
grandness *n* [U].
□ ˌ**Grand** ˈ**Canyon** deep gorge formed by the Colorado River in Arizona, USA. It is about 350 km (217 miles) long, 8-24 km (5-15 miles) wide, and, in some places, 1 800 m (6 000 ft) deep.
ˌ**grand** ˈ**duke** hereditary ruler of various European countries.
ˌ**grand fi**ˈ**nale** /fɪˈnɑːlɪ/ last part of a theatrical or similar performance, in which all the performers reassemble on stage.
Grand Guignol /ˌgrɒn giːˈnjɒl/ type of theatrical entertainment, originating in France, which consists of (usu short) plays with horrifying or violent themes.
ˌ**grand** ˈ**jury** (in the US) jury that has to decide whether there is enough evidence against an accused person for him to be tried.
ˈ**grand master 1** chess champion. **2** ˈ**Grand Master** head of an order of knighthood, group of Freemasons, etc.
the ˌ**Grand** ˈ**National** annual horse-race at Liverpool, England, with high fences to jump. ⇨ articles at ANIMAL, SPORT.
ˌ**grand** ˈ**opera** opera in which there are no spoken parts, everything being sung.
ˌ**grand** ˈ**piano** large piano with horizontal strings. ⇨ illus at MUSIC.
ˌ**grand** ˈ**slam** (*sport*) **(a)** victory in every single part of a contest, or in all the main tournaments in a year. **(b)** (in cards, esp bridge) winning all 13 tricks in a hand.
ˈ**grandstand** *n* large building with rows of seats for spectators at races, sports meetings, etc: [attrib] *have a grandstand view of sth,* ie be able to see sth clearly, as if from a grandstand. ˌ**grandstand** ˈ**finish** exciting end of a race, in which the leading cars, horses, etc reach the finishing line close together. Cf STAND[1] 7.
ˌ**grand** ˈ**total** complete total when other totals have been added together.
ˌ**grand** ˈ**tour** (in former times) tour of the chief towns, countries, etc of Europe, considered as completing the education of a wealthy young person.
grand- (forming compound *ns* indicating family relationships).
□ ˈ**grandchild** (*pl* **-children**), ˈ**granddaughter**, ˈ**grandson** *ns* daughter or son of one's child. ⇨ App 8.
ˈ**grandfather**, ˈ**grandmother**, ˈ**grandparent** *ns* **1** father or mother of either of one's parents. ⇨ App 8. **2** (idm) **teach one's grandmother to suck eggs** ⇨ TEACH. ˈ**grandfather clock** clock worked by weights in a tall wooden case.
grand-dad (also **grandad**) /ˈgrændæd/ *n* (*Brit infml*) = GRANDFATHER (GRAND-).
grandee /grænˈdiː/ *n* (formerly) Spanish or Portuguese nobleman of high rank.
grandeur /ˈgrændʒə(r)/ *n* [U] **1** greatness; magnificence; impressiveness: *the grandeur of the Swiss alps.* **2** (idm) **delusions of grandeur** ⇨ DELUSION.
grandiloquent /grænˈdɪləkwənt/ *adj* (*fml derog*) using or being a pompous style of speech, full of words which ordinary people do not understand: *a grandiloquent speaker, speech.* ▷ **grandiloquence** /-əns/ *n* [U].
grandiose /ˈgrændɪəʊs/ *adj* (*usu derog*) planned on a large scale; (intended to seem) imposing: *a grandiose building, style, etc* ○ *She had some grandiose* (ie overambitious) *plan to start up her own company.*
grandma /ˈgrænmɑː/ *n* (*infml*) = GRANDMOTHER (GRAND-).
grand mal /ˌgrɒn ˈmæl/ (*French*) severe form of epilepsy with convulsions and loss of consciousness. Cf PETIT MAL.
grandpa /ˈgrænpɑː/ *n* (*infml*) = GRANDFATHER (GRAND-).
Grand Prix /ˌgrɑːn ˈpriː/ (*French*) any of a series of races for the international motor-racing championship.
grange /greɪndʒ/ *n* country house with farm buildings attached.
graniferous /grəˈnɪfərəs/ *adj* (of a plant) producing grain or grain-like seeds.
granite /ˈgrænɪt/ *n* [U] hard, usu grey, stone used for building.
granny (also **grannie**) /ˈgrænɪ/ *n* (*infml*) = GRANDMOTHER (GRAND-).
□ ˈ**granny bond** (*infml*) (in Britain) form of National Savings certificate originally issued to men and women over the age of retirement. In 1981 granny bonds became available to people below this age.
ˈ**granny flat** (*Brit infml*) flat for an old person, esp in a relative's house. ⇨ article at RETIREMENT.
ˈ**granny knot** reef-knot (REEF[1]) that is incorrectly tied, so that it easily comes undone.
ˌ**Granny** ˈ**Smith** type of crisp green apple, with a hard skin.
granola /grəˈnəʊlə/ *n* [U] (*US*) type of breakfast cereal similar to muesli.
Grant[1] /grɑːnt; *US* grænt/ Cary (1904-86), American film actor, born in Britain, famous for his charm and elegant acting in sophisticated comedies like *His Girl Friday* or *Hitchcock's thriller, *North by Northwest.*
Grant[2] /grɑːnt; *US* grænt/ Ulysses S(impson) (1822-1885), American general and president. He was responsible for many of the victories through which the Union won the Civil War. He succeeded *Lincoln as president, but is considered to have failed in this office. ⇨ App 2.
grant /grɑːnt; *US* grænt/ *v* **1 (a)** [Tn, Dn·n] agree to give or allow (what is asked for): *grant a favour, request, etc* ○ *They granted him permission to go.* ○ *The minister granted journalists an interview.* **(b)** [Dn·n, Dn·pr] ~ **sth (to sb)** give sth formally or legally: *These lands were granted to our family in perpetuity.* ○ *She was granted a pension.* **2** [Tn, Tf, Dn·f] (*fml*) agree or admit (that sth is true): *grant the truth of what sb says* ○ *I grant he's been ill, but that doesn't excuse him.* ○ *I grant you she's a clever woman, but I wouldn't want to work for her.* **3** (idm) **take sb/sth for** ˈ**granted** be so familiar with sb/sth that one no longer appreciates his/its full value: *He never praises his wife: he just takes her for granted.* **take sth for** ˈ**granted** assume sth to be true: *I take it for granted you have read this book.*
▷ **grant** *n* ~ **(to do sth/towards sth)** thing given for a particular purpose, esp money from the government: *student grants,* ie to pay for their education ○ *award sb a research grant* ○ *You can get a grant to repair/towards the repair of your house.*
granted *adv* (used to admit the truth of a statement before introducing a contrary argument): *Granted, it's a splendid car, but have you seen how much it costs!*
grantor /grɑːnˈtɔː(r); *US* grænˈtɔːr/ *n* (*law*) person who makes a legal arrangement to transfer property to sb else.
granular /ˈgrænjʊlə(r)/ *adj* **1** like, containing or consisting of small hard pieces: *a granular substance.* **2** rough to the touch or in appearance: *a granular surface, texture, etc.*
granulate /ˈgrænjʊleɪt/ *v* [I, Tn esp passive] (cause sth to) form into grains or have a granular surface or texture.
□ ˌ**granulated** ˈ**sugar** sugar in the form of small crystals.
granule /ˈgrænjuːl/ *n* small hard piece; small grain(3): *instant-coffee granules.*
grape /greɪp/ *n* **1** green or purple berry growing in clusters on vines, used for making wine or eaten as fruit: *a bunch of grapes* ○ [attrib] *grape juice.* ⇨ illus. **2** (idm) **sour grapes** ⇨ SOUR.
□ ˌ**grape** ˈ**hyacinth** small garden or indoor plant with clusters of (usu blue) flowers like very small grapes.
ˈ**grape-shot** *n* [U] (formerly) cluster of small iron balls fired together from a cannon.
ˈ**grape-sugar** *n* [U] dextrose or glucose, a type of sugar found in ripe grapes and other kinds of fruit.

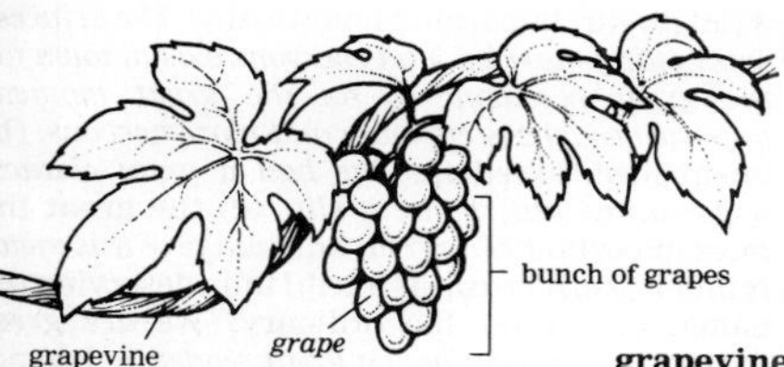

ˈ**grapevine** *n* **1** type of vine on which grapes grow. ⇨ illus. **2** (usu **the grapevine**) [sing] (*fig*) means by which news is passed on from person to person, eg in an office, a school or a group of friends: *I heard on the grapevine that Jill is to be promoted.*

grapefruit /ˈgreɪpfru:t/ *n* (*pl* unchanged or ~**s**) large round yellow citrus fruit with acid juicy flesh: [attrib] ˈ*grapefruit juice.*

graph /grɑ:f; *US* græf/ *n* (*mathematics*) (diagram consisting of a) line or lines (often curved) showing the variation of two quantities, eg the temperature at each hour: *the rising graph of crime statistics.* ⇨ illus at CHART.
□ ˈ**graph paper** paper with small squares of equal size, used for drawing graphs.

-graph *comb form* (forming *ns*) **1** instrument that writes or records: *telegraph* ○ *pantograph* ○ *phonograph.* **2** writing, record or drawing: *autograph* ○ *monograph* ○ *photograph* ○ *lithograph.*
▷ **-graphic(al)** *comb form* (forming *adjs* from *ns* ending in *-graph* or *-graphy*).

graphic /ˈgræfɪk/ *adj* **1** [attrib] of visual symbols (eg lettering, diagrams, drawings): *a graphic artist* ○ *graphic displays* ○ *the graphic arts.* **2** (of descriptions) giving one a clear detailed picture in the mind; vivid: *a graphic account of a battle* ○ *She kept telling us about her operation, in the most graphic detail.*
▷ **graphically** /-klɪ/ *adv* **1** by writing or diagrams. **2** (*fig*) vividly.
graphics *n* [pl] lettering, drawings, diagrams, etc, esp as used to illustrate or explain a written or spoken text, and often produced by a computer: *a striking use of graphics* ○ [attrib] *a graphics package.*

graphite /ˈgræfaɪt/ *n* [U] soft black substance (a form of carbon) used in making lead pencils, in lubrication, and for slowing down neutrons in atomic reactors.

graphology /grəˈfɒlədʒɪ/ *n* [U] scientific study of handwriting, esp to determine the writer's personality.
▷ **graphological** /ˌgræfəˈlɒdʒɪkl/ *adj.*
graphologist /-dʒɪst/ *n* expert in this.

-graphy *comb form* (forming *ns*) **1** indicating a form of writing, representation, etc: *calligraphy* ○ *photography.* **2** indicating an art or a descriptive science: *choreography* ○ *geography.*
▷ **-grapher** *comb form* (forming *ns*) person who does such an activity: *photographer* ○ *geographer.*

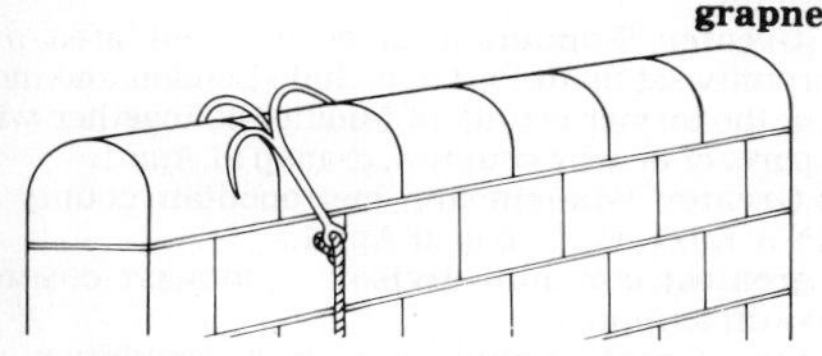
grapnel

grapnel /ˈgræpnəl/ *n* (*nautical*) **1** (also **grappling-iron**, **grappling-hook**) (formerly) instrument with hooks for holding an enemy ship in order to climb on board. **2** hooked anchor for holding a boat still, esp in a lake, river, etc. ⇨ illus.

Grappelli /ˌgræˈpelɪ/ Stéphane (1908-), French jazz violinist. He played with Django *Reinhardt in the Hot Club Quintet, and is famous for the elegance of his improvisation.

grapple /ˈgræpl/ *v* [I, Ipr] ~ (**with sb/sth**) **1** seize (an opponent) firmly and try to fight: *She grappled with her assailant but he got away.* **2** (*fig*) work hard to overcome (a difficulty): *He has been grappling with the problem for a long time.*
▷ **grapple** *n* **1** wrestling hold. **2** contest in which two or more people grapple with each other.
□ ˈ**grappling-iron** (also ˈ**grappling-hook**) *n* = GRAPNEL 1.

grasp /grɑ:sp; *US* græsp/ *v* **1** [Tn] (**a**) seize (sb/sth) firmly with hand(s), finger(s), teeth, etc: *She grasped the rope and pulled herself up.* ○ *He grasped my hand warmly,* ie to shake it. ○ *He grasped her firmly by the arm.* (**b**) (*fig*) take advantage of (sth); not lose: *grasp an opportunity.* **2** [Tn, Tw] understand (sth) fully: *I don't think you've quite grasped the seriousness of the situation.* ○ *She never could grasp how to do it.* **3** (idm) **grasp the ˈnettle** deal with a difficult matter firmly and boldly. **4** (phr v) **grasp at sth** try to seize sth: *grasp at a swinging rope* ○ (*fig*) *grasp at an opportunity.*
▷ **grasp** *n* (usu *sing*) **1** (**a**) hold; grip: *Take a firm grasp of the handle and pull.* (**b**) (*fig*) power; control: *in the grasp of powerful emotions he could not control* ○ *They had fled to America, and were living beyond the grasp of their enemies.* **2** understanding: *difficulties within/beyond sb's grasp* ○ *She has a good grasp of the subject.*

grasping /ˈgrɑ:spɪŋ; *US* ˈgræspɪŋ/ *adj* greedy for money, possessions, etc; avaricious: *a grasping miser, capitalist, etc.* ▷ **graspingly** *adv.*

grass[1] /grɑ:s; *US* græs/ *n* **1** [U] various kinds of common wild low-growing plants of which the thin green leaves and stalks are eaten by cattle, horses, sheep, etc: *a blade* (ie leaf) *of grass* ○ *a meadow covered with/planted with grass* ○ [attrib] *grass seed* ○ *a grass skirt,* ie made of long dried grass, as worn in the S Pacific. **2** [C] any species of this plant (including, in botanical use, cereals, reeds and bamboos): *a study of different grasses.* **3** [U] ground covered with grass; lawn; pasture: *Don't walk on the grass.* ○ *mow the grass* ○ *cattle put out to grass,* ie put in a field to eat the grass. **4** [U] (*sl*) marijuana. **5** [C] (*Brit sl usu derog*) (used by criminals) person who informs the police of criminal activities and plans. **6** (idm) **the grass is (always) greener on the other ˈside (of the fence)** (*saying*) (said of people who never seem satisfied and always think that others have a better situation than they have). **(not) let the grass grow under one's feet** (not) delay in getting sth done. **put sb out to ˈgrass** (*infml*) force sb to retire, esp because of old age. **a snake in the grass** ⇨ SNAKE.
▷ **grassy** *adj* (**-ier**, **-iest**) covered with grass: *a grassy meadow.*
□ **grassland** /-lænd, -lənd/ *n* [U] (also **grasslands** [pl]) land covered with grass, esp as used for grazing.
ˌ**grass ˈroots** (*esp politics*) ordinary people in society, as opposed to those who make decisions: *We must not forget about the grass roots.* ○ *dissatisfaction at the grass roots* ○ [attrib] *grass-roots opposition to the party's policy.*
ˈ**grass snake** small harmless type of snake.
ˌ**grass ˈwidow** (*often joc*) woman whose husband is temporarily absent.

grass[2] /grɑ:s; *US* græs/ *v* **1** (**a**) [Tn, Tn·p] ~ **sth (over)** cover sth with turf. (**b**) [Tn] (*US*) feed (animals) with grass. **2** [I, Ipr] ~ (**on sb**) (*Brit sl usu derog*) (used by criminals) inform the police of sb's criminal plans or activities: *If anyone grasses on us, his life won't be worth living!*

grasshopper /ˈgrɑ:shɒpə(r); *US* ˈgræs-/ *n* **1** jumping insect that makes a shrill chirping noise. **2** (idm) **knee-high to a grasshopper** ⇨ KNEE-HIGH (KNEE).

grate[1] /greɪt/ *n* (metal frame for holding coal, etc in a) fireplace.

grate[2] /greɪt/ *v* **1** [esp passive: Tn, Tn·pr] ~ **sth (into sth)** rub sth into small pieces, usu against a rough surface; rub small bits off sth: *Grate the carrot finely/into small pieces.* ○ *grated cheese, carrot, etc* ○ *Grate the nutmeg into the mixture/over the pudding.* **2** (**a**) [I] make a harsh noise by rubbing: *The hinges grated as the gate swung back.* (**b**) [I, Ipr] ~ (**on sb/sth**) (*fig*) have an irritating effect (on a person, or his nerves): *His voice grates (on my ears).* ○ *His bad manners grate on my nerves.* ○ *It's her ingratitude that grates on me.*
▷ **grater** *n* device with a rough surface for grating food: *a nutmeg grater.*
grating *adj* irritating: *her grating voice.* **gratingly** *adv.*

grateful /ˈgreɪtfl/ *adj* **1** ~ (**to sb**) (**for sth**); ~ (**that...**) feeling or showing appreciation for sth good done to one, for sth fortunate that happens, etc; thankful: *I am grateful to you for your help.* ○ *I was grateful that they didn't ask me.* **2** (*dated*) pleasant; agreeable; comforting: *trees that afford a grateful shade.* **3** (idm) **be grateful/thankful for small mercies** ⇨ SMALL.
▷ **gratefully** /-fəlɪ/ *adv* in a thankful manner: *I offered help, and she accepted gratefully.*

gratify /ˈgrætɪfaɪ/ *v* (*pt, pp* **-fied**) (*fml*) **1** [Tn esp passive] give pleasure or satisfaction to (sb): *I was most gratified at/by/with the outcome of the meeting.* ○ *It gratified me to hear of your success.* ○ *I was gratified that they appreciated what I did for them.* **2** [Tn] give (sb) what is desired; indulge: *gratify a person's whims* ○ *To gratify my curiosity, do tell me what it is.*
▷ **gratification** /ˌgrætɪfɪˈkeɪʃn/ *n* (*fml*) **1** [U] gratifying or being gratified; state of being pleased or satisfied: *the gratification of knowing one's plans have succeeded* ○ *sexual gratification.* **2** [C] thing that gives one pleasure or satisfaction: *one of the few gratifications of an otherwise boring job.*
gratifying *adj* ~ (**to do sth/that...**) (*fml*) pleasing; satisfying: *It is gratifying to see one's efforts rewarded.* **gratifyingly** *adv.*

grating /ˈgreɪtɪŋ/ *n* framework of wooden or metal bars, either parallel or crossing one another, placed across an opening, eg a window, to prevent people or animals from climbing through or to allow air to flow easily.

gratis /ˈgreɪtɪs/ *adv* without payment; free: *be admitted to the exhibition gratis.*

gratitude /ˈgrætɪtju:d; *US* -tu:d/ *n* [U] ~ (**to sb**) (**for sth**) being grateful; thankfulness: *She felt eternal gratitude to him for saving her life.* ○ *I owe you a debt of gratitude for what you've done.*

gratuitous /grəˈtju:ɪtəs; *US* -ˈtu:-/ *adj* (*fml derog*) done, given or acting unnecessarily, purposely and without good reason: *a gratuitous insult* ○ *a gratuitous lie/liar* ○ *scenes of gratuitous violence on TV.* ▷ **gratuitously** *adv.* **gratuitousness** *n* [U].

gratuity /grəˈtju:ətɪ; *US* -ˈtu:-/ *n* **1** (*fml*) money given to sb who has done one a service; tip. **2** (*Brit*) money given to a retiring employee.

grave[1] /greɪv/ *adj* (**-r**, **-st**) **1** (*fml*) (of situations, etc) needing careful consideration; serious: *This could have grave consequences.* ○ *grave news, danger, etc* ○ *There is a grave risk of flooding.* ○ *a sick person in a grave condition* ○ *a situation that is graver/more grave than expected* ○ *a grave mistake, error, etc.* **2** (of people) serious or solemn in manner: *He looked grave. 'Is there anything wrong?' I asked.* ▷ **gravely** *adv*: *gravely ill* ○ *If you think that, you are gravely mistaken.*

grave[2] /greɪv/ *n* **1** hole dug in the ground for a dead body; mound of earth or monument over it: *strewing flowers on her grave.* **2 the grave** [sing] (*rhet*) death; being dead: *from the cradle to the grave,* ie from birth till death ○ *Is there life beyond the grave* (ie after death)? **3** (idm) **dig one's own grave** ⇨ DIG[1]. **from the cradle to the grave** ⇨ CRADLE. **have one foot in the grave** ⇨ FOOT[1]. **turn in one's ˈgrave** (*saying*) of a person who is already dead, likely to be offended or angry: *You can't go out dressed like that. It's enough to make your grandmother turn in her grave!*
□ ˈ**gravestone** *n* stone on top of or at the head of a grave, with the name, etc of the person buried there. ⇨ illus at CHURCH.
ˈ**graveyard** *n* burial ground; cemetery.

grave[3] /grɑ:v/ *n* (also ˌ**grave ˈaccent**) mark (`) placed over a vowel to indicate how it is to be sounded (as in French *mère*).

gravel /ˈgrævl/ *n* [U] small stones, as used to make the surface of roads and paths: *a load of gravel* ○ [attrib] *a gravel path* ○ *a gravel pit,* ie from which

gravel is dug.
▷ **gravel** *v* (-ll-; *US also* -l-) [Tn esp passive] cover (sth) with gravel: *gravel a road* ○ *a gravelled path.*
gravelly /ˈgrævəlɪ/ *adj* **1** (full) of gravel: *This gravelly soil is well drained and good for growing root crops.* **2** (*fig esp approv*) (of a voice) deep and rough.

graven /ˈgreɪvn/ *adj* [pred] ~ **(in/on sth)** (*arch*) carved: (*fig*) *graven on* (ie permanently fixed in) *my memory.*
□ ˌ**graven** ˈ**image** (*Bible*) idol.

Graves /greɪvz/ Robert (1895-1985), English author. His output was huge, including historical novels, eg *I, Claudius* and *Claudius the God*, and many volumes of poetry. His autobiography, *Goodbye to All That*, tells of his experiences in the First World War.

gravid /ˈgrævɪd/ *adj* (*fml or medical*) pregnant.

graving dock /ˈgreɪvɪŋ dɒk/ *n* dry dock in which the outside of a ship's hull may be cleaned.

gravitas /ˈgrævɪtæs/ *n* [U] (*Latin*) seriousness and dignity (of behaviour, manner, speech, etc): *displaying all the gravitas of a professional diplomat.*

gravitate /ˈgrævɪteɪt/ *v* [Ipr] ~ **towards/to sb/sth** move towards or be attracted to sb/sth, gradually and irresistibly; turn to sb/sth: *When she arrived, all the men in the room gravitated towards her.* ○ *The conversation gravitated to sport.*
▷ **gravitation** /ˌgrævɪˈteɪʃn/ *n* [U] force of attraction; gravity(1): *effects of gravitation on bodies in space.* According to *Newton's theory of gravitation all particles in the universe attract each other with a force which depends on the mass of each particle and which is inversely proportional to the square of the distance between them. This was considered to be completely true until *Einstein produced his theory of relativity, which states that space-time is 'curved' near matter. On Earth the two theories give virtually the same practical results. **gravitational** /-ʃənl/ *adj*: *a gravitational field.*

gravity /ˈgrævətɪ/ *n* [U] **1** force that attracts objects in space towards each other, and on the earth pulls them towards the centre of the planet, so that things fall to the ground when dropped. **2** (**a**) importance (of a worrying kind); seriousness: *I don't think you realize the gravity of the situation.* ○ *For an offence of this gravity, imprisonment is the usual punishment.* ○ *news of considerable, unusual, etc gravity.* (**b**) solemnity: *behave with due gravity in a court of law, at a funeral, etc* ○ *a twinkle in his eye which belied the gravity of his demeanour.*
□ ˈ**gravity feed** system for supplying material, fuel, etc by the effect of gravity rather than by a pump, etc.

gravy /ˈgreɪvɪ/ *n* [U] **1** juice that comes from meat while it is cooking; sauce made from this: *a typical English meal of meat, vegetables, potatoes and gravy.* **2** (*sl esp US*) unearned or unexpected money (or profit).
□ ˈ**gravy-boat** *n* vessel in which gravy is served at table.
ˈ**gravy train** (*sl esp US*) means of getting a lot of money without much effort (eg through corruption): *be/get on the gravy train.*

Gray /greɪ/ Thomas (1716-71), English poet. He is most famous for his *Elegy written in a Country Church-Yard.* His works were first published by his friend Horace *Walpole.

gray[1] /greɪ/ *n* (*abbr* **Gy**) (*physics*) SI unit of the absorbed dose of ionizing radiation.

gray[2] /greɪ/ *adj, n, v* (*esp US*) = GREY.

grayling /ˈgreɪlɪŋ/ *n* (*pl* unchanged) silver-grey freshwater fish with a long high dorsal fin.

graze[1] /greɪz/ *v* **1** [I, Ipr] ~ **(in/on sth)** (of cattle, sheep, etc) eat growing grass: *cattle grazing in the fields.* **2** (**a**) [Tn, Tn·pr] ~ **sth (in/on sth)** put (cattle, etc) in a field to eat grass: *graze sheep.* (**b**) [Tn] use (grassland) to feed cattle, etc.
▷ **grazier** /ˈgreɪzɪə(r)/ *n* **1** person who farms grazing animals. **2** (*Austral*) sheep-farmer.
ˈ**grazing** *n* [U] land used for grazing cattle; pasturage: *cows put out to grazing.*

graze[2] /greɪz/ *v* **1** [Tn, Tn·pr] ~ **sth (against/on sth)** touch and scrape the skin from sth: *graze one's arm, leg, etc against/on a rock* ○ *I fell and grazed my knee.* **2** [I, Tn, Tn·pr] ~ **(sth) (against/along sth)** touch or scrape (sth) lightly while passing: *Our bumpers just grazed* (ie touched each other) *as we passed.* ○ *A bullet grazed his cheek.* ○ *a missile which flies so low that it almost grazes the tops of the hedgerows* ○ *The car's tyres grazed (against) the kerb.*
▷ **graze** *n* raw place where the skin is scraped.

grease /gri:s/ *n* [U] **1** animal fat that has been softened by cooking or heating: *The grease from pork can be used for frying.* **2** any thick semi-solid oily substance: *axle-grease*, ie used to lubricate axles ○ *He smothers his hair with grease*, eg hair-oil. ○ [attrib] *Grease marks or spots can be removed with liquid detergent.*
▷ **grease** *v* **1** [Tn] put or rub grease on or in (esp parts of a machine). **2** (idm) **grease sb's** ˈ**palm** (*infml*) bribe sb. **like greased lightning** ⇨ LIGHTNING[1]. **greaser** *n* (*Brit*) **1** person who greases machinery, eg a ship's engines. **2** (*US sl offensive*) person from Latin America, esp a Mexican.
□ ˈ**grease-gun** *n* device for forcing grease into the parts of an engine, a machine, etc.
ˈ**grease-paint** *n* [U] coloured make-up used by actors.
ˌ**grease-proof** ˈ**paper** paper that does not let grease pass through it, and is used esp for cooking or wrapping food in.

greasy /ˈgri:sɪ/ *adj* (**-ier, -iest**) **1** (**a**) covered with grease; slippery: *greasy fingers* ○ *a greasy road.* (**b**) producing an excessive amount of oily secretions: *greasy skin/hair.* (**c**) (*derog*) containing or cooked with too much fat or oil: *greasy food.* **2** (*fig infml derog*) (of people or their behaviour) insincerely flattering and smooth; unctuous: *He greeted me with a greasy smile.* ▷ **greasily** /-ɪlɪ/ *adv.* **greasiness** *n* [U].
□ ˌ**greasy** ˈ**spoon** (*joc sl derog esp US*) cheap café or restaurant, esp one that is dirty and serves poor food.

great /greɪt/ *adj* (**-er, -est**) **1** (**a**) [attrib] well above average in size, extent or quantity: *The great ship sank below the waves.* ○ *a great expanse of forest* ○ *dive to a great depth* ○ *all creatures great and small* ○ *A great crowd had turned up.* ○ *People had turned up in great numbers.* ○ *The great majority (of people)* (ie Most people) *approve.* ○ *The greater part* (ie Most) *of the area is flooded.* (**b**) far away in space or time: *He lives a great distance away.* ○ *That was a great while ago.* (**c**) [usu attrib] exceptional in degree or intensity; considerable: *of great value, importance, relevance, significance, etc* ○ *He described it in great detail.* ○ *Take great care to do it properly.* ○ *You have my greatest* (ie very great) *sympathy.* ○ *be in great demand*, ie much wanted. (**d**) in a very good state of health, morale or well-being; fine: *I feel great today!* ○ *in great form*, ie very fit and active ○ *in great spirits*, ie very cheerful. (**e**) [attrib] with very good or bad effects: *It's a great relief to know you're safe.* ○ *You've been a great help.* ○ *the greatest disaster that has ever befallen us.* ⇨ Usage at BIG. **2** (**a**) of remarkable ability or quality; outstanding: *a great man, artist, musician, etc* ○ *her great deeds* ○ *No one would deny that Beethoven's symphonies are great masterpieces.* ○ *the world's greatest novelist.* (**b**) [attrib] of high rank or status: *a great lady* ○ *the great powers*, ie important and powerful countries ○ *Alexander the Great.* (**c**) (*infml*) very remarkable; splendid: *He's great!* ○ *She's the greatest!* ○ *It's great that you can come!* ○ *What a great party!* ○ *He scored a great goal.* (**d**) (*infml*) ~ **(to do sth)** very enjoyable or satisfactory: *We had a great time in Majorca.* ○ *It's great to know you!* ○ *It's great to have met you!* **3** (**a**) ~ **for sth** (*infml*) very suitable for sth; ideal or useful for sth: *This little gadget's great for opening tins.* ○ *These are great shoes for muddy weather.* (**b**) [pred] ~ **at sth** (*infml*) clever or skilful at sth: *She's great at tennis, chess, etc.* (**c**) (*ironic*) (used to express exasperation, scorn, etc): *Oh great, I've missed the bus again!* ○ *You've been a great help, you have!* **4** [attrib] (**a**) important; noteworthy: *The princes[s] was getting married, and everyone was in town fo[r] the great occasion.* ○ *As the great momen[t] approached, she grew more and more nervous.* (**b**) unequalled; excellent: *She had a great chance[/] opportunity, but she let it slip.* (**c**) **the great** th[e] most important: *The great advantage of this meta[l] is that it doesn't rust.* **5** [attrib] fully deserving th[e] name of; beyond the ordinary: *We are grea[t] friends.* ○ *I've never been a great reader*, ie I do no[t] read much. ○ *He's a great one for complaining*, i[e] He constantly complains. **6** [attrib] (*infml*) (use[d] to intensify another *adj* of size, etc) very: *What [a] great big idiot!* ○ *You great fat pig!* ○ *That's a grea[t] thick slice of cake!* **7** [attrib] (used to name th[e] larger of two types, species, etc): *the great auk*, i[e] contrasted with the little auk. **8** (added to word[s] for relatives beginning with *grand-* to show [a] further stage in relationship): *one's* ˌ*grea[t]*ˈ*grandfather*, ie one's father's or mother'[s] grandfather ○ *one's* ˌ*great-*ˈ*grandson*, ie th[e] grandson of one's son or daughter. ⇨ App [8]. **9** (*dated infml*) (in exclamations of surprise) *Great Scott!* ○ *Great heavens!* **10** (idm) **be no grea[t] shakes** (*infml*) not be very good, efficien[t], suitable, etc: *She's no great shakes as an actress.* **going great guns** (*infml*) proceeding vigorousl[y] and successfully. **a good/great deal** ⇨ DEAL[2]. **great and small** rich and poor, powerful an[d] weak, etc: *Everyone, great and small, is affected b[y] these changes.* **make great/rapid strides** ⇨ STRIDE. **of great price** very valuable. **your need i[s] greater than mine** ⇨ NEED[3].
▷ **great** *n* **1** (usu *pl*) (*infml*) person of outstandin[g] ability: *one of boxing's all-time greats.* **2 the grea[t]** [pl *v*] great(2) people: *a fashionable affair attende[d] by all the great and the good*, ie important an[d] influential people. **3 Greats** [sing *v*] (**a**) course a[t] Oxford University for a BA degree in classics an[d] philosophy. (**b**) final examinations in this course. **greatly** *adv* much; by much: *We were greatl[y] amused.* ○ *The reports were greatly exaggerated.* **greatness** *n* [U]: *achieve greatness in one's lifetim[e].*
□ **the** ˌ**Great Au**ˌ**stralian** ˈ**Bight** wide bay on th[e] southern coast of Australia, forming part of th[e] Indian Ocean.
the ˌ**Great** ˌ**Barrier** ˈ**Reef** largest coral reef in th[e] world, parallel to the north-east coast of Australi[a] and about 2 000 km (1 250 miles) long.
the ˌ**Great** ˈ**Bear** large constellation near th[e] North Pole. Cf THE LITTLE BEAR (LITTLE[1]).
ˌ**Great** ˈ**Britain** (*abbr* **GB**) (also **Britain**) England, Wales and Scotland. ⇨ Usage.
great ˈ**circle** circle drawn round a sphere in suc[h] a way that one of its diameters passes through th[e] centre of the sphere.
ˈ**greatcoat** *n* (esp military) heavy overcoat.
ˌ**Great** ˈ**Dane** breed of large short-haired do[g] originally used for hunting.
the ˌ**Great Di**ˌ**viding** ˈ**Range** crest of the easter[n] highlands of Australia, which follows the curve [of] the coast as it crosses the country from north t[o] south.
ˌ**Greater** ˈ**London** local government area an[d] county set up in 1963 to include London and mo[st] of the former county of Middlesex, together wit[h] parts of nearby counties. ⇨ map at App 1.
ˌ**Greater** ˈ**Manchester** metropolitan county i[n] NW England. ⇨ map at App 1.
greatest common divisor = HIGHEST COMMO[N] FACTOR (HIGH[1]).
the ˌ**Great Exhi**ˈ**bition** first exhibition [of] industrial products from all over the worl[d] organized largely by Prince *Albert and held in th[e] *Crystal Palace in London in 1851.
the ˌ**Great** ˌ**Fire of** ˈ**London** fire that destroye[d] 13 000 buildings (including the old *St Paul['s] Cathedral) over a wide area of London in 1666.
ˌ**great-**ˈ**hearted** *adj* (*fml*) brave or generou[s]. ˌ**great-**ˈ**heartedness** *n* [U].
the ˌ**Great** ˈ**Lakes** five large lakes in Nort[h] America between Canada and the USA. Lak[e] Michigan is entirely within the USA; Lake Superior, Huron, Erie and Ontario are on th[e]

border between the two countries. They are connected to the Atlantic Ocean by the St Lawrence Seaway and form an important commercial waterway.

the ˌGreat ˈPlague epidemic of bubonic plague that killed many people in and around London in 1664-65.

the ˌGreat ˈPlains vast area of plains in Canada and the USA, stretching from the Rocky Mountains to the Mississippi valley.

the ˌGreat ˌSalt ˈLake large lake in northern *Utah, USA, containing salt water.

the ˌGreat ˌSandy ˈDesert large area of desert in northern central Western Australia.

the ˌGreat ˈSchism 1 split that separated the Eastern and Western Churches in 1054, caused partly by a disagreement over a theological point about the Trinity. **2** split within the Western Church from 1378 to 1417 when rival popes were elected by cardinals from different countries. The rival to the pope in Rome had his seat at Avignon in France.

ˌGreat ˈSeal official seal of a country used on documents of national importance. In Britain it is kept by the *Lord Chancellor and in the USA by the Secretary of State.

the ˌGreat ˈTrek journey made by *Boers in 1835-37 migrating northwards from the Cape Colony of South Africa to escape from British rule. They eventually founded the Transvaal Republic and the Orange Free State.

the ˌGreat Vicˌtoria ˈDesert large area of desert on either side of the border between Western Australia and South Australia.

the ˌGreat ˈWar the First World War, 1914-18.

NOTE ON USAGE: **Britain** or **Great Britain (GB)** consists of the geographical areas of England, Scotland and Wales. It is often also used to refer to the political state, officially called the **United Kingdom of Great Britain and Northern Ireland** and usually abbreviated to the **United Kingdom** or the **UK**. The **British Isles** are the islands of Britain and Ireland. People from Wales, Scotland and Northern Ireland are often offended when the terms *England* and *English* are used to refer to the whole country or its citizens. There is no noun in British English commonly used to refer to the nationality of the people of Britain; instead the adjective is used: *She's British.* ○ *The British are said to have an unusual sense of humour.* **Britisher** is used in American English. **Briton** is found in newspaper, etc reports of incidents concerning British people and in statistical information. It is also used of the early inhabitants of Britain: *10 Britons in hijacked plane.* ○ *According to the latest surveys many Britons suffer from heart disease.* ○ *the ancient Britons.* The distinctive national flag, usu called the *Union Jack*, is made up of the designs of three flags placed on top of each other: the flag of Saint George for England, of Saint Patrick for Ireland and of Saint Andrew for Scotland.

greaves /gri:vz/ *n* [pl] pieces of armour worn (esp formerly) to protect the shins.

grebe /gri:b/ *n* water bird similar to a duck but without webbed feet.

Grecian /ˈgri:ʃn/ *adj* (suggestive) of the art or culture of ancient Greece: *a Grecian* (ie an ancient Greek) *urn* ○ *his handsome Grecian profile.*

□ **ˌGrecian ˈnose** straight nose that continues in a straight line from the forehead. ⇨ illus at NOSE.

Greece /gri:s/ country in SE Europe, a member of the European Community since 1981; pop approx 10 013 000; official language Greek; capital Athens; unit of currency drachma (= 100 lepta). The country is mountainous, making road communications difficult, and over 400 islands lie around its coasts. Besides its typically Mediterranean crops of grapes, olives and wheat, it also grows tobacco. Industry in Greece developed much later than in the rest of Europe, giving it less importance in the economy. The

Greece

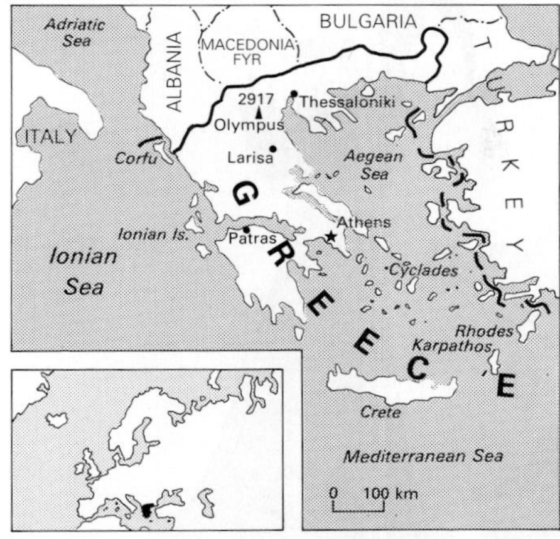

country's shipping industry is however one of the largest in the world and the sunny climate and the cultural heritage of ancient Greece have helped to make tourism important. For 400 years Greece was ruled by Turkey and relations with this country remain difficult, esp over *Cyprus. ⇨ map.

greed /gri:d/ *n* [U] ~ **(for sth)** (*derog*) **1** excessive desire for food, esp when one is not hungry. **2** excessive and selfish desire for wealth, power, etc: *the greed with which large companies swallow up their smaller competitors* ○ *consumed with greed and envy.*

▷ **greedy** *adj* **(-ier, -iest)** ~ **(for sth)** filled with greed or desire: *a greedy little boy* ○ *not hungry, just greedy* ○ *looking at the cakes with greedy eyes* ○ *greedy for power* ○ *greedy for information.* **greedily** *adv.* **greediness** *n* [U]. **ˈgreedy-guts** *n* (*pl* unchanged) (*joc infml*) person who is very greedy about food: *You little greedy-guts — you've eaten all the biscuits!*

Greek /gri:k/ *adj* of Greece or its people or language.

▷ **Greek** *n* **1** [C] member of the people living in ancient or modern Greece. **2** [U] language spoken in ancient or modern Greece. Classical Greek, like Latin, developed as one of the *Indo-European languages. It was used by the great philosophers like Plato and Aristotle and for Greek tragic drama, and it was regarded as a language of cultured people even in the Roman Empire. It continued to be the official language of the Byzantine Empire, though many aspects of grammar and pronunciation changed. Modern Greek still uses the ancient alphabet, but the letters do not all have the sound value they once had. It has two forms: *demotic*, which is used in everyday language, and *katharevousa*, which is closer to classical Greek and much less commonly used. **3** (idm) **it's all Greek to me** (*infml saying*) it's impossible to understand.

□ **ˌGreek ˈcross** cross with four equal arms.

Greek ˈgod very attractive young man.

green[1] /gri:n/ *adj* **(-er, -est) 1** of the colour between blue and yellow in the spectrum; of the colour of growing grass, and the leaves of most plants and trees: *as green as grass* ○ *fresh green peas.* ⇨ illus at SPECTRUM. **2** covered with grass or other plants: *green fields, hills, etc.* **3 (a)** (of fruit) not yet ripe: *green bananas* ○ *apples too green to eat.* **(b)** (of wood) not yet dry enough for use: *Green wood does not burn well.* **(c)** (of tobacco) not dried. **4** (*infml*) immature; inexperienced; easily fooled: *a green young novice* ○ *You must be green to believe that!* **5** [usu pred] (of the complexion) pale; sick-looking: *The passengers turned quite green with sea-sickness.* **6** [pred] extremely envious: *I was absolutely green (with envy) when I saw his splendid new car.* **7** (*fig rhet*) flourishing; full of vigour; fresh (used esp in the expressions shown): *live to a green old age* ○ *keep sb's memory green*, ie not allow sb (dead) to be forgotten. **8** [usu attrib] (*esp politics*) (favouring the party that is) particularly concerned about protecting the environment and the plants and animals that grow in it: *green politics.* ⇨ articles at ENVIRONMENT, POLITICS. **9** (idm) **give sb/get the green ˈlight** (*infml*) give sb/get permission to do sth. **the grass is greener on the other side** ⇨ GRASS[1].

▷ **greenish** /ˈgri:nɪʃ/ *adj* somewhat green: *a greenish-yellow tinge.*

greenness *n* [U].

□ **ˈgreenback** *n* (*US infml*) US banknote.

ˌgreen ˈbelt area of open land around a city, where building is strictly controlled. ⇨ article at COUNTRYSIDE.

ˌgreen ˈcard 1 international insurance document needed by motorists who take their cars abroad. **2** (*US*) identity card given to non-Americans who have been given permission to live and work in the USA.

the ˌGreen Cross ˈCode (in Britain) set of rules for teaching road safety to children.

ˌgreen-eyed ˈmonster [sing] (*rhet*) envy; jealousy.

ˈgreenfinch *n* finch with green and yellow feathers.

ˌgreen ˈfingers (*infml*) skill in gardening: *Mother has green fingers.*

ˈgreenfly *n* (*pl* unchanged) any of various kinds of small insects (*aphids*) that are harmful to plants.

ˈgreengage /-geɪdʒ/ *n* type of small yellowish-green plum.

ˈgreengrocer *n* (*Brit*) shopkeeper selling vegetables and fruit.

ˈgreenhouse *n* building with sides and roof of glass, used for growing plants that need protection from the weather. **the ˈgreenhouse effect** gradual warming of the earth's atmosphere, thought to be caused by carbon dioxide, methane and other gases preventing infra-red radiation from the sun escaping from the earth's atmosphere. Cf GLOBAL WARMING (GLOBAL).

ˌGreen ˈPaper (in Britain) preliminary report of government proposals, for discussion. Cf WHITE PAPER (WHITE[1]).

the ˈGreen Party (in Britain) political party whose aims are to protect the countryside, atmosphere, etc from pollution and other dangers.

ˌgreen ˈpound value of the pound as a currency exchange for agricultural produce in the EC.

ˌgreen revoˈlution greatly increased production of crops in developing countries, resulting from improved agricultural methods, pest control, etc.

ˌgreen ˈsalad salad made chiefly from lettuce and other raw green vegetables.

ˌgreen-stick ˈfracture fracture, common in children, in which the bone does not break completely but bends and cracks on one side.

ˈgreenstuff *n* [U] green vegetables or plants.

green ˈtea light-coloured tea made from incompletely fermented leaves.

ˈgreenwood *n* (*arch*) forest in summer.

green[2] /gri:n/ *n* **1** [U, C] green colour: *the green of the English countryside in spring* ○ *curtains of bright emerald green* ○ *a picture in greens and blues*, ie with various shades of green and blue. **2** [U] green clothes: *a girl dressed in green.* **3 greens** [pl] **(a)** vegetables with large edible green leaves, eg cabbage, spinach. **(b)** (*US*) vegetation; greenery: *Christmas greens*, eg branches of fir and holly for decoration. **4** [C] area of land with grass growing: *the village ˈgreen*, ie public or common land ○ *a ˈbowling-green*, ie for the game of bowls. **5** [C] area with grass cut short surrounding a hole on a golf-course: *a ˈputting-green* ○ *the 13th ˈgreen.* ⇨ illus at GOLF. **6 Green** [C] (usu *pl*) member of a green[1](8) political party. **7** (idm) **the rub of the green** ⇨ RUB[2].

□ **ˈgreen-fee** *n* amount of money charged for playing a round of golf on a golf-course.

Greenaway /ˈgri:nəweɪ/ Kate (1846-1901), English artist, famous for her illustrations for children's books, which show idealized children in early 19th-century dress playing in pretty surroundings. ⇨ illus.

Kate Greenaway: The Pied Piper of Hamelin

Greene /gri:n/ Graham (1904-91), English novelist. He became a Catholic in 1926 and his characters are often involved in moral or religious conflicts, as in *The Power and the Glory*. He travelled widely and the locations of many of his novels reflect international events. He also wrote plays, travel books and essays.

greenery /ˈgri:nəri/ *n* [U] attractive green foliage, either on growing plants or cut for decoration: *The hall looks more festive with all that greenery in pots.*

greenhorn *n* inexperienced and easily deceived person.

Greenland /ˈgri:nlənd/ island in the Arctic Circle, the largest in the world. It is a self-governing part of Denmark; pop approx 55 000; capital Godthaab (or Nuuk). Most of Greenland is covered in ice and uninhabited. Fishing is the main economic activity. ⇨ map at CANADA.

green-room *n* room in a theatre, TV studio, etc where the performers can relax.

Greensleeves /ˈgri:nsli:vz/ famous English song, probably Elizabethan, in which a lover complains that the lady Greensleeves does not return his love. It has been said that Henry VIII wrote it but there is no evidence for this. The tune has been adapted and arranged in many musical styles.

Greenwich /ˈgrenɪdʒ/ district of SE London, England. It was the site of the original Royal Observatory founded in 1675 by King *Charles II and designed by Christopher *Wren. The Observatory was moved to E Sussex in 1948 and the buildings are now part of the National Maritime Museum.

□ ˌ**Greenwich** ˈ**Mean Time** (*abbr* **GMT**) (also **Universal Time**) time on the line of 0° longitude (which passes through Greenwich) used as a basis for calculating time throughout the world. It is used in Britain from October to March; for the rest of the year *British Summer Time, one hour ahead of Greenwich Mean Time, is used.

Greenwich Village /ˌgrenɪdʒ ˈvɪlɪdʒ/ district in Manhattan, New York City, famous for its old buildings and its intellectual and artistic life.

greet[1] /gri:t/ *v* **1** (**a**) [Tn, Tn·pr] ~ **sb** (**with sth**) give a conventional sign or word of welcome or pleasure when meeting sb or receiving a (guest): *He greeted me in the street with a friendly wave of the hand.* ○ *greeting her guests at the door.* (**b**) [Tn·pr esp passive] ~ **sth with sth** receive sth with a particular reaction: *The news was greeted by/with cheering, booing, etc.* ○ *This appointment was greeted with relief, dismay, etc.* **2** [Tn] (of sights and sounds) be suddenly seen or heard by (sb): *the view that greeted us at the top of the hill.*

▷ **greeting** *n* **1** first words used on seeing sb or in writing to sb; expression or act with which sb is greeted: *'Hello!' and 'Dear Sir' are greetings.* ○ *exchange, send greetings* ○ [attrib] *a* ˈ*greetings card*, ie a decorative card sent at Christmas, on sb's birthday, etc. ⇨ article. **2** (idm) **the season's greetings** ⇨ SEASON.

greet[2] /gri:t/ *v* [I] (*Scot*) cry; weep.

gregarious /grɪˈgeərɪəs/ *adj* **1** liking to be with other people. **2** (*biology*) (of animals, birds, etc) living in groups or communities. ▷ **gregariously** *adv.* **gregariousness** *n* [U].

Gregorian /grɪˈgɔ:rɪən/ *adj.*

□ **Gre**ˌ**gorian** ˈ**calendar** system now in general use of arranging the months in the year and the days in the month, introduced by Pope Gregory XIII (1502-85). Cf JULIAN CALENDAR.

Greˌ**gorian** ˈ**chant** kind of medieval church music named after Pope Gregory I (540-604).

gremlin /ˈgremlɪn/ *n* imaginary mischievous creature supposed to cause mechanical or other failure: *The gremlins have got into the computer again.*

Grenada /grɪˈneɪdə/ group of Caribbean islands, an independent state and member of the Commonwealth since 1974; pop approx 100 000; official language English; capital Saint George's; unit of currency dollar (= 100 cents). The main island is densely forested and has several volcanic mountains. The economy is based on agriculture, the main crops being cocoa and nutmeg, and tourism is increasingly important. ⇨ map at CARIBBEAN.

grenade /grəˈneɪd/ *n* small bomb thrown by hand or fired from a rifle: *a* ˈ*hand-grenade* ○ [attrib] *a grenade attack.*

grenadier /ˌgrenəˈdɪə(r)/ *n* (formerly) soldier who threw grenades; (now) soldier in the Grenadiers (or Grenadier Guards), a British infantry regiment.

Gresham /ˈgreʃəm/ Sir Thomas (c 1519-79), English merchant. He was an early economist and advised the government of *Elizabeth I on financial matters. He founded the *Royal Exchange in London.

□ ˌ**Gresham's** ˈ**law** economic principle attributed to Gresham, often expressed as 'Bad money drives out good': money of lower intrinsic value tends to be used more widely than money of higher intrinsic value, when both are available, since people save the latter and pass on the former in payment of debts, etc.

Gretna Green /ˌgretnə ˈgri:n/ village near Carlisle, just north of the border between England and Scotland. It is famous as the place where couples came from England to be married by the local blacksmith without the formalities required by English law. The tradition ended in 1940, when such marriages were made illegal.

grew *pt* of GROW.

Grey[1] /greɪ/ Lady Jane (1537-54), granddaughter of the sister of *Henry VIII. The Duke of

Greetings Cards

In Britain, greetings cards are sold in chain stores and supermarkets, in newsagents' shops, corner shops and, increasingly, in shops that specialize in the sale of cards and paper for wrapping presents in. The variety of cards available represents the many aspects of British family life, with cards that are appropriate for every conceivable occasion.

The most common cards are birthday and Christmas cards. Many Christmas cards are sold in aid of charity and special 'charity card shops' are often set up in temporary premises in the weeks before Christmas. A wide variety of birthday cards is available, to cater for different ages and tastes. Some, especially ones for young children or for people celebrating a particular birthday, have the person's age on the front. Many have comic, often risqué, messages printed on them, and cartoon-style illustrations. Others are more sober, with reproductions of famous paintings or attractive original designs. The usual greeting on a birthday card is 'Happy Birthday', 'Many Happy Returns' or 'Best Wishes for a Happy Birthday'.

Some people also send special cards for Easter and New Year. Easter cards either portray images of spring, such as chicks, eggs, lambs, spring flowers, etc, or have a religious theme.

Cards are produced for every 'milestone' in a person's life. There are special cards for an engagement, a marriage, a new home, a birth, success in an examination, retirement, a death in the family, etc. Some are 'good luck' or 'congratulations' cards. Others, for example 'get well' cards for people who are ill, express sympathy.

Birthday and Christmas cards often have words like 'For Mum', 'For a Lovely Wife', 'For my Darling Husband', 'To a Wonderful Grandad' printed on the front of the card. There are also special cards for Mother's Day and Father's Day, as well as cards for St Valentine's Day (14 February) with hearts, cupids, etc. Many of these contain rather banal sentimental verses. Although they are often laughed at as examples of bad taste, they are still very popular.

Northumberland forced her to marry his son and persuaded the Protestant king Edward VI to declare that she should succeed to the throne rather than his half-sister Mary Tudor. Jane was queen for nine days before being deposed by forces loyal to Mary, and later executed to avoid possible rebellions by Protestants.

Grey[2] /greɪ/ Zane (1875-1939), American novelist. He wrote over 60 books, mainly about life in the American West. He is regarded as the founder of the western novel and many of his works were made into films.

grey (also *esp US* **gray**) /greɪ/ *adj* **1** (**a**) of the colour between black and white; coloured like ashes, slate, lead, etc: *grey eyes, hair, etc* ○ *a grey suit.* (**b**) [usu pred] having grey hair: *She has turned quite grey recently.* ○ *I'm going grey.* (**c**) dull; cloudy: *a grey day.* **2** (*fig*) (**a**) depressing; monotonous: *a grey existence* ○ *Life seemed grey and pointless after she'd gone.* (**b**) (*derog*) having no life or attractive features; anonymous: *a government department run by little grey men.*

▷ **grey** (*esp US* **gray**) *n* **1** [U, C] grey colour: *a suit of dark/light/medium grey.* **2** [U] grey clothes: *dressed in grey.* **3** [C] grey or white horse.

grey (*esp US* **gray**) *v* [I, Tn] (cause sth to) become grey: *He/His hair has greyed a lot.* ○ *He was 50 and greying.* ○ *Worry had greyed her hair.*

greyish (*esp US* **grayish**) *adj* somewhat grey.

□ ˌ**grey** ˈ**area** aspect, topic, etc that does not fit into a particular category, and is therefore difficult to deal with: *When the rules for police procedure were laid down, a lot of grey areas remained.*

ˈ**greybeard** *n* (*rhet*) old man.

ˈ**Grey Friars** Franciscan friars (so called because of their grey cloaks).

ˌ**grey-**ˈ**headed** *adj* with grey hair; old.

ˈ**grey matter** (**a**) material of the brain. (**b**) (*fig infml*) intelligence: *a boy without much grey matter.*

ˌ**grey** ˈ**squirrel** common squirrel, brought to Europe from the USA in the 19th century.

greyhound /ˈgreɪhaʊnd/ *n* large thin fast-running dog used in racing: [attrib] *ˈgreyhound racing.* ⇨ illus at DOG.

greylag /ˈgreɪlæg/ *n* (also **greylag goose**) European wild goose.

grid /grɪd/ *n* **1** framework of crossing or parallel metal or wooden bars; grating: *a ˈcattle-grid*, ie one placed at a gate, etc to prevent cattle from straying onto a main road, etc. **2** (**a**) network of lines, esp crossing at right angles: [attrib] *New York is laid out on a grid pattern.* (**b**) network of squares on a map, numbered for reference: [attrib] *the grid reference of a place on a map.* ⇨ illus at MAP. **3** system of electric-power cables or gas-supply lines for distributing power evenly over a large area: *the National Grid*, ie the network of electricity supply in Britain. **4** pattern of lines marking the starting-places on a car-racing track.

griddle /ˈgrɪdl/ *n* (*Scot* **girdle**) circular iron plate heated for cooking flat cakes.

gridiron /ˈgrɪdaɪən/ *n* **1** framework of metal bars used for cooking meat or fish over an open fire. **2** (*US*) field for American football (the area of play being marked by a pattern of parallel lines). ⇨ article at SPORT.

grief /gri:f/ *n* **1** [U] ~ (**over/at sth**) deep or violent sorrow: *driven almost insane by grief over/at his death* ○ *die of grief.* **2** [C] event causing such feelings: *His marriage to someone outside their faith was a great grief to his parents.* **3** (idm) **come to** ˈ**grief** (*infml*) (**a**) end in failure: *All his little schemes for making money seem to come to grief.* (**b**) have an accident; fall down, crash, etc: *Several pedestrians had come to grief on the icy pavement.* **good** ˈ**grief!** (*infml*) (exclamation of surprise and (usu mild) dismay).

□ ˈ**grief-stricken** *adj* overcome by deep sorrow: *trying to console the grief-stricken relatives.*

Grieg /gri:g/ Edvard (1843-1907), Norwegian composer. Much of his music, like the popular piano concerto and the suite for *Ibsen's *Peer Gynt*, was inspired by his country's folk-music, though he rarely used its tunes directly.

grievance /ˈgri:vns/ *n* ~ (**against sb**) real or imagined cause for complaint or protest (used esp with the *vs* shown): *inviting the members to air* (ie express) *their grievances* ○ *He'd been harbouring/nursing a grievance against his boss.* ○ *Management agreed to settle the workers' grievances.*

grieve /gri:v/ *v* (*fml*) **1** [Tn] cause great sorrow to (sb): *Your mother is very grieved by your refusal to return home.* ○ *It grieves me to hear how disobedient you've been.* ○ *It grieves me to have to say it, but* (ie It is regrettably true that) *you have only yourself to blame.* **2** (**a**) [I, Ipr] ~ (**for sb**); ~ (**over/about sb/sth**) feel a deep sorrow because of loss: *Their daughter died over a year ago, but they are still grieving.* ○ *grieve for one's (dead, lost) child* ○ *grieve over the death of sb.* (**b**) [Ipr] ~ **at/about/over sth** feel deep regret (about sth): *It's no use grieving about past errors.*

grievous /ˈgri:vəs/ *adj* **1** causing grief or suffering: *grievous news, losses, wrongs.* **2** (*fml*) (of sth bad) severe; serious: *grievous pain, wounds, etc* ○ *a grievous error, fault, sin, crime, etc.* ▷ **grievously** *adv*: *If you think that, you are grievously in error.*

□ ˌ**grievous** ˌ**bodily** ˈ**harm** (*law*) (*abbr* **GBH**) serious injury caused by a criminal attack.

griffin /ˈgrɪfɪn/ (also **griffon**, **gryphon** /ˈgrɪfən/) *n* mythical creature with the head and wings of an eagle and a lion's body.

Griffith /ˈgrɪfɪθ/ D(avid) W(ark) (1875-1948), American film director. He was one of the great figures of the early cinema and invented or developed many basic film techniques, such as the flashback and fade-out. He made many remarkable silent films, including *The Birth of a Nation* on the American Civil War.

griffon /ˈgrɪfn/ *n* **1** breed of dog similar to a terrier, with coarse hair. **2** type of large vulture. **3** = GRIFFIN.

grill /grɪl/ *n* **1** (**a**) device on a cooker that directs heat downwards for cooking meat, toasting bread, etc: *an electric grill* ○ *an eye-level grill* ○ *Put it under the grill for a minute to brown the top.* ○ [attrib] *a grill pan.* (**b**) gridiron (for cooking on). (**c**) dish of meat, etc cooked directly over or under great heat: *a mixed grill*, ie grilled steak, liver, bacon, etc served together. (**d**) (also ˈ**grill-room**) room in a hotel or restaurant where such dishes are cooked and served: *Let's meet in the first-floor grill-room.* **2** = GRILLE.

▷ **grill** *v* **1** (**a**) [I, Tn, Dn·n] be cooked or cook (sth) over or under great heat: *grilled steak* ○ *I'll grill you some fish.* ⇨ Usage at COOK. (**b**) [I, Tn] (*infml*) expose (oneself) to great heat: *sit grilling (oneself) in front of a fire, in the sun, under a sun-ray lamp, etc.* **2** [Tn] (*fig infml*) question (sb) intensively and for a long time, often hostilely: *The police grilled him (with non-stop questions) for over an hour.*

grille (also **grill**) /grɪl/ *n* protective screen of metal bars or wires: *The bank clerk peered at the customer through/from behind the grille.* ○ *Ensure that the grille is in place while the machinery is in operation.*

grim /grɪm/ *adj* (**-mmer, -mmest**) **1** very serious and unsmiling in appearance: *a grim face, look, etc* ○ *He looked grim; I could tell something was wrong.* **2** severe; unrelenting: *their grim day-to-day struggle for survival.* **3** unpleasant; depressing: *grim news* ○ *We face the grim prospect of still higher unemployment.* **4** determined in spite of fear: *a grim smile.* **5** containing disturbing or horrific material: *a grim little tale of torture and murder.* **6** (of a place) depressingly plain; gloomy: *the grim walls of the prison.* **7** [pred] (*infml*) ill: *I feel pretty grim.* **8** [usu pred] (*infml*) very bad or unpleasant: *I've seen her so-called paintings; they're fairly grim, I can tell you!* **9** (idm) **like grim** ˈ**death** with great determination or perseverance in spite of difficulties: *He held onto the branch like grim death.* ○ *She stuck to her task like grim death.* ▷ **grimly** *adv*: *grimly determined.* **grimness** *n* [U].

grimace /grɪˈmeɪs; *US* ˈgrɪməs/ *n* ugly twisted expression (on the face), expressing pain, disgust, etc or intended to cause laughter: *make/give a grimace of pain.*

▷ **grimace** *v* [I, Ipr] ~ (**at sb/sth**) make grimaces: *She grimaced in/with distaste at the thought of it.* ⇨ Usage at SMIRK.

Grimaldi /grɪˈmɔ:ldɪ/ Joseph (1779-1837), English actor and creator of the English clown (in circuses, etc), in whose honour all later clowns have the nickname 'Joey'. He was famous for his comic inventiveness, yet despite the laughter he created, in private he was an unhappy man.

grime /graɪm/ *n* [U] dirt, esp in a layer on a surface: *the soot and grime of a big manufacturing town* ○ *a face covered with grime and sweat.*

▷ **grime** *v* [Tn esp passive] make (sb/sth) dirty: *a face grimed with dust.*

grimy /ˈgraɪmɪ/ *adj* (**-ier, -iest**) covered with grime: *grimy hands, windows.* **griminess** *n* [U].

Grimm /grɪm/ Jacob (1785-1863) and his brother Wilhelm (1786-1859), German scholars. They worked together on a historical German dictionary and their famous collection of German fairy-tales. Jacob also produced a historical German grammar in which Grimm's law appeared.

□ ˈ**Grimm's law** statement of how certain consonants in the German languages correspond regularly with other consonants in the other Indo-European languages.

grin /grɪn/ *v* (**-nn-**) **1** [I, Ipr] ~ (**at sb**) smile broadly, so as to show the teeth, expressing amusement, foolish satisfaction, contempt, etc: *He grinned at me, as if sharing a secret joke.* ○ *grin with delight* ○ *grin from ear to ear*, ie very broadly. **2** [Tn] express (sth) by grinning: *He grinned his approval.* **3** (idm) **grin and** ˈ**bear it** endure pain, disappointment, etc without complaining.

▷ **grin** *n* act of grinning: *a broad, foolish, silly, etc grin* ○ *With a nasty grin on his face he took out a knife.*

grind /graɪnd/ *v* (*pt, pp* **ground** /graʊnd/) **1** (**a**) [Tn, Tn·pr, Tn·p] ~ **sth (down/up) (to/into sth)** crush sth to very small pieces or to powder between millstones, the teeth, etc or using an electrical or a mechanical apparatus: *The elephant grinds its food with/between its powerful molars.* ○ *grind coffee beans* ○ *grind corn (down/up) into flour* ○ *grind sth to dust, to (a fine) powder, etc.* (**b**) [I, Ipr, Ip] ~ (**down**) (**to/into sth**) be able to be crushed finely: *The corn grinds easily.* ○ *It won't grind down any finer than this.* (**c**) [Tn] (*US*) mince (meat): *ground beef.* **2** [Tn, Tn·pr] ~ **sth (from sth)** produce sth by crushing: *grind flour from corn.* **3** [esp passive: Tn, Tn·p] ~ **sb (down)** (*fig*) treat sb extremely harshly; oppress sb: *people ground (down) by poverty, taxation, tyranny, etc* ○ *tyrants who grind down the poor.* **4** [Tn, Tn·pr] ~ **sth (on/with sth)** polish or sharpen sth by rubbing it on or with a rough hard surface: *grind a knife, lens, etc on a stone, etc.* **5** [Tn, Tn·pr, Tn·p] ~ **sth (together)**; ~ **sth in/into sth** press or rub sth firmly and often noisily: *He ground his teeth (together) in frustration.* ○ *dirt that had become ground into the surface* ○ (*fig*) *grind one's heel into the fragments*, ie crush them very hard. **6** [I, Ip] ~ (**away**) make a harsh noise (as if) from friction: *The old engine ground and shuddered.* **7** [Tn] work (sth) by turning a handle: *grind a coffee-mill, barrel-organ.* **8** [I, Ipr, Ip] ~ (**away**) (**at sth**) (*infml*) work or study hard and long: *grind away at one's studies.* **9** (idm) **bump and grind** ⇨ BUMP. **grind the faces of the** ˈ**poor (into the** ˈ**dust)** (*rhet*) deliberately cause poor people to suffer more than necessary, taking pleasure in doing so. **grind to a** ˈ**halt/**ˈ**standstill** (**a**) (of a vehicle) stop slowly and noisily. (**b**) (*fig*) (of a process) gradually stop: *The strike brought industry grinding to a halt.* **have an axe to grind** ⇨ AXE. **10** (phr v) **grind on** continue for a long time boringly and monotonously: *The speaker ground on, oblivious of his listeners' boredom.* **grind sth out** (**a**) produce sth by turning a handle: *grind out music from a barrel-organ.* (**b**) (*derog*) play (music) heavily, tediously or monotonously: *The jukebox ground out an incessant stream of pop music.* (**c**) (*derog*) produce (books, stories, etc) with sustained but uninspired effort: *He has been grinding out cheap romantic stories at the rate of one a week.*

▷ **grind** *n* **1** [sing] act of grinding. **2** [sing] size of ground particles: *a coarse grind.* **3** [sing] (*infml*) long, steady, tiring or monotonous effort (physical or mental): *a long uphill grind in a cycle race* ○ *Marking examination papers is a real grind.*

grinding *adj* **1** making a harsh noise (as if) from friction: *The car screeched to a halt with grinding brakes.* **2** (idm) **bring sth/come to a grinding ˈhalt** (*infml*) (cause sth to) stop completely. **grinding ˈpoverty** (*rhet*) extreme poverty that causes suffering.

□ **grindstone** /ˈgraɪndstəʊn/ *n* **1** stone shaped like a wheel, turned on an axle, against which one holds knives or other tools to sharpen them. **2** (idm) **keep one's/sb's nose to the grindstone** ⇨ NOSE[1].

grinder /ˈgraɪndə(r)/ *n* **1** thing that grinds, eg a molar tooth; apparatus for grinding: *a ˈcoffee-grinder.* **2** (in compounds) person who grinds: *a ˈknife-grinder* ○ *an ˈorgan-grinder*, ie sb who plays a barrel-organ.

gringo /ˈgrɪŋgəʊ/ *n* (*pl* ~**s**) (*infml derog*) (used esp by Latin-Americans) foreigner, esp an American or English person.

grip /grɪp/ *v* (**-pp-**) **1** [I, Tn] take and keep a firm hold of (sth/sb): *The frightened child gripped its mother's hand.* ○ *The brakes failed to grip* (ie engage with and stop the wheels) *and the car ran into a wall.* **2** [Tn esp passive] (*fig*) seize the attention, imagination, etc of (sb): *an audience gripped by a play* ○ *gripped by/with fear.*

▷ **grip** *n* **1** [sing] ~ (**on sb/sth**) (**a**) action of gripping; firm hold: *take a grip on a rope* ○ *I let go/released my grip and he ran away.* ○ *The climber relaxed her grip and fell.* ○ (*fig*) *The play's exciting at first, but in the third act it loses its grip on one's attention.* (**b**) way or power of gripping: *a grip like iron, like a vice, like a bulldog, etc* ○ *tyres which give (a) good grip on the road.* (**c**) (*fig*) force that paralyses or disables: *the icy grip of winter* ○ *people in the grip of disease, despair, etc.* **2** [C] part that is to be gripped; handle: *a wooden, metal, etc (hand-)grip.* **3** [C] wire pin with two prongs for keeping hair tidy; hair-grip. **4** [C] (*US*) large strong bag with handles: *a leather grip.* **5** (idm) **come/get to grips with sb/sth** (**a**) seize (an opponent) and begin to fight: *She was unable to get to grips with her assailant.* (**b**) (*fig*) begin to deal with (a problem, challenge, etc). **get/keep/take a ˈgrip/ˈhold on oneself** (*infml*) gain control of oneself and improve one's behaviour (eg after being afraid, lazy, out of control, etc). **lose one's grip** ⇨ LOSE.

gripping *adj* exciting; holding the attention: *a gripping account, film, story, etc* ○ *gripping yarns.* **grippingly** *adv.*

gripe[1] /graɪp/ *v* [I] feel or cause sudden sharp pain in the stomach or intestines: *a griping pain in the stomach* ○ *medicine to take when your stomach gripes.*

▷ **the gripes** *n* [pl] (*infml*) sharp pain in the intestines, etc.

□ **ˈgripe-water** *n* [U] medicine to cure stomach or intestinal pain in babies.

gripe[2] /graɪp/ *v* [I, Ipr] ~ (**about sb/sth**) (*infml derog*) complain (about sb/sth); grumble (habitually): *He keeps griping about having no money.*

▷ **gripe** *n* (*infml*) **1** [C] complaint; expression of discontent: *Bring all your gripes to the boss.* **2** (*derog*) [sing] act of complaining: *He likes to have a good gripe from time to time.*

grisly /ˈgrɪzlɪ/ *adj* causing horror or terror; ghastly: *the grisly remains of the half-eaten corpses.*

grist /grɪst/ *n* **1** [U] (*arch*) grain to be ground. **2** (idm) **grist to the/sb's ˈmill** useful or profitable, esp in addition to or as a contribution to sth larger: *I never refuse odd jobs to supplement my income — it's all grist to the mill.*

gristle /grɪsl/ *n* [U] tough unappetizing tissue (esp cartilage) in meat: *I can't eat this meat — it's all gristle*, ie full of gristle.

▷ **gristly** /-lɪ/ *adj* like or full of gristle.

grit /grɪt/ *n* [U] **1** tiny hard bits of stone, sand, etc: *spread grit on icy roads* ○ *I've got some grit/a piece of grit in my shoe.* **2** quality of courage and endurance: *Mountaineering in a blizzard needs a lot of grit.*

▷ **grit** *v* (**-tt-**) **1** [Tn] cover (sth) with grit; spread grit on (esp icy roads). **2** (idm) **grit one's ˈteeth** (**a**) keep one's jaws tight together. (**b**) (*fig*) summon up one's courage and determination: *When things get difficult, you just have to grit your teeth and persevere.*

gritty *adj* (**-ier**, **-iest**) full of grit: *cheap gritty bread* ○ *a gritty fighter.* **grittiness** *n* [U].

grits /grɪts/ *n* [pl] coarse oatmeal.

grizzle /ˈgrɪzl/ *v* (*infml derog*) [I] ~ (**about sth**) (esp of children) keep complaining (about sth) in a whining way: *Stop grizzling!*

▷ **grizzly** *adj* grizzling or inclined to grizzle.

grizzled /ˈgrɪzld/ *adj* grey(-haired).

grizzly /ˈgrɪzlɪ/ *n* (also ˌ**grizzly ˈbear**) large fierce grey-brown bear of N America. ⇨ illus at BEAR.

Gro *abbr* (in street names) Grove: *6 Lime Gro.*

groan /grəʊn/ *v* **1** [I, Ipr] ~ (**at sb/sth**); ~ (**with sth**) make a deep sad sound when in pain, or to express despair, disapproval or distress: *'I've been hit,' he groaned*, ie said with a groan. ○ *She groaned with pain.* ○ *The audience groaned at his terrible jokes.* **2** (**a**) [I, Ipr] ~ (**with sth**) (of things) make a noise like that of groaning: *The ship's timbers groaned during the storm.* (**b**) [Ipr] ~ **with sth** (*fig*) be heavily laden with sth: *a table groaning with food.* **3** [I, Ipr, Ip] ~ (**on**) (**about/over sth**) (*derog*) complain irritably; moan: *She's always groaning on about how much work she has to do.* **4** [Ipr] ~ **beneath/under sth** (*fig esp rhet*) suffer or be oppressed by sth: *poor people groaning beneath/under the weight of heavy taxes.* **5** (idm) ˌ**groan ˈinwardly** feel like groaning at sth but remain silent: *She groaned inwardly as she saw the fresh pile of work on her desk.*

▷ **groan** *n* **1** deep sound made when in pain, etc: *the groans of an injured man* ○ *give a groan of dismay* ○ *The chair gave a groan as he sat down in it.* **2** (usu *sing*) (*fig infml*) person or thing that makes people groan: *a joke, story, person that is a bit of a groan.*

groat /grəʊt/ *n* English silver coin worth four old pence, not in use since the 17th century.

groats /grəʊts/ *n* [pl] (crushed) grain, esp oats, that has had the outer covering removed.

grocer /ˈgrəʊsə(r)/ *n* shopkeeper who sells food in packets, tins or bottles and general small household goods: *Go down to the grocer's* (ie grocer's shop) *and get me some sugar.*

▷ **groceries** *n* [pl] things sold by a grocer.

grocery *n* **1** [U] grocer's trade: [attrib] *a grocery store.* **2** [C] (*esp US*) grocer's shop.

grog /grɒg/ *n* [U] (*nautical or infml*) drink of spirits (esp rum) mixed with water.

groggy /ˈgrɒgɪ/ *adj* (**-ier**, **-iest**) weak and dizzy (after illness, shock, lack of sleep, etc); unsteady: *The attack of flu left her feeling very groggy.* ○ *He's still groggy from the anaesthetic.* ▷ **groggily** *adv.* **grogginess** *n* [U].

groin /grɔɪn/ *n* **1** (*anatomy*) lower part of the abdomen, where the tops of the legs meet, containing the sexual organs: *She kicked her attacker in the groin.* ⇨ illus at HUMAN. **2** (*architecture*) curved edge where two arches supporting a roof meet. **3** (*US*) = GROYNE.

grommet /ˈgrɒmɪt/ (also **grummet** /ˈgrʌmɪt/) *n* ring-shaped piece of metal or other strong material used to strengthen a hole (eg in a piece of fabric).

groom /gru:m/ *n* **1** person in charge of horses. **2** = BRIDEGROOM.

▷ **groom** *v* **1** (**a**) [Tn] clean and look after (horses), esp by brushing. (**b**) [I, Tn] (of an ape, a monkey, etc) clean the fur and skin of (another or itself): *a female ape grooming her mate.* **2** [esp passive: Tn, Tn·pr, Cn·n/a] ~ **sb** (**for/as sth**) (*infml*) select, prepare and train (a young person) for a particular career, etc: *groomed for stardom by ambitious parents* ○ *He had been groomed for a career in the Civil Service/groomed as a future civil servant.* **groomed** *adj* (usu preceded by an *adv*) having the stated appearance of dress, hair-style and general neatness: *She is always perfectly groomed.*

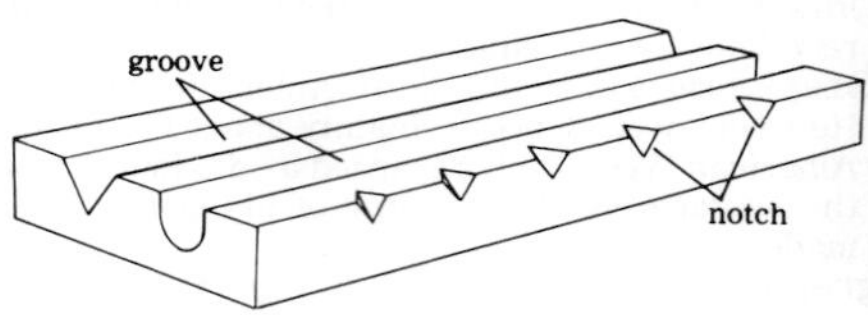

groove /gru:v/ *n* **1** long narrow cut or depression in the surface of hard material: *a groove for a sliding door.* ⇨ illus. **2** spiral cut on a gramophone disc for the needle or stylus: *The needle has jumped several grooves.* **3** (idm) **get into/be stuck in a groove** become set in a particular way of life.

▷ **grooved** *adj* having a groove or grooves.

groovy /ˈgru:vɪ/ *adj* (*dated sl*) attractive or excellent, esp because fashionable or modern.

grope /grəʊp/ *v* **1** [Ipr, Ip] ~ (**about**) (**for/after sth**) feel or search about (for sth) as one does in the dark: *grope about in the dark* ○ *grope for the door-handle, light-switch, etc* ○ (*fig*) *a tricky question which left him groping for an answer* ○ *scientists groping blindly after the secrets of the atom.* **2** [I, Tn] (*infml derog*) (attempt to) touch or fondle (sb) sexually. **3** (phr v) **grope (one's way) across, along, past, etc (sth)** make one's way in the stated direction by feeling or searching: *grope one's way along a darkened corridor.*

▷ **gropingly** *adv* in the manner of sb who gropes.

Gropius /ˈgrəʊpɪəs/ Walter (1883-1969), German architect. He was the director of the *Bauhaus school 1919-28, and had a great influence on modern urban design. ⇨ article at ARCHITECTURE.

gross[1] /grəʊs/ *n* (*pl* unchanged or ~**es**) (*esp commerce*) twelve dozen; 144: *two gross of best apples* ○ *sell sth by the gross/in grosses.* ⇨ App 9.

gross[2] /grəʊs/ *adj* (**-er**, **-est**) **1** repulsively fat: *a gross person* ○ *He's not just fat. He's positively gross!* **2** (*fml*) not refined; vulgar; coarse: *gross behaviour, language, manners* ○ *indulging in the grosser pleasures.* **3** [usu attrib] (*esp law fml*) glaringly obvious; flagrant: *gross negligence, indecency, vice, etc* ○ *a gross error, injustice, etc.* **4** [attrib] total; whole: *gross weight, profit, etc* ○ *sb's gross income*, ie before deduction of tax, etc. Cf NET[2] 1. **5** (idm) **in (the) gross** in a general or large-scale way rather than in detail.

▷ **gross** *v* [Tn, Tn·p] ~ **sth** (**up**) make sth as a total amount: *Her last film grossed* (ie earned) *a million pounds.* ○ *work out the grossed-up interest on a loan.*

grossly *adv* (of sth bad) extremely: *grossly fat, extravagant, unfair, exaggerated.*

grossness *n* [U] coarseness; vulgarity.

□ ˌ**gross doˌmestic ˈproduct** (*abbr* **GDP**) annual total value of goods produced, and services provided, in a country.

ˌ**gross ˌnational ˈproduct** (*abbr* **GNP**) annual total value of goods produced, and services provided, in a country, taken together with net income from abroad.

grotesque /grəʊˈtesk/ *adj* **1** strangely distorted so as to arouse fear or laughter; fantastic: *tribal dancers wearing grotesque masks.* **2** (*art*) combining human, animal and plant forms in a fantastic design. **3** ridiculously exaggerated or unreasonable; absurd: *a grotesque distortion of the truth* ○ *It's grotesque to expect a person of her experience to work for such little money.* **4** offensively incongruous: *the grotesque sight of an old man trying to flirt with a young girl.*

▷ **grotesque** *n* **1** [C] with fantastic or incongruous clothes, make-up, features, etc. **2 the grotesque** [sing] grotesque style used in a painting, carving, etc.

grotesquely *adv.*

grotesqueness *n* [U].

grotto /ˈgrɒtəʊ/ *n* (*pl* ~**es** or ~**s**) cave, esp one made artificially as a garden shelter.

grotty /ˈgrɒtɪ/ *adj* (**-ier, -iest**) (*infml*) unpleasant: *a grotty little man living in a grotty little room in a grotty part of town* ○ *I feel pretty grotty*, ie unwell.

grouch /graʊtʃ/ *v* [I, Ipr] ~ (**about sth**) (*derog*) complain: *Stop grouching about everything!*
▷ **grouch** *n* **1** (**a**) [sing] ~ (**about sth**) (*derog*) fit of bad-tempered complaining: *He's always having a grouch about sth.* (**b**) [C] ~ (**against sth/sb**) complaint: *One of my main grouches against the council is that they don't run enough buses.* **2** [C] (*derog*) sulky discontented person: *You're nothing but an old grouch!* **grouchy** *adj* (**-ier, -iest**) sullenly discontented: *in a grouchy mood.*

ground[1] /graʊnd/ *n* **1 the ground** [sing] solid surface of the earth (esp contrasted with the air above): *sit on the ground* ○ *He slipped off the ladder and fell to the ground.* ○ *The aircraft hadn't enough power to get off the ground*, ie take off. ○ [attrib] *at ground level.* **2** [U] (**a**) area or distance on the earth's surface; land: *have more ground than one's next-door neighbour* ○ *buy up some ground for building on* ○ *The land near the border is disputed ground.* ○ *measure the ground between two points.* (**b**) soil; earth: *solid, marshy, stony, etc ground.* ⇨ Usage at EARTH. **3** (esp in compounds) (**a**) [C] piece of land (often with associated buildings) used for a particular purpose: *a ˈfootball, ˈcricket, ˈsports, recreˈation ground* ○ *a paˈrade-ground* ○ *a ˈplayground* ○ *The cheers of the fans echoed round the ground as the team appeared.* (**b**) **grounds** [pl] large area of land or sea used for the stated purpose: *ˈfishing, ˈhunting grounds.* **4 grounds** [pl] land or gardens round a building, often enclosed with walls, hedges or fences: *The house has extensive grounds.* ○ *the grounds of Buckingham Palace.* **5** [U] (*fig*) area of interest, discussion, etc: *They managed to cover quite a lot of ground in a short programme.* ○ *go over the same ground*, ie discuss a familiar topic ○ *trying to find some common ground between the two sides*, ie points on which they can agree ○ *You're on dangerous ground when you criticize his daughter*, ie because he will react angrily. **6** [C esp *pl*] ~ (**for sth/doing sth/to do sth**) reason(s) or justification for saying, doing or believing sth: *You have no grounds for complaint/for complaining.* ○ *If you continue to behave like this you will give them/provide them with grounds for dismissing you.* ○ *Desertion is a ground* (ie legally sufficient reason) *for divorce.* ○ *They had no grounds to arrest him.* ○ *I had to retire on medical grounds/on the grounds of ill health*, ie because I was ill. ○ *Her claim was disallowed on the ground(s) that she had not paid her premium.* ○ *On what grounds do you make that accusation?* ⇨ Usage at REASON[1]. **7** [C] surface on which a design is painted, printed, cut, etc; undecorated part; background: *a design of pink roses on a white ground.* **8** [U] bottom of the sea: *The ship touched ground a few yards from the shore.* **9 grounds** [pl] ground coffee beans after they have been brewed. **10** (idm) **above ˈground** above the surface of the earth. **be on firm ground** ⇨ FIRM[1]. **below ˈground** beneath the surface of the earth: *Their missile silos are below ground.* **break fresh/new ˈground** introduce or discover a new method, system, etc; innovate. **cut the ground from under sb's ˈfeet** spoil sb's plan, argument, defence, etc by anticipating it. **forbidden ground** ⇨ FORBID. **gain/make up ground** (**on sb/sth**) get gradually closer to sb/sth going in the same direction as oneself: *The police car was gaining ground on the robbers.* ○ (*fig*) *How can we make up ground on our competitors?* **get off the ˈground** (of activities, enterprises, etc) make a successful start. **give/lose ˈground** (**to sb/sth**) (**a**) retreat. (**b**) get gradually less far ahead of sb/sth going in the same direction: *The leader is losing ground as the rest of the runners accelerate.* ○ (*fig*) *The gas lamp gradually lost ground to* (ie was replaced by) *electric lighting.* **go/run to earth/ground** ⇨ EARTH. **have/keep a/one's ear to the ground** ⇨ EAR[1]. **have, etc one's/both feet on the ground** ⇨ FOOT[1]. **hold/keep/stand one's ˈground** maintain one's claim, intention, argument, etc; not yield or give way. **keep both/one's feet on the ground** ⇨ FOOT[1]. **on the ˈground** amongst ordinary people: *There's a lot of support for our policies on the ground.* **prepare the ground** (**for sth**) make the development of sth possible or easier: *Early experiments with military rockets prepared the ground for space travel.* **run sb/sth into the ˈground** (*infml*) wear sb/sth out completely; exhaust sb/sth: *By working 13 hours a day she is running herself into the ground.* ○ *We couldn't afford to buy a new car, so we had to run the old one into the ground.* **shift one's ˈground** ⇨ SHIFT[1]. **suit sb down to the ground** ⇨ SUIT[2]. **thin on the ground** ⇨ THIN. **to the ˈground** (of destroying, demolishing, etc) completely; utterly: *The building was burned to the ground.*
□ **ˈground-bait** *n* [U] food thrown to the bottom of a river, lake, etc by an angler to attract fish.
ground ˈbass (*music*) short theme that is constantly repeated in the bass, common in 16th- and 17th-century music.
ˈground control personnel, system or equipment (stationed on the ground) whose job is to ensure the safe flight of aircraft or spacecraft.
ˈground cover plants covering the surface of the earth, esp low spreading ones grown in gardens to check the growth of weeds.
ˈground crew people at an airfield whose job is to repair, refuel, etc aircraft.
ground ˈfloor 1 (*US* **first floor**) floor of a building at ground level, not upstairs: [attrib] *at ground-floor level* ○ *a ground-floor flat.* ⇨ Usage at FLOOR[1]. **2** (idm) **be/get in on the ground ˈfloor** (*infml*) join an enterprise at its beginning.
ˈgroundhog N American marmot or woodchuck.
ˈGroundhog Day (*US*) 2 February, the day when groundhogs are supposed to come out of their holes after the winter. There is a tradition that if it is sunny and they can see their shadows, there will be another six weeks of winter weather.
ˈground-nut *n* = PEANUT.
ˈground-plan *n* (drawing representing the) lay-out of a building at ground level.
ˈground-rent *n* [U, C] rent paid for the use of land leased for building.
ˈground rule (usu *pl*) basic principle: *The new code of conduct lays down the ground rules for management-union relations.*
ˈgroundsheet *n* (*US* also **ˈground cloth**) waterproof sheet for spreading on the ground, eg under bedding in a tent.
ˈgroundsman /-zmən/ *n* person who maintains a sports ground.
ˈground speed speed of an aircraft relative to the ground. Cf AIR SPEED (AIR[1]).
ˈground staff 1 people at a sports ground whose job is to maintain the condition of grass, equipment, etc. **2** = GROUND CREW.
ˈground state (also **ˈground level**) (*physics*) lowest energy state of an atom, a molecule, a nucleus, etc.
ˈground stroke (in tennis) stroke with which a player hits a ball that has just bounced and is not far from the ground.
ˈground swell 1 heavy slow-moving waves caused by a distant or recent storm or earthquake. **2** (*fig*) rapidly developing general feeling or opinion: *Opinion polls have detected a ground swell of support for the Socialists.*
ˈgroundwork *n* [U] ~ (**for sth**) preparatory work that provides the basis for sth.

ground[2] /graʊnd/ *v* **1** (**a**) [I, Ipr, Tn, Tn·pr] ~ (**sth**) (**in/on sth**) (of a ship) touch the sea bottom; cause (a ship) to do this: *Our ship grounded in shallow water/on a sandbank.* (**b**) [Tn esp passive] require or force (an aircraft) to stay on the ground: *All aircraft at London Airport were grounded by fog today.* **2** [Tn] (*esp US*) = EARTH *v.* **3** (idm) **ground arms** (of soldiers) lay (esp rifles) on the ground. **4** (phr v) **ground sb in sth** give sb good teaching or basic training (in a subject): *She grounded her pupils well in arithmetic.* **ground sth on sth** base beliefs, etc on sth: *ground one's arguments on facts* ○ *a well-grounded theory.*
▷ **grounding** *n* [sing] ~ (**in sth**) teaching of the basic elements of a subject: *a thorough grounding in grammar.*

ground[3] *pt, pp* of GRIND: ˌ*ground ˈrice*, ie reduced to a fine powder ○ ˌ*ground ˈglass*, ie made non-transparent by rubbing the surface to make it rough.

groundless /ˈgraʊndlɪs/ *adj* without foundation or good reason: *groundless anxiety, rumours, allegations* ○ *Our fears proved groundless.* ▷ **groundlessly** *adv.*

groundsel /ˈgraʊnsl/ *n* [U] weed with yellow flowers, sometimes used as food for certain cage-birds.

group /gru:p/ *n* [CGp] **1** number of people or things gathered, placed or acting together, or naturally associated: *a group of girls, trees, houses, etc* ○ *A group of us are going up to London for the day.* ○ *people standing about in groups* ○ *an ˈage group*, ie people of the same age ○ *Our diˈscussion group is/are meeting this week.* ○ *a ˈdrama group*, ie small club for acting ○ *the Germanic group of languages* ○ *What ˈblood group are you?* ○ [attrib] *a group acˈtivity*, ie done by people in a group. **2** set of jointly-controlled business companies, eg as the result of a merger: *a ˈnewspaper group* ○ *the ˈBurton Group* ○ [attrib] *the group sales director.* **3** set of musicians performing pop music together. **4** division of an air force, consisting of several squadrons. **5** mathematical set, with an operation combining any pair of its elements to yield a third, in which certain conditions are fulfilled. **6** (*chemistry*) combination of atoms that form a distinct unit and are found in a number of compounds.
▷ **group** *v* [I, Ipr, Ip, Tn, Tn·pr, Tn·p] ~ (**sb/sth**) (**round sb/sth**); ~ (**sb/sth**) (**together**) gather or form (sb/sth) into a group or groups: *The police grouped (themselves) round the demonstrators.* ○ *Group together in fours!*
groupie /ˈgru:pɪ/ *n* (*infml*) keen supporter (esp a young girl) who follows pop groups to concerts given on tour.
grouping *n* set of individuals with sth in common, esp acting together within a larger organization: *various anti-leadership groupings within the party.*
□ **ˈgroup captain** officer in the British air force between the ranks of wing commander and air commodore. ⇨ App 4.
ˌ**group ˈpractice** set of doctors who work jointly, use the same premises, etc.
ˌ**group ˈtherapy** form of treatment in which people with similar psychological problems meet together to discuss them.

grouper /ˈgru:pə(r)/ *n* type of large sea fish with a heavy body, large head and wide mouth.

grouse[1] /graʊs/ *n* (*pl* unchanged) (**a**) [C] small dark bird of northern hilly areas, shot for sport and food: [attrib] *ˈgrouse shooting on the moors of Scotland and northern England.* ⇨ illus at BIRD. (**b**) [U] its flesh as food: *roast grouse.*

grouse[2] /graʊs/ *v* (*infml usu derog*) [I, Ipr] ~ (**about sb/sth**) grumble; complain: *He's always grousing about the work-load.*
▷ **grouse** *n* complaint: *If you've got any grouses, you'd better tell me about them.*

grout /graʊt/ *n* [U] thin liquid mortar, used esp to fill the gaps between tiles.
▷ **grout** [Tn] provide or fill (eg a tiled wall) with grout.

grove /grəʊv/ *n* group of trees; small wood: *an olive grove.*

grovel /ˈgrɒvl/ *v* (**-ll-**; *US* **-l-**) (*derog*) **1** [I, Ipr] ~ (**to/before sb**) lie or crawl with the face downwards in a show of humility or fear: *Those who wished a favour of the emperor had to grovel on hands and knees before him.* **2** (*fig*) [I, Ipr] ~ (**to sb**) (**for sth**) behave with a show of humility or shame: *You will just have to grovel to the bank manager for a loan.* **3** (phr v) **grovel about/around** move about on one's hands and knees; crawl about: *grovelling around under the table* *looking for a pin.*

▷ **grovelling** /ˈgrɒvəlɪŋ/ *adj* excessively humble; abject: *a grovelling apology.*

grow /grəʊ/ *v* (*pt* **grew** /gruː/, *pp* **grown** /grəʊn/) **1** [La, I] increase in size or quantity; become greater: *How tall you've grown!* ○ *A growing child needs plenty of sleep.* ○ *She wants to let her hair grow,* ie not have it cut short. ○ *You must invest if you want your business to grow.* **2** [I, Ipr] ~ **(from sth) (into sth)** develop, esp into a mature or an adult form: *Rice does not grow in a cold climate.* ○ *Plants grow from seeds.* ○ *Tadpoles grow into frogs.* ○ (*fig*) *grow in stature, wisdom, etc.* **3** [La] become (gradually): *grow old(er), rich(er), etc* ○ *grow small(er), weak(er), etc* ○ *It began to grow dark.* ○ *I grew tired of waiting, and left.* **4** [Tn, Tn·pr] ~ **sth (from sth)** cause or allow sth to grow: *grow roses* ○ *grow a beard* ○ *grow onions from seed.* **5** [It] reach the point or stage at which one does the specified thing: *He grew increasingly to rely on her.* ○ *She has a hot temper, but you will soon grow to like her.* **6** (idm) **big, etc oaks from little acorns grow** ⇨ OAK. **let the grass grow under one's feet** ⇨ GRASS[1]. **(not) grow on trees** be (not) plentiful, easily obtained, etc: *Don't spend so much — money doesn't grow on trees, you know.* **7** (phr v) **grow away from sb** come to have a less close, less easy relationship with sb: *a teenage girl growing away from her mother.* **grow into sth** (no passive) **(a)** become sth (gradually, with the passage of time): *She is growing into a beautiful young woman.* ○ *He has grown into an old miser.* **(b)** become big enough to fit (clothes): *The coat is too big for him now, but he will grow into it.* **(c)** become accustomed to (a new job, role or activity): *She is a good actress, but still needs time to grow into the part she is playing.* **grow on sb** (no passive) **(a)** become more firmly established in sb: *a habit that grows on you if you are not careful.* **(b)** come to have a greater attraction for sb; win the liking of sb: *a book, piece of music, etc that grows on you.* **grow out of sth (a)** become too big to wear sth: *grow out of one's clothes.* **(b)** become too old for sth and stop doing it: *grow out of children's games, etc.* **(c)** (no passive) have sth as a source: *My interest in the art of India grew out of the time I spent there during the war.* **grow up (a)** (of people or animals) reach the stage of full development; become adult or mature: *She's growing up fast.* ○ *Oh, grow up!* ie Behave in a more mature way! Cf GROWN UP (GROWN). **(b)** develop: *A close friendship gradually grew up between them.* ○ *Nobody knows exactly how the practice grew up.*

▷ **grower** *n* (usu in compounds) **1** person who grows things: *a* ˈ*fruit-grower* ○ ˈ*rose-growers.* **2** plant that grows in a certain way: *a quick grower.*

growing *adj* increasing: *his growing indifference to her* ○ *a growing problem* ○ *a popular club with a growing membership.* ˈ**growing pains (a)** pains in the limbs of young children, popularly believed to be caused by rapid growth. **(b)** (*fig*) problems arising while a new enterprise is developing: *The business is still suffering from growing pains.*

growl /graʊl/ *v* **1** [I, Ipr] ~ **(at sb/sth)** (of animals or thunder) make a low threatening sound: *The dog growled at the intruder.* ○ *The thunder growled in the distance.* ○ (*fig*) *He's in a really bad mood today, growling at* (ie speaking angrily to) *everyone.* **2** [Tn, Tn·p] ~ **sth (out)** say sth in a low threatening voice: *He growled out an answer.*

▷ **growl** *n* low threatening sound or remark.

grown /grəʊn/ *adj* [attrib] adult; mature: *a grown man* ○ *a full-grown/fully grown elephant.* Cf GROW 2.

□ ˌ**grown** ˈ**up** adult; mature: *What do you want to be when you're grown up?* [attrib] *his* ˌ*grown-up* ˈ*son* ○ *Try to behave in a more grown-up way.*

grown-up /ˈgrəʊnʌp/ *n* adult person (contrasted with a child).

growth /grəʊθ/ *n* **1** [U] **(a)** (process of) growing; development: *the rapid growth of plants, of hair, of inflation, of the economy* ○ *Lack of water will stunt the plant's growth.* ○ *a phenomenon of comparatively recent growth,* ie that has developed recently ○ [attrib] *a growth industry,* ie one which is developing faster than most others. **(b)** ~ **(in/of sth)** increase: *the recent growth in/of violent crime.* **2** [U] increase in economic activity, profitability, etc: *The government has decided to go for growth,* ie a policy of increased production, spending, etc. ○ [attrib] *Japan's growth rate.* **3** [sing] thing that grows or has grown: *a thick growth of weeds* ○ *a week's growth of beard.* **4** [C] abnormal or diseased formation in the body (eg a tumour or cancer): *a (non-)malignant growth.*

groyne (*US* **groin**) /grɔɪn/ *n* structure of wood, stone or concrete, built to prevent sand and pebbles from being washed away by the sea, the current of a river, etc. ⇨ illus at COAST.

grub[1] /grʌb/ *n* **1** [C] larva of an insect. **2** [U] (*infml*) food: *Grub's up!* ie The meal is ready!

□ ˈ**grub-screw** *n* small screw without a head, used eg to fix a handle to a spindle.

grub[2] /grʌb/ *v* (**-bb-**) **1** [I, Ipr, Ip] ~ **(around/about) (for sth) (a)** dig or poke at the soil; search (for sth) by digging: *pigs grubbing around/about in the bushes* ○ *a dog grubbing for a bone.* **(b)** (*fig*) search for (esp information) intently but usu unmethodically: *He found what he wanted by grubbing around in the library.* **2** [Tn, Tn·p] ~ **sth (up) (a)** remove (roots, etc) from ground to clear it. **(b)** remove roots, etc from (ground). **3** (phr v) **grub sth up/out** dig sth up: *birds grubbing up worms* ○ *grub out a dead tree.*

grubby /ˈgrʌbɪ/ *adj* (**-ier, -iest**) (*infml*) dirty; unwashed: *grubby hands* ○ (*fig*) *a grubby* (ie unsavoury) *scandal.* ▷ **grubbiness** *n* [U].

grubstake /ˈgrʌbsteɪk/ *n* (*US infml*) money, equipment, etc supplied for an enterprise (originally gold-mining) in return for a share of any profit that may result from it.

▷ ˈ**grubstake** *v* [Tn] (*US infml*) give (sb) a grubstake.

Grub Street /ˈgrʌb striːt/ (writers of) works of poor quality, produced solely to earn a living: [attrib] ˌ*Grub Street* ˈ*journalism.*

grudge /grʌdʒ/ *v* [Tn, Tg, Tsg, Dn·n, Dn·pr] ~ **sth (to sb)** feel resentful about sth; do or give sth very unwillingly: *He grudges every penny he has to spend.* ○ *I grudge paying so much for such inferior goods.* ○ *He grudges her earning more than he does.* ○ *I don't grudge him his success,* ie I admit he deserves it. ○ *She would grudge a penny even to the poorest beggar,* ie She is very mean.

▷ **grudge** *n* ~ **(against sb)** feeling of ill will, envy, resentment, spite, etc: *I bear him no grudge.* ○ *He has a grudge against me.* ○ *He has been harbouring/nursing a grudge against me.* ○ [attrib] *a grudge fight,* ie when one boxer, etc has a grudge against the other.

grudging *adj* unwilling; reluctant: *a grudging admission* ○ *grudging praise.* **grudgingly** *adv*: *The boss grudgingly raised my salary.*

gruel /ˈgruːəl/ *n* [U] simple dish made of oatmeal, etc boiled in milk or water.

gruelling (*US* **grueling**) /ˈgruːəlɪŋ/ *adj* severe; exhausting: *a gruelling climb, race, ordeal, etc.*

gruesome /ˈgruːsəm/ *adj* filling one with horror or disgust; frightful: *After the slaughter, the battlefield was a gruesome sight.* ▷ **gruesomely** *adv.* **gruesomeness** *n* [U].

gruff /grʌf/ *adj* (of a person, his voice or behaviour) rough; surly: *Beneath his gruff exterior he's really very kind-hearted.* ▷ **gruffly** *adv.* **gruffness** *n* [U].

grumble /ˈgrʌmbl/ *v* **1** [I, Ipr] ~ **(at/to sb) (about/at/over sth)** complain or protest in a bad-tempered way: *Stop grumbling! You've got nothing to complain about.* ○ *Why grumble at me about your own stupid mistakes?* ○ *grumble at one's low pay/at being badly paid.* **2** [I, Ip] ~ **(away)** make a deep continuous sound: *thunder grumbling (away) in the distance* ○ *the sound of one's stomach grumbling* ○ (*fig*) *a grumbling* (ie intermittently painful) *appendix.*

▷ **grumble** *n* **1** complaint: *a person full of grumbles* ○ *I don't want to hear another grumble from you.* **2** rumble: *a distant grumble of thunder.*

grumbler /ˈgrʌmblə(r)/ *n* person who grumbles: *He's a dreadful grumbler.*

grummet /ˈgrʌmɪt/ *n* = GROMMET.

grumpy /ˈgrʌmpɪ/ *adj* (**-ier, -iest**) (*infml*) bad-tempered; surly. ▷ **grumpily** /-ɪlɪ/ *adv.* **grumpiness** *n* [U].

grunt /grʌnt/ *v* **1** [I] **(a)** (of animals, esp pigs) make a low rough sound from deep in the throat. **(b)** (of people) make a similar sound expressing pain, boredom, irritation, etc or indicating inattention or distraction: *He grunted as the bullet hit him.* ○ *I asked him what he thought, but he just grunted.* ○ *grunting with pain, pleasure, etc.* **2** [Tn, Tn·pr] ~ **sth (to sb)** utter sth in a grunting way: *She grunted some incomprehensible reply.*

▷ **grunt** *n* low rough sound made by an animal or a person: *give a grunt of approval, pain, pleasure, etc.*

gruyère /ˈgruːjeə(r)/ *n* [U] type of pale firm cheese with large holes.

gryphon /ˈgrɪfən/ *n* = GRIFFIN.

G-string /ˈdʒiːstrɪŋ/ *n* narrow piece of cloth (worn esp by female dancers) that covers the sexual organs and is held up by a string round the hips.

GT /ˌdʒiː ˈtiː/ *abbr* (of cars) large tourer (Italian *gran turismo*): *a Renault 5 Turbo GT.*

Gt *abbr* Great: *Gt Britain.*

guacamole /ˌgwɑːkəˈməʊlɪ/ *n* [U] thick paste made from mashed avocados, tomatoes, onions and other ingredients.

guano /ˈgwɑːnəʊ/ *n* [U] dung from sea-birds, poultry, etc, used as fertilizer.

guarantee[1] /ˌgærənˈtiː/ *n* **1 (a)** ~ **(against sth)** promise (usu in writing) that certain conditions agreed to in a transaction will be fulfilled: *The watch comes with a year's guarantee,* ie a promise to repair it free for a year after purchase. ○ *It's still under guarantee* (ie The guarantee is still valid), *so the manufacturer will repair it.* ○ *provide a guarantee against rust* ○ *You have our guarantee.* ○ *The Soviets are demanding certain guarantees about verification before signing the treaty.* **(b)** ~ **(of sth/that...)** promise given by one person to another that he will be responsible for seeing that sth is done (eg payment of a debt by another person): *give a guarantee of (one's/sb's) good behaviour.* **(c)** document, property, etc offered as security for carrying out the conditions in a guarantee: *'What guarantee can you offer?' 'I can offer my house as a guarantee.'* Cf SECURITY 3. **2** person who promises to be responsible for seeing that sth is done: *Are you willing to be a guarantee of your friend's good behaviour* (ie undertake to make sure that he behaves himself properly)? ○ *be sb's guarantee for a loan from the bank.* **3** ~ **(of sth/that...)** (*infml*) thing that makes an event likely to happen: *Blue skies are not a guarantee of continuing fine weather.* ○ *There's no guarantee she won't reject them all,* ie She may well do so.

guarantee[2] /ˌgærənˈtiː/ *v* **1** [Tn, Tf, Tt, Cn·a usu passive, Cn·t usu passive, Dn·n, Dn·pr] ~ **sth (to sb)** promise sth with certainty (to sb): *We cannot guarantee the punctual arrival of trains in foggy weather.* ○ *I can guarantee it's true — I saw it myself.* ○ *We guarantee to deliver within a week.* ○ *This food is guaranteed additive-free,* ie The manufacturer officially promises that it contains no additives. ○ *We guarantee you delivery within one day.* **2** [Tn, Tf, Tt] undertake to be legally responsible for (sth/doing sth): *guarantee sb's debts/the payment of sb's debts* ○ *guarantee that the debts will be paid* ○ *guarantee to pay debts.* **3** [Tn, Tn·pr] ~ **sth (against sth)** undertake to pay the cost of repairs resulting from a fault in (an article which has been bought): *a clock guaranteed for one year against mechanical failure or faulty workmanship.* **4** [Tn] make (an event) likely to happen: *His turning up will guarantee the success of the meeting.* **5** (idm) **be guaranteed to do sth** (*infml ironic*) be certain to do sth: *It's guaranteed to rain when you want to go out.*

guarantor /ˌgærənˈtɔː(r)/ *n* (*law*) person who gives a guarantee[1](1).

guaranty /ˈgærəntɪ/ *n* (*law*) guarantee[1](1).

guard[1] /gɑːd/ *n* **1** [U] state of watchfulness against attack, danger or surprise: *a soldier, sentry, etc on* *guard*, ie at his post, on duty ○ *The escaped prisoner was brought back under (close) guard*, ie (closely) guarded. ○ *policemen keeping guard outside the building* ○ [attrib] *guard duty* ○ *a guard dog*, ie kept to guard a building, etc. **2** [U] position of readiness to defend oneself, eg in boxing, fencing, bayonet-drill: *drop/keep up one's guard* ○ *(fig) an awkward question which got through/ penetrated the minister's guard.* **3** [C] **(a)** person (esp a soldier or policeman) who watches over sb or sth: *The prisoner slipped past the guards on the gate and escaped.* ○ *a se'curity guard*, ie one responsible for protecting property, a building, its grounds, etc against entry by intruders, burglars, etc ○ *'border guards.* **(b)** *(esp US)* (*Brit* **warder**) person who watches over prisoners in gaol. **4** **(a)** **the guard** [Gp] group of soldiers who protect buildings, etc: *the changing of the guard*, ie replacing of one such group by another, eg at Buckingham Palace ○ *The guard are being inspected today.* ○ *double the guard (in an emergency)*, ie have twice the usual number of sentries on duty. **(b)** [CGp] body of soldiers with the duty of protecting, honouring or escorting sb: *On his arrival the president inspected the guard of honour.* **5 the Guards** [pl] (in Britain and some other countries) regiments whose original duty was to protect the sovereign: *the Royal 'Horse Guards* ○ [attrib] *a Guards officer.* **6** [C] *(Brit)* person in charge of a railway train. **7** [C] (esp in compounds) (part of an) article or apparatus designed to prevent injury or loss: *Ensure the guard is in place before operating the machine.* ○ *a 'fire-guard*, ie in front of a fireplace ○ *a 'mudguard*, ie over the wheel of a bicycle, etc. **8** (idm) **mount guard** ⇨ MOUNT². **off/on one's 'guard** unprepared/prepared for an attack, a surprise or a mistake: *be on one's guard against saying the wrong thing* ○ *put sb on his guard* ○ *The lawyer's seemingly innocent question caught the witness off his guard.* **stand 'guard (over sb/sth)** act as a sentry: *Four soldiers stood guard over the coffin.*

□ **'guardhouse** *n* building with the same function as a guardroom.

'guard-rail *n* protective rail, eg to prevent people falling off a staircase or to separate them from dangerous traffic.

'guardroom *n* room for soldiers on guard or for keeping military prisoners.

'guardsman /-mən/ *n* (*pl* **-men** /-mən/) soldier in the Guards.

'guard's van *(Brit)* (*US* **caboose**) carriage in which the guard on a train travels.

guard² /gɑ:d/ *v* **1** [Tn] **(a)** keep (sb/sth) safe from danger, theft, etc; protect: *soldiers guarding the president* ○ *A dragon guarded the treasure.* ○ *(fig) a woman who jealously guarded her reputation.* **(b)** watch over (sb) and prevent him from escaping: *guard prisoners closely.* **2** (phr v) **guard against sth** use care and caution to prevent sth: *guard against disease* ○ *They've been doing very well, but they should guard against over-confidence*, ie not become over-confident.

▷ **guarded** *adj* (of statements, etc) cautious: *a guarded reply* ○ *be guarded in what one says.* **guardedly** *adv.*

guardian /'gɑ:dɪən/ *n* **1** one who guards or protects sth: *The police are guardians of law and order.* ○ *a self-appointed guardian of public morality.* **2** *(law)* person who is legally responsible for sb who cannot manage his own affairs, eg an orphaned child.

▷ **'guardianship** *n* [U] position or office of a guardian.

□ **,guardian 'angel 1** spirit that supposedly protects and guides a person or place. **2** person who behaves like this.

Guatemala /,gwɑ:tə'mɑ:lə/ country in Central America; pop approx 8 681 000; official language Spanish; capital Guatemala City; unit of currency quetzal (= 100 centavos). Much of the country is mountainous and most of the population, the largest in Central America, lives on the high plateaus in the south. Agriculture is based on crops like coffee, maize and cotton. The economy has suffered from Guatemala's history of political instability and the conflict with its neighbour Belize over territory. ⇨ map at CENTRAL AMERICA.

▷ **Guatemalan** *n, adj.*

guava /'gwɑ:və; *US* 'gwɔ:və/ *n* (tropical tree with a) fruit having a light yellow skin and pink or white edible flesh.

gubernatorial /,gu:bənə'tɔ:rɪəl/ *adj (fml)* (in the USA, Nigeria, etc) of a (state) governor.

gudgeon¹ /'gʌdʒən/ *n* small freshwater fish used as bait.

gudgeon² /'gʌdʒən/ *n* **1** pivot or metal pin at the end of an axle, for a wheel, etc. **2** socket into which a rudder is fitted at the stern of a boat.

guelder rose /,geldə 'rəʊz/ shrub with round bunches of white flowers.

Guernsey /'gɜ:nzɪ/ second largest of the *Channel Islands; capital Saint Peter Port. It is famous for its milk products and as a tourist centre. ⇨ map at UNITED KINGDOM. ▷ **Guernsey** *n* **1** breed of dairy cattle, originally from Guernsey. **2 guernsey** thick sweater with a distinctive design, originally produced on Guernsey.

guerrilla (also **guerilla**) /gə'rɪlə/ *n* person (not a member of a regular army) engaged in fighting in small secret groups: *urban guerrillas*, ie those who fight in towns only ○ [attrib] *guerrilla war/ warfare*, ie fought on one side or both sides by guerrillas.

guess /ges/ *v* **1** **(a)** [I, Ipr, Tn, Tf, Tw, Tnt] ~ **(at sth)** give an answer, form an opinion or make a statement about (sth) without calculating or measuring and without definite knowledge: *You don't know. You're just guessing!* ○ *guess at an answer* ○ *guess right/wrong* ○ *'Can you guess her age/guess how old she is?' 'I'd guess that she's about 30/guess her to be about 30.'* **(b)** [Tn, Tf, Tw no passive] do this correctly: *She guessed the answer straight away.* ○ *I knew by her smile that she had guessed what I was thinking.* ○ *You'll never guess how they got in!* **2** [no passive: Tn, Tf] *(infml esp US)* suppose (sth); consider likely: *I guess you're feeling tired after your journey.* ○ *'Will you be there?' 'I guess so.'* **3** (idm) **keep sb 'guessing** *(infml)* keep sb uncertain about one's plans, etc.

▷ **guess** *n* **1** ~ **(at sth)**; ~ **(that...)** opinion formed by guessing: *have/make a guess (at sth)* ○ *If I might hazard a guess, I'd say she was about 30.* ○ *My guess is that it will rain soon.* ○ *Your guess is as good as mine*, ie I do not know. ○ *I'll give you three guesses!* ie The answer is fairly obvious and you should guess it easily. **2** (idm) **'anybody's guess** fact that no one can be sure about: *What will happen is anybody's guess!* **at a 'guess** making a guess: *'How old is she?' 'At a guess, about 30.'* **an educated guess** ⇨ EDUCATE.

□ **guesstimate** /'gestɪmət/ *n (infml)* estimate made by combining guessing with reasoning.

'guesswork *n* [U] guessing: *obtain an answer by pure guesswork.*

guest /gest/ *n* **1** person invited to visit one's house or being entertained at one's expense: *We are expecting guests this weekend.* ○ *He invited her to be his guest for the evening at the theatre.* ○ *an uninvited guest* ○ *the guest of honour* (ie most important guest) *at a banquet.* **2** person staying at a hotel, boarding house, etc: *This hotel has accommodation for 500 guests.* ○ *a paying guest*, ie one living in a private house, but paying as if in a hotel. **3** visiting performer taking part in an entertainment: *tonight's guests on the chat show* ○ [attrib] *a guest artist, singer, conductor, etc.* **4** person specially invited to visit a place, participate in a conference, etc: *The scientists are visiting this country as guests of the government.* ○ [attrib] *a guest speaker.* **5** (idm) **be my 'guest** *(infml)* (used as a response to a request) please do: *'May I see the newspaper?' 'Be my guest!'*

▷ **guest** *v* [I, Ipr] ~ **(on sth)** *(infml)* appear as a guest(3) on a television or radio programme.

□ **'guest-house** *n* boarding house. ⇨ article at ACCOMMODATION.

'guest-night *n* evening on which members of a club or other society may invite guests.

'guest-room *n* bedroom kept for the use of guests.

guff /gʌf/ *n* [U] *(infml derog)* insincere or meaningless talk: *They gave us the usual guff about the need to cut costs.*

guffaw /gə'fɔ:/ *v (derog)* [I] give a noisy laugh.

▷ **guffaw** *n* such a laugh: *let out a loud guffaw.*

guidance /'gaɪdns/ *n* [U] guiding or being guided; leadership; direction: *be under sb's guidance* ○ *parental guidance*, ie guidance by parents ○ *child guidance*, ie (system of) help given to children with social or psychological problems ○ [attrib] *a missile guidance system.*

guide¹ /gaɪd/ *n* **1** person who shows others the way, esp a person employed to point out interesting sights on a journey or visit: *I know the place well, so let me be your guide.* ○ *The tour guide gave a running commentary from the front of the coach.* ○ *We engaged a guide to show us the way across the mountains.* **2** thing that helps one form an opinion, make a calculation, etc: *The essay needn't be too long; as a rough guide, you should write about three pages.* **3** adviser; person or thing that directs or influences one's behaviour: *His elder sister had been his guide, counsellor and friend.* ○ *Instinct is not always a good guide.* **4** ~ **(to sth)** **(a)** (also **'guidebook**) book for travellers, tourists, etc with information about a place: *a guide to Italy, to the British Museum, etc.* **(b)** book giving information about a subject: *a guide to French wines* ○ *a gardening guide.* **5 Guide** = GIRL GUIDE (GIRL).

□ **'guide-dog** *n* dog trained to guide a blind person. ⇨ article at ANIMAL.

'guide-line *n* (usu *pl*) advice (usu from sb in authority) on policy: *drawing up guide-lines on prices and incomes* ○ *follow the guide-lines closely.*

guide² /gaɪd/ *v* **1** [Tn, Tn·pr, Tn·p] ~ **sb (to...)** (go with sb and) show the way (to a place): *If you haven't a compass, use the stars to guide you.* ○ *I guided him to his chair.* **2** [Tn] direct (sb); influence: *Be guided by your sense of what is right and just.*

▷ **guided** *adj* [usu attrib] accompanied or led by a guide: *a guided tour/visit.* **,guided 'missile** rocket (for use in war) which can be guided to its destination while in flight by electronic devices.

guild /gɪld/ *n* [CGp] society of people with similar interests and aims, esp one of the associations of craftsmen or merchants in the Middle Ages: *the guild of barber-surgeons* ○ *the Townswomen's Guild.* Guilds of merchants selling the same goods and of craftsmen with the same trade became very powerful in Europe in the Middle Ages, controlling commerce and often running local government. The modern livery companies are descended from these medieval guilds.

□ **,guild-'hall** **(a)** hall in which members of a guild met in the Middle Ages. **(b)** **the 'Guild-hall** hall of the Corporation of the City of London, used for banquets, receptions, etc.

guilder /'gɪldə(r)/ *n* (also **gulden**) unit of money in the Netherlands.

guile /gaɪl/ *n* [U] deceit; cunning: *a man full of guile* ○ *get sth by guile.* ▷ **guileful** /-fl/ *adj.* **guilefully** /-fəlɪ/ *adv.* **guileless** *adj.* **guilelessly** *adv.*

guillemot /'gɪlɪmɒt/ *n* type of northern sea-bird with black and white plumage and a long narrow beak.

guillotine

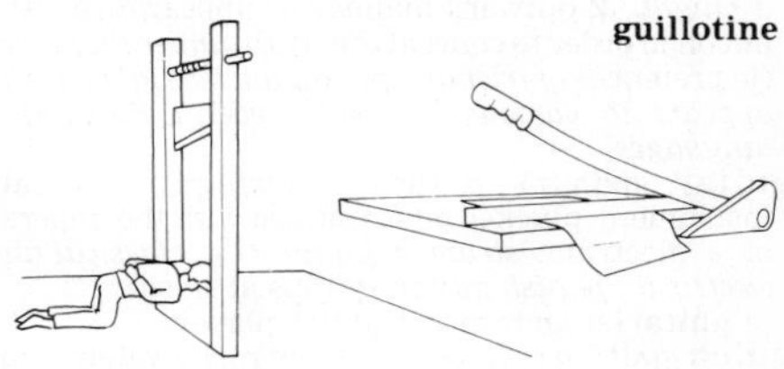

guillotine /'gɪləti:n/ *n* **1** machine of French origin for cutting people's heads off, consisting of a heavy blade which slides in grooves and is dropped from a height. **2** machine with a long blade for cutting or trimming large quantities of paper (eg in book-binding) or for cutting metal. ⇨ illus. **3** (*fig Brit politics*) setting of a time limit for discussion of a bill in Parliament so as to prevent it being obstructed by too much debate. Cf CLOSURE 2.

▷ **guillotine** *v* [Tn] use the guillotine on (sb/sth).

guilt /gɪlt/ *n* [U] **1** (*law*) condition or fact of having done wrong: *The police established his guilt beyond all doubt.* **2** blame or responsibility for wrongdoing: *find out where the guilt lies*, ie who is to blame ○ *Guilt was written all over her face*, ie She was obviously to blame. **3** anxiety or unhappiness caused by the knowledge of having done wrong: *racked by feelings of guilt because he had not done enough to help his sick friend* ○ [attrib] *a guilt complex*, ie an obsession with the idea that one is guilty of sth.

▷ **guiltless** *adj* ~ (**of sth**) innocent; without guilt: *guiltless of the offence.*

guilty *adj* (**-ier, -iest**) **1** ~ (**of sth**) (*esp law*) having done wrong; being to blame (for sth): *plead guilty to a crime* ○ *The verdict of the jury was 'not guilty'*, ie innocent. ○ *be found guilty of negligence* ○ *the guilty party*, ie person to blame. **2** showing or feeling guilt: *look guilty* ○ *I feel guilty about visiting her so rarely.* ○ *guilty looks* ○ *a guilty conscience*, ie conscience troubled by feelings of guilt. **guiltily** /-ɪlɪ/ *adv*: *She looked up guiltily as I came in.* **guiltiness** *n* [U].

Guinea /ˈgɪnɪ/ country on the west coast of Africa; pop approx 5 071 000; official language French; capital Conakry; unit of currency franc. It has a varied climate and landscape. Agriculture is the main activity, but the country is not self-sufficient: rice and ground-nuts are the chief crops. There are also important reserves of bauxite, the country's main export. ⇨ map at NIGERIA.

guinea /ˈgɪnɪ/ *n* (formerly in Britain) (gold coin worth the) sum of 21 shillings (now £1.05), used in stating professional fees (eg legal, medical), prices, etc: *the 2 000 Guineas*, ie a British horse-race with an original prize of this amount.

Guinea-Bissau /ˌgɪnɪbɪˈsaʊ/ country in W Africa; pop approx 945 000; official language Portuguese; capital Bissau; unit of currency peso (= 100 centavos). The coastal area is marshy, with high plateaus inland. The country's economy is chiefly agricultural and ground-nuts are the main crop. Oil has been discovered off the coast, but production is not yet economically possible. ⇨ map at NIGERIA.

guinea-fowl /ˈgɪnɪfaʊl/ *n* (*pl* unchanged) bird of the pheasant family, with dark grey feathers spotted with white, often used as food.

guinea-pig /ˈgɪnɪpɪg/ *n* **1** short-eared animal like a big rat, often kept as a pet. **2** person or animal used in medical or other experiments: *local residents who were unwitting guinea-pigs in the government's nuclear power programme.*

Guinevere /ˈgwɪnɪvɪə(r)/ (in English legend) wife of King *Arthur and mistress of *Lancelot.

Guinness[1] /ˈgɪnɪs/ *n* [U, C] (*propr*) type of dark bitter beer; glass of this: *a pint of draught Guinness.*

Guinness[2] /ˈgɪnɪs/ Sir Alec (1914-), British actor. A successful stage actor, he turned to the cinema, acting in several of the *Ealing comedies. He is now best known for his characterization in films like *Bridge on the River Kwai.*

guise /gaɪz/ *n* **1** (*arch*) style of dress: *in the guise of a knight.* **2** outward manner or appearance, esp put on in order to conceal the truth: *under the guise* (ie pretence) *of friendship* ○ *an ancient tale which appears in various guises in several European languages.*

guitar /gɪˈtɑː(r)/ *n* (usu six-stringed) musical instrument, plucked or strummed with the fingers or a plectrum: *strum a guitar* ○ *a classical/an electric/a Spanish guitar.* ⇨ illus at MUSIC.

▷ **guitarist** /gɪˈtɑːrɪst/ *n* guitar player.

gulch /gʌltʃ/ *n* (*US*) deep narrow rocky valley, esp one through which a torrent of water flows.

gulden /ˈgʊldən/ *n* (*pl* unchanged or ~**s**) = GUILDER.

gulf /gʌlf/ *n* **1** part of the sea almost surrounded by land: *the Gulf of Mexico.* **2** (**a**) (*rhet*) deep hollow in the ground; chasm; abyss: *a yawning gulf opened up by an earthquake.* (**b**) ~ (**between A and B**); ~ (**in sth**) (*fig*) area of difference; division (in opinions, etc): *The gulf between the two leaders cannot be bridged*, ie Their opinions are so far apart that they cannot be reconciled.

□ **the ˈGulf Stream** warm current flowing across the Atlantic Ocean from the Gulf of Mexico towards Europe. ⇨ article at WEATHER.

gull[1] /gʌl/ (also ˈ**seagull**) *n* any of several types of large long-winged sea-bird with usu white and grey or black feathers. ⇨ illus at BIRD.

gull[2] /gʌl/ *v* [Tn, Tn·pr] ~ **sb** (**into/out of sth**) (*arch*) cheat sb (so that he has to do or give up sth); deceive sb.

▷ **gull** *n* (*arch*) person who is easily deceived; simpleton.

gullet /ˈgʌlɪt/ *n* food passage from the mouth to the stomach; throat: *a bone stuck in one's gullet.* ⇨ illus at DIGESTIVE.

gullible /ˈgʌləbl/ *adj* willing to believe anything or anyone; easily deceived: *He must have been pretty gullible to fall for that old trick.* ▷ **gullibility** /ˌgʌləˈbɪlətɪ/ *n* [U]. **gullibly** /-əblɪ/ *adv.*

Gulliver's Travels /ˌgʌlɪvəz ˈtrævlz/ novel by Jonathan *Swift, in which he satirized the society and politics of his time. Lemuel Gulliver, an English traveller, visits strange lands, including Lilliput (whose people are all tiny), Brobdingnag (where they are all giants) and the country of the Houyhnhnms (where the horses are wise and the humans ignorant brutes). Despite the book's pessimism, it has remained popular with all ages since it was first published.

gully /ˈgʌlɪ/ *n* **1** narrow channel cut or formed by rain-water, eg on a hillside, or made for carrying water away from a building. **2** (in cricket) close fielding position between cover point and slip.

gulp /gʌlp/ *v* **1** [Tn, Tn·p] ~ **sth** (**down**) swallow (food or drink) quickly or greedily: *gulp one's food* ○ *gulp down a cup of tea.* **2** [I] make a swallowing motion: *She gulped nervously, as if the question bothered her.* **3** [Tn, Tn·p] ~ **sth** (**in**) breathe (air) deeply, (as if) to recover from partial suffocation: *She crawled onto the river bank and lay there gulping in air.* **4** (phr v) **gulp sth back** prevent (the expression of emotion) by swallowing: *She gulped back her tears and tried to smile.*

▷ **gulp** *n* **1** act of gulping: *swallow/sob with loud gulps.* **2** mouthful, esp of sth liquid: *a gulp of cold milk.* **3** (idm) **at a ˈgulp** with one gulp: *empty a glass at a gulp.*

gum[1] /gʌm/ *n* (usu *pl*) firm pink flesh at the base of the teeth: *The dog bared its gums at me.* ⇨ illus at TOOTH.

▷ **gummy** /ˈgʌmɪ/ *adj* (**-ier, -iest**) with no teeth; toothless: *a gummy smile.*

□ **gumboil** /ˈgʌmbɔɪl/ *n* boil or abscess on the gums.

gumshield /ˈgʌmʃiːld/ *n* (usu plastic) pad placed inside the mouth to protect the teeth of a boxer, Rugby player, etc.

gum[2] /gʌm/ *n* **1** [U] (**a**) sticky substance which oozes from certain trees, used for making glue. (**b**) glue used for sticking light things (eg paper) together. **2** [U] = CHEWING-GUM (CHEW). **3** (also ˈ**gum-drop**) [C] transparent sweet made of a firm jelly-like substance: *fruit gums.* **4** [C] = GUM-TREE.

▷ **gum** *v* (**-mm-**) **1** [Tn, Tn·pr, Tn·p] ~ **A to/onto B**; ~ **A and B together**; ~ **sth** (**down**) spread gum on the surface of sth; stick (one thing to another) with gum: *gum (the edges of) a piece of paper* ○ *gum down the flap of an envelope* ○ *gum paper to/onto card* ○ *Cut out two pieces of cardboard and gum them together.* **2** (idm) **gum up the ˈworks** (*infml*) make a machine or system unable to operate. **3** (phr v) **gum sth up** fill sth with a sticky substance and stop it moving.

ˈ**gummy** *adj* (**-ier, -iest**) sticky.

□ ˈ**gumboot** *n* rubber boot that extends up the leg; wellington.

ˈ**gum-tree** *n* **1** eucalyptus tree. **2** (idm) **up a ˈgum-tree** (*infml*) in difficulties.

gum[3] /gʌm/ *n* [U] (*Brit infml euph*) (used in oaths, etc, esp in N England) God: *By gum!*

gumbo /ˈgʌmbəʊ/ *n* [U] (*US*) thick soup made with the vegetable okra.

gumption /ˈgʌmpʃn/ *n* [U] (*infml*) common sense and initiative; qualities likely to bring success: *He's a nice enough lad, but he doesn't seem to have much gumption.*

gumshoe /ˈgʌmʃuː/ *n* (*US infml*) detective.

guns

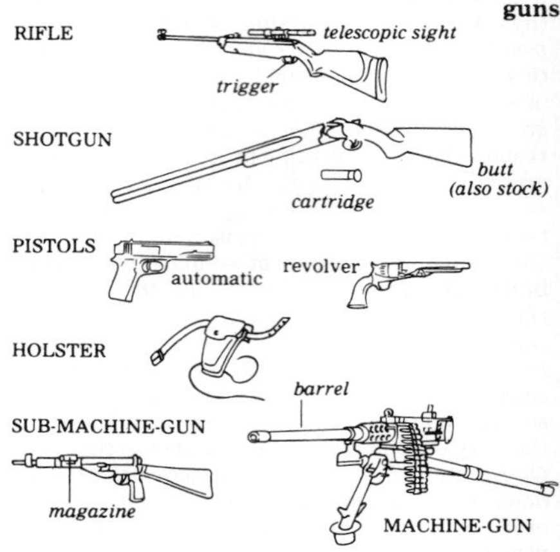

gun /gʌn/ *n* **1** [C] any type of firearm that fires bullets or shells from a metal tube: *Look out, he's got a gun!* ○ *a warship with 16-inch guns* ○ *maˈchine-guns.* ⇨ illus. **2 the gun** [sing] signal to begin a race, given with a starting pistol: *Wait for the gun!* **3** [C] tool that forces out a substance for injecting; device for fixing sth: *a ˈgrease-gun* ○ *a ˈstaple-gun.* **4** [C] person using a sporting gun as a member of a shooting party. **5** [C] (*US infml*) gunman: *a hired gun.* **6** (idm) **big gun** ⇨ BIG. **going great guns** ⇨ GREAT. **jump the gun** ⇨ JUMP[2]. **smoking gun** ⇨ SMOKE[2]. **spike sb's guns** ⇨ SPIKE *v.* **stick to one's guns** ⇨ STICK[2].

▷ **gun** *v* (**-nn-**) **1** [I, Tn] (*infml*) accelerate (an engine or a vehicle). **2** (idm) **be gunning for sb** (*infml*) be looking for an opportunity to attack or criticize sb. **3** (phr v) **gun sb down** (*infml*) shoot sb, esp so as to kill or seriously injure him.

□ ˈ**gunboat** *n* small warship carrying heavy guns or long-range missiles. ˌ**gunboat diˈplomacy** (*fig*) diplomacy backed by the threat of force.

ˈ**gun-carriage** *n* wheeled support of a big gun, or part on which a gun slides when it recoils.

ˈ**gun cotton** cellulose material impregnated with nitric acid, used as an explosive.

ˈ**gun dog** dog trained to help in the sport of shooting (eg by collecting shot birds).

ˈ**gunfight** *n* (*esp US*) fight between people shooting at each other with guns. ˈ**gunfighter** *n.*

ˈ**gunfire** *n* [U] firing of a gun or guns.

ˈ**gunman** /-mən/ *n* (*pl* **-men** /-mən/) man who uses a gun to rob or kill people: *terrorist gunmen.*

ˈ**gun-metal** *n* [U] alloy of copper and tin or zinc: [attrib] *gun-metal grey*, ie a dull blue-grey colour.

ˈ**gunpoint** *n* (idm) **at ˈgunpoint** while threatening or being threatened with a gun: *rob a bank at gunpoint.*

ˈ**gunpowder** *n* [U] explosive powder used in guns, fireworks, blasting, etc.

the Gunpowder ˈPlot conspiracy to blow up the Houses of Parliament in 1605. A number of Catholic opponents of *James I smuggled gunpowder into the cellars before the opening of Parliament by the king on 5 November. The plot was discovered, however, and Guy *Fawkes, one of the conspirators, was arrested and tortured into giving the names of his associates, who were later executed. The incident was the origin of the celebrations of *Bonfire Night.

ˈ**gunroom** *n* room in a large country house, in which sporting guns are kept.

ˈ**gun-runner** *n* person engaged in the secret and illegal importation of firearms into a country, eg to help a revolt. ˈ**gun-running** *n* [U] activity of a gun-runner.

ˈ**gunship** *n* aircraft, esp a helicopter, that is heavily armed with automatic weapons.
ˈ**gunshot** *n* **(a)** [C] shot fired from a gun: *the sound of gunshots* ○ [attrib] *gunshot wounds.* **(b)** [U] range of a gun: *be out of/within gunshot.*
ˈ**gunslinger** *n* (*sl esp US*) gunman or gunfighter, esp in the days of the American West.
ˈ**gunsmith** *n* person who makes and repairs small firearms.

gunge /gʌndʒ/ *n* [U] (*Brit infml*) unpleasant messy semi-liquid substance: *What's this horrible gunge in the bottom of the bucket?*

gung-ho /ˌgʌŋˈhəʊ/ *adj* (*infml derog*) enthusiastic in a reckless way, esp about fighting: *display a gung-ho attitude to war.*

gunner /ˈgʌnə(r)/ *n* **1** (in the British army) soldier in the artillery: *Gunner Jones.* **2** (in the British navy) chief petty officer in charge of a battery of guns. ⇨ App 4.
▷ **gunnery** /ˈgʌnərɪ/ *n* [U] operation of large military guns: [attrib] *gunnery practice* ○ *the gunnery officer.*

gunwale /ˈgʌnl/ *n* (*nautical*) upper edge of the side of a boat or small ship.

guppy /ˈgʌpɪ/ *n* small West Indian freshwater fish, often kept as a pet in aquariums.

gurgle /ˈgɜ:gl/ *n* bubbling sound like water flowing from a narrow-necked bottle (esp that made by babies when happy): *gurgles of delight.*
▷ **gurgle** *v* [I] make this sound: *The water gurgled as it ran down the plug-hole.* ○ *The baby was gurgling happily.*

Gurkha /ˈgɜ:kə/ *n* member of a regiment in the British or Indian army made up of soldiers from Nepal.

gurnard /ˈgɜ:nəd/ *n* sea fish with a large spiny head and rays resembling fingers on its underside, used for crawling along the sea bed, etc.

guru /ˈgʊru:; *US* gəˈru:/ *n* **1** Hindu spiritual leader. **2** (*fig infml*) respected and influential teacher or authority.

gush /gʌʃ/ *v* **1** [I, Ipr, Ip] ~ **(out) (from sth)** flow or pour out suddenly in great quantities: *gushing water* ○ *oil gushing out (from a well)* ○ *blood gushing from a wound.* **2** [I, Ipr] ~ **over sb/sth** (*fig derog*) talk with excessive enthusiasm: *Don't gush!* ○ *a young mother gushing over a baby.*
▷ **gush** *n* **1** (esp *sing*) sudden outflow or outburst: *a gush of oil, anger, enthusiasm.* **2** [U] (*infml*) excessive display of enthusiasm or sentimentality.
gusher *n* oil-well with a strong natural flow (so that pumping is not needed).
gushing *adj*: *gushing compliments.* **gushingly** *adv.*

gusset /ˈgʌsɪt/ *n* (usu triangular or diamond-shaped) piece of cloth inserted in a garment to strengthen or enlarge it.

gust /gʌst/ *n* **(a)** sudden violent rush of wind: *the wind blowing in gusts* ○ *fitful gusts of wind.* **(b)** (*fig*) outburst of feeling: *a gust of temper.*
▷ **gust** *v* [I] (of the wind) blow in gusts: *winds gusting up to 60 mph.*
gusty *adj* (**-ier**, **-iest**) with wind blowing in gusts: *a gusty day, wind.*

gusto /ˈgʌstəʊ/ *n* [U] (*infml*) enthusiastic vigour in doing sth: *singing the choruses with great gusto.*

gut /gʌt/ *n* **1 guts** [pl] (*infml*) **(a)** internal organs of the abdomen: *a pain in the guts.* **(b)** (*fig*) essential (mechanical) parts of sth: *remove the guts of a clock.* **2 guts** [pl] (*fig infml*) courage and determination: *a man with plenty of guts* ○ *have the guts to do sth.* **3** [C] **(a)** (*anatomy*) lower part of the alimentary canal; intestine: *dissecting a frog's gut.* **(b)** (*infml*) abdomen; stomach: *his huge beer gut*, ie made fat by drinking beer. **4** [U] thread made from the intestines of animals, used surgically for sewing wounds, and for violin and tennis-racket strings; catgut. **5** [C] narrow passage or channel for water. **6** (idm) **bust a gut** ⇨ BUST². **hate sb's guts** ⇨ HATE. **have sb's** ˌ**guts for** ˈ**garters** (*infml often joc*) punish sb severely: *If that work's not done on time, I'll have your guts for garters!* **slog/sweat one's** ˈ**guts out** (*infml*) work very hard, to the point of exhaustion.
▷ **gut** *v* (**-tt-**) [Tn] **1** take the guts out of (a fish, etc). **2** destroy the inside or contents of (a building, room, etc): *a warehouse gutted by fire.*
gut *adj* [attrib] instinctive rather than based on thought: *a gut feeling/reaction.*
gutless *adj* cowardly.
gutsy /ˈgʌtsɪ/ *adj* (**-ier**, **-iest**) (*infml*) **1** full of courage and determination. **2** greedy about food: *You gutsy beast!*

gutta-percha /ˌgʌtəˈpɜ:tʃə/ *n* [U] rubber-like substance made from the juice of various Malayan trees.

gutter[1] /ˈgʌtə(r)/ *n* **1** long (usu semicircular) metal or plastic channel fixed under the edge of a roof to carry away rain-water. ⇨ illus at HOME. **2** **(a)** (channel at the) side of a road, next to the kerb: *cigarette packets thrown into the gutter.* **(b)** **the gutter** [sing] (*fig*) poor or debased state of life: *the language of the gutter*, ie vulgar language ○ *He picked her out of the gutter and made her a great lady.*
▷ **guttering** /ˈgʌtərɪŋ/ *n* [U] system of gutters.
□ ˈ**gutter press** (*derog*) newspapers that print a lot of sensational stories, scandal, etc.
ˈ**guttersnipe** /-snaɪp/ *n* (*derog*) poor, badly-dressed, badly-behaved child.

gutter[2] /ˈgʌtə(r)/ *v* [I] (of a candle) burn fitfully, as if about to go out.

guttural /ˈgʌtərəl/ *adj* (of a sound) (seeming to be) produced in the throat: *a low guttural growl* ○ *guttural consonants.*

guv, **guvnor** ⇨ GOVERNOR³.

guy[1] /gaɪ/ *n* rope or chain used to keep sth steady or secured, eg to hold a tent in place.
□ ˈ**guy rope** such a rope.

guy[2] /gaɪ/ *n* **1** (*infml*) **(a)** [C] man: *He's a great guy.* ○ *the guys at the office* ○ *her guy*, ie boy-friend, husband, etc ○ *Come on, (you) guys, let's get going!* **(b) guys** [pl] (*US*) group of people of either sex, esp friends or colleagues: *Have any of you guys seen Helen?* **2** [C] figure in the form of a man, dressed in old clothes, burned in Britain on 5 November in memory of Guy *Fawkes.
▷ **guy** *v* [Tn] (*fml*) ridicule (sb/sth), esp by comic imitation.
□ **Guy** ˈ**Fawkes Night** = BONFIRE NIGHT (BONFIRE).

Guyana, Suriname and French Guiana

Guyana /gaɪˈænə/ country on the north-east coast of S America, a member of the Commonwealth; pop approx 1 007 000; official language English; capital Georgetown; unit of currency dollar (= 100 cents). Most of the country inland is covered with tropical forest. Agriculture is the principal activity, the main crops being rice and sugar-cane. Mineral reserves include bauxite and manganese. The country's economic difficulties have led to large-scale emigration. ⇨ map. ▷ **Guyanese** /ˌgaɪəˈni:z/ *n, adj.*

guzzle /ˈgʌzl/ *v* [I, Ip, Tn, Tn·p] ~ **(away)**; ~ **sth (down/up)** (*infml*) eat or drink sth greedily: *He's always guzzling.* ○ *guzzle beer* ○ *The children guzzled down all the cakes.*
▷ **guzzler** /-zlə(r)/ *n* person who guzzles.

Gwent /gwent/ county of SE Wales. ⇨ map at App 1.

Gwynedd /ˈgwɪnəð/ county of NW Wales. ⇨ map at App 1.

Gwynn /gwɪn/ Nell (1650-87), English actress and mistress of King *Charles II. One of their sons was given the title of Duke of Saint Albans.

Gy *abbr* (*physics*) gray¹.

gybe (*US* **jibe**) /dʒaɪb/ *v* [I] (*nautical*) change direction when the wind is behind, by swinging the sail from one side of a boat to the other.

gym /dʒɪm/ *n* (*infml*) **1** [C] gymnasium: *exercises in the gym.* **2** [U] gymnastics, esp at school: *I don't like gym.* ○ [attrib] *gym-shoes*, ie esp plimsolls ○ *a gym mistress.*
□ ˈ**gym-slip** (also **slip**) *n* sleeveless tunic worn in Britain by some girls as part of school uniform.

gymkhana /dʒɪmˈkɑ:nə/ *n* public competitive display of horse-riding or vehicle-driving.

gymnasium /dʒɪmˈneɪzɪəm/ *n* (*pl* ~**s** or **-ia** /-zɪə/) room or hall with apparatus for physical exercise.

gymnast /ˈdʒɪmnæst/ *n* expert in gymnastics.

gymnastic /dʒɪmˈnæstɪk/ *adj* of physical exercises and training.
▷ **gymnastics** *n* [pl] (forms of) exercises performed to develop the muscles or fitness or to demonstrate agility: (*fig*) *mental gymnastics*, ie mental agility, elaborate reasoning.

gynaecology (*US* **gyne-**) /ˌgaɪnəˈkɒlədʒɪ/ *n* [U] scientific study and treatment of diseases and disorders of the female reproductive system.
▷ **gynaecological** (*US* **gyne-**) /-kəˈlɒdʒɪkl/ *adj.*
gynaecologist (*US* **gyne-**) *n* expert in gynaecology.

gyp /dʒɪp/ *n* (idm) **give sb** ˈ**gyp** (*Brit infml*) **(a)** scold or punish sb very severely. **(b)** cause sb much pain: *My rheumatism's been giving me gyp.*

gypsum /ˈdʒɪpsəm/ *n* [U] mineral (calcium sulphate) from which plaster of Paris is made, also used as fertilizer.

gypsy (also **gipsy**, **Gypsy**) /ˈdʒɪpsɪ/ *n* member of a wandering, originally Asiatic, people who live in caravans: (*fig*) *I've never lived in one place for long; it must be the Gypsy in me*, ie my desire to wander round the world. ○ [attrib] *a gypsy camp* ○ *the gypsy life*, ie wandering from place to place.
📖 Gypsies are believed to have originated in India. They are found in most parts of the world and share a common language, Romany. They often refer to themselves as 'travellers'. Gypsies have often been persecuted (a quarter of a million were killed by the Nazis) and they still suffer from social prejudice. However, gypsies also have a romantic image in Britain, which is of the nomad who, free of the restrictions of material possessions, travels from site to site, practising rural crafts, telling fortunes and selling sprigs of 'lucky' heather. This image has been reinforced by such writers as George Borrow, and by the general nostalgia that the British have for the English countryside.
□ ˌ**gypsy** ˈ**moth** type of moth whose larvae do great damage to the leaves of trees.

gyrate /ˌdʒaɪˈreɪt; *US* ˈdʒaɪreɪt/ *v* [I] move around in circles or spirals; revolve.
▷ **gyration** /ˌdʒaɪˈreɪʃn/ *n* [U, C] act of revolving.

gyrfalcon (also **gerfalcon**) /ˈdʒɜ:fɔ:lkən/ *n* large northern falcon.

gyro /ˈdʒaɪərəʊ/ *n* (*pl* ~**s**) (*infml*) gyroscope.

gyrocompass /ˈdʒaɪərəʊkʌmpəs/ *n* compass that uses a gyroscope to keep itself aligned with the earth's axis, so that it indicates true north and bearings from it.

gyroscope /ˈdʒaɪərəskəʊp/ *n* device containing a heavy metal wheel held in a structure which allows it, when it spins fast, to maintain the same orientation regardless of any movement of the supporting structure. Gyroscopes are used in compasses on aircraft, ships, etc and in stabilizer systems. ▷ **gyroscopic** /ˌdʒaɪərəˈskɒpɪk/ *adj*: *a gyroscopic compass.*

H, h

H, h /eɪtʃ/ *n* (*pl* **H's, h's** /ˈeɪtʃɪz/) the eighth letter of the English alphabet: *'Hat' begins with (an) H/'H'.* Cf AITCH.

H /eɪtʃ/ *abbr* (of lead used in pencils) hard: *an H/an HH/a 2H pencil.* Cf B, HB.

H *symb* hydrogen.

Ha *symb* hahnium.

ha /hɑː/ *interj* **1** (used to express surprise, joy, triumph, suspicion, etc) **2** (also **ha! ha!**) (used in print to indicate laughter; when spoken used ironically). ▷ **ha** *v* (idm) **hum and ha** ⇨ HUM.

ha *abbr* hectare(s).

habeas corpus /ˌheɪbɪəs ˈkɔːpəs/ (also **writ of habeas corpus**) (*law*) order requiring a person to be brought before a judge or into court, esp to investigate the right of the authorities to keep him in prison.

haberdasher /ˈhæbədæʃə(r)/ *n* **1** (*Brit*) shopkeeper who sells small articles for sewing such as pins, cotton, buttons, zips, etc. **2** (*US*) shopkeeper who sells men's clothing.
▷ **haberdashery** *n* **1** [U] goods sold by a haberdasher. **2** [C] haberdasher's shop.

Haber process /ˈhɑːbə prəʊses; *US* prɒses/ (also **Haber-Bosch process** /ˌhɑːbə ˈbɒʃ prəʊses/) industrial process for making ammonia by reacting hydrogen and nitrogen.

habit /ˈhæbɪt/ *n* **1** (**a**) [C] thing that a person does often and almost without thinking, esp sth that is hard to stop doing: *He has the irritating habit of smoking during meals.* ○ *It's all right to borrow money occasionally, but don't let it become a habit.* (**b**) [U] usual behaviour: *I only do it out of habit.* **2** [C] long garment worn by a monk or nun. **3** (idm) **be in/fall into/get into the habit of doing sth** have/acquire the habit of doing sth: *He's not in the habit of drinking a lot.* ○ *I've got into the habit of switching on the TV as soon as I get home.* **break sb/oneself of a habit** succeed in getting sb/oneself to give a habit up. **a creature of habit** ⇨ CREATURE. **fall/get into bad ˈhabits** acquire bad habits. **fall/get out of the habit of doing sth** lose the habit of doing sth: *I've got out of the habit of having a cooked breakfast.* **force of ˈhabit** ⇨ FORCE[1]. **kick the habit** ⇨ KICK[1]. **make a habit/practice of sth/doing sth** develop the habit of (doing) sth: *I make a habit of never lending money to strangers.*
□ **ˈhabit-forming** *adj* causing addiction: *habit-forming drugs.*

habitable /ˈhæbɪtəbl/ *adj* suitable for living in: *This house is no longer habitable.* ▷ **habitability** /ˌhæbɪtəˈbɪlətɪ/ *n* [U].

habitat /ˈhæbɪtæt/ *n* natural environment of an animal or a plant; home: *This creature's (natural) habitat is the jungle.*

habitation /ˌhæbɪˈteɪʃn/ *n* **1** [U] inhabiting or being inhabited: *houses unfit for (human) habitation.* **2** [C] (*fml*) place to live in; house or home: *wildlife undisturbed by human habitations.*

habitual /həˈbɪtʃʊəl/ *adj* **1** [attrib] regular; usual: *his habitual place at the table.* **2** done constantly or as a habit: *their habitual moaning.* **3** [attrib] doing sth by habit: *a habitual drunkard, cinema-goer, etc.*
▷ **habitually** /-tʃʊəlɪ/ *adv* usually; regularly: *Tom is habitually late for school.*

habituate /həˈbɪtʃʊeɪt/ *v* [Tn·pr] ~ **sb/oneself to sth** (*fml*) accustom sb/oneself to sth: *habituate oneself to* (ie get used to) *hard work, a cold climate.*

habitué /həˈbɪtʃʊeɪ/ *n* (*French*) person who visits a place regularly: *a habitué of the Café Royal.*

hacienda /ˌhæsɪˈendə/ *n* (in Spanish-speaking countries) large landed estate with a house.

hack[1] /hæk/ *v* **1** [Ipr] ~ **at sth/sb** strike heavy cutting blows at sth/sb: *He hacked (away) at the branch until it fell off.* ⇨ Usage at CUT[1]. **2** [Tn] kick (sth) roughly: *hack the ball/sb's shin.* **3** [I] cough harshly. **4** (phr v) **hack sth off (sth)** remove sth with rough heavy blows: *hack a leg off the carcass.* **hack one's way across, out of, through, etc, sth** make a path by hacking at sth: *We hacked our way through the undergrowth.*
▷ **hack** *n* **1** act of chopping. **2** kick with the toe of a boot. **3** miner's pickaxe.
□ ˌ**hacking ˈcough** short dry persistent cough.
ˈhack-saw *n* saw with a short narrow blade in a frame, used for cutting metal.

hack[2] /hæk/ *v* [I, Ipr, Tn] ~ **(into) (sth)** (*computing infml*) gain unauthorized access to (the contents of a computerized storage system, eg a database).
▷ **hacker** *n* (*infml*) **1** person whose hobby is programming or using computers. **2** person who hacks (HACK[2]).

hack[3] /hæk/ *n* **1** horse for ordinary riding or one that may be hired. **2** person paid to do hard and uninteresting work, esp as a writer: *a publisher's hack* ○ *hack journalist* ○ *hack work.* **3** (*US infml*) (**a**) taxi. (**b**) taxi driver.
▷ **hack** *v* [I, Ip] **1** (*Brit*) ride on horseback at an ordinary pace, esp along roads: *go hacking.* **2** (*US infml*) drive a taxi.
□ **ˈhacking jacket** (*esp Brit*) jacket with slits at the side and slanting pockets, originally designed to be worn while riding on horseback.

hackberry /ˈhækberɪ/ *n* purple cherry-like edible fruit of a N American tree.

hackles /ˈhæklz/ *n* [pl] **1** long feathers on the neck of the domestic cock, etc or hairs on the neck of a dog. **2** (idm) **make sb's ˈhackles rise/raise sb's ˈhackles** make sb angry. **with one's ˈhackles up** angry and ready to fight.

hackney carriage /ˈhæknɪ kærɪdʒ/ (also **hackney cab**) (*dated Brit*) taxi.

hackneyed /ˈhæknɪd/ *adj* (of a phrase, saying, etc) used so often that it has become trite and dull.

had *pt, pp* of HAVE.

haddock /ˈhædək/ *n* (*pl* unchanged) [C, U] sea-fish like cod but smaller, used for food.

Hades /ˈheɪdiːz/ *n* [sing] (in Greek mythology) place where the spirits of the dead go; the underworld.

hadj (also **hajj**) /hædʒ/ *n* journey to Mecca, which Muslims must make as a religious duty.
▷ **hadji** (also **hajji**) /ˈhædʒiː/ *n* Muslim who has been on a hadj.

Hadrian's Wall /ˌheɪdrɪənz ˈwɔːl/ wall built in 122 AD across northern England, from the Solway Firth to the mouth of the River Tyne, on the orders of the Roman emperor Hadrian. Its purpose was to prevent tribes from the north invading the Roman province of Britain.

haematite /ˈhiːmətaɪt/ *n* [U] red or black mineral from which iron is obtained.

haematology (also *esp US* **hem-**) /hiːməˈtɒlədʒɪ/ *n* [U] scientific study of the blood and its diseases. ▷ **haematologist** (esp *US* **hem-**) *n.*

haem(o)- (also *esp US* **hem(o)-**) *comb form* of blood: *haematology* ○ *haemophilia.*

haemoglobin (also *esp US* **hem-**) /ˌhiːməˈgləʊbɪn/ *n* [U] substance carrying oxygen in the red blood-cells of vertebrates.

haemophilia (also *esp US* **hem-**) /ˈhiːməˈfɪlɪə/ *n* [U] disease, usu inherited, that causes the sufferer to bleed severely from even a slight injury, because the blood fails to clot normally.
▷ **haemophiliac** (also *esp US* **hem-**) /ˌhiːməˈfɪlɪæk/ *n* person who suffers from haemophilia.

haemorrhage (also *esp US* **hem-**) /ˈhemərɪdʒ/ *n* **1** [U] (esp heavy) bleeding. **2** [C] escape of blood.
▷ **haemorrhage** *v* [I] bleed heavily; undergo a haemorrhage.

haemorrhoids (also *esp US* **hem-**) /ˈhemərɔɪdz/ (also **piles**) *n* [pl] swollen veins at or near the anus.

hafnium /ˈhæfnɪəm/ *n* [U] (*symb* **Hf**) chemical element, a metal used in the manufacture of the control rods in nuclear reactors. ⇨ App 11.

haft /hɑːft; *US* hæft/ *n* handle of an axe, a knife, etc.

hag /hæg/ *n* (*derog*) ugly old woman or witch.

Haggard /ˈhægəd/ Sir Henry Rider (1856-1925), English writer of adventure stories. The best-known, *King Solomon's Mines* and *She*, are set in southern Africa.

haggard /ˈhægəd/ *adj* looking tired and unhappy, esp from worry, lack of sleep, etc: *a haggard face* ○ *He looks haggard.*

haggis /ˈhægɪs/ *n* [C, U] Scottish dish made from sheep's heart, lungs and liver: *Would you like some more haggis?*

haggle /ˈhægl/ *v* [I, Ipr] ~ **(with sb) (over/about sth)** argue (esp about the price, etc when agreeing upon the terms of a sale or other transaction): *It's not worth haggling over a few pence.*

hagiography /ˌhægɪˈɒgrəfɪ/ *n* [U, C] **1** writing about the lives of saints. **2** biographical writing that is too full of praise for its subject.

hagridden /ˈhægrɪdn/ *adj* **1** troubled by bad dreams. **2** very worried: *a hagridden look.*

Hague /heɪg/ **The Hague** city in the Netherlands where most of the Dutch government departments are situated, and also the *International Court of Justice.

ha-ha /ˈhɑːhɑː/ *n* ditch with a wall or fence in it, forming a boundary to a park or garden without interrupting the view.

hahnium /ˈhɑːnɪəm/ *n* [U] (*symb* **Ha**) artificially produced radioactive chemical element. ⇨ App 11.

Haig /heɪg/ Douglas, 1st Earl Haig of Bemersyde (1861-1928), British soldier who commanded the British Army in France during the First World War. After the war he founded the *Royal British Legion and organized *Poppy Day.

haiku /ˈhaɪkuː/ *n* (*pl* unchanged) type of very short Japanese poem having 17 syllables, often about a subject in nature.

hail[1] /heɪl/ *n* **1** [U] frozen rain falling in a shower. **2** [sing] (*fig*) thing coming in great numbers and force: *a hail of bullets, blows, curses.*
▷ **hail** *v* **1** [I] fall as hail in a shower: *It is hailing.* **2** [I, Ip, Tn, Tn·p] ~ **(sth) down (on sb)** (*fig*) come or send (sth) down hard and fast: *Stones hailed down on them.* ○ *They hailed curses down on us.*
□ **ˈhailstone** *n* (usu *pl*) small ball of hail.
ˈhailstorm *n* period of heavy hail.

hail[2] /heɪl/ *v* **1** [Tn] (**a**) call to (a person or ship) in order to attract attention: *within ˈhailing distance*, ie close enough to be hailed. (**b**) signal to (a taxi, etc) to stop. **2** [Cn·n/a] ~ **sb/sth as sth** enthusiastically acknowledge sb/sth as sth: *crowds hailing him as king, as a hero* ○ (*fig*) *The book was hailed as a masterpiece/as masterly.* **3** [Ipr] ~ **from...** originate from (a place): *She hails* (ie comes) *from India.* ○ *Where does the ship hail from?* ie Which is her home port? **4** (idm) **be ˌhail-fellow-well-ˈmet (with sb)** be very friendly or too friendly (with people, esp strangers).
▷ **hail** *interj* (*arch*) welcome!: *Hail, Caesar!* — *n* [U] (idm) **within ˈhail** close enough to be hailed..
□ ˌ**Hail ˈMary** = AVE MARIA.

Haile Selassie /ˌhaɪlɪ səˈlæsɪ/ (1891-1975), emperor of Ethiopia 1930-74. He was forced to leave the country following an Italian invasion in 1936. He returned in 1941, but was deposed in the Communist coup of 1974. Among his many titles was 'Lion of Judah', the one used by the *Rastafarians, who revere him as a spiritual leader.

hair /heə(r)/ *n* **1** (a) [C] one of the fine thread-like strands that grow from the skin of people and animals: *two blonde hairs on his coat collar* ○ *There's a hair in my soup.* (b) [U] mass of these, esp on the human head: *have one's ˈhair cut* ○ *have long, black hair* ○ *a cat with a fine coat of hair.* (c) [C] thread-like growth on the stems and leaves of some plants. **2** (idm) **(by) a ˈhair/a ˌhair's ˈbreadth** (by) a very small amount or distance: *She won by a ˈhair.* ○ *We escaped by a hair's ˈbreadth.* ○ [attrib] *a ˌhair's-breadth eˈscape.* **get/have sb by the short hairs** ⇨ SHORT[1]. **get in sb's ˈhair** be a burden to or annoy sb. **a/the hair of the ˈdog (that ˈbit you)** (*infml*) another alcoholic drink to cure the effects of drink. **hang by a hair/a thread** ⇨ HANG[1]. **(not) harm, etc a hair of sb's ˈhead** (not) injure sb, even in the slightest way. **have a good, etc head of hair** ⇨ HEAD[1]. **keep your ˈhair on** (*catchphrase*) don't become angry; remain calm. **let one's ˈhair down** (*infml*) relax after a period of being formal. **make sb's ˈhair curl** (*infml*) horrify sb: *The clothes some young people wear nowadays really make your hair curl.* **make one's ˈhair stand on end** fill one with fright or horror. **neither hide nor hair of sb/sth** ⇨ HIDE[2]. **not turn a ˈhair** not show fear, dismay, surprise, etc when such a reaction might be expected. **put ˈhairs on sb's chest** (*joc infml*) (of an alcoholic drink) be very strong: *Try some of my home-made wine — it'll put hairs on your chest.* **split hairs** ⇨ SPLIT. **tear one's hair** ⇨ TEAR[2].

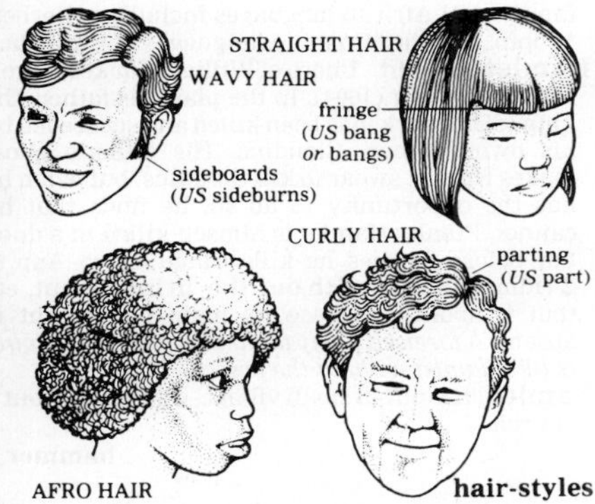

hair-styles

▷ **-ˈhaired** (in compound *adjs*) with hair of the specified kind: *a ˌcurly-haired ˈgirl.*

hairless *adj* without hair; bald.

hairy *adj* (**-ier, -iest**) **1** of or like hair. **2** having much hair: *a hairy chest.* **3** (*sl*) difficult; unpleasant: *Driving on icy roads can be pretty hairy.* **hairiness** *n* [U].

□ **ˈhairbrush** *n* brush for the hair. ⇨ illus at BRUSH.

ˈhaircloth *n* cloth made of a mixture of fabric and animal's hair.

ˈhaircut *n* **1** cutting the hair: *You ought to have a haircut.* **2** style in which hair is cut: *That's a nice haircut.*

ˈhair-do *n* (*pl* ~s) (*infml*) style or process of arranging (esp a woman's) hair: *She has a new hair-do.*

ˈhairdresser *n* person whose business is to arrange and cut hair. Cf BARBER. **ˈhairdressing** *n* [U].

ˈhair-drier (also **ˈhair-dryer**) *n* device for drying the hair by blowing hot air over it.

ˈhair-grip (also **grip**) *n* (*Brit*) flat clip with two ends close together, used for holding the hair in place.

ˈhair-line *n* **1** edge of a person's hair round the face. **2** (*fig*) very thin line: [attrib] *a ˌhair-line ˈcrack/ˈfracture.*

ˈhair-net *n* net for keeping the hair in place.

ˈhair-oil *n* oil for dressing the hair.

ˈhair-piece *n* false hair worn to increase the amount of a person's natural hair.

ˈhairpin *n* U-shaped pin for keeping the hair in position. **ˌhairpin ˈbend** very sharp bend in a road, esp a very steep road.

ˈhair-raising *adj* terrifying.

ˈhair-restorer *n* [C, U] substance used to promote growth of hair.

ˌhair ˈshirt shirt made of rough cloth and therefore uncomfortable, worn by penitents or ascetics.

ˈhair-slide (also **slide**) *n* (*Brit*) clip for keeping the hair in position.

ˈhair-splitting *n* [U] making small unimportant distinctions.

ˈhair-style *n* particular way of arranging or cutting the hair. ⇨ illus. **ˈhair-stylist** *n* hairdresser.

ˈhair-trigger *n* trigger that causes a gun to fire at the very slightest pressure.

hairspring /ˈheəsprɪŋ/ *n* fine spring in a watch, controlling the balance-wheel.

Haiti /ˈheɪtɪ/ country in the Caribbean occupying the western part of the island of Hispaniola, pop approx 5 523 000; official language French; capital Port-au-Prince; unit of currency gourde (= 100 centimes). Formerly a French colony, it became independent in 1804 after a slaves' rebellion. Between 1957 and 1986 it was ruled by the dictator 'Papa Doc' Duvalier and then by his son. Voodoo is practised there. ⇨ map at CARIBBEAN.

hake /heɪk/ *n* (*pl* unchanged) [C, U] fish of the cod family, used as food.

Hakluyt /ˈhæklu:t/ Richard (c 1552-1616), English geographer whose *Principall Navigations*, a collection of accounts of famous voyages of discovery around the world, made the exploits of the great 16th-century explorers (eg *Drake) more widely known.

halal (also **hallal**) /hɑ:ˈlɑ:l/ *v* [Tn] kill (animals for meat) as prescribed by Muslim law.

▷ **halal** *n* [U] meat prepared in this way.

halberd /ˈhælbəd/ *n* weapon used in former times, a combination of a spear and a battleaxe.

halcyon /ˈhælsɪən/ *adj* (*dated or rhet*) peaceful and happy: *the halcyon days of youth.*

hale /heɪl/ *adj* (idm) **hale and ˈhearty** (esp of an old person) strong and healthy.

half[1] /hɑ:f; *US* hæf/ *n* (*pl* **halves** /hɑ:vz; *US* hævz/) **1** either of two equal or corresponding parts into which a thing is divided: *I broke the chocolate into halves — here's your half.* ○ *John and Liz shared the prize money between them — John used his half to buy a word processor.* ○ *Two halves make a whole.* ○ *The second half of the book is more exciting than the first.* ○ *two and a half ounces, hours, miles.* ⇨ Usage at ALL[1]. **2** either of two (usu equal) periods of time into which a sports match, concert, etc is divided: *No goals were scored in the first half.* **3** half-price ticket, esp for a child, on a bus or train: *Two and two halves to the city centre, please.* **4** = HALF-BACK (HALF[2]): *playing (at) left half.* **5** (*infml esp Brit*) half a pint (esp of beer): *Two halves of bitter, please.* **6** (idm) **and a ˈhalf** (*infml*) of more than usual importance, excellence, size, etc: *That was a game and a half!* **one's better half** ⇨ BETTER[1]. **break, chop, cut, tear, etc sth in ˈhalf** cause sth to become separated into two parts by breaking, cutting, chopping, tearing, etc: *I once saw a man tear a telephone directory in half.* **do nothing/not do anything by ˈhalves** do everything one is engaged in completely and thoroughly: *He's not a man who does things by halves — either he donates a huge sum to a charity or he gives nothing.* **go half and ˈhalf/go ˈhalves (with sb)** share the cost (of sth) equally: *That was an expensive meal — let's go halves.* **the ˈhalf of it** (*infml*) the most important part: *You don't know the half of it.* **how the other half lives** (knowledge or experience of a) way of life of a different social group, esp one much richer or poorer than oneself: *He's been lucky all his life and has never had to find out how the other half lives.*

NOTE ON USAGE: **Quarter**, **half** and **whole** can all be nouns: *Cut the apple into quarters.* ○ *Two halves make a whole.* **Whole** is also an adjective: *I've been waiting here for a whole hour.* **Half** is also a determiner: *Half the work is already finished.* ○ *They spent half the time looking for a parking space.* ○ *Her house is half a mile down the road.* It can be used as an adverb: *This meal is only half cooked.*

half[2] /hɑ:f; *US* hæf/ *indef det* **1** amounting to or forming a half: *half the men* ○ *half an hour/a half-hour*, ie thirty minutes ○ *half a pint/a half-pint* ○ *half a dozen/a half-dozen*, ie six ○ *He has a half share in the firm.* ○ *Half the fruit was bad.* Cf ALL[1], BOTH[1]. ⇨ Usage at ALL[1]. **2** (idm) **half a minute, second, tick, etc** (*infml*) a short time: *I'll be ready in half a minute.* **half past ˈone, ˈtwo, etc**; *US* **half after ˈone, ˈtwo, etc** thirty minutes after (any hour on the clock). **half ˈone, ˈtwo, etc** (*Brit infml*) = HALF PAST ONE, TWO, ETC.

▷ **half** *indef pron* **1** quantity or amount that constitutes a half: *Half of six is three.* ○ *Half of the plums are rotten.* ○ *Half of the money is mine.* ○ *I only need half.* ○ *Out of 36 children, half passed.* **2** (idm) **too clever, etc by ˈhalf** far too clever, etc.

□ **ˌhalf-and-ˈhalf** *adj* [usu pred] being half one thing and half another: *'How do you like your coffee?' 'Half-and-half* (ie Half coffee and half milk), *please.'*

ˈhalf-back *n* (position of a) player between the forwards and the full back in football, hockey, etc.

ˈhalf-binding *n* binding of a book with pieces of leather down the back and at the corners.

ˌhalf ˈboard provision of bed, breakfast and one main meal at a hotel, etc. Cf FULL BOARD (FULL).

ˈhalf-brother *n* brother with only one parent in common with another.

ˈhalf-caste (also **ˈhalf-breed**) *n* (*sometimes derog*) person of mixed race.

ˌhalf ˈcock 1 position of the hammer of a gun when pulled half-way back. **2** (idm) **go off at half ˈcock** (of an event) fail because of being only half ready or badly prepared.

ˌhalf-ˈcrown *n* (also **ˌhalf a ˈcrown**) (*Brit*) (before 1971) coin or amount of $2\frac{1}{2}$ shillings.

ˈhalf-hitch *n* simple knot made by passing the end of a piece of rope round itself and then through the loop made by doing this. ⇨ illus at KNOT.

ˌhalf ˈholiday day of which the afternoon is taken as a holiday.

ˌhalf-ˈhourly *adj*, *adv* (done or occurring) every thirty minutes: *a half-hourly news bulletin* ○ *The buses run half-hourly.*

ˌhalf-ˈlength *adj* (of a portrait) of the upper half of a person.

ˈhalf-life *n* time taken for the radioactivity of a substance to fall to half its original value. It varies enormously in different substances, from a millionth of a second to billions of years, and is used as a measure of radioactivity.

ˈhalf-light *n* [sing] dim imperfect light.

ˌhalf-ˈmast *n* (idm) **at half-mast** (a) (of a flag) half-way up a mast, as a mark of respect for a dead person: *Flags were (flown) at half-mast everywhere on the day of the king's funeral.* (b) (*joc*) (of full-length trousers) too short, so that the ankles are seen.

ˌhalf ˈmoon 1 moon when only half its disc is illuminated. **2** time when this occurs. **3** object shaped like a half moon.

half nelson /ˌhɑ:f ˈnelsn/ hold in wrestling with an arm under the opponent's arm and behind his back.

ˈhalf-note *n* (*US*) = MINIM.

ˌhalf ˈpay reduced pay given to sb who is not fully employed but not yet retired.

halfpenny /ˈheɪpnɪ/ *n* (*pl* usu **halfpennies** for separate coins, **halfpence** /ˈheɪpəns/ for a sum of money) (*Brit*) obsolete coin, either (before 1971) one worth half a penny, or (after 1971) a smaller one worth half a (new) penny. **halfpennyworth** /ˈheɪpnɪwɜ:θ/ (*Brit* **ha'p'orth**) *n* amount this would buy; very small amount.

ˈhalf-pint *n* (*infml usu joc or derog*) small or unimportant person.

ˌhalf-ˈprice *adv* at half the usual price: *Children are (admitted) half-price.*

ˌhalf-seas-ˈover *adj* [pred] (*dated infml*) half

drunk.
ˈ**half-sister** *n* sister with only one parent in common with another.
ˌ**half-ˈsize** *adj* half the usual or regular size.
ˈ**half-step** *n* (*US*) = SEMITONE.
ˌ**half-ˈterm** *n* short holiday half-way through a school term.
ˌ**half-ˈtime** *n* [sing] interval between the two halves of a game of football, hockey, etc: *The score at half-time was 2-2.* ○ [attrib] *the* ˌ*half-time* ˈ*score.*
ˈ**half-tone** *n* **1** black-and-white illustration (eg in a book) in which light and dark shades are reproduced by small and large dots. **2** (*US*) = SEMITONE.
ˈ**half-track** *n* vehicle, esp one for carrying troops, with wheels at the front and tracks (TRACK 7) at the back.
ˈ**half-truth** *n* statement that gives only a part of the truth, and is intended to mislead.
ˌ**half-ˈvolley** *n* (*sport*) ball that is hit or kicked just after it bounces.
ˌ**half-ˈway** *adj, adv* **1** situated between and at an equal distance from two places: *reach the half-*ˈ*way point* ○ *meet* ˌ*half-*ˈ*way.* **2** (idm) **a** ˌ**half-way** ˈ**house** compromise between opposite attitudes, plans, etc. **meet sb half-way** ⇨ MEET[1].
ˈ**half-wit** *n* stupid or foolish person. ˌ**half-ˈwitted** *adj.*
ˌ**half-ˈyearly** *adj, adv* (done or occurring) every half year: *meetings held at* ˌ*half-yearly* ˈ*intervals.*

half[3] /hɑ:f; *US* hæf/ *adv* **1** to the extent of half: *half full.* **2** partly: *half cooked* ○ *half built* ○ *I'm half inclined to agree.* **3** (idm) ˌ**half as** ˌ**many**, ˌ**much**, **etc aˈgain** an increase of 50% of the existing number, amount, etc: *There aren't enough chairs for the meeting — we need half as many again.* ○ *I'd like the photograph enlarged so that it's half as big again.* ˌ**not** ˈ**half** (**a**) (*infml*) not at all: *It's* ˌ*not half* ˈ*bad, your new flat*, ie I like it. (**b**) (*sl*) to the greatest possible extent: *He didn't half swear*, ie He swore violently. ○ *'Was she annoyed?' 'Not half!'*, ie She was extremely annoyed.
□ ˌ**half-ˈbaked** *adj* (*infml*) stupid; foolish: *a* ˌ*half-baked i*ˈ*dea.*
ˌ**half-ˈcrazed** = CRAZED.
ˌ**half-ˈhardy** *adj* (of plants) able to grow in the open air at all times except in severe frost.
ˌ**half-ˈhearted** *adj* lacking enthusiasm; feeble. ˌ**half-ˈheartedly** *adv.*
ˌ**half-ˈtimbered** *adj* (of a building) having walls of a wooden framework filled in with brick, stone or plaster.

halibut /ˈhælɪbət/ *n* (*pl* unchanged) [C, U] large flat sea-fish used as food.

halide /ˈheɪlaɪd/ *n* (*chemistry*) chemical compound of a halogen with another element or radical.

halitosis /ˌhælɪˈtəʊsɪs/ *n* [U] breath that smells unpleasant.

hall /hɔ:l/ *n* **1** (also ˈ**hallway**) [C] space or passage on the inside of the main entrance or front door of a building: *Leave your coat in the hall.* **2** [C] building or large room for meetings, meals, concerts, etc: *the Town* ˈ*Hall* ○ ˈ*dance halls.* **3** (**a**) [C] = HALL OF RESIDENCE. (**b**) [U] (in colleges at some English universities) large room for meals: *dine in hall.* **4** [C] (in England) large country house, esp one that belongs to the chief landowner in the district. **5** (idm) **Liberty Hall** ⇨ LIBERTY.
□ ˌ**hall of** ˈ**fame** (esp in the USA) building or room containing small statues or similar memorials of people who have become famous in a particular activity.
ˌ**hall of** ˈ**residence** (also **hall**) building for university students to live in.
ˈ**hall-stand** *n* piece of furniture in the hall of a house, for hats, coats, umbrellas, etc.
ˈ**hallway** *n* **1** = HALL 1. **2** (*esp US*) corridor.

hallal = HALAL.

hallelujah = ALLELUIA.

Halley /ˈhælɪ *or, rarely,* ˈhɔ:lɪ/ Edmond (1656-1742), English astronomer and mathematician, most famous for his successful prediction that Halley's comet, named after him, would return in 1758.
□ ˌ**Halley's** ˈ**comet** bright comet which reappears about every 76 years. It was first recorded in 240 BC, and the fact of its regular return was established by Edmond Halley. Its next appearance is due in 2061.

halliard = HALYARD.

hallmark /ˈhɔ:lmɑ:k/ *n* **1** mark used for indicating the standard of gold, silver and platinum on articles made of these metals. **2** (*fig*) distinctive feature, esp of excellence: *Attention to detail is the hallmark of a fine craftsman.*
▷ **hallmark** *v* [Tn] stamp (sth) with a hallmark.

hallo (also **hello**, **hullo**) /həˈləʊ/ *interj* (used in greeting, or to attract attention or express surprise, or to answer a telephone call): *Hello, how are you?* ○ *Hallo, can you hear me?* ○ *Hullo, hullo, hullo, what's going on here?* ○ *Hallo, is that Oxford 56767?*
▷ **hallo** (also **hello**, **hullo**) *n* (*pl* ~**s**) the cry 'hallo': *He gave me a cheery hallo.*

halloo /həˈlu:/ *interj, n* cry used to urge on hounds or to attract attention.
▷ **halloo** *v* [I] shout 'halloo', esp to hounds.

hallow /ˈhæləʊ/ *v* [Tn usu passive] make (sb/sth) holy; honour as holy: *ground hallowed by sacred memories.*

Hallowe'en /ˌhæləʊˈi:n/ *n* 31 October, the eve of All Saints' Day, when according to ancient superstition the spirits of the dead arise from their graves. In the USA it is traditional to have Hallowe'en parties at which people wear weird masks or costumes, and for children to go from house to house demanding small gifts in return for not playing tricks on the people inside (the game being known as 'trick or treat'). These customs are now common in Britain.

hallucinate /həˈlu:sɪneɪt/ *v* [I] imagine one is seeing or hearing sth when no such thing is present: *Drug addicts often hallucinate.*

hallucination /həˌlu:sɪˈneɪʃn/ *n* **1** [C, U] illusion of seeing or hearing sth when no such thing is actually present: *suffer from/have hallucinations.* **2** [C] thing seen or heard in this way.
▷ **hallucinatory** /həˈlu:sɪnətrɪ, həˌlu:sɪˈneɪtərɪ; *US* həˈlu:sɪnətɔ:rɪ/ *adj* of or causing hallucinations: *a hallucinatory experience/drug.*

hallucinogen /həˈlu:sɪnədʒen/ *n* drug causing hallucinations. ▷ **hallucinogenic** /həˌlu:sɪnəˈdʒenɪk/ *adj.* ⇨ article at DRUG.

halma /ˈhælmə/ *n* [U] board game, popular in the late 19th and early 20th centuries, in which the object is to move one's pieces to the opposite corner of the board.

halo /ˈheɪləʊ/ *n* (*pl* ~**es** or ~**s**) (also **aureola**, **aureole**) **1** (in paintings, etc) circle of light shown round or above the head of a sacred figure. **2** = CORONA.

halogen /ˈhælədʒən/ *n* (*chemistry*) any of the chemical elements fluorine, chlorine, bromine, iodine and astatine, which form salts by simple union with a metal: [attrib] *halogen lamps/headlights.*

Hals /hæls/ Frans (c 1581-1666), Dutch painter of portraits and domestic scenes. His most famous work is *The Laughing Cavalier.*

halt /hɔ:lt/ *n* **1** (**a**) [sing] temporary stop; interruption of progress: *Work was brought/came to a halt when the machine broke down.* (**b**) [C] (esp of soldiers) short stop on a march or journey. **2** [C] (*Brit*) place on a railway line where local trains stop, but where there are no station buildings. **3** (idm) **bring sth/come to a grinding halt** ⇨ GRIND. **call a halt** ⇨ CALL[2]. **grind to a halt/standstill** ⇨ GRIND.
▷ **halt** *v* [I, Tn] (cause sb/sth to) stop temporarily: *Platoon, halt!* ○ *The officer halted his troops for a rest.*

halter /ˈhɔ:ltə(r)/ *n* **1** rope or leather strap put round the head of a horse for leading or fastening it. **2** rope used for hanging a person. **3** (also **halter-neck**) style of woman's dress with the top held up by a strap passing round the back of the neck, leaving the back and shoulders bare.

halting /ˈhɔ:ltɪŋ/ *adj* [usu attrib] slow and hesitant, as if lacking in confidence: *speak in a halting voice* ○ *a halting reply* ○ *a toddler's first few halting steps.* ▷ **haltingly** *adv*: *speak haltingly.*

halve /hɑ:v; *US* hæv/ *v* [Tn] **1** divide (sth) into two equal parts: *halve an apple.* **2** reduce (sth) by a half: *The latest planes have halved the time needed for crossing the Atlantic.* **3** (in golf) make the same score as one's opponent at (a particular hole) or in (a match): *I won four holes, she won two, and the rest were halved.*

halves *pl* of HALF[1].

halyard (also **halliard**) /ˈhæljəd/ *n* rope for raising or lowering a sail or flag.

ham /hæm/ *n* **1** (**a**) [C] upper part of a pig's leg, salted and dried or smoked for food: *several hams hanging on hooks.* (**b**) [U] meat from this: *a slice of ham* ○ [attrib] *a ham sandwich.* Cf BACON, GAMMON, PORK. **2** [C] (esp of animals) back of the thigh; thigh and buttock. **3** [C] (*sl*) person who acts or performs badly: *He's a terrible ham.* ○ [attrib] *ham actors/acting.* **4** [C] (*infml*) operator of an amateur radio station: *a radio ham.*
▷ **ham** *v* (-**mm**-) [I, Ip, Tn, Tn·p] ~ (**it/sth**) (**up**) (*sl*) act in a deliberately artificial or exaggerated way; overact: *Do stop hamming!* ○ *The actors were really hamming it up to amuse the audience.*
□ ˌ**ham-ˈfisted**, ˌ**ham-ˈhanded** *adjs* (*infml derog*) clumsy in using the hands.

hamburger /ˈhæmbɜ:gə(r)/ *n* **1** (also **burger**) [C] flat round cake of minced beef, usu fried and eaten with onions, often in a bread roll. **2** [U] (*US*) = MINCE *n.*

Hamite /ˈhæmaɪt/ *n* member of a group of N African peoples, including the *Berbers and the ancient Egyptians.
▷ **Hamitic** /həˈmɪtɪk/ *adj* **1** of the Hamites. **2** of a family of N African languages including *Berber, *Coptic and the *Cushitic languages of Ethiopia.

Hamlet /ˈhæmlɪt/ **1** hero of William Shakespeare's tragedy *Hamlet* (1604). In the play, his father, the king of Denmark, has been killed and succeeded by his own brother, Claudius. His father's ghost makes Hamlet swear to kill Claudius, but when he has the opportunity to do so, he finds that he cannot. Finally Hamlet is himself killed in a duel, but before he dies he kills Claudius. ⇨ App 6. **2** (idm) ˌ**Hamlet with**ˌ**out the** ˈ**prince** event, etc that is spoiled because its main participant is absent: *A farewell party without the person leaving is like Hamlet without the prince.*

hamlet /ˈhæmlɪt/ *n* small village, esp one without a church.

hammer

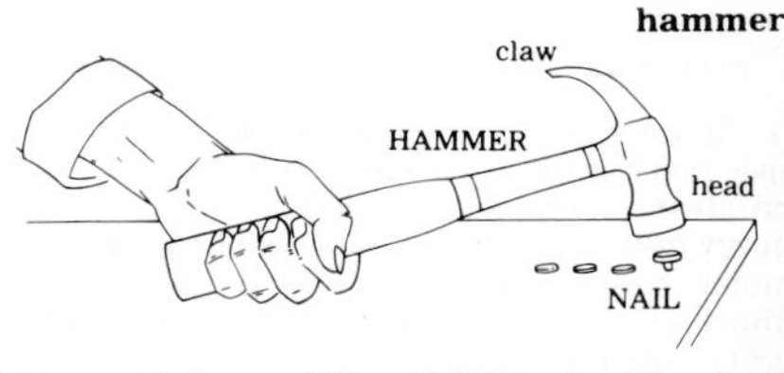

hammer[1] /ˈhæmə(r)/ *n* **1** [C] tool with a heavy metal head at right angles to the handle, used for breaking things, driving nails in, etc: [attrib] (*fig*) *The decision was a hammer blow to his hopes*, ie It destroyed them. ⇨ illus. **2** [C] any of the parts of a piano that strike the strings. **3** [C] part of the firing device of a gun that explodes the charge. **4** [C] instrument like a small wooden hammer used by an auctioneer to indicate with a rap that an article is sold. **5** (**a**) [C] (in athletics) metal ball attached to a wire for throwing. (**b**) **the hammer** [sing] event in which this is thrown. **6** [C] (*anatomy*) one of the three bones in the middle ear. **7** (idm) **be/go at it/each other** ˌ**hammer and** ˈ**tongs** (of two people) argue or fight violently and noisily: *We could hear the neighbours going at each other hammer and tongs.* **come/go under the** ˈ**hammer** be sold at auction: *This painting came under the hammer at Christie's today.*
□ **hammer and sickle** symbols of the industrial worker and the peasant, used as the emblem of the USSR.
ˈ**hammer-beam** *n* beam that sticks out into a room from the top of a wall.
ˈ**hammer-head** *n* type of shark with long extensions on each side of its head, like the head of

a hammer.

ˌ**hammer-ˈtoe** *n* toe that is deformed, being bent permanently downwards.

hammer[2] /ˈhæmə(r)/ *v* **1** [I, Ip, Tn] hit or beat (sth) with a hammer or as if with a hammer: *I could hear him hammering (away) in the house next door.* ○ *hammer a sheet of copper.* **2** [Ipr] ~ **at/on sth** strike sth loudly: *hammer at the door*, ie with one's fists, a stick, etc ○ *He hammered on the table with his fist.* **3** [Tn] (*infml*) defeat (sb) utterly: *Manchester United were hammered 5-1.* **4** (phr v) **hammer away at sth** work hard at sth: *hammer away at a difficult problem.* **hammer sth down, off, etc** cause sth to fall down, off, etc by hammering: *hammer the door down.* **hammer sth flat, straight, etc** make sth flat, etc by hammering. **hammer sth home (a)** hammer (a nail) in fully. **(b)** stress (a point, an argument, etc) so that it is fully understood. **hammer sth in** force sth inwards by hammering: *hammer a nail in/hammer in a nail.* **hammer sth into sb** force sb to learn sth by repeating it many times: *They have had English grammar hammered into them.* **hammer sth into sth (a)** force sth to enter sth by hammering: *hammer a nail into a wall.* **(b)** fashion sth by hammering (esp metal): *hammer copper into pots and pans.* **hammer sth out (a)** remove (a dent, etc) by hammering. **(b)** devise (a plan, solution, etc); achieve sth by great effort: *After much discussion the negotiators hammered out a compromise settlement.*

▷ **hammering** /ˈhæmərɪŋ/ *n* **1** noisy beating or striking, esp with a hammer. **2** (*infml*) total defeat: *Our team took a terrible hammering.*

Hammerstein /ˈhæməstaɪn/ Oscar (1895-1960), American librettist who wrote the words for many Richard *Rodgers musicals (eg *Oklahoma!* and *South Pacific*).

Hammett /ˈhæmɪt/ Dashiell (1894-1961), American writer of tough detective stories (eg *The Maltese Falcon* and *The Thin Man*). He created the character Sam Spade.

hammock /ˈhæmək/ *n* bed made of canvas or rope netting, suspended by cords at the ends, used esp on board ship.

hamper[1] /ˈhæmpə(r)/ *n* **1** large basket with a hinged lid, esp one containing food, wine, etc. **2** (*esp Brit*) box or parcel containing food, wine, etc sent as a gift: *a Christmas hamper.*

hamper[2] /ˈhæmpə(r)/ *v* [Tn] prevent the free movement or activity of (sb); hinder (sb/sth): *Our progress was hampered by the bad weather.*

Hampshire /ˈhæmpʃə(r)/ (*abbr* **Hants**) rural county on the south coast of England, which contains the ports of Southampton and Portsmouth. ⇨ map at App 1.

Hampton Court /ˌhæmptən ˈkɔːt/ palace beside the Thames, to the west of London. Cardinal *Wolsey had it built in 1515. He gave it to *Henry VIII, and it has been a royal palace ever since. The gardens contain a well-known maze.

hamster /ˈhæmstə(r)/ *n* small rat-like rodent kept as a pet, with pouches in its cheeks for carrying grain.

hamstring /ˈhæmstrɪŋ/ *n* **1** any of the five tendons at the back of the human knee. **2** thick tendon at the back of an animal's hock.

▷ **hamstring** *v* (*pt, pp* **hamstringed** or **hamstrung** /ˈhæmstrʌŋ/) [Tn] **1** cripple (a person or an animal) by cutting the hamstring(s). **2** (*fig*) destroy the activity or efficiency of (sb/sth): *The project was hamstrung by lack of funds.*

the hand

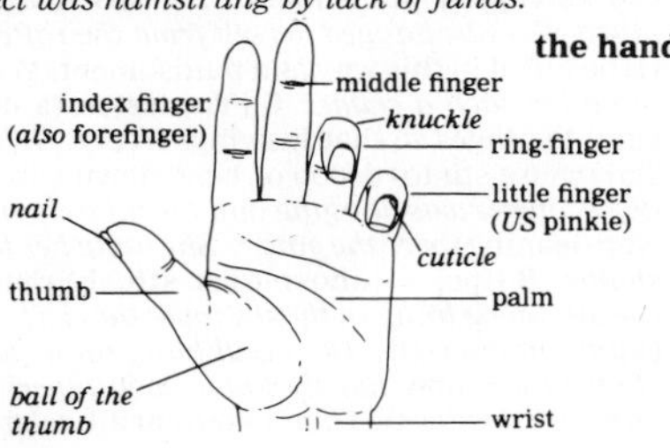

hand[1] /hænd/ *n* **1** [C] end part of the human arm below the wrist: *take/lead sb by the hand* ○ *have one's hands in one's pockets.* ⇨ illus. **2 a hand** [sing] (*infml*) active help: *Please lend a hand.* ○ *Give (me) a hand with the washing-up.* ○ *Do you want/need a hand?* **3** [C] pointer on a clock, dial, etc: *the ˈhour/ˈminute/ˈsecond hand of a watch.* **4** [C] **(a)** manual worker on a farm or in a factory, dockyard, etc: *ˈfarm-hands.* **(b)** member of a ship's crew: *All hands* (ie All seamen are needed) *on deck!* **5** [sing] skill in using the hands: *He has a light hand with pastry*, ie makes it well. **6** [C] **(a)** set of cards dealt to a player in a card-game: *have a good, bad, poor, etc hand.* **(b)** one round in a game of cards: *Let's play one more hand.* **7** [sing] style of handwriting: *He has/writes a good/legible hand.* **8** [sing] (*dated or fml*) promise to marry: *He asked for her hand.* ○ *She gave him her hand (in marriage).* **9** [C] unit of measurement, about four inches (10.16 cm), used for measuring the height of a horse. **10** [C] bunch (of bananas). **11** (idm) ˌ**all** ˌ**hands to the ˈpump** (*saying*) everyone must help: *We've an urgent job on this week, so it's (a case of) all hands to the pump.* **at first, second, etc ˈhand** directly/indirectly from the original source: *I only heard the news at second hand.* **(close/near) at ˈhand (a)** near; close by: *He lives close at hand.* **(b)** (*fml*) about to happen: *Your big moment is at hand.* **at sb's hands** from sb: *I did not expect such unkind treatment at your hands.* **be a dab, an old, a poor, etc hand (at sth)** have (or lack) the specified skill or experience: *He's an old hand at this game.* ie very experienced ○ *I was never much of a hand* (ie never very good) *at cookery.* **bind/tie sb hand and ˈfoot (a)** tie sb's hands and feet together. **(b)** (*fig*) take away sb's freedom of action. **a bird in the hand is worth two in the bush** ⇨ BIRD. **bite the hand that feeds one** ⇨ BITE[1]. **blood on one's hands** ⇨ BLOOD[1]. **bring sb/sth up by hand** rear (a person or an animal) by feeding from a bottle: *The lamb had to be brought up by hand.* **by ˈhand (a)** by a person, not a machine: *made by hand.* **(b)** by a messenger (not through the post): *The note was delivered by hand.* **by one's own fair hand** ⇨ FAIR[1]. **cap in hand** ⇨ CAP. **change hands** ⇨ CHANGE[1]. **the dead hand of sth** ⇨ DEAD. **the devil makes work for idle hands** ⇨ DEVIL[1]. **eat out of sb's hand** ⇨ EAT. **fall, etc into sb's, etc ˈhands** be taken or obtained (esp by an enemy): *The town fell into enemy hands.* ○ *I would hate my diary to get into the wrong hands.* **a firm hand** ⇨ FIRM[1]. **fold one's hands** ⇨ FOLD[1]. **force sb's hand** ⇨ FORCE[2]. **from** ˌ**hand to ˈhand** from one person to another: *Buckets of water were passed from hand to hand to put the fire out.* **gain/win sb's hand** (*fml*) make sb promise to marry one. **gain, get, etc the upper hand** ⇨ UPPER. **get one's eye/hand in** ⇨ EYE[1]. **get, have, etc a free hand** ⇨ FREE[1]. **give sb/get a big hand** ⇨ BIG. **give sb/get the glad hand** ⇨ GLAD. **give one's ˈhand on sth** (*fml*) take sb's hand and clasp it when agreeing to sth. **(be)** ˌ**hand in ˈglove (with sb)** working in close association: *He was found to be hand in glove with the enemy.* ˌ**hand in ˈhand (a)** holding each other's hand. ⇨ illus at ARM. **(b)** (*fig*) closely associated; linked together: *War and suffering go hand in hand.* ˌ**hand over ˈhand** using one's hands alternately (as when climbing). ˌ**hands ˈoff (sth/sb)** (*infml*) don't touch (sth/sb); don't interfere: ˌ*Hands off my ˈsandwiches!* ˌ**hands ˈup (a)** (said when addressing a group of people) raise one hand (eg to show agreement or to answer a question): *Hands up, anyone who knows the answer.* **(b)** raise both hands (eg to show that one is surrendering): *Hands up and drop your gun!* ˌ**hand to ˈhand** (of fighting) involving physical contact with one's opponent: [attrib] *hand-to-hand combat.* **have/take a hand in sth** participate in sth; be partly responsible for sth: *I bet he had a ˈhand in it.* **have one's ˈhands free/tied** be/not be in a position to do as one likes. **have one's ˈhands full** be so busy that one cannot undertake anything else. **have sb in the palm of one's hand** ⇨ PALM[1]. **have time on one's hands/time to kill** ⇨ TIME[1]. **have, etc the whip hand** ⇨ WHIP. **a heavy hand** ⇨ HEAVY. **a helping hand** ⇨ HELP[1]. **hold sb's ˈhand** comfort or help sb in a sad or difficult situation. **hold ˈhands (with sb)** sit, walk, etc beside another person with hands linked, usu as a sign of affection: *two lovers holding hands.* **in capable, good, etc ˈhands** being well managed, etc: *I've left the department in Bill's very efficient hands.* **in ˈhand (a)** in one's possession and available for use: *I still have some money in hand.* ○ *Cash in hand, £37.25.* **(b)** in control: *We have the situation well in hand.* **(c)** receiving attention and being dealt with: *the job in hand* ○ *The work is in hand and will soon be completed.* **in one's/sb's ˈhands** in one's/sb's possession, control or care: *The affair is no longer in my hands.* ○ *Put the matter in the hands of a solicitor.* **an iron fist/hand in a velvet glove** ⇨ IRON[1]. **join hands** ⇨ JOIN. **keep one's ˈhand in** retain one's skill by practice: *I like to play tennis regularly, just to keep my hand in.* **know (a place) like the back of one's hand** ⇨ KNOW. **lay one's ˈhands on sb/sth (a)** find sb/sth: *The book's here somewhere, but I can't lay my hands on it just now.* **(b)** (*infml*) catch sb/sth: *If I ever lay my hands on the thief, he'll be sorry.* **(c)** (of a priest) put the hands on the head of sb, to bless, confirm or ordain him. **lend a hand** ⇨ LEND. **lift/raise a finger/hand (to do sth)** ⇨ LIFT. **lift/raise a/one's ˈhand against sb** threaten or attack sb. **live from** ˌ**hand to ˈmouth** satisfy only one's present basic needs (esp for food): [attrib] *a hand-to-mouth existence.* **make money hand over fist** ⇨ MONEY. **many hands make light work** (*saying*) a task is soon completed if many people help. **not do a hand's ˈturn** not do any work: *He never does a hand's turn around the house — his wife does everything.* **off one's ˈhands** no longer one's responsibility: *They'll be glad to get their son off their hands.* **offer one's hand** ⇨ OFFER. **on either/every ˈhand** (*fml*) on both/all sides. **on ˈhand** available. **on one's ˈhands** resting on one as a responsibility: *I have an empty house on my hands*, eg one for which I want to find a buyer or tenant. **on the ˈone hand... on the ˈother (hand)...** (used to indicate contrasting points of view, opinions, etc). **out of ˈhand (a)** out of control; undisciplined: *The football fans have got completely out of hand.* **(b)** at once; without further thought: *The proposal was rejected out of hand.* ˌ**out of one's ˈhands** no longer under one's control: *I can't help you, I'm afraid — the matter is out of my hands.* **overplay one's hand** ⇨ OVERPLAY. ˌ**play into sb's ˈhands** do sth that is to (an opponent's) advantage. **put one's** ˌ**hand in one's ˈpocket** be ready to spend or give money. **putty in sb's hands** ⇨ PUTTY. **see, etc sb's hand in sth** notice sb's (esp unfriendly or harmful) influence in sth: *Do I detect your hand in this?* **set one's hand to sth** (*dated or fml*) sign (esp a formal document): *set one's hand to a treaty.* **shake sb's hand/shake hands/shake sb by the hand** ⇨ SHAKE[1]. **show one's hand/cards** ⇨ SHOW[2]. **a show of hands** ⇨ SHOW[1]. **sit on one's hands** ⇨ SIT. **sleight of hand** ⇨ SLEIGHT. **take one's courage in both hands** ⇨ COURAGE. ˌ**take sb in ˈhand** take control of sb in order to improve his behaviour: *Those dreadful children need to be taken in hand.* **take the law into one's own hands** ⇨ LAW. **take one's life in one's hands** ⇨ LIFE. **take matters into one's own hands** ⇨ MATTER[1]. **throw one's ˈhand in** (*infml*) abandon sth in which one is engaged. **time hangs/lies heavy on one's hands** ⇨ TIME[1]. **to ˈhand (a)** within reach; readily available: *I don't have the information to hand.* ○ *I used whatever materials came to hand*, ie were available. **(b)** (*commerce*) received: *Your letter is to hand*, ie has reached me and is receiving attention. **try one's hand** ⇨ TRY[1]. **turn one's hand to sth** (be able to) undertake sth: *She can turn her hand to all sorts of jobs.* **wait on sb hand and foot** ⇨ WAIT[1]. **wash one's hands of sb/sth** ⇨ WASH[2]. **win hands down** ⇨ WIN. **wring one's hands** ⇨ WRING.

▷ **-handed** (in compound *adjs*) **1** having hands as specified: *big-handed.* **2 (a)** using the specified hand usually, in preference to the other: *right-handed people.* **(b)** made by or for the specified hand: *a left-handed blow* ○ *a one-handed* *catch.*

handful /ˈhændfʊl/ *n* (*pl* **-fuls**) **1** [C] ~ (**of sth**) as much or as many as can be held in one hand: *pick up a handful of sand.* **2** [sing] ~ (**of sb/sth**) small number: *a handful of people.* **3 a handful** [sing] (*infml*) person or animal that is difficult to control: *That young lad is quite a handful*, ie is lively and troublesome.

□ ˈ**hand-axe** *n* prehistoric tool consisting of a sharpened stone, used for chopping, cutting and scraping.

ˈ**handbag** (*US* **purse**) *n* small bag for money, keys, etc, carried esp by women. ⇨ illus at LUGGAGE.

ˈ**hand-baggage** *n* [U] (*US*) = HAND-LUGGAGE.

ˈ**handball** *n* [U] any of several games in which players throw a ball to each other or hit it (usu with a gloved hand) against a wall.

ˈ**hand-barrow** *n* light two-wheeled barrow.

ˈ**handbell** *n* small bell with a handle, esp one of a tuned set used for playing music.

ˈ**handbill** *n* printed advertisement or announcement distributed by hand.

ˈ**handbook** *n* small book giving useful facts; guidebook: *a car handbook* ○ *a handbook of wild flowers.* Cf MANUAL *n* 1.

ˈ**handbrake** *n* (in a motor vehicle) brake operated by hand, used when the vehicle is stationary: *Don't drive with the handbrake on.* ⇨ illus at CAR.

ˈ**handcart** *n* = CART 1b.

ˈ**handclap** *n* [sing] clapping of the hands: *give sb a slow handclap*, ie clap slowly and rhythmically to show impatience.

ˈ**handcuffs** *n* [pl] pair of metal rings joined by a chain, for fastening round the wrists of prisoners: *The prisoner wore (a pair of) handcuffs.* ⇨ illus at SHACKLE. ˈ**handcuff** *v* [esp passive: Tn, Tn·pr] ~ **sb** (**to sth/sb**) put handcuffs on sb: *The demonstrator had handcuffed herself to the railings.*

ˈ**hand-grenade** *n* grenade thrown by hand.

ˈ**hand-gun** *n* (*esp US*) gun that is held and fired with one hand; pistol.

ˌ**hand-ˈheld** *adj* held in the hand: *film taken with a ˌhand-held ˈcamera.*

ˈ**handhold** *n* thing that a climber may grip, eg on a rock face.

ˈ**hand-luggage** (*US* ˈ**hand-baggage**) *n* [U] luggage that is light enough to be carried by hand.

ˌ**handˈmade** *adj* made by hand: *ˌhandmade ˈpottery.* Cf MACHINE-MADE (MACHINE).

ˈ**handmaid** (also ˈ**handmaiden**) *n* (*arch*) female servant.

ˈ**hand-organ** *n* = BARREL-ORGAN (BARREL).

ˌ**hand-ˈpicked** *adj* carefully chosen.

ˈ**hand puppet** (*US*) = GLOVE PUPPET (GLOVE).

ˈ**handrail** *n* narrow rail for holding as a support, eg when going up or down stairs. ⇨ illus at STAIR.

ˈ**handsaw** *n* saw used with one hand only.

ˈ**handset** *n* part of a telephone which one holds close to one's ear and mouth so that one can both hear and speak.

ˈ**handshake** *n* **1** shaking of sb's hand with one's own, as a greeting, etc. **2** (idm) **a ˌgolden ˈhandshake** ⇨ GOLDEN.

ˌ**hands-ˈon** *adj* [attrib] practical: *have ˌhands-on exˈperience of a computer keyboard.*

ˈ**handspring** *n* somersault in which a person lands first on his hands and then on his feet.

ˈ**handstand** *n* balancing on one's hands with one's feet in the air: *do a handstand.*

ˈ**handwriting** *n* [U] **1** writing with a pen, pencil, etc. **2** person's particular style of this: *I can't read his handwriting.*

ˈ**handwritten** *adj* written by hand (ie not printed or typed): *Letters of application must be handwritten.*

hand[2] /hænd/ *v* **1** [Tn·p, Dn·n, Dn·pr] ~ **sth** (**to sb**) give or transfer sth with one's hand or hands: *He handed round the biscuits.* ○ *Please hand me that book.* ○ *She handed it to the boy.* **2** (idm) **hand/give sb sth on a plate** ⇨ PLATE[1].

3 (phr v) **hand sth down** (**to sb**) (**a**) pass sth on by tradition, inheritance, etc: *stories handed down from generation to generation* ○ *Most of my clothes were handed down to me by my older brother.* (**b**) (*esp US*) announce sth formally or publicly: *hand down a budget, legal decision, verdict.*

hand sth in (**to sb**) bring or give sth; offer or submit sth: *Hand in your examination papers now, please.* ○ *She handed in her resignation.*

hand sb off (in Rugby football) push away (an opponent) with one's hand.

hand sth on (**to sb**) send or give sth to another person: *Please hand on the magazine to your friends.*

hand sth out (**to sb**) distribute sth: *Relief workers were handing out emergency rations (to the survivors).*

hand (**sth**) **over** (**to sb**) transfer (a position of authority or power) to sb: *I am resigning as chairman and handing over to my deputy.* ○ *hand over power to an elected government.* **hand sb over to sb** (esp at a meeting, on TV, etc or on the telephone) let sb listen or speak to another person: *I'm handing you over now to our home affairs correspondent.* **hand sb/sth over** (**to sb**) deliver sb/sth, esp to authority: *They handed him/their weapons over to the police.*

hand it to sb (*infml*) (always with *must* or *have (got) to*) give sb the praise that he deserves: *You've got to hand it to her — she's damned clever.*

□ ˈ**hand-me-downs** (also ˈ**reach-me-downs**) *n* [pl] used or unwanted things (esp clothes) that are given to another person, esp a younger brother or sister: *I don't want your old hand-me-downs!*

ˈ**hand-out** *n* **1** (esp) food, money or clothes given free to a needy person. **2** (**a**) leaflet, etc distributed free of charge. (**b**) prepared statement given, eg by a politician, to newspaper men. (**c**) duplicated sheet containing examples, etc distributed by a teacher.

ˈ**hand-over** *n* (period of) transfer, esp of power or responsibility.

h and c /ˌeɪtʃ ənd ˈsiː/ *abbr* hot and cold (running water); supply of hot and cold water from taps (eg in a hotel room).

Handel /ˈhændl/ George (1685-1759), German composer who in 1712 came to live in England. His most familiar works are oratorios, musical dramas based on stories from the Bible. These include *Saul* and *Judas Maccabaeus*, but the best-known is the *Messiah*, about the coming of Christ, which is regularly performed by choirs in Britain. He also wrote ceremonial music for King George I, such as the *Water Music* and the *Music for the Royal Fireworks*. He was blind for the last seven years of his life.

handicap /ˈhændɪkæp/ *n* **1** thing that makes progress or success difficult. **2** physical or mental disability: *Deafness can be a serious handicap.* **3** (**a**) race or competition in which the competitors are given disadvantages in order to make their chances of success more equal. (**b**) disadvantage given in this way, eg a weight to be carried by a horse. **4** number of strokes by which a golfer normally exceeds par for the course.

▷ **handicap** *v* (**-pp-**) [Tn esp passive] give or be a disadvantage to (sb): *be handicapped by a lack of education.* **handicapped** *adj* suffering from a serious physical or mental disability. **the handicapped** *n* [pl *v*] handicapped people: *a school for the severely handicapped.*

handicraft /ˈhændɪkrɑːft; *US* -kræft/ *n* [U, C] work that needs both skill with the hands and artistic skill, eg needlework, pottery, woodwork: *an exhibition of handicraft(s).*

handiwork /ˈhændɪwɜːk/ *n* [U] **1** work done by the hands. **2** (*often ironic*) thing done by a particular person: *Is that drawing on the board your handiwork, Clare?*

handkerchief /ˈhæŋkətʃɪf, *also* -tʃiːf/ *n* (*pl* ~**s** or **handkerchieves** /-tʃiːvz/) (usu square) piece of cloth or paper tissue for blowing the nose into, wiping the face, etc.

handle /ˈhændl/ *n* **1** part of a tool, cup, bucket, door, drawer, etc, by which it may be held, carried or controlled. **2** fact that may be taken advantage of: *His indiscretions gave his enemies a handle to use against him.* **3** (*sl*) title: *have a handle to one's name*, ie have a title, eg 'Sir' or 'Lord'. **4** (idm) **fly off the handle** ⇨ FLY[2].

▷ **handle** *v* **1** [Tn] touch (sth) with or hold (sth) in the hand(s): *Gelignite is dangerous stuff to handle.* ○ *Wash your hands before you handle food.* ○ *Fragile* — handle with care. **2** [Tn] deal with, manage or control (people, a situation, a machine, etc): *An officer must know how to handle his men.* ○ *This port handles 100 million tons of cargo each year.* ○ *I was impressed by her handling of the affair.* **3** [I] (with an *adv*) (esp of a vehicle) be able to be operated in the specified way: *This car handles well.* **4** [Tn] treat (a person or an animal) as specified: *The speaker was roughly handled by the mob.* **5** [Tn] buy and sell (sth): *This shop does not handle such goods.* **6** [Tn] discuss or write about (a subject). **handler** /ˈhændlə(r)/ *n* person who trains and controls an animal, esp a police-dog.

-handled (in compound *adjs*) having a handle of the specified type: *a ˌbone-handled ˈknife.*

□ ˈ**handlebar** *n* (usu *pl*) bar with a handle at each end, for steering a bicycle, etc. ⇨ illus at BICYCLE.

ˌ**handlebar mouˈstache** thick moustache with curved ends.

handsome /ˈhænsəm/ *adj* **1** (**a**) (of men) good-looking. (**b**) (of women) having a fine figure and a strong dignified appearance: *I would describe her as handsome rather than beautiful.* (**c**) of fine appearance: *a handsome horse, building, car.* ⇨ Usage at BEAUTIFUL. **2** (of gifts, behaviour, etc) generous: *a handsome present.* **3** considerable: *a handsome profit, price, fortune, etc.* **4** (idm) ˌ**handsome ˈis as ˌhandsome ˈdoes** (*saying*) a person's quality can only be judged from his behaviour, not from his appearance. **high, wide and handsome** ⇨ HIGH[1]. ▷ **handsomely** *adv*: *She was handsomely rewarded for her efforts.* **handsomeness** *n* [U].

handy /ˈhændɪ/ *adj* (**-ier, -iest**) **1** (of gadgets, etc) convenient to handle or use; useful: *A good tool-box is a handy thing to have in the house.* **2** [pred] conveniently placed for being reached or used: *Our flat is very handy for the schools.* ○ *Always keep a first-aid kit handy.* **3** [usu pred] clever with one's hands: *He's handy about the house.* **4** (idm) ˌ**come in ˈhandy** be useful some time or other: *My extra earnings came in very handy.* ○ *Don't throw that cardboard box away — it may come in handy.* ▷ **handily** *adv*: *We're handily placed for* (ie within a short distance of) *the shopping centre.* **handiness** *n* [U].

□ **handyman** /ˈhændɪmæn/ *n* (*pl* **-men** /-men/) person who is clever at doing household repairs, etc or who is employed to do odd jobs.

hang[1] /hæŋ/ *v* (*pt, pp* **hung** /hʌŋ/; in senses 5 and 9 **hanged**) **1** (**a**) [Ipr, Ip, Tn, Tn·pr, Tn·p] be supported, or support (sth), from above, esp so that the lower end is free: *A towel hung from the rail.* ○ *Hang your coat (up) on that hook.* ○ *She was hanging her washing (out) on the line.* (**b**) [Ipr, Ip] (of material, clothing, etc) drape or fall as specified: *The curtains were hanging in folds.* ○ *How does the dress hang at the back?* **2** [I, Tn] be left hanging, or leave (sth) hanging, until ready for eating: *How long has this meat (been) hung for?* **3** (**a**) [I, Tn] be fastened, or fasten (sth), to a wall esp in an exhibition: *His portrait (was) hung above the fireplace.* ○ *Her paintings hang in the National Gallery.* (**b**) [Tn·pr esp passive] ~ **sth with sth** decorate sth with (pictures, ornaments, etc): *The rooms were hung with tapestries.* **4** [Tn] stick (wallpaper) to a wall. **5** (**a**) [Tn, Tn·pr] kill (sb/oneself) by hanging from a rope around the neck, esp as capital punishment: *He was hanged for murder.* ○ *She hanged herself from the rafters.* (**b**) [I] be killed in this way as a punishment: *You can't hang for such a crime.* **6** [Tn] fasten (a door or gate) to hinges so that it swings freely. **7** [Ipr, Ip, Tn] (cause sth to) droop or bend downwards: *The dog's tongue was hanging out.* ○ *Children hung* (ie were leaning) *over the gate.* ○ *She hung her head in shame.* **8** [Ipr] ~ (**above/over sth/sb**) remain in the air: *Smog hung in the sky (over the city).* **9** [Tn] (*infml*) damn (sth): *Do it and hang the expense!* ○ *Hang it all, they hardly know each other!* ○ *I'm hanged if I know* (ie I don't know at all) *what to do.*

10 (idm) **go hang** (*sl*) (used to express defiance or lack of concern) be damned: *He can go hang for all I care.* **hang by a ˈhair/a (single) ˈthread** (of a person's fate, etc) depend on sth small. **hang ˈfire** (**a**) (of a gun) be slow in firing. (**b**) be slow in taking action or making progress: *The project had hung fire for several years because of lack of funds.* **hang in the ˈbalance** (of events) have reached a critical point, where the result may go either way. **hang on sb's ˈlips/ˈwords/on sb's every ˈword** listen attentively to sb. **let it all hang ˈout** (*sl catchphrase*) be completely uninhibited. **one may/might as well be hanged/hung for a ˌsheep as (for) a ˈlamb** (*saying*) if the penalty for a more serious offence is no greater than that for a less serious one, one might as well continue to commit the more serious one. **a peg to hang sth on** ⇨ PEG. **(and) thereby hangs a tale** there is an interesting (often surprising) story or piece of further information about what has just been mentioned. **time hangs/lies heavy on one's hands** ⇨ TIME[1]. **with one's tongue hanging out** ⇨ TONGUE. **11** (phr v) **hang aˈbout/aˈround (...)** (*infml*) be standing about (a place), doing nothing definite; not move away: *unemployed people hanging about (the ˈstreets).* **hang back (from sth)** show unwillingness to do sth; hesitate: *She volunteered to help but he was afraid and hung ˈback.* **hang ˈin** (*infml esp US*) refuse to give up in spite of difficulties; persevere: *Keep hanging in there!* **ˌhang ˈon** (**a**) grip sth firmly: *ˌHang on ˈtight — we're off!* (**b**) (*infml*) wait for a short time: *Hang ˈon a minute — I'm nearly ready.* (**c**) (*infml*) (on the telephone) not replace the receiver: *The line was engaged and the operator asked if I'd like to hang ˈon.* **hang on sth** depend on sth: *A great deal hangs on this decision.* **hang on to sth** (**a**) hold sth tightly: *ˌHang on to that ˈrope and don't let go.* (**b**) (*infml*) keep sth; not sell or give sth away: *I should ˌhang on to those old ˈphotographs — they may be valuable.* **hang ˈout** (**a**) (*infml*) visit a place often; have one's home: *Where does he hang out these days?* (**b**) (*US sl*) pass one's time idly, talking to friends, looking around, thinking, etc. **hang sth out** put (washing) on a clothes-line so that it can dry: *He ˌhung out her ˈblouses.* **hang over sb** (of sth bad) seem to be about to happen to sb; threaten sb: *I have this awful fear of failure hanging over me.* **hang toˈgether** (**a**) (of people) support or help one another. (**b**) (of statements) be consistent: *Their accounts of what happened don't hang together.* **hang ˈup (on sb)** (*infml*) end a telephone conversation by replacing the receiver. **be/get hung ˈup (about/on sb/sth)** (*sl*) be emotionally upset or inhibited: *She's really hung up on that guy.* **be/get hung ˈup (by sth)** be delayed by some difficulty.

▷ **hanging** *n* **1** [U, C] death by hanging: *sentence sb to death by hanging* ○ *There were two hangings here today.* **2 hangings** [pl] curtains, draperies, etc hung on walls.

□ **hanger-on** /ˌhæŋər ˈɒn/ *n* (*pl* **hangers-on** /ˌhæŋəz ˈɒn/) (*usu derog*) person who tries to become or appear friendly with others, esp in the hope of personal gain: *The great actor was surrounded by his usual crowd of hangers-on.*

hang-gliding

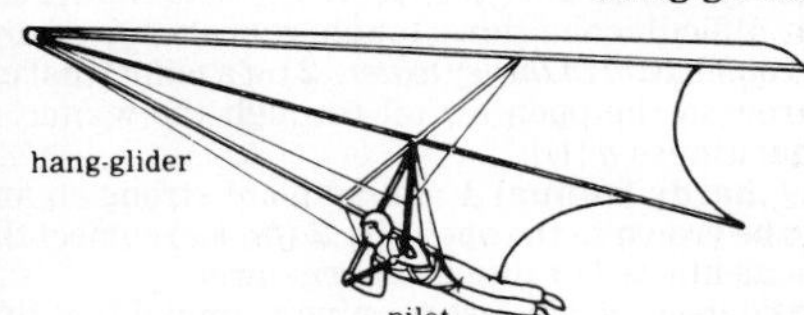

ˈ**hang-gliding** *n* [U] sport of flying while hanging from a frame like a large kite controlled by one's own movements. Cf GLIDING (GLIDE). ˈ**hang-glider** *n* frame used in this sport.

ˌ**hanging ˈvalley** valley that stops suddenly when it meets the side of another, steeper valley.

ˈ**hangman** /-mən/ *n* (*pl* **-men** /-mən/) person whose job is to hang people condemned to death.

ˈ**hang-out** *n* (*sl*) place where one lives or which one visits often.

ˈ**hang-up** *n* (*sl*) emotional inhibition or problem: *She's got a real hang-up about her freckles.*

hang[2] /hæŋ/ *n* [sing] **1** way in which sth hangs: *the hang of a coat, skirt, etc.* **2** (idm) **get the hang of sth** (*infml*) (**a**) learn how to operate or do sth: *I'm trying to get the hang of the new telephone system.* (**b**) grasp the meaning of sth said or written: *I didn't quite get the hang of his argument.* **not care/give a ˈhang (about sth/sb)** (*infml*) not care at all.

hangar /ˈhæŋə(r)/ *n* large shed in which aircraft are kept.

hangdog /ˈhæŋdɒg/ *adj* [attrib] (of sb's look) sly and ashamed, as if guilty: *his hangdog expression.*

hanger /ˈhæŋə(r)/ *n* **1** (also ˈ**clothes-hanger**, ˈ**coat-hanger**) curved piece of wood, plastic or wire with a hook, used for hanging up a garment. **2** loop or hook on or by which sth is hung.

hangnail /ˈhæŋneɪl/ (also **agnail** /ˈægneɪl/) *n* (soreness caused by) torn skin near the root of a finger-nail.

hangover /ˈhæŋəʊvə(r)/ *n* **1** unpleasant after-effects of drinking too much alcohol: *The next morning he was suffering from/had a hangover.* **2** thing left from an earlier time: *This procedure is a hangover from the old system.*

hank /hæŋk/ *n* coil or length of wool, thread, etc: *wind a hank of wool into balls.*

hanker /ˈhæŋkə(r)/ *v* [Ipr, It] ~ **after/for sth/to do sth** have a strong desire for sth: *hanker after wealth* ○ *hanker to become famous.*

▷ **hankering** *n* ~ **(after/for sth)** strong desire: *have a hankering for a cigarette.*

hanky /ˈhæŋkɪ/ *n* (*infml*) handkerchief.

hanky-panky /ˌhæŋkɪ ˈpæŋkɪ/ *n* [U] (*infml*) **1** dishonest dealing; trickery. **2** naughty (esp sexual) behaviour.

Hanna /ˈhænə/ Bill (1910-), American cartoon maker. With Joe Barbera he produced many witty short animated features, including those featuring their greatest creations, the cat and mouse team of Tom and Jerry.

Hannibal /ˈhænɪbl/ (247-c 183 BC), Carthaginian general who in 218 BC led an army from Spain across the Alps, accompanied by elephants, to attack Rome. The Romans were defeated several times, but Hannibal was unable to capture Rome, and he returned to Africa. He defended Carthage against Roman invasion, but was finally defeated and sent into exile.

Hanover /ˈhænəʊvə(r)/ **1** town in northern Germany, spelt **Hannover** in German. **2** former state in northern Germany, whose leader (called *Elector*) succeeded to the British throne in 1714 as George I. Until the death of Queen Victoria in 1901 the British royal family was known as the House of Hanover.

▷ **Hanoverian** /ˌhænəʊˈvɪərɪən/ *adj* of Hanover or the British House of Hanover.

Hansard /ˈhænsɑːd/ *n* [sing] official report of the proceedings of the British Parliament. ⇨ article at PARLIAMENT.

hansom /ˈhænsəm/ *n* (also ˌ**hansom ˈcab**) old type of horse-drawn carriage with two wheels, for carrying two passengers inside, having the driver's seat high at the back outside, and the reins going over the roof.

Hants /hænts/ *abbr* Hampshire.

Hanukka /ˈhɑːnəkə, *also* ˈhænuːkə/ *n* eight-day Jewish religious festival beginning in December.

haphazard /hæpˈhæzəd/ *adj* without plan or order; random: *books piled on shelves in a haphazard fashion.* ▷ **haphazardly** *adv.*

hapless /ˈhæplɪs/ *adj* [attrib] (*arch or rhet*) unlucky; unfortunate: *our hapless hero* ○ *a hapless fate.*

haploid /ˈhæplɔɪd/ *adj* (of a cell, esp an egg or a sperm cell) having a single set of chromosomes.

ha'p'orth /ˈheɪpəθ/ *n* (*Brit infml*) = HALFPENNY-WORTH (HALF).

happen /ˈhæpən/ *v* **1** (**a**) [I] occur (by chance or otherwise); take place: *How did the accident happen?* ○ *What happened next?* ○ *I'd stay if they promoted me, but I can't see that happening.* (**b**) [Ipr] ~ **to sb/sth** be the experience or fate of sb/sth: *If anything happens to him* (ie If he has an accident), *let me know.* ○ *What's happened to my clothes?* ie Do you know where they are? **2** have the (good or bad) fortune (to do sth); chance: *She happened to be out/It happened that she was out when he called.* ⇨ Usage at APPEAR. **3** [Ipr] ~ **on sth** (*fml*) find sth by chance: *I happened on just the thing I'd been looking for.* **4** (idm) **accidents will happen** ⇨ ACCIDENT. **as it happens/happened** by coincidence or chance: *We met her only yesterday, as it happens.*

▷ **happening** /ˈhæpənɪŋ/ *n* (**a**) (usu *pl*) thing that happens; event; occurrence: *There have been strange happenings here lately.* (**b**) special event, esp a spontaneous theatrical performance.

NOTE ON USAGE: Compare **happen**, **occur** and **take place. Happen** and **occur** refer to accidental or unplanned events; **occur** is more formal than **happen**: *The accident happened/occurred at about 9.30.* **Happen** can also indicate one event resulting from another: *What happened when you told him the news?* (ie What did he do?). **Take place** suggests that an event is/was planned: *The funeral took place on 24 April at 3 pm.*

happenstance /ˈhæpənstæns/ *n* [C, U] (*esp US*) (thing that happens by) chance.

happy /ˈhæpɪ/ *adj* (**-ier, -iest**) **1** ~ **(about/in/with sth/sb)** feeling or expressing pleasure, contentment, satisfaction, etc: *a happy marriage, scene, memory, child, ending (to a book, etc)* ○ *I won't be happy until I know she's safe.* ○ *Are you happy in your work/with your life?* **2** (in greetings) full of joy: *Happy Christmas!* ○ *After she'd cut the cake we all sang 'Happy Birthday'*, ie a special song sung on sb's birthday. **3** [pred] ~ **to do sth** (*fml*) pleased to do sth: *I am happy to be of service.* **4** fortunate; lucky: *He is in the happy position of never having to worry about money.* **5** (of words, ideas, behaviour, etc) well suited to the situation; pleasing: *That wasn't a very happy choice of words.* **6** (idm) **(as) happy as the day is ˈlong/as a ˈsandboy/as ˈLarry** very happy. **a happy eˈvent** the birth of a child. **a/the happy ˈmedium** thing that achieves a satisfactory avoidance of excess; balance between extremes: *be/find/seek a happy medium.* **many happy reˈturns (of the ˈday)** (used as a greeting to sb on his or her birthday).

▷ **happily** *adv* **1** contentedly: *They lived happily ever after.* **2** fortunately: *Happily this never happened.* **3** appropriately: *His message was not very happily worded.*

happiness *n* [U].

□ ˌ**happy ˈfamilies** card-game using a special pack of cards with the pictures of members of various families on them. The aim of the game is to collect as many complete families as possible.

ˌ**happy-go-ˈlucky** *adj* accepting events cheerfully as they happen; carefree: *She goes through life in a happy-go-lucky fashion.*

ˈ**happy hour** (*esp US*) time, usu in early evening, when drinks, etc are served at reduced prices in a bar, etc.

hara-kiri /ˌhærə ˈkɪrɪ/ *n* [U] ritual suicide using a sword to cut open one's stomach, formerly practised by Japanese samurai to avoid dishonour when they believed they had failed in their duty.

harangue /həˈræŋ/ *n* long, loud, serious and usu angry speech.

▷ **harangue** *v* [I, Tn] give a harangue to (sb): *haranguing the troops before a battle.*

harass /ˈhærəs; *US* həˈræs/ *v* [Tn] **1** trouble and annoy (sb) continually: *Political dissidents complained of being harassed by the police.* ○ *He always looks harassed*, ie tired and irritated by constant worry. **2** make repeated attacks on (an enemy).

▷ **harassment** *n* [U] harassing or being harassed.

harbinger /ˈhɑːbɪndʒə(r)/ *n* ~ **(of sb/sth)** (*rhet*) person or thing that announces or shows that sb/sth is coming: *The crowing of the cock is a harbinger of dawn.* ○ *The cuckoo is a harbinger of* *spring.*

harbour (*US* **harbor**) /ˈhɑːbə(r)/ *n* [C, U] **1** place of shelter for ships: *Several boats lay at anchor in the harbour.* ○ *We reached (the) harbour at sunset.* **2** (*fig*) place of safety or shelter.

▷ **harbour** (*US* **harbor**) *v* **1** [Tn] give shelter to (a criminal, etc); protect; conceal: *be convicted of harbouring a wanted man* ○ *Dirt harbours germs.* **2** [Tn] keep (sth) secretly in one's mind: *harbour a grudge, suspicions, thoughts of revenge, etc.* **3** [I, Ipr] (of a sailor or ship) shelter in a harbour.

harbourage (*US* **-bor-**) /ˈhɑːbərɪdʒ/ *n* [U] shelter.

□ ˈ**harbour-master** *n* official in charge of a harbour.

ˈ**harbour seal** small seal[1] common in the northern hemisphere.

hard[1] /hɑːd/ *adj* (**-er, -est**) **1** not soft or yielding to the touch or easily cut; solid; firm: *ground made hard by frost* ○ *Their bodies were hard and muscular after much training.* Cf SOFT. **2** ~ (**for sb**) (**to do sth**) difficult to do or understand or answer; not easy: *a hard task, book, language* ○ *She found it hard to decide.* ○ *Whether it's true or not is hard to tell.* ○ *It's hard for old people to change their ways.* ○ *You are hard to please/a hard person to please.* **3** (**a**) requiring much effort of body or mind; tough: *It's hard work shifting snow.* ○ *Some hard bargaining is called for.* ○ *We must take a hard look at our finances.* (**b**) [attrib] showing much effort; energetic: *a hard worker.* (**c**) of or like a strict or extreme political faction: *the hard left/right.* **4** forceful; violent; harsh: *hard knocks* ○ *hard words.* **5** causing unhappiness, discomfort or pain; difficult to endure: *have a hard childhood* ○ *be given/have a hard time,* ie experience difficulties, misfortunes, etc ○ *in these hard times,* ie when life is difficult because of poverty, unemployment, etc. **6** (of the weather) severe: *a hard winter/frost.* **7** (esp of a person) unfeeling; unsympathetic; harsh: *a hard father,* ie one who treats his children severely. **8** (of sounds or colours) unpleasant to the ear or eye; harsh: *a hard voice.* **9** (of consonants) sounding sharp, not soft: *The letter 'g' is hard in 'gun' and soft in 'gin'.* **10** (of drinks) strongly alcoholic: *hard liquor* ○ (*joc*) *a drop of the hard stuff,* ie alcoholic drink. **11** (idm) **be hard on sb** (**a**) treat or criticize sb severely: *Don't be too hard on her — she's very young.* (**b**) be unfair to sb: *The new law is a bit hard on those who were born abroad.* **drive a hard bargain** ⇨ DRIVE[1]. ˌ**hard and** ˈ**fast** (of rules, etc) that cannot be altered to fit special cases; inflexible: *hard and fast regulations, categories* ○ *This distinction isn't hard and fast.* (**as**) **hard as** ˈ**nails** (of a person) without sentiment or sympathy; hard-hearted. (**as**) **hard as** ˈ**stone** very hard or firm: *The ground is as hard as stone after the drought.* **hard** ˈ**at it** working hard. **hard** ˈ**facts** accurate information, not expressions of opinion, etc. **hard** ˈ**going** difficult to understand or enjoy; boring: *I'm finding this book very hard going.* **hard** ˈ**lines**; **hard, etc luck** (**on sb**) (*infml*) (used as an exclamation or a sympathetic comment on sb's misfortune): *You failed your driving test, I hear — hard lines!* ○ *It's hard luck on those who were beaten in the first round of the competition.* **a hard-**ˈ**luck story** version of events told by sb wanting sympathy. **a hard/tough nut to crack** ⇨ NUT. ˌ**hard of** ˈ**hearing** rather deaf: *TV subtitles for the hard of hearing.* **the hard/soft sell** ⇨ SELL *n.* **hard to** ˈ**take** difficult to accept without annoyance, grief or bitterness: *I find his attitude very hard to take.* **the** ˈ**hard way** using the most difficult or least convenient method to do or achieve sth: *do sth/find out/learn/grow up the hard way.* **make hard** ˈ**work of sth** make an activity seem more difficult than it is. **no hard** ˈ**feelings** no resentment or bitterness: *We were enemies once, but there are no hard feelings between us now.* **play hard to** ˈ**get** (*infml*) try to increase one's status and desirability by not readily accepting an offer or invitation, esp from the opposite sex. **take a hard line** (**on/over sth**) remain fixed and uncompromising in one's attitude, policy, etc. **too much like hard** ˈ**work** (of an activity) too demanding or wearisome to undertake: *I don't want to go for a walk on such a hot day — it's too much like hard work for me.* ▷ **hardness** *n* [U].

□ ˈ**hardback** *n* [C, U] book bound in a stiff cover: *Hardbacks are expensive.* ○ *My novel has just appeared in hardback.* ○ [attrib] *a hardback book.* Cf PAPERBACK (PAPER). ⇨ article at PUBLISHING.

ˈ**hardboard** *n* [U] stiff board made of compressed and treated wood-pulp.

ˈ**hard case** (*infml*) tough or unsentimental person.

ˌ**hard** ˈ**cash** coins and notes (ie not a cheque or promise to pay later).

ˌ**hard** ˈ**cheese** (*dated Brit sl sometimes ironic*) (used to express sympathy for sb) bad luck.

ˌ**hard** ˈ**copy** (*computing*) printed material produced by a computer or from a microfilm, etc and able to be read without a special device.

ˈ**hard core** (**a**) rubble, broken bricks, etc (used for foundations, roadmaking, etc). (**b**) central, basic or most enduring part (of a group, etc): *the hard core of the opposition.* ˈ**hard-core** *adj* [attrib] (of pornography) showing or describing sexual activity in great detail, with nothing hidden. Cf HARD PORN.

ˈ**hard court** tennis court with a hard surface, not of grass.

ˌ**hard** ˈ**cover** stiff binding for a book: [attrib] ˌ*hard-cover* ˈ*books.*

ˌ**hard** ˈ**currency** currency that is not likely to fall suddenly in value.

ˌ**hard** ˈ**disk** (*computing*) rigid disk, capable of holding more data than a floppy disk (FLOP).

ˌ**hard** ˈ**drug** drug that is strong and likely to lead to addiction: *Heroin and cocaine are hard drugs.* Cf SOFT DRUG (SOFT).

ˈ**hard hat** **1** (**a**) light protective helmet worn by building workers. (**b**) (*US*) building worker. **2** (*infml*) person opposed to (esp political) progress or reform.

ˌ**hard-**ˈ**headed** *adj* not sentimental; practical: *a* ˌ*hard-headed* ˈ*realist.*

ˌ**hard-**ˈ**hearted** *adj* lacking in feeling or sympathy; unkind.

ˌ**hard** ˈ**labour** (imprisonment with) heavy physical labour as a punishment: *be sentenced to ten years' hard labour.*

ˌ**hard-**ˈ**line** *adj* uncompromising in one's beliefs or policies: *a* ˌ*hard-line* ˈ*socialist.* ˌ**hard-**ˈ**liner** *n*: *socialist hard-liners.*

ˌ**hard-**ˈ**nosed** *adj* (*infml esp US*) tough and unyielding: *a* ˌ*hard-nosed* ˈ*businessman.*

ˈ**hard-on** *n* (*sl*) erection of the penis.

ˈ**hard pad** infectious disease of dogs, a form of distemper[2].

ˌ**hard** ˈ**palate** front part of the roof of the mouth. ⇨ illus at THROAT.

ˌ**hard** ˈ**porn** very obscene pornography.

ˌ**hard** ˈ**sauce** (*esp US*) butter and sugar creamed with a flavouring (eg vanilla, rum or brandy) and served with plum pudding, etc.

ˌ**hard** ˈ**shoulder** strip of ground with a hard surface beside a motorway where vehicles may stop in an emergency. ⇨ illus at MOTORWAY.

ˈ**hard tack** hard biscuit formerly eaten on ships.

ˈ**hard-top** *n* car with a metal roof.

ˈ**hardware** *n* [U] (**a**) metal tools and household implements, eg pans, nails, locks; ironmongery. (**b**) heavy machinery or weapons: *military hardware.* (**c**) (*computing*) mechanical and electronic parts of a computer. Cf SOFTWARE (SOFT).

ˌ**hard** ˈ**water** water containing mineral salts that prevent soap from lathering freely and produce a hard coating inside pipes, tanks, etc.

ˈ**hardwood** *n* [U] hard heavy wood from a deciduous tree, eg oak, teak, beech: [attrib] *hardwood doors, floors, etc.* Cf SOFTWOOD (SOFT).

hard[2] /hɑːd/ *adv* **1** with great effort, energy or concentration; strenuously; intently: *work, think, pull, push, etc hard* ○ *try hard to succeed.* **2** with difficulty; with a struggle: *enjoy a hard-earned rest* ○ *Our victory was hard won.* **3** severely; heavily: *freezing/raining/snowing hard.* **4** at a sharp angle: *Turn hard left.* **5** (idm) **be hard** ˈ**put** (**to it**) (**to do sth**) find it difficult: *He was hard put (to it) to explain her disappearance.* **be hard** ˈ**up** be short of money. **be hard up for sth** have too few of sth; need sth: *He's hard up for ideas.* **die hard** ⇨ DIE[2]. **hard by** (**sth**) (*arch*) near by: ˌ*hard by the* ˈ*river* ○ *There was an inn hard* ˈ*by.* **hard** ˈ**done by** unfairly treated: *She feels (she's been) rather hard done by.* **hard on sth** (*fml*) soon after sth: *His death followed hard on hers.* **hard on sb's** ˈ**heels** closely following sb: *He ran ahead, with the others hard on his heels.* **hit sb/sth hard** ⇨ HIT[1]. **take sth hard** be very grieved or upset by sth: *When their child died they took it very hard.*

□ ˌ**hard**ˈ**bitten** *adj* (of people) made tough by bitter experience.

ˌ**hard-**ˈ**boiled** *adj* **1** (of eggs) boiled until solid inside. **2** (*infml*) (of people) callous; tough; unsentimental.

ˌ**hard-**ˈ**hitting** *adj* not sparing the feelings of others; vigorous; direct: *a* ˌ*hard-hitting* ˈ*speech.*

ˌ**hard-**ˈ**pressed** *adj* **1** closely pursued. **2** very busy.

ˌ**hard-**ˈ**wearing** *adj* able to stand much wear and use: *a* ˌ*hard-wearing ma*ˈ*terial.*

ˌ**hard-**ˈ**working** *adj* working with care and energy.

harden /ˈhɑːdn/ *v* **1** (**a**) [I, Tn] (cause sth to) become hard, strong, unyielding, etc: *The varnish takes a few minutes to harden.* ○ *Attitudes to the strike have hardened on both sides.* ○ *For her own good, you must harden your heart,* ie not allow yourself to show love, pity, etc. (**b**) [esp passive: Tn, Tn·pr] ~ **sb** (**to sth**) make sb less sensitive (to sth): *a hardened criminal,* ie one who shows no sign of shame or repentance ○ *He became hardened to the suffering around him.* **2** (phr v) **harden** (**sth**) **off** (cause young plants, esp seedlings to) become strong enough for planting outside.

Hardie /ˈhɑːdɪ/ James Keir (1856-1915), Scottish politician, one of the founders of the British Labour Party and its first leader in Parliament.

hardly /ˈhɑːdlɪ/ *adv* **1** only just; scarcely: *I hardly know her.* ○ *We had hardly begun/Hardly had we begun our walk when it began to rain.* ○ *I'm so tired I can hardly* (ie only with difficulty) *stay awake.* **2** (used to suggest that sth is improbable, unlikely or unreasonable): *He can hardly* (ie cannot possibly) *have arrived yet.* ○ *You can hardly expect me to lend you money again.* **3** almost no; almost not: *There's hardly any coal left.* ○ *Hardly anybody* (ie Very few people) *came.* ○ *He hardly ever* (ie very seldom) *goes to bed before midnight.* ○ *I need hardly say* (ie It is almost unnecessary for me to say) *that I was very upset.* ⇨ Usage at ALMOST.

hardship /ˈhɑːdʃɪp/ *n* **1** [U] severe suffering or discomfort; privation: *bear/suffer great hardship.* **2** [C] circumstance causing this: *During the war we suffered many hardships.*

Hardy /ˈhɑːdɪ/ Thomas (1840-1928), English novelist and poet. Born in Dorset, he set most of his stories in that county (which he called 'Wessex'). The underlying theme of most of them (eg *Far from the Madding Crowd, The Mayor of Casterbridge, Tess of the D'Urbervilles* and *Jude the Obscure*) is the way in which human lives are controlled by the often cruel whims of fate. Later in his life Hardy turned to writing poetry, which some recent critics regard more highly than his novels.

hardy /ˈhɑːdɪ/ *adj* (**-ier, -iest**) **1** able to endure cold or difficult conditions; tough, robust: *A few hardy people swam in the icy water.* **2** (of a plant) that can grow in the open air all through the winter. ▷ **hardiness** *n* [U].

□ ˌ**hardy** ˈ**annual** **1** annual plant strong enough to be grown in the open air. **2** (*fig joc*) subject that is mentioned or discussed regularly.

hare /heə(r)/ *n* **1** fast-running mammal that lives in fields, like a rabbit but larger, with long ears and a divided upper lip. Cf LEVERET. ⇨ illus at ANIMAL. **2** (idm) ˌ**mad as a March** ˈ**hare** ⇨ MAD. ˌ**raise**/ˌ**start a** ˈ**hare** introduce a subject for discussion to stimulate conversation or to divert people's minds from the main subject. ˌ**run with the** ˌ**hare and** ˌ**hunt with the** ˈ**hounds** try to remain friendly with both sides in a dispute.

▷ **hare** *v* [Ipr, Ip] run very fast: *He hared off* (ie ran away at great speed) *down the street.*

□ **ˈhare-brained** *adj* foolish; crazy: *a hare-brained scheme, person.*

ˈhare lip *n* condition in which a person's (usu upper) lip is deformed at birth, with a vertical split in it.

harebell /ˈheəbel/ (*Scot* **bluebell**) *n* wild plant with blue bell-shaped flowers and round leaves.

Hare Krishna /ˌhærɪ ˈkrɪʃnə/ love-chant used by members of an Oriental-style religion (the International Society for Krishna Consciousness) founded in the USA in 1966.

harem /ˈhɑːriːm; *US* ˈhærəm/ *n* **1** separate part of a traditional Muslim house in which the women live. **2** women living in this.

Hargreaves /ˈhɑːgriːvz/ James (1720-78), English inventor whose machine for spinning cotton (known as the 'spinning-jenny') enabled one worker to spin as much yarn as eight could do before, and contributed to the *Industrial Revolution in Britain.

haricot /ˈhærɪkəʊ/ *n* (also ˌ**haricot ˈbean**) white dried seed of a type of bean plant, eaten as a vegetable.

hark /hɑːk/ *v* **1** [I] (*arch*) listen. **2** (phr v) **hark at sb** (*infml joc*) (usu imperative) listen to sb (implying that the previous speaker is being arrogant, silly, etc): *Just hark at him! Who does he think he is?* **hark back (to sth)** mention again or remember an earlier subject, event, etc: *To hark back to what we were discussing earlier....*

Harlem /ˈhɑːləm/ area of New York City, in upper Manhattan, where many black people live.

Harlequin /ˈhɑːlɪkwɪn/ *n* (formerly) comic character in pantomime, usu dressed in a costume of many colours and wearing a mask. ⇨ illus at COMMEDIA DELL'ARTE.

▷ **harlequin** *adj* [usu attrib] gaily coloured.

harlequinade /ˌhɑːlɪkwɪˈneɪd/ *n* part of a pantomime in which a Harlequin plays the main part. It originated in a type of Italian drama of the 16th century called *commedia dell'arte,* in which the characters Harlequin, Columbine and Pantaloon played comic scenes. It was later incorporated into English pantomimes, but has now disappeared.

Harley Street /ˈhɑːlɪ striːt/ street in central London where many fashionable specialists have their practices. It is associated with the most expensive private medical treatment: [attrib] *a Harley Street consultant, practice, surgery.*

harlot /ˈhɑːlət/ *n* (*arch or derog*) prostitute.

Harlow /ˈhɑːləʊ/ Jean (1911-37), American film actor. Famed for her part as the vulgar heroine in Capra's *Platinum Blonde,* Harlow had become an accomplished comedienne before her early death.

harm /hɑːm/ *n* **1** [U] damage; injury: *He meant no harm,* ie did not intend to hurt or upset anyone. ○ *A few late nights never did anyone any harm.* **2** (idm) ˌ**come to ˈharm** (usu negative) be injured physically, mentally or morally: *I'll go with her to make sure she comes to no harm.* ˌ**do more ˌharm than ˈgood** have an effect which is more damaging than helpful: *If we interfere, it may do more harm than good.* **out of harm's way** in a safe place: *Put that vase out of harm's way so the children can't break it.* **there is no harm in (sb's) doing sth/it does no harm (for sb) to do sth** nothing is lost by doing sth (and some good may result from it): *He may not be able to help but there's no harm in asking him.*

▷ **harm** *v* **1** [Tn] cause harm to (sb/sth): *an event which has harmed relations between the two countries* ○ *Were the hostages harmed?* **2** (idm) **not harm/hurt a fly** ⇨ FLY[1].

harmful /ˈhɑːmfl/ *adj* ~ (**to sb/sth**) causing harm: *the harmful effects of smoking* ○ *Smoking is harmful to your health.* **harmfully** /ˈhɑːmfəlɪ/ *adv.*

harmless *adj* **1** not able or likely to cause harm: *harmless snakes.* **2** (**a**) (*infml*) unlikely to be difficult or unpleasant; inoffensive: *harmless fun* ○ *He's a harmless enough chap.* (**b**) innocent: *The bomb blast killed several harmless passers-by.* **harmlessly** *adv.* **harmlessness** *n* [U].

harmonic /hɑːˈmɒnɪk/ *n* (*music*) higher note produced (eg by the vibration of a string) when a note is played that has a fixed relation to it.

▷ **harmonic** *adj* of or full of harmony: *harmonic tones/overtones.*

□ **harˌmonic ˈmotion** (also **simple harmonic motion**) (*physics*) form of regular to-and-fro movement (eg the swing of a pendulum or sound vibration).

harˌmonic ˈseries (*music*) set of tones consisting of a fundamental tone and the overtones produced by it.

harmonica /hɑːˈmɒnɪkə/ *n* = MOUTH-ORGAN (MOUTH[1]).

harmonious /hɑːˈməʊnɪəs/ *adj* **1** free from disagreement or ill feeling: *a harmonious community, relationship, atmosphere.* **2** arranged together in a pleasing, orderly way: *a harmonious group of buildings* ○ *harmonious colour combinations.* **3** sweet-sounding; tuneful: *harmonious sounds.* ▷ **harmoniously** *adv.*

harmonium /hɑːˈməʊnɪəm/ *n* musical instrument with a keyboard (like an organ), in which notes are produced by air pumped through metal reeds.

harmonize, -ise /ˈhɑːmənaɪz/ *v* **1** [I, Ipr, Tn, Tn·pr] ~ (**sth**) (**with sth**) be or make (sth) harmonious: *colours that harmonize well,* ie together produce a pleasing artistic effect ○ *The cottages harmonize well with the landscape.* ○ *It would be sensible if we could harmonize our plans (with yours).* **2** (*music*) (**a**) [Tn, Tn·pr] ~ **sth (with sth)** add notes to (a melody) to produce harmony. (**b**) [I, Ipr] ~ (**with sb**) sing in harmony with another singer or singers: *That group harmonizes well.* ▷ **harmonization, -isation** /ˌhɑːmənaɪˈzeɪʃn; *US* -nɪˈz-/ *n* [U, C].

harmony /ˈhɑːmənɪ/ *n* **1** [U] agreement (of feelings, interests, opinions, etc): *working towards harmony in international affairs.* **2** [C, U] (instance of a) pleasing combination of related things: *the harmony of colour in nature* ○ *The designer's aim is to produce a harmony of shape and texture.* **3** (**a**) [U] (*music*) (study of the) combination of different notes at the same time to produce chords: *The two sang in harmony.* (**b**) [C] sweet or melodious sound. Cf CONCORD, DISCORD. **4** (idm) **in harmony (with sb/sth)** agreeing; matching: *live together in perfect harmony,* ie peacefully and happily ○ *His tastes are in harmony with mine.*

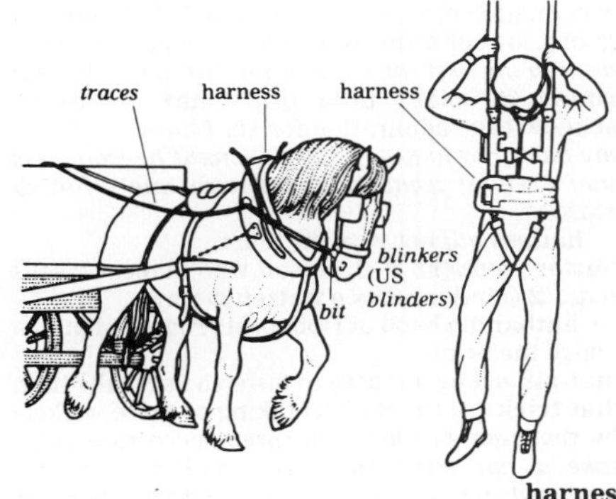

harness

harness /ˈhɑːnɪs/ *n* **1** equipment consisting of leather straps and saddle and metal fittings by which a horse is controlled and fastened to the cart, plough, etc that it pulls. **2** similar equipment, eg as worn by a parachutist or for controlling a small child. ⇨ illus. **3** (idm) **die in harness** ⇨ DIE[2]. **in double ˈharness** ⇨ DOUBLE[1].

▷ **harness** *v* **1** [Tn, Tn·pr] ~ **sth (to sth)** put a harness on (a horse, etc); attach (a horse, etc) by a harness: *harness a horse to a wagon.* **2** [Tn] control and use (a natural force) to produce electrical power, etc: *harness a river, a waterfall, the sun's rays as a source of energy.*

Harold I /ˈhærəld/ (died 1040), king of England 1035-40. He was the illegitimate son of King *Canute. ⇨ App 3.

Harold II /ˈhærəld/ (c 1019-66), king of England 1066, the last Anglo-Saxon king. He succeeded *Edward the Confessor, and immediately had to take an army north to repel a Viking invasion. Immediately after that the Normans attacked. Harold led his army south to meet them, but it was defeated at the Battle of *Hastings, and Harold himself was killed. ⇨ App 3. Cf BAYEUX TAPESTRY.

harp /hɑːp/ *n* large upright musical instrument with strings stretched on a triangular frame and played with the fingers. ⇨ illus at MUSIC.

▷ **harp** *v* (phr v) **harp on (about) sth** talk repeatedly and tiresomely about sth: *She's always harping on (about) my faults.*

harpist *n* person who plays the harp.

□ **ˈharp-seal** *n* type of seal[1] that lives in the North Atlantic and Arctic Oceans. It has a harp-shaped mark on its back.

harpoon /hɑːˈpuːn/ *n* missile like a spear with a rope attached, thrown by hand or fired from a gun, used for catching whales, etc: [attrib] *a ˈharpoon gun.*

▷ **harpoon** *v* [Tn] strike (sth) with a harpoon.

harpsichord /ˈhɑːpsɪkɔːd/ *n* musical instrument similar to a piano, but with strings that are plucked mechanically.

harpy /ˈhɑːpɪ/ *n* **1** (in Greek mythology) cruel monster with a woman's head and body and a bird's wings and claws. **2** cruel greedy hard-hearted woman.

harquebus /ˈhɑːkwɪbəs/ (also **arquebus** /ˈɑːkwɪ-/) *n* long heavy portable gun used in the 15th and 16th centuries. The musket developed from it.

harridan /ˈhærɪdən/ *n* bad-tempered old woman.

harrier /ˈhærɪə(r)/ *n* **1** hound used for hunting hares. **2** cross-country runner. **3** type of falcon.

Harris tweed /ˌhærɪs ˈtwiːd/ *n* [U] (*propr*) rough woollen cloth made in the Outer *Hebrides, used for jackets, coats, etc: [attrib] *a ˌHarris tweed ˈskirt.*

Harrods /ˈhærədz/ fashionable department store in *Knightsbridge, west London. ⇨ article at SHOP.

Harrow /ˈhærəʊ/ (also ˌ**Harrow ˈSchool**) public school (PUBLIC) for boys in Harrow, a borough of north-west London. Founded in 1571, it is a traditional rival of *Eton College (eg in sporting contests).

▷ **Harrovian** /həˈrəʊvɪən/ *n* pupil of Harrow School: *an Old Harrovian,* ie a former pupil of the school.

harrow /ˈhærəʊ/ *n* heavy frame with metal spikes or discs dragged over ploughed land to break up lumps of earth, cover seeds, etc.

▷ **harrow** *v* **1** [I, Tn] pull a harrow over (land). **2** [Tn] distress (sb) greatly. **harrowing** /ˈhærəʊɪŋ/ *adj* very distressing: *a harrowing experience, story, film.*

harrumph /həˈrʌmf/ *interj* (used in writing to indicate the noise made by sb expressing disapproval or doubt).

▷ **harrumph** *v* [I] express disapproval or doubt by saying 'harrumph', or by clearing one's throat.

harry /ˈhærɪ/ *v* (*pt, pp* **harried**) [Tn] **1** annoy (sb) with repeated requests, questions, etc; harass: *harried by press reporters wanting a story.* **2** raid and plunder (sth) repeatedly: *The Vikings harried the English coast.*

harsh /hɑːʃ/ *adj* (**-er, -est**) **1** ~ (**to sb/sth**) unpleasantly rough or sharp, esp to the senses: *a harsh texture, voice, light, colour* ○ *be harsh to the ear/eye/touch.* **2** stern; cruel; severe: *a harsh judge, judgement, punishment.* ▷ **harshly** *adv*: *be harshly treated.* **harshness** *n* [U].

hart /hɑːt/ *n* (*pl* unchanged or ~**s**) adult male of (esp red) deer; stag. Cf HIND[2].

hartebeest /ˈhɑːtəbiːst/ *n* large African antelope with curving horns.

Hartley /ˈhɑːtlɪ/ L(eslie) P(oles) (1895-1972), English novelist who wrote vividly about childhood. His best-known works are *Eustace and Hilda* and *The Go-Between.*

harum-scarum /ˌheərəm ˈskeərəm/ *adj* (*infml*) (of a person or his behaviour) wild and reckless.

Harvard /ˈhɑːvəd/ university at Cambridge, near

Boston, Massachusetts. Founded in 1636, it is the oldest university in the USA. ⇨ article at POST-SCHOOL.

harvest /ˈhɑːvɪst/ *n* **1** (**a**) [C] cutting and gathering of grain and other food crops. (**b**) [C, U] season when this is done: *Farmers are very busy during (the) harvest.* (**c**) [C] (amount of the) crop obtained: *gather in the harvest* ○ *a succession of good harvests* ○ *This year's wheat harvest was poor.* **2** [C] (*fig*) consequences of any action: *reap the harvest of* (ie be rewarded for) *one's hard work.*

▷ **harvest** *v* [I, Tn] gather (a crop); reap: *The farmers are out harvesting (the corn).* **harvester** *n* **1** person who harvests crops; reaper. **2** machine for cutting and gathering grain, esp the type that also binds the grain into sheaves or threshes the grain. Cf COMBINE[2] 2.

□ ˌ**harvest** ˈ**festival** service of thanksgiving in Christian churches after the harvest has been gathered. People bring fruit, vegetables, loaves of bread and other produce to decorate their church for the service.

ˌ**harvest** ˈ**home** (*esp Brit*) celebration organized by farmers for their workers after the harvest has been gathered.

ˌ**harvest** ˈ**moon** full moon nearest to the autumn equinox (22 or 23 September).

ˈ**harvest mouse** very small European and Asian mouse that makes its nest in fields of corn.

Harvey /ˈhɑːvɪ/ William (1578-1657), English physician who discovered the circulation of blood. He also served in the court of *James I and *Charles I.

Harwell /ˈhɑːwel/ atomic energy research station near the village of Harwell in Oxfordshire, England. It was established in 1947.

has ⇨ HAVE.

has-been /ˈhæz biːn/ *n* (*infml derog*) person or thing that is no longer as famous, successful, popular, etc as formerly.

hash[1] /hæʃ/ *n* **1** [U] (dish of) cooked meat cut into small pieces and recooked. **2** [C] mixture or jumble; reused material. **3** (idm) **make a hash of sth** (*infml*) do sth badly. **settle sb's hash** ⇨ SETTLE[2].

▷ **hash** *v* [Tn, Tn·p] ~ **sth** (**up**) **1** chop (meat) into small pieces. **2** (*sl*) make a mess of sth; do sth badly: *I'm sorry I hashed up the arrangements.*

□ ˌ**hash** ˈ**browns** (*US*) chopped boiled potatoes mixed with onion and then fried until they form a brown cake.

hash[2] /hæʃ/ *n* (*infml*) = HASHISH.

hashish /ˈhæʃiːʃ/ (also **hash**) *n* [U] top leaves and tender parts of the hemp plant dried for smoking or chewing as a narcotic drug. Cf CANNABIS, MARIJUANA.

hasp /hɑːsp; *US* hæsp/ *n* part of a fastening for a door, window, etc consisting of a hinged metal strip that fits over a staple and is secured by a padlock.

hassle /ˈhæsl/ *n* [C, U] (*infml*) (**a**) difficulty; struggle: *Changing trains with all that luggage was a real hassle.* (**b**) argument; quarrel: *Do as you're told and don't give me any hassle!*

▷ **hassle** *v* (*infml*) **1** [I, Ipr] ~ (**with sb**) argue; quarrel. **2** [Tn] harass (sb); bother; jostle: *Don't keep hassling me!*

hassock /ˈhæsək/ *n* **1** thick firm cushion for kneeling on, esp in church. **2** small thick clump of grass.

haste /heɪst/ *n* **1** [U] quickness of movement; hurry: *Why all the haste?* **2** (idm) **in haste** quickly. **make haste** (*dated or fml*) act quickly; hurry. **marry in haste, repent at leisure** ⇨ MARRY. ˌ**more** ˌ**haste**, ˌ**less** ˈ**speed** (*saying*) one makes more real progress if one does things less hurriedly. **with all speed/haste** ⇨ SPEED.

hasten /ˈheɪsn/ *v* **1** [Ipr, Ip, It] move or act with speed; hurry: *He hastened (away) to the office.* ○ *I have important news for you — good news, I hasten to add.* **2** [Tn] cause (sth) to be done or to happen earlier: *Artificial heating hastens the growth of plants.*

Hastings[1] /ˈheɪstɪŋz/ town on the coast of East Sussex, in southern England. The Normans under Duke William of Normandy landed near by in 1066 and defeated the Anglo-Saxons at what has come to be known as the Battle of Hastings (although in fact it took place several miles inland). Hastings is one of the *Cinque Ports.

Hastings[2] /ˈheɪstɪŋz/ Warren (1732-1818), British colonial administrator who was the first British Governor-General of India. When he returned to England in 1785 after his period of office he was accused of corruption. After a trial that lasted for seven years, he was eventually found not guilty.

hasty /ˈheɪstɪ/ *adj* (**-ier, -iest**) (**a**) said, made or done quickly or too quickly; hurried: *a hasty departure, meal, farewell* ○ *hasty words that are soon regretted.* (**b**) [usu pred] ~ (**in doing sth/to do sth**) (of a person) acting quickly; too fast: *You shouldn't be too hasty in deciding to get married.* ▷ **hastily** /-ɪlɪ/ *adv.* **hastiness** *n* [U].

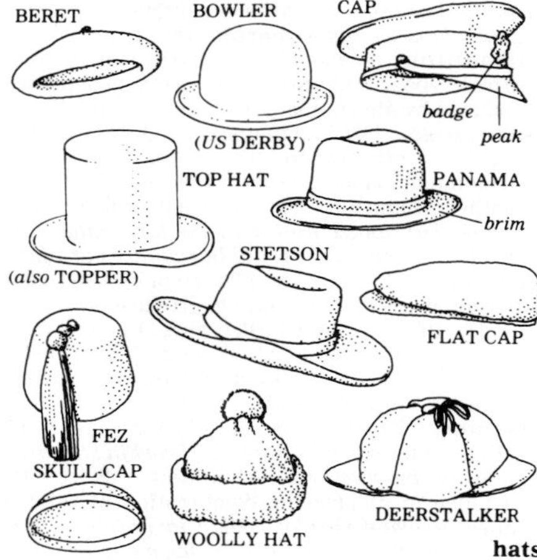

hats

hat /hæt/ *n* **1** covering made to fit the head, usu with a brim, worn out of doors: *put on/take off one's hat.* Cf BONNET. **2** (*infml*) symbol of a person's official position: *wear two hats*, ie have two official or professional roles. **3** (idm) **at the drop of a hat** ⇨ DROP[1]. **I'll eat my hat** ⇨ EAT. ˌ**keep sth under one's** ˈ**hat** keep sth secret. **knock sb/sth into a cocked hat** ⇨ KNOCK[2]. ˌ**my** ˈ**hat** (used as an exclamation of astonishment or disbelief). **old hat** ⇨ OLD. ˌ**out of a/the** ˈ**hat** picked at random: *Prizes went to the first three out of the hat.* **pass the hat round** ⇨ PASS[2]. **take one's hat off to sb** acknowledge admiration for sb: *I must say I take my hat off to him — I never thought he would get into the first team.* **talk through one's hat** ⇨ TALK[2].

▷ **hatless** *adj* not wearing a hat.

hatter /ˈhætə(r)/ *n* **1** person who makes or sells hats. **2** (idm) **mad as a hatter** ⇨ MAD.

□ ˈ**hatband** *n* band of ribbon, etc round a hat just above the brim.

ˈ**hat-pin** *n* long pin used to fasten a hat to the hair.

ˈ**hat trick** (**a**) (in cricket) taking of three wickets by the same bowler with three successive balls: *take a hat trick.* (**b**) three similar successes achieved by one person in another sport or activity: *score a hat trick of goals.*

hatch[1] /hætʃ/ *n* **1** (**a**) opening in a door, floor or ceiling. (**b**) (also ˈ**hatchway**) opening in a ship's deck through which cargo is lowered or raised: *under hatches*, ie below deck. (**c**) opening in a wall between two rooms, esp a kitchen and dining-room, through which dishes, etc are passed. (**d**) door in an aircraft or a spacecraft. **2** movable cover over any of these openings. **3** (idm) ˌ**down the** ˈ**hatch** (*infml*) (said before esp drink is swallowed) down the throat.

hatch[2] /hætʃ/ *v* **1** [I, Ip] ~ (**out**) (**a**) (of a young bird or fish, etc) emerge from an egg: *The chicks/caterpillars/grubs have hatched (*ˈ*out).* (**b**) (of an egg) produce a young bird, etc: *When will the eggs hatch (*ˈ*out)?* **2** [Tn, Tn·p] ~ **sth** (**out**) (**a**) cause (sth) to emerge from an egg: *The hen hatches (out) her young by sitting on the eggs.* (**b**) cause (eggs) to produce young birds, etc. **3** [Tn, Tn·p] ~ **sth** (**out**/**up**) think out and produce (a plot, plan, etc): *What mischief are those children hatching (*ˈ*up)?*

▷ **hatchery** *n* place for hatching eggs, esp of fish: *a* ˈ*trout hatchery.* Cf INCUBATOR (INCUBATE).

hatch[3] /hætʃ/ *v* [Tn] mark (a surface) with close parallel lines.

▷ **hatching** *n* [U] lines drawn or engraved in this way.

hatchback /ˈhætʃbæk/ *n* car with a large sloping back, hinged at the top, that opens like a door. ⇨ illus at CAR.

hatchet /ˈhætʃɪt/ *n* **1** light short-handled axe. ⇨ illus at AXE. **2** (idm) **bury the hatchet** ⇨ BURY.

□ ˈ**hatchet-faced** *adj* having a long face and sharp features.

ˈ**hatchet job** (*infml esp US*) destructive or malicious attack on sb, esp in speech or writing: *Two newspapers did a very effective hatchet job on the Prime Minister's achievements.*

ˈ**hatchet man** (*infml*) (**a**) person employed to discredit and remove opponents or to carry out criminal tasks. (**b**) person employed to reduce staff and expenditure in a firm, etc.

hatchway /ˈhætʃweɪ/ *n* = HATCH[1] 1.

hate /heɪt/ *v* **1** (**a**) [Tn] feel hatred towards (sb/sth): *My cat hates dogs.* ○ *her hated rival.* (**b**) [Tn, Tt, Tnt, Tg, Tsg] strongly dislike (sb/sth): *I hate fried food.* ○ *I hate delays/to be delayed/being delayed.* ○ *She hates anyone listening when she's telephoning.* (**c**) [Tt, Tnt no passive, Tg] (*infml*) be reluctant; regret: *I hate to trouble you.* ○ *I would hate you to think I didn't care.* **2** (idm) ˌ**hate sb's** ˈ**guts** (*infml*) dislike sb intensely.

▷ **hate** *n* (**a**) [U] strong dislike; hatred: *feel hate for sb* ○ *a look (full) of hate.* (**b**) [C] (*infml*) hated person or thing: *one of my pet hates* ○ *Plastic flowers are a particular hate of mine.*

hateful /ˈheɪtfl/ *adj* ~ (**to sb**) causing sb to feel hatred or strong dislike; detestable; very unpleasant: *a hateful person, remark, deed* ○ *All tyranny is hateful to us.* ▷ **hatefully** /-fəlɪ/ *adv.* **hatefulness** *n* [U].

Hathaway /ˈhæθəweɪ/ Anne (?1557-1623), wife of William *Shakespeare, whom she married in 1582. Her cottage near Stratford-upon-Avon is a popular tourist attraction.

hatred /ˈheɪtrɪd/ *n* [U] ~ (**for/of sb/sth**) very strong dislike; hate: *feel hatred for the enemy* ○ *He looked at me with hatred.* ○ *She has a profound hatred of fascism.*

hatter ⇨ HAT.

haughty /ˈhɔːtɪ/ *adj* (**-ier, -iest**) (of a person or his manner) arrogant while despising others; proud and disdainful: *The nobles treated the common people with haughty contempt.* ▷ **haughtily** /-ɪlɪ/ *adv.* **haughtiness** *n* [U].

haul /hɔːl/ *v* **1** [I, Ipr, Ip, Tn, Tn·pr, Tn·p] pull or drag (sth) with effort or force: *sailors hauling (away) (on the ropes)* ○ *elephants hauling logs* ○ *haul a car out of the mud* ○ *They hauled the boat up the beach.* ⇨ Usage at PULL[2]. **2** [Tn] transport (sth) by lorry, etc. **3** (idm) ˌ**haul sb over the** ˈ**coals** (*infml*) reprimand sb severely: *I was hauled over the coals for being late.* **4** (phr v) **haul sb up** (**before sb**) (*infml*) bring sb to be tried or reprimanded: *He was hauled up before the local magistrates for disorderly conduct.*

▷ **haul** *n* **1** act of hauling. **2** (usu *sing*) distance to be travelled: *short/medium/long haul aircraft* ○ *Our camp is only a short haul from here.* **3** (**a**) quantity of fish caught in a net at one time: *The fishermen had a good haul.* (**b**) (*fig*) amount gained by effort: *The thief got away with a huge haul.* **4** (idm) **a long haul** ⇨ LONG[1].

haulage /ˈhɔːlɪdʒ/ *n* [U] **1** transport of goods: *the road haulage industry*, ie the business of transporting goods by road in lorries, etc ○ *a haulage contractor.* **2** money charged for this: *How much is haulage?*

haulier /ˈhɔːlɪə(r)/ *n* (*Brit*) (*US* **hauler**) person or firm whose trade is transporting goods by road.

haunch /hɔːntʃ/ *n* **1** (usu *pl*) (in man and animals) fleshy part of the buttock and thigh: *The dog was sitting on its haunches.* **2** leg and loin of deer, etc as food: *a haunch of venison.*

haunt /hɔ:nt/ *v* [Tn] **1** (of ghosts) visit (a place) regularly: *a haunted house* ○ *A spirit haunts the castle.* **2** be in (a place) very often: *This is one of the cafés I used to haunt.* **3** return repeatedly to the mind of (sb): *a haunting melody* ○ *a wrongdoer haunted by fear of discovery* ○ *The memory still haunts me.*

▷ **haunt** *n* (often *pl*) place visited frequently by the person or people named: *This pub is a favourite haunt of artists.* ○ *revisit the haunts of one's youth*, ie the places where one spent one's time then.

haute couture /ˌəʊt ku:ˈtjʊə(r)/ (*French*) leading companies making fashionable clothes, or their products; high fashion.

haute cuisine /ˌəʊt kwɪˈzi:n/ (*French*) high-class cookery.

hauteur /əʊˈtɜ:(r)/ *n* [U] (*fml*) haughtiness.

Havana /həˈvænə/ *n* cigar made in Cuba.

have[1] /həv; *strong form* hæv/ ⇨ Guide to Entries 5.2, 5.3 *aux v* ⇨ Usage at HAVE[3]; (used with the *past participle* to form perfect tenses): *I've finished my work.* ○ *He's gone home, hasn't he?* ○ *Have you seen it? Yes I have/No I haven't.* ○ *He'll have had the results by then.* ○ *She may not have told him yet.* ○ *Had they left before you got there?* ○ *She'd fallen asleep by that time, hadn't she?* ○ *If I hadn't seen it with my own eyes I wouldn't have believed it.* ○ *Had I known that* (ie If I had known that), *I would never have come.*

have[2] /hæv/ *v* ⇨ Usage at HAVE[2,3]. (*Brit* also **have got**) (not used in the continuous tenses)

► POSSESSING **1** (Cf MY, YOUR, HIS, HER, ITS, OUR, THEIR) (a) [Tn] possess or own (sth): *He has a house in London and a cottage near the sea.* ○ *Do you have any pets?* ○ *They've got two cars.* ○ *How many glasses have we got?* ○ *Do you have/Have you got a 50p piece?* (b) [Tn, Tn·pr, Cn·a] possess or display (a mental quality or physical feature): *You must have a lot of courage.* ○ *She has a good memory.* ○ *Giraffes have long necks.* ○ *The house has* (ie contains) *three bedrooms.* ○ *You've got a cut on your chin.* ○ *have a tooth loose/missing.* **2** [Tn] (indicating a relationship): *I have two sisters.* ○ *They have four children.* ○ *Does he have any friends?* **3** [Tn] (be able to) make use of or exercise (sth): *She has no real power.* ○ *I don't have the authority to send them home.* ○ *I haven't as much responsibility as before.* ○ *Have you got time to phone him?*

► EXPERIENCING **4** [Tn] experience or feel (sth); keep in the mind (used esp with the *ns* shown): *I have no doubt* (ie I am sure) *that you are right.* ○ *She had the impression that she had seen him before.* ○ *Do you have any idea where he lives?* ○ *What reason have you (got) for thinking he's dishonest?* **5** [Tng] experience the results of sb's actions: *We've got people phoning up from all over the world.* ○ *They have orders coming in at the rate of 30 an hour.* **6** [Tn] suffer from (an illness or a disease): *She's got appendicitis.* ○ *He says he has a headache.* ○ *Have you got problems at work?* ○ *How often do you have a bad back?*

► SHOWING OR DISPLAYING **7** [Tnt] show or demonstrate (a quality) by one's actions: *He has the impudence to take things behind my back!* ○ *Surely she didn't have the nerve to say that to him?* ○ (*fml*) *Would you have the goodness* (ie Please be good or kind enough) *to help me with my cases?*

► TAKING OR ACCEPTING SOMEBODY **8** [Tn] (sometimes in the *-ing* form to indicate an intention or arrangement for the future) attend to the needs of (sb/sth) for a limited period; take care of; look after: *Are you having the children tomorrow afternoon?* ○ *We've got the neighbours' dog while they're away.* ○ *We usually have my mother* (ie staying in our house) *for a month in the summer.* **9** [Cn·n/a] take or accept (sb) in a specified function: *We'll have Jones as our spokesman.* ○ *Who can we have as treasurer?*

► OTHER MEANINGS **10** [Tn, Tn·pr, Tn·p] be holding or displaying (sb/sth) in a specified way: *She's got him by the collar.* ○ *Why did you have your back to the camera?* ○ *He had his head down as he walked out of the court.* **11** [Tn, Tnt] be aware of (sth) as a duty or necessity: *He has a lot of homework (to do) tonight.* ○ *I must go — I have a bus to catch.* ○ *She's got a family to feed.* **12** (idm) ˈ**have it (that)...** claim to be a fact that...; say that...: *Rumour has it that we'll have a new manager soon.* **have (got) it/that** ˈ**coming** can expect unpleasant consequences to follow: *It was no surprise when he was sent to prison — everyone knew he had it coming (to him).* **have it** ˈ**in for sb** (*infml*) intend to punish or do sth unpleasant to sb: *She's had it in for him ever since he called her a fool in public.* **have it** ˈ**in one (to do sth)** (*infml*) be capable of (sth): have the ability (to do sth): *Do you think she's got it in her to be a dancer?* **13** (phr v) **have sth in** have a stock of sth in one's home, etc: *Have we got enough food in?* **have sth on** be wearing sth: *She has a red jacket on.* ○ *He's got a tie on today.* **have sth on sb** (*infml*) [no passive] have (evidence) to show that sb is guilty of a crime, etc: *Have the police got anything on him?* **have sb/sth to oneself** be able to use, enjoy, etc sb/sth without others: *With my parents away I've got the house to myself.*

NOTE ON USAGE: When indicating possession, the most commonly used verb in British English is **have got** (in present tense forms): *'Have you got any pets?' 'Yes, I've got three rabbits and a tortoise.'* In US English (and commonly in tenses other than the present in British English) **have** is used: *I have an apartment in downtown Manhattan.* ○ *I haven't got a car now but I'll have one next week.* **Have** when used in the present tense in British English is more formal than **have got**: *I have no objection to your proposal.* In British English **have got**, indicating possession, behaves like an auxiliary verb and a *pp*: *'Have you got a computer?' 'Yes, I have.'* In US English questions and negatives are formed with **do**: *'Do you have a computer?' 'Yes I do.'* This construction is common in British English in tenses other than the present: *I didn't have any money so I couldn't get a newspaper.* It is also increasingly found in the present tense.

have[3] /hæv/ *v* ⇨ Usage.

► PERFORMING AN ACTION **1** [Tn] (a) perform (the action indicated by the following *n*) for a limited period: *have a swim, walk, ride, etc* (Cf *go for a swim, walk, ride, etc*) ○ *have a wash, rest, talk* ○ *Let me have a try.* ○ *She usually has a bath in the morning.* (b) consume (sth) by eating, drinking, smoking, etc: *have breakfast/lunch/dinner* ○ *I usually have a sandwich for lunch.* ○ *We have coffee at 11.*

► RECEIVING OR UNDERGOING **2** [Tn] (a) (not used in the continuous tenses) receive (sth); experience: *I had a letter from my brother this morning.* ○ *She'll have an accident one day.* ○ *I had a shock when I heard the news.* (b) undergo (sth): *I'm having treatment for my lumbago.* ○ *She's having an operation on her leg.* **3** [Tn] experience (sth): *We're having a wonderful time, holiday, party.* ○ *I've never had a worse morning than today.* ○ *They seem to be having some difficulty in starting the car.*

► PRODUCING **4** [Tn] give birth to (sb/sth); produce: *My wife's having a baby.* ○ *Our dog has had puppies twice already.* ○ *have a good effect/result/outcome* ○ *His paintings had a strong influence on me as a student.*

► CAUSING OR ALLOWING SOMETHING TO HAPPEN **5** [Cn·i no passive] order or arrange (that sb does sth): *I'll have the gardener plant some trees.* ○ *Have the driver bring the car round at 4.* **6** (a) (used with a *n* + past participle) cause sth to be done: *Why don't you have your hair cut?* ○ *They're going to have their house painted.* ○ *We're having our car repaired.* (b) (used with a *n* + past participle) suffer the consequences of another person's action: *He had his pocket picked*, ie Something was stolen from his pocket. ○ *She's had her wallet taken.* ○ *Charles I had his head cut off.* ○ *They have had their request refused.* (c) [Tn, Cn·g] (used in negative sentences, esp after *will not, cannot*, etc) allow or tolerate (sth): *I cannot have such behaviour in my house.* ○ *She won't have boys arriving late.* **7** (a) [Cn·g no passive] cause sb to do sth: *She had her audience listening attentively.* ○ *The film had us all sitting on the edges of our seats with excitement.* (b) [Cn·a no passive] cause sb to be in a certain state: *The news had me worried.* **8** [no passive: Tn·pr, Tn·p] cause (sb) to come in a specified direction as a visitor, guest, etc: *We're having friends (over) for dinner.* ○ *We had her up here last term to give a lecture.*

► OTHER MEANINGS **9** [Tn] (*infml*) (a) (esp passive) trick (sb); deceive: *I'm afraid you've been had.* (b) win an advantage over (sb); beat: *She certainly had me in that argument.* ○ *You had me there!* **10** [Tn] (⚠ *sl*) (esp of a man) have sexual intercourse with (sb): *Have you had her yet?* **11** (idm) **have** ˈ**had it** (*sl*) (a) not be going to receive or enjoy sth: *If he was hoping for a lift home I'm afraid he's had it.* (b) be going to experience sth unpleasant: *When they were completely surrounded by police they realized they'd had it.* **have it** ˈ**off**/**a**ˈ**way (with sb)** (⚠ *sl*) have sexual intercourse with sb: *She was having it off with a neighbour while her husband was away on business.* **what** ˈ**have you** (*infml*) other things, people, etc of the same kind: *There's room in the cellar to store unused furniture and what have you.* **12** (phr v) **have sb back** allow (a spouse, etc from whom one is separated) to return: *I'll never have her back.* **have sth back** receive sth that has been borrowed, stolen, etc from one: *Let me have it back soon.* ○ *You can have your files back after we've checked them.* **have sb in** have sb working in one's house: *We had the builders in all last week.*

have sb ˈ**on** (*infml*) persuade sb of the truth of sth, usu to make fun of him: *You really won all that money on a horse? You're not having me on?*

have sth ˈ**out** cause sth to be removed, etc: *have a tooth, one's appendix, one's tonsils out.* **have sth out (with sb)** settle (a dispute, etc) by open (often angry) discussion: *After weeks of silent hostility they've at last had it out with each other.*

have sb ˈ**up (for sth)** (*infml*) (esp passive) cause sb to be accused of a crime, etc in a lawcourt: *He was had up for exceeding the speed limit.*

NOTE ON USAGE: **Have** is used as an auxiliary verb (**have**[1]) and as two separate main verbs (**have**[2] and **have**[3]). Except for the negative forms **haven't, hasn't** and **hadn't**, the following written and spoken forms are common to all three verbs: **have** (*pres t* with *I, you, we, they*) /həv, əv, v/, *strong form* /hæv/; written contractions **I've** /aɪv/, **you've** /ju:v/, **we've** /wi:v/, **they've** /ðeɪv/; negative **haven't** /ˈhævnt/. **has** (*pres t* with *he, she, it*) /həz, əz, s, z/, *strong form* /hæz/; written contractions **he's** /hi:z/, **she's** /ʃi:z/, **it's** /ɪts/, **Jack's** /dʒæks/, **Sam's** /sæmz/; negative **hasn't** /ˈhæznt/. **had** (*pt*) /həd, əd, d/, *strong form* /hæd/; written contractions **I'd** /aɪd/, **we'd** /wi:d/, **she'd** /ʃi:d/, etc; negative **hadn't** /ˈhædnt/. **had** (*pp*) /hæd/. When **have**[2] refers to a regular state or habitual feature, etc, negatives and questions are formed with **do** in both British and US English: *People don't have central heating in their houses in my country.* ○ *Does the referee have the power to send him off the field?* However, when **have**[2] refers to a specific object, fact or feature, etc, British speakers tend to form negatives and questions without an auxiliary verb (informally they use **have got**), while US speakers invariably form them with **do**: (*Brit*) *We haven't (got) many wine glasses.* ○ (*US*) *We don't have many wine glasses.* ○ (*Brit*) *Have you got a £1 coin?* ○ (*US*, and sometimes *Brit*) *Do you have a £1 coin?* As regards **have**[3], British and US speakers form negatives and questions in the same way, with **do**: *She didn't have any letters last week.* ○ *Did this have a good effect?* Note that, as a general rule, the continuous tenses can be used with **have**[3] but not with **have**[2]. As a present tense form of the auxiliary, **has** is often contracted to **'s** /s, z/, as in *She's gone to Scotland.* But **has** is seldom reduced in this way when it is a part of a main verb, except in set phrases such as: *He's no head for heights.* ○ *She's no right to say that.*

haven /ˈheɪvn/ *n* **1** place of safety or rest; refuge: *Terrorists will not find a safe haven here.* **2** (*dated*) harbour.

haver /ˈheɪvə/ *v* [I] **1** keep changing one's mind; hesitate. **2** (*esp Scot*) talk foolishly.

haversack /ˈhævəsæk/ *n* strong (usu canvas) bag carried on the back or over the shoulder. Cf RUCKSACK.

have to /ˈhæv tə; *strong form* ˈhæf tə/ *modal v* (*3rd pers sing pres t* **has to** /ˈhæz tə, ˈhæs tə/, *pt* **had to** /ˈhæd tə, *also* ˈhæt tə/) (in negative sentences and questions usu formed with *do*) **1** (indicating obligation): *I have to type letters and answer the phone.* ○ *He has to pass an examination before he can start work.* ○ (*fml*) *Have we to make our own way to the conference?* ○ *You don't have to knock — just walk in.* ○ *They don't have to have finished the work before I arrive.* ○ *Does she have to stay at home every night?* ○ *Did you have to pay a fine?* ⇨ Usage 1 at MUST. **2** (indicating advice or recommendation): *You simply have to get a new job.* ⇨ Usage 2 at MUST. **3** (drawing a logical conclusion): *There has to be a solution.* ○ *This has to be part of the original manuscript.* ⇨ Usage 3 at MUST. **4** (idm) **have/has got to** (*Brit infml*) **(a)** (indicating obligation): *I've got to go to work by bus tomorrow.* ○ *Why have you got to take these tablets?* ○ *You haven't got to take flowers but many people do.* ⇨ Usage 1 at MUST. **(b)** (indicating advice or recommendation): *You've got to try this new recipe — it's delicious.* ⇨ Usage 2 at MUST.

havoc /ˈhævək/ *n* [U] **1** widespread damage; great destruction: *The floods created havoc.* **2** (idm) **make havoc of sth; play/wreak havoc with sth** damage or upset sth: *The bad weather played havoc with our plans.*

haw[1] /hɔː/ *n* red berry of the hawthorn bush.

haw[2] /hɔː/ *v* (idm) **hum and haw** ⇨ HUM.

Hawaii /həˈwaɪiː/ 50th state of the USA, consisting of a group of volcanic islands in the North Pacific Ocean. They were discovered by Captain *Cook in 1778. It is a centre for tourism, and is popular with surfers. Its capital is Honolulu. ⇨ map at UNITED STATES OF AMERICA. **Hawaiian** /həˈwaɪən/ *adj, n.* **Haˌwaiian guiˈtar** type of guitar held horizontally and played by moving a metal bar up and down the strings after they have been plucked (PLUCK 4).

hawfinch /ˈhɔːfɪntʃ/ *n* large European finch with a powerful beak.

hawk[1] /hɔːk/ *n* **1** strong swift bird of prey with sharp eyesight. **2** (*politics*) person who favours aggressive policies in foreign affairs. Cf DOVE[1] 2.

▷ **hawkish** *adj* (*politics*) favouring aggressive policies rather than negotiation and compromise. **hawkishness** *n* [U].

□ ˌ**hawk-ˈeyed** *adj* **1** having very good eyesight. **2** (of a person) watching closely and carefully.

ˈ**hawk-moth** any of several types of large moth which hover and dart.

hawk[2] /hɔːk/ *v* [Tn, Tn·p] ~ **sth (about/around)** **1** offer (goods) for sale by going from house to house, street to street, etc. **2** (*fig*) spread (news) by talking: *Who's been hawking gossip about?*

▷ **hawker** *n* person who hawks goods.

Hawks /hɔːks/ Howard (1896-1977), American film director. A versatile director, he made many different types of film: adventures, detective mysteries (eg *The Big Sleep* with Humphrey Bogart), westerns and comedies (eg *Bringing up Baby*).

hawser /ˈhɔːzə(r)/ *n* thick heavy rope or thin steel cable, used for mooring or towing a ship.

hawthorn /ˈhɔːθɔːn/ *n* thorny shrub or tree with white, red or pink blossom and small dark red berries: [attrib] *a hawthorn hedge.*

Hawthorne /ˈhɔːθɔːn/ Nathaniel (1804-64), American author best known for *The Scarlet Letter*, a novel about public and private morality in the Puritan New England of the 17th century, and *Tanglewood Tales*, classic stories retold for children.

hay /heɪ/ *n* [U] **1** grass cut and dried for use as animal food: *make hay*, ie turn it over to be dried by the sun. **2** (idm) **hit the hay/sack** ⇨ HIT[1]. **make hay of sb/sth** destroy sb/sth; throw sb/sth into confusion: *She made hay of my argument.* **make hay while the ˈsun shines** (*saying*) make good use of opportunities, favourable conditions, etc while they last.

□ ˈ**hay fever** allergic illness affecting the nose and throat, caused by pollen or dust.

ˈ**hay-fork** *n* two-pronged fork for turning or lifting hay.

ˈ**haymaking** *n* [U] cutting grass and spreading it to dry. ˈ**haymaker** *n* **1** person or machine employed in making hay. **2** (*infml esp US*) powerful swinging blow with the fist.

ˈ**hayseed** *n* (*US derog*) country person; yokel.

ˈ**haystack** (also ˈ**hayrick**) *n* **1** large pile of hay firmly packed for storing, with a pointed or ridged top. **2** (idm) **a needle in a haystack** ⇨ NEEDLE.

Haydn /ˈhaɪdn/ Franz Joseph (1732-1809), Austrian composer who did much to establish the classical form of the symphony (he wrote over 100 of them). He also wrote oratorios (including *The Creation* and *The Seasons*) and much chamber music. *Mozart and *Beethoven were his pupils.

haywire /ˈheɪwaɪə(r)/ *adj* (idm) **be/go haywire** (*infml*) be/become disorganized or out of control: *Since I dropped it on the floor my watch has gone completely haywire.*

Hayworth /ˈheɪwəθ/ Rita (1918-87), American film actress. She became a Hollywood sex symbol in *Gilda*, but revealed her dramatic potential in *The Lady from Shanghai*, by Orson Welles, who was her husband at the time.

hazard /ˈhæzəd/ *n* **1** ~ **(to sb/sth)** (thing that can cause) danger; risk: *Smoking is a serious health hazard.* ○ *Wet roads are a hazard to drivers.* **2** obstacle on a golf-course.

▷ **hazard** *v* [Tn] **1** expose (sth) to danger; risk: *Rock-climbers are hazarding their lives.* **2** venture to make (sth); suggest tentatively: *I don't know where he is but I could hazard a guess.*

hazardous *adj* dangerous; risky: *hazardous work, conditions* ○ *The journey was hazardous.* **hazardously** *adv.*

haze[1] /heɪz/ *n* [C, U] **1** thin mist. ⇨ Usage at FOG. **2** (*fig*) mental confusion or uncertainty: *I/My mind was in a complete haze.*

▷ **haze** *v* (phr v) **haze over (a)** become covered with a thin mist. **(b)** lose focus; become dreamy: *His eyes hazed over when he thought of her.*

haze[2] /heɪz/ *v* [Tn] (*US*) harass (sb) by making him perform humiliating jobs; bully; persecute.

hazel /ˈheɪzl/ *n* bush or small tree with small edible nuts. ⇨ illus at TREE.

▷ **hazel** *adj* (esp of eyes) reddish brown or greenish brown.

□ ˈ**hazel-nut** *n* edible nut of the hazel. ⇨ illus at NUT.

Hazlitt /ˈhæzlɪt/ William (1778-1830), British essayist and critic. He was the first author in Britain to make most of his living from writing and lecturing about literature, and his judgements on the work of contemporary poets were often sharp and outspoken.

hazy /ˈheɪzɪ/ *adj* (**-ier, -iest**) **1** misty: *We couldn't see far because it was so hazy.* **2** not clear; vague: *hazy memories.* **3** (of a person) rather confused; uncertain: *I'm a bit hazy about what to do next.* ▷ **hazily** *adv*: *remember sth hazily.* **haziness** *n* [U].

HB /ˌeɪtʃ ˈbiː/ *abbr* (of lead used in pencils) hard black (ie medium hard): *an HB pencil.* Cf B, H.

H-block /ˈeɪtʃ blɒk/ *n* any of a group of prison buildings, each in the shape of an H, in the Maze Prison near Belfast, Northern Ireland.

H-bomb /ˈeɪtʃ bɒm/ *n* hydrogen bomb.

HCF /ˌeɪtʃ siː ˈef/ *abbr* highest common factor.

HE *abbr* **1** (on labels, notices, etc) high explosive. **2** /ˌeɪtʃ ˈiː/ His/Her Excellency: *HE the British Ambassador* ○ *HE Governor Robert Mount* ○ (*infml*) *HE is coming.*

He *symb* helium.

he /hiː/ ⇨ Guide to Entries 5.2 *pers pron* (used as the subject of a *v*) **1** male person or animal mentioned earlier or being observed now: *'Where's your brother?' 'He's in Paris.'* ○ *Look! He* (ie The man we are watching) *is climbing the fence.* **2** (male or female) person: (*fml*) *If a member wishes to bring a guest into the club, he must sign the visitors' book.* ○ (*saying*) *He who* (ie Anyone who) *hesitates is lost.* Cf HIM.

▷ **he** *n* [sing] male animal: *What a sweet puppy! Is it a he or a she?*

he- (forming compound *ns*) male: *a ˈhe-goat.*

□ ˈ**he-man** /-mæn/ *n* (*pl* **-men** /-men/) strong virile man.

NOTE ON USAGE: Frequently, **he**, **him**, and **his** are used to refer to a member of a group which includes both males and females: *Everybody knows what he wants.* ○ *A good teacher always prepares his lessons well.* Many people think that this discriminates against women and the use of **he or she**, **him or her**, etc is becoming more common. In writing, **he/she**, **s/he** or **(s)he** can be used: *Everybody knows what's best for him or herself.* ○ *If in doubt, ask your doctor. He/She can give you further information.* ○ *When a baby cries, it means that s/he is tired, hungry or just unhappy.* In informal language **they**, **them**, or **their** can be used: *Everybody knows what they want.* Alternatively, the sentence can be rephrased, using a plural noun: *Babies cry when they are tired.* Note that, to save space in this dictionary, we use **he/him/his** when referring to 'sb' (somebody) in definitions, although the person may be either female or male. This is usually made clear by the examples which follow such definitions.

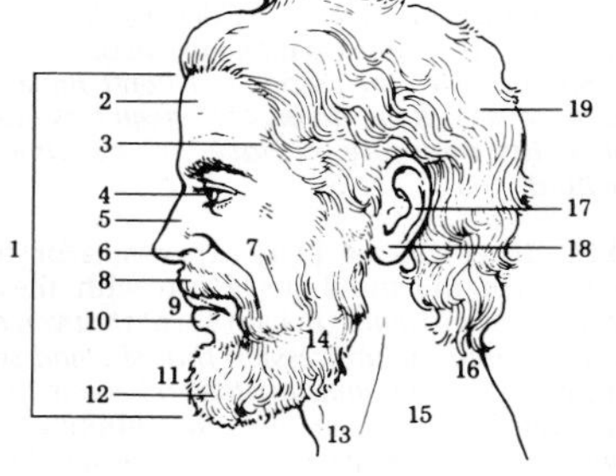

1 face
2 forehead (*also* brow)
3 temple
4 eye
5 nose
6 nostril
7 cheek
8 moustache (*US* mustache)
9 mouth
10 lip
11 chin
12 beard
13 throat
14 jaw
15 neck
16 nape of the neck
17 ear
18 ear lobe
19 hair

head[1] /hed/ *n* **1 (a)** [C] part of the body containing the eyes, nose, mouth and brain: *He fell and hit his head.* ○ *The ball hit her on the head.* ○ *My head aches.* ⇨ illus. **(b) a head** [sing] this as a measure of length: *The Queen's horse won by a head.* ○ *Tom is taller than John by a head.* **2** [C] (*infml*) headache: *I've got a terrible head this morning.* **3** [C] ability to reason; intellect; imagination; mind: *Use your head*, ie Think. ○ *The thought never entered my head.* **4** [sing] mental ability or natural talent as specified: *have a good head for business, figures, etc* ○ *have no head for heights*, ie feel giddy and frightened in high places, eg on top of a cliff. **5 heads** [sing *v*] side of a coin with the head of a person on it: *We tossed a coin* (eg to decide sth by chance) *and it came down heads.* Cf TAILS (TAIL 6). **6 (a) a head** [sing] individual person: *dinner at £15 a head.* **(b)** [pl *v*] individual animal in a herd or flock: *50 head of cattle.* **7** [C] thing like a head in form or position, eg the flattened end of a pin etc, the striking or cutting part of a tool, the mass of leaves or flowers at the top of a stem: *the head of a nail, hammer, axe, etc* ○ *cut off the dead heads (of the roses)* ○ *a cabbage-head.* **8** [C] foam on the top of poured beer, etc. **9** [C] device on a tape-recorder that touches the moving magnetic tape and converts the electrical signals into sound. **10** [C] top part of a boil or swelling on the skin: *The pimple came to a head before bursting.* **11** [C usu *sing*] top or highest part: *the title at the head of the page* ○ *stand at the head of the stairs* ○ *at the head of the poll*, ie having received most votes in an election. **12** [C] more important or prominent end: *My father took his place at the head of the table.* ○ *Place the pillows at the head of the bed.* ○ *the head of the lake*, ie where a river enters it. **13** [sing] (a) leading part in a procession or army; front: *be at the head of a queue* ○ *march at the head of the regiment.* (b) (*fig*) chief position: *be at the head of one's profession.* **14** [C] (a) chief person of a group or organization, etc: *the head of the family* ○ *a meeting of the heads of government* ○ *a gathering of the crowned heads* (ie kings or queens) *of Europe* ○ [attrib] *head waiter* ○ *head office*, ie chief place of a business. (b) (also **Head**) chief person in a school or college; headmaster or headmistress: *Report to the Head immediately!* **15** [C usu *sing*] (a) mass of water kept at a certain height (eg for a water-mill or a hydroelectric power-station). (b) confined body of steam for exerting pressure: *They kept up a good head of steam.* **16** [C usu *sing*] (in place-names) promontory; cape: *Beachy Head.* **17** [C] main division in a lecture, an essay, etc; heading: *a speech arranged under five heads.* **18** (idm) **above/over one's ˈhead** too difficult to understand: *The lecture was/went way above my head.* **bang, etc one's head against a brick ˈwall** (*infml*) continue vainly trying to achieve sth in spite of several unsuccessful attempts. **be/stand head and ˈshoulders above sb/sth** be very much better, cleverer, etc than (others). **bite sb's head off** ⇨ BITE[1]. **bother one's head/oneself about sth** ⇨ BOTHER. **bring sth/come to a ˈhead** bring sth to/reach a climax: *The atmosphere in the office had been tense for some time but this latest dismissal brought matters to a head.* **bury/hide one's head in the sand** pretend not to see an obvious danger, etc. **by a short head** ⇨ SHORT[1]. **drive sth into sb's head** ⇨ DRIVE[1]. **drum sth into sb/sb's head** ⇨ DRUM[2]. **enter one's head** ⇨ ENTER. **from ˌhead to ˈfoot/ˈtoe** over the whole length of one's body: *The children were covered in mud from head to toe.* Cf FROM TOP TO TOE (TOP[1]). **get one's ˈhead down** (*infml*) go to bed or to sleep. **get it into one's head that...** understand fully...; realize...: *I wish he'd get it into his head that exams are important.* **give sb his ˈhead** let sb move or act freely. **go to one's ˈhead** (a) (of alcoholic drink) make one dizzy or slightly drunk: *The whisky went straight to my head.* (b) (of success) make one conceited or too confident: *All that praise has really gone to her head.* **harm, etc a hair of sb's head** ⇨ HAIR. **have eyes in the back of one's head** ⇨ EYE[1]. **have a good, etc head of ˈhair** have a full, etc covering of hair on the head. **have a good ˈhead on one's shoulders** have practical ability, common sense, etc. **have one's head in the ˈclouds** have one's thoughts far away; be day-dreaming. **have one's ˈhead screwed on (the right way)** (*infml*) be sensible. **have a level head** ⇨ LEVEL[1]. **have a swollen head** ⇨ SWELL. **have, etc a thick head** ⇨ THICK. **head ˈfirst** (a) (plunging, etc) with one's head before the rest of one's body: *She fell head first down the stairs.* (b) with too much haste; rashly. **head over ˈheels** (a) rolling the body over in a forward direction. (b) completely: *She's head over heels in ˈlove (with him).* **ˌheads I ˈwin, ˌtails you ˈlose** (*saying*) I win whatever happens. **heads or ˈtails?** (said when spinning a coin to decide sth by chance). **ˈheads will roll (for sth)** some people will be punished (because of sth). **heap coals of fire on sb's head** ⇨ HEAP *v*. **hit the nail on the head** ⇨ HIT[1]. **hold one's ˈhead high** show pride in one's achievements, worth, ability, etc; not feel ashamed. **hold a pistol to sb's head** ⇨ PISTOL. **in one's ˈhead** in one's memory (not in writing): *How do you keep all those telephone numbers in your head?* **keep one's ˈhead** remain calm in a crisis. **keep one's head above water** stay out of debt, difficulty, etc: *I'm managing to keep my head above water, though I'm not earning much.* **keep one's ˈhead down** avoid danger or distraction. **knock sb's block/head off** ⇨ KNOCK[2]. **knock sb/sth on the head** ⇨ KNOCK[2]. **knock your/their heads together** ⇨ KNOCK[2]. **laugh, scream, etc one's ˈhead off** (*infml*) laugh, scream, etc loudly. **like a bear with a sore head** ⇨ BEAR[1]. **lose one's ˈhead** ⇨ LOSE. **make head or ˈtail of sth** understand sth: *I can't make head (n)or tail of these instructions.* **need, etc (to have) one's ˈhead examined** (*infml*) show oneself to be stupid or crazy: *He swims in the sea in winter — he ought to have his head examined!* **not right in the/one's head** ⇨ RIGHT[1]. **off one's ˈhead** (*infml*) crazy; very foolish: *He's (gone) off his head!* **off the top of one's head** ⇨ TOP[1]. **an old head on young shoulders** ⇨ OLD. **on sb's/one's (own) head be it** sb/one will be responsible for any unpleasant consequences: *You wanted to try this new route, not me, so on your head be it.* **ˌout of one's ˈhead** (a) invented or made up by oneself, without help. (b) forgotten: *Her name's gone completely out of my head.* (c) (*infml esp US*) mad; crazy. **ˌover sb's ˈhead** to a position of authority higher than sb: *I couldn't help feeling jealous when she was promoted over my head.* ○ *When her boss refused to listen to her she went over his head to the managing director.* **a price on sb's head** ⇨ PRICE. **put one's ˈhead in the noose** allow oneself to be caught. **put our/your/their ˈheads together** exchange ideas or advice; consult together: *I'm sure we can solve the problem if we all put our heads together.* **put sth into sb's ˈhead** make sb believe sth; suggest sth to sb: *Who's been putting such ideas into your head?* **put sth out of one's ˈhead** stop thinking about sth; give up (a plan, etc): *You'd better put the idea of marriage out of your head.* **put sth out of sb's/one's ˈhead** make sb/one forget sth: *An interruption put it quite out of my head.* **scratch one's head** ⇨ SCRATCH[1]. **shake one's head** ⇨ SHAKE[1]. **(do sth) standing on one's ˈhead** (*infml*) (do sth) very easily: *She could pass the exam standing on her head.* **stand/turn sth on its ˈhead** reverse the expected order of sth: *She stood our argument on its head.* **take it into one's head to do sth/that...** decide (esp sth unexpected or foolish): *She suddenly took it into her head to dye her hair green.* ○ *He's taken it into his head that I'm spreading rumours about him.* **talk one's/sb's head off** ⇨ TALK[2]. **turn sb's ˈhead** make sb conceited: *The success of his first novel completely turned his head.* **two heads are better than ˈone** (*saying*) two people working together achieve more than one person working alone. **weak in the head** ⇨ WEAK. **wet the baby's head** ⇨ WET *v*.

▷ **-headed** (in compound *adjs*) having a head or heads as specified: *a bald-headed man.*

headless *adj* having no head.

ˈheadship *n* position of headmaster or headmistress: *apply for a headship.*

□ **ˈheadache** *n* **1** continuous pain in the head: *suffer from headaches* ○ *have a splitting headache.* **2** person or thing that causes worry: *Their son is a constant headache to them.*

ˈheadband *n* strip of material worn around the head. ⇨ illus at SQUASH.

ˈheadboard *n* upright panel along the head of a bed. ⇨ illus at FURNITURE.

ˈhead cheese (*US*) = BRAWN 2.

ˈhead-dress *n* ornamental covering or band worn on the head.

ˈheadgear *n* [U] hat, cap or head-dress.

ˈhead-hunter *n* **1** member of a tribe that collects the heads of its enemies as trophies. **2** person or firm paid to find and recruit staff at a senior level. **ˈhead-hunting** *n* [U].

ˈheadlamp *n* = HEADLIGHT.

headland /ˈhedlənd/ *n* high piece of land that juts into the sea; promontory. ⇨ illus at COAST.

ˈheadlight *n* (a) lamp at the front of a motor vehicle or railway engine. ⇨ illus at CAR. (b) beam from this: *Driving without headlights at night is illegal.*

ˈheadline *n* **1** [C] line of words printed in large type at the top of a page, esp in a newspaper: [attrib] *headline news.* **2 the headlines** [pl] brief summary on TV or radio of the most important items of news. **3** (idm) **hit/make/reach the ˈheadlines** become important or much-publicized news. **ˈheadliner** *n* (*US*) leading performer; star(4).

ˈheadlong *adv, adj* [attrib] **1** with the head first: *fall headlong.* **2** in a hasty and rash way: *rush headlong into danger.*

ˈheadman /-mæn/ *n* (*pl* **-men** /-men/) chief man of a village, tribe, etc.

headˈmaster, headˈmistress *ns* principal man or woman in a school, responsible for organizing it.

ˌHead of ˈState (*pl* **Heads of State**) chief public representative of a country, who may also be the head of government.

ˌhead-ˈon *adj, adv* (a) with the front parts of two vehicles colliding: *a ˌhead-on ˈcrash* ○ *The lorries crashed head-ˈon.* (b) with the front part of a vehicle hitting a stationary object: *The car hit the tree head-ˈon.* ○ (*fig*) *tackle a problem head-ˈon*, ie without trying to avoid it.

ˈheadphones *n* [pl] radio or telephone receivers held over the ears by a band fitting over the head; earphones: *a pair of headphones.*

ˌheadˈquarters *n* [sing or pl *v*] (*abbr* **HQ**) place from which an organization is controlled: *The firm's headquarters are in London.*

ˈhead-rest *n* thing that supports the head of a person sitting down, eg in a car. ⇨ illus at CAR.

ˈheadroom *n* [U] overhead space, esp above a vehicle; clearance: *There is not enough headroom for buses to go under this bridge.*

ˈheadscarf *n* (*pl* **-scarves**) scarf tied round the head, usu with a knot under the chin, worn instead of a hat.

ˈhead-set *n* headphones.

ˈhead-shrinker *n* (*sl*) psychiatrist.

ˈheadsquare *n* square headscarf, worn by women.

ˌhead ˈstart advantage given or gained at an early stage: *Being already able to read gave her a head start over the other pupils.*

ˈheadstock *n* non-moving part which supports a revolving part in a machine (eg the part of a lathe that holds the rotating spindle).

ˈheadstone *n* piece of stone placed to mark the head of a grave.

ˈhead-waters *n* [pl] tributary stream or streams forming the sources of a river.

ˈheadway *n* [U] progress, esp in difficult circumstances: *We are making little headway with the negotiations.* ○ *The boat made slow headway against the tide.*

ˈhead wind wind blowing from directly in front. Cf TAIL WIND (TAIL).

ˈheadword *n* word forming a heading, eg the first word, in heavy type, of a dictionary entry.

head[2] /hed/ *v* **1** [Tn] (a) be at the front or top of (sth): *head a procession* ○ *Smith's name headed the list.* (b) be in charge of or lead (sth): *head a rebellion, government, delegation.* **2** [Tn esp passive] give a heading to (a letter, etc): *The chapter was headed 'My Early Life'.* **3** [Ipr, Ip] move in the specified direction: *Where are you heading/headed?* ○ *head south, back to camp, away from the town, towards home, etc.* **4** [Tn] strike (the ball) with one's head in football. **5** (idm) **head/top the bill** ⇨ BILL[1]. **6** (phr v) **head for...** move towards (a place): *The boat was heading for some rocks.* ○ *He headed straight for the bar.* ○ (*fig*) *Is the world heading for disaster?* **head sb/sth off** get in front of sb/sth so as to turn him/it back or aside: *head off enemy troops, reporters, an angry mob, etc* ○ *head off a flock of sheep*, ie to prevent them from going the wrong way ○ (*fig*) *head off* (ie prevent or forestall) *a quarrel.*

header /ˈhedə(r)/ *n* **1** (*infml*) dive or fall (esp into water) with the head first: *take a header into the swimming-pool.* **2** (in football) act of hitting

Health

Most health care in Britain is provided by the National Health Service (NHS), which was introduced in 1948 to provide free medical treatment for all who need it. Most of the cost of the service is paid from the taxes the government collects, but a small percentage comes from direct charges and the National Insurance contributions paid by everybody in employment. The NHS is responsible for most of the country's hospitals, doctors and medical services.

People register as patients of a family doctor, called a general practitioner (GP), and when they are ill it is the GP who makes a diagnosis and decides on the treatment necessary or refers the patient to a specialist doctor in a hospital. GPs usually work in a group practice and see patients at a surgery or health centre. The GP prescribes medicines when necessary, giving the patient a prescription so that the drugs needed can be obtained from a chemist. There is a standard charge for drugs which are obtained on prescription, but drugs are free for those patients who are in hospital.

The funding of the NHS is one of the most important political issues in Britain. The Secretary of State for Health, a Cabinet minister, is responsible for the NHS budget. The service is administered at the local level by District Health Authorities, which are in turn responsible to the Regional Health Authorities. There is a continuing public debate about the way the service should be funded and managed, and what the priorities in health care should be. In general, the Conservative Party is in favour of encouraging people to pay for private health insurance whereas the Labour Party supports the principle of the NHS as a service for all.

Most doctors and dentists also have private patients, ie people who pay for their treatment. NHS hospitals have facilities for private patients and there are also private hospitals owned by health insurance companies. An increasing number of people pay for private health insurance, partly as a way of avoiding the National Health waiting lists for non-urgent operations. Many employers pay for private health insurance for their employees.

Medical research is financed both by the government and by the many charities that raise funds for research into particular diseases. There is a government programme of health education. In recent years campaigns have been aimed at warning of the dangers of smoking, informing people about AIDS, encouraging them to take part in a sporting activity to keep fit, and persuading them to eat a healthier diet in order to reduce the risk of heart disease.

In the USA, where there is no public health service, most people have private health insurance. There are two government schemes which provide some help with medical costs: Medicare, an insurance scheme for people over 65 and the disabled, and Medicaid, which funds medical care for the poor.

the ball with the head. **3** brick or stone laid in a wall so that its end shows, not its long side. Cf STRETCHER 3.

heading /ˈhedɪŋ/ *n* word or words put at the top of a page, section of a book, etc as a title.

headstrong /ˈhedstrɒŋ; *US* -strɔːŋ/ *adj* obstinately determined to do things in one's own way without listening to others; self-willed.

heady /ˈhedɪ/ *adj* (**-ier, -iest**) **1 (a)** (of alcoholic drinks) likely to make people drunk quickly; potent: *a heady wine.* **(b)** having a quick effect on the senses; very exciting: *a heady perfume* ○ *the heady days of one's youth.* **2 (a)** (of a person) excited and acting rashly: *be heady with success.* **(b)** (of an action) done impulsively or rashly.

heal /hiːl/ *v* **1** [I, Ip, Tn] ~ **(over/up)** (cause sth to) become healthy again: *The wound healed slowly.* ○ *The cut soon healed over/up, but it left a scar.* ○ *the healing powers of sleep* ○ *The wound is not yet healed*, ie has not yet been covered by new skin. **2 (a)** [Tn] cause (sth) to end; make easier to bear: *heal a quarrel* ○ *Time heals all sorrows.* **(b)** [Tn, Tn·pr] ~ **sb (of sth)** (*arch*) restore sb to health; cure sb (of a disease): *The holy man healed them of their sickness.*

▷ **healer** *n* person or thing that heals: *Time is a great healer.*

health /helθ/ *n* [U] **1** condition of a person's body or mind: *have poor health* ○ *be in/enjoy the best of health* ○ *Exercise is good for the health.* ○ *Your (very) good health!* eg said when drinking a toast to sb ○ [attrib] *health insurance/care* ○ *He retired early for health reasons.* ⇨ article. **2** state of being well and free from illness: *be restored to health* ○ *be bursting with health and vitality.* **3** (idm) **a clean bill of health** ⇨ CLEAN[1]. **drink sb's health; drink a health to sb** ⇨ DRINK[2]. **in rude health** ⇨ RUDE. **propose a toast/sb's health** ⇨ PROPOSE.

▷ **healthful** /ˈhelθfl/ *adj* (*fml*) good for the health.

□ ˈ**health centre** (*Brit*) headquarters of a group of local medical services.

ˈ**health farm** place where people go in order to try to improve their health by dieting, exercising, etc.

ˈ**health food** (often *pl*) natural food, usu free of artificial substances, that is thought to be especially good for the health: [attrib] *a health food restaurant, shop, etc.*

ˈ**health service** public service providing medical care.

ˈ**health visitor** (*Brit*) trained nurse who visits people in their homes, giving advice on how to avoid illness.

healthy /ˈhelθɪ/ *adj* (**-ier, -iest**) **1** having good health; well and able to resist disease: *a healthy child, animal, tree* ○ (*fig*) *a healthy bank balance.* **2** likely to produce good health: *a healthy climate, life-style, environment.* **3** indicating good health: *have a healthy appetite.* **4** natural and beneficial: *The child showed a healthy curiosity.* ○ *She has a healthy respect for her rival's talents.* ▷ **healthily** *adv.* **healthiness** *n* [U].

NOTE ON USAGE: **1 Healthy** and **fit** both indicate that a person is physically strong and rarely suffers from any physical illness. **Healthy** also refers to the conditions which are good for somebody's health, or the outward signs of somebody having good health: *They have very healthy children.* ○ *This damp climate isn't very healthy.* ○ *She has a healthy appetite.* **2 Fit** suggests that someone is in good physical condition particularly as a result of taking regular exercise: *'How do you stay so fit?' 'I go to keep-fit classes.'* **3 Well** generally refers to somebody's health on a particular occasion. It is used in answer to inquiries about health: *He's been quite ill. I hope he gets well soon.* ○ *I think I'll go to bed. I don't feel at all well.* ○ *'How are you?' 'Very well, thank you.'*

heap /hiːp/ *n* **1** number of things or mass of material lying piled up: *a heap of books, sand, rubbish* ○ *clothes left in heaps on the ground* ○ *The building was reduced to a heap of rubble.* ○ (*fig*) *She collapsed on the floor in a heap.* **2 heaps** [pl] ~ **(of sth)** (*infml*) great number or amount; plenty: *We have heaps of time.* ○ *She's been there heaps of times.* ○ *I've got heaps to tell you.* **3** (*infml joc*) motor car that is old and in poor condition. **4** (idm) **heaps better, more, older, etc** (*infml*) much better, etc: *Do have a second helping — there's heaps more.*

▷ **heap** *v* **1** [Tn, Tn·p] ~ **sth (up)** put (things) in a pile: *heap (up) stones to form a dam* ○ (*fig*) *heap up riches* ○ *a heaped spoonful of flour.* **2** [Tn·pr] ~ **sth on sb/sth**; ~ **sb/sth with sth** load or place sth in a pile on sb/sth: *heap food on one's plate/heap one's plate with food* ○ (*fig*) *heap praises, insults, etc on sb.* **3** (idm) **heap coals of ˈfire on sb's head** make sb feel remorse for treating one badly by treating him well in return.

hear /hɪə(r)/ *v* (*pt, pp* **heard** /hɜːd/) **1** [I, Tn, Tng, Tni] perceive (sounds) with the ears: *She doesn't/can't hear very well*, ie is rather deaf. ○ *We listened but could hear nothing.* ○ *Have you ever heard that song sung in Italian?* ○ *I heard someone laughing.* ○ *Did you hear him go out?* ○ *He was heard to groan.* **2** [Tn, Tw] listen or pay attention to (sb/sth): *You're not to go — do you hear me!* ○ *We'd better hear what they have to say.* ⇨ Usage at FEEL[1]. **3** [Tn] listen to and try (a case) in a lawcourt: *The court heard the evidence.* ○ *Which judge will hear the case?* **4** [I, Tn, Tf] be told or informed about (sth): *You sing very well, I hear.* ○ *Have you heard the news?* ○ *I heard (that) he was ill.* ○ *I've heard (say) that it's a good film.* **5** [Tn] grant (a prayer). **6** (idm) ˌ**hear!** ˈ**hear!** (used to express agreement and approval). **hear/see the last of sb/sth** ⇨ LAST[1]. **hear a ˈpin drop** hear the slightest noise: *The audience was so quiet you could have heard a pin drop.* **hear tell of sth** hear people talking about sth: *I've often heard tell of such things.* **make one's voice heard** ⇨ VOICE. **not/never hear the end of sth** not be finished with sth as the subject of discussion or matter that affects one: *If we don't give her what she wants we'll never hear the end of it.* **7** (phr v) **hear about sth** be given information about sth: *I've only just heard about his dismissal.* ○ *You will hear about this* (ie will receive a formal rebuke about it) *later.* **hear from sb** receive a letter, telephone call, etc from sb: *How often do you hear from your sister?* **hear of sb/sth** be told about or have knowledge of sb/sth: *I've never heard of the place.* ○ *She disappeared and was never heard of again.* **not ˈhear of sth** (usu with *will* or *would*) refuse to allow sth: *He wouldn't hear of my walking home alone.* ○ *I can't let you pay my debts — I won't hear of such a thing.* **hear sb out** listen until sb has finished saying what he wants to say: *I know you don't believe me but please hear me out!*

▷ **hearer** /ˈhɪərə(r)/ *n* person who hears sth, esp a member of an audience.

hearing /ˈhɪərɪŋ/ *n* **1** [U] ability to hear; sense(1) with which sound is perceived: *Her hearing is poor*, ie She is rather deaf. **2** [U] distance within which one can hear: *He said so in my hearing*, ie in my presence so that I could hear. ○ *Please keep within hearing (distance)*, ie stay near enough to hear. **3** [C] **(a)** opportunity to be heard: *be given a fair hearing* ○ *I never gained a hearing*, ie Nobody was willing to listen to me. **(b)** trial of a case in a lawcourt, esp before a judge without a jury: *The defendant's family were present at the hearing.* **4** (idm) **hard of hearing** ⇨ HARD[1].

□ ˈ**hearing-aid** *n* small device that amplifies sound and helps a deaf person to hear: *have/wear a hearing-aid.*

hearken /ˈhɑːkən/ *v* [I, Ipr] ~ **(to sb/sth)** (*arch*) listen.

hearsay /ˈhɪəseɪ/ *n* [U] things one has heard another person or other people say, which may or may not be true; rumour: *You shouldn't believe that — it's just hearsay.* ○ [attrib] *hearsay evidence.*

hearse /hɜːs/ *n* vehicle for carrying a coffin at a funeral.

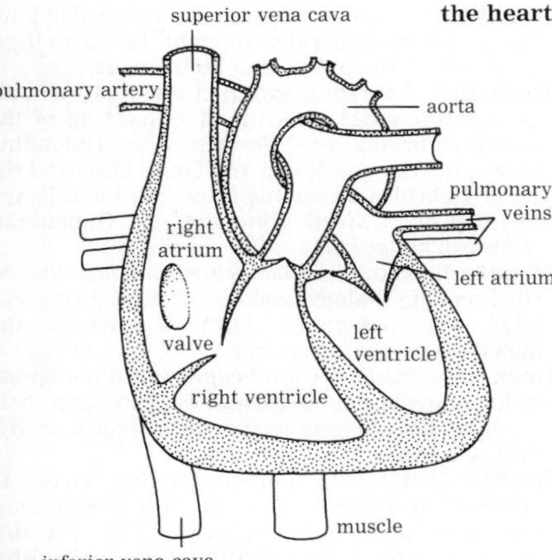

heart /hɑːt/ *n* **1** [C] **(a)** hollow muscular organ that pumps blood through the body. Blood returning to it is pumped by the right side of the heart into the lungs, where the carbon dioxide it has collected in the body is exchanged for oxygen. It then flows back to the left side of the heart, from where it is pumped around the body through arteries, providing a supply of oxygen for the body to use. It returns to the right side of the heart through veins, and the whole process starts again. The heart is traditionally thought of as the place from which feelings come, esp love, and also courage: *His heart stopped beating and he died soon afterwards.* ○ [attrib]: *have heart trouble/disease* ○ *a heart hospital.* ⇨ illus, ⇨ illus at RESPIRE. Cf AURICLE 2, VENTRICLE 1. **(b)** part of the body where this is: *He pressed her hand against his heart.* **2** [C] centre of a person's thoughts and emotions, esp of love; ability to feel emotion: *I have everything my heart desires.* ○ *She knew it in her heart.* ○ *He has a kind heart.* ○ *The princess captured the hearts of the nation.* **3** [U] enthusiasm: *I want you to put more heart into your singing.* **4** [C] **(a)** central, innermost or most important part of sth: *in the heart of the forest* ○ *get to the heart of the matter, subject, mystery.* **(b)** inner compact part of a cabbage, lettuce, etc. **5 (a)** [C] thing shaped like a heart, esp a regular red shape used to represent a heart, eg to symbolize love or on a playing-card. **(b) hearts** [sing or pl *v*] suit of playing-cards marked with these: *the ten of hearts* ○ *Hearts is/are trumps.* ⇨ illus at PLAYING-CARD. **(c)** [C] playing-card of this suit: *play a heart.* **6** [C] (used as a term of endearment) beloved person: *dear heart.* **7** (idm) **after one's own ˈheart** of exactly the type one likes best: *He likes good wine too — he's obviously a man after my own heart.* **at ˈheart** in one's real nature; basically: *I'm a country girl at heart.* **bare one's heart/soul** ⇨ BARE[2]. **break sb's/one's ˈheart** make sb/one feel very sad: *It breaks my heart to see him crying.* ○ *It broke her heart when he left.* **by ˈheart** from memory: *learn/know a poem by heart.* **a change of heart** ⇨ CHANGE[2]. **close/dear/near to sb's ˈheart** of deep interest and concern to sb: *This subject is very close to my heart.* **cross my heart** ⇨ CROSS[2]. **cry one's eyes/heart out** ⇨ CRY[1]. **do one's ˈheart good** cause one to feel encouraged, cheerful, etc: *It does my heart good to see the children enjoying themselves.* **eat one's heart out** ⇨ EAT. **find it in one's heart/oneself to do sth** ⇨ FIND[1]. **from the (bottom of one's) ˈheart** sincere(ly): *This advice comes from the heart.* **give one's heart to sb/sth** come to love sb/sth. **have sth at ˈheart** be anxious to support or defend sth: *He has your welfare at heart,* ie wants you to be happy, etc. **have a ˈheart** (*infml*) be sympathetic or kind; show mercy. **have the heart (to do sth)** (usu in negative sentences or questions with *can* or *could*) be cruel or unfeeling enough (to do sth): *I hadn't the heart to refuse.* **have one's heart in one's ˈboots** be very gloomy and depressed. **have one's heart in one's ˈmouth** be badly frightened: *My heart was in my mouth.* **have one's ˈheart in the right place** have true or kind feelings. **have one's heart set on sth** = SET ONE'S HEART ON STH. **heart and ˈsoul** enthusiastically; energetically: *devote oneself heart and soul to one's work.* **one's heart ˈbleeds for sb** (*often ironic*) one pities or feels sorry for sb. **one's heart goes out to sb** one feels compassion for sb. **one's heart is in sth** one is enthusiastic about sth: *I want her to take the exam again but her heart's not in it.* **a heart of ˈgold** a very kind nature: *He sometimes seems bad-tempered but really he's got a heart of gold.* **a heart of ˈstone** a pitiless and unfeeling nature. **one's heart sinks** one feels disappointed: *When I saw the pile of dirty dishes, my heart sank.* **in good ˈheart** in good condition or spirits. **in one's ˌheart (of ˈhearts)** in one's inmost feelings: *He knew in his heart that he was doing the wrong thing.* **lose heart** ⇨ LOSE. **lose one's heart to sb/sth** ⇨ LOSE. **open one's heart/mind to sb** ⇨ OPEN[2]. **search one's heart/conscience** ⇨ SEARCH *v*. **set one's heart on (having/doing) sth** want sth greatly. **sick at heart** ⇨ SICK. **sob one's heart out** ⇨ SOB. **strike fear, etc into sb/sb's heart** ⇨ STRIKE[2]. **take ˈheart (at sth)** become encouraged or more confident. **take sth to ˈheart** be much affected or upset by sth: *I took your criticism very much to heart.* **to one's heart's conˈtent** as much as one wishes. **wear one's heart on one's sleeve** ⇨ WEAR[2]. **with ˌall one's ˈheart/one's whole ˈheart** completely; sincerely: *I hope with all my heart that you succeed.* **young at heart** ⇨ YOUNG.

▷ **-hearted** (in compound *adjs*) having feelings or a nature as specified: *kind-hearted* ○ *faint-hearted.* **heartless** *adj* unkind; without pity. **heartlessly** *adv.* **heartlessness** *n* [U].

□ **ˈheartache** *n* [U, C] great sorrow.

ˈheart attack sudden illness with irregular and violent beating of the heart: *have/suffer a heart attack.* Cf CORONARY THROMBOSIS (CORONARY).

ˈheartbeat *n* pulsating movement of the heart or the sound it makes: *Your heartbeat is quite normal.*

ˈheart-break *n* [C, U] (cause of) very great unhappiness: *She's had her share of heart-break(s).* **ˈheart-breaking** *adj.*

ˈheart-broken *adj* (of a person) feeling great sadness: *He was heart-broken when she left.*

ˈheartburn *n* [U] burning sensation in the lower part of the chest, caused by indigestion.

ˈheart failure sudden failure of the heart to function properly.

ˈheartfelt *adj* deeply felt; sincere: *heartfelt sympathy/thanks.*

heartland /ˈhɑːtlænd/ *n* central or most important part of an area: *Germany's industrial heartland.*

ˌheart-ˈlung machine machine that can temporarily perform the functions of the heart and lungs, esp during a surgical operation.

ˈheart-rending *adj* very distressing: *a heart-rending sight, scream, appeal.*

ˈheart-searching *n* [U] examination of one's own feelings and motives: *After much heart-searching they decided to separate.*

ˈheartsick *adj* sad and dejected.

ˈheart-strings *n* [pl] deepest feelings of love or pity: *play upon sb's heart-strings,* ie move him emotionally.

ˈheart-throb *n* (*infml*) attractive person who arouses strong feelings of love; sweetheart: *He's my heart-throb.* ○ *He's a real heart-throb.*

ˌheart-to-ˈheart *n* frank conversation about personal matters: *have a heart-to-heart with sb* ○ [attrib] *a ˌheart-to-heart ˈchat.*

ˈheart-warming *adj* causing feelings of happiness and pleasure: *a heart-warming reunion, gesture, gift.*

ˈheartwood *n* [U] wood that makes up the hard inner part of a tree-trunk.

hearten /ˈhɑːtn/ *v* [Tn esp passive] make (sb) feel cheerful and encouraged: *We are much heartened by the latest developments.* ▷ **heartening** *adj*: *heartening news.* **hearteningly** *adv.*

hearth /hɑːθ/ *n* **1 (a)** floor of a fireplace: *a fire burning in the hearth.* **(b)** area in front of this: *slippers warming on/by the hearth.* **2** (*fig*) home: *a longing for hearth and home.*

□ **ˈhearthrug** *n* rug laid in front of a fireplace.

heartily /ˈhɑːtɪlɪ/ *adv* **1** with obvious enjoyment and enthusiasm; vigorously: *laugh, sing, eat, etc heartily.* **2** very; truly: *be heartily glad, pleased, relieved, upset, etc* ○ *I'm heartily sick of this wet weather.*

hearty /ˈhɑːtɪ/ *adj* (**-ier, -iest**) **1** [usu attrib] showing warm and friendly feelings; enthusiastic: *a hearty welcome, reception, greeting, etc* ○ *give one's hearty approval and support to a plan.* **2** (*sometimes derog*) loud and (too) cheerful: *a hearty person, laugh.* **3** [attrib] large: *eat a hearty breakfast* ○ *have a hearty appetite.* **4** (esp of older people) strong and healthy. **5** (idm) **hale and hearty** ⇨ HALE.

▷ **heartiness** *n* [U].

hearty *n* **1** hearty person, esp one who is fond of sport. **2** (idm) **my hearties** (*dated infml*) (used as a form of address, esp among sailors): *Heave ho, my hearties!*

heat[1] /hiːt/ *n* **1** [U] **(a)** high temperature; hotness: *feel the heat of the sun's rays* ○ *This fire doesn't give out much heat.* **(b)** hot weather: *suffer from the heat* ○ *Never go out in the heat* (ie at the hottest time) *of the day without a hat.* **2** [U] (*fig*) intense feeling, esp of anger or excitement: *speak with considerable heat* ○ *in the heat of the argument* ○ *This topic generates a lot of heat.* ○ *He tried to take the heat out of the situation,* ie reduce the tension. **3** [C] preliminary contest, the winners of which take part in further contests or the final: *be eliminated in the first heat.* **4** (idm) **be on heat**; *US* **be in heat** (of female mammals) be in the time or condition of sexual excitement and ready for mating. **the ˈheat is on/off** (*infml*) intense activity intended to find sb, persuade sb, etc is continuing/has stopped: *The hunted criminal stayed in hiding until the heat was off.* **in the ˌheat of the ˈmoment** while (temporarily) very angry, excited, upset, etc.

□ **ˈheat barrier** limit on the speed of aircraft, etc caused by heat resulting from air friction.

ˈheat engine engine that uses heat to produce mechanical movement (eg a steam-engine or an internal-combustion engine).

ˈheat pump machine that extracts heat from a source (eg water or air), and transfers it to a hotter place. Heat pumps are used in refrigerators.

ˈheat rash itchy red rash caused by blockage of the sweat glands in hot weather.

ˈheat shield device on a spacecraft that protects it against excessive heat, esp when it re-enters the earth's atmosphere.

ˈheat-stroke *n* [U] sudden illness caused by too much exposure to heat or sun.

ˈheat treatment use of heat to change the physical properties of sth, esp metal.

ˈheatwave *n* time of unusually hot weather.

heat[2] /hiːt/ *v* [I, Ip, Tn, Tn·p] ~ **(sth) (up)** (cause sth to) become hot or warm: *The office will soon heat up.* ○ *Heating these offices is expensive.* ○ *The pie has already been cooked — it just needs heating up.* ○ *Is it a heated swimming-pool?*

▷ **heated** *adj* (of a person or discussion) angry; excited: *a heated argument.* **heatedly** *adv.*

heater *n* device for supplying warmth to a room or for heating water: *a gas heater* ○ *a water-heater* ○ *The heater in my car doesn't work properly.* Cf FIRE[1] 3, STOVE[1] 2. ⇨ illus at CAR.

heating *n* [U] means or system of supplying heat: *Switch the heating on — I'm cold!* ○ [attrib] *heating costs.*

heath /hiːθ/ *n* **1** [C] area of flat uncultivated land, esp one covered with shrubs; moorland. **2** [C, U] small evergreen shrub that grows on a heath. Cf HEATHER.

heathen /ˈhi:ðn/ *n* **1** person who does not believe in any of the world's chief religions, esp one who is neither Christian, Muslim nor Jew; pagan: [attrib] *heathen customs.* **2** (*infml*) wild or bad-mannered person: *Some young heathen has vandalized the bus shelter.*

▷ **heathenish** /ˈhi:ðənɪʃ/ *adj* of or like heathens; barbarous.

heather /ˈheðə(r)/ *n* [U] low evergreen plant or shrub with small purple, pink or white bell-shaped flowers, common on moorland. Cf HEATH 2.

Heath Robinson /ˌhi:θ ˈrɒbɪnsən/ William (1872-1944), English cartoonist and illustrator who specialized in drawings of absurdly complicated mechanical devices that are unlikely to work. His name is now used to describe such devices: *Your plumbing looks a bit Heath Robinson to me.* ○ [attrib] *a Heath Robinson contraption.*

Heathrow /ˌhi:θˈrəʊ/ Britain's largest international airport, to the west of London. It is known officially as London Airport.

heave /hi:v/ *v* (*pt, pp* **heaved** or, esp in nautical use, **hove** /həʊv/) **1** (**a**) [Tn·pr, Tn·p] lift or drag (sth heavy) with great effort: *We heaved the wardrobe up the stairs.* (**b**) [I, Ipr] ~ (**at/on sth**) pull (at a rope, etc): *heave (away) at the capstan* ○ *'Heave ho!' cried the sailors as they raised the anchor.* **2** [Tn, Tn·pr, Tn·p] (*infml*) throw (esp sth heavy): *heave a brick through a window* ○ *heave sth overboard.* **3** [Tn] utter (sth) with effort: *heave a sigh of relief/a groan.* **4** [I] rise and fall regularly: *his heaving chest.* **5** [I, Ip] ~ (**up**) be violently sick; vomit. **6** (idm) ˌ**heave in** ˈ**sight** become visible: *A ship hove in sight.* **7** (phr v) ˌ**heave (sth)** ˈ**to** (of a ship) stop; cause (a ship) to stop without anchoring or mooring: *The vessel/We hove to.* ○ *We hove the vessel to.*

▷ **heave** *n* [C, U] (act of) heaving: *with a mighty heave*, ie a strong pull or throw ○ *the steady heave of the waves.*

□ **heave-**ˈ**ho** *n* **the heave-ho** [sing] (*infml*) dismissal: *I got the (old) heave-ho from my last job.*

heaven /ˈhevn/ *n* **1** [sing] (without *a* or *the*) place believed to be the home of God and the angels and of good people after death: *ascend into/go to heaven.*

Many people retain in adulthood a mental picture of heaven as a place in the sky where God reigns, and where angels sit on clouds playing harps. This image can often be seen in the illustrations in religious books from Victorian times, and in the stained glass windows in the churches of that period.

2 (also **Heaven**) [sing] God; Providence: *It was the will of Heaven.* ○ *If that's the way he treats his friends, heaven help his enemies!* **3** [U, C] place or state of very great happiness: *She was in heaven when he kissed her.* ○ *Sitting here with you is heaven.* ○ *If there's a heaven on earth, this is it!* **4 the heavens** [pl] the sky, as seen from the earth: *Rain fell from the heavens all day long.* **5** (idm) **for God's/goodness'/Heaven's sake** ⇨ SAKE. **God/Heaven forbid** ⇨ FORBID. **God/Heaven help sb** ⇨ HELP[1]. **God in Heaven** ⇨ GOD. **God/goodness/Heaven knows** ⇨ KNOW. (**Good**) ˈ**Heavens!**; ˌ**Heavens a**ˈ**bove!** (used to express surprise). **the heavens opened** it began to rain heavily. **move heaven and earth** ⇨ MOVE[2]. **pennies from heaven** ⇨ PENNY. **seventh heaven** (*infml*) state of great happiness: *Just give him a bucket and spade and he's in seventh heaven!* **smell, etc to high heaven** ⇨ HIGH[1]. **to God/goodness/Heaven** ⇨ GOD.

▷ **heavenward** /-wəd/ (also **heavenwards** /-wədz/) *adv* towards heaven.

□ ˌ**heaven-**ˈ**sent** *adj* happening at a most favourable time; very lucky: *a* ˌ*heaven-sent oppor*ˈ*tunity.*

heavenly /ˈhevnlɪ/ *adj* **1** [attrib] of or from heaven; divine: *a heavenly angel, vision.* **2** [attrib] of the sky: *heavenly bodies*, ie the sun, moon, stars, etc. **3** (*infml*) very pleasing: *This cake is heavenly.*

Heaviside /ˈhevɪsaɪd/ Oliver (1850-1925), English physicist who made advances in the field of telegraphy and suggested the existence of the layer in the atmosphere later named after him.

□ ˈ**Heaviside layer** (also ˌ**Kennelly-**ˈ**Heaviside layer**, ˈ**E-layer**) (*physics*) part of the earth's atmosphere that reflects medium-frequency waves. Cf IONOSPHERE.

heavy /ˈhevɪ/ *adj* (**-ier, -iest**) **1** having weight (esp great weight); difficult to lift or move: *How heavy is it?* ie How much does it weigh? ○ *Lead is a heavy metal.* ○ *The box is too heavy for me to carry.* **2** (**a**) of more than the usual size, amount, force, etc: *heavy guns, artillery*, ie of the largest type ○ *a heavy* (ie abundant) *crop* ○ *Traffic on the roads is heaviest at weekends.* ○ *Fighting was heavy.* ○ *suffer heavy casualties/losses* ○ *have heavy expenses* ○ *a heavy frost* ○ *have a heavy cold* ○ *heavy* (ie loud) *breathing* ○ *a heavy sleeper*, ie one who is difficult to wake ○ *a heavy drinker/smoker*, ie one who drinks/smokes a lot. (**b**) [usu attrib] full of activity; busy: *a very heavy day, programme, schedule.* (**c**) [pred] ~ **on sth** (*infml*) using large quantities of sth: *My car is rather heavy on petrol.* ○ *Don't go so heavy on the sauce!* **3** falling or striking with force: *a heavy blow, fall of snow* ○ *heavy rain, seas.* **4** (**a**) dense; solid: *a heavy mist* ○ *heavy bread*, ie doughy from not having risen. (**b**) (of the ground) muddy and sticky; hard to work or travel over: *heavy soil* ○ *The going was heavy at the racecourse.* **5** (**a**) (of food) difficult to digest: *a heavy meal.* (**b**) (*fig*) serious: *the heavier newspapers.* (**c**) (*derog*) (of a person, book, style, etc) serious and tedious; dull: *This article is/makes heavy reading.* **6** stern: *He can be very heavy with/on his children.* **7** (of a person's appearance or way of moving) clumsy or ungraceful: *heavy features.* **8** drowsy: *be heavy with sleep/wine.* **9** (of the sky) dark with clouds. **10** (*sl esp US*) dangerous; threatening: *a heavy scene.* **11** sad: *a heavy heart.* **12** (idm) ˌ**heavy** ˈ**going** difficult or boring: *She's heavy going*, ie hard to talk to in an easy, friendly way. ○ *I find the work heavy going.* **a heavy hand** harsh or firm control: *He runs his department with a heavy hand.* **make heavy** ˈ**weather of sth** make a task more difficult than it really is. **take a heavy toll/take its toll** ⇨ TOLL[1].

▷ **heavily** *adv*: *a heavily loaded lorry* ○ *smoke/drink heavily* ○ *be heavily taxed* ○ *heavily armed terrorists* ○ *rely heavily on sb* ○ *He fell heavily and twisted his ankle.* ○ *She lost heavily at cards.* **heaviness** *n* [U].

heavy *adv* (idm) **lie heavy on sth** ⇨ LIE[2]. **time hangs/lies heavy on one's hands** ⇨ TIME[1].

heavy *n* **1** villainous or serious role or actor in a play, film, etc. **2** (*sl*) big, strong man employed as a bodyguard, etc: *a gangster protected by his heavies.*

□ ˌ**heavier-than-**ˈ**air** *adj* (of an aircraft) heavier than an equivalent volume of air, and so needing wings, rotors, etc to fly.

ˌ**heavy-**ˈ**duty** *adj* intended to withstand hard use, bad weather, etc: *a* ˌ*heavy-duty* ˈ*battery*, ˈ*tyre.*

ˌ**heavy-**ˈ**handed** *adj* **1** clumsy; awkward: ˌ*heavy-handed inter*ˈ*ference*, ˈ*compliments*, ˈ*humour.* **2** oppressive: *a heavy-handed regime.* ˌ**heavy-**ˈ**handedly** *adv.* ˌ**heavy-**ˈ**handedness** *n* [U].

ˌ**heavy-**ˈ**hearted** *adj* sad.

ˌ**heavy** ˈ**hydrogen** isotope of hydrogen with atoms twice the normal weight.

ˌ**heavy** ˈ**industry** industry producing metal, large machines, etc.

ˌ**heavy-**ˈ**laden** *adj* carrying a heavy load.

ˌ**heavy** ˈ**metal 1** [C] very dense metal (eg gold or lead). **2** [U] type of very loud rock music with a strong beat.

ˌ**heavy** ˈ**water** water whose molecules consist of two heavy hydrogen atoms and one ordinary oxygen atom.

ˈ**heavyweight** *n* **1** boxer weighing 79.5 kg or more; next above light-heavyweight: [attrib] *a heavyweight contest.* **2** person of more than average weight. **3** (*fig*) person of great influence or importance: *a literary heavyweight.*

Hebraic /hi:ˈbreɪɪk/ *adj* of the Hebrew language or people.

Hebrew /ˈhi:bru:/ *n* **1** [C] member of a Semitic people in ancient Palestine. **2** [U] (**a**) language of the Hebrews. A member of the Semitic family of languages, it had largely died out as an everyday spoken language by 200 AD, but was retained by the Jews as a religious language. (**b**) modern form of this revived in the 19th century and used esp in Israel. Cf YIDDISH. **3 Hebrews** (also **Epistle to the Hebrews**) book of the New Testament, traditionally included among the letters of St Paul but now not generally thought to have been written by him. ⇨ App 5. ▷ **Hebrew** *adj.*

Hebrides /ˈhebrədi:z/ group of about 500 islands off the NW coast of Scotland, consisting of the Outer Hebrides or *Western Isles (including Lewis, Harris, and North and South Uist) and the Inner Hebrides (including Skye, Mull and Islay). ⇨ map at UNITED KINGDOM. ▷ **Hebridean** /ˌhebrəˈdi:ən/ *adj, n.*

Hecate /ˈhekətɪ, *in Shakespeare sometimes* ˈhekət/ (in Greek mythology) goddess of the underworld, who was associated with witchcraft, the supernatural and the moon.

heck /hek/ *interj, n* (*infml euph*) (used to express mild annoyance or surprise or for emphasis) hell: *Oh heck, I'm going to be late.* ○ *We had to wait a heck of a long time.*

heckle /ˈhekl/ *v* [Tn] interrupt and harass (a speaker) at a public meeting with troublesome questions and rude remarks: *The Socialist candidate was heckled continuously.* ▷ **heckler** /ˈheklə(r)/ *n.*

hectare /ˈhekteə(r), hektɑ:(r)/ *n* (*abbr* **ha**) measure of area in the metric system, equal to 100 ares or 10 000 square metres (2.471 acres). ⇨ App 10.

hectic /ˈhektɪk/ *adj* with much confused activity and excitement; very busy: *hectic last-minute preparations* ○ *lead a hectic life* ○ *Today was hectic.*

▷ **hectically** /-klɪ/ *adv.*

hect(o)- *comb form* hundred: *hectare* ○ *hectogram.* ⇨ App 12.

hectogram /ˈhektəgræm/ *n* unit of mass in the metric system, equal to 100 grams.

hector /ˈhektə(r)/ *v* [Tn] try to frighten (sb) by bullying: *a hectoring tone of voice.*

he'd /hi:d/ *contracted form* ⇨ Guide to Entries 5.3 **1** he had ⇨ HAVE[3]. **2** he would ⇨ WILL[1], WOULD[1].

hedge /hedʒ/ *n* **1** row of bushes or shrubs planted close together and forming a boundary for a field, garden, etc: *a privet hedge.* ⇨ illus at HOME. **2** ~ (**against sth**) means of defence against possible loss: *buy gold as a hedge* (ie to protect one's money) *against inflation.*

▷ **hedge** *v* **1** [Tn] put a hedge round (a field, garden, etc). **2** [I] make or trim hedges. **3** [I] avoid giving a direct answer to a question; refuse to commit oneself: *Answer 'yes' or 'no' — stop hedging!* **4** (idm) ˌ**hedge one's** ˈ**bets** protect oneself against loss or error by not committing oneself to a single course of action, opinion, etc: *hedge one's bets by backing both teams to win the game.* **5** (phr v) **hedge sb/sth about/around** (**with sth**) restrict or limit sb/sth: *My life is hedged about with petty regulations.* **hedge sb in** restrict the freedom of sb.

□ ˈ**hedge-hop** *v* (**-pp-**) [I] fly an aircraft very low, eg when spraying crops.

ˈ**hedgerow** *n* row of bushes, etc forming a hedge.

ˈ**hedge-sparrow** (also **sparrow**) *n* small brown bird common in Europe and America.

hedgehog /ˈhedʒhɒg; *US* -hɔ:g/ *n* small insect-eating animal covered with stiff spines, that rolls itself up into a ball to defend itself. ⇨ illus at ANIMAL.

hedonism /ˈhi:dənɪzəm/ *n* [U] (behaviour based on the) belief that pleasure should be the main aim in life.

▷ **hedonist** *n* believer in hedonism.

hedonistic /ˌhi:dəˈnɪstɪk/ *adj.*

heebie-jeebies /ˌhi:bɪ ˈdʒi:biz/ *n* [pl] (*infml*) feeling of discomfort or nervous fear: *Being alone in the dark gives me the heebie-jeebies.*

heed /hi:d/ *v* [Tn, Tw] (*fml*) pay attention to (advice, etc); take notice of (sth): *heed a warning* ○ *heed what sb says.*

▷ **heed** *n* **1** [U] (*fml*) careful attention. **2** (idm) **pay heed** ⇨ PAY². **take heed (of sth)** note sth carefully and act accordingly: *Take heed of your doctor's advice.* **heedful** /-fl/ *adj* [usu pred] ~ **(of sth/sb)** (*fml*) attentive: *You should be more heedful of advice.* **heedless** *adj* [usu pred] ~ **(of sth/sb)** (*fml*) disregarding; inattentive: *heedless of danger*. **heedlessly** *adv*.

hee-haw /ˈhiː hɔː/ *n* cry of a donkey.

heel¹ /hiːl/ *n* **1** (**a**) back part of the human foot. ⇨ illus at FOOT. (**b**) part of a sock, stocking, etc covering this. (**c**) part of a boot or shoe supporting this. ⇨ illus at SHOE. **2** thing like a heel in shape or position: *the heel of the hand*, ie the front part next to the wrist. **3** (*sl*) dishonourable man; rogue; villain. **4** crusty end of a loaf of bread. **5** act of heeling the ball in Rugby football: *a good quick heel.* **6** (idm) **an/one's Achilles' heel** ⇨ ACHILLES. **at/on sb's ˈheels; on the heels of sth** following closely after sb/sth: *The thief ran off with an angry crowd at his heels.* ○ *Famine often follows on the heels of war.* **bring sb/sth to ˈheel/come to ˈheel** (**a**) (force sb to) submit to discipline and control: *The rebels have been brought to heel.* (**b**) (cause a dog to) come close behind its owner: *I'm training my dog to come to heel.* **cool one's heels** ⇨ COOL². **dig one's heels/toes in** ⇨ DIG¹. **ˌdown at ˈheel** (**a**) (of shoes) with the heels worn down by wear. (**b**) (of a person) untidy and poorly dressed; shabby. **drag one's feet/heels** ⇨ DRAG². **hard on sb's heels** ⇨ HARD². **head over heels** ⇨ HEAD¹. **hot on sb's heels** ⇨ HOT. **kick one's heels** ⇨ KICK¹. **ˌkick up one's ˈheels** ⇨ KICK¹. **show a clean pair of heels** ⇨ SHOW². **ˌtake to one's ˈheels** run away: *We took to our heels and ran.* **tread on sb's heels** ⇨ TREAD. **ˌturn on one's ˈheel** turn sharply round and go in the opposite direction. **under the heel of sb** dominated by sb.

▷ **heel** *v* [Tn] **1** repair the heel of (a shoe, etc): *These shoes need soling and heeling.* **2** (in Rugby football) kick (the ball) backwards using the heel or sole of the boot.

-ˈheeled (forming compound *adjs*) with heels of the specified type: *ˌhigh-heeled ˈshoes.*

□ **ˈheel bar** small shop or counter in a large shop where shoes are repaired quickly.

heel² /hiːl/ *v* [I, Ip] ~ **(over)** (of a ship) lean over to one side: *The boat heeled over in the strong wind.*

hefty /ˈheftɪ/ *adj* (**-ier, -iest**) (*infml*) **1** (of a person) big and strong. **2** [usu attrib] (**a**) (of a thing) large and heavy: *a hefty suitcase.* (**b**) powerful: *deal sb a hefty blow.* (**c**) (*fig*) extensive; substantial: *She earns a hefty salary.* ▷ **heftily** *adv*: *a heftily-built fellow.*

Hegel /ˈheɪg(ə)l/ Georg Wilhelm Friedrich (1770-1831), German philosopher who saw human history as 'the development of the idea of freedom'. He had great influence on many religious and political thinkers, including Karl *Marx.

hegemony /hɪˈgemənɪ; *US* ˈhedʒəməʊnɪ/ *n* [U, C] (*fml*) leadership, esp by one state in a group of states.

Hegira (also **Hejira**) /ˈhedʒɪrə, hɪˈdʒaɪərə/ *n* **the Hegira** [sing] Muhammad's flight from Mecca to Medina in AD 622, from which date the Muslim era is reckoned.

heifer /ˈhefə(r)/ *n* young cow, esp one that has not yet had a calf. Cf cow¹ 1.

heigh-ho /ˌheɪ ˈhəʊ/ *interj* (used to express disappointment, boredom, etc).

height /haɪt/ *n* **1** (**a**) [U, C] measurement from the bottom to the top of a thing or from head to foot of a standing person: *What is the height of the mountain?* ○ *State your height*, ie how tall are you. ○ *He is two metres in height.* ⇨ App 9. ⇨ illus at DIMENSION. (**b**) [U] being tall: *She can see over the wall because of her height.* **2** [C, U] distance (of an object or a position) above ground or sea-level: *fly at a height of 6 000 metres (above sea-level)* ○ *The aircraft was gaining height.* **3** [C esp *pl*] high place or area: *be afraid of heights.* **4** [sing] main point or highest degree of sth: *the height of summer* ○ *The storm was at its height.* ○ *the height of folly* ○ *be dressed in the height of fashion* ○ *the height of one's ambition.* **5** (idm) **draw oneself up to one's full height** ⇨ DRAW².

NOTE ON USAGE: **Height** can be **1** the vertical measurement of a person or object: *Please state your height.* ○ *What's the height of that wall?* or **2** the distance of somebody or something from ground/sea-level: *The climber fell from a great height.* ○ *The aircraft was flying at a height of 2 000 feet.* The adjective **tall** relates to sense 1 and is used mainly of people, trees and buildings: *How tall are you/is the building/tree?* **High** relates to senses 1 and 2 (but is not used for the vertical measurement of people): *How high is that jump?* ○ *That poster is too high — nobody can read it.*

heighten /ˈhaɪtn/ *v* [I, Tn] (cause sth to) become higher or more intense: *heightening tension* ○ *her heightened colour*, ie the increased colour in her face, eg caused by emotion ○ *music to heighten the dramatic effect.*

heinous /ˈheɪnəs/ *adj* very wicked: *a heinous crime, criminal.* ▷ **heinously** *adv*. **heinousness** *n* [U].

heir /eə(r)/ *n* ~ **(to sth)** person with the legal right to receive property, etc when the owner dies: *be heir to a large fortune, a title, the throne* ○ *She made her stepson (her) heir.*

▷ **heiress** /ˈeərɪs, eəˈres/ *n* female heir, esp one who inherits great wealth.

□ **ˌheir apˈparent** (*pl* **heirs apparent**) heir whose legal right cannot be cancelled by the birth of another with a stronger claim.

ˌheir preˈsumptive (*pl* **heirs presumptive**) heir who may lose his legal right if another heir with a stronger claim is born.

heirloom /ˈeəluːm/ *n* (usu valuable) object that has been handed down in a family for several generations: *That clock is a family heirloom.*

heist /haɪst/ *n* (*sl esp US*) robbery; burglary.

▷ **heist** *v* [Tn] (*sl esp US*) rob or steal (sth).

Hejira = HEGIRA.

held *pt, pp* of HOLD¹.

Helen /ˈhelɪn/ (in Greek mythology) daughter of Zeus and Leda. In the poems of *Homer, her abduction by Paris led to the Trojan War.

helical /ˈhelɪkl, *also* ˈhiːlɪkl/ *adj* like a helix.

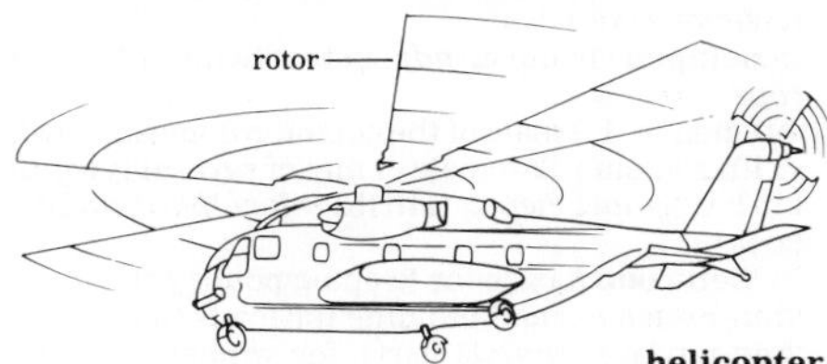

helicopter

helicopter /ˈhelɪkɒptə(r)/ *n* type of aircraft with horizontal revolving blades or rotors, able to take off and land vertically and remain stationary in the air. *Leonardo da Vinci drew a design for one, but the first practical helicopter was not built until 1939: *rescued from the sea by (a) helicopter* ○ [attrib] *a helicopter pilot.* ⇨ illus.

helio- *comb form* sun: *heliocentric* ○ *heliotrope.*

heliocentric /ˌhiːlɪəʊˈsentrɪk/ *adj* having or regarding the sun as the centre: *a heliocentric universe.*

heliotrope /ˈhiːlɪətrəʊp/ *n* **1** [C, U] plant with small sweet-smelling purple flowers. **2** [U] light purple colour.

heliport /ˈhelɪpɔːt/ *n* place where helicopters take off and land.

helium /ˈhiːlɪəm/ *n* [U] (*symb* **He**) chemical element, a light colourless gas that does not burn, used in airships. ⇨ App 11.

helix /ˈhiːlɪks/ *n* (*pl* **helices** /ˈhiːlɪsiːz/) spiral, either like a corkscrew or flat like a watch-spring: *Some biological molecules have the form of a helix.*

hell /hel/ *n* **1** [sing] (without *a* or *the*) place believed in some religions to be the home of devils and of wicked people after death.

📖 Hell is often portrayed in Christian imagery as a place below the earth where there is eternal fire and torment, and where the Devil, an evil-looking creature with horns and a forked tail, reigns supreme. This image has been expressed in great works of literature, such as *Dante's *Inferno*, and in art, as in the paintings of Hieronymus *Bosch.

2 [U, C] state or place of great suffering or wickedness; very unpleasant experience: *suffer hell on earth* ○ *She made his life (a) hell.* ○ *The journey was absolute hell.* **3** [U] (*infml*) (used as an exclamation of annoyance or surprise or for emphasis): *Oh hell, I've broken it!* ○ *Bloody hell!* ○ *Oh go to hell!* ○ *Who the hell is he?* ○ *What the hell* (ie It doesn't matter), *I can go tomorrow instead.* **4** (idm) **a/one hell of a...** (also **a helluva** /ˈheləvə/) (*sl*) (**a**) (used for emphasis): *one hell of a row*, ie a dreadful row. (**b**) very: *It's a hell of a long way.* ○ *He's a helluva (nice) guy.* **all ˈhell broke/was let loose** suddenly there was great noise and confusion. **beat/knock hell out of sb/sth** (*infml*) hit sb/sth very hard. **a cat in hell's chance** ⇨ CAT¹. **for the ˈhell of it** (*infml*) just for fun: *steal a car for the hell of it.* **give sb ˈhell** (*infml*) scold, punish or harass sb: *The boss really gave me hell today.* ○ *This tooth is giving me hell*, ie is very painful. **hell for ˈleather** as quickly as possible: *drive, ride, run, etc hell for leather.* **(come) ˌhell or high ˈwater** no matter what the difficulties. **ˌhell's ˈbells** (*infml*) (used as an *interj* to express anger or annoyance). **like a bat out of hell** ⇨ BAT¹. **like ˈhell** (**a**) (*infml*) (used for emphasis): *drive like hell*, ie very fast. (**b**) (*sl ironic*) (used before a clause) not at all: *'You can pay.' 'Like hell I will* (ie I certainly will not)*!'* **not have a hope in hell** ⇨ HOPE *n.* **play hell with sth/sb** (*infml*) seriously upset sth/sb: *That curry is playing hell with my insides!* **raise Cain/hell/the roof** ⇨ RAISE. **the road to hell is paved with good intentions** ⇨ ROAD. **see sb (damned) in ˈhell first** (*infml*) (used when emphatically rejecting a suggestion): *Lend him money? I'll see him in hell first.* **there will be/was ˈhell to pay** (*infml*) sb will be/was punished severely: *There'll be hell to pay if we're caught.* **to hell with sb/sth** damn sb/sth: *To hell with the lot of you, I'll do what I please!*

▷ **hellish** *adj* **1** of or like hell. **2** (*infml*) extremely unpleasant: *His schooldays were hellish.* — *adv* (*infml*) extremely: *hellish expensive.* **hellishly** *adv* **1** very badly: *be hellishly treated.* **2** (*infml*) extremely: *a hellishly difficult problem.*

□ **ˈhell-bent** *adj* [pred] ~ **on sth** recklessly determined to do sth: *He seems hell-bent on drinking himself to death.*

ˈhell-cat *n* spiteful or furious woman.

ˈhell-hole *n* (*infml*) extremely unpleasant place: *I can't wait to get out of this hell-hole.*

ˈhell-raiser *n* person who causes trouble by behaving wildly, etc.

ˌHell's ˈAngel member of a gang of youths who ride motor cycles, wear leather clothing, and have a reputation for aggressive behaviour.

he'll /hiːl/ *contracted form* he will ⇨ WILL¹.

hellebore /ˈhelɪbɔː(r)/ *n* any of several European and Asian plants with white or green flowers, some of which are poisonous.

Hellene /ˈheliːn/ *n* **1** native of modern Greece. **2** person of genuine Greek race in ancient times.

▷ **Hellenic** /heˈliːnɪk; *US* heˈlenɪk/ *adj* of the ancient or modern Greeks, their arts, culture, etc.

Hellenistic /ˌhelɪˈnɪstɪk/ *adj* of the Greek language and culture of the 4th-1st centuries BC.

Heller /ˈhelə(r)/ Joseph (1923-), American novelist whose best-known work, *Catch-22*, describes the stupidities of military life.

Hellespont /ˈhelɪspɒnt/ ancient name for the *Dardanelles, a stretch of water separating Europe from Asia Minor.

hello ⇨ HALLO.

helluva /ˈheləvə/ ⇨ HELL 4.

helm /helm/ *n* **1** handle or wheel for moving the rudder of a ship or boat: (*fig*) *the helm of state*, ie government of a country. Cf TILLER. **2** (idm) **at the ˈhelm** at the head of an organization, etc; in control.

□ **ˈhelmsman** (/-zmən/) *n* (*pl* **-men** /-mən/) person

who steers a ship. Cf STEERSMAN (STEER[1]).

helmet /ˈhelmɪt/ *n* protective head-covering such as that worn by firemen, miners, motor-cyclists, policemen and sportsmen, and by soldiers when they are fighting. ⇨ illus at AMERICAN FOOTBALL (AMERICAN).

▷ **helmeted** *adj* wearing or provided with a helmet.

help[1] /help/ *v* **1** [I, Ipr, It, Tn, Tn·pr, Tn·p, Cn·t, Cn·i] ~ **(sb) (with sth)** be of use or service to (sb); make it easier for (sb) to do sth; aid; assist: *Help! I'm stuck.* ○ *May I help with the washing-up?* ○ *Your advice helped (me) a lot.* ○ *We must all help each other.* ○ *A man is helping the police with their enquiries.* ○ *Please help me up/down the stairs with this heavy case,* ie help me to carry it up/down. ○ *Would it help you to know* (ie if I told you) *that...?* ○ *This charity aims to help people to help themselves.* ○ *I helped (him) (to) find his things.* **2 (a)** [Tn, Tn·pr] ~ **oneself/sb (to sth)** serve oneself/sb with food, drink, etc: *Help yourself (to a cigarette).* ○ *May I help you to some more meat?* **(b)** [Tn·pr] ~ **oneself to sth** take sth without permission: *He's been helping himself to my stationery.* **3** [I, It, Tn] make it easier for sth to happen: *This latest development doesn't exactly help (matters).* ○ *drugs that help to take away pain* ○ *stiffer measures to help fight terrorism.* **4** (idm) **can/could (not) help (doing) sth** can/could (not) prevent or avoid sth: *It can't/couldn't be helped,* ie There was no way of avoiding it and we must accept that. ○ *Can I help it* (ie Is it my fault) *if people don't read the instructions?* ○ *He can't help having big ears.* ○ *I wouldn't live there; well, not if I could help it.* ○ *We can't help thinking he's still alive.* ○ *She burst out laughing; she couldn't help it/herself,* ie could not stop herself. ○ *Don't tell him more than you can help,* ie more than you must. ○ *She never does more work than she can help,* ie She does as little as possible. **God/Heaven ˈhelp sb** (used when expressing fears for sb's safety): *God help you* (ie You will be in trouble) *if the teacher finds out!* **help a lame dog over a stile** give help to sb who is in difficulty or trouble. **a ˌhelping ˈhand** assistance: *give/lend (sb) a helping hand.* **so ˈhelp me (God)** I swear it: *I never stole the money, so help me (I didn't)!* **5** (phr v) **help sb off/on with sth** help sb to take off/put on (a garment): *Can I help you on with your coat?* **help (sb) ˈout** help sb esp in a difficult situation or a crisis: *He's always willing to help (us) out when we're short of staff.*

▷ **helper** *n* person who helps.

helping *n* portion of food at a meal: *take a third helping* ○ *She had two generous helpings of pie.*

help[2] /help/ *n* **1** [U] helping or being helped: *Thank you for all your kind help.* ○ *Can I be of (any) help to you?* ○ *The map wasn't much help.* ○ *She came to our help,* ie helped us. **2** [sing] **a** ~ **(to sb)** person or thing that helps: *The servants were more of a hindrance than a help (to me).* ○ *Her advice was a great help.* ○ (*ironic*) *You're a great help* (ie no help at all), *I must say!* **3** [C] person employed to help with the housework: *The help hasn't come this morning.* **4** [C] way of avoiding or preventing sth (used esp in the expression shown): *There's no help for it.*

▷ **helpful** /-fl/ *adj* giving help; useful: *a helpful person, suggestion, map* ○ *He's always very helpful to his mother.* **helpfully** /-fəlɪ/ *adv.* **helpfulness** *n* [U].

helpless *adj* **1** unable to act without help; needing the help of others: *a helpless baby, invalid, drunkard* ○ *be helpless with laughter.* **2** without help; defenceless: *Without their weapons they were helpless.* **helplessly** *adv.* **helplessness** *n* [U].

helpmate /ˈhelpmeɪt/ *n* helpful partner or companion, esp a husband or wife.

helter-skelter /ˌheltə ˈskeltə(r)/ *adv* in disorderly haste.

▷ **helter-skelter** *n* tall tower at a fun-fair, etc with a spiral track outside it that people slide down on mats.

helve /helv/ *n* handle of a weapon or tool, esp an axe.

hem[1] /hem/ *n* edge of a piece of cloth which has been turned under and sewn or fixed down: *I took the hems of my dresses up to make them shorter.*

▷ **hem** *v* (**-mm-**) **1** [Tn] make a hem on (sth): *hem a skirt, handkerchief, etc.* **2** (phr v) **hem sb about/around** (esp passive) surround sb: *be hemmed about by obstacles.* **hem sb in** surround and restrict the movement of sb; confine sb: *The enemy troops were hemming us in.* ○ (*fig*) *He felt hemmed in by convention.*

□ **ˈhem-line** *n* lower edge of a dress or skirt: *lower/raise the hem-line,* ie make a skirt, etc longer/shorter.

ˈhem-stitch *n* [U] ornamental stitching used esp on hems. — *v* [Tn] decorate (sth) with such stitching.

hem[2] /hem/ (also **h'm** /hm/) *interj* (used to call attention or express doubt or hesitation).

▷ **hem** *v* (**-mm-**) [I] say *hem*; hesitate while speaking.

Hemingway /ˈhemɪŋweɪ/ Ernest Miller (1899-1961), American novelist whose books deal with themes such as physical courage and man's struggle against nature. They include *Death in the Afternoon, For Whom the Bell Tolls* and *The Old Man and the Sea.* He was awarded the Nobel prize for literature in 1954. He committed suicide.

hemiplegia /ˌhɪmɪˈpli:dʒə/ *n* [U] paralysis of one side of the body. ▷ **hemiplegic** /-ˈpli:dʒɪk/ *adj.*

hemipterous /heˈmɪptərəs/ *adj* of a large group of insects (eg aphids, cicadas and bugs) which have piercing or sucking mouth-parts.

hemisphere /ˈhemɪsfɪə(r)/ *n* **1** half a sphere. **2** any half of the earth, esp as divided by the equator (**the Northern/Southern hemisphere**) or by a line passing through the poles (**the Eastern hemisphere**, ie Europe, Africa, Asia, Australia, and **the Western hemisphere**, ie N and S America). ⇨ illus at GLOBE. **3** (*anatomy*) either half of the cerebrum.

▷ **hemispherical** /ˌhemɪˈsferɪkl/ *adj* shaped like a hemisphere.

hemlock /ˈhemlɒk/ *n* **1** [C, U] poisonous plant with small white flowers. **2** [U] poison made from this plant.

hem(o)- ⇨ HAEM(O)-.

hemp /hemp/ *n* [U] **1** plant from which coarse fibres are obtained for making rope and cloth. **2** narcotic drug made from this plant. Cf CANNABIS, HASHISH, MARIJUANA.

▷ **hempen** /ˈhempən/ *adj* made of hemp: *a hempen rope.*

hen /hen/ *n* **1** female of the common domestic fowl. ⇨ illus at BIRD. **2** female of any of several types of bird: *a ˈguinea-hen* ○ [attrib] *a hen ˈpheasant.* Cf COCK[1].

□ **ˈhen-coop** *n* cage for keeping poultry in.

ˈhen-house *n* small building for fowls to roost in.

ˈhen-party *n* (*infml*) party for women only. Cf STAG-PARTY (STAG).

ˈhenpecked *adj* (*infml*) (of a husband) nagged by a fussy and domineering wife.

henbane /ˈhenbeɪn/ *n* poisonous European and Asian plant with unpleasant-smelling yellow flowers.

hence /hens/ *adv* **1** from this time: *a week hence,* ie in a week from now. **2** for this reason: *I fell off my bike yesterday — hence the bruises.* **3** (*arch*) from here.

□ **henceforth** /ˌhensˈfɔ:θ/ (also **henceforward** /ˌhensˈfɔ:wəd/) *adv* (*fml*) from this time on; in future: *Henceforth I expect you to be punctual for meetings.*

henchman /ˈhentʃmən/ *n* (*pl* **-men** /-mən/) faithful follower or political supporter who always obeys the orders of his leader: *the dictator and his henchmen.*

Hengist /ˈheŋgɪst/ legendary leader, with his brother Horsa, of the *Jutes who settled in SE England around 450 AD.

Henley /ˈhenlɪ/ (also **ˌHenley-on-ˈThames**) town on the River Thames in Oxfordshire where every June/July the Henley Royal Regatta is held. This is a five-day contest of rowing races, in which many of the best crews from around the world compete. It is fashionable to go as a spectator. ⇨ article at SEASON.

henna /ˈhenə/ *n* [U] **1** reddish-brown dye used esp on the hair. **2** tropical plant from which this dye is obtained.

▷ **hennaed** /ˈhenəd/ *adj* dyed with henna.

henry /ˈhenrɪ/ *n* (*pl* ~**s** or **-ies**) SI unit of inductance, which gives an electromotive force of one volt in a closed circuit with a rate of change of current of one ampere per second.

Henry I /ˈhenrɪ/ (1068-1135), king of England 1100-35. Youngest son of *William I, he established a bureaucracy to support the English monarchy and set up a system of travelling judges. ⇨ App 3.

Henry II /ˈhenrɪ/ (1133-89), king of England 1154-89. He restored order to the kingdom after the civil war of 1139-53, but his reign was overshadowed by his dispute with Thomas *Becket over the rights of the Church and the Crown, which ended with the murder of Becket. ⇨ App 3.

Henry III /ˈhenrɪ/ (1207-72), king of England 1216-72. Unpopular because of his financial mismanagement and his reliance on foreign advisers, he was deposed by Simon de Montfort's revolt in 1264. He was restored the following year, but most of the real power in the kingdom passed to his son, later Edward I. ⇨ App 3.

Henry IV /ˈhenrɪ/ (1367-1413), king of England 1399-1413. As Henry Bolingbroke he was exiled in 1398 for his opposition to Richard II, but returned the following year to overthrow Richard and establish the *Lancastrian dynasty. His reign was troubled by rebellions in Wales and the north of England. ⇨ App 3.

Henry V /ˈhenrɪ/ (1387-1422), king of England 1413-22. Son of Henry IV, he enhanced an already high reputation as a soldier by leading an English invasion of France in 1415, winning a notable victory at *Agincourt and bringing Normandy back under English control. ⇨ App 3.

Henry VI /ˈhenrɪ/ (1421-71), king of England 1422-61 and 1470-1. Son of Henry V, he was a weak and unpopular king. During his reign the *Hundred Years War with France was lost, and at home increasing opposition led to the *Wars of the Roses, in which Henry was deposed by the *Yorkists. He briefly regained the throne in 1470, but was deposed again and killed. ⇨ App 3.

Henry VII /ˈhenrɪ/ (1457-1509), king of England 1485-1509. Born Henry Tudor, he inherited the *Lancastrian claim to the throne. In 1485 he returned from exile in France to defeat and kill Richard III at the Battle of Bosworth. As king he modernized and strengthened the system of royal government. ⇨ App 3.

Henry VIII /ˈhenrɪ/ (1491-1547), king of England 1509-47. Son of Henry VII, his efforts to divorce his first wife, Catherine of Aragon, led eventually to a break with the Roman Catholic church, the abolition of all monasteries, and the establishment of Protestantism in England. He was married five more times, to Anne Boleyn (whom he had beheaded), Jane Seymour, Anne of Cleves, Catherine Howard (also beheaded), and Catherine Parr. He was an impressively large man, fond of sport and hunting in his youth. ⇨ App 3. ⇨ article at CHURCH OF ENGLAND.

hepatitis /ˌhepəˈtaɪtɪs/ *n* [U] inflammation of the liver.

Hepburn /ˈhepbən/ Katharine (1909-), American actress. She had a long career both on Broadway and in Hollywood, and had a famous partnership with Spencer *Tracy, as in *Adam's Rib.*

Hepplewhite /ˈheplwaɪt; *US* ˈheplhwaɪt/ *adj* of a simple elegant style of English furniture developed by the cabinet-maker George Hepplewhite (died 1786). Hepplewhite chairs typically have oval or shield-shaped backs.

heptagon /ˈheptəgən; *US* -gɒn/ *n* geometric figure with seven sides and angles. ▷ **heptagonal** /hepˈtægənl/ *adj.*

Barbara Hepworth: Forms in Movement

Hepworth /ˈhepwəθ/ Barbara (1903-75), British sculptor who specialized in large rounded abstract forms, many of them containing holes with wires stretched across them. She lived and worked in Cornwall, where her studio is now a museum. ⇨ illus.

her[1] /hɜ:(r)/ ⇨ Guide to Entries 5.2 *pers pron* (used as the object of a *v* or of a *prep*; also used independently and after *be*) female person or animal mentioned earlier or being observed now: *We're going to call her Diana.* ○ *Please give her my regards.* ○ *The manager will be free soon — you can wait for her here.* ○ (*infml*) *That must be her now.* ○ (*fig*) *I know that ship well — I've often sailed in her.* Cf SHE. ⇨ Usage at HE.

her[2] /hɜ:(r)/ ⇨ Guide to Entries 5.2 *possess det* of or belonging to a female person or animal mentioned earlier: *Mary's mother is dead but her father is still alive.* ○ *Jane's here, I think — isn't that her coat?* ○ *Fiona has broken her leg.*
▷ **hers** /hɜ:z/ *possess pron* of or belonging to her: *If this isn't Susan's book that one must be hers.* ○ *My mother has a lot of hats so I borrowed one of hers.* ⇨ Usage at HE.

Hera /ˈhɪərə/ (in Greek mythology) wife and sister of *Zeus, worshipped as queen of heaven and goddess of marriage. Her Roman equivalent was *Juno.

Heracles /ˈherəkli:z/ ⇨ HERCULES.

herald /ˈherəld/ *n* **1** (formerly) person who made important announcements and carried messages from a ruler. **2** person or thing that announces or shows that sb/sth is coming: *In England the cuckoo is the herald of spring.* **3** (*Brit*) official who keeps records of families that have coats of arms (COAT).
▷ **herald** *v* [Tn, Tn·p] ~ **sb/sth (in)** announce the approach of sb/sth: *This invention heralded (in) the age of the computer.*
heraldic /heˈrældɪk/ *adj* of heralds or heraldry: *heraldic arms, devices, etc.*
heraldry *n* [U] study of the coats of arms and the history of old families. The use of special pictorial designs relating to particular families originated in western Europe in the 12th century with the need to identify knights in battle. The designs were painted on the knights' shields. Aristocratic families retain them to this day, even though their original purpose has long been superseded. Over the centuries their design has become much more complicated, because when members of two families marry, their coats of arms are combined. In modern times commercial companies have adopted their own coats of arms.

herb /hɜ:b; *US* ɜ:rb/ *n* (**a**) plant with a soft stem that dies down to the ground after flowering. (**b**) plant of this kind whose leaves or seeds, etc are used in medicines and perfumes or for flavouring food: *Sage, mint and dill are all herbs.* ○ [attrib] *a herb garden* ○ *herb tea*, ie drink made by pouring hot water onto dried herbs.
▷ **herbal** /ˈhɜ:bl; *US* ˈɜ:rbl/ *adj* [usu attrib] of herbs used in medicine or for flavouring: *herbal remedies.* — *n* book containing descriptions of these. **herbalist** /ˈhɜ:bəlɪst; *US* ˈɜ:rb-/ *n* person who grows, sells or specializes in herbs for medical use.

herbaceous /hɜ:ˈbeɪʃəs; *US* ɜ:r-/ *adj* of or like herbs.
□ **her,baceous ˈborder** flower-bed in a garden with plants that flower year after year.

herbage /ˈhɜ:bɪdʒ; *US* ˈɜ:r-/ *n* [U] herbs collectively, esp as pasture for cattle, etc; grass and other field plants.

Herbert[1] /ˈhɜ:bət/ A(lan) P(atrick) (1890-1970), English humorous writer who was for 15 years a Member of Parliament.

Herbert[2] /ˈhɜ:bət/ George (1593-1633), English metaphysical poet. He was a clergyman, and much of his poetry is on religious and spiritual themes. It was published in a collection called *The Temple* in the year of his death.

herbicide /ˈhɜ:bɪsaɪd; *US* ˈɜ:r-/ *n* substance that is poisonous to plants, used to destroy weeds, etc.

herbivore /ˈhɜ:bɪvɔ:(r); *US* ˈɜ:r-/ *n* animal that feeds on plants. Cf CARNIVORE.
▷ **herbivorous** /hɜ:ˈbɪvərəs; *US* ɜ:r-/ *adj* (of animals) feeding on plants.

herculean /ˌhɜ:kjʊˈli:ən/ *adj* having or needing very great strength (like that of Hercules): *a herculean task.*

Hercules /ˈhɜ:kjʊli:z/ (in Greek and Roman mythology) extremely strong man who was given, and succeeded in doing, twelve almost impossible tasks (or 'labours') by the king of Argos (eg cleaning the Augean stables and killing the many-headed Hydra). He is shown in pictures with a lion-skin, a club and a bow. The Greek form of his name is Heracles.

herd /hɜ:d/ *n* **1** [C] number of animals, esp cattle, feeding or staying together: *a herd of cows, deer, elephant(s), etc.* **2 the herd** [sing] (*usu derog*) large number of people; mob: *the common herd* ○ *He preferred to stick with the herd* (ie do the same as everyone around him) *so as not to be noticed.*
▷ **herd** *v* **1** [Ipr, Ip, Tn·pr, Tn·p] move or drive (sb/sth) forward as a herd in the specified direction: *The prisoners were herded (together) onto the train.* **2** [Tn] look after (sth) in a herd: *a shepherd herding his flock.*
□ **ˈherd instinct** instinct in people or animals to behave and think like the majority.
herdsman /-mən/ *n* (*pl* **-men** /-mən/) person who looks after a herd of animals.

here /hɪə(r)/ *adv* **1** (**a**) (with a *v* or after a *prep*) in, at or to this position or place: *I live here.* ○ *We leave here tomorrow.* ○ *Fill it up to here.* ○ *Let's get out of here.* ○ *Put the box here.* ○ *Come (over) here.* (**b**) (placed for emphasis at the beginning of a sentence and followed by the finite *v* if the subject is a *n*, but not if the subject is a *pers pron*): *Here comes the bus!* ○ *Here it comes!* ○ *Here are the others!* ○ *Here they are!* ○ *Here we are* (ie We've arrived)*!* **2** at this point (in an activity, a series of events or a situation): *Here the speaker paused to have a drink.* **3** (used for emphasis immediately after a *n* or informally before a *n*): *My friend here saw it happen.* ○ (*infml*) *What do you make of this here letter?* **4** (idm) **(the) ˌhere and ˈnow** (at) the present time. **ˌhere and ˈthere** in various places. **here below** (*rhet*) on earth (contrasted with being in heaven): *Life goes on for those of us who remain here below.* **ˌhere ˈgoes** (*infml*) (used to announce that one is about to do something exciting, risky, etc). **here's to sb/sth** (used when drinking to a person's health or to the success of an enterprise, etc): *Here's to the bride!* ○ *Here's to your future happiness!* **ˌhere, there and ˈeverywhere** in many different places; all around. **here we go again** ⇨ GO[1]. **neither ˈhere nor ˈthere** not important; irrelevant: *The fact that I don't like your fiancé is neither here nor there — what matters is what you feel.*
▷ **here** *interj* **1** (used to call attention to sth or as a command): *Here, let me carry it.* **2** (used as a reply in a roll-call) I am present.
□ **hereabouts** /ˌhɪərəˈbaʊts/ (also **hereabout**) *adv* (*fml*) near this place; around here.
hereafter /ˌhɪərˈɑ:ftə(r); *US* -ˈæf-/ *adv* (*fml*) **1** (in legal documents, etc) from now on; following this. **2** in future. — *n* **the hereafter** [sing] the future; life after death.
hereby /ˌhɪəˈbaɪ/ *adv* (*fml*) by this means; as a result of this.
herein /ˌhɪərˈɪn/ *adv* (*fml*) in this place or document.
hereof /ˌhɪərˈɒv/ *adv* (*arch*) of this.
hereto /ˌhɪəˈtu:/ *adv* (*arch*) to this.
heretofore /ˌhɪətu:ˈfɔ:(r)/ *adv* (*fml*) until now; formerly.
herewith /ˌhɪəˈwɪð, -ˈwɪθ/ *adv* (*fml*) (esp in commercial use) with this (letter, etc): *Please fill in the form enclosed herewith.*

hereditary /hɪˈredɪtrɪ; *US* -terɪ/ *adj* **1** passed on from parent to child, or from one generation to following generations: *hereditary characteristics, features, beliefs* ○ *The disease is hereditary.* **2** holding a position by inheritance: *a hereditary ruler, peer.* ⇨ article at ARISTOCRAT.

heredity /hɪˈredətɪ/ *n* [U] (**a**) passing on of physical or mental characteristics from parents to children by means of information built into the genes. The DNA of which each parent's chromosomes are made carries a set of instructions which determine what their offspring will be like — in the case of a human being, whether he or she will be tall or short, what colour the eyes will be, etc. The mechanism of heredity was discovered by Gregor *Mendel: [attrib] *heredity factors.* (**b**) such characteristics in a particular person: *part of one's heredity.*

Hereford /ˈherɪfəd/ *n* any of a breed of reddish-brown and white cattle reared for their meat.

Hereford and Worcester /ˌherɪfəd ən ˈwʊstə(r)/ county in the West Midlands of England, on the Welsh border, created in 1974 by joining the former counties of Herefordshire and Worcestershire. It is mainly agricultural, producing much fruit. ⇨ map at App 1.

heresy /ˈherəsɪ/ *n* **1** [C] belief or opinion that is contrary to what is generally accepted, esp in religion: *the heresies of the early Protestants.* **2** [U] holding of such an opinion: *be guilty of heresy.*
▷ **heretic** /ˈherətɪk/ *n* person who is guilty of heresy or who supports a heresy.
heretical /hɪˈretɪkl/ *adj* of heresy or heretics: *heretical beliefs.* **heretically** *adv.*

Hereward the Wake /ˌherɪwəd ðə ˈweɪk/ semi-legendary leader of Anglo-Saxon resistance to the invading Normans. He is thought to have organized a revolt at Ely in 1070.

heritable /ˈherɪtəbl/ *adj* (*law*) **1** (of property, etc) that can be inherited. **2** (of a person) able to inherit.

heritage /ˈherɪtɪdʒ/ *n* [C usu *sing*] **1** things such as works of art, cultural achievements and folklore that have been passed on from earlier generations: *our literary heritage* ○ *These ancient buildings are part of the national heritage.* **2** (*dated or fml*) property that has been or may be inherited by an heir.

hermaphrodite /hɜ:ˈmæfrədaɪt/ *n* person or animal that has both male and female sexual organs or characteristics. Cf BISEXUAL, EPICENE. ▷ **hermaphroditic** /hɜ:ˌmæfrəˈdɪtɪk/ *adj.*

Hermes /ˈhɜ:mi:z/ (in Greek mythology) son of *Zeus who acted as messenger of the gods and was also the god of merchants, thieves, heralds, etc. He is shown in pictures as having a broad-brimmed hat, winged shoes, and a winged rod. His Roman equivalent was *Mercury.

hermetic /hɜ:ˈmetɪk/ *adj* tightly closed so that air cannot escape or enter; completely airtight. ▷ **hermetically** /-klɪ/ *adv*: *hermetically sealed containers.*

hermit /ˈhɜ:mɪt/ *n* person (esp a man in early Christian times) who has withdrawn from society and lives completely alone; recluse.
▷ **hermitage** /-ɪdʒ/ *n* place where a hermit or a group of hermits lives.
□ **ˈhermit-crab** *n* type of soft-bodied crab that makes its home in a mollusc's discarded shell.

hernia /ˈhɜ:nɪə/ *n* [U, C] rupture, esp one caused by a part of the bowel being pushed through a weak point of the muscle wall of the abdomen.

hero /ˈhɪərəʊ/ *n* (*pl* ~**es**) **1** person who is admired by many for his noble qualities or his bravery: *receive a hero's welcome*, ie such as is given to returning heroes ○ *He died a hero/a hero's death*, ie died while doing sth very brave or noble. ○ *You're*

my hero, ie I admire you greatly. **2** chief male character in a story, poem, play, etc: *the hero of the novel*. Cf VILLAIN.
▷ **heroine** /ˈherəʊɪn/ *n* female hero.
heroism /ˈherəʊɪzəm/ *n* [U] brave and noble conduct; courage: *an act of great heroism*.
□ ˈ**hero-worship** *n* [U] excessive devotion to a person one admires. — *v* (**-pp-**) [Tn] be excessively devoted to (sb): *pop-stars hero-worshipped by their fans*.

Hero and Leander /ˌhɪərəʊ ən lɪˈændə(r)/ pair of lovers in ancient Greek legend. Leander swam across the *Hellespont every night to be with Hero, a priestess of Aphrodite. One stormy night Leander was drowned; in her grief Hero threw herself into the sea and drowned too.

Herod /ˈherəd/ (also **Herod the Great**) (c 73 BC-4 BC), king of Judea 37 BC-4 BC who according to the Bible had every child in Bethlehem under the age of two killed in an attempt to destroy the newly born Christ.

Herod Antipas /ˌherəd ˈæntɪpæs/ (died c 40 AD), son of Herod the Great and governor of Galilee 4 BC-39 AD who had *John the Baptist beheaded.

heroic /hɪˈrəʊɪk/ *adj* **1** (**a**) having the characteristics of a hero; very brave: *heroic deeds*. (**b**) of heroes: *heroic myths*. **2** of a size larger than in real life: *a statue on a heroic scale*.
▷ **heroically** /-klɪ/ *adv*.
heroics *n* [pl] **1** talk or behaviour that is excessively dramatic: *There is no need to indulge in such heroics*. **2** = HEROIC VERSE.
□ **heˌroic ˈverse** (also **heˌroic ˈcouplets**) verse form used in epic poetry, with lines of ten syllables and five stresses, in rhyming pairs.

heroin /ˈherəʊɪn/ *n* [U] narcotic drug made from morphine, used medically to cause sleep or relieve pain, or by drug addicts. ⇨ article at DRUG.

heroine ⇨ HERO.

heron /ˈherən/ *n* water-bird with a long neck and long legs that lives in marshy places. ⇨ illus at BIRD.
▷ **heronry** *n* place where herons breed.

herpes /ˈhɜːpiːz/ *n* [U] (*medical*) virus disease that causes blisters on the skin.
□ ˌ**herpes ˈsimplex** form of herpes characterized by blisters on the face or genitals.
ˌ**herpes ˈzoster** = SHINGLES.

Herr /heə(r)/ *n* (*pl* **Herren** /ˈherən/) German word for *Mr*; title of a German man.

Herrick /ˈherɪk/ Robert (1591-1674), English poet and friend of Ben *Jonson, best remembered today for his often light-hearted lyrical verse, including 'Cherry Ripe' and 'Gather Ye Rosebuds'.

herring /ˈherɪŋ/ *n* (*pl* unchanged or ~**s**) **1** [U, C] N Atlantic fish, usu swimming in very large shoals, used for food: *a catch of mackerel and herring* ○ *a couple of fresh herring(s)* ○ [attrib] *herring fishermen*. Cf KIPPER, BLOATER. **2** (idm) **neither fish, flesh nor good red herring** ⇨ FISH[1]. **a red herring** ⇨ RED[1].
□ ˈ**herring-bone** *n* [U] zigzag pattern used in stitching and weaving. ⇨ illus at PATTERN.
ˈ**herring gull** large N Atlantic gull with dark wing-tips.

hers ⇨ HER[2].

Herschel /ˈhɜːʃl/ Sir William (1738-1822), German-born astronomer who settled in England and became official astronomer to George III. A careful observer of the sky at night who made his own telescopes, he recorded hundreds of stars and nebulae, and discovered the planet Uranus.

herself /hɜːˈself/ *reflex, emph pron* (only taking the main stress in sentences when used emphatically) **1** (*reflex*) (used when the female doer of an action is also affected by it): *She* ˈ*hurt herself*. ○ *She must be* ˈ*proud of herself*. **2** (*emph*) (used to emphasize the female subject or object of a sentence): *The Prime Minister her*ˈ*self was at the meeting*. ○ *She told me the news her*ˈ*self*. ○ *I saw Jane her*ˈ*self in the supermarket*. **3** (idm) (**all**) **by her**ˈ**self** (**a**) alone: *She lives by herself*. (**b**) without help: *She can mend the fridge by herself*. ⇨ Usage at HE.

Hertfordshire /ˈhɑːfədʃə(r)/ county of England, to the north of London, which is mainly residential and agricultural but also contains some light industry. ⇨ map at App 1.

hertz /hɜːts/ *n* (*pl* unchanged) (*abbr* **Hz**) unit of frequency, equal to one cycle per second.

Herzog /ˈhɜːtzɒg/ Werner (1942-), German film director. His work shows his preoccupation with characters in extreme situations, and gives an epic and pessimistic view of humanity, as in *Aguirre, Wrath of God* and *Fitzcarraldo*.

he's /hiːz/ ⇨ Guide to Entries 5.3 *contracted form* **1** he is ⇨ BE. **2** he has ⇨ HAVE[3].

hesitant /ˈhezɪtənt/ *adj* tending to be slow in speaking or acting because of uncertainty or unwillingness: *a hesitant reply, manner, voice, speaker* ○ *I'm rather hesitant about signing this*.
▷ **hesitancy** /-ənsɪ/ *n* [U] state or quality of being hesitant.
hesitantly *adv*.

hesitate /ˈhezɪteɪt/ *v* **1** [I, Ipr] ~ (**at**/**about**/**over sth**) be slow to speak or act because one feels uncertain or unwilling; pause in doubt: *She replied without hesitating*. ○ *She hesitated before replying*. ○ *He's still hesitating about joining/over whether to join the expedition*. ○ *He hesitates at nothing*. ○ *I'd hesitate before accepting such an offer*. **2** [It] be reluctant: *I hesitate to spend so much money on clothes*. ○ *Don't hesitate to tell us if you have a problem*.
▷ **hesitation** /ˌhezɪˈteɪʃn/ *n* **1** [U] state of hesitating: *She agreed without the slightest hesitation*. ○ *There's no room for hesitation*. **2** [C] instance of hesitating: *His frequent hesitations annoyed the audience*.

hessian /ˈhesɪən; *US* ˈheʃn/ *n* [U] strong coarse cloth of hemp or jute; sack-cloth.

het /het/ *adj* (phr v) (**be**/**get**) **het up** (**about**/**over sth**) (*infml*) (of a person) upset; excited: *What are you getting so het up about?*

hetero- *comb form* other; different: *heterogeneous* ○ *heterosexual*. Cf HOMO-.

heterodox /ˈhetərədɒks/ *adj* not conforming with accepted standards or beliefs: *a heterodox opinion, person*. Cf ORTHODOX, UNORTHODOX. ▷ **heterodoxy** *n* [U, C].

heterogeneous /ˌhetərəˈdʒiːnɪəs/ *adj* made up of different kinds; varied in composition: *the heterogeneous population of the USA*, ie of many different races. ▷ **heterogeneity** /-dʒɪˈniːətɪ/ *n* [U]. **heterogeneously** *adv*. Cf HOMOGENEOUS.

heterosexual /ˌhetərəˈsekʃʊəl/ *adj* feeling sexually attracted to people of the opposite sex. Cf BISEXUAL, HOMOSEXUAL.
▷ **heterosexual** *n* heterosexual person.
heterosexuality /ˌhetərəˌsekʃʊˈælətɪ/ *n* [U].

heterotrophic /ˌhetərəˈtrəʊfɪk/ *adj* (of organisms) that take in organic substances (eg plants or flesh) as food: *Animals are heterotrophic*. Cf AUTOTROPHIC.

heuristic /hjʊəˈrɪstɪk/ *adj* (of a method of teaching) that helps or allows a learner to discover and learn things for himself.
▷ **heuristically** /hjʊəˈrɪstɪklɪ/ *adv*.
heuristics *n* [U] method of solving problems by evaluating past experience and moving by trial and error to a solution.

hew /hjuː/ *v* (*pt* **hewed**, *pp* **hewed** or **hewn** /hjuːn/) **1** [Tn, Tn·pr] chop or cut (sth/sb) with an axe, sword, etc: *hewing wood* ○ *He hewed his enemy to pieces*. **2** [Tn, Tn·p] ~ **sth** (**down**) cause sth to fall by chopping: *hewing (down) trees*. **3** [Tn] shape (sth) by chopping: *roughly hewn timber*. **4** [I, Ipr, Ip] ~ (**away**) (**at**/**among sth**) aim cutting blows at sth: *He was hewing away at the trunk of the tree*. **5** (phr v) **hew sth across, through, etc** (**sth**) make sth by chopping: *They hewed a path through the jungle*. **hew sth away, off, etc** remove sth by chopping: *hew off dead branches*. **hew sth out** make sth by hard work: *hew out a career for oneself*.
▷ **hewer** *n* person who hews, esp one who cuts out coal in a mine.

HEW *abbr* (*US*) Department of Health, Education and Welfare.

hex /heks/ *n* (*US*) **1** magic spell, esp one causing harm: *put a hex on sb*. **2** person who practises witchcraft; witch.
▷ **hex** *v* [Tn] (*US*) put a hex on (sb/sth); harm with an evil spell.

hex(a)- *comb form* having or made up of six of sth: *hexagon* ○ *hexameter*.

hexagon /ˈheksəgən; *US* -gɒn/ *n* geometric figure with six sides and angles.
▷ **hexagonal** /heksˈægənl/ *adj* six-sided.

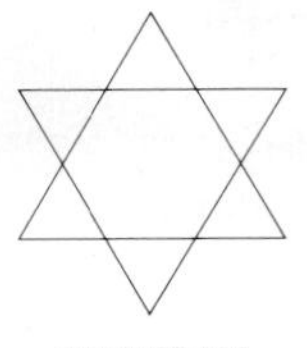
HEXAGRAM

PENTAGRAM

hexagram /ˈheksəgræm/ *n* six-pointed star formed by combining two triangles. Cf STAR OF DAVID (STAR).

hexameter /hekˈsæmɪtə(r)/ *n* line of verse with six metrical feet.

hey /heɪ/ *interj* **1** (also **hi**) (used to call attention or express surprise or inquiry): *Hey, come and look at this!* **2** (idm) **hey presto** (said by a conjuror as he completes a trick successfully, or by sb commenting on or announcing sth that has been done surprisingly easily or quickly): *I just turned the piece of wire in the lock and hey presto, the door opened*.

heyday /ˈheɪdeɪ/ *n* [sing] time of greatest success, prosperity, power, etc: *She was a great singer in her heyday*. ○ *Steam railways had their heyday in the 19th century*.

HF /ˌeɪtʃ ˈef/ *abbr* (*radio*) high frequency. Cf LF.

Hf *symb* hafnium.

HG *abbr* His/Her Grace: *HG the Duke/Duchess of Kent*.

Hg *symb* mercury.

HGV /ˌeɪtʃ dʒiː ˈviː/ *abbr* (*Brit*) heavy goods vehicle, eg a lorry, bus, etc: *have an HGV licence*.

HH *abbr* **1** His/Her Highness: *HH the Prince/Princess of Wales*. **2** His Holiness: *HH the Pope*.

hi /haɪ/ *interj* (*infml*) **1** (*esp US*) = HALLO: *Hi there!* **2** (*Brit*) = HEY.

hiatus /haɪˈeɪtəs/ *n* **1** gap in a series or sequence, making it incomplete; break in continuity. **2** (*linguistics*) break between two vowels coming together but not in the same syllable.

Hiawatha /ˌhaɪəˈwɒθə/ legendary 16th-century North American Indian chieftain. He is the hero of a long poem, *The Song of Hiawatha*, by *Longfellow, which tells the story of his life. The poem's memorably repetitive rhythm, of four beats per line, has often been imitated and parodied.

hibernate /ˈhaɪbəneɪt/ *v* [I] (of animals) spend the winter in a state like deep sleep. ▷ **hibernation** /ˌhaɪbəˈneɪʃn/ *n* [U]: *go into hibernation*.

Hibernian /haɪˈbɜːnɪən/ *n, adj* (*arch*) (native or inhabitant) of Ireland.

hibiscus /hɪˈbɪskəs; *US* haɪ-/ *n* plant or shrub with large brightly coloured flowers, grown esp in tropical countries.

hiccup (also **hiccough**) /ˈhɪkʌp/ *n* **1** (**a**) [C] sudden involuntary stopping of the breath with a sharp gulp-like sound, often recurring at short intervals: *give a loud hiccup*. (**b**) **hiccups** [pl] persistent repetition of these: *She laughed so much she got (the) hiccups*. **2** [C] (*infml*) temporary small problem or stoppage: *There's been a slight hiccup in our mailing system*.
▷ **hiccup** (also **hiccough**) *v* [I] make a hiccup(1).

hick /hɪk/ *n* (*infml derog esp US*) **1** awkward or foolish country person; bumpkin. **2** [attrib] provincial; not sophisticated: *a hick town*.

hickey /ˈhɪkɪ/ *n* (*US infml*) **1** gadget; device **2** pimple; blemish.

hickory /ˈhɪkərɪ/ *n* (**a**) N American tree with edible nuts. (**b**) its hard wood: [attrib] *a hickory walking-stick*.

hide[1] /haɪd/ *v* (*pt* **hid** /hɪd/, *pp* **hidden** /ˈhɪdn/) **1** (**a**)

[Tn, Tn·pr, Tn·p] prevent (sth/sb/oneself) from being seen; put or keep out of sight: *The sun was hidden by the clouds.* ○ *The trees hid the house from view.* ○ *He hid the gun in his pocket.* ○ *She's hidden my book (away) somewhere.* **(b)** [I, Ipr, Ip] be or get out of sight; be or become concealed: *Quick, run and hide!* ○ *The child was hiding behind the sofa.* ○ *(fig) She hid behind a false identity.* ○ *The wanted man hid (away) in the forest.* **2** [Tn, Tn·pr] ~ **sth (from sb)** prevent sth from being known; keep sth secret: *She tried to hide her feelings.* ○ *The future is hidden from us.* ○ *His words had a hidden meaning.* **3** (idm) **bury/hide one's head in the sand** ⇨ HEAD[1]. **cover/hide a multitude of sins** ⇨ MULTITUDE. **hide one's ˌlight under a ˈbushel** hide one's talents, abilities or good qualities because of modesty, etc.

▷ **hide** *n* (*Brit*) (*US* **blind**) place where naturalists, hunters, etc can watch wild animals or birds without being seen by them.

hiding *n* [U] (idm) **ˌgo into/ˌcome out of ˈhiding** hide/reveal oneself. **in ˈhiding** hidden: *He stayed in hiding for a year.*

□ **hide-and-seek** /ˌhaɪdnˈsiːk/ *n* [U] children's game in which one player hides and the others try to find him.

ˈhide-out (*US* also **ˈhideaway**) *n* hiding-place for people: *a guerrilla hide-out in the mountains.*

ˈhiding-place *n* place where sb/sth is or could be hidden.

hide[2] /haɪd/ *n* **1** [C, U] animal's skin, esp when bought and sold or used for making sth: *boots made of buffalo hide.* **2** [U] (*infml joc*) human skin. **3** (idm) **have, etc a hide/skin like a rhinoceros** ⇨ RHINOCEROS. **neither hide nor ˈhair of sb/sth** no trace of sb/sth: *I've not seen hide nor hair of him all week.* **save one's hide** ⇨ SAVE[1]. **tan sb's hide** ⇨ TAN.

hidebound /ˈhaɪdbaʊnd/ *adj* (*derog*) not willing to consider new ideas, methods, etc; too conventional and narrow-minded: *hidebound bureaucrats, views* ○ *a society hidebound by convention.*

hideous /ˈhɪdɪəs/ *adj* filling the mind with horror; very ugly; frightful: *a hideous crime, face, noise, creature* ○ (*infml*) *I think the colour scheme they've chosen is hideous.* ▷ **hideously** *adv*: *be hideously deformed.* **hideousness** *n* [U].

hiding[1] ⇨ HIDE[1].

hiding[2] /ˈhaɪdɪŋ/ *n* **1** (*infml*) beating; thrashing: *His dad gave him a good hiding.* **2** (idm) **on a ˌhiding to ˈnothing** (*infml*) with no chance at all of succeeding.

hie /haɪ/ *v* (*pt* **hied**, *pres part* **hieing** or **hying**) [Ipr, Tn·pr] ~ **oneself to sth** (*arch or joc*) go quickly: *Hie (thee) to thy chamber.*

hierarchy /ˈhaɪərɑːkɪ/ *n* system with grades of authority or status from the lowest to the highest: *She's high up in the management hierarchy.* ○ *There is a hierarchy in the classification of all living creatures.*

▷ **hierarchical** /ˌhaɪəˈrɑːkɪkl/ *adj* of or arranged in a hierarchy: *a hierarchical society, system, organization, etc.*

hieroglyph /ˈhaɪərəglɪf/ *n* **1** picture or symbol of an object, representing a word, syllable or sound, as used in ancient Egyptian and other writing. **2** written symbol with a secret or hidden meaning. ▷ **hieroglyphic** /ˌhaɪərəˈglɪfɪk/ *adj* of or written in hieroglyphs.

hieroglyphics *n* [pl] hieroglyphs: *deciphering Egyptian hieroglyphics* ○ *His writing is so bad it just looks like hieroglyphics to me.*

hi-fi /ˈhaɪfaɪ/ *adj* [usu attrib] (*infml*) = HIGH FIDELITY (HIGH[1]): *hi-fi records, tapes, radios.*

▷ **hi-fi** *n* [C, U] (*infml*) hi-fi equipment: *You must hear my new hi-fi.*

higgledy-piggledy /ˌhɪgldɪ ˈpɪgldɪ/ *adv, adj* [usu pred] (*infml*) without order; completely mixed up: *Files were scattered (all) higgledy-piggledy about the office.*

high[1] /haɪ/ *adj* (**-er**, **-est**) **1 (a)** (of things) extending far upwards; having a relatively big distance from the base to the top: *a high fence, forehead, mountain* ○ *high heels* ○ *How high is Mt Everest?* **(b)** having a specified distance from the base to the top: *knee-high boots* ○ *The wall is six feet high.* **(c)** situated far above the ground or above sea-level: *a high ceiling, shelf* ○ *fly at a high altitude.* **(d)** being above the normal level: *a jersey with a high neck.* **(e)** (of a physical action) performed at or reaching a considerable distance above ground: *a high dive, kick.* ⇨ Usage at HEIGHT. Cf LOW[1]. **2** [usu attrib] ranking above others in importance or quality: *a high official* ○ *a man of high standing* ○ *refer a case to a higher court* ○ *high society*, ie the upper classes ○ *I have this information on the highest authority.* **3 (a)** above the normal; extreme; intense: *a high price, temperature, fever, speed, wind, living standard* ○ *high voltage, blood pressure, praise* ○ *The cost in terms of human life was high.* ○ *I have high hopes of passing the exam.* ○ *A high degree of accuracy is needed.* ○ *be in high spirits*, ie be very cheerful ○ *a high Tory*, ie one holding traditional Conservative opinions. **(b)** of great value: *play for high stakes* ○ *My highest card is a ten.* **(c)** [attrib] extravagant; luxurious: *indulge in high living* ○ *enjoy the high life.* **(d)** [usu attrib] (of aims, ideas, etc) morally good; noble; virtuous: *have high ideals* ○ *a woman of high principle.* **(e)** [usu attrib] very favourable: *have a high opinion of/high regard for sb.* **(f)** [attrib] (most) enjoyable: *the high point of the evening.* **4** (of a sound) at or near the top of the musical scale; not deep or low: *the high voice of a child* ○ *The note was too high for him.* **5** [attrib] (of time) fully reached: *high noon* ○ *high summer*, ie the middle of the summer. **6** (of a gear) allowing greater speed of a vehicle in relation to its engine speed: *You can change into a higher gear now you're going faster.* **7** [pred] (of meat, etc) beginning to go bad: *Some game-birds are kept until they are high before cooking.* **8** [usu pred] ~ **(on sth)** (*infml*) under the influence of (esp drugs or alcohol): *be/get high on cannabis.* **9** (idm) **be/get on one's ˌhigh ˈhorse** (*infml*) act haughtily. **have/give sb a ˈhigh old time** (*infml*) enjoy oneself/entertain sb in a very exuberant or jolly way. **hell or high water** ⇨ HELL. **ˌhigh and ˈdry** (of a ship) stranded; aground: *(fig) He left her high and dry in a strange country without any money.* **ˌhigh and ˈmighty** (*infml*) arrogant; haughty: *There's no need to be/get so high and mighty with me!* **ˌhigh days and ˈholidays** festivals and special occasions. **ˌhigh ˈjinks** (*infml*) noisy and mischievous fun. **a high/low profile** ⇨ PROFILE. **high/about time** ⇨ TIME[1]. **high, wide and handsome** in a carefree or stylish manner: *riding her horse all high wide and handsome.* **in ˌhigh ˈdudgeon** angry and indignant: *He stalked off in high dudgeon.* **in ˌhigh ˈplaces** among people of power and influence: *She has friends in high places.* **smell, stink, etc to high ˈheaven** (*infml*) **(a)** have a strong unpleasant smell. **(b)** seem to be very dishonest, corrupt, etc: *The whole scheme stinks to high heaven — don't get involved in it.*

□ **ˈhighbinder** *n* (*US infml*) **1** gangster hired to kill sb. **2** corrupt politician.

ˈhigh-born *adj* of noble birth.

ˌhigh ˈchair infant's chair with long legs and an attached tray, for use at meals. ⇨ illus at FURNITURE.

ˌHigh ˈChurch section of the Church of England that emphasizes ritual, the authority of bishops and priests, and historical links with the Catholic Church. It originated in the mid 19th-century *Oxford Movement: (*infml*) *The whole family is very High Church.* **ˌHigh-ˈChurchman** /-mən/ *n* (*pl* **-men** /-mən/).

ˌhigh-ˈclass *adj* **1** of high quality; excellent: *a ˌhigh-class ˈrestaurant.* **2** of high social class.

ˌhigh ˈcolour unusually red complexion.

ˌhigh comˈmand (headquarters of the) commander of an army and his staff.

ˌHigh Comˈmission embassy of one Commonwealth country in another. Cf CONSULATE 1. **ˌHigh Comˈmissioner** head of this (equivalent to an ambassador). Cf CONSUL 1.

ˌHigh ˈCourt (also **ˌHigh Court of ˈJustice**) supreme court for civil cases.

ˌhigher ˈanimals, ˈplants, etc animals, plants, etc that are highly developed and have a complex structure.

ˌhigher eduˈcation education and training at universities, polytechnics, etc.

ˌhighest ˌcommon ˈfactor (*abbr* **HCF**) (also **ˌgreatest ˌcommon diˈvisor**) largest number that can be divided exactly into each of two or more other numbers: *7 is the highest common factor of 21 and 35.*

ˌhigh exˈplosive very powerful explosive with a violent shattering effect.

ˌhigh-faˈlutin /ˌhaɪ fəˈluːtn/ *adj* (*infml*) pompous; pretentious: *high-falutin ideas, language.*

ˌhigh fiˈdelity (also **ˈhi-fi**) reproduction of sound (by radios, record-players, tape-recorders, etc) that is of high quality, with little or no distortion of the original sound.

ˌhigh ˈfinance professional handling of large financial transactions (eg by merchant banks or stockbrokers).

ˌhigh-ˈflown *adj* (of language, etc) extravagantly grand and pretentious.

ˌhigh-ˈflyer (also **high-flier**) *n* person with the ability or ambition to be very successful. **ˌhigh-ˈflying** *adj.*

ˌhigh ˈfrequency (*abbr* **HF**) radio frequency of 3 to 30 megahertz.

ˌHigh ˈGerman standard written and spoken German.

ˌhigh-ˈgrade *adj* of high quality: *ˌhigh-grade ˈpetrol.*

ˌhigh-ˈhanded *adj* using power or authority without considering the opinions and wishes of others: *a ˌhigh-handed ˈperson, ˈaction.* **ˌhigh-ˈhandedly** *adv.* **ˌhigh-ˈhandedness** *n* [U].

ˌhigh-ˈhat *adj* (*infml*) behaving as if one were better than others; supercilious. — *v* (**-tt-**) [I, Tn] (*infml esp US*) behave or treat (sb) in a high-hat way.

ˌhigh ˈholiday either of two Jewish religious holidays, New Year or *Yom Kippur.

the ˈhigh jump 1 athletic contest of jumping as high as possible, over an adjustable horizontal bar: *enter for the high jump.* **2** (idm) **be for the high jump** (*infml*) be likely to be severely punished: *If you're caught stealing you'll be for the high jump.*

ˈhighland /-lənd/ *adj* **1** of or in mountainous regions. **2 Highland** of or in the Scottish Highlands: *Highland cattle* ○ *Highland dress.* — *n* **1** [C usu *pl*] mountainous part of a country. **2 the Highlands** [pl] the mountainous part of Scotland. ⇨ map at UNITED KINGDOM. **ˈhighlander** *n* person who lives in the Scottish Highlands.

ˌHighland ˈfling lively Scottish dance.

ˌHighland ˈGames (also **ˌHighland ˈGathering**) traditional Scottish outdoor event which includes various sports (eg tossing the caber) and also dancing, playing the bagpipes, etc.

ˈHighland Region administrative area of northern Scotland, to the north of the *Grampian mountains.

the ˌHighlands and ˈIslands northern Scotland, including Highland Region and the major island groups (the *Hebrides, the *Orkneys and the *Shetlands).

ˌhigh-ˈlevel *adj* [usu attrib] (of negotiations, etc) involving very senior people: *ˌhigh-level ˈtalks, ˈconferences, etc.*

ˌhigh-level ˈlanguage computer language that is close to ordinary language and usu not machine-readable.

ˈhigh life (in W Africa) popular style of music and dance.

ˌhigh ˈmass formal celebration of a Roman Catholic mass that is sung.

high-minded /ˌhaɪ ˈmaɪndɪd/ *adj* having or showing a noble and virtuous character. **ˌhigh-ˈmindedly** *adv.* **ˌhigh-ˈmindedness** *n* [U].

ˌhigh-ˈoctane *adj* (of petrol) having a high percentage of a certain octane and thus of good quality.

ˌhigh-ˈpitched *adj* **1** (of sounds) shrill; high in pitch[3](3a): *a ˌhigh-pitched ˈwhine.* **2** (of roofs) steeply sloping.

ˌhigh-ˈpowered *adj* [usu attrib] **1** (of things) having great power: *a ˌhigh-powered ˈcar, ˈrifle, ˈengine.* **2** (of people) forceful and energetic: *high-powered business executives.*

ˌhigh ˈpressure 1 condition of the atmosphere with pressure above average: *a ridge of high pressure.* **2** energetic activity and effort: *work at high pressure* ○ [attrib] *ˌhigh-pressure* (ie aggressive and persistent) *ˈsalesmanship.*

ˌhigh-ˈpriced *adj* expensive.

ˌhigh ˈpriest chief priest: (*fig*) *the high priest of modern technology.*

ˌhigh-ˈprincipled *adj* honourable: *a ˌhigh-principled ˈperson, ˈdeed.*

ˌhigh-ˈranking *adj* of high rank; senior: *a ˌhigh-ranking ˈarmy officer.*

ˈhigh-rise *adj* [attrib] (of a building) very tall, with many storeys: *a high-rise office block.* — *n* such a building.

ˈhigh road main road: (*fig*) *take the high road* (ie the most direct way) *to happiness.*

ˈhigh school (*esp US*) secondary school; school providing more advanced education than a primary or middle school.

the ˌhigh ˈsea (also **the high seas**) the open seas beyond the legal control of any one country.

ˌhigh ˈseason time of year when most visitors regularly come to a resort, etc: *Hotels usually raise their prices in (the) high season.*

ˈhigh-sounding *adj* (of language, etc) pretentious; high-flown.

ˌhigh-ˈspeed *adj* [usu attrib] (that can be) operated at great speeds.

ˌhigh-ˈspirited *adj* **1** lively and cheerful; vivacious. **2** (of a horse) frisky.

ˈhigh spot (*infml*) outstanding event, memory, etc; most important feature: *The excursion was the high spot of our holiday.*

ˈhigh street (esp in names) main street of a town, with shops, etc: *Oxford High Street* ○ [attrib] *high-street banks, shops, etc.*

ˌhigh ˈtable table on a raised platform where the most important people at a public dinner or in a college sit to eat: *dine on high table.*

hightail /ˈhaɪteɪl/ *v* (idm) **hightail it** (*sl esp US*) leave in a hurry; run (away) quickly: *The robbers hightailed it out of town.*

ˌhigh ˈtea (*Brit*) early evening meal of cooked food, usu with tea.

ˌhigh-ˈtech *adj* (*infml*) **1** involving high technology. **2** (of interior design, etc) imitating styles more common in industry, etc.

ˌhigh techˈnology advanced technological development.

ˌhigh ˈtension high voltage: [attrib] *ˌhigh-tension ˈcables.*

ˌhigh ˈtide (**a**) tide when at its highest level. (**b**) time when this occurs.

ˌhigh ˈtreason treason against one's country or ruler.

ˈhigh-up *n* (*infml*) person of high rank.

ˌhigh ˈwater = HIGH TIDE. **ˌhigh-ˈwater mark 1** mark showing the highest level reached by the sea or by flood waters. **2** (*fig*) highest point of achievement.

ˌhigh ˈwire high tightrope.

high² /haɪ/ *n* **1** high or highest level or number: *Profits reached a new high last year.* **2** area of high barometric pressure; anticyclone: *A high over southern Europe is bringing fine sunny weather to all parts.* **3** (*sl*) feeling of extreme pleasure or excitement caused by a drug. **4** (idm) **on ˈhigh** (**a**) in a high place: *The climbers gazed down from on high.* (**b**) in heaven: *God on high* ○ *The disaster was seen as a judgement from on high.*

high³ /haɪ/ *adv* **1** at or to a high position or level: *An eagle circled high overhead.* ○ *I can't jump any higher.* ○ *He never got very high in the company.* ○ *aim high*, ie be ambitious ○ *pay high*, ie pay a high price. **2** (of sound) at or to a high pitch: *I can't sing that high.* **3** (idm) **be/stand ˌhigh in sb's ˈfavour** be well regarded by sb. **fly high** ⇨ FLY². **ˌhigh and ˈlow** everywhere: *I've searched high and low for my lost pen.* **hold one's head high** ⇨ HEAD¹. **play ˈhigh** play a card of high value. **ride high** ⇨ RIDE². **run ˈhigh** (**a**) (of the sea) have a strong current with a high tide. (**b**) (esp of feelings) be intense: *Passions ran high as the election approached.*

highball /ˈhaɪbɔːl/ *n* (*US*) drink of spirits mixed with soda water, ginger ale, etc and served with ice in a tall glass.

highboy /ˈhaɪbɔɪ/ *n* (*US*) = TALLBOY.

highbrow /haɪbraʊ/ *n* (*often derog*) person who has or is thought to have superior intellectual and cultural tastes. ▷ **highbrow** *adj*: *highbrow drama, books, interests.* Cf LOWBROW, MIDDLE-BROW (MIDDLE).

highlight /ˈhaɪlaɪt/ *n* **1** best, most interesting or most exciting part of something: *The highlight of our tour was seeing the palace.* ○ *The highlights of the match will be shown on TV tonight.* **2** (usu *pl*) (**a**) light or bright part of a picture, photograph, etc. (**b**) bright tint in the hair.

▷ **highlight** *v* [Tn] **1** give special attention to (sth); emphasize: *a TV programme highlighting the problems of the unemployed.* **2** bleach or tint (parts of the hair) so that it reflects the light. **highlighter** *n* marker pen used to draw attention to a written or printed word by covering it with a transparent colouring.

highly /ˈhaɪlɪ/ *adv* **1** to an unusually great extent; very: *a highly amusing film* ○ *be highly probable, contagious, inflammable* ○ *The goods on display are all very highly priced.* **2** very favourably: *think highly of sb*, ie have a high opinion of sb ○ *speak highly of sb*, ie praise sb.

□ **ˌhighly-ˈstrung** *adj* (of a person) very sensitive and nervous; easily upset.

highness /ˈhaɪnɪs/ *n* (usu **Highness**) title used in speaking to or of a member of the royal family: *His/Her/Your Royal Highness* ○ *Their Royal Highnesses the Duke and Duchess of Kent.*

highway /ˈhaɪweɪ/ *n* **1** (*esp US*) main public road. **2** direct route by air, sea or land: (*fig*) *We are on the highway to progress.*

□ **ˌHighway ˈCode** (*Brit*) set of official rules for users of public roads; book containing these. ⇨ Usage at ROAD.

ˈhighwayman /-mən/ *n* (*pl* **-men** /-mən/) (formerly) man, usu armed and on horseback, who robbed travellers on public roads.

Highwaymen are often imagined to have been courageous adventurers who led exciting and colourful lives. This romantic image comes from fanciful stories about the lives of famous highwaymen in British history, such as Dick *Turpin, whose exploits made them legendary figures.

hijack /ˈhaɪdʒæk/ *v* [Tn] **1** seize control of (a vehicle, esp an aircraft) in order to force it to go to a new destination, to take its passengers hostage or to steal its cargo: *The plane was hijacked while on a flight to Delhi.* **2** steal (goods) from a vehicle.

▷ **hijack** *n* instance of hijacking.

hijacker *n* person who hijacks a vehicle.

hijacking *n* [C, U]: *prevent (a) hijacking.*

hike /haɪk/ *n* **1** long walk, esp in the country, taken for pleasure or exercise: *go on a ten-mile hike.* Cf RAMBLE 1.

Hiking used to be a favourite British weekend or holiday pastime. In the 1930s especially, the image of hikers enjoying the healthy outdoor life was often used in advertising. Hikers were shown walking in pairs or groups with walking shoes and sturdy walking-sticks, and carrying knapsacks on their backs. Cross-country walking of this type is still popular, but is now generally called 'rambling'.

2 (*infml*) rise in prices, costs, etc: *The union demands a 7% wage hike.*

▷ **hike** *v* **1** [I] go for a long walk: *a hiking holiday.* **2** [Tn, Tn·p] ~ **sth** (**up**) (*infml*) (*esp US*) raise (prices, etc): *hike (up) an insurance claim.* **hiker** *n* person who hikes.

hilarious /hɪˈleərɪəs/ *adj* (**a**) extremely amusing; very funny: *a hilarious account of their camping holiday.* (**b**) noisily merry: *a hilarious party.*

▷ **hilariously** *adv*: *be hilariously funny.*

hilarity /hɪˈlærətɪ/ *n* [U] loud laughter; great amusement: *The announcement was greeted with much hilarity and mirth.*

Hilary term /ˈhɪlərɪ tɜːm/ (at Oxford and some other universities) term that begins in January.

hill /hɪl/ *n* **1** natural elevation on the earth's surface, not as high or rugged as a mountain: *a range of hills* ○ *The house is on the side of a hill.* **2** slope in a road, etc: *push one's bike up a steep hill* **3** (esp in compounds) heap of earth; mound: *an ˈanthill* ○ *a ˈmolehill.* **4** (idm) **a hill of ˈbeans** (*US infml*) thing of little value: *It's not worth a hill of beans*, ie It is worth very little. **old as the hills** ⇨ OLD. **over the ˈhill** (*infml*) (of a person) past one's prime; old. **up ˌhill and down ˈdale** everywhere: *We've been chasing up hill and down dale trying to find you.*

▷ **hilly** /ˈhɪlɪ/ *adj* having many hills: *hilly countryside.* **hilliness** *n* [U].

□ **ˈhill figure** figure (eg of a human being or a horse) cut into a chalk or limestone hillside, so that it appears white against the green grass Several such figures were made by prehistoric people in southern England.

ˈhill-fort *n* ancient settlement on top of a hill protected by a high earth wall, built by European *Iron Age peoples.

ˈhillside *n* sloping side of a hill.

ˈhill-station *n* (esp during British rule in India) settlement in the hills of northern India used for holidays, etc during the very hot weather of summer.

ˈhilltop *n* top of a hill.

Hillary /ˈhɪlərɪ/ Sir Edmund Percival (1919-), New Zealand mountaineer who in 1953 became one of the first two men (with the Sherpa Tenzing Norgay) to reach the top of Mount *Everest.

hill-billy /ˈhɪl bɪlɪ/ *n* **1** [C] (*US infml usu derog*) unsophisticated person from a remote rural area esp the mountains in the south-eastern US. **2** [U] folk music like that of the southern US.

Hilliard /ˈhɪlɪəd/ Nicholas (1537-1619), English painter who specialized in very small pictures (*miniatures*), mainly portraits.

hillock /ˈhɪlək/ *n* small hill; mound.

hilt /hɪlt/ *n* **1** handle of a sword, dagger, etc. ⇨ illus at SWORD. **2** (idm) (**up**) **to the ˈhilt** completely: *be up to the hilt in debt* ○ *be mortgaged up to the hilt* ie have an extremely high mortgage ○ *I'll support you to the hilt.*

him /hɪm/ *pers pron* (used as the object of a *v* or of a *prep*; also used independently or after *be*) male person or animal mentioned earlier or being observed now: *When did you see him?* ○ *I'm taller than him.* ○ (*infml*) *That's him over there.* ○ *Oh, not ˈhim again!* ⇨ Usage at HE.

Himalayas /ˌhɪməˈleɪəz *or, rarely*, hɪˈmɑːlɪəz/ **the Himalayas** range of mountains extending along the northern border of India. It includes Mount *Everest, the highest mountain in the world, and several other very tall peaks. ▷ **Himalayan** /ˌhɪməˈleɪən/ *adj.*

himself /hɪmˈself/ *reflex, emph pron* (only taking the main stress when used emphatically) **1** (*reflex*) (used when the male doer of an action is also affected by it): *He ˈcut himself.* ○ *Peter ought to be aˈshamed of himself.* **2** (*emph*) (used to emphasize the male subject or object of a sentence): *The doctor said so himˈself.* ○ *Did you see the manager himˈself?* **3** (idm) (**all**) **by himˈself** (**a**) alone: *He lives all by himself in that large house.* (**b**) without help: *John managed to repair his car by himself.* ⇨ Usage at HE.

hind¹ /haɪnd/ *adj* **1** (of things in pairs) situated at the back: *a dog's hind legs.* Cf FORE¹. **2** (idm) **on one's hind ˈlegs** (*joc*) on one's feet; standing: *Get up on your hind legs and do some work!* **talk the hind legs off a donkey** ⇨ TALK².

▷ **ˈhindmost** *adj* (*dated*) **1** furthest behind **2** (idm) **the devil take the hindmost** ⇨ DEVIL¹.

□ **ˌhindˈquarters** *n* [pl] back parts of a four-legged animal including the back legs. ⇨ illus at HORSE

hind² /haɪnd/ *n* (*pl* unchanged or ~**s**) female deer esp red deer. Cf DOE, HART.

hinder /ˈhɪndə(r)/ *v* [Tn, Tn·pr] ~ **sb/sth** (**from sth/doing sth**) prevent the progress of sb/sth; obstruct or delay sb/sth: *hinder sb (from working,*

○ *hinder sb in his work* ○ *Production was hindered by lack of materials.*

Hindi /ˈhɪndi:/ *adj, n* [U] (of) one of the official languages of India, spoken esp in N India.

hindrance /ˈhɪndrəns/ *n* **1** ~ (**to sth/sb**) thing or person that hinders: *Some kitchen gadgets are more of a hindrance than a help.* **2** (idm) **without let or hindrance** ➪ LET[3].

hindsight /ˈhaɪndsaɪt/ *n* [U] wisdom about an event after it has occurred: *We failed, and with (the benefit of) hindsight I now see where we went wrong.* Cf FORESIGHT.

Hindu /ˌhɪnˈdu:; *US* ˈhɪndu:/ *n* person whose religion is Hinduism.

▷ **Hindu** *adj* of the Hindus or Hinduism.

Hinduism /ˈhɪndu:ɪzəm/ *n* [U] Indian religion, philosophy and social system characterized by belief in reincarnation, worship of several gods, and the caste system. Its three main gods are *Brahma, *Siva and *Vishnu. Hindus consider that all the things they do in their lives have an effect on the form in which they will be reincarnated. ➪ article at RELIGION.

Hindustani /ˌhɪndʊˈstɑ:ni:/ *n* [U] (former name for) dialect of Hindi spoken in Delhi, and also used widely throughout the rest of India, containing many Arabic and Persian words. ▷ **Hindustani** *adj.*

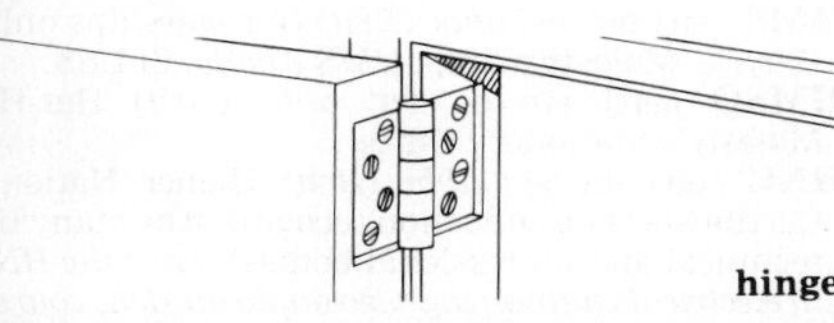

hinge

hinge /hɪndʒ/ *n* piece of metal, etc on which a lid, door, or gate turns or swings as it opens and closes: *take the door off its hinges and rehang it* ○ *The gate hinges need oiling — they're squeaking.* ➪ illus.

▷ **hinge** *v* **1** [I, Tn esp passive] be attached or attach (sth) by a hinge or hinges: *The rear door hinges/is hinged at the top so that it opens upwards.* **2** (phr v) **hinge on sth** depend on sth: *Everything hinges on the outcome of these talks.*

hinny /ˈhɪnɪ/ *n* animal whose female parent is an ass and whose male parent is a horse.

hint /hɪnt/ *n* **1** subtle way of indicating to sb what one is thinking or what one wants; indirect suggestion: *a strong, broad, gentle, delicate, etc hint* ○ *She coughed to give him the hint that he should go.* **2** slight indication; trace: *There was more than a hint of sadness in his voice.* ○ *The calm sea gave no hint of the storm that was coming.* **3** small piece of practical information or advice; tip: *helpful hints for plant lovers.* **4** (idm) **drop a hint** ➪ DROP[2]. **take a ˈhint** understand and do what has been indirectly suggested: *I thought they'd never go — some people just can't take a hint!*

▷ **hint** *v* [Ipr, Tn, Dn·pr, Dpr·f] ~ **at sth**; ~ **sth (to sb)** suggest sth slightly or indirectly: *The possibility of an early election has been hinted at.* ○ *She has already hinted (to me) that I've won the prize.*

hinterland /ˈhɪntəlænd/ *n* (usu *sing*) **1** area lying inland from the coast or away from a river. **2** part of a country that is served by a port or some other centre.

hip[1] /hɪp/ *n* **1** part on either side of the body below the waist where the bone of a person's leg is joined to the trunk: *He stood with his hands on his hips.* ○ *I'm quite wide round/in the hips.* ○ *break one's hip,* ie break the top of one's thigh-bone. ○ [attrib] *the hip-bone* ○ *one's hip measurement.* **2** (idm) **shoot from the hip** ➪ SHOOT[1].

▷ **-hipped** (forming compound *adjs*) having hips of the specified size, shape, etc: *a large-hipped girl.*

□ **ˈhip-bath** *n* portable tub in which one sits immersed up to the hips.

ˈhip-flask *n* small bottle for spirits, with flat or curved sides for carrying in the hip-pocket.

ˌhip-ˈpocket *n* trouser pocket just behind the hips.

hip[2] /hɪp/ (also **ˈrose-hip**) *n* berry-like fruit of the wild rose, red when ripe.

hip[3] /hɪp/ *interj* (idm) **hip, hip, hurrah/hurray** (used as a cheer to express general satisfaction or approval).

hip[4] /hɪp/ *adj* (*dated sl*) fashionable; trendy; up-to-date.

hippie (also **hippy**) /ˈhɪpɪ/ *n* young person who rejects the conformity, materialism and aggression of modern society. Since coming to prominence in the 1960s hippies have typically become associated with unconventional dress, long hair, the use of drugs and belief in universal peace and love. Cf BEATNIK.

hippo /ˈhɪpəʊ/ *n* (*pl* ~**s**) (*infml*) = HIPPOPOTAMUS.

Hippocratic oath /ˌhɪpəkrætɪk ˈəʊθ/ **the Hippocratic oath** oath to observe the medical code of ethical and professional behaviour, sworn by doctors when they become qualified.

hippodrome /ˈhɪpədrəʊm/ *n* **1** (esp in names) dance-hall or music-hall; theatre or cinema: *the Brighton Hippodrome.* **2** (in ancient Greece or Rome) course for horse or chariot races.

hippopotamus

hippopotamus /ˌhɪpəˈpɒtəməs/ *n* (*pl* **-muses** /-məsɪz/ or **-mi** /-maɪ/) (also **hippo**) large African river animal with short legs and thick dark skin. ➪ illus.

hippy = HIPPIE.

hipster /ˈhɪpstə(r)/ *adj* [attrib] (of a garment) having its top part around the hips rather than the waist: *hipster jeans, briefs, etc.*

hire /ˈhaɪə(r)/ *v* **1** [Tn, Tn·pr] ~ **sth/sb (from sb)** obtain the use of sth or the services of sb temporarily and esp for a short period of time, in return for payment: *hire a bicycle, hall, wedding-dress* ○ *a hired car* ○ *a hired assassin* ○ *hire a dozen men to dig a ditch.* **2** [Tn, Tn·pr, Tn·p] ~ **sth (out) (to sb)** allow the temporary use of sth, in return for payment: *We hire out our vans by the day,* ie at a cost of a certain amount per day. ➪ Usage at LET[2].

▷ **hire** *n* [U] **1** hiring: *have the hire of a car for a week* ○ *bicycles for hire, £1 an hour* ○ *pay for the hire of a hall* ○ *This suit is on hire.* ○ [attrib] *a car hire firm* ○ *a hire car.* **2** payment for hiring sth/sb: *work for hire.* **3** (idm) **ply for hire** ➪ PLY[2].

hireable /ˈhaɪərəbl/ *adj* (of an object) that may be hired.

hireling /ˈhaɪəlɪŋ/ *n* (*usu derog*) person whose services may be hired.

□ **ˌhired ˈhand** (*US*) person hired to work as a labourer on a farm.

ˌhire-ˈpurchase *n* [U] (*Brit*) (*abbr* **hp**) (also *esp US* **inˈstalment plan**) method of purchase by which the buyer pays for an article in instalments, is allowed to use it immediately and becomes the owner of it after a certain number of instalments have been paid: *We're buying a TV on hire-purchase.* ○ [attrib] *a hire-purchase agreement.*

Hiroshima /hɪˈrɒʃɪmə; *US* ˌhɪrəˈʃi:mə/ Japanese city on which the USA dropped an atom bomb on 6 August 1945, the first such bomb used in war. This, together with the bombing of *Nagasaki, forced Japan to surrender, so ending the Second World War.

hirsute /ˈhɜ:sju:t; *US* -su:t/ *adj* (*fml*) (esp of a man) covered with hair; hairy; shaggy: (*joc*) *You're looking very hirsute, Richard — are you growing a beard?*

his /hɪz/ ➪ Guide to Entries 5.2 *possess det* of or belonging to a male person or animal mentioned earlier: *James has sold his car.* ○ *He claims it was ˈhis idea.* ○ *His speech on unemployment was well received.*

▷ **his** *possess pron* of or belonging to him: *My address is No 22 Laburnum Close so his must be No 26.* ○ *Learning to ski has always been an ambition of his.* ➪ Usage at HE.

Hispanic /hɪˈspænɪk/ *adj* **1** of Spain and Portugal. **2** of Spain and other Spanish-speaking countries.

Hispaniola /ˌhɪspænˈjəʊlə/ large island in the *Caribbean, containing the modern states of *Haiti and the *Dominican Republic. ➪ map at CARIBBEAN.

hiss /hɪs/ *v* **1** [I, Ipr] ~ **(at sb/sth)** make a sound like that of a long 's': *The steam escaped with a loud hissing noise.* ○ *A fire hisses if water is thrown on it.* ○ *The goose hissed at me angrily.* **2** (**a**) [Ipr, Tn] ~ **(at) sb/sth** make this sound to show disapproval of sb/sth: *hiss (at) a new play.* (**b**) [Tn] say (sth) with an angry hissing voice: *'Stay away from me!' she hissed.* **3** (phr v) **hiss sb off (sth)** (of an audience) force (a performer or speaker) to leave (the stage, etc) by hissing in disapproval: *The politician was hissed off (the platform).*

▷ **hiss** *n* hissing sound: *The crowd greeted the performers with boos and hisses.*

histamine /ˈhɪstəmi:n/ *n* [U] (*medical*) chemical compound that is present in all body tissues and causes (usu unpleasant) reactions in people with certain allergies.

histogram /ˈhɪstəgræm/ *n* = BAR CHART (BAR[1]).

histology /hɪˈstɒlədʒɪ/ *n* [U] scientific study of animal and plant tissues.

historian /hɪˈstɔ:rɪən *or, rarely,* ɪˈs-/ *n* person who studies or writes about history.

historic /hɪˈstɒrɪk *or, rarely,* ɪˈs-; *US* -ˈstɔ:r-/ *adj* famous or important in history: *the historic spot on which the first pilgrims landed in America* ○ *This is a(n) historic occasion,* ie will be regarded as a significant event in history. ○ *historic times,* ie those of which the history is known and recorded.

▷ **historicity** /ˌhɪstəˈrɪsətɪ/ *n* [U] quality of being historically true: *an event of doubtful historicity.*

□ **hiˌstoric ˈpresent** (*grammar*) simple present tense used when describing events in the past to make the description more vivid.

historical /hɪsˈtɒrɪk *or, rarely,* ɪˈs-; *US* -ˈstɔ:r-/ *adj* [usu attrib] **1** concerning past events: *historical records, research.* **2** based on the study of history: *We have no historical evidence for it.* ○ *It's a historical fact.* **3** (**a**) that have actually occurred or existed (as contrasted with legend or fiction): *historical* (ie real, not imaginary) *events, people.* (**b**) (of a book, film, etc) dealing with real events in history: *a historical novel.* **4** (of a subject of study) showing development over a period of time: *historical linguistics.* ▷ **historically** /-klɪ/ *adv*: *The book is historically inaccurate.*

history /ˈhɪstrɪ/ *n* **1** (**a**) [U] study of past events, esp the political, social and economic development of a country, a continent or the world: *a student of Russian history.* ○ *ancient/medieval/modern history.* (**b**) this as a subject at school or university: *a degree in history and geography* ○ [attrib] *my history teacher.* **2** [U] past events, esp when considered as a whole: *Throughout history men have waged war.* ○ *a people with no sense of history.* **3** [C] systematic description of past events: *writing a new history of Europe* ○ [attrib] *Shakespeare's history plays.* **4** [C usu *sing*] series of past events or experiences connected with an object, a person or a place: *This house has a strange history.* ○ *sb's medical history,* ie the record of his past illnesses ○ *There is a history of heart disease in my family.* ○ *He has a history of violent crime.* **5** [U] (*infml*) fact, event, etc that is no longer relevant or important: *They had an affair once, but that's ancient history now.* **6** (idm) **make/go down in ˈhistory** be or do sth so important or unusual that it will be recorded in history: *a discovery that made medical history.*

histrionic /ˌhɪstrɪˈɒnɪk/ *adj* **1** (*usu derog*) very theatrical in manner; excessively dramatic; affected: *histrionic behaviour.* **2** (*fml*) of acting or the theatre: *her histrionic talents.*

▷ **histrionically** /-klɪ/ *adv* (*usu derog*): *wave one's arms around histrionically.*

histrionics *n* [pl] (*usu derog*) theatrical manners or behaviour, esp when exaggerated in order to impress others: *indulge in histrionics.*

hit[1] /hɪt/ *v* (**-tt-**, *pt, pp* **hit**) **1** (**a**) [I, Tn, Tn·pr] strike sb/sth with a blow, missile, etc: *hit the nail with the hammer* ○ *She hit him on the head with a book.* ○ *I was hit by a falling stone.* ○ *The car was hit by a grenade.* ○ *He's been hit* (ie wounded) *in the leg by a sniper's bullet.* ○ *All her shots hit the target.* ○ (*fig*) *The family likeness really hits you,* ie is very noticeable. ○ *He hit himself a nasty blow on the head.* (**b**) [Tn] come against (sth/sb) with force: *The lorry hit the lamp-post with a crash.* (**c**) [Tn, Tn·pr] ~ **sth** (**on**/**against sth**) knock (part of the body) against sth: *He hit his forehead (against the wall) as he fell.* ⇨ Usage. **2** (**a**) [Tn, Tn·pr] drive (a ball, etc) forward by striking it with a bat or club: *hit a ball over the fence.* (**b**) [Tn] (in cricket) score (runs) in this way: *He's already hit two sixes,* ie scored two boundaries worth six runs each. **3** [Tn] have a bad or sudden effect on (a person, thing or place); cause to suffer; affect: *How will the new law hit the unemployed?* ○ *The rent increase will hit the pockets of the poor.* ○ *Rural areas have been worst hit by the strike.* ○ *News of the disaster hit the Stock Exchange around noon.* **4** [Tn] (**a**) find (sth sought), esp by chance: *Follow the footpath and you'll eventually hit the road.* (**b**) (*infml*) arrive in or at (a place): *When does the new show hit town?* (**c**) achieve (sth); reach: *I can't hit the high notes.* ○ *The yen hit a record high in trading today.* **5** [Tn] (*infml*) encounter (sth); experience: *If you go now, you're likely to hit the rush hour.* ○ *hit a snag, problem, etc* ○ *Everything was going well but then we hit trouble.* **6** [Tn] (*infml*) attack (sb/sth); raid: *hit the enemy when they least expect it.* **7** [Tn] (*US sl*) kill (sb); murder. **8** (idm) ˌ**hit the** ˈ**bottle** (*infml*) drink too much alcohol regularly: *After she died he began to hit the bottle.* **hit the** ˈ**ceiling**/ˈ**roof** (*infml*) become suddenly very angry. Cf GO THROUGH THE ROOF (ROOF). **hit the** ˈ**deck** (*US infml*) (**a**) fall to the ground. (**b**) get out of bed. (**c**) get ready for action. **hit/knock sb for six** deal a severe blow to sb; affect deeply: *He was knocked completely for six by his sudden dismissal.* **hit sb/sth** ˈ**hard** affect sb/sth badly: *Television has hit the cinema industry very hard.* ○ *Old people are hardest hit by the rising cost of living.* **hit the** ˈ**hay**/ˈ**sack** (*infml*) go to bed. **hit/make/reach the headlines** ⇨ HEADLINES (HEAD[1]). **hit/strike home** ⇨ HOME[3]. **hit sb in the** ˈ**eye** be very obvious to sb. **hit it** = HIT THE NAIL ON THE HEAD. **hit it** ˈ**off** (**with sb**) (*infml*) have a good and harmonious relationship (with sb); get on well. **hit the** ˈ**jackpot** make a lot of money unexpectedly. **hit/kick a man when he's down** ⇨ MAN[1]. **hit/miss the mark** ⇨ MARK[1]. **hit the nail on the** ˈ**head** express the truth precisely; guess correctly. **hit/touch a nerve** ⇨ NERVE. **hit/strike the right/wrong note** ⇨ NOTE[1]. **hit the** ˈ**road**; *esp US* **hit the** ˈ**trail** (*infml*) start on a journey. **not know what hit one** ⇨ KNOW. **9** (phr v) **hit at sb/sth** aim a blow at sb/sth. **hit back** (**at sb/sth**) reply forcefully to (esp verbal) attacks; retaliate: *In a TV interview she hit back at her critics.* **hit sb/sth off** (*infml*) describe sb/sth briefly and accurately (in words). **hit on/upon sth** think up (a plan, solution, etc) unexpectedly and by inspiration; find sth by luck: *She hit upon a good title for her new novel.* **hit out** (**at sb/sth**) attack sb/sth vigorously or violently with words or blows: *In a rousing speech the President hit out against the trade union.*

□ ˌ**hit-and-**ˈ**run** *adj* [attrib] (**a**) (of a motorist) causing an accident and driving away immediately so as not to be identified. (**b**) (of a road accident) caused by a driver who does not stop to help, call an ambulance, etc.

ˌ**hit-or-**ˈ**miss** (also ˌ**hit-and-**ˈ**miss**) *adj* done haphazardly or carelessly; liable to error; random: *Long-term planning is always rather a hit-or-miss affair.*

NOTE ON USAGE: **Hit** is used in a more general way than **strike** or **beat.** A person, an animal or a thing can be **hit** by a hand or by an object held or thrown. When used with this meaning, **strike** is more formal than **hit.** One can hit or strike a person with the intention of hurting them: *She hit/struck him hard on the face.* One can also hit or strike a person or thing accidentally: *The car hit/struck a lamp-post.* In addition we can hit or strike things with a purpose: *hit/strike a nail with a hammer.* **Beat** means 'hit repeatedly'. We cannot **beat** people or things accidentally: *He was beaten to death by thugs.* ○ *beat eggs, a carpet, a drum.*

hit[2] /hɪt/ *n* **1** (**a**) act of hitting; blow or stroke: *That was a clever hit!* ○ *a direct hit on an enemy ship.* (**b**) point scored by a shot, etc that reaches its target: *a final score of two hits and six misses.* **2** ~ **at sb** (*fig*) sarcastic comment made to or about sb: *That last remark was a hit at me.* **3** person or thing that is very popular; success: *He's a hit with everyone.* ○ *Her new film is quite a hit.* ○ *They sang their latest hit.* ○ [attrib] *hit songs, records.* **4** (idm) **make a hit** (**with sb**) (*infml*) make a very favourable impression (on sb): *You've made quite a hit with Bill.*

□ ˈ**hit list** (*sl*) list of people who are to be killed or against whom some action is being planned.

ˈ**hit man** (*sl esp US*) hired assassin; person who is paid to kill another person.

ˈ**hit parade** list of best-selling popular records; record charts.

hitch /hɪtʃ/ *v* **1** [I, Ipr, Tn, Tn·pr] get (free rides) in other people's cars as a way of travelling: *hitch round Europe* ○ *hitch a ride to London on a lorry* ○ *Can I hitch a lift with you as far as the station?* Cf HITCH-HIKE. **2** [Tn·pr, Tn·p] fasten (sth) to sth with a loop, hook, etc: *hitch a horse to a fence* ○ *hitch a rope round a branch* ○ *a car with a trailer hitched on (to it) at the back* ○ *She tied her horse to the hitching post.* **3** (idm) **get** ˈ**hitched** (*dated sl*) get married. **4** (phr v) **hitch sth up** pull (esp one's clothes) up with a quick movement: *He hitched up his trousers before sitting down.* ○ *She hitched up her skirt so as not to get it wet.*

▷ **hitch** *n* **1** temporary difficulty or problem; snag: *The ceremony went off without a hitch.* ○ *The launch was delayed by a technical hitch.* **2** sudden pull or push. **3** any of various types of noose or knot: *a clove hitch.* **4** (*US sl*) period of (esp military) service.

□ ˈ**hitch-hike** *v* [I, Ipr] travel by obtaining free rides in other people's cars: *hitch-hike through France to Spain.* ˈ**hitch-hiker** *n.*

Hitchcock /ˈhɪtʃkɒk/ Sir Alfred (1899-1980), British film director who specialized in stories of suspense and mystery. He introduced many new techniques of narrative and camerawork to the cinema. His most famous films include *The Thirty-Nine Steps, Rebecca, North by Northwest* and *Psycho.* He often made a brief appearance in his own films.

hither /ˈhɪðə(r)/ *adv* **1** (*arch*) to or towards this place. **2** (idm) ˌ**hither and** ˈ**thither** in various directions: *blown hither and thither by the wind.*

hitherto /ˌhɪðəˈtu:/ *adv* (*fml*) until now: *a woman referred to hitherto as Mrs X* ○ *a hitherto unknown species of moth.*

Hitler /ˈhɪtlə(r)/ Adolf (1889-1945), German dictator, born in Austria. He served in the German Army in the First World War, and in the 1920s became involved in right-wing politics. He was put in prison in 1923 for leading an uprising, and while there wrote *Mein Kampf,* which set out his political aims. His *Nazi party won increasing support, and in 1933 he became Chancellor of Germany. He improved the German economy and built up the German armed forces, starting a series of invasions of neighbouring countries which led in 1939 to the Second World War. During the war he developed his racist ideas by attempting to exterminate the Jews. After early successes the war went badly for Germany, and Hitler, increasingly out of touch with reality, was unable to provide the coherent leadership needed. He killed himself in Berlin just before the invading Russian forces arrived. ▷ **Hitlerian** /hɪtˈlɪərɪən/ *adj.*

Hittite /ˈhɪtaɪt/ *n* **1** (**a**) [C] member of an ancient people who lived in the area of modern Turkey and Syria between about 1900 and 700 BC. (**b**) [U] *Indo-European language spoken by the Hittites, written with wedge-shaped (*cuneiform*) marks. **2** [C] (in the Bible) member of a *Canaanite or Syrian tribe which may have been related to the Hittites.

HIV /ˌeɪtʃ aɪ ˈvi:/ *abbr* human immunodeficiency virus (the virus that causes AIDS): *HIV positive.*

hive /haɪv/ *n* **1** (**a**) (also ˈ**beehive**) box or other container for bees to live in. ⇨ illus at BEE. (**b**) bees living in a hive. **2** place full of busy people: *a hive of activity/industry.*

▷ **hive** *v* **1** [Tn] place (bees) in a hive: *hive a swarm.* **2** [I] (of bees) enter or live in a hive. **3** (phr v) **hive off** become separate from a large group; form an independent body. **hive sth off** (**to/into sth**) transfer (work) to another section or firm; make (part of an organization) independent: *hive off parts of a nationalized industry to private ownership.*

hives /haɪvz/ *n* [pl] skin disease with itchy red patches; nettle-rash.

hiya /ˈhaɪjə/ *interj* (*US infml*) (used as a greeting)

h'm = HEM[2].

HM *abbr* Her/His Majesty: *HM the Queen.*

HMG *abbr* Her/His Majesty's Government: (*infml*) *HMG should be kept informed.*

HMI /ˌeɪtʃ em ˈaɪ/ *abbr* (*Brit*) Her/His Majesty's Inspector (of schools): *a visit from (the) HMI.*

HMS /ˌeɪtʃ em ˈes/ *abbr* (*Brit*) (for warships only) Her/His Majesty's Ship: *HMS Apollo.* Cf USS.

HMSO /ˌeɪtʃ em es ˈəʊ/ *abbr* (*Brit*) Her/His Majesty's Stationery Office.

HNC /ˌeɪtʃ en ˈsi:/ *abbr* (*Brit*) Higher National Certificate (a qualification recognized by many UK technical and professional bodies): *have the HNC in electrical engineering* ○ *go on/do an HNC course*

HND /ˌeɪtʃ en ˈdi:/ *abbr* (*Brit*) Higher National Diploma (a qualification in technical subjects equal to a bachelor's degree without honours): *have the HND in fashion design* ○ *go on/do an HND course.*

Ho *symb* holmium.

ho /həʊ/ *interj* **1** (used to express surprise, scorn, admiration, amusement, etc). **2** (used to draw attention to sth): *Land ho!*

hoar /hɔ:(r)/ *adj* (*dated*) = HOARY 1: *a hoar-headed old man.*

hoard /hɔ:d/ *n* carefully collected and guarded store of money, food or other treasured objects: *a miser's hoard* ○ *a squirrel's hoard of nuts.*

▷ **hoard** *v* [I, Tn, Tn·p] ~ **sth** (**up**) collect (sth in quantity) and store it away: *People found hoarding (food) during the famine were punished.* ○ *hoard up treasure.* **hoarder** *n* person who hoards.

hoarding /ˈhɔ:dɪŋ/ *n* **1** (*Brit*) (*US* ˈ**billboard**) large board used for displaying advertisements. **2** temporary fence of light boards around a building site, etc.

hoar-frost /ˈhɔ: frɒst; *US* frɔ:st/ *n* [U] white frost, frozen dew on grass, leaves, roofs, etc.

hoarse /hɔ:s/ *adj* (**a**) (of the voice) sounding rough and harsh. (**b**) (of a person) having a hoarse voice: *He shouted himself hoarse.* ▷ **hoarsely** *adv.* **hoarseness** *n* [U].

hoary /ˈhɔ:rɪ/ *adj* (**-ier**, **-iest**) **1** (also **hoar**) (esp of hair) grey or white with age. **2** very old: *a hoary old joke.* ▷ **hoariness** *n* [U].

hoax /həʊks/ *n* mischievous trick played on sb for a joke: *The fire brigade answered the emergency call but there was no fire — it was all a hoax.* ○ [attrib] *a hoax phone call.*

▷ **hoax** *v* [Tn, Tn·pr] ~ **sb** (**into doing sth**) deceive sb as a joke: *I was hoaxed into believing their story.* **hoaxer** *n.*

hob /hɒb/ *n* (**a**) flat heating surface for a pan, kettle, etc on the top of a cooker. (**b**) (esp formerly) flat metal shelf at the side of a fireplace, where a pan, kettle, etc can be heated.

Hobbes /hɒbz/ Thomas (1588-1679), English philosopher who developed a wide-ranging set of theories concerning the nature of matter, of human beings and of society. He believed that all human motives are essentially selfish, and that therefore the only way to keep society from falling

Hobbies

In Britain, one of the most popular hobbies is do-it-yourself (DIY). People choose to maintain and improve their homes by doing their own building work, carpentry, painting, electrical work and plumbing. Almost every town has a large DIY store where all the necessary materials can be bought. Gardening is also very popular and one reason why the British prefer houses to flats is that they like to have a garden. Some people grow their own vegetables, others take pride in their lawn or specialize in growing a particular type of plant, for example roses or alpine flowers. Most towns have at least one garden centre, at which everything needed for the garden can be bought. (Cf article at GARDEN.)

Collecting is a hobby that can become an obsession. People collect all kinds of objects, from beer-mats and matchbox labels to antiques and old cars. There are collectors of stamps, coins, medals, first editions of books, records, prints, picture postcards, etc. Some people specialize in objects from a particular period or region, for example Victorian dolls or Chinese stamps. Train-spotters visit stations and collect the numbers of the locomotives they see, and autograph hunters collect the signatures of famous people.

Creative hobbies include photography, painting, brass-rubbing and model-making. People who want to write can join a local writers' group to discuss their work with other enthusiasts. People with musical talent can join a local choir, choral society or orchestra. Many communities, even quite small ones, have their own amateur dramatic societies, which perform plays locally. Similar groups, organized nationally, include the Sealed Knot Society, whose members dress up and re-enact battles of the English Civil War. (Cf articles at LEISURE and SPORT.)

apart is to have strong social institutions and a single all-powerful ruler. His book *Leviathan* sets out these views. ▷ **Hobbesian** /ˈhɒbzɪən/ *adj*.

hobble /ˈhɒbl/ *v* **1** [I, Ipr, Ip] walk with difficulty because the feet or legs hurt or are disabled; walk lamely; limp: *The old man hobbled along (the road) with the aid of his stick.* ⇨ Usage at SHUFFLE. **2** [Tn] tie together two legs of (a horse, etc) to prevent it from going far away.

▷ **hobble** *n* [sing] limping way of walking.

hobby /ˈhɒbɪ/ *n* favourite activity that a person does for pleasure and not as his regular business: *My hobby is stamp-collecting/collecting stamps.* ⇨ article.

hobby-horse /ˈhɒbɪ hɔːs/ *n* **1** long stick with a horse's head, used as a toy. **2** subject that a person likes to discuss; favourite topic of conversation: *You've got me onto* (ie talking about) *one of my favourite hobby-horses.*

hobgoblin /hɒbˈgɒblɪn/ *n* (in folklore) mischievous little creature; ugly and evil spirit; goblin.

hobnail /ˈhɒbneɪl/ *n* short nail with a heavy head used for the soles of heavy shoes: [attrib] *hobnail boots.*

▷ **hobnailed** *adj* (of boots, etc) fitted with hobnails.

hob-nob /ˈhɒb nɒb/ *v* (**-bb-**) [I, Ipr, Ip] ~ (**with sb**); ~ (**together**) (*sometimes derog*) spend time (with sb) in a friendly way; associate (with sb): *I've seen you two hob-nobbing (together) a lot recently.* ○ *hob-nob with the rich and famous.*

hobo /ˈhəʊbəʊ/ *n* (*pl* ~**s** or ~**es** /-bəʊz/) (*esp US*) (**a**) unemployed worker who wanders from place to place. (**b**) tramp; vagrant.

Hobson's choice /ˌhɒbsnz ˈtʃɔɪs/ situation in which a person must accept what is offered because there is no alternative other than taking nothing at all.

hock[1] /hɒk/ *n* middle joint of an animal's hind leg. ⇨ illus at HORSE.

hock[2] /hɒk/ *n* [U, C] type of German white wine: *a fine dry hock.*

hock[3] /hɒk/ *v* [Tn] (*sl*) give (an object of some value) as security for the repayment of a loan; pawn.

▷ **hock** *n* (*sl*) **1** [U] state of being pawned: *get sth out of hock.* **2** (idm) **in hock** (**a**) pawned: *Her jewellery is all in hock.* (**b**) in prison. (**c**) in debt: *I'm in hock to the tune of* (ie I owe a total of) *£5000.*

hockey /ˈhɒkɪ/ *n* [U] **1** (*Brit*) (*US* usu ˈ**field hockey**) game played on a field by two teams of eleven players each, with curved sticks and a small hard ball. ⇨ illus. **2** (*US*) = ICE HOCKEY (ICE[1]).

Hockey is sometimes jokingly associated with hearty schoolgirls, and the expression 'jolly hockey sticks' reflects the connotations of the word. This expression came from a popular radio show of the 1960s, in which one of the characters, a snobbish schoolgirl, used it as a catchphrase.

□ ˈ**hockey stick 1** long stick curved at the bottom, used to hit the ball in hockey. **2** (idm) **jolly hockey sticks** ⇨ JOLLY.

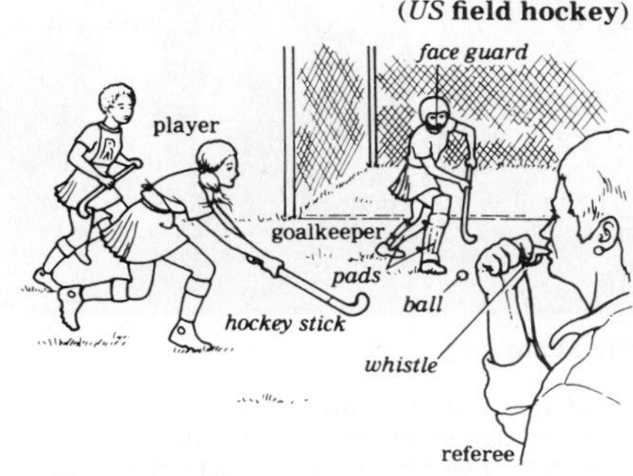

David Hockney: A Bigger Splash

Hockney /ˈhɒknɪ/ David (1937-), English painter. He is best known for portraits and for a series of studies, produced in California, of swimming-pools and modern architecture, which reflect his interest in light and colour. ⇨ illus.

hocus-pocus /ˌhəʊkəs ˈpəʊkəs/ *n* [U] talk or behaviour designed to draw one's attention away from what is actually happening; trickery; deception.

hod /hɒd/ *n* **1** light open box attached to a pole, used by builders for carrying bricks, etc on the shoulder. **2** container for coal used in the home; coal-scuttle.

hodgepodge = HOTCHPOTCH.

Hodgkin's disease /ˈhɒdʒkɪnz dɪziːz/ *n* [U] malignant disease that causes the lymph nodes, spleen and liver to become enlarged.

hoe /həʊ/ *n* long-handled tool with a blade, used for loosening the soil and removing weeds.

▷ **hoe** *v* (*pres p* **hoeing**, *pt, pp* **hoed**) (**a**) [Tn] loosen (ground) with a hoe: *hoe the soil, the flower beds, etc.* (**b**) [Tn, Tn·p] ~ **sth** (**up**) remove (weeds) with a hoe. (**c**) [Tn] remove weeds from around (crops, plants, etc) with a hoe: *hoeing the lettuces.*

hoedown /ˈhəʊdaʊn/ *n* (*US*) (**a**) type of lively country dance. (**b**) party with dances of this type.

Hoffmann /ˈhɔːfmən/ Dustin (1937-), American film actor. Since his first major starring role in *The Graduate* he has shown a meticulous approach to characterization in a wide range of films, including *Rain Man.*

hog /hɒg; *US* hɔːg/ *n* **1** pig reared for meat, esp a castrated male pig. Cf BOAR, SOW[1]. **2** (*infml*) selfish or greedy person. **3** (idm) **go the whole hog** ⇨ WHOLE.

▷ **hog** *v* (**-gg-**) [Tn] (*infml*) take more than one's fair share of (sth); use (sth) selfishly, excluding others: *hog (the middle of) the road*, ie drive near the middle of the road so that others cannot overtake ○ *hog the bathroom*, ie spend a long time in it preventing others from using it ○ *hog the fire*, ie sit in front of it so that others do not feel the heat ○ *Stop hogging the biscuits and pass them round!*

hoggish *adj* greedy and selfish.

□ ˈ**hog cholera** (*US*) = SWINE FEVER (SWINE).

ˈ**hog's back** ridge of land sloping steeply on each side.

ˈ**hog-tie** *v* [Tn] (*infml esp US*) prevent (an animal or a person) from acting freely by tying the feet, or hands and feet, together.

ˈ**hog-wash** *n* [U] nonsense; bilge.

Hogarth /ˈhəʊgɑːθ/ William (1697-1764), English painter and engraver, best known for his sets of paintings which tell a moral story, such as *A Rake's Progress* and *Marriage à la Mode.* ⇨ illus.

hogmanay /ˈhɒgmənei/ *n* (usu **Hogmanay**) (*Scot*) last day of the year and the celebrations that occur on it, esp in Scotland.

hogshead /ˈhɒgzhed; *US* ˈhɔːg-/ *n* **1** large barrel for beer. **2** liquid or dry measure, about 50 gallons in Britain, 62 gallons in the US.

hogweed /ˈhɒgwiːd/ *n* [C, U] tall plant with a thick hollow stem and flat clusters of small white or pink flowers.

ho-ho /həʊˈhəʊ/ *interj* (used to express surprise, scorn or amusement).

ho-hum /həʊˈhʌm/ *interj* (used to express boredom, indifference or resigned acceptance).

hoick /hɔɪk/ *v* [Tn·pr, Tn·p] (*infml*) lift or bring (sth) in the specified direction, esp with a jerk: *She hoicked her bike onto the car roof.* ○ *He tried to hoick the meat out of the tin with a fork.*

hoi polloi /ˌhɔɪ pəˈlɔɪ/ [pl] **the hoi polloi** (*derog*) the common people; the masses.

hoist /hɔɪst/ *v* **1** [Tn, Tn·pr, Tn·p] raise (sth) by means of ropes, special apparatus, etc: *hoist a flag, the sails* ○ *hoisting crates aboard ship* ○ *hoist in the boats*, ie raise them from the water up to the deck ○ *The fireman hoisted the boy (up) onto his shoulders.* **2** (idm) (**be**) **hoist with one's own petard** /peˈtɑːd/ (be) caught or injured by what one

William Hogarth: scene from the series 'Marriage à la Mode'

intended as a trick for others.

▷ **hoist** *n* **1** (usu *sing*) pull or push up; lift: *Give me a hoist (up)*, eg when climbing a wall. **2** apparatus for hoisting things.

hoity-toity /ˌhɔɪtɪ ˈtɔɪtɪ/ *adj* (*infml derog*) behaving in an arrogant way as if one thinks one is superior to others; haughty: *a hoity-toity person, manner*.

hokum /ˈhəʊkəm/ *n* [U] (*infml esp US*) **1** poor or crude theatrical writing: *a piece of second-rate hokum*. **2** nonsense: *talking complete hokum*.

Holbein /ˈhɒlbaɪn/ Hans (1497/8-1543), German painter who from 1526 worked extensively in England. He was made the official royal painter, and is best known for his portraits of Henry VIII and his court.

hold[1] /həʊld/ *v* (*pt, pp* **held** /held/) **1** [Tn, Tn·pr] take and keep or support (sb/sth) in one's arms, hands, teeth, etc: *The girl was holding her father's hand.* ○ *The lovers held each other tight.* ○ *They were holding hands*, ie holding each other's hands. ○ *She was holding an umbrella.* ○ *She held me by the sleeve.* ○ *She was holding the baby in her arms.* ○ *He held the rope in his teeth as he climbed the tree.* **2** [Tn] (**a**) bear the weight of (sb/sth); support: *Is that branch strong enough to hold you/your weight?* (**b**) restrain or control (sb/sth): *Try to hold the thief until the police arrive.* ○ *The dam gave way; it was not strong enough to hold the flood waters.* **3** [Tn·pr, Tn·p, Cn·a] keep (oneself/sb/sth) in the specified position or condition: *The wood is held in position by a clamp.* ○ *Hold your head up.* ○ *Hold your arms out.* ○ *It took three nurses to hold him down while they gave him the injection.* ○ *She held out her hand to take the rope.* ○ *Hold yourself still for a moment while I take your photograph.* **4** (**a**) [I] remain secure or in position: *How long will the anchor hold?* ○ *I don't think the shelf will hold if we put anything else on it.* (**b**) remain unchanged; last: *How long will this fine weather hold?* ○ *If their luck holds, they could still win the championship.* (**c**) continue to be true or valid: *The offer I made to you last week still holds.* ○ *The argument still holds.* **5** [Tn] (of the wheels of a car, etc) maintain a grip of (a corner, road, etc): *My new car holds the road well.* **6** [Tn] have enough space for (sth/sb); contain: *This barrel holds 25 litres.* ○ *Will this suitcase hold all my clothes?* ○ *I don't think the car will hold you all.* ○ *My brain can't hold so much information at one time.* ○ (*fig*) *Who knows what the future holds for us?* **7** [Tn] defend (sth) against military attack; keep possession of: *hold a fort, garrison, etc* ○ *The town was held against frequent enemy attacks.* ○ *The Tory candidate held the seat, but with a greatly reduced majority.* **8** [Tn, Cn·n] keep (sb) and not allow him to leave: *Police are holding two men in connection with last Thursday's bank robbery.* ○ *The terrorists are holding three men hostage.* ○ *He was held prisoner throughout the war.* **9** [Tn] have ownership of (sth); possess: *An American conglomerate holds a major share in the company.* **10** [Tn] have the position of (sth); occupy: *She has now held the post of Prime Minister longer than anyone else this century.* ○ *How long has he held office?* **11** [Tn] have (sth) as sth one has gained: *She holds the world record for the long jump.* **12** [Tn] keep (sb's attention or interest) by being interesting: *A good teacher must be able to hold her pupils' attention.* **13** [Tn] have (a belief, an opinion, a view, etc): *He holds strange views on religion.* ○ *I hold the view that the plan cannot work.* **14** [Tf, Cn·a, Cn·t] (*fml*) believe, consider or regard: *I hold that the government's economic policies are mistaken.* ○ *I hold the parents responsible for their child's behaviour.* ○ *I hold him to be a fool.* **15** [Tn] cause (a meeting, conference, etc) to take place: *The meeting will be held in the community centre.* ○ *We hold a general election every four or five years.* ○ *The Motor Show is usually held in October.* **16** [Tn] (**a**) (of a ship or an aircraft) continue to move in (a particular direction): *The ship is holding a south-easterly course.* (**b**) (of a singer) continue to sing (a note): *hold a high note.* **17** [I, Tn] wait until the person one has telephoned is ready to speak: *Mr Crowther's extension is engaged at the moment; will you hold (the line)?* **18** (idm) **hold ˈgood** remain true or valid: *the same argument doesn't hold good in all cases.* **ˈhold it** (*infml*) (used to ask sb to wait, or not to move): *Hold it a second — I don't think everyone's arrived yet.* **there is no holding sb** sb cannot be prevented from doing sth: *Once she gets onto the subject of politics there's no holding her.* (For other idioms containing **hold**, see entries for *ns, adjs*, etc, eg **hold the fort** ⇨ FORT; **hold sb/sth dear** ⇨ DEAR.)

19 (phr v) **hold sth against sb** (*infml*) allow sth to influence one's judgement or opinion of sb: *He's afraid that his criminal record will be held against him when he applies for jobs.* ○ *I don't hold it against him that he votes Conservative.*

hold ˈback (from sth) hesitate to act or speak because of fear or reluctance: *She held back, not knowing how to break the terrible news.* ○ *She held back from telling him what she thought of him.* **hold sb ˈback** prevent the progress or development of sb: *Do you think that mixed-ability teaching holds the brighter children back?* **hold sb/sth back** prevent sb/sth from advancing; control or restrain sb/sth: *The police cordon was unable to hold back the crowd.* ○ *The dam was not strong enough to hold back the flood waters.* **hold sth back** (**a**) not release or grant sth; withhold sth: *hold back information* ○ *I think he's holding something back; he knows more than he admits.* (**b**) not express or reveal (an emotion); control sth: *She just managed to hold back her anger.* ○ *He bravely held back his tears.*

hold sb ˈdown control the freedom of sb; oppress sb: *The people are held down by a vicious and repressive military regime.* **hold sth ˈdown** (**a**) keep sth at a low level; keep sth down: *The rate of inflation must be held down.* (**b**) (be competent enough to) remain in (a job) for some time: *He couldn't hold down a job after his breakdown.* ○ *What's the longest she's held down a job?*

hold ˈforth speak pompously and lengthily about sth: *He loves holding forth on any subject once he has an audience.*

hold sth/oneself in restrain, control or check sth/oneself: *hold in one's feelings, temper, anger, etc* ○ *He's incapable of holding himself in.*

hold ˈoff (**a**) (of rain, a storm, etc) not occur; be delayed: *The rain held off just long enough for us to have our picnic.* (**b**) restrain oneself from doing sth, esp attacking sb: *Let's hope the gunmen will hold off for the duration of the cease-fire.* **hold sb/sth off** resist (an attack or advance by sb): *Though outnumbered, they held off (repeated attacks by) the enemy.* **hold off sth/doing sth** delay sth: *Could you hold off (making) your decision until next week?*

hold ˈon (**a**) (*infml*) (usu in the imperative) wait or stop: *Hold on a minute while I get my breath back.* (**b**) survive in a difficult or dangerous situation; hang on: *They managed to hold on until help arrived.* ○ *I don't think I can hold on much longer.* **hold sth on** keep sth in position: *These nuts and bolts hold the wheels on.* ○ *This knob is only held on by Sellotape.* **hold on(to sb/sth)** keep grasping or gripping sb/sth; not let go of sb/sth: *He held on(to the rock) to stop himself slipping.* ○ *hold onto one's hat on a windy day.* **hold onto sth** (*infml*) not give or sell sth to sb else; keep or retain sth: *You should hold onto your oil shares.* ○ *I'd hold onto that house for the time being; house prices are rising sharply at the moment.*

hold ˈout (**a**) last; remain: *We can stay here for as long as our supplies hold out.* ○ *I can't hold out* (ie retain my urine) *much longer; I must find a toilet.* (**b**) resist an attack: *They held out bravely against repeated enemy bombing.* **hold sth out** offer (a chance, hope, possibility, etc): *The forthcoming talks hold out the hope of real arms reductions.* ○ *Doctors hold out little hope of her recovering.* **hold out for sth** (*infml*) deliberately delay reaching an agreement in the hope of gaining sth: *Union negotiators are holding out for a more generous pay settlement.* **hold out on sb** (*infml*) refuse to give information, etc to sb: *I'm not holding out on you. I honestly don't know where he is.*

hold sth ˈover (often passive) postpone or defer sth: *The matter was held over until the next meeting.*

ˈhold to sth not abandon or change (a principle, an opinion, etc); remain loyal to sth: *She always holds to her convictions.* ○ *beliefs that were firmly held to.* **hold sb to sth** make sb keep (a promise): *He promised her a honeymoon in Paris when they got married, and she held him to it.* ○ *We must hold the contractors to* (ie not allow them to exceed) *their estimates.*

Holidays

In Britain, there is no legal requirement for an employer to give paid leave, but in practice most workers have three or four weeks' holiday per year. As well as this annual leave, there are national holidays, when most people do not work. These are the public holidays, called bank holidays, most of them on varying dates: New Year's Day (1 January), Good Friday, Easter Monday, May Day Holiday (the first Monday after 1 May), Spring Bank Holiday (the last Monday in May), Summer Bank Holiday (the last Monday in August), Christmas Day (25 December) and Boxing Day (26 December). The bank holidays vary in Scotland and Northern Ireland. (2 January is a holiday in Scotland, for example, and 12 July, Orangeman's Day, is a public holiday in Northern Ireland.) Schools and universities have three holiday periods in the year, around Christmas, around Easter and in the summer.

Most British people spend at least part of their holidays away from home and many go abroad. A traditional holiday is one spent at the seaside and many people prefer to go to a warmer climate. The most popular holiday areas in Britain are in the south, because of the warmer climate and the many south-coast seaside resorts. (Cf article at ACCOMMODATION.) The most popular tourist region in southern England is the West Country, in particular Devon and Cornwall. Other destinations for holiday-makers in Britain are the Lake District, North Wales, the Norfolk Broads, and the Highlands and Lowlands of Scotland. The offshore islands also attract visitors, notably the Isle of Man, the Isle of Wight, the Scilly Isles, and the many Scottish island groups.

More and more people now travel further afield for their holiday, and in 1989 Britain was third in the word (after Canada and Japan) in the number of tourists who visited the USA. Tourist companies usually offer 'package' holidays at specially favourable rates.

An increasing trend is for people to take two breaks in the year, with the first a leisurely and relaxing holiday, and the second an 'activity' holiday, such as walking or climbing or winter sports. Seaside holiday camps, like Butlins, are a popular choice with families, and provide an 'all-in' holiday with a wide choice of daily entertainment.

In the USA, there are no public holidays as such, since each state has jurisdiction over its holidays. In practice, however, most states observe the ten federal legal public holidays: New Year's Day (1 January), Martin Luther King Day (15 January, his birthday, a holiday introduced in 1988), Washington's Birthday (the third Monday in February), Memorial Day (the last Monday in May), Independence Day (4 July), Labor Day (the first Monday in September), Columbus Day (the second Monday in October), Veterans' Day (11 November), Thanksgiving Day (the fourth Thursday in November) and Christmas Day (25 December). When a holiday falls on a Saturday or Sunday, it is usually observed on the following Monday or preceding Friday. Thanksgiving Day owes its origin to the Pilgrim Fathers who sailed from England to America on board the *Mayflower* in 1620 to found a community where they could practise their religion without interference. A year after their arrival, the Pilgrim Fathers held a feast to give thanks to God for a good harvest, cooking wild turkey as one of the main dishes. Today Thanksgiving Day is celebrated with a traditional meal of roast turkey. It is also a day when Americans give gifts of food to the needy, and when families living near military bases invite service personnel to dinner. Many also attend a religious service. Confederate Heroes' Day, or Robert E Lee Day (19 January), is observed in various southern states, and Texas keeps Texas Independence Day (2 March).

In the USA, there is a vast choice of popular holiday resorts and tourist attractions, both natural, such as the beaches of Florida and California, and man-made, such as Disneyland. Most Americans are keen travellers, however, and many of them go abroad for their holidays. One of the most popular destinations is Britain, partly because of the common language and the historical ties between the two countries.

hold toˈgether (a) remain whole: *The car's bodywork scarcely holds together.* (b) remain united: *The Tory party always holds together in times of crisis.* **hold sth together** cause sth to remain together; unite sth: *The country needs a leader who will hold the nation together.*

hold sb/sth up (a) put sb/sth forward as an example: *She's always holding up her children as models of behaviour.* (b) obstruct or delay the progress of sb/sth: *Road-works on the motorway are holding up traffic.* ○ *My application was held up by the postal strike.* ○ *Our flight was held up by fog.* **hold up sth** rob sth using the threat of force or violence: *hold up a bank, post office, etc* ○ *Masked men held up a security van in South London yesterday.*

hold with sth (used in negative sentences or in questions) agree with or approve of sth: *I don't hold with his views on education.* ○ *Do you hold with nudity on the stage?*

□ **ˈhold-up** *n* (a) stoppage or delay: *a hold-up on the motorway* ○ *We should arrive in half an hour, barring hold-ups.* (b) robbery by armed robbers: *After the hold-up, the gang made their getaway in a stolen car.*

hold[2] /həʊld/ *n* **1** (a) [sing] act or manner of holding sb/sth; grasp; grip: *She kept a firm hold of her little boy's hand as they crossed the road.* ○ *He lost his hold on the rope.* (b) [C] particular way of holding an opponent, etc: *wrestling holds.* **2** [sing] ~ **(on/over sb/sth)** influence: *He has a tremendous hold over his younger brother.* **3** [sing] ~ **(on sb/sth)** power or control of sb/sth: *The military has tightened its hold on the country.* **4** [C] place where a climber can put his hands or feet when climbing: *There are very few holds on the cliff face.* Cf FOOTHOLD (FOOT[1]). **5** (idm) **catch, get, grab, seize, take, etc ˈhold of sb/sth** take sb/sth in the hands: *I threw the rope and he caught hold of it.* ○ *I managed to grab hold of the jug before it fell.* **get hold of sb/sth** (*infml*) (a) find and use sth: *Do you know where I can get hold of a second-hand carpet cleaner?* ○ *Wherever did you get hold of that idea?* (b) contact or find sb: *I've been trying to get hold of her for days but she's never at home.*

hold[3] /həʊld/ *n* hollow part of a ship below the deck, where cargo is stored.

holdall /ˈhəʊldɔːl/ (*US* **ˈcarry-all**) *n* large (usu soft) bag for holding clothes, etc when travelling.

holder /ˈhəʊldə(r)/ *n* (often forming compound *ns*) **1** person who holds sth; person who has sth at his disposal or in his possession: *an account-holder* ○ *a licence-holder* ○ *a ticket-holder* ○ *the holder of the world record/the world record-holder* ○ *holders of high office* ○ *the holder of a French passport.* **2** thing that supports or holds sth: *a pen-holder* ○ *a cigarette-holder* ○ *a plant pot holder.*

holding /ˈhəʊldɪŋ/ *n* **1** land held by a tenant. **2** (often *pl*) thing owned, such as land, stocks, shares, etc; personal property: *She has a 40% holding* (ie share) *in the company.*

□ **ˈholding company** company formed to hold the shares of other companies, which it then controls.

hole /həʊl/ *n* **1** [C] (a) sunken or hollow place in a solid mass or surface; cavity: *a hole in a tooth* ○ *roads full of holes.* (b) opening through sth; gap: *The prisoner escaped through a hole in the wall.* ○ *I've worn holes in my socks.* ○ *My socks are in holes/full of holes*, ie worn so much that holes have formed. ○ *a hole in the heart*, ie a defect at birth in the membrane of the heart. **2** [C] (a) animal's burrow: *a ˈmouse hole* ○ *a fox's hole.* (b) (usu *sing*) (*fig infml*) small, dark or unpleasant room, flat, district, etc: *Why do you want to live here — it's a dreadful hole!* **3** [sing] (*sl*) awkward or difficult situation: *be in (a bit of) a hole.* **4** [C] (*sport*) (a) hollow or cavity into which a ball, etc must be hit in various games: *an ˌeighteen-hole ˈgolf-course.* (b) (in golf) section of a golf-course between a tee and a hole; point scored by a player who reaches the hole with the fewest strokes: *win the first hole.* **5** (idm) **have an ace in the hole** ⇨ ACE. **a hole in the ˈwall** very small dingy shop, café, etc, esp in a row of buildings. **make a hole in sth** (*infml*) use a large amount of (one's money, supplies, etc): *The hospital bills made a big hole in his savings.* **money burns a hole in sb's pocket** ⇨ MONEY. **pick holes in sth** ⇨ PICK[3].

▷ **hole** *v* **1** [Tn] make a hole or holes in (sth): *The ship was holed by an iceberg.* **2** [I, Ip, Tn] ~ **(out)** (in golf, etc) hit (the ball) into a hole: *She holed out from forty yards.* **3** (phr v) **hole up** (also **be holed up**) (*sl esp US*) hide oneself: *The gang (was) holed up in the mountains somewhere.*

□ **ˌhole-and-ˈcorner** *adj* [usu attrib] (*derog*) (of an activity) secret because dishonest or illegal; underhand: *a hole-and-corner affair, business, method.*

holiday /ˈhɒlədeɪ/ *n* **1** (a) day of rest, recreation or festivity, when no work is done: *Sunday is a holiday in Christian countries.* ⇨ article. (b) (*esp Brit*) (also *esp US* **vacation**) (often *pl*) period of time away from everyday work, used esp for travel, recreation and rest: *the school holidays* ○ *the Christmas holidays* ○ *We're going to Spain for our summer holiday(s).* ○ *I'm taking two weeks' holiday.* ○ *I'm entitled to 20 days' holiday a year.* ○ [attrib] *a holiday resort, brochure.* **2** (idm) **a busman's holiday** ⇨ BUSMAN (BUS). **high days and holidays** ⇨ HIGH[1]. **on ˈholiday/on one's ˈholidays** having a holiday: *The typist is away on holiday this week.*

▷ **holiday** *v* (*esp Brit*) (also *esp US* **vacation**) [I, Ipr, Ip] spend a holiday: *They're holidaying on the west coast.*

□ **ˈholiday camp** (also **ˈholiday centre**) (*esp Brit*) place with accommodation and organized amusements for people on holiday.

ˈholiday-maker *n* person who is on holiday: *The plane was full of holiday-makers.*

NOTE ON USAGE: **Holiday**, **vacation** and **leave** all indicate a period of absence from work or duty. There are differences between British and American usage. **1 Holiday** is used in both Britain and the US to mean a single day without work because of a religious or national festival: *Friday is a holiday in Muslim countries.* ○ *The shops are closed tomorrow because it is a bank holiday.* ○ *In* *this country New Year's Day is a national holiday.* **2 Holiday** is used in Britain and **vacation** in the US when talking about the regular period of time taken away from work each year: *Where are you going for your summer holidays/vacation?* ○ *I was on holiday/vacation last month.* **3** In Britain **vacation** is used mainly for the period of time when universities and lawcourts do not work: *In Britain the long vacation is from June to October.* **4 Leave** means permission given to an employee to be absent from work for a special reason: *She's been given sick/compassionate/maternity leave.* ○ *They've refused him leave of absence.* ○ *He's taken unpaid leave for a month.* **5 Leave** also means the period away from official duties of those working overseas, eg soldiers and diplomats: *He gets home leave every two years.*

holier-than-thou /ˌhəʊlɪə ðən ˈðaʊ/ *adj* (*infml derog*) thinking that one is more virtuous than others; self-righteous: *a holier-than-thou preacher, attitude.*

holiness /ˈhəʊlɪnɪs/ *n* **1** [U] state of being holy or sacred. **2 His/Your Holiness** title used of or to the Pope.

Holinshed /ˈhɒlɪnʃed/ Raphael (died c 1580), English writer of historical chronicles. Shakespeare used his account of 14th- to 16th-century English history in writing many of his plays.

holistic /həʊˈlɪstɪk, *also* hɒˈlɪstɪk/ *adj* including or dealing with the whole, rather than with individual parts. ▷ **holistically** /hɒˈlɪstɪklɪ/ *adv.*
□ **hoˌlistic ˈmedicine** form of medical treatment that takes account of every aspect of a patient's life in attempting to cure illness.

Holland /ˈhɒlənd/ **1** = THE NETHERLANDS. **2** former province of the Netherlands, now divided into North and South Holland. ⇨ map at BENELUX.

hollandaise sauce /ˌhɒləndeɪz ˈsɔːs/ sauce made from butter, egg yolks and lemon juice or vinegar, served esp with vegetables or fish.

holler /ˈhɒlə(r)/ *v* [I, Tn] (*infml esp US*) shout (sth); yell.

hollow /ˈhɒləʊ/ *adj* **1** having a hole or empty space inside; not solid: *a hollow tree, ball.* **2** sunken; deeply set: *hollow cheeks* ○ *ˌhollow-ˈeyed from lack of sleep.* **3** [usu attrib] (of sounds) echoing, as if coming from a hollow place: *a hollow groan.* **4** (*fig*) **(a)** false; insincere: *a hollow promise* ○ *hollow* (ie forced and cynical) *laughter* ○ *His words rang hollow.* **(b)** without real value; worthless: *hollow joys and pleasures*, ie not giving true happiness ○ *win a hollow victory.* **5** (idm) **beat sb hollow** ⇨ BEAT[1]. **have hollow legs** (*Brit joc*) have a large appetite.
▷ **hollow** *n* **(a)** sunken place, esp a small valley: *a wooded hollow.* **(b)** hole or enclosed space within sth: *She held the small bird in the hollow of her hand.*
hollow *v* **1** [Tn, Tn·p] ~ **sth (out)** form (sth) into a hollow shape: *river banks hollowed out by rushing water.* **2** (phr v) **hollow sth out** form sth by making a hole in sth else: *hollow out a nest in a tree trunk.*
hollowly *adv.*
hollowness *n* [U].

holly /ˈhɒlɪ/ *n* **(a)** [C] evergreen shrub with hard shiny sharp-pointed leaves and, in winter, red berries. **(b)** [U] its branches used for Christmas decorations.

hollyhock /ˈhɒlɪhɒk/ *n* tall garden plant with brightly coloured flowers. ⇨ illus at PLANT.

Hollywood /ˈhɒlɪwʊd/ district of Los Angeles, California, USA, where many American film companies have their headquarters and many film studios are situated: [attrib] *Hollywood stars.*

Holmes[1] /həʊmz/ Oliver Wendell (1809-94), American doctor and essayist who wrote a series of books (eg *The Autocrat of the Breakfast Table* and *The Professor at the Breakfast Table*) describing mealtime conversation full of wit and wisdom.

Holmes[2] /həʊmz/ Sherlock, fictional English

Sherlock Holmes

private detective created by Sir Arthur Conan *Doyle. Using his acute intelligence and powers of observation and deduction, he solved (together with his friend Dr Watson) cases which mystified the police. He is usu pictured wearing a cape and deerstalker hat, and smoking a curved pipe. The Sherlock Holmes stories are still immensely popular and have been filmed many times. ⇨ illus.

holm-oak /ˈhəʊm əʊk/ *n* = ILEX 2.

holocaust /ˈhɒləkɔːst/ *n* **(a)** [C] large-scale destruction, esp by fire; great loss of human life: *fear a nuclear holocaust.* **(b) the Holocaust** [sing] the mass killing of Jews by the Nazis before and during the Second World War.

hologram /ˈhɒləgræm/ *n* (*physics*) photographic representation that gives a three-dimensional image when suitably lit.

holograph /ˈhɒləgrɑːf; *US* -græf/ *n* document that is entirely written by hand by the named author. Cf AUTOGRAPH 2.

hols /hɒlz/ *n* [pl] (*Brit infml*) holidays (HOLIDAY 1b).

Holst /həʊlst/ Gustav (1874-1934), English composer. His music, which was strongly influenced by folk music, is marked by a visionary quality combined with a strong sense of rhythm. His best-known piece is the orchestral suite *The Planets*, and others include *The Hymn of Jesus* and the *Choral Symphony*.

Holstein /ˈhɒlstaɪn/ *n* (*US*) = FRIESIAN.

holster /ˈhəʊlstə(r)/ *n* leather case for a pistol, usu fixed to a belt or saddle. ⇨ illus at GUN.

holy /ˈhəʊlɪ/ *adj* (**-ier, -iest**) **1 (a)** associated with God or with religion; of God: *the Holy Bible/Scriptures.* **(b)** regarded as sacred; consecrated: *holy ground* ○ *holy water*, ie water blessed by a priest ○ *a holy war*, ie one fought to defend what is sacred ○ *Yom Kippur is a holy day* (ie a religious festival) *for the Jews.* **2** devoted to the service of God; morally and spiritually pure: *a holy man* ○ *live a holy life.* **3** (idm) **a holy ˈterror** (*infml*) **(a)** (*joc*) naughty or cheeky child. **(b)** formidable or dominating person.
□ **the ˌHoly ˈCity** Jerusalem.
ˌHoly Comˈmunion = COMMUNION 1.
the ˌHoly ˈFamily Mary, Joseph and the young Jesus.
the ˌHoly ˈFather the Pope.
the ˌHoly ˈGhost = THE HOLY SPIRIT.
the ˌHoly ˈGrail ⇨ GRAIL.
the ˈHoly Land 1 country west of the river Jordan, revered by Christians as the place where Christ lived. **2** any region revered in non-Christian religions.
the ˌholy of ˈholies (a) sacred inner chamber of the Jewish temple at Jerusalem. **(b)** (*fig often joc*) sacred place: *To the children, their father's study was the holy of holies.*
ˌholy ˈorders ⇨ ORDER[1].
the ˌHoly ˈSee 1 the papal court; the Vatican. **2** the office of the pope; the papacy.
the ˌHoly ˈSpirit (also **the ˌHoly ˈGhost**) the Third Person in the Trinity.
ˈHoly Week week before Easter Sunday.
ˌHoly ˈWrit the Bible: *You shouldn't treat the newspapers as if they were Holy Writ.*

Holy Island /ˈhəʊlɪ aɪlənd/ = LINDISFARNE.

Holy Roman Empire /ˌhəʊlɪ ˌrəʊmən ˈempaɪə(r)/, **the Holy Roman Empire** European empire set up by the Catholic Church to create a unified stable area under secular power and Christian influence. Its first emperor, *Charlemagne, was crowned in Rome in 800 AD. At its largest it included much of western and central Europe. From the 10th century onwards it was closely identified with the German Empire. *Napoleon abolished it in 1806.

Holyrood House /ˌhɒlɪruːd ˈhaʊs/ royal palace in Edinburgh, Scotland, used by members of the British royal family when they visit Scotland.

homage /ˈhɒmɪdʒ/ *n* [U] (*fml*) things said or done to show great respect; tribute to a person or his qualities (used esp with the *vs* shown): *They stood in silent homage round her grave.* ○ *Many came to do the dead man homage.* ○ *We pay homage to the genius of Shakespeare.*

Homburg /ˈhɒmbɜːg/ *n* man's soft felt hat with a narrow curled brim and a lengthwise dent in the top.

home[1] /həʊm/ *n* **1 (a)** [C, U] place where one lives, esp with one's family: *The nurse visits patients in their homes.* ○ *He left home* (ie left his parents and began an independent life) *at sixteen.* ○ [attrib] *my home address.* **(b)** [C] house, flat, etc: *Homes for Sale*, eg on an estate agent's notice. ○ [attrib] *a home improvement grant.* ⇨ article at HOUSE. **(c)** [C] (*infml*) place where an object is stored: *I must find a home for all these tins.* **2** [C, U] district or country where one was born or where one has lived for a long time or to which one feels attached: *She was born in London, but she now looks on Paris as her home.* ○ *She lives a long way from home.* ○ *He left India for home*, ie for his own country. **3** [C] **(a)** institution for people needing care or rest: *a children's home* ○ *a home for the blind* ○ *an old people's home.* **(b)** institution providing accommodation for workers: *a sailor's home.* **4** [C] **(a)** place where an animal or a plant is native or most common; habitat: *The tiger's home is in the jungle.* **(b)** place from which sth originates: *Greece is the home of democracy.* ○ [attrib] *Liverpool is the ship's home port*, ie where it is registered. **5** [U] **(a)** (in sport and in various games) place where a player is safe, cannot be caught, etc. **(b)** finishing point in a race. **6** (idm) **at home (a)** in the house, flat, etc: *Is there anybody at home?* **(b)** at one's ease, as if in one's own home: *Make yourself at home!* ○ *They always make us feel very much at home.* **(c)** (of football matches, etc) played in the town, etc to which the team belongs: *Is our next match at home or away?* **(d)** (*fml*) expecting and ready to receive visitors: *Mrs Hill is not at home to anyone except close relatives.* **at home in sth** familiar and relaxed with sth: *Is it difficult to feel at home in* (ie confident when using) *a foreign language?* **charity begins at home** ⇨ CHARITY. **close/near to home** close to the point at which one is directly affected: *Her remarks were embarrassingly close to home.* ○ *The threat of war is coming steadily nearer to home.* **eat sb out of house and home** ⇨ EAT. **an Englishman's home is his castle** ⇨ ENGLISHMAN (ENGLISH). **a ˈhome bird** person who likes to spend as much time as possible at home because he is happiest there. **a ˌhome from ˈhome** place where one is as happy, comfortable, etc as in one's own home: *You will find our hotel a true home from home!* **a ˌhome ˈtruth** unpleasant fact about a person told to him by sb else: *It's time you listened to a few home truths about yourself.* **one's spiritual home** ⇨ SPIRITUAL. **there's no place like home** ⇨ PLACE[1]. **when he's, it's, etc at ˈhome** (*joc*) (used facetiously to emphasize a question): *Who's Gloria Button when she's at home?*
▷ **homeless** *adj* having no home: *homeless families.* **the homeless** *n* [pl *v*] homeless people: *provide emergency accommodation for the homeless.* **homelessness** *n* [U]. ⇨ article at ACCOMMODATION.

homeward /ˈhəʊmwəd/ *adj, adv* going towards home: *the homeward journey* ○ *We're homeward*

SOME TYPICAL BRITISH HOMES

Row of terraced houses/terrace

1 lintel
2 lamp-post
3 knocker
4 doorbell
5 door
6 doorstep
7 drain-pipe
8 drain
9 letter-box
10 sash-window
11 window-sill or -ledge
12 brick
13 slate
14 window-pane

Semi-detached houses

1 skylight
2 roof
3 pane
4 wall
5 porch
6 hanging basket
7 path
8 fence
9 bay window
10 garden gate
11 casement window

Bungalow

1 cowl
2 aerial
3 conservatory
4 French window
5 parasol
6 clothes-line
7 crazy paving
8 deck-chair
9 vegetable garden
10 garden shed
11 back door
12 tiles

Detached house

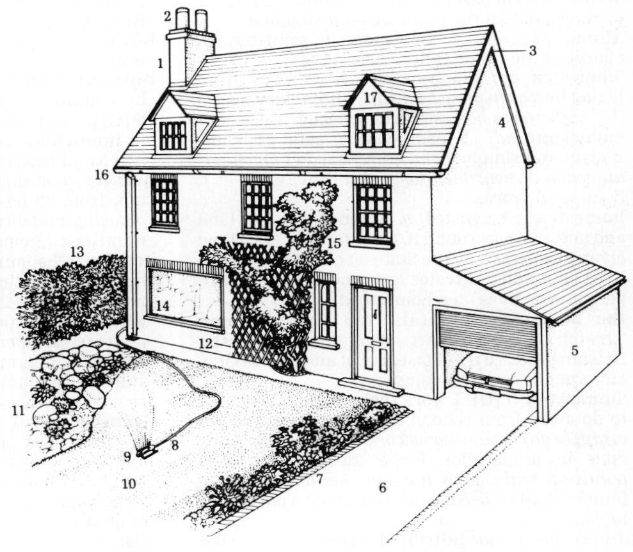

1 chimney
2 chimney-pot
3 eaves
4 gable
5 garage
6 drive
7 border
8 hose
9 sprinkler
10 lawn
11 rockery
12 trellis
13 hedge
14 picture window
15 climber
16 gutter
17 dormer window

bound.

homewards /-wədz/ *adv* towards home: *travel homewards.* ⇨ Usage at FORWARD².

□ ˌ**home-ˈbrewed** *adj* (of beer, etc) made at home (contrasted with beer from a brewery).

the ˌHome ˈCounties the counties round London. ⇨ map at App 1.

ˌ**home-ˈcured** *adj* (of food, esp bacon) treated by smoking, salting, etc.

ˌ**home ecoˈnomics** study of household management.

ˈ**home farm** farm worked by the owner of an estate on which there are other farms.

the ˌhome ˈfront the civilians (in a country at war).

ˌ**home-ˈgrown** *adj* (of food, esp fruit and vegetables) grown in one's own country, garden, etc: *Are these lettuces home-grown or did you buy them in the market?* ○ (*fig*) *The team includes several foreign players because of the shortage of ˌhome-grown ˈtalent.*

the ˌHome ˈGuard (formerly) British volunteer army formed in 1940 to defend the country against invaders.

ˌ**home ˈhelp** person whose job is to help others with housework, etc, esp one employed by a local authority to help the elderly, disabled, etc in this way.

ˈ**homeland** /-lænd/ *n* **1** one's native country. **2** (usu *pl*) any of the nine areas reserved for black people in the Republic of S Africa. They include Transkei and Bophuthatswana.

ˌ**home-ˈmade** *adj* made at home: *a ˌhome-made ˈcake* ○ *Home-made jam is usually better than the kinds you buy in the shops.*

the ˈHome Office British Government department dealing with law and order, immigration, etc in England and Wales. Cf THE FOREIGN AND COMMONWEALTH OFFICE (FOREIGN).

ˌ**Home ˈRule** government of a country or region by its own citizens, esp the independence of Ireland from Britain, which was the aim of a long and sometimes violent Irish campaign between 1870 and 1921.

ˌ**home ˈrun** (in baseball) hit that allows the batter to run round all the bases without stopping.

ˌ**Home ˈSecretary** Government minister in charge of the Home Office.

ˈ**homesick** *adj* sad because one is away from home: *He was homesick for Italy.* ˈ**homesickness** *n* [U]: *suffer from homesickness when abroad.*

ˈ**homespun** *adj* **1** made of yarn spun at home. **2** plain and simple: *homespun remedies for minor ailments* ○ *sensible homespun advice.* — *n* homespun fabric.

homestead /ˈhəʊmsted/ *n* **1** house with the land and outbuildings round it, esp a farm. **2** (*US*) land given to a person by the State on condition that he lives on it and cultivates it. **homesteader** *n* (*US*) person who lives on a homestead.

the home ˈstraight (also *esp US* **the home ˈstretch**) (**a**) last part of a race, near the finishing-line. (**b**) (*fig*) last part of an undertaking, etc, when it is nearly completed.

ˈ**homework** *n* [U] **1** work that a pupil is required to do away from school: *The teacher gave us an essay (to do) for our homework.* **2** (*fig infml*) work done in preparation for a meeting, etc: *The politician had clearly not done his homework,* ie found out all he needed to know about a particular topic.

home² /həʊm/ *adj* [attrib] **1** (**a**) of or connected with one's home: *have a happy home life* ○ *home comforts.* (**b**) done or produced at home: *home cooking* ○ *home movies.* **2** in one's own country; not foreign; domestic: *home industries* ○ *the home market* ○ *home news.* **3** (*sport*) played on or connected with one's own ground: *a home match, win, defeat* ○ *the home team,* ie the one playing at home ○ *playing in front of their home crowd.*

home³ /həʊm/ *adv* **1** at, in or to one's home or country: *Is he home yet?* ○ *She's on her way home.* ○ *He went home.* ○ *Will the Spanish authorities send him home for trial?* ○ (*US*) *stay home,* ie stay at home. **2** to the point aimed at; as far as possible: *drive a nail home.* **3** (idm) **be, etc nothing to write home about** ⇨ WRITE. **bring home the ˈbacon** (*infml*) achieve sth successfully. **bring sth ˈhome to sb** make sb realize sth fully: *The television pictures brought home to us all the plight of the refugees.* **come ˈhome (to sb)** become fully (and often painfully) clear. **come home to ˈroost** (of words) take effect upon the person who has said them. **drive sth home** ⇨ DRIVE¹. **drive the point home** ⇨ DRIVE¹. **hit/strike ˈhome** (of remarks, etc) have the intended (often painful) effect: *I could see from her expression that his sarcastic comments had hit home.* (**be**) **home and ˈdry** safe and successful, esp after a difficult time. **invalid sb home** ⇨ INVALID² *v.* **press sth home** ⇨ PRESS². **romp home/in** ⇨ ROMP. **till the cows come home** ⇨ COW¹. **when one's ship comes home/in** ⇨ SHIP¹.

□ ˈ**home-coming** *n* [C, U] arrival at home (esp of sb who has been away for a long time).

home⁴ /həʊm/ *v* **1** [I] (of a trained pigeon) fly home. **2** (phr v) **home in (on sth)** be directed or move towards sth: *The torpedo homed in on its target.* ○ *Pop fans are homing in on the concert site from miles around.*

homely /ˈhəʊmlɪ/ *adj* (**-ier, -iest**) **1** (*approv esp Brit*) (**a**) simple and plain: *a homely woman.* (**b**) making sb feel comfortable: *a homely place, atmosphere.* **2** (*US derog*) (of a person's appearance) not good-looking; plain. ▷ **homeliness** *n* [U].

homeopath, homeopathy (*US*) = HOMOEOPATH (HOMOEOPATHY), HOMOEOPATHY.

Homer /ˈhəʊmə(r)/ **1** (?c 700 BC), ancient Greek poet traditionally regarded as the author of the **Iliad* and the **Odyssey,* long epic poems about the deeds of Greek heroes. It is now thought that, although such a man may have existed, the poems as they have come down to us are the product of constant retelling by oral storytellers over many centuries. **2** (idm) **Homer (sometimes) ˈnods** (*saying*) even the best, greatest, etc people occasionally make mistakes.

▷ **Homeric** /həʊˈmerɪk/ *adj* [usu attrib] of Homer or the period of ancient Greek history when he lived: *Homeric heroes* ○ *the Homeric age.*

homey /ˈhəʊmɪ/ *adj* (**-mier, -miest**) (*US infml*) = HOMY.

homicide /ˈhɒmɪsaɪd/ *n* **1** [U] killing of one person by another: *be accused of homicide.* Cf MURDER. **2** [C] person who kills another.

▷ **homicidal** /ˌhɒmɪˈsaɪdl/ *adj* of homicide: *have homicidal tendencies* ○ *a homicidal maniac.*

homily /ˈhɒmɪlɪ/ *n* **1** (*often derog*) long and boring talk from sb on the correct way to behave, etc: *preach/give/deliver a homily.* **2** (*fml*) sermon. ▷ **homiletic** /ˌhɒmɪˈletɪk/ *adj.*

homing /ˈhəʊmɪŋ/ *adj* [attrib] **1** (of a pigeon) having the instinct or trained to fly home from a great distance. **2** (of a torpedo, missile, etc) fitted with an electronic device that enables it to find and hit a target: *ˈhoming devices.*

hominid /ˈhɒmɪnɪd/ *n* any of a family of two-legged animals including human beings and their prehistoric ancestors.

Homo /ˈhəʊməʊ/ *n* (*pl* ~**s**) any of a genus (*Homo*) of two-legged animals that includes modern human beings (*Homo sapiens*) and their prehistoric ancestors. The first known species, *Homo habilis,* originated in E Africa about 2 million years ago. About half a million years later *Homo erectus* began to populate other parts of Africa and also Asia and Europe. *Homo sapiens* is about 80 000 years old.

homo- *comb form* the same: *homosexual* ○ *homophone* ○ *homogeneous.* Cf HETERO-.

homoeopathy (*US* **homeo-**) /ˌhəʊmɪˈɒpəθɪ/ *n* [U] treatment of a disease by very small amounts of drugs that, if given to a healthy person, would produce symptoms like those of the disease itself.

▷ **homoeopath** (*US* **homeo-**) /ˈhəʊmɪəpæθ/ *n* person who practises homoeopathy.

homoeopathic (*US* **homeo-**) /ˌhəʊmɪəˈpæθɪk/ *adj*: *homoeopathic remedies, treatment, medicines, etc.*

homogeneous /ˌhɒməˈdʒiːnɪəs/ *adj* formed of parts that are all of the same type. Cf HETEROGENEOUS.

▷ **homogeneity** /ˌhɒmədʒɪˈniːətɪ/ *n* [U] quality of being alike.

homogenize, -ise /həˈmɒdʒənaɪz/ *v* [Tn] **1** treat (milk) so that the particles of fat are broken down and the cream is blended with the rest. **2** make (sth) homogeneous.

homograph /ˈhɒməgrɑːf; *US* -græf/ *n* word spelt like another word but with a different meaning or pronunciation, eg *bow*¹ /baʊ/, *bow*² /bəʊ/.

homologous /həˈmɒləgəs/ *adj* ~ (**with sth**) in a similar position or performing a similar function (to sth else).

□ **hoˌmologous ˈchromosome** (*biology*) either of a pair of chromosomes that are identical in their shape, size and distribution of their genes. One is from the female parent and one from the male. They pair up during cell division (*meiosis*).

hoˌmologous ˈseries (*chemistry*) series of organic compounds, each of which differs from the previous one by a particular fixed amount, esp by having one extra carbon and two extra hydrogen atoms.

homonym /ˈhɒmənɪm/ *n* word spelt and pronounced like another word but with a different meaning, eg *see*¹, *see*².

homophone /ˈhɒməfəʊn/ *n* word pronounced like another word but with a different meaning or spelling, eg *some, sum* /sʌm/; *knew, new* /njuː/.

Homo sapiens /ˌhəʊməʊ ˈsæpɪenz/ (*Latin*) modern man regarded as a species.

homosexual /ˌhɒməˈsekʃʊəl/ *adj* sexually attracted only to people of the same sex as oneself: *homosexual relationships, tendencies.* Cf GAY 1, HETEROSEXUAL, BISEXUAL.

▷ **homosexual** *n* homosexual person. Cf LESBIAN.

homosexuality /ˌhɒməsekʃʊˈælətɪ/ *n* [U] condition of being homosexual.

homy (*US* **homey**) /ˈhəʊmɪ/ *adj* (**-ier, -iest**) (*approv*) like home; cosy.

Hon *abbr* **1** /ɒn/ Honorary: *the Hon Sec,* ie Honorary Secretary ○ *the Hon Treasurer.* **2** Honourable: *the Hon Emily Smythe.* Cf RT HON. ⇨ article at ARISTOCRAT.

Honduras /hɒnˈdjʊərəs; *US* -ˈdʊə-/ country in Central America, between Guatemala and Nicaragua; pop approx 4 802 000; official language Spanish; capital Tegucigalpa; unit of currency lempira or peso (= 100 centavos). It is mountainous, and nearly half of it is covered in forests. Coffee, bananas and timber are its main exports. ⇨ map at CENTRAL AMERICA. ▷ **Honduran** /hɒnˈdjʊərən; *US* -ˈdʊə-/ *adj.*

hone /həʊn/ *n* stone used for sharpening the cutting edges of tools, etc.

▷ **hone** *v* [Tn] sharpen (sth) on a hone.

honest /ˈɒnɪst/ *adj* **1** (**a**) (of a person) telling the truth; not cheating or stealing: *an honest witness, businessman.* (**b**) (of a statement) frank, sincere and direct: *give an honest opinion* ○ *Do you like my dress? Please be honest!* (**c**) showing or resulting from an honest mind: *an honest face* ○ *He looks honest enough, but can we trust him?* ○ *She's never done an honest day's work* (ie worked hard and conscientiously) *in her life.* **2** (of wages, etc) fairly earned: *make an honest living.* **3** (of actions, etc) sincere but undistinguished. **4** (idm) **earn/turn an honest ˈpenny** earn money by working hard and fairly. **honest to ˈGod/ˈgoodness** (*infml*) truthfully: *Honest to goodness, I didn't do it.* **make an honest ˈwoman of sb** (*dated joc*) marry sb after having had a sexual relationship with her. **to be (quite) ˈhonest (about it/with you)** (*catch-phrase*) (used to emphasize that one is speaking frankly): *To be honest, I don't think we have a chance of winning.*

▷ **honest** *adv* (*infml*) truthfully: *It wasn't me, honest!*

honestly *adv* **1** in a truthful and fair way: *deal honestly with sb.* **2** (used for emphasis) really: *I don't honestly know.* ○ *Honestly, that's all the money I've got!* **3** (used to show disapproval and impatience): *Honestly! What a fuss!*

□ ˌ**honest ˈbroker** neutral person who attempts

to settle a dispute between two others.
ˌ**honest-to-ˈgoodness** *adj* [attrib] plain and simple; genuine; straightforward: *a bit of honest-to-goodness hard work.*

honesty /ˈɒnəstɪ/ *n* [U] **1** quality of being honest; truthfulness. **2** plant with purple flowers and flat round semi-transparent seed-pods. **3** (idm) **in all ˈhonesty** honestly: *I can't in all honesty* (ie if I must be honest) *deny it.*

honey /ˈhʌnɪ/ *n* **1** [U] **(a)** sweet sticky yellowish substance made by bees from nectar. **(b)** its colour: *honey-coloured hair.* **2** [U] sweetness; pleasantness. **3** [C] (*infml esp US*) **(a)** (used to address or refer to a person one likes or loves): *You look great tonight, honey!* ○ *Our baby-sitter is an absolute honey.* **(b)** thing that is excellent or delightful: *That computer game's a honey.*
▷ **honeyed** /ˈhʌnɪd/ *adj* (of words) sentimental and flattering.
□ ˈ**honey-bee** *n* ordinary type of bee that lives in hives.

honeycomb /ˈhʌnɪkəʊm/ (also **comb**) *n* **1** [C, U] wax structure of six-sided cells made by bees for holding their honey and eggs: *a piece of honeycomb.* **2** [C] pattern or arrangement of six-sided sections. ˈ**honeycombed** *adj* ~ **(with sth)** filled with holes, tunnels, etc: *The Rock of Gibraltar is honeycombed with caves.*

honeydew /ˈhʌnɪdjuː/ *n* [U] sweet sticky substance found on leaves and stems in hot weather.
□ ˌ**honeydew ˈmelon** cultivated variety of melon with pale skin and sweet green flesh.

honeymoon /ˈhʌnɪmuːn/ *n* **1** holiday taken by a newly married couple: *They went to Italy for their honeymoon.* ○ *We're on our honeymoon.* ⇨ article at WEDDING. **2** (*fig*) period of enthusiastic goodwill at the start of an undertaking, a relationship, etc: [attrib] *The honeymoon period for the new government is over, and they must now start to tackle the country's many problems.*
▷ **honeymoon** *v* [I, Ipr] spend a honeymoon: *They are honeymooning in Paris.* **honeymooner** *n.*

honeysuckle /ˈhʌnɪsʌkl/ *n* [U] climbing shrub with sweet-smelling yellow or pink flowers.

Hong Kong /ˌhɒŋ ˈkɒŋ/ British colony on the SE coast of China; pop approx 5 681 000; official languages English and Chinese; unit of currency Hong Kong dollar (HK$). The island of Hong Kong came under British rule in 1841, and an area on the mainland of China, known as the New Territories, was leased to Britain for 99 years in 1898. The whole colony is to be returned to Chinese rule in 1997. Hong Kong is a major financial centre, and has the world's third largest container port. ⇨ map at CHINA.

honk /hɒŋk/ *n* **1** cry of the wild goose. **2** sound made by a car horn, esp of the old-fashioned type.
▷ **honk** *v* [I, Ipr, Tn, Tn·pr] ~ **(sth) (at sb/sth)** (cause sth to) make a honk: *the honking cry of migrating geese* ○ *The driver honked (his horn) at me to get out of the way.*

honkie (also **honky**) /ˈhɒŋkɪ/ *n* (*US derog sl offensive*) (used by Blacks) white person.

honky-tonk /ˈhɒŋkɪ tɒŋk/ *n* (*infml*) **1** [U] type of ragtime music played on a piano: [attrib] *a honky-tonk rhythm.* **2** [C] cheap night-club.

honorarium /ˌɒnəˈreərɪəm/ *n* (*pl* ~**s**) voluntary payment made for professional services for which a fee is not normally paid or required by law.

honorary /ˈɒnərərɪ; *US* ˈɒnərerɪ/ *adj* [usu attrib] **1** (of a degree, rank, etc) given as an honour: *be awarded an honorary doctorate, title.* **2** (in titles **Honorary**, *abbr* **Hon**) (of a position or its holder) unpaid: *the honorary (post of) President* ○ *the Honorary Secretary Mrs Hill.*

honor, honorable (*US*) = HONOUR, HONOURABLE.

honorific /ˌɒnəˈrɪfɪk/ *n, adj* (expression) indicating respect for the person being addressed, esp in Oriental languages.

honour[1] (*US* **honor**) /ˈɒnə(r)/ *n* **1** [U, sing] source of pride and pleasure; privilege: *the seat of honour at the head of the table* ○ *It is a great honour to be invited.* **2** [U] **(a)** good personal character; strong sense of what is morally right: *a man of honour* ○ *Honour demands that he should resign.* **(b)** reputation for greatness, good behaviour, truthfulness, etc: *fight for the honour of one's country* ○ *My honour is at stake.* **3** [U] great respect; high public regard: *They stood in silence as a mark of honour to her.* **4** [sing] **an** ~ **to sth/sb** a person or thing that brings credit to sth/sb: *She is an honour to her profession.* **5** [C usu *pl*] thing given as a distinction or mark of respect, esp an official award for achievement or bravery: *bury a person with full military honours*, ie with a special ceremony to honour the dead soldier ○ *Birthday/New Year Honours*, ie titles, decorations, etc awarded in Britain by the Sovereign on his or her birthday or on 1 January each year. ⇨ article at ARISTOCRAT. **6 honours** [pl] specialized course for a university degree or high level of distinction reached in it: [attrib] *an honours degree course in French literature.* **7 your/his/her Honour** [sing] (used to or about certain judges or people of importance as a title of respect): *I plead innocent, your Honour.* **8** [C esp *pl*] (in card-games) any of the cards of highest value: *hold five spades to* (ie of which the highest is) *an honour.* **9** [U] (in golf) right of driving off first: *It's ˈyour honour, partner.* **10** (idm) **a debt of honour** ⇨ DEBT. **do sb ˈhonour** (*fml*) show respect for sb: *Fifty heads of state attended the Queen's coronation to do her honour.* **do sb an honour; do sb the honour (of doing sth)** (*fml*) give sb a privilege: *You do us a great honour by attending.* ○ *Will you do me the honour of dining with me?* **do the ˈhonours** (*infml*) act as host or hostess; perform some social duty or small ceremony: *Who's going to pour the tea — shall I do the honours?* **have the honour (of sth)** (*fml*) be granted the privilege specified: *May I have the honour of this dance?* ○ *To whom do I have the honour of speaking?* **(there is) honour among ˈthieves** (*saying*) criminals often have their own standards of behaviour that they live by. **honours are ˈeven** the contest is level: *Both teams have won the same number of games so honours are even between them.* **(in) honour ˈbound (to do sth)** required to do sth as a moral duty but not by law: *I feel honour bound to attend because I promised I would.* **in honour of sb/sth; in sb's/sth's honour** out of respect for sb/sth: *a ceremony in honour of those killed in battle.* **on one's honour (to do sth)** under a moral obligation (to do sth). **on my ˈhonour** I swear it: *I promise I'll pay you back, on my honour.* **a point of honour** ⇨ POINT[1]. **put sb on his, etc ˈhonour** make sb promise solemnly to do sth. **one's word of honour** ⇨ WORD.
□ ˈ**honours list** (*Brit*) list of people given titles, decorations, etc by the Sovereign.

honour[2] (*US* **honor**) /ˈɒnə(r)/ *v* **1** [Tn, Tn·pr] ~ **sb/sth (with sth)** show great respect for sb/sth; give public praise and distinction to sb: *I feel highly honoured by your trust.* ○ (*fml*) *Will you honour me with a visit?* **2** [Tn] (*commerce*) accept and pay (sth) when due: *honour a cheque/bill/draft.*

honourable (*US* **honorable**) /ˈɒnərəbl/ *adj* **1** deserving, bringing or showing honour: *an honourable person, deed, calling* ○ *conclude an honourable peace* ○ *do the honourable thing by resigning.* **2** (in titles **the Honourable**, *abbr* **Hon**) **(a)** (title given to certain high officials). **(b)** (title used in Parliamentary debates by members of Parliament when speaking of or to each other): *my Honourable friend, the member for Chester.* Cf RIGHT HONOURABLE (RIGHT[2]). **(c)** (title given to the children of peers below the rank of marquis): *the Honourable Mrs Craig Holmes.* ▷ **honourably** /-əblɪ/ *adv*: *acquit oneself honourably.*
□ ˌ**honourable ˈmention** praise or credit given to sb for doing well, though not winning.

Hons /ɒnz/ *abbr* Honours (in Bachelor degrees): *Jim West BSc (Hons)* ○ *a degree with Hons* ○ *degree class: Hons 2(i).*

Hon Sec /ˌɒn ˈsek/ *abbr* Honorary Secretary.

hooch /huːtʃ/ *n* [U] (*US infml*) (esp cheap or illegally made) alcoholic liquor.

hood[1] /hʊd/ *n* **1** **(a)** covering for the head and neck, often fastened to a coat, etc, so that it can hang down at the back, or be detached, when not in use. **(b)** garment of coloured silk, fur, etc similar to a hood and worn over a university gown to show the degree held by the wearer. **2** thing resembling a hood in shape or use: *The robbers all wore hoods to hide their faces.* **3** **(a)** (*Brit*) folding waterproof top of a motor car, carriage, pram, etc: *In fine weather I can drive my car with the hood down.* **(b)** cover placed over a machine to protect it or sb using it: *a soundproof hood for the computer printer.* **4** (*US*) = BONNET 3.
▷ **hooded** *adj* **1** having a hood: *a hooded raincoat.* **2** wearing a hood: *hooded monks.*

hood[2] /hʊd/ *n* (*US sl*) = HOODLUM 2.

-hood *suff* (with *ns* or *adjs* forming *ns*) **1** state or condition of: *childhood* ○ *brotherhood* ○ *falsehood.* **2** group of: *priesthood.*

hoodlum /ˈhuːdləm/ *n* **1** destructive and rowdy youth. **2** violent criminal; gangster.

hoodoo /ˈhuːduː/ *n* (*pl* ~**s**) ~ **(on sb/sth)** (*esp US*) person or thing that brings or causes bad luck; jinx: *My car seems to have a hoodoo on it — it keeps breaking down.*
▷ **hoodoo** *v* [Tn] (*esp US infml*) make (sb) unlucky.

hoodwink /ˈhʊdwɪŋk/ *v* [Tn, Tn·pr] ~ **sb (into doing sth)** deceive sb; trick sb: *I was hoodwinked into buying fake jewels.*

hooey /ˈhuːɪ/ *n* [U], *interj* (*sl*) false or foolish talk; nonsense: *That's a lot of hooey!* ○ *What hooey!*

hoof /huːf/ *n* (*pl* ~**s** or **hooves** /huːvz/) **1** horny part of the foot of a horse, an ox or a deer. ⇨ illus at HORSE. **2** (idm) **on the ˈhoof** (of cattle) alive: *bought on the hoof and then slaughtered.*
▷ **hoof** *v* (idm) ˈ**hoof it** (*sl*) go on foot: *The last bus had gone so we had to hoof it home.*

hoo-ha /ˈhuː hɑː/ *n* [U, sing] (*infml*) noisy or excited protest, esp about sth unimportant; commotion; fuss: *The photo caused a real hoo-ha.* ○ *What are they making such a hoo-ha about?* ○ *There was a terrific hoo-ha (going on) about who should pay.*

hook

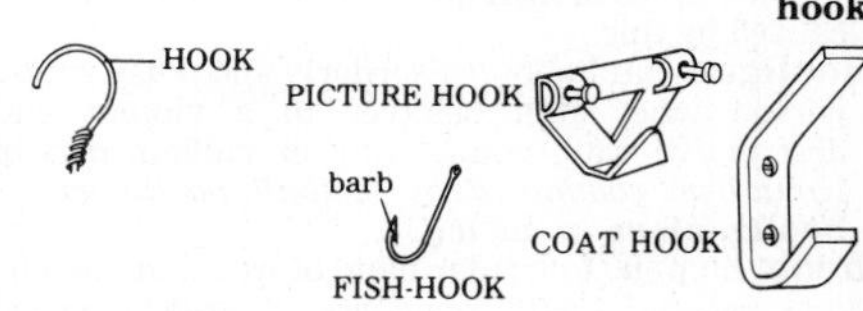

hook[1] /hʊk/ *n* **1** curved or bent piece of wire, plastic, etc for catching hold of sth or for hanging sth on: *a ˈfish-hook* ○ *a ˈcrochet hook* ○ *Hang your towel on a hook.* **2** (esp in compounds) curved tool for cutting (grain, etc) or for chopping (branches): *a ˈreaping-hook* ○ *a ˈbillhook.* **3** thing shaped like a hook, eg a sharp bend in a river, etc or a curving point of land: *the Hook of Holland.* **4** **(a)** (in cricket or golf) type of stroke that hooks (HOOK[2] 4a) the ball. **(b)** (in boxing) short blow with the elbow bent: *a left hook to the jaw.* **5** (idm) **by ˌhook or by ˈcrook** by one means or another, no matter what happens. ˌ**hook, line and ˈsinker** entirely; completely: *What I said was untrue but he fell for it/swallowed it* (ie believed it) *hook, line and sinker.* **off the ˈhook** (of a telephone receiver) not replaced, thus preventing incoming calls: *He left the phone off the hook so that he wouldn't be disturbed.* **(let sb/get) off the ˈhook** (*infml*) out of difficulty or trouble: *She was winning easily, but then she started to get careless and let her opponent off the hook*, ie allowed her to avoid being defeated. **sling one's hook** ⇨ SLING *v.*
□ ˌ**hook and ˈeye** small metal hook and loop which together form a fastening for clothes, etc: *a row of hooks and eyes.*
ˈ**hook-nose** *n* nose with a curved shape; aquiline nose. ˈ**hook-nosed** *adj.*

hook[2] /hʊk/ *v* **1** **(a)** [I, Ipr, Tn, Tn·pr] ~ **(sth) (on/onto/over/round sth)** (cause sth to) be fastened with or as if with a hook or hooks: *These two pieces of the chain hook together.* ○ *a dress that hooks/is hooked at the back* ○ *hook the caravan (on)to the car*

○ *My shirt got hooked on a thorn.* **(b)** [Tn] catch (sth) with a hook: *hook a large fish* ○ *(fig joc) hook a husband/wife.* **2** [Tn] make (sth) into the form of a hook: *hook one's finger.* **3** [Tn] *(sl)* steal (sth). **4** [Tn] *(sport)* **(a)** hit (a ball) in a curving path or with a curving stroke. **(b)** (in Rugby football) kick (the ball) backwards in a scrum(1). **5** (idm) **be hooked (on sb)** *(sl)* be in love (with sb). **be/get hooked (on sth)** *(sl)* be/become addicted (to sth); be/become completely committed (to sth): *get hooked on heroin, gambling, television* ○ *She's completely hooked on the idea of a camping holiday.* **6** (phr v) **hook sth/sb up** fasten (a garment) by means of hooks and eyes: *hook up a dress* ○ *Please will you hook me up* (ie fasten my dress up) *at the back?* **hook (sth) up (with sth)** link broadcasting facilities for special transmissions: *The BBC is hooked up with Australian television by satellite.*

▷ **hooked** *adj* **(a)** curved like a hook: *a hooked nose, beak.* **(b)** having a hook or hooks.

□ ˈ**hook-up** *n* link between two or more radio or television stations for the transmission of the same programme: *a satellite hook-up between the major European networks.*

hookah /ˈhʊkə/ (also **hubble-bubble**) *n* pipe used esp in Arab countries for smoking tobacco, with a long flexible tube to a container of water which cools the smoke as it is drawn through it.

Hooke /hʊk/ Robert (1635-1703), English scientist who invented the spirit-level, the marine barometer and the balance-spring for watches. He was also the first to use the term 'cell' in biology.

Hooker /ˈhʊkə(r)/ Sir Joseph Dalton (1817-1911), English botanist who made important discoveries about the distribution of plants around the world.

hooker /ˈhʊkə(r)/ *n* **1** *(sl esp US)* prostitute. **2** player in the front row of a scrum in Rugby football, who tries to hook[2](4) the ball.

hookey (also **hooky**) /ˈhʊkɪ/ *n* (idm) **play ˈhookey** *(sl esp US)* stay away from school, etc without permission; play truant.

hookworm /ˈhʊkwɜːm/ *n* **(a)** [C] worm that infests the intestines of men and animals. **(b)** [U] disease caused by this.

hooligan /ˈhuːlɪɡən/ *n* disorderly and noisy young person who often behaves in a violent and destructive way; young thug or ruffian: *acts of vandalism committed by football hooligans.* ▷ **hooliganism** /-ɪzəm/ *n* [U].

hoop /huːp/ *n* **1** circular band of wood, metal, etc: *a barrel bound with iron hoops.* **2** large ring used at a circus for riders or animals to jump through. **3** large (usu wooden) ring used (esp formerly) as a child's toy. **4** (in croquet) small iron arch fixed in the ground, through which balls are hit. **5** (idm) **put sb/go through the ˈhoops** make sb/be made to endure a test or an ordeal.

▷ **hoop** *v* [Tn] bind or encircle (a barrel, etc) with hoops.

hoop-la /ˈhuːp lɑː/ *n* [U] game in which players try to throw rings over objects in order to win them as prizes.

hoopoe /ˈhuːpuː/ *n* bird with a large fan-like crest and striped wing and tail feathers.

hooray /hʊˈreɪ/ *interj* = HURRAH.

hoosegow /ˈhuːsɡaʊ/ *n (US sl)* gaol; prison.

hoot /huːt/ *n* **1** cry of an owl. **2** sound made by a vehicle's horn, factory siren, etc. **3** shout expressing disapproval or scorn: *His suggestion was greeted with hoots of laughter.* **4** *(infml)* **(a)** loud laugh of delight and amusement. **(b)** thing that causes this: *What a hoot!* ○ *She looked an absolute hoot!* **5** (idm) **not care/give a hoot/two hoots** *(infml)* not care at all.

▷ **hoot** *v* **1** [I, Ipr] ~ **(at sb/sth)** make a hoot or hoots: *the eery sound of an owl hooting* ○ *The driver hooted at the sheep in the road.* ○ *The crowd was hooting and jeering at the speaker.* ○ *He hooted with laughter.* **2** [Tn] make scornful hoots at (sb); greet with jeers: *hoot a bad actor.* **3** [Tn, Tn·pr] ~ **sth (at sb/sth)** sound (a horn): *The driver hooted his horn (at us).* **4** (phr v) **hoot sth/sb down/off; hoot sb off sth** reject sth or drive sb away (from a place) by jeering: *The proposal was hooted down.* ○ *hoot a speaker off (a platform).* **hooter** *n* **1** *(esp Brit)* siren or steam whistle, esp as a signal for work to start or stop at a factory, etc. **2** *(dated esp Brit)* car horn. **3** *(Brit sl)* nose.

Hoover /ˈhuːvə(r)/ *n (propr)* vacuum cleaner.

▷ **hoover** *v* [Tn] *(Brit)* clean (a carpet, etc) with a vacuum cleaner: *hoover the rug, floor, hall, whole house.*

hooves *pl* of HOOF.

hop[1] /hɒp/ *v* **(-pp-)** **1** [I, Ipr, Ip] **(a)** (of a person) move by jumping on one foot: *He had hurt his left foot and had to hop along.* **(b)** (of an animal or a bird) move by jumping with both or all feet together: *Several frogs were hopping about on the lawn.* **2** [Tn] cross (a ditch, etc) by jumping. **3** [Ip] ~ **across/over (to...)** *(infml)* make a short quick trip to a place: *I'm hopping over to Paris for the weekend.* **4** (idm) **hop it** *(sl)* go away: *Go on, hop it!* ○ *When the burglar heard their car he hopped it out of the window.* **hopping ˈmad** *(infml)* very angry. **5** (phr v) **hop in/into sth; hop out/out of sth** get into/out of (a car): *Hop in, I'll give you a lift to the station.* **hop on/onto sth; hop off (sth)** jump (esp quickly) onto/off (a bus, etc).

▷ **hop** *n* **1** act of hopping; short jump, esp on one leg. **2** *(infml)* short flight or one stage in a long-distance flight: *the long flight across the Atlantic, then the final hop from New York to Boston* ○ *We flew from London to Bombay in one hop.* **3** *(infml)* informal dance party: *Are you coming to the hop tonight?* **4** (idm) **on the ˈhop** *(infml)* active; busy: *I've been on the hop all day.* **(catch sb) on the ˈhop** unprepared; taken by surprise: *You've caught me on the hop, I'm afraid — give me five minutes to get ready.*

□ **hopped-up** /ˌhɒpt ˈʌp/ *adj (US sl)* **1** excited, esp by drugs. **2** supercharged: *a ˌhopped-up ˈengine.*

ˌ**hop, skip and ˈjump** (also **hop, step and jump**) *(dated)* = TRIPLE JUMP (TRIPLE).

hop[2] /hɒp/ *n* **(a)** [C] climbing plant with flowers growing in clusters. **(b) hops** [pl] dried flowers of this plant, used for giving a bitter flavour to beer.

▷ **hopper** *n* = HOP-PICKER.

□ ˈ**hop-field** (also **hop-garden**) *n* field in which hops are grown.

ˈ**hop-picker** *n* worker or machine employed to pick hops.

ˈ**hop-pole** *n* tall pole for supporting wires on which hop plants are trained to grow.

Hope /həʊp/ Bob (1903-), British-born American film actor and comedian. His most famous comic roles have been as the cowardly dentist in *The Paleface* and (with his partner Bing *Crosby) in the series of *Road* films beginning with *Road to Singapore.*

hope /həʊp/ *n* **1** [C, U] ~ **(of/for sth);** ~ **(of doing sth/that...)** desire for sth to happen, combined with the expectation that it will: *cherish a/the hope that he will recover* ○ *a ray of hope,* ie a slight hope ○ *Our hopes for fine weather were not disappointed.* ○ *We've set/pinned all our hopes on you.* ○ *She has (high) hopes* (ie is very confident) *of winning.* ○ *Don't give up hope yet.* ○ *There is not much hope that they are/hope of their being still alive.* ○ *All hope (of finding them) was abandoned and the search was called off.* **2** [C usu *sing*] person, thing or circumstance that encourages hope: *You are my last hope; if you can't help, I'm ruined.* ○ *Does our only hope of survival lie in disarmament?* **3** (idm) **be beyond hope** have no chance of succeeding, recovering, etc. **build up/raise sb's hopes** encourage sb to expect better fortune, etc: *Don't raise his hopes too much.* **dash/shatter sb's hopes** cause sb to lose hope: *All our hopes were dashed by the announcement.* **a forlorn hope** ⇨ FORLORN. **have a hope (of doing sth)** have a chance of succeeding, recovering, etc: *He has no hope of winning.* **hold out (some, not much, little, no, etc) hope (of sth/that...)** provide (some, etc) reason to expect sth: *The doctors held out no hope of recovery.* **hope springs eˈternal (in the human ˈbreast)** *(saying)* people never stop being hopeful, even in the worst situations. **in the hope of sth/that...** because of the wish for sth/that...: *I called in the hope of finding her at home.* **live in ˈhope; live in hope(s) of sth** ⇨ LIVE[2]. **not have a hope in hell** have no chance at all. **not a ˈhope; ˌsome ˈhope!** (there is) no chance at all (that that will happen): *'He might turn up with the cash.' 'Some hope!'*

▷ **hope** *v* [I, Ipr, Tf, Tt] ~ **(for sth)** **1 (a)** desire and expect (sth) or feel confident (about sth): *We haven't heard from him for weeks but we're still hoping (for a letter).* ○ *I hope to announce the winner shortly.* **(b)** wish (sth); desire: *'Will it rain tomorrow?' 'I hope not/so.'* ○ *We hope (that) you're well.* **2** (idm) ˌ**hope against ˈhope (that)...** continue to hope for sth even though it is very unlikely. ˌ**hope and ˈpray** hope very much: *I just hope and pray we aren't too late.* ˌ**hope for the ˈbest** hope for a favourable result.

□ ˈ**hope chest** *(US)* = BOTTOM DRAWER (BOTTOM).

NOTE ON USAGE: Compare **hope** and **wish** as verbs. **1 Hope (that)** indicates a desire relating to the past, present or future: *I hope you weren't late.* ○ *I hope you're ready.* ○ *We hope you'll be very happy.* **Wish (that)** expresses regret about the past, present or future: *I wish I hadn't gone to that party,* ie but I went. ○ *I wish I could speak Chinese,* ie but I can't. ○ *I wish I was going on holiday next month,* ie but I'm not. **2 Hope** and **wish** can also be used with an infinitive, in which case their meanings are closer. *She hopes to get a job overseas* means she has a strong desire to get one and there's a good possibility that she will. *She wishes to get a job overseas* is a formal way of saying that she wants to get one.

hopeful /ˈhəʊpfl/ *adj* **1** [usu pred] ~ **(of/about sth);** ~ **(that...)** (of a person) having hope: *be hopeful about the future* ○ *I feel hopeful of success/that we shall succeed.* **2** (of a sign, situation, etc) giving hope; likely to be favourable or successful; promising: *The future does not seem very hopeful.*

▷ **hopeful** *n* person who hopes or seems likely to succeed: *the young hopefuls, lined up before the judges* ○ *Many a young hopeful went to Hollywood.*

hopefully *adv* **1** in a hopeful way: *'I'm sure we'll find it,' he said hopefully.* **2** it is to be hoped; let us hope: *Hopefully, we'll arrive before dark.*

hopefulness *n* [U].

NOTE ON USAGE: There is a group of adverbs and adverbial phrases (eg **frankly**, **obviously**, **to begin with**) which can be used in two distinct ways: **1** They may modify the whole sentence: *Frankly, you are wrong.* ○ *Obviously, I'd prefer a better job.* ○ *To begin with, I don't like his attitude.* **2** They may simply modify the verb: *He spoke frankly* (= in a frank way) *about his past life.* ○ *He pointed very obviously at the woman in the fur coat.* ○ *I liked it in America to begin with.* Other examples are **generally**, **hopefully**, **personally**, **really**, **sadly**, **seriously**, **thankfully.** Some careful speakers use **hopefully** only in pattern 2, but its use in pattern 1 is now widely accepted.

hopeless /ˈhəʊplɪs/ *adj* **1** most unlikely to improve, succeed, be settled, etc; causing despair: *a hopeless situation, struggle, attempt, etc* ○ *It's hopeless trying to convince her.* ○ *Most of the students are making good progress but Jeremy seems a hopeless case,* ie he cannot or will not learn anything. **2** ~ **(at sth)** *(infml)* (of a person) lacking in ability or skill; incompetent: *a hopeless cook, teacher, etc* ○ *He's hopeless at maths.*

▷ **hopelessly** *adv*: *a hopelessly ill patient* ○ *be hopelessly lost* ○ *be hopelessly in love, in debt.* **hopelessness** *n* [U].

Hopkins /ˈhɒpkɪnz/ Gerard Manley (1844-89), English poet. Much of his verse is concerned with religious themes and with the beauty of nature. He often used what he called 'sprung rhythm' (fixed stress patterns combined with a varying number of syllables), to capture the rhythms of natural speech. The quality of his work was not fully recognized until the 20th century. His best-known poems are 'The Wreck of the Deutschland' and 'Windhover'.

hopper[1] /ˈhɒpə(r)/ *n* **(a)** V-shaped structure for

holding (esp) grain or coal, with an opening at its base through which the contents can pass into a mill, furnace, etc below. (**b**) any similar device for feeding materials into a machine, etc.

hopper[2] /ˈhɒpə(r)/ *n* any hopping insect, eg a flea.

hopper[3] /ˈhɒpə(r)/ ⇨ HOP[2].

hopsack /ˈhɒpsæk/ *n* [U] type of loosely woven cloth.

hopscotch /ˈhɒpskɒtʃ/ *n* [U] children's game of hopping into and over squares marked on the ground in order to retrieve a stone thrown into one of these squares.

Horace /ˈhɒrɪs; *US* ˈhɔ:rəs/ (Quintus Horatius Flaccus, 65 BC-8 BC), Roman poet whose works include a collection of *Odes*, modelled on early Greek lyrics, and *Satires*, in which he reflected on life, literature and morality. ▷ **Horatian** /həˈreɪʃn/ *adj*.

horde /hɔ:d/ *n* (*sometimes derog*) very large group (esp of people); huge crowd; throng: *hordes of fans, tourists, football supporters, shoppers, etc* ○ *There were hordes of people at the jumble sale.* ○ *Fans had descended on the concert hall in their hordes*, ie in large numbers.

horizon /həˈraɪzn/ *n* **1 the horizon** [sing] the line at which the earth and sky appear to meet: *The sun sank below the horizon.* ○ *A ship appeared on the horizon.* **2** [C usu *pl*] (*fig*) limit of a person's knowledge, experience, interest, etc: *a woman of narrow horizons* ○ *Travel broadens one's horizons.* **3** (idm) **on the hoˈrizon** about to happen; just becoming apparent; imminent: *There's trouble on the horizon.*

horizontal /ˌhɒrɪˈzɒntl; *US* ˌhɔ:r-/ *adj* parallel to the horizon; flat; level: *a horizontal line.* ⇨ illus at VERTICAL.

▷ **horizontal** *n* [C, sing] horizontal line, bar, etc: *He shifted his position from the horizontal.*

horizontally /-təlɪ/ *adv*: *Lay it horizontally on the floor.*

hormone /ˈhɔ:məʊn/ *n* (**a**) substance produced within the body of an animal and carried by the blood to an organ which it stimulates to assist growth, etc; similar substance produced by a plant and transported in the sap: [attrib] *hormone deficiency, imbalance.* (**b**) synthetic substance that has a similar effect.

▷ **hormonal** /hɔ:ˈməʊnl/ *adj* of a hormone or hormones.

Hormuz /ˌhɔ:ˈmu:z/ small island in the **Strait of Hormuz**, a narrow stretch of water at the southern end of the *Persian Gulf through which oil-tankers coming from the Arabian Sea to the oil ports of the Gulf must pass. ⇨ map at ARABIAN PENINSULA.

horn /hɔ:n/ *n* **1** (**a**) [C] bony outgrowth, usu curved and pointed and one of a pair, on the heads of cattle, deer, rams and various other animals. ⇨ illus at SHEEP. (**b**) [U] hard smooth substance of which this is made. **2** [C] any of the various wind instruments with a trumpet-shaped end: *a French ˈhorn* ○ *a ˈhunting horn.* **3** [C] device for sounding a warning signal: *a ˈcar horn* ○ *sound the horn to alert a cyclist* ○ (*joc*) *He's got a voice like a ˈfog-horn.* ⇨ illus at CAR. **4** [C] thing resembling an animal's horn, eg the projection on the head of a snail. **5** [C] either of the ends of the crescent moon. **6** (idm) **draw in one's horns** ⇨ DRAW[2]. **on the horns of a diˈlemma** faced with a choice between things that are equally undesirable. **take the bull by the horns** ⇨ BULL[1].

▷ **horn** *v* (phr v) **horn in (on sth)** (*sl*) join in (an attractive or a profitable undertaking, etc) without being invited; intrude.

horned *adj* (often in compound *adjs*) having horns, esp of the specified type: *horned cattle* ○ *long-horned cattle.* **horned ˈowl** owl with hornlike tufts of feathers by its ears. **horned ˈtoad** small burrowing N American lizard with a flattened spiny body.

hornless *adj* without horns.

hornlike *adj* **1** similar to a horn(1a) in shape. **2** hard like horn(1b).

horny *adj* (**-ier, -iest**) **1** made of horn. **2** made hard and rough, eg by hard work: *horny hands.* **3** (*sl*) sexually aroused: *feeling horny.*

□ ˈ**hornbill** *n* tropical bird with a hornlike growth on its beak.

the ˌHorn of ˈAfrica triangular region at the NE corner of Africa, containing Somalia and parts of Ethiopia.

horn of ˈplenty = CORNUCOPIA.

ˈ**horn-rimmed** *adj* (of spectacles) with frames made of a material like horn.

hornbeam /ˈhɔ:nbi:m/ *n* type of tree with smooth grey bark and hard tough wood, often used in hedges.

hornet /ˈhɔ:nɪt/ *n* **1** large type of wasp that can give a severe sting. **2** (idm) **a ˈhornet's nest** attacks, criticism or abuse from several people, or angry quarrelling: *His letter to the newspaper about racialism in schools has stirred up a real hornet's nest.*

hornpipe /ˈhɔ:npaɪp/ *n* **1** lively dance usu performed by one person and traditionally associated with sailors. **2** music for such a dance.

horoscope /ˈhɒrəskəʊp; *US* ˈhɔ:r-/ *n* **1** forecast of a person's future based on a diagram showing the relative positions of the planets, etc at a particular time, eg the time of his birth: *read one's horoscope.* Cf ASTROLOGY, ZODIAC. ⇨ article at SUPERSTITION. **2** such a diagram, made by an astrologer.

horrendous /hɒˈrendəs/ *adj* (*infml*) horrifying; horrific: *horrendous queues, prices, clothes* ○ *That colour scheme is horrendous.* ▷ **horrendously** *adv*: *horrendously expensive.*

horrible /ˈhɒrəbl; *US* ˈhɔ:r-/ *adj* **1** causing horror: *a horrible crime, nightmare, death.* **2** (*infml*) very unpleasant: *horrible weather, food, people.* ○ *It tastes horrible.* ○ *Don't be so horrible (to me).* ▷ **horribly** /-əblɪ/ *adv*: *horribly burnt* ○ *He died horribly and in great pain.*

horrid /ˈhɒrɪd; *US* ˈhɔ:rɪd/ *adj* **1** terrible; frightful; horrible: *horrid cruelty, crimes.* **2** (*infml*) very unpleasant: *horrid weather, food, children* ○ *Don't be so horrid to your little sister.* ▷ **horridly** *adv*. **horridness** *n* [U].

horrific /həˈrɪfɪk/ *adj* **1** causing horror; horrifying: *a horrific crash, murder.* **2** (*infml*) excessive; causing horror: *horrific prices.* ▷ **horrifically** /-klɪ/ *adv* (*infml*): *The hotel was horrifically expensive.*

horrify /ˈhɒrɪfaɪ; *US* ˈhɔ:r-/ *v* (*pt, pp* **-fied**) [Tn] fill (sb) with horror; shock greatly: *We were horrified by what we saw.* ▷ **horrifying** *adj*: *a horrifying sight, experience* ○ (*infml*) *I find their ignorance horrifying.* **horrifyingly** *adv*.

horror /ˈhɒrə(r); *US* ˈhɔ:r-/ *n* **1** [U] feeling of intense fear or dismay; terror: *I recoiled in horror from the snake.* ○ *To her horror she saw him fall.* ○ *I have a/this horror of being trapped in a broken lift.* **2** [U] (**a**) feeling of intense dislike; hatred: *I have a deep horror of cruelty.* (**b**) horrifying nature: *It's hard to appreciate the full horror of life in a prison camp.* **3** [C] thing or person that causes hatred or fear: *the horrors of war.* **4** [C] (*infml*) bad or mischievous person, esp a naughty child: *Her son is a right little horror.* **5 the horrors** [pl] (*infml*) fit of depression or nervousness, etc: *Having to address an audience always gives me the horrors.*

▷ **horror** *adj* [attrib] designed to entertain by arousing pleasurable feelings of horror, shock, etc: *horror films/stories/comics.*

horrors *interj* (*usu joc*) used to express fear or dislike: *Oh horrors! Not another invitation to tea with Aunt Muriel!*

□ ˈ**horror-stricken** (also ˈ**horror-struck**) *adj* overcome with horror; very shocked.

Horsa /ˈhɔ:sə/ ⇨ HENGIST.

hors de combat /ˌɔ: də ˈkɒmbɑ:/ (*French*) unable to continue fighting because one is wounded: (*fig*) *I can't play you at squash this week — I'm hors de combat with a twisted ankle.*

hors-d'oeuvre /ˌɔ:ˈdɜ:vrə; *US* -ˈdɜ:v/ *n* (*pl* unchanged or **-d'oeuvres**) food served at the beginning of a meal as an appetizer.

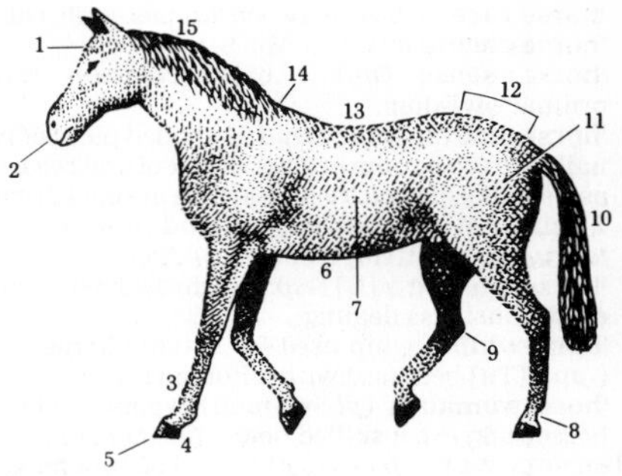

1 forelock	6 belly	11 croup
2 muzzle	7 flank	12 hindquarters
3 shank	8 fetlock	13 back
4 pastern	9 hock	14 withers
5 hoof	10 tail	15 mane

horse /hɔ:s/ *n* **1** (**a**) [C] large four-legged animal with a flowing mane and tail, used for riding on or to carry loads, pull carts, etc. ⇨ illus. Cf COLT 1, FILLY, FOAL, GELDING (GELD), MARE, STALLION. (**b**) [C] adult male horse; stallion. (**c**) [Gp, U] mounted soldiers; cavalry: *a detachment of horse.* **2** [C] = VAULTING HORSE (VAULT[2]). **3** [C] frame on which sth is supported: *a ˈclothes-horse.* **4** [U] (*sl*) heroin. **5** (idm) **back the wrong horse** ⇨ BACK[4]. **be/get on one's high horse** ⇨ HIGH[1]. **change/swap horses in midˈstream** transfer one's preference for or trust in sb/sth to another in the middle of an undertaking. **a dark horse** ⇨ DARK[2]. **drive a coach and horses through sth** ⇨ DRIVE[1]. **eat like a horse** ⇨ EAT. **flog a dead horse** ⇨ FLOG. **(straight) from the horse's ˈmouth** (of advice, information) given by sb who is directly involved or very reliable. **hold one's ˈhorses** (*infml*) wait a moment; restrain one's impatience, enthusiasm, etc. **a ˌhorse of a ˌdifferent ˈcolour** person or thing that is significantly different from the one being discussed (although perhaps related or relevant to him/it). **lock, etc the stable door after the horse has bolted** ⇨ STABLE[2]. **look a gift horse in the mouth** ⇨ GIFT. **put the cart before the horse** ⇨ CART. **a willing horse** ⇨ WILLING. **you can ˌtake, etc a horse to ˈwater, but you ˌcan't make him ˈdrink** (*saying*) one can give a person the opportunity to do sth but he may still refuse to do it.

▷ **horse** *v* (phr v) **horse about/around** (*infml*) act in a noisy rough playful way.

□ ˌ**horse-and-ˈbuggy** *adj* [attrib] (*US infml*) of times before motorized vehicles; old-fashioned: (*fig*) *ˌhorse-and-buggy eduˈcational methods.*

ˈ**horseback** *n* (idm) **on ˈhorseback** mounted on a horse: *riding on horseback.* — *adv, adj* [attrib] (*esp US*): *Do you like to ride horseback?* ○ *horseback riding.*

ˈ**horse-box** *n* closed vehicle for transporting a horse.

ˌ**horse-ˈchestnut** *n* **1** large tree with widely spreading branches and tall clusters of white or pink flowers. ⇨ illus at TREE. **2** its reddish-brown nut.

ˈ**horseflesh** *n* [U] **1** (also ˈ**horsemeat**) flesh of a horse, used as food. **2** horses collectively: *He's a good judge of horseflesh.*

ˈ**horse-fly** *n* any of various large insects that bite horses, cattle, etc.

ˈ**Horse Guards** (*Brit*) cavalry brigade of troops guarding the sovereign.

ˈ**horsehair** *n* [U] hair from the mane or tail of a horse, used esp for padding furniture, etc.

ˈ**horse latitudes** areas of the oceans around 30°N and 30°S, where there is often very little wind.

ˈ**horse laugh** loud coarse laugh.

ˈ**horseman** /-mən/ *n* (*pl* **-men** /-mən/, *fem* ˈ**horsewoman**) rider on horseback, esp a skilled one. ˈ**horsemanship** *n* [U] art of or skill in riding horses.

ˈ**horseplay** *n* [U] rough noisy fun or play.

ˈ**horse-race** *n* race between horses with riders. ˈ**horse-racing** *n* [U]. ⇨ App 9.

ˈ**horse sense** (*infml*) basic common sense; ordinary wisdom.

ˈ**horseshoe** (also **shoe**) *n* **1** U-shaped piece of iron nailed to the bottom of a horse's hoof and regarded as a symbol of good luck. ⇨ article at SUPERSTITION. **2** thing having this shape: *Stand in a horseshoe facing me.* ○ [attrib] *a horseshoe bend.*

ˈ**horse-trading** *n* [U] (*esp US*) shrewd bargaining; clever business dealing.

ˈ**horsewhip** *n* whip used for driving horses. — *v* (**-pp-**) [Tn] beat (sb) with a horsewhip.

ˈ**horsewoman** *n* (*pl* **-women**) woman rider on horseback, esp a skilled one: *a fine horsewoman.*

horsepower /ˈhɔːspaʊə(r)/ *n* (*pl* unchanged) (*abbr* **hp**) unit for measuring the power of an engine, etc (550 foot-pounds per second, about 750 watts): [attrib] *a twelve horsepower engine.*

horse-radish /ˈhɔːs rædɪʃ/ *n* [U] (plant with a) hot-tasting root which is grated to make a cold sauce: [attrib] *roast beef with horse-radish sauce.*

horsy /ˈhɔːsɪ/ *adj* **1** of or like a horse: *He had a long, rather horsy face.* **2** interested in or involved with horses and horse-racing; showing this in one's dress, conversation, etc: *She comes from a very horsy family.*

horticulture /ˈhɔːtɪkʌltʃə(r)/ *n* [U] art of growing flowers, fruit and vegetables; gardening.

▷ **horticultural** /ˌhɔːtɪˈkʌltʃərəl/ *adj*: *a horticultural show, society, expert.*

horticulturist /ˌhɔːtɪˈkʌltʃərɪst/ *n* person who practises horticulture; skilled gardener.

hosanna /həʊˈzænə/ *interj, n* shout of praise and worship to God.

hose[1] /həʊz/ (also ˈ**hose-pipe**) *n* [C, U] flexible tube made of rubber, plastic or canvas and used for directing water onto fires, gardens, etc: *a length of hose* ○ *The firemen played their hoses on* (ie directed them at) *the burning building.* ⇨ illus at HOME.

▷ **hose** *v* [Tn, Tn·p] ~ **sth/sb (down)** wash or water sth/sb using a hose: *hose the flower-beds* ○ *hose down the car.*

hose[2] /həʊz/ *n* [pl *v*] **1** (esp in shops) stockings, socks and tights. **2** garment covering the body from the waist to the knees or feet, formerly worn by men; breeches: *doublet and hose.*

hosier /ˈhəʊzɪə(r); *US* -ʒər/ *n* (*dated or fml*) person who sells stockings and socks.

▷ **hosiery** /ˈhəʊzɪərɪ; *US* ˈhəʊʒərɪ/ *n* [U] (esp in shops) stockings, socks and knitted or woven underwear: [attrib] *the hosiery department.*

hospice /ˈhɒspɪs/ *n* **1** (**a**) hospital for dying people. (**b**) home for very poor people in need of food and shelter. **2** (*arch*) house where travellers could stay and rest, esp one kept by a religious order.

hospitable /hɒˈspɪtəbl, *also* ˈhɒspɪtəbl/ *adj* ~ (**to/towards sb**) (of a person) pleased to welcome and entertain guests; giving hospitality: *She is always hospitable to visitors from abroad.* ▷ **hospitably** /-əblɪ/ *adv.*

hospital /ˈhɒspɪtl/ *n* institution providing medical and surgical treatment and nursing care for ill or injured people: *go to hospital*, ie as a patient ○ *I'm going to the hospital to visit my brother.* ○ *be admitted to/be taken to/be released from/be discharged from hospital* ○ *The injured were rushed to hospital in an ambulance.* ○ *He died in hospital.* ○ *I've never been in hospital*, ie as a patient. ○ [attrib] *a hospital nurse* ○ *receive hospital treatment.* ⇨ Usage at SCHOOL[1].

▷ **hospitalize, -ise** *v* [Tn esp passive] send or admit (sb) to hospital. **hospitalization, -isation** /ˌhɒspɪtəlaɪˈzeɪʃn; *US* -lɪˈz-/ *n* [U]: *a long period of hospitalization.*

hospitality /ˌhɒspɪˈtælətɪ/ *n* [U] friendly and generous reception and entertainment of guests or strangers, esp in one's own home: *Thank you for your kind hospitality.* ○ [attrib] *a hospitality room, suite, coach*, ie one reserved for the use of guests in a hotel, TV studio, etc.

host[1] /həʊst/ *n* **1** ~ **of sb/sth** large number of people or things: *He has hosts of friends.* ○ *I can't come, for a whole host of reasons.* **2** (*arch*) army.

host[2] /həʊst/ *n* **1** (*fem* **hostess** /ˈhəʊstɪs, -tes/) person who receives and entertains one or more other people as guests: *I was away so my son acted as host.* ○ *Mr and Mrs Hill are such good hosts.* ○ [attrib] *the host nation*, eg for an international conference, etc. **2** (*fem* **hostess**) compere of a television programme, etc: *Your host on tonight's show is Max Astor.* **3** (*dated or joc*) landlord of an inn; publican: *mine host.* **4** animal or plant on which a parasite lives: [attrib] *host organisms.* **5** (idm) **be/play host to sb** receive and entertain sb as a guest: *The college is (playing) host to a group of visiting Russian scientists.*

▷ **host** *v* [Tn] act as host at (an event) or to (a person): *Which country is hosting the Games this year?* ○ *Hosting our show this evening is the lovely Gloria Monroe.*

host[3] /həʊst/ *n* **the Host** [sing] the bread that is blessed and eaten at Holy Communion.

hostage /ˈhɒstɪdʒ/ *n* **1** person held as a captive by one or more others who threaten to keep, harm or kill him unless certain demands are met: *The hijackers kept the pilot on board the plane as (a) hostage.* **2** (idm) **a** ˌ**hostage to** ˈ**fortune** (*fml*) person or thing that one acquires and may then suffer by losing, esp a husband or wife or child. **take/hold sb** ˈ**hostage** seize/keep sb as a hostage: *The gunman is holding two children hostage in the building.*

hostel /ˈhɒstl/ *n* building in which (usu cheap) food and lodging are provided for students, certain groups of workers, the homeless, travellers, etc: *a youth hostel.* ⇨ article at ACCOMMODATION.

▷ **hosteller** (*US* **hosteler**) /ˈhɒstələ(r)/ *n* person who travels around staying in youth hostels.

hostelry /ˈhɒstəlrɪ/ *n* (*arch or joc*) inn; public house: *Why don't we adjourn to the local hostelry?*

hostess /ˈhəʊstɪs/ *n* **1** woman who receives and entertains one or more other people as guests. **2** woman employed to welcome and entertain people at a night-club, etc, or to provide information at an exhibition, etc. **3** = AIR HOSTESS (AIR[1]). **4** female compere of a television programme, etc. Cf HOST[2] 2.

hostile /ˈhɒstaɪl; *US* -tl/ *adj* **1** ~ (**to/towards sb/sth**) (**a**) showing strong dislike or enmity; very unfriendly: *a hostile crowd, glance, review, reception* ○ *She found his manner towards her distinctly hostile.* (**b**) [usu pred] showing rejection of sth; opposed to sth: *be hostile to reform.* **2** of an enemy; warlike: *hostile aircraft.* ▷ **hostilely** *adv.*

hostility /hɒˈstɪlətɪ/ *n* **1** [U] ~ (**to/towards sb/sth**) (**a**) being hostile (to sb/sth); antagonism; enmity: *feelings of hostility* ○ *feel no hostility towards anyone* ○ *show hostility to sb/sth.* (**b**) opposition; rejection: *His suggestion met with some hostility.* **2 hostilities** [pl] acts of war; fighting: *at the outbreak of hostilities* ○ *suspend hostilities*, ie stop fighting.

hot /hɒt/ *adj* (**-tter, -ttest**) **1** (**a**) having a relatively or noticeably high temperature; giving off heat: *a hot day, meal* ○ *hot weather, water* ○ *Cook in a very hot oven.* ○ *This coffee is too hot to drink.* Cf COLD[1], WARM[1]. (**b**) (of a person) feeling heat: *I am/feel hot.* (**c**) causing the sensation of heat: *be in a hot sweat.* **2** (of spices, etc) producing a burning sensation to the taste: *a hot curry* ○ *Pepper and mustard are hot.* **3** intense; fiery; passionate: *have a hot temper*, ie be easily angered ○ *in the hottest part of the election campaign* ○ *The current debate about privatization is likely to grow hotter in the coming weeks.* **4** (**a**) (of the scent in hunting) fresh and strong. (**b**) (of news) fresh, very recent and usu sensational: *a hot tip* ○ *a story that is hot off the press*, ie has just appeared in the newspapers. **5** (*infml*) (of a competitor, performer or feat) very skilful or impressive. **6** (*sl*) (of goods) stolen and difficult to dispose of because of determined efforts made by the police to recover them: *This painting is too hot to handle.* **7** (of music, esp jazz) rhythmical and emotional; stirring. **8** (*sl*) radioactive. **9** (*infml*) (in children's games, etc) very near the object sought; very close to guessing correctly: *You're getting really hot!* **10** (idm) **be hot at/in/on sth** (*infml*) be skilled, gifted or knowledgeable in sth: *I'm good at history but not so hot at arithmetic.* **be hot on sb** (*infml*) be infatuated with sb; admire sb. **be in/get into hot** ˈ**water** (*infml*) be in/get into trouble or disgrace. **blow hot and cold** ⇨ BLOW[1]. **go/sell like hot** ˈ**cakes** sell quickly or in great numbers or quantity: *The new portable computers are going like hot cakes.* **have the** ˈ**hots for sb** (*sl*) be sexually attracted to sb. **hot** ˈ**air** (*infml*) empty or boastful talk. **(all) hot and** ˈ**bothered** (*infml*) harassed because of fear, the pressure of work, the need to hurry, etc. **(too) hot for sb** (*infml*) (too) difficult for sb to cope with: *When the pace got too hot for him, he disappeared.* ○ *They're making things very hot for her*, ie making her life difficult or dangerous. **(be) hot on sb's** ˈ**heels** following sb very closely. **(be) hot on sb's** ˈ**tracks/**ˈ**trail**; **(be) hot on the trail (of sth)** (*infml*) pursuing sb or searching for sth so closely that one has almost caught him or found it. **a hot po**ˈ**tato** (*infml*) thing or situation that is difficult or unpleasant to deal with: *The racial discrimination issue is a political hot potato.* **the** ˈ**hot seat** (*infml*) the vulnerable position of a person who has important responsibilities and must face criticism, answer questions, etc. **a hot spot** (*infml*) difficult or dangerous situation; place where (eg political) trouble is likely. **hot** ˈ**stuff** (*sl*) (**a**) person or thing of first-rate quality: *She's really hot stuff at tennis.* (**b**) sexually attractive person. **hot under the** ˈ**collar** (*infml*) angry, indignant or embarrassed. **like a cat on hot bricks** ⇨ CAT[1]. **not so/too/that** ˈ**hot** (*infml*) not well; not good: *'How do you feel?' 'Not so hot.'* ○ *Her exam results aren't too hot.* **piping hot** ⇨ PIPING. **strike while the iron is hot** ⇨ STRIKE[2].

▷ **hot** *v* (**-tt-**) (phr v) **hot up** (*infml*) become more exciting or critical; intensify; increase: *With only a week to go before the election things are really hotting up.*

hotly *adv* (**a**) passionately; excitedly; angrily: *a hotly debated topic* ○ *Recent reports in the press have been hotly denied.* ○ *'Nonsense!' he replied hotly.* (**b**) closely and determinedly: *a hotly contested match* ○ *The pickpocket ran off, hotly pursued by the police.*

□ **hot-**ˈ**air balloon** = BALLOON 2.

ˈ**hotbed** *n* **1** bed of earth heated by rotting manure to help plants to grow. **2** (*fig*) ~ **of sth** place where sth evil or undesirable is able to develop easily and freely: *a hotbed of vice, crime, intrigue, etc.*

ˌ**hot-**ˈ**blooded** *adj* (**a**) easily angered; excitable. (**b**) passionate; ardent: *a* ˌ*hot-blooded* ˈ*lover.*

ˈ**hot cake** (*US*) = PANCAKE 1.

ˌ**hot cross** ˈ**bun** sweet bun (usu containing currants) marked with a cross and eaten toasted on Good Friday.

ˌ**hot** ˈ**dog** **1** hot sausage served in a soft bread roll, often with onions and mustard. **2** (*US infml*) (used as an *interj* to express pleasure or surprise).

ˌ**hot** ˈ**favourite** competitor most fancied to win a race, etc.

ˌ**hot**ˈ**foot** *adv* in great haste; quickly and eagerly: *The children came running hotfoot when they heard tea was ready.* — *v* (idm) ˈ**hotfoot it** (*infml*) walk or run hurriedly and eagerly: *We hotfooted it down to the beach.*

ˌ**hot** ˈ**gospeller** (*infml often derog*) eager and enthusiastic preacher.

ˈ**hothead** *n* person who often acts too hastily or rashly; impetuous person. ˌ**hot-**ˈ**headed** *adj* rash; impulsive; impetuous. ˌ**hot-**ˈ**headedly** *adv.* ˌ**hot-**ˈ**headedness** *n* [U].

ˈ**hothouse** *n* heated building, usu made of glass, used for growing delicate plants in; greenhouse.

ˈ**hot line** direct and exclusive communication link between heads of government, eg those of Moscow and Washington.

ˌ**hot** ˈ**money** funds moved frequently from one financial centre to another by speculators seeking high interest rates and the greatest opportunity for profit.

ˈ**hotplate** *n* flat heated metal surface on a cooking stove, etc used for cooking food or keeping it hot.

ˈ**hotpot** *n* stew of meat and vegetables cooked in the oven in a dish with a lid.

ˈ**hot rod** (*sl*) motor vehicle modified to have extra power and speed.

ˈ**hotshot** *n* (*US infml*) person who is skilful or talented in a showy or aggressive way: [attrib] *a hotshot young lawyer*.

ˌ**hot** ˈ**spring** spring[1](2) of naturally hot mineral water.

ˌ**hot-**ˈ**tempered** *adj* easily becoming very angry.

ˌ**hot-**ˈ**water bottle** container, usu made of rubber, that is filled with hot water and put in a bed, etc to warm it.

hotchpotch /ˈhɒtʃpɒtʃ/ (also **hodgepodge** /ˈhɒdʒpɒdʒ/) *n* (usu *sing*) number of things mixed together without order; confused jumble: *His essay was a hotchpotch of other people's ideas.*

hotel /həʊˈtel/ *n* building where rooms and usu meals are provided for people in return for payment: *staying at/in a(n) hotel.* Cf INN.

▷ **hotelier** /həʊˈtelɪə(r), -lɪeɪ; *US* ˌhəʊtelˈjeɪ/ *n* person who owns or manages a hotel.

Hottentot /ˈhɒtntɒt/ *n* member of a now almost extinct people of SW Africa. They are quite short and have yellow-brown skin.

Houdini /hu:ˈdi:nɪ/ Harry (real name Eric Weiss, 1874-1926), American conjuror and escapologist. He achieved fame by staging escapes from apparently impossible situations (eg locked into a box which was lowered under water). His name is often used for any person or animal that makes amazing escapes.

hound /haʊnd/ *n* **1** type of dog used in hunting; foxhound: *The hounds lost the scent of the fox.* **2** (idm) **follow hounds** ⇨ FOLLOW. **ride to hounds** ⇨ RIDE[2]. **run with the hare and hunt with the hounds** ⇨ HARE.

▷ **hound** *v* **1** [Tn] pursue (sb) relentlessly and energetically (esp in order to obtain sth); harass: *be hounded by reporters, one's creditors, the press.* **2** (phr v) **hound sb/sth down** find sb/sth after a persistent chase. **hound sb out (of sth/...)** force sb to leave (sth/a place): *He was hounded out of his job by jealous rivals.*

hour /ˈaʊə(r)/ *n* **1** [C] twenty-fourth part of a day and night; 60 minutes: *The film starts at 7.30 and lasts two hours.* ○ *work a forty-hour week* ○ *a three hours' journey/a three-hour journey.* ⇨ App 10. **2** (**a**) [C] number of hours past midnight, eg 1 o'clock, 2 o'clock, etc, as indicated by a clock, watch, etc: *The clock strikes the hours but not the half-hours.* (**b**) **hours** [pl] (*fml*) (used when calculating time according to the 24-hour clock): *It's eighteen hundred hours,* ie 6 pm. ○ *It's twenty-one thirty hours,* ie 9.30 pm. **3 hours** [pl] fixed period of time for work, use of facilities, etc: *hours of business* ○ *Office hours are from 9 am to 5 pm.* ○ *Doctors work long hours.* **4** [C usu *sing*] period of about an hour, usu set aside for a specified purpose: *a long lunch hour.* **5** [C] distance that can be travelled in an hour: *London's only two hours away.* **6** [C] point in time: *He came at the agreed hour.* ○ *Who can be ringing us at this late hour?* **7** [C usu *sing*] indefinite period of time: *the country's finest hour* ○ *She helped me in my hour of need.* **8** (idm) ˌ**after** ˈ**hours** after a period of regular business, etc: *Staff must stay behind after hours to catch up on their work.* **at/till** ˈ**all hours** at/till any time, however unsuitable or inconvenient: *She stays out till all hours,* ie very late. ○ *He's inclined to telephone at all hours of the day or night.* **at the e**ˌ**leventh** ˈ**hour** at the last possible moment; only just in time: *The president's visit was called off at the eleventh hour* ○ [attrib] *an e*ˌ*leventh-hour de*ˈ*cision.* **the early hours** ⇨ EARLY. **keep late, early, regular, etc** ˈ**hours** go to bed or work late, early, for a normal and regular period of time, etc. **on the** ˈ**hour** at exactly 1 o'clock, 2 o'clock, 3 o'clock, etc: *My appointment was for 9 am and I arrived on the hour,* ie at 9 am precisely. ○ *The London bus departs every hour on the hour.* ˌ**out of** ˈ**hours** (**a**) before or after one's regular work time. (**b**) (*esp Brit*) during times when alcohol may no longer be sold in bars. **the small hours** ⇨ SMALL. **one's waking hours** ⇨ WAKE[1].

▷ **hourly** /ˈaʊəlɪ/ *adv* **1** every hour: *This medicine is to be taken hourly.* **2** at any time: *We're expecting news hourly.* — *adj* **1** done or occurring every hour: *an hourly bus service* ○ *Trains leave at hourly intervals.* **2** calculated by the hour: *be paid on an hourly basis.* **3** continual; frequent: *live in hourly dread of being discovered.*

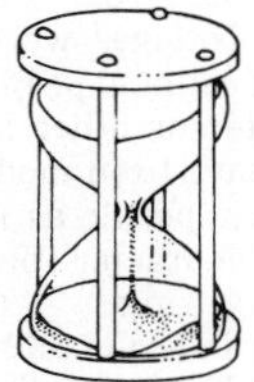

hourglass

□ ˈ**hourglass** *n* glass container holding fine sand that takes an hour to pass through the narrow gap from the upper to the lower section.

ˈ**hour-hand** *n* small hand on a clock or watch, indicating the hour.

houri /ˈhʊərɪ/ *n* beautiful young woman of the Muslim paradise.

house[1] /haʊs/ *n* (*pl* ~**s** /ˈhaʊzɪz/) **1** [C] (**a**) building made for people to live in, usu for one family or for a family and lodgers. ⇨ article. (**b**) (usu *sing*) people living in such a building: *Be quiet or you'll wake the whole house!* **2** [C] (in compounds) building made or used for some special purpose or for keeping animals or goods in: *an* ˈ*opera-house* ○ *a* ˈ*schoolhouse* ○ *a* ˈ*hen-house* ○ *a* ˈ*store-house.* **3** [C] (**a**) building in which a religious community or a section of a boarding-school or college lives. (**b**) (group of pupils in) each of the divisions of a day-school for competitive purposes, esp sport. **4** (usu **House**) [C] (building used by a) group of people who meet to discuss or pass laws: *the* ˌ*House of* ˈ*Commons/*ˈ*Lords* ○ *the* ˌ*Houses of* ˈ*Parliament* ○ *This house condemns the Prime Minister's action,* eg said in a debate. **5 the House** [sing] (*infml*) (**a**) (*Brit*) the House of Commons or the House of Lords: *enter the House,* ie become an MP. (**b**) (*Brit*) the Stock Exchange. (**c**) (*US*) the House of Representatives. **6** [C] business firm: *a fashion house* ○ *a banking house* ○ [attrib] *house style,* ie written style established by a newspaper, publishing firm, etc ○ *a house magazine,* ie one produced by a firm for its employees. **7** (usu **House**) [C] royal family or dynasty: *the House of Windsor,* ie the British Royal Family. **8** [C] (**a**) (usu *sing*) audience in a theatre, concert hall, etc: *Is there a doctor in the house?* (**b**) theatre, etc building: *a full house,* ie with every seat occupied ○ *an orchestra playing to packed houses,* ie full concert halls. (**c**) performance in a theatre, etc: *The second house starts at 8 o'clock.* **9** [C usu *sing*] establishment where guests are received (eg a hotel, restaurant, pub, club, etc): *The house* (ie The hotel management) *reserves the right to require guests to present their passports.* ○ *Goulash is the speciality of the house.* ○ *a* ˈ*steak-house,* ie a restaurant where meat steaks are served ○ [attrib] *A glass of the house red, please,* ie of the ordinary, comparatively cheap, red wine recommended by the restaurant. **10** [C] each of the twelve parts into which the heavens are divided in astrology. **11** (idm) **bring the** ˈ**house down** make an audience laugh or applaud loudly. **eat sb out of house and home** ⇨ EAT. **get on like a** ˈ**house on fire** (*infml*) (of people) quickly become very friendly; have an agreeable and cheerful relationship. **a half-way house** ⇨ HALF-WAY (HALF[2]). **keep** ˈ**house** manage the affairs of a household. **keep open house** ⇨ OPEN[1]. **the lady of the house** ⇨ LADY. **master in one's own house** ⇨ MASTER[1]. **move house** ⇨ MOVE[2]. **not a dry eye in the house** ⇨ DRY[1]. **on the** ˈ**house** paid for by the pub, firm, etc; free: *The landlord gave us a drink on the house.* **put/set one's (own)** ˈ**house in order** organize one's own affairs efficiently. **safe as houses** ⇨ SAFE[1]. **set up** ˈ**house (together)** live together as man and wife.

▷ ˈ**houseful** /-fʊl/ *n* as much or many as a house can contain or accommodate: *have a houseful of guests.*

□ ˈ**house-agent** *n* = ESTATE AGENT (ESTATE).

ˈ**house arrest** detention in one's own house, not in prison: *be (kept) under house arrest.*

ˈ**houseboat** *n* boat, usu stationary on a river, equipped as a place to live in.

ˈ**house-bound** *adj* unable to leave one's house, eg because of illness.

ˈ**housebreaking** *n* [U] entering a building without right or permission in order to commit a crime. ˈ**housebreaker** *n.*

ˈ**housecoat** *n* woman's long dress-like garment for informal wear in the house.

ˈ**housecraft** *n* [U] theory and practice of running a home.

ˈ**house-dog** *n* dog kept to guard a house.

ˈ**house-father** *n* man in charge of children in an institution, esp a children's home.

ˈ**house-fly** *n* (*pl* **-flies**) common fly found in and around houses.

ˈ**house-husband** *n* man who stays at home and does housework, looks after children, etc while his wife goes out to work.

ˈ**housekeeper** *n* person (esp a woman) employed to manage a household. ˈ**housekeeping** *n* [U] **1** management of household affairs. **2** money allowed for this.

ˈ**house lights** lights in the auditorium of a theatre, cinema, etc.

ˈ**housemaid** *n* woman servant in a house, esp one who cleans rooms, etc. **housemaid's** ˈ**knee** inflammation of the kneecap, caused by kneeling too much.

ˈ**houseman** /-mən/ *n* (*pl* **-men** /mən/) (*Brit*) (*US* **intern** /ˈɪntɜ:n/) resident junior doctor at a hospital, etc.

ˈ**house-martin** *n* bird that builds its nest of mud in the walls of houses and in cliffs.

ˈ**housemaster** *n* (*fem* ˈ**housemistress**) teacher in charge of a house(3a) at a boarding-school.

ˈ**house-mother** *n* woman in charge of children in an institution, esp a children's home.

ˌ**house of** ˈ**cards 1** tower-like structure built by balancing playing-cards against and on top of each other. **2** (*fig*) scheme, etc that is likely to collapse.

Chamber of the House of Commons

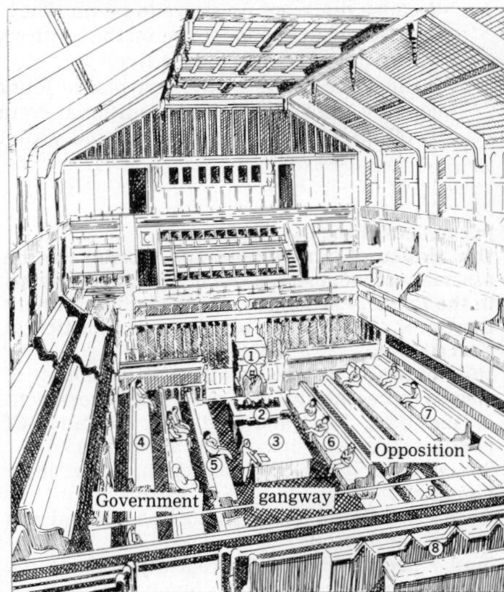

1 Speaker's chair 2 clerks' chairs 3 Table of the House
4 Government back benches 5 Government front bench
6 Opposition front bench 7 Opposition back benches
8 Public Gallery

the ˌ**House of** ˈ**Commons** (also **the** ˈ**Commons**) (**a**) the assembly of elected representatives of the British or the Canadian Parliament. ⇨ illus. ⇨ illus at BARRY. (**b**) the building where they meet. Cf THE HOUSE of LORDS. ⇨ article at PARLIAMENT.

ˌ**House of** ˈ**God** (*fml*) church or chapel.

the ˌ**House of** ˈ**Keys** the elected branch of the

House and Home

In Britain, government policy has for many years been to encourage people to buy their own homes by offering tax relief on mortgage interest payments, with the result that the number of owner-occupiers has increased from 4 million in 1951 to 15 million in 1989. The majority of homes are houses, which outnumber flats by four to one.

Many of the houses in Britain today date from the 1930s. In 1939 out of a total housing stock of 13 million, 4.5 million homes had been built in the previous ten years. The houses that today line the roads out of many towns and cities often date from this period. The 1950s and 1960s also saw a great increase in house building as the homes destroyed in the Second World War as well as the inner-city slums were replaced.

In towns, there are three main types of houses: detached, semi-detached and terraced. A detached house, standing in its own plot of land, is usually more expensive than the others. A semi-detached house (also called a 'semi') is similar, but shares one wall with its neighbour, which is its 'mirror image'. It is normally smaller than a detached house. Most of these houses have two storeys, with two rooms and a kitchen downstairs and the bedrooms and bathroom upstairs. A terraced house (or terrace-house) is one of a row of houses, often built in blocks of four or more and sometimes extending the entire length of a street. Many small terraced houses were cheaply built in the 19th and early 20th centuries as towns were rapidly expanding. Some houses built in this way are, however, much older, for example the large Georgian or Regency terraces, several storeys high, that are a feature of Bath and London in particular.

Bungalows (single-storey detached houses) are popular, especially with elderly people because there are no stairs to climb. They are often found in seaside towns on the south coast, where many retired people live.

Houses of all these kinds can also be found in country villages, but the traditional country dwelling is the cottage. This is usually a small, old, detached or semi-detached house, often picturesque with old wooden beams inside, and perhaps a thatched roof and an attractive flower garden. Cottages were originally the simple homes of country people, and often had no running water or other facilities. Today, many of them have been modernized and are regarded by some people as ideal homes, not only for their 'character' but also for their attractive rural setting.

Some of the grandest of all houses are found in the country. These are the large country-houses or 'stately homes', which in some cases are still occupied by members of the land-owning families who originally built them. Many such houses are of historical and architectural importance, and stand in extensive grounds. Old or architecturally interesting houses may be designated as 'listed buildings' by the government. (Cf article at ARCHITECTURE.)

Flats are found mainly in towns, although they can also be self-contained units in converted country-houses or hotels, etc. Modern flats are often 'purpose-built' in the form of large apartment blocks or tower blocks, but many large houses in towns have also been converted into flats. Flats may be owned by the people who live in them, or rented from a private landlord or local authority. Local authorities are the main providers of rented accommodation. Most towns have 'council estates', groups of council houses laid out some way from the town centre. A typical council house is either semi-detached or terraced. Many large blocks of flats were built in the 1960s as part of a programme to improve the housing situation.

There has been a steady increase in home ownership in recent years, partly because council house tenants are now able to buy their house after living in it for a certain number of years. The building of new council houses, on the other hand, declined sharply in the 1980s. A recent development has been the growth of 'sheltered housing'. (Cf article at RETIREMENT.) This consists of blocks of modern flats or groups of small houses specially designed for elderly people. They are usually situated near the centre of a town, close to shops and other amenities, and have a resident warden. As with council houses, the residents rent their homes from the local council. Similar housing also exists for private tenants, who can purchase or rent their sheltered homes.

Most home owners have bought their house by means of a mortgage loan through a building society or bank. 'First-time buyers' (people such as young married couples setting up home for the first time) almost always buy their houses this way. A typical loan is for up to 90 per cent of the price of house, repaid over 20 or 25 years in monthly instalments. The house itself is security for the loan.

Some people prefer not to live in a council house, yet cannot afford to buy a home of their own. In such cases they may turn to a housing association. This is a non-profit-making body that converts or improves existing houses, or builds new ones, then rents them out at rates which people can afford. A small housing association may own a group of sheltered homes for elderly people, while a large one can own literally thousands of homes. Another alternative for people in this category is to rent or buy a 'mobile home', which is actually a fixed caravan-type home on a caravan site (usually called a 'home park').

In Britain, house prices have generally risen faster than other prices and incomes and houses have been a good investment, so that people often move house in order to own a bigger property. By the end of the 1980s, however, the rapid rise in house values seemed to have come to an end.

Houses are usually bought and sold in Britain through an estate agent, using the legal services of a solicitor. In the USA, they are conveyed through a real estate broker or agent. (A general word for such a broker is 'realtor', although this term properly applies to a member of the National Association of Realtors.)

parliament of the Isle of Man.

the ˌHouse of ˈLords (also **the ˈLords**) **(a)** the assembly of members of the nobility and bishops in the British Parliament. **(b)** the building where they meet. Cf THE HOUSE OF COMMONS. ⇨ article at PARLIAMENT.

the ˌHouse of ˌRepreˈsentatives the assembly of elected representatives in the central government of the USA, Australia and New Zealand. Cf CONGRESS 2, SENATE 1. ⇨ article at POLITICS.

ˈhouse party group of guests staying at a country house, etc.

ˈhouse physician doctor living in a hospital as a member of its staff.

ˈhouse-proud *adj* giving great attention to the care and appearance of one's home.

ˈhouse-room *n* [U] (idm) **not give sb/sth ˈhouse-room** not want to have sb/sth in one's house, etc: *I wouldn't give that table house-room.*

the ˌHouses of ˈParliament (a) the House of Commons and the House of Lords, regarded together. **(b)** the group of buildings in London where these two assemblies meet.

ˈhouse-sparrow (also **sparrow**) *n* common grey and brown bird. ⇨ illus at BIRD.

ˈhouse surgeon surgeon living in a hospital as a member of its staff.

ˌhouse-to-ˈhouse *adj* [attrib] calling at each house in turn: *The police made house-to-house enquiries.*

ˈhouse-tops *n* (idm) **(proclaim, shout, etc sth) from the ˈhouse-tops** (announce sth) publicly so that many people know about it.

ˈhouse-trained *adj* (of pet cats, dogs, etc) trained not to defecate and urinate inside the house: (*fig joc*) *His manners were appalling before he got married, but his wife soon got him house-trained.*

ˈhouse-warming *n* party given to celebrate the move into a new home: [attrib] *have/throw a house-warming party.*

ˈhousewife *n* (*pl* **-wives**) woman whose occupation is looking after her family, cleaning the house, etc, and who usu does not have full-time paid work outside the home. **ˈhousewifely** *adj* of a housewife: *housewifely skills.* **ˈhousewifery** /-wɪfərɪ/ *n* [U] work of a housewife.

ˈhousework *n* [U] work done in a house, eg cleaning and cooking.

house[2] /haʊz/ *v* [Tn] **1 (a)** provide permanent or temporary accommodation for (sb): *be poorly housed* ○ *We can house you if the hotels are full.* **(b)** provide shelter for (an animal). **2** store (goods, etc): *house one's old books in the attic.* **3** enclose or contain (a part or fitting), esp in order to protect it: *The gas meter is housed in the cupboard under the stairs.*

household /ˈhaʊshəʊld/ *n* **1** all the people (family, lodgers, etc) living together in a house: *I grew up as part of a large household.* ○ [attrib] *household* (ie domestic) *expenses, duties, goods.* **2** (idm) **a ˌhousehold ˈname/ˈword** name of a person or thing that has become very well known because it is so often used: *The product was so successful that its name became a household word.*

▷ **ˈhouseholder** *n* /-həʊldə(r)/ **1** person who rents or who owns and occupies a house (ie not a person who lives in a hotel, etc). **2** head of a household.

□ **ˌhousehold ˈtroops** soldiers employed to guard the sovereign.

housing /ˈhaʊzɪŋ/ *n* **1** [U] houses, flats, etc, considered collectively; accommodation: *More housing is needed for old people.* ○ [attrib] *poor housing conditions.* **2** [U] providing accommodation for people: [attrib] *the council's housing policy.* **3** [C] hard casing that protects machinery, etc: *a car's rear axle housing.*

□ **ˈhousing association** society formed by a group of people with the aim of building and providing housing at reasonable cost and without making a profit.

ˈhousing estate area in which a number of houses for living are planned and built together.

Housman /ˈhaʊsmən/ A(lfred) E(dward) (1859-1936), English poet and scholar who was professor of Latin at London and Cambridge universities. His best-known work is *A Shropshire Lad*, a collection of short ballad-like poems, many of which look back to the happiness of a lost past. Several 20th-century English composers have set a selection of the poems to music.

hove ⇨ HEAVE.

hovel /ˈhɒvl; *US* ˈhɑːvl/ *n* (*derog*) small house that is unfit to live in; very poor and squalid dwelling.

hover /ˈhɒvə(r); *US* ˈhʌvər/ *v* [I, Ipr, Ip] **1** (of birds, etc) remain in the air in one place: *a hawk hovering above/over its prey* ○ *There was a helicopter hovering overhead.* **2** **(a)** (of a person) wait in a timid and uncertain manner: *I can't work with you hovering over me like that.* ○ *She's always hovering around the place annoying people.* ○ *He hovered about outside, too afraid to go in.* **(b)** remain near sth or in an uncertain state: *hovering between life and death* ○ *a country hovering on the brink of war.*

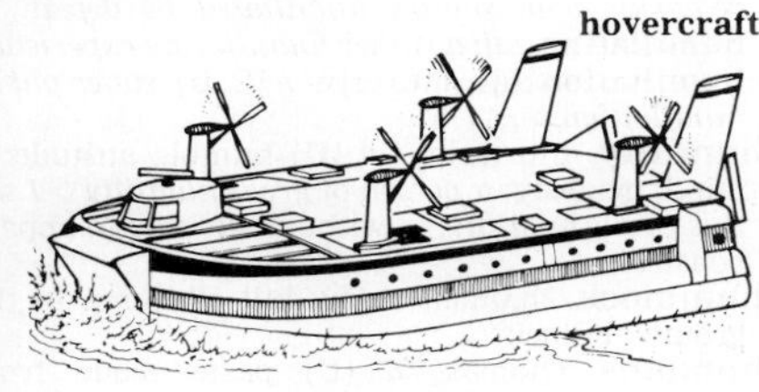

□ **ˈhovercraft** *n* (*pl* unchanged) vehicle that is capable of moving over land or water while supported on a cushion of air made by jet engines.

how /haʊ/ *interrog adv* **1** in what way or manner: *How is the word spelt?* ○ *Tell me how to spell it.* ○ *How did you escape?* ○ *Tell us how you escaped.* ○ *How are things going* (ie Is your life good or bad) *at the moment?* **2** in what state of health; in what condition: *How are the children?* ○ *How is* (ie What is your opinion of) *your job?* **3** (used before an *adj* or *adv*) to what extent or degree: *How old is she?* ○ *How long did you wait?* ○ *How often do you go swimming?* ○ *How fast can she run?* ○ *How much money have you got?* **4** (used in exclamations to comment on extent or degree): *How dirty that child is!* ○ *How kind of you to help!* ○ *How pale she looks!* ○ *How well he plays the violin!* ○ *How he snores!* ie He snores very loudly. **5** (idm) ˌ**and ˈhow!** (*infml*) (used to agree strongly and sometimes ironically): *'He's done very well, hasn't he?' 'And how!'* **how about?** (used to make a suggestion): *How about going for a walk?* ○ *How about a hot bath?* ˌ**how's ˈthat?** **(a)** what is the explanation for that? **(b)** (used when asking sb's opinion of sth): *How's that for punctuality?* **(c)** (used by the fielding side in cricket to ask the umpire if the batsman is out or not).

▷ **how** *conj* (*infml*) the/any way in which: *She described to me how he ran up to her and grabbed her handbag.* ○ *I can dress how I like in my own house!*

Howard[1] /ˈhaʊəd/ Catherine (?1521-42), fifth wife of *Henry VIII of England. He had her beheaded after only two years of marriage, because she was said to have had love affairs with other men.

Howard[2] /ˈhaʊəd/ John (?1726-90), English prison reformer whose campaigning brought about improvements in the building and management of gaols. He gave his name to the Howard League for Penal Reform, a 20th-century British organization concerned with criminal justice.

howdah /ˈhaʊdə/ *n* seat, usu with a canopy, for riding on the back of an elephant or a camel.

however /haʊˈevə(r)/ *adv* **1** (used before an *adj* or *adv*) to whatever extent or degree: *You won't move that stone, however strong you are.* ○ *She leaves her bedroom window open, however cold it is.* ○ *He will never succeed however hard he tries.* ○ *However short the journey is, you always get something to eat on this airline.* **2** (used to comment on a previously stated fact) although sth is, was or may be true; nevertheless: *She felt ill. She went to work, however, and tried to concentrate.* ○ *His first response was to say no. Later, however, he changed his mind.* ○ *I thought those figures were correct. However, I have recently heard they were not.* ⇨ Usage at ALTHOUGH.

▷ **however** *conj* in any way; regardless of how: *You can travel however you like.* ○ *However I approached the problem, I couldn't find a solution.*

however *interrog adv* (expressing surprise) in what way; by what means: *However did you get here without a car?* ○ *However does he manage to write music when he is so deaf?*

howitzer /ˈhaʊɪtsə(r)/ *n* short gun for firing shells at a high angle and at short range.

howl /haʊl/ *n* **(a)** long loud wailing cry of a dog, wolf, etc. **(b)** loud cry of a person expressing pain, scorn, amusement, etc: *let out a howl of laughter, agony, rage* ○ (*fig*) *The proposed changes caused howls of protest from the public.* **(c)** similar noise made by a strong wind, an electrical amplifier, etc.

▷ **howl** *v* **1** [I, Ipr] make a howl: *wolves howling in the forest* ○ *howl in agony* ○ *howl with laughter* ○ *The wind howled through the trees.* **2** [I] weep loudly: *The baby howled all night.* **3** [Tn] utter (sth) with a howl: *'I hate you all!' she howled.* ○ *The crowd howled its displeasure.* **4** (phr v) **howl sb down** (of an audience, etc) prevent a speaker from being heard by shouting scornfully.

howler /ˈhaʊlə(r)/ *n* **1** (also ˈ**howler monkey**) tropical S American monkey with a loud howling cry. **2** (*dated infml*) foolish and obvious mistake, esp in the use of words: *schoolboy howlers.*

howling /ˈhaʊlɪŋ/ *adj* [attrib] (*infml*) very great; extreme: *a howling success* ○ *Shut the door — there's a howling draught in here!*

hoyden /ˈhɔɪdn/ *n* (*fml derog*) girl who behaves in a wild noisy manner. ▷ **hoydenish** /-dənɪʃ/ *adj.*

Hoyle /hɔɪl/ **1** Edmond (1672-1769), English author of books on card-games, esp whist. **2** (idm) **according to ˈHoyle** correct(ly); according to the rules.

hp (also **HP**) /ˌeɪtʃ ˈpiː/ *abbr* **1** (*Brit*) hire-purchase: *buy a new television on (the) hp.* **2** horsepower (of an engine).

HQ /ˌeɪtʃ ˈkjuː/ *abbr* headquarters: *see you back at HQ* ○ *police HQ.*

hr *abbr* (*pl* **hrs**) hour: *fastest time 1 hr* ○ *The train leaves at 15.00 hrs.* Cf MIN 2.

HRH /ˌeɪtʃ ɑːr ˈeɪtʃ/ *abbr* His/Her Royal Highness: *HRH the Duke of Edinburgh* ○ (*infml*) *HRH was there.*

hub /hʌb/ *n* **1** central part of a wheel from which the spokes radiate. ⇨ illus at BICYCLE. **2** (*fig*) central point of activity, interest or importance: *a hub of industry, commerce, etc* ○ *He thinks that Boston is the hub of the universe.*

□ ˈ**hub-cap** *n* round metal cover over the hub of a car wheel. ⇨ illus at CAR.

hubble-bubble /ˈhʌbl bʌbl/ *n* (*infml*) = HOOKAH.

hubbub /ˈhʌbʌb/ *n* [sing, U] **(a)** loud confused noise, eg of many voices; din. **(b)** disturbance; uproar.

hubby /ˈhʌbɪ/ *n* (*Brit infml*) husband.

hubris /ˈhjuːbrɪs/ *n* [U] (*fml*) arrogant pride.

huckleberry /ˈhʌklbərɪ; *US* -berɪ/ *n* **1** low shrub common in N America. **2** its small dark-blue berry.

Huckleberry Finn /ˌhʌklbrɪ ˈfɪn/ hero of Mark *Twain's novel *The Adventures of Huckleberry Finn* (1884), the sequel to *Tom Sawyer* and generally regarded as his masterpiece. The story describes young Huckleberry (or Huck) Finn's journey down the river Mississippi and the things that happen to him on the way.

huckster /ˈhʌkstə(r)/ *n* person who sells goods in the street; hawker.

huddle /ˈhʌdl/ *v* **1** [Ipr, Ip, Tn·pr esp passive, Tn·p esp passive] (cause sb/sth to) crowd or be heaped together, esp in a small space: *sheep huddling (up) together for warmth* ○ *We all huddled around the radio to hear the news.* ○ *The clothes lay huddled up in a pile in the corner.* **2** (phr v) ~ **up (against/to sb/sth)** curl one's body up into a small space; snuggle: *Tom was cold so he huddled up against the radiator.*

▷ **huddle** *n* **1** number of people or things close together without order: *People stood around in small huddles, sheltering from the rain.* ○ *Their clothes lay in a huddle on the floor.* **2** (idm) **go into a ˈhuddle (with sb)** (*infml*) hold a private or secret conference.

Hudson /ˈhʌdsn/ Henry (died 1611), English explorer who discovered a large inland sea in NE Canada (**Hudson Bay**). His crew mutinied there, setting him adrift in a small boat, and he was never seen again.

Hudson's Bay Company /ˌhʌdsnz ˌbeɪ ˈkʌmpənɪ/ trading company founded in 1670 to exploit northern Canada commercially (eg by buying and selling furs trapped there). At first British-owned, it was handed over to Canadian control in 1869.

hue[1] /hjuː/ *n* (*fml*) colour; variety or shade of colour: *birds of many different hues* ○ *Add orange paint to get a warmer hue.*

▷ **-hued** /hjuːd/ (forming compound *adjs*) having the specified colour: ˈ*dark-hued* ○ ˈ*many-hued.*

hue[2] /hjuː/ *n* (idm) ˌ**hue and ˈcry** general alarm or loud public protest; outcry: *A terrific hue and cry was raised against the new tax proposals.*

huff[1] /hʌf/ *n* (usu *sing*) fit of bad temper or annoyance (used esp in the expressions shown): *be in a huff* ○ *get/go into a huff* ○ *go off in a huff.*

▷ **huffish, huffy** *adjs* **(a)** in a bad temper. **(b)** easily offended. **huffily** *adv.*

huff[2] /hʌf/ *v* [I] **1** blow; puff. **2** (idm) ˌ**huff and ˈpuff** **(a)** breathe heavily because one is exhausted: *When I got to the top I was huffing and puffing.* **(b)** show one's annoyance in a self-important or threatening way without actually achieving anything.

hug /hʌg/ *v* (**-gg-**) [Tn] **1** put the arms round (sb/sth) tightly, esp to show love. **2** (of a bear) squeeze (sb/sth) between its front legs. **3** (of a ship, car, etc) keep close to (sth): *hug the shore, kerb* ○ *tyres that help a vehicle to hug the road.* **4** fit tightly round (sth): *a figure-hugging dress.* **5** cling firmly to and take pleasure in (opinions): *hug one's cherished beliefs.*

▷ **hug** *n* strong clasp with the arms, esp to show love; tight embrace: *She gave her mother an affectionate hug.*

huge /hjuːdʒ/ *adj* very large in size or amount; enormous: *a huge elephant* ○ *Canada is a huge country.* ○ *have a huge appetite* ○ *huge debts, profits.*

▷ **hugely** *adv* enormously, very much: *be hugely successful* ○ *enjoy oneself hugely.*

hugeness *n* [U].

hugger-mugger /ˈhʌgə mʌgə(r)/ *adj, adv* **1** secret(ly). **2** confused(ly); in disorder.

▷ **hugger-mugger** *n* [U] **1** secrecy. **2** confusion.

Hughes /hjuːz/ Ted (1930-), English poet whose work (eg *The Hawk in the Rain*) vividly and forcefully evokes the beauty and violence of the natural world. He was made Poet Laureate in 1984. The American poet Sylvia *Plath was his wife.

Hugo /ˈhjuːgəʊ/ Victor-Marie (1802-85), French novelist, poet and playwright who was one of the leading figures in the Romantic movement in France. He lived in exile between 1851 and 1870, mainly in Guernsey. His best-known novels are *Notre Dame de Paris* (called in English *The Hunchback of Notre Dame*) and *Les Misérables.*

Huguenot /ˈhjuːgənəʊ/ *n* French Protestant in the 16th and 17th centuries. The Huguenots were involved in civil war with the Catholic majority, and were constantly persecuted for their beliefs. In the late 17th century many emigrated to England and elsewhere.

huh /hʌ/ *interj* (used to express scorn, disgust, enquiry, etc): *You think you know the answer, huh?*

hulk /hʌlk/ *n* **1** body of an old ship which is no longer in use: *rotting hulks on the beach.* **2** very large and usu clumsy person or thing.

▷ **hulking** *adj* [attrib] (*infml*) (of a person or thing) very big or heavy and usu awkward or clumsy: *a hulking great brute of a man.*

hull[1] /hʌl/ *n* body of a ship: *a fully-loaded tanker* *with its hull low in the water.* ⇨ illus at CATAMARAN, YACHT.

hull[2] /hʌl/ *n* **1** outer covering of some fruits and seeds, esp the pods of peas and beans. **2** cluster of leaves on a strawberry, raspberry, etc.

▷ **hull** *v* [Tn] remove the hulls of (peas, beans, fruit, etc).

hullabaloo /ˌhʌləbəˈluː/ *n* (*pl* ~**s**) (usu *sing*) continuous loud noise, esp of people shouting; uproar; din: *make a hullabaloo (about sth).*

hullo = HALLO.

hum /hʌm/ *v* (**-mm-**) **1** (**a**) [I] make a low steady continuous sound like that made by bees. (**b**) [I] utter a slight sound, esp of hesitation. (**c**) [I, Ip, Tn, Tn·pr] ~ (**sth**) (**to sb**) sing (a tune) with closed lips: *She was humming (away) to herself.* ○ *I don't know the words of the song but I can hum it to you.* **2** [I, Ipr] (*infml*) be in a state of activity: *make things hum* ○ *The whole place was humming (with life) when we arrived.* **3** [I] (*sl*) smell unpleasantly. **4** (idm) ˌ**hum and** ˈ**ha**; ˌ**hum and** ˈ**haw** (*infml*) take a long time to make a decision; hesitate: *We hummed and ha'd for ages before deciding to buy the house.*

▷ **hum** *n* (usu *sing*) **1** humming sound, esp of an insect; indistinct murmur, esp of many voices: *the hum of bees, of distant traffic, of machines* ○ *the hum of conversation in the next room.* **2** (*sl*) bad smell.

hum *interj* (used to indicate hesitation).

□ ˈ**humming-bird** *n* any of various types of tropical bird, usu very small and brightly coloured, that make a humming sound by vibration of the wings.

ˈ**humming-top** *n* top[3](1) that makes a humming sound when it spins.

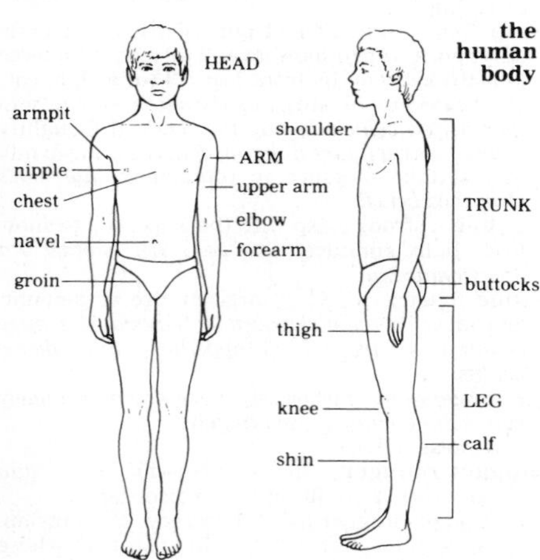

human /ˈhjuːmən/ *adj* **1** of or characteristic of man (contrasted with God, animals or machines): *a human skull* ○ *human anatomy, affairs, behaviour* ○ *a terrible loss of human life* ○ *This food is not fit for human consumption.* ○ *We must allow for human error.* ○ *Even she makes mistakes occasionally — she's only human.* **2** (*approv*) having or showing the better qualities of man; kind; good: *She'll understand and forgive; she's really quite human.* **3** (idm) **the milk of human kindness** ⇨ MILK[1]. **to err is human** ⇨ ERR.

▷ **human** *n* = HUMAN BEING.

humankind /ˌhjuːmənˈkaɪnd/ *n* [U] (*fml*) = MANKIND.

humanly *adj* **1** in a human way. **2** by human means; within human ability: *The doctors did all that was humanly possible.*

□ ˌ**human** ˈ**being** man, woman or child; person.

ˌ**human** ˈ**interest** aspect of a newspaper story, etc that interests people because it describes the experiences, feelings, etc of individuals.

ˌ**human** ˈ**nature** general characteristics and feelings common to all people: *You can't change human nature.*

the ˌ**human** ˈ**race** human beings collectively; mankind. ⇨ Usage at MAN[1].

ˌ**human** ˈ**rights** rights which it is generally thought that every living person should have, eg the right to freedom, justice, etc.

humane /hjuːˈmeɪn/ *adj* **1** having or showing sympathy, kindness and understanding: *a humane person, act, penal system* ○ *humane killing.* **2** [attrib] (*dated fml*) (of areas of learning) tending to civilize: *humane studies.* ▷ **humanely** *adv.*

□ ˌ**humane** ˈ**killer** instrument for the painless killing of animals.

humanism /ˈhjuːmənɪzəm/ *n* [U] **1** (**a**) system of beliefs that concentrates on common human needs and seeks rational (rather than divine) ways of solving human problems. (**b**) study of mankind and human affairs (contrasted with theological subjects). **2** literary culture (esp in the Renaissance) based on Greek and Roman learning.

▷ **humanist** /ˈhjuːmənɪst/ *n* supporter of humanism.

humanistic /ˌhjuːməˈnɪstɪk/ *adj.*

humanitarian /hjuːˌmænɪˈteərɪən/ *adj* concerned with improving the lives of mankind and reducing suffering, esp by social reform: *humanitarian deeds, ideals, work.*

▷ **humanitarian** *n* humanitarian person.

humanitarianism /-ɪzəm/ *n* [U].

humanity /hjuːˈmænətɪ/ *n* **1** [U] human beings collectively; the human race; people: *crimes against humanity.* ⇨ Usage at MAN[1]. **2** [U] being humane; kind-heartedness: *treat people and animals with humanity.* **3** [U] human nature; being human. **4 humanities** [pl] subjects of study concerned with human culture, esp literature, language, history and philosophy.

humanize, -ise /ˈhjuːmənaɪz/ *v* [Tn] **1** make (sth) human: *animal characters humanized in cartoons.* **2** make (sb) humane: *have a humanizing influence on a barbaric system.* ▷ **humanization, -isation** /ˌhjuːmənaɪˈzeɪʃn; *US* -nɪˈz-/ *n* [U].

Humberside /ˈhʌmbəsaɪd/ county of NE England, formed in 1974 from parts of Lincolnshire and the East and West Ridings of Yorkshire. Its main centre of population is Hull. ⇨ map at App 1.

humble /ˈhʌmbl *or, rarely, US* ˈʌm-/ *adj* (**-r** /-blə(r)/, **-st** /-blɪst/) **1** (of a person or his words or actions) having or showing a low or modest opinion of one's own importance; not proud: *my humble apologies* ○ *in my humble opinion.* **2** (**a**) (of a person, his position in society, etc) low in rank; unimportant: *men of humble birth* ○ *a humble occupation.* (**b**) (of a thing) not large or elaborate; poor: *a humble home, meal, offering.* **3** (idm) **eat humble pie** ⇨ EAT.

▷ **humble** *v* [Tn] make (sb/sth/oneself) humble; lower the rank or self-importance of: *humble one's enemies* ○ *humble sb's pride* ○ *humble oneself before God* ○ *a humbling experience.*

humbly /ˈhʌmblɪ *or, rarely, US* ˈʌm-/ *adv*: *beg most humbly for forgiveness* ○ *live humbly* ○ *humbly born*, ie of a poor or an unimportant family.

Humboldt /ˈhʌmbəʊlt/ Friedrich Heinrich Alexander, Baron von (1769-1859), German explorer and scientist who made several important discoveries in S America (showing eg that the *Amazon and *Orinoco river systems are connected).

□ **the** ˌ**Humboldt** ˈ**Current** (also **the Peru Current**) cold ocean current that flows north along the coasts of Chile and Peru.

humbug /ˈhʌmbʌg/ *n* **1** (**a**) [U] dishonest behaviour or talk that is intended to deceive people and win their support or sympathy. (**b**) [C] dishonest and deceitful person. **2** [C] (*Brit*) hard boiled sweet, usu flavoured with peppermint.

▷ **humbug** *v* (**-gg-**) [Tn, Tn·pr] ~ **sb** (**into/out of sth/doing sth**) deceive or trick sb; cheat sb.

humdinger /ˌhʌmˈdɪŋə(r)/ *n* (*sl*) excellent or remarkable person or thing: *His girl-friend is a real humdinger.* ○ *We had a humdinger of an argument.*

humdrum /ˈhʌmdrʌm/ *adj* lacking excitement or variety; dull; monotonous: *humdrum chores* ○ *Her life is humdrum.*

Hume /hjuːm/ David (1711-76), Scottish philosopher and historian who maintained that human beings cannot know anything for certain which is not directly perceived through their senses. His main philosophical work was *A Treatise of Human Nature*, and he also wrote a *History of Great Britain.*

humerus /ˈhjuːmərəs/ *n* (*pl* **humeri** /ˈhjuːməraɪ/) (*anatomy*) bone in the upper arm, from shoulder to elbow. ⇨ illus at SKELETON.

humid /ˈhjuːmɪd/ *adj* (of the air or climate) containing moisture; damp: *humid heat, atmosphere.*

▷ **humidify** /hjuːˈmɪdɪfaɪ/ *v* (*pt, pp* **-fied**) [Tn] make (the air, etc) damp. **humidifier** *n* device for keeping the air moist in a room, etc.

humidity /hjuːˈmɪdətɪ/ *n* [U] degree of moisture, esp in the air; dampness.

humiliate /hjuːˈmɪlɪeɪt/ *v* [Tn] make (sb) feel ashamed or disgraced; lower the dignity or self-respect of: *He felt humiliated by her scornful remarks.* ○ *a country humiliated by defeat.* ▷ **humiliating** *adj*: *a rather humiliating experience.* **humiliation** /hjuːˌmɪlɪˈeɪʃn/ *n* [C, U]: *suffer public humiliation.*

humility /hjuːˈmɪlətɪ/ *n* [U] humble attitude of mind; modesty: *a person of great humility* ○ *I say this in all humility*, ie without wishing to appear boastful.

hummock /ˈhʌmək/ *n* low hill or hump in the ground; hillock.

hummus /ˈhʊməs/ *n* [U] paste made from chick-peas and oil flavoured with garlic, etc, used for spreading or as a dip. It originated in the Middle East.

humorist /ˈhjuːmərɪst/ *n* person who is known for his humorous writing or talk.

humorous /ˈhjuːmərəs/ *adj* having or showing a sense of humour; amusing; funny: *a humorous writer, remark* ○ *see the humorous side of a situation.* ▷ **humorously** *adv.*

humour (*US* **humor**) /ˈhjuːmə(r)/ *n* **1** [U] quality of being amusing or comic: *a story full of humour* ○ *recognize the humour of a situation.* ⇨ article. **2** [U] ability to appreciate things, situations or people that are comic; ability to be amused: *She lacks humour.* ○ *He has a good sense of humour.* **3** [U, sing] (*fml*) person's state of mind; mood; temper: *be in (an) excellent humour* ○ *I'll do it when the humour takes me.* **4** [C] (*arch*) any of the four liquids (blood, phlegm, choler, melancholy) in the body that were once thought to determine a person's mental and physical qualities. **5** (idm) ˌ**out of** ˈ**humour** (*dated fml*) in a bad mood.

▷ **humour** (*US* **humor**) *v* [Tn] keep (sb) happy or contented by accepting or agreeing to his wishes, even if they seem unreasonable: *It's always best to humour him when he's in one of his bad moods.*

-humoured (*US* **-humored**) (forming compound *adjs*) having or showing the specified mood: *good-humoured* ○ *ill-humoured.*

humourless (*US* **humorless**) *adj* lacking a sense of humour: *a humourless person, style of writing.*

hump /hʌmp/ *n* **1** (**a**) round projecting part on the back of a camel, etc. ⇨ illus at CAMEL. (**b**) deformity on a person's back, where there is an abnormal curvature of the spine. **2** rounded raised mound of earth, etc: *a dangerous hump in the road.* **3** (idm) **give sb the** ˈ**hump** (*Brit infml*) make sb feel depressed or annoyed. **over the** ˈ**hump** past the most difficult part (of a task, etc).

▷ **hump** *v* **1** [Tn, Tn·p] ~ **sth** (**up**) form sth into a hump: *hump up the bedclothes.* **2** [Tn·pr, Tn·p] carry (sth) on one's shoulder or back: *I don't enjoy humping heavy furniture around all day.* ⇨ Usage at CARRY. **3** [Tn] (⚠ *sl*) have sexual intercourse with (sb).

□ ˈ**humpback** *n* = HUNCHBACK (HUNCH).

ˈ**humpbacked** *adj* = HUNCHBACKED (HUNCH).

ˌ**humpback** ˈ**bridge** small bridge with an arch that rises and falls steeply.

humph /hʌmpf, həh/ *interj* (light grunting sound usu made with the lips closed and used to express doubt or dissatisfaction).

Humour

The British sense of humour takes many different forms. At its most basic level, humour is seen in the British love of 'slapstick', in physical and often purely visual comedy, as performed by clowns in a circus, two comedians in a double act (for example, in a pantomime or television show), or a single comedian acting out a ridiculous scene. Even in Shakespeare's tragedies, scenes of slapstick comedy are inserted after scenes of powerful emotion in order to break the tension.

Such visual humour often has an extreme or even surreal aspect, and in this form can range from a 'drag act' (with a man dressed as a woman) to an absurd impersonation of a well-known personality. At its most sophisticated, humour of this type combines comedy with satire, as in the popular television series *Spitting Image*, where grotesque puppets represent famous people who are respected establishment figures (such as politicians and members of the royal family) in a comically exaggerated manner.

At a lower level, the British enjoy 'smutty' or 'lavatorial' humour, especially when it takes the form of barely disguised innuendo, or a play on words. The subjects of such humour are sex or excretion, and the language is often puerile, with much use of 'naughty' words and names such as 'knickers', 'bum', 'wee' and 'willy'. The double entendre is an essential feature of such humour, in particular the use of very common words like 'have' or 'it' that are often used with a sexual meaning. Humour of this type is seen on car stickers, badges and T-shirts. A typical example of such double entendre is 'skiers do it standing up'.

Puns are very prominent in British humour. The English language, which contains various words and expressions that have several senses, adapts well to this sort of humour. Shakespeare was very fond of using puns, both in comic and serious contexts. British people generally find using puns very entertaining, although in everyday speech some puns have been over-used, such as the remark, 'Did you enjoy your trip?' said when a person trips up. The usual response to such corny puns is to groan.

At its highest level, British humour is represented not by puns but by witty observations on life and society, such as those by Oscar Wilde. Humour of this kind is more clever than comic. Examples are 'There is one thing in the world worse than being talked about, and that is not being talked about,' and 'Work is the curse of the drinking classes.'

There is a British tradition that the English spoken by foreigners is amusing and a suitable subject for humour. An English person speaking a foreign language, especially French, is also an object of fun. 'Franglais', the literal translation of English, and especially English idioms, into French, for example 'C'est un morceau de gâteau' for 'It's a piece of cake' (meaning 'It's an easy task') is one form of this humour.

British children's traditional humour has to some extent been adopted by adults, in particular riddles with punning answers. An example is: 'What's grey, has four legs and a trunk? A mouse on holiday.' A special type of children's humour is the 'Knock knock' joke, involving the comic distortion of a person's name. A typical joke of this type has dialogue that runs: 'Knock knock.' 'Who's there?' 'Robert.' 'Robert who?' 'Robert out (ie Rub it out) and do it again.' Another favourite distortion of language is the spoonerism, named after the Oxford college head and clergyman who is said to have invented it. 'It's roaring with pain' instead of 'It's pouring with rain' and 'the weight of rages' instead of 'the rate of wages' are spoonerisms.

Graffiti, in the form of witty but often punning, nonsensical or surreal slogans (typically written in places such as public toilets), are a modern American form of humour that has become popular in Britain. An example is: 'Nostalgia isn't what it used to be.'

Cartoons appear in most British and American newspapers and magazines. The humour may be 'angled' in a particular way, usually to make a political point. Children's comics are full of cartoons of the purely 'funny' or 'crazy' type. Like all humour, cartoons can be indecent, with the milder forms traditionally seen in the 'naughty postcard' sold at seaside resorts. Many of these depict men with big stomachs or women with large breasts, and link the garishly drawn picture to an 'innocent' remark spoken by one of the characters that can also have an indecent meaning. Cartoons in popular newspapers often involve pairs of stock characters, such as a wife with a rolling-pin and her drunken husband, an office boss and his secretary, or two neighbours chatting over a garden fence.

An especially American type of humour is 'sick' or 'black' humour in which jokes are made about subjects like nuclear war, disability or disease that people otherwise find too painful to think about. This type of humour has traditionally been avoided in the British media but recently 'alternative' comedians, already popular working in clubs and bars, have become television entertainers. Zany and eccentric humour is also very popular on British radio and television.

Much humour is very 'low key' and relies for its effect on a casual amusing contrast or an inconsequential 'punchline'. One particular type of joke is the 'shaggy dog story', in which a speaker recounts a lengthy, boring tale with an unexpectedly tame ending.

Both the British and Americans value a sense of humour (not for nothing has the word 'humour' been adopted by many other languages), and often resort to it when in trouble or difficulties. A high value is placed on the ability to laugh in the face of adversity. Expressions that reflect this attitude are 'grin and bear it' (for example, on hearing bad news), 'see the funny side' (for example, in an embarrassing or disastrous situation) and the saying 'laughter is the best medicine'.

humus /ˌhju:məs/ *n* [U] rich dark organic material formed by the decay of dead leaves, etc and essential to the fertility of soil.

Hun /hʌn/ *n* **1** member of one of the Asiatic peoples who ravaged Europe in the 4th and 5th centuries AD. **2** (*dated derog offensive*) German.

hunch /hʌntʃ/ *n* idea based on intuition or instinct and not on evidence: *He had a hunch that she was lying.* ○ *play/follow one's hunch*, ie act according to one's intuition.

▷ **hunch** *v* [Tn, Tn·p] ~ **sth (up)** bend forward (part of the body, esp the back and shoulders) into a rounded shape: *Stand straight, don't hunch your shoulders!* ○ *She sat all hunched up over the small fire.*

□ ˈ**hunchback** (also ˈ**humpback**) *n* **1** rounded part on a person's back where there is an abnormal curvature of the spine; hump. **2** person with such a deformity. ˈ**hunchbacked** (also ˈ**humpbacked**) *adj* having such a hump on the back.

hundred /ˈhʌndrəd/ *pron, det* (after *a* or *one* or an indication of quantity) 100; one more than ninety-nine: *one, two, three, etc hundred* ○ *a few hundred* ○ *There were a/one hundred (people) in the room.* ○ *I could give you a hundred reasons for not going.* ○ *This antique is worth several hundred pounds.* ○ *If I've said it once, I've said it a hundred times.* ○ *He's a hundred (years old) today.* ⇨ App 9.

▷ **hundred** *n* (after *a* or *one*, a number or an indication of quantity) the number 100: *How many hundreds are there in a thousand?* ○ *Her coat cost hundreds (of pounds).* ○ *There are hundreds (of people) (ie very many) who need new housing.* ○ *The cake was decorated with a large (one) hundred.*

hundred- (in compounds) having one hundred of the thing specified: *a hundred-year lease.*

hundredth /ˈhʌndrətθ/ *pron, det* 100th; next after ninety-ninth. — *n* one of one hundred equal parts of sth.

□ ˈ**hundredfold** *adj, adv* **1** one hundred times as much or as many. **2** having one hundred parts.

ˈ**hundredweight** *n* (*pl* unchanged) (*abbr* **cwt**) one twentieth of one ton; 112 lb (in US 100 lb). ⇨ App 10.

Hundred Years War /ˌhʌndrəd jɪəz ˈwɔ:(r)/ **the Hundred Years War** war between France and England which lasted intermittently from the 1340s to the 1450s. The English wanted to gain control of France, and conducted military campaigns in the north of the country, winning notable victories in the battles of *Crécy (1346) and *Agincourt (1415). Some territory was gained, but by the time the war ended all of it except the area around Calais had been lost.

hung *pt, pp* of HANG[1].

□ ˌ**hung-**ˈ**over** *adj* [pred] (*infml*) having a hangover: *I feel a bit hung-over this morning.*

ˌ**hung** ˈ**parliament** parliament in which no party has a clear majority.

Hungary /ˈhʌŋgərɪ/ country in central Europe, with borders on Austria and Romania; pop approx 10 597 000; official language Hungarian; capital Budapest; unit of currency forint (= 100 fillér). It was part of the Austro-Hungarian Empire until 1918, when it became independent. After the Second World War it became a Communist state. A liberal reform movement was crushed in 1956 by a Soviet invasion. At the end of the 1980s democratic institutions were restored, and in 1990 parliamentary elections were held. Hungary's main exports are machinery and chemicals. ⇨ map.

▷ **Hungarian** /hʌŋˈgeərɪən/ *adj* of Hungary. — *n* **1** [C] native or inhabitant of Hungary. **2** [U] non-Indo-European language spoken in Hungary. Cf FINNO-UGRIC.

hunger /ˈhʌŋgə(r)/ *n* **1** [U] (**a**) state of not having enough to eat; lack of food: *He died of hunger.* (**b**) desire for food: *satisfy one's hunger.* **2** [sing] ~ **for sth** (*fig*) strong desire for sth: *have a hunger for adventure.*

▷ **hunger** *v* **1** [I] (*arch*) feel a lack of or desire for food. **2** (phr v) **hunger for/after sth/sb** have a

Hungary

Holman Hunt: Our English Coasts (Strayed Sheep)

strong desire for sth/sb; long for sth/sb: *She hungered for his love.*
□ ˈ**hunger march** long walk undertaken by unemployed people to make others aware of their sufferings.
ˈ**hunger strike** refusal to take food, esp by a prisoner, as a form of protest: *be/go on (a) hunger strike.* ˈ**hunger striker**.

hungry /ˈhʌŋgrɪ/ *adj* (**-ier**, **-iest**) **1** (**a**) suffering from weakness, pain, etc because of lack of food; starving: *the hungry masses.* (**b**) feeling a desire for food: *Let's eat soon — I'm hungry!* **2** [pred] ~ **for sth** (*fig*) in need of sth; feeling a strong desire for sth: *The orphan was hungry for affection.* **3** [usu attrib] showing hunger: *He had a hungry look.* **4** [attrib] causing hunger: *Haymaking is hungry work.* **5** (idm) **go** ˈ**hungry** remain unfed: *Thousands are going hungry because of the failure of the harvest.* ○ *I'd rather go hungry than eat that!*
▷ **hungrily** /ˈhʌŋgrəlɪ/ *adv.*

hunk /hʌŋk/ *n* **1** large piece (esp of food) cut from a larger piece: *a hunk of bread, cheese, meat.* **2** (*sl usu approv*) big strong man, esp an attractive one.

hunkers /ˈhʌŋkəz/ *n* [pl] (*infml*) haunches: *on one's hunkers*, ie in a squatting position.

hunky-dory /ˌhʌŋkɪ ˈdɔːrɪ/ *adj* [usu pred] (*infml esp US*) satisfactory; fine: *Everything's just hunky-dory!*

Hunt[1] /hʌnt/ William Holman (1827-1910), English painter of the *Pre-Raphaelite school who specialized in landscapes, biblical scenes and paintings with a moral message. His work is characterized by bright colours and attention to fine detail. ⇨ illus.

Hunt[2] /hʌnt/ (James Henry) Leigh (1784-1859), English poet, essayist and editor who was a friend and supporter of *Keats, *Shelley and other Romantic poets.

hunt[1] /hʌnt/ *v* **1** [I, Tn] chase (wild animals or game) and try to kill or capture them, for food or sport: *go hunting* ○ *Wolves hunt* (ie pursue their prey) *in packs.* **2** [I, Ipr, Ip, Tn] ~ (**for sth/sb**) search for (sth/sb); try to find (sth/sb): *hunt for a lost book* ○ *I've hunted everywhere but I can't find it.* ○ *Police are hunting an escaped criminal.* **3** [Tn·pr, Tn·p] drive or chase (sth) away; pursue (sth) with hostility: *hunt the neighbour's cats out of the garden.* **4** [Tn] (*Brit*) (**a**) (in fox-hunting) follow the hounds through or in (a district): *hunt the country.* (**b**) use (a horse or hounds) in hunting. (**c**) act as master or huntsman of (a pack of hounds). **5** [I] (of an engine) run alternately too fast and too slow. **6** (idm) **run with the hare and hunt with the hounds** ⇨ HARE. **7** (phr v) **hunt sb/sth down** pursue sb/sth until he/it is found: *hunt down a criminal.* **hunt sth out** search for sth (esp an object that has been put away or is no longer in use) until it is found: *hunt out an old diary.* **hunt sth up** search for sth (esp sth hidden and difficult to find): *hunt up references in the library.*
▷ **hunter** *n* **1** (often in compounds) person who hunts: *hunters of big game in Africa* ○ ˈ*bargain-hunters in the sales.* **2** horse used in hunting. **3** watch with a metal cover over the glass face. ˌ**hunter's** ˈ**moon** first full moon after the harvest moon (HARVEST).
hunting *n* [U] chasing and capturing or killing of wild animals, etc as a sport; (esp in Britain) fox-hunting: [attrib] *a* ˈ*hunting jacket* ○ *a* ˈ*hunting crop.* **hunting-ground** *n* **1** place where one hunts for sth. **2** (idm) **a happy, etc hunting-ground (for/of sb)** favourable place, etc where sb may do or observe or acquire what he wants: *Crowded shops are a happy hunting-ground for pickpockets.*
huntress /ˈhʌntrɪs/ *n* (*dated*) woman hunter.

NOTE ON USAGE: **1** In British English **go hunting** refers to the sport of chasing and killing foxes with dogs while on horseback. The riders in charge of the hunt are called **huntsmen** and the event is a **hunt.** A **hunter** chases big game, eg lions, elephants, etc. **Shooting** is the killing of game birds, deer and other animals for sport. **2** In US English **hunting** relates to the shooting of deer or game birds by a **hunter.**

hunt[2] /hʌnt/ *n* **1** [C] (often in compounds) act of hunting wild animals; chase: *a* ˈ*fox-hunt.* ⇨ articles at ANIMAL, PROTEST. **2** [C usu *sing*] act of looking for sth; search: *I had a good hunt for that key.* ○ *He found it after a long hunt.* ○ *The police are on the hunt for further clues.* ○ *The hunt is on for the culprit.* **3** (*esp Brit*) (**a**) [CGp] group of people who regularly hunt foxes, etc with horses and hounds: [attrib] *a hunt* ˈ*ball*, ie a dance held by a hunt. (**b**) [C] district in which they hunt.

huntsman /ˈhʌntsmən/ *n* (*pl* **-men** /-mən/) **1** man who hunts wild animals, esp foxes. **2** man in charge of the hounds during a hunt.

hurdle /ˈhɜːdl/ *n* **1** (**a**) [C] (in athletics or horse-racing) each of a series of upright frames to be jumped over in a race: *five furlongs over hurdles* ○ [attrib] *a* ˈ*hurdle-race.* ⇨ illus. (**b**) **hurdles** [pl] race over these: *He won the 400 metres hurdles.* **2** [C] (*fig*) difficulty to be overcome; obstacle: *I'v[e] passed the written test; the interview is the nex[t] hurdle.* **3** [C] portable oblong frame with bars use[d] for making temporary fences (eg for sheep pens).
▷ **hurdle** *v* [I] (in athletics) run in a hurdle-race. **hurdler** /ˈhɜːdlə(r)/ *n* person who runs i[n] hurdle-races.

hurdy-gurdy /ˈhɜːdɪ gɜːdɪ/ *n* **1** portable musica[l] instrument with a droning sound, played by turning a handle. **2** (*infml*) = BARREL-ORGA[N] (BARREL).

hurl /hɜːl/ *v* [Tn, Tn·pr, Tn·p] **1** throw (sth/sb/ oneself) violently; fling: *rioters hurling stones a[t] the police* ○ *He hurled himself into his work.* ○ *Sh[e] was hurled to her death.* **2** (*fig*) utter (sth) wit[h] force; shout; yell: *hurl insults at sb.*

hurling /ˈhɜːlɪŋ/ (also **hurley** /ˈhɜːlɪ/) *n* [U] Iris[h] ball game similar to hockey.

hurly-burly /ˈhɜːlɪ bɜːlɪ/ *n* [U] noisy and energeti[c] activity (esp of many people together).

Huron[1] /ˈhjʊərən/ *n* member of any of a group of N American Indian tribes living in the area of Lak[e] Huron.

Huron[2] /ˈhjʊərən/ **Lake Huron** second largest o[f] the *Great Lakes of N America.

hurrah /hʊˈrɑː/ (also **hurray**, **hooray** /hʊˈreɪ/) *interj* **1** ~ (**for sb/sth**) (used to express joy, approval, etc): *Hurrah for the holidays!* **2** (idm) **hip, hip, hurrah/hurray** ⇨ HIP[3].
▷ **hurrah** (also **hurray**) *n* shout of 'hurrah'.

hurricane /ˈhʌrɪkən; *US* -keɪn/ *n* **1** storm with a violent wind, esp a West Indian cyclone. **2** wind o[f] 73 miles per hour or more: [attrib] *gales o[f] hurricane force.* Cf CYCLONE, TYPHOON.
□ ˈ**hurricane lamp** (also ˈ**storm-lantern**) type o[f] lamp with glass sides to protect the flame from th[e] wind.

hurry /ˈhʌrɪ/ *n* **1** [U] need or wish to get somethin[g] done quickly; eager haste: *In his hurry to leave, h[e] forgot his passport.* ○ *There's no hurry, so do i[t] slowly and carefully.* ○ *What's the hurry?* ○ *Why a[ll] the hurry?* **2** (idm) **in a** ˈ**hurry** (**a**) quickly; hastily: *She dressed in a hurry.* (**b**) eager; impatient: *He wa[s] in a hurry to leave.* (**c**) (*infml*) (usu with a negative) soon; readily: *I shan't invite him again in a hurr[y] — he behaved very badly.* ○ *She won't forget that i[n] a hurry.* **in no** ˈ**hurry/not in any** ˈ**hurry** (**a**) no[t] eager or under pressure to act: *I don't min[d] waiting — I'm not in any particular hurry.* (**b**) unwilling: *I'm in no hurry to see him again.*
▷ **hurry** *v* (*pt, pp* **hurried**) **1** (**a**) [I, Ipr, Ip] do st[h] or move quickly or too quickly; rush: *Don't hurr[y], there's plenty of time.* ○ *It's no use trying to mak[e] her hurry.* ○ *He picked up his bag and hurried o[n] along the platform.* ○ *Hurry along, children!* (**b**

[Tn, Tn·pr, Tn·p] make (sb) do sth or move quickly or too quickly: *We're late; I must hurry you.* ○ *They hurried him into hospital.* ○ *I was hurried into making an unwise decision.* **2** [Tn, Tn·p] ~ **sth (along/up)** hasten the progress of sth: *This work needs care; it mustn't be hurried.* ○ *A good meal should never be hurried.* **3** (phr v) **hurry up** (*infml*) move more quickly or too quickly; do sth more quickly: *I wish the train would hurry up and come.* ○ *Hurry up and get ready — we're waiting!* **hurry sb/sth up** make sb/sth do sth or move quickly or too quickly; speed sth up: *He's a good worker but he needs hurrying up.* **hurried** *adj* done quickly or too quickly: *a hurried meal* ○ *write a few hurried lines.* **hurriedly** *adv*: *We had to leave rather hurriedly.*

hurt /hɜ:t/ *v* (*pt, pp* **hurt**) **1** (a) [I, Tn] cause physical injury or pain to (sb/oneself, a part of the body, an animal, etc): *Did you hurt yourself?* ○ *Are you badly hurt?* ○ *She was more frightened than hurt.* ○ *He hurt his back when he fell.* (b) [I] feel or cause pain: *My leg hurts.* ○ *My shoes hurt; they're too tight.* ○ *It hurts when I move my leg.* ⇨ Usage at WOUND[1]. **2** [Tn] cause mental pain to (a person, his feelings); distress; upset: *These criticisms have hurt him/his pride deeply.* ○ *It hurts/I am hurt not to have been invited.* ○ *I hope we haven't offended him; he sounded rather hurt on the phone.* **3** [Tn] have a bad effect on (sth); harm: *Sales of the product have been seriously hurt by the adverse publicity.* **4** (idm) **it, etc won't/wouldn't hurt (sb/sth) (to do sth)** (*esp ironic*) it, etc will/would not cause harm or inconvenience: *It won't hurt to postpone the meeting.* ○ *A bit of weeding wouldn't hurt (this garden).* ○ *It wouldn't hurt (you) to say sorry for once.* **not harm/hurt a fly** ⇨ FLY[1].

▷ **hurt** *n* **1** [U, sing] ~ **(to sth)** mental pain or suffering: *The experience left me with a feeling of deep hurt.* ○ *It was a severe hurt to her pride.* **2** [C] physical injury or pain. **hurtful** /-fl/ *adj* ~ **(to sb)** causing (esp mental) suffering; unkind: *hurtful remarks* ○ *She can be very hurtful sometimes.* **hurtfully** /-fəlɪ/ *adv.* **hurtfulness** *n* [U].

hurtle /ˈhɜ:tl/ *v* [Ipr, Ip] move violently, noisily or with great speed in the specified direction: *During the gale roof tiles came hurtling down.* ○ *The van hurtled round the corner.* ○ *She slipped and went hurtling downstairs.*

husband /ˈhʌzbənd/ *n* **1** man to whom a woman is married: *her new husband* ○ *He'll make someone a very good husband.* ⇨ App 8. **2** (idm) ˌ**husband and** ˈ**wife** married couple: *They lived together as husband and wife for years.*

▷ **husband** *v* [Tn] (*fml*) use (sth) sparingly and economically; try to save: *husband one's strength, resources.*

husbandry /ˈhʌzbəndrɪ/ *n* [U] (*fml*) **1** farming: *animal husbandry.* **2** management of resources: *Through careful husbandry we survived the hard winter.*

hush /hʌʃ/ *v* **1** (a) [I] become silent: *Hush!* ie Be quiet! (b) [Tn, Tn·pr] make (sb) silent or calm; quieten (sb): *He hushed the baby to sleep.* **2** (phr v) **hush sth up** prevent sth from becoming generally known, esp sth shameful: *The government hushed the affair up to avoid a public outcry.*

▷ **hush** *n* [U, sing] stillness; silence: *in the hush of the night* ○ *There was a sudden deathly hush.*

□ ˌ**hush-**ˈ**hush** *adj* (*infml*) very secret or confidential: *a hush-hush affair* ○ *His job is very hush-hush.*

ˈ**hush-money** *n* [U] money paid to prevent sth scandalous from becoming known publicly.

husk /hʌsk/ *n* **1** dry outer covering of certain seeds and fruits, esp grain: *rice in the husk*, ie brown rice, with the husks not removed. Cf BRAN, CHAFF. **2** (*fig*) worthless outside part of anything.

▷ **husk** *v* [Tn] remove the husk(s) from (seeds or fruit).

husky[1] /ˈhʌskɪ/ *adj* (**-ier, -iest**) **1** (of a person or voice) dry in the throat; sounding slightly hoarse: *I'm still a bit husky after my recent cold.* **2** (*infml*) (of a person) big and strong. ▷ **huskily** *adv*: *speak huskily.* **huskiness** *n* [U].

husky[2] /ˈhʌskɪ/ *n* strong breed of dog with a thick coat, used in the Arctic for pulling sledges.

Huss /hʌs/ John (c 1372-1415), Czech religious reformer who attacked abuses in the Catholic Church, for which he was tried and burned at the stake.

▷ **Hussite** /ˈhʌsaɪt/ *n* follower of John Huss. The Hussites fought wars against Catholic religious and secular authority in central Europe in the 15th and 16th centuries.

huss /hʌs/ *n* [U] flesh of the dogfish used as food: *a nice piece of fresh huss.*

hussar /hʊˈzɑ:(r)/ *n* soldier of a cavalry regiment, carrying light weapons.

hussy /ˈhʌsɪ/ *n* (*dated derog*) **1** bold cheeky girl. **2** sexually immoral woman: *You brazen hussy!*

hustings /ˈhʌstɪŋz/ *n* [pl] **the hustings** the political campaigning leading up to a parliamentary election, eg canvassing votes and making speeches: *Most politicians will be at/on the hustings in the coming week.*

hustle /ˈhʌsl/ *v* **1** [Tn·pr, Tn·p] push (sb) roughly and hurriedly; jostle; shove: *The police hustled the thief out of the house and into their van.* ○ *The thief was hustled off (to gaol).* **2** [Tn, Tn·pr] ~ **sb (into sth/doing sth)** make sb act quickly and without time to consider things: *I was hustled into (making) a hasty decision.* **3** [I] hurry; push one's way: *people hustling and bustling all around us.* **4** [Tn] (*infml esp US*) sell or obtain (sth) by energetic (and sometimes deceitful) activity. **5** [I] (*US sl*) work as a prostitute.

▷ **hustle** *n* [U] busy energetic activity: *I hate all the hustle (and bustle) of Saturday shopping.*

hustler /ˈhʌslə(r)/ *n* **1** (*infml esp US*) person who hustles (HUSTLE 4). **2** (*US sl*) prostitute.

Huston /ˈhju:stən/ John (1906-87), American director, writer and actor. His work covers a vast range of themes from his début, *The Maltese Falcon*, to the intimacy of his adaptation of James Joyce's *The Dead*, often examining situations of human grandeur and defeat.

hut /hʌt/ *n* small roughly-built house or shelter, usu made of wood or metal. Cf SHED[1].

▷ **hutment** /ˈhʌtmənt/ *n* group of huts, esp for soldiers.

hutted having huts: *a hutted camp.*

hutch /hʌtʃ/ *n* box or cage with a front of wire netting, esp one used for keeping rabbits in.

Huxley[1] /ˈhʌkslɪ/ Aldous Leonard (1894-1963), English novelist and essayist whose early wittily satirical novels *Crome Yellow*, *Antic Hay* and *Point Counter Point* were followed by the more serious futuristic *Brave New World*. From 1937 he lived in California and became deeply interested in mysticism and parapsychology.

Huxley[2] /ˈhʌkslɪ/ Sir Julian (1887-1975), English biologist who made advances in the study of animal behaviour.

Huxley[3] /ˈhʌkslɪ/ Thomas Henry (1825-95), English biologist who did much to support and publicize *Darwin's ideas about evolution. A doubter of the existence of God, he coined the word 'agnostic'.

Huygens /ˈhaɪgənz/ Christiaan (1629-95), Dutch physicist, mathematician and astronomer who invented the pendulum clock, discovered the rings of Saturn and proposed the theory that light travels in waves.

hyacinth /ˈhaɪəsɪnθ/ *n* plant with sweet-smelling bell-shaped flowers, growing from a bulb. ⇨ illus at PLANT.

hyaena = HYENA.

hybrid /ˈhaɪbrɪd/ *n* **1** animal or plant that has parents of different species or varieties: *A mule is a hybrid of a male donkey and a female horse.* **2** thing made by combining two different elements, esp a word with parts from different languages.

▷ **hybrid** *adj* **1** produced as a hybrid; cross-bred: *a hybrid animal, plant.* **2** composed of unrelated parts.

hybridize, -ise /-aɪz/ *v* **1** [I] (of animals or plants) produce hybrids; interbreed. **2** [Tn] cause (animals or plants) to produce hybrids; cross-breed.

Hyde Park /ˌhaɪd ˈpɑ:k/ large public park in central London, containing a large lake called the Serpentine, Speakers' Corner (where people can make speeches on topics that interest or concern them) and Rotten Row, a track for riding horses.

□ ˌ**Hyde Park** ˈ**Corner** busy road junction at the north-east corner of Hyde Park.

hydra /ˈhaɪdrə/ *n* **1** (in Greek mythology) snake-like monster with many heads that grew again if they were cut off. **2** (*fig*) thing that is hard to get rid of; recurring problem.

hydrangea /haɪˈdreɪndʒə/ *n* shrub with white, pink or blue flowers growing in large round clusters.

hydrant /ˈhaɪdrənt/ *n* pipe (esp in a street) with a nozzle to which a hose can be attached, for drawing water from a water-main to clean streets, put out fires, etc.

hydrate /ˈhaɪdreɪt/ *n* chemical compound of water with another substance.

▷ **hydrate** /ˈhaɪdreɪt, haɪˈdreɪt/ *v* **1** [I] combine chemically with water. **2** [Tn] cause (a substance) to absorb water. **hydration** /haɪˈdreɪʃn/ *n* [U].

hydraulic /haɪˈdrɔ:lɪk/ *adj* **1** of water moving through pipes. **2** operated by the movement of liquid: *a hydraulic lift* ○ *hydraulic brakes* ○ *a hydraulic engineer*, ie one concerned with the use of water in this way. **3** hardening under water: *hydraulic cement.*

▷ **hydraulically** /-klɪ/ *adv.*

hydraulics *n* [sing or pl *v*] science of using water to produce power.

hydride /ˈhaɪdraɪd/ *n* [C, U] chemical compound of hydrogen with another element, esp a metal.

hydr(o)- *comb form* **1** of water or liquid: *hydroelectricity.* **2** combined with hydrogen: *hydrochloric.*

hydrocarbon /ˌhaɪdrəˈkɑ:bən/ *n* any of a class of compounds of hydrogen and carbon that are found in petrol, coal and natural gas.

hydrocephalus /ˌhaɪdrəʊˈsefələs/ *n* [U] abnormal increase of fluid in the brain, esp in young children, causing enlargement of the head and sometimes mental deficiency. ▷ **hydrocephalic** /ˌhaɪdrəʊsɪˈfælɪk/ *adj.*

hydrochloric /ˌhaɪdrəˈklɒrɪk; *US* -ˈklɔ:r-/ *adj* containing hydrogen and chlorine: ˌ*Hydrochloric* ˈ*acid is very corrosive.*

hydroelectric /ˌhaɪdrəʊɪˈlektrɪk/ *adj* (a) using water-power to produce electricity: *a hydroelectric plant.* (b) (of electricity) produced by the pressure of rushing water: *hydroelectric power.* ▷ **hydroelectrically** /-klɪ/ *adv.* **hydroelectricity** /ˌhaɪdrəʊˌɪlekˈtrɪsətɪ/ *n* [U].

hydrofoil /ˈhaɪdrəfɔɪl/ *n* **1** boat equipped with a device which raises the hull out of the water when the boat is moving, enabling it to travel fast and economically. **2** such a device.

hydrogen /ˈhaɪdrədʒən/ *n* [U] (*symb* **H**) (*chemistry*) gas that has no colour, taste or smell and is the lightest substance known, combining with oxygen to form water. ⇨ App 11.

▷ **hydrogenate** /haɪˈdrɒdʒɪneɪt/ *v* [Tn] cause (sth) to combine chemically with hydrogen: *hydrogenated gases.*

□ ˈ**hydrogen bomb** (also ˈ**H-bomb**) immensely powerful type of bomb which explodes when the nuclei of deuterium (an isotope of hydrogen) fuse.

ˌ**hydrogen** ˈ**carbonate** = BICARBONATE.

ˌ**hydrogen pe**ˈ**roxide** = PEROXIDE 2.

ˌ**hydrogen** ˈ**sulphide** unpleasant-smelling poisonous gas formed by rotting animal matter.

hydrography /haɪˈdrɒgrəfɪ/ *n* [U] scientific study of seas, lakes, rivers, etc. ▷ **hydrographic** /ˌhaɪdrəˈgræfɪk/ *adj.*

hydrolysis /haɪˈdrɒləsɪs/ *n* [U] chemical change of a substance through reaction with water.

▷ **hydrolyse** (*US* **hydrolyze**) /ˈhaɪdrəlaɪz/ *v* [I, Tn] (cause sth to) change chemically by hydrolysis.

hydrometer /ˌhaɪˈdrɒmɪtə(r)/ *n* scientific instrument that measures the density of liquids.

hydrophilic /ˌhaɪdrəˈfɪlɪk/ *adj* (*chemistry*) that can be wetted by or dissolved in water.

hydrophobia /ˌhaɪdrəˈfəʊbɪə/ *n* [U] **1** abnormal fear of water and of drinking, esp as a symptom of rabies in humans. **2** rabies, esp in humans.

hydroplane /ˈhaɪdrəpleɪn/ *n* **1** light motor boat with a flat bottom, that can travel fast over the surface of the water. **2** device on a submarine enabling it to rise or descend.

hydroponics /ˌhaɪdrəˈpɒnɪks/ *n* [sing *v*] art of growing plants without soil in water or sand to which chemical food is added.

hydrostatic /ˌhaɪdrəˈstætɪk/ *adj* of the condition or properties of liquids when they are not moving.
▷ **hydrostatics** /-ˈstætɪks/ *n* [sing *v*] scientific study of the behaviour and properties of stationary liquids.

hydrotherapy /ˌhaɪdrəʊˈθerəpɪ/ *n* [U] treatment of disease and abnormal physical conditions by exercising the body in water and applying water internally.

hydrous /ˈhaɪdrəs/ *adj* (*chemistry*) (of a substance) containing water.

hydroxide /haɪˈdrɒksaɪd/ *n* [C, U] chemical compound of an element with a combination of hydrogen and oxygen: *potassium hydroxide*.

hyena (also **hyaena**) /haɪˈi:nə/ *n* flesh-eating animal of Africa and Asia, like a wolf, with a howl that sounds like wild laughter.

hygiene /ˈhaɪdʒi:n/ *n* [U] study and practice of cleanliness as a way of maintaining good health and preventing disease: *Wash regularly to ensure personal hygiene.* ○ *In the interests of hygiene, please do not smoke in this shop.*
▷ **hygienic** /haɪˈdʒi:nɪk; *US* ˌhaɪdʒɪˈenɪk; *US also* haɪˈdʒenɪk/ *adj* free from germs that cause disease; clean: *hygienic conditions*. **hygienically** /-klɪ/ *adv*.

hygrometer /haɪˈgrɒmɪtə(r)/ *n* scientific instrument for measuring the amount of water vapour in the air.

hygroscope /ˈhaɪgrəskəʊp/ *n* scientific instrument that shows changes in the amount of water vapour in the air (but does not measure it).
▷ **hygroscopic** /ˌhaɪgrəˈskɒpɪk/ *adj* (of a substance) that tends to absorb water vapour from the air.

hymen /ˈhaɪmən/ *n* (*anatomy*) piece of skin-like tissue partly closing the external opening of the vagina of a virgin girl or woman.

hymenopterous /ˌhaɪməˈnɒptərəs/ *adj* (of an insect such as a bee or wasp) having a narrow waist between thorax and abdomen.

hymn /hɪm/ *n* song of praise, esp one praising God sung by Christians.
▷ **hymn** *v* [Tn] praise (God) in hymns.
hymnal /ˈhɪmnəl/ (also ˈ**hymnbook**) *n* book of hymns.

Hymns are often sung at school assemblies and heard on television and on the radio, so many people know quite a lot of hymn tunes, even if they never go to church. Christmas carols are even better known than hymns. Many hymns and carols were written in Victorian times and are generally still as popular now as they were when they were written. Hymn-singing is especially popular in Wales and there are many fine Welsh hymn tunes.

hype /haɪp/ *n* [C, U] (*sl*) (piece of) misleading and exaggerated publicity: *The public were not fooled by all the hype the press gave the event.*
▷ **hype** *v* (phr v) **hype sth up** (*sl*) publicize sth in a wildly exaggerated way: *The movie has been hyped up far beyond its worth.* **hyped up** *adj* (*sl*) **1** exaggerated. **2** (of a person) stimulated (as if) by drugs.

hyper- *pref* (with *adjs* and *ns*) to an excessive degree; above; over: *hypercritical* ○ *hypersensitive* ○ *hypertension*. Cf OVER-.

hyperactive /ˌhaɪpə(r)ˈæktɪv/ *adj* (esp of a child) abnormally and excessively active; unable to relax. ▷ **hyperactivity** /ˌhaɪpərækˈtɪvətɪ/ *n* [U].

hyperbola /haɪˈpɜ:bələ/ *n* (*geometry*) curve produced when a cone is cut by a plane that makes a larger angle with the base than the side of the cone makes. ⇨ illus. ▷ **hyperbolic** /ˌhaɪpəˈbɒlɪk/ *adj*.

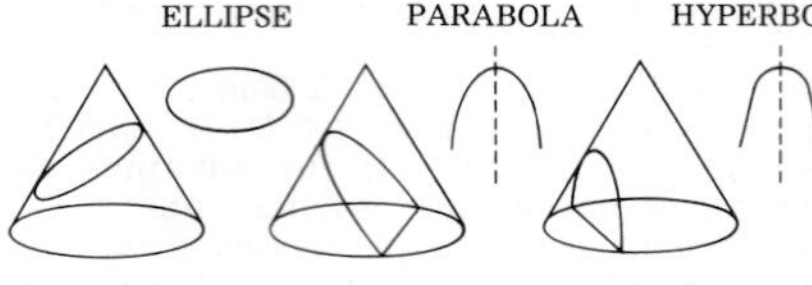

hyperbole /haɪˈpɜ:bəlɪ/ *n* [U, C] exaggerated statement that is made for special effect and is not meant to be taken literally, eg *I've invited millions of people to my party.* ▷ **hyperbolical** /ˌhaɪpəˈbɒlɪkl/ *adj*.

hyperborean /ˌhaɪpəˈbɔ:rɪən, ˌhaɪpəbɔ:ˈri:ən/ *n* (usu **Hyperborean**) (in Greek mythology) member of a race of people who lived in the far north, in a land where the sun always shone.
▷ **hyperborean** *adj* (*fml or rhet*) of the far north.

hypercritical /ˌhaɪpəˈkrɪtɪkl/ *adj* too critical, esp of small faults. ▷ **hypercritically** /-klɪ/ *adv*.

hypermarket /ˈhaɪpəmɑ:kɪt/ *n* (*Brit*) very large self-service shop, selling a wide range of goods and offering a number of services (eg hairdressing), usu situated outside a town. ⇨ article at SHOP.

hypersensitive /ˌhaɪpəˈsensətɪv/ *adj* **1** ~ (**to**/**about sth**) extremely sensitive emotionally. **2** ~ (**to sth**) abnormally sensitive to certain drugs, etc.
▷ **hypersensitivity** /ˌhaɪpəˌsensəˈtɪvətɪ/ *n* [U].

hypertension /ˌhaɪpəˈtenʃn/ *n* [U] **1** (*medical*) abnormally high blood pressure. Cf HYPOTENSION. **2** great emotional tension.

hyperventilation /ˌhaɪpəˌventɪˈleɪʃn/ *n* [U] action of breathing too rapidly or too deeply, which may lead to dizziness and fainting.

hyphen /ˈhaɪfn/ *n* short line (-) used to join two words together (as in *ex-wife*; *co-operated*; *long-legged*; *a ten-dollar bill*) or to show that a word has been divided into parts, eg between the end of one line and the beginning of the next. ⇨ App 14.
▷ **hyphen, hyphenate** /ˈhaɪfəneɪt/ *vs* [Tn] join or write (words) with a hyphen. **hyphenation** /ˌhaɪfəˈneɪʃn/ *n* [U].

hypnosis /hɪpˈnəʊsɪs/ *n* [U] state like deep sleep in which a person's actions may be controlled by another person: *put a person under hypnosis*.
▷ **hypnotic** /hɪpˈnɒtɪk/ *adj* **1** of or producing hypnosis or a similar condition: *be in a hypnotic trance*. **2** (of a drug) producing sleep. — *n* hypnotic drug or influence.
hypnotism /ˈhɪpnətɪzəm/ *n* [U] production or practice of hypnosis. **hypnotist** /ˈhɪpnətɪst/ *n* person who produces hypnosis in another person or who practices hypnosis.
hypnotize, -ise /ˈhɪpnətaɪz/ *v* [Tn] **1** produce hypnosis in (sb). **2** (*fig*) fascinate (sb); charm: *He was hypnotized by her beauty.*

hypo /ˈhaɪpəʊ/ *n* (*pl* ~**s**) (*infml*) = HYPODERMIC *n*.

hyp(o)- *pref* under; beneath: *hypodermic* ○ *hypothesis*.

hypocaust /ˈhaɪpəkɔ:st/ *n* form of heating used in ancient Roman houses, consisting of underfloo passages along which hot air was sent from a furnace.

hypochondria /ˌhaɪpəˈkɒndrɪə/ *n* [U] abnormal and unnecessary anxiety about one's health.
▷ **hypochondriac** /-drɪæk/ *n* person who suffers from hypochondria. Cf VALETUDINARIAN. — *adj* of or suffering from hypochondria.

hypocrisy /hɪˈpɒkrəsɪ/ *n* [U] practice of misrepresenting one's real character, opinions etc, esp by pretending to be more virtuous than one really is; insincerity.
▷ **hypocrite** /ˈhɪpəkrɪt/ *n* person who pretends to have opinions which he does not have or to be what he is not.
hypocritical /ˌhɪpəˈkrɪtɪkl/ *adj* of hypocrisy or a hypocrite: *hypocritical words, behaviour, people*. **hypocritically** /-klɪ/ *adv*.

hypodermic /ˌhaɪpəˈdɜ:mɪk/ *adj* (**a**) (of drugs, etc) injected beneath the skin. (**b**) (of a syringe) used for such injections: *a hypodermic needle*.
▷ **hypodermic** *n* **1** (also *infml* **hypo**) hypodermic syringe. **2** hypodermic injection.
□ ˌ**hypodermic syˈringe** (also **syringe**) syringe with a hollow needle used for injecting a liquid beneath the skin, taking blood samples, etc. ⇨ illus at INJECTION.

hypotension /ˌhaɪpəˈtenʃn/ *n* [U] (*medical*) abnormally low blood pressure. Cf HYPERTENSION.

hypotenuse /haɪˈpɒtənju:z; *US* -tnu:s/ *n* (*geometry*) side opposite the right angle of a right-angled triangle. ⇨ illus at TRIANGLE.

hypothalamus /ˌhaɪpəʊˈθæləməs/ *n* (*pl* **-mi** /-maɪ/) part of the brain that controls body temperature, hunger and thirst, production of hormones, etc. ⇨ illus at BRAIN.

hypothermia /ˌhaɪpəˈθɜ:mɪə/ *n* [U] (*medical*) condition of having an abnormally low body-temperature.

hypothesis /haɪˈpɒθəsɪs/ *n* (*pl* **-ses** /-si:z/) idea or suggestion that is based on known facts and is used as a basis for reasoning or further investigation: *put sth forward as a hypothesis* ○ *prove/disprove a hypothesis*.
▷ **hypothesize, -ise** /haɪˈpɒθəsaɪz/ *v* [I, Tn, Tf] form a hypothesis; assume (sth) as a hypothesis.
hypothetical /ˌhaɪpəˈθetɪkl/ *adj* of or based on a hypothesis; not necessarily true or real. **hypothetically** /-klɪ/ *adv*.

hyrax /ˈhaɪræks/ *n* small plant-eating mammal of Africa and SW Asia which looks like a hamster but is distantly related to the elephants.

hysterectomy /ˌhɪstəˈrektəmɪ/ *n* [C, U] (*medical*) surgical operation for removing a woman's womb.

hysteria /hɪˈstɪərɪə/ *n* [U] (**a**) wild uncontrollable emotion or excitement, with eg laughter, crying or screaming: *crowds of football supporters gripped by mass hysteria*. (**b**) disturbance of the nervous system, esp with emotional outbursts.
▷ **hysterical** /hɪˈsterɪkl/ *adj* **1** caused by hysteria: *hysterical laughter, weeping, screaming, etc* ○ *hysterical behaviour*. **2** suffering from hysteria: *hysterical fans at a rock concert*. **3** (*infml*) very amusing. **hysterically** /-klɪ/ *adv*: *laughing hysterically* ○ (*infml*) *It was hysterically funny.*
hysterics /hɪˈsterɪks/ *n* [pl] **1** fit of hysteria: *go into hysterics* ○ (*infml*) *Your mother would have hysterics* (ie be very angry and upset) *if she knew you were using her car.* **2** (*infml*) wild uncontrolled laughter: *She had the audience in hysterics.*

Hz *abbr* hertz. Cf KHz.

I, i

I[1], **i** /aɪ/ *n* (*pl* **I's, i's** /aɪz/) **1** the ninth letter of the English alphabet: *'Idiot' begins with an I/'I'.* **2** (idm) **dot one's/the i's and cross one's/the t's** ⇨ DOT *v*.

I[2] /aɪ/ *pers pron* (used as the subject of a *v*) person who is the speaker or writer: *I think I'd like a bath.* ○ *When he asked me to marry him I said yes.* Cf ME.

I *abbr* Island(s); Isle(s): *CI*, ie (the) Channel Islands, eg in an address ○ *I* (ie Isle) *of Man*, eg on a map. Cf Is *abbr*.

I *symb* **1** (also **i**) Roman numeral for 1. **2** iodine.

-ial *suff* (with *ns* forming *adjs*) characteristic of: *dictatorial* ○ *managerial* ○ *editorial*. ▷ **-ially** (forming *advs*): *officially*.

iambus /aɪˈæmbəs/ *n* (*pl* ~**es** or **-bi** /-baɪ/) (also **iamb** /ˈaɪæm, ˈaɪæmb/) metrical foot in poetry consisting of one short or unstressed syllable followed by one long or stressed syllable.
▷ **iambic** /aɪˈæmbɪk/ *adj* of or using iambuses: *iambic feet*, eg I ˈsaw three ˈships come ˈsailing ˈby.
iambics *n* [pl] lines of poetry in iambic metre.

-ian (also **-an**) *suff* **1** (with proper *ns* forming *ns* and *adjs*): *Bostonian* ○ *Brazilian* ○ *Shakespearian* ○ *Libran*. **2** (with *ns* ending in *-ics* forming *ns*) specialist in: *optician* ○ *paediatrician*.

-iana (also **-ana**) *suff* (with proper *ns* forming uncountable *ns*) collection of objects (esp publications), facts, anecdotes, etc relating to: *Victoriana* ○ *Mozartiana* ○ *Americana*.

-iatrics *comb form* (forming *ns*) medical treatment of: *paediatrics*. ▷ **-iatric**, **-iatrical** (forming *adjs*). Cf -IATRY.

-iatry *comb form* (forming *ns*) healing or medical treatment of: *psychiatry*. ▷ **-iatric** (forming *adjs*). Cf -IATRICS.

IBA /ˌaɪ biː ˈeɪ/ *abbr* (*Brit*) Independent Broadcasting Authority. Cf BBC, ITV, articles at ADVERTISING, RADIO, TELEVISION.

Iberian /aɪˈbɪərɪən/ *adj* of the large area of land at the south-west corner of Europe (the **Iberian peninsula**) which contains Spain and Portugal.

ibex /ˈaɪbeks/ *n* (*pl* unchanged or ~**es**) type of mountain goat with long curved horns.

ibidem /ˈɪbɪdem/ *adv* (*Latin*) (*abbr* **ibid**) in the same book, article, passage, etc (previously mentioned).

ibis /ˈaɪbɪs/ *n* wading bird like a heron with a long curved beak, found in warm climates.

Ibiza /ɪˈbiːθə/ most westerly of the *Balearic Islands. ▷ **Ibizan** *n*, *adj*. ⇨ map at SPAIN.

-ible ⇨ -ABLE.

IBM /ˌaɪ biː ˈem/ *abbr* International Business Machines (a large computer company): *work for IBM*.

Ibsen /ˈɪbsn/ Henrik (1828-1906), Norwegian dramatist. His powerful realistic prose plays dealing with personal and social themes set the pattern for European drama in modern times. Many of them (eg *A Doll's House*, *Ghosts* and *Hedda Gabler*) are about the position of women in marriage.

i/c /ˌaɪ ˈsiː/ *abbr* in charge (of); in command (of): (*infml*) *Who's i/c ticket sales?*

-ic /-ɪk/ *suff* **1** (with *ns* forming *adjs* and *ns*) of or concerning: *poetic* ○ *scenic* ○ *Arabic*. **2** (with *vs* ending in *-y* forming *adjs*) that performs the specified action: *horrific* ○ *specific*. ▷ **-ical** /-ɪkl/ (forming *adjs*): *comical*. **-ically** /-ɪklɪ/ (forming *advs*): *economically*.

NOTE ON USAGE: Both **-ic** and **-ical** form adjectives from nouns: *scene/scenic*; *sociology/sociological*. Some nouns form pairs of adjectives with both **-ic** and **-ical** which have different meanings: *history/historic* (of great significance)/ *historical* (belonging to history); *economy/economic* (concerned with the economy)/ *economical* (not wasteful). Other examples are *comic/comical*, *politic/political*, *classic/classical*, *poetic/poetical*. Sometimes the pairs are almost synonymous: *rhythmic/rhythmical*. Note that the adverb is derived from the **-ical** form: *comically*, *poetically*, *rhythmically*, *etc*.

Icarus /ˈɪkərəs/ (in Greek mythology) a young man who flew using wings made by his father Daedalus. They were attached with wax, which melted when he flew too near the sun. The wings dropped off, and Icarus fell into the sea and was killed.

ICBM /ˌaɪ siː biː ˈem/ *abbr* intercontinental ballistic missile. Cf IRBM, MRBM.

ice[1] /aɪs/ *n* **1** [U] (**a**) water frozen so that it has become solid: *pipes blocked by ice in winter*. (**b**) sheet or layer of this: *Is the ice thick enough for skating?* **2** [C] (**a**) = WATER ICE (WATER): *Can I have a strawberry-ice?* (**b**) portion of ice-cream: *Two ˈchoc-ices, please.* **3** [U] (*sl*) diamonds. **4** (idm) **be skating on thin ice** ⇨ SKATE[1]. **ˌbreak the ˈice** do or say sth to remove or reduce awkwardness or tension, esp at a first meeting or at the start of a party, etc. **ˌcut no ˈice (with sb)** have little or no effect or influence; be unconvincing: *His excuses cut no ice with me.* **on ˈice** (**a**) (of wine, etc) kept cold by being surrounded by ice. (**b**) (*fig*) in reserve for later use or consideration. (**c**) (of entertainment, etc) performed by skaters: *Cinderella on ice*. (**d**) (*infml*) absolutely certain: *The deal's on ice.*
□ **ˈice age** period when much of the northern hemisphere was covered with glaciers.
ˈice-axe (also *esp US* **ice-ax**) *n* axe used by mountaineers for cutting steps and holds in ice. ⇨ illus at AXE.
ˌice-ˈblue *adj*, *n* [U] (of a) very pale blue colour.
ˈice-bound *adj* surrounded by ice or unable to function because of ice: *an ice-bound ship, harbour*.
ˈicebox *n* (**a**) box with ice in, used for keeping food cool; freezing compartment of a refrigerator. (**b**) (*esp US*) = REFRIGERATOR.
ˈice-breaker *n* strong ship designed to break a passage through ice.
ˈice-cap *n* permanent covering of ice, esp in polar regions.
ˌice-ˈcold *adj* as cold as ice; very cold: *an ˌice-cold ˈdrink*.
ˌice-ˈcream /*esp US* ˈaɪskriːm/ *n* [C, U] (portion of) frozen food made from sweetened and flavoured cream or custard: *a/some strawberry ice-cream*.
ˈice-cube *n* small cube of ice made in a mould in the refrigerator, for drinks, etc.
ˌice ˈdancing art or sport of dancing on ice-skates.
ˈice-fall *n* very steep part of a glacier, like a frozen waterfall.
ˈice-field *n* large area of floating ice, esp in polar regions.
ˈice-floe *n* large sheet of floating ice: *In spring the ice-floes break up.*
ˈice-free *adj* (of a harbour) free from ice.
ˈice hockey (*US* **hockey**) form of hockey played on ice by two teams of skaters, using long sticks to hit a hard rubber disc.
ˈice-house *n* building or room for storing ice, esp one built partly or wholly underground.
ˌice ˈlolly (*US propr* **Popsicle**) flavoured ice on a small stick.
ˈice-pack *n* bag filled with ice, used medically to cool parts of the body, esp the head.
ˈice-pick *n* tool for breaking ice.
ˈice-rink *n* specially prepared sheet of ice, often indoors, for skating, playing ice hockey, etc.
ˈice-show *n* variety entertainment performed by skaters on an ice-rink.
ˈice-skate *n* boot fitted with a thin metal blade for skating on ice. ⇨ illus at SKATE. — *v* [I] skate on ice.
ˈice-skating *n* [U].
ˈice-tray *n* small tray divided into sections for making ice-cubes.
ˈice-water *n* (*esp US*) water made very cold and used for drinking.

ice[2] /aɪs/ *v* **1** [Tn] make (esp a liquid) very cold: *iced water/beer*. **2** [Tn] cover (a cake) with sugar icing. **3** (phr v) **ˌice (sth) ˈover/ˈup** cover (sth) or become covered with ice: *The pond (was) iced over during the cold spell.* ○ *The wings of the aircraft had iced up.*

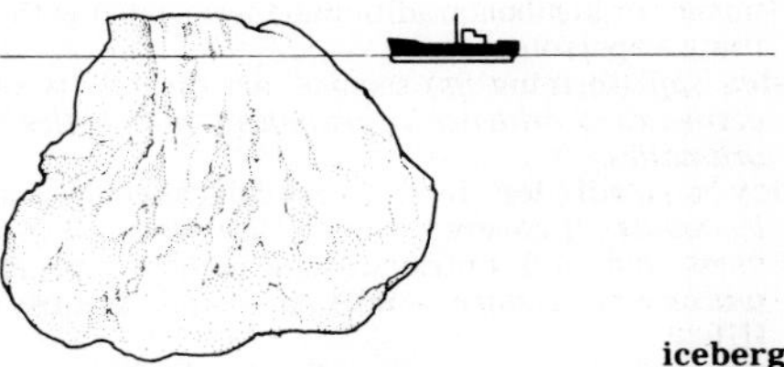

iceberg

iceberg /ˈaɪsbɜːg/ *n* **1** huge mass of ice floating in the sea. ⇨ illus. **2** (*fig*) unemotional person. **3** (idm) **the tip of the iceberg** ⇨ TIP[1].

Iceland

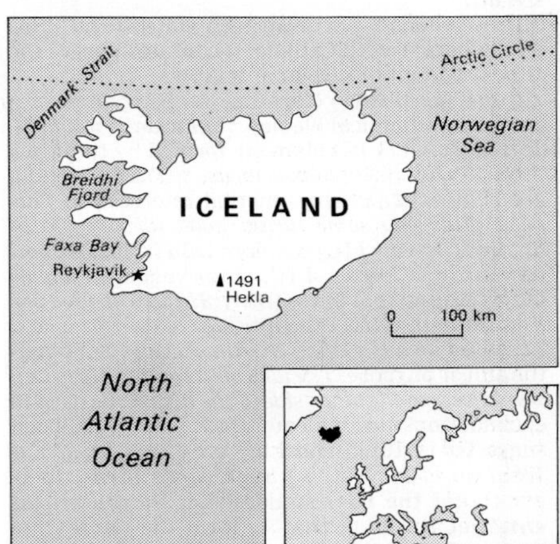

Iceland /ˈaɪslənd/ island and country in the North Atlantic ocean, to the north-west of Britain; pop approx 249 000; official language Icelandic; capital Reykjavik; unit of currency króna (= 100 aurar). It was settled by people from Scandinavia in the Middle Ages, and until the 20th century it was a Danish colony. Its main industry is fishing. ⇨ map.
▷ **Icelander** /ˈaɪsləndə(r)/ *n* native or inhabitant of Iceland.
Icelandic /aɪsˈlændɪk/ *adj* of Iceland — *n* [U] Scandinavian language spoken in Iceland.

Iceni /aɪˈsiːnaɪ/ *n* [pl] ancient British tribe that inhabited the east of Britain at the time of the Roman invasion. Cf BOUDICCA.

ichneumon /ɪkˈnjuːmən; *US* -ˈnuː-/ *n* **1** (also **ichˈneumon-fly**) small winged insect that lays its eggs in or on the larvae of other insects. **2** type of African mongoose that eats crocodiles' eggs.

ichthyosaurus /ˌɪkθɪəˈsɔːrəs/ *n* large extinct reptile with a fish-shaped body that lived in the sea.

ICI /ˌaɪ siː ˈaɪ/ *abbr* Imperial Chemical Industries: *work for ICI.*

-ician ⇨ -IAN 2.

icicle /ˈaɪsɪkl/ *n* pointed piece of ice formed by the freezing of dripping water.

icing /ˈaɪsɪŋ/ (*US* **frosting**) *n* [U] **1** mixture of sugar, egg white, flavouring, etc for covering and decorating cakes: *chocolate icing.* **2** (idm) **the ˌicing on the ˈcake** extra thing, factor, etc that is not necessary but is very welcome: *What really matters to me is getting the job; the high salary is just the icing on the cake.*

□ **ˈicing sugar** finely powdered sugar used esp for icing.

icon (also **ikon**) /ˈaɪkɒn/ *n* (in the Orthodox Church) painting, carving, etc of a holy person, itself regarded as sacred.

iconoclast /aɪˈkɒnəklæst/ *n* **1** person who attacks popular beliefs or established customs. **2** (formerly) person who destroyed religious images. ▷ **iconoclasm** /aɪˈkɒnəklæzəm/ *n* [U]. **iconoclastic** /aɪˌkɒnəˈklæstɪk/ *adj.*

iconography /ˌaɪkəˈnɒgrəfɪ/ *n* [U] **1** illustration of a subject by pictures, drawings, etc. **2** pictorial images or symbols traditionally associated with a thing or person.

-ics *suff* (forming *ns*) science, art or activity of: *aesthetics* ○ *athletics* ○ *graphics* ○ *acrobatics* ○ *dramatics.*

icy /ˈaɪsɪ/ *adj* (**-ier, -iest**) **1** very cold; as cold as ice: *icy winds.* **2** covered with ice: *icy roads.* **3** (*fig*) very cold and unfriendly in manner: *an icy welcome, voice, stare.* ▷ **icily** /ˈaɪsɪlɪ/ *adv.* **iciness** *n* [U].

id /ɪd/ *n* (*psychology*) part of the mind relating to a person's unconscious instincts and impulses. Cf EGO 1, SUPEREGO.

I'd /aɪd/ *contracted form* **1** I had ⇨ HAVE. **2** I would ⇨ WILL[1], WOULD[2].

ID /ˌaɪ ˈdiː/ *abbr* (*esp US*) identification; identity: *an ID card.*

Idaho /ˈaɪdəhəʊ/ north-western state of the USA, on the border with Canada. It contains part of the *Rocky Mountains. ⇨ map at App 1.

-ide *suff* (*chemistry*) (forming *ns*) compound of a particular chemical element: *chloride* ○ *sulphide.*

idea /aɪˈdɪə/ *n* **1** [C] plan, etc formed by thinking; thought: *He's full of good ideas.* ○ *That's an* (ie a good) *idea.* **2** [U, sing] mental impression: *This book gives you some idea/a good idea of life in ancient Greece.* **3** [C] opinion; belief: *He has some very strange ideas.* **4** [U, sing] vague notion or fancy; feeling that sth is likely: *He had no idea she was like that.* ○ *Have you any idea what time it is?* ○ *I have an idea it's going to rain.* **5 the idea** [sing] the aim or purpose: *The idea of the game is to get all your pieces to the other side of the board.* **6** (used in exclamations to indicate that what has been suggested is stupid, shocking, etc): *The idea of it!* ○ *What an idea!* **7** (idm) **buck one's ideas up** ⇨ BUCK[2]. **get the iˈdea** understand: *Do you get the idea?* **get the idea that...** form the impression that...: *Where did you get the idea that she doesn't like you?* **give sb ideas** give sb expectations or hopes which may not be realized: *Don't give her ideas — you know how difficult it is to get into films.* **have no iˈdea** not know; be incompetent: *He has no idea how to manage people.* **not have the first idea about sth** know nothing at all about sth. **one's idea of sth** what one thinks of as representing sth. **run away with the idea that...** (*infml*) (often used in the negative imperative) be mislead by or accept a false idea: *Don't run away with the idea that this job is going to be easy.* **what's the big idea?** ⇨ BIG. **the young idea** ⇨ YOUNG.

ideal /aɪˈdɪəl/ *adj* **1** satisfying one's idea of what is perfect; most suitable: *ideal weather for a holiday* ○ *He's the ideal husband for her.* **2** existing only in the imagination or as an idea; unrealistic and so not likely to be achieved: *ideal plans for reform* ○ *ideal happiness* ○ *in an ideal world.*

▷ **ideal** *n* **1** [C usu *sing*] person or thing regarded as perfect: *She's looking for a job, but hasn't found her ideal yet.* **2** [C usu *pl*] standard of perfection: *He finds it hard to live up to his ideals.*

ideally /aɪˈdɪəlɪ/ *adv*: *She's ideally suited to the job.* ○ *Ideally, everyone would be given equal opportunities.*

idealism /aɪˈdɪəlɪzəm/ *n* [U] **1** forming, pursuing or believing in ideals (IDEAL *n* 2), esp unrealistically: *Idealism has no place in modern politics.* **2** (esp in art and literature) imaginative treatment of objects or ideas in an ideal and often unrealistic way. Cf CLASSICISM, ROMANTICISM (ROMANTIC). **3** (*philosophy*) belief that ideas are the only things that are real or about which we can know anything. Cf REALISM.

▷ **idealist** /aɪˈdɪəlɪst/ *n* person who has high ideals and tries (often in an unrealistic way) to achieve them. **idealistic** /ˌaɪdɪəˈlɪstɪk/ *adj.* **idealistically** /ˌaɪdɪəˈlɪstɪklɪ/ *adv.*

idealize, -ise /aɪˈdɪəlaɪz/ *v* [Tn] consider or represent (sb/sth) as perfect or ideal: *an idealized account of village life.* ▷ **idealization, -isation** /aɪˌdɪəlaɪˈzeɪʃn; *US* -lɪˈz-/ *n* [U, C].

idée fixe /ˌiːdeɪ ˈfiːks/ *n* (*pl* **idées fixes** /ˌiːdeɪ ˈfiːks/) (*French*) strong idea or thought that one cannot dispel from one's mind, esp a false or misleading one; obsession.

identical /aɪˈdentɪkl/ *adj* **1 the ~** [attrib] the same: *This is the identical room we stayed in last year.* **2 ~ (to/with sb/sth)** similar in every detail; exactly alike: *They're wearing identical clothes.* ○ *Their clothes are identical.* ○ *This picture is identical to one my mother has.* ▷ **identically** /-klɪ/ *adv.*

□ **iˌdentical ˈtwins** twins born from a single egg and therefore of the same sex and very similar in appearance.

identify /aɪˈdentɪfaɪ/ *v* (*pt, pp* **-fied**) **1** [Tn, Cn·n/a] **~ sb/sth as sb/sth** show, prove, etc who or what sb/sth is; recognize sb/sth (as being the specified person or thing): *Can you identify your umbrella among this lot?* ○ *She identified the man as her attacker.* **2** [Tn·pr] **~ sth with sth** consider sth to be identical with sth; equate two things: *One cannot identify happiness with wealth.* **3** (phr v) **identify (oneself) with sb/sth** give support to sb/sth; be associated with sb/sth: *He refused to identify himself/become identified with the new political party.* **identify with sb** regard oneself as sharing the characteristics or fortunes of sb; take sb as a model: *I found it hard to identify with any of the characters in the film.*

▷ **identification** /aɪˌdentɪfɪˈkeɪʃn/ *n* [U] **1** (process of) identifying or being identified: *The identification of the accident victims took some time.* **2** (*abbr* **ID**) means of proving who one is; official papers that do this: *Can I see some identification, please?* **iˌdentifiˈcation parade** number of people, including one suspected of a crime, arranged in a row for viewing by witnesses who may be able to identify the suspect.

Identikit /aɪˈdentɪkɪt/ *n* (*propr*) set of pictures of different features that can be fitted together to form the face of a person (esp sb wanted by the police) with the help of descriptions given by people who have seen him.

identity /aɪˈdentətɪ/ *n* **1** [C, U] who or what sb/sth is: *There is no clue to the identity of the thief.* ○ *The cheque will be cashed on proof of identity.* ○ *This is a clear case of mistaken identity*, eg when the wrong person is arrested by mistake. ○ [attrib] *She's going through an identity crisis*, ie She is anxious and depressed because of uncertainty about how she fits into society, relates to other people, etc. **2** [U] (state of) exact likeness or sameness.

□ **iˈdentity card** (also **ID card** /ˌaɪˈdiː kɑːd/), **iˈdentity disc** card or disc, often with a photograph, carried or worn by sb to show who he is.

Identity cards were issued in Britain during the Second World War but were abolished in 1952. Because they are unused to carrying identity cards, the British tend to regard them as a restriction of personal liberty, so there is a general resistance to any idea of reintroducing them. Nowadays, ID cards are only carried by members of the armed forces and by employees of certain large companies and corporations like the BBC. In such cases they are used only for work purposes most commonly to allow employees access to their place of work.

ideogram /ˈɪdɪəgræm/ (also **ideograph** /ˈɪdɪəgrɑːf; *US* -græf/) *n* **1** symbol used in a writing system that represents the idea (rather than the sounds forming the name) of a thing, eg Chinese characters. **2** any sign or symbol for sth: *In this dictionary the ideogram ⚠ is used to mean 'taboo'.* ▷ **ideographic** /ˌɪdɪəˈgræfɪk/ *adj.*

ideology /ˌaɪdɪˈɒlədʒɪ/ *n* [C, U] (set of) ideas that form the basis of an economic or political theory or that are held by a particular group or person: *Our ideologies differ.* ○ *according to Marxist, bourgeois, monetarist, etc ideology.* ▷ **ideological** /ˌaɪdɪəˈlɒdʒɪkl/ *adj.* **ideologically** /-klɪ/ *adv.*

Ides /aɪdz/ *n* [sing or pl *v*] (in the ancient Roman calendar) 15th day of March, May, July or October, or the 13th day of the other months: *Julius Caesar was killed on the Ides of March.*

idiocy /ˈɪdɪəsɪ/ *n* **1** [U] (**a**) extreme stupidity: *It's sheer idiocy to go climbing in such bad weather.* (**b**) state of being an idiot; imbecility. **2** [C] extremely stupid act, remark, etc.

idiolect /ˈɪdɪəlekt/ *n* (*linguistics*) total amount of a language that any one person knows and uses: *Is the word 'psychosis' part of your idiolect?*

idiom /ˈɪdɪəm/ *n* **1** [C] phrase or sentence whose meaning is not clear from the meaning of its individual words and which must be learnt as a whole unit, eg *give way, a change of heart, be hard put to it*: *The English language has many idioms.* **2** [U] (**a**) language or dialect of a people or country: *the French idiom.* (**b**) use of language that is typical of or natural to speakers of a particular language. (**c**) use of language peculiar to a period or an individual: *Shakespeare's idiom.* **3** [C] style which shows that sth, esp a work of art, belongs to a particular period, place, person, etc: *a piece of music in the modern idiom.*

▷ **idiomatic** /ˌɪdɪəˈmætɪk/ *adj* (**a**) in accordance with the particular nature or structure of a language, dialect, etc: *She speaks fluent and idiomatic French.* (**b**) containing an idiom or idioms: *an idiomatic expression, language.* **idiomatically** /-klɪ/ *adv.*

idiosyncrasy /ˌɪdɪəˈsɪŋkrəsɪ/ *n* person's particular way of thinking, behaving, etc that is clearly different from that of others: *One of her little idiosyncrasies is always washing in cold water.* ▷ **idiosyncratic** /ˌɪdɪəsɪŋˈkrætɪk/ *adj.*

idiot /ˈɪdɪət/ *n* **1** (*infml*) very foolish person; fool: *What an idiot I was to leave my suitcase on the train!* **2** person with very limited intelligence who cannot think or behave normally: *an idiot since birth.*

▷ **idiotic** /ˌɪdɪˈɒtɪk/ *adj* stupid: *Don't be idiotic!* **idiotically** /-klɪ/ *adv.*

idle /ˈaɪdl/ *adj* (**-r, -st**) **1** (**a**) doing or having no work; not employed: *Many people were idle during the depression.* (**b**) not active or in use: *The factory machines lay idle during the workers' strike.* **2** (of time) not spent in doing sth: *We spent many idle hours just sitting in the sun.* **3** (of people) avoiding work; lazy: *an idle, useless student.* **4** [usu attrib] worthless or having no special purpose or effect; useless: *an idle threat/promise* ○ *idle curiosity, gossip/speculation* ○ *It's idle to expect help from him.* **5** (idm) **the devil makes work for idle hands** ⇨ DEVIL[1].

▷ **idle** *v* **1** [I, Ip] **~ (about)** do nothing; waste time; be idle: *Stop idling and help me clean up.* **2** [I] (of an engine) run slowly in neutral gear or without doing work. **3** (phr v) **idle sth away** waste (time): *idle away the hours watching TV.*

idler /ˈaɪdlə(r)/ *n.*

idleness *n* [U].

idly /ˈaɪdlɪ/ *adv.*

idol /ˈaɪdl/ *n* **1** image of a god, often carved in stone, wood, etc and used as an object of worship. **2** person or thing that is greatly loved or admired: *As an only child he was the idol of his parents.* ○ *The Beatles were the pop idols of the 60s.*

idolater /aɪˈdɒlətə(r)/ (*fem* **idolatress**

/aɪˈdɒlətrɪs/) *n* person who worships an idol or idols.

▷ **idolatrous** /aɪˈdɒlətrəs/ *adj* (**a**) worshipping idols. (**b**) of or like the worship of idols: *an idolatrous love of material wealth.* **idolatrously** /-lɪ/ *adv.*

idolatry /aɪˈdɒlətrɪ/ *n* [U] (**a**) worship of idols. (**b**) too much devotion or admiration: *He supports his local team with a fervour that borders on idolatry.*

idolize, -ise /ˈaɪdəlaɪz/ *v* [Tn] (**a**) treat (sb/sth) as an idol. (**b**) love or admire (sb/sth) very much: *idolize a pop group.*

▷ **idolization, -isation** /ˌaɪdəlaɪˈzeɪʃn/ *n* [U] idolizing or being idolized.

idyll /ˈɪdɪl; *US* ˈaɪdl/ *n* **1** short piece of poetry or prose that describes a happy and peaceful scene or event, esp of country life. **2** simple pleasant scene or event.

▷ **idyllic** /ɪˈdɪlɪk; *US* aɪˈd-/ *adj* like an idyll; peaceful and pleasant: *an idyllic setting, holiday, marriage.* **idyllically** /-klɪ/ *adv*: *idyllically happy.*

ie /ˌaɪ ˈiː/ *abbr* that is to say; in other words (Latin *id est*): *Hot drinks, ie tea and coffee, are charged for separately.* ⇨ Usage at VIZ.

-ie ⇨ -Y².

if /ɪf/ *conj* **1** on condition that; supposing. (**a**) (used with the present and present perfect tenses for highly predictable situations): *I'll only stay if you offer me more money.* ○ *If you have finished eating you may leave the table.* ○ *If (it is) necessary I will come at 6.* ○ *You can stay to dinner if you like.* ○ *If anyone calls tell them I'm not at home.* ○ (*fml*) *If the patient should vomit, turn him over with his head to the side.* (**b**) (used with a past tense for imaginary situations): *If you learned to type you would easily find a job.* ○ *If he were here I could explain to him myself.* ○ *If I was a man they would have given me the job.* ○ *Would she tell us the truth if we asked her?* ○ *If you liked* (ie With your approval) *I could ask my brother to look at your car.* ○ *They would have been here by now if they'd caught the early train.* ○ *I wouldn't have believed it possible, if I hadn't seen it happen.* ⇨ Usage at UNLESS. **2** when(ever): *If metal gets hot it expands.* ○ *She glares at me if I go near her desk.* **3** (used with *will* and *would* as the first part of a sentence when making a polite request): *If you will sit down for a few moments* (ie Please sit down and) *I'll tell the manager you're here.* ○ *If you would care to leave your name, we'll get in touch as soon as possible.* **4** (used after *ask, know, find out, wonder,* etc to introduce alternatives) whether: *Do you know if he's married?* ○ *I wonder if I should wear a hat.* ○ *He couldn't tell if she was laughing or crying.* ○ *Listen to the tune — see if you can remember the words.* **5** (used after *vs* or *adjs* expressing feelings): *I am sorry if I'm disturbing you.* ○ *I'd be grateful if you would keep it a secret* ○ *Do you mind if I switch the radio off?* **6** (also **even if**) (used when admitting that sth may be true or may happen) although: *If he said that, he didn't expect you to take it personally.* ○ *Even if you saw him pick up the money, you can't be sure he stole it.* **7** (used before an *adj* to introduce a contrast) although also: *It was thoughtless if well-meaning.* ○ *He's a real gentleman, if a little pompous at times.* **8** (used to express surprise, astonishment, dismay, etc): *If it isn't my old friend Bob Thomson — what a coincidence!* ○ *If that's not the best idea I've heard in a long time!* ○ *If he hasn't gone and got into trouble with the police!* **9** (used before *you think, ask, remember, etc* to invite sb to listen to one's opinion): *If you ask me, she's too scared to do it.* ○ *If you think about it, those children must be grown-up by now.* ○ *If you remember, Mary was always fond of animals.* **10** (idm) ˌ**if and** ˈ**when** (used to express uncertainty about a possible event in the future): *If and when we ever meet again I hope he remembers to thank me.* **if** ˌ**I were** ˈ**you; if** ˌ**I was/were in** ˈ**your shoes/place** (used to introduce a piece of advice to sb): *If I were you I'd start looking for another job.* ○ *If I were in your shoes, he'd soon know what I thought of him.* **if** ˈ**anything** (used to express a tentative opinion or after a negative statement to say that the opposite is true) if anything definite can be said, this is it: *I'd say he was more like his father, if anything.* ○ *He's not thin — if anything he's rather on the plump side.* **if** ˈ**not** (**a**) (used after *if* and a *v* in the present or present perfect tense) otherwise: *I'll go if you're going — if not I'd rather stay at home.* ○ *If you've finished we can have a coffee — if not, you'd better keep working.* (**b**) (used after a *yes/no* question to give a promise, warning, etc): *Are you ready? If not, I'm going without you.* **if** ˈ**only** (**a**) (used to express a wish with reference to present or future time): *If only I were rich.* ○ *If only I could swim.* ○ *If only I knew her name.* ○ *If only it would stop raining.* ○ *If only they would tell me what they've decided.* (**b**) (used to express a wish that past events had been different): *If only he'd remembered to buy some fruit.* ○ *If only I had gone by taxi.* **only if** (when used at the beginning of a sentence, making the *v* in the following clause precede its subject) only on condition that: *Only if a teacher has given permission is a student allowed to enter this room.* ○ *Only if the red light comes on is there any danger to employees.*

▷ **if** *n* (*infml*) **1** uncertainty: *If he wins — and it's a big if — he'll be the first Englishman to win for twenty years.* **2** (idm) ˌ**ifs and** ˈ**buts** reservations; arguments against sth: *Now I'm not having any ifs and buts — it's cold showers for everyone before breakfast tomorrow.*

NOTE ON USAGE: Both **if** and **whether** are used in reporting questions which invite yes/no answers or offer a choice between alternatives: (*'Do you want a drink?'*) *He asked whether/if we wanted a drink.* ○ *He didn't know whether/if we should write or phone.* **Whether** (NOT **if**) can be followed by an infinitive: *I'm not sure whether to resign or stay on.* After a preposition **whether** must be used: *It depends on whether the letter arrives in time.* **Whether** is also used when the clause it begins is the subject of a sentence: *Whether they win or lose is all the same to me.* **Whether** (NOT **if**) can be immediately followed by 'or not': *I'll be happy whether or not I get the job* (compare: *I'll be happy whether/if I get the job or not).*

iffy /ˈɪfɪ/ *adj* (**-ier, -iest**) (*infml*) full of unpredictable possibilities; uncertain: *It may succeed, but it's a bit iffy.*

-ify (also **-fy**) *suff* (with *ns* and *adjs* forming *vs*) make or become: *solidify* ○ *speechify.*

igloo /ˈɪgluː/ *n* (*pl* ~**s**) small dome-shaped house built by Eskimos from blocks of hard snow as a temporary shelter.

igneous /ˈɪgnɪəs/ *adj* (*geology*) (of rocks) formed by molten matter (esp from volcanoes) that has become solid. Cf METAMORPHIC.

ignis fatuus /ˌɪgnɪs ˈfætjʊəs; *US* ˌɪgnəs ˈfætʃʊəs/ *n* (*pl* **ignes fatui** /ˌɪgneɪz ˈfætjʊiː; *US* ˌɪgniːz ˈfætʃʊaɪ/) (*arch or rhet*) will-o'-the-wisp.

ignite /ɪgˈnaɪt/ *v* [I, Tn] (cause sth to) catch fire: *Petrol ignites very easily.* ○ *He struck a match and ignited the fuse.*

▷ **ignition** /ɪgˈnɪʃn/ *n* **1** [U] causing sth to catch fire. **2** [C] electrical mechanism that ignites the mixture of explosive gases in a petrol engine: *switch/turn on the ignition.* ⇨ illus at CAR.

ignoble /ɪgˈnəʊbl/ *adj* not honourable in character or purpose; shameful: *an ignoble person, action.* ▷ **ignobly** /-nəʊblɪ/ *adv.*

ignominy /ˈɪgnəmɪnɪ/ [U] (esp public) shame or humiliation; disgrace: *the ignominy of defeat.*

▷ **ignominious** /ˌɪgnəˈmɪnɪəs/ *adj* shameful or humiliating; causing disgrace: *an ignominious defeat.* **ignominiously** *adv.*

ignoramus /ˌɪgnəˈreɪməs/ *n* (*pl* ~**es** /-sɪz/) ignorant person.

ignorance /ˈɪgnərəns/ *n* [U] ~ (**of sth**) lack of knowledge or information (about sth): *We are in complete ignorance of your plans.* ○ *If he did wrong it was only through ignorance.*

ignorant /ˈɪgnərənt/ *adj* **1** (**a**) ~ (**of sth**) knowing little or nothing; lacking education or information; unaware: *He's not stupid, just ignorant.* ○ *To say you were ignorant of the rules is no excuse.* (**b**) showing or resulting from lack of knowledge: *an ignorant stare, look, etc.* **2** (*infml*) rude through lack of knowledge about good manners: *His ignorant behaviour at the dinner table caused much embarrassment.* ▷ **ignorantly** *adv.*

ignore /ɪgˈnɔː(r)/ *v* [Tn] **1** take no notice of (sb/sth): *You've been ignoring me.* ○ *I can't ignore his rudeness any longer.* ○ *ignore criticism.* **2** deliberately refuse to greet or acknowledge (sb): *I said hello to her, but she ignored me completely!*

iguana /ɪˈgwɑːnə/ *n* type of large tree-climbing lizard of tropical America.

ikon = ICON.

il- ⇨ IN-².

ILEA /ˈɪlɪə, ˌaɪ el: iː ˈeɪ/ Inner London Education Authority (abolished in 1990). ⇨ article at LONDON.

ileum /ˈɪlɪəm/ *n* (*pl* **ilea** /ˈɪlɪə/) (*anatomy*) last section of the small intestine, before it joins the large intestine.

ilex /ˈaɪleks/ *n* (*pl* ~**es**) **1** (*botany*) (plant of the) genus of trees that includes holly. **2** (also **holm-oak**) type of evergreen oak-tree with leaves like holly.

Iliad /ˈɪlɪæd/ **the Iliad** long poem said to have been composed by the ancient Greek poet *Homer. It tells the story of the Greek campaign to capture Troy, and in particular of the exploits of the Greek hero *Achilles.

ilk /ɪlk/ *n* (idm) **of that/the same/his, her, etc ilk** (*infml joc*) of that, the same, his, etc kind, sort or type: *I can't stand him, or any others of that/his ilk.*

ill¹ /ɪl/ *adv* (esp in compounds) **1** badly; wrongly: *an* ˌ*ill-written* ˈ*book* ○ *Their children are ill* ˈ*cared for,* ie neglected. Cf WELL³ 1a. **2** unfavourably; unkindly: *speak/think ill of sb.* Cf WELL³ 1b. **3** only with difficulty; scarcely: *We can ill afford the time or money for a holiday.* **4** (idm) **augur well/ill for sb/sth** ⇨ AUGUR. **bode well/ill** ⇨ BODE. **deserve well/ill of sb** ⇨ DESERVE. ˌ**ill at** ˈ**ease** uncomfortable; embarrassed. **wish sb well/ill** ⇨ WISH *v.*

□ **ill-advised** *adj* unwise: *an* ˌ*ill-advised* ˈ*meeting.* ˌ**ill-ad**ˈ**visedly** /ˌɪlədˈvaɪzɪdlɪ/ *adv.*

ˌ**ill-as**ˈ**sorted** *adj* badly matched; mixed: *an ill-assorted collection of shoes* ○ *They make an* ˌ*ill-assorted* ˈ*couple,* ie don't seem well suited to each other.

ˌ**ill-**ˈ**bred** *adj* badly brought up; badly behaved; rude: *an* ˌ*ill-bred* ˈ*child.* Cf WELL-BRED (WELL³). ˌ**ill** ˈ**breeding** bad manners.

ˌ**ill-con**ˈ**sidered** *adj* not carefully or sufficiently thought about: *an* ˌ*ill-considered* ˈ*act.*

ˌ**ill-de**ˈ**fined** *adj* **1** not accurately described: *an* ˌ*ill-defined* ˈ*job.* **2** not distinct in outline: *an ill-defined lump of rock on the horizon.*

ˌ**ill-dis**ˈ**posed** *adj* ~ (**towards sb/sth**) (*fml*) not friendly or pleasant; not favouring: *She's very ill-disposed towards her neighbours.* Cf WELL-DISPOSED (WELL³).

ˌ**ill-**ˈ**fated** *adj* bringing or having bad luck or misfortune: *an ill-fated expedition.*

ˌ**ill-**ˈ**favoured** *adj* (*fml*) (esp of people) unattractive in appearance; ugly.

ˌ**ill-**ˈ**founded** *adj* not based on fact or truth: ˌ*ill-founded* ˈ*claims, as*ˈ*sumptions, su*ˈ*spicions, etc.*

ˌ**ill-**ˈ**gotten** *adj* (*dated or joc*) obtained dishonestly: ˌ*ill-gotten* ˈ*gains.*

ˌ**ill-**ˈ**judged** *adj* not well timed; unwise: *an* ˌ*ill-judged* ˈ*rescue attempt.*

ˌ**ill-**ˈ**mannered** *adj* having bad manners; rude: *He's an ill-mannered brute!*

ˌ**ill-**ˈ**natured** *adj* bad-tempered; unkind: *an* ˌ*ill-natured* ˈ*person,* ˈ*comment.*

ˌ**ill-**ˈ**omened,** ˌ**ill-**ˈ**starred** *adjs* (*rhet*) unlucky.

ˌ**ill-**ˈ**tempered** *adj* often cross or irritable; peevish; bad-tempered.

ˌ**ill-**ˈ**timed** *adj* done or happening at a wrong or unsuitable time: *Our visit was ill-timed — my mother had guests already.* Cf WELL-TIMED (WELL³).

ˌ**ill-**ˈ**treat,** ˌ**ill-**ˈ**use** *vs* [Tn] treat or use (sb/sth) unkindly or badly: *ill-treat one's dog.* ˌ**ill-**ˈ**treatment,** ˌ**ill-**ˈ**usage** *ns* [U].

ill² /ɪl/ *adj* **1** (*US* usu **sick**) [usu pred] physically or mentally unwell; sick: *He's been ill for two weeks.* ○

She fell ill/was taken ill suddenly. ⇨ Usage at SICK. **2** [attrib] (**a**) not good; bad: *ill health* ○ *people of ill repute*, ie with a bad reputation. (**b**) harmful; intending harm: *suffer no ill effects.* (**c**) unkind; resentful: *bear sb no ill will* ○ *You ought to apologize and show there is no ill feeling between you.* **3** [attrib] not favourable: *ill luck* ○ *a bird of ill omen*, ie one thought to bring bad luck. **4** (idm) **it's an ˌill ˈwind (that blows nobody any good)** (*saying*) few things are so bad that they don't offer some good to sb.
▷ **ill** *n* (*fml*) **1** [U] harm; evil: *I wish him no ill.* **2** [C usu *pl*] problem; misfortune: *the various ills of life.*

I'll /aɪl/ *contracted form* I will ⇨ WILL.

illegal /ɪˈliːgl/ *adj* against the law; not legal.
▷ **illegality** /ˌɪlɪˈgælətɪ/ *n* **1** [U] state of being illegal. **2** [C] illegal act.
illegally /-gəlɪ/ *adv*: *an illegally parked car.*

illegible /ɪˈledʒəbl/ (also **unreadable**) *adj* difficult or impossible to read; not legible: *an illegible signature.* ▷ **illegibility** /ɪˌlədʒəˈbɪlətɪ/ *n* [U]. **illegibly** /-əblɪ/ *adv*.

illegitimate /ˌɪlɪˈdʒɪtɪmət/ *adj* **1** born of parents not married to each other; not legitimate by birth: *an ˌillegitimate ˈchild* ○ *She's illegitimate.* **2** not allowed by the law or by the rules: *illegitimate use of company property.* **3** (of a conclusion in an argument, etc) not logical. ▷ **illegitimacy** /ˌɪlɪˈdʒɪtɪməsɪ/ *n* [U]. **illegitimately** *adv*.

illiberal /ɪˈlɪbərəl/ *adj* (*fml*) **1** (**a**) not tolerant; narrow-minded: *illiberal attitudes.* (**b**) lacking culture: *an illiberal upbringing.* **2** mean or stingy; not generous: *illiberal helpings of food.* ▷ **illiberality** /ɪˌlɪbəˈrælətɪ/ *n* [U]. **illiberally** /-rəlɪ/ *adv*.

illicit /ɪˈlɪsɪt/ *adj* (**a**) not allowed by law; illegal: *the illicit sale of drugs.* (**b**) not approved by the normal rules of society: *an illicit relationship.* ▷ **illicitly** *adv*.

Illinois /ˌɪlɪˈnɔɪ/ state in the *Mid West of the USA. Much of it is agricultural, but it also contains the city of *Chicago. ⇨ map at App 1.

illiterate /ɪˈlɪtərət/ *adj* **1** (**a**) not able to read or write: *an illiterate child.* Cf UNLETTERED. (**b**) showing such ignorance: *an illiterate letter*, ie one that contains many mistakes of spelling and grammar. **2** (**a**) showing little or no education: *You must be illiterate if you've never heard of Marx.* (**b**) ignorant in a particular field: *be scientifically illiterate.*
▷ **illiteracy** /ɪˈlɪtərəsɪ/ *n* [U] state of being illiterate: *Illiteracy is a major problem in some developing countries.*
illiterate *n* illiterate person.

illness /ˈɪlnɪs/ *n* **1** [U] state of being ill in body or mind; lack of health: *We've had a lot of illness in the family.* **2** [C] type or period of illness: *serious illnesses* ○ *recovering after a long illness.*

illogical /ɪˈlɒdʒɪkl/ *adj* **1** without reason or logic; not sensible: *It seems illogical to change the timetable so often.* **2** contrary to the rules of logic: *an illogical conclusion.* ▷ **illogicality** /ɪˌlɒdʒɪˈkælətɪ/ *n* [C, U]. **illogically** /-klɪ/ *adv*.

illuminate /ɪˈluːmɪneɪt/ *v* [Tn] **1** provide (sth) with light: *a football pitch illuminated with floodlights.* **2** decorate (sth) with bright lights for a special occasion: *illuminate a street, building, etc.* **3** (esp formerly) decorate (a book) with gold, silver and bright colours, usu by hand: *an illuminated manuscript.* **4** (*fml*) make (sth) clear; help to explain: *illuminate a difficult passage in a book.*
▷ **illuminating** *adj* particularly revealing or helpful: *an illuminating analysis, talk, etc.*
illumination /ɪˌluːmɪˈneɪʃn/ *n* **1** [U] illuminating or being illuminated; (source of) light. **2 illuminations** [pl] (*Brit*) bright colourful lights used to decorate a town for a special occasion: *the Christmas illuminations in the high street.* **3** [C usu *pl*] coloured decoration, usu painted by hand, in an old book.

illusion /ɪˈluːʒn/ *n* **1** (**a**) [C] false idea, belief or impression; delusion: *I have no illusions about my ability*, ie I know that I am not very able. ○ *We're left with few illusions about our ally.* (**b**) [U] state of mind in which one is deceived in this way: *You think that, do you? Pure illusion!* **2** [C] thing that a person wrongly believes to exist; false perception: *an optical illusion* ○ *In the hot sun the surface of the road seems wet, but that is only an illusion.* **3** (idm) **be under an/the illusion (that...)** believe wrongly: *I was under the illusion that he was honest until he was caught stealing some money.*
▷ **illusionist** /-ʒənɪst/ *n* person who does clever tricks on stage that deceive the audience; conjurer.

illusive /ɪˈluːsɪv/, **illusory** /ɪˈluːsərɪ/ *adjs* based on illusion; deceptive: *The upturn in the company's fortunes proved illusory.* ie did not last.

illustrate /ˈɪləstreɪt/ *v* [Tn] **1** supply (sth) with pictures, diagrams, etc: *illustrate a book, magazine, lecture* ○ *a well-illustrated textbook.* **2** (**a**) explain or make (sth) clear by examples, diagrams, pictures, etc: *To illustrate my point I have done a comparative analysis.* (**b**) be an example of (sth): *This behaviour illustrates your selfishness.*
▷ **illustration** /ˌɪləˈstreɪʃn/ *n* **1** [U] illustrating or being illustrated: *the art of book illustration* ○ *Illustration is often more useful than definition for showing what words mean.* **2** [C] drawing, diagram or picture in a book, magazine, etc: *colour illustrations.* **3** [C] example used to explain sth.
illustrative /ˈɪləstrətɪv; *US* ɪˈlʌs-/ *adj* serving as an example or illustration: *an illustrative quotation* ○ *That outburst was illustrative of her bad temper.*
illustrator *n* person who draws and paints pictures for books, etc.

illustrious /ɪˈlʌstrɪəs/ *adj* very famous and distinguished. ▷ **illustriously** *adv*.

ILO /ˌaɪ el ˈəʊ/ *abbr* International Labour Organization.

im- ⇨ IN-[1], IN-[2].

I'm /aɪm/ *contracted form* I am ⇨ BE.

image /ˈɪmɪdʒ/ *n* **1** (**a**) [C] copy of the shape of a person or thing, esp one made in stone or wood; statue: *carved images.* (**b**) [sing] (*arch*) close likeness: *According to the Bible, God created man in his image.* **2** [C] mental picture or idea: *I have this image of you as always being cheerful.* **3** [C] general impression that a person, firm, product, etc gives to the public; reputation: *How can we improve our (public) image?* **4** [C] figure of speech; simile; metaphor: *a poem full of startling images.* **5** [C] appearance of sb or sth when seen in a mirror or through the lens of a camera. **6** [C] (*mathematics*) set[1](4) formed by mapping. **7** (idm) **be the (very/living/spitting) image of sb/sth** (*infml*) be or look exactly like sb/sth: *She's the (spitting) image of her mother.*
▷ **imagery** /ˈɪmɪdʒərɪ/ *n* [U] **1** use of figurative language to produce pictures in the minds of readers or hearers: *poetic imagery.* **2** statues; images as a group.

imaginable /ɪˈmædʒɪnəbl/ *adj* that can be imagined: *We had the greatest difficulty imaginable getting here in time.*

imaginary /ɪˈmædʒɪnərɪ; *US* -ənerɪ/ *adj* existing only in the mind or imagination; not real: *imaginary fears.*

imagination /ɪˌmædʒɪˈneɪʃn/ *n* **1** (**a**) [U, C] ability to form mental images or pictures: *He hasn't much imagination.* ○ *Her talk captured* (ie gripped and stimulated) *the imagination of the whole class.* (**b**) [C] part of the mind that does this: *In my imagination, I thought I heard her calling me.* **2** [U] use of this ability in a practical or creative way: *His writing lacks imagination.* ○ *Use your imagination to find an answer.* **3** [U] thing experienced in the mind and not in reality: *I can't have seen a ghost — it must have been imagination.* ○ *Is it my imagination or have you lost a lot of weight?* **4** (idm) **the mind/imagination boggles** ⇨ BOGGLE. **not by any/by no stretch of the imagination** ⇨ STRETCH *n*.
▷ **imaginative** /ɪˈmædʒɪnətɪv; *US* -ənetɪv/ *adj* having or showing imagination: *an imaginative child, writer, production.* **imaginatively** *adv*.

imagine /ɪˈmædʒɪn/ *v* **1** [Tn, Tf, Tw, Tg, Tsg, Cn·a, Cn·t] form a mental image of (sth): *Imagine a house with a big garden.* ○ *Imagine that you are in London.* ○ *Can you imagine what it would be like to live without electricity?* ○ *She imagined walking into the office and telling everyone what she thought of them.* ○ *Imagine yourself (to be) rich and famous.* **2** [Tf, Tw, Tg, Tsg] think of (sth) as probable or possible: *I can't imagine that anyone cares what I do.* ○ *I can't imagine living* (ie don't think I shall ever live) *anywhere but England.* ○ *Would you ever have imagined him/his becoming a politician?* **3** [Tn, Tf] suppose (sth); assume: *I imagine (that) he'll be there.*

imagist /ˈɪmədʒɪst/ *n* member of an early 20th-century movement in British and American poetry which tried to get away from the vagueness of *Romanticism by using precise images. Ezra *Pound was a leading imagist. ▷ **imagism** /ˈɪmədʒɪzəm/ *n* [U].

imago /ɪˈmeɪgəʊ/ *n* (*pl* **~es** or **imagines** /ɪˈmeɪdʒɪniːz/) insect in its adult, sexually mature form, after metamorphosis of the larval stage.

imam /ɪˈmɑːm/ *n* **1** person who leads the prayers in a mosque. **2 Imam** title of various Muslim religious leaders.

imbalance /ˌɪmˈbæləns/ *n* lack of balance or proportion; inequality: *The current trade deficit indicates a serious imbalance between our import and export trade.*

imbecile /ˈɪmbəsiːl; *US* -sl/ *n* (**a**) (esp adult) person with abnormally low intelligence. (**b**) (*infml*) stupid or silly person; fool.
▷ **imbecile, imbecilic** *adjs* [usu attrib] stupid; foolish: *an imbecile remark* ○ *imbecile behaviour.*
imbecility /ˌɪmbəˈsɪlətɪ/ *n* **1** [U] stupidity. **2** [C] stupid act, remark, etc.

imbibe /ɪmˈbaɪb/ *v* **1** [I, Tn] (*fml or joc*) drink (sth, esp alcohol): *Are you imbibing?* **2** [Tn] (*fig*) take in or absorb (sth): *imbibe fresh air, knowledge.*

imbroglio /ɪmˈbrəʊlɪəʊ/ *n* (*pl* **~s** /-z/) complicated, confused or embarrassing situation, esp a political or an emotional one.

imbue /ɪmˈbjuː/ *v* [Tn·pr esp p] **~ sb/sth with sth** (*fml*) fill or inspire sb/sth with (feelings, etc): *imbued with patriotism, ambition, love, etc* ○ *politicians imbued with a sense of their own importance.*

IMF /ˌaɪ em ˈef/ *abbr* International Monetary Fund.

imitate /ˈɪmɪteɪt/ *v* [Tn] **1** copy the behaviour of (sb/sth); take or follow as an example: *Decide what you want to do; don't just imitate others.* **2** copy the speech, actions, dress, etc of (sb); mimic: *He's very clever at imitating his friends.* **3** be like (sb/sth); look like: *The stage was designed to imitate a prison cell.*
▷ **imitator** *n* person who imitates (esp other people).

imitation /ˌɪmɪˈteɪʃn/ *n* **1** [C] thing produced as a copy of the real thing: *That's not an original Rembrandt, it's an imitation.* ○ [attrib] *imitation leather, jewellery, etc*, ie material made to look like leather, jewellery, etc. **2** [U] imitating: *learn sth by imitation* ○ *The house was built in imitation of a Roman villa.* **3** [C] impersonation or mimicking of a person's speech or behaviour: *an entertainer who does hilarious imitations of politicians' voices.*

imitative /ˈɪmɪtətɪv; *US* -teɪtɪv/ *adj* copying or following a model or example: *His style of public speaking is imitative of the prime minister.* ○ *Sculpture is an imitative art*, ie it copies people, things, etc from real life.

immaculate /ɪˈmækjʊlət/ *adj* (*approv*) **1** perfectly clean and tidy; spotless: *an immaculate uniform.* **2** right in every detail; having no mistakes: *an immaculate performance.* ▷ **immaculately** *adv*: *immaculately dressed.*
□ **the Imˌmaculate Conˈception** Roman Catholic teaching that the Virgin Mary was without sin from the moment of her conception.

immanent /ˈɪmənənt/ *adj* **~ (in sth)** **1** (*fml*) (of qualities) naturally present; inherent: *He believed that beauty was not something imposed, but something immanent.* **2** (of God) permanently present throughout the whole universe. ▷ **immanence** /-əns/ *n* [U].

Immanuel (also **Emmanuel**) /ɪˈmænjʊəl/ name

given to Christ in the Bible, esp as the saviour of Judah whose birth was foretold by *Isaiah.

immaterial /ˌɪməˈtɪərɪəl/ *adj* **1** ~ **(to sb)** not important; irrelevant: *The cost is immaterial.* ○ *It is immaterial (to me) whether he stays or leaves.* **2** without physical form or substance: *as immaterial as a ghost.*

immature /ˌɪməˈtjʊə(r); *US* -tʊər/ *adj* **1** not sensible in behaviour or in controlling one's feelings; less mature than one would expect: *He's very immature for his age.* **2** not (yet) fully developed or grown: *immature plants.* ▷ **immaturity** /ˌɪməˈtjʊərətɪ; *US* -tʊər-/ *n* [U].

immeasurable /ɪˈmeʒərəbl/ *adj* that cannot be measured, esp because of largeness in size or extent: *the immeasurable depths of the universe.* ▷ **immeasurably** /-blɪ/ *adv*: *Your presence has enriched our lives immeasurably.* ○ *The task seems immeasurably difficult.*

immediate /ɪˈmi:dɪət/ *adj* **1** (**a**) happening or done at once: *I want an immediate reply.* ○ *The response of the people to the famine appeal was immediate.* ○ *take immediate action.* (**b**) [usu attrib] existing at the present time: *Our immediate concern is for/with the families of those who died.* **2** [attrib] nearest in time, space or relationship: *What are your plans for the immediate future?* ○ *There's no post office in the immediate neighbourhood.* ○ *his immediate predecessor* ○ *one's immediate family*, ie parents, children, brothers and sisters. **3** [attrib] with nothing coming in between; direct: *The immediate cause of death is unknown.*

▷ **immediacy** /-əsɪ/ (also **immediateness**) *n* [U] closeness or reality of sth, so that one feels directly involved or has to deal with it at once: *the immediacy of the war, as seen on television* ○ *the immediacy of the problem.*

immediately *adv* **1** at once; without delay: *She answered almost immediately.* ○ *The purpose may not be immediately evident.* **2** being nearest in time or space; directly: *in the years immediately after the war* ○ *fix the lock immediately below the handle.* **3** directly or very closely: *the houses most immediately affected by the motorway.* — *conj* (esp *Brit*) as soon as; the moment that: *I recognized her immediately I saw her.*

immemorial /ˌɪməˈmɔ:rɪəl/ *adj* (*fml or rhet*) **1** going back beyond the reach of human memory or written records. **2** (idm) **from/since time immemorial** ⇨ TIME.

immense /ɪˈmens/ *adj* extremely large: *immense difficulties, problems, possibilities, etc* ○ *of immense importance.*

▷ **immensely** *adv* to a very great extent; extremely: *immensely popular, rich, successful, etc* ○ *They enjoyed the film immensely.*

immensity /ɪˈmensətɪ/ *n* [U] largeness; great size: *the immensity of the universe.*

immerse /ɪˈmɜ:s/ *v* [Tn, Tn·pr] **1** ~ **sth (in sth)** put sth under the surface of a liquid: *Immerse the plant (in water) for a few minutes.* **2** ~ **oneself (in sth)** involve oneself deeply (in sth); absorb oneself: *be immersed in thought, one's business, a book* ○ *He immersed himself totally in his work.*

▷ **immersion** /ɪˈmɜ:ʃn; *US* -ʒn/ *n* [U] **1** immersing; being immersed. **2** baptism by putting the whole body under water. **immersion heater** electric heater fixed inside a hot-water tank in a home.

immigrate /ˈɪmɪgreɪt/ *v* [I, Ipr] ~ **(to/into...)** enter a foreign country in order to live there permanently. Cf EMIGRATE.

▷ **immigrant** /ˈɪmɪgrənt/ *n* person who has come to live permanently in a foreign country: *Irish immigrants* ○ *illegal immigrants* ○ [attrib] *the immigrant population.*

immigration /ˌɪmɪˈgreɪʃn/ *n* **1** [U, C] (instance of) moving of people from one country to come to live in another country permanently: *restrictions on immigration* ○ [attrib] *immigration officials* ○ *immigration controls.* ⇨ article at ETHNIC. **2** [U] (also **immiˈgration control**) control point at an airport, sea terminal, etc at which the passports and other documents of people wanting to come into a country are checked: *go/pass through immigration.*

imminent /ˈɪmɪnənt/ *adj* (esp of unpleasant events) about to happen; likely to happen very soon: *no warning of imminent danger* ○ *An announcement of further cuts in government expenditure is imminent.* ▷ **imminence** /-əns/ *n* [U]: *the imminence of nuclear war.* **imminently** *adv.*

immiscible /ɪˈmɪsəbl/ *adj* (*fml*) (of liquids) that cannot be mixed: *Oil and water are immiscible.*

immobile /ɪˈməʊbaɪl; *US* -bl/ *adj* **1** unable to move or be moved: *Her illness has made her completely immobile.* **2** not moving: *The deer stood immobile among the trees.*

▷ **immobility** /ˌɪməˈbɪlətɪ/ *n* [U] state of being immobile.

immobilize, -ise /ɪˈməʊbəlaɪz/ *v* [Tn] **1** prevent (sth) from moving or operating normally: *A whole tank regiment was completely immobilized by enemy air attacks.* ○ *This alarm immobilizes the car.* ○ *The firm has been immobilized by a series of strikes.* **2** keep (a patient, a broken limb, etc) completely still, in order to help recovery. **immobilization, -isation** /ɪˌməʊbəlaɪˈzeɪʃn; *US* -lɪˈz-/ *n* [U].

immoderate /ɪˈmɒdərət/ *adj* too extreme or excessive; not moderate: *immoderate eating/drinking habits.* ▷ **immoderately** *adv.*

immodest /ɪˈmɒdɪst/ *adj* **1** indecent or not proper; not modest, esp concerning sexual behaviour: *an immodest dress* ○ *immodest talk, behaviour, etc.* **2** showing or expressing too high an opinion of oneself; conceited: *If I may be immodest for a moment, let me tell you about the latest book that I've written.* ▷ **immodestly** *adv.* **immodesty** *n* [U].

immolate /ˈɪməleɪt/ *v* [Tn] (*fml*) kill (sb) as a sacrifice. ▷ **immolation** /ˌɪməˈleɪʃn/ *n* [U].

immoral /ɪˈmɒrəl; *US* ɪˈmɔ:rəl/ *adj* **1** not following accepted standards of morality; not moral: *It's immoral to steal.* **2** not following accepted standards of sexual behaviour: *Some people still think it is immoral to have sex before marriage.* ○ *an immoral young man* ○ *immoral earnings*, eg from prostitution.

▷ **immorality** /ˌɪməˈrælətɪ/ *n* [U] immoral behaviour: *a life of immorality.*

immorally /-rəlɪ/ *adv*: *behave immorally.* Cf AMORAL.

immortal /ɪˈmɔ:tl/ *adj* **1** living for ever; not mortal: *The soul is immortal.* **2** (**a**) famous for ever; that will be remembered for ever: *the immortal Shakespeare.* (**b**) that will last for a long time or for ever; unfading: *immortal fame/glory.*

▷ **immortal** *n* (usu *pl*) **1** person of lasting fame: *Beethoven is regarded as one of the immortals of classical music.* **2** immortal being, esp a god of ancient Greece and Rome.

immortality /ˌɪmɔ:ˈtælətɪ/ *n* [U] state of being immortal: *man's belief in immortality.*

immortalize, -ise /ɪˈmɔ:təlaɪz/ *v* [Tn] give endless life or fame to (sb/sth): *Wigan pier, as immortalized in George Orwell's book 'The Road to Wigan Pier'.*

immovable /ɪˈmu:vəbl/ *adj* **1** that cannot be moved; impossible to move; fixed: *an immovable stone column* ○ (*law*) *immovable property*, eg buildings and land. **2** not changing; steadfast; firm: *immovable in purpose, intent, etc.* ▷ **immovably** /-əblɪ/ *adv.*

immune /ɪˈmju:n/ *adj* [usu pred] **1** ~ **(to/against sth)** that cannot be harmed by a disease or illness, either because of inoculation or through natural resistance: *I'm immune to smallpox as a result of vaccination.* **2** ~ **(to sth)** not affected by sth; not susceptible to sth: *immune to criticism, abuse, opposition, etc.* **3** ~ **(from sth)** protected or exempt from sth: *immune from additional taxes* ○ *immune from prosecution.*

▷ **immunity** /ɪˈmju:nətɪ/ *n* [U] **1** ~ **(to/against sth)** ability to resist infection, disease, etc: *immunity to measles* ○ *This vaccine will give you immunity for two years.* **2** ~ **(to sth)** ability to be unaffected by sth: *immunity to criticism.* **3** ~ **(from sth)** ability to be protected or exempt from sth: *immunity from prosecution* ○ *diplomatic immunity.*

immunize, -ise /ˈɪmjʊnaɪz/ *v* [Tn, Tn·pr] ~ **sb (against sth)** make sb immune (to a disease or infection), esp by injecting him with a vaccine: *Have you been immunized (against smallpox) yet?* Cf INOCULATE, VACCINATE. **immunization, -isation** /ˌɪmjʊnaɪˈzeɪʃn; *US* -nɪˈz-/ *n* [U, C]: *government plans for (a) mass immunization against measles.*

immunology /ˌɪmjʊˈnɒlədʒɪ/ *n* [U] scientific study of protection against and resistance to infection.

□ **imˈmune response** natural reaction of the body to harmful bacteria, viruses, etc (*antigens*), in which substances (*antibodies*) are produced in the blood to make the antigens harmless.

immuno- *comb form* of immunity, immunology or the immune response: *immunosuppressant drugs*, ie that stop the body rejecting transplanted organs.

immure /ɪˈmjʊə(r)/ *v* [Tn] (*fml*) imprison (sb); shut in: *immured in a cold dungeon* ○ *He immured himself in a small room to work undisturbed.*

immutable /ɪˈmju:təbl/ *adj* (*fml*) that cannot be changed; that will never change: *an immutable decision* ○ *immutable principles/laws.* ▷ **immutability** /ɪˌmju:təˈbɪlətɪ/ *n* [U]. **immutably** /-əblɪ/ *adv.*

imp /ɪmp/ *n* **1** small devil or evil spirit. **2** mischievous child: *What a little imp you are!*

impact /ˈɪmpækt/ *n* **1** [U] (**a**) hitting of one object against another: *the impact of a collision* ○ *The bomb exploded on impact*, ie at the moment of collision. (**b**) force with which one object hits another: *He collapsed under the full impact of the blow.* **2** [C usu *sing*] ~ **on/upon sb/sth** strong impression or effect on sb/sth: *Her speech made a tremendous impact on everyone.* ○ *the impact of new methods, technology, etc on modern industry.*

▷ **impact** /ɪmˈpækt/ *v* **1** [I, Tn] press, drive or wedge (sth) firmly into sth; press, etc (two things) together. **2** [Ipr, Tn] ~ **(on) sth** (*esp US*) have an effect on sth. **impacted** *adj* (of a tooth) wedged in the jaw so that it cannot grow through the gum normally: *an impacted wisdom tooth.* **impaction** /ɪmˈpækʃn/ *n* [C, U].

impair /ɪmˈpeə(r)/ *v* [Tn] weaken or damage (sth): *Loud noise can impair your hearing.* ○ *Today's attack has seriously impaired attempts to achieve peace in the area.* ○ *impaired vision.* ▷ **impairment** *n* [U].

impala /ɪmˈpɑ:lə/ *n* (*pl* unchanged or ~**s**) type of African antelope.

impale /ɪmˈpeɪl/ *v* [Tn, Tn·pr] ~ **sb/sth (on sth)** pierce sb/sth with a sharp-pointed object: *In former times, prisoners' heads were impaled on pointed stakes.* ▷ **impalement** *n* [U].

impalpable /ɪmˈpælpəbl/ *adj* (*fml*) **1** that cannot be touched or felt physically: *impalpable darkness, horror, fear.* **2** not easily understood or grasped by the mind.

impanel = EMPANEL.

impart /ɪmˈpɑ:t/ *v* (*fml*) **1** [Tn, Tn·pr] ~ **sth (to sth)** give (a quality) to sth: *Her presence imparted an air of elegance (to the ceremony).* ○ *impart spin to a cricket ball.* **2** [Tn, Dn·pr] ~ **sth (to sb)** make known (information) to sb; reveal sth: *I have no news to impart (to you).*

impartial /ɪmˈpɑ:ʃl/ *adj* not favouring one person or thing more than another; fair or neutral: *an impartial judge/judgement.* Cf PARTIAL 2. ▷ **impartiality** /ˌɪmˌpɑ:ʃɪˈælətɪ/ *n* [U]: *They showed complete impartiality in discussing these sensitive issues.* **impartially** /-ʃəlɪ/ *adv*: *treat prisoners impartially.*

impassable /ɪmˈpɑ:səbl; *US* -ˈpæs-/ *adj* (of a road, route, etc) impossible to travel on or over: *country lanes that are often impassable in winter* ○ *roads made impassable by fallen trees.*

impasse /ˈæmpɑ:s; *US* ˈɪmpæs/ *n* difficult position or situation from which there is no way out; deadlock: *The negotiations had reached an impasse, with both sides refusing to compromise.*

impassioned /ɪmˈpæʃnd/ *adj* showing strong deep feeling: *an impassioned plea for mercy.*

impassive /ɪmˈpæsɪv/ *adj* showing no sign of

feeling: *an impassive expression.* ▷ **impassively** *adv*: *The accused sat impassively as the judge sentenced him to ten years in prison.* **impassiveness**, **impassivity** /ˌɪmpæˈsɪvətɪ/ *ns* [U].

impatient /ɪmˈpeɪʃnt/ *adj* **1** (**a**) ~ (**at sth/with sb**) unable to deal calmly with sth/sb or to wait for sth; easily irritated by sb/sth; not patient: *Don't be so impatient! The bus will be here soon.* ○ *You're too impatient with her; she's only a child.* (**b**) showing a lack of patience: *another impatient glance at his watch.* **2** [pred] ~ (**to do sth**); ~ (**for sth**) very eager to do sth or for sth to happen; anxious: *Many graduates are impatient to become managers.* ○ *impatient for the summer holidays to come.* **3** [pred] ~ **of sth** (*fml*) intolerant of sth: *impatient of delay.* ▷ **impatience** /ɪmˈpeɪʃns/ *n* [U]: *the government's growing impatience with the unions.* **impatiently** *adv*: *We sat waiting impatiently for the film to start.*

impeach /ɪmˈpiːtʃ/ *v* **1** [Tn, Tn·pr] ~ **sb** (**for sth**) accuse (a public official or politician) of committing a serious crime, esp one against the State: *The committee decided to impeach the President.* ○ *impeach a judge for taking bribes.* **2** [Tn] (*fml*) raise doubts about (sth); question: *impeach sb's motives.*
▷ **impeachable** *adj* (of a crime) for which a public official or politician can be impeached: *an impeachable offence.*
impeachment *n* [U].

impeccable /ɪmˈpekəbl/ *adj* free from mistakes; excellent or faultless: *Your English is impeccable!* ○ *impeccable behaviour, manners, style, etc.* ▷ **impeccably** /-blɪ/ *adv*: *He was impeccably dressed for the occasion.*

impecunious /ˌɪmpɪˈkjuːnɪəs/ *adj* (*fml*) having little or no money. ▷ **impecuniously** *adv.* **impecuniousness** *n* [U].

impedance /ɪmˈpiːdəns/ *n* [U] resistance of an electric circuit to the flow of alternating current. Cf ADMITTANCE 2.

impede /ɪmˈpiːd/ *v* [Tn] hinder or obstruct the progress or movement of (sb/sth): *The development of the project was seriously impeded by a reduction in funds.*

impediment /ɪmˈpedɪmənt/ *n* **1** ~ (**to sb/sth**) person or thing that hinders or obstructs the progress or movement of sth: *The main impediment to growth was a lack of capital.* **2** physical disability of a specified type; defect: *a speech impediment*, eg a lisp or a stammer.

impedimenta /ɪmˌpedɪˈmentə/ *n* [pl] (*fml or joc*) baggage and other supplies that slow down an army on a long journey: *He came with his wife, six children, four dogs and various other impedimenta.*

impel /ɪmˈpel/ *v* (**-ll-**) [Tn, Tn·pr, Cn·t] ~ **sb** (**to sth**) force or urge sb to do sth: *Impelled by feelings of guilt, John wrote to apologize.* ○ *The President's speech impelled the nation to greater efforts.* ○ *I felt impelled to investigate the matter further.* Cf COMPEL.

impending /ɪmˈpendɪŋ/ *adj* [esp attrib] about to happen; imminent: *his impending arrival, departure, retirement, visit, etc.*

impenetrable /ɪmˈpenɪtrəbl/ *adj* **1** ~ (**to sth**) that cannot be entered, passed through, etc: *an impenetrable jungle, swamp, fortress, etc* ○ *impenetrable darkness, fog, etc*, ie that cannot be seen through ○ (*fig*) *his impenetrable ignorance.* **2** impossible to understand or solve: *an impenetrable difficulty, mystery, problem, etc* ○ *This history book is completely impenetrable to me.* ▷ **impenetrability** /ɪmˌpenɪtrəˈbɪlətɪ/ *n* [U]. **impenetrably** /-blɪ/ *adv.*

impenitent /ɪmˈpenɪtənt/ *adj* (*fml*) not sorry for or ashamed of one's misdoings; not penitent. ▷ **impenitence** /-əns/ *n* [U]. **impenitently** *adv.*

imperative /ɪmˈperətɪv/ *adj* **1** [usu pred] very urgent or important; needing immediate attention: *It is imperative that we make a quick decision.* **2** expressing a command; authoritative: *an imperative tone of voice that had to be obeyed.* **3** (*grammar*) of the verb form that expresses a command: *'Go!' is in the imperative mood.* Cf INDICATIVE, INFINITIVE, SUBJUNCTIVE.
▷ **imperative** *n* **1** (*grammar*) (verb in the) mood[2] that expresses a command: *In 'Go away!' the verb is in the imperative.* ○ *'Go!' is an imperative.* **2** thing that is essential or urgent: *Survival is our first imperative.* ○ *a moral imperative.*
imperatively *adv.*

imperceptible /ˌɪmpəˈseptəbl/ *adj* that cannot be noticed or felt because so small, slight or gradual: *an imperceptible change in temperature* ○ *an almost imperceptible shift of opinion.* ▷ **imperceptibly** /-əblɪ/ *adv*: *Almost imperceptibly her expression changed.*

imperfect /ɪmˈpɜːfɪkt/ *adj* **1** faulty or defective; not perfect: *an imperfect copy* ○ *imperfect knowledge, understanding, etc of sth.* **2** [attrib] (*grammar*) of the verb tense that expresses incomplete action in the past (more usually called *continuous* or *progressive*): *the imperfect tenses in French.*
▷ **imperfect** *n* **the imperfect** [sing] (*grammar*) (verb in the) tense that expresses incomplete action in the past; continuous aspect: *'I was speaking' is in the imperfect.*
imperfection /ˌɪmpəˈfekʃn/ *n* **1** [U] being imperfect: *My father never tolerated imperfection.* **2** [C] fault or defect that makes sb/sth imperfect; blemish: *The only slight imperfection in this painting is a scratch in the corner.* ○ *the house's structural imperfections.*
imperfectly *adv.*

imperial /ɪmˈpɪərɪəl/ *adj* **1** [usu attrib] (**a**) of an empire or its ruler(s): *the imperial palace, guards, servants* ○ *imperial power, trade.* (**b**) like or characteristic of such rulers; majestic: *with imperial generosity.* **2** [attrib] belonging to a legal non-metric system of weights and measures formerly used in the United Kingdom for all goods and still used for certain goods: *an imperial pint, gallon, pound, etc.* ▷ **imperially** /-rɪəlɪ/ *adv.*

imperialism /ɪmˈpɪərɪəlɪzəm/ *n* [U] (*usu derog*) (belief in the) policy of extending a country's power and influence in the world through diplomacy or military force, and esp by acquiring colonies.
▷ **imperialist** /ɪmˈpɪərɪəlɪst/ *n* (*usu derog*) person who supports or believes in imperialism: [attrib] *imperialist policies.*
imperialistic /ɪmˌpɪərɪəˈlɪstɪk/ *adj.*

imperil /ɪmˈperəl/ *v* (**-ll-**; *US also* **-l-**) [Tn] (*fml*) put (sb/sth) in danger; endanger: *The security of the country had been imperilled.*

imperious /ɪmˈpɪərɪəs/ *adj* (*fml*) proud and arrogant; domineering; expecting obedience: *an imperious look, command, gesture.* ▷ **imperiously** *adv*: *The envoys were dismissed imperiously.* **imperiousness** *n* [U].

imperishable /ɪmˈperɪʃəbl/ *adj* (*fml*) that will not decay; that will never disappear: *imperishable goods* ○ (*fig*) *imperishable glory.*

impermanent /ɪmˈpɜːmənənt/ *adj* (*fml*) not permanent; temporary. ▷ **impermanence** /-əns/ *n* [U].

impermeable /ɪmˈpɜːmɪəbl/ *adj* (of a substance) not allowing a liquid to pass through: *an impermeable membrane.* Cf PERMEABLE (PERMEATE).

impermissible /ˌɪmpəˈmɪsəbl/ *adj* (*fml*) not allowed or permitted.

impersonal /ɪmˈpɜːsənl/ *adj* **1** (*usu derog*) not influenced by, showing or involving human feelings: *a vast impersonal organization* ○ *a cold impersonal stare* ○ *Giving people time to get to know one another will make the meeting less impersonal.* **2** (*usu approv*) not referring to any particular person; objective: *an impersonal discussion.* ▷ **impersonally** /-sənəlɪ/ *adv.*

impersonate /ɪmˈpɜːsəneɪt/ *v* [Tn] **1** pretend to be (another person) in order to entertain others: *He can impersonate many well-known politicians.* **2** imitate the behaviour of (another person) in order to deceive others: *He was caught trying to impersonate a military officer.*
▷ **impersonation** /ɪmˌpɜːsəˈneɪʃn/ *n* [C, U]: *He does some brilliant impersonations of the president.*
impersonator *n* person who impersonates other people: *a famous female impersonator*, ie a man who impersonates women on the stage.

impertinent /ɪmˈpɜːtɪnənt/ *adj* ~ (**to sb**) not respectful; rude: *impertinent remarks* ○ *an impertinent child* ○ *It would be impertinent to suggest that he was always wrong.* ▷ **impertinence** /-əns/ *n* [C usu *sing*, U]: *I've had enough of your impertinence.* **impertinently** *adv.*

imperturbable /ˌɪmpəˈtɜːbəbl/ *adj* not easily troubled or worried; calm: *She was one of those imperturbable people who never get angry or upset.* ▷ **imperturbability** /ˌɪmpəˌtɜːbəˈbɪlətɪ/ *n* [U]. **imperturbably** /-əblɪ/ *adv.*

impervious /ɪmˈpɜːvɪəs/ *adj* ~ (**to sth**) **1** not allowing water, gas, etc to pass through: *This material is impervious to rain-water.* **2** not affected or influenced by sth: *impervious to criticism, argument, fear.*

impetigo /ˌɪmpɪˈtaɪgəʊ/ *n* [U] type of contagious skin disease that causes crusty yellow sores.

impetuous /ɪmˈpetʃʊəs/ *adj* acting or done quickly and with little thought or care; rash or impulsive: *an impetuous young man* ○ *impetuous behaviour* ○ *It would be foolish and impetuous to resign over such a small matter.* ▷ **impetuosity** /ɪmˌpetʃʊˈɒsətɪ/ *n* [U]. **impetuously** *adv.*

impetus /ˈɪmpɪtəs/ *n* **1** [u *sing*] ~ (**to sth/to do sth**) thing that encourages a process to develop more quickly: *The treaty gave (a) fresh impetus to trade.* **2** [U] force with which sth moves.

impi /ˈɪmpɪ/ *n* (*S African*) group of Bantu (esp Zulu) warriors.

impiety /ɪmˈpaɪətɪ/ *n* (**a**) [U] lack of respect, esp for God and religion. (**b**) [C usu *pl*] act, remark, etc showing a lack of such respect.

impinge /ɪmˈpɪndʒ/ *v* [Ipr] ~ **on/upon sth** (*fml*) have an effect on sth: *In his sleepy state, the sound of a car driving up to the house scarcely impinged on his consciousness.*

impious /ˈɪmpɪəs/ *adj* (*fml*) showing a lack of respect, esp for God and religion; not pious. ▷ **impiously** *adv.*

impish /ˈɪmpɪʃ/ *adj* of or like an imp; mischievous. ▷ **impishly** *adv.* **impishness** *n* [U].

implacable /ɪmˈplækəbl/ *adj* that cannot be changed or satisfied: *implacable hatred, fury, opposition* ○ *an implacable enemy, rival, etc.* ▷ **implacably** /-əblɪ/ *adv*: *implacably opposed to the plan.*

implant /ɪmˈplɑːnt; *US* -ˈplænt/ *v* **1** [Tn, Tn·pr] ~ **sth** (**in sth**) (**a**) deliberately introduce or fix (ideas, etc) into a person's mind: *implant religious beliefs in young children.* (**b**) insert (tissue, etc) into a part of the body: *In this operation the surgeons implant a new lens (in the eye).* **2** [I, Ipr] ~ (**in/into sth**) (of a newly fertilized egg) become attached to the inside of the uterus.
▷ **implant** /ˈɪmplɑːnt; *US* -plænt/ *n* [C] thing that has been implanted in the body.
implantation /ˌɪmplɑːnˈteɪʃn; *US* -plænt-/ *n* [C, U].

implausible /ɪmˈplɔːzəbl/ *adj* unlikely to be true; not convincing: *an implausible story, excuse, theory, etc.* Cf PLAUSIBLE.

implement[1] /ˈɪmplɪmənt/ *n* tool or instrument: *farm implements* ○ *Man's earliest implements were carved from stone and bone.* ⇨ Usage at MACHINE.

implement[2] /ˈɪmplɪment/ *v* [Tn] put (sth) into effect; carry out: *implement plans, policies, a programme of reforms, etc.* ▷ **implementation** /ˌɪmplɪmenˈteɪʃn/ *n* [U].

implicate /ˈɪmplɪkeɪt/ *v* [Tn, Tn·pr] ~ **sb** (**in sth**) show that sb is involved in sth, esp a crime: *His enemies tried to implicate him (in the murder).* ○ *He was deeply implicated* (ie involved) *in the plot.*

implication /ˌɪmplɪˈkeɪʃn/ *n* **1** [C, U] ~ (**for sb/sth**) thing that is suggested or implied; thing not openly stated: *Study the implications of the president's statement.* ○ *The new report has far-reaching implications for the future of broadcasting.* ○ *Failure to say 'No' may, by implication, be taken to mean 'Yes'.* **2** [U] involving or being involved, esp in a crime: *The trial resulted in the implication of several major figures in the organization.*

implicit /ɪmˈplɪsɪt/ *adj* **1** ~ **(in sth)** implied, but not expressed directly; not explicit: *implicit assumptions* ○ *an implicit threat* ○ *obligations which are implicit in the contract.* **2** unquestioning and absolute: *I have implicit faith in your abilities.* ▷ **implicitly** *adv*: *trust sb implicitly.*

implode /ɪmˈpləʊd/ *v* [I, Tn] (cause sth to) burst or collapse inwards: *The light bulb imploded.* Cf EXPLODE 1. ▷ **implosion** /ɪmˈpləʊʒn/ *n* [C, U].

implore /ɪmˈplɔː(r)/ *v* [Tn, Dn·t] ask or beg (sb) earnestly; beseech: *'Help me,' he implored.* ○ *implore sb's forgiveness, mercy, etc* ○ *They implored her to stay.* ⇨ Usage at ASK. ▷ **imploring** *adj*: *She gave him an imploring look.* **imploringly** *adv.*

imply /ɪmˈplaɪ/ *v* (*pt, pp* **implied**) **1** [Tn, Tf] suggest (sth) indirectly rather than state it directly; hint: *His silence implied agreement.* ○ *implied criticism* ○ *I don't wish to imply that you are wrong.* **2** [Tn] suggest (sth) as a logical consequence; entail: *Freedom does not necessarily imply responsibility.* ○ *The fact she was here implies a degree of interest.* Cf INFER.

impolite /ˌɪmpəˈlaɪt/ *adj* rude; not polite: *Some people still think it is impolite for men not to stand up when a woman comes into the room.* ▷ **impolitely** *adv.* **impoliteness** *n* [U].

impolitic /ɪmˈpɒlətɪk/ *adj* (*fml*) not wise; not politic: *It might be impolitic to refuse his offer.*

imponderable /ɪmˈpɒndərəbl/ *adj* of which the effect or importance cannot be measured or estimated.

▷ **imponderable** *n* (usu *pl*) thing, eg a quality or an emotion, that is imponderable: *the great imponderables of love and power.*

import[1] /ɪmˈpɔːt/ *v* [Tn, Tn·pr] ~ **sth (from...)**; ~ **sth (into...)** bring (goods, ideas, etc) from a foreign country into one's own country: *The country has to import most of its raw materials.* ○ *cars imported from Japan* ○ *meat imported (into the United Kingdom)* ○ *the latest pop music imported from America.* Cf EXPORT[2].

▷ **importation** /ˌɪmpɔːˈteɪʃn/ *n* [U, C]: *a ban on the importation of drugs.*

importer *n* person, company, etc that imports goods or services: *the country's largest importer of tobacco.*

import[2] /ˈɪmpɔːt/ *n* **1** [C esp *pl*] imported goods, services, etc: *Britain's food imports (from the rest of the world)* ○ *restrict cheap foreign imports.* **2** [U] action of importing goods: *the import of coal* ○ *tariffs on the import of manufactured goods* ○ [attrib] *import controls.* Cf EXPORT[1].

import[3] /ɪmˈpɔːt/ *v* [Tn, Tn·pr] ~ **sth (to sb)** (*fml*) mean or convey sth (to sb): *What did these developments import to them?*

▷ **import** /ˈɪmpɔːt/ *n* (*fml*) **1** [U] importance or significance: *matters of no great import.* **2** [sing] meaning (of sth), esp when not directly stated: *the hidden import of his speech.*

important /ɪmˈpɔːtnt/ *adj* **1** ~ **(to sb/sth)** very serious and significant; of great value or concern: *an important decision, announcement, meeting* ○ *It is vitally important to cancel the order immediately.* ○ *It is important that students (should) attend/for students to attend all the lectures.* ○ *They need more money now but, more important, they need long-term help.* ○ *It's important to me that you should be there.* **2** (of a person) having great influence or authority; influential: *She was clearly an important person.* ○ *It's not as if he was very important in the company hierarchy.*

▷ **importance** /-tns/ *n* **1** [U] ~ **(to sb/sth)** being important; significance or value: *the importance of industry to the economy* ○ *They attached very great importance to the project,* ie They considered it to be very important. ○ *a matter of the utmost political importance* ○ *These issues now assume even greater importance.* **2** (idm) **full of one's own importance** ⇨ FULL.

importantly *adv*: *strut about importantly* ○ *More importantly, can he be depended on?*

importunate /ɪmˈpɔːtʃʊnət/ *adj* (*fml*) persistent, esp in making requests or demands: *an importunate beggar.* ▷ **importunately** *adv.* **importunity** /ˌɪmpɔːˈtjuːnətɪ/ *n* [U, C esp *pl*]: *irritated by his constant importunities.*

importune /ˌɪmpɔːˈtjuːn/ *v* (*fml*) **1** [Tn, Tn·pr, Dn·t] ~ **sb (for sth)** ask sb persistently (for sth), usu in an annoying manner; beg or demand insistently: *importune one's creditors for an extension of the borrowing period/to extend the borrowing period.* **2** [I, Tn] (of a prostitute) attempt to attract (clients): *arrested for importuning.*

impose /ɪmˈpəʊz/ *v* **1** [Tn, Tn·pr] ~ **sth (on sb/sth)** (**a**) place (a penalty, tax, etc) officially on sb/sth: *impose a fine, sentence, term of imprisonment, etc* ○ *impose a further tax on wines and spirits.* (**b**) place (sth unwelcome or unpleasant) on sb/sth; inflict: *impose one's rule (on a people)* ○ *impose restrictions, limitations, restraints, etc (on trade).* **2** [Tn, Tn·pr] ~ **sth (on sb)** try to make sb accept (an opinion or a belief); inflict sth: *She imposed her ideas on the group.* **3** [Tn, Tn·pr] ~ **oneself/sth (on sb)** force sb to accept (oneself, one's company, etc): *She'd never think of imposing herself.* ○ *He imposed his presence on us for the weekend.* **4** (phr v) **impose on/upon sb/sth** win a favour from sb, esp by using undue pressure: *I hope it's not imposing on you/your hospitality, but could I stay to dinner?*

▷ **imposing** *adj* impressive in appearance or manner; grand: *an imposing façade, building, person, personality.* **imposingly** *adv.*

imposition /ˌɪmpəˈzɪʃn/ *n* ~ **(on sb/sth)** **1** [U] action of imposing: *The imposition of the new tax on books caused a sharp rise in prices.* **2** [C] unfair or unpleasant thing that sb is obliged to accept: *I'd like to stay if it's not too much of an imposition (on you).* **3** [C] (*Brit*) piece of work (eg copying a sentence many times) given to a school pupil as a punishment. **4** [C] (*dated*) act of deception; imposture.

impossible /ɪmˈpɒsəbl/ *adj* **1** that cannot be done or exist; not possible: *It's impossible for me to be there before 8.00 pm.* ○ *It is virtually impossible to predict the future accurately.* ○ *an almost impossible task* ○ *It's an impossible story,* ie it cannot be believed. **2** very difficult to bear; hopeless: *an impossible situation* ○ *Their son is impossible,* eg He is very badly behaved.

▷ **impossibility** /ɪmˌpɒsəˈbɪlətɪ/ *n* [U, C]: *the impossibility of any improvement* ○ *a logical impossibility.*

the impossible *n* [sing] thing that cannot be achieved: *ask for, want, attempt, do the impossible.*

impossibly /-əblɪ/ *adv*: *impossibly difficult.*

impost[1] /ˈɪmpəʊst/ *n* ~ **(on sth)** (*fml*) tax or duty imposed on sth.

impost[2] /ˈɪmpəʊst/ *n* upper part of a pillar or column, supporting an arch.

impostor /ɪmˈpɒstə(r)/ *n* person pretending to be sb else, usu in order to deceive others.

imposture /ɪmˈpɒstʃə(r)/ *n* [C, U] (*fml*) (action of) deliberately deceiving by pretending to be sb else.

impotent /ˈɪmpətənt/ *adj* **1** [usu pred] unable to take effective action; powerless or helpless: *Without the chairman's support, the committee is impotent.* **2** (of men) unable to have sexual intercourse or reach an orgasm.

▷ **impotence** /-əns/ *n* [U] being impotent: *political impotence* ○ *fear of impotence.*

impotently *adv.*

impound /ɪmˈpaʊnd/ *v* [Tn] **1** take legal possession of (sth): *impound goods, property, belongings, etc.* **2** put (an illegally parked car or a stray animal) in a pound(2) until it is claimed.

impoverish /ɪmˈpɒvərɪʃ/ *v* [Tn] **1** make (sb) poor: *an elderly impoverished writer.* **2** make (sth) poorer or worse in quality: *Heavy rain and excessive use have impoverished the soil.* ○ *Our lives would have been greatly impoverished if we had not known our dear friend.* ▷ **impoverishment** *n* [U].

impracticable /ɪmˈpræktɪkəbl/ *adj* impossible to put into practice; not practicable: *an impracticable scheme.* ▷ **impracticability** /ɪmˌpræktɪkəˈbɪlətɪ/ *n* [U]. **impracticably** /-əblɪ/ *adv.*

impractical /ɪmˈpræktɪkl/ *adj* **1** not sensible, useful or realistic: *It was impractical to think that we could build the house in one month.* **2** not skilled at doing practical work: *an academically clever but totally impractical young man.* ▷ **impracticality** /ɪmˌpræktɪˈkælətɪ/ *n* [U, C]. **impractically** /-klɪ/ *adv.*

imprecation /ˌɪmprɪˈkeɪʃn/ *n* (*fml*) oath or curse: *muttering imprecations.* ▷ **imprecatory** /ˌɪmprɪˈkeɪtərɪ; *US also* ɪmˈprekətɔːrɪ/ *adj.*

imprecise /ˌɪmprɪˈsaɪs/ *adj* not exact or accurate; not correctly or clearly stated; not precise: *imprecise thoughts, statements, measurements.* ▷ **imprecisely** *adv.* **imprecision** /ˌɪmprɪˈsɪʒn/ *n* [U]: *imprecision in his use of legal terms.*

impregnable /ɪmˈpregnəbl/ *adj* (**a**) so strong and well-constructed that it cannot be entered or captured: *an impregnable fortress.* (**b**) (*fig*) so strong that it cannot be overcome or broken down: *impregnable arguments, defences, reserve.* ▷ **impregnability** /ɪmˌpregnəˈbɪlətɪ/ *n* [U]. **impregnably** /-əblɪ/ *adv.*

impregnate /ˈɪmpregneɪt; *US* ɪmˈpreg-/ *v* **1** [Tn, Tn·pr] ~ **sth (with sth)** (**a**) cause (one substance) to be filled in every part with another substance; saturate sth: *water impregnated with salt.* (**b**) cause sth to be affected or influenced in every part by sth: *The drawing is impregnated with the artist's personality.* **2** [Tn] (*fml*) fertilize (an egg or ovum) with sperm or pollen; make pregnant.

impresario /ˌɪmprɪˈsɑːrɪəʊ/ *n* manager or director of a ballet, concert, theatre or opera company.

impress /ɪmˈpres/ *v* **1** [Tn, Tn·pr] ~ **sb (with sth)** have a favourable effect on sb; make sb feel admiration and respect: *The sights of the city never fail to impress foreign tourists.* ○ *The girl impressed her fiancé's family with her liveliness and sense of humour.* ○ *We were most impressed with/by your efficiency.* **2** [Tn·pr] ~ **sth on/upon sb** fix sth in sb's mind; make sb keenly aware of sth: *His words impressed themselves on my memory.* ○ *The manager impressed on his office staff the importance of keeping accurate records.* **3** [Tn, Tn·pr] ~ **sth (in/on sth)** press sth hard into a soft surface, leaving a mark: *designs impressed on/in wax.*

▷ **impress** /ˈɪmpres/ *n* (*fml*) mark left by pressing sth hard, eg a seal, into a soft surface.

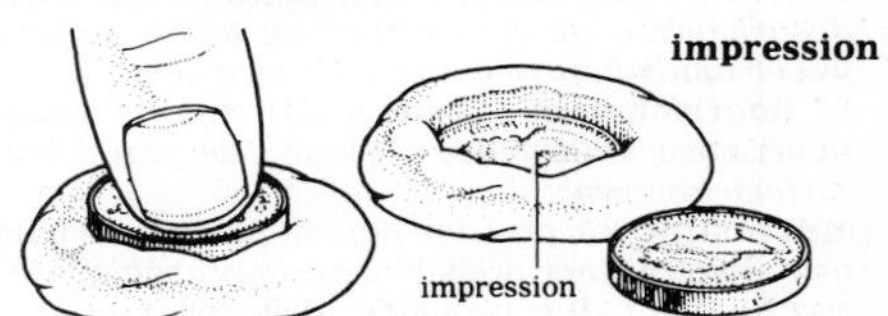

impression /ɪmˈpreʃn/ *n* **1** ~ **(on sb)** deep lasting effect on the mind or feelings of sb: *His first speech as president made a strong impression on his audience.* ○ *create an unfavourable impression.* **2** (esp *sing*) ~ **(of sth/doing sth/that...)** (unclear or uncertain) idea, feeling or opinion: *My general impression was that he seemed a pleasant man.* ○ *I had the distinct impression that I was being followed.* ○ *one's first impressions of* (ie one's immediate reaction to) *the new headmaster* ○ *He gives the impression of being a hard worker/that he works hard,* ie It seems as if he works hard. ○ *'I always thought you were a nurse.' 'I wonder how you got that impression?'* **3** appearance or effect of sb/sth: *The room's lighting conveys an impression of spaciousness.* **4** ~ **(of sb)** funny imitation of the behaviour or way of talking of a well-known person: *The students did some marvellous impressions of the teachers at the end-of-term party.* **5** mark left by pressing an object hard into a surface: *the impression of a leaf in a fossil.* ⇨ illus. **6** reprint of a book made with few or no alterations to its contents: *the fifth impression.* Cf EDITION 2. **7** (idm) **be under the impression that...** have the (usu mistaken) idea that...: *I was under the impression that you were coming tomorrow.*

▷ **impressionism** /-ʃənɪzəm/ *n* (usu **Impressionism**) [U] style of painting, developed in France in the late 19th century, which creates the general impression of a subject by using the effects of colour and light, without realistic detail. At first it was much criticized, but today it is very popular. Among the leading painters in this style were *Monet, *Renoir, *Cézanne and *Degas. **impressionist** /-ʃənɪst/ *n* **1** (usu **Impressionist**) artist who paints in the style of Impressionism. **2** person who does impressions (IMPRESSION 4) of other people. — *adj* (usu **Impressionist**) of or relating to the style of Impressionism: *Impressionist painters, works, exhibitions.* **impressionistic** giving a general idea rather than specific facts or detailed knowledge: *a purely impressionistic description of the incident.*

impressionable /ɪmˈpreʃənəbl/ *adj* easily influenced or affected: *children at an impressionable age* ○ *impressionable young people.* ▷ **impressionability** /ɪmˌpreʃənəˈbɪlətɪ/ *n* [U].

impressive /ɪmˈpresɪv/ *adj* having a strong effect on sb, esp through size, grandeur, or importance: *an impressive ceremony, building, speech, performance* ○ *His collection of paintings is most impressive.* ▷ **impressively** *adv*. **impressiveness** *n* [U].

imprimatur /ˌɪmprɪˈmeɪtə(r), -ˈmɑːtə(r)/ *n* (**a**) official permission to print a book, esp as given by the Roman Catholic Church. (**b**) (*fig*) permission or approval: *give the scheme one's imprimatur.*

imprint /ɪmˈprɪnt/ *v* [Tn·pr] ~ **sth in/on sth** (**a**) press (sth hard) onto a surface, leaving an impression or mark: *imprint one's hand in soft cement.* (**b**) (*fig*) fix sth firmly in sb's mind: *details imprinted on his memory/mind.*

▷ **imprint** /ˈɪmprɪnt/ *n* **1** ~ (**in/on sth**) mark made by pressing or stamping a surface: *the imprint of a foot in the sand.* **2** (usu *sing*) ~ (**on sb/sth**) lasting characteristic mark or effect: *Her face bore the deep imprint of suffering.* **3** name and address of the publisher, usu printed on the title-page of a book.

imprinting /ɪmˈprɪntɪŋ/ *n* [U] learning process in which young animals recognize and have a strong attachment to members of their own species, esp their mothers.

imprison /ɪmˈprɪzn/ *v* [esp passive: Tn, Tn·pr] ~ **sb** (**in sth**) put or keep sb in or as if in prison: *Several of the rioters were imprisoned for causing a disturbance.* ○ *conditions in which young mothers feel virtually imprisoned in their own homes.*

▷ **imprisonment** /-mənt/ *n* [U] state of being imprisoned: *sentenced to one year's, ten years', life, etc imprisonment.*

improbable /ɪmˈprɒbəbl/ *adj* not likely to be true or to happen; not probable: *an improbable idea, event, result* ○ *It is very/most improbable that the level of unemployment will fall.*

▷ **improbability** /ɪmˌprɒbəˈbɪlətɪ/ *n* (**a**) [U] state of being improbable: *the improbability of his being recaptured.* (**b**) [C] event that is improbable: *Don't worry about such improbabilities as floods and earthquakes.*

improbably /-əblɪ/ *adv*.

impromptu /ɪmˈprɒmptjuː; *US* -tuː/ *adj, adv* (done) without preparation, rehearsal or thought in advance: *an impromptu speech, news conference, performance, etc* ○ *He spoke impromptu.*

▷ **impromptu** *n* musical composition, etc that is or appears to be improvised: *an impromptu by Schubert.*

improper /ɪmˈprɒpə(r)/ *adj* **1** wrong or incorrect: *improper use of a tool, word, drug, etc.* **2** not suited or appropriate to the situation or circumstances; unseemly or indecent: *Laughing and joking are considered improper behaviour at a funeral.* **3** dishonest; irregular: *improper business practices.* Cf PROPER. ▷ **improperly** *adv*.

□ **improper ˈfraction** numerical fraction in which the value above the line is greater than the value below the line, eg $\frac{720}{63}$. Cf PROPER FRACTION (PROPER).

impropriety /ˌɪmprəˈpraɪətɪ/ *n* (*fml*) (**a**) [U] indecent or unsuitable behaviour; dishonest practice: *The investigation revealed no impropriety.* (**b**) [C] instance of this.

improve /ɪmˈpruːv/ *v* **1** [I, Tn] (cause sth to) become or make (sth) better: *His work is improving slowly.* ○ *Her health is gradually improving,* ie after an illness. ○ *The Post Office aims to improve its quality of service.* ○ *The soil has been greatly improved by the use of fertilizers.* ○ *He studied harder to improve his French.* ○ *a new improved washing-powder.* **2** (phr v) **improve on/upon sth** achieve or produce sth of a better standard or quality than sth else: *The German girl improved on her previous best performance in the 100 metres.* ○ *This achievement has never been improved on.*

▷ **improvement** *n* **1** [C, U] ~ (**on/in sth**) action or process of improving; state of being improved: *cause a distinct/significant/marked improvement in working conditions* ○ *a slight, gradual, etc improvement in the weather* ○ *This year's car is an improvement on* (ie is better than) *last year's model.* ○ *There is room for further improvement in your English.* **2** [C] addition or alteration that improves sth or adds to its value: *home improvements* ○ [attrib] *a road improvement scheme.*

improvident /ɪmˈprɒvɪdənt/ *adj* (*fml*) not preparing for future needs; wasteful: *improvident spending habits.* ▷ **improvidence** /-əns/ *n* [U]. **improvidently** *adv*.

improvise /ˈɪmprəvaɪz; *US also* ˌɪmprəˈvaɪz/ *v* [I, Tn] **1** compose or play (music), speak or act without previous preparation: *The pianist forgot his music and had to improvise (the accompaniment).* ○ *an improvised speech.* **2** make (sth) from whatever is available, without preparation: *As we've not got the proper materials, we'll just have to improvise.* ○ *a hastily improvised meal.* ▷ **improvisation** /ˌɪmprəvaɪˈzeɪʃn; *US also* ɪmˌprɒvəˈzeɪʃn/ *n* [U, C].

imprudent /ɪmˈpruːdnt/ *adj* (*fml*) not wise or discreet; not prudent: *It would be imprudent (of you) to resign from your present job before you are offered another.* ▷ **imprudence** /-ns/ *n* [U]. **imprudently** *adv*.

impudent /ˈɪmpjʊdənt/ *adj* very rude and disrespectful: *an impudent child, grin, question.*

▷ **impudence** /-əns/ *n* [U] being impudent; impudent behaviour or speech: *I've had enough of your impudence!*

impudently *adv*.

impugn /ɪmˈpjuːn/ *v* [Tn] (*fml*) express doubts about (sth): *impugn sb's motives, actions, morals, etc.*

impulse /ˈɪmpʌls/ *n* **1** (**a**) [C] ~ (**to do sth**) sudden urge to act without thinking about the results: *He felt an irresistible impulse to jump.* ○ *check/curb/resist an impulse.* (**b**) [U] tendency to act in this way: *a man of impulse.* **2** [C] push or thrust; stimulus; impetus: *give an impulse to industrial expansion.* **3** [C] stimulating force in a nerve or an electric circuit that causes a reaction: *nerve impulses.* **4** (idm) **on impulse** suddenly and without previous thinking or planning: *On impulse, I picked up the phone and rang my sister in Australia.*

□ **ˈimpulse buying** buying goods on impulse.

impulsion /ɪmˈpʌlʃn/ *n* [C] ~ (**to do sth**) (*fml*) strong urge (to do sth): *the impulsion to break away and make a new life.*

impulsive /ɪmˈpʌlsɪv/ *adj* (of people or their behaviour) marked by sudden action that is undertaken without careful thought: *an impulsive man, comment, decision, departure.* ▷ **impulsively** *adv*: *react, behave impulsively.* **impulsiveness** *n* [U].

impunity /ɪmˈpjuːnətɪ/ *n* (idm) **with impunity** with freedom from punishment or injury: *You cannot break the law with impunity.*

impure /ɪmˈpjʊə(r)/ *adj* **1** (*dated*) morally wrong, esp in one's sexual behaviour: *impure thoughts, motives, actions.* **2** not clean; dirty or contaminated. **3** not consisting of one substance, but mixed with another substance of poorer quality: *impure metals.*

▷ **impurity** /ɪmˈpjʊərətɪ/ *n* **1** [U] state or quality of being impure. **2** [C] substance present in another substance that makes it of poor quality: *remove impurities from silver.*

impute /ɪmˈpjuːt/ *v* [Tn·pr] ~ **sth to sb/sth** (*fml*) put the responsibility for sth on sb/sth; attribute sth to sb/sth: *He imputed the failure of his marriage to his wife's shortcomings.*

▷ **imputation** /ˌɪmpjuːˈteɪʃn/ *n* [U, C] (*fml*) action of imputing; accusation: *imputation of guilt.*

In *symb* indium.

in[1] /ɪn/ *adv part* (For special uses with many *vs*, eg *come in, give in,* see the *v* entries.) **1** (to a position) within a particular area or volume: *The top drawer is the one with the cutlery in.* ○ *I'm afraid I can't drink coffee with milk in.* ○ *She opened the bedroom door and went in.* ○ *The children were playing by the river when one of them slipped and fell in.* ○ *The door opened and in walked my father.* **2** (of people) at home or at a place of work: *Nobody was in when we called.* ○ *She's usually in by seven o'clock.* ○ *I'm afraid the manager isn't in today.* Cf OUT 2. **3** (of trains, buses, etc) at the station or terminus: *The train was in when we got to the station.* ○ *It's due in* (ie It should arrive) *at 6 o'clock.* **4** (of farm animals or crops) brought to the farm from the fields: *The cows will be in for milking soon.* ○ *We need help to get the wheat in.* **5** (of the tide) at or towards its highest point on land: *It's one o'clock. The tide must be in.* ○ *Is the tide coming in or going out?* ○ (*fig*) *My luck's in — I won a new car in a raffle.* **6** (of letters, cards, etc) delivered to the destination; received: *Applications must be in by 30 April.* ○ *Entries should be in on Monday morning.* **7** fashionable; popular: *Miniskirts are (coming) in again.* **8** (of fruit, fish, etc) on sale or obtainable: *Strawberries are never in for long.* ○ *Do you have any fresh salmon in at the moment?* **9** elected to office: *Labour came in after the war.* ○ *The club president has been in since 1979.* **10** (*sport*) (**a**) (in cricket, baseball, etc) batting: *England were in first.* ○ *He had only been in for 10 minutes when Jones bowled him out.* (**b**) (in tennis, badminton, etc) (of a ball, etc) having landed inside the line: *Her service was in.* (**c**) (of the ball in football, hockey, etc) between and behind the goalposts: *It's in — we've got a goal!* Cf OUT 16. **11** (of a coal or wood fire) burning: *The fire was still in when we got home.* **12** (idm) **be in for sth** (*infml*) (**a**) be about to experience (esp sth unpleasant): *He's in for a nasty shock/surprise!* ○ *I'm afraid we're in for a storm.* (**b**) having agreed to take part in sth: *Are you in for this game of whist?* ○ *I'm in for the 1 000 metres.* **be/get in on sth** (*infml*) participate in sth; have a share or knowledge of sth: *I'd like to be in on the scheme.* ○ *Are you in on her secret?* **be (well) ˈin with sb** (*infml*) be (very) friendly with sb (and likely to benefit from the friendship): *He's well in with the boss.* **have (got) it ˈin for sb** (*infml*) want to take revenge on sb; bear ill will towards sb: *That teacher has always had it in for me.* **ˌin and ˈout (of sth)** sometimes in and sometimes out (of a place): *He's been in and out of hospital* (ie often ill and in hospital) *all year.*

▷ **in-** (forming compound *ns*) **1** (*infml*) popular and fashionable: *It's the in-thing to do at the moment.* ○ *the in-place to go.* **2** shared by or appealing to a small group: *an in-joke.*

□ **ˈin-tray** *n* tray for holding letters, etc that are waiting to be read or answered. Cf OUT-TRAY (OUT).

in[2] /ɪn/ *prep* (For special uses with many *ns* and *vs*, eg *in place, in memory of, end in sth,* see the *n* and *v* entries.) **1** (indicating place) (**a**) at a point within the area or volume of (sth): *the highest mountain in the world* ○ *a country in Africa* ○ *She lives in a small village in France.* ○ *the biggest shop in town* ○ *islands in the Pacific Ocean* ○ *children playing in the street* ○ *not a cloud in the sky* ○ *swimming in the pool* ○ *standing in the corner of a room* (Cf *standing at the corner of the street*) ○ *It's in a drawer.* ○ *I read about it in the newspaper.* ○ *Can you see the dog in the picture?* (**b**) within the shape of (sth); enclosed by: *lying in bed* (Cf *sitting on the bed*) ○ *sitting in a chair,* ie an armchair ○ *Leave the key in the lock.* ○ *a cigarette in her mouth* ○ *What have you got in your hand/pocket?* **2** (indicating movement) into (sth): *He dipped his pen in the ink.* ○ *Throw it in the fire.* ○ *She got in her car and drove off.* **3** during (a period of time): *in the twentieth century* ○ *in 1999* ○

in spring, summer, etc ○ in March (Cf on 18 March) ○ in the morning/afternoon/evening ○ It happened in the past. ⇨ Usage at TIME². **4** (**a**) after (a maximum length of time): return in a few minutes, hours, days, months, etc ○ It will be ready in a week. ○ She learnt to drive in three weeks, ie After 3 weeks she could drive. (**b**) (used after a negative or first, last, etc) during; for: I haven't seen him in years. ○ It's the first/only letter I've had in 10 days. **5** forming the whole or part of (sth); contained within: seven days in a week ○ eight pints in a gallon ○ There's a cover charge included in the total. ○ I recognize his father in him, ie His character is partly similar to his father's. **6** (indicating ratio): a slope/gradient of one in five ○ taxed at the rate of 15p in the pound ○ One in ten said they preferred their old brand of margarine. **7** wearing (clothes, colours, etc): dressed/clothed in rags ○ the man in the hat ○ the woman in white ○ in uniform, mourning, disguise, armour ○ in high-heeled shoes ○ in a silk shirt. **8** (indicating physical surroundings, circumstances, etc): go out in the rain, sun, cold, etc. **9** (indicating the state or condition of sb/sth): in order ○ in a mess ○ in good repair ○ in poor health ○ in a rage ○ in a hurry ○ in fun ○ in poverty ○ in ruins ○ in anger, ie angrily. **10** (indicating form, shape, arrangement or quantities): a novel in three parts ○ stand in groups ○ sit in rows ○ her hair in a pony-tail ○ curtains hanging in folds ○ Tourists queue in (their) thousands to see the tomb. **11** (indicating the medium, means, material, etc): speak in English ○ write a message in code ○ written in biro, ink, pencil, etc ○ printed in italics, capitals, etc ○ say it in a few words ○ speak in a loud voice ○ pay in cash (Cf by cheque). **12** (used to introduce the name of a particular person): We have lost a first-rate teacher in Jim. ○ You've got a real trouble-maker in Wilkins. ○ You will always find a good friend in me, ie I will always be a good friend to you. **13** with reference to (sth); regarding: He's behind the others in reading but a long way ahead in arithmetic. ○ lacking in courage ○ equal in strength ○ a country rich/poor in minerals ○ blind in one eye ○ three feet in length, depth, diameter, etc. **14** (indicating sb's occupation, activity, etc): in the army/navy/air force ○ in business, insurance, computers, journalism, etc ○ He's been in politics (ie a politician) all his life. ○ killed in action, ie While fighting as a soldier ○ In (ie while) attempting to save a child from drowning, she nearly lost her own life. **15** (idm) **in that** /ɪn ðət/ (never taking stress) for the reason that; because: Privatization is thought to be beneficial in that it promotes competition.

in³ /ɪn/ n (idm) **the ins and outs (of sth)** the details and complexities (of an activity or a procedure): know all the ins and outs of a problem ○ He's been here for years; he should know the ins and outs of the job by now.

in abbr (pl unchanged or **ins**) (also symb ″) inch: 4 in × (ie by) 2 in (4 × 2) ○ He is 6ft 2 in (tall). Cf FT, YD.

in-¹ (also **im-**) pref **1** (with vs forming ns and vs) in; on: intake ○ imprint. **2** (with ns forming vs) put into a certain state or condition: inflame ○ imperil.

in-² (also **il-**, **im-**, **ir-**) pref (forming adjs, advs and ns) not: infinite ○ illogical ○ immorally ○ irrelevance. ⇨ Usage at UN-.

-in /ɪn/ (forming compound ns) (becoming dated) (added to another word (usu a v) to indicate an activity in which many people participate): a ˈsit-in ○ ˈteach-ins.

inability /ˌɪnəˈbɪlətɪ/ prep [U] ~ (**to do sth**) lack of power, skill or ability; being unable: his inability to understand mathematics.

in absentia /ˌɪn æbˈsentɪə/ adv when absent: He was found guilty in absentia, ie although he was not present at the trial.

inaccessible /ˌɪnækˈsesəbl/ adj ~ (**to sb**) very difficult or impossible to reach, approach, or be contacted (by sb); not accessible: an inaccessible mountain retreat ○ His busy schedule made him completely inaccessible to his students. ○ (fig) philosophical theories that are inaccessible to (ie cannot be understood by) ordinary people. ▷ **inaccessibility** /ˌɪnækˌsesəˈbɪlətɪ/ n [U]. **inaccessibly** /ˌɪnækˈsesəblɪ/ adv.

inaccurate /ɪnˈækjərət/ adj having errors; not correct or accurate: an inaccurate report, statement, description, etc.
▷ **inaccuracy** /ɪnˈækjərəsɪ/ n (**a**) [U] being inaccurate: an unacceptable level of inaccuracy. (**b**) [C] inaccurate statement; mistake or error: There are so many inaccuracies in this report that it will have to be written again.
inaccurately adv.

inaction /ɪnˈækʃn/ n [U] lack of action; doing nothing; idleness.

inactive /ɪnˈæktɪv/ adj **1** not (physically) active; idle: If you weren't so inactive you wouldn't be so fat! ○ Some animals are inactive during the daytime. **2** not working or operating any more; not in use: an inactive machine. **3** not participating fully (in a club, etc): inactive members of the music society. ▷ **inactivity** /ˌɪnækˈtɪvətɪ/ n [U]: A holiday need not mean inactivity.

inadequate /ɪnˈædɪkwət/ adj **1** not sufficient or enough; not good enough for a particular purpose: The safety precautions are totally inadequate. ○ inadequate supplies, income, preparation. **2** not sufficiently able or confident to deal with a difficult situation: feel inadequate when faced by a difficult problem.
▷ **inadequacy** /ɪnˈædɪkwəsɪ/ n **1** [C, U] (instance or example of) being inadequate: the inadequacy of our resources ○ realize one's personal inadequacy. **2** [C] fault or failing; weakness: the inadequacies of the present voting system.
inadequately /ɪnˈædɪkwətlɪ/ adv.

inadmissible /ˌɪnədˈmɪsəbl/ adj that cannot be allowed or admitted, esp in a court of law: inadmissible evidence. ▷ **inadmissibility** /ˌɪnədˌmɪsəˈbɪlətɪ/ n [U]. **inadmissibly** /ˌɪnədˈmɪsəblɪ/ adv.

inadvertent /ˌɪnədˈvɜːtənt/ adj (of actions) done without thinking or not deliberately: an inadvertent slip, omission, etc.
▷ **inadvertence** n [U].
inadvertently adv by accident; unintentionally: She inadvertently telephoned the wrong person.

inadvisable /ˌɪnədˈvaɪzəbl/ adj [usu pred] unwise; not sensible: It is inadvisable to have too much sugar in your diet. ▷ **inadvisability** /ˌɪnədˌvaɪzəˈbɪlətɪ/ n [U].

inalienable /ɪnˈeɪlɪənəbl/ adj [usu attrib] (fml) that cannot be taken away: inalienable rights.

inane /ɪˈneɪn/ adj without meaning; silly or stupid: an inane remark, question, etc ○ inane conversation.
▷ **inanely** adv: They grinned inanely.
inanity /ɪˈnænətɪ/ n (**a**) [U] being inane. (**b**) [C] inane remark or act.

inanimate /ɪnˈænɪmət/ adj **1** not alive, esp in the way that humans and animals are: A rock is an inanimate object. **2** lacking energy and vitality; dull: inanimate conversation.

inanition /ˌɪnəˈnɪʃn/ n [U] (fml) feeling of emptiness and tiredness, esp from lack of food.

inapplicable /ɪnˈæplɪkəbl, also ˌɪnəˈplɪkəbl/ adj ~ (**to sb/sth**) that is not relevant or cannot be applied: The rules seem to be inapplicable to this situation. ▷ **inapplicability** /ɪnˌæplɪkəˈbɪlətɪ, also ˌɪnəˌplɪkəˈbɪlətɪ/ n [U]. **inapplicably** /ɪnˈæplɪkəblɪ, also ˌɪnəˈplɪkəblɪ/ adv.

inappropriate /ˌɪnəˈprəʊprɪət/ adj ~ (**to/for sb/sth**) not suitable or appropriate (for sb/sth): an inappropriate comment, name, moment ○ clothes inappropriate to the occasion ○ It seems inappropriate for us to intervene at this stage. ▷ **inappropriately** adv: inappropriately dressed for the funeral. **inappropriateness** n [U].

inapt /ɪnˈæpt/ adj not relevant, appropriate or useful: an inapt remark, question, translation.
▷ **inaptitude** /ɪnˈæptɪtjuːd; US -tuːd/ n [U] ~ (**for sth**) lack of ability or suitability (for sth).
inaptness n [U] being inapt.

inarticulate /ˌɪnɑːˈtɪkjʊlət/ adj **1** unable to express one's words, ideas or feelings clearly: a clever but inarticulate mathematician. **2** not clearly or well expressed: an inarticulate speech, essay, sound ○ speaking in an inarticulate mumble. **3** not expressed as spoken words: Her actions were an inarticulate cry for help. ▷ **inarticulately** adv. **inarticulateness** n [U].

inartistic /ˌɪnɑːˈtɪstɪk/ adj not having or appreciating skill in art. ▷ **inartistically** adv.

inasmuch as /ˌɪnəzˈmʌtʃ əz/ conj (fml) since; because; to the extent that: He is a Dane inasmuch as he was born in Denmark, but he became a British citizen at the age of 30.

inattention /ˌɪnəˈtenʃn/ n [U] ~ (**to sb/sth**) lack of attention; neglect: work marred by inattention to detail.
▷ **inattentive** /ˌɪnəˈtentɪv/ adj ~ (**to sb/sth**) not paying attention (to sb/sth); not attentive: inattentive to the needs of others. **inattentively** adv. **inattentiveness** n [U].

inaudible /ɪnˈɔːdəbl/ adj not loud enough to be heard; not audible: speak in an almost inaudible voice. ▷ **inaudibility** /ɪnˌɔːdəˈbɪlətɪ/ n [U]. **inaudibly** /ɪnˈɔːdəblɪ/ adv.

inaugural /ɪˈnɔːgjʊrəl/ adj [attrib] of or for an inauguration: an inaugural speech, lecture, meeting, etc.

inaugurate /ɪˈnɔːgjʊreɪt/ v **1** [Tn, Cn·n/a] ~ **sb** (**as sth**) introduce (a new public official or leader) at a special ceremony: inaugurate the President ○ He will be inaugurated as president in January. **2** [Tn] mark the beginning of (an organization or undertaking) or open (a building, an exhibition, etc) with a special ceremony: inaugurate a conference, an organization, a scheme, etc ○ The city library was inaugurated by the mayor. **3** [Tn] be the beginning of (sth); introduce: Concorde inaugurated a new era in aeroplane travel.
▷ **inauguration** /ɪˌnɔːgjʊˈreɪʃn/ n [C, U] (act of) inaugurating or being inaugurated: the President's inauguration ○ [attrib] the President's inauguration speech.
inaugurator n person who inaugurates sth.

inauspicious /ˌɪnɔːˈspɪʃəs/ adj having signs which show that future success is unlikely; not favourable: an inauspicious occasion, event, meeting, etc. ▷ **inauspiciously** adv. **inauspiciousness** n [U].

inboard /ˈɪnbɔːd/ adj, adv (situated) within the sides of or towards the centre of a boat or aircraft: an inboard motor.

inborn /ˌɪnˈbɔːn/ adj existing in a person or animal from birth; natural; innate: an ˌinborn ˌtalent for ˈmusic.

inbred /ˌɪnˈbred/ adj **1** natural; innate: an ˌinbred ˌsense of ˈduty. **2** produced by inbreeding: The long nose on these dogs is an ˌinbred characteˈristic.
▷ **inbreeding** /ˈɪnbriːdɪŋ/ n [U] breeding among closely related people or animals: deformities caused by inbreeding.

in-built /ˌɪnˈbɪlt/ adj = BUILT-IN (BUILD).

Inc (also **inc**) /ɪŋk/ abbr (US) Incorporated: Manhattan Drugstores Inc. Cf LTD, PLC.

Inca /ˈɪŋkə/ n member of a S American people who once inhabited the area of modern Peru. They had a highly developed civilization and were skilled builders and engineers. At its height their empire stretched over large parts of western S America, but it was weakened in the early 16th century by civil war, and in 1532 the Incas were defeated by the invading Spanish.

incalculable /ɪnˈkælkjʊləbl/ adj **1** too large or great to be calculated: do incalculable harm to sb's reputation. **2** that cannot be predicted; uncertain: a person of incalculable moods. ▷ **incalculably** /-əblɪ/ adv.

in camera /ˌɪn ˈkæmərə/ adv (law) without members of the public being present; in secret: The case was tried in camera.

incandescent /ˌɪnkænˈdesnt/ adj glowing or shining when heated. ▷ **incandescence** /-sns/ n [U].
□ **ˌincanˌdescent ˈlamp** electric lamp with a heated filament that gives off white light.

incantation /ˌɪnkænˈteɪʃn/ n (**a**) [C] series of words used as a magic spell or charm: chant incantations to the evil spirits. (**b**) [U] saying or use of these.

incapable /ɪnˈkeɪpəbl/ *adj* **1** [pred] ~ **of sth/doing sth** not able to do sth: *The children seem to be totally incapable of working quietly by themselves.* ○ *incapable of telling a lie*, ie too honest to do so ○ *incapable of sympathy.* **2** unable to do anything well; helpless; not capable: *As a lawyer she's totally incapable.* **3** (idm) **drunk and incapable** ⇨ DRUNK². ▷ **incapability** /ɪnˌkeɪpəˈbɪlətɪ/ *n* [U]. **incapably** *adv.*

incapacitate /ˌɪnkəˈpæsɪteɪt/ *v* [Tn, Tn·pr] ~ **sb (for sth/from doing sth)** **1** make sb unable (to do sth); weaken or disable sb: *be incapacitated by an accident* ○ *Poor health incapacitated him for work/from working all his life.* **2** deprive sb of the legal ability (to do sth); disqualify sb.

incapacity /ˌɪnkəˈpæsətɪ/ *n* [U] ~ **(to do sth)**; ~ **(for sth/doing sth)** lack of ability and necessary strength (to do sth); weakness or inability: *his increasing incapacity for work* ○ *society's incapacity to deal with the growing numbers of the elderly.*

incarcerate /ɪnˈkɑːsəreɪt/ *v* [Tn, Tn·pr] ~ **sb (in sth)** (*fml*) put sb in prison: *He was incarcerated (in the castle dungeon) for years.* ▷ **incarceration** /ɪnˌkɑːsəˈreɪʃn/ *n* [U].

incarnate /ɪnˈkɑːneɪt/ *adj* (following *ns*) **1** in the physical form of a human being: *The guards were sadistic beasts and their leader was the devil incarnate.* **2** (of ideas, qualities, etc) appearing in a human form: *virtue incarnate.*

▷ **incarnate** /ˈɪnkɑːneɪt/ *v* [Tn] (*fml*) **1** give human form to (sth). **2** put (an idea, a quality, etc) into real or physical form. **3** (of a person) be a living form of (a quality): *He incarnates all the qualities of a successful manager.*

incarnation /ˌɪnkɑːˈneɪʃn/ *n* **1** [C] person that prominently displays a particular quality: *She's the very incarnation of goodness.* **2** [C, U] (instance of) being alive in human form: *the nine incarnations of Vishnu* ○ *He believed he had been a prince in a previous incarnation.* **3 the Incarnation** [sing] (in Christianity) the act of God becoming a man in Jesus.

incautious /ɪnˈkɔːʃəs/ *adj* acting or done without enough care or thought; not cautious; rash. ▷ **incautiously** *adv.*

incendiary /ɪnˈsendɪərɪ; *US* -dɪerɪ/ *adj* **1** designed to set buildings, etc on fire: *an incendiary bomb, device, attack.* **2** tending to create public disturbances or violence: *an incendiary speech.*

▷ **incendiary** *n* bomb that causes a fire.

incense¹ /ˈɪnsens/ *n* [U] (smoke from a) substance that produces a pleasant smell when burnt, used esp in religious ceremonies.

incense² /ɪnˈsens/ *v* [Tn esp passive] make (sb) very angry: *The decision to reduce pay levels incensed the work-force.* ○ *He felt deeply incensed by/at the way he had been treated.*

incentive /ɪnˈsentɪv/ *n* [C, U] ~ **(to do sth)** thing that encourages sb to do sth; stimulus: *the offer of cash incentives* ○ *an incentive to work harder* ○ *They don't try very hard, but then there's no incentive.* ○ [attrib] *an incentive scheme.*

inception /ɪnˈsepʃn/ *n* [sing] (*fml*) start or beginning of sth: *He had been director of the project since its inception.*

incessant /ɪnˈsesnt/ *adj* not stopping; continual: *a week of almost incessant rain* ○ *an incessant stream of visitors.* ▷ **incessantly** *adv*: *complain incessantly.*

incest /ˈɪnsest/ *n* [U] sexual intercourse between people who are too closely related to marry, eg brother and sister or father and daughter.

▷ **incestuous** /ɪnˈsestjʊəs; *US* -tʃʊəs/ *adj* **1** involving incest; guilty of incest: *an incestuous relationship.* **2** (*derog*) of a group of people that have close relationships with one another and do not include people outside their group: *Theatre people are a rather incestuous group, I find.* **incestuously** *adv.*

inch /ɪntʃ/ *n* **1** (*abbr* **in**) measure of length equal to 2.54 cm or one twelfth of a foot: *a pile of books 12 inches high.* ⇨ App 9, 10. **2** small amount or distance: *He escaped death by an inch.* ○ *We argued for an hour but he wouldn't budge* (ie change his attitude or ideas) *an inch.* **3** amount of rain or snow that would cover a surface one inch deep: *Three inches of rain fell in Manchester last night.* **4** (idm) **by inches** only just: *The car missed me by inches.* **every inch (a)** the whole area: *The police examined every inch of the house for clues.* **(b)** completely; entirely: *He looked every inch a gentleman.* **ˌgive sb an ˈinch (and he'll ˌtake a ˈmile/ˈyard)** (*saying*) if you surrender a little to sb, he will increase his demands greatly. **ˌinch by ˈinch** very slowly and in small steps; by degrees: *They climbed the steep mountain inch by inch.* **within an inch of sth/doing sth** very close to sth/doing sth: *He came within an inch of being killed.*

inch² /ɪntʃ/ *v* [I, Ipr, Ip, Tn·pr, Tn·p] ~ **(sth) forward, past, through etc (sth)** move (sth) slowly and carefully in the specified direction: *inch the car forward* ○ *he inched (his way) through the narrow passage.*

inchoate /ɪnˈkəʊeɪt, ˈɪnkəʊeɪt/ *adj* (*fml*) just begun and therefore not fully formed or developed: *inchoate ideas, attitudes, wishes, etc.*

incidence /ˈɪnsɪdəns/ *n* [sing] **1** ~ **of sth** extent to which sth happens or has an effect: *This area has a high incidence of crime, disease, unemployment, etc.* **2** way in which a ray of light strikes a surface: *the angle of incidence.*

incident¹ /ˈɪnsɪdənt/ *n* **1** event or happening, often of minor importance: *He could remember every trivial incident in great detail.* **2** hostile military activity between countries, opposing forces, etc: *border incidents.* **3** [C, U] public disturbance, accident or violence: *The demonstration proceeded without incident.* ⇨ Usage at OCCURRENCE.

incident² /ˈɪnsɪdənt/ *adj* [pred] ~ **to/upon sb/sth** (*fml*) forming a natural or expected part of sb/sth; naturally connected with sb/sth: *the risks incident to the life of a test pilot* ○ *responsibilities incident upon one as a parent.*

incidental /ˌɪnsɪˈdentl/ *adj* **1** small and relatively unimportant; minor: *incidental expenses.* **2** accompanying, but not a major part of sth; supplementary: *incidental music for a play.* **3** [pred] ~ **(to sth)** liable to occur because of sth or in connection with sth: *the risks that are incidental to exploration* ○ *additional responsibilities that are incidental to the job.* **4** occurring by chance in connection with sth else.

▷ **incidentally** /-tlɪ/ *adv* **1** (used to introduce sth additional that the speaker has just thought of) by the way: *Some people, and incidentally that includes Arthur, just won't look after themselves properly.* **2** in an incidental way.

incinerate /ɪnˈsɪnəreɪt/ *v* [Tn] destroy (sth) completely by burning; burn to ashes.

▷ **incineration** /ɪnˌsɪnəˈreɪʃn/ *n* [U].

incinerator /ɪnˈsɪnəreɪtə(r)/ *n* furnace or enclosed container for burning rubbish, etc.

incipient /ɪnˈsɪpɪənt/ *adj* (*fml*) in its early stages; beginning to happen: *signs of incipient tooth decay.*

incise /ɪnˈsaɪz/ *v* [Tn] **(a)** make a cut in (a surface). **(b)** carve designs into (a surface); engrave.

▷ **incision** /ɪnˈsɪʒn/ *n* [C, U] (act or instance of) cutting, esp by a surgeon into the flesh for an operation: *make a deep incision in the thigh.*

incisive /ɪnˈsaɪsɪv/ *adj* clear and precise; direct or sharp: *incisive comments, criticism, advice, etc* ○ *an incisive mind.* ▷ **incisively** *adv.* **incisiveness** *n* [U].

incisor /ɪnˈsaɪzə(r)/ *n* each of the eight sharp cutting teeth at the front of the mouth. ⇨ illus at TOOTH.

incite /ɪnˈsaɪt/ *v* **1** [Tn·pr, Dn·t] ~ **sb (to sth)** urge or persuade sb to do sth by making him very angry or excited: *incite the workers to violence/against the government* ○ *The captain was accused of inciting other officers to mutiny.* **2** [Tn] create or cause (sth): *incite a riot/breach of the peace.*

▷ **incitement** *n* [U, C] ~ **(to sth)** action that incites certain behaviour: *incitement to defy authority.*

incivility /ˌɪnsɪˈvɪlətɪ/ *n* (*fml*) **1** [U] lack of politeness. Cf UNCIVIL. **2** [C] impolite act or remark.

incl *abbr* including; inclusive: *total £29.53 incl tax.*

inclement /ɪnˈklemənt/ *adj* (*fml*) cold and stormy; bad: *inclement weather.* ▷ **inclemency** /-ənsɪ/ *n* [U].

inclination /ˌɪŋklɪˈneɪʃn/ *n* **1** [C, U] ~ **(to/for/towards sth)**; ~ **(to do sth)** feeling that makes sb want to behave in a particular way; disposition: *I have little inclination to listen to you all evening.* ○ *She is not free to follow her own inclination in the matter of marriage.* **2** [C] ~ **to sth**; ~ **to be/do sth** event that regularly happens; tendency: *He has an inclination to stoutness/to be fat.* ○ *The car has an inclination to stall on cold mornings.* **3 (a)** [U] degree of sloping; slant. **(b)** [C] sloping surface; slope: *a small inclination just beyond the trees.* **4** [C usu *sing*] bending or bowing movement: *an inclination of his head.*

incline¹ /ɪnˈklaɪn/ *v* **1** [Ipr] ~ **towards sth** lean or slope in the direction of sth: *The land inclines towards the shore.* **2** [Tn] bend (usu a part of the body) forward: *She inclined her head in prayer.* **3** (*fml*) **(a)** [Tn·pr, Cn·t] ~ **sb towards sth** persuade sb to do sth; cause a certain tendency in sb; influence sb: *His love of languages inclined him towards a career as a translator.* ○ *His sincerity inclines me to trust him.* **(b)** [Ipr] ~ **to/towards sth** have a physical or mental tendency towards sth: *He inclines to laziness.* ○ *She inclines towards depression.*

▷ **inclined** *adj* [pred] **1** ~ **(to do sth)** wanting to behave in a particular way; disposed: *I'm inclined to trust him.* ○ *We can go for a walk, if you feel so inclined.* **2** ~ **to do sth** having a tendency to be/do sth; likely to be/do sth: *He's inclined to be lazy.* ○ *The car is inclined to stall when it's cold outside.* **3** ~ **to do sth** (used to make what is said sound less strong) holding a particular opinion: *I'm inclined to believe he's innocent.* ○ *Generally speaking, I'm inclined to agree with you.* **4** having a natural ability in a specified subject: *Louise is very musically inclined.*

□ **inˌclined ˈplane** (*mathematics*) plane whose angle to the horizontal is less than 90°; upward or downward-sloping surface.

incline² /ˈɪnklaɪn/ *n* sloping surface; slope: *a gentle/steep incline.*

inclinometer /ˌɪŋklɪˈnɒmɪtə(r)/ *n* **1** instrument for measuring the angle that the earth's magnetic field makes with the horizon. **2** instrument for measuring the angle that an aircraft or a ship makes with the horizontal (eg when pitching).

inclose = ENCLOSE.

inclosure = ENCLOSURE.

include /ɪnˈkluːd/ *v* **1** [Tn, Tg] have (sb/sth) as part of a whole: *The conference delegates included representatives from abroad.* ○ *The tour included a visit to the Science Museum.* ○ *Does the price include VAT?* ○ *Your duties include checking the post and distributing it.* **2** [Tn, Tn·pr] ~ **sb/sth (in/among sth)** make sb/sth part of a larger group or set: *include an article (in a newspaper)* ○ *We all went, me/myself included*, ie I was among those who went. ○ *Detailed instructions are included in the booklet.*

▷ **including** /ɪnˈkluːdɪŋ/ *prep* having (sb/sth) as a part: *£57.50, including postage and packing* ○ *The band played many songs, including some of my favourites.* ○ *Sales up to and including last month amounted to £10 000.*

inclusion /ɪnˈkluːʒn/ *n* [U] ~ **(in sth)** including or being included: *the inclusion of the clause in the contract.*

inclusive /ɪnˈkluːsɪv/ *adj* **1** ~ **(of sth)** including sth; including much or all: *The price is £800, inclusive of tax.* ○ *inclusive terms*, ie with no extra charges, eg at a hotel. **2** (following *ns*) including the limits stated: *from Monday to Friday inclusive* ○ *pages 7 to 26 inclusive.* ▷ **inclusively** *adv.*

incognito /ˌɪŋkɒgˈniːtəʊ; *US* ɪŋˈkɒgnətəʊ/ *adj* [pred], *adv* with one's true identity hidden; in disguise: *He didn't want to be recognized, so he travelled incognito.*

▷ **incognito** *n* (*pl* ~**s**) pretended identity.

incoherent /ˌɪŋkəʊˈhɪərənt/ *adj* **1** not clear or

logical: *an incoherent explanation.* **2** not expressed clearly: *talk incoherent gibberish.* ▷ **incoherence** /-əns/ *n* [U]. **incoherently** *adv.* Cf COHERENT (COHERE).

incombustible /ˌɪŋkəmˈbʌstəbl/ *adj* (*fml*) that cannot be burnt.

income /ˈɪŋkʌm/ *n* [C, U] money received over a certain period, esp as payment for work or as interest on investments: *a family with two incomes*, eg when the husband and wife both do paid work ○ *Tax is payable on all income over £2 000.* ○ *high/low income groups* ○ *a useful source of income for the charity* ○ [attrib] *the government's incomes policy*, eg for limiting increases in income.
□ ˈ**income tax** tax payable according to the level of one's income: *reduce the standard rate of income tax.* Cf CAPITAL LEVY (CAPITAL²), article at TAX.

NOTE ON USAGE: **1 Income** is the most general word for money we receive from work, investments, etc. It can be **earned** or **unearned income. 2 Pay** is a general word for money we regularly receive from an employer for work done. **Pay-day** is the day of the week/month when this money is received. **3 Wages** are paid weekly (sometimes daily) and usually in cash. They are based on an hourly, daily or weekly rate or on a certain amount of work done. **Wage-earners** are usually manual workers: *A postman's wages are £180 per week.* **4** A **salary** is paid monthly, often directly into a bank account. The amount of **salary** received is quoted at a yearly rate: *a salary of £12 000 a year/per annum.* Professional people and those who work in offices receive a **salary:** *The company is offering a salary of £20 000 per annum.* **5** A **fee** is a payment to a lawyer, doctor, etc for professional services: *I thought the accountant's fee rather high.*

incoming /ˈɪnkʌmɪŋ/ *adj* [attrib] **1** coming in: *the incoming tide* ○ *incoming* (ie enemy) *artillery fire* ○ *incoming telephone calls* ○ *incoming passengers.* **2** recently elected or appointed; new or succeeding: *the incoming president.*

incommensurable /ˌɪŋkəˈmenʃərəbl/ *adj* [usu pred] (also **incommensurate**) ~ **(with sb/sth)** (*fml*) that cannot be judged or measured by the same standard (as sb/sth).

incommensurate /ˌɪŋkəˈmenʃərət/ *adj* [usu pred] (*fml*) **1** ~ **(to/with sth)** not in proportion to sth; inadequate: *His abilities are incommensurate to the task.* **2** = INCOMMENSURABLE.

incommode /ˌɪŋkəˈməʊd/ *v* [Tn] (*fml*) inconvenience or trouble (sb).
▷ **incommodious** /ˌɪŋkəˈməʊdɪəs/ *adj* (*fml*) uncomfortable, usu because too small; inconvenient. **incommodiously** *adv.*

incommunicable /ˌɪŋkəˈmju:nɪkəbl/ *adj* that cannot be communicated.

incommunicado /ˌɪŋkəˌmju:nɪˈkɑ:dəʊ/ *adj* [pred], *adv* without being allowed to communicate with other people: *The prisoner was held incommunicado.*

incomparable /ɪnˈkɒmprəbl/ *adj* too good, great, etc to have an equal; beyond comparison: *incomparable singing, hospitality, food.* ▷ **incomparability** /ɪnˌkɒmpərəˈbɪlətɪ/ *n* [U]. **incomparably** /ɪnˈkɒmprəblɪ/ *adv.*

incompatible /ˌɪŋkəmˈpætəbl/ *adj* **1** ~ **(with sb)** not able to live or work happily with sb: *temperamentally, sexually, socially incompatible* ○ *I've never seen such an incompatible couple.* **2** ~ **(with sth)** not consistent or in logical agreement with sth: *behaviour that is totally incompatible with the aims of the society.* ▷ **incompatibility** /ˌɪŋkəmˌpætəˈbɪlətɪ/ *n* [U, C].

incompetent /ɪnˈkɒmpɪtənt/ *adj* **1** not having or showing the necessary skills to do sth successfully: *I suppose my application has been lost by some incompetent bureaucrat.* ○ *criticized for his incompetent handling of the problem.* **2** not (esp legally) qualified: *incompetent to judge.*
▷ **incompetence** /-əns/ *n* [U] lack of skill or ability to do a task successfully: *He was dismissed for incompetence.*
incompetent *n* incompetent person.
incompetently *adv.*

incomplete /ˌɪŋkəmˈpli:t/ *adj* not having all its parts; not complete: *an incomplete set of results.* ▷ **incompletely** *adv.* **incompleteness** *n* [U].

incomprehensible /ɪnˌkɒmprɪˈhensəbl/ *adj* that cannot be understood; not comprehensible: *technical expressions that are incomprehensible to ordinary people.* ▷ **incomprehensibility** /ɪnˌkɒmprɪˌhensəˈbɪlətɪ/ *n* [U]. **incomprehensibly** /-səblɪ/ *adv.*

incomprehension /ɪnˌkɒmprɪˈhenʃn/ *n* [U] failure to understand sth: *Her explanations were met with blank incomprehension.*

incompressible /ˌɪŋkəmˈpresəbl/ *adj* that cannot be compressed; unyielding: *incompressible gases/liquids.*

inconceivable /ˌɪŋkənˈsi:vəbl/ *adj* **1** (*infml*) very difficult to believe: *It seems inconceivable that the accident could have happened so quickly.* **2** that cannot be imagined; not conceivable: *the inconceivable vastness of space.*
▷ **inconceivably** *adv* in a way that is very difficult to believe or understand: *The task proved inconceivably more difficult than we had imagined.*

inconclusive /ˌɪŋkənˈklu:sɪv/ *adj* not leading to a definite decision, conclusion or result: *inconclusive arguments, discussions, evidence, etc.*
▷ **inconclusively** *adv.* **inconclusiveness** *n* [U].

incongruous /ɪnˈkɒŋgrʊəs/ *adj* strange because not in harmony with the surrounding features; out of place: *slow traditional methods that seem rather incongruous in this modern technical age.*
▷ **incongruity** /ˌɪŋkɒŋˈgru:ətɪ/ *n* **1** [U] state of being incongruous: *the apparent incongruity of a scientist having a simple religious faith.* **2** [C] something that is incongruous.
incongruously *adv.*

inconsequent /ɪnˈkɒnsɪkwənt/ *adj* **1** not following logically. **2** = INCONSEQUENTIAL. ▷ **inconsequence** /ɪnˈkɒnsɪkwəns/ *n* [U]. **inconsequently** *adv.*

inconsequential /ɪnˌkɒnsɪˈkwenʃl/ *adj* (also **inconsequent**) trivial or irrelevant; not important: *inconsequential details, events, questions.* ▷ **inconsequentially** /-ʃəlɪ/ *adv.*

inconsiderable /ˌɪŋkənˈsɪdrəbl/ *adj* small in size or value; not worth considering: *a not inconsiderable sum of money*, ie a large sum of money.

inconsiderate /ˌɪŋkənˈsɪdərət/ *adj* not caring about the feelings of other people; thoughtless; not considerate: *How could you have been so inconsiderate?* ○ *inconsiderate behaviour, remarks.*
▷ **inconsiderately** *adv.* **inconsiderateness** *n* [U].

inconsistent /ˌɪnkənˈsɪstənt/ *adj* **1** [usu pred] ~ **(with sth)** not in harmony (with sth); containing parts that do not agree with one another: *Such behaviour is inconsistent with her high-minded principles.* ○ *His account of the events was inconsistent.* **2** not staying the same; changeable: *He is inconsistent in his loyalty: sometimes he supports us, sometimes he's against us.*
▷ **inconsistency** /-ənsɪ/ *n* **(a)** [U] quality of being inconsistent: *inconsistency in the standard of his work.* **(b)** [C] instance of this: *She noticed several minor inconsistencies in his argument.*
inconsistently *adv.*

inconsolable /ˌɪŋkənˈsəʊləbl/ *adj* that cannot be comforted: *inconsolable grief* ○ *The children were inconsolable when their father died.* ▷ **inconsolably** /-əblɪ/ *adv*: *weep inconsolably.*

inconspicuous /ˌɪŋkənˈspɪkjʊəs/ *adj* not very noticeable or obvious; not conspicuous: *a small inconspicuous crack in the vase* ○ *The newcomer tried to make herself as inconspicuous as possible*, ie tried to avoid attention. ▷ **inconspicuously** *adv.* **inconspicuousness** *n* [U].

inconstant /ɪnˈkɒnstənt/ *adj* (*fml*) **1** (of people) having feelings and intentions that change often; not faithful: *an inconstant lover.* **2** having a quantity or value that changes; not fixed. ▷ **inconstancy** /-ənsɪ/ *n* [U, C].

incontestable /ˌɪŋkənˈtestəbl/ *adj* that cannot be disputed or disagreed with: *an incontestable fact.* ▷ **incontestably** /-əblɪ/ *adv.*

incontinent /ɪnˈkɒntɪnənt/ *adj* **1** unable to control the bladder or bowels in passing waste matter from the body: *People often become incontinent when they get very old.* **2** lacking self-control, esp in sexual matters. ▷ **incontinence** /-əns/ *n* [U].

incontrovertible /ˌɪŋkɒntrəˈvɜ:təbl/ *adj* so obvious and certain that it cannot be disputed or denied: *We have incontrovertible evidence.* ▷ **incontrovertibility** /ɪnˌkɒntrəvɜ:təˈbɪlətɪ/ *n* [U]. **incontrovertibly** /ˌɪŋkɒntrəˈvɜ:təblɪ/ *adv*: *incontrovertibly true.*

inconvenience /ˌɪŋkənˈvi:nɪəns/ *n* **(a)** [U] trouble, difficulty or discomfort: *He apologized for the inconvenience he had caused.* ○ *put sb to, suffer great inconvenience.* **(b)** [C] person or thing that causes inconvenience: *Having to change trains is a small inconvenience.* ○ *put up with slight inconveniences.*
▷ **inconvenience** *v* [Tn] cause inconvenience to (sb/sth): *We were greatly inconvenienced by the postal delays.*

inconvenient /ˌɪŋkənˈvi:nɪənt/ *adj* causing trouble, difficulty or discomfort; awkward: *They arrived at an inconvenient time — we had just started the meal.* ○ *Living such a long way from the shops can be very inconvenient.* ▷ **inconveniently** *adv.*

incorporate /ɪnˈkɔ:pəreɪt/ *v* **1 (a)** [Tn, Tn·pr] ~ **sth (in/into sth)** make sth part of a whole; include: *Many of your suggestions have been incorporated in the new plan.* **(b)** [Tn] have (sth) as part of a whole: *The new car design incorporates all the latest safety features.* **2** [Tn] (*US*) form a legal corporation(2b): *We had to incorporate the company for tax reasons.* ○ *a company incorporated in the USA.*
▷ **incorporate** /ɪnˈkɔ:pərət/ *adj* formed into a corporation; incorporated.
incorporated /ɪnˈkɔ:pəreɪtɪd/ *adj* (*US*) (following the name of a company) (*abbr* **Inc**) formed into a legal organization: *Nelson Inc.*
incorporation /ɪnˌkɔ:pəˈreɪʃn/ *n* [U] incorporating or being incorporated.

incorporeal /ˌɪŋkɔ:ˈpɔ:rɪəl/ *adj* (*fml*) without a body or material form.

incorrect /ˌɪŋkəˈrekt/ *adj* **1** not correct or true: *an incorrect answer* ○ *incorrect conclusions.* **2** not according to accepted standards; improper: *incorrect behaviour.* ▷ **incorrectly** *adv*: *answer incorrectly.* **incorrectness** *n* [U].

incorrigible /ɪnˈkɒrɪdʒəbl; *US* -ˈkɔ:r-/ *adj* (of people or their faults) that cannot be corrected or improved: *an incorrigible liar, gambler, gossip, etc* ○ *incorrigible habits.* ▷ **incorrigibility** /ɪnˌkɒrɪdʒəˈbɪlətɪ/ *n* [U]. **incorrigibly** /ɪnˈkɒrɪdʒəblɪ/ *adv.*

incorruptible /ˌɪŋkəˈrʌptəbl/ *adj* **1** unable to be corrupted morally, eg with bribes: *Judges should be incorruptible.* **2** that cannot decay or be destroyed. ▷ **incorruptibility** /ˌɪŋkəˌrʌptəˈbɪlətɪ/ *n* [U]. **incorruptibly** /ˌɪŋkəˈrʌptəblɪ/ *adv.*

increase¹ /ɪnˈkri:s/ *v* [I, Ipr, Tn, Tn·pr] ~ **(sth) (from A) (to B)** become or make (sth) greater in number, quantity, size, etc: *The population has increased from 1.2 million 10 years ago to 1.8 million now.* ○ *The rate of inflation has increased by 2%.* ○ *increased profits* ○ *He increased his speed to overtake the lorry.*
▷ **increasingly** /ɪnˈkri:sɪŋlɪ/ *adv* more and more: *increasingly difficult, important, popular* ○ *Increasingly, people are realizing that our basic problems are not economic ones.*

increase² /ˈɪŋkri:s/ *n* **1** [C, U] ~ **(in sth)** amount by which sth increases: *Greater spending on education is expected to lead to a large increase in the number of students.* ○ *an increase of nearly 50% over/on last year* ○ *a wage increase* ○ *Some increase in working hours may soon be needed.* **2** (idm) **on the** ˈ**increase** (*infml*) increasing: *The number of burglaries in the area seems to be on the increase.*

incredible /ɪnˈkredəbl/ *adj* **1** impossible to believe: *What an incredible story!* **2** (*infml*) difficult to believe; amazing or fantastic: *He earns*

an incredible amount of money. ○ *We had an incredible* (ie extremely good) *holiday!* ○ *She's an incredible actress.*
▷ **incredibility** /ɪnˌkredəˈbɪlətɪ/ *n* [U].
incredibly /ɪnˈkredəblɪ/ *adv* **1** to a great degree; extremely or unusually: *incredibly hot weather.* **2** in a way that is difficult to believe; amazingly: *Incredibly, no one had ever thought of such a simple idea before.*

incredulous /ɪnˈkredjʊləs; *US* -dʒuːl-/ *adj* not willing or able to believe; showing disbelief: *an incredulous look, stare, gaze, etc.* ▷ **incredulity** /ˌɪŋkrɪˈdjuːlətɪ; *US* -ˈduː-/ *n* [U]: *an expression of shock and utter incredulity.* **incredulously** *adv.*

increment /ˈɪŋkrəmənt/ *n* increase, esp in money paid as a salary; added amount: *Your salary will be £12 000 a year, with annual increments of £500.* ▷ **incremental** /ˌɪŋkrəˈmentl/ *adj*: *incremental increases.* **incrementally** /-təlɪ/ *adv.*

incriminate /ɪnˈkrɪmɪneɪt/ *v* [Tn] make (sb) appear to be guilty of wrongdoing: *She refused to make a statement to the police in case she incriminated herself.* ○ *incriminating evidence.*
▷ **incrimination** /ɪnˌkrɪmɪˈneɪʃn/ *n* [U].
incriminatory /ɪnˈkrɪmɪnətrɪ, -neɪtərɪ/ *adj* tending to incriminate sb.

incrustation /ˌɪnkrʌˈsteɪʃn/ *n* **1** [U] formation of a hard outer covering; encrusting. **2** [C] hard outer covering or layer, esp one that forms gradually: *incrustations of barnacles on the hull.*

incubate /ˈɪŋkjʊbeɪt/ *v* **1** (**a**) [I, Tn] keep (eggs) warm, usu by sitting on them, until they hatch: *a bird incubating (her eggs).* (**b**) [I] (of eggs) be kept warm until ready to hatch. **2** [I, Tn] (*medical or biology*) (of bacteria, etc) develop under favourable conditions, esp heat; cause (bacteria, etc) to develop: *Some viruses incubate very rapidly.* ○ *incubate germs in a laboratory.* **3** [I, Tn] (*fig*) (cause sth to) develop slowly and patiently: *plans for revolution that had long been incubating in their minds.*
▷ **incubation** /ˌɪnkjʊˈbeɪʃn/ *n* **1** [U] hatching (of eggs): *artificial incubation*, ie hatching by artificial warmth. **2** [C] (also **incuˈbation period**) (**a**) (*medical*) period between being infected with a disease and the appearance of the first symptoms. (**b**) (*fig*) (period for) developing plans, etc.
incubator /ˈɪŋkjʊbeɪtə(r)/ *n* boxlike apparatus for hatching eggs by artificial warmth or for rearing small, weak babies (esp those born prematurely). Cf HATCHERY (HATCH[2]).

incubus /ˈɪŋkjʊbəs/ *n* (*pl* ~**es** or **-bi** /-baɪ/) (**a**) male evil spirit formerly supposed to have sex with a sleeping woman. Cf SUCCUBUS. (**b**) (*rhet*) thing (eg an approaching examination, an unpaid debt) that oppresses sb like a nightmare.

inculcate /ˈɪnkʌlkeɪt; *US* ɪnˈkʌl-/ *v* [Tn, Tn·pr] ~ **sth (in/into sb)**; ~ **sb with sth** (*fml*) fix (ideas, principles, etc) firmly in sb's mind, esp by repetition: *inculcate in young people a respect for the law* ○ *inculcate young people with a respect for the law.*

incumbent /ɪnˈkʌmbənt/ *adj* **1** [pred] ~ **on/upon sb** (*fml*) necessary as part of sb's duty: *It is incumbent upon all users of this equipment to familiarize themselves with the safety procedure.* **2** [usu attrib] holding the specified official position; current: *the incumbent president.*
▷ **incumbent** *n* person holding an official position, esp in the church: *the present incumbent of the White House*, ie the US President.
incumbency /-ənsɪ/ *n* position of an incumbent.

incur /ɪnˈkɜː(r)/ *v* (**-rr-**) [Tn] cause oneself to suffer (sth bad); bring upon oneself: *incur debts, great expense, sb's anger.*

incurable /ɪnˈkjʊərəbl/ *adj* that cannot be cured: *incurable diseases, habits.*
▷ **incurable** *n* person with an incurable disease: *a home for incurables.*
incurably /-əblɪ/ *adv*: *incurably ill, stupid, optimistic.*

incurious /ɪnˈkjʊərɪəs/ *adj* (*fml*) having no curiosity; not inquisitive.

incursion /ɪnˈkɜːʃn; *US* -ʒn/ *n* ~ **(into/on/upon sth)** (*fml*) **1** sudden attack on or invasion of a place (not usu made in order to occupy it permanently): *repel a sudden incursion of enemy troops (into/on one's territory).* **2** (*fig*) inconvenient interruption of sb's time, privacy, etc; intrusion: *I resent these incursions into/upon my leisure time.*

incurved /ˌɪnˈkɜːvd/ *adj* curved inwards; bent into a curve.

Ind *abbr* (*politics*) Independent (candidate): *Tom Lee (Ind).*

indebted /ɪnˈdetɪd/ *adj* ~ **to sb (for sth)** owing money or gratitude to sb: *be (deeply, greatly, etc) indebted to sb for his help, advice, encouragement, etc.* ▷ **indebtedness** *n* [U].

indecent /ɪnˈdiːsnt/ *adj* **1** (of behaviour, talk, etc) offending against accepted standards of decency or morality; obscene: *That short skirt of hers is positively indecent.* **2** [usu attrib] improper; undue: *leave a party in indecent haste*, ie too early or too soon to be polite. Cf DECENT.
▷ **indecency** /-nsɪ/ *n* **1** [U] being indecent; indecent behaviour: *arrested by the police for gross indecency*, eg indecent exposure. **2** [C] indecent act, gesture, expression, etc..
indecently *adv.*
□ **inˌdecent asˈsault** sexual attack on sb that does not involve sexual intercourse.
inˌdecent exˈposure crime of showing one's sexual organs in public.

indecipherable /ˌɪndɪˈsaɪfrəbl/ *adj* that cannot be deciphered: *an indecipherable code, signature, scribble, etc.*

indecision /ˌɪndɪˈsɪʒn/ *n* [U] ~ **(about sth)** state of being unable to decide; hesitation: *He stood outside the door in an agony of indecision.*

indecisive /ˌɪndɪˈsaɪsɪv/ *adj* (**a**) not final or conclusive: *an indecisive battle, answer, meeting.* (**b**) unable to make decisions; hesitating; uncertain: *He's too indecisive to make a good leader.* ▷ **indecisively** *adv.*

indecorous /ɪnˈdekərəs/ *adj* (*fml*) not in accordance with dignity, good manners or good taste: *forced to make a hasty and indecorous departure without his trousers.* ▷ **indecorously** *adv.*

indecorum /ˌɪndɪˈkɔːrəm/ *n* [U] (*fml*) improper or undignified behaviour; lack of decorum.

indeed /ɪnˈdiːd/ *adv* **1** truly; really; certainly. (**a**) (used to emphasize an affirmative reply): *'Did he complain?' 'Indeed he did.'* ○ *'Do you agree?' 'Yes indeed!'* (**b**) (intensifying an *adj*, an *adv* or a *n* in an exclamation): *That is indeed remarkable!* ○ *That is indeed a remarkable thing!* **2** (used after *very* + *adj* or *adv* to emphasize a statement, description, etc) really: *Thank you very much indeed!* ○ *I was very sad indeed to hear about it.* ○ *a very big elephant indeed.* **3** (*fml*) in fact: *I don't mind. Indeed, I am delighted to help.* ○ *I was annoyed, indeed furious, over what happened.* **4** (as a comment or response) (**a**) (expressing surprise, but not disbelief): *'I saw a ghost!' 'Indeed? Where was it?'* (**b**) (expressing disbelief and even scorn): *'A ghost indeed! I've never heard anything so ridiculous!'* (**c**) (showing interest of a critical or an ironical kind): *'When will the weather improve?' 'When, indeed!'*

indefatigable /ˌɪndɪˈfætɪgəbl/ *adj* (*fml approv*) never giving up or stopping in spite of tiredness or difficulty; tireless: *indefatigable workers* ○ *an indefatigable campaigner for civil rights.*

indefensible /ˌɪndɪˈfensəbl/ *adj* that cannot be defended, justified or excused: *indefensible behaviour, rudeness, harshness, etc.* ▷ **indefensibly** /-əblɪ/ *adv*: *indefensibly rude.*

indefinable /ˌɪndɪˈfaɪnəbl/ *adj* that cannot be defined: *an indefinable air of mystery.* ▷ **indefinably** /-əblɪ/ *adv.*

indefinite /ɪnˈdefɪnət/ *adj* **1** not clearly defined or stated; vague: *He has rather indefinite views on the question.* ○ *He gave me an indefinite answer*, ie neither 'yes' nor 'no'. **2** lasting an unspecified time: *She'll be away for an indefinite period.* **3** (*grammar*) not referring to a specific person or thing: *the indefinite pronoun 'anyone'.* ▷ **indefinitely** *adv*: *You may have to wait indefinitely.*
□ **inˌdefinite ˈarticle** (*grammar*) the word 'a' or 'an'. Cf DEFINITE ARTICLE (DEFINITE).

indelible /ɪnˈdeləbl/ *adj* (of marks, stains, ink, etc) that cannot be rubbed out or removed: *an indelible pencil*, ie one that makes such marks ○ (*fig*) *indelible shame* ○ *an indelible memory.* ▷ **indelibly** /-əblɪ/ *adv.*

indelicate /ɪnˈdelɪkət/ *adj* (*fml often euph*) (of a person, his speech, behaviour, etc) lacking in tact or refinement; rather rude or embarrassing: *indelicate remarks* ○ *It was indelicate of you to mention her marriage problems.*
▷ **indelicacy** /-kəsɪ/ *n* **1** [U] being indelicate. **2** [C] indelicate act, remark, etc.

indemnify /ɪnˈdemnɪfaɪ/ *v* (*pt, pp* **-fied**) **1** [Tn, Tn·pr] ~ **sb (from/against sth)** (*law or commerce*) promise to compensate sb for any harm he may suffer: *indemnify sb against harm, damage, loss, etc.* **2** [Tn, Tn·pr] ~ **sb (for sth)** (*fml*) repay sb (for sth): *I undertook to indemnify them for expenses incurred on my behalf.*
▷ **indemnification** /ɪnˌdemnɪfɪˈkeɪʃn/ *n* (*fml*) **1** [U] indemnifying or being indemnified. **2** [C] thing given or received as compensation or repayment.

indemnity /ɪnˈdemnətɪ/ *n* **1** [U] ~ **(against/for sth)** guarantee against damage or loss; compensation for these: [attrib] *an indemnity fund.* **2** [C] money, goods, etc given as compensation for damage or loss: *The victorious nations are demanding huge indemnities from their former enemies.*

indent /ɪnˈdent/ *v* **1** [Tn] make a mark or set of marks (as if) by cutting into the edge or surface of (sth): *an indented* (ie very irregular) *coastline.* **2** [I, Tn] start (a line of print or writing) further in from the margin than the other lines: *Please indent the first line of each paragraph.* **3** [Ipr] ~ **(on sb) for sth** (*commerce*) (*esp Brit*) make an official order for goods or stores: *indent on the firm for new equipment*, ie place an order for which the firm will pay.
▷ **indent** /ˈɪndent/ *n* (*commerce esp Brit*) official order for stores or equipment.
indentation /ˌɪndenˈteɪʃn/ *n* **1** [U] indenting (INDENT 1, 2) or being indented. **2** [C] (**a**) ~ **(in sth)** mark made by indenting: *the deep indentations of the Norwegian coastline.* (**b**) space left at the beginning of a line of print or writing.

indentures /ɪnˈdentʃəz/ *n* [pl] (esp formerly) written contract according to which an apprentice works for and is trained by a particular employer.
▷ **indenture** *v* [Tn, Tn·pr] ~ **sb (to sb)** contract sb to work as an apprentice: *His son was indentured to the local blacksmith.*

independence /ˌɪndɪˈpendəns/ *n* [U] ~ **(from sb/sth)** state of being independent: *young people who want independence from their parents* ○ [attrib] *independence celebrations*, eg of a newly independent country.
□ **Indeˈpendence Day** 4 July, celebrated in the USA as the anniversary of the day in 1776 on which the American colonies declared themselves independent of Britain.

independent /ˌɪndɪˈpendənt/ *adj* **1** ~ **(of sb/sth)** not dependent (on other people or things); not controlled (by other people or things): *old enough to be independent of one's parents* ○ *She never borrows anything; she's far too independent for that.* ○ *Barbados was once a British colony, but now it's independent.* **2** ~ **(of sb/sth)** not connected with each other; separate: *Two independent investigators have reached virtually the same conclusions.* **3** financed by private rather than government money: *independent television* ○ *the independent sector in education* ○ *independent schools.* ⇨ article at SCHOOL. **4** not depending for its validity or operation on the thing(s) involved: *independent evidence, proof, etc.* **5** not unfairly influenced by the people who are involved; impartial: *an independent witness, observer, etc* ○ *We demand an independent inquiry into the government's handling of the affair.*
▷ **independent** *n* (*abbr* **Ind**) (*politics*) MP,

candidate, etc who does not belong to a political party: *stand as an independent*.
independently *adv*: *Scientists in different countries, working independently of each other, have come up with very similar results.*
□ ˌ**independent ˈmeans** private income sufficiently large for one not to have to rely financially on anyone else: *a woman of independent means.*
in-depth /ˌɪn ˈdepθ/ *adj* [attrib] making a careful examination of all details; thorough: *an in-depth investigation, survey, report, etc.*
indescribable /ˌɪndɪˈskraɪbəbl/ *adj* too bad or good to be described: *indescribable squalor.* ▷ **indescribably** /-əblɪ/ *adv*: *indescribably beautiful, awful, filthy, etc.*
indestructible /ˌɪndɪˈstrʌktəbl/ *adj* that cannot be destroyed: *Furniture for young children needs to be indestructible.* ○ (*fig joc*) *I'm pretty indestructible; it takes more than a bout of flu to lay me low.* ▷ **indestructibility** /ˌɪndɪˌstrʌktəˈbɪlətɪ/ *n* [U].
indeterminable /ˌɪndɪˈtɜ:mɪnəbl/ *adj* (*fml*) that cannot be decided or settled.
indeterminate /ˌɪndɪˈtɜ:mɪnət/ *adj* (a) not fixed or exact; vague; indefinite: *a sort of indeterminate colour, half-way between grey and brown.* (b) (*mathematics*) of no fixed value: *an indeterminate quantity.* ▷ **indeterminacy** /-nəsɪ/ *n* [U].
index /ˈɪndeks/ *n* (*pl* ~**es**; in sense 2, ~**es** or **indices** /ˈɪndɪsi:z/; in sense 3, **indices**) **1** (a) list of names or topics referred to in a book, etc, usu arranged at the end in alphabetical order. (b) (also ˈ**card index**) set of names, book titles, etc filed on cards, usu in alphabetical order (eg in a library). **2** (a) figure showing the relative level of prices or wages compared with that of a previous date: *the cost-of-ˈliving index.* (b) ~ (**of sth**) (*fig*) thing that is a sign of sth else, esp because it increases or decreases proportionately; measure: *The increasing sale of luxury goods is an index of the country's prosperity.* **3** (*mathematics*) small number or letter showing the power to which a quantity is raised; exponent: *In* $b^3 = b \times b \times b$, *3 is an index.*
▷ **index** *v* **1** (a) [Tn] make an index for (sth): *The book is not well indexed.* (b) [Tn, Tn·pr] ~ **sth** (**in sth**) enter sth in an index: *index all the quoted names in a book.* **2** [Tn, Tn·pr] ~ **sth** (**to sth**) link (wages, pensions, etc) to increases in prices, etc.
indexation /ˌɪndekˈseɪʃn/ *n* [U] indexing (INDEX 2a) of wages, pensions, etc.
□ ˈ**index finger** *n* finger next to the thumb, used for pointing. ⇨ illus at HAND.
ˈ**index-linked** *adj* (of wages, pensions, etc) increased according to increases in the cost of living.
India /ˈɪndɪə/ country in southern Asia, occupying most of the Indian subcontinent; pop approx 797 000 000; official languages Hindi and English; capital New Delhi; unit of currency rupee (= 100 paise). The most densely populated democracy in the world, it is a republic made up of 25 States and 6 Union Territories. Its main religions are Hinduism, Islam and Sikhism. It began to be colonized by European countries in the 17th century. From the mid 18th century large parts of it were ruled by the British East India Company, and in the mid 19th century the British government took over control (British rule being known as the 'Raj'). In 1877 Queen Victoria was proclaimed Empress of India. After a long campaign led by Mahatma *Gandhi, India became independent in 1947, its former territory being divided into India and Pakistan, which was itself later divided into Pakistan and Bangladesh. Its economy depends heavily on agriculture, though since 1947 it has built up a considerable industrial base, including textile and jute industries. ⇨ map.
□ **Indiaman** /ˈɪndɪəmən/ *n* (*pl* **-men**) (formerly) sailing ship carrying goods to and from India and the East Indies.
Indian /ˈɪndɪən/ *n*, *adj* **1** (native or inhabitant) of the Republic of India. **2** = AMERICAN INDIAN (AMERICAN): *an Indian ceremony, encampment.*

India and its neighbours

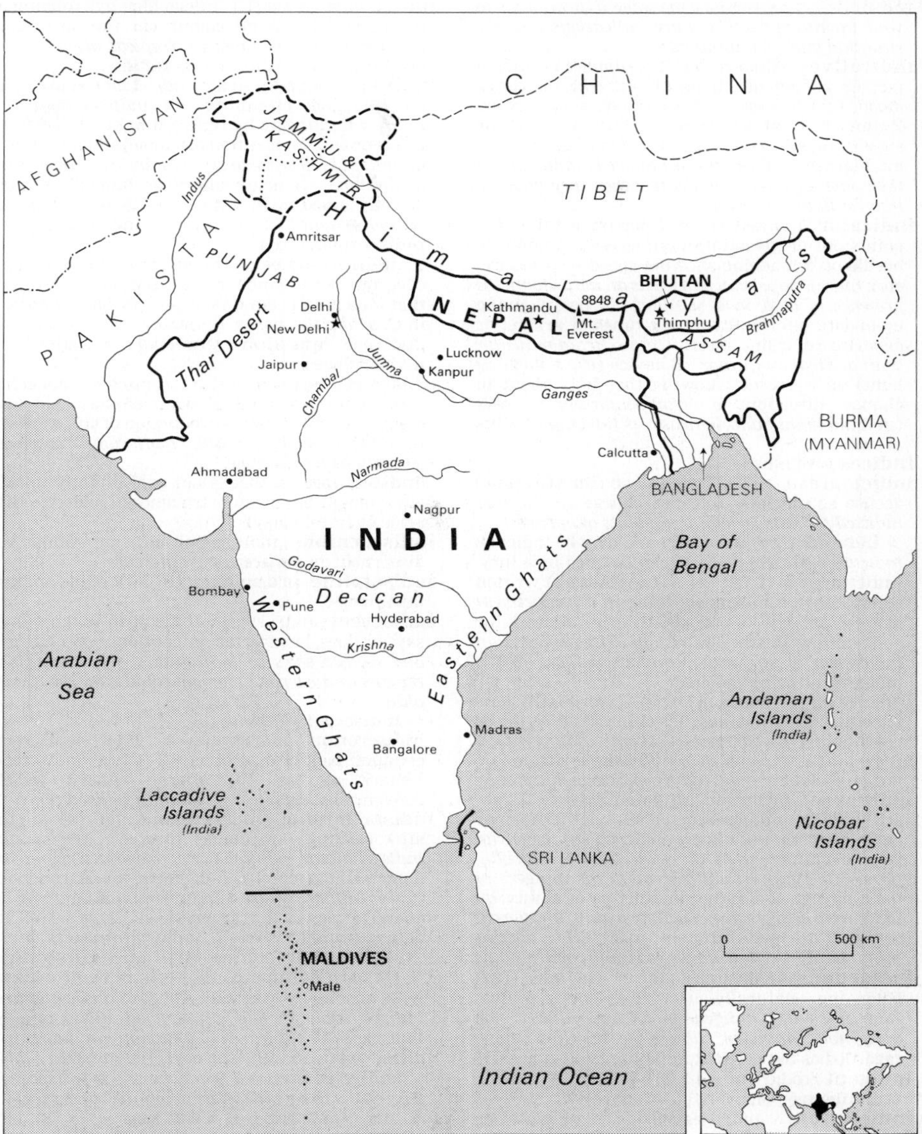

3 (idm) **Indian/single file** ⇨ FILE[3]. **an** ˌ**Indian** ˈ**summer** (a) period of calm dry sunny weather in late autumn. (b) (*fig*) period of late success or improvement.
□ ˌ**Indian** ˈ**club** bottle-shaped object for use in juggling, gymnastic exercises, etc.
ˌ**Indian** ˈ**corn** maize.
ˌ**Indian** ˈ**hemp** = CANNABIS.
ˌ**Indian** ˈ**ink** (*US* ˌ**India** ˈ**ink**) thick black ink, used esp for drawing.
the ˌ**Indian** ˈ**Mutiny** revolt by Indian troops against British rule in India in 1857-58. It originated in a number of British garrison towns and was largely confined to the northern part of the country. The revolt was defeated, but it led to the replacement of the controlling British East India Company with direct rule by the British government.
ˌ**Indian** ˈ**rope trick** trick of climbing up an unsupported rope, thought to have originated in India.
Indiana /ˌɪndɪˈænə/ state in the *Mid West of the USA. It is mainly agricultural, but also has large centres of manufacturing industry. ⇨ map at App 1.
indiarubber /ˌɪndɪəˈrʌbə(r)/ *n* piece of rubber for removing pencil or ink marks; eraser.
indicate /ˈɪndɪkeɪt/ *v* **1** (a) [Tn, Tf, Tw, Dn·pr, Dpr·f, Dpr·w] ~ **sth** (**to sb**) show sth, esp by pointing: *a sign indicating the right road to follow* ○ *With a nod of his head he indicated to me where I should sit.* (b) [Tn, Tf, Tw] be a sign of (sth); suggest the possibility or probability of: *A red sky at night indicates fine weather the following day/ indicates that the following day will be fine.* (c) [Tn] give (the specified reading or measurement) on a scale: *The speedometer was indicating 95 mph.* **2** [Tn, Tf, Tw, Dn·pr, Dpr·f, Dpr·w] ~ **sth** (**to sb**) state sth briefly or indirectly: *The minister has indicated that he may resign next year.* ○ *She has not indicated how she proposes to react.* **3** [Tn esp passive] show the need for or advisability of (sth); call for: *With the government's failure to solve the problem of unemployment, a fresh approach is indicated.* ○ *a diagnosis of advanced cancer indicating an emergency operation.* **4** [I, Tf] signal that one's vehicle is going to change direction: *Why don't you indicate?* ○ *He indicated that he was turning right, but then he turned left!*
▷ **indication** /ˌɪndɪˈkeɪʃn/ *n* **1** [U] indicating or being indicated. **2** [C, U] ~ (**of sth/doing sth**); ~ (**as to sth/that...**) remark, gesture, sign, etc that

indicates sth: *She gave no indication of having heard us.* ○ *Can you give me some indication as to your intentions?* ○ *There are indications that the situation may be improving.*

indicative /ɪnˈdɪkətɪv/ *adj* **1** (*grammar*) stating a fact or asking questions of fact: *the indicative mood.* Cf IMPERATIVE 3, INFINITIVE, SUBJUNCTIVE. **2** [pred] ~ **of sth/that...** (*fml*) showing or suggesting sth: *Is a large head indicative of high intelligence?* ○ *Their failure to act is indicative of their lack of interest/indicative that they have no interest in the problem.*

indicator /ˈɪndɪkeɪtə(r)/ *n* **1** person or thing that points out or gives information (eg a pointer or needle on a machine showing speed or pressure, etc): *Litmus paper can be used as an indicator of the presence of acid in a solution.* **2** board giving up-to-date information about times of arrival or departure of trains, aircraft, etc: *a ˈtrain indicator* ○ *an arˈrivals indicator.* **3** device (esp a flashing light) on a vehicle showing that it is about to change direction: *a ˈtraffic-indicator* ○ *His left-hand/right-hand indicator is flashing.* ⇨ illus at CAR.

indices *pl* of INDEX.

indict /ɪnˈdaɪt/ *v* [Tn, Tn·pr] ~ **sb (for sth)** (*law*) accuse sb officially (of sth); charge sb: *He was indicted for murder/on three counts of murder.*

▷ **indictable** *adj* for which one may be indicted: *indictable offences*, ie that may be tried by a jury.

indictment *n* **1** [C] **(a)** ~ **(against sb)** written statement that indicts sb: *bring in an indictment against sb.* **(b)** ~ **of sb/sth** (*fig*) reason for condemning sb/sth: *The rise in delinquency is an indictment of our society and its values.* **2** [U] indicting or being indicted.

indifference /ɪnˈdɪfrəns/ *n* [U] ~ **(to sb/sth)** state of being indifferent; absence of interest, feeling or reaction: *He treated my request with indifference.* ○ *It's a matter of complete indifference to me*, ie I do not care about it. ○ *her indifference to their appeals.*

indifferent /ɪnˈdɪfrənt/ *adj* **1** [usu pred] ~ **(to sb/sth)** having no interest in sb/sth; neither for nor against sb/sth; not caring about sb/sth: *How can you be indifferent to the sufferings of starving people?* ○ *explorers indifferent to the dangers of their journey.* **2** of rather low quality or ability: *an indifferent book, wine, meal* ○ *a very indifferent athlete.* ▷ **indifferently** *adv*: *He nodded indifferently.* ○ *The team played indifferently today.*

indigenous /ɪnˈdɪdʒɪnəs/ *adj* ~ **(to sth)** (*fml*) belonging naturally (to a place); native: *Kangaroos are indigenous to Australia.* ○ *the indigenous language, culture, etc*, ie of the people regarded as the original inhabitants of an area.

indigent /ˈɪndɪdʒənt/ *adj* (*fml*) poor.

▷ **indigence** /-əns/ *n* [U] (*fml*) poverty.

indigestible /ˌɪndɪˈdʒestəbl/ *adj* difficult or impossible to digest: *Fried onions can be indigestible.* ○ (*fig*) *indigestible statistics*, ie hard to understand. ▷ **indigestibility** /ˌɪndɪˌdʒestəˈbɪlətɪ/ *n* [U].

indigestion /ˌɪndɪˈdʒestʃən/ *n* [U] (pain from) difficulty in digesting food: *suffer from indigestion* ○ *have an attack of indigestion* ○ [attrib] *indigestion pills/tablets*, ie taken to cure indigestion.

indignant /ɪnˈdɪgnənt/ *adj* ~ **(with sb)/(at/over/about sth)** angry and scornful, esp at injustice or because of undeserved blame, etc: *She was most indignant with me when I suggested she might try a little harder.* ○ *He was terribly indignant at what he saw as false accusations.* ▷ **indignantly** *adv.*

indignation /ˌɪndɪgˈneɪʃn/ *n* [U] ~ **(against sb)/(at/over/about sth)** anger caused by sth thought to be unjust, unfair, etc: *general indignation at the sudden steep rise in bus fares* ○ *arouse sb's indignation* ○ *Much to my indignation, he sat down in my seat.* ○ *righteous indignation*, ie which one considers appropriate and justified (but others usu do not).

indignity /ɪnˈdɪgnətɪ/ *n* **1** [U] rude or unworthy treatment causing shame or loss of respect: *be subjected to indignity and humiliation.* **2** [C] thing said or done that humiliates sb: *The hijackers inflicted all kinds of indignities on their captives.*

indigo /ˈɪndɪgəʊ/ *n* [U] **1** deep blue dye (obtained from plants). **2** its colour (in the spectrum between blue and violet): *a tropical night sky of deepest indigo.* ⇨ illus at SPECTRUM.

indirect /ˌɪndɪˈrekt, -daɪˈr-/ *adj* **1** not going in a straight line; circuitous: *an indirect route* ○ *indirect lighting*, ie by reflected light. **2** avoiding direct or explicit mention of a topic; allusive: *make an indirect reference to sth* ○ *an indirect answer to a question.* **3** not primary or immediate; not directly aimed at sth; secondary: *an indirect cause, reason, result.* Cf DIRECT. ▷ **indirectly** *adv.* **indirectness** *n* [U].

□ ˌ**indirect** ˈ**object** (*grammar*) additional object of certain verbs which refers to the person or thing that an action is done to or for *eg him (= to him)* in *Give him the money.* Cf OBJECT[1] 5.

ˌ**indirect** ˈ**question** (*grammar*) question in indirect speech.

ˌ**indirect** ˈ**speech** (also **reported speech**) (*grammar*) reporting of what sb has said (as compared with direct reproduction of sb's words): *In indirect speech, 'He said, "I will come"' becomes 'He said he would come.'*

ˈ**indirect tax** tax that is not paid directly to the government but as an extra amount added to the price of certain goods.

indiscernible /ˌɪndɪˈsɜːnəbl/ *adj* that cannot be discerned: *an indiscernible difference.*

indiscipline /ɪnˈdɪsɪplɪn/ *n* [U] lack of discipline; unruliness.

indiscreet /ˌɪndɪˈskriːt/ *adj* too open in what one says or does; lacking tact or caution: *Don't tell her any secrets; she's so indiscreet.* ○ *One indiscreet remark at the wrong moment could ruin the whole plan.*

▷ **indiscreetly** *adv.*

indiscretion /ˌɪndɪˈskreʃn/ *n* **1** [U] indiscreet conduct; lack of discretion. **2** [C] **(a)** indiscreet remark or act. **(b)** offence against social conventions: *committing youthful indiscretions.*

indiscriminate /ˌɪndɪˈskrɪmɪnət/ *adj* **(a)** ~ **(in sth)** acting without careful judgement: *indiscriminate in his choice of friends.* **(b)** given or done without careful judgement, or at random: *indiscriminate praise* ○ *indiscriminate bombing of enemy targets*, eg that might kill civilians as well as damage military sites. ▷ **indiscriminately** *adv.*

indispensable /ˌɪndɪˈspensəbl/ *adj* ~ **(to sb/sth);** ~ **(for sth/doing sth)** that cannot be dispensed with; absolutely essential: *Air, food and water are indispensable to life.* ○ *A good dictionary is indispensable for learning a foreign language.*

indisposed /ˌɪndɪˈspəʊzd/ *adj* [pred] **1** (*often euph*) (slightly) ill: *She has a headache and is indisposed.* **2** [pred] ~ **to do sth** (*fml*) not inclined or willing to do sth: *I felt indisposed to help him.*

▷ **indisposition** /ˌɪndɪspəˈzɪʃn/ *n* [C, U] **1** (*often euph*) slight illness; ill health. **2** ~ **to do sth** (*fml*) feeling of unwillingness or disinclination to do sth.

indisputable /ˌɪndɪˈspjuːtəbl/ *adj* that cannot be disputed or denied. ▷ **indisputably** *adv*: *indisputably the best tennis player in the world.*

indissoluble /ˌɪndɪˈsɒljʊbl/ *adj* (*fml*) that cannot be dissolved or broken up; firm and lasting: *indissoluble bonds of friendship between the two men* ○ *The Roman Catholic Church regards marriage as indissoluble.* ▷ **indissolubility** /ˌɪndɪˌsɒljʊˈbɪlətɪ/ *n* [U]. **indissolubly** /ˌɪndɪˈsɒljʊblɪ/ *adv.*

indistinct /ˌɪndɪˈstɪŋkt/ *adj* not distinct; vague: *indistinct speech* ○ *indistinct sounds, memories.* ▷ **indistinctly** *adv.* **indistinctness** *n* [U].

indistinguishable /ˌɪndɪˈstɪŋgwɪʃəbl/ *adj* ~ **(from sth)** that cannot be identified as different or distinct; (virtually) identical: *Its colour makes the moth indistinguishable from the branch it rests on.*

▷ **indistinguishably** /-əblɪ/ *adv.*

indium /ˈɪndɪəm/ *n* [U] (*symb* **In**) (*chemistry*) soft silvery metallic element found in small quantities in zinc ores and used in the manufacture of transistors. ⇨ App 11.

individual /ˌɪndɪˈvɪdʒʊəl/ *adj* **1** [attrib] (esp after *each*) single; separate: *Each individual person is responsible for his own arrangements.* **2** [usu attrib] **(a)** of or for one person: *food served in individual portions* ○ *It is difficult for a teacher to give individual attention to children in a large class.* **(b)** by or from one person: *an individual effort, contribution, etc.* Cf COLLECTIVE. **3** [usu attrib] characteristic of a single person, animal, plant or thing; particular: *an individual style of dress* ○ (*approv*) *He writes in a very individual way*, ie an original way, not derived or imitative.

▷ **individual** *n* **1** single human being: *the rights of an/the individual compared with those of society as a whole.* **2** (*infml*) person of the specified sort: *a pleasant, unpleasant, etc individual* ○ *What a strange individual!* **3** (*approv or derog*) unusual or eccentric person: *He's quite an individual!*

individually /-dʒʊəlɪ/ *adv* separately; one by one: *speak to each member of a group individually.*

individualism /ˌɪndɪˈvɪdʒʊəlɪzəm/ *n* [U] **1** feeling or behaviour of a person who likes to do things his/her own way, regardless of what other people do. **2** theory that favours free action and complete liberty of belief for each individual person (contrasted with the theory that favours the supremacy of the state).

▷ **individualist** /-əlɪst/ *n* **1** person who behaves with individualism(1): *a rugged individualist.* **2** supporter of the theory of individualism(2).

individualistic /ˌɪndɪˌvɪdʒʊəˈlɪstɪk/ *adj* of individualism or its principles. **individualistically** /-klɪ/ *adv.*

individuality /ˌɪndɪˌvɪdʒʊˈælətɪ/ *n* **1** [U] all the characteristics that belong to a particular person and that make him/her different from others: *a man of marked individuality* ○ *the individuality of sb's work, style, etc.* **2** [U] state of separate existence: *The state often presents a threat to individuality.* **3 individualities** [pl] individual tastes, preferences, etc: *cater for different people's individualities.*

individualize, -ise /ˌɪndɪˈvɪdʒʊəlaɪz/ *v* **1** [Tn] give an individual, a distinct or a personal character to (sth); characterize; personalize: *Does your style of writing individualize your work?* ○ *Prisoners try to individualize their cells by hanging up pictures, etc.* ○ *individualized writing paper*, ie made for a particular person with his/her address, etc printed on it. **2** [I, Tn] treat (sth) separately; specify; particularize.

indivisible /ˌɪndɪˈvɪzəbl/ *adj* that cannot be divided. ▷ **indivisibility** /ˌɪndɪˌvɪzɪˈbɪlətɪ/ *n* [U]. **indivisibly** /ˌɪndɪˈvɪzəblɪ/ *adv.*

Indo- *comb form* Indian; of India: *the Indo-Pakistan border.*

□ **Indo-European** /ˌɪndəʊˌjʊərəˈpiːən/ *adj* of the family of languages spoken in most of Europe and parts of western Asia (including eg English, French, German, Latin, Greek, Swedish and Hindi). They are descended from an ancestor language that was spoken about 8 000 years ago in the general area to the north of the Black Sea, though no actual records of this language survive.

Indo-China /ˌɪndəʊ ˈtʃaɪnə/ area of SE Asia that includes Burma, Thailand, Laos, Cambodia, Vietnam and the Malayan peninsula.

indoctrinate /ɪnˈdɒktrɪneɪt/ *v* [Tn, Tn·pr, Cn·t] ~ **sb (with sth/against sb/sth)** (*usu derog*) cause sb to have (a particular set of beliefs), esp by teaching which excludes any other points of view: *teachers who indoctrinate children with antisocial theories* ○ *a religious organization which indoctrinates young people against their parents/to disobey their parents.*

▷ **indoctrination** /ɪnˌdɒktrɪˈneɪʃn/ *n* [U] ~ **(with/in/against sth)** indoctrinating: *the indoctrination of prisoners* ○ *indoctrination of converts in the ways of their new religion.*

indolent /ˈɪndələnt/ *adj* (*fml*) lazy; inactive. ▷ **indolence** /-əns/ *n* [U]. **indolently** *adv.*

indomitable /ɪnˈdɒmɪtəbl/ *adj* (*fml approv*) that cannot be subdued or defeated; unyielding: *indomitable courage* ○ *an indomitable will.* ▷ **indomitably** /-əblɪ/ *adv.*

Industry

The development of industry in Britain at the time of the Industrial Revolution was closely associated with coal. Coal was the fuel used in the factories and foundries which were built near the coalfields. Traditionally Yorkshire was associated with the woollen industry, Staffordshire with the potteries, Lancashire with cotton spinning, Birmingham with mechanical engineering, the north-east with shipbuilding, Scotland with steel manufacture and shipbuilding, and south Wales with steel. Traditional industries in Northern Ireland were shipbuilding and linen production. In the 19th century, at the height of the British Empire, raw materials were imported from British colonies and finished manufactured goods exported to them.

The 20th century has seen a decline both in these traditional industries and in Britain's share of world markets. Adjusting to these changes has been a cause of many of the social and economic problems that the country has experienced. By the end of the 1980s, manufacturing industry employed one fifth of the workforce and accounted for less than a quarter of Gross Domestic Product (GDP), while service industries accounted for nearly three quarters. Traditional industries have been replaced by more modern industries, such as chemicals, electronics, aeronautics, and the offshore oil and gas industry. The social cost of the decline of traditional heavy industries has been severe in those areas where a high proportion of the local population was employed in them, and unemployment is a particular problem, for example in the north-west and north-east of England.

The government has established special 'assisted areas' in regions where major industries have declined, such as south Wales, the Midlands, north-east England, south-west Scotland and Northern Ireland. In each area, the government encourages new industrial enterprise and investment by making loans and granting special tax concessions.

After the Second World War, some major industries were nationalized, including the steel industry, mining and, later, car manufacturing. During the 1980s, under the Conservative government, a programme of denationalization or privatization was undertaken and British Steel, British Aerospace, Rolls Royce, Jaguar, British Telecom, BP, British Gas, the British Airports Authority and the water and electricity industries have all become private sector companies, with shares offered for sale to the public. The few remaining state-owned companies include British Coal, British Rail, the Post Office and London Transport.

In the private sector, companies may be public limited companies (PLCs), with shares quoted on the Stock Exchange and available for sale to the public, or private companies owned by a group of individuals who usually act as the directors of the company. Britain's largest manufacturers include ICI (chemicals), British Steel, BP and Shell (oil and oil products), Pilkington (glass), English China Clays, British Aerospace (which includes Rover, the car manufacturer), Rolls Royce (aero-engines), Unilever (food and chemicals), and Coats Viyella (textiles), as well as the conglomerates that own many firms producing a wide range of goods, such as Hanson and BAT Industries.

The employers' organization is the Confederation of British Industry (CBI), which aims to keep the government and the public informed about the needs and problems of industry. Regular surveys of its members are conducted to gain a picture of the economic outlook for companies.

Indonesia

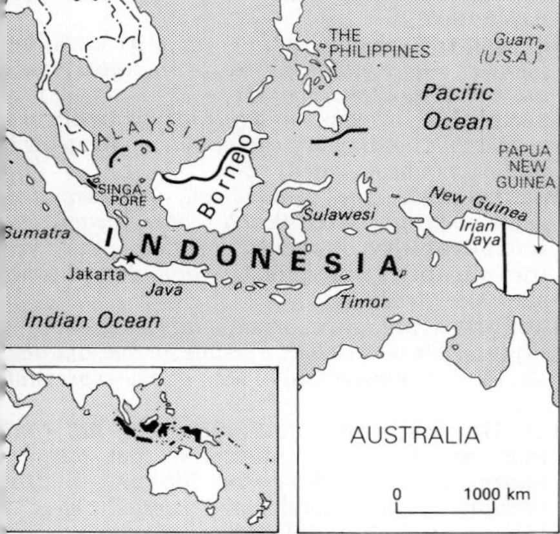

Indonesia /ˌɪndəˈniːzɪə; *US* ˌɪndəˈniːʒə/ country in SE Asia consisting of several islands (the largest being *Java, *Sumatra, South *Borneo, West *New Guinea and *Sulawesi); pop approx 174 951 000; official language Indonesian; capital Jakarta; unit of currency rupiah (= 100 sen). Between the early 17th and mid 20th centuries it was a Dutch colony. Its main products are oil, timber and rubber. ⇨ map.

▷ **Indonesian** /ˌɪndəˈniːzɪən; *US* ˌɪndəˈniːʒn/ *adj* of Indonesia. — *n* 1 [C] native or inhabitant of Indonesia. 2 [U] Malay language that is the official language of Indonesia.

indoor /ˈɪndɔː(r)/ *adj* [attrib] carried on or situated inside a building; used in or suitable for the inside of a building: *indoor games, photography, activities* ○ *an indoor swimming-pool* ○ *indoor clothes*. Cf OUTDOOR.

indoors /ˌɪnˈdɔːz/ *adv* in or into a building: *go/stay indoors* ○ *kept indoors all week by bad weather*. Cf OUTDOORS.

indorse *v* = ENDORSE.

indrawn /ˌɪnˈdrɔːn/ *adj* [attrib] drawn in, esp inhaled: *All that betrayed his surprise was a sharply indrawn breath.*

indubitable /ɪnˈdjuːbɪtəbl; *US* -ˈduː-/ *adj* (*fml*) that cannot be doubted; without doubt. ▷ **indubitably** /-əblɪ/ *adv*: *That is indubitably the best course of action.*

induce /ɪnˈdjuːs; *US* -duːs/ *v* **1** [Cn·t] **(a)** persuade or influence (sb) to do sth: *We couldn't induce the old lady to travel by air.* **(b)** lead or cause (sb) to do sth: *What induced you to do such a stupid thing?* **2** [Tn] **(a)** bring (sth) about; cause: *illness induced by overwork.* **(b)** (*medical*) cause (a woman) to begin (childbirth) by means of drugs: *an induced labour* ○ *We'll have to induce her.*

▷ **inducement** *n* [C, U] ~ **(to do sth)** **(a)** that which persuades; incentive: *They have little inducement to work harder.* **(b)** (*euph*) bribe; bribery: *offer sb an inducement.*

inducible *adj* that can be induced.

induct /ɪnˈdʌkt/ *v* **1** [Tn, Tn·pr, Cn·n/a] ~ **sb (into/to/as sth)** install sb formally or with ceremony in a position or an office; admit sb as a member of sth: *He was inducted as Vicar of Bassingbourne.* ○ *The president-elect cannot approve new laws until he has been inducted into office.* **2** [Tn, Tn·pr] ~ **sb (into sth)** (*US*) force sb by law to join the armed forces; conscript sb.

▷ **inductee** /ɪndʌkˈtiː/ *n* (*US*) person who has been inducted into the armed forces.

inductance /ɪnˈdʌktəns/ *n* [U] (*physics*) **(a)** ability of an electric circuit to produce an electric current by induction(4). **(b)** measure of this (in henries).

induction /ɪnˈdʌkʃn/ *n* [U] **1** ~ **(into sth/as sb/sth)** inducting or being inducted; initiation: *the induction of new employees into their jobs* ○ *his induction as a priest* ○ [attrib] *an induction course*, ie to give a new employee, entrant, etc general knowledge of future activities, requirements, etc. **2** inducing: *the induction of labour*, ie in childbirth. **3** method of logical reasoning which obtains or discovers general laws from particular facts or examples. Cf DEDUCTION 1. **4** (*physics*) production of an electric or a magnetic state in an object (eg a circuit) by bringing an electrified or a magnetic object close to but not touching it, or by varying a magnetic field. Cf INDUCTANCE. **5** (*engineering*) drawing a fuel mixture into the cylinder(s) of an internal-combustion engine: [attrib] *a fuel-induction system.*

□ **inˈduction-coil** *n* (*physics*) transformer for producing a high voltage from a low voltage.

inˈduction motor (*physics*) type of electric motor in which a magnetic field is created that produces an electric current.

inductive /ɪnˈdʌktɪv/ *adj* **1** (of logic, mathematics) based on induction: *inductive reasoning.* **2** (*physics*) of magnetic or electrical induction. ▷ **inductively** *adv*.

indulge /ɪnˈdʌldʒ/ *v* **1** **(a)** [Tn, Tn·pr] ~ **oneself/sb (with sth)** allow oneself/sb to have whatever one/he likes or wants: *They indulge their child too much; it's bad for his character.* ○ *I'm really going to indulge myself tonight with a bottle of champagne.* **(b)** [Tn] (*fml*) allow (sb) to proceed without interrupting or hindering him: *If you will indulge me for one moment* (ie allow me to continue to speak), *I think I can explain the matter to you.* **2** [Tn] satisfy (a perhaps unwarranted or illicit desire): *Will you indulge my curiosity and tell me how much it cost?* ○ *She indulges his every whim.* **3** [I, Ipr] ~ **(in sth)** allow oneself to enjoy the pleasure of sth: *I shall forget about dieting today. I'm just going to indulge*, ie eat and drink what I like. ○ *indulge in (the luxury of) a long hot bath* ○ (*rhet or joc*) *'Whisky?' 'No thanks, I don't indulge* (ie don't drink alcohol).*'*

▷ **indulgent** /-ənt/ *adj* inclined to indulge: *indulgent parents*, ie parents who allow their children to have or do anything. **indulgently** *adv*.

indulgence /ɪnˈdʌlgəns/ *n* **1** [U] state of being allowed whatever one wants: *a life of (self-)indulgence*, ie gratifying oneself ○ *If I may crave your indulgence for one moment....* **2** [U] ~ **in sth** (habit of) satisfying one's own desires: *Constant indulgence in bad habits brought about his ruin.* **3** [C] thing in which a person indulges: *A cigar after dinner is my only indulgence.* **4** **(a)** [U] (in the Roman Catholic Church) granting of freedom from punishment for sin. **(b)** [C] instance of this: *selling indulgences.*

industrial /ɪnˈdʌstrɪəl/ *adj* **1** [attrib] of or engaged in industry: *industrial workers* ○ *industrial development.* **2** for use in industry: *industrial diamonds.* **3** having many well-developed industries: *an industrial country, society, etc* ○ *the industrial areas of England.*

▷ **industrialism** /-ɪzəm/ *n* social system in which large industries have an important part.

industrialist /-ɪst/ *n* owner of a large industrial firm.

industrialize, -ise /-aɪz/ *v* [Tn] develop (a country or an area) extensively with industries: *the industrialized nations.* **industrialization, -isation** /ɪnˌdʌstrɪəlaɪˈzeɪʃn; *US* -lɪˈz-/ *n* [U].

industrially /-əlɪ/ *adv.*

□ **inˌdustrial ˈaction** refusing to work normally; striking: *take industrial action,* ie strike.

inˌdustrial ˈalcohol alcohol for industrial use (not for drinking).

inˌdustrial deˈmocracy democratic control of a business company by all the people who work for it.

inˌdustrial diˈspute disagreement between workers and management.

inˌdustrial eˈstate area of land, usu on the edge of a town, containing factories. Cf TRADING ESTATE (TRADE[2]).

inˌdustrial reˈlations dealings between employers and employees: *setting up a combined workers/management committee to foster good industrial relations.*

the Inˌdustrial Revoˈlution development of Britain and other western nations into industrial societies in the 18th and 19th centuries. In the mid 18th century new machinery, much of it run on the newly discovered steam power, allowed one worker to do what had previously been the work of many people. Large factories were built, and industrial production rose dramatically, making Britain a very rich nation. The population of cities increased greatly as people came from country areas to work in the factories, and problems of overcrowding, poverty, etc grew. New methods of transportation (eg canals and railways) were developed to move goods around.

industrious /ɪnˈdʌstrɪəs/ *adj* hard-working; diligent. ▷ **industriously** *adv.* **industriousness** *n* [U].

industry /ˈɪndəstrɪ/ *n* **1** [C, U] **(a)** (branch of) manufacture or production: *Britain's coal industry* ○ *heavy industry,* ie producing large goods, eg steel or cars ○ *nationalized industries.* ⇨ article. **(b)** commercial undertaking that provides services: *the catering, hotel, tourist, entertainment, etc industry.* **2** [U] *(fml)* quality of being hard-working: *praise sb for his industry* ○ *The industry of these little ants is wonderful to behold.* **3** (idm) **a captain of industry** ⇨ CAPTAIN.

inebriated /ɪˈni:brɪeɪtɪd/ *adj* [usu pred] *(fml or joc)* drunk; intoxicated: *(fig) inebriated* (ie uncontrollably excited) *by his success.*

▷ **inebriate** /ɪˈni:brɪət/ *adj, n (fml)* habitually drunk (person).

inebriation /ɪˌni:brɪˈeɪʃn/ *n* [U] *(fml or joc)* drunkenness.

inedible /ɪnˈedɪbl/ *adj (fml)* not suitable to be eaten: *The fish was quite inedible.* Cf UNEATABLE.

ineducable /ɪnˈedjʊkəbl/ *adj* that cannot be educated, eg because of mental deficiency.

ineffable /ɪnˈefəbl/ *adj (fml)* too great to be described in words: *ineffable joy, beauty, etc.* ▷ **ineffably** /-əblɪ/ *adv.*

ineffective /ˌɪnɪˈfektɪv/ *adj* not producing the required effect(s): *use ineffective methods* ○ *She is totally ineffective as a teacher,* ie She cannot teach satisfactorily. ▷ **ineffectively** *adv.* **ineffectiveness** *n* [U].

ineffectual /ˌɪnɪˈfektʃʊəl/ *adj* lacking confidence and unable to get things done; without effect: *make ineffectual attempts to do sth* ○ *ineffectual as a leader, teacher, etc* ○ *a well-meaning but ineffectual person.* ▷ **ineffectually** /-tʃʊəlɪ/ *adv.*

inefficient /ˌɪnɪˈfɪʃnt/ *adj* **1** (of a machine, process, etc) not producing adequate results; wasteful: *an inefficient system, method, use of resources, etc.* **2** (of a person) wasting time, energy, etc in what one does, and therefore failing to do it well or quickly enough: *dismissed for being inefficient* ○ *an inefficient management, administration, body of workers, etc.* ▷ **inefficiency** /-nsɪ/ *n* [U]: *dismissed for inefficiency.* **inefficiently** *adv.*

inelastic /ˌɪnɪˈlæstɪk/ *adj* not flexible or adaptable; unyielding: *(fig) This timetable is too inelastic. You must allow for possible modifications.*

inelegant /ˌɪnˈelɪgənt/ *adj* not graceful or refined; ugly: *an inelegant gesture, reply.* ▷ **inelegance** /-əns/ *n* [U]. **inelegantly** *adv.*

ineligible /ɪnˈelɪdʒəbl/ *adj* ~ **(for sth/to do sth)** not having the appropriate or necessary qualifications (for sth): *ineligible for the job, for promotion* ○ *Any person under the age of 18 is ineligible for benefit.* ▷ **ineligibility** /ɪnˌelɪdʒəˈbɪlətɪ/ *n* [U].

ineluctable /ˌɪnɪˈlʌktəbl/ *adj (fml)* that cannot be escaped from: *the victim of ineluctable fate.* ▷ **ineluctably** /-əblɪ/ *adv.*

inept /ɪˈnept/ *adj* **(a)** ~ **(at sth/doing sth)** completely unskilful (at sth): *I've never heard anyone so inept at making speeches.* ○ *His inept handling of a minor problem turned it into a major crisis.* **(b)** said or done at the wrong time; not appropriate or tactful: *an inept remark.*

▷ **ineptitude** /ɪˈneptɪtju:d; *US* -tu:d/ *n* **(a)** [U] quality of being inept. **(b)** [C] inept action, remark, etc.

ineptly *adv.*

inequality /ˌɪnɪˈkwɒlətɪ/ *n* **(a)** [U] lack of equality in size, degree, circumstances, etc, esp unfair difference in rank, wealth, opportunity, etc: *fight against political, racial, etc inequality.* **(b)** [C] instance of this: *Inequalities in wealth cause social unrest.*

inequitable /ɪnˈekwɪtəbl/ *adj (fml)* unjust; unfair: *an inequitable division of the profits.* ▷ **inequitably** /-əblɪ/ *adv.*

inequity /ɪnˈekwətɪ/ *n (fml)* **(a)** [U] injustice or unfairness: *the inequity of the system.* **(b)** [C] instance of this.

ineradicable /ˌɪnɪˈrædɪkəbl/ *adj* (esp of sth bad) that cannot be got rid of; firmly and deeply established: *ineradicable faults, failings, prejudices, etc.* ▷ **ineradicably** /-əblɪ/ *adv.*

inert /ɪˈnɜ:t/ *adj* **1** without power to move or act: *She lay there inert; I thought she must be dead.* ○ *(physics) inert matter.* **2** *(derog)* heavy and slow in action, thought, etc; without vigour: *an inert management team.* ▷ **inertly** *adv.* **inertness** *n* [U].

□ **iˌnert ˈgas** gas (eg helium, neon) that does not react chemically with other substances.

inertia /ɪˈnɜ:ʃə/ *n* [U] **1** *(usu derog)* **(a)** lack of vigour; lethargy: *I'm unable to throw off this feeling of inertia.* **(b)** tendency to remain unchanged: *Because of the sheer inertia of the system many badly needed reforms were never introduced.* **2** *(physics)* property of matter by which it remains in a state of rest or, if in motion, continues moving in a straight line, unless acted upon by an external force.

▷ **inertial** /ɪˈnɜ:ʃl/ *adj* of or by inertia: *a missile's inertial guidance system.*

□ **iˌnertia ˈreel** type of reel round which one end of a safety-belt is wound so that the belt will tighten automatically over the wearer if it is pulled suddenly.

iˌnertia ˈseat-belt seat-belt incorporating an inertia reel.

iˌnertia ˈselling *(esp Brit)* sending of goods to a person who has not ordered them, in the hope that he will not refuse them and will therefore later have to pay for them.

inescapable /ˌɪnɪˈskeɪpəbl/ *adj* that cannot be avoided; inevitable: *be forced to the inescapable conclusion that he is a liar.* ▷ **inescapably** /-əblɪ/ *adv.*

inessential /ˌɪnɪˈsenʃl/ *adj* not essential; unnecessary.

▷ **inessential** *n* (usu *pl*) inessential thing: *Don't waste money on inessentials.*

inestimable /ɪnˈestɪməbl/ *adj (fml)* too great, precious, etc to be estimated: *The value of your assistance is inestimable.* ▷ **inestimably** /-əblɪ/ *adv.*

inevitable /ɪnˈevɪtəbl/ *adj* **1** that cannot be avoided; that is sure to happen: *an inevitable disaster* ○ *It seems inevitable that they'll lose.* **2** [attrib] *(infml often joc)* so frequently seen, heard, etc that it is familiar and expected: *a tourist with his inevitable camera.*

▷ **inevitability** /ɪnˌevɪtəˈbɪlətɪ/ *n* [U].

the inevitable *n* [sing] that which is inevitable: *accept the inevitable.*

inevitably /-əblɪ/ *adv* as is or was sure to happen: *The train was inevitably delayed by the accident.*

inexact /ˌɪnɪgˈzækt/ *adj* not exact or precise: *Weather forecasting is an inexact science.*

▷ **inexactitude** /ˌɪnɪgˈzæktɪtju:d; *US* -tɪtu:d/ *n* **(a)** [U] being inexact. **(b)** [C] instance of this: *(joc euph) a terminological inexactitude,* ie a lie.

inexcusable /ˌɪnɪkˈskju:zəbl/ *adj* too bad to be excused: *inexcusable conduct, delays, inefficiency.* ▷ **inexcusably** /-əblɪ/ *adv*: *inexcusably rude, late, etc.*

inexhaustible /ˌɪnɪgˈzɔ:stəbl/ *adj* that will always continue; that cannot be used up: *an inexhaustible supply of sth* ○ *My patience is not inexhaustible,* ie I will eventually become angry or impatient. ▷ **inexhaustibly** /-əblɪ/ *adv.*

inexorable /ɪnˈeksərəbl/ *adj* continuing unstoppably; relentless: *inexorable demands, pressures, etc* ○ *the inexorable march of progress.* ▷ **inexorability** /ɪnˌeksərəˈbɪlətɪ/ *n* [U]. **inexorably** /ɪnˈeksərəblɪ/ *adv.*

inexpedient /ˌɪnɪkˈspi:dɪənt/ *adj (fml)* not serving a useful purpose; unwise; not expedient: *It would be inexpedient to inform them at this stage.* ▷ **inexpediency** /-ənsɪ/ *n* [U].

inexpensive /ˌɪnɪkˈspensɪv/ *adj* low priced; not expensive. ▷ **inexpensively** *adv.*

inexperience /ˌɪnɪkˈspɪərɪəns/ *n* [U] ~ **(in sth)** lack of experience: *failure due to inexperience* ○ *You must forgive my inexperience in these matters.* ▷ **inexperienced** *adj* ~ **(in sth)** lacking experience: *inexperienced in love, business negotiation.*

inexpert /ɪnˈekspɜ:t/ *adj* ~ **(at sth)** unskilled: *inexpert advice, guidance, etc.* ▷ **inexpertly** *adv*: *an inexpertly executed stroke.*

inexpiable /ɪnˈekspɪəbl/ *adj (fml)* (of an offence) so bad that nothing one can do can make up for it; that cannot be expiated.

inexplicable /ˌɪnɪkˈsplɪkəbl/ *adj* that cannot be explained: *an inexplicable phenomenon.* ▷ **inexplicability** /ˌɪnɪkˌsplɪkəˈbɪlətɪ/ *n* [U]. **inexplicably** /ˌɪnɪkˈsplɪkəblɪ/ *adv*: *Inexplicably she never turned up.*

inexpressible /ˌɪnɪkˈspresəbl/ *adj* too great to be expressed in words: *inexpressible sorrow, anguish, joy, etc.* ▷ **inexpressibly** /-əblɪ/ *adv*: *inexpressibly sad.*

inextinguishable /ˌɪnɪkˈstɪŋgwɪʃəbl/ *adj (fml)* that cannot be extinguished or put out: *the inextinguishable flame of liberty* ○ *(fig) inextinguishable hope, love, desire, etc.* ▷ **inextinguishably** /-əblɪ/ *adv.*

in extremis /ˌɪnɪkˈstri:mɪs/ *(Latin)* **1** *(fml)* (as a last resort when) in an emergency: *This alarm button is only to be used in extremis.* **2** *(religion)* (in the Roman Catholic Church) about to die: *administer the last sacrament to sb in extremis.*

inextricable /ˌɪnɪkˈstrɪkəbl, ɪnˈekstrɪkəbl/ *adj* **1** so closely linked that separation is impossible: *In the Middle Ages, philosophy and theology were inextricable.* **2** that cannot be escaped from: *inextricable difficulties.* ▷ **inextricably** *adv*: *Her career was inextricably linked with his.*

inf *abbr* below; further on (in a book, etc) (Latin *infra*). Cf SUP *abbr.*

infallible /ɪnˈfæləbl/ *adj* **1** incapable of making mistakes or doing wrong: *None of us is infallible.* **2** extremely accurate: *a journalist with an infallible nose* (ie instinct) *for a story.* **3** never failing; always effective: *an infallible remedy, cure, method, test.*

▷ **infallibility** /ɪnˌfæləˈbɪlətɪ/ *n* [U] **1** complete freedom from the possibility of being wrong: *the doctrine of Papal infallibility.* **2** absolute certainty of effectiveness: *I can't claim infallibility for this method.*

infallibly /-əblɪ/ *adv* **1** in a manner that cannot fail: *infallibly accurate.* **2** without exception; always: *Every day she arrives, infallibly, five minutes late. I could set my watch by her!*

infamous /ˈɪnfəməs/ *adj* **1** ~ **(for sth)** well-known as being wicked or immoral; notorious: *an infamous traitor* ○ *a king infamous for his cruelty.* **2** (*fml*) wicked; disgraceful: *his infamous treatment of her.*
▷ **infamously** *adv.*

infamy /ˈɪnfəmɪ/ *n* (*fml*) **1** (a) [U] infamous behaviour; wickedness. (b) [C] wicked act: *guilty of many infamies.* **2** [U] public dishonour or disgrace: *His name will live in infamy,* ie He will always be held in disgrace.

infancy /ˈɪnfənsɪ/ *n* [U] **1** (a) state or period of being an infant; early childhood: *in early infancy.* (b) (*Brit law*) period before one reaches the age of 18; minority. **2** (*fig*) early stage of development or growth: *The project was cancelled while it was still in its infancy.*

infant /ˈɪnfənt/ *n* **1** child during the first few years of life: *infants, older children and adults* ○ [attrib] *our infant ˈson* ○ *infant ˈvoices* ○ *infant morˈtality rate,* ie percentage of children that die in the first few years of life ○ *an ˈinfant teacher,* ie one who teaches infants ○ (*fig*) *In its first general election, the infant* (ie newly-formed) *Social Democratic Party won few seats.* **2** (*Brit law*) person under the age of 18; minor.
□ ˌ**infant ˈprodigy** unusually talented child that shows signs of genius from an early age.
ˈ**infant school** (part of a) primary school for children up to the age of 7.

infanticide /ɪnˈfæntɪsaɪd/ *n* **1** [U] (a) crime of killing an infant: *commit infanticide.* (b) (formerly) custom among some people of killing unwanted new-born children. **2** person who kills an infant.

infantile /ˈɪnfəntaɪl/ *adj* **1** [usu attrib] of infants or infancy: *infantile diseases.* **2** (*derog*) (esp of older children or adults) childish: *infantile behaviour.*
▷ **infantilism** /ɪnˈfæntɪlɪzəm/ *n* [U] (of older children and adults) mentally and physically underdeveloped state.
□ ˌ**infantile paˈralysis** (*dated*) poliomyelitis.

infantry /ˈɪnfəntrɪ/ *n* [U, Gp] soldiers who fight on foot: *We have less infantry and armour than the enemy.* ○ *The infantry is/are defending well.* ○ [attrib] *an infantry regiment.* Cf CAVALRY.
□ ˈ**infantryman** /-mən/ *n* (*pl* **-men**) soldier in an infantry regiment.

infatuated /ɪnˈfætʃʊeɪtɪd/ *adj* ~ **(with/by sb/sth)** (*usu derog*) (temporarily) filled with an intense but usu foolish love: *It's no use talking to him: he's completely infatuated.* ○ *She's infatuated by his good looks.* ○ (*fig*) *He's so infatuated with the idea that he can't talk about anything else.*
▷ **infatuation** /ɪnˌfætʃʊˈeɪʃn/ *n* [U, C] ~ **(with/for sb/sth)** being infatuated: *His infatuation with her lasted six months.* ○ *This is only a passing infatuation, not to be taken too seriously.* ○ *develop an infatuation for sb.*

infect /ɪnˈfekt/ *v* [esp passive: Tn, Tn·pr] ~ **sb/sth (with sth) 1** cause sb/sth to have a disease; contaminate sb/sth: *The laboratory animals had been infected with the bacteria.* ○ *an infected wound* ○ *Clean the infected area with disinfectant.* ○ *Police have sealed off infected areas of the country.* **2** (*fig derog*) fill (sb's mind) with undesirable ideas: *a mind infected with racial prejudice.* **3** (*fig approv*) fill (sb's mind or spirit) with happy and positive ideas or feelings: *Her cheerful spirits and bubbling laughter infected the whole class,* ie They became happy too.

infection /ɪnˈfekʃn/ *n* **1** [U] ~ **(with sth)** (a) becoming ill through contact with bacteria, etc: *be exposed to infection* ○ *the infection of the body with bacteria.* (b) (*fig derog*) filling the mind with undesirable ideas: *the infection of young people with dangerous ideologies.* **2** [C] disease caused by a micro-organism: *spread/pass on an infection* ○ *People catch all kinds of infections in the winter.* ○ *an airborne/a waterborne infection.* Cf CONTAGION.

infectious /ɪnˈfekʃəs/ *adj* **1** (of a disease) caused by bacteria, etc that are passed on from one person to another: *Flu is highly infectious.* **2** [usu pred] (of a person) in danger of infecting others (with a disease): *While you have this rash you are still infectious.* **3** (*fig approv*) quickly influencing others; likely to spread to others: *infectious enthusiasm* ○ *an infectious laugh.* ▷ **infectiously** *adv*: *laugh infectiously.* **infectiousness** *n* [U]. Cf CONTAGIOUS.

infelicity /ˌɪnfəˈlɪsətɪ/ *n* (*fml or rhet*) **1** [C, U] (instance of) unsuitability or inappropriateness: *infelicities of style in his new novel.* **2** [U] unhappiness; misfortune.
▷ **infelicitous** /ˌɪnfəˈlɪsɪtəs/ *adj* (*fml*) not suitable or appropriate.

infer /ɪnˈfɜː(r)/ *v* (**-rr-**) [Tn, Tn·pr, Tf] ~ **sth (from sth)** reach (an opinion) from facts or reasoning; conclude sth: *It is possible to infer two completely opposite conclusions from this set of facts.* ○ *Am I to infer (from your remarks) that you think I'm not telling the truth?* Cf IMPLY.
▷ **inference** /ˈɪnfərəns/ *n* **1** [U] process of inferring: *If he is guilty then by inference so is she,* ie This conclusion follows logically from the same set of facts. **2** [C] ~ **(from sth) (that...)** that which is inferred; conclusion: *Is that a fair inference (to draw) from his statement?* ○ *She'd begun spending a lot of money, and the obvious inference was that she'd stolen it.* **inferential** /ˌɪnfəˈrenʃl/ *adj* that may be inferred: *inferential proof.* **inferentially** /-ʃəlɪ/ *adv.*

inferior /ɪnˈfɪərɪə(r)/ *adj* ~ **(to sb/sth)** low(er) in rank, social position, importance, quality, etc: *A captain is inferior to a major.* ○ *be socially inferior* ○ *make sb feel inferior* ○ *inferior goods, workmanship.* Cf SUPERIOR.
▷ **inferior** *n* person who is inferior (in rank, etc): *one's social inferior* ○ *We should not despise our intellectual inferiors.*
inferiority /ɪnˌfɪərɪˈɒrətɪ; *US* -ˈɔːr-/ *n* [U] state of being inferior: *feelings of inferiority.* **inferiˈority complex** (*psychology*) state of mind in which sb feels less important, clever, admired, etc than other people, and often tries to compensate for this by boasting and being aggressive. Cf SUPERIORITY COMPLEX (SUPERIOR).

infernal /ɪnˈfɜːnl/ *adj* **1** (*rhet*) (a) of hell: *the infernal regions.* (b) devilish; abominable: *infernal cruelty.* **2** [attrib] (*infml*) annoying; tiresome: *That infernal telephone hasn't stopped ringing all day!* ○ *an infernal nuisance.* ▷ **infernally** /-nəlɪ/ *adv*: *infernally rude.*

inferno /ɪnˈfɜːnəʊ/ *n* (*pl* ~**s** /-z/) **1** place or situation like hell, esp in being full of horror and confusion: *the inferno of war.* **2** (place affected by a) large destructive fire: *The place was a blazing, raging, roaring, etc inferno.*

infertile /ɪnˈfɜːtaɪl; *US* -tl/ *adj* not fertile; barren: *infertile land* ○ *an infertile couple,* ie unable to have children. ▷ **infertility** /ˌɪnfəˈtɪlətɪ/ *n* [U].

infest /ɪnˈfest/ *v* [usu passive: Tn, Tn·pr] ~ **sth (with sth)** (*derog*) (of pests, vermin, insects, etc) live in (a place) persistently and in large numbers: *a warehouse infested by rats* ○ *clothing infested with lice* ○ *a garden infested with weeds.*
▷ **infestation** /ˌɪnfeˈsteɪʃn/ *n* [C, U] (instance of) infesting or being infested: *an infestation of cockroaches.*

infidel /ˈɪnfɪdəl/ *n* (*arch derog*) person with no belief in a religion, esp in what is considered to be the true religion.

infidelity /ˌɪnfɪˈdelətɪ/ *n* [C, U] (*fml*) (act of) disloyalty or unfaithfulness, esp adultery: *willing to forgive her husband's little infidelities.*

infield /ˈɪnfiːld/ *n* **the infield 1** (a) [sing] (in cricket) part of the ground near the wicket. (b) [pl *v*] fielders stationed there. **2** (a) [sing] (in baseball) area within the diamond(4). (b) [pl *v*] fielders stationed there. Cf OUTFIELD.
▷ **infielder** *n* person fielding in the infield.

infighting /ˈɪnfaɪtɪŋ/ *n* [U] **1** (in boxing) fighting in which the opponents are very close to or holding on to each other. **2** (*fig infml*) fierce competition between rivals (eg involving intrigue, betrayal, etc): *I gather a lot of political infighting went on before he got the top job.*

infill /ˈɪnfɪl/ (also **infilling**) *n* [U] **1** act of filling gaps (eg in a row of buildings). **2** material used to fill a hole or gap (eg in a wall).

infiltrate /ˈɪnfɪltreɪt/ *v* **1** [I, Ipr] ~ **(through sth) (into sth)** (of liquids, gases, etc) pass slowly by filtering; penetrate: *The thick fog seemed to have infiltrated through the very walls into the room.* ○ (*fig*) *the depths of the ocean, where no light can infiltrate.* **2** [Tn·pr] ~ **A into B**/~ **B with A** cause sth to pass slowly by filtering it into sth else: *infiltrate poison into the water-supply/infiltrate the water-supply with poison.* **3** [Ipr, Tn] ~ **(through sth) (into sth)** (*esp military or politics*) enter (sth) stealthily without being noticed: *troops infiltrating through enemy lines into occupied territory* ○ *Our entire organization had been infiltrated by enemy agents.* **4** [Tn·pr] (*esp military or politics*) ~ **sb/sth into sth;** ~ **sth with sb/sth** introduce sb/sth stealthily into sth: *infiltrate spies into a country* ○ *infiltrate an organization with one's own men.*
▷ **infiltration** /ˌɪnfɪlˈtreɪʃn/ *n* **1** [U] ~ **(of sth) (into sth)** infiltrating or being infiltrated: *infiltration of poisonous chemicals into the water-supply.* **2** ~ **(of sb/sth into sth);** ~ **(of sth with sb/sth)** (*esp military or politics*) (a) [U] infiltrating of people, ideas, etc: *the infiltration of spies, troops, etc into an area, organization, etc* ○ *the infiltration of an organization with one's agents.* (b) [C] instance of this.
infiltrator /ˈɪnfɪltreɪtə(r)/ *n* person who infiltrates: *left-wing infiltrators.*

infinite /ˈɪnfɪnət/ *adj* **1** (a) without limits; endless: *infinite space.* (b) that cannot be measured, calculated or imagined; very great: *the infinite goodness of God* ○ *have infinite faith/an infinite amount of faith in sb* ○ *a painting restored with infinite care* ○ *You need infinite patience for this job.* **2** (*mathematics*) (a) greater than any number that can be counted. (b) (of a series of numbers) that can go on being extended for ever, and never reaches an end.
▷ **the Infinite** *n* [sing] (*rhet*) God.
infinitely *adv* **1** to an infinite degree: *The particles in an atom are infinitely small.* **2** (esp with comparatives) very much: *infinitely better, taller, wiser, etc (than sb/sth else)* ○ *infinitely preferable (to sb/sth else).*

infinitesimal /ˌɪnfɪnɪˈtesɪml/ *adj* extremely small: *an infinitesimal increase.* ▷ **infinitesimally** /-məlɪ/ *adv.*
□ ˌ**infiniˌtesimal ˈcalculus** (*mathematics*) differential calculus and integral calculus together regarded as one subject.

infinitive /ɪnˈfɪnətɪv/ *n* (*grammar*) **1** basic form of a verb, without inflections, etc (in English used with or without *to,* as in *he can go; ask him to go*): *a verb in the infinitive* ○ [attrib] *the infinitive form.* **2** (idm) **split an infinitive** ⇨ SPLIT.

infinitude /ɪnˈfɪnɪtjuːd; *US* -tuːd/ *n* (*fml*) (a) [U] state of being endless or boundless; boundless number or extent: *the infinitude of God's mercy.* (b) [C] infinite number, quantity or extent: *an infinitude of small particles.*

infinity /ɪnˈfɪnətɪ/ *n* **1** [U] state of being endless or boundless; infinite nature: *the infinity of space.* **2** [U] infinite distance or point in space: *gaze into infinity,* ie vaguely into the distance ○ *Parallel lines meet at infinity.* **3** [U] (*mathematics*) number larger than any other that can be thought of (expressed by the symbol ∞); infinite quantity: *1/n tends to infinity as n gets very small.* ⇨ App 9. **4** [sing] indefinitely large amount: *an infinity of stars, of troubles, of things to do.*

infirm /ɪnˈfɜːm/ *adj* **1** physically weak (esp from old age or illness): *walk with infirm steps.* **2** ~ **of sth** (*fml*) without strength of sth: *infirm of purpose, will, etc,* ie not purposeful, not resolute.
▷ **the infirm** *n* [pl *v*] infirm people: *support for the aged and infirm.*
infirmity /ɪnˈfɜːmətɪ/ *n* [C, U] (particular form of) weakness: *Old age and infirmity had begun to catch up with him.* ○ *infirmity of purpose* ○

Deafness and failing eyesight are among the infirmities of old age.

infirmary /ɪnˈfɜːmərɪ/ *n* **1** hospital. **2** (in a school or some other institution) room used for people who are ill or injured.

in flagrante delicto /ˌɪn fləˌgræntɪ dɪˈlɪktəʊ/ (also **in flagrante**) while actually committing a crime or misdeed; red-handed: *The murderer was caught in flagrante delicto.*

inflame /ɪnˈfleɪm/ *v* [Tn, Tn·pr] ~ **sb/sth (with/to sth)** cause sb/sth to become angry or over-excited: *a speech that inflamed the crowd with anger/to a high pitch of fury.*

▷ **inflamed** *adj* ~ **(by/with sth) 1** (of a part of the body) red, hot and sore (eg because of infection): *inflamed eyes* ○ *an inflamed boil* ○ *a nose inflamed by an infection.* **2** (*fig*) roused to anger, indignation, etc: *inflamed by sb's words* ○ *inflamed with passion.*

inflammable /ɪnˈflæməbl/ *adj* **1** that can be set on fire: *Petroleum — highly inflammable*, eg on a notice. Cf NON-FLAMMABLE. ⇨ Usage at INVALUABLE. **2** (*fig infml*) easily excited or aroused: *a man with an inflammable temper.*

inflammation /ˌɪnfləˈmeɪʃn/ *n* [C, U] condition in which a part of the body is red, swollen and sore or itchy, esp because of infection: *(an) inflammation of the lungs, liver, etc.*

inflammatory /ɪnˈflæmətrɪ; *US* -tɔːrɪ/ *adj* **1** (*derog*) tending to make people angry or over-excited: *inflammatory remarks, speeches, words, etc.* **2** of, being or tending to produce inflammation: *an inflammatory condition of the lungs.*

inflate /ɪnˈfleɪt/ *v* **1** (**a**) [Tn, Tn·pr] ~ **sth (with sth)** fill (a tyre, balloon, etc) with air or gas: *a fully inflated tyre.* (**b**) [I] become filled with air or gas; swell: *With a supply of compressed air the large balloon inflated in a matter of seconds.* **2** [Tn] (*fig*) cause (sb's self-opinion) to become too great: *flattery that would inflate the most modest person's ego.* **3** [I, Tn] (*finance*) take action to increase the amount of money in circulation in (an economy) so that prices rise. Cf DEFLATE, REFLATE.

▷ **inflatable** /-əbl/ *adj* that can be or must be inflated: *an inflatable dinghy.*

inflated *adj* **1** filled with air, gas, etc. **2** (*derog*) exaggerated: *an inflated opinion of oneself* ○ *inflated language*, ie full of impressive words, but little meaning. **3** (of prices) raised artificially or as a result of financial inflation: *having to pay inflated prices.*

inflation /ɪnˈfleɪʃn/ *n* [U] **1** process of inflating (INFLATE 1a); being inflated. **2** rise in prices resulting from an increase in the supply of money, credit, etc: *control/curb inflation* ○ *galloping* (ie severe and rapid) *inflation.* **inflationary** /ɪnˈfleɪʃnrɪ; *US* -nerɪ/ *adj* of, caused by or causing financial inflation: *the inflationary spiral*, ie economic situation in which prices and wages rise in turn as the supply of money is increased ○ *inflationary wage claims.*

inflect /ɪnˈflekt/ *v* [Tn] **1** (*grammar*) change the ending or form of (a word) to show its grammatical function in a sentence: *Most English verbs are inflected with '-ed' in the past tense.* **2** make (the voice) higher or lower in speaking: *By inflecting the voice more one can hold the attention of an audience.*

▷ **inflected** *adj* (of a language) having many inflected words: *Latin is a more inflected language than English.*

inflection (also **inflexion**) /ɪnˈflekʃn/ *n* **1** (*grammar*) (**a**) [U] inflecting. (**b**) [C] suffix used to inflect a word (eg *-ed, -ing*). **2** [U] rise and fall of the voice in speaking. Cf INTONATION, STRESS 3.

▷ **inflectional** /-ʃənl/ *adj* of or being inflections: *inflectional endings/forms*, eg *-ed.*

inflexible /ɪnˈfleksəbl/ *adj* (**a**) that cannot be bent or turned: *made of an inflexible plastic.* (**b**) (*fig*) that cannot be changed, influenced, etc; unyielding: *an inflexible will, determination, purpose, etc* ○ *an inflexible attitude, rule, system.* ▷ **inflexibility** /ɪnˌfleksəˈbɪlətɪ/ *n* [U]. **inflexibly** /-əblɪ/ *adv.*

inflict /ɪnˈflɪkt/ *v* **1** [Tn, Tn·pr] ~ **sth (on sb)** cause (a blow, penalty, etc) to be suffered (by sb): *inflict a severe wound on sb* ○ *inflict a crushing defeat on the enemy.* **2** [Tn·pr] ~ **sb/sth on sb** (*infml often joc*) force sb to accept one's unwelcome presence: *apologize for inflicting oneself/one's company on sb* ○ *My uncle is inflicting himself on* (ie visiting) *us again this weekend.*

▷ **infliction** /ɪnˈflɪkʃn/ *n* (**a**) [U] inflicting or being inflicted: *the unnecessary infliction of pain and suffering.* (**b**) [C] thing inflicted; painful or troublesome experience.

in-flight /ˌɪnˈflaɪt/ *adj* [usu attrib] occurring or provided during the flight of an aircraft: *ˌin-flight reˈfuelling, enterˈtainment.*

inflorescence /ˌɪnflɔːˈresəns/ *n* (*botany*) arrangement of a plant's flowers on the stem; collective flower of a plant.

inflow /ˈɪnfləʊ/ *n* **1** [U] flowing in. **2** [C, U] (**a**) that which flows in: *an inflow of 25 litres per hour* ○ [attrib] *an inflow pipe.* (**b**) (*fig*) influx: *an inflow of cash, capital, etc.*

influence /ˈɪnflʊəns/ *n* **1** [U] ~ **(on sth)** power to produce an effect; action of natural forces: *the influence of the moon (on the tides), of the climate (on agricultural production), etc.* **2** (**a**) [sing] ~ **(on sb/sth)** (exercising of) power to affect sb's actions, character or beliefs through example, fear, admiration, etc: *the influence of parents on their children* ○ *have a good, bad, beneficial, harmful, civilizing, pernicious, etc influence on sb's behaviour, character, etc* ○ *a young ruler under the influence of his chief minister* ○ *escape sb's influence.* (**b**) [C] ~ **(on sb/sth)** person, fact, etc that exercises such power: *Those so-called friends of hers are a bad influence on her.* ○ *Religion has been an influence for good in her life.* ○ *We are subject to many influences.* ○ *The influences at work in this case* (ie factors causing it to develop in a particular way) *are hard to disentangle.* **3** [U] ~ **(over sb/sth)** power to control sb's behaviour: *His parents no longer have any real influence over him.* **4** [U] ~ **(with sb)** ability to obtain favourable treatment from sb, usu by means of acquaintance, status, wealth, etc: *use one's influence (with sb)* ○ *She has great influence with the manager and could no doubt help you.* **5** (idm) **under the ˈinfluence (of ˈalcohol)** (*fml or joc*) (showing signs of) having had too much to drink: *be charged with driving under the influence.*

▷ **influence** *v* **1** [Tn] have an effect or influence on (sb/sth); cause (sb/sth) to act, behave, think, etc in a particular way: *the belief of astrologers that planets influence human character* ○ *I don't want to influence you either way, so I won't tell you my opinion.* ○ *It's clear that her painting has been influenced by Picasso.* **2** [Cn·t] cause or persuade (sb) to do sth: *What influenced you to behave like that?*

influential /ˌɪnflʊˈenʃl/ *adj* **1** ~ **(in sth/doing sth)** having influence; persuasive: *factors that are influential* (ie have an important effect) *in reaching a decision* ○ *an influential speech.* **2** having the status, wealth, etc that enables one to persuade others to do sth: *a committee of influential businessmen, union leaders, etc.*

influenza /ˌɪnflʊˈenzə/ *n* [U] (*fml*) (also *infml* **flu** /fluː/) infectious virus disease causing fever, muscular pain and catarrh.

influx /ˈɪnflʌks/ *n* ~ **(into…)** arrival of people or things, esp suddenly and in large numbers or quantities: *frequent influxes of visitors* ○ *an influx of wealth.*

info /ˈɪnfəʊ/ *n* [U] ~ **(on/about sb/sth)** (*infml*) = INFORMATION 2.

inform /ɪnˈfɔːm/ *v* **1** [Tn, Tn·pr, Dn·f] ~ **sb (of/about sth)** give sb knowledge (of sth); tell sb: *'Some money is missing.' 'Have you informed the police?'* ○ *Keep me informed (of/about what happens).* ○ *inform oneself of the facts*, ie find out all that needs to be known ○ *He informed the police that some money was missing.* **2** [Ipr] ~ **against/on sb** (*law*) give evidence or make an accusation against sb (to the police): *One of the criminals informed against/on the rest of the gang.* **3** [Tn] (*fml*) give (sth) its essential features; pervade: *th sense of justice which informs all her writings.*

▷ **informant** /-ənt/ *n* **1** person who give information: *The journalist did not want to revea the identity of his informant.* **2** (*linguistics*) nativ speaker of a language who helps a scholar make a analysis of the language.

informed *adj* having or showing knowledge: *ar informed critic, member of the public, etc* ○ *informed criticism* ○ *an informed guess*, ie based or some knowledge.

informer *n* person who informs, esp against a criminal or fugitive.

informal /ɪnˈfɔːml/ *adj* **1** not formal; withou formality: *an informal* (ie friendly) *manner, tone atmosphere, person* ○ *an informal* (ie not official *arrangement, gathering, meeting, occasion, visit* **2** (of dress, behaviour, etc) chosen to show personal taste rather than follow social conventions of formality. **3** (of language, speech writing) conversational in style (and markec (*infml*) in this dictionary): *an informal letter.* C COLLOQUIAL, SLANG.

▷ **informality** /ˌɪnfɔːˈmælətɪ/ *n* **1** [U] being informal. **2** [C] informal act.

informally /ɪnˈfɔːməlɪ/ *adv*: *They told m informally* (ie unofficially) *that I had got the job.*

□ **inˌformal ˈvote** (*Austral and NZ*) vote that is not valid because the voting paper has not beer filled in properly.

information /ˌɪnfəˈmeɪʃn/ *n* **1** [U] informing or being informed: *For your information* (ie This is sth you may wish to know), *the library is on the first floor.* ○ (*ironic*) *I'm perfectly able to look after myself, for your information.* ○ (*fml*) *My information is that* (ie I have been told that) *they have all left.* **2** [U] ~ **(on/about sb/sth)** facts told heard or discovered (about sb/sth): *give, pass on receive, obtain, seek, find, collect, etc information (on/about sb/sth)* ○ *For further information please write to…* ○ *a useful bit/piece of information* ○ [attrib] *an information bureau, desk, etc.* **3** [C] ~ **(against sb)** (*law*) charge or complaint officially made against sb in a lawcourt. **4** (idm) **a mine of information** ⇨ MINE[2].

□ **inforˈmation science** (also **inforˈmation technology**) study or use of processes (esp computers, telecommunications, etc) for storing retrieving and sending information of all kinds (eg words, numbers, pictures).

informative /ɪnˈfɔːmətɪv/ *adj* giving much information; instructive: *an informative book film, lecture, speaker.*

infra /ˈɪnfrə/ *adv* (*Latin fml*) further on (in a book etc); below: *see infra.* Cf VIDE.

□ **ˌinfra ˈdig** /dɪg/ [pred] (*infml often joc*) beneath one's dignity; demeaning: *Dancing in the street is rather infra dig for a bank manager!*

infra- *pref* (with *adjs*) below: *infra-sonic.* Cf ULTRA-.

infraction /ɪnˈfrækʃn/ *n* (*fml*) (**a**) [U] breaking of a rule, law, etc. (**b**) [C] instance of this: *a minor infraction of the rules.*

infra-red /ˌɪnfrə ˈred/ *adj* of the (invisible heat-giving) rays below the red in the spectrum: *an ˌinfra-red ˈheater* ○ *ˌinfra-red phoˈtography*, ie used for taking pictures in darkness.

infrastructure /ˈɪnfrəstrʌkʃə(r)/ *n* (**a**) subordinate parts, installations, etc that form the basis of a system, an organisation or an enterprise (eg of an army). (**b**) (*economics*) facilities such as roads, railways, power-stations, water supply, telephones, etc which form the basis for a country's economic growth.

infrequent /ɪnˈfriːkwənt/ *adj* not frequent; rare: *infrequent visits, performances, etc.* ▷ **infrequency** /-kwənsɪ/ *n* [U]. **infrequently** *adv.*

infringe /ɪnˈfrɪndʒ/ *v* **1** [Tn] (**a**) break (a rule, an agreement, etc): *infringe the regulations, a copyright agreement, etc.* (**b**) interfere with (sth); violate: *infringe sb's liberty, rights, etc.* **2** [Ipr] ~ **on/upon sth** affect sth so as to limit or restrict it; encroach on: *infringe upon the rights of other people.*

▷ **infringement** /-mənt/ *n* (**a**) [U] infringing or being infringed: *laws subject to frequent* *infringement.* **(b)** [C] instance of this: *an infringement of the highway code, of copyright, of sb's privacy.*

infuriate /ɪnˈfjʊərɪeɪt/ *v* [Tn] make (sb) extremely angry: *I was infuriated by/with their constant criticism.*
▷ **infuriating** *adj* that infuriates: *infuriating delays.* **infuriatingly** *adv*: *Infuriatingly, I just missed my plane.*

infuse /ɪnˈfju:z/ *v* **1** [Tn·pr] ~ **sth into sb/sth;** ~ **sb/sth with sth** put (a quality) into sb/sth; fill sb/sth with (a quality): *infuse new life, energy, etc into the workers* ○ *infuse the workers with new life, energy, etc.* **2 (a)** [Tn] soak (tea or herbs) in a liquid (usu hot water) to extract flavour or ingredients for a drink or medicine. **(b)** [I] (of tea or herbs) undergo this process: *Don't drink the tea until it has finished infusing.*

infusion /ɪnˈfju:ʒn/ *n* **1** [U] ~ **of sth (into sb/sth)** infusing a quality or being infused into sb/sth: *infusion of new life (into the enterprise)* ○ *This company needs an infusion of new blood,* ie needs new employees to give it vigour. **2 (a)** [U] infusing of tea, herbs, etc or being infused. **(b)** [C] liquid made by infusing.

-ing *suff* **1** (with *vs* forming [U] *ns* denoting the action of the verb): *Her hobby is sailing.* **2** (forming the *pres p* of *vs*): *The ship was sailing along.* ▷ **-ingly** /ɪŋlɪ/ *suff* (forming *advs* from *vs*): *She spoke soothingly.*

ingenious /ɪnˈdʒi:nɪəs/ *adj* **(a)** ~ **(at sth/doing sth)** (of a person) clever at finding new or simple solutions for complex problems: *So you fitted that wire through that little hole there: that's very ingenious!* ○ *ingenious at solving difficult crossword puzzles.* **(b)** (of a thing) original in design and well suited to its purpose: *an ingenious device, gadget, etc.* **(c)** (of an idea) very clever and original: *an ingenious plan, method, solution, etc.* ▷ **ingeniously** *adv.*
ingenuity /ˌɪndʒɪˈnju:ətɪ; *US* -ˈnu:-/ *n* [U] cleverness and originality in solving problems.

ingénue /ˈænʒeɪnju:; *US* ˈændʒənu:/ *n* simple innocent girl, esp as portrayed in plays, films, etc: [attrib] *an ingénue role.*

ingenuous /ɪnˈdʒenjʊəs/ *adj (fml)* not attempting to deceive or conceal; open; innocent: *an ingenuous smile.* ▷ **ingenuously** *adv.* **ingenuousness** *n* [U].

ingest /ɪnˈdʒest/ *v* [Tn] *(fml)* **1** take (food, etc) into the body, typically by swallowing. **2** *(fig)* take (sth) in; absorb: *ingest information.*

ingle-nook /ˈɪŋgl nʊk/ *n* small opening beside a wide old-fashioned fireplace in which one can sit close to the fire.

inglorious /ɪnˈglɔ:rɪəs/ *adj* **1** shameful; ignominious: *an inglorious defeat* ○ *a new play which suffered the inglorious fate of being taken off after only three days.* **2** [usu attrib] *(rhet)* unknown; obscure: *an inglorious name.* ▷ **ingloriously** *adv.*

ingoing /ˈɪŋgəʊɪŋ/ *adj* [attrib] going in: *the ingoing* (ie new) *tenant of a flat.*

ingot /ˈɪŋgət/ *n* (usu brick-shaped) lump of metal, esp gold and silver, cast in a mould.

ingrained /ɪnˈgreɪnd/ *adj* **1** (of habits, tendencies, etc) deeply fixed; thorough: *ingrained prejudices, suspicions, assumptions, etc.* **2** (of dirt, stains, etc) going deeply into a substance, and therefore difficult to clean off: *deeply ingrained dirt.*

ingratiate /ɪnˈgreɪʃɪeɪt/ *v* [no passive: Tn, Tn·pr] *(fml derog)* ~ **oneself (with sb)** (attempt to) gain the favour of sb by flattering him, doing things that will please him, etc: *She tried to ingratiate herself with the director, in the hope of getting promotion.*
▷ **ingratiating** *adj (derog)* attempting to please, flatter or gain favour: *an ingratiating smile.* **ingratiatingly** *adv.*

ingratitude /ɪnˈgrætɪtju:d; *US* -tu:d/ *n* [U] lack of gratitude.

ingredient /ɪnˈgri:dɪənt/ *n* **1** any of the foods that are combined to make a particular dish: *the ingredients of a cake* ○ *Mix all the ingredients in a bowl.* **2** *(fig)* any of the qualities of which sth is made: *the ingredients of a/sb's character, of success, of happiness, etc.*

ingress /ˈɪŋgres/ *n* [U] *(fml)* going in; (right of) entrance: *a means of ingress.* Cf EGRESS.

in-group /ˈɪn gru:p/ *n (usu derog)* group within an organization or in society that behaves in an exclusive way and gives favoured treatment to its own members; clique.

ingrowing /ˈɪŋgrəʊɪŋ/ *adj* [usu attrib] growing inwards: *an ingrowing toenail,* ie one growing into the flesh.

inhabit /ɪnˈhæbɪt/ *v* [Tn] live in (sth); occupy: *an island inhabited only by birds.*
▷ **inhabitable** *adj* that can be lived in.
inhabitant /-ənt/ *n* person or animal living in a place: *the local inhabitants* ○ *the oldest inhabitants of the island.*

inhale /ɪnˈheɪl/ *v* [I, Tn, Tn·pr] ~ **sth (into sth) (a)** breathe sth in: *inhale deeply* ○ *Inhale! Exhale!* ie breathe in; breathe out ○ *miners who have inhaled coal dust into their lungs.* **(b)** take (tobacco smoke) into the lungs: *Smokers who inhale are likely to become addicted to nicotine.*
▷ **inhalant** *n* /-ənt/ medicinal substance that is inhaled, eg to help sb who has difficulty in breathing.
inhalation /ˌɪnhəˈleɪʃn/ *n* [U].
inhaler *n* device that emits medicine in a fine spray to be inhaled, eg by sb with asthma.

inharmonious /ˌɪnhɑ:ˈməʊnɪəs/ *adj (fml)* not harmonious. ▷ **inharmoniously** *adv.* **inharmoniousness** *n* [U].

inherent /ɪnˈhɪərənt, -ˈher-/ *adj* ~ **(in sb/sth)** existing as a natural or permanent feature or quality of sth/sb: *an inherent distrust of foreigners* ○ *an inherent weakness in a design* ○ *the power inherent in the office of President.* ▷ **inherently** *adv*: *a design which is inherently weak.*

inherit /ɪnˈherɪt/ *v* [Tn, Tn·pr] ~ **sth (from sb) 1** receive (property, a title, etc) as a result of the death of the previous owner: *a son inheriting an estate, a title, etc (from his father)* ○ *She inherited a little money from her grandfather.* **2** derive (qualities, etc) from an ancestor: *She inherited her mother's good looks and her father's bad temper.* **3** *(fig)* receive (sth) from a predecessor: *This government has inherited many problems from the previous one.*
▷ **inheritance** /-əns/ *n* **1** [U] ~ **(of sth) (from sb/sth)** inheriting (sth from sb): *The title passes by inheritance to the eldest son.* ○ *(fig) the inheritance of good looks from one's parents* ○ [attrib] *inheritance tax.* ⇨ article at TAXATION. **2** [C] ~ **(from sb)** what is inherited: *When she was 21 she came into* (ie received) *her inheritance.* ○ *(fig) a bitter dispute which left an inheritance of ill-feeling.* Cf LEGACY.
inheritor *n* person who inherits.

inhibit /ɪnˈhɪbɪt/ *v* **1** [Tn, Tn·pr] ~ **sb (from sth/doing sth)** prevent sb from doing sth that should be natural or easy to do: *Shyness inhibited him from speaking.* **2** [Tn] hinder or prevent (a process or an action): *an enzyme which inhibits a chemical reaction.*
▷ **inhibited** *adj* **(a)** (of people) unable to relax or express one's feelings in a natural and spontaneous way: *She's too inhibited to laugh at jokes about sex.* **(b)** (of behaviour) not relaxed or spontaneous: *a nervous inhibited laugh.* **inhibitedly** *adv.*
inhibition /ˌɪnhɪˈbɪʃn, ˌɪnɪˈb-/ *n* **1** [U] inhibiting or being inhibited: *Inhibition of natural impulses may cause psychological problems.* **2** [C] inability to act naturally or spontaneously: *Alcohol weakens a person's inhibitions,* ie makes him behave more naturally. ○ *(infml) She had no inhibitions about asking for more,* ie did so without hesitation.
inhibitor *n* substance that prevents or slows down chemical change. Cf CATALYST 1.

inhospitable /ˌɪnhɒˈspɪtəbl/ *adj* **(a)** (of people) not giving a friendly or polite welcome to guests: *It was inhospitable of you not to offer her a drink.* **(b)** *(fig)* (of places) not giving shelter; unpleasant to be in: *an inhospitable coast.* ▷ **inhospitably** *adv.*

inhuman /ɪnˈhju:mən/ *adj* lacking normal human qualities of kindness, pity, etc; extremely cruel or brutal: *inhuman behaviour, treatment, etc* ○ *That man is an inhuman monster!* ○ *It was inhuman to refuse him permission to see his wife.*
▷ **inhumanity** /ˌɪnhju:ˈmænətɪ/ *n* [U] inhuman conduct or behaviour: *man's inhumanity to man.*

inhumane /ˌɪnhju:ˈmeɪn/ *adj* insensitive to the suffering of others; cruel: *inhumane treatment of animals, prisoners, the mentally ill, etc* ○ *an inhumane law, policy, decision, etc.* ▷ **inhumanely** *adv*: *animals slaughtered inhumanely.*

inimical /ɪˈnɪmɪkl/ *adj* [usu pred] ~ **(to sb/sth)** *(fml)* **1** unfriendly; hostile: *countries that are inimical to us/to our interests.* **2** tending to prevent or discourage sth; harmful: *actions that are inimical to friendly relations between countries.* ▷ **inimically** /-klɪ/ *adv.*

inimitable /ɪˈnɪmɪtəbl/ *adj* impossible to imitate; too good, clever, etc to imitate: *Frank Sinatra's inimitable style of singing.* ▷ **inimitably** /-əblɪ/ *adv.*

iniquitous /ɪˈnɪkwɪtəs/ *adj* **1** *(fml)* very wicked or unjust: *an iniquitous system, regime, etc.* **2** (of a price, charge, etc) unfairly or ridiculously high: *Have you seen this bill? It's iniquitous!*
▷ **iniquitously** *adv.*
iniquity /ɪˈnɪkwətɪ/ *n* **1 (a)** [U] *(rhet)* wickedness and unjustness: *He regards the city as a place where all forms of iniquity are practised.* **(b)** [C] wicked and unjust act. **2** (idm) **a den of iniquity/vice** ⇨ DEN.

initial /ɪˈnɪʃl/ *adj* [attrib] of or at the beginning; first: *the initial letter of a word* ○ *in the initial stages* (ie at the beginning) *(of sth)* ○ *My initial reaction was to refuse.*
▷ **initial** *n* (usu *pl*) initial letter (of a name): *George Bernard Shaw was well-known by his initials GBS.* ○ *Sign your name and initials,* ie your surname and the initial letters of your other names.
initial *v* (-ll-; *US* usu -l-) [I, Tn] mark or sign (sth) with one's initials: *Initial here, please.* ○ *initial a note, document, treaty, etc.*
initially /-ʃəlɪ/ *adv* at the beginning; at first: *She came initially to spend a few days, but in the end she stayed for a whole month.*
□ **iˌnitial ˈteaching alphabet** phonetic alphabet with 44 letters devised to help (esp young) people learning to read and write English.

initiate /ɪˈnɪʃɪeɪt/ *v* **1** [Tn] *(fml)* put (a scheme, etc) into operation; cause (sth) to begin: *initiate plans, schemes, social reforms, etc* ○ *(law) initiate proceedings against sb,* ie begin a legal action against sb. **2** [Tn, Tn·pr] ~ **sb (into sth) (a)** admit or introduce sb to membership of a group, etc, often by means of a special ceremony: *initiate sb into a religious sect, secret society, etc.* **(b)** give sb elementary instruction (in sth) or secret knowledge (of sth): *an older woman who had initiated him into the mysteries of love.*
▷ **initiate** /ɪˈnɪʃɪət/ *n* person who has (just) been initiated into a group.
the initiated /ɪˈnɪʃɪeɪtɪd/ *n* [pl *v*] people who share special knowledge, secrets, etc known only to a few: *the government's secret defence committee, known to the initiated as DefCom.*
initiation /ɪˌnɪʃɪˈeɪʃn/ *n* [U] **1** ~ **(of sth)** *(fml)* bringing sth into effect; starting: *the initiation of an investigation.* **2** ~ **(into sth)** initiating or being initiated (into sth): [attrib] *an initiation ceremony.*

initiative /ɪˈnɪʃətɪv/ *n* **1** [C] action taken to resolve a difficulty: *It is hoped that the government's initiative will bring the strike to an end.* **2 the initiative** [sing] power or right to take action: *The initiative has passed to us.* ○ *Because of the general's indecisiveness, our armies have lost the initiative to the enemy.* **3** [U] *(approv)* capacity to see what needs to be done and enterprise enough to do it, esp without others' help: *a man who lacks the initiative to be a leader* ○ *The child showed/displayed great initiative in going to fetch the police.* ○ [attrib] *an initiative test.* **4** [C] power or right of ordinary citizens to make proposals for new laws (as in Switzerland). **5** (idm) **on one's**

own i'nitiative without anyone else ordering one to do sth, or suggesting that one should do it: *In the absence of my commanding officer, I acted on my own initiative.* **take the initiative** take the first step in an undertaking, esp one that encourages others to act: *It's up to this country to take the initiative in banning nuclear weapons.*

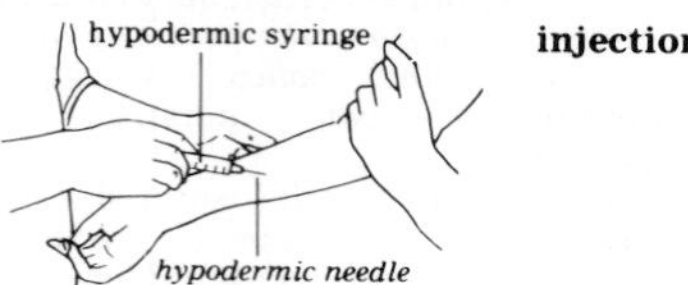

injection

inject /ɪnˈdʒekt/ *v* **1** [Tn, Tn·pr] ~ **sth (into sb/sth)**; ~ **sb/sth (with sth)** force (a drug or other liquid) into sb/sth with a syringe or similar implement: *a drug that can be injected or taken by mouth* ○ *inject penicillin into sb/sb's arm, leg, etc* ○ *inject sb/sb's arm, leg, etc with penicillin* ○ *inject foam into a cavity wall.* **2** [Tn, Tn·pr] ~ **sth (into sb/sth)** (*fig*) introduce (new thoughts, feelings, etc) into sb/sth: *inject a few new ideas into the project* ○ *Try to inject a bit of enthusiasm into your performance.*

▷ **injection** /ɪnˈdʒekʃn/ *n* ~ **(of sth) (into sb/sth)** **1** [U] injecting: *The morphine was administered by injection.* ○ [attrib] *a fuel-injection system.* **2** [C] instance of this: *a lethal injection of the drug* ○ *a course of injections* ○ *If you're going abroad, have you had your injections yet?* ○ *The firm would be revitalized by an injection of new funds.*

in-joke /ˈɪn dʒəʊk/ *n* joke whose meaning can be understood only by a small group of people.

injudicious /ˌɪndʒuːˈdɪʃəs/ *adj* (*fml*) not appropriate or tactful: *injudicious remarks* ○ *Now would be an injudicious moment to ask for a rise.* ▷ **injudiciously** *adv.* **injudiciousness** *n* [U].

injunction /ɪnˈdʒʌŋkʃn/ *n* (*fml*) official order, esp a written order from a lawcourt, demanding that sth shall or shall not be done: *The government has sought an injunction preventing the paper from publishing the story.*

injure /ˈɪndʒə(r)/ *v* [Tn] hurt (sb); harm: *injure oneself (by falling)* ○ *be slightly/seriously/badly injured in the crash* ○ (*fig*) *injure one's health (by smoking, drinking, etc)* ○ *malicious gossip which seriously injured her reputation.*

▷ **injured** *adj* **1** wounded; hurt: *an injured man* ○ *an injured leg.* **2** treated unfairly; wronged: (*law*) *the injured party*, ie person who has been wronged. **3** offended: *an injured look, voice, etc.* **the injured** *n* [pl *v*] people injured (in an accident, battle, etc): *counting the dead and injured* ○ *All 14 injured were later discharged from hospital.* ○ [attrib] *on the injured list*, ie the list of people injured. ⇨ Usage at WOUND[1].

injurious /ɪnˈdʒʊərɪəs/ *adj* (*fml*) **1** ~ **(to sb/sth)** causing or likely to cause injury; harmful: *Smoking is injurious to the health.* **2** wrongful; insulting: *injurious treatment by sb* ○ *injurious remarks.*

injury /ˈɪndʒərɪ/ *n* ~ **(to sb/sth)** **1** [U] **(a)** physical harm to a living being: *Excessive dosage of this drug can result in injury to the liver.* ○ *a person prone to injury*, ie one who is easily or often injured. **(b)** (*fig*) damage (to sb's feelings, reputation, etc): *injury to one's pride.* **2** [C] instance of harm to one's body or reputation: *In the crash he suffered severe injuries to the head and arms.* ○ *an eye injury* ○ (*fig*) *injuries to one's reputation.* **3** (idm) **add insult to injury** ⇨ ADD. **do sb/oneself an ˈinjury** (*often joc*) cause sb/oneself (physical) harm: *If you try and lift that suitcase you'll do yourself an injury!*

□ **ˈinjury time** (*sport*) time added on by the referee at the end of a (football, rugby, etc) match, if the game has been interrupted because of injuries to players.

injustice /ɪnˈdʒʌstɪs/ *n* **1** [U] lack of justice: *a fierce opponent of injustice.* **2** [C] unjust act, etc. **3** (idm) **do sb an inˈjustice** **(a)** judge sb unfairly: *In saying this you do her an injustice.* **(b)** (*fig*) fail to show sb's true merits: *His latest novel does him an injustice*, ie does not show how well he can write.

ink /ɪŋk/ *n* **1** [U, C] coloured liquid for writing, drawing and printing: *written in ink* ○ *different coloured inks* ○ [attrib] *an ink blot* ○ *a pen-and-ink drawing.* **2** [U] black liquid produced by cuttlefish, squids, etc.

▷ **ink** *v* **1** [Tn] cover (sth) with ink (for printing): *ink the roller of a duplicating machine.* **2** (phr v) **ink sth in** write or draw over (a pencilled word, outline, etc) with ink.

inky /ˈɪŋkɪ/ (**-ier, -iest**) *adj* **1** made dirty with ink: *inky fingers.* **2** black like ink: *the inky darkness of a moonless night.*

□ **ˈink-bottle** *n* bottle in which ink is sold.

ˈink-pad (also **pad**) *n* pad for ink used on rubber stamps.

ˈink-pot *n* pot for holding ink.

ˈinkstand *n* stand for one or more ink-bottles.

ˈink-well *n* ink-pot that fits into a hole in a desk.

inkling /ˈɪŋklɪŋ/ *n* [sing] ~ **(of sth/that...)** slight knowledge (of sth secret or not previously known); hint: *Can you give me some inkling of what is going on?* ○ *The first inkling I had that all was not well was when the share prices began to fall.*

inlaid *pt, pp* of INLAY.

inland /ˈɪnlənd/ *adj* [usu attrib] **1** **(a)** situated in the interior of a country, not by the sea or by a frontier: *inland areas, towns, waterways, etc.* Cf COASTAL (COAST[1]). **(b)** (of a sea) (almost) surrounded by land or islands: *an inland sea such as the Caspian.* **2** (*commerce esp Brit*) carried on or obtained inside a country: *inland trade*, ie domestic trade, as opposed to imports and exports.

▷ **inland** /ˌɪnˈlænd/ *adv* in or towards the interior: *They live inland.* ○ *move further inland.*

□ ˌ**Inland ˈRevenue** (in Britain) government department responsible for collecting taxes. Cf INTERNAL REVENUE SERVICE (INTERNAL). ⇨ article at TAXATION.

in-laws /ˈɪn lɔːz/ *n* [pl] (*infml*) relatives by marriage: *All my in-laws live far away.*

inlay /ˌɪnˈleɪ/ *v* (*pt, pp* **inlaid** /ˌɪnˈleɪd/) [esp passive: Tn, Tn·pr] ~ **A (with B)**; ~ **B (in/into A)** make a design on (a surface) by putting pieces of wood, metal, etc into it in such a way that the resulting surface is smooth; insert (pieces of wood, metal, etc) in this way: *ivory inlaid with gold* ○ *gold inlaid into ivory.*

▷ **inlaid** *adj* **1** embedded in a substance: *a floor with inlaid tiles.* **2** decorated with inlaid designs: *an inlaid floor.*

inlay /ˈɪnleɪ/ *n* [C, U] **1** design or pattern made by inlaying: *a wooden jewel-box with (a) gold inlay.* **2** (in dentistry) (method of making a) solid filling of gold, plastic, etc for a hole in a tooth.

inlet /ˈɪnlet/ *n* **1** strip of water extending into the land from the sea or a lake, or between islands. **2** opening to allow esp liquid to enter: *the fuel inlet* ○ [attrib] *an inlet pipe.* **3** something put in, eg a piece of material inserted into a garment to make it larger.

in loco parentis /ɪn ˌləʊkəʊ pəˈrentɪs/ (*Latin*) acting for or instead of a parent; having the responsibility of a parent: *I stand towards her in loco parentis.*

inmate /ˈɪnmeɪt/ *n* one of a number of people living together, esp in a hospital, prison or some other institution.

in memoriam /ˌɪn məˈmɔːrɪəm/ (*Latin*) (used in epitaphs, on gravestones, etc) in memory of sb; as a memorial to sb.

inmost /ˈɪnməʊst/ *adj* [attrib] **1** most inward; furthest from the surface: *the inmost recesses of the cave.* **2** (*fig*) most private or secret: *my inmost thoughts, feelings, etc.*

inn /ɪn/ *n* (*Brit*) public house or small old hotel where lodgings, drink and meals may be had, now usu in the country. Cf HOTEL. ⇨ article at ACCOMMODATION.

□ **ˈinnkeeper** *n* person who manages an inn.

ˌ**Inn of ˈCourt** (building occupied by) any of four law societies in London having the exclusive right of admitting people to the rank of barrister in England.

innards /ˈɪnədz/ *n* [pl] (*infml*) **1** stomach and/or bowels: *a pain in my innards.* **2** any inner parts: *To mend this engine I'll have to have its innards out.*

innate /ɪˈneɪt/ *adj* (of a quality, feeling, etc) in one's nature; possessed from birth: *innate ability, beauty, etc* ○ *an innate desire.*

▷ **innately** *adv* naturally: *innately honest.*

inner /ˈɪnə(r)/ *adj* [attrib] **1** (of the) inside: *an inner room.* Cf OUTER. **2** (of feelings) unexpressed: *If she had inner doubts, it was not apparent to anyone else.* **3** (idm) **the ˌinner ˈman/ˈwoman** **(a)** (*rhet*) a person's mind or soul. **(b)** (*joc*) one's appetite: *satisfy the inner man/woman.*

▷ **innermost** /-məʊst/ *adj* [attrib] most inward; inmost: *the innermost depths of a forest* ○ *encouraging her to express her innermost feelings.*

□ ˌ**inner ˈcircle** small, often secretive, controlling group of people within an organization.

ˌ**inner ˈcity** oldest parts of a city, at or near its centre: [attrib] ˌ*inner-city ˈslums, deˈcay, ˈhousing problems.*

ˌ**inner ˈear** part of the hearing organ furthest inside the head, from which sounds are sent by nerve impulses to the brain. ⇨ illus at EAR.

ˌ**inner ˈlane** = INSIDE LANE (INSIDE).

ˌ**inner-ˈspring** *adj* (*US*) = INTERIOR-SPRUNG (INTERIOR[1]).

ˌ**inner ˈtube** inflatable rubber tube inside a tyre.

innings /ˈɪnɪŋz/ *n* (*pl* unchanged) **1** (in cricket) time during which a team or single player is batting: *England made 300 runs in their first innings.* **2** (idm) **have had a good ˈinnings** (*Brit infml*) have had a long and happy life.

▷ **inning** *n* (*pl* ~**s**) (in baseball) time during which one team is batting; division of a game in which both teams have a turn to bat.

innocent /ˈɪnəsnt/ *adj* **1** ~ **(of sth)** not guilty (of wrongdoing): *They have imprisoned an innocent man.* ○ *innocent of a crime, a charge, an accusation.* **2** [attrib] suffering harm although not involved: *an innocent bystander* ○ *innocent victims of the bomb blast.* **3** harmless; innocuous: *innocent amusement, enjoyment, etc* ○ *It was a perfectly innocent question. Why get so worked up about it?* **4** knowing nothing of evil or wrong: *as innocent as a new-born babe.* **5** foolishly simple: *Don't be so innocent as to believe everything the politicians tell you.* **6** [pred] ~ **of sth** (*fml*) lacking sth: *a bare room, innocent of any decoration.*

▷ **innocence** /-sns/ *n* [U] ~ **(of sth)** quality or state of being innocent(1, 4, 5): *do sth in all innocence*, ie without any evil intention or knowledge ○ *She protested her innocence*, ie kept saying she was innocent. ○ *Children lose their innocence as they grow older.*

innocent *n* innocent person, esp a young child: *He's a complete innocent as far as sex is concerned.* ○ *the Massacre of the Innocents*, ie the killing of all male babies in Bethlehem on the orders of *Herod, in an attempt to kill Jesus.

innocently *adv.*

innocuous /ɪˈnɒkjʊəs/ *adj* (*fml*) **1** causing no harm: *innocuous snakes, drugs.* **2** not intended to offend: *a fairly innocuous remark, statement, etc.* ▷ **innocuously** *adv.* **innocuousness** *n* [U].

innovate /ˈɪnəveɪt/ *v* [I] make changes; introduce new things: *prepared to innovate in order to make progress.*

▷ **innovation** /ˌɪnəˈveɪʃn/ *n* **(a)** [U] innovating: *a period of innovation.* **(b)** [C] instance of this; new technique, idea, etc: *one innovation after another* ○ *technical innovations in industry.*

innovative /ˈɪnəvətɪv/ (also **innovatory** /ˌɪnəˈveɪtərɪ/) *adj* (*approv*) introducing or using new ideas, techniques, etc: *an innovative firm.*

innovator /ˈɪnəveɪtə(r)/ *n* person who innovates.

innuendo /ˌɪnjuːˈendəʊ/ *n* [C, U] (*pl* ~**s** or ~**es** /-z/) (*derog*) indirect reference (usu suggesting sth bad or discreditable about sb): *There have been too many unpleasant innuendoes in this debate and not enough facts.* ○ *He had been subject to a campaign of innuendo in the press.*

Innuit (also **Inuit**) /ˈɪnuːɪt, -njuː-/ *n* (*pl* unchanged) = ESKIMO.

innumerable /ɪˈnjuːmərəbl; *US* ɪˈnuː-/ *adj* too

many to be counted. ⇨ Usage at INVALUABLE.

innumerate /ɪˈnju:mərət/ *adj* without a basic knowledge of mathematics; unable to count or do sums.
▷ **innumeracy** /-rəsɪ/ *n* [U] state of being innumerate: *the problem of innumeracy and illiteracy among young people.*

inoculate /ɪˈnɒkjʊleɪt/ *v* [Tn, Tn·pr] ~ **sb (with sth) (against sth)** inject sb with a mild form of a disease, so that he will not catch the disease itself: *inoculate sb (with a vaccine)* ○ *inoculate sb against cholera.* Cf IMMUNIZE (IMMUNE), VACCINATE.
▷ **inoculation** /ɪˌnɒkjʊˈleɪʃn/ *n* ~ **(with sth) (against sth)** (a) [U] inoculating or being inoculated. (b) [C] instance of this: *have inoculations against cholera and yellow fever.*

inoffensive /ˌɪnəˈfensɪv/ *adj* not giving offence; not objectionable: *an inoffensive remark, person.* ▷ **inoffensively** *adv.* **inoffensiveness** *n* [U].

inoperable /ɪnˈɒpərəbl/ *adj* **1** (of tumours, etc) that cannot be cured by a surgical operation. **2** (*fml*) that cannot be made to work; not practicable: *an inoperable solution to a problem.*

inoperative /ɪnˈɒpərətɪv/ *adj* (of laws, rules, etc) not working or taking effect; invalid: *a bus, train, air service that is inoperative* ○ *This rule is inoperative until further notice.*

inopportune /ˌɪnˈɒpətju:n; *US* -tu:n/ *adj* (esp of time) not appropriate or convenient: *at an inopportune moment.* ▷ **inopportunely** *adv*: *arrive inopportunely.*

inordinate /ɪnˈɔ:dɪnət/ *adj* (*fml*) beyond proper or normal limits; excessive: *the inordinate demands of the tax collector* ○ *inordinate delays.* ▷ **inordinately** *adv*: *inordinately fond of sth.*

inorganic /ˌɪnɔ:ˈgænɪk/ *adj* **1** not composed of living substances: *Rocks and minerals are inorganic.* **2** (*fig*) not the result of natural growth; artificial: *an inorganic form of society.* Cf ORGANIC 2. ▷ **inorganically** /-klɪ/ *adv.*
□ ˌ**inorganic** ˈ**chemistry** branch of chemistry that deals with substances which do not contain carbon. Cf ORGANIC CHEMISTRY (ORGANIC).

in-patient /ˈɪn peɪʃnt/ *n* person who lives in hospital while receiving treatment.

input /ˈɪnpʊt/ *n* ~ **(into/to sth) 1** (a) [U] action of putting sth in: *the input of additional resources into the project.* (b) [C, U] that which is put in: *an input of energy (to a system)* ○ *electrical input.* (c) [C] place in a system where this happens. **2** (*computing*) (a) [U] putting of data into a computer for processing or storage. (b) [C, U] data that is put in. (c) [C] place in a computer where this is done: [attrib] *an input key, code, level.* Cf OUTPUT 3.
▷ **input** *v* (-tt-, *pt, pp* **input** or **inputted**) [Tn, Tn·pr] ~ **sth (into/to sth)** (*computing*) put (data) into a computer. Cf OUTPUT *v.*
□ ˈ**input circuit** (*computing*) circuit that controls input.
ˈ**input device** (*computing*) equipment by which data is transferred from a memory store to a computer.

inquest /ˈɪŋkwest/ *n* ~ **(on/into sth) 1** official inquiry to discover facts, esp about a death which may not have been the result of natural causes. **2** (*infml*) discussion about sth which has been unsatisfactory: *hold an inquest on the team's performance in the match.*

inquietude /ɪnˈkwaɪətju:d; *US* -tu:d/ *n* [U] (*fml*) uneasiness of mind; anxiety.

inquire (also **enquire**) /ɪnˈkwaɪə(r)/ *v* (*fml*) **1** [Tn, Tn·pr, Tw] ~ **sth (of sb)** ask to be told sth (by sb): *inquire sb's name* ○ *'How are you?' she inquired.* ○ *inquire where to go, how to do sth, etc* ○ *She inquired of me most politely whether I wished to continue.* **2** [I, Ipr] ~ **(about sb/sth)** ask for information: *'How much are the tickets?' 'I'll inquire.'* ○ *inquire at the information desk* ○ *inquire about trains to London.* **3** (phr v) **inquire after sb** ask about sb's health or welfare: *People called to inquire after the baby.* **inquire into sth** try to learn the facts about sth; investigate sth: *We must enquire further into the matter.*
▷ **inquirer** /ɪnˈkwaɪərə(r)/ *n* person who inquires.
inquiring /ɪnˈkwaɪərɪŋ/ *adj* [usu attrib] **1** showing an interest in learning: *an inquiring mind.* **2** suggesting that information is needed: *an inquiring look.* **inquiringly** *adv.*

inquiry (also **enquiry**) /ɪnˈkwaɪərɪ; *US* ˈɪnkwərɪ/ *n* **1** (a) [C] ~ **(about/concerning sb/sth)** (*fml*) request for help or information (about sb/sth): *In answer to your recent inquiry, the book you mention is not in stock.* ○ *I've been making (some) inquiries* (ie trying to find out) *about it.* ○ [attrib] *an inquiry desk/office.* (b) **inquiries** [pl] place from which one can get information: *'How do I apply for this licence?' 'You want inquiries.'* ○ *directory inquiries,* ie giving information about telephone numbers. **2** [U] (*fml*) asking; inquiring: *learn sth by inquiry* ○ *The police are following several lines of inquiry.* ○ *On inquiry* (ie Having asked) *I found it was true.* **3** [C] ~ **(into sth)** investigation: *hold an official inquiry* ○ *call for a public inquiry into safety standards.*
□ **inˈquiry agent** private detective.

inquisition /ˌɪnkwɪˈzɪʃn/ *n* **1 the Inquisition** (also **the Holy ˈOffice**) [sing] organization appointed by the Roman Catholic Church in the Middle Ages to discover and punish heretics, esp the very severe one in Spain, also called the Spanish Inquisition. **2** [C] ~ **(into sth)** (*fml or joc*) investigation or interrogation, esp one that is severe and looks closely into details: *I was subjected to a lengthy inquisition into the state of my marriage and the size of my bank balance.*

inquisitive /ɪnˈkwɪzətɪv/ *adj* (too) fond of inquiring into other people's affairs: *'What's that you're hiding?' 'Don't be so inquisitive!'* ▷ **inquisitively** *adv.* **inquisitiveness** *n* [U].

inquisitor /ɪnˈkwɪzɪtə(r)/ *n* investigator, esp an officer of the Inquisition.
▷ **inquisitorial** /ɪnˌkwɪzɪˈtɔ:rɪəl/ *adj* of or like an inquisitor: *the inquisitorial system,* ie the legal system (as in many European countries) in which the judge acts as prosecutor in criminal cases. Cf ACCUSATORIAL. **inquisitorially** /-rɪəlɪ/ *adv.*

inroad /ˈɪnrəʊd/ *n* (esp *pl*) **1** ~ **(into sth)** sudden attack on another's territory; raid: *inroads into enemy territory.* **2** (idm) **make inroads into/on sth** gradually use up or consume more and more of sth; lessen the amount of sth available: *Hospital bills had made deep inroads into her savings.* ○ *Already the children had made considerable inroads on the food.*

inrush /ˈɪnrʌʃ/ *n* (usu *sing*) rushing in (of sth); sudden arrival in large numbers: *an inrush of air, water, etc* ○ *an inrush of tourists, visitors, etc.*

insalubrious /ˌɪnsəˈlu:brɪəs/ *adj* (*fml*) unhealthy: *insalubrious alleys and slums.*

insane /ɪnˈseɪn/ *adj* not sane; mad; senseless: *an insane person* ○ *an insane desire, idea, decision, policy.*
▷ **the insane** *n* [pl v] insane people: *an institution for the insane.*
insanely *adv*: *insanely jealous.*
insanity /ɪnˈsænətɪ/ *n* [U] madness; being mad: *a plea of insanity,* ie a plea in a court of law that a crime was due to the defendant having a mental disorder.
□ **insane asylum** (*dated*) = MENTAL HOME (MENTAL).

insanitary /ɪnˈsænɪtrɪ; *US* -terɪ/ *adj* not sanitary: *insanitary living conditions.*

insatiable /ɪnˈseɪʃəbl/ *adj* ~ **(for sth)** that cannot be satisfied; very greedy: *Another cake? You're insatiable!* ○ *an insatiable appetite, curiosity, desire, thirst (for knowledge), etc* ○ *a politician who is insatiable for power.* ▷ **insatiably** /-ʃəblɪ/ *adv.*

insatiate /ɪnˈseɪʃɪət/ *adj* (*fml*) never satisfied.

inscribe /ɪnˈskraɪb/ *v* [Tn, Tn·pr, Cn·n] ~ **A (on/in B)**/~ **B (with A)** write (words, one's name, etc) on or in sth, esp as a formal or permanent record: *inscribe verses on a tombstone/inscribe a tombstone with verses* ○ *inscribe one's name in a book/inscribe a book with one's name* ○ *The book was inscribed 'To Cyril, with warmest regards.'*
▷ **inscription** /ɪnˈskrɪpʃn/ *n* words written on sth, cut in stone (eg on a monument) or stamped on a coin or medal: *an illegible inscription carved on the doorpost* ○ *What does the inscription say?*

inscrutable /ɪnˈskru:təbl/ *adj* that cannot be understood or known; mysterious: *the inscrutable ways of Providence* ○ *his inscrutable face,* ie which does not show what he is thinking. ▷ **inscrutability** /ɪnˌskru:təˈbɪlətɪ/ *n* [U]. **inscrutably** /ɪnˈskru:təblɪ/ *adv.*

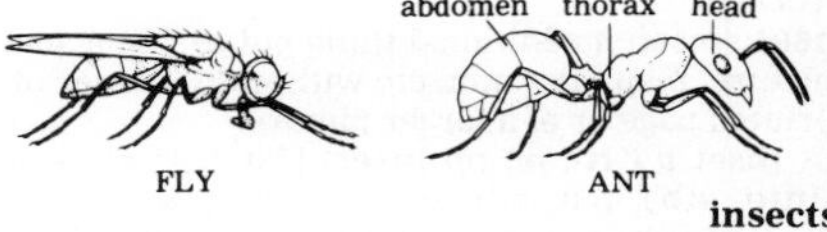

insects

insect /ˈɪnsekt/ *n* **1** type of small animal (eg an ant, a fly, a wasp) having six legs, no backbone and a body divided into three parts (head, thorax and abdomen): [attrib] *an insect bite.* ⇨ illus. **2** (in incorrect but common usage) any small, crawling creature (eg a spider).
▷ **insecticide** /ɪnˈsektɪsaɪd/ *n* [C, U] substance used for killing insects (eg DDT): [attrib] *an insecticide spray, powder, etc.* Cf PESTICIDE. **insecticidal** /ɪnˌsektɪˈsaɪdl/ *adj.*
insectivore /ɪnˈsektɪvɔ:(r)/ *n* animal that eats insects. **insectivorous** /ˌɪnsekˈtɪvərəs/ *adj* that eats insects: *Swallows are insectivorous.*

insecure /ˌɪnsɪˈkjʊə(r)/ *adj* **1** not secure or safe; not providing good support; that cannot be relied on: *have an insecure hold/grip on sth,* eg when climbing ○ (*fig*) *an insecure arrangement, plan, etc* ○ *an insecure job,* ie from which one may be dismissed at any time ○ *insecure evidence,* ie not reliable enough to convict sb in a court of law. **2** ~ **(about sb/sth)** not feeling safe or protected; lacking confidence: *an insecure person* ○ *She feels very insecure about her marriage.* ▷ **insecurely** *adv*: *insecurely fastened.* **insecurity** /ˌɪnsɪˈkjʊərətɪ/ *n* [U]: *suffer from feelings of insecurity.*

inseminate /ɪnˈsemɪneɪt/ *v* [Tn] put sperm into (a female, esp a female animal) either naturally or artificially: *inseminate a cow.*
▷ **insemination** /ɪnˌsemɪˈneɪʃn/ *n* [U] inseminating.

insensate /ɪnˈsenseɪt/ *adj* (*fml*) **1** without the power to feel or experience: *insensate rocks.* **2** unfeeling, esp in a foolish way: *insensate rage, cruelty, etc.* ▷ **insensately** *adv.*

insensibility /ɪnˌsensəˈbɪlətɪ/ *n* [U] (*fml*) **1** unconsciousness: *lying in a state of drugged insensibility.* **2** ~ **(to sth)** (a) lack of physical feeling: *insensibility to pain, cold, etc.* (b) (*derog*) lack of ability to respond emotionally: *insensibility to art, music, beauty, etc.* (c) (*derog*) indifference: *He showed total insensibility to the animal's fate.*

insensible /ɪnˈsensəbl/ *adj* (*fml*) **1** unconscious as the result of injury, illness, etc: *knocked insensible by a falling rock.* **2** [pred] ~ **(of sth)** without knowledge (of sth); unaware: *be insensible of (one's) danger* ○ *I'm not insensible how much I owe to your help.* **3** [pred] ~ **(to sth)** not able to feel (sth); insensitive(2): *insensible to pain, cold, etc.* **4** [attrib] (of changes) too small or gradual to be noticed; imperceptible: *by insensible degrees.* ▷ **insensibly** /-əblɪ/ *adv.*

insensitive /ɪnˈsensətɪv/ *adj* **1** not realizing or caring how other people feel, and therefore likely to offend them: *It was rather insensitive of you to mention his dead wife.* **2** ~ **(to sth)** not able to feel sth: *insensitive to pain, cold, etc* ○ (*fig*) *He's insensitive to criticism.* ▷ **insensitively** *adv.* **insensitivity** /ɪnˌsensəˈtɪvətɪ/ *n* [U].

inseparable /ɪnˈseprəbl/ *adj* ~ **(from sb/sth)** that cannot be separated: *Rights are inseparable from duties.* ○ *inseparable* (ie extremely close) *friends.* ▷ **inseparability** /ɪnˌseprəˈbɪlətɪ/ *n* [U]. **inseparably** /ɪnˈseprəblɪ/ *adv.*

insert /ɪnˈsɜ:t/ *v* [Tn, Tn·pr] ~ **sth (in/into/between sth)** put, fit or place sth into sth or between two things: *insert an additional paragraph in an essay, an advertisement in a newspaper, etc* ○ *insert a key into a lock* ○ *Insert your fingers between the layers and press them apart.*

▷ **insert** /ˈɪnsɜːt/ *n* ~ **(in sth)** thing inserted (esp an additional section in a book, newspaper, etc): *an eight-page insert.*
insertion /ɪnˈsɜːʃn/ *n* **1** [U] ~ **(into sth)** inserting or being inserted: *the insertion of a coin into a slot.* **2** [C] thing inserted, eg an announcement or advertisement put in a newspaper.
in-service /ˈɪnsɜːvɪs/ *adj* [attrib] carried out while actually working at a job: *the in-service training of teachers.*
inset /ˈɪnset/ *n* additional thing put in, esp a small picture, map, diagram, etc within the border of a printed page or of a larger picture.
▷ **inset** *v* (-tt-; *pt, pp* **inset**) [Tn, Tn·pr] ~ **sth (into sth)** put sth in as an inset: *For an explanation of the symbols see the key, inset left.*
inshore /ˌɪnˈʃɔː(r)/ *adj* [usu attrib] (of sth at sea) close to the shore: *an ˌinshore ˈcurrent* ○ *ˌinshore ˈfisheries.* ▷ **inshore** *adv*: *fishing inshore or out at sea.*
inside[1] /ɪnˈsaɪd/ *n* **1** (**a**) [C usu *sing*] inner side or surface; part within: *The inside of the box was lined with silk.* ○ *This cup is stained on the inside.* ○ *chocolates with a creamy inside* ○ *Which paint is suitable for the inside of a house?* ○ *The room had been locked from/on the inside.* ○ *The insides of the cylinders must be carefully cleaned.* (**b**) [sing] part of a road or track nearest to the inner side of a curve: *Daley Thomson is coming up on the inside.* (**c**) [sing] side of a pavement or footpath that is furthest away from the road: *Walk on the inside to avoid the traffic fumes.* Cf OUTSIDE[1]. **2** [sing] (also **insides** /ɪnˈsaɪdz/ [pl]) (*infml*) stomach and bowels: *a pain in his inside* ○ *My insides are crying out for food.* **3** (idm) **ˌinside ˈout** (**a**) with the normal inner side on the outside: *wearing his socks inside out* ○ *Turn the blouse inside out before drying it.* ○ *My umbrella has blown inside out.* ⇨ illus at BACK[1]. (**b**) thoroughly; completely: *know a subject inside out* ○ *turn a cupboard, drawer, etc inside out*, ie search thoroughly by emptying it and looking through its contents. **on the inˈside** (**a**) within a group or an organization so that one has direct access to information, etc: *The thieves must have had someone on the inside to help them break in.* (**b**) (of motorists, motor vehicles, etc) using the lane that is furthest away from the centre of the road or motorway: *The driver behind me tried to overtake on the inside.*
▷ **inside** *adj* [attrib] **1** forming the inner part of sth; not on the outer side: *He kept his wallet in an ˌinside ˈpocket.* ○ *What does your inside leg* (ie from the crutch to the inner side of the foot) *measure?* ○ *the inside pages of a newspaper* ○ *choosing to run on the inside track.* **2** told or performed by sb who is in a building, a group or an organization: *Acting on inside information, the police were able to arrest the gang before the robbery occurred.* ○ *The robbery appeared to have been an inside job.*
insider /ɪnˈsaɪdə(r)/ *n* person who, as a member of a group or an organization, is able to obtain information not available to others. **inˌsider ˈdealing** (also **inˌsider ˈtrading**) buying or selling with the help of information known only by those connected with the business.
□ **ˌinside ˈlane** section of a road or motorway where the traffic moves more slowly: *After overtaking you should move back into the inside lane.*
ˌinside ˈleft, ˌinside ˈright player (in football, etc) in the forward line who is immediately to the left/right of the centre-forward.
inside[2] /ɪnˈsaɪd/ (also *esp US* **inside of**) *prep* **1** on or to the inner side of (sb/sth); within: *go inside the house* ○ *put it inside its cage* ○ *Inside the box there was a gold coin.* ○ *You'll feel better with a good meal inside you*, ie when you've eaten a good meal. Cf OUTSIDE[2]. **2** (of time) in less than (sth): *The job is unlikely to be finished inside (of) a year.*
▷ **inside** *adv* **1** on or to the inside: *The coat has a detachable lining inside.* ○ *She shook it to make certain there was nothing inside.* ○ *The guests had to move inside* (ie indoors) *when it started to rain.* **2** (*sl*) in prison.
insidious /ɪnˈsɪdɪəs/ *adj* (*fml derog*) spreading or acting gradually and unnoticed but with harmful effects: *an insidious disease* ○ *insidious jealousy.* ▷ **insidiously** *adv*: *He had insidiously wormed his way into her affections.* **insidiousness** *n* [U].
insight /ˈɪnsaɪt/ *n* ~ **(into sth) 1** (**a**) [U] (*approv*) ability to see into the true nature (of sth); deep understanding: *a person of insight* ○ *show insight into human character.* (**b**) [C] instance of this: *a book full of remarkable insights.* **2** [C] (sudden) perception or understanding of the true nature (of sth): *She was given an unpleasant insight into what life would be like as his wife.* ○ *have/gain an insight into a problem.*
▷ **insightful** /-fʊl/ *adj* (*approv*) showing insight: *an insightful remark.*
insignia /ɪnˈsɪgnɪə/ *n* [pl] (**a**) symbols of rank or authority, eg the crown and sceptre of a king or queen: *the insignia of office.* (**b**) identifying badge of a military regiment, squadron, etc.
insignificant /ˌɪnsɪgˈnɪfɪkənt/ *adj* having little or no value, use, meaning or importance: *The rate has fallen by an insignificant* (ie too small to be important) *amount.* ○ *an insignificant-looking little man who turned out to be the managing director.* ▷ **insignificance** /-kəns/ *n* [U]: *reduced to insignificance.* **insignificantly** *adv*.
insincere /ˌɪnsɪnˈsɪə(r)/ *adj* not sincere. ▷ **insincerely** *adv*. **insincerity** /ˌɪnsɪnˈserətɪ/ *n* [U].
insinuate /ɪnˈsɪnjʊeɪt/ *v* **1** [Tn, Dn·pr, Tf, Dpr·f] ~ **sth (to sb)** suggest sth (to sb) unpleasantly and indirectly: *What are you insinuating?* ○ *Are you insinuating that I am a liar?* **2** [Tn·pr] ~ **sth/oneself into sth** (*fml*) place sth/oneself smoothly and stealthily into sth: *insinuate one's body/person into a narrow opening* ○ (*fig derog*) *insinuate oneself into sb's favour*, ie ingratiate oneself with sb.
▷ **insinuation** /ɪnˌsɪnjʊˈeɪʃn/ *n* (**a**) [U] insinuating: *blacken sb's character by insinuation.* (**b**) [C] ~ **(that...)** thing that is insinuated; indirect suggestion: *I object to your (unpleasant) insinuations!*
insipid /ɪnˈsɪpɪd/ *adj* (*derog*) **1** having almost no taste or flavour: *insipid food.* **2** (*fig*) lacking in interest or vigour: *painted in pale, insipid colours* ○ *an insipid performance of the symphony* ○ *a good-looking but insipid young man.* ▷ **insipidity** /ˌɪnsɪˈpɪdɪtɪ/ (also **insipidness**) *n* [U]. **insipidly** *adv*.
insist /ɪnˈsɪst/ *v* **1** [I, Ipr, Tf] ~ **(on sth)** demand (sth) forcefully, not accepting a refusal: *'You really must go!' 'All right, if you insist.'* ○ *I insist on your taking/insist that you take immediate action to put this right.* **2** [Ipr] ~ **on sth/doing sth** require or demand (the specified thing), refusing to accept an alternative: *I always insist on wholemeal bread.* ○ (*fig*) *She will insist on getting up early and playing her radio loud*, ie She always does this, annoyingly. **3** [Ipr, Tf] ~ **on sth** state or declare sth forcefully, esp when other people oppose or disbelieve one: *She kept insisting on her innocence/insisting that she was innocent.*
▷ **insistent** /-ənt/ *adj* ~ **(about/on sth)**; ~ **(that...)** tending to insist; not allowing refusal or opposition: *She's a most insistent person; she won't take 'no' for an answer.* ○ *You mustn't be late; he was most insistent about that.* ○ (*fig*) *this job's insistent demands* ○ (*fig*) *the insistent* (ie constantly and noticeably repeated) *horn phrase in the third movement of the symphony.* **insistence** /-əns/ *n* [U] ~ **(about/on sth)**; ~ **(that...)**. **insistently** *adv*.
in situ /ˌɪn ˈsɪtjuː/ (*Latin*) in its original or proper place.
insobriety /ˌɪnsəˈbraɪətɪ/ *n* [U] (*fml*) excessive drinking of alcohol; intemperance.
insofar as /ˌɪnsəˈfɑːr əz/ = IN SO FAR AS (FAR[2]).
insolation /ˌɪnsəˈleɪʃn/ *n* [U] exposure to sunlight.
insole /ˈɪnsəʊl/ *n* inside surface of the bottom of a shoe.
insolent /ˈɪnsələnt/ *adj* ~ **(to/towards sb)** extremely rude, esp in expressing contempt: *insolent children, remarks, behaviour.*
▷ **insolence** /-əns/ *n* [U] ~ **(to/towards sb)** being insolent: *That's enough of your insolence, boy!* ○ *dumb insolence*, ie expressed by behaviour rather than verbally.
insolently *adv*.
insoluble /ɪnˈsɒljʊbl/ *adj* **1** (of substances) that cannot be dissolved; not soluble. **2** (*fig*) that cannot be solved or explained: *an insoluble problem, mystery, riddle, etc.*
insolvent /ɪnˈsɒlvənt/ *adj* unable to pay debts; bankrupt.
▷ **insolvency** /-ənsɪ/ *n*.
insolvent *n* insolvent person. [U].
insomnia /ɪnˈsɒmnɪə/ *n* [U] inability to sleep: *suffer from insomnia.*
▷ **insomniac** /ɪnˈsɒmnɪæk/ *n* person who finds it difficult to go to sleep.
insomuch /ˌɪnsəʊˈmʌtʃ/ *adv* ~ **as...** because of the fact that...; to the degree or extent that...; inasmuch as...: *This statement was important insomuch as it revealed the extent of their knowledge.*
insouciance /ɪnˈsuːsɪəns/ *n* [U] (*fml*) state of being unconcerned, esp in a light-hearted way; nonchalance. ▷ **insouciant** /-sɪənt/ *adj*.
Insp *abbr* Inspector (esp in the police force): *Chief Insp (Paul) King.*
inspect /ɪnˈspekt/ *v* **1** [Tn] (**a**) examine (sth) closely: *The customs officer inspected my passport suspiciously.* (**b**) visit (sth) officially to see that rules are obeyed, that work is done properly, etc: *inspect a school, factory, regiment, etc.* **2** [Tn·pr] ~ **sb/sth for sth** examine sb/sth in order to detect the presence of sth: *inspect sb/sb's head for lice, dandruff, etc* ○ *inspect an object for fingerprints.*
▷ **inspection** /ɪnˈspekʃn/ *n* **1** [U] inspecting or being inspected: *On inspection* (ie When inspected) *the notes proved to be forgeries.* ○ *after inspection (of the factory) for signs of inefficiency.* **2** [C] instance of this: *carry out frequent inspections.*
inspector /ɪnˈspektə(r)/ *n* **1** official who inspects eg schools, factories, mines. **2** (*Brit*) police officer between the ranks of chief-inspector and sergeant: *Inspector Davies.* **3** official who examines bus or train tickets to ensure that they are valid.
▷ **inspectorate** /ɪnˈspektərət/ *n* [CGp] inspectors collectively: *the primary schools inspectorate.*
□ **inˌspector of ˈtaxes** (also **ˈtax inspector**) official who examines statements of people's income and decides the tax to be paid on it.
inspiration /ˌɪnspəˈreɪʃn/ *n* **1** [U] ~ **(to do sth)** stimulation of the mind, feelings, etc to do sth beyond a person's usual ability, esp creative ability in art, literature, music, etc; state or quality of being inspired: *Wordsworth found (his) inspiration in/drew (his) inspiration from the Lake District scenery. It was a great source of inspiration to him.* ○ *Her work shows real inspiration.* ○ *I sat down to write my essay, but found I was completely without inspiration*, ie could think of nothing to write. ○ (*saying*) *Genius is 10% inspiration and 90% perspiration*, ie hard work. **2** [C] ~ **(to/for sb)** person or thing that causes this state: *This woman's an inspiration to all of us*, ie is so excellent that she inspires us. **3** [C] (*infml*) (sudden) good idea resulting from such a state: *I've just had an inspiration: why don't we try turning it the other way!*
▷ **inspirational** /-ʃənl/ *adj* providing inspiration: *an inspirational piece of writing.*
inspire /ɪnˈspaɪə(r)/ *v* **1** [Tn, Tn·pr, Cn·t] ~ **sb (to sth)** fill sb with the ability or urge to do, feel, etc sth beyond his usual ability, esp to write, paint, compose, etc: *His noble example inspired the rest of us to greater efforts.* ○ *The Lake District scenery inspired Wordsworth to write his greatest poetry.* **2** [Tn, Tn·pr] ~ **sb (with sth)**/~ **sth (in sb)** fill sb with thoughts, feelings or aims: *Our first sight of the dingy little hotel did not inspire us with much confidence/inspire much confidence in us.* ○ *inspire hope, loyalty, enthusiasm, etc in sb* ○ *gloomy statistics which inspired panic in the stock market/among the stockbrokers.*
▷ **inspired** *adj* (*approv*) **1** filled with creative power: *an inspired poet, artist, etc.* **2** full of a spirit that leads to outstanding achievements: *act like a man/woman inspired.* **3** produced (as if) by or with

the help of inspiration: *an inspired work of art* ○ *an inspired effort* ○ *an inspired guess*, ie made by intuition rather than logic, but usu correct.

inspiring /ɪnˈspaɪərɪŋ/ *adj* **1** that inspires (sb to do sth): *an inspiring thought.* **2** (usu with negatives) (*infml*) filling one with interest and enthusiasm: *a book on a not very inspiring subject.*

inspirit /ɪnˈspɪrɪt/ *v* [Tn] fill (sb) with courage, cheerfulness, etc; hearten. ▷ **inspiriting** /ɪnˈspɪrɪtɪŋ/ *adj*: *an inspiriting speech, victory, etc.*

inst /ɪnst/ *abbr* (*dated or fml commerce*) instant (of this month): *your letter of the 6th inst.*

Inst *abbr* Institute; Institution.

instability /ˌɪnstəˈbɪlətɪ/ *n* [U] lack of stability: *mental instability*, ie liability to fits of madness ○ *the inherent instability of this chemical*, eg one which may blow up or catch fire.

install (*US* also **instal**) /ɪnˈstɔːl/ *v* **1** [Tn, Tn·pr] ~ **sth (in sth)** fix equipment, furniture, etc in position for use, esp by making the necessary connections with the supply of electricity, water, etc: *install a heating or lighting system (in a building)* ○ *I'm having a shower installed.* **2** [Tn, Tn·pr] ~ **sb/oneself (in sth)** settle sb/oneself in a place: *be comfortably installed in a new home* ○ *She installed herself in her father's favourite armchair.* **3** [Tn, Tn·pr] ~ **sb (in sth)** place sb in a new position of authority with the usual ceremony: *install a priest (in office).*

▷ **installation** /ˌɪnstəˈleɪʃn/ *n* **1** (**a**) [U] installing or being installed: *Installation requires several days.* ○ *the installation of the new vice-chancellor* ○ [attrib] *installation costs/charges.* (**b**) [C] instance of this: *carry out several installations.* **2** [C] (**a**) that which is installed: *a heating installation.* (**b**) site housing military equipment: *attacking the enemy's missile installations.*

instalment (*US* usu **installment**) /ɪnˈstɔːlmənt/ *n* **1** any one of the separate but connected parts in which a story is presented over a period of time: *a story that will appear in instalments* ○ *Don't miss the next instalment!* **2** ~ (**on sth**) any one of the parts of a payment spread over a period of time: *pay for a house by monthly instalments* ○ *keep up the instalments* (ie maintain regular payments) *on the house.*

□ **inˈstalment plan** (*esp US*) = HIRE PURCHASE (HIRE).

instance /ˈɪnstəns/ *n* **1** ~ (**of sth**) particular occurrence of sth that happens generally or several times; example; case: *I can quote you several instances of her being deliberately rude.* ○ *In most instances* (ie Mostly) *the pain soon goes away.* **2** (idm) **at the instance of sb** (*fml*) at sb's (urgent) request or suggestion. **for ˈinstance** as an example; for example: *Several of his friends came: Ben, Carol and Mike, for instance.* **in the ˈfirst instance** (*fml*) at the beginning; initially: *In the first instance I was inclined to refuse, but then I reconsidered.* **in ˈthis instance** on this occasion; in this case.

▷ **instance** *v* [Tn] give (sth) as an example.

instant[1] /ˈɪnstənt/ *adj* **1** [usu attrib] coming or happening at once: *a new book that was an instant success* ○ *feel instant relief after treatment* ○ *instant hot water*, ie as soon as the tap is turned on. **2** (of food preparations) that can very quickly and easily be made ready for use: *instant coffee*, ie made by adding hot water or milk to a powder. **3** (*abbr* **inst**) (*dated commerce*) (after dates) of the present month: *in reply to your letter of the 9th inst.* **4** [attrib] (*fml*) urgent: *attend to sb's instant needs* ○ *in instant need of help.*

▷ **instantly** *adv* at once; immediately: *an instantly recognizable face.* — *conj* as soon as: *Tell me instantly he arrives.*

instant[2] /ˈɪnstənt/ *n* (esp *sing*) **1** precise point of time: *Come here this instant!* ie at once! ○ *He left (at) that (very) instant.* ○ *leave on the instant of six o'clock*, ie not a second later than six ○ *I recognized her the instant (that)* (ie as soon as) *I saw her.* **2** short space of time; moment: *I shall be back in an instant.* ○ *Help came not an instant too soon.* ○ *Just for an instant I thought he was going to refuse.*

instantaneous /ˌɪnstənˈteɪnɪəs/ *adj* happening or done immediately: *Death was instantaneous*, eg in a fatal accident. ▷ **instantaneously** *adv.*

instead /ɪnˈsted/ *adv* as an alternative or replacement: *We've no coffee. Would you like tea instead?* ○ *It will take days by car, so let's fly instead.* ○ *Stuart was ill so I went instead.*

□ **instead of** *prep* as an alternative or replacement to (sb/sth): *Let's play cards instead of watching television.* ○ *We sometimes eat rice instead of potatoes.* ○ *Instead of Graham, it was Peter who moved in.*

instep /ˈɪnstep/ *n* (**a**) upper surface of the human foot between the toes and the ankle. ⇨ illus at FOOT. (**b**) part of a shoe, etc covering this. ⇨ illus at SHOE.

instigate /ˈɪnstɪgeɪt/ *v* [Tn] cause (sth) to begin or happen; initiate: *instigate a strike, strike action, etc* ○ *The minister has instigated a full official inquiry into the incident.*

▷ **instigation** /ˌɪnstɪˈgeɪʃn/ *n* [U] instigating or being instigated: *At his instigation we concealed the facts from the authorities*, ie He encouraged us to do so.

instigator /ˈɪnstɪgeɪtə(r)/ *n* person who instigates (esp sth bad): *the instigators of violence in our society.*

instil (*US* **instill**) /ɪnˈstɪl/ *v* (-**ll**-) [Tn, Tn·pr] ~ **sth (in/into sb)** cause sb gradually to acquire (a particular desirable quality): *instilling a sense of responsibility (in/into one's children).* ▷ **instillation** /ˌɪnstɪˈleɪʃn/ *n* [U].

instinct /ˈɪnstɪŋkt/ *n* ~ (**for sth/doing sth**); ~ (**to do sth**) [U, C] **1** natural inborn tendency to behave in a certain way without reasoning or training: *Birds learn to fly by instinct.* ○ *Birds have the instinct to learn to fly.* **2** natural feeling that makes one choose to act in a particular way: *When I saw the flames I acted on instinct and threw a blanket over them.* ○ *My first instinct was to refuse, but later I reconsidered.* ○ *have an instinct for survival* ○ *Trust your instincts and marry him!* ○ *I'm afraid I gave way to my worst instincts and hit him.* ○ *The sight of the helpless little boy aroused her maternal instinct(s).* ○ (*ironic*) *have an instinct for doing or saying the wrong thing* ○ (*fig*) *I'm afraid he lacks the killer instinct*, ie ability to be ruthless.

▷ **instinctive** /ɪnˈstɪŋktɪv/ *adj* based on instinct; not coming from training or based on reasoning: *an instinctive fear of fire* ○ *an instinctive dislike of sb* ○ *an instinctive reaction.* **instinctively** *adv*: *I instinctively raised my arm to protect my face.*

institute[1] /ˈɪnstɪtjuːt; *US* -tuːt/ *n* **1** (building that contains a) society or organization for a special (usu social, professional or educational) purpose: *the Working Men's institute* ○ *the Institute of Chartered Surveyors.* **2** (*esp US*) short course of instruction, eg for teachers, on a particular topic.

institute[2] /ˈɪnstɪtjuːt; *US* -tuːt/ *v* (*fml*) **1** [Tn] establish or start (an inquiry, a custom, a rule, etc): *institute legal proceedings against sb* ○ *Police have instituted inquiries into the matter.* **2** [Tn] place (sb, esp a clergyman) officially in a new post with a formal ceremony.

institution /ˌɪnstɪˈtjuːʃn; *US* -tuːʃn/ *n* **1** [U] instituting (INSTITUTE 1) or being instituted: *the institution of rules, customs, etc* ○ *institution of a bishop/of sb as a bishop.* **2** [C] (building of an) organization for helping people with special needs, eg an orphanage, a home for old people: *living in an institution.* **3** [C] long-established custom, practice or group (eg a club or society): *Marriage is a sacred institution.* ○ *Drinking tea at 4 pm is a popular British institution.* **4** [C] (*infml usu approv or joc*) person who is a very familiar figure in some activity or place: *My uncle has become quite an institution at the club!*

▷ **institutional** /-ʃənl/ *adj* of, from or connected with an institution: *institutional food* ○ *old people in need of institutional care.* **institutionalize**, **-ise** /-ʃənəlaɪz/ *v* **1** [Tn] make (sth) into an institution(3). **2** [Tn] place (sb) in an institution(2). **3** [Tn esp passive] cause (sb) to become accustomed to living in an institution, esp so as to lose self-reliance. **institutionalization**, **-isation** /ˌɪnstɪˌtjuːʃənəlaɪˈzeɪʃn; *US* -lɪˈz/ *n* [U].

instruct /ɪnˈstrʌkt/ *v* **1** [Tn, Tn·pr] ~ **sb (in sth)** teach sb a school subject, a skill, etc: *instruct a class (in history), recruits (in drill), etc.* ⇨ Usage at TEACH. **2** [Tn·pr, Dn·w, Dn·t] ~ **sb (about sth)** give orders or directions to sb: *instruct sb about his duties* ○ *They haven't instructed us where to go.* ○ *I've instructed them to keep the room locked.* ⇨ Usage at ORDER[2]. **3** [Dn·f esp passive] (*esp law*) inform: *We are instructed by our clients that you owe them £300.* **4** [Tn] (*law*) employ (a solicitor or barrister) to act on one's behalf: *Who are the instructing solicitors* (ie solicitors who are employing a barrister to act) *in this case?*

▷ **instructor** *n* (**a**) person who instructs; trainer: *a driving instructor.* (**b**) (*US*) college teacher below the rank of professor.

instruction /ɪnˈstrʌkʃn/ *n* **1** [U] ~ (**in sth**) process of teaching; knowledge or teaching given: *In this course, students receive instruction in basic engineering.* **2** [C] ~ (**to do sth/that...**) (**a**) order or direction given: *leave, give detailed instructions* ○ *understand, carry out an instruction.* (**b**) (*computing*) word, code, etc that, when input into a computer, makes it perform a particular operation. **3 instructions** [pl] ~ (**to do sth/that...**) statements telling sb what he should or must do: *follow the instructions on a tin of paint, in a car repair manual, etc* ○ *My instructions are that I am not to let anyone in*, ie I have been ordered not to. ○ *instructions to a lawyer.*

▷ **instructional** /-ʃənl/ *adj* giving instruction; educational: *instructional films.*

instructive /ɪnˈstrʌktɪv/ *adj* (*approv*) giving much useful information: *instructive books* ○ *The minister's visit to the prison was not instructive.* ▷ **instructively** *adv.*

instrument /ˈɪnstrʊmənt/ *n* **1** implement or apparatus used in performing an action, esp for delicate or scientific work: *a surgical instrument*, eg a scalpel ○ *an optical instrument*, eg a microscope ○ *instruments of torture.* **2** apparatus for producing musical sounds, eg a piano, violin, flute or drum: *learning to play an instrument* ○ *the instruments of the orchestra.* **3** measuring device giving information about the operation of an engine, etc or in navigation: *a ship's instruments* ○ [attrib] *an instrument panel* ○ *instrument flying/landing*, ie controlled by the aircraft's instruments rather than by the pilot. ⇨ Usage at MACHINE. **4** (**a**) ~ **of sb/sth** person used and controlled by another person, organization, etc, often without being aware of it: *We humans are merely the instruments of fate.* (**b**) ~ **of sth** person or thing that brings sth about: *The organization he had built up eventually became the instrument of his downfall.* **5** ~ (**of sth**) formal (esp legal) document: *The king signed the instrument of abdication.*

▷ **instrumentation** /ˌɪnstrʊmenˈteɪʃn/ *n* [U] **1** arrangement of music for instruments: *The instrumentation of the work is particularly fine.* **2** instruments (INSTRUMENT 3): *monitoring the spacecraft's instrumentation.*

instrumental /ˌɪnstrʊˈmentl/ *adj* **1** [pred] ~ **in doing sth** being the means of bringing sth about: *Our artistic director was instrumental in persuading the orchestra to come and play for us.* **2** of or for musical instruments: *instrumental music.*

▷ **instrumentalist** /-təlɪst/ *n* player of a musical instrument. Cf VOCALIST (VOCAL).

instrumentality /ˌɪnstrʊmenˈtælətɪ/ *n* [U] (*fml*) condition of being instrumental(1); means: *by the instrumentality of sb*, ie by means of sb.

insubordinate /ˌɪnsəˈbɔːdɪnət/ *adj* disobedient; rebellious.

▷ **insubordination** /ˌɪnsəˌbɔːdɪˈneɪʃn/ *n* (**a**) [U] being insubordinate: *gross/rank insubordination.* (**b**) [C] instance of this.

insubstantial /ˌɪnsəbˈstænʃl/ *adj* **1** not solid or real; imaginary: *an insubstantial vision, figure, creature.* **2** not firmly or solidly made; weak: *Early aircraft were insubstantial constructions of wood and glue.* ○ (*fig*) *an insubstantial argument,* *accusation, claim, etc.*

insufferable /ɪnˈsʌfrəbl/ *adj* **1** too extreme to be tolerated; unbearable: *insufferable insolence.* **2** (of a person) extremely annoying and unpleasant, esp because of conceit: *He really is insufferable!* ▷ **insufferably** /-əblɪ/ *adv.*

insufficient /ˌɪnsəˈfɪʃnt/ *adj* ~ **(for sth/to do sth)** not sufficient: *The case was dismissed because of insufficient evidence.* ▷ **insufficiency** /-ʃnsɪ/ *n* [U]. **insufficiently** *adv.*

insular /ˈɪnsjʊlə(r); *US* -sələr/ *adj* **1** of an island: *an insular climate, way of life.* **2** (*derog*) narrow-minded and avoiding contact with others: *an insular attitude* ○ *insular habits and prejudices.* ▷ **insularity** /ˌɪnsjʊˈlærətɪ; *US* -səˈl-/ *n* [U] state of being insular(2).

insulate /ˈɪnsjʊleɪt; *US* -səl-/ *v* **1** [I, Ipr, Tn, Tn·pr] ~ **(sth) (from/against sth) (with sth)** protect (sth) by covering it with a material that prevents sth (esp heat, electricity or sound) from passing through: *material which insulates well* ○ *insulate pipes from loss of heat with foam rubber.* **2** [Tn·pr] ~ **sb/sth from/against sth** (*fig*) protect sb/sth from the unpleasant effects of sth: *children carefully insulated from harmful experiences* ○ *Index-linked pay rises insulated them against inflationary price increases.*

▷ **insulated** *adj* protected in this way: *an insulated wire*, ie to avoid an electric shock ○ *a well-insulated house*, ie to avoid loss of heat.

insulating *adj* giving this kind of protection: *insulating materials.*

insulation /ˌɪnsjʊˈleɪʃn; *US* -səˈl-/ *n* [U] (**a**) insulating or (state of) being insulated: *Foam rubber provides good insulation.* (**b**) materials used for this: *pack the wall cavity with insulation.*

insulator /ˈɪnsjʊleɪtə(r); *US* -səl-/ *n* substance or device for insulating, esp a porcelain support for bare electric wires and cables.

□ **ˈinsulating tape** tape used for covering joins in electrical wires, preventing the possibility of an electrical shock.

insulin /ˈɪnsjʊlɪn; *US* -səl-/ *n* [U] substance (a hormone) produced in the pancreas, controlling the absorption of sugar by the body: [attrib] *People suffering from diabetes have to have insulin injections, because they cannot produce their own.*

insult /ɪnˈsʌlt/ *v* [Tn] speak or act in a way that hurts or is intended to hurt the feelings or dignity of (sb); be extremely rude to (sb): *I felt most insulted when they made me sit at a little table at the back.*

▷ **insult** /ˈɪnsʌlt/ *n* **1** [C] ~ **(to sb/sth)** remark or action that insults: *She hurled insults at the unfortunate waiter.* ○ *Don't take it as an insult if I go to sleep during your speech; I'm very tired.* **2** [U] (*medical*) injury to the body. **3** (idm) **add insult to injury** ⇨ ADD. **a calculated insult** ⇨ CALCULATE. **an insult to sb's inˈtelligence** task, explanation, etc that is too easy to be worthy of sb's attention. **insulting** *adj* uttering or being an insult: *He was most insulting to my wife.* ○ *insulting remarks, behaviour.*

insuperable /ɪnˈsuːpərəb *or, in British use* -ˈsjuː-/ *adj* (*fml*) (of difficulties) that cannot be overcome: *insuperable barriers, obstacles, etc.* Cf INSURMOUNTABLE. ▷ **insuperably** /-əblɪ/ *adv.*

insupportable /ˌɪnsəˈpɔːtəbl/ *adj* (*fml*) unbearable; too bad to be endured: *insupportable behaviour, rudeness, etc.*

insurance /ɪnˈʃɔːrəns; *US* -ˈʃʊər-/ *n* **1** [U, sing] ~ **(against sth)** (contract made by a company or society, or by the state, to provide a) guarantee of compensation for loss, damage, sickness, death, etc in return for regular payment: *People without insurance had to pay for their own repairs.* ○ *an insurance against theft, fire, etc* ○ *household, personal, etc insurance* ○ [attrib] *an insurance company*, ie one that provides this ○ *an insurance salesman.* Cf ASSURANCE 3. **2** [U] business of providing such contracts: *Her husband works in insurance.* **3** [U] payment made by or to such a company, etc: *When her husband died, she received £50 000 in insurance.* **4** [C, U] ~ **(against sth)** (*fig*) any measure taken as a safeguard against loss, failure, etc: *He's applying for two other jobs as an insurance against not passing the interview for this one.*

□ **inˈsurance broker** person whose business is providing insurance.

inˈsurance policy contract between the company insuring and the insured person: (*fig*) *They regard nuclear weapons as an insurance policy against conventional attack.*

inˈsurance premium one of the regular sums paid in order to be insured.

insure /ɪnˈʃɔː(r); *US* ɪnˈʃʊər/ *v* **1** [Tn, Tn·pr] ~ **sb/sth (against sth)** make a contract that promises to pay sb an amount of money in case of accident, injury, death, etc, or damage to or loss of sth: *insure oneself/one's life for £50 000* ○ *insure one's house against fire.* **2** (*esp US*) = ENSURE.

▷ **the insured** *n* [sing or pl *v*] person or people to whom payment will be made in the case of loss, etc. **insurer** /ɪnˈʃɔːrə(r); *US* ɪnˈʃʊərər/ *n* person or company undertaking to make payment in case of loss, etc.

insurgent /ɪnˈsɜːdʒənt/ *adj* [usu attrib] in revolt; rebellious: *insurgent troops* ○ *an insurgent mob.*

▷ **insurgent** *n* rebel soldier: *an attack by armed insurgents.*

insurmountable /ˌɪnsəˈmaʊntəbl/ *adj* (*fml*) (of obstacles, difficulties, etc) that cannot be overcome: *The problems are not insurmountable.* Cf INSUPERABLE.

insurrection /ˌɪnsəˈrekʃn/ *n* **1** [U] sudden, usu violent, action taken by (part of) the population to try to remove the government. **2** [C] instance of this; revolt.

▷ **insurrectionist** /-ʃənɪst/ *adj* of or taking part in an insurrection.

int *abbr* **1** interior; internal. Cf EXT 1. **2** international.

intact /ɪnˈtækt/ *adj* undamaged; complete: *a box recovered from an accident with its contents intact* ○ *He can scarcely survive this scandal with his reputation intact.*

intaglio /ɪnˈtɑːlɪəʊ/ *n* (*pl* ~**s** /-z/) **1** [U] (process or technique of) carving deeply into stone or metal. **2** [C] (gem with a) figure or design made by cutting into the surface.

intake /ˈɪnteɪk/ *n* **1** (**a**) [U] process of taking liquid, gas, etc into a machine, etc. (**b**) [C] place where liquid, etc enters: *the fuel intake* ○ [attrib] *an intake pipe.* **2** (**a**) [C, U] quantity, number, etc of people entering or taken in (during a particular period): *an annual intake of 100 000 men for military service* ○ *Intake in state primary schools is down by 10%.* (**b**) [CGp] such people: *This year's intake seems/seem to be quite bright.*

intangible /ɪnˈtændʒəbl/ *adj* **1** that cannot be clearly or definitely understood or grasped; indefinable: *The old building had an intangible air of sadness about it.* **2** (*commerce*) (of a business asset) that has no physical existence: *the intangible value of a good reputation.* ▷ **intangibility** /ɪnˌtændʒəˈbɪlətɪ/ *n* [U]. **intangibly** *adv.*

integer /ˈɪntɪdʒə(r)/ *n* (*mathematics*) whole number (contrasted with a *fraction*): *1, 2 and 3 are integers;* $\frac{3}{4}$ *is not an integer.*

integral /ˈɪntɪgrəl/ *adj* **1** ~ **(to sth)** necessary for completeness: *The arms and legs are integral parts of the human body; they are integral to the human body.* **2** [usu attrib] having or containing all parts that are necessary for completeness; whole: *an integral design.* **3** [usu attrib] included as part of the whole, rather than supplied from outside: *a machine with an integral power source.* **4** (*mathematics*) of or being an integer; made up of integers.

▷ **integral** *n* (*mathematics*) quantity of which a given function is a derivative.

integrally /-grəlɪ/ *adv.*

□ **ˌintegral ˈcalculus** (*mathematics*) branch of calculus concerned with finding out the sum total of a lot of extremely small numbers, and with applying this knowledge to calculating areas, volumes, etc. Cf DIFFERENTIAL CALCULUS (DIFFERENTIAL).

integrate /ˈɪntɪgreɪt/ *v* **1** [Tn, Tn·pr] ~ **sth (into sth)**; ~ **A and B**/~ **A with B** combine sth in such a way that it becomes fully a part of sth else: *integrating private schools into the state education system* ○ *The buildings are well integrated with the landscape/The buildings and the landscape are well integrated.* **2** [I, Tn, Tn·pr] ~ **(sb) (into sth/with sth)** (cause sb to) become fully a member of a community, rather than remaining in a separate (esp racial) group: *foreign immigrants who don't integrate well* ○ *integrating black people into a largely white community.* Cf SEGREGATE. **3** [Tn] (*mathematics*) find the integral of (a quantity, an equation, etc).

▷ **integrated** /-tɪd/ *adj* with various parts fitting well together: *an integrated transport scheme*, eg including buses, trains, taxis, etc ○ *an integrated personality*, ie sb who is psychologically stable.

integration /ˌɪntɪˈgreɪʃn/ *n* [U] ~ **(into sth)** integrating or being integrated: *the integration of black children into the school system in the Southern States of America.* Cf SEGREGATION (SEGREGATE).

□ **ˌintegrated ˈcircuit** very small electronic circuit(2b) made of a single small piece of semiconductor material (eg a silicon chip), designed to replace a conventional electric circuit of many parts.

integrity /ɪnˈtegrətɪ/ *n* [U] **1** quality of being honest and morally upright: *He's a man of integrity; he won't break his promise.* ○ *personal, commercial, intellectual, etc integrity.* **2** condition of being whole or undivided: *respect, preserve, threaten, etc a nation's territorial integrity.*

integument /ɪnˈtegjʊmənt/ *n* (*fml*) (usu natural) outer covering, eg a skin, husk, rind or shell.

intellect /ˈɪntəlekt/ *n* **1** [U] power of the mind to reason and acquire knowledge (contrasted with feeling and instinct): *a man of (great) intellect* ○ *Intellect distinguishes humans from other animals.* **2** [C] person of high intelligence and reasoning power: *He was one of the most formidable intellects of his time.*

intellectual /ˌɪntɪˈlektʃʊəl/ *adj* **1** [usu attrib] of the intellect: *the intellectual faculties.* **2** of, interested in or able to deal with things of the mind (eg the arts, ideas for their own sake) rather than practical matters: *intellectual people* ○ *intellectual interests, pursuits, etc.*

▷ **intellectual** *n* intellectual person: *a play, book, etc for intellectuals.*

intellectually *adv.*

intellectualism /ˌɪntəˈlektʃʊəlɪzəm/ *n* [U] **1** (*derog*) too great reliance on or use of the intellect, ignoring feelings or practical considerations. **2** (*philosophy*) theory that knowledge comes from the reasoning power of the mind.

intelligence /ɪnˈtelɪdʒəns/ *n* **1** [U] power of learning, understanding and reasoning; mental ability: *a person of high, great, average, little, low intelligence* ○ *When the water pipe burst, she had the intelligence to turn off the water at the main.* **2** (**a**) [U] information, esp of military value: *an intelligence-gathering satellite* ○ [attrib] *the government's Secret Intelligence Service*, ie organization that gathers such information, esp by spying. (**b**) [Gp] people engaged in gathering such information: *Intelligence has/have reported that the enemy is planning a new attack.*

▷ **intelligent** /-dʒənt/ *adj* having or showing intelligence: *an intelligent child* ○ *an intelligent expression on sb's face* ○ *intelligent questions, answers, remarks, etc* ○ *take an intelligent interest in sth.* **intelligently** *adv.*

□ **inˈtelligence quotient** (*abbr* **IQ**) comparative measure of a person's intelligence.

inˈtelligence test test to measure sb's mental ability. Cf APTITUDE TEST (APTITUDE).

intelligentsia /ɪnˌtelɪˈdʒentsɪə/ *n* **the intelligentsia** [Gp] those people within a community who are of high intelligence and concern themselves with matters of culture, learning, etc; intellectuals as a class.

intelligible /ɪnˈtelɪdʒəbl/ *adj* that can be (easily)

understood: *intelligible speech* ○ *a muddled explanation which was scarcely intelligible.*
▷ **intelligibility** /ɪnˌtelɪdʒəˈbɪlətɪ/ *n* [U] quality of being intelligible.
intelligibly *adv.*

intemperate /ɪnˈtempərət/ *adj (fml)* showing lack of self-control: *intemperate habits*, ie esp excessive drinking of alcohol ○ *His intemperate* (ie thoughtlessly angry or rude) *remarks got him into trouble.* ▷ **intemperance** /-pərəns/ *n* [U]. **intemperately** *adv.*

intend /ɪnˈtend/ *v* **1 (a)** [Tn, Tf, Tt, Tnt, Tg, Cn·n/a, Dn·n] ~ **sth (as sth)** have (a particular purpose or plan) in mind; mean: *I meant it to be an informal discussion, but it didn't turn out as I intended (it should).* ○ *It's not what I intended (it to be).* ○ *I hear they intend to marry/intend marrying.* ○ *I intended to do it, but I'm afraid I forgot.* ○ *I don't intend to listen to this rubbish any longer!* ○ *I intended it as a joke.* ○ *He intends you no harm*, ie does not plan to harm you. **(b)** [Tf, Tnt] have (sth) as a fixed plan or purpose for sb else: *I intend that you shall take over the business.* ○ *I intend you to take over.* ○ *You weren't intended* (ie supposed) *to hear that remark.* **2** [Dn·pr] ~ **sth for sb** plan that sb should receive or be affected by sth: *I think the bomb was intended for* (ie planned to harm) *me.* **3** [Cn·n/a] ~ **sth as sth** plan that sth should be or become sth: *Was that remark intended as* (ie supposed to be) *a joke?* **4** [Tn·pr] ~ **sth by sth** plan that sth should have the specified meaning: *What did he intend by that remark?*
▷ **intended** /-dɪd/ *adj* **1** [attrib] planned; meant; desired: *the intended meaning, result, effect, purpose.* **2** ~ **for sb/sth** [pred] planned or designed for sb/sth: *a book, course, programme, etc intended for children, adults, beginners, etc* ○ *water (not) intended for drinking.*

intense /ɪnˈtens/ *adj* (**-r, -st**) **1** (of sensations) very great or severe; extreme: *intense heat, pain, etc.* **2** (of emotions, etc) very strong: *intense interest, anger, jealousy, convictions, etc.* **3** (of people) highly emotional.
▷ **intensely** *adv.*
intensify /-sɪfaɪ/ *v* (*pt, pp* **-fied**) [I, Tn] (cause sth to) become more intense or intensive: *Her anger intensified.* ○ *The terrorists have intensified their campaign of violence.* **intensification** /ɪnˌtensɪfɪˈkeɪʃn/ *n* [U]. **intensifier** /ɪnˈtensɪfaɪə(r)/ *n (grammar)* word (esp an *adj* or *adv*, eg *so, such, very*) that strengthens the meaning of another word.
intensity /-sətɪ/ *n* **1** [U] state or quality of being intense: *work with greater intensity.* **2** [U] strength of emotion: *I didn't realize the intensity of people's feelings on this issue.* **3** [U, C] (*esp physics*) **(a)** amount of energy or force being exerted. **(b)** degree of brightness of a colour, light, etc.

intensive /ɪnˈtensɪv/ *adj* **1 (a)** concentrating all one's effort on a specific area: *intensive bombardment of a town.* **(b)** involving hard work concentrated into a limited amount of time: *They teach you English in an intensive course lasting just a week; it's quite an intensive few days!* **2** extremely thorough: *An intensive search failed to reveal any clues.* **3** (of farming methods) concentrating labour and care in small areas, in order to produce large quantities of food. Cf EXTENSIVE. **4** *(grammar)* giving force and emphasis: *In 'It's a bloody miracle!', 'bloody' is used as an intensive word.*
▷ **intensive** *n (grammar)* intensive word; intensifier.
-intensive (forming compound *adjs*) using or requiring a lot of the stated thing: *a capital-intensive/labour-intensive industry.*
intensively *adv.*
□ **inˌtensive ˈcare** (part of a hospital giving) constant attention in the treatment of seriously ill patients: *The accident victims are in/have been taken into intensive care.*

intent[1] /ɪnˈtent/ *adj* **1** (of looks, attention, etc) full of eager interest and concentration: *watch with an intent gaze, look, expression, etc.* **2** [pred] ~ **on/upon sth/doing sth (a)** having the stated firm intention: *He's intent on getting promotion, and no one's going to stop him!* **(b)** occupied in doing sth with great concentration: *I was so intent (up)on my work that I didn't notice the time.* ▷ **intently** *adv*: *I listened intently to what she had to say.* **intentness** *n* [U].

intent[2] /ɪnˈtent/ *n* **1** [U] ~ **(to do sth)** (*esp law*) intention; purpose: *act with criminal intent* ○ *fire a weapon with intent to kill* ○ *arrest sb for loitering with intent*, ie for apparently intending to commit a crime. **2** (idm) **to all intents (and purposes)** in all important respects; virtually: *Although there was still a faint heartbeat, he was to all intents and purposes dead.*

intention /ɪnˈtenʃn/ *n* **1 (a)** [C, U] ~ **(of doing sth/that...)** that which one proposes or plans to do: *What are your intentions?* ie What do you plan to do? ○ *She's keeping her intentions to herself*, ie not telling anyone what she plans to do. ○ *I came with the/every intention of staying, but now I've decided to leave.* ○ *My intention was to stay.* ○ *I have no intention of coming* (ie I shall certainly not come) *to this terrible place again!* ○ (*dated*) *Peter asked the young man if his intentions were honourable*, ie if he intended to marry his daughter, whom he was courting. **(b)** [U] *(fml)* intending: *I'm sorry I offended you; it wasn't my intention.* **2** [C] purpose or aim; meaning: *What do you think was the author's intention in this passage?* **3** (idm) **the road to hell is paved with good intentions** ⇨ ROAD. **with the best of intentions** ⇨ BEST[3].
▷ **-intentioned** (forming compound *adjs*) having the specified intentions: *ill-intentioned* ○ *well-intentioned.*

intentional /ɪnˈtenʃənl/ *adj* done on purpose; not accidental; intended: *If I hurt your feelings, it was not intentional.* ○ *an intentional foul in football.*
▷ **intentionally** /-ʃənəlɪ/ *adv* deliberately: *I would never intentionally hurt your feelings.*

inter /ɪnˈtɜː(r)/ *v* (**-rr-**) [Tn] *(fml)* put (a corpse) in a grave or tomb; bury. Cf INTERMENT.

inter- *pref* (with *vs, ns* and *adjs*) **1** between; from one to another: *interleave* ○ *interface* ○ *international.* **2** together; mutually: *interconnect* ○ *interlink.*

interact /ˌɪntərˈækt/ *v* **1** [I, Ipr] ~ **(with sth)** act or have an effect on each other: *chemicals that interact to form a new compound* ○ *ideas that interact.* **2** [I, Ipr] ~ **(with sb)** (of people) act together or co-operatively, esp so as to communicate with each other: *a sociologist studying the complex way in which people interact (with each other) at parties.*
▷ **interaction** /-ˈækʃn/ *n* **(a)** [U] ~ **(among/between sb/sth);** ~ **(with sb/sth)** interacting; co-operation: *Increased interaction between different police forces would improve the rate of solving crimes.* **(b)** [C] instance of this.
interactive /-ˈæktɪv/ *adj* **1** ~ **(with sb/sth)** (of two or more people or things) interacting: *The psychotherapy is carried out in small interactive groups.* **2** *(computing)* allowing a continuous two-way transfer of information between a computer and the person using it.

inter alia /ˌɪntər ˈeɪlɪə/ *(Latin)* among other things.

interbreed /ˌɪntəˈbriːd/ *v* [I, Ipr, Tn, Tn·pr] ~ **(sth) (with sth)** (cause individuals of different species to) breed together, so producing a hybrid: *These two types of dog can interbreed/be interbred (with each other).*

intercede /ˌɪntəˈsiːd/ *v (fml)* **1** [I, Ipr] ~ **(with sb) (for/on behalf of sb)** plead (with sb) to be merciful (to sb): *We have interceded with the authorities on behalf of people unfairly imprisoned there*, ie asked them to release the prisoners. **2** [I, Ipr] ~ **(between A and B)** act as an intermediary (between two people, groups, countries that cannot agree), trying to help them settle their differences.
▷ **intercession** /ˌɪntəˈseʃn/ *n* **(a)** [U] interceding. **(b)** [C] plea on behalf of sb.

intercept /ˌɪntəˈsept/ *v* [Tn] stop or catch (sb travelling or sth in motion) before he or it can reach a destination: *Reporters intercepted him as he tried to leave by the rear entrance.* ○ *Effective defence is a matter of intercepting their missiles before they can reach us.* ○ *The police had been intercepting my mail*, ie reading it before it was delivered.
▷ **intercept** /ˈɪntəsept/ *n (mathematics)* part of a line or surface cut off by another line or surface.
interception /ˌɪntəˈsepʃn/ *n* **(a)** [U] intercepting. **(b)** [C] instance of this.
interceptor /-tə(r)/ *n* person or thing that intercepts (esp a fast military plane which attacks incoming bombers).

interchange /ˌɪntəˈtʃeɪndʒ/ *v* **1** [Tn, Tn·pr] ~ **sth (with sb)** (of two people, etc) give sth to and receive sth from each other; exchange: *We interchanged partners; he danced with mine, and I danced with his.* **2** [Tn, Tn·pr] ~ **sth/sb (with sth/sb)** put each of two things or people in the other's place: *interchange the front and rear tyres of a car* ○ *interchange the front tyres with the rear ones.* **3** [I, Tn] (cause sth to) alternate: *the city's brightly-lit Christmas decorations, with their constantly interchanging colours.*
▷ **interchange** /ˈɪntətʃeɪndʒ/ *n* **1 (a)** [U] interchanging: *a regular interchange of letters.* **(b)** [C] instance of this. **2** [C] junction (eg on a motorway) where vehicles leave or join a road without crossing other lines of traffic.
interchangeable /ˌɪntəˈtʃeɪndʒəbl/ *adj* ~ **(with sth)** that can be interchanged, esp without affecting the way in which sth works: *a machine with interchangeable parts* ○ *True synonyms are entirely interchangeable (with one another).*
interchangeably *adv.*

inter-city /ˌɪntəˈsɪtɪ/ *adj* [usu attrib] (of fast transport) operating between cities, esp without making stops on the way: *an inter-city train, coach, etc* ○ *an inter-city air shuttle.*
▷ **inter-city** *n* **(a)** [U] such a service: *travel by inter-city.* **(b)** [C] *(infml)* such a train, coach, etc: *catch the inter-city.*

intercollegiate /ˌɪntəkəˈliːdʒɪət/ *adj* existing or done between colleges: *intercollegiate games, debates, etc.*

intercom /ˈɪntəkɒm/ *n* system of communication by means of microphones and loud speakers, as used on an aircraft, in a large building (eg a factory), etc: *make an announcement on/over the intercom* ○ [attrib] *an intercom system.*

intercommunicate /ˌɪntəkəˈmjuːnɪkeɪt/ *v* **1** [I, Ipr] ~ **(with sb)** communicate with one another; give messages to each other: *The lack of a common language made it very difficult to intercommunicate (with each other).* **2** [I, Ipr] ~ **(with sth)** (also **interconnect**) (of two or more rooms, compartments, etc) have a means (eg door or corridor) of passing from one to another: *We had intercommunicating rooms.* ▷ **intercommunication** /ˌɪntəkəˌmuːnɪˈkeɪʃn/ *n* [U].

intercommunion *n* [U] mutual communion, esp between different Churches, eg Catholic and Orthodox.

interconnect /ˌɪntəkəˈnekt/ *v* [I, Ipr] ~ **(with sth)** **1** be connected with each other: *It's strange how people's lives interconnect.* **2** = INTERCOMMUNICATE 2.
▷ **interconnected** /-tɪd/ *adj* ~ **(with sth)** that have a connection (with one another); not independent: *I see these two theories as somehow interconnected.*
interconnecting *adj* [attrib] joining two or more things together: *an interconnecting corridor.*
interconnection /-ˈnekʃn/ *n* **(a)** [U] connecting two or more things together. **(b)** [C] mutual connection between two or more things.

intercontinental /ˌɪntəˌkɒntɪˈnentl/ *adj* between continents: *intercontinental travel.*
□ **ˌintercontiˌnental balˌlistic ˈmissile** (*abbr* **ICBM**) missile capable of being fired a very long distance, from one continent to another, and typically having a nuclear warhead.

intercourse /ˈɪntəkɔːs/ *n* [U] ~ **(with sb);** ~ **(between sb and sb)** *(fml)* **1** = SEXUAL INTERCOURSE (SEXUAL). **2** dealings with people, nations, etc: *a shy person who avoids all human intercourse.*

interdenominational /ˌɪntədɪˌnɒmɪˈneɪʃənl/ *adj* common to or shared by different religious denominations, eg Methodist, Baptist, Catholic.

interdepartmental /ˌɪntəˌdiːpɑːtˈmentl/ *adj* of or done by more than one department. ▷ **interdepartmentally** /-təlɪ/ *adv.*

interdependent /ˌɪntədɪˈpendənt/ *adj* depending on each other: *All nations are interdependent in the modern world.* ▷ **interdependence** /-əns/ *n* [U]. **interdependently** *adv.*

interdict /ˌɪntəˈdɪkt/ *v* [Tn] *(fml)* **1** *(esp law)* prohibit (an action); forbid the use of (sth). **2** (in the Roman Catholic Church) forbid sb from taking part in church services and receiving Communion.

▷ **interdict** /ˈɪntədɪkt/ *n (fml)* **(a)** *(law)* prohibition from doing sth by an official order of the court. **(b)** (in the Roman Catholic Church) order forbidding sb from taking part in church services, etc.

interdiction /ˌɪntəˈdɪkʃn/ *n* [C, U] (instance of) interdicting.

interdisciplinary /ˌɪntəˌdɪsɪˈplɪnərɪ/ *adj* of or covering more than one area of study: *interdisciplinary studies* ○ *an interdisciplinary course, qualification, degree, etc.*

interest¹ /ˈɪntrəst/ *n* **1** [U, sing] ~ **(in sb/sth)** state of wanting to learn or know (about sb/sth); curiosity; concern: *feel, have, show, express (an) interest in sb or sth* ○ *a topic that arouses, provokes, stimulates, etc a lot of interest* ○ *Now he's grown up he no longer takes any interest in his stamp collection: he's lost all interest in it.* ○ *do sth (just) for interest/out of interest/for interest's sake,* ie (just) to satisfy a desire for knowledge. **2** [U] quality that arouses concern or curiosity; power to hold one's attention: *The subject may be full of interest to you, but it holds no interest for me.* ○ *Suspense adds interest to a story.* **3** [C] thing with which one concerns oneself or about which one is enthusiastic: *a person of wide, varied, narrow, limited interests* ○ *Her main interests in life are music, tennis and cooking.* **4** [C usu *pl*] advantage; benefit: *look after, protect, safeguard, etc one's own interests,* ie make sure that nothing is done to one's disadvantage ○ *He has your best interests at heart,* ie is acting for your advantage. **5** [C usu *pl*] ~ **(in sth)** legal right to share in sth (eg a business), esp in its profits: *He has considerable business interests.* ○ *American interests in Europe,* eg capital invested in European countries ○ *sell one's interest in a company.* **6** [C] ~ **(in sth)** personal connection with sth from which one may benefit, esp financially: *If a Member of Parliament wishes to speak about a company with which he is connected, he must declare his interest.* **7** [U] ~ **(on sth)** *(finance)* money charged for borrowing money, or paid to sb who invests money: *pay interest on a capital sum* ○ *the rate of interest,* ie payment made by the borrower expressed as a percentage of capital ○ *interest at 10%* ○ [attrib] *the interest rate* ○ *an interest-free loan,* ie on which one does not have to pay interest. **8** [C usu *pl*] *(often derog)* group of people engaged in the same business, etc or having sth in common: *landed interests,* ie landowners ○ *Powerful business interests* (ie large business firms collectively) *are influencing the government's actions.* ○ [attrib] *influential interest groups.* **9** (idm) **in sb's interest(s)** for or to sb's advantage: *sth that is not in the public interest* ○ *It would be in your interests to accept.* **in the interest(s) of sth** for the sake of sth: *In the interest(s) of safety, no smoking is allowed.* **a vested interest** ⇨ VEST². **(repay, return, etc sth) with interest (a)** *(finance)* (give back a sum of money) adding a percentage of interest. **(b)** *(fig infml)* (respond to an action, good or bad, by doing it to the doer) with added force: *return a blow, a kindness with interest.*

interest² /ˈɪntrəst/ *v* [Tn, Tn·pr] ~ **oneself/sb (in sth) (a)** cause oneself/sb to give one's/his attention (to sth) or to be concerned (about sth): *a topic that interests me greatly* ○ *Having lost his job, he'd begun to interest himself in local voluntary work.* ○ *It may interest you to know that she's since died.* **(b)** arouse sb's desire to do, buy, eat, etc sth: *Can I interest you in our latest computer?*

▷ **interested** /-tɪd/ *adj* **1** ~ **(in sth/sb)** showing curiosity or concern (about sb or sth): *Are you interested in history?* ○ *I tried to tell him about it, but he just wasn't interested.* ○ *interested listeners* ○ *an interested look* ○ *I shall be interested to know what happens.* **2** ~ **(in sth)** in a position to obtain an advantage (from sth); not impartial: *As an interested party* (ie sb likely to profit), *I was not allowed to vote.*

interesting *adj* holding the attention; arousing curiosity: *interesting people, books, conversation.* **interestingly** *adv*: *She was there but her husband, interestingly, wasn't.*

NOTE ON USAGE: The adjective **interested** can mean **1** 'desiring to learn or know (about something)': *I am very interested in local history.* **2** 'having an involvement (in something)': *The lawyer invited the interested parties to discuss the problem.* **Uninterested** relates to sense 1: *She seemed completely uninterested in what I had to tell her about my new job.* **Disinterested** relates to sense 2: *In financial matters it is important to get disinterested advice,* ie from somebody who is not directly involved.

interface /ˈɪntəfeɪs/ *n* **1** surface common to two areas. **2** *(computing)* electrical circuit linking one device with another or software linking two systems, enabling data coded in one format to be transmitted in another. **3** *(fig)* place where two subjects, etc meet and affect each other: *at the interface of art and science* ○ *at the art/science interface.*

interfere /ˌɪntəˈfɪə(r)/ *v* **1** [I, Ipr] ~ **(in sth);** ~ **(between sb and sb)** concern oneself with or take action affecting sb else's affairs without the right to do so or being invited to do so: *Don't interfere in matters that do not concern you!* ○ *It's unwise to interfere between husband and wife.* **2** [Ipr] ~ **with sth (a)** handle, adjust, etc sth without permission, esp so as to cause damage: *Who's been interfering with the clock? It's stopped.* **(b)** obstruct sth wholly or partially; prevent sth from being done or carried out properly: *interfere with sb else's plans* ○ *Don't allow pleasure to interfere with duty.* **3** [Ipr] ~ **with sb (a)** distract or hinder sb: *Don't interfere with him while he's working.* **(b)** *(Brit euph)* assault sb sexually: *The police reported that the murdered child had not been interfered with.*

▷ **interference** /ˌɪntəˈfɪərəns/ *n* [U] **1** ~ **(in/with sth)** interfering: *I don't want any interference from you!* **2 (a)** *(radio)* prevention of clear reception because a second signal is being transmitted on a wavelength close to the first: *interference from foreign broadcasting stations.* **(b)** *(computing)* presence of unwanted signals in a communications circuit. **(c)** *(sport esp US)* (in ice hockey, American football, etc) unlawful obstruction of an opposing player.

interfering *adj* [attrib] likely to concern oneself annoyingly with other people's affairs, to try to control what they do, etc: *She's an interfering old busybody!*

interferon /ˌɪntəˈfɪərɒn/ *n* [U] type of protein produced by the body cells when attacked by a virus which acts to prevent the further development of the virus.

interglacial /ˌɪntəˈɡleɪsɪəl; *US* -ˈɡleɪʃl/ *n* period of relatively warm weather, coming between two ice ages, when it is very cold.

interim /ˈɪntərɪm/ *n* (idm) **in the interim** during the time that comes between; meantime: *'My new job starts in May.' 'What are you doing in the interim?'*

▷ **interim** *adj* [attrib] existing or in force only for a short time; temporary; provisional: *interim arrangements, measures, proposals, etc* ○ *an interim loan, payment, etc* ○ *an interim report,* ie one made before the main or final report.

interior¹ /ɪnˈtɪərɪə(r)/ *n* **1** [C usu *sing*] inner part; inside: *the interior of a house* ○ *a house with a classical exterior and a modern interior.* Cf EXTERIOR. **2 the interior** [sing] inland part of a country or continent: *the jungles of the interior of Africa* ○ *explorers who penetrated deep into the interior.* **3 the Interior** [sing] domestic affairs of a country, as dealt with by its government (in the UK, the responsibility of the Home Office): *the Department/Minister of the Interior.*

□ **inˌterior ˈdecorator** person who decorates the inside of a house or other building with paint, wallpaper, etc.

inˌterior deˈsign planned choice of style, colour, furnishing, etc for the inside of a house, flat, etc. **inˌterior deˈsigner** person who is expert in this. **inˌterior-ˈsprung** (*US* ˌ**inner-ˈspring**) *adj* (esp of a mattress) having springs inside.

interior² /ɪnˈtɪərɪə(r)/ *adj* [usu attrib] **1** situated inside or indoors: *an interior room.* **2** far from the borders of a country; inland. **3** of a country's domestic affairs: *the Department of Interior Affairs.* **4** existing deep within sth, and usu partly hidden: *the poem's interior meaning.*

□ **inˌterior ˈmonologue** form of writing that expresses a person's private thoughts, eg in a novel. Cf STREAM OF CONSCIOUSNESS (STREAM).

interject /ˌɪntəˈdʒekt/ *v* [Tn, Tn·pr, Tf] ~ **sth (into sth)** make (a sudden remark) that interrupts what sb else is saying: *If I may interject a note of caution into the discussion...* ○ *When I brought up the question of funding, he quickly interjected that it had been settled.*

▷ **interjection** /ˌɪntəˈdʒekʃn/ *n (grammar)* word or phrase used as an exclamation (eg *Oh!, Hurray!* or *For goodness sake!*).

interlace /ˌɪntəˈleɪs/ *v* [I, Ipr, Tn, Tn·pr] ~ **(sth) (with sth)** (cause things to) be joined by weaving or lacing together; cross (one thing with another) as if woven: *interlacing branches* ○ *interlace sb's hair with ribbons.*

interlard /ˌɪntəˈlɑːd/ *v* [Tn·pr] ~ **sth with sth** *(rhet often derog)* mix (ordinary writing, speech, etc) with unusual or striking expressions, eg quotations or foreign phrases: *essays liberally interlarded with quotations from the poets.*

interleave /ˌɪntəˈliːv/ *v* [Tn, Tn·pr] ~ **B (between A)/** ~ **A (with B)** insert (extra pages, usu blank ones) between the pages of a book: *The exercise book has plain pages interleaved between its lined ones/has lined pages interleaved with plain ones.*

interline /ˌɪntəˈlaɪn/ *v* [Tn, Tn·pr] ~ **sth (with sth) 1** put an extra layer of material between the fabric of (a garment) and its lining in order to give firmness or extra warmth: *interline a coat (with wool, acrylic fibre, etc).* **2** (also **interlineate** /ˌɪntəˈlɪnɪeɪt/) write or print additional material between the lines of (a text): *interline a book with notes, glosses, etc.*

▷ **interlining** /ˈɪntəlaɪnɪŋ/ *n* (usu *sing*) material used to interline a garment.

interlinear /ˌɪntəˈlɪnɪə(r)/ *adj* (written or printed) between the lines of a text.

interlink /ˌɪntəˈlɪŋk/ *v* [I, Ipr, Tn, Tn·pr] ~ **(sth) (with sth) (a)** link (sth) (with sth): *chains which interlink/are interlinked.* **(b)** *(fig)* connect (sth) or be connected closely (with sth): *transport systems that interlink with each other* ○ *destinies that are interlinked.*

interlock /ˌɪntəˈlɒk/ *v* [I, Ipr, Tn, Tn·pr] ~ **(sth) (with sth)** fit (things which are joined together) firmly so they do not come apart: *a system of interlocking parts* ○ *two pieces of machinery, pipe, etc that interlock* ○ *They walked along holding hands, their fingers interlocked.* ○ *interlock one pipe with another.*

▷ **interlock** /ˈɪntəlɒk/ *n* **1** [C] *(computing)* device used in a logic circuit to prevent certain operations from occurring unless preceded by certain events. **2** [U] machine-knitted fabric with fine stitches.

interlocutor /ˌɪntəˈlɒkjʊtə(r)/ *n (fml)* person taking part in a conversation or discussion: *my interlocutor,* ie the person talking to me.

▷ **interlocutory** /ˌɪntəˈlɒkjʊtərɪ; *US* -tɔːrɪ/ *adj* **1** *(fml)* of or occurring in a conversation between two people. **2** (*law*) issued during a legal action, and liable to be changed or withdrawn later; provisional: *an interlocutory order*.

interloper /ˈɪntələʊpə(r)/ *n* person who is present in a place where he does not belong, interferes in sth which is not his affair, etc; intruder: *Security guards were stationed at the door to deal with any interlopers.*

interlude /ˈɪntəluːd/ *n* **1** **(a)** short period of time separating the parts of a play, film, etc; interval: *There will now be a 15-minute interlude.* **(b)** piece performed during this: *a musical interlude.* **2** period of time coming between two events: *a brief interlude of peace between two wars.* **3** event or phase of a different kind occurring in the middle of something: *a comic interlude*, ie during a serious drama or during sb's life. ⇨ Usage at BREAK[2].

intermarry /ˌɪntəˈmærɪ/ *v* (*pt, pp* **-ried**) [I, Ipr] ~ **(with sb)** **1** (of racial, religious, etc groups) become connected by marriage with other groups: *blacks intermarrying with whites* ○ *Catholics intermarrying with Protestants.* **2** marry sb within one's own family or group: *cousins who intermarry (with one another)*, eg in a royal family.

▷ **intermarriage** /ˌɪntəˈmærɪdʒ/ *n* [U] such marriage.

intermediary /ˌɪntəˈmiːdɪərɪ; *US* -dɪerɪ/ *n* ~ **(between sb and sb)** person who acts as a means of communication between two or more others: *They disliked each other too much to meet, so they conducted all their business through an intermediary.*

▷ **intermediary** *adj* acting in such a way: *play an intermediary role in a dispute.*

intermediate /ˌɪntəˈmiːdɪət/ *adj* ~ **(between A and B)** **(a)** situated or coming between (two people, things, etc) in time, space, degree, etc: *at an intermediate point, level, stage, etc* ○ *The pupa is at an intermediate stage of development; it is intermediate between the egg and the adult butterfly.* **(b)** between elementary and advanced: *an intermediate course, book, level.*

▷ **intermediate** *n* **1** intermediate thing or person. **2** (*chemistry*) compound formed by one chemical reaction and then taking part in another reaction.

intermediately *adv.*

□ **interˌmediate-range (balˌlistic) ˈmissile** (typically nuclear) missile designed to attack targets between long-range and short-range.

interment /ɪnˈtɜːmənt/ *n* (*fml*) [C, U] burying of a dead body. Cf INTER.

intermezzo /ˌɪntəˈmetsəʊ/ *n* (*pl* ~**s** or **-zzi** /-tsɪ/) (*music*) **(a)** short composition to be played between the acts of a drama or an opera, or one that comes between the main movements of a symphony or some other large work. **(b)** short instrumental piece in one movement: *two intermezzi by Brahms.*

interminable /ɪnˈtɜːmɪnəbl/ *adj* (*usu derog*) going on too long, and usu therefore annoying or boring: *an interminable argument, debate, sermon, etc.* ▷ **interminably** /-əblɪ/ *adv*: *We had to wait interminably.*

intermingle /ˌɪntəˈmɪŋgl/ *v* [I, Ipr, Tn, Tn·pr] ~ **(sb/sth) (with sb/sth)** (cause people, ideas, substances, etc to) mix together: *Oil and water will not intermingle.* ○ *a busy trading port, where people of all races intermingle (with each other)* ○ *a book which intermingles fact with fiction.*

intermission /ˌɪntəˈmɪʃn/ *n* [C, U] period of time during which sth stops before continuing; interval; pause: *a short intermission halfway through a film* ○ *The fever lasted five days without intermission.* ⇨ Usage at BREAK[2].

intermittent /ˌɪntəˈmɪtənt/ *adj* continually stopping and then starting again; not constant: *intermittent flashes of light from a lighthouse* ○ *intermittent bursts of anger, energy, interest, etc* ○ *an intermittent fever.* ▷ **intermittently** *adv.*

intermix /ˌɪntəˈmɪks/ *v* [I, Ipr, Tn, Tn·pr] ~ **(sb/sth) (with sb/sth)** (cause people, things, ideas, etc to) mix together; intermingle.

▷ **intermixture** /ˌɪntəˈmɪkstʃə(r)/ *n* [C, U] (instance of) intermixing: *a confusing intermixture of fact and fiction.*

intern[1] /ɪnˈtɜːn/ *v* [Tn, Tn·pr] ~ **sb (in sth)** put sb (eg a terrorist or sb from an enemy country) in prison, a camp, etc, esp during a war and without trial.

▷ **internee** /ˌɪntɜːˈniː/ *n* person who is interned.

internment /ɪnˈtɜːnmənt/ *n* [U]: *the internment of enemy aliens* ○ [attrib] *an internment camp.*

intern[2] (also **interne**) /ˈɪntɜːn/ *n* (*US*) (*Brit* **ˈhouseman**) young doctor who is completing his training by living in a hospital and acting as an assistant physician or surgeon there.

internal /ɪnˈtɜːnl/ *adj* **1** of or on the inside: *the internal workings of a machine* ○ *holding an internal inquiry* (ie within an organization) *to find out who is responsible* ○ (*mathematics*) *an internal angle*, eg one of the three inside a triangle. Cf EXTERNAL. **2** (*medical*) of the inside of the body: *internal organs* ○ *internal medicine*, ie medical study of the interior of the body ○ (*infml*) *She's been having some internal problems.* **3** of the mind, but not outwardly expressed: *wrestling with internal doubts.* **4** (of examinations, etc) set and marked within a school, university, college, etc: *an internal examiner*, ie one who marks papers from his own college, etc. **5** of political, economic, etc affairs within a country, rather than abroad; domestic: *internal trade, revenue, etc.* **6** (derived from) within the thing itself: *a theory which lacks internal consistency*, ie of which the parts do not fit together ○ *internal evidence*, eg of when a book was written.

▷ **internalize**, **-ise** /-nəlaɪz/ *v* [Tn] (*psychology*) make (attitudes, behaviour, language, etc) fully part of one's nature or mental capacity, by learning or unconsciously assimilating them. **internalization**, **-isation** /ɪnˌtɜːnəlaɪˈzeɪʃn; *US* -lɪˈz-/ *n* [U, C].

internally /-nəlɪ/ *adv*: *medicine that is not to be taken internally*, ie not swallowed ○ *a theory which is not internally consistent.*

□ **inˌternal comˈbustion** process by which power is produced by the explosion of gases or vapours inside a cylinder (as in a car engine): [attrib] *an internal-combustion engine.*

Internal Revenue Service (*US*) government department responsible for collecting domestic taxes. Cf INLAND REVENUE (INLAND).

inˌternal ˈrhyme rhyme between two words in the same line of poetry.

international /ˌɪntəˈnæʃnəl/ *adj* of, carried on by or existing between two or more nations: *international sport, trade, law* ○ *an international agreement, conference, flight* ○ *an international call*, ie a telephone call to another country ○ *an international incident*, ie a crisis between two or more nations ○ *a pianist with an international reputation.*

▷ **international** *n* **1** (*sport*) **(a)** contest involving teams from two or more countries: *the France-Scotland Rugby international.* **(b)** player who takes part in an international contest: *a retired Welsh Rugby international.* **2** **International** any of four socialist or communist associations for workers of all countries, formed in 1864, 1889, 1919 and 1937.

internationalize, **-ise** /ˌɪntəˈnæʃnəlaɪz/ *v* [Tn] bring (sth) under the combined control or protection of all or many nations; make international: *Should the Suez and Panama Canals be internationalized?* **internationalization**, **-isation** /ˌɪntəˌnæʃnəlaɪˈzeɪʃn; *US* -lɪˈz-/ *n* [U].

internationally /-nəlɪ/ *adv*: *an internationally known pianist.*

□ **the ˌInternational ˌCourt of ˈJustice** United Nations court which makes judgements on disputes between member nations. It is based in The Hague, Holland.

the ˌinternational ˈdate-line = DATE-LINE 1 (DATE[1]).

the ˌInternational ˈLabour Organization (*abbr* **ILO**) United Nations organization that tries to ensure proper conditions for workers in countries around the world.

the ˌInternational ˈMonetary Fund (*abbr* **IMF**) international financial organization which seeks to stabilize the exchange rates of the world's currencies. It makes loans to member nations when they are in economic difficulty.

the ˌInternational Phoˌnetic ˈAlphabet (*abbr* **IPA**) alphabet consisting of letters and symbols that stand for individual speech sounds, and can be used for representing the pronunciation of words in all the world's languages. IPA is used in this dictionary to show how English words are pronounced.

Internationale /ˌɪntənæʃəˈnɑːl/ *n* **the Internationale** [sing] (revolutionary) socialist song.

internationalism /ˌɪntəˈnæʃnəlɪzəm/ *n* [U] belief in the need for friendly co-operation between nations.

▷ **internationalist** /-ʃnəlɪst/ *n* person who supports or believes in internationalism.

interne = INTERN[2].

internecine /ˌɪntəˈniːsaɪn/ *adj* causing destruction to both sides: *internecine strife, war, conflict, etc.*

internist /ɪnˈtɜːnɪst/ *n* (*esp US*) doctor who specializes in internal diseases.

interpellate /ɪnˈtɜːpeleɪt; *US* ˌɪntərˈpeleɪt/ *v* [Tn] (in some parliaments, eg the French and Japanese) question (a government minister) about a matter of government policy, thus interrupting parliamentary proceedings.

▷ **interpellation** /ɪnˌtɜːpəˈleɪʃn/ *n* [C, U] (instance of) interpellating.

interpenetrate /ˌɪntəˈpenɪtreɪt/ *v* [I, Tn] penetrate (each other), esp so as to lose individuality; spread through (sth) thoroughly in each direction: *two cultures, originally distinct, which have so interpenetrated (each other) as to become virtually a single culture.*

▷ **interpenetration** /ˌɪntəˌpenɪˈtreɪʃn/ *n* [C, U] (instance of) interpenetrating or being interpenetrated.

interpersonal /ˌɪntəˈpɜːsənl/ *adj* existing or done between two people: *ˌinterpersonal reˈlations.*

interplanetary /ˌɪntəˈplænɪtrɪ; *US* -terɪ/ *adj* between planets: *an interplanetary flight.*

interplay /ˈɪntəpleɪ/ *n* [U] ~ **(of A and B/between A and B)** way in which two or more things have an effect on each other; interaction: *the subtle interplay of colours* (ie their combined effect) *in Monet's painting* ○ *the interplay between generosity and self-interest which influences people's actions.*

Interpol /ˈɪntəpɒl/ *n* [Gp] International Police Commission, an organization through which national police forces can co-operate with each other.

interpolate /ɪnˈtɜːpəleɪt/ *v* [Tn, Tn·pr] ~ **sth (into sth)** (*fml*) **1** make (a remark, etc) which interrupts a conversation, speech, etc: *If I may interpolate a comment, before you continue your speech....* **2** add (sth) to a text, book, etc, sometimes misleadingly: *Close inspection showed that many lines had been interpolated into the manuscript at a later date.* **3** (*mathematics*) **(a)** put (additional terms) into a mathematical series. **(b)** estimate (a value) between two values that are already known.

▷ **interpolation** /ɪnˌtɜːpəˈleɪʃn/ *n* **(a)** [U] interpolating or being interpolated. **(b)** [C] thing interpolated.

interpose /ˌɪntəˈpəʊz/ *v* (*fml*) **1** [Tn, Tn·pr] ~ **sb/sth (between A and B)** place sb/sth between others: *He interposed his considerable bulk* (ie body) *between me and the window, so that I could not see out.* **2** [I, Tn] interrupt, esp by making (a remark): *'But how do you know that?' he interposed.*

▷ **interposition** /ˌɪntəpəˈzɪʃn/ *n* (*fml*) **(a)** [U] interposing or being interposed. **(b)** [C] thing interposed.

interpret /ɪnˈtɜːprɪt/ *v* **1** [Tn] **(a)** explain (sth which is not easily understandable): *interpret a difficult text, an inscription, sb's dream, etc.* **(b)** make clear or bring out the intended meaning of (a character, composition, etc): *interpret a role in a* *play* ○ *interpret a piece of music,* ie as player or conductor ○ *Poetry helps us to interpret life.* **2** [Cn·n/a] ~ **sth as sth** understand sth in a particular way: *'How would you interpret his silence?' 'I would interpret it as a refusal.'* **3** [I, Ipr] ~ (**for sb**) give a simultaneous spoken translation from one language to another: *Will you please interpret for me?* Cf TRANSLATE.

▷ **interpretation** /ɪnˌtɜːprɪˈteɪʃn/ *n* (**a**) [U] interpreting. (**b**) [C] result of this; explanation or meaning: *the conductor's controversial interpretation of the symphony* ○ *These facts allow of/may be given many possible interpretations.* ○ *What interpretation would you put/place on them?* ie How would you explain them?

interpretative /ɪnˈtɜːprɪtətɪv/ *adj* (*Brit*) (also *esp US* **interpretive** /ɪnˈtɜːprɪtɪv/) of or concerning interpretation: *the pianist's considerable interpretative skills.*

interpreter *n* **1** person who gives a simultaneous translation of words spoken in another language. Cf TRANSLATOR (TRANSLATE). **2** computer program which converts instructions in real time (REAL) into a form that can be understood by the computer.

interpreting *n* [U] activity of an interpreter.

interracial /ˌɪntəˈreɪʃl/ *adj* between or involving different races: *interracial conflict, harmony, cooperation, etc.*

interregnum /ˌɪntəˈregnəm/ *n* (*pl* ~**s** or **-na** /-nə/) **1** (**a**) period when a state has no normal or lawful ruler, esp at the end of a sovereign's reign and before the appointment of a successor. (**b**) period in an organization when no appointed head or leader is in charge, after the resignation or death of the previous one, until a new appointment is made. **2** (*fig*) interval or pause; gap in continuity.

interrelate /ˌɪntərɪˈleɪt/ *v* [I, Ipr, Tn, Tn·pr] ~ (**sth**) (**with sth**) (cause parts, etc to) be connected very closely so that they have an effect on each other: *Many would say that crime and poverty interrelate/are interrelated (with one another).*

▷ **interrelated** *adj* mutually related: *a complex network of interrelated parts.*

interrelation /ˌɪntərɪˈleɪʃn/ (also **interrelationship**) *n* [U, C] ~ (**of A and B/between A and B**) mutual relationship.

interrogate /ɪnˈterəgeɪt/ *v* [Tn, Tn·pr] ~ **sb** (**about sth**) question sb aggressively or closely and for a long time: *interrogate a prisoner* ○ *He refused to be interrogated about his friends.*

▷ **interrogation** /ɪnˌterəˈgeɪʃn/ *n* [C, U] (instance of) interrogating or being interrogated: *several interrogations by police officers* ○ *The prisoner gave way under interrogation.* ○ [attrib] *interrogation techniques.*

interrogator *n* person who interrogates.

interrogative /ˌɪntəˈrɒgətɪv/ *adj* **1** (*fml*) asking or seeming to ask a question; inquiring: *an interrogative look, glance, remark, etc* ○ *in an interrogative tone, manner, etc.* **2** (*grammar*) used in questions: *interrogative pronouns, determiners, adverbs, eg who, which, why.*

▷ **interrogative** *n* (*grammar*) interrogative word, esp a pronoun or a determiner. **interrogatively** *adv.*

interrogatory /ˌɪntəˈrɒgətrɪ; *US* -tɔːrɪ/ *adj* (*fml*) interrogative(1): *in an interrogatory tone, voice, manner, etc.*

interrupt /ˌɪntəˈrʌpt/ *v* **1** [Tn] break the continuity of (sth) temporarily: *Trade between the two countries was interrupted by the war.* ○ *We interrupt this programme to bring you a news flash.* **2** [I, Ipr, Tn, Tn·pr] ~ (**sb/sth**) (**with sth**) (*derog*) stop (sb) speaking, etc or (sth) happening by speaking oneself or by causing some other sort of disturbance: *Don't interrupt (me) while I'm busy!* ○ *Don't interrupt the speaker now; he will answer questions later.* ○ *Hecklers interrupted her speech with jeering.* **3** [Tn] destroy the uniformity of (sth): *a vast flat plain interrupted only by a few trees.* **4** [Tn] obstruct (sth): *These new flats will interrupt our view of the sea.*

▷ **interrupter** *n* person or thing that interrupts.

interruption /ˌɪntəˈrʌpʃn/ *n* (**a**) [U] interrupting or being interrupted. (**b**) [C] instance of this; thing that interrupts: *Numerous interruptions have prevented me from finishing my work.*

intersect /ˌɪntəˈsekt/ *v* **1** [Tn esp passive] divide (sth) by going across it: *a landscape of small fields intersected by hedges and streams.* **2** [I, Ipr, Tn] ~ (**sth**) (**with sth**) (of lines, roads, etc) meet and go past (another or each other) forming a cross shape: *The lines AB and CD intersect at E.* ○ *The line AB intersects the line CD at E.* ○ *How many times do the road and railway intersect (with one another) on this map?*

▷ **intersecting** *adj* that intersect: *intersecting lines.*

intersection /ˌɪntəˈsekʃn/ *n* **1** [U] intersecting or being intersected. **2** [C] point where two lines, etc intersect. **3** [C] place where two or more roads intersect; crossroads.

intersperse /ˌɪntəˈspɜːs/ *v* [Tn·pr] ~ **B among/between/in/throughout A;** ~ **A with B** vary sth by placing other things at irregular intervals among it: *intersperse flower-beds among/between the trees* ○ *a landscape of trees interspersed with a few flower-beds* ○ *a day of sunshine interspersed with occasional showers.*

interstate /ˌɪntəˈsteɪt/ *adj* [usu attrib] between states, esp in the USA: ˌ*interstate* ˈ*rivalry,* ˈ*tensions,* ˈ*highways.*

interstellar /ˌɪntəˈstelə(r)/ *adj* between the stars: *interstellar matter,* eg the masses of gas between stars ○ *interstellar communication.* Cf STELLAR.

interstice /ɪnˈtɜːstɪs/ *n* (usu *pl*) ~ (**of/between/in sth**) (*fml*) very small gap or crack: *The interstices between the bricks let in cold air.* ▷ **interstitial** /ˌɪntəˈstɪʃl/ *adj.*

intertribal /ˌɪntəˈtraɪbl/ *adj* between tribes: *intertribal wars.*

intertwine /ˌɪntəˈtwaɪn/ *v* [I, Ipr, Tn, Tn·pr] ~ (**sth**) (**with sth**) be twisted so as to become joined; twist (things) so as to join them: *Their fingers intertwined.* ○ *His fingers intertwined with hers.* ○ *They intertwined their fingers.* ○ *He intertwined his fingers with hers.* ○ (*fig*) *Our fates seemed inextricably intertwined,* ie linked.

interval /ˈɪntəvl/ *n* **1** ~ (**between sth**) (**a**) time between two events: *the interval between a flash of lightning and the sound of thunder* ○ *go out, and return after an interval of half an hour.* (**b**) space between two or more things: *They planted trees in the intervals between the houses.* **2** (*Brit*) short period of time separating parts of a play, film, concert, etc: *an interval of 15 minutes after the second act.* **3** pause; break in activity: *an interval of silence to show respect for the dead* ○ *He returned to work after an interval in hospital.* ⇨ Usage at BREAK². **4** (esp *pl*) limited period during which sth occurs: *sunny/showery intervals,* ie non-continuous periods of sunshine/rain ○ *She's delirious, but has lucid intervals.* **5** (*music*) difference in pitch between two notes: *an interval of one octave.* **6** (idm) **at intervals** (**a**) with time between: *At intervals she would stop for a rest.* ○ *He comes back to see us at regular intervals.* ○ *The runners started at 5-minute intervals.* (**b**) with spaces between: *The trees were planted at 20 ft intervals.*

intervene /ˌɪntəˈviːn/ *v* (*fml*) **1** [I] (of time) come or be between: *during the years that intervened.* **2** [I] (of events, circumstances) happen in such a way as to hinder or prevent sth from being done: *I will come if nothing intervenes.* ○ *We should have finished harvesting, but a storm intervened.* **3** [I, Ipr] ~ (**in sth/between A and B**) (of people) interfere so as to prevent sth happening or to change the result: *When rioting broke out, the police were obliged to intervene.* ○ *intervene in a dispute, quarrel, etc* ○ *intervene between two people who are quarrelling* ○ *I intervened on her behalf to try and get the decision changed.*

▷ **intervening** *adj* coming between: *When she came back, she found that much had changed in the intervening years.*

intervention /ˌɪntəˈvenʃn/ *n* ~ (**in sth**) [C, U] (instance of) interfering or becoming involved, eg to prevent sth happening: *armed intervention by one country in the affairs of other countries* ○ *He had been saved from death as if by divine intervention,* ie as though God had taken action to save him. **interventionist** /-ʃənɪst/ *n* person in favour of intervening in the affairs of another: [attrib] *interventionist policies.*

interview /ˈɪntəvjuː/ *n* ~ (**with sb**) **1** meeting at which sb (eg sb applying for a job) is asked questions to find out if he is suitable: *a job interview* ○ *I've got an interview with National Chemicals.* ○ *Applicants will be called for interview in due course.* ○ [attrib] *an interview panel.* **2** meeting at which a reporter, etc asks sb questions in order to find out his views: *a TV interview* ○ *I never give interviews.* ○ *In an exclusive interview with David Frost, the former president made many revelations.* **3** meeting between two people to discuss important matters, usu rather formally: *a careers interview* ○ *I asked for an interview with my boss to discuss my future.*

▷ **interview** *v* **1** [I, Tn, Tn·pr] ~ **sb** (**for sth**) conduct an interview with sb (eg a job applicant): *I'm interviewing all this afternoon.* ○ *interview a number of candidates* ○ *We interviewed 20 people for the job.* **2** [Tn, Tn·pr] ~ **sb** (**about sth**) (of a reporter, etc) ask sb questions in an interview: *interview the Prime Minister (about government policy).*

interviewee /ˌɪntəvjuːˈiː/ *n* person who is interviewed.

interviewer /ˈɪntəvjuːə/ *n* person who conducts an interview.

interweave /ˌɪntəˈwiːv/ *v* (*pt* **-wove** /-ˈwəʊv/, *pp* **-woven** /-ˈwəʊvn/) **1** [I, Ipr, Tn, Tn·pr] ~ (**sth**) (**with sth**) be woven or weave sth together: *threads that interweave (with one another)* ○ *interweave wool with cotton/wool and cotton.* **2** [usu passive: Tn, Tn·pr] ~ **sth** (**with sth**) (*fig*) (**a**) join (two or more lives, etc) together so that they seem to be no longer separate or independent: *Our lives are interwoven.* ○ *Your destiny is interwoven with mine.* (**b**) combine different features in writing, artistic creation, etc: *primitive dance rhythms interwoven with folk melody.*

intestate /ɪnˈtesteɪt/ *adj* [usu pred] (*law*) not having made a will before death occurs: *die intestate.*

▷ **intestacy** /ɪnˈtestəsɪ/ *n* [U] (*law*) condition of being intestate.

intestine /ɪnˈtestɪn/ *n* (usu *pl*) long tube in the body which helps to digest food and carries it from the stomach to the anus: *a pain in the intestines* ○ *Food passes from the stomach to the small intestine and from there to the large intestine.* Cf ABDOMEN. ⇨ illus at DIGESTIVE.

▷ **intestinal** /ɪnˈtestɪnl, *or, in British use* ˌɪntesˈtaɪnl/ *adj* of the intestines: *intestinal disorders.*

intimate¹ /ˈɪntɪmət/ *adj* **1** ~ (**with sb**) (**a**) having or being a very close and friendly relationship: *intimate friends* ○ *an intimate friendship* ○ *We had been intimate* (ie very close friends) *for some time.* (**b**) (*euph*) having a sexual relationship, esp outside marriage: *She was accused of being intimate with several men.* **2** likely or intended to encourage close relationships, esp sexual ones, typically by being small, quiet, and private: *an intimate restaurant, atmosphere.* **3** private and personal: *tell a friend the intimate details of one's life* ○ *an intimate diary,* ie one in which sb records private experiences, thoughts, emotions, etc. **4** [attrib] (*fml*) (of knowledge) detailed and obtained by deep study or long experience: *an intimate knowledge of African religions.* **5** (idm) **be/get on intimate** ˈ**terms** (**with sb**) (come to) know sb very well and be friendly with him: *We're not exactly on intimate terms, but we see each other fairly often.*

▷ **intimacy** /ˈɪntɪməsɪ/ *n* **1** [U] (**a**) state of being intimate; close friendship or relationship. (**b**) (*euph*) sexual activity. **2 intimacies** [pl] (*rhet*) intimate actions, eg caresses or kisses.

intimate *n* intimate friend: *Sir Reginald, known to his intimates as 'Porky'*

intimately *adv.*

intimate[2] /ˈɪntɪmeɪt/ *v* [Tn, Tf, Tw, Dn·pr, Dpr·f, Dpr·w] ~ **sth (to sb)** *(fml)* make sth known (to sb), esp discreetly or indirectly: *He intimated his wishes with a slight nod of his head.* ○ *She has intimated (to us) that she no longer wishes to be considered for the post.* ○ *The judge has not intimated (to the jury) whether they will be allowed to reach a majority verdict.*

▷ **intimation** /ˌɪntɪˈmeɪʃn/ *n (fml)* **(a)** [U] intimating. **(b)** [C] ~ **(of sth/that...)** something intimated; hint; notification: *He has given us no intimation of his intentions/what he intends to do.*

intimidate /ɪnˈtɪmɪdeɪt/ *v* [Tn, Tn·pr] ~ **sb (into sth/doing sth)** frighten sb (in order to make him do sth): *intimidate a witness (into silence, into keeping quiet, etc)*, eg by threatening him.

▷ **intimidating** *adj* frightening, esp because of seeming difficulty or impossibility: *The intimidating bulk of Mt Everest rose up before the climbers.*

intimidation /ɪnˌtɪmɪˈdeɪʃn/ *n* [U] intimidating or being intimidated: *give way to intimidation* ○ *keep people in order by intimidation.*

intimidatory /ɪnˌtɪmɪˈdeɪtərɪ/ *adj* tending to intimidate: *intimidatory tactics.*

into /ˈɪntə, *before vowels and finally* ˈɪntu:/ *prep* **1 (a)** (moving) to a point within (an enclosed space or volume): *Come into the house.* ○ *Throw it into the fire.* ○ *go into town* ○ *She dived into the swimming-pool.* ○ *(fig) He turned and walked off into the night.* ○ *put money into an account.* Cf OUT OF. **(b)** in the direction of (sth): *Speak clearly into the microphone.* ○ *Driving into the sun, we had to shade our eyes.* **(c)** to a point at which one hits (sb/sth): *I nearly ran into a bus when it stopped suddenly in front of me.* ○ *A lorry drove into a line of parked cars.* **2** until a point during (sth): *He carried on working long into the night.* ○ *She didn't get married until she was well into middle age.* ○ *We're usually into May before the weather changes.* **3 (a)** (indicating a change in form as the result of an action): *turn the spare room into a study* ○ *cut the paper into strips* ○ *fold the napkin into a triangle* ○ *collect the rubbish into a heap.* Cf OUT OF. **(b)** (indicating a change to a specified condition or action): *frighten sb into submission* ○ *shocked into a confession of guilt* ○ *She came into power in 1979.* (See *n* entries for similar examples.). **4** (used to express division in mathematics): *5 into 25 = 5.* **5** (idm) **be into sth** *(infml)* be enthusiastic about sth in which one takes an active interest: *be (heavily) into yoga, science fiction, stamp collecting.*

intolerable /ɪnˈtɒlərəbl/ *adj* too bad to be borne or endured: *intolerable heat, noise, etc* ○ *intolerable insolence, behaviour, etc* ○ *This is intolerable: I've been kept waiting for three hours!* ▷ **intolerably** /-əblɪ/ *adv*: *intolerably rude.*

intolerant /ɪnˈtɒlərənt/ *adj* ~ **(of sb/sth)** *(usu derog)* not tolerant: *intolerant of opposition.* ▷ **intolerance** /-əns/ *n* [U]: *religious intolerance.* **intolerantly** *adv.*

intonation /ˌɪntəˈneɪʃn/ *n* **1** [U] intoning: *the intonation of a prayer.* **2 (a)** [C, U] rise and fall of the pitch of the voice in speaking, esp as this affects the meaning of what is said: *In English, some questions have a rising intonation.* ○ *a change of intonation* ○ [attrib] *intonation patterns.* Cf INFLECTION 2, STRESS 3. **(b)** [C] slight accent in speaking: *speak English with a Welsh intonation.* **3** [U] *(music)* quality of playing or singing in tune: *The violin's intonation was poor.*

intone /ɪnˈtəʊn/ *v* **1** [I, Tn] recite (a prayer, psalm, etc) in a singing tone. **2** [Tn] *(fig)* say (sth) in a solemn voice.

in toto /ɪnˈtəʊtəʊ/ *(Latin fml)* totally; altogether.

intoxicant /ɪnˈtɒksɪkənt/ *n* intoxicating substance, esp alcoholic drink.

intoxicate /ɪnˈtɒksɪkeɪt/ *v (fml)* **1** [esp passive: Tn, Tn·pr] ~ **sb (with sth)** cause sb to lose self-control as a result of the effects of a drug, a gas (or esp alcoholic) drink: *He'd been in the bar all night, and was thoroughly intoxicated.* **2** [Tn·pr usu passive] ~ **sb with sth** *(fig)* excite sb greatly, beyond self-control: *intoxicated by success, by a sense of power, etc* ○ *intoxicated with joy, with the fresh air.*

▷ **intoxication** /ɪnˌtɒksɪˈkeɪʃn/ *n* [U] state of being intoxicated, esp drunkenness.

intra- *pref* (with *adjs*) on the inside; within: *intramuscular* ○ *intramural.*

intractable /ɪnˈtræktəbl/ *adj (fml)* not easily controlled or dealt with; hard to manage: *intractable children* ○ *an intractable problem.* ▷ **intractability** /ɪnˌtræktəˈbɪlətɪ/ *n* [U]. **intractably** /ɪnˈtræktəblɪ/ *adv.*

intramural /ˌɪntrəˈmjʊərəl/ *adj* **1** intended for full-time students living within a college: *intramural courses, studies, staff.* **2** *(US)* between teams or players from the same school: *an intramural game, league.*

intramuscular /ˌɪntrəˈmʌskjʊlə(r)/ *adj (medical)* within a muscle or muscles: *an intramuscular injection.*

intransigent /ɪnˈtrænsɪdʒənt/ *adj (fml derog)* unwilling to change one's views or be co-operative; stubborn: *Owing to their intransigent attitude we were unable to reach an agreement.* ▷ **intransigence** /-əns/ *n* [U]. **intransigently** *adv.*

intransitive /ɪnˈtrænsətɪv/ *adj (grammar)* (of verbs) used without an object. Cf TRANSITIVE. ▷ **intransitively** *adv.*

intrastate /ˌɪntrəˈsteɪt/ *adj* (existing) within one state, esp of the USA: *intrastate highways.*

intra-uterine /ˌɪntrəˈju:təraɪn/ *adj (medical)* within the uterus.

□ **ˌintra-uterine deˈvice** *(abbr* **IUD)** (also **coil**) loop or spiral inserted in the uterus as a contraceptive.

intravenous /ˌɪntrəˈvi:nəs/ *adj (medical)* within a vein or veins: *an intravenous injection*, ie into the bloodstream. ▷ **intravenously** *adv.*

in-tray ⇨ IN[1].

intrench = ENTRENCH.

intrepid /ɪnˈtrepɪd/ *adj (esp rhet)* fearless; brave: *our intrepid hero.*

▷ **intrepidity** /ˌɪntrɪˈpɪdətɪ/ *n* [U] fearlessness. **intrepidly** /ɪnˈtrepɪdlɪ/ *adv.*

intricate /ˈɪntrɪkət/ *adj* made up of many small parts put together in a complex way, and therefore difficult to follow or understand: *an intricate piece of machinery* ○ *a novel with an intricate plot* ○ *the intricate windings of a labyrinth* ○ *an intricate design, pattern, etc.*

▷ **intricacy** /ˈɪntrɪkəsɪ/ *n* **(a)** [U] quality of being intricate. **(b) intricacies** [pl] intricate things, events, etc: *unable to follow the intricacies of the plot.*

intricately /-ətlɪ/ *adv.*

intrigue /ɪnˈtri:g/ *v* **1** [I, Ipr] ~ **(with sb) (against sb)** make and carry out secret plans or plots to do sth bad: *She was intriguing with her sister against her mother.* ○ *Some of the members had been intriguing to get the secretary dismissed.* **2** [Tn, Tn·pr] ~ **sb (with sth)** arouse sb's interest or curiosity: *What you say intrigues me; tell me more.* ○ *intrigue sb with an exciting story, a piece of news, etc.*

▷ **intrigue** /ˈɪntri:g, ɪnˈtri:g/ *n* **1** [U] making of secret plans to do sth bad; conspiracy: *a novel of mystery and intrigue.* **2** [C] **(a)** secret plan to do sth bad. **(b)** secret arrangement: *amorous intrigues.*

intriguer /ɪnˈtri:gə/ *n* person who intrigues (INTRIGUE 1).

intriguing *adj* full of interest, esp because unusual; fascinating: *What an intriguing story!*

intrinsic /ɪnˈtrɪnsɪk, -zɪk/ *adj* (of a value or quality) belonging naturally; existing within, not coming from outside: *a man's intrinsic worth*, eg arising from such qualities as honour and courage, rather than how much he owns, etc ○ *the intrinsic value of a coin*, ie the value of the metal in it, usu less than the value of what it will buy. Cf EXTRINSIC. ▷ **intrinsically** /-klɪ/ *adv*: *He is not intrinsically bad.*

intro /ˈɪntrəʊ/ *n (pl* ~**s)** *(infml)* introduction: *I'd like an intro to that girl you were talking to!* ○ *(music) There's an intro of eight bars before you come in.*

introduce /ˌɪntrəˈdju:s; *US* -ˈdu:s/ *v* **1** [Tn, Tn·pr] ~ **sb (to sb)** make sb known formally to sb else by giving the person's name, or by giving each person's name to the other: *Allow me to introduce my wife.* ○ *I don't think we've been introduced*, ie and therefore I do not know your name. ○ *I was introduced to the president at the party.* **2** [Tn, Tn·pr] ~ **sth (to sb)** announce and give (details of a speaker or broadcast, programme, etc) to listeners or viewers: *The next programme is introduced by Mary Davidson.* **3** [Tn] present (sth new) formally for discussion: *introduce a bill before Parliament.* **4** [Tn·pr] ~ **sb to sth (a)** lead sb up to the main part of sth: *The first lecture introduces new students to the broad outlines of the subject.* ○ *It was she who first introduced me to the pleasures of wine-tasting.* **(b)** cause sb to start using or experiencing sth: *introduce young people to alcohol, tobacco, drugs, etc.* **5** [Tn, Tn·pr] ~ **sth (in/into sth)** bring sth into use or operation for the first time: *The company is introducing a new family saloon this year.* ○ *introduce computers (into schools)* ○ *introduce a ban on smoking in public places.* **6** [Tn, Tn·pr] ~ **sth (into sth)** *(fml)* put sth (into sth): *introduce a hypodermic needle into a vein* ○ *(fig) introduce a subject into a conversation.* **7** [Tn] begin (a piece of music, book, play, etc): *A slow theme introduces the first movement.*

introduction /ˌɪntrəˈdʌkʃn/ *n* **1** [C, U] ~ **(to sb)** formal presentation of one person to another, in which each is told the other's name: *It is time to make introductions all round*, ie introduce many people to one another. ○ *a person who needs no introduction*, ie who is already well-known ○ *a letter of introduction*, ie which tells sb who you are, written by a mutual acquaintance. **2** [C] **(a)** ~ **(to sth)** something that leads up to the main part of sth (eg an explanatory article at the beginning of a book): *a short, brief, detailed, general, long, etc introduction* ○ *The introduction explains how the chapters are organized.* Cf PREFACE. **(b)** ~ **(to sth)** textbook for people beginning a subject: *'An Introduction to Astronomy'* **3** [sing] ~ **to sth** first experience of sth: *his introduction to modern jazz.* **4** [U] bringing into use or operation for the first time: *the introduction of new manufacturing methods.* **5** [C] ~ **(in/into sth)** thing introduced, esp a new animal or plant species: *The rabbit is a relatively recent introduction in Australia.* **6** [C] *(music)* short section at the beginning of a musical composition, leading up to the main part: *an eight-bar introduction.*

introductory /ˌɪntrəˈdʌktərɪ/ *adj* acting as an introduction(2): *some introductory remarks by the chairman* ○ *an introductory chapter.*

introspect /ˌɪntrəˈspekt/ *v* [I] *(fml)* examine or be concerned with one's own thoughts, feelings and motives.

▷ **introspection** /ˌɪntrəˈspekʃn/ *n* [U] introspecting.

introspective /-ˈspektɪv/ *adj* **(a)** inclined to introspect: *an introspective person.* **(b)** characteristic of sb who does this: *in an introspective mood* ○ *introspective writing.*

introvert /ˈɪntrəvɜ:t/ *n* person who is more interested in his own thoughts and feelings than in things outside himself, and is often shy and unwilling to speak or join in activities with others. Cf EXTROVERT.

▷ **introverted** /ˈɪntrəvɜ:tɪd/ *adj* having the quality of an introvert.

introversion /ˌɪntrəˈvɜ:ʃn; *US* -ˈvɜ:rʒn/ *n* [U] state of being introverted.

intrude /ɪnˈtru:d/ *v* [I, Ipr, Tn·pr] ~ **(oneself) on/upon sb/sth;** ~ **(oneself/sth) into sth** *(esp fml)* put (oneself/sth) into a place or situation where one/it is unwelcome or unsuitable: *I don't wish to intrude, but could I talk to you for a moment?* ○ *I felt as though I was intruding on their private grief.* ○ *If I could intrude a note of seriousness into this frivolous conversation....*

▷ **intruder** *n* person or thing that intrudes, esp sb who enters another's property illegally.

intrusion /ɪnˈtru:ʒn/ *n* ~ **(on/upon/into sth) (a)** [U] intruding: *guilty of intrusion upon sb's privacy.* **(b)** [C] instance of this: *This newspaper article is a disgraceful intrusion into my private life.*

▷ **intrusive** /ɪnˈtruːsɪv/ *adj* intruding: *intrusive neighbours* ○ *the intrusive 'r' often heard between vowel sounds*, eg in 'law and order'

intuit /ɪnˈtjuːɪt; *US* ˈtuː-/ *v* [I, Tn, Tf] *(fml)* sense (sth) by intuition: *incapable of intuiting (sb's intentions, feelings, etc).*

intuition /ˌɪntjuːˈɪʃn; *US* ˈtuː-/ *n* (*often approv*) **1** [U] (power of) understanding things (eg a situation, sb's feelings) immediately, without the need for conscious reasoning or study: *know sth by intuition* ○ *Nobody told me where to find you. It was sheer intuition.* ○ *Intuition told me you were here.* **2** [C] ~ **(about sth/that...)** piece of knowledge gained by this power: *I had a sudden intuition about the missing jewels.* ○ *I had an intuition that we would find them there.* ○ *My intuitions proved correct.*

▷ **intuitive** /ɪnˈtjuːɪtɪv; *US* -tuː-/ *adj* **(a)** of or coming from intuition: *intuitive knowledge* ○ *an intuitive feeling (about sb), approach (to sth), assessment (of sth), etc.* **(b)** possessing intuition: *Are woman more intuitive than men?* **intuitively** *adv*: *He seemed to know intuitively how to do it.*

intumescence /ˌɪntjuːˈmesns; *US* -tuː-/ *n* [U, C] *(medical)* (process or condition of) swelling.

Inuit = INNUIT.

inundate /ˈɪnʌndeɪt/ *v* **1** [Tn, Tn·pr] ~ **sth (with sth)** *(fml)* cover sth with water by overflowing; flood: *When the river burst its banks the fields were inundated.* **2** [esp passive: Tn, Tn·pr] ~ **sb (with sth)** *(fig)* give or send sb so many things that he can hardly deal with them all; overwhelm: *We were inundated with enquiries.*

▷ **inundation** /ˌɪnʌnˈdeɪʃn/ *n* [C, U] *(fml)* (instance of) flooding.

inure /ɪˈnjʊə(r)/ *v* [usu passive: Tn, Tn·pr] ~ **oneself/sb (to sth)** *(fml)* accustom oneself/sb (usu to sth unpleasant): *After living here for years I've become inured to the cold climate.* ○ *One cannot inure oneself altogether to such malicious criticism.*

invade /ɪnˈveɪd/ *v* **1 (a)** [I, Ipr, Tn, Tn·pr] ~ **(sth) (with sth)** enter (a country or territory) with armed forces in order to attack, damage or occupy it: *He ordered the army to invade at dawn.* ○ *Alexander the Great invaded India with a large army.* **(b)** [Tn esp passive] *(fig)* enter (sth) in large numbers, esp so as to cause damage; crowd into: *The cancer cells may invade other parts of the body.* ○ *a city invaded by tourists* ○ *a mind invaded with worries, anxieties, etc.* **2** [Tn] interfere with (sth); intrude on: *invade sb's rights, privacy, etc.*

▷ **invader** *n* person or thing that invades.

invalid[1] /ɪnˈvælɪd/ *adj* **1** not properly based or able to be upheld by reasoning: *an invalid argument, assumption, claim, etc.* **2** not usable; not officially acceptable (because of an incorrect detail or details); not legally recognized: *A passport that is out of date is invalid.* ○ *an invalid will* ○ *declare a marriage invalid.*

▷ **invalidate** /ɪnˈvælɪdeɪt/ *v* [Tn] make (sth) invalid: *faulty logic which invalidated her argument.* **invalidation** /ɪnˌvælɪˈdeɪʃn/ *n* [U] (action of) making sth invalid: *The making of false statements could result in the invalidation of the contract.*

invalidity /ˌɪnvəˈlɪdətɪ/ *n* [U] state of being invalid[1]: *the invalidity of his passport.*

invalid[2] /ˈɪnvəlɪd, ˈɪnvəliːd/ *n* person weakened through illness or injury; one who suffers from ill health for a very long time: *He has been an invalid all his life.* ○ [attrib] *her invalid mother, father, etc* ○ *an invalid diet*, ie one planned for an invalid ○ *an invalid chair*, ie one with wheels on for moving an invalid easily.

▷ **invalid** *v* **1** (idm) **invalid sb ˈhome** send sb (esp a soldier) home (esp from abroad) because of ill health. **2** (phr v) **invalid sb out (of sth)** cause sb to leave (esp the armed forces) because of ill health: *He was invalided out of the army because of the wounds he received.*

invalidism /-ɪzəm/ *n* [U] long-lasting ill health: *a life of invalidism.*

invalidity /ˌɪnvəˈlɪdətɪ/ *n* [U] state of being an invalid[2]: [attrib] *an invalidity pension.*

invaluable /ɪnˈvæljʊəbl/ *adj* ~ **(to sb/sth)** of value too high to be measured; extremely valuable: *an invaluable collection of paintings* ○ *invaluable help, advice, etc* ○ *Your help has been invaluable to us.*

NOTE ON USAGE: A few adjectives have misleading 'negative' affixes such as *in -* or *-less*. **1 Invaluable** means 'extremely valuable'. It is not the opposite of **valuable**, which is **valueless** (or **worthless**). **2 Priceless** means 'too valuable to be priced', ie 'having a very high price'. **3 Innumerable** and **numberless** mean 'too many to be counted' or 'very numerous'. **4 Flammable** and **inflammable** have the same meaning (opposite: **non-flammable**).

invariable /ɪnˈveərɪəbl/ *adj* never changing; always the same; constant: *an invariable pressure, temperature, amount* ○ *a noun with an invariable plural* ○ *his invariable courtesy.* ▷ **invariability** /ɪnˌveərɪəˈbɪlətɪ/ *n* [U]. **invariably** /ɪnˈveərɪəblɪ/ *adv*: *She invariably* (ie always) *arrives late.*

invasion /ɪnˈveɪʒn/ *n* **(a)** [U] invading or being invaded: *suffer invasion by enemy forces* ○ *the invasion of Poland by Germany in 1939.* **(b)** [C] instance of this: *an outrageous invasion of privacy.*

invasive /ɪnˈveɪsɪv/ *adj* tending to spread harmfully: *invasive cancer cells.*

invective /ɪnˈvektɪv/ *n* [U] *(fml)* violent attack in words; abusive language: *a speech full of invective* ○ *let out a stream of invective.*

inveigh /ɪnˈveɪ/ *v* [Ipr] ~ **against sb/sth** *(fml)* attack sb or sth violently in words: *inveigh against God, destiny, the elements, the system.*

inveigle /ɪnˈveɪgl/ *v* [Tn·pr] ~ **sb into sth/doing sth** persuade sb to go somewhere or do sth by using flattery and deception: *She inveigled him into the house and robbed him while he slept.* ○ *He inveigled them into buying a new car, even though they didn't really want one.*

invent /ɪnˈvent/ *v* [Tn] **1** make or design (sth that did not exist before); create by thought: *Laszlo Biro invented the ball-point pen.* Cf DISCOVER 1. **2** (*often derog*) make up or think of (esp sth that does not exist or is not true): *Use an invented name, such as Anytown, not a real one.* ○ *Can't you invent a better excuse than that?*

▷ **inventive** /ɪnˈventɪv/ *adj* **1** [attrib] of or for invention: *using one's inventive powers.* **2** *(approv)* having or showing the ability to invent things and think originally: *an inventive mind* ○ *an inventive design.*

inventor *n* person who invents things.

invention /ɪnˈvenʃn/ *n* **1** [U] **(a)** action of inventing: *the invention of radio by Marconi* ○ *a story of one's own invention*, ie invented by oneself. **(b)** capacity for inventing. **(c)** *(euph)* making up of untrue or unreal things; lying: *I'm afraid he is guilty of a good deal of invention.* **2** [C] thing that is invented: *the scientific inventions of the 20th century.* **3** (idm) **necessity is the mother of invention** ⇨ NECESSITY.

inventory /ˈɪnvəntrɪ; *US* -tɔːrɪ/ *n* detailed list, eg of goods, furniture, jobs to be done: *keep/make a full, complete, careful inventory (of sth).*

▷ **inventory** *v* (*pt, pp* **-ried**) [Tn] make an inventory of (sth); put in an inventory: *inventory the contents of a house* ○ *These items have not been inventoried yet.*

inverse /ˌɪnˈvɜːs/ *adj* [usu attrib] reversed in position, direction or relation: *The number of copies the paper sells seems to be in ˌinverse ˈratio/proˈportion to the amount of news it contains*, ie The more news, the fewer copies it sells.

▷ **inverse** /ˈɪnvɜːs/ *n* **the inverse** [sing] **1** (*esp mathematics*) inverted state: *The inverse of 2 ($\frac{2}{1}$) is* $\frac{1}{2}$. **2** direct opposite: *This is the inverse of his earlier proposition.*

inversely /ɪnˈvɜːslɪ/ *adv*: *inversely proportional to each other.*

inversion /ɪnˈvɜːʃn; *US* ɪnˈvɜːrʒn/ *n* [U, C] **(a)** inverting or being inverted; instance of this: *(an) inversion of word order.* **(b)** *(music)* (arrangement of a) chord[1] in which the lowest note of the chord is not the root: *A chord of C major with E in the bass is in the 1st inversion.*

invert /ɪnˈvɜːt/ *v* [Tn] put (sth) upside down or in the opposite order, position or arrangement: *invert a glass* ○ *invert the word order in a sentence.*

□ **inˌverted ˈcommas** *(Brit)* quotation-marks, ie ' ' or " ". ⇨ App 14.

inˌverted ˈsnob *(derog)* person who unnecessarily finds fault with things of good quality or things which suggest wealth or social superiority; one who wishes to prove that he is not a snob. **inˌverted ˈsnobbery** attitude or behaviour of such a person.

invertebrate /ɪnˈvɜːtɪbreɪt/ *n, adj* (animal) not having a backbone or spinal column: *Molluscs, insects and worms are all invertebrates.*

invest /ɪnˈvest/ *v* **1** [I, Ipr, Tn, Tn·pr] ~ **(sth) (in sth/with sb)** use (money) to buy shares, property, etc, in order to earn interest or bring profit: *The best time to invest is now.* ○ *invest £1 000 (in government bonds)* ○ *invest (one's money) in a business enterprise* ○ *invest (money) with a firm.* **2** [Tn·pr] ~ **sth in sth/doing sth** give (time, effort, etc) to a particular task, esp in a way that involves commitment or self-sacrifice: *invest one's time in learning a new language* ○ *invest all one's efforts in passing an exam* ○ *She's invested a lot of emotional energy in that business.* **3** [Ipr] ~ **in sth** *(infml)* buy sth expensive but useful: *I'm thinking of investing in a new car.* **4** [Tn·pr, Cn·n/a] ~ **sb (with sth/as sth)** *(fml)* confer a rank, an office or power on sb: *The governor has been invested with full authority to act.* ○ *Prince Charles was invested as Prince of Wales in 1969.* **5** [Tn·pr] ~ **sb/sth with sth** *(fml)* cause sb/sth to have a quality: *The crimes committed there invested the place with an air of mystery and gloom.* **6** [Tn] *(dated)* surround (a fort, town, etc) with armed forces.

▷ **investment** *n* **1** [U] ~ **(in sth)** investing of money: *make a profit by careful investment.* **2** [C] ~ **(in sth) (a)** sum of money that is invested: *an investment of £500 in oil shares.* **(b)** company, etc in which money is invested: *Those oil shares were a good investment*, ie have been profitable. **3** = INVESTITURE.

investor *n* person who invests money.

investigate /ɪnˈvestɪgeɪt/ *v* **1** [I, Tn, Tw] find out and examine (all the facts about sth) in order to obtain the truth: *The police were baffled, and Sherlock Holmes was called in to investigate.* ○ *Scientists are investigating to find out the cause of the crash/are investigating how the crash occurred.* ○ *The police are investigating the murder.* **2** [Tn] find out detailed facts about (sb or his character) by questioning, observation, etc: *Applicants for government posts are always thoroughly investigated before being appointed.* **3** [Tn] try to discover (sth) by detailed study, research, etc: *investigate the market for a product, ways of increasing profits, etc* ○ *We might be able to help you; I'll investigate the possibilities.* **4** [I] *(infml)* make a brief check: *'What was that noise outside?' 'I'll just go and investigate.'*

▷ **investigation** /ɪnˌvestɪˈgeɪʃn/ *n* **(a)** [U] investigating or being investigated: *The matter is under investigation.* ○ *It is subject to investigation*, ie It must be investigated. **(b)** [C] ~ **(into sth)** instance of this: *Scientists are conducting an investigation into the causes of the accident.* ○ *carry out fresh investigations.*

investigative /ɪnˈvestɪgətɪv; *US* -geɪtɪv/, **investigatory** /ɪnˈvestɪgeɪtərɪ; *US* -gətɔːrɪ/ *adjs* of or concerned with investigating: *investigative/investigatory methods used by the police* ○ *investigative journalism*, ie in which reporters try to uncover important facts of public interest which have been concealed.

investigator /ɪnˈvestɪgeɪtə(r)/ *n* person who investigates: *accident investigators who find out the causes of air crashes* ○ *insurance investigators*

investiture /ɪnˈvestɪtʃə(r); *US* -tʃʊər/ (also **investment**) *n* [U, C] ceremony of conferring an office, a rank or power on sb: *the investiture of the Prince of Wales.*

inveterate /ɪnˈvetərət/ *adj* *(derog)* **1** (of bad feelings, habits, etc) that have lasted a long time and seem likely to continue: *inveterate hatred, prejudice, drunkenness, etc.* **2** (of people) habitually doing the specified bad thing; addicted: *an inveterate smoker, drinker, gambler, liar, etc.* ▷ **inveterately** *adv.*

invidious /ɪnˈvɪdɪəs/ *adj* likely to cause resentment or unpopularity (esp because it is or seems to be unjust): *an invidious comparison, distinction, argument, etc* ○ *You put me in an invidious position by asking me to comment on my colleague's work.* ▷ **invidiously** *adv.* **invidiousness** *n* [U].

invigilate /ɪnˈvɪdʒɪleɪt/ *v* [I, Ipr, Tn] ~ **(at sth)** (*Brit*) be present during (an examination) to make sure that it is properly conducted, that no cheating occurs, etc: *invigilate (at) a history exam.*
▷ **invigilation** /ɪnˌvɪdʒɪˈleɪʃn/ *n* [C, U] (instance of) invigilating or being invigilated: *pupils under invigilation.*
invigilator /ɪnˈvɪdʒɪleɪtə(r)/ *n* person who invigilates.

invigorate /ɪnˈvɪɡəreɪt/ *v* [I, Tn] make (sb) feel more lively and healthy: *I feel invigorated by all this fresh air!*
▷ **invigorating** *adj* that invigorates: *an invigorating climate, morning, swim, walk.* **invigoratingly** *adv.*

invincible /ɪnˈvɪnsəbl/ *adj* too strong to be overcome or defeated: *an invincible army* ○ (*fig*) *an invincible will.* ▷ **invincibility** /ɪnˌvɪnsəˈbɪlətɪ/ *n* [U]: *the apparent invincibility of their forces.* **invincibly** /ɪnˈvɪnsəblɪ/ *adv.*

inviolable /ɪnˈvaɪələbl/ *adj* (*fml*) that must not be violated or dishonoured: *The people possess inviolable rights.* ○ *an inviolable oath, law, treaty.*
▷ **inviolability** /ɪnˌvaɪələˈbɪlətɪ/ *n* [U]. **inviolably** /ɪnˈvaɪələblɪ/ *adv.*

inviolate /ɪnˈvaɪələt/ *adj* [usu pred] ~ **(from sth)** (*fml*) that has not been or cannot be violated or harmed: *The treaty remained/stood inviolate*, ie was not broken. ○ *They considered themselves inviolate from attack.*

invisible /ɪnˈvɪzəbl/ *adj* **1** ~ **(to sb/sth)** that cannot be seen; not visible: *distant stars that are invisible to the naked eye*, ie that cannot be seen except with a telescope or binoculars. **2** [usu attrib] (*commerce*) in the form of services (eg banking, insurance, tourism, etc) rather than goods or raw materials: *invisible exports/trade.* ▷ **invisibility** /ɪnˌvɪzəˈbɪlətɪ/ *n* [U]. **invisibly** /ɪnˈvɪzəblɪ/ *adv.*
□ **inˌvisible ˈink** ink which, when used for writing, cannot be seen until specially treated, eg by heat.
inˌvisible ˈmending repair of woven materials, etc by interweaving threads so that the repair is hardly noticeable.

invite /ɪnˈvaɪt/ *v* **1** [Tn, Tn·pr, Dn·t] ~ **sb (to/for sth)** **(a)** ask sb in a friendly way to go somewhere or do sth: *'Are you coming to the party?' 'No, I haven't been invited.'* ○ *invite sb for/to dinner/to have dinner* ○ *invite sb home/to one's house* ○ *invite sb to a party/to come to a party.* **(b)** ask sb formally to go somewhere or do sth: *Candidates will be invited for interview early next month.* ○ *I've been invited to give a talk at the conference.* **2** [Tn, Tn·pr] ~ **sth (from sb)** ask for (comments, suggestions, etc): *After his speech he invited questions and comments (from the audience).* **3** [Tn] act so as to be likely to cause (sth bad) usu without intending to: *Leaving your car unlocked is just inviting trouble!* ○ *behaviour that is sure to invite criticism, hostility, ridicule, etc.* **4** [Tn, Cn·t] attract (sb/sth); tempt: *Cover the jam! It's sure to invite the wasps.* ○ *Leaving the windows open is inviting thieves to enter.* **5** (phr v) **invite sb along** ask sb to accompany one. **invite sb away** ask sb to go away with one, eg on holiday. **invite sb back** **(a)** ask sb to return with one to one's home: *Shall we invite them back after the theatre?* **(b)** ask sb who has been one's host to come to one's home as a guest. **invite sb down** ask sb to come for a visit at some distance, esp in the country or by the sea: *They've invited us down to their country cottage for the weekend.* **invite sb in** ask sb to enter a room, house, etc. **invite sb out** ask sb to come out with one for a walk, a ride, entertainment, etc, esp for the purpose of courting. **invite sb over/round** ask sb to visit one's home: *I've invited the Smiths round for drinks next Friday.* **invite sb up** ask sb to come upstairs.
▷ **invitation** /ˌɪnvɪˈteɪʃn/ *n* **1** [U] inviting or being invited: *a letter of invitation* ○ *Admission is by invitation only.* **2** [C] ~ **(to sth/to do sth)** request to go or come somewhere, or do sth: *send out invitations to a party* ○ *I gladly accepted their invitation to open the fête.* ○ [attrib] *an invitation card.* **3** [C usu *sing*] ~ **to sb/sth (to do sth)** that which tempts or encourages sb to do sth: *An open window is an invitation to burglars/an invitation to crime.*
invite /ˈɪnvaɪt/ *n* (*infml*) invitation, eg to a party: *Did you get an invite?*
inviting /ɪnˈvaɪtɪŋ/ *adj* tempting; attractive: *an inviting look, smell, prospect, idea* ○ *an inviting smile, place, meal.* **invitingly** *adv.*

in vitro /ˌɪn ˈviːtrəʊ/ (*Latin*) (*biology*) (of the fertilization of an egg) by artificial means outside the body of the mother: *ˌin vitro fertiliˈzation* ○ *an egg fertilized in vitro.*

invocation ⇨ INVOKE.

invoice /ˈɪnvɔɪs/ *n* ~ **(for sth)** (*commerce*) list of goods sold or services provided with the price(s) charged, esp sent as a bill: *make out an invoice for the goods.*
▷ **invoice** *v* (*commerce*) **1** [Tn] make a list of (such goods): *invoice the orders, goods, etc.* **2** [Tn, Tn·pr] ~ **sb (for sth)**/~ **sth to sb** send such a list to sb, esp as a request for payment: *invoice sb (for an order, for goods, etc).*

invoke /ɪnˈvəʊk/ *v* (*fml*) **1** [Tn] use (sth) as a reason for one's action: *The government has invoked the Official Secrets Act in having the book banned.* **2** [Tn] **(a)** call upon (God, the power of the law, etc) for help or protection. **(b)** summon (sth) up (as if) by magic: *invoke evil spirits.* **3** [Tn, Tn·pr] ~ **sth (on/upon sb/sth)** beg for sth (as if) by praying: *invoke help, assistance, etc in a desperate situation* ○ *invoke vengeance (up)on one's enemies.*
▷ **invocation** /ˌɪnvəˈkeɪʃn/ *n* **1** ~ **(to sb)** **(a)** [U] invoking or being invoked. **(b)** [C] instance of this. **2** [C] prayer that calls upon God for help or protection, esp at the beginning of a religious service.

involuntary /ɪnˈvɒləntrɪ; *US* -terɪ/ *adj* done without intention; done unconsciously: *an involuntary movement of surprise*, eg jumping when startled. Cf VOLUNTARY[1]. ▷ **involuntarily** /ɪnˈvɒləntrəlɪ; *US* ɪnˌvɒlənˈterəlɪ/ *adv.* **involuntariness** *n* [U].

involute /ˈɪnvəluːt/ (also **involuted**) *adj* **1** complex or intricate. **2** (*botany*) (esp of leaves or petals in bud and of shells) curling inwards at the edges. ▷ **involution** /ˌɪnvəˈluːʃn/ *n* [U, C].

involve /ɪnˈvɒlv/ *v* **1** [Tn, Tg, Tsg] make (sth) necessary as a condition or result; entail: *The scheme involves computers.* ○ *The job involved me/my living in London.* **2** [Tn] include or affect (sb/sth) in its operation: *The strike involved many people.* ○ *a situation in which national security is involved.* **3** [Cn·pr] **(a)** ~ **sb/sth in (doing) sth** cause sb/sth to take part in (an activity or a situation): *Don't involve me in solving your problems!* **(b)** ~ **sb/sth in sth** bring sb/sth into (a difficult situation): *involve sb in expense, a lot of trouble* ○ *He was involved in a heated argument.* **(c)** ~ **sb in sth** show sb to be concerned in (a crime, etc): *The witness's statement involves you in the robbery.*
▷ **involved** *adj* **1** complicated in thought or form: *an involved sentence, explanation, style of writing, etc.* **2** **(a)** ~ **(in sth)** concerned (with sth): *be/become/get involved in politics, criminal activities, etc.* **(b)** ~ **(with sb)** (closely) connected (with sb): *become emotionally involved with sb* ○ *He sees her often but doesn't want to get too involved.*
involvement *n* [U, C].

invulnerable /ɪnˈvʌlnərəbl/ *adj* **1** ~ **(to sth)** that cannot be wounded, hurt or damaged by attack: *a fortification that is invulnerable to attack.* **2** (*fig*) secure; safe: *in an invulnerable position.* ▷ **invulnerability** /ɪnˌvʌlnərəˈbɪlətɪ/ *n* [U].

inward /ˈɪnwəd/ *adj* **1** situated within; inner (esp in the mind or spirit): *inward thoughts, feelings, doubts, etc* ○ *sb's inward nature.* **2** turned towards the inside: *an inward curve.* Cf OUTWARD.
▷ **inward** (also **inwards**) *adv* **1** towards the inside: *toes turned inwards.* **2** into or towards the mind or soul: *thoughts turned inwards* ○ *be inward-looking*, ie introvert. ⇨ Usage at FORWARD[2].
inwardly *adv* **1** in mind or spirit: *inwardly grateful, relieved, etc* ○ *grieve inwardly*, ie not show one's grief. **2** (idm) **groan inwardly** ⇨ GROAN.
inwardness *n* [U] spiritual quality: *the true inwardness of Christ's teaching.*

iodide /ˈaɪədaɪd/ *n* (*chemistry*) compound of iodine with another chemical.

iodine /ˈaɪədiːn; *US* -daɪn/ *n* [U] **1** (*symb* **I**) (*chemistry*) non-metallic element found in sea water and seaweed. It forms black crystals, and gives off a purple vapour when heated. It is used in chemical analysis, photography and medicine. ⇨ App 11. **2** solution of this used as an antiseptic.

iodize, -ise /ˈaɪədaɪz/ *v* [Tn] treat (a substance) with iodine or a compound of iodine.

IOM *abbr* Isle of Man.

ion /ˈaɪən; *US also* ˈaɪɒn/ *n* (*chemistry or physics*) atom or group of atoms bearing an electrical charge due to a gain or loss of electrons. Ions are responsible for electrical conduction in liquids and gases.
▷ **ionic** /aɪˈɒnɪk/ *adj* of, using or containing ions: *an ionic gas.*
ionize, -ise /ˈaɪənaɪz/ *v* [I, Tn esp passive] be converted or convert (sth) into ions. **ionization, -isation** /ˌaɪənaɪˈzeɪʃn; *US* -nɪˈz-/ *n* [U].
□ **ˈion exchange** process in which the ions in a solid and in a solution are interchanged. It is used for removing mineral substances from water.

-ion (also **-ation**, **-ition**, **-sion**, **-tion**, **-xion**) *suff* (with *vs* forming *ns*) action or condition of: *confession* ○ *hesitation* ○ *competition.*

Iona /aɪˈəʊnə/ small island in the Inner *Hebrides, off the north-west coast of Scotland, which was a centre of early Celtic Christianity in the 6th century AD.

Ionesco /jɒˈneskəʊ/ Eugene (1912-), French playwright, born in Romania, a leading exponent of the *Theatre of the Absurd. His best known play, *The Bald Prima Donna*, has been performed continuously in Paris since its publication in 1950.

Ionia /aɪˈəʊnɪə/ ancient region on the west coast of Asia Minor.
▷ **Ionian** /aɪˈəʊnɪən/ *adj.* **Iˌonian ˈIslands** group of islands off the west coast of Greece, including *Corfu, Cephalonia, and Ithaca.

Ionic /aɪˈɒnɪk/ *adj* (*architecture*) of the type of column(1) in ancient Greek architecture having scrolls on the capital[1](3). Cf CORINTHIAN 2, DORIC. ⇨ illus at ORDER.

ionosphere /aɪˈɒnəsfɪə(r)/ *n* [sing] set of layers of the earth's atmosphere that reflect radio waves round the earth. Cf HEAVISIDE LAYER, STRATOSPHERE.

iota /aɪˈəʊtə/ *n* **1** the Greek letter I, ι. **2** (*fig*) (esp in negative expressions) smallest amount: *not an iota of truth* (ie no truth at all) *in the story.*

IOU /ˌaɪ əʊ ˈjuː/ *n* (*infml*) (*abbr* of *I owe you*) signed paper acknowledging that one owes the sum of money stated: *give sb an IOU for £20.*

IOW *abbr* Isle of Wight.

Iowa /ˈaɪəwə/ state in the *Mid West of the USA. It is mainly agricultural.

IPA /ˌaɪ piː ˈeɪ/ *abbr* International Phonetic Alphabet/Association.

ipso facto /ˌɪpsəʊ ˈfæktəʊ/ (*Latin*) (*fml*) by that very fact: *He was an outstanding pupil and, ipso facto, disliked by the rest of the class.*

IQ /ˌaɪ ˈkjuː/ *abbr* intelligence quotient (a comparative measure of a person's intelligence): *have a high/low IQ* ○ *an IQ of 120.*

Ir *symb* iridium.

ir- ⇨ IN-[2].

IRA /ˌaɪ ɑːr ˈeɪ/ *abbr* Irish Republican Army: *an IRA attack* ○ *a member of the IRA.*

Iran

Iran /ɪˈrɑːn; *US* ɪˈræn/ country in the Middle East, between the Caspian Sea and the Persian Gulf, formerly known as *Persia; pop approx 52 522 000; official language Persian (Farsi); capital Tehran; unit of currency rial (= 100 dinars). It was ruled by a Shah until 1979, when a fundamentalist Islamic republic was declared, led by the Ayatollah *Khomeini. It was at war with its neighbour *Iraq 1980-88. Its main export is oil. ⇨ map.

▷ **Iranian** /ɪˈreɪnɪən/ *adj* of Iran. — *n* native or inhabitant of Iran.

Iraq

Iraq /ɪˈrɑːk, *also* ɪˈræk/ country in the Middle East, to the north-west of the Persian Gulf; pop approx 17 657 000; official language Arabic; capital Baghdad; unit of currency dinar (= 1000 fils). Formerly part of the *Ottoman Empire, it did not become fully independent until 1932. It was at war with its neighbour *Iran 1980-88. In 1990 under President Saddam Hussein it occupied the neighbouring country of Kuwait. This led to the Gulf War in 1991 which forced Iraq to withdraw to its own territory. Its main export is oil. ⇨ map.

▷ **Iraqi** /ɪˈrɑːkɪ, *also* ɪˈrækɪ/ *adj* of Iraq. — *n* native or inhabitant of Iraq.

irascible /ɪˈræsəbl/ *adj* (*fml*) (of a person) easily made angry.

▷ **irascibility** /ɪˌræsəˈbɪlətɪ/ *n* [U] tendency to become angry; angry behaviour.

irascibly /ɪˈræsəblɪ/ *adv.*

irate /aɪˈreɪt/ *adj* (*fml*) angry. ▷ **irately** *adv.*

IRBM /ˌaɪ ɑː biː ˈem/ *abbr* intermediate-range ballistic missile. Cf ICBM, MRBM.

ire /ˈaɪə(r)/ *n* [U] (*fml*) anger.

Republic of Ireland

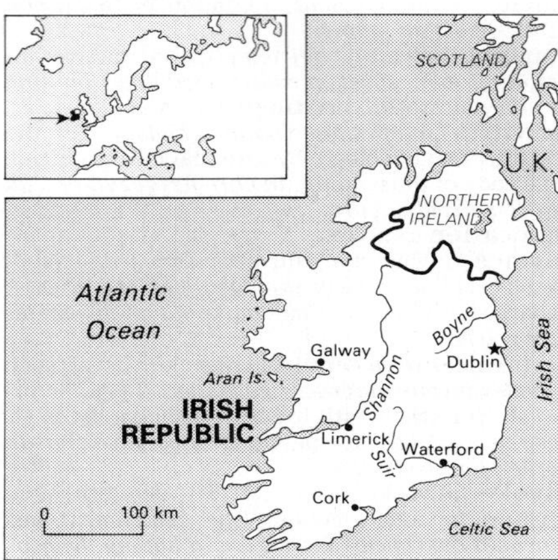

Ireland /ˈaɪələnd/ **1** island of the British Isles, to the west of Britain. Formerly consisting of a number of independent Celtic kingdoms, from the 12th century onwards it was gradually brought under English control. In 1921 the island was divided into *Northern Ireland, which remains in the United Kingdom, and a self-governing Irish state. Its damp climate encourages the growth of grass, and the cattle which feed on it form the basis of a large dairy industry. ⇨ article. ⇨ map. **2** (also **the Reˌpublic of ˈIreland, the ˌIrish Reˈpublic**) country occupying the southern four-fifths of the island of Ireland; pop approx 3 538 000; official languages Irish and English; capital Dublin; unit of currency pound (punt) (= 100 pence). It became an independent state in 1921, and between 1937 and 1949 it was known as Eire. It joined the European Community in 1973.

iridescent /ˌɪrɪˈdesnt/ *adj* (*fml*) **1** showing colours like those of the rainbow. **2** changing colour as its position changes: *jewels sparkling with iridescent colours.* ▷ **iridescence** /-ˈdesns/ *n* [U].

iridium /ɪˈrɪdɪəm/ *n* [U] (*symb* **Ir**) (*chemistry*) white metallic element of the platinum group. It is extremely hard and resistant to corrosion, and it is mixed with other metals to give these qualities to them. ⇨ App 11.

iris /ˈaɪərɪs/ *n* **1** (*anatomy*) coloured circular membrane surrounding the pupil of the eye. ⇨ illus at EYE. **2** any of various types of tall plant with sword-shaped leaves and large bright flowers. Cf FLAG[4]. ⇨ illus at PLANT. **3** (*photography*) device made from thin overlapping sheets of metal which can be adjusted to make a hole at the centre larger or smaller. It is used to vary the amount of light let into a camera.

Irish /ˈaɪərɪʃ/ *adj* of Ireland, its culture, language or people: *the Irish Republic*, ie Eire.

▷ **Irish** *n* **1 the Irish** [pl] the Irish people. **2** (also **Erse**) [U] the Celtic language of Ireland. ⇨ article at LANGUAGE.

□ **ˌIrish ˈcoffee** hot coffee mixed with whiskey and having thick cream on top.

ˈIrishman (*pl* **-men** /-mən/, **-women** /-wɪmɪn/) *ns* (*pl*) native of Ireland.

the ˌIrish Reˌpublican Army (*abbr* **IRA**) secret military organization formed in Ireland in 1919 to fight for Irish independence from Britain. It has remained active since then, seeking to have *Northern Ireland united with the Irish Republic. In 1970, it split into two sections: the official IRA and the Provisional IRA, which has conducted bombing and shooting campaigns in Northern Ireland, England and elsewhere.

the ˌIrish ˈSea sea that separates Ireland from England and Wales.

ˌIrish ˈsetter (also **red setter**) type of dog with a silky reddish-brown coat.

ˌIrish ˈstew stew of mutton boiled with onions and other vegetables.

ˌIrish ˈwolfhound very large type of dog with rough hair, originally bred in Ireland for hunting wolves.

irk /ɜːk/ *v* [Tn] (esp in constructions with *it*) be tiresome to (sb); annoy: *It irks me to see money being wasted.* ○ *It irked him that she had thought of it first.*

▷ **irksome** /ˈɜːksəm/ *adj* tiresome; annoying: *an irksome task* ○ *irksome complaints.*

iron

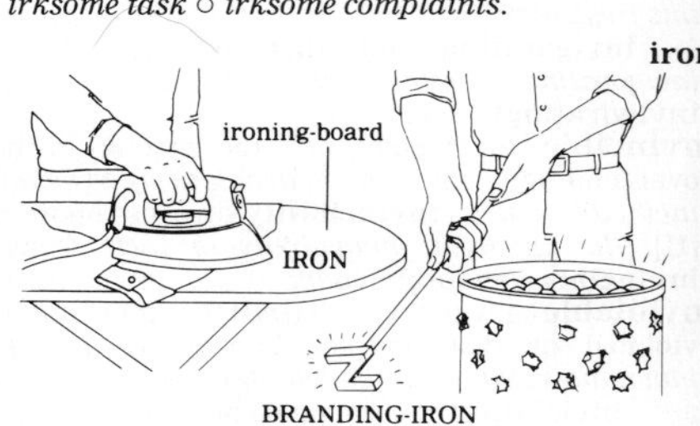

iron[1] /ˈaɪən; *US* ˈaɪərn/ *n* **1** [U] (*symb* **Fe**) (*chemistry*) common hard silver-white metallic element capable of being magnetized and used in various forms of steel: *cast iron* ○ *wrought iron* ○ *scrap iron* ○ *as hard as iron* ○ [attrib] *iron ore*, ie rock containing iron ○ *an iron bar, gate, railing*, ie made of iron. ⇨ App 11. **2** [C] implement with a smooth flat base that can be heated to smooth clothes, etc: *a ˈsteam-iron.* ⇨ illus. **3** [C] (esp in compounds) tool made of iron: *ˈfire-irons*, ie poker, tongs, etc used at a fireplace ○ *a ˈbranding-iron*, eg for marking cattle, etc. ⇨ illus. **4** [C] golf-club with an iron or steel head. Cf WOOD 4. **5** [C usu *pl*] metal splint or support worn on the leg. **6 irons** [pl] fetters: *put/clap sb in irons*, ie fasten his wrists and ankles in chains. **7** [U] a preparation of iron as a tonic. **8** [U esp attrib] (*fig*) (showing) physical strength or moral firmness or harshness: *have an iron constitution*, ie very good health ○ *a man of iron* ○ *have a will of iron/an iron will* ○ *impose an iron rule*, ie rule very strictly. **9** (idm) **an ˌiron ˌfist/ˌhand in a ˌvelvet ˈglove** an appearance of gentleness concealing severity, determination, etc. **have many, etc irons in the fire** have many resources available or be involved in many undertakings at the same time. **rule with a rod of iron** ⇨ RULE. **strike while the iron is hot** ⇨ STRIKE[2].

□ **the ˈIron Age** prehistoric period following the Bronze Age, when iron began to be used for making tools and weapons.

the ˌIron ˈCurtain (*dated*) frontier that separated the USSR and other Communist countries of Eastern Europe from the West, formerly seen by the West as a barrier to information and trade: *life behind the Iron Curtain* ○ [attrib] *Iron Curtain countries*, ie countries of the Soviet bloc.

the ˌIron ˈDuke name given to the first Duke of *Wellington.

ˈiron foundry foundry where cast iron is produced.

ˌiron-ˈgrey *adj*, *n* (of the) colour of freshly broken cast iron: *ˌiron-grey ˈhair.*

ˌiron ˈlung metal case fitted over the whole body except the head, to provide a person with prolonged artificial respiration by the use of mechanical pumps.

ˈiron-mould (*US* **-mold**) *n* [U] brown mark caused

Ireland

The relationship between the island of Ireland and mainland Britain has mostly been an unhappy one, chiefly because of the two inherent ethnic and religious differences between them. The Irish are a Celtic and largely Roman Catholic race, whereas the British are mostly Anglo-Saxon and Protestant. Many would add that the Irish are by nature a peace-loving people, whereas the English, who came to dominate the rest of the British Isles, have been seen more as 'empire-builders'.

The Danes invaded Ireland in the 8th century, but were ultimately defeated in the 11th. The English began their invasions in the 12th century, and waged a long and bitter struggle against the Irish in their bid for supremacy. They eventually conquered Ireland in the 16th and early 17th centuries, populating Ulster in the north with many English and Scottish Protestant settlers, and ruled the country as a dependency until 1801, when it was united with Great Britain. Fierce rebellions by the Irish against British dominance continued, however, one of the most violent being the Easter Rising of 1916. Its harsh suppression by British troops, known as the 'Black and Tans', was followed by civil war.

In 1921 the British granted the status of a dominion to Ireland, dividing it into the largely Protestant six counties of Ulster (Northern Ireland), which became part of the United Kingdom but with their own Parliament at Stormont, and the predominantly Catholic 26 counties of southern Ireland, which was established as the Irish Free State (reconstituted as Eire in 1937, and the Republic of Ireland in 1949, the year that Ireland left the Commonwealth).

From that time on, Britain has maintained her claim on Northern Ireland, a claim that has never been recognized by the Irish. Successive Irish governments have favoured peaceful reunification with Northern Ireland, while more militant groups, in particular the Irish Republican Army (IRA), have tried to achieve Irish unity by force. The Protestant majority of Northern Ireland has remained firmly opposed to unification.

There has been serious unrest in the province of Northern Ireland since 1968, when British troops moved in to help maintain law and order. 'The Troubles' as this unrest has come to be called, resulted largely from claims by Roman Catholics, who form about a third of the population, that they were discriminated against in voting rights, housing and employment. The dispute was taken up as an armed struggle by the IRA (who are outlawed in the Republic of Ireland) on the one hand, and British Protestant groups, police and troops on the other. The Royal Ulster Constabulary (RUC) are the police force in Northern Ireland, and are aided by the Ulster Defence Regiment, a local paramilitary force, set up by the British government in 1969, and British soldiers posted in the province from the mainland. Since 1968, over 2 000 people have died as a result of bombing and shooting related to the unrest, mainly in Northern Ireland, but also in mainland Britain and other European countries.

Britain has governed Northern Ireland by 'direct rule' since 1972, but despite attempts to find a way of governing the province acceptable to both 'Loyalist' Protestants and 'Republican' Catholics, no solution to the problem has been found. The Anglo-Irish Agreement of 1985 gave the Republic of Ireland a say in the governing of Northern Ireland, but it was bitterly opposed by Ulster Protestants.

Northern Ireland has suffered not only from the Troubles but in recent years also from economic decline and a level of unemployment higher than anywhere else in Britain. It has been badly affected by the decline of the shipbuilding industry, formerly an important part of the economy.

As a result of Ireland's troubled economic and political history, in particular the great potato famine (1845-49), when nearly a million Irish people died of starvation, millions of Irish people have emigrated. At the time of the famine around one and a half million emigrated to the USA. Today many people in Britain and the USA are the descendants of Irish immigrants.

The Irish have a popular reputation for charm, the gift of persuasiveness or cajolery (a person with this gift is said to have 'kissed the Blarney stone') and a tendency to ignore logic, so that a statement that is absurdly inconsistent is sometimes said to be 'Irish'.

by iron-rust or an ink-stain.

ˌ**iron pyˈrites** (also **fool's gold**) shiny mineral sometimes mistaken for gold.

ˌ**iron ˈrations** small supply of (esp tinned) food to be used only in an emergency (by troops, explorers, etc).

ˈ**Ironsides** *n* [pl] soldiers (esp the cavalry) of Oliver *Cromwell's army during the English Civil War.

ˈ**ironstone** *n* [U] **1** (also ˌ**ironstone ˈchina**) type of hard-wearing white pottery. **2** hard iron ore.

ˈ**ironware** /-weə(r)/ *n* [U] (esp domestic) articles made of iron.

ˈ**ironwork** *n* [U] things made of iron, eg gratings, rails, railings.

ˈ**ironworks** *n* [pl usu sing *v*] (*Brit*) place where iron is smelted or where heavy iron goods are made.

iron² /ˈaɪən; *US* ˈaɪərn/ *v* **1** [I, Ip, Tn] smooth (clothes, etc) with an iron¹(2): *This material irons well/easily*, ie the creases come out quickly. ○ *She was ironing (away) all evening.* ○ *I prefer to iron my shirts while they are still damp.* **2** (phr v) **iron sth out** (**a**) remove sth by ironing: *iron out creases.* (**b**) (*fig*) resolve sth by discussion: *iron out misunderstandings, problems, difficulties, etc.*

▷ **ironing** *n* [U] **1** action of smoothing clothes with an iron. **2** clothes that need to be or have just been ironed: *do the ironing.* ˈ**ironing-board** *n* padded board, usu fitted with adjustable legs, on which clothes are ironed. ⇨ illus at IRON.

ironic /aɪˈrɒnɪk/ (also **ironical** /aɪˈrɒnɪkl/) *adj* using or expressing irony; full of irony: *an ironic expression, smile, remark etc*, ie one showing that you do not expect to be taken seriously or literally ○ *His death gave an ironic twist to the story*, eg because he died before he could enjoy the money he had stolen.

▷ **ironically** /-klɪ/ *adv* **1** in an ironic manner: *He smiled ironically.* **2** it seems ironic (that): *Ironically, most people came to watch the match on the day it poured with rain.*

ironmonger /ˈaɪənmʌŋgə(r)/ *n* (*Brit*) (*US* ˈ**hardware dealer**) dealer in tools, household implements, etc. ▷ ˈ**ironmongery** /-mʌŋgərɪ/ *n* [U] (*Brit*) (*US* **hardware**).

irony /ˈaɪərənɪ/ *n* **1** [U] expression of one's meaning by saying the direct opposite of one's thoughts in order to be emphatic, amusing, sarcastic, etc: *'That's really lovely, that is!' he said with heavy irony.* **2** [U, C] situation, event, etc that is desirable in itself but so unexpected or ill-timed that it appears to be deliberately perverse: *the irony of fate* ○ *He inherited a fortune but died a month later; one of life's little ironies.*

Iroquois /ˈɪrəkwɔɪ/ *n* (*pl* unchanged) member of a group of native American peoples formerly living in what is now New York State.

▷ **Iroquoian** /ˌɪrəˈkwɔɪən/ *adj* of the Iroquois. — *n* [U] family of native American languages of the north-eastern USA.

irradiate /ɪˈreɪdɪeɪt/ *v* (*fml*) **1** [Tn, Tn·pr] ~ **sth** (**with sth**) send rays of light upon sth; subject sth to sunlight, ultraviolet rays, or radioactivity. **2** [Tn·pr esp passive] ~ **sth with sth** (*fig*) light up or brighten sth: *faces irradiated with joy.*

irrational /ɪˈræʃənl/ *adj* **1** not guided by reason; illogical or absurd: *irrational fears, behaviour, arguments.* **2** not capable of reasoning: *behave like an irrational animal.* ▷ **irrationality** /ɪˌræʃəˈnælətɪ/ *n* [U]. **irrationally** /ɪˈræʃnəlɪ/ *adv.*

□ **irˌrational ˈnumber** number (eg the square root of 2) that cannot be expressed as a rational number or fraction.

irreconcilable /ɪˈrekənsaɪləbl, ɪˌrekənˈsaɪləbl/ *adj* (*fml*) ~ (**with sb/sth**) (**a**) (of people) that cannot be reconciled. (**b**) (of ideas or actions) that cannot be brought into harmony with each other: *We can never agree — our views are irreconcilable.*

▷ **irreconcilably** /-əblɪ/ *adv.*

irrecoverable /ˌɪrɪˈkʌvərəbl/ *adj* (*fml*) that cannot be recovered or remedied: *suffer irrecoverable losses*, eg in business. ▷ **irrecoverably** /-əblɪ/ *adv.*

irredeemable /ˌɪrɪˈdiːməbl/ *adj* **1** (*finance*) (**a**) (of government annuities, bonds, shares, etc) that cannot be terminated by repayment. (**b**) (of paper money) that cannot be exchanged for money in coins. **2** (*fml*) that cannot be restored, reclaimed or saved: *an irredeemable loss, misfortune, etc.* ▷ **irredeemably** /-əblɪ/ *adv* (*fml*).

irreducible /ˌɪrɪˈdjuːsəbl; *US* -ˈduːs-/ *adj* (*fml*) **1** that cannot be reduced or made smaller: *Expenditure on road repairs has been cut to an irreducible minimum.* **2** that cannot be made simpler: *a problem of irreducible complexity.* ▷ **irreducibly** /-əblɪ/ *adv.*

irrefutable /ˌɪrɪˈfjuːtəbl, *also* ɪˈrefjʊtəbl/ *adj* (*fml*) that cannot be proved false: *an irrefutable argument* ○ *irrefutable evidence, proof, etc.* ▷ **irrefutably** /-əblɪ/ *adv*: *irrefutably the greatest living violinist.*

irregular /ɪˈregjʊlə(r)/ *adj* ~ (**in sth**) **1** not regular in shape, arrangement, etc; uneven: *a coast with an irregular outline*, eg with many bays, inlets, etc. **2** not happening, coming, going, etc regularly; varying or unequal: *an irregular pulse* ○ *occur at irregular intervals* ○ *be irregular in attending class.* **3** contrary to the rules or to what is normal or established: *an irregular practice, situation* ○ *keep irregular hours*, eg get up and go to bed at unusual times ○ *His behaviour is highly irregular.* **4** (*grammar*) not inflected in the usual way: *'Child' has an irregular plural, ie 'children'.* ○ *irregular verbs.* ⇨ App 13. **5** (of troops) not belonging to the regular armed forces.

▷ **irregular** *n* (usu *pl*) member of an irregular military force.

irregularity /ɪˌregjʊˈlærətɪ/ *n* **1** [U] state or quality of being irregular. **2** [C] thing that is irregular: *the irregularities of the earth's surface* ○ *There were some irregularities in the accounts*, eg

figures that were not correct.
irregularly *adv.*

irrelevant /ɪˈreləvənt/ *adj* ~ (**to sth**) not connected (with sth); not relevant (to sth): *irrelevant remarks* ○ *What you say is irrelevant to the subject.*
▷ **irrelevance** /-əns/ *n* [U] state of being irrelevant.
irrelevancy /-ənsɪ/ *n* **1** [U] = IRRELEVANCE. **2** [C] irrelevant remark, question, etc: *Let us ignore these irrelevancies.*
irrelevantly *adv.*

irreligious /ˌɪrɪˈlɪdʒəs/ *adj* feeling no interest in, or feeling hostile to, religion; irreverent: *an irreligious act, person.*

irremediable /ˌɪrɪˈmi:dɪəbl/ *adj* (*fml*) that cannot be remedied or corrected: *an irremediable loss, mistake.* ▷ **irremediably** /-əblɪ/ *adv.*

irremovable /ˌɪrɪˈmu:vəbl/ *adj* that cannot be removed.

irreparable /ɪˈrepərəbl/ *adj* (of a loss, an injury, etc) that cannot be put right, restored or repaired: *irreparable damage, harm, etc.* ▷ **irreparably** /-əblɪ/ *adv.*

irreplaceable /ˌɪrɪˈpleɪsəbl/ *adj* that cannot be replaced if lost or damaged: *an irreplaceable antique vase, the only one of its kind.*

irrepressible /ˌɪrɪˈpresəbl/ *adj* that cannot be held back or controlled: *irrepressible laughter, envy, high spirits, etc* ○ *You cannot keep her quiet for long; she's irrepressible!* ▷ **irrepressibly** /-əblɪ/ *adv.*

irreproachable /ˌɪrɪˈprəʊtʃəbl/ *adj* free from blame or fault: *irreproachable conduct.* ▷ **irreproachably** /-əblɪ/ *adv.*

irresistible /ˌɪrɪˈzɪstəbl/ *adj* **1** too strong to be resisted: *an irresistible temptation, urge, impulse, etc* ○ *His arguments were irresistible.* **2** too delightful or attractive to be resisted: *On such a hot day, the sea was irresistible,* ie We couldn't resist the desire to swim in it. ○ *With her beauty, wit and charm, he found her irresistible.* ▷ **irresistibly** /-əblɪ/ *adv.*

irresolute /ɪˈrezəlu:t/ *adj* (*fml*) feeling or showing uncertainty; hesitating. ▷ **irresolutely** *adv.* **irresolution** /ɪˌrezəˈlu:ʃn/ *n* [U].

irrespective /ˌɪrɪˈspektɪv/ **irrespective of** *prep* not taking account of or considering (sth/sb): *The laws apply to everyone irrespective of race, creed or colour.*

irresponsible /ˌɪrɪˈspɒnsəbl/ *adj* (of people, actions, etc) not showing a proper sense of responsibility: *an irresponsible child* ○ *irresponsible behaviour* ○ *It is irresponsible of you not to prepare students properly for their exams.* Cf RESPONSIBLE 4. ▷ **irresponsibility** /ˌɪrɪˌspɒnsəˈbɪlətɪ/ *n* [U]. **irresponsibly** /-əblɪ/ *adv.*

irretrievable /ˌɪrɪˈtri:vəbl/ *adj* (*fml*) that cannot be retrieved or remedied: *an irretrievable loss* ○ *The breakdown of their marriage was irretrievable.* ▷ **irretrievably** /-əblɪ/ *adv.*

irreverent /ɪˈrevərənt/ *adj* feeling or showing no respect for sacred things or for conventional standards of behaviour. ▷ **irreverence** /-rəns/ *n* [U]. **irreverently** *adv.*

irreversible /ˌɪrɪˈvɜ:səbl/ *adj* that cannot be reversed or revoked; unalterable: *He suffered irreversible brain damage in the crash.* ▷ **irreversibly** /-əblɪ/ *adv.*

irrevocable /ɪˈrevəkəbl/ *adj* (*fml*) that cannot be changed or revoked; final: *an irrevocable decision, judgement, etc* ○ (*finance*) *an irrevocable letter of credit.* ▷ **irrevocably** /-əblɪ/ *adv.*

irrigate /ˈɪrɪgeɪt/ *v* [Tn] **1** supply (land or crops) with water (by means of streams, reservoirs, channels, pipes, etc): *irrigate desert areas to make them fertile.* **2** (*medical*) wash (a wound, etc) with a constant flow of liquid.
▷ **irrigable** /ˈɪrɪgəbl/ *adj* that can be irrigated.
irrigation /ˌɪrɪˈgeɪʃn/ *n* [U attrib]: *an irrigation project* ○ *irrigation canals.*

irritable /ˈɪrɪtəbl/ *adj* easily annoyed or made angry; touchy. ▷ **irritability** /ˌɪrɪtəˈbɪlətɪ/ *n* [U]. **irritably** /-əblɪ/ *adv.*

irritant /ˈɪrɪtənt/ *adj* causing irritation; irritating: *a substance that is irritant to sensitive skins.*
▷ **irritant** *n* (**a**) substance that irritates, eg pepper in the nose. (**b**) (*fig*) thing that annoys: *The noise of traffic is a constant irritant to city dwellers.*

irritate /ˈɪrɪteɪt/ *v* [Tn] **1** make (sb) angry, annoyed or impatient: *irritated by/at the delay* ○ *It irritates me to have to shout to be heard.* **2** (**a**) (*biology*) cause discomfort to a part of the body: *Acid irritates the stomach lining.* (**b**) make sore or inflamed: *The smoke irritates my eyes.*
▷ **irritation** /ˌɪrɪˈteɪʃn/ *n* (**a**) [U] irritating or being irritated. (**b**) [C] instance of this.

irruption /ɪˈrʌpʃn/ *n* [C] (*fml*) ~ (**into sth**) sudden and violent entry; bursting in: *the irruption of a noisy group of revellers.*

Irving[1] /ˈɜ:vɪŋ/ Sir Henry (1838-1905), real name John Henry Brodribb, English actor famous for his playing of Shakespearean roles.

Irving[2] /ˈɜ:vɪŋ/ Washington (1783-1859), American writer who invented the character *Rip Van Winkle. His books include *A History of New York, The Sketch Book* and a biography of George Washington.

is ⇨ BE.

Is *abbr* Island(s); Isle(s): *(the) Windward Is,* ie Islands ○ *(the) British Is,* ie Isles. Cf I *abbr.*

Isaac /ˈaɪzək/ (in the Old Testament) son of *Abraham and father of Esau and Jacob, from whose 12 sons come the 12 tribes of Israel. God commanded Abraham to sacrifice Isaac, but then relented.

Isaiah /aɪˈzaɪə/ **1** (in the Old Testament) Hebrew prophet of the 8th century BC who told of a saviour and ruler who would come to the people of Israel (later interpreted as Christ). **2** book of the Old Testament partially written by Isaiah. ⇨ App 5.

ISBN /ˌaɪ es bi: ˈen/ *abbr* International Standard Book Number: *ISBN 0 19 861131 5,* eg on the cover of a book.

ISD /ˌaɪ es ˈdi:/ *abbr* international subscriber dialling.

-ise ⇨ -IZE.

-ish *suff* **1** (with *ns* forming *adjs* and *ns*) (language or people) of the specified nationality: *Danish* ○ *Irish.* **2** (with *ns* forming *adjs*) (*esp derog*) of the nature of; resembling: *childish* ○ *bookish* ○ *oafish* ○ *stand-offish.* **3** (with *adjs*) somewhat; approximately: *reddish* ○ *twentyish.* ▷ **-ishly** (with sense 2 forming *advs*).

Isherwood /ˈɪʃəwʊd/ Christopher William Bradshaw (1904-86), English novelist whose best-known works, *Mr Norris Changes Trains* and *Goodbye to Berlin* (on which the musical *Cabaret* was based) reflect the time he spent in Germany in the early 1930s. He later settled in the USA.

Ishmael /ˈɪʃmeɪl/ (in the Old Testament) son of *Abraham by his wife's servant. He was forced to leave home because of Abraham's wife's jealousy. He is regarded as the ancestor of *Muhammad and the Arab people.

isinglass /ˈaɪzɪŋglɑ:s; *US* -glæs/ *n* [U] clear white jelly from the air bladders of some freshwater fish, used for making jellies, glue, etc.

Islam /ɪzˈlɑ:m; *US* ˈɪslɑ:m/ *n* **1** [U] Muslim religion, based on the teaching of the prophet *Muhammad. He founded it in Arabia in the 7th century AD. A single god (known as *Allah*) is worshipped. Islam's holy book is the *Koran. There are two main sects: the *Sunni and the *Shi'ites. Muslims are expected to pray regularly, to give alms to the poor, to eat nothing during the daytime in the month of *Ramadan, and to go on a pilgrimage to the holy city of *Mecca. Islam is the main religion of the Arab world, and it is also widespread in Africa and southern Asia. **2** [sing] all Muslims; all the Muslim world. ⇨ Usage at CHRISTIAN. ▷ **Islamic** /ɪzˈlæmɪk; *US* ɪsˈlɑ:mɪk/ *adj.*

island /ˈaɪlənd/ *n* **1** (*abbrs* **I, Is**) piece of land surrounded by water: *a group of tropical islands* ○ [attrib] *The Shetlanders are an island race.* **2** = TRAFFIC ISLAND (TRAFFIC).
▷ **islander** *n* person living on an island, esp a small or an isolated one.
□ **the ˈislands area** administrative area of Scotland including the islands of *Orkney, *Shetland and the *Hebrides.

isle /aɪl/ *n* (*abbrs* **I, Is**) (esp in poetry and proper names) island: *the Isle of Wight* ○ *the British Isles.*
▷ **islet** /ˈaɪlɪt/ *n* small island. **the islets of Langerhans** /ˌaɪlɪts əv ˈlæŋəhæns/ small groups of cells in the pancreas which produce insulin.

Isle of Man /ˌaɪl əv ˈmæn/ **the Isle of Man** island in the *Irish Sea which is a possession of the British Crown but is self-governing, with its own parliament; pop approx 66 000; capital Douglas. Its ancient Celtic language, *Manx, is now only used for ceremonial purposes. ⇨ map at UNITED KINGDOM.

Isle of Wight /ˌaɪl əv ˈwaɪt/ **the Isle of Wight** island off the coast of Hampshire, in the south of England; pop approx 123 000. It has been a county since 1974. It has many tourist resorts, and yacht races are held every year at Cowes. ⇨ map at UNITED KINGDOM. ⇨ map at App 1.

ism /ˈɪzəm/ *n* (*usu derog*) any distinctive doctrine or practice: *behaviourism and all the other isms of the twentieth century.*

-ism *suff* **1** (with *vs* ending in *-ize* forming *ns*): *baptism* ○ *criticism.* **2** (**a**) (with *ns* forming *ns*) showing qualities typical of: *heroism* ○ *Americanism.* (**b**) (with proper *ns* forming uncountable *ns*) doctrine, system or movement: *Buddhism* ○ *Communism.* (**c**) (with *ns*) medical condition or disease: *alcoholism.* (**d**) (with *ns*) practice of showing prejudice or discrimination because of: *sexism* ○ *racism.*

isn't ⇨ BE.

is(o)- *comb form* equal: *isobar* ○ *isometric.*

ISO /ˌaɪ es ˈəʊ/ *abbr* International Standardization Standards Organization. Cf ASA 2, BSI.

isobar /ˈaɪsəbɑ:(r)/ *n* line on a map, esp a weather chart, joining places with the same atmospheric pressure at a particular time.

isolate /ˈaɪsəleɪt/ *v* [Tn esp passive, Tn·pr] **1** ~ **sb/sth (from sb/sth)** put or keep sb/sth entirely apart from other people or things; separate sb/sth: *isolate a problem,* ie in order to deal with it separately ○ *When a person has an infectious disease, he is usually isolated (from other people).* ○ *Several villages have been isolated by heavy snowfalls.* **2** ~ **sth (from sth)** (*biology or chemistry*) separate (a single substance, germ, etc) from its combination with others: *Scientists have isolated the virus causing the epidemic.*
▷ **isolated** *adj* **1** separate; single or unique: *an isolated outbreak of smallpox* ○ *an isolated case, instance, occurrence, etc.* **2** standing alone; solitary: *an isolated building* ○ *lead an isolated existence,* eg as a lighthouse-keeper.

isolation /ˌaɪsəˈleɪʃn/ *n* [U] **1** ~ (**from sb/sth**) isolating or being isolated. **2** (idm) **in isolation (from sb/sth)** separately; alone: *examine each piece of evidence in isolation,* ie without considering the others ○ *Looked at in isolation, these facts are not encouraging.*
□ **isoˈlation hospital, isoˈlation ward** hospital or ward for people with infectious diseases.

isolationism /ˌaɪsəˈleɪʃənɪzəm/ *n* [U] ~ (**from sth**) policy of not participating in the affairs of other countries or groups.
▷ **isolationist** /-ʃənɪst/ *n, adj* (person) supporting isolationism.

isomer /ˈaɪsəmə(r)/ *n* any of two or more chemical substances whose molecules have the same atoms, but differently arranged.
▷ **isomeric** /ˌaɪsəˈmerɪk/ *adj.*
isomerism /aɪˈsɒmərɪzəm/ *n* [U] existence of isomers of the same substance.

isometric /ˌaɪsəˈmetrɪk/ *adj* **1** having equal dimensions and measurements. **2** (in physiology) (of muscle action) contracting and developing tension while the muscle is prevented from shortening. **3** (of a drawing, etc) without perspective, so that lines along the three axes are of equal length.

isomorph /ˈaɪsəmɔ:f/ *n* substance or organism with the same form or structure as another. ▷ **isomorphic** /ˌaɪsəˈmɔ:fɪk/ (also **isomorphous** /ˌaɪsəˈmɔ:fəs/) *adj.*

isosceles /aɪˈsɒsəli:z/ *adj* (*geometry*) (of a triangle) having two sides equal in length. ⇨ illus at TRIANGLE.

isotherm /ˈaɪsəθɜːm/ *n* line on a map joining places that have the same average temperature.

isotope /ˈaɪsətəʊp/ *n* one of two or more forms of a chemical element with different atomic weight and different nuclear properties but the same chemical properties: *radioactive isotopes*, ie unstable forms of atoms used in medicine and industry.

I-spy /ˌaɪ ˈspaɪ/ *n* [U] children's game in which one player calls out the first letter of the name of an object he can see, and the others have to guess what the object is.

Israel

Israel /ˈɪzreɪl/ **1** modern Jewish state at the eastern end of the Mediterranean, founded in 1948; pop approx 4 437 000; official languages Hebrew and Arabic; capital Jerusalem; unit of currency new shekel. It was set up after the Second World War to provide a homeland for the Jewish people. Most neighbouring Arab states have been hostile to its existence, and this led to the Arab-Israeli wars of 1948, 1956, 1967 and 1973. Cf PALESTINE. ⇨ map. **2** (**a**) (in the Bible) the Hebrew nation descended from the 12 sons of *Jacob. (**b**) kingdom at the eastern end of the Mediterranean formed by the northern Hebrew tribes in the 10th century BC and conquered by the *Assyrians in 721 BC.

▷ **Israeli** /ɪzˈreɪlɪ/ *adj* of the modern state of Israel. — *n* inhabitant of Israel(1).

Israelite /ˈɪzrəlaɪt/ *n* (**a**) (in the Bible) Hebrew person. (**b**) citizen of the ancient kingdom of Israel.

issue /ˈɪʃuː, ˈɪsjuː/ *n* **1** (**a**) [U] outgoing; outflow: *the place/point of issue.* (**b**) [sing] instance of flowing out: *an issue of blood*, eg from a wound. **2** (**a**) [U] supply and distribution of items for use or sale: *buy new stamps on the day of issue* ○ *the issue of rifles and ammunition to troops* ○ *the issue of a new edition of this dictionary.* (**b**) [C] number, quantity or set of items supplied and distributed at one time: *a special issue of stamps/banknotes/shares* ○ *emergency issues of blankets to refugees.* (**c**) [C] one of a regular series of publications: *the July issue*, eg of a magazine. **3** [sing] (*fml*) result or outcome: *await the issue* ○ *bring a campaign to a successful issue.* **4** [C] important topic for discussion; point in question: *a vital, political, topical, etc issue* ○ *debate an issue* ○ *raise a new issue* ○ *evade/avoid the issue* ○ *confuse the issue.* **5** [U] (*law*) children considered as part of one's family: *die without issue*, ie childless. **6** (idm) **(the matter, point, etc) at issue** (the matter, point, etc) being discussed or debated: *What's at issue here is the whole future of the industry.* **force the issue** ⇨ FORCE². **make an issue (out) of sth** treat (a minor matter) as if it needed serious discussion like a major matter: *It's only a small disagreement — let's not make an issue of it.* **take issue with sb (about/on/over sth)** proceed to disagree or argue with sb (about sth).

▷ **issue** *v* (*fml*) **1** [Ipr, Ip] ~ **from sth**; ~ **out/forth (from sth)** come, go or flow out: *blood issuing from a wound* ○ *smoke issuing (forth) from a chimney.* **2** [Tn, Tn·pr] ~ **sth (to sb)/sb with sth** supply or distribute sth to sb for use: *issue visas to foreign visitors* ○ *issue warm clothing to the survivors* ○ *issue them with warm clothing.* **3** [Tn] publish (books, articles, etc) or put into circulation (stamps, banknotes, shares, etc). **4** [Tn, Tn·pr] ~ **sth (to sb)** send sth out; make sth known: *issue orders, instructions, etc* ○ *The minister issued a statement to the press.* **5** [Ipr] ~ **from sth** (*fml*) result or be derived from sth.

-ist *suff* **1** (with *vs* ending in *-ize* forming *ns*): *dramatist* ○ *publicist.* **2** (with *ns* ending in *-ism*) believer in; practiser of: *atheist* ○ *socialist.* **3** (with *ns* forming *ns*) person concerned with: *physicist* ○ *motorist* ○ *violinist.*

NOTE ON USAGE: Both **-ist** and **-ite** form nouns indicating people who have certain beliefs. **-ist** suggests a strong belief in a theory, religion, etc: *She's a convinced Marxist, Buddhist, etc.* Nouns with **-ite** generally indicate a follower of someone or a member of a group. They are often used in a derogatory way: *a committee full of Unionites, Thatcherites, etc.*

isthmus /ˈɪsməs/ *n* (*pl* ~**es**) narrow strip of land joining two larger areas of land that would otherwise be separated by water: *the Isthmus of Panama.*

IT /ˌaɪ ˈtiː/ *abbr* (*computing*) Information Technology.

it¹ /ɪt/ *pers pron* (used as the subject or object of a *v* or after a *prep*) **1** (**a**) animal or thing mentioned earlier or being observed now: *'Where's your car?' 'It's in the garage.'* ○ *Did you hit it?* ○ *Fill a glass with water and dissolve this tablet in it.* ○ *We've got £500. Will it be enough for a deposit?* (**b**) baby, esp one whose sex is not known or unimportant: *Her baby's due next month. She hopes it will be a boy.* ○ *The baby next door kept me awake. It cried all night.* **2** fact or situation already known or implied: *When the factory closes it,* (ie this event) *will mean 500 redundancies.* ○ *Yes, I was at home on Sunday. What about/of it?* **3** (used to identify a person): *It's the milkman.* ○ *It's Peter on the phone.* ○ *Was it you who put these books on my desk?* **4** (idm) **this/that is ˈit** (**a**) this/that is what is required: *We've been looking for a house for months and I think this is it.* (**b**) this/that is the reason for the lack of success: *That's just it — I can't work when you're making so much noise.* (**c**) this/that is the end: *I'm afraid that's it — we've lost the match.*

▷ **its** /ɪts/ *possess det* of or belonging to a thing, an animal or a baby: *We wanted to buy the table but its surface was damaged.* ○ *Have you any idea of its value?* ○ *The dog was howling — its paw was hurt.* ○ *The baby threw its food on the floor.*

it² /ɪt/ *pron* **1** (used in the normal subject or object position to indicate that a longer subject or object has been placed at the end of a sentence): *It appears that the two leaders are holding secret talks.* ○ *Does it matter what colour it is?* ○ *It's impossible (for us) to get there in time.* ○ *It's no use shouting.* ○ *She finds it boring staying/to stay at home.* ○ *I find it strange that she doesn't want to travel.* **2** (used in the normal subject position to make a statement about time, distance or weather): *It's ten past twelve.* ○ *It's our anniversary.* ○ *It's two miles to the beach.* ○ *It's a long time since they left.* ○ *It was raining this morning.* ○ *It's quite warm at the moment.* ○ *It's stormy out at sea.* **3** circumstances or conditions; things in general: *If it's convenient I can see you tomorrow.* ○ *It's getting very competitive in the car industry.* **4** (used to emphasize any part of a sentence): *It's ˈJim who's the clever one.* ○ *It's ˈSpain that they're going to on holiday.* ○ *It was three weeks ˈlater that he heard the news.*

ita /ˌaɪ tiː ˈeɪ/ *abbr* initial teaching alphabet (a partially phonetic system used to teach reading).

Italian /ɪˈtælɪən/ *adj* of Italy, its culture, language or people.

▷ **Italian** *n* native of Italy.

Italianate /ɪˈtæljəneɪt/ *adj* of Italian style or appearance.

italic /ɪˈtælɪk/ *adj* **1** (of printed letters) sloping forwards: *This sentence is in italic type.* Cf ROMAN 3. **2** of or for a compact pointed style of handwriting: *write in italic script* ○ *an italic pen-nib.*

▷ **italicize, -ise** /ɪˈtælɪsaɪz/ *v* [Tn] print (sth) in italic type.

italics *n* [pl] printed italic letters: *Examples in this dictionary are in italics.* ⇨ App 14.

Italo- *comb form* Italian; of Italy: *the Italo-Swiss frontier.*

Italy

Italy /ˈɪtəlɪ/ country of southern Europe consisting of a peninsula that sticks out into the Mediterranean Sea; pop approx 57 441 000; official language Italian; capital Rome; unit of currency lira. A unified area under the Roman Empire, it broke up in the Middle Ages into a number of small states. These were not brought back together into a single country until the mid 19th century, as a result of the nationalist movement led by *Garibaldi and others. The kingdom of Italy was created in 1861. It became a republic in 1946. Italy was the birthplace of the *Renaissance, and has contributed significantly to the development of literature, music, and particularly painting in Europe. Today its main exports are agricultural produce (including wine), textiles, and motor vehicles. ⇨ map.

itch /ɪtʃ/ *n* **1** [C usu *sing*] feeling of irritation on the skin, causing a desire to scratch: *suffer from, have, feel an itch.* **2** [sing] ~ **for sth/to do sth** (*infml*) restless desire or longing: *have an itch for adventure* ○ *She cannot resist the/her itch to travel.* **3** (idm) **the seven-year ˈitch** (*joc infml*) the desire for new sexual experience that is thought to be felt after about seven years of marriage.

▷ **itch** *v* **1** [I] have or cause an itch: *scratch where it itches* ○ *Scratch yourself if you itch!* ○ *Are your mosquito bites still itching?* **2** [Ipr, It] ~ **for sth/to do sth** (*infml*) feel a strong restless desire for sth: *pupils itching for the lesson to end* ○ *I'm itching to tell you the news!* **3** (idm) **have an itching ˈpalm** be greedy for money.

itchy *adj* (**-ier** /ˈɪtʃɪə(r)/, **-iest** /ˈɪtʃɪɪst/) **1** having or producing irritation on the skin: *an itchy scalp*, eg caused by dandruff. **2** (idm) **(get/have) itchy feet** (*infml*) (feel a) restless desire to travel or move from place to place. **itchiness** *n* [U].

it'd /ˈɪtəd/ *contracted form* **1** it had ⇨ HAVE. **2** it would ⇨ WILL¹, WOULD².

-ite *suff* (with proper *ns* forming *ns*) follower or supporter of: *Labourite* ○ *Thatcherite.* ⇨ Usage at -IST.

item /ˈaɪtəm/ *n* **1** single article or unit in a list, etc: *the first item on the agenda* ○ *number the items in a catalogue.* **2** single piece of news: *There's an important news item/item of news in today's paper.*

▷ **item** *adv* (used to introduce each of several articles in a list) also: *item, one chair; item, two carpets, etc.*

itemize, -ise /ˈaɪtəmaɪz/ *v* [Tn] give or write every item of (sth): *an itemized list, account, bill, etc.*

iterate /ˈɪtəreɪt/ *v* [Tn, Tn·pr, Tf, Tw, Dpr·f, Dpr·w] ~ **sth (to sb)** (*fml*) say sth again and again; make (an accusation, a demand, etc) repeatedly. Cf REITERATE. ▷ **iteration** /ˌɪtəˈreɪʃn/ *n* [U].

itinerant /aɪˈtɪnərənt, ɪˈtɪnərənt/ *adj* [usu attrib] travelling from place to place: *an itinerant musician, entertainer, preacher, etc.*

itinerary /aɪˈtɪnərərɪ, ɪˈtɪnərərɪ; *US* -rerɪ/ *n* plan for, or record of, a journey; route: *keep to, depart from, follow one's itinerary.*

-ition ⇨ -ION.

-itis *suff* (with *ns* forming uncountable *ns*) **1** (*medical*) inflammatory disease of: *appendicitis* ○ *tonsillitis.* **2** (*infml esp joc*) excessive interest in or exposure to: *World Cup-itis.*

it'll /ɪtl/ *contracted form* it will ⇨ WILL¹.

ITN /ˌaɪ tiː ˈen/ *abbr* (*Brit*) Independent Television News: *news at 10 on ITN.* ⇨ article at TELEVISION.

its ⇨ IT¹.

it's /ɪts/ *contracted form* **1** it is. ⇨ BE. **2** it has. ⇨ HAVE.

itself /ɪtˈself/ *reflex, emph pron* (only taking the main stress in sentences when used emphatically) **1** (*reflex*) (used when the animal, thing, etc causing the action is also affected by it): *The wounded horse could not ˌraise itself from the ˈground.* ○ *The committee decided to aˌward itself a ˈpay increase.* **2** (*emph*) (used to emphasize an animal, a thing, etc): *The name itˈself sounds foreign.* **3** (idm) **by itˈself** (**a**) automatically: *The machine will start by itself in a few seconds.* (**b**) alone: *The statue stands by itself in the square.*

itsy-bitsy /ˌɪtsɪ ˈbɪtsɪ/ (also **itty-bitty** /ˌɪtɪ ˈbɪtɪ/) *adj* (*infml esp joc or derog*) extremely small.

ITT /ˌaɪ tiː ˈtiː/ *abbr* International Telephone and Telegraph Corporation: *work for ITT.*

ITV /ˌaɪ tiː ˈviː/ *abbr* (*Brit*) Independent Television: *watch a film on ITV* ○ *an ITV documentary.* Cf BBC, IBA. ⇨ article at TELEVISION.

-ity *suff* (with *adjs* forming *ns*): *purity* ○ *oddity.*

IUD /ˌaɪ juː ˈdiː/ (also **IUCD** /ˌaɪ juː siː ˈdiː/) *abbr* intra-uterine (contraceptive) device.

I've /aɪv/ *contracted form* I have ⇨ HAVE[1, 2].

-ive *suff* (with *vs* forming *ns* and *adjs*) (person or thing) having a tendency to or the quality of: *explosive* ○ *captive* ○ *descriptive.*

Ivory /ˈaɪvərɪ/ James (1928-), American film director. Influenced by Satyajit *Ray, he set his first films (eg *Shakespeare-Wallah*) in India, but later made notable adaptations of works by Henry *James, eg *The Europeans*, and of E.M.Forster's *A Room with a View*. He has directed most of his films in partnership with the producer Ismail Merchant.

ivory /ˈaɪvərɪ/ *n* **1** [U] creamy-white bone-like substance forming the tusks of elephants, walruses, etc: [attrib] *an ivory statuette.* **2** [C] object made of this: *a priceless collection of ivories.* **3** [U] colour of ivory: [attrib] *an ivory skin, complexion, etc* ○ *ivory-coloured silk.* **4 ivories** [pl] (*infml*) (**a**) piano keys: *tickling the ivories*, ie playing the piano. (**b**) (*dated*) teeth. **5** (idm) **an ˌivory ˈtower** place or situation where people retreat from the unpleasant realities of everyday life and pretend that these do not exist: *live in an ivory tower* ○ [attrib] *lead an ˌivory-tower eˈxistence.*

Ivory Coast /ˌaɪvərɪ ˈkəʊst/ country on the coast of West Africa; pop approx 11 613 000; official language French; capital Abidjan; unit of currency franc. Formerly a French colony, it became fully independent in 1960. Large parts of it are covered in tropical rain forest, and timber is one of its main exports. ⇨ map at NIGERIA.

ivy /ˈaɪvɪ/ *n* [U] any of various types of climbing evergreen plant, esp one with dark shiny five-pointed leaves: [attrib] *an ivy leaf.*

▷ **ivied** /ˈaɪvɪd/ *adj* covered with ivy: *ivied walls.*

□ **the ˌIvy ˈLeague** group of old-established universities in the eastern USA (Harvard, Yale, Princeton, Pennsylvania, Columbia, Brown, Cornell and Dartmouth) with a reputation for high academic standards and social prestige. ⇨ article at POST-SCHOOL.

-ize, -ise *suff* (with *ns* and *adjs* forming *vs*) **1** become or make like: *dramatize* ○ *miniaturize.* **2** act or treat with the qualities of: *criticize* ○ *deputize.* **3** place in: *containerize* ○ *hospitalize.* ▷ **-ization, -isation** (forming *ns*): *immunization.* **-izationally, -isationally** (forming *advs*): *organizationally.*

NOTE ON USAGE: **1** In some words ending with the sound /aɪz/ **-ize** and **-ise** are equally acceptable spellings: *emphasize/emphasise, criticize/criticise.* **-ise** is more common in British than in US English. In this dictionary both spellings are shown when both are possible. **2** There are some words which, because of their origin, are always spelt with **-ise**: *advertise* (*US* also *advertize*), *advise, comprise, despise, exercise, etc.* **3** Some people criticize the over-use of **-ize** or **-ise** to form words such as *burglarize* (= 'burgle') or *hospitalize* (= 'send to hospital').

J, j

J, j /dʒeɪ/ *n* (*pl* **J's, j's** /dʒeɪz/) the tenth letter of the English alphabet: *'Joker' begins with (a) J/'J'.*

J *abbr* joule(s).

jab /dʒæb/ *v* (**-bb-**) **1** [I, Ipr, Ip, Tn, Tn·pr] ~ (**at sb/sth**) (**with sth**); ~ **sb/sth** (**with sth**) poke or push at sb/sth roughly, usu with sth sharp or pointed: *He kept jabbing (away) at the paper cup with his pencil.* ○ *a blackbird jabbing at a worm*, ie using its beak ○ *He jabbed at his opponent*, eg of a boxer aiming a quick blow. ○ *She jabbed me in the ribs with her elbow.* **2** (phr v) **jab sth into sb/sth** force sth into sb/sth: *He jabbed his elbow into my side.* **jab sth out** force or push sth out by jabbing: *Be careful with that umbrella — you nearly jabbed my eye out!* ⇨ Usage at NUDGE.

▷ **jab** *n* (**a**) sudden rough blow or thrust, usu with sth pointed: *a jab in the arm.* (**b**) (*infml*) injection or inoculation: *Have you had your cholera jabs yet?*

jabber /ˈdʒæbə(r)/ *v* **1** [I, Ip] ~ (**away/on**) talk rapidly in what seems to be a confused manner: *Listen to those children jabbering away!* **2** [Tn, Tn·p] utter (words, etc) rapidly and indistinctly: *He jabbered out what I assumed was an apology.*

▷ **jabber** *n* [U] jabbering; chatter: *the jabber of monkeys.*

jabot /ˈʒæbəʊ/ *n* ornamental frill on the front of a woman's blouse or a man's shirt.

jack[1] /dʒæk/ *n* **1** (usu portable) device for raising heavy weights off the ground, esp one for raising the axle of a motor vehicle so that a wheel may be changed. **2** ship's flag flown to show nationality: *the Union Jack*, ie the flag of the United Kingdom. **3 Jack** familiar form of the name *John.* **4** (also **knave**) (in a pack of playing-cards) card between the ten and the queen: *the jack of clubs.* **5** (in the game of bowls) small white ball towards which bowls are rolled. **6** socket into which a (usu single-pronged) plug can be fitted to connect an electric circuit. ⇨ illus at PLUG. **7** device for turning a spit[2] (1). **8** (*sl*) policeman, esp a detective. **9** (idm) **before you can/could say Jack Robinson** ⇨ SAY. **every man jack** ⇨ MAN[1]. **a jack of 'all trades** person who can do many different kinds of work but not necessarily well.

□ **Jack 'Frost** (*joc*) frost considered as a person: *Look what pretty patterns Jack Frost has painted on the windows.*

jackhammer /ˈdʒækhæmə(r)/ *n* (*US*) portable drill, worked by compressed air, for drilling rock, etc.

'jack-in-office *n* (*derog*) self-important official.

'jack-in-the-box *n* (*pl* **-boxes**) toy in the form of a box with a figure inside that springs up when the lid is opened.

jack-o'-'lantern *n* pumpkin with holes cut in it so that it looks like a face, used as a lantern (by placing a candle inside) for fun.

'jack-rabbit *n* large hare of Western N America.

Jack 'Russell breed of small lively terrier dog.

jackstraws /ˈdʒækstrɔ:z/ *n* [sing or pl *v*] = SPILLIKINS.

Jack 'tar (also **tar**) (*dated nautical*) sailor.

jack[2] /dʒæk/ *v* (phr v) **jack sth in** (*sl*) leave sth readily; abandon (work, etc): *I can't concentrate any more. I'm going to jack it in.* **jack sth up** (**a**) raise sth using a jack[1](1): *to jack up a car.* (**b**) (*fig infml*) increase (salary, payment, etc); raise: *It's time you jacked up my allowance.* (**c**) (*infml*) arrange or organize sth that is in disorder: *Everything's falling apart; the whole system needs jacking up.*

jackal /ˈdʒækɔ:l; *US* -kl/ *n* wild animal of Africa and Asia that is related to the dog.

jackanapes /ˈdʒækəneɪps/ *n* (*pl* unchanged) (*dated*) impertinent fellow; mischievous child: *Come here, you young jackanapes!*

jackass /ˈdʒækæs/ *n* **1** male ass. **2** (*fig infml*) foolish person.

jackboot /ˈdʒækbu:t/ *n* **1** tall boot, esp one worn by certain soldiers. **2** (*fig*) military oppression; tyranny: *under the jackboot of a dictatorial regime.*

jackdaw /ˈdʒækdɔ:/ *n* bird of the crow family (noted for stealing small bright objects).

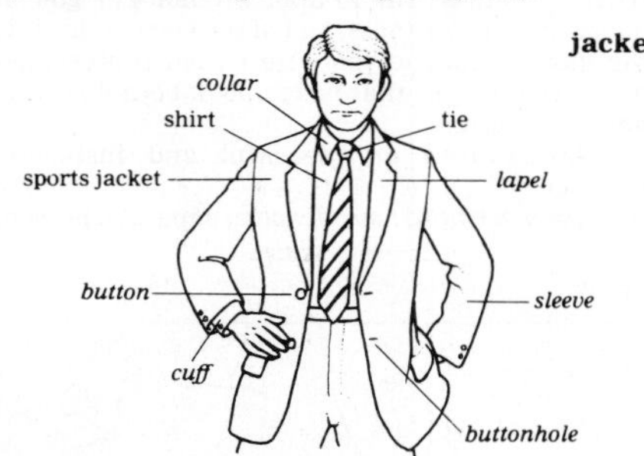

jacket /ˈdʒækɪt/ *n* **1** short coat with sleeves: *a tweed jacket.* ⇨ illus. **2** outer cover round a boiler, tank, pipe, etc to reduce loss of heat: *a water jacket*, ie cover used to cool an engine. **3** (also **'dust-jacket**) loose paper cover for a hardback book. **4** (of a potato) skin: [attrib] *ˌjacket poˈtatoes*, ie potatoes baked without being peeled.

jack-knife /ˈdʒæknaɪf/ *n* (*pl* **~s**) /-naɪvz/ **1** large pocket-knife with a folding blade. **2** (*sport*) dive in which the body is first bent double and then straightened.

▷ **jack-knife** *v* [I] (esp of an articulated lorry) bend sharply in the middle into a V-shape, usu as the result of an accident: *A heavy lorry has jack-knifed on the motorway, causing long delays.*

jackpot /ˈdʒækpɒt/ *n* **1** (in various games, esp poker) stake or prize that continues to be added to until won. **2** (idm) **hit the jackpot** ⇨ HIT[1].

Jackson[1] /ˈdʒæksn/ Andrew (1767-1845), 7th President of the USA 1829-37. After a career as a soldier he entered politics, and while in office extended the powers of the US presidency. His nickname was 'Old Hickory'. ⇨ App 2.

Jackson[2] /ˈdʒæksn/ Thomas Jonathan ('Stonewall') (1824-63), Confederate general in the American Civil War who got his nickname from the firmness of his resistance to the Northern army at the battle of Bull Run in 1861. He was shot and killed accidentally by one of his own soldiers at the battle of Chancellorsville.

Jack the Ripper /ˌdʒæk ðə ˈrɪpə(r)/ name given to an unknown man who brutally murdered several prostitutes in the *East End of London in 1888. People have tried ever since to find out who he was, but without success.

Jacob /ˈdʒeɪkəb/ (in the Old Testament) son of *Isaac, who tricked his twin bother Esau into giving him the right of seniority. His 12 sons founded the 12 tribes of Israel.

□ **ˌJacob's 'ladder 1** ladder between heaven and earth, with angels going up and down it, which Jacob saw in a dream. **2** ladder made of rope or wire with wooden cross-pieces, used on ships.

Jacobean /ˌdʒækəˈbi:ən/ *adj* of the reign of the English king James I (1603-25): *ˌJacobean ˈliterature, ˈarchitecture, ˈfurniture, etc.*

Jacobin /ˈdʒækəbɪn/ *n* member of an extreme political party during the *French Revolution, which had a policy of equality for all but used violence and terror to get rid of its opponents. *Robespierre was one of its leaders.

Jacobite /ˈdʒækəbaɪt/ *n* supporter of the English king *James II after his overthrow, or of his descendants who claimed the throne. Most Jacobites were Scottish, and they rebelled against England three times, in 1689, 1715 and 1745 (when they invaded England under *Bonny Prince Charlie). They were finally defeated at the battle of Culloden in 1746: [attrib] *the first Jacobite rebellion.* ⇨ article at SCOTLAND.

Jacquard /ˈdʒækɑ:d/ *n* (also **Jacquard loom**) loom on which patterned fabrics can be woven.

Jacuzzi /dʒəˈku:zɪ/ *n* (*propr*) bath with underwater jets of water that massage the body.

jade[1] /dʒeɪd/ *n* [U] **1** hard, usu green, stone from which ornaments, etc are carved: [attrib] *a jade vase, necklace, etc* ○ *jade-green eyes.* **2** ornaments, etc made of jade: *a collection of Chinese jade.*

jade[2] /dʒeɪd/ *n* **1** tired or worn-out horse. **2** (*dated derog or joc*) woman: *You saucy little jade!*

jaded /ˈdʒeɪdɪd/ *adj* (*derog or joc*) tired and lacking zest, usu after too much of sth: *looking jaded after an all-night party* ○ (*fig*) *a jaded appetite.*

Jaffa /ˈdʒæfə/ *n* (also **ˌJaffa ˈorange**) large thick-skinned type of orange, grown originally in the area near Jaffa in Israel.

jag[1] /dʒæg/ *n* sharp part that sticks out from sth (eg a projecting piece of rock).

▷ **jag** *v* (**-gg-**) [Tn, Tn·pr] ~ **sth** (**on sth**) cut or tear sth unevenly.

jag[2] /dʒæg/ *n* (*infml*) **1** bout of heavy drinking; spree. **2** period of concentrated activity, strong emotion, etc.

jagged /ˈdʒægɪd/ *adj* with rough, uneven, often sharp, edges; notched: *jagged rocks* ○ *a piece of glass with a jagged edge.*

jaguar /ˈdʒægjʊə(r)/ *n* large spotted member of the cat family inhabiting parts of central America.

jail = GAOL.

jalopy /dʒəˈlɒpɪ/ *n* (*infml*) battered old car.

jalousie /ˈʒælu:zi:; *US* ˈdʒæləsɪ/ *n* hinged framework containing horizontal bars with gaps between, fitted over a window to let in air and some light but not rain, etc.

jam[1] /dʒæm/ *n* **1** [U] sweet substance made by boiling fruit with sugar until it is thick, usu preserved in jars, etc: *He spread some strawberry jam on his toast.* **2** [C] type of this: *recipes for jams and preserves.* **3** (idm) **jam toˈmorrow** pleasant thing that is continually promised but never provided. **money for jam/old rope** ⇨ MONEY. **want ˈjam on it** (*infml usu derog*) want more even though one already has or has gained an advantage.

▷ **jammy** /ˈdʒæmɪ/ *adj* (**-ier, -iest**) (*infml*) **1** covered with jam: *Don't wipe your jammy fingers on the table-cloth.* **2** (*Brit infml*) (**a**) lucky: *You jammy so-and-so!* (**b**) easy: *This is one of the jammiest jobs I've ever had.*

jam[2] /dʒæm/ *v* (**-mm-**) **1** [esp passive: Tn·pr, Tn·p] ~ **sb/sth in, under, between, etc sth**; ~ **sb/sth in** (**a**) squeeze sb/sth (into a space) so that he/it cannot move out: *sitting in a railway carriage, jammed between two fat men* ○ *The ship was jammed in the ice.* ○ *Don't park there — you'll probably get jammed in.* (**b**) thrust sth forcibly or clumsily into a space: *The newspapers were so tightly jammed in the letter-box he could hardly get them out.* ○ *He jammed his key into the lock.* **2** [I, Tn, Tn·p] ~ **sth** (**up**) (cause sth to) become immovable or unworkable because sth has stuck: *The key turned halfway and then jammed.* ○ *There's something jamming (up) the lock.* **3** [Tn, Tn·p] ~ **sth** (**up**) crowd (an area, etc) so as to block; obstruct: *The holiday traffic is jamming the roads.* ○ *a river jammed up with logs* ○ *a corridor jammed full of people and luggage.* **4** [Tn] (*broadcasting*) make (a message, programme, etc) difficult to understand by sending out a signal at the same time: *The government tried to jam the guerrillas' transmissions.* **5** [I] (*infml*) take part in a jam session (JAM *n*). **6** (phr v) **jam sth on** apply (esp brakes) suddenly and forcibly: *As soon as she saw the child in the road, she jammed on her brakes.*

▷ **jam** *n* **1** crowding together of people, things, etc so that movement is difficult or impossible; congestion: *a ˈtraffic jam in a town* ○ *a ˈlog-jam on a river.* **2** failure or stoppage of a system, machine, etc caused by jamming: *a jam in the dispatch department.* **3** (*infml*) difficult or embarrassing situation: *How am I going to get out of this jam?* ○ *be in/get into a jam.*

□ **ˈjam session** performance of improvised jazz.

Jamaica /dʒəˈmeɪkə/ island and country in the Caribbean; pop approx 2 447 000; official language English; capital Kingston; unit of currency dollar (= 100 cents). Between 1655 and 1962 it was a British colony. Its chief exports are sugar, bananas and bauxite, and tourism is also important. ⇨ map at CARIBBEAN.

▷ **Jamaican** /dʒəˈmeɪkən/ *n, adj* (native or inhabitant) of Jamaica: *Jamaican rum.*

jamb /dʒæm/ *n* vertical post at the side of a doorway, window frame, fireplace, etc.

jamboree /ˌdʒæmbəˈriː/ *n* **1** large party; celebration. **2** large rally of Scouts or Guides.

James[1] /dʒeɪmz/ Henry (1843-1916), American novelist who from 1876 lived and worked in England. His novels, many of which deal with the impact of European civilization on Americans, include *Portrait of a Lady, Washington Square, The Ambassadors* and *The Golden Bowl.* He also wrote the ghost story *The Turn of the Screw.*

James[2] /dʒeɪmz/ Saint (1st century AD), 'the Less', leader of the Christian church in Jerusalem and, according to St Paul, the brother of Jesus. He may have been the same person as an apostle called James. He wrote the book of the New Testament known as the Epistle of St James.

James[3] /dʒeɪmz/ Saint (died 44 AD), 'the Great', one of Christ's apostles, brother of St *John, who was put to death because of his Christian faith. He is the patron saint of Spain.

James I /dʒeɪmz/ (1566-1625), king of England 1603-25 and of Scotland (as James VI) 1567-1625. The son of *Mary Queen of Scots, he succeeded to the throne of Scotland at the age of only one, when she abdicated. In the 1580s he established strong royal authority. In 1603 he succeeded *Elizabeth I, uniting the crowns of Scotland and England. He was not a popular king in England, however, and his quarrels with Parliament foreshadowed the Civil War of the mid 17th century. ⇨ App 3.

James II /dʒeɪmz/ (1633-1701), king of Britain 1685-88. The younger son of *Charles I, he succeeded his brother *Charles II as king, but he faced much opposition because he was a Roman Catholic, and in 1688 he was replaced by *William III. James fled to France. He went to Ireland in 1689 to try to start a rebellion, but it was defeated, and he returned to France to live in exile. ⇨ App 3.

Jammu and Kashmir /ˈdʒæmuː ən kæʃˈmɪə(r)/ area in the extreme north of India, formerly part of disputed *Kashmir and since 1972 an Indian state; pop approx 5 987 389; official language Urdu; capitals Jammu (winter) and Srinagar (summer). The region is traversed by the Himalayas and is known for its beauty.

jam-packed /ˌdʒæmˈpækt/ *adj* [usu pred] (*infml*) ~ (**with sb/sth**) very full or crowded: *a stadium jam-packed with spectators.*

Jan /*in informal use* dʒæn/ *abbr* January: *1 Jan 1932.*

Jane Doe /ˌdʒeɪn ˈdəʊ/ ⇨ JOHN DOE.

jangle /ˈdʒæŋgl/ *v* **1** [I, Ip, Tn] (cause sth to) make a harsh metallic noise: *The fire-alarm kept jangling (away).* **2** (phr v) **jangle on sth** irritate (nerves, etc) by making an unpleasant noise: *Her voice jangles on my ears.*

▷ **jangle** *n* [sing] harsh, usu metallic, noise.

janissary /ˈdʒænɪsərɪ/ *n* member of a specially chosen group of soldiers in the Turkish army between the 14th and the 19th centuries, which guarded the sultan and formed the main fighting force of the army.

janitor /ˈdʒænɪtə(r)/ *n* (*US*) = CARETAKER.

Jansenism /ˈdʒænsənɪzəm/ *n* [U] (ideas of a) 16th- and 17th-century movement in the Roman Catholic Church, esp in France, which held that the elect, ie those who would enjoy salvation, were chosen in advance, and that their number was limited. The philosopher *Pascal was influenced by Jansenism.

▷ **Jansenist** /ˈdʒænsənɪst/ *n, adj* (follower) of Jansenism.

January /ˈdʒænjʊərɪ; *US* -jʊerɪ/ *n* [U, C] (*abbr* **Jan**) the first month of the year, coming before February.

For the uses of *January* see the examples at *April.*

Janus /ˈdʒeɪnəs/ (in Roman mythology) god of doorways, of entrances, and of the start of the day, the month and the year. He is usu represented with two faces, so that he can look both forwards and backwards.

□ **ˈJanus-faced** *adj* deceitful and insincere; two-faced.

Jap /dʒæp/ *n* (*infml usu offensive*) Japanese person.

Japan

Japan /dʒəˈpæn/ country in eastern Asia consisting of four large and over 1000 smaller islands off the coast of China and Korea; pop approx 122 613 000; official language Japanese; capital Tokyo; unit of currency yen. Since ancient times it has been a centralized empire, but from the 12th century it was ruled by military leaders called *shoguns.* The imperial system was restored in the 19th century, and to this day the Emperor remains head of state. Japan did not become a powerful and influential country until the 20th century. In the Second World War it allied itself with Germany, and made many conquests in SE Asia and the Pacific before finally being defeated. Its cities Hiroshima and Nagasaki were the targets of the first atomic bombs used in war. Today Japan is one of the richest countries in the world, its economic power based on a vigorous export trade in electronic equipment, cars, ships, etc. ⇨ map.

▷ **Japanese** /ˌdʒæpəˈniːz/ *adj* of Japan. — *n* (*pl* unchanged) **1** [C] native or inhabitant of Japan. **2** [U] Japanese language, written in characters similar to those of Chinese.

japan /dʒəˈpæn/ *n* [U] hard shiny black varnish.

▷ **japan** *v* [Tn usu passive] (-**nn**-) cover (esp sth made of wood or metal) with japan.

jape /dʒeɪp/ *n* (*dated infml*) joke played on sb.

japonica /dʒəˈpɒnɪkə/ *n* ornamental type of quince tree, with red flowers.

jar[1] /dʒɑː(r)/ *n* **1** (**a**) cylindrical container, usu made of glass: *I keep my paint-brushes in old ˈjam jars.* ⇨ illus at POT. (**b**) this and its contents: *a jar of plum jam.* **2** tall vessel with a wide mouth, usu cylindrical, with or without handles: *large jars of olive oil* ○ *a ˈwine-jar* ○ *a jar of cookies.* **3** (*Brit infml*) glass (of beer): *We're going down to the pub for a few jars.*

jar[2] /dʒɑː(r)/ *v* (-**rr**-) **1** [I, Ipr] ~ (**on sb/sth**) have a harsh or an unpleasant effect: *His tuneless whistling jarred on my nerves.* **2** [I, Ipr] ~ (**with sth**) be out of harmony; clash: (*fig*) *Her comments on future policy introduced a jarring note to the proceedings.* ○ *His harsh criticism jarred with the friendly tone of the meeting.* **3** [Tn] give a sudden or painful shock to (sb/sth); jolt: *He jarred his back badly when he fell.* **4** (phr v) **jar against/on sth** strike sth with a harsh unpleasant sound: *The ship jarred against the quayside.*

▷ **jar** *n* [sing] **1** unpleasant sound or vibration: *The side of the boat hit the quay with a grinding jar.* **2** sudden unpleasant shock; jolt: *He gave his back a nasty jar when he fell.*

jardinière /ˌʒɑːdɪˈnjeə(r)/ *n* **1** large ornamental pot for holding indoor plants. **2** dish of mixed vegetables chopped small, cooked, and served as an accompaniment to a main dish.

jargon /ˈdʒɑːgən/ *n* [U] (*often derog*) technical or specialized words used by a particular group of people and difficult for others to understand: *scientific jargon* ○ *She uses so much jargon I can never understand her explanations.*

Jarrow /ˈdʒærəʊ/ town in *Tyne and Wear, in north-east England, on the banks of the river Tyne. In the 1930s unemployment was extremely bad in the area, and in 1936 many of the unemployed workers walked from Jarrow to London on a 'hunger march', as a way of drawing attention to their plight.

jasmine /ˈdʒæsmɪn; *US* ˈdʒæzmən/ *n* [U] shrub with white or yellow sweet-smelling flowers.

Jason /ˈdʒeɪsn/ (in Greek mythology) leader of the *Argonauts, who sailed to Colchis to try to find the *Golden Fleece.

jasper /ˈdʒæspə(r)/ *n* [U] red, yellow or brown semi-precious stone.

jaundice /ˈdʒɔːndɪs/ *n* [U] **1** disease caused by an excess of bile in the blood which makes the skin and the whites of the eyes become abnormally yellow. **2** (*fig*) state of mind in which one is jealous, spiteful or suspicious: *Do I detect a touch of jaundice* (ie a slight hint of jealousy, etc) *in that remark?*

▷ **jaundiced** *adj* affected by jealousy, spite, etc; bitter: *a jaundiced mind, opinion, outlook, etc* ○ *He has rather a jaundiced view of life.*

jaunt /dʒɔːnt/ *n* short journey, made for pleasure: *She's gone on a jaunt into town.*

jaunty /ˈdʒɔːntɪ/ *adj* (-**ier**, -**iest**) feeling or showing cheerfulness and self-confidence; sprightly: *wear one's hat at a jaunty angle,* ie tipped to one side, as a sign of high spirits, etc. ▷ **jauntily** *adv*: *swagger jauntily.* **jauntiness** *n* [U]..

Java /ˈdʒɑːvə/ large island in the Malay Archipelago, between *Sumatra and *Bali. Colonized by the Dutch in the 17th century, in 1950 it became part of the republic of *Indonesia.

▷ **Javanese** /ˌdʒɑːvəˈniːz/ *adj* of Java. — *n* (*pl* unchanged) **1** [C] native or inhabitant of Java. **2** [U] Indonesian language of Java.

□ ˌ**Java** ˈ**man** type of prehistoric human being whose remains were found in Java.

javelin

javelin /ˈdʒævlɪn/ *n* **1** [C] light spear for throwing (usu in sport). **2 the javelin** [sing] sporting contest in which competitors try to throw this the furthest: *She came second in the javelin.* ⇨ illus.

jaw /dʒɔː/ *n* **1** (**a**) [C usu *pl*] either of the bone structures containing the teeth: *the upper/lower jaw.* (**b**) **jaws** [pl] the mouth with its bones and teeth: *The crocodile's jaws snapped shut.* ○ (*fig*) *into/out of the jaws of death,* ie into/out of great danger. (**c**) [sing] lower part of the face; lower jaw: *a handsome man with a strong square jaw* ○ *The punch broke the boxer's jaw.* ○ *The pain was terrible, but she set her jaw* (ie thrust it forwards, as a sign of determination) *and carried on.* ⇨ illus at HEAD. **2 jaws** [pl] narrow mouth of a valley, channel, etc: *the jaws of a gorge, canyon, etc.* **3 jaws** [pl] part of a tool, machine, etc that grips or crushes things: *the jaws of a vice.* ⇨ illus at VICE. **4** [U, C] (*infml*) (**a**) long dull talk, usu giving moral advice. (**b**) gossip; talkativeness. **5** (idm) **one's ˈjaw drops** (*infml*) one shows sudden surprise or disappointment: *My jaw dropped when I saw how much the meal had cost.*

▷ **jaw** *v* (*infml*) **1** [I, Ipr, Ip] ~ (**on**) (**at sb**) talk at length about sb's faults, behaviour, etc. **2** [I, Ip] ~ (**on**) gossip.

□ **ˈjaw-bone** *n* either of the two bones forming the lower jaw in most mammals.

jay /dʒeɪ/ *n* noisy European bird with brightly coloured feathers.

jay-walk /ˈdʒeɪ wɔːk/ *v* [I] walk carelessly across or along town streets without paying enough attention to traffic or traffic signals. ▷ **ˈjay-walker** *n.*

jazz /dʒæz/ *n* **1** [U] music of American Negro origin, characterized by the use of improvisation and strong, often syncopated, rhythms. Since its origin in the southern USA in the early 20th century, jazz has developed many different styles, including *Dixieland, swing, be-bop and blues: *traditional jazz* ○ *modern jazz* ○ [attrib] *jazz music/musicians* ○ *a ˈjazz band.* **2** [U] (*sl derog*) pretentious talk; nonsense: *Don't give me that jazz!* **3** (idm) **and all that jazz** (*sl usu derog*) and similar things: *She lectured us about the honour of the school and all that jazz.*

▷ **jazz** *v* **1** [Tn, Tn·p] ~ **sth** (**up**) play or arrange (music) in the style of jazz: *a jazzed-up version of an old tune.* **2** (phr v) **jazz sth up** make sth more lively: *jazz up a party, a magazine, a dress.*

jazzy *adj* (*infml*) **1** of or like jazz. **2** flashy or showy: *jazzy clothes, colours, etc* ○ *a jazzy sports car.*

□ **the ˈJazz Age** (esp in the USA) the 1920s, when jazz became popular. Following the grimness of the First World War, it was a period of gaiety and self-indulgence, particularly for the rich, and it was marked by a general relaxation in social formality. It was brought to an end by the depression of the 1930s.

JCR /ˌdʒeɪ siː ˈɑː(r)/ *abbr* junior common room.

jealous /ˈdʒeləs/ *adj* **1** feeling or showing fear or resentment of possible rivals in love or affection: *a jealous husband* ○ *jealous looks.* **2** ~ (**of sb/sth**) feeling or showing resentment of sb's advantages, achievements, etc; envious: *He was jealous of Tom/of Tom's success.* **3** ~ (**of sth**) anxiously protective (of one's rights, belongings, etc); possessive: *keeping a jealous eye on one's property* ○ *She's jealous of her privileges.*

▷ **jealously** *adv.*

jealousy /ˈdʒeləsɪ/ *n* (**a**) [U] being jealous: *a lover's jealousy.* (**b**) [C] instance of this; act or remark that shows a person to be jealous: *She grew tired of his petty jealousies.* Cf ENVY[1].

jeans /dʒiːnz/ *n* [pl] trousers of strong cotton for informal wear: *She was wearing a pair of tight blue jeans.*

Jeep /dʒiːp/ *n* (*prop*) small sturdy motor vehicle with four-wheel drive. ⇨ illus.

jeer /dʒɪə(r)/ *v* [I, Ipr, Tn] ~ (**at sb/sth**) laugh at or mock (sb/sth): *a jeering crowd* ○ *jeer at a defeated opponent* ○ *They jeered (at) the speaker.*

▷ **jeer** *n* jeering remark; taunt: *He ran off, their jeers ringing in his ears.*

JEEP

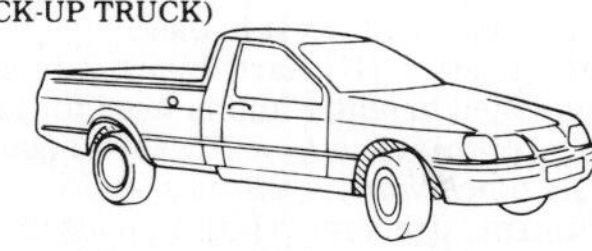
PICK-UP (*also* PICK-UP TRUCK)

jeering *n* [U]: *He had to face the jeering of his classmates.*

Jeeves /dʒiːvz/ Reginald, the valet of Bertie Wooster in the stories of P G *Wodehouse. He is often taken as the perfect example of a resourceful and discreet personal servant.

Jefferson /ˈdʒefəsn/ Thomas (1743-1826), 3rd president of the USA 1801-9. He drafted the Declaration of Independence and played a key role in the American leadership during the Revolution. A man of wide learning and liberal philosophy, he was against putting too much power into the hands of the president. ⇨ App 2. ⇨ article at POLITICS.

Jeffreys /ˈdʒefrɪz/ George (c1648-89) British judge who became notorious for condemning to death over 150 followers of the Duke of *Monmouth found guilty of treason at the 'Bloody Assizes'. He was later imprisoned himself and died in the *Tower of London.

Jehovah /dʒɪˈhəʊvə/ *n* (*Bible*) name of God used in the Old Testament.

□ **Jeˌhovah's ˈWitness** member of a religious organization which believes that the end of the world is near and that everyone will be damned except its own members. Its members go from house to house trying to persuade others to join. It was founded in the USA around 1879 by Charles Taze Russell. ⇨ article at RELIGION.

jejune /dʒɪˈdʒuːn/ *adj* (*fml*) **1** (of writings) dull and uninteresting; unsatisfying to the mind. **2** childish; unsophisticated.

Jekyll and Hyde /ˌdʒekl ən ˈhaɪd/ single person with two personalities, one good (*Jekyll*) and one bad (*Hyde*), named after a character in Robert Louis *Stevenson's story *The Strange Case of Dr Jekyll and Mr Hyde* who could turn himself into an evil person by drinking a special substance: *I'd never have expected her to behave like that; she's a real Jekyll and Hyde.*

jell /dʒel/ *v* [I] **1** become like jelly; set: *This strawberry jam is still runny: I can't get it to jell.* **2** (*fig*) take shape; become definite: *My ideas are beginning to jell.*

jelly /ˈdʒelɪ/ *n* **1** (**a**) [U, C] clear (fruit-flavoured) food substance made of liquid set with gelatine, usu prepared in a mould, which shakes when moved: *Can I have some more jelly, please?* ○ *All the strawberry jellies had been eaten* ○ (*fig*) *She went into the interview room, her legs shaking like jelly,* ie She was so nervous that she was unsteady. ○ [attrib] *a jelly mould.* (**b**) [U] savoury food like this made from the juices of meat and gelatine. **2** [U] type of jam made of strained fruit juice and sugar: *blackcurrant jelly.* **3** [U] jelly-like substance: *petroleum jelly.* **4** [U] (*sl*) = GELIGNITE.

▷ **jellied** *adj* [usu attrib] set in jelly; prepared in jelly; like jelly: *jellied eels.*

□ **ˈjelly baby** small fruit-flavoured sweet in the shape of a baby, made from gelatine.

ˈjellyfish *n* (*pl* unchanged or ~**es**) sea animal with a jelly-like body and stinging tentacles.

jemmy /ˈdʒemɪ/ (*US* **jimmy** /ˈdʒɪmɪ/) *n* short heavy steel bar used by burglars to force open doors and windows.

je ne sais quoi /ʒə nə seɪ ˈkwɑː/ (*French*) (usu pleasing) quality that is difficult to describe: *His new play has a certain je ne sais quoi.*

Jenner /ˈdʒenə(r)/ Edward (1749-1823), English physician who pioneered vaccination. He discovered that by deliberately infecting people with the disease cowpox, they could be prevented from catching the related but much more serious disease smallpox.

jeopardize, -ise /ˈdʒepədaɪz/ *v* [Tn] cause (sth) to be harmed, lost or destroyed; put in danger: *The security of the whole operation has been jeopardized by one careless person.*

jeopardy /ˈdʒepədɪ/ *n* (idm) **in jeopardy** in danger of harm, loss or destruction: *A fall in demand for oil tankers has put/placed thousands of jobs in the shipbuilding industry in jeopardy.*

jerboa /dʒɜːˈbəʊə/ *n* small rat-like animal of Asia and the N African deserts with long hind legs and the ability to jump well.

jeremiad /ˌdʒerɪˈmaɪæd/ *n* (*fml*) long, sad and complaining story of troubles, misfortunes, etc.

Jeremiah /ˌdʒerɪˈmaɪə/ *n* **1** (**a**) (in the Old Testament) Hebrew prophet (c 650-c 585 BC) who foretold the defeat and capture of the Israelites by the Babylonians and the destruction of Jerusalem. (**b**) book of the Old Testament containing his prophecies. ⇨ App 5. **2** [C] pessimistic person: *Don't be such a Jeremiah!*

Jericho /ˈdʒerɪkəʊ/ ancient city to the north of the *Dead Sea, in the *West Bank territory now occupied by Israel. In Old Testament times it was occupied by the *Canaanites. The Israelites attacked it and were able to capture it when, according to the Bible story, *Joshua destroyed its walls with the sound of trumpets. Modern archaeology has shown that its walls were destroyed many times.

jerk /dʒɜːk/ *n* **1** sudden pull, push, start, stop, twist, lift or throw: *He gave his tooth a sharp jerk and it came out.* ○ *The bus stopped with a jerk.* **2** sudden involuntary twitch of a muscle or muscles: *a jerk of an eyelid.* **3** (*infml derog*) foolish person.

▷ **jerk** *v* **1** [Tn·pr, Tn·p] pull (sth/sb) suddenly and quickly in the specified direction: *He jerked the fishing-rod out of the water.* ○ *She jerked her hand away when he tried to touch it.* **2** [I, Ipr, Ip, Tn, Tn·pr, Tn·p] (cause sth/sb to) move with a short sudden action or a series of short uneven actions: *His head keeps jerking.* ○ *The train jerked to a halt.* ○ *She jerked upright in surprise.* ○ *Try not to jerk the camera when taking a photograph.* ○ *He jerked his head towards the door.* **3** (phr v) **jerk (oneself) off** (⚠ *sl*) (of a man) masturbate. **jerk sth out** utter sth in an abrupt nervous manner: *jerk out a request, an apology, etc.*

jerky *adj* (**-ier**, **-iest**) making abrupt starts and stops; not moving or talking smoothly: *The toy robot moved forward with quick jerky steps.* ○ *his jerky way of speaking.* **jerkily** /-ɪlɪ/ *adv.* **jerkiness** *n* [U].

jerkin /ˈdʒɜːkɪn/ *n* short close-fitting jacket without sleeves, worn by men or women. ⇨ illus at DRESS.

jeroboam /ˌdʒerəˈbəʊəm/ *n* very large wine bottle containing four or (for claret) five times the amount of an ordinary bottle.

Jerome /dʒəˈrəʊm/ Saint (c 342-420), early Christian scholar who translated the Bible into Latin (in a translation known as the *Vulgate). He was born in the former Yugoslavia.

jerry-build /ˈdʒerɪbɪld/ *v* [I, Tn] (*derog*) build (houses, etc) quickly and cheaply without concern for quality.

▷ **ˈjerry-builder** *n* person who builds in this way. **ˈjerry-building** *n* [U]. **ˈjerry-built** *adj*: *jerry-built houses.*

jerrycan /ˈdʒerɪkæn/ *n* type of large flat-sided metal or plastic container used for storing or carrying liquids, usu petrol or water.

Jersey /ˈdʒɜːzɪ/ *n* **1** small island off the north coast of France that is one of the *Channel Islands. ⇨ map at UNITED KINGDOM. **2** [C] type of light-brown cow that produces creamy milk.

jersey /ˈdʒɜːzɪ/ *n* (*pl* ~**s**) **1** (*also* **jumper**, **pullover**, **sweater**) [C] close-fitting knitted (esp woollen) garment without fastenings, usu worn over a shirt or blouse: *a thick green jersey.* **2** (*also* **jersey-wool**) [U] soft fine knitted woollen fabric used for making clothes.

Jerusalem[1] /dʒəˈru:sələm/ city at the eastern end of the Mediterranean, near the river *Jordan, now the capital of *Israel. An ancient city, it was captured from the *Canaanites by King *David, who made it the Israelites' capital. *Solomon built his temple there. Jesus was crucified there, and between the 7th and the 11th centuries it was under Islamic control. As a result of its history it is regarded as a holy city by Jews, Christians and Muslims, and this has made it the centre of much conflict. The *Crusades were fought to recapture Jerusalem for Christianity, and in modern times Arab states do not recognize Israel's right to have it as a capital.

□ **Jeˌrusalem ˈartichoke** = ARTICHOKE 2.

the Jeˌrusalem ˈBible modern English translation of the Bible used by Roman Catholics.

Jerusalem[2] /dʒəˈru:sələm/ hymn written by Hubert *Parry to words by William *Blake, which describe a vision of England as an idealized Christian country. It is often sung as a patriotic song.

Jesse /ˈdʒesɪ/ (in the Old Testament) father of *David, regarded as the ancestor of Christ.

□ **ˈJesse window** stained-glass window in a church, which shows the descent of Christ from Jesse, representing it in the form of a tree (called a **tree of Jesse**).

jest /dʒest/ *n* **1** thing said or done to cause amusement; joke. **2** (idm) **in jest** in fun; not seriously: *His reply was taken half seriously, half in jest.* ○ (*saying*) *Many a true word is spoken in jest.*

▷ **jest** *v* [I, Ipr] ~ **(with sb) (about sth)** make jokes (to sb) (about sth); speak or act without seriousness: *Stop jesting and be serious for a moment!* ○ *Don't jest about such important matters!*

jester *n* (formerly) man whose job was to make jokes to amuse a court or noble household: *the court/king's/queen's jester.*

Jesu /ˈdʒi:zju:/ (*arch*) (used as a form of the name *Jesus* when addressing Christ, eg in a prayer).

Jesuit /ˈdʒezjʊɪt; *US* ˈdʒeʒəwət/ *n* **1** member of the Society of Jesus, a Roman Catholic religious order founded in France in 1534 to do missionary work. It took the lead in opposing the *Reformation in Europe, and became known for the uncompromising zeal with which it taught and spread Roman Catholic beliefs. **2** (*derog*) person who uses clever but false reasoning to persuade others to do as he wishes.

▷ **Jesuitical** /ˌdʒezjʊˈɪtɪkl; *US* ˌdʒeʒʊ-/ *adj* (*derog*) involving deception or dishonesty: *a Jesuitical scheme, reply.*

Jesus /ˈdʒi:zəs/ (also **Jesus Christ** /ˌdʒi:zəs ˈkraɪst/) founder of the Christian religion. He was a Jew born in Palestine at the beginning of the first century AD. The *New Testament describes how he went round preaching and healing the sick, how he was arrested and executed, and how belief in his resurrection spread among his followers, who saw him as the Christ or Messiah foretold in the *Old Testament.

jet[1] /dʒet/ *n* **1** (also **jet aircraft**) aircraft powered by a jet engine: *The accident happened as the jet was about to take off.* ○ *travel by jet* ○ [attrib] *a jet fighter, airliner, etc* ○ *the age of jet travel.* **2** (**a**) strong narrow stream of gas, liquid, steam or flame, forced out of a small opening: *The pipe burst and jets of water shot across the kitchen.* (**b**) narrow opening from which this comes: *clean the gas jets on the cooker.*

▷ **jet** *v* (**-tt-**) **1** [I, Ipr, Ip] (*infml*) travel by jet airliner: *politicians who constantly jet around the world.* **2** (phr v) **jet (sth) from/out of sth; jet (sth) out** (cause sth to) come out in a jet or jets: *Flames jetted out (of the nozzles).*

□ **ˈjet engine** engine that gives forward movement by sending out a high-speed jet of hot gases, etc at the back. ⇨ illus at AIRCRAFT.

ˈjet lag delayed physical effects of tiredness, etc felt after a long flight by plane, esp when there is a great difference in the local times at which the journey begins and ends. **ˈjet-lagged** *adj* affected by jet lag.

ˌjet-proˈpelled *adj* powered by jet engines. **ˌjet proˈpulsion** [U].

the ˈjet set rich fashionable social group who travel about the world for business or pleasure: *I see she's joining the jet set!* **ˈjet-setter** *n* member of the jet set.

ˈjet stream (usu narrow) current of very strong wind blowing high above the surface of the earth, typically from west to east.

jet[2] /dʒet/ *n* [U] hard black mineral that can be polished brightly and is used for jewellery.

□ **ˌjet-ˈblack** *adj, n* [U] (of a) deep glossy black: *ˌjet-black ˈhair, ˈeyebrows, etc.*

jetsam /ˈdʒetsəm/ *n* [U] **1** goods thrown overboard from a ship in distress to lighten it; such goods washed up ashore. Cf FLOTSAM. **2** (idm) **flotsam and jetsam** ⇨ FLOTSAM.

jettison /ˈdʒetɪsn/ *v* [Tn] **1** throw or eject (unwanted goods or material) from a ship in distress, or from an aeroplane, a spacecraft, etc: *The first-stage vehicle is used to launch the rocket and is then jettisoned in the upper atmosphere.* **2** abandon or reject (sth that is not wanted): *to jettison a plan, an idea, a theory, etc.*

jetty /ˈdʒetɪ/ *n* stone wall or wooden platform built out into a sea, river, etc as a breakwater or landing-place for boats. Cf PIER.

Jew /dʒu:/ *n* person of the Hebrew people or religion. Jews are a *Semitic people who inhabited ancient *Palestine perhaps as long ago as the 18th century BC. In modern times they have migrated widely round the world. They have been subjected to much discrimination and persecution in their adopted countries. Their religion, Judaism, is based on a belief in one God as the creator of all things and the source of all righteousness. ⇨ article at RELIGION.

▷ **Jewess** /ˈdʒu:ɪs, dʒu:ˈes/ *n* (*sometimes offensive*) Jewish woman.

Jewish /ˈdʒu:ɪʃ/ *adj* of the Jews: *the local Jewish community.*

Jewry /ˈdʒʊərɪ/ *n* **1** [Gp] Jewish people collectively: *world Jewry.* **2** [U] Jewish religion or culture. ⇨ Usage at CHRISTIAN.

□ **ˌJew's ˈharp** small musical instrument held between the teeth with a projecting metal strip that is struck with a finger.

jewel /ˈdʒu:əl/ *n* **1** (**a**) precious stone (eg a diamond or a ruby). (**b**) ornament with such a stone or stones set in it: [attrib] *a jewel thief.* **2** small precious stone, or piece of special glass, used in the machinery of a watch or compass: *a watch with 17 jewels.* **3** person or thing that is greatly valued: *He's always saying his wife is a real jewel.* ○ *a painting by Goya, the brightest jewel in his collection of art treasures.*

▷ **jewelled** (*US* **jeweled**) *adj* decorated with or having jewels: *a jewelled ring, dagger, snuff-box, etc.*

jeweller (*US* **jeweler**) *n* person who sells, makes or repairs jewellery or watches.

jewellery (also **jewelry**) /ˈdʒu:əlrɪ/ *n* [U] ornaments, eg rings and necklaces, esp made of a valuable metal and sometimes set with jewels.

□ **ˈjewel box**, **ˈjewel case** box for keeping jewels in.

Jezebel /ˈdʒezəbl, -bel/ *n* (*derog*) shameless scheming woman.

jib[1] /dʒɪb/ *n* **1** small triangular sail in front of the mainsail. ⇨ illus at YACHT. **2** projecting arm of a crane. **3** (idm) **the cut of his jib** ⇨ CUT[2].

□ **ˈjib-boom** *n* pole to which the lower part of a jib(1) is fastened.

jib[2] /dʒɪb/ *v* (**-bb-**) **1** [I] (of a horse, etc) stop suddenly; refuse to go forwards. **2** [I, Ipr] ~ **(at sth/doing sth)** (*fig*) refuse to proceed with (an action); be reluctant to do or accept sth: *He jibbed when he heard how much the tickets would cost.* ○ *The staff don't mind the new work schedule but they would jib at taking a cut in wages.*

jibe[1] /dʒaɪb/ *v* [I, Ipr] ~ **(with sth/sb)** (*US infml*) fit in (with sth/sb); be made to agree, esp when apparently in conflict: *How does their claim to support disarmament jibe with their increased spending on weapons?*

jibe[2] /dʒaɪb/ **1** = GIBE. **2** (*US*) = GYBE.

jiffy /ˈdʒɪfɪ/ *n* [C] (*infml*) moment: *I'll be with you in a couple of jiffies*, ie very soon.

jig /dʒɪg/ *n* **1** (music for a) quick lively dance. **2** device that holds a piece of work in position and guides the tools that are working on it.

▷ **jig** *v* (**-gg-**) **1** [I] dance a jig. **2** [I, Ip, Tn, Tn·p] (cause sb/sth to) move up and down in a quick jerky way: *jigging up and down in excitement* ○ *to jig a baby (up and down) on one's knee.*

jigger /ˈdʒɪgə(r)/ *n* small measure for alcoholic drinks; small glass holding this amount.

jiggered /ˈdʒɪgəd/ *adj* [pred] (*infml*) **1** (*dated*) (used as a mild expression of surprise, anger, etc): *Well I'm jiggered!* **2** exhausted: *I was completely jiggered.*

jiggery-pokery /ˌdʒɪgərɪ ˈpəʊkərɪ/ *n* [U] (*infml esp Brit*) secret and mischievous or dishonest behaviour; mischief or trickery: *He began to suspect that some jiggery-pokery was going on.*

jiggle /ˈdʒɪgl/ *v* [I, Tn] (*infml*) (cause sth to) move lightly and quickly from side to side or up and down: *jiggling in time to the music* ○ *jiggle a key in a lock.*

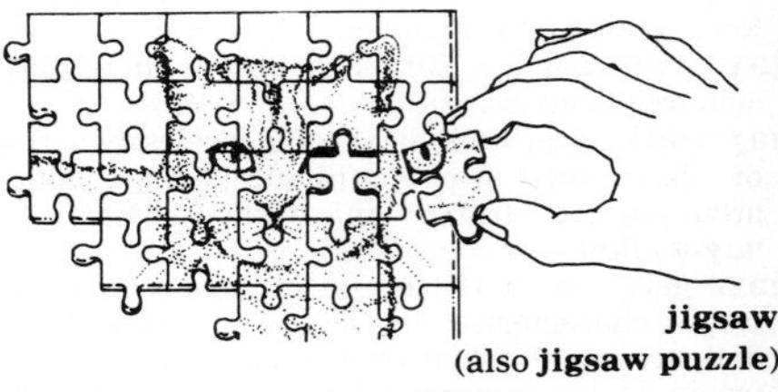

jigsaw
(also jigsaw puzzle)

jigsaw /ˈdʒɪgsɔ:/ *n* **1** (also **ˈjigsaw puzzle**) picture, map, etc pasted on cardboard or wood and cut into irregular shapes that have to be fitted together again: *do a jigsaw* ○ *Have you finished the jigsaw yet?* ○ (*fig*) *a complex jigsaw of interlocking social and economic factors.* ⇨ illus. **2** mechanically operated fretsaw.

jihad /dʒɪˈhɑ:d/ *n* holy war fought by Muslims against those who reject Islam.

jilt /dʒɪlt/ *v* [Tn] leave (a man or woman) with whom one has had a close emotional relationship, esp suddenly and unkindly: *a jilted lover.*

Jim Crow /ˌdʒɪm ˈkrəʊ/ (*US derog offensive*) Black; negro: [attrib] *Jim Crow laws*, ie ones unfair to Black Americans ○ *Jim Crow schools, buses, etc*, ie for American Blacks only, and usu of poor quality.

jim-jams /ˈdʒɪmdʒæmz/ *n* **the jim-jams** [pl] (*sl*) feelings of extreme nervousness; the jitters: *Steady on: you're giving me the jim-jams!*

jimmy (*US*) = JEMMY.

jingle /ˈdʒɪŋgl/ *n* **1** [sing] metallic ringing or clinking sound, as of coins, keys or small bells: *the jingle of coins in his pocket.* **2** [C] short simple rhyme or song that is designed to attract attention and be easily remembered, esp one used in advertising on radio or television: *an advertising jingle.*

▷ **jingle** *v* [I, Tn] (cause sth to) make a gentle ringing or clinking sound: *The coins jingled in his pocket* ○ *the sound of jingling bracelets and bangles* ○ *Stop jingling your keys like that!*

jingoism /ˈdʒɪŋgəʊɪzəm/ *n* [U] (*derog*) extreme and unreasonable belief that one's own country is best, together with a warlike attitude towards other countries.

▷ **jingoist** /ˈdʒɪŋgəʊɪst/ *n* person who has such a belief.

jingoistic /ˌdʒɪŋgəʊˈɪstɪk/ *adj*: *ˌjingoistic reˈmarks.*

jink /dʒɪŋk/ *v* [I, Ipr, Ip] (*infml*) move quickly or suddenly with sharp turns, usu to avoid being caught; dodge.

▷ **jink** *n* **1** quick turning movement: *a sharp jink to the right.* **2** (idm) **high jinks** ⇨ HIGH[1].

Jinnah /ˈdʒɪnə/ Muhammad Ali (1876-1948), Muslim politician in India who pressed for the creation of a separate Muslim state after independence, and in 1947 was appointed the first

Governor-General of the newly created Pakistan.

jinnee /dʒɪˈniː/ (also **djinn, jinn** /dʒɪn/) *n* (*pl* **jinn**) **1** (in Muslim mythology) spirit with supernatural power which is able to appear in human and animal forms. **2** = GENIE.

jinx /dʒɪŋks/ *n* (usu *sing*) ~ **(on sb/sth)** (*infml*) (person or thing that is thought to bring) bad luck (to sb/sth); curse: *There's a jinx on/Someone's put a jinx on this car: it's always giving me trouble.*
▷ **jinx** *v* [Tn usu passive] (*infml*) bring bad luck to (sb/sth): *I've been jinxed!* ○ *I think this computer must be jinxed — it's always breaking down.*

jitter /ˈdʒɪtə(r)/ *v* [I] (*infml*) feel nervous; behave nervously: *jittering with fright.*
▷ **the jitters** *n* [pl] (*infml*) feelings of extreme nervousness; the jim-jams: *give sb/have/get the jitters* ○ *I always get the jitters before I go on stage.* **jittery** /ˈdʒɪtərɪ/ *adj* (*infml*) nervous; frightened.
□ **ˈjitterbug** *n* performer of a lively popular dance of the 1940s to swing music. — *v* [I] perform such a dance.

jive /dʒaɪv/ *n* (usu **the jive**) [sing] fast lively form of music with a strong beat; dance done to this.
▷ **jive** *v* [I] dance to jive music.

Jnr (also **Jr, Jun**) *abbr* (*esp US*) Junior: *John F Davis Jnr*, ie to distinguish him from his father with the same name. Cf SEN 3.

Joan of Arc /ˌdʒəʊn əv ˈɑːk/ Saint (1412-31), French peasant girl who, believing she had heard 'divine' voices telling her to act, led the French armies which defeated the English in 1429 and 1430, during the *Hundred Years' War. She was captured and handed over to the English, who burned her at the stake for heresy and witchcraft. She was canonized in 1920.

Job /dʒəʊb/ **1 (a)** (in the Old Testament) virtuous man who kept his faith in God in spite of many misfortunes. **(b)** book of the Old Testament which tells the story of Job. ➩ App 5. **2** (idm) **the patience of Job** ➩ PATIENCE.
□ **ˌJob's ˈcomforter** person who increases the unhappiness or distress of the person he is attempting to comfort.

job /dʒɒb/ *n* **1** regularly paid position or post: *Thousands of workers lost their jobs when the factory closed.* ○ *He got a part-time job as a gardener.* ○ *Should she give up her job when she has a baby?* ○ *The government is trying to create new jobs.* ➩ Usage at TRADE¹. **2** piece of work; task or assignment: *The shipyard is working on three different jobs*, ie building three ships. ○ *They've done a fine job (of work) sewing these curtains.* ○ *pay sb by the job*, ie separately for each job done ○ *Writing a book was a more difficult job than he'd thought.* ○ *It was quite a job* (ie a difficult task) *finding his flat.* ➩ Usage at WORK¹. **3** (usu *sing*) responsibility or function of sb/sth: *It's not my job to lock up!* ○ *It's the job of the church to help people lead better lives.* **4** (*computing*) piece of work (to be) done by a computer, consisting of a set of programs and the data to be manipulated by them. **5** (*infml*) thing that is completed; product: *Your new car is a neat little job, isn't it?* **6** (*infml*) criminal act, esp theft; dishonest or unfair action: *He got three years for a job he did in Leeds.* **7** (idm) **do the ˈjob/ˈtrick** (*infml*) succeed in doing what is required or desired: *This extra strong glue should do the job nicely.* **give sb/sth up as a bad ˈjob** (*infml*) decide that one can no longer help sb or be concerned for sb/sth because there seems no hope of success: *His parents have given him up as a bad job.* ○ *After waiting an hour for the bus she decided to give it up as a bad job.* **a good ˈjob** (*infml*) (used as a comment on actions or events) a fortunate state of affairs: *She's stopped smoking, and a good job too!* ○ *It's a good job you were there to help — we couldn't have managed without you.* **have a devil of a job doing sth** ➩ DEVIL¹. **jobs for the ˈboys** (*infml*) the giving of paid employment to favoured groups, usu friends or relations. **just the ˈjob/ˈticket** (*infml approv*) exactly what is wanted or needed: *Thanks for lending me your big lawn-mower. It was just the job for the long grass.* **make a bad, excellent, good, poor, etc job of sth** do sth badly, well, etc: *Mark's a difficult child and I think they're making a good job of bringing him up.* ○ *You've certainly made an excellent job of the kitchen*, eg decorating it. **make the best of a bad job** ➩ BEST³. **on the ˈjob (a)** working; at work: *lie down/go to sleep on the job*, ie not work energetically and continuously ○ [attrib] *on-the-job training*, ie training given to workers at their place of work. **(b)** (*Brit sl*) having sexual intercourse. **out of a ˈjob** unemployed: *He was out of a job for six months.*
▷ **jobless** *adj* unemployed. **the jobless** *n* [pl *v*] people who are unemployed: *The government's new scheme is designed to help the jobless.* **joblessness** *n* [U].
□ **ˈjobcentre** *n* (*Brit*) (also *dated Brit* **Labour Exchange**) government office displaying information about available jobs. ➩ article at EMPLOYMENT.
ˈjob creation process of providing opportunities for paid work, esp for those who are currently unemployed: [attrib] *a ˌjob-creation ˈscheme, ˈproject, ˈprogramme, etc.*
ˈjob description written description of the exact responsibilities of a job.
ˌjob ˈlot mixed collection of articles, esp of poor quality, offered together for sale.
ˈjob satisfaction fulfilment gained from doing one's job.
ˈjob sharing arrangement by which two or more people are employed on a part-time basis to do work that would otherwise have been done by one person working full-time.

jobber /ˈdʒɒbə(r)/ *n* (*Brit*) (formerly) trader on the Stock Exchange who buys and sells shares without dealing directly with the public.

jobbery /ˈdʒɒbərɪ/ *n* [U] (*derog*) use of unfair or corrupt methods in order to gain a financial or political advantage.

jobbing /ˈdʒɒbɪŋ/ *adj* [attrib] doing single, specific (and esp small) pieces of work for payment: *a jobbing printer, gardener, etc.*

Jock /dʒɒk/ *n* (*infml sometimes offensive*) (often used as a term of address) Scotsman.

jockey¹ /ˈdʒɒkɪ/ *n* (*pl* ~**s**) person who rides a horse, usu a professional competing in races.

jockey² /ˈdʒɒkɪ/ *v* (phr v) **jockey for sth** manoeuvre to gain (an advantage, a favour, etc): *jockey for position, power, favours, etc.* **jockey sb into/out of sth** persuade sb by skilful management or unfair manoeuvring to do/give up sth: *They jockeyed Fred out of his position on the board.*

jock-strap /ˈdʒɒkstræp/ *n* close-fitting under-garment worn by sportsmen to support or protect the genitals.

jocose /dʒəʊˈkəʊs/ *adj* (*dated fml*) humorous; playful. ▷ **jocosely** *adv.* **jocosity** /dʒəʊˈkɒsətɪ/ *n* [U].

jocular /ˈdʒɒkjʊlə(r)/ *adj* **1** meant as a joke; humorous: *jocular remarks.* **2** fond of joking; playful: *a jocular fellow.* ▷ **jocularity** /ˌdʒɒkjʊˈlærətɪ/ *n* [U]. **jocularly** *adv*: *Philip, jocularly known as Flip.*

jocund /ˈdʒɒkənd/ *adj* (*dated*) merry; cheerful. ▷ **jocundity** /dʒəʊˈkʌndətɪ/ *n* [U].

jodhpurs /ˈdʒɒdpəz/ *n* [pl] trousers worn for horse-riding, loose above the knee and close fitting from the knee to the ankle: *a pair of jodhpurs.*

Jodrell Bank /ˌdʒɒdrəl ˈbæŋk/ place in Cheshire, England, where several large radio telescopes are sited. They are owned and run by Manchester University.

Joe Bloggs /ˌdʒəʊ ˈblɒgz/ (*Brit infml*) (*US* **Joe Blow** /ˌdʒəʊ ˈbləʊ/, **Joe Doakes** /ˌdʒəʊ ˈdəʊks/) (used as the name of an imaginary average ordinary man): *Joe Bloggs is usually more interested in sport than in politics.*

Joe Soap /ˌdʒəʊ ˈsəʊp/ (*Brit infml*) (used as a name for an imaginary foolish person who is easily deceived).

joey /ˈdʒəʊɪ/ *n* (*Austral infml*) young kangaroo.

jog /dʒɒg/ *v* (**-gg-**) **1** [Tn] push or knock (sb/sth) slightly: *Don't jog me, or you'll make me spill something!* **2** [I] (usu **go jogging**) run slowly and steadily for a time, for physical exercise: *He goes jogging every evening.* ➩ Usage at RUN¹. **3** [Ipr, Ip] move unsteadily, esp up and down, in a shaky manner: *The wagon jogged along (a rough track).* **4** [I] (of a horse) move at a jogtrot. **5** (idm) **jog sb's memory** help sb to recall sth: *This photograph may jog your memory.* **6** (phr v) **jog along/on** continue in a steady manner, with little or no excitement or progress: *For years the business just kept jogging along.*
▷ **jog** *n* [sing] **1** slight push, knock or shake; nudge: *He gave the pile of tins a jog and they all fell down.* ○ (*fig*) *give sb's memory a jog.* **2** spell of jogging as exercise: *Are you coming for a jog tomorrow morning?*
jogger /ˈdʒɒgə(r)/ *n* person who jogs for exercise. **jogging** /ˈdʒɒgɪŋ/ *n* [U].
□ **ˈjogtrot** *n* slow regular trot.

joggle /ˈdʒɒgl/ *v* [I, Ip, Tn, Tn·p] (cause sb/sth to) move or shake slightly, usu up and down.

John¹ /dʒɒn/ (1165-1216), king of England 1199-1216. The youngest son of *Henry II, he succeeded his brother *Richard I on his death, having previously tried to take the throne from him. He was an unpopular and unsuccessful king: he lost most of the English territory in France, and his methods of raising large amounts of money by taxation annoyed the barons so much that they forced him to sign *Magna Carta, which limited royal powers. ➩ App 3.

Augustus John: Madame Suggia

John² /dʒɒn/ Augustus (1878-1961), British painter of portraits and landscapes who was noted for his flamboyant appearance and bohemian life-style. He painted in a vigorous and sometimes almost visionary representational style. ➩ illus.

John³ /dʒɒn/ Gwen (1876-1939), British painter who lived most of her life in France. For a long time overshadowed by the work of her brother Augustus John, the quality of her painting is being increasingly recognized. She specialized in quiet interior scenes. ➩ illus.

John⁴ /dʒɒn/ **1** Saint, one of Christ's apostles, who is said to have written the fourth Gospel, three New Testament epistles and the Book of *Revelation. He was traditionally identified as the disciple 'whom Jesus loved' but many modern scholars have questioned this. **2** the fourth Gospel. **3** any of the three New Testament epistles said to have been written by St John. ➩ App 5.

john /dʒɒn/ *n* (*US sl*) lavatory: *go to the john.*

John Bull /ˌdʒɒn ˈbʊl/ (*dated*) typical Englishman, representing English people as a whole. He is usually shown in pictures as a stout red-faced farmer wearing a top hat and high boots. ➩ article at NATIONAL.

John Doe /ˌdʒɒn ˈdəʊ/ *n* **1** (*fem* **Jane Doe**) (used in US law as the name of a person whose real name is unknown) **2** (*US*) average ordinary man.

Gwen John: Young Woman Holding a Black Cat

John Dory /ˌdʒɒn ˈdɔːrɪ/ *n* European sea fish that has a round flat body with a dark spot on each side, and is often used for food.

johnny /ˈdʒɒnɪ/ *n* (*Brit*) **1** (*dated infml*) man; fellow. **2** (*sl*) condom: *a rubber johnny.*

□ **ˌjohnny-come-ˈlately** *n* (*pl* **johnnies-come-lately**, **johnny-come-latelys**, **johnny-come-latelies**) (*infml often derog*) person who has just arrived, esp one who quickly makes use of advantages earned by those who were there before; upstart.

John of Gaunt /ˌdʒɒn əv ˈgɔːnt/ (1340-99), English statesman, son of *Edward III, who acted as head of government towards the end of Edward's reign and before his successor *Richard II was old enough to rule. *Henry IV was his son.

John o' Groats /ˌdʒɒn ə ˈgrəʊts/ **1** village in north-east Scotland, traditionally regarded as the most northerly point on the British mainland. Cf LAND'S END. **2** (idm) **from Land's End to John O' Groats** ⇨ LAND'S END.

Johns Hopkins /ˌdʒɒnz ˈhɒpkɪnz/ university in Baltimore, Maryland, USA, founded in 1876.

Johnson[1] /ˈdʒɒnsn/ Amy (1903-41), English pilot who flew solo to Australia, Japan and South Africa in the 1930s. She is believed to have been drowned in the Thames estuary when her plane crashed there during the Second World War.

Johnson[2] /ˈdʒɒnsn/ Samuel (1709-84), English critic, poet and lexicographer. Born in Lichfield, he came to London and began to earn a living as a writer, contributing essays to journals, producing poems, etc. He was engaged to compile a comprehensive dictionary of English, which was published in 1755. His *Lives of the English Poets* is his outstanding critical work. As his biographer *Boswell recorded, in later life he became the leading figure on the London literary scene, famous for his eloquent and witty conversation. ⇨ illus at REYNOLDS.

Johnson[3] /ˈdʒɒnsn/ Andrew (1808-75), 17th president of the USA 1865-69, succeeding *Lincoln who had been assassinated. A Southerner, he allowed the *Confederate states to rejoin the Union after the Civil War, and was unsuccessfully impeached for doing so. ⇨ App 2.

Johnson[4] /ˈdʒɒnsn/ Lyndon Baines (1908-73), 36th president of the USA 1963-69. As vice-president, he succeeded the assassinated John *Kennedy. At home he introduced a series of social reforms, known as the 'Great Society' (eg new civil rights laws), but he became unpopular for involving the USA in the Vietnam War, and did not stand for re-election. ⇨ App 2.

John the Baptist /ˌdʒɒn ðə ˈbæptɪst/ Saint (c 12 BC-c 27 AD), (in the New Testament) preacher who lived and worked in the wilderness. He told of the coming of Christ, and baptized him in the River *Jordan. He was beheaded by King *Herod at the request of *Salome.

joie de vivre /ˌʒwɑː də ˈviːvrə/ (*French*) [U] cheerful enjoyment of life: *full of joie de vivre.*

join /dʒɔɪn/ *v* **1** [Tn, Tn·pr, Tn·p] ~ **sth onto sth/on**; ~ **A to B**; ~ **A and B (together/up)** fasten one thing to another; connect or combine two things: *Two extra carriages were joined onto the train/joined on at York.* ○ *join one section of pipe to the next* ○ *join two sections of pipe together* ○ *The island is joined to the mainland by a bridge.* ○ (*fig*) *join two people (together) in marriage*, ie make them man and wife. **2** [I, Ipr, Ip, Tn] ~ **up with sb/sth**; ~ **up** meet and unite with (sb/sth) to form one group or thing: *the place where the rivers join* ○ *The firm joined up with a small delivery company to reduce costs.* ○ *The M62 joins up with the M1/The M62 and the M1 join up south of Leeds.* ○ *The two groups of walkers joined up for the rest of the holiday.* ○ *The road joins the motorway at Newtown.* **3** [Tn] come into the company of (sb); meet: *I'll join you in a minute.* ○ *Ask him to join us for lunch.* ○ *Mary has just joined her family in Australia.* ○ *They joined* (ie got on) *the train at Watford.* **4** [I, Tn] become a member of (sth); become an employee in (sth): *Membership is free, so join today!* ○ *join a union, choir, club, etc* ○ *join the army, navy, police, etc.* **5** (**a**) [Tn] take part in (sth); take one's place in (sth): *join a demonstration, procession, queue, etc.* (**b**) [Ipr, Tn·pr] ~ **(with) sb in doing sth/to do sth**; ~ **together in doing sth/to do sth** take part with sb in an activity: *Mother joins (with) me in sending you our best wishes.* ○ *The class all joined together to sing 'Happy Birthday' to the teacher.* **6** (idm) **if you can't beat them join them** ⇨ BEAT[1]. **join battle (with sb)** (*fml*) begin fighting sb. **join the ˈclub** (said when sth bad that has already happened to oneself now happens to sb else): *You've got a parking-ticket? Well join the club!* **join ˈforces (with sb)** come together in order to achieve a common aim: *The two firms joined forces to win a major contract.* **join ˈhands** hold each other's hands. **7** (phr v) **join in (sth/doing sth)** take part in (an activity): *Can I join in (the game)?* ○ *They all joined in singing the Christmas carols.* **join up** become a member of the armed forces: *We both joined up in 1939.*

▷ **join** *n* place or line where two things are joined: *The two pieces were stuck together so well that you could hardly see the join.*

joiner /ˈdʒɔɪnə(r)/ *n* (*Brit*) skilled workman who makes the wooden fittings of a building, eg window frames and doors. Cf CARPENTER.

▷ **joinery** /ˈdʒɔɪnərɪ/ *n* [U] work of a joiner.

joint[1] /dʒɔɪnt/ *n* **1** structure in the body of an animal by which bones are fitted together: *ankle, knee, elbow, etc joints* ○ *suffer from stiff joints.* **2** place, line or surface at which two or more things are joined: *Check that the joints of the pipes are sealed properly.* **3** any of the parts into which a butcher cuts an animal's carcass; this cooked and served as meat: *a joint of beef* ○ *carve the Sunday joint.* **4** (*sl derog*) low or shabby bar, club, etc; house or shop. **5** (*sl*) cigarette containing marijuana. **6** (idm) **case the joint** ⇨ CASE[2]. **out of joint** (**a**) (of bones) pushed out of position; dislocated: *She fell and put her knee out of joint.* (**b**) (*fig*) in disorder; disorganized: *The delays put the whole schedule out of joint.* **put sb's nose out of joint** ⇨ NOSE[1].

▷ **joint** *v* [Tn esp passive] **1** provide (sth) with a joint or joints: *a jointed doll, fishing-rod.* **2** divide (a carcass) into joints or at the joints: *a jointed chicken.*

joint[2] /dʒɔɪnt/ *adj* [attrib] **1** shared, held or done by two or more people together: *a joint account*, ie a bank account in the name of more than one person (eg husband and wife) ○ *joint ownership, responsibility, consultation* ○ *a joint effort.* **2** sharing in an activity, a position, an achievement, etc: *joint authors, owners, winners, etc.* ▷ **jointly** *adv*: *a jointly owned business.*

□ **joint-ˈstock company** = STOCK COMPANY (STOCK[1]).

joist /dʒɔɪst/ *n* one of the long thick pieces of wood or metal that are used to support a floor or ceiling in a building.

joke /dʒəʊk/ *n* **1** thing said (eg a story with a funny ending) or done to cause amusement, laughter, etc: *tell (sb) a joke* ○ *cracking jokes with one's friends.* **2** [sing] ridiculous person, thing or situation: *His attempts at cooking are a complete joke.* **3** (idm) **be no ˈjoke**; **be/get beyond a ˈjoke** be/become a serious matter: *Trying to find a job these days is no joke, I can tell you.* ○ *All your teasing of poor Michael is getting beyond a joke.* **have a joke with sb** share the pleasure of laughing at sth with sb: *He's someone I have an occasional chat and joke with.* **the joke's on sb** (*infml*) sb who tried to make another person look foolish now looks ridiculous instead. **make a joke about/of sb/sth** speak lightly or amusingly about sb/sth. **play a joke/prank/trick on sb** trick sb, in order to make him appear ridiculous. **see the ˈjoke** understand why sth said or done is amusing: *I'm sorry but I can't see the joke.* **take a ˈjoke** accept playful remarks or tricks with good humour: *Can't you take a joke?*

▷ **joke** *v* **1** [I, Ipr] ~ **(with sb) (about sth)** tell jokes (to sb) (about sth); talk in a light-hearted, frivolous way: *I was only joking.* ○ *For Pat to lose his job is nothing to joke about*, ie is a serious matter. **2** (idm) **joking aˈpart** speaking seriously: *Joking apart, you ought to smoke fewer cigarettes, you know.* **you must be/have got to be ˈjoking** (used to express mocking disbelief): *'Jackie's passed her driving test.' 'You must be joking — she can't even steer straight!'*

jokey *adj* joking; amusing or ridiculous.

jokingly *adv* in a joking manner.

joker /ˈdʒəʊkə(r)/ *n* **1** (*infml*) person who is fond of making jokes; foolish irresponsible person: *Some joker's been playing around with my car aerial!* **2** (*infml*) person who is not treated seriously: *I don't want that joker in my sales team.* **3** extra playing-card used in certain card-games. **4** (*US*) clause added without warning to a document (eg a contract), which changes its effectiveness in a way that may not become immediately apparent.

jolly /ˈdʒɒlɪ/ *adj* (**-ier**, **-iest**) **1** happy and cheerful: *a jolly person, manner, laugh.* **2** (*dated infml*) lively and very pleasant; delightful or enjoyable; merry: *a jolly party, song, time.* **3** cheerful because slightly drunk: *feel/look jolly.* **4** (idm) **ˌjolly ˈhockey sticks** (*Brit catchphrase*) (used to suggest the cheerful athletic style of life associated with (esp private) girls' schools).

▷ **jollification** /ˌdʒɒlɪfɪˈkeɪʃn/ *n* [U, C] (*dated*) merry-making; festivity.

jollity /ˈdʒɒlətɪ/ *n* [U] (*dated*) state of being jolly.

jolly *adv* (*Brit infml*) **1** very: *She's a jolly good teacher.* ○ *He can cook, and he does it jolly well.* **2** (idm) **ˈjolly well** (used to emphasize a statement) certainly: *'Will you come back for me?' 'No — if you don't come now, you can jolly well walk home.'*

jolly *v* (*pt, pp* **jollied**) (phr v) **jolly sb along** (*infml*) keep sb in a good/friendly mood so that he will help, work, etc: *You'll have to jolly him along a bit, but he'll do a good job.* **jolly sth up** make sth bright and pleasant to look at; cheer sth up: *This room needs jollying up - how about yellow and red wallpaper?*

□ **the ˌJolly ˈRoger** the black flag of a pirate ship (with skull and cross-bones).

jolly-boat /ˈdʒɒlɪ bəʊt/ *n* type of ship's boat.

jolt /dʒəʊlt/ *v* **1** [I, Ipr, Ip, Tn, Tn·pr, Tn·p] (cause sb/sth to) move with sudden jerky movements: *The old bus jolted along (a rough track).* **2** (phr v) **jolt sb into/out of sth** make sb act by giving him a sudden shock: *He was jolted out of his lethargy and into action when he realized he had only a short time to finish the article.*

▷ **jolt** *n* (esp *sing*) **1** sudden bump or shake; jerk: *stop with a jolt.* **2** (*fig*) surprise; shock: *The news of the accident gave her an unpleasant jolt/quite a jolt.* **jolty** *adj* jolting.

Jonah /ˈdʒəʊnə/ *n* **1** (**a**) (in the Old Testament) Hebrew prophet who, as a punishment for disobeying God, was thrown overboard from his boat and swallowed by a huge fish. He later escaped. (**b**) book of the Old Testament which tells the story of Jonah. ⇨ App 5. **2** (*infml*) person who is thought to or seems to bring bad luck.

the Queen's House, Greenwich, designed by Inigo Jones

Jones[1] /dʒəʊnz/ Inigo (1573-1652), English architect and stage designer who introduced the Italian (or *Palladian) style to Britain. His best-known buildings are the Queen's House, Greenwich and the Banqueting Hall, Whitehall. ⇨ illus. ⇨ article at ARCHITECTURE.

Jones[2] /dʒəʊnz/ Robert Tyre ('Bobby') (1902-71), American golfer. Though he played competitively for only 8 years and as an amateur, he is generally regarded as the greatest golfer ever.

Joneses /ˈdʒəʊnzɪz/ *n* [pl] (idm) **keep up with the Joneses** ⇨ KEEP[1].

jonquil /ˈdʒɒŋkwɪl/ *n* type of narcissus with white or yellow sweet-smelling flowers.

Jonson /ˈdʒɒnsn/ Ben (1572-1637), English playwright and poet, best known for his great comedies *Every Man in his Humour, Volpone, The Alchemist* and *Bartholomew Fair.* He was a contemporary and friend of Shakespeare.

Joplin /ˈdʒɒplɪn/ Scott (1868-1917), American jazz pianist and composer who created ragtime.

Jordan

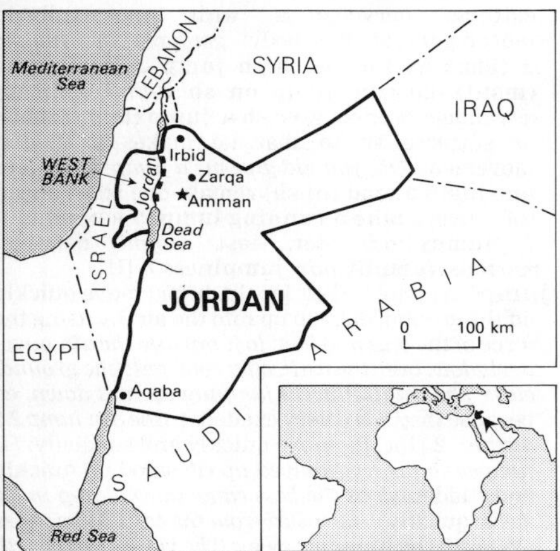

Jordan /ˈdʒɔːdn/ **1** country in the Middle East, bordering Saudi Arabia, Israel and Syria; pop approx 3 943 000; official language Arabic; capital Amman; unit of currency dinar (= 1 000 fils). It was created from former territory of the *Ottoman Empire after the Second World War, and its king since 1952 has been Hussein. ⇨ map. **2** river that passes through Syria and the Lebanon, forms part of the boundary between Israel and Jordan, and flows into the *Dead Sea. *John the Baptist baptized Christ in it. ▷ **Jordanian** /dʒɔːˈdeɪnɪən/ *adj, n.*

Joseph[1] /ˈdʒəʊzɪf, ˈdʒəʊsɪf/ (in the Old Testament) son of *Jacob, who was sold into captivity in Egypt by his jealous brothers but rose to become a high official there.

Joseph[2] /ˈdʒəʊzɪf, ˈdʒəʊsɪf/ (in the New Testament) husband of the Virgin *Mary.

josh /dʒɒʃ/ *v* (*US infml*) **1** [I] joke. **2** [Tn] tease (sb).

Joshua /ˈdʒɒʃʊə/ (**a**) (in the Old Testament) 13th-century BC leader of the *Israelites who succeeded *Moses and led his people into *Canaan. He attacked the city of *Jericho, whose walls collapsed when he ordered trumpets to be blown. (**b**) book of the Old Testament that tells the story of Joshua. ⇨ App 5.

joss-stick /ˈdʒɒstɪk/ *n* thin stick that burns slowly and produces a smell of incense.

jostle /ˈdʒɒsl/ *v* [I, Ipr, Tn] **1** ~ (**against sb**) push roughly against (sb), usu in a crowd: *The youths jostled (against) an old lady on the pavement.* **2** ~ (**with sb**) (**for sth**) compete with (other people) in a forceful manner in order to gain sth: *advertisers jostling (with each other) for the public's attention.*

jot[1] /dʒɒt/ *v* (**-tt-**) (phr v) **jot sth down** make a quick, usu short, written note of sth: *I'll just jot down their phone number before I forget it.*

▷ **jotter** *n* notebook or pad for short written notes. **jot·tings** *n* [pl] short written notes.

jot[2] /dʒɒt/ *n* [sing] (usu with a negative) very small amount: *I don't care a jot for their feelings.* ○ *There's not a jot of truth in his story.*

joule /dʒuːl/ *n* (*abbr* **J**) (*physics*) unit of energy or work.

journal /ˈdʒɜːnl/ *n* **1** newspaper or periodical, esp one that is serious and deals with a specialized subject: *a medical, a scientific, an educational, etc journal* ○ *a trade journal* ○ *The Wall Street Journal* ○ *The Architects' Journal* ○ *subscribe to a journal.* **2** daily record of news, events, business transactions, etc: *He kept a journal of his wanderings across Asia.*

▷ **journalese** /ˌdʒɜːnəˈliːz/ *n* [U] (*derog*) style of language thought to be typical of newspapers, containing many clichés. Cf OFFICIALESE (OFFICIAL).

journalism /ˈdʒɜːnəlɪzəm/ *n* [U] work of collecting, writing, editing and publishing material in newspapers and magazines or on television and radio: *a career in journalism.*

journalist /-nəlɪst/ *n* person whose profession is journalism: *He's a journalist on the 'Daily Telegraph'.* Cf REPORTER (REPORT[1]).

journalistic /ˌdʒɜːnəˈlɪstɪk/ *adj* [attrib] of journalism; characteristic of journalism.

journey /ˈdʒɜːnɪ/ *n* (*pl* ~**s**) (**a**) (distance covered in) travelling, usu by land, from one place to another, often far away: *Did you have a good journey?* ○ *go on a long train journey* ○ *break one's journey,* ie interrupt it by stopping briefly at a place ○ *the journey from Edinburgh to London* ○ (*fig*) *our great journey through life.* (**b**) time taken in going from one place to another: *It's a day's journey by car.*

▷ **journey** *v* [Ipr, Ip] go on a journey; travel: *journeying overland across North America.*

NOTE ON USAGE: **Journey** may indicate a long distance or a short one travelled regularly: *'How long is your journey to work?' 'Only about 15 minutes.'* A **voyage** is a long journey by sea or in space. The word **travels** [pl] suggests a fairly long period of travelling from place to place, especially abroad, for pleasure or interest. It is often used with a possessive adjective: *She's gone off on her travels again.* **Travel** is an uncountable noun indicating the action of travelling: *Travel broadens the mind.* A **tour** is a (short or long) journey for pleasure, spent visiting several places: *They're going on a world tour.* A **trip** and (more formal) an **excursion** are short journeys and visits from and returning to a particular place. **Excursion** suggests a group of people travelling together: *During our holiday in Venice we went on a few trips/excursions to places near by.*

journeyman /ˈdʒɜːnɪmən/ *n* (*pl* **-men** /-mən/) **1** trained worker who works for an employer: [attrib] *a journeyman printer.* **2** reliable and competent but not outstanding worker: [attrib] *a journeyman artist.*

joust /dʒaʊst/ *v* [I] (of knights in medieval times) fight on horseback with lances.

Jove /dʒəʊv/ *n* (idm) **by Jove** (*dated infml*) (used to express surprise or to emphasize a statement): *By Jove, I think you're right!*

jovial /ˈdʒəʊvɪəl/ *adj* very cheerful and good-humoured; merry: *a friendly jovial fellow* ○ *in a jovial mood.* ▷ **joviality** /ˌdʒəʊvɪˈælətɪ/ *n* [U]. **jovially** /-ɪəlɪ/ *adv.*

jowl /dʒaʊl/ *n* **1** (usu *pl*) jaw; lower part of the face: *a man with heavy jowls/a heavy-jowled man,* ie one with heavy jaws, with a fold or folds of flesh hanging from the chin. **2** (idm) **cheek by jowl** ⇨ CHEEK.

joy /dʒɔɪ/ *n* **1** [U] feeling of great happiness: *the sheer joy of seeing you again after all these years* ○ *overcome with (a deep sense of) joy* ○ *to dance, jump, shout, etc for joy,* ie because of feeling great joy. **2** [C] person or thing that makes one feel very happy: *He is a great joy to listen to.* ○ *one of the simple joys of life.* **3** (idm) **full of the joys of spring** ⇨ FULL. **(get/have) no joy (from sb)** (obtain) no success or satisfaction: *They complained about the bad service, but got no joy from the manager.* **sb's pride and joy** ⇨ PRIDE.

▷ **joyful** /-fl/ *adj* filled with, showing or causing joy: *joyful celebrations* ○ *on this joyful occasion.* **joyfully** /-fəlɪ/ *adv.* **joyfulness** *n* [U].

joyless *adj* without joy; gloomy or miserable: *a joyless marriage, childhood, etc.* **joylessly** *adv.* **joylessness** *n* [U].

joyous /ˈdʒɔɪəs/ *adj* (*fml*) filled with, showing or causing joy: *a joyous sense of freedom.* **joyously** *adv.* **joyousness** *n* [U].

□ **ˈjoy-ride** *n* (*infml*) car ride taken for fun and excitement, usu without the owner's permission: *teenagers going for joy-rides round town.* **ˈjoy-rider** *n.* **ˈjoy-riding** *n* [U].

Joyce /dʒɔɪs/ James Augustine Aloysius (1882-1941), Irish novelist who lived abroad for most of his life. His two greatest works, *Ulysses* (originally banned in Britain for obscenity) and *Finnegans Wake,* revolutionized the techniques of fiction-writing, introducing the 'stream of consciousness' (which represents a continuous flow of thoughts), inventing words, and experimenting with syntax. His earlier books include *The Dubliners,* a collection of short stories, and the autobiographical *Portrait of the Artist as a Young Man.*

joystick /ˈdʒɔɪstɪk/ *n* control-lever on an aircraft, a computer, etc.

JP /ˌdʒeɪ ˈpiː/ *abbr* (*law*) Justice of the Peace: *Clive Small JP.*

Jr *abbr* = JNR.

jubilant /ˈdʒuːbɪlənt/ *adj* (*fml*) ~ (**about/at/over sth**) showing great happiness, esp because of a success: *Liverpool were in a jubilant mood after their cup victory.*

▷ **jubilantly** *adv.*

jubilation /ˌdʒuːbɪˈleɪʃn/ *n* [U] great happiness, esp because of a success: *express great jubilation.*

jubilee /ˈdʒuːbɪliː/ *n* (celebration of a) special anniversary of an event. Cf DIAMOND JUBILEE (DIAMOND), GOLDEN JUBILEE (GOLDEN), SILVER JUBILEE (SILVER).

Judaism /ˈdʒuːdeɪɪzəm; *US* -dɪɪzəm/ *n* [U] religion of the Jewish people; their culture.

▷ **Judaic** /dʒuːˈdeɪɪk/ *adj* [attrib] of Jews and Judaism. ⇨ Usage at CHRISTIAN.

Judas /ˈdʒuːdəs/ *n* **1** (also **Judas Iscariot** /ˌdʒuːdəs ɪˈskærɪət/) one of Christ's apostles, who betrayed Christ to the Jewish authorities so that he was arrested and crucified. Judas later killed himself. **2** person who betrays a friend; traitor: *You Judas!*

judder /ˈdʒʌdə(r)/ *v* [I, Ipr, Ip] shake violently: *The plane juddered to a halt,* ie shook violently and then stopped.

▷ **judder** *n* [sing] violent shaking: *The engine gave a sudden judder.*

Jude /dʒu:d/ **1** Saint, one of Christ's apostles. **2** last epistle in the New Testament, said to have been written by St Jude. ⇨ App 5.

judge[1] /dʒʌdʒ/ *n* **1** public officer with authority to decide cases in a lawcourt: *a High Court judge* ○ *The case came before Judge Cooper last week.* ○ *The judge found him guilty and sentenced him to five years*, ie in gaol. Cf MAGISTRATE. ⇨ article at LAW. **2** person who decides who has won a competition, contest, etc: *a panel of judges at the flower show* ○ (in the rules of many competitions) *The judges' decision is final*, ie It cannot be changed or challenged. **3** person qualified and able to give an opinion on the value or merits of sth: *a good judge of art, wine, character* ○ *I thought that the third violinist was the best player — not that I'm any judge*, ie though I do not know much about the subject. **4** (idm) **sober as a judge** ⇨ SOBER.

judge[2] /dʒʌdʒ/ *v* **1** [I, Ipr, Tn, Tn·pr, Tf no passive, Tw no passive, Cn·a, Cn·t] ~ (**sb/sth**) **by/from sth** form an opinion about (sb/sth); estimate (the value, amount, etc of sth); consider: *As far as I can judge, they are all to blame.* ○ *to judge by appearances* ○ *Judging from previous experience, he will be late.* ○ *It is difficult to judge the full extent of the damage.* ○ *The performance was good, when judged by their usual standards.* ○ *He judged that it was time to open the proceedings.* ○ *I find it hard to judge how the election will go*, ie who will win. ○ *The committee judged it advisable to postpone the meeting.* ○ *I judged him to be about 50.* **2** [I, Tn] **(a)** decide (a case) in a lawcourt; make a decision about (sb) in a lawcourt; try[1](3a): *judge fairly, harshly, leniently, etc* ○ *judge a murder case.* **(b)** speak critically and harshly about (sb): *You're no better than they are: who are you to judge other people?* **3** [Tn] decide the result or winner in (a competition): *The flower show was judged by the local MP.*

judgement (also, *esp in legal use*, **judgment**) /ˈdʒʌdʒmənt/ *n* **1** [C] ~ (**of/about sth**) opinion about sth: *make an unfair judgement of sb's character* ○ *My judgement is that/In my judgement the plan is ill-conceived.* **2** [C, U] decision of a lawcourt or judge; verdict: *The judgement was given in favour of the accused*, ie the accused was declared not guilty. ○ *The court has still to pass judgement* (ie give a decision) *in this case.* **3 (a)** [U] ability to come to sensible conclusions and make wise decisions; good sense; discernment: *He lacks sound judgement.* ○ *display/exercise/show excellent judgement.* **(b)** [U, C] action or process of judging: *errors of judgement.* **4** [sing] **a** ~ (**on sb**) misfortune considered to be a punishment from God for doing sth wrong: *This failure is a judgement on you for being so lazy.* **5** (idm) **against one's better judgement** ⇨ BETTER[1]. **an error of judgement** ⇨ ERROR. **reserve judgement** ⇨ RESERVE[1]. **sit in judgement** ⇨ SIT.

□ ˈ**Judgement Day** (also **the Day of ˈJudgement**, **the Last ˈJudgement**) the day at the end of the world when God will judge everyone who has ever lived.

Judges /ˈdʒʌdʒɪz/ [sing *v*] book of the Old Testament that tells the story of how the *Israelites conquered *Canaan under various leaders (known as *judges*). ⇨ App 5.

judicature /ˈdʒu:dɪkətʃə(r)/ *n* (*law*) **1** [U] administration of justice. **2** [CGp] group of judges; judiciary.

judicial /dʒu:ˈdɪʃl/ *adj* [attrib] **1** of or by a court of law; of a judge or of judgement: *a judicial inquiry, review, system* ○ *the judicial process* ○ *take judicial proceedings against sb*, ie bring a case against him in court. **2** able to judge things wisely; critical; impartial: *a judicial mind.* ▷ **judicially** /-ʃəlɪ/ *adv.*

□ **juˌdicial ˈmurder** (*law*) sentence of death that is legal but considered unjust.

juˌdicial sepaˈration (*law*) order that forbids a man and wife to live together but does not end the marriage.

judiciary /dʒu:ˈdɪʃərɪ; *US* -ʃɪerɪ/ *n* [CGp] judges of a country collectively.

judicious /dʒu:ˈdɪʃəs/ *adj* showing or having good sense: *a judicious choice, decision, remark.* ▷ **judiciously** *adv.* **judiciousness** *n* [U].

judo /ˈdʒu:dəʊ/ *n* [U] sport of wrestling and self-defence between two people who try to throw each other to the ground.

jug[1] /dʒʌg/ *n* **1** [C] (*Brit*) (*US* **pitcher**) **(a)** deep vessel, with a handle and a lip, for holding and pouring liquids: *pour milk into/from a jug* ○ *a milk/coffee/water jug.* **(b)** amount of liquid contained in this: *spill a whole jug of juice.* **2** [U] (*sl*) prison: *three months in jug.*

▷ **jugful** /-fʊl/ *n* amount of liquid contained in a jug.

jug[2] /dʒʌg/ *v* (**-gg-**) [Tn usu passive] stew (hare) in a covered dish: *jugged hare.*

juggernaut /ˈdʒʌgənɔ:t/ *n* **1** (*Brit esp derog*) very large articulated lorry: *juggernauts roaring through our country villages.* **2** large, powerful and destructive force or institution: *the juggernaut of bureaucracy.*

juggling

juggler

juggle /ˈdʒʌgl/ *v* **1** [I, Ipr, Tn] ~ (**with sth**) throw (a number of objects, usu balls) up into the air, catch them and throw them into the air again and again, keeping one or more in the air at the same time: *When did you learn to juggle?* ○ *to juggle (with) plates, balls, hoops, etc.* **2** [Ipr, Tn] ~ **with sth** change the arrangement of sth constantly in order to achieve a satisfactory result or to deceive people: *juggling with one's timetable to fit in the extra classes* ○ *The government has been juggling (with) the figures to hide the latest rise in unemployment.*

▷ **juggler** /ˈdʒʌglə(r)/ *n* person who juggles (JUGGLE 1). ⇨ illus.

jugular /ˈdʒʌgjʊlə(r)/ *adj* of the neck or throat.

▷ **jugular** *n* **1** (also **jugular ˈvein**) any of several veins in the neck that return blood from the head to the heart. **2** (idm) **go for the ˈjugular** (*infml*) make a fierce destructive attack on the weakest point in an opponent's argument.

juice /dʒu:s/ *n* **1** [U, C] **(a)** liquid obtained from a fruit; drink made from this: *squeeze some more juice from a lemon* ○ *a carton of fresh orange, pineapple, grapefruit, etc juice* ○ *One tomato juice and one soup, please.* **(b)** liquid that comes from a piece of meat when it is cooked: *Wrapping aluminium foil round a joint allows the meat to cook in its own juice/juices.* **2** [C usu *pl*] liquid in the stomach or another part of the body that helps sb to digest food: *gastric/digestive juices.* **3** [U] (*infml*) electric current: *turn on the juice.* **4** [U] (*infml*) petrol: *We ran out of juice on the motorway.* **5** (idm) **stew in one's own juice** ⇨ STEW.

juicy /ˈdʒu:sɪ/ *adj* (**-ier, -iest**) **1** containing a lot of juice and being enjoyable to eat; succulent: *fresh juicy oranges.* **2** (*infml*) interesting (esp because scandalous): *juicy gossip, stories, scenes, etc* ○ *Tell me all the juicy details!* **3** (*infml*) producing a lot of money; profitable: *a nice juicy contract.* ▷ **juiciness** *n* [U].

ju-jitsu /dʒu:ˈdʒɪtsu:/ *n* [U] Japanese art of self-defence from which judo was developed.

ju-ju /ˈdʒu:dʒu:/ *n* **(a)** [C] W African charm believed to have magic power; fetish. **(b)** [U] its magic power.

jujube /ˈdʒu:dʒu:b/ *n* small flavoured jelly-like sweet.

juke-box /ˈdʒu:kbɒks/ *n* large record-player in a café, bar, etc that automatically plays chosen records when a coin is inserted.

Jul *abbr* July: *21 Jul 1965.*

julep /ˈdʒu:lɪp/ *n* [C, U] (*US*) alcoholic drink made from spirit (usu whisky), sugar, mint and ice: *mint julep.*

Julian calendar /ˌdʒu:lɪən ˈkælɪndə(r)/ **the Julian calendar** calendar introduced by Julius Caesar in Rome in 46 BC. Cf GREGORIAN CALENDAR (GREGORIAN). ⇨ App 10.

Julius Caesar /ˌdʒu:lɪəs ˈsi:zə(r)/ (also **Caesar**) Gaius (100-44 BC), Roman general and statesman. He led the Roman army which conquered Gaul, and in 55 BC invaded Britain. He returned to Rome in triumph, defeating his enemy Pompey, and taking over control of the city and its empire as a virtual dictator. He was murdered on the *Ides of March in 44 BC by conspirators led by Brutus and Cassius (an episode portrayed by Shakespeare in his play *Julius Caesar*). They were republican supporters who feared that he was trying to make himself into a king. The name Caesar was taken by later Roman emperors.

July /dʒu:ˈlaɪ/ *n* [U, C] (*abbr* **Jul**) the seventh month of the year, next after June.

For the uses of *July* see the examples at *April.*

jumble /ˈdʒʌmbl/ *v* [usu passive: Tn, Tn·p] ~ [illegible] (**up**) mix (things) in a confused way: *Toys, books, shoes and clothes were jumbled (up) on the floor.* ○ (*fig*) *Details of the accident were all jumbled up in his mind.*

▷ **jumble** *n* **1** [sing] ~ (**of sth**) confused or untidy group of things; muddle: *a jumble of books and papers on the table.* **2** [U] (*Brit*) mixed collection of old unwanted goods for a jumble sale.

□ ˈ**jumble sale** (*Brit*) (*US* ˈ**rummage sale**) sale of a mixed collection of old unwanted goods in order to raise money, usu for a charity: *hold a jumble sale in aid of hospital funds.*

jumbo /ˈdʒʌ[illegible]/ *adj* [attrib] (*infml*) unusually large; [illegible] *jumbo(-sized) packet of washing-pow[illegible].*

▷ **jumbo** *n* (*pl* ~**s**) (also ˌ**jumbo ˈjet**) very large aircraft that can carry several hundred passengers.

jump[1] /dʒʌmp/ *n* **1** [C] act of jumping: *a parachute jump* ○ *a superb jump.* **2** [C] obstacle to be jumped over: *The horse fell at the last jump.* ○ *The water-jump is the most difficult part of the race.* **3** [C] ~ (**in sth**) sudden rise in amount, price or value: *The company's results show a huge jump in profits.* **4** [C] sudden change to a different condition or set of circumstances; leap: *the country's great j[illegible]rward to a new technological era.* [illegible] [pl] (*infml*) state of extreme nervousness with uncontrollable movements of the body: *get/have the jumps.* **6** (idm) **be for the high jump** ⇨ HIGH JUMP (HIGH[1]). **get the jump on sb** (*infml*) gain an advantage over sb. **give sb a ˈjump** (*infml*) shock or surprise sb so that he makes a sudden movement: *Oh, you did give me a jump!* **keep, etc one jump ahead (of sb)** remain one stage ahead (of a rival). **take a running jump** ⇨ RUNNING.

▷ **jumpy** *adj* (**-ier, -iest**) (*infml*) nervous; anxious. **jumpily** *adv.* **jumpiness** *n* [U].

jump[2] /dʒʌmp/ *v* **1** [I, Ipr, Ip, In/pr] move quickly off the ground, etc, esp up into the air, by using the force of the legs and feet: *to jump into the air, out of a window, over the wall, off a roof, onto the ground, etc* ○ *The children were jumping up and down*, eg because they were very excited. ○ *She can jump 2.2 metres.* **2** [Ipr, Ip] move quickly and suddenly: *He jumped to his feet/jumped up* (ie stood up quickly and suddenly) *as the boss came in.* ○ *'Jump in* (ie get in quickly)*', he called from the car.* **3** [Tn] pass over (sth) by jumping; clear: *The horses jumped all the fences.* **4** [I] move suddenly with a jerk because of excitement, surprise, shock, etc; start: *The loud bang made me jump.* ○ *Her heart jumped when she heard the news.* ⇨ Usage. **5** [I, Ipr, Ip] (of a device) move suddenly and unexpectedly, esp out of its correct position: *a typewriter that jumps*, ie omitting letters ○ *The needle jumps on this record.* **6** [Ipr] ~ **from sth to sth** change suddenly from discussing one subject to another subject: *I couldn't understand his lecture because he kept* *jumping from one topic to the next.* **7** [Ipr, It, Tn] ~ **from sth to sth** pass over sth to a further point; omit or skip: *The film suddenly jumped from the events of 1920 to those of 1930.* ○ *jump several steps in an argument.* **8** [I, In/pr] ~ **(by) sth** rise suddenly by a very large amount: *Prices jumped (by) 60% last year.* **9** [Tn] (*infml*) attack (sb) suddenly: *The gang jumped an old woman in the subway.* **10** [Tn] (*infml usu US*) travel illegally on (a train): *jump a freight train.* **11** (idm) **climb/jump on the bandwagon** ⇨ BANDWAGON (BAND). **go (and) jump in the/a ˈlake** (usu in the imperative) (*dated infml*) go away. **jump ˈbail** fail to appear for a trial after being released on bail. **jump down sb's ˈthroat** (*infml*) speak to sb in an angry, critical way. **jump for ˈjoy** show one's delight at sth by excited movements: *The children are jumping for joy at the thought of an extra day's holiday.* **jump the ˈgun (a)** start a race before the starting-gun has been fired. **(b)** do sth too soon, before the proper time: *They jumped the gun by building the garage before permission had been given.* **jump the ˈlights** ignore and pass a red traffic-light. **jump out of one's ˈskin** be extremely surprised: *The shock of seeing her again made me nearly jump out of my skin.* **jump the ˈqueue** (*Brit*) **(a)** go to the front of a queue of people without waiting for one's proper turn. **(b)** obtain sth unfairly without waiting for one's proper turn. **jump the ˈrails/ˈtrack** (of a train, etc) leave the rails suddenly. **jump ˈship** leave the ship on which one is serving, without having obtained permission. **jump to conˈclusions** come to a decision about sb/sth too quickly, before one has thought about all the facts: *I know I was standing near the till when you came back into the shop, but don't jump to conclusions.* **jump ˈto it** (usu in the imperative) (*infml*) hurry up: *The bus will be leaving in five minutes, so jump to it!* **wait for the cat to jump/to see which way the cat jumps** ⇨ WAIT[1]. **12** (phr v) **jump at sth** seize (an opportunity, a chance, etc) eagerly: *If they offered me a job in the USA, I'd jump at the chance.* **jump on sb** (*infml*) criticize or challenge sb sharply: *My maths teacher really used to jump on us when we got our answers wrong.*

□ **ˈjumped-up** *adj* [attrib] (*Brit infml derog*) thinking of oneself as more important than one really is; upstart: *that new jumped-up boss of ours.*

jumping-ˈoff place (also **jumping-ˈoff point**) place from where a journey, plan, campaign, etc is begun or launched.

ˈjump-jet *n* jet aircraft that can take off and land vertically.

ˈjump-lead *n* (usu *pl*) one of two cables used for carrying electric current from one car battery to another one that has no power in it.

ˈjump-off *n* (in show-jumping) extra round held to decide the winner when two or more horses have the same score.

ˈjump-rope *n* (*US*) = SKIPPING-ROPE (SKIP[1]).

ˈjump seat (*esp US*) folding seat in a car or an aircraft.

ˈjump-start *v* [Tn] start (a car) by pushing or rolling it and then engaging the gears instead of using the starter motor. **ˈjump-start** *n.*

ˈjump suit one-piece garment of trousers and jacket or shirt.

NOTE ON USAGE: **Leap** and **spring** suggest a more energetic movement than **jump. Spring** usually indicates a deliberate movement forward: *The cat sprang forward and caught the mouse.* We can **leap** and **jump** in any direction: *jump/leap into the car, onto the platform, to one's feet, up the stairs* ○ *jump/leap up, down, forwards, back, etc.* We also **jump** in surprise: *The sudden noise made me jump.* **Bounce** indicates repeated movement up and down, often while jumping on a springy surface: *bounce on a bed/trampoline.*

jumper /ˈdʒʌmpə(r)/ *n* **1** (*Brit*) = JERSEY 1. **2** (*US*) pinafore. **3** person, animal or insect that jumps. **4** short wire used for completing or breaking an electrical circuit.

Jun *abbr* **1** June: *12 Jun 1803.* **2** = JNR.

junction /ˈdʒʌŋkʃn/ *n* **1** [C] place where roads or railway lines meet: *a pub near the junction of London Road and Chaucer Avenue* ○ *Join the M1 at Junction 11.* ○ *The accident happened at one of the country's busiest railway junctions.* **2** [C, U] (*fml*) (instance of) joining or being joined: *effect a junction of two armies.*

□ **ˈjunction box** box containing a connection between electric circuits.

juncture /ˈdʒʌŋktʃə(r)/ *n* (idm) **at this juncture** (*fml*) at a particular, esp important, stage in a series of events: *It is very difficult at this juncture to predict the company's future.*

June /dʒu:n/ *n* [U, C] (*abbr* **Jun**) the sixth month of the year, next after May.

For the uses of *June* see the examples at *April.*

Jung /jʊŋ/ Carl Gustav (1875-1961), Swiss psychologist who developed the theory of the 'collective unconscious'. This states that the unconscious mind contains memories and instincts inherited from earlier in human history. In the first part of his career he was a colleague of *Freud.

▷ **Jungian** /ˈjʊŋɪən/ *n, adj* (supporter) of Jung or his ideas.

jungle /ˈdʒʌŋgl/ *n* **1** [U, C] area of land, usu in a tropical country, that is covered with a thick growth of trees and tangled plants: *There's not much jungle 100 miles inland.* ○ *The new road was hacked out of the jungle.* ○ *the dense jungles of Africa and South America* ○ [attrib] *jungle warfare*, ie war fought in the jungle, where surprise attacks by small groups are difficult to anticipate or avoid. **2** [sing] confused, disordered and complicated mass of things: *a jungle of welfare regulations.* **3** [C] place of intense or confusing struggle: *the blackboard jungle*, ie school(s) where pupils are very disruptive and hostile to their teachers ○ *the concrete jungle*, ie a typical modern city with a dense mass of ugly high-rise concrete buildings and in which life is bewildering and sometimes violent. **4** (idm) **the law of the jungle** ⇨ LAW.

▷ **jungly** /ˈdʒʌŋglɪ/ *adj* (*infml*) of, like or from the jungle or its inhabitants.

□ **ˌjungle ˈfever** type of severe malarial fever.

junior /ˈdʒu:nɪə(r)/ *adj* **1** ~ **(to sb)** lower in rank or standing (than sb): *a junior clerk in an office* ○ *He is several years junior to Mrs Cooper.* **2 Junior** (*abbrs* **Jnr**, **Jr**, **Jun**) (*esp US*) (used after a name to refer to a son who has the same name as his father or to the younger of two boys having the same name in a school, university, etc): *Sammy Davies, Jnr.* Cf MINOR 2. **3** (*Brit*) of or intended for children from the ages of 7 to 11: *junior school.* Cf SENIOR.

▷ **junior** *n* **1** person who holds a low rank in a profession; person with an unimportant job: *the office junior.* **2** [sing] (used with *his, her, your,* etc) person who is a specified number of years younger than sb else: *He is three years her junior/her junior by three years.* **3** (*Brit*) child who goes to junior school: *The juniors' Christmas party is on Tuesday.* **4** (*US*) student in his third year of a four-year course at college or high school. **5** (*US infml*) way of addressing a son in a family: *Come here, Junior!*

□ **ˌjunior ˈcollege** (in the USA) college that provides a two-year course equivalent to the first two years of a four-year undergraduate course.

ˌjunior ˈcommon room (also **ˌjunior combiˈnation room**) (*abbr* **JCR**) room used by the undergraduates in a college eg for reading, watching television, etc.

juniper /ˈdʒu:nɪpə(r)/ *n* evergreen bush with purple berries which are used in medicine and as a flavouring in gin.

junk[1] /dʒʌŋk/ *n* [U] **1** (*infml*) things that are considered useless or of little value: *all that junk in the boot of the car* ○ *You read too much junk*, ie low-quality books. **2** old or unwanted things that are sold cheaply: *pick up some interesting junk* ○ [attrib] *a junk shop.* **3** (*sl*) narcotic drug; heroin.

□ **ˈjunk food** (*infml derog*) food (eg potato crisps) eaten as a snack and usu thought to be not good for one's health.

ˈjunk mail (*infml derog*) advertising material, circulars, etc which are sent to large numbers of people by post and which they have not asked for.

junk[2] /dʒʌŋk/ *n* flat-bottomed Chinese sailing-ship.

junket /ˈdʒʌŋkɪt/ *n* **1** [C, U] (dish of) sweet custard-like pudding made of milk curdled with rennet, and often sweetened and flavoured. **2** [C] (*infml derog esp US*) trip made esp for pleasure by a government official and paid for with government money. **3** social gathering for a feast; picnic.

▷ **junket** *v* [I] make merry; feast. **junketing** *n* **1** [U] (*infml derog esp US*) party or celebration for visiting government officials, paid for with government money. **2** [C, U] (period of) feasting or merry-making.

junkie /ˈdʒʌŋkɪ/ *n* (*sl*) drug addict, esp one who is addicted to heroin.

Juno /ˈdʒu:nəʊ/ chief goddess of ancient Rome, wife and sister of *Jupiter, and protecting goddess of women. She was the equivalent of the Greek goddess Hera.

▷ **Junoesque** /ˌdʒu:nəʊˈesk/ *adj* (of a woman) having a graceful dignified beauty.

junta /ˈdʒʌntə; *US* ˈhʊntə/ *n* [CGp] (*esp derog*) group, esp of military officers, who rule a country after taking power by force in a revolution.

Jupiter /ˈdʒu:pɪtə(r)/ *n* **1** chief god of ancient Rome, originally a sky-god but later king of all the gods. He was the equivalent of the Greek god *Zeus. **2** (*astronomy*) largest planet of the solar system, fifth in order from the sun. It is mainly composed of hydrogen and helium. Its surface is marked by different coloured bands and patterns caused by weather systems, including the Great Red Spot, a vast circulating mass of gas. Jupiter has at least 16 moons and takes nearly 12 years to go round the sun.

Jurassic /ˌdʒʊəˈræsɪk/ *adj* of the period of the earth's history between 213 and 144 million years ago, when large dinosaurs existed. Cf MESOZOIC.

juridical /dʒʊəˈrɪdɪkl/ *adj* of law or legal proceedings.

jurisdiction /ˌdʒʊərɪsˈdɪkʃn/ *n* [U] **(a)** authority to carry out justice and to interpret and apply laws; right to exercise legal authority: *The court has no jurisdiction over foreign diplomats living in this country.* **(b)** limits within which legal authority may be exercised: *to come within/fall outside sb's jurisdiction.*

jurisprudence /ˌdʒʊərɪsˈpru:dns/ *n* [U] science or philosophy of law.

jurist /ˈdʒʊərɪst/ *n* expert in law.

juror /ˈdʒʊərə(r)/ *n* member of a jury.

jury /ˈdʒʊərɪ/ *n* [CGp] **1** group of people in a lawcourt who have been chosen to listen to the facts in a case and to decide whether the accused person is guilty or not guilty: *Seven men and five women sat on* (ie were members of) *the jury.* ○ *The jury returned a verdict of* (ie reached a decision that the accused was) *not guilty.* ○ *The jury is/are still out*, ie Members of the jury are still thinking about their decision. ○ *trial by jury.* ⇨ article at LAW. **2** group of people chosen to decide the winner or winners in a competition: *The jury is/are about to announce the winners.*

□ **ˈjury-box** *n* enclosure where a jury sits in a court.

juryman /ˈdʒʊərɪmən/ *n* (*fem* **jurywoman** /ˈdʒʊərɪwʊmən/) member of a jury.

jury-mast /ˈdʒʊərɪ mɑ:st/ *n* temporary mast put up to replace one that has been broken or lost.

just[1] /dʒʌst/ *adj* **1** acting or being in accordance with what is morally right and proper; fair: *a just and honourable ruler* ○ *a just decision, law, solution, society* ○ *a just* (ie legally right) *sentence/verdict* ○ *be just in one's dealings with sb.* **2** reasonable; well-founded: *a just complaint* ○ *just demands* ○ *criticized without just cause.* **3** deserved; right: *a just reward/punishment* ○ *get one's just deserts.*

▷ **the just** *n* [pl *v*] **1** just people. **2** (idm) **sleep the sleep of the just** ⇨ SLEEP[2].

justly *adv*: *to act justly* ○ *You can be justly proud of your achievement.*

justness *n* [U].

just[2] /dʒʌst/ *adv* **1** exactly. **(a)** (before *ns* and *n* phrases): *It's just two o'clock.* ○ *This hammer is just the thing I need.* ○ *It's just my size.* ○ *Just my luck!* (**b**) (before *adjs, advs* and prepositional phrases): *just right* ○ *just here/there* ○ *just on target.* (**c**) (before clauses): *just what I wanted* ○ *just where I expected it to be.* **2** ~ **as** (**a**) exactly as; the same as: *It's just as I thought.* (**b**) at the same moment as: *just as I arrived.* (**c**) (before an *adj/adv* followed by *as*) no less (than); equally: *just as beautiful as her sister* ○ *You can get there just as cheaply by air as by train.* **3** (esp after *only*) (**a**) barely; scarcely; narrowly: *I can (only) just reach the shelf, if I stand on tiptoe.* ○ *She (only) just caught the train with one minute to spare.* ○ *just manage to pass the entrance exam* ○ *just miss a target, fail a test, reach the top.* (**b**) (with perfect tenses; in US English with the simple past tense) very recently; in the immediate past: *I have (only) just seen John.* ○ *When you arrived he had (only) just left,* ie He left immediately before you arrived. ○ *By the time you arrive, he will have just finished.* ○ *He has just been speaking.* ○ (*US*) *I just saw him (a moment ago).* **4** at this/that moment; now; immediately. (**a**) (esp with the present and past continuous tenses): *Please wait: I am just finishing a letter.* ○ *I was just having lunch when Bill rang.* ○ *Just/I'm just coming!* ○ *I'm just off,* ie I'm leaving now. (**b**) ~ **about/going to do sth** (referring to the immediate future): *I was just about to tell you when you interrupted.* ○ *The clock is just going to strike noon.* **5** (**a**) simply: *Why not just wait and see what happens?* ○ *You ˈcould just ask me for ˈhelp,* ie instead of making a great fuss, giving a long explanation, etc. (**b**) (used, esp with the imperative, to cut short a possible argument or delay or to appeal for attention or understanding): *Just listen to what I'm saying!* ○ *Just try to understand!* ○ *Just let me say something!* ○ *Just look at this!* ○ *Just listen to him* (ie and you will see how clever, funny, stupid, unusual, etc he is)*!* **6** ~ (**for sth/to do sth**) only; simply: *There is just one way of saving him.* ○ *I waited an hour just to see you,* ie solely for that purpose. ○ *just for fun, a laugh, a joke, etc.* **7** (*infml*) really; truly; emphatically: *The weather is just marvellous!* ○ *It's just a miracle that he survived the accident!* ○ *'He's rather pompous.' 'Isn't he just?*(ie He certainly is!)*'* **8** (idm) **it is just as ˈwell (that...)** it is a good thing: *It's just as well that we didn't go out in this rain.* **it is/would be just as well (to do sth)** it is advisable: *It would be just as well to lock the door when you go out.* **just about** (*infml*) (**a**) almost; very nearly: *I've met just about everyone.* ○ *That's just about the limit!* ie That makes the situation almost unbearable. (**b**) approximately: *He should be arriving just about now.* **(not) just ˈany** (not) simply at random: *You can't ask just anybody to the party.* **just as one/it ˈis** without any special decoration or alteration: *The trousers are rather long, but I'll take them just as they are.* ○ *Tell her to come to the party (dressed) just as she is.* **ˌjust in ˈcase** as a precaution: *The sun is shining, but I'll take an umbrella just in case.* **ˌjust like ˈthat** suddenly, without warning or explanation: *He walked out on his wife just like that!* **ˌjust ˈnow** (**a**) at this very moment: *Come and see me later, but not just now.* (**b**) during this present period: *Business is good just now.* (**c**) only a short time ago: *I saw him just now.* **ˌjust on** (*infml*) (esp with numbers) exactly; only just: *It's ˌjust on ˌsix oˈclock* ○ *She's ˌjust on ˌninety years ˈold.* **ˌjust the ˈsame** (**a**) identical: *These two pictures are just the same (as one another).* (**b**) nevertheless: *The sun's out, but I'll take a raincoat just the same.* **ˌjust ˈso** (**a**) (*fml esp Brit*) quite true: *'Your name is Smythe, is it?' 'Just so.'* (**b**) performed or arranged with precision: *She cannot bear an untidy desk. Everything must be just so.* **just such a sth** sth exactly like this: *It was on just such a day (as this) that we left for France.* **(it's/that's) ˌjust too ˈbad** (*infml*) (often used to show lack of sympathy) the situation cannot be helped; one must simply manage as best one can: *'I've left my purse at home.' 'That's just too bad, I'm afraid!'* **one might just as well be/do sth** one would not benefit from being or doing otherwise: *The weather was so bad on holiday we might just as well have stayed at home.* **not just ˈyet** not at this present moment but probably quite soon: *'Are you ready?' 'Not just yet.'*

justice /ˈdʒʌstɪs/ *n* **1** [U] (**a**) right and fair behaviour or treatment: *laws based on the principles of justice* ○ *efforts to achieve complete social justice.* (**b**) quality of being reasonable or fair: *He demanded, with some justice, that he should be given an opportunity to express his views.* **2** [U] the law and its administration: *a court of justice* ○ *a miscarriage of justice,* ie a wrong legal decision. **3 Justice** [C] (used as a title of a High Court Judge): *Mr Justice Smith.* **4** [C] (*US*) judge of a lawcourt. **5** (idm) **bring sb to ˈjustice** arrest, try and sentence (a criminal). **ˌdo oneself ˈjustice** behave in a way that is worthy of one's abilities: *He didn't do himself justice in the exams,* ie did not perform as well as he was capable of doing. **do justice to sb/sth** (**a**) recognize the true value of sb/sth; treat sb/sth fairly: *To do her justice, we must admit that she did deserve to win.* ○ *The photograph does not do full justice to* (ie does not truly reproduce) *the rich colours of the gardens.* (**b**) deal with sb/sth adequately: *Since we'd already eaten, we couldn't do justice to her cooking,* ie could not eat all the food she had cooked.

□ **ˌJustice of the ˈPeace** (*abbr* **JP**) person who judges less serious cases in a local lawcourt; magistrate. ⇨ article at LAW.

justify /ˈdʒʌstɪfaɪ/ *v* (*pt, pp* **-fied**) **1** [Tn, Tg, Tsg] show that (sb/sth) is right, reasonable or just: *Such action can be justified on the grounds of greater efficiency.* ○ *You shouldn't attempt to justify yourself.* ○ *You can't justify neglecting your wife and children.* ○ *They found it hard to justify their son's giving up a secure well-paid job.* **2** [Tn, Tg, Tsg] be a good reason for (sth): *Improved productivity justifies an increase in wages.* ○ *Tiredness cannot possibly justify your treating staff this way.* **3** [Tn] arrange (lines of type) so that the margins are even: *a justified text.* **4** (idm) **the end justifies the means** ⇨ END[1].

▷ **justifiable** /ˌdʒʌstɪˈfaɪəbl, *also* ˈdʒʌstɪfaɪəbl/ *adj* that can be justified: *a justifiable explanation, action, use* ○ *justifiable homicide,* eg killing in self-defence. **justifiably** /-əblɪ/ *adv*: *justifiably cautious, indignant, proud, etc.*

justification /ˌdʒʌstɪfɪˈkeɪʃn/ *n* **1** [U, C] ~ (**for sth/doing sth**) acceptable reason (for doing sth): *I can see no justification for dividing the company into smaller units.* ○ *He was getting angry — and with some justification.* ⇨ Usage at REASON[1]. **2** [U] arrangement of lines of type so that the margins are even. **3** (idm) **in justification (for/of sb/sth)** as a defence (of sb/sth): *I suppose that, in justification, he could always claim he had a family to support.*

justified *adj* **1** ~ (**in doing sth**) having good reasons for doing sth: *As the goods were damaged, she felt fully justified in asking for her money back.* **2** for which there is a good reason: *justified criticism, suspicion, anger.*

jut /dʒʌt/ *v* (**-tt-**) (phr v) **jut out** stand out (from sth); be out of line (with the surrounding surface); stick out: *a balcony that juts out (over the garden)* ○ *a headland that juts out into the sea* ○ *His chin juts out rather a lot.*

Jute /dʒuːt/ *n* member of a Germanic people from the area of modern Denmark who settled in SE England in the 5th century AD.

jute /dʒuːt/ *n* [U] fibre from the outer skin of certain tropical plants, used for making sacking, rope, etc: *the jute mills of Bangladesh.*

juvenile /ˈdʒuːvənaɪl/ *n* **1** (*fml or law*) young person who is not yet adult. **2** actor or actress who plays such a part: [attrib] *play the juvenile lead.*

▷ **juvenile** *adj* **1** [attrib] (*fml or law*) of, characteristic of or suitable for young people who are not yet adults: *juvenile crime* ○ *juvenile offenders* ○ *juvenile books.* **2** (*derog*) immature and foolish; childish: *a juvenile sense of humour* ○ *Stop being so juvenile!* **juvenility** /ˌdʒuːvəˈnɪlətɪ/ *n* [U].

□ **ˌjuvenile ˈcourt** court that tries young people who are not yet adults.

ˌjuvenile deˈlinquent young person not yet an adult, who is guilty of a crime, eg vandalism. **ˌjuvenile deˈlinquency** criminal or antisocial behaviour by juvenile delinquents.

juvenilia /ˌdʒuːvəˈnɪlɪə/ *n* [pl] works produced by an artist, author, etc when very young.

juxtapose /ˌdʒʌkstəˈpəʊz/ *v* [Tn] (*fml*) place (people or things) side by side or very close together, esp to show a contrast: *juxtapose the classical style of architecture with the modern.* ▷ **juxtaposition** /ˌdʒʌkstəpəˈzɪʃn/ *n* [U]: *the juxtaposition of (different) ideas, civilizations, traditions.*

K, k

K, k /keɪ/ *n* (*pl* **K's, k's** /keɪz/) the eleventh letter of the English alphabet: *'King' begins with (a) K/'K'.*

K /keɪ/ *abbr* **1** kelvin(s). **2** (**a**) (*computing*) unit of capacity in a computer's memory, equal to 1000 (or more strictly 1 024) words, bits or bytes: *a 64K RAM machine.* Cf KILOBYTE. (**b**) (*infml*) one thousand (Greek *kilo-*): *She earns 12K* (ie £12 000) *a year.*

K *symb* potassium.

Kaaba /ˈkɑːbə/ building in the courtyard of the Great Mosque in *Mecca, the Muslim holy city. In its wall is a black stone said to have been given to *Abraham by the archangel *Gabriel. It is a very sacred place for Muslims, who turn towards it when they pray.

Kaddish /ˈkædɪʃ; *US* ˈkɑːdɪʃ/ *n* (*pl* **Kaddishim** /kæˈdɪʃɪm/) Jewish prayer of mourning.

kaffir /ˈkæfə(r)/ *n* (*S African* ⚠ *offensive*) black African person.

Kafka /ˈkæfkə/ Franz (1883-1924), Czech novelist whose works (written in German) include *The Trial, The Castle,* and the short story *The Metamorphosis,* in which a man turns into a beetle. Much of his writing depicts a single individual alone and threatened by unexplained forces in a nightmarish impersonal world.
▷ **Kafkaesque** /ˌkæfkəˈesk/ *adj* characterized by the feeling of being controlled by unexplained sinister forces, as described in Franz Kafka's novels.

kaftan = CAFTAN.

Kaiser /ˈkaɪzə(r)/ *n* title of the German and Austro-Hungarian emperors until 1918.

kale (also **kail**) /keɪl/ *n* [U] type of cabbage with curly leaves.

kaleidoscope /kəˈlaɪdəskəʊp/ *n* (**a**) toy consisting of a tube containing small loose pieces of coloured glass, etc and mirrors which reflect these to form changing patterns when the tube is turned. (**b**) (usu *sing*); (*fig*) constantly and quickly changing pattern: *His paintings are a kaleidoscope of gorgeous colours.* ○ *The bazaar was a kaleidoscope of unfamiliar sights and impressions.*
▷ **kaleidoscopic** /kəˌlaɪdəˈskɒpɪk/ *adj.* **kaleidoscopically** /-klɪ/ *adv.*

Kama Sutra /ˌkɑːmə ˈsuːtrə/ book written in Sanskrit between the 4th and the 7th centuries AD, describing the art of sexual love.

kamikaze /ˌkæmɪˈkɑːzɪ/ *n* (in the Second World War) (pilot of a) Japanese aircraft deliberately crashed on enemy ships, etc: [attrib] *a kamikaze attack* ○ (*fig*) *kamikaze* (ie suicidal) *tactics.*

Kampuchea /ˌkæmpʊˈtʃɪə/ ➪ CAMBODIA.

kangaroo /ˌkæŋɡəˈruː/ *n* (*pl* ~**s**) Australian animal that jumps along on its strong hind legs, the female carrying its young in a pouch on the front of its body. ➪ illus.
□ ˌ**kangaroo** ˈ**court** illegal court formed by a group of prisoners, striking workers, etc to settle disputes among themselves.

Kansas /ˈkænzəs, ˈkænsəs/ state in the *Mid West of the USA, an important producer of wheat and cattle. ➪ map at App 1.

Kant /kænt; *US* kɑːnt/ Immanuel (1724-1804), German philosopher who considered that human beings can never grasp the ultimate nature of reality, because they interpret the world according to a set of in-built mental concepts of space and time. His best-known book is the *Critique of Pure Reason.*

kaolin /ˈkeɪəlɪn/ *n* [U] (also **china** ˈ**clay**) fine white clay used in making porcelain and in medicine.

kapok /ˈkeɪpɒk/ *n* [U] substance like cotton wool, used for stuffing cushions, soft toys, etc.

kaput /kəˈpʊt/ *adj* [pred] (*sl*) broken; ruined; not working properly: *The car's kaput — we'll have to walk.*

karakul (also **caracul**) /ˈkærəkʊl/ *n* **1** [C] Asian sheep whose young have a dark curly coat. **2** [U] (also **Persian lamb**) fur made from this, used for clothing.

karat (*US*) = CARAT 2.

karate /kəˈrɑːtɪ/ *n* [U] Japanese system of unarmed combat in which the hands, feet, etc are used as weapons: [attrib] *a karate chop,* ie a blow with the side of the hand.

karma /ˈkɑːmə/ *n* [U] (**a**) (in Buddhism and Hinduism) sum of a person's actions in one of his successive lives, believed to decide his fate in the next. (**b**) (*esp joc*) destiny; fate: *It's my karma always to fall in love with brunettes.*

kart /kɑːt/ *n* = GO-KART.

kasbah (also **casbah**) /ˈkæzbɑː/ *n* **1** citadel of an Arab city in N Africa. **2** old crowded part of the city near this, esp in Algiers.

Kashmir /ˌkæʃˈmɪə(r); *US* ˈkæʃmɪər/ disputed territory in S Asia, bounded by India, Pakistan, China and Tibet. Since 1972 the area has been divided into Indian *Jammu and Kashmir, and Pakistani Azad Kashmir. ▷ **Kashmiri** /kæʃˈmɪərɪ/ *n, adj.*

kayak /ˈkaɪæk/ *n.* ➪ illus at CANOE. (**a**) Eskimo canoe made of light wood covered with sealskins. (**b**) small covered canoe resembling this.

Kazakhstan /ˌkæzəkˈstɑːn/ country in central Asia between the Caspian Sea and China; pop approx 16 700 000; official language Kazakh; capital Alma-Ata; unit of currency rouble. Part of the Russian empire from the 18th century, it became a member of the USSR before gaining independence as a republic in 1991. Its economy is rich in minerals and has a developed agriculture. ➪ map at UNION OF SOVIET SOCIALIST REPUBLICS.

Kazan /ˈkəzæn/ Elia (1909-), American film director. A pioneer of method acting (METHOD) in American cinema, he brought its students to public attention, esp Marlon *Brando in *On the Waterfront* and James *Dean in *East of Eden.*

kazoo /kəˈzuː/ *n* (*pl* ~**s**) toy musical instrument that gives a buzzing sound when sb blows through it while humming.

KB /ˌkeɪ ˈbiː/ *abbr* **1** (*computing*) kilobyte. **2** (*Brit law*) King's Bench. Cf QB.

KBE /ˌkeɪ biː ˈiː/ *abbr* (*Brit*) Knight Commander (of the Order) of the British Empire: *be made a KBE* ○ *Sir John Brown KBE.* Cf CBE, DBE, MBE.

KC /ˌkeɪ ˈsiː/ *abbr* (*Brit law*) King's Counsel. Cf QC.

KCB /ˌkeɪ siː ˈbiː/ *abbr* (*Brit*) Knight Commander (of the Order) of the Bath. ➪ article at ARISTOCRAT.

KCMG /ˌkeɪ siː em ˈdʒiː/ *abbr* (*Brit*) Knight Commander (of the Order) of St Michael and St George. ➪ article at ARISTOCRAT.

KCVO /ˌkeɪ siː viː ˈəʊ/ *abbr* (*Brit*) Knight Commander of the Royal Victorian Order. ➪ article at ARISTOCRAT.

Kean /kiːn/ Edmund (1787-1833), English actor who was famous for his portrayal of Shakespearean villains, such as Shylock and Iago.

Keaton /ˈkiːtn/ Buster (Joseph Francis) (1895-1966), American comedian whose masterly silent films are characterized by his unsmiling, pale face and complicated gags and stunts.

Keats /kiːts/ John (1795-1821), English Romantic poet. His best-known works include 'Hyperion', 'Ode on a Grecian Urn', 'Ode to a Nightingale', 'To Autumn', and 'The Eve of St Agnes'. He is generally regarded as one of the greatest of the Romantic poets, and his poems are still widely read for the richness and sensuousness of their language. He died in Rome of tuberculosis.

kebab /kɪˈbæb/ *n* (often *pl*) small pieces of meat and vegetables cooked and (often) served on a skewer: *lamb kebabs* ○ *shish kebab.*

Keble /ˈkiːbl/ John (1792-1866), English clergyman. He was one of the leaders of the *Oxford Movement, which aimed to restore Catholic doctrine in the Church of England.

kedgeree /ˈkedʒəriː, ˌkedʒəˈriː/ *n* [U, C] cooked dish of rice and fish, with hard-boiled eggs and sometimes onions, all mixed together.

keel /kiːl/ *n* **1** timber or steel structure along the bottom of a ship, on which the framework is built up: *lay down a keel,* ie start building a ship. **2** (idm) **on an even keel** ➪ EVEN[1].
▷ **keel** *v* (phr v) **keel over 1** (of a ship) capsize. **2** (*infml*) fall over; collapse: *After a couple of drinks he just keeled over on the floor.* ○ *The structure had keeled over in the high winds.*
□ **keelhaul** /ˈkiːlhɔːl/ *v* [Tn] **1** pull (sb) underneath a ship from one side to the other as a naval punishment. **2** (*fig*) scold (sb) severely.

keelson /ˈkelsn, *also* ˈkiːlsn/ (also **kelson** /ˈkelsn/) *n* long piece of wood or metal fixed to the bottom of a boat to strengthen it.

keen[1] /kiːn/ *adj* (**-er, -est**) **1** ~ (**to do sth/that ...**) eager; enthusiastic: *a keen swimmer* ○ *I'm not keen to go again.* ○ *She's keen that we should go.* **2** (of feelings, etc) intense; strong; deep: *a keen desire, interest, sense of loss.* **3** (of the senses) highly developed: *Dogs have a keen sense of smell.* **4** (of the mind) quick to understand: *a keen wit, intelligence.* **5** [esp attrib] (of the points and cutting edges of knives, etc) sharp: *a keen blade, edge.* **6** (of a wind) bitterly cold. **7** (*Brit*) (of prices) low; very competitive. **8** (idm) (**as**) ˌ**keen as** ˈ**mustard** (*infml*) extremely eager or enthusiastic. **keen on sth/sb** (*infml*) (**a**) interested in sth: *keen on (playing) tennis.* (**b**) fond of sb/sth: *He seemed mad keen on* (ie very interested in) *my sister.* ○ *I'm not too keen on jazz.* (**c**) enthusiastic about sth: *She's not very keen on the idea.* ○ *Mrs Hill is keen on Tom's marrying Susan.* ▷ **keenly** *adv.* **keenness** *n* [U].

keen[2] /kiːn/ *v* [I] (usu in the continuous tenses) lament a dead person by wailing: *keening over her murdered son.*
▷ **keen** *n* Irish funeral song accompanied by wailing.

keep[1] /kiːp/ *v* (*pt, pp* **kept** /kept/) **1** (**a**) [La, Ipr, Ip] continue to be in the specified condition or position; remain or stay: *She has the ability to keep calm in an emergency.* ○ *Please keep quiet — I'm trying to get some work done.* ○ *You ought to keep indoors with that heavy cold.* ○ *The notice said 'Keep off* (ie Do not walk on) *the grass'.* ○ *Keep back! The building could collapse at any moment.* (**b**) [Ip] ~ (**on**) **doing sth** continue doing sth; do sth repeatedly or frequently: *keep eating, laughing, smiling, walking* ○ *Keep (on) talking amongst yourselves, I'll be back in a minute.* ○ *How can I trust you if you keep lying to me?* ○ *I do wish you wouldn't keep interrupting me!* ○ *My shoe laces keep (on) coming undone.* ○ *Keep going* (ie Do not stop) *until you reach a large roundabout.* ○ *This is exhausting work, but I manage to keep going somehow.* (**c**) [Ipr, Ip] continue to move in the specified direction: *Traffic in Britain keeps to the left,* ie drives on the left-hand side of the road. ○

Keep straight on until you get to the church. ○ *The sign says 'Keep Left', so I don't think we can turn right here.* **2** [Tn·pr, Tn·p, Cn·a, Cn·g] cause sb/sth to remain in the specified condition or position: *If your hands are cold, keep them in your pockets.* ○ *Extra work kept him (late) at the office.* ○ *Don't keep us in suspense any longer — what happens at the end of the story?* ○ *keep sb amused, cheerful, happy, etc* ○ *These gloves will keep your hands warm.* ○ *Give the baby her bottle; that'll keep her quiet for a while.* ○ *He's in a coma and is being kept alive by a life-support machine.* ○ *I'm sorry to keep you waiting.* ○ *Add some more coal to keep the fire going.* **3** [Tn] detain or delay (sb): *You're an hour late; what kept you?* Cf KEEP SB FROM STH/DOING STH. **4** [Tn] **(a)** continue to have (sth); retain: *You can keep that book I lent you; I don't want it back.* ○ *Here's a five-pound note — you can keep the change.* **(b)** [Tn, Tn·pr, Dn·n] ~ **sth (for sb)** look after sth (for sb); retain sth: *Could you keep my place in the queue (for me)*(ie prevent anybody else from taking it)*?* ○ *Please keep me a place in the queue.* **(c)** [Tn, Tn·pr] have (sth) in a particular place; store: *Where do you keep the cutlery?* ○ *We haven't enough shelves to keep all our books on.* ○ *Always keep your driving licence in a safe place.* **(d)** [Tn] retain (sth) for future use or reference: *These trousers are so worn they're hardly worth keeping.* ○ *Let's not eat all the sandwiches now — we can keep some for later.* ○ *I keep all her letters.* **5** [Tn] own and manage (a shop, restaurant, etc): *Her father kept a grocer's shop for a number of years.* ○ *He plans to keep a pub when he retires.* **6** [Tn] own and look after (animals) for one's use or enjoyment: *keep bees, goats, hens, etc.* **7** [Tn] have (sth) regularly on sale or in stock: *'Do you sell Turkish cigarettes?' 'I'm sorry, we don't keep them.'* **8** [Tn] not reveal (a secret): *Can you keep a secret?* ie If I tell you one, can I be sure that you will not tell it to sb else? **9** [I] (of food) remain in good condition: *Do finish off the fish pie; it won't keep.* ○ *(fig) The news will keep*, ie can be told later rather than immediately. **10** [I] (used with an *adv*, or in questions after *how*) be in the specified state of health: *'How are you keeping?' 'I'm keeping well, thanks.'* **11** [Tn] **(a)** make written entries in (sth): *She kept a diary for over twenty years.* **(b)** write down (sth) as a record: *keeping an account/a record of what one spends each week.* **12** [Tn] provide what is necessary for (sb); support (sb) financially: *He scarcely earns enough to keep himself and his family.* **13** **(a)** [Tn] guard or protect (sth): *keep goal*, ie in football ○ *keep wicket*, ie in cricket. Cf GOALKEEPER (GOAL), Cf WICKET-KEEPER (WICKET). **(b)** [Tn, Tn·pr] ~ **sb (from sth)** *(fml)* protect sb (from sth): *May the Lord bless you and keep you*, ie used in prayers in the Christian Church. ○ *She prayed to God to keep her son from harm.* **14** [Tn] be faithful to (sth); respect or observe: *keep an appointment, the law, a promise, a treaty.* **15** (idm) **ˌkeep it ˈup** maintain a high standard of achievement: *Excellent work, Cripps — keep it up!* **ˌkeep up with the ˈJoneses** /ˈdʒəʊnzɪz/ *(infml often derog)* try to maintain the same social and material standards as one's neighbours (For other idioms containing **keep**, see entries for *ns, adjs*, etc, eg; **keep house** ⇨ HOUSE[1]; **keep the ball rolling** ⇨ BALL[1].). **16** (phr v) **keep (sb) at sth** (cause sb to) continue to work at sth: *Come on, keep ˈat it, you've nearly finished!* ○ *The teacher kept us at our ˈwork all morning.*

keep (sb/sth) away (from sb/sth) (cause sb/sth) not to go near sb/sth: *Police warned bystanders to keep away from the blazing building.* ○ *Her illness kept her away from* (ie caused her to be absent from) *work for several weeks.*

keep sth back **(a)** prevent sth from moving; restrain sth: *Millions of gallons of water are kept back by the dam.* ○ *She was unable to keep back her tears.* **(b)** not pay sth to sb: *A certain percentage of your salary is kept back by your employer as an insurance payment.* **keep sth ˈback (from sb)** refuse to tell sb sth; hold sth back: *I'm sure she's keeping something back (from us).* **keep (sb) ˈback (from sb/sth)** (cause sb to) remain at a distance from sb/sth: *Keep well back from the road.* ○ *Barricades were erected to keep back the crowds.*

keep ˈdown not show where one is; not stand up: *Keep down! You mustn't let anybody see you.* **keep sb ˈdown** repress or oppress (a people, nation, etc): *The people have been kept down for years by a brutal régime.* **keep sth ˈdown** **(a)** not raise (a part of the body): *Keep your head down!* **(b)** retain sth in the stomach: *The medicine was so horrid I couldn't keep it down*, ie I was sick. **(c)** cause sth to remain at a low level; not increase sth: *keep down wages, prices, the cost of living, etc* ○ *Keep your voices down; your mother's trying to get some sleep.* **(d)** not allow sth to multiply or grow: *use chemicals to keep pests down.*

keep oneself/sb from sth/doing sth prevent oneself/sb from doing sth: *The church bells keep me from sleeping.* ○ *I hope I'm not keeping you from your work.* **keep (oneself) from doing sth** prevent oneself from doing sth; stop (oneself) doing sth: *She could hardly keep (herself) from laughing.* ○ *I just managed to keep myself from falling.* **keep sth from sb** not tell sb sth: *I think we ought to keep the truth from him until he's better.* ○ *They don't keep anything from each other.*

keep sb ˈin detain (a child) after normal school hours as a punishment: *She was kept in for an hour for talking in class.* **keep sth in** not express (an emotion); restrain sth: *He could scarcely keep in his indignation.* **keep oneself/sb in sth** give or allow oneself/sb a regular supply of sth: *She earns enough to keep herself and all the family in good clothes.* **keep in with sb** *(infml)* continue to be friendly with sb, esp in order to gain some advantage: *Have you noticed how he tries to keep in with the boss?*

keep ˈoff (of rain, snow, etc) not begin: *The fête will go ahead provided the rain keeps off.* **keep off (sb/sth)** not approach, touch, etc sb/sth. **keep off sth** **(a)** not eat, drink or smoke sth: *keep off cigarettes, drugs, drink, fatty foods.* **(b)** not mention (the specified subject); avoid: *Please keep off (the subject of) politics while my father's here.* **keep sb/sth off (sb/sth)** cause sb/sth not to approach, touch, etc sb/sth: *They lit a fire to keep wild animals off.* ○ *Keep your hands off* (ie Do not touch) *me!*

keep ˈon continue one's journey: *Keep on past the church; the stadium is about half a mile further on.* **keep on (doing sth)** continue (doing sth): *The rain kept on all night.* ○ *She kept on working although she was tired.* **keep sb ˈon** continue to employ sb: *He's incompetent and not worth keeping on.* **keep sth on** **(a)** continue to wear sth: *You don't need to keep your hat on indoors.* **(b)** continue to rent or be the owner of (a house, flat, etc): *We're planning to keep the cottage on over the summer.* **keep ˈon (at sb) (about sb/sth)** continue talking (to sb) in an irritating way (about sb/sth): *He does keep on so!* ○ *I will mend the lamp — just don't keep on at me about it!*

keep ˈout (of sth) not enter (a place); remain outside: *The sign said 'Ministry of Defence - Danger - Keep Out!'* **keep sb/sth out (of sth)** prevent sb/sth from entering (a place): *Keep that dog out of my study!* ○ *She wore a hat to keep the sun out of her eyes.* **keep (sb) out of sth** not expose oneself/sb to sth; (cause sb to) avoid sth: *Do keep out of the rain if you haven't a coat.* ○ *That child seems incapable of keeping out of* (ie not getting into) *mischief.* ○ *Keep the children out of harm's way if you take them to the match.*

keep to sth **(a)** not wander from or leave (a path, road, etc): *Keep to the track — the moor is very boggy around here.* ○ *(fig) keep to the point/subject.* **(b)** follow or observe (a plan, schedule, etc): *Things will only work out if we all keep to the plan.* **(c)** remain faithful to (a promise, etc): *keep to an agreement, an undertaking.* **(d)** remain in and not leave (the specified place or position): *She's old and infirm and has to keep to the house.* **(e)** (used esp in the imperative when rebuking sb) not express (a comment, view, etc): *Keep your opinions to yourself in future!* **keep (oneself) to oneself** avoid meeting people socially; not concern oneself with other people's affairs: *Nobody knows much about him; he keeps himself (very much) to himself.* **keep sth to oneˈself** not tell other people about sth: *I'd be grateful if you kept this information to yourself.*

keep sb ˈunder oppress sb: *The local population i kept under by a brutal army of mercenaries.* **keep sth under** control or suppress sth: *Firemer managed to keep the fire under.*

keep ˈup (of rain, snow, good weather, etc continue without stopping: *Let's hope the sunny weather keeps up for Saturday's tennis match* **keep sb up** prevent sb from going to bed: *I do hop we're not keeping you up.* **keep sth up** **(a)** preven sth from falling down: *wear a belt to keep one' trousers up.* **(b)** cause sth to remain at a high level *The high cost of raw materials is keeping prices up* **(c)** not allow (one's spirits, strength, etc) to decline; maintain: *They sang songs to keep their morale up.* **(d)** continue sth at the same (usu high level: *The enemy kept up their bombardment day and night.* ○ *We're having difficulty keeping up our mortgage payments.* ○ *You're all doing a splendid job; keep up the good work!* **(e)** continue to practise or observe sth: *keep up old customs, traditions, etc* ○ *Do you still keep up your Spanish?* **(f)** maintain (a house, garden, etc) in good condition by spending money or energy on it: *The house is becoming to expensive for them to keep up.* Cf UPKEEP. **keep ˈup (with sb/sth)** move or progress at the same rate (as sb/sth): *Slow down — I can't keep up (with you)* ○ *I can't keep up with all the changes in compute technology.* **keep up (with sth)** rise at the same rate (as sth): *Workers' incomes are not keeping up with inflation.* **keep up with sb** continue to be in contact with sb: *How many of your old schoo friends do you keep up with?* **keep up with sth** inform oneself or learn about (the news, curren events, etc): *She likes to keep up with the lates fashions.*

□ **ˌkept ˈwoman** *(dated or joc)* woman who is provided with money and a home by a man with whom she is having a sexual relationship.

keep[2] /kiːp/ *n* **1** [U] (cost of providing) food and other necessities of life: *It's time you got a job and started paying for your keep!* ○ *(fig) Does that old car still earn its keep?* ie Is it useful enough to be worth the cost of keeping it? **2** [C] strongly buil tower of an ancient castle. **3** (idm) **for ˈkeeps** *(infml)* permanently; for ever: *Can I have it for keeps or do you want it back?*

keeper /ˈkiːpə(r)/ *n* **1** person who looks after animals in a zoo or a collection of items in a museum. **2** (esp in compounds) person who is in charge of or looks after sth: *a ˈlighthouse-keeper* ○ *a ˈgamekeeper* ○ *a ˈshopkeeper.* **3** *(infml)* **(a)** = GOALKEEPER (GOAL). **(b)** = WICKET-KEEPER (WICKET) **4** = ARMATURE 2. **5** (idm) **finders keepers** ⇨ FINDER (FIND[1]).

keeping /ˈkiːpɪŋ/ *n* (idm) **for safe keeping** ⇨ SAFE[1]. **in sb's keeping** in sb's care or custody: *I'l leave the keys in your keeping.* **in/out of keeping (with sth)** in/not in conformity or harmony: *a development wholly in keeping with what we expected* ○ *That tie is not quite in keeping.* **in safe keeping** ⇨ SAFE[1].

keepsake /ˈkiːpseɪk/ *n* gift, usu small and often not very costly, that is kept in memory of the giver or previous owner: *My aunt gave me one of her brooches as a keepsake.*

keg /keg/ *n* small barrel, usu containing less than 10 British or 30 US gallons of liquid. ⇨ illus at BARREL.

□ **keg beer** *(Brit)* beer served from kegs, using gas pressure.

Keller /ˈkelə(r)/ Helen Adams (1880-1968) American author and social reformer, who raised money for the education of handicapped people despite being herself blind and deaf from early childhood.

Kelly /ˈkelɪ/ Ned (1855-80), Australian outlaw who became a national folk hero. Wanted for stealing horses and cattle, he hid in the bush, but was captured by the police and hanged. He and his gang often wore metal armour for protection.

kelp /kelp/ *n* [U] type of large brown seaweed.

kelpie /ˈkelpɪ/ *n* (in Scottish folklore) water-spirit in the shape of a horse, believed to drown travellers.

kelson = KEELSON.

Kelvin /ˈkelvɪn/ William Thomson, 1st Baron

(1824-1907), British physicist who introduced an absolute temperature scale (named after him), established the principle that perpetual motion is impossible, was involved in the laying of the first Atlantic cable, and invented several scientific instruments.

kelvin /ˈkelvɪn/ *n* (*abbr* **K**) unit (equal to the Celsius degree) of an international scale of temperature (the **Kelvin scale**) with 0° at absolute zero (–273.15°C). ➪ App 11.

ken[1] /ken/ *n* (idm) **beyond/outside one's ken** not within one's range of knowledge: *The workings of the Stock Exchange are beyond most people's ken.*

ken[2] /ken/ *v* (**-nn-**, *pt* **kenned** or **kent**, *pp* **kenned**) [Tn, Tf, Tw] (*Scot*) know.

kendo /ˈkendəʊ/ *n* [U] Japanese martial art in which people fight with bamboo sticks.

Kennedy /ˈkenədɪ/ John Fitzgerald (1917-63), 35th president of the USA 1961-63. The youngest ever US president, he introduced liberal reforms and supported the widening of civil rights. He defeated the attempt by the USSR to establish missile sites in Cuba. He was shot while driving through Dallas, Texas. ➪ App 2.

kennel /ˈkenl/ *n* **1** [C] shelter for a pet dog: *Rover lives in a kennel in the back garden.* **2** [C] shelter for a pack of hounds. **3 kennels** [sing or pl *v*] place where dogs are bred, cared for, etc: *We put the dog into kennels when we go on holiday.* Cf CATTERY.
▷ **kennel** *v* (**-ll-**; *US also* **-l-**) [Tn] put or keep (a dog) in a kennel or kennels: *She kennels her dog in the yard.*

Kennelly-Heaviside layer /ˌkenəlɪ ˌhevɪsaɪd ˈleɪə(r)/ = HEAVISIDE LAYER (HEAVISIDE).

Kent /kent/ county in SE England, through which much passenger and freight traffic passes to the continent of Europe. Fruit is its main product (it is known as the 'Garden of England'), and hops are also grown. Traditionally, natives of Kent are divided into 'Kentish men' (those born west of the river Medway) and 'men of Kent' (those born east of it). ➪ map at App 1.
▷ **Kentish** /ˈkentɪʃ/ *adj* of Kent.

Kentucky /kenˈtʌkɪ/ state in the central south-eastern USA, nicknamed the 'Blue Grass State' because of the large areas of bluish-coloured grass that grow there and are used for pasture. ➪ map at App 1.
□ **the Kenˌtucky ˈDerby** annual horse-race held at Louisville, Kentucky.

Kenya /ˈkenjə; *US* ˈkiːnjə/ country in East Africa, bordered by Ethiopia, Sudan, Tanzania and Uganda; pop approx 23 883 000; official languages Swahili and English; capital Nairobi; unit of currency shilling (= 100 cents). Formerly a British colony, it became independent in 1963. Its main exports are coffee and tea, and tourism is also important, centred on the many wildlife reserves. ➪ map at TANZANIA. ▷ **Kenyan** /ˈkenjən; *US* ˈkiːnjən/ *adj, n.*

Kenyatta /kenˈjætə/ Jomo (c1894-1978), Kenyan statesman who led his country's fight for independence and became president of Kenya in 1964.

kepi /ˈkeɪpɪ/ *n* type of French military cap with a horizontal peak.

Kepler /ˈkeplə(r)/ Johannes (1571-1630), German astronomer who explained the motion of the planets round the sun and is regarded as one of the founders of modern astronomy.

kept *pt, pp of* KEEP[1].

keratin /ˈkerətɪn/ *n* [U] hard fibrous protein that forms the outer layer of hair, finger-nails and toe-nails, claws, etc.

kerb (also *esp US* **curb**) /kɜːb/ *n* stone or concrete edge of a pavement at the side of a road: *Stop at the kerb and look both ways before crossing (the road).*
□ **ˈkerb-crawling** *n* [U] driving slowly along trying to persuade sb on the pavement to enter one's car, esp for sexual purposes: *be arrested for kerb-crawling.*
ˈkerb drill set of rules for crossing the road safely.
ˈkerbstone *n* block of stone or concrete forming part of a kerb.

kerchief /ˈkɜːtʃɪf/ *n* (*arch*) **1** square piece of cloth worn on the head or round the neck, esp by women. **2** handkerchief.

kerfuffle /kəˈfʌfl/ *n* [U] (*Brit infml*) fuss; noise; excitement: *What's all the kerfuffle (about)?*

Kern /kɜːn/ Jerome (1885-1945), American composer of many popular songs, including 'Ol' Man River' and 'Smoke gets in your Eyes'.

kernel /ˈkɜːnl/ *n* **1** soft and usu edible part inside a nut or fruit stone. ➪ illus at NUT. **2** part of a grain or seed within the hard outer shell. **3** (*fig*) central or essential part (of a subject, plan, problem, etc): *the kernel of her argument.*

kerosene (also **kerosine**) /ˈkerəsiːn/ *n* [U] (*esp US*) = PARAFFIN 1: [attrib] *a kerosene lamp.*

Kerouac /ˈkerʊæk; *US* ˈkerəwæk/ Jack (1922-69), American writer whose best-known books (including *On the Road* and *Big Sur*) are autobiographical. He was a leading member of the *Beat Generation, and established a genre of writing about casual travel and the adventures, friendships, etc that occur along the way.

kestrel /ˈkestrəl/ *n* type of small falcon. ➪ illus at BIRD.

Ketch /ketʃ/ Jack (died 1686), English executioner who had a reputation for being cruel and incompetent. His name was formerly used as a general term for a hangman.

ketch /ketʃ/ *n* small sailing-boat with two masts.

ketchup /ˈketʃəp/ (also *esp US* **catsup** /ˈkætsəp/) *n* [U] thick sauce made from tomatoes, vinegar, etc and used cold as a seasoning.

ketone /ˈkiːtəʊn/ *n* any of a small group of related chemical compounds which includes acetone (also called *propanone*).

kettle /ˈketl/ *n* **1** container with a spout, lid and handle, used for boiling water: *boil (water in) the kettle and make some tea.* **2** (idm) **a different kettle of fish** ➪ DIFFERENT. **a ˈfine, ˈpretty, etc kettle of fish** messy, unpleasant or confusing situation. **the pot calling the kettle black** ➪ POT[1].

kettledrum /ˈketldrʌm/ *n* large brass or copper bowl-shaped drum with skin stretched over the top, that can be tuned to an exact pitch. ➪ illus at MUSIC.

Kew Gardens /ˌkjuː ˈgɑːdnz/ park near Richmond, Surrey, England which contains a large collection of flowering plants, trees, etc and is a centre of botanical research in Britain. ➪ article at GARDEN.

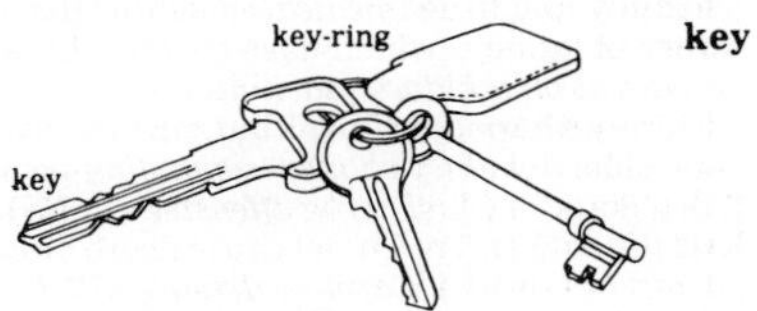

key[1] /kiː/ *n* **1** [C] metal instrument shaped so that it will move the bolt of a lock (and so lock or unlock sth): *turn the key in the lock* ○ *the car keys* ○ *the key to the front door* ○ *have a duplicate key cut*, ie made. ➪ illus. **2** [C] similar instrument for grasping and turning sth, eg for winding a clock: *Where's the key for turning off the radiator?* **3** [C] (**a**) (*music*) set of related notes, based on a particular note, and forming the basis of (part of) a piece of music: *a sonata in the key of E flat major/A minor* ○ *This piece changes key many times.* (**b**) (*fig*) general tone or style of sth: *Her speech was all in the same key*, ie monotonous. **4** [C] any of the set of levers that are pressed by the fingers to operate a typewriter, piano, etc. ➪ illus at MUSIC, ➪ illus at PIANO. **5** [C] (**a**) set of answers to exercises or problems: *a book of language tests, complete with key.* (**b**) explanation of the symbols used in a coded message or on a map, diagram, etc. **6** [C usu *sing*] ~ (**to sth**) thing that provides access, control or understanding: *Diet and exercise are the key (to good health).* ○ *The key to the whole affair was his jealousy.* **7** [sing] roughness given to a surface so that plaster or paint will stick to it: *Gently sand the plastic to provide a key for the paint.* **8** [C] (*botany*) winged fruit of some trees, eg the ash and elm. ➪ illus at TREE. **9** (idm) **under lock and key** ➪ LOCK[2].
▷ **key** *adj* [attrib] very important or essential: *a key figure in the dispute* ○ *a key industry, speech, position.*
□ **ˈkeyboard** *n* set of keys (KEY[1] 4) on a typewriter, piano, etc. ➪ illus at COMPUTER. — *v* **1** [I] operate a keyboard (eg for setting printing type). **2** [Tn] enter (data) in a computer by means of a keyboard. **ˈkeyboarder** *n* person who operates a keyboard.
ˈkeyhole *n* hole through which a key is put into a lock.
ˈkey money payment illegally demanded from a new tenant of a house or flat before he is allowed to move in.
ˈkeynote *n* **1** central theme of a speech, book, etc: *Unemployment has been the keynote of the conference.* ○ [attrib] *a keynote speech*, ie one setting the tone for or introducing the theme of a meeting, etc. **2** (*music*) note on which a musical key is based.
ˈkey-pad *n* small keyboard of numbered buttons used instead of a dial on a telephone, for selecting a channel, etc on a television set, or for entering data in a computer.
ˈkey-ring *n* ring on which keys are kept. ➪ illus.
ˈkey signature (*music*) sharps and flats shown on a piece of music indicating the key in which it is written. ➪ illus at MUSIC.
ˈkeystone *n* **1** (*architecture*) central stone at the top of an arch locking the others into position. **2** (usu *sing*); (*fig*) most important part of a plan, an argument, etc on which all the other parts depend: *Belief in a life after death is the keystone of her religious faith.* Cf CORNER-STONE (CORNER[1]).
keyword /ˈkiːwɜːd/ *n* **1** word that enables one to understand or break a code. **2** important or significant word.

key[2] /kiː/ *v* **1** [Tn, Tn·p] ~ **sth (in)** (*computing*) type in (data) using a keyboard: *I've keyed this sentence (in) three times, and it's still wrong!* **2** [Tn] roughen (a surface) so that plaster or paint will stick to it. **3** (phr v) **key sth to sth** (**a**) make sth similar to sth else: *She keyed her mood to that of the other guests.* (**b**) make sth suitable for sth else: *The farm was keyed to the needs of the local people.* **key sb up** (usu passive) make sb excited, nervous or tense: *The manager warned us not to get too keyed up before the big match.*

key[3] (also **cay**) /kiː/ *n* low island or reef, esp in the W Indies and off the coast of Florida.

Keynes /keɪnz/ John Maynard (1883-1946), English economist who put forward the view that governments should manage demand in national economies and where necessary borrow money to finance public spending.
▷ **Keynesian** /ˈkeɪnzɪən/ *n, adj* (supporter) of John Maynard Keynes: *Keynesian economics.* **Keynesianism** /ˈkeɪnzɪənɪzəm/ *n* [U].

Keystone Cops, the Keystone Cops incompetent police department, the heroes of a series of American silent slapstick comedies by Mack Sennett's Keystone Studios. They are still referred to as examples of comic disorganization.

KG /ˌkeɪ ˈdʒiː/ *abbr* (in Britain) Knight (of the Order) of the Garter: *be made a KG* ○ *Sir Thomas Bell KG.*

kg *abbr* kilogram(s): *10 kg.*

KGB /ˌkeɪ dʒiː ˈbiː/ *abbr* USSR Intelligence Agency which has survived the break-up of the Soviet Union (Russian *Komitet Gosudarstvennoi Bezopasnosti*): *a KGB agent* ○ *dealing with the KGB.*

khaki /ˈkɑːkɪ/ *n* [U], *adj* (cloth of a) dull brownish-yellow colour, used esp for military uniforms.

Khmer /kmeə(r)/ *n* **1** [C] member of a Cambodian people who from the 9th to the 14th centuries AD had a powerful empire in SE Asia. **2** [U] language spoken by this people.
□ **the Khmer ˈRouge** communist guerrilla organization which seized power in Cambodia in 1975 and ruled the country until 1979.

Khomeini /hɒˈmeɪnɪ/ Ruholla (1900-89), Iranian Shi'ite religious leader (ayatollah). As an opponent of the Shah of Iran, he was exiled from

1964 to 1979, but then returned to set up a fundamentalist Muslim regime, acting as virtual head of state until his death.

Khrushchev /krʊsˈtʃɒf, *also* ˈkru:ʃtʃɒf/ Nikita Sergevich (1894-1971), Russian statesman, Communist Party secretary and Soviet leader 1958-64. He was forceful in his dealings with the West, but economic failures at home led to his removal from office.

Khyber Pass /ˌkaɪbə ˈpɑ:s; *US* -ˈpæs/ **the Khyber Pass** major mountain pass on the border between Pakistan and Afghanistan. It is of great strategic importance as a route for invading India, and has been the scene of much fighting.

kHz *abbr* kilohertz. Cf Hz.

kibbutz /kɪˈbʊts/ *n* (*pl* **kibbutzim** /kɪbʊˈtsi:m/) communal farm or settlement in Israel.

▷ **kibbutznik** /-nɪk/ *n* member of a kibbutz.

kick[1] /kɪk/ *v* **1** (**a**) [Tn, Tn·pr] hit (sb/sth) with the foot: *Mummy, Peter kicked me (on the leg)!* (**b**) [Tn, Tn·pr, Tn·p] move (sth) by doing this: *He kicked the ball into the river.* ○ *Can we kick the ball around for a while?* (**c**) [Tn·pr] make (sth) by kicking: *He kicked a hole in the fence.* (**d**) [I, Ip] move the foot or feet in a jerky violent way: *The child was screaming and kicking.* ○ *Be careful of that horse — it often kicks.* ○ *(fig) She kicks out when she's angry.* **2** [Tn] ~ **oneself** be very annoyed with oneself because one has done sth stupid, missed an opportunity, etc: *When I discovered I'd come for the appointment on the wrong day, I could have kicked myself.* **3** [Tn] (esp in Rugby football) score (a goal or conversion) by kicking the ball: *That's the twentieth goal he's kicked this season.* **4** [I] (of a gun) jerk backwards when fired. **5** (idm) **alive and kicking** ⇨ ALIVE. **hit/kick a man when he's down** ⇨ MAN. **ˌkick against the ˈpricks** hurt oneself by useless resistance or protest. **ˌkick the ˈbucket** (*sl*) die. **ˈkick the habit** (*infml*) give up an addiction: *Doctors should try to persuade smokers to kick the habit.* **ˌkick one's ˈheels** have nothing to do while waiting for sth: *She had to kick her heels for hours because the train was so late.* **ˌkick over the ˈtraces** (of a person) refuse to accept discipline or control (from parents, etc). **kick up/raise a dust** ⇨ DUST[1]. **ˌkick up a ˈfuss, ˈrow, shindy, stink, etc** (*infml*) cause a disturbance, esp by protesting about sth. **ˌkick up one's ˈheels** (*infml*) enjoy oneself enthusiastically. **ˌkick sb upˈstairs** (*infml*) get rid of sb by promoting him to a position that seems more important but in fact is less so. **6** (phr v) **kick against sth** protest about or resist sth: *It's no use kicking against the rules.* **kick around** (*infml*) be present, alive or in existence: *I've been kicking around Europe since I saw you last.* ○ *My shirt is kicking around on the floor somewhere.* ○ *an idea which has been kicking around for some considerable time.* **kick sth around/round** (*infml*) discuss (plans, ideas, etc) informally: *We'll kick some ideas around and make a decision tomorrow.* **kick sth in** break sth inwards by kicking: *kick in a door* ○ *kick sb's teeth in.* **kick ˈoff** start a football match (by kicking the ball): *United kicked off and scored almost immediately.* [Tn] **kick (sth) off** begin (a meeting, etc): *I'll ask Tessa to kick off (the discussion).* **kick sth off** remove sth by kicking: *kick off one's slippers, shoes, etc.* **kick sb out (of sth)** (*infml*) expel sb or send him away by force: *They kicked him out (of the club) for fighting.*

▷ **kicker** *n* person who kicks.

□ **ˈkick-off** *n* start of a football match.

kick[2] /kɪk/ *n* **1** [C] (**a**) act of kicking: *give sb a kick up the backside* ○ *If the door won't open give it a kick.* (**b**) leg movement in swimming. **2** [C] (*infml*) thrill; feeling of pleasure: *I get a big kick from motor racing.* ○ *She gets her kicks from windsurfing and skiing.* ○ *do sth (just) for kicks.* **3** [C] (*infml*) (usu temporary) interest or activity: *(be on) a health-food kick.* **4** [U, sing] (*infml*) strength; effectiveness: *He has no kick left in him.* ○ *This drink has (quite) a kick (to it),* ie is strong. **5** (idm) **a kick in the teeth** (*infml*) unpleasant and often unexpected action: *The Government's decision is a real kick in the teeth for the unions.*

□ **ˈkick-start** *v* [Tn] start (a motor cycle, etc) by pushing down a lever with one's foot. **kick-start** (also **ˈkick-starter**) *n* this lever.

kickback /ˈkɪkbæk/ *n* (*infml*) money paid to sb who has helped one to make a profit, often illegally.

kid[1] /kɪd/ *n* **1** (**a**) [C] (*infml*) child or young person: *How are your wife and kids?* ○ *Half the kids round here are unemployed.* (**b**) [attrib] (*infml esp US*) younger: *his kid sister/brother.* **2** (**a**) [C] young goat. ⇨ illus at GOAT. (**b**) [U] leather made from its skin: *a bag made of kid* ○ [attrib] *a pair of kid gloves.* **3** (idm) **handle, treat, etc sb with kid ˈgloves** deal with sb very gently or tactfully. **ˈkid's stuff** (*infml*) thing, activity, etc that is very simple: *You should be solving cryptic crosswords — these elementary ones are just kid's stuff.*

▷ **kiddy** (also **kiddie**) *n* (*infml*) child.

□ **ˈkid-glove** *adj* [attrib] gentle; tactful: *Kid-glove methods haven't worked — it's time to get tough.*

kid[2] /kɪd/ *v* (**-dd-**) **1** [I, Tn] (*infml*) deceive (sb), esp playfully; tease: *You're kidding!* ○ *Don't kid yourself — it won't be easy.* **2** (idm) **ˌno ˈkidding** (*infml*) (used to express surprise at what has been said): (*ironic*) *'It's raining.' 'No kidding! I wondered why I was getting wet!'*

Kidd /kɪd/ William (1645-1701), British pirate, known as 'Captain Kidd'. He was hanged for his crimes, but is reputed to have buried a large hoard of stolen treasure which has never been found.

kidnap /ˈkɪdnæp/ *v* (**-pp-**; *US* **-p-**) [Tn] steal (sb) away by force and illegally, esp in order to obtain money or other (esp political) demands: *Two businessmen have been kidnapped by terrorists.*

▷ **kidnap** *n* [attrib]: *a kidnap attempt, plot, victim.*

kidnapper *n*: *The kidnappers have demanded £1 million for his safe release.*

kidnapping *n* [C, U] (act of) stealing sb away in this way: *The kidnapping occurred in broad daylight.*

kidney /ˈkɪdnɪ/ *n* (*pl* ~**s**) **1** [C] either of a pair of organs in the body that remove waste products from the blood and produce urine. **2** [U, C] kidney(s) of certain animals used as food: *two kilos of lamb's kidney* ○ [attrib] *steak and kidney pie.* **3** [sing] (*rhet*) type; sort (used esp as in the expressions shown): *men of the same/of a different kidney.*

□ **ˈkidney bean** (plant producing a) reddish-brown kidney-shaped bean.

ˈkidney machine (*medical*) machine that does the work of kidneys which have become diseased: *put a patient on a kidney machine.*

ˈkidney-shaped *adj* oval but curved inwards on one side: *a ˌkidney-shaped ˈswimming-pool.*

kike /kaɪk/ *n* (⚠ *sl derog offensive esp US*) Jew.

kill /kɪl/ *v* **1** [I, Tn, Tn·pr] cause death or cause the death of (sb/sth): *Careless driving kills!* ○ *Cancer kills thousands of people every year.* ○ *The guard was killed with a high-powered rifle.* ○ *(fig infml) My mother will kill me* (ie be very angry with me) *when she finds out where I've been.* **2** [Tn] (*infml*) (usu in the continuous tenses) cause pain to (sb): *My feet are killing me.* **3** [Tn] (**a**) (esp in football) stop (a ball) suddenly and completely with one's foot. (**b**) (esp in tennis) hit (a ball) so that it cannot be returned. **4** [Tn] bring (sth) to an end: *kill sb's affection, interest, appetite* ○ *the goal that killed Brazil's chances of winning.* **5** [Tn, Cn·a] (*infml*) cause (sth) to fail or be rejected: *kill a project, a proposal, an idea, etc (stone dead)* ○ *The play was killed by bad reviews.* **6** [Tn] (*infml*) switch or turn off: *kill a light, the radio, a car engine.* **7** [Tn] make (one colour) appear ineffective by contrast with another: *The bright red of the curtains kills the brown of the carpet.* **8** (idm) **be dressed to kill** ⇨ DRESS[2]. **curiosity killed the cat** ⇨ CURIOSITY. **have time to kill** ⇨ TIME[1]. **ˌkill the fatted ˈcalf** (*fml or joc saying*) joyfully celebrate sb's return or arrival. **ˌkill the ˌgoose that ˌlays the ˌgolden ˈeggs** (*saying*) destroy (through greed or carelessness) sth that would have produced continuous profit in the future. **kill oneself (doing sth/to do sth)** (*infml*) try too hard: *The party's at eight, but don't kill yourself getting here/to get here on time.* **ˌkill or ˈcure** [esp attrib] (likely to) be either completely successful or a total failure: *a kill-or-cure approach to the problem* ○ *The tough new measures on drug abuse are likely to be a case of kill or cure.* **kill ˈtime; kill two, a few etc hours** spend time as pleasantly as possible but unprofitably, esp while waiting for sth: *My flight was delayed, so I killed time/killed two hours reading a book.* **kill ˌtwo ˌbirds with ˌone ˈstone** achieve two aims with a single action or simultaneously. **ˌkill sb with ˈkindness** harm sb by being excessively or mistakenly kind. **9** (phr v) **kill sb/sth off** destroy or get rid of sb/sth: *kill off weeds, insects, rats* ○ *He killed off all his political opponents.* ○ *(fig) The author kills off her hero in Chapter 7.*

▷ **kill** *n* **1** act of killing: *The lion made only one kill that day.* **2** (usu *sing*) animal(s) killed: *The hunters brought their kill back to camp.* **3** (idm) **go/move in for the ˈkill** prepare to finish off an opponent. **(be) ˌin at the ˈkill** (be) present at the climax of a struggle, etc: *She wants to be in at the kill when his business finally collapses.*

killer *n* person, animal or thing that kills: *Police are hunting her killer.* ○ *Heroin is a killer.* ○ [attrib] *a killer disease* ○ *Sharks have the killer instinct.*

□ **ˈkilljoy** *n* (*derog*) person who spoils the enjoyment of others.

killing /ˈkɪlɪŋ/ *n* (idm) **ˌmake a ˈkilling** have a great financial success: *She's made a killing on the stock market.*

▷ **killing** *adj* (*infml*) **1** exhausting: *walk at a killing pace.* **2** very amusing: *a killing joke.*

killingly *adv* (*infml*) extremely: *a killingly funny film.*

kiln /kɪln/ *n* oven for baking pottery or bricks, drying hops or wood, burning lime, etc.

kilo /ˈki:ləʊ/ *n* (*pl* ~**s**) kilogram. ⇨ App 12.

kilo- *comb form* thousand: *kilogram* ○ *kilometre.*

kilobyte /ˈkɪləbaɪt/ *n* (*abbrs* **K, KB**) unit of size of a computer's memory; 1 000 or 1 024 bytes.

kilocycle /ˈkɪləsaɪkl/ *n* (*dated*) = KILOHERTZ.

kilogram (also **kilogramme**) /ˈkɪləgræm/ *n* (*abbr* **kg**) basic unit of mass in the SI system; 1 000 grams. ⇨ App 10, 12.

kilohertz /ˈkɪləhɜ:ts/ *n* (*pl* unchanged) (*abbr* **kHz**) (also **kilocycle**) unit of frequency of electromagnetic waves; 1 000 hertz.

kilolitre (*US* **-liter**) /ˈkɪləli:tə(r)/ *n* (*abbr* **kl**) metric unit of capacity; 1 000 litres.

kilometre (*US* **-meter**) /ˈkɪləmi:tə(r), kɪˈlɒmɪtə(r)/ *n* (*abbr* **km**) metric unit of length; 1 000 metres. ⇨ App 9, 10.

kiloton (also **kilotonne**) /ˈkɪlətʌn/ *n* unit of explosive force equal to 1 000 tons of TNT.

kilowatt /ˈkɪləwɒt/ *n* (*abbrs* **kW, kw**) unit of electrical power; 1 000 watts.

□ **ˌkilowatt-ˈhour** *n* (*abbr* **kWh**) unit of electrical energy equal to 1 000 watts working for one hour.

kilt /kɪlt/ *n* (**a**) pleated knee-length skirt of tartan wool, worn by men as part of Scottish national costume. ⇨ illus at BAGPIPES. ⇨ articles at CLOTHES, SCOTLAND. (**b**) similar skirt worn by women or children.

▷ **kilted** *adj* wearing a kilt.

kilter /ˈkɪltə(r)/ *n* (idm) **ˌout of ˈkilter** not working properly or in proper condition.

kimono /kɪˈməʊnəʊ; *US* -nə/ *n* (*pl* ~**s**) (**a**) long loose Japanese robe with wide sleeves, worn with a sash. (**b**) dressing-gown resembling this.

kin /kɪn/ *n* **1** [pl *v*] (*dated or fml*) one's family and relatives: *All his kin were at the wedding.* ○ *He's my kin,* ie related to me. ○ *We are near kin,* ie closely related. Cf KINDRED 2. **2** (idm) **kith and kin** ⇨ KITH. **no kin to sb** not related to sb. Cf NEXT OF KIN (NEXT[1]).

□ **kinsfolk** /ˈkɪnzfəʊk/ *n* [pl *v*] = KIN.

ˈkinship *n* [U] **1** blood relationship: *claim kinship with sb.* **2** (*fig*) close sympathy or similarity of character: *Even after meeting only once, they felt a kinship.*

kinsman /ˈkɪnzmən/ *n* (*pl* **-men** /-mən/) (*fml*) male relative.

ˈkinswoman *n* (*pl* **-women**) (*fml*) female relative.

-kin *suff* (with *ns* forming *ns*) small or young one:

lambkin.

kind[1] /kaɪnd/ *adj* **1** friendly and thoughtful to others: *Would you be kind enough to/be so kind as to help me?* ○ *a kind man, gesture, face, thought* ○ *She always has a kind word for* (ie stops to speak kindly to) *everyone.* **2** (idm) **be cruel to be kind** ⇨ CRUEL.

▷ **kindly** *adv* **1** in a kind manner: *treat sb kindly* ○ *He spoke kindly to them.* **2** (used when making polite requests or ironically when ordering sb to do sth) please: *Would you kindly hold this for a moment?* ○ *Kindly leave me alone!* **3** (idm) **take kindly to sb/sth** (usu in negative sentences) be pleased by sth; accept sb/sth willingly: *She didn't take (at all) kindly to being called plump.* ○ *I don't think he takes kindly to foreign tourists.*

kindness *n* **1** [U] quality of being kind: *She always shows kindness to children and animals.* ○ *He did it entirely out of kindness, not for the money.* **2** [C] kind act: *I can never repay her many kindnesses to me.* **3** (idm) **do/show sb a ˈkindness** do sth kind for sb. **kill sb with kindness** ⇨ KILL. **the milk of human kindness** ⇨ MILK[1].

□ **ˌkind-ˈhearted** *adj* having a kind nature; sympathetic.

kind[2] /kaɪnd/ *n* **1** [C] group having similar characteristics; sort; type; variety: *fruit of various kinds/various kinds of fruit* ○ *Do you want all the same kind, or a mixture?* ○ *Don't trust him: I know his kind*, ie what sort of person he is. ○ *She's not the kind (of woman/person) to lie.* **2** [U] nature; character: *They differ in size but not in kind.* **3** (idm) **in kind** (a) (of payment) in goods or natural produce, not in money: *When he had no money, the farmer sometimes used to pay me in kind*, eg with a sack of potatoes. (b) (*fig*) with something similar: *repay insults in kind*, ie by being insulting in return. **a kind of** (*infml*) (used to express uncertainty): *I had a kind of* (ie a vague) *feeling this might happen.* ○ *He's a kind of unofficial adviser, but I'm not sure exactly what he does.* **kind of** (*infml*) slightly; to some extent: *I'm not sure why, but I feel kind of sorry for him.* ○ *'Is she interested?' 'Well, kind of.'* **nothing of the ˈkind/sort** not at all like it: *People had told me she was very pleasant but she's nothing of the kind.* **of a kind** (a) very similar: *They look alike, talk alike, even think alike — they're two of a kind/they're very much of a kind.* (b) (*derog*) of an inferior kind: *The town offers entertainments of a kind, but nothing like what you'll find in the city.* **something of the kind** something like what has been said: *Did you say they're moving? I'd heard something of the kind myself.*

NOTE ON USAGE: **1** After **kind of/sort of** it is usual to have a singular noun: *What kind of/sort of tree is that?* ○ *There are many different kinds of/sorts of snake in South America.* Informally, it is possible to use a plural noun thus: *I have met all kinds of/sorts of salesmen, tourists, etc.* In more formal usage the plural noun can be put in front: *People of that kind/sort never apologize.* ○ *Snakes of many kinds/sorts are found in South America.* **2 Kind of/sort of** are also used informally to indicate that somebody or something is not genuine or of good quality, or to suggest vagueness: *I had a kind of/sort of holiday in the summer but I couldn't really relax.* ○ *He gave a kind of/sort of smile and left the room.* **3 Kind of** and **sort of** are used in very informal English as adverbs. They mean 'to some extent': *She kind of/sort of likes him.*

kindergarten /ˈkɪndəgɑ:tn/ *n* school for very young children; nursery school.

kindle /ˈkɪndl/ *v* **1** [I, Tn] (cause sth to) catch fire: *This wood is too wet to kindle.* ○ *The sparks kindled the dry grass.* **2** (*fig*) (a) [Tn] arouse or stimulate (feelings, etc): *kindle hopes, interest, anger.* (b) [I, Ipr] ~ (**with sth**) become bright; shine or glow: *Her eyes kindled with excitement.*

▷ **kindling** /ˈkɪndlɪŋ/ *n* [U] small dry pieces of wood, etc for lighting fires.

kindly[1] /ˈkaɪndlɪ/ *adj* [usu attrib] (**-ier**, **-iest**) kind or friendly in character, manner or appearance: *a kindly man, voice, smile* ○ *give sb some kindly advice.* ▷ **kindliness** *n* [U].

kindly[2] ⇨ KIND[1].

kindred /ˈkɪndrɪd/ *n* (*fml*) **1** [U] family relationship: *claim kindred with sb.* **2** [pl *v*] one's family and relatives: *Most of his kindred still live in Ireland.* Cf KIN 1.

▷ **kindred** *adj* [attrib] (*fml*) **1** having a common source; related: *kindred families* ○ *English and Dutch are kindred languages.* **2** similar: *hunting and shooting and kindred activities.* **3** (idm) **a kindred ˈspirit** person whose tastes, feelings, etc are similar to one's own: *We immediately realized that we were kindred spirits.*

kinetic /kɪˈnetɪk/ *adj* [esp attrib] of or produced by movement.

▷ **kinetically** /-klɪ/ *adv.*

kinetics *n* [sing *v*] science of the relations between the movement of bodies and the forces acting on them.

□ **kiˌnetic ˈart** art (esp sculpture) that depends for its effect on the movement of some of its parts, eg in air currents.

kiˌnetic ˈenergy energy that sth moving has; ability of sth moving to do work (eg drive a machine).

kiˌnetic ˈtheory theory of physics which accounts for the properties of matter in terms of the movement of the atoms and molecules of which the matter is made.

Martin Luther King

King /kɪŋ/ Martin Luther (1929-68), black American clergyman and civil rights leader whose powerful and moving speeches inspired the movement for black equality. He was awarded the Nobel Peace prize in 1964, and was assassinated in 1968 in Memphis, Tennessee. In his honour the third Monday in January, named 'Martin Luther King Day', is now a public holiday in the USA. ⇨ illus.

king /kɪŋ/ *n* **1** (title of the) male ruler of an independent state, usu inheriting the position by right of birth: *the King of Denmark* ○ *King Edward VII* ○ *be made/crowned king.* Cf QUEEN. **2** person, animal or thing regarded as best or most important in some way: *To his fans, Elvis will always be 'the King'.* ○ *the king of beasts/of the jungle*, ie the lion ○ *Barolo is the king of Italian red wines.* **3** [attrib] largest variety of a species: *king cobra, penguin, prawn, etc.* **4** (a) (in chess) the most important piece. ⇨ illus at CHESS. (b) (in draughts) piece that has been crowned on reaching the opponent's side of the board. (c) (in playing-cards) any of four cards with the picture of a king on: *the king of spades.* **5** (idm) **the King's/Queen's English** ⇨ ENGLISH. **a ˌking's ˈransom** very large amount of money: *That painting must be worth a king's ransom.* **turn King's/Queen's evidence** ⇨ EVIDENCE. **the uncrowned king/queen** ⇨ UNCROWNED.

▷ **kingly** *adj* of, like or suitable for a king; regal. **kingliness** *n* [U].

kingship /-ʃɪp/ *n* [U] condition of being, or official position of, a king.

□ **ˌKing Charles ˈspaniel** small breed of spaniel dog with a short nose.

the ˌKing ˌJames ˈversion = THE AUTHORIZED VERSION (AUTHORIZE).

ˈkingmaker *n* person who controls appointments to positions of high (esp political) authority.

ˌking of the ˈcastle 1 children's game in which one player stands on a mound or heap and the others try to take his place. **2** (*infml*) person in a position of advantage or control: *She'll be king of the castle when her boss retires.*

ˈkingpin *n* **1** (*engineering*) vertical bolt used as a pivot. **2** (*fig*) essential person or thing: *He's the kingpin of the whole team.*

ˈking-post *n* vertical post supporting the top of an angled roof.

ˌking's ˈevil [U] (*arch*) = SCROFULA.

ˈking-size (also **-sized**) *adj* [esp attrib] larger than normal; extra large: *a king-size bed, cigarette, hamburger* ○ *king-sized portions.*

King's/Queen's ˈBench (*abbrs* **KB**, **QB**) (*Brit law*) division of the High Court of Justice.

King's/Queen's ˈCounsel (*abbrs* **KC**, **QC**) (*Brit law*) senior barrister appointed as legal adviser to the Crown.

kingcup /ˈkɪŋkʌp/ *n* large variety of buttercup; marsh marigold.

kingdom /ˈkɪŋdəm/ *n* **1** country or state ruled by a king or queen: *the United Kingdom.* **2** any one of the three divisions of the natural world: *the animal, plant/vegetable and mineral kingdoms.* **3** (*fig*) area belonging to or associated with a particular thing or person: *the kingdom of the imagination* ○ *the kingdom under the waves*, ie the sea. **4** (idm) **till/until kingdom ˈcome** (*infml*) for ever: *Don't mention politics or we'll be here till kingdom come.* **to kingdom ˈcome** (*infml*) into the life after death: *gone to kingdom come*, ie dead ○ *The bomb exploded and blew them all to kingdom come.*

kingfisher /ˈkɪŋfɪʃə(r)/ *n* small brightly-coloured bird that dives to catch fish in rivers, etc. ⇨ illus at BIRD.

King Kong /ˌkɪŋ ˈkɒŋ/ monster like a huge gorilla, capable of destroying buildings, which appeared in an American film (original version 1933).

Kings /kɪŋz/ *n* [sing *v*] either of two books of the Old Testament which tell the history of the Jews from the time of *Solomon to the destruction of the Temple in 586 BC. ⇨ App 5.

Kingsley /ˈkɪŋzlɪ/ Charles (1819-75), English author and clergyman, whose writings combine elements of strict moral teaching with a concern for social justice. His best-known works are the historical novel *Westward Ho!* and the children's book *The Water-Babies.*

kink /kɪŋk/ *n* **1** sharp twist in sth that is normally straight, eg a wire, rope, pipe, hair, etc. **2** (*fig usu derog*) mental or moral peculiarity: *He's got a few kinks in his personality, if you ask me.*

▷ **kink** *v* [I, Tn, Tn·pr] (cause sth to) form kinks: *Keep the wire stretched tight — don't let it kink.*

kinky *adj* (*infml derog*) bizarre or abnormal, esp in sexual behaviour: *There's lots of straight sex in the film, but nothing kinky.* **kinkiness** *n* [U].

Kinnock /ˈkɪnək/ Neil Gordon (1942-), British Labour politician, leader of the Labour party since 1983.

kinsfolk, **kinsman**, **kinswoman** ⇨ KIN.

kiosk /ˈki:ɒsk/ *n* **1** small open structure where

newspapers, refreshments, etc are sold. **2** (*dated Brit*) public telephone box or booth.

kip /kɪp/ *n* [C usu *sing*, U] (*Brit sl*) sleep: *have a kip* ○ *get some kip.*

▷ **kip** *v* (**-pp-**) [I, Ipr, Ip] (*Brit sl*) lie down to sleep: *Could I kip here tonight?* ○ *kip down (on the floor)* ○ *kip out in a field.*

Kipling /ˈkɪplɪŋ/ Rudyard (1865-1936), English author. He was born in India, where several of his books are set (eg *The Jungle Book, Kim,* and many of the poems in *Barrack-Room Ballads*). He wrote in a wide range of forms, in verse and prose, for children and adults, and a particular theme of his was the details of people's working lives. Today it is his sometimes enigmatic short stories that are most highly regarded. He was the first English writer to be awarded the Nobel prize for literature (in 1907).

kipper /ˈkɪpə(r)/ *n* salted herring, split open and dried or smoked.

Kirgyzstan /kɪəgizˈstɑːn/ (formerly **Kirghizia**) country in east central Asia; pop approx 4 367 000; official language Kirghiz; capital Bishkek; unit of currency som. Part of the Russian empire in the 19th century, it became a member of the USSR and gained independence in 1991. There has since been tension between rural and urban ethnic populations, and also over market reforms. ⇨ map at UNION OF SOVIET SOCIALIST REPUBLICS.

Kiribati /ˌkɪrɪˈbæs *or, more commonly,* ˌkɪrɪˈbɑːtɪ/ country consisting of a group of 36 islands in the SW Pacific; pop approx 67 000; official languages English and the local *Micronesian language; capital Bairiki; unit of currency dollar (= 100 cents). Until 1975 it was part of the British colony of the Gilbert and Ellice Islands. It became fully independent in 1979. Its main exports are copra and fish. ⇨ map at MICRONESIA.

kirk /kɜːk/ *n* (*Scot*) **1** [C, U] church: *go to (the) kirk.* **2 the Kirk** [sing] = THE CHURCH OF SCOTLAND (CHURCH).

□ ˈ**Kirk-session** *n* lowest court of the Church of Scotland.

kirsch /kɪəʃ/ *n* [U] colourless liqueur made from cherries.

kismet /ˈkɪzmet, ˈkɪs-/ *n* [U] (*rhet*) destiny; fate.

kiss /kɪs/ *v* [I, Tn, Tn·pr] **1** touch (sb/sth) with the lips to show affection or as a greeting: *They kissed passionately when she arrived.* ○ *kiss the children good night* ○ *She kissed him on the lips.* **2** (idm) **kiss sth goodbye/kiss goodbye to sth** (*sl*) accept the loss or failure of sth as certain: *You can kiss goodbye to a holiday this year — we've no money!* **3** (phr v) **kiss sth away** remove sth with kisses: *Let mummy kiss your tears away,* ie help you to stop crying by kissing you.

▷ **kiss** *n* **1** touch or caress given with the lips: *give sb a kiss.* **2** (idm) **blow a kiss** ⇨ BLOW[1]. **the kiss of ˈdeath** (*infml esp joc*) apparently favourable action that makes failure certain: *one of those polite lukewarm reviews that are the kiss of death for a commercial film.*

kissable *adj* (*approv*) inviting kisses: *kissable lips* ○ *Darling, you look so kissable tonight.*

kisser *n* (*sl*) mouth: *a punch in the kisser.*

□ ˈ**kiss-curl** *n* small bunch of hair that curls down in a circular shape, esp over the forehead.

the ˌkiss of ˈlife mouth-to-mouth method of restoring breathing to save the life of sb injured or rescued from drowning: (*fig*) *the Government's £2 million kiss of life for the ailing cotton industry.*

kit /kɪt/ *n* **1** [U] clothing and personal equipment of a soldier, etc or a traveller: *They marched twenty miles in full kit.* **2** [C, U] equipment needed for a particular (esp sporting) activity, situation or trade: *a ˈtool-kit* ○ *a first-ˈaid kit* ○ *a reˈpair kit* ○ *ˈshaving kit* ○ *ˈriding-kit* ○ *ˈtennis kit* ○ *ˈsports kit.* **3** [C] set of parts sold together to be assembled by the purchaser: *a kit to build a model railway locomotive* ○ [attrib] *furniture in kit form.*

▷ **kit** *v* (**-tt-**) (phr v) **kit sb out/up (with sth)** equip sb: *Kit this man out with everything he needs.* ○ *He was all kitted out to go skiing.*

□ ˈ**kitbag** *n* long canvas bag in which soldiers, etc carry their kit.

kitchen /ˈkɪtʃɪn/ *n* **1** room or building in which meals are cooked or prepared: [attrib] *the kitchen table* ○ *kitchen units,* ie cupboards, etc forming part of a fitted kitchen. **2** (idm) **everything but the kitchen ˈsink** (*infml joc*) every possible (movable) object: *We always seem to take everything but the kitchen sink when we go on holiday.*

▷ **kitchenette** /ˌkɪtʃɪˈnet/ *n* small room or part of a room used as a kitchen, eg in a flat.

□ ˌ**kitchen ˈcabinet** (*sometimes derog*) group of unofficial but influential advisers to a political leader.

ˌ**kitchen ˈgarden** garden or part of a garden where fruit and vegetables are grown.

ˌ**kitchen ˈsink drama** type of British drama of the 1950s and 1960s (eg John *Osborne's *Look Back in Anger* and Arnold *Wesker's *Roots*) that attempts to show realistic working-class family life.

Kitchener /ˈkɪtʃɪnə(r)/ Horatio Herbert, Earl Kitchener (1850-1916), British soldier who led British armies with success in the Sudan and during the *Boer War. At the beginning of the First World War he was appointed Secretary for War, and organized a large recruitment programme for the army with the slogan 'Your Country Needs You'. He was drowned when the ship taking him on a mission to Russia was sunk by a mine.

kite /kaɪt/ *n* **1** toy consisting of a light framework covered with paper, cloth, etc that is flown in the wind at the end of a long string. **2** bird of prey of the hawk family. **3** (*sl*) cheque that is not valid or fraudulent, eg one forged from a stolen cheque-book. **4** (idm) **fly a kite** ⇨ FLY[2]. **fly a/one's kite** ⇨ FLY[2].

▷ **kite** *v* [I] (*sl*) get money by writing an invalid cheque.

□ ˈ**kite-flying** *n* [U] **1** (sport of) flying kites in the wind. **2** (*infml*) testing public reaction to sth by starting a rumour about it.

Kitemark /ˈkaɪtmɑːk/ *n* (in Britain) official mark, in the form of a kite, on goods approved by the British Standards Institution.

kith /kɪθ/ *n* (idm) **kith and kin** friends and relations.

kitsch /kɪtʃ/ *n* [U] (*derog*) **(a)** cheap and showy vulgarity or pretentiousness in art, design, etc: *That new lamp they've bought is pure kitsch.* **(b)** art, design, etc of this type.

kitten /ˈkɪtn/ *n* **1** young cat. **2** (idm) **have ˈkittens** (*Brit infml*) be very anxious, tense, etc: *My mum'll have kittens if I'm not home by midnight.*

▷ **kittenish** *adj* playful like a kitten.

kittiwake /ˈkɪtɪweɪk/ *n* type of small seagull of northern regions, commonly nesting on sea cliffs.

kitty[1] /ˈkɪtɪ/ *n* **1** (in some card-games) pool of money to be played for. **2** (*infml*) any form of money for joint use, eg the savings of a club: *We each put £2 in the kitty, and then sent John to buy food for everybody.*

kitty[2] /ˈkɪtɪ/ *n* (*infml*) (used by or to young children) cat or kitten.

kiwi /ˈkiːwiː/ *n* **1** New Zealand bird that cannot fly, with a long bill, short wings and no tail. **2 Kiwi** (*infml*) New Zealander, esp a soldier or member of a national sports team.

□ ˈ**kiwi fruit** small oval fruit with thin brown skin, soft green flesh and black seeds.

KKK /ˌkeɪ keɪ ˈkeɪ/ *abbr* (*US*) Ku-Klux-Klan.

kl *abbr* (*pl* unchanged or **kls**) kilolitre.

klaxon /ˈklæksn/ *n* (*propr*) powerful electric warning horn or siren.

Kleenex /ˈkliːneks/ *n* [U, C] (*pl* unchanged or ~**es**) (*propr*) (sheet of) soft paper tissue, used as a handkerchief, etc: *a packet of Kleenex.*

kleptomania /ˌkleptəˈmeɪnɪə/ *n* [U] illness that causes an uncontrollable desire to steal things, often with no wish to possess the things stolen.

▷ **kleptomaniac** /-nɪæk/ *n* person suffering from kleptomania. — *adj* [attrib]: *display kleptomaniac tendencies.*

Klondike /ˈklɒndaɪk/ river and district in *Yukon, north-western Canada, where gold was discovered in 1896, causing thousands of people to go there to look for more.

km *abbr* (*pl* unchanged or **kms**) kilometre(s): *a 10 km walk* ○ *distance to beach 2 kms.*

kn *abbr* (*nautical*) knot(s) (KNOT[2]): *35 kn.*

knack /næk/ *n* [sing] **1** skill at performing some special task; ability: *Making an omelette is easy once you've got the knack (of it).* ○ *There's a knack in/to locking this door which takes a while to master.* ○ *I used to be able to skate quite well, but I've lost the knack.* **2** ~ **of doing sth** (often annoying) habit of doing sth: *My car has a knack of breaking down just when I need it most.*

knacker[1] /ˈnækə(r)/ *n* **1** person who buys and slaughters useless horses to sell the meat and hides. **2** person who buys and breaks up old buildings, etc to sell the materials in them.

□ ˈ**knacker's yard** knacker's place of business.

knacker[2] /ˈnækə(r)/ *v* [Tn] (*Brit sl*) exhaust (sb); wear out: *All this hard work is knackering me.*

▷ **knackered** *adj* [esp pred] (*Brit sl*) exhausted; worn out: *I'm completely knackered — I ran all the way!*

knapsack /ˈnæpsæk/ *n* (*dated*) = RUCKSACK.

knapweed /ˈnæpwiːd/ *n* plant with purple thistle-like flowers.

knave /neɪv/ *n* **1** (*fml*) = JACK[1] 4: *the knave of hearts.* **2** (*arch*) dishonest man; man without honour.

▷ **knavery** /ˈneɪvərɪ/ *n* [U] (*arch*) dishonesty; trickery.

knavish /ˈneɪvɪʃ/ *adj* (*arch*) deceitful. **knavishly** *adv.*

knead /niːd/ *v* **1** [Tn, Tn·pr] press and stretch (bread dough, wet clay, etc) with the hands to form a firm smooth paste: *Knead the dough (into a ball).* **2** [Tn] massage (muscles, etc) firmly to relieve tension or pain.

knee /niː/ *n* **1 (a)** joint between the thigh and lower part of the human leg; corresponding joint in animals. ⇨ illus at HUMAN. **(b)** upper surface of a sitting person's thigh: *sit on my knee* ○ *You'll have to eat your dinner off your knees, I'm afraid!* **2** part of a garment covering the knee: *These trousers are torn at the knee.* **3** (idm) **be/go (down) on one's ˈknees** kneel or be kneeling (down), esp when praying or to show that one accepts defeat. **the bee's knees** ⇨ BEE[1]. **bring sb to his ˈknees** force sb to submit: (*fig*) *The country was almost brought to its knees by the long strike.* **on bended knee** ⇨ BEND[1]. **weak at the knees** ⇨ WEAK.

▷ **knee** *v* (*pt, pp* **kneed**) [Tn, Tn·pr, Cn·a] strike or push with the knee: *knee sb (in the groin)* ○ *knee the door open.*

□ ˈ**knee-breeches** *n* [pl] breeches reaching to or just below the knee.

ˈ**kneecap** *n* small bone covering the front of the knee joint. ⇨ illus at SKELETON. — *v* (**-pp-**) [Tn] (of terrorist groups) lame (sb) by breaking the kneecaps, esp by shooting at them. ˈ**kneecapping** *n* [C, U] (instance of) this practice.

ˌ**knee-ˈdeep** *adj* **1** deep enough to reach the knees: *The snow was knee-deep in places.* **2** ~ **in sth** (*fig*) deeply involved in or very busy with sth: *be knee-deep in trouble, work.* — *adv*: *He went knee-deep in the icy water.*

ˌ**knee-ˈhigh** *adj* **1** high enough to reach the knees: *ˌknee-high ˈgrass.* **2** (idm) **knee-high to a**

ˈgrasshopper (*joc*) still just a very small child: *I've known him since he was knee-high to a grasshopper.*

ˈ**knee-jerk** *n* **1** involuntary jerk of the leg when a tendon below the knee is struck. **2** [attrib] (*fig derog*) done or produced automatically and without thought: *a knee-jerk reaction to the mention of Communism.*

ˈ**knee-length** *adj* long enough to reach the knee: *a knee-length skirt.*

ˈ**knees-up** *n* (*Brit infml*) lively party, usu with dancing.

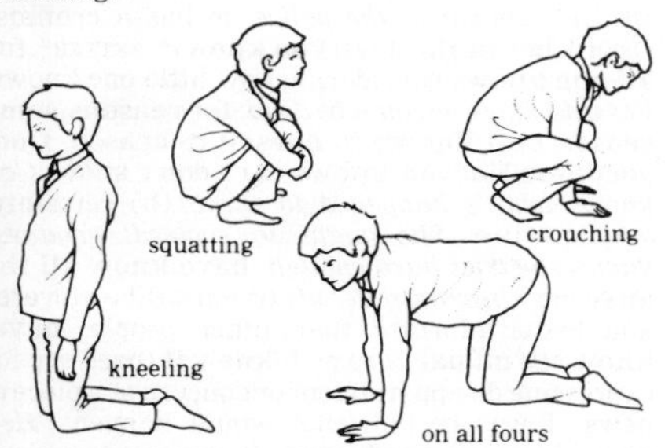

kneel /ni:l/ *v* (*pt, pp* **knelt** /nelt/ or *esp US* **kneeled**) ➩ Usage at DREAM[1]. [I, Ipr, Ip] ~ **(down)** go down on one or both knees; rest on the knee(s): *She knelt in prayer.* ○ *kneel down (on the grass) to examine a flower.*

▷ **kneeler** /ˈni:lə(r)/ *n* thing for kneeling on, eg a hassock.

knell /nel/ *n* (usu *sing*) **1** sound of a bell rung slowly after a death or at a funeral. **2** (*fig rhet*) sign that sth has ended for ever: *It sounded the (death-)knell of all her hopes.*

Knesset /ˈkneset/ *n* **the Knesset** [Gp] parliament of the modern state of Israel.

knew *pt of* KNOW.

knickerbockers /ˈnɪkəbɒkəz/ (*US* **knickers** /ˈnɪkəz/) *n* [pl] (esp formerly) loose wide breeches gathered just below the knee.

knickers /ˈnɪkəz/ *n* [pl] **1** (*Brit*) woman's or girl's underpants: *a pair of knickers.* **2** (*US*) = KNICKERBOCKERS. **3** (idm) **get one's ˈknickers in a twist** (*Brit sl*) become angry, confused, nervous, etc; react to sth more strongly than is necessary.

knick-knack (also **nick-nack**) /ˈnɪk næk/ *n* (esp *pl*) (*sometimes derog*) small ornamental article, usu of little value.

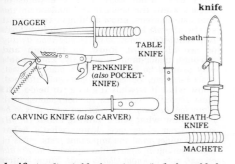

knife

DAGGER
TABLE KNIFE
sheath
PENKNIFE (*also* POCKET-KNIFE)
CARVING KNIFE (*also* CARVER)
SHEATH-KNIFE
MACHETE

knife /naɪf/ *n* (*pl* **knives** /naɪvz/) **1** sharp blade with a handle, used for cutting or as a weapon: *a ˈtable-knife* ○ *a ˈcarving-knife* ○ *a ˈpaper-knife* ○ *He'd been stabbed four times with a kitchen knife.* **2** cutting blade in a machine or tool. **3** (idm) **you could ˌcut it with a ˈknife** (*infml*) it was very obvious or heavy: *His accent is so thick you could cut it with a knife — I can hardly understand a word he says.* **get one's knife into sb/have one's knife in sb** try to harm sb spitefully (not usu physically). **like a knife through butter** easily; without meeting any resistance or difficulty: *The power saw sliced the logs like a knife through butter.* ○ *His strong voice cut through the hum of conversation like a knife through butter.* **under the ˈknife** (*dated or joc*) having surgery.

▷ **knife** *v* [Tn, Tn·pr] cut or stab (sb) with a knife: *The victim had been knifed (in the chest).*

□ ˈ**knife-edge** *n* (usu *sing*) **1** cutting edge of the blade of a knife. **2** (idm) **on a knife-edge** (**a**) (of a person) nervous (about the outcome of sth): *He's on a knife-edge about his exam results.* (**b**) (of a situation, etc) at a critical point: *The success of the project is still very much on a knife-edge.*

knight /naɪt/ *n* **1** (*abbr* **Kt**) man to whom the sovereign has given a rank of honour, lower than that of baronet, having the title 'Sir' used before the first name, with or without the surname: *Sir James Hill (Kt)* ○ *Good morning, Sir James.* ➩ article at ARISTOCRAT. **2** (in the Middle Ages) man raised to honourable military rank, serving as a heavily armed horseman. **3** (*abbr* **Kt**) chess piece, usu shaped liked a horse's head. ➩ illus at CHESS. **4** (idm) **a ˌknight in ˌshining ˈarmour** brave or admirable person who saves another (esp a woman) from danger, a difficult situation, etc.

▷ **knight** *v* [esp passive: Tn, Tn·pr] make (sb) a knight: *He was knighted in the last Honours List (for services to industry).*

knighthood /-hʊd/ *n* **1** [C] title and rank of a knight: *The Queen conferred a knighthood on him.* **2** [U] rank, character or dignity of a knight: *Knighthood was an ideal in medieval Europe.*

knightly *adj* [usu attrib] (*fml*) of or like a knight; chivalrous: *knightly qualities, virtues, etc.*

□ ˌ**knight ˈerrant** (*pl* **knights errant**) medieval knight who wandered in search of adventure.

ˌ**knights of the Round ˈTable** [pl] group of knights (eg Sir *Lancelot, Sir Galahad, Sir Gawain) at the court of King *Arthur.

Knightsbridge /ˈnaɪtsbrɪdʒ/ fashionable area of west London with many shops, including *Harrods.

knit /nɪt/ *v* (**-tt-**, *pt, pp* **knitted**; in sense 3, usu **knit**) **1** [I, Tn, Dn·n, Dn·pr] ~ **sth (for sb)** make (a garment or fabric) by forming wool, silk, etc yarn into connecting loops, either by hand (using long needles) or on a machine: *Do you know how to knit?* ○ *She knitted her son a sweater.* **2** [I, Tn] (in knitting instructions) make a plain (ie not a purl) stitch: *knit one, purl one.* **3** [I, Ip, Tn, Tn·p] ~ **(sth) (together)** (cause sth to) join or grow firmly together: *The broken bones have knit (together) well.* ○ *a well-knit frame*, ie a compact sturdy body ○ (*fig*) *a closely-knit argument* ○ (*fig*) *The two groups are knit together by common interests.* **4** (idm) **knit one's ˈbrow(s)** frown.

▷ **knitter** *n* person who knits.

knitting *n* [U] material that is being knitted: *Oh dear, I've left my knitting on the bus!* ˈ**knitting-machine** *n* machine that knits. ˈ**knitting-needle** *n* long thin pointed rod used esp in pairs for knitting by hand.

□ ˈ**knitwear** *n* [U] knitted garments: [attrib] *a knitwear factory.*

knob /nɒb/ *n* **1** (**a**) round handle (of a door, drawer, etc). (**b**) round control button (for adjusting a radio, TV, etc). **2** round lump on the surface of sth, eg a tree trunk. **3** small lump (of butter, coal, etc). **4** (idm) **with knobs on** (*Brit sl*) (used to indicate the return of an insult, or emphatic agreement): *'You're a selfish pig!' 'And the same to you, with knobs on!'*

knobbly /ˈnɒblɪ/ *adj* having many small hard lumps on: *knobbly knees.*

knock[1] /nɒk/ *n* **1** (sound of a) sharp blow: *Did I hear a knock at the door?* ○ *If you're not up by eight o'clock I'll give you a knock*, ie wake you by knocking at your door. ○ *She fell off her bike and got a nasty knock.* ○ *In football you have to get used to hard knocks.* **2** (in an engine) sound of knocking (KNOCK[2] 4): *What's that knock I can hear?* **3** (*infml*) (in cricket) innings: *That was a good knock: 86 not out.* **4** (idm) **take a ˈknock** (*infml*) suffer a financial or an emotional blow: *She took a bad knock when her husband died.*

knock[2] /nɒk/ *v* **1** [Tn, Tn·pr] strike (sth) with a sharp blow: *Mind you don't knock your head (on this low beam).* **2** [I, Ipr] make a noise by striking sth: *knock three times (at the door, on the window, etc).* ➩ Usage at BANG[1]. **3** (**a**) [Cn·a, Cn·g] cause (sb/sth) to be in a certain state or position by striking (him/it): *The fall knocked me senseless.* ○ *He knocked me flat with one punch.* ○ *He knocked my drink flying.* (**b**) [Tn·pr] make (sth) by striking: *knock a hole in the wall.* **4** [I] (of a faulty petrol engine) make a tapping or thumping noise. **5** [Tn] (*infml*) say critical or insulting things about (sb/sth): *The newspapers are too fond of knocking the England team.* ○ *He's always knocking the way I do things.* **6** (idm) **beat/knock the daylights out of sb** ➩ DAYLIGHTS. **beat/knock hell out of sb/sth** ➩ HELL. **get/knock sb/sth into shape** ➩ SHAPE[1]. **hit/knock sb for six** ➩ HIT[1]. **knock sb's ˈblock/ˈhead off** (*sl*) (used esp when threatening sb) strike sb in anger: *Call me that again and I'll knock your block off!* **knock the bottom out of sth** cause sth to collapse: *It knocked the bottom out of the coffee market*, ie caused the price of coffee to fall sharply. ○ *She knocked the bottom out of our argument.* **knock sb/sth galley-west** ➩ GALLEY-WEST. **knock sb/sth on the ˈhead** (**a**) strike sb/sth hard on the head, in order to stun or kill. (**b**) stop sth from developing further: *She said something about buying an electric guitar, but I soon knocked that idea on the head!* **knock your/their ˈheads together** (*infml*) force people to stop quarrelling and behave sensibly: *I often feel that politicians should have their heads knocked together, like naughty children.* **knock sb/sth into a cocked ˈhat** defeat or outclass sb/sth: *A true professional could knock my efforts into a cocked hat.* **knock it ˈoff** (*sl*) (esp imperative) stop a noise, an argument, etc: *Knock it off, kids, I'm trying to sleep!* **knock sb off his ˈpedestal/perch** (*infml*) defeat sb; show that sb is no longer best at sth. **knock sb ˈsideways** (*infml*) defeat sb; astonish sb. **knock ˈspots off sb/sth** (*infml*) be much better than sb/sth: *In learning foreign languages, the girls knock spots off the boys every time.* **knock the stuffing out of sb** (*infml*) make sb feeble, weak or demoralized: *His failure in the exam has knocked all the stuffing out of him.* **knock them in the ˈaisles** (*infml*) (of a theatre performance, etc) be very successful with the audience. **you could have knocked me down with a ˈfeather** (*infml*) (used esp as an exclamation) I was amazed.

7 (phr v) **knock about (...)** (*infml*) lead an unsettled life, travelling and living in various places: *spend a few years knocking about (in) Europe.* **knock about with sb/together** (*infml*) be often in sb's/each other's company. **knock sb/sth about** (*infml*) hit sb/sth repeatedly; treat sb/sth roughly: *She gets knocked about by her husband.* ○ *The car's been knocked about a bit, but it still goes.*

knock sth back (*infml*) drink sth quickly: *knock back a pint of beer.*

knock sb down strike sb to the ground or the floor: *She was knocked down by a bus.* ○ *He knocked his opponent down three times in the first round.* **knock sth down** demolish sth: *These old houses are going to be knocked down.* **knock sth down (to sb)** (*infml*) (at an auction sale) sell sth (to a bidder): *The painting was knocked down (to an American dealer) for £5000.* **knock sth/sb down** (force sb to) reduce (a price or charge): *I managed to knock his price/him down (from £500 to £450).*

knock sth in; knock sth into sth make sth enter sth by striking it: *knock in a few nails.*

knock off (sth) (*infml*) stop doing sth (esp work): *What time do you knock off (work)?* **knock sb off** (*sl*) (**a**) murder sb. (**b**) have sexual intercourse with (a woman). **knock sth off** (**a**) deduct sth from a price or charge: *It cost me £10 but I'll knock off 20% as it's no longer new.* (**b**) (*infml*) complete sth quickly: *knock off two whole chapters in an hour.* (**c**) (*sl*) steal (from) sth: *knock off some watches from a shop* ○ *knock off a bank.* **knock sth off (sth)** remove sth by striking it: *knock sb's glass off the table.*

knock (sth) on (in Rugby football) illegally knock (the ball) forward with the hands: *He accidentally knocked on (the pass from Jones).*

knock sb out (**a**) (in boxing) strike (an opponent) so that he cannot rise or continue in a specified time and so loses the fight. (**b**) make sb unconscious by means of a blow, alcoholic drink, etc: *Don't drink too much of this — it'll knock you out!* (**c**) (*infml*) overwhelm or astonish sb: *The film*

just knocked me out — it's the best thing I've ever seen. **knock sb/oneself out** make sb/oneself exhausted, ill, etc: *She's knocking herself out with all that work.* **knock sb out (of sth)** eliminate sb (from a competition) by defeating him: *France knocked Belgium out (of the European Cup).* **knock sth out (on sth)** empty (a tobacco pipe) by knocking it (against sth).
knock sb/sth over upset sb/sth by striking him/it: *You've knocked over my drink!*
knock sth together make or complete sth quickly and often not very well: *knock bookshelves together from old planks* ○ *knock a few scenes together to make a play.*
knock up (in tennis, badminton, etc) practise hitting the ball before the start of a match. **knock sb up (a)** (*Brit infml*) awaken sb by knocking on his door, etc: *Would you please knock me up at 7 o'clock?* **(b)** (⚠ *sl esp US*) make (a woman) pregnant. **knock sth up (a)** prepare or make sth quickly and without much planning: *Even though they weren't expecting us, they managed to knock up a marvellous meal.* **(b)** (in cricket) score (runs): *knock up a quick fifty.*

□ **ˈknockabout** *adj* (esp of a theatrical performance) rough and boisterous in a funny way; slapstick: *knockabout humour/comedy/farce.*
ˈknock-down *adj* [attrib] **(a)** (of prices) very low. **(b)** (of furniture) easy to dismantle and reassemble.
ˌknock-for-ˈknock *adj* [attrib] (of an insurance agreement) in which each insurance company agrees to pay its own policy holder without trying to decide who was responsible (eg for an accident involving more than one vehicle).
ˈknocking-shop *n* (*Brit sl*) brothel.
ˌknock-ˈkneed *adj* having legs abnormally curved so that the knees touch when standing or walking.
ˌknock-ˈon *n* (in Rugby football) act of knocking the ball on. **ˌknock-ˈon effect** indirect result of an action: *The closure of the car factory had a knock-on effect on the tyre manufacturers.*
ˈknock-out *n* **1** blow that knocks a boxer out: *He has won most of his fights by knock-outs.* ○ [attrib] *a knock-out punch.* **2** [attrib] (of a drug) causing sleep or unconsciousness: *knock-out drops/pills.* **3** competition in which the loser of each successive round is eliminated: [attrib] *a knock-out tournament.* **4** (*infml*) outstandingly impressive person or thing: *She's an absolute knock-out*, ie very beautiful. ○ [attrib] *a knock-out idea.*
ˈknock-up *n* [sing] (in tennis, badminton, etc) period of practice before a match: *have a quick knock-up.*

knocker /ˈnɒkə(r)/ *n* **1** [C] hinged metal hammer attached to a door, used for knocking by sb outside who wants the door to be opened. ⇨ illus at HOME. **2** [C] (*infml*) person who constantly criticizes. **3 knockers** [pl] (⚠ *Brit sl sexist*) woman's breasts: *a nice pair of knockers.*

knoll /nəʊl/ *n* small round hill or mound.

knot[1] /nɒt/ *n* **1** fastening made by tying a piece or pieces of string, rope, etc: *make a knot at the end of the rope* ○ *tie the two ropes together with a secure knot.* ⇨ illus. **2** ornament or decoration made of ribbon, etc twisted and tied. **3** tangle; twisted piece: *comb a knot out of one's hair.* **4** hard round spot in timber where a branch used to join the trunk or another branch. ⇨ illus at GRAIN. **5** small gathering (of people or things): *a knot of people arguing outside the pub.* **6** (idm) **cut the Gordian knot** ⇨ GORDIAN KNOT. **tie sb/oneself in knots** ⇨ TIE[2]. **tie the knot** ⇨ TIE[2].

▷ **knot** *v* (**-tt-**) **1** [I, Tn, Tn·p] (cause sth to) form knots: *My hair knots easily.* ○ *knot two ropes together.* **2** [Tn] fasten (sth) with a knot or knots: *knot one's tie loosely.* **3** (idm) **get ˈknotted** (*Brit sl*) (used to express contempt, annoyance, etc): *If he asks you for money again just tell him to get knotted.*
knotty *adj* (**-ier, -iest**) **1** (of timber) full of knots. **2** puzzling; difficult: *a knotty problem, question, etc.*

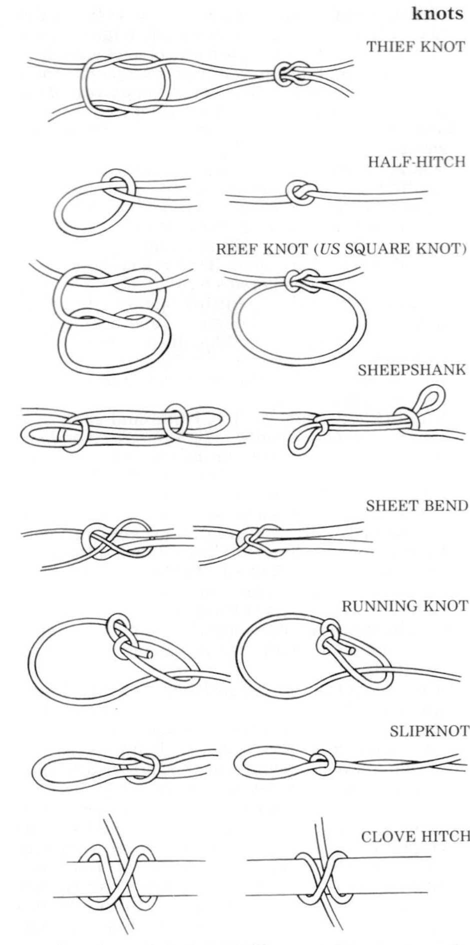

□ **ˈknot-grass** *n* weed with creeping stems and small pink flowers.
ˈknot-hole *n* hole in a piece of timber where a knot[1](4) has fallen out.

knot[2] /nɒt/ *n* (usu *pl*) (*nautical*) **1** unit of speed (one nautical mile per hour) used by ships and aircraft. ⇨ App 10. **2** (idm) **at a rate of knots** ⇨ RATE.

know /nəʊ/ *v* (*pt* **knew** /njuː; *US* nuː/, *pp* **known** /nəʊn/) **1 (a)** [I, Tn, Tf, Tw, Tt, Cn·t] have (sth) in one's mind or memory as a result of experience or learning or information: *I'm not guessing — I know!* ○ *She doesn't know your address.* ○ *Every child knows (that) two and two make four.* ○ *I knew where he was hiding.* ○ *Do you know who Napoleon was?* ○ *Does he know to come here* (ie that he should come here) *first?* ○ *We knew her to be honest.* **(b)** [Tnt, Tni] (only in the past and perfect tenses) have seen, heard, etc: *I've never known it (to) snow in July before.* ○ *He's sometimes been known to sit there all day.* **2** [Tf] feel certain: *I know (that) it's here somewhere — it must be!* **3 (a)** [Tn] be acquainted with (sb): *Do you know Bob Hill?* ie Have you met him, talked with him, etc? ○ *I know him by sight, but not to talk to*, ie I have seen him but never spoken to him. ○ *We've known each other since we were children.* **(b)** [Tn, Cn·n/a] ~ **sth (as sth)** be familiar with (a place): *I know Paris better than Rome.* ○ *I know London as the place where I spent my childhood.* **4** [Cn·n/a, only passive] ~ **sb/sth as sth** regard sb/sth as (being) sth: *It's known as the most dangerous part of the city.* ○ *We know John Smith as a fine lawyer and a good friend.* **5** [Cn·n/a, usu passive] ~ **sb/sth as sth** call, nickname or label sb/sth as sth: *a heavyweight boxer known as 'The Greatest'* ○ *This area is known as the 'Cornish Riviera'.* **6** [Tn, Tn·pr] ~ **sb/sth (from sb/sth)** be able to distinguish (one person or thing) from another; recognize: *She knows a bargain when she sees one.* ○ *know right from wrong* ○ *I met so many people at the party that I wouldn't know half of them again.* **7** [Tn, Tw] understand and be able to use (a language, skill, etc): *know Japanese* ○ *know how to swim.* **8** [Tn] have personal experience of (sth): *a man who has known both poverty and riches.* **9** (idm) **beˌfore one ˌknows where one ˈis** very quickly or suddenly: *We were whisked off in a taxi before we knew where we were.* **be known to sb** be familiar to sb: *He's known to the police*, ie has a criminal record. **better the devil you know** ⇨ BETTER[2]. **for all one knows** considering how little one knows: *For all I know he could be dead.* **for reasons/some reason best known to oneself** ⇨ REASON. **God/goodness/Heaven knows (a)** I don't know: *God knows what's happened to them.* **(b)** certainly; emphatically: *She ought to succeed; goodness knows she tries hard enough.* **have/know all the answers** (*infml esp derog*) (seem to) be cleverer and better-informed than other people. **have/know sth off pat** ⇨ PAT[1]. **I ˈknew it** (used esp for expressing disappointment or concern at a piece of news) I was certain that would happen: *'He's phoned to say he can't come.' 'I knew it - he's never available when we need him.'* **know sth as well as ˈI/ˈyou do** understand sth perfectly well: *You know as well as I do that you're being unreasonable.* **know sth ˈbackwards** (*infml*) be thoroughly familiar with sth: *You've read that book so many times you must know it backwards by now!* **know ˈbest** know what should be done, etc better than other people: *The doctor told you to stay in bed, and he knows best.* **know better (than that/than to do sth)** be wise or sensible (enough not to do it): *You ought to know better (than to trust her).* **know sb by sight** recognize who sb is without knowing him as a personal friend. **know ˈdifferent/ˈotherwise** (*infml*) have information or evidence to the contrary: *He says he was at the cinema, but I know different.* **know how many beans make five** be shrewd and sensible in practical matters. **know sth inside ˈout/like the back of one's ˈhand** (*infml*) be thoroughly familiar with a place, subject, etc: *He's a taxi driver, so he knows London like the back of his hand.* **know no ˈbounds** (*fml*) be very great or too great: *When she heard the news her fury knew no bounds.* **know one's ˈonions/ˈstuff** (*infml*) be good at one's work, etc. **know one's own ˈmind** know what one wants or intends. **know the ˈscore** (*infml*) understand the true state of affairs. **know a thing or two (about sb/sth)** (*infml*) know a lot (about sb/sth): *She's been married five times, so she should know a thing or two about men.* **know sb through and ˈthrough** understand sb perfectly. **know one's way around** be familiar with a place, subject, procedure, etc; be capable and well-informed. **know what it is/what it's like (to be/do sth)** have personal experience (of being/doing sth): *Many famous people have known what it is to be poor.* **know what one's ˈtalking about** (*infml*) speak from experience. **know what's ˈwhat** (*infml*) understand the important facts, rules of behaviour, etc in a particular situation: *You're old enough now to know what's what.* **know which side one's ˈbread is buttered** (*infml saying*) know where one's interests lie or what will be to one's advantage. **let sb ˈknow** inform sb about sth: *I don't know if I can come yet, but I'll let you know tomorrow.* **make oneself known to sb** introduce oneself to sb: *There's our host; you'd better make yourself known to him.* **not be to know (a)** not be allowed to find out (about sth): *I'll pay his bill, but he's not to know about it*, ie don't tell him that I have. **(b)** have no way of knowing: *It wasn't your fault the chair collapsed; you weren't to know* (ie no one had told you) *it had a damaged leg.* **not know ˈany ˈbetter** not behave well, through lack of experience, bad upbringing, etc: *Don't blame the children for their bad manners — they don't know any better.* **not know ˈbeans (about sth)** (*US infml*) know nothing (about sth). **not know ˌone**

end of ˌsth from the ˈother (*infml*) be unable to do the activity associated with sth: *Me play tennis? I don't know one end of a racket from the other*(ie I cannot play tennis at all)*!* **not know one is ˈborn** (*infml*) have an easy life (and not realize how easy it is). **not know one's ˌarse from one's ˈelbow** (⚠ *sl derog*) be totally ignorant, stupid or inefficient. **not know the first thing about sb/sth/doing sth** know nothing at all about sb/sth/doing sth: *I'm afraid I don't know the first thing about gardening.* **not know sb from ˈAdam** (*infml*) not know at all who sb is. **not know what ˈhit one** (**a**) be suddenly injured or killed: *The bus was moving so fast she never knew what hit her.* (**b**) (*infml fig*) be amazed or confused: *The first time I heard their music I didn't know what had hit me.* **not know where/which way to look** (*infml*) be embarrassed, awkwardly self-conscious, etc: *When he started undressing in public I didn't know where to look.* **not want to know** ➪ WANT[1]. **old enough to know better** ➪ OLD. **show sb/know/learn the ropes** ➪ ROPE. **see/know better days** ➪ BETTER[1]. **tell/know A and B apart** ➪ APART. **that's what I'd like to know** ➪ LIKE[2]. **there's no ˈknowing** it's difficult or impossible to know: *There's absolutely no knowing how he'll react.* (**well**) **what do you ˈknow (about ˈthat)?** (*infml esp US*) (used to express surprise on hearing news, etc) **you know** (*infml*) (**a**) (used when reminding sb of sth): *Guess who I've just seen? Marcia! You know — Jim's ex-wife!* (**b**) (used as an almost meaningless expression when the speaker is thinking what to say next): *'I was feeling a bit bored, you know, and so ...'.* **you know something/what?** (*infml*) (used to introduce an item of news, expression of opinion, etc): *You know something? Cathy and Tim are engaged.* **you never know** you cannot be certain: *'It's sure to rain tomorrow.' 'Oh, you never know, it could be a lovely day.'* ○ *You should keep those old jam jars — you never know when you might need them.* **10** (phr v) **know about sth** have knowledge of sth; be aware of sth: *Not much is known about his background.* ○ *Do you know about Jack getting arrested?* **know of sb/sth** have information about or experience of sb/sth: *'Isn't tomorrow a holiday?' 'Not that I know of* (ie Not as far as I am aware)*.'* ○ *Do you know of any way to stop a person snoring?* ○ *I don't know him personally, though I know ˈof him.*

▷ **know** *n* (idm) **in the ˈknow** (*infml*) (of a person) having information not possessed by others; well informed.

□ **ˈknow-all** *n* (*infml derog*) person who behaves as if he knows everything: *one of those young know-alls fresh from university.*

ˈknow-how *n* [U] (*infml*) practical (contrasted with theoretical) knowledge or skill in an activity.

knowing /ˈnəʊɪŋ/ *adj* [usu attrib] **1** showing or suggesting that one has information which is secret or not known to others: *a knowing look, glance, expression, etc.* **2** shrewd; cunning: *She's a bit too knowing for me to feel relaxed with her.*

▷ **knowingly** *adv* **1** intentionally: *It appears that what I said was untrue, but I did not knowingly lie to you.* **2** in a knowing(1) manner: *He winked at her knowingly.*

knowledge /ˈnɒlɪdʒ/ *n* **1** [U] understanding: *A baby has no knowledge of good and evil.* **2** [U, sing] all that a person knows; familiarity gained by experience: *I have only (a) limited knowledge of computers.* ○ *My knowledge of French is poor.* **3** [U] everything that is known; organized body of information: *all branches of knowledge* ○ *the sum of human knowledge on this subject.* **4** (idm) **be common/public knowledge** be known by everyone in a community or group: *It's pointless trying to keep your friendship secret — it's common knowledge already.* **come to sb's ˈknowledge** (*fml*) become known by sb: *It has come to our knowledge that you have been cheating the company.* **to one's ˈknowledge** (**a**) as far as one knows: *To my knowledge, she has never been late before.* (**b**) as one knows to be true: *That is impossible, because to my (certain) knowledge he was in France at the time.* **to the best of one's belief/knowledge** ➪ BEST[3]. **with/without sb's ˈknowledge** having/not having informed sb: *He sold the car without his wife's knowledge.*

▷ **knowledgeable** /-əbl/ *adj* ~ (**about sth**) well-informed: *She's very knowledgeable about art.* **knowledgeably** /-əblɪ/ *adv*: *speak knowledgeably on the subject.*

Knox /nɒks/ John (c 1505-72), Scottish religious reformer who introduced Protestantism into Scotland. Exiled for a time in Geneva, where he met *Calvin, he returned to Scotland and led the opposition to the Catholic *Mary Queen of Scots by writing tracts and preaching fiercely hostile sermons.

knuckle /ˈnʌkl/ *n* **1** bone at the finger-joint: *graze/skin one's knuckles.* ➪ illus at HAND. **2** (of animals) knee-joint, or the part joining the leg to the foot, esp as a joint of meat: *pig's knuckles.* **3** (idm) **a rap on/over the knuckles** ➪ RAP[1]. **near the ˈknuckle** (*infml*) on the borderline of indecency and therefore likely to offend: *Some of his jokes are a bit too near the knuckle for my taste.*

▷ **knuckle** *v* (phr v) **knuckle down (to sth)** (*infml*) begin to work seriously (at sth): *If you want to pass that exam, you'll have to knuckle down (to some hard work).* **knuckle under** (*infml*) accept or admit defeat; surrender.

□ **ˈknuckleduster** *n* (*US* **brass ˈknuckles**) metal cover worn over the knuckles to increase the injury caused by a blow with the fist.

ˈknucklehead *n* (*infml derog*) fool.

KO /ˌkeɪ ˈəʊ/ *abbr* (*infml*) knock-out (esp in boxing): *He was KO'd* (ie knocked out) *in the second round.*

koala /kəʊˈɑːlə/ *n* (also **koala bear**) Australian tree-climbing mammal with thick grey fur, large ears and no tail.

kobo /ˈkɒbəʊ/ *n* (*pl* unchanged) unit of currency in Nigeria; 100th part of a naira.

Koh-i-noor /ˈkəʊɪnʊə(r)/ *n* [sing] large Indian diamond, now part of the British crown jewels.

kohl /kəʊl/ *n* [U] cosmetic powder used in the East to darken the eyelids.

kohlrabi /ˌkəʊlˈrɑːbɪ/ *n* [C, U] cabbage with an edible turnip-shaped stem.

kola = COLA.

koodoo /ˈkuːduː/ *n* = KUDU.

kook /kuːk/ *n* (*US derog sl*) peculiar, eccentric or crazy person. ▷ **kooky** *adj.*

kookaburra /ˈkʊkəbʌrə/ *n* (also **laughing jackass**) Australian giant kingfisher.

kopeck (also **kopek**) = COPECK.

koppie (also **kopje**) /ˈkɒpɪ/ *n* (in S Africa) small hill.

Koran /kəˈrɑːn; *US* -ˈræn/ *n* **the Koran** [sing] sacred book of the Muslims, written in Arabic, said to contain the word of God communicated to the Prophet Muhammad by the archangel *Gabriel. It contains 114 sections, and deals with Islamic religious doctrine, social organization, morality, etc. Traditional Islamic education involves learning it by heart. ▷ **Koranic** /kəˈrænɪk/ *adj.*

Korda /ˈkɔːdə/ Sir Alexander (1893-1956), Hungarian-born film producer and director who settled in England. His films include *The Private Life of Henry VIII, Rembrandt* and *Things to Come.*

Korea /kəˈrɪə/ peninsula on the eastern coast of Asia, containing two states, both created in 1948: **North Korea** (also **the People's Democratic Republic of Korea**), a communist state; pop approx 21 902 000; official language Korean; capital Pyongyang; unit of currency won (= 100 jun); and **South Korea** (also **the Republic of Korea**), a capitalist state which exports large quantities of manufactured consumer goods to the West; pop approx 41 975 000; official language Korean; capital Seoul; unit of currency won. ➪ map.

▷ **Korean** /kəˈrɪən/ *adj* of Korea, its people or its language. — *n* **1** [C] native or inhabitant of Korea. **2** [U] language spoken in Korea, perhaps related to Mongolian.

□ **the Koˌrean ˈWar** war (1950-53) between North and South Korea. The North, supported by China, invaded the South. The United Nations opposed this, and sent (mainly US) troops to support the South. After extensive but inconclusive fighting up and down the peninsula a peace treaty was signed.

Korea

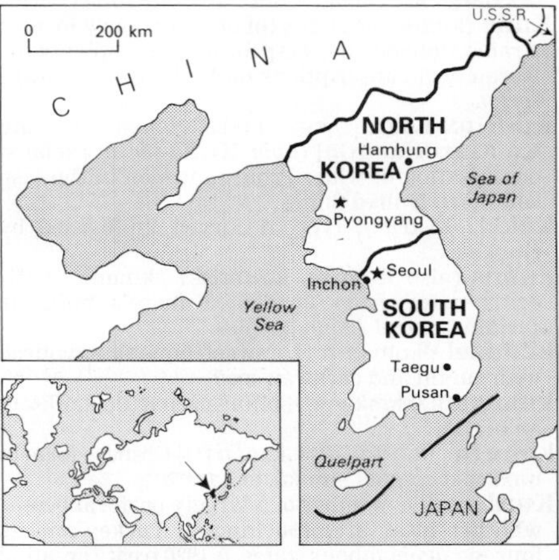

kosher /ˈkəʊʃə(r)/ *adj* **1** (of food, food shops, etc) fulfilling the requirements of Jewish dietary law: *a kosher butcher's, restaurant, meal.* **2** (*infml*) genuine or legitimate: *the real kosher article, not just any old rubbish* ○ *something not quite kosher about the way he made his money.*

koumiss = KUMIS.

kowtow /ˌkaʊˈtaʊ/ *v* [I, Ipr] ~ (**to sb/sth**) be submissive, humble or respectful (to sb/sth): *a refusal to kowtow (to the government's wishes on this issue).*

kph /ˌkeɪ piː ˈeɪtʃ/ *abbr* kilometres per hour. Cf MPH.

Kr *symb* krypton.

kraal /krɑːl; *US* krɔːl/ *n* (in S Africa) **1** village of huts enclosed by a fence. **2** enclosure for cattle, sheep, etc.

krait /kraɪt/ *n* highly poisonous snake found in India and SE Asia.

kraken /ˈkrɑːkən/ *n* mythical monster said to live in the sea off the Norwegian coast.

Kraut /kraʊt/ *n* (⚠ *sl derog offensive*) German person.

Krebs cycle /ˈkrebz saɪkl/ *n* cyclical series of biochemical reactions by which organisms break down food using oxygen, so as to be able to use its energy. It is named after the British scientist Sir Hans Krebs.

kremlin /ˈkremlɪn/ *n* **1** [C] citadel within a Russian town. **2 the Kremlin** (**a**) [Gp] government of the former USSR, or of Russia: *the Kremlin's latest proposals on arms control.* (**b**) [sing] the citadel of Moscow.

▷ **Kremlinology** /ˌkremlɪˈnɒlədʒɪ/ *n* [U] study and analysis of Soviet or of Russian policies and actions. **Kremlinologist** *n.*

krill /krɪl/ *n* [pl *v*] mass of tiny shellfish eaten by whales.

kris /kriːs/ *n* Malay or Indonesian dagger.

Kriss Kringle /ˌkrɪs ˈkrɪŋgl/ (*US*) Santa Claus.

krona /ˈkrəʊnə/ *n* **1** (*pl* **-nor** /-nə(r)/) unit of money in Sweden. **2** (*pl* **-nur** /-nə(r)/) unit of money in Iceland.

krone /ˈkrəʊnə/ *n* (*pl* **-ner** /-nə(r)/) unit of money in Denmark and Norway.

krugerrand /ˈkruːgərænd/ *n* South African gold coin weighing one ounce.

krypton /ˈkrɪptɒn/ *n* [U] (*symb* **Kr**) chemical element, an inert colourless and odourless gas. ➪ App 11.

Kt *abbr* Knight: *Sir James Bailey Kt.*

Kubrick /ˈkjuːbrɪk/ Stanley (1928-), American film director. An intellectual film maker, he has chosen deliberately varied subject matter for each of his pictures, from the futuristic *2001: A Space Odyssey* to the period drama of *Barry Lyndon.*

kudos /ˈkjuːdɒs; *US* ˈkuː/ *n* [U] (*infml*) honour and glory; credit[1](2): *She did most of the work but all the kudos went to him.*

kudu (also **koodoo**) /ˈkuːduː/ *n* (*pl* unchanged or ~**s**) large African antelope with long spiral horns.

Kufic /ˈkuːfɪk/ *adj*, *n* [U] (of or in an) early form of Arabic alphabet, used esp for making copies of the Koran or for inscriptions on buildings, etc: *Kufic script.*

Ku-Klux-Klan /ˌkuː klʌks ˈklæn/ *n* **the Ku-Klux-Klan** [Gp] (*abbr* **KKK**) secret racialist organization of white Protestant men in the (esp southern) United States.

kukri /ˈkʊkrɪ/ *n* type of curved knife used by Gurkhas.

kumis (also **kumiss**, **koumiss**) /ˈkuːmɪs/ *n* [U] drink made from fermented mare's milk by certain Central Asian peoples.

kümmel /ˈkʊməl/ *n* [U] sweet liqueur flavoured with cumin and caraway seeds.

kumquat /ˈkʌmkwɒt/ *n* plum-sized fruit similar to an orange.

kung fu /ˌkʊŋ ˈfuː, *also* ˌkʌŋ/ *n* [U] Chinese form of unarmed combat similar to karate.

Kurd /kɜːd/ *n* member of a largely pastoral people who live in an area touching on Turkey and its four Asian neighbour states. A 1920 treaty creating the Kurds a unified homeland was never ratified; their recent history has been one of armed resistance and of exploitation by outside powers. After the Gulf War in 1991 many refugee Kurds were resettled in 'safe havens' in N Iraq. Their political ambitions all focus on a fully independent and unified country of **Kurdistan**.
▷ **Kurdish** *n* [U] language of the Kurds.—*adj* of the Kurds or their language.

Kurosawa /kʊərəˈsɑːwə/ Akira (1910-), Japanese film director. His early films concentrated on post-war Japan, but his more famous films like *The Seven Samurai* have historical settings, and some, eg *Ran*, are adaptations of Shakespeare.

Kuwait /kʊˈweɪt/ country at the northern end of the *Persian Gulf, bordered by Iraq and Saudi Arabia; pop approx 1 958 000; official language Arabic; capital Kuwait City; unit of currency dinar (= 1 000 fils). It is ruled by a sheikh, and is one of the world's leading producers of oil. In 1990 it was invaded by Iraq but coalition forces led by the USA liberated it in 1991. ⇨ map at ARABIAN PENINSULA.
▷ **Kuwaiti** /kʊˈweɪtɪ/ *adj*, *n*.

kvass /kvæs/ *n* [U] type of weak beer made in Russia and other parts of the former USSR.

kvetch /kvetʃ/ *v* [I] (*US sl*) complain continuously and annoyingly; gripe.
▷ **kvetch** *n* (*US sl*) person who complains a lot.

kW (also **kw**) *abbr* kilowatt(s): *a 2 kW electric heater.*

kwashiorkor /kwæʃɪˈɔːkɔː(r)/ *n* [U] severe tropical disease of children whose diet does not contain enough protein.

kwela /ˈkweɪlə/ *n* [U] type of South African jazz music.

kWh *abbr* kilowatt-hour(s).

kybosh (also **kibosh**) /ˈkaɪbɒʃ/ *n* (idm) **put the kybosh on sb/sth** (*sl*) prevent sb/sth from continuing; stop sb/sth: *When he broke his leg it put the kybosh on his holiday.*

Kyd /kɪd/ Thomas (1558-94), English dramatist, best known for his play *Spanish Tragedy*, published anonymously, which was very popular with Elizabethan audiences.

kyle /kaɪl/ *n* (esp in Scottish place-names) narrow channel between two islands or between an island and the mainland.

Kyrie /ˈkɪrɪeɪ/ *n* (also ˌ**Kyrie eˈleison** /ɪˈleɪɪzɒn/) (**a**) short prayer in Greek, used esp at the beginning of Mass in Roman Catholic and Greek Orthodox Churches. It means 'Lord, have mercy'. (**b**) musical setting of this prayer.

L, l

L, l /el/ (*pl* **L's, l's** /elz/) *n* the twelfth letter of the English alphabet: *'London' begins with (an) L/'L'.*

L *abbr* **1** Lake: *L Windermere*, eg on a map. **2** /el/ (*Brit*) (on a motor vehicle) learner-driver. Cf L-PLATE. **3** (esp on clothing, etc) large (size). **4** (*Brit politics*) Liberal (party). Cf LIB. **5** lira: *L6 000.* **6** (esp on electric plugs) live (connection).

L (also **l**) *symb* Roman numeral for 50.

l *abbr* **1** left. Cf R 2. **2** (*pl* **ll**) line: *p* (ie page) *2, l 19* ○ *verse 6, ll 8-10.* **3** litre(s).

LA /ˌel ˈeɪ/ *abbr* Los Angeles (California).

La *symb* lanthanum.

la = LAH.

laager /ˈlɑːgə(r)/ *n* (*S African*) **1** (formerly) camp inside a circle of wagons. **2** (*fig*) defensive position: *retreat into the laager.*

Lab /læb/ *abbr* (*Brit politics*) Labour (party): *Tom Warner (Lab).*

lab /læb/ *n* (*infml*) laboratory: *I'll meet you outside the science lab.* ○ [attrib] *a lab coat*, ie one worn to protect clothes in a laboratory.

label /ˈleɪbl/ *n* **1** piece of paper, cloth, metal, etc on or beside an object and describing its nature, name, owner, destination, etc: *put a label on a piece of clothing, a specimen, one's luggage* ○ *I read the information on the label before deciding which jam to buy.* **2** (*fig*) descriptive word or phrase applied to a person, group, etc: *hang, stick, slap, etc a label on sb/sth* ○ *A reviewer called her first novel 'super-romantic' and the label has stuck.* **3** (brand name appearing on the products of a) company, esp a recording or clothing company: *They've reissued it on their budget label*, ie in a series of recordings at a lower price. ○ [attrib] *designer label* (ie fashionably styled) *jeans.*

▷ **label** *v* (**-ll-**; *US* **-l-**) **1** [Tn] put a label or labels on (sth): *a machine for labelling wine bottles.* **2** [Tn, Cn·n, Cn·n/a] ~ **sb/sth as sth** (*fig*) describe or classify sb/sth: *His work is difficult to label accurately.* ○ *She is usually labelled (as) an Impressionist.*

labia /ˈleɪbɪə/ *n* [pl] lip-shaped folds of the female genitals, including the **labia majora** /məˈdʒɔːrə/ (the larger outer pair) and the **labia minora** /mɪˈnɔːrə/ (the smaller inner pair).

labial /ˈleɪbɪəl/ *adj* **1** of the lips. **2** (*phonetics*) made with the lips: *labial sounds*, eg /m, p, v/.

▷ **labial** *n* (*phonetics*) sound made with the lips.

labiate /ˈleɪbɪeɪt/ *n, adj* (*botany*) (plant) with a corolla or calyx divided into two parts that look like lips.

labium /ˈleɪbɪəm/ *n* (*pl* **-ia** /-ɪə/) lower part of an insect's mouth.

laboratory /ləˈbɒrətrɪ; *US* ˈlæbrətɔːrɪ/ *n* room or building used for (esp scientific) research, experiments, testing, etc.

laborious /ləˈbɔːrɪəs/ *adj* **1** (of work, etc) needing much effort: *a laborious task.* **2** showing signs of great effort; not fluent or natural: *a laborious style of writing.* Cf LABOURED (LABOUR²). ▷ **laboriously** *adv.* **laboriousness** *n* [U].

labour¹ (*US* **labor**) /ˈleɪbə(r)/ *n* **1** [U] physical or mental work: *manual labour* ○ *Workers are paid for their labour.* **2** [C usu *pl*] task; piece of work: *tired after one's labours.* ⇨ Usage at WORK¹. **3** [U] workers as a group or class, esp as contrasted with capital, management, etc: *skilled/unskilled labour* ○ [attrib] *labour relations*, ie between workers and employers ○ *labour leaders*, ie trade union leaders. **4** [U, sing] contractions of the womb during the process of childbirth: *begin, go into, be in labour* ○ *She had a difficult labour.* ○ [attrib] *a labour ward*, ie a set of rooms in a hospital for childbirth. **5 Labour** (*abbr* **Lab**) (*Brit politics*) [Gp] the Labour Party: [attrib] *the Labour vote* ○ *Labour supporters.* ⇨ article at TRADE UNION, POLITICS. **6** (idm) **a ˌlabour of ˈHercules** task needing great strength or effort. **a ˌlabour of ˈlove** task done out of enthusiasm or devotion, not from necessity or for profit.

□ **ˈlabor union** (*US*) = TRADE UNION (TRADE).

ˈlabour camp prison camp with physical labour as a punishment.

ˈLabour Day (*US* **Labor Day**) public holiday in honour of workers (1 May; in US the first Monday in September). ⇨ article at HOLIDAY.

ˈLabour Exchange (*dated Brit*) = JOBCENTRE (JOB).

ˌlabour-inˈtensive *adj* (of an industrial process, etc) needing to employ many people. Cf CAPITAL-INTENSIVE (CAPITAL²).

the ˈLabour Party (*Brit politics*) one of the major political parties in Britain, founded to represent esp the interests of workers and traditionally supported by the trade union movement. It is the only large party of the left and covers a wide range of political opinion, from those favouring a mixed economy to those wanting nationalization of industry on a large scale. Cf THE CONSERVATIVE PARTY (CONSERVATIVE), THE LIBERAL DEMOCRATS (LIBERAL).

ˈlabour-saving *adj* [usu attrib] designed to reduce the amount of work or effort needed to do sth: *labour-saving devices*, eg a lawn-mower, a washing-machine.

labour² (*US* **labor**) /ˈleɪbə(r)/ *v* **1** [I, Ipr, Ip, It] work or try hard: *labour on/at a task* ○ *I've been labouring (away) over a hot stove all morning.* ○ *He laboured to finish the job on time.* **2** (**a**) [I, Ipr, It] do sth only with difficulty and effort: *The old man laboured up the hillside.* ○ *The ship laboured through the rough seas.* ○ *labouring to breathe.* (**b**) [I] (of an engine) work slowly and with difficulty: *You should change gear — the engine's starting to labour.* **3** (idm) **ˈlabour the point** continue to repeat or explain sth that has already been said and understood: *Your argument was clear to us from the start — there's no need to labour the point.* **4** (phr v) **labour under sth** (*fml*) (**a**) suffer because of (a disadvantage or difficulty): *people labouring under the handicaps of ignorance and superstition.* (**b**) be deceived or misled by sth: *He labours under the delusion that he's a fine actor.*

▷ **laboured** (*US* **labored**) *adj* **1** slow and difficult: *laboured breathing.* **2** showing signs of too much effort; not natural or spontaneous: *a laboured style of writing.* Cf LABORIOUS 2.

labourer (*US* **laborer**) /ˈleɪbərə(r)/ *n* person who does heavy unskilled work: *a farm labourer.*

Labrador¹ /ˈlæbrədɔː(r)/ peninsula in NE Canada, from Hudson Bay to the mouth of the St Lawrence river, esp the part belonging to the province of Newfoundland. The climate is extremely cold, and the population consists mainly of native Eskimos and Indians, with workers from outside mining the large iron reserves.

□ **the ˌLabrador ˈcurrent** cold ocean current coming from the Arctic Ocean along the east coast of North America.

Labrador² /ˈlæbrədɔː(r)/ *n* breed of dog with a smooth black or golden coat.

labrum /ˈleɪbrəm/ *n* (*pl* **-bra** /-brə/) upper lip of an insect.

laburnum /ləˈbɜːnəm/ *n* [C, U] small ornamental tree with hanging clusters of yellow flowers.

labyrinth /ˈlæbərɪnθ/ *n* complicated network of winding passages, paths, etc through which it is difficult to find one's way: *The old building was a labyrinth of dark corridors.* ○ (*fig*) *go through a real labyrinth of procedures to get a residence permit.* Cf MAZE. ▷ **labyrinthine** /ˌlæbəˈrɪnθaɪn; *US* -θɪn/ *adj*

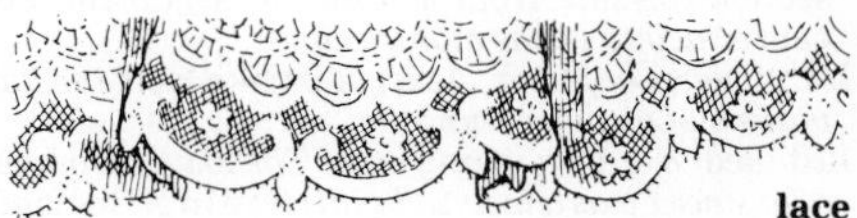

lace

lace /leɪs/ *n* **1** [U] delicate fabric with an ornamental openwork design of threads: *a wedding dress made of lace* ○ [attrib] *lace curtains.* ⇨ illus. **2** [C] string or cord threaded through holes or hooks in shoes, etc to pull and hold two edges together: *a pair of ˈshoe-laces* ○ *a broken lace.* ⇨ illus at SHOE.

▷ **lace** *v* **1** [I, Ip, Tn, Tn·p] ~ **(sth) (up)** fasten (sth) with laces: *a blouse that laces (up) at the front* ○ *lace (up) one's shoes.* **2** [Tn, Tn·pr] ~ **sth (with sth)** flavour or strengthen (a drink) with a small amount of spirits: *a glass of milk laced with rum* ○ *My drink has been laced.* **3** (phr v) **lace into sb** (*infml*) attack sb physically or with words.

□ **ˈlace-ups** *n* [pl] shoes that are fastened with laces: *She has to wear lace-ups at school.*

lacerate /ˈlæsəreɪt/ *v* [Tn] **1** injure (flesh) by tearing: *The sharp stones lacerated his feet.* **2** (*fig fml*) hurt (the feelings).

▷ **laceration** /ˌlæsəˈreɪʃn/ *n* (**a**) [U] tearing of the flesh. (**b**) [C] injury caused by this: *facial lacerations.*

lachrymal /ˈlækrɪml/ *adj* [attrib] (*anatomy*) producing or concerned with tears or weeping: *lachrymal glands, ducts, etc.*

lachrymose /ˈlækrɪməʊs/ *adj* (*fml*) in the habit of weeping; tearful; mournful: *a lachrymose disposition.*

lack /læk/ *v* **1** [Tn no passive] be without (sth); have less than enough of: *lack creativity, self-discipline, courage* ○ *They lacked the money to send him to university.* ○ *What he lacks in experience he makes up for in enthusiasm.* **2** [Ipr no passive] ~ **for sth** (*fml*) need sth: *They lacked for nothing*, ie had everything they wanted. **3** (idm) **be ˈlacking** not be available when needed: *Money for the project is still lacking.* **be lacking in sth** not have enough of sth: *be lacking in warmth, courage, strength* ○ *The film was lacking in pace.* **have/lack the courage of one's convictions** ⇨ COURAGE.

▷ **lack** *n* [U, sing] absence or shortage (of sth that is needed): *a lack of care, money, water* ○ *The project had to be abandoned for* (ie because of) *lack of funds.*

□ **ˈlack-lustre** *adj* dull; uninspiring; lifeless: *lack-lustre eyes* ○ *They gave a lack-lustre performance.*

lackadaisical /ˌlækəˈdeɪzɪkl/ *adj* lacking vigour and determination; unenthusiastic: *a lackadaisical approach to his studies.* ▷ **lackadaisically** /-klɪ/ *adv.*

lackey /ˈlækɪ/ *n* **1** (formerly) footman or manservant, usu in special uniform. **2** (*fig derog*) person who acts or is treated like a servant: *The singer was surrounded by the usual crowd of lackeys and hangers-on.*

laconic /ləˈkɒnɪk/ *adj* using few words; terse: *a laconic person, remark, style.* ▷ **laconically** /-klɪ/ *adv*: *'Too bad,' she replied laconically.*

lacquer /ˈlækə(r)/ *n* [U] **1** varnish used on metal or wood to give a hard glossy surface. **2** (*becoming dated*) liquid sprayed on the hair to keep it in place.

▷ **lacquer** *v* [Tn] coat (sth) with lacquer: *a lacquered table* ○ *lacquered hair.*

lacrosse /ləˈkrɒs; *US* -ˈkrɔːs/ *n* [U] game like hockey, played by two teams of 10 players each who use rackets to catch, carry and throw the ball.

lactation /lækˈteɪʃn/ *n* [U] (*medical or biology*) **1** production of milk in the breasts of women or the udders of female animals. **2** time during which this happens.

lactic /ˈlæktɪk/ *adj* [esp attrib] of or from milk.

□ ˌ**lactic** ˈ**acid** (*chemistry*) acid that forms in sour milk.

lactose /ˈlæktəʊs, -əʊz/ *n* [U] (*chemistry*) type of sugar found in milk and used in some baby foods.

lacuna /ləˈkju:nə/ *n* (*pl* **-nae** /-ni:/ or ~**s**) (*fml*) section missing from a book, an argument, etc; gap: *a lacuna in the manuscript.*

lacy /ˈleɪsɪ/ *adj* (**-ier, -iest**) of or like lace: *the lacy pattern of a spider's web.*

lad /læd/ *n* **1** boy; young man: *The town's changed a lot since I was a lad.* **2** (*infml*) (esp in N England) fellow; chap: *The lads at the office have sent you a get-well card.* **3** (*Brit infml approv*) lively, daring or reckless man (used esp in the expressions shown): *He's quite a lad/a bit of a lad.*

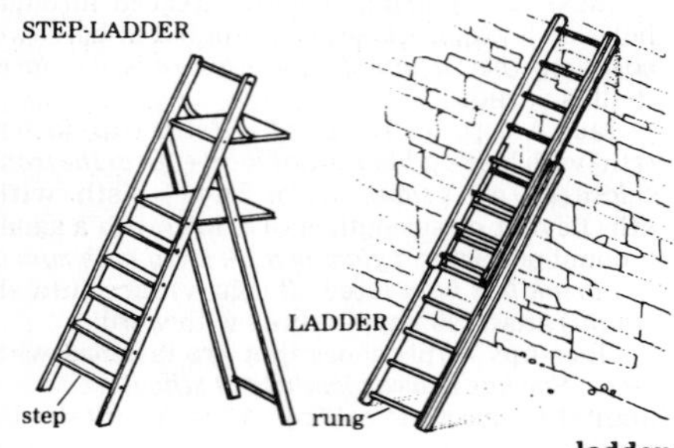

ladder

ladder /ˈlædə(r)/ *n* **1** structure for climbing up and down sth, consisting of two upright lengths of wood, metal or rope joined to each other by crossbars (*rungs*) used as steps. ⇨ illus. **2** (*US* **run**) fault in a stocking, etc where some stitches have come undone, causing a vertical ladder-like flaw. **3** (*fig*) series of stages by which a person may advance in his career, etc: *climbing the ladder of success* ○ *He is still on the bottom rung of the political ladder.*

▷ **ladder** *v* (**a**) [I] (of stockings, etc) develop a ladder(2): *Have you any tights that won't ladder?* (**b**) [Tn] cause (stockings, etc) to develop a ladder: *She laddered her new tights climbing the fence.*

laddie /ˈlædɪ/ *n* (*infml esp Scot*) boy; young man. Cf LASS.

laden /ˈleɪdn/ *adj* [usu pred] **1** ~ (**with sth**) loaded or weighted: *trees laden with apples* ○ *a lorry laden with supplies* ○ *Shoppers with their baskets fully laden.* **2** ~ **with sth** (*fig*) (of a person) troubled or burdened with sth: *laden with guilt, grief, remorse, etc.*

la-di-da /ˌlɑ:dɪˈdɑ:/ *adj* (*infml usu derog*) having an affected manner or pronunciation; pretentious: *I can't stand her or her la-di-da friends.*

ladle /ˈleɪdl/ *n* long-handled cup-shaped spoon for serving or transferring liquids: *a* ˈ*soup ladle.* ⇨ illus at KITCHEN.

▷ **ladle** *v* **1** [Tn, Tn·pr, Tn·p] ~ **sth** (**out**) serve (food) with a ladle or in large quantities: *She ladled cream over her pudding.* ○ *ladling out the stew.* **2** (phr v) **ladle sth out** (*infml*) distribute sth (too) lavishly: *He isn't one to ladle out praise, so when he says 'Good,' he means it.*

lady /ˈleɪdɪ/ *n* **1** [C] woman of good manners and dignified behaviour: *She's a real lady — never loses her temper.* Cf GENTLEMAN. **2** [C] (esp formerly) woman of good family and social position: *She was a lady by birth.* **3** [C] (esp in polite use) woman: *Ask that lady to help you.* ○ *The lady at the tourist office told me it opened at 1 pm.* ○ *the old lady next door* ○ *the* ˈ*tea-lady* ○ [attrib] *a lady doctor.* **4** [C] (*US infml*) (used as a term of address) woman: *Hey lady — you can't park there!* **5 Lady** (**a**) (esp in the UK) title used with the surname of the wives of some nobles: *Lady (Randolph) Churchill.* (**b**) (esp in the UK) title used with the first name of the daughters of some nobles: *Lady Philippa (Stewart).* (**c**) part of an official title of respect: *Lady* ˈ*Mayoress* ○ *Lady* ˈ*President.* **6 Ladies** [sing v] (*Brit*) women's public lavatory: *Is there a Ladies near here?* **7** (idm) **the** ˌ**lady of the** ˈ**house** woman with authority in a household: *Might I speak to the lady of the house?* **one's young lady/young man** ⇨ YOUNG.

□ ˈ**ladies' fingers** = OKRA.

ˈ**Lady Chapel** chapel in a large church, dedicated to the Virgin Mary.

ˈ**Lady Day** the Feast of the Annunciation, 25 March.

ˈ**ladyfinger** *n* (*esp US*) long thin sponge biscuit.

ˌ**lady-in-**ˈ**waiting** *n* (*pl* **ladies-in-waiting**) lady attending a queen or princess.

ˈ**lady-killer** *n* (*infml often derog*) man with the reputation of being very popular and successful with women.

ˈ**ladylike** *adj* (*approv*) like or suitable for a lady; polite; dignified; delicate: *ladylike behaviour, speech* ○ *She drank her wine with small ladylike sips.*

ˈ**ladyship** (also **Ladyship**) *n* title used in speaking to or about a titled lady: *their ladyships* ○ *If your ladyship will step this way, please.* ○ (*ironic or joc*) *Watch out, Jill — her ladyship is in one of her moods!*

ˈ**lady's maid** (esp formerly) personal maid reponsible for a lady's clothes, room, etc.

ˈ**lady's man** (also **ladies' man**) man who is fond of the company of women.

ˌ**lady's** ˈ**slipper** type of wild or garden orchid with a flower shaped like a pouch.

1 POLITE ADDRESS **Ladies** and **gentlemen** are used as the plural forms of **sir** and **madam**.

OCCASION	SINGULAR	PLURAL
giving a public speech		**Ladies and gentlemen,** I would like to thank ...
in a shop	Yes, **sir/madam**, will there be anything else?	Good morning, **ladies/gentlemen**, can I help you?
writing formal letters	Dear **Sir/Madam**, Thank you for your ...	**Gentlemen,** (very formal) Dear **Sirs,** ..(less formal) (There is no plural form of **madam**)

2 REFERRING TO PEOPLE **Lady** and **gentleman** are used instead of **woman** and **man** to show politeness.

with the person present	Mr Smith, this **lady/gentleman** wishes to make a complaint.
describing behaviour	He's very **gentlemanly**. She's very **ladylike**.
approving behaviour	He's/She's a real **gentleman/lady**.
referring to public toilets	the **Gents** (*US* the **men's room**) the **Ladies** (*US* the **ladies' room**) Where's the **Gents**, please? Where's the **Ladies**, please?

ladybird /ˈleɪdɪbɜ:d/ (*US* **ladybug** /ˈleɪdɪbʌg/) *n* small flying beetle, reddish-brown or yellow with black spots.

lag[1] /læg/ *v* (**-gg-**) [I, Ipr, Ip] ~ (**behind sb/sth**); ~ (**behind**) go too slow; fail to keep pace with others: *The small boy soon became tired and lagged far behind (the rest of the walkers).* ○ (*fig*) *Prices are rising sharply, while incomes are lagging far behind.*

▷ **lag** (also ˈ**time-lag**) *n* period of time separating two events, esp an action and its effect; delay: *a lag of several seconds between the lightning and the thunder.*

lag[2] /læg/ *v* (**-gg-**) [Tn, Tn·pr] ~ **sth** (**with sth**) cover (pipes, boilers, etc) with insulating material to prevent freezing of water or loss of heat.

▷ **lagging** *n* [U] material used for this.

lag[3] /læg/ ⇨ OLD LAG (OLD).

lager /ˈlɑ:gə(r)/ *n* **1** [U] type of light pale beer. **2** [C] glass or bottle of this.

laggard /ˈlægəd/ *n* person who lags behind: *He's no laggard when it comes to asking for more money*, ie He is very quick to do this.

lagoon /ləˈgu:n/ *n* **1** salt-water lake separated from the open sea by sandbanks or coral reefs. **2** (*US and Austral and NZ*) small shallow freshwater lake near a larger lake or river.

lah (also **la**) /lɑ:/ *n* (*music*) sixth note in the sol-fa scale.

laid *pt, pp* of LAY[1].

laid-back /ˌleɪd ˈbæk/ *adj* (*infml*) (of a person or his behaviour) calm and relaxed: *She always seems so laid-back* ○ *a* ˌ*laid-back* ˈ*style,* ˈ*manner etc.*

lain *pp* of LIE[2].

lair /leə(r)/ *n* **1** sheltered place where a wild animal regularly sleeps or rests; den. **2** (*fig*) person's hiding place: *The kidnappers' lair was an old farm in the hills.*

laird /leəd/ *n* (*Scot*) landowner.

laisser-faire (also **laissez-faire**) /ˌleɪseɪ ˈfeə(r)/ *n* [U] (*French*) policy of freedom from government control, esp for private commercial interests: [attrib] *a* ˌ*laisser-faire e*ˈ*conomy.*

laity /ˈleɪətɪ/ *n* **the laity** [Gp] **1** all the members of a Church who are not ordained clergymen; laymen. Cf CLERGY. **2** people outside a particular profession (contrasted with those inside it).

lake[1] /leɪk/ *n* **1** large area of water surrounded by land: *We sail on the lake in summer.* ○ *Lake Victoria* ○ *the Great Lakes.* **2** (idm) **jump in the/a lake** ⇨ JUMP 2.

□ **the** ˈ**Lake District** (also **the Lakes**) region of lakes and mountains in NW England. ⇨ map at UNITED KINGDOM.

the ˈ**Lake Poets** English romantic poets, esp Wordsworth, Coleridge and Southey, who lived in the Lake District. ⇨ article at COUNTRYSIDE.

lake[2] /leɪk/ *n* [U] (also ˌ**crimson** ˈ**lake**) dark red colouring material.

lakh /læk, lɑ:k/ *n* (in India and Pakistan) one hundred thousand: *50 lakhs of rupees.*

lam[1] /læm/ *v* (**-mm-**) (*sl*) **1** [Tn] hit (sb/sth) hard; thrash. **2** (phr v) **lam into sb** attack sb, physically or verbally: *My father really lammed into me for damaging his car.*

lam[2] /læm/ *n* (*US sl*) **1** sudden escape. **2** (idm) **on the lam** escaping or hiding, esp from the police.

lama /ˈlɑ:mə/ *n* Buddhist priest or monk in Tibet or Mongolia.

▷ **lamasery** /ˈlɑ:məsərɪ; *US* -serɪ/ *n* building or group of buildings where lamas live together; monastery.

Lamb /læm/ Charles (1775-1834), English essayist and critic. His best-known works are *Tales from Shakespear* (written esp for children with his sister Mary) and the entertaining *Essays of Elia.* His writings on drama and literature had an important influence on literary taste.

lamb /læm/ *n* **1** (**a**) [C] young sheep. ⇨ illus at SHEEP. Cf EWE. (**b**) [U] its flesh as food: *a leg of lamb* ○ [attrib] *lamb chops.* Cf MUTTON. **2** (*infml*) gentle or dear person. **3** (idm) **one may/might as well be hanged/hung for a sheep as a lamb** ⇨ HANG[1]. **like a lamb** (**to the slaughter**) without resisting or protesting: *She surprised us all on her first day of school by going off like a lamb.* **mutton dressed as lamb** ⇨ MUTTON.

▷ **lamb** *v* [I] **1** (of a ewe) give birth to lambs: *lambing ewes.* **2** (of a farmer) tend ewes doing this: *the lambing season*, ie when lambs are born.

□ **the** ˌ**Lamb of** ˈ**God** Jesus Christ, seen as having been sacrificed to save humanity.

ˈ**lambskin** *n* **1** [C] skin of a lamb with its wool on (used to make coats, gloves, etc). **2** [U] leather made from this.

ˈ**lamb's-wool** *n* [U] soft fine fluffy wool from lambs, used for making knitted clothes: *a scarf made of lamb's-wool* ○ [attrib] *a lamb's-wool cardigan.*

lambaste /læmˈbeɪst/ *v* [Tn] (*infml*) **1** hit (sb) hard and repeatedly; thrash. **2** reprimand (sb) severely.

lambda /ˈlæmdə/ *n* the eleventh letter of the Greek alphabet, written λ or Λ and corresponding to 'l'.

lambent /ˈlæmbənt/ *adj* [esp attrib] **1** (of a flame) moving over a surface with soft flickering radiance. **2** (of the eyes, sky, etc) shining or glowing softly. **3** (of humour, style, etc) witty in a brilliant but gentle way. ▷ **lambency** /-ənsɪ/ *n* [U].

Lambeth Palace /ˌlæmbəθ ˈpælɪs/ the London home of the archbishop of Canterbury.

□ **the ˌLambeth ˈConference** conference of Anglican bishops from all over the world, held every ten years (formerly always at Lambeth Palace).

lame /leɪm/ *adj* **1** unable to walk normally because of an injury or defect: *The accident made him lame in the left leg.* ○ *Halfway through the race the horse went lame.* **2** (of an excuse or argument) weak and unconvincing. **3** (idm) **help a lame dog over a stile** ⇨ HELP¹. **a ˌlame ˈduck (a)** person, organization or thing that is in difficulties and unable to manage without help: *The government should not waste money supporting lame ducks.* **(b)** (*esp US*) elected official in his final period of office: [attrib] *a ˌlame duck ˈPresident.*

▷ **lame** *v* [Tn] make (a person or an animal) lame; disable: *lamed in a riding accident.*

lamely *adv.*

lameness *n* [U].

lamé /ˈlɑːmeɪ; *US* lɑːˈmeɪ/ *n* [U] fabric in which gold or silver thread is interwoven with silk, wool or cotton: [attrib] *a silver lamé evening gown.*

lament /ləˈment/ *v* **(a)** [I, Ipr, Tn] ~ **(for/over sb/sth)** feel or express great sorrow or regret for (sb/sth): *lament loudly* ○ *lament (for) a dead friend* ○ *lament (over) one's misfortunes* ○ *lament the passing of old ways.* **(b)** [I, Tn] complain (about sth): *She's always lamenting the lack of sports facilities in town.*

▷ **lament** *n* **1** strong expression of grief. **2** song or poem expressing grief; dirge: *a funeral lament.*

lamentable /ˈlæməntəbl/ *adj* regrettable; deplorable: *a lamentable loss of life, lack of foresight.* **ˈlamentably** /-əblɪ/ *adv.*

lamentation /ˌlæmenˈteɪʃn/ *n* **1** [U] lamenting: *Much lamentation followed the death of the old king.* **2** [C] expression of grief; lament. **3 Lamentations** [sing *v*] book of the Old Testament, once thought to have been written by the prophet *Jeremiah, which describes the sorrow of Judah after the destruction of Jerusalem in 586 BC. ⇨ App 5.

lamented *adj* (*rhet or joc*) mourned for; regretted: *the much lamented pound note* ○ *our late lamented friend.*

laminate /ˈlæmɪneɪt/ *v* [Tn] **1** make (material) by bonding thin layers together: *laminated plastic.* **2** beat or roll (metal) into thin sheets.

▷ **laminate** /ˈlæmɪnət/ *n* [U] laminated material.

lamp /læmp/ *n* **1** device for giving light, either by the use of electricity or (esp formerly) by burning gas or oil: *a street, table, bicycle lamp.* **2** electrical device producing radiation (for medical, etc purposes): *an infra-red/ultraviolet lamp.*

□ **ˈlampblack** *n* [U] black colouring matter made from soot.

ˈlamplight *n* [U] light from a lamp.

ˈlamplighter *n* (formerly) person whose job was to light and extinguish gas street lamps.

ˈlamp-post *n* tall post supporting a street lamp. ⇨ illus at HOME.

ˈlampshade *n* cover (made of glass, cloth, etc) placed over a lamp to soften or screen its light.

lampoon /læmˈpuːn/ *n* piece of writing that attacks and ridicules a person, a book, an institution, etc.

▷ **lampoon** *v* [Tn] publicly ridicule (sb/sth) in a lampoon, etc: *His cartoons mercilessly lampooned the leading politicians of the day.*

lamprey /ˈlæmprɪ/ *n* eel-like water animal with a round sucking mouth which it uses to attach itself to other creatures.

Lancashire /ˈlæŋkəʃə(r)/ county in NW England. After the *Industrial Revolution it became one of Britain's great manufacturing centres, famous esp for its cotton mills. Most of these have now closed, but Lancashire remains an important industrial area. ⇨ map at App 1.

Lancaster /ˈlæŋkəstə(r)/ name of the English royal house descended from *John of Gaunt, Duke of Lancaster, which ruled England from 1399 (Henry IV) to the death of Henry VI in 1471. The British monarch still has the title Duke of Lancaster. ⇨ App 3.

Lancastrian /læŋˈkæstrɪən/ *n, adj* **1** (native or inhabitant) of Lancashire. **2** (member or supporter) of the House of Lancaster.

lance¹ /lɑːns; *US* læns/ *n* **1** weapon used for catching fish, etc with a long wooden shaft and a pointed steel head. **2** (formerly) similar weapon used by mounted knights, cavalry, etc.

▷ **lancer** *n* soldier of a cavalry regiment formerly armed with lances.

□ **ˌlance-ˈcorporal** *n* (in the British army or US Marines) non-commissioned officer of the lowest rank. ⇨ App 4.

lance² /lɑːns; *US* læns/ *v* [Tn] prick or cut open (sth) with a lancet: *lance an abscess, a boil, a swelling, etc.*

Lancelot /ˈlɑːnsəlɒt/ most famous of the knights of King *Arthur's Round Table, who became the lover of Queen Guinevere.

lancet /ˈlɑːnsɪt; *US* ˈlæn-/ *n* **1** (*medical*) sharp pointed two-edged surgical instrument used for opening abscesses, etc. **2** (*architecture*) tall narrow pointed arch or window.

land¹ /lænd/ *n* **1** [U] solid part of the earth's surface (contrasted with sea or water): *travel over land* ○ *be on, reach, come to land* ○ *The journey to the far side of the island is quicker by land than by sea,* ie by car, train, etc than by boat. ○ *On land the turtle is ungainly, but in the water it is very agile.* **2** [U] expanse of country: *The land west of the mountains stretched as far as the eye could see.* **3** [U] **(a)** ground or soil of the same type: *rich, stony, forest land.* **(b)** ground or soil as used for a particular purpose: *farming land* ○ *arable land* ○ *The city suffers from a shortage of building land,* ie land on which to build houses. **4 the land** [U] **(a)** ground or soil used for farming: *working the land.* **(b)** rural areas as contrasted with cities and towns: *Many farmers are leaving the land to work in industry.* **5 (a)** [U] property in the form of land: *How far does your land extend?* ○ *a house with a hundred acres of land adjoining it* ○ *land for sale.* **(b) lands** [pl] estates. **6** [C] (*rhet*) country, state or nation: *my native land* ○ *the finest orchestra in the land* ○ (*fig*) *the land of dreams.* ⇨ Usage at COUNTRY. **7** (idm) **in the ˌland of the ˈliving** (*joc*) alive. **the ˌland of ˈNod** (*joc*) sleep. **the lie of the land** ⇨ LIE². **live off/on the fat of the land** ⇨ LIVE². **live off the land** ⇨ LIVE². **make ˈland** (*nautical*) see or reach the shore. **(be/go) on the ˈland** work as a farmer: *He left his office job to try to make a living on the land.* **the promised land** ⇨ PROMISE². **see, etc how the ˈland lies** learn what the situation is, how matters stand, etc: *We'd better find out how the land lies before taking any action.* **spy out the land** ⇨ SPY *v.*

▷ **landed** *adj* [attrib] owning much land: *the landed classes/gentry.*

landless *adj* not owning land.

ˈlandward *adj* /ˈlændwəd/ towards the land: *on the landward side of the island.*

ˈlandwards *adv* going or facing towards the land.

□ **ˈland-agent** *n* (*esp Brit*) person employed to manage an estate.

ˈland-breeze *n* light wind blowing from the land towards the sea, usu after sunset.

ˈlandfall *n* **(a)** first sight of or approach to land after a journey by sea: *We made a landfall at dusk after three weeks at sea.* **(b)** land sighted or reached: *Our next landfall should be Jamaica.*

ˈlandfill *n* [U] **(a)** process of burying waste material, rather than burning or recycling it, esp in order to reclaim land: [attrib] *a landfill site.* **(b)** waste material used in this way.

ˈland-form *n* (*geology*) natural feature of the surface of the earth.

ˈlandholder *n* owner or (esp) tenant of land.

ˈland-locked *adj* almost or entirely surrounded by land: *a land-locked harbour, bay, inlet, etc* ○ *Switzerland is completely land-locked.*

ˈlandlubber *n* (*derog or joc*) person who is not accustomed to ships or to being at sea.

ˈlandmark *n* **1** object, etc easily seen and recognized from a distance: *The Empire State Building is a famous landmark on the New York skyline.* **2** (*fig*) event, discovery, invention, etc that marks an important stage or turning-point: *a landmark in the history of modern art* ○ [attrib] *a landmark decision, victory, speech.*

ˈland mass large area of land: *several small islands separated from the main land mass by a deep channel.*

ˈland-mine *n* explosive charge laid in or on the ground, detonated by vehicles, etc passing over it.

ˈland office (*US*) office that records sales of public land. **land-office business** (*US infml*) fast and active business.

ˈlandowner *n* person who owns (esp a large area of) land: *one of the biggest single landowners* (ie individual people owning the most land) *in England.*

ˈLandrover *n* (*propr*) strongly-built motor vehicle designed for use over rough ground or farm land.

ˈlandslide *n* **1** (also **ˈlandslip**) sliding of a mass of earth, rock, etc down the side of a mountain, cliff, etc. **2** (*fig*) overwhelming majority of votes for one side in an election: *Opinion polls forecast a Conservative landslide.* ○ [attrib] *a landslide victory.*

ˈlandsman /-mən/ *n* (*pl* **-men** /-mən/) person who is not a sailor.

land² /lænd/ *v* **1** [I, Ipr, Tn, Tn·pr] ~ **(sb/sth) (at...)** (cause sb/sth to) go on land from a ship; disembark: *We landed at Dover.* ○ *Troops have been landed at several points.* **2 (a)** [Tn, Tn·pr] bring (an aircraft) down to the ground, etc: *The pilot managed to land the damaged plane safely.* **(b)** [I, Ipr] come down in this way: *We shall be landing (at Gatwick airport) shortly — please fasten your seat-belts.* **3** [I, Ipr] reach the ground after a jump or fall: *Try to catch the ball before it lands.* ○ *He fell down the stairs, landing in a heap at the bottom.* **4** [Tn] bring (a fish) to land: *Fewer herring than usual have been landed this year.* **5** [Tn] (*infml*) succeed in obtaining sth, esp against strong competition: *land a good job, a big contract, the prize.* **6** [Tn] (*sl*) strike (a blow): *unable to land any good punches in the early rounds.* **7** (idm) **fall/land on one's feet** ⇨ FOOT¹. **land sb one** (*sl*) hit or punch sb: *She landed him one in the eye.* **8** (phr v) **land sb/oneself in sth** (*infml*) get sb/oneself into difficulties, etc: *This is a fine mess you've landed us in!* ○ *He's really landed himself in it this time.* **land up (in...)** (*infml*) reach a final position or situation: *Her hat flew off and landed up in the river.* ○ *You'll land up in prison at this rate,* ie if you continue to act in this way. **land up doing sth** (*infml*) do sth in the end, esp reluctantly: *They landed up not only having to apologize but also offering to pay.* ○ *Why is it that I always land up cleaning the bath?* **land sb with sth/sb** (*infml*) give sb (a task or burden) to deal with: *I found myself landed with three extra guests for dinner.* ○ *Don't try and land me with your responsibilities!*

landau /ˈlændɔː/ *n* four-wheeled carriage pulled by horses. The roof is in two halves, each of which can be lowered separately.

landing /ˈlændɪŋ/ *n* **1** act of coming or bringing to land: *during the Queen's landing from the Royal Yacht* ○ *Because of engine trouble the plane had to make an emergency landing,* ie come to land suddenly to avoid further danger or damage. ○ *She slipped and fell, but had a soft landing on some cushions.* **2** (also **ˈlanding-place**) place where people and goods may be landed from a boat or ship: *There is no safe landing on that coast.* ○ *a convenient landing-place in a nearby sheltered cove.* **3** level area at the top of a flight of stairs, or between one flight and another: *Your room opens off the top landing.* ⇨ illus at STAIR.

Language

English is the main language of the British Isles, including Ireland, and there are few people who do not speak it as their first language. The other languages of the British Isles belong to the Celtic family. The main ones are Welsh (in Wales), Gaelic (in Scotland), and Irish (in Ireland).

Welsh is spoken by about 20 per cent of the population of Wales, mostly in the rural areas in the north and west. Of Scotland's population of 5 million, about 80 000 speak Gaelic, mainly in the islands and the north west. In Ireland, Irish (also known as Irish Gaelic or, less commonly, Erse) is the country's first official language, but is spoken only by a minority of about five per cent, almost all of them in the Republic of Ireland. Its official status means, however, that it is taught in schools and is used for government publications, road signs etc.

In Britain's 'Celtic fringe' there is an enthusiastic interest in encouraging the use of the Celtic languages which had been in danger of dying out. Wales, in particular, has seen vigorous and even violent 'anti-English' campaigns in recent years, with acts of protest ranging from a refusal to complete English-language government forms to the obliteration of English road signs. Most of these 'pro-Welsh' activists are members of the principality's nationalist party, Plaid Cymru ('Party of Wales'). Legislation has given equal official status to Welsh and English. The Welsh Language Board was set up by the government in 1988 to ensure the survival of Welsh. The first language in many schools is Welsh. (Cf article at WALES.)

In Scotland the campaign for the promotion of Scots Gaelic has been less militant than the Welsh campaign, and is carried on by members either of a Gaelic cultural organization such as An Comunn Gaidealach ('The Gaelic Society') or of the Scottish Nationalist Party (SNP), the political party that aims to achieve home rule for Scotland.

Ireland has a number of nationalist organizations that promote the use of Irish. Their activities are coordinated by the Comhdháil Náisiúnta na Gaeilge ('National Gaelic Convention') in Dublin.

Two further Celtic languages in Britain are now virtually extinct, although they also have their active promoters. These are Manx, once spoken in the Isle of Man, and Cornish, the former language of Cornwall. There are no native speakers left in either, although Manx is sometimes used for ceremonial purposes, and members of Mebyon Kernow ('Sons of Cornwall'), the county's independent political party, support the revival of Cornish.

The survival of Celtic languages in Britain has been supported by the media, in particular radio and television. In Wales, for example, the independent television service S4C (Sianel 4 Cymru, 'Channel 4 Wales'), the equivalent of the national Channel 4, transmits Welsh programmes for an average of three hours daily, and there are several Celtic language newspapers.

□ ˈ**landing-craft** *n* flat-bottomed naval craft designed for putting ashore troops and equipment. ˈ**landing-field** (also ˈ**landing-strip**) *n* = AIRSTRIP (AIR[1]).
ˈ**landing-gear** *n* [U] = UNDERCARRIAGE.
ˈ**landing-net** *n* (in angling) long-handled net used for landing a fish caught on a hook.
ˈ**landing-stage** *n* (usu floating) platform on which people and goods are landed from a boat.

landlady /ˈlændleɪdɪ/ *n* **1** woman who lets rooms, etc to tenants. **2** woman who keeps a public house or a boarding-house. Cf LANDLORD. ⇨ article at ACCOMMODATION.

landlord /ˈlændlɔ:d/ *n* **1** person who lets land, a house, a room, etc to a tenant. **2** person who keeps a public house or a boarding-house: *It's a nice pub, except for the landlord.* Cf LANDLADY. ⇨ Usage at TENANT.

Landor /ˈlændɔ:(r)/ Walter Savage (1775-1864), English writer of poetry and prose. His most famous work is his *Imaginary Conversations* between famous figures of the past.

landscape /ˈlændskeɪp/ *n* **1** [C] scenery of an area of land: *a bleak urban landscape* ○ *Mountains dominate the Welsh landscape.* **2** (**a**) [C] picture showing a view of the countryside: *an exhibition of landscapes by local artists.* (**b**) [U] this type of art. Cf PORTRAIT 1. **3** (idm) **a blot on the landscape** ⇨ BLOT[1].
▷ **landscape** *v* [Tn] improve the appearance of (a garden, park, etc) by means of landscape gardening.
□ ˌ**landscape** ˈ**architecture** planning and designing public parks, gardens, etc and often also the buildings and roads near them. ˌ**landscape** ˈ**architect**.
ˌ**landscape** ˈ**gardening** laying out a garden, etc in a way that imitates natural scenery. ˌ**landscape** ˈ**gardener**.

Landseer /ˈlænsɪə(r)/ Sir Edwin (1802-73), English painter and sculptor, best known for painting animals, often in Highland settings. He carved the lions at the foot of *Nelson's Column in London, and was Queen Victoria's favourite painter. ⇨ illus.

Land's End /ˌlændz ˈend/ **1** most southerly point in England, at the tip of Cornwall, about 1 400 km (876 miles) from *John o' Groats, the most northerly point in Scotland. **2** (idm) **from** ˌ**Land's** ˌ**End to** ˌ**John o'**ˈ**Groats** all over Britain: *People from Land's End to John o' Groats have written to complain.*

the lions at Trafalgar Square, designed by Sir Edwin Landseer

lane /leɪn/ *n* **1** narrow country road or track, usu between hedges or banks. **2** (esp in place names) narrow street or alley between buildings: ˌ*Drury* ˈ*Lane.* ⇨ Usage at ROAD. **3** strip of road marked out for a single line of traffic: *the inside/near side lane* ○ *the outside/off side lane* ○ *the slow/fast/overtaking lane of a motorway.* **4** route intended for or regularly used by ships or aircraft: ˈ*shipping lanes* ○ ˈ*ocean lanes.* **5** marked strip of track, water, etc for a competitor in a race: *The world champion is in lane four.* ⇨ Usage at PATH. **6** (idm) **memory lane** ⇨ MEMORY.

Lang /læŋ/ Fritz (1890-1976), Austrian film director. His early films, esp *M* and *Metropolis*, were moral fables in the style of German expressionism. He left Nazi Germany to make films in Hollywood, including *Fury* and *The Woman in the Window*.

Langland /ˈlæŋlənd/ William (c 1330-c 1386), English poet. His only known work is *Piers Plowman*, an allegorical poem describing a spiritual journey in search of truth. It vividly describes the corruption of the Church and the suffering of the poor.

language /ˈlæŋgwɪdʒ/ *n* **1** [U] system of sounds, words, patterns, etc used by humans to communicate thoughts and feelings: *the origins of language* ○ [attrib] *the development of language skills in young children.* **2** [C] form of language used by a particular group, nation, etc: *the Bantu group of languages* ○ *one's native language* ○ *a second, a foreign, an acquired language.* ⇨ article. **3** [U] manner of expressing oneself: *His language was uncompromising: he told them their work must improve or they would be fired.* ○ *bad/strong/foul language*, ie words considered improper, eg those marked ⚠ in this dictionary ○ *everyday language*, ie not specialized or technical. **4** [U] words, phrases, etc used by a particular group of people: *the language of science, drug users, the courtroom* ○ *medical language.* **5** [C, U] system of signs, symbols, gestures, etc used for conveying information: *Music has been called the universal language.* ○ *the language of flowers* ○ *body, sign language* ○ *This theory can only be expressed in mathematical language.* **6** [C, U] (*computing*) system of coded instructions used in programming: *BASIC is the language most programmers learn first.* **7** (idm) **speak the same language** ⇨ SPEAK.
□ ˈ**language laboratory** room equipped with a special tape-recording system for language learning.

languid /ˈlæŋgwɪd/ *adj* lacking vigour or energy; slow-moving: *languid movements* ○ *speak with a languid drawl.* ▷ **languidly** *adv.*

languish /ˈlæŋgwɪʃ/ *v* [I] (*fml*) **1** lack or lose vitality: *Since the war the industry has gradually languished.* ○ *The children soon began to languish in the heat.* **2** ~ (**for sb/sth**) be or become weak and miserable because of unfulfilled longings; pine[2](1): *languish for love, company, sympathy.* **3** ~ (**in/under sth**) live wretchedly: *He languished in poverty for years.* ○ *languishing under foreign domination.*
▷ **languishing** *adj* (of looks, etc) trying to win sympathy or affection: *a languishing sigh.*

languor /ˈlæŋgə(r)/ *n* **1** [U] tiredness or laziness of mind and body; listlessness. **2** [sing] feeling of dreamy peacefulness: *music that induces a delightful languor.* **3** [U] oppressive stillness (of the air, etc): *the hazy languor of a summer's afternoon.* ▷ **languorous** /ˈlæŋgərəs/ *adj.* **languorously** *adv.*

lank /læŋk/ *adj* **1** (of hair) straight and limp. **2** (of a person) tall and thin.

lanky /ˈlæŋkɪ/ *adj* (**-ier**, **-iest**) (of a person) ungracefully tall and thin: *a lanky teenager.* ▷ **lankiness** *n* [U].

lanolin (also **lanoline**) /ˈlænəlɪn/ *n* [U] fat extracted from sheep's wool and used in making skin creams.

lantern /ˈlæntən/ *n* **1** (usu portable) light for use outdoors in a transparent case that protects it from the wind, etc. **2** (*architecture*) structure with windows or openings to admit light or air at the top of a dome or room.

□ ˈ**lantern jaws** long thin jaws that give the face a hollow look. ˌ**lantern-ˈjawed** *adj*.

lanthanide /ˈlænθənaɪd/ *n* (*chemistry*) any of the 15 elements in the lanthanide series, with atomic numbers from 57 (lanthanum) to 71 (lutetium).

lanthanum /ˈlænθənəm/ *n* [U] (*symb* **La**) (*chemistry*) silver-white metallic element, used in certain alloys and in glass-making. ⇨ App 11.

lanyard /ˈlænjəd/ *n* **1** cord worn round the neck to hold a knife, whistle, etc. **2** (*nautical*) short rope or line attached to sth to secure it.

Laos /ˈlɑːɒs/ country in SE Asia; pop approx 3 875 000; official language, Laotian; capital Vientiane; unit of currency kip (= 100 att). It is a mountainous country covered in forests, and has an agricultural economy based largely on the growing of rice. For much of its recent history there has been civil war, but since 1975 the country has been a Marxist republic. ⇨ map at VIETNAM.

▷ **Laotian** /ˈlɑːɒʃn; *US* leɪˈəʊʃn/ *n* **1** [C] native or inhabitant of Laos. **2** [U] (also **Lao** /laʊ/) language of Laos. — *adj*.

lap[1] /læp/ *n* **1** area formed by the upper part of a seated person's thighs: *Come and sit on Grandpa's lap!* ○ *She had fallen asleep with an open book in her lap.* **2** part of a dress, etc covering this: *She gathered the fallen apples and carried them in her lap.* **3** (idm) **drop/dump sth in sb's lap** (*infml*) make sth the responsibility of sb else: *You've got to deal with this — don't try and dump it in my lap.* **in the lap of the ˈgods** (of future events) uncertain. **in the lap of ˈluxury** in conditions of great luxury.

□ ˈ**lap-dog** *n* small pampered pet dog.

ˈ**lap-robe** *n* (*US*) = TRAVELLING RUG (TRAVEL).

lap[2] /læp/ *v* (**-pp-**) **1** [Tn·pr] ~ **A round B**/~ **B in A** wrap or fold (cloth, etc) round sth: *lap a bandage round the wrist/the wrist in a bandage.* **2** [I, Tn] (cause sth to) overlap: *Each row of tiles laps the one below.* **3** [Tn] be one or more laps ahead of (another competitor) in a race: *She's lapped all the other runners.*

▷ **lap** *n* **1** part that overlaps or amount by which it overlaps. **2** single circuit of a track or racecourse: *The leading car crashed midway through the tenth lap.* ○ *do a lap of honour*, ie make a ceremonial circuit of a race-track, etc after winning a contest. **3** one section of a journey: *The next lap of our trip takes us into the mountains.* **4** (idm) **the last lap** ⇨ LAST[1].

lap[3] /læp/ *v* (**-pp-**) **1** [Tn, Tn·p] ~ **sth (up)** (esp of animals) drink sth by taking it up with the tongue: *a dog noisily lapping water.* **2** [I, Ipr] (of water) make gentle splashing sounds: *waves lapping on a beach, against the side of a boat, etc.* **3** (phr v) **lap sth up** (*infml*) receive (praise, news, good fortune, etc) eagerly, uncritically or greedily: *He tells her all those lies and she just laps them up.* ○ *The film got terrible reviews but the public are lapping it up*, ie going to see it in great numbers. ○ *lap up sunshine, knowledge, company.* ▷ **lapping** *n* [U]: *the gentle lapping of the waves.*

laparotomy /ˌlæpəˈrɒtəmɪ/ *n* (*medical*) act of cutting through the abdominal wall during a surgical operation on the internal organs of the body.

lapel /ləˈpel/ *n* front part of the collar of a coat or jacket that is folded back over the chest: *What is that badge on your lapel?* ⇨ illus at JACKET.

lapidary /ˈlæpɪdərɪ; *US* -derɪ/ *adj* (*fml*) **1** [attrib] of gems or stones, esp of their cutting, polishing or engraving. **2** (*approv*) dignified and concise: *a lapidary inscription, proverb, speech, etc.*

▷ **lapidary** *n* person who cuts, polishes, sets or engraves gems.

lapis lazuli /ˌlæpɪs ˈlæzjʊlɪ; *US* ˈlæzəlɪ/ *n* **(a)** [U, C] bright-blue semi-precious stone. **(b)** [U] colour of this: [attrib] *a sea of ˌlapis lazuli ˈblue.*

Lapland /ˈlæplənd/ region in the extreme northern part of Scandinavia, from the Norwegian coast to the *White Sea.

▷ **Lapp** /læp/ **1** [C] native of Lapland. **2** [U] language of Lapland.

lappet /ˈlæpɪt/ *n* **1** flap or fold in the cloth of a garment. **2** loose or hanging piece of flesh, eg a lobe(1) or wattle[2].

lapse /læps/ *n* **1** small error, esp one caused by forgetfulness or inattention: *A brief lapse in the final set cost her the match.* ○ *It was a superb performance, despite occasional lapses of intonation.* **2** ~ **(from sth) (into sth)** fall or departure from correct or usual standards; backsliding: *Wives were expected to forgive their husbands' lapses*, ie forgive them when they were unfaithful. ○ *The debate was marred by a brief lapse into unpleasant name-calling.* ○ *a lapse from grace*, ie becoming out of favour. **3** passing of a period of time: *after a lapse of six months.* **4** (*law*) ending of a right, etc because of disuse.

▷ **lapse** *v* **1** [I, Ipr] ~ **(from sth) (into sth)** fail to maintain one's position or standard: *lapse back into bad habits* ○ *a lapsed Catholic.* **2** [Ipr] ~ **into sth** sink or pass gradually into sth: *She lapsed into a coma.* **3** [I] (*law*) (of rights and privileges) be lost or invalid because not used, claimed or renewed: *He didn't get any compensation because his insurance policy had lapsed.*

□ ˈ**lapse rate** rate at which the temperature of the air falls in relation to its height above the earth.

lapwing /ˈlæpwɪŋ/ (also **peewit, pewit**) *n* type of small black and white wading bird.

larceny /ˈlɑːsənɪ/ *n* [C, U] (*dated law*) (instance of) theft of personal goods. In 1968 larceny was replaced by *theft* as a statutory crime in English law. ▷ **larcenous** /ˈlɑːsənəs/ *adj*.

larch /lɑːtʃ/ *n* **(a)** [C] tall deciduous tree of the pine family, with small cones and needle-like leaves. ⇨ illus at TREE. **(b)** [U] its wood.

lard /lɑːd/ *n* [U] white greasy substance made from the melted fat of pigs and used in cooking.

▷ **lard** *v* **1** [Tn] prepare (meat) for roasting by putting strips of bacon in or on it: *Lean meat can be larded to keep it moist in the oven.* **2** [Tn·pr] ~ **sth with sth** (*often derog*) embellish (speech or writing) with sth: *a lecture larded with obscure quotations.*

larder /ˈlɑːdə(r)/ *n* (esp formerly) cupboard or small room used for storing food. Cf PANTRY.

lardy-cake /ˈlɑːdɪkeɪk/ *n* [C, U] (*Brit*) breadlike cake made with lard and currants.

large /lɑːdʒ/ *adj* (**-r, -st**) **1** of considerable size, extent or capacity: *A large family needs a large house.* ○ *She inherited a large fortune.* ○ *He has a large appetite*, ie eats a lot. ○ ˌ*large-print* ˈ*books*, ie printed in large type for people who cannot see well ○ (*euph*) *a large* (ie fat) *lady.* **2** wide in range, scope or scale; broad: *an official with large powers* ○ *take the large view* ○ *a book dealing with large themes* ○ *large and small farmers.* ⇨ Usage at BIG. **3** (idm) **(as) large as ˈlife** (*joc*) seen or appearing in person, with no possibility of error or doubt: *And there she was as large as life!* **bulk large** ⇨ BULK *v*. **by and ˈlarge** taking everything into consideration: *By and large, the company's been pretty good to me.* **larger than ˈlife** exaggerated in size, so as to seem more impressive: [attrib] *The hero appears as a larger-than-life character.* **writ large** ⇨ WRIT.

▷ **large** *n* (idm) **at ˈlarge (a)** (of a criminal, animal, etc) free; not confined: *The escaped prisoner is still at large.* **(b)** at full length; thoroughly and in great detail: *The question is discussed at large in my report.* **(c)** (used after a *n*) as a whole; in general: *the opinion of students, voters, society, etc at large.*

largely *adv* to a great extent; chiefly: *His success was largely due to luck.*

largeness *n* [U].

largish *adj* fairly large.

□ ˌ**large inˈtestine** part of the alimentary canal consisting of the caecum, the vermiform appendix, the colon and the rectum. It is mainly concerned with absorbing water from the material passed from the small intestine.

ˈ**large-scale** *adj* [esp attrib] **1** extensive: *a large-scale police search.* **2** (of a map, model, etc) drawn or made to a large scale so that many details can be shown.

largess (also **largesse**) /lɑːˈdʒes/ *n* [U] **1** generous giving of money or gifts, esp to sb of lower rank or status. **2** money or gifts given in this way.

largo /ˈlɑːgəʊ/ *n* (*pl* ~**s**), *adv* (*music*) (piece or movement) played in slow and solemn time: *The second movement is a largo.*

lariat /ˈlærɪət/ *n* (*esp US*) length of rope for catching or tethering a horse; lasso.

lark[1] /lɑːk/ *n* **1** any of several small songbirds, esp the skylark. **2** (idm) **be/get ˌup with the ˈlark** get up early in the morning.

lark[2] /lɑːk/ *n* (usu *sing*) (*infml*) **1** bit of adventurous fun: *The boys didn't mean any harm — they were only having a lark.* ○ *They stole the car for a lark, but now they're in trouble.* ○ *What a lark!* ie How amusing! **2** (*Brit ironic*) (esp) unpleasant or irritating type of activity: *I don't much like this queuing lark.*

▷ **lark** *v* [I, Ip] ~ **(about/around)** behave playfully or irresponsibly: *Stop larking about and get on with your work.*

Larkin /ˈlɑːkɪn/ Philip Arthur (1922-85), English poet and novelist. His early poems show the influence of *Yeats but his own distinctive style soon emerged. This shows a witty but often gloomy stoicism about suburban life and a preoccupation with death. In much of his work Larkin adapted everday speech rhythms and vocabulary with subtle elegance.

larkspur /ˈlɑːkspɜː(r)/ *n* tall garden plant with blue, pink or white flowers.

larva /ˈlɑːvə/ *n* (*pl* **larvae** /ˈlɑːviː/) insect in the first stage of its life, after coming out of the egg: *A caterpillar is the larva of a butterfly.* ⇨ illus at BUTTERFLY. ▷ **larval** /ˈlɑːvl/ *adj* [attrib]: *in a larval state.*

larynx /ˈlærɪŋks/ *n* (*pl* **larynges** /læˈrɪndʒiːz/) (*anatomy*) (also ˈ**voice-box**) boxlike space at the top of the windpipe, containing the vocal cords which produce the voice. ⇨ illus at THROAT.

▷ **laryngitis** /ˌlærɪnˈdʒaɪtɪs/ *n* [U] (*medical*) inflammation of the larynx.

lasagne (also **lasagna**) /ləˈzænjə/ *n* [U] **(a)** pasta made in broad flat strips. **(b)** dish made from layers of this with meat sauce, tomatoes and cheese, baked in the oven.

Lascar /ˈlæskə(r)/ *n* seaman from the E Indies.

lascivious /ləˈsɪvɪəs/ *adj* feeling, expressing or causing sexual desire. ▷ **lasciviously** *adv*. **lasciviousness** *n* [U].

laser /ˈleɪzə(r)/ *n* device that generates an intense and highly controlled beam of light: [attrib] *laser beams, radiation, physics* ○ *a laser-guided missile.*

lash[1] /læʃ/ *n* **1** [C] flexible part of a whip. **2** [C] blow given with or as with a whip, etc: (*fig*) *feel the lash of sb's tongue*, ie be spoken to harshly or cruelly by sb. **3 the lash** [sing] (formerly) punishment by flogging: *sailors sentenced to the lash.* **4** [C] = EYELASH (EYE[1]).

lash[2] /læʃ/ *v* **1** [Ipr, Ip, Tn, Tn·pr] strike (sb/sth) with or as with a whip: *rain lashing (down) on the roof, against the windows, etc* ○ *waves lashing the shore* ○ *lashed the horses with a stick* ○ (*fig*) *politicians regularly lashed* (ie strongly criticized) *in the popular press.* **2** [Tn, Tn·pr, Tn·p] move (a limb, etc) like a whip: *a tiger lashing its tail angrily to and fro/from side to side.* **3** [Tn, Tn·pr] ~ **sb (into sth)** rouse or incite sb: *a speech cleverly designed to lash the audience into a frenzy.* **4** [Tn·pr, Tn·p] ~ **A to B/A and B together** fasten things together securely with ropes, etc. **5** (phr v) **lash sth down** tie sth securely in position with ropes, etc: *lash down the cargo on the deck.* **lash out (at/against sb/sth)** make a sudden violent attack with blows or words: *The horse lashed out with its back legs.* ○ *He lashed out at the opposition's policies.* **lash out (on sth)** (*infml*) spend money freely or extravagantly: *Let's lash out and have champagne.* ○ *This is no time to lash out on a new stereo.*

lashing /ˈlæʃɪŋ/ *n* **1** [C] whipping or beating: *He gave the poor donkey a terrible lashing.* **2** [C] rope, etc used to fasten things together or in position. **3 lashings** [pl] ~**s** (**of sth**) (*Brit infml*) a lot: *lashings of cream on one's fruit salad.*

lass /læs/ (also **lassie** /ˈlæsɪ/) *n* (esp in Scotland and N England) girl; young woman. Cf LADDIE.

Lassa fever /ˌlæsə ˈfiːvə(r)/ serious (often fatal) disease caused by a virus, with fever, severe pain in the muscles and multiple organ damage.

lassitude /ˈlæsɪtjuːd; *US* -tuːd/ *n* [U] (*fml*) tiredness of mind or body.

lasso /læˈsuː; *US also* ˈlæsəʊ/ *n* (*pl* ~**s** or ~**es**) long rope with a noose at one end, used for catching horses and cattle.

▷ **lasso** *v* [Tn] catch (esp an animal) using a lasso: *lassoing wild horses.*

last[1] /lɑːst; *US* læst/ *adj* **1** coming after all others in time or order: *December is the last month of the year.* ○ *the last Sunday in June* ○ *the last time I saw her* ○ *the last two/the two last people to arrive.* Cf FIRST[1] 1. **2** [attrib] latest; most recent: *last night, week, month, summer, year, etc* ○ *last Tuesday/on Tuesday last* ○ *in/for/during the last fortnight, few weeks, two decades, etc* ○ *I thought her last book was one of her best.* ⇨ Usage at LATE[1]. **3** [esp attrib] only remaining; final: *This is our last bottle of wine.* ○ *He knew this was his last hope of winning.* ○ *I wouldn't marry you if you were the last person on earth.* **4** least likely or suitable: *the last thing I'd expect him to do* ○ *She's the last person to trust with a secret.* **5** (idm) **at one's last ˈgasp** making one's final effort or attempt before exhaustion or death: *The team were at their last gasp when the whistle went.* **be on one's/its last ˈlegs** be weak or in poor condition: *My car's on its last legs — it keeps breaking down.* **the day, week, month, etc before last** the day, etc immediately before the most recent one; two days, etc ago: *I haven't seen him since the Christmas before last.* **draw one's first/last breath** ⇨ DRAW[2]. **every last/single ˈone, etc** every person or thing (in a group) included: *We spent every last penny we had on the house.* **famous last words** ⇨ FAMOUS. **first/last/next but one, two, three, etc** ⇨ FIRST[1]. **first/last thing** ⇨ THING. **have the last ˈlaugh** triumph over one's rivals, critics, etc in the end. **have, etc the last ˈword** make, etc the final and decisive contribution to an argument, a dispute, etc: *We can all make suggestions, but the manager has the last word.* **in the last/final analysis** ⇨ ANALYSIS. **in the last reˈsort; (as) a/one's last reˈsort** (person or thing one turns to) when everything else has failed: *In the last resort we can always walk home.* ○ *I've tried everyone else and now you're my last resort.* **one's last/dying breath** ⇨ BREATH. **the ˌlast ˈditch** the last effort one can make to ensure one's safety, avoid defeat, etc: [attrib] *a ˌlast-ditch ˈstand.* **the last ˈminute/ˈmoment** the latest possible time before an important event, etc: *change one's plans at the last minute* ○ *We always leave our packing to/till the last moment.* ○ [attrib] *a last-minute dash for the train.* **the last ˈlap** final stage of a journey, contest, project, etc: *We're on the last lap, so don't slacken!* **the last/final straw** ⇨ STRAW. **the last ˈword (in sth)** most recent, fashionable, advanced, etc thing: *Ten years ago this dress was considered the last word in elegance.* **the last ˈword (on sth)** definitive statement, account, etc: *a book which may fairly claim to be the last word on the subject.* **say/be one's last ˈword (on sth)** give/be one's final opinion or decision: *I've said my last word — take it or leave it.* ○ *I hope that's not your last word on the subject.* **to a man/to the last man** ⇨ MAN. **a week last Monday, etc** ⇨ WEEK.

▷ **last** *n* **1 the** ~ (**of sb/sth**) (*pl* unchanged) person or thing that is last or mentioned last: *These are the last of our apples.* ○ *We invited Bill, Tom and Sue — the last being Bill's sister.* **2** (idm) **at (long) ˈlast** after (much) delay, effort, etc; in the end: *At last we were home!* ○ *At long last a compromise was agreed on.* **breathe one's last** ⇨ BREATHE. **from first to last** ⇨ FIRST[3]. **hear/see the last of sb/sth (a)** hear/see sb/sth for the last time: *That was the last I ever saw of her.* **(b)** not have to deal with or think about sb/sth again: *It would be a mistake to assume we've heard the last of this issue.* **to/till the ˈlast** consistently, until the last possible moment (esp death): *He died protesting his innocence to the last.*

lastly *adv* in the last place; finally: *Lastly, we're going to visit Athens, and fly home from there.*

□ **the ˌLast ˈJudgement** = JUDGEMENT DAY (JUDGEMENT).

ˈlast name surname.

the ˌlast ˈpost military bugle-call sounded at sunset, military funerals, etc.

the ˌlast ˈrites religious ceremony for a person near death: *administer the last rites to sb.*

the ˌLast ˈSupper (*religion*) meal eaten by Christ and his disciples on the day before the Crucifixion.

the ˌlast ˈtrump trumpet-call to wake the dead on *Judgement Day (JUDGEMENT): (*joc*) *She's sleeping so soundly that the last trump wouldn't wake her.*

last[2] /lɑːst; *US* læst/ *adv* **1** after all others: *He came last in the race.* ○ *This country ranks last in industrial output.* Cf FIRST[2]. **2** on the occasion before the present time; most recently: *I saw him last/last saw him in New York two years ago.* ○ *They last defeated England in 1972.* **3** (idm) **first and last** ⇨ FIRST[2]. **he who laughs last laughs longest** ⇨ LAUGH. **ˌlast but not ˈleast** (used before the final item in a list) last but no less important(ly) than the others: *And last but not least there is the question of adequate funding.* **ˌlast ˈin, ˌfirst ˈout** those most recently employed, included, etc will be the first to be dismissed, excluded, etc if such action should become necessary: *The firm will apply the principle of 'last in, first out'.*

EXPRESSING TIME

When referring to days, weeks, etc in the past, present and future the following expressions are used, speaking from a point of view in the present.

	PAST	PRESENT	FUTURE
morning afternoon evening	yesterday morning, etc	this morning, etc	tomorrow morning, etc
night	last night	tonight	tomorrow night
day	yesterday	today	tomorrow
week	last week	this week	next week
month	last month	this month	next month
year	last year	this year	next year

last[3] /lɑːst; *US* læst/ *v* **1** [I, In/pr] ~ (**for**) **sth** continue for a period of time; endure: *The pyramids were really built to last.* ○ *How long do you think this fine weather will last?* ○ *She won't last long in that job — it's too tough.* ○ *The war lasted (for) five years.* **2** [I, Ip, In/pr] ~ (**out**); ~ (**for**) **sth** be adequate or enough: *Will the petrol last (out) till we reach London?* ○ *enough food to last (us) three days.* ⇨ Usage at TAKE[1]. **3** [no passive: Tn, Tn·p] ~ **sth** (**out**) be strong enough to survive or endure sth: *He's very ill and probably won't last (out) the night,* ie will probably die before the morning.

▷ **lasting** *adj* continuing for a long time: *a lasting effect, interest, relationship* ○ *a work of lasting significance.*

last[4] /lɑːst; *US* læst/ *n* **1** block of wood or metal shaped like a foot, used in making and repairing shoes. **2** (idm) **stick to one's last** ⇨ STICK[2].

lat *abbr* latitude: *lat 70°N/S,* ie North/South. Cf LONG *abbr*.

latch /lætʃ/ *n* **1** fastening for a gate or door, consisting of a bar that is lifted from its catch, groove, hole, etc by a lever. **2** spring lock on a door that catches when the door is closed, and that needs a key to open it from the outside. ⇨ illus. **3** (idm) **on the ˈlatch** (esp of a door) closed but not locked.

▷ **latch** *v* **1** [I, Tn] be fastened or fasten (sth) with a latch: *This door won't latch properly.* ○ *Please latch the front gate when you leave.* **2** (phr v) **latch on (to sth)** (*infml*) understand an idea, sth said, etc: *He's a bit slow but in the end he latches on.* ○ *I haven't really latched on to what you mean — could you explain it again?* **latch on to sb** (*infml*) become sb's constant (and often unwelcome) companion: *He always latches on to me when he sees me at a party.*

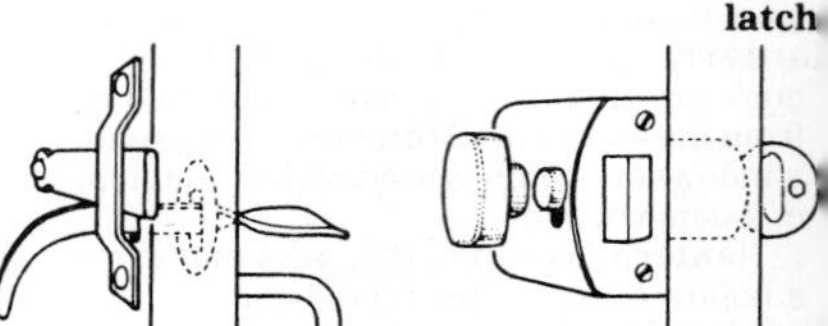
latch

□ **ˈlatchkey** *n* key of an outer door, esp the front door of a house or flat. **ˈlatchkey child** (*becoming dated*) child who has to let himself into his house or flat and look after himself, esp after returning from school, because both parents are out at work.

late[1] /leɪt/ *adj* (**-r, -st**) **1** [esp pred] after the proper or usual time: *My flight was an hour late.* ○ *Because of the cold weather the crops are late this year.* ○ *It's never too late to stop smoking.* ○ *a late marriage* ○ *a late riser,* ie sb who gets out of bed late in the morning. Cf EARLY 2. **2** far on in the day or night, a period of time, a series, etc: *till a late hour* ○ *in the late afternoon* ○ *in late summer* ○ *She married in her late twenties,* eg when she was 28. ○ *the late nineteenth century* ○ *a late Victorian house* ○ *Beethoven's late quartets,* ie the last ones he wrote. Cf EARLY 1. **3** [attrib] (esp in the superlative) recent: *the latest news* ○ *There were several clashes before this latest incident.* ○ *the latest craze, fashion, vogue, etc* ○ *her latest novel* ○ (*fml*) *during the late political unrest.* **4** [attrib] **(a)** no longer alive: *her late husband.* **(b)** no longer holding a certain position; former: *The late prime minister attended the ceremony.* **5** (idm) **at the ˈlatest** no later than: *Passengers should check in one hour before their flight time at the latest.* **an early/late night** ⇨ NIGHT. **it's ˌnever too ˌlate to ˈmend** (*saying*) it is always possible to improve one's character, habits, etc. **of ˈlate** lately; recently.

▷ **latish** /ˈleɪtɪʃ/ *adj, adv* fairly late.

□ **ˈlatecomer** *n* person who arrives late: *Latecomers will not be admitted until the interval.*

NOTE ON USAGE: **The last** may indicate the final item in a sequence, after which there are no more: *The last bus leaves at 11.15 pm.* ○ *That was the last novel he wrote before he died.* It may also refer to the item before the one being discussed: *I much prefer this job to my last one/the last one I had.* ○ *The last time we met you had a beard.* **The latest** means 'the most recent': *She always dressed in the latest fashion.* ○ *His latest novel is a great success.* **The latter** refers to the second of two items already mentioned and is rather more formal: *One can travel there by ship or plane. Most people choose the latter.*

late[2] /leɪt/ *adv* **1** after the proper or usual time: *get up, go to bed, arrive home late* ○ *I sat* (ie stayed) *up late last night.* ○ *She married late.* Cf EARLY 2. **2** far on in a period of time: *It happened late last century — in 1895, to be exact.* ○ *As late as the 1950s tuberculosis was still a threat.* ○ *He became an author quite late in life,* ie when he was quite old. Cf EARLY 1. **3** formerly but not now (used esp as in the expression shown): *Jane Wood, late of* (ie who used to live in) *Cedar Gardens, Oxford.* **4** (idm) **better late than never** ⇨ BETTER[2]. **ˌlate in the ˈday** later than is proper or desirable: *It's rather late in the day to say you're sorry — the harm's done now.* **later ˈon** at a later time or stage: *a few days later on* ○ *At first things went well, but later on we ran into trouble.* **sooner or later** ⇨ SOON.

lately /ˈleɪtlɪ/ *adv* in recent times; recently: *Have you seen her lately?* ○ *It's only lately that she's been well enough to go out.* ○ *We've been doing a lot of gardening lately.* ⇨ Usage at RECENT.

latent /ˈleɪtnt/ *adj* [esp attrib] existing but not yet active, developed or visible: *latent abilities* ○ *a latent infection.*
▷ **latency** /ˈleɪtnsɪ/ *n* [U]. **latency period** (*psychology*) stage of personal development from the age of about five to the start of puberty.
□ ˌ**latent** ˈ**heat** heat lost or gained when a substance changes state (from solid to liquid, liquid to vapour, etc) without a change of temperature.
ˌ**latent** ˈ**image** (in photography) image on a film that is not visible until the film has been developed.
ˈ**latent period** period between catching a disease and the appearance of symptoms.

lateral /ˈlætərəl/ *adj* [esp attrib] of, at, from or towards the side(s): *a lateral vein, artery, limb, etc* ○ *lateral buds, shoots, branches, etc.*
▷ **lateral** *n* lateral shoot or branch.
laterally /-rəlɪ/ *adv.*
□ ˌ**lateral** ˈ**thinking** way of solving problems by letting the mind consider unusual and apparently illogical approaches to them.

Lateran /ˈlætərən/ site in Rome of the **Lateran Palace**, where the popes lived in former times, and of the **Basilica of Saint John Lateran**, the city's cathedral, largely designed by *Borromini.
□ **the** ˌ**Lateran** ˈ**Treaty** agreement reached in 1929 between the papacy and *Mussolini formally recognizing the Vatican State.

laterite /ˈlætəraɪt/ *n* [U] type of red soil occurring in tropical regions and widely used there for making roads.

latex /ˈleɪteks/ *n* [U] **1** milky fluid produced by (esp rubber) plants. **2** synthetic product resembling this, used in paints, adhesives, etc.

lath /lɑːθ; *US* læθ/ *n* (*pl* ~**s** /lɑːðz; *US* læðz/) **1** [C] thin narrow strip of wood. **2** [U] (esp formerly) building material consisting of such strips used as a support for plaster: [attrib] *a lath-and-plaster wall.*

lathe

lathe /leɪð/ *n* machine that shapes pieces of wood, metal, etc by holding and turning them against a fixed cutting tool.

lather /ˈlɑːðə(r), *also* ˈlæð-; *US* ˈlæð-/ *n* **1** [U] white foam or froth produced by soap or detergent mixed with water: *work up a lather on one's chin*, ie before shaving. **2** [U] frothy sweat, esp on a horse. **3** (idm) **be in/get into a** ˈ**lather** (*infml*) (**a**) be/become excited and nervous: *She's in a lather about having to speak to such a large crowd.* (**b**) be/become angry, agitated and upset: *Calm down — there's no need to get into a lather about it!*
▷ **lather** *v* **1** [I, Ip] ~ (**up**) form lather: *Soap will not lather in sea-water.* **2** [Tn] cover (sth) with lather: *lather one's chin before shaving.* **3** [Tn] (*dated infml*) thrash (a person or an animal).

Latimer /ˈlætɪmə(r)/ Hugh (c 1485-1555), English bishop. A witty and influential preacher, he became one of the leading figures of the *Reformation in England. When *Mary Tudor became queen, he opposed her Catholic policies and was burnt at the stake with *Ridley at Oxford.

Latin /ˈlætɪn; *US* ˈlætn/ *n* [U] language of ancient Rome and the official language of its empire. The Latin written by *Cicero and *Virgil and taught in schools is of the classical period (up to 200 AD). The Romance languages of Europe developed from the form spoken by the less educated citizens of the empire (called Vulgar Latin). Latin remained the language of learning and of the law for many centuries. The Catholic Church continued to use it in all services until the 1960s.
▷ **Latin** *adj* **1** of or in Latin: *Latin poetry.* **2** of the countries or peoples using languages developed from Latin, eg France, Italy, Portugal, Spain: *the Latin temperament, landscape.* Cf ROMANCE.
Latinate /-eɪt/ *adj* (of words, writing, etc) like or influenced by Latin: *Latinate expressions*, ie using words that come from Latin.
Latinist *n* scholar of Latin.
□ ˌ**Latin A**ˈ**merica** parts of Central and South America in which Spanish or Portuguese is the official language. ˌ**Latin-A**ˈ**merican** *n, adj* (native) of these parts.
the Latin ˈ**Church** the Roman Catholic Church.
Latin ˈ**cross** plain cross with the lowest arm longer than the other three. ➪ illus at CROSS.
the ˈ**Latin Quarter** area of Paris on the south bank of the Seine around the *Sorbonne, traditionally frequented by students and artists.

latitude /ˈlætɪtjuːd; *US* -tuːd/ *n* **1** (*abbr* **lat**) [U] distance of a place north or south of the equator, measured in degrees. ➪ illus at GLOBE, Cf LONGITUDE. **2 latitudes** [pl] region, esp with reference to climate: *high/low latitudes*, ie regions far from/near to the equator. **3** [U] freedom to behave and hold opinions without restriction: *They allow their children too much latitude, in my view; they should be stricter.*
▷ **latitudinal** /ˌlætɪˈtjuːdɪnl; *US* -ˈtuːdənl/ *adj* [attrib]: *latitudinal variation.*
latitudinarian /ˌlætɪtjuːdɪˈneərɪən; *US* -ˌtuːdnˈeər-/ *n, adj* (*fml*) (person who is) tolerant and broad-minded, esp in religious matters.

latrine /ləˈtriːn/ *n* lavatory in a camp, barracks, etc, esp one made by digging a trench or hole in the earth.

latter /ˈlætə(r)/ *adj* (*fml*) [attrib] near to the end of a period: *the latter half of the year* ○ *in the latter part of her life.*
▷ **the latter** *pron* the second of two things or people already mentioned: *Many support the former alternative, but personally I favour the latter (one).* ➪ Usage at LATE[1].
latterly *adv* lately; nowadays. Cf FORMER.
□ ˌ**latter-**ˈ**day** *adj* [attrib] modern; recent: *latter-day technology* ○ *They see themselves as latter-day crusading knights.* ˌ**Latter-day** ˈ**Saints** Mormons' name for themselves.

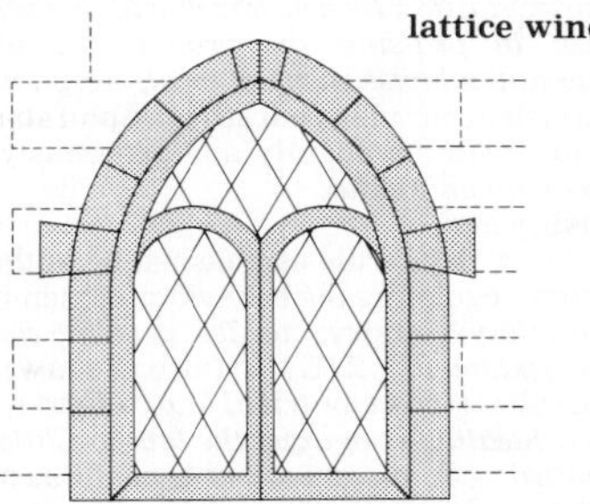
lattice window

lattice /ˈlætɪs/ (also ˈ**lattice-work**) [C, usu *sing*] **1** framework of crossed laths or bars with spaces between, used as a screen, fence, support for climbing plants, etc: *a steel lattice-work placed around dangerous machinery.* **2** structure or design resembling this: *peering through the lattice of tall reeds.* **3** (*chemistry*) regular pattern in which the atoms or molecules of crystals are arranged.
□ ˌ**lattice** ˈ**window** window with small diamond-shaped panes set in a framework of lead strips. ➪ illus.

Latvia /ˈlætvɪə/ country on the east coast of the Baltic Sea; pop approx 2 606 000; official language Lettish; capital Riga; unit of currency Latvian rouble. An independent republic from 1918, it became part of the USSR in 1940 and regained independence in 1991. ➪ map at UNION OF SOVIET SOCIALIST REPUBLICS.
▷ **Latvian** *adj* of Latvia, its culture or its people. ~ *n* [C] (native or) inhabitant of Latvia. Cf LETT.

Laud /lɔːd/ William (1573-1645), Archbishop of Canterbury from 1633 under Charles I. Although a Protestant, he tried to force churches to return to the type of Catholic services held before the *Reformation. Opposition in both England and Scotland eventually led to his being executed for treason.

laud /lɔːd/ *v* [Tn] (*fml or rhet*) praise (sb/sth); glorify: *a much-lauded production.*
▷ **lauds** *n* [sing or pl *v*] traditional morning prayer of the Roman Catholic Church. Cf MATINS.

laudable /ˈlɔːdəbl/ *adj* (*fml*) deserving praise; praiseworthy: *a laudable ambition, endeavour, enterprise, etc* ○ *Her work for charity is highly laudable.* ▷ **laudably** /-əblɪ/ *adv.*

laudanum /ˈlɔːdənəm/ *n* [U] (esp formerly) opium prepared for use as a sedative.

laudatory /ˈlɔːdətərɪ; *US* -tɔːrɪ/ *adj* (*fml*) expressing or giving praise.

laugh /lɑːf; *US* læf/ *v* **1** [I] make the sounds and movements of the face and body that express lively amusement, joy, contempt, etc: *laugh aloud/out loud* ○ *He's so funny — he always makes me laugh.* ○ *Don't laugh* (ie think me ridiculous), *but I've decided to teach myself Chinese.* **2** [I] have these emotions: *a man who laughs in the face of danger* ○ *She hasn't got much to laugh about, poor woman.* **3** (idm) **he who laughs last laughs** ˈ**longest** (*saying*) (used as a warning against expressing joy or triumph too soon). **laugh in sb's** ˈ**face** openly show one's contempt for sb. **laugh like a** ˈ**drain** (*infml*) laugh loudly. **laugh on the other side of one's face** (*infml*) be forced to change from joy or triumph to disappointment or regret: *He'll be laughing on the other side of his face when he reads this letter.* **laugh sb/sth out of** ˈ**court** (*infml*) dismiss sb/sth scornfully: *Their allegations were simply laughed out of court.* **laugh oneself** ˈ**silly/**ˈ**sick** become hysterical or ill by laughing excessively. **laugh till/until one** ˈ**cries** laugh so long or hard that one's eyes water. **laugh sb/sth to scorn** (*fml*) mock or ridicule sb/sth. **laugh up one's** ˈ**sleeve (at sb/sth)** (*infml*) be secretly amused: *She knew the truth all along and was laughing up her sleeve at us.* **4** (phr v) **laugh at sb/sth** (**a**) show that one is amused by sb/sth: *laugh at a comedian, a joke.* (**b**) mock or ridicule sb/sth: *We all laughed at Jane when she said she believed in ghosts.* (**c**) disregard sb/sth; treat sb/sth with indifference: *laugh at danger.* **laugh sth away** dismiss (an unpleasant feeling, etc) by laughing: *He tried without success to laugh her fears away.* **laugh sb/sth down** silence or reject sb/sth by laughing scornfully: *laugh down a speaker, a proposal.* **laugh sth off** (*infml*) show that one does not care about sth: *An actor has to learn to laugh off bad reviews.* ○ *There was an embarrassing silence after her indiscreet remark but she was able to laugh it off.* **laugh sb out of sth** cause sb to forget their problems, etc by making them laugh: *He could tell she was in a bad mood, and tried to laugh her out of it.*
▷ **laugh** *n* **1** act, sound or manner of laughing: *give, let out, break into, utter, etc a (loud) laugh* ○ *a cynical, gentle, polite, hearty, etc laugh* ○ *I recognized him by his raucous, penetrating laugh.* **2** (*infml*) amusing incident or person: *And he didn't realize it was you? What a laugh!* ○ (*ironic*) *Her, offer to help? That's a laugh!* ○ *He's a real laugh — such fun to be with.* **3** (idm) **have the last laugh** ➪ LAST[1]. **raise a laugh/smile** ➪ RAISE.
laughable /-əbl/ *adj* (*derog*) causing people to laugh; ridiculous: *a laughable attempt to discredit the Government.* **laughably** /-əblɪ/ *adv.*

laughing /ˈlɑːfɪŋ; *US* ˈlæfɪŋ/ *adj* **1** showing amusement, happiness, etc: *laughing faces.* **2** (idm) **be** ˈ**laughing** (*sl*) be in a satisfactory or enviable situation: *It's all right for you, with a good job and a nice house — you're laughing.* **be no laughing matter** be sth serious, not to be joked about. **die laughing** ➪ DIE[2].
▷ **laughingly** *adv* **1** in an amused manner. **2** (*often derog*) in an amusing manner; ridiculously: *They're fond of holding what are laughingly known as literary soirées.*
□ ˈ**laughing-gas** *n* [U] = NITROUS OXIDE (NITROUS).
laughing-stock *n* (esp *sing*) person or thing that is ridiculed: *His constant blunders made him the laughing-stock of the whole class.*

laughter /ˈlɑːftə(r); *US* ˈlæf-/ *n* [U] act, sound or manner of laughing: *roar with laughter* ○ *tears of laughter* ○ *a house full of laughter*, ie with a happy relaxed atmosphere.

Laughton /ˈlɔːtən/ Charles (1899-1962), British

actor. A dominant but sensitive performer, he worked in England, often with *Korda, before making films like *Mutiny on the Bounty* in Hollywood.

launch[1] /lɔ:ntʃ/ *v* **1** [Tn, Tn·pr] put (sth) into motion; send on its course: *launch a blow, a missile, a torpedo, a satellite* ○ *(fig) launch threats, insults, gibes, etc at sb.* **2** [Tn] cause (a ship, esp one newly built) to move into the water: *The Queen is to launch a new warship today.* ○ *The lifeboat was launched immediately to rescue the four men.* **3** [Tn, Tn·pr] put (sth/sb) into action; set going: *launch an attack/offensive (against the enemy)* ○ *The company is launching a new model next month.* ○ *He's launching his son on a career in banking.* **4** (phr v) **launch (out) into sth** enter boldly or freely into (a course of action): *He launched into a long series of excuses for his behaviour.* ○ *She wants to be more than just a singer and is launching out into films,* ie starting a career as a film actress. **launch out at sb** attack sb, physically or verbally: *He suddenly launched out at me for no reason at all.*
▷ **launch** *n* (esp *sing*) process of putting into motion a ship, spacecraft or new product: *the launch of their new saloon received much media coverage.*
launcher *n* structure or device used for launching missiles: *a rocket launcher.*
□ ˈ**launching pad** (also ˈ**launch pad**) base or platform from which spacecraft, etc are launched.
ˈ**launch window** period during which it is possible for spacecraft, etc to be launched successfully (because of the position of the planets, etc).

launch[2] /lɔ:ntʃ/ *n* large motor boat.

launder /ˈlɔ:ndə(r)/ *v* **1** [Tn] *(fml)* wash and iron (clothes, etc): *Send these shirts to be laundered.* **2** [Tn, Tn·pr] *(fig)* transfer (money obtained from crime) to foreign banks, legitimate businesses, etc so as to disguise its source: *The gang laundered the stolen money through their chain of restaurants.*
▷ **laundress** /ˈlɔ:ndrɪs/ *n* woman who earns money by laundering.

launderette (also **laundrette**) /ˌlɔ:ndəˈret, lɔ:nˈdret/ *n* business where the public may wash and dry their clothes, etc in coin-operated machines.

laundromat /ˈlɔ:ndrəmæt/ *n* *(propr esp US)* launderette.

laundry /ˈlɔ:ndrɪ/ *n* **1** [C] **(a)** business where clothes, sheets, etc are laundered: *sent to the laundry,* ie attrib ○ *a laundry van.* **(b)** room in a house, hotel, etc where clothes, sheets, etc are laundered. **2** [U] clothes, sheets, etc that have been or need to be laundered: *There's not much laundry this week* ○ *Did you do the laundry today?* ○ [attrib] *a laundry basket.*

Laureate /ˈlɒrɪət; *US* ˈlɔ:r-/ *n* = POET LAUREATE (POET).

laurel /ˈlɒrəl; *US* ˈlɔ:rəl/ *n* **1** [C] evergreen shrub with smooth glossy leaves. **2** (also **laurels** [pl]) wreath of laurel leaves, used by the ancient Greeks and Romans as an emblem of victory or honour. **3** (idm) **gain/win one's** ˈ**laurels** win fame or honour. **look to one's** ˈ**laurels** beware of losing one's position of superiority: *There are so many good new actors around that the older ones will soon have to look to their laurels.* **rest on one's laurels** ⇨ REST[1].

Laurel and Hardy /ˌlɒrəl ənd ˈhɑ:dɪ/ Stanley (usu Stan) Laurel (1890-1965) and Oliver (or Ollie) Hardy (1892-1957), American film actors (though Laurel was born in England). For over 25 years they formed the most successful comic partnership in the history of the cinema. Stan (the thin one) played an incompetent innocent who created chaos for the fat pompous Ollie: *(fig) You should have seen us trying to get the crate upstairs — it was pure Laurel and Hardy!* ⇨ illus.

lav /læv/ *n* *(infml)* lavatory.

lava /ˈlɑ:və/ *n* [U] **1** hot liquid rock that comes out of a volcano: *a stream of lava.* ⇨ illus at VOLCANO. **2** type of rock formed from this when it has cooled and hardened.

Laurel and Hardy

lavatory /ˈlævətrɪ; *US* -tɔ:rɪ/ *n* **1** (also **also** *dated* ˈ**water-closet**) device, usu consisting of a bowl connected to a drain, used for disposing of waste matter from the body. **2** room, building, etc equipped with this device. ⇨ Usage at TOILET.

lavender /ˈlævəndə(r)/ *n* [U] **1** **(a)** plant with sweet-smelling pale purple flowers. **(b)** its dried flowers and stalks used to give linen, etc a pleasant smell. **2** pale purple colour.
□ ˈ**lavender-water** *n* [U] delicate perfume made from lavender.

lavish /ˈlævɪʃ/ *adj* **1** ~ **(in/of/with sth)**; ~ **(in doing sth)** giving or producing generously or in large quantities: *He was lavish with his praise for/lavish in praising the project.* **2** plentiful; abundant: *a lavish display, meal, reception.*
▷ **lavish** *v* (phr v) **lavish sth on/upon sb/sth** give sth to sb/sth abundantly and generously: *lavish care on an only child.*
lavishly *adv.*

law /lɔ:/ *n* **1** [C] rule established by authority or custom, regulating the behaviour of members of a community, country, etc: *The new law comes into force next month.* **2** [U] **(a)** (also **the law**) body of such rules: *respect for tribal law* ○ *observe/obey the law* ○ *Stealing is against the law.* ○ *Children not admitted — by law.* ○ *I didn't know I was breaking the law,* ie doing sth illegal. ○ *be within/outside the law* ○ *She acts as if she's above the law,* ie as if the law does not apply to her. ○ *The law is on our side,* ie We are right according to the law. ⇨ article. **(b)** **the Law** (also **the law of Moses**, **Mosaic Law**) (in Judaism) the first five books of the Bible; the Pentateuch. **3** [U] such rules as a science or subject of study: *read* (ie study) *law at university.* ○ *He gave up law to become a writer.* ○ [attrib] *a law student.* **4** [C] rule of action or procedure, esp in the arts or a game: *the laws of perspective, harmony* ○ *the laws of tennis.* **5** [C] factual statement of what always happens in certain circumstances; scientific principle: *the law of gravity* ○ *the laws of motion.* **6 the law** [sing] *(infml)* the police: *Watch out — here comes the law!* **7** (idm) **the arm of the law** ⇨ ARM[1]. **be a law unto one**ˈ**self/it**ˈ**self** behave in an unconventional or unpredictable fashion: *My car's a law unto itself — I can't rely on it.* **go to** ˈ**law (against sb)** ask the lawcourts to decide about a problem, claim, etc. **have the** ˈ**law on sb** *(infml)* report sb to the police; start legal proceedings against sb: *If you do that again I'll have the law on you.* **law and** ˈ**order** situation in which the law is obeyed: *a breakdown in/of law and order* ○ *establish, maintain, uphold, etc law and order* ○ [attrib] *a law-and-order policy.* **the law of** ˈ**averages** principle according to which one believes that if one extreme occurs it will be matched by the other extreme occurring, so that a normal average is maintained. **the law of the** ˈ**jungle** the survival or success of the strongest or the most unscrupulous. **lay down the** ˈ**law** say with (real or assumed) authority what should be done: *He's always laying down the law about gardening but he really doesn't know much about it.* **the letter of the law** ⇨ LETTER. **possession is nine points of the law** ⇨ POSSESSION. **take the law into one's own** ˈ**hands** disregard the law and take independent (and usu forceful) action to correct sth believed to be wrong. **there's no law against sth** *(infml)* (doing) sth is allowed: *I'll stay in bed as long as I like — there's no law against it.*
▷ **lawful** /-fl/ *adj* **1** allowed by law; legal: *take power by lawful means.* **2** [esp attrib] recognized by law: *his lawful heir.* **lawfully** /-fəlɪ/ *adv.*
lawless *adj* **(a)** (of a country or area) where laws do not exist or are not enforced. **(b)** (of people or actions) without respect for the law: *a lawless mob looting and destroying shops.* **lawlessly** *adv.* **lawlessness** *n* [U].
□ ˈ**law-abiding** *adj* obeying the law: *law-abiding citizens.*
ˈ**law agent** *(Scot)* solicitor.
ˈ**law-breaker** *n* person who disobeys the law; criminal.
ˈ**lawcourt** (also ˌ**court of** ˈ**law**) *n* room or building in which legal cases are heard and judged. Cf COURT[1] 1.
ˈ**Law Lord** (in Britain) member of the House of Lords who is qualified to perform its legal work.
ˈ**lawmaker** *n* person who makes laws; legislator.
ˈ**lawman** /-mən/ *n* *(pl* **-men** /-mən/) *(esp US)* person responsible for enforcing the law, esp a sheriff.
ˌ**law of** ˈ**nature** = NATURAL LAW (NATURAL): *(joc) All men are selfish: it's a law of nature.*
the ˈ**Law Society** professional body to which all British solicitors belong.
ˈ**lawsuit** (also **suit**) *n* process of bringing a dispute, claim, etc before a court of law for settlement.

lawn[1] /lɔ:n/ *n* [C, U] area of closely-cut grass in the garden of a house or a public park, or used for a game: *In summer we mow our lawn once a week.* ○ *The house has half an acre of lawn.* ○ *a* ˈ*croquet lawn.* ⇨ illus at HOME.
📖 Lawns are a special feature of most country houses and of Oxford and Cambridge colleges. Lawns used for sporting purposes, such as tennis or croquet, are tended with extra care, being regularly mown, rolled and watered. The word 'lawn' is not always used to describe an area of grass used for sports. For example, we talk about a cricket *pitch* and a bowling *green.*
ˈ**lawn-mower** *n* machine for cutting the grass on lawns.
ˌ**lawn** ˈ**tennis** *(fml)* = TENNIS.

lawn[2] /lɔ:n/ *n* [U] type of fine linen used for dresses, etc.

Lawrence[1] /ˈlɒrəns/ D(avid) H(erbert) (1885-1930), English novelist and poet. He came from a working-class mining background which he sometimes used in his stories. The theme present in most of his work is the repression of individuality and sexuality by society, and many of his books were originally regarded as obscene. His novel *Lady Chatterley's Lover* was not published in full in Britain until 1960, after a celebrated court case. ⇨ article at TABOO. ▷ **Lawrentian** /ləˈrenʃn/ *adj.*

Lawrence[2] /ˈlɒrəns/ Thomas Edward (1888-1935), British archaeologist, soldier and writer, known as 'Lawrence of Arabia'. In the First World War he helped to plan and lead a guerrilla campaign which ended Turkish rule in the Middle East and won him fame and a romantic reputation. He describes the campaign in *The Seven Pillars of Wisdom.* Dissatisfaction with official policy and with life as a public figure later led him to join the Royal Air Force and then the tank corps under false names. People continue to be fascinated by

Law

The main sources of British law are common law, legislation and, more recently, European Community law. Scotland and Northern Ireland have their own legal system and lawcourts, distinct from those in England and Wales.

Common law is the ancient 'law of the land' that has been passed down by precedent and custom. It is unwritten. Judgements are based on judgements made in previous cases and this forms the basis of all law that is not specifically legislation. Legislation consists of Acts passed by Parliament and there are also by-laws made by local authorities. European Community law is mainly concerned with economic and social affairs. In some circumstances it can reverse judgements made in the British courts.

A distinctive ancient British law is that of habeas corpus. This Latin phrase literally means 'you must have the body', and is the opening words of a 17th-century writ guaranteeing a person a fair trial. A person who believes that he is being wrongly held by the police can issue a writ of habeas corpus to have his complaint heard by a court. This is also part of the US Constitution.

The decision to bring a person to court in the first place is usually made by the police. If a criminal charge is made, the papers go to the Crown Prosecution Service, which then decides whether to prosecute or not.

Criminal offences are prosecuted either in a magistrates' court or at a Crown Court. A magistrate, also called a Justice of the Peace (JP), is a member of the public who is not legally qualified; normally three magistrates sit together as a court. There are also some full-time legally qualified magistrates who normally sit alone in town courts where the number of prosecutions is usually higher.

Magistrates' courts deal with less important offences. More serious offences are committed to a Crown Court, which also passes sentence on criminals convicted by magistrates' courts, and hears appeals from people tried in those courts. It sits at various centres around the country and is presided over either by a visiting High Court judge, a 'circuit judge' (a former barrister or solicitor serving as a full-time judge on a 'circuit', one of six administrative districts for legal purposes), or a recorder (a part-time judge). All Crown Court trials are heard by a judge and a jury, or by a judge alone if the accused pleads guilty. Circuit judges and recorders sit with magistrates in the Crown Court to deal with appeals.

Non-criminal cases, ie civil disputes (for example, a claim for damages as a result of a traffic accident or a dispute about custody of children) are usually heard by a circuit judge in a county court without a jury. The judge normally sits alone, but may very rarely in special cases order a trial by jury.

A trial in a criminal court is a contest between the prosecution, who put the case and call the evidence against the defendant, and the defence. The defendant normally has a lawyer to represent him and act as his legal adviser. An accused person pleads 'guilty' or 'not guilty'. It is a principle of English law that a person is presumed to be innocent until proved guilty, and the Prosecution have to satisfy the Court of the defendant's guilt so that the Court is sure of it, otherwise he must be found 'not guilty'.

The jury, who make the eventual decision in the Crown Court as to whether the defendant is actually 'guilty' or 'not guilty', is normally composed of 12 people chosen at random from the list of local people who have a right to vote in the area. Their decision is called a verdict.

The lawyers who speak for the prosecution or the defence in magistrates' courts and county courts are normally solicitors, while in the Crown Courts they are barristers. In Scotland a barrister is known as an 'advocate'. Barristers are so called because they have been 'called to the Bar' by one of the Inns of Court.

Young people under 17 are tried in a special juvenile court, a kind of magistrates' court which is held separately from the other courts. Sudden or suspicious deaths are investigated in a special coroner's court.

The Crown Court can only hear criminal appeals from the magistrates' courts in criminal cases; it cannot hear appeals from them in civil matters, such as the adoption of a child. These go to the High Court of Justice, which itself is divided into the Chancery Division, the Queen's Bench Division and the Family Division, where, for example, an appeal against an adoption or custody order would be heard. Appeals from the High Court and the county courts go to the Civil Division of the Court of Appeal, while appeals from the Crown Court go to its Criminal Division. The Civil Division is presided over by the Master of the Rolls, and the Criminal Division by the Lord Chief Justice.

Appeals in both civil and criminal cases may then go on to the final court of appeal. This is the House of Lords, where the judges are the nine 'Lords of Appeal'. Five of them usually sit at one time. Solicitors have much wider duties than merely speaking in court. They are qualified lawyers who not only appear in court but draft legal documents, such as wills, and give advice on legal matters. They are paid either by the client or by the state if the client's low income qualifies him for legal aid. Some solicitors also work in local government, or as legal advisers to a company. One of their most frequent jobs is to supervise the legal procedures involved in conveyancing (the buying or selling of a house), although this can now also be carried out through a building society or bank.

US law is based on English law and is represented by common law, statute law, and the US Constitution. There are two types of court, state and federal, with each state having its own distinctive laws, courts and prisons. Federal law cases are first heard before a federal district judge in a district court presided over by a Chief Judge. Appeals are made to one of 13 Courts of Appeal or to the Supreme Court, the highest in the country. The federal legal system has its own police force, the Federal Bureau of Investigation (FBI).

Routine criminal and civil cases are heard in local, district and county courts, with some states having a Supreme Court. Even small villages may have a local judge, called a 'justice of the peace', who can deal with minor legal matters. There are both federal and state judges, with the former, as well as judges of the Supreme Court, being appointed by the President with the advice and consent of the Senate. The Supreme Court itself at present comprises the Chief Justice of the United States and eight Associate Justices. Juries are used in civil cases as well as in criminal trials.

A sheriff in the USA is the chief law enforcement officer in a county, with the power of a police officer in the matter of enforcing criminal law. In his judicial role he is entitled to serve writs. He is elected by the local people in all states except Rhode Island.

In England and Wales the sheriff is the principal officer of the Crown in a county, with mainly ceremonial duties. In Scotland, however, he is a judge in a sheriff court, which deals with most types of crime. (The most serious cases are heard in a High Court, which is similar to an English Crown Court, and the minor ones in a district court). (Cf articles at CRIME and PUNISHMENT.)

his enigmatic personality and there have been many biographies of him.

lawrencium /lə'rensɪəm/ *n* [U] (*symb* **Lr**) (*chemistry*) artificial radioactive metallic element.

lawyer /'lɔːjə(r)/ *n* person who is trained and qualified in legal matters, esp a solicitor: *Don't sign anything until you've consulted a lawyer.* Cf ADVOCATE *n* 2, ATTORNEY 2, BARRISTER.

lax /læks/ *adj* not sufficiently strict or severe; negligent: *lax security, behaviour, regulations* ○ *He's too lax with his pupils.* ▷ **laxity** /'læksətɪ/ *n* [U]. **laxly** *adv*.

laxative /'læksətɪv/ *n, adj* (medicine, food or drink) causing or helping the bowels to empty: *If you're constipated you may need a laxative.*

lay[1] /leɪ/ *v* (*pt, pp* **laid** /leɪd/)

► PLACING SOMETHING IN A CERTAIN POSITION OR ON A SURFACE **1** (**a**) [Tn·pr, Tn·p, Cn·a] put (sth/sb) in a certain position or on a surface: *lay the book on the table* ○ *lay the blanket over the sleeping child* ○ *lay oneself down to sleep* ○ *He laid his hand on my shoulder.* ○ *The horse laid back its ears.* ○ *The storm laid the crops flat.* (**b**) [Tn, Tn·pr] put (sth) in the correct position for a particular purpose: *lay a carpet, cable, pipe* ○ *lay the foundations of a house* ○ *lay the table,* ie put plates, cutlery, etc on it for a meal ○ *A bricklayer lays bricks to make a wall.* ○ *They are laying new sewers along the road.* **2** [Tn, Tn·pr] ~ **A** (**on/over B**); ~ **B with A** spread sth (on sth); cover or coat sth with sth: *lay the paint evenly* ○ *lay straw everywhere* ○ *lay carpeting on the floor/lay the floor with carpeting.* ⇨ Usage at LIE[2].

► CAUSING SOMEBODY OR SOMETHING TO BE IN A CERTAIN STATE **3** [Tn·pr] (*fml*) cause (sb/sth) to be in a certain state or situation: *lay sb under an obligation* (ie oblige sb) *to do sth* ○ *lay new laws before parliament.* **4** [Tn] cause (sth) to settle: *sprinkle water to lay the dust.* **5** [Tn] make (sth) smooth or flat: *using hair cream to lay the hair sticking up at the back.* **6** [Tn] (*fml*) cause (sth) to be less strong; allay: *lay sb's fears, doubts, suspicions, etc.*

► OTHER MEANINGS **7** [Tn, Tn·pr, Dn·n, Dn·f no passive] ~ **sth** (**on sth**) bet (money) on sth; place (a bet): *gamblers laying their stakes in roulette* ○ *How much did you lay on that race?* ○ *I'll lay you £5 that she won't come.* **8** [Tn esp passive] (⚠ *sl*) (of a man) have sexual intercourse with (a woman): *get laid.* **9** [I, Tn] (of birds, insects, etc) produce (eggs): *The hens are not laying well* (ie not producing many eggs) *at the moment.* ○ *The cuckoo*

lays its eggs in other birds' nests. ○ new-laid eggs at 90p a dozen. **10** (in some combinations of *lay* + *n* + *prep*/infinitive, having the same meaning as a *v* related in form to the *n*, eg *lay the emphasis on certain points* = *emphasize certain points*): *lay stress on neatness*, ie stress it ○ *Who should we lay the blame on?* ie Who should we blame? ○ *lay (one's) plans* (ie plan) *to do sth* ○ *lay a trap for* (ie prepare to trap) *sb.* **11** (idm) **lay it ˈon (ˈthick/with a ˈtrowel)** (*infml*) use exaggerated praise, flattery, etc: *To call him a genius is laying it on a bit (too thick)!* (For other idioms containing **lay**, see entries for *ns, adjs*, etc, eg **lay one's hands on sb/sth** ⇨ HAND[1]; **lay sth bare** ⇨ BARE[1].).
12 (phr v) **lay aˈbout one (with sth)** hit out in all directions: *As we approached her, she laid about her with a stick.* **lay about sb/sth (with sth)** attack sb/sth with words or blows: *She laid about him, calling him a liar and a cheat.*
lay sth aside (*fml*) **(a)** put sth aside: *I laid my book aside, turned off the light and went to sleep.* **(b)** abandon sth; give sth up: *lay aside one's studies, one's responsibilities.* **(c)** (also **lay sth by**) keep sth for future use; save sth: *lay some money aside for one's old age.*
lay sth away (*US*) pay a deposit on sth to reserve it until full payment is made.
lay sth down (a) store (wine) in a cellar, etc: *lay down claret.* **(b)** (begin to) build sth: *lay down a new ship, railway track.* **(c)** (*fml*) cease to perform sth; give sth up: *lay down one's office, duties.* **lay sth down; lay it ˈdown that...** give sth as a rule, principle, etc; establish: *You can't lay down hard and fast rules.* ○ *It is laid down that all applicants must sit a written exam.*
lay sth in provide oneself with a stock of sth: *lay in food, coal, supplies, etc.*
lay into sb/sth (*infml*) attack sb/sth violently, with words or blows: *He really laid into her, saying she was arrogant and unfeeling.*
lay ˈoff (sb) (*infml*) stop doing sth that irritates, annoys, etc: *Lay off! You're messing up my hair!* ○ *Lay off him! Can't you see he's badly hurt?* **lay ˈoff (sth)** (*infml*) stop doing or using sth harmful, etc: *I've smoked cigarettes for years, but now I'm going to lay off (them).* ○ *You must lay off alcohol for a while.* **lay sb ˈoff** dismiss (workers), usu for a short time: *They were laid off because of the lack of new orders.*
lay sth ˈon (a) supply (gas, water, etc) for a house, etc: *We can't move in until the electricity has been laid on.* **(b)** (*infml*) provide sth; arrange sth: *lay on a party, show, trip* ○ *lay on food and drink* ○ *Sightseeing tours are laid on for visitors.*
lay sb ˈout knock sb unconscious: *The boxer was laid out in the fifth round.* **lay sth ˈout (a)** spread sth out ready for use or to be seen easily: *beautiful jewellery laid out in the shop window* ○ *Please lay out all the clothes you want to take on holiday.* **(b)** (often passive) arrange sth in a planned way: *lay out a town, garden* ○ *a well laid out magazine.* **(c)** (*infml*) spend (money): *I had to lay out a fortune on that car.* **(d)** prepare (a corpse) for burial.
lay ˈover (*US*) stop at a place on a journey: *We laid over in Arizona on the way to California.* Cf STOP OVER (STOP[1]).
lay sb ˈup (usu passive) cause sb to stay in bed, not be able to work, etc: *She's laid up with a broken leg.* ○ *I've been laid up with flu for a week.* **lay sth up (a)** save sth; store sth: *lay up supplies, fuel, etc.* **(b)** put (a vehicle, ship, etc) out of use: *lay a ship up for repairs* ○ *My car's laid up at the moment.* **lay sth up (for oneself)** ensure by what one does or fails to do that one will have trouble in the future: *You're only laying up trouble (for yourself) by not mending that roof now.*
▷ **lay** *n* (⚠ *sl esp sexist*) partner in sexual intercourse (esp a woman): *an easy lay*, ie a person who is ready and willing to have sexual intercourse.
□ ˈ**layaway** *n* [U] (*US*) system of reserving goods by putting a deposit on them until full payment is made: *She buys her Xmas presents on layaway.*
ˈ**lay-off** *n* **(a)** dismissal of a worker, usu for a short time: *many lay-offs among factory workers.* **(b)** period of this: *a long lay-off over the winter.*
ˈ**layout** *n* way in which the parts of sth are arranged according to a plan: *the layout of rooms in a building* ○ *a magazine's attractive new page layout.*
ˈ**lay-over** *n* (*US*) short stop on a journey. Cf STOPOVER (STOP[1]).

lay[2] /leɪ/ *adj* [attrib] **1** not belonging to the clergy: *a lay preacher.* **2 (a)** not having expert knowledge of a subject: *lay opinion* ○ *speaking as a lay person.* **(b)** not professionally qualified, esp in law or medicine. Cf LAITY.
□ ˈ**layman** /-mən/ *n* (*pl* **-men** /-mən/, *fem* **laywoman**, *pl* **-women**) **1** person who does not have an expert knowledge of a subject: *a book written for professionals and laymen alike.* **2** Church member who is not a clergyman or priest.
lay ˈreader = READER 6.

lay[3] /leɪ/ *n* (*arch*) poem that was written to be sung; ballad.

lay[4] *pt* of LIE[2].

layabout /ˈleɪəbaʊt/ *n* (*Brit infml*) lazy person who avoids work.

lay-by /ˈleɪ baɪ/ *n* (*pl* **lay-bys**) (*Brit*) (*US* **rest stop**) area at the side of a road where vehicles may stop without obstructing the flow of traffic.

layer /ˈleɪə(r)/ *n* **1** thickness of material (esp one of several) laid over a surface or forming a horizontal division: *Several thin layers of clothing will keep you warmer than one thick one.* ○ *a layer of dust on the furniture* ○ *a layer of clay in the earth* ○ *remove layers of old paint.* ⇨ illus. **2** (preceded by an *adj*) hen that lays eggs: *a poor, good, etc layer.* **3** (in gardening) shoot[2](1) fastened down for layering.
▷ **layer** *v* [Tn] **1** arrange (sth) in layers: *layer lime and garden clippings to make compost* ○ *layered hair*, ie cut to several differing lengths. **2** (in gardening) cause (a shoot[2](1)) to take root while still attached to the parent plant.

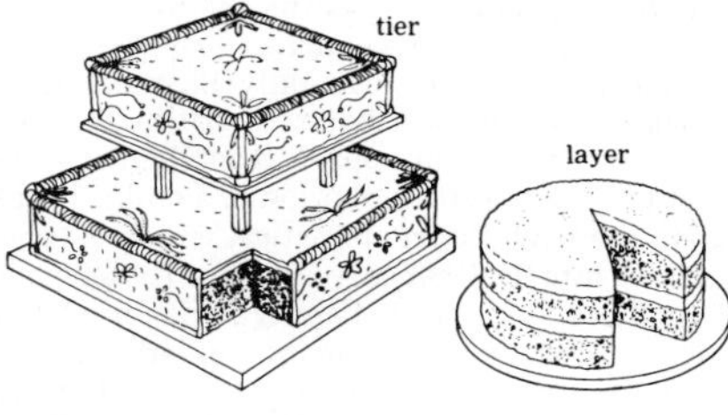

□ ˈ**layer cake** cake consisting of layers with fillings of cream, etc between.

layette /leɪˈet/ *n* set of clothes, nappies, rugs, etc for a new-born baby.

lay figure /ˌleɪ ˈfɪgə(r)/ **1** wooden figure of the human body with jointed movable limbs, used as a model by artists. **2** unconvincing character in a novel, etc.

layman ⇨ LAY[2].

laze /leɪz/ *v* **1** [I, Ipr, Ip] ~ **(about/around)** be lazy; rest; relax: *lazing by the river all day* ○ *spend the afternoon lazing around (the house).* **2** (phr v) **laze sth away** spend (time) idly: *You can't go on lazing your life away.*

lazy /ˈleɪzɪ/ *adj* (**-ier**, **-iest**) **1** unwilling to work; doing little work: *He's not stupid, just lazy.* **2** showing or causing a lack of energy or activity: *a lazy yawn* ○ *a lazy summer evening* ○ *We spent a lazy day at the beach.* ▷ **lazily** *adv*: *a river flowing lazily beside the meadow.* **laziness** *n* [U].
□ ˈ**lazy-bones** *n* (*infml*) lazy person.
ˌ**lazy ˈSusan** (*US*) = DUMB WAITER (DUMB).

lb *abbr* (*pl* unchanged or **lbs**) pound (weight) (Latin *libra*): *apples 20p* (ie 20 pence) *per lb* ○ *Add 2lb sugar.* Cf oz.

lbw /ˌel biː ˈdʌbljuː/ *abbr* (in cricket) leg before wicket.

LCD /ˌel siː ˈdiː/ *abbr* (*electronics*) liquid crystal display.

lcm /ˌel siː ˈem/ *abbr* lowest (or least) common multiple.

L/Cpl *abbr* Lance-Corporal: *L/Cpl (Colin) Small.*

LEA /ˌel iː ˈeɪ/ *abbr* (*Brit*) Local Education Authority: *an ˌLEA ˈstudy grant.* ⇨ articles at POST-SCHOOL, SCHOOL.

lea /liː/ *n* (*arch*) area of open grassland; meadow.

leach /liːtʃ/ *v* **1** [Tn] make (liquid) percolate through soil, ore, ash, etc. **2** [Tn·pr, Tn·p] ~ **sth from sth**; ~ **sth out/away** remove (soluble matter) from sth by the action of a percolating fluid: *leach minerals/nutrients from the soil.*

lead[1] /led/ *n* **1** [U] (*symb* **Pb**) (*chemistry*) heavy soft metal of dull greyish colour, used in car batteries, in roofing, as a radiation shield, etc and mixed with other metals to form alloys. ⇨ App 11. **2** [C, U] (thin stick of) graphite used as the part of a pencil that makes a mark. **3** [C] (*nautical*) lump of lead fastened to a cord, used for measuring the depth of water beneath a ship. **4 leads** /ledz/ [pl] **(a)** strips of lead used to cover a roof. **(b)** area of roof (esp flat) covered with these. **(c)** framework of lead strips holding glass panes, eg in a lattice window. **5** (idm) **swing the lead** ⇨ SWING[1].
▷ **leaded** /ˈledɪd/ *adj* [usu attrib] covered or framed with lead: *leaded windows, glass.* ˌ**leaded ˈlight** small panel of leaded glass, esp coloured, forming part of a larger window.
leaden /ˈledn/ *adj* **1** dull, heavy or slow: *the leaden atmosphere of the museum* ○ *a leaden heart* ○ *moving at a leaden pace.* **2** lead-coloured; dull grey: *leaden clouds promising rain.* **3** [attrib] (*dated*) made of lead: *leaden pipes.*
leading /ˈledɪŋ/ *n* [U] (in printing) space between lines of print.
□ ˌ**lead ˈpencil** stick of graphite enclosed in a wooden or metal holder, used for writing or drawing.
ˌ**lead-ˈpoisoning** *n* diseased condition caused by taking lead into the body.

lead[2] /liːd/ *n* **1** [U, sing] guidance given by going first or in front; example: *He's the chief trouble-maker; the others just follow his lead.* **2** [sing] distance by which one competitor, etc is in front: *have a lead of three metres, two lengths, half a lap, etc* ○ *The company has built up a substantial lead in laser technology.* **3 the lead** [sing] first place or position: *move/go into the lead* ○ *take (over) the lead (from sb)/lose the lead (to sb).* **4** [C] principal part in a play, etc; person who plays this part: *play the lead in the new West End hit* ○ [attrib] *the lead guitarist of the group.* **5** [C] (also **lead story**) item of news printed most prominently in a newspaper or coming first in a news broadcast. **6** [C] (in card-games) act or right of playing first: *Whose lead is it?* **7** [C] piece of information or evidence that might provide the solution to a problem; clue: *The police are investigating an important new lead.* **8** [C] (also **leash**) strap or cord for leading or controlling a dog: *You must keep your dog on a lead in the park.* **9** [C] length of wire conveying electrical current from a source to a place of use. **10** (idm) **follow sb's example/lead** ⇨ FOLLOW. **give (sb) a ˈlead (a)** encourage others by doing sth first: *The Church should give more of a lead on basic moral issues.* **(b)** provide a hint towards the solution of a problem. **take the ˈlead (in doing sth)** set an example for others to follow.

lead[3] /liːd/ *v* (*pt, pp* **led** /led/) **1** [Tn, Tn·pr, Tn·p] **(a)** show (sb) the way, esp by going in front: *lead a guest to his room* ○ *He led the group out into the garden.* **(b)** guide or take (sb/sth) by holding, pulling, etc: *lead a blind man across the road* ○ *She grasped the reins and led the horse back.* **2** [Tn, Tn·pr, Tn·p, Cn·t] ~ **sb (to sth)** influence the actions or opinions of sb: *He's too easily led.* ○ *What led you to this conclusion?* ○ *Don't be led astray* (ie tempted to do wrong) *by him.* ○ *Her constant lying led me to distrust everything she said.* **3** [Ipr, Ip] be a route or means of access: *This door leads into the garden.* **4** [Ipr] ~ **to sth** have sth as its result: *This misprint led to great confusion.* ○ *Your work seems to be leading nowhere*, ie achieving nothing. **5** [Tn] have a certain kind of life (used esp with the *ns* shown): *lead a miserable existence, a life of luxury, a double life, etc* ○ *decide to lead a new life.* **6** [I, Ipr, Tn, Tn·pr] ~ **(sb/sth) (in sth)** be in first place or ahead of (sb/sth): *The champion is leading by* *eighteen seconds.* ○ *lead the world in cancer research.* **7** [I, Tn, Tn·pr] ~ (**sb/sth**) (**into sth**) be the leader or head of (sb/sth); direct; control: *I'll take part, but I won't want to lead.* ○ *lead an army, an expedition, a strike* ○ *lead a discussion, the singing, the proceedings* ○ *Who is to lead the party into the next election?* **8** [Tn] (in card-games) play (sth) as one's first card: *lead trumps, the two of clubs, etc.* **9** [Ipr] ~ **with sth** (**a**) (*journalism*) have (sth) as the main news item: *We'll lead with the dock strike.* (**b**) (in boxing) use (a particular punch) to begin an attack: *lead with one's left/right.* **10** (idm) **all roads lead to Rome** ⇨ ROAD. **the blind leading the blind** ⇨ BLIND[1]. **lead sb by the ˈnose** make sb do everything one wishes; control sb completely. **lead sb a (merry) ˈdance** cause sb a lot of trouble, esp by making him follow from place to place. **lead a ˈdog's life** be constantly worried, troubled or miserable. **lead sb a ˈdog's life** make sb's life wretched. **lead sb to the ˈaltar** (*dated or joc*) marry sb. **lead sb to believe (that)...** cause sb to believe (sth that is false or uncertain). **lead sb up the garden ˈpath** deceive sb. **lead the ˈway (to sth)** go first; show the way: *Our scientists are leading the way in space research.* **11** (phr v) **lead (sth) off** start (sth): *Her recital led off/She led off her recital with a Haydn sonata.* **lead sb on** (*infml*) persuade sb to believe or do sth by making false promises or claims: *The salesman tried to lead me on with talk of amazing savings on heating bills.* **lead up to sth** prepare, introduce or go before sth: *the events leading up to the outbreak of war.*

□ **ˈlead-in** *n* **1** introduction to a subject, etc: *He told an amusing story as a lead-in to the serious part of his speech.* **2** wire connecting an aerial to a radio or television set.

leader /ˈli:də(r)/ *n* **1** person or thing that leads: *the leader of an expedition, a gang, etc* ○ *the leader of the Opposition*, eg in the British Parliament ○ *He is well up with the leaders* (ie the leading competitors) *at the half-way stage of the race.* ○ *the brand leader*, ie the brand of a product that has the highest sales. **2** (*music*) (*US* **ˈconcert-master**) principal first violinist of an orchestra. **3** (*law*) principal counsel in a court case. **4** = LEADING ARTICLE (LEADING). **5** blank strip at the beginning of a tape, film, etc used to help when threading into a machine. **6** (*botany*) long thin shoot growing from a stem or branch, esp of fruit trees, usu cut back in pruning.

▷ **leaderless** *adj*: *a leaderless rabble.*

leadership *n* **1** [U] being a leader: *the responsibilities of leadership* ○ [attrib] *a leadership crisis.* **2** [U] ability to be a leader: *qualities of leadership necessary in a team captain* ○ [attrib] *leadership potential.* **3** [CGp] group of leaders: *calling for firm action by the union leadership.*

□ **ˌLeader of the ˈHouse** (in Britain) member of the government in the House of Commons or Lords who arranges and announces the business of the House.

leading /ˈli:dɪŋ/ *adj* [attrib] **1** most important; chief: *one of the leading writers of her day* ○ *play a leading role in sth.* **2** in first positions: *the leading runners.*

□ **ˌleading ˈarticle** (also **leader**) (*Brit journalism*) principal newspaper article by the editor, giving opinions on events, policies, etc; editorial.

ˌleading ˈedge forward edge of an aircraft's wing.

ˌleading ˈlady, ˌleading ˈman actor taking the chief part in a play, etc.

ˌleading ˈlight (*infml approv*) prominent member of a group: *one of the leading lights of our club.*

ˌleading ˈquestion question that is worded so as to prompt the desired answer.

ˈleading-rein *n* (**a**) long rein used for leading a horse. (**b**) (also **ˈwalking rein**) strap attached to a lightweight harness worn by a young child who has just learnt to walk.

leaf /li:f/ *n* (*pl* **leaves** /li:vz/) **1** [C] one of the (usu green and flat) parts of a plant, growing from a stem or branch or directly from the root: *lettuce, cabbage, etc leaves* ○ *sweep up the dead leaves.* **2** [C] sheet of paper (esp forming two pages of a book): *carefully turn over the leaves of the precious volume* ○ *a loose leaf of paper lying on the desk.* **3** [U] metal, esp gold or silver, in the form of very thin sheets: *gold leaf.* **4** [C] hinged flap or detachable section used to extend a table-top. **5** (idm) **come into/be in ˈleaf** grow/be covered with leaves. **shake like a leaf** ⇨ SHAKE[1]. **take a leaf out of sb's ˈbook** copy sb; act or behave in a similar way to sb. **turn over a new leaf** ⇨ NEW.

▷ **leaf** *v* (phr v) **leaf through sth** turn over the pages of (a book, etc) quickly; glance through sth: *leaf idly through a magazine while waiting.*

leafage /ˈli:fɪdʒ/ *n* [U] leaves collectively; foliage.

leafless *adj* having no leaves.

leafy *adj* (**-ier, -iest**) (**a**) covered in or having many leaves: *a leafy forest, branch, bush.* (**b**) consisting of leaves: *leafy vegetables.* (**c**) made or caused by leaves: *a leafy shade.*

□ **ˈleaf-insect** type of insect with a flattened body that looks like a plant leaf.

ˈleaf-mould *n* [U] soil or compost consisting mostly of decayed leaves.

leaflet /ˈli:flɪt/ *n* **1** printed sheet of paper, usu folded and free of charge, containing information: *pick up a leaflet about care of the teeth.* **2** (*botany*) small leaf.

league[1] /li:g/ *n* **1** group of people or countries combined for a particular purpose: *the Arab League.* **2** group of sports clubs competing against each other for a championship: *the local darts league* ○ [attrib] *the league champions.* **3** (*infml*) class or category of excellence: *They're not in the same league.* ○ *I'm not in his league.* ○ *be out of one's league*, ie outclassed. **4** (idm) **in league (with sb)** conspiring together; allied: *He pretended not to know her but in fact they were in league (together).*

▷ **league** *v* (phr v) **league together** form a league; unite: *We must league together against this threat.*

□ **the ˌLeague of ˈNations** international organization formed after the First World War to promote cooperation and peace between the member countries. Despite a hopeful start, it proved helpless when faced with the rise of nationalism in Germany, Italy and Japan which led to the Second World War. It was dissolved in 1946. Cf THE UNITED NATIONS (UNITE).

ˈleague table list of teams, contestants, etc arranged according to performance, with the best at the top: *at the bottom of the league table* ○ (*fig*) *a league table of unit trusts*, ie showing which make the biggest profits.

league[2] /li:g/ *n* (*arch*) former measure of distance (about 3 miles or 4.8 km.) ⇨ App 10.

leak /li:k/ *n* **1** (**a**) hole, crack, etc through which liquid or gas may wrongly get in or out: *a leak in the roof*, ie allowing rain to enter ○ *a leak in the gas pipe*, ie allowing gas to escape ○ *a slow leak in a bicycle tyre.* (**b**) liquid or gas that passes through this: *smell a gas leak.* **2** similar escape of an electric charge, caused by faulty insulation, etc. **3** (*fig*) accidental or deliberate disclosure of secret or confidential information: *the latest in a series of damaging leaks.* **4** (⚠ *sl*) act of urination: *have/take/go for a leak.* **5** (idm) **spring a leak** ⇨ SPRING[3].

▷ **leak** *v* **1** (**a**) [I] (of a container) allow liquid or gas to get in or out wrongly: *This boat leaks like a sieve*, ie very badly. (**b**) [I, Ipr, Ip] (of liquid or gas) get in or out in this way: *The rain's leaking in* ○ *Air leaked out of the balloon.* ⇨ Usage at DRIP[1]. **2** [Tn, Tn·pr] ~ **sth (to sb)** reveal (information): *Who leaked this to the press?* **3** (phr v) **leak out** (of information) become known: *The details were supposed to be secret but somehow leaked out.*

leakage /ˈli:kɪdʒ/ *n* **1** [C, U] (instance of) leaking: *a leakage of toxic waste* ○ (*fig*) *The leakage of technological secrets is reaching alarming proportions.* **2** [C] thing that has leaked.

leaky *adj* having holes or cracks that leak: *a leaky ship, kettle, roof.*

Lean /li:n/ Sir David (1908-91), British film director. He had one of the longest and most successful careers in the British cinema, and was most famous for such spectacular epics as *Lawrence of Arabia* and *A Passage to India.*

lean[1] /li:n/ *adj* (**-er, -est**) **1** (of people and animals) without much flesh; thin and healthy: *a lean athletic body.* **2** (of meat) containing little or no fat: *lean beef.* **3** [esp attrib] (**a**) small in amount or quality; meagre: *a lean diet, harvest.* (**b**) (of a period of time) not productive: *lean years* ○ *a lean season for good films.*

▷ **lean** *n* [U] lean part of meat: *a lot of fat but not much lean.*

leanness /ˈli:nnɪs/ *n* [U].

lean[2] /li:n/ *v* (*pt, pp* **leant** /lent/ or **leaned** /li:nd/) ⇨ Usage at DREAM[2]. **1** [I, Ipr, Ip] be in a sloping position; bend: *lean out of the window, back in one's chair, over to one side, etc* ○ *Just lean forward for a moment, please.* **2** [Ipr] ~ **against/(up)on sth** rest on sth in a sloping position for support: *a ladder leaning against the wall* ○ *The old man leant upon his stick.* ○ *lean on sb's arm, one's elbows, etc.* **3** [Tn·pr] ~ **sth against/on sth** cause sth to rest against sth: *The workmen leant their shovels against the fence and went to lunch.* **4** (idm) **bend/lean over backwards** ⇨ BACKWARDS (BACKWARD). **5** (phr v) **lean on sb** (*infml esp US*) try to influence sb by threats: *If they don't pay soon we'll have to lean on them a little.* **lean (up)on sb/sth (for sth)** depend on sb/sth: *lean upon others for guidance* ○ *lean on his friends' advice.* **lean towards sth** have a tendency towards sth: *He leans towards more lighthearted subjects in his later works.*

▷ **leaning** *n* tendency; inclination: *have a leaning towards socialism/have socialist leanings.*

□ **ˈlean-to** *n* small building or shed with its roof resting against the side of a larger building, wall or fence: *They keep hens in a lean-to at the end of the garden.* ○ [attrib] *a lean-to greenhouse.*

Leander /lɪˈændə(r)/ ⇨ HERO AND LEANDER.

leap /li:p/ *v* (*pt, pp* **leapt** /lept/ or **leaped** /li:pt/) ⇨ Usage at DREAM[2]. **1** [I, Ipr, Ip] jump vigorously: *The cat leapt from the chair.* ○ (*fig*) *My heart leapt for joy at the news.* ○ *A frog leapt out.* **2** [I, Ipr, Ip] move quickly in the specified direction; rush: *leap to the telephone, into one's car, upstairs* ○ (*fig*) *They leapt to stardom with their first record.* **3** (**a**) [Tn] jump over (an obstacle): *leap a gate, puddle, ditch, etc.* (**b**) [Tn·pr] ~ **sth over sth** cause (a horse, etc) to jump over (an obstacle): *leap a horse over a fence.* ⇨ Usage at JUMP[2]. **4** (idm) **jump/leap to conˈclusions** ⇨ CONCLUSION. **ˌlook before you ˈleap** (*saying*) consider the possible consequences before taking action. **5** (phr v) **leap at sth** accept sth eagerly, without hesitation: *She leapt at the chance to go to America.* ○ *leap at an opportunity, offer, invitation, etc.*

▷ **leap** *n* **1** vigorous jump: *He crossed the garden in three leaps.* **2** (*fig*) rapid increase or change: *a leap in prices, oil production, the number of people out of work.* **3** (idm) **by/in ˌleaps and ˈbounds** very rapidly: *Her health is improving in leaps and bounds.* **a leap/shot in the dark** ⇨ DARK[1].

leaping *adj* [attrib] moving up and down quickly and irregularly: *leaping waves, flames, etc.*

leap-frog

□ **ˈleap-frog** *n* [U] game in which each player in turn leaps with parted legs over another who is bending down. — *v* (**-gg-**) **1** [Tn] leap over (sb/sth) in this way. **2** [I, Ipr, Tn] ~ (**over/past**) (**sb/sth**) advance ahead of (sb/sth) before being overtaken in turn oneself: *The two cars kept leap—frogging (past) each other on the motorway.* ○ (*fig*) *leap-frogging wage demands.*

ˈleap year one year in every four years, with an extra day (29 February): [attrib] *a ˌleap-year proˈposal*, ie made on 29 February, when women are traditionally allowed to ask men to marry them.

There was an Old Man with a beard,
Who said, "It is just as I feared!—
Two Owls and a Hen,
Four Larks and a Wren,
Have all built their nests in my beard!"

from Edward Lear's 'Book of Nonsense'

Lear /lɪə(r)/ Edward (1812-88), English poet and painter. Through his ability to draw and paint animals he worked for the Earl of Derby and wrote *A Book of Nonsense* for the Earl's grandchildren. This was the first of a series of nonsense verses, including limericks, written and illustrated by Lear, for which he is best remembered, though his reputation as a water-colour artist has risen steadily since his death. ⇨ illus.

learn /lɜːn/ *v* (*pt, pp* **learnt** /lɜːnt/ or **learned** /lɜːnd/) ⇨ Usage at DREAM². **1** [I, Ipr, Tn, Tn·pr, Tw, Tt] ~ **(sth) (from sb/sth)** gain knowledge or skill by study, experience or being taught: *I can't drive yet — I'm still learning.* ○ *learn from one's mistakes* ○ *learn a poem by heart*, ie memorize it ○ *She learns languages with ease.* ○ *learn (how) to swim, to walk, to fly, etc.* **2** [Ipr, Tn, Tf, Tw] ~ **(of/about) sth** become aware (of sth) through information or observation; realize: *I'm sorry to learn of/about your illness.* ○ *I never learned his name.* ○ *learn (that) it's no use blaming other people* ○ *learn what it means to be poor.* **3** (idm) **learn one's ˈlesson** learn what to do or not to do in future by noting the results of one's actions: *I'll never do that again; I've learned my lesson!* **show sb/know/learn the ropes** ⇨ ROPE. **you/we live and learn** ⇨ LIVE².
▷ **learned** /ˈlɜːnɪd/ *adj* **1** having much knowledge acquired by study: *learned men* ○ *He's very learned but rather absent-minded.* **2** of or for learned people: *learned journals, societies, language* ○ *the learned professions*, eg law, medicine ○ (*law*) *my learned friend*, ie legal colleague (a term of courtesy). **learnedly** *adv*: *speak learnedly and at length.*
learner *n* person who is gaining knowledge or skill: *I'm still only a learner, so don't expect perfection!* ○ *a quick/slow learner* ○ *That car's being driven by a learner*, ie a learner driver.
learning *n* [U] knowledge obtained by study: *a man of great learning.*
□ ˌ**learner ˈdriver** person who is learning to drive but has not yet passed the driving test.

lease /liːs/ *n* **1** contract by which the owner of land, a building, etc allows another person to use it for a specified time, usu in return for rent: *take out a lease on a holiday home* ○ *When does the lease expire?* ○ *The lease has four years left to run.* ○ (*esp Brit*) *have a flat on a 99-year lease.* ⇨ Usage at TENANT. **2** (idm) **a new lease of life** ⇨ NEW.
▷ **lease** *v* [Tn, Tn·pr, Dn·n] ~ **sth (to/from sb)** grant or obtain the use of (sth) in this way: *lease a car, building, field* ○ *The firm leases an office with views over the river.*
□ ˈ**leaseback** *n* [C, U] sale of a property, etc made so that the owner selling it may lease it back from the new owner.
ˈ**leasehold** ~ **(of/on sth)** *n* (*esp Brit*) holding of property by means of a lease: *have the leasehold on a house, etc.* — *adj, adv*: *a leasehold property* ○ *own a flat leasehold.* ˈ**leaseholder** *n*. Cf FREEHOLD (FREE¹).
ˈ**lease-lend** *n* [U] = LEND-LEASE (LEND).

leash /liːʃ/ *n* **1** = LEAD² 7. **2** (idm) **hold sth in ˈleash** restrain sth: *I managed to hold my anger in leash until she had gone.* **strain at the leash** ⇨ STRAIN¹.

least /liːst/ *indef det, indef pron* (used as the superlative of LITTLE²) smallest in size, amount, extent, etc. (**a**) (*det*): *He's the best teacher even though he has the least experience.* ○ *The least worry we have is about the weather.* ○ *If you had only the least thought for others you would not have spoken out in that way.* ⇨ Usage at MUCH. (**b**) (*pron*): *That's the least of my anxieties.* ○ *It's the least I can do to help.* ○ *She gave (the) least of all towards the wedding-present.*
▷ **least** *adv* **1** to the smallest extent: *just when we least expected it* ○ *He disliked many of his teachers and Miss Smith he liked (the) least.* ○ *She chose the least expensive of the hotels.* ○ *one of the least performed of Shakespeare's plays.* **2** (idm) **at least** (**a**) if nothing else is true; at any rate: *She may be slow but at least she's reliable.* (**b**) not less than: *at least 3 months, £3, 10 inches.* ˌ**least of ˈall** to an insignificant degree: *Nobody need worry, you least of all/least of all you.* ○ *Least of all would I lie to you.* ˌ**not in the ˈleast** absolutely not; not at all: *It doesn't matter in the least.* ○ *'Would you mind if I put the television on?' 'No, not in the least.'* **not least** especially; in particular: *The film caused a lot of bad feeling, not least among the workers whose lives it described.* **last but not least** ⇨ LAST².
□ ˈ**leastways**, ˈ**leastwise** *advs* (*dialect or infml*) or at least: *There's no pub round here, leastways not that I know of.*

leather /ˈleðə(r)/ *n* [U] **1** material made by tanning animal skins: *This sofa is covered in real leather.* ○ [attrib] *leather shoes, gloves, belts, etc.* **2** [C] = CHAMOIS-LEATHER (CHAMOIS). **3 leathers** [pl] leather jacket and trousers, esp as worn by motor-cyclists. **4** (idm) **hell for leather** ⇨ HELL.
▷ **leather** *v* [Tn] beat (sb), esp as a punishment; thrash.
leatherette /ˌleðəˈret/ *n* [U] imitation leather.
leathery /ˈleðərɪ/ *adj* as tough as leather: *leathery skin, meat.*
□ ˈ**leatherback** *n* largest of the turtles, with a flexible shell.
ˈ**leather-jacket** *n* grub of the crane-fly.
ˈ**leather-neck** *n* (*US sl*) member of the US Marine Corps.

leave¹ /liːv/ *v* (*pt, pp* **left** /left/) **1** [I, Ipr, Tn, Tn·pr] go away from (a person or a place): *It's time for us to leave/time we left.* ○ *The plane leaves Heathrow for Orly at 12.35.* **2** [I, Tn] cease to live at (a place), belong to (a group), work for (an employer), etc: *He left England in 1964 and never returned.* ○ *Many children leave school at 16.* ○ *My secretary has threatened to leave.* **3** [Cn·a, Cn·g] cause or allow (sb/sth) to remain in a certain condition, place, etc: *Leave the door open, please.* ○ *Don't leave her waiting outside in the rain.* **4** [Tn, Tn·pr] neglect or fail to take or bring (sth): *I've left my gloves on the bus.* **5** [Tn, Tn·pr] cause (sth) to remain as a result: *Red wine leaves a stain.* ○ *The accident left a scar on her leg.* **6** [Tn, Dn·n, Dn·pr] ~ **sth (for sb)** hand over (sth) and then go away: *Did the postman leave anything?* ○ *Someone left you this note/left this note for you.* **7** [Tn, Dn·n, Dn·pr] ~ **sth to sb** give sth as a legacy to sb: *How much did he leave?* ○ *She left you £500.* ○ *leave all one's money to charity.* **8** [Tn·pr] entrust (sth) to another person: *You can leave the cooking to me.* ○ *leave an assistant in charge of the shop/leave the shop in an assistant's charge.* **9** [Tn, Tn·pr] ~ **sth (till/until sth)** delay doing or having sth: *Let's leave the washing-up till the morning.* ○ *I like to leave the best bits till last.* **10** [Tn] (*mathematics*) have (a certain amount) remaining: *Seven from ten/Ten minus seven leaves three*, ie 10 − 7 = 3. ○ *There are six days left before we go.* **11** [Tn] have (sb) remaining alive: *He leaves a widow and two children.* **12** (idm) **be left at the ˈpost** be left far behind from the start (of a contest, etc). **keep/leave one's options open** ⇨ OPTION. **leave/let sb/sth aˈlone/ˈbe** not disturb or interfere with sb/sth: *Leave me be! Go away!* ○ *I've told you to leave my things alone.* **leave a bad/nasty ˈtaste in the mouth** (of experiences) be followed by feelings of disgust, anger or shame. **leave sb ˈcold** fail to move, interest or impress sb: *Her emotional appeal left him completely cold.* ○ *Jellied eels leave me cold!* **leave the ˈdoor open** allow for the possibility of further discussion, negotiation, etc: *Although talks have broken down the door has been left open.* **leave ˈgo/ˈhold (of sth)** release (sth): *Leave go of my arm — you're hurting!* Cf LET SB/STH GO (LET¹). **leave sb holding the ˈbaby** (*infml*) give sb unwanted responsibilities. **leave sb in the ˈlurch** (*infml*) abandon sb in an awkward situation. **leave/make one's, its, etc, mark** ⇨ MARK¹. **leave it at ˈthat** (*infml*) say or do nothing more: *We'll never agree, so let's just leave it at that.* **leave a lot, much, something, nothing, etc to be deˈsired** be very, etc (un)satisfactory: *Your conduct leaves a lot to be desired*, ie is extremely unsatisfactory. **leave the ˈroom** (*euph*) go to the lavatory to relieve oneself. **leave no stone unˈturned (to do sth)** try every possible means: *They left no stone unturned in their search for the child's mother.* **leave sth out of acˈcount/considerˈration** fail to allow for sth; treat sth as unimportant. **leave sb/be/go out on a limb** ⇨ LIMB. **leave sb to his own deˈvices/to himˈself** allow or force sb to deal with problems unaided; not try to control sb: *He leaves his staff to their own devices — as long as the work gets done he's happy.* **leave sb/sth to the tender mercy/mercies of sb/sth** (*ironic*) expose sb/sth to cruel or rough treatment by sb/sth: *Never leave a silk shirt to the tender mercies of an automatic washing-machine.* **leave/let well alone** ⇨ WELL³. **leave word (with sb)** give a message (to sb): *Please leave word with my secretary if you can't come.* **13** (phr v) **leave sth aside** not consider sth; disregard: *Leaving the expense aside, do we actually need a second car?* **leave sb/sth behind** (**a**) fail or forget to bring or take sb/sth: *Wait — don't leave me behind!* ○ *It won't rain: you can leave your umbrella behind.* (**b**) (*fml*) cause (signs of one's actions, an event, etc) to remain: *a ruler who left behind a legacy of bitterness* ○ *The storm left a trail of destruction behind.* **leave sb/sth for sb/sth** abandon sb/sth in favour of sb/sth else: *He left his wife for one of his students.* ○ *leave advertising for a job in publishing.* **leave ˈoff** stop: *Hasn't the rain left off yet?* **leave off sth/doing sth** (*infml*) stop sth/doing sth: *It's time to leave off work.* ○ *I wish you'd leave off whistling like that.* **leave sth off** no longer wear sth: *Pullovers can be left off in this warm weather.* **leave sb/sth out (of sth)** not include or mention; exclude; omit: *Leave me out of this quarrel, please — I don't want to get involved.* ○ *This word is wrongly spelt; you've left out a letter.* **leave sth over** postpone sth: *These matters will have to be left over until the next meeting.*

leave² /liːv/ *n* **1** [U] time absent from duty or work: *sick, shore, annual leave* ○ *a fortnight's leave.* **2** [U] ~ **to do sth** (*fml*) (**a**) official permission to be absent from duty or work: *be given leave to visit one's mother.* (**b**) permission: *She has my leave to see him.* ⇨ Usage at HOLIDAY. **3** (idm) **beg leave to do sth** ⇨ BEG. ˌ**by/ˌwith your ˈleave** (*fml*) with your permission. **take French leave** ⇨ FRENCH. ˌ**leave of ˈabsence** permission to be absent (esp from an official or a military post): *ask for leave of absence to attend a wedding.* **on ˈleave** absent with permission: *He's just gone on leave.* **take (one's) leave (of sb)** (*fml*) say goodbye. **take ˌleave of one's ˈsenses** (*rhet or joc*) go mad: *Have you all taken leave of your senses?* **without as/so much as a ˌby your ˈleave** (*infml*) without asking permission; rudely.
□ ˈ**leave-taking** *n* (*fml*) act of saying goodbye: *a tearful leave-taking.*

-leaved (forming compound *adjs*) having leaves of the specified type or number: *a broad-leaved plant* ○ *a three-leaved clover.*

leaven /ˈlevn/ *n* [U] **1** substance (eg yeast) used to make dough rise before it is baked to make bread. **2** (*fig*) quality or influence that makes people, an atmosphere, etc less serious, more lively, etc: *a lively artistic community, acting as the leaven in society.*

▷ **leaven** *v* [Tn] **1** add leaven to (sth): *leavened bread.* **2** (*fig*) enliven (sth).

leaves *pl* of LEAF.

leavings /ˈliːvɪŋz/ *n* [pl] what is left, esp sth unwanted or of little value; left-overs: *Give our leavings* (ie unwanted food) *to the dog.*

Lebanon /ˈlebənən; *US* ˈlebənɒn/ country at the eastern end of the Mediterranean Sea; pop approx 2 828 000; official language Arabic; capital Beirut; unit of currency pound (= 100 piastres). Until the mid-1970s it was the commercial and cultural centre of the Middle East, with an important tourist industry. Since then the country has been devastated by armed conflict between different religious groups, complicated by the involvement of neighbouring powers. ⇨ map at SYRIA. ▷ **Lebanese** /ˌlebəˈniːz/ *n, adj.*

Le Carré /lə ˈkæreɪ/ John, pen-name of David Cornwell (1931-), English novelist. His works, like *The Spy Who Came in from the Cold*, give a vivid picture of the complex world of spies and double agents.

Le Chatelier's principle /lə ʃæˈtelɪeɪz prɪnsəpl/ (*chemistry*) principle stating that if a system is in equilibrium, any change made to it will modify the equilibrium so that the effect of the change is counteracted.

lechery /ˈletʃərɪ/ *n* [C, U] (instance of) excessive interest in sexual pleasure.

▷ **lecher** /ˈletʃə(r)/ *n* (*derog*) man who is always thinking about and looking for sexual pleasure.

lecherous /ˈletʃərəs/ *adj* having or showing an excessive interest in and desire for sexual pleasure. **lecherously** *adv.*

lecithin /ˈlesɪθɪn/ *n* [U] complex fatty substance containing phosphorus, often used in commercial emulsifiers.

Leclanché cell /ləˈklɑːnʃeɪ sel/ (*chemistry*) primary cell consisting of a carbon rod and a zinc rod, whose ends are placed in a solution of ammonium chloride, with the carbon rod in contact with a mixture of manganese dioxide and crushed carbon.

Le Corbusier /lə kɔːˈbuːzɪeɪ/ (1887-1965), French architect (real name Charles-Edouard Jeanneret). He was a leading member of the functionalist movement, famous for his use of concrete and buildings supported on pillars. His designs have had an important influence on modern architecture.

lectern /ˈlektən/ *n* high sloping desk made to hold a lecturer's notes, a Bible in church, etc. ⇨ illus at CHURCH.

lectionary /ˈlekʃənrɪ; *US* -nerɪ/ *n* book that lists or contains the readings from the Bible to be read at church services during the year.

lecture /ˈlektʃə(r)/ *n* **1** ~ **(to sb) (on sth)** talk giving information about a subject to an audience or a class, often as part of a teaching programme: *give/deliver/read a lecture* ○ *a course of lectures on Greek philosophy* ○ [attrib] *a lecture tour.* **2** long reproach or scolding: *The policeman let me off with a lecture about speeding.* ○ *give sb a lecture*, ie scold sb.

▷ **lecture** *v* **1** [I, Ipr] ~ **(on sth)** give a lecture or series of lectures: *Professor Jones is not lecturing this term.* ○ *He is lecturing on Russian literature.* **2** [Tn, Tn·pr] ~ **sb (for/about sth)** scold or warn sb (about sth): *Do stop lecturing me!* ○ *lecture one's children for being untidy/about the virtues of tidiness.* **lecturer** /ˈlektʃərə(r)/ *n* person who gives lectures, esp at a college or university.

lectureship *n* post of lecturer (the lowest teaching grade at a British college or university).

LED /ˌel iː ˈdiː/ *abbr* (*electronics*) light-emitting diode.

led *pt, pp* of LEAD[3].

ledge /ledʒ/ *n* **1** narrow horizontal shelf coming out from a wall, cliff, etc: *a window-ledge* ○ *The climbers rested on a sheltered ledge jutting out from the cliff.* ○ *a ledge for chalk beneath the blackboard.* **2** ridge of rocks under water, esp near the shore.

ledger /ˈledʒə(r)/ *n* **1** book in which a bank, business firm, etc records its financial accounts. **2** (*music*) = LEGER.

Lee /liː/ Robert E(dward) (1807-70), American general who commanded the Confederate forces in the American Civil War and was considered its greatest military leader. After early victories he was defeated at *Gettysburg, but continued his resistance at Richmond.

lee /liː/ *n* [sing] **1** part or side of sth providing shelter against the wind: *shelter in/under the lee of a hedge.* **2** [attrib] (*nautical*) of or on the part or side away from the wind: *the lee side of the ship.* Cf WINDWARD (WIND[1]).

□ ˈ**lee shore** (*nautical*) shore towards which the wind is blowing from the sea.

leech /liːtʃ/ *n* **1** small blood-sucking worm usu living in water and formerly used by doctors to remove blood from sick people. **2** (*fig derog*) person who hangs about other people hoping to obtain money, food, alcohol, etc. **3** (*arch or joc*) doctor. **4** (idm) **cling/stick to sb like a ˈleech** stay very close to sb; be difficult for sb to get rid of.

leek /liːk/ *n* vegetable related to the onion but with wider green leaves above a long white bulb. It is the national emblem of Wales. ⇨ illus at ONION. ⇨ article at NATIONAL.

leer /lɪə(r)/ *n* (usu *sing*) sly unpleasant look suggesting lust or ill will: *He has a most unpleasant leer.*

▷ **leer** *v* [I, Ipr, Ip] ~ **(at sb)** look with a leer: *Go away; I don't enjoy being leered at.*

leery /ˈlɪərɪ/ *adj* [pred] ~ **(of sb/sth)** (*infml*) wary; suspicious: *I tend to be a bit leery of cut-price 'bargains'.*

lees /liːz/ *n* [pl] sediment at the bottom of a bottle of wine, etc; dregs: *Don't shake the bottle or you will disturb the lees.*

leeward /ˈliːwəd *or, in nautical use,* ˈluːəd/ *adj, adv* on or to the side sheltered from the wind: *sandhills on the leeward side of the island.* Cf WINDWARD (WIND[1]).

▷ **leeward** *n* [U] (*nautical*) side or direction towards which the wind blows: *steer to leeward.* Cf WINDWARD *n* (WIND[1]).

Leeward Islands /ˈliːwəd aɪləndz/ **the Leeward Islands** group of islands in the West Indies, including the Virgin Islands, Guadeloupe, Antigua, Saint Kitts-Nevis and Montserrat. ⇨ map at WEST INDIES.

leeway /ˈliːweɪ/ *n* [U] **1** amount of freedom to move, change, etc that is left to sb: *This itinerary leaves us plenty of leeway.* ○ *The parking space was big enough, but there wasn't much leeway*, ie margin for error. **2** sideways drift of a ship or aircraft, due to the wind. **3** (idm) **make up ˈleeway** recover lost time; get back into position: *She's been off school for a month, so she has a lot of leeway to make up.*

left[1] *pt, pp* of LEAVE[1].

□ **left-ˈluggage office** (*Brit*) (*US* ˈ**baggage room**) place (at railway stations, etc) where luggage may be temporarily deposited.

ˈ**left-overs** *n* [pl] things remaining when the rest is finished, esp food at the end of a meal; leavings. ⇨ Usage at REST[3].

left[2] /left/ *adj, adv* **1** of, on or towards the side of the body which is towards the west when a person faces north: *Fewer people write with their left hand than with their right.* ○ *Turn left here.* ○ [attrib] (*sport*) *left half, back, wing(er), etc.* Cf RIGHT[5]. **2** (idm) **about/left/right face** ⇨ FACE[2]. **eyes right/left/front** ⇨ EYE[1]. **have two left ˈfeet** (*infml*) be very clumsy. ˌ**left, right and ˈcentre** (*infml*) everywhere: *I've been looking for it left, right and centre — where did you find it?* **right and left** ⇨ RIGHT[5].

▷ **left** *n* **1** [U] left side or region: *In Britain cars are driven on the left.* ○ *She was sitting immediately to my left.* **2** [C] (in boxing and fist-fighting) (blow given with the) left hand: *He knocked down his opponent with a powerful left.* **3 the Left** [Gp] (*politics*) **(a)** the left wing of a party or other group. **(b)** supporters of socialism in general: *a history of the Left in Europe/of the European Left.*

leftist *n, adj* (*politics*) (supporter) of socialism.

lefty (also **leftie**) *n* (*infml*) **1** (*derog*) leftist. **2** (*esp US*) left-handed person.

□ ˌ**left ˈbank 1** bank of a river on the left side of a person facing downstream. **2 the ˌLeft ˈBank** part of Paris south of the Seine, esp in or near the *Latin Quarter.

ˈ**left-hand** *adj* [attrib] of or on the left: *the left-hand side of the street* ○ *a left-hand drive car*, ie one with the steering wheel and other controls on the left-hand side. ˌ**left-ˈhanded** *adj* **1** (of a person) using the left hand more easily or usually than the right. **2** (of a blow) delivered with the left hand. **3** (of a tool) designed for use with the left hand: ˌ*left-handed* ˈ*scissors.* **4** (of a screw) to be tightened by turning towards the left. **5** (idm) **a ˌleft-handed ˈcompliment** compliment that is ambiguous in meaning and possibly ironic. — *adv* with the left hand: *Do you always write left-handed?* ˌ**left-ˈhandedness** *n* [U]. ˌ**left-ˈhander** left-handed person or blow.

ˌ**left ˈwing 1** (*politics*) supporters of a more extreme form of socialism than others in their party, group, etc: *the left wing of the Labour Party.* **2 (a)** (in football, hockey, etc) left side of a team on the playing field. **(b)** player in this position. ˌ**left-ˈwing** *adj*: ˌ*left-wing iˈdeas, intelˈlectuals,* ˈ*policies.* ˌ**left-ˈwinger** *n* **1** supporter of the left wing. **2** player on the left wing.

leg /leg/ *n* **1** [C] one of the limbs of an animal's or person's body used for standing and walking: *have long, short, straight, crooked, skinny, sturdy, bandy, shapely, etc legs* ○ *the powerful back legs of a frog* ○ *the long thin legs of a spider* ○ *a gammy* (ie lame) *leg.* ⇨ illus at HUMAN. **2** [C, U] this part of an animal used as food: *a leg of lamb* ○ *Would you like some leg or some breast* (eg of turkey) *?* **3** [C] part of a garment covering this limb: *The leg of my tights has torn.* ○ *a trouser leg.* **4** [C] one of the supports of a chair, table, etc: *a chair with one leg missing.* **5** [C] either branch of a pair of compasses, dividers, etc. **6** [C] **(a)** section of a journey: *The last leg of our trip was the most tiring.* **(b)** (*sport*) one of a series of matches between the same opponents. **7** [U] (in cricket) part of the field to the left of the wicket-keeper and behind the batsman: *long, short, square leg*, ie fieldsmen at various positions there ○ [attrib] *a leg break*, ie a ball bowled so as to move away from this side ○ *a leg glance*, ie a stroke by batsman that sends the ball there ○ *the leg stump*, ie the stump nearest this. **8** (idm) **as fast as one's legs can carry one** ⇨ FAST[1] *adv.* **be all ˈlegs** (*derog*) have legs that are disproportionately long and thin. **be on one's/its last legs** ⇨ LAST[1]. **be on one's ˈlegs** (*joc*) **(a)** be standing, esp to make a speech. **(b)** (*infml*) (after an illness) be well enough to walk about. Cf ON ONE'S HIND LEGS (HIND[1]). **give sb a ˈleg up** (*infml*) **(a)** help sb to mount a horse, climb a wall, etc. **(b)** (*fig*) use money or influence to help sb. **have hollow legs** ⇨ HOLLOW. **have, etc one's tail between one's legs** ⇨ TAIL. ˌ**leg before ˈwicket** (*abbr* **lbw**) (in cricket) way in which a batsman may be out because of illegally obstructing, with a leg or some other part of the body, a ball that would otherwise have hit the wicket. **not have a ˌleg to ˈstand on** (*infml*) have nothing to support one's opinion, justify one's actions, etc. **not have the ˈlegs** (*infml*) (esp of a ball in sport) stop before reaching the place the player was aiming for: *I thought my shot had reached the green* (ie in golf) *but it didn't quite have the legs.* **pull sb's leg** ⇨ PULL[2]. **shake a leg** ⇨ SHAKE[1]. **show a leg** ⇨ SHOW[2]. **stretch one's legs** ⇨ STRETCH. **talk the hind legs off a donkey** ⇨ TALK[2]. **walk one's legs off** ⇨ WALK[1]. **walk sb off his feet/legs** ⇨ WALK[1].

▷ **leg** *v* (-gg-) (idm) ˈ**leg it** (*infml*) go on foot: *It's no use, the car won't start — we'll have to leg it.*

□ ˌ**leg-of-mutton ˈsleeve** sleeve that is wide around the arm but fits closely around the wrist.

ˈ**leg-pull** *n* (*infml*) hoax. ˈ**leg-pulling** *n* [U].

ˈ**leg-rest** *n* support for a seated person's leg.

ˈ**leg-room** *n* [U] space available for a seated person's legs: *There's not much leg-room in these* *aircraft.*

ˈ**leg-warmers** *n* [pl] outer coverings, usu woollen, for each leg from knee to ankle.

ˈ**leg work** (*infml*) work involving much walking or travelling about to collect information, deliver messages, etc: *Being a detective involves a lot of leg work.*

legacy /ˈlegəsɪ/ *n* **1** money or property left to sb in a will. **2** (*fig*) thing passed to sb by predecessors or from earlier events, etc: *the cultural legacy of the Renaissance* ○ *His weak chest was a legacy of a childhood illness.* Cf INHERITANCE (INHERIT).

legal /ˈli:gl/ *adj* **1** [attrib] of or based on the law: *my legal adviser/representative*, eg a solicitor ○ *seek legal advice*, ie consult a solicitor ○ *take legal action*, ie sue or prosecute ○ *the legal age for drinking, driving, voting, etc*, ie the minimum age for doing these things legally. **2** allowed or required by the law: *Should euthanasia be made legal?* ○ (*joc*) *Why shouldn't I take a holiday? It's perfectly legal.*

▷ **legalism** /ˈli:gəlɪzəm/ *n* [U] (*usu derog*) strict adherence to or excessive respect for the law. **legalistic** *adj.*

legally /ˈli:gəlɪ/ *adv*: *be legally responsible for sth* ○ *a legally witnessed will.*

□ ˌ**legal** ˈ**aid** payment from public funds for or towards the cost of legal advice or representation. ⇨ article at LAW.

ˌ**legal** ˈ**holiday** (*US*) public holiday.

ˌ**legal pro**ˈ**ceedings** lawsuit: *take, begin, threaten, etc legal proceedings (against sb).*

ˌ**legal** ˈ**tender** form of money that must be accepted if offered in payment: *The old pound note is no longer legal tender.*

legality /li:ˈgælətɪ/ *n* [U] state of being legal: *the legality of this action will be decided by the courts.*

legalize, -ise /ˈli:gəlaɪz/ *v* [Tn] make (sth) legal: *Some people want to legalize the possession of cannabis.*

legate /ˈlegɪt/ *n* ambassador of the Pope to a foreign country.

legatee /ˌlegəˈti:/ *n* (*law*) person who receives a legacy.

legation /lɪˈgeɪʃn/ *n* **1** [CGp] minister below the rank of ambassador, and his staff, representing his government in a foreign country. **2** [C] this minister's official residence.

legato /ləˈgɑ:təʊ/ *adj, adv* (*music*) (to be played) in a smooth even manner.

legend /ˈledʒənd/ *n* **1** [C] story handed down from the past, esp one that may not be true: *the legend of Robin Hood.* **2** [U] such stories gathered together: *exploits famous in legend and song* ○ *the heroes of Greek legend.* **3** [C] (*infml*) famous event or person: *Her daring work behind the enemy lines is now legend.* ○ *one of the great legends of pop music, Elvis Presley.* **4** [C] **(a)** inscription on a coin or medal. **(b)** (*fml*) words accompanying and explaining a map, picture, etc. **5** [C] (*infml*) person who achieves great fame while still alive: *a legend in one's (own)* ˈ*lifetime.* **6** (idm) **a** ˌ**living** ˈ**legend** ⇨ LIVING[1].

▷ **legendary** /ˈledʒəndrɪ; *US* -derɪ/ *adj* **1** of or mentioned in legend: *legendary heroes.* **2** (*infml*) very well known; famous: *a legendary recording* ○ *Her patience and tact were legendary.*

leger /ˈledʒə(r)/ *n* (also ˈ**leger line, ledger, ledger line**) (*music*) short line added above or below the the staff to take notes which are outside its range. ⇨ illus at MUSIC.

legerdemain /ˌledʒədəˈmeɪn/ *n* [U] (*fml*) **1** skilful performance of tricks using the hands; juggling; conjuring. **2** cunning or deceitful way of arguing.

-legged (forming compound *adjs*) having legs of the specified number or type: *a* ˌ*three-legged* ˈ*stool* ○ ˌ*bare-*ˈ*legged* ○ ˌ*long-*ˈ*legged* ○ ˌ*cross-*ˈ*legged.*

leggings /ˈlegɪŋz/ *n* [pl] protective outer coverings for the legs: *a pair of leggings.*

leggy /ˈlegɪ/ *adj* **1** having noticeably long legs: *a tall leggy girl in a short dress* ○ *a leggy newborn foal.* **2** (of a plant) having a long thin stem.

leghorn /ˈleghɔ:n/ *n* **1** type of fine plaited straw: [attrib] *a leghorn hat.* **2 Leghorn** small but strong type of hen that lays white eggs.

legible /ˈledʒəbl/ *adj* (of print or handwriting) clear enough to be read easily: *The inscription was still legible.* Cf READABLE (READ). ▷ **legibility** /ˌledʒəˈbɪlətɪ/ *n* [U]. **legibly** /-əblɪ/ *adv*: *Please write more legibly.*

legion /ˈli:dʒən/ *n* **1** **(a)** battle unit of the ancient Roman army: *Caesar's legions.* **(b)** special military unit, esp of volunteers serving in the army of another country: *the French Foreign Legion.* **2** large number of people: *This new film will please his legions of admirers.*

▷ **legion** *adj* [pred] (*rhet*) very many; numerous: *Their crimes are legion.*

legionary /ˈli:dʒənərɪ; *US* -nerɪ/ *n, adj* (member) of a legion(1).

legionnaire /ˌli:dʒəˈneə(r)/ *n* member of a legion, esp of the French Foreign Legion.

□ ˌ**legion**ˈ**naires' disease** (*medical*) form of bacterial pneumonia.

legislate /ˈledʒɪsleɪt/ *v* [I, Ipr] ~ (**for/against sth**) make laws: *It is the job of Parliament to legislate.* ○ *It's impossible to legislate for every contingency.* ○ *legislate against racial discrimination.*

▷ **legislation** /ˌledʒɪsˈleɪʃn/ *n* [U] **(a)** action of making laws: *Legislation will be difficult and take time.* **(b)** the laws made: *New legislation is to be introduced to help single-parent families.*

legislative /ˈledʒɪslətɪv; *US* -leɪtɪv/ *adj* [esp attrib] law-making: *a legislative assembly, chamber, body, etc* ○ *Legislative reform is long overdue.*

legislator /ˈledʒɪsleɪtə(r)/ *n* (*fml*) member of a legislature.

legislature /ˈledʒɪsleɪtʃə(r)/ *n* [CGp] (*fml*) body of people with the power to make and change laws. ⇨ article at LAW.

legit /lɪˈdʒɪt/ *adj* (*sl*) legitimate(1): *all legit and above-board* ○ *a legit excuse.*

legitimate /lɪˈdʒɪtɪmət/ *adj* **1** in accordance with the law or rules; lawful: *the legitimate heir* ○ *I'm not sure that his business is strictly legitimate*, ie is legal. **2** that can be defended; reasonable: *a legitimate argument, reason, case, etc* ○ *Politicians are legitimate targets for satire.* **3** (of a child) born to parents who are legally married to each other. Cf ILLEGITIMATE. **4** genuine: *legitimate theatre*, ie serious drama, not musicals, revues, etc.

▷ **legitimacy** /lɪˈdʒɪtɪməsɪ/ *n* [U] (*fml*): *question the legitimacy of his actions.*

legitimately *adv.*

legitimize, -ise /lɪˈdʒɪtɪmaɪz/ *v* (*fml*) [Tn] make (sth) lawful or regular: *a court ruling that legitimized the position taken by the protestors.*

legless /ˈleglɪs/ *adj* **1** without legs. **2** [pred] (*sl*) very drunk.

Lego /ˈlegəʊ/ *n* [U] (*propr*) small coloured plastic blocks, etc that children play with, fitting them together to make models or toys: [attrib] *a Lego house.*

legume /ˈlegju:m, lɪˈgju:m/ *n* **1** type of plant that has its seeds in pods, eg the pea and bean. **2** edible pod or seed of this.

▷ **leguminous** /lɪˈgju:mɪnəs/ *adj* of this family of plants.

lei /ˈleɪi:/ *n* (esp in Polynesian countries) garland of flowers worn around the neck.

Leibniz /ˈlaɪbnɪts/ Gottfried Wilhelm (1646-1716), German rationalist philosopher. He worked on the laws of motion and discovered the principles of calculus at about the same time as *Newton. His philosophical ideas on the essential goodness of the world were satirized by *Voltaire in *Candide.*

Leicestershire /ˈlestəʃə(r)/ (*abbr* **Leics**) county in the *Midlands of England. ⇨ map at App 1.

Leigh /li:/ Vivien (1913-67), British actress. After her success in the London theatre, she went to Hollywood with her husband Laurence *Olivier, where she became a star in films like *Gone with the Wind* and *A Streetcar Named Desire.*

Leighton /ˈleɪtn/ Frederic, Lord (1830-96), English painter and sculptor. He was very popular in Victorian times for his large-scale works on mythological subjects.

leisure /ˈleʒə(r); *US* ˈli:ʒər/ *n* [U] **1** time free from work or other duties; spare time: *We've been working all week without a moment's leisure.* ○ [attrib] *leisure activities*, eg sport, hobbies ○ *leisure wear*, ie casual clothing. ⇨ article. **2** (idm) **at leisure (a)** (*fml*) not occupied: *They're seldom at leisure.* **(b)** without hurrying: *I'll take the report home and read it at leisure.* **at one's** ˈ**leisure** when one has free time. **marry in haste, repent at leisure** ⇨ MARRY.

▷ **leisured** /ˈleʒəd/ *adj* [attrib] having plenty of leisure: *the leisured classes.*

leisurely *adj, adv* without hurry: *walk at a leisurely pace* ○ *work leisurely.*

□ ˈ**leisure centre** public building with facilities for sports and recreational activities.

leitmotiv (also **leitmotif**) /ˈlaɪtməʊti:f/ *n* **1** (*music*) short repeated theme in an opera, symphony, etc associated with a particular person, thing or idea. The technique was developed by *Wagner in his *Ring* cycle. **2** (*fig*) any recurring feature: *The leitmotiv of her speech was the need to reduce expenditure.*

Lely /ˈli:lɪ/ Sir Peter (1618-80), painter born in Germany of Dutch parents. He became court painter to Charles II and produced many portraits of the English aristocracy.

lemming /ˈlemɪŋ/ *n* small mouse-like rodent of the arctic regions which migrates in large numbers, often with many of the animals drowning in the sea: *a lemming-like readiness to follow their leaders into certain disaster.*

lemon /ˈlemən/ *n* **1** **(a)** [C, U] oval yellow fruit with acidic juice used for drinks and flavouring. ⇨ illus at FRUIT. **(b)** [C] (also ˈ**lemon tree**) tree with glossy green leaves on which this fruit grows. **2** (also ˌ**lemon** ˈ**yellow**) [U] pale yellow colour. **3** [C] (*sl*) unsatisfactory or defective thing, esp a car.

□ ˌ**lemon** ˈ**curd** (also ˌ**lemon** ˈ**cheese**) thick smooth jam made from lemons, sugar, eggs and butter.

ˌ**lemon** ˈ**sole** type of edible flatfish.

ˌ**lemon** ˈ**squash** (*Brit*) sweet lemon-flavoured drink that is diluted with water.

ˈ**lemon-squeezer** *n* device for pressing the juice out of a lemon.

lemonade /ˌleməˈneɪd/ *n* [U, C] **(a)** sweet fizzy drink. **(b)** drink made from lemon juice, sugar and water.

lemur /ˈli:mə(r)/ *n* monkey-like animal of Madagascar that lives in trees and is active at night.

lend /lend/ *v* (*pt, pp* **lent** /lent/) **1** [Tn, Dn·n, Dn·pr] ~ **sth (to sb) (a)** give or allow the use of sth temporarily, on the understanding that it will be returned: *Can you lend me £5? I'll pay you back tomorrow.* ○ *I lent that record to John but never got it back.* **(b)** provide (money) for a period of time in return for payment of interest: *The banks are lending money at a competitive rate of interest.* Cf BORROW. **2** [Tn, Dn·n, Dn·pr] ~ **sth (to sth)** contribute or add sth to sth: *lend one's services* ○ *lend the occasion a little glamour* ○ *His presence lent dignity to the occasion.* ○ *A little garlic lends flavour to a sauce.* **3** [Tn·pr] ~ **sth to sth** (*fml*) make an event, development, report, etc more believable, significant, etc (used esp with the *ns* shown): *lend credibility, credence, plausibility, etc to a report* ○ *This news lends some support to earlier reports of a ceasefire.* **4** (idm) **give/lend colour to sth** ⇨ COLOUR[1]. **lend an** ˈ**ear (to sb/sth)** listen patiently and sympathetically (to sb/sth). **lend (sb) a (helping) hand (with sth)** give (sb) help (with sth). **lend oneself/one's name to sth** (*fml*) allow oneself to be associated with sb: *a man who would never lend himself to violence* ○ *She lent her name to many worthy causes.* **5** (phr v) **lend itself to sth** be suitable for sth: *a novel which lends itself well to dramatization for television.*

▷ **lender** *n* person who lends. Cf BORROWER (BORROW).

□ ˈ**lend-lease** (also **lease-lend**) *n* [U] arrangement made during the Second World War, by which the USA supplied military equipment to its allies in return for the use of some of their naval bases.

length /leŋθ/ *n* **1** [U] measurement or extent from end to end: *a river 300 miles in length* ○ *This room*

Leisure

With a gradual decrease in working hours, and longer holidays than formerly, the British have a fair amount of leisure time, and a wide choice of ways to spend it. People use their free time to relax, but many people also do voluntary work, especially for charities or political parties, or further their education by attending evening classes or working for a degree at the Open University.

A lot of free time is spent in the home, where the most popular leisure activity is watching television, the average viewing time being 25 hours a week. Many families have a second television set so that different programmes can be watched or so that children can watch separately from their parents. People often record programmes on video so that they can watch them later, and video recorders are also widely used for watching videos hired from a video rental shop.

Reading is also a favourite way of spending leisure time and many people borrow books regularly from their local library to read at home. The British also spend a lot of time reading newspapers and magazines; they buy more of them per head than any other nation in the world. Most daily and weekly newspapers include at least one daily crossword puzzle, to satisfy a widespread demand among their readers for this form of pastime.

In the summer gardening is popular, and in winter it is often replaced by 'do-it-yourself', when people spend time improving or repairing their homes. Many people have pets to look after; taking the dog for a daily walk is a regular routine.

Some leisure activities are mostly or entirely social. Inviting friends for a drink or a meal at home is the most usual one. Keep-fit classes are often an opportunity to meet friends. For many people a regular evening out is something to look forward to, whether it is joining friends for a drink in a pub, or dining out at a restaurant. A visit to a pub often includes a game, for example bar billiards or darts. The most popular time for drinking or dining out is Friday or Saturday evening, when the working week is over.

The extra leisure time available at weekends means that some leisure activities, many of them to do with sport, normally take place only then. Traditional spectator sports include football, cricket, horse racing, motor racing (including stock-car racing) and motor cycle racing. Popular forms of exercise are swimming, tennis, ice-skating or roller-skating, cycling, climbing, and hill or country walking.

Families often have a 'day out' at the weekend, especially in summer, with a visit to a local event such as a fête, festival, fair or show. A country show is an agricultural event centred on the judging of cattle, sheep, etc, but also with a wide range of other attractions to give 'fun for all the family'. These may include displays of show-jumping, go-kart racing, country dancing, tug-of-war contests, children's fancy dress competitions, parachute jumping, a brass band or other musical groups, and demonstrations of crafts as well as stalls with goods for sale.

Family visits to country-houses, gardens, leisure parks, wildlife reserves or the seaside are also popular. Older people often go on day trips by coach, sightseeing or shopping. Young people especially go to clubs and discos, while people of all ages go to the theatre, the cinema, art exhibitions and concerts.

is twice the length of the other, but much narrower. ○ *a book the length of* (ie as long as) *'War and Peace'* ○ *He jogged the length of the beach.* ⇨ App 10, 12. ⇨ illus at DIMENSION. **2** [U] amount of time occupied by sth: *You spend a ridiculous length of time in the bath.* ○ *Size of pension depends on length of service with the company.* ○ *a speech, symphony, ceremony, etc of considerable length.* **3** [C] extent of a thing used as a unit of measurement: *This car will turn in its own length.* ○ *The horse/boat won the race by two lengths,* ie by a distance equal to twice its own length. **4** (a) [sing] (in cricket) distance between the batsman and the point where a bowled ball bounces on the ground: *bowl a good length.* (b) ideal such distance (for a bowler): *bowling on a length.* **5** [C] piece (of sth): *timber sold in lengths of 5, 10 or 20 metres* ○ *I need a length of wire or string to tie it with.* ○ *a ˈdress length,* ie a piece of cloth long enough to make a dress. **6** (idm) **at arm's length** ⇨ ARM[1]. **at length** (a) *(fml)* after a long time; eventually; at last: *At length the bus arrived, forty minutes late.* (b) taking a long time; in great detail; fully: *discuss sth at some, great, excessive, etc length* ○ *He went on at tedious length about his favourite hobby.* (**at**) **full length** ⇨ FULL. **go to any, some, great, etc ˈlengths (to do sth)** be prepared to do anything, something, a lot, etc to achieve sth: *They went to absurd lengths to keep the affair secret.* ○ *There are no lengths to which an addict will not go to obtain his drug.* ○ *She even went to the length of driving me home.* **keep sb at arm's length** ⇨ ARM[1]. **the length and breadth of sth** in or to all parts of sth: *travel the length and breadth of the British Isles.* **measure one's length** ⇨ MEASURE[1].

▷ **-length** (forming compound *adjs*): *a ˌknee-length ˈdress* ○ *ˌfloor-length ˈcurtains* ○ *a ˌfeature-length ˈfilm,* ie about two hours long.

lengthen *v* [I, Tn] (cause sth to) become longer: *The days start to lengthen in March.* ○ *lengthen a skirt.* Cf SHORTEN.

ˈlengthways (also **ˈlengthwise, longways, longwise**) *adv, adj* with the shortest sides placed together; end to end: *The tables were laid lengthways.*

lengthy /ˈleŋθɪ/ *adj* (**-ier, -iest**) **1** very long: *Lengthy negotiations must take place before any agreement can be reached.* **2** *(derog)* tiresomely long; long and boring: *lengthy explanations, speeches, etc.* ▷ **lengthily** *adv.*

lenient /ˈliːnɪənt/ *adj* not severe (esp in punishing people); merciful: *a lenient fine, law, view* ○ *I hope the judge will be lenient.*

▷ **lenience** /-əns/ (also **leniency** /-ənsɪ/) *n* [U] being lenient: *a magistrate known for her leniency with first-time offenders.*

leniently *adv*: *treat sb leniently.*

Lenin /ˈlenɪn/ Nicolai (1870-1924), real name Vladimir Ilyich Ulyanov, Russian revolutionary leader. After the overthrow of the Tsar in 1917 he established control by the Bolshevik party and became leader of the new Communist state.

Lennon /ˈlenən/ John (1940-1980), British composer, writer and guitarist. A founder-member of the *Beatles, he wrote many of the group's most successful songs together with Paul *McCartney. He was murdered in New York.

lens /lenz/ *n* (*pl* ~**es**) **1** piece of glass or other transparent material with one or more curved surfaces used to make things appear clearer, larger or smaller when viewed through it, and used in spectacles, cameras, telescopes, etc. ⇨ illus at CAMERA, GLASSES (GLASS). **2** *(anatomy)* transparent part of the eye, behind the pupil, that focuses light. ⇨ illus at EYE.

Lent /lent/ *n* (in the Christian religion) period from Ash Wednesday to Easter Eve, the 40 weekdays observed as a time of fasting and penitence: *give up chocolates, smoking, meat for Lent.*

▷ **Lenten** /ˈlentən/ *adj* [attrib] of Lent: *Lenten services.*

□ **ˌLent ˈterm** second of the three terms at Cambridge and some other universities, in which Lent occurs.

lent *pt, pp* of LEND.

lentil /ˈlentl/ *n* (a) plant grown for its small bean-like seeds. (b) its seed, usu dried, prepared as food: [attrib] *lentil soup.*

lento /ˈlentəʊ/ *adj, adv* *(music)* (played or to be played) slowly.

Leo /ˈliːəʊ/ *n* **1** [U] the fifth sign of the zodiac, the Lion. **2** [C] (*pl* ~**s**) person born under the influence of this sign. ⇨ Usage at ZODIAC. ⇨ illus at ZODIAC.

Leonardo da Vinci /liːəˈnɑːdəʊ dɑː ˈvɪntʃɪ/ (1452-1519), Italian artist, scientist and writer. One of the greatest painters of the *Renaissance, he was also an engineer, mathematician, musician, naturalist and philosopher, as well as an architect and sculptor. His work had great influence both on his contemporaries and on succeeding generations of artists. His most famous paintings include the *Mona Lisa* and *The Last Supper.*

Leone /leɪˈəʊnɪ/ Sergio (1921-1990), Italian film director. He is most famous for the new style of western he made in the 1960s (called 'Spaghetti Westerns'), like *The Good, the Bad and the Ugly,* with their violent and menacing atmosphere.

leonine /ˈlɪənaɪn/ *adj (fml)* of or like a lion: *leonine dignity.*

leopard /ˈlepəd/ *n* **1** large African and S Asian flesh-eating animal of the cat family with a yellowish coat and dark spots, or a completely black coat. The black leopard is usu called a panther. ⇨ illus at CAT. **2** (idm) **a/the ˌleopard can't ˌchange its/his ˈspots** *(saying)* it is almost impossible for sb to change his old habits or faults.

▷ **leopardess** /ˈlepədes, ˌlepəˈdes/ *n* female leopard.

leotard /ˈliːətɑːd/ *n* close-fitting one-piece garment worn by acrobats, dancers, etc.

leper /ˈlepə(r)/ *n* **1** person suffering from leprosy. **2** *(fig)* person who is rejected and avoided by others; outcast: *His unpopular views made him a social leper.*

Lepidoptera /ˌlepɪˈdɒptərə/ *n* [pl] order of insects, including the moths and butterflies, having two pairs of membranous wings covered with scales.

▷ **lepidopterist** /-tərɪst/ *n* person who studies moths and butterflies.

lepidopterous /-tərəs/ *adj* of Lepidoptera.

leprechaun /ˈleprəkɔːn/ *n* (in Irish folklore) fairy in the shape of a little old man.

leprosy /ˈleprəsɪ/ *n* [U] infectious disease affecting the skin and nerves, causing disfigurement and deformity.

lesbian /ˈlezbɪən/ *n* homosexual woman.

▷ **lesbian** *adj* of or concerning lesbians: *a lesbian relationship.*

lesbianism *n* [U].

lèse-majesté (also **lese-majesty**) /ˌleɪzˈmæʒesteɪ; *US* ˌliːzˈmædʒɪstɪ/ *n* [U] *(French)* **1** *(law)* crime or offence against a sovereign or government; treason. **2** *(joc)* presumptuous behaviour from a junior person: *Firing senior staff without reference to the boss comes pretty close to lèse-majesté.*

lesion /ˈliːʒn/ *n (medical)* **1** wound; injury: *painful lesions on his arms and legs.* **2** harmful change in the tissue of a bodily organ, caused by injury or disease: *a lesion of the left lung.*

Lesotho /ləˈsuːtuː/ small African country, completely surrounded by the Republic of South Africa; pop approx 1 676 000; official languages

English and Sesotho; capital Maseru; unit of currency loti (= 100 lisente). Lesotho has been an independent state since 1966 and is a member of the Commonwealth. Most of the active population is either involved in agriculture or employed in mining in South Africa. ⇨ map at NAMIBIA.

less /les/ *indef det, indef pron* ~ **(sth) (than...)** (used with [U] *ns* as the comparative of LITTLE[2]) not as much (as...); a smaller amount (of). **(a)** (*det*): *less butter, sugar, time, significance* ○ *less coffee than tea* ○ *I received less money than the others did.* ○ *You ought to smoke fewer cigarettes and drink less beer.* ⇨ Usage at MUCH. **(b)** (*pron*): *It seems less of a threat than I'd expected.* ○ *There's less to do in this job than the last.* ○ *'You must have paid £3000 for your car.' 'No, (it was) less.'* ○ *It's not far — it'll take less than an hour to get there.* ○ *The receptionist was less than* (ie not at all) *helpful when we arrived.* ○ *It took less than no* (ie very little) *time to write a reply.*

▷ **less** *adv* ~ **(than...)** **1** to a smaller extent; not so much (as): *I read much less now than I did at school.* ○ *It rains less in London than in Manchester.* ○ *less colourful, expensive, hungry, intelligent, tired, etc* ○ *less awkwardly, enthusiastically, often.* **2** (idm) **any (the) less** (used after *not*) to a smaller extent: *She wasn't any (the) less happy for being on her own.* **even/much/still less** and certainly not: *He's too shy to ask a stranger the time, still less speak to a room full of people.* **less and less** at a continually decreasing rate: *She found the job less and less attractive.* ○ *He played the piano less and less as he grew older.* **the less, more, etc... the less, more, etc...** ⇨ THE. **more or less** ⇨ MORE. **no less (than...)** as much as: *We won £500, no less, in a competition.* ○ *We won no less than £500 in a competition.*

less *prep* before subtracting (sth); minus: *a monthly salary of £450, less tax and national insurance* ○ *send a cheque for the catalogue price, less 10% discount.*

NOTE ON USAGE: **Less**, instead of **fewer**, is now commonly and increasingly used with plural nouns: *There have been less accidents on this road since the speed limit was introduced.* However, this is still thought to be incorrect English, and careful speakers prefer **fewer**: *fewer accidents.*

-less /-lɪs/ *suff* (used widely with *ns* to form *adjs*) without: *treeless* ○ *hopeless.* ▷ **-lessly** (forming *advs*): *meaninglessly.* **-lessness** (forming uncountable *ns*): *helplessness.*

lessee /leˈsiː/ *n* (*law*) person who holds a building, land, etc on a lease. Cf LESSOR. ⇨ Usage at TENANT.

lessen /ˈlesn/ *v* **1** [I] become less: *The pain was already lessening.* **2** [Tn] reduce (sth): *lessen the impact, likelihood, risk of sth.*

lesser /ˈlesə(r)/ *adj* [attrib] **1** not as great as the other(s): *one of the author's lesser works* ○ *He's stubborn, and so is she, but to a lesser degree,* ie not as much. ○ *one of the lesser lights* (ie less prominent members) *of his profession.* **2** (idm) **the ˌlesser of two ˈevils** the less harmful of two bad choices.

Lessing /ˈlesɪŋ/ Doris (1919-), British novelist. Her early novels used the background of Zimbabwe (then Rhodesia) where she spent her early years, while later novels like *The Golden Notebook* reflect her socialist and feminist concerns.

lesson /ˈlesn/ *n* **1** thing to be learnt by a pupil: *The first lesson in driving is how to start the car.* **2** period of time given to learning or teaching: *My yoga lesson begins in five minutes.* ○ *She gives piano lessons.* **3** ~ **(to sb)** experience from which one can learn; example: *Let this be a lesson to you never to play with matches!* ○ *His courage is a lesson to us all.* ○ *We are still absorbing the lessons of this disaster.* **4** (*religion*) passage from the Bible read aloud during a church service: *The first lesson is taken from St John's Gospel.* **5** (idm) **learn one's lesson** ⇨ LEARN.

lessor /ˈlesɔː(r)/ *n* (*law*) person who lets a property on lease. Cf LESSEE. ⇨ Usage at TENANT.

lest /lest/ *conj* (*fml*) **1** for fear that; in order that...not: *He ran away lest he (should/might) be seen.* ○ *Lest anyone should think it strange, let me assure you that it is quite true.* **2** (used after *fear, be afraid, be anxious,* etc): *She was afraid lest he might drown.*

let[1] /let/ *v* (**-tt-**, *pt, pp* **let**) **1** [Cn·i no passive] (often with the infinitive omitted when the context is clear) allow (sb/sth) to: *Don't let your child play with matches.* ○ *My father's only just had his operation and they won't let me see him yet.* ○ *She asked me if she could leave but I wouldn't let her (leave).* **2** [Tn·pr, Tn·p] allow (sb/oneself/sth) to go or pass in, etc: *let sb into the house* ○ *I'll give you a key to the flat so that you can let yourself in.* ○ *You've let all the air out of the tyres.* ○ *Let her past (you).* ○ *Don't let the dog out (of the room).* ○ *The roof lets water through.* ○ *Windows let in light and air.* **3** [Cn·i no passive] (used as an imperative) **(a)** (with the first person plural to make a suggestion): *Let's go to the cinema.* ○ *I don't think we'll succeed but let's try anyway.* **(b)** (in requests and commands): *Let the work be done immediately.* ○ *Let there be no mistake about it,* ie Don't misunderstand me. **(c)** (used to express an assumption, eg in mathematics): *Let line AB be equal to line CD.* ○ *Let ABC be an angle of 90°.* **(d)** (used to express defiance): *Let them do their worst.* ○ *Let them attack: we'll defeat them anyway.* **4** [Tn, Tn·pr, Tn·p] ~ **sth (out/off) (to sb)** allow sb to use (a house, room, etc) in return for regular payments: *I let (out) my spare rooms (to lodgers).* ○ *They decided to let (off) the smaller flats at lower rents.* **5** (idm) **ˌlet sb/sth ˈbe** not disturb or interfere with sb/sth: *Let me be, I want a rest.* ○ *Let the poor dog be,* ie Don't tease it. **let it ˈgo (at that)** say or do no more about sth: *I don't agree with all you say, but I'll let it go at that.* ○ *I thought she was hinting at something but I let it go.* **ˌlet oneself ˈgo** **(a)** no longer restrain one's feelings, desires, etc: *Go on, enjoy yourself, let yourself go.* **(b)** stop being careful, tidy, conscientious, etc: *He has let himself go a bit since he lost his job.* **let sb/sth go; let go of sb/sth** release (one's hold of) sb/sth: *let the rope go/let go of the rope* ○ *Let me go!* ○ *Will they let the hostages go?* **let sb ˈhave it** (*sl*) shoot, punish, etc sb: *Hold this bucket of water, and when he comes round the corner let him have it,* ie throw the water at him. **let me ˈsee** I'm thinking or trying to remember: *Let me see — where did I leave my hat?* **let us ˈsay** for example: *If the price is £500, let us say, is that too much?* **to ˈlet** available for renting: *Rooms to let,* eg on a sign outside a house. (For other idioms containing **let**, see entries for *ns, adjs,* etc, eg **let alone** ⇨ ALONE; **let rip** ⇨ RIP.).

6 (phr v) **let sb down** fail to help sb; disappoint sb: *Please come and support me. Don't let me down.* ○ *This machine won't let you down,* ie is very reliable.

let sth down **(a)** lower sth: *We let the bucket down by a rope.* ○ *This skirt needs letting down,* ie lengthening by lowering the hem-line. **(b)** deflate sth: *let sb's tyres down.*

let sth in make (a garment, etc) narrower: *This skirt needs letting in at the waist.* **let sb/oneself in for sth** (*infml*) cause sb/oneself to suffer (sth unpleasant): *You're letting yourself in for trouble by buying that rusty old car.* **let sb in on/into sth** (*infml*) allow sb to share (a secret, etc): *Are you going to let them in on the plans?*

let sth into sth put sth into the surface of sth: *a window let into a wall.*

let sb off (with sth) not punish sb (severely): *She was let off with a fine instead of being sent to prison.* ○ *Don't let these criminals off lightly,* ie Punish them severely. **let sb off (sth)** not compel sb to do (sth): *We've been let off school today because our teacher is ill.* **let sth off** fire sth off; explode sth: *The boys were letting off fireworks.*

let ˈon (about sth/that...) (to sb) (*infml*) reveal a secret: *I'm getting married next week, but please don't let on (to anyone) (about it), will you?*

let sb out release sb from sth, esp sth unpleasant: *The teacher said only Janet, George and Sue were to be punished, so that let me out.* **let sth out** **(a)** make (a garment, etc) looser or larger: *He's getting so fat that his trousers have to be let out round the waist.* **(b)** utter (a cry, etc): *She let out a scream of terror.* **(c)** reveal (a secret, etc): *Don't let it out about me losing my job, will you?*

let sb through allow sb to pass an exam or a test: *I'm a hopeless driver, but the examiner let me through.*

let ˈup become less strong, intense, etc; relax one's efforts: *Will the rain ever let up?* ○ *We mustn't let up, even though we're winning.*

□ **ˈlet-down** *n* disappointment: *The party was a big let-down.*

ˈlet-up *n* reduction in strength, intensity, etc; relaxation of efforts: *There is no sign of a let-up in the hijack crisis.*

let[2] /let/ *n* (*Brit*) letting of property; lease: *I can't get a let for my house,* ie find anyone to rent it from me.

▷ **letting** *n* (*Brit*) property that is let or to be let: *a furnished letting,* ie a furnished house or flat that is let ○ *a holiday letting.*

NOTE ON USAGE: Compare **let**, **rent** and **hire**. In British English these three verbs indicate a person giving permission for someone else to use something in return for money: *X lets (out)/rents (out)/hires (out) Z to Y.* Additionally, the user (Y) can be the subject of **rent** and **hire**: *Y rents/hires Z from X.* We usually **let (out)** accommodation, buildings or land: *He lets (out) his house to tourists during the summer.* ○ *The biggest factory in town is to let.* We **rent (out)** houses, cars, etc usually for fairly long periods of time: *She decided to rent out a room to get extra income.* ○ *I don't own my video. I rent it from a shop.* We **hire (out)** a building, car, suit, etc, usually for a short period and for a particular purpose: *They hire out boats by the hour.* ○ *The Labour party hired a concert hall for the election meeting.* In US English **rent (out)** is used in all the above meanings and **hire** can mean 'employ': *The company's hiring more men next week.* This use is less common in British English.

let[3] /let/ *n* **1** (in tennis) ball which, when it is served, hits the top of the net and drops into the opponent's court. **2** (idm) **without ˌlet or ˈhindrance** (*fml or law*) unimpeded; without obstruction: *Please allow the bearer of this passport to pass freely without let or hindrance.*

-let *suff* (with *ns* forming *ns*) **1** little: *booklet* ○ *piglet.* **2** unimportant; minor: *starlet.*

lethal /ˈliːθl/ *adj* **1** causing or able to cause death: *a lethal dose of poison* ○ *lethal weapons.* **2** damaging; harmful: (*fig*) *The closure of the factory dealt a lethal blow to the town.* ○ (*joc*) *This wine's pretty lethal!* ie very strong. ▷ **lethally** /ˈliːθəlɪ/ *adv.*

lethargy /ˈleθədʒɪ/ *n* [U] extreme lack of energy or vitality; inactivity; apathy: *She suffers from bouts of lethargy and depression.* ○ *government lethargy on this issue.* ▷ **lethargic** /ləˈθɑːdʒɪk/ *adj*: *Hot weather makes me lethargic.* **lethargically** /-klɪ/ *adv.*

let's *contracted form* of let us ⇨ LET[1] 3a.

Lett /let/ *n* native of Latvia.

▷ **Lettish** *n* [U] language of the Letts. ~ *adj* of the Letts or their language.

letter /ˈletə(r)/ *n* **1** [C] written or printed sign representing a sound used in speech: *'B' is the second letter of the alphabet.* ○ *Fill in your answers in capital letters, not small letters.* **2** [C] written message addressed to a person or an organization usu in an envelope, and sent by post: *Are there any letters for me?* ○ *Please inform me by letter of your plans.* ⇨ App 14. **3** (*US*) initial letter or letters of the name of a school or college awarded to a student who has performed well in sports, etc: [attrib] *a letter sweater, jacket, etc,* ie one with a large letter on it, worn by such a student. **4 letters** [pl] (*dated or fml*) literature as a profession or an academic study: *the profession of letters* ○ *a man/woman of letters.* **5** (idm) **a bread-and-butter letter** ⇨ BREAD. **a dead letter** ⇨ DEAD. **the ˌletter of the ˈlaw** the exact requirements or form of words of a law, rule, etc (as opposed to its general meaning or spirit). **to the ˈletter** paying strict attention to every detail: *carry out an order to the letter* ○ *keep to the letter of an agreement, a contract, etc.*

▷ **lettered** /ˈletəd/ *adj* well-educated or well-read.

lettering /ˈletərɪŋ/ *n* [U] letters or words, esp with reference to their visual appearance: *The lettering on the poster is very eye-catching.*

□ ˈ**letter-bomb** *n* terrorist explosive device disguised as a letter and sent by post.

ˈ**letter-box** *n* (a) (*Brit*) opening in a door, covered by a movable flap, through which letters are delivered. (b) (*US* ˈ**mailbox**) box near or at the entrance to or inside a building, in which letters and other articles brought by the postman are placed. ⇨ illus at HOME. (c) = POST-BOX (POST³).

ˈ**letterhead** *n* (a) [C] name and address of a person or an organization printed as a heading on stationery. (b) [U] stationery printed with such a heading.

ˌ**letter of** ˈ**credit** (*finance*) letter from a bank authorizing the bearer to draw money from another bank.

ˈ**letterpress** *n* [U] 1 printed text in a book, etc (as opposed to illustrations). 2 method of printing from raised type.

lettuce /ˈletɪs/ *n* 1 [C] garden plant with crisp green leaves. 2 [U] its leaves used as food (esp in salads): [attrib] *a lettuce and tomato salad.* ⇨ illus at SALAD.

leucocyte (*US* **leukocyte**) /ˈlu:kəsaɪt/ *n* (*medical*) white blood cell.

leucotomy /lu:ˈkɒtəmɪ/ *n* (*Brit*) = LOBOTOMY.

leukaemia (*US* **leukemia**) /lu:ˈki:mɪə/ *n* [U] disease in which there is an uncontrollable increase in the numbers of white corpuscles.

Levant /lɪˈvænt/ *n* **the Levant** [sing] (*arch*) countries and islands in the eastern part of the Mediterranean Sea, eg Cyprus and Lebanon.

▷ **Levantine** /ˈlevəntaɪn; *US* ləˈvænti:n/ *n, adj* (*arch*) (native or inhabitant) of the Levant.

levee¹ /ˈlevɪ/ *n* (*arch*) assembly of visitors, esp at a formal reception.

levee² /ˈlevɪ/ *n* (*esp US*) embankment built to prevent a flooded river from overflowing: *the levees along the Mississippi.*

level¹ /ˈlevl/ *adj* 1 having a horizontal surface; flat; not sloping: *Find level ground for the picnic table.* ○ *Add one level* (ie not heaped) *tablespoon of sugar.* 2 of the same height, standard or position on a scale: *The two pictures are not quite level — that one is higher than the other.* ○ *France took an early lead but Wales drew level* (ie equalized the score) *before half-time.* 3 (of voices, looks, etc) steady: *a level stare.* 4 (idm) **have a level head** be able to judge well. ˌ**level** ˈ**pegging** making progress at the same rate.

□ ˌ**level-**ˈ**crossing** *n* (*US* ˈ**grade crossing**) place where a road and a railway cross each other at the same level. Cf CROSSING 2.

ˌ**level-**ˈ**headed** *adj* able to judge well; sensible; calm.

level² /ˈlevl/ *n* 1 [C] line or surface parallel to the horizon, esp with reference to its height: *1 000 metres above sea-level* ○ *a multi-level car-park*, ie one with two or more storeys ○ *The controls are at eye-level.* 2 [C] position on a scale of quantity, strength, value, etc: *the level of alcohol in the blood* ○ *Levels of unemployment vary from region to region.* ○ (*fig*) *I could use threats too, but I refuse to sink to your level*, ie behave as badly as you. 3 [U] relative position in rank, class or authority: *discussions at Cabinet level*, ie involving members of the Cabinet ○ *high-/low-level negotiations.* 4 [C] (a) more or less flat surface, layer or area: *The archaeologists found gold coins and pottery in the lowest level of the site.* (b) **levels** [pl] (*Brit*) wide area of flat open country. 5 [C] = SPIRIT-LEVEL (SPIRIT). 6 (idm) **find one's/its level** ⇨ FIND¹. **on a level (with sb/sth)** at the same level: *Technically, both players are on a level*, ie of the same standard. ○ *The water rose until it was on a level with the river banks.* **on the** ˈ**level** (*infml*) honest(ly): *Are you sure this deal is on the level?* ○ *I'd like to help, but I can't — on the level!*

level³ /ˈlevl/ *v* (-ll-; *US* -l-) 1 [Tn] make (sth) level, equal or uniform: *The ground should be levelled before you plant a lawn.* ○ *She needs to win this point to level the score.* ○ *level social differences.* 2 [Tn esp passive] demolish (a building, etc): *a town levelled by an earthquake.* 3 [Tn] ~ **sth (at sb)** aim (a gun, etc): *The hostage had a rifle levelled at his head.* 4 (phr v) **level sth at sb** bring (a charge or an accusation) against sb: *level criticism at the council* ○ *accusations levelled at the directors.* **level sth down/up** make (surfaces, scores, incomes, etc) equal by lowering the higher/raising the lower: *Marks at the lower end need to be levelled up.* **level off/out** (a) (of an aircraft, etc or its pilot) fly horizontally after a climb or dive: *level off at 20 000 feet.* (b) (*fig*) become level after rising or falling: *House prices show no sign of levelling off*, ie are continuing to rise or fall. ○ *Share values have levelled off after yesterday's steep rise.* **level with sb** (*infml*) speak or deal with sb in an honest and frank way.

▷ **leveller** (*US* **leveler**) /ˈlevələ(r)/ *n* person who wants to abolish social distinctions: (*fig*) *death, the great leveller.*

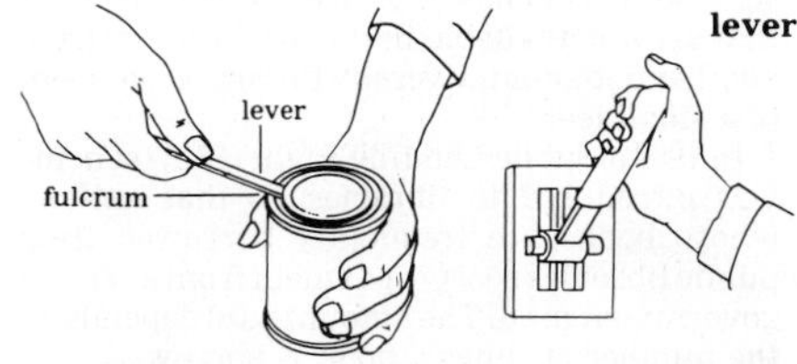

lever /ˈli:və(r); *US* ˈlevər/ *n* 1 bar or other device turning on a fixed point (the *fulcrum*) which lifts or opens sth with one end when pressure is applied to the other end. 2 handle used to operate or control machinery: *Move this lever to change gear.* ⇨ illus. 3 (*fig*) means of exerting moral pressure: *This latest incident may be the lever needed to change government policy.*

▷ **lever** *v* [Tn, Tn·pr, Cn·a] move (sth) with a lever: *They levered the rock into the hole.* ○ *lever a crate open.*

leverage /-ərɪdʒ/ *n* [U] 1 action or power of a lever. 2 (*fig*) power; influence: *Her wealth gives her enormous leverage in social circles.*

leveret /ˈlevərɪt/ *n* young hare.

leviathan /lɪˈvaɪəθn/ *n* 1 (*Bible*) sea-monster. 2 thing of enormous size and power.

Levis /ˈli:vaɪz/ *n* [pl] (*propr*) jeans.

levitate /ˈlevɪteɪt/ *v* [I, Tn, Tn·pr] (cause sb/sth to) rise and float in the air, esp by means of supernatural powers. ▷ **levitation** /ˌlevɪˈteɪʃn/ *n* [U]: *powers of levitation.*

Leviticus /ləˈvɪtɪkəs/ third book of the Old Testament, containing details of laws and rituals. ⇨ App 5.

levity /ˈlevətɪ/ *n* [U] (*fml*) lack of proper seriousness or respect.

levy /ˈlevɪ/ *v* (*pt, pp* **levied**) 1 [Tn, Tn·pr] ~ **sth (on sb)** collect (a payment, etc) by authority or force; impose sth: *a departure tax levied on all travellers.* 2 [Tn] (*fml*) wage (war). 3 [Tn] enlist (troops, etc). 4 (phr v) **levy on sth** (*law*) seize sth in order to force payment of a debt: *levy on sb's property, estate, etc.*

▷ **levy** *n* 1 [C] (a) act of levying money, etc. (b) money, etc so obtained. 2 **levies** [pl] troops that have been enlisted.

lewd /lju:d; *US* lu:d/ *adj* 1 treating sexual matters in a vulgar or indecent way: *a story full of lewd innuendos.* 2 lustful: *a lewd expression, glance, gesture, etc.* ▷ **lewdly** *adv.* **lewdness** *n* [U].

Lewis¹ /ˈlu:ɪs/ C(live) S(taples) (1898-1963), English writer. He taught at both Oxford and Cambridge Universities, but became famous through his popular books on Christian life and the *Narnia* series of fantasy novels for children.

Lewis² /ˈlu:ɪs/ (Harry) Sinclair (1885-1951), American novelist. His works, like *Babbitt*, give a vivid satirical view of life and society in the small towns of the American Midwest. He was the first American to be awarded the Nobel prize for literature (in 1930).

Lewis³ /ˈlu:ɪs/ (Percy) Wyndham (1882-1957), British novelist and painter. His novels and essays attacked the hypocrisy he found in the artistic and literary establishment of his day. He was one of the founders of vorticism, an artistic movement similar to *futurism.

lexical /ˈleksɪkl/ *adj* (*linguistics*) of the vocabulary of a language: *lexical items*, ie words and phrases.

▷ **lexically** /-klɪ/ *adv.*

lexis /ˈleksɪs/ *n* [U] vocabulary.

lexicography /ˌleksɪˈkɒgrəfɪ/ *n* [U] theory and practice of compiling dictionaries.

▷ **lexicographer** /ˌleksɪˈkɒgrəfə(r)/ *n* person who compiles dictionaries.

lexicographical /ˌleksɪkəˈgræfɪkl/ *adj.*

lexicon /ˈleksɪkən; *US* -kɒn/ *n* 1 dictionary, esp of an ancient language (eg Greek or Hebrew). 2 (*linguistics*) vocabulary (contrasted with grammar).

ley¹ /leɪ/ *n* land that is temporarily sown with grass.

ley² /leɪ/ *n* (also ˈ**ley line**) supposed straight line of a prehistoric track connecting prominent features of the landscape, usu hilltops.

Leyden jar /ˈleɪdn dʒɑ:(r)/ early type of capacitor consisting of a glass jar with layers of metal foil on the inside and the outside. It was invented at Leyden University in Holland in 1745.

LF /ˌel ˈef/ *abbr* (*radio*) low frequency. Cf HF.

lh *abbr* left hand. Cf RH.

Lhasa /ˈlɑ:sə/ capital of Tibet, sometimes called the Forbidden City. It is situated high in the Himalayas, and is the spiritual centre of Tibetan Buddhism. Many of its temples were closed or destroyed by the Chinese after the Tibetan revolt in 1959. ⇨ map at CHINA.

Li *symb* lithium.

liability /ˌlaɪəˈbɪlətɪ/ *n* 1 [U] ~ **(for sth)** state of being liable: *liability for military service* ○ *Don't admit liability for the accident.* 2 [C] (*infml*) handicap: *Because of his injury Jones was just a liability to the team.* Cf ASSET. 3 **liabilities** [pl] debts; financial obligations.

liable /ˈlaɪəbl/ *adj* [pred] 1 ~ **(for sth)** responsible by law: *Is a wife liable for her husband's debts?* ○ *Be careful — if you have an accident I'll be liable.* 2 ~ **to sth** subject to sth: *a road liable to subsidence* ○ *Offenders are liable to fines of up to £100.* 3 ~ **to do sth** likely to do sth: *We're all liable to make mistakes when we're tired.*

liaise /lɪˈeɪz/ *v* [I, Ipr] ~ **(with sb)**; ~ **(between A and B)** (*infml*) act as a link or go-between.

liaison /lɪˈeɪzn; *US* ˈlɪəzɒn/ *n* 1 [U] communication and co-operation between units of an organization: *excellent liaison between our two departments* ○ [attrib] *a liaison officer.* 2 [C] (*often derog*) person who liaises. 3 [C] (*often derog*) illicit sexual relationship: *a brief liaison.*

liana /lɪˈɑ:nə/ *n* tropical climbing plant.

liar /ˈlaɪə(r)/ *n* person who tells lies, esp habitually: *a good/bad liar*, ie sb who can/cannot easily deceive others by telling lies.

Lib /lɪb/ *abbr* (*Brit politics*) Liberal (Party): *Joan Wells (Lib)* ○ *a Lib-Lab pact*, ie between the Liberal and Labour Parties. Cf L 4.

lib /lɪb/ *n* [U] (*infml*) (in compounds) liberation: *gay, women's, animal, etc lib.* ▷ **libber** *n* (in compounds): *Is she a women's libber?*

libation /laɪˈbeɪʃn/ *n* 1 (pouring out of an) offering of wine, etc to a god in former times. 2 (*joc*) alcoholic drink.

libel /ˈlaɪbl/ *n* 1 [C] false written or printed statement that damages sb's reputation. 2 [U] (*law*) act of publishing such a statement: *sue a newspaper for libel* ○ [attrib] *libel proceedings.* 3 [C] ~ **(on sb)** (*infml*) thing that tends to harm the reputation of sb/sth: *That interview was an absolute libel on a honest man.* Cf SLANDER.

▷ **libel** *v* (-ll-; *US* -l-) [Tn] harm the reputation of (sb) by publishing a false statement.

libellous (*US* **libelous**) /ˈlaɪbələs/ *adj* 1 being or containing a libel: *a libellous statement.* 2 in the habit of publishing libels: *a libellous magazine.*

liberal /ˈlɪbərəl/ *adj* 1 tolerant and open-minded; free from prejudice: *a liberal attitude to divorce and remarriage.* 2 giving or given generously: *She's very liberal with promises but much less so*

Libraries

Almost every town in Britain has a public library, funded by the local authority, where local people may borrow books free of charge.

Most libraries divide their books into two main sections, lending and reference. The lending section normally offers a good range of fiction and non-fiction, while the reference section contains encyclopedias, dictionaries, atlases, etc. Books from the lending section can be borrowed, usually for a period of two or three weeks, while books in the reference section may normally be consulted only in the library. Libraries are usually open daily from Monday to Friday, including some evenings, as well as on Saturday mornings.

Other facilities besides books usually include: a selection of newspapers and magazines, often in a special 'reading room'; desks for private reading and study; a children's book section, where story-reading sessions are sometimes held; access to current catalogues, including *British Books In Print*, and many other sources of information by means of a computer terminal; bus timetables, local guides, maps etc; a coin-operated photocopier; a collection of sheet music, music scores, records, audio-cassettes and videos that may be borrowed, and, in larger libraries, special audio booths for listening to cassettes, for example when studying a foreign language. Most libraries also put on exhibitions of local interest, for example paintings by local artists or displays about local history. Some have a meeting room which can be booked by individuals or organizations.

Many libraries also contain a local tourist information desk, while the main book stock often includes a section on local history, where special records such as local census returns and minutes of council meetings are also kept.

Borrowers are normally allowed to have up to ten or even more books out at any one time. A system of fines operates when books are not returned by the end of the borrowing period. People living in rural areas can use a 'mobile library', a van that tours these areas regularly with a selection of books from the local library.

All libraries operate an inter-library loan scheme. This makes it possible to obtain books that are not available in the local library from another public or university library on payment of a small fee.

In 1982 a Public Lending Right (PLR) scheme was introduced in libraries, so that authors whose books are frequently borrowed from public libraries receive payment from a central government fund. The amount paid depends on the number of times a book is borrowed.

Britain's national library is the British Library (formerly the British Museum Library), one of the world's largest libraries, with its headquarters, from 1993, in a new building in St Pancras, London. The British Library, the National Libraries of Scotland and Wales, the Bodleian Library at Oxford and the Cambridge University Library are all copyright libraries. This means that they receive by right a copy of every book published in Britain.

Copies of all daily and weekly newspapers and magazines published are held at the Newspaper Library in north London, as part of the British Library. The Public Record Office in London holds all government and legal documents, including Cabinet papers, which are not made public until 30 years have passed.

Apart from the public libraries, there are several important private libraries in Britain. Many of them are in London, such as the London Library and the libraries of learned bodies like the Royal Geographical Society and the Royal Academy of Music. Others belong to universities such as the John Rylands University Library, Manchester, and the Oxford and Cambridge libraries already mentioned. Most important libraries, whether public or private, will allow serious readers and students to consult or borrow their books. However, no book may ever be borrowed from the British Library.

In the USA public libraries operate on the same principles as in Britain, and are funded from taxes. The national equivalent of the British Library is the Library of Congress in Washington, which must similarly be supplied with a copy of all books published in the USA. The Harvard University Library is the largest of its kind in the world.

---

with money. ○ *a liberal sprinkling of sugar.* **3** (of education) concerned chiefly with broadening the mind, not simply with technical or professional training. **4** not strict, literal or exact: *a liberal translation giving a general idea of the writer's intentions.* **5 Liberal** (*politics*) of the Liberal Party: *Liberal housing policy.* ⇨ article at POLITICS.

▷ **liberal** *n* **1** tolerant and open-minded person. **2 Liberal** (*Brit politics*) (*abbr* **Lib**) member of the Liberal Party.

liberalism /-ɪzəm/ *n* [U] liberal opinions and principles.

liberally /-rəlɪ/ *adv*: *rolls spread liberally with butter* ○ *interpret the ruling liberally.*

□ **liberal ˈarts** (*esp US*) the arts (ART¹2), esp as a subject of study, as distinct from science and technology.

the Liberal ˈDemocrats (*Brit politics*) political party in Britain (formerly called **the Liberal Party**) favouring moderate political and social reform. The (former) Liberal Party succeeded the old *Whig party in the 1860s and under *Gladstone and *Lloyd George it became the party of radical social reform. It declined with the rise of the Labour Party and in 1988 merged with the Social Democratic Party to form the Social and Liberal Democrats, later renamed the Liberal Democrats. Cf THE CONSERVATIVE PARTY (CONSERVATIVE), THE LABOUR PARTY (LABOUR).

liberality /lɪbəˈrælətɪ/ *n* [U] **1** free giving; generosity. **2** quality of being tolerant and open-minded: *a period remarkable for its liberality.*

liberalize, -ise /ˈlɪbrəlaɪz/ *v* [Tn] free (sb/sth) from political or moral restrictions: *There is a move to liberalize literature and the Arts.* ▷ **liberallization, -isation** /lɪbrəlaɪˈzeɪʃn; *US* -lɪˈz-/ *n* [U].

liberate /ˈlɪbəreɪt/ *v* [Tn, Tn·pr] ~ **sb/sth (from sth)** set (sb/sth) free: *liberate prisoners, an occupied country.*

▷ **liberated** *adj* showing freedom from traditional ideas in social and sexual matters: *a liberated male, mother, lifestyle.*

liberation /lɪbəˈreɪʃn/ *n* [U]: *the liberation of Europe by Allied troops* ○ *The break-up of their marriage was an enormous liberation for her.*

liberator *n*: *hailing the soldiers as liberators.*

Liberia /laɪˈbɪərɪə/ country in W Africa; pop approx 2 705 000; official language English; capital Monrovia; unit of currency dollar (= 100 cents). It was founded in 1822 as a settlement for freed American slaves and became independent in 1847. Agriculture is based on rice and rubber plantations, but the main strength of the country's economy lies in its large reserves of iron ore. Many ships are registered in Liberia, which provides them with a flag of convenience. The 1990s saw a prolonged power-struggle between three factions and civil war that resulted in intervention by a five-nation peacekeeping force. ⇨ map at NIGERIA.

▷ **Liberian** *adj, n*: *a Liberian tanker.*

libertarian /lɪbəˈteərɪən/ *n, adj* (person) believing in complete freedom in matters of politics, religion, morality, etc.

libertine /ˈlɪbəti:n/ *n* man who lives an irresponsible and immoral life.

liberty /ˈlɪbətɪ/ *n* **1** [U] freedom from captivity, slavery, or oppressive control. **2** [C, U] right or power to do as one chooses: *They give their children a great deal of liberty.* **3** [C esp *pl*] right or privilege granted by authority: *liberties enjoyed by all citizens.* **4** (idm) **at liberty (to do sth) (a)** (of a person) free; allowed: *You are at liberty to leave.* **(b)** free from restrictions or control: *You're at liberty to say what you like.* ˌ**Liberty ˈHall** place or condition of complete freedom: *Wear what you like for the party — it's Liberty Hall.* **set sb free/at liberty** ⇨ FREE. **take liberties (with sb/sth)** behave in a presumptuous disrespectful way: *She told him to stop taking liberties*, ie treating her with too much familiarity. ○ *The film takes considerable liberties with the novel on which it is based*, eg by shortening or changing it. **take the liberty of doing sth** do sth without permission: *I took the liberty of borrowing your lawn-mower while you were away.*

□ **the ˈLiberty Bell** bell rung at the adoption of the Declaration of Independence. It is now on display near Independence Hall in Philadelphia, USA.

ˈ**liberty bodice** type of close-fitting vest with buttons at the front, worn (esp formerly) by women and young children.

libidinous /lɪˈbɪdɪnəs/ *adj* (*fml*) having or showing strong sexual feelings; lustful.

libido /lɪˈbi:dəʊ, *also* ˈlɪbɪdəʊ/ *n* (*pl* ~**s**) [U, C] (*psychology*) emotional energy or urge, esp sexual.

Lib-Lab /ˈlɪblæb/ *adj* [usu attrib] (esp formerly) involving the Liberal and Labour Parties: *a* ˌ*Lib-Lab* ˈ*pact.*

Libra /ˈli:brə/ *n* **1** [U] the seventh sign of the zodiac, the Scales. **2** [C] person born under the influence of this sign. ▷ **Libran** *n, adj.* ⇨ Usage at ZODIAC. ⇨ illus at ZODIAC.

library /ˈlaɪbrərɪ; *US* -brerɪ/ *n* **1 (a)** collection of books for reading or borrowing: *a public, reference, university, etc library* ○ *He has many foreign books in his library.* ○ [attrib] *When is that library book due back?* ie When must it be returned to the public library? ⇨ article. **(b)** room or building where these are kept: *Let's meet outside the library.* **2** similar collection of records, films, etc: *a recording to add to your library* ○ *a photographic library.*

▷ **librarian** /laɪˈbreərɪən/ *n* person in charge of or assisting in a library. **librarianship** *n* [U] work of being a librarian.

□ **the** ˌ**Library of** ˈ**Congress** US national library in Washington DC.

libretto /lɪˈbretəʊ/ *n* (*pl* ~**s** or **-retti** /-ti:/) words that are sung and spoken in an opera or musical play.

▷ **librettist** /lɪˈbretɪst/ *n* author of a libretto.

Libya /ˈlɪbɪə/ country in N Africa; pop approx 4 232 000; official language Arabic; capital Tripoli; unit of currency dinar (= 1 000 millemes). Most of the country is desert and agriculture is limited to sheep-farming. The main economic resource is oil, but production has declined. In 1969 after a coup d'état the country became a republic with a radical revolutionary leadership. ⇨ map at ALGERIA.

lice *pl* of LOUSE.

licence (*US* **license**) /ˈlaɪsns/ *n* **1** [C] official document showing that permission has been given to own, use or do sth: *a driving licence* ○ *a licence to practise as a doctor* ○ *This used to be a pub but the landlord has lost his licence,* ie is no longer permitted to sell alcoholic drinks. ⇨ radio TELEVISION. **2** [U] (*fml*) permission: *Why give these people licence to enter the place at will?* **3** [U] **(a)** irresponsible use of freedom, esp to behave in an offensive way. **(b)** freedom to rearrange or exaggerate words or images: *artistic/poetic licence.* **4** (idm) **a ˌlicence to print ˈmoney** (*infml*) scheme, etc that has been officially approved but is likely to be excessively costly, with little or no control over the money spent.

□ **ˈlicence plate** (*US* **license plate**) *n* (*esp US*) = NUMBER-PLATE (NUMBER).

license (also **licence**) /ˈlaɪsns/ *v* [Tn, Cn·t] give a licence to (sb/sth): *shops licensed to sell tobacco* ○ *licensed premises,* ie where the sale of alcoholic drinks is permitted.

▷ **licensee** /ˌlaɪsənˈsiː/ *n* person who has a licence, esp to sell alcoholic drinks.

□ **ˈlicensing laws** (*Brit*) laws limiting the places and times at which alcoholic drinks may be sold.

licentiate /laɪˈsenʃɪət/ *n* person who has a certificate showing that he is competent to practise a certain profession: *a licentiate in dental surgery.*

licentious /laɪˈsenʃəs/ *adj* (*fml*) disregarding the rules of behaviour, esp in sexual matters. ▷ **licentiously** *adv.* **licentiousness** *n* [U].

lichen /ˈlaɪkən/ *n* [U] dry-looking plant, usu yellow, grey or green, that grows on rocks, walls, tree-trunks, etc. Cf MOSS.

lich-gate (also **lych-gate**) /ˈlɪtʃgeɪt/ *n* roofed gateway to a churchyard.

lick /lɪk/ *v* **1** [Tn, Cn·a] pass the tongue over (sb/sth): *He licked his fingers.* ○ *The cat was licking its fur.* ○ *lick the back of a postage stamp,* ie to moisten the glue ○ *He licked the spoon clean.* **2** [Tn] (of waves or flames) touch (sth) lightly: *flames beginning to lick the furniture.* **3** [Tn] (*sl*) defeat (sb). **4** (idm) **lick sb's ˈboots** (*infml*); **lick sb's ˈarse** (⚠ *sl*) be servile towards sb. **lick sb/sth into ˈshape** (*infml*) make sb/sth efficient or presentable: *The new recruits will be fine once they've been licked into shape.* **lick/smack one's ˈlips/ˈchops** (*infml*) show eager enjoyment or anticipation of sth: *The children licked their lips as the cake was cut.* ○ (*fig*) *She's licking her chops at the thought of spending all that money!* **lick one's ˈwounds** try to restore one's strength or spirits after a defeat: *The disappointed losers crawled home to lick their wounds.* **5** (phr v) **lick sth from/off sth** remove sth by licking: *lick blood from a cut, honey off a spoon.* **lick sth up** take sth into the mouth by licking: *The cat licked up its milk.*

▷ **lick** *n* **1** [C] stroke of the tongue in licking: *One last lick and the milk was gone.* ○ *a lick of ice-cream.* **2** [sing] slight application (of paint, etc): *The boat would look better with a lick of paint.* **3** [sing] (*sl*) speed: *going at quite a, a fair old, a full, etc lick,* ie quite, fairly, extremely fast. **4** = SALT-LICK (SALT). **5** (idm) **a ˌlick and a ˈpromise** (*infml*) quick and careless attempt to clean or wash sth.

licking *n* (esp *sing*) (*sl*) **1** defeat: *give sb/get a (right) licking.* **2** beating: *If your father hears about this he'll give you such a licking!*

licorice = LIQUORICE.

lid /lɪd/ *n* **1** hinged or removable cover for a box, pot, etc. ⇨ illus at PAN. **2** = EYELID (EYE). **3** (idm) **flip one's lid** ⇨ FLIP. **put the lid on sth** (*Brit infml*) stop or control sth threatening or troublesome: *I'm determined to put the lid on these rumours.* **put the (tin) ˈlid on sth/things** (*Brit infml*) be the final event that provokes an outburst. **take, lift, blow, etc the lid off sth** reveal unpleasant secrets concerning sth: *an article that lifts the lid off the world of professional gambling.*

▷ **lidded** *adj* [usu attrib] **1** (of a box, pot, etc) having a lid. **2** (of eyes) having lids of a particular type: *heavily lidded eyes.*

lidless *adj.*

lido /ˈliːdəʊ/ *n* (*pl* ~**s**) public bathing beach or open air swimming-pool.

lie[1] /laɪ/ *v* (*pt, pp* **lied**, *pres p* **lying**) **1** [I, Ipr] ~ **(to sb) (about sth)** make a statement one knows to be untrue: *He's lying.* ○ *Don't you dare lie to me!* ○ *She lies about her age.* **2** [I] give a false impression; be deceptive: *The camera cannot lie.* ○ *lying smiles.* **3** (idm) **lie in one's ˈteeth/ˈthroat** (*infml*) lie grossly and shamelessly. **lie one's way into/out of sth** get (oneself) into or out of a situation by lying: *He's lied his way into a really plum job.* ⇨ Usage at LIE[2].

▷ **lie** *n* **1** statement one knows to be untrue: *His story is nothing but a pack of lies.* Cf FIB. **2** (idm) **give the lie to sth** show sth to be untrue: *These figures give the lie to reports that business is declining.* **live a lie** ⇨ LIVE[2]. **nail a lie** ⇨ NAIL. Cf WHITE LIE (WHITE[1]).

□ **ˈlie-detector** *n* instrument that can detect changes in the pulse-rate, breathing, etc, thought to result from the stress caused by lying in response to questions.

lie[2] /laɪ/ *v* (*pt* **lay** /leɪ/, *pp* **lain** /leɪn/, *pres p* **lying**) **1** [Ipr] have or put one's body in a flat or resting position on a horizontal surface: *The corpse lay face down in a pool of blood.* ○ *lie on one's back/side/front* ○ *Don't lie in bed all morning!* ○ *a dog lying at his master's feet.* **2** [La, Ipr] (of a thing) be at rest on a surface: *The letter lay open on his desk.* ⇨ Usage. **3** [La, Ipr] be, remain or be kept in a certain state: *snow lying thick on the ground* ○ *These machines have lain idle since the factory closed.* ○ *I'd rather use my money than leave it lying in the bank.* **4** [Ipr] be spread out to view; extend: *The valley lay at our feet.* ○ (*fig*) *You're still young — your whole life lies before you!* **5** [Ipr] be situated: *The town lies on the coast.* ○ *a ship lying at anchor, at its moorings, alongside, etc.* **6** [Ipr] (of abstract things) exist or be found: *I only wish it lay within my power to* (ie that I could) *help you.* ○ *The cure for stress lies in learning to relax.* ○ *It's obvious where our interest lies,* ie which option, development, etc would be to our advantage. **7** [I] (*law*) be admissible or able to be upheld: *The objection will not lie.* **8** (idm) **as/so far as in me lies** ⇨ FAR[2]. **as one makes one's bed so one must lie in it** ⇨ BED[1]. **keep/lie close** ⇨ CLOSE[1]. **let sleeping dogs lie** ⇨ SLEEP[2]. **lie at sb's ˈdoor** be attributable to sb: *I accept that the responsibility for this lies squarely at my door.* **lie doggo** (*infml*) lie without moving or making a sign. **lie heavy on sth** cause sth to feel uncomfortable: *The rich meal lay heavy on my stomach.* ○ *a crime lying heavy on one's conscience.* **lie in ˈstate** (of a corpse) be placed on view in a public place before burial. **lie in ˈwait (for sb)** be hidden waiting to surprise sb: *arrested by the police who had been lying in wait.* **lie ˈlow** (*infml*) keep quiet or hidden: *He's been lying low ever since I asked him for the money he owes me.* **see, etc how the land lies** ⇨ LAND[1]. **take sth lying ˈdown** accept an insult, etc without protest; submit meekly. **time hangs/lies heavy on one's hands** ⇨ TIME[1]. **9** (phr v) **lie back** get into or be in a resting position; relax: *You don't have to do anything — just lie back and enjoy the journey.* **lie behind sth** be the explanation for sth: *What lay behind this strange outburst?* **lie down** be or move into a horizontal position on a bed, etc in order to sleep or rest: *Go and lie down for a while.* ○ *He lay down on the sofa and soon fell asleep.* **lie down under sth** (*infml*) accept (an insult etc) without protest; submit meekly: *We have no intention of lying down under these absurd allegations.* **lie ˈin** **(a)** (*Brit*) (*US* **sleep in**) (*infml*) stay in bed after the normal time for getting up: *It's a holiday tomorrow, so you can lie in.* **(b)** (*dated*) stay in bed to await the birth of a child: *a lying-ˈin hospital.* **lie over** (of problems, business, etc) await attention or action at a later date: *These items can lie over till our next meeting.* **lie ˈto** (*nautical*) (of a vessel) come to a stop facing the wind; be anchored or moored. **lie up** stay in bed to rest during an illness. **lie with sb (to do sth)** (*fml*) be sb's duty or responsibility: *The decision on whether to proceed lies with the Minister.* ○ *It lies with you to accept or reject the proposal.*

▷ **lie** *n* **1** [sing] way or position in which sth lies. **2** [C usu *sing*] (in golf) where the ball comes to rest after a shot: *a good, poor, etc lie.* **3** (idm) **the ˌlie of the ˈland** (*US* **the ˌlay of the ˈland**) **(a)** the natural features (esp rivers, mountains, etc) of an area. **(b)** (*infml fig*) assessment of the state of a situation: *I'll need several weeks to discover the lie of the land before I can make any decisions about the future of the business.*

□ **ˈlie-down** *n* (usu *sing*); (*Brit infml*) a short rest, usu in bed.

ˈlie-in *n* (usu *sing*); (*infml esp Brit*) act of staying in bed longer than usual, esp in the morning: *look forward to a nice long lie-in on Sunday.*

NOTE ON USAGE: Note the difference between the intransitive verb **lie** (**lying**, **lay**, **lain**), meaning 'be in a resting position': *I was feeling ill, so I lay down on the bed for a while* and the transitive verb **lay** (**laying**, **laid**, **laid**), meaning 'put on a surface': *She laid her dress on the bed to keep it neat.* There is another intransitive verb **lie** (**lying**, **lied**, **lied**), meaning 'say something untrue': *He lied about his age to join the army.*

Liebig condenser /ˈliːbɪg kəndensə(r)/ simple form of condenser used in laboratories, consisting of one glass tube surrounded by another, with cooling water flowing between them. It is named after the German chemist Baron Justus von Liebig (1803-73).

Liechtenstein /ˈlɪktənstaɪn/ small country in western Europe between Austria and Switzerland; pop approx 28 000; official language German; capital Vaduz; unit of currency franc (= 100 centimes). It is used as a tax haven by many companies and is one of the world's richest countries. ⇨ map at SWITZERLAND.

Lied /liːt/ *n* (*pl* **Lieder** /ˈliːdə(r)/) (*German music*) German song for solo voice and piano, esp of the Romantic period.

liege /liːdʒ/ *n* **1** (also **ˈliege lord**) (in feudal times) sovereign or lord, entitled to loyal service. **2** (also **ˈliegeman** /-mən/) man or servant bound to give loyal service to such a sovereign or lord.

lien /lɪən/ *n* [C] ~ **(on/upon sth)** (*law*) right to keep sb's property until a debt owed in connection with it (for repair, transport, etc) is paid.

lieu /luː *or, in British use,* ljuː/ *n* (idm) **in lieu (of sth)** instead: *accept a cheque in lieu of cash.*

Lieut (also **Lt**) *abbr* Lieutenant: *Lieut (James) Brown.*

lieutenant /lefˈtenənt; *US* luːˈt-/ *n* **1** army officer next below a captain. ⇨ App 4. **2** navy officer next below a lieutenant-commander. ⇨ App 4. **3** (in compounds) officer ranking next below the one specified: *lieuˌtenant-ˈgeneral* ○ *lieuˌtenant-ˈgovernor,* ie official next below a governor-general. **4** (*US*) police officer next in rank below captain. **5** deputy; chief assistant.

▷ **lieutenancy** /-ənsɪ/ *n* rank of a lieutenant.

life /laɪf/ *n* (*pl* **lives** /laɪvz/) **1** [U] ability to function and grow that distinguishes living animals and plants from dead ones and from rocks, metals, etc: *the origins of life on earth* ○ *The motionless body showed no signs of life.* **2** [U] living things: *Is there life on Mars?* ○ *animal and plant life.* **3** [U] state of being alive as a human being: *The riot was brought under control without loss of life,* ie without anyone being killed. **4** [U] qualities, events and experiences that characterize existence as a human being: *He does not want much from life.* ○ *What do you expect? That's life!* ie These things happen and must be expected and accepted. **5** [C] existence of an individual human being: *Doctors worked through the night to save the life of the injured man.* ○ *Three lives were lost* (ie Three people died) *in the accident.* **6** **(a)** [C] period between birth and death: *She lived her whole life in the country.* ○ *He spent his adult life in Canada.* **(b)** [C] period between birth and the present: *I've lived here all my life.* **7** [U] **(a)** period between the present and death: *a friend, job, membership for life.* **(b)** (*infml*) (also **life sentence**) sentence of imprisonment for the rest of one's life made by a court of law: *be given/get/do life.* **8** [U] (**a**) business, pleasure and social activities of the world: *As a taxi-driver you really see life.* (**b**) activity; movement: *There are few signs of life here in the evenings.* **9** [U] liveliness; interest: *Children are always so full of life.* ○ *Put more life into your work.* **10** [U, C] way of living: *private/public life* ○ *Village life is too dull for me.* ○ *have an easy/hard life* ○ *Singing is her life,* ie the most important thing in her existence. ○ *That's the life (for me)!* ie the best way to live ○ *This is the life!* ie a very enjoyable way of living ○ *He's decided to emigrate and start a new life in America.* **11** [C] biography: *He's writing a life of Newton.* **12** [U] living model: *a portrait drawn/taken from life* ○ [attrib] *a ˈlife class,* ie one in which art students draw, etc from living models. **13** [C] period during which sth continues to exist or function: *throughout the life of the present government* ○ [attrib] *a long-life battery.* **14** [C] (**a**) fresh start or opportunity after a narrow escape: *The batsman was given a life* (eg because a fielder missed an easy catch) *when his score was 24.* (**b**) (in children's games) one of a set number of chances before a player is out of the game. **15** (idm) **at one's time of life** ⇨ TIME[1]. **the bane of sb's existence/life** ⇨ BANE. **bet one's life that...** ⇨ BET[1]. **the breath of life** ⇨ BREATH. **bring sb/sth to ˈlife** give sb/sth vitality: *Let's invite Ted — he knows how to bring a party to life.* **a cat-and-dog life** ⇨ CAT[1]. **the change of life** ⇨ CHANGE[2]. **come to ˈlife** become animated: *You're very cool with your brother, but with your friends you really come to life.* ○ *Sunrise — and the farm comes to life again.* **depart this life** ⇨ DEPART. **end one's days/life** ⇨ END[2]. **expectation of life** ⇨ EXPECTATION. **a fact of life** ⇨ FACT. **the facts of life** ⇨ FACT. **for dear ˈlife/one's ˈlife** (as if) in order to escape death: *Run for your life!* **for the ˈlife of one** (*infml*) however hard one tries: *I cannot for the life of me remember her name.* **frighten the life out of sb** ⇨ FRIGHTEN. **full of beans/life** ⇨ FULL. **have the time of one's life** ⇨ TIME[1]. **in fear of one's life** ⇨ FEAR[1]. **in peril of one's life** ⇨ PERIL. **large as life** ⇨ LARGE. **larger than life** ⇨ LARGE. **lay down one's life (for sb/sth)** (*rhet*) sacrifice one's life: *He laid down his life for the cause of freedom.* **lead a dog's life** ⇨ LEAD[3]. **lead sb a dog's life** ⇨ LEAD[3]. **ˌlife and ˈlimb** one's survival from accident or injury: *Fire-fighters risk life and limb every day in their work.* **the life and soul of sth** (*infml*) the most lively and amusing person present at a party, etc. **the love of sb's life** ⇨ LOVE[1]. **make (sb's) life a ˈmisery** cause sb to be unhappy or suffer pain in daily life: *Having unpleasant neighbours can make one's life an absolute misery.* **make one's way in life** ⇨ WAY[2]. **a matter of life and death** ⇨ MATTER[1]. **a new lease of life** ⇨ NEW. **not on your (sweet) ˈlife!** (*infml*) certainly not. **put an end to one's life/oneself** ⇨ END[1]. **sell one's life dearly** ⇨ SELL. **spring to life** ⇨ SPRING[3]. **the staff of life** ⇨ STAFF. **take one's (own) ˈlife** commit suicide. **take one's life in one's hands** risk being killed: *You take your life in your hands simply crossing the road these days!* **take sb's ˈlife** kill sb. **to the ˈlife** exactly like the original: *draw, imitate, resemble sb to the life.* **true to life** ⇨ TRUE. **walk of life** ⇨ WALK[2]. **a/sb's way of life** ⇨ WAY[1].

▷ **lifeless** *adj* **1** never having had life: *lifeless stones* ○ *a lifeless planet.* **2** dead: *the lifeless bodies of the slaughtered animals.* **3** lacking vitality; dull: *a lifeless performance.* **lifelessly** *adv.* **lifelessness** *n* [U].

lifer /ˈlaɪfə(r)/ *n* (*sl*) **1** person sentenced to life imprisonment. **2** (*US*) person who joins the armed forces as a career.

□ **ˌlife-and-ˈdeath** (also **ˌlife-or-ˈdeath**) *adj* [attrib] serious; crucial; deciding between life and death: *desert animals locked in a life-and-death struggle with the elements* ○ (*fig*) *a life-or-death attempt to reach the grand final.*

ˌlife anˈnuity (*finance*) annuity paid for the rest of a person's life.

ˈlife assurance, ˈlife insurance type of insurance policy providing a specified payment on the death of the holder.

lifebelt (*also* lifebuoy) life-jacket

ˈlifebelt (also **ˈlifebuoy**) *n* ring of buoyant or inflatable material used to keep afloat a person who has fallen into water.

ˈlife-blood *n* [U] **1** blood necessary to life. **2** (*fig*) thing that gives strength and vitality: *Credit is the life-blood of the consumer society.*

ˈlifeboat *n* (**a**) small boat carried on a ship for use if the ship has to be abandoned at sea. (**b**) boat specially built for going to the help of people in danger in the sea along a coast.

ˈlife cycle (*biology*) series of forms into which a living thing changes as it develops: *the life cycle of the butterfly.*

ˈlife expectancy (**a**) number of years that a person is likely to live, esp as statistically determined for insurance purposes: *Women have a higher life expectancy than men.* (**b**) length of time sth is likely to exist or function: *the life expectancy of the average car, the present government.*

ˈlife-giving *adj* [esp attrib] that restores life or vitality.

ˈlife-guard *n* expert swimmer employed to rescue bathers in difficulty or danger.

the ˈLife Guards cavalry regiment in the British army.

ˌlife ˈhistory (*biology*) record of the life cycle of an organism.

ˌlife ˈinterest (*law*) benefit (from property, etc) valid during sb's life.

ˈlife-jacket *n* sleeveless jacket of buoyant or inflatable material used to keep afloat a person in danger of drowning. ⇨ illus.

ˈlifelike *adj* exactly like a real person or thing: *a lifelike statue, drawing, toy.*

ˈlifeline *n* **1** (*nautical*) (**a**) line or rope for saving life such as that attached to a lifebelt, or fastened along the deck of a ship in a storm for sailors to hold on to. (**b**) line attached to a deep-sea diver. **2** (*fig*) anything on which sb/sth depends for continued existence: *Public transport is a lifeline for many rural communities.*

ˈlifelong *adj* [attrib] extending throughout one's life: *a lifelong interest, friendship, wish.*

ˌlife ˈpeer peer whose title is granted only to himself, and is not inherited by his heirs. ⇨ article at ARISTOCRAT.

ˈlife-preserver *n* (*US*) life-jacket.

ˈlife-raft *n* raft (esp inflatable) for emergency use at sea.

ˈlife-saver *n* (**a**) (*Austral or NZ*) life-guard. (**b**) thing that restores, benefits or is of great assistance: *The clothes-dryer was a life-saver during the wet weather.*

ˈlife sciences biology and related subjects.

ˈlife-size(d) *adj* of the same size as the person or thing represented: *The statue is twice life-size.*

ˈlife-span *n* length of time that sth is likely to live, continue or function: *Some insects have a life-span of no more than a few hours.*

ˈlife story biography: *She told me her life story.*

ˈlife-style *n* way of life of an individual or group: *He and his brother have quite different life-styles.*

ˌlife-supˈport *adj* [attrib] (of equipment) enabling sb to live in a hostile environment (eg a spacecraft) or when natural bodily functions have failed (eg following an accident). **ˌlife-supˈport system** such equipment used to keep a person alive.

ˈlifetime *n* **1** duration of sb's life or sth's existence: *a lifetime of service* ○ *In your lifetime you must have seen many changes.* ○ [attrib] *a lifetime subscription (to a magazine, etc).* **2** (idm) **the chance, etc of a ˈlifetime** an exceptional opportunity, etc: *Book now for the holiday of a lifetime!*

ˌlife-ˈwork (also **ˌlife's-ˈwork**) *n* (usu *sing*) activity that occupies one's whole life.

lift /lɪft/ *v* **1** [Tn, Tn·pr, Tn·p] ~ **sb/sth (up)** raise sb/sth to a higher level or position: *Lift me up, mummy — I can't see.* ○ *Three men were lifted by helicopter from the burning ship.* ○ (*fig*) *This piece of luck lifted his spirits.* **2** [Tn·pr] take (sth) from its resting-place in order to move it: *lift a box into a lorry, out of a train, down from a shelf, etc.* **3** [I] (of clouds, fog, etc) rise; disperse: *The mist began to lift.* ○ (*fig*) *Her heart lifted at the sight of him.* **4** [Tn] dig up (vegetables); remove (plants) from the ground: *lift potatoes, turnips, etc.* **5** [Tn, Tn·pr] ~ **sth (from sb/sth)** (*infml*) (**a**) steal sth: *She was caught lifting make-up from the supermarket.* (**b**) copy (material) from another source without permission or acknowledgement: *Many of his ideas were lifted from other authors.* **6** [Tn] remove or abolish (restrictions): *lift a ban, embargo, curfew, etc.* **7** [Tn, Tn·pr, Tn·p] transport (goods, livestock, people) esp by air: *fresh tomatoes lifted in from the Canary Islands.* **8** (idm) **have one's face lifted** ⇨ FACE[1]. **lift/raise a finger/hand (to do sth)** (*infml*) (usu negative) give help (with sth): *He never lifts a finger round the house,* ie never helps with the housework. **lift/raise a hand/one's hand against sb** ⇨ HAND[1]. **lift (up) one's eyes (to sth)** (*rhet*) look up. **lift/raise one's voice** ⇨ VOICE. **9** (phr v) **lift off** (of a rocket or spacecraft) rise from the launching site.

▷ **lift** *n* **1** [sing] lifting; being lifted: *Give him a lift: he's too small to see anything.* **2** [C] (*Brit*) (*US* **elevator**) box-like device for moving people or goods from one floor of a building to another: *It's on the sixth floor — let's take the lift.* **3** [C] free ride in a private vehicle: *I'll give you a lift to the station.* ○ *thumb/hitch a lift,* ie hitch-hike. **4** [U] upward pressure that air exerts on an aircraft in flight. Cf DRAG[1] 2. **5** [sing] feeling of elation: *Winning the scholarship gave her a tremendous lift.*

□ **ˈlift-off** *n* vertical take-off of a rocket or spacecraft: *We have lift-off.*

ˈlift-attendant *n* (*US* **elevator operator**) person who operates a lift(2).

ligament /ˈlɪɡəmənt/ *n* tough flexible tissue in a person's or an animal's body that connects bones and holds organs in position: *tear/pull a ligament.*

ligature /ˈlɪɡətʃə(r)/ *n* **1** thread, bandage, etc used for tying, esp in surgical operations. **2** (*music*) smooth combination of two or more notes of different pitch, or mark indicating this; slur; tie. **3** (in printing) two or more joined letters, such as œ or fl.

light[1] /laɪt/ *n* **1** [U] (**a**) kind of natural radiation that makes things visible: *the light of the sun, a lamp, the fire, etc.* (**b**) amount or quality of this: *The light was beginning to fail,* ie It was getting dark. ○ *This light is too poor to read by.* ○ *the flickering light of candles* ○ (*fig*) *A soft light* (ie expression) *came into her eyes as she looked at him.* Cf DARK[1]. **2** [C] source of light, esp an electric lamp: *turn/switch the lights on/off* ○ *Far below the plane we could see the lights of London.* ○ *A light was still burning in his study.* ○ *That car hasn't got its lights* (ie headlights) *on.* ○ *Keep going, the lights* (ie traffic lights) *are green.* **3** [C] (thing used to produce a) flame or spark: *Have you got a light?* eg for a cigarette. **4** [U] understanding; enlightenment: *I wrestled with the crossword clue for ages before light finally dawned,* ie I understood the solution. **5** [C] (esp in compounds) (*architecture*) window or opening to admit light: *skylight* ○ *leaded light.* **6** [U, C usu *sing*] (*art*) part of a picture shown as lighted up: *light and shade.* **7** (idm) **according to one's ˈlights** (*fml*) in conformity with one's beliefs, attitudes or abilities: *We can't blame him: he did his best according to his lights.* **at first light** ⇨ FIRST. **be/stand in sb's ˈlight** be placed between sb and a source of light: *Can you move? You're in my light and I can't read.* **the bright lights** ⇨ BRIGHT. **bring sth to ˈlight** reveal sth; make sth known: *New facts have been brought to light.* **by the light of nature** without special guidance or teaching. **cast/shed/throw light on sth** make sth clearer: *Recent research has shed new light on the causes of the disease.* **come to light** be revealed; become known: *New evidence has recently come to light.* **give sb/get the green light** ⇨ GREEN[1]. **go out like a ˈlight** (*infml*) faint or fall asleep suddenly. **hide one's light under a bushel** ⇨ HIDE[1]. **in a good, bad, favourable, etc ˈlight** (a) (of a picture, etc) so as to be seen well, badly, etc: *Two pictures have been hung in a bad light.* (b) (*fig*) well, badly, favourably, etc: *Press reports make his actions appear in the worst possible light.* ○ *It is hard to view his conduct in a favourable light.* **in the cold light of day** ⇨ COLD[1]. **in the light of sth** (*US* **in light of sth**) in view of sth; considering sth: *review the proposals in the light of past experience.* **jump the lights** ⇨ JUMP[2]. **light at the end of the tunnel** success, happiness, etc after a long period of difficulty or hardship. **lights out** (in barracks, dormitories, etc) time when lights are (to be) turned out: *Lights out!* ○ *No talking after lights out.* **see the ˈlight** (a) understand or accept sth after much difficulty or doubt. (b) be converted to religious belief. **see the light (of ˈday)** (a) (*rhet*) be born. (b) (of abstract things) be conceived or made public: *The notion of a Channel Tunnel first saw the light of day more than a century ago.* **set light to sth** cause sth to start burning. **strike a light** ⇨ STRIKE[2]. **sweetness and light** ⇨ SWEETNESS (SWEET[1]).

▷ **light** *adj.* Cf DARK[2]. **1** full of light; not in darkness: *a light airy room* ○ *In spring the evenings start to get lighter.* **2** pale: *Light colours suit you best.* ○ *light-green eyes.* **ˈlight-coloured** *adj*: *I prefer light-coloured fabrics.*

□ **ˈlight bulb** = BULB[2].

ˈlighthouse *n* tower or other structure containing a beacon light to warn or guide ships.

ˈlight meter = EXPOSURE METER (EXPOSURE).

ˈlight pen (*computing*) (also **wand**) photoelectric device, shaped like a pen, that can communicate with a computer either by making marks on the screen of a visual display unit or by reading the pattern of a bar code.

ˈlightship *n* moored or anchored ship with a beacon light, serving the same purpose as a lighthouse.

ˈlight-year *n* **1** (*astronomy*) distance that light travels in one year (about 6 million million miles). **2 light-years** [pl] (*infml fig*) a very long time: *Genuine racial equality still seems light-years away.*

light[2] /laɪt/ *v* (*pt, pp* **lit** /lɪt/ or **lighted**) (*Lighted* is used esp as an attributive *adj*, as in *a lighted candle*, but Cf *He lit the candle* and *The candles were lit.*) **1** [I, Tn, Tn·pr] (cause sth to) begin burning: *This wood is so damp it won't light.* ○ *light a cigarette* ○ *Let's light a fire in the living-room tonight.* **2** [Tn] turn on (an electric lamp, etc): *Light the torch — I can't see the path.* **3** [Tn, Tn·pr] provide (sth) with light: *These streets are very poorly lit.* ○ *Nowadays, houses are mostly lit by electricity.* **4** [Tn·pr] guide (sb) with a light: *a candle to light your way.* **5** (phr v) **light (sth) up** (*infml*) begin to smoke (a cigarette, etc): *light up a pipe.* **light up (with sth)** (of a person's face, etc) become bright or animated: *Her eyes lit up with joy.* **light sth up** (a) illuminate sth: *a castle lit up with floodlights* ○ *flashes of lightning lit up the sky.* (b) make (a person's face, etc) bright or animated: *A rare smile lit up his stern features.*

▷ **ˈlighting** *n* [U] **1** equipment for providing light for a room, building, etc: *street lighting.* **2** the light itself: *Subtle lighting helps people relax.* **ˌlighting-ˈup time** time when road vehicle lights must be turned on.

□ **lit up** /ˌlɪt ˈʌp/ (*sl*) drunk.

light[3] /laɪt/ *adj* (**-er, -est**) **1** easy to lift or move; not heavy: *He's lost a lot of weight: he's three kilos lighter than he used to be.* ○ *Carry this bag — it's the lightest.* **2** (a) [esp attrib] of less than average weight: *This coat is light but very warm.* ○ *light shoes, clothing*, ie for summer wear ○ *The old bridge can only be used by light vehicles.* ○ *a light aircraft.* (b) [attrib] designed for small loads: *a light railway.* **3** (following *ns*) less than the expected weight: *This sack of potatoes is five kilos light.* **4** [esp attrib] gentle; delicate: *a light tap on the shoulder, a light patter of rain on the window* ○ *a light knock on the door*, ie not loud ○ *be light on one's feet*, ie agile or nimble. **5** [esp attrib] (a) easy to carry out or perform: *Since her accident she can only do light work.* ○ *take a little light exercise.* (b) easy to understand: *I took some light reading* (eg a thriller) *for the train journey.* ○ *light music, comedy, entertainment*, ie not serious or difficult. **6** easy to bear; not severe: *The company was fined £1 000, which critics said was too light.* ○ *a light attack of flu.* **7** not intense: *The wind is very light.* ○ *Trading on the Stock Exchange was light today.* ○ *light showers of rain.* **8** [esp attrib] not dense: *light traffic* ○ *The river was visible through a light mist.* ○ *This plant will only grow in light* (ie sandy) *soil.* **9** (a) (of meals) small in quantity: *a light snack, supper, etc.* (b) (of food) that is easy to digest: *a light pudding* ○ *Her soufflés are always so light.* **10** [attrib] (of sleep) not deep: *Please don't make any noise — my mother's a very light sleeper*, ie wakes easily. **11** [esp attrib] (of drinks) low in alcohol: *light ale* ○ *a light white wine.* **12** [esp attrib] cheerful; free from worry: *with a light heart.* **13** (idm) **(as) ˌlight as ˈair/as a ˈfeather** very light. **light reˈlief** words or actions that relax tension or relieve concentration: *His humour provided some welcome light relief.* **make light of sth** treat sth as unimportant: *He made light of his injury*, ie said it was not serious. **make light work of sth** do sth with little effort: *We made light work of the tidying up.* **many hands make light ˈwork** ⇨ HAND[1].

▷ **light** *adv* with little luggage or possessions (used esp in the expression shown): *travel light.*

lightly *adv* **1** in a light manner. **2** without serious consideration: *Marriage is not something to be undertaken lightly.* **3** (idm) **get off ˈlightly/ˈcheaply** (*infml*) escape serious punishment or inconvenience.

lightness *n* [U]: *great lightness of touch*, eg when playing the piano.

□ **ˌlighter-than-ˈair** *adj* (of an aircraft, eg a balloon) weighing less than the volume of air it takes up.

ˌlight-ˈfingered *adj* (*infml*) in the habit of stealing (esp small) things.

ˌlight-ˈheaded *adj* feeling slightly faint or dizzy. **ˌlight-ˈheadedly** *adv*, **ˌlight-ˈheadedness** *n* [U].

ˌlight-ˈhearted *adj* (a) without cares; cheerful. (b) (*derog*) not serious or sensible enough; casual. **ˌlight-ˈheartedly** *adv*, **ˌlight-ˈheartedness** *n* [U].

ˌlight-ˈheavyweight *n* boxer weighing between 72.5 and 79.5 kg, next above middleweight.

ˌlight ˈindustry industry producing small consumer goods or components.

ˈlightweight *n, adj* **1** (boxer) weighing between 57 and 61 kg, next above featherweight: *the European lightweight champion.* **2** (*infml*) (person or thing) of little influence or importance: *a political lightweight* ○ *a lightweight news item.*

light[4] /laɪt/ *v* (*pt, pp* **lit** /lɪt/ or **lighted**) (phr v) **light into sb** (*sl*) attack sb (physically or verbally). **light on/upon sb/sth** find sb/sth by chance: *Luckily, I lit on a secondhand copy of the book.* **light out** (*US sl*) leave quickly: *I lit out for home.*

lighten[1] /ˈlaɪtn/ *v* [I, Tn] **1** (cause sth to) become lighter in weight: *lighten a burden, cargo, pack, etc.* **2** (cause sth to) be relieved of care or worry: *My mood gradually lightened.* ○ *lighten sb's duties.*

lighten[2] /ˈlaɪtn/ *v* **1** [Tn] make (sth) brighter: *These new windows have lightened the room considerably.* **2** [I] (*fig*) become brighter: *His face lightened as she apologized.*

lighter[1] /ˈlaɪtə(r)/ *n* = CIGARETTE-LIGHTER (CIGARETTE): *a ciˈgar lighter.*

lighter[2] /ˈlaɪtə(r)/ *n* flat-bottomed boat used for loading and unloading ships not brought to a quay or in transporting goods for short distances. Cf PINNACE.

▷ **ˈlighterage** /ˈlaɪtərɪdʒ/ *n* [U] (a) transport of goods by lighter. (b) charge for this.

□ **ˈlighterman** /-mən/ *n* (*pl* **ˈlightermen** /-mən/) person who works on a lighter.

lightning[1] /ˈlaɪtnɪŋ/ *n* **1** [U] flash of brilliant light in the sky produced by natural electricity passing between clouds or from clouds to the ground, usu followed by thunder: *be struck by lightning* ○ *a flash of lightning.* **2** (idm) **lightning never strikes in the same place twice** (*saying*) an unusual event, or one that happens by chance, is not likely to occur again in exactly the same circumstances or to the same people. **like (greased) ˈlightning; like a streak of lightning; (as) quick as ˈlightning** very fast.

□ **ˈlightning-bug** *n* (*US*) firefly.

ˈlightning conductor (*Brit*) (*US* **lightning rod**) metal rod or wire fixed to an exposed part of a building, etc to prevent damage by lightning.

lightning[2] /ˈlaɪtnɪŋ/ *adj* [attrib] **1** rapid, brief or sudden: *Police made a lightning raid on the house.* **2** (idm) **with lightning ˈspeed** very fast.

□ **lightning ˈstrike** sudden industrial stoppage taken without warning: *a lightning strike called to protest about the dismissal of a workmate.*

lights /laɪts/ *n* [pl] lungs of sheep, pigs, etc used as food.

lightsome /ˈlaɪtsəm/ *adj* (*arch or rhet*) moving with grace and ease.

ligneous /ˈlɪgnɪəs/ *adj* (of plants) woody.

lignite /ˈlɪgnaɪt/ *n* [U] soft brownish coal.

lignum vitae /ˌlɪgnəm ˈvaɪtiː, ˈviːtaɪ/ [C, U] (very hard wood of a) type of tropical American tree.

like[1] /laɪk/ *v* **1** (a) [Tn, Tg, Tsg] find (sb/sth) pleasant or satisfactory; enjoy: *Do you like fish?* ○ *She likes him* (ie is fond of him) *but doesn't love him.* ○ *She's never liked swimming.* ○ *I didn't like him/his taking all the credit.* (b) [Tt, Tnt] (no passive) [Cn·a] regularly choose (to do sth); prefer (to do sth): *On Sundays I like to sleep late.* ○ *He likes his guests to be punctual.* ○ *'How do you like your tea?' 'I like it rather weak.'* **2** [Tt, Tg] (in negative sentences) be unwilling or reluctant to do sth: *I didn't like* (ie felt reluctant) *to disturb you.* ○ *He doesn't like asking for help.* **3** [Tn, Tt, Tnt] (used with *should/would/'d* to express a wish or preference at a particular time): *Would you like something to eat?* ○ *I'd like to think it over before deciding.* ○ *We would like you to come and visit us.* ○ (*ironic*) *So he thinks it's easy, does he? I'd like to see him try!* ie He would find it difficult. ⇨ Usage at WANT[1]. **4** [Tn] (*infml*) (of food) not suit sb's health: *I like lobster but it doesn't like me.* **5** (idm) **if you ˈlike** (used as a polite form of agreement or suggestion): *'Shall we stop now?' 'If you like'* ○ *If you like, we could go out this evening.* **I like his ˈnerve, ˈcheek, etc** (*ironic*) (used as an exclamation to complain that sb's behaviour is too impudent): *'She has written to demand an apology.' 'I like her nerve!'* **I like ˈthat!** (*ironic*) (used to protest that sth that has been said is untrue or unfair): *'She called you a cheat.' 'Well, I like that!'* **like the look/sound of sb/sth** be favourably impressed by what one has seen of/heard about sb/sth: *I like the look of your new assistant — she should do very well.* ○ *I don't like the sound of that cough — oughtn't you to see a doctor?* **that's what I'd like to know** (*infml*) (used to express disbelief, suspicion, etc): *Where's all the money coming from? That's what I'd like to know.*

▷ **likeable** (also **likable**) /ˈlaɪkəbl/ *adj* easy to like; pleasant: *He's likeable enough, but a bit boring.*

likes *n* [pl] (idm) **ˌlikes and ˈdislikes** things one does and does not like: *He has so many likes and dislikes that it's impossible to please him.*

NOTE ON USAGE: Note these ways of using **Would you like?**: **1** *'Would you like to come to dinner tomorrow?' 'Yes, thank you.'* (invitation). **2** *'Would you like to clear the table?' 'Okay.'* (request). Sometimes the speaker uses pattern **2** in order to make a complaint: *'Would you like to turn that music down?' 'Yes, sorry.'*

like[2] /laɪk/ *prep* **1** similar to (sb/sth); resembling: *wearing a hat like mine* ○ *a house built like an*

Indian palace ○ *I've always wanted a garden like theirs.* ○ *I'm going to be a pop star like Michael Jackson* ○ *He's like his father*, ie in character or looks. ○ *She looks a bit like the Queen.* ○ *That sounds like* (ie I think I can hear) *the postman.* **2** characteristic of (sb/sth): *It's just like her to tell everyone about it.* **3** in the manner of (sb/sth); to the same degree as: *chatter like monkeys* ○ *behave like children* ○ *run like the wind*, ie very fast. ⇨ Usage at AS. **4** for example: *We could look at some modern poets, like Eliot and Hughes.* ○ *Practical lessons, like woodwork and cookery, are not considered as important as maths.* **5** (idm) **like ˈanything** (*infml*) very fast, hard, much, etc: *I had to run like anything to catch the bus.* ○ *We must work like anything to finish on time.* **like ˈso** in this way: *You place the paper like so, and it feeds into the printer automatically.*

▷ **like** *conj* (*infml*) **1** in the same manner as: *No one sings the blues like she did.* ○ *Don't think you can learn grammatical rules like you learn multiplication tables.* **2** (*esp US*) as if: *She acts like she owns the place*, ie is very bossy.

like³ /laɪk/ *adj* **1** having some or all of the qualities or features of; similar: *They're not twins, but they're very like.* ○ *Like causes tend to produce like results.* ○ *mice, rats and like creatures.* **2** (idm) **(as) ˌlike as two ˈpeas/as ˌpeas in a ˈpod** virtually identical.

▷ **like** *adv* (idm) **(as) ˌlike as ˈnot; ˌlike eˈnough; most/very ˈlike** (*dated*) (quite/very) probably: *It'll rain this afternoon, as like as not.*

like *n* **1** [sing] person or thing that is like another: *You should only compare like with like.* ○ *jazz, rock and the like*, ie similar kinds of music ○ *a man whose like we shall not see again* ○ *I've never seen the like of it!* ie anything so strange, etc. **2** (idm) **the likes of sb/sth** (*infml*) a similar person or thing: *He's a bit of a snob — won't speak to the likes of me.*

□ **ˌlike-ˈminded** *adj* having similar tastes or opinions: *I have complained to my MP, and urge all ˌlike-minded ˈpeople to do the same.*

-like *suff* (used widely with *ns* to form *adjs*) similar to; resembling: *childlike* ○ *ladylike* ○ *shell-like* ○ *snake-like.*

likely /ˈlaɪklɪ/ *adj* **(-ier, -iest) 1** ~ **(to do sth/that...)** that is expected; probable: *the likely outcome, winner* ○ *It isn't likely to rain.* ○ *She's very likely to ring me tonight.* ○ *It's very likely that she'll ring me tonight.* **2** that seems suitable for a purpose: *This looks a likely field for mushrooms.* ○ *a likely-looking candidate*, ie one expected to succeed. **3** (idm) **a ˈlikely story** (*ironic*) (used to express scorn and disbelief about what sb has said): *He says he just forgot about it — a likely story!*

▷ **likelihood** /ˈlaɪklɪhʊd/ *n* [U] probability: *There's no likelihood of that happening.* ○ *In all likelihood* (ie Very probably) *the meeting will be cancelled.*

likely *adv* (idm) **as ˌlikely as ˈnot; most/very likely** (very) probably: *as likely as not she's forgotten all about it.* **not (bloody, etc) ˈlikely!** (*infml*) certainly not: *Me? Join the army? Not likely!*

liken /ˈlaɪkən/ *v* [Tn·pr] ~ **sth to sth** (*fml*) show the resemblance between one thing and another: *Life has often been likened to a journey.*

likeness /ˈlaɪknɪs/ *n* **1 (a)** [U] being alike; resemblance: *I can't see much likeness between him and his father.* **(b)** [C usu *sing*] instance of this: *All my children share a strong family likeness.* **2** [sing] (following an *adj*) extent to which a portrait, photograph, etc resembles the person portrayed: *That photo is a good likeness of David.*

likewise /ˈlaɪkwaɪz/ *adv* (*fml*) **1** similarly: *I'm going to bed and you would be well advised to do likewise.* **2** also: *The food was excellent, (and) likewise the wine.*

liking /ˈlaɪkɪŋ/ *n* (idm) **for one's liking** (used after an expression with *too* to show the speaker's dislike of sth): *It's too hot for my liking*, ie It's hotter than I like it to be. ○ *She's too much of a boaster for my liking.* **have a liking for sth** be fond of sth: *I've always had a liking for the sea.* **to sb's liking** (*fml*) giving sb satisfaction; pleasing sb: *I trust the meal was to your liking.*

lilac /ˈlaɪlək/ *n* **1 (a)** [C] shrub with sweet-smelling pale purple or white blossom: *The lilacs are in flower.* **(b)** [U] its blossom: *a bunch of lilac.* **2** [U] pale purple colour.

▷ **lilac** *adj* of a pale purple colour.

Lillibullero (also **Lilliburlero**) /ˌlɪlɪbəˈleərəʊ/ signature tune of the BBC World Service, originally a 17th-century satirical song.

lilliputian /ˌlɪlɪˈpjuːʃn/ *adj* (*fml*) on a small scale; tiny: *a model railway layout peopled with lilliputian figures.*

lilo /ˈlaɪləʊ/ *n* (*pl* ~**s**) (*Brit propr*) type of lightweight inflatable mattress for lying on, eg at the beach.

lilt /lɪlt/ *n* [sing] **1** rise and fall of the voice while speaking: *She has a faint Irish lilt.* **2** regular rising and falling pattern in music, usu accompanied by a lively rhythm.

▷ **lilting** *adj* having a lilt.

lily /ˈlɪlɪ/ *n* **1 (a)** any of various types of plant growing from a bulb, with large white or reddish flowers: *ˈwater lilies.* **(b)** type of lily with white flowers: *daffodils and lilies flowering in the spring.* **2** (idm) **gild the lily** ⇨ GILD.

□ **lily-livered** /ˈlɪlɪ lɪvəd/ *adj* (*dated*) cowardly.

ˈlily pad large round leaf of a water-lily floating on the surface of the water.

ˌlily of the ˈvalley plant with small sweet-smelling bell-shaped white flowers.

ˌlily-ˈwhite *adj* **1** (*rhet*) perfectly white, like the flower of the lily: *her ˌlily-white ˈhands.* **2** (*fig*) completely clean, pure or honest: *Few politicians are absolutely lily-white.*

limb /lɪm/ *n* **1** leg, arm or wing: *I need to sit down and rest my weary limbs.* **2** main branch of a tree. **3** (idm) **life and limb** ⇨ LIFE. **out on a ˈlimb** (*infml*) isolated and vulnerable; without supporters (used esp in the expressions shown): *leave sb/be/go out on a limb.* **sound in wind and limb** ⇨ SOUND¹. **tear sb limb from limb** ⇨ TEAR².

▷ **-limbed** /lɪmd/ (forming compound *adjs*) having limbs of the kind specified: *ˌlong-ˈlimbed* ○ *ˌweary-ˈlimbed* ○ *ˌloose-ˈlimbed*, ie supple.

limber¹ /ˈlɪmbə(r)/ *adj* (*dated*) supple; flexible.

▷ **limber** *v* (phr v) **ˌlimber ˈup** exercise in preparation for sport, etc; warm up (WARM²): *I always do a few easy exercises to limber up before a match.*

limber² /ˈlɪmbə(r)/ *n* detachable front part of a wheeled artillery gun, consisting of a frame and two wheels.

▷ **limber** [Tn, Tn·p] ~ **sth (up)** attach a limber to (a gun).

limbo¹ /ˈlɪmbəʊ/ *n* **1** (usu **Limbo**) [U] (in the Christian religion) place where it was once thought the souls of good people and young children went if they died without being baptized. **2** (idm) **in limbo** in an intermediate or uncertain state; neglected: *The project must remain in limbo until the committee makes its decision.*

limbo² /ˈlɪmbəʊ/ *n* (*pl* ~**s** /-bəʊz/) West Indian dance in which the dancer bends back and passes under a bar that is gradually lowered.

lime¹ /laɪm/ *n* [U] **1** (also **ˈquicklime**) white substance (calcium oxide) obtained by heating limestone, used in making cement and mortar and as a fertilizer. **2** = BIRDLIME (BIRD).

▷ **lime** *v* [Tn] treat (fields, etc) with lime to improve the soil.

□ **ˈlime-kiln** *n* kiln in which lime is produced.

ˈlimestone *n* [U] type of rock, eg chalk, composed esp of the remains of prehistoric plants and animals.

lime² /laɪm/ (also **ˈlime-tree, linden**) *n* tree with smooth heart-shaped leaves and fragrant yellow flowers.

lime³ /laɪm/ *n* **1** [C] (tree bearing) round fruit like a lemon but smaller and more acid. **2** [U] (also **lime green**) yellowish-green colour of this fruit.

□ **ˈlime-juice** *n* [U] juice of limes used for flavouring or as a drink.

limelight /ˈlaɪmlaɪt/ *n* [U] publicity or attention: *She claims she never sought the limelight.* ○ *When I was President, I was always in the limelight — there was no privacy.*

limerick /ˈlɪmərɪk/ *n* type of humorous poem with five lines, the first two rhyming with the last. The most famous writer of limericks was Edward *Lear. His humour was based on absurd situations, but most modern limericks are either satirical or indecent. ⇨ article at NURSERY RHYME.

limey /ˈlaɪmɪ/ *n* (*pl* ~**s**) (*US sl usu derog*) British person, usu male.

limit¹ /ˈlɪmɪt/ *n* [C] **1** point or line beyond which sth does not extend; boundary: *within the city limits* ○ (*fig*) *He tried my patience to its limits.* ○ *No fishing is allowed within a twenty-mile limit.* **2** greatest amount allowed or possible: *The speed limit on this road is 70 mph.* ○ *There's a limit to how much I'm prepared to spend.* **3** (idm) **(be) the limit** (*sl*) as much or more than one can tolerate: *You really are the (absolute) limit!* **ˌoff ˈlimits** (*US*) = OUT OF BOUNDS (BOUNDS). **the sky's the limit** ⇨ SKY. **within ˈlimits** in moderation; up to a point: *I'm willing to help, within limits.* **without ˈlimit** to any extent or degree.

▷ **limitless** *adj* without limit: *limitless ambition, greed, wealth.*

limit² /ˈlɪmɪt/ *v* [Tn, Tn·pr] ~ **sb/sth (to sth)** set a limit or limits to sb/sth; restrict sb/sth: *We must try and limit our expenditure.* ○ *I shall limit myself to three aspects of the subject.*

▷ **limited** *adj* restricted; few or small: *Only a limited number of places is available.* ○ *His intelligence is rather limited.* **ˌlimited eˈdition** (production of only a) fixed, usu small, number of copies. **ˌlimited liaˈbility company** (*abbr* **Ltd**) business company whose members are liable for its debts only to the extent of the capital sum they have provided: *Acme Interiors Ltd.* **ˌlimited ˈtrain** (*US*) fast train that makes few stops.

limiting *adj* imposing limits; restrictive: *Time is the limiting factor.*

limitation /ˌlɪmɪˈteɪʃn/ *n* **1** [U] limiting; being limited: *resist any limitation of their powers.* **2** [C] condition, fact or circumstance that limits: *impose limitations on imports, expenditure, reporting.* **3** [C] lack of ability: *He knows his limitations*, ie knows what he can and cannot achieve.

limousine /ˈlɪməziːn, ˌlɪməˈziːn/ *n* large luxurious car, esp with a glass partition separating driver and passengers.

limp¹ /lɪmp/ *adj* **1** not stiff or firm: *a limp edition*, ie a book with a flexible binding. **2** lacking strength or energy: *a limp handshake, gesture, response* ○ *The flowers looked limp in the heat.* ▷ **limply** *adv.* **limpness** *n* [U].

limp² /lɪmp/ *v* **1** [I, Ipr, Ip] walk unevenly, as when one foot or leg is hurt or stiff: *That dog must be hurt — he's limping.* ○ *The injured footballer limped slowly off the field.* ○ *limp about, along, away, off* ○ (*fig*) *The third act limps badly.* ⇨ Usage at SHUFFLE. **2** [Ipr] (of a ship, etc) proceed with difficulty in a specified direction, esp after an accident: *After the collision both vessels managed to limp into harbour.*

▷ **limp** *n* [sing] limping walk: *walk with/have a bad, slight, etc limp.*

limpet /ˈlɪmpɪt/ *n* small shellfish that sticks tightly to rocks: *cling, hold on, etc (to sb/sth) like a limpet*, ie very tenaciously.

□ **ˈlimpet mine** mine²(2b) that is attached to a ship, usu by magnets, and explodes after a certain time.

limpid /ˈlɪmpɪd/ *adj* (of liquids, etc) clear; transparent: *limpid eyes.* ▷ **limpidity** /lɪmˈpɪdətɪ/ *n* [U]. **limpidly** *adv.*

linchpin /ˈlɪntʃpɪn/ *n* **1** pin passed through the end of an axle to keep the wheel in position. **2** (*fig*) person or thing that is vital to an organization, plan, etc: *Controlling wages is the linchpin of the Government's policies.*

Lincoln /ˈlɪŋkən/ Abraham (1809-65), American politician, 16th president of the USA 1861-65. As president he supported the policy of ending slavery in the USA. The southern states left the Union because of this, and eventually it led to the American Civil War. Lincoln issued a proclamation in 1861 freeing all slaves, and Congress later amended the Constitution to end slavery. He won great popularity through the simplicity and directness of his speeches. He was assassinated shortly after the end of the Civil War. ⇨ App 2.

□ **the ˈLincoln Center** (also **the ˌLincoln ˌCenter for the PerˌformingˈArts**) set of theatres, concert halls, etc in New York, including the New York Theater, used by the city's opera and ballet companies, the Metropolitan Opera, the Philharmonic Hall and the Juilliard School of Music.

Lincoln green /ˌlɪŋkən ˈgri:n/ bright green, supposed to have been the colour of the clothes worn by *Robin Hood and his outlaws.

Lincolnshire /ˈlɪŋkənʃə(r)/ eastern county of England. Much of it is flat agricultural land: grain, vegetables and bulbs are grown. ⇨ map at App 1.

Lincoln's Inn /ˌlɪŋkənz ˈɪn/ one of the four *Inns of Court.

linctus /ˈlɪŋktəs/ *n* [U] (*Brit*) syrupy medicine to soothe coughs.

Lindbergh /ˈlɪndbɜ:g/ Charles (1902-74), American aviation pioneer. He won international fame when he made the first solo flight across the Atlantic in 1927. He later opposed the entry of the USA into the Second World War.

linden /ˈlɪndən/ *n* = LIME².

Lindisfarne /ˈlɪndɪsfɑ:n/ (also **Holy Island**) small island off the coast of Northumberland, NE England. A monastery was founded there in the 7th century AD which became a centre of the Celtic Church.

□ **the ˌLindisfarne ˈGospels** illustrated manuscript of the Gospels produced about 700 AD, which contains early examples of the northern dialect of Old English.

line¹ /laɪn/ *n* **1** [C] **(a)** long narrow mark, either straight or curved, traced on a surface: *a straight line* ○ *Sign your name on the dotted line.* ○ *Don't park on the double yellow lines*, ie those painted at the side of a road in Britain. ○ *Draw a line from A to B.* **(b)** mark like a line on the skin: *The old man's face was covered in lines and wrinkles.* **2** [U] use of lines in art: *Line and colour are both important in portrait painting.* **3 lines** [pl] overall shape; outline: *the graceful lines of the ship.* **4 (a)** [C] (usu **the line**) (in sport) mark on the ground to show the limits of a pitch, court, race-track, etc: *first across the line*, ie in a race ○ *If the ball crosses the line it is out.* **(b)** [C] boundary: *cross the line* (ie border) *from Mexico into the US.* **(c) the Line** [sing] the equator. **5** [C] series of connected defence posts, trenches, etc: *the front line*, ie that nearest to the enemy ○ *a safe position well behind the lines.* **6** [C] row of people or things: *a line of customers queuing* ○ *lines of trees in an orchard* ○ *a long line of low hills.* **7** [C usu *sing*] series of people following one another in time, esp generations of the same family: *a line of kings* ○ *the Stuart line* ○ *in the male/female line* ○ *descended from King David in a direct line.* **8 (a)** [C] row of words on a page of writing or in print: *page 5, line 13* ○ *The last two lines* (ie of verse) *rhyme.* **(b)** [C] (*infml*) letter: *Just a short line to say thanks.* **(c) lines** [pl] words spoken by a particular actor: *Have you learnt your lines yet?* **(d) lines** [pl] (in schools) punishment in which a pupil is required to write out a specified number of lines: *The maths teacher was furious and gave me 50 lines.* **9** [C] **(a)** piece or length of thread, rope, etc used for a particular purpose: *a ˈfishing-line* ○ *Hang (out) the clothes on the line.* **(b)** (*esp nautical*) rope. **10** [C] (equipment providing a) telephone connection: *Our firm has twenty lines.* ○ *I'm sorry, the line is engaged.* ○ *a bad* (eg noisy) *line.* **11** [C] **(a)** single track of a railway: *The train was delayed because of ice on the line.* **(b)** one section of a railway system: *a ˈbranch line* ○ *the main ˈline* ○ *the second stop from Oxford on the Worcester line.* **12** [sing] course of action, behaviour or thought: *Don't take that line with me.* ○ *I absolutely reject the management's line on this.* ○ *She always takes a Marxist line.* **13** [sing] ~ (**of sth**) direction or course: *the line of ˈmarch (of an army, etc).* **14** [C] system of ships, buses, aircraft, etc regularly moving passengers or goods between certain places: *a ˈshipping line* ○ *an ˈair line.* **15 the lines** [pl] (esp in the army) row of tents, huts, etc. **16 the line** [sing] **(a)** (*Brit*) (in the army) regular infantry regiments (excluding the Guards). **(b)** (*US*) (in the army) regular regiments of all kinds. **17** [sing] (in the army) double row of soldiers standing side by side: *attack in extended line.* **18** [sing] **(a)** department of activity; type of business: *He's something in the ˈbanking line.* ○ *Her line is more selling than production.* ○ *That's not (much in) my line*, ie not one of my skills or interests. **(b)** type of product: *This shop has a nice line in winter coats.* **19** (idm) **all along the ˈline** (*infml*) in every way; at every point: *I've trusted you all along the line and now you've let me down.* **along/on the same, etc ˈlines** in the way specified: *Could you write another programme on the same lines?* ○ *The novel develops along traditional lines.* **be in the firing line** ⇨ FIRE². **bring sth, come, fall, get, move, etc into ˈline (with sb/sth)** (cause sth to) conform: *He'll have to fall into line with the others.* **draw the line at sth/doing sth** ⇨ DRAW². **drop sb a line** ⇨ DROP². **the end of the line/road** ⇨ END¹. **get, have, etc one's ˈlines crossed (a)** be unable to contact sb by telephone because of a technical fault: *I can't get through — the lines must be crossed.* **(b)** (*infml*) fail to communicate with or understand sb else correctly. **give sb/get/have a line on sth** (*infml*) give sb/get/have information about sth. **hard lines** ⇨ HARD¹. **hold the ˈline** keep a telephone connection open: *Hold the line while I see if she's here.* **hook, line and sinker** ⇨ HOOK¹. **in (a) line (with sth)** so as to form a straight line with sth; level with sth else: *Place your right toe in line with your left heel.* **(stand) in/on line** (*US*) in a queue. **in line for sth** likely to get sth: *She's in line for promotion.* **in the ˌline of ˈduty** while doing one's duty. **in line with sth** similar to sth; in accordance with sth: *in line with the others/with the latest research.* **ˌlay it on the ˈline** (*infml*) talk frankly and openly: *Let me lay it on the line — I think you're cheating.* **(choose, follow, take, etc) the line of least reˈsistance** the easiest way of doing sth. **(put sth) on the line** (*infml*) at risk: *If this goes wrong your job's on the line.* **out of ˈline (with sb/sth) (a)** not forming a straight line: *One of the soldiers is out of line.* **(b)** unacceptably different: *Our prices are out of line with those of our competitors.* **read between the lines** ⇨ READ. **shoot a line** ⇨ SHOOT¹. **sign on the dotted line** ⇨ SIGN². **somewhere, etc along the ˈline** at a certain stage during a process: *He started off enthusiastically but at some point along the line boredom set in.* **step out of line** ⇨ STEP¹. **take a firm, etc line (on/over sth)** deal with a problem or an issue in a firm, etc way. **take a hard line** ⇨ HARD¹. **toe the line** ⇨ TOE *v.*

□ **ˈline-drawing** *n* drawing done with a pen, pencil, etc.

ˌline of ˈfire direction in which guns, etc are fired: *Our patrol came into their line of fire.*

ˌline of ˈvision (also **ˌline of ˈsight**) imaginary straight line from a person's eyes to the thing being looked at: *Wait till the target crosses your line of vision.*

ˈline printer (*computing*) high-speed printer producing a complete line of text at a time.

line² /laɪn/ *v* **1** [esp passive: Tn, Tn·pr] mark (sth) with lines: *lined paper*, ie with lines printed on it ○ *a face lined with age and worry.* **2** [Tn, Tn·pr] form a line along (sth): *a road lined with trees* ○ *Crowds of people lined the route of the procession.* **3** (phr v) **line up (for sth)** (*US*) form a queue. **line (sb) up** (cause sth to) form a line: *line up the suspects/get the suspects to line up.* **line sth up** (*infml*) arrange or organize sth: *I've got rather a lot lined up* (ie I'm very busy) *this week.* ○ *He's lined up a live band for the party.*

□ **ˈline-out** *n* (in Rugby football) two parallel lines of opposing forwards jumping for the ball when it is thrown in from the touchline.

ˈline-up *n* **1** line of people formed for inspection, etc: *a line-up of men in an identification parade.* **2** any set of people, items, etc arranged for a purpose: *Jones will be missing from the team line-up.* ○ *A film completes this evening's TV line-up.*

line³ /laɪn/ *v* **1** [esp passive: Tn, Tn·pr] ~ **sth (with sth)** cover the inside surface of sth with a layer of different material: *an overcoat lined with silk* ○ *fur-lined gloves* ○ *Line the drawers with paper before you use them.* ○ *The walls of the room were lined with books.* **2** (idm) **line one's (own)/sb's ˈpocket(s)** (cause sb to) make a lot of money, esp by dishonest or corrupt methods.

lineage /ˈlɪnɪɪdʒ/ *n* [U] (*fml*) line of descent from an ancestor; ancestry: *trace one's lineage back many centuries* ○ *be of humble lineage.*

lineal /ˈlɪnɪəl/ *adj* [usu attrib] **1** (*fml*) in the direct line of descent: *a lineal heir to the title.* **2** = LINEAR. ▷ **lineally** /-ɪəlɪ/ *adv*: *lineally descended from sb.*

lineaments /ˈlɪnɪəmənts/ *n* [pl] (*fml*) features of the face, etc: (*fig*) *the lineaments* (ie main factors) *of the situation.*

linear /ˈlɪnɪə(r)/ *adj* **1** of or in lines: *a linear design* ○ *linear perspective*, ie using real or imaginary converging lines to show distance. **2** [attrib] of length: *linear measure*, eg metres, feet, inches. ⇨ App 10. ▷ **linearity** /ˌlɪnɪˈærətɪ/ *n* [U].

□ **ˌlinear acˈcelerator** (*physics*) apparatus used in nuclear research which makes charged particles move at high speed in a straight line.

ˌlinear eˈquation (*mathematics*) equation between two variables which appears as a straight line when it is presented on a graph.

ˌlinear ˈprogramming mathematical technique used esp for efficient planning by maximizing or minimizing a function (eg output or cost) of several variables (eg resources).

lineman (*esp US*) = LINESMAN.

linen /ˈlɪnɪn/ *n* [U] **1** cloth made of flax: [attrib] *linen handkerchiefs.* **2** household articles (eg sheets, table-cloths, clothing) formerly made of this: [attrib] *a linen cupboard.* **3** (idm) **wash one's dirty linen in public** ⇨ WASH².

liner¹ /ˈlaɪnə(r)/ *n* **1** large passenger or cargo ship travelling on a regular route: *a transatlantic cruise liner.* **2** = FREIGHTLINER (FREIGHT). **3** = EYE-LINER (EYE¹).

liner² /ˈlaɪnə(r)/ *n* (esp in compounds) removable lining: *ˈnappy-liners* ○ *ˈbin-liners*, ie plastic bags used to line a rubbish bin.

linesman /ˈlaɪnzmən/ (also *esp US* **lineman** /ˈlaɪnmən/) *n* (*pl* **-men** /-mən/) **1** official helping the referee in certain games, esp in deciding whether or where a ball crosses one of the lines. **2** person whose job is to repair and maintain electrical or telephone lines.

ling¹ /lɪŋ/ *n* [U] type of heather.

ling² /lɪŋ/ *n* sea-fish of N Europe used (usu salted) for food.

-ling *suff* **1** (with *ns* forming *ns*) little: *duckling.* **2** (with *vs* forming *ns*) (*usu derog*) person or thing connected with: *hireling* ○ *nursling.*

linger /ˈlɪŋgə(r)/ *v* [I, Ipr, Ip] **1** stay for a long time; be unwilling to leave: *She lingered after the concert, hoping to meet the star.* ○ *linger about/around/on.* **2** be slow; dawdle: *There's no time to linger — it'll soon be dark.* ○ *linger (long) over one's meal.* **3** remain in existence although becoming weaker: *Though desperately ill he could linger on* (ie not die) *for months.* ○ *The custom still lingers (on) in some villages.* ○ *The smell of her perfume lingered in the empty house.*

▷ **lingerer** *n* person who lingers.

lingering *adj* [esp attrib] **(a)** long; protracted: *a lingering illness* ○ *a last lingering look.* **(b)** remaining: *a few lingering doubts* ○ *a lingering sense of guilt.* **lingeringly** *adv.*

lingerie /ˈlænʒəri:; *US* ˌlɑ:ndʒəˈreɪ/ *n* [U] (in shops, etc) women's underwear.

lingo /ˈlɪŋgəʊ/ *n* (*pl* ~**es**) (*infml joc or derog*) **1** foreign language: *If you live abroad it helps to know the local lingo.* **2** special words or expressions used by a particular group; jargon: *Don't use all that technical lingo — try and explain in plain English.*

lingua franca /ˌlɪŋgwə ˈfræŋkə/ language used

for communicating between the people of an area in which several languages are spoken: *Swahili is the principal lingua franca in East Africa.*

linguist /ˈlɪŋɡwɪst/ *n* **1** person who knows several foreign languages well: *She's an excellent linguist.* ○ *I'm afraid I'm no linguist,* ie I am poor at foreign languages. **2** person who studies language(s) scientifically.

linguistic /lɪŋˈɡwɪstɪk/ *adj* of language or linguistics.

▷ **linguistics** *n* [sing *v*] scientific study of language or of particular languages. Cf PHILOLOGY.

liniment /ˈlɪnɪmənt/ *n* [C, U] liquid, esp one made with oil, for rubbing on the body to relieve aches or bruises.

lining /ˈlaɪnɪŋ/ *n* **1** (**a**) [C] layer of material used to cover the inside surface of sth: *a coat with a fur lining.* (**b**) [U] material used for this. **2** [U] tissue covering the inner surface of an organ of the body: *the stomach lining.* **3** (idm) **every cloud has a silver lining** ⇨ CLOUD[1].

link /lɪŋk/ *n* **1** one ring or loop of a chain. **2** person or thing that connects two others: *Police suspect there may be a link between the two murders.* ○ *commercial, cultural, diplomatic, etc links (between two countries).* **3** (formerly) measure of length, one hundredth of a chain, equal to 7.92 inches or about 20 centimetres.

▷ **link** *v* **1** [Tn, Tn·pr, Tn·p] ~ **A with B**/~ **A and B (together)**; ~ **sth (up)** make or suggest a connection between people or things: *The crowd linked arms to form a barrier.* ○ *Television stations around the world are linked by satellite.* ○ *The newspapers have linked his name with hers,* ie implied that they are having an affair. ○ *a new road to link (up) the two motorways.* **2** (phr v) **link up (with sb/sth)** form a connection: *The two spacecraft will link up (with each other) in orbit.*

□ ˈ**linkman** /-mæn/ *n* (*pl* **-men** /-men/) person providing connecting links between parts of a radio or television programme or between programmes.

ˈ**link-up** *n* connection or joining: *the first link-up of two satellites in space.*

linkage /ˈlɪŋkɪdʒ/ *n* **1** [U, C] action or manner of linking or being linked. **2** [C] device, etc that links. **3** [U] (*biology*) association of two or more genetic characteristics when the genes responsible for them occur on the same chromosome.

links /lɪŋks/ *n* **1** = GOLF-LINKS (GOLF). **2** [pl] (*esp Scot*) grassy sand-hills near the sea.

Linnaean /lɪˈneɪən/ *adj* of the Swedish naturalist Carl Linné (Latinized name Carolus Linnaeus, 1707-78) or his binomial system of Latin scientific names for animals and plants, using a genus name and a species name.

linnet /ˈlɪnɪt/ *n* small brown songbird, common in Europe.

lino /ˈlaɪnəʊ/ *n* [U] (*infml*) = LINOLEUM.

□ ˈ**linocut** *n* (**a**) design cut into the surface of a piece of thick linoleum as a form of art. (**b**) print made from this.

linoleum /lɪˈnəʊlɪəm/ (also *infml* **lino**) *n* [U] type of tough floor-covering made of canvas coated with powdered cork and linseed oil, etc.

linseed /ˈlɪnsiːd/ *n* [U] seed of flax.

□ ˌ**linseed** ˈ**oil** oil pressed from this, used in paint, varnish, etc.

linsey-woolsey /ˌlɪnzɪ ˈwʊlzɪ/ *n* [U] type of rough cloth made (esp formerly) from a mixture of wool and cotton.

lint /lɪnt/ *n* [U] **1** soft material used for dressing wounds: [attrib] *a lint bandage.* **2** fluff.

lintel /ˈlɪntl/ *n* horizontal piece of wood or stone over a door or window, forming part of the frame. ⇨ illus at HOME.

lion /ˈlaɪən/ *n* **1** [C] large powerful flesh-eating animal of the cat family, found in Africa and parts of southern Asia. ⇨ illus at CAT. ⇨ article at NATIONAL. **2** [C] (*becoming dated*) brave or famous person: *a literary lion,* ie a celebrated author. **3 the Lions** [pl] = THE BRITISH LIONS (BRITISH). **4** (idm) **beard the lion in his den** ⇨ BEARD[2]. **the** ˈ**lion's share (of sth)** the largest or best part of sth when it is divided: *As usual, the lion's share of the budget is for defence.*

▷ **lioness** /-es/ *n* female lion.

lionize, -ise /-aɪz/ *v* [Tn] treat (sb) as a celebrity: *Marilyn wanted to be loved, not lionized.*

□ ˌ**lion-**ˈ**hearted** *adj* very brave.

lip /lɪp/ *n* **1** [C] either of the fleshy edges of the opening of the mouth: *the lower/upper lip* ○ *kiss sb on the lips* ○ *She had a cigarette between her lips.* ○ *He put the bottle to his lips and drank deeply.* ⇨ illus at HEAD, ⇨ Usage at BODY. **2** [C] edge of a hollow container or opening: *the lip of a cup, saucer, crater.* **3** [U] (*sl*) impudence: *Less of your lip!* ie Don't be so cheeky! **4** (idm) **bite one's lip** ⇨ BITE[1]. **button one's lip** ⇨ BUTTON. **curl one's lip** ⇨ CURL[2]. **hang on sb's lips** ⇨ HANG[1]. **lick/smack one's lips/chops** ⇨ LICK. **one's lips are sealed** one will not or must not discuss or reveal sth: *I'd like to tell you what I know but my lips are sealed.* **a stiff upper lip** ⇨ STIFF. **there's many a slip 'twixt cup and lip** ⇨ SLIP[1].

▷ **-lipped** (forming compound *adjs*) having lips of the specified kind: *thin-lipped* ○ *tight-lipped.*

□ ˈ**lip-read** *v* (*pt, pp* ˈ**lip-read** /-red/) [I, Tn] understand (what sb is saying) by watching his lip movements, not by hearing (eg because one is deaf). ˈ**lip-reading** *n* [U].

ˈ**lipsalve** *n* [C, U] ointment for sore lips.

ˈ**lip-service** *n* (idm) **give/pay lip-service to sth** say that one approves of or supports sth while not doing so in practice: *He pays lip-service to feminism but his wife still does all the housework.*

ˈ**lipstick** *n* [C, U] (stick of) cosmetic for colouring the lips.

liquefy /ˈlɪkwɪfaɪ/ *v* (*pt, pp* **-fied**) [I, Tn] (cause sth to) become liquid: *liquefied wax.* ▷ **liquefaction** /ˌlɪkwɪˈfækʃn/ *n* [U]: *the liquefaction of gases.*

liquescent /lɪˈkwesnt/ *adj* (of a gas or solid) becoming or apt to become liquid; melting.

liqueur /lɪˈkjʊə(r); *US* -ˈkɜːr/ *n* strong (usu sweet) alcoholic spirit, drunk in small quantities esp after a meal: [attrib] *liqueur* ˈ*brandy,* ie one of special quality for drinking as a liqueur ○ *a li*ˈ*queur glass,* ie a small one for liqueurs.

liquid /ˈlɪkwɪd/ *n* **1** [C, U] substance that flows freely but is not a gas, eg water or oil: *Air is a fluid but not a liquid, while water is both a fluid and a liquid.* ○ *If you add too much liquid the mixture will not be thick enough.* **2** [C] (*phonetics*) either of the consonants /r/ or /l/.

▷ **liquid** *adj* [usu attrib] **1** in the form of a liquid; not gaseous or solid: *liquid food/nourishment,* ie easily swallowed, eg by sick people ○ (*joc*) *a liquid lunch,* ie beer, etc rather than food. **2** clear and clean, like water: *eyes of liquid blue.* **3** (of sounds) clear, pure and flowing: *the liquid song of a blackbird.* **4** (*finance*) easily converted into cash: *one's liquid assets.*

□ ˌ**liquid** ˈ**gas** gas reduced to liquid form by intense cold.

liquidate /ˈlɪkwɪdeɪt/ *v* [Tn] **1** pay or settle (a debt). **2** close down (a business) and divide up the proceeds to pay its debts. **3** get rid of (sb), esp by killing: *liquidated his political opponents.*

▷ **liquidation** /ˌlɪkwɪˈdeɪʃn/ *n* [U] **1** liquidating or being liquidated. **2** (idm) ˌ**go into liqui**ˈ**dation** (of a business) be closed down, esp because of bankruptcy.

liquidator *n* person responsible for liquidating a business.

liquidity /lɪˈkwɪdətɪ/ *n* [U] **1** (*finance*) state of having assets that can easily be changed into cash: *The company has good liquidity.* **2** state of being liquid.

liquidize, -ise /ˈlɪkwɪdaɪz/ *v* [Tn] (**a**) cause (sth) to become liquid. (**b**) crush (vegetables, fruit, etc) into a thick liquid.

▷ **liquidizer, -iser** (also *esp US* **blender**) *n* (usu electric) device for liquidizing food.

liquor /ˈlɪkə(r)/ *n* [U] **1** (**a**) (*Brit*) any alcoholic drink: *under the influence of liquor,* ie drunk. (**b**) (*esp US*) any distilled alcoholic drink; spirits: *hard liquor* ○ *She drinks wine and beer but no liquor.* **2** liquid produced by cooking food.

liquorice (*US* **licorice**) /ˈlɪkərɪs/ *n* **1** [U] (**a**) black substance used in medicine and as a sweet. (**b**) sweet made with this. **2** [U] plant from whose root this is obtained.

lira /ˈlɪərə/ *n* (*pl* **lire** /ˈlɪərə/ or **liras**) (abbr **L**) unit of money in Italy and Turkey.

lisle /laɪl/ *n* [U] fine smooth cotton thread, used esp for stockings and gloves.

lisp /lɪsp/ *n* speech defect in which /s/ is pronounced as /θ/ and /z/ as /ð/: *speak with a lisp* ○ *have a bad, pronounced, slight, etc lisp.*

▷ **lisp** *v* [I, Tn] speak or say (sth) with a lisp. **lispingly** *adv.*

lissom (also **lissome**) /ˈlɪsəm/ *adj* quick and graceful in movement; lithe. ▷ **lissomness** *n* [U].

list[1] /lɪst/ *n* **1** series of names, items, figures, etc written or printed: *a shopping list* ○ *make a list of things one must do* ○ *put sb/sth on the list* ○ *take sb/sth off the list.* **2** (idm) **on the danger list** ⇨ DANGER.

▷ **list** *v* [Tn] (**a**) make a list of (things): *list one's engagements for the week.* (**b**) put (things) on a list: *The books are listed alphabetically.* **listed** ˈ**building** (*Brit*) building officially registered as being of architectural or historical importance (and therefore protected from demolition, etc). ⇨ article at ARCHITECTURE.

□ ˈ**list price** (*commerce*) published or advertised price of goods: *selling sth for less than the list price.*

list[2] /lɪst/ *v* [I, Ipr] (of a ship) lean over to one side: *The damaged vessel was listing badly to port.*

▷ **list** *n* [sing] listing position; tilt: *develop a heavy list.*

listen /ˈlɪsn/ *v* **1** [I, Ipr] ~ **(to sb/sth)** try to hear sb, sth; pay attention: *We listened carefully but heard nothing.* ○ *You're not listening to what I'm saying.* **2** [Ipr] ~ **to sb/sth** allow oneself to be persuaded by (a suggestion, request, etc): *I never listen to* (ie believe) *what salesmen tell me.* **3** (phr v) **listen (out) for sth** wait alertly in order to hear (a sound): *Please listen out for the phone while I'm in the bath.* **listen** ˈ**in (to sth)** (**a**) listen to a radio broadcast: *listening in to the BBC World Service.* (**b**) overhear (a conversation, etc): *She loves listening in to other people's gossip.* ○ *The criminals did not know the police were listening in,* eg by tapping their telephone.

▷ **listen** *n* (usu *sing*); (*infml*) act of listening: *Have a listen and see if you can hear anything — I can't.*

listener *n* (**a**) person who listens: *a good listener* ie one who can be relied on to listen attentively or sympathetically. (**b**) person listening to a radio programme: *Good evening to all our listeners!*

Lister /ˈlɪstə(r)/ Joseph, 1st Baron (1827-1912), English surgeon. Influenced by *Pasteur's discoveries, he introduced the use of antiseptics in surgery in 1865. Aseptic techniques became common about 20 years later.

listeria /lɪˈstɪərɪə/ *n* [C, U] type of bacterium that causes disease, esp through infected food.

listless /ˈlɪstlɪs/ *adj* having no energy, vitality or enthusiasm: *She was very listless after her illness.*

▷ **listlessly** *adv.* **listlessness** *n* [U].

lists /lɪsts/ *n* [pl] **1** (formerly) area used for contests between men on horseback armed with lances. **2** (idm) **enter the lists** ⇨ ENTER.

Liszt /lɪst/ Franz (1811-86), Hungarian composer. He was internationally famous as a virtuoso pianist, and this is shown in the great technical difficulty of some of his piano compositions, such as the *Hungarian Rhapsodies.* He also wrote many orchestral and choral works, eg *A Faust Symphony.*

lit *pt, pp* of LIGHT[2, 4].

litany /ˈlɪtənɪ/ *n* **1** (**a**) [C] series of prayers to God for use in church services, spoken by a priest with set responses by the congregation. (**b**) **the Litany** [sing] that in the Book of Common Prayer of the Church of England. **2** [C] (*fig*) ~ **(of sth)** long boring recital: *a litany of complaints.*

litchi = LYCHEE.

liter (*US*) = LITRE.

literacy /ˈlɪtərəsɪ/ *n* [U] ability to read and write.

literal /ˈlɪtərəl/ *adj* **1** [esp attrib] (**a**) corresponding exactly to the original: *a literal transcript of a speech* ○ *a literal* (ie word-for-word) *translation.* Cf FREE[1] 11. (**b**) concerned with the basic or usual meaning of a word or phrase: *His story is incredible in the literal sense of the word,* ie It is impossible to believe him, so he must be lying. Cf FIGURATIVE, METAPHORICAL (METAPHOR). **2** (*esp derog*) unimaginative; prosaic: *His interpretation* *of the music was rather too literal.* ○ *Don't be so literal-minded — you know what I meant!*

▷ **literal** *n* (also **literal error**) misprint.

literalism /-ɪzəm/ [U] (*often derog*) tendency to interpret sth, eg the Bible or the law, in a very literal way. **literalist** /-rəlɪst/ *n*.

literally /ˈlɪtərəlɪ/ *adv* **1** in a literal manner; exactly: *Idioms usually cannot be translated literally in another language.* ○ *When he said he never wanted to see you again I'm sure he didn't mean it literally.* **2** (*infml*) (used loosely, to intensify meaning): *I was literally bored to death!*

literalness *n*.

literary /ˈlɪtərərɪ; *US* ˈlɪtərerɪ/ *adj* of or concerned with literature: *literary criticism* ○ *a literary agent*, ie one acting on behalf of writers ○ *His style is a bit too literary* (ie formal or rhetorical) *for my taste.*

literate /ˈlɪtərət/ *adj* **1** able to read and write: *Though nearly twenty he was barely literate.* Cf NUMERATE. **2** cultured; well-read: *Every literate person should read this book.*

literati /ˌlɪtəˈrɑːtiː/ *n* [pl] (*fml*) educated and intelligent people who have learned much from literature and books.

literature /ˈlɪtrətʃə(r); *US* -tʃʊər/ *n* [U] **1** (**a**) writings that are valued as works of art, esp fiction, drama and poetry (as contrasted with technical books and journalism). (**b**) activity of writing or studying these: *a degree in American literature.* (**c**) writings of this kind from a particular country or period: *French literature* ○ *18th century (English) literature.* **2** writings on a particular subject: *I've read all the available literature on poultry-farming.* ○ *There is now an extensive literature on the use of computers in the home.* **3** (*infml*) pamphlets or leaflets: *Please send me any literature you have on camping holidays in Spain.*

-lith *comb form* (forming *ns*) of stone or rock: *monolith* ○ *megalith.* ▷ **-lithic** (forming *adjs*): *palaeolithic.*

lithe /laɪð/ *adj* (of a person, the body, etc) bending or turning easily; supple: *The lithe grace of a gymnast.*

lithium /ˈlɪθɪəm/ *n* [U] (*symb* **Li**) chemical element, a soft silver-white metal similar to sodium and used in alloys and certain fuels. ⇨ App 11.

litho /ˈlaɪθəʊ/ *n* [U] (*infml*) lithography.

lithograph /ˈlɪθəgrɑːf; *US* -græf/ *n* picture, etc printed by lithography.

▷ **lithograph** *v* [Tn] print (sth) by lithography.

lithography /lɪˈθɒgrəfɪ/ (also *infml* **litho** /ˈlaɪθəʊ/) *n* [U] process of printing from a smooth surface (eg a metal plate) treated so that ink adheres only to the design to be printed: *a book printed by offset litho.* ▷ **lithographic** /ˌlɪθəˈgræfɪk/ *adj*.

Lithuania /ˌlɪθjʊˈeɪnɪə/ country bordering on the eastern Baltic Sea; pop approx 3 761 000; official language Lithuanian; capital Vilnius; unit of currency Lithuanian rouble. An independent republic from 1918, it became part of the USSR in 1940 and regained independence in 1991. ⇨ map at UNION OF SOVIET SOCIALIST REPUBLICS.

▷ **Lithuanian** *adj* of Lithuania, its culture or its people. ~ *n* **1** [C] native or inhabitant of Lithuania. **2** [U] language of Lithuania.

litigant /ˈlɪtɪgənt/ *n* (*law*) person involved in a lawsuit.

litigate /ˈlɪtɪgeɪt/ *v* (*law*) (**a**) [I] engage in a lawsuit; go to law. (**b**) [Tn] contest (a claim, etc) in a lawsuit.

▷ **litigation** /ˌlɪtɪˈgeɪʃn/ *n* (*law*) (**a**) [U] process of going to law. (**b**) [C] lawsuit.

litigious /lɪˈtɪdʒəs/ *adj* (*esp law*) **1** of lawsuits. **2** that can result in a lawsuit. **3** (*often derog*) fond of going to law; disputatious.

litmus /ˈlɪtməs/ *n* [U] blue colouring-matter that is turned red by acid and can be turned blue again by alkali: [attrib] *a litmus test*, ie showing the acidity of a solution, etc ○ (*fig*) *The local elections will be a litmus test for the Government*, ie show if they are still popular.

□ **ˈlitmus paper** paper stained with litmus, used to test if a solution is acid or alkaline.

litotes /ˈlaɪtəʊtiːz/ (also **meiosis**) *n* [U] ironical understatement, esp using a negative to emphasize the contrary, eg 'It wasn't easy' meaning 'It was very difficult'.

litre (*US* **liter**) /ˈliːtə(r)/ *n* (*abbr* **l**) unit of capacity in the metric system, equal to about $1\frac{3}{4}$ pints, used for measuring liquids. ⇨ App 10.

Litt D /ˌlɪt ˈdiː/ *abbr* = D LITT.

litter /ˈlɪtə(r)/ *n* **1** (**a**) [U] light rubbish (eg bits of paper, wrappings, bottles) left lying about, esp in a public place: *Please do not leave litter.* ⇨ article at ENVIRONMENT. (**b**) [sing] state of untidiness: *Her desk was covered in a litter of books and papers.* ○ *His room was a litter of old clothes, dirty crockery and broken furniture.* **2** [U] straw, etc used as bedding for animals. **3** [CGp] all the young born to an animal at one time: *a litter of puppies.* **4** [C] (**a**) type of stretcher(1). (**b**) (formerly) couch carried on men's shoulders or by animals as a means of transport.

▷ **litter** *v* **1** [Tn, Tn·pr, Tn·p] ~ **sth** (**up**) (**with sth**) make (a place) untidy with scattered rubbish: *Newspapers littered the floor.* ○ *He's always littering up the room with his old magazines.* **2** [Tn, Tn·p] ~ **sth** (**down**) supply straw, etc as bedding for (an animal). **3** [I] (of animals) bring forth young: *The sow's about to litter.*

□ **ˈlitter-bin**, **ˈlitter-basket** *ns* container for rubbish.

ˈlitter-lout (*Brit*) (also *esp US* **ˈlitter-bug**) *n* (*infml derog*) person who leaves litter untidily in public places.

little[1] /ˈlɪtl/ *adj* [usu attrib] (The comparative and superlative forms, **littler** /ˈlɪtlə(r)/ and **littlest** /ˈlɪtlɪst/, are rare. It is more common to use *smaller, smallest.*) **1** not big; small: *six little puppies* ○ *a little coffee-table* ○ *a little movement of impatience* ○ *a little group of tourists* ○ *There's a little mark on your sleeve.* ○ *a house with a little garden* ○ *little holes to let air in.* **2** (of distance or time) short: *It's only a little way now.* ○ *You may have to wait a little while.* ○ *Shall we go for a little walk?* **3** (used usu after *nice, pretty, sweet, nasty*, etc to express the speaker's feeling of affection, pleasure, annoyance, etc): *a nice little room* ○ *a sweet little child* ○ *a funny little restaurant* ○ *What a nasty little man!* ○ *A (dear) little old lady helped me find my way.* ○ *There's a little shop on the corner that sells bread.* **4** not important; insignificant: *a little mistake* ○ *We only had a little snack at lunchtime.* **5** young: *I had curly hair when I was little.* ○ *My little* (ie younger) *brother is 18.* **6** small when compared with others: *one's little finger* ○ *the little hand of the clock* ○ *'Which packet would you prefer?' 'I'll take the little one.'* ⇨ Usage at SMALL. **7** (idm) **big, etc oaks from little acorns grow** ⇨ OAK. **in little** (*fml*) on a small scale. **a little bird told me (that...)** (*joc*) I know but will not tell you how, or from whom, I know. **twist sb round one's little finger** ⇨ TWIST.

□ **the ˌLittle ˈBear** small constellation near the north pole. Cf THE GREAT BEAR (GREAT).

ˌLittle ˈJohn one of the companions of *Robin Hood, famous for his great height and strength.

Little Lord Fauntleroy /ˌlɪtl lɔːd ˈfɔːntlərɔɪ/ (*usu derog*) young boy who is unusually polite and well-behaved (from a character in a popular Victorian children's story).

the ˈlittle people, **the ˈlittle folk** small people with supernatural powers; fairies or elves.

little[2] /ˈlɪtl/ *indef det* (used with [U] *ns*) a small amount (of sth); not enough: *I have very little time for reading.* ○ *We had little rain all summer.* ○ *There's little point in telling her now.* ⇨ Usage at MUCH[1].

▷ **little** *indef pron* (used as a *n* when preceded by *the*) a small amount: *Little of the music was recognizable.* ○ *I understood little of what he said.* ○ *We read a lot of poetry at school — I remember very little now.* ○ *The little that I have seen of his work is satisfactory.*

little *adv* **1** not much; only slightly: *He is little known as an artist.* ○ *She left little more than an hour ago.* ○ *I slept very little last night.* ○ *Little does he know* (ie He doesn't know) *what trouble he's in.* **2** (idm) **ˌlittle by ˈlittle** making progress slowly, gradually: *Little by little the snow disappeared.* ○ *His English is improving little by little.* **ˌlittle or ˈnothing** hardly anything: *She said little or nothing about her experience.* **make little of sth** (**a**) = MAKE LIGHT OF STH (LIGHT[3]). (**b**) understand or read hardly anything of sth: *It's in Chinese — I can make little of it.* Cf LESS.

little[3] /ˈlɪtl/ **a little** *indef det* (used with [U] *ns*) a small amount (of sth); some but not much: *a little milk, sugar, tea, etc* ○ *Could you give a little more attention to spelling?* ○ *I need a little help to move these books.* ○ *It caused not a little* (ie a great deal of) *confusion.*

▷ **a little** *indef pron* **1** a small amount of sth; some but not much. (**a**) (referring back): *There was a lot of food but I only ate a little.* ○ *If you've got any spare milk, could you give me a little?* (**b**) (referring forward): *I've only read a little of the book.* ○ *A little of the conversation was about politics.* **2** (idm) **after/for a ˈlittle** after/for a short distance or time: *After a little he got up and left.* ○ *We left the car and walked for a little.*

a little *adv* to some extent: *She seemed a little afraid of going inside.* ○ *These shoes are a little too big for me.* ○ *She was not a little* (ie very) *worried about the expense.*

littoral /ˈlɪtərəl/ *n, adj* (*fml*) (part of a country that is) along the coast.

liturgy /ˈlɪtədʒɪ/ *n* fixed form of public worship used in churches. ▷ **liturgical** /lɪˈtɜːdʒɪkl/ *adj*. **liturgically** /-ˈklɪ/ *adv*.

live[1] /laɪv/ *adj* [usu attrib] **1** having life: *live fish.* **2** (used esp of surprising or unusual experiences, etc) actual; not pretended: *We saw a real live rattlesnake!* **3** glowing or burning: *live coals.* **4** not yet exploded or lit; ready for use: *a live bomb* ○ *several rounds of live ammunition* ○ *a live match.* **5** (of a wire, etc) charged with or carrying electricity: *That terminal is live.* ○ *the live rail*, eg on an electric railway. **6** of interest or importance at the present time: *Pollution is still very much a live issue.* **7** (**a**) (of a broadcast) transmitted while actually happening, not recorded or edited: *live coverage of the World Cup.* (**b**) (of a musical performance or recording) given or made during a concert, not in a studio: *a live recording made at Covent Garden in 1962.* Cf PRE-RECORD. **8** (idm) **a live ˈwire** lively and energetic person.

▷ **live** *adv* broadcast, played or recorded at an actual performance, etc without being edited: *This show is going out live.*

□ **ˈlive birth** baby born alive. Cf STILLBIRTH (STILL[1]).

live[2] /lɪv/ *v* **1** [I] (less common than *be alive* in this sense) have life; be alive. **2** [I, Ipr, It] remain alive: *live to be old/to a great age* ○ *The doctors don't think he will live through the night.* ○ *Some trees can live for hundreds of years.* ○ *How long do elephants live?* ○ *live to see many changes.* **3** [I, Ipr] make one's home; reside: *Where do you live?* ○ *live at home, in London, in a flat, abroad.* **4** [Ln, I, Tn] conduct one's life in a specified way: *live and die a bachelor* ○ *live honestly, happily* ○ *He lives well*, ie enjoys the luxuries of life. ○ *live like a saint* ○ *live a peaceful life.* **5** [I] (*fig*) (of things without life) remain in existence; survive: *The memory will live in my heart for ever*, ie I will never forget it. **6** [I] enjoy life fully: *I don't call that living.* ○ *I don't want to work in an office all my life — I want to live!* **7** (idm) **how the other half lives** ⇨ HALF[1]. **live and ˈlet live** (*saying*) be tolerant of others so that they will be tolerant in turn. **live beˌyond/withˌin one's ˈmeans** spend more/less than one earns or can afford. **ˌlive by one's ˈwits** earn money by clever and sometimes dishonest means. **live from hand to mouth** ⇨ HAND[1]. **live in hope(s) (of sth)** remain hopeful: *live in hopes of better times to come* ○ *The future looks rather gloomy, but we live in hope.* **live in the ˈpast** behave as though circumstances, values, etc have not changed from what they were earlier. **live in ˈsin** (*dated or joc*) live together as if married. **live it ˈup** (*infml*) live in a lively and extravagant way: *Now you've been left some money you can afford to live it up a bit.* **live a ˈlie** suggest by one's way of living that sth untrue is true: *She lived a lie for 20 years by pretending to be his wife.* **live like ˈfighting cocks** enjoy the best possible food. **live like a ˈlord** enjoy a luxurious style of living. **live off/on the ˌfat of the ˈland** enjoy the best food, drink, lodging, entertainment, etc. **live off the ˈland** use agricultural products for one's food needs. **live ˈrough** live without comforts or amenities, esp out of doors: *He's a tramp and used to living rough.* **you/we ˌlive and ˈlearn** (used to express surprise at some new or unexpected information, etc.) **8** (phr v) **live by doing sth** earn one's living by doing sth. **live sth ˈdown** live in such a way that (a past embarrassment, scandal, crime, etc) is forgotten: *Beaten by the worst team in the league? They'll never live it down!* **live for sth** regard sth as the aim of one's life: *She lives for her work.* ○ *After she died he had nothing to live for.* **live in/out** (of an employee) live on/off the premises where one works: *They both go out to work and have a nanny living in.* **live on** continue to live or exist: *She lived on for many years after her husband died.* ○ *Mozart is dead but his music lives on.* **live on sth** (**a**) have sth as one's food: *live on (a diet of) fruit and vegetables* ○ *You can't live on 200 calories a day.* (**b**) depend on sth for financial support: *live on one's salary, on £8 000 a year, on charity.* **live through sth** experience sth and survive: *He lived through both world wars.* **live together** (**a**) live in the same house, etc. (**b**) share a home and have a sexual relationship. **live up to sth** behave in accordance with sth: *failed to live up to his principles, his reputation, his parents' expectations.* **live with sb** = LIVE TOGETHER. **live with sth** accept or tolerate sth: *You'll have to learn to live with it, I'm afraid.*

□ **ˈlived-in** *adj* (of a room, house, etc) occupied, or showing signs of people living there: *There were no pictures or plants to give the place a lived-in look.*

ˈlive-in *adj* [attrib] living with a person as if married: *one's live-in lover.*

liveable /ˈlɪvəbl/ *adj* (of life) worth living; tolerable.

□ **ˈliveable-in** *adj* [pred] (*infml*) (of a house, etc) fit to live in.

ˈliveable-with *adj* [pred] (*infml*) (of a person, etc) easy to live with.

livelihood /ˈlaɪvlɪhʊd/ *n* (usu *sing*) (**a**) means of living; income: *earn one's livelihood by teaching* ○ *deprive sb of his livelihood.* (**b**) way of earning a living; occupation: *Farming is his sole livelihood.*

livelong /ˈlɪvlɒŋ; *US* ˈlɪvlɔːŋ/ *adj* (idm) **the livelong ˈday/ˈnight** (*dated or rhet*) the whole length of the day/night.

lively /ˈlaɪvlɪ/ *adj* (**-ier**, **-iest**) **1** full of life and energy; high-spirited; vigorous: *She's a lively child and popular with everyone.* ○ *The patient seems a little livelier/more lively this morning.* ○ *one of the liveliest parties I've been to* ○ *a lively melody* ○ *She has a lively interest in everything around her.* **2** vivid or striking: *a lively imagination* ○ *a lively shade of pink* ○ *She gave a lively account of her adventures.* **3** moving vigorously or roughly: *The sea is quite lively today.* ○ *We batted on a lively pitch*, ie a cricket pitch that caused the ball to move sharply. **4** (idm) **ˌlook ˈlively** move, etc more quickly; show more energy: *We'd better look lively if we're to finish in time.* **make it/things lively for sb** (*esp ironic*) make things exciting and perhaps dangerous for sb. ▷ **liveliness** *n* [U].

liven /ˈlaɪvn/ *v* (phr v) **ˌliven (sb/sth) ˈup** (cause sb/sth to) become lively: *Put on some music to liven things up.* ○ *Do liven up a bit!*

liver[1] /ˈlɪvə(r)/ *n* **1** [C] large organ in the abdomen that produces bile and purifies the blood. ⇨ illus at DIGESTIVE. **2** [U, C] liver of certain animals, used as food: *pig's liver* ○ *chicken livers.*

▷ **liverish** (also **livery**) *adj* **1** suffering from a disorder of the liver. **2** irritable; peevish.

□ **ˈliver salts** powder that can be dissolved and swallowed to relieve discomfort when one has eaten or drunk too much.

ˈliver sausage (also *esp US* **liverwurst** /ˈlɪvəwɜːst/) sausage containing cooked and finely chopped liver, usu eaten cold on bread.

liver[2] /ˈlɪvə(r)/ *n* person who lives in a specified way: *a fast, quiet, loose, etc liver.*

Liverpudlian /ˌlɪvəˈpʌdlɪən/ *n, adj* (native or inhabitant) of Liverpool, England.

liverwort /ˈlɪvəwɜːt/ *n* [C, U] round flat plant without stems or leaves.

livery /ˈlɪvərɪ/ *n* **1** [U, C] special uniform such as that worn by male servants in a great household or by members of the London trade guilds: *in/out of* (ie wearing/not wearing) *livery.* **2** [U] (*rhet*) covering: *trees in their spring livery*, ie with new leaves.

▷ **liveried** /ˈlɪvərɪd/ *adj* wearing livery: *a liveried chauffeur.*

□ **ˈlivery company** any of the London trade guilds with their own special uniforms.

ˈliveryman /-mən/ *n* (*pl* **-men** /-mən/) **1** member of a livery company. **2** person who works in a livery stable.

ˈlivery stable stable where horses are kept for their owners in return for payment, or where horses may be hired.

lives *pl* of LIFE.

livestock /ˈlaɪvstɒk/ *n* [U] animals kept on a farm for use or profit, eg cattle or sheep.

livid /ˈlɪvɪd/ *adj* **1** [usu attrib] of the colour of lead; bluish-grey: *a livid bruise.* **2** [usu pred] (*infml*) furiously angry: *livid with rage* ○ *He'd be livid if he found out what you're doing.* ▷ **lividly** *adv.*

living[1] /ˈlɪvɪŋ/ *adj* **1** alive, esp now: *all living things* ○ *the finest living pianist* ○ *No man living could have done better.* **2** used or practised; active: *living languages*, ie those still spoken ○ *a living hope, faith, reality.* **3** (idm) **a ˌliving ˈlegend** person who has achieved great fame during his lifetime and is still alive. **be living proof of sth** show sth by the fact that one is alive: *He is living proof of the wonders of modern medicine.* **within/in ˌliving ˈmemory** at a time, or during the time, remembered by people still alive: *Wages were sixpence a week within living memory.* ○ *the coldest winter in living memory.*

▷ **the living** *n* [pl *v*] **1** people who are now alive: *the living and the dead.* **2** (idm) **in the land of the living** ⇨ LAND[1].

□ **ˌliving ˈdeath** time of continuous misery: *Exile was for him a living death.*

living[2] /ˈlɪvɪŋ/ *n* **1** [C usu *sing*] (**a**) means of keeping alive or of living in a certain style; income: *earn one's living as a journalist, by/from writing* ○ *make a good, an adequate, a meagre, etc living.* (**b**) way of earning this: *It may not be the best job in the world, but it's a living.* **2** [U] manner of life: *Both the cost and the standard of living were lower before the war.* ○ *understand the art of living*, ie how to live a worthwhile, satisfying life. **3** [C] (*Brit*) clergyman's position, providing his income; benefice. **4** (idm) **scrape a living** ⇨ SCRAPE[1].

□ **ˈliving-room** (also *esp Brit* **ˈsitting-room**) *n* room in a private house for general use during the daytime. Cf DRAWING-ROOM.

ˌliving ˈwage lowest wage on which sb can afford a reasonable standard of living.

Livingstone /ˈlɪvɪŋstən/ David (1813-73), Scottish missionary and explorer. He became a national hero through his travels in Africa, discovering the Zambezi river and the Victoria Falls. He learned much about native customs and campaigned against the slave trade. ⇨ illus at STANLEY.

lizard

lizard /ˈlɪzəd/ *n* (usu small) reptile with a rough skin, four legs and a long tail.

LJ *abbr* (*pl* **LJJ**) Lord Justice.

ll *pl* of L 2.

llama /ˈlɑːmə/ *n* S American animal with soft woolly hair, used for carrying loads.

LL B, LL D, LL M *abbrs* Bachelor, Doctor, Master of Laws: *have/be an LL B* ○ *David Grafton LL B.*

Lloyd /lɔɪd/ Marie (1870-1922), real name Matilda Wood, English music-hall performer. She was famous for her cockney humour and comic songs.

Lloyd /lɔɪd/ Harold (1893-1971), American film actor. Along with *Chaplin and *Keaton he was one of the great comedians of the silent cinema, famous for the spectacular stunts of films like *Safety Last.*

Lloyd George /ˌlɔɪd ˈdʒɔːdʒ/ David (1863-1945), Welsh Liberal politician, prime minister of Britain 1916-22. He was a passionate speaker and social reformer. As Chancellor of the Exchequer (1908-15) he introduced national insurance and old-age pensions. He became prime minister during the First World War, but after the war opposition to his policy on Irish independence forced him to resign. He remained in Parliament for the rest of his life, but neither he nor the Liberals ever returned to power. ⇨ App 2.

Lloyd's /lɔɪdz/ association of insurance underwriters in the City of London. The first members used to meet at Edward Lloyd's coffee-house in the late 17th century. It was originally concerned with insuring ships, but now handles insurance of all kinds all over the world.

□ **ˌLloyd's ˈRegister** classified list of ships from all over the world, compiled and published each year by Lloyd's. ⇨ article at FINANCE.

lo /ləʊ/ *interj* **1** (*arch*) look; see. **2** (idm) **ˌlo and beˈhold** (*esp joc or ironic*) (used to indicate surprise): *As soon as we went out, lo and behold, it began to rain.*

load[1] /ləʊd/ *n* **1** [C] thing that is being carried or to be carried, esp if heavy: *a load of sand.* **2** [C] (esp in compounds) quantity that can be carried, eg by a vehicle: *coach-loads of tourists* ○ *a boat-load of survivors.* **3** [C] (**a**) amount of work that a dynamo, a motor, an engine, etc is required to do. (**b**) amount of electric current supplied by a dynamo or generating station. **4** [C usu *sing*] (*fig*) weight of responsibility, worry, grief, etc: *a heavy load of guilt.* **5 loads (of sth)** [pl] (*infml*) plenty (of sth): *loads of friends, money, time* ○ *'Have you got any change?' 'Loads!'* **6** (idm) **be/take a ˌload/ˌweight off sb's ˈmind** ⇨ MIND[1]. **a ˌload of (old) ˈrubbish, etc** (*infml*) nonsense: *I've never heard such a load of garbage!* **get a load of sb/sth** (*infml*) take notice of sb/sth: *Get a load of that old bloke with the funny hat!*

□ **ˈload-shedding** *n* [U] cutting off the supply of electric current on certain lines when the general demand is greater than the available supply.

load[2] /ləʊd/ *v* **1** (**a**) [I, Ip, Tn, Tn·pr, Tn·p] ~ **(up)**; ~ **(up with sth)**; ~ **sth/sb (down/up) (with sth)**; ~ **sth (into/onto sth/sb)** put a load in or on (sth/sb): *We're still loading.* ○ *load a lorry (up) with bricks/load bricks onto a lorry* ○ *loaded down with shopping* ○ (*fig*) *load sb with honours.* (**b**) [I] receive a load: *The boat is still loading.* **2** [Tn esp passive] weight (sth) with lead, etc: *a loaded cane, stick, etc*, ie for use as a weapon ○ *loaded dice*, ie one weighted so as to fall in a certain way, eg with the six uppermost. **3** (**a**) [I, Tn, Tn·pr] ~ **sth (with sth)** put film into (a camera) or ammunition into (a gun): *Be careful, that gun's loaded.* (**b**) [Tn, Tn·pr] ~ **sth (into sth)** place (film or ammunition) thus: *load a new film into the camera.* **4** [Tn] (*computing*) transfer (data or a program) from a storage medium into the memory of a computer. **5** (idm) **load the dice (against sb)** (usu passive) put sb at a disadvantage: *Having lost both his parents when he was a child he always felt that the dice were loaded against him.*

▷ **loaded** *adj* **1** carrying a load. **2** [pred] (*sl*) (**a**) very rich. (**b**) drunk. (**c**) (*esp US*) under the influence of a drug. **3** (idm) **a ˌloaded ˈquestion** question intended to trap sb into saying sth which he does not want to say or which could harm him.

loadstar = LODESTAR (LODE).

loadstone (also **lodestone**) /ˈləʊdstəʊn/ *n* (**a**) [U] magnetic oxide of iron. (**b**) [C] piece of this used as a magnet: (*fig*) *She seems to be a loadstone for people in trouble*, ie They come to her regularly for help.

loaf[1] /ləʊf/ *n* (*pl* **loaves** /ləʊvz/) **1** mass of bread shaped and baked in one piece: *Two brown loaves and one large white one, please.* **2** (idm) **half a loaf is better than none/than no bread** (*saying*) having to accept less than one expects, or feels that one deserves, is better than having nothing. **use one's loaf** ⇨ USE[1].

□ ˈ**loaf sugar** sugar in small lumps or cubes.

loaf[2] /ləʊf/ *v* [I, Ipr, Ip] (*infml*) spend time idly: *Don't stand there loafing — there's work to be done.* ○ *loaf around (the house all day).*

▷ **loafer** *n* **1** idler. **2** (*esp US*) flat shoe, similar to a moccasin, for casual wear.

loam /ləʊm/ *n* [U] rich soil containing clay, sand and decayed vegetable matter. ▷ **loamy** *adj*: *loamy land.*

loan /ləʊn/ *n* **1** [C] thing that is lent, esp a sum of money: *I'm only asking for a loan — I'll pay you back.* ○ *a bank loan*, ie money lent by a bank. **2** [U] lending or being lent (used esp as in the expressions shown): *May I have the loan of* (ie borrow) *your bicycle?* ○ *Can we ask your father for the loan of his car?* ○ *It's not my book — I've got it on loan from the library.*

▷ **loan** *v* [Tn, Dn·n, Dn·pr] ~ **sth (to sb)** (*esp US*) (*Brit fml*) lend sth: *a painting graciously loaned by Her Majesty the Queen.*

□ ˈ**loan-collection** *n* several works of art, etc lent by their owners for exhibition.

ˈ**loan shark** (*infml derog*) person who lends money at high rates of interest and in a dishonest way.

ˈ**loan-word** *n* word taken into one language from another.

loath (also **loth**) /ləʊθ/ *adj* [pred] (*fml*) **1** ~ **to do sth** unwilling; reluctant: *He seemed somewhat loath to depart.* **2** (idm) ˌ**nothing** ˈ**loath** quite willing; eager.

loathe /ləʊð/ *v* **(a)** [Tn] feel great hatred or disgust for (sb/sth): *loathe the smell of fried fish.* **(b)** [Tn, Tg] (*infml*) dislike (sth) greatly: *I loathe having to go to these conferences.*

▷ **loathing** *n* [U] disgust: *have a loathing of sth* ○ *feel intense loathing for sb/sth.*

loathsome /-səm/ *adj* causing one to feel disgusted or shocked; repulsive: *a loathsome disease* ○ *What a loathsome creature he is!*

loaves *pl* of LOAF[1].

lob /lɒb/ *v* (**-bb-**) [I, Tn, Tn·pr, Tn·p] (in tennis, cricket, etc) send or strike (a ball) in a high arc: *She lobbed the ball over her opponent's head to the back of the court.*

▷ **lob** *n* **(a)** lobbed ball. **(b)** slow underarm delivery in cricket.

lobby /ˈlɒbɪ/ *n* **1** [C] porch, entrance-hall or ante-room: *the lobby of a hotel, theatre, etc.* **2** [C] (in the House of Commons, etc) large hall open to the public and used for interviews with Members of Parliament. **3** [CGp] group of people who try to influence politicians, esp to support or oppose proposed legislation: *The anti-nuclear lobby is/are becoming stronger.* **4** [C] = DIVISION LOBBY (DIVISION).

▷ **lobby** *v* (*pt, pp* **lobbied**) **1** [I, Ipr, Tn, Tn·pr] ~ **(sb) (for sth)** try to persuade (a politician, etc) to support or oppose proposed legislation: *lobby (MPs) for higher farm subsidies.* **2** (phr v) **lobby sth through (sth)** get (a bill, etc) passed or rejected by lobbying: *lobby a bill through Parliament/the Senate.* **lobbyist** /-ɪst/ *n* person who lobbies.

lobe /ləʊb/ *n* **1** lower soft part of the outer ear. ⇨ illus at HEAD. **2** rounded flattish part or projection of a body organ, esp the lungs or brain.

▷ **lobed** *adj* having lobes.

lobelia /ləˈbiːlɪə/ *n* [C, U] garden plant with brightly coloured flowers, usu grown in borders.

lobotomy /ləˈbɒtəmɪ/ (also *Brit* **leucotomy**) *n* (*medical*) [C, U] (operation involving) cutting into the brain tissue to treat severe mental disorders. Such treatment is now rarely used.

lobster /ˈlɒbstə(r)/ *n* **(a)** [C] large bluish-black shellfish with eight legs and two long claws that turns scarlet when it is boiled. ⇨ illus at SHELLFISH. **(b)** [U] its flesh as food.

□ ˈ**lobster-pot** *n* device for trapping lobsters, esp one like a basket.

lobworm /ˈlɒbwɜːm/ *n* large earthworm used by anglers as bait.

local /ˈləʊkl/ *adj* [esp attrib] **1** belonging to a particular place or district: *Following the national news we have the local news and weather.* ○ *the local farmer, doctor, shopkeeper, etc* ○ *local knowledge*, ie detailed knowledge of an area that one gets esp by living there ○ *She's a local girl*, ie from this area. ○ *a local train/bus*, ie not long-distance. **2** (*esp medical*) affecting a particular place; not general: *local inflammation* ○ *Is the pain local?*

▷ **local** *n* **1** (*usu pl*) inhabitant of a particular place or district: *The locals tend to be suspicious of strangers.* **2** (*Brit infml*) public house, esp near one's home: *pop into the local for a pint* ○ *Which is your local?* **3** (*US*) branch of a trade union, etc. **4** (*esp US*) local train or bus. **locally** /-kəlɪ/ *adv.*

□ ˌ**local anaesˈthetic** (*medical*) anaesthetic that affects only a specific part of the body.

ˌ**local auˈthority** (*Brit*) group of people responsible for the administration of local government.

ˈ**local call** telephone call to a nearby place, charged at a low rate.

ˌ**local ˈcolour** details that are typical of the place and time in which a novel, etc is set, used to make the story seem more real.

ˌ**local ˈgovernment** system of administration of a district, county, etc by elected representatives of the people who live there.

ˌ**local ˈoption** (esp in Scotland, New Zealand and the USA) right of local residents to decide sth (eg whether alcohol should be sold there) by voting.

ˈ**local time** (according to the) system of time being used in a given part of the world: *We reach Delhi at 1400 hours local time.*

locale /ləʊˈkɑːl; *US* -ˈkæl/ *n* scene of events, operations, etc: *The director is looking for a suitable locale for his new film.*

locality /ləʊˈkælətɪ/ *n* position of sth; place or district in which sth happens: *trying to pinpoint the ship's exact locality* ○ *The entire locality has been affected by the new motorway.*

localize, -ise /ˈləʊkəlaɪz/ *v* [Tn] **1** find out the place of (sth): *It can localize pirate radio transmitters.* **2** restrict (sth) to a particular area or part; make local: *try to localize an outbreak of disease, violence, unrest* ○ *a localized infection.* **3** move (eg the offices of an organization) away from a capital, city centre, etc; decentralize. ▷ **localization, -isation** /ˌləʊkəlaɪˈzeɪʃn; *US* -lɪˈz-/ *n* [U].

locate /ləʊˈkeɪt; *US* ˈləʊkeɪt/ *v* **1** [Tn] discover the exact position or place of (sb/sth): *locate an electrical fault* ○ *locate a town on a map* ○ *I'm trying to locate Mr Smith. Do you know where he is?* **2** [esp passive: Tn, Tn·pr] establish (sth) in a place; situate: *A new factory is to be located on this site.* ○ *The information office is located in the city centre.* **3** [Ipr] (*US*) settle in a place; establish oneself: *The company has located on the West Coast.*

location /ləʊˈkeɪʃn/ *n* **1** [C] place or position: *a suitable location for new houses.* **2** [U] finding the position of sb/sth: *responsible for the location of the missing yacht.* **3** [C] (*computing*) basic unit of a computer's memory, able to store a single item of data. **4** (idm) **on location** (*cinema*) being filmed in suitable surroundings instead of in a film studio.

loc cit /ˌlɒk ˈsɪt/ *abbr* in the passage, etc already quoted (Latin *loco citato*). Cf OP CIT.

loch /lɒk, lɒx/ *n* (*Scot*) (often in names) **1** lake: *Loch Tay.* **2** long narrow inlet of the sea. Cf LOUGH.

□ **the** ˌ**Loch Ness** ˈ**monster** (also *infml* **Nessie**) large animal that is said to live in Loch Ness in the north of Scotland. Many people claim to have seen it, but there is no convincing proof that it exists.

loci *pl* of LOCUS.

lock[1] /lɒk/ *n* **1** [C] portion of hair that hangs or lies together: *He kept a lock of her hair as a memento.* **2 locks** [pl] (*esp rhet or joc*) hair of the head: *He gazed ruefully in the mirror at his greying locks.*

lock[2] /lɒk/ *n* **1** [C] device for fastening a door, lid, etc, with a bolt that needs a key to work it. **2** [C] section of a canal or river where the water level changes, enclosed by gates fitted with sluices so that water can be let in or out to raise or lower boats from one level to another. **3** [C] (in wrestling) hold that keeps an opponent's arm, leg, etc from moving: *have sb's arm in a lock.* **4** [U] condition in which parts are jammed or fixed together so that movement is impossible. **5** [U, sing] (maximum extent of the) turning of a motor vehicle's front wheels by use of the steering-wheel: *on full lock*, ie with the steering-wheel turned as far as it will go one way or the other ○ *My car has a good lock*, ie can turn within a short distance. **6** [C] mechanism for exploding the charge in a gun. **7** [C] (also ˌ**lock** ˈ**forward**) (in Rugby football) player in the second row of a scrum. **8** (idm) ˌ**lock, stock and** ˈ**barrel** including everything; completely. **(keep sth/put sth/be) under** ˌ**lock and** ˈ**key** locked up: *The criminals are now safely under lock and key.*

□ ˌ**lock-**ˈ**gate** *n* gate on a canal or river lock.

ˈ**lockjaw** *n* [U] form of tetanus in which the jaws become rigidly closed.

ˈ**lock-keeper** *n* person in charge of a canal or river lock.

ˈ**lock-nut** *n* extra nut screwed over another to prevent it becoming loose.

ˈ**locksmith** *n* person who makes and mends locks.

ˈ**lock-stitch** *n* [U] sewing-machine stitch that locks threads firmly together.

lock[3] /lɒk/ *v* **1 (a)** [Tn] fasten (a door, lid, etc) with a lock: *Is the gate locked?* **(b)** [Tn] make (a house, box, etc) secure in this way: *Be sure to lock your bicycle.* **(c)** [I] be able to be fastened or secured with a lock: *This suitcase doesn't lock*, ie has no lock or has a lock that is broken. ⇨ Usage at CLOSE[4]. **2** [I, Ipr, Ip, Tn, Tn·pr] ~ **(sth/sb) (in/into sth)**; ~ **(sb/sth) (together)** (cause sb/sth to) become rigidly fixed; jam: *The brakes locked, causing the car to skid.* ○ *The pieces of the puzzle lock into each other/lock together*, ie interlock. ○ (*fig*) *two nations locked in mortal combat*, ie at war ○ *two lovers locked in each other's arms*, ie embracing. **3** (idm) **lock, etc the stable door after the horse has bolted** ⇨ STABLE[2]. **4** (phr v) **lock sth away** store sth securely and safely: *lock away one's jewellery.* **lock onto sth** (of a missile, etc) automatically find and follow (a target). **lock sb/oneself out (of sth)/in** prevent sb/oneself from entering or leaving by locking a door, etc (intentionally or unintentionally): *At 9 pm the prisoners are locked in for the night.* ○ *I've lost my key and I'm locked out!* ○ *lock oneself out of the house.* **lock (sth) up** make (a house, etc) secure by locking the doors and windows: *Don't forget to lock up before leaving home.* **lock sb up** put sb in prison, a mental institution, etc. **lock sth up (a)** = LOCK STH AWAY. **(b)** invest (money) so that it cannot easily be converted into cash: *All their capital is locked up in land.*

▷ ˈ**lockable** *adj* that can be locked: *a lockable steering-wheel.*

□ ˈ**lock-out** *n* refusal by an employer to let workers enter a factory, etc until they agree to certain conditions.

ˈ**lock-up** *n* **(a)** place where prisoners can be kept temporarily. **(b)** (*infml*) prison. **(c)** (*Brit*) (usu small) shop whose owner does not live in it. — *adj* [attrib] that can be locked up: *a lock-up garage.*

Locke[1] /lɒk/ John (1632-1704), English philosopher. His most famous work, *An Essay concerning Human Understanding*, is an attempt to show what can and what cannot be known, so as to guide human conduct. He is considered to be the founder of empiricism, claiming that all knowledge comes from experience through the senses, so that our understanding of the world is limited and must be helped by faith.

Locke[2] /lɒk/ Matthew (c 1630-77), English composer. After the *Restoration he became court composer to Charles II and wrote many works for the theatres that had just reopened.

locker /ˈlɒkə(r)/ *n* **1 (a)** small cupboard, esp one of several where clothes can be kept, eg at a swimming-pool: *left-ˈluggage lockers*, ie for depositing luggage in, eg at a railway station. **(b)** (*nautical*) box or compartment for storing clothes, ammunition, etc in a ship. **2** (idm) **be in/go to**

ˌ**Davy Jones's ˈlocker** be drowned at sea.

□ ˈ**locker-room** *n* (*esp US*) room at a sports club, etc for changing in, with lockers for clothes, etc.

locket /ˈlɒkɪt/ *n* small ornamental case, usu of gold or silver, holding a portrait, lock of hair, etc and worn on a chain round the neck.

loco[1] /ˈləʊkəʊ/ *n* (*pl* ~**s**) (*infml*) locomotive engine: [attrib] *loco-spotting*, ie as a hobby.

loco[2] /ˈləʊkəʊ/ *adj* [pred] (*sl esp US*) mad.

locomotion /ˌləʊkəˈməʊʃn/ *n* [U] (*fml or joc*) moving, or the ability to move, from place to place.

▷ **locomotive** /ˈləʊkəməʊtɪv/ *adj* of, having or causing locomotion: *locomotive power.* — *n* = ENGINE 2: *electric, diesel, steam, etc locomotives.*

locum /ˈləʊkəm/ *n* (also *fml* ˌ**locum ˈtenens** /ˈtiːnenz, ˈtenenz/) deputy acting for a doctor or priest in his absence: *When they are on holiday the work of doctors is often done by locums.*

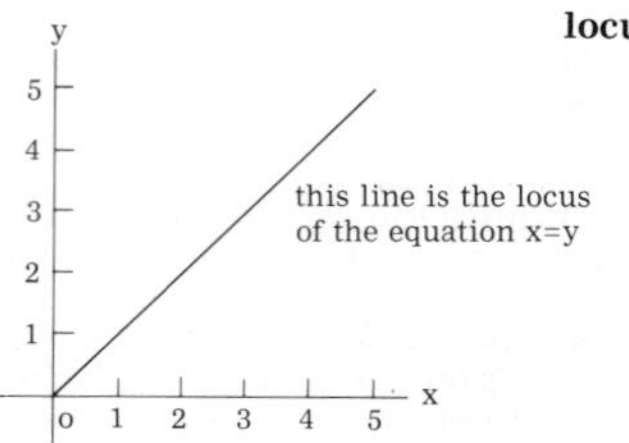

locus /ˈləʊkəs/ *n* (*pl* **loci** /ˈləʊsaɪ/) **1** exact place of sth. **2** (*mathematics*) line or curve formed by all the points that satisfy a particular rule: *A circle is the locus of points which are the same distance from a fixed point.* ⇨ illus.

□ ˌ**locus ˈclassicus** /ˈklæsɪkəs/ (*Latin*) best-known or most authoritative passage on a subject.

locust /ˈləʊkəst/ *n* **1** type of African and Asian winged insect that migrates in huge swarms which destroy all the vegetation of a district. **2** (*US*) = CICADA.

locution /ləˈkjuːʃn/ *n* **1** [U] (*fml*) style of speech; way of using words. **2** [C] (*esp linguistics*) phrase or idiom.

lode /ləʊd/ *n* vein of metal ore.

□ ˈ**lodestar** (also **loadstar**) *n* (**a**) star used as a guide in navigation, esp the pole-star. (**b**) (*fig*) principle that guides one's behaviour and actions.

ˈ**lodestone** *n* = LOADSTONE.

lodge[1] /lɒdʒ/ *n* **1** small house at the gates of a park or in the grounds of a large house, occupied by a gate-keeper or other employee. **2** country house or cabin for use in certain seasons: *a ˈhunting/ˈfishing/ˈskiing lodge.* **3** porter's room at the main entrance to a block of flats, college, factory, etc. **4** members or meeting-place of a branch of a society such as the Freemasons. **5** beaver's or otter's lair. **6** N American Indian dwelling or household.

□ ˌ**lodge-pole ˈpine** type of N American pine tree.

lodge[2] /lɒdʒ/ *v* **1** [Tn, Tn·pr] provide (sb) with a place to sleep or live in for a time: *The refugees are being lodged in an old army camp.* **2** [I, Ipr] ~ (**with sb/at...**) live for payment in sb's house: *Where are you lodging?* ○ *I'm lodging at Mrs Brown's (house)/with Mrs Brown.* **3** [Ipr, Tn·pr] ~ (**sth**) **in sth** (cause sth to) enter and become fixed in sth: *The bullet (was) lodged in his brain.* **4** [Tn·pr] ~ **sth with sb/in sth** leave (money, etc) with sb/in sth for safety: *lodge one's valuables in the bank.* **5** [Tn, Tn·pr] ~ **sth** (**with sb**) (**against sb**) present (a statement, etc) to the proper authorities for attention: *lodge a complaint with the police against one's neighbours* ○ *lodge an appeal, a protest, an objection, etc.* **6** (**a**) [Tn] (of wind or rain, etc) beat down or flatten (crops in a field). (**b**) [I] (of crops) be flattened by wind, rain, etc.

▷ **lodger** *n* person who pays to live in (part of) sb's house: *She makes a living by taking in lodgers.*

lodgement (also **lodgment**) /ˈlɒdʒmənt/ *n* (*fml*) **1** [U] action or process of lodging (LODGE[2] 5): *the lodgement of a complaint.* **2** [C] mass of material that collects in or blocks sth: *a lodgement of dirt in a pipe.*

lodging /ˈlɒdʒɪŋ/ *n* **1** [U, C] temporary accommodation: *full board and lodging*, ie a room to stay in and all meals provided ○ *find a lodging for the night.* **2 lodgings** [pl] room or rooms (not in a hotel) rented for living in: *It's cheaper to live in lodgings than in a hotel.*

□ ˈ**lodging-house** *n* house in which lodgings are let, usu by the week.

loess /ˈləʊes/ *n* [U] layer of fine fertile light-coloured soil, found in large areas of Asia, Europe and America.

loft[1] /lɒft; *US* lɔːft/ *n* **1** (**a**) room or space directly under the roof of a house, used for storing things: [attrib] *a loft conversion*, ie one that has been made into a room or rooms for living in. (**b**) space under the roof of a stable or barn, used for storing hay, etc. **2** (*US*) one of the upper floors of a warehouse, etc. **3** gallery or upper level in a church or hall: *the ˈorgan-loft.*

loft[2] /lɒft; *US* lɔːft/ *v* [Tn, Tn·pr] (*esp sport*) hit, kick or throw (a ball) in a high arc: *loft the ball over the goalkeeper* ○ *a lofted drive*, eg at cricket or golf.

▷ **lofted** *adj* (of a golf-club) shaped to hit the ball high.

lofty /ˈlɒftɪ; *US* ˈlɔːftɪ/ *adj* (**-ier, -iest**) **1** [usu attrib] (of thoughts, aims, etc) noble; exalted: *lofty sentiments.* **2** (*derog*) seeming to be proud and superior; haughty: *in a lofty manner.* **3** (*rhet*) (not used of people) very tall: *a lofty mountain* ○ *lofty halls.* ▷ **loftily** /-ɪlɪ/ *adv.* **loftiness** *n* [U].

log[1] /lɒg; *US* lɔːg/ *n* **1** (**a**) length of tree-trunk that has fallen or been cut down: *birds nesting in a hollow log.* (**b**) short piece of this, esp one used as firewood: *Put another log on the fire.* **2** (idm) **easy as falling off a log** ⇨ EASY[1]. **sleep like a log/top** ⇨ SLEEP.

▷ **logging** *n* [U] (*US*) work of cutting down forest trees for timber: [attrib] *a logging camp.*

□ ˈ**log cabin** hut built of logs.

ˈ**log-jam** *n* (*esp US*) deadlock; standstill.

ˈ**log-rolling** *n* [U] (*derog esp US*) practice of helping others in return for their help, as when authors review each other's books favourably.

log[2] /lɒg; *US* lɔːg/ *n* **1** (formerly) floating device pulled behind a ship to measure its speed: *sail by the log*, ie calculate a ship's position using this. **2** log-book of a ship or an aircraft.

▷ **log** *v* (**-gg-**) [Tn] **1** enter (facts) in a log-book. **2** achieve (a certain speed, distance, number of hours worked, etc) as recorded in a log-book or similar record: *The pilot had logged over 200 hours in the air.* **3** (phr v) **log in/on** (*computing*) open one's on-line access to a database, etc. **log off/out** (*computing*) end one's on-line access to a database, etc.

□ ˈ**log-book** *n* **1** detailed record of a ship's voyage or an aircraft's flight; any similar record. **2** motor vehicle's registration book.

log[3] /lɒg; *US* lɔːg/ *n* (*infml mathematics*) logarithm: [attrib] *log tables.*

-log (*US*) = -LOGUE.

loganberry /ˈləʊgənbrɪ; *US* -berɪ/ *n* large dark-red berry from a plant that is a cross[2](7) between a blackberry and a raspberry.

logarithm /ˈlɒgərɪðəm; *US* ˈlɔːg-/ *n* (*mathematics*) any of a series of numbers set out in tables which make it possible to work out problems in multiplication and division by adding and subtracting. ⇨ App 9. ▷ **logarithmic** /ˌlɒgəˈrɪðmɪk; *US* ˌlɔːg-/ *adj*: *a logarithmic function.* **logarithmically** /-klɪ/ *adv.*

loggerheads /ˈlɒgəhedz/ *n* (idm) **at loggerheads** (**with sb**) disagreeing or quarrelling: *He and his wife are always at loggerheads.* ○ *His father's will has set him at loggerheads with his brother*, ie caused them to quarrel.

loggia /ˈləʊdʒə, ˈlɒdʒɪə/ *n* open-sided gallery or arcade, esp one that forms part of a house and has one side open to the garden.

logic /ˈlɒdʒɪk/ *n* [U] **1** science of reasoning. **2** particular method or system of reasoning. **3** chain of reasoning (regarded as good or bad): *You have to accept the logic of his argument.* **4** ability to reason correctly. **5** (*computing*) (**a**) principles used in designing a computer. (**b**) the circuit(s) involved in this.

▷ **logician** /ləˈdʒɪʃn/ *n* person who is skilled in logic.

logical /ˈlɒdʒɪkl/ *adj* **1** in accordance with the rules of logic; correctly reasoned: *a logical argument, conclusion.* **2** (of an action, event, etc) in accordance with what seems reasonable or natural: *the logical outcome* ○ *It seemed the only logical thing to do.* **3** capable of reasoning correctly: *a logical mind.*

▷ **logicality** /ˌlɒdʒɪˈkælətɪ/ *n* [U] being logical. **logically** /-klɪ/ *adv*: *argue logically.*

□ ˌ**logical ˈpositivism** school of philosophy which claims that a statement only has meaning if it can be empirically proved to be true or false, and which aims to develop formal methods, similar to those of mathematics, for carrying out this kind of proof. ˌ**logical ˈpositivist.**

logistics /ləˈdʒɪstɪks/ *n* [sing or pl *v*] organization of supplies and services, etc for any complex operation. ▷ **logistic, logistical** /ləˈdʒɪstɪkl/ *adjs*: *Organizing famine relief presents huge logistical problems.* **logistically** /-klɪ/ *adv.*

logo /ˈləʊgəʊ/ *n* (*pl* ~**s**) printed symbol designed for and used by a business, company, etc as its emblem, eg in advertising.

logos /ˈlɒgɒs/ *n* [sing] (*religion*) the Word of God, which became human in Jesus Christ.

-logue (*US* **-log**) *comb form* (forming *ns*) talk or speech: *monologue* ○ *travelogue.*

-logy *comb form* (forming *ns*) **1** subject of study: *mineralogy* ○ *sociology* ○ *theology* ○ *zoology.* **2** speech or writing: *trilogy* ○ *phraseology* ○ *tautology.*

▷ **-logic(al)** *comb form* (forming *adjs*): *physiologic(al)* ○ *pathological.*

-logist *comb form* (forming *ns*) person skilled in a subject of study: *biologist* ○ *geologist.*

loin /lɔɪn/ *n* **1** [C] (*anatomy*) side and back of the body between the ribs and the hip-bone. **2** [C, U] (joint of) meat from this part of an animal: *some loin of pork.* **3 loins** [pl] (*dated*) (**a**) lower part of the body on both sides below the waist and above the legs. (**b**) (*euph*) reproductive organs. **4** (idm) **gird one's loins** ⇨ GIRD.

□ ˈ**loincloth** *n* piece of cloth worn around the body at the hips, esp as the only garment worn.

loiter /ˈlɔɪtə(r)/ *v* **1** [I, Ipr, Ip] ~ (**about/around**) stand about idly: *loitering at street corners.* **2** [I] go slowly, with frequent stops: *Don't loiter on the way home!* ▷ **loiterer** *n.*

Lolita /lɒˈliːtə/ *n* (*often derog*) young girl regarded as sexually desirable, esp by an older man. The term comes from the name of such a girl in Vladimir *Nabokov's novel *Lolita.*

loll /lɒl/ *v* **1** [I, Ipr, Ip] ~ (**about/around**) rest, sit or stand lazily, often while leaning against sth: *loll around the house.* **2** (phr v) **loll out** (of the tongue) hang loosely.

Lollard /ˈlɒlɑːd/ *n* follower of any of the medieval English preachers like John *Wyclif who attacked abuses in the Church and believed in a life of poverty and prayer. The term 'Lollard' was used by opponents of Wyclif, whose followers were often persecuted for their beliefs.

lollipop /ˈlɒlɪpɒp/ *n* large (usu flat and round) boiled sweet on a small stick, held in the hand and sucked.

□ ˈ**lollipop man** (*fem* ˈ**lollipop woman,** ˈ**lollipop lady**) (*Brit infml*) person who carries a circular sign marked 'Stop! Children Crossing' as a warning to traffic to stop, allowing children to cross a busy road, esp on their way to and from school.

lollop /ˈlɒləp/ *v* [I, Ipr, Ip] (*infml esp Brit*) move in clumsy jumps; flop about: *lolloping along (the road).*

lolly /ˈlɒlɪ/ *n* (*Brit*) **1** [C] (*infml*) lollipop. **2** [U] (*sl*) money.

London /ˈlʌndən/ capital of England and the United Kingdom, in the south-east of the country. It is one of the world's largest cities with a population of 6 700 000, not counting those who come to the capital to work or as tourists. **Greater**

London

London is the capital of Britain, and the buildings of Buckingham Palace, Whitehall (especially No 10 Downing Street), the Houses of Parliament, and the City of London represent respectively the seats of the British monarchy, government, parliament, and the financial and business world. London is also the country's cultural capital, with world-famous institutions such as the British Museum, the National Gallery, the BBC (at Broadcasting House) and the Royal Albert Hall. The familiar sights of the Tower of London and Tower Bridge on the River Thames, are also visible reminders of the city's historic past and its former importance as the country's principal commercial port.

The historic centre of London is the City of London, sometimes known as 'the square mile', around which the capital has grown and expanded since the Roman occupation of Britain. Only sixty years ago London was the largest city in the world, with a population of over 8 million. Today it has under 7 million inhabitants and the trend is for people and firms to move away from the capital.

Greater London extends over about 1 579 sq km (610 sq miles), from Enfield in the north to Croydon in the south, and Uxbridge in the west to Romford in the east. It was formed in 1965 from the City of London and parts of the Home Counties (the surrounding counties, eg Surrey, Kent and Essex), and consists of the City and 32 boroughs, the 13 boroughs of Inner London and the 19 of Outer London.

The civic government of the City is the responsibility of the Corporation of London, led by the Lord Mayor. Until it was abolished in 1986, Greater London was administered by the Greater London Council (GLC). Most of its work passed to the individual boroughs and government departments.

Many of London's most famous buildings and institutions are in the City, including St Paul's Cathedral, the Bank of England, Lloyd's, and the Central Criminal Court (the Old Bailey). The City lies between the fashionable West End, centred on Piccadilly Circus with high-class shops and hotels, prestigious clubs, and many cinemas and theatres, and the East End, historically the poorer area, where there were once many slums.

London has altered considerably in recent years. Not only have many industries and businesses moved out of London since the 1960s, but the last of the docks closed in the early 1980s, and the docking and shipping facilities moved down the Thames to Tilbury. The old dockland site is being converted into a business and residential area with its own airport. A ring-road, the M25, was built in the 1980s to enable traffic to avoid central London, but it immediately proved inadequate for the number of vehicles that use it. London's skyline has been radically altered by the many tall buildings that have appeared, especially in the City. Many important institutions have been relocated. The old fruit and vegetable market at Covent Garden moved to a bigger site south of the Thames in the mid-1970s, Lloyd's was rehoused in a striking modern building in the City in the 1980s, and the British Library is being reconstructed near St Pancras station, where its new premises are due for completion in the mid-1990s. By the end of the 1980s, too, most of the newspaper offices that were formerly in Fleet Street had moved to other sites (notably Wapping in the East End) or out of London altogether. Many Civil Service departments have also moved to other cities.

London's transport is the responsibility of London Regional Transport (LRT), which oversees the operation of the Underground, the London buses (the famous red 'double-deckers') and the recently constructed Docklands Light Railway, built in the new Docklands development as an extension of the Underground. The Underground links London's main line railway termini and also extends for some distance out of Greater London in several directions. The construction of the Channel Tunnel will make it possible for trains to run direct from London to Paris.

With its numerous famous buildings and historic sites, London is an important tourist attraction. Its appeal is enhanced by the River Thames, which runs through it, and by its many public parks and gardens. Most of these, including Hyde Park, Green Park, St James's Park, Regent's Park and Kensington Gardens, are 'royal parks', so called because they belong to the Crown.

London, ie the centre along with the suburbs, divided into the 32 boroughs and the *City, covers a vast area in which a large part of Britain's economic activity goes on. **Central London** contains the older parts: the *Houses of Parliament and *Buckingham Palace, historical and cultural attractions like the *Tower of London, *Westminster Abbey and the *National Gallery, and financial institutions like *Lloyd's and the *Bank of England. ⇨ article.

▷ **Londoner** *n* person who lives in or comes from London.

lone /ləʊn/ *adj* [attrib] (*usu rhet*) **1** without companions; solitary: *a lone figure trudging through the snow.* Cf ALONE 1, LONELY 3. **2** (idm) **a ˌlone ˈwolf** person who prefers to be, work, etc alone.

▷ **loner** *n* (*infml*) person who avoids the company of others: *She's been a loner all her life.*

lonely /ˈləʊnlɪ/ *adj* **1** sad because one lacks friends or companions: *I live all alone but I never feel lonely.* ○ *a lonely-looking child* ○ *Living in a big city can be* (ie make one feel) *very lonely.* ○ *Hers is a lonely life.* **2** [attrib] (of places) far from inhabited places; not often visited; remote: *Antarctica is the loneliest place on earth.* **3** [attrib] without companions: *a lonely traveller.* **4** (idm) **plough a lonely furrow** ⇨ PLOUGH *v.* ⇨ Usage at ALONE. ▷ **loneliness** *n* [U]: *suffer from loneliness.*

□ **ˌlonely ˈhearts** people who are seeking friendship, esp with a view to marriage: [attrib] *a lonely hearts column,* ie a section of a newspaper, etc containing messages from such people.

lonesome /ˈləʊnsəm/ *adj* (*esp US*) **1** lonely: *I get lonesome when you're not here.* ○ *a lonesome mountain village.* **2** causing loneliness: *a lonesome journey.* ⇨ Usage at ALONE. **3** (idm) **by/on one's ˈlonesome** (*infml*) on one's own; alone.

long[1] /lɒŋ; *US* lɔːŋ/ *adj* (**-er** /-ŋgə(r)/, **-est** /-ŋgɪst/) **1** having a great or specified extent in space: *How long is the River Nile?* ○ *Your hair is longer than mine.* ○ *Is it a long way* (ie far) *to your house?* ○ *These trousers are two inches too long.* Cf SHORT[1] 1. **2** having a great or specified duration or extent in time: *He's been ill for a long time.* ○ *How long are the holidays?* ○ *They're six weeks long.* ○ *Don't be too long about it,* ie Do it soon or quickly. ⇨ Usage at LONG[3]. **3** (*phonetics*) (of vowel sounds) taking relatively more time to utter than the corresponding short vowel sound: *The vowel sound in 'caught' is long; in 'cot' it is short.* **4** seeming to be longer than it really is: *ten long years, miles, etc.* **5** (of memory) able to recall events distant in time. **6** (idm) **at the ˈlongest** not longer than the specified time: *He's only away for short periods — a week at the longest.* **go ˈfar/go a long ˈway** become very successful: *That girl will go a long way, I'm sure.* **go far/go a long way towards doing sth** make a considerable contribution towards sth: *concessions which go a long way towards satisfying his critics* ○ *The new legislation does not go far enough towards solving the problem.* **go a long way** (**a**) (of money, food, etc) last a long time: *She makes a little money go a long way,* ie buys many things by careful spending. ○ *A little of this paint goes a long way,* ie covers a large area. (**b**) be as much as one can bear: *A little of his company goes a long way,* ie One can tolerate his company for a short time only. **happy as the day is long** ⇨ HAPPY. **have come a long way** have made much progress: *We've come a long way since those early days of the project.* **have a long ˈarm** be able to make one's power or authority felt even at a distance. **in long/short pants** ⇨ PANTS. **in the ˈlong run** ultimately; eventually: *In the long run prices are bound to rise.* **in the long/short term** ⇨ TERM. **it's as broad as it's long** ⇨ BROAD[1]. (**put on, have, wear, etc**) **a long ˈface** sad expression. **a long ˈhaul** long and difficult activity, etc: *It's been a long haul but at last this dictionary is published.* **a ˈlong shot** wild guess or attempt. **ˌlong in the ˈtooth** (*joc*) rather old: *He's getting a bit long in the tooth to be playing football.* **long time no ˈsee** (*infml*) (used as a greeting) it's a long time since we last met. **not by a ˈlong chalk**; *Brit* **not by a ˈlong shot** not at all: *We're not beaten yet, (not) by a long chalk.* **take a long (cool/hard) ˈlook at sth** consider a possibility, problem, etc carefully and at length. **take the ˈlong view** consider events, effects, factors, etc a long time in the future, rather than the immediate situation. **to cut a long story short** to get to the point of what one is saying quickly.

□ **ˈlongboat** *n* largest boat carried on a sailing-ship.

ˈlongbow *n* bow drawn by hand, equal in length to the height of the archer and used to shoot feathered arrows. Cf CROSSBOW.

ˌlong-ˈdistance *adj, adv* travelling or operating between distant places: *a ˌlong-distance ˈlorry driver, ˈphone call, ˈrunner* ○ *to phone long-distance.*

ˌlong diˈvision (*mathematics*) (process of) dividing one number by another with all the calculations written down: *Can you do long division?* ○ [attrib] *a long-division sum.*

ˈlong drink drink that is large in quantity, filling a tall glass, eg beer.

ˌlong-ˈhaired *adj* [usu attrib] (*infml derog*) **1** concerned with intellectual or artistic matters in a pretentious or impractical way: *ˌlong-haired intelˈlectuals/muˈsicians.* **2** wearing long hair as a sign of an unconventional way of life: *ˌlong-haired ˈhippies.*

ˈlonghand *n* [U] ordinary writing (contrasted with shorthand, typing, etc): *all written in longhand.*

ˈlong-haul *adj* [attrib] (esp of an aircraft flight) covering a long distance.

ˈlong hop (in cricket) ball that pitches short and is easy to hit.

ˈlonghorn *n* one of a breed of domestic cattle with long horns.

ˌlong ˈjohns (*infml*) underpants with legs that extend to the ankles: *a warm pair of long johns.*

ˈlong jump (*US* **ˈbroad jump**) athletic contest of jumping as far forward as possible: *competing in the long jump.*

ˌlong-ˈlife *adj* (esp of dairy products) remaining usable for a long time: *ˌlong-life ˈmilk.*

long ˈodds (in betting) very uneven odds, eg 50 to 1.

the ˌLong ˈParliament English parliament first summoned to meet by Charles I in 1640. Its opposition to the king led eventually to the Civil War. *Cromwell dismissed it in 1653. It reassembled briefly as the *Rump Parliament before being finally dissolved at the *Restoration in 1660.

ˌlong-ˈrange *adj* [attrib] (**a**) of or for a period of time far in the future: *ˌlong-range ˈplanning* ○ *a ˌlong-range ˈweather forecast.* (**b**) (of vehicles, missiles, etc) that can be used over great distances: *a ˌlong-range ˈbomber.*

ˈlongship *n* long narrow ship with a sail and oars, used by the Vikings and later Scandinavian peoples.

ˌlong-ˈsighted (also *esp US* **ˌfar-ˈsighted**) *adj* [usu pred] (**a**) only able to see clearly what is at a distance: *She's long-sighted and needs glasses to read.* (**b**) (*fig*) having foresight; prudent.

ˈlongstop *n* (in cricket) fielder standing directly behind the wicket-keeper.

ˌlong ˈsuit 1 many playing-cards of one suit in a hand: *Play the highest card in your longest suit.* **2** (*fig*) thing at which one excels: *Modesty is not his long suit.*

ˈlong-time *adj* [attrib] that has lasted for a long time: *a long-time friendship.*

ˌlong-ˈterm *adj* [usu attrib] of or for a long period of time: *a ˌlong-term comˈmitment.*

ˌlong ˈton measure of weight, equal to 2240 pounds.

ˈlong wave (*abbr* **LW**) radio wave having a wavelength of more than 1000 metres: [attrib] *a long-wave broadcast.*

ˌlong weekˈend weekend that is made longer (as a holiday) by an extra day at the beginning or the end of it.

ˌlong-ˈwinded *adj* talking or writing at tedious length: *a ˌlong-winded ˈspeaker, ˈspeech, ˈstyle.* **ˌlong-ˈwindedness** *n* [U].

long[2] /lɒŋ; *US* lɔːŋ/ *n* **1** [U] long time or interval (used esp as in the expressions shown): *This won't take long.* ○ *Will you be away for long?* ○ *I hope to write to you before long.* ⇨ Usage at LONG[3]. **2** [C] long signal (eg in Morse code); long vowel or syllable (esp in Latin verse): *a long and two shorts.* **3** (idm) **the ˌlong and (the) ˈshort of it** all that need be said about it; the general effect or result of it.

long[3] /lɒŋ; *US* lɔːŋ/ *adv* (**-er** /-ŋgə(r)/, **-est** /-ŋgɪst/) **1** for a long time: *Were you in Rome long?* ○ *Stay as long as you like.* ○ *long into the next century* ○ *I shan't be long*, ie will come, go, etc soon. **2** at a time distant from a specified point of time (used esp in the expressions shown): *long ago/before/after/since* ○ *He died not long* (ie soon) *after (that).* ⇨ Usage at RECENT. **3** (with *ns* indicating duration) throughout the specified time: *all day long* ○ *I've waited for this moment my whole life long.* **4** (idm) **as/so long as** (used as a *conj*) (**a**) on condition that; provided that: *As long as it doesn't rain we can play.* (**b**) (*US*) since; inasmuch as. **be not long for this world** be likely to die soon. **no/any/much ˈlonger** after a certain point in time: *I can't wait any/much longer.* ○ *He no longer lives here.* **he who laughs last laughs longest** ⇨ LAUGH. **so long** (*dated infml*) goodbye.

□ **ˌlong-drawn-ˈout** *adj* made to last too long; unnecessarily extended: *long-drawn-out negotiations.*

ˌlong-ˈlived *adj* having a long life; lasting for a long time: *My family tend to be quite long-lived.*

ˌlong-playing ˈrecord (also *dated* **ˌlong-ˈplayer**) (*abbr* **LP**) type of gramophone record that plays for up to about 30 minutes on each side.

ˌlong-ˈstanding *adj* [esp attrib] that has existed or lasted for a long time: *ˌlong-standing ˈgrievances* ○ *a ˌlong-standing arˈrangement.*

ˌlong-ˈsuffering *adj* patiently bearing problems, troubles, etc, esp those caused by another person: *I pity his ˌlong-suffering ˈwife.*

NOTE ON USAGE: Both **long** and **a long time** are used as adverbial expressions of time. **1 Long** is not used in positive sentences unless it is modified by another adverb, eg *too, enough, ago*: *You've been sleeping too long/long enough.* ○ *She waited there (for) a long time.* **2** Both can be used in questions: *Have you been here long/a long time?* **3** In negative sentences there can be a difference in meaning. Compare: *I haven't been here for a long time* (ie It is a long time since I was last here) and *I haven't been here long* (ie I arrived here only a short time ago).

long[4] /lɒŋ; *US* lɔːŋ/ *v* [Ipr, It] ~ **for sth**/ ~ **(for sb) to do sth** have an intense desire for sth; want sth very much: *The children are longing for the holidays.* ○ *a (much) longed-for rest* ○ *She longed for him to ask her to dance.* ○ *I'm longing to see you again.*

▷ **longing** /ˈlɒŋɪŋ; *US* ˈlɔːŋɪŋ/ *n* [C, U] ~ **(for sb/sth)** intense desire: *a longing for home* ○ *a deep sense of longing.* — *adj* [attrib] having or showing longing: *a longing look* ○ *gaze with longing eyes.* **longingly** *adv*: *speak longingly of one's native land* ○ *The children were gazing longingly at the toys in the shop window.*

long *abbr* longitude: *long 23°E/W*, ie East/West. Cf LAT.

longevity /lɒnˈdʒevətɪ/ *n* [U] (*fml*) long life: *a family noted for its longevity.*

Longfellow /ˈlɒŋfeləʊ/ Henry Wadsworth (1807-82), American poet. He won great popularity with his poems and stories based on history and folklore, as in his most famous work, *Hiawatha*, which uses an American Indian legend.

longitude /ˈlɒndʒɪtjuːd; *US* -tuːd/ *n* [U] (*abbr* **long**) distance east or west of the Greenwich meridian, measured in degrees: *lines of longitude marked on a map.* ⇨ illus at GLOBE. Cf LATITUDE 1.

▷ **longitudinal** /ˌlɒndʒɪˈtjuːdɪnl; *US* -ˈtuːdnl/ *adj* **1** of longitude. **2** of or in length; measured lengthwise: *longitudinal stripes*, eg on a flag. **longitudinally** /-nəlɪ/ *adv*.

long-shoreman /ˈlɒŋʃɔːmən; *US* ˈlɔːŋ-/ *n* (*pl* **-men** /-mən/) (*esp US*) person employed to work on shore loading and unloading ships.

longways /ˈlɒŋweɪz; *US* ˈlɔːŋ-/ (also **longwise** /ˈlɒŋwaɪz; *US* ˈlɔːŋ-/) *adv* = LENGTHWISE (LENGTH).

loo /luː/ *n* (*pl* ~**s**) (*Brit infml euph*) lavatory: *I need to go to the loo.* ⇨ Usage at TOILET.

loofah (also *esp US* **luffa**) /ˈluːfə/ *n* [C] rough bath sponge made from the dried pod of a type of gourd.

look[1] /lʊk/ *v* **1** [I, Ipr, Ip] ~ **(at sb/sth)** turn one's eyes in a particular direction (in order to see sb/sth): *If you look carefully you can just see the church from here.* ○ *We looked but saw nothing.* ○ *'Has the postman been yet?' 'I'll just look and see.'* ○ *Look to see whether the road is clear before you cross.* ○ *I was looking the other way when the goal was scored.* ○ *She looked at me and smiled.* ○ *She looked out of the window and saw the postman coming up the path.* ○ *They looked across the room at each other.* ○ *She blushed and looked down at the floor.* **2** [Ipr, Tw] ~ **at sth** (esp imperative) pay attention to sth; observe sth: *Look at the time! We should have been at the theatre ten minutes ago.* ○ *Can't you look where you're going? You nearly knocked me over!* ○ *Look what Denise has given me for Christmas!* ○ *Look who's here!* **3** (**a**) [La, Ln] seem to be; appear: *look healthy, ill, pale, puzzled, sad, tired* ○ *That book looks interesting/That looks an interesting book.* ○ *That pie looks good*, ie good to eat. ○ *The town always looks deserted on Sunday mornings.* ○ *'How do I look in this dress?' 'You look very nice (in it).'* ○ *You made me look a complete fool!* (**b**) [Ipr] ~ **(to sb) like sb/sth**; ~ **(to sb) as if.../as though...** (usu not in the continuous tenses) have the appearance of sb/sth; suggest by appearance that...: *It looks like salt and it is salt.* ○ *That photograph doesn't look like her at all.* ○ *This looks to me like the right door.* ○ *It looks like rain/It looks as if it's going to rain.* ○ *It looks like being/as if it's going to be a nice day.* ○ *You look as if you slept badly.* ○ *It doesn't look to me as if the Socialists will win the election.* ⇨ Usage at FEEL[1]. **4** [I, Ipr] ~ **(for sb/sth)** search for or try to find sb/sth: *'I can't find the papers.' 'Well, keep looking!'* ○ *Where have you been? We've been looking for you everywhere.* ○ *Are you still looking for a job?* ○ *Negotiators are looking for a peaceful settlement to the dispute.* ○ *The youths were clearly looking for* (ie were intending to start) *a fight.* **5** [Ipr, Ip] face in, or give a view in, a particular direction: *The house looks east.* ○ *The hotel looks towards the sea.* ○ *My bedroom looks onto the garden.* **6** (idm) **be looking to do sth** try to do sth: *The government will be looking to reduce inflation by a further two per cent this year.* **look ˈbad; not look ˈgood** be not right according to convention, and likely to make others have a bad opinion of one: *It looks bad not going to your own brother's wedding.* **look ˈbad (for sb)** suggest probable failure, trouble or disaster; be ominous: *He's had a severe heart attack; things are looking bad for him, I'm afraid*, ie he is probably going to die. **look ˈgood** seem to be promising; seem to be making satisfactory progress: *This year's sales figures are looking good.* **look ˈhere** (used to express protest or to ask sb to pay attention or listen to sth): *Now look here, it wasn't my fault that we missed the train.* ○ *Look here, I'm not having you make remarks like that about my sister.* **(not) look oneˈself** (not) have one's normal (healthy) appearance: *You're not looking yourself today*, eg You look tired or ill. **look sb ˌup and ˈdown** examine sb in a careful or contemptuous way: *I didn't like the way he looked me up and down before speaking to me.* **never/not look ˈback** (*infml*) continue to prosper or be successful: *Her first novel was published three years ago and since then she hasn't looked back.* **to ˈlook at sb/sth** judging by the appearance of sb/sth: *To look at him you'd never think he was a successful businessman.* **not be much to ˈlook at** (*infml*) not have an attractive appearance: *The house isn't much to look at but it's quite spacious inside.* (For other idioms containing **look**, see entries for *ns, adjs*, etc, eg **look one's age** ⇨ AGE; **look sharp** ⇨ SHARP.)

7 (phr v) **look ˈafter oneself/sb** make sure that one/sb is safe and well; take care of oneself/sb: *He needs to be properly looked after.* ○ *Who will look after the children while their mother is in hospital?* ○ *He's good at looking after himself/his own interests.* **look after sth** be responsible for sth: *Our neighbours are looking after the garden while we are away.*

look aˈhead think about what is going to happen in the future: *Have you looked ahead to what you'll be doing in five years' time?*

look at sth (**a**) examine sth, esp closely: *Your ankle is badly swollen; I think the doctor ought to look at it.* ○ *I haven't had time to look at* (ie read) *your essay yet.* ○ *I'm taking my car to the garage to be looked at.* (**b**) think about, consider or study sth: *The implications of the new legislation will need to be looked at.* ○ *The committee wouldn't even look at my proposal.* (**c**) view or regard sth: *The Americans look at life differently from the British.* ○ *Looked at from that point of view, the job becomes easy.*

look ˈback (on sth) think about (sth in) one's past: *look back on one's childhood, past, life.*

look down on sb/sth (*infml*) regard sb/sth with contempt; consider sb/sth inferior to oneself; despise sb/sth: *She looks down on people who've never been to university.* ○ *He was looked down on because of his humble background.*

look for sth hope for sth; expect sth: *We shall be looking for an improvement in your work this term.*

look forward to sth/doing sth anticipate sth with pleasure: *look forward to one's holidays, the weekend, a trip to the theatre* ○ *We're so much looking forward to seeing you again.*

look ˈin (on sb/at...) make a short visit to sb's house/a place: *The doctor will look in again this evening.* ○ *Why don't you look in (on me) next time you're in town?* ○ *I may look in at the party on my way home.*

look into sth investigate or examine sth: *A working party has been set up to look into the problem.* ○ *His disappearance is being looked into by the police.*
look ˈon be a spectator at an event or incident; watch sth without taking part in it oneself: *Passers-by just looked on as a man was viciously attacked.* **look on sb/sth as sb/sth** regard or consider sb/sth to be sb/sth: *She's looked on as the leading authority on the subject.* **look on sb/sth with sth** regard sb/sth in the specified way: *I look on him/his behaviour with contempt.* ○ *She was always looked on with distrust.* ○ *How do people in general look on her?*
look ˈout (used in the imperative) be careful; watch out: *Look out! There's a car coming.* **look out (for sb/sth)** be alert or watchful in order to see, find or be aware of sb/sth: *Will you go to the station and look out for Mr Hill?* ○ *Look out for pickpockets.* ○ *Police will be looking out for trouble-makers at today's match.* ○ *Do look out for spelling mistakes when you check your work.* **look sth out (for sb/sth)** search for sth and find it: *I must look out some bits and pieces for the church jumble sale.*
look over sth inspect or examine sth: *We must look over the house before we decide to rent it.* **look sth over** examine sth one by one or part by part: *Here's the mail. I've looked it over.*
look ˈround (a) turn one's head in order to see sb/sth: *She looked round when she heard the noise behind her.* **(b)** examine various options or possibilities: *We're going to look round a bit before deciding where to buy a house.* **look round sth** visit (a place or building) as a tourist or sightseer: *Shall we look round the cathedral this afternoon?*
look through sb deliberately ignore sb whom one can see clearly: *She just looked straight through me.* **look through sth** examine or read sth quickly: *She looked through her notes before the examination.* **look sth through** examine or read sth carefully; examine or read (a number of things) one by one: *Always look your work through before handing it in.* ○ *He looked the proposals through before approving them.*
look to sb for sth; look to sb to do sth rely on or expect sb to provide sth or do sth: *We are looking to you for help.* ○ *She's regularly looked to for advice.* ○ *Many people are looking to the new government to reduce unemployment.* **look to sth** make sure that sth is safe or in good condition; be careful about sth: *The country must look to its defences.* ○ *You should look to your health.*
look ˈup (a) raise one's eyes: *She looked up (from her book) as I entered the room.* **(b)** (*infml*) (of business, sb's prospects, etc) become better; improve: *Inflation is coming down; unemployment is coming down; things are definitely looking up!* **look sb up** (*infml*) visit or contact sb, esp after not having seen him for a long time: *Do look me up the next time you're in London.* **look sth up** search for (a word or fact) in a dictionary or reference book: *If you want to know how a word is used, look the word up in the Advanced Learner's Dictionary.* ○ *Look up the time of the next train in the timetable.* **look up to sb** admire or respect sb: *She has always looked up to her father.*
▷ **look** *interj* (used to make sb listen to sth important that one is saying): *Look, don't you think you're over-reacting slightly?*
looker *n* (*infml approv sexist*) attractive girl or woman: *She's a real looker!* **looker-on** /ˌlʊkərˈɒn/ *n* (*pl* **lookers-on** /ˌlʊkəzˈɒn/) person who watches sth but does not take part in it; spectator; onlooker.
-looking (forming compound *adjs*) having the specified appearance: *a ˌstrange-looking ˈplace* ○ *She's not ˌbad-ˈlooking*, ie quite attractive.
□ **ˈlook-alike** *n* (often used after a person's name) person who has a very similar appearance to sb else: *the Prime Minister's look-alike* ○ [attrib] *a Marilyn Monroe look-alike contest.*
ˈlook-in *n* (idm) **(not) give sb/get/have a ˈlook-in** (*infml*) (not) give sb/have a chance to participate or succeed in sth: *She talks so much that the rest of us never get a look-in.* ○ *He'd love to play for the school team but he never gets a look-in*, ie is never chosen.
ˈlooking-glass *n* (*dated*) mirror.
ˈlook-out *n* **1** [C] place from which sb watches carefully in order to see an enemy, intruder, etc: [attrib] *a look-out tower.* **2** [C] person who watches from such a place: *We posted several look-outs.* **3** (idm) **be a bad, grim, poor, etc look-out (for sb/sth)** prospects are bad, etc for sb/sth: *It's a bleak look-out for the coal industry as the number of pit closures increases.* **be ˈsb's look-out** (*infml*) (used to describe an action that is considered irresponsible) be sb's concern or responsibility: *If you want to waste your money, that's your ˈown look-out.* **be on the look-out for sb/sth; keep a look-out for sb/sth** = LOOK OUT FOR SB/STH.
ˈlook-over *n* [sing] brief examination or inspection: *Would you give these figures a look-over to check my calculations?*
ˈlook-through *n* [sing] act of reading sth quickly: *I gave her article a quick look-through.*

NOTE ON USAGE: **1 Look (at)** means to direct one's eyes towards a particular object: *Just look at this beautiful present.* ○ *I looked in the cupboard but I couldn't find a clean shirt.* **2 Gaze (at)** means to keep one's eyes turned in a particular direction for a long time. We can gaze at something without looking at it if our eyes are not focussed: *He spent hours gazing into the distance.* ○ *She sat gazing unhappily out of the window.* **3 Stare (at)** suggests a long, deliberate, fixed look. Staring is more intense than gazing and the eyes are often wide open. It can be impolite to stare at somebody: *I don't like being stared at.* ○ *She stared at me in astonishment.* **4 Peer (at)** means to look very closely and suggests that it is difficult to see well: *We peered through the fog at the house numbers.* ○ *He peered at me through thick glasses.* **5 Gawp (at)** means to look at someone or something in a foolish way with the mouth open: *What are you gawping at?* ○ *He just sits there gawping at the television all day!*

look² /lʊk/ *n* **1** [C usu *sing*] act of looking: *Have/Take a look at this letter.* **2** [C usu *sing*] search; inspection: *I've had a good look (for it) but I can't find it anywhere.* **3** [C] way of looking; expression or appearance: *a look of pleasure, fear, relief, etc* ○ *I knew something was wrong: everyone was giving me funny looks*, ie looking at me strangely. ○ *The house has a Mediterranean look.* **4** [C] fashion; style: *The broad-shouldered look is in this year.* ○ *They've given the shop a completely new look*, ie redesigned it. ○ [attrib] *I like your new-look hair-style.* **5 looks** [pl] person's appearance: *She's got her father's good looks.* ○ *She's starting to lose her looks*, ie become less beautiful. **6** (idm) **by/from the look of sb/sth** judging by sb's/sth's appearance, etc: *Taxes are going to go up, by the look of it.* **give sb/get a dirty look** ⇨ DIRTY¹. **like the look/sound of sb/sth** ⇨ LIKE¹. **take a long look at sth** ⇨ LONG¹.
loom¹ /lu:m/ *n* machine for weaving cloth.
loom² /lu:m/ *v* **(a)** [Ipr, Ip] appear in an indistinct and often threatening way: *an enormous shape looming (up) in the distance, out of the darkness, through the mist, etc.* **(b)** [La, I] (*fig*) appear important or threatening: *The prospect of war loomed large in everyone's mind.* ○ *the looming threat of a strike.*
loony /ˈlu:nɪ/ *n, adj* (*sl*) (person who is) crazy or eccentric; lunatic: *He does have some pretty loony ideas.*
□ **ˈloony-bin** *n* (*sl joc offensive*) mental home or hospital.

loop

loop

loop

loop

loop /lu:p/ *n* **1 (a)** shape produced by a curve crossing itself: *a double loop like a figure eight* ○ *handwriting with loops on many of the letters.* **(b)** any path or pattern shaped roughly like this: *The plane flew round and round in wide loops.* **(c)** length of string, wire, etc in such a shape, usu fastened at the crossing: *a loop of ribbon to carry the package by.* **2** complete circuit for electric current. **3** (*computing*) set of instructions carried out repeatedly until some specified condition is satisfied. **4** contraceptive coil.
▷ **loop** *v* **1** [I, Tn, Tn·pr, Tn·p] form or bend (sth) into a loop or loops: *strings of lanterns looping/looped between the branches of the trees* ○ *looped threads* ○ *loop (up) a rope.* **2** [Tn, Tn·pr, Tn·p] fasten or join (sth) with a loop or loops: *loop the rope round the post* ○ *loop the curtains back.* **3** (idm) **ˌloop the ˈloop** (of an aircraft) fly in a complete circle vertically; (of a pilot) cause an aircraft to do this.
□ **ˈloop-line** *n* railway or telegraph line that leaves the main line and then joins it again.
loophole /ˈlu:phəʊl/ *n* **1** way of escaping a rule, the terms of a contract, etc, esp one provided by vague or careless wording: *A good lawyer can always find a loophole.* **2** narrow vertical opening in the wall of a fort, etc for looking or shooting through, or to let light and air in.
loopy /ˈlu:pɪ/ *adj* (*sl*) crazy: *It sounds a pretty loopy idea to me.*
loose¹ /lu:s/ *adj* (**-r, -st**) **1** freed from control; not tied up: *The cows had got out of the field and were (roaming) loose in the road.* ⇨ Usage. **2** (that can be) detached from its place; not firmly fixed: *Be careful with that saucepan — the handle's loose.* ○ *a rope hanging loose* ○ *a loose tooth, thread, screw.* **3** not fastened together; not held or contained in sth: *loose change*, ie coins carried eg in a pocket ○ *nails sold loose by weight*, ie not in a packet. **4** not organized strictly: *a loose confederation of states* ○ *a loose symphonic structure.* **5** not exact; vague: *a loose translation* ○ *loose thinking.* **6 (a)** physically slack; not tense: *loose skin* ○ *have loose bowels*, ie suffer from diarrhoea. **(b)** not tight or constricting: *a loose collar.* ⇨ Usage. **7** not compact or dense in texture: *cloth with a loose weave* ○ *loose soil.* **8** [esp attrib] (of talk, behaviour, etc) not sufficiently controlled: *loose conduct* ○ *lead a loose and dissolute life* ○ *a loose* (ie immoral) *woman.* **9** (of play in a game) careless and inaccurate: *some rather loose bowling*, ie in cricket. **10** (idm) **all hell broke/was let loose** ⇨ HELL. **at a loose ˈend**; *US* also **at loose ends** having nothing to do; not knowing what to do: *Come and see us if you're at a loose end.* **break ˈloose (from sb/sth)** escape confinement or restriction: *The dog has broken loose*, ie got free from its chain. ○ *break loose from tradition.* **come/work ˈloose** (of a fastening, bolt, etc) become unfastened or insecure. **cut ˈloose** (*infml*) act, speak, etc freely and without restraint: *He really cut loose and told me what he thought of me.* **cut sth/sb loose (from sth)** make sth/sb separate or free: *cut a boat loose* ○ *cut oneself loose from one's family.* **have a loose ˈtongue** be in the habit of talking too freely. **have a screw loose** ⇨ SCREW *n.* **let sb/sth loose** release sb/sth: *Don't let that dog loose among the sheep.* ○ *Just close your eyes and let loose your imagination.* **let sb loose on sth** allow sb to do as he likes with sth: *I daren't let Bill loose on the garden — he'd pull up all the flowers.* **play fast and ˈloose (with sb)** behave dishonestly or deceitfully.
▷ **loose-** (in compounds) loosely: *loose-fitting clothes.*
loosely *adv* in a loose manner: *loosely speaking*, ie in general ○ *loosely translated.*
looseness *n* [U].
□ **ˈloose box** stall in which a horse can move about freely.
ˈloose covers removable covers for chairs, etc.
ˌloose-ˈleaf *adj* [esp attrib] (of a note-book, etc) with pages that can be removed separately and replaced.

NOTE ON USAGE: The adjective **loose** has

several senses. Two of these are **1** 'not tied up' and **2** 'not tight': *The dogs are loose in the garden.* ○ *a tight/loose shirt, dress, belt, etc.* The verb **loose** (also **unloose**) relates to the first sense and means 'set free': *The guard loosed the dogs when the burglar alarm went off.* The verb **loosen** (also **unloosen**) relates to the second sense and means 'make loose': *After the huge meal he loosened his belt and went to sleep.* Note that the verb **lose** (*pt* **lost**, *pp* **lost**) is unconnected with **loose** or **loosen**.

loose[2] /luːs/ *v* **1** [Tn] release (an animal, etc): *loose the dogs.* **2** (phr v) **loose (sth) off (at sb/sth)** fire (a gun or missile): *Men were loosing off at shadows* ○ *loose off a few bullets (at the enemy).* ⇨ Usage at LOOSE[1].

loose[3] /luːs/ *n* (idm) **(be) on the ˈloose** enjoying oneself freely.

loosen /ˈluːsn/ *v* **1** [I, Tn] become or make loose or looser: *Can you loosen the lid of this jar?* ○ *This knot keeps loosening.* ○ *medicine to loosen a cough*, ie help bring up the phlegm. ⇨ Usage at LOOSE[1]. **2** (idm) **loosen/tighten the purse-strings** ⇨ PURSE[1]. **loosen sb's ˈtongue** make sb talk freely: *Wine soon loosened his tongue.* **3** (phr v) **loosen (sth) up** (cause sth to) relax: *You should loosen up (your muscles) before playing any sport.* ○ *Don't be so nervous — loosen up a bit.*

loot /luːt/ *n* [U] **1** goods (esp private property) taken from an enemy in war, or stolen by thieves. **2** (*infml*) money; wealth.

▷ **loot** *v* **(a)** [I] carry off loot: *soldiers killing and looting wherever they went.* **(b)** [Tn] take (sth) as loot; take loot from (buildings, etc left unprotected, eg after a violent event): *The mob looted many shops in the area.* Cf PILLAGE, PLUNDER. **looter** *n*: *Looters will be shot on sight.*

lop /lɒp/ *v* (**-pp-**) **1** [Tn] cut branches, twigs, etc off (a tree). **2** (phr v) **lop sth off/away** remove (branches, twigs, etc) from a tree, etc by cutting: *He had his arm lopped off by an electric saw.*

lope /ləʊp/ *v* [I, Ip] run fairly fast with long bounding strides: *The tiger loped off into the jungle.*

▷ **lope** *n* (usu *sing*) long bounding step or stride: *move at a steady lope.*

lop-eared /ˌlɒp ˈɪəd/ *adj* having drooping ears: *a ˌlop-eared ˈrabbit.*

lopsided /ˌlɒp ˈsaɪdɪd/ *adj* with one side lower, smaller, etc than the other; unevenly balanced: *a ˌlopsided ˈgrin.*

loquacious /ləˈkweɪʃəs/ *adj* (*fml*) fond of talking; talkative. ▷ **loquaciously** *adv.* **loquaciousness**, **loquacity** /ləˈkwæsətɪ/ *ns* [U].

loquat /ˈləʊkwɒt, ˈlɒkwæt/ *n* [C] **(a)** ornamental tree, common in China and Japan, having small yellow edible fruit. **(b)** fruit of this tree.

lord /lɔːd/ *n* **1** [C] master; male ruler: *our sovereign lord the king.* **2** [sing] **(a) the Lord** God; Christ. **(b) Our Lord** Christ. **3 (a)** [C] nobleman: *She married a lord.* **(b)** [C] **the Lords** [sing or pl *v*] (*Brit*) (members of) the House of Lords (HOUSE[1] 4): *The Lords is/are debating the issue.* ⇨ article at PARLIAMENT. **4 Lord** (*Brit*) **(a)** title of certain high officials: *the Lords of the Treasury* ○ *the First Lord of the Admiralty* ○ *the Lord Mayor of London.* **(b)** title prefixed to the names of peers and barons: *Lord Derby*, ie the title of the Earl of Derby. ⇨ article at ARISTOCRAT. **(c) My Lord** respectful form of address to certain noblemen, judges and bishops. **5** (idm) **drunk as a lord** ⇨ DRUNK[2]. **good ˈLord** *interj* (expressing surprise, etc). **live like a lord** ⇨ LIVE[2]. **one's ˌlord and ˈmaster** (*joc*) one's husband. **ˈLord knows** nobody can say: *Lord knows where he dug up that dreadful story.* **year of our Lord** ⇨ YEAR.

▷ **lord** *v* (phr v) **lord it over sb** behave in a superior or domineering way to sb: *He likes to lord it over the junior staff.*

□ **ˌLord ˈAdvocate** senior legal official in Scotland (equivalent to the Attorney-General in England and Wales) who is responsible for advising Parliament and the monarch on the law and prosecutes for the Crown in some important cases.

ˌLord ˈJustice (*abbr* **LJ**) title of a judge in the Court of Appeal (COURT[4]).

the ˌLord Mayor's ˈShow annual parade held in London on the second Saturday in November, when the new Lord Mayor rides in a horse-drawn carriage to the Royal Courts of Justice.

ˌlord of the ˈmanor (in the Middle Ages) master from whom men held land and to whom they owed service.

the ˈLord's Day Sunday.

the ˌLord's ˈPrayer the prayer taught by Christ to his disciples, beginning 'Our Father'.

ˌLords ˈspiritual (*Brit*) bishops and archbishops in the House of Lords.

ˌLords ˈtemporal (*Brit*) noblemen in the House of Lords who inherit their titles or are given them for life.

lordly /ˈlɔːdlɪ/ *adj* (**-ier, -iest**) **1** haughty; insolent in a superior way: *dismiss people with a lordly gesture.* **2** suitable for a lord; magnificent: *a lordly mansion.* ▷ **lordliness** *n* [U].

lordship /ˈlɔːdʃɪp/ *n* **1** [C] title used in speaking to or about a man of the rank of 'Lord': *his/your lordship* ○ *their lordships* ○ (*joc*) *Would your lordship like a cup of tea?* **2** [U] ~ **(over sb/sth)** (*dated fml*) authority; rule.

lore /lɔː(r)/ *n* [U] knowledge and traditions about a subject or possessed by a particular group of people: *ˈbird lore* ○ *ˈfolklore* ○ *ˈgypsy lore* ○ *ˈCeltic lore.*

lorgnette /lɔːˈnjet/ *n* pair of eye-glasses held to the eyes on a long handle.

lorn /lɔːn/ *adj* (*arch or joc*) lonely and sad.

lorry
(also *esp US* **truck**)

lorry /ˈlɒrɪ; *US* ˈlɔːrɪ/ *n* (*Brit*) (also *esp US* **truck**) large strong motor vehicle for transporting goods, soldiers, etc by road: *an army lorry* ○ [attrib] *a lorry driver.* ⇨ illus.

lose /luːz/ *v* (*pt, pp* **lost** /lɒst; *US* lɔːst/) **1** [Tn] have (sth/sb) taken away from one by accident, misfortune, old age, death, etc: *lose all one's money at cards* ○ *lose a leg in an industrial accident* ○ *lose one's hair, teeth, good looks*, ie as a result of ageing ○ *He lost both his sons* (ie They were killed) *in the war.* ○ *She's just lost her husband*, ie He has died recently. ○ *lose one's job.* **2** [Tn] no longer have or maintain (esp a moral or mental quality): *lose one's confidence, composure, etc* ○ *The train was losing speed.* ○ *lose interest in sth/sb*, ie cease to be interested or attracted ○ *He's lost ten pounds in weight.* ○ *lose one's balance/equilibrium* ○ *She's losing colour*, ie becoming pale. ○ *I warn you, I'm rapidly losing patience*, ie becoming impatient. **3** [Tn] become unable to find: *I've lost my keys.* ○ *The books seem to be lost/to have got lost.* ○ *She lost her husband in the crowd.* **4** [Tn] **(a)** fail to obtain or catch (sth): *His words were lost* (ie could not be heard) *in the applause.* **(b)** (*infml*) be no longer understood by (sb): *I'm afraid you've lost me.* **5** [Tn] (*infml*) escape from (sb/sth); elude: *We managed to lose our pursuers in the darkness.* ○ *You see that car following us? Well, lose it!* **6 (a)** [I, Ipr, Tn, Tn·pr] ~ **(sth) (to sb)** be defeated; fail to win (a contest, a lawsuit, an argument, etc): *It's only the second time the team has lost (a match) this season.* ○ *We lost to a stronger side.* ○ *They won the battle but lost the war.* ○ *lose a motion*, ie fail to carry it in a debate. **(b)** [Tn, Tn·pr] ~ **sth (to sth/sb)** have sth taken away (by sth/sb): *Railways have lost much of their business to the bus companies.* **7** [Tn] have to give up or forfeit (sth): *The Labour candidate lost his deposit*, ie did not obtain the minimum number of votes necessary in an election. ○ *lose one's no-claim bonus*, eg by making an insurance claim following an accident. **8** [Tn] waste (time or an opportunity): *We lost twenty minutes through having to change a tyre.* ○ *There's no time to lose*, ie We must hurry. **9 (a)** [I, Ipr, Tn, Tn·pr] ~ **(sth) (on sth/by doing sth)** become poorer (as a result of sth): *We lost (a lot) on that deal.* ○ *Poetry always loses (something) in translation.* ○ *You will lose nothing by telling the truth.* **(b)** [Dn·n] cause (sb) to be without or forfeit (sth): *His carelessness lost him the job.* ○ *Such behaviour will lose you everyone's sympathy.* **10** [I, Tn] (of a watch or clock) go too slowly by (an amount of time): *A good watch neither gains nor loses.* ○ *This clock loses two minutes* (ie becomes two minutes behind the correct time) *a day.* **11** (idm) **fight a losing battle** ⇨ FIGHT[1]. **find/lose favour with sb/in sb's eyes** ⇨ FAVOUR[1]. **find/lose one's voice/tongue** ⇨ FIND[1]. **give/lose ground** ⇨ GROUND[1]. **heads I win, tails you lose** ⇨ HEAD[1]. **keep/lose one's balance** ⇨ BALANCE[1]. **keep/lose one's cool** ⇨ COOL[1]. **keep/lose count** ⇨ COUNT[2]. **keep/lose one's temper** ⇨ TEMPER[1]. **keep/lose track of sb/sth** ⇨ TRACK. **lose all ˈreason** become irrational or illogical: *He lost all reason and started abusing his opponent.* **lose one's ˈbearings** become lost or confused. **lose one's ˈbreath** pant for breath, eg after running hard. **lose ˈcaste (with/among sb)** lose status or respect. **lose ˈcourage** become depressed or fearful; despair. **lose ˈface** be humiliated; lose credit or reputation. **lose one's grip (on sth)** be unable to understand or control a situation, etc: *I think the Prime Minister may be losing his grip.* **lose one's ˈhead** become confused or over-excited: *Don't lose your head — just keep calm!* **lose ˈheart** become discouraged. **lose one's ˈheart (to sb/sth)** fall in love. **lose one's ˈlife** be killed. **lose one's ˈmarbles** (*sl*) go mad; no longer behave sensibly or rationally. **lose/waste no time in doing sth** ⇨ TIME[1]. **lose one's ˈplace** (in a book, etc) be unable to find the point at which one stopped reading. **lose one's ˈrag** (*infml*) express one's anger, impatience, etc in an uncontrolled way. **lose one's ˈseat (a)** have the place where one was sitting taken by another person. **(b)** (of a Member of Parliament) fail to be re-elected. **lose one's ˈshirt** (*infml*) lose all one's money, esp as a result of gambling or speculation: *He lost his shirt on the horses.* **lose sight of sb/sth (a)** no longer be able to see sb/sth: *lose sight of land.* **(b)** overlook sth; fail to consider sth: *We must not lose sight of the fact that…* ○ *Our original aims have been lost sight of.* **lose the thread (of sth)** be unable to follow an argument, a story, etc. **lose one's ˈtouch** no longer have the abilities, etc that once made one successful. **lose touch (with sb/sth)** no longer be in contact with sb/sth: *I've lost touch with all my old friends.* ○ *Let us not lose touch with reality.* **lose one's ˈway** become lost: *We lost our way in the dark.* **lose/take off weight** ⇨ WEIGHT. **a losing ˈbattle/ˈgame** struggle/contest in which defeat seems certain: *It's a losing battle trying to persuade Henry to take more exercise.* **not lose sleep/lose no sleep over sth** not worry unduly about sth: *It's not worth losing sleep over.* **win/lose by a neck** ⇨ NECK. **win or lose** ⇨ WIN. **a winning/losing streak** ⇨ STREAK *n.* **win/lose the toss** ⇨ TOSS *n.* **12** (phr v) **lose oneself in sth** become totally absorbed in sth: *I soon lost myself in the excitement of the film.* **lose ˈout (on sth)** (*infml*) be unsuccessful; suffer loss: *If things go wrong I'm the one who'll lose out, not you.* **lose out to sb/sth** (*infml*) be overcome or replaced by sb/sth: *Has the cinema lost out to TV?* ⇨ Usage at LOOSE[1].

▷ **loser** *n* person who loses or is defeated, esp habitually: *a good/bad loser*, ie one who accepts defeat well/badly ○ *a born loser*, ie sb who regularly fails in life.

Losey /ˈləʊzɪ/ Joseph (1909-84), American film director. After early successes in Hollywood (eg *The Prowler*), the *McCarthy persecution forced him to continue his career in Europe with films like *The Servant* and *Accident* (with screenplays by *Pinter).

loss /lɒs; *US* lɔːs/ *n* **1** [U] act, instance or process of losing: *loss of blood, health, prestige, money* ○ *The loss* (ie death) *of his wife was a great blow to him.* ○ *without (any) loss of time* ○ *a temporary loss of power* ○ *The loss of this contract would be very serious.* **2** [C] **(a)** person or thing lost: *heat loss* ○ *The enemy suffered heavy losses,* ie many men killed, etc or much equipment destroyed. ○ *The car was so badly damaged that it had to be abandoned as a total loss.* **(b)** money lost in a business deal, etc: *made a loss on the deal* ○ *sell sth at a loss,* ie for less than it cost ○ *suffer losses in the export market.* **3** [sing] suffering caused by losing sb/sth; disadvantage: *Her departure is a great loss to the orchestra.* ○ *It's no loss,* ie Its loss does not matter. **4** (idm) **at a ˈloss** not knowing what to do or say; perplexed or puzzled: *It left him at a complete loss (for words).* ○ *I'm at a loss what to do next.* **cut one's ˈlosses** abandon a scheme that causes loss before one loses too much. **a dead loss** ⇨ DEAD.

□ **ˈloss adjuster** person employed by an insurance company who estimates how much damage has been done by a fire, storm, etc, so that the amount of compensation can be calculated.

ˌloss-ˈleader *n* (*commerce*) article sold at a loss to attract customers to buy other goods.

lost[1] *pt, pp* of LOSE.

lost[2] /lɒst; *US* lɔːst/ *adj* **1** that cannot be found or recovered: *recalling her lost youth* ○ *The art of good conversation seems lost.* ○ *lost tribes of Africa.* **2** [esp pred] (*fig*) confused or puzzled: *I got rather lost trying to find the station.* ○ *We would be totally lost without your help.* ○ *They spoke so quickly I just got lost.* **3** (idm) **ˌall is not ˈlost** (*saying*) there is still some hope of success, recovery, etc. **be lost in sth** be absorbed in sth: *lost in thought/wonder/admiration.* **be lost on sb** fail to influence sb: *Our hints were not lost on him,* ie He noticed them and acted accordingly. **be lost to sth** be no longer affected or influenced by sth: *When he listens to music he's lost to the world,* ie unaware of what is happening around him. **get ˈlost** (*sl*) go away: *Tell him to get lost.* **give sb up for ˈlost** no longer expect sb to be found alive. **a lost ˈcause** project, ideal, etc that has failed or is certain to fail. **make up for lost ˈtime** hurry, etc in order to compensate for time wasted earlier: *He didn't have a girl-friend till he was 18, but now he's making up for lost time,* ie he has had many girl-friends since then. **there's little/no love lost between A and B** ⇨ LOVE[1].

□ **ˌlost ˈproperty** possessions mislaid in a public place and not yet claimed by their owners: [attrib] *a ˌlost-ˈproperty office.*

lot[1] /lɒt/ *n* [Gp] (*infml*) **the ˈlot, all the ˈlot, the whole ˈlot** the whole number or amount (of sb/sth): *That's the lot!* ○ *Take all the lot if you want.* ○ *The whole lot was/were discovered in a field.* ○ *I want the lot* (ie all) *of you to get out of my house.* ○ *He expects a good salary, a company car, first-class air travel — the lot.*

lot[2] /lɒt/ *pron* **a lot, lots** (*infml*) large number or amount: *Have some more pie, there's lots left.* ○ *'How many do you want?' 'A lot/Lots.'*

□ **a lot of** *det* (also *infml* **lots of**) a large number or amount of sth/sb: *What a lot of presents!* ○ *I haven't got a lot of time.* ○ *There was lots of money in the safe.* ○ *A lot of people were queuing for the film.* ○ *I saw quite a lot of her* (ie I saw her quite often) *during the holidays.* ⇨ Usage at MUCH[1].

lot[3] /lɒt/ *adv* (*infml*) **1 a lot, lots** (used with *adjs* and *advs*) considerably: *I'm feeling a lot better today.* ○ *I eat lots less than I used to.* **2 a lot** (used with *vs*) **(a)** a great amount: *I care about you a lot.* **(b)** often: *I play tennis quite a lot in the summer.* Cf A FAT LOT (FAT[1] 7).

lot[4] /lɒt/ *n* **1 (a)** [C] item or number of items sold, esp at an auction sale: *Lot 46: six chairs.* **(b)** [CGp] group, collection or set of people or things of the same kind: *Nobody in the first lot of applicants was suitable for the job.* ○ *I have several lots of essays to mark this weekend.* ○ *This next lot of washing is the last.* **2** [C] **(a)** piece of land. **(b)** (*esp US*) area used for a particular purpose: *a ˈparking lot,* ie a car-park ○ *a vacant ˈlot,* ie a building site ○ *a ˈfilm lot,* ie a film studio and the land around it. **3** [sing] person's fortune, destiny or share: *Her lot has been a hard one.* ○ *I would not want to share his lot.* **4** [U] method of deciding sth or selecting sb/sth by chance: *She was chosen by lot to represent us.* **5** (idm) **a bad egg/lot** ⇨ EGG. **cast/draw ˈlots (for sth)** make a selection by lot: *They drew lots for the right to go first.* **fall to sb's lot to do sth** (*fml*) become sb's task or responsibility. **throw in one's lot with sb** decide to join sb and share his fortunes.

loth = LOATH.

lotion /ˈləʊʃn/ *n* [C, U] liquid medicine or cosmetic for use on the skin: *soothing lotions for insect bites* ○ *a bottle of cleansing lotion for the face.*

lottery /ˈlɒtərɪ/ *n* **1** [C] way of raising money by selling numbered tickets and giving prizes to the holders of numbers selected at random: [attrib] *a ˈlottery ticket.* Cf DRAW[1] 1, RAFFLE. **2** [sing] (*fig*) thing whose success, outcome, etc is determined by luck: *Some people think that marriage is a lottery.*

lotto /ˈlɒtəʊ/ *n* [U] game of chance similar to bingo but with the numbers drawn by the players instead of being called.

lotus /ˈləʊtəs/ *n* (*pl* ~**es**) **1** type of tropical water-lily: [attrib] *lotus flowers/blooms* ○ *lotus blossom.* **2** (in Greek legends) fruit that makes those who eat it lazily and dreamily contented.

□ **ˈlotus-eater** *n* person who enjoys himself in a lazy way, forgetting or ignoring serious matters.

ˈlotus position way of sitting cross-legged, used when meditating, in yoga, etc.

loud /laʊd/ *adj* (**-er, -est**) **1** producing much noise; easily heard: *loud voices, screams, laughs, etc* ○ *That music's too loud; please turn it down.* **2** (*derog*) (of colours, behaviour, etc) forcing people to notice them/it: *That dress is a bit loud* (ie gaudy), *isn't it?* ○ *His manner is too loud.* **3** (idm) **be loud in one's praise(s) (of sb/sth)** praise sb/sth very highly.

▷ **loud** *adv* (**-er, -est**) **1** (used esp with *talk, sing, laugh,* etc) in a loud manner: *laugh loud and long* ○ *Speak louder — I can't hear you.* ○ *Their baby screamed loudest of all.* **2** (idm) **actions speak louder than words** ⇨ ACTION. **for crying out loud** ⇨ CRY[1]. **ˌout ˈloud** aloud: *Don't whisper; if you've got something to say, say it out loud.*

loudly *adv*: *a dog barking loudly* ○ *loudly dressed.*

loudness *n* [U].

loudhailer (*US* **bullhorn**)

□ **ˌloudˈhailer** *n* (*US* **bullhorn**) portable electronic device for amplifying the sound of sb's voice so that it can be heard at a great distance: *use a loudhailer to address the crowd.*

ˈloud-mouth *n* (*infml*) person who talks too loudly or too much, esp boastingly. **ˈloud-mouthed** *adj.*

ˌloudˈspeaker (also **speaker**) *n* part of a radio, record-player, etc that changes electrical impulses into audible sounds.

lough /lɒk, lɒ/ *n* (*Irish*) lake or long inlet of the sea. Cf LOCH.

Louis /ˈluːɪ/ Joe (real name Joseph Louis Barrows, 1914-81), American boxer. He was the heavyweight champion of the world from 1937 to 1949.

Louis XIV /ˈluːɪ/ (1638-1715), king of France 1643-1715. He ruled the country with unlimited power, and led it into several wars to try to increase its influence in Europe. The magnificence of his court earned him the name 'the Sun King'. His reign was marked by splendid achievements in the arts. He had the Palace of Versailles built.

Louis XVI /ˈluːɪ/ (1754-93), king of France 1774-93. He was a weak ruler and unable to stop the discontent that led to the *French Revolution. He was executed for treason.

Louisiana /luːˌiːzɪˈænə/ state of the south-west USA. New Orleans, its largest city, still shows the state's origins as a French colony. The economy is based on agriculture and its great mineral resources, including oil and natural gas. ⇨ map at App 1.

lounge /laʊndʒ/ *v* [I, Ipr, Ip] sit or stand in a lazy way, esp leaning against sth; loll: *lounge about/around (the house)* ○ *lounging at street corners.*

▷ **lounge** *n* **1** waiting-room at an airport, etc: *the departure lounge.* **2** public sitting-room in a hotel, club, etc. **3** (*Brit*) sitting-room, with comfortable chairs, in a private house. **4** = LOUNGE BAR. **5** (*esp US*) sofa, esp one with a head-rest at one end but no back.

lounger *n* lazy or idle person.

□ **ˈlounge bar** (*Brit*) (*US* **saˈloon bar**) smarter, and usu more expensive, bar in a pub, hotel, etc. Cf PUBLIC BAR (PUBLIC).

ˈlounge-suit *n* (*Brit*) man's suit with matching jacket and trousers, worn esp in offices and on more formal occasions.

lour (also **lower**) /ˈlaʊə(r)/ *v* [I, Ipr] ~ **(at/on sb/sth) (a)** look threatening; frown: *louring looks.* **(b)** (of the sky, clouds, etc) look dark, as if threatening a storm.

louse /laʊs/ *n* **1** (*pl* **lice** /laɪs/) **(a)** small insect living on the bodies of animals and human beings, esp in dirty conditions. **(b)** similar insect living on plants. **2** (*pl* ~**s**) (*sl*) contemptible person.

▷ **louse** *v* (phr v) **louse sth up** (*infml*) spoil sth; ruin sth: *You've really loused things up this time.*

lousy /ˈlaʊzɪ/ *adj* (**-ier, -iest**) **1** infested with lice. **2** (*infml*) very bad or ill: *a lousy holiday* ○ *I feel lousy.* **3** [pred] ~ **with sth/sb** (*sl*) having more than enough of sth/sb: *In August the place is lousy with tourists.*

lout /laʊt/ *n* clumsy vulgar man or youth with bad manners.

▷ **loutish** *adj* of or like a lout: *loutish behaviour.*

louvre (also **louver**) /ˈluːvə(r)/ *n* **(a)** one of a set of fixed or movable strips of wood, metal, etc arranged to let air in while keeping light or rain out. **(b)** set of such strips inside a supporting frame. ▷ **louvred** (also **louvered**) *adj*: *a louvred door.*

lovable /ˈlʌvəbl/ *adj* easy to love; worthy of love: *a lovable puppy* ○ *He's such a lovable rascal!*

love[1] /lʌv/ *n* **1** [U] warm liking or affection; affectionate devotion: *a mother's love for her children* ○ *love of (one's) country,* ie patriotism ○ *She has a great love for animals.* ○ *He shows little love towards her.* **2** [U] sexual affection or passion: *marry for love, not money* ○ *Their love has cooled,* ie is no longer strong. **3** [U] (*religion*) (in Christianity) God's benevolence towards mankind. **4** [U, sing] strong liking for sth: *a love of learning, adventure, music.* **5** [C] person who is loved; sweetheart: *Take care, my love.* ○ *one of my former loves* ○ (*joc*) *with his lady love,* ie his girlfriend or wife. **6** [C] (*infml*) delightful person or thing: *What a love her daughter is!* ○ *Isn't this hat a perfect love?* **7** [C] (*Brit infml*) (form of address used by a man to a woman or child (not necessarily a friend), or by a woman to a person of either sex): *Mind your head, love!* **8** [U] (in tennis) no score; nil: *love all,* ie neither player or pair has scored ○ *The score in the game on Court One is thirty-love.* **9** (idm) **be in love (with sb)** feel affection and desire (for sb): *They're very much in love (with each other).* ○ *I'm madly in love with her.* **be in love with sth** be very fond of sth: *a city in love with its own past* ○ *He's in love with the sound of his own voice,* ie talks too much. **cupboard love** ⇨ CUPBOARD. **fall in love (with sb)** feel a sudden strong attraction for sb. **(just) for ˈlove/for the ˈlove of sth** without payment or other reward: *They're all volunteers, doing it just for the love of the thing.* **for the ˌlove of ˈGod, etc (a)** (expressing surprise, dismay, etc): *For the love of God, not another bill!* **(b)** (used when urging sb to do sth): *For the love of Mike let's get out of here!* **ˌgive/ˌsend sb one's ˈlove** give/send an affectionate greeting to sb: *Please give your sister my love.* ○ *My parents* *send their love.* **a labour of love** ⇨ LABOUR[1]. **ˌlove is ˈblind** (*saying*) people who are in love cannot see each other's faults. **the ˌlove of sb's ˈlife (a)** person's most dearly loved sweetheart: *I think I've met the love of my life.* **(b)** person's favourite possession, activity, etc: *Sailing is the love of his life.* **make love (to sb) (a)** have sexual intercourse: *He refused to make love before they were married.* **(b)** (*dated*) behave amorously (towards sb), esp by being specially attentive. **not for ˌlove or ˈmoney** not by any means: *We couldn't find a hotel room for love or money.* **there's little/no ˈlove lost between A and B** they dislike each other: *There's never been much love lost between her and her sister.*

▷ **loveless** *adj* without love: *a loveless marriage.*

□ **ˈlove-affair** *n* romantic or sexual relationship between two people who are in love.

ˈlove-bird *n* **1** small brightly-coloured parrot that seems to show great affection for its mate. **2** (usu *pl*) (*infml*) person who is very much in love: *Come along, you two love-birds!*

ˈlove-child *n* (*euph*) child of unmarried parents.

ˌlove-ˈhate relationship intense emotional relationship involving feelings of both love and hate.

ˌlove-in-a-ˈmist *n* [U] garden plant with thin feathery leaves and usu blue flowers.

ˈlove-letter *n* letter between two people expressing the love of one for the other.

ˌlove-lies-ˈbleeding *n* [U] garden plant with spikes of small reddish-purple flowers which hang downwards.

ˈlovelorn /-lɔːn/ *adj* unhappy because one's love is not returned.

ˈlove-making *n* [U] sexual play between two lovers, esp including sexual intercourse.

ˈlove-match *n* marriage made because the two people are in love with each other.

ˈlove-potion (also **ˈlove-philtre**) *n* (in stories) magic drink supposed to make the person who drinks it fall in love.

ˈlove-seat *n* small sofa in the shape of an S, with two seats facing in opposite directions.

ˈlovesick *adj* weak or ill because of being in love.

ˈlove-song *n* song expressing or describing love.

ˈlove-story *n* story or novel in which the main theme is romantic love.

love[2] /lʌv/ *v* **1** [Tn] have a strong affection or deep tender feelings for (sb/sth): *love one's parents, country, wife* ○ *love God,* ie worship Him. **2** [Tn, Tt, Tnt, Tg, Tsg] like (sb/sth) greatly; take pleasure in: *She's always loved horses.* ○ *He loves his pipe,* ie smoking it. ○ *Children love to play/playing.* ○ *'Will you come?' 'I'd love to!'* ○ *We'd love you to come to dinner.* ○ *I love him reading to me in bed.* **3** (idm) **ˌlove ˈme, ˌlove my ˈdog** (*saying*) if one loves sb, one will or should love everyone and everything associated with him.

Lovelace /ˈlʌvleɪs/ Richard (1618-58), English poet. He was one of the so-called 'Cavalier poets', a supporter of *Charles I. He was put in prison during the Civil War, and wrote some of his finest works there (eg 'To Althea from Prison').

lovely /ˈlʌvlɪ/ *adj* (**-ier, -iest**) **1** beautiful; attractive: *a lovely view, voice, woman* ○ *lovely hair, weather, music.* **2** (*infml*) enjoyable; pleasant: *a lovely dinner, time, story* ○ *It's lovely and warm* (ie pleasant because warm) *in here.* **3** loved or respected for good qualities: *Everyone in the village thinks he's a lovely man.* **4** (idm) **everything in the garden is lovely** ⇨ GARDEN.

▷ **loveliness** *n* [U].

lovely *n* (*infml sexist*) pretty woman: *a couple of television lovelies.*

lover /ˈlʌvə(r)/ *n* **1** [C] partner (usu a man) in a sexual relationship outside marriage: *They say he used to be her lover.* ○ *She's taken a new lover.* Cf MISTRESS 4. **2 lovers** [pl] two people who are in love or having a sexual relationship though not married to each other: *young lovers strolling in the park* ○ *They met on holiday and soon became lovers.* **3** [C] (often in compounds) person who likes or enjoys sth specified: *a lover of music, horses, good wine* ○ *art-lovers.*

lovey-dovey /ˌlʌvɪˈdʌvɪ/ *adj* (*infml often derog*) showing affection in a sentimental or ridiculous way: *They're very lovey-dovey now they're just married, but what will things be like in a year's time?*

loving /ˈlʌvɪŋ/ *adj* [esp attrib] feeling or showing love: *a loving friend* ○ *loving words.* ▷ **lovingly** *adv.*

□ **ˈloving-cup** *n* large wine-cup passed from person to person at a banquet, etc, so that everyone may drink from it.

ˌloving-ˈkindness *n* [U] (*arch*) tender consideration or care.

low[1] /ləʊ/ *adj* (**-er, -est**) **1** not high or tall; not extending far upwards: *a low wall, ceiling, tree* ○ *a low range of hills* ○ *flying at a low altitude* ○ *The sun is low in the sky.* ○ *a low brow,* ie with hair-line and eyebrows close together ○ *a dress low in the neck/a low-necked dress,* ie one leaving the upper part of the breasts and much of the shoulders bare. **2** below the usual or normal level, amount, intensity, etc: *low wages, taxes, prices, etc* ○ *low temperature* ○ *low pressure,* eg of the atmosphere, of gas or water piped to houses, of blood ○ *low cloud* ○ *The surrounding land is low* (ie not far above sea-level) *and marshy.* ○ *a low-density housing estate,* ie one with comparatively few houses in the space available ○ *The reservoir was very low after the long drought.* **3** ranking below others in importance or quality: *upper and lower classes of society* ○ *of low birth* ○ *low forms of life,* ie creatures having a relatively simple structure ○ *low-grade fuel.* **4** vulgar or coarse: *low manners, tastes, etc* ○ *He keeps low company.* ○ *low comedy,* ie a crude form of farce ○ *low cunning,* ie immoral and selfish cleverness. **5** (of sound or a voice) not high in pitch; deep: *A man's voice is usually lower than a woman's.* **6** not loud: *a low rumble of thunder* ○ *Keep your voice low.* **7** lacking in vigour; feeble or depressed: *in a low state of health* ○ *feel low/in low spirits/low-spirited.* **8** (of a gear) allowing a slower speed of a vehicle in relation to its engine speed: *You'll need to change into a lower gear when going up this hill.* **9** (idm) **at a low ˈebb** in a poor state; worse than usual: *Her spirits were at a very low ebb,* ie She was very depressed. **be/run ˈlow (on sth)** (of supplies) be/become almost exhausted; have almost exhausted the supplies (of sth): *The petrol's running low.* ○ *We're (running) low on petrol.* **a high/low profile** ⇨ PROFILE. **lay sb/sth ˈlow (a)** bring sb/sth into a flat or horizontal position: *He laid his opponent low with a single punch.* **(b)** weaken or destroy: *The whole family was laid low by/with* (ie was ill and in bed with) *flu.*

▷ **ˈlowermost** *adj* lowest.

lowness *n* [U].

□ **ˈlow-boy** *n* (*esp US*) low table with drawers.

ˌLow ˈChurch section of the Church of England that gives little importance to ritual and the authority of bishops and priests: *My family is Low Church.* **ˌLow-ˈChurchman** *n* member or supporter of this. ⇨ article at CHURCH OF ENGLAND.

ˌlow-ˈclass *adj* of poor quality or low social class: *ˌlow-class ˈmerchandise.* ⇨ article at CLASS.

the ˈLow Countries (esp formerly) the Netherlands, Belgium and Luxembourg.

ˌlower ˈcase (in printing) small letters, not capitals: [attrib] *ˌlower-case ˈlettering.*

ˌLower ˈChamber (also **ˌLower ˈHouse**) larger, usu elected, branch of a legislative assembly (eg the House of Commons in Britain, the House of Representatives in the US).

the ˌlower ˈdeck (in the Navy) petty officers and lower ranks (not the officers).

the ˌlower ˈclass (also **the ˌlower ˈclasses, the ˌlower ˈorders**) = THE WORKING CLASS (WORKING).

ˌlower-ˈclass *adj.* ⇨ article at CLASS.

ˌlowest common deˈnominator 1 (*mathematics*) smallest number that can be divided exactly by the lower number in a set of fractions. **2** (*often derog*) position, belief, taste, etc, that is shared by the greatest number of people: *Catering for the lowest common denominator does not produce great art.*

ˌlow ˈfrequency (*abbr* **LF**) radio frequency of 30 to 300 kilohertz.

ˌlow-ˈkey (also **ˌlow-ˈkeyed**) *adj* not intense or emotional; restrained: *The wedding was a very ˌlow-key afˈfair.*

lowland /ˈləʊlənd/ *n* (usu *pl*) low-lying land. **ˈlowlander** /-ləndə(r)/ *n* **(a)** person who lives in a lowland area. **(b)** (also **ˈLowlander**) native of the Scottish Lowlands.

ˌlow-level ˈlanguage computer language using instructions that correspond closely to the operations which the computer will perform.

ˈlow life way of life of people who are not socially respectable: *Dickens's picture of London low life* ○ [attrib] *drinking in low-life bars.*

ˌlow-ˈpitched *adj* (of sounds) low in pitch[3](3a): *a ˌlow-pitched ˈvoice.*

ˈlow season time of year when fewest visitors come to a resort, etc.

ˌLow ˈSunday the Sunday after Easter.

ˌlow ˈtide (also **ˌlow ˈwater**) **(a)** tide when at its lowest level. **(b)** time when this occurs. **ˌlow-ˈwater mark (a)** lowest point reached by the water at low tide. **(b)** (*fig*) lowest or worst point: *the low-water mark of the company's fortunes.*

low[2] /ləʊ/ *adv* (**-er, -est**) **1** in, at or to a low level or position: *aim, shoot, throw, etc low* ○ *bow low to the Queen* ○ *play low,* ie play a card with a low value ○ *The simplest way to succeed in business is to buy low* (ie at low prices) *and sell high.* **2** not at a high pitch; quietly: *I can't sing as low as that.* ○ *Speak lower or she'll hear you!* **3** (idm) **be brought ˈlow** be reduced in health, wealth or position: *Many rich families were brought low by the financial crisis.* **high and low** ⇨ HIGH[3]. **lie low** ⇨ LIE[2]. **stoop so low** ⇨ STOOP[1].

□ **ˌlow-ˈborn** *adj* of humble birth: *a ˌlow-born ˈleader.*

ˌlow-ˈlying *adj* near to the ground or to sea-level: *fog in ˌlow-lying ˈareas.*

ˌlow-ˈpaid *adj* paid low wages: *They are among the ˌlowest-paid (ˌworkers) in the ˈcountry.*

ˌlow-ˈrise *adj* [attrib] (of a building) having few storeys: *ˌlow-rise deˈvelopments.*

low[3] /ləʊ/ *n* **1** low level or figure: *The (value of the) pound has fallen to a new low against the dollar,* ie is worth less in exchange for dollars than ever before. **2** area of low barometric pressure: *another low moving in from the Atlantic.*

low[4] /ləʊ/ *n* deep sound made by cattle.

▷ **low** *v* [I] make this sound; moo.

lowbrow /ˈləʊbraʊ/ *adj* (*esp derog*) not cultured or intellectual: *a lowbrow programme, discussion, person.*

▷ **lowbrow** *n* lowbrow person. Cf HIGHBROW, MIDDLE-BROW (MIDDLE).

low-down /ˈləʊdaʊn/ *adj* [attrib] (*infml*) dishonourable; underhand: *That was a pretty low-down trick to play!*

▷ **low-down** *n* (idm) **give sb/get the low-down (on sb/sth)** (*infml*) tell sb/be told the true facts (about sb/sth): *Give me the low-down on her divorce.*

Lowell[1] /ˈləʊəl/ Amy Lawrence (1874-1925), American poet. She was influenced by the French *Symbolists and Ezra *Pound and produced works in an 'imagist' style, using precise images to express her ideas.

Lowell[2] /ˈləʊəl/ Robert (1917-77), American poet. His poems reflect his troubled life as an intellectual, a Catholic convert, an anti-war campaigner and an alcoholic. They use themes from American history and his own experiences.

lower[1] /ˈləʊə(r)/ *v* **1** [Tn, Tn·pr] **(a)** let or bring (sb/sth) down: *lower supplies to the stranded men,* eg from a helicopter ○ *lower the sails, a flag, a window* ○ *He lowered his gun slowly.* ○ *lower one's eyes (to the ground),* ie look down ○ (*infml*) *He lowered* (ie drank) *four pints of beer in an hour.* **(b)** make less high: *lower the roof of a house* ○ *lower (the height of) the ceiling.* **2** [I, Ipr, Tn, Tn·pr] (cause sth to) become less in amount or quantity: *Stocks generally lowered in value.* ○ *lower one's voice to a whisper* ○ *A poor diet lowers one's resistance to illness.* **3** [Tn, Tn·pr] ~ **oneself (by doing sth)** (*infml*) reduce one's dignity or self-respect: *Don't lower yourself by asking ˈhim for help.* ○ *Speak to*

L S Lowry: Coming from the Mill

her? I'd never lower myself. 4 (idm) **raise/lower one's sights** ⇨ SIGHT[1]. 5 (phr v) **lower (sth) away** (*nautical*) lower (a boat, sail, etc).

lower[2] = LOUR.

lowly /ˈləʊlɪ/ *adj* (**-ier, -iest**) (*dated*) of humble rank or condition. ▷ **lowliness** *n* [U].

Lowry /ˈlaʊrɪ/ L(awrence) S(tephen) (1887-1976), English painter. He is famous for his paintings of the industrial landscape of northern England where he lived, with 'matchstick' figures of people represented in a few thin lines. ⇨ illus.

lox[1] /lɒks/ *n* [U] liquid oxygen, used esp as a fuel for rockets.

lox[2] /lɒks/ *n* [U] (*US*) smoked salmon.

loyal /ˈlɔɪəl/ *adj* ~ (**to sb/sth**) true and faithful: *remain loyal to one's principles* ○ *a loyal supporter of the Labour Party.*

▷ **loyalist** /ˈlɔɪəlɪst/ *n* 1 person who is loyal, esp to the established ruler or government during a revolt: [attrib] *loyalist troops.* 2 **Loyalist** person from Northern Ireland who wishes it to remain part of the United Kingdom. ⇨ article at IRELAND.

loyally /ˈlɔɪəlɪ/ *adv.*

□ ˌ**loyal** ˈ**toast** (in Britain) toast to the king or queen at a formal dinner, after which people are traditionally allowed to smoke.

loyalty /ˈlɔɪəltɪ/ *n* (**a**) [U] being true and faithful; loyal behaviour: *swear an oath of loyalty to the King* ○ *Can I count on your loyalty?* (**b**) [C often *pl*] bond that makes a person faithful to sb/sth: *We all have a loyalty to the company.* ○ *a case of divided loyalties,* ie of being loyal to two different and often conflicting causes, etc.

lozenge /ˈlɒzɪndʒ/ *n* 1 four-sided figure in the shape of a diamond. 2 small tablet of flavoured sugar, esp one containing medicine, which is dissolved in the mouth: *a throat lozenge,* ie for a sore throat.

LP /ˌel ˈpiː/ *abbr* long-playing (record): *a collection of LPs.* Cf EP, SINGLE *n* 5.

L-plate /ˈel pleɪt/ *n* (in Britain) sign with a large red letter L, fixed to a motor vehicle that is being driven by a learner-driver. Cf L *abbr* 2.

LPN /ˌel piː ˈen/ *abbr* (*US*) Licensed Practical Nurse.

Lr *symb* lawrencium.

LSD /ˌel es ˈdiː/ *abbr* 1 (also *sl* **acid**) lysergic acid diethylamide, a powerful drug that produces hallucinations. 2 (also **£sd**) (*dated Brit infml*) (in former British currency) pounds, shillings and pence (Latin *librae, solidi, denarii*); money: *I'm rather short of LSD — can you lend me some?*

LSE /ˌel es ˈiː/ *abbr* London School of Economics.

LST /ˌel es ˈtiː/ *abbr* (*US*) Local Standard Time.

Lt *abbr* Lieutenant: *Lt-Cdr/-Col/-Gen/-Gov.*

LTA /ˌel tiː ˈeɪ/ *abbr* (*Brit*) Lawn Tennis Association.

Ltd *abbr* (*Brit*) Limited (ie 'limited liability company', now used only by private companies): *Canning Bros Ltd* ○ *Pearce and Co Ltd.* Cf INC, PLC.

Lu *symb* lutetium.

lubber /ˈlʌbə(r)/ *n* (*dated*) big clumsy stupid boy or man. ▷ **lubberly** *adj.*

Lubitsch /ˈluːbɪtʃ/ Ernst (1892-1947), German film director. After making a series of historical spectaculars in Germany, he introduced a new subtlety into Hollywood comedy in films like *Ninotchka* and *To Be or Not To Be.*

lubricate /ˈluːbrɪkeɪt/ *v* [Tn] put oil or grease on or in (machinery, etc) so that it moves easily: *lubricate the wheels, bearings, hinges, etc* ○ *(fig) My throat needs lubricating,* ie with a drink.

▷ **lubricant** /ˈluːbrɪkənt/ *n* [U, C] substance that lubricates.

lubrication /ˌluːbrɪˈkeɪʃn/ *n* [C, U] (action of) lubricating or being lubricated.

lubricious /luːˈbrɪʃəs/ *adj* (*fml*) showing an unpleasant enjoyment of sexual matters; lewd. ▷ **lubricity** /-ˈbrɪsətɪ/ *n* [U].

lucerne /luːˈsɜːn/ *n* (*US* **alfalfa**) plant similar to clover, used for feeding animals.

lucid /ˈluːsɪd/ *adj* 1 clearly expressed; easy to understand: *a lucid explanation* ○ *His style is very lucid.* 2 clear in one's mind; sane: *lucid intervals,* ie periods of sanity during mental illness. ▷ **lucidity** /luːˈsɪdətɪ/ *n* [U]. **lucidly** *adv*: *lucidly explained.*

Lucifer /ˈluːsɪfə(r)/ Satan; the Devil.

luck /lʌk/ *n* [U] 1 chance, esp thought of as a force that brings good or bad fortune: *have good, poor, hard* (ie bad), *little, bad, etc luck.* 2 good fortune: *I hope this charm will bring you luck.* ○ *I always carry one for luck.* ○ *I had the luck to find him at home.* ○ *Any luck with* (ie Did you manage to get) *the job?* ○ *Our luck has run out,* ie has ended. 3 (idm) **as (good/ill) luck would have it** fortunately/unfortunately. **(what) bad, rotten, etc** ˈ**luck!** (used to show sympathy). **be bad/hard** ˈ**luck (on sb)** be unfortunate: *It was very hard luck (on you) to get ill on your holiday.* **be** ˌ**down on one's** ˈ**luck** (*infml*) have a period of misfortune. **beginner's luck** ⇨ BEGINNER (BEGIN). **be in/out of** ˈ**luck** be fortunate/unfortunate. **better luck next time** ⇨ BETTER[1]. **the** ˌ**devil's** ˌ**own** ˈ**luck** (also **the** ˌ**luck of the** ˈ**devil**) ⇨ DEVIL[1]. ˌ**good** ˈ**luck (to sb)** may sb be fortunate and successful: *Good luck in your exams!* **just one's** ˈ**luck** (indicating that sth unfortunate or inconvenient has happened to one, as usual): *It was just my luck to go to the play on the day the star was ill.* **one's** ˈ**luck is in** one is lucky. **the luck of the draw** the way in which chance decides what some people become, do, get, etc and others not. **the luck of the game** the element of luck, as opposed to skill, that operates in a game, an activity, etc. ˌ**no such** ˈ**luck** unfortunately not. **push one's luck** ⇨ PUSH[2]. **take pot luck** ⇨ POT[1]. ˌ**tough** ˈ**luck** (**a**) (used to show sympathy) (**b**) (*ironic*) (used to show that one does not really care about sb's misfortune). **try one's luck/fortune** ⇨ TRY[1]. **worse luck** ⇨ WORSE.

▷ **luck** *v* (phr v) **luck out** (*US infml*) be lucky or successful.

luckless *adj* unlucky.

lucky /ˈlʌkɪ/ *adj* (**-ier, -iest**) 1 having, bringing or resulting from good luck: *You're very lucky to be alive after that accident.* ○ *It's lucky she's still here.* ○ *a lucky charm* ○ *Seven is my lucky number.* ○ *a lucky guess* ○ *a lucky break,* ie a piece of good fortune ○ *It's my, your, etc lucky day,* ie one on which I am, you are, etc having good fortune. 2 (idm) **strike lucky** ⇨ STRIKE[2]. **thank one's lucky stars** ⇨ THANK. **you'll be lucky; you should be so lucky** (*ironic catchphrase*) what you expect, wish for, etc is very unlikely to happen. ▷ **luckily** /ˈlʌkɪlɪ/ *adv*: *I arrived late but luckily the meeting had been delayed.*

□ ˌ**lucky** ˈ**dip** (*Brit*) (*US* **grab-bag**) barrel, etc containing small prizes of various values which people pick out at random for a payment, hoping to get sth that is worth more than they have paid.

lucrative /ˈluːkrətɪv/ *adj* producing much money; profitable: *a lucrative business.* ▷ **lucratively** *adv.* **lucrativeness** *n* [U].

lucre /ˈluːkə(r)/ *n* [U] 1 (*derog*) profit or money-making, as a motive for doing sth: *the lure of lucre.* 2 (idm) **filthy lucre** ⇨ FILTHY.

Luddite /ˈlʌdaɪt/ *n, adj* (*derog*) (person) opposed to change or improvement in working methods, machines, etc in industry. The original Luddites were early 19th-century British craftsmen who destroyed machinery which they thought would threaten their jobs.

ludicrous /ˈluːdɪkrəs/ *adj* causing laughter; ridiculous; absurd: *a ludicrous idea.* ▷ **ludicrously** *adv*: *His trousers were ludicrously short.* **ludicrousness** *n* [U].

ludo /ˈluːdəʊ/ *n* [U] simple game played with dice and counters on a special board.

luff /lʌf/ *v* [I, Tn] (*nautical*) steer (a sailing boat or ship) so that its front moves nearer to the direction from which the wind is blowing.

luffa = LOOFAH.

lug[1] /lʌg/ *v* (**-gg-**) [Tn, Tn·pr, Tn·p] drag or carry (sth) with great effort: *lugging a heavy suitcase up the stairs* ○ *(fig infml) She had to lug the kids around/about/along all day.* ⇨ Usage at CARRY.

lug[2] /lʌg/ *n* 1 projecting part of an object, by which it may be carried or fixed in place. 2 (also ˈ**lug-hole**) (*Brit sl*) ear.

luge /luːʒ/ *n* small toboggan for one person.

luggage

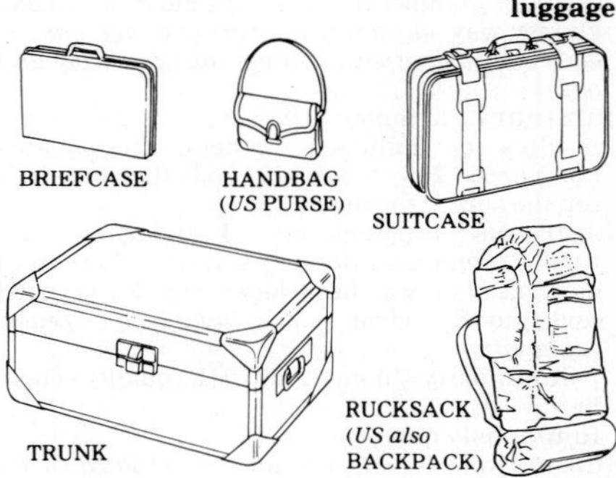

luggage /ˈlʌgɪdʒ/ (*US* **baggage**) *n* [U] bags, suitcases, etc containing sb's belongings and taken on a journey: *six pieces of luggage* ○ *clear one's luggage through customs* ○ *Have you any hand-luggage?* ⇨ illus.
□ ˈ**luggage-rack** *n* (**a**) shelf for luggage above the seats in a railway carriage, coach, etc. (**b**) = ROOF-RACK (ROOF).
ˈ**luggage-van** *n* (*US* **baggage car**) carriage for passengers' luggage on a railway train.

lugger /ˈlʌgə(r)/ *n* (*nautical*) small ship with one or more four-cornered sails.

lugubrious /ləˈgu:brɪəs/ *adj* dismal; mournful: *Why are you looking so lugubrious?* ▷ **lugubriously** *adv*. **lugubriousness** *n* [U].

lugworm /ˈlʌgwɜ:m/ *n* large worm living in the sand on the sea-shore, used as bait by fishermen.

Luke /lu:k/ **1** Saint (1st century AD), companion of Saint Paul. According to tradition he was a Greek doctor and wrote the third gospel and the Acts of the Apostles. **2** St Luke's gospel, the third in the New Testament.

lukewarm /ˌlu:kˈwɔ:m/ *adj* **1** (of liquids) only slightly warm; tepid: *Heat the milk until it is just lukewarm.* **2** ~ (**about sb/sth**) (*fig*) not eager or enthusiastic: *get a ˌlukewarm reˈception* ○ *Her love had grown lukewarm.*

lull /lʌl/ *v* **1** [Tn, Tn·pr] (**a**) ~ **sb/sth** (**to sth**) make (a person or an animal) quiet or less active; soothe sb/sth: *lull a baby to sleep*, ie by rocking it or singing to it. (**b**) ~ **sb/sth** (**into sth**) calm (sb, sb's fears, etc), esp by deception: *lull his suspicions* ○ *lulled us into a false sense of security.* **2** [I] (of a storm or noise) become quiet; lessen: *By dawn the wind had lulled.*
▷ **lull** *n* (usu *sing*) interval of quiet or inactivity: *a lull before the storm, in the conversation, during the battle.*

lullaby /ˈlʌləbaɪ/ *n* soft gentle song sung to make a child go to sleep. ⇨ article at NURSERY RHYME.

lumbago /lʌmˈbeɪgəʊ/ *n* [U] pain in the muscles of the lower part of the back, caused by rheumatism.

lumbar /ˈlʌmbə(r)/ *adj* [usu attrib] of the lower part of the back: *lumbar pains* ○ *the lumbar regions.*
□ ˈ**lumbar puncture** (*medical*) removing fluid from the base of the spine by means of a hollow needle.

lumber[1] /ˈlʌmbə(r)/ *n* [U] **1** (*esp Brit*) unwanted pieces of furniture, etc that are stored away or take up space. **2** (*esp US*) = TIMBER 1.
▷ **lumber** *v* **1** (**a**) [esp passive: Tn, Tn·pr] ~ **sb** (**with sb/sth**) give as a burden or an inconvenience to sb: *He got lumbered with the job of finding accommodation for the whole team.* ○ *It looks as though we're going to be lumbered with Uncle Bill for the whole weekend.* (**b**) [esp passive: Tn, Tn·pr, Tn·p] ~ **sth** (**up**) (**with sth**) fill up (space) inconveniently: *a room lumbered up with junk* ○ *a mind lumbered with useless facts.* **2** [I, Tn] (*esp US*) cut and prepare (timber) for use.
□ ˈ**lumberjack** (also ˈ**lumberman** /-mən/) *n* (esp in the US and Canada) man whose job is felling trees or cutting or transporting timber.
ˈ**lumber-jacket** *n* hip-length jacket fastening up to the neck, usu of thick checked material.
ˈ**lumber-room** *n* (*esp Brit*) room in which lumber[1](1) is kept.

lumber[2] /ˈlʌmbə(r)/ *v* [Ipr, Ip] move in a heavy clumsy way: *elephants lumbering along, past, by, etc* ○ *Look where you're going, you lumbering great oaf!*

luminary /ˈlu:mɪnərɪ; *US* -nerɪ/ *n* **1** person who inspires or influences others: *leading/lesser luminaries.* **2** (*fml*) heavenly body that gives light, esp the sun or the moon.

luminous /ˈlu:mɪnəs/ *adj* **1** giving out light; bright: *luminous paint*, ie paint that glows in the dark, used on watches, clocks, etc. **2** (*fig*) easily understood; clear: *a luminous speaker, explanation.*
▷ **luminosity** /ˌlu:mɪˈnɒsətɪ/ *n* [U] quality of being luminous.
luminously *adv*.

lumme (also **lummy**) /ˈlʌmɪ/ *interj* (*dated Brit sl*) (expressing surprise).

lump[1] /lʌmp/ *n* **1** hard or compact mass, usu without a regular shape: *a lump of clay* ○ *a sugar lump* ○ *break a piece of coal into small lumps* ○ *How many lumps* (ie of sugar) *do you take in your tea?* **2** swelling, bump or bruise: *a nasty lump on her neck.* **3** (*infml*) heavy, clumsy or stupid person: *Do hurry up, you great lump!* **4 the Lump** [sing] (*Brit*) (system of using) workers in the British building trade who are paid in cash, pay no taxes and are not properly insured by their employers. **5** (idm) **have, etc a ˈlump in one's/the throat** feel pressure in the throat as a result of strong emotion caused by love, sadness, etc.
▷ **lump** *v* **1** [Tn, Tn·pr, Tn·p] ~ **sb/sth** (**together**) put or consider people or things together; treat people or things as alike or under the same heading: *We've lumped all the advanced students into a single class.* ○ *Can we lump all these items together as 'incidental expenses'?* **2** [I] form lumps: *Stir the sauce to prevent it lumping.*
lumpish /-ɪʃ/ *adj* (of a person) heavy; clumsy; stupid.
lumpy *adj* (**-ier, -iest**) full of lumps; covered in lumps: *lumpy gravy* ○ *a lumpy mattress.*
□ **lump ˈsugar** sugar in the form of small lumps or cubes.
ˈ**lump sum** one payment for a number of separate items; one sum paid all at once rather than in several smaller amounts.

lump[2] /lʌmp/ *v* (idm) ˈ**lump it** (*infml*) reluctantly accept sth unpleasant or unwanted: *If you don't like the decision you'll just have to lump it.*

lumpen /ˈlʌmpən/ *adj* [attrib] (*derog*) stupid and uninterested in matters that need serious thought: *The average lumpen consumer does not worry about the environment.*
□ **lumpenproletariat** /ˌlʌmpənˌprəʊlɪˈteərɪət/ *n* [Gp] (esp in Marxist thought) the lower classes of society who are unorganized and have no interest in politics.

lunacy /ˈlu:nəsɪ/ *n* [U] **1** unsoundness of mind; insanity; madness. **2** very foolish behaviour: *It's sheer lunacy driving in this weather.* **3** [C usu *pl*] mad or foolish act.

lunar /ˈlu:nə(r)/ *adj* [usu attrib] of the moon: *lunar rocks* ○ *a lunar eclipse.*
□ ˌ**lunar ˈmodule** (also ˌ**lunar exˈcursion module**) part of a spacecraft circling the moon that can be detached to make a journey to the moon's surface and back.
ˌ**lunar ˈmonth** average time between one new moon and the next (about $29\frac{1}{2}$ days). ⇨ App 10. Cf CALENDAR MONTH (CALENDAR).

lunatic /ˈlu:nətɪk/ *n* **1** (*dated*) insane person. **2** wildly foolish person: *You're driving on the wrong side of the road, you lunatic!*
▷ **lunatic** *adj* **1** (*dated*) insane. **2** wildly foolish: *a lunatic proposal.* **3** (idm) **the ˌlunatic ˈfringe** (*derog*) those members of a political or some other group whose views are regarded as wildly extreme or eccentric: *The lunatic fringe is/are ignored by most members of the party.*
□ ˈ**lunatic asylum** (*dated*) home for the mentally ill; mental hospital.

lunch /lʌntʃ/ *n* [C, U] **1** meal taken in the middle of the day: *We serve hot and cold lunches.* ○ *He's gone to/for lunch.* ○ [attrib] *a one-hour lunch break.* **2** (*US*) light meal taken at any time: *We'll have a lunch after the show.* ⇨ Usage at DINNER.
▷ **lunch** *v* **1** [I, Ipr, Ip] eat lunch: *Where do you usually lunch?* ○ *We lunched (out) on cold meat and salad.* **2** [Tn] entertain (sb) to lunch.
□ ˈ**lunch-room** *n* (*esp US*) place where light meals are served or eaten.
ˈ**lunch-time** *n* [C, U] time around the middle of the day when lunch is normally eaten.

luncheon /ˈlʌntʃən/ *n* [C, U] (*fml*) lunch.
□ ˈ**luncheon meat** tinned cooked meat made from pork, ham, etc and usu eaten cold.
ˈ**luncheon voucher** (*abbr* **LV**) (*Brit*) (*US* ˈ**meal-ticket**) ticket, given to an employee as part of his pay, that can be exchanged for food at certain restaurants.

lung /lʌŋ/ *n* either of the two respiratory organs of air-breathing vertebrates located in the thorax, within the rib-cage: [attrib] *lung cancer* ○ *a singer with good lungs*, ie a powerful voice. ⇨ illus at RESPIRE.
□ ˈ**lung-fish** *n* (*pl* unchanged) freshwater fish that has a simple breathing organ like a lung as well as or instead of gills.
ˈ**lung-power** *n* [U] ability to shout, sing, etc strongly.

lunge /lʌndʒ/ *n* sudden forward movement of the body (eg when trying to attack sb); thrust.
▷ **lunge** *v* [I, Ipr, Ip] make a lunge: *He lunged wildly at his opponent.* ○ *She lunged out with a knife.* ⇨ illus at FENCING.

lupin (*US* **lupine**) /ˈlu:pɪn/ *n* garden plant with tall spikes of flowers, bearing seeds in pods.

lupine /ˈlu:paɪn/ *adj* of or like wolves.

lupus /ˈlu:pəs/ *n* [U] disease that causes ulcers on the skin, esp tuberculosis of the skin.

lurch[1] /lɜ:tʃ/ *n* (idm) **leave sb in the lurch** ⇨ LEAVE[1].

lurch[2] /lɜ:tʃ/ *n* **1** [C] sudden lean or roll to one side: *The ship gave a lurch to starboard.* **2** [sing] unsteady swaying movement; stagger.
▷ **lurch** *v* [I, Ipr, Ip] lean or roll suddenly; stagger: *a drunken man lurching along the street.*

lurcher /ˈlɜ:tʃə(r)/ *n* type of dog bred from a collie or sheep-dog crossed with a greyhound.

lure /lʊə(r)/ *n* **1** (**a**) thing that attracts or invites: *She used all her lures to attract his attention.* (**b**) (usu *sing*) power of attracting: *the lure of adventure.* **2** (**a**) bait or decoy used to attract wild animals. (**b**) device used to make a trained hawk return to its trainer or master.
▷ **lure** *v* [Tn, Tn·pr, Tn·p] attract or tempt (a person or an animal): *lure sb into a trap* ○ *Greed lured him on.*

lurid /ˈlʊərɪd/ *adj* **1** having bright glaring colours or combinations of colour: *a lurid sky, sunset* ○ *the lurid glow of the blazing warehouse.* **2** violent and shocking; sensational: *the lurid details of the murder* ○ *a lurid tale.* ▷ **luridly** *adv*. **luridness** *n* [U].

lurk /lɜ:k/ *v* [Ipr, Ip] **1** (**a**) be or stay hidden, esp when waiting to attack: *a suspicious-looking man lurking in the shadows.* (**b**) wait near a place trying not to attract attention: *He's usually lurking somewhere near the bar.* **2** (*fig*) linger (esp in the mind) without being clearly shown: *a lurking suspicion.* ⇨ Usage at PROWL.

luscious /ˈlʌʃəs/ *adj* **1** rich and sweet in taste or smell: *the luscious taste of ripe peaches.* **2** (of art, music, etc) very rich and suggesting sensual pleasures: *the luscious tones of the horns.* **3** sensually attractive; voluptuous: *a luscious blonde.* ▷ **lusciously** *adv*. **lusciousness** *n* [U].

lush[1] /lʌʃ/ *adj* **1** growing thickly and strongly; luxuriant: *lush pastures, vegetation, etc.* **2** (*fig*) luxurious: *lush carpets.*

lush[2] /lʌʃ/ *n* (*US sl*) person who is often drunk.

lust /lʌst/ *n* (*often derog*) **1** [C, U] ~ (**for sb**) strong sexual desire, esp when thought to be sinful: *curb one's lust* ○ *gratify one's lusts.* **2** [C, U] ~ (**for/of sth**) intense desire for sth or enjoyment of sth: *a lust for power, gold, adventure* ○ *filled with the lust of battle.*
▷ **lust** *v* [Ipr] ~ **after/for sb/sth** (*often derog*) feel a strong desire for sb/sth: *lust after women* ○ *He lusted for revenge.*
lustful /-fl/ *adj* (*often derog*) filled with lust: *lustful glances.* **lustfully** /-fəlɪ/ *adv*.

lustre (*US* **luster**) /ˈlʌstə(r)/ *n* [U] **1** soft brightness of a smooth or shining surface; sheen: *the deep lustre of pearls.* **2** (*fig*) glory; distinction: *brave deeds adding lustre to one's name.* **3** [U] (**a**) glaze on pottery that shines with many colours when light is reflected in it. (**b**) (also ˈ**lustreware**) pottery with such a glaze.
▷ **lustrous** /ˈlʌstrəs/ *adj* having lustre: *lustrous eyes, hair.* **lustrously** *adv*.

lusty /ˈlʌstɪ/ *adj* healthy, vigorous and full of vitality: *lusty youngsters at play* ○ *give a lusty cheer.* ▷ **lustily** /-ɪlɪ/ *adv*: *sing lustily.*

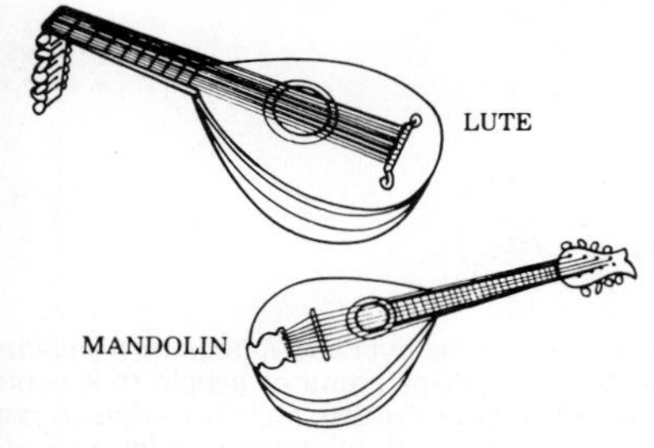

lute[1] /lu:t/ *n* stringed musical instrument with a pear-shaped body, used mainly from the 14th to the 18th centuries and played by plucking with the fingers.

lute[2] /lu:t/ *n* [U] type of clay or cement used for filling holes, sealing joints, etc.
▷ **lute** *v* [Tn] treat (sth) with lute[2].

lutenist (also **lutanist**) /ˈlu:tənɪst/ *n* person who plays the lute[1].

lutetium /lu:ˈti:ʃɪəm/ *n* [U] (*symb* **Lu**) rare metallic element with no known uses.

Luther /ˈlu:θə(r)/ Martin (1483-1546), German Protestant theologian. He is considered to have started the *Reformation with a statement of his ideas at Wittenberg, esp by claiming that salvation was only possible through faith. He organized a new Church for whose services *Bach and others composed great music, and his translation of the Bible into German had a great influence on the development of German language and literature.
▷ **Lutheran** /-ən/ *n, adj* (member) of the Protestant Church named after Luther. ➪ article at RELIGION.

Lutine Bell /ˌlu:ti:n ˈbel/ **the Lutine Bell** bell rung at *Lloyd's in London to halt business for an important announcement, esp about the loss of a ship insured there. The bell was recovered from the *Lutine*, a ship insured at Lloyd's which sank in 1799 with a large cargo of gold.

Lutyens /ˈlʌtjənz/ Sir Edwin (1869-1944), English architect. His early work on private houses adapted traditional English styles. His later designs for public buildings, as in New Delhi, show a more classical influence. ➪ illus. ➪ article at ARCHITECTURE.

Luxembourg /ˈlʌksəmbɜ:g/ small country in western Europe, founder member of the European Community and one of the three *Benelux countries; pop approx 374 000; official language French; capital Luxembourg (city); unit of currency franc (= 100 centimes). The economy is based on financial services and the chemical industry, with a very small agricultural sector. Its

The Deanery, Berkshire, designed by Sir Edwin Lutyens

landscape of hills and forests also makes it attractive to tourists. ➪ map at BENELUX.

luxuriant /lʌgˈʒʊərɪənt/ *adj* growing thickly and strongly; lush: *luxuriant tropical vegetation* ○ (*fig*) *the poem's luxuriant imagery*. Cf LUXURIOUS.
▷ **luxuriance** /-əns/ *n* [U] luxuriant growth. **luxuriantly** *adv*.

luxuriate /lʌgˈʒʊərɪeɪt/ *v* [Ipr] ~ **in sth** take great pleasure in sth; enjoy sth as a luxury: *a cat luxuriating in the warm sunshine* ○ *luxuriate in a hot bath*.

luxurious /lʌgˈʒʊərɪəs/ *adj* 1 supplied with luxuries; very comfortable: *live in luxurious surroundings* ○ *This car is our most luxurious model*. 2 [usu attrib] fond of luxury; self-indulgent: *luxurious habits*. Cf LUXURIANT. ▷ **luxuriously** *adv*.

luxury /ˈlʌkʃərɪ/ *n* 1 [U] (regular use and enjoyment of) the best and most expensive food and drink, clothes, surroundings, etc: *live in luxury* ○ *lead/live a life of luxury* ○ [attrib] *a luxury hotel, flat, liner*. 2 [C] thing that is expensive and enjoyable, but not essential: *caviar, champagne and other luxuries* ○ *We can't afford many luxuries*. 3 (idm) **in the lap of luxury** ➪ LAP[1].

LV /ˌel ˈvi:/ *abbr* (*Brit*) luncheon voucher.

LW *abbr* (*radio*) long wave.

-ly /-lɪ/ *suff* 1 (used fairly widely with *ns* to form *adjs*) having the qualities of: *cowardly* ○ *scholarly*. 2 (with *ns* forming *adjs* and *advs*) occurring at intervals of: *hourly* ○ *daily*. 3 (used widely with *adjs* to form *advs*) in the specified manner: *happily* ○ *stupidly*.

lycée /ˈli:seɪ; *US* li:ˈseɪ/ *n* (*French*) state secondary school in France.

lychee (also **litchi**) /ˌlaɪˈtʃi:, ˈlaɪtʃi:/ *n* (**a**) fruit with a sweetish white pulp and a single seed in a thin brown shell. (**b**) tree (originally from China) that bears this.

lych-gate = LICH-GATE.

lye /laɪ/ *n* [U] alkaline solution, esp one obtained by passing water through wood ashes and used for washing things.

lying *pres p of* LIE[1, 2].

Lyly /ˈlɪlɪ/ John (c 1554-1606), English author and playwright. The elaborate ornamental style of his prose romances became known as 'euphuism' after the title of one of them, *Euphues*.

lymph /lɪmf/ *n* [U] 1 (*anatomy*) colourless fluid from the tissues or organs of the body, containing white blood-cells. 2 (*medical*) this fluid taken from cows and used in vaccination against smallpox.
▷ **lymphatic** /lɪmˈfætɪk/ *adj* 1 (*anatomy*) of or carrying lymph: *the lymphatic vessels*, ie those that carry lymph from the tissues with any waste matter. 2 (*fml*) (of people) slow in thought and action; sluggish.
□ ˈ**lymph node** (also ˈ**lymph gland**) mass of tissue in which the lymph is filtered and bacteria and other impurities are removed, and which produces some of the white blood cells the body uses to fight infection.

lynch /lɪntʃ/ *v* [Tn] put to death or punish violently (sb believed to be guilty of a crime) without a lawful trial: *innocent men lynched by the angry mob*.
□ ˈ**lynch law** procedure followed when sb is lynched.

lynx /lɪŋks/ *n* wild animal of the cat family with spotted fur and a short tail, noted for its keen sight.
□ ˌ**lynx-ˈeyed** *adj* having keen eyesight.

lyre /ˈlaɪə(r)/ *n* ancient musical instrument with strings fixed in a U-shaped frame, played by plucking with the fingers.
□ ˈ**lyre-bird** *n* Australian bird, the male having a long tail shaped like a lyre when spread out.

lyric /ˈlɪrɪk/ *adj* 1 (of poetry) expressing direct personal feelings. 2 of or composed for singing.
▷ **lyric** *n* 1 lyric poem. 2 (esp *pl*) words of a song, eg in a musical play: [attrib] *a fine lyric-writer/writer of lyrics*.

lyrical /ˈlɪrɪkl/ *adj* 1 = LYRIC. 2 eagerly enthusiastic: *She started to become/wax lyrical about health food*. ▷ **lyrically** /-klɪ/ *adv*.

lyricism /ˈlɪrɪsɪzəm/ *n* 1 [U] quality of being lyric, esp in poetry. 2 [C] expression of strong emotion or enthusiasm.

lyricist /ˈlɪrɪsɪst/ *n* person who writes the words of (esp popular) songs.

M, m

M, m /em/ *n* (*pl* **M's, m's** /emz/) the thirteenth letter of the English alphabet: *'Moscow' starts with (an) M/'M'.*

M *abbr* **1** (also **med**) (esp on clothing, etc) medium (size). **2** (also **m**) Roman numeral for 1000 (Latin *mille*). **3** /em/ (*Brit*) motorway: *heavy traffic on the M25.*

m *abbr* **1** (esp on forms) male (sex). **2** (esp on forms) married (status). **3** (also **masc**) (*grammar*) masculine (gender). **4** (**a**) metre(s): *run in the 5000 m*, ie a race over that distance. (**b**) (*radio*) metres: *800 m long wave.* **5** million(s): *population 10m.*

MA /ˌem ˈeɪ/ (*US* **AM**) Master of Arts: *have/be an MA in Modern Languages* ○ *Marion Bell MA (London).* ⇨ article at POST-SCHOOL.

ma /mɑː/ *n* (*infml*) (usu used to address sb) mother: *I'm going now, ma.* ○ *He always does what his ma tells him to.*

ma'am /mæm *or, rarely*, mɑːm/ *n* [sing] **1** (used to address the Queen, a noblewoman, a female superior officer in the army, etc) madam. **2** (*US*) (used as a polite form of address to a woman): *Can I help you, ma'am?*

Mabinogion /ˌmæbɪˈnɒgɪən/ collection of medieval Welsh prose stories containing Celtic legends.

mac[1] (also **mack**) /mæk/ *n* (*Brit infml*) = MACKINTOSH.

mac[2] /mæk/ *n* [sing] (*US infml*) (used to address a man whose name one does not know): *Hey, mac! What do you think you're doing?*

macabre /məˈkɑːbrə/ *adj* connected with death, and thus causing fear; gruesome: *a macabre ghost story.*

macadam /məˈkædəm/ *n* [U] road surface made of layers of compressed broken stones: [attrib] *a macadam road.* Cf TARMAC.

▷ **macadamize, -ise** /-aɪz/ *v* [Tn] make or cover (a road) with macadam: *macadamized roads.*

Macao /məˈkaʊ/ Portuguese territory on the South China Sea, west of Hong Kong. It has a free port and is a centre of tourism noted for gambling. The territory is to be returned to Chinese rule in 1999. ⇨ map at CHINA.

macaque /məˈkæk/ *n* short-tailed monkey of SE Asia, India and N Africa. The rhesus monkey and the Barbary ape are types of macaque.

macaroni /ˌmækəˈrəʊnɪ/ *n* [U] long hard tubes of pasta, often chopped into short pieces and boiled in water before eating.

□ ˌ**macaroni** ˈ**cheese** dish of macaroni with a cheese sauce.

macaronic /mækəˈrɒnɪk/ *adj* (of poetry) containing foreign (esp Latin) words and phrases for humorous effect.

macaroon /ˌmækəˈruːn/ *n* small flat cake or biscuit made of sugar, egg white and crushed almonds or coconut.

MacArthur /məˈkɑːθə(r)/ Douglas (1880-1964), American general who commanded the US forces in the south-western Pacific during the Second World War, and after accepting the Japanese surrender commanded the Allied forces in Japan from 1945 to 1950. He later commanded United Nations forces in the early phase of the Korean War.

Macaulay /məˈkɔːlɪ/ Thomas Babington, 1st Baron (1800-59), English historian, politician and poet. His best-known works are his uncompleted *History of England*, which was very influential on the writing of history, and the *Lays of Ancient Rome.*

macaw /məˈkɔː/ *n* type of large long-tailed tropical American parrot.

Macbeth /məkˈbeθ/ play (1606) by *Shakespeare which tells the story of Macbeth, a Scottish general who, urged on by his ambitious wife, murders the king and becomes king himself. In the end Macbeth is himself killed. It is traditionally regarded as an unlucky play by actors, who avoid mentioning it by name, calling it 'the Scottish play'. ⇨ App 6.

Maccabees /ˈmækəbiːz/ *n* [pl] four books of Jewish history and theology, of which the first two (whose hero is Judas Maccabaeus) are in the *Apocrypha. ⇨ App 5.

MacDonald[1] /məkˈdɒnəld/ Flora (1722-90), Scottish heroine who in 1746 helped Charles Edward *Stuart ('Bonny Prince Charlie') to escape from Scotland in a small boat after his defeat by the English at *Culloden. Cf SKYE.

MacDonald[2] /məkˈdɒnəld/ James Ramsay (1866-1937), British politician, leader of the Labour Party 1911-14 and 1922-31, prime minister 1924, 1929-31 and 1931-35. He was the first British Labour prime minister. His second government failed to deal with economic difficulties, and was replaced by a coalition government, which he led. This came to be increasingly dominated by the Conservatives, and MacDonald became unpopular among Labour supporters. ⇨ App 2.

Mace /meɪs/ *n* [U] (*propr*) chemical substance that causes tears, dizziness, etc and is sprayed on rioters, attackers, etc to make them go away.

mace[1] /meɪs/ *n* **1** large heavy club formerly used as a weapon, usu having a head with metal spikes. **2** staff or rod, usu ornamented, carried or displayed as a sign of the authority of an official, eg a mayor.

□ ˈ**mace-bearer** *n* person who carries an official mace.

mace[2] /meɪs/ *n* [U] dried outer covering of nutmegs, used for flavouring foods.

Macedonia /ˌmæsɪˈdəʊnɪə/ **1** (also **Macedon** /ˈmæsɪdən/) ancient country in NE Greece, which under *Philip of Macedon and *Alexander the Great became the centre of a powerful empire. **2** one of the federal republics of the former Yugoslavia, now an independent country; capital Skopje.

macerate /ˈmæsəreɪt/ *v* [I, Tn] (*fml*) (cause sth to) become soft or break up by soaking. ▷ **maceration** /ˌmæsəˈreɪʃn/ *n* [U].

Mach /mɑːk, mæk/ *n* [U] (followed by a number) ratio of the speed of sth (esp an aircraft) to the speed of sound: *an aircraft flying at Mach two*, ie twice the speed of sound.

machete /məˈtʃetɪ; *US* -ˈʃetɪ/ *n* broad heavy knife used as a cutting tool and as a weapon, esp in Latin America and the West Indies. ⇨ illus at KNIFE.

Machiavelli /ˌmækɪəˈvelɪ/ Niccolò (1469-1527), Italian politician and author who in his best-known book, *The Prince*, described the subtle, cunning and sometimes deceitful methods a statesman or politician should use to become successful.

▷ **machiavellian** (also **Machiavellian**) /-ɪən/ *adj* cunning and deceitful in gaining what one wants; showing such cunning or deceit: *a machiavellian person, scheme, plot.*

machination /ˌmækɪˈneɪʃn/ *n* (**a**) [C usu *pl*] evil plot or scheme: *attempts to counter their machinations.* (**b**) [U] plotting.

machine /məˈʃiːn/ *n* **1** [C] (often in compounds) apparatus with several moving parts, designed to perform a particular task, and driven by electricity, steam, gas, etc, or by human power: *The scrap merchant has a machine which crushes cars.* ○ *a* ˈ*sewing-machine*, ˈ*washing-machine, etc* ○ *office machines*, eg computers, word processors, photocopiers, etc ○ *Machines have replaced human labour in many industries.* ⇨ Usage. **2** [C] (*fig*) person who acts automatically, without thinking: *Years of doing the same dull job can turn you into a machine.* **3** [CGp] group of people that control (part of) an organization, etc: *the (political) party machine* ○ *The public relations machine covered up the firm's heavy losses.* **4** (idm) **a cog in the machine** ⇨ COG.

▷ **machine** *v* [Tn] **1** cut, shape, polish, etc (sth) with a machine: *The edge of the disc had been machined flat/smooth.* **2** make (clothes) using a sewing-machine: *I have to machine the hem.*

machinery /məˈʃiːnərɪ/ *n* [U] **1** (**a**) moving parts (of a machine): *the machinery of a clock.* (**b**) machines collectively or in general: *Much new machinery has been installed.* **2** ~ (**of sth/for doing sth**) organization or structure (of sth/for doing sth): *reform the machinery of government* ○ *We have no machinery for dealing with complaints.* ○ *All this will be processed by the Home Office machinery.*

machinist /məˈʃiːnɪst/ *n* **1** person who operates a machine, esp a sewing-machine. **2** person who makes, repairs or operates machine tools.

□ **ma**ˈ**chine code** (also **ma**ˈ**chine language**) (*computing*) binary code in which instructions are written that a computer can understand and act on.

maˈ**chine-gun** *n* gun that fires bullets continuously while the trigger is pressed: *operate, set up a machine-gun* ○ [attrib] *accurate machine-gun fire.* ⇨ illus at GUN. — *v* (-**nn**-) [Tn] shoot (sb) with a machine-gun: *They machine-gunned the advancing troops.*

maˌ**chine-**ˈ**made** *adj* made by machine. Cf HAND-MADE (HAND[1]).

maˌ**chine-**ˈ**readable** *adj* (*computing*) (of data) in a form that a computer can understand: *convert a book into machine-readable form.*

maˈ**chine tool** tool for cutting or shaping materials, driven by a machine.

NOTE ON USAGE: Compare **machine, tool**, etc. A **machine** consists of moving parts powered by electricity, etc and is designed for a specific job. An (**electrical**) **appliance** is a machine used in the house, such as a washing-machine or dishwasher. An **apparatus** is a system of connected machines, wires, etc: *the apparatus for lighting the stage.* A **tool** is an object held in the hand, often used by people in their jobs, eg a hammer, drill or spanner. An **instrument** is a tool designed for a technical task, eg a surgeon's knife. It may have some moving parts and be used in a technical operation, eg a microscope or meter. An **implement** is a tool generally used outdoors, especially in gardening or farming, eg a plough, rake or spade. **Device** and **gadget** are more general terms. **Device** is often used implying approval of a useful machine or instrument: *a labour-saving device* ○ *a clever device for locking windows.* **Gadget** is more informal and can suggest disapproval: *Their kitchen is full of the latest gadgets.* ○ *All these modern gadgets are more trouble than they're worth.*

machismo /məˈtʃɪzməʊ, *also* məˈkɪzməʊ/ *n* [U] (*esp derog*) exaggerated or aggressive pride in being male.

macho /ˈmætʃəʊ/ *adj* (*infml esp derog*) aggressively masculine: *He thinks it's macho to drink a lot and get into fights.*

Mackenzie[1] /məˈkenzɪ/ Sir Alexander (1764-1820), Scottish explorer of Canada who discovered the Mackenzie River, the longest river in Canada, and was the first white man to reach the Pacific Ocean by land along a northern route.

Mackenzie[2] /məˈkenzɪ/ Sir (Edward Montague)

Compton (1883-1972), British novelist, essayist and critic whose best-known books include the semi-autobiographical *Sinister Street* and the humorous novel *Whisky Galore*.

mackerel /ˈmækrəl/ *n* (*pl* unchanged) **1** striped fish that lives in the sea and is eaten as food: *a good catch of mackerel.* **2** (idm) **a sprat to catch a mackerel** ➪ SPRAT.
□ ˌ**mackerel** ˈ**sky** sky covered with strips of fleecy cloud, similar to the stripes on a mackerel's back.

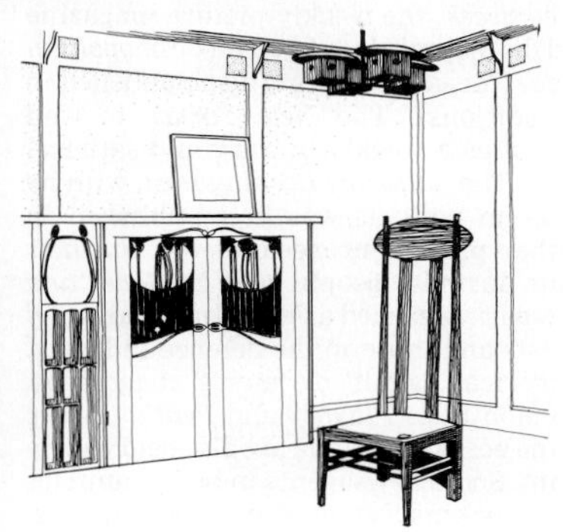

Mackintosh /ˈmækɪntɒʃ/ Charles Rennie (1868-1928), Scottish architect and designer who produced buildings, furniture, etc in the art nouveau (ART[1]) style. His best-known building is the Glasgow School of Art. ➪ illus. ➪ article at ARCHITECTURE.

mackintosh /ˈmækɪntɒʃ/ (also **mac**, **mack** /mæk/) *n* (*Brit*) coat made of rainproof material.

Macmillan /məkˈmɪlən/ Maurice Harold, 1st Earl of Stockton (1894-1986), British politician, leader of the Conservative Party and prime minister 1957-63. He encouraged the growth of the British economy, using the catchphrase 'You've never had it so good' to refer to people's wealth, and tried unsuccessfully to get Britain into the *European Economic Community.

MacNeice /məkˈni:s/ (Frederick) Louis (1907-63), British poet, born in Northern Ireland. His books of verse include *Blind Fireworks* and *Holes in the Sky*, but he is perhaps best known for his radio play *The Dark Tower* and his collaboration with W H *Auden in *Letters from Iceland*.

macramé /məˈkrɑ:mɪ/ *n* [U] art of knotting string in decorative patterns.

macro- *comb form* large; large-scale: *macrobiotic* ○ *macroeconomic(s).* Cf MICRO-, MINI-.

macrobiotics /ˌmækrəʊbaɪˈɒtɪks/ *n* [sing *v*] science of diets that consist of whole grains and vegetables grown without chemical treatment. ▷ **macrobiotic** *adj* [esp attrib]: *macrobiotic food.*

macrocosm /ˈmækrəʊkɒzəm/ *n* **1 the macrocosm** [sing] the universe. **2** [C] any large complete structure containing smaller structures. Cf MICROCOSM.

macroeconomics /ˈmækrəʊi:kənɒmɪks, -ekə-/ *n* [sing *v*] study of the behaviour of a large-scale economic system (eg the economy of a country). ▷ **macroeconomic** *adj.*

macromolecule /ˈmækrəʊmɒlɪkju:l/ *n* molecule containing a very large number of atoms.

mad /mæd/ *adj* (**-dder**, **-ddest**) **1** (a) mentally ill; insane: *a mad person, act* ○ *be/go mad* ○ *drive/send sb mad.* (b) (*infml esp derog*) very foolish; crazy: *What a mad thing to do!* ○ *You must be mad to drive so fast!* ○ *He's quite mad: he goes round in very odd clothes.* **2** (*infml*) (a) ~ **about/on sth/sb** very interested in sth/sb; enthusiastic about sth/sb: *mad on football, pop music, etc* ○ *He's mad about her*, ie likes/loves her very much. (b) (following *ns*) very keen on (sth/sb): *be cricket mad, photography mad, pop music mad, etc* ○ *a crowd of football-mad little boys.* **3** ~ **(with sth)** (*infml*) very excited; wild; frenzied: *a mad dash, rush, etc* ○ *mad with pain* ○ *The crowd is mad with excitement!* **4** (*infml*) ~ **(at/with sb)** angry; furious: *His obstinacy drives me mad!* ○ *She was mad at/with him for losing the match.* ○ *mad at/with the dog for eating her shoe* ○ *Don't get mad (about the broken window).* **5** (of a dog) suffering from rabies. **6** (idm) **hopping mad** ➪ HOP[1]. **like** ˈ**mad** (*infml*) very much, quickly, etc: *smoke, run, work, etc like mad.* **(as) mad as a** ˈ**hatter/a March** ˈ**hare** (*infml*) completely insane. **mad** ˈ**keen (on sb/sth)** (*infml*) very interested (in sb/sth) or enthusiastic (about sb/sth): *She's mad keen on hockey/on Arthur Higgins.* **stark raving/staring mad** ➪ STARK.
▷ **madly** *adv* **1** in an insane manner: *madly bent on further conquests.* **2** (*infml*) extremely: *madly excited, jealous, etc* ○ *She's madly in love with him.*
madness *n* [U] **1** state of being insane; insane behaviour: *His madness cannot be cured.* **2** extreme foolishness: *It is madness to climb in such bad weather.* **3** (idm) **method in one's madness** ➪ METHOD. **midsummer madness** ➪ MIDSUMMER.
□ ˈ**madhouse** *n* **1** (*infml derog*) place where there is much confusion or noise: *This classroom is a madhouse: be quiet!* **2** (*dated*) mental hospital.
ˈ**madman** /-mən/, ˈ**madwoman** *ns* person who is insane.

Madagascar /ˌmædəˈgæskə(r)/ island and country in the Indian Ocean, off SE Africa; pop approx 11 238 000; official language Malagasy; capital Antananarivo; unit of currency franc. It was a French colony between 1896 and 1960, when it became an independent republic. Its economy is mainly agricultural. Many plants and animals of the island are found nowhere else. ➪ map at NAMIBIA.

madam /ˈmædəm/ *n* **1** (also **Madam**) [sing] (*fml*) (polite form of address to a woman, whether married or unmarried, usu sb one does not know personally): *Can I help you, madam?* ○ *Dear Madam*, ie used like *Dear Sir* in a letter ○ *Madam Chairman, may I be allowed to speak?* Cf MISS[2] 2. **2** [C] (*infml derog*) girl or young woman who likes to get her own way: *She's a real little madam!* **3** [C esp *sing*] woman who is in charge of a brothel.

Madame /məˈdɑ:m; *US* məˈdæm/ *n* (*abbr* **Mme**) (*pl* **Mesdames** /meɪˈdɑ:m/, *abbr* **Mmes**) (French title given to an older, esp married or widowed, woman or to an older woman who is not British or American): *Madame Lee from Hong Kong.*

madcap *adj* [attrib], *n* (typical of a) person who acts recklessly or impulsively: *some madcap adventure* ○ *a complete madcap.*

madden /ˈmædn/ *v* [Tn] make (sb) mad(4); irritate; annoy: *It maddens me that she was chosen instead of me!*
▷ **maddening** /ˈmædnɪŋ/ *adj* annoying; irritating: *maddening delays* ○ *Her laziness is quite maddening.* **maddeningly** *adv*: *maddeningly unhelpful, stupid, inefficient, etc.*

madder /ˈmædə(r)/ *n* [U] (red dye obtained from the root of a) climbing plant with yellowish flowers.

made *pt, pp* of MAKE[1].

Madeira[1] /məˈdɪərə/ largest of a group of islands (the **Madeira Islands** or the **Madeiras**) in the Atlantic Ocean, off NW Africa, which belong to Portugal. ➪ map at PORTUGAL.

Madeira[2] /məˈdɪərə/ *n* [U, C] white dessert wine from the island of Madeira.
□ **Ma**ˈ**deira cake** type of sponge-cake.

Madison Avenue /ˌmædɪsn ˈævnju:/ **1** street in New York where many American advertising agencies have their offices. **2** (*fig*) the American advertising industry.

madonna /məˈdɒnə/ *n* **1 the Madonna** [sing] the Virgin Mary, mother of Jesus Christ. **2** [C] statue or picture of the Virgin Mary: *There was a madonna on the altar.*

madrigal /ˈmædrɪgl/ *n* (esp 16-century) song for several voices, usu without instrumental accompaniment, on the themes of love and/or nature.

Maecenas /maɪˈsi:nəs/ *n* (*rhet*) person who helps and encourages artists, esp poets. The term comes from the name of Gaius Maecenas (c 70-8 BC), a wealthy friend and patron of *Virgil, *Horace, etc.

maelstrom /ˈmeɪlstrɒm/ *n* (usu *sing*) **1** great whirlpool. **2** (*fig*) state of violent confusion: *the maelstrom of war* ○ *She was drawn into a maelstrom of revolutionary events.*

maestro /ˈmaɪstrəʊ/ *n* (*pl* ~**s** or **maestri** /ˈmaɪstrɪ/) (with a capital letter when followed by a name) (title given to a) master in the arts, esp a great musical composer, conductor or teacher: *Maestro Giulini* ○ *the maestri of the seventeenth century.*

Mae West /ˌmeɪ ˈwest/ *n* (*infml*) inflatable life-jacket, esp as worn by airman during the Second World War. It was named after the American film actress Mae West, who was famous for her large bust.

Mafeking /ˈmæfəkɪŋ/ town in South Africa where British forces were besieged for 215 days in 1899-1900 during the *Boer War. The end of the siege (the 'Relief of Mafeking') was the cause of great rejoicing in Britain. In 1980 the town's name was changed to Mafikeng.

Mafia /ˈmæfɪə; *US* ˈmɑ:f-/ *n* [CGp] **1 the Mafia** (a) secret organization of criminals in Sicily. (b) similar organization active esp in Italy and the USA: [attrib] *a Mafia boss, gang, killing, plot.* **2 mafia** (*derog or joc*) group of people who (are thought to) exert great influence secretly: *The town hall mafia will prevent this plan going through.*
▷ **Mafioso** /ˌmæfɪˈəʊsəʊ/ *n* (*pl* **Mafiosi** /-si:/) member of the Mafia.

magazine[1] /ˌmægəˈzi:n; *US* ˈmægəzi:n/ *n* (*infml abbr* **mag** /mæg/) paper-covered periodical, usu weekly or monthly, with articles, stories, etc by various writers: *women's magazines* ○ *a literary magazine* ○ [attrib] *a magazine article.* ➪ article.
□ **maga**ˈ**zine programme** radio or television programme containing various brief items, usu of topical interest.

magazine[2] /mægəˈzi:n; *US* ˈmægəzi:n/ *n* **1** store for arms, ammunition, explosives, etc. **2** chamber holding the cartridges of a rifle or pistol before they are fed into the breech. ➪ illus at GUN. **3** place that holds the roll or cartridge of film in a camera.

Magellan /məˈgelən/ Ferdinand (c1480-1521), Portuguese explorer who tried to find a western route to the East Indies. He sailed round the southern tip of South America, through what is now called the Strait of Magellan, and across the Pacific Ocean, which he named, but he was killed in the Philippines. His crew returned to Spain, completing the first voyage round the world.

Magellanic cloud /ˌmædʒəˌlænɪk ˈklaʊd/ *n* either of two small galaxies that can be faintly seen in the southern hemisphere.

magenta /məˈdʒentə/ *adj*, *n* [U] bright purplish-red (dye).

maggot /ˈmægət/ *n* larva or grub (esp of the bluebottle or cheese-fly), which lays its eggs in meat, cheese, etc: *People use maggots as bait when they go fishing.*
▷ **maggoty** *adj* full of maggots: *maggoty cheese, meat, etc.*

Magi /ˈmeɪdʒaɪ/ **the Magi** *n* [pl] the three wise men from the East who brought gifts to the infant Jesus.

magic /ˈmædʒɪk/ *n* [U] **1** power of apparently using supernatural forces to change the form of things or influence events; superstitious practices based on this: *They believe that it was all done by magic.* ○ *black/white magic* ○ *This soap works like magic — the stains just disappear.* ○ *The paper turned green as if by magic.* Cf SORCERY (SORCERER), WITCHCRAFT (WITCH). **2** (art of performing) tricks with mysterious results, done to entertain: *She's very good at magic; she can conjure a rabbit out of a hat.* **3** (*fig approv*) (a) charming or enchanting quality: *the magic of Shakespeare's poetry, of the woods in autumn.* (b) thing that has this quality: *Her piano playing is absolute magic.*
▷ **magic** *adj* **1** used in or using magic: *a magic spell, word, trick, etc* ○ *the magic arts.* **2** (*sl*) wonderful; excellent: *That music is really magic!* ○ *We had a magic time today!* ○ *You got the tickets? Magic!*

Magazines

The British are avid magazine readers, and a very wide range of magazines are published to cater for their many interests. Most of them are published weekly, but some appear fortnightly, and others monthly. Most newsagents display their magazines under different headings, such as 'leisure interest', 'sport', 'motoring', 'music and hi-fi', and 'women's interest'.

A heading such as 'general interest' or 'leisure interest' may cover a great variety of specialized subjects, from photography to gardening, computers to country life, children's comics to 'adult' (ie sex) magazines. In each area there are usually several competing magazines. For those with an interest in photography, for example, the range includes *Amateur Photographer*, *Creative Camera*, *Photo Answers*, *Photography*, and *Practical Photography*.

The magazines with the largest circulations, often over a million copies, are women's and family magazines. Examples are *Woman* and *Woman's Weekly*. One of the magazines with the highest circulation of all is *Radio Times* which, despite its name, gives details of all the week's programmes on television and radio.

Many children's magazines are comics. Two of the best known and longest running are *Beano* and *Dandy*. Some of them are of an educational nature. There are relatively few magazines specifically for boys, but a wide choice of weeklies for girls is available. One of the best known boys' magazines is *Victor*, containing stories about war, sport and adventure. Girls have such weeklies as *Jackie*, *Judy*, and *Just Seventeen*.

Some of the serious weekly magazines have been published for many years. *New Statesman and Society*, an established left-wing magazine, was first published (as the *New Statesman*) in 1913, and the right-wing weekly *The Spectator*, founded in 1828, is one of the oldest in Britain. *The Economist*, an influential economic and financial journal, has been published since 1843.

Punch, a weekly founded in 1841, has long been famous as a humorous magazine, while more recently *Private Eye*, a fortnightly first issued in 1961, has gained a reputation for its satirical content, and for the many writs for libel it has attracted. *Time Out*, founded in 1968, and *City Limits*, are popular weekly 'listing' magazines that give details and reviews of events of all kinds in London.

Most Sunday newspapers publish an accompanying magazine and many daily papers issue one with their Saturday edition. (Cf article at NEWSPAPER.) These magazines are included in the price of the newspaper.

Americans are equally keen magazine readers, and have a similarly wide choice. Excluding comics, the most popular magazines, all with a circulation of 10 million or more, are currently *Modern Maturity*, *NRTA/AARP News Bulletin*, *TV Guide* and *National Geographic Magazine*. The first two of these are for retired people and are subscription papers, not on sale to the general public. ('NRTA' stands for 'National Retired Teachers Association' and 'AARP' for 'American Association of Retired Persons'.) The US edition of the monthly magazine *Reader's Digest* is also a best seller, as the British edition is in Britain.

Some American magazines have gained a high reputation in their field. They include the women's monthlies *McCall's* and *Harper's Bazaar*, the weekly news magazine *Time*, its rival *Newsweek*, the weekly picture magazine *Life*, and the magazines for women *Cosmopolitan* and *Vogue* (the last two being also published in British editions). The *New Yorker* is well established as a weekly literary and satirical magazine. The *Saturday Evening Post*, with its emphasis on politics, was first published in 1821. Other prominent weeklies are *Business Week*, for business people, and *US News and World Report*, regarded as essential reading by economists and those in the defence industry.

Of American 'adult' or 'men's' magazines, the two monthlies *Playboy* and *Penthouse* are among the best known, and are also sold widely in Britain. Some newsagents in both countries no longer stock magazines of this type, however, partly as a result of pressure from women's groups.

Magazines accompanying American newspapers are usually syndicated. The popular weekly *Parade*, for example, is distributed with over 300 different Sunday newspapers.

Almost all magazines, both British and American, and especially the more popular ones, have a high proportion of advertisements, aimed specifically at the type of reader who takes a particular magazine. The British weekly *Exchange and Mart*, founded in 1868, is devoted entirely to advertisements of 'sales and wants'.

magic *v* (*pt*, *pp* **magicked**) (phr v) **magic sth away** cause sth to disappear by magic: *The conjurer magicked the bird away.* ○ (*fig*) *As soon as the trouble began, his bodyguards magicked him away.* **magic sth from/out of sth** produce sth by magic from sth: *She magicked a rabbit out of a hat.*

magical /-kl/ *adj* **1** of, used in or like magic: *a wizard's magical hat.* **2** (*infml*) charming; enchanting: *a magical view over the calm waters of the bay.* **magically** /-klɪ/ *adv*.

magician /məˈdʒɪʃn/ *n* person who is skilled in magic(2). Cf CONJURER (CONJURE[1]).

□ ˌ**magic ˈcarpet** (in fairy stories) carpet that is able to fly and carry people.

ˌ**magic ˈeye** (*infml*) photoelectric device which shows that sb/sth is present or which is used to control an electric or electronic device: *lifts opened and closed by a magic eye.*

ˌ**magic ˈlantern** early form of slide projector, with which pictures printed on glass were shown on a screen by means of a beam of light.

magisterial /ˌmædʒɪˈstɪərɪəl/ *adj* (*fml*) **1** having or showing authority: *a magisterial manner, statement, pronouncement.* **2** of or conducted by a magistrate: *magisterial decisions, proceedings.* ▷ **magisterially** /-ɪəlɪ/ *adv*: *dismiss the servants magisterially.*

magistrate /ˈmædʒɪstreɪt/ *n* official who acts as a judge in the lowest courts; Justice of the Peace: *the Magistrates' Courts* ○ *come up before the magistrate.* ➪ article at LAW.

▷ **magistracy** /ˈmædʒɪstrəsɪ/ *n* **1** [C] position of a magistrate. **2 the magistracy** [Gp] magistrates as a group: *He's been elected to the magistracy.*

magma /ˈmægmə/ *n* [U] molten rock found beneath the earth's crust. ➪ illus at VOLCANO.

Magna Carta (also **Magna Charta**) /ˌmægnə ˈkɑːtə/ political charter which King *John was forced to accept by the English barons in 1215, granting certain political and civil liberties which have been fundamental principles of the British constitution ever since (eg no one may be illegally imprisoned).

magnanimous /mægˈnænɪməs/ *adj* having or showing great generosity (esp towards a rival, an enemy, etc): *a magnanimous person, gesture, gift* ○ *a leader who was magnanimous in victory*, ie when he won.

▷ **magnanimity** /ˌmægnəˈnɪmətɪ/ *n* [U] being magnanimous: *show great magnanimity towards an opponent.*

magnanimously *adv*.

magnate /ˈmægneɪt/ *n* wealthy and powerful landowner or industrialist: *an industrial magnate.*

magnesia /mægˈniːʃə/ *n* [U] white tasteless powder (carbonate of magnesium) used in liquid form as a medicine, and in industry.

magnesium /mægˈniːzɪəm; *US* mægˈniːʒəm/ *n* [U] (*symb* **Mg**) (*chemistry*) silver-white metallic element that burns with a very bright flame and is used in making alloys and fireworks. ➪ App 11.

magnet

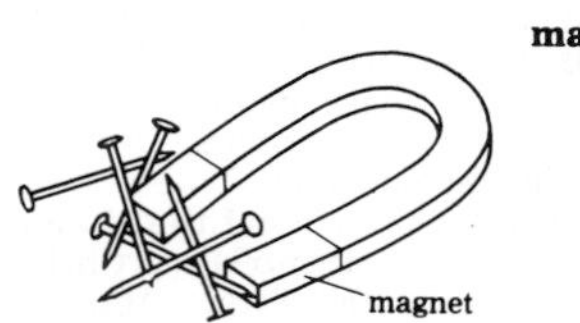

magnet /ˈmægnɪt/ *n* **1** piece of iron, often in a horseshoe shape, which can attract iron, either naturally or because of an electric current passed through it, and which points roughly north and south when freely suspended. ➪ illus. **2** (*fig*) person or thing that has a powerful attraction: *This disco is a magnet for young people.*

▷ **magnetism** /ˈmægnɪtɪzəm/ *n* [U] **1** (science of the) properties and effects of magnetic substances. **2** (*fig*) great personal charm and attraction: *the magnetism of a great cinema performer.*

magnetize, -ise /ˈmægnətaɪz/ *v* [Tn] **1** cause (sth) to become magnetic: *This screwdriver has been magnetized.* **2** (*fig*) attract (sb) strongly, as if by magnetism: *She can magnetize a theatre audience.*

magnetic /mægˈnetɪk/ *adj* **1** with the properties of a magnet: *The block becomes magnetic when the current is switched on.* **2** (*fig*) having a powerful attraction: *a magnetic smile, personality.* **3** of magnetism: *magnetic properties, forces, etc.* ▷ **magnetically** /-klɪ/ *adv*.

□ **magˌnetic ˈcompass** = COMPASS[1].

magˌnetic eˈquator ➪ EQUATOR.

magˌnetic ˈfield area round a magnet where a magnetic force is exerted.

magˌnetic ˈmine underwater mine[2](2) that explodes when a large mass of iron, eg a ship, approaches it.

magˌnetic ˈneedle needle that points roughly north and south, used on a compass.

magˌnetic ˈnorth northerly direction indicated by a magnetic needle: *magnetic north pole*, ie close to the geographical North Pole but not identical with it.

magˌnetic ˈtape plastic tape coated with iron oxide, used for recording sound or television pictures.

magneto /mægˈniːtəʊ/ *n* (*pl* ~**s**) electric apparatus that produces the sparks for the ignition of an internal combustion engine.

Magnificat /mægˈnɪfɪkæt/ *n* [sing] **the Magnificat** song of the Virgin Mary praising God, used in Church of England services.

magnificent /mægˈnɪfɪsnt/ *adj* splendid; remarkable; impressive: *a magnificent Renaissance palace* ○ *her magnificent generosity.* ▷ **magnificence** /-sns/ *n* [U]: *the magnificence of the ceremonies.* **magnificently** *adv*.

magnify

magnify /ˈmægnɪfaɪ/ *v (pt, pp* **-fied**) **1** [Tn, Tn·pr] make (sth) appear larger, as a lens or microscope does: *bacteria magnified to 1000 times their actual size.* ⇨ illus. **2** [Tn] *(fml)* exaggerate (sth): *magnify the dangers, risks, uncertainties, etc.* **3** [Tn] *(arch)* give praise to (God): *My soul doth magnify the Lord.*

▷ **magnification** /ˌmægnɪfɪˈkeɪʃn/ *n* **1** [U] (power of) magnifying: *a lens with excellent magnification.* **2** [C] amount of increase in apparent size: *This object has been photographed at a magnification of × 3,* ie three times actual size.

magnifier /-faɪə(r)/ *n* device, etc that magnifies.

□ ˈ**magnifying glass** hand-held lens used for magnifying objects. ⇨ illus.

magniloquent /mægˈnɪləkwənt/ *adj (fml)* **(a)** (of words or speech) pompous-sounding. **(b)** (of a person) using pompous-sounding words. ▷ **magniloquence** /-əns/ *n* [U]. **magniloquently** *adv.*

magnitude /ˈmægnɪtjuːd; *US* -tuːd/ *n* [U] **1** *(fml)* (usu large) size: *The magnitude of the epidemic was frightening.* **2** (degree of) importance: *You don't appreciate the magnitude of her achievement.* ○ *a discovery of the first magnitude,* ie a most important discovery. **3** *(astronomy)* degree of brightness of a star: *a star of the first, second, etc magnitude.*

magnolia /mægˈnəʊlɪə/ *n* tree with large sweet-smelling wax-like flowers, usu white or pink.

magnum /ˈmægnəm/ *n* (bottle containing) 1.5 litres of wine or spirits: *a magnum of champagne.*

magnum opus /ˌmægnəm ˈəʊpəs/ *(Latin)* work of art or literature regarded as its author's greatest.

magpie /ˈmægpaɪ/ *n* **1** noisy black-and-white bird that is attracted by, and often takes away, small bright objects. ⇨ illus at BIRD. ⇨ article at SUPERSTITION. **2** *(fig derog)* **(a)** person who collects or hoards things. **(b)** person who chatters a lot.

Magyar /ˈmægjɑː(r)/ *n, adj* (member or language) of the main ethnic group in Hungary.

maharaja (also **maharajah**) /ˌmɑːhəˈrɑːdʒə/ *n* (title of an) Indian prince.

▷ **maharani** (also **maharanee**) /ˌmɑːhəˈrɑːniː/ *n* wife of a maharaja; queen or princess with a position like that of a maharaja.

maharishi /ˌmɑːhəˈrɪʃiː; *US* məˈhɑːrəʃiː/ *n* Hindu wise man.

mahatma /məˈhɑːtmə, məˈhætmə/ *n* (in India) title given to a person regarded with great reverence because of his wisdom and holiness: *Mahatma Gandhi.*

Mahdi /ˈmɑːdɪ/ *n* (in Islam) title given to a leader sent by God to prepare human society for the end of the world, esp by converting everyone to Islam. It was adopted by Muhammad Ahmad (c1843-85), who led Sudanese resistance to Egyptian rule.

mah-jong (also **mah-jongg**) /ˌmɑːˈʒɒŋ, -ˈdʒɒŋ/ *n* [U] game of Chinese origin which is similar to certain card-games but is played with small pieces called *tiles*. It became popular in the West in the 1920s.

Mahler /ˈmɑːlə(r)/ Gustav (1860-1911), Austrian composer best known for his nine large symphonies written in late-romantic style for a big orchestra and in many cases singers too. His work was neglected after his death, but the 1960s saw a revival of interest, and it is now very popular. Mahler was also a conductor, and Director of the Viennese Opera 1897-1907. ▷ **Mahlerian** /mɑːˈlɪərɪən/ *adj.*

mahlstick = MAULSTICK.

mahogany /məˈhɒgənɪ/ *n* **1** [C, U] (tropical tree with) hard reddish-brown wood used esp for making furniture: *I'm going to use mahogany to make the bookcase.* ○ *This table is mahogany.* ○ [attrib] *a mahogany chair, desk, etc.* **2** [U] reddish-brown colour: *with skin tanned to a deep mahogany.*

▷ **mahogany** *adj* of a reddish-brown colour: *mahogany skin.*

maid /meɪd/ *n* **1** (often in compounds) woman servant: *We have a maid to do the housework.* ○ *a ˈdairy-maid, ˈhousemaid, ˈnursemaid, etc.* **2** *(arch)* young unmarried woman; girl: *love between a man and a maid.*

□ ˌ**maid of ˈhonour (a)** principal bridesmaid. **(b)** unmarried woman attending a queen or princess.

ˈ**maidservant** *n (dated)* maid(1). Cf MANSERVANT (MAN).

maiden /ˈmeɪdn/ *n* **1** *(arch)* girl or unmarried woman. **2** (also ˌ**maiden ˈover**) (in cricket) over[3] in which no runs are scored. **3** horse that has not yet won a race: [attrib] *a maiden chase.*

▷ ˈ**maidenhood** /-hʊd/ *n* [U] *(fml)* **(a)** state of being a maiden; virginity. **(b)** period when one is a maiden.

maidenly *adj (approv)* gentle and modest; of or like a maiden: *her maidenly shyness.*

□ ˌ**maiden ˈaunt** unmarried aunt.

ˈ**maidenhair** *n* [U] type of fern with fine stalks and delicate fronds.

ˈ**maidenhead** /-hed/ *n (arch)* **1** [C] hymen. **2** [U] virginity.

ˈ**maiden name** woman's family name before her marriage.

ˌ**maiden ˈspeech** first speech in Parliament by a Member of Parliament. ⇨ article at PARLIAMENT.

ˌ**maiden ˈvoyage** ship's first voyage.

mail[1] /meɪl/ *n* **1** [U] official system of collecting, transporting and delivering letters and parcels: *send a letter by airmail* ○ *The letter is in the mail.* ○ [attrib] *the mail van, service, train* ○ *the ˈmail-coach,* ie horse-drawn coach formerly used for carrying letters, etc. **2 (a)** [U] letters, parcels, etc sent by post: *Post office workers sort the mail.* ○ *There isn't much mail today.* ○ *The office mail is opened in the morning.* **(b)** [C] letters, parcels, etc delivered or collected at one time: *I want this letter to catch the afternoon mail.* ○ *Is there another mail in the afternoon?* Cf POST[3].

▷ **mail** *v* [Tn, Dn·n, Dn·pr] ~ **sth (to sb)** *(esp US)* send sth (to sb) by post: *Mail me a new form, please.* ○ *I'll mail it to you tomorrow.* Cf POST[4].

mailer *n (US)* (usu small) container or envelope in which sth is sent by post.

mailing *n* = MAILSHOT b: *We do several mailings each year to teachers in the area.* ˈ**mailing list** list of names and addresses of persons to whom advertising material, etc is to be sent regularly: *Please add my name to your mailing list.*

□ ˈ**mail-bag** *n* strong sack in which letters, parcels, etc are carried.

ˈ**mailbox** *n (US)* **1** = LETTER-BOX (LETTER). **2** = POST-BOX (POST[3]).

ˈ**mailman** /-mæn/ *n (pl* **-men** /-mən/) *(US)* = POSTMAN (POST[3]).

ˈ**mail order** system of buying and selling goods by post: *buy sth by mail order* ○ [attrib] *a mail-order business,* ie one dealing in mail-order goods ○ *a mail-order catalogue,* ie one which lists mail-order goods and their prices.

ˈ**mailshot** *n* **(a)** piece of advertising material sent to potential customers by post. **(b)** (also **mailing**) act of sending these.

mail[2] /meɪl/ *n* [U] body armour made of metal rings or plates linked together: *a coat of mail.*

▷ **mailed** *adj* (idm) **the mailed fist** *(dated or rhet)* (threat of) armed force.

Mailer /ˈmeɪlə(r)/ Norman (1923-), American novelist whose best-known work is *The Naked and the Dead*, based on his experiences in the Pacific during the Second World War. His other books include *The American Dream* and *The Armies of the Night.*

maim /meɪm/ *v* [Tn usu passive] wound or injure (sb) so that part of the body cannot be used: *He was maimed in a First World War battle.*

main[1] /meɪn/ *adj* [attrib] (no comparative or superlative forms) **1** most important; chief; principal: *the main thing to remember* ○ *the main street of a town* ○ *Be careful crossing that main road.* ○ *the main meal of the day* ○ *the main course (of a meal)* ○ *My main concern is the welfare of the children.* **2** (idm) **have an eye for/on/to the main chance** ⇨ EYE[1]. **in the ˈmain** for the most part; on the whole: *These businessmen are in the main honest.*

▷ **mainly** *adv* chiefly; primarily: *You are mainly to blame.* ○ *The people in the streets were mainly tourists.*

□ ˌ**main ˈclause** *(grammar)* clause(1) that can stand on its own to make a sentence.

ˈ**main deck** upper deck of a ship.

ˌ**main ˈdrag** *(infml esp US)* main street of a town or city.

ˈ**mainframe** *n* (also ˌ**mainframe comˈputer**) large powerful computer with an extensive memory. Cf MICROCOMPUTER, MINICOMPUTER.

ˈ**mainland** /-lænd/ *n* [sing] large mass of land forming a country, continent, etc without its islands.

ˌ**main ˈline** principal railway line between two places: *the main line from London to Coventry* ○ [attrib] *a ˌmain-line ˈtrain, ˈstation.*

ˈ**mainline** *v* [Ipr, Tn, Tn·pr] ~ **sth (into sth)** *(sl)* inject (a drug) into a large vein for stimulation, often because of addiction: *be mainlining on hard drugs* ○ *She mainlined heroin (into a vein in her arm).*

ˈ**mainmast** *n* principal mast of a sailing-ship.

ˈ**mainsail** /ˈmeɪnsl, ˈmeɪnseɪl/ *n* principal sail on a sailing-ship, usu attached to the mainmast. ⇨ illus at YACHT.

ˈ**mainspring** *n* **1** principal spring of a clock or watch. **2** *(fml fig)* chief motive or reason (for sth): *Her jealousy is the mainspring of the novel's plot.*

ˈ**mainstay** /-steɪ/ *n* **1** rope from the top of the mainmast to the base of the foremast. **2** *(fig)* chief support(er): *He is the mainstay of our theatre group.*

ˈ**mainstream** *n* [sing] **1** dominant trend, tendency, etc: *the mainstream of political thought* ○ [attrib] *mainstream politics.* **2** style of jazz that is neither traditional nor modern: [attrib] *a mainstream band, player.*

ˈ**main street (a)** chief street of a small town, esp in America. **(b)** (usu **Main Street**) *(US)* (place characterized by the) boring money-loving culture of small towns.

main[2] /meɪn/ *n* **1** [C] **(a)** principal pipe bringing water or gas, or principal cable carrying electric current, from the source of supply into a building: *a burst water main* ○ *The gas main exploded and set fire to the house.* **(b)** principal sewer to which pipes from a building are connected. **2** [sing] *(arch or rhet)* open sea: *ships on the main* ○ *the Spanish Main.* **3 the mains** [sing or pl *v*] source of water, gas or electricity supply to a building or area: *My new house is not yet connected to the mains.* ○ *The electricity supply has been cut off/disconnected at the mains.* ○ [attrib] *mains gas/water/electricity,* ie (supplied) from the mains ○ *a mains/battery shaver,* ie one which can be operated either from a mains electricity supply or by batteries.

main[3] /meɪn/ *n* (idm) **with might and main** ⇨ MIGHT[3].

mainbrace /ˈmeɪnbreɪs/ *n* (idm) **splice the main brace** ⇨ SPLICE.

Maine /meɪn/ state in the north-eastern corner of the USA, on the Atlantic coast. It has many hills and forests. Agriculture, fishing and tourism are economically important. ⇨ map at App 1.

maintain /meɪnˈteɪn/ *v* **1** [Tn, Tn·pr] ~ **sth (with sth)** cause sth to continue; keep sth in existence at the same level, standard, etc: *maintain friendly relations, contacts, etc (with sb)* ○ *enough food to maintain one's strength* ○ *maintain law and order* ○ *maintain prices,* ie prevent them falling ○ *maintain one's rights* ○ *Maintain your speed at 60 mph.* ○ *The improvement in his health is being* *maintained.* **2** [Tn] support (sb) financially: *earn enough to maintain a family in comfort* ○ *This school is maintained by a charity.* ○ *She maintains two sons at university.* **3** [Tn] keep (sth) in good condition or working order: *maintain the roads, a house, a car, etc* ○ *Engineers maintain the turbines.* ○ *a well-maintained house.* **4** [Tn, Tf] assert (sth) as true: *maintain one's innocence* ○ *maintain that one is innocent of a charge.*

maintenance /ˈmeɪntənəns/ *n* [U] **1** maintaining or being maintained: *the maintenance of good relations between countries* ○ *price maintenance* ○ *money for the maintenance of one's family* ○ *He's taking classes in car maintenance.* ○ [attrib] *a maintenance man, gang, van.* **2** (*law*) money that one is legally ordered to pay or pays voluntarily to support sb: *He has to pay maintenance to his ex-wife.* Cf ALIMONY.

□ ˈ**maintenance order** (*law*) order to pay maintenance(2).

maisonette (also **maisonnette**) /ˌmeɪzəˈnet/ *n* **1** self-contained dwelling on two floors, part of a larger building or block. **2** (*dated*) small house.

maître d' /ˌmeɪtrə ˈdiː/ *n* (*pl* **maître d's**) (*US*) = MAÎTRE D'HÔTEL 1.

maître d'hôtel /ˌmeɪtrə dəʊˈtel/ *n* (*pl* **maîtres d'hôtel** /ˌmeɪtrə dəʊˈtel/) (*French*) **1** head waiter. **2** manager of a hotel.

maize /meɪz/ *n* [U] tall cereal plant bearing yellow grain on large ears (EAR[2]). Cf CORN ON THE COB (CORN[1]), SWEET CORN (SWEET[1]).

Maj *abbr* Major: *Maj (James) Williams* ○ *Maj-Gen* (ie Major-General) *(Tom) Phillips.*

majestic /məˈdʒestɪk/ *adj* having or showing majesty; stately; grand: *majestic views, scenery, etc* ○ *The great ship looked majestic in her new colours.*

▷ **majestically** /-klɪ/ *adv*: *She strode majestically through the palace.*

majesty /ˈmædʒəstɪ/ *n* **1** [U] (**a**) impressive dignity and stateliness; grandeur, as of a king or queen: *all the majesty of royal ceremonies* ○ (*fig*) *the majesty of the mountain scenery.* (**b**) royal power. **2 Majesty** [C] (used with a preceding *possess det* to address or speak of a royal person or royal people): *Thank you, Your Majesty.* ○ *at His/Her Majesty's command* ○ *Their Majesties have arrived.*

majolica /məˈdʒɒlɪkə, -ˈjɒl-/ *n* [U] brightly coloured Italian pottery, esp as made in Renaissance times.

major[1] /ˈmeɪdʒə(r)/ *adj* **1** [usu attrib] (more) important; great(er): *a major road* ○ *the major portion* ○ *a major operation*, ie a surgical operation that could be dangerous to a person's life ○ *a major suit*, ie (in cards, esp bridge) either spades or hearts ○ *We have encountered major problems.* ○ *She has written a major novel*, ie one of high quality and great importance. Cf MINOR. **2** (*Brit dated or joc*) (in private schools) first or older of two brothers or boys with the same surname (esp in the same school): *Smith major.* Cf MINOR, SENIOR. **3** (*music*) (of a key or scale) having two full tones between the first and third notes: *the major key* ○ *a major scale* ○ *the key of C major, E flat major, etc.* Cf MINOR.

▷ **major** *v* [Ipr] ~ **in sth** (*US*) specialize in a certain subject (at college or university): *She majored in math and physics (at university).*

major *n* **1** [sing] (*music*) major key: *shift from major to minor.* **2** [C] (*US*) (**a**) principal subject or course of a student at college or university: *Her major is French.* (**b**) student studying such a subject: *She's a French major.* **3 majors** [pl] (also **major ˈleagues**) (*US sport*) senior and most important leagues, esp in baseball and ice hockey: [attrib] *major league baseball.*

□ ˌ**major ˈpremise** the first, more general statement of a syllogism.

major[2] /ˈmeɪdʒə(r)/ *n* army officer ranking between a captain and a lieutenant-colonel. ⇨ App 4.

□ ˌ**major-ˈgeneral** *n* army officer ranking between a brigadier and a lieutenant-general. ⇨ App 4.

Majorca /məˈjɔːkə/ largest of the *Balearic Islands. The capital is Palma. ▷ **Majorcan** *n, adj.* ⇨ map at SPAIN.

major-domo /ˌmeɪdʒə ˈdəʊməʊ/ *n* (*pl* ~**s**) chief male servant in a large house.

majority /məˈdʒɒrətɪ; *US* -ˈdʒɔːr-/ *n* **1** [Gp] the greater number or part; most: *A/The majority of people seem to prefer TV to radio.* ○ *The majority was/were in favour of the proposal.* ○ [attrib] *majority opinion.* Cf MINORITY. **2** [C] ~ (**over sb**) (**a**) number by which votes for one side exceed those for the other side: *She was elected by a majority of 3749.* ○ *They had a large majority over the other party at the last election.* ○ *The government does not have an overall majority*, ie a majority over all other parties together. (**b**) (*US*) number by which votes for one candidate exceed those for all other candidates together. Cf PLURALITY 3. **3** [sing] legal age of full adulthood: *The age of majority is eighteen.* ○ *She reaches her majority next month.* **4** (idm) **be in the/a majority** form the greater part/the larger number: *Among the members of the committee those who favour the proposed changes are in the majority.* **the silent majority** ⇨ SILENT.

□ **maˌjority ˈrule** political principle that the greater number voting in a certain way should thereby acquire the right to impose their will on all.

maˌjority ˈverdict (*law*) verdict of the majority of a jury.

make[1] /meɪk/ *v* (*pt, pp* **made** /meɪd/)

►CONSTRUCTING OR CREATING **1** (**a**) [Tn, Tn·pr, Dn·n, Dn·pr] ~ **sth (from/(out) of sth)**; ~ **sth (for sb)** construct, create or prepare sth by combining materials or putting parts together: *make a car, a dress, a cake* ○ *make bread, cement, wine* ○ *make* (ie manufacture) *paper* ○ *God made man.* ○ *She makes her own clothes.* ○ *Wine is made from grapes.* ○ *'What is your bracelet made of?' 'It's made of gold.'* ○ *I made myself a cup of tea.* ○ *She made coffee for all of us.* ○ *This car wasn't made* (ie is not big enough) *to carry eight people.* (**b**) [Tn·pr esp passive] ~ **sth into sth** put (materials or parts) together to produce sth: *Glass is made into bottles.* (**c**) [Tn] arrange (a bed) so that it is ready for use: *Please make your beds before breakfast.* **2** [Tn, Tn·pr] cause (sth) to appear by breaking, tearing, removing material or striking: *The stone made a dent in the roof of my car.* ○ *The holes in the cloth were made by moths.* **3** [Tn] create (sth); establish: *These regulations were made to protect children.* ○ *Who made this ridiculous rule?* **4** [Tn] write, compose or prepare (sth): *make one's will* ○ *make a treaty with sb* ○ *She has made* (ie directed) *several films.* ○ *I'll ask my solicitor to make a deed of transfer.*

►CAUSING TO BECOME, DO OR APPEAR **5** [Tn] cause (sth): *make a noise, disturbance, mess* ○ *She's always making trouble (for her friends).* **6** [Cn·a] cause (sb/sth) to be or become: *The news made her happy.* ○ *She made clear her objections/made it clear that she objected to the proposal.* ○ *His actions made him universally respected.* ○ *Can you make yourself understood in English?* ○ *The full story was never made public.* ○ *She couldn't make herself/her voice heard above the noise of the traffic.* **7** [Cn·i] (**a**) force or compel (sb) to do sth: *They made me repeat/I was made to repeat the story.* ○ *She must be made to comply with the rules.* ○ *He never tidies his room and his mother never tries to make him (do it).* ⇨ Usage at CAUSE. (**b**) cause (sb/sth) to do sth: *Onions make your eyes water.* ○ *Her jokes made us all laugh.* ○ *I couldn't make my car start this morning.* ○ *What makes you say that?* ○ *I rang the doorbell several times but couldn't make anyone hear.* ○ *Nothing will make me change my mind.* **8** [Cn·a, Cn·n, Cn·i] represent (sb/sth) as being or doing sth: *You've made my nose too big*, eg in a drawing or painting. ○ *The novelist makes his heroine commit suicide at the end of the book.* **9** [Cn·n] elect (sb); appoint: *make sb king, an earl, a peer, etc* ○ *He was made spokesman by the committee.* ○ *She made him her assistant.* **10** [Tn·pr, Cn·n] ~ **sth of sb/sth** cause sb/sth to be or become sth: *We'll make a footballer of him yet*, ie turn him into a good footballer despite the fact that he is not a good one now. ○ *This isn't very important — I don't want to make an issue of it.* ○ *Don't make a habit of it/Don't make it a habit.* ○ *She made it her business* (ie special task) *to find out who was responsible.*

►BEING OR BECOMING SOMETHING **11** [Ln] be or become (sth) through development; turn out to be: *If you train hard, you'll make a good footballer.* ○ *He'll never make an actor.* ○ *She would have made an excellent teacher.* **12** [Ln] serve or function as (sth); constitute: *That will make a good ending to the book.* ○ *This hall would make an excellent theatre.* **13** [Ln] add up to (sth); equal; amount to; constitute: *5 and 7 make 12.* ○ *A hundred pence make one pound.* ○ *How many members make a quorum?* ○ *His thrillers make enthralling reading.* ○ *The play makes a splendid evening's entertainment.* **14** [Ln] count as (sth): *That makes the tenth time he's failed his driving test!*

►GAINING OR WINNING **15** [Tn] earn (sth); gain; acquire: *She makes £15 000 a year.* ○ *make a profit/loss* ○ *He made a fortune on the stock market.* ○ *How much do you stand to make?* **16** [Tn] (in cricket) score (sth): *England made 235 for 5.* ○ *Botham made a century.* **17** (in card-games, esp bridge) (**a**) [Tn] win a trick with (a particular card): *She made her ten of hearts.* (**b**) [Tn] win (a trick) or fulfil (a contract). (**c**) [I, Tn] shuffle (the cards): *It's my turn to make.* **18** [Tn] (*sl sexist*) succeed in having sex with (a woman): *The guy doesn't make the girl until the last chapter.*

►OTHER MEANINGS **19** [no passive: Cn·a, Cn·n, Cn·t] calculate or estimate (sth) to be (sth): *What time do you make it?/What do you make the time?* ○ *How large do you make the audience?* ○ *I make the total (to be) about £50.* ○ *I make the distance about 70 miles.* **20** [Tn no passive] (**a**) travel over (a distance): *We've made 100 miles today.* (**b**) reach or maintain (a speed): *Can your car make a hundred miles per hour?* (**c**) manage to reach (a place): *Do you think we'll make Oxford by noon?* ○ *The train leaves in five minutes — we'll never make it*, ie reach the station in time to catch it. ○ *I'm sorry I couldn't make your party last night.* ○ *Her new novel has made* (ie sold enough copies to be in) *the best-seller lists.* ○ *She'll never make* (ie win a place in) *the team.* ○ *He made* (ie reached the rank of) *sergeant in six months.* ○ *The story made* (ie appeared on) *the front page of the national newspapers.* **21** [Tn, Dn·n] put (sth) forward; propose; offer: *Has she made you an offer* (ie said how much money she would pay you) *for your car?* ○ *make a proposal* ○ *The employers made a new offer* (ie of a rise in wages) *to the work-force.* ○ *I made him a bid for the antique table.* **22** [Tn] cause or ensure the success of (sth): *A good wine can make a meal.* ○ *It was the beautiful weather that really made the holiday.* **23** [It] behave as if one is about to do sth: *He made as if to strike her.* ○ *She made to go but he told her to stay.* **24** eat or have (a meal): *We make a good breakfast before leaving.* ○ *She made a hasty lunch.* **25** (Often used in a pattern with a *n*, in which *make* and the *n* have the same meaning as a *v* similar in spelling to the *n*, eg *make a decision*, ie decide; *make a guess (at sth)*, ie guess (at sth); for other expressions of this kind, see entries for *ns*.) **26** (idm) **make do with sth**; **make (sth) ˈdo** manage with sth that is not really adequate or satisfactory: *We were in a hurry so we had to make do with a quick snack.* ○ *There isn't much of it but you'll have to make (it) do.* **make ˈgood** become rich and successful: *a local boy made good*, eg as a businessman. **make sth good** (**a**) pay for, replace or repair sth that has been lost or damaged: *She promised to make good the loss.* ○ *make good the damage* ○ *The plaster will have to be made good before you paint it.* (**b**) carry sth out; fulfil sth: *make good a promise, threat, etc.* ˈ**make it** (*infml*) be successful in one's career: *He's never really made it as an actor.* **make the most of sth/sb/oneself**

sb/oneself profit as much as one can from sth/sb/oneself: *make the most of one's chances, opportunities, talents, etc* ○ *It's my first holiday for two years so I'm going to make the most of it.* ○ *She really tries to make the most of herself,* eg by dressing well. **make much of sth/sb** (**a**) (in negative sentences and questions) understand sth: *I couldn't make much of his speech — it was all in Russian.* (**b**) treat sth/sb as very important; stress or emphasize sth: *He always makes much of his humble origins.* ○ *She was always made much of by her adoring friends.* **make nothing of sth** easily achieve sth that appears to be difficult; treat sth as trifling. **make or break sb/sth** be crucial in making sb/sth either a success or a failure: *The council's decision will make or break the local theatre.* ○ [attrib] *It's make-or-break time for the local theatre.* (For other idioms containing **make**, see entries for *ns, adjs*, etc, eg **make love** ⇨ LOVE[1]; **make merry** ⇨ MERRY.)

27 (phr v) **make after sb/sth** chase or pursue sb/sth: *The policeman made after the burglar.*

make at sb move towards sb (as if) to attack him: *His attacker made at him with a knife.*

make a'way with oneself commit suicide. **make away with sth** = MAKE OFF WITH STH.

make for sb/sth move in the direction of sb/sth; head for sb/sth: *The ship made for the open sea.* ○ *It's getting late; we'd better turn and make for home.* ○ *When the interval came everyone made for the bar.* ○ *I turned and ran when I saw the bull making for* (ie charging towards) *me.* **make for sth** help to make sth possible; contribute to sth: *The large print makes for easier reading.* ○ *Constant arguing doesn't make for a happy marriage.* **be 'made for sb/each other** be well suited to sb/each other: *Ann and Robert seem (to be) made for each other.*

make sb/sth into sb/sth change or convert sb/sth into sb/sth: *We're making our attic into an extra bedroom.* ○ *The local cinema has been made into a bingo hall.*

make sth of sb/sth understand the meaning or nature of sb/sth to be sth: *What do you make of it all?* ○ *What are we to make of her behaviour?* ○ *What do you make of* (ie think of) *the new manager?* ○ *I can make nothing of this scribble.*

make 'off (*infml*) hurry or rush away, esp in order to escape: *The thieves made off in a stolen car.* **make off with sth** (*infml*) steal sth and hurry away with it: *Two boys made off with our cases while we weren't looking.*

make 'out (*infml*) (usu in questions after *how*) manage; survive; fare: *How did he make out while his wife was away?* ○ *How are you making out with Mary?* ie How is your relationship with her developing? **make sb 'out** understand (sb's character): *What a strange person she is! I can't make her out at all.* **make sb/sth out** manage to see sb/sth or read sth: *I could just make out a figure in the darkness.* ○ *The dim outline of a house could be made out.* ○ *Can you make out what that sign says?* **make sth out** write out sth; complete sth: *make out a cheque for £10* ○ *Applications must be made out in triplicate.* ○ *The doctor made me out a prescription.* **make sth out; make out if/whether...** understand sth: *I can't make out what she wants.* ○ *How do you make that out?* ie How did you reach that conclusion? ○ *I can't make out if she enjoys her job or not.* **make out that...; make oneself/sb/sth out to be...** claim; assert; maintain: *He made out that he had been robbed.* ○ *She's not as rich as people make out/as people make her out to be.* ○ *He makes himself out to be cleverer than he really is.*

make sb/sth over (into sth) change or convert sb/sth: *The basement has been made over into a workshop.* **make sth over (to sb/sth)** transfer the ownership of sth: *The estate was made over to the eldest son.* ○ *He has made over the whole property to the National Trust.*

make 'up; make oneself/sb up put powder, lipstick, greasepaint, etc on the face, etc to make it more attractive or to prepare it for an appearance in the theatre, on television, etc: *She spent an hour making (herself) up before the party.* ○ *She's always very heavily made up,* ie She puts a lot of make-up on her face. **make sth up** (**a**) form, compose or constitute sth: *Animal bodies are made up of cells.* ○ *What are the qualities that make up her character?* ○ *These arguments make up the case for the defence.* ○ *Society is made up of people of widely differing abilities.* (**b**) put sth together from several different things: *make up a bundle of old clothes for a jumble sale* ○ *She made up a basket of food for the picnic.* (**c**) prepare (a medicine) by mixing different ingredients together: *The pharmacist made up the prescription.* (**d**) fashion (material) into a garment: *Can you make up this dress length for me?* (**e**) prepare (a bed) for use; set up (a temporary bed): *We made up the bed in the spare room for our guest.* ○ *They made up a bed for me on the sofa.* (**f**) add fuel to (a fire): *The fire needs making up,* ie needs to have more coal put on it. (**g**) (esp passive) put a hard surface on (a road) to make it suitable for motor vehicles. (**h**) arrange (type, illustrations, etc) in columns or pages for printing. (**i**) invent sth, esp in order to deceive sb: *make up an excuse* ○ *I couldn't remember a story to tell the children, so I made one up as I went along.* ○ *Stop making things up!* (**j**) complete sth: *We still need £100 to make up the sum required.* ○ *We have ten players, so we need one more to make up a team.* (**k**) replace sth: *Our losses will have to be made up with more loans.* ○ *You must make up the time you wasted this afternoon by working late tonight.* **make up for sth** compensate for sth: *Hard work can make up for a lack of intelligence.* ○ *Nothing can make up for the loss* (ie death) *of a child.* ○ *The beautiful autumn made up for the wet summer.* **make up (to sb) for sth** compensate sb for the trouble or suffering one has caused him: *How can I make up for the way I've treated you?* **make up to sb** (*infml*) be pleasant to sb in order to win favours: *He's always making up to the boss.* **make it up to sb** (*infml*) compensate sb for sth he has missed or suffered or for money he has spent: *Thanks for buying my ticket — I'll make it up to you later.* **make (it) 'up (with sb)** end a quarrel or dispute with sb: *Why don't you two kiss and make up?* ○ *Has he made it up with her yet/Have they made it up yet?* **make with sth** (*US sl*) (esp imperative) produce or supply sth quickly: *Make with the beers, buster!* **make it with sb** (*sl*) succeed in having sex with sb: *Terry made it with Sharon on the back seat of his car.*

□ **'make-believe** *n* [U] (**a**) pretending or imagining things; fantasizing: *indulge in make-believe.* (**b**) things thus imagined: *live in a world of make-believe* ○ [attrib] *a make-believe world.*

'make-up *n* **1** [U] cosmetics such as powder, lipstick, etc used by a woman to make herself more attractive, or by an actor: *She never wears make-up.* ○ *Her make-up is smudged.* **2** [sing] (**a**) combination of qualities that form a person's character or temperament: *Jealousy is not part of his make-up.* (**b**) combination of things, people, etc that form sth; composition of sth: *There are plans to change the make-up of the committee,* ie to replace some of the people who work on it. **3** [C usu *sing*] arrangement of type, illustrations, etc on a printed page.

make[2] /meɪk/ *n* ~ (**of sth**) **1** [U] way a thing is made: *a coat of excellent make.* **2** [C] origin of manufacture; brand: *cars of all makes* ○ *What make of radio is it?* **3** (idm) **on the 'make** (*infml derog*) (**a**) trying to gain an advantage or profit for oneself. (**b**) trying to win favour with sb for sexual pleasure.

maker /ˈmeɪkə(r)/ *n* **1 the/our Maker** [sing] the Creator; God. **2** [C] (esp in compounds) person who makes sth: *a 'dressmaker* ○ *a 'cabinet-maker.* **3** (idm) **meet one's Maker** ⇨ MEET[1].

makeshift /ˈmeɪkʃɪft/ *n, adj* (thing that is) used temporarily until sth better is available: *use an empty crate as a makeshift (table).*

makeweight /ˈmeɪkweɪt/ *n* **1** small quantity added to get the weight required. **2** (*fig*) thing or person, usu of little value, that supplies a deficiency, fills a gap, etc.

making /ˈmeɪkɪŋ/ *n* (idm) **be the making of sb** make sb succeed or develop well: *These two years of hard work will be the making of him.* **have the makings of sth** have the qualities needed to become sth: *She has the makings of a good lawyer.* **in the 'making** in the course of being made, formed or developed: *This first novel is the work of a writer in the making,* ie not yet an expert writer. ○ *This model was two years in the making,* ie took two years to make.

mal- *comb form* bad(ly); not; incorrect(ly): *maladjusted* ○ *maladministration* ○ *malfunction.*

Malacca cane /məˌlækə ˈkeɪn/ (walking-stick made from a) cane from the stem of an Asian palm-tree.

Malachi /ˈmæləkaɪ/ last book of the Old Testament. ⇨ App 5.

malachite /ˈmæləkaɪt/ *n* [U] green mineral that can be polished and used for ornaments, decoration, etc.

maladjusted /ˌmæləˈdʒʌstɪd/ *adj* (of a person) unable for psychological reasons to behave acceptably or deal satisfactorily with other people: *a school for maladjusted children.*

▷ **maladjustment** /ˌmæləˈdʒʌstmənt/ *n* [U] state of being maladjusted.

maladministration /ˌmælədˌmɪnɪˈstreɪʃn/ *n* [U] (*fml*) poor or dishonest management (of public affairs, business dealings, etc).

maladroit /ˌmæləˈdrɔɪt/ *adj* [usu pred] (*fml*) not clever or skilful; clumsy; bungling: *His handling of the negotiations was maladroit.* Cf ADROIT. ▷ **maladroitly** *adv.* **maladroitness** *n* [U].

malady /ˈmælədɪ/ *n* (*fml usu fig*) disease; illness: *Violent crime is only one of the maladies afflicting modern society.*

Malagasy /ˌmæləˈgæsɪ/ *adj* of *Madagascar.

▷ **Malagasy** *n* [C] native or inhabitant of Madagascar. **2** [U] language of Madagascar, which is related to Malay.

malaise /mæˈleɪz/ *n* [U, sing] (*fml*) (**a**) general feeling of illness, without clear signs of a particular disease. (**b**) feeling of uneasiness whose exact cause cannot be explained: *You can see signs of (a creeping) malaise in our office.* ○ *a deeply-felt malaise among the working classes.*

malapropism /ˈmæləprɒpɪzəm/ *n* comical confusion of a word with another, similar-sounding, word which has a quite different meaning, eg *'an ingenuous* (for *ingenious*) *machine for peeling potatoes'.*

malaria /məˈleərɪə/ *n* [U] fever produced when germs are introduced into the blood by a bite from certain mosquitoes: *a bad attack of malaria* ○ [attrib] *a malaria sufferer.*

▷ **malarial** /-ɪəl/ *adj* (**a**) of malaria: *malarial symptoms.* (**b**) having malaria: *a malarial patient.*

malarkey (also **malarky**) /məˈlɑːkɪ/ *n* [U] (*infml*) foolish or slightly dishonest talk: *He said he'd lost all his money gambling or some such malarkey.*

Malawi /məˈlɑːwɪ/ country in southern central Africa, between Tanzania, Zambia and Mozambique; pop approx 7 755 000; official language English; capital Lilongwe; unit of currency kwacha (= 100 tambala). Formerly a British colony, called Nyasaland, it became independent in 1964. Its main exports are tea and tobacco. ⇨ map at NAMIBIA. ▷ **Malawian** *adj, n.*

Malay /məˈleɪ/ *adj* of a people who form most of the population of Malaysia and Indonesia: *the Malay Peninsula.*

▷ **Malay** *n* **1** [C] Malay person. **2** [U] language of the Malays, spoken mainly in Malaysia. It is almost the same as Indonesian.

□ **the Maˌlay Archiˈpelago** very large group of islands between SE Asia and Australia, including Sumatra, Java, Borneo, the Philippines and New Guinea.

Malaya /məˈleɪə/ former name for the southern part of a long peninsula in SE Asia, formerly consisting of several independent states which were united under British rule, and now forming part of Malaysia. ▷ **Malayan** *adj, n.*

Malaysia /məˈleɪzɪə; *US* məˈleɪʒə/ country in SE Asia consisting of the southern part of the Malay

Malaysia and its neighbours

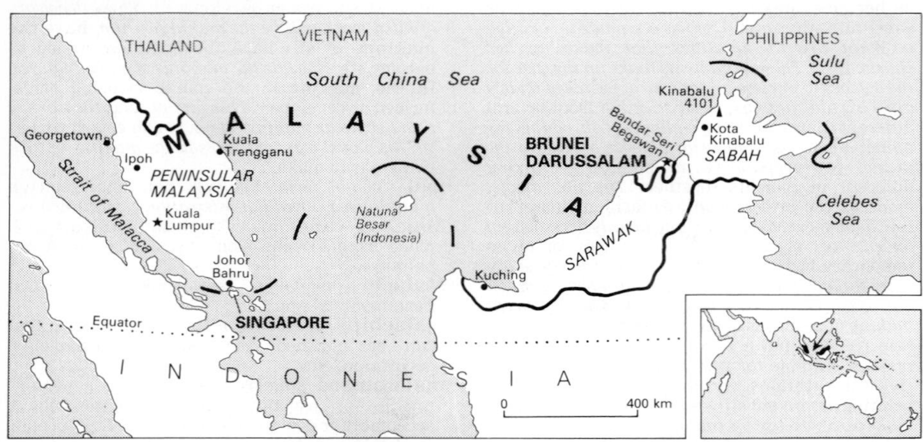

peninsula, to the south of Thailand, and the northern part of Borneo; pop approx 16 921 000; official language Malay; capital Kuala Lumpur; unit of currency dollar (ringgit) (= 100 cents). It was formed in 1963 from former British colonies in the area. It is the world's leading producer of rubber and leading exporter of tin; oil is also an important export. ⇨ map. ▷ **Malaysian** *adj, n.*

malcontent /ˈmælkəntent/ *n, adj* (person who is) discontented and rebellious: *All the trouble is being caused by a handful of malcontents.*

Maldives /ˈmɔːldɪvz/ **the Maldives** country in the Indian Ocean, to the south-west of India, consisting of about 2 000 coral islands; pop approx 202 000; official language Divehi, related to Sinhalese; capital Malé; unit of currency rufiyaa (= 100 laari). Formerly a British protectorate, it became independent in 1965. ⇨ map at INDIA.

the male reproductive system

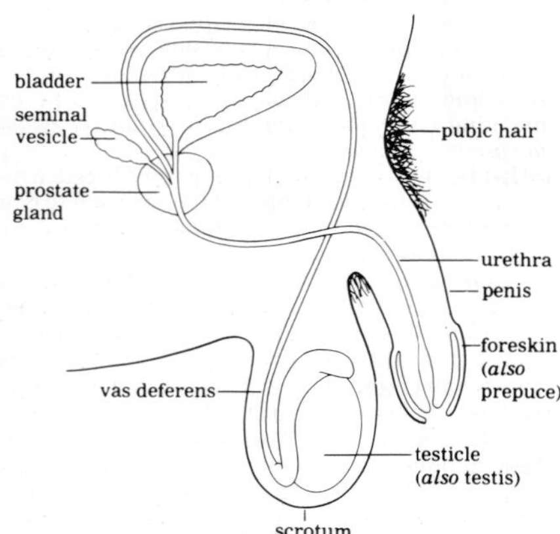

male /meɪl/ *adj* **1** of the sex that does not give birth to offspring: *a male horse, human, bird.* **2** (of a plant) having flowers that contain pollen-bearing organs and not seeds. **3** (of electrical plugs, parts of tools, etc) having a projecting part which is inserted into a socket, hole, etc.
▷ **male** *n* male person, animal, plant, etc. ⇨ Usage at FEMALE.
□ ˌ**male** ˈ**alto** = COUNTER-TENOR.
ˌ**male** ˈ**chauvinism** *(derog)* prejudiced attitude of certain men who believe that they are superior to women. ˌ**male** ˈ**chauvinist**: *She was so angry at his sexist remarks that she called him a male chauvinist pig.*
ˌ**male voice** ˈ**choir** choir of men who sing tenor, baritone or bass.

malediction /ˌmælɪˈdɪkʃn/ *n (fml)* prayer that sb or sth may be destroyed, hurt, etc; curse.

malefactor /ˈmælɪfæktə(r)/ *n (fml)* wrongdoer; criminal: *Malefactors will be pursued and punished.*

maleficent /məˈlefɪsnt/ *adj (fml)* causing or doing evil. ▷ **maleficence** /-sns/ *n* [U].

malevolent /məˈlevələnt/ *adj* ~ **(to/towards sb)** [usu attrib] wishing to do evil or cause harm to others; spiteful: *a malevolent person, look, smile.*
▷ **malevolence** /-əns/ *n* [U] desire to do evil or cause harm to others; ill-will.
malevolently *adv.*

malformation /ˌmælfɔːˈmeɪʃn/ *n* **1** [U] state of being badly formed or shaped: *This treatment could result in malformation of the arms.* **2** [C] badly formed part, esp of the body; deformity: *a malformation of the spine.*
▷ **malformed** /ˌmælˈfɔːmd/ *adj* badly formed or shaped.

malfunction /ˌmælˈfʌŋkʃn/ *v* [I] *(fml)* (of a machine) fail to work normally or properly: *The computer malfunctioned and printed out the wrong data.*
▷ **malfunction** *n* [C, U] *(fml)* failure of this kind: *a major malfunction* ○ *several instances of malfunction.*

Mali /ˈmɑːlɪ/ inland country in W Africa, to the south of Algeria; pop approx 8 918 000; official language French; capital Bamako; unit of currency franc. Formerly a French colony, it became independent in 1960. The northern part is desert. Most of the population are semi-nomadic herders of livestock. ⇨ map at NIGERIA. ▷ **Malian** *adj, n.*

malice /ˈmælɪs/ *n* **1** [U] ~ **(towards sb)** desire to harm others: *She certainly bears you no malice.* ○ *harbour no malice towards sb* ○ *a look of pure malice* ○ *She did it out of malice.* **2** (idm) **with** ˌ**malice a**ˈ**forethought** *(law)* with the conscious intention to commit a crime.
▷ **malicious** /məˈlɪʃəs/ *adj* intended to harm others: *(a) malicious gossip* ○ *a malicious act, comment.* **maliciously** *adv.* **maliciousness** *n* [U] malicious nature (of sth): *the sheer maliciousness of the gossip.*

malign /məˈlaɪn/ *v* [Tn] say unpleasant or untrue things about (sb): *malign an innocent person.*
▷ **malign** *adj (fml)* harmful: *a malign influence, intention, effect.* Cf BENIGN.
malignity /məˈlɪgnətɪ/ *n* [U].

malignant /məˈlɪgnənt/ *adj* **1** (of people or their actions) feeling or showing great desire to harm others; malevolent: *a malignant slander, attack, thrust.* **2** (a) (of a tumour) growing uncontrollably, and likely to prove fatal: *The growth is not malignant.* (b) (of diseases) harmful to life.
▷ **malignancy** /-nənsɪ/ *n* **1** [U] state of being malignant. **2** [C] malignant tumour.
malignantly *adv.*

malinger /məˈlɪŋgə(r)/ *v* [I] *(derog)* (usu in the continuous tenses) pretend to be ill in order to avoid work or duty.
▷ **malingerer** *n (derog)* person who malingers.

mall /mæl, mɔːl/ *n (esp US)* street or covered area with rows of shops, closed to traffic: *a shopping mall.* ⇨ article at SHOP.

mallard /ˈmælɑːd; *US* ˈmælərd/ *n (pl* unchanged) type of common wild duck.

malleable /ˈmælɪəbl/ *adj* **1** (of metals) that can be beaten or pressed into different shapes easily. **2** *(fig)* (of a person, his ideas, etc) easily influenced or changed: *The young are more malleable than the old.* ▷ **malleability** /ˌmælɪəˈbɪlətɪ/ *n* [U].

mallet /ˈmælɪt/ *n* **1** hammer with a wooden head, eg for striking the handle of a chisel. ⇨ illus at CHISEL. **2** long-handled hammer with a wooden head, used for striking the ball in croquet or polo.

mallow /ˈmæləʊ/ *n* plant with hairy stems and leaves and pink, purple or white flowers.

malmsey /ˈmɑːmzɪ/ *n* [U] strong sweet wine from Greece, Spain, Madeira, etc.

malnourished /ˌmælˈnʌrɪʃt; *US* -ˈnɜː-/ *adj* suffering from malnutrition. Cf UNDERNOURISHED.

malnutrition /ˌmælnjuːˈtrɪʃn; *US* -nuː-/ *n* [U] condition resulting from a lack of (the right type of) food: *children suffering from severe malnutrition.*

malodorous /ˌmælˈəʊdərəs/ *adj (fml)* smelling unpleasant: *malodorous drains, ditches, bogs, etc.*

Malory /ˈmælərɪ/ Sir Thomas (died 1471), English author who, while in prison, wrote *Le Morte D'Arthur*, a collection of stories about King *Arthur and the knights of the Round Table. It was one of the first books to be printed by *Caxton.

Malpighi /mælˈpiːgɪ/ Marcello (c1628-94), Italian biologist who pioneered the use of the microscope in the fields of comparative anatomy and plant anatomy.
□ **the Malpighian layer** /mælˌpiːgɪən ˈleɪə(r)/ deepest layer of the epidermis of the skin, from which the upper layers develop.

malpractice /ˌmælˈpræktɪs/ *n (law)* **(a)** [U] careless, illegal or unethical behaviour by sb in a professional or official position: *lawyers, doctors, etc sued for malpractice.* **(b)** [C] instance of this: *Various malpractices by police officers were brought to light by the enquiry.*

malt /mɔːlt/ *n* **1** [U] grain (usu barley) that has been soaked in water and allowed to germinate and then dried, used for making beer, whisky, etc: [attrib] *malt liquors* ○ *malt whisky.* **2** [C] variety of malt whisky: *an excellent 12-year-old malt.*
▷ **malt** *v* **(a)** [Tn] make (grain) into malt. **(b)** [I] (of grain) become malt.
□ ˌ**malted** ˈ**milk** drink made from malt and dried milk.

Malta /ˈmɔːltə/ island and country in the Mediterranean Sea, to the south of Sicily; pop approx 348 000; official languages Maltese and English; capital Valletta; unit of currency lira (= 100 cents). In the 16th, 17th and 18th centuries it was the headquarters of the Knights of St John, an order of religious knights. In 1814 it was taken over by Britain, and became an important naval base. In the Second World War it was awarded the George Cross for its resistance to heavy German air attacks. It became independent in 1964 and is a member of the Commonwealth ⇨ map at ITALY.
▷ **Maltese** /mɔːlˈtiːz/ *adj* of Malta. — *n (pl* unchanged) **1** [C] native or inhabitant of Malta. **2** [U] language of Malta, an Arab dialect much influenced by Italian. ˌ**Maltese** ˈ**cross** cross with the arms of equal length, each of which tapers towards the centre. ⇨ illus at CROSS.

Malthus /ˈmælθəs/ Thomas Robert (1766-1834), English clergyman and economist who in his *Essay on the Principle of Population* proposed the idea that human populations grow faster than the supply of food, and that unless population growth was artificially controlled, it would eventually be checked by an increased death rate so that, in the long term, wages would settle at a level sufficient for subsistence. ▷ **Malthusian** /mælˈθjuːzɪən; *US* mɔːˈθuːʒn/ *adj.*

maltreat /ˌmælˈtriːt/ *v* [Tn] *(fml)* treat (a person or an animal) with violence or cruelty; mistreat.
▷ **maltreatment** *n* [U] maltreating or being maltreated: *the man's maltreatment of his dog* ○ *the*

dog's maltreatment by his owner.

mama /məˈmɑː/ *n* (*dated Brit infml*) mother.

mamba /ˈmæmbə/ *n* black or green poisonous African snake.

mamma /ˈmɑːmə/ *n* (*US infml*) mother.

mammal /ˈmæml/ *n* any of the class of animals that give birth to live offspring and feed their young on milk from the breast. ▷ **mammalian** /mæˈmeɪlɪən/ *adj.*

mammary /ˈmæmərɪ/ *adj* [attrib] (*biology*) of the breasts: *the mammary gland,* ie the one which produces milk.

mammon (also **Mammon**) /ˈmæmən/ *n* [sing] (*usu derog*) god of wealth, regarded as evil or immoral: *those who worship mammon,* ie greedy people who value money (too) highly.

mammoth /ˈmæməθ/ *n* large hairy type of elephant, now extinct.

▷ **mammoth** *adj* [attrib] immense; huge: *a mammoth project, corporation, undertaking.*

mammy /ˈmæmɪ/ *n* (*US*) **1** (word for *mother* used by or to children) **2** (*dated now offensive*) black nursemaid for white children.

man[1] /mæn/ *n* (*pl* **men** /men/) **1** [C] adult male human being: *clothes for men.* **2** [C] human being of either sex; person: *All men must die.* ○ *Growing old is something a man has to accept.* **3** [sing] (without *the* or *a*) the human race; mankind: *Man is mortal.* ○ *the origin of man* ○ *medieval man,* ie all people in the Middle Ages. ⇨ Usage. **4** [C] husband, male lover, boy-friend, etc: *Her man's been sent overseas by his employers.* ○ *be made man and wife,* ie be married. **5** [C usu *pl*] male person under the authority of sb else: *officers and men in the army, navy, etc* ○ *The manager gave the men* (ie the workers) *their instructions.* **6** [sing] (*fml*) manservant; valet: *My man will drive you home.* **7** [C] (*fml*) present or former member of a named university: *a Cambridge man* ○ *a Yale man.* **8** [sing] (*infml*) (used as a form of address, usu in a lively or an impatient way): *Hey, man, are you coming?* ○ *Be quiet, man!* **9** [C] male person with the qualities of courage, toughness, etc often associated with men: *Be a man!* ie Be brave. ○ *They acquitted themselves like men.* **10** [C] piece used in games such as chess, draughts, etc: *capture all sb's men.* **11 the Man** [sing] (*US sl*) (**a**) the police. (**b**) (*derog*) (used by Blacks) white-skinned people. **12** (idm) **as good, etc as the next man** ⇨ NEXT[1]. **as one man** acting unanimously; with everyone agreeing: *The staff speak as one man on this issue.* **be sb's man** be the person required or ideally suited for a task: *If you need a driver, I'm your man.* ○ *If you want a good music teacher, he's your man.* **be man enough (to do sth)** be brave enough: *You're not man enough to fight me!* **be one's own ˈman** be able to arrange and decide things independently: *He's his own man, but he doesn't ignore advice.* **be twice the man/woman** ⇨ TWICE. **the best-laid schemes/plans of mice and men** ⇨ BEST[2]. **the child is father of the man** ⇨ CHILD. **dead men's shoes** ⇨ DEAD. **dead men tell no tales** ⇨ DEAD. **a dirty old man** ⇨ DIRTY. **ˌevery man for himˈself (and the devil take the hindmost)** (*saying*) everyone must look after his own interests, safety, etc: *In business, it's every man for himself.* **ˌevery man ˈjack** (*rhet esp derog*) every single person: *Every man jack of them ran off and left me!* **the grand old man** ⇨ GRAND. **hit/kick a man when he's down** continue to attack or injure sb who is already defeated. **the inner man** ⇨ INNER. **make a ˈman (out) of sb** turn a young man into an adult: *The army will make a man of him.* **a ˌman about ˈtown** man who spends much time at fashionable parties, clubs, theatres, etc. **ˌman and ˈboy** from boyhood onwards: *He has worked for the firm, man and boy, for thirty years.* **the ˌman in the ˈmoon** shape of a face that can be seen in the patterns of light and dark on the surface of the moon: (*fig infml*) *She knows as much about it as the man in the moon,* ie knows nothing about it. **the ˌman in the ˈstreet; the ˌman on the ˌClapham ˈomnibus** (*Brit*) the average ordinary person of either sex: *The man in the street is opposed to this idea.* **a ˌman of ˈGod** (*fml or rhet*) clergyman. **a man/woman of parts** ⇨ PART[1]. **the ˌman of the ˈmatch** man who gives the best performance in a particular game of cricket, football, etc: *be voted man of the match.* **a ˌman of ˈstraw** (*rhet*) (**a**) person of apparent, but not real, power. (**b**) imaginary or very weak person presented as an opponent. **a man/woman of his/her word** ⇨ WORD. **a man/woman of the world** ⇨ WORLD. **ˌman to ˈman** frankly; openly: *Let's talk man to man.* ○ [attrib] *a ˌman-to-man ˈtalk.* **a marked man** ⇨ MARK[2]. **the odd man/one out** ⇨ ODD. **the poor man's sb/sth** ⇨ POOR. **sort out the men from the boys** ⇨ SORT[2]. **time and tide wait for no man** ⇨ TIME[1]. **to a ˈman; to the last ˈman** all, without exception: *To a man, they answered 'Yes'.* ○ *They were killed, to the last man, in a futile attack.* **one's young lady/young man** ⇨ YOUNG.

▷ **man** *interj* (*infml esp US*) (used to express surprise, admiration, etc): *Man! That's huge!*

-man (forming compound *ns*) **1** (**a**) (with *ns*) person who lives in: *countryman.* (**b**) (with *adjs* and *ns*) native of: *Irishman.* **2** (with *ns*) man concerned with: *ˈbusinessman* ○ *doorman* ○ *ˈpostman.* Cf -WOMAN (WOMAN). ⇨ Usage at CHAIR.

-manship (forming uncountable *ns*) skill or quality of: *craftsmanship* ○ *sportsmanship.* Cf -SHIP.

□ **ˌman-at-ˈarms** *n* (*pl* **ˌmen-at-ˈarms**) (in the Middle Ages) mounted soldier with heavy armour and weapons.

ˈman-eater *n* lion, tiger, etc that attacks men: (*fig joc*) *My sister's a real man-eater!* **ˈman-eating** *adj* [attrib]: *a man-eating lion, tiger, etc.*

ˌman ˈFriday male general assistant in an office, etc. The term comes from Friday, the name of the faithful servant in *Defoe's novel *Robinson Crusoe.*

ˈmanhole *n* hole in a street fitted with a lid, through which sb can enter a sewer, etc to inspect it: [attrib] *manhole cover.*

ˈman-hour *n* work done by one person in one hour: *The builder reckons 15 man-hours for the job.*

ˈman-hunt *n* large-scale search for a (male or female) criminal, etc: *Police have launched a man-hunt for the bullion robbers.*

ˌman of ˈletters, ˌwoman of ˈletters person who does literary work, eg as a writer or critic.

ˌman-ˈmade *adj* not naturally made; artificial: *ˌman-made ˈfibres, ˈchemicals.*

ˌman-of-ˈwar *n* (*pl* **ˌmen-of-ˈwar**) armed sailing-ship of a country's navy.

ˈmanservant *n* (*pl* **menservants**) male servant. Cf MAIDSERVANT (MAID).

ˈman-size (also **ˈman-sized**) *adj* of a size suitable for a man; large: *a man-size(d) handkerchief, beefsteak, portion.*

ˈmanslaughter *n* [U] crime of killing a person unlawfully but not intentionally: *commit manslaughter.* Cf HOMICIDE 1, MURDER 1.

ˈmantrap *n* trap with large jaws formerly used for catching poachers, trespassers, etc.

NOTE ON USAGE: **Man** can be used, in a similar way to **mankind**, to mean 'all men and women'. Many people consider this biased against women and avoid it by using **humanity**, **the human race** (singular) or **humans**, **human beings**, **people** (plural).

man[2] /mæn/ *v* (-nn-) [Tn, Tn·pr] ~ **sth (with sb)** supply sth (with men or, sometimes, women) for service or to operate something: *man the boat with a replacement crew* ○ *a warship manned by experienced officers* ○ *Barbara will man the telephone switchboard till we get back.*

manacle /ˈmænəkl/ *n* (usu *pl*) one of a pair of chains or metal bands for binding the hands or feet; fetter.

▷ **manacle** *v* [Tn] bind (sb/sth) with manacles.

manage /ˈmænɪdʒ/ *v* **1** (**a**) [Tn] be in charge of (sth); run: *manage a shop, business, factory, etc* ○ *manage a department, project* ○ *Jones manages the finances here.* (**b**) keep (a child, an animal, etc) in order; control: *manage a difficult horse* ○ *Can you manage children well?* ○ *He's good at managing his money,* ie at controlling how much he spends. **2** (**a**) [I, Ipr, Tn, Tt] ~ **(on sth)**; ~ **(without sb/sth)** succeed in doing (sth); cope (with sth): *I just can't manage* (ie live) *on £50 a week.* ○ *I can't borrow the money so I'll have to manage without.* ○ *I shan't be able to manage (the job) (without help).* ○ *In spite of these insults, she managed not to get angry.* ○ *I just about managed to get up the stairs.* (**b**) [Tn] (used often with *can, could*) succeed in producing, achieving or doing (sth): *I haven't been learning French for long, so I can only manage* (ie speak) *a few words.* ○ *Even a schoolboy could manage* (ie write) *a better story than that.* ○ *I couldn't manage* (ie eat) *another thing, I'm afraid.* ○ *Despite his disappointment, he managed a smile,* ie succeeded in smiling. ○ *Can you manage lunch* (ie come to lunch) *on Tuesday?*

▷ **manageable** *adj* that can be managed; easily controlled: *a business of manageable size.*

□ **ˌmanaging diˈrector** person who controls the business operations of a company.

management /ˈmænɪdʒmənt/ *n* **1** [U] control and organization (of a business, etc): *The failure was caused by bad management.* ○ [attrib] *a management course, consultant.* **2** [CGp] all those who control a business, enterprise, etc: *Management/The management is/are considering closing the factory.* ○ *joint consultation between workers and management* ○ *The business is under new management.* ○ [attrib] *a top management job.* **3** [U] skill in dealing with people: *She gets them to accept these changes by tactful management.*

manager /ˈmænɪdʒə(r)/ *n* **1** (**a**) person controlling a business, etc: *a shop, cinema, hotel, etc manager* ○ *departmental managers.* (**b**) person dealing with the business affairs of an entertainer, a sportsman, etc. (**c**) person who controls a sports team: *the England football manager.* **2** (usu preceded by an *adj*) person who controls people, a household, money, etc in the way specified: *She's not a very good manager — she always spends more money than she earns.*

▷ **manageress** /ˌmænɪdʒəˈres/ *n* woman who is in charge of a business, esp a shop, restaurant, hotel, etc.

managerial /ˌmænəˈdʒɪərɪəl/ *adj* of managers or management: *a managerial job, meeting, decision* ○ *managerial skills, expertise, etc.*

mañana /mænˈjɑːnə/ *adv* (*Spanish*) (used for suggesting continual delay, esp in Spain and other southern European countries) tomorrow; at some unspecified or uncertain time in the future.

manatee /ˌmænəˈtiː/ *n* large seal-like animal that lives in the sea on the Atlantic coasts of tropical America and Africa.

Manchu /mænˈtʃuː/ *n* **1** [C] member of a Tartar people who conquered China and founded the *Ch'ing dynasty. **2** [U] language of the Manchus, which is related to *Mongolian.

Manchuria /mænˈtʃʊərɪə/ region of NE China, from which the Manchu conquerors of China originally came. ▷ **Manchurian** *adj, n.*

Mancunian /mæŋˈkjuːnɪən/ *n, adj* (person) of or from Manchester, a city in NW England.

mandamus /mænˈdeɪməs/ *n* [U] order issued by a court of law, instructing a public authority or lower court to do sth: *a writ of mandamus.*

mandarin /ˈmændərɪn/ *n* **1 Mandarin** [U] official standard spoken language of China. **2** [C] (formerly) high-ranking government official in China. **3** [C] high-ranking official who behaves and writes in a remote and difficult way: *Whitehall mandarins,* ie top British civil servants ○ [attrib] *pages and pages of mandarin prose.* **4** [C] (also **ˌmandarin ˈorange**) type of small orange with loose skin. **5** [C] (also **ˌmandarin ˈduck**) small (originally Chinese) duck with brightly coloured feathers.

mandate /ˈmændeɪt/ *n* (usu *sing*) **1** ~ **(to do sth)** (**a**) authority given to a party, trade union, etc by the people who support it: *Our election victory has given us a mandate to reform the economy.* ○ *We have a mandate from the union membership to proceed with strike action.* (**b**) order (given to sb to do sth); mission: *The government gave the police a* *mandate to reduce crime.* **2** (formerly) power given to a country to administer a territory.

▷ **mandate** *v* **1** [Tn esp passive] put (a territory) under a mandate(2): *the mandated territories.* **2** (a) [Dn·t] give (sb) the power (to do sth) by mandate(2): *Britain was mandated to govern the former colony of German East Africa.* (b) [Tn esp passive] order (sb) to do sth.

mandatory /ˈmændətərɪ; *US* -tɔːrɪ/ *adj* (*fml*) required by law; compulsory: *a mandatory payment* ○ *Attendance is mandatory at all meetings.*

Mandela /mænˈdelə/ Nelson Rolihlahla (1918-), South African black politician, deputy president of the *African National Congress. He was found guilty of plotting against the government in 1964, and while in prison became a focus for the anti-apartheid movement. In 1990 he was released, and began talks with the South African government aimed at resolving the country's racial problems.

mandible /ˈmændɪbl/ *n* (*anatomy*) **1** jaw, esp the lower jaw of mammals and fishes. ⇨ illus at SKELETON. **2** upper or lower part of a bird's beak. **3** (in insects, etc) either half of the upper pair of jaws, used for biting and seizing.

mandolin /ˈmændəlɪn, ˌmændəˈlɪn/ *n* musical instrument with 6 or 8 metal strings arranged in pairs, and a rounded back. ⇨ illus at LUTE.

mandragora /mænˈdrægərə/ (also **mandrake** /ˈmændreɪk/) *n* [U] poisonous plant used to make drugs, esp ones which make people sleep.

mandrill /ˈmændrɪl/ *n* large W African baboon.

mane /meɪn/ *n* **1** long hair on the neck of a horse, lion, etc. ⇨ illus at HORSE. **2** (*joc*) person's long hair: *A young man with a thick mane hanging over his shoulders.*

Manet /ˈmæneɪ/ Edouard (1832-83), French painter. Rebelling against traditional academic style, he pioneered a frank realism. (One of his best-known works, *Déjeuner sur l'herbe*, shows a naked woman having a picnic with men in modern dress, and this caused a scandal when it was first shown.) Manet was an early inspirer of the *Impressionists and is sometimes called the 'father of modern art'.

maneuver *n*, *v* (*US*) = MANOEUVRE.

manful /ˈmænfl/ *adj* brave; determined: *manful resistance, defence, etc.* ▷ **manfully** /-fəlɪ/ *adv*: *He strove manfully to overcome his speech defect.*

manganese /ˈmæŋɡəniːz/ *n* [U] (*symb* **Mn**) (*chemistry*) hard brittle light-grey metallic element used in making steel, glass, etc ⇨ App 11.

mange /meɪndʒ/ *n* [U] skin disease of hairy animals, caused by a parasite.

▷ **mangy** /ˈmeɪndʒɪ/ *adj* (**-ier, -iest**) **1** suffering from mange: *a mangy dog.* **2** (*fig*) shabby and becoming worn and threadbare: *a mangy old chair, blanket, etc.*

mangel-wurzel /ˈmæŋɡl wɜːzl/ *n* type of large root vegetable used as cattle food.

manger /ˈmeɪndʒə(r)/ *n* **1** long open box or trough from which horses or cattle can feed. **2** (idm) **a dog in the manger** ⇨ DOG[1].

mange-tout /ˌmɒnʒ ˈtuː/ (also **sugar-pea**) *n* type of pea with an edible pod.

mangle[1] /ˈmæŋɡl/ *v* [Tn esp passive] **1** damage (sth) greatly, (almost) beyond recognition; mutilate: *the badly mangled bodies of those killed by the explosion.* **2** (*fig*) (of a writer, an actor, etc) badly spoil (a piece of work, performance, etc: *a mangled translation* ○ *The symphony was dreadfully mangled.*

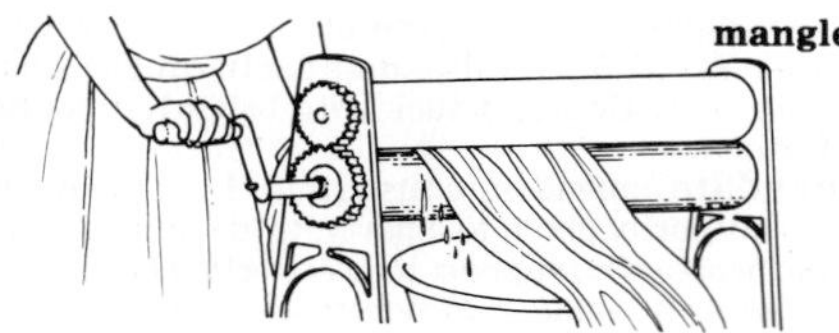

mangle[2] /ˈmæŋɡl/ *n* machine with rollers used (esp formerly) for squeezing water from or smoothing clothes, etc that have been washed; wringer.

▷ **mangle** *v* [Tn] put (clothes, etc) through a mangle.

mango /ˈmæŋɡəʊ/ *n* (*pl* **~es** or **~s**) (a) pear-shaped fruit with flesh which is yellow when ripe: [attrib] *mango chutney*, ie chutney made with green unripe mangoes. (b) tropical tree bearing these.

mangrove /ˈmæŋɡrəʊv/ *n* tropical tree that grows in swamps and sends roots down from its branches.

mangy ⇨ MANGE.

manhandle /ˈmænhændl/ *v* **1** [Tn, Tn·pr] move (sth) by physical strength: *We manhandled the piano up the stairs.* **2** [Tn] treat (sb) roughly: *The drunk had been manhandled by a gang of youths.*

Manhattan /mænˈhætn/ island at the mouth of the Hudson River, forming a borough of New York City. It is the commercial and cultural centre of the city.

□ **the Manˈhattan Project** (code name for the) secret American project set up in 1942 to produce the first atomic bomb.

manhood /ˈmænhʊd/ *n* [U] **1** state of being a man: *reach manhood.* **2** qualities of a man, eg courage, virility, etc: *have doubts about one's manhood.* **3** all the men collectively, esp of a country: *Our nation's manhood died on the battlefield.*

mania /ˈmeɪnɪə/ *n* **1** [U] (*medical*) any phase of mental disorder marked by extreme excitement or violence. **2** [C] ~ (**for sth**) (*infml*) extreme or abnormal enthusiasm: *have a mania for sweets, for collecting things.*

▷ **maniac** /ˈmeɪnɪæk/ *n* **1** mad person. **2** (*derog or joc*) (a) person with an extreme liking (for sth): *She's a football maniac.* (b) wild or foolish person: *That maniac drives far too fast.* **maniacal** /məˈnaɪəkl/ *adj* (*fml*) **1** violently mad: *maniacal behaviour* ○ *a maniacal expression on his face.* **2** (*derog or joc*) extremely enthusiastic: *He's maniacal about sex.* **maniacally** /məˈnaɪəklɪ/ *adv.*

-mania *comb form* (forming *ns*) madness or abnormal behaviour of a particular type: *kleptomania* ○ *nymphomania.*

▷ **-maniac** (forming *ns* and *adjs*) (person) affected with a mania of a particular type: *dipsomaniac* ○ *pyromaniac.*

manic /ˈmænɪk/ *adj* (of a person, his moods, etc) changing quickly and often between extremes of depression and cheerfulness.

□ **ˌmanic-deˈpressive** *n* (*medical*) person who is manic.

Manichaeism /ˌmænɪˈkiːɪzəm/ *n* [U] medieval religious system, containing Christian and pagan elements. It taught that the material world is the scene of a continuous conflict between good and evil, which are equal.

▷ **Manichaean** /-ˈkiːən/ *adj* of Manichaeism. — *n* believer in Manichaeism.

manicure /ˈmænɪkjʊə(r)/ *n* [C, U] (a) treatment for the hands and finger-nails: *have a manicure once a week* ○ *do a course in manicure.* Cf PEDICURE.

▷ **manicure** *v* [Tn] give such treatment to (sb/sb's hands): *beautifully manicured nails.*

manicurist /-kjʊərɪst/ *n* person who practises manicure as a profession.

manifest[1] /ˈmænɪfest/ *adj* ~ (**to sb**) (*fml*) clear and obvious: *a manifest truth, lie, difference* ○ *sth that is manifest to all of us.*

▷ **manifest** *v* [Tn] (*fml*) **1** show (sth) clearly; demonstrate: *manifest the truth of a statement* ○ *manifest fear, hatred, etc* ○ *She manifested little interest in her studies.* **2** ~ **itself/themselves** show itself/themselves; appear: *The symptoms manifested themselves ten days later.* ○ *Has the ghost manifested itself recently?* **manifestation** /ˌmænɪfeˈsteɪʃn/ *n* (*fml*) **1** [U] showing clearly; manifesting. **2** [C usu *pl*] action or statement that shows sth clearly: *This riot is only one manifestation of people's discontent.* **3** [C] appearance of a ghost, spirit, etc: *She claims to have seen manifestations of dead people in the haunted house.*

manifestly *adv*: *The statement is manifestly false.*

manifest[2] /ˈmænɪfest/ *n* list of cargo, passengers, etc on a ship, an aircraft, etc: *the passenger manifest of a ship.*

manifesto /ˌmænɪˈfestəʊ/ *n* (*pl* **~s** or **~es**) (publication containing a) public declaration by a political party, ruler, etc of principles and policy: *an election manifesto* ○ *publish/issue a manifesto.*

manifold /ˈmænɪfəʊld/ *adj* (*fml*) of many types; many and various: *a person with manifold interests* ○ *a versatile machine with manifold uses.*

▷ **manifold** *n* pipe or chamber with several openings that connect with other parts, eg for taking gases into or out of cylinders in an internal combustion engine: *the exhaust manifold.*

manikin /ˈmænɪkɪn/ *n* (*dated*) abnormally small man; dwarf.

Manila (also **Manilla**) /məˈnɪlə/ *n* [U] **1** (also **Manila ˈhemp**) plant fibre used for making ropes, mats, etc. **2 manila** (also **manila ˈpaper**) strong brown wrapping-paper made from Manila hemp: [attrib] *manila envelopes.*

manioc /ˈmænɪɒk/ *n* [U] cassava.

manipulate /məˈnɪpjʊleɪt/ *v* [Tn] **1** control or handle (sth) with skill: *manipulate the gears and levers of a machine* ○ *Primitive man quickly learned how to manipulate tools.* **2** control or influence (sb) cleverly or by unfair means: *a clever politician who knows how to manipulate public opinion* ○ *She uses her charm to manipulate people.* **3** (*medical*) examine or treat (a part of the body, eg a broken limb) with the hands.

▷ **manipulation** /məˌnɪpjʊˈleɪʃn/ *n* [C, U] (act of) manipulating or being manipulated: *His clever manipulation of the stock markets makes him lots of money.*

manipulative /məˈnɪpjʊlətɪv; *US* -leɪtɪv/ *adj* (*esp derog*) tending to manipulate(2): *manipulative skill, power, ability, etc.*

manipulator /məˈnɪpjʊleɪtə(r)/ *n* (*esp derog*) person who manipulates (MANIPULATE 2): *an unscrupulous manipulator.*

Manitoba /ˌmænɪˈtəʊbə/ province of central Canada, between Ontario and Saskatchewan. It produces large amounts of wheat. ⇨ map at App 1.

mankind *n* [U] **1** /ˌmænˈkaɪnd/ the human race: *an invention that benefits mankind* ⇨ Usage at MAN[1]. **2** /ˈmænkaɪnd/ men collectively (contrasted with ˈ*womankind*).

man-like /ˈmænlaɪk/ *adj* like a man in appearance, characteristics, etc: *a man-like creature about four feet tall.*

manly /ˈmænlɪ/ *adj* (**-ier, -iest**) **1** (a) (*approv*) (of a man) having the qualities or appearance expected of a man: *I've always thought he looked very manly in his uniform.* (b) (*derog*) (of a woman) having the qualities or appearance more appropriate to a man; mannish. **2** (*approv*) (of things) suitable for a man: *manly clothes* ○ *a manly pose.* ▷ **manliness** *n* [U].

Mann /mæn; *US* mɑːn/ Thomas (1875-1955), German writer whose main theme is the role of the artist in relation to society. Among his best-known works are the novels *Buddenbrooks, The Magic Mountain* and *Dr Faustus*, and the short story *Death in Venice.*

manna /ˈmænə/ *n* [U] **1** (in the Bible) food provided by God for the Israelites during their forty years in the desert. **2** (idm) **like manna (from ˈheaven)** as an unexpected and beneficial gift: *I needed that money so desperately, it was like manna from heaven when it arrived!*

mannequin /ˈmænɪkɪn/ *n* **1** (*dated*) woman employed to display new styles of clothes by wearing them; fashion model. **2** life-size dummy of a human body, used by tailors when making clothes, or by shops for displaying them.

manner /ˈmænə(r)/ *n* **1** [sing] (*fml*) way in which a thing is done or happens: *the manner in which he died* ○ *the manner of his death*, ie the way he died ○ *I don't object to what she says, but I strongly disapprove of her manner of saying it.* ○ *Do it in a businesslike manner.* ○ *He objected in a forceful manner.* **2** [sing] person's way of behaving towards others: *He has an aggressive manner.* ○ *I don't like her manner — she's very hostile.*

3 manners [pl] (**a**) social behaviour: *good/bad manners* ○ *It's bad manners to stare at people.* ○ *He has no manners at all*, ie behaves very badly. ○ *Aren't you forgetting your manners* (ie being rude)? (**b**) habits and customs: *eighteenth-century aristocratic manners.* **4** [sing] (*fml or rhet*) kind (of person or thing); sort: *What manner of man is he?* **5** (idm) **all manner of sb/sth** (*fml*) every kind of sb/sth: *All manner of vehicles were used.* **bedside manner** ⇨ BEDSIDE (BED[1]). **a comedy of manners** ⇨ COMEDY. **in a manner of speaking** to some extent; if regarded in a certain way: *His success is in a manner of speaking our success, too.* **in the manner of sb** in the style of literature or art typical of sb: *a painting in the manner of Raphael.* **not by ˈany manner of means/by ˈno manner of means** (used for emphasis) not at all: *She hasn't won yet, (not) by any manner of means.* **(as/as if) to the manner ˈborn** as if one has long experience of doing sth: *She isn't a practised public speaker, but she faced her audience as (if) to the manner born.*

▷ **mannered** *adj* having an unnatural style of speaking, writing, etc; affected: *Her prose is far too mannered and self-conscious.*

-mannered (forming compound *adjs*) having manners of the specified type: *ˌill-/ˌwell-/ˌrough-ˈmannered.*

mannerism /ˈmænərɪzəm/ *n* **1** [C] peculiar habit of behaviour, speech, etc: *an eccentric with many odd mannerisms.* **2** [U] (*derog*) excessive use of a distinctive style in art or literature: *painting that is not free of mannerism.* **3 Mannerism** [U] style of 16th-century Italian art which challenged some of the traditional classical rules of painting (eg by altering perspectives, showing people in distorted poses and using violently rich colours). It can be seen in the later works of *Michelangelo. The term is also applied to architecture of the same period.

▷ **mannerist** *n.*

mannish /ˈmænɪʃ/ *adj* (*derog*) **1** (of a woman) looking, sounding or behaving like a man. **2** (of things) more suitable for a man than for a woman: *a mannish jacket, voice, walk.* ▷ **mannishly** *adv.* **mannishness** *n* [U].

manoeuvre (*US* **maneuver**) /məˈnuːvə(r)/ *n* **1** (*military*) (**a**) [C] planned and controlled movement of armed forces: *a flanking manoeuvre*, ie round the sides of an enemy army. (**b**) **manoeuvres** [pl] large-scale exercises by troops or ships: *The army is on* (ie taking part in) *manoeuvres in the desert.* **2** [C] (**a**) movement performed with care and skill: *A rapid manoeuvre by the driver prevented an accident.* (**b**) (*usu fig*) (esp deceptively) skilful plan or movement: *This was a crafty manoeuvre to outwit his pursuers.* ○ *These shameful manoeuvres were aimed at securing his election.*

▷ **manoeuvre** (*US* **maneuver**) *v* **1** (**a**) [I, Ipr, Tn, Tn·pr] (cause sth to) move about by using skill and care: *Cyclists were manoeuvring on the practice track.* ○ *The yachts were manoeuvring for position*, ie moving around to get good positions (eg in a race). ○ *his skill in manoeuvring a motor cycle* ○ *The driver manoeuvred (the car) into the garage, over to the side of the road.* (**b**) [Tn, Tn·pr, Tn·p] (*fig*) guide (sb/sth) skilfully and craftily (in a specified direction): *She manoeuvred her friends into positions of power*, ie used her influence, etc to put them there. ○ *manoeuvre the conversation round to money.* **2** [I] (*military*) perform manoeuvres(1b): *The fleet is manoeuvring in the Baltic.* **manoeuvrable** (*US* **maneuverable**) /-vrəbl/ *adj* that can be manoeuvred (easily): *a highly manoeuvrable aircraft, motorboat, etc.* **manoeuvrability** (*US* **maneuverability**) /məˌnuːvrəˈbɪlətɪ/ *n* [U].

manometer /məˈnɒmɪtə(r)/ *n* instrument for measuring pressure in gases and liquids.

manor /ˈmænə(r)/ *n* **1** (formerly) unit of land under the feudal system, part of which was used by the lord of the manor (LORD), the rest being farmed by tenants. **2** (**a**) (also ˈ**manor-house**) large country house surrounded by an estate. (**b**) this estate. **3** (*Brit sl*) (used esp by policemen) area for which a particular police station is responsible.

▷ **manorial** /məˈnɔːrɪəl/ *adj* of a manor(1,2).

manpower /ˈmænpaʊə(r)/ *n* [U] **1** number of people working or available for work: *There's not enough qualified manpower to staff all the hospitals* ○ [attrib] *a manpower shortage.* **2** power supplied by human physical effort: *a treadmill driven by manpower rather than water-power.*

manqué /ˈmɒŋkeɪ/ *adj* (following *ns*) (*French*) (of a person) who could have followed the career mentioned, but who failed or lacked the opportunity to do so: *a teacher, an actor, a writer, etc manqué.*

mansard /ˈmænsɑːd/ *n* (also ˌ**mansard** ˈ**roof**) roof with a double slope, the lower part being more steep than the upper part.

manse /mæns/ *n* church minister's house, esp in Scotland.

Mansfield /ˈmænsfiːld/ Katherine (real name Kathleen Mansfield Beauchamp, 1888-1923), New Zealand short-story writer who lived most of her life in England. Her stories (eg *In a German Pension* and *Bliss*) are full of intensity and poetic feeling.

mansion /ˈmænʃn/ *n* **1** [C] large and stately house. **2 Mansions** [pl] (used in proper names for a block of flats): *49 Victoria Mansions, Grove Road, London.*

□ **the** ˈ**Mansion House** official home of the Lord Mayor of London, in the City of London.

manslaughter ⇨ MAN[1].

manta /ˈmæntə/ *n* (also ˈ**manta ray**) very large flat fish that swims by flapping its wing-like fins.

Mantegna /mænˈteɪnjə/ Andrea (1431-1506), Italian painter best known for his large wall-paintings depicting historical and other scenes.

mantel /ˈmæntl/ *n* (*dated*) mantelpiece.

mantelpiece /ˈmæntlpiːs/ (also ˈ**chimney-piece**) *n* shelf above a fireplace: *A clock and two vases stood on the mantelpiece.*

mantilla /mænˈtɪlə/ *n* lace veil or scarf worn (esp by Spanish women) to cover the hair and shoulders.

mantis /ˈmæntɪs/ *n* (also ˌ**praying** ˈ**mantis**) insect like a grasshopper, which holds its front legs together as if in prayer.

mantissa /mænˈtɪsə/ *n* part of a logarithm that follows the decimal point. Cf CHARACTERISTIC *n* 4.

mantle /ˈmæntl/ *n* **1** [C] (**a**) loose sleeveless cloak. (**b**) (*fig*) covering: *hills with a mantle of snow.* **2** [sing] **the ~ of sth** (*rhet*) the responsibilites of an important job, etc: *assume/take on/inherit the mantle of supreme power.* **3** [C] lace-like cover round the flame of a gas lamp that becomes very bright when heated. **4** [sing] (*geology*) part of the Earth below the crust and surrounding the core. ⇨ illus at EARTH.

▷ **mantle** *v* (*fig rhet*) [Tn] cover (sth) as if with a mantle: *an ivy-mantled wall* ○ *Snow mantled the hills.*

mantra /ˈmæntrə/ *n* (in Hinduism and Buddhism) sacred word or phrase which has magic powers, and which one says to oneself when meditating.

manual /ˈmænjʊəl/ *adj* of, done with or controlled by the hands: *Making small models requires manual skill.* ○ *manual labour* ○ *a manual gear-box*, ie one operated by the hand with a gear-lever, not automatically. Cf MECHANICAL 1.

▷ **manual** *n* **1** book containing information or practical instructions (on a given subject): *a training manual* ○ *a workshop manual gives diagrams and instructions for repairing your car.* Cf HANDBOOK (HAND[1]). **2** keyboard of an organ, played with the hands: *a two-manual organ.*

manually /-jʊəlɪ/ *adv*: *manually operated.*

manufacture /ˌmænjʊˈfæktʃə(r)/ *v* [Tn] **1** make (goods) on a large scale using machinery: *manufacture shoes, cement, cookers* ○ *manufacturing industry*, eg in contrast with industries which do not make products. **2** (*usu derog*) invent (evidence, an excuse, etc): *She manufactured a false story to hide the facts.*

▷ **manufacture** *n* **1** [U] activity of manufacturing: *firms engaged in the manufacture of plastics* ○ *goods of foreign manufacture*, ie made abroad. **2 manufactures** [pl] manufactured goods or articles.

manufacturer *n* person or firm that manufactures things: *Send these faulty goods back to the manufacturer.* ○ *a clothing, a car, an electronics, etc manufacturer.*

manumit /ˌmænjʊˈmɪt/ *v* (-tt-) [Tn] (*fml*) (formerly) free (a slave). ▷ **manumission** /ˌmænjʊˈmɪʃn/ *n* [U].

manure /məˈnjʊə(r)/ *n* [U] animal dung or other material, natural or artificial, spread over or mixed with soil to make it fertile: *dig manure into the soil.* Cf FERTILIZER (FERTILIZE).

▷ **manure** *v* [Tn] put manure on or in (soil).

manuscript /ˈmænjʊskrɪpt/ *n* (*abbr* **MS**) **1** thing written by hand, not typed or printed: [attrib] *a manuscript copy of a typed letter.* **2** author's work when written or typed (ie not yet a printed book): *submit a manuscript to an editor.* **3** (idm) **in** ˈ**manuscript** not yet printed: *Her poems are still in manuscript.*

Manx /mæŋks/ *adj* of the *Isle of Man, its people or its language.

▷ **Manx** *n* [U] language of the Isle of Man. ⇨ article at LANGUAGE.

□ **Manx** ˈ**cat** breed of cat with no tail, thought to have originated on the Isle of Man.

ˈ**Manxman** /-mən/ (*pl* **-men**), ˈ**Manxwoman** (*pl* **-women**) *ns* native of the Isle of Man.

many /ˈmenɪ/ *indef det, indef pron* (used with *pl ns* or *vs*) **1** a large number of people or things. (**a**) (*det*): *Many people agree with nationalization.* ○ *I didn't see many houses under £50 000.* ○ *Were there many pictures by British artists?* ○ *How many children have you got?* ○ *There are too many mistakes in this essay.* ○ *I don't need many more.* (**b**) (*pron*): *Many of the students were from Japan.* ○ *I have some classical records but not very many.* ○ *Did you know many of them?* ○ *How many do you want?* ○ *I wouldn't have offered to water the plants if I'd known there were so many.* ○ *He made ten mistakes in as many* (ie ten) *lines.* ⇨ Usage at MUCH[1]. **2 many a** a large number of (used with a *sing n* + *sing v*): *Many a strong man has weakened before such a challenge.* ○ *Many a famous pop star has been ruined by drugs.* ○ *I've been to the top of the Eiffel Tower many a time.* ○ (*saying*) *Many a true word is spoken in jest.* **3** (idm) **be 'one, etc too** ˈ**many (for sth)** be one, etc more than the correct or needed number: *There are six of us — two too many for a game of whist.* **a good/great many** very many. **have had** ˌ**one too** ˈ**many** (*infml*) be slightly drunk. **many's the sb/sth who/that...** there are many people/things that...: *Many's the promise that has been broken.* (Cf *Many a promise has been broken.*) ○ *Many's the time that I heard him use those words.* (Cf *I heard him use those words many a time.*).

▷ **the many** *n* most people; the masses or majority: *a government which improves conditions for the many.* Cf THE FEW (FEW[1]).

□ ˌ**many-**ˈ**sided** *adj* having many sides: (*fig*) *We are faced with a* ˌ*many-sided* ˈ*problem.*

Maoism /ˈmaʊɪzəm/ *n* [U] Communist political ideas and practices developed by *Mao Tse-tung, emphasizing the role of peasants and agricultural workers in bringing about the perfect socialist state. ▷ **Maoist** /ˈmaʊɪst/ *adj, n.*

Maori /ˈmaʊrɪ/ *n* **1** [C] member of the aboriginal race of New Zealand. The Maoris arrived from Tahiti, probably in the 9th century AD, and by 1200 had established settlements in various parts of New Zealand. There are now about 25 000 of them. **2** [U] *Polynesian language of the Maoris.

▷ **Maori** *adj* of the Maoris or their language: *Maori dress, customs, words.*

Mao Tse-tung /ˌmaʊ tsɪˈtʊŋ/ (also **Mao Zedong** /ˌmaʊ dzəˈdʊŋ/) (1893-1976), Chinese statesman. He organized and led the revolution which resulted in the establishment of Communist rule in China in 1949. He became president, and remained in control of China until his death. His political ideas have had considerable influence on left-wing revolutionary movements around the world. Cf MAOISM.

map /mæp/ *n* **1** (**a**) representation on paper, etc of the earth's surface or part of it, showing countries, rivers, mountains, oceans, roads, etc: *a map of France* ○ *find a place on the map* ○ *a street map of London* ○ *I'll draw you a map of how to get to my house.* ⇨ illus. (**b**) similar plan showing the position of the stars, etc in the sky: *a map of the heavens.* Cf CHART, PLAN 2. **2** (idm) **put sb/sth on the ˈmap** make sb/sth famous or important: *Her performance in that play really put her on the map as a comedy actress.* **wipe sth off the map** ⇨ WIPE.
▷ **map** *v* (**-pp-**) [Tn] **1** make a map of (an area, etc); show on a map: *an unexplored country that hasn't yet been mapped.* **2** (phr v) **map sth out** (**a**) plan or arrange sth: *He's already mapped out his whole future career.* (**b**) present sth in detail: *She mapped out her ideas on the new project.*
□ **ˈmap-reader** *n* person who follows a route on a map: *a good, poor, etc map-reader* ○ *You drive and I'll be (the) map-reader.*

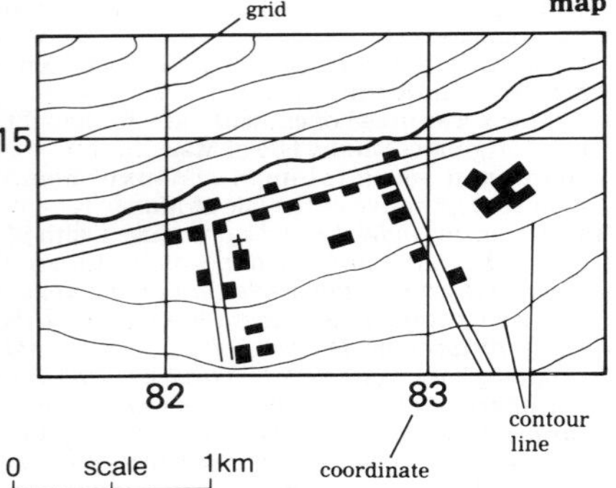

maple /ˈmeɪpl/ *n* (**a**) [C] (also **ˈmaple tree**) any of various types of tree of the northern hemisphere, grown for timber and ornament. The maple leaf is used as the emblem of Canada. (**b**) [U] hard wood of the maple tree, sometimes used for furniture: [attrib] *a maple desk.*
□ **maple ˈsugar**, **maple ˈsyrup** sugar/syrup obtained from the sap of one kind of maple.

maquis /ˈmæki:; *US* ˈmɑ:ki:/ *n* **the maquis** (also **the Maquis**) [Gp] the secret army of French patriots who fought in France against the Germans in the Second World War.

mar /mɑ:(r)/ *v* (**-rr-**) [Tn] **1** damage (sth); spoil: *a mistake that could mar his career* ○ *Nothing happened to mar the old man's happiness.* **2** (idm) **make or mar sb/sth** make sb/sth a success or a failure: *His handling of the crisis could make or mar his career.*

Mar *abbr* March: *3 Mar 1941.*

marabou /ˈmærəbu:/ *n* **1** [C] large W African stork. **2** [U] its soft feathers used as trimming, eg for a hat.

maraca /məˈrækə/ *n* (usu *pl*) musical instrument consisting of a container (often a gourd) with beans, beads, etc in it that makes a noise when shaken. Maracas are usu played in pairs.

maraschino /ˌmærəˈski:nəʊ/ *n* (*pl* ~**s** /-nəʊz/) **1** [U] sweet liqueur made from a small black cherry. **2** [C] (also ˌ**maraschino ˈcherry**) cherry soaked in this liqueur, used in drinks, puddings, etc.

Marat /ˈmærɑ:/ Jean-Paul (1743-93), French revolutionary who was a strong supporter of the working classes, and opposed the more moderate right-wing revolutionaries. He was murdered in his (medicinal) bath by Charlotte Corday.

Marathon /ˈmærəθən; *US* -θɒn/ site of a battle in Greece in 490 BC where the Athenians defeated an invading Persian army. The news of their victory was brought to Athens by a messenger; the distance he covered (about 26 miles) is used for the modern marathon race.

marathon /ˈmærəθən; *US* -θɒn/ *n* **1** (also **Marathon**) long-distance running race (of about 42 km or 26 miles): *I've never run a marathon.* ○ *She won the gold medal in the women's marathon at this year's Olympic Games.* **2** (*fig*) long-lasting event which is hard to endure: *My job interview was a real marathon.* ○ [attrib] *a marathon session, exam, etc.*

marauding /məˈrɔ:dɪŋ/ *adj* [attrib] (of soldiers, armies, etc) going about searching for things to steal, people to attack, etc: *The countryside was overrun by marauding bands.*
▷ **marauder** /məˈrɔ:də(r)/ *n* person or animal that does this.

marble /ˈmɑ:bl/ *n* **1** [U] type of hard limestone used, when cut and polished, for building and sculpture: *a slab of unpolished marble* ○ *These steps are made of marble.* ○ [attrib] *a marble statue, tomb, etc.* **2 marbles** [pl] collection of marble sculptures; works of art in marble. **3** (**a**) [C] small ball of glass, clay, etc used by children in games. (**b**) **marbles** [pl] game played with these: *Let's have a game of marbles.* **4** (idm) **lose one's marbles** ⇨ LOSE.
▷ **marble** *adj* [attrib] (*fig*) like marble: *marble* (ie smooth and white) *skin* ○ *a marble* (ie cold and unfeeling) *heart.*
marbled /ˈmɑ:bld/ *adj* **1** having a pattern of streaks in different colours, resembling marble: *a book with marbled covers.* **2** (of meat) streaked with fat.
marbling /ˈmɑ:blɪŋ/ *n* [U] (technique of producing) a marbled pattern on paper.
□ ˌ**Marble ˈArch** large arch with three gates, erected at the north-east corner of *Hyde Park, London, in 1851.

marcasite /ˈmɑ:kəsaɪt/ *n* [C, U] (piece of a) type of crystallized mineral, used in jewellery: [attrib] *a marcasite ring*, ie a ring with a marcasite set into it.

March /mɑ:tʃ/ *n* **1** [U, C] (*abbr* **Mar**) the third month of the year, next after February. **2** (idm) **mad as a March hare** ⇨ MAD.
For the uses of *March* see the examples at *April.*

march[1] /mɑ:tʃ/ *v* **1** (**a**) [I, Ipr, Ip] walk as soldiers do, with regular steps of equal length: *Quick march!* ie a military command to start marching ○ *Demonstrators marched through the streets.* ○ *They marched in and took over the town.* ○ *march by, past, in, out, off, away, etc* ○ *The army has marched thirty miles today.* (**b**) [I, Ipr, Ip] walk purposefully and determinedly: *She marched in and demanded an apology.* (**c**) [Tn·pr, Tn·p] cause (sb) to march: *march the troops up and down* ○ *They marched the prisoner away.* ○ *She was marched into a cell.* **2** (idm) **get one's marching orders**; **give sb his marching orders** (*infml or joc*) be told/tell sb to go; be dismissed/dismiss sb: *She was totally unreliable, so she got/was given her marching orders.* **3** (phr v) **march past** (**sb**) (of troops) march ceremonially past (an honoured guest, a high-ranking officer, etc), eg in a parade. ▷ **marcher** *n*: *freedom marchers* ○ *civil-rights marchers.*
□ **ˈmarch past** act or event of marching past sb ceremonially: *a march past by the light infantry.*

march[2] /mɑ:tʃ/ *n* **1** (**a**) [C] act of marching: *a long, an arduous, etc march* ○ *a ten-mile march.* (**b**) [sing] progress when marching; advance: *their steady march towards the enemy* ○ *the line of march*, ie route followed by troops when marching. **2** [C] procession from one place to another by many people, esp as a protest: *a peace march* ○ *an anti-nuclear (weapons) march.* Cf DEMONSTRATION 3. **3** [C] piece of music written for marching to: *military marches* ○ *a dead march*, ie a slow one for a funeral ○ [attrib] *a march tune* ○ *in march tempo.* **4** [sing] **the ~ of sth** the steady development or onward movement of sth: *the march of progress/events/time.* **5** (idm) **on the march** marching: *The enemy are on the march at last.* **steal a march** ⇨ STEAL.

marches /ˈmɑ:tʃɪz/ *n* [pl] historical borders, esp between England and Scotland or England and Wales.

marchioness /ˌmɑ:ʃəˈnes/ *n* (**a**) wife or widow of a marquis. (**b**) woman holding the same rank as a marquis.

Marconi /mɑ:ˈkəʊnɪ/ Guglielmo (1874-1937), Italian physicist and electrical engineer who developed the practical use of radio. Using the work of previous researchers, such as Hertz, he transmitted long-wave radio signals over a mile in 1895, and in 1901 he transmitted a signal across the Atlantic Ocean from Cornwall to Newfoundland. He later developed long-distance short-wave transmission, and was awarded the Nobel prize for physics in 1909. He was successful in exploiting his work commercially.

Marco Polo /ˌmɑ:kəʊ ˈpəʊləʊ/ (c1254-c1324), Venetian traveller who made a journey through central Asia to China, staying there for 15 years before returning home. His account of his travels was for centuries the only reliable description of the Far East available in the West.

Marcus Aurelius /ˌmɑ:kəs ɔ:ˈri:lɪəs/ ⇨ AURELIUS.

Mardi Gras /ˌmɑ:dɪ ˈgrɑ:/ carnival held in some countries to celebrate the last day (Shrove Tuesday) or days before Lent.

mare[1] /meə(r)/ *n* **1** female horse or donkey. Cf FILLY, FOAL, STALLION. **2** (idm) **a ˈmare's nest** discovery that seems interesting but turns out to be false or worthless. **on Shank's pony/mare** ⇨ SHANK.

mare[2] /ˈmɑ:rɪ/ *n* (*pl* **maria** /ˈmɑ:rɪə/) (*astronomy*) large flat dark area on the moon or Mars, once thought to be a sea.

margarine /ˌmɑ:dʒəˈri:n; *US* ˈmɑ:rdʒərɪn/ (also *Brit infml* **marge** /mɑ:dʒ/) *n* [U] food like butter, made from animal or vegetable fats.

margin /ˈmɑ:dʒɪn/ *n* **1** (**a**) blank space round the written or printed matter on a page: *wide/narrow margins* ○ *notes written in the margin.* (**b**) edge or border: *the margin of a lake, pool, pond, etc.* **2** (**a**) amount of space, time, votes, etc by which sth is won: *a wide margin between the winner and the loser*, eg a big difference in points scored ○ *He beat the other runners by a margin of ten seconds/by a wide margin.* ○ *She won the seat by a margin of ten votes.* (**b**) amount of space, time, etc which is allowed for success or safety: *Leave a good safety margin between your car and the next.* **3** (*commerce*) difference between cost price and selling price: *a business operating on tight* (ie small) *(profit) margins.*
▷ **marginal** /-nl/ *adj* **1** [attrib] of or in a margin(1a): *marginal notes, marks, etc.* **2** small; slight: *There's only a marginal difference between the two estimates.* **3** insignificant: *This once important social group is becoming more and more marginal (to the way the country is run).* **4** (of land) not fertile enough for profitable farming except when prices of farm products are high. **5** (*politics esp Brit*) that is won by only a small majority of votes: *a marginal seat/constituency.* — *n* seat or constituency of this type: *a Labour marginal.* **marginally** /-nəlɪ/ *adv* slightly: *a marginally bigger area.* ˌ**marginal ˈcost** cost of producing one additional item.
marginalia /ˌmɑ:dʒɪˈneɪlɪə/ *n* [pl] notes, etc written in the margin of a text.
□ ˌ**margin of ˈerror** additional amount (of time, money, etc) allowed in case of a mistake or an accident: *The schedule is very tight and allows no margin of error.*

marguerite /ˌmɑ:gəˈri:t/ *n* any of various types of daisy, esp the ox-eye daisy with white petals round a yellow centre.

Mariana Trench /ˌmærɪɑ:nə ˈtrentʃ/ **the Mariana Trench** deep valley on the floor of the NW Pacific Ocean. Its depth is 11 033 m (36 198 ft), making it the deepest place on earth.

Maria Theresa /məˌri:ə təˈreɪzə/ (1717-80), archduchess of Austria, queen of Hungary and Bohemia 1740-80. She succeeded to her titles on the death of her father, the Holy Roman Emperor Charles VI, but disputes over her claim to them led to the War of the Austrian Succession (1740-48) and the *Seven Years War (1756-63). The later part of her reign was peaceful.

Marie Antoinette /ˌmærɪ ɑ:ntwəˈnet/ (1755-93), queen of France 1774-93. An Austrian princess, she married the heir to the French throne, later *Louis

XVI, in 1770. She became unpopular because of her extravagant spending, and when the Revolution came she was imprisoned and eventually executed.

marigold /ˈmærɪgəʊld/ *n* any of various types of garden plant with orange or yellow flowers.

marijuana (also **marihuana**) /ˌmærɪjuˈɑːnə/ *n* [U] dried leaves and flowers of Indian hemp, usu smoked as a drug. Cf CANNABIS, HASHISH. ⇨ article at DRUG.

marimba /məˈrɪmbə/ *n* musical instrument like a xylophone.

marina /məˈriːnə/ *n* harbour (often with leisure facilities, hotels, etc) built for yachts and pleasure-boats.

marinade /ˌmærɪˈneɪd/ *n* [C, U] sauce of wine, herbs, etc in which fish or meat is soaked before it is cooked; fish or meat soaked in this: *a marinade of pork and lamb.*

▷ **marinade** (also **marinate** /ˈmærɪneɪt/) *v* [Tn, Tn·pr] ~ **sth (in sth)** soak (food) in a marinade: *marinated pork* ○ *Marinate the veal in white wine for two hours.*

marine[1] /məˈriːn/ *adj* **1** of, near, found in or produced by the sea: *a marine creature, plant, etc* ○ *a marine painter*, ie an artist who paints seascapes ○ *a marine biologist*, ie a scientist who studies life in the sea. **2** of ships, sea-trade, the navy, etc: *marine insurance*, ie insurance of ships and cargo ○ *marine stores*, ie materials and supplies for ships.

marine[2] /məˈriːn/ *n* **1 (a)** [C] member of a body of soldiers trained to fight on land or sea. **(b) the Marines** [pl] body of such soldiers belonging to the forces of a country. ⇨ App 4. **2** (idm) **tell that to the marines** ⇨ TELL.

Mariner /ˈmærɪnə(r)/ any of a series of unmanned US spacecraft sent to make observations of various planets between 1962 and 1977.

mariner /ˈmærɪnə(r)/ *n* (*dated or fml*) sailor: *a master mariner.*

marionette /ˌmærɪəˈnet/ *n* jointed puppet moved by strings. ⇨ illus at PUPPET.

marital /ˈmærɪtl/ *adj* [attrib] of a husband or wife; of marriage: *marital vows*, ie to be faithful, etc ○ *marital problems, disagreements, disharmony, etc.*

□ ˌ**marital** ˈ**status** (*fml*) whether one is married, single or divorced.

maritime /ˈmærɪtaɪm/ *adj* **1** of the sea, sailing or shipping: *maritime law* ○ *the great maritime powers*, ie countries with powerful navies. **2** situated or found near the sea: *maritime species.*

□ **the** ˈ**Maritime Provinces** the Canadian provinces of New Brunswick, Nova Scotia, Prince Edward Island, and sometimes Newfoundland.

marjoram /ˈmɑːdʒərəm/ *n* [U] sweet-smelling herb used as a seasoning in cooking.

Mark /mɑːk/ **1** Saint (1st century AD), one of Christ's apostles and companion of St Peter and St Paul. **2** second gospel in the New Testament, named after St Mark, who may have written it.

mark[1] /mɑːk/ *n* **1 (a)** stain, spot, line, etc, esp one that spoils the appearance of sth: *black marks on white trousers* ○ *Who made these dirty marks on my new book?* **(b)** noticeable spot or area on the body by which a person or animal may be recognized: *a horse with a white mark on its head* ○ *This scar is her main distinguishing mark.* Cf BIRTHMARK (BIRTH). **2 (a)** written or printed symbol; figure, line, etc made as a sign or an indication of sth: *ˌpunctuˈation marks* ○ *Put a mark in the margin to show the omission.* ○ *White marks painted on the trees show the route.* **(b)** symbol on sth to show its origin, ownership or quality: *ˈlaundry marks*, ie showing which laundry items have been sent to ○ *cattle branded with a distinctive mark*, ie of ownership. Cf TRADE MARK (TRADE[1]). **3** visible trace; sign or indication (of a quality, feeling, etc): *marks of suffering, old age* ○ *Please accept this gift as a mark of our respect.* **4** number or letter, eg B+, used as an assessment of sb's work or conduct: *get a good/poor mark in maths* ○ *give sb high/low marks (for sth)* ○ *She got 80 marks out of 100 for geography.* **5** cross made on a document instead of a signature by an illiterate person: *put/make one's mark (on sth).* **6 Mark** (followed by a number) model or type (of a machine, vehicle, etc): *the Jaguar XJ6, Mark II* ○ *a Mark IV Cortina.* **7** (*fml*) thing aimed at; target: *The arrow reached its mark and the bird fell dead.* **8** (in sport) line from which a race starts; point from which a bowler, jumper, etc begins his run: *be quick/slow off the mark.* **9** (idm) **be/fall wide of the mark** ⇨ WIDE. **an easy mark** ⇨ EASY[1]. **full marks** ⇨ FULL. **give sb full marks** ⇨ FULL. ˌ**hit**/ˌ**miss the** ˈ**mark** succeed/fail in an attempt to do sth. **leave/make one's, its, etc mark (on sth/sb)** leave a lasting (good or bad) impression: *War has left its mark on the country.* ○ *Two unhappy marriages have left their mark on her.* ˌ**make one's** ˈ**mark** become famous, successful, etc: *an actor who has made his mark in films.* **not be/feel (quite)** ˌ**up to the** ˈ**mark** not feel as well, lively, etc as usual: *I've got flu, so I'm not quite up to the mark.* **on your** ˈ**marks, (get)** ˈ**set,** ˈ**go!** (words said by the official starter of an athletics race). **overshoot the mark** ⇨ OVERSHOOT. **overstep the mark** ⇨ OVERSTEP. ˈ**up to the** ˈ**mark** equal to the required standard: *Her school work isn't quite up to the mark.*

mark[2] /mɑːk/ *v* **1** [Tn, Tn·pr] ~ **A (with B);** ~ **B on A** make (a mark or marks) on sth: *mark one's name on one's clothes/mark one's clothes with one's name* ○ *The route has been marked so that it is easy to follow.* ○ *Prices are marked on the goods.* ○ *a face marked* (ie scarred) *by smallpox.* **2** [Tn] indicate or denote (sth): *This cross marks the spot where she died.* ○ *His death marked the end of an era.* ○ *There will be ceremonies to mark* (ie celebrate) *the Queen's birthday.* **3** [Tn] give marks (MARK[1] 4) to (pupils' work, etc): *mark examination papers* ○ *I have twenty essays to mark tonight.* **4** [Cn·a] show (sth) by putting a mark, eg a tick by sb's name: *mark sb absent/present* ○ *Why have you marked the sentence wrong?* **5** [Tn, Cn·n/a] ~ **sth (as sth)** be a distinguishing feature of (sth): *a style marked by precision and wit* ○ *These are qualities which mark the film as quite exceptional.* **6** [Tn, Tw] (*fml*) pay attention to (sth); note carefully: *You mark/Mark my words*, ie You will find that what I say is correct. ○ *Mark carefully how it is done.* **7** [Tn] (*sport*) stay close to (an opposing player) so that he cannot play easily: *Our defence had him closely marked throughout the first half.* **8** (idm) **a marked** ˈ**man** man whose conduct, etc has caused him to be disliked and selected for punishment, etc: *By breaking the rule of absolute secrecy, he became a marked man.* **mark** ˈ**time (a)** march without moving forward. **(b)** (*fig*) pass one's time doing sth routine until one can do sth more interesting, etc: *I'm just marking time in this job; I'm hoping to become an actor.* **mark you** nevertheless; all the same; however: *She hasn't had much success yet. Mark you, she does try hard.* **9** (phr v) **mark sb down** reduce the marks given to sb in an examination, etc: *She was marked down because her answers were too short.* **mark sth down** reduce the price of sth: *All goods have been marked down by 15%.* **mark sth off** separate sth by marking a boundary: *We have marked the playing area off with a white line.* **mark sb out for sth** (esp passive) choose sb to receive sth special: *a woman marked out for early promotion* ○ *He was marked out for special training.* **mark sth out** draw lines to show the boundaries of sth: *mark out a tennis court, car-park, etc.* **mark sb up** increase the marks given to sb in an examination: *If we mark him up a tiny bit, he'll just get through.* **mark sth up (a)** add a percentage to the cost/wholesale price of sth in calculating the selling/retail price: *Whisky is marked up by 150%.* **(b)** increase the price of sth: *Cars have been marked up recently.*

▷ **marked** /mɑːkt/ *adj* clear; noticeable; easily seen: *a marked difference, similarity, improvement, etc* ○ *a woman of marked intelligence.* **markedly** /ˈmɑːkɪdlɪ/ *adv* (*fml*) in a marked manner; noticeably: *He was markedly more pleasant than before.*

marker *n* **1 (a)** person or tool that makes marks: [attrib] *a* ˈ*marker pen.* **(b)** person who keeps the score in certain games. **(c)** examiner. **2** flag, post, etc, that marks a position: [attrib] *a* ˈ*marker buoy.*

marking *n* (usu *pl*) pattern of marks, esp the colours of skin, fur or feathers: *a dog with white markings on its chest.*

□ ˈ**mark-down** *n* (usu *sing*) reduction in price: *a mark-down of 20%.*

ˈ**marking-ink** *n* [U, C] indelible ink used for marking names on clothes, etc.

ˈ**mark-up** *n* (usu *sing*) **1** percentage of the wholesale/cost price added when calculating the retail/selling price of sth: *The mark-up on food in a restaurant is usually at least 100%.* **2** increase in price: *a 10% mark-up on cigarettes after the Budget.*

mark[3] /mɑːk/ *n* unit of currency in Germany: *a ten-mark note.*

Mark Antony /ˌmɑːk ˈæntənɪ/ (83-30 BC), Roman soldier and statesman. After the murder of *Julius Caesar he ruled Rome jointly with *Octavius and Lepidus. Following the battle of Philippi he took charge of the eastern part of the empire, including Egypt. He fell in love with the Egyptian queen, *Cleopatra. He quarrelled with Octavius, and after his defeat at the sea-battle of Actium he killed himself.

market[1] /ˈmɑːkɪt/ *n* **1** [C] gathering of people for buying and selling goods; place where they meet: *She went to (the) market to sell what she had made.* ○ *The next market is on the 15th.* ○ *There is a covered market in the town centre.* ○ [attrib] *a market stall, trader, day.* ⇨ article at SHOP. **2** [C] the state of trade (in a particular type of goods), as shown by prices or the rate at which things are bought and sold: *a dull/lively market (in coffee)* ○ *a rising/falling market (in shares)*, ie in which prices are rising/falling ○ *The (gold) market is steady*, ie Prices are not changing much. **3** [sing, U] ~ **(for sth)** demand: *a good/poor market for motor cars* ○ *There's not much (of a) market for these goods.* **4** [C] area, country, section of the population, etc to which goods may be sold: *We must find new (foreign) markets for our products.* ○ *This clothing sells well to the teenage market.* **5 the market** [sing] buyers and sellers: *The market determines what goods are made.* ○ *This product did not appeal to the German market.* **6** (idm) **come onto the** ˈ**market** be offered for sale: *This house only came onto the market yesterday.* **a drug on the market** ⇨ DRUG. **flood the market** ⇨ FLOOD[1]. **in the market for sth** (*infml*) interested in buying sth: *I'm not in the market for a big, expensive car.* **on the** ˈ**market** offered for sale; on sale: *These computers are not yet on the market.* ○ *put a car, house, etc on the market.* **play the** ˈ**market** (*infml*) buy and sell stocks and shares to make a profit. **price oneself/sth out of the market** ⇨ PRICE *v.*

□ ˈ**market-day** *n* day on which a market is regularly held: *Thursday is market-day in Wetherford.*

ˌ**market** ˈ**forces** effects of supply and demand, which determine the level of prices.

ˌ**market** ˈ**garden** (*Brit*) (*US* ˈ**truck farm**) farm where vegetables are grown for sale in markets. ˌ**market** ˈ**gardener** person who owns or works in a market garden. ˌ**market** ˈ**gardening** [U].

ˈ**market hall** large roofed area where a market is held.

ˈ**market-place** *n* **1** (also ˌ**market-**ˈ**square**) [C] open space in a town where a market is held. **2 the market-place** [sing] commercial buying and selling: *Companies must be able to compete in the market-place.*

ˌ**market** ˈ**price** price for which sth is or can be sold when publicly offered for sale.

ˌ**market re**ˈ**search** study of why and what people buy, to make the sale of goods more successful.

ˌ**market** ˈ**share** proportion that one company, etc has of the total volume of trading in one kind of goods or services: *Thomsons have a 48% market share.*

ˈ**market town** town where a market is held regularly.

ˈ**market value** price at which sth would be sold if offered publicly: *offer a car at £500 below (its) market value.*

market[2] /ˈmɑːkɪt/ *v* **(a)** [Tn] sell (sth) in a market:

market vegetables, fruit, etc. (**b**) [Tn, Dn·pr] ~ **sth (to sb)** offer sth for sale, esp by advertising, etc: *We need somebody to market our products (to retailers, in Germany, etc).*

▷ **marketable** *adj* that can be sold; suitable to be sold: *a highly marketable new product.* **marketability** /ˌmɑːkɪtəˈbɪlətɪ/ *n* [U].

marketeer /ˌmɑːkɪˈtɪə(r)/ *n* (usu in compounds): *black marketeers.*

marketing *n* [U] (**a**) theory and practice of commercial selling. (**b**) division of a company which markets its products: *Do you work in marketing?* ○ [attrib] *the marketing department.*

Markova /mɑːˈkəʊvə/ Dame Alicia (real name Lilian Alicia Marks, 1910-), English ballet-dancer. She was trained by *Pavlova, danced with Diaghilev's company, and took the leading role in the first British productions of many classic ballets.

Marks and Spencer /ˌmɑːks ən ˈspensə(r)/ (also *infml* **Marks, Marks and Sparks** /ˌmɑːks ən ˈspɑːks/, **M and S** /ˌem ənd ˈes/) (any of a) chain of large British shops selling mainly clothes and food.

marksman /ˈmɑːksmən/ *n* (*pl* **-men** /-mən/) person skilled in accurate shooting.

▷ **marksmanship** *n* [U] skill in shooting.

marl /mɑːl/ *n* [U] soil consisting of clay and lime, used as a fertilizer.

Marlborough /ˈmɔːlbrə/ John Churchill, 1st Duke of (1650-1722), English soldier. He commanded the British and Austrian armies in the *War of Spanish Succession, defeating the French forces at the battles of Blenheim, Ramillies, Oudenarde and Malplaquet and ending Louis XIV's attempts to dominate Europe. He was rewarded with a palace in Oxfordshire, named after his victory at Blenheim, but in 1711 he quarrelled with Queen *Anne and was dismissed from all his posts.

marlin /ˈmɑːlɪn/ *n* (*pl* unchanged) type of large sea fish with a long nose, similar to the swordfish.

marlinspike /ˈmɑːlɪnspaɪk/ *n* pointed tool used, esp by sailors, to separate strands of rope or wire.

Marlowe /ˈmɑːləʊ/ Christopher (1564-93), English playwright and poet, whose development of blank-verse drama influenced the early plays of Shakespeare. His best-known works are the plays *Tamburlaine the Great*, *The Jew of Malta*, *Edward II* and *Dr Faustus*, and the poem *Hero and Leander*. He was killed in a fight in a tavern.

marmalade /ˈmɑːməleɪd/ *n* [U] type of jam made from citrus fruit, esp oranges.

marmoreal /mɑːˈmɔːrɪəl/ *adj* (*fml*) of or like marble: *marmoreal* (ie white and smooth) *skin.*

marmoset /ˈmɑːməzet/ *n* type of small tropical American monkey with a bushy tail.

marmot /ˈmɑːmət/ *n* type of small burrowing animal of the squirrel family.

maroon[1] /məˈruːn/ *adj, n* [U] (of a) brownish red: *a maroon jacket.*

maroon[2] /məˈruːn/ *v* [Tn usu passive] abandon (sb) in a place from which he cannot escape, eg a desert island: *sailors marooned on a remote island* ○ (*fig*) *Without a car, she was marooned at home for days.*

maroon[3] /məˈruːn/ *n* small rocket that makes a loud bang, used as a warning signal.

marque /mɑːk/ *n* (*fml approv*) (famous or particularly good) make or brand of product, esp of a car: *the Mercedes marque.*

marquee /mɑːˈkiː/ *n* **1** large tent used for garden parties, flower shows, circuses, etc. **2** (*esp US*) canopy over the entrance to a theatre, cinema, hotel, etc.

marquetry /ˈmɑːkɪtrɪ/ *n* [U] pattern of pieces of wood, ivory, etc set into the surface of furniture as decoration.

marquis (also **marquess**) /ˈmɑːkwɪs/ *n* **1** (in the UK) nobleman next in rank above an earl and below a duke. **2** (in other countries) nobleman next in rank above a count. Cf MARCHIONESS.

marram /ˈmærəm/ *n* [U] (also ˈ**marram grass**) *n* type of coarse grass that grows esp in sand-dunes.

marriage /ˈmærɪdʒ/ *n* **1** [U, C] legal union between a man and a woman as husband and wife; state of being married: *an offer of marriage* ○ *After ten years of marriage, they are divorcing.* ○ [attrib] *a marriage feast, settlement* ○ *Her first marriage ended after five years.* **2** [C] ceremony at which a couple are married; wedding: *Her second marriage was held/took place in St John's Church.* ○ *a marriage in a registry office.* ⇨ article at WEDDING. **3** (idm) **give sb in** ˈ**marriage (to sb)** (*fml*) offer (usu one's daughter) as a wife. **take sb in** ˈ**marriage** (*fml*) marry sb.

▷ **marriageable** *adj* (*fml*) old enough to marry; suitable for marriage: *a woman of marriageable age.* **marriageability** /ˌmærɪdʒəˈbɪlətɪ/ *n* [U].

□ ˈ**marriage bureau** organization that arranges meetings between people wanting a husband or a wife.

ˈ**marriage certificate** legal document which shows that two people are married.

ˌ**marriage** ˈ**guidance** advice given by qualified people on the problems of married couples: [attrib] *a marriage guidance counsellor.*

ˈ**marriage licence** licence permitting a legal ceremony of marriage.

ˈ**marriage lines** (*Brit infml*) marriage certificate.

ˌ**marriage of con**ˈ**venience** marriage made not for love, but for the personal benefit of one or both partners.

ˈ**marriage settlement** arrangement that establishes the ownership of property between people about to marry each other.

married /ˈmærɪd/ *adj* **1** (**a**) ~ **(to sb)** having a husband or wife; united in marriage: *a married man, woman, couple, etc* ○ *They like being married.* ○ *be/get married (to sb)* ○ *He's married to a famous writer.* (**b**) [attrib] of marriage; marital: *married life, bliss.* **2** [pred] ~ **to sth** (*fig*) dedicated to sth: *married to one's work.*

marron glacé /ˌmærɒŋ ˈglæseɪ; *US* glæˈseɪ/ (*pl* **marrons glacés** /ˌmærɒŋ ˈglæseɪ; *US* glæˈseɪ/) (*French*) edible chestnut preserved in sugar.

marrow[1] /ˈmærəʊ/ *n* **1** [U] soft fatty substance that fills the hollow parts of human and animal bones. **2** [U] (*fig*) essential part; inner meaning: *the marrow of his statement.* **3** (idm) **to the** ˈ**marrow** right through: *I felt frozen to the marrow.* ○ *She was shocked to the marrow by his actions.*

□ ˈ**marrowbone** *n* bone containing edible marrow: [attrib] *marrowbone jelly.*

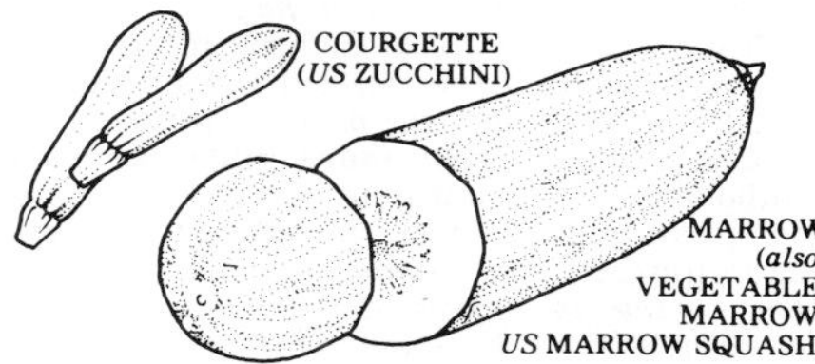

marrow[2] /ˈmærəʊ/ *n* [C, U] (also *Brit* ˈ**vegetable marrow**, *US* **marrow** ˈ**squash**) (**a**) [C] vegetable of the gourd family, with white flesh and green skin. (**b**) [U] its flesh used as food. ⇨ illus.

marrowfat /ˈmærəʊfæt/ *n* (also ˌ**marrowfat** ˈ**pea**) type of large pea.

marry /ˈmærɪ/ *v* (*pt, pp* **married**) **1** [I, Tn] take (sb) as a husband or wife: *They married (when they were) young.* ○ *She didn't marry until she was over fifty.* ○ *He married again six months after the divorce.* **2** [Tn] (of a clergyman or civil official, etc) join (a couple) in marriage at a ceremony: *Which priest is going to marry them?* ○ *They were married by her* (ie the bride's) *father, who's a bishop.* ○ *Jane is going to marry John.* **3** [I, Ipr, Tn, Tn·p] ~ **(sth) with sth** (*fig*) combine (sth) successfully with sth else: *training that marries well with the needs of the job* ○ *She marries wit and/with scholarship in her writing.* **4** (idm) ˌ**marry in** ˈ**haste, re**ˌ**pent at** ˈ**leisure** (*saying*) if one gets married too hurriedly one may regret it for a long time. **marry money** (*infml*) marry a rich person. **5** (phr v) **marry into sth** become a part of (a family, etc) by marrying: *He married into the French aristocracy.* **marry sb off** get rid of (a daughter) by finding a husband for her. **marry up** (*infml*) (of parts) join up or assemble correctly; match(3): *The two halves of the structure didn't marry up.* ○ (*fig*) *The two versions of the story don't quite marry up.*

Marryat /ˈmærɪət/ Captain Frederick (1792-1848), English naval officer and novelist who wrote stories about the sea (eg *Mr Midshipman Easy*) and children's books (eg *The Children of the New Forest*).

Mars /mɑːz/ *n* **1** (in Roman mythology) god of war. **2** (*astronomy*) planet fourth in order from the sun, next to the Earth. It has iron-rich minerals on its surface, which give it a red colour. Grooves and channels, visible from earth, suggest that water may once have existed there.

Marsala /mɑːˈsɑːlə/ *n* [U] light sweet Sicilian dessert wine.

Marseillaise /ˌmɑːseɪˈjeɪz/ **the Marseillaise** national anthem of France.

marsh /mɑːʃ/ *n* [C, U] (area of) low-lying wet land: *miles and miles of marsh* ○ *We had to cross the marshes.*

▷ **marshy** *adj* (**-ier, -iest**) of, like or containing a marsh: *marshy ground, fields, countryside, etc.*

□ ˈ**marsh gas** = METHANE.

ˌ**marsh** ˈ**marigold** plant with yellow flowers that grows in wet areas.

marshal[1] /ˈmɑːʃl/ *n* **1** (usu in compounds) officer of high rank: ˌ*Field-*ˈ*Marshal*, ie in the Army ○ ˌ*Air-*ˈ*Marshal*, ie in the Air Force. ⇨ App 4. **2** official responsible for arranging or controlling crowds at certain public events, eg motor races, ceremonies, etc. **3** (*US*) (**a**) officer with duties similar to a sheriff's. (**b**) head of a police or fire department.

marshal[2] /ˈmɑːʃl/ *v* (**-ll-**; *US* **-l-**) **1** [Tn, Tn·pr] arrange (sb/sth) in proper order; gather: *marshal troops, forces, crowds, etc* ○ *The children were marshalled into straight lines.* ○ (*fig*) *marshal one's facts, thoughts, etc.* **2** (phr v) **marshal sb into, out of, past, etc sth** lead or guide (people) ceremoniously in the specified direction: *marshal people into the presence of the Queen* ○ *marshal them in/out.*

□ ˈ**marshalling yard** railway yard in which goods trains, etc are assembled.

Marshall /ˈmɑːʃl/ George Catlett (1880-1959), American general and diplomat who as Secretary of State (1947-49) introduced the Marshall Plan.

□ **the** ˈ**Marshall Plan** programme of American financial help (**Marshall Aid**) for Europe after the Second World War.

Marshall Islands /ˈmɑːʃl aɪləndz/ country of 34 atolls and islands in the central Pacific; pop approx 45 000; official languages Marshallese and English; capital Majuro; unit of currency US dollar. After German and Japanese colonization, the islands were administered from 1947 by the US within a United Nations Trust Territory of Micronesia. Since 1990 they have been independent except in US-handled defence matters. ⇨ map at MICRONESIA.

marshmallow /ˌmɑːʃˈmæləʊ/ *n* [C, U] soft sweet made from sugar and gelatine.

Marston Moor /ˌmɑːstən ˈmɔː(r); *US* ˈmʊər/ moor near York, N England, where the largest battle of the English *Civil War took place in 1644. The Parliamentarians, under *Cromwell, defeated the Royalists.

marsupial /mɑːˈsuːpɪəl/ *n, adj* (animal) of the class of mammals which includes the kangaroo, the female of which has a pouch on its body to hold its young.

mart /mɑːt/ *n* (*dated*) **1** market: *A model railway mart will be held on Friday.* **2** centre of trade: *London is an international mart for stocks and shares.*

marten /ˈmɑːtɪn; *US* -tn/ *n* **1** [C] small animal of the weasel family. **2** [U] its fur.

Martha /ˈmɑːθə/ (in the Bible) friend of Jesus Christ, who occupied herself with household duties while her sister Mary listened to Jesus.

Martial /ˈmɑːʃl/ (Marcus Valerius Martialis, c 40-c 104 AD), Roman writer of epigrams, short poems with witty endings, on all aspects of Roman life.

martial /ˈmɑːʃl/ *adj* (*fml*) of or associated with war: *martial music.*

□ ˌ**martial** ˈ**arts** fighting sports such as judo and karate.

ˌ**martial** ˈ**law** military rule imposed on a country

temporarily, eg during a rebellion: *declare/impose martial law.*

Martian /ˈmɑːʃn/ *n, adj* (supposed inhabitant) of the planet Mars.

martin /ˈmɑːtɪn; *US* -tn/ *n* bird of the swallow family. Cf HOUSE-MARTIN (HOUSE[1]).

martinet /ˌmɑːtɪˈnet; *US* -tnˈet/ *n* (*usu derog*) person who imposes strict discipline and demands obedience to orders.

Martini (also **martini**) /mɑːˈtiːnɪ/ *n* [C, U] (*propr*) (cocktail made of a) mixture of gin and vermouth: *mix two martinis.*

martyr /ˈmɑːtə(r)/ *n* **1** person who is killed or made to suffer greatly because of his (esp religious) beliefs: *the early Christian martyrs* ○ *She died a martyr in the cause of progress,* ie died trying to achieve progress. **2** (*usu derog*) person who suffers or makes sacrifices, or pretends to do so, in order to be admired or pitied: *He always acts the martyr when he has to do the housework.* ○ *Don't make such a martyr of yourself!* **3** ~ **to sth** (*infml*) constant sufferer from sth: *She's a martyr to rheumatism.*

▷ **martyr** *v* [Tn, usu passive] kill (sb) or make (sb) suffer as a martyr: *He was martyred by the Romans.*

martyrdom /ˈmɑːtədəm/ *n* [U, C] martyr's suffering or death: *suffer martyrdom at the stake,* ie by burning.

marvel /ˈmɑːvl/ *n* **1** [C] wonderful or miraculous thing; thing causing (pleased) astonishment: *the marvels of modern science* ○ *It's a marvel that he escaped unhurt.* **2** [C esp *sing*] ~ **(of sth)** person or thing that is surprisingly good, pleasing, etc: *She works so hard in spite of her illness: she's a marvel!* ○ *He's a marvel of patience.* ○ *Your room is a marvel of neatness and order.* **3 marvels** [pl] wonderful results (used esp with the *vs* shown): *The doctor's treatment has worked marvels: the patient has recovered completely.* ○ *perform/do marvels at the kitchen stove.*

▷ **marvel** *v* (-ll-; *US* -l-) [Ipr, Tf] ~ **at sth** (*fml*) be very surprised (and often admiring): *marvel at sb's boldness* ○ *I marvelled at the maturity of such a young child/at the beauty of the landscape.* ○ *I marvel that she agreed to do something so dangerous.*

marvellous (*US* **marvelous**) /ˈmɑːvələs/ *adj* **1** (*infml*) very good; excellent: *a marvellous writer, car, dog.* **2** astonishing; wonderful: *It's marvellous how he's managed to climb that far.* **marvellously** (*US* **marvelously**) *adv.*

Marvell /ˈmɑːvl/ Andrew (1621-78), English poet. His metaphysical lyrics (eg *To His Coy Mistress*) have earned him a high reputation in the 20th century, but in his own time he was better known as a satirist of *Charles II and his ministers, and as a politician — he was Member of Parliament for Hull.

Marx[1] /mɑːks/ Karl Heinrich (1818-83), German political philosopher and economist. As a student he was a radical follower of *Hegel. With his colleague *Engels he wrote the *Communist Manifesto,* a pamphlet setting out a programme for a workers' socialist revolution. In 1848 he came to live in England, and spent much of the rest of his life developing his theories. The result of his work is the three-volume *Das Kapital,* the fundamental work of Marxist economics.

Marx[2] /mɑːks/ Chico (1891-1961), Harpo (1893-64) and Groucho (1895-1977), known as the Marx Brothers, American comedians, famous for their absurd verbal and visual humour in films like *Duck Soup.* They brought some of the traditions of the circus to the cinema, esp in the clowning musical performances of Chico and Harpo. ⇨ illus.

Marxism /ˈmɑːksɪzəm/ *n* [U] political and economic theory of Karl *Marx, stating that class struggle is the force behind historical change and that capitalism will inevitably be replaced by socialism and a classless society: *Communism is based on Marxism.*

▷ **Marxist** /ˈmɑːksɪst/ *n* supporter of Marxism. — *adj* characterized by, supporting or relating to Marxism: *have Marxist views* ○ *a Marxist government, régime, etc.*

the Marx Brothers

□ **Marxism-Leninism** /-ˈlenɪnɪzəm/ *n* [U] Marxism as developed by Lenin. **Marxist-Leninist** *n, adj.*

Mary /ˈmeərɪ/ (in the Bible) the mother of Jesus. She is also known as the 'Virgin Mary', 'Mary the Virgin' and the 'Blessed Virgin (Mary)'.

Mary Celeste /ˌmeərɪ səˈlest/ ship that was discovered empty in the N Atlantic Ocean in 1872, in perfect condition but with its crew all gone. Their disappearance has never been explained: *It was so quiet and deserted in there — really eerie, just like the Mary Celeste.*

Mary I /ˈmeərɪ/ Mary Tudor (1516-58), queen of England 1553-58. A daughter of *Henry VIII, she tried to restore England to Roman Catholicism, and her persecution of Protestants earned her the nickname 'Bloody Mary'. She married Philip II of Spain but died childless. ⇨ App 3.

Mary II /ˈmeərɪ/ (1662-94), queen of England 1688-94. Daughter of *James II, she married William of Orange, and when he took the English throne, as *William III, she reigned jointly with him. ⇨ App 3.

Maryland /ˈmeərɪlənd/ state of the north-eastern USA, on the Atlantic coast. It was one of the 13 original states of the USA. ⇨ map at App 1.

Mary Magdalene /ˌmeərɪ ˈmægdəlɪn/ Saint. In the Bible she was present when Jesus was crucified, and was the first to see him when he came back from the dead. Jesus cured her of possession by evil spirits. According to tradition she had been a prostitute.

Mary, Queen of Scots /ˌmeərɪ ˌkwiːn əv ˈskɒts/ Mary Stuart (1542-87), queen of Scotland 1542-67. She became queen shortly after her birth, but did not begin to rule in person until 1561. A Roman Catholic, she was unable to control her Protestant lords, and two unsuccessful marriages made her position even more difficult. After her supporters were defeated, she abdicated and fled to England. There were several Roman Catholic plots to make her queen of England in place of *Elizabeth I, so Elizabeth put her in prison and eventually (with some reluctance) had her executed.

Mary Tudor /ˌmeərɪ ˈtjuːdə(r)/ ⇨ MARY I.

marzipan /ˈmɑːzɪpæn, ˌmɑːzɪˈpæn/ *n* [U] thick paste of ground almonds, sugar, etc used to make sweets, decorate cakes, etc.

Masada /məˈsɑːdə/ fortress on a hill near the *Dead Sea, which was besieged by the Romans in 72 AD. Rather than surrender, its defenders (about 1 000 of them) all committed suicide.

Masai /ˈmæsaɪ/ *n* (*pl* unchanged) **1** [C] member of an African people of Tanzania and Kenya, traditionally nomadic breeders of cattle but now adopting a more settled way of life. **2** [U] language of the Masai.

masc *abbr* masculine. Cf FEM.

mascara /mæˈskɑːrə; *US* -ˈskærə/ *n* [U] cosmetic substance for darkening the eyelashes: *apply the mascara thickly.*

mascot /ˈmæskət, -skɒt/ *n* person, animal or thing thought to bring good luck: *The regimental mascot is a goat.* ○ *His little son is the mascot for the local football team.* ⇨ article at SUPERSTITION.

masculine /ˈmæskjʊlɪn/ *adj* **1** having the qualities or appearance thought to be typical of men: *masculine looks, attitudes* ○ *She looks rather masculine in that suit.* **2** (*grammar*) referring to the male gender: *'He' and 'him' are masculine pronouns.*

▷ **masculine** *n* (*grammar*) **1** [C] a masculine(2) word or word form. **2 the masculine** [sing] the class of these: *a French adjective in the masculine.*

masculinity /ˌmæskjʊˈlɪnətɪ/ *n* [U] quality of being masculine. ⇨ Usage at FEMALE.

Masefield /ˈmeɪsfiːld/ John Edward (1878-1967), English poet, best known for his poems about the sea, esp *Sea Fever.* He also wrote adventure novels (eg *Odtaa*) and stories for children (eg *The Box of Delights*). He was Poet Laureate from 1930.

maser /ˈmeɪzə(r)/ *n* device for producing or amplifying microwaves.

mash /mæʃ/ *n* **1** [U] grain, bran, etc cooked in water until soft, used as food for animals. **2 (a)** [U, C] any substance made by crushing sth into a soft mass: *a mash of wet paper and paste.* **(b)** [U] (*infml*) boiled potatoes crushed into a soft mass: *bangers* (ie sausages) *and mash.* **3** [C, U] mixture of malt and hot water used in brewing beer.

▷ **mash** *v* [Tn, Tn·pr, Tn·p] ~ **sth (up)** beat or crush sth into a mash: *mashed potatoes, turnips, etc* ○ *Mash the fruit up (with a fork) so that the baby can eat it.* **masher** *n* cooking utensil for mashing potatoes, etc.

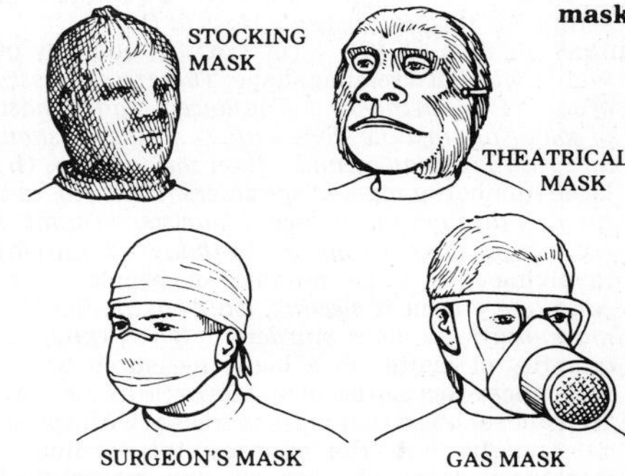

mask[1] /mɑːsk; *US* mæsk/ *n* **1** covering for the face, or part of it, worn as a disguise: *a bank robber wearing a stocking mask.* **2 (a)** likeness of a face carved in wood, ivory, etc, or made of papier mâché, plastic, card, etc: *a child wearing a gorilla mask* ○ *an actor wearing the mask of tragedy,* eg in Greek drama. **(b)** likeness of a face made by taking a mould in wax: *a death mask,* ie such a mould taken when a person is dead. **3** = GAS MASK. ⇨ illus. **4** pad of sterile material worn over the mouth and nose, eg by doctors and nurses during a surgical operation, to protect against infection. ⇨ illus. **5** (usu *sing*) (*fml fig*) thing that hides the truth; pretence: *Her sociable manner is really a mask for a very shy nature.* ○ *He conceals his worries behind a mask of nonchalance.*

mask[2] /mɑːsk; *US* mæsk/ *v* [Tn] **1** cover (the face) with a mask; cover the face of (sb) with a mask: *The thief masked his face with a stocking.* ○ *a masked robber, woman, etc.* **2** (*fig*) conceal (sth); disguise: *mask one's fear by a show of confidence* ○ *This perfume won't mask the unpleasant smell.*

□ ˌ**masked** ˈ**ball** ie formal dance at which masks are worn to disguise the guests.

ˈ**masking tape** adhesive tape used when painting sth to cover up the parts that one does not want to get paint on: *He put masking tape round the edges of the glass while he painted the window frame.*

masochism /ˈmæsəkɪzəm/ *n* [U] **1** getting (esp sexual) pleasure from one's own pain or humiliation. Cf SADISM. **2** (*infml*) apparent enjoyment of sth annoying, painful, etc: *Only a masochist would run five miles before breakfast every day!* ▷ **masochist** /-kɪst/ *n*. **masochistic** /ˌmæsəˈkɪstɪk/ *adj*.

mason /ˈmeɪsn/ *n* **1** person who builds in or works with stone. **2 Mason** Freemason.
▷ **masonic** (also **Masonic**) /məˈsɒnɪk/ *adj* of Freemasons: *masonic ritual*.
masonry /ˈmeɪsənrɪ/ *n* [U] **1** that part of a building that is made of stone and mortar; stonework: *crumbling masonry*. **2 Masonry** Freemasonry.

Mason-Dixon Line /ˌmeɪsn ˈdɪksn laɪn/ **the Mason-Dixon line** (also **the Mason and Dixon Line**) boundary between the northern and southern states of the USA. Originally it was the southern boundary of *Pennsylvania, fixed in the 18th century by the surveyors Charles Mason and Jeremiah Dixon, but during the 19th century it came to be regarded as the line separating the slave-owning South from the North.

masque /mɑːsk; *US* mæsk/ *n* (**a**) [C] verse drama, often with music and dancing, popular in England in the 16th and 17th centuries. (**b**) [U] this theatrical form: *the study of Elizabethan masque*.

masquerade /ˌmɑːskəˈreɪd; *US* ˌmæsk-/ *n* **1** false show; pretence: *Her sorrow is just a masquerade.* **2** formal dance at which masks and other disguises are worn.
▷ **masquerade** *v* [I, Ipr] ~ (**as sth**) pretend to be sth one is not; disguise oneself as sth or sb else: *masquerade as a policeman* ○ *The prince masqueraded as a peasant.* **masquerader** *n*.

Mass (also **mass**) /mæs/ *n* **1** [C, U] celebration of Christ's Last Supper, esp in the Roman Catholic Church: *go to Mass* ○ *hear Mass* ○ *High Mass*, ie with incense, music and much ceremony ○ *The priest says two Masses each day.* **2** [C] musical setting for this: *Beethoven's Mass in D*.

mass /mæs/ *n* **1** [C] ~ (**of sth**) (**a**) quantity of matter without a regular shape: *There were masses of dark clouds in the sky.* ○ *The flowers made a mass of colour against the stone wall.* ○ *A mass of snow and rock broke away and fell on the climbers.* (**b**) large number: *a mass of spectators* ○ *She elbowed her way through the masses of tourists.* ○ (*infml*) *I got masses of cards on my birthday.* **2** [attrib] involving/of a large number of people: *mass education* ○ *a mass meeting, walk-out, audience* ○ *mass murder/a mass murderer.* **3** [U] (*physics*) quantity of matter in a body, measured by its resistance to acceleration by a force (ie its inertia). *Einstein showed that mass increases with speed. ➪ App 12. **4 the masses** [pl] ordinary, working-class people, esp as seen by political leaders or thinkers: *a revolutionary who urged the masses to overthrow the government.* **5** [sing] **the ~ of...** the majority of (people): *The mass of workers do not want this strike.* **6** (idm) **be a mass of sth** be full of or covered with: *The garden was a mass of colour.* ○ *His face was a mass of bruises after the fight.* **in the ˈmass** (*fml*) as a whole: *She says she doesn't like children in the mass.*
▷ **mass** *v* [I, Ipr, Tn, Tn·pr] assemble/gather (sb/sth) into a mass: *clouds massing on the horizon* ○ *The general massed his troops for a final attack.* ○ *the massed pipes and bands of several regiments.*
□ **ˌmass communiˈcations**, **ˌmass ˈmedia** means, such as newspapers, television and radio, of communicating with very large numbers of people.
ˌmass hyˈsteria hysteria that affects many people at the same time.
ˌmass-proˈduce *v* [Tn] manufacture (identical articles) in very large quantities by mechanical processes: *mass-produced cars, fridges, etc.* **ˌmass proˈduction** manufacturing in this way.
ˌmass specˈtrometer apparatus that analyses the composition of a substance by separating atoms and molecules electromagnetically according to their mass.

Massachusetts /ˌmæsəˈtʃuːsɪts/ state of the north-eastern USA, on the Atlantic coast. The *Pilgrim Fathers landed there in 1620. It was one of the 13 original states of the USA. ➪ map at App 1.
□ **MassaˌchusettsˌInstitute of Techˈnology** (*abbr* **MIT**) university in *Cambridge, Massachusetts that has a reputation for academic excellence in science.

massacre /ˈmæsəkə(r)/ *n* **1** cruel killing of a large number (of people or animals): *the massacre of thousands of people for their religious beliefs.* **2** (*infml*) defeat (of a team) by a large number of points, etc: *The game was a 10-0 massacre.*
▷ **massacre** *v* [Tn] **1** kill large numbers of (people or animals). **2** (*infml*) defeat (a team) by a large number of points, etc: *We were massacred in the final.*

massage /ˈmæsɑːʒ; *US* məˈsɑːʒ/ *n* [C, U] (act of) rubbing and pressing the body, usu with the hands, to relieve or prevent stiffness or pain in muscles, joints, etc: *give sb a relaxing massage* ○ *The doctor recommended massage for my back pain.*
▷ **massage** *v* [Tn] **1** give massage to (sb, sb's muscles, etc). **2** (*infml*) alter the way of presenting (data, statistics, etc) so as to make them seem more acceptable: *He accused the government of massaging the unemployment figures.*
masseur /mæˈsɜː(r)/ (*fem* **masseuse** /mæˈsɜːz/) *ns* person who practises massage as a profession.

massif /mæˈsiːf/ *n* compact group of mountain peaks.

massive /ˈmæsɪv/ *adj* **1** (**a**) large, heavy and solid: *a massive monument, rock, etc.* (**b**) (of the features of a person or animal) heavy-looking: *The gorilla had a massive forehead.* **2** substantial; very large: *a massive increase, crowd* ○ *She drank a massive amount of alcohol.* ○ *He suffered a massive* (ie very severe) *heart attack.* ▷ **massively** *adv*. **massiveness** *n* [U].

mast[1] /mɑːst; *US* mæst/ *n* **1** upright post of wood or metal used to support a ship's sails. ➪ illus at YACHT. **2** tall pole, eg for a flag. **3** tall steel structure for the aerials of a radio or TV transmitter. **4** (idm) **at half-mast** ➪ HALF. **before the ˈmast** (*dated or rhet*) serving as an ordinary seaman: *He spent ten years before the mast.* **nail one's colours to the mast** ➪ NAIL *v*.
▷ **-masted** (forming compound *adjs*) having the specified number or type of mast(s): *a two-/three-masted ship* ○ *a tall-masted yacht.*
□ **ˈmast-head** *n* **1** highest part of a mast, often used as a look-out post. **2** display title of a newspaper, etc at the top of the front page.

mast[2] /mɑːst; *US* mæst/ *n* [U] fruit of forest trees, eg the beech, oak, etc, used as food for pigs.

mastectomy /məˈstektəmɪ/ *n* (*medical*) surgical removal of a woman's breast.

master[1] /ˈmɑːstə(r); *US* ˈmæs-/ *n* **1** man who has others working for him or under him; employer: *master and servant* ○ *The slaves feared their master.* Cf MISTRESS[1]. **2** [attrib] skilled workman or one who has his own business: *a master carpenter, builder, etc.* **3** male head of a household: *the master of the house.* **4** captain of a merchant ship: *obtain a master's certificate/ticket*, ie licence that gives the holder the right to be a ship's captain ○ *the master of HMS Britain* ○ [attrib] *a master mariner.* **5** male owner of a dog, horse, etc: *That dog is devoted to his master.* **6** (**a**) (*esp Brit*) male schoolteacher: *the ˈFrench master*, ie person who teaches French ○ *ˈschoolmaster.* (**b**) (esp in compounds) teacher of other subjects taught outside school: *a ˈdancing-master* ○ *riding-master.* **7 Master** holder of the second university degree: *She's a Master of Arts/Sciences.* ○ *a Master of Engineering.* **8 Master** (used as a title for boys too young to be called Mr): *Master Charles Smith.* **9 Master** title of the heads of certain colleges: *the Master of Balliol College, Oxford.* **10** great artist: *a painting by a Dutch master.* **11** (**a**) ~ **of sth** (*fml*) person who has control of sth: *He is master of the situation.* ○ *be master of a subject*, ie know it thoroughly ○ *He has made himself master of the language*, ie He speaks it very well. ○ *You cannot be the master of* (ie decide) *your own fate.* ○ (*dated*) *He is the master of a large fortune*, ie can use it as he wishes. (**b**) person who is superior: *We shall see which of us is master*, eg which of us will win (a fight, competition, etc). ○ *He has met his master*, ie has been overcome, defeated, etc. **12** film, tape, etc from which copies are made: *Take the master and make 20 copies by tomorrow.* ○ [attrib] *the master tape, film, copy, etc.* **13** [attrib] (**a**) commanding; superior; excellent: *This painting is the work of a master hand*, ie a superior and skilful artist. (**b**) overall; complete: *a master plan of the building.* (**c**) main; principal: *the master bedroom* ○ *the master cylinder.* **14** (idm) **one's lord and master** ➪ LORD. **master in one's own ˈhouse** person who can manage his own affairs without interference. (**be**) **one's own ˈmaster/ˈmistress** (be) free and independent: *She likes being her own mistress, and not having to work for someone else.* **serve two masters** ➪ SERVE.
□ **ˈmaster class** lesson, esp in music, given by a famous expert to highly skilled students.
ˈmaster-key *n* (also **ˈpass key**) key made to open many different locks, each also opened by a separate key.
ˈmastermind *n* person who is unusually intelligent, esp one who plans the work of others: *the mastermind behind the project.* — *v* [Tn] plan and/or direct (a scheme, etc): *mastermind a campaign, robbery, project* ○ *A major criminal masterminded the huge fraud.*
ˌMaster of ˈCeremonies (*abbr* **MC**) person in charge of certain social occasions, who introduces guests, etc.
ˌMaster of the ˈRolls (*abbr* **MR**) (in England and Wales) senior judge, presiding over the Court of Appeal. ➪ article at LAW.
ˈmasterpiece *n* task done with great skill, esp an artist's greatest work.
ˈMaster's degree (also **ˈMaster's**) higher degree between a Bachelor of Arts, etc and a Doctor of Philosophy.
ˌmaster ˈsergeant (*US*) senior non-commissioned officer in the army, air force, or marines. ➪ App 4.
ˈmaster-stroke *n* very skilful act which ensures success: *Settling the dispute needed a diplomatic master-stroke.*
ˈmaster-switch *n* switch controlling a supply, esp of electricity, to an entire system.

master[2] /ˈmɑːstə(r); *US* ˈmæs-/ *v* [Tn] **1** gain control of (sth); overcome (sth): *master one's temper, feelings, etc.* **2** gain considerable knowledge of or skill in (sth): *master a foreign language* ○ *She has fully mastered the technique.* ○ *He has mastered the saxophone.*

masterful /ˈmɑːstəfl; *US* ˈmæs-/ *adj* able to control others; dominating: *a masterful person, character, tone* ○ *speak in a masterful manner.* ▷ **masterfully** /-fəlɪ/ *adv*.

masterly /ˈmɑːstəlɪ; *US* ˈmæs-/ *adj* (*approv*) very skilful: *their masterly handling of a difficult situation.*

mastery /ˈmɑːstərɪ/ *n* [U] **1** ~ (**of sth**) (complete) knowledge; great skill: *demonstrate a mastery of Arabic* ○ *She showed complete mastery in her handling of the discussion.* **2** ~ (**over sb/sth**) control: *Which side will get the mastery?* ○ *gain mastery (over an opponent).*

mastic /ˈmæstɪk/ *n* [U] **1** gum or resin from the bark of certain trees, used in making varnish. **2** type of pliable cement used for waterproofing joints in window-frames, roofs, etc.

masticate /ˈmæstɪkeɪt/ *v* [I, Tn] (*fml*) chew (food).
▷ **mastication** /ˌmæstɪˈkeɪʃn/ *n* [U].

mastiff /ˈmæstɪf/ *n* type of large strong dog with drooping ears, often used as a watchdog.

mastitis /mæˈstaɪtɪs/ *n* [U] (*medical*) inflammation, usu with swelling, of the breast or udder.

mastodon /ˈmæstədɒn/ *n* large animal like an elephant, now extinct.

mastoid /ˈmæstɔɪd/ *n* part of a bone behind the ear.
▷ **mastoiditis** /ˌmæstɔɪˈdaɪtɪs/ *n* [U] inflammation of the mastoid.

Mastroianni /mæstrɔɪˈænɪ/ Marcello (1924-),

Italian actor famous for the subtlety and sensitivity of his performances. He has appeared in many of the films of *Fellini, including *La Dolce Vita*.

masturbate /ˈmæstəbeɪt/ *v* [I, Tn] give (oneself/sb) sexual pleasure by stimulating the genitals, esp by hand. ▷ **masturbation** /ˌmæstəˈbeɪʃn/ *n* [U]. **masturbatory** /ˌmæstəˈbeɪtərɪ; *US* -bəˈtɔ:rɪ/ *adj* [usu attrib]: *masturbatory fantasies*.

mat[1] /mæt/ *n* **1** (**a**) piece of material, made of straw, rushes, fibre, etc, used to cover part of a floor: *a* ˈ*doormat*. (**b**) thick pad, usu of foam, rubber, etc, used in gymnastics or wrestling for competitors to land on. **2** small piece of material placed under a hot dish, or a glass, vase, etc to protect the surface underneath: *a cork* ˈ*table-mat* ○ *a beer mat*. **3** mass of things tangled thickly together: *a mat of weeds, hair, threads*.

▷ **mat** *v* (-tt-) [I, Tn esp passive] (cause sth to) become thickly tangled or knotted: *matted hair*.

mat[2] = MATT.

matador /ˈmætədɔ:(r)/ *n* bullfighter whose task is to fight and kill the bull.

match[1] /mætʃ/ *n* short piece of wood or pasteboard with a head made of material that bursts into flame when rubbed against a rough or specially prepared surface: *strike a match* ○ *a box of matches* ○ *put a match to sth*, ie set it alight.

□ ˈ**matchbox** *n* box for holding matches.

ˈ**matchstick** *n* stem of a match: *two thin legs, like matchsticks*.

ˈ**matchwood** *n* [U] **1** wood suitable for making matches. **2** splinters or small pieces of wood: *a boat smashed to matchwood*, ie completely broken up.

match[2] /mætʃ/ *n* **1** [C] game in which individuals or teams compete against each other; contest: *a* ˈ*football,* ˈ*wrestling, etc match* ○ *a* ˈ*boxing match of twenty rounds*. ⇨ Usage at SPORT. **2** [sing] ~ **for sb; sb's** ~ person equal to sb else in skill, strength, etc: *He's no match for her (in tennis).* ○ *She's his match* (ie as good as or better than him) *when it comes to chess.* **3** [C] marriage: *She made a good match when she married him.* **4** [sing] (**a**) ~ (**for sb/sth**) person or thing combining well with another: *The new curtains are a perfect match for the carpet.* (**b**) ~ (**of sb/sth**) person or thing similar or identical to another: *I've found a vase that's an exact match of the one we already have.* **5** (idm) **find/meet one's match (in sb)** meet sb who has as much skill, determination, etc as oneself, and perhaps more: *He thought he could beat anyone at tennis, but he's met his match in her.* **a good, bad, etc match** (*dated*) person considered as a suitable, unsuitable, etc husband or wife: *The young heiress was a good match.* **the man of the match** ⇨ MAN. **a slanging match** ⇨ SLANG *v*.

▷ **matchless** *adj* unequalled: *matchless beauty, skill, etc*.

□ ˈ**matchmaker** *n* person who likes trying to arrange marriages for others. ˈ**matchmaking** *n* [U].

ˈ**match play** (in golf) form of play in which the match is won by the player or team winning the greater number of holes. Cf MEDAL PLAY (MEDAL).

ˌ**match** ˈ**point** final point needed to win a match, eg in tennis.

match[3] /mætʃ/ *v* **1** [I, Tn] (**a**) combine well with (sth), esp in colour: *The curtains and the carpets match perfectly.* ○ *These curtains won't match your carpet.* ○ (*fig*) *a well-matched couple.* (**b**) be like or correspond to (sth else): *a brown dress and gloves to match.* **2** [Tn] find sth that is like or corresponds to (sth else): *Can you match this wallpaper?* **3** [Tn] (**a**) be equal to (sb): *No one can match her at chess.* ○ *The two players are well-matched*, ie roughly equal in ability. (**b**) find (sb/sth) equal to sb/sth else: *Can you match that story?* ie Can you tell one that is equally good, amusing, etc? **4** [Tn·pr] ~ **sb/sth with sb/sth** find sb/sth that fits or corresponds to sb/sth else: *We try to match the applicants with appropriate vacancies.* **5** (phr v) **match sth/sb against/with sth/sb** cause sth/sb to compete with sth/sb else: *I'm ready to match my strength against yours.* ○ *Match your skill against the experts in this quiz.* **match up** be in agreement; tally: *The two statements don't match up.* **match sth up (with sth)** fit sth (to sth else) to form a complete whole: *matching up the torn pieces of the photograph.* **match up to sb/sth** be as good as or equal to sb/sth: *The film didn't match up to my expectations.*

mate[1] /meɪt/ *n* **1** (**a**) (*infml*) (male) friend, companion or fellow-worker: *He's an old mate of mine.* ○ *I'm off for a drink with my mates.* (**b**) (*Brit sl*) (used as a form of address to a man): *Where are you off to, mate?* (**c**) (in compounds) person participating in the same named activity, organization, etc or sharing the same accommodation: *my room-mate/flat-mate* ○ *her team-mates, class-mates, playmates.* **2** (in job names) assistant of a skilled workman: *a plumber's mate.* **3** (in the merchant navy) ship's officer below the rank of captain: *the chief mate*, ie ranking just below the captain ○ *the first/second/third mate.* **4** (**a**) either of a pair of birds or animals: *The blackbird sat on the nest waiting for the return of her mate.* (**b**) (*infml*) husband or wife.

mate[2] /meɪt/ *v* [I, Ipr, Tn, Tn·pr] ~ **(sth) (with sth)** (of birds or animals) (cause to) come together to have sexual intercourse and produce young: *Pandas rarely mate (with each other) in captivity.* ○ *Our bitch should produce a fine litter. We mated her with John's dog.* ▷ **mating** *n* [U]: [attrib] *the mating season*, ie time when birds, etc mate.

mate[3] /meɪt/ *n* = CHECKMATE.

material[1] /məˈtɪərɪəl/ *n* **1** [C, U] substance or things from which sth else is or can be made; thing with which sth is done: *raw materials for industry*, eg iron ore, oil, etc ○ *building materials*, eg bricks, timber, sand ○ *writing materials*, eg pens, paper, ink ○ *We use high-quality raw material for our goods.* ○ (*fig*) *He is not officer material*, ie will not become a good officer. **2** [U, C] fabric; cloth: *enough material to make two dresses* ○ *tough cotton material* ○ *We sell the best materials.* **3** [U] facts, information, etc to be used in writing a book, as evidence, etc: *She's collecting material for a newspaper article.*

material[2] /məˈtɪərɪəl/ *adj* **1** [attrib] composed of or connected with physical substance rather than the mind or spirit: *the material world.* **2** [attrib] of bodily comfort; of physical needs: *our material needs*, eg food and drink ○ *You think too much of material comforts.* Cf SPIRITUAL 1. **3** ~ **(to sth)** (*esp law*) important; essential; relevant: *material evidence* ○ *The witness held back material facts*, ie ones that might influence a decision. ○ *Is this point material to your argument?*

▷ **materially** /-ɪəlɪ/ *adv* in a significant way; essentially: *This isn't materially different from the old system.*

materialism /məˈtɪərɪəlɪzəm/ *n* [U] **1** (*usu derog*) obsession with material possessions, bodily comforts, etc while neglecting spiritual values: *the rampant materialism of modern society.* **2** (*philosophy*) theory or belief that only material things exist.

▷ **materialist** /məˈtɪərɪəlɪst/ *n* **1** person excessively interested in material things. **2** believer in materialism(2).

materialistic /məˌtɪərɪəˈlɪstɪk/ *adj* of materialism: *a materialistic person, theory, society.* **materialistically** /-klɪ/ *adv*.

materialize, -ise /məˈtɪərɪəlaɪz/ *v* [I] **1** become a reality; happen: *Our plans did not materialize.* ○ *The threatened strike never materialized.* **2** take bodily form; become visible; appear: *He claimed that he could make ghosts materialize.* ○ (*infml*) *He failed to materialize*, ie did not come. ▷ **materialization, -isation** /məˌtɪərɪəlaɪˈzeɪʃn; *US* -lɪˈz-/ *n* [U].

maternal /məˈtɜ:nl/ *adj* **1** of or like a mother: *maternal affection, feelings, duties, etc* ○ *She feels very maternal towards him.* **2** [attrib] related through the mother's side of the family: *my maternal grandfather, aunt, etc.* Cf PATERNAL. ▷ **maternally** /-nəlɪ/ *adv*.

maternity /məˈtɜ:nətɪ/ *n* [U] motherhood: [attrib] *a maternity dress*, ie one for a pregnant woman ○ *a maternity ward, hospital, etc*, ie for women who have just given birth.

matey /ˈmeɪtɪ/ *adj* ~ **(with sb)** (*infml*) sociable; familiar; friendly: *Don't get too matey with him — he's a rogue.*

mathematics /ˌmæθəˈmætɪks/ *n* [sing or pl *v*] (also *Brit infml* **maths** /mæθs/ [sing or pl *v*]; *US* **math** /mæθ/[sing *v*]) science of numbers, quantity and space, of which eg arithmetic, algebra, trigonometry and geometry are branches: *His mathematics are weak*, ie He is not very good at doing calculations, etc. ○ *Maths is her strongest subject.* ○ *I don't understand the mathematics* (eg the complicated calculations) *here.*

▷ **mathematical** /ˌmæθəˈmætɪkl/ *adj* of mathematics: *a mathematical calculation, formula, etc.* **mathematically** /-klɪ/ *adv*: *She's not mathematically inclined*, ie not interested in mathematics.

mathematician /ˌmæθəməˈtɪʃn/ *n* expert in mathematics.

Matilda /məˈtɪldə/ (1102-67), queen of England for a few months in 1135. She was the only legitimate child of *Henry I, but soon after she came to the throne, *Stephen overthrew her.

matinée (*US* also **matinee**) /ˈmætneɪ; *US* ˌmætnˈeɪ/ *n* afternoon performance at a cinema or theatre: [attrib] *a matinée idol*, ie an actor greatly admired by women.

matins (also **mattins**) /ˈmætɪnz; *US* ˈmætnz/ *n* [sing or pl *v*] service of morning prayer, esp in the Church of England. Cf VESPERS.

Matisse /mæˈti:s/ Henri Emile Benoît (1869-1954), French painter whose style, based on simple flowing lines and rich colour, has had a considerable influence on 20th-century art.

matri- *comb form* of a mother: *matricide* ○ *matriarch.* Cf PATRI-.

matriarch /ˈmeɪtrɪɑ:k/ *n* female head of a family or tribe. Cf PATRIARCH.

▷ **matriarchal** /ˌmeɪtrɪˈɑ:kl/ *adj*: *a matriarchal society, tribe, etc.*

matriarchy /ˈmeɪtrɪɑ:kɪ/ *n* type of society in which women are the heads of families, own property and have most of the authority.

matrices *pl* of MATRIX.

matricide /ˈmætrɪsaɪd/ *n* **1** [C, U] (act of) killing one's own mother. **2** [C] person who does this. Cf PATRICIDE.

matriculate /məˈtrɪkjʊleɪt/ *v* [I, Tn] be admitted or admit (sb) as a student to a university.

▷ **matriculation** /məˌtrɪkjʊˈleɪʃn/ *n* [C, U] (instance of) matriculating or being matriculated.

matrimony /ˈmætrɪmənɪ; *US* -məʊnɪ/ *n* [U] (*fml*) state of being married; marriage: *unite a couple in holy matrimony.*

▷ **matrimonial** /ˌmætrɪˈməʊnɪəl/ *adj* [usu attrib] of matrimony: *a matrimonial dispute, problem, etc.*

$$\begin{pmatrix} 3 & 12 & 8 \\ 4 & 8 & 13 \\ 12 & 9 & 3 \end{pmatrix}$$

matrix

matrix /ˈmeɪtrɪks/ *n* (*pl* **matrices** /ˈmeɪtrɪsi:z/ or ~**es**) **1** mould into which molten metal, liquid, etc is poured to form shapes for eg printer's type, gramophone records, etc. **2** mass of rock, etc in which minerals, etc are found in the ground. **3** place where sth begins or develops: *bacteria growing in a matrix of nutrients.* **4** (*mathematics*) arrangement of numbers, symbols, etc in a rectangular grid, treated as a single quantity in mathematical operations. ⇨ illus. **5** (*computing*) group of circuit elements arranged to look like a lattice or grid.

□ ˈ**matrix printer** (*computing*) printer that forms the letter, number, etc to be printed from an arrangement of tiny dots.

matron /ˈmeɪtrən/ *n* **1** woman who manages the domestic affairs of a school, etc. **2** (formerly) woman in charge of the nurses in a hospital (now called a *senior nursing officer*). **3** middle-aged or

elderly married woman, esp one with a dignified appearance.
▷ **matronly** *adj* like or suitable for a matron(3); sedate: *a matronly manner.*
□ ˌ**matron of ˈhonour** (*esp US*) married woman acting as a bride's attendant at a wedding.

matt, mat (*US* also **matte**) /mæt/ *adj* (of surfaces, eg paper, photographs) not shiny or glossy; dull: *Will this paint give a gloss or a matt finish?* Cf GLOSS[1] 1.

matter[1] /ˈmætə(r)/ *n* **1** [C] (**a**) affair, topic or situation being considered: *the heart/core/crux/root etc of the matter* ○ *the matter in hand, under discussion, etc* ○ *a matter I know little about* ○ *ˈmoney matters* ○ *I don't discuss private matters with my colleagues.* ○ *We have several important matters to deal with at our next meeting.* ○ (*ironic*) *There's the small matter of the money you owe me.* (**b**) ~ **of sth** (**to sb**) situation, problem or result that arouses the specified emotion: *matters of growing public concern* ○ *This discussion is on a matter of considerable interest to me.* **2** [U] (**a**) physical substance in general (contrasted with mind or spirit): *inert matter* ○ *to study the properties of matter* ○ *The universe is composed of matter.* (**b**) substance, material or things of a specified kind: *decaying vegetable matter* ○ *waste matter*, eg human excreta ○ *reading matter*, ie books, newspapers, etc ○ *printed matter*, ie forms, leaflets, etc. **3** [U] (*fml*) ideas or topic of a book, speech, etc (contrasted with its language or style). **4** [U] discharge from the body; pus. **5** (idm) **as a matter of fact** (used for emphasis) in reality; to tell the truth: *I'm going there tomorrow, as a matter of fact.* **be no laughing matter** ⇨ LAUGHING. **for ˈthat matter** (used to indicate that a second category, topic, etc is as relevant as the first): *Don't talk like that to your mother, or to anyone else for that matter.* **in the matter of sth** (*dated fml*) concerning sth: *I want to speak to her in the matter of my salary.* **it's all, only, etc a matter of ˈtime** (**before . . .**) this consequence is inevitable though it may not happen immediately: *It's simply a matter of time before the rebels are crushed.* **let the matter ˈdrop/ˈrest** stop mentioning sth or trying to change it: *She reluctantly agreed to let the matter drop.* **make matters ˈworse** make an already difficult situation more difficult: *Her attempts to calm them down only made matters worse.* (**as**) **a matter of ˈcourse** (as) a regular habit or usual procedure: *I check my in-tray every morning as a matter of course.* (**be**) **the matter** (**with sb/sth**) (*infml*) the reason for unhappiness, pain, problems, etc (used esp as in the expressions shown): *What's the matter with him?* ○ *Is anything the matter?* ○ *There's nothing the matter with it.* **a matter of ˈhours, ˈminutes, ˈdays, etc; a matter of ˈpounds, ˈfeet, ˈounces, etc** (**a**) not more than: *I'll be back in a matter of hours.* ○ *It's a matter of a few more miles, that's all.* (**b**) not less than: *It may be a matter of months before it's ready.* ○ *You realize it'll be a matter of days* (ie two days or more) *before we get news?* **a** ˌ**matter of** ˌ**life and ˈdeath** issue that is crucial to survival, success, etc: *Of course this must have priority — it's a matter of life and death.* **a matter of oˈpinion** issue on which there is disagreement: *'She's a fine singer.' 'That's a matter of opinion.'* (**be**) **a matter of sth/doing sth** situation, question or issue that depends on sth else: *Dealing with these problems is all a matter of experience.* ○ *Success in business is simply a matter of knowing when to take a chance.* **mind over matter** ⇨ MIND[1]. **no matter; be/make no matter** (**to sb**) (**that/whether . . .**) be of no importance (to sb): *'I can't do it.' 'No matter, I'll do it myself.'* ○ *It's no matter to me whether you arrive early or late.* **no matter who, what, where, etc** whoever, whatever, wherever, etc: *Don't open the door, no matter who comes.* ○ *Don't trust him, no matter what he says.* **not mince matters/words** ⇨ MINCE. **take matters into one's own hands** take action oneself rather than waiting for others to act.
□ ˌ**matter-of-ˈfact** *adj* showing no emotion or imagination: *She told us the news in a very* ˌ*matter-of-fact* ˈ*way.*

matter[2] /ˈmætə(r)/ *v* [I, Ipr] ~ (**to sb**) (used esp in negative sentences and questions; in sentences containing *what, who, where, if*, etc, usu with *it* as the subject) be important: *What does it matter (whether he comes or goes)?* ○ *Some things matter more than others.* ○ *Does it matter if we're a bit late?* ○ *It doesn't matter to me what you do.*

Matterhorn /ˈmætəhɔːn/ **the Matterhorn** mountain with a distinctive pointed peak in the *Alps, on the border between Switzerland and Italy. It is 4477 m (14688 ft) high.

Matthew /ˈmæθjuː/ **1** Saint (1st century AD), one of Christ's apostles. He was originally a tax-collector from Capernaum in *Galilee. **2** first gospel in the New Testament, named after St Matthew but not written by him.

matting /ˈmætɪŋ/ *n* [U] rough woven material used for making mats or for packing goods: *floors covered with coconut-matting.*

mattins = MATINS.

mattock /ˈmætək/ *n* heavy tool with a long handle and a metal head, one end of which is sharp and the other blunt, used for breaking up soil, cutting roots, etc.

mattress /ˈmætrɪs/ *n* fabric case filled with soft or springy material (eg wool, hair, feathers, foam rubber, etc) and used for sleeping on. ⇨ illus at FURNITURE.

mature[1] /məˈtjʊə(r); *US* -ˈtʊər/ *adj* **1** (**a**) fully grown or developed mentally or physically; having achieved one's full potential: *a mature person, oak, starling* ○ *a house with a mature garden*, ie one where the plants, trees, etc are fully grown and well established ○ *He's not mature enough to be given too much responsibility.* (**b**) (of wine or cheese) having reached a stage where its flavour has fully developed. **2** (of thought, intentions, etc) careful and thorough: *after mature consideration.* **3** (*commerce*) (of insurance policies, etc) due for payment.
▷ **maturely** *adv.*
maturity /məˈtjʊərətɪ; *US* -ˈtʊə-/ *n* [U] state of being mature: *reach maturity.*

mature[2] /məˈtjʊə(r); *US* -ˈtʊər/ *v* **1** [I, Tn] (cause sb/sth to) become mature: *Her character matured during these years.* ○ *cheese/wine that matures slowly* ○ *My plan gradually matured.* ○ *Experience has matured him greatly.* **2** [I] (*commerce*) (of insurance policies, etc) become due.
▷ **maturation** /ˌmætʃʊˈreɪʃn/ *n* [U, C] process of becoming or being made mature: *a slow maturation.*

maudlin /ˈmɔːdlɪn/ *adj* foolishly or tearfully sentimental or self-pitying, esp when drunk.

Maugham /mɔːm/ (William) Somerset (1874-1965), English short-story writer and novelist. His novels include *Of Human Bondage* and *The Razor's Edge*, but he is best known for his short stories (eg *Rain* and *The Alien Corn*), in many of which he cynically observes human frailties.

maul /mɔːl/ *v* **1** [Tn, Tn·p] ~ **sb/sth** (**about**) handle sb/sth roughly or brutally: (*fig*) *Her novel has been badly mauled by the critics.* **2** [Tn] injure (a person or an animal) by tearing his or its flesh: *He died after being mauled by a tiger.*

maulstick /ˈmɔːlstɪk/ (also **mahlstick** /ˈmɑːlstɪk/) *n* stick held by a painter in one hand to support the other hand, which holds the brush.

Mau Mau /ˈmaʊ maʊ/ secret African terrorist organization operating in Kenya between 1953 and 1957 with the aim of gaining independence from Britain.

maunder /ˈmɔːndə(r)/ *v* [I, Ip] **1** ~ (**on**) talk in a rambling way: *The drunk sat there maundering (on) about his troubles.* **2** ~ (**about**) move around listlessly or idly: *Don't just maunder about: do some work!*

Maundy /ˈmɔːndɪ/ *n* [U] **1** giving of specially made coins by the British sovereign to a certain number of old people in a religious ceremony on Maundy Thursday. **2** (also **ˈMaundy money**) these coins.
□ ˌ**Maundy ˈThursday** the Thursday before Easter.

Maupassant /ˈməʊpæsɒŋ; *US* ˌməʊpəˈsɑːn/ Guy de (1850-93), French short-story writer and novelist. His work is in the naturalistic style pioneered by *Zola. He wrote over 300 short stories, portraying a wide range of French society. The best known is *Boule de Suif*.

Mauritania /ˌmɒrɪˈteɪnɪə; *US* ˌmɔːrəˈt-/ country in NW Africa, to the west of Mali; pop approx 1077000; official language Arabic; capital Nouakchott; unit of currency ouguiya (= 5 khoums). Formerly a French colony, it became independent in 1961. The northern part is mainly desert, but the south is more fertile. ⇨ map at ALGERIA. ▷ **Mauritanian** *adj, n.*

Mauritius /məˈrɪʃəs/ island and country in the Indian Ocean, to the east of Madagascar; pop approx 1077000; official language English; capital Port Louis; unit of currency rupee (= 100 cents). Successively colonized by the Netherlands, France and Britain, it became independent in 1968. Its main export is sugar, and tourism is also important. ▷ **Mauritian** /məˈrɪʃn/ *adj, n.*

mausoleum /ˌmɔːsəˈliːəm/ *n* large, finely built tomb.

mauve /məʊv/ *adj, n* (of a) pale purple colour.

maverick /ˈmævərɪk/ *n* **1** (*US*) unbranded calf. **2** person with independent or unorthodox views: *Politically, she's a bit of a maverick.*

maw /mɔː/ *n* (*fml*) animal's stomach or throat: (*fig*) *swallowed up in the maw of battle.*

mawkish /ˈmɔːkɪʃ/ *adj* sentimental in a feeble or sickly way. ▷ **mawkishly** *adv.* **mawkishness** *n* [U].

max /mæks/ *abbr* maximum: *temperature 60° max.* Cf MIN 1.

maxim /ˈmæksɪm/ *n* saying that expresses a general truth or rule of conduct, eg 'Waste not, want not'.

maximize, -ise /ˈmæksɪmaɪz/ *v* [Tn] **1** increase (sth) as much as possible: *We must maximize profits.* **2** make the best use of (sth): *maximize one's opportunities.* Cf MINIMIZE. ▷ **maximization, -isation** /ˌmæksɪmaɪˈzeɪʃn; *US* -mɪˈz-/ *n* [U].

maximum /ˈmæksɪməm/ *n* (*pl* **maxima** /ˈmæksɪmə/) (*abbr* **max**) greatest amount, size, intensity, etc possible or recorded: *obtain 81 marks out of a maximum of 100* ○ *The July maximum* (ie the highest temperature recorded in July) *was 30°C.* ○ *This hall holds a maximum of seventy people.* Cf MINIMUM.
▷ **maximal** /ˈmæksɪml/ *adj* [usu attrib] as great as can be achieved: *She obtained maximal benefit from the course.*
maximum *adj* [attrib] as high, great, intense, etc as possible: *the maximum temperature, voltage, volume* ○ *The maximum load for this lorry is one ton.*

Maxwell /ˈmækswel/ James Clerk (1831-79), Scottish physicist. His electromagnetic theory had a major influence on the development of modern theoretical physics. He also worked on thermodynamics, the theory of Saturn's rings, and colour vision. In 1861 he demonstrated one of the earliest colour photographs.

May /meɪ/ *n* [U, C] the fifth month of the year, next after April: *the first of May* ○ *go on holiday in May.* For the uses of *May* see the examples at *April.*
□ **ˈMay Day** 1st of May, celebrated as a spring festival and, in some countries, as a day for socialist and labour demonstrations. Cf MAYDAY.
ˈMay-beetle, **ˈMay-bug** *ns* = COCKCHAFER.
ˈmayfly *n* short-lived insect that appears in May.
ˈmaypole *n* decorated pole around which people dance on May Day.

may[1] /meɪ/ *modal v* (*neg* **may not**, *rare contracted form* **mayn't** /ˈmeɪənt/; *pt* **might** /maɪt/, *neg* **might not**, *rare contracted form* **mightn't** /ˈmaɪtnt/) **1** (indicating permission): *You may come if you wish.* ○ *May I come in?* ○ *Passengers may cross by the footbridge.* ⇨ Usage 1. **2** (indicating possibility): *This coat may be Peter's.* ○ *That may or may not be true.* ○ *He may have* (ie Perhaps he has) *missed his train.* ○ *This medicine may cure your cough.* ⇨ Usage 2. **3** (indicating purpose): *I'll write today so that he may know when to expect us.* ⇨ Usage 3. **4** (*dated*) (asking for information):

Well, who may ˈ*you be?* ○ *How old may* ˈ*she be?* ⇨ Usage 4. **5** (used to express wishes and hopes): *May you both be very happy!* ○ *Long may she live to enjoy her good fortune!*

NOTE ON USAGE: **1** PERMISSION (**can**[2], **could**[1], **may**[1], **might**[1]) (**a**) British speakers normally use **can** to give or request permission: *You can come if you want to.* ○ *Can I come too?* **Could** is more polite but is only used in questions: *'Could I use your telephone?' 'Yes, of course.'* **May** is formal: *You may come if you wish.* However, US speakers often use **may** where British English has **can**: *May I sit down?* Both British and US speakers use **could** or **might** to suggest doubt, shyness, etc: *Might I suggest another time?* ○ *Could I arrange a meeting with the director?* (**b**) In indirect questions, **can** becomes **could** and **may** becomes **might**: *John asked if he could/might come too.* **2** POSSIBILITY (**can**[2], **could**[1], **may**[1], **might**[1]) (**a**) **Could** or **might** express more doubt or hesitation than **may**: *That may be our taxi now!* ○ *That could/might be our taxi (but I doubt it).* (**b**) In questions and negative sentences **can** replaces **may**. Compare: *It may be Bill's.* ○ *Can it be Bill's?* ○ *It can't be Bill's.* (**c**) **Could have, may have** or **might have** are used to show the possibility of something having happened in the past: *She could have forgotten to tell him.* ○ *He may have lost his way.* ○ *He might just possibly have lost his keys.* **3** PURPOSE (**may**[1], **would**[1]) (**a**) **May** can be used after *so that, in order that,* to express present purpose: *I'll write so that he may know when to expect us.* (**b**) To indicate a purpose in the past, **might** or **would** are used: *I wrote so that he might/would know when to expect us.* ○ *He died so that others might/would live.* **4** ASKING FOR INFORMATION (**may**[1], **might**[1]) (**a**) **May** (rather dated) and **might** are used to request information in an uncertain or a superior way: *Well, and who may/might* ˈ*you be?* (**b**) In indirect questions, only **might** is used: *Bill asked who* ˈ*she might be.*

may[2] /meɪ/ *n* [U] hawthorn blossom.

Maya /ˈmɑːjə/ *n* (*pl* unchanged or ~**s**) (**a**) (also **Mayan**) [C] member of an American Indian people of Yucatan and Central America who still retain aspects of their ancient culture and civilization. This was at its height from the 4th to the 8th centuries with a spectacular flowering of art and learning. Stone temples built on pyramids remain from this period. (**b**) (usu **the Maya**) [pl] this people. (**c**) [U] their language.
▷ **Maya** (also **Mayan**) *adj* of the Maya or their language.

maya /ˈmɑːjə/ *n* [U] **1** (in Hinduism) supernatural or magical power used by gods and demons. **2** (in Hindu and Buddhist philosophy) power creating the illusion that the world is real.

maybe /ˈmeɪbiː/ *adv* **1** perhaps; possibly: *Maybe he'll come, maybe he won't.* ○ *'Is that true?' 'Maybe, I'm not sure.'* **2** (idm) **as soon as maybe** ⇨ SOON.

mayday (also **Mayday**) /ˈmeɪdeɪ/ *n* (*radio*) international distress signal, used by ships and aircraft: [attrib] *a mayday call/signal.* Cf SOS.

Mayer /ˈmeɪə(r)/ Louis B(urt) (1885-1967), American film producer. With Samuel *Goldwyn and Marcus Loew he founded Metro-Goldwyn-Mayer (MGM), the studios whose successful films included *Gone With the Wind.*

Mayfair /ˈmeɪfeə(r)/ fashionable area of west central London, containing expensive shops, galleries, hotels, etc.

Mayflower /ˈmeɪflaʊə(r)/ ship in which the Pilgrim Fathers sailed from Plymouth to N America in order to found a colony in New England. It arrived at Cape Cod on 21 November 1620.

mayhem /ˈmeɪhem/ *n* [U] **1** violent disorder or confusion; havoc: *There was absolute mayhem when the farmer's bull got into the village hall.* **2** (*dated or US*) crime of maiming a person: *commit mayhem.*

mayn't /ˈmeɪənt/ *contracted form* may not ⇨ MAY[1].

mayonnaise /ˌmeɪəˈneɪz; *US* ˈmeɪəneɪz/ *n* [U] (**a**) thick creamy sauce made with egg-yolks, oil and vinegar, used esp on cold foods, eg salads. (**b**) dish made with this: *Egg mayonnaise is made with mayonnaise and hard-boiled eggs.*

mayor /meə(r); *US* ˈmeɪər/ *n* head of the council of a city or borough, usu elected yearly.
▷ **mayoral** /ˈmeərəl; *US* ˈmeɪə-/ *adj* [attrib] of a mayor or mayoress: *mayoral robes, duties.*
mayoralty /ˈmeərəltɪ; *US* ˈmeɪər-/ *n* (period of) office of a mayor.
mayoress /meəˈres; *US* ˈmeɪərəs/ *n* **1** (also ˌ**lady** ˈ**mayor**) woman holding the office of mayor. **2** mayor's wife or other woman helping a mayor or mayoress(1) to perform mayoral duties.

maze

maze /meɪz/ *n* (usu *sing*) **1** network of paths or hedges designed as a puzzle in which one must find one's way: *We got lost in Hampton Court maze.* ⇨ illus: (*fig*) *A maze of narrow alleys leads down to the sea.* **2** confused collection or complicated mass (of facts, etc): *finding one's way through the maze of rules and regulations.* Cf LABYRINTH.

mazurka /məˈzɜːkə/ *n* (piece of music for a) lively Polish dance for four or eight couples.

MB /ˌem ˈbiː/ *abbr* Bachelor of Medicine: *have/be an MB* ○ *Philip Watt MB, ChB.*

MBA /ˌem biː ˈeɪ/ *abbr* Master of Business Administration: *have/be an MBA* ○ *Marion Strachan MBA.*

MBE /ˌem biː ˈiː/ *abbr* (*Brit*) Member (of the Order) of the British Empire: *be made an MBE* ○ *William Godfrey MBE.* Cf CBE, KBE, MBE.

MC /ˌem ˈsiː/ *abbr* **1** master of ceremonies. Cf EMCEE. **2** (*US*) Member of Congress: *Senator Karl B Kaufman (MC).* **3** (*Brit*) Military Cross: *be awarded the/an MC for bravery.*

MCC /ˌem siː ˈsiː/ *abbr* (*Brit*) Marylebone Cricket Club (the former governing body of English cricket, and owner of Lord's cricket ground).

McCarthy /məˈkɑːθɪ/ Joseph ('Joe') Raymond (1908-57), American politician who as chairman of a Senate investigating committee accused many Americans of being Communists and of being disloyal to America. This encouraged a public mood in which left-wing people were persecuted.
▷ **McCarthyism** /məˈkɑːθɪɪzəm/ *n* [U] (*derog*) persecution of left-wing people (such as was) encouraged by Joe McCarthy.

McCartney /məˈkɑːtnɪ/ (James) Paul (1942-), English pop musician who was one of the *Beatles pop group. With John *Lennon he wrote many of their songs (eg 'She Loves You' and 'Yesterday'), and since the Beatles disbanded he has continued to write and perform songs solo or with other groups..

McCoy ⇨ THE REAL McCOY (REAL[1]).

MCP /ˌem siː ˈpiː/ *abbr* (*infml*) male chauvinist pig.

MD /ˌem ˈdiː/ *abbr* **1** Doctor of Medicine (Latin *Medicinae Doctor*): *be an MD* ○ *D W Walker MD.* **2** (*infml*) Managing Director: *the MD's office.* **3** mentally deficient.

Md *symb* mendelevium.

MDT /ˌem diː ˈtiː/ *abbr* (*US*) Mountain Daylight Time. Cf MST.

me[1] /miː/ ⇨ Guide to Entries 5.2. *pers pron* (used as the object of a *v* or of a *prep*; also used independently or after *be*) person who is the speaker or writer: *Don't hit me.* ○ *Give it to me.* ○ *Hello, it's me.* ○ *'Who's there?' 'Only me.'* Cf I[2].

me[2] /miː/ *n* (*music*) = MI.

mead[1] /miːd/ *n* [U] alcoholic drink made from fermented honey and water.

mead[2] /miːd/ *n* (*arch*) meadow.

meadow /ˈmedəʊ/ *n* [C, U] (area or field of) grassland, esp used for growing hay; (area of) low, often boggy, land near a river: *cattle grazing in the meadows* ○ *20 acres of meadow.*
□ ˈ**meadow lark** type of N American songbird.
ˈ**meadowsweet** *n* [U] plant with large masses of small sweet-smelling creamy-white flowers.

meagre (*US* **meager**) /ˈmiːgə(r)/ *adj* **1** small in quantity and poor in quality: *a meagre meal of bread and cheese* ○ *her meagre contribution to our funds* ○ *Our appeal for help met with a meagre response.* **2** thin; lacking in flesh: *the meagre faces of the starving children.* ▷ **meagrely** *adv.* **meagreness** *n* [U].

meal[1] /miːl/ *n* **1** occasion when food is eaten: *be present at all family meals* ○ *breakfast, the first meal of the day.* **2** food eaten on such an occasion: *a meal of fish and chips* ○ *eat a big meal,* ie a lot of food for one meal. **3** (idm) **make a** ˈ**meal of sth** (*infml*) give sth more attention, effort, etc than it deserves or needs: *She always makes such a meal of it — I could do it in half the time!* **a square meal** ⇨ SQUARE[1].
□ ˌ**meals-on-**ˈ**wheels** *n* [pl] (*Brit*) service, usu provided by a women's voluntary organization, by which meals are taken by car to old or sick people in their own homes. ⇨ article at RETIREMENT.
ˈ**meal-ticket** *n* **1** (*US*) = LUNCHEON VOUCHER (LUNCHEON). **2** (*infml fig*) person, position, etc that provides a basic income: *His rich wife is his meal ticket.*
ˈ**mealtime** *n* time at which a meal is usu eaten.

meal[2] /miːl/ *n* [U] (often in compounds) coarsely ground grain: ˈ*oatmeal.*
▷ **mealy** *adj* (**-ier, -iest**) **1** of, like, containing or covered with meal. **2** (of boiled potatoes) dry and powdery.

mealie /ˈmiːlɪ/ *n* (*S African*) **1 mealies** [pl] maize. **2** [C] ear of maize.

mealy-mouthed /ˌmiːlɪˈmaʊðd/ *adj* (*derog*) not willing to speak plainly: *Don't be so mealy-mouthed, say what you mean!*

mean[1] /miːn/ *v* (*pt, pp* **meant** /ment/) **1** [Tn, Tn·pr, Tf] ~ **sth** (**to sb**) (intend to) convey sth; signify sth: *A dictionary tells you what words mean.* ○ *What does this sentence mean?* ○ *These symbols mean nothing to me.* ○ *The flashing lights mean that the road is blocked.* **2** [Tn, Tf, Tg, Tsg] (be likely to) result in (sth) ; be a sign (that); involve: *Spending too much now will mean a shortage of cash next year.* ○ *The sudden thaw means that spring is here.* ○ *This new order will mean (us) working overtime.* **3** (**a**) [Tn, Tn·pr, Tf no passive, Tt, Tnt, Cn·n/a, Dn·n, Dn·pr] ~ **sth for sb**; ~ **sth** (**as sth**); ~ **sth** (**to sb**) have sth as a purpose; intend sth: *What does she mean by cancelling her performance?* ie Why has she done it? ○ *He means what he says,* ie is not joking, exaggerating, etc. ○ *Don't laugh! I mean it!* ie I am serious. ○ *He means (to cause) trouble.* ○ *She meant this gift for you.* ○ *I never meant that you should come alone.* ○ *She means to succeed.* ○ *I'm sorry I hurt you: I didn't mean to.* ○ *I wasn't serious. I meant it as a joke.* ○ *I didn't mean you to read the letter.* ○ *You're meant to* (ie You are supposed to) *pay before you come in.* ○ *I mean you no harm.* ○ *He means no harm to anyone.* (**b**) [Tn, Tf no passive] intend to say (sth) on a particular occasion: *What did he mean by that remark?* ○ *Do you mean Miss Anne Smith or Miss Mary Smith?* ○ *Did he mean (that) he was dissatisfied with our service?* **4** [Tn·pr esp passive, Tnt] ~ **sb for sth** intend or destine sb to be or do sth: *I was never meant for the army,* ie did not have the qualities needed to become a soldier. ○ *She was never meant to be a teacher.* ○ *His father meant him to be an engineer.* **5** [Tn·pr no passive] ~ **sth to sb** be of value or importance to sb: *Your friendship means a great deal to me.* ○ *£20 means a lot* (ie seems to be a lot of money) *to a poor person.* ○ *Money means nothing to him.* ○ *You don't know how much you mean to me,* ie how much I like you. **6** (idm) **mean** ˈ**business** (*infml*) be serious in one's intentions: *He means business: he really will shoot us if we try to escape.* **mean ˈmischief** intend to do sth wrong or harmful. **ˈmean well** (*derog*) have good intentions, though perhaps not the will or ability to carry them out: *He's hopelessly inefficient, but I suppose he means well.* **mean well by sb** have kindly intentions towards sb.

mean[2] /miːn/ *adj* (**-er**, **-est**) **1** ~ (**with sth**) ungenerous; selfish (esp with money): *be very mean with money* ○ *She's too mean to make a donation.* **2** ~ (**to sb**) (of people or their behaviour) unworthy; unkind: *That was a mean trick!* ○ *It was mean of you to eat all the food.* ○ *Don't be so mean to your little brother!* ○ *I feel rather mean for not helping more.* **3** (*esp US*) nasty; vicious: *A rattlesnake is a really mean creature.* ○ *He looks like a mean character.* **4** poor in appearance, quality, etc; shabby-looking: *the mean little houses where the poorest people live.* **5** (esp of the understanding or abilities) inferior: *This should be clear even to the meanest intelligence.* **6** (*dated*) of humble birth or low social rank: *The meanest labourer has the same rights as the richest landowner.* **7** (*infml approv*) very skilful, effective, etc: *a mean golfer, chess-player, etc* ○ *a new tennis champion with a mean service.* **8** (idm) **no mean sth** (*approv*) a very good or great performer or performance: *She's no mean chess player.* ○ *That was no mean achievement.*

▷ **meanie** (also **meany**) /ˈmiːnɪ/ *n* (*joc*) ungenerous person: *Give me some more, you meanie!*

meanly *adv.*

meanness *n* [U].

mean[3] /miːn/ *n* **1** condition, quality, course of action, etc that is halfway between two extremes: *You must find a mean between frankness and rudeness.* **2** (*mathematics*) midway point, quantity, etc between two extremes; average: *The mean of 13, 5 and 27 is found by adding them together and dividing by 3.* **3** (idm) **the happy/golden mean** a moderate course of action.

▷ **mean** *adj* [attrib] midway between two extremes; average: *the mean annual temperature.* **ˌmean ˈsea-level** level of the sea half-way between high tide and low tide.

meander /mɪˈændə(r)/ *v* **1** [I] (of a river, etc) follow a winding course, flowing slowly. **2** [I, Ipr, Ip] (**a**) (of a person) wander aimlesssly: *meander through the park* ○ *meander around/along.* (**b**) (*fig*) (of conversation) proceed in an aimless way; ramble: *The discussion meandered (on) for hours.*

▷ **meander** *n* (usu *pl*) winding bend of a river, etc.

meanderingly /mɪˈændrɪŋlɪ/ *adv.*

meanderings /mɪˈændrɪŋz/ *n* [pl] winding course; aimless wandering.

meaning /ˈmiːnɪŋ/ *n* **1** [U, C] what is conveyed or signified; sense: *You can't say that these sounds have no meaning.* ○ *a word with many distinct meanings* ○ *signals with certain fixed meanings.* **2** [U] purpose; significance: *My life seems to have lost all meaning.* ○ *a glance full of meaning.*

▷ **meaning** *adj* full of meaning; significant: *a meaning look, gesture, etc.*

meaningful /-fl/ *adj* full of purpose; significant: *a meaningful relationship, discussion, look.*

meaningfully /-fəlɪ/ *adv.*

meaningless *adj* without sense or motive: *meaningless chatter* ○ *meaningless violence.*

means[1] /miːnz/ *n* [sing or pl *v*] **1** action by which a result is brought about; method(s): *use illegal means to get a passport* ○ *This money wasn't earned by honest means.* ○ *There is no means of finding out what happened.* ○ *All possible means have been tried.* **2** (idm) **by ˈall means** (*fml*) yes, of course; certainly: *'Can I see it?' 'By all means.'* **by fair means or foul** ⇨ FAIR[1]. **by means of sth** (*fml*) by using sth; with the help of sth: *lift the load by means of a crane.* **by no manner of means** ⇨ MANNER. **by ˈno means; not by ˈany means** (*esp fml*) not at all: *She is by no means poor: in fact, she's quite rich.* **the end justifies the means** ⇨ END[1]. **a ˌmeans to an ˈend** thing or action not important in itself but as a way of achieving sth: *He regarded his marriage merely as a means to an end: he just wanted his wife's wealth.* **ways and means** ⇨ WAY[1].

means[2] /miːnz/ *n* [pl] **1** money; wealth; resources: *a man of means*, ie a wealthy man ○ *She lacks the means to support a large family.* ○ *A person of your means can afford it.* **2** (idm) **live beyond/within one's means** ⇨ LIVE[2].

□ **ˈmeans test** official inquiry into a person's wealth or income before support is given from public funds (eg unemployment benefit).

meant *pt, pp* of MEAN[1].

meantime /ˈmiːntaɪm/ *adv* meanwhile: *I continued working. Meantime, he went out shopping.*

▷ **meantime** *n* (idm) **in the ˈmeantime** meanwhile: *The next programme starts in five minutes: in the meantime, here's some music.*

meanwhile /ˈmiːnwaɪl; *US* -hwaɪl/ *adv* in the time between two events; at the same time: *She's due to arrive on Thursday. Meanwhile, what do we do?* ○ *I went to college. Meanwhile, all my friends got well-paid jobs.*

measles /ˈmiːzlz/ *n* [sing *v*] infectious disease, esp of children, with a fever and small red spots that cover the whole body. Cf GERMAN MEASLES (GERMAN).

measly /ˈmiːzlɪ/ *adj* (*infml derog*) ridiculously small in size, amount or value: *He gave us measly little portions of cake.* ○ *What a measly birthday present!*

measure[1] /ˈmeʒə(r)/ *v* **1** (**a**) [I, Ip, Tn, Tn·pr, Tn·p] ~ (**sth**) (**up**) find the size, length, volume, etc of (sth) by comparing it with a standard unit: *Can you measure accurately with this ruler?* ○ *First measure (it) up, then cut the timber to the correct length.* ○ *measure the width of a door, the level of an electric current, the speed of a car* ○ *The tailor measured me (up) for a suit*, ie measured my chest, arms, legs, etc. (**b**) [Tn] (*fig*) assess (sth); gauge: *It's hard to measure his ability when we haven't seen his work.* **2** [In/pr] be (a certain size, length, volume, etc): *The room measures 10 metres across.* **3** [Tn] carefully consider (sth): *He's a man who measures his words.* ○ *She failed to measure the effect of her actions on her family.* **4** [Tn·pr] ~ **sth against/with sth/sb** test sth through competition, conflict, etc: *measure one's strength against sb else* ○ *You have to measure your determination with that of other people.* **5** (idm) **measure one's ˈlength** (*joc*) fall flat on the ground. **measure one's strength** (**with/against sb**) compete with sb to see who is the stronger. **6** (phr v) **measure sth off** mark out a length or lengths of sth: *She measured off two metres of cloth.* **measure sth out** give a measured quantity of sth: *measure out a dose of medicine.* **measure up** (**to sth**) reach the standard required or expected: *The discussions didn't measure up (to my expectations).*

▷ **measurable** /ˈmeʒərəbl/ *adj* **1** that can be measured. **2** noticeable; significant: *There's been a measurable improvement in his work.*

measurably /-əblɪ/ *adv.*

measured *adj* **1** (of language) carefully considered: *measured words.* **2** slow and with a regular rhythm: *with a measured tread* ○ *with measured steps.*

measureless *adj* that cannot be measured; limitless.

measurement *n* **1** [U] measuring: *the metric system of measurement.* **2** [C usu *pl*] width, length, etc found by measuring: *What is your waist measurement?* ○ *The measurements of the room are 20 feet by 15 feet.* ○ *The width measurement is 80 cm.*

□ **ˈmeasuring-tape** *n* = TAPE-MEASURE (TAPE).

measure[2] /ˈmeʒə(r)/ *n* **1** (**a**) [U, C] standard or system used in stating the size, quantity or degree of sth: *liquid measure* ○ *dry measure* ○ *Which measure of weight do pharmacists use?* ⇨ App 10. (**b**) [C] unit used in such a standard or system: *The metre is a measure of length.* **2** [C] standard quantity of sth: *a measure of grain*, eg a bushel ○ *a measure of whisky*, ie in England usu $\frac{1}{6}$ gill, in Scotland usu $\frac{1}{5}$. **3** [C] instrument such as a rod, tape or container marked with standard units, used for testing length, volume, etc: *The barman uses a small silver measure for brandy.* **4** [sing] ~ **of sth** way of assessing sth: *His resignation is a measure of how angry he is.* ○ *Words cannot always give the measure of one's feelings*, ie show how strong they are. **5** [sing] ~ **of sth** degree of sth; some: *She achieved a measure of success with her first book.* **6** [C usu *pl*] action taken to achieve a purpose: *measures against crime* ○ *safety measures* ○ *The authorities took measures to prevent tax fraud.* ○ *The government has suggested measures* (ie proposed laws) *to reduce crime.* **7** [C] layer of rock containing minerals; seam(2): *coal measures.* **8** [U] (*dated*) verse-rhythm; metre; tempo of a piece of music. **9** (idm) **beyond ˈmeasure** (*fml*) very great(ly): *Her joy was beyond measure.* ○ *He fascinates me beyond measure.* **for good ˈmeasure** as an extra amount of sth or as an additional item: *The pianist gave a long and varied recital, with a couple of encores for good measure.* **get/take the measure of sb** assess sb's character or abilities: *It took the tennis champion a few games to get the measure of his opponent.* **give full/short ˈmeasure** give exactly/less than the correct amount: *I'm sure the shopkeeper gave me short measure when she weighed out the potatoes.* **ˌhalf ˈmeasures** policy that lacks thoroughness: *This job must be done properly — I want no half measures.* **in great, large, some, etc ˈmeasure** (*fml*) to a great, some, etc extent or degree: *His failure is in great/large measure due to lack of confidence.* ○ *Her success is in no small measure the result of luck.* **make sth to ˈmeasure** make (a garment) after taking individual measurements: *Do you make suits to measure?* ○ *a made-to-measure suit.*

meat /miːt/ *n* **1** [U, C] flesh of animals, esp mammals rather than fish or birds, used as food: *meat-eating animals* ○ *fresh meat*, ie from a recently killed animal ○ *frozen meat*, ie meat frozen to keep it in good condition ○ *cooked meat* ○ [attrib] *a meat pie* ○ *a joint/slice of meat* ○ (*joc*) *a skinny boy without much meat on him.* **2** [U] edible part inside the hard inedible outer part of sth (eg a nut). **3** [U] chief or important part (of sth): *This chapter contains the meat of the writer's argument.* **4** [U] (*arch*) food in general: *meat and ˈdrink.* **5** (idm) **meat and ˈdrink to sb** source of great enjoyment to sb; what sb lives for: *Scandal and gossip are meat and drink to him.*

▷ **meaty** *adj* (**-ier**, **-iest**) **1** (**a**) like meat: *a meaty smell, taste, etc.* (**b**) full of meat: *a meaty pork chop* ○ *a meaty steak pie.* **2** (*fig*) important; significant: *a meaty book, discussion.*

□ **ˈmeatball** *n* small ball of minced meat or sausage-meat.

Mecca /ˈmekə/ **1** city in Saudi Arabia, birthplace of Muhammad and the spiritual centre of Islam: Thousands of Muslim pilgrims visit it each year and Muslims face towards it when they pray. **2** [C] (also **mecca**) place that very many people wish to visit, esp people with a shared interest: *This exhibition is a mecca for stamp collectors.* ○ *Stratford-on-Avon, the Mecca of tourists in Britain.*

Meccano /mɪˈkɑːnəʊ/ *n* (*propr*) [U] child's construction set of small metal or plastic parts for making mechanical models: *build a crane out of Meccano* ○ [attrib] *a Meccano model crane.*

mechanic /mɪˈkænɪk/ *n* worker skilled in using or repairing machines or tools: *a ˈcar mechanic.*

mechanical /mɪˈkænɪkl/ *adj* **1** of, connected with, produced by or operated by a machine or machines: *I have little mechanical knowledge*, ie I know little about machines. ○ *mechanical power, transport, engineering* ○ *a mechanical device, toy, etc.* Cf MANUAL. **2** (**a**) (of people) acting (as if) without thinking, in a machine-like way: *She was quite mechanical and unthinking in the way she ironed the shirts.* (**b**) (of actions) done (as if) without thought; automatic: *a mechanical movement, gesture, response, etc.*

▷ **mechanically** /-klɪ/ *adv* in a mechanical way: *mechanically-operated equipment* ○ *He performed the movements very mechanically.*

□ **meˌchanical adˈvantage** ratio of the force produced by a machine to the effort applied to it to make it produce the force.

mechanics /mɪˈkænɪks/ *n* **1** [sing *v*] (**a**) science that deals with the movement of objects and with the forces that act on moving and stationary objects: *a course in mechanics.* (**b**) science of machinery. **2 the mechanics** [pl] (**a**) working parts (of sth): *The mechanics of the pump are very old.* (**b**) (*fig*) processes by which sth is done or operates: *The mechanics of staging a play are very complicated.*

mechanism /ˈmekənɪzəm/ *n* **1** working parts of a machine, etc: *a delicate watch mechanism* ○ *the firing mechanism of a rifle.* **2** parts of an organism or system which work together: *the mechanisms of the body.* **3** method or procedure for getting things done: *There are no mechanisms for transferring funds from one department to another.*

mechanistic /ˌmekəˈnɪstɪk/ *adj* of the theory that all things in the universe are the result of physical and chemical processes: *a mechanistic explanation of the origin of life.*

mechanize, -ise /ˈmekənaɪz/ *v* [I, Tn] change (a process, factory, etc) so that it is run by machines rather than people, etc: *We are mechanizing rapidly.* ○ *mechanize a factory, procedure* ○ *highly mechanized industrial processes* ○ *mechanized forces* ○ *a mechanized army unit*, ie equipped with tanks, armoured cars, etc, rather than eg horses.
▷ **mechanization, -isation** /ˌmekənaɪˈzeɪʃn; *US* -nɪˈz-/ *n* [U].

Med /med/ *n* **the Med** [sing] (*infml*) the Mediterranean Sea: *The ship was returning home after a tour of duty in the Med.*

MEd /ˌem ˈed/ *abbr* Master of Education: *have/be an MEd* ○ *Janet White MEd.*

med *abbr* = M *abbr* 1.

medal /ˈmedl/ *n* flat piece of metal, usu shaped like a coin and stamped with words and a design, which commemorates an event etc, or is awarded to sb for bravery, sporting achievement, etc: *present/award medals for long service* ○ *win a silver medal for shooting.*
▷ **medallist** (*US* **medalist**) /ˈmedəlɪst/ *n* person who has been awarded a medal, eg for sporting achievement: *an Olympic gold medallist.*
□ ˈ**medal play** (in golf) form of play in which the match is won by the player who takes the lowest number of strokes to complete all the holes. Cf MATCH PLAY (MATCH[2]).

medallion /mɪˈdæliən/ *n* (**a**) large medal. (**b**) thing similar in shape, eg a piece of jewellery, design on a carpet, cut of meat, etc: *medallions of veal.*

meddle /ˈmedl/ *v* [I, Ipr] (*derog*) (**a**) ~ (**in sth**) interfere (in sth that is not one's concern): *You're always meddling.* ○ *Don't meddle in my affairs.* (**b**) ~ (**with sth**) handle sth that one ought not to, or about which one has no specialized knowledge: *Who's been meddling with my papers?* ○ *Don't meddle with the electrical wiring: you're not an electrician.*
▷ **meddler** *n* person who meddles.
meddlesome /-səm/ *adj* (*fml*) fond of or in the habit of meddling: *Get rid of that meddlesome fool!*

Medea /mɪˈdiːə/ (in Greek mythology) princess with magical powers who helped Jason to obtain the Golden Fleece. She avenged herself on him when he deserted her by killing their two children.

media /ˈmiːdiə/ *n* **the media** [pl] means of mass communication, eg TV, radio, newspapers: *a book that is often mentioned in the media* ○ *The media are to blame for starting the rumours.* ○ [attrib] *a media personality* ○ *good media coverage of the event.* ⇨ Usage at DATA.

mediaeval = MEDIEVAL.

medial /ˈmiːdiəl/ *adj* (*fml*) **1** situated in the middle: *occupy a medial position.* **2** of average size. ▷ **medially** /-iəli/ *adv.*

median /ˈmiːdiən/ *adj* (*mathematics*) situated in or passing through the middle: *a median point, line, value.*
▷ **median** *n* (*mathematics*) **1** straight line drawn from a corner of a triangle to the middle of the opposite side. **2** middle number or point in a series. **3** (in statistics) middle value of a set of values when arranged in order.
□ ˌ**median** ˈ**strip** (*US*) = CENTRAL RESERVATION (CENTRAL).

mediate /ˈmiːdieɪt/ *v* **1** [I, Ipr] ~ (**between sb and sb**) act as a peacemaker or go-between for two or more people, groups, etc who disagree: *mediate in an industrial dispute* ○ *mediate between two countries which are at war.* **2** [Tn] bring about (sth) by doing this: *mediate a peace, settlement, etc.*
▷ **mediation** /ˌmiːdiˈeɪʃn/ *n* [U]: *All offers of mediation were rejected.*
mediator *n* person, organization, etc that mediates.

medic /ˈmedɪk/ *n* (*infml*) medical student or doctor.

Medicaid /ˈmedɪkeɪd/ *n* [U] US government health insurance scheme for the poor. Cf MEDICARE. ⇨ articles at HEALTH, SOCIAL SECURITY.

medical /ˈmedɪkl/ *adj* **1** of the art of medicine; of curing disease: *a medical student, school* ○ *medical skill, treatment, etc* ○ *a medical examination*, ie to discover sb's state of health ○ *a medical practitioner*, ie a doctor ○ *a medical certificate*, ie one that states whether one is healthy or not. **2** of treatment (of disease) that does not involve surgery: *The hospital has a medical ward and a surgical ward.*
▷ **medical** *n* (*infml*) thorough physical examination (eg before joining the army): *have a medical.*
medically /-kli/ *adv*: *medically sound.*
□ ˈ**medical officer** (also **director of public health**) person in charge of health services.
ˈ**medical orderly** = ORDERLY[2].

medicament /məˈdɪkəmənt/ *n* (*fml*) substance used in or on the body to cure illness.

Medicare /ˈmedɪkeə(r)/ *n* [U] US government scheme providing medical care, esp for old people. Cf MEDICAID. ⇨ articles at HEALTH, SOCIAL SECURITY.

medicated /ˈmedɪkeɪtɪd/ *adj* containing a medicinal substance: *medicated shampoo, soap, gauze, etc.*
▷ **medication** /ˌmedɪˈkeɪʃn/ *n* **1** [U] adding or giving of medicinal substances: *need, prescribe, administer medication.* **2** [C] medicinal substance; medicine: *What is the best medication for this condition?*

Medici /ˈmedɪtʃɪ/ Italian family, the most important one in Florence during the 15th century, esp during the lifetimes of Cosimo (1389-1464) and Lorenzo (1449-92). The family became Grand Dukes of Tuscany in the 16th century. Two of its members became Popes (Leo X and Clement IV) and two were married to kings of France (Catherine to Henry II, Marie to Henry IV).

medicinal /məˈdɪsɪnl/ *adj* having healing properties; (used for) healing: *medicinal herbs* ○ *a medicinal preparation* ○ *used for medicinal purposes.*

medicine /ˈmedsn; *US* ˈmedɪsn/ *n* **1** [U] (art and science of the) prevention and cure of disease, esp by drugs, diet, etc, but sometimes including surgery also: *study medicine at the university* ○ *practise medicine* ○ *a Doctor of Medicine* ○ *ethical problems in medicine.* **2** [C, U] (type of) substance, esp one taken through the mouth, used in curing disease: *Has nurse given you your medicine?* ○ *Don't take too much medicine.* ○ *cough medicine(s).* **3** (idm) **some, a little, a taste, etc of one's own** ˈ**medicine** the same bad treatment one has given to others: *The smaller boys badly wanted to give the bully a dose of his own medicine.* **take one's** ˈ**medicine (like a** ˈ**man)** (*esp joc*) submit to punishment, sth unpleasant, etc (without complaining): *He really hates shopping but he goes anyway, and takes his medicine like a man.*
□ ˈ**medicine chest** chest or box containing medicines, bandages, etc.
ˈ**medicine-man** *n* = WITCH-DOCTOR (WITCH).

medico /ˈmedɪkəʊ/ *n* (*pl* ~**s**) (*infml*) medical student or doctor.

medieval (also **mediaeval**) /ˌmediˈiːvl; *US* ˌmiːd-, *also* mɪˈdiːvl/ *adj* of the Middle Ages, about AD 1100-1400: *medieval history, literature, etc* ○ *The conditions were positively medieval*, ie very primitive.

Medina /meˈdiːnə/ oasis in NW Arabia, the second holiest city of Islam and the place where Muhammad is buried. Cf MECCA.

mediocre /ˌmiːdiˈəʊkə(r), *also* ˌmed-/ *adj* not very good; second-rate: *His films are mediocre.* ○ *a mediocre actor, display, meal.*
▷ **mediocrity** /ˌmiːdiˈɒkrəti, *also* ˌmed-/ *n* **1** [U] quality of being mediocre: *His plays are distinguished only by their stunning mediocrity.* **2** [C] person who is mediocre in ability, personal qualities, etc: *a government of mediocrities.*

meditate /ˈmedɪteɪt/ *v* **1** [I, Ipr] ~ (**on/upon sth**) think deeply, esp about spiritual matters: *I meditate in order to relax.* ○ *meditate on the sufferings of Christ.* **2** [Tn, Tg] (*fml*) plan (sth) in one's mind; consider: *meditate revenge, mischief, etc* ○ *She is meditating leaving home.*
▷ **meditation** /ˌmedɪˈteɪʃn/ *n* **1** [U] deep thought, esp about spiritual matters: *religious meditation* ○ *Meditation is practised by some Eastern religions.* **2** [C usu *pl*] ~ (**on sth**) (usu written) expression of deep thought: *meditations on the causes of society's evils.*
meditative /ˈmedɪtətɪv; *US* -teɪt-/ *adj* of meditation; engrossed in thought: *a meditative mood* ○ *You're looking very meditative today.*
meditatively *adv.*

Mediterranean Sea /ˌmedɪtəˈreɪniən ˈsiː/ **the Mediterranean Sea** sea between southern Europe and N Africa, connected with the Atlantic Ocean by the Strait of Gibraltar and with the Red Sea by the Suez Canal.
▷ **Mediterranean** *adj* of or like the Mediterranean Sea or the countries, etc bordering it: *a Mediterranean(-type) climate.*

medium /ˈmiːdiəm/ *n* (*pl* ~**s** or **media** /ˈmiːdiə/) **1** (*pl* usu **media**) means by which sth is expressed or communicated: *Commercial television is an effective medium for advertising.* ○ *She chose the medium of print* (eg published a book) *to make her ideas known.* ○ *The artist chose the medium of oil* (ie used oil paints) *for the portrait.* ○ *In this country English is the medium of instruction*, ie all subjects are taught in English. **2** (*pl* **mediums**) something that is in the middle between two extremes: *find the medium between severity and leniency.* **3** (*pl* usu **media**) substance or surroundings in which sth exists or moves or is transmitted: *bacteria growing in a sugar medium* ○ *Sound travels through the medium of air.* **4** (*pl* **mediums**) person who claims to be able to communicate with the spirits of the dead. ⇨ Usage at DATA. **5** (idm) **a/the happy medium** ⇨ HAPPY.
▷ **medium** *adj* [usu attrib] in the middle between two amounts, extremes, etc; average: *a man of medium height* ○ *a medium-sized firm* ○ *clothes to be washed at medium temperature.*
□ ˈ**medium wave** (*abbr* **MW**) (*radio*) radio wave with a length of between 100 and 1000 metres: [attrib] *a medium-wave station, broadcast, etc.*

medlar /ˈmedlə(r)/ *n* (**a**) fruit like a small brown apple, eaten when it begins to decay. (**b**) tree on which this grows.

medley /ˈmedli/ *n* **1** piece of music made up of passages from other musical works. **2** mixture of people or things of different kinds: *the medley of races in Hawaii.*
□ ˌ**medley** ˈ**relay** swimming relay race between teams in which each team member swims a different stroke.

medulla /mɪˈdʌlə/ *n* (*anatomy*) **1** central part of an animal organ that differs from the outer part, esp the marrow of a bone or the substance within the spinal cord: *the medulla of the kidney.* Cf CORTEX. **2** (also **me**ˌ**dulla oblon**ˈ**gata** /ɒblɒŋˈɡɑːtə/) hindmost part of the brain ⇨ illus at BRAIN. ▷ **medullary** *adj.*

Medusa /mɪˈdjuːsə/ (in Greek mythology) one of the Gorgons. She was the only mortal one and was killed by Perseus, who cut off her head.

medusa /mɪˈdjuːsə/ *n* (*pl* **-ae** or ~**s**) jellyfish.

meek /miːk/ *adj* (**-er, -est**) humble and obedient; submissive: *She's as meek as a lamb.* ▷ **meekly** *adv*: *He meekly did everything he was told to.* **meekness** *n* [U].

meerschaum /ˈmɪəʃəm/ *n* (also ˌ**meerschaum** ˈ**pipe**) tobacco pipe with a bowl made of a type of white clay.

meet[1] /miːt/ *v* (*pt, pp* **met** /met/) **1** (**a**) [I, Ip, Tn] come face to face with (sb); come together: *Goodbye till we meet again.* ○ *We write regularly but seldom meet (up)*, ie see each other. ○ *We met (each other) quite by chance.* ○ *I met her in the street.* ○ (*fig*) *A terrible scene met their eyes as they entered the room.* (**b**) [I] come together formally for discussion, etc: *The Cabinet meets regularly.* ○ *The Debating Society meets on Fridays.* (**c**) [Tn no passive] (*fig*) experience (sth unpleasant); encounter: *meet disaster, one's death, etc* ○ *meet a problem, difficulty, etc.* **2** [I, Tn no passive] make the acquaintance of (sb); be introduced to (sb): *I know Mrs Hill by sight, but we've never met.* ○ *He's an interesting man, would you like to meet him?* ○ *Meet my wife Susan*, ie as an informal style of introduction. ○ *Pleased to meet you.* **3** [Tn] go to a place and await the arrival of (a person, train, etc): *Will you meet me at the station?* ○ *I'll meet your bus.* ○ *The hotel bus meets all the trains.* **4** [I, Tn no passive] come together with (sb) as opponent(s) in a contest, etc: *The champion and the challenger meet next week.* ○ *City met United in the final last year, and City won.* **5** [I, Tn] come into contact with (sth); touch; join: *Their hands met.* ○ *His hand met hers.* ○ *The vertical line meets the horizontal one here.* ○ *These trousers won't meet* (ie fasten) *round my waist any more!* **6** [Tn] fulfil (a demand, etc); satisfy: *meet sb's wishes, conditions, needs, etc* ○ *Can we meet all their objections?* **7** [Tn] pay (sth): *meet all the expenses, bills, etc* ○ *The cost will be met by the company.* **8** (idm) **find/meet one's match** ⇨ MATCH[2]. **make ends meet** ⇨ END[1]. **meet the ˈcase** be adequate or satisfactory: *This proposal of yours hardly meets the case.* **meet sb's ˈeye** look into sb's eyes: *She was afraid to meet my eye.* **meet the ˈeye/ˈear** be seen/heard: *All sorts of strange sounds met the ear.* **meet sb half-ˈway** make a compromise with sb: *If you can drop your price a little, I'll meet you half-way.* **meet one's ˈMaker** (*esp joc*) die: *Poor Fred: he's gone to meet his Maker.* **ˌmeet one's Waterˈloo** lose a decisive contest. **there is more in/to sb/sth than meets the eye** sb/sth is more complex, interesting, etc than one might at first think. **9** (phr v) **meet up (with sb)** meet (sb), esp by chance: *I met up with him/We met up at the supermarket.* **meet with sb** (*US*) meet sb, esp for discussion: *The President met with senior White House aides at breakfast.* **meet with sth** encounter sth; experience sth: *meet with obstacles, difficulties, misfortune* ○ *She met/was met with much hostility, criticism, kindness, etc.*

meet[2] /miːt/ *n* **1** (*esp Brit*) gathering of riders and hounds at a fixed place for fox-hunting. **2** (*esp US*) sporting contest where many competitors gather: *an athˈletics meet* ○ *a ˈtrack, ˈswimming meet.* Cf MEETING 3.

meet[3] /miːt/ *adj* [pred] (*arch*) suitable; appropriate.

meeting /ˈmiːtɪŋ/ *n* **1** coming together of people, esp for discussion: *We've had three meetings, and still we haven't reached agreement.* ○ *The meeting between the two families was a joyful one.* **2** (**a**) assembly of people for a particular purpose: *hold, conduct a meeting* ○ *a ˈprayer meeting* ○ *a political meeting* ○ *a staff meeting.* (**b**) the people gathered together in this way: *Miss Smith will now address the meeting.* **3** gathering of people for a sporting contest: *a ˈrace-meeting* ○ *an athˈletics meeting.* Cf MEET[2]. **4** (idm) **a meeting of ˈminds** close understanding between people, esp as soon as they meet for the first time.

□ **ˈmeeting-house** *n* building for meetings, esp those held by Quakers.

ˈmeeting-place *n* place arranged for a meeting.

mega- *comb form* **1** million: *ˈmegabyte* ○ *ˈmegacycle* ○ *ˈmegawatt.* **2** very large or great: *ˈmegaphone* ○ *a ˈmegastar*, ie a very famous person from films, etc. ⇨ App 12.

megadeath /ˈmegədeθ/ *n* death of one million people in (esp nuclear) war.

megahertz /ˈmegəhɜːts/ (also **megacycle** /ˈmegəsaɪkl/) *n* (*abbr* **MHz**) one million hertz.

megalith /ˈmegəlɪθ/ *n* large stone, esp one erected as (part of) a monument in ancient times.

▷ **megalithic** /ˌmegəˈlɪθɪk/ *adj* **1** made of megaliths: *a megalithic circle, tomb, etc.* **2** (of a period of the past, etc) marked by the use of megaliths: *the megalithic era.*

megal(o)- *comb form* of very great size or importance: *megalomania* ○ *megalopolis.*

megalomania /ˌmegələˈmeɪnɪə/ *n* [U] form of madness in which a person has an exaggerated view of his own importance, power, etc: *The dictator was suffering from megalomania.*

▷ **megalomaniac** /-nɪæk/ *n* (*medical or fig*) person suffering from megalomania.

megalopolis /ˌmegəˈlɒpəlɪs/ *n* urban region that includes several large towns forming one great city.

megaphone /ˈmegəfəʊn/ *n* funnel-shaped device for speaking through, that allows the voice to be heard at a distance.

megaton /ˈmegətʌn/ *n* explosive force equal to one million tons of TNT: [attrib] *a one-megaton bomb.*

meiosis /maɪˈəʊsɪs/ *n* (*pl* **meioses** /maɪˈəʊsiːz/) **1** [U, C] (*biology*) process in which a reproductive cell divides into two new cells, each of these having half a set of chromosomes. It leads to the production of sperm and eggs, and allows genetic material to be exchanged between the chromosomes of father and mother. Cf MITOSIS. **2** [U] = LITOTES.

Meissen /ˈmaɪsn/ **1** German town near Dresden, famous for its porcelain factory. **2** [U] (also **Dresden china**) porcelain made in this factory.

Mekong /ˈmiːkɒŋ/ major river of SE Asia that rises in Tibet and flows south-east and south for 4 180 km (2 600 miles). It forms the borders between Burma and Laos and between Thailand and Laos, and flows through Cambodia and Vietnam to its delta on the South China Sea.

melamine /ˈmeləmiːn/ *n* [U] tough resilient type of plastic material, used eg for the surface of kitchen cupboards: [attrib] *a melamine chopping board.*

melancholy /ˈmelənkɒlɪ/ *n* [U] (tendency towards) deep sadness which lasts for some time; depression.

▷ **melancholia** /ˌmelənˈkəʊlɪə/ *n* [U] (*medical*) mental disease marked by melancholy.

melancholic /ˌmelənˈkɒlɪk/ *adj* (having a tendency to be) melancholy: *have a melancholic nature.*

melancholy *adj* (**a**) very sad; depressed: *a melancholy mood, person.* (**b**) causing sadness: *melancholy news* ○ *A funeral is a melancholy occasion.*

Melanesia

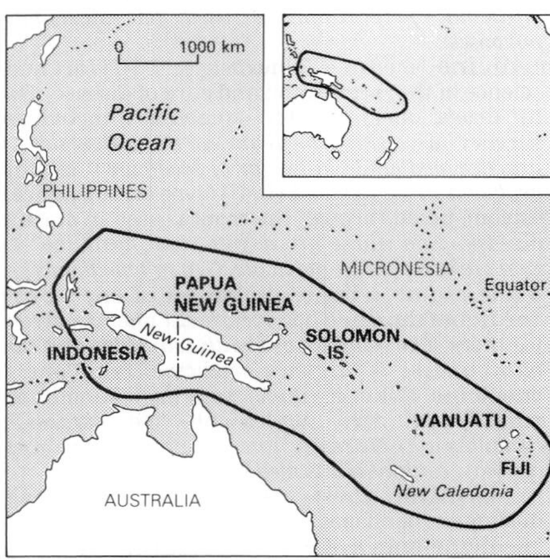

Melanesia /ˌmeləˈniːʃə/ group of islands in the SW Pacific that includes New Guinea, divided between Irian Jaya, a peninsula of Indonesia, and Papua New Guinea, the Solomon Islands, Vanuatu, New Caledonia and Fiji. ⇨ map.

mélange /ˈmeɪlɑːnʒ; *US* meɪˈlɑːnʒ/ *n* (*French*) mixture; medley.

melanin /ˈmelənɪn/ *n* [U] (*biology*) dark pigmen[t] found in the skin, hair, etc of humans and animals.

melan(o)- *comb form* black or dark: *melanin* ○ *melanism* ○ *melanoma.*

Melba toast /ˈmelbə təʊst/ very thin crisp toast.

Melbourne /ˈmelbən, ˈmelbɔːn/ second-larges[t] city in Australia, the capital of Victoria.

Melchior /ˈmelkɪɔː(r)/ (in Christian tradition) on[e] of the three *Magi, supposedly an African king.

meld[1] /meld/ *v* [I, Tn] (*US*) (cause sth to) blend combine or merge.

meld[2] /meld/ *v* [I, Tn] (in certain card-games, e[g] canasta) lay (one's cards) on the table so that the[y] score points.

mêlée /ˈmeleɪ; *US* meɪˈleɪ/ *n* (*French*) confuse[d] struggle; confused crowd of people: *There was [a] scuffle and I lost my hat in the mêlée.*

mellifluous /meˈlɪflʊəs/ (also **mellifluen[t]** /meˈlɪflʊənt/) *adj* (of a voice, speech, music, etc) sweet-sounding; (almost) musical: *speak i[n] mellifluous tones.* ▷ **mellifluence** /-flʊəns/ *n* [U] **mellifluously, mellifluently** *advs.*

mellow /ˈmeləʊ/ *adj* (**-er, -est**) **1** (**a**) fully ripe i[n] flavour or taste: *mellow wine, fruit, etc.* (**b**) soft pure and rich in colour or sound: *the mello[w] colours of the dawn sky* ○ *the mellow tones of [a] violin.* **2** (more) wise and sympathetic through ag[e] or experience (than previously): *a mellow attitud[e] to life.* **3** (*infml*) genial, cheerful, etc, esp as a resul[t] of being slightly drunk: *I'd had two glasses of win[e] and I was feeling quite mellow.*

▷ **mellow** *v* [I, Tn] (cause sb/sth to) becom[e] mellow: *Wine mellows with age.* ○ *Age ha[s] mellowed his attitude to some things.*

mellowly *adv.*

mellowness *n* [U].

melodeon /mɪˈləʊdɪən/ *n* (*music*) **1** (als[o] **American organ**) type of keyboard instrumen[t] similar to a harmonium. **2** type of accordion o[n] which the notes are produced by pressing buttons.

melodrama /ˈmelədrɑːmə/ *n* [U, C] **1** drama full o[f] sensational events and exaggerated characters often with a happy ending: *I love Victorian melodrama(s).* ○ (*derog*) *The critics dismissed he[r] new play as mere melodrama.* **2** (*fig*) events behaviour, language, etc resembling (a) drama o[f] this kind: *all the melodrama of a major murde[r] trial* ○ *We really don't need all this ridiculou[s] melodrama!*

▷ **melodramatic** /ˌmelədrəˈmætɪk/ *adj* (*ofte[n] derog*) of, like or suitable for (a) melodrama: *[a] sudden melodramatic outburst of temper* **melodramatically** /-klɪ/ *adv.*

melody /ˈmelədɪ/ *n* **1** [C] arrangement of word[s] put to music; song or tune: *old Irish melodies.* **2** [C] main part within a piece of harmonized music, us[ually] more distinctly heard than the rest; theme: *Th[e] melody is next taken up by the flutes.* **3** [U] arrangement of musical notes in an expressiv[e] order; tunefulness: *There's not much melody in thi[s] piece, is there?*

▷ **melodic** /mɪˈlɒdɪk/ *adj* of melody; melodious.

melodious /mɪˈləʊdɪəs/ *adj* of or producin[g] pleasant music; tuneful: *a melodious cello* ○ *th[e] melodious notes of a thrush.* **melodiously** *adv* **melodiousness** *n* [U].

melon /ˈmelən/ *n.* (**a**) [C] large juicy round fruit o[f] various types of plant that trail along the ground (**b**) [U] flesh of this fruit, used as food: *Would yo[u] like some melon?* ⇨ illus at FRUIT.

melt /melt/ *v* **1** [I, Tn] (cause sth to) become liqui[d] through heating: *The ice melted when the sun shon[e] on it.* ○ *The hot sun soon melted the ice.* ○ *It is eas[y] to melt butter.* **2** (**a**) [I] (*fig*) (of food) become soft dissolve: *a sweet that melts on the tongue* ○ *Thi[s] cake melts in the mouth!* (**b**) [I, Tn] (of a solid in [a] liquid) dissolve; cause (a solid) to dissolve: *Suga[r] melts in hot tea.* ○ *The hot coffee melts the sugar.* ⇨ Usage at WATER[1]. **3** [I, Ipr, Tn] (*fig*) (cause sb, sb' feelings, etc to) soften because of pity, love, etc *Her anger melted*, ie disappeared. ○ *His hear[t] melted with pity.* ○ *She melted into tears.* ○ *Pit[y] melted her heart.* **4** (idm) **butter wouldn't melt i[n] sb's mouth** ⇨ BUTTER. **5** (phr v) **melt (sth) awa[y]** (cause sth to) disappear by melting or dissolving

The sun has melted the snow away. ○ *(fig) The crowd melted away when the storm broke.* ○ *All his support melted away when he really needed it.* **melt sth down** melt (a metal object) to be used again as raw material: *Many of the gold ornaments were melted down to be made into coins.* **melt into sth** **(a)** change by gradual degrees into sth else: *One colour melted into another*, eg in the sky at sunset. **(b)** slowly disappear into sth: *He melted into the thick fog.* ○ *The ship melted into the darkness.*

▷ **melting** *adj* [usu attrib] *(fig)* cause feelings of love, pity, etc; tender: *a melting voice, mood, etc.*

□ **ˈmeltdown** *n* melting of the overheated core of a nuclear reactor, causing the escape of radioactivity.

ˈmelting-point *n* temperature at which a solid melts: *Lead has a lower melting-point than iron.*

ˈmelting-pot *n* **1** (usu *sing*) place where large numbers of immigrants from many different countries live together: *New York is a vast melting-pot of different nationalities.* **2** (idm) **be in/go into the ˈmelting-pot** be likely to change/be in the process of changing: *All our previous ideas are now in the melting-pot; our jobs are bound to change radically.*

ˈmelt water water formed by the melting of snow and ice, esp from a glacier.

Melville /ˈmelvɪl/ Herman (1819-91), American novelist and poet. He went to sea as a cabin-boy and a voyage on a whaler in the South Seas provided the material for his best-known novel *Moby Dick*. His novella *Billy Budd* was the basis for *Britten's opera of that name.

member /ˈmembə(r)/ *n* **1** person belonging to a group, society, etc: *Every member of her family came to the wedding.* ○ *an active, an honorary, a founding, etc member of the club.* **2** part of a larger structure: *a steel supporting member* ○ *a cross-member*, ie diagonally or horizontally positioned. **3** *(fml)* **(a)** part of a human or animal body; limb: *lose a vital member, such as an arm.* **(b)** *(euph)* male sexual organ; penis. **4 Member** Member of Parliament: *the Member for Leeds North-East.*

▷ **membership** *n* **1** [U] state of being a member of a group, society, etc: *apply for membership of the association.* **2** [Gp] (number of) members: *The membership numbers 800.* ○ *The membership is/are very annoyed at your suggestion.* ○ *a club with a large membership.*

□ **ˌMember of ˈCongress** (*abbr* **MC**) elected representative in the US Congress.

ˌMember of ˈParliament (*abbr* **MP**) elected representative in the House of Commons. ⇨ articles at PARLIAMENT, POLITICS.

membrane /ˈmembreɪn/ *n* [C, U] (piece of) thin pliable skin-like tissue connecting, covering or lining parts of an animal or a vegetable body: *rupture a membrane.*

▷ **membranous** /ˈmembrənəs/ *adj* of or like a membrane.

memento /mɪˈmentəʊ/ *n* (*pl* ~**s** or ~**es**) thing given, bought, etc and kept as a reminder (of a person, a place or an event): *a little gift as a memento of a visit.*

□ **memento mori** /mɪˌmentəʊ ˈmɔːrɪ/ thing, event, etc that makes one uncomfortable or frightened by reminding one of death.

memo /ˈmeməʊ/ *n* (*pl* ~**s**) *(infml)* memorandum: *an inter-office memo* ○ [attrib] *a memo pad.*

memoir /ˈmemwɑː(r)/ *n* **1** [C] written record of (esp important) events, usu based on personal knowledge: *She wrote a memoir of her stay in France.* **2 memoirs** [pl] person's written account of his life and experiences: *the memoirs of a retired politician.*

memorabilia /ˌmemərəˈbɪlɪə/ *n* [pl] noteworthy objects, esp those connected with a particular famous person or event: *a large collection of Dickens memorabilia.*

memorable /ˈmemərəbl/ *adj* deserving to be remembered; easily remembered: *a memorable experience, concert, trip* ○ *memorable verses by Keats.* ▷ **memorably** /-əblɪ/ *adv.*

memorandum /ˌmeməˈrændəm/ *n* (*pl* **-da** /-də/ or ~**s**) **1 (a)** note made for future use, esp to help oneself remember sth: *write a memorandum about sth.* **(b)** ~ **(to sb)** informal written business communication: *circulate a memorandum to all sales personnel.* **2** *(law)* record of an agreement that has been reached but not yet formally drawn up and signed.

memorial /məˈmɔːrɪəl/ *n* ~ **(to sb/sth)** monument, plaque, ceremony, etc that reminds people of an event or a person: *erect a war memorial* ○ *This statue is a memorial to a great statesman.* ○ *The church service was a memorial to the disaster victims.* ○ [attrib] *a memorial tablet, plaque, service.*

□ **Meˈmorial Day** holiday, usu at the end of May, observed in the USA to commemorate troops who died in war.

memorize, -ise /ˈmeməraɪz/ *v* [Tn] put (sth) into one's memory; learn (sth) well enough to remember it exactly: *She can memorize facts very quickly.* ○ *An actor must be able to memorize his lines.*

memory /ˈmemərɪ/ *n* **1 (a)** [U] power of the mind by which facts can be remembered: *devices which aid memory.* **(b)** [C] individual person's power to remember: *He has a good/poor memory (for dates)*, ie remembers (them) easily/with difficulty. ○ *speak from memory*, ie without referring to notes, etc ○ *commit sth to memory*, ie memorize it ○ *paint from memory*, ie without a model, photograph, etc ○ *I'm afraid the fact slipped my memory*, ie I forgot it. **2** [U] period over which people's memory extends; recollection: *This hasn't happened before within memory.* **3** [C] thing, event, etc that is remembered: *happy memories of childhood.* **4** [U] what is remembered about sb after his death: *His memory will always remain with us*, ie We will always remember him. **5** [C] *(computing)* part of a computer where information is processed. **6** (idm) **have a memory/mind like a sieve** ⇨ SIEVE. **if memory serves** if I remember correctly. **in memory of sb/to the memory of sb** serving to remind people of sb, esp as a tribute: *He founded the charity in memory of his late wife.* **jog sb's memory** ⇨ JOG. **ˌmemory ˈlane** imaginary path or journey that reminds one of pleasant past events: *a trip/stroll down memory lane.* **refresh one's/sb's memory** ⇨ REFRESH. **to the best of my memory** ⇨ BEST[3]. **within/in living memory** ⇨ LIVING[1].

memsahib /ˈmemsɑːb/ *n (dated)* (used in India as a respectful term of address) madam; lady.

men *pl* of MAN[1].

menace /ˈmenəs/ *n* **1** [U] threatening quality, tone, feeling, etc: *in a speech filled with menace* ○ *a film that creates an atmosphere of menace.* **2** [sing] **(a)** ~ **(to sb/sth)** person or thing that threatens: *These weapons are a menace (to world peace).* **(b)** *(infml or joc)* person or thing that is a nuisance, a danger, etc: *That woman is a menace! Keep her away from this machine!* ○ *That low beam is a menace! I keep hitting my head on it.*

▷ **menace** *v* [Tn, Tn·pr] ~ **sb/sth (with sth)** threaten sb/sth; endanger sb/sth: *countries menaced by/with war* ○ *Your vicious dog is menacing my cat!* **menacing** *adj* threatening: *a menacing look.* **menacingly** *adv.*

ménage /meɪˈnɑːʒ/ *n (fml)* household.

□ **ménage à trois** /ˌmeɪnɑːʒ ɑː ˈtrwɑː/ *(French)* household consisting of a husband and wife and the lover of one of them.

menagerie /mɪˈnædʒərɪ/ *n* collection of wild animals in captivity, esp in a travelling circus or for exhibition.

Menai Strait /ˌmenaɪ ˈstreɪt/ **the Menai Strait** channel that separates Anglesey from NW Wales.

mend /mend/ *v* **1 (a)** [Tn] return (sth broken, worn out or torn) to good condition or working order; repair: *mend shoes, a watch, a broken toy.* Cf FIX[1] 4. **(b)** [Tn] make (sth) better; improve: *Mend your manners!* ie Don't be so rude! ○ *That won't mend matters*, ie improve the situation. **2** [I] return to health; heal: *The injury is mending slowly.* **3** (idm) **it's ˌnever too ˌlate to ˈmend** *(saying)* one can always improve one's habits, etc. **least said, soonest mended** ⇨ SAY. **mend one's ˈfences** restore good relations, eg after a quarrel or dispute. **mend one's ˈways** improve one's habits, way of living, etc: *There's no sign of him mending his ways.*

▷ **mend** *n* **1** damaged or torn part of sth (esp clothing, etc) that has been mended: *The mends were almost invisible.* **2** (idm) **on the ˈmend** *(infml)* getting better after an illness, injury, etc: *She's been very unwell, but she's on the mend now.*

mender *n* (usu in compounds) person who mends sth: *a ˈroad-mender* ○ *a ˈwatch-mender*.

mending *n* [U] **1** work of repairing (esp clothes): *do the mending.* **2** clothes, etc to be mended: *a pile of mending.*

mendacious /menˈdeɪʃəs/ *adj (fml)* untruthful; lying: *a mendacious story, report, etc.*

▷ **mendaciously** *adv.*

mendacity /menˈdæsətɪ/ *n (fml)* **1** [U] untruthfulness. **2** [C] untrue statement; lie.

Mendel /ˈmendl/ Gregor Johann (1822-84), Moravian biologist, the 'father of genetics'. From his experiments with peas he argued that hybrids of plants showing different characters produced second-generation offspring in which parental characters were inherited in precise ratios. The importance of his work lies in the fact that he recognized that it was not the characters themselves that are inherited but the predisposing factors that underlie them.

▷ **Mendelian** /ˌmenˈdiːlɪən/ *adj* of Mendel or his theory of heredity by genes.

Mendelism *n* [U] part of genetics that is concerned with the way in which certain characteristics are passed on to successive generations.

Mendelssohn /ˈmendlsn/ Felix (1809-47), German composer. He produced many works, including 13 string symphonies, the incidental music to *A Midsummer Night's Dream*, the descriptive *Fingal's Cave*, and two oratorios. His music is greatly admired for its poetic elegance and melodic freshness.

mendicant /ˈmendɪkənt/ *n, adj (fml)* (person) getting a living by begging: *mendicant friars.*

Menelaus /ˌmenəˈleɪəs/ (in Greek legend) king of Sparta, who was the brother of *Agamemnon and husband of *Helen of Troy.

menfolk /ˈmenfəʊk/ *n* [pl] *(fml)* men, esp the men of a family considered together: *The menfolk have all gone out fishing.* Cf WOMENFOLK.

menhir /ˈmenhɪə(r)/ *n* tall upright stone set in place as a monument in prehistoric times.

menial /ˈmiːnɪəl/ *adj (usu derog)* (of work) suitable to be done by servants; unskilled: *a menial task, job, etc* ○ *menial chores like dusting and washing up.*

▷ **menial** *n (fml usu derog)* servant.

meninges /mɪˈnɪndʒiːs/ *n* [pl] (*sing* **meninx** /ˈmiːnɪŋks/) *(anatomy)* membranes that surround the brain and spinal cord in vertebrates. In man and other mammals there are three: the *dura mater*, the *arachnoid* and the *pia mater*.

meningitis /ˌmenɪnˈdʒaɪtɪs/ *n* [U] inflammation of the meninges.

meniscus /məˈnɪskəs/ *n* (*pl* **-ci** /-ˈnɪsaɪ/ or **-cuses** /-kəsɪz/) **1** curved upper surface of a liquid in a tube. **2** lens that is convex on one side and concave on the other. **3** *(anatomy)* piece of cartilage between the bones in a joint, which stops the bones rubbing against each other.

Mennonite /ˈmenənaɪt/ *n* member of a Protestant Christian sect that is opposed to infant baptism, the swearing of oaths, military sevice and the holding of civic office. Cf ANABAPTIST.

menopause /ˈmenəpɔːz/ *n* **the menopause** [sing] time when a woman ceases to menstruate, usu around the age of 50: *reach the menopause.*

▷ **menopausal** /ˌmenəˈpɔːzl/ *adj* **(a)** of the menopause. **(b)** experiencing the menopause.

menorah /mɪˈnɔːrə/ *n* (usu seven-branched) candle-holder used in Jewish worship.

menses /ˈmensiːz/ *n* **the menses** [pl] *(fml or medical)* monthly flow of blood, etc from the lining of the uterus.

menstruate /ˈmenstrʊeɪt/ *v* [I] discharge blood,

etc from the uterus, usu once a month.

▷ **menstrual** /ˈmenstrʊəl/ *adj* of the menses or menstruation: *menstrual pain.*

menstruation /ˌmenstrʊˈeɪʃn/ *n* [U] process or time of menstruating.

mensuration /ˌmensjʊˈreɪʃn/ *n* [U] (*dated or fml*) (**a**) mathematical rules for finding length, area and volume. (**b**) process of measuring.

menswear /ˈmenzweə(r)/ *n* [U] clothes worn by men: [attrib] *the menswear department.*

-ment *suff* (with *vs* forming *ns*) result or means of: *development* ○ *government.* ▷ **-mental** (forming *adjs*). **-mentally** (forming *advs*).

mental /ˈmentl/ *adj* **1** of, in or to the mind: *an enormous mental effort* ○ *a mental process, illness, deficiency* ○ *This experience caused him much mental suffering.* ○ *make a mental note of sth*, ie fix sth in one's mind to be remembered later. **2** (*infml derog*) mad: *You must be mental to drive so fast!*

▷ **mentally** /ˈmentəlɪ/ *adv* in the mind; with regard to the mind: *mentally alert, aware, active, etc* ○ *mentally deficient/defective*, ie medically subnormal in the power of the brain ○ *mentally deranged*, ie mad.

□ ˈ**mental age** level of sb's intellectual ability, expressed in terms of the average ability for a certain age: *She is sixteen years old but has a mental age of five.*

ˌ**mental aˈrithmetic** calculation(s) done in the mind, without writing down figures or using a calculator, etc.

ˌ**mental ˈcruelty** causing of extreme unhappiness: *Mental cruelty is grounds for divorce in the USA.*

ˈ**mental home**, ˈ**mental hospital** home/hospital for mental patients.

ˈ**mental patient** person suffering from mental illness.

mentality /menˈtælətɪ/ *n* **1** [C] characteristic attitude of mind; way of thinking: *He has many years' experience of the criminal mentality.* **2** [U] (*fml*) intellectual ability: *a woman of poor mentality.*

menthol /ˈmenθɒl/ *n* [U] solid white substance obtained from oil of peppermint, used to relieve pain and as a flavouring, eg in cigarettes or toothpaste: [attrib] *menthol cigarettes.*

▷ **mentholated** /ˈmenθəleɪtɪd/ *adj* containing menthol.

mention /ˈmenʃn/ *v* [Tn, Tf, Tw, Tg, Cn·n/a, Dn·pr, Dpr·f, Dpr·w] ~ **sth/sb (as sth)**; ~ **sth/sb (to sb)** **1** write or speak about sth/sb briefly; say the name of sth/sb; refer to sth/sb: *Did she mention it (to the police)?* ○ *Did I hear my name mentioned?* ie Was somebody talking about me? ○ *He mentioned (to John) that he had seen you.* ○ *Did she mention when she would arrive?* ○ *Whenever I mention playing football, he says he's too busy.* ○ *They mentioned you as a good source of information.* **2** (idm) **don't ˈmention it** (used to indicate that thanks, an apology, etc are not necessary): *'You are so kind!' 'Don't mention it.'* **mentioned in dispatches** mentioned by name in the official report of a battle, etc because of one's bravery. **not to mention** (*infml*) as well as: *He has a big house and an expensive car, not to mention a villa in France.*

▷ **mention** *n* **1** [U] reference to sb/sth (in speech or writing): *He made no mention of your request.* ○ *There was no mention of her contribution.* **2** [C] (*infml*) act of mentioning; brief reference: *Did the concert get a mention in the paper?*

-mentioned (forming compound *adjs*) referred to in the specified place: *aˌbove-/beˌlow-ˈmentioned*, ie mentioned before/after the current passage in a book, an article, etc.

mentor /ˈmentɔ:(r)/ *n* experienced and trusted adviser of an inexperienced person.

menu /ˈmenju:/ *n* **1** list of dishes available at a restaurant or to be served at a meal: *What's on the menu tonight?* ○ *Fish has been taken off the menu.* **2** (*computing*) list of options from which a user can choose, displayed on a computer screen.

MEP /ˌem i: ˈpi:/ *abbr* Member of the European Parliament.

Mephistopheles /ˌmefɪˈstɒfɪli:z/ (in German legend) the evil demon to whom *Faust sold his soul.

▷ **mephistophelean** (also **mephistophelian**) /ˌmefɪstəˈfi:lɪən/ *adj* (*fml*) **1** of or like Mephistopheles. **2** devilish; evil: *a mephistophelean plan, trick, etc* ○ *mephistophelean cunning.*

mercantile /ˈmɜ:kəntaɪl; *US* -ti:l, -tɪl/ *adj* of trade and commerce; of merchants.

□ ˌ**mercantile maˈrine** merchant navy.

mercantilism /ˈmɜ:kəntɪlɪzm/ *n* [U] (*economics*) belief or theory that bullion is the only form of wealth and that foreign trade should be regulated by the state to ensure that exports exceed imports.

Mercator's projection /məˌkeɪtəz prəˈdʒekʃn/ method of drawing maps of the world in which the globe is represented on a flat grid of squares formed by lines of latitude and longitude, making areas far from the equator exaggerated in size.

mercenary /ˈmɜ:sɪnərɪ; *US* -nerɪ/ *adj* interested only in making money, etc; done from this motive: *a mercenary act, motive, etc* ○ *His actions are entirely mercenary.*

▷ **mercenary** *n* soldier hired to fight in a foreign army.

mercerize, -ise /ˈmɜ:səraɪz/ *v* [Tn esp passive] treat (cotton thread) so that it becomes stronger and glossy like silk: *mercerized cotton.*

merchandise /ˈmɜ:tʃəndaɪz/ *n* [U] goods bought and sold; goods for sale: *the merchandise on display in the shop window.*

▷ **merchandise** *v* [Tn] buy and sell (goods); promote sales of (goods): *The fabrics are merchandised through a network of dealers.* ○ *We merchandise our furniture by advertising in newspapers.* **merchandising** *n* [U].

merchant /ˈmɜ:tʃənt/ *n* **1** (**a**) wholesale trader, esp one who trades with foreign countries: *an ˌimport-ˈexport merchant.* (**b**) (in compounds) trader in the goods stated: *a ˈcoal-merchant* ○ *a ˈwine-merchant.* ➪ Usage at DEALER. **2** (*derog sl*) person who is fond of a specified activity, etc: *a ˈspeed merchant*, ie sb who likes to drive (too) fast.

□ ˌ**merchant ˈbank** bank that specializes in (often large) commercial loans and finance for industry.

ˌ**merchant maˈrine**, ˌ**merchant ˈnavy** the merchant ships and seamen of a country collectively. ➪ article at SEA.

ˌ**merchant ˈseaman** sailor in the merchant navy.

ˌ**merchant ˈship**, ˌ**merchant ˈshipping** ship(s) used for transporting goods.

Mercia /ˈmɜ:ʃə/ kingdom that was founded in central England by the *Angles in the 6th century and became powerful under *Offa in the 8th century. The name has been revived in 'West Mercia Authority', an area of police administration covering the counties of Hereford and Worcester, and Shropshire.

merciful ➪ MERCY.

mercurial /mɜ:ˈkjʊrɪəl/ *adj* **1** (**a**) (of people or their moods, etc) often changing: *a mercurial temperament.* (**b**) lively; quick-witted: *She has a mercurial turn of conversation.* **2** (*fml or medical*) of, like, containing or caused by mercury: *a mercurial ointment, compound, etc* ○ *mercurial poisoning.*

Mercury /ˈmɜ:kjʊrɪ/ *n* **1** (in Roman mythology) messenger of the gods, the equivalent of the Greek *Hermes. **2** (*astronomy*) the planet nearest to the sun.

mercury /ˈmɜ:kjʊrɪ/ *n* [U] (also **quicksilver**) (*symb* **Hg**) chemical element, a heavy silver-coloured metal usu found in liquid form. It is used in electrical equipment, in thermometers and barometers, and in alloys with other metals. It is toxic, and mercury pollution of lakes and seas has occurred. ➪ App 11.

□ ˌ**mercury baˈrometer** barometer in which atmospheric pressure is measured by the height of a column of mercury.

mercy /ˈmɜ:sɪ/ *n* **1** [U] kindness, forgiveness, restraint, etc shown to sb one has the right or power to punish: *They showed mercy to their enemies.* ○ *We were given no/little mercy.* ○ *He threw himself on my mercy*, ie begged me to show mercy. ○ *a tyrant without mercy.* **2** [C usu *sing*] (*infml*) event to be grateful for; piece of good luck: *It's a mercy she wasn't hurt in the accident.* ○ *His death was a mercy*, eg He was in such pain that it was best that he died. **3** (idm) **at the mercy of sb/sth** in the power of sb/sth; under the control of sb/sth: *The ship was at the mercy of the storm*, ie out of control or helpless. **be grateful/thankful for small mercies** ➪ SMALL. **an errand of mercy** ➪ ERRAND. **leave sb/sth to the mercy/mercies of sb/sth** ➪ LEAVE[1]. **throw oneself on sb's mercy** (*fml*) beg sb to treat one kindly or leniently.

▷ **merciful** /-fl/ *adj* ~ (**to/towards sb**) having, showing or feeling mercy: *She was merciful to the prisoners.* ○ *a merciful gesture, action, etc.* **mercifully** /-fəlɪ/ *adv* **1** in a merciful way: *treat sb mercifully.* **2** (*infml*) fortunately: *The play was very bad, but mercifully it was also short!*

merciless *adj* ~ (**to/towards sb**) showing no mercy; pitiless: *a merciless killer, beating* ○ *This judge is merciless towards anyone found guilty of murder.* **mercilessly** *adv.*

mercy *interj* (*dated*) (used to express surprise or (pretended) terror): *Mercy (on us)! What a noise!*

□ ˈ**mercy killing** (*infml*) euthanasia.

mere[1] /mɪə(r)/ *adj* [attrib] (no comparative form) **1** nothing more than; no better or more important than: *She's a mere child.* ○ *He's not a mere boxer: he's world champion.* ○ *Mere words* (ie Words without acts) *won't help.* **2** (idm) **the merest sth** the smallest or most unimportant thing: *The merest noise is enough to wake him.*

▷ **merely** *adv* only; simply: *I merely asked his name.* ○ *I meant it merely as a joke.*

mere[2] /mɪə(r)/ *n* (esp in place names) pond; small lake.

Meredith /ˈmerədɪθ/ George (1828-1909), English novelist and poet, known esp for his novel *The Egoist.* Though he was much praised in his lifetime, his difficult style of writing has caused his reputation to suffer.

meretricious /ˌmerɪˈtrɪʃəs/ *adj* apparently attractive but in fact valueless: *a meretricious style, book, argument.* ▷ **meretriciously** *adv.* **meretriciousness** *n* [U].

merganser /mɜ:ˈgænsə(r)/ *n* any of several types of diving duck with a long narrow bill, which feeds on fish.

merge /mɜ:dʒ/ *v* **1** [I, Ipr, Ip, Tn, Tn·pr, Tn·p] ~ (**with/into sth**); ~ (**together**); ~ **A with B**/~ **A and B (together)** (*esp commerce*) (cause two things to) come together and combine: *The two marching columns moved closer and finally merged (together).* ○ *traffic merging* (ie joining a larger stream of traffic) *from the left* ○ *Where does this stream merge into the Rhine?* ○ *The bank merged with its major rival.* ○ *We can merge our two small businesses (together) into one larger one.* **2** [I, Ipr] ~ (**into sth**) fade or change gradually (into sth else): *One end is blue, one end is red, and the colours merge in the middle.* ○ *Twilight merged into total darkness.*

▷ **merger** /ˈmɜ:dʒə(r)/ *n* [C, U] (act of) joining together (esp two commercial companies): *a merger between two breweries* ○ *The two companies are considering merger as a possibility.* ○ [attrib] *merger discussions.*

meridian /məˈrɪdɪən/ *n* **1** imaginary circle round the earth, passing through (a given place and) the North and South Poles: *the Greenwich meridian*, ie longitude 0°, which passes through the North and South Poles and Greenwich, England. **2** highest point reached by the sun or other star, as viewed from a given point on the earth's surface.

meridiem ➪ AM *abbr*, PM *abbr*.

meridional /məˈrɪdɪənl/ *adj* of the south (esp the south of Europe).

meringue /məˈræŋ/ *n* (**a**) [U] mixture of whites of egg and sugar baked until crisp and used as a covering over sweet pies, tarts, etc. (**b**) [C] small cake made of this.

merino /məˈri:nəʊ/ *n* (*pl* ~**s**) **1** [C] (also **merino sheep**) breed of sheep with long fine wool. **2** [U] (**a**) yarn or cloth made from this wool. (**b**) similar soft wool and cotton material.

meristem /ˈmerɪstem/ *n* (*botany*) area of growing tissue in plants, consisting of small cells that divide and form new tissue.

merit /ˈmerɪt/ *n* **1** [U] quality of deserving praise or reward; worth; excellence: *a man/woman of merit* ○ *There's no merit in keeping what you don't really want.* ○ *I don't think there's much merit in the plan.* ○ *She was awarded a certificate of merit for her piano-playing.* ○ [attrib] *a merit award.* **2** [C usu *pl*] fact, action, quality, etc that deserves praise or reward: *The merits of the scheme are quite obvious.* ○ *consider, judge, etc sb/sth on his/its (own) merits,* ie according to his/its own qualities, worth, etc, regardless of one's personal feelings.
▷ **merit** *v* [Tn] (*fml*) be worthy of (sth); deserve: *merit reward, praise, punishment, etc* ○ *I think the suggestion merits consideration.*

meritocracy /ˌmerɪˈtɒkrəsɪ/ *n* (*politics*) **1** (**a**) [U] system of government by people of high achievement. (**b**) [CGp] such people in a society. **2** [C] country with such a system of government: *Is Britain a meritocracy?*

meritorious /ˌmerɪˈtɔ:rɪəs/ *adj* (*fml*) deserving praise or reward: *a prize for meritorious conduct.*
▷ **meritoriously** *adv.*

Merlin /ˈmɜ:lɪn/ (in Arthurian legend) magician who helped and supported King Arthur. The stones that form *Stonehenge are said to have been brought from Ireland with his help.

merlin /ˈmɜ:lɪn/ *n* type of small falcon.

mermaid /ˈmɜ:meɪd/ *n* mythical creature having the body of a woman, but a fish's tail instead of legs.
▷ **merman** /ˈmɜ:mæn/ *n* (*pl* **-men** /-men/) male mermaid.

merry /ˈmerɪ/ *adj* (**-ier**, **-iest**) **1** (*dated*) happy and cheerful; full of joy and gaiety: *a merry laugh, party, group* ○ *wish sb a merry Christmas.* **2** (*infml*) slightly drunk: *We were already merry after only two glasses of wine.* **3** (*arch*) pleasant: *the merry month of May* ○ *Merry England.* **4** (idm) **eat, drink and be merry**; **make ˈmerry** (*dated*) sing, laugh, feast, etc; celebrate.
▷ **merrily** /ˈmerəlɪ/ *adv.*
merriment /ˈmerɪmənt/ *n* [U] (*fml*) gaiety, laughter, celebration, etc.
□ **ˈmerry-go-round** *n* (*Brit*) (*US* **carousel**) = ROUNDABOUT *n* 1.
ˈmerry-maker *n* (*dated*) person who celebrates (sth). **ˈmerry-making** *n* [U].

Mersey /ˈmɜ:zɪ/ **1** English river that rises in the Peak district and flows into the Irish Sea near Liverpool. ⇨ article at RIVER. **2** [attrib] of Liverpool and the area around it: *the Mersey sound,* ie the music of pop groups that performed in Liverpool in the 1960s, esp the *Beatles ○ *the Mersey poets,* ie a group of contemporary poets from Liverpool.
□ **Merseyside** /ˈmɜ:zɪsaɪd/ **1** area around Liverpool. **2** metropolitan county that was formed from parts of Lancashire and Cheshire. ⇨ map at App 1.

mesa /ˈmeɪsə/ *n* (*US*) flat-topped hill with steep sides, common in south-western USA.

mésalliance /ˌmeɪˈzælɪɑ:ns/ *n* (*French derog*) marriage with sb of a lower social position.

mescaline (also **mescalin**) /ˈmeskəlɪn/ *n* [U] hallucinatory drug obtained from a type of cactus.

Mesdames *pl of* MADAME.

Mesdemoiselles *pl of* MADEMOISELLE.

mesh /meʃ/ *n* **1** (**a**) [C, U] (piece of) material made of a network of wire, thread, etc: *(a) wire mesh on the front of the chicken coop* ○ *stockings made of fine silk mesh.* (**b**) [C] any of the spaces in such material: *a net with half-inch meshes/with a half-inch mesh.* **2** [C esp *pl*] network, esp for trapping sth: *a fish tangled in the mesh(es) of the net* ○ (*fig*) *entangled in the meshes/a mesh of political intrigue.* **3** (idm) **in mesh** (of the teeth of gears) engaged; interlocked.
▷ **mesh** *v* [I, Ipr] ~ (**with sth**) (**a**) (of toothed gears) engage; interlock (with others): *The cogs don't quite mesh.* (**b**) (*fig*) harmonize; be compatible; fit in: *Our future plans must mesh with existing practices.*

mesmerism /ˈmezmərɪzəm/ *n* [U] (*dated*) hypnotism.
▷ **mesmeric** /mezˈmerɪk/ *adj* hypnotic.
mesmerist /ˈmezmərɪst/ *n* hypnotist.
mesmerize, -ise /ˈmezməraɪz/ *v* [Tn esp passive] hold the attention of (sb) completely: *an audience mesmerized by her voice.*

mes(o)- *comb form* middle; intermediate: *mesolithic* ○ *mesomorph.*

mesolithic /ˌmesəˈlɪθɪk/ *adj* of the *Stone Age, in the period of transition between the palaeolithic and the neolithic periods, esp in Europe where it occurred between the end of the last glacial period and the beginnings of agriculture.

mesomorph /ˈmesəmɔ:f/ *n* type of person whose body is of a compact muscular build. Cf ECTOMORPH, ENDOMORPH.

Mesopotamia /ˌmesəpəˈteɪmɪə/ region of SW Asia that lies between the rivers Tigris and Euphrates and is now part of Iraq.

Mesozoic /ˌmesəˈzəʊɪk/ *adj* (*geology*) of the geological era between the Palaeozoic and the Cainozoic, comprising the Triassic, Jurassic and Cretaceous periods and lasting from about 248 to 65 million years ago. It was a time of abundant vegetation when the reptiles were dominant.

mess[1] /mes/ *n* **1** [C usu *sing*] dirty or untidy state: *This kitchen's a mess!* ○ *The children have made an awful mess in the lounge.* ○ *The spilt milk made a terrible mess on the carpet.* **2** [U] (*infml euph*) excrement of a dog, cat, etc: *Who will clean up the cat's mess in the bedroom?* **3** [sing] difficult or confused state or situation; disorder: *My life's (in) a real mess!* ○ *You've made a mess of the job,* ie done it very badly. ○ (*ironic*) *A nice/fine mess you've made of that!* **4** [sing] person/people who is/are untidy or dirty: *Get cleaned up! You're a mess!/You two are a mess!*
▷ **mess** *v* (*infml*) **1** [Tn] (*US*) put (sth) into an untidy, etc state: *Don't mess your hair!* **2** (phr v) **mess about/around** (**a**) behave in a foolish or boisterous way: *Stop messing about and come and help!* (**b**) work in a pleasantly casual or disorganized way; potter: *I just love messing about in the garden.* **mess sb about/around; mess about/around with sb** treat sb inconsiderately: *Be nicer to him. You shouldn't mess around with him like that.* ○ *Stop messing me about! Tell me if I've got the job or not!* **mess sth about/around; mess about/around with sth** handle sth roughly or incompetently; make a muddle of sth: *Don't mess the files around, I've just put them in order.* ○ *Somebody's been messing about with the radio and now it doesn't work.* **mess sth up** (**a**) make sth untidy, disordered or dirty: *Don't mess up my hair: I've just combed it.* ○ *Who messed up my clean kitchen?* (**b**) do sth incompetently; bungle sth: *I was asked to organize the trip, but I messed it up.* **mess with sb/sth** (*infml*) interfere with sb/sth: *Don't mess with her: she's got a violent temper.*
messy *adj* (**-ier**, **-iest**) **1** in a state of disorder; dirty: *a messy kitchen.* **2** causing dirt or disorder: *a messy job.*

mess[2] /mes/ *n* **1** [CGp] group of people who take meals together and share living quarters, esp in the armed forces: *The mess has ordered some new furniture.* **2** (*US* also **ˈmess hall**) building in which these meals are taken: *the officers'/sergeants' mess.*
▷ **mess** *v* [Ipr, Ip] ~ (**in**) **with sb**; ~ (**in**) **together** eat meals: *He messed with me/We messed together when we were in the Navy.*
□ **ˈmess-jacket** *n* short jacket worn by officers in their mess on formal occasions.
ˈmess kit soldier's cooking and eating utensils.

message /ˈmesɪdʒ/ *n* **1** [C] information, news, request, etc sent to sb in writing, speech, by radio, etc: *We've had a message (to say) that your father is ill.* ○ *The ship sent a radio message asking for help.* **2** [sing] statement (said to be) of political, moral or social significance made by a prophet, writer, book, etc: *a film with a message* ○ *the prophet's message to the world.* **3** (idm) **get the ˈmessage** (*sl*) understand (what sb is hinting at, trying to say, etc): *She said it was getting late: I got the message, and left.*

messenger /ˈmesɪndʒə(r)/ *n* person carrying a message.

Messiah /mɪˈsaɪə/ *n* **1** (also **messiah**) [C] person expected to come and save the world: *He believes in every new political messiah.* **2 the Messiah** [sing] (*religion*) (**a**) Jesus Christ regarded as this saviour. (**b**) similar person expected by the Jews.

Messieurs *pl of* MONSIEUR.

Messina /meˈsi:nə/ Sicilian city and harbour situated on the **Strait of Messina** which separates Sicily from Italy.

Messrs /ˈmesəz/ *abbr* (used as the *pl* of *Mr* (French *Messieurs*) before a list of men's names, eg *Messrs Smith, Brown and Robinson,* and before names of business firms, eg *Messrs T Brown and Co*).

messy ⇨ MESS[1].

Met[1] /met/ *adj* [attrib] (*Brit infml*) meteorological: *the ˈMet Office* ○ *the latest Met report,* ie weather report from the Meteorological Office.

Met[2] /met/ **the Met** *n* **1** [Gp] (*Brit infml*) the Metropolitan Police. **2** [sing] the Metropolitan Opera House, New York City.

met *pt, pp of* MEET[1].

meta- *comb form* **1** above; beyond; behind: *metalanguage* ○ *metacarpal* ○ *metaphysics.* **2** of change: *metabolism* ○ *metamorphosis.*

metabolism /məˈtæbəlɪzəm/ *n* [U] (*biology*) chemical process by which food is built up into living matter in an organism or by which living matter is broken down into simpler substances.
▷ **metabolic** /ˌmetəˈbɒlɪk/ *adj* of metabolism: *a metabolic process, rate, etc.*
metabolize, -ise /məˈtæbəlaɪz/ *v* [Tn] (*biology*) break down (food) chemically for use in the body: *Our bodies constantly metabolize the food we eat.*

metacarpus /ˌmetəˈkɑ:pəs/ *n* (*anatomy*) point of the hand containing the five bones between the wrist and the fingers.
▷ **metacarpal** *adj, n* (*anatomy*) (of a) bone between the wrist and the fingers. ⇨ illus at SKELETON.

metal /ˈmetl/ *n* **1** [C, U] any of a class of mineral substances such as tin, iron, gold, copper, etc, which are usu opaque and good conductors of heat and electricity, or any alloy of these: *Various metals are used to make the parts of this machine.* ○ *There isn't much metal in the bodywork of this new car; it's mainly plastic.* ○ [attrib] *a metal support, fitting, container.* **2** [U] = ROAD METAL (ROAD). **3 metals** [pl] railway-lines: *These locomotives ran on Great Western Railway metals until 1940.*
▷ **metal** *v* (**-ll-**; *US* **-l-**) [Tn esp passive] (*dated*) make or repair (a road) with broken stone: *This rough track will soon be a metalled road.*
metallic /mɪˈtælɪk/ *adj* [esp attrib] of or like metal: *a metallic plate, sheet, etc* ○ *metallic paint,* ie looking like metal ○ *metallic sounds, clicks, etc,* eg made (as if) by metal objects struck together.
□ **ˈmetalwork** *n* [U] artistic or skilled work done using metal. **ˈmetalworker** *n.*

metalanguage /ˈmetəlæŋgwɪdʒ/ *n* [C, U] language or set of symbols used in talking about or describing another language, etc.

metallurgy /mɪˈtælədʒɪ; *US* ˈmetəlɜ:rdʒɪ/ *n* [U] science of the properties of metals, their uses, methods of obtaining them from their ores, etc.
▷ **metallurgical** /ˌmetəˈlɜ:dʒɪkl/ *adj* of metallurgy.
metallurgist /mɪˈtælədʒɪst; *US* ˈmetəlɜ:rdʒɪst/ *n* expert in metallurgy.

metamorphic /ˌmetəˈmɔ:fɪk/ *adj* **1** of or characterized by metamorphosis. **2** (*geology*) (of rock) that has been changed into its present structure, texture or chemical composition by natural forces such as heat or pressure, as in the transformation of limestone into marble or shale into slate. Cf IGNEOUS, SEDIMENTARY.
▷ **metamorphism** /ˌmetəˈmɔ:fɪzm/ *n* [U] (*geology*) process of metamorphic change in rock.

metamorphose /ˌmetəˈmɔ:fəʊz/ *v* [I, Ipr, Tn, Tn·pr] ~ (**sb/sth**) (**into sth**) (*fml*) (cause sb/sth to) change in form or nature: *A larva metamorphoses into a chrysalis and then into a butterfly.* ○ *The magician metamorphosed the frog into a prince.*
▷ **metamorphosis** /ˌmetəˈmɔ:fəsɪs/ *n* (*pl* **-oses** /-əsi:z/) (*fml*) change of form or nature, eg by natural growth or development: *the*

metamorphosis of a larva into a butterfly ○ *(fig) the social metamorphosis that has occurred in China.*

metaphor /ˈmetəfə(r)/ *n* [C, U] (example of the) use of a word or phrase to indicate sth different from (though related in some way to) the literal meaning, as in 'I'll make him *eat* his words' or 'She has a heart *of stone*': *striking originality in her use of metaphor.* Cf SIMILE.
▷ **metaphorical** /ˌmetəˈfɒrɪkl; *US* -ˈfɔ:r-/ *adj* of or like a metaphor; containing metaphors: *a metaphorical use, expression, phrase, etc.* Cf FIGURATIVE, LITERAL 1a.
metaphorically /-klɪ/ *adv.* Cf MIXED METAPHOR (MIXED).

metaphysics /ˌmetəˈfɪzɪks/ *n* [sing *v*] **1** branch of philosophy dealing with the nature of existence, truth and knowledge. It discusses eg whether existence is only in the mind or if there is an independent external physical reality. **2** (*esp derog*) speculative philosophy; any type of abstract talk, writing, etc.
▷ **metaphysical** /ˌmetəˈfɪzɪkl/ *adj* **1** of metaphysics. **2** (of poetry) using complex imagery (applied esp to certain 17th-century poets).
ˌ**metaˌphysical** ˈ**poet** any of a number of 17th-century English poets, including *Donne, *Herbert and *Marvell, who used complex imagery and elaborate metaphors.

metatarsus /ˌmetəˈtɑ:səs/ *n* (*pl* **-tarsi** /-tɑ:saɪ/) (*anatomy*) part of the foot containing the five bones between the ankle and the toes. ▷ **metatarsal** *adj.* ➪ illus at SKELETON.

mete /mi:t/ *v* (phr v) **mete sth out (to sb)** (*fml*) give or administer (punishment, rewards, etc): *The judge meted out severe penalties.* ○ *Justice was meted out to the offenders.*

meteor /ˈmi:tɪɔ:(r)/ *n* small mass of matter that enters the earth's atmosphere from outer space, making a bright streak across the night sky as it is burnt up. Cf SHOOTING STAR (SHOOT[1]).
▷ **meteoric** /ˌmi:tɪˈɒrɪk; *US* -ˈɔ:r-/ *adj* **1** of meteors. **2** (*fig*) (of a career, etc) rapidly successful: *a meteoric rise to fame.* **meteorically** *adv.*

meteorite /ˈmi:tɪəraɪt/ *n* piece of rock or metal that has reached the earth's surface from outer space.

meteorology /ˌmi:tɪəˈrɒlədʒɪ/ *n* [U] scientific study of the earth's atmosphere and its changes, used esp for forecasting weather.
▷ **meteorological** /ˌmi:tɪərəˈlɒdʒɪkl; *US* ˌmi:tɪɔ:r-/ *adj* of meteorology: *a meteorological chart, forecast, etc* ○ *weather forecasts from the Central Meteorological Office.*
meteorologist /ˌmi:tɪəˈrɒlədʒɪst/ *n* expert in meteorology.

meter[1] /ˈmi:tə(r)/ *n* (esp in compounds) device that measures the volume of gas, water, etc passing through it, time passing, electrical current, distance, etc: *an* ˌ*elecˈtricity meter* ○ *a* ˈ*gas meter* ○ *a* ˈ*water meter* ○ *an exˈposure meter*, ie for measuring how long a photographic film should be exposed ○ *a* ˈ*parking-meter*, ie one into which coins are put to pay for parking a car for a certain period of time ○ *fares mounting up on the meter*, ie of a taxi-cab.
▷ **meter** *v* [Tn] measure (sth) with a meter: *meter sb's consumption of gas.*
□ ˈ**meter maid** (*infml*) female traffic warden.

meter[2] (*US*) = METRE.

-meter *comb form* (forming *ns*) **1** device for measuring (sth): *thermometer* ○ *voltameter.* **2** poetic metre with a given number of feet (FOOT[1] 6): *pentameter* ○ *hexameter.*

methadone /ˈmeθədəʊn/ *n* [U] drug used as a substitute in treating heroin addiction and as a pain-killer.

methane /ˈmi:θeɪn/ *n* [U] (also **marsh gas**) odourless colourless inflammable gas that occurs in coalmines and in marshes. Cf FIREDAMP (FIRE[1]).

methinks /mɪˈθɪŋks/ *v* (*pt* **methought** /mɪˈθɔ:t/) [I] (*arch*) it seems to me: *Methought I heard a voice.*

method /ˈmeθəd/ *n* **1** [C] way (of doing sth): *modern methods of teaching arithmetic* ○ *various methods of payment*, eg cash, cheques, credit card. **2** [U] orderly arrangement, habits, etc: *We must get some method into our office filing.* ○ *He's a man of accuracy and strict method.* **3** (idm) (**have, etc**) **method in one's madness** behaviour that is not as irrational, strange, etc as it seems.
▷ **methodical** /mɪˈθɒdɪkl/ *adj* (**a**) done in an orderly logical way: *methodical work, study, etc.* (**b**) (of a person) doing things in an orderly or systematic way: *a methodical worker, organizer, etc.* **methodically** /-klɪ/ *adv.*
methodology /ˌmeθəˈdɒlədʒɪ/ *n* **1** [C] set of methods used (in doing sth): *a methodology for statistical analysis.* **2** [U] science or study of methods. **methodological** /ˌmeθədəˈlɒdʒɪkl/ *adj.* **methodologically** /-klɪ/ *adv.*
□ ˈ**method acting** type of acting in which the actor tries to achieve a realistic interpretation by pretending to be the character he is acting. It was developed in America and based on the techniques of *Stanislavsky.

Methodism /ˈmeθədɪzəm/ *n* [U] Nonconformist Protestant religious denomination that originated in the teachings of John *Wesley. ➪ article at RELIGION.
▷ **Methodist** /ˈmeθədɪst/ *n, adj* (member) of this denomination. Cf WESLEYAN.

meths /meθs/ *n* [U] (*infml esp Brit*) methylated spirits.

Methuselah /mɪˈθju:zələ/ **1** Hebrew patriarch, the grandfather of *Noah, described in the Old Testament as living for 969 years. **2** (idm) **old as Methuselah** ➪ OLD.

methyl alcohol /ˌmeθɪl ˈælkəhɒl, *also* ˌmi:θaɪl/ (also ˈ**wood spirit**) type of alcohol present in many organic compounds.

methylated spirits /ˌmeθəleɪtɪd ˈspɪrɪts/ type of alcohol (made unfit for drinking) used as a fuel for lighting and heating.

meticulous /mɪˈtɪkjʊləs/ *adj* ~ (**in sth/doing sth**) giving or showing great precision and care; very attentive to detail: *a meticulous worker, researcher, etc* ○ *meticulous work* ○ *She is meticulous in her presentation of facts.* ▷ **meticulously** *adv.* **meticulousness** *n* [U].

métier /ˈmetɪeɪ/ *n* (*French*) profession, trade or main area of activity, expertise, etc: *Don't ask me how to make an omelette; cooking isn't my métier.*

metonymy /mɪˈtɒnɪmɪ/ *n* [C, U] (instance of the) substitution of the name of an attribute or adjunct of sth for the thing itself, eg *the crown* for *the queen* or *the cloth* for *the clergy.* Cf SYNECDOCHE.

metre[1] (*US* **meter**) /ˈmi:tə(r)/ *n* (*abbr* **m**) unit of length in the metric system, equal to 39.37 inches. ➪ App 9, 10, 12.

metre[2] (*US* **meter**) /ˈmi:tə(r)/ *n* (**a**) [U] verse rhythm. (**b**) [C] particular form of this; fixed arrangement of accented and unaccented syllables: *a metre with six beats to a line.*

-metre (*US* **-meter**) *comb form* (used in *ns* expressing a given fraction or multiple of a metre[1]): *centimetre* ○ *millimetre* ○ *kilometre.*

metric /ˈmetrɪk/ *adj* **1** of or based on the metre[1]: *metric measurement, dimensions, scale, etc.* **2** made, measured, etc according to the metric system: *These screws are metric*, ie have been measured in fractions of a metre. ○ *The petrol pumps have gone metric*, ie measure petrol in litres. **3** = METRICAL.
▷ **metricate** /ˈmetrɪkeɪt/ *v* [Tn] convert (sth) to the metric system: *The UK metricated its currency in 1971.* **metrication** /ˌmetrɪˈkeɪʃn/ *n* [U]: *metrication of the currency.*
□ **the** ˈ**metric system** the decimal measuring system, using the metre, the kilogram and the litre as basic units.
ˌ**metric** ˈ**ton** 1 000 kilograms; tonne.

metrical /ˈmetrɪkl/ (also **metric**) *adj* of or composed in verse, not prose: *a metrical translation of the Iliad.*

Metro /ˈmetrəʊ/ *n* **the Metro** underground railway system, esp in Paris: [attrib] *a Metro station, sign, train.* Cf TUBE, UNDERGROUND.

metronome /ˈmetrənəʊm/ *n* (*music*) device, usu with an inverted pendulum that can move back and forward at various speeds, which is used by a musician to mark time.

metropolis /məˈtrɒpəlɪs/ *n* (*pl* **-lises**) chief city of a region or country; capital: *a great metropolis like Tokyo* ○ *working in the metropolis*, ie for British people, in London.
▷ **metropolitan** /ˌmetrəˈpɒlɪtən/ *adj* of or in a large or capital city: *the population of metropolitan New York*, ie not including its suburbs. — *n* **1** person who lives in a metropolis. **2 Metropolitan** (also **metroˌpolitan** ˈ**bishop**) bishop (usu an archbishop) having authority over the bishops in his province. **metroˌpolitan** ˈ**county** any of six large urban areas created in England in 1974 with local-government powers similar to those of counties, and abolished in 1986. They included Greater Manchester, Merseyside, South Yorkshire, Tyne and Wear, West Midlands and West Yorkshire. They remain as territorial regions. **metroˌpolitan** ˈ**district** any of the areas into which a metropolitan county was divided. **Metroˌpolitan** ˈ**France** France itself, not including its colonies, etc. **the Metroˌpolitan Poˈlice** (also **the Met**) the London police force. ➪ article at POLICE.

-metry *comb form* (forming *ns*) procedure or system involving measurement: *geometry.*

mettle /ˈmetl/ *n* [U] **1** quality of endurance or courage, esp in people or horses: *a man of mettle* ○ *test sb's mettle* ○ *She showed her mettle by winning in spite of her handicap.* **2** (idm) **be on one's** ˈ**mettle; put sb on his** ˈ**mettle** be encouraged or forced to do one's best; encourage or force sb to do his best: *You'll be on your mettle during the training period.* ○ *The next race will put him on his mettle.*
▷ **mettlesome** /-səm/ *adj* (*approv*) (usu of horses, etc) high-spirited; courageous.

mew /mju:/ *n* cry characteristic of a (usu young) cat or a sea-bird: *We heard the mew of a cat.*
▷ **mew** *v* [I] make this sound.

mews /mju:z/ *n* (*pl* unchanged) (*usu Brit*) square or street of stables, converted into garages or flats, etc: *live in a Chelsea mews* ○ [attrib] *a mews flat.*

Mexico

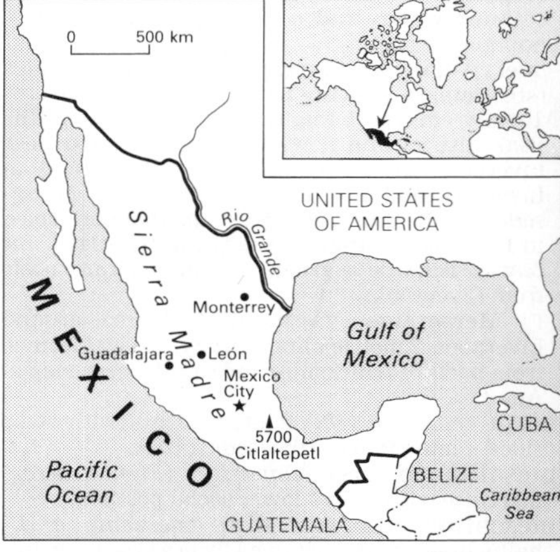

Mexico /ˈmeksɪkəʊ/ central American country, bordered by the USA to the north, with extensive coastlines on the Atlantic and Pacific Oceans; pop approx 82 734 000; official language Spanish; capital Mexico City; unit of currency peso. Mexico was the centre of the *Aztec and *Mayan civilizations. It was colonized by Spain from the early 16th century until 1821. Part of its territory, including Texas, was lost to the USA in the 19th century. Although a major oil-producing country, Mexico still has huge international debts. ➪ map.
▷ **Mexican** *adj, n* (native or inhabitant) of Mexico.

mezzanine /ˈmezəni:n/ *n* **1** floor between the ground floor and the first floor of a building, often in the form of a balcony: [attrib] *a mezzanine floor, department, etc.* **2** (*US*) (first few rows of the) lowest balcony in a theatre. Cf DRESS-CIRCLE (DRESS[1]).

mezzo /ˈmetsəʊ/ *adv* (*music*) moderately; half: *mezzo forte*, ie moderately loud(ly) ○ *mezzo piano*, ie moderately quiet(ly).
▷ **mezzo** *n* (*infml*) mezzo-soprano.
□ ˌ**mezzo-soˈprano** *n* **1** (**a**) voice between soprano and contralto. (**b**) singer with such a voice. **2** part in a piece of music for such a voice.

mezzotint /ˈmetsəʊtɪnt/ *n* [C, U] (print produced by a) method of printing from a metal plate, parts of which are roughened to give darker areas, and parts of which are smoothed to give lighter areas.

MF /ˌem ˈef/ *abbr* (*radio*) medium frequency.

MG /ˌem ˈdʒiː/ *abbr* (name of a sports car formerly manufactured by) Morris Garages. Cf NUFFIELD, LORD.

Mg *symb* magnesium.

mg *abbr* milligram(s): *100 mg*.

Mgr *abbr* **1** Monsignor. **2** Monseigneur.

MHR /em eɪtʃ ˈɑː(r)/ *abbr* Member of the House of Representatives (in the USA and Australia).

MHz *abbr* megahertz.

mi (also **me**) /miː/ *n* (*music*) third note in the sol-fa scale.

mi *abbr* (*US*) = ML 1.

MI5 /ˌem aɪ ˈfaɪv/ *abbr* (*Brit*) Military Intelligence, section five, the former name (still often used unofficially) of the security service of the British Government, which deals with counter-intelligence.

MI6 /ˌem aɪ ˈsɪks/ *abbr* (*Brit*) Military Intelligence, section six, the former name (still often used unofficially) of the intelligence and espionage agency of the British Government. Cf MI5.

miaou /miːˈaʊ/ *n* cry characteristic of a cat.
▷ **miaow** *v* [I] make this cry.

miasma /mɪˈæzmə/ *n* (esp *sing*) (*fml*) **1** unhealthy or unpleasant mist, etc: *A miasma rose from the marsh.* **2** (*fig*) bad atmosphere or influence: *a miasma of despair*.

mica /ˈmaɪkə/ *n* [U] transparent mineral easily divided into thin layers, used as an electrical insulator, etc.

Micah /ˈmaɪkə/ (**a**) Hebrew prophet. (**b**) book of the Old Testament that bears his name, foretelling the destruction of Jerusalem. ⇨ App 5.

Micawber /mɪˈkɔːbə(r)/ person who is always hoping that something good will happen so that his difficulties will be resolved without any effort made by him (named after a character in *David Copperfield* by Charles *Dickens).
▷ **Micawberism** *n* [C, U] (instance of or words that express the) attitude to life of such a person.

mice *pl* of MOUSE.

Michael /ˈmaɪkl/ Saint, one of the archangels, usu represented in art, etc killing a dragon.

Michaelmas /ˈmɪklməs/ *n* the festival of St Michael, 29 September.
□ ˌ**Michaelmas ˈdaisy** perennial plant that flowers in autumn, with blue, white, pink or purple flowers.
ˈ**Michaelmas term** autumn term at some British universities, colleges, etc.

Michelangelo /ˌmaɪkəlˈændʒələʊ/ (1475-1564), Italian sculptor, painter, architect and poet who worked in Rome and Florence (full name Michelangelo Buonarroti). Among his most famous works are his statues of *David* and the *Pietà*, the painted ceiling of the Sistine chapel in the Vatican, and his design for the rebuilding of St Peter's basilica. As a genius who worked in many fields, he is seen as the embodiment of *Renaissance man and has had a profound influence on later artists.

Michigan /ˈmɪʃɪgən/ (*abbrs* **MI**, **Mich**) **1** state in the north-western USA. Its northern boundary is formed by Lakes Huron and Superior. ⇨ map at App 1. **2** (also **Lake Michigan**) one of the five *Great Lakes of N America, the only one that is wholly within the USA. The cities of Chicago and Milwaukee are on its shores.

mick /mɪk/ *n* (*usu offensive*) Irishman.

mickey /ˈmɪkɪ/ *n* (idm) **take the mickey (out of sb)** (*infml*) ridicule or tease sb: *Stop taking the mickey (out of poor Susan)!*

Mickey Finn /ˌmɪkɪ ˈfɪn/ (*infml*) strong alcoholic drink, esp one that also contains a drug.

Mickey Mouse /ˌmɪkɪ ˈmaʊs/ **1** popular cartoon character created by Walt *Disney. **2** [attrib] (*infml*) unimportant; petty or trivial: *Who's going to vote for a party with a Mickey Mouse manifesto like theirs?*

micro /ˈmaɪkrəʊ/ *n* (*pl* **~s**) (*infml*) microcomputer.

micro- *comb form* **1** very small: *microchip* ○ *microfiche*. **2** one millionth part of: *microgram*, ie one millionth of a gram. ⇨ App 12. Cf MACRO-, MINI-.

microbe /ˈmaɪkrəʊb/ *n* tiny organism that can only be seen under a microscope, esp one that causes disease or fermentation. Cf VIRUS.

microbiology /ˌmaɪkrəʊbaɪˈɒlədʒɪ/ *n* [U] study of micro-organisms.
▷ **microbiologist** /-lədʒɪst/ *n* expert in microbiology.

microchip /ˈmaɪkrəʊtʃɪp/ (also **chip**) *n* very small piece of silicon or similar material carrying a complex electrical circuit.

microcircuit /ˈmaɪkrəʊsɜːkɪt/ *n* integrated circuit or other very small electronic circuit (eg on a microchip).

microclimate /ˈmaɪkrəʊklaɪmɪt/ *n* climate of a small area immediately surrounding sth, eg plants in a greenhouse.

microcomputer /ˌmaɪkrəʊkəmˈpjuːtə(r)/ *n* small domestic or business computer in which the central processor is a microprocessor. Cf MAINFRAME (MAIN[1]), MINICOMPUTER.

microcosm /ˈmaɪkrəʊkɒzəm/ *n* **1** thing or being regarded as representing the universe, or mankind, on a small scale; miniature representation (of a system, etc): *Man is a microcosm of the whole of mankind.* ○ *This town is a microcosm of our world.* Cf MACROCOSM. **2** (idm) **in microcosm** in miniature; on a small scale: *This small island contains the whole of nature in microcosm.* ▷ **microcosmic** *adj*.

microdot /ˈmaɪkrəʊdɒt/ *n* photograph, usu of secret documents, etc, reduced to the size of a dot.

micro-electronics /ˌmaɪkrəʊˌɪlekˈtrɒnɪks/ *n* [sing *v*] design, manufacture and use of electrical devices with very small components.

microfiche /ˈmaɪkrəʊfiːʃ/ (also **fiche**) *n* [C, U] sheet of microfilm: *documents stored on microfiche*.

microfilm /ˈmaɪkrəʊfɪlm/ *n* [C, U] (piece of) film on which extremely small photographs are stored, esp of documents, printed matter, etc: *scientific papers on microfilm*.
▷ **microfilm** *v* [Tn] photograph (sth) using such film: *microfilm secret papers, bank accounts, etc*.

microform /ˈmaɪkrəʊfɔːm/ *n* [U] any or all of the forms in which documents, etc are reproduced in miniature, eg microfiche, microfilm, etc.

microlight /ˈmaɪkrəʊlaɪt/ *n* type of very light miniature aircraft.

micrometer /maɪˈkrɒmɪtə(r)/ *n* device for measuring very small objects, angles or distances.

micron /ˈmaɪkrɒn/ *n* one millionth of a metre; micrometre.

Micronesia /ˌmaɪkrəʊˈniːzɪə/ area of the western Pacific Ocean that includes the Mariana, Caroline and Marshall Islands, and Kiribati. ⇨ map.
□ ˌ**Federated** ˌ**States of** ˌ**Microˈnesia** country of over 600 islands that span the Caroline archipelago in the western Pacific Ocean; pop approx 101 000; official language English; capital Palikir (on Pohnpei Island); unit of currency US dollar. After German and Japanese colonization, it was administered from 1947 by the US as a United Nations Trust Territory, but since 1986 it has been independent except in US-handled defence matters. ⇨ map.

Micronesia

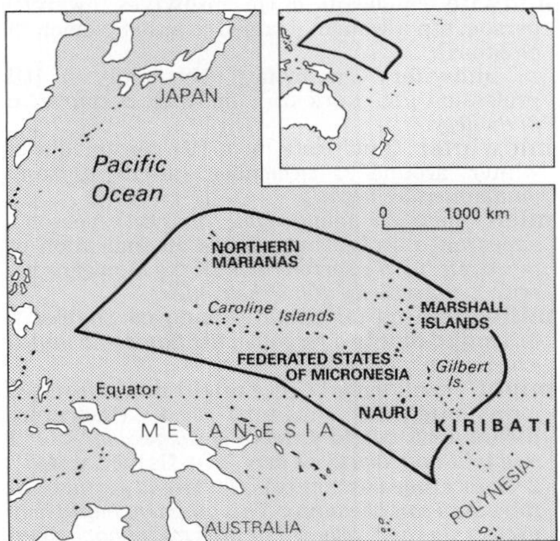

micro-organism /ˌmaɪkrəʊˈɔːgənɪzəm/ *n* organism so small that it can be seen only under a microscope.

microphone /ˈmaɪkrəfəʊn/ *n* instrument that changes sound waves into electrical current (used in recording or broadcasting speech, music, etc).

microprocessor /ˈmaɪkrəʊprəʊsesə(r)/ *n* (*computing*) central data processing unit of a computer, contained on one or more microchips.

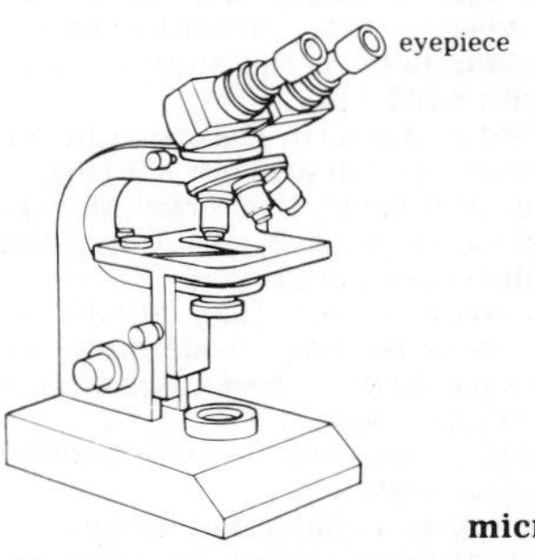

microscope

microscope /ˈmaɪkrəskəʊp/ *n* instrument with lenses for making very small objects appear larger. The modern microscope, with at least two lenses, was developed in the 17th century. The lenses are mounted in a tube: the one at the far end magnifies the object looked at, and the one nearer the eye enlarges this image further: *examine bacteria under a microscope* ○ (*fig*) *put politicians under the microscope*, ie examine them closely. Cf ELECTRON MICROSCOPE (ELECTRON), ⇨ illus.
▷ **microscopic** /ˌmaɪkrəˈskɒpɪk/, **microscopical** /-kl/ *adjs* **1** too small to be seen without the help of a microscope: *a microscopic creature, particle* ○ *of microscopic size*. **2** of or using a microscope: *microscopic examination of traces of blood*.
microscopically /-klɪ/ *adv*.
microscopy /maɪˈkrɒskəpɪ/ *n* [U] use of microscopes.

microsurgery /ˈmaɪkrəʊsɜːdʒərɪ/ *n* [U] intricate surgery that requires the use of a microscope because the body tissue and instruments involved are so small.

microwave /ˈmaɪkrəweɪv/ *n* **1** very short electromagnetic wave used esp in radio and radar, and also in cooking. **2** (also ˌ**microwave ˈoven**) type of oven that cooks food very quickly using microwaves: [attrib] *microwave cookery*.
▷ **microwave** *v* [Tn] cook (sth) in a microwave oven.

mid /mɪd/ *adj* [attrib] the middle of: *from mid July to mid August* ○ *in mid winter* ○ *a collision in mid Channel/in mid air*.

mid- *comb form* in the middle of: *mid-morning coffee* ○ *a mid-air collision* ○ *midsummer/midwinter*.
□ **the** ˌ**Midˈwest** *n* [sing] (also **the Middle West**) loosely, the northern central part of the USA, from the Great Lakes to the Ohio River, Kansas and Missouri.

Midas /ˈmaɪdəs/ **1** (in Greek mythology) king of Phrygia who had the power of turning everything he touched into gold. **2** (idm) **(have) the ˈMidas touch** (have) the skill or good fortune to be financially successful in what one does: *an investor with the Midas touch who turned a small legacy into a fortune*.

midday /ˌmɪdˈdeɪ/ *n* [U] middle of the day; noon: *finish work at midday* ○ [attrib] *the* ˌ*midday* ˈ*meal*, ie lunch.

midden /ˈmɪdn/ *n* heap of dung or rubbish.

middle /ˈmɪdl/ *n* **1 the middle** [sing] point, position or part which is at an equal distance from two or more points, etc; point between the beginning and the end: *the middle of the room* ○ *in the middle of the century* ○ *in the very middle of the night* ○ *a pain in the middle of his back* ○ *They were in the middle of dinner* (ie were having dinner) *when I called.* ○ *I was right in the middle of reading it* (ie was busy reading it) *when she phoned.* **2** [C] (*infml*) waist: *seize sb round the/his middle* ○ *fifty inches round the middle.* **3** (idm) **the middle of ˈnowhere** (*infml*) somewhere very remote or isolated: *She lives on a small farm in the middle of nowhere.* **pig in the middle** ⇨ PIG.

▷ **middle** *adj* [attrib] **1** (occupying a position) in the middle: *the middle house of the three* ○ *He wears a ring on his middle finger.* **2** (idm) (**take/follow**) **a middle ˈcourse** (make) a compromise between two extreme courses of action.

□ ˌ**middle ˈage** period between youth and old age. ˌ**middle-ˈaged** /-eɪdʒd/ *adj* of middle age: *a* ˌ*middle-aged* ˈ*man.* ˌ**middle-age(d) ˈspread** (*infml*) stoutness of the stomach that tends to come with middle age.

the ˌ**Middle ˈAges** (in European history) period from about AD 1100 to about AD 1400.

ˌ**Middle Aˈmerica 1** = THE MIDWEST (MID-). **2** middle classes of the USA, esp regarded as politically conservative.

ˈ**middle-brow** *n, adj* [usu attrib] (*esp derog*) (person who is) only moderately intellectual: *middle-brow writers, books, music, interests.* Cf HIGHBROW, LOWBROW.

ˌ**middle ˈC** (*music*) note C situated near the middle of the piano keyboard.

ˌ**middle ˈclass** social class between the lower/working and upper classes, including professional and business people: [attrib] *a* ˌ*middle-class* ˈ*neighbourhood.* ⇨ article at CLASS.

ˌ**middle-ˈdistance** *adj* [attrib] (**a**) (in athletics) of a running race which is between a sprint and a long-distance race in length, eg 800 or 1 500 metres. (**b**) of a runner who takes part in such races.

the ˌ**middle ˈdistance** that part of a landscape scene, painting, etc that is between the foreground and the background.

ˌ**middle ˈear** cavity of the central part of the ear, behind the eardrum: *an infection of the middle ear.* ⇨ illus at EAR.

the ˌ**Middle ˈEast** loosely, an area comprising Egypt, Iran and the countries between them.

ˌ**Middle ˈEnglish** English as spoken between about 1150 and 1500.

ˌ**middle ˈfinger** longest finger. ⇨ illus at HAND.

ˌ**middle ˈground** position midway between extremes; moderate position: *occupy the middle ground.*

ˈ**middleman** /-mæn/ *n* (*pl* **-men** /-men/) **1** trader who passes goods from the producer to the final buyer: *She wants to buy direct from the manufacturer and cut out the middleman.* **2** intermediary; go-between: *He acted as a middleman in discussions between the two companies.*

ˌ**middle ˈmanagement** business executives of middle rank, in charge of the day-to-day running of a company.

ˌ**middle ˈname 1** second of two given names, eg *Bernard* in *George Bernard Shaw.* **2** (idm) **be sb's middle ˈname** (*infml*) be sb's chief characteristic: *Charm is her middle name.*

ˌ**middle-of-the-ˈroad** *adj* (of people, policies, etc) moderate; avoiding extremes: *Her political beliefs are very middle-of-the-road.* ○ *a middle-of-the-road taste in music.*

ˈ**middle school** (*esp Brit*) school for children aged between 9 and 13 years.

ˈ**middleweight** *n* boxer weighing between 67 and 72.5 kg, next above welterweight.

the ˌ**Middle ˈWest** = THE MIDWEST (MID-).

Middlesex /ˈmɪdlseks/ (*abbr* **Middx**) former English county, now forming part of Greater London and Hertfordshire since the local government reorganization of 1974.

Middleton /ˈmɪdltn/ Thomas (1580-1627), English dramatist, author of many satirical comedies. He is best known today for his tragedies *The Changeling* (written in collaboration with William Rowley) and *Women Beware Women.*

middling /ˈmɪdlɪŋ/ *adj* **1** of medium size, quality, etc: *a man of middling height* ○ *'Is it big or small?' 'Middling'.* **2** [pred] in fairly good health: *He says he's only (feeling) middling today.* cf FAIR-TO-MIDDLING (FAIR[1]).

midfield /ˌmɪdˈfi:ld/ *n* middle part of a football, etc pitch; part of a pitch equally distant from the two goals: [attrib] *a midfield player.* ⇨ illus at ASSOCIATION FOOTBALL (ASSOCIATION).

midge /mɪdʒ/ *n* small winged insect like a gnat.

midget /ˈmɪdʒɪt/ *n* extremely small person. ▷ **midget** *adj* [attrib] very small: *a midget submarine.*

Mid Glamorgan /ˌmɪd ɡləˈmɔ:ɡən/ county of S Wales. ⇨ map at App 1.

midland /ˈmɪdlənd/ *adj* [attrib] of the middle part of the country: *the midland region, economy, accent.*

▷ **the Midlands** *n* [sing or pl *v*] central inland counties of England: [attrib] *a Midlands firm.* ⇨ map at UNITED KINGDOM.

midnight /ˈmɪdnaɪt/ *n* [U] **1** 12 o'clock at night: *at/before/after midnight* ○ [attrib] *a midnight visit*, ie one made around midnight. **2** (idm) **burn the midnight oil** ⇨ BURN[2].

□ **the** ˌ**midnight ˈsun** sun seen at midnight in summer near the North and South Poles.

midriff /ˈmɪdrɪf/ *n* **1** middle part of the human body, between the waist and the chest; belly: *a punch in the midriff.* **2** (*anatomy*) diaphragm.

midshipman /ˈmɪdʃɪpmən/ *n* (*pl* **-men** /-mən/) **1** (*Brit*) rank below that of sub-lieutenant in the Royal Navy. **2** (*US*) student training to be an officer in the US Navy. ⇨ App 4.

midships /ˈmɪdʃɪps/ *adv* = AMIDSHIPS.

midst /mɪdst/ *n* (used after a *prep*) middle part: *in the midst of the crowd* ○ *A fox darted out of the midst of the thicket.* ○ *There is a thief in our/your/their midst*, ie among or with us, you, etc.

midstream /ˌmɪdˈstri:m/ *n* [U] **1** part of a stream, river, etc half-way between its banks: *There's a fast current in midstream.* **2** (idm) **change/swap horses in midstream** ⇨ HORSE. **in midstream** in the middle of an action, etc: *The speaker stopped in midstream, coughed, then started up again.*

midsummer /ˌmɪdˈsʌmə(r)/ *n* [U] **1** the middle of summer, around 21 June: [attrib] *a warm* ˌ*midsummer('s)* ˈ*day.* **2** (idm) ˌ**midsummer ˈmadness** very great madness or foolishness.

□ ˌ**Midsummer's ˈDay** 24 June.

midway /ˌmɪdˈweɪ/ *adj, adv* ~ (**between sth and sth**) (situated) in the middle; half-way: *The two villages are a mile apart, and my house lies midway between them.*

midweek /ˌmɪdˈwi:k/ *n* [U] middle of the week, ie Tuesday, Wednesday and Thursday, but esp Wednesday: *Midweek is a good time to travel to avoid the crowds.* ○ [attrib] *a* ˌ*midweek* ˈ*holiday,* ˈ*meeting.*

▷ **midweek** *adv* in the middle of the week: *meet, travel, call, etc midweek.*

midwife /ˈmɪdwaɪf/ *n* (*pl* **midwives** /-waɪvz/) person, esp a woman, trained to assist women in childbirth.

▷ **midwifery** /ˈmɪdwɪfərɪ; *US* -waɪf-/ *n* [U] profession and work of a midwife: *a course in midwifery.*

midwinter /ˌmɪdˈwɪntə(r)/ *n* [U] the middle of winter, around 21 December: [attrib] *a frosty* ˌ*midwinter('s)* ˈ*night.*

mien /mi:n/ *n* [sing] (*fml or rhet*) person's appearance or bearing, esp as an indication of mood, etc: *with a sorrowful mien* ○ *a man of proud mien* ○ *the severity of his/their mien.*

miffed /mɪft/ *adj* (*sl*) (slightly) annoyed: *She was (a bit) miffed that he'd forgotten her name.* ○ *a miffed expression.*

might[1] /maɪt/ *modal v* (*neg* **might not**, *contracted form* **mightn't** /ˈmaɪtnt/) **1** (indicating permission): *Might I make a suggestion?* ○ *If I might just put in a word here....* ⇨ Usage 1 at MAY[1]. **2** (indicating possibility): *He ˈmight get here in time, but I can't be sure.* ○ *This ointment might help to clear up your rash.* ○ *The pills might have cured him, if only he'd taken them regularly.* ⇨ Usage 2 at MAY[1]. **3** (asking for information): *And who might ˈshe be?* ○ *How long might ˈthat take?* ⇨ Usage 4 at MAY[1]. **4** (used to make polite requests or appeals): *You might just* (ie Please) *call in at the supermarket for me.* ○ *I think you might at least offer to help!* ⇨ Usage at WOULD.

might[2] *pt* of MAY[1].

might[3] /maɪt/ *n* [U] **1** great strength or power: *I pushed the rock with all my might.* ○ *We fear the military might of the enemy.* **2** (idm) ˌ**might is ˈright** (*saying*) having the power to do sth gives one the right to do it. **with** ˌ**might and ˈmain** (*rhet*) with all one's physical strength.

mighty /ˈmaɪtɪ/ *adj* (**-ier, -iest**) **1** (*esp fml*) powerful; strong: *a mighty army, nation, ruler* ○ (*infml*) *She gave him a mighty thump.* **2** great and imposing: *mighty mountain peaks* ○ *the mighty ocean.* **3** (idm) **high and mighty** ⇨ HIGH[1]. **the pen is mightier than the sword** ⇨ PEN[1].

▷ **mightily** /-ɪlɪ/ *adv* **1** (*fml*) powerfully; forcefully: *He struck it mightily with his sword.* **2** very: *mightily pleased, relieved, etc.*

mighty *adv* (*infml esp US*) very: *mighty good, clever, etc* ○ *He's mighty pleased with himself.*

mignonette /ˌmɪnjəˈnet/ *n* annual plant with small sweet-smelling flowers.

migraine /ˈmi:ɡreɪn; *US* ˈmaɪɡreɪn/ *n* [U, C] severe recurring type of headache, usu on one side of the head or face, often accompanied by nausea and disturbance of the eyesight.

migrate /maɪˈɡreɪt; *US* ˈmaɪɡreɪt/ (also **transmigrate**) *v* [I, Ipr] ~ (**from...**) (**to...**) **1** move from one place to go to live or work in another. **2** (of animals, etc) go from one place to another with the seasons, esp to spend the winter in a warmer place: *These birds migrate to North Africa in winter.*

▷ **migrant** /ˈmaɪɡrənt/ *n, adj* [attrib] (of a) person or animal who migrates: *migrant workers*, ie those who travel to another region or country to work ○ *migrant sea-birds.*

migration /maɪˈɡreɪʃn/ *n* (**a**) (also **transmigration**) [C, U] (action of) migrating. (**b**) [C] number of migrating people, animals, etc: *a huge migration of people into Europe.*

migratory /ˈmaɪɡrətrɪ, maɪˈɡreɪtərɪ; *US* ˈmaɪɡrətɔ:rɪ/ *adj* having or of the habit of migrating: *migratory birds* ○ *the migratory instinct.*

mikado /mɪˈkɑ:dəʊ/ *n* (*pl* ~**s**) (name formerly used outside Japan for the) Emperor of Japan.

mike /maɪk/ *n* (*infml*) microphone.

milage = MILEAGE.

milch /mɪltʃ/ *adj* [attrib] (*dated*) (of domestic mammals, esp cows) giving or kept for milk: *a milch cow, goat, etc.*

mild /maɪld/ *adj* (**-er, -est**) **1** (**a**) (of a person or his manner) gentle; soft: *He's the mildest man you could wish to meet.* ○ *She's a very mild-mannered person.* ○ *He gave a mild answer, in spite of his annoyance.* (**b**) not severe or harsh: *mild weather, a mild climate, etc*, ie not cold ○ *a mild punishment* ○ *the mild action of the soap.* **2** (of a flavour) not strong or bitter: *mild cheese* ○ *a mild cigar, curry.*

▷ **mild** *n* [U] (also **mild ale**) (*Brit*) type of beer not strongly flavoured with hops: *two pints of mild.*

mildly *adv* **1** in a gentle manner: *She spoke mildly to us.* **2** (idm) **to put it ˈmildly** without exaggerating; using understatement: *At 6' 4", she's tall, to put it mildly*, ie She's extremely tall.

mildness *n* [U].

□ ˌ**mild ˈsteel** tough malleable type of steel with a low percentage of carbon.

mildew /ˈmɪldju:; *US* -du:/ *n* [U] tiny fungus forming a (usu white) coating on plants, leather, food, etc in warm and damp conditions: *roses ruined by mildew.*

▷ **mildew** *v* [I, Tn esp passive] (cause sth to) be affected by mildew: *mildewed canvas, leaves, fruit.*

mile /maɪl/ *n* **1** [C] unit of distance equal to 1.6 km: *For miles and miles there's nothing but desert.* ○ *a 39-mile journey.* ⇨ App 9, 10. Cf NAUTICAL MILE (NAUTICAL). **2** [C esp *pl*] (*infml*) a great amount or distance; much: *She's feeling miles* (ie very much) *better today.* ○ *He's miles older than she is.* ○ *There's no one within miles/a mile of her* (ie No one can rival her) *as a tennis player.* ○ *You missed the target by a mile/by miles.* **3** (esp **the mile**) [sing] race over one mile: *Who's running in the mile?* ○ *He can run a four-minute mile,* ie run a mile in four minutes or less. ○ [attrib] *the world mile record.* **4** (idm) **ˌmiles from ˈanywhere/ˈnowhere** in a remote or isolated place, position, etc. **a miss is as good as a mile** ⇨ MISS¹. **run a mile (from sb/sth)** be anxious or careful to avoid sb/sth: *I'd sooner run a mile than be interviewed on television.* **see/tell sth a ˈmile off** (*infml*) see/tell sth very easily: *He's lying: you can see that a mile off.* **stand/stick out a ˈmile** be very striking or noticeable: *Her honesty sticks out a mile.* ○ *It stands out a mile that she's telling the truth.*

□ **ˈmilestone** *n* **1** stone put at the side of a road showing distances in miles. **2** (*fig*) very important stage or event: *This victory was a milestone in our country's history.*

mileage (also **milage**) /ˈmaɪlɪdʒ/ *n* **1** [C, U] distance travelled, measured in miles: *a used car with a low/high mileage,* ie one that has not/has been driven many miles. **2** [U] (also **ˈmileage allowance**) allowance paid for the expenses of travelling by (one's own) car: *Have you claimed your mileage?* **3** [U] (*fig infml*) (amount of) benefit or advantage: *He doesn't think there's any mileage in that type of advertising.*

miler /ˈmaɪlə(r)/ *n* (*infml*) person or horse specializing in races of one mile: *He's our best miler.*

milfoil /ˈmɪlfɔɪl/ *n* plant of the yarrow family with small white flowers and finely divided leaves.

milieu /ˈmiːljɜː; *US* ˌmiːˈljɜː/ *n* (*pl* **~s** or **~x** /-z/) (usu *sing*) social surroundings; environment: *Coming from another milieu, she found life as an actor's wife very strange at first.*

militant /ˈmɪlɪtənt/ *adj* using force or strong pressure, or supporting their use, to achieve one's aims: *The strikers were in a militant mood,* ie ready to take strong action.

▷ **militancy** /-ənsɪ/ *n* [U].

militant *n* militant person, esp in trade unionism or politics.

□ **ˌMilitant ˈTendency** (also **Militant**) extreme left-wing group formed within the British Labour Party in the 1970s. It enjoyed some influence and electoral success in the late 1970s and early 1980s, but it was expelled in the mid 1980s for having policies incompatible with those of the party.

militarism /ˈmɪlɪtərɪzəm/ *n* [U] (*usu derog*) believing in or depending on military strength and methods, esp as a government policy.

▷ **militarist** /ˈmɪlɪtərɪst/ *n* person who supports militarism.

militaristic /ˌmɪlɪtəˈrɪstɪk/ *adj.*

militarize, -ise /ˈmɪlɪtəraɪz/ *v* [Tn esp passive] use (esp land) for military purposes: *a militarized zone.*

military /ˈmɪlɪtrɪ; *US* -terɪ/ *adj* [usu attrib] of or for soldiers or an army; of or for (all the) armed forces: *military training, discipline, etc* ○ *in full military uniform* ○ *be called up for/do military service,* ie go to be trained or serve as a soldier, etc for a fixed period of time ○ *the military police.*

▷ **the military** *n* [sing or pl *v*] soldiers or the army; the armed forces (as distinct from police or civilians): *The military were called in to deal with the riot.*

militate /ˈmɪlɪteɪt/ *v* [Ipr] **~ against sth** (*fml*) (of evidence, facts, etc) have great force or influence to prevent sth: *Many factors militated against the success of our plan.*

militia /mɪˈlɪʃə/ *n* [CGp] force of civilians who are trained as soldiers and reinforce the regular army in the internal defence of the country in an emergency.

□ **militiaman** /-mən/ *n* (*pl* **-men**) member of a militia.

milk¹ /mɪlk/ *n* [U] **1** white liquid produced by female mammals as food for their young, esp that of cows, goats, etc drunk by human beings and made into butter and cheese: *milk fresh from the cow* ○ *skimmed milk* ○ *dried/powdered milk* ○ [attrib] *milk products,* eg butter, cheese, yoghurt ○ *a milk bottle.* **2** milk-like juice of some plants and trees, eg that found inside a coconut. **3** milk-like preparation made from herbs, drugs, etc. **4** (idm) **cry over spilt milk** ⇨ CRY¹. **ˌmilk and ˈwater** (*derog*) feeble or sentimental talk, ideas, etc: *His speech was nothing but milk and water.* ○ [attrib] *I found it a disappointing thriller — very milk-and-water stuff.* **the milk of human ˈkindness** the kindness that should be natural to human beings.

□ **ˈmilk bar** (*esp Brit*) bar for the sale of non-alcoholic drinks (esp those made from milk), ice-cream, etc.

ˌmilk ˈchocolate chocolate (for eating) made with milk and usu sold in wrapped bars: *Do you prefer milk chocolate or plain (chocolate)?*

ˈmilk churn (*Brit*) large tall metal container, fitted with a lid, for carrying milk. ⇨ illus at BARREL.

ˈmilk-float *n* (*Brit*) light low vehicle, usu electrically powered, used for delivering milk to people's houses.

ˈmilk-loaf *n* (*pl* **-loaves**) (*Brit*) sweet-tasting white bread made with milk.

ˈmilkmaid *n* woman who milks cows and works in a dairy.

ˈmilkman /-mən/ *n* (*pl* **-men**) man who goes from house to house delivering and selling milk. ⇨ article at SERVICE.

ˌmilk ˈpudding (*esp Brit*) rice, sago, tapioca, etc baked in milk in a dish.

ˈmilk round milkman's route from house to house and from street to street: *go on/do a milk round.*

ˈmilk run (*fig infml*) regular and uneventful journey providing a service: *I do the milk run every day taking the children to school.*

ˌmilk ˈshake drink made of milk and flavouring (sometimes ice-cream) mixed or shaken until frothy.

ˈmilktooth *n* (*pl* **-teeth**) (also *esp US* **baby tooth**) any of the first (temporary) teeth in young mammals.

ˈmilkweed *n* any of various wild plants with a milky juice.

ˌmilk-ˈwhite *adj* of a white colour like milk: *The prince rode a ˌmilk-white ˈhorse.*

milk² /mɪlk/ *v* **1** [I, Tn] draw milk from (a cow, goat, etc): *The farmer hasn't finished milking.* **2** [I] yield milk: *The cows are milking well,* ie giving large quantities of milk. **3** [Tn, Tn·pr] **~ A (of B)/ ~ B (from A)** (a) draw (juice) from (a plant or tree): *milk a tree of its sap* ○ *milk the sap from a tree.* (b) draw (venom) from (a snake). **4** [Tn, Tn·pr] **~ sb/sth (of sth); ~ sth (out of/from sb/sth)** (*fig*) extract (money, information, etc) dishonestly from (a person or an institution): *milking the Welfare State (of money, resources, etc)* ○ *His illegal deals were steadily milking the profits from the business.* **5** (idm) **milk/suck sb/sth dry** ⇨ DRY¹.

▷ **milker** *n* **1** person who milks an animal. **2** animal that gives milk: *That cow is a good milker.*

□ **ˈmilking-machine** *n* apparatus for milking cows mechanically.

milksop /ˈmɪlksɒp/ *n* (*derog*) man or boy who is weak and timid.

milky /ˈmɪlkɪ/ *adj* (**-ier, -iest**) **1** of or like milk: *a milky white skin.* **2** mixed with or made of milk: *milky tea, coffee, etc* ○ *I like a hot milky drink at bedtime.* **3** (of a jewel or a liquid) not clear; cloudy: *Opals are milky gems.* ▷ **milkiness** *n* [U].

□ **the ˌMilky ˈWay** = THE GALAXY (GALAXY 2).

Mill /mɪl/ John Stuart (1806-73), English philosopher and economist. He is best known for his political and moral works (eg *On Liberty* and *The Subjection of Women*), in which he argued for representative democracy, advocated the replacement of the socio-economic class structure by a system of worker ownership, and criticized the treatment of married women in the society of his day.

mill¹ /mɪl/ *n* **1** (building fitted with) machinery or apparatus for grinding grain into flour: *a ˈwater-mill* ○ *a ˈwindmill.* **2** machine for grinding or crushing a solid substance into powder: *a ˈcoffee-mill* ○ *a ˈpepper-mill.* **3** (building fitted with) machinery for processing materials of certain kinds: *a ˈcotton-mill* ○ *a ˈpaper-mill* ○ *a ˈsteel-mill* ○ *a ˈsaw-mill,* ie for timber. ⇨ Usage at FACTORY. **4** (idm) **grist to the/sb's mill** ⇨ GRIST. **put sb/go through the ˈmill** (cause sb to) undergo hard training or an unpleasant experience. Cf RUN-OF-THE-MILL (RUN²).

□ **ˈmill-dam** *n* dam built across a stream to make water available for a mill.

ˈmill-hand *n* factory worker.

ˈmill-pond *n* still water held by a mill-dam to flow to a mill: *The sea was as calm as a mill-pond.*

ˈmill-race *n* current of water that turns a mill-wheel.

ˈmillstone *n* **1** either of a pair of flat circular stones between which grain is ground. **2** (idm) **a millstone round one's/sb's ˈneck** heavy burden or responsibility: *My debts were like a millstone round my neck.*

ˈmill-wheel *n* wheel used to drive a water-mill.

ˈmillwright *n* man who designs, builds and repairs water-mills and windmills.

mill² /mɪl/ *v* [Tn esp passive] **1** (a) grind or crush (sth) in a mill: *The grain was coarsely milled.* (b) produce (sth) in a mill: *milled flour.* **2** produce regular markings on the edge of (a coin): *English pound coins have milled edges.* **3** cut or shape (metal) with a rotating tool. **4** (phr v) **mill about/around** (of people or animals) move round and round in a confused mass: *Groups of fans were milling about in the streets after the match.*

Sir John Everett Millais: Bubbles

Millais /ˈmɪleɪ/ Sir John Everett (1829-96), English painter, a founder member of the *Pre-Raphaelite Brotherhood when he was a young man. He later became a highly successful Victorian painter of portraits, landscapes and sentimental pictures (such as *Bubbles*). ⇨ illus.

millboard /ˈmɪlbɔːd/ *n* [C, U] (piece of) strong pasteboard used in bookbinding.

millefeuille /miːlˈfɜːj/ *n* (*French*) small iced cake made of puff pastry filled with jam, cream, etc.

millenarian /ˌmɪlɪˈneərɪən/ *n* person who believes that the millennium(3) will come.

millennium /mɪˈlenɪəm/ *n* (*pl* **-nia** /-nɪə/ or **~s**) **1** [C] period of 1 000 years: *the first millennium AD.* **2 the millennium** [sing] (*religion*) the 1 000-year reign of Christ on earth prophesied in the Bible. **3 the millennium** [sing] future time of great happiness and prosperity for everyone. ▷ **millennial** *adj.*

millepede (also **millipede**) /ˈmɪlɪpiːd/ *n* small worm-like creature resembling a centipede, but with two pairs of legs on each segment of its body.

Miller[1] /ˈmɪlə(r)/ Arthur (1915-), American playwright. His tragedy *Death of a Salesman*, a powerful attack on contemporary American values, established him as a major writer. His other plays include *The Crucible* and *A View from the Bridge*. He was married to Marilyn *Monroe from 1955 to 1961. ⇨ article at PERFORMING ARTS.

Miller[2] /ˈmɪlə(r)/ Glenn (1904-44), American trombonist, bandleader, composer and arranger. The band he led from 1937 to 1942 was one of the most popular in the world.

Miller[3] /ˈmɪlə(r)/ Henry (1891-1980), American writer famous for his satires of modern society. His early works, including *Tropic of Cancer* and *Tropic of Capricorn*, were published in Paris, and banned for many years in Britain and America.

miller /ˈmɪlə(r)/ *n* person who owns or runs a mill for grinding corn, esp a windmill or a water-mill.

millet /ˈmɪlɪt/ *n* [U] (**a**) type of cereal plant growing 3 to 4 feet high and producing a large crop of small seeds. (**b**) these seeds used as food.

milli- *comb form* (in the metric system) one thousandth part of: ˈ*milligram* ○ ˈ*millimetre*. ⇨ App 12.

milliard /ˈmɪlɪɑːd/ *n* (*Brit*) one thousand million(s), 1 000 000 000. Cf BILLION.

millibar /ˈmɪlɪbɑː(r)/ *n* unit of atmospheric pressure equal to one thousandth of a bar[4].

milligram /ˈmɪlɪgræm/ *n* (*abbr* **mg**) one-thousandth of a gram.

millilitre /ˈmɪlɪliːtə(r)/ *n* (*abbr* **ml**) one-thousandth of a litre.

millimetre /ˈmɪlɪmiːtə(r)/ *n* (*abbr* **mm**) one-thousandth of a metre.

milliner /ˈmɪlɪnə(r)/ *n* person who makes or sells (trimmings for) women's hats.

▷ **millinery** /-nərɪ; *US* -nerɪ/ *n* [U] (business of making or selling) (trimmings for) women's hats: [attrib] *the millinery department*, eg in a large store.

million /ˈmɪljən/ *pron, det* (after *a* or *one*, used to indicate quantity; no *pl* form) 1 000 000; one thousand thousand. ⇨ App 9.

▷ **million** *n* **1** (*sing* after *a* or *one*, but often *pl*) the number 1 000 000: *She made her first million* (eg pounds or dollars) *before she was thirty.* **2** (idm) **one, etc in a ˈmillion** person or thing of rare or exceptional quality: *She's a wife in a million.* ○ *We haven't a chance in a million* (ie We have almost no chance) *of winning.*

million- (in compounds) having a million of the thing specified: *a million-dollar law-suit*, ie one costing one million dollars or more.

millionth *pron, det* 1 000 000th. — *n* one of one million equal parts of sth.

For the uses of *million* and *millionth* see examples at *hundred* and *hundredth*.

millionaire /ˌmɪljəˈneə(r)/ (*fem* **millionairess** /ˌmɪljəˈneəres/) *ns* person who has a million pounds, dollars, etc; very rich person.

millipede = MILLEPEDE.

Mills and Boon /ˌmɪlz ən ˈbuːn/ British firm that publishes light romantic fiction, eg historical romances or love stories set in hospitals. Its name has become synonymous with the genre of popular trivial romantic fiction: [attrib] *The film treats their affair in terms of a Mills and Boon romance.*

Milne /mɪln/ A(lan) A(lexander) (1882-1956), British writer noted for his verses and books for children, including *Winnie-the-Pooh* and *The House at Pooh Corner*.

milometer *n* (also **mileometer**) /maɪˈlɒmɪtə(r)/ (*US* **odometer**) instrument in a vehicle or on a bicycle for measuring the number of miles travelled.

milord /mɪˈlɔːd/ *n* (French word formerly used for an) English lord or wealthy Englishman.

milt /mɪlt/ *n* [U] (also **soft roe**) fish sperm.

Milton /ˈmɪltən/ John (1608-74), English *Puritan poet, author of the epic poems *Paradise Lost* and *Paradise Regained*, and the drama *Samson Agonistes*, all written after he had gone blind.

mime /maɪm/ *n* (**a**) [U] (in the theatre, etc) use of only facial expressions and gestures to tell a story: *a play acted entirely in mime* ○ [attrib] *a mime artist.* (**b**) [C] performance using this.

▷ **mime** *v* **1** [I] act using mime: *mime to a recording of a song*, ie pretend that one is singing the words. **2** [Tn] express (sth) by mime: *He mimed the part of a drunken man.*

mimeograph /ˈmɪmɪəgrɑːf; *US* -græf/ *n* (*dated*) apparatus for making copies of written or typed material from a stencil.

▷ **mimeograph** *v* [Tn] copy (sth) with a mimeograph.

mimetic /mɪˈmetɪk/ *adj* (fml) of imitating or mimicking: *mimetic skills*, eg of some birds.

mimic /ˈmɪmɪk/ *v* (*pt, pp* **mimicked**) [Tn] **1** copy the appearance or manner of (sb/sth) in a mocking or amusing way: *Tom mimicked his uncle's voice and gestures perfectly.* **2** (of things) resemble (sth) closely: *wood painted to mimic marble.*

▷ **mimic** *n* person, animal, etc clever at mimicking others: *This parrot is an amazing mimic.*

mimic *adj* [attrib] imitated or pretended: *mimic warfare*, eg in peacetime manoeuvres ○ *mimic colouring*, eg of animals, birds and insects, etc whose colours blend with their natural surroundings.

mimicry *n* [U] mimicking: *protective mimicry*, ie resemblance of animals, birds, insects, etc to the colours and patterns of their natural surroundings, as a means of hiding from their enemies.

mimosa /mɪˈməʊzə; *US* -məʊsə/ *n* (**a**) [U, C] type of tropical tree or shrub with clusters of small, ball-shaped, sweet-smelling, yellow flowers. (**b**) [U] these flowers: *a bunch, spray, etc of mimosa.*

min *abbr* **1** minimum: *temperature 50° min.* Cf MAX. **2** minute(s): *fastest time 6 mins.* Cf HR.

mina = MYNAH.

minaret /ˌmɪnəˈret/ *n* tall slender spire forming part of a mosque, with a balcony from which people are called to prayer by a muezzin.

minatory /ˈmɪnətərɪ; *US* -tɔːrɪ/ *adj* (*fml*) threatening: *minatory actions, gestures, etc.*

mince /mɪns/ *v* **1** [Tn] chop or cut (esp meat) into very small pieces in a machine with revolving blades. **2** [I, Ipr, Ip] (*usu derog*) walk or speak in an affected manner, trying to appear delicate or refined: *She minced into the room wearing very high heels.* **3** (idm) **not ˈmince matters; not mince (one's) ˈwords** speak plainly or bluntly, esp when condemning sb/sth: *I didn't mince matters: I said he was an idiot.* ○ *I won't mince words (with you): I think your plan is stupid.*

▷ **mince** *n* [U] (*esp Brit*) (*US* **hamburger**) minced meat: *a pound of mince.*

mincer *n* device for mincing food, esp meat.

mincing *adj* (*usu derog*) affected: *take small, mincing steps.* **mincingly** *adv.*

□ **ˌmince ˈpie** small round pie containing mincemeat and eaten esp at Christmas. ⇨ article at CHRISTMAS.

mincemeat /ˈmɪnsmiːt/ *n* [U] **1** mixture of currants, raisins, sugar, candied peel, apples, suet, etc used esp as a filling for a mince pie. **2** (idm) **make mincemeat of sb/sth** (*infml*) defeat sb/sth completely in a fight or an argument: *The Prime Minister made mincemeat of his opponent's arguments.*

mind[1] /maɪnd/ *n* **1** [U] ability to be aware of things and to think and feel: *have the right qualities of mind for the job* ○ *have complete peace of mind.* **2** [C] (**a**) ability to reason; intellectual powers: *have a brilliant, logical, simple, etc mind.* (**b**) person who uses his reasoning or intellectual powers well: *He is one of the greatest minds of the age.* **3** [C] person's thoughts or attention: *Are you quite clear in your own mind what you ought to do?* ○ *Don't let your mind wander!* **4** [C] ability to remember; memory: *I can't think where I've left my umbrella; my mind's a complete blank!* **5** [U, C] normal condition of one's mental faculties; sanity: *be sound in mind and body* ○ *He's 94 and his mind is going*, ie he is becoming senile. **6** (idm) **absence of mind** ⇨ ABSENCE. **at the back of one's mind** ⇨ BACK[1]. **be in one's right mind** ⇨ RIGHT[1]. **be in two ˈminds about sth/doing sth** feel doubtful about or hesitate over sth: *I was in two minds about leaving London: my friends were there, but the job abroad was a good one.* **be/take a load/weight off sb's mind** cause one/sb great relief: *Paying my mortgage was an enormous weight off my mind!* **be of one ˈmind (about sb/sth)** agree or have the same opinion (about sb/sth). **be on one's ˈmind; have sth on one's ˈmind** (cause sb to) worry about sth: *My deputy has resigned, so I've got a lot on my mind just now.* **be ˌout of one's ˈmind** (*infml*) be crazy or mad: *You must be out of your mind if you think I'm going to lend you £50!* **bear in mind that...** ⇨ BEAR[2]. **bear/keep sb/sth in ˈmind** remember sb/sth: *We have no vacancies now, but we'll certainly bear your application in mind.* **bend one's mind to sth** ⇨ BEND[1]. **blow one's/sb's mind** ⇨ BLOW[1]. **boggle sb's/the mind** ⇨ BOGGLE. **bring/call sb/sth to mind** recall sb/sth to one's memory: *I know her face but I can't call her name to mind.* **cast one's mind back** ⇨ CAST[1]. **change one's/sb's mind** ⇨ CHANGE[1]. **close one's mind to sth** ⇨ CLOSE[4]. **come/spring to ˈmind** present itself to one's thoughts: *'Have you any suggestions?' 'Nothing immediately springs to mind.'* **concentrate one's/the mind** ⇨ CONCENTRATE. **cross one's mind** ⇨ CROSS[2]. **ease sb's conscience/mind** ⇨ EASE[2]. **enter sb's head/mind** ⇨ ENTER. **frame of mind** ⇨ FRAME[1]. **give one's mind to sth** concentrate on or direct all one's attention to sth. **give sb a piece of one's mind** ⇨ PIECE[1]. **go out of/slip one's ˈmind** be forgotten. **have, etc an enquiring, etc turn of mind** ⇨ TURN[2]. **have half a mind to do sth** (*infml*) feel a moderate desire to do sth. **have/keep an open mind** ⇨ OPEN[1]. **have it in mind to do sth** (*fml*) intend to do sth: *I have it in mind to ask her advice when I see her.* **have sb/sth in mind (for sth)** be considering sb/sth as suitable (for sth): *Who do you have in mind for the job?* **have a memory/mind like a sieve** ⇨ SIEVE. **have a mind of one's ˈown** be capable of forming opinions, making decisions, etc independently. **have a (good) mind to do sth** (*infml*) have a (strong) desire to do sth: *I'd a good mind to smack him for being so rude!* **in one's mind's ˈeye** in one's imagination; in one's memory: *In my mind's eye, I can still see the house where I was born.* **keep one's mind on sth** continue to pay attention to sth; not be distracted from sth: *Keep your mind on the job!* **know one's own mind** ⇨ KNOW. **make up one's ˈmind** come to a decision: *I've made up my mind to be a doctor.* ○ *Have you made your mind up where to go for your holiday?* **make up one's mind to (doing) sth** (*fml*) come to accept sth that cannot be changed, etc: *As we can't afford a bigger house we must make up our minds to staying here.* **a meeting of minds** ⇨ MEETING. **the mind/imagination boggles** ⇨ BOGGLE. **ˌmind over ˈmatter** mental powers regarded as being stronger than those of the body or physical objects: *Keeping to a strict diet is a question of mind over matter.* **of the same mind** ⇨ SAME[1]. **of unsound mind** ⇨ UNSOUND. **open one's heart/mind to sb** ⇨ OPEN[2]. **out of sight, out of mind** ⇨ SIGHT[1]. **pissed out of one's head/mind** ⇨ PISS. **poison A's mind against B** ⇨ POISON. **presence of mind** ⇨ PRESENCE. **prey on sb's mind** ⇨ PREY *v.* **put sb in mind of sb/sth** cause sb to think of or remember sb/sth: *Her way of speaking put me in mind of her mother.* **put/set one's/sb's ˈmind at ease/rest** cause or enable one/sb to stop worrying. **put/set/turn one's mind to sth** give all one's attention to (achieving) sth: *You could be a very good writer if you set your ˈmind to it.* **speak one's mind** ⇨ SPEAK. **stick in one's mind** ⇨ STICK[2]. **take one's/sb's mind off sth** help one/sb not to think or worry about sth: *Hard work always takes your mind off domestic problems.* **time out of mind** ⇨ TIME[1]. **to ˈmy mind** according to my way of thinking; in my opinion: *To ˈmy mind, it's all a lot of nonsense!* **turn sth over in one's ˈmind** consider or think carefully about sth for some time.

□ **ˈmind-bending** *adj* (*infml*) strongly influencing the mind: *a mind-bending problem.*

ˈ**mind-blowing** *adj* (*infml*) (of drugs or extraordinary sights, experiences, etc) causing mental excitement, ecstasy, hallucinations, etc.
ˈ**mind-boggling** *adj* (*infml*) alarming; extraordinary or astonishing: *Distances in space are quite mind-boggling.* Cf BOGGLE SB'S MIND (BOGGLE).
ˈ**mind-reader** *n* person who claims to know what another person is thinking. ˈ**mind-reading** *n* [U].

mind[2] /maɪnd/ *v* **1** [Tn] take care of or attend to (sb/sth): *mind the baby* ○ *Mind my bike while I go into the shop, please.* ○ *Could you mind the phone* (ie answer it if it rings) *for five minutes?* **2** [I, Ipr, Tn, Tf, Tw no passive, Tg, Tsg] ~ **about sth/doing sth** (esp in questions, negative and conditional sentences, and in affirmative sentences that answer a question) feel annoyance or discomfort at (sth); object to (sth): *Did she mind (about) not getting the job?* ○ *Do you mind the noise?* ○ *I wouldn't mind* (ie I would very much like) *a drink.* ○ *She minded very much that he had not come.* ○ *I don't mind how cold it is.* ○ *Do you mind if I smoke?* ○ *Would you mind helping me?* ie Would you please help me? ○ *Do you mind my closing the window?* **3** [no passive: Tn, Tw] pay attention to or care about (sth): *There's no need to mind the expense if you're not paying!* ○ *Don't mind me! I promise not to disturb you.* ○ *I mind what people think about me.* ○ *I mind whether you like me or not.* **4** [I, Tn, Tf, Tw] be careful about (sb/sth): *Mind* (ie Don't trip over) *that step!* ○ *Mind your head!* eg Be careful not to hit it on the low doorway. ○ *Mind the dog!* ie It may be fierce. ○ *This knife is sharp. Mind you don't cut yourself!* ○ *Mind you come home before 11 o'clock.* ○ *Mind where you put those glasses!* **5** (idm) ˌ**do you** ˈ**mind?** (*ironic*) please stop that: *'Do you mind?' she said, as he pushed into the queue in front of her.* **I don't mind if I** ˈ**do** (*infml ironic*) (used when accepting esp a drink gratefully): *'Will you have a drink?' 'I don't mind if I do* (ie Yes, please).*'* ˌ**mind one's** ˌ**own** ˈ**business** (esp imperative) not interfere in other people's affairs. ˌ**mind one's** ˌ**p's and** ˈ**q's** be careful and polite about what one says or does. **mind/watch one's step** ⇨ STEP[2]. ˌ**mind** ˈ**you; mind** (used as an *interj*) please note: *They're getting divorced, I hear — mind you, I'm not surprised.* ˌ**never** ˈ**mind** don't worry: *'Did you miss the bus? Never mind, there'll be another one in five minutes.'* **never mind (doing) sth** stop, or don't start, doing sth: ˌ*Never mind* ˌ*saying you're* ˈ*sorry, who's going to pay for the damage you've done?* ˌ**never you** ˈ**mind** (*infml*) don't ask (because you will not be told): *Never you mind how I found out — it's true, isn't it?* **6** (phr v) ˌ**mind** ˈ**out** (*infml*) (esp imperative) allow sb to pass: *Mind out (of the way) — you're blocking the passage.* **mind out (for sb/sth)** beware (of danger, etc): *Mind out for the traffic when you cross the road.*
▷ **minder** *n* **1** (esp in compounds) person whose duty it is to attend to sth: *a ma*ˈ*chine-minder* ○ *a* ˈ*child-minder.* **2** (*Brit sl*) person who protects sb from attack; bodyguard, esp for a criminal.

minded /ˈmaɪndɪd/ *adj* **1** [pred] ~ **(to do sth)** (*fml*) disposed or inclined (to do sth): *He could do it if he were so minded.* **2** (forming compound *adjs* or following *advs*) having the kind of mind specified: *a* ˌ*strong-minded,* ˌ*narrow-minded,* ˌ*feeble-minded,* ˌ*high-minded, etc* ˈ*person* ○ *I appeal to all* ˌ*like-minded* ˈ*people to support me.* ○ *be com*ˌ*mercially, po*ˌ*litically,* ˌ*technically, etc* ˈ*minded.* **3** (with *ns* forming compound *adjs*) conscious of the value or importance of the thing specified: *She has become very* ˈ*food-minded since her holiday in France.*

mindful /ˈmaɪndfl/ *adj* [pred] ~ **of sb/sth** (*fml*) giving thought and care or attention to sb/sth: *mindful of one's family, one's duties, one's reputation, the need for discretion.*

mindless /ˈmaɪndlɪs/ *adj* **1** not requiring intelligence: *mindless drudgery.* **2** (*derog*) lacking in intelligence; thoughtless: *mindless vandals.* **3** [pred] ~ **of sb/sth** (*fml*) not thinking of sb/sth; heedless of sb/sth: *mindless of personal risk.* ▷ **mindlessly** *adv.* **mindlessness** *n* [U].

mine[1] /maɪn/ *possess pron* of or belonging to me: *I think that book is mine.* ○ *He's a friend of mine,* ie one of my friends. Cf MY.

mine[2] /maɪn/ *n* **1** excavation (with shafts, galleries, etc) made in the earth for extracting coal, mineral ores, precious stones, etc: *a* ˈ*coal-mine* ○ *a* ˈ*gold-mine* ○ *The inspector went down the mine.* ○ [attrib] *a* ˈ*mine worker.* Cf QUARRY[2]. **2** (a) tunnel for a charge of high explosive to destroy eg enemy fortifications. (b) container filled with explosive, placed in or on the ground, and designed to explode when sth strikes it or passes near it, or after a fixed time, to destroy eg enemy troops, vehicles, etc. (c) such a container placed in water to damage or destroy eg enemy ships: *magnetic, acoustic, etc mines* ○ *lay mines* ○ *clear the coastal waters of mines* ○ [attrib] *mine warfare.* Cf DEPTH CHARGE (DEPTH). **3** (idm) **a mine of information (about/on sb/sth)** rich or abundant source of knowledge: *My grandmother is a mine of information about our family's history.*
□ ˈ**mine-detector** *n* electromagnetic device for finding explosive mines.
ˈ**minefield** *n* **1** area of land or sea where explosive mines have been laid. **2** (*fig*) area presenting many unseen difficulties: *International law is a minefield for anyone not familiar with its complexity.*
ˈ**minelayer** *n* ship or aircraft used for laying explosive mines at sea. ˈ**minelaying** *n* [U].
ˈ**minesweeper** *n* naval vessel used for detecting and clearing explosive mines. ˈ**minesweeping** *n* [U].
ˈ**mineworker** *n* person who works in a mine[2](1).

mine[3] /maɪn/ *v* **1** (a) [I, Ipr] ~ **(for sth)** dig in the ground (for coal, ores, precious stones, etc): *mining for gold, diamonds, etc.* (b) [Tn, Tn·pr] ~ **A (for B)**/~ **B (from A)** extract (coal, etc) from (the earth) by digging: *mine the earth for iron ore* ○ *Gold is mined from deep under ground.* **2** [Tn] make tunnels in the earth under (sth); undermine: *mine enemy trenches, forts, etc.* **3** [Tn] (a) lay explosive mines in (sth): *The enemy had mined the entrance to the harbour.* (b) destroy (sth) by means of explosive mines: *The cruiser was mined, and sank in five minutes.*

miner /ˈmaɪnə(r)/ *n* person who works in a mine underground: ˈ*coal-miners.*

mineral /ˈmɪnərəl/ *n* **1** [C, U] substance that is not vegetable or animal, esp one with a constant chemical composition and usu a characteristic crystalline structure, which is found naturally in the earth: *substances classified as mineral(s)* ○ [attrib] *mineral salts* ○ *the mineral kingdom.* Cf ANIMAL, VEGETABLE. **2** [C, U] any substance got from the earth by mining, esp a metal ore: *Coal and iron are minerals.* ○ [attrib] *mineral deposits, resources, wealth, etc.* **3** [C usu *pl*] (*Brit*) (a) = MINERAL WATER. (b) (*US* **soda**) non-alcoholic canned or bottled drink containing flavouring and soda-water: *Soft drinks and minerals sold here.*
□ ˈ**mineral oil 1** (*Brit*) any oil of mineral origin, esp petroleum. **2** (*US*) liquid paraffin.
ˈ**mineral water** water that naturally contains dissolved mineral salts or gases, and is drunk for its medicinal value.

mineralogy /ˌmɪnəˈrælədʒɪ/ *n* [U] scientific study of minerals.
▷ **mineralogical** /ˌmɪnərəˈlɒdʒɪkl/ *adj* of or concerning mineralogy.
mineralogist /ˌmɪnəˈrælədʒɪst/ *n* student of or expert in mineralogy.

Minerva /mɪˈnɜːvə/ (in Roman mythology) goddess of handicrafts, often identified with *Athene and therefore regarded also as the goddess of war.

minestrone /ˌmɪnɪˈstrəʊnɪ/ *n* [U] thick rich meat soup (of Italian origin) containing chopped mixed vegetables and pasta or rice.

Ming /mɪŋ/ name of the Chinese dynasty that lasted from 1368 to 1644, a period of expansion and exploration in which the arts flourished. Cf CH'ING.
▷ **Ming** *n* [U] Chinese porcelain of this period: *a priceless collection of Ming* ○ [attrib] *a Ming vase.*

mingle /ˈmɪŋgl/ *v* **1** (a) [I, Ipr, Ip] ~ **with sth**/~ **(together)** form a mixture with sth; combine: *The waters of the two rivers mingled (together) to form one river.* (b) [Tn, Tn·pr, Tn·p] ~ **A with B**/~ **A and B (together)** mix one thing with another; combine things together: *truth mingled with falsehood* ○ *The priest mingled the water with the wine.* ○ *He mingled the water and wine (together).* **2** [I, Ipr, Ip] ~ **with sb/sth**; ~ **(together)** go about among sb/sth; associate with sb/sth: *Security men mingled with the crowd.*

mingy /ˈmɪndʒɪ/ *adj* (**-ier, -iest**) (*Brit infml*) mean; ungenerous; stingy: *He's so mingy with his money.* ○ *This restaurant serves very mingy portions.*

mini /ˈmɪnɪ/ *n* (*pl* ~**s**) (*infml*) **1 Mini** (*propr*) type of small car. **2** miniskirt.

mini- *comb form* of small size, length, etc; miniature: ˈ*minibus* ○ ˈ*minicab* ○ ˈ*miniskirt* ○ ˈ*minigolf.* Cf MACRO-, MICRO-.

miniature /ˈmɪnətʃə(r); *US* ˈmɪnɪətʃʊər/ *n* **1** (a) [C] very small detailed painting, usu of a person. (b) [U] art of painting in this way: [attrib] *a miniature artist,* ie one who specializes in this type of art. **2** [C] very small copy or model of sth: *a detailed miniature of the Titanic* ○ [attrib] *miniature dogs,* ie very small breeds ○ *miniature bottles of brandy, etc* ○ *a miniature railway,* ie a small model one on which people may ride for short distances. **3** (idm) **in miniature** on a very small scale: *copy sth in miniature* ○ *She is just like her mother in miniature.*
▷ **miniaturist** /ˈmɪnɪtʃərɪst/ *n* painter of miniatures.

minibus /ˈmɪnɪbʌs/ *n* (*esp Brit*) small vehicle like a bus with seats for only a few people: *hire a self-drive minibus.*

minicab /ˈmɪnɪkæb/ *n* (*Brit*) car like a taxi but available only if ordered in advance.

minicomputer /ˌmɪnɪkəmˈpjuːtə(r)/ *n* comparatively cheap computer that is small in size and storage capacity. Cf MAINFRAME (MAIN[1]), MICROCOMPUTER.

minim /ˈmɪnɪm/ *n* **1** (*Brit*) (*US* **half note**) (*music*) note with half the time-value of a semibreve. ⇨ illus at MUSIC. **2** unit of liquid measure equal to one sixtieth of a dram (about one drop).

minimal /ˈmɪnɪməl/ *adj* **1** smallest in amount or degree: *We stayed with friends, so our expenses were minimal.* **2** (of art, etc) characterized by the use of simple or primary forms or structures, etc.
▷ **minimalism** *n* [U] practice in art, music, etc, esp in the late 20th century, of using simple abstract forms and motifs to create an impersonal unemotional style.
minimalist *n* **1** person who practises or supports minimalism. **2** person in favour of doing, using, etc as little as possible.
minimally *adv.*

minimize, -ise /ˈmɪnɪmaɪz/ *v* [Tn] **1** reduce (sth) to the smallest amount or degree: *To minimize the risk of burglary, install a good alarm system.* **2** estimate (sth) at the smallest possible amount; reduce the true value or importance of (sth): *He minimized the value of her contribution to his research so that he got all the praise.* Cf MAXIMIZE.

minimum /ˈmɪnɪməm/ *n* (*pl* **minima** /-mə/) [C usu *sing*] **1** least or smallest amount, degree, etc possible: *a minimum of work, effort, etc* ○ *keep/reduce sth to the (absolute) minimum* ○ *Repairing your car will cost a minimum of £100,* ie at least £100. **2** (*abbr* **min**) least or smallest amount, degree, etc allowed or recorded: *The class needs a minimum of 6 pupils to continue.* ○ *Temperatures will reach a minimum of 50°F.* Cf MAXIMUM.
▷ **minimum** *adj* that is a minimum: *20p is the minimum fare on buses.*
□ ˌ**minimum** ˈ**lending rate** (*abbr* **MLR**) (*finance*) lowest rate of interest at which the central bank lends money at any particular time.
ˌ**minimum ther**ˈ**mometer** thermometer that automatically records the lowest temperature within a particular period.
ˌ**minimum** ˈ**wage** lowest wage that an employer is allowed, by law or a union agreement, to pay: *earn the minimum wage.*

mining /ˈmaɪnɪŋ/ *n* [U] (often in compounds)

process of getting coal, ores, precious stones, etc from mines: ˈ*tin-mining* ○ *open-cast mining*, ie getting coal, etc that is near the surface, using mechanical shovels, etc ○ [attrib] *the* ˈ*mining industry* ○ *a* ˈ*mining engineer*.

minion /ˈmɪnɪən/ *n* (esp *pl*) (*derog or joc*) subordinate or assistant, esp one who tries to win favour by obeying a superior slavishly: *the dictator and his minions* ○ *Can you send one of your minions to collect this file?*

miniskirt /ˈmɪnɪskɜːt/ *n* very short skirt. ⇨ illus at DRESS.

minister[1] /ˈmɪnɪstə(r)/ *n* **1** (*US* **secretary**) person at the head of a government department or a main branch of one (and often a member of the Cabinet): *the Minister of Education* ○ *a minister of state for finance* ○ *the Prime Minister*. **2** person, usu of lower rank than an ambassador, representing his government in a foreign country. **3** Christian clergyman, esp in the Presbyterian and some Nonconformist churches: *a minister of religion*. Cf PRIEST, VICAR.

□ ˌ**Minister of** ˈ**State** (*Brit*) departmental senior minister between a departmental head and a junior minister.

ˌ**Minister of the** ˈ**Crown** (*Brit*) senior government minister, usu in the Cabinet.

minister[2] /ˈmɪnɪstə(r)/ *v* **1** [Ipr] ~ **to sb/sth** (*fml*) give active help or service to sb/sth: *nurses ministering to (the needs of) the sick and wounded*. **2** (idm) **a ministering** ˈ**angel** person (esp a woman) who helps or serves others with tenderness and care.

ministerial /ˌmɪnɪˈstɪərɪəl/ *adj* **1** of a minister, his position, duties, etc: *hold ministerial office/rank* ○ *a decision taken at ministerial level*. **2** of or for a government ministry (or the Cabinet): *the ministerial benches*. ▷ **ministerially** /-ɪəlɪ/ *adv*.

ministrant /ˈmɪnɪstrənt/ *adj* [attrib] (*fml*) giving help or service, esp in religious ceremonies.

▷ **ministrant** *n* (*fml*) supporter or helper; attendant.

ministration /ˌmɪnɪˈstreɪʃn/ *n* (*fml*) **(a)** [U] helping or serving, eg at a religious ceremony: *the ministration of the sacraments*. **(b)** [C usu *pl*] instance of this.

ministry /ˈmɪnɪstrɪ/ *n* **1** (*US* **department**) [C] (buildings containing a) government department: *the* ˈ*Air Ministry* ○ *the* ˌ*Ministry of De*ˈ*fence*. **2 (a) the ministry** [Gp] the ministers of (esp the Protestant) religion as a body: *His parents intended him for the ministry*, ie wanted him to become a minister. **(b)** [C usu *sing*] duties or (period of) service of a minister of religion: *enter/go into/take up the ministry*, ie train to become a minister of religion.

mink /mɪŋk/ *n* **1** [C] small stoat-like animal of the weasel family. **2 (a)** [U] its valuable thick brown fur: [attrib] *a mink stole, coat*. **(b)** [C] coat made from this fur: *wearing her new mink*.

Minn *abbr* Minnesota.

minnesinger /ˈmɪnɪsɪŋə(r)/ *n* (*pl* unchanged) German lyric poet and singer of the 12th-14th centuries. Cf TROUBADOUR, MINSTREL 1.

Minnesota /mɪnɪˈsəʊtə/ (*abbrs* **Minn, MN**) state of northern central USA on the Canadian border.

minnow /ˈmɪnəʊ/ *n* (*pl* unchanged or ~**s**) any of several types of very small freshwater fish of the carp family.

Minoan /mɪˈnəʊən/ *adj* of the *Bronze Age civilization of *Crete (c 3000-1100 BC) or its people, culture or language. The Minoan civilization was the earliest in Europe and is noted particularly for its script and its art and architecture. It greatly influenced the *Mycenaeans who succeeded the Minoans in the control of the Aegean c 1400 BC.

▷ **Minoan** *n* **1** [C] inhabitant of Minoan Crete or any other part of the Minoan world. **2** [U] language or script associated with the Minoan civilization.

minor /ˈmaɪnə(r)/ *adj* **1** [usu attrib] smaller, less serious, less important, etc: *a minor road*, eg in the country ○ *minor repairs, alterations, etc* ○ *a minor operation*, ie one that does not risk the patient's life ○ *minor injuries, burns, fractures, etc* ○ *a minor part/role in a play* ○ *minor poets*. Cf MAJOR. **2** (*Brit dated or joc*) (in private schools) second or younger of two brothers or boys with the same surname (esp in the same school): *Smith minor*. Cf MAJOR, JUNIOR 2. **3** (*music*) of or based on a scale that has a semitone above its second note: *a minor third*, ie an interval of three semitones ○ *a song in a minor key*, ie one based on a minor scale ○ *a symphony in C minor*. Cf MAJOR.

▷ **minor** *n* **1** (*law*) person under the age of full legal responsibility (18 in the UK). **2** (*US*) subsidiary subject or course of a student at college or university.

minor *v* [Ipr] ~ **in sth** (*US*) (of a student) study sth as a subsidiary subject.

□ **minor** ˈ**planet** asteroid.

minor ˈ**suit** (in card-games, esp bridge) diamonds or clubs.

Minorca /mɪˈnɔːkə/ second largest of the *Balearic Islands. The capital and chief port is Mahon. ⇨ map at SPAIN.

minority /maɪˈnɒrətɪ; *US* -ˈnɔːr-/ *n* **1 (a)** [CGp] (usu *sing*) smaller number or part (esp of people voting or of votes cast): *Only a minority of British households do/does not have a car*. ○ *A small minority voted against the motion*. ○ [attrib] *a minority vote, opinion, point of view, etc*, ie one cast, held, etc by a smaller number of people. **(b)** [C] small group in a community, nation, etc, differing from others in race, religion, language, etc: *the rights of ethnic minorities* ○ [attrib] *belong to a minority group* ○ *minority rights*. Cf MAJORITY. **2** [U] (*law*) state or period of being a minor: *be in one's minority*, eg under 18 in the UK. **3** (idm) **be in a/the minority** be in the smaller of esp two voting groups: *We're in the minority*, ie More people are against us than with us. ○ *I'm in a minority of one*, ie No one agrees with me.

□ **mi**ˌ**nority** ˈ**government** government that has fewer seats in a legislative assembly than the total number held by the opposition parties.

Minos /ˈmaɪnɒs/ (in Greek mythology) king of Crete, a cruel tyrant who every year demanded 14 young men and women to be sent from Athens to be killed and eaten by the Minotaur.

Minotaur /ˈmaɪnətɔː(r)/ (in Greek mythology) fierce creature, half man and half bull, which lived in a labyrinth in Crete. It was killed by *Theseus.

minster /ˈmɪnstə(r)/ *n* (*Brit*) large or important church, esp one that once belonged to a monastery: *York Minster*.

minstrel /ˈmɪnstrəl/ *n* **1** (in the Middle Ages) travelling composer, player and singer of songs and ballads. **2** (usu *pl*) one of a company of public entertainers with blackened faces, etc performing supposedly Negro songs and music: [attrib] *a minstrel show*.

▷ **minstrelsy** /ˈmɪnstrəlsɪ/ *n* [U] art, songs, etc of minstrels (MINSTREL 1).

mint[1] /mɪnt/ *n* **1** [U] any of various types of aromatic herb whose leaves are used for flavouring food, drinks, toothpaste, chewing-gum, etc: *a sprig of mint*, eg in a cocktail ○ [attrib] *mint* ˈ*sauce*, ie mint leaves chopped up in vinegar and sugar, usu eaten with roast lamb. **2** [U, C] = PEPPERMINT: *Do you like mints?* ▷ **minty** /ˈmɪntɪ/ *adj*.

mint[2] /mɪnt/ *n* **1** [C] place where coins are made, usu under State authority: *coins fresh from the mint* ○ *the Royal Mint*, ie that of the UK, in Wales. **2** [sing] (*infml*) very large amount of money: *She made an absolute mint (of money) in the fashion trade*. **3** (idm) **in mint condition** (as if) new; unsoiled; perfect: *coins, banknotes, postage stamps, books, etc in mint condition*.

▷ **mint** *v* [Tn] **1** make (a coin) by stamping metal: *newly-minted £1 coins*. **2** (*fig*) invent (a word, phrase, etc): *I've just minted a new word!*

minuet /ˌmɪnjʊˈet/ *n* (piece of music for a) slow graceful dance in triple time.

minus /ˈmaɪnəs/ *prep* **1** (*mathematics*) with the deduction of; less: *Seven minus three equals four (7 − 3 = 4)*. **2** below zero: *a temperature of minus ten degrees centigrade (−10°C)*. **3** (*infml*) without or lacking; deprived of: *He came back from the war minus a leg*. ○ *I'm minus my car today*, eg because it's being repaired. Cf PLUS.

▷ **minus** *adj* **1** (*mathematics*) negative: *a minus quantity*, ie a quantity less than zero (eg $-2x^2$). **2** [pred] (of marks or grades) of a standard slightly lower than the one stated: *I got B minus (B−) in the test*.

minus *n* **1** (also **minus sign**) the mathematical symbol −. ⇨ App 9. **2** (*infml*) disadvantage or drawback: *Let's consider the pluses and minuses of moving house*. Cf PLUS.

minuscule /ˈmɪnəskjuːl/ *adj* very small; tiny.

minute[1] /ˈmɪnɪt/ *n* **1 (a)** [C] one sixtieth part of an hour, equal to 60 seconds: *It's ten minutes to/past six*. ○ *I arrived a couple of minutes early/late*. ○ *My house is ten minutes (away) from* (ie It takes ten minutes to drive, walk, etc from it to) *the shops*. ○ *We caught the bus with only minutes to spare*. ⇨ App 10. **(b)** [sing] very short time; moment: *It only takes a minute to make a salad*. ○ *Will you wait for me? I shan't be a minute*. **(c)** [sing] exact point of time; instant: *Stop it this minute!* ie immediately ○ *At that very minute, Tom opened the door*. **2** [C] one sixtieth part of a degree, used in measuring angles: *37 degrees 30 minutes (37°30′)*. **3** [C] official note that records a decision or comment, or gives authority for sth to be done: *make a minute of sth*. **4 minutes** [pl] brief summary or record of what is said and decided at a meeting, esp of a society or committee: *We read (through) the minutes of the last meeting*. ○ *Who will take* (ie make notes for) *the minutes?* **5** (idm) **(at) any minute/moment (now)** (*infml*) very shortly or soon: *The leading cyclist will be coming round that corner any minute now!* **in a** ˈ**minute** very soon: *Our guests will be here in a minute!* ˌ**just a** ˈ**minute** (*infml*) wait for a short time (usu while the speaker says or does sth): *Just a minute! Let me put your tie straight*. **the last minute/moment** ⇨ LAST[1]. ˌ**not for a/one** ˈ**minute**/ˈ**moment** (*infml*) not at all: *I never suspected for a minute that you were married*. **the minute/moment (that)...** as soon as...: *I want to see him the minute (that) he arrives*. **there's one born every minute** ⇨ BORN. **to the** ˈ**minute** exactly: *The train arrived at 9.05 to the minute*. ˌ**up to the** ˈ**minute** (*infml*) **(a)** fashionable: *Her clothes are always right up to the minute*. ○ [attrib] *an* ˌ*up-to-the-*ˈ*minute look, dress, style, etc*. **(b)** having the latest information: [attrib] *an* ˌ*up-to-the-minute* ˈ*news bulletin, summary, etc*.

▷ **minute** *v* [Tn] make a note of (sth) in an official memorandum; record (sth) in the minutes (MINUTE[1] 4): *minute an action point, comment, etc* ○ *Your suggestion will be minuted*.

□ ˈ**minute-book** *n* book in which minutes (MINUTE[1] 4) are written.

ˈ**minute-gun** *n* gun fired at intervals of a minute, eg at a funeral.

ˈ**minute-hand** *n* hand on a watch or clock indicating the minutes.

ˈ**minute-man** *n* (*pl* **-men**) (*US*) (formerly) militiaman or armed civilian ready to fight immediately if required.

ˌ**minute** ˈ**steak** thin piece of (usu beef) steak that can be cooked very quickly.

minute[2] /maɪˈnjuːt; *US* -ˈnuːt/ *adj* (**-r, -st**) **1** very small in size or amount: *minute particles of gold dust* ○ *water containing minute quantities of lead*. **2** very detailed; accurate or precise: *a minute description, inquiry, examination, inspection, etc* ○ *The detective studied the fingerprints in the minutest detail*. ▷ **minutely** *adv*. **minuteness** *n* [U].

minutiae /maɪˈnjuːʃiː; *US* mɪˈnuːʃiː/ *n* [pl] very small or unimportant details: *I won't discuss the minutiae of the contract now*.

minx /mɪŋks/ *n* (*derog or joc*) cunning, cheeky or mischievous girl: *She can be a proper little minx when she wants to get her own way!*

Miocene /ˈmaɪəsiːn/ *adj* (*geology*) of the fourth epoch of the *Tertiary period, lasting from about 24.6 to 5.1 million years ago.

▷ **Miocene** *n* (*geology*) this epoch, a period of great earth movements, during which the *Alps and *Himalayas were being formed. It followed the

*Oligocene and preceded the *Pleiocene.

miracle /ˈmɪrəkl/ *n* **1** [C] good or welcome act or event which does not follow the known laws of nature and is therefore thought to be caused by some supernatural power: *perform/work/accomplish miracles* ○ *Her life was saved by a miracle.* ○ *The doctors said her recovery was a miracle.* **2** [sing] (*infml fig*) remarkable or unexpected event: *It's a miracle you weren't killed in that car crash!* ○ *It'll be a miracle if he ever gives up smoking!* ○ [attrib] *a miracle cure, drug, etc.* **3** [C] ~ **of sth** remarkable example or specimen of sth: *miracles of ingenuity, craftsmanship, etc* ○ *The compact disc is a miracle of modern technology.* **4** (idm) **do/work miracles/wonders (for/with sb/sth)** (*infml*) be remarkably successful in achieving positive results (for/with sb/sth): *This tonic will work miracles for your depression.* ○ *He can do miracles with a few kitchen left-overs*, eg by making them into a tasty meal.

▷ **miraculous** /mɪˈrækjʊləs/ *adj* **1** like a miracle; contrary to the laws of nature: *make a miraculous recovery.* **2** (*infml*) remarkable or unexpected: *It's miraculous how much weight you've lost!* **miraculously** *adv*.

□ ˈ**miracle play** medieval drama showing the miracles performed by the saints. Cf MYSTERY PLAY (MYSTERY).

mirage /ˈmɪrɑːʒ, mɪˈrɑːʒ/ *n* **1** optical illusion caused by hot air conditions, esp that of a sheet of water seeming to appear in the desert or on a hot road. **2** (*fig*) any illusion or hope that cannot be fulfilled.

mire /ˈmaɪə(r)/ *n* [U] **1** swampy ground or bog; soft deep mud: *sink into/get stuck in the mire.* **2** (idm) **drag sb/sb's name through the mire/mud** ⇨ DRAG².

▷ **miry** /ˈmaɪərɪ/ *adj* swampy or boggy; muddy.

Miró /mɪˈrəʊ/ Joan (1893-1983), Spanish painter, a major artist of a type of *Surrealism rooted in abstract art.

mirror /ˈmɪrə(r)/ *n* **1** (often in compounds) polished surface, usu of coated glass or of metal, that reflects images: *a* ˈ*driving-mirror*, eg in a car, to enable the driver to see what is behind ○ *a* ˈ*hand mirror*, ie a small one, esp as used by women ○ *She glanced at herself in the mirror.* ⇨ illus at FURNITURE. **2** (*fig*) thing that reflects or gives a likeness of sth: *Pepys's 'Diary' is a mirror of/holds up a mirror to the times he lived in.*

▷ **mirror** *v* [Tn] reflect (sth) as in a mirror: *The trees were mirrored in the still water of the lake.* ○ (*fig*) *a novel that mirrors modern society.*

□ ˌ**mirror** ˈ**image** reflection or copy of sth with the right and left sides of the original reversed.

ˈ**mirror writing** writing in which words and letters are back to front and appear as they would if reflected in a mirror.

mirth /mɜːθ/ *n* [U] (*fml*) merriment or happiness; laughter: *Her funny costume caused much mirth among the guests.* ▷ **mirthful** /-fl/ *adj*. **mirthless** *adj*: *a mirthless laugh*, ie showing that one is not really amused.

MIRV *abbr* multiple independently-targeted re-entry vehicle (a type of missile).

mis- *comb form* **1** (with *vs* and derivatives of *vs*, *adjs* and *ns*) bad(ly) or wrong(ly); amiss: *mislead* ○ *mispronounce* ○ *misshapen* ○ *mistakes* ○ *misdeed.* **2** (with *vs* and *ns*) lack of; absence of: *mistrust* ○ *misfortune.*

misadventure /ˌmɪsədˈventʃə(r)/ *n* **1** [C, U] (*fml*) (piece of) bad luck; misfortune: *Their holiday was ruined by a whole series of misadventures.* **2** [U] (*law*) accidental cause of death not involving crime or negligence: *death by misadventure.*

misalliance /ˌmɪsəˈlaɪəns/ *n* unsuitable alliance, esp marriage with sb of a lower social class: *make a misalliance.*

misanthropist /mɪˈsænθrəpɪst/ (also **misanthrope** /ˈmɪsənθrəʊp/) *n* person who hates mankind and avoids human society. Cf PHILANTHROPIST (PHILANTHROPY).

▷ **misanthropic** /ˌmɪsənˈθrɒpɪk/ *adj* hating or distrusting mankind or human society.

misanthropy /mɪˈsænθrəpɪ/ *n* [U] hatred or distrust of mankind.

misapply /ˌmɪsəˈplaɪ/ *v* (*pt, pp* **-lied**) [Tn] (*fml*) use (esp public funds) wrongly: *misapplied* (ie wasted) *efforts, talents.*

▷ **misapplication** /ˌmɪsæplɪˈkeɪʃn/ *n* [U, C] wrong or unjust use of sth.

misapprehend /ˌmɪsæprɪˈhend/ *v* [Tn] (*fml*) understand (words or a person) wrongly.

▷ **misapprehension** /ˌmɪsæprɪˈhenʃn/ *n* (idm) **under a misappreˈhension** not understanding correctly: *I thought you wanted to see me but I was clearly under a complete misapprehension.*

misappropriate /ˌmɪsəˈprəʊprɪeɪt/ *v* [Tn] take (sb else's money) wrongly, esp for one's own use: *The treasurer misappropriated the society's funds.* ▷ **misappropriation** /ˌmɪsəˌprəʊprɪˈeɪʃn/ *n* [U].

misbegotten /ˌmɪsbɪˈgɒtn/ *adj* [usu attrib] **1** badly planned; ill-advised: ˌ*misbegotten* ˈ*schemes, i*ˈ*deas,* ˈ*notions, etc.* **2** **(a)** (*dated*) illegitimate; bastard. **(b)** (of a person) contemptible.

misbehave /ˌmɪsbɪˈheɪv/ *v* [I, Tn] ~ **(oneself)** behave badly or improperly. ▷ **misbehaviour** (*US* **misbehavior**) /ˌmɪsbɪˈheɪvɪə(r)/ *n* [U].

misc *abbr* miscellaneous.

miscalculate /ˌmɪsˈkælkjʊleɪt/ *v* [I, Tn, Tw] calculate (amounts, distances, measurements, etc) wrongly: *There's too much meat. I must have miscalculated the amount/how much I needed.* ▷ **miscalculation** /ˌmɪskælkjʊˈleɪʃn/ *n* [C, U]: *I made a slight miscalculation.*

miscarriage /ˌmɪsˈkærɪdʒ, ˈmɪskærɪdʒ/ *n* **1** **(a)** [U] spontaneous premature loss of a foetus from the womb. **(b)** [C] instance of this: *have/suffer a miscarriage.* Cf ABORTION 1. **2** **(a)** [U, C] (*commerce*) (instance of) failure to arrive at, or deliver goods to, the right destination: *miscarriage of goods, freight, letters, etc.* **(b)** [U, C] failure of a plan, etc: *the miscarriage of one's hopes, schemes, etc.*

□ **mis**ˌ**carriage of** ˈ**justice** (*law*) failure of a court to administer justice properly: *Sending an innocent man to prison is a clear miscarriage of justice.*

miscarry /ˌmɪsˈkærɪ/ *v* (*pt, pp* **-ried**) [I] **1** (of a pregnant woman) have a miscarriage. **2** (of plans, etc) fail; have a result different from what was hoped for. **3** (of goods, letters, etc) fail to reach the right destination.

miscast /ˌmɪsˈkɑːst; *US* -ˈkæst/ *v* (*pt, pp* **miscast**) **1** [usu passive: Tn, Cn·n/a] ~ **sb (as sb/sth)** give (an actor, etc) a role for which he is not suitable: *The young actor was badly miscast as Lear/in the role of Lear.* **2** [Tn usu passive] allocate the parts in (a play, etc) unsuitably: *The film was thoroughly miscast.*

miscegenation /ˌmɪsɪdʒɪˈneɪʃn/ *n* [U] mixture of races; production of offspring by two people of different (esp white and non-white) races.

miscellaneous /ˌmɪsəˈleɪnɪəs/ *adj* [usu attrib] **1** of various kinds: *miscellaneous items, goods, expenses.* **2** of mixed composition or character: *a miscellaneous collection, assortment, selection, etc* ○ *Milton's miscellaneous prose works*, eg essays, tracts, etc.

miscellany /mɪˈselənɪ; *US* ˈmɪsəleɪnɪ/ *n* ~ **(of sth)** **1** varied collection of items: *The show was a miscellany of song and dance.* **2** book containing a collection of writings, esp by different authors about different subjects.

mischance /ˌmɪsˈtʃɑːns; *US* -ˈtʃæns/ *n* [C, U] (*fml*) (piece of) bad luck: *a series of mischances* ○ *I lost your file by pure mischance.*

mischief /ˈmɪstʃɪf/ *n* **1** [U] behaviour (esp of children) that is annoying or does slight damage, but is not malicious (used esp as in the expressions shown): *act out of mischief* ○ *Those girls are fond of mischief*, ie of playing tricks, etc. ○ *Tell the children to keep out of mischief.* ○ *He's up to* (ie planning) *some mischief again!* ○ *She's always getting into mischief.* **2** [C] person who is fond of mischief: *Where have you hidden my book, you little mischief?* **3** [U] tendency to tease or annoy playfully: *There was mischief in her eyes.* ○ *The kittens were full of mischief.* **4** [U] moral harm or injury, esp caused by a person: *His malicious gossip caused much mischief until the truth became known.* **5** (idm) ˌ**do sb/oneself a** ˈ**mischief** (*infml or joc*) hurt sb/oneself physically: *You could do yourself a mischief on that barbed-wire fence!* **make** ˈ**mischief** do or say sth to upset, annoy or provoke others: *Don't let her make mischief between you — she's only jealous.* **mean mischief** ⇨ MEAN¹.

□ ˈ**mischief-maker** *n* person who deliberately causes trouble or discord. ˈ**mischief-making** *n* [U].

mischievous /ˈmɪstʃɪvəs/ *adj* **1** (of a person) filled with, fond of or engaged in mischief: *He's as mischievous as a monkey!* **2** (of behaviour) showing a spirit of mischief: *a mischievous look, smile, trick.* **3** (*fml*) (of a thing) causing harm or damage: *a mischievous letter, rumour.* ▷ **mischievously** *adv*. **mischievousness** *n* [U].

miscible /ˈmɪsəbl/ *adj* ~ **(with sth)** (*fml*) (of liquids) that can be mixed: *Oil and water are not miscible.*

misconceive /ˌmɪskənˈsiːv/ *v* [Tn esp passive] (*fml*) have a wrong idea or understanding of (sth): *The housing needs of our inner cities have been misconceived from the start.* ▷ **misconception** /ˌmɪskənˈsepʃn/ *n* [U, C]: *dispel misconceptions* ○ *It is a popular misconception* (ie Many people wrongly believe) *that all Scotsmen are mean.* Cf PRECONCEPTION.

misconduct /ˌmɪsˈkɒndʌkt/ *n* [U] (*fml*) **1** (*esp law*) improper behaviour, esp of a sexual or professional kind: *guilty of grave/serious misconduct* ○ *She sued for divorce on the grounds of her husband's alleged misconduct with his secretary.* **2** bad management; professional negligence: *misconduct of the company's affairs.*

▷ **misconduct** /ˌmɪskənˈdʌkt/ *v* (*fml*) **1** [Tn, Tn·pr] ~ **oneself (with sb)** behave improperly, esp with a member of the opposite sex. **2** [Tn] manage (sth) badly.

misconstruction /ˌmɪskənˈstrʌkʃn/ *n* [C, U] (*fml*) (instance of) false or inaccurate interpretation or understanding: *What you say is open to misconstruction*, ie could easily be misunderstood. ○ *It is possible to place/put a misconstruction on these words*, ie assume them to mean what they do not.

misconstrue /ˌmɪskənˈstruː/ *v* [Tn, Tw] (*fml*) get a wrong idea of or misinterpret (sb's words, acts, etc): *You have completely misconstrued me/my words/what I said.*

miscount /ˌmɪsˈkaʊnt/ *v* [I, Tn] count (sth) wrongly: *We've got too many chairs — I must have miscounted.*

▷ **miscount** /ˈmɪskaʊnt/ *n* wrong count, esp of votes at an election.

miscreant /ˈmɪskrɪənt/ *n* (*dated*) villain; wrongdoer.

misdate /ˌmɪsˈdeɪt/ *v* [Tn] **1** give a wrong date to (an event, etc). **2** write a wrong date on (a letter, cheque, etc).

misdeal /ˌmɪsˈdiːl/ *v* (*pt, pp* **misdealt** /-ˈdelt/) [I, Tn] deal (playing-cards) wrongly.

▷ **misdeal** *n* error in dealing cards; hand of cards wrongly dealt: *I've got 14 cards; it's a misdeal!*

misdeed /ˌmɪsˈdiːd/ *n* (usu *pl*) (*fml*) wicked act; crime: *punished for one's many misdeeds.*

misdemeanour (*US* **misdemeanor**) /ˌmɪsdɪˈmiːnə(r)/ *n* **1** (*infml or joc*) minor wrongdoing; misdeed: *petty misdemeanours.* **2** (*law*) (formerly, in England and Wales) punishable offence less serious than a felony.

misdirect /ˌmɪsdɪˈrekt, -daɪˈrekt/ *v* **1** [Tn, Tn·pr] ~ **sb/sth (to sth)** instruct sb to go or send sth to the wrong place: *misdirect sb to the bus station instead of the coach station* ○ *The letter was misdirected to our old address.* **2** [Tn esp passive] use (sth) in a wrong or pointless way: *misdirected energies, abilities, etc* ○ *misdirected* (ie undeserved) *criticism, sarcasm, etc* ○ *Your talents are misdirected — study music, not maths!* **3** [Tn] (*law*) (of a judge in a lawcourt) give (the jury) wrong instruction on a point of law or about the evidence, when summing up the case. ▷ **misdirection** /ˌmɪsdɪˈrekʃn, -daɪˈrek-/ *n* [U].

misdoing /ˌmɪsˈduːɪŋ/ *n* (usu *pl*) (*fml*) wicked act;

misdeed.

mise-en-scène /ˌmiːz ɒn ˈseɪn/ *n* [sing] (*French*) **1** (arrangement of) scenery, furniture, etc of a play on a stage; dramatic setting. **2** (*fig*) general surroundings of an event: *the magnificent mise-en-scène of the Royal Wedding.*

miser /ˈmaɪzə(r)/ *n* person who loves wealth for its own sake and spends as little as possible: (*infml fig*) *Why don't you buy me a drink for a change, you old miser!*
▷ **miserly** *adj* (*derog*) **1** like a miser; mean or selfish: *miserly habits.* **2** barely adequate; meagre: *a miserly allowance, share, portion, etc.* **miserliness** *n* [U].

miserable /ˈmɪzrəbl/ *adj* **1** very unhappy or uncomfortable; wretched: *miserable from cold and hunger* ○ *Refugees everywhere lead miserable lives.* ○ *He makes her life miserable*, eg by his cruelty, selfishness, etc. ○ *Don't look so miserable!* **2** causing unhappiness or discomfort; unpleasant: *miserable* (eg cold and wet) *weather* ○ *a miserable afternoon* ○ *live in miserable conditions.* **3** poor in quality or quantity; too small or meagre: *What a miserable meal that was!* ○ *How can I keep a family on such a miserable wage?* **4** [attrib] mean; contemptible: *What a miserable old devil Scrooge was!* ○ *The plan was a miserable failure.* **5** (idm) **miserable/ugly as sin** ⇨ SIN. ▷ **miserably** /-əblɪ/ *adv*: *die miserably* ○ *a miserably wet day* ○ *be miserably poor* ○ *We failed miserably to agree.*

misericord /mɪˈzerɪkɔːd/ *n* ledge or projection under a hinged seat in a church, which when the seat is raised can be used as a support by a standing person. In many medieval churches the wooden misericords are elaborately carved.

misery /ˈmɪzərɪ/ *n* **1** [U] great suffering or discomfort (of mind or body): *suffer the misery of toothache* ○ *living in misery and want*, ie in wretched conditions and poverty ○ *lead a life of misery.* **2** [C usu *pl*] painful happening; great misfortune: *the miseries of unemployment.* **3** [C] (*Brit infml*) person who is always miserable and complaining: *It's no fun being with you, you old misery!* **4** (idm) **make sb's life a misery** ⇨ LIFE. **put an animal, bird, etc out of its ˈmisery** end the suffering of an animal, etc by killing it. **put sb out of his ˈmisery** (**a**) end sb's sufferings by killing him. (**b**) (*joc*) end sb's anxiety or suspense: *Put me out of my misery — tell me if I've passed or not!*

misfire /ˌmɪsˈfaɪə(r)/ *v* **1** [I] (of a gun, rocket, etc) fail to go off correctly. **2** [I, Ipr] (of an engine, etc) fail to start or function properly: *The engine is misfiring badly on one cylinder.* **3** [I] (*fig infml*) fail to have the desired effect: *The joke misfired completely.* Cf BACKFIRE (BACK³). ▷ **misfire** *n.*

misfit /ˈmɪsfɪt/ *n* **1** person not well suited to his work or his surroundings: *a social misfit* ○ *He always felt a bit of a misfit in the business world.* **2** article of clothing which does not fit well.

misfortune /ˌmɪsˈfɔːtʃuːn/ *n* **1** [U] bad luck: *suffer great misfortune* ○ *companions in misfortune* ○ *Misfortune struck early in the voyage.* ○ *They had the misfortune to be hit by a violent storm.* **2** [C] instance of this; unfortunate condition, accident or event: *She bore her misfortunes bravely.*

misgiving /ˌmɪsˈɡɪvɪŋ/ *n* [U, C esp *pl*] (*fml*) (feeling of) doubt, worry, suspicion or distrust: *a heart/mind full of misgiving(s)* ○ *I have serious misgivings about taking the job.*

misgovern /ˌmɪsˈɡʌvn/ *v* [Tn] govern (a country, etc) badly or unjustly. ▷ **misgovernment** *n* [U].

misguided /ˌmɪsˈɡaɪdɪd/ *adj* [usu attrib] (*fml*) **1** led by sb/sth to be mistaken in one's opinions, thoughts, etc: *His untidy clothes give one a misguided impression of him.* **2** wrong or foolish in one's actions (because of bad judgement): *misguided zeal, energy, ability, etc* ○ *The thief made a misguided attempt to rob a policewoman.* ▷ **misguidedly** *adv.*

mishandle /ˌmɪsˈhændl/ *v* [Tn] **1** handle or treat (sb/sth) roughly: *damage* (eg to a parcel) *caused by mishandling* ○ *A sensitive child should not be mishandled.* **2** (*fig*) deal with (sth) wrongly or inefficiently: *mishandle a situation, an affair, a business deal, etc* ○ *He mishandled the meeting badly and lost the vote.*

mishap /ˈmɪshæp/ *n* (**a**) [C] unlucky accident (usu not serious): *arrive home after many mishaps* ○ *We had a slight mishap with the car*, eg a puncture. (**b**) [U] bad luck: *Our journey ended without (further) mishap.*

mishear /ˌmɪsˈhɪə(r)/ *v* (*pt, pp* **misheard** /-ˈhɜːd/) [Tn, Tw] hear (sb/sth) incorrectly: *Was she asking for a lift? I must have misheard her/what she was saying.*

mishit /ˌmɪsˈhɪt/ *v* (**-tt-**, *pt, pp* **mishit**) [Tn] (in cricket, golf, etc) hit (the ball) badly or in a faulty way.
▷ **mishit** /ˈmɪshɪt/ *n* bad or faulty hit.

mishmash /ˈmɪʃmæʃ/ *n* [sing] ~ (**of sth**) (*infml derog*) confused mixture: *not a proper plan, just a mishmash of vague ideas.*

Mishnah /ˈmɪʃnɑː/ *n* first part of the *Talmud, containing commentaries on Jewish law.

misinform /ˌmɪsɪnˈfɔːm/ *v* [esp passive: Tn, Tn·pr] ~ **sb** (**about sth**) (*fml*) give wrong information to sb; mislead sb intentionally or unintentionally: *I regret to say you have been misinformed (about that).* ▷ **misinformation** /ˌmɪsɪnfəˈmeɪʃn/ *n* [U]. Cf DISINFORMATION.

misinterpret /ˌmɪsɪnˈtɜːprɪt/ *v* [Tn, Tw] interpret (sb/sth) wrongly; make a wrong inference from (sth): *misinterpret sb's remarks/what sb says* ○ *He misinterpreted her silence as indicating agreement.*
▷ **misinterpretation** /ˌmɪsɪntɜːprɪˈteɪʃn/ *n* [U, C]: *comments, actions, views, etc open to misinterpretation*, ie likely to be misinterpreted.

misjudge /ˌmɪsˈdʒʌdʒ/ *v* [Tn, Tw] **1** form a wrong opinion of (sb/sth): *I'm sorry I misjudged you/your motives.* **2** estimate (eg time, distance, quantity) wrongly: *I misjudged how wide the stream was and fell in.* ▷ **misjudgement** (also **misjudgment**) *n* [U, C].

mislay /ˌmɪsˈleɪ/ *v* (*pt, pp* **mislaid** /-ˈleɪd/) [Tn] (*often euph*) put (sth) where it cannot easily be found; lose (sth), usu for a short time only: *I seem to have mislaid my passport — have you seen it?*

mislead /ˌmɪsˈliːd/ *v* (*pt, pp* **misled** /-ˈled/) **1** [Tn, Tn·pr] ~ **sb** (**about/as to sth**) cause sb to have a wrong idea or impression about sb/sth: *You misled me as to your intentions.* **2** [Tn esp passive] (**a**) lead or guide (sb) in the wrong direction: *We were misled by the guide.* (**b**) (*fig*) lead or guide (sb) into wrong behaviour or beliefs: *misled by bad companions.* **3** (phr v) **mislead sb into doing sth** cause sb to do sth by deceiving him: *He misled me into thinking he was rich.*
▷ **misleading** *adj* giving wrong ideas, etc; deceptive: *misleading comments, advertisements, instructions.* **misleadingly** *adv.*

mismanage /ˌmɪsˈmænɪdʒ/ *v* [Tn] manage (sth) badly or wrongly: *mismanage one's business affairs, finances, accounts, etc* ○ *The company had been mismanaged for years.* ▷ **mismanagement** *n* [U].

mismatch /ˌmɪsˈmætʃ/ *v* [Tn usu passive] match (people or things) wrongly or unsuitably: *mismatching colours* ○ *The two players were badly mismatched*, eg one was much better than the other.
▷ **mismatch** /ˈmɪsmætʃ/ *n* act or result of mismatching: *Their marriage was a mismatch — they had little in common.*

misname /ˌmɪsˈneɪm/ *v* [Tn usu passive] call (sb/sth) by a wrong or an unsuitable name: *That tall man is misnamed Mr Short!*

misnomer /ˌmɪsˈnəʊmə(r)/ *n* wrong use of a name, word or description: *'First-class hotel' was a complete misnomer for the tumbledown farmhouse we stayed in.*

mis(o)- *comb form* hating or hatred of: *misanthropy* ○ *misogynist.*

misogynist /mɪˈsɒdʒɪnɪst/ *n* person who hates women. ▷ **misogyny** *n* [U].

misplace /ˌmɪsˈpleɪs/ *v* (*fml*) [Tn esp passive] **1** put (sth) in the wrong place: *I've misplaced my glasses — they're not in my bag.* **2** give (love, affection, etc) wrongly or unwisely: *misplaced admiration, trust, confidence, etc.* **3** use (words or actions) unsuitably: *If you think deafness is funny, you've got a very misplaced sense of humour.*
□ ˌ**misplaced** ˈ**modifier** = DANGLING PARTICIPLE (DANGLE).

misprint /ˌmɪsˈprɪnt/ *v* [Tn, Tn·pr] ~ **sth** (**as sth**) make an error in printing sth: *They misprinted John as Jhon.*
▷ **misprint** /ˈmɪsprɪnt/ *n* error in printing: *Jhon is a misprint for John.*

mispronounce /ˌmɪsprəˈnaʊns/ *v* [Tn, Tn·pr] ~ **sth** (**as sth**) pronounce (words or letters) wrongly: *She mispronounced 'ship' as 'sheep'.* ▷ **mispronunciation** /ˌmɪsprəˌnʌnsɪˈeɪʃn/ *n* [U, C].

misquote /ˌmɪsˈkwəʊt/ *v* [Tn, Tw] quote (sth written or spoken) wrongly, either intentionally or unintentionally: *misquote a price, figure, etc* ○ *He is frequently misquoted in the press.* ○ *You misquoted me/what I said.* ▷ **misquotation** /ˌmɪskwəʊˈteɪʃn/ *n* [C, U]: *misquotations from Shakespeare.*

misread /ˌmɪsˈriːd/ *v* (*pt, pp* **misread** /-ˈred/) **1** [Tn, Tn·pr, Tw] ~ **sth** (**as sth**) read sth wrongly: *I misread the instructions/what the instructions said.* ○ *He misread 'the last train' as 'the fast train'.* **2** [Tn] interpret (sb/sth) wrongly: *His tactlessness showed that he had completely misread the situation.* ▷ **misreading** *n* [C, U]: *a misreading of the gas meter.*

misrepresent /ˌmɪsˌreprɪˈzent/ *v* [esp passive: Tn, Tn·pr] ~ **sb/sth** (**as sb/sth**) represent (sb/sth) wrongly; give a false account of sb/sth: *She was misrepresented in the press as (being) a militant.* ▷ **misrepresentation** /ˌmɪsˌreprɪzenˈteɪʃn/ *n* [C, U]: *a gross misrepresentation of the facts.*

misrule /ˌmɪsˈruːl/ *n* [U] bad government; disorder or confusion: *The country suffered years of misrule under a weak king.*

miss¹ /mɪs/ *n* **1** failure to hit, catch or reach sth aimed at: *score ten hits and one miss* ○ *The ball's gone right past him — that was a bad miss*, ie one he ought to have stopped, caught, etc. **2** (idm) **give sb/sth a ˈmiss** (*infml*) (**a**) omit sb/sth: *I think I'll give the fish course a miss.* (**b**) not do sth, not go somewhere, not see sb, etc as one is in the habit of doing: *give yoga, the cinema, my boy-friend a miss tonight.* **a ˌmiss is as ˌgood as a ˈmile** (*saying*) (**a**) an escape by a narrow margin (from danger, defeat, etc) is just as successful as an escape by a wide margin. (**b**) a failure by a narrow margin (to achieve success, etc) is just as disappointing as a failure by a wide margin. **a near miss** ⇨ NEAR¹.

miss² /mɪs/ *n* **1 Miss** (**a**) (title used with the name of an unmarried woman or kept by a married woman eg for professional reasons): *Miss (Gloria) Kelly* ○ *the Miss Hills* ○ (*fml*) *the Misses Hill.* Cf MRS, MS. (**b**) (title given to the winner of a beauty contest in the specified country, town, etc): *Miss England* ○ *Miss Brighton* ○ *the Miss World contest.* **2 Miss** (**a**) (used as a polite form of address to a young woman, eg by taxi-drivers, hotel staff, etc): *I'll take your luggage to your room, Miss.* Cf MADAM. (**b**) (used as a form of address by schoolchildren to a woman teacher): *Good morning, Miss!* Cf SIR 1. **3** (*joc or derog*) young girl or schoolgirl; young unmarried woman: *She's a saucy little miss!*

miss³ /mɪs/ *v* **1** [I, Tn, Tg] fail to hit, catch, reach, etc (sth aimed at): *He shot at the bird but missed.* ○ *miss the target, mark, goal, etc* ○ *The goalkeeper just missed (stopping) the ball.* ○ *miss one's footing*, ie slip or stumble, eg while climbing ○ *The plane missed the runway by several yards.* **2** [Tn, Tw] fail to see, hear, understand, etc (sb/sth): *The house is on the corner; you can't miss it.* ○ *I'm sorry, I missed that/what you said.* ○ *He missed the point of my joke.* **3** [Tn, Tg] fail to be present at (sth); arrive too late for (sth): *miss a meeting, a class, an appointment, etc* ○ *He missed the 9.30 train.* ○ *We only missed (seeing) each other by five minutes.* **4** [Tn, Tg] fail to take advantage of (sth): *miss the chance/opportunity of doing sth* ○ *Don't miss our bargain offers!* **5** (**a**) [Tn] notice the absence or loss of (sb/sth): *When did you first miss your purse?* ○ *He's so rich that he wouldn't miss £100.* ○ *We seem to be missing two chairs.* (**b**) [Tn, Tg, Tsg] feel regret at the absence or loss of (sb/sth): *Old Smith won't be missed*, eg when he is away, retires, dies, etc. ○ *I miss you bringing me cups of tea in the mornings!* **6** [Tn, Tg] avoid or escape (sth): *If you go early you'll miss the traffic.* ○ *We only just missed having a nasty accident.* **7** [I] (of an engine) misfire. **8** (idm) **hit/miss the mark** ⇨ MARK[1]. ˌ**miss the ˈboat/ˈbus** (*infml*) be too slow to take an opportunity: *If we don't offer a good price for the house now, we'll probably miss the boat altogether*, ie It will be sold to someone else. **not ˈmiss much**; **not miss a ˈtrick** (*infml*) be very aware or alert: *Jill will find out your secret — she never misses a trick!* **(be) too good to ˈmiss** (be) too attractive or profitable to reject: *The offer of a year abroad with all expenses paid seemed too good to miss.* **9** (phr v) **miss sb/sth out** not include sb/sth: *I'll miss out the sweet course*, ie not take it at a meal. ○ *We'll miss out* (eg not sing) *the last two verses.* ○ *The printers have missed out a whole line here.* **miss ˈout (on sth)** (*infml*) lose an opportunity to benefit from sth or enjoy oneself: *If I don't go to the party, I shall feel I'm missing out.*

▷ **missing** *adj* **1** **(a)** that cannot be found or that is not in its usual place; lost: *The book had two pages missing/two missing pages.* ○ *The hammer is missing from my tool-box.* **(b)** not present: *He's always missing when there's work to be done.* **2** that cannot be found; absent from home: *a police file on missing persons* ○ *The child had been missing for a week.* **3** (of a soldier, etc) neither present after a battle nor known to have been killed: *Two planes were reported (as) missing.* ˌ**missing ˈlink** **1** thing needed to complete a series or solve a problem. **2** type of animal thought to have existed between the apes and early human beings. The idea originated in the 19th century, when people thought humans were directly descended from monkeys: (*fig derog*) *Who's that missing link* (ie ugly or ape-like man) *your sister goes out with?* **the missing** *n* [pl *v*]: *Captain Jones is among the missing.*

missal /ˈmɪsl/ *n* book containing the prayers, etc for Mass throughout the year in the Roman Catholic Church.

missel-thrush (also **mistle-thrush**) /ˈmɪslθrʌʃ/ *n* type of large thrush that feeds on mistletoe and other berries.

misshapen /ˌmɪsˈʃeɪpən/ *adj* (esp of the body or a limb) badly shaped; deformed.

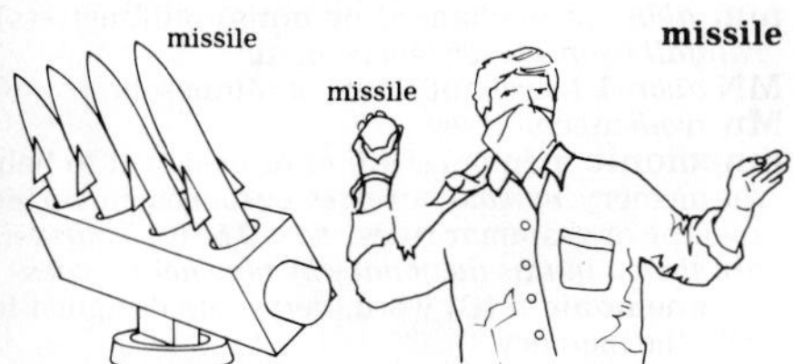

missile

missile /ˈmɪsaɪl; *US* ˈmɪsl/ *n* **1** object or weapon that is thrown or fired at a target: *Missiles thrown at the police included stones and bottles.* **2** (esp explosive) weapon directed at a target by remote control or automatically: *ballistic, guided, nuclear, etc missiles* ○ [attrib] *missile bases, sites, launching pads, etc.* ⇨ illus.

mission /ˈmɪʃn/ *n* **1** (work done by a) group of people sent abroad, esp on political or commercial business: *a British trade mission to China* ○ *go/come/send sb on a mission of inquiry* ○ *The delegation completed its mission successfully.* **2** **(a)** (work done by a) group of religious teachers sent to convert people: *a Catholic, Methodist, etc mission in Africa.* **(b)** building or settlement where the work of such a mission is done, esp among poor people: *The doctor works at the mission.* ○ [attrib] *a mission station, school, hospital, etc.* **3** **(a)** particular task or duty undertaken by an individual or a group: *a top-secret mission* ○ *My mission in life is to help poor people.* **(b)** such a task or duty performed by an individual or a unit of the armed forces: *The squadron flew a reconnaissance mission.* ○ [attrib] *mission control, headquarters, etc.*

missionary /ˈmɪʃənrɪ; *US* -nerɪ/ *n* person sent to preach (usu the Christian) religion, esp among people who are ignorant of it: *Catholic, Anglican, etc missionaries* ○ [attrib] *speak with missionary zeal*, ie great enthusiasm and commitment.

□ **the ˈmissionary position** (*infml*) standard position in sexual intercourse, in which the man lies on top of the woman facing her.

missis = MISSUS.

Mississippi /ˌmɪsɪˈsɪpɪ/ **1** largest river in N America, rising near the Canadian border and flowing south to the Gulf of Mexico. With its chief tributary, the Missouri, it is 5970 km (3710 miles) long. ⇨ article at RIVER. **2** state of the USA situated east of the lower Mississippi River. ⇨ map at App 1.

missive /ˈmɪsɪv/ *n* (*fml or joc*) letter, esp a long or official one.

Missouri /mɪˈzʊrɪ/ **1** N American river, one of the main tributaries of the Mississippi, which rises in the Rocky Mountains and flows into the Mississippi from the west. ⇨ article at RIVER. **2** (*abbrs* **MO**, **Mo**) state of the USA situated west of the Mississippi River. ⇨ map at App 1.

misspell /ˌmɪsˈspel/ *v* (*pt*, *pp* **misspelled** or **misspelt** /-ˈspelt/) [Tn] spell (sth) wrongly. ⇨ Usage at DREAM[2]. ▷ **misspelling** *n* [U, C].

misspend /ˌmɪsˈspend/ *v* (*pt*, *pp* **misspent** /-ˈspent/) [Tn esp passive, Tn·pr] ~ **sth (on sb/sth)** spend or use (money, time, etc) wrongly, foolishly or wastefully: ˌ*misspent* ˈ*energy*, ˈ*talent*, *enˈthusiasm, etc* ○ *a* ˌ*misspent* ˈ*youth*, ie one wasted on foolish pleasures.

misstate /ˌmɪsˈsteɪt/ *v* [Tn] (*fml*) state (facts, etc) wrongly: *Be careful not to misstate your case.* ▷ **misstatement** *n*: *I wish to correct my earlier misstatement.*

missus (also **missis**) /ˈmɪsɪz/ *n* **1** (*infml or joc*) (used esp by uneducated speakers; with *the, my, your, his*) wife: *How's the missus* (ie your wife)*?* ○ *My missis hates me smoking indoors.* **2** (*sl*) (used as a form of address to a woman): *Are these your kids, missis?*

missy /ˈmɪsɪ/ *n* (*dated infml*) (used as a polite or affectionate form of address to a young girl): *Well, missy, what do you want?*

mist /mɪst/ *n* **1** **(a)** [U, C] cloud of minute drops of water vapour hanging just above the ground, less thick than fog but still difficult to see through: *hills hidden/shrouded in mist* ○ *early morning mists in autumn* ○ [attrib] *mist patches on the motorway.* **(b)** [C usu *pl*] (*fig*) thing that is difficult to penetrate: *dispel the mists of ignorance* ○ *lost in the mists of time.* ⇨ Usage at FOG. **2** [U] water vapour condensed on a cold surface, eg a window, mirror, etc making it look cloudy. **3** [sing] dimness or blurring of the sight: *She saw his face through a mist of tears.* **4** [U] fine spray of liquid, eg from an aerosol: *A mist of perfume hung in the air.*

▷ **mist** *v* **1** [I, Tn] (cause sth to) be covered with mist or as if with mist: *His eyes (were) misted with tears.* ○ *mist the plants*, ie with an aerosol of water. **2** (phr v) ˌ**mist ˈover** become covered with mist: *The scene misted over.* ○ *When I drink tea, my glasses mist over.* ○ *His eyes misted over.* **mist (sth) up** cover or become covered by a film of water vapour: *Our breath is misting up the car windows.* **misty** *adj* (**-ier**, **-iest**) **1** full of or covered with mist: *a misty morning* ○ *misty weather* ○ *a misty view.* **2** (*fig*) not clear; blurred or indistinct: *a misty photograph.* **mistily** *adv.* **mistiness** *n* [U]. ˌ**misty-ˈeyed** *adj* dreamily sentimental: *going all misty-eyed at the thought of meeting his favourite pop star.*

mistake[1] /mɪˈsteɪk/ *n* **1** wrong idea or opinion; misconception: *You can't arrest me! There must be some mistake!* **2** thing done incorrectly through ignorance or wrong judgement; error: *spelling mistakes* ○ *learn by one's mistakes* ○ *The waiter made a mistake over the bill.* ○ *It was a big mistake to leave my umbrella at home.* **3** (idm) **and** ˌ**no miˈstake** (*infml*) without any doubt: *It's hot today and no mistake!* **by miˈstake** as a result of carelessness, forgetfulness, etc; in error: *I took your bag instead of mine by mistake.* ˌ**make no miˈstake (about sth)** (*infml*) do not be misled into thinking otherwise: *Sue seems very quiet, but make no mistake (about it), she has a terrible temper!*

NOTE ON USAGE: **Mistake**, **error**, **blunder**, **fault** and **defect** all refer to something done incorrectly or improperly. **Mistake** is the most general, used of everyday situations: *Your essay is full of mistakes.* ○ *It was a mistake to go there on holiday.* **Error** is more formal: *an error in your calculations* ○ *a technical error.* A **blunder** is a careless mistake, often unnecessary or resulting from misjudgement: *I made a terrible blunder in introducing her to my husband.* **Fault** emphasizes a person's responsibility for a mistake: *The child broke the window, but it was his parents' fault for letting him play football indoors.* **Fault** can also indicate an imperfection in a person or thing: *He has many faults, but vanity is not one of them.* ○ *an electrical fault.* A **defect** is more serious: *The new car had to be withdrawn from the market because of a mechanical defect.*

mistake[2] /mɪˈsteɪk/ *v* (*pt* **mistook** /mɪˈstʊk/, *pp* **mistaken** /mɪsˈteɪkən/) **1** [Tn, Tw] be wrong or get a wrong idea about (sb/sth): *I must have mistaken your meaning/what you meant.* ○ *Don't mistake me, I mean what I say.* ○ *We've mistaken the house*, ie come to the wrong house. **2** [Tn·pr] ~ **sb/sth for sb/sth** wrongly suppose that sb/sth is sb/sth else: *mistake a toadstool for a mushroom* ○ *She is often mistaken for her twin sister.* **3** (idm) **there's no mistaking sb/sth** there is no possibility of being wrong about sb/sth: *There's no mistaking what ought to be done.*

▷ **mistaken** *adj* **1** [usu pred] ~ **(about sb/sth)** wrong in opinion: *If I'm not mistaken, that's the man we saw on the bus.* ○ *You're completely mistaken.* **2** wrongly judged; not correct: *a case of mistaken identity* ○ *mistaken ideas, views, etc* ○ *I helped him in the mistaken belief that he needed me.* **3** applied unwisely: *mistaken kindness, zeal, etc.* **mistakenly** *adv.*

mister /ˈmɪstə(r)/ *n* **1** (full form, rarely used in writing, of the abbreviation *Mr*). Cf MR. **2** (*sl*) (used as a form of address to a man, esp by children, tradespeople, etc): *Please mister, can I have my ball back?* ○ *Now listen to me, mister!*

mistime /ˌmɪsˈtaɪm/ *v* [Tn esp passive] say or do (sth) at a wrong or an unsuitable time: *a mistimed remark, comment, etc* ○ *a mistimed shot*, eg in golf ○ *The government's intervention was badly mistimed.*

mistletoe /ˈmɪsltəʊ/ *n* [U] evergreen plant with small white berries that grows as a parasite esp on apple trees and is hung indoors as a Christmas decoration: *the tradition of kissing under the mistletoe.* ⇨ article at CHRISTMAS.

mistook *pt* of MISTAKE.

mistral /ˈmɪstrəl, mɪˈstrɑːl/ *n* **the mistral** [sing] strong cold dry N or NW wind that blows in S France, usu in winter.

mistranslate /ˌmɪstrænsˈleɪt/ *v* [I, Tn] translate (eg words) wrongly. ▷ **mistranslation** /-ˈleɪʃn/ *n* [U, C].

mistreat /ˌmɪsˈtriːt/ *v* [Tn esp passive] treat (sb/sth) badly or unkindly: *I hate to see books being mistreated.* ▷ **mistreatment** *n* [U].

mistress /ˈmɪstrɪs/ *n* **1** woman in a position of authority or control: *mistress of the situation* ○ *She wants to be mistress of her own affairs*, ie organize her own life. ○ (*dated*) *Is the mistress of the house* (ie the female head of the household) *in?* ○ (*fig*) *Venice was called the 'Mistress of the Adriatic'.* Cf MASTER[1] 1. **2** female owner of a dog or other animal. **3** (*esp Brit*) female schoolteacher: *the ˈFrench mistress*, ie teacher of French (but not necessarily a Frenchwoman) ○ *We've got a new ˈgames mistress* (ie one in charge of sport) *this year.* **4** woman having an illicit but regular sexual relationship, esp with a married man: *have/keep a mistress.* Cf LOVER 1. **5** (*arch*) woman loved and courted by a man; sweetheart: *O mistress mine!*

6 (idm) **be one's own master/mistress** ⇨ MASTER[1].

mistrial /ˌmɪsˈtraɪəl/ *n* (*law*) **1** trial that is invalid because of some error in the proceedings. **2** (*US*) trial in which the jury cannot agree on a verdict.

mistrust /ˌmɪsˈtrʌst/ *v* [Tn] **1** feel no confidence in (sb/sth): *mistrust one's own judgement.* **2** be suspicious of (sb/sth): *mistrust sb's motives.*
▷ **mistrust** *n* [U, sing] **(a)** ~ **(of sb/sth) 1** lack of confidence in sb/sth. **2** suspicion of sb/sth: *She has a deep mistrust of anything new or strange.* **mistrustful** /-fl/ *adj* ~ **(of sb/sth)**: *be mistrustful of one's ability to make the right decision.* **mistrustfully** /-fəlɪ/ *adv.*

misty ⇨ MIST.

misunderstand /ˌmɪsʌndəˈstænd/ *v* (*pt, pp* **-stood** /-ˈstʊd/) [Tn, Tw] interpret (instructions, messages, etc) incorrectly; form a wrong opinion of (sb/sth): *Don't misunderstand me/what I'm trying to say.* ○ *She had always felt misunderstood,* ie that people did not appreciate her.
▷ **misunderstanding** *n* **1** [U, C] failure to understand rightly or correctly: *There must be some misunderstanding!* **2** [C] minor disagreement or quarrel: *clear up* (eg by discussion) *a misunderstanding between colleagues* ○ *We had a slight misunderstanding over the time.*

misuse /ˌmɪsˈjuːz/ *v* [Tn esp passive] **1** use (sth) in the wrong way or for the wrong purpose: *misuse a word, expression, etc* ○ *misuse public funds.* **2** treat (sb/sth) badly: *He felt misused by the company.* Cf ABUSE.
▷ **misuse** /ˌmɪsˈjuːs/ *n* [C, U] (instance of) wrong or incorrect use: *the misuse of power, authority, etc.*

MIT /ˌem aɪ ˈtiː/ *abbr* Massachusetts Institute of Technology.

mite[1] /maɪt/ *n* **1** [C usu *sing*] very small or modest contribution or offering: *offer a mite of comfort to sb* ○ *give one's mite to a good cause.* **2** [C] small child or animal (usu when treated as an object of sympathy): *Poor little mite!*
▷ **a mite** *adv* (*infml*) a little; somewhat: *This curry is a mite too hot for me!*

mite[2] /maɪt/ *n* small spider-like creature that may be found in food, and may carry disease: *ˈcheese-mites.*

Mitford /ˈmɪtfəd/ Nancy (1904-73), English novelist and biographer. In an essay in *Noblesse Oblige* (1956) she helped to originate the 'U' and 'non-U' classification of behaviour and use of language. Cf U[2], NON-U.

Mithras /ˈmɪθræs/ (in Persian mythology) god of light and truth. He was widely worshipped in ancient Rome and throughout the Roman Empire, and in the first three centuries AD the cult of Mithras was a serious rival to Christianity.

mitigate /ˈmɪtɪgeɪt/ *v* [Tn] (*fml*) make (sth) less severe, violent or painful; moderate: *mitigate sb's suffering, anger, anxiety, etc* ○ *mitigate the severity of a punishment, sentence, etc* ○ *mitigate the effects of inflation,* eg by making credit easily obtainable.
▷ **mitigating** *adj* [attrib] reducing the severity, violence or pain of sth; moderating: *mitigating circumstances,* ie those that partially excuse a mistake, crime, etc ○ *the mitigating effect of pain-killing drugs.*
mitigation /ˌmɪtɪˈgeɪʃn/ *n* [U]: *say sth in mitigation of sb's faults, crimes, etc,* ie to make them seem less serious.

mitosis /maɪˈtəʊsɪs, mɪt-/ *n* (*pl* **-es** /-siːz/) (*biology*) process of division of a cell or its nucleus, in which each chromosome splits lengthways into two identical sets, one for each of the two new cells. Cf MEIOSIS. ▷ **mitotic** /-ˈtɒtɪk/ *adj.*

mitral valve /ˈmaɪtrəl vælv/ heart valve between the left atrium and the left ventricle, which stops blood flowing backwards.

mitre (*US* **miter**) /ˈmaɪtə(r)/ *n* **1** tall pointed head-dress worn by bishops and abbots on ceremonial occasions as a symbol of their office. **2** (also **ˈmitre-joint**) corner joint esp of two pieces of wood with their ends evenly tapered so that together they form a right angle.
▷ **mitre** (*US* **miter**) *v* [Tn esp passive] join (esp two pieces of wood) with a mitre-joint: *mitred corners.*

mitt /mɪt/ *n* **1** = MITTEN. **2** (in baseball) large padded leather glove worn by the catcher. **3** (*infml*) boxing-glove. **4** (usu *pl*) (*sl*) hand; fist: *Take your mitts off me!*

mitten /ˈmɪtn/ *n* **1** (also **mitt**) type of glove covering four fingers together and the thumb separately. ⇨ illus at GLOVE. **2** covering for the back and palm of the hand only, leaving most of the thumb and fingers bare.

Mitty /ˈmɪtɪ/ Walter, hero of a story by James *Thurber, who enjoyed having extravagant daydreams about his own success: *He's a bit of a Walter Mitty character.*

mix[1] /mɪks/ *v* **1** [Tn, Tn·p, Dn·n, Dn·pr] ~ **sth (up) (for sb/sth)** make or prepare sth by putting substances, etc together so that they are no longer distinct: *mix cement, mortar, etc* ○ *mix cocktails, drinks, etc* ○ *He mixed his guests a salad.* ○ *She mixed a cheese sauce for the fish.* ○ *The chemist mixed (up) some medicine for me.* **2 (a)** [I, Ipr, Ip] ~ **with sth/** ~ **(together)** be able to be combined; make a suitable combination: *Oil and water don't mix.* ○ *Oil won't mix with water.* ○ *Pink and blue mix well together.* **(b)** [Tn, Tn·pr, Tn·p] ~ **A with B/** ~ **A and B (together)** combine one thing with another; blend things together: *mix the sugar with the flour* ○ (*fig*) *Don't try to mix business with pleasure.* ○ *Don't mix your drinks* (ie have different ones in close succession) *at parties!* ○ *If you mix red and yellow, you get orange.* ○ *Many women successfully mix marriage and a career.* ○ *Many races are mixed together in Brazil.* **3** [I, Ipr] ~ **(with sb/sth)** (of people) come or be together socially: *He finds it hard to mix at parties.* ○ *In my job, I mix with all sorts of people.* **4** (idm) **be/get mixed ˈup in sth** (*infml*) be/become involved in or connected with sth: *I don't want to be mixed up in the affair.* **be/get mixed ˈup with sb** (*infml*) be/become associated with sb (esp sb disreputable): *Don't get mixed up with him — he's a crook!* **mix it (with sb)**; *US* **mix it up (with sb)** (*sl*) start a quarrel or a fight: *Don't try mixing it with me — I've got a gun!* **5** (phr v) **mix sth in** (esp in cooking) combine one ingredient with another: *Mix the eggs in slowly.* ○ *Mix in the butter when melted.* **mix sth into sth (a)** add (another ingredient) to sth and combine the two: *mix the yeast into the flour.* **(b)** make sth by blending (one or more ingredients): *mix the flour and water into a smooth paste.* **mix sb up (about/over sth)** cause sb to become confused: *Now you've mixed me up completely!* **mix sb/sth up (with sb/sth)** confuse sb/sth with sb/sth else; be unable to distinguish between (people or things): *You're always mixing me up with my twin sister!* ○ *I got the tickets mixed up and gave you mine.*
□ **ˈmix-up** *n* (*infml*) confused situation; misunderstanding: *There's been an awful mix-up over the dates!*

mix[2] /mɪks/ *n* **1** [C usu *sing*] mixture or combination of things or people: *a good social, racial, etc mix,* eg in a group of students. **2** [C, U] mixture of ingredients sold for making kinds of food, etc: *a packet of ˈcake mix.*

mixed /mɪkst/ *adj* **1** composed of different qualities or elements: *The critics gave the new play a mixed reception,* ie one of criticism and praise. ○ *The weather has been very mixed recently.* **2** of different shapes, flavours, etc: *a tin of mixed biscuits, sweets, etc.* **3** having or showing various races or social classes: *live in a mixed society* ○ *people of mixed blood.* **4** for members of both sexes: *a mixed school* ○ *mixed changing rooms,* eg at a sports centre. **5** (idm) **have ˌmixed ˈfeelings (about sb/sth)** react to sb/sth with confused or conflicting feelings, eg joy and sorrow.
□ **ˌmixed ˈbag** (*infml*) assortment of things or people, esp of varying quality: *The competition entries were a very mixed bag.*
ˌmixed ˈblessing thing that has advantages and also disadvantages.
ˌmixed ˈdoubles game (esp of tennis) in which a man and a woman are partners on each side.
ˌmixed eˈconomy national economy in which some businesses are privately owned and some are state-controlled.
ˌmixed ˈfarming farming of both crops and livestock.
ˌmixed ˈgrill dish of various grilled meats, often with tomatoes and mushrooms.
ˌmixed ˈmarriage marriage between people of different races or religions.
ˌmixed ˈmetaphor combination of two or more metaphors that do not fit together and therefore produce a ludicrous effect, eg *The hand that rocks the cradle has kicked the bucket.*
ˌmixed-ˈup *adj* (*infml*) mentally or emotionally confused; not well-adjusted socially: *She feels very mixed-up about life since her divorce.* ○ *ˌmixed-up ˈkids who take drugs.*

mixer /ˈmɪksə(r)/ *n* **1** (esp electrical) device for mixing things: *a ceˈment-mixer* ○ *a ˈfood-mixer.* **2** (*infml*) person able or unable (as specified) to mix easily with others, eg at parties: *be a good/bad mixer.* **3** drink that can be mixed with another, eg to make cocktails: *use fruit juice as a mixer.* **4 (a)** (in films and TV) person or device that combines shots onto one length of film or videotape. **(b)** (in sound recording) person or device that combines sounds onto one tape.

mixture /ˈmɪkstʃə(r)/ *n* **1** [U] mixing or being mixed. **2** [C] thing made by mixing: *a ˈcough mixture,* ie containing several medicines ○ *The city was a mixture of old and new buildings.* **3** [sing] (*chemistry*) combination of two or more substances which do not alter their composition: *Air is a mixture, not a compound, of gases.* Cf COMPOUND[1] 1, ELEMENT 3.

mizzen (also **mizen**) /ˈmɪzn/ *n* (*nautical*) **1** = MIZZEN-MAST. **2** (also **ˈmizzen-sail**) lowest square fore-and-aft sail set on the mizzen-mast.
□ **ˈmizzen-mast** *n* third mast from the bow on a sailing-ship with three or more masts; mast nearest the stern on smaller ships.

Mk *abbr* **1** mark (currency): *Mk 300.* **2** (on cars) mark (ie model or type): *Ford Granada Ghia Mk II.*

ml *abbr* (*pl* unchanged or **mls**) **1** (*US* **mi**) mile(s): *distance to village 3mls.* **2** millilitre(s): *25ml.*

MLitt /ˌem ˈlɪt/ *abbr* Master of Letters (Latin *Magister Litterarum*): *have/be an MLitt in philosophy* ○ *Debra Kahn MLitt.*

MLR *abbr* minimum lending rate.

m'lud /məˈlʌd/ (*Brit*) form of address to a judge in a court of law, meaning 'My Lord'.

mm *abbr* (*pl* unchanged or **mms**) millimetre(s): *rainfall 6 mm* ○ *a 35 mm camera.*

MN *abbr* **1** Merchant Navy. **2** Minnesota.

Mn *symb* manganese.

mnemonic /nɪˈmɒnɪk/ *adj* of or designed to help the memory: *mnemonic verses,* eg for remembering spelling or grammar rules, etc ○ *The verb patterns are shown in this dictionary by mnemonic codes.*
▷ **mnemonic** *n* [C] word, verse, etc designed to help the memory.
mnemonics [usu sing *v*] art of or system for improving the memory.

MO /ˌem ˈəʊ/ *abbr* **1** Medical Officer. **2** (also **Mo**) Missouri. **3** money order.

Mo *symb* molybdenum.

mo /məʊ/ *n* (*pl* **mos**) (*Brit infml*) short period of time; moment: *Half a mo* (ie Wait a little), *I'm not quite ready.*

mo *abbr* (*US*) = MTH.

moan /məʊn/ *n* **1 (a)** [C] long low mournful sound, usu expressing regret, pain or suffering: *the moans of the wounded.* **(b)** [sing] similar sound as made by eg the wind. **2** [C] (*infml*) grumble or complaint: *We had a good moan about the weather.*
▷ **moan** *v* **1 (a)** [I, Ip, Tn] utter moans or say (sth) with moans: *He was moaning (away) all night long.* ○ *'Where's the doctor?' he moaned.* **(b)** [I, Ipr] make a moaning sound: *The wind was moaning through the trees.* **2** [I, Ipr, Ip] ~ **(about sth)** (*infml*) grumble or complain: *moaning and groaning (away)* ○ *He's always moaning (on) about how poor he is.*

moat /məʊt/ *n* deep wide ditch filled with water, dug round a castle, etc as a defence. ⇨ illus at

CASTLE.
▷ **moated** *adj* having a moat: *a moated manor house.*

mob /mɒb/ *n* **1** [CGp] large disorderly crowd, esp one that has gathered to attack or cause mischief: *The fans rushed onto the pitch in an excited mob.* ○ [attrib] *mob law/rule*, ie that imposed or enforced by a mob ○ *mob oratory*, ie speech-making that appeals to the emotions of the masses, not to their intellect. **2 the mob** [sing] (*derog*) the masses or the common people. **3** [C esp *sing*] (*sl*) gang of criminals: *Whose mob is he with?*
▷ **mob** *v* (**-bb-**) [Tn esp passive] crowd round (sb) noisily in great numbers, either to attack or admire: *The pop singer was mobbed by teenagers.*

mob-cap /ˈmɒb kæp/ *n* large round cotton cap covering the whole of the hair, worn indoors by women in the 18th century.

mobile /ˈməʊbaɪl; *US* -bl, also -bi:l/ *adj* **1** (**a**) that can move or be moved easily and quickly from place to place: *mobile troops, artillery, etc* ○ *a mobile library*, ie one inside a vehicle. (**b**) (of people) able to change class, occupation or place of residence easily: *a mobile work-force.* Cf STATIONARY. **2** (of a face, its features, etc) changing shape or expression easily and often. **3** [pred] (*infml*) having transport, esp a car: *Can you give me a lift if you're mobile?*
▷ **mobile** *n* ornamental hanging structure of metal, plastic, cardboard, etc, whose parts move freely in currents of air.
mobility /məʊˈbɪlətɪ/ *n* [U] being mobile.
□ ˌ**mobile** ˈ**home** large caravan that can be towed by a vehicle but is normally parked in one place and used as a home.

mobilize, -ise /ˈməʊbɪlaɪz/ *v* **1** [I, Tn] (cause sb/sth to) become ready for service or action, esp in war: *The troops received orders to mobilize.* **2** [Tn] organize or assemble (resources, etc) for a particular purpose: *They are mobilizing their supporters to vote at the election.*
▷ **mobilization, -isation** /ˌməʊbɪlaɪˈzeɪʃn; *US* -lɪˈz-/ *n* [U] mobilizing or being mobilized: [attrib] *mobilization orders.*

Möbius strip /ˈmɜ:bɪəs strɪp/ (*mathematics*) surface with only one side and one edge, formed by twisting a long narrow rectangular strip through 180° and joining the ends.

mobster /ˈmɒbstə(r)/ *n* member of a gang of criminals; gangster.

Moby Dick /ˌməʊbɪ ˈdɪk/ name of a huge fierce white whale, the subject of a novel by Herman *Melville published in 1851.

moccasin /ˈmɒkəsɪn/ *n* flat-soled shoe made from soft leather, as originally worn by N American Indians.

mocha /ˈmɒkə; *US* ˈməʊkə/ *n* [U] **1** type of strong fine-quality coffee, originally shipped from the Arabian port of Mocha. **2** flavouring made by mixing this and chocolate: [attrib] *mocha ice-cream.*

mock[1] /mɒk/ *v* **1** [I, Ipr, Tn] ~ (**at sb/sth**) make fun of (sb/sth), esp by mimicking him/it contemptuously; ridicule: *a mocking smile, voice, laugh* ○ *mock (at) sb's fears, efforts, attempts* ○ *It is wrong to mock cripples.* **2** [Tn] (*fml esp fig*) defy (sb/sth) contemptuously: *The heavy steel doors mocked our attempts to open them.*
▷ **mock** *n* (idm) **make (a)** ˈ**mock of sb/sth** make sb/sth seem foolish; ridicule sb/sth.
mocker *n* **1** person who mocks. **2** (idm) **put the** ˈ**mockers on sb** (*sl*) bring bad luck to sb.
mockingly *adv.*
□ ˈ**mocking-bird** *n* type of American bird of the thrush family that mimics the calls of other birds.
ˈ**mock-up** *n* **1** full-scale experimental model or replica, eg of a machine, made for testing, etc. **2** arrangement of text, pictures, etc of sth to be printed: *do a mock-up of a book cover.*

mock[2] /mɒk/ *adj* [attrib] (**a**) not real; substitute: *a mock battle, exam*, eg for training or practice. (**b**) not genuine; counterfeit: ˌ*mock* ˈ*modesty*, ie pretence of being modest ○ ˌ*mock-he*ˈ*roic style*, ie making fun of the heroic style in art or literature.
□ **mock** ˌ**turtle** ˈ**soup** soup made from calf's head or other meat to resemble turtle soup.

mockery /ˈmɒkərɪ/ *n* **1** [U] action of mocking sb/sth; scorn or ridicule: *He replied with a note of mockery in his voice.* **2** [C] ~ (**of sth**) completely inadequate or ridiculous action or representation (of sth); travesty: *The performance was an utter mockery.* ○ *The trial was a mockery of justice.* **3** [sing] person or thing that is mocked; occasion when this happens. **4** (idm) **make a mockery of sth** make sth appear foolish or worthless: *The unfair and hasty decision of the court made a mockery of the trial.*

MOD /ˌem əʊ ˈdi:/ *abbr* (*Brit*) Ministry of Defence.

mod /mɒd/ *n* (also **Mod**) (*Brit*) member of a group of young people, prominent in Britain in the 1960s, who liked to wear neat and fashionable clothes and to ride motor-scooters. Cf ROCKER (ROCK[2]).

modal /ˈməʊdl/ *n* (also **modal verb**, **modal auˈxiliary**, **modal auˈxiliary verb**) (*grammar*) verb that is used with another verb (not a modal) to express possibility, permission, obligation, etc: *'Can', 'may', 'might', 'must' and 'should' are all modals.*
▷ **modal** *adj* [usu attrib] **1** (*grammar*) of a modal. **2** relating to mode or manner, in contrast to substance.

mod cons /ˌmɒd ˈkɒnz/ (*Brit infml approv*) (used esp by advertisers of houses) modern installations in a house (eg hot water, electricity, heating, telephone) that make the house easier and more comfortable to live in: *a house with all mod cons.*

mode /məʊd/ *n* **1** ~ (**of sth**) (*fml*) way or manner in which sth is done: *a mode of life, living, operation, thought, transport* ○ *The level of formality determines the precise mode of expression.* **2** (usu *sing*) style or fashion in clothes, art, drama, etc: *the latest mode.* **3** any of several arrangements of musical notes, esp the major or minor scale system in modern music. Other modes often produce a characteristic sound, as in the traditional scales used in early music, church music and folk music. **4** arrangement or setting of equipment to perform a certain task: *a spacecraft in re-*ˈ*entry mode* ○ *a tape-recorder in* ˈ*play-back/re*ˈ*cording mode.* **5** (in statistics) the most commonly occurring value of a variable. Cf MEAN[3], MEDIAN.

model

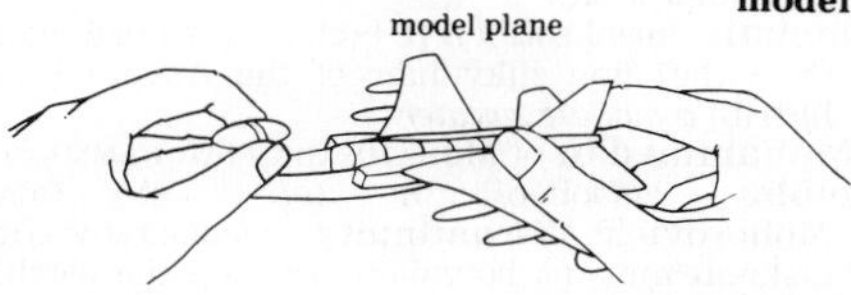

model[1] /ˈmɒdl/ *n* **1** (**a**) representation of sth, usu smaller than the original: *a model of the proposed new airport* ○ *construct a scale model of the Eiffel Tower* ○ [attrib] *a model train, aeroplane, car, etc.* ⇨ illus. (**b**) design of sth that is made so that it can be copied in another material: *a clay/wax model for a statue*, eg to be copied in stone or metal. **2** particular design or type of product: *All this year's new models are displayed at the motor show.* ○ *This is the most popular model in our whole range.* **3** simplified description of a system used in explanations, calculations, etc: *a model of a molecule* ○ *a statistical/mathematical/economical model*, eg used to forecast future trends. **4** system used as a basis for a copy; pattern: *The nation's constitution provided a model that other countries followed.* **5** ~ (**of sth**) (*approv*) person or thing regarded as excellent of his/its kind and worth imitating: *a model of tact, fairness, accuracy, etc* ○ [attrib] *a model pupil, husband, teacher, etc* ○ *model behaviour* ○ *a model farm, prison, etc*, ie one that has been specially designed to be very efficient. **6** (**a**) person employed to pose for an artist, photographer, etc. (**b**) person employed to display clothes, hats, etc to possible buyers, by wearing them: *She is one of the country's top models.* ○ *a male* ˈ*model* ○ *a* ˈ*fashion model.* **7** (copy of a) garment, hat, etc fashioned by a well-known designer and shown in public: *see, buy, wear, etc the latest Paris models.*

model[2] /ˈmɒdl/ *v* (**-ll-**; *US* **-l-**) **1** [Tn.pr] ~ **oneself/sth on sb/sth** take sb/sth as an example for one's action, plans, etc: *She models herself on her favourite novelist.* ○ *The design of the building is modelled on classical Greek forms.* **2** [I, Tn] work as a model[1](6); display (clothes, hats, etc) by wearing them: *She earns a living by modelling (dresses, swim-suits, etc).* **3** [I, Tn] make a model of (sth) in clay, wax, etc; shape (clay, wax, etc) to form sth: *modelling (in) plasticine.*
▷ **modeller** (*US* **modeler**) *n* person who practises modelling: *a railway modeller.*
modelling (*US* **modeling**) *n* [U] **1** art of making models (MODEL[1] 1a); way in which this is done: *clay modelling* ○ *by skilful modelling.* **2** working as a model[1](6): *She did some modelling as a student to earn a bit of money.*

modem /ˈməʊdem/ *n* device linking a computer system and eg a telephone line so that data can be transmitted at high speeds from one computer to another.

moderate[1] /ˈmɒdərət/ *adj* **1** average in amount, intensity, quality, etc; not extreme: *moderate price increases* ○ *travelling at a moderate speed* ○ *a moderate-sized bathroom* ○ *give a moderate performance*, ie neither very good nor very bad ○ *a moderate sea*, ie neither calm nor rough ○ *a moderate breeze*, ie a wind of medium strength. **2** of or having (usu political) opinions that are not extreme: *a man with moderate views* ○ *moderate policies.* **3** keeping or kept within limits that are not excessive: *a moderate drinker* ○ *moderate wage demands.*
▷ **moderate** /ˈmɒdərət/ *n* person with moderate opinions, esp in politics.
moderately *adv* to a moderate extent; not very; quite: *a moderately good performance* ○ *a moderately expensive house* ○ *She only did moderately well in the exam.*

moderate[2] /ˈmɒdəreɪt/ *v* [I, Tn] (cause sb/sth to) become less violent, extreme or intense: *The wind has moderated, making sailing safer.* ○ *He must learn to moderate his temper.* ○ *exercise a moderating* (ie controlling, restraining) *influence on sb.*

moderation /ˌmɒdəˈreɪʃn/ *n* **1** [U] quality of being moderate; freedom from excess; restraint: *They showed a remarkable degree of moderation in not quarrelling publicly on television.* **2** (idm) **in modeˈration** (of smoking, drinking alcohol, etc) in a moderate manner; not excessively: *Whisky can be good for you if taken in moderation.*

moderator /ˈmɒdəreɪtə(r)/ *n* **1** person who arbitrates in a dispute; mediator. **2** person who makes sure that the same standards are used by different examiners when marking an examination. **3** Presbyterian minister presiding over a church court. **4** (*physics*) substance, eg graphite, beryllium or heavy water (HEAVY), which slows down neutrons in a nuclear reactor. The neutrons lose some of their energy when they collide with the moderator and so are more likely to cause nuclear fission.

modern /ˈmɒdn/ *adj* **1** [attrib] of the present or recent times; contemporary: *Unemployment is one of the major problems of modern times.* ○ *in the modern world/age* ○ *modern history*, eg of Europe from about 1475 onwards. **2** (*esp approv*) using or having the newest methods, equipment, buildings, etc; up to date: *modern marketing techniques* ○ *one of the most modern shopping centres in the country.* **3** [attrib] of a contemporary style of art, fashion, etc, esp one that is experimental and not traditional: *modern dance.* ⇨ Usage at NEW.
▷ **modern** *n* (*dated or fml*) person living in modern times.
modernity /məˈdɜ:nətɪ/ *n* [U] being modern.
□ ˌ**modern** ˈ**language** (*esp Brit*) language that is spoken or written now, esp a European language such as French, German or Spanish: *study modern languages at university.*
ˌ**modern penˈtathlon** athletic contest in which competitors take part in five sports: running,

swimming, riding, fencing and pistol shooting.

modernism /ˈmɒdənɪzəm/ *n* [U] modern ideas or methods in contrast to traditional ones, esp in art, literature or religion. In English literature, the term Modernism refers to an early 20th-century movement including writers such as *Pound, T S *Eliot, Virginia *Woolf, *Joyce and *Conrad. Despite the great differences in their styles, they all reacted against traditional forms of poetry and prose, developing new techniques like the use of the 'stream of consciousness' (STREAM). The movement had parallels in the other arts, as in the early paintings of Paul *Nash.

▷ **modernist** /ˈmɒdənɪst/ *n* believer in or supporter of modernism. — *adj* [attrib] of or associated with modernism. **modernistic** /ˌmɒdəˈnɪstɪk/ *adj* noticeably modern; showing modernism: *modernistic furniture designs.*

modernize, -ise /ˈmɒdənaɪz/ *v* **1** [Tn] make (sth) suitable for modern needs or habits; bring up to date: *modernize a transport system, a factory, farming methods* ○ *a fully modernized shop.* **2** [I] adopt modern ways or views: *If the industry doesn't modernize it will not survive.* ▷ **modernization, -isation** /ˌmɒdənaɪˈzeɪʃn; *US* -nɪˈz-/ *n* [U]: *the modernization of the telephone system* ○ [attrib] *embark on a major modernization programme.*

modest /ˈmɒdɪst/ *adj* **1** (**a**) not large in amount, size, etc; moderate: *live on a modest income* ○ *make very modest demands* ○ *a modest improvement, success.* (**b**) not showy or splendid in appearance; not expensive: *live in a modest little house.* **2** (**a**) ~ (**about sth**) (*approv*) having or showing a not too high opinion of one's abilities, qualities, etc; not vain or boastful: *be modest about one's achievements.* (**b**) rather shy; not putting oneself forward; bashful: *Might I make a modest suggestion?* **3** (esp of women or their appearance or behaviour) having or showing respect for conventional ideas of decency and purity: *a modest dress, blouse, neckline, etc,* ie one that is not sexually provocative.

▷ **modestly** *adv.*

modesty /ˈmɒdɪstɪ/ *n* [U] (*esp approv*) state of being modest: *speak with genuine modesty/without (a trace of) false modesty* ○ *I'd like to tell you all about my success but modesty forbids.*

modicum /ˈmɒdɪkəm/ *n* [sing] ~ (**of sth**) small or moderate amount of sth: *achieve success with a modicum of effort* ○ *Anyone with even a modicum of intelligence would have realized that!*

modify /ˈmɒdɪfaɪ/ *v* (*pt, pp* **-fied**) [Tn] **1** change (sth) slightly, esp to make it less extreme or to improve it: *The union has been forced to modify its position.* ○ *The policy was agreed by the committee, but only in a modified form.* ○ *The heating system has recently been modified to make it more efficient.* ⇨ Usage at CHANGE¹. **2** (*grammar*) (esp of an *adj* or *adv*) limit the sense of (another word): *In 'the black cat' the adjective 'black' modifies the noun 'cat'.*

▷ **modification** /ˌmɒdɪfɪˈkeɪʃn/ *n* (**a**) [U] modifying or being modified: *The design of the spacecraft is undergoing extensive modification.* (**b**) [C] instance of this; change or alteration: *The plan was approved, with some minor modifications.*

modifier /-faɪə(r)/ *n* (*grammar*) word or phrase that modifies (MODIFY 2) another word or phrase.

modish /ˈməʊdɪʃ/ *adj* (*sometimes derog*) fashionable. ▷ **modishly** *adv.*

modiste /məʊˈdiːst/ *n* (*dated*) person, usu a woman, who makes women's dresses or hats.

modulate /ˈmɒdjʊleɪt; *US* -dʒʊ-/ *v* **1** [Tn] vary the strength, volume or pitch of (one's voice): *the actor's clearly modulated tones.* **2** [I, Ipr] ~ (**from sth**) (**to sth**) change from one musical key to another: *music that modulates frequently* ○ *to modulate from C major to A minor.* **3** [Tn] (*fml*) adjust or moderate (sth). **4** [Tn] vary the amplitude, phase or frequency of (a radio wave) so as to convey a particular signal.

▷ **modulation** /ˌmɒdjʊˈleɪʃn; *US* -dʒʊˈl-/ *n* **1** [C, U] modulating or being modulated. **2** [U] any of various ways of altering a radio wave so as to make it carry a signal. Cf AMPLITUDE MODULATION (AMPLITUDE), FREQUENCY MODULATION (FREQUENCY).

module /ˈmɒdjuːl; *US* -dʒuːl/ *n* **1** (**a**) any one of a set of standardized parts or units that are made separately and are joined together to construct a building or piece of furniture. (**b**) unit, esp of a computer or computer program, that has a particular function: *a software module.* **2** (*aerospace*) independent self-contained unit of a spacecraft: *a service module* ○ *the command module,* ie for the astronaut in command ○ *a lunar module,* ie used for landing on the moon. **3** any one of several independent units or options that make up a course of study, esp at a college or university.

▷ **modular** /ˈmɒdjʊlə(r); *US* -dʒʊ-/ *adj* **1** using a module or modules as the basis of design or construction: *modular components* ○ *modular furniture.* **2** (of a course of study) composed of a number of separate units from which students may select a certain number.

modulus /ˈmɒdjʊləs; *US* ˈmɒdʒələs/ *n* (*pl* **-li** /-laɪ/) (*mathematics*) value of a number, regardless of whether it represents a positive or a negative quantity. It can be expressed as the positive square root of the square of the number.

modus operandi /ˌməʊdəs ˌɒpəˈrændiː/ (*Latin*) (**a**) person's method of dealing with a task. (**b**) way in which a thing operates.

modus vivendi /ˌməʊdəs vɪˈvendiː/ (*Latin*) **1** temporary practical arrangement by which people who are opposed or quarrelling can continue to live or work together while waiting for their dispute to be settled: *We managed to achieve a kind of modus vivendi.* **2** way of living or coping.

moggie (also **moggy**) /ˈmɒɡɪ/ (also **mog** /mɒɡ/) *n* (*Brit infml esp joc*) cat.

Mogul (also **Moghul**) /ˈməʊɡl/ *n* member of a dynasty of Muslim rulers of India, esp one of the **Great Moguls** from Babur (1483-1530) to Aurangzeb (1618-1707), who were famous for the magnificence of their courts and for their patronage of art and architecture. The *Taj Mahal was built in this period.

mogul /ˈməʊɡl/ *n* very rich, important or influential person: *Hollywood moguls* ○ *a television mogul.*

MOH /ˌem əʊ ˈeɪtʃ/ *abbr* (*Brit*) Medical Officer of Health (eg a doctor in charge of public health in a particular area).

mohair /ˈməʊheə(r)/ *n* [U] (cloth or thread made from the) fine silky hair of the Angora goat: [attrib] *a mohair sweater.*

Mohammedan = MUHAMMADAN (MUHAMMAD).

moho /ˈməʊhəʊ/ *n* (*pl* ~**s**) (also **Mohorovičić discontinuity** /məʊhəˌrəʊvətʃɪtʃ dɪskɒntəˈnjuːətɪ/) boundary between the earth's crust and the layer of rocks beneath it, the mantle(4). The waves produced in an earthquake travel faster through the rocks beneath the moho. It lies about 10-12 km (6-7 miles) beneath the oceans and 40-50 km (25-30 miles) beneath the continents.

moiety /ˈmɔɪətɪ/ *n* (usu *sing*) ~ (**of sth**) (*fml or law*) either of two parts into which sth is divided; half.

moiré /ˈmwɑːreɪ; *US* ˈmɔɪər/ *n* [U] fabric, esp silk, that has a shiny wavy look.

moist /mɔɪst/ *adj* slightly wet: *moist eyes, lips, etc* ○ *a rich moist fruit-cake* ○ *Water the plant regularly to keep the soil moist.*

▷ **moisten** /ˈmɔɪsn/ *v* [I, Tn] (cause sth to) become moist: *His eyes moistened (with tears).* ○ *She moistened her lips with her tongue.* ○ *Moisten the cloth slightly before applying the lotion.*

moisture /ˈmɔɪstʃə(r)/ *n* [U] (thin layer of) tiny drops of water on a surface, in the air, etc: *The rubber seal is designed to keep out all the moisture.* ○ *Humidity is a measure of moisture in the atmosphere.*

▷ **moisturize, -ise** /ˈmɔɪstʃəraɪz/ *v* [Tn] make (the skin) less dry by the use of certain cosmetics: *moisturizing cream for the face and hands.* **moisturizer, -iser** *n* [C, U] cream used for moisturizing the skin.

moke /məʊk/ *n* (*Brit infml esp joc*) donkey.

molar¹ /ˈməʊlə(r)/ *n* any of the teeth at the back of the jaw used for grinding and chewing food: *upper/lower/front/back molars.* ⇨ illus at TOOTH.

▷ **molar** *adj* of such teeth: *molar cavities.*

molar² /ˈməʊlə(r)/ *adj* (*chemistry*) containing a mole⁴ of a substance: *Measure the molar volume of this gas.*

molasses /məˈlæsɪz/ *n* [U] **1** thick dark syrup drained from raw sugar during the refining process. **2** (*US*) treacle.

mold (*US*) = MOULD.

molder (*US*) = MOULDER.

molding (*US*) = MOULDING.

Moldova /mɒlˈdəʊvə/ (formerly **Moldavia**) country between Ukraine and Romania; pop approx 4 361 000; official language Moldovan; capital Kishinev; unit of currency rouble. As Bessarabia it became part of the Russian empire in the 19th century, and subsequently a member of the USSR. Independence in 1991 led to tension between ethnic-majority Romanians wishing to rejoin that country, and native Ukranians and Russians who form a majority in the east of Moldova. This delayed a permanent political solution and economic reform. ⇨ map at UNION OF SOVIET SOCIALIST REPUBLICS.

moldy (*US*) = MOULDY (MOULD³).

mole¹ /məʊl/ *n* small permanent dark spot on the human skin. Cf FRECKLE.

mole² /məʊl/ *n* **1** small dark-grey fur-covered animal with tiny eyes, living in tunnels which it makes underground. ⇨ illus at ANIMAL. **2** (*infml*) person who works within an organization and secretly passes confidential information to another organization or country: *The authorities believe there is a mole at the Treasury.* Cf SPY.

□ ˈ**molehill** *n* **1** small pile of earth thrown up by a mole²(1) when it is digging underground. **2** (idm) **make a mountain out of a molehill** ⇨ MOUNTAIN.

ˈ**moleskin** *n* [U] **1** fur of a mole. **2** type of strong cotton cloth that looks like this, used for making clothes: [attrib] *moleskin trousers.*

mole³ /məʊl/ *n* stone wall built from the shore into the sea as a breakwater or causeway.

mole⁴ /məʊl/ *n* (*abbr* **mol**) unit of amount of substance, which contains the same number of atoms, molecules, ions, etc as there are atoms in 0.012 kilogram of carbon 12. Cf MOLAR⁴.

molecule /ˈmɒlɪkjuːl/ *n* smallest unit (usu consisting of a group of atoms) into which a substance can be divided without a change in its chemical nature: *A molecule of water consists of two atoms of hydrogen and one atom of oxygen.*

▷ **molecular** /məˈlekjʊlə(r)/ *adj* [attrib] of or relating to molecules: *molecular structure, mass, etc.* **molecularity** /-ˈlærətɪ/ *n* [U]. **moˌlecular biˈology** study of the structure and function of large molecules associated with living organisms. **moˌlecular ˈformula** way of representing the number and type of atoms present in a molecule of a chemical compound. Cf EMPIRICAL FORMULA (EMPIRICAL). **moˌlecular ˈweight** weight of a molecule of a substance, consisting of the total of the atomic weights of all the atoms in the molecule.

molest /məˈlest/ *v* [Tn] (**a**) trouble or annoy (sb) in a hostile way or in a way that causes injury: *an old man molested and robbed by a gang of youths.* (**b**) attack or annoy (usu a woman or child) sexually; interfere with: *He was found guilty of molesting a young girl.* ▷ **molestation** /ˌməʊleˈsteɪʃn/ *n* [U]. **molester** /məˈlestə(r)/ *n*: *a child molester.*

Molière /ˈmɒlɪeə(r); *US* məʊlˈjeər/ (real name Jean-Baptiste Poquelin, 1622-73), French comic dramatist and actor. His plays, based on characters with such classic human vices as greed, pretentiousness and hypocrisy, have always had an immediate theatrical appeal. They include *Le Bourgeois gentilhomme, Le Malade imaginaire* and *Tartuffe.*

moll /mɒl/ *n* (*sl*) woman companion of a gangster.

mollify /ˈmɒlɪfaɪ/ *v* (*pt, pp* **-fied**) [Tn] lessen the anger of (sb); make calmer; soothe: *He tried to find ways of mollifying her.* ▷ **mollification** /ˌmɒlɪfɪˈkeɪʃn/ *n* [U].

mollusc (*US* also **mollusk**) /ˈmɒləsk/ *n* any of the class of animals, including oysters, mussels, snails and slugs, that have a soft body, no backbone, and usu a hard shell.

mollycoddle /ˈmɒlɪkɒdl/ *v* [Tn] (*derog*) treat (sb) with too much kindness and protection; pamper: *He doesn't believe that children should be mollycoddled.*

Molotov cocktail /ˌmɒlətɒf ˈkɒkteɪl/ type of simple bomb that consists of a bottle filled with petrol and stuffed with a rag which is lit.

molt (*US*) = MOULT.

molten /ˈməʊltən/ *adj* [usu attrib] melted or made liquid by heating to a very high temperature: *molten rock, steel, lava.*

molto /ˈmɒltəʊ; *US* ˈməʊltəʊ/ *adv* (*music*) very: *molto adagio*, ie very slowly.

Molucca Islands /məˈlʌkə aɪləndz/ **the Molucca Islands** (also **the Moluccas**) group of Indonesian islands, south-east of the Philippines, formerly called the Spice Islands.

molybdenum /məˈlɪbdənəm/ *n* [U] (*symb* **Mo**) chemical element, a silvery-white hard metal used in alloys for making high-speed tools. ⇨ App 11.

mom /mɒm/ *n* (*US infml*) = MUM².

□ **ˌmom-and-ˈpop** *adj* [attrib] (*US infml*) (eg of a store) run by a married couple.

moment /ˈməʊmənt/ *n* **1** [C] very brief period of time: *He thought for a moment and then spoke.* ○ *It was all over in a few moments.* ○ *Can you wait a moment or two, please?* ○ *She answered without a moment's hesitation.* ○ *One moment, please*, ie Please wait a short time. ○ *I shall only be a moment.* ○ *I'll be back in a moment*, ie very soon. ○ *Extra police arrived not a moment too soon*, ie It was almost too late when they arrived. **2** [sing] exact point in time: *At that (very) moment, the phone rang.* ○ *the moment of birth* ○ *'Could you go to the post office for me, please?' 'I've only this moment come in'*, ie I came in a very short time ago. **3** [C] time for doing something; occasion: *This is a suitable moment to ask for the afternoon off.* ○ *wait for the right moment* ○ *in moments of great happiness.* **4** [C usu *sing*] (*physics*) tendency to cause movement, esp rotation about a point: *the moment of a force.* **5** (idm) **any minute/moment** ⇨ MINUTE¹. **at the ˈmoment** at the present time; now, considered as a shorter or longer period: *The number is engaged at the moment. Try again in five minutes.* ○ *He's unemployed at the moment and has been for over six months.* **for the ˈmoment/ ˈpresent** temporarily; for now: *We're happy living in a flat for the moment but we may want to move to a house soon.* **have one's/its ˈmoments** (*infml*) have short times that are more interesting than the ordinary usual times: *My job is not a very glamorous one but it does have its moments.* **in the heat of the moment** ⇨ HEAT¹. **in a ˈmoment** very soon: *I'll come in a moment.* **the last minute/ moment** ⇨ LAST¹. **the man, woman, boy, girl, etc of the ˈmoment** person who is highly praised, most popular or most important at present. **the minute/moment (that...)** ⇨ MINUTE¹. **the ˌmoment of ˈtruth** point at which the reality of the condition of sb/sth has to be faced and an important decision has to be made. **not for a/one minute/moment** ⇨ MINUTE¹. **of ˈmoment** (*fml*) of importance: *This is a matter of great/some/little/no small moment.* **on the spur of the moment** ⇨ SPUR. **the psychological moment** ⇨ PSYCHOLOGICAL (PSYCHOLOGY). **a weak moment** ⇨ WEAK.

□ **ˌmoment of iˈnertia** measure of the tendency of a spinning body to resist any change in its rotational speed.

momentary /ˈməʊməntrɪ; *US* -terɪ/ *adj* lasting for a very short time: *a momentary pause, interruption, success.*

▷ **momentarily** /ˈməʊməntrəlɪ; *US* ˌməʊmənˈterəlɪ/ *adv* **1** for a very short time: *He shuddered momentarily.* **2** (*esp US*) very soon; immediately: *The doctor will see you momentarily.*

momentous /məˈmentəs, məʊˈm-/ *adj* very important; serious: *a momentous decision, occasion, event* ○ *momentous changes.*

momentum /məˈmentəm, məʊˈm-/ *n* [U] **1** force that increases the rate of development of a process; impetus: *The movement to change the union's constitution is slowly gathering momentum.* **2** (*physics*) quantity of motion of a moving object, measured as its mass multiplied by its velocity: *The sledge gained momentum as it ran down the hill.*

momma /ˈmɒmə/ (also **mommy** /ˈmɒmɪ/) *n* (*US infml*) = MUMMY².

Mon *abbr* Monday: *Mon 21 June.*

Monaco /ˈmɒnəkeʊ/ small independent state on the northern Mediterranean coast, near the French-Italian border; pop approx 28 000 (of whom only about 5 000 are actual citizens); official language French; capital Monaco; unit of currency franc (= 100 centimes). It has been ruled by the Grimaldi family since 1297, and is surrounded by French territory. France is responsible for its foreign affairs and defence. Its small size prevents any agricultural activity and the economy is based on tourism and small-scale industry. ⇨ map at FRANCE.

▷ **Monacan** /mɒˈnɑːkən/, (also **Monégasque** /ˌmɒneˈgæsk/) *adj, n* (native or inhabitant) of Monaco.

Mona Lisa /ˌməʊnə ˈliːzə/ (also **La Gioconda**) painting by Leonardo da *Vinci, now in the Louvre in Paris, of a woman with a mysterious smiling expression.

monarch /ˈmɒnək/ *n* **1** supreme ruler; king, queen, emperor or empress: *the reigning monarch.* **2** (also **monarch butterfly**) large N American butterfly with a black pattern on its orange wings.

▷ **monarchic** /məˈnɑːkɪk/, **monarchical** /məˈnɑːkɪkl/ *adjs* [attrib] of a monarch or monarchy: *the system of monarchical government.*

monarchist /ˈmɒnəkɪst/ *n* person who believes that a country should be ruled by a monarch. **monarchism** /-kɪzəm/ *n* [U].

monarchy /ˈmɒnəkɪ/ *n* **1** (usu **the monarchy**) [sing] system of government by a monarch: *plans to abolish the monarchy.* **2** [C] state governed by such a system: *The United Kingdom is a constitutional monarchy.* Cf REPUBLIC.

monastery /ˈmɒnəstrɪ; *US* -terɪ/ *n* building in which monks live as a community. Cf CONVENT, NUNNERY (NUN).

monastic /məˈnæstɪk/ *adj* **1** of or relating to monks, nuns, or the monasteries or convents where they live. **2** like life in a monastery; simple and quiet: *lead a monastic life.*

▷ **monasticism** /məˈnæstɪsɪzəm/ *n* [U] way of life of monks in monasteries.

monaural /ˌmɒnˈɔːrəl/ *adj* ⇨ MONOPHONIC.

Monday /ˈmʌndɪ/ *n* [C, U] (*abbr* **Mon**) the second day of the week, next after Sunday: *He was born on a Monday.* ○ *They met on the Monday and were married on the Friday*, ie on those days in a particular week. ○ *last/next Monday* ○ *the Monday before last* ○ *'What's today?' 'It's Monday.'* ○ *We'll meet on Monday.* ○ (*Brit infml or US*) *We'll meet Monday*, ie on the day before next Tuesday. ○ *'When did they meet?' '(On) Monday* (ie On the day before last Tuesday).*'* ○ *I work Monday(s) to Friday(s).* ○ *(On) Monday(s)* (ie Every Monday) *I do the shopping.* ○ *I always do the shopping on a Monday.* ○ [attrib] *Monday morning/afternoon/ evening* ○ *Monday week*, ie a week after next Monday.

□ **ˌMonday-morning ˈquarterback** (*US infml derog*) person who criticizes the actions of others after it becomes clear what they should have done.

Mondrian /ˈmɒndrɪɑːn/ Piet (1872-1944), Dutch abstract painter whose works are characterized by geometric patterns of intersecting straight lines and blocks of simple primary colours.

Monégasque /ˌmɒneˈgæsk/ *adj, n* = MONACAN (MONACO).

Monet /ˈmɒneɪ; *US* məʊˈneɪ/ Claude (1840-1926), French painter. His *Impression: Sunrise* gave *Impressionism its name. He is famous for series of paintings showing the different effects of light on the subjects painted, eg the water-lilies of his garden and Rouen cathedral.

monetary /ˈmʌnɪtrɪ; *US* -terɪ/ *adj* [attrib] of money or currency: *the government's monetary policy* ○ *the international monetary system* ○ *The monetary unit of Japan is the yen.*

▷ **monetarism** /-tərɪzəm/ *n* [U] policy of controlling the amount of money available as the chief method of stabilizing a country's economy. Economists who believe in monetarism claim that stable monetary growth prevents high inflation. Cf KEYNES. **monetarist** /-tərɪst/ *n* person favouring monetarism. — *adj* of or relating to monetarism: *monetarist policies.*

money /ˈmʌnɪ/ *n* (*pl* in sense 3 **moneys** or **monies**) **1** [U] means of payment, esp coins and banknotes, given and accepted in buying and selling: *have money in one's pocket* ○ *earn, borrow, save, etc a lot of money* ○ *How much money is there in my (bank) account?* ○ *change English money into French money/francs.* ⇨ App 9. **2** [U] wealth; (total value of) sb's property: *inherit money from sb* ○ *lose all one's money* ○ *marry sb for his money*, ie for the sake of wealth and possessions that he has or will inherit later. **3 moneys** or **monies** [pl] (*arch or law*) sum of money: *to collect all monies due.* **4** (idm) **be in the ˈmoney** (*infml*) have a lot of money to spend; be rich. **coin it/money** ⇨ COIN. **easy money** ⇨ EASY¹. **even chances/odds/money** ⇨ EVEN¹. **a fool and his money are soon parted** ⇨ FOOL¹. **for ˈmy money** (*infml*) in my opinion: *For my money, Ann's idea is better than Mary's.* **get one's ˈmoney's-worth** get the full value in goods or services for the money one has spent. **good ˈmoney** a lot of money; money that is hard-earned and not to be wasted: *earn, pay, cost good money.* **have ˈmoney to burn** have so much money that one can spend it freely. **a licence to print money** ⇨ LICENCE. **ˈmade of money** (*infml*) very wealthy: *I'm not made of money, you know!* **make ˈmoney** make a profit; earn a lot of money. **make money ˌhand over ˈfist** make big profits from business, etc. **marry money** ⇨ MARRY. **money burns a hole in sb's pocket** sb is eager to spend money or spends it quickly or extravagantly. **money for ˈjam/old ˈrope** (*infml*) money or profit earned from a task that requires very little effort. **money talks** (*saying*) if one is wealthy it enables one to get special treatment, influence people, promote one's own interests, etc. **not for love or money** ⇨ LOVE¹. **put money into sth** invest money in (an enterprise, etc): *put money into stocks and shares, the Channel tunnel project, property.* **put one's money on sb/sth** (a) place a bet that (a horse, dog, etc) will win a race. (b) confidently expect sb/sth to succeed: *I'll put my money on him.* **put one's money where one's ˈmouth is** (*infml*) show one's support in a practical way, not just by one's words. **a run for one's money** ⇨ RUN¹. **see the colour of sb's money** ⇨ COLOUR¹. **the smart money** ⇨ SMART¹. **there's money in sth** profit can be obtained from sth. **throw one's money about** (*infml*) spend one's money recklessly and ostentatiously. **time is money** ⇨ TIME. **you pays your money and you takes your choice** ⇨ PAY².

▷ **moneyed** /ˈmʌnɪd/ *adj* (*dated*) having a lot of money; wealthy: *the moneyed classes.*

moneyless *adj* having no money.

□ **ˈmoney-back guarantee** guarantee to return the money paid if the buyer is not satisfied.

ˈmoney-bags *n* (*pl* unchanged) (*infml esp derog*) rich person.

ˈmoney-box *n* small closed box with a slot in the top, into which coins are put as a method of saving money.

ˈmoney-changer *n* person whose business is to change money of one country for that of another, usu at the official rate.

ˈmoney-grubber *n* person who greedily wants to gain money, usu by dishonest methods. **ˈmoney-grubbing** *adj.*

ˈmoney-lender *n* person whose business is to lend money, usu at a high rate of interest.

ˈmoney-maker *n* **1** person who works to gain a lot of money. **2** (*infml usu approv*) product or business investment that produces a large profit. **ˈmoney-making** *adj*: *a money-making plan.*

ˈmoney-market *n* place of operation of dealers in short-term loans.

ˈmoney order official document for payment of a specified sum of money, issued by a bank or Post Office.

ˈ**money spider** type of small garden spider. There is an old superstition that if such a spider crawls on to sb, he or she will become rich.

ˈ**money-spinner** *n* (*infml esp Brit*) thing that earns a lot of money: *Her new book is a real money-spinner.*

the ˈmoney supply total amount of money that exists in the economy of a country at a particular time: *control, reduce, increase, etc the money supply.*

monger /ˈmʌŋgə(r)/ *n* (only in compounds) **1** trader or dealer: *fishmonger* ○ *ironmonger*, ie sb who sells hardware. **2** (*derog*) person who makes something unpleasant widely known: *a gossip monger* ○ *a scandalmonger* ○ *a warmonger.*

mongol /ˈmɒŋgəl/ *n* (*usu offensive*) person suffering from Down's syndrome. ▷ **mongolism** /-ɪzəm/ *n* [U] (*usu offensive*) = DOWN'S SYNDROME.

Mongolia /mɒŋˈgəʊlɪə/ formerly ˌ**Outer Monˈgolia**) large Central Asian country; pop approx 2 156 000; official language Mongolian; capital Ulan Bator; unit of currency tugrik (= 100 mongo). It is part of a larger region also called Mongolia which includes part of China. The country is a large plateau with mountains in the north and west, and the Gobi desert covers a large area. The economy is based on livestock farming and on mining. Since the break-up of the USSR (to which it was very close politically and economically) Mongolia has had a democratic constitution; trade now focuses on Western countries, Japan and South Korea. ➪ map at CHINA.

▷ **Mongolian** /mɒŋˈgəʊlɪən/, **Mongol** /ˈmɒŋgl/ *adj* of Mongolia. — *n* **1** [C] native or inhabitant of Mongolia. **2** [U] Mongolian language, which is distantly related to Turkish.

Mongoloid /ˈmɒŋgəlɔɪd/ *adj* having facial characteristics like those of the Mongolians, esp a broad flat face with slightly yellow skin.

mongoose

mongoose /ˈmɒŋgu:s/ *n* (*pl* ~**s** /-sɪz/) small furry tropical mammal that kills snakes, birds, rats, etc.

mongrel /ˈmʌŋgrəl/ *n* **1** dog of mixed breed. **2** any plant or animal of mixed origin: [attrib] *a mongrel breed* ○ *of mongrel stock.*

monism /ˈmɒnɪzəm; *US* ˈməʊ-/ *n* [U] belief that reality is ultimately based on a single principle, rather than separated into eg spirit and matter. Cf DUALISM. ▷ **monist** /ˈmɒnɪst; *US* ˈməʊ-/ *n*. **monistic** /mɒˈnɪstɪk; *US* məʊ-/ *adj.*

monitor /ˈmɒnɪtə(r)/ *n* **1** device used to observe, record or test sth: *a heart monitor* ○ *a monitor for radioactivity.* **2** person who listens to and reports on foreign radio broadcasts and signals. **3** (**a**) TV screen used in a studio to check or choose the broadcast picture. (**b**) (*computing*) screen or other device used for checking the progress and operation of a computer system. ➪ illus at COMPUTER. **4** (*fem* **monitress** /ˈmɒnɪtrɪs/) pupil with special duties in a school: *the homework monitor.* **5** any of various large lizards of Africa, Asia or Australia.

▷ **monitor** *v* [Tn] **1** make continuous observation of (sth); record or test the operation of (sth): *monitor sb's performance/progress* ○ *monitor a patient's pulse.* **2** listen to and report on (foreign radio broadcasts and signals).

Monk /mʌŋk/ Thelonius (1920-82), American jazz pianist. With Gillespie and *Parker he was one of the originators of the be-bop style and had a great influence on modern jazz.

monk /mʌŋk/ *n* member of a religious community of men who live apart from the rest of society and who have made solemn promises, esp not to marry and not to have any possessions. Cf FRIAR, NUN.
The popular image of a monk is often of a fat and jolly person who likes good food. A typical example is Friar Tuck, the jovial, plump chaplain in the legends about *Robin Hood.

▷ **monkish** *adj* of or like monks.

□ ˈ**monkfish** *n* (**a**) (also **angler fish**) [C] deep-sea fish with a large flat head and wide mouth. (**b**) [U] its flesh used as food.

ˈ**monkshood** *n* [U, C] poisonous plant with hood-shaped flowers.

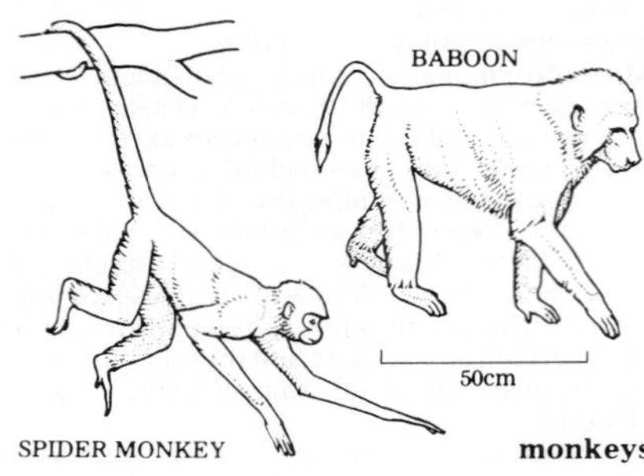

monkeys

monkey /ˈmʌŋkɪ/ *n* **1** member of the group of animals most similar to humans in appearance, esp a type of small long-tailed tree-climbing animal. ➪ illus. **2** (*infml*) lively mischievous child: *Come here at once, you little monkey!* **3** (*sl*) £500 or $500. **4** (idm) **have a ˈmonkey on one's back** (*sl*) be a drug addict. **make a monkey out of sb** (*infml*) make sb look or feel foolish.

▷ **monkey** *v* (phr v) **monkey about/around** (*infml*) behave in a foolish mischievous way: *Stop monkeying about!* **monkey about/around with sth** (*infml*) play or interfere with sth in a careless way: *monkeying about with a fire extinguisher.*

□ ˈ**monkey business** mischievous or dishonest activity or behaviour: *There's been some monkey business going on here!*

ˈ**monkey-nut** *n* peanut.

ˈ**monkey-puzzle** *n* (also ˈ**monkey-puzzle tree**) evergreen tree with narrow stiff sharp leaves and interlaced branches.

ˈ**monkey-wrench** *n* spanner with a jaw that can be adjusted to hold things of different widths.

Monmouth /ˈmɒnməθ, ˈmʌn-/ James Scott, 1st Duke of (1649-85), illegitimate son of *Charles II, who claimed the English throne. He led a rebellion in 1685, but was defeated at the battle of Sedgemoor and executed.

mono /ˈmɒnəʊ/ *adj* (*infml*) = MONOPHONIC.

▷ **mono** *n* [U] (*infml*) monophonic sound or reproduction: *a recording in mono.* Cf STEREO.

mon(o)- *comb form* one; single: *monogamy* ○ *monomania* ○ *monorail.*

monochrome /ˈmɒnəkrəʊm/ *adj* **1** having or using images in black, white and shades of grey; black and white: *a monochrome photograph, print, drawing, etc* ○ *monochrome television.* **2** having or using varying shades of one colour.

▷ **monochromatic** /ˌmɒnəkrəʊˈmætɪk/ *adj* (of light or other radiation) containing only one colour or wavelength.

monochrome *n* (**a**) [U] monochrome reproduction: *painting in monochrome.* (**b**) [C] monochrome painting, photograph, etc.

monocle /ˈmɒnəkl/ *n* single glass lens for one eye, kept in position by the muscles round the eye.

monocotyledon /ˌmɒnəˌkɒtɪˈli:dən/ *n* (*botany*) flowering plant that has one leaf at the embryonic stage.

monocular /mɒˈnɒkjʊlə(r)/ *adj* with or of one eye: *monocular vision.*

monoculture /ˈmɒnəkʌltʃə(r)/ *n* [U] system of growing a single agricultural crop.

monody /ˈmɒnədɪ/ *n* **1** poem in which the writer mourns sb who has died. **2** composition, esp a type of 16th-century song, written for a single voice part.

monogamy /məˈnɒgəmɪ/ *n* [U] practice or custom of being married to only one person at a time. Cf POLYGAMY. ▷ **monogamous** /məˈnɒgəməs/ *adj*

monogram /ˈmɒnəgræm/ *n* two or more letters (esp a person's initials) combined in one design and marked on handkerchiefs, notepaper, etc. ▷ **monogrammed** *adj*: *a monogrammed shirt* ➪ illus.

monogram

monograph /ˈmɒnəgrɑ:f; *US* -græf/ *n* detailed scholarly study of one subject.

monolingual /ˌmɒnəˈlɪŋgwəl/ *adj* using only one language: *a monolingual dictionary.* Cf BILINGUAL, MULTILINGUAL.

monolith /ˈmɒnəlɪθ/ *n* large single upright block of stone, usu shaped into a pillar or monument.

▷ **monolithic** /ˌmɒnəˈlɪθɪk/ *adj* **1** consisting of one or more monoliths: *a monolithic monument.* **2** single, massive and unchangeable: *the monolithic structure of the state.*

monologue (*US* also **monolog**) /ˈmɒnəlɒg; *US* -lɔ:g/ *n* **1** [C] long speech by one person in a conversation, which prevents other people from talking; soliloquy. **2** [C, U] (**a**) long speech in a play, film, etc spoken by one actor, esp when alone; soliloquy. (**b**) dramatic story, esp in verse, recited or performed by one person.

monomania /ˌmɒnəʊˈmeɪnɪə/ *n* [U] state of mind in which a person is obsessed with one idea or subject.

▷ **monomaniac** /ˌmɒnəʊˈmeɪnɪæk/ *n* sufferer from monomania.

monophonic /ˌmɒnəˈfɒnɪk/ *adj* (also *infml* **mono**) (of sound reproduction) using only one channel of transmission: *a monophonic recording.* Cf STEREOPHONIC.

monophthong /ˈmɒnəfθɒŋ/ *n* simple or pure vowel sound, in which the speech organs remain in the same position as the sound is pronounced. Cf DIPHTHONG.

monoplane /ˈmɒnəpleɪn/ *n* aeroplane with only one set of wings. Cf BIPLANE.

monopolize, -ise /məˈnɒpəlaɪz/ *v* [Tn] have a very large share of (sth), so preventing others from sharing it; dominate: *monopolize a conversation* ○ *trying to monopolize the supply of oil* ○ (*fig*) *Don't monopolize our special guest — there are others who would like to talk to her.* ▷ **monopolization, -isation** /məˌnɒpəlaɪˈzeɪʃn; *US* -lɪˈz-/ *n* [U].

monopoly /məˈnɒpəlɪ/ *n* **1** (**a**) ~ (**of/on sth**) sole right to supply or trade in some commodity or service: *gain/hold/secure a monopoly* ○ *They could lose their monopoly on the supply of coal.* (**b**) commodity or service controlled in this way: *In some countries tobacco is a government monopoly.* **2** ~ (**of/on sth**) sole possession or control of sth: *A good education should not be the monopoly of the rich.* ○ *You can't have a complete monopoly of the car — I need to use it occasionally.* **3 Monopoly** (*propr*) board game in which players use imitation money to try to buy property marked on the board and obtain rent from other players. The winning player succeeds in leaving the others with no money: [attrib] (*joc*) *Monopoly money*, ie money treated as if it had no real value.

▷ **monopolist** /-lɪst/ *n* person who has a monopoly. **monopolistic** /məˌnɒpəˈlɪstɪk/ *adj.*

□ **the Moˌnopolies and ˈMergers Commission** British government body which investigates proposed mergers and takeovers of companies, so as to prevent situations where a single person or company gains control of too large a proportion of the supply of particular goods or services.

monorail /ˈmɒnəʊreɪl/ *n* [U, C] railway system in which trains travel along a track consisting of a single rail usu placed high above the ground.

monosodium glutamate /ˌmɒnəʊˌsəʊdɪəm ˈglu:təmeɪt/ (*abbr* **MSG**) white chemical compound that is added to foods, esp meat, to make their flavour stronger.

monosyllable /ˈmɒnəsɪləbl/ *n* word with only one syllable, eg *it, and, no*: *speak in monosyllables*, eg when not wanting to talk to sb. Cf DISYLLABLE.

▷ **monosyllabic** /ˌmɒnəsɪˈlæbɪk/ *adj* **1** having only one syllable: *a monosyllabic word.* **2** made up of words of only one syllable: *monosyllabic* *answers*, eg saying only 'Yes' or 'No' when not wanting to give sb any information. **monosyllabically** /-klɪ/ *adv.*

monotheism /ˈmɒnəʊθiːɪzəm/ *n* [U] belief that there is only one God. Cf POLYTHEISM.
▷ **monotheist** /ˈmɒnəʊθiːɪst/ *n* believer in monotheism.
monotheistic /ˌmɒnəʊθiːˈɪstɪk/ *adj.*

monotone /ˈmɒnətəʊn/ *n* [sing] **1** (sound in a) way of speaking in which the pitch of the voice remains level and unchanging: *to speak in a monotone.* **2** lack of variety, as in a style of writing.
▷ **monotone** *adj* [attrib] without changing the pitch of the voice or the shade of colour: *monotone concrete buildings.*

monotonous /məˈnɒtənəs/ *adj* not changing and therefore uninteresting; boring or tedious: *a monotonous voice*, ie one with little change of pitch ○ *monotonous work.* ▷ **monotonously** *adv.*

monotony /məˈnɒtənɪ/ *n* [U] state of being monotonous; lack of variety that causes weariness and boredom: *relieve the monotony of everyday life.*

monoxide /mɒˈnɒksaɪd/ *n* [U, C] chemical compound whose molecules contain one atom of oxygen combined with one or more other atoms: *carbon monoxide.*

Monroe /mʌnˈrəʊ/ Marilyn (1926-62), American actress. Her blonde hair and glamorous charm brought her roles as a naive object of male desire in film comedies (eg *Some Like It Hot* and *The Seven Year Itch*). Her troubled private life ended in early death, which established her as a Hollywood legend.

Monroe doctrine /mʌnˈrəʊ dɒktrɪn/ **the Monroe doctrine** policy adopted by James Monroe (1758-1831) as US president in 1823, which stated that European nations could establish no further colonies in N or S America, and that they must recognize the new republics in S America. In return, the USA could not interfere in Europe.

Monseigneur /ˌmɒnseɪˈnjɜː(r)/ *n* (*abbr* **Mgr**) (*French*) (used as a title or form of address for a French cardinal or bishop, or formerly as a form of address to an important French nobleman).

Monsieur /məˈsjɜː(r)/ *n* (*abbr* **M**) (*pl* **Messieurs** /meɪˈsjɜː(r)/) (*French*) (title used before the name of a man to refer to him, or used alone as a formal and polite term of address) Mr; sir: *M Hercule Poirot* ○ *Yes, monsieur.*

Monsignor /mɒnˈsiːnjə(r)/ *n* (*abbr* **Mgr**) (used as a title or form of address for certain Catholic priests and bishops).

monsoon /ˌmɒnˈsuːn/ *n* **1** seasonal wind in S Asia, esp in the Indian Ocean, blowing from the south-west from April to October and from the north-east from October to April. During summer the inland parts of the continent heat the air and create an area of low pressure which brings in sea air and heavy rainfall. The combination of this rain with cyclones can cause great destruction. During the winter, cool air moves out from inland areas and a dry wind blows towards the coast. **2** very rainy season that comes with the SW monsoon: [attrib] *monsoon forests*, ie with trees that grow during this season and lose their leaves after it.

monster /ˈmɒnstə(r)/ *n* **1** (**a**) large, ugly and frightening creature, esp an imaginary one: *A hideous monster attacked the helpless villagers.* ○ *prehistoric monsters* ○ *Do you believe in the Loch Ness monster?* (**b**) (usu ugly) animal or plant that is abnormal in form.
People are often fascinated by the idea of monsters and this is reflected in the enormous popularity of comics, books and films which feature them. Famous monsters in English literature include Mary *Shelley's Frankenstein and Lewis *Carroll's Jabberwock from *Through the Looking Glass*. Famous American monsters include **King Kong*, a gigantic ape in a film of this name, and 'the Incredible Hulk', a comic-book character which first appeared in the 1960s. Monsters also exist in popular legend, such as the *Loch Ness monster. **2** cruel or evil person: *Let go of me, you vicious monster!* **3** thing that is extremely large: [attrib] *monster high-rise blocks of flats.*

monstrous /ˈmɒnstrəs/ *adj* **1** shocking, unjust or absurd; outrageous: *a monstrous lie* ○ *monstrous crimes* ○ *It's absolutely monstrous to pay men more than women for the same job.* **2** like a monster in appearance; ugly and frightening: *the monstrous form of a fire-breathing dragon.* **3** extremely large; gigantic.
▷ **monstrosity** /mɒnˈstrɒsətɪ/ *n* thing that is large and very ugly: *That new multi-storey car-park is an utter monstrosity!*
monstrously *adv.*

montage /ˈmɒntɑːʒ; *US* mɒnˈtɑːʒ/ *n* **1** (**a**) [C] picture, film or piece of music or writing made up of many separate items put together, esp in an interesting combination. (**b**) [U] process of making such a picture, film, etc. **2** [U] choosing, cutting and joining of different pieces of film to indicate a passage of time, change of place, etc: [attrib] *a montage sequence*, ie series of very short shots.

Montaigne /mɒnˈteɪn/ Michel Eyquem de (1533-92), French writer. His *Essays*, the first of their kind, use a personal style of self-examination to explore matters of morality and human experience.

Montana /mɒnˈtænə/ state in the north-western USA. Much of it lies in the *Great Plains with the *Rocky Mountains in the west. The economy is based on agriculture and important mineral resources including coal and copper. ⇨ map at App 1.

Mont Blanc /mɒn ˈblɒŋ/ highest mountain in Europe (4 180 m, 15 781 ft), in the Alps on the border between France and Italy.

monte /ˈmɒntɪ/ *n* [U] card-game in which players bet on the cards that are to be dealt.

Monte Carlo /ˌmɒntɪ ˈkɑːləʊ/ town in *Monaco famous for its casino and as the finishing-point of an international car rally.

Montenegro /ˌmɒntəˈniːgrəʊ/ one of the federal republics of the former Yugoslavia.

Montessori /ˌmɒntɪˈsɔːrɪ/ Maria (1870-1952), Italian educationist. She developed the **Montessori method** which aims to stimulate young children's minds and senses through play.
□ **ˌMontesˈsori school** school using the Montessori method.

Monteverdi /ˌmɒntɪˈveədɪ/ Claudio (1567-1643), Italian composer. He was one of the most remarkable figures of Renaissance music, transforming existing musical styles. His *Orfeo* is regarded as the first great modern opera.

Montezuma's revenge /ˌmɒntɪˌzuːməz rɪˈvendʒ/ (*infml joc*) diarrhoea suffered by travellers in hot countries, esp Mexico.

Montgolfier /mɒntˈgɒlfɪeɪ/ Joseph Michel (1740-1810) and his brother Jacques *Étienne (1745-99), French pioneers of the hot-air balloon. After experiments with animals they organized the first manned balloon flight in 1783.

Montgomery /mɒntˈgʌmərɪ/ Bernard Law, 1st Viscount Montgomery of Alamein (1887-1976), British soldier. Known as 'Monty' to the public and his troops, his strong personality and superior forces were as important as his tactical skill in defeating the German army in N Africa during the Second World War. He received the official German surrender in 1945.

month /mʌnθ/ *n* **1** (also ˌ**calendar ˈmonth**) any of the twelve periods of time into which the year is divided, eg May and June: *We're going on holiday next month.* ○ *She earns £1000 a month.* ○ *The rent is £300 per calendar month.* **2** period of time between a day in one month and the corresponding day in the next month, eg 3 June to 3 July: *The baby is three months old.* ○ *several months later* ○ *the first few months of marriage* ○ [attrib] *a six-month contract* ○ *a seven-month-old baby.* **3** (idm) **for/in a ˌmonth of ˈSundays** (esp in negative sentences) for a very long time: *I've not seen her for/in a month of Sundays.*
▷ **monthly** *adj* **1** done, happening, published, etc once a month or every month: *a monthly meeting, visit, magazine.* **2** payable, valid or calculated for one month: *a monthly season ticket* ○ *a monthly income of £800.* — *adv* every month; once a month: *to be paid monthly.* — *n* **1** magazine published once a month: *a literary monthly.* **2** season-ticket valid for a month: *A monthly is more economical than 4 weeklies.*

Montserrat /ˌmɒntsəˈræt/ small island in the *Leeward Islands, a British dependency; pop approx 12 000; official language English; capital Plymouth. The economy is based on tourism.

monument /ˈmɒnjʊmənt/ *n* **1** building, column, statue, etc built to remind people of a famous person or event: *a monument erected to soldiers killed in the war.* **2** building, etc that is preserved because of its historical importance to a country: *an ancient monument.* **3** ~ **to sth** notable thing that stands as a lasting reminder of sb's deeds, achievements, etc: *This whole city is a monument to his skill as a planner and administrator.*

monumental /ˌmɒnjʊˈmentl/ *adj* **1** [attrib] of, related to or serving as a monument: *a monumental inscription*, ie inscribed on a monument ○ *monumental brasses, sculptures, figures, etc.* **2** [attrib] (of buildings, sculptures, etc) very large and impressive: *a monumental arch, column, façade, etc.* **3** [usu attrib] (of a literary or musical work) large and of lasting value: *a monumental production.* **4** [usu attrib] exceptionally great: *a monumental achievement, success, blunder, failure, etc* ○ *What monumental ignorance!*
▷ **monumentally** /-təlɪ/ *adv* extremely: *monumentally boring, stupid, successful.*
□ **ˌmonumental ˈmason** maker of tombstones, etc.

moo /muː/ *n* long deep sound made by a cow.
▷ **moo** *v* [I] make this sound.
□ **ˈmoo-cow** *n* (used by or to young children) cow.

mooch /muːtʃ/ *v* **1** [Tn, Tn·pr] ~ **sth (off/from sb)** (*US infml*) get sth by asking; cadge sth: *mooch money off sb.* **2** (phr v) **mooch about/around (...)** (*infml*) wander aimlessly around (a place): *mooching around the house with nothing to do.*

mood[1] /muːd/ *n* **1** state of one's feelings or mind at a particular time: *She's in a good mood* (ie happy) *today.* ○ *He's always in a bad mood* (ie irritable and angry) *on Mondays.* ○ *His mood suddenly changed and he became calm.* **2** fit of bad temper; depression: *He's in a mood/in one of his moods today.* **3** (usu *sing*) way a group or community feels about sth; atmosphere: *The film captured* (ie described very well) *the mood of quiet confidence at the hospital.* **4** (idm) **(be) in the mood for (doing) sth/to do sth** feeling like doing sth; inclined to do sth: *I'm not in the mood to disagree with you.* **(be) in no mood for (doing) sth/to do sth** not feeling like doing sth; not inclined to sth: *He's in no mood for (telling) jokes/to tell jokes.*
▷ **moody** *adj* (**-ier, -iest**) **1** having moods that change quickly: *moody and unpredictable.* **2** bad-tempered; gloomy or sullen. **moodily** /-ɪlɪ/ *adv.* **moodiness** *n* [U].

mood[2] /muːd/ *n* (*grammar*) any of the three sets of verb forms that show whether what is said or written is considered certain, possible, doubtful, necessary, desirable, etc: *the indicative/imperative/subjunctive mood.*

Moog /muːg, məʊg/ *n* (also **ˈMoog synthesizer**) (*propr*) synthesizer that can imitate the sound of various musical instruments electronically.

moon[1] /muːn/ *n* **1** [sing] (**a**) (usu **the moon**) the natural body that moves round the earth once every 28 days and shines at night by light reflected from the sun: *explore the surface of the moon* ○ [attrib] *a moon landing.* (**b**) this body as it appears in the sky at a particular time: *There's no moon tonight*, ie No moon can be seen. ○ *a crescent moon* ○ *a new moon* ○ *a full moon.* **2** [C] body that moves round a planet other than the earth: *How many moons does Jupiter have?* **3** (idm) **many ˈmoons ago** a long time ago: *All that happened many moons ago.* **once in a blue moon** ⇨ ONCE. **over the ˈmoon** (*infml*) absolutely delighted; ecstatic: *The whole team were over the moon at winning the competition.* **promise the earth/moon** ⇨ PROMISE[2]. **shoot the moon** ⇨ SHOOT[1].
▷ **moonless** *adj* without a visible moon: *a dark, moonless sky/night.*
□ **ˈmoonbeam** *n* ray of moonlight.
ˈmoon-face *n* round face like a moon when seen as a complete circle.
ˈmoonlight *n* [U] light of the moon: *a walk by*

moonlight/in the moonlight. — *v* (*pt, pp* **-lighted**) [I] (*infml*) have a second job, esp at night, in addition to one's regular one during the day. **ˈmoonlighting** *n* [U]. — *adj* [attrib] **1** lit by the moon; moonlit: *a moonlight night.* **2** (idm) **do a moonlight ˈflit** (*Brit infml*) leave a place quickly, secretly and at night to avoid paying one's debts, rent, etc.
ˈmoonlit *adj* lit by the moon: *a moonlit night.*
ˈmoonshine *n* [U] **1** foolish talk, ideas, etc; nonsense. **2** (*US*) whisky or other spirits illegally distilled.
ˈmoon-shot *n* launch of a spacecraft to the moon.
ˈmoonstone *n* semi-precious stone with a pearly appearance used in making jewellery.
ˈmoonstruck *adj* slightly mad; wild and wandering in the mind (supposedly as a result of the moon's influence).

moon[2] /mu:n/ *v* **1** [I, Ip] ~ (**about/around**) (*infml*) wander about aimlessly or listlessly: *Stop mooning and get on with some work!* ○ *She spent the whole summer mooning about at home.* **2** (phr v) **moon over sb** (*infml*) spend one's time dreamily thinking about sb one loves.
▷ **moony** *adj* foolishly dreamy: *a moony person, look.*

Moonie /ˈmu:nɪ/ *n* (*often derog*) member of the Unification Church, a religious organization founded in 1954 by the Korean industrialist Sun Myung Moon (1920-), which has been accused of using unscrupulous methods to recruit and keep members.

moor[1] /mɔ:(r); *US* mʊər/ *n* (often *pl*) open uncultivated high area of land, esp one covered with heather: *go for a walk on the moor/the moors* ○ *the Yorkshire moors* ○ *a grouse moor*, ie where grouse are reared for shooting in sport.
□ **ˈmoorhen** *n* small water-hen.
ˈmoorland /-lənd/ *n* [U, C usu *pl*] land that consists of moor: [attrib] *moorland regions.*

moor[2] /mɔ:(r); *US* mʊər/ *v* [I, Tn, Tn·pr] ~ **sth** (**to sth**) attach (a boat, ship, etc) to a fixed object or the land with a rope or an anchor, etc: *We moored alongside the quay.* ○ *The boat was moored to (a post on) the river bank.*
▷ **mooring** /ˈmɔ:rɪŋ; *US* ˈmʊərɪŋ/ *n* **1 moorings** [pl] ropes, anchors, chains, etc by which a ship, boat, etc is moored: *Let go your moorings!* **2** [C usu *pl*] place where a ship, boat, etc is moored: *private moorings* ○ [attrib] *mooring ropes.*

Moor /mʊə(r)/ *n* (**a**) member of a Muslim people living in NW Africa. (**b**) one of the Muslim Arabs who invaded Spain in the 8th century.
▷ **Moorish** /ˈmʊərɪʃ/ *adj* of the Moors and their culture.

Henry Moore: King and Queen

Moore /mɔ:(r); *US* mʊər/ Henry (1898-1986), English sculptor. He is famous for his large sculptures, usu in stone or wood, with smooth curves and hollows. They are his interpretation of the human figure, often designed to be seen as part of a landscape. ⇨ illus.

moose /mu:s/ *n* (*pl* unchanged) (*US*) = ELK.

moot /mu:t/ *adj* (idm) **a moot ˈpoint/ˈquestion** (**a**) matter about which there is uncertainty: *It's a moot point whether men or women are better drivers.* (**b**) (*US law*) purely hypothetical point or question.
▷ **moot** *v* [Tn usu passive] (*fml*) raise (a matter) for discussion; propose: *The question was first mooted many years ago.*
moot *n* (*law*) formal discussion in the form of a mock trial as an academic exercise.

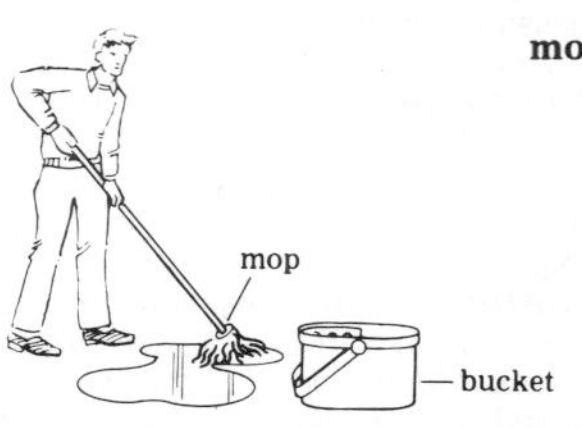

mop /mɒp/ *n* **1** (**a**) tool consisting of a bundle of thick strings or a piece of sponge fastened to a long handle, used for cleaning floors. (**b**) similar tool with a short handle, used for various purposes, eg cleaning dishes: *a dish mop.* **2** mass of thick (usu untidy) hair: *a mop of curly red hair.*
▷ **mop** *v* (**-pp-**) **1** [Tn] clean (sth) with a mop: *mop the floor.* **2** (**a**) [Tn] wipe (the face), esp with a handkerchief, to remove sweat, tears, etc: *mop one's brow (with a handkerchief).* (**b**) [I, Ipr, Tn, Tn·pr] ~ (**sth**) **with sth**; ~ **sth** (**from sth**) wipe (a liquid) from a surface using an absorbent cloth: *keep mopping (with a towel)* ○ *mop tears (from one's face) (with a handkerchief).* **3** (phr v) **mop sth/sb up** (**a**) remove (spilt or unwanted liquid) by wiping it with an absorbent cloth, a mop, etc: *She mopped up the pools of water on the bathroom floor.* ○ (*Brit*) *mop up* (ie soak up, absorb) *one's gravy with a piece of bread.* (**b**) complete (the final parts of a task); deal with (the final members of a group): *mop up the last few bits of work.* (**c**) capture or kill (the remaining small groups of people who continue to fight an army): *mop up isolated pockets* (ie small areas) *of resistance* ○ *engaged in mopping-up operations.*

mope /məʊp/ *v* **1** [I] feel very unhappy and pity oneself: *Stop moping!* **2** (phr v) **mope about/around** (**...**) wander about (a place) in an unhappy or listless mood: *He's been moping around (the house) all day.*
▷ **mope** *n* **1** [C] person who mopes. **2** [sing] act of moping: *have a bit of a mope.*

moped /ˈməʊped/ *n* motor cycle with pedals and a petrol engine of low power. ⇨ illus at MOTOR CYCLE (MOTOR).

moppet /ˈmɒpɪt/ *n* (*Brit infml*) (used esp as an affectionate term for a child) darling; poppet: *The poor moppet's thirsty.*

moquette /mɒˈket; *US* məʊ-/ *n* [U] thick velvety fabric used for carpets and furniture covers: [attrib] *a moquette sofa.*

moraine /mɒˈreɪn, məˈreɪn/ *n* mass of earth, stones, etc carried along and deposited by a glacier. ⇨ illus at ESKER.

moral[1] /ˈmɒrəl; *US* ˈmɔ:rəl/ *adj* **1** [attrib] concerning principles of right and wrong behaviour; ethical: *the decline of moral standards* ○ *a moral question, problem, judgement, dilemma, etc* ○ *moral philosophy* ○ *challenge sth on moral grounds* ○ *strong moral fibre*, ie the courage to face opposition bravely when doing what is right. **2** [attrib] based on people's sense of what is right and just, not on legal rights and obligations: *a moral law, duty, obligation, etc* ○ *show moral courage.* **3** following standards of right behaviour; good or virtuous: *lead a moral life* ○ *a very moral person.* **4** [attrib] able to understand the differences between right and wrong: *Human beings are moral individuals.* **5** teaching or illustrating good behaviour: *a moral story, tale, poem, etc.*
▷ **morally** /-rəlɪ/ *adv* **1** in a moral manner: *to behave morally.* **2** with respect to standards of right and wrong: *morally wrong, unacceptable, reprehensible, etc* ○ *hold sb morally responsible.*
□ ˌ**moral ˈcertainty** thing that is so probable that there is little room for doubt.
ˌ**Moral Reˈarmament** Christian organization aiming to revive conservative moral values.
ˌ**moral supˈport** expression of sympathy or encouragement, rather than practical or financial help: *give sb moral support.*
ˌ**moral ˈtutor** university teacher who is responsible for giving guidance to students on personal matters.
ˌ**moral ˈvictory** defeat that is in some ways as satisfying as a victory, eg when the principles that one is fighting for are shown to be right.

moral[2] /ˈmɒrəl; *US* ˈmɔ:rəl/ *n* **1** [C] practical lesson that a story, an event or an experience teaches: *The moral of this story is 'Better late than never'.* **2 morals** [pl] standards of behaviour; principles of right and wrong: *question sb's morals* ○ *the corruption of public morals* ○ *a person of loose morals*, ie one who has had many casual sexual partners.

morale /məˈrɑ:l; *US* -ˈræl/ *n* [U] state of confidence, enthusiasm, determination, etc of a person or group at a particular time: *affect/raise/boost/lower/undermine sb's morale* ○ *The news is good for (the team's) morale.*

moralist /ˈmɒrəlɪst; *US* ˈmɔ:r-/ *n* (*often derog*) person who expresses or teaches moral principles, esp one who tells people how they should behave.

moralistic /ˌmɒrəˈlɪstɪk; *US* ˌmɔ:r-/ *adj* (*usu derog*) having or showing definite but narrow beliefs and judgements about right and wrong actions: *a moralistic attitude.*

morality /məˈrælətɪ/ *n* **1** [U] principles of good behaviour: *matters of public/private morality* ○ *Have standards of morality improved?* **2** [U] (degree of) conforming to moral principles; goodness or rightness: *discuss the morality of abortion.* **3** particular system of morals: *Muslim, Hindu, Christian, etc morality.*
□ **moˈrality play** form of drama, popular in the 15th and 16th centuries, in which good behaviour is taught and in which the characters represent good and bad qualities. The most famous morality play is *Everyman*, in which the hero Everyman is called by Death; characters like Fellowship and Goods refuse to go with him on his journey, and he has to rely on Knowledge and Good Deeds.

moralize, -ise /ˈmɒrəlaɪz; *US* ˈmɔ:r-/ *v* [I, Ipr] ~ (**about/on sth**) (*esp derog*) talk or write (usu critically) about right and wrong behaviour, esp in a self-righteous way: *He's always moralizing about the behaviour of young people.*

morass /məˈræs/ *n* (usu *sing*) **1** stretch of low soft wet land; marsh. **2** ~ (**of sth**) (*fig*) thing that confuses people or prevents progress: *a morass of confusion, doubt, despair, etc* ○ *be caught up in, bogged down in, floundering in a morass of bureaucratic procedures.*

moratorium /ˌmɒrəˈtɔ:rɪəm; *US* ˌmɔ:r-/ *n* (*pl* ~**s**) **1** ~ (**on sth**) temporary stopping of an activity, esp by official agreement: *declare a moratorium on arms sales.* **2** legal authorization to delay payment of a debt.

Moravian /məˈreɪvɪən/ *n* member of a Christian group founded in 1722 by emigrants from Moravia in Czechoslovakia, who follow a very simple way of life based on the teachings of the Bible.

moray /ˈmɒreɪ/ *n* (also ˌ**moray ˈeel**) large eel of tropical seas.

morbid /ˈmɔ:bɪd/ *adj* **1** (of sb's mind or ideas) having or showing an interest in gloomy or unpleasant things, esp disease or death: *a morbid imagination* ○ *'He might even die.' 'Don't be so morbid.'* **2** (*medical*) diseased: *a morbid growth*, eg a cancer or tumour. ▷ **morbidity** /mɔ:ˈbɪdətɪ/ *n* [U]. **morbidly** *adv.*

mordant /ˈmɔ:dnt/ *adj* (*fml*) very sarcastic; biting:

mordant criticism/humour/wit.
▷ **mordancy** /-dənsɪ/ *n* [U].
mordant *n* substance, usu a salt, that makes a fabric dye permanent.
mordent /ˈmɔːdnt/ *n* (*music*) ornament produced by playing an extra note very quickly just above or below the one indicated in the score.
More /mɔː(r)/ Sir Thomas (1478-1535), English statesman and saint. He was a brilliant scholar and writer, esp on religious matters; his most famous work, *Utopia*, describes an ideal society and satirizes abuses of the time. He was the first lawyer and layman to become Lord Chancellor of England, but his opposition to *Henry VIII's claim to be head of the English Church led to his execution.
more /mɔː(r)/ *indef det, indef pron* ~ **(sth) (than...)** **1** a greater or additional number or amount (of). **(a)** (*det*): *more people, cars, money, imagination* ○ *more accuracy than originality* ○ *more food than could be eaten at one time* ○ *Would you like some more coffee?* ○ *There are two more students here than yesterday.* ○ *I know many more people who'd like to come.* **(b)** (*pron*): *Thank you, I couldn't possibly eat any more.* ○ *Is there much more of this film?* ○ *What more can I say* (ie in addition to what has already been said)? ○ *We need a few more.* ○ *I'll take three more.* ○ *room for no more than three cars* ○ *I hope we'll see more of you*, ie see you more often. ➪ Usage at MUCH[1]. **2** an increasing number or amount (of sb/sth): *She spends more and more time alone in her room.* ○ *He's always hungry — he seems to want more and more to eat.*
▷ **more** *adv* **1** (used to form the comparative of *adjs* and *advs* with two or more syllables): *more expensive, intelligent, generous, frightened, anxiously* ○ *She read the letter more carefully the second time.* **2** to a greater extent: *I like her more than her husband.* ○ *Try and concentrate more on your work.* ○ *This costs more than that.* ○ *Please repeat it once more*, ie one more time. ○ *It had more the appearance of a deliberate crime than of an accident.* **3** (idm) ˌ**more and** ˈ**more** increasingly: *I am becoming more and more irritated by his selfish behaviour.* ○ *He speaks more and more openly about his problem.* ˌ**more or** ˈ**less** **(a)** almost: *I've more or less finished reading the book.* **(b)** approximately: *It took more or less a whole day to paint the ceiling.* ○ *I can earn £20 a night, more or less, as a waiter.* **more than happy, glad, willing, etc (to do sth)** very happy, etc: *I'm more than happy to take you there in my car.* **no more** **(a)** neither: *He couldn't lift the table and no more could I.* **(b)** not more: *You're no more capable of speaking Chinese than I am.* ○ *It's no more than a mile to the shops.* **that's more** ˈ**like it** (*infml*) that is better, more acceptable, etc. **what is** ˈ**more** in addition; more importantly: *They are getting married, and what's more they are setting up in business together.* ○ *He's dirty, and what's more he smells.*
moreover /mɔːˈrəʊvə(r)/ *adv* (used to introduce sth new that adds to or supports the previous statement) further; besides; in addition: *They knew the painting was a forgery. Moreover, they knew who had painted it.*
mores /ˈmɔːreɪz/ *n* [pl] (*fml*) customs or conventions considered typical of or essential to a group or community: *social mores.*
morganatic /ˌmɔːgəˈnætɪk/ *adj* (of a marriage) between a man of high rank (eg a prince) and a woman of lower rank who keeps her lower status, the children having no claim to the property, titles, etc of their father. ▷ **morganatically** /-klɪ/ *adv.*
Morgan le Fay /ˌmɔːgən lə ˈfeɪ/ 'Morgan the fairy', the half-sister of King *Arthur.
morgue /mɔːg/ *n* building in which dead bodies are kept before being buried or cremated; mortuary.
MORI /ˈmɒrɪ/ *abbr* Market and Opinion Research International (an organization that conducts opinion polls). Cf GALLUP, NOP.
Moriarty /ˌmɒrɪˈɑːtɪ/ Professor, the evil enemy of Sherlock Holmes in the stories by Conan *Doyle.
moribund /ˈmɒrɪbʌnd; *US* ˈmɔːr-/ *adj* (*fml*) at the point of death; about to come to an end: *a moribund civilization, industry, custom.*
Morisot /ˈmɒriːsəʊ/ Berthe (1841-95), French painter. One of the *Impressionists, she specialized in paintings of women and children in harmonious outdoor settings. Her brush strokes often suggest the effects of dazzling sunlight.
Mormon /ˈmɔːmən/ *n, adj* (member) of a religious group founded in the USA in 1830, officially called 'The Church of Jesus Christ of Latter-day Saints'.
▷ **Mormonism** /-ɪzəm/ *n* [U]. ➪ article at RELIGION.
morn /mɔːn/ *n* (usu *sing*) (*arch*) (esp in poetry) morning.
mornay /ˈmɔːneɪ/ *n* [U] (also ˌ**mornay** ˈ**sauce**) cheese-flavoured white sauce (WHITE).
morning /ˈmɔːnɪŋ/ *n* [C, U] **1 (a)** early part of the day between dawn and noon or before the midday meal: *They left for Spain early this morning.* ○ *The taxi came at 8 o'clock the next morning.* ○ *The discussion group meets in the mornings.* ○ *(on) one fine summer morning* ○ *They stayed till Monday morning.* ○ *I'll see him tomorrow morning.* ○ *He swims every morning.* ○ *on the morning of the wedding* ○ *I've been painting the room all morning.* ○ *She works hard from morning to night.* ○ [attrib] *an early morning run* ○ *the fresh morning air* ○ *read the morning papers* ○ *Morning coffee is now being served.* **(b)** period from midnight to noon: *He died in the early hours of Sunday morning.* **2** (idm) **good** ˈ**morning** (used as a polite greeting or reply to a greeting when people first see each other in the morning and sometimes also when people leave in the morning): *Good morning, Rosalind/Miss Dixon.* (In informal use the greeting *Good morning* is often shortened to just *Morning.*). **in the** ˈ**morning** **(a)** during the morning of the next day: *I'll ring her up in the morning.* **(b)** between midnight and noon, not in the afternoon or evening: *The accident must have happened at about 11 o'clock in the morning.* **the morning** ˈ**after (the night be**ˈ**fore)** (*infml*) the effects of drinking too much alcohol the previous evening; hangover.
▷ **mornings** *adv* (*esp US*) in the morning; every morning: *I only work mornings.*
□ ˌ**morning-**ˈ**after pill** pill taken by a woman some hours after sexual intercourse to prevent conception.
ˈ**morning coat** long black or grey tailcoat with the front part cut away, worn as part of morning dress.
ˈ**morning dress** clothes worn by a man on very formal occasions, eg a wedding, including a morning coat, (usu striped) grey trousers and a top hat.
ˌ**morning** ˈ**glory** climbing plant with trumpet-shaped flowers that usu close in the afternoons.
ˌ**Morning** ˈ**Prayer** service in the Church of England for morning worship.
ˈ**morning sickness** feeling of sickness in the morning during the first few months of pregnancy.
the ˌ**morning** ˈ**star** bright star or planet, esp Venus, seen in the east before sunrise.

NOTE ON USAGE: Usually the preposition **in** is used with **morning/afternoon/evening**, on their own and in combination with other time expressions: *in the morning/afternoon/evening* ○ *at 3 o'clock in the afternoon* ○ *on the 4th of September in the morning.* **In** is also used with the adjectives **early** and **late:** *in the early/late morning.* With other adjectives and in certain other expressions **on** is used: *on a cool morning in spring* ○ *on Monday afternoon* ○ *on the previous/following evening* ○ *on the morning of the 4th of September.* No preposition is used in combination with **tomorrow/this/yesterday afternoon:** *We arrived yesterday afternoon.* ○ *They'll leave this evening.* ○ *I'll start work again tomorrow morning.* See also usage note at TIME[1].

Morocco /məˈrɒkəʊ/ country in N Africa on the Mediterranean and Atlantic coasts; pop approx 27 575 000; official language Arabic; capital Rabat; unit of currency dirham (= 100 centimes). Much of the country is covered in desert and the north is crossed by the *Atlas mountains. The economy is based on agriculture, chemical industries and mining, particularly of phosphates in the *Sahara. Territory to the south of the country in the former Spanish Sahara (now Western Sahara) is claimed by the Polisario independence movement, and there has been fighting since the 1970s. A referendum to determine its status was discussed in 1993. ➪ map at ALGERIA. ▷ **Moroccan** /məˈrɒkən/ *n, adj.*
morocco /məˈrɒkəʊ/ *n* [U] fine soft leather made from goatskins, or an imitation of this, used for making shoes and covers for books.
moron /ˈmɔːrɒn/ *n* **1** (*infml derog*) very stupid person: *He's an absolute moron!* ○ *They're a load of morons.* **2** adult with the intelligence of an average child of 8-12 years.
▷ **moronic** /məˈrɒnɪk/ *adj* (*infml derog*) (behaving) like a moron: *a moronic laugh.*
morose /məˈrəʊs/ *adj* very unhappy, bad-tempered and silent; sullen: *a morose person, manner, expression.* ▷ **morosely** *adv.* **moroseness** *n* [U].
morpheme /ˈmɔːfiːm/ *n* (*linguistics*) smallest meaningful unit into which a word can be divided: *'Run-s' contains two morphemes and 'un-like-ly' contains three.*
Morpheus /ˈmɔːfɪəs/ **1** (in Roman mythology) god of dreams. **2** (idm) **in the arms of Morpheus** ➪ ARM[1].
morphia /ˈmɔːfɪə/ *n* [U] (*dated*) = MORPHINE.
morphine /ˈmɔːfiːn/ *n* [U] drug made from opium, used for relieving pain.
morphogenesis /ˌmɔːfəʊˈdʒenəsɪs/ *n* [U] development of form and structure in living organisms.
morphology /mɔːˈfɒlədʒɪ/ *n* [U] **1** (*biology*) scientific study of the (esp external) form and structure of animals and plants. Cf ANATOMY. **2** (*linguistics*) study of the morphemes of a language and how they are combined to make words. Cf GRAMMAR 1, SYNTAX. ▷ **morphological** /ˌmɔːfəˈlɒdʒɪkl/ *adj.*

William Morris: 'Norwich', a design for wallpaper

Morris[1] /ˈmɒrɪs/ William (1834-96), English writer, artist and designer. He was influenced by the *Pre-Raphaelites' love of the Middle Ages, seen in his early poetry and his dislike of Victorian mass-production. He set up Morris and Company and the Kelmscott Press to restore the role of the craftsman in home decoration and printing. He was a leading figure in the *Arts and Crafts and early socialist movements. ➪ illus.
Morris[2] /ˈmɒrɪs/ ➪ NUFFIELD, LORD.

morris dance /ˈmɒrɪs dɑːns; *US* ˈmɔːrɪs dæns/ old English folk-dance traditionally performed by men wearing special (usu white) costumes often with ribbons and small bells around the knees. Dances from some parts of England involve waving handkerchieves; in others the dancers bang sticks together. The tradition nearly died out in the 19th century, but was revived as a hobby in the 20th century. ▷ **ˈmorris dancer**.

morrow /ˈmɒrəʊ; *US* ˈmɔːr-/ *n* **1 the morrow** [sing] (*dated or rhet*) the next day after the present or after any given day: *on the morrow* ○ *They wondered what the morrow had in store for them.* **2** (idm) **good ˈmorrow** (*arch*) (used as a greeting).

Morse /mɔːs/ *n* [U] (also ˌ**Morse ˈcode**) system of sending messages, using dots and dashes or short and long sounds or flashes of light to represent letters of the alphabet and numbers: *send a message in Morse.*

morsel /ˈmɔːsl/ *n* ~ (**of sth**) small amount or piece of sth, esp food: *a tasty/dainty/choice morsel of food* ○ *not have a morsel of common sense.*

mortal /ˈmɔːtl/ *adj* **1** that must die; that cannot live for ever: *All human beings are mortal.* ○ *Here lie the mortal remains of George Chapman*, eg as an inscription on a tombstone. **2** causing death; fatal: *a mortal wound, injury, etc* ○ (*fig*) *The collapse of the business was a mortal blow* (ie a great emotional shock) *to him and his family.* **3** [attrib] lasting until death; marked by great hatred; deadly: *mortal enemies* ○ *locked in mortal combat*, ie a fight that is only ended by the death of one of the fighters. **4** [attrib] extreme or intense: *live in mortal fear, terror, danger, etc.* **5** [attrib] (*dated infml*) (used to emphasize what follows and to show annoyance): *They stole every mortal thing in the house.*

▷ **mortal** *n* human being: (*joc*) *They're so grand these days that they probably don't talk to ordinary mortals like us any more.*

mortally /-təlɪ/ *adv* **1** resulting in death: *mortally wounded.* **2** greatly; intensely: *mortally afraid.*

□ ˌ**mortal ˈsin** (in the Roman Catholic Church) sin that causes the loss of God's grace and leads to damnation unless it is confessed and forgiven.

mortality /mɔːˈtælətɪ/ *n* [U] **1** state of being mortal. **2** (also **morˈtality rate**) number of deaths in a specified period of time: *Infant mortality* (ie The rate at which babies die) *was 20 deaths per thousand live births in 1986.* **3** large number of deaths caused by a disease, disaster, etc.

□ **morˈtality table** (esp in insurance) table showing how long people at various ages may normally be expected to live.

mortar[1] /ˈmɔːtə(r)/ *n* [U] mixture of lime or cement, sand and water, used to hold bricks, stones, etc together in building.

▷ **mortar** *v* [Tn] join (bricks, etc) with mortar.

mortar[2] /ˈmɔːtə(r)/ *n* **1** short cannon that fires shells at a high angle: [attrib] *under mortar fire/attack*, ie being fired at by a mortar or mortars. **2** strong bowl in which substances are crushed and ground with a pestle. ⇨ illus at PESTLE.

mortar-board /ˈmɔːtə bɔːd/ *n* (usu black) cap with a stiff square top, worn by certain university teachers and students on formal occasions.

mortgage /ˈmɔːgɪdʒ/ *n* (**a**) agreement in which money is lent by a building society, bank, etc for buying a house or other property, the property being the security: *apply for/take out a mortgage* ○ *It's difficult to get a mortgage on an old house.* ○ [attrib] *a mortgage agreement/deed.* ⇨ articles at BANK, HOUSE. (**b**) sum of money lent in this way: *We've got a mortgage of £40 000.* ○ [attrib] *monthly mortgage payments*, ie money to repay the sum borrowed and the interest on it.

▷ **mortgage** *v* [Tn, Tn·pr, Dn·pr] ~ **sth** (**to sb**) (**for sth**) give sb the legal right to take possession of (a house or some other property) as a security for payment of money lent: *He mortgaged his house in order to start a business*, ie borrowed money with his house as a security. ○ *The house is mortgaged (to the bank) (for £30 000).* **mortgagee** /ˌmɔːgɪˈdʒiː/ *n* person or firm that lends money in mortgage agreements. **mortgager** /ˈmɔːgɪdʒə(r)/ (also, in legal use, **mortgagor** /ˌmɔːgɪdʒɔː(r)/) *n* person who borrows money in a mortgage agreement.

Grandma Moses: A Beautiful World

mortician /mɔːˈtɪʃn/ *n* (*US*) = UNDERTAKER.

mortify /ˈmɔːtɪfaɪ/ *v* (*pt, pp* **-fied**) **1** [Tn usu passive] cause (sb) to be very ashamed or embarrassed: *He was/felt mortified.* ○ *a mortifying failure, defeat, mistake, etc.* **2** [Tn] (*fml or joc*) control (human desires or needs) by discipline or self-denial: *mortify the flesh*, ie one's body. ▷ **mortification** /ˌmɔːtɪfɪˈkeɪʃn/ *n* [U]: *To his mortification, he was criticized by the managing director in front of all his junior colleagues.*

mortise (also **mortice**) /ˈmɔːtɪs/ *n* (usu rectangular) hole cut in a piece of wood, etc to receive the end of another piece so that the two are held together. Cf TENON. ⇨ illus at TENON.

▷ **mortise** (also **mortice**) *v* **1** [Tn·pr, Tn·p] ~ **A to/into B**; ~ **A and B together** join or fasten things with a mortise: *The cross-piece is mortised into the upright post.* **2** [Tn] cut a mortise in (sth).

□ ˈ**mortise lock** lock that is fitted inside a hole cut into the edge of a door, not one that is screwed onto the surface.

Morton /ˈmɔːtn/ 'Jelly Roll' (real name Ferdinand La Menthe, 1885-1941), American jazz pianist and composer. With his band, the Red Hot Peppers, he was a link between the New Orleans ragtime style and classic jazz.

mortuary /ˈmɔːtʃərɪ; *US* ˈmɔːtʃʊerɪ/ *n* room or building (eg part of a hospital) in which dead bodies are kept before being buried or cremated.

▷ **mortuary** *adj* [attrib] (*fml*) of death or burial: *mortuary rites.*

mosaic /məʊˈzeɪɪk/ *n* **1** [C, U] picture or pattern made by placing together small pieces of glass, stone, etc of different colours: *ancient Greek mosaics* ○ *a design in mosaic* ○ [attrib] *a mosaic design, pavement, ceiling.* **2** [C usu *sing*] ~ (**of sth**) design or pattern made up of many different individual items; patchwork: *a rich mosaic of meadows, rivers and woods.*

Mosaic /məʊˈzeɪɪk/ *adj* [usu attrib] of or associated with Moses: *Mosaic law.*

Moscow /ˈmɒskəʊ; *US also* -kaʊ/ capital and largest city of the Russian federation. The city contains the *Kremlin, the country's seat of government, and its other landmarks include Red Square, the distant Lenin hills, and the Bolshoi Ballet theatre. ⇨ map at UNION OF SOVIET SOCIALIST REPUBLICS. Cf MUSCOVITE (MUSCOVY).

moselle /məʊˈzel/ *n* [C, U] (type of) dry white wine from the valley of the river Moselle in Germany.

Moses[1] /ˈməʊzɪz/ (*Bible*) Hebrew patriarch who was born in Egypt and led his people out of captivity there and through the desert towards the Promised Land. He received the *Ten Commandments from God on Mount Sinai.

□ ˈ**moses basket** wicker basket used as a bed for a small baby.

Moses[2] /ˈməʊzɪz/ Anna Mary Robertson ('Grandma Moses') (1860-1961), American artist. She did not begin to paint seriously until she was over 70. Her paintings, in the primitive style, are enormously popular in the USA, and her birthday, 7 September, is celebrated in New York State as 'Grandma Moses Day'.

mosey /ˈməʊzɪ/ *v* [Ipr, Ip] (*US infml*) walk aimlessly (in the specified direction); amble: *I'd best be moseying along*, ie leaving. ○ *Why don't you mosey round to my place?*

Moslem = MUSLIM.

Mosley /ˈməʊzlɪ/ Sir Oswald (1896-1980), English fascist leader. He was a Conservative and a Labour member of Parliament before starting the unsuccessful fascist movement in Britain. He was put in prison for most of the Second World War.

mosque /mɒsk/ *n* building in which Muslims worship. ⇨ article at RELIGION.

mosquito /məsˈkiːtəʊ, *also, in British use*, mɒs-/ *n* (*pl* ~**es**) small flying insect (esp the type that spreads malaria), the female of which sucks the blood of people and animals.

□ **mosˈquito-net** *n* net hung over a bed, etc to keep mosquitoes away.

Moss /mɒs/ Stirling (1929-), English racing driver. He won a number of grand prix races before an accident ended his career in 1962.

moss /mɒs; *US* mɔːs/ *n* **1** [U, C] very small green or yellow flowerless plant growing in thick masses on damp surfaces or trees or stones: *moss-covered rocks, walls.* Cf LICHEN. **2** (idm) **a rolling stone gathers no moss** ⇨ ROLL[2].

▷ **mossy** *adj* **1** covered with moss: *mossy bark.* **2** like moss: *mossy green.*

□ ˈ**moss-grown** *adj* covered with moss.

Mossad /ˈmɒsæd/ the Israeli secret service.

mossback /ˈmɒsbæk; *US* ˈmɔːs-/ *n* (*US infml*) old-fashioned person with very conservative ideas.

Moss Bros /ˈmɒs brɒs/ British clothing firm, famous for hiring out men's formal clothes for weddings and similar occasions.

most[1] /məʊst/ *indef det, indef pron* (used as the superlative of MANY, MUCH[2]) **1** greatest in number, amount or extent. **(a)** (*det*): *Who do you think will get (the) most votes?* ○ *Peter made the most mistakes of all the class.* ○ *When we toured Italy we spent most time in Rome.* ○ *Most racial discrimination is based on ignorance.* **(b)** (*pron*): *We all had some of the cake; I probably ate (the) most*, ie more than the others ate. ○ *Harry got 6 points, Susan got 8 points but Alison got most.* ○ *The person with the most to lose is the director.* ⇨ Usage at MUCH[1]. **2** more than half of sb/sth; the majority of sb/sth. **(a)** (*det*): *Most European countries are democracies.* ○ *Most classical music sends me to sleep.* ○ *The new tax laws affect most people.* ○ *I like most vegetables.* **(b)** (*pron*): *It rained for most of the summer.* ○ *As most of you know, I've decided to resign.* ○ *There are hundreds of verbs in English and most are regular.* ○ *He has a lot of free time — he spends most of it in the garden.* **3** (idm) **at (the) ˈmost** as a maximum; not more than: *At (the) most I might earn £250 a night.* ○ *There were 50 people there, at the very most.*
▷ **mostly** *adv* almost all; generally: (*infml*) *The drink was mostly lemonade.* ○ *We're mostly out on Sundays.*

most[2] /məʊst/ *adv* **1** **(a)** (used to form the superlative of *adjs* and *advs* of two or more syllables): *most boring, beautiful, impressive, etc* ○ *The person who gave most generously to the scheme has been blind from birth.* ○ *It was the most exciting holiday I've ever had.* **(b)** to the greatest extent: *What did you most enjoy?* ○ *She helped me (the) most when my parents died.* ○ *I saw her most* (ie most often) *when we were at university.* **2** **(a)** very: *We heard a most interesting talk about Japan.* ○ *I received a most unusual present from my aunt.* ○ *It was most kind of you to take me to the airport.* ○ *He spoke most bitterly of his experiences in prison.* **(b)** absolutely: *'Can we expect to see you at church?' 'Most certainly.'* **3** (*infml esp US*) almost: *I go to the store most every day.*

-most *suff* (with *preps* and *adjs* of position forming *adjs*): *inmost* ○ *topmost* ○ *uppermost*.

MOT /ˌem əʊ ˈtiː/ *abbr* (*Brit*) **(a)** Ministry of Transport. **(b)** (also **MOT test**) (*infml*) compulsory annual test of cars, etc over a certain age: *She took her car in for its MOT.* ○ *Has your car been MOT'd/had its MOT?*

mot /məʊ/ *n* (*French*) clever or witty remark.
□ **the mot juste** /ðə ˌməʊ ˈʒuːst/ (*French*) expression that is exactly appropriate.

mote /məʊt/ *n* **1** small particle, usu of dust; speck. **2** (idm) **the mote in sb's ˈeye** (*dated*) the minor fault that sb has committed, when compared with one's own much greater fault.

motel /məʊˈtel/ *n* hotel for motorists, with space for parking cars near the rooms.

motet /məʊˈtet/ *n* short piece of church music, usu for voices only. Cf ANTHEM.

moth /mɒθ; *US* mɔːθ/ *n* **1** insect like a butterfly but less brightly coloured, flying mainly at night and attracted to bright lights. **2** (also **clothes moth**) small similar insect that breeds in cloth, fur, etc, its young feeding on the cloth and making holes in it.
□ **ˈmothball** *n* **1** small ball made of a strong-smelling substance, used for keeping moths away from stored clothes. **2** (idm) **in ˈmothballs** stored and not used for a long time: *old aircraft kept in mothballs.*
ˈmoth-eaten *adj* **1** eaten, damaged or destroyed by moths: *moth-eaten old clothes.* **2** (*infml derog*) **(a)** looking very old; shabby or worn out: *moth-eaten armchairs.* **(b)** old-fashioned; out of date: *moth-eaten ideas.*
ˈmothproof *adj* (of clothes) treated chemically against damage by moths. — *v* [Tn] make (clothes) mothproof.

mother /ˈmʌðə(r)/ *n* **1** female parent of a child or animal: *My mother died when I was 6.* ○ *the relationship between mother and baby* ○ *How are you, Mother?* ○ *an expectant* (ie a pregnant) *mother* ○ [attrib] *Look how the mother chimpanzee cares for her young.* ⇨ App 8. **2** (way of addressing the) head of a female religious community: *Pray for me, Mother.* **3** (way of addressing an old woman). **4** (⚠ *sl esp US*) = MOTHERFUCKER. **5** (idm) **necessity is the mother of invention** ⇨ NECESSITY. **old enough to be sb's father/mother** ⇨ OLD.
▷ **mother** *v* [Tn] **1** care for (sb/sth) as a mother does; rear: *piglets mothered by a sow.* **2** treat (sb) with too much protection or care: *He likes being mothered by his landlady.* **ˈMothering Sunday** (also *Brit* **ˈMother's Day**) the fourth Sunday in Lent, when mothers traditionally receive gifts and cards from their children, originally a day when servants were given a holiday to visit their families.
motherhood /-hʊd/ *n* [U] state of being a mother: *She finds motherhood very rewarding.*
motherless *adj* having no mother.
motherlike *adj* in the manner of a mother: *a motherlike smile, embrace.*
motherly *adj* having or showing the kind and tender qualities of a mother: *motherly love, affection, care, etc* ○ *a motherly kiss.* **motherliness** *n* [U].
□ **ˈmother country** (*fml*) **1** one's native country. **2** country in relation to its colonies.
ˈmotherfucker *n* (⚠ *sl esp US*) contemptible or annoying person or thing: *The motherfucker's got a gun!*
ˈmother goddess (in many ancient religions) goddess controlling the whole cycle of birth and growth.
ˌMother ˈGoose rhyme (*US*) = NURSERY RHYME (NURSERY). ⇨ article at NURSERY RHYME.
ˈmother-in-law *n* (*pl* **mothers-in-law**) mother of one's wife or husband. ⇨ App 8.
ˈmotherland /-lænd/ *n* one's native country.
ˌMother ˈNature (*often joc*) nature considered as a force that affects the world and human beings: *Leave the cure to Mother Nature. She knows best.*
ˌmother-of-ˈpearl (also **nacre**) *n* [U] hard smooth shiny rainbow-coloured substance that forms the lining of some shells (eg oysters, mussels) and is used for making buttons, ornaments, etc: [attrib] *a mother-of-pearl ear-ring, necklace, brooch, etc.*
ˈmother's boy (also **ˈmummy's boy**, *US* **ˈmama's boy**) (*infml derog*) boy or man, esp one considered emotionally weak, whose character and behaviour are influenced too much by the protection of his mother.
ˈMother's Day **(a)** (*Brit*) = MOTHERING SUNDAY. **(b)** (*US*) similar day held in the USA on the second Sunday in May.
ˈmother ship ship from which smaller ships get supplies.
ˌmother's ˈruin (*dated sl*) = GIN.
ˌMother Suˈperior head of a convent.
ˌmother-to-ˈbe *n* (*pl* **mothers-to-be**) woman who is pregnant.
ˈmother tongue language that one first learned to speak as a child; one's native language.

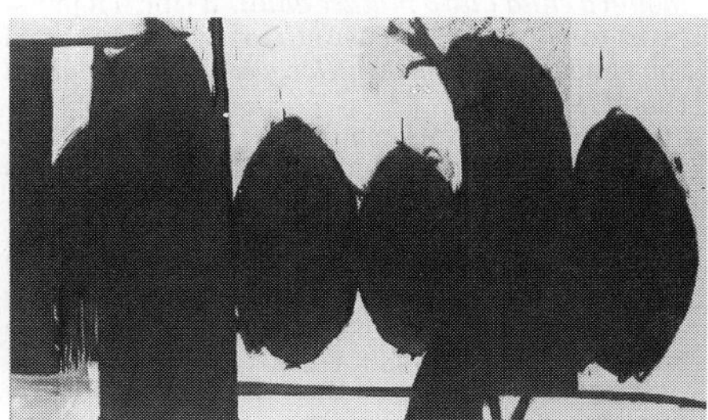

Robert Motherwell: Elegy to the Spanish Republic, 70

Motherwell /ˈmʌðəwel/ Robert (1915-91), American painter. One of the major figures of abstract expressionism (ABSTRACT), he is famous for his use of black and white paint applied freely with a heavily loaded brush and for his enormous canvases. ⇨ illus.

motif /məʊˈtiːf/ *n* **1** decorative design or pattern: *an eagle motif on the curtains.* **2** theme or idea that is repeated and developed in a work of music or literature.

motion /ˈməʊʃn/ *n* **1** [U] (manner of) moving: *the swaying motion of the ship* ○ *The object is no longer in motion*, ie has stopped moving. **2** [C] particular movement; way of moving part of the body; gesture: *with a sudden, single, upward, downward, etc motion of the hand.* **3** [C] formal proposal to be discussed and voted on at a meeting: *propose, put forward, reject, etc a motion* ○ *The motion was adopted/carried by a majority of six votes.* **4** [C] (*fml*) **(a)** act of emptying the bowels: *regular motions.* **(b)** waste matter emptied from the bowels; faeces: *solid motions.* **5** (idm) **go through the motions (of doing sth)** (*infml*) pretend to do sth; do sth but without sincerity or serious intention: *He went through the motions of welcoming her friends but then quickly left the room.* **put/set sth in ˈmotion** cause sth to start moving or operating: *set machinery in motion* ○ (*fig*) *put the new campaign in motion.* Cf SLOW MOTION (SLOW[1]).
▷ **motion** *v* **1** [Ipr, Dpr·t, Dn·t no passive] ~ **to sb** indicate to sb by a gesture: *He motioned to the waiter.* ○ *He motioned (to) me to sit down.* **2** [Tn·pr, Tn·p] direct (sb) in the specified direction by a gesture: *motion sb to a chair, away, in, etc.*
motionless *adj* not moving; still: *standing motionless.*
□ **ˌmotion ˈpicture** (*esp US*) cinema film.
ˈmotion sickness (*esp US*) = TRAVEL-SICKNESS (TRAVEL).

motivate /ˈməʊtɪveɪt/ *v* **1** [Tn usu passive] be the reason for (sb's action); cause (sb) to act in a particular way; inspire: *be motivated by greed, fear, love, etc.* **2** [Tn, Cn·t] stimulate the interest of (sb); cause to want to do sth: *a teacher who can motivate her pupils (to work harder).* ▷ **motivated** *adj*: *a politically motivated murder* ○ *be highly motivated*, ie very keen to do sth. **motivation** /ˌməʊtɪˈveɪʃn/ *n* [C, U]: *the basic financial motivations for the decision* ○ *They lack the motivation to study.*

motive /ˈməʊtɪv/ *n* ~ **(for sth)** that which causes sb to act in a particular way; reason: *The police could not find a motive for the murder.* ○ *question sb's motives* ○ *the profit motive*, ie the desire to make a profit. ⇨ Usage at REASON[1].
▷ **motive** *adj* [attrib] causing movement or action: *motive force/power*, eg electricity, to operate machinery.
motiveless *adj*: *an apparently motiveless crime.*

motley /ˈmɒtlɪ/ *adj* **1** (*derog*) of many different types of people or things: *wearing a motley collection of old clothes* ○ *a motley crowd/crew*, ie a group of many different types of people. **2** [attrib] of various colours: *a motley coat*, eg one worn by a jester in former times.
▷ **motley** *n* [U] (formerly) clothes worn by a jester: *put on/wear the motley*, ie dress as or play the part of a jester.

motocross /ˈməʊtəkrɒs; *US* -krɔːs/ *n* [U] cross-country motor-cycle racing over an enclosed track of rough ground.

motor /ˈməʊtə(r)/ *n* **1** **(a)** device that changes (usu electric) power into movement, used for making machines work: *an electric motor.* **(b)** device that changes fuel (eg petrol) into energy to provide power for a vehicle, boat, etc: *an outboard motor*, ie one attached to the back of a small boat. **2** (*Brit dated or joc*) car.
▷ **motor** *adj* [attrib] **1** having or driven by a motor(1): *motor vehicles* ○ *a motor mower.* **2** of or for vehicles driven by a motor: *motor racing* ○ *motor insurance* ○ *the motor trade* ○ *the Motor Show* ○ *a motor mechanic.* **3** giving or producing motion: *motor nerves*, ie those that carry impulses from the brain to the muscles.
motor *v* [I, Ipr, Ip] (*dated Brit*) travel by car: *They spent a pleasant afternoon motoring through the countryside.* **motoring** /ˈməʊtərɪŋ/ *n* [U] driving in a car: [attrib] *a motoring offence.*

motorist /ˈməʊtərɪst/ *n* person who drives a car. Cf PEDESTRIAN.

motorize, -ise /ˈməʊtəraɪz/ *v* [Tn usu passive] **1** equip (sth) with a motor: *motorized vehicles.* **2** equip (troops, etc) with motor vehicles: *motorized infantry.*

□ **ˈmotor bike** (*infml*) = MOTOR CYCLE.

ˈmotor boat (usu small) fast boat driven by an engine.

motorcade /ˈməʊtəkeɪd/ *n* procession of motor vehicles, often with important people travelling in them.

ˈmotor car (*Brit fml*) = CAR 1.

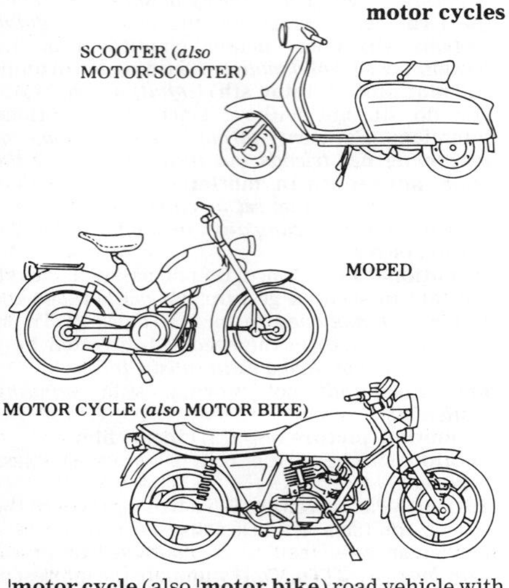

ˈmotor cycle (also **ˈmotor bike**) road vehicle with two wheels, driven by an engine, with one seat for the driver and usu with space for a passenger behind the driver. **ˈmotor-cyclist** *n* rider of a motor cycle.

📖 The motor cycle is often associated with violent and lawless young people, especially the gangs of *Hell's Angels who flourished from the 1960s, with their distinctive black leather clothes and long hair.

ˈmotor home (*esp US*) large vehicle equipped like a caravan for people to live in on holiday or permanently.

ˈmotor-scooter = SCOOTER 1.

ˈmotorway *n* (*Brit*)(*abbr* **M**) (*US* **exˈpressway**) *n* wide road specially built for fast-moving traffic, with a restricted number of places for entry and exit, and separate carriageways for vehicles travelling in opposite directions: *join/leave a motorway* ○ *You're not allowed to stop on motorways.* ○ [attrib] *a motorway service station.* ⇨ Usage at ROAD. ⇨ illus. ⇨ article at ROAD.

motte /mɒt/ *n* mound on which a medieval castle is built.

mottled /ˈmɒtld/ *adj* marked with patches of different colours without a regular pattern: *the mottled skin of a snake.*

motto /ˈmɒtəʊ/ *n* (*pl* ~**es**) **1** short sentence or phrase chosen and used as a guide or rule of behaviour or as an expression of the aims or ideals of a family, a country, an institution, etc: *My motto is: 'Live each day as it comes.'* ○ *What's your school motto?* **2** (*esp Brit*) witty remark or riddle or short saying printed on a piece of paper, esp inside a Christmas cracker.

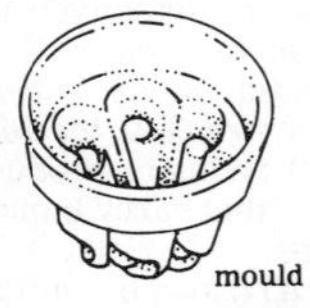

mould¹ (*US* **mold**) /məʊld/ *n* **1** (**a**) hollow container with a particular shape, into which a soft or liquid substance (eg jelly or molten metal) is poured to set or cool into that shape: *a jelly mould in the shape of a racing car.* ⇨ illus. (**b**) jelly, pudding, etc made in such a container. **2** (usu *sing*) particular type of (a person's) character: *He doesn't fit (into) the traditional mould of a university professor.* ○ *They are all cast in the same/a similar mould*, ie They all have similar attitudes and ways of behaving.

▷ **mould** *v* **1** [Tn, Tn·pr] (**a**) ~ **sth (into sth)** shape (a soft substance) into a particular form or object: *mould plastic (into drain-pipes).* (**b**) ~ **sth (from/out of/in sth)** make sth by shaping it: *mould a head out of/in clay.* **2** [Tn, Tn·pr] ~ **sb/sth (into sb/sth)** guide or control the development of sb/sth; shape or influence sb/sth: *mould sb's character* ○ *Television moulds public opinion.* ○ *mould a child into a mature adult.* **3** [Ipr, Tn·pr] ~ **(sth) to/round sth** (cause sth to) fit tightly round the shape of (an object): *Her wet clothes moulded round her body.*

mould² (*US* **mold**) /məʊld/ *n* [U, C] fine furry growth of fungi that forms on old food or on objects left in moist warm air.

▷ **mouldy** (*US* **moldy**) *adj* **1** covered with mould; smelling of mould: *mouldy cheese.* **2** (*infml derog*) old and decaying; fusty: *Let's get rid of this mouldy old furniture.* **3** (*Brit infml*) unpleasant because dull, mean or miserable: *We had a mouldy holiday — it rained every day.* ○ *They've given us a pretty mouldy pay increase this year.*

mould³ (*US* **mold**) /məʊld/ *n* [U] soft fine loose earth, esp from decayed vegetable matter: *leaf mould*, ie from decayed leaves and twigs that have fallen off trees.

moulder (*US* **molder**) /ˈməʊldə(r)/ *v* [I, Ip] ~ **(away)** crumble to dust; decay slowly: *the mouldering ruins of an old castle.*

moulding (*US* **molding**) /ˈməʊldɪŋ/ *n* **1** [U] action of shaping; way in which sth is shaped: (*fig*) *the moulding of young people's characters.* **2** [C] (*architecture*) line of ornamental plaster, carved woodwork, etc, typically along the top of sth, eg a wall.

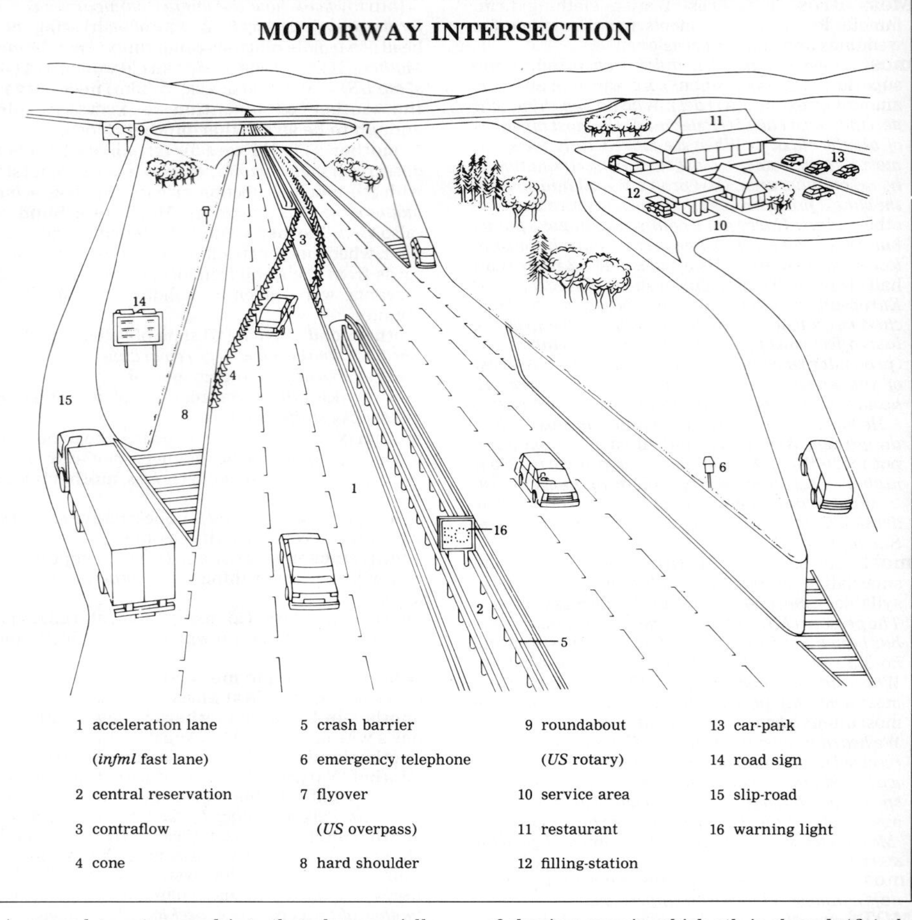

Moulin Rouge /ˌmuːlæn ˈruːʒ/ **the Moulin Rouge** cabaret in the Montmartre district of Paris, famous for its shows with attractive female dancers. Around 1900 it was a popular meeting-place for artists and poets. *Toulouse-Lautrec made many paintings of scenes there.

moult (*US* **molt**) /məʊlt/ *v* [I] (**a**) (of birds) lose feathers before a new growth. (**b**) (of dogs, cats, etc) lose hair: *a dog that moults all over the house.* (**c**) (of some insects, snakes and some other animals) lose the outer layer of skin, shell, etc before a new one grows.

▷ **moult** *n* [C, U] process or time of moulting.

mound /maʊnd/ *n* **1** mass of piled-up earth; small hill. **2** pile or heap; quantity of things to do: *a mound of mashed potato* ○ *a mound of washing and ironing.*

mount¹ /maʊnt/ *n* (*arch*, except in place names, usu written *Mt*) mountain; hill: *Mt Etna, Everest, etc* ○ *the Mount of Olives* ○ *St Michael's Mount.*

mount² /maʊnt/ *v* **1** [I, Ipr, Tn] ~ **(to sth)** go up; ascend: *The climbers mounted higher and higher.* ○ *a staircase that mounts to the top of a building* ○ *A blush mounted to the child's face*, ie The blood spread to the child's cheeks. ○ *mount the stairs.* **2** [I, Tn, Tn·pr] ~ **sb (on sth)** get onto or put (sb) onto a horse, etc for riding; provide (sb) with a horse for riding: *He quickly mounted (his horse) and rode away.* ○ *He mounted the boy on the horse.* ○ *The policemen were mounted on* (ie rode) *black horses.* **3** [I, Ipr, Ip] ~ **(up) (to sth)** increase in amount or intensity: *The death toll mounted (to 100).* ○ *Concern is mounting over the fate of the lost* *expedition.* ○ *bills, debts, expenses, etc that mount up.* **4** [Tn, Tn·pr] ~ **sth (on/onto/in sth)** put sth into place on a support; fix sth in position for use, display or study: *mount a collection of stamps onto card/in an album* ○ *mount specimens on slides* ○ *a brooch of diamonds mounted in silver.* **5** [Tn, Tn·pr] ~ **sth (in sth)** set sth up; organize sth; begin sth: *mount an exhibition, a production, a display, etc* ○ *mount a protest, a demonstration, an attack, an offensive, etc* ○ *The pop concert was mounted in a sports stadium.* **6** [Tn, Tn·pr] ~ **sb (on/around sth)** place sb on guard: *mount sentries on a wall, round a palace, etc.* **7** [I, Tn] (esp of large male animals, eg bulls) get up on (a female) in order to copulate. **8** (idm) **mount guard (at/over sb/sth)** act as a guard or sentinel: *soldiers mounting guard at/over the palace.* **mount the ˈthrone** become king, queen, etc.

▷ **mount** *n* thing on which a person or thing is mounted (eg a card for a picture, a glass slide for a specimen, a horse for riding, etc).

mounted *adj* provided with a mount: *a mounted photograph,* ie fixed on a card ○ *mounted policemen,* ie on horses.

mounting *adj* increasing: *mounting tension.*

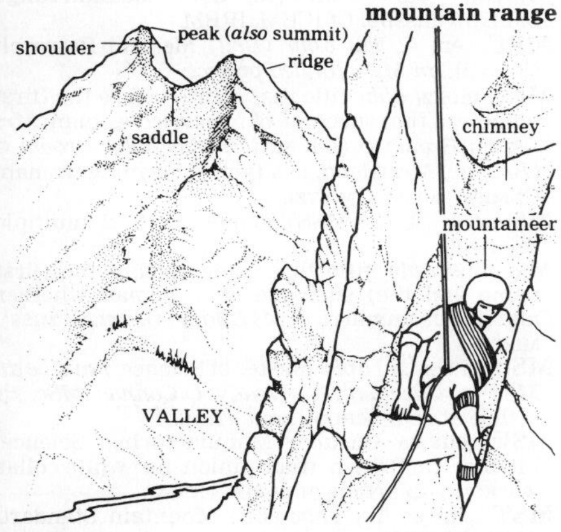

mountain /ˈmaʊntɪn; *US* -ntn/ *n* **1** [C] mass of very high rock going up to a peak: *Everest is the highest mountain in the world.* ○ [attrib] *mountain peaks, paths, streams, etc* ○ *the refreshing mountain air.* **2** [sing] ~ **of sth** *(fig)* **(a)** large heap or pile, esp of work needing attention: *a mountain of paperwork, unanswered letters, correspondence, washing and ironing, etc.* **(b)** large overwhelming amount (of difficulties): *a mountain of debts, complaints, queries.* **3** [C usu *sing*] large surplus stock: *the butter mountain,* ie the large unsold amount of butter in the EC. **4** (idm) **make a ˌmountain out of a ˈmolehill** *(derog)* make a trivial matter seem important.

▷ **mountaineer** /ˌmaʊntɪˈnɪə(r); *US* -ntnˈɪər/ *n* person who is skilled at climbing mountains.

mountaineering /ˌmaʊntɪˈnɪərɪŋ; *US* -ntnˈɪə-/ *n* [U] climbing mountains (as a sport): [attrib] *a mountaineering expedition.*

mountainous /ˈmaʊntɪnəs; *US* -ntənəs/ *adj* **1** having many mountains: *mountainous country.* **2** huge; rising like mountains: *mountainous waves.*

□ **ˌmountain ˈash** type of tree with scarlet berries; rowan.

ˌmountain ˈchain, ˌmountain ˈrange row or series of mountains more or less in a straight line. ⇨ illus.

ˌmountain ˈdew *(joc)* whisky or other spirits made illegally in the countryside.

ˌmountain ˈgoat 1 white goat-like animal that lives in the *Rocky Mountains of America. **2** any goat that lives in the mountains.

ˌmountain ˈlion = PUMA.

ˈmountain sickness nausea and difficulty in breathing felt by people in high mountain regions, caused by the reduced pressure of oxygen in the air.

ˈmountainside *n* side or slope of a mountain.

ˌMountain ˈStandard Time *(abbr* **MST)** standard time in parts of Canada and the USA around the *Rocky Mountains, eight hours behind *Greenwich Mean Time.

Mountbatten /ˌmaʊntˈbætn/ Louis, 1st Earl Mountbatten of Burma (1900-79), British admiral. During the Second World War he commanded the Allied forces in SE Asia, defeating the Japanese in Burma and the Indian Ocean. He was the last viceroy of India before it achieved independence, remaining as its first Governor-General. He was killed by the IRA.

mountebank /ˈmaʊntɪbæŋk/ *n (dated or rhet derog)* person who tries to cheat others by clever talk; swindler.

Mountie /ˈmaʊntɪ/ *n (infml)* member of the Royal Canadian Mounted Police.

mourn /mɔːn/ *v* [I, Ipr, Tn] ~ **(for/over sb/sth)** feel or show sorrow or regret for the loss of sb/sth: *She mourned (for/over) her dead child for many years.* ○ *We all mourn the destruction of a well-loved building.*

▷ **mourner** *n* person who mourns, esp one who attends a funeral as a friend or relative of the dead person.

mournful /-fl/ *adj (often derog)* sad; sorrowful: *a mournful look on her face* ○ *I wish you'd stop playing that mournful music.* **mournfully** /-fəlɪ/ *adv.* **mournfulness** *n* [U].

mourning *n* [U] black or dark clothes worn as a (conventional) sign of grief at sb's death: *When grandmother died they went into* (ie started to wear) *mourning.* ○ *She was in mourning for a month.*

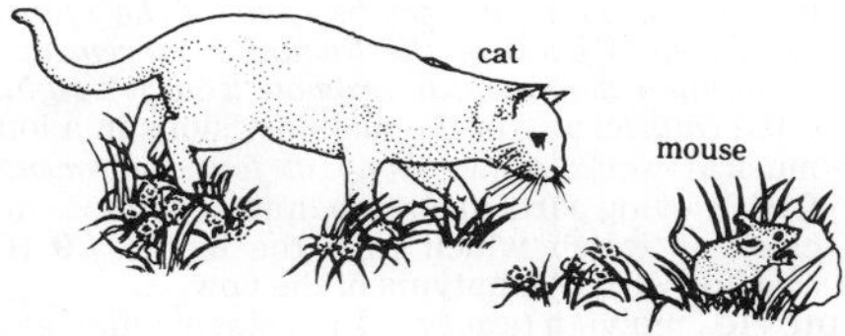

mouse /maʊs/ *n (pl* **mice** /maɪs/) **1** (often in compounds) (any of several types of) small rodent with a long thin tail: *a ˈhouse mouse* ○ *a ˈfield-mouse* ○ *a ˈharvest-mouse.* ⇨ illus. **2** *(fig esp joc or derog)* shy, timid person: *His wife, a strange little mouse, never said anything.* ○ *Are you a man or a mouse* (ie brave or cowardly)*?* **3** *(computing)* small hand-held device that is moved across a desk-top, etc to produce a corresponding movement of the cursor, with a button for entering commands. ⇨ illus at COMPUTER. **4** (idm) **the best-laid schemes/plans of mice and men** ⇨ BEST[2]. **play cat and mouse/a cat-and-mouse game with sb** ⇨ CAT[1]. **quiet as a mouse** ⇨ QUIET.

▷ **mouser** /ˈmaʊsə(r), ˈmaʊzə(r)/ *n* cat that hunts for or catches mice.

mousy /ˈmaʊsɪ/ *adj* **(-ier, -iest)** *(derog)* **1** (esp of hair) dull brown. **2** (of people) timid; shy.

□ **ˈmousetrap** *n* trap for catching mice. **ˌmousetrap ˈcheese** *(joc)* cheese of poor quality or taste, not good to eat.

moussaka /muːˈsɑːkə/ *n* [U] Greek dish made of minced meat and vegetables (usu including aubergine and tomato), cooked in the oven.

mousse /muːs/ *n* [U, C] **1** cold dish made of cream, egg whites, etc mixed lightly and flavoured with sth sweet (fruit or chocolate) or sth savoury (fish or meat): *a/some banana, strawberry, raspberry, etc mousse* ○ *salmon mousse.* **2** thick creamy liquid put on the hair to shape it or improve its condition: *styling/conditioning mousse.*

moustache /məˈstɑːʃ/ *(US* **mustache** /ˈmʌstæʃ/) *n* **1** [C] hair allowed to grow on the upper lip. ⇨ illus at HEAD. Cf BEARD[1] a, WHISKER 1. **2 moustaches** [pl] long moustache.

📖 Certain types of moustache have had distinctive associations in Britain. Small, bristly moustaches (called 'toothbrush' moustaches) are often associated with junior officials. Pointed moustaches with ends that can be twirled are traditionally associated with either military men, such as sergeant-majors or colonels, or with circus ringmasters; and handlebar moustaches (thick with curved ends) were once popular among Royal Air Force officers.

mouth[1] /maʊθ/ *n (pl* ~**s** /maʊðz/) **1** [C] opening through which animals take in food; space behind this containing the teeth, tongue, etc: *'Open your mouth a little wider,' said the dentist.* ○ *Don't talk with your mouth full.* ○ *(fig) Every time I open my mouth* (ie speak) *he contradicts me.* ○ *(derog) She's got a big mouth,* ie talks a lot and (esp) reveals secrets. ⇨ illus at HEAD. **2** [U] *(infml derog)* **(a)** meaningless or ineffectual talk: *He's all mouth and no action.* **(b)** impudent talk; rudeness: *I don't want any mouth from you!* **3** [C] place where sth (eg a bag, bottle, tunnel, etc) opens: *inside/in/at the mouth of a cave.* **4** [C] place where a river enters the sea. **5** [C] (used esp as in the expressions shown) person requiring to be fed: *He left her with three hungry mouths* (ie children) *to feed.* ○ *If she comes to live with us, it'll mean another mouth to feed.* **6** (idm) **born with a silver spoon in one's mouth** ⇨ BORN. **butter wouldn't melt in sb's mouth** ⇨ BUTTER. **by word of mouth** ⇨ WORD. **down in the mouth** dejected; depressed. **from the horse's mouth** ⇨ HORSE. **keep one's ˈmouth shut** *(infml)* not reveal a secret, esp of dishonest or criminal activity: *He'd better keep his mouth shut, or else...!* **leave a bad/nasty taste in the mouth** ⇨ LEAVE[1]. **live from hand to mouth** ⇨ LIVE[2]. **look a gift horse in the mouth** ⇨ GIFT. **out of the mouths of babes and ˈsucklings** *(saying)* children often speak wisely. **put one's money where one's mouth is** ⇨ MONEY. **put words into sb's mouth** ⇨ WORD. **shoot one's mouth off** ⇨ SHOOT[1]. **shut one's mouth/face** ⇨ SHUT. **shut sb's mouth** ⇨ SHUT. **take the bread out of sb's mouth** ⇨ BREAD. **take the words out of sb's mouth** ⇨ WORD.

▷ **-mouthed** /maʊðd/ (forming compound *adjs*) **1** having the specified type of mouth: *small-mouthed, wide-mouthed, open-mouthed, etc.* **2** *(usu derog)* having the specified way of speaking: *loud-mouthed, foul-mouthed, etc.*

mouthful /-fʊl/ *n* **1** [C] as much as can easily be put into the mouth at one time: *eat a few mouthfuls of food* ○ *swallow sth in a/one mouthful.* **2** [sing] *(infml joc)* word or phrase that is too long or difficult to pronounce: *Timothy Thistlethwaite? That's a bit of a mouthful!*

□ **ˈmouth-organ** (also **harmonica**) *n* small musical instrument played by passing it along the lips while blowing or sucking air.

ˈmouthparts *n* jaw-like parts on animals like insects and crabs that can be used for feeding.

ˈmouthpiece *n* **1** part of a musical instrument, pipe, telephone, etc that is placed at or between the lips. ⇨ illus at MUSIC. **2** *(usu derog)* person, newspaper, etc that expresses the opinions of others: *a newspaper which is merely the mouthpiece of the Tory party.*

ˌmouth-to-ˈmouth *adj* [usu attrib] done by placing one's mouth over a dying (esp drowning) person's mouth and breathing into the lungs: *mouth-to-mouth resuscitation.*

ˈmouthwash *n* [U] liquid for cleaning the mouth.

ˈmouthwatering *adj (approv)* that makes one want to eat; extremely delicious: *the mouthwatering smell of freshly baked bread.*

mouth[2] /maʊð/ *v* **1** [I, Tn] speak or say (sth) with movement of the jaw but no sound: *silently mouthing curses.* **2** [Tn] *(derog)* say (sth) insincerely or without understanding: *mouthing the usual platitudes about the need for more compassion.*

movable /ˈmuːvəbl/ *adj* **1** that can be moved: *a machine with a movable arm for picking up objects.* **2** *(law)* (of property) that can be taken from place to place (eg furniture, as distinct from buildings or land, called *real property*). **3** varying in date from year to year: *Christmas is fixed, but Easter is a movable feast.*

▷ **movables** *n* [pl] *(esp law)* personal property; articles that can be removed from a house;

chattels. Cf FITTING[2] 2, FIXTURE 1.

move[1] /muːv/ *n* **1** change of place or position: *She sat in the corner, watching my every move.* ○ *'One false move and you're dead!' he said, pointing a gun at me.* **2** ~ **(from...) (to/into...)** action or process of changing the place where one lives, works, etc: *a move from the town into the country* ○ *a move to a new job/office* ○ *The move took six hours with a team of three men.* **3 (a)** act of changing the position of a piece in chess or other board game: *Do you know all the possible moves in chess?* **(b)** player's turn to do this: *Whose move is it?* **4** ~ **(towards sth/to do sth)** action (to be) done to achieve a purpose: *We've tried peaceful persuasion; what's our next move?* ○ *The government's announcement is seen as a move towards settling the strike.* ○ *In a move to restrict imports, the government raised custom duties.* **5** (idm) **a false move** ⇨ FALSE. **get a ˈmove on** (*infml*) hurry up. **make a ˈmove (a)** set off on a journey; leave: *It's getting dark; we'd better make a move.* **(b)** take action: *We're waiting to see what our competitors do before we make a move.* **on the ˈmove** moving: *The army is on the move.* ○ *Don't jump off a train when it's on the move.*

move[2] /muːv/ *v* **1** [I, Ipr, Ip, Tn, Tn·pr, Tn·p] ~ **(sb/sth) (about/around)** (cause sb/sth to) be in motion, or change position or place: *Don't move; stay perfectly still.* ○ *The leaves were moving in the breeze.* ○ *I could hear someone moving (about/around) in the room above.* ○ *move one's head, arm, leg, etc* ○ *move a chair nearer to the fire* ○ *Has someone moved my book? I left it on this desk.* ○ *She is too ill to be moved.* ○ (*fig*) *That car was really moving!* ie travelling fast. **2** [I, Ipr, Ip] ~ **(from...) (to...)** change residence: *We're moving to Scotland.* ○ *The new neighbours moved in yesterday.* ○ *He couldn't pay his rent, so he had to move out.* **3** [I, Ip] ~ **(ahead/on)** make progress: *work which moves (ahead) steadily, quickly, etc* ○ *Time moves (on)* (ie passes) *slowly.* ○ *Share prices moved ahead* (ie rose) *today.* ○ *Things are not moving as fast as we hoped.* **4** [I, Tn] (in chess and other board games) change the position of (a piece): *It's your turn to move.* **5** [Tn, Tn·pr] ~ **sb (to sth)** cause sb to have very powerful feelings, esp of sadness: *The story of their sufferings moved us deeply.* ○ *move sb to laughter, tears, etc.* **6** [Tn, Cn·t] cause or prompt (sb) (to do or not do sth): *He works as the spirit moves him,* ie when he feels the desire to do so. ○ *It was so odd that I was moved to ask her where she got it.* **7** [Tn, Tf] propose (sth) formally for discussion and decision (at a meeting): *The MP moved an amendment to the Bill.* ○ *Mr Chairman, I move that the matter be discussed after lunch.* **8** [I, Tn] (cause or persuade sb/sth to) change one's attitude: *The government won't move on this issue.* ○ *She's made up her mind and nothing can move her.* **9** [I] take action; do sth: *Unless the employers move quickly, there will be a strike.* ○ *The government has moved to dispel the rumours.* **10** [I, Tn] (*medical or fml*) (of the bowels) be emptied; (of people) empty (the bowels). **11** (idm) **get ˈmoving** begin, leave, etc quickly: *It's late; we'd better get moving.* **get sth ˈmoving** cause sth to make vigorous progress: *A new director in this department will really get things moving.* **go/move in for the kill** ⇨ KILL *n.* **move the ˈgoal-posts** (*Brit infml*) change the accepted conditions within which a particular matter is being discussed or a particular action taken. **move heaven and ˈearth** do everything one possibly can in order to achieve sth. **move ˈhouse** move one's furniture, goods, etc to another place to live in. **12** (phr v) **move across/along/down/over/up** move further in the direction indicated so as to make space for others: *'Move along, please,' said the bus conductor.* ○ *Move over so I can get into bed.* **move for sth** (*US esp law*) request sth formally: *Your honour, I move for an adjournment.* **move in sth** live, be active, pass one's time, etc in a particular social group: *move in high society* ○ *She only moves in the best circles.* **move in on sb/sth** converge on sb/sth, esp in a menacing way: *The police moved in on the (house occupied by the) terrorists.* **move off** (esp of a vehicle) start a journey; leave: *The signal was given, and the procession moved off.* **move on (a)** continue one's journey: *It's time we moved on.* **(b)** move to another place; stop loitering (eg when ordered by the police). **move sb on** (of police) order sb to move away from the scene of an accident, etc.

▷ **mover** /ˈmuːvə(r)/ *n* **1** person who moves: *She's a lovely mover,* ie moves (eg dances) elegantly. **2** person who formally makes a proposal.

moving *adj* **1** [attrib] that moves: *a moving staircase* ○ *a mechanism with no moving parts* ○ *a moving picture,* ie cinema film. **2** causing one to have deep feelings, esp of sadness or sympathy: *a moving story, film, tragedy, etc* ○ *His speech was very moving.* **movingly** *adv.*

movement /ˈmuːvmənt/ *n* **1 (a)** [U, C] moving or being moved: *the movement of his chest as he breathes* ○ *lie still without (making) any movement* ○ *Loose clothing gives you greater freedom of movement.* ○ *I detected a slight movement in the undergrowth.* **(b)** [U] action; activity: *a play, novel, etc that lacks movement.* **2** [C] act of changing position, esp as a military manoeuvre: *Troop movements can be observed from space by a satellite.* **3 movements** [pl] actions, journeys, etc over a period of time (esp as observed and/or recorded by sb else): *The police have been keeping a close watch on the suspects' movements.* **4** [sing] ~ **(away from/towards sth)** trend (in society): *the movement towards greater freedom in fashion styles.* **5** [U, C] ~ **(in sth)** change in amount (esp the rise or fall of prices in a stock market): *not much movement in oil shares.* **6** [CGp, C] ~ **(to do sth)** (group of people with a) shared set of aims or principles: *the aims, members, etc of the Labour Movement* ○ *poets of the Romantic movement* ○ *founding a movement to promote women's rights.* **7** [C] (*music*) any of the main divisions in a long musical work: *a symphony in four movements.* **8** [C] moving parts in a mechanism, esp those in a clock or watch which turn the hands. **9** [C] (*medical or fml*) emptying of the bowels.

movie /ˈmuːvɪ/ *n* (*esp US*) **1** [C] cinema film: *go to (see) a movie* ○ [attrib] *a movie producer* ○ *movie stars.* **2 the movies** [pl] **(a)** (also **movie house, movie theatre**) the cinema: *go to the movies.* **(b)** the film industry: *She is in/works in the movies.*

▷ **ˈmovie-goer** *n* (*esp US*) person who (regularly) goes to the cinema.

mow /məʊ/ *v* (*pt* **mowed**, *pp* **mown** /məʊn/ or **mowed**) **1** [I, Tn] cut (grass, etc) using a machine with blades, or a scythe: *mow the lawn* ○ *mow a field,* ie cut the crops or vegetation in it ○ *the smell of new-mown hay.* **2** (phr v) **mow sb down** kill (people) in large numbers, as if by making a sweeping movement: *soldiers mown down by machine-gun fire* ○ *The lorry's brakes failed, and it mowed down several people in the bus queue.*

▷ **mower** *n* (esp in compounds) machine or person that mows: *a ˈlawn-mower* ○ *an electric mower* ○ *mowers and reapers.*

Mozambique /ˌməʊzæmˈbiːk/ country on the east coast of Africa; pop approx 16 084 000; official language Portuguese; capital Maputo; unit of currency metical (= 100 centavos). The country is generally low-lying, with a long coastal plain. Traditionally it has provided Malawi and Zimbabwe with access to the sea. However, after independence in 1975, a civil war continued to 1993, with both government and rebel forces then delaying the United Nations' timetable for demobilization followed by elections. This has seriously damaged Mozambique's economy, agriculture and transport system. There is little export trade. ⇨ map at NAMIBIA. ▷ **Mozambican** /ˌməʊzæmˈbiːkən/ *n, adj.*

Mozart /ˈməʊtsɑːt/ Wolfgang Amadeus (1756-91), Austrian composer. He was a child prodigy on the harpsichord and violin, and wrote his first works when he was six. His music, regarded as some of the finest ever written, combined an Italian gift for melody with a German sense of technique. It includes over 40 symphonies, 30 concertos and great operas like *The Marriage of Figaro, Don Giovanni* and *The Magic Flute.* ▷ **Mozartian** /ˌməʊtˈzɑːtɪən/ *adj.*

MP /ˌem ˈpiː/ *abbr* **1** (*esp Brit*) Member of Parliament (esp in the House of Commons): *Annie Hill MP* ○ *become an MP.* **2** military police(man).

mpg /ˌem piː ˈdʒiː/ *abbr* miles per gallon: *This car does 40 mpg,* ie of petrol.

mph /ˌem piː ˈeɪtʃ/ *abbr* miles per hour: *a 70 mph speed limit* ○ *driving at a steady 35 mph.* Cf KPH.

MPhil /ˌem ˈfɪl/ *abbr* Master of Philosophy: *have/be an MPhil in English* ○ *Mary Karlinski MPhil.* ⇨ article at POST-SCHOOL.

Mr /ˈmɪstə(r)/ *abbr* **1** title that comes before the (first name and the) surname of a man; Mister: *Mr (John) Brown* ○ *Mr and Mrs Brown.* **2** (*fml*) title for certain men in official positions: *Mr Chairman* ○ (*esp US*) *Mr President.* **3** (*often joc*) title for a man who represents the quality, activity, etc that is mentioned: *Mr Clean,* eg a politician who is considered not to be corrupt ○ (*ironic*) *So what would you do, Mr Clever?* ○ *Mr Baseball,* ie a famous figure in the sport ○ *Mr and Mrs Average,* ie an ordinary married couple ○ *Mr Right,* ie the right man for a woman to marry ○ *Mr Big,* ie a very important person, esp in organized crime.

MRBM /ˌem ɑː biː ˈem/ *abbr* medium-range ballistic missile. Cf ICBM, IRBM.

MRC /ˌem ɑː ˈsiː/ *abbr* (*Brit*) Medical Research Council: *an MRC-funded project.*

Mrs /ˈmɪsɪz/ *abbr* title that comes before the (first name and the) surname of a married woman: *Mrs (Jane) Brown* ○ (*fml sexist*) *Mrs John Brown* ○ (*Brit joc*) *Mrs Mopp,* ie a typical cleaning woman. Cf MISS[2], MISSUS, MISTER.

MS *abbr* **1** (*pl* **MSS**) manuscript. **2** multiple sclerosis.

Ms /mɪz/ *abbr* title that comes before the (first name and the) surname of a woman whether married or unmarried: *Ms (Mary) Green.* Cf MISS[2], MISTER.

MSc /ˌem es ˈsiː/ *abbr* Master of Science: *have/be an MSc in Chemistry* ○ *Wendy O'Connor MSc.* ⇨ article at POST-SCHOOL EDUCATION.

MSF /ˌem es ˈef/ *abbr* Manufacturing, Science, Finance (a British trade union for white-collar workers). ⇨ article at TRADE UNION.

MST /ˌem es ˈtiː/ *abbr* (*US*) Mountain Standard Time. Cf MDT.

Mt *abbr* Mount: *Mt Kenya,* eg on a map.

mth *abbr* (*US* **mo**) (*pl* **mths**; *US* **mos**) month: *6 mths old.*

much[1] /mʌtʃ/ *indef det, indef pron* (used with [U] *ns*; esp with negative and interrogative *vs* or after *as, how, so, too*) **1** a large amount or quantity (of sth). **(a)** (*det*): *I haven't got much money.* ○ *There's never very much news on Sundays.* ○ *Did you have much difficulty finding the house?* ○ *How much* (ie What volume of) *petrol do you need?* ○ *Take as much time as you like.* ○ *There was so much traffic that we were stationary for half an hour.* ○ *I have much pleasure in introducing our speaker.* ○ *After much applause the audience went home.* **(b)** (*pron*): *He sat at his desk all morning but he didn't write much.* ○ *'Is there any mail?' 'Not (very) much.'* ○ *She never eats much for breakfast.* ○ *Did the President say much to you?* ○ *How much is it?* ie What is its price? ○ *Eat as much as you can.* ○ *He drank (far) too much last night.* ○ *You'll find you have much to learn in your new job.* ○ *I lay awake much of the night.* ○ *We have much to be thankful for.* **2** (idm) **not much of a** not a good (sth): *He's not much of a cricketer.* ○ *I'm not much of a correspondent,* ie I rarely write letters. **(with) not/without so much as** ⇨ SO[1]. **ˈthis much** what I am about to say: *I will say this much for him — he never leaves a piece of work unfinished.* ○ *This much is certain, you will never walk again.*

▷ **muchness** *n* (idm) **ˌmuch of a ˈmuchness** very similar; almost alike: *It's hard to choose between the two candidates: they're both much of a muchness.*

much[2] /mʌtʃ/ *adv* to a great extent or degree. **1** (often used with negative *vs*): *She didn't enjoy the film (very) much.* ○ *He isn't in the office (very) much,* ie often. ○ *I would very much like you to come to dinner next week.* ○ *It doesn't much matter what* you wear. ○ *Much to her surprise he came back next day.* **2** (**a**) (with past participles used adjectivally and *afraid, alive, aware,* etc): *I was very much frightened by the report.* ○ *He was (very) much surprised to find us there.* ○ *I'm very much aware of the lack of food supplies.* (**b**) (used with comparatives and superlatives): *much slower, bigger, heavier, etc* ○ *much harder, faster, louder, etc* ○ *much more expensive* ○ *much more confidently* ○ *She's much better today.* ○ *That was much the best meal I've ever tasted.* ○ *My favourite is usually much the most expensive.* ○ *I would never willingly go anywhere by boat, much less go on a cruise.* ⇨ Usage at VERY. **3** (idm) **as much** the same; equal(ly): *Please help me get this job — you know I would do as much for you.* ○ *That is as much as saying I am a liar.* ○ *I thought/said/knew as much.* ie My thoughts/statements/beliefs are confirmed. **as much as sb can do** the maximum that sb can do: *I won't have a pudding — it was as much as I could do to finish the very large first course.* **much as** although: *Much as I would like to stay, I really must go home.* ˌ**much the ˈsame** in about the same condition: *The patient is much the same this morning.* **not much good at sth** (*infml*) not very good at (doing) sth: *I'm not much good at tennis.* **not so much sth as sth** ⇨ so[1].

EXPRESSING QUANTITY

	uncountable nouns	countable nouns
positive statements	lots of money (*less fml*)	lots of coins (*less fml*)
	a lot of money	a lot of coins
	much money (*more fml*)	many coins (*more fml*)
negative statements	not much money	not many coins
	little money (*more fml*)	few coins (*more fml*)
questions	How much money?	How many coins?

1 Notice the difference between **little**/**few** and **a little**/**a few**. If we say, *'I have little money and few interests'*, we sound disappointed and negative. If we say, *'I have a little money and a few interests'*, we sound more positive. Compare: *He's lived here a long time but has few friends* and *He's lived here a short time but already has a few friends.*

2 **A lot of** can also be used in questions: *Have we got a lot of time/cards left?* It suggests that the speaker knows that there is/are some left and wants to know whether the amount/number is big or small.

3 The comparative and superlative forms of **much**, **many**, and **a lot of** are **more** and (**the**) **most**. For **little** the comparative and superlative forms are **less** and (**the**) **least** and for **few** they are **fewer** and (**the**) **fewest**.

mucilage /ˈmju:sɪlɪdʒ/ *n* [U] thick sticky fluid produced by plants, esp seaweed.

▷ **mucilaginous** /ˌmju:sɪˈlædʒɪnəs/ *adj* **1** producing mucilage. **2** (*fml*) (of liquid) (unpleasantly) thick and sticky.

muck /mʌk/ *n* **1** [U] excrement of farm animals, esp as used for fertilizing; manure: *spreading muck on the fields* ○ [attrib] *a ˈmuck heap.* **2** [U] (*infml esp Brit*) dirt; filth; anything disgusting: *Don't come in here with your boots all covered in muck.* ○ *Do you call that food? I'm not eating that muck!* ○ (*fig*) *You shouldn't believe all the muck and scandal you read in the Sunday papers.* ○ *I don't want my name dragged through the muck,* ie mentioned contemptuously, in connection with scandal. **3** (idm) **common as dirt/muck** ⇨ COMMON[1]. **in a ˈmuck** (*Brit infml*) in an untidy state: *You can't leave your room in a muck like that.* **make a muck of sth** (*infml*) (**a**) make sth dirty. (**b**) do sth badly; spoil sth; bungle sth: *I made a real muck of that exam.* ˌ**where there's ˌmuck there's ˈbrass** (*Brit saying*) money can usu be made from work which makes people dirty.

▷ **muck** *v* (phr v) **muck about/around** (*Brit infml*) behave in an aimless and silly way; waste time in useless activity: *Stop mucking about and finish your work!* **muck in** (*Brit infml*) share tasks or accommodation equally: *Let's all muck in together, and we'll soon finish the job.* ○ *The officers had to muck in with their men.* **muck (sth) out** clean out (stables, etc) by removing excrement. **muck sth up** (*infml esp Brit*) (**a**) make sth dirty: *muck up one's clothes.* (**b**) do sth badly; spoil sth; bungle sth: *I really mucked up my chances by doing badly in the interview.*

mucky *adj* (**-ier, -iest**) **1** dirty: *My hands are all mucky.* **2** obscene; rude: *telling those mucky stories of his.*

□ ˈ**muck-raker** *n* (*derog*) person who tries to find out bad things that people have done and spread scandal about them. ˈ**muck-raking** *n* [U] (*derog*) activity of a muck-raker.

ˈ**muck-up** *n* (usu *sing*) (*infml esp Brit*) act of bungling or spoiling sth; mess: *make a complete muck-up of sth.*

mucous /ˈmju:kəs/ *adj* of, like or covered with mucus.

□ ˌ**mucous ˈmembrane** (*anatomy*) moist skin that lines the nose, mouth and certain internal organs and produces mucus.

mucus /ˈmju:kəs/ *n* [U] **1** sticky slimy substance produced by the mucous membrane which protects and lubricates the interior of the nose, breathing passages, etc: *a nose blocked with mucus.* **2** any similar slimy substance: *a trail of mucus left by a snail or slug.*

mud /mʌd/ *n* [U] **1** soft wet earth: *rain that turns dust into mud* ○ *My shoes were covered/plastered in/with mud.* ○ *The armies got bogged down in the thick squelching mud.* **2** (idm) **clear as mud** ⇨ CLEAR[1]. **drag sb/sb's name through the mire/mud** ⇨ DRAG[2]. **fling, sling, throw, etc ˈmud (at sb)** try to damage sb's reputation (by slander, libel, etc). ˌ**mud ˈsticks** (*saying*) people tend to believe and remember bad or slanderous things said about sb. **sb's name is mud** ⇨ NAME[1].

▷ **muddy** *adj* (**-ier, -iest**) **1** full of or covered in mud: *muddy roads, shoes.* **2** (**a**) (of liquids or colours) coloured by or like mud; not clear; thick like mud: *a muddy stream* ○ *muddy water* ○ *muddy coffee* ○ *clothes of a muddy* (ie brownish) *green.* (**b**) (*fig derog*) not clear; confused: *muddy thinking.* **muddiness** *n* [U].

muddy *v* (*pt, pp* **muddied**) **1** [Tn] make (sb/sth) muddy: *muddy one's face, clothes.* **2** (idm) **muddy the ˈwaters** (*derog*) make a situation confused and unclear.

□ ˈ**mud-bath** *n* bath in mud believed to have health-giving qualities (eg in treating rheumatism): (*fig*) *The pitch was a mud-bath after the heavy rain.*

ˈ**mud-flat** *n* (often *pl*) (stretch of) muddy land covered by the sea at high tide.

ˈ**mudguard** *n* curved cover over a wheel (of a bicycle, etc). ⇨ illus at BICYCLE.

ˌ**mud ˈhut** simple hut made of mud that has dried and hardened.

ˈ**mud pack** paste applied thickly to the face, for improving the health and appearance of the skin.

ˈ**mud-slinging** *n* [U] (*derog*) trying to damage sb's reputation by saying bad things about him: *There's too much mud-slinging by irresponsible journalists.*

ˌ**mud volˈcano** cone-shaped hill of hardened mud usu formed by the pressure of underground gas.

muddle /ˈmʌdl/ *v* **1** [Tn, Tn·p] (**a**) ~ **sth (up)** put sth into disorder; mix sth up: *The cleaner had muddled my papers, and I couldn't find the one I wanted.* ○ *My papers were all muddled up together.* (**b**) ~ **sb (up)** confuse sb mentally: *Stop talking, or you'll muddle me (up) completely.* (**c**) ~ **sb/sth (up)** be confused about two or more things, people, etc and therefore make mistakes in arrangements: *I muddled (up) the dates and arrived three days late.* **2** [Tn·pr, Tn·p] ~ **A (up) with B**; ~ **A and B (up)** fail to distinguish two people or things: *You must be muddling me up with my twin brother.* **3** (phr v) **muddle along** (*derog*) live one's life in a foolish or helpless way, with no clear purpose or plan: *We muddle along from day to day.* **muddle through** (*often joc*) achieve one's aims even though one does not act efficiently, have the proper equipment, etc: *I expect we shall muddle through somehow!*

▷ **muddle** *n* ~ (**about/over sth**) **1** [C] state of untidiness or confusion: *Your room's in a real muddle.* ○ *There was a muddle over our hotel accommodation.* **2** [sing] mental confusion: *The old lady gets in(to) a muddle trying to work the video.*

muddled *adj* confused: *muddled thinking.*

muddling *adj* confusing: *These government forms are very muddling.*

□ ˌ**muddle-ˈheaded** *adj* lacking clearness of thought; confused: *muddle-headed people, ideas, arguments.* ˌ**muddle-ˈheadedness** *n* [U].

muesli /ˈmju:zlɪ/ *n* [U] breakfast food that is a mixture of uncooked cereal, nuts, dried fruit, etc.

muezzin /mu:ˈezɪn; *US* mju:-/ *n* man who calls out the hours of prayer for Muslims, usu from the minaret of a mosque.

muff[1] /mʌf/ *n* hollow roll of fur or other warm material used to keep the hands warm in cold weather. ⇨ illus at DRESS.

muff[2] /mʌf/ *v* [Tn] (*infml derog*) fail to catch or seize (sth); miss; bungle: *The fielder muffed an easy catch.* ○ *She had a wonderful opportunity, but she muffed it.*

muffin /ˈmʌfɪn/ *n* **1** (*Brit*) (*US* ˌ**English ˈmuffin**) small flat round bun, usu toasted and eaten hot with butter. **2** (*US*) small sweet bread roll or cake, often eaten with butter.

muffle /ˈmʌfl/ *v* **1** [Tn, Tn·pr, Tn·p] ~ **sb/sth (up) (in sth)** wrap or cover sb/sth for warmth or protection: *He walked out into the snow, heavily muffled (up) in a thick scarf and warm overcoat.* **2** [Tn, Tn·pr] ~ **sth (with sth)** make the sound of sth (eg a bell or a drum) quieter by wrapping it, covering it in cloth, etc: *muffle the oars of a boat,* ie wrap the blades to stop them splashing noisily.

▷ **muffled** *adj* (of sounds) heard indistinctly, because an obstacle is in the way: *muffled voices coming from the next room.*

muffler /ˈmʌflə(r)/ *n* **1** (*dated*) scarf or other cloth worn round the neck for warmth. **2** (*US*) = SILENCER.

mufti /ˈmʌftɪ/ *n* [U] ordinary clothes worn by people (eg soldiers) who normally wear uniform in their job: *Soldiers wear mufti on leave, not uniform.* ○ *officers in mufti.*

mug[1] /mʌg/ *n* **1** (**a**) (usu straight-sided, fairly large) drinking vessel of china, metal or plastic with a handle, for use without a saucer: *a coffee mug.* (**b**) its contents: *a mug of coffee.* ⇨ illus at CUP. **2** (*sl derog or joc*) face: *What an ugly mug!*

▷ ˈ**mugful** /-fʊl/ *n* amount (of tea, coffee, etc) contained in a mug: *drink two mugfuls.*

□ ˈ**mug shot** (*sl*) photograph of sb's face, esp one kept in police records.

mug[2] /mʌg/ *n* (*infml*) **1** person who is easily deceived. **2** (idm) **a ˈmug's game** (*derog esp Brit*) activity unlikely to be successful or profitable: *Trying to sell overcoats in midsummer is a real mug's game.*

mug[3] /mʌg/ *v* (**-gg-**) (phr v) **mug sth up** (*Brit infml*) (try to) learn sth, usu in a short time for a special purpose (eg an exam): *mugging up the Highway Code before a driving-test.*

mug[4] /mʌg/ *v* (**-gg-**) [Tn] (*infml*) attack and rob (sb) violently out of doors: *an old lady mugged by a gang of youths in the park.*

▷ **mugger** *n* person who does this.

mugging *n* [C, U] such an attack or attacks: *several reported muggings.*

muggins /ˈmʌgɪnz/ *n* [sing] (*Brit infml joc*) (used esp self-mockingly) foolish person: *Don't do that, you silly muggins!* ○ *Muggins here locked his keys in the car!*

muggy /ˈmʌgɪ/ *adj* (**-ier, -iest**) (of weather) oppressively warm and damp: *a muggy August day.* ▷ **mugginess** *n* [U].

mugwump /ˈmʌgwʌmp/ *n* (*esp US usu derog*) person who does not wish to be committed or involved, esp in political matters.

Muhammad (also **Mohammed**) /məˈhæmɪd/ (c 570-632 AD), founder of *Islam, born in *Mecca. He began his teaching after visions in which he received from God the words of the *Koran. Rejected and exiled from Mecca, he later returned to begin the conversion of the Arabian peninsula to Islam. He replaced the tribal and pagan society with a new social and monotheistic religious structure. Muslims call him the Prophet, last in the line of Abraham, Moses and Jesus.

▷ **Muhammadan** (also **Muhammedan, Mohammedan**) /-ən/ *adj, n* (of or being a) Muslim. **Muhammadanism** (also **Muhammedanism, Mohammedanism**) /məˈhæmɪdənɪzəm/ *n* [U] Islam (the preferred name). ⇨ Usage at CHRISTIAN.

mulatto /mju:ˈlætəʊ; *US* məˈl-/ *n* (*pl* ~**s** or *esp US* ~**es**) person who has one black parent and one white.

mulberry /ˈmʌlbrɪ; *US* ˈmʌlberɪ/ *n* (**a**) tree with broad, dark-green leaves on which silkworms feed. (**b**) its purple or white fruit: [attrib] *mulberry juice.*

mulch /mʌltʃ/ *n* protective covering (eg of straw, rotting leaves, or plastic sheeting) spread over the roots of trees and bushes, to retain moisture, kill weeds, etc.

▷ **mulch** *v* [Tn] cover (plant roots or the ground round them) with a mulch.

mule[1] /mju:l/ *n* **1** animal that is the offspring of a donkey and a horse, used for carrying loads and noted for its stubbornness. **2** (*fig infml*) stubborn person. **3** (idm) **(as) ˌobstinate/ˌstubborn as a ˈmule** very obstinate or stubborn.

▷ **muleteer** /ˌmju:ləˈtɪə(r)/ *n* (*dated*) person who leads mules.

mulish *adj* stubborn; obstinate. **mulishly** *adv.* **mulishness** *n* [U].

mule[2] /mju:l/ *n* slipper that is open around the heel.

mull[1] /mʌl/ *v* [Tn] make (wine, beer, etc) into a hot drink with sugar, spices, etc: *mulled claret.*

mull[2] /mʌl/ *n* (*Scot*) (esp in place-names) long piece of land sticking out into the sea: *the Mull of Kintyre.*

mull[3] /mʌl/ *v* (phr v) **mull sth over** think about or consider sth long and carefully: *I haven't decided yet; I'm mulling it over in my mind.*

mullah /ˈmʌlə/ *n* Muslim teacher of theology and sacred law.

mullet /ˈmʌlɪt/ *n* (*pl* unchanged) any of several types of seafish used as food, esp **red mullet** and **grey mullet**.

mulligan /ˈmʌlɪgən/ *n* [U, C] (also ˌ**mulligan** ˈ**stew**) (*US*) stew made from food left over from previous meals.

mulligatawny /ˌmʌlɪgəˈtɔ:nɪ/ *n* [U] thick, highly seasoned soup with curry powder in it.

mullion /ˈmʌlɪən/ *n* vertical (stone, wood or metal) division between two parts of a window, esp in a large old building. ⇨ illus at CHURCH.

▷ **mullioned** /ˈmʌlɪənd/ *adj* having mullions.

multi- *comb form* having many of: *multicoloured* ○ *a ˌmultimillioˈnaire*, ie a person having more than two million pounds, dollars, etc ○ *a ˌmultiracial comˈmunity, soˈciety, ˈcountry, etc*, ie with many different races ○ *a ˌmulti-storey ˈcar-park*, ie consisting of a building with several floors.

multicellular /ˌmʌltɪˈseljʊlə(r)/ *adj* (of tissue, organs or organisms) made up of many cells. Cf UNICELLULAR.

multifarious /ˌmʌltɪˈfeərɪəs/ *adj* (*fml*) of many different kinds; having great variety: *the multifarious life-forms that can be found in a coral reef* ○ *the multifarious rules and regulations of the bureaucracy.*

multilateral /ˌmʌltɪˈlætərəl/ *adj* involving two or more participants: *a ˌmultilateral aˈgreement* ○ *ˌmultilateral nuclear disˈarmament*, ie involving all or most countries which have nuclear weapons. Cf BILATERAL, UNILATERAL.

multilingual /ˌmʌltɪˈlɪŋgwəl/ *adj* **1** speaking or using many languages: *India is a ˌmultilingual ˈcountry.* **2** written or printed, in many languages: *a ˈmultilingual ˈdictionary, ˈphrasebook, eˈdition, etc* ○ *electrical goods sold with ˌmultilingual ˈoperating instructions.* Cf BILINGUAL, MONOLINGUAL.

multinational /ˌmʌltɪˈnæʃnəl/ *adj* involving many countries: *a multinational organization, operation, agreement.*

▷ **multinational** *n* (usu very large) company that does business in many different countries: *Some people believe that the multinationals have too much power.*

multiple /ˈmʌltɪpl/ *adj* [attrib] having or involving many individuals, items or types: *a multiple crash on a motorway*, ie one involving many vehicles ○ *person with multiple injuries*, ie with many cuts, broken bones, etc.

▷ **multiple** *n* **1** (*mathematics*) quantity which contains another quantity an exact number of times: *14, 21 and 28 are multiples of 7.* ○ *30 is a common multiple of 2, 3, 5, 6, 10 and 15.* ○ *least/lowest common multiple*, ie smallest quantity that contains two or more given quantities exactly (usu shortened to *LCM*, eg *The LCM of 4, 5, 6, 10 and 12 is 60*). **2** (also ˌ**multiple** ˈ**store**) (*esp Brit*) shop with many branches throughout a country.

□ ˌ**multiple-ˈchoice** *adj* (of examination questions) showing several possible answers from which the correct one must be chosen.

ˌ**multiple scleˈrosis** (*abbr* **MS**) disease of the nervous system causing gradual paralysis.

multiplex /ˈmʌltɪpleks/ *adj* [usu attrib] (*fml*) having many parts or forms; consisting of many (usu complex) elements.

multiplicand /ˌmʌltɪplɪˈkænd/ *n* number or mathematical expression that is to be multiplied by another.

multiplication /ˌmʌltɪplɪˈkeɪʃn/ *n* **1** [U] multiplying or being multiplied: *children learning to do multiplication and division* ○ *an organism that grows by the multiplication of its cells* ○ [attrib] *the multiplication sign/symbol* ×. **2** [C] instance of this: *2 × 3 is an easy multiplication.*

□ ˌ**multiplicˈation table** list showing the results when a number is multiplied by a set of other numbers (esp 1 to 12) in turn.

multiplicity /ˌmʌltɪˈplɪsətɪ/ *n* [sing] ~ **of sth** large number or great variety of things: *a computer with a multiplicity of* (ie many) *uses.*

multiply /ˈmʌltɪplaɪ/ *v* (*pt, pp* **-lied**) **1** [I, Tn, Tn·pr, Tn·p] ~ **A by B**/~ **A and B (together)** add a number to itself a particular number of times: *children learning to multiply and divide* ○ *2 and 3 multiply to make 6*, ie 2 × 3 = 2 + 2 + 2 = 6. ○ *2 multiplied by 4 makes 8*, ie 2 × 4 = 8. ○ *One can make 12 by multiplying 2 and 6 (together) or 4 and 3 (together)*, ie 12 = 2 × 6 or 4 × 3. **2** [I, Tn] increase (sth) in number or quantity: *Our problems have multiplied since last year.* ○ *Buy lots of raffle tickets and multiply your chances of success.* **3** [I, Tn] (*biology*) (cause sb/sth to) produce large numbers of offspring by procreation, fertilization, etc: *Rabbits multiply rapidly.* ○ *It is possible to multiply bacteria and other living organisms in the laboratory.*

▷ **multiplier** /ˈmʌltɪplaɪə(r)/ *n* **1** number or mathematical expression by which another is multiplied. **2** (*economics*) number expressing the relationship between an amount of extra money invested in sth and the amount of extra income it eventually produces. **3** instrument that increases a small current, etc, so that it can be used or measured more easily.

multitude /ˈmʌltɪtju:d; *US* -tu:d/ *n* (*fml*) **1** [C] ~ **(of sb/sth)** extremely large number of people or things (esp of people gathered or moving about in one area): *A large multitude had assembled to hear him preach.* ○ *Vast multitudes of birds visit this lake in spring.* ○ *just one of a multitude of problems, reasons, etc.* **2 the multitude** [Gp] (*sometimes derog*) ordinary people; the masses: *special qualities which mark her out from the multitude* ○ *demagogues who appeal to the multitude.* **3** (idm) **cover/hide a multitude of sins** (*often joc*) conceal a (usu unpleasant) reality: *The description 'produce of more than one country' can cover a multitude of sins.*

▷ **multitudinous** /ˌmʌltɪˈtju:dɪnəs; *US* -ˈtu:dɪnəs/ *adj* (*fml*) extremely large in number: *multitudinous crowds, problems, debts.*

multi-user /ˌmʌltɪ ˈju:zə(r)/ *adj* (of a computer system) that allows several users at different terminals to use the central processor at the same time.

mum[1] /mʌm/ *adj* (*Brit infml*) **1** silent: *keep mum*, ie say nothing. **2** (idm) ˌ**mum's the** ˈ**word!** (*Brit infml*) (used when asking sb to keep a secret) say nothing about this.

mum[2] /mʌm/ (*US* usu **mom** /mɒm/) *n* (*infml*) mother: *This is my mum.* ○ *Hello, mum!*

mumble /ˈmʌmbl/ *v* [I, Ipr, Tn, Tf, Dn·pr] ~ **(about sth)**; ~ **sth (to sb)** speak or say sth unclearly and usu quietly, so that people cannot hear what is said: *He always mumbles when he's embarrassed.* ○ *What are you mumbling about? I can't understand a word!* ○ *He mumbled something to me which I didn't quite catch.* ○ *She mumbled that she didn't want to get up yet.*

▷ **mumble** *n* [sing] speech that is not heard clearly; noise like this: *a mumble of voices, conversation, etc* ○ *an incoherent, indistinct, distant, etc mumble.*

mumbler /ˈmʌmblə(r)/ *n.*

mumbo-jumbo /ˌmʌmbəʊ ˈdʒʌmbəʊ/ *n* [U] (*infml derog*) **1** complicated but meaningless ritual: *go through the mumbo-jumbo of joining a secret society.* **2** meaningless or unnecessarily complicated language: *These government forms are full of such mumbo-jumbo, I can't understand them at all.*

mummer /ˈmʌmə(r)/ *n* actor in an old form of drama without words.

▷ **mumming** /ˈmʌmɪŋ/ *n* [U] performance of such drama.

□ ˈ**mummers' play** traditional English folk play that originated in country areas. The plot involves a fight between St George and a Turkish knight; one of them is killed and a doctor brings him back to life. This suggests the theme of the earth's death in winter and resurrection in spring. Mummers' plays were very popular in the 19th century.

mummify /ˈmʌmɪfaɪ/ *v* (*pt, pp* **-fied**) [Tn] preserve (a corpse) by treating it with special oils and wrapping it in cloth: *a mummified body.* Cf EMBALM.

▷ **mummification** /ˌmʌmɪfɪˈkeɪʃn/ *n* [U] this method of preservation.

mummy[1] /ˈmʌmɪ/ *n* body of a human being or animal that has been mummified for burial: *an Egyptian mummy.*

mummy[2] /ˈmʌmɪ/ (*US* usu **mommy** /ˈmɒmɪ/) *n* (*infml*) (used mainly by young children) mother.

mumps /mʌmps/ *n* [sing *v*] disease with painful swellings in the neck, caught esp by children.

munch /mʌntʃ/ *v* [I, Ipr, Tn] ~ **(at/on sth)** chew (sth) with much movement of the jaw: *munch (at/on) an apple.*

Münchausen /ˈmʊntʃaʊzn/ Baron, hero of a series of amazing adventures in a book by the German writer Rudolph Raspe (1737-94). He is based on a real 18th-century German soldier who was said to have exaggerated his deeds of bravery, and the name is now used for people who tell incredible stories about themselves.

munchies /ˈmʌntʃɪz/ *n* [pl] (*infml*) **1** light snacks. **2** (idm) **have the** ˈ**munchies** (*US*) be slightly hungry.

mundane /mʌnˈdeɪn/ *adj* (*often derog*) ordinary and typically unexciting: *I lead a pretty mundane life; nothing interesting ever happens to me.* ○ *a mundane book, film, etc.*

mung bean /ˌmʌŋ ˈbi:n/ type of bean grown esp to produce bean sprouts.

Munich /ˈmju:nɪk/ city in SW Germany, the capital of *Bavaria; German name **München**. It is an important economic and cultural centre, famous for its October beer festival.

□ **the** ˈ**Munich agreement** agreement signed in Munich in 1938 between Britain, France, Germany and Italy, which allowed Hitler's Germany to take

Museums

In both Britain and the USA, museums are considered an important part of the national heritage. Britain's most frequently visited museum, the British Museum in London, is also its largest. It was founded in 1753 and is especially famous for its collection of antiquities and as the home, until the early 1990s, of the British Library.

The oldest museum in Britain is the Ashmolean in Oxford, founded in 1683. It has collections of ancient history, fine art and archaeology. Many of the most important specialist museums, however, are in London. They include the museums built in South Kensington after the Great Exhibition of 1851: the Victoria and Albert Museum, which specializes in applied art, the Science Museum, especially popular with children, and the Natural History Museum. Also in London are the Museum of London, illustrating the capital's history, the Imperial War Museum and the London Transport Museum. One of the most recently founded museums is the Museum of the Moving Image, which specializes in the history of film and television. Important art collections in London are those of the National Gallery and the National Portrait Gallery, next door to each other in Trafalgar Square, and the Tate Gallery, with its collections of British art and international modern art.

Outside London, well-known museums and collections include the Fitzwilliam Museum in Cambridge, the City Museum and Art Gallery in Birmingham, the City Art Gallery in Leeds, and the Yorvik Centre in York, a reconstruction of the city's Viking settlement. Liverpool has the Tate Gallery of the North as an extension of the Tate Gallery in London. It also has the Walker Art Gallery, one of the finest in the country. Museums of specialist interest outside London include the National Railway Museum in York and the National Museum of Photography, Film and Television in Bradford.

Scottish collections include those of the National Gallery of Scotland, the Scottish National Portrait Gallery and the Scottish National Gallery of Modern Art, which are all in Edinburgh. Glasgow has the important Burrell Collection, donated to the city in 1944 by the ship-owner and collector Sir William Burrell.

Many famous museums began as private collections. The Ashmolean houses the collection donated to Oxford University by Elias Ashmole. The Tate opened in 1897 with the financial support of Sir Henry Tate. The Fitzwilliam was built to house the collection bequeathed to Cambridge University in 1816 by Viscount Fitzwilliam.

Smaller museums in Britain include the town museums owned by many local councils, often showing collections of local history. The homes of famous people, especially writers, are often preserved as museums. One of the most frequently visited is Shakespeare's birthplace in Stratford-upon-Avon. The homes of Jane Austen, Dickens, Wordsworth, Keats and Samuel Johnson are also preserved.

Many of the newer museums are 'living' museums that aim to recreate the lives of ordinary people or show how things were made in the past. An example of the latter is the Gladstone Pottery Museum near Stoke-on-Trent where potters can be seen at work in a Victorian pottery.

The first public museum to open in the USA was the Charlestown Museum in South Carolina, which was founded in 1773. The country's largest museum complex, however, is the Smithsonian Institution in Washington DC, a group of 14 individual museums, including the Frier Gallery of Art, the Cooper-Hewitt Museum of Decorative Arts and Design, the National Museum of History and Technology, and a number of other scientific collections. The Smithsonian's National Air and Space Museum, which was opened in 1976, is one of the most popular museums in the USA. Important art collections include those of the Metropolitan Museum of Art, the Museum of Modern Art and the Guggenheim Museum of Modern Art, which are all in New York.

As in Britain, the houses of famous people are often preserved as museums. Among the best known are Arlington House, Virginia, the home of Robert E Lee, Abraham Lincoln's birthplace at Hodgenville in Kentucky, Franklin D Roosevelt's birthplace and home, including the 'Summer White House' in New York, and Longfellow's home in Cambridge, Massachusetts.

possession of part of Czechoslavakia. It is remembered as an act of appeasement which failed to prevent Hitler from further acts of aggression.

municipal /mju:ˈnɪsɪpl/ *adj* [usu attrib] of a town or city with its own local government: *municipal buildings*, eg town hall, public library ○ *municipal affairs, elections*, ie of the local council and its members ○ *the municipal transport system, rubbish dump*.

▷ **municipality** /mju:ˌnɪsɪˈpælətɪ/ *n* town, city or district with its own local government; governing body of such a town, etc.

munificent /mju:ˈnɪfɪsnt/ *adj* (*fml*) extremely generous; (of sth given) large in amount or splendid in quality: *a munificent giver, gift*.

▷ **munificence** /-sns/ *n* [U] (*fml*) great generosity: *overwhelmed by their munificence*.

munificently *adv*.

muniments /ˈmju:nɪmənts/ *n* [pl] (*law*) documents kept as evidence of rights or privileges.

munitions /mju:ˈnɪʃnz/ *n* [pl] military supplies, esp guns, shells, bombs, etc: *The war was lost because of a shortage of munitions.* ○ [attrib] *a munitions worker, factory*.

▷ **munition** *v* [Tn, Tn·pr] ~ **sth (with sth)** provide sth with munitions: *munitioning the fleet (with fresh supplies of shells)*.

muntjak (also **muntjac**) /ˈmʌntdʒæk/ *n* small SE Asian deer.

muon /ˈmju:ɒn/ *n* unstable elementary particle, similar to the electron but having a mass 200 times greater.

Muppet /ˈmʌpɪt/ *n* any of a range of puppet characters in a popular television comedy series.

mural /ˈmjʊərəl/ *n* (usu large) painting done on a wall.

▷ **mural** *adj* of or on a wall: *mural art, tiles etc.*

murder /ˈmɜ:də(r)/ *n* **1** (**a**) [U] unlawful killing of a human being intentionally: *commit murder* ○ *be guilty of murder* ○ *the murder of a six-year-old child* ○ [attrib] *Her latest book's a murder mystery.* (**b**) [C] instance of this: *six murders in one week.* Cf HOMICIDE 1, MANSLAUGHTER (MAN[1]). **2** [U] (*derog*) sacrifice of large numbers of people (esp in war): *10 000 men died in one battle: it was sheer murder.* **3** [U] (*fig infml*) (**a**) very difficult or frustrating experience: *It's murder trying to find a parking place for the car.* (**b**) ~ (**on sth**) thing that causes great harm or discomfort (to sth): *This hot weather's murder on my feet.* **4** (idm) ˌ**get away with** ˈ**murder** (*infml esp joc*) succeed in ignoring rules, ordinary standards, etc without being punished, corrected, etc: *His latest book is rubbish. He seems to think that because he's a famous author he can get away with murder!* ˌ**murder will** ˈ**out** (*saying*) a crime such as murder cannot be hidden. **scream, etc blue murder** ⇨ BLUE[1].

▷ **murder** *v* **1** [I, Tn, Tn·pr] ~ **sb (with sth)** kill sb unlawfully and intentionally: *He murdered his wife with a knife.* **2** [Tn] (*fig infml*) spoil (sth) by lack of skill or knowledge: *murder a piece of music*, ie play it very badly ○ *murder the English language*, ie speak or write in a way that shows ignorance of correct usage. **3** [Tn] (*sl*) defeat (eg an opponent) heavily: *I murdered him at chess.* ○ *murder the opposition*, eg an opposing team.

murderer /ˈmɜ:dərə(r)/ *n* person guilty of murder: *a mass murderer*, ie one who has killed many people.

murderess /ˈmɜ:dərɪs/ *n* female murderer.

murderous /ˈmɜ:dərəs/ *adj* **1** intending or likely to murder: *a murderous villain, look, attack* ○ *a murderous-looking knife.* **2** (*infml*) very severe or unpleasant: *I couldn't withstand the murderous heat.* **murderously** *adv*.

Murdoch /ˈmɜ:dɒk/ Iris (1919-), British novelist. She was a lecturer in philosophy at Oxford University and has written on *Sartre. The complex plots of novels like *The Good Apprentice* and *A Severed Head* deal with the themes of good and evil in modern society.

murk /mɜ:k/ *n* [U] darkness; gloom: *peering through the murk*.

▷ **murky** *adj* (**-ier, -iest**) **1** unpleasantly dark; gloomy: *a murky night, with no moon* ○ *The light was too murky to continue playing.* ○ *London's streets, murky with November fog.* **2** (of water) dirty; unclear: *She threw it into the river's murky depths.* **3** (*fig derog or joc*) (of people's actions or character) not known but suspected of being immoral or dishonest: *She had a decidedly murky past.* **murkily** /-ɪlɪ/ *adv*.

murmur /ˈmɜ:mə(r)/ *n* **1** low continuous indistinct sound: *the murmur of bees in the garden* ○ *the distant murmur of the sea, of a brook, of traffic, etc.* **2** quietly spoken word(s): *a murmur of conversation, of voices from the next room, etc.* **3** quiet expression of feeling: *There were murmurs of discontent from the work-force.* **4** (*medical*) faint blowing sound in the chest, usu a sign of disease or damage in the heart. **5** (idm) **with**ˌ**out a** ˈ**murmur** without complaining: *He paid the extra cost without a murmur.*

▷ **murmur** *v* **1** [I] make a murmur: *The wind murmured in the trees.* ○ *a murmuring brook.* **2** [Ipr, Tn, Tf] ~ **about sth** say (sth) in a low voice: *He was delirious, murmuring about his childhood.* ○ *murmuring words of love into her ear* ○ *He murmured that he wanted to sleep.* **3** [Ipr] ~ **against sb/sth** complain about sb/sth quietly, not openly: *For some years the people had been murmuring against the government.*

murmurous /ˈmɜ:mərəs/ *adj* (*esp rhet*) consisting of a low continuous indistinct sound: *the murmurous hum of bees*.

Murphy bed /ˈmɜ:fɪ bed/ (*US*) type of bed that fits vertically into a cupboard and can be pulled down when needed. ⇨ illus at FURNITURE.

Murphy's law /ˈmɜ:fɪz lɔ:/ (*joc*) principle that if anything can go wrong it will, used for explaining accidents and failures. Cf SOD'S LAW (SOD[2]).

muscat /ˈmʌskæt/ *n* type of grape used for eating

and making wine.

muscatel /ˌmʌskəˈtel/ *n* [C, U] raisin or wine made from muscat grapes.

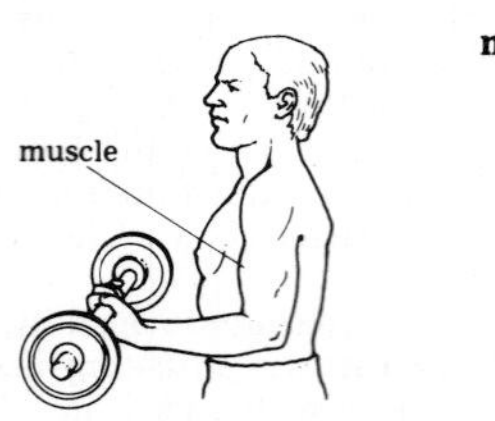

muscle /ˈmʌsl/ *n* **1** (**a**) [C] length of stretchable tissue in an animal body that is attached at each end to bone and can be tightened or relaxed to produce movement: *arm, leg, face, etc muscles* ○ *strain/tear/pull a muscle* ○ *exercises to develop the muscles* ○ *Don't move a muscle!* ie Stay completely still. (**b**) [U] such tissue: *The heart is made of muscle.* ○ [attrib] *muscle fibres.* **2** [U] muscular power: *have plenty of muscle but no brains.* **3** [U] (*fig*) power to make others do as one wishes: *political, industrial, etc muscle* ○ *a trade union with plenty of muscle.* **4** (idm) **flex one's muscles** ⇨ FLEX².

▷ **muscle** *v* (phr v) **muscle in** (**on sb/sth**) (*infml derog*) join in sth when one has no right to do so, for one's own advantage: *I wrote the book, and now she's trying to muscle in on its success by saying she gave me the ideas.*

□ ˈ**muscle-bound** *adj* having large stiff muscles as the result of excessive exercise.

ˈ**muscleman** /-mæn/ *n* (*pl* **-men** /-men/) (*infml sometimes derog*) man with large muscles and

MUSIC: SOME BAND INSTRUMENTS

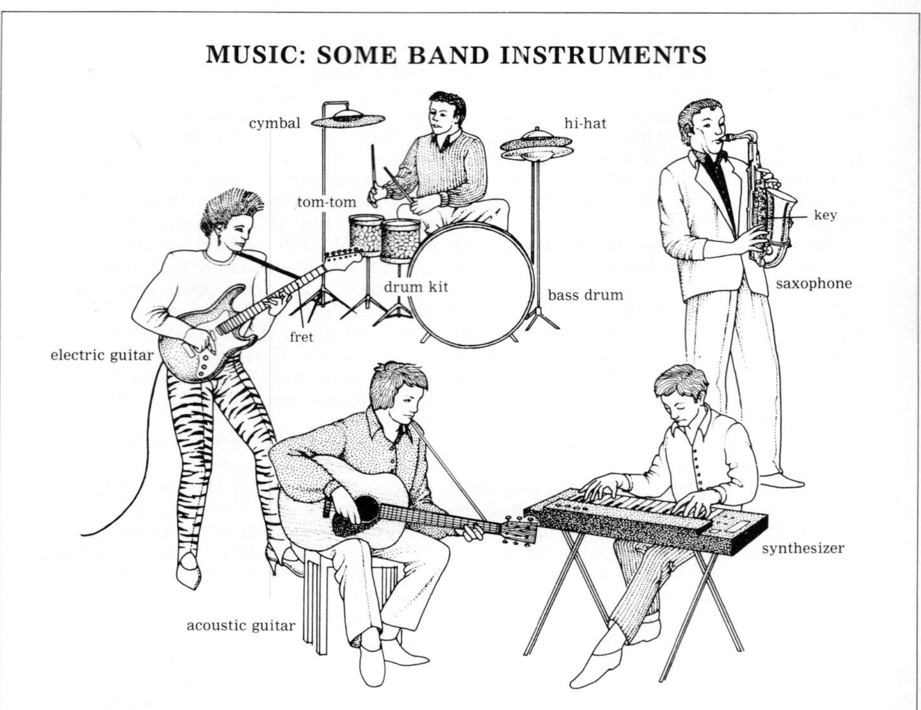

Music

The British have not been regarded as a particularly musical people and, from the end of the 17th century until the 20th century, there were relatively few British composers of international renown.

Before the 16th century, musical life was centred on the church, especially the cathedrals and the royal chapels. The choral works of John Taverner, William Byrd and Thomas Tallis are still performed today, most notably by the choirs of King's College, Cambridge and Christ Church in Oxford. Secular music in the 16th century included the instrumental work of William Byrd and Orlando Gibbons and the madrigals of Gibbons and Thomas Morley.

Henry Purcell, famous for his opera *Dido and Aeneas* (1689), has been described as the last great English composer before the 20th century. John Gay's *The Beggar's Opera* (1728), is still occasionally performed, and the comic operas of Gilbert and Sullivan are among the few 19th century British works that are still part of the repertoire.

The 20th century saw a renaissance in British music with the work of composers such as Delius, Holst, Elgar, Vaughan Williams, Walton, Tippett, Maxwell Davies and Britten. Britten in particular came to be regarded as a specially 'English' composer, partly through the English themes of several of his operas but also through the folk songs and church music that provided the inspiration for many of his other works.

There is now a flourishing musical life in Britain, with more people going to concerts than ever before. The BBC plays an important part in the development of music both by commissioning new work and by supporting orchestras. The BBC Radio 3 programme, which is broadcast throughout the day and evening, is devoted mainly to music. Many British orchestras and musical groups have an international reputation. They include the London Philharmonic Orchestra (LPO), the London Symphony Orchestra (LSO), the BBC Symphony Orchestra, the Philharmonia, the Royal Liverpool Philharmonic, the Hallé (based in Manchester), the City of Birmingham Orchestra and the Bournemouth Symphony Orchestra. Among more specialized orchestras are the English Chamber Orchestra, the Academy of St Martin-in-the-Fields, the Northern Sinfonia and the London Sinfonietta. Famous choirs include the Bach Choir and the Royal Choral Society. Music festivals held annually include those at Bath and Aldeburgh, and the Three Choirs Festival, held at Gloucester, Hereford and Worcester in turn. The popular series of Promenade Concerts held every summer in the Royal Albert Hall, London, are broadcast by the BBC, with the 'Last Night of the Proms' forming a spirited climax to the season.

At a more modest level, almost all schools and colleges have an orchestra or other music-making group, and many towns have a choral society. Music in the home is more likely to be listened to than played, but many homes have a piano.

Almost all American composers of note belong to the 20th century, and include such names as Charles Ives, Aaron Copland, Samuel Barber, Roger Sessions and Virgil Thomson. Edgard Varèse and John Cage have gained fame as experimental composers.

It is through the development of popular music in the 20th century that the USA has dominated the western world. Jazz, a style of music created at the end of the 19th century by black Americans out of their gospel and blues songs, was being played all over the USA by both black and white musicians by the 1920s, and influenced the development of both dance music and popular songs in the 1930s and 1940s. After the Second World War jazz and popular music developed in separate directions. Black musicians created a more sophisticated style called bebop. The rhythm and blues music that derived from jazz, combined with aspects of country and western music, developed into rock 'n' roll in the 1950s with the music of Bill Haley, Chuck Berry, Elvis Presley, Buddy Holly and others. In the 1960s some British groups, especially the Beatles and the Rolling Stones, became internationally famous and for a brief period popular music was dominated by developments in Britain. Since that time, rock has incorporated folk music, soul music has developed, and many social phenomena, such as drug culture, the civil rights movement and the peace movement, have found their expression in rock music.

The musical has also made an important contribution to popular music. Developing from the British music hall and American vaudeville early in the 20th century, composers such as George Gershwin, Cole Porter, Rodgers and Hammerstein, Stephen Sondheim and Leonard Bernstein on Broadway, and Ivor Novello, Noël Coward and more recently Andrew Lloyd Webber in Britain, have made the musical into one of the most important forms of popular music.

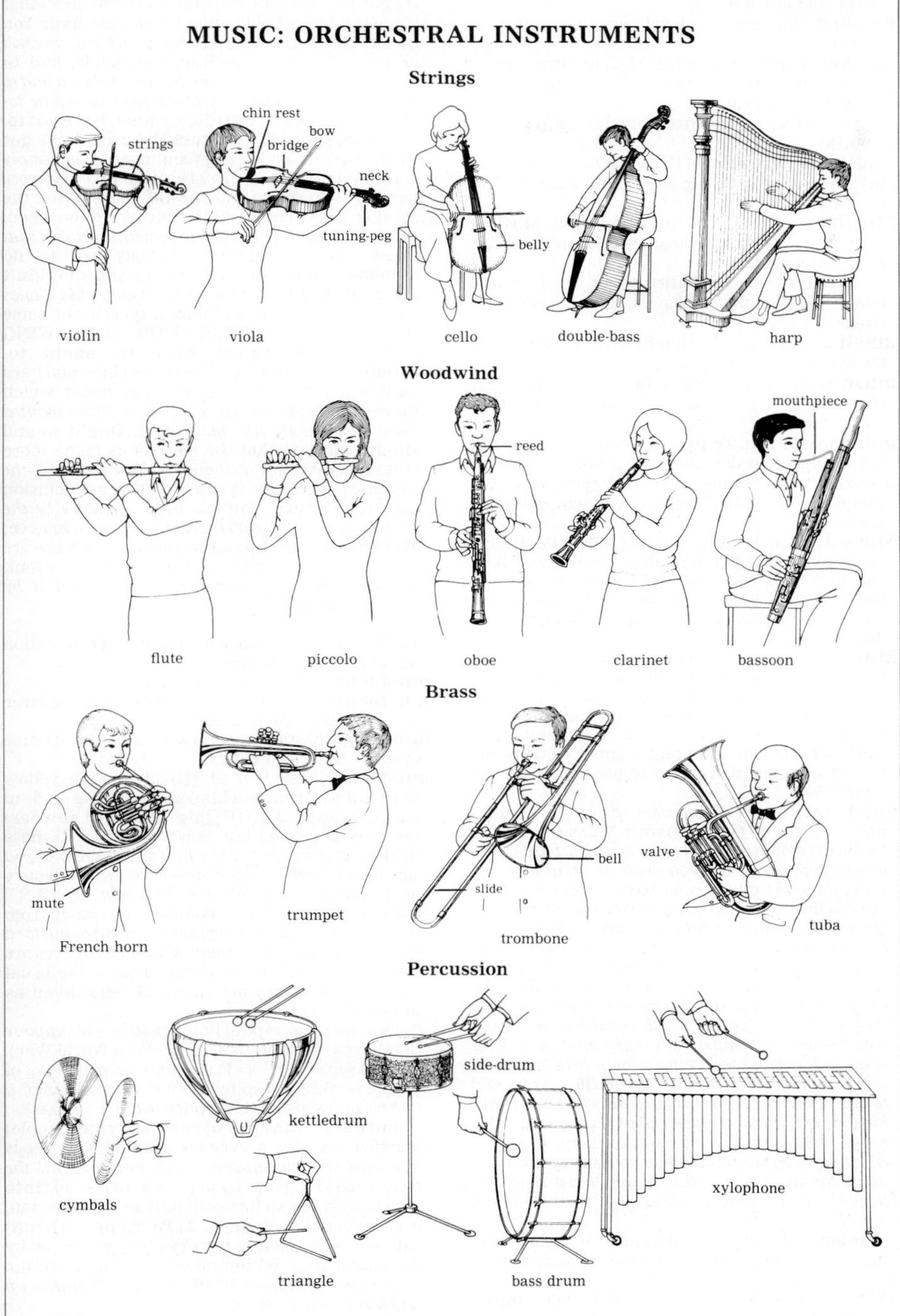

often great strength.

Muscovy /ˈmʌskəvɪ/ *(arch)* Russia.

▷ **Muscovite** /-vaɪt/ *n, adj* (person) of or from Moscow.

□ ˈ**Muscovy duck** tropical American duck, widely domesticated.

muscular /ˈmʌskjʊlə(r)/ *adj* **1** of the muscles: *muscular effort, contraction* ○ *muscular tissue.* **2** having large strong muscles: *his powerful muscular arms.* ▷ **muscularity** /ˌmʌskjʊˈlærətɪ/ *n* [U].

□ ˌ**muscular** ˈ**dystrophy** long-lasting illness in which the muscles become gradually weaker.

muse[1] /mju:z/ *n* **1 the Muses** [pl] (in Greek mythology) nine goddesses, daughters of Zeus, each of whom protected and encouraged one of the arts or sciences. They were: Calliope (epic poetry), Clio (history), Euterpe (music), Terpsichore (dance), Erato (lyric arts), Melpomene (tragedy), Thalia (comedy), Polyhymnia (poetry) and Urania (astronomy). **2** [C] *(rhet)* spirit that inspires a creative artist, esp a poet: *His muse had deserted him, and he could no longer write.*

muse[2] /mju:z/ *v* **1** [I, Ipr] ~ **(about/over/on/upon sth)** think in a deep or concentrated way, ignoring what is happening around one: *sit musing on the events of the day, memories of the past, etc.* **2** [Tn] say (sth) to oneself in a thoughtful way: *'I wonder if I shall ever see them again,' he mused.*

museum /mju:ˈzɪəm/ *n* building in which objects of artistic, cultural, historical or scientific importance and interest are displayed: *a museum of natural history* ○ *an anthropological museum.* ⇨ article.

□ **mu**ˈ**seum piece 1** fine specimen suitable for a museum. **2** *(joc derog)* out-of-date or obsolete thing or person: *This old radio of yours is a bit of a museum piece; it's about time you got a new one!*

mush[1] /mʌʃ/ *n* **1** [U, sing] *(usu derog)* soft thick mixture or mass: *The vegetables had been boiled to a mush, and were quite uneatable.* **2** [U] *(US)* boiled corn meal. **3** [U] *(infml derog)* (speech or writing full of) weak sentimentality: *I've never read such a load of mush!*

▷ **mushy** *adj* **1** like mush. **2** *(infml derog)* weakly sentimental: *a mushy film, book, etc.*

mush[2] /mʊʃ/ *v (esp US and Canadian)* **1** [I, Ipr] travel over snow in a sledge pulled by dogs: *We mushed over to the next camp.* ○ *Mush!* ie a cry used by the driver of the sledge to encourage the dogs. **2** [Tn] make (dogs) pull a sledge over snow.

▷ **mush** *n* journey by sledge.

mushroom /ˈmʌʃrʊm, -ru:m/ *n* fast-growing fungus with a round flattish head and a stalk, of which some kinds can be eaten: *grilled/fried mushrooms* ○ *a button mushroom,* ie a small one with a round head like a button ○ *Computers started springing up round the office like mushrooms,* ie A large number of them appeared suddenly. ○ [attrib] *mushroom soup.* ⇨ illus at FUNGUS. Cf TOADSTOOL.

▷ **mushroom** *v* [I] **1** (usu **go mushrooming**) gather mushrooms (in a field or wood). **2** *(sometimes derog)* spread or increase in number rapidly: *new blocks of flats and offices mushrooming all over the city.*

□ ˌ**mushroom** ˈ**cloud** cloud (shaped like a mushroom) that forms after a nuclear explosion.

music /ˈmju:zɪk/ *n* [U] **1 (a)** art of arranging the sounds of voice(s) or instrument(s) or both in a pleasing sequence or combination: *study music* ○ [attrib] *a music lesson, teacher.* **(b)** compositions made by doing this: *Mozart's music* ○ *play a piece of music* ○ [attrib] *a music lover.* ⇨ article. **(c)** (book, sheets of paper, etc containing) written or printed signs representing such compositions: *I'd left my music at home.* ○ *read music.* **2** (idm) **face the music** ⇨ FACE[2]. **music to one's** ˈ**ears** information that pleases one very much: *The news of his resignation was music to my ears.* **put/set sth to** ˈ**music** write music to go with words (eg of a poem) so that they can be sung.

□ ˈ**music box** *(US)* = MUSICAL BOX (MUSICAL).

ˈ**music centre** equipment combining a radio, record player and tape recorder.

ˈ**music-hall** *n* **(a)** [C] theatre used for popular entertainment, eg songs, acrobatics or juggling, esp in the late 19th and early 20th centuries. The earliest halls were simply bars with a stage for the performers, but they became gradually more elaborate. Leading performers like Marie *Lloyd were famous all over Britain and many of their songs are still sung today. **(b)** [U] the entertainment itself: [attrib] *music-hall songs, entertainers.*

ˈ**music-stand** *n* light (usu folding) framework for holding sheets of printed music.

ˈ**music-stool** *n* seat without a back (usu adjustable in height) used when playing a piano. ⇨ illus.

musical /ˈmju:zɪkl/ *adj* **1** [usu attrib] of or for music: *a musical entertainment* ○ *musical instruments,* ie for producing music, eg piano, violin, flute, horn ○ *musical talent* ○ *She has no formal musical qualifications.* ○ *a musical society,* ie for people to listen to music or perform music together. **2** fond of or skilled in music: *She's very musical.* **3** melodious; pleasant to listen to: *He has quite a musical voice.*

▷ **musical** *n* (also ˌ**musical** ˈ**comedy**) theatrical or film entertainment similar to a light opera, with both singing and spoken dialogue, and often with dancing. The subjects are usu, but not always, comic and romantic. The best and most famous

musical notation

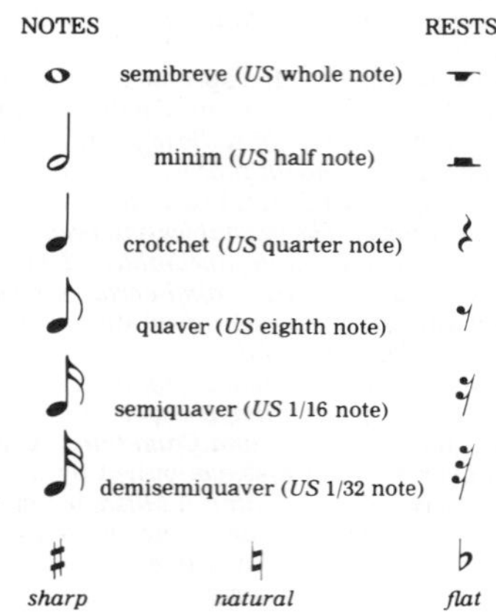

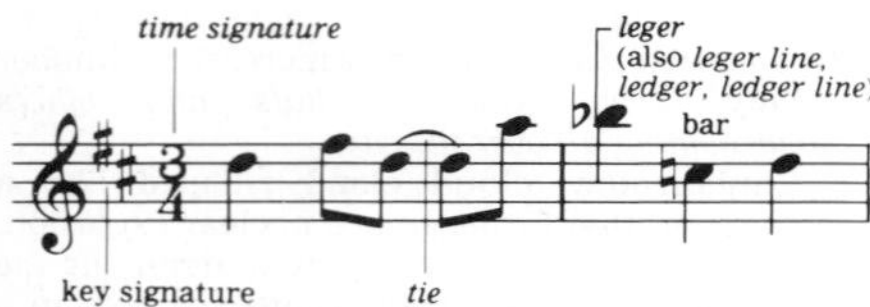

examples are American, written by Irving *Berlin, Cole *Porter, Jerome *Kern, Richard *Rodgers (with Hammerstein or Hart), and more recently, Stephen *Sondheim: *Broadway musicals*. ⇨ article at MUSIC.

musically /-klɪ/ **1** in or of music: *musically gifted, talented, ignorant.* **2** in a way that is pleasing to listen to: *play, sing, speak, etc musically.*

□ ˈ**musical box** (also ˈ**music box**) box with a mechanical device that produces a tune when the box is opened.

ˌ**musical** ˈ**chairs 1** game in which players go round a row of chairs (one fewer than the number of players) until the music stops, when the one who finds no chair to sit on has to leave the game. **2** (*fig often derog*) situation in which people frequently take turns to have sth, esp a job: *He had come out on top in the game of musical chairs by which senior posts seemed to be filled.*

musician /mju:ˈzɪʃn/ *n* person who makes music by playing or conducting: *She is a fine musician.*

▷ **musicianship** *n* [U] art and skill in (performing) music: *the pianist's sensitive musicianship.*

musicology /ˌmju:zɪˈkɒlədʒɪ/ *n* [U] academic study of music. ▷ **musicological** /ˌmju:zɪkəˈlɒdʒɪkl/ *adj.* **musicologist** /ˌmju:zɪˈkɒlədʒɪst/ *n.*

musique concrète /mju:ˌzi:k kɒŋˈkret/ (*French*) = CONCRETE MUSIC (CONCRETE).

musk /mʌsk/ *n* [U] **1** strong-smelling substance produced in glands by the male musk-deer, used in the manufacture of perfume. **2** any of several plants with a similar smell.

▷ **musky** *adj* (**-ier, -iest**) (smelling) like musk: *a musky odour.*

□ ˈ**musk-deer** *n* small hornless deer of Central Asia.

ˈ**musk-melon** *n* sweet juicy type of melon.

ˈ**musk-ox** *n* shaggy ox with curved horns that lives in N Canada and Greenland.

ˈ**musk-rat** (also ˈ**musquash**) *n* large rat-like water animal of N America, valuable for its fur.

ˈ**musk-rose** *n* rambling rose with large, sweet-smelling flowers.

muskeg /ˈmʌskeg/ *n* level swamp or bog in Canada.

musket /ˈmʌskɪt/ *n* long-barrelled firearm used by soldiers from the 16th to the 19th centuries (now replaced by the rifle).

▷ **musketeer** /ˌmʌskɪˈtɪə(r)/ *n* soldier armed with a musket.

musketry /ˈmʌskɪtrɪ/ *n* [U] (*dated*) (science of or instruction in) shooting with rifles: *learn skill in musketry.*

Muslim /ˈmʊzlɪm; *US* ˈmʌzləm/ (also **Moslem** /ˈmɒzləm/) *n* person whose religion is Islam. ⇨ article at RELIGION.

▷ **Muslim** (also **Moslem**) *adj* of Muslims and Islam: *Muslim historians, holidays, leaders.* ⇨ Usage at CHRISTIAN.

muslin /ˈmʌzlɪn/ *n* [U] thin fine cotton cloth, used for dresses, curtains, etc.

musquash /ˈmʌskwɒʃ/ *n* **(a)** [C] = MUSK-RAT (MUSK). **(b)** [U] fur of the musk-rat: [attrib] *a musquash coat.*

muss /mʌs/ *v* [Tn, Tn·p] ~ **sth (up)** (*infml esp US*) put sth into disorder: *Don't muss (up) my hair!*

mussel /ˈmʌsl/ *n* any of several types of edible shellfish with a black shell in two parts. ⇨ illus at SHELLFISH.

Mussolini /ˌmʊsəˈli:nɪ/ Benito (1883-1945), Italian dictator. He founded the Italian fascist movement and took power in 1922. He took Italy into the Second World War on the side of Germany, and was hanged by communist partisans just before the war ended.

Mussorgsky /mʊˈsɔ:gskɪ/ Modest (1839-81), Russian composer. His technique of making music follow the natural rhythms of speech in his operas (eg *Boris Godunov* and *Khovanshchina*) and songs shocked composers of his time, and many of his works are known in arrangements by others (eg *Ravel's orchestral version of his *Pictures at an Exhibition*).

must[1] /məst, *strong form* mʌst/ *modal v* (*neg* **must not**, *contracted form* **mustn't** /ˈmʌsnt/) **1 (a)** (indicating obligation): *I must go to the bank to get some money.* ○ *When you enter the building you must show the guard your pass.* ○ *Cars must not park in front of the entrance.* ○ *You mustn't open the oven door before the cake is ready.* ○ *We mustn't be late, must we?* ○ *'Must you go so soon?' 'Yes, I must.'* ⇨ Usage 1. **(b)** (indicating advice or recommendation): *We must see what the authorities have to say.* ○ *I must ask you not to do that again.* ⇨ Usage 2. **2** (drawing a logical conclusion): *You must be hungry after your long walk.* ○ *She must be having a lot of problems with the language.* ○ *You must be Mr Smith — I was told to expect you.* ○ *They must be twins.* ○ *He must have known* (ie Surely he knew) *what she wanted.* ○ *We must have read the same report.* ⇨ Usage 3. **3** (indicating insistence): *You* ˈ*must put your name down for the team.* ○ *You simply* ˈ*must read this book — it's so funny.* ○ ˈ*Must you make so much noise?*

▷ **must** *n* (*infml*) thing that must be done, seen, heard, etc: *a must for all lovers of crime fiction.*

NOTE ON USAGE: **1** OBLIGATION (**must, need**[1,2], **have to, ought to, should**[1]) **(a) Must** is used to show that the speaker orders or expects something to be done: *The children must be back by 4 o'clock.* ○ *I must go now*, ie I feel obliged to go. **Need to** (informal **have to**) is used when somebody else is giving orders or controlling events: *You need to/have to pass a special exam to get into the school.* ○ *I have to go now*, ie something (or somebody else) requires it. **Ought to** and **should** indicate that the speaker is giving an order, but suggest that he or she is not sure it will be obeyed: *She really ought to/should be leaving now.* ○ *You ought to/should apologize* (though I'm not sure you will). **(b) Mustn't** (and **oughtn't to, shouldn't**) are used when the speaker wants somebody *not* to do something: *You mustn't leave the gate open.* ○ *You oughtn't to/shouldn't neglect the garden.* **Needn't** and **don't have to** mean that there is a lack of obligation to do something: *You needn't/don't have to arrive early.* (Cf *You mustn't arrive early.*) **(c)** In indirect commands, **had to** replaces **must**: *Mother said that the children had to be back by 4 o'clock.* (Cf *Mary said he ought to/should apologize.*) **2** ADVICE (**must, have got to, ought to, should**[1]) **(a) Must** (informal **have got to**) is used to advise or recommend: *You simply must see that film.* ○ *You've got to take life more seriously.* **Ought to** and **should** suggest that the speaker is less confident the advice will be taken: *You really ought to/should do something about that cough!* **(b)** To advise somebody not to do something, **mustn't, oughtn't to** and **shouldn't** are used: *You mustn't/oughtn't to/shouldn't miss this opportunity.* **(c)** In indirect speech, the same rules apply as for OBLIGATION. **3** DRAWING CONCLUSIONS (**must, have to, ought to, should**[1]) **(a) Must** and **have to** (informal) are used when drawing a conclusion about which there is no doubt: *He must be/has to be the wanted man: he's exactly like his picture.* **Ought to** and **should** indicate that the speaker is being more tentative: *He ought to/should be here in time — he started early enough.* **(b)** To show that a conclusion cannot be drawn, **can't** is used: *He can't be the wanted man.* ○ *He can't (surely) get here in time.* **(c) Must have, ought to have** and **should have** are used to draw a conclusion from some past event: *She must have received the parcel: I sent it by registered post.*

must[2] /mʌst/ *n* [U] grape juice before fermentation has changed it into wine.

mustache *n* (*US*) = MOUSTACHE.

mustachio /məˈstɑ:ʃɪəʊ; *US* -stæʃ-/ *n* (*pl* ~**s**) large (usu long-haired) moustache.

mustang /ˈmʌstæŋ/ *n* small wild or half-wild horse of the N American plains.

mustard /ˈmʌstəd/ *n* **1** [U] plant with yellow flowers and (black or white) sharp-tasting seeds in long thin pods. **2 (a)** [U] (also ˈ**mustard powder**) these seeds ground into powder. **(b)** [U, C] these seeds or this powder mixed into a strong-flavoured sauce with (esp) vinegar and served with savoury food: [attrib] *a mustard pot/jar/spoon, etc.* **3** [U] darkish yellow colour (like the sauce made from the seeds of the mustard plant): [attrib] *a mustard (yellow) sweater.* **4** [U] plant whose seed leaves are eaten as a salad: *mustard and cress*, ie the usual form in which they are eaten. **5** (idm) **keen as mustard** ⇨ KEEN[1].

□ ˈ**mustard gas** type of liquid poison with vapour that burns the skin (used in the First World War).

muster /ˈmʌstə(r)/ *n* **1** assembly or gathering of people or things, esp for review or inspection: *a muster of troops.* **2** (idm) **pass muster** ⇨ PASS[2].

▷ **muster** *v* **1 (a)** [I, Tn] come or bring (people) together, esp for a military parade: *The troops mustered (on the square).* ○ *He mustered all the troops.* **(b)** [Tn, Tn·p, Tn·pr] ~ **sb (in)**; ~ **sb (into sth)** (*US*) bring sb formally into an organization, esp the army; enrol, enlist. **2** [Tn, Tn·p] ~ **sth (up)** gain sth by collecting it from other people or by drawing it from within oneself; summon sth up: *muster public support for sth* ○ *I couldn't muster up much enthusiasm for it.*

musty /ˈmʌstɪ/ *adj* (**-ier, -iest**) **1** smelling or tasting stale, mouldy and damp: *musty old books* ○ *a musty room full of damp* ○ *The wine tastes musty.* **2** (*fig derog*) out-of-date; obsolete: *the same musty old ideas presented as if they were new.* ▷ **mustiness** /ˈmʌstɪnɪs/ *n* [U].

mutable /ˈmju:təbl/ *adj* (*rhet*) liable to change; likely to change. ▷ **mutability** /ˌmju:təˈbɪlətɪ/ *n* [U].

mutant /ˈmju:tənt/ *n* **1** (*biology*) living thing that differs basically from its parents as a result of genetic change; mutation(c). **2** (*infml*) (esp in science fiction) living thing that is deformed or disfigured as a result of genetic change.

▷ **mutant** *adj* differing as a result of genetic change: *a mutant gene* ○ *a mutant strain of a virus.*

mutation /mju:ˈteɪʃn/ *n* **(a)** [U] change; alteration:

(*biology*) *Mutation of cells, involving changes in genetic material, often leads to cancer and other diseases.* ○ (*linguistics*) *mutation of sounds* ○ *vowel mutation.* (**b**) [C] instance of this: *mutations in plants caused by radiation.* (**c**) [C] new organism resulting from such a change; mutant(1).

▷ **mutate** /mju:ˈteɪt; *US* ˈmju:teɪt/ *v* [I, Ipr, Tn] ~ **(into sth)** (cause sth to) undergo mutation: *cells that mutate/are mutated* ○ *organisms that mutate into new forms.*

mutatis mutandis /mu:ˌtɑ:tɪs mu:ˈtændɪs/ (*Latin*) with appropriate changes (when comparing cases): *What I have said about the army also applies, mutatis mutandis, to the navy.*

mute /mju:t/ *adj* **1** silent; making no sound: *stare in mute amazement, admiration, astonishment, etc* ○ *remain mute.* **2** (*dated*) (of people) unable to speak; dumb: *mute from birth.* **3** (of a letter in a written word) not pronounced when spoken: *The 'b' in 'dumb' is mute.*

▷ **mute** *n* **1** (**a**) piece of metal, plastic, etc used to soften the sounds produced from a stringed instrument. (**b**) pad placed in the opening of a wind instrument to change the quality of the sounds produced. ⇨ illus at MUSIC. **2** (*dated*) dumb person.

mute *v* [Tn esp passive] make the sound of (esp a musical instrument) quieter or softer, esp with a mute: *The strings are muted throughout the closing bars of the symphony.* **muted** *adj* **1** (of sounds) quiet and often indistinct: *They spoke in muted voices.* **2** not openly or vigorously expressed: *muted excitement* ○ *muted criticism.* **3** (of musical instruments) fitted with a mute: *muted strings.* **4** (of colours) not bright; subdued: *muted greens and blues.*

mutely *adv* silently; dumbly.

muteness *n* [U].

□ ˌ**mute** ˈ**swan** common white swan of Europe and W Asia.

mutilate /ˈmju:tɪleɪt/ *v* [Tn] injure, damage or disfigure (sb/sth) by breaking, tearing or cutting off a necessary part: *The invaders cut off their prisoners' arms and legs and threw their mutilated bodies into the ditch.* ○ *A madman mutilated the painting by cutting holes in it.* ○ (*fig*) *The editor mutilated my text by removing whole paragraphs from it.*

▷ **mutilation** /ˌmju:tɪˈleɪʃn/ *n* (**a**) [U] mutilating or being mutilated: *Thousands suffered death or mutilation as a result of the bomb attacks.* (**b**) [C] injury, damage or loss caused by this.

mutinous /ˈmju:tɪnəs/ *adj* guilty of mutiny; refusing to obey; rebellious: *mutinous sailors, workers, children, etc* ○ *mutinous behaviour.* ▷ **mutinously** *adv.*

mutiny /ˈmju:tɪnɪ/ *n* [C, U] rebellion against lawful authority, esp by soldiers or sailors: *The crew tried to seize control of the ship, and were shot for mutiny.* ○ *If the manager hadn't accepted some of the team's demands he could have had a mutiny on his hands.*

▷ **mutineer** /ˌmju:tɪˈnɪə(r)/ *n* person guilty of mutiny.

mutiny *v* (*pt, pp* **-nied**) [I, Ipr] ~ **(against sb/sth)** be guilty of mutiny; revolt (against sb/sth): *a crew that mutinies (against its captain, against bad living conditions).*

mutt /mʌt/ *n* **1** (*infml*) foolish, incompetent and awkward person: *You silly big mutt!* **2** (*derog*) mongrel dog: *What an ugly mutt!*

mutter /ˈmʌtə(r)/ *v* **1** [I, Ipr, Tn, Tn·pr, Tf, Dn·pr] ~ **(sth) (to sb) (about sth)** speak or say (sth) in a low voice that is hard to hear: *Don't mutter! I can't hear you.* ○ *Sarah was muttering away to herself as she did the washing-up.* ○ *He muttered something (to the cashier) (about losing his wallet).* **2** [I, Ipr] ~ **(about/against/at sb/sth)** complain or grumble privately or in a way that is not openly expressed: *For some time people had been muttering about the way she ran the department.* **3** [I] (of thunder) be heard distantly; rumble.

▷ **mutter** *n* (usu *sing*) indistinct utterance or sound.

mutterer /ˈmʌtərə(r)/ *n* person who mutters.

muttering /ˈmʌtərɪŋ/ *n* [U] (also **mutterings** [pl]) complaints that are privately or not openly expressed.

mutton /ˈmʌtn/ *n* **1** [U] meat from a fully grown sheep: *a leg/shoulder of mutton* ○ *roast, boiled, stewed mutton* ○ [attrib] *mutton stew* ○ *a mutton chop*, ie a piece of rib of mutton. Cf LAMB 2. **2** (idm) **dead as mutton** ⇨ DEAD. **mutton dressed (up) as** ˈ**lamb** (*infml derog*) older person dressed in a style suitable for a younger person.

□ ˌ**mutton** ˈ**chops** (also ˌ**mutton-chop** ˈ**whiskers**) hair growing on each side of a man's face, extending down past the ears and growing thickly round the jaws.

ˈ**mutton-head** *n* (*infml derog*) stupid person.

mutual /ˈmju:tʃʊəl/ *adj* **1** (of a feeling or an action) felt or done by each towards the other: *mutual affection, suspicion, etc*, ie A is fond/suspicious of B, and B is fond/suspicious of A. ○ *mutual aid, assistance, etc.* **2** [attrib] (of people) having the same specified relationship to each other: *We are mutual friends, enemies, etc.* **3** [attrib] (*infml*) shared by two or more people: *our mutual friend, Smith*, ie Smith, a friend of both of us. **4** (idm) **a mutual admiration society** (*derog*) situation in which two or more people praise or openly admire each other.

▷ **mutualism** /-əlɪzəm/ *n* [U] **1** belief that society is based on the mutual dependence of its members. **2** form of symbiosis in which both organisms benefit.

mutually /-ʊəlɪ/ *adv*: *The two assertions are mutually exclusive*, ie cannot both be true.

□ ˌ**mutual** ˈ**funds** (*US*) = UNIT TRUSTS (UNIT).

ˌ**mutual in**ˈ**surance company** insurance company in which some or all of the profits are divided among the policy-holders.

Muzak /ˈmju:zæk/ *n* [U] (*propr often derog*) continuous recorded light music often played in shops, restaurants, factories, etc.

muzzle /ˈmʌzl/ *n* **1** (**a**) nose and mouth of an animal (eg a dog or fox). (**b**) guard of straps or wires placed over this part of an animal's head to prevent it biting, etc. **2** open end of a firearm, out of which the bullets, etc come: *a* ˌ*muzzle-loading* ˈ*gun.* Cf BREECH.

▷ **muzzle** *v* [Tn esp passive] **1** put a muzzle on (a dog, etc): *Such a fierce animal ought to be muzzled.* **2** (*fig derog*) prevent (a person, society, newspaper, etc) from expressing opinions freely: *accuse the government of muzzling the press, freedom of speech, etc.*

□ ˈ**muzzle velocity** speed of a bullet, shell, etc as it leaves the muzzle of a firearm.

muzzy /ˈmʌzɪ/ *adj* (**-ier, -iest**) **1** unable to think clearly; confused: *After a couple of whiskies my head felt all muzzy.* **2** blurred. ▷ **muzzily** *adv.* **muzziness** *n* [U].

MV /ˌem ˈvi:/ *abbr* motor vessel.

MW *abbr* (*radio*) medium wave.

my /maɪ/ *possess det* **1** of or belonging to the speaker or writer: *Where's my hat?* ○ *My feet are cold.* ○ *He always forgets my birthday.* **2** (used before a *n* or an *adj* as a form of address): *my dear, darling, love, etc* ○ *my dear fellow, chap, man, girl, woman, etc* ○ *Come along, my boy.* **3** (used in exclamations): *My goodness, what a surprise!* ○ *My God, look at the time!* Cf MINE[1].

Myanmar /ˈmɪənmɑ:(r)/ = BURMA.

Mycenae /maɪˈsi:ni:/ city in ancient Greece, near the sea in the NW Peloponnese. It was the site of the earliest great civilization on the Greek mainland, c 1400-1200 BC. After the fall of the *Minoan civilization, Mycenae controlled the Aegean shipping routes. The ruins and jewellery discovered by archaeologists have revealed the extent of its artistic and architectural development. ▷ **Mycenaean** /ˌmaɪsəˈni:ən/ *adj, n.*

mycology /maɪˈkɒlədʒɪ/ *n* [U] science or study of fungi.

myelitis /ˌmaɪəˈlaɪtɪs/ *n* [U] (*medical*) inflammation of the spinal cord.

mynah (also **myna, mina**) /ˈmaɪnə/ *n* any of several types of starling of SE Asia, known for their ability to copy human speech.

myopia /maɪˈəʊpɪə/ *n* [U] **1** (*medical*) short-sightedness. **2** (*derog*) inability to look into the future: *ministers charged with myopia.*

▷ **myopic** /maɪˈɒpɪk/ *adj* **1** (*medical*) short-sighted: *myopic eyes, vision, etc.* **2** (*fig derog*) showing inability to look ahead into the future: *a myopic outlook, attitude, etc* ○ *a government with myopic policies.* **myopically** /-klɪ/ *adv.*

myriad /ˈmɪrɪəd/ *n* extremely large number: *Each galaxy contains myriads of stars.*

▷ **myriad** *adj* [attrib] uncountably many: *a butterfly's wing, with its myriad tiny scales.*

myriapod /ˈmɪrɪəpɒd/ *n* animal like the centipede or millipede with many body segments, each bearing one or two pairs of legs.

myrmidon /ˈmɜ:mɪdən; *US* -dɒn/ *n* (*derog or joc*) person who carries out orders without question: *myrmidons of the law*, eg bailiffs.

myrrh /mɜ:(r)/ *n* [U] sweet-smelling, bitter-tasting type of gum or resin obtained from shrubs and used for making incense and perfumes.

myrtle /ˈmɜ:tl/ *n* [U] any of several types of evergreen shrub with shiny leaves and sweet-smelling white flowers.

myself /maɪˈself/ *reflex, emph pron* (only taking the main stress in sentences when used emphatically) **1** (*reflex*) (used when the speaker or writer is also the person affected by an action): *I* ˌ*cut myself with a* ˈ*knife.* **2** (*emph*) (used to emphasize the speaker or writer): *I my*ˈ*self will present the prizes.* ○ *I said so my*ˈ*self only last week.* **3** (idm) **(all) by my**ˈ**self** (**a**) alone. (**b**) without help: *I finished the crossword (all) by myself.*

mysterious /mɪˈstɪərɪəs/ *adj* **1** full of mystery; hard to understand or explain: *a mysterious event, crime, etc* ○ *a mysterious letter, parcel, etc*, ie whose contents or sender are unknown. **2** keeping or liking to keep things secret: *He was being very mysterious, and wouldn't tell me what he was up to.* ○ *She gave me a mysterious look*, ie suggesting secret knowledge. ▷ **mysteriously** *adv*: *The main witness had mysteriously disappeared.* ○ *Mysteriously, there was no answer when I rang.* **mysteriousness** *n* [U].

mystery /ˈmɪstərɪ/ *n* **1** [C] (**a**) thing of which the cause or origin is hidden or impossible to explain: *the mystery/mysteries of life* ○ *a crime that is an unsolved mystery* ○ *It's a mystery to me why they didn't choose him.* ○ [attrib] *a mystery guest, visitor*, ie kept secret until a certain moment. (**b**) (*infml*) person about whom not much is known or can be found out: *He's a bit of a mystery!* **2** [U] condition of being secret or obscure: *His past is shrouded in mystery*, ie One cannot find out the truth about it. **3** [U] practice of or fondness for making things secret; secrecy: *You're full of mystery tonight; what's going on?* ○ [attrib] *a* ˈ*mystery man/woman.* **4** [C] religious truth or belief that is beyond human understanding: *the mystery of the Incarnation, of the Eucharist, etc.* **5 mysteries** [pl] secret religious ceremonies (of the ancient Greeks, Romans, etc): (*fig*) *initiating the new recruit into the mysteries* (ie customs and practices) *of army life.* **6** [C] story or play about a puzzling crime: *a murder mystery* ○ [attrib] *a mystery thriller.*

□ ˈ**mystery play** medieval drama based on stories from the Bible. They were usu performed by members of trade guilds. Originally, the performances took place in a church, but later they were given outdoors, often in the streets. Many towns put on mystery plays, but the ones that have survived come from four English cities: York, Chester, Wakefield and Coventry. Cf MIRACLE PLAY (MIRACLE).

ˈ**mystery tour** organized trip on which the travellers are not told where they are going: (*fig joc*) *I'd forgotten the map so the journey turned into a bit of a mystery tour.*

mystic /ˈmɪstɪk/ (also **mystical** /ˈmɪstɪkl/) *adj* **1** of hidden meaning or spiritual power, esp in religion: *mystic rites and ceremonies.* **2** of or based on mysticism: *the world's mystic religions* ○ *the mystical writings of St John of the Cross.* **3** causing feelings of awe and wonder: *mystic beauty* ○ *For me, standing before the temple door as the sun rose was a mystical experience.*

▷ **mystic** *n* person who tries to be united with God and, through that, to reach truths beyond human understanding.
mystically /-klɪ/ *adv.*

mysticism /ˈmɪstɪsɪzəm/ *n* [U] belief or experiences of a mystic; teaching and belief that knowledge of God and of real truth may be reached through meditation or spiritual insight, independently of reason and the senses: *Christian mysticism* ○ *A strain of mysticism runs through his poetry.*

mystify /ˈmɪstɪfaɪ/ *v* (*pt, pp* **-fied**) [Tn] make (sb) confused through lack of understanding; puzzle; bewilder: *I'm mystified; I just can't see how he did it.* ○ *her mystifying disappearance.*
▷ **mystification** /ˌmɪstɪfɪˈkeɪʃn/ *n* [U] **1** mystifying or being mystified. **2** (*derog*) deliberately making sth mysterious or hard to understand, so as to prevent people finding out about it.

mystique /mɪˈsti:k/ *n* [sing] quality of sth which is not fully known about or understood but is seen to be admirable or special: *the mystique of the British monarchy* ○ *a simple, straightforward textbook that helps to dispel some of the mystique surrounding computers* ○ *There is a certain mystique about eating oysters.*

myth /mɪθ/ *n* **1** [C] story that originated in ancient times, esp one dealing with ideas or beliefs about the early history of a race, or giving explanations of natural events, such as the seasons: *the Creation myth* ○ *ancient Greek myths.* **2** [U] such stories collectively: *famous in myth and legend.* **3** [C] thing, person, etc that is imaginary, fictitious or impossible: *the myth of racial superiority, of a classless society, of human perfectibility* ○ *The rich uncle he boasts about is only a myth.*
▷ **mythical** /ˈmɪθɪkl/ *adj* **1** existing (only) in myth: *mythical heroes.* **2** imaginary; fictitious: *mythical wealth* ○ *that mythical 'rich uncle' he boasts about.*

mythology /mɪˈθɒlədʒɪ/ *n* **1** [U] study or science of myths. **2** [U] myths collectively: *Greek mythology.* **3** [C] body or collection of myths: *the mythologies of primitive races.*
▷ **mythological** /ˌmɪθəˈlɒdʒɪkl/ *adj* of or in mythology or myths: *mythological literature* ○ *Pluto, the mythological king of the underworld.*
mythologist /mɪˈθɒlədʒɪst/ *n* person who studies myths.

myxomatosis /ˌmɪksəməˈtəʊsɪs/ *n* [U] fatal infectious disease of rabbits.

N, n

N, n /en/ *n* (*pl* **N's, n's** /enz/) the fourteenth letter of the English alphabet: *'Nicholas' begins with (an) N/'N'.*

N *abbr* **1** (*US* also **No**) north(ern): *N Yorkshire* ○ *London N14 6BS*, ie as a postal code. **2** (esp on electric plugs) neutral (connection).

N *symb* nitrogen.

n *abbr* **1** (esp on forms) name. **2** (*grammar*) neuter (gender).

n *symb* (*mathematics*) indefinite number.

Na *symb* sodium.

NAACP /ˌen eɪ eɪ siː ˈpiː/ *abbr* (*US*) National Association for the Advancement of Colored People.

NAAFI /ˈnæfɪ/ *abbr* (*Brit*) Navy, Army and Air Force Institutes (providing canteens, shops, etc for British servicemen in England and abroad). Cf PX.

nab /næb/ *v* (**-bb-**) [Tn] (*Brit infml*) catch (sb) doing wrong; seize: *He was nabbed (by the police) for speeding.*

Nabokov /nəˈbəʊkɒf/ Vladimir (1899-1977), Russian-born novelist and critic. He left Russia in 1919 and later started writing in English. His best-known novel is *Lolita*, about a middle-aged man's infatuation with a 12-year-old girl.

nacelle /næˈsel/ *n* outer casing for an aircraft engine.

nacho /ˈnætʃəʊ/ *n* (*pl* ~**s**) (*US*) tortilla chip with a topping of cheese and chillies.

nacre /ˈneɪkə(r)/ *n* [U] (*arch*) = MOTHER-OF-PEARL (MOTHER).

nadir /ˈneɪdɪə(r); *US* ˈneɪdər/ *n* **1** point in the heavens directly beneath an observer. Cf ZENITH. **2** (*fig*) lowest point; time of greatest depression, despair, etc: *This failure was the nadir of her career.*

naff /næf/ *adj* (*Brit sl*) lacking taste or style; worthless; unfashionable: *That suit's pretty naff.*

nag[1] /næg/ *n* (*infml often derog*) horse: *It's a waste of money betting on that old nag!*

nag[2] /næg/ *v* (**-gg-**) **1** [I, Ipr, Tn] ~ **at sb** scold or criticize (sb) continuously: *He nagged (at) her all day long.* **2** [Tn] worry or hurt (sb) persistently: *a nagging pain* ○ *The problem had been nagging me for weeks.*

Nagasaki /ˌnægəˈsɑːkɪ/ city in Japan, destroyed by a US atomic bomb in August 1945. Cf HIROSHIMA.

Nahuatl /ˈnɑːwɑːtl/ *n* (*pl* unchanged or **Nahuatls**) **1** [C] member of a group of American Indian peoples of Central America. **2** [U] language of these peoples, formerly spoken by the *Aztecs. ▷ **Nahuatl** *adj.*

Nahum /ˈneɪhəm/ **(a)** minor prophet of the Old Testament. **(b)** book of the Old Testament containing his prophecy of the destruction of *Nineveh. ⇨ App 5.

naiad /ˈnaɪæd/ *n* (*pl* ~**s** or ~**es** /ˈnaɪədiːz/) (in Greek mythology) water-nymph.

nail /neɪl/ *n* **1** layer of horny substance over the outer tip of a finger or toe: *ˈfinger-nails* ○ *a ˈtoe-nail* ○ *cut one's nails.* ⇨ illus at HAND. **2** small thin piece of metal with a sharp point at one end and a (usu) flat head at the other, hammered into articles to hold them together, or into a wall, etc for use as a peg to hang things on. ⇨ illus at HAMMER. **3** (idm) **a nail in sb's/sth's ˈcoffin** thing that hastens or ensures sb's death, or the end, failure, etc of sb/sth: *The long and costly strike proved to be the last nail in the company's coffin.* **fight, etc tooth and nail** ⇨ TOOTH. **hard as nails** ⇨ HARD. **hit the nail on the head** ⇨ HIT[1]. **on the nail** (*infml*) (of payment) without delay: *I want cash on the nail.* **(as) tough as ˈnails** ⇨ TOUGH.

▷ **nail** *v* **1** [Tn] (*infml*) catch or arrest (sb): *Have the police nailed the man who did it?* ○ *She finally nailed me in the corridor.* **2** [Tn] (*infml*) reveal (sth) to be untrue: *I've finally nailed the myth of his infallibility*, ie shown that he can make mistakes. **3** (idm) **nail one's colours to the ˈmast** declare openly and firmly what one believes, whom one supports, etc. **nail a lie (to the counter)** prove that a statement is untrue. **4** (phr v) **nail sth down (a)** make (a carpet, lid, etc) secure with nails. **(b)** define sth precisely. **nail sb down (to sth)** make sb say precisely what he believes or wants to do: *She says she'll come, but I can't nail her down to a specific time.* **nail sth on; nail sth on/onto/to sth** fasten sth to sth with nails: *nail a lid on (the crate)* ○ *nail a sign to the wall.* **nail sth up (a)** fasten sth with nails so that it hangs from a wall, post, etc. **(b)** make (a door, window, etc) secure with nails so that it cannot easily be opened.

□ **ˈnail-biting** *adj* (*infml*) causing great nervous excitement or tension: *the nail-biting wait for the verdict.*

ˈnail-brush *n* small brush with stiff bristles for cleaning the finger-nails. ⇨ illus at BRUSH.

ˈnail-file *n* small flat file[1] for shaping the finger-nails.

ˈnail-punch *n* tool with a small point, placed between a nail and a hammer to drive the head of the nail below the surface.

ˈnail-scissors *n* [pl] small scissors for trimming the finger-nails and toe-nails: *a pair of nail-scissors.*

ˈnail varnish (also **varnish**) (*Brit*) (*US* **ˈnail polish**) varnish for giving a shiny tint to the finger-nails and toe-nails.

Naipaul /ˈnaɪpɔːl/ V(idiadhar) S(urajprasad) (1932-), West Indian novelist, born of an Indian family. His early novels are comedies set in his native Trinidad (eg *A House for Mr Biswas*), but his later novels and travel writings give a harsh view of the problems of the Third World.

naira /ˈnaɪrə/ *n* (*pl* unchanged) unit of Nigerian currency, 100 kobo.

naive (also **naïve**) /naɪˈiːv/ *adj* **1** natural and innocent in speech and behaviour; unaffected. **2** (*esp derog*) **(a)** too ready to believe what one is told; credulous: *You weren't so naive as to believe him, were you?* **(b)** showing lack of experience, wisdom or judgement: *a naive person, remark.*

▷ **naively** (also **naïvely**) *adv.*

naivety (also **naïvety** /naɪˈiːvtɪ/, **naïveté** /naɪˈiːvteɪ/) *n* **1** [U] quality of being naive. **2** [C] naive remark, action, etc.

naked /ˈneɪkɪd/ *adj* **1 (a)** without clothes on: *a naked body* ○ *as naked as the day he was born.* **(b)** [usu attrib] without the usual covering: *a naked sword*, ie one without its sheath ○ *fight with naked fists*, ie without boxing-gloves ○ *naked trees*, ie without leaves ○ *a naked light*, eg an electric bulb without a lampshade. **2** (*fig*) not disguised: *the naked truth.* **3** (idm) **the naked ˈeye** eyesight without the use of a telescope, a microscope, etc: *Microbes are too small to be seen by the naked eye.* ▷ **nakedly** *adv.* **nakedness** *n* [U].

NALGO /ˈnælgəʊ/ *abbr* (*Brit*) National and Local Government Officers' Association. ⇨ article at TRADE UNION.

namby-pamby /ˌnæmbɪ ˈpæmbɪ/ *adj* (*derog*) (of people or their talk) foolishly sentimental.

▷ **namby-pamby** *n* such a person: *Don't be such a namby-pamby!*

name[1] /neɪm/ *n* **1** [C] word or words by which a person, an animal, a place or thing is known and spoken to or of: *My name is Peter.* ○ *What is the name of the town where you live?* **2 (a)** [sing] reputation; fame: *a shop with a (good, bad, etc) name for reliability.* **(b)** [attrib] (*esp US*) having a well-known name or an established reputation: *a name brand of soap* ○ *a big-name company.* **3** [C] famous person: *the great names of history* ○ *All the big names in the pop music world were at the party.* **4** (idm) **answer to the name of sth** ⇨ ANSWER[2]. **be sb's middle name** ⇨ MIDDLE. **by name** having or using a name or names: *A strange man, Fred by name, came to see me.* ○ *The teacher knows all his students by name.* ○ *I only know her by name*, ie from hearing others speak of her, not personally. **by/of the name of** named: *He goes by the name of Henry.* ○ *Someone of the name of Henry wants to see you.* **call sb names** ⇨ CALL[2]. **drag sb/sb's name through the mire/mud** ⇨ DRAG[2]. **drop names** ⇨ DROP[2]. **enter one's name/put one's name down (for sth)** apply to enter (a school, college, course, etc). **give a dog a bad name** ⇨ DOG[1]. **give one's name to sth** invent or originate sth which then becomes known by one's own name: *He gave his name to a well-known brand of frozen food.* **a household name/word** ⇨ HOUSEHOLD. **in ˌall but ˈname** so in reality, although not officially; virtually: *She retired last year, but she's still the leader in all but name.* **in the name of sb/sth (a)** on behalf of sb/sth: *I greet you in the name of the President.* **(b)** by the authority of sth: *I arrest you in the name of the law.* **(c)** calling sb/sth to witness: *In God's name, what are you doing?* **(d)** for the sake of sth: *They did it all in the name of friendship.* **in name only** not in reality: *He is leader in name only: his deputy has effectively taken over.* **lend one's name to sth** ⇨ LEND. **make a ˈname for oneself/make one's ˈname** become well known: *She first made a name for herself as an actress.* **sb's name is mud** sb is disliked or (often temporarily) unpopular because of sth he has done. **name names** ⇨ NAME[2]. **the name of the ˈgame** the main purpose or most important aspect of an activity: *Hard work is the name of the game if you want to succeed in business.* **a name to conjure with** name of a person, group, company, etc that is respected and influential. **no names, no pack drill** ⇨ PACK[1]. **not have sth to one's ˈname** not possess even a small amount of (esp money): *She hasn't a penny to her name*, ie is very poor. **put a name to sb/sth** know or remember what sb/sth is called: *I've heard that tune before but I can't put a name to it.* **take sb's name in vain** use a name, esp God's, disrespectfully. **under the name (of) sth** using sth as a name instead of one's real name: *He writes under the name of Nimrod.*

□ **ˈname-day** *n* feast day of the saint whose name one was given at christening.

ˈname-dropping *n* [U] practice of casually mentioning the names of famous people one knows or pretends one knows in order to impress others. **ˈname-drop** *v* (**-pp**) [I] talk in this way.

ˈname-part *n* title-role in a play, etc: *He's got the name-part in 'Hamlet'.*

ˈname-plate *n* plaque on or near the door of a room, building, etc, showing the name of the occupant.

ˈnamesake *n* person or thing having the same name as another: *She's my namesake but we're not related.*

ˈname-tape *n* small tape with the owner's name on it, sewn into clothing.

NOTE ON USAGE: Your **first name** (*US* often **given name**) is, in English-speaking countries, the name given to you by your parents at birth. The name common to your family is your **family name** or, more usually, **surname.** In Christian countries **Christian name** is often used for **first name. Forename**, also meaning **first name** is formal and is often found on documents, application forms, etc.

Names

In both Britain and the USA, people usually have two or three names: a first name, also called a forename or Christian name, a middle name and a last name, also called a surname or family name. First names and middle names are often chosen because they have been used in the family in the past. For example, a child may have the name of a parent or grandparent as a middle name. The choice of names is also influenced by fashion. In the USA when a boy has the same name as his father 'Junior' is often added after his name. There are no legal restrictions on the choice or number of a person's first names. Any words may be used as names. Within a family children are called by their first names, but they usually call their parents Dad, Daddy or Father and Mum (in the USA Mom), Mummy or Mother. Grandparents are often addressed as Grandad, Grandpa or Grandfather and Granny, Grandma, Nan or Grandmother. Aunts and uncles may be addressed as Uncle and Aunt or Aunty, sometimes followed by the first name, eg Aunty Jane, Uncle Jack. Children sometimes address adult friends of the family as aunts or uncles even though they are not related. Parents of a boy may occasionally address him as 'son', but a daughter is no longer ever addressed as 'daughter'. There are no special forms of address for parents-in-law and step-parents; they are usually addressed either in the same way as parents or by their first names.

The use of a person's first name was, until fairly recently, a sign of familiarity, but it is now the usual custom. People at work, for example, usually call each other and refer to each other by their first names, although a young person in a junior position might use Mr, Mrs, etc when speaking to or about a senior colleague. Mr, Mrs, etc is also used whenever people wish to be formal. In some professions, job titles are used as forms of address. Army officers, for example, are addressed as Colonel, General, etc followed by their family name. Medical doctors are addressed as Dr Smith, etc (although surgeons are addressed as Mr, Mrs, etc). A clergyman in the Church of England may be addressed as 'Vicar', while a priest in the Roman Catholic Church is addressed as 'Father'. Inspectors and Chief Inspectors of Police are also addressed by their rank. There are no special titles for lawyers, except for judges (Judge followed by the family name).

When women marry, they may be called 'Mrs' followed by their husband's name, but may also, if they prefer, continue to use their own name. There are, in fact, no legal restrictions on the name one uses. Unmarried women are called 'Miss' followed by their family name, but the form 'Ms' is increasingly used by both married and unmarried women as a convenient female equivalent to 'Mr'.

When writing to a person one has never met, it is usual to use the formal form with Mr, etc, but it is also possible (and common practice in the USA) to use the first name and surname, for example 'Dear Mary Burton'. If the name of the person being written to is unknown to the writer, the usual form is 'Dear Sir' or 'Dear Sir or Madam'. In the USA, 'Sir' is frequently used also when addressing a man who is a stranger. In Britain, its use now is limited to the armed forces, where officers of senior rank are addressed as 'Sir', some schools where boys call male teachers 'Sir', and situations where a service is being offered to customers, for example by shop assistants or waiters.

In the past it was usual for men to address each other using the family name only, and the custom survived until recently in boarding schools and in the legal profession. Elsewhere it has now almost entirely disappeared. Nicknames, once frequently used in schools and in the army, are now mostly restricted to use in families and between lovers. (Cf Appendix 7.)

name[2] /neɪm/ *v* **1** [Tn, Tn·pr, Cn·n] ~ **sb/sth (after sb)** *US*; ~ **sb/sth (for sb)** give a name to sb/sth: *The child was named after its father*, ie given its father's first name. ○ *Tasmania was named after its discoverer, A J Tasman.* ○ *They named their child John.* **2** [Tn] give the name(s) of (sb/sth); identify: *Can you name all the plants in this garden?* ○ *Police have named a man they would like to question.* **3** [Tn] state (sth) precisely; specify: *We have named a date for the party.* ○ *Name your price*, ie Say what price you want to charge. ○ *The young couple have named the day*, ie chosen the day on which they will get married. **4** [Tn, Tn·pr, Cn·n/a] ~ **sb (for sth)**; ~ **sb as sth** nominate sb for, or appoint sb to, a position: *Ms X has been named for the directorship/named as the new director.* **5** (idm) **name the ˈday** tell people the date on which one has decided to hold an important event, esp one's wedding. **name ˈnames** give the name of a person or people being criticized, accused, praised, etc: *He said someone had lied but wouldn't name names.* **to ˌname but a ˈfew** giving only these as examples: *Lots of our friends are coming: Anne, Ken and George, to name but a few.* **you ˈname it** (*infml*) every thing, place, etc you can name or think of: *She can make anything: chairs, tables, cupboards — you name it.*

nameless /ˈneɪmlɪs/ *adj* **1** (**a**) [esp attrib] having no name or no known name; anonymous: *a nameless grave* ○ *a nameless 13th century poet* ○ *the nameless thousands who built the pyramids.* (**b**) not mentioned by name: *He had received information from a nameless source in the government.* ○ *a well-known public figure, who shall be/remain nameless*, ie whose name I will not mention. **2** [esp attrib] (**a**) (esp of emotions) not easy to describe: *a nameless longing, fear, etc.* (**b**) too terrible to describe; unmentionable: *the nameless horrors of the prison camp.*

namely /ˈneɪmlɪ/ *adv* that is to say; specifically: *Only one boy was absent, namely Harry.* ⇨ Usage at VIZ.

Namibia /nəˈmɪbɪə/ country in SW Africa, a member of the Commonwealth; pop approx 1 761 000; official languages English and Afrikaans; capital Windhoek; unit of currency dollar (= 100 cents). Much of the country is desert, with mountains in the centre. Agriculture, based on livestock, is important, and there are large mineral reserves. From 1920 it was administered by South Africa, and was called South West Africa. In 1990, after a long military struggle, it became the last African colony to receive full independence. ⇨ map (SOUTHERN AFRICA). ▷ **Namibian** *adj, n.*

nanny /ˈnænɪ/ *n* (*Brit*) **1** child's nurse. **2** (*infml*) grandmother.

nanny-goat /ˈnænɪ ɡəʊt/ *n* female goat. ⇨ illus at GOAT. Cf BILLY-GOAT.

Nansen /ˈnænsn/ Fridtjof (1861-1930), Norwegian explorer and statesman. He became famous through his expeditions to the North Pole, and was awarded the Nobel Peace prize in 1922 for his work for refugees during the First World War.

nap[1] /næp/ *n* short sleep, esp during the day: *have/take a quick nap after lunch.*

▷ **nap** *v* (**-pp-**) [I] **1** have a short sleep. **2** (idm) **catch sb napping** ⇨ CATCH[1].

nap[2] /næp/ *n* [U] short fibres on the surface of cloth, felt, etc, usu smoothed and brushed in one direction: *with/against the nap*, ie in the same direction as/the opposite direction to that of the nap. Cf PILE[4].

nap[3] /næp/ *n* (*Brit*) type of card-game.

napalm /ˈneɪpɑːm/ *n* [U] petrol in jellied form, used in making fire-bombs.

nape /neɪp/ *n* (usu *sing*) back part of the neck: *He kissed her on the nape of her neck.* ⇨ illus at HEAD.

naphtha /ˈnæfθə/ *n* [U] type of inflammable oil obtained from coal tar and petrol.

▷ **naphthalene** /-liːn/ *n* [U] strong-smelling substance obtained from coal tar and petrol, used in making dyes and mothballs.

Napier /ˈneɪpɪə(r)/ John (1550-1617), Scottish mathematician who discovered logarithms. His form of logarithms (known as **Napierian logarithms**) are calculated on the base e, but decimal logarithms, based on 10, were soon developed from them.

napkin /ˈnæpkɪn/ *n* **1** (also ˈ**table napkin**) piece of cloth or paper used at meals for protecting one's clothes and wiping one's lips and fingers. **2** (*Brit fml*) = NAPPY.

Napoleon I /nəˈpəʊlɪən/ (1769-1821), Emperor of France 1804-14, born (in Corsica) Napoleone Buonaparte. He was an officer in the army of the new French republic and took power in 1799. He reorganized France, founding its modern legal and education systems. As Emperor, he conquered most of Europe, failing only in his attempts on Russia and Britain. He was exiled in 1814 but returned, only to be defeated at the battle of *Waterloo. He surrendered to the British and died on St Helena. His nephew Louis Napoleon Bonaparte (1808-73) became the Emperor of France 1852-70 as Napoleon III.

nappy /ˈnæpɪ/ *n* (*Brit infml*) (also *fml* **napkin**) (*US* **diaper**) piece of towelling cloth or similar soft padding folded round a baby's bottom and between its legs to absorb or hold its urine and excreta: *a disposable nappy*, ie one that is made to be thrown away after being used once.

narcissism /ˈnɑːsɪsɪzəm/ *n* [U] (*psychology*) abnormal and excessive love or admiration for oneself. ▷ **narcissistic** /ˌnɑːsɪˈsɪstɪk/ *adj.*

narcissus /nɑːˈsɪsəs/ *n* (*pl* ~**es** /nɑːˈsɪsəsɪz/ or **-cissi** /nɑːˈsɪsaɪ/) any of several types of spring flowering bulbs, including the daffodil.

narcosis /nɑːˈkəʊsɪs/ *n* [U] (*medical*) state of unconsciousness, esp as caused by narcotic drugs.

narcotic /nɑːˈkɒtɪk/ *n* **1** substance causing sleep or (sometimes extreme) drowsiness: *The juice of this fruit is a mild narcotic.* **2** (often *pl*) drug that affects the mind: *Narcotics are a major threat to health.* ○ [attrib] *a narcotics agent*, ie one investigating the illegal trade in narcotics.

▷ **narcotic** *adj* of or having the effect of a narcotic: *a narcotic effect, substance.*

nark[1] /nɑːk/ *n* (*Brit sl*) police informer or spy.

nark[2] /nɑːk/ *v* [Tn usu passive] (*Brit sl*) annoy: *feeling narked about being ignored.*

narrate /nəˈreɪt; *US* ˈnæreɪt/ *v* [Tn] tell (a story); give a written or spoken account of: *narrate one's adventures* ○ *The story is narrated by its hero.*

▷ **narration** /nəˈreɪʃn/ *n* **1** [U] activity of telling a story, etc. **2** [C] story; account of events.

narrator *n* person who narrates.

narrative /ˈnærətɪv/ *n* **1** [C] spoken or written account of events; story: *a gripping narrative*

Southern Africa

about the war. **2** [U] **(a)** story-telling: *a master of narrative.* **(b)** narrated parts of a book, etc: *The novel contains more narrative than dialogue.*

▷ **narrative** *adj* [attrib] of, or in the form of, story-telling: *narrative literature*, ie stories and novels ○ *narrative poems* ○ *a writer of great narrative power*, ie able to describe events vividly.

narrow /ˈnærəʊ/ *adj* (**-er, -est**) **1** of small width compared with length: *a narrow bridge, path, ledge* ○ *The road was too narrow for cars to pass.* Cf BROAD[1] 1, THIN 1, WIDE 1. **2** of limited range or variety; small or restricted: *a narrow circle of friends* ○ *the narrow confines of small-town life.* **3** [usu attrib] with only a small margin; barely achieved: *a narrow escape from death* ○ *elected by a narrow majority*, eg when voting is 67 to 64 ○ *The favourite had a narrow lead over* (ie was not far ahead of) *the rest.* **4** limited in outlook; having little sympathy for the ideas, etc of others: *He has a very narrow mind.* ○ *She takes a rather narrow view of the subject.* **5** strict; exact: *What does the word mean in its narrowest sense?* **6** (idm) **a narrow ˈsqueak** situation in which one barely avoids failure or escapes danger. **the straight and narrow** ⇨ STRAIGHT[1].

▷ **narrow** *v* [I, Tn] (cause sth to) become narrower: *The road narrows here.* ○ *Her eyes narrowed* (ie She partly closed them) *menacingly.* ○ *The gap between the two parties has narrowed considerably.* ○ *In order to widen the road they had to narrow the pavement.*

narrowly *adv* **1** only just; by only a small margin: *We won narrowly.* ○ *He narrowly escaped drowning.* **2** closely; carefully: *observe someone narrowly.*

narrowness *n* [U].

narrows *n* [pl] **1** narrow strait or channel connecting two larger bodies of water. **2** narrow place in a river or pass.

□ **ˈnarrow boat** (*Brit*) traditonal long narrow barge used on canals. ⇨ illus at BARGE.

ˌnarrow-ˈminded /ˈmaɪndɪd/ *adj* not ready to listen to or tolerate the views of others: *a ˌnarrow-minded ˈbigot.* **ˌnarrow-ˈmindedly** *adv.* **ˌnarrow-ˈmindedness** *n* [U].

narwhal /ˈnɑːwəl/ *n* Arctic animal like a whale, the male of which has a long spiral tusk.

NASA /ˈnæsə/ *abbr* (*US*) National Aeronautics and Space Administration.

nasal /ˈneɪzl/ *adj* of, for or in the nose: *nasal sounds*, eg /m, n, ŋ/ ○ *a nasal spray*, ie one sprayed into the nose to make breathing easier ○ *a nasal voice*, ie one which produces sounds through both the nose and the mouth.

▷ **nasal** *n* nasal sound.

nasalize, -ise /ˈneɪzəlaɪz/ *v* [Tn] make (a sound) with the air stream, or part of it, passing through the nose.

nasally /ˈneɪzəlɪ/ *adv.*

nascent /ˈnæsnt/ *adj* (*fml*) beginning to exist; not yet well developed: *a nascent industry, talent, suspicion.*

Nash[1] /næʃ/ John (1752-1835), English architect. He worked in several different styles, but is most famous for the Royal Pavilion at Brighton with its Chinese influence, and for the neoclassical terraces around Regent's Park in London. ⇨ illus at REGENCY.

Nash[2] /næʃ/ Ogden (1902-71), American comic poet. His verse is famous for its witty comments and his use of unexpected rhymes and rhythms.

Nash[3] /næʃ/ Paul (1889-1946), English painter, illustrator and photographer. He was a war artist in the First and Second World Wars. His early work included scenes of destruction in a *Modernist style. In the 1930s he was influenced by Surrealism, as can be seen in his pictures of the *Battle of Britain. ⇨ illus.

Nash[4] /næʃ/ Richard (1674-1762), known as 'Beau Nash', a fashionable figure of English society in the 18th century. He was a professional gambler who dictated fashion and etiquette in Bath in the early Georgian age.

Nashville /ˈnæʃvɪl/ capital of the state of *Tennessee, USA. It is famous as the home of country-and-western music (COUNTRY).

nasturtium /nəˈstɜːʃəm; *US* næ-/ *n* garden plant with red, orange or yellow flowers and round flat leaves.

nasty /ˈnɑːstɪ; *US* ˈnæ-/ *adj* (**-ier, -iest**) **1** unpleasant; disgusting: *a nasty smell, taste, sight* ○ *I don't like the colour they've chosen for their new carpet — it looks really nasty.* Cf NICE. **2** **(a)** unkind; spiteful: *What a nasty man!* ○ *Don't be nasty to your little brother.* ○ *She has a nasty temper.* **(b)** morally bad: *a person with a nasty mind* ○ *nasty stories.* **3** **(a)** dangerous; threatening: *The weather is too nasty for sailing.* ○ *He had a nasty look in his eye.* ○ *This is a nasty corner*, ie is dangerous for cars going fast. **(b)** painful; severe: *a nasty cut, wound, etc* ○ *She had a nasty skiing accident.* ○ *The news gave me a nasty shock.* **4** (idm) **cheap and nasty** ⇨ CHEAP. **leave a bad/nasty taste in the mouth** ⇨ LEAVE[1]. **a nasty piece of work** (*infml*) unpleasant or untrustworthy person. ▷ **nastily** *adv.* **nastiness** *n* [U].

NAS/UWT /ˌen eɪ ˈes ˌjuː ˌdʌbljuː ˈtiː/ *abbr* (*Brit*) National Association of Schoolmasters and Union of Women Teachers. ⇨ article at TRADE UNION.

natch /nætʃ/ *adv* (*sl*) (used esp as a reply) naturally; of course.

Paul Nash: Totes Meer (Dead Sea)

National Symbols

Both Britain and the USA are often represented by national symbols. The symbols may signify the country as a whole or a region of it. The most obvious are the national flags. Britain's Union Jack contains the intersecting crosses of three of her patron saints: St George's cross, red on white, for England, St Andrew's cross, white on blue, for Scotland, and St Patrick's cross, red on white, for Ireland. The crosses represent the union of England with Scotland in 1707, and the union of both with Ireland in 1801. (The patron saint of Wales, St David, is not represented in the Union Jack.) St George is traditionally depicted on horseback slaying a dragon, and is also portrayed on some coins.

The US national flag is the Stars and Stripes, also known as the Star-Spangled Banner (after a patriotic song). The 13 red and white stripes represent the 13 original states of the North American Union, while the 50 white stars represent the present 50 states of the USA.

There are two personifications of Britain: John Bull and Britannia. John Bull represents the typical Englishman, supposed to have a 'bullish' appearance and characteristics. These may be seen as favourable, ie suggesting a strong, loyal, upright and persevering person, or unfavourable, suggesting someone who is stubborn, unfeeling, cruel and mean. The character was popularized (but not invented) by John Arbuthnot's collection of satirical pamphlets *The History of John Bull*, published in 1712.

Britannia is a female personification of Britain. She is depicted on coins leaning on a shield and holding a trident in one hand. She represents Britain as a victorious maritime nation. Her name is familiar from the patriotic song 'Rule, Britannia', composed in 1740.

The national personification of the USA is Uncle Sam, depicted as a tall, thin, elderly man with a grey goatee beard, wearing a dark morning coat and tails, a tall top hat covered in stars, and bright striped trousers. His top hat and trousers represent the Stars and Stripes. He is said to get his name from the abbreviation 'US Am' marked on military supplies and standing for 'United States of America'.

Britain is also represented by two animals, the lion and the bulldog. The lion, which with the unicorn is one of the two animal 'supporters' on the royal coat of arms, represents pride, bravery and valour. It is also, as 'king of the animals', a symbol of power and royalty. The bulldog, like John Bull, represents both tenacity and brute force.

The bald-headed eagle is a symbol for the USA and is used on the currency. The two main political parties, the Republicans and the Democrats, are respectively represented by an elephant and a donkey. The elephant represents power and strength; the donkey humility and patient hard work.

Britain is further symbolized by different plants and flowers: the rose for England, the leek and daffodil for Wales, the thistle for Scotland and the shamrock for Ireland. Another symbol for Ireland is the harp, which is also regarded as the national musical instrument of Wales. The oak is sometimes depicted as the traditional tree of England, partly for its connotations of strength and endurance, and partly for its royal associations. Not only is it regarded as the 'monarch of the forest' but it also has specific historic links with individual English kings. (Edward I held a parliament under an oak in the 14th century, and during the Civil War Charles II hid in an oak after his defeat at the Battle of Worcester in 1651.)

Well-known or historic buildings also serve as national symbols. In Britain, Tower Bridge, the Houses of Parliament, Big Ben and Parliament's clock tower are often used. Other popular symbolic sites are Piccadilly Circus, with its statue of 'Eros', and Nelson's Column in Trafalgar Square. The USA is often represented by two New York landmarks, the Statue of Liberty and the Empire State Building.

Both countries are sometimes identified by what is regarded as a typical inhabitant. This usually means, for an Englishman, a businessman wearing a bowler hat and pin-striped trousers and carrying a rolled umbrella. A ceremonially dressed guardsman, wearing a busby, or a policeman with characteristic blue helmet, are also used. Equivalent American stereotypes include the cowboy and the tourist abroad with his cheerful manner and brightly coloured shirt.

nation /ˈneɪʃn/ *n* large community of people, usu sharing a common history, language, etc, and living in a particular territory under one government: *the nations of Western Europe* ○ *the United Nations Organization.* ⇨ Usage at COUNTRY.

□ ˌ**nation-ˈwide** *adj, adv* over the whole of a nation: *a ˌnation-wide ˈsurvey, camˈpaign, etc* ○ *Police are looking for him nation-wide.*

national /ˈnæʃnəl/ *adj* [usu attrib] **1** of a nation; common to or characteristic of a whole nation: *a national treasure, institution, campaign, trait* ○ *national and local newspapers* ○ *the British national character* ○ *national opposition* (ie that expressed by all the citizens) *to government policy* ○ *a national holiday*, ie in all parts of a country ○ *national and international issues*, ie those that concern only one's own nation and those that concern many nations. **2** owned, controlled or financially supported by the State: *a national theatre.*

▷ **national** *n* **1** citizen of a particular nation: *He's a French national working in Italy.* **2 the National** (*infml*) = THE GRAND NATIONAL (GRAND).

nationally /ˈnæʃnəlɪ/ *adv.*

□ ˌ**national ˈanthem** song or hymn adopted by a nation, used to express loyalty and patriotism, esp on ceremonial occasions.

ˌ**national asˈsistance** (*Brit*) (formerly) money given by the government to people in need through illness, old age, etc (now called *supplementary benefit*).

ˌ**national ˈbank** (*US*) bank that has received a charter from the federal government.

the ˌ**National ˈDebt** total amount of money owed by a country to those who have lent it money.

the ˌ**National Economic Deˈvelopment Council** (*abbrs* **NEDC**, *infml* **Neddy**) (in Britain) organization with members representing the government, industry and the trade unions, and giving advice on economic development. Influential in the 1960s and 1970s, its power was reduced in the 1980s.

the ˌ**National ˈFront** British political party with extreme right-wing views, noted for its hostility to ethnic minorities. It has no MPs.

ˌ**National ˈGallery** gallery showing works of art that belong to a nation. The National Gallery in London, now in Trafalgar Square, was founded in 1824, and the National Gallery in Washington in 1937. ⇨ article at MUSEUM.

the ˌ**National ˈGrid 1** network supplying electric power throughout England, Scotland and Wales. **2** system of co-ordinates used on British Ordnance Survey maps. Every place has its own distinctive National Grid reference.

the ˌ**National ˈGuard** (in the USA) state militia that can be called into active service by the state or federal government. ⇨ article at ARMED FORCES.

the ˌ**National ˈHealth Service** (*abbr* **NHS**) (in Britain) public service providing medical care, paid for by taxation: *I got my hearing aid on the National Health (Service).* ⇨ articles at HEALTH, SOCIAL SECURITY.

ˌ**National Inˈsurance** (*abbr* **NI**) (*Brit*) system of compulsory payments made by employees and employers to provide State assistance to people who are ill, unemployed, retired, etc. ⇨ article at SOCIAL SECURITY.

ˌ**national ˈpark** area of countryside or historic interest whose natural beauty is maintained by the government for the public to enjoy.

ˌ**national ˈservice** period of compulsory service in the armed forces: *do one's national service.* ⇨ article at ARMED FORCES.

ˌ**National ˈSocialism** = NAZISM (NAZI).

the ˌ**National ˈTrust** (in Britain) society founded in 1895 to preserve places of natural beauty or historic interest. ⇨ articles at COUNTRYSIDE, CHARITY.

nationalism /ˈnæʃnəlɪzəm/ *n* [U] **1** devotion to one's own nation; patriotic feelings, principles or efforts. **2** movement favouring political independence in a country that is controlled by another or is part of another.

▷ **nationalist** /ˈnæʃnəlɪst/ *n* **1** supporter of nationalism(2): *Scottish nationalists*, ie those who want Scotland to have more self-government ○ [attrib] *nationalist sympathies.* **2** person in Northern Ireland who wishes to see it become part of the Irish Republic. Cf LOYALIST (LOYAL).

nationalistic /ˌnæʃnəˈlɪstɪk/ *adj* strongly favouring nationalism: *nationalistic fervour during the World Cup.*

nationality /ˌnæʃəˈnælətɪ/ *n* **1** [U, C] membership of a particular nation: *What is your nationality?* ○ *He has French nationality.* ○ *There were diplomats of all nationalities in Geneva.* **2** [C] ethnic group forming part of a political nation: *the two main nationalities of Czechoslovakia.*

nationalize, -ise /ˈnæʃnəlaɪz/ *v* [Tn] **1** transfer (sth) from private to public ownership: *nationalize the railways, the coal-mines, the steel industry, etc* ○ *a nationalized industry.* Cf DENATIONALIZE, PRIVATIZE. **2** make (sb) a national: *nationalized Poles and Greeks in the USA.*

▷ **nationalization, -isation** /ˌnæʃnəlaɪˈzeɪʃn; *US* -lɪˈz-/ *n* [U] nationalizing or being nationalized: *the nationalization of the railways.*

native /ˈneɪtɪv/ *n* **1** (**a**) person born in a place, country, etc, and associated with it by birth: *a native of London, Wales, India, Kenya.* (**b**) local inhabitant: *When we're on holiday in Greece, we live like the natives.* **2** (*esp offensive*) local inhabitant as distinguished from immigrants, visitors, etc, when the race to which he belongs is regarded as less civilized: *The white people here don't mix socially with the natives.* ○ *the first meeting between Captain Cook and the natives* (ie the aboriginal inhabitants) *of Australia.* **3** animal or plant that lives or grows naturally in a certain area: *The kangaroo is a native of Australia.*

▷ **native** *adj* **1** associated with the place and circumstances of one's birth: *one's native land, city, etc* ○ *Her native language/tongue is German.* **2** of natives (NATIVE 1a): *native customs, rituals,* *etc.* **3** (of qualities) belonging to a person's basic personality or character, not acquired by education, training, etc: *He has a great deal of native intelligence, ability, charm, etc.* **4** (**a**) [attrib] being a member of the people originally inhabiting a place: *native Americans*, ie American Indians. (**b**) ~ **to...** (of plants, animals, etc) originating in a place: *plants native to America*, eg tobacco, potatoes ○ *The tiger is native to India.* **5** (idm) **go ˈnative** (*esp joc*) (of an immigrant, a visitor, etc) adopt the customs of the local people and abandon one's own: *He's emigrated to the USA and gone completely native.*

□ **ˌnative ˈspeaker** person who has spoken (a particular language) since birth, rather than learning it later: *a native speaker of French, Italian, etc* ○ *Her English accent is so good, you would think she was a native speaker.*

nativity /nəˈtɪvətɪ/ *n* **1 the Nativity** [sing] the birth of Jesus Christ. **2 Nativity** [C] painting of the birth of Christ.

□ **naˈtivity play** play about the birth of Christ.

NATO (also **Nato**) /ˈneɪtəʊ/ *abbr* North Atlantic Treaty Organization (an alliance of several European countries, USA, Canada and Iceland agreeing to give each other military help if necessary). Cf SEATO. ⇨ article at ARMED FORCES.

natter /ˈnætə(r)/ *v* [I, Ipr, Ip] ~ **(on) (about sth)** (*Brit infml*) talk informally and aimlessly; chatter: *He nattered (on) about his work.*

▷ **natter** *n* [sing] (*Brit infml*) informal conversation: *have a quick natter.*

natterjack /ˈnætədʒæk/ *n* (also **ˌnatterjack ˈtoad**) small European toad with a yellow stripe down its back, which runs rather than hops.

natty /ˈnætɪ/ *adj* (**-ier**, **-iest**) (*infml*) **1** (*often derog*) smart and tidy; neat: *natty new uniforms for policewomen.* **2** well thought out; clever: *a natty little machine* ○ *a natty solution to a problem.* ▷ **nattily** *adv* (*often derog*): *nattily dressed.*

natural /ˈnætʃrəl/ *adj* **1** [attrib] of, concerned with or produced by nature(1), not by human beings: *natural phenomena, forces, etc*, eg thunderstorms, earthquakes, gravity ○ *the natural world*, ie of trees, rivers, animals and birds ○ *animals living in their natural state*, ie in the wild ○ *a country's natural resources*, ie its coal, oil, forests, etc ○ *land in its natural state*, ie not used for industry, farming, etc. **2** of or in agreement with the character or personality of a living thing: *natural charm, ability, etc* ○ *She has the natural grace of a born dancer.* ○ *It is natural for a bird to fly.* **3** [attrib] (of people) born with a certain skill, ability, etc: *He's a natural orator*, ie is very good at making speeches. ○ *She's a natural linguist*, ie learns languages easily. **4** as (might be) expected; normal: *die a natural death/of natural causes*, ie not by violence, etc, but normally, of old age ○ *It's only natural that she should be upset by the insult.* **5** not exaggerated or self-conscious; straightforward: *natural behaviour, manners, speech, etc* ○ *It is difficult to be natural when one is tense.* **6** (*music*) (used after the name of the note) (of notes) neither sharp nor flat: *B natural.* ⇨ illus at MUSIC, Cf FLAT[4] 2, SHARP *n.* **7** (**a**) (of a son or daughter) related by blood: *He's not our natural son — we adopted him when he was three.* (**b**) illegitimate: *her natural child.* **8** based on human reason alone: *natural justice* ○ *natural religion*, ie not based on divine revelation.

▷ **natural** *n* **1** (*music*) (**a**) musical note that is neither sharp nor flat: *There are two naturals in this chord.* (**b**) the sign (♮) placed before a note in printed music to show that it is neither sharp nor flat. **2** ~ **(for sth)** person considered ideally suited for a role, a job, an activity, etc: *He's a natural for the role of Lear.* ○ *She didn't have to learn how to run: she's a natural.*

naturalness *n* [U] state or quality of being natural.

□ **ˌnatural ˈchildbirth** method of childbirth in which the mother is given no anaesthetic and does breathing and relaxation exercises.

ˌnatural ˈgas gas found in the earth's crust, not manufactured. ⇨ article at ELECTRICITY.

ˌnatural ˈhistory study of plants and animals: *the natural history of the Gobi desert* ○ [attrib] *a natural history programme on TV.*

ˌnatural ˈlaw (also **law of nature**) rule for behaviour considered to be basic to human nature.

ˌnatural ˈnumber any whole number greater than zero.

ˌnatural phiˈlosophy (*dated*) science of physics, or physics and dynamics.

ˌnatural seˈlection evolutionary theory that animals survive or become extinct according to their ability to adapt themselves to their environment.

ˌnatural ˈwastage (also *esp US* **attrition**) gradual reduction in the number of workers through people leaving, dying, etc (as opposed to the sudden dismissal of many workers).

naturalism /ˈnætʃrəlɪzəm/ *n* [U] **1** style of art and literature in which there is faithful representation of real life. **2** (*philosophy*) theory that rejects the supernatural and claims that natural causes and laws explain everything. ▷ **naturalistic** /ˌnætʃrəˈlɪstɪk/ *adj*: *a naturalistic style, writer, painter.*

naturalist /ˈnætʃrəlɪst/ *n* person who studies animals, plants, birds and other living things.

naturalize, -ise /ˈnætʃrəlaɪz/ *v* [Tn usu passive] ~ **sb/sth (in...)** **1** make (sb from another country) a citizen (of the specified country): *a naturalized American who was born in Poland* ○ *She's a German who was naturalized in Canada.* **2** adopt (a foreign word, expression, etc) into a language: *English sporting terms have been naturalized in many languages.* **3** introduce (a plant or an animal) into a country where it is not native.

▷ **naturalization, -isation** /ˌnætʃrəlaɪˈzeɪʃn; *US* -lɪˈz-/ *n* [U] naturalizing or being naturalized: [attrib] *naturalization papers*, ie documents that prove that a person has been made a citizen of a country.

naturally /ˈnætʃrəlɪ/ *adv* **1** by nature(4a): *a naturally gifted actor* ○ *She's naturally musical.* **2** of course; as might be expected: *'Did you answer her letter?' 'Naturally!'* ○ *Naturally, as a beginner I'm not a very good driver yet.* **3** without artificial help, special treatment, etc: *Her hair curls naturally.* ○ *Plants grow naturally in such a good climate.* **4** without exaggeration; unselfconsciously: *She speaks and behaves naturally.* ○ *Try to act naturally, even if you're tense.* **5** easily; instinctively: *He's such a good athlete that most sports come naturally to him.*

nature /ˈneɪtʃə(r)/ *n* **1** [U] the whole universe and every created, not man-made, thing: *the wonders of nature* ○ *This phenomenon is unique in (the whole of) nature.* ○ [attrib] *nature worship.* **2** [U] simple life of man before he became civilized: *He wants to give away all his modern possessions and return to nature.* **3** [U] (esp **Nature**) force(s) controlling the events of the physical world: *Man is engaged in a constant struggle with Nature.* ○ *Miracles are contrary to nature.* **4** (**a**) [C, U] typical qualities and characteristics of a person or an animal: *It's his nature* (ie It's his natural reaction) *to be kind to people.* ○ *There is no cruelty in her nature.* ○ *Cats and dogs have quite different natures — dogs like company, cats are independent.* ○ *She is proud by nature.* (**b**) [sing] qualities of a material or non-material thing: *Chemists study the nature of gases.* ○ *He knows nothing of the nature of my work.* **5** [sing] sort; kind: *Things of that nature do not interest me.* **6** (idm) **against ˈnature** unnatural; immoral. **one's better feelings/nature** ⇨ BETTER[1]. **a call of nature** ⇨ CALL[1]. **in the nature of sth** similar to/like sth; a type of sth: *His speech was in the nature of an apology.* **in the ˈnature of things** because things are the way they are; inevitably: *It's in the nature of things that children misbehave; you can't change it.* **in a state of nature** ⇨ STATE[1]. **second ˈnature (to sb)** what seems natural or instinctive, but has been learned: *After a while, driving becomes second nature to you.*

▷ **-natured** (forming compound *adjs*) having qualities or characteristics of the specified kind: *ˌgood-ˈnatured* ○ *pleasant-natured.*

□ **ˈnature study** (in school) study of plants, animals, insects, etc.

ˈnature trail path through woods or countryside, along which interesting plants, animals, etc can be seen.

naturism /ˈneɪtʃərɪzəm/ *n* [U] = NUDISM. ▷ **naturist** /ˈneɪtʃərɪst/ *n* = NUDIST.

naturopath /ˈneɪtʃrəpæθ/ *n* person who treats illness by suggesting changes of diet, exercise, etc and without using medicines. ▷ **naturopathic** /ˌneɪtʃrəˈpæθɪk/ *adj.* **naturopathically** /-klɪ/ *adv.* **naturopathy** /ˌneɪtʃəˈrɒpəθɪ/ *n* [U].

naught = NOUGHT 2.

naughty /ˈnɔːtɪ/ *adj* (**-ier**, **-iest**) **1** (*infml*) (used by adults when talking to or about children) disobedient; bad; causing trouble: *He's a terribly naughty child.* ○ *You were naughty to pull the cat's tail.* **2** shocking or intended to shock people through mild indecency: *a naughty joke, story, etc.* ▷ **naughtily** *adv.* **naughtiness** *n* [U].

Nauru /ˈnaʊruː/ island and country in the SW Pacific; pop approx 8 000; official language English; capital Yaren; unit of currency dollar (= 100 cents). Formerly administered by Australia, New Zealand and Britain, it became independent in 1968. Its economy is based on its rich phosphate mines. ⇨ map at MICRONESIA.

nausea /ˈnɔːsɪə; *US* ˈnɔːʒə/ *n* [U] feeling of sickness or disgust: *overcome by nausea after eating raw meat* ○ *filled with nausea at the sight of cruelty to animals.*

▷ **nauseate** /ˈnɔːsɪeɪt; *US* ˈnɔːz-/ *v* [Tn] make (sb) feel nausea: *The idea of eating raw shellfish nauseates me.* **nauseating** *adj*: *nauseating food* ○ *a nauseating person* ○ *The smell is quite nauseating.* **nauseatingly** *adv.*

nauseous /ˈnɔːsɪəs; *US* ˈnɔːʃəs/ *adj* **1** causing nausea; disgusting. **2** (*esp US*) feeling nausea or disgust: *She felt/was nauseous during the sea crossing.*

nautical /ˈnɔːtɪkl/ *adj* of ships, sailors or navigation: *nautical terms*, ie used by sailors ○ *A nautical almanac gives information about the sun, moon, tides, etc.*

□ **ˌnautical ˈmile** (also **sea mile**) measure of distance at sea, about 1 852 m (6 080 ft). ⇨ App 10.

nautilus /ˈnɔːtɪləs; *US* ˈnɔːtələs/ *n* (*pl* ~**es**) small sea animal that has a spiral-shaped shell, the female's being very thin.

naval /ˈneɪvl/ *adj* of a navy; of warships: *a naval officer, uniform, battle* ○ *a naval power*, ie a country with a strong navy.

nave /neɪv/ *n* long central part of a church, where the congregation(1) sits. ⇨ illus at CHURCH.

navel /ˈneɪvl/ *n* (in humans) small hollow in the middle of the belly where the umbilical cord was attached at birth. ⇨ illus at HUMAN.

□ **ˌnavel ˈorange** large orange with a navel-like formation at the top.

navigable /ˈnævɪgəbl/ *adj* **1** (of seas, rivers, etc) suitable for ships, boats, etc to sail on: *The Rhine is navigable from Strasbourg to the sea.* **2** (of ships, etc) that can be steered and sailed: *not in a navigable condition.* ▷ **navigability** /ˌnævɪgəˈbɪlətɪ/ *n* [U].

navigate /ˈnævɪgeɪt/ *v* **1** [I] find the position and plot the course of a ship, an aircraft, a car, etc, using maps and instruments: *Which officer in the ship navigates?* ○ *I'll drive the car: you navigate*, ie tell me which way to go. **2** [Tn, Tn·pr] steer (a ship); pilot (an aircraft): *navigate the tanker round the Cape* ○ (*fig*) *navigate a Bill through Parliament.* **3** [Tn] (**a**) sail along, over or through (a sea, river, etc): *Who first navigated the Atlantic?* ○ *the first woman to navigate the Amazon alone.* (**b**) (*fig*) find one's way through, over, etc (sth): *I don't like having to navigate London's crowded streets.*

▷ **navigation** /ˌnævɪˈgeɪʃn/ *n* [U] **1** action of navigating. **2** art or science of navigating: *an expert in navigation.* **3** movement of ships over water or aircraft through the air: *There has been an increase in navigation through the canal*, ie More ships use it. ○ [attrib] *navigation lights*, ie on a ship or aircraft, showing its position and direction at night. **navi'gation satellite** man-made satellite in a fixed orbit that sends signals for use in navigation.

navigator *n* **1** person who navigates. **2** early explorer travelling by ship: *the 16th-century Spanish and Portuguese navigators.*

navvy /ˈnævɪ/ *n* (*Brit*) unskilled manual labourer who works on a building site, etc.

navy /ˈneɪvɪ/ *n* **1** (a) [C] country's force of ships and their crews: *naval exercises involving six navies.* (**b**) **the navy, the Navy** [Gp] warships of a specific country with their crews and the organization that administers them: *join the navy*, ie of one's own country ○ *an officer/sailor in the Royal Navy* ○ *The navy is/are introducing a new class of warship this year.* ⇨ App 4. ⇨ article at ARMED FORCES. **2** [U] = NAVY BLUE.

□ ˌ**navy 'blue** (also **navy**) dark blue as used for naval uniforms: *Where's my navy (blue) suit?*

nay /neɪ/ *adv* (*dated or rhet*) **1** and more than that; and indeed: *I suspect, nay, I am certain, that he is wrong.* **2** (*arch*) no. Cf YEA.

Nazi /ˈnɑːtsɪ/ *n, adj* (member) of the German National Socialist Party founded by *Hitler: *the rise of the Nazis* ○ *a Nazi meeting, newspaper.*

▷ **Nazism** /ˈnɑːtsɪzəm/ *n* [U] ideology of the Nazis, including belief in German racial superiority.

NB (also **nb**) /ˌen ˈbiː/ *abbr* (used before a written note) take special notice of; note well (Latin *nota bene*).

Nb *symb* niobium.

NBC /ˌen biː ˈsiː/ *abbr* (*US*) National Broadcasting Company: *heard it on NBC.* ⇨ article at TELEVISION.

NCO /ˌen siː ˈəʊ/ *abbr* (*Brit*) non-commissioned officer.

Nd *symb* neodymium.

NE *abbr* North-East(ern): *NE Kent.*

Ne *symb* neon.

Neanderthal /niːˈændətɑːl/ *adj* of an extinct type of man living in Europe in the Stone Age: *Neanderthal man* ○ *Neanderthal culture, artefacts, etc.*

neap /niːp/ (also **'neap-tide**) *n* tide when there is least difference between high and low water. Cf SPRING-TIDE (SPRING[1]).

Neapolitan /nɪəˈpɒlɪtən/ **1** *n, adj* (inhabitant) of Naples. **2 neapolitan** *adj* (of ice cream) in layers of different colours and flavours.

near[1] /nɪə(r)/ *adj* (**-er** /ˈnɪərə(r)/, **-est** /ˈnɪərɪst/) ~ (**to sb/sth**) **1** [usu pred except *nearest*] within a short distance or time from sb/sth; not far (from sb/sth): *His flat's very near* ○ *Where's the nearest bus-stop?* ○ *The supermarket is very near (to) the station.* ○ *We hope to move to the country in the near future*, ie very soon. ○ *4.15 is too near to the time of departure.* **2** closely related: *a near relation/relative* ○ *The nearest member of my family still alive is a rather distant cousin.* **3** [pred except *nearest*] similar: *We don't have that colour in stock — this is the nearest.* ○ *This copy is nearer the original than the others I've seen.* ⇨ Usage at NEXT[1]. **4** = NEARSIDE. **5** (idm) **close/dear/near to sb's heart** ⇨ HEART. **a close/near thing** ⇨ THING. **close/near to home** ⇨ HOME[1]. **one's ˌnearest and 'dearest** (*joc*) one's close family: *I always spend Christmas with my nearest and dearest.* **or ˌnear(est) 'offer** (*abbr* **ono**) or an amount that is less than the specified price but more than other offers: *I'll accept £350 for the car, or nearest offer.* **a ˌnear 'miss** (**a**) bomb, shot, etc that lands near the target but not quite on it. (**b**) situation where one just avoids, or escapes from, some mishap: *Luckily the van ahead of us skidded off the road on our left, but it was a very near miss.*

▷ **near** *v* [I, Tn] come closer to (sth) in space or time; approach: *The day is nearing when we'll have to decide.* ○ *The job is at last nearing completion.* ○ *The ship was nearing land.* ○ *The old man was nearing his end.*

nearness *n* [U].

□ **the ˌnear 'distance** part of a scene between the foreground and the background: *You can see the river in the near distance and the mountains beyond.*

the ˌNear 'East = THE MIDDLE EAST (MIDDLE).

'nearside (also **near**) *adj* [attrib] (*Brit*) (of a part of a vehicle, a road or an animal) on the left-hand side: *the nearside front wheel, door, lane of traffic, etc* ○ *the near foreleg of a horse* ○ *He didn't see the car approaching on his nearside.* Cf OFFSIDE[2].

ˌ**near-'sighted** *adj* only able to see clearly things that are close to one's eyes; short-sighted: *I'm very near-sighted without my glasses on.* ˌ**near-'sightedness** *n* [U]

NOTE ON USAGE: Compare **near**, **nearby** and **near by**. Only **near** has a comparative and superlative form and can relate to time as well as space. **1** Both **near** and **nearby** are adjectives. **Nearby**, not **near**, is used attributively when space, not time, is referred to: *the near future* ○ *Those shops are nearer/the nearest.* ○ *a nearby village.* **2** Both **near** and **near by** can be used adverbially. **Near by** sometimes modifies the whole sentence: *Do you live near/near by?* ○ *My exams are getting nearer.* ○ *Near by, the cars could be heard speeding past on the motorway.* **3 Near** (**to**) is a preposition: *Is there a cinema near here?*

near[2] /nɪə(r)/ *prep* **1** with only a short distance or time between: *Bradford is near Leeds.* ○ *Don't sit near the door.* ○ *My birthday is very near Christmas.* **2** (idm) **be, come, etc near to sth/doing sth** almost experience, reach or do sth: *I came near to screaming.* ○ *She was near to tears*, ie almost crying ○ *He felt near to death.*

▷ **near** *adv* **1** at a short distance away; near by: *We found some shops quite near.* ○ *Are you all sitting near enough to see the screen?* **2** (idm) **as near as** as accurately as: *There were about 500 people there, as near as I could judge.* **as ˌnear as 'dammit; as ˌnear as ˌmakes no 'difference** (*infml*) an amount, a measurement, etc that is not significantly more or less: *It's going to cost £200 or as near as dammit.* ○ *It's 500 miles from here, or as near as makes no difference.* **far and near/wide** ⇨ FAR[2]. **not anywhere/nowhere 'near** certainly not; far from: *The hall was nowhere near full.* ○ *I've nowhere near enough for the fare.* ○ *There wasn't anywhere near enough to eat and drink* ○ *It's nowhere near the colour I'm looking for.* **so ˌnear and ˌyet so 'far** (used to comment on an attempt that was nearly successful but failed finally).

near- (forming compound *adjs*) almost: *near-'perfect* ○ *near-'vertical* ○ *a near-'featureless ˌlandscape.*

□ **'nearby** *adj* [attrib] near in position; not far away: *a nearby church, river, town.*

near 'by *adv* at a short distance from sb/sth: *They live near by.* ○ *The beach is quite near by.* ⇨ Usage at NEAR[1].

nearly /ˈnɪəlɪ/ *adv* **1** not completely; almost; very close to: *nearly empty, full, finished, etc* ○ *It's nearly one o'clock.* ○ *It's nearly time to leave.* ○ *We're nearly there.* ○ *There's nearly £1 000 here.* ○ *She nearly won first prize.* **2** (idm) **not nearly** far from; much less than: *There isn't nearly enough time to learn all these new words* ○ *We aren't nearly ready for the inspection.* **pretty much/nearly/well** ⇨ PRETTY. ⇨ Usage at ALMOST.

neat /niːt/ *adj* **1** (a) (of things) arranged in an orderly way; done carefully; tidy: *a neat cupboard, room, row of books, garden* ○ *neat work, writing, etc.* (**b**) (of people) liking to keep order and do things carefully; tidy: *a neat worker, dresser, etc.* **2** (a) (of clothes) simple and elegant: *a neat uniform, dress, etc.* (**b**) having a pleasing shape or appearance: *She has a neat figure.* **3** economical with time and effort; skilful; efficient: *a neat way of doing the job* ○ *a neat solution to the problem* ○ *He gave a neat summary of the financial situation.* **4** (*infml esp US*) fine; splendid: *a neat movie, idea, car.* **5** (*US* usu **straight**) (of spirits or wines) unmixed with water; undiluted: *a neat whisky, vodka, etc* ○ *drink one's whisky neat.* ▷ **neatly** *adv.* **neatness** *n* [U].

Nebraska /nəˈbræskə/ state in the central USA. Most of it is a vast plain with the Bad Lands (BAD[1]) in the north-west; its economy is based largely on agriculture. ⇨ map at App 1.

nebula /ˈnebjʊlə/ *n* (*pl* ~**e** /-liː/ or ~**s**) light or dark patch in the night sky caused by a cluster of very distant stars or a cloud of dust or gas: *the Crab nebula.*

▷ **nebular** /-lə(r)/ *adj* of nebulas.

nebulous /ˈnebjʊləs/ *adj* **1** cloudlike; hazy. **2** (*fig*) vague; unclear: *nebulous ideas, plans, concepts, etc.*

necessarily /ˌnesəˈserəlɪ *or, in British use,* ˈnesəsərəlɪ/ *adv* as an inevitable result: *Big men aren't necessarily strong men.*

necessary /ˈnesəsərɪ; *US* -serɪ/ *adj* **1** essential for a purpose; that cannot be done without or avoided: *I haven't got the necessary tools.* ○ *Is it necessary for us to meet/necessary that we meet?* ○ *She hasn't the experience necessary for the job.* ○ *Sleep is necessary to/for one's health.* **2** that must be; inevitable: *If a = b, and b = c, then the necessary conclusion is that a = c.* ○ *the necessary consequences.* **3** (idm) **a ˌnecessary 'evil** thing that is undesirable and possibly harmful but must be accepted for practical reasons: *The loss of jobs is regarded by some as a necessary evil in the fight against inflation.*

▷ **necessary** *n* **1 necessaries** [pl] things needed for living: *the little necessaries of life.* **2 the necessary** [sing] (*infml*) what is needed, esp the money needed to pay for sth: *I'd like a car, but I just haven't got the necessary.*

necessitate /nɪˈsesɪteɪt/ *v* [Tn, Tg, Tsg] (*fml*) make (sth) necessary: *It's an unpopular measure, but the situation necessitates it.* ○ *Your proposal will necessitate borrowing more money.*

necessitous /nɪˈsesɪtəs/ *adj* (*fml*) poor; needy: *in necessitous circumstances*, ie in poverty.

necessity /nɪˈsesətɪ/ *n* **1** [U] ~ (**for sth/to do sth**) circumstances that force one to do sth; state of being necessary; need: *He felt a great necessity to talk about his problems.* ○ *She was driven by necessity to steal food for her starving children.* ○ *We will always come in cases of extreme necessity*, ie if we are very much needed. ○ *There's no necessity (for you) to write to your mother every single day.* ○ *We must all bow to necessity*, ie accept what is inevitable. **2** [C] necessary thing: *Food, clothing and shelter are all basic necessities of life.* **3** [sing] natural law that is seen as governing human action: *Is it a logical necessity that higher wages will lead to higher prices?* **4** (idm) **make a virtue of necessity** ⇨ VIRTUE. **neˌcessity is the ˌmother of inˈvention** (*saying*) the need for sth forces people to find a way of getting it. **of neˈcessity** necessarily; unavoidably; inevitably.

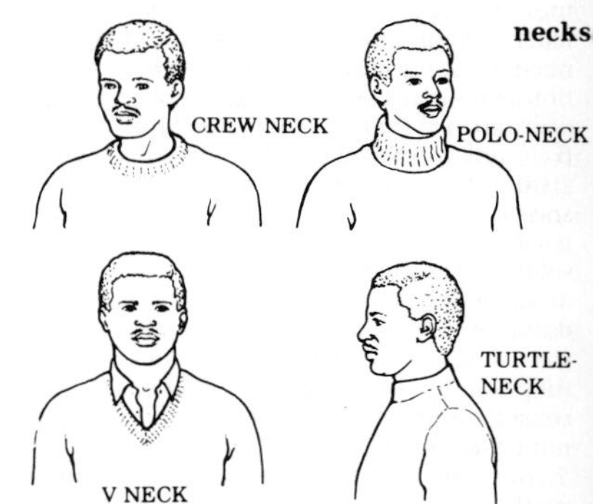

neck /nek/ *n* **1** [C] (a) part of the body that connects the head to the shoulders: *wrap a scarf round one's neck* ○ *She fell and broke her neck.* ○ *Giraffes have very long necks.* ⇨ illus at HEAD. (**b**) part of a garment round this: *a V-neck sweater* ○ *My shirt is rather tight in the neck.* ⇨ illus. **2** [U, C] flesh of an animal's neck as food: *buy some neck of lamb.* **3** [C] narrow part of sth, like a neck in shape or position: *the neck of a bottle/violin* ○ *a neck of land*, eg an isthmus. ⇨ illus at MUSIC. **4** (idm) **break one's 'neck (doing sth/to do sth)** (*infml*) work especially hard at sth: *I'm not going to break* *my neck to finish my essay today — my teacher doesn't want it until next week.* **breathe down sb's neck** ⇨ BREATHE. **dead from the neck up** ⇨ DEAD. ˌ**get it in the ˈneck** (*infml*) be severely scolded or punished for sth: *You'll get it in the neck if you're caught stealing.* **a millstone round one's neck** ⇨ MILLSTONE (MILL[1]). ˌ**neck and ˈcrop** completely: *His shot beat the goalkeeper neck and crop.* ˌ**neck and ˈneck (with sb/sth)** (in horse-racing or in a contest, struggle, etc) with neither one nor the other having an advantage or a lead; level: *The two contestants are neck and neck with 20 points each.* ˌ**neck of the ˈwoods** (*infml*) area; neighbourhood: *What are you doing in this neck of the woods?* ˌ**neck or ˈnothing** taking great risks: *She drove neck or nothing to get there on time.* **a pain in the neck** ⇨ PAIN. **risk/save one's ˈneck** risk/save one's life; risk/avoid great misfortune: *He saved his own neck by fleeing the country.* **stick one's neck out** ⇨ STICK[2]. **(be) up to one's neck in sth** very deeply involved in sth: *Even as a young man he was up to his neck in crime.* **win/lose by a ˈneck** (in horse-racing, etc) win/lose by a small margin. **wring sb's neck** ⇨ WRING.

▷ **neck** *v* [I] (*infml*) (of couples) hug and kiss each other intimately: *The two of them were necking on a park bench.*

□ ˈ**neckband** *n* narrow strip of material round the neck of a garment.

neckerchief /ˈnekətʃɪf/ *n* scarf or piece of cloth worn round the neck.

necklace /ˈneklɪs/ *n* ornament of pearls, beads, etc worn round the neck.

necklet /ˈneklɪt/ *n* ornament or fur worn round the neck.

ˈ**neckline** *n* outline of the edge of (esp) a woman's garment at or below the neck: *a dress with a high/ low/ plunging neckline.*

ˈ**necktie** *n* (*dated or US*) = TIE[1] 1.

ˈ**neckwear** *n* [U] (in shops) ties, scarves, etc.

necr(o)- *comb form* of death or the dead: *necromancer* ○ *necropolis.*

necromancy /ˈnekrəʊmænsɪ/ *n* [U] art or practice of communicating by magic with the dead in order to learn about the future.

▷ **necromancer** /-sə(r)/ *n* person who practises necromancy.

necrophilia /ˌnekrəˈfɪlɪə/ *n* [U] abnormal (and usu sexual) attraction to dead bodies.

▷ **necrophiliac** /-ˈfɪlɪæk/ *n* person who is affected by necrophilia.

necropolis /nɪˈkrɒpəlɪs/ *n* (*pl* ~**es** /-lɪsɪz/) cemetery, esp a large ancient one.

necrosis /nɪˈkrəʊsɪs/ *n* [U] (*medical*) death of body tissue in localized areas.

nectar /ˈnektə(r)/ *n* [U] **1** sweet liquid produced by flowers and collected by bees for making honey. **2** (in Greek and Roman mythology) the drink of the gods: (*fig*) *On a hot summer day a long cool drink is like nectar.* Cf AMBROSIA.

nectarine /ˈnektərɪn/ *n* type of peach with a thin smooth skin and firm flesh.

nectary /ˈnektərɪ/ *n* organ in a plant that produces nectar.

NEDC /ˌen iː diː ˈsiː/ (also *infml* **Neddy** /ˈnedɪ/) *abbr* (*Brit*) National Economic Development Council.

née /neɪ/ *adj* (used after the name of a married woman and before her father's family name) having had the maiden name; born with the name: *(Mrs) Jane Smith, née Brown.*

need[1] /niːd/ *modal v* (*neg* **need not**, *contracted form* **needn't** /ˈniːdnt/) (used only in negative sentences and questions, after *if* and *whether* or with *hardly, scarcely, no one,* etc) **1** (indicating obligation): *You needn't finish that work today.* ○ *'Need you go yet?' 'No, I needn't.'* ○ *He wondered whether they need send a deposit.* ○ *If she wants anything, she need only ask.* ○ *I need hardly tell you* (ie You must already know) *that the work is dangerous.* ○ *Nobody need be afraid of catching the disease.* ⇨ Usage 1 at MUST[1]. **2** (used with *have* + a past participle to indicate that actions in the past were or may have been unnecessary): *You needn't have hurried.* ○ *She needn't have come in person — a letter would have been enough.* ○ *Need you have paid so much?* ○ *Need they have sold the farm?*

need[2] /niːd/ *v* **1** [Tn, Tt, Tg] require (sth/sb); want; lack: *That dog needs a bath.* ○ *Do you need any help?* ○ *Don't go — I may need you.* ○ *I need to consult a dictionary.* ○ *This plant needs to be watered twice a week.* ○ *The garden doesn't need watering — it rained last night.* ○ (*ironic*) *What that child needs* (ie deserves) *is a good spanking.* **2** [Tt] (indicating obligation): *She needs to have access to our files.* ○ *What do you need to take with you on holiday?* ○ *I didn't need to go to the bank — I borrowed some money from Mary.* ○ *I didn't need to go out but I wanted a breath of fresh air.* ○ *A dog needs to be taken out for a walk every day.* ○ *Will we need to show our passports?* ⇨ Usage 1 at MUST[1].

need[3] /niːd/ *n* **1** [sing, U] ~ **(for sth)**; ~ **(for sb) to do sth** circumstances in which sth is lacking, or necessary, or which require sth to be done; necessity: *There's a great need for a new book on the subject.* ○ *I feel a need to talk to you about it.* ○ *There's no need for you to start yet.* **2 needs** [pl] basic necessities or requirements: *supply a baby's needs* ○ *I don't live in luxury but I have enough to satisfy my needs.* ○ *Will £20 be enough for your immediate needs?* **3** [U] poverty; misfortune; adversity: *He helped me in my hour of need.* **4** (idm) **a friend in need** ⇨ FRIEND. **have need of sth** (*fml*) need sth: *I have no need of your help, thank you.* **if need be** if necessary: *There's always the food in the freezer if need be.* ○ *If need be, I can do extra work at the weekend.* ˌ**your need is** ˌ**greater than ˈmine** (*saying*) we both want this but you must have it because you need it more than I do.

▷ **needful** /-fl/ *adj* **1** necessary: *promise to do what is needful.* **2** (idm) **do the ˈneedful** do what is required, esp by providing money for sth. **needfully** /-fəlɪ/ *adv.*

needless *adj* **1** without need; unnecessary: *needless work, trouble, worry.* **2** (idm) ˌ**needless to ˈsay** as you already know or would expect: *Needless to say, I survived.* ○ *Needless to say, he kept his promise.* **needlessly** *adv.*

needs *adv* (*arch or rhet*) (used only with *must*, often indicating sarcasm) **1** of necessity; from a sense of personal obligation: *He must needs break a leg just before we go on holiday*, ie It was a foolish action causing great inconvenience. **2** (idm) ˌ**needs** ˌ**must when the** ˌ**devil ˈdrives** (*saying*) one is sometimes forced by circumstances to do what one does not want to do.

needy *adj* without the things that are needed for life, ie food and shelter; very poor: *a needy family* ○ *help the poor and needy.*

needle /ˈniːdl/ *n* **1** [C] small thin piece of polished steel with a point at one end and a hole for thread at the other, used in sewing. **2** [C] long thin piece of plastic, metal, polished wood, etc without a hole but with a pointed end (for knitting) or a hook (for crocheting): ˈ*knitting needles* ○ *a* ˈ*crochet needle.* **3** [C] thin, usu metal pointer on a dial, eg of a compass, meter, etc. **4** [C] **(a)** pointed hollow end of a syringe used for giving injections. ⇨ illus at INJECTION. **(b)** (*US infml*) injection: *She was given a needle for whooping cough.* **5** [C] thing like a needle(1) in shape, appearance or use, eg the thin pointed leaf of a pine tree, a pointed rock or peak, an obelisk, etc. ⇨ illus at TREE. **6** [C] stylus used in playing gramophone records. **7** [U] (*infml*) anger or hositility, esp in situations of rivalry: *A certain amount of needle has crept into* (ie gradually appeared in) *this game.* ○ [attrib] *a needle match/ game*, ie one in which there is particularly fierce rivalry between the two sides. **8** (idm) **give sb/get the ˈneedle** (*sl*) (cause sb to) become annoyed. **look for a needle in a ˈhaystack** (*saying*) look for one thing among many others, without hope of finding it: *Searching for one man in this big city is like looking for a needle in a haystack.* **sharp as a needle** ⇨ SHARP. Cf PINS AND NEEDLES (PIN[1]).

▷ **needle** *v* [Tn] (*infml*) provoke or annoy (sb), esp with words: *Stop needling him or he might hit you.*

needlecraft [U] skill in sewing or embroidery.

ˈ**needle-point** *n* [U] embroidery done on canvas.

ˈ**needlewoman** *n* (*pl* **-women**) woman who sews (usu skilfully); seamstress: *a good, poor, etc needlewoman.*

ˈ**needlework** *n* [U] sewing or embroidery.

needlecord /ˈniːdlkɔːd/ *n* [U] type of corduroy with a pattern of close narrow ridges.

needy /ˈniːdɪ/ *adj* (**-ier, -iest**) lacking the necessities of life; very poor: *a needy family* ○ *food for the poor and needy.*

ne'er /neə(r)/ *adv* (*arch*) never.

ne'er-do-well /ˈneə duː wel/ *n* useless, lazy or irresponsible person: [attrib] *How is that ne'er-do-well brother of yours?*

nefarious /nɪˈfeərɪəs/ *adj* (*fml*) wicked; unlawful: *nefarious deeds, activities, etc.* ▷ **nefariously** *adv.* **nefariousness** *n* [U].

neg *abbr* negative.

negate /nɪˈgeɪt/ *v* [Tn] (*fml*) **1** deny or disprove the existence of (sb/sth): *How can you negate God?* **2** cancel the effect of (sth); nullify: *These facts negate your theory.*

▷ **negation** /nɪˈgeɪʃn/ *n* (*fml*) **1** [U] action of denying: *Shaking the head is a sign of negation.* **2** [C] denial: *This theory is a negation of all traditional beliefs.*

negative /ˈnegətɪv/ *adj* **1** (of words, sentences, etc) expressing denial or refusal; indicating 'no' or 'not': *a negative sentence, question, adverb* ○ *give sb a negative answer* ○ *a negative decision on an application.* Cf AFFIRMATIVE. **2** lacking in definite, constructive or helpful qualities or characteristics: *He has a very negative attitude to his work*, ie is not interested in trying to do it well or properly. ○ *negative criticism*, ie that does not suggest how the thing criticized could be improved ○ *a negative definition*, ie one that defines a word, etc by saying what it does not mean ○ *The results of her pregnancy test were negative*, ie showed that she was not pregnant. **3** (*mathematics*) (of a quantity) less than zero; (of a number) that has to be subtracted from other numbers or from zero. **4** containing or producing the type of electric charge carried by electrons: *the negative terminal of a battery*, ie the one through which current enters from an external circuit. **5** (of a photograph) with the light areas of the actual object(s) or scene appearing as dark, and the dark areas as light. Cf POSITIVE.

▷ **negative** *n* **1** word or statement that expresses or means denial or refusal: *'No', 'not' and 'neither' are negatives.* **2** developed photographic film, etc on which the light and dark areas of the actual object(s) or scene are reversed and from which positive pictures can be made. **3** (idm) **in the ˈnegative** (*fml*) (of a sentence, etc) containing a negative word; expressing denial, refusal, etc: *She answered in the negative*, ie said 'no'.

negative *v* [Tn] (*fml*) **1** refuse to approve or grant (sth); veto: *negative a request, an application, etc.* **2** prove (sth) to be untrue; disprove. **3** neutralize (an effect).

negatively *adv.*

neglect /nɪˈglekt/ *v* **1** [Tn] give no or not enough care or attention to (sb/sth): *neglect one's studies, children, health.* **2** [no passive: Tt, Tg] fail or forget to do sth, esp carelessly; leave undone (what one ought to do): *He neglected to write and say 'Thank you'.* ○ *Don't neglect writing to your mother.*

▷ **neglect** *n* [U] neglecting or being neglected: *She was severely criticized for neglect of duty.* ○ *The car shows signs of neglect.* ○ *The garden was in a state of total neglect.*

neglected *adj* showing a lack of care or attention: *a neglected appearance* ○ *The house looks very neglected.*

neglectful /-fl/ *adj* ~ **(of sth/sb)** in the habit of neglecting things or people: *neglectful of one's appearance, responsibilities, family.* **neglectfully** /-fəlɪ/ *adv.* **neglectfulness** *n* [U].

négligé (also **negligee**) /ˈneglɪʒeɪ; *US* ˌneglɪˈʒeɪ/ *n* woman's light flimsy dressing-gown.

negligence /ˈneglɪdʒəns/ *n* [U] lack of proper care or attention; carelessness: *The accident was due to her negligence.*

negligent /ˈneglɪdʒənt/ *adj* not giving proper attention or care to sth; careless: *She was negligent* *in her work.* ○ *He was negligent of his duties.* ▷ **negligently** *adv.*

negligible /ˈneglɪdʒəbl/ *adj* of little importance or size; not worth considering: *a negligible amount, error, effect* ○ *Losses in trade this year were negligible.*

negotiable /nɪˈgəʊʃɪəbl/ *adj* **1** that can be settled by discussion: *The salary is negotiable.* **2** (of a cheque, bond, etc) that can be exchanged for cash or passed to another person instead of cash: *negotiable securities.* **3** (of rivers, roads, etc) that can be crossed, passed along or over, etc: *The mountain track is negotiable, but only with difficulty.*

negotiate /nɪˈgəʊʃɪeɪt/ *v* **1** (**a**) [I, Ipr] ~ (**with sb**) try to reach agreement by discussion: *We've decided to negotiate with the employers about our wage claim.* (**b**) [Tn, Tn·pr] ~ **sth** (**with sb**) arrange or settle sth in this way: *negotiate a sale, loan, treaty* ○ *a negotiated settlement.* **2** [Tn] get or give money for (cheques, bonds, etc). **3** [Tn] get over or past (an obstacle, etc) successfully: *The climber had to negotiate a steep rock face.* ○ *The horse negotiated* (ie jumped over) *the fence with ease.* **4** (idm) **the neˈgotiating table** formal meeting to discuss wages, conditions, etc: *Both sides still refuse to come to the negotiating table.*

▷ **negotiator** *n* person who negotiates.

negotiation /nɪˌgəʊʃɪˈeɪʃn/ *n* [U, C often *pl*] discussion aimed at reaching an agreement; negotiating: *be in negotiation with sb* ○ *The price is a matter of/for negotiation.* ○ *Negotiation of the sale took a long time.* ○ *enter into/open/carry on/resume negotiations with sb* ○ *A settlement was reached after lengthy negotiations.*

Negress /ˈni:gres/ *n* (*sometimes offensive*) Negro woman or girl.

Negro /ˈni:grəʊ/ *n* (*pl* ~**es** /-rəʊz/) (*sometimes offensive*) member of the black-skinned race of mankind that originated in Africa.

Negroid /ˈni:grɔɪd/ *adj* having the physical characteristics that are typical of Negroes: *a Negroid face, nose, etc.*

▷ **Negroid** *n* Negroid person.

Nehemiah /ˌni:ɪˈmaɪə/ book of the Old Testament telling of the work of the Hebrew leader Nehemiah, who rebuilt the walls of Jerusalem and introduced moral and social reforms. ➪ App 5.

Nehru /ˈneəru:/ Pandit Jawaharlal (1889-1964), first prime minister of India 1947-64. He was involved with *Gandhi in independence negotations. He was the father of Indira Gandhi, India's first woman prime minister 1966-84.

neigh /neɪ/ *n* long high-pitched cry of a horse.

▷ **neigh** *v* [I] make this cry.

neighbour (*US* **neighbor**) /ˈneɪbə(r)/ *n* **1** (**a**) person living next to or near another: *Turn your radio down, or you'll wake the neighbours.* ○ *We're next-door neighbours,* ie Our houses are side by side. ○ *They are close neighbours of ours,* ie live not far from us. (**b**) person, thing or country that is next to or near another: *We were neighbours* (ie sat side by side) *at dinner.* ○ *When the big tree fell, it brought down two of its smaller neighbours,* ie two smaller trees near it. ○ *Britain's nearest neighbour is France.* **2** fellow human being: *Love your neighbour* ○ *be a good neighbour,* ie treat others kindly.

▷ **neighbour** (*US* **-bor**) *v* [Ipr] ~ **on sth** be next or near to sth: *The garden neighbours on a golf-course.* **neighbouring** (*US* **-boring**) /ˈneɪbərɪŋ/ *adj* [attrib] situated or living next or near to sb/sth: *the neighbouring country, town, village, etc* ○ *neighbouring families.*

neighbourhood (*US* **-borhood**) /ˈneɪbəhʊd/ *n* **1** [CGp] (people living in a) district; area near a particular place: *She is liked by the whole neighbourhood.* ○ *We live in a rather rich neighbourhood.* ○ *There's some beautiful scenery in our neighbourhood.* ○ *We want to live in the neighbourhood of London.* **2** (idm) **in the neighbourhood of** approximately: *a sum in the neighbourhood of £500.*

neighbourly (*US* **-borly**) *adj* kind and friendly, as neighbours should be. **neighbourliness** (*US* **-borliness**) *n* [U].

neither /ˈnaɪðə(r), ˈni:ðə(r)/ *indef det, indef pron* not one nor the other of two. (**a**) (*det*): *Neither boy is to blame.* ○ *Neither answer is correct.* ○ *I saw neither Mr nor Mrs Smith at church.* ○ *Neither one of us could understand German.* ○ *In neither case was a decision reached.* (**b**) (*pron*): *I chose neither of them.* ○ *'Which is your car?' 'Neither, mine's being repaired.'*

▷ **neither** *adv* **1** not either (used before a *modal v* or *aux v* placed in front of its subject): *He doesn't like Beethoven and neither do I.* ○ *I haven't been to New York before and neither has my sister.* ○ *'Did you see it?' 'No.' 'Neither did I.'* **2 neither...nor** not...and not: *He neither knows nor cares what happened.* ○ *The hotel is neither spacious nor comfortable.*

nelly /ˈnelɪ/ *n* (idm) ˌ**not on your ˈnelly** (*Brit sl*) certainly not.

Nelson /ˈnelsn/ Horatio, Viscount Nelson (1758-1805), British admiral. His victories during the wars against *Napoleon ensured Britain's superiority at sea and prevented a French invasion. He put an end to Napoleon's power at sea at *Trafalgar, but was killed in the battle.

□ ˌ**Nelson's ˈColumn** tall column, nearly 44 m (185 ft) high, in Trafalgar Square, London, erected in 1840-43 as a memorial to Nelson. It has four large bronze lions by *Landseer around its base.

nelson /ˈnelsn/ *n* wrestling hold in which one arm is passed under the opponent's arm from behind, while the other hand presses his neck forward. Cf HALF NELSON (HALF[2]).

nematode /ˈnemətəʊd/ *n* (also ˈ**nematode worm**) type of long thin unsegmented worm, esp one found as a parasite in the human digestive system.

nem con /ˌnem ˈkɒn/ *abbr* without any objection being raised; unanimously (Latin *nemine contradicente*): *The resolution was carried nem con.*

nemesis /ˈneməsɪs/ *n* (*pl* **-eses** /-əsi:z/) (usu *sing*) (*fml*) deserved and unavoidable punishment for wrongdoing: *to meet one's nemesis.*

neo- *comb form* new; modern; in a later form: *neolithic* ○ *neoclassical.*

neoclassical /ˌni:əʊˈklæsɪkl/ *adj* of or in a style of art, literature or music that is based on or influenced by the classical style.

neo-colonialism /ˌni:əʊ kəˈləʊnɪəlɪzəm/ *n* [U] use of economic or political pressure by powerful countries to obtain or keep influence over other countries, esp former colonies.

neodymium /ˌnɪəˈdɪmɪəm/ *n* [U] (*symb* **Nd**) soft silvery metallic element, used in certain alloys and for colouring glass.

neolithic /ˌni:əˈlɪθɪk/ *adj* of the later part of the Stone Age, when people began to form settled agricultural communities and to tame wild animals, leading to the growth of human population. Neolithic civilization may first have appeared in the Middle East, around the *Fertile Crescent: *neolithic man* ○ *neolithic tools.* Cf MESOLITHIC, PALAEOLITHIC.

neologism /ni:ˈɒlədʒɪzəm/ *n* **1** [C] newly-invented word. **2** [U] creating or using new words: *an author with a fondness for neologism.*

neon /ˈni:ɒn/ *n* [U] (*symb* **Ne**) chemical element, a colourless inert gas much used in illuminated signs because it glows with a bright light when an electric current is passed through it: [attrib] *a neon lamp/light/sign.* ➪ App 11.

neophyte /ˈni:əfaɪt/ *n* (*fml*) **1** person recently converted to some belief or religion. **2** beginner learning a new skill.

Neoplatonism /ˌnɪəʊˈpleɪtənɪzəm/ *n* [U] school of philosophy developed in the non-Christian world around 250 AD, based on the teachings of *Plato, *Aristotle and other Greek philosophers, and influenced by mystical religions of the Near East. Its basic belief was that all things came from the ultimate being called the One, to which the human soul sought to return. It had a strong influence on medieval and Renaissance philosophy.

Nepal /nɪˈpɔ:l/ country in southern Asia, between India and China; pop approx 18 234 000; official language Nepali; capital Kathmandu; unit of currency rupee (= 100 pice). Most of the country is mountainous, with the *Himalayas and *Everest in the north. Its geographical position has isolated it from contact with the rest of the world and its traditional way of life remains largely unchanged. Its economy is based on agriculture and there is no real industry. There are plans to develop hydroelectric power. ➪ map at INDIA.

▷ **Nepalese** /ˌnepəˈli:z/ *adj, n* (*pl* unchanged) [C, U] Nepali.

Nepali /nɪpɔ:lɪ/ *adj* of Nepal. — *n* **1** [U] language of Nepal, an Indo-European language related to Hindi and other Indian languages. **2** [C] native or inhabitant of Nepal.

nephew /ˈnevju:, ˈnefju:/ *n* son of one's brother or sister, or son of one's brother-in-law or sister-in-law. ➪ App 8. Cf NIECE.

nephritis /nɪˈfraɪtɪs/ *n* [U] inflammation of the kidneys.

nepotism /ˈnepətɪzəm/ *n* [U] (*derog*) practice among people with power or influence of favouring their own relatives, esp by giving them jobs.

Neptune /ˈneptju:n; *US* -tu:n/ *n* **1** (in Roman mythology) god of the sea. His Greek equivalent was Poseidon. **2** (*astronomy*) the planet eighth in order from the sun, one of the furthest in the solar system.

neptunium /ˌnepˈtju:nɪəm; *US* -ˈtu:n-/ *n* [U] (*symb* **Np**) radioactive metallic element.

nerd (also **nurd**) /nɜ:d/ *n* (*sl derog*) stupid or irritating person; idiot.

nerve /nɜ:v/ *n* **1** [C] fibre or bundle of fibres carrying impulses of sensation or of movement between the brain and all parts of the body: *pain caused by a trapped nerve.* ➪ illus at EPIDERMIS, TOOTH. **2 nerves** [pl] (*infml*) condition in which one is very nervous, irritable, worried, etc; nervousness: *suffer from nerves,* ie be easily upset, worried, etc ○ *She doesn't know what nerves are,* ie is never worried, upset, etc by events. ○ *He has nerves of steel,* ie a very calm temperament in times of stress, danger, etc. **3** (**a**) [U] boldness; courage: *lose/regain one's nerve* ○ *a first-class skier with a lot of nerve* ○ *It takes nerve to be a racing driver.* ○ *Rock-climbing is a test of nerve and skill.* ○ *I wouldn't have the nerve to try anything so dangerous.* (**b**) [sing] (*derog infml*) impudence (used esp as in the expressions shown): *What a nerve! She just walked off with my radio!* ○ *He's got a nerve, going to work dressed like that.* ○ *She had the nerve to say I was cheating.* **4** [C] (*botany*) rib of a leaf. **5** (idm) **a bundle of nerves** ➪ BUNDLE. **get on sb's ˈnerves** (*infml*) irritate or annoy sb: *Stop whistling! It's/You're getting on my nerves!* **hit/touch a** (**raw**) **ˈnerve** refer to a subject that causes sb pain, anger, etc: *You hit a raw nerve when you mentioned his first wife.* **strain every nerve** ➪ STRAIN[1]. **a war of nerves** ➪ WAR.

▷ **nerve** *v* [Tn·pr, Cn·t] ~ **sb/oneself for sth** give sb/oneself the courage, strength or determination to do sth: *Her support helped nerve us for the fight.* ○ *I nerved myself to face my accusers.*

nerveless *adj* lacking strength; unable to move: *The knife fell from her nerveless fingers.* **nervelessly** *adv.*

□ ˈ**nerve-cell** *n* cell that carries impulses in nerve tissue.

ˈ**nerve-centre** *n* **1** group of closely connected nerve-cells. **2** (*fig*) place from which a large factory, organization, project, etc is controlled and instructions sent out: *the nerve-centre of an election campaign.*

ˈ**nerve gas** poisonous gas that affects the central nervous system.

ˈ**nerve-racking** *adj* causing great mental strain: *a nerve-racking wait for exam results.*

nervous /ˈnɜ:vəs/ *adj* **1** of the nerves (NERVE 1): *a nervous disorder* ○ *the nervous system of the human body.* **2** ~ (**of sth/doing sth**) fearful; timid: *a frail, nervous little person* ○ *I'm nervous of (being in) large crowds.* ○ *Are you nervous in the dark?* ○ *She gave a nervous laugh.* **3** tense; excited; unstable: *full of nervous energy* ○ *a nervous style of writing.*

▷ **nervously** *adv*: *smile, fidget, whisper nervously.*

nervousness *n* [U].

□ ˌ**nervous ˈbreakdown** (time of) mental illness that causes depression, tiredness and general physical weakness.

ˈ**nervous system** system of nerves throughout the body of a person or an animal.

nervy /ˈnɜːvɪ/ *adj* (**-ier, -iest**) (*infml*) **1** (*Brit*) excitable; uneasy; jumpy. **2** (*US*) impudent; cheeky.

Nesbit /ˈnezbɪt/ Edith (1858-1924), English writer of children's stories. Her books, esp *The Railway Children*, remain popular, combining everyday detail with elements of magic.

-ness /nɪs/ *suff* (with *adjs* forming uncountable *ns*) quality, state or character of: *dryness* ○ *silliness*.

nest /nest/ *n* **1** (**a**) place or structure chosen or made by a bird for laying its eggs and sheltering its young: *sparrows building a nest of straw and twigs*. (**b**) place where certain other creatures live, or produce and keep their young: *an ants' nest* ○ *a wasps' nest*. **2** snug, comfortable or sheltered place: *make oneself a nest of cushions*. **3** secret or protected place, esp for criminals and their activities: *a nest of thieves* ○ *a nest of vice, crime, etc*. **4** group or set of similar things of different sizes made to fit inside each other: *a nest of boxes/tables/bowls*. **5** site where guns, etc are placed: *a machine-gun nest*. **6** (idm) **feather one's nest** ⇨ FEATHER[2]. **foul one's nest** ⇨ FOUL[2]. **a hornet's nest** ⇨ HORNET. **a mare's nest** ⇨ MARE[1].

▷ **nest** *v* [I] **1** make and use a nest: *nesting robins* ○ *Swallows are nesting in the garage*. **2** (usu **go nesting**) search for the nests of wild birds and take the eggs. **3** [I, Tn] (cause things to) fit together so that smaller items are contained inside larger ones: *The cases are made to nest inside each other*. ○ *a set of nesting tables*.

□ ˈ**nest-egg** *n* sum of money saved for future use: *a tidy little nest-egg of £5 000*.

nestle /ˈnesl/ *v* **1** [Ipr, Ip] settle comfortably and warmly in a soft place: *nestle (down) among the cushions* ○ *nestle into bed*. **2** [Ipr] lie in a half-hidden or sheltered position: *The egg nestled in the long grass*. ○ *The village nestled at the foot of the hill*. **3** [Tn] hold (sb/sth) snugly, as if in a nest; cradle: *She nestled the baby in her arms*. ○ *The cat lay nestled in the cushions*. **4** [Tn·pr] ~ **sth against, on, etc sth** push (one's head, shoulder, etc) lovingly against, etc sth: *She nestled her head on his shoulder*. **5** (phr v) **nestle up (against/to sb/sth)** settle oneself against sb/sth comfortably: *The child nestled up to its mother and fell asleep*. ○ *The dog nestled up against the warm radiator*.

nestling /ˈnestlɪŋ/ *n* bird that is too young to leave the nest.

net[1] /net/ *n* **1** (**a**) [U] loose open material made of string, thread, wire, etc knotted or woven together: *a large piece of net* ○ [attrib] *net curtains* ○ *a wire-net fence*. (**b**) [C] piece of this used for a particular purpose, eg catching fish, holding hair in place, etc: ˈ*fishing-nets* ○ *a* ˈ*tennis net* (⇨illus at TENNIS) ○ *a* ˈ*hair-net* ○ *a mos*ˈ*quito net* ○ *kick/hit the ball into the net*, eg in football, hockey, etc. **2** [C] (*esp fig*) trap or snare: *caught in a net of crime* ○ *The wanted man has so far escaped the police net*. **3** (**a**) **the nets** [pl] (in cricket) one or more wickets set up inside a net or nets for practice: *have an hour in the nets*. (**b**) [sing] period of practice in these: *The players had a short net before the game*. **4** [C] network (esp of communications). **5** (idm) **cast one's net wide** ⇨ CAST[1]. **spread one's net** ⇨ SPREAD.

▷ **net** *v* (**-tt-**) **1** [Tn, Dn·n, Dn·pr] ~ **sth/sb (for sb)** catch or obtain sth/sb with or as if with a net: *They netted a good haul of fish*. ○ *The deal netted (him) a handsome profit*. **2** [Tn] cover (eg fruit trees) with a net or nets: *If you don't net your peas the birds will eat them*. **3** [Tn] (*sport*) kick, hit, etc (a ball) into the goal net. **4** [Tn] make (eg cord) into net.

□ ˈ**netball** *n* [U] team game in which a ball has to be thrown so that it falls through a high horizontal ring with a net hanging from it.

ˈ**network** *n* **1** complex system of roads, etc crossing each other: *a network of roads, railways, canals, etc*. **2** (**a**) closely linked group of people, companies, etc: *a spy network* ○ *a network of shops all over the country* ○ *a communications network*, eg for radio and TV, using satellites. (**b**) group of broadcasting stations that link up to broadcast the same programmes at the same time: *the three big US television networks*. **3** (idm) **the old-boy network** ⇨ OLD.

net[2] (also **nett**) /net/ *adj* **1** ~ **(of sth)** remaining when nothing more is to be taken away: *a net price*, ie one from which a discount has been deducted ○ *net profit*, ie one that remains when working expenses have been deducted ○ *net weight*, ie that of the contents only, excluding the weight of the wrappings, the container, etc ○ *What do you earn, net of tax* (ie after tax has been paid)? Cf GROSS[2] 4. **2** [attrib] (of an effect, etc) final, after all the major factors have been considered: *The net result of the long police investigation is that the identity of the killer is still a complete mystery*.

▷ **net** *v* (**-tt-**) [Tn] gain (sth) as a net profit: *net a profit, sum, etc* ○ *She netted £5 from the sale*.

nether /ˈneðə(r)/ *adj* (*arch or joc*) lower: *the nether regions/world*, ie the world of the dead, hell ○ *nether garments*, ie trousers. ▷ **nethermost** /-məʊst/ *adj*.

Netherlands /ˈneðələndz/ **the Netherlands** (also **Holland**) country in western Europe on the North Sea, a founder member of the European Economic Community and one of the *Benelux countries; pop approx 14 758 000; official language Dutch; capital Amsterdam; seat of government the Hague; unit of currency guilder (= 100 cents). Most of the country is low-lying, at or below sea-level. It has one of the most efficient systems of agriculture in the world, esp for dairy products. There are reserves of oil and natural gas. Industries include petrochemicals and electronics. ⇨ map at BENELUX.

netsuke /ˈnetsʊkɪ/ *n* carved button-like ornament, often in ivory, worn with traditional Japanese dress, eg to fix a purse to a belt.

netting /ˈnetɪŋ/ *n* [U] string, wire, etc knotted or woven into a net: *five yards of wire netting* ○ *windows screened with netting*.

nettle /ˈnetl/ *n* **1** common wild plant with hairs on its leaves that sting and redden the skin when touched. **2** (idm) **grasp the nettle** ⇨ GRASP.

▷ **nettle** *v* [Tn] make (sb) angry; annoy; irritate: *My remarks clearly nettled her*.

□ ˈ**nettle-rash** *n* [U] condition caused by an allergy, producing red patches on the skin like nettle stings.

network ⇨ NET[1].

Neumann /ˈnɔɪmən/ John von (1903-57), American mathematician born in Hungary. He worked on the mathematics of quantum physics in its early stages, and established games theory (GAME). He took part in early nuclear research and the development of the modern computer.

neural /ˈnjʊərəl/ *adj* (*anatomy*) of the nerves.

neuralgia /njʊəˈrældʒə; *US* nʊ-/ *n* [U] (*medical*) intermittent sharp pain felt along a nerve, usu in the head or face.

▷ **neuralgic** /njʊəˈrældʒɪk/ *adj* (*medical*) of neuralgia: *neuralgic pain*.

neurasthenia /ˌnjʊərəsˈθiːnɪə; *US* ˌnʊr-/ *n* [U] (*medical*) weak condition attributed to nervous origins, expressed as tiredness worry, dizziness, etc.

▷ **neurasthenic** /-ˈθenɪk/ *adj* (*medical*) of or suffering from neurasthenia. — *n* (*medical*) person suffering from neurasthenia.

neuritis /njʊəˈraɪtɪs; *US* nʊ-/ *n* [U] (*medical*) inflammation of a nerve or nerves.

neur(o)- *comb form* of nerves or the nervous system: *neuralgia* ○ *neuritis* ○ *neurosis*.

neurology /njʊəˈrɒlədʒɪ; *US* nʊ-/ *n* [U] scientific study of nerves and their diseases.

▷ **neurological** /ˌnjʊərəˈlɒdʒɪkl; *US* ˌnʊ-/ *adj*: *neurological research*.

neurologist /njʊəˈrɒlədʒɪst; *US* nʊ-/ *n* expert in neurology.

neurone /ˈnjʊərəʊn; *US* ˈnʊ-/ (also **neuron** /ˈnjʊərɒn; *US* ˈnʊ-/) *n* nerve cell with its branches which send impulses to the central nervous system or from it to muscles.

neurosis /njʊəˈrəʊsɪs; *US* nʊ-/ *n* (*pl* **-oses** /-əʊsiːz/) (*medical*) emotional disorder, primarily characterized by anxiety, which does not involve gross distortions of external reality or disorganization of personality.

neurotic /njʊəˈrɒtɪk; *US* nʊ-/ *adj* caused by or suffering from neurosis; abnormally anxious or obsessive: *neurotic worries, outbursts, letters* ○ (*infml*) *She's neurotic about switching lights off at home to save electricity*.

▷ **neurotic** *n* neurotic person.

neurotically /-klɪ/ *adv*.

neuter /ˈnjuːtə(r); *US* ˈnuː-/ *adj* **1** (*grammar*) (of a word) neither masculine nor feminine in gender: *a neuter noun*. **2** (of plants) having neither male nor female parts. **3** (of insects) sexually undeveloped; sterile.

▷ **neuter** *n* **1** neuter noun or gender. **2** (**a**) sexually undeveloped insect. (**b**) castrated animal: *My cat is a neuter*.

neuter *v* [Tn] castrate (an animal): *a neutered tom-cat*.

neutral /ˈnjuːtrəl; *US* ˈnuː-/ *adj* **1** (**a**) not supporting or helping either side in a dispute, contest, war, etc; impartial: *a neutral country, judge, assessment* ○ *be/remain neutral*. (**b**) of a country that remains neutral in war: *neutral territory, ships, etc*. **2** (**a**) having no distinct or positive qualities: *He is rather a neutral character*, ie has no obvious virtues or faults. (**b**) (of colours) not strong or vivid, eg grey or fawn: *A neutral tie can be worn with a shirt of any colour*. **3** (of a gear) in which the engine is not connected with the parts driven by it: *leave a car in neutral gear* ○ *Put the gear lever in the neutral position*. **4** (*chemistry*) neither acidic nor alkaline.

▷ **neutral** *n* **1** [C] person, country, etc that is neutral. **2** [U] neutral(3) position of the gears: *slip (the gears) into neutral* ○ *The car's in neutral*.

neutrality /njuːˈtrælətɪ; *US* nuː-/ *n* [U] state of being neutral, esp in war: *armed neutrality*, ie readiness to fight if attacked, while remaining neutral until this happens.

neutralize, -ise *v* [Tn] **1** take away the effect or special quality of (sth) by using sth with the opposite effect or quality: *neutralize a poison, an acid*. **2** make (a region, country, etc) neutral by agreement; keep free or exclude from fighting: *a neutralized zone*. **neutralization, -isation** /ˌnjuːtrəlaɪˈzeɪʃn; *US* -lɪˈz-/ *n* [U].

neutrally /-rəlɪ/ *adv*.

neutrino /njuːˈtriːnəʊ; *US* ˈnuː-/ *n* (*pl* ~**s**) (*physics*) elementary particle with no electric charge, which travels at the speed of light and probably has zero mass.

neutron /ˈnjuːtrɒn; *US* ˈnuː-/ *n* particle carrying no electric charge, with about the same mass as a proton, and forming part of the nucleus of an atom. Cf ELECTRON, PROTON.

□ ˈ**neutron bomb** bomb that kills people by intense radiation, but does little damage to buildings, etc.

Nevada /nəˈvɑːdə; *US* nəˈvædə/ state of the western USA, acquired from Mexico in 1848. It is mountainous and arid. Agriculture is limited, but there are metal deposits. The state is famous for its liberal gambling laws and the casinos of Las Vegas. ⇨ map at App 1.

never /ˈnevə(r)/ *adv* **1** at no time; on no occasion; not ever: *She never goes to the cinema*. ○ *He has never been abroad*. ○ *I will never agree to their demands*. ○ *I'm tired of your never-ending complaints*. ○ *'Would you do that?' 'Never.'* ○ *Never in all my life have I heard such nonsense!* ○ *I shall never (ever) stay at that hotel again*. ○ *Such a display has never been seen before/never before been seen*. **2** (used for emphasis) not (used esp as in the expressions shown): *That will never do*, ie is completely unacceptable. ○ *He never so much as smiled*, ie didn't smile even once. ○ *You never did!* ie Surely you didn't! ○ *Never fear!* ie Don't be afraid! **3** (idm) **on the** ˌ**never-**ˈ**never** (*sl joc*) on the hire-purchase system: *buy sth on the never-never*. **well, I never (did)!** (expressing surprise, disapproval, etc): *Well, I never! Fancy getting married and not telling us!*

▷ **never** *interj* (*infml*) surely not: *'I got the job.' 'Never!'*

nevermore /ˌnevəˈmɔː(r)/ *adv* (*arch*) never again; at no future time.

□ **the ˌNever ˈNever Land 1** imaginary ideal place (from J M *Barrie's novel **Peter Pan**): *They dreamt of retiring to some Never Never Land by the Mediterranean.* **2** (also **the ˌNever ˈNever**) desertlike parts of the outback in Australia.

nevertheless /ˌnevəðəˈles/ *adv, conj* (*fml*) in spite of this; however; still: *Though very intelligent, she is nevertheless rather modest.* ○ *There was no news; nevertheless we went on hoping.* ○ *He is often rude to me, but I like him nevertheless.*

new /njuː; *US* nuː/ *adj* (**-er, -est**) **1** not existing before; seen, introduced, made, invented, etc recently or for the first time: *a new school, idea, film, novel, invention, car* ○ *new clothes, furniture* ○ *new potatoes*, ie ones dug from the soil early in the season ○ *new* (ie freshly baked) *bread* ○ *the newest* (ie latest) *fashions.* ⇨ Usage. **2 (a)** ~ **(to sb)** already existing but not seen, experienced, etc before; unfamiliar to sb: *learn new words in a foreign language* ○ *a new* (ie recently discovered) *star* ○ *As a beginner, everything is very new to him.* **(b)** ~ **(to sth)** not yet accustomed to sth; unfamiliar with sth: *I am new to this town.* ○ *They are still new to the work.* ○ *You're new here, aren't you?* **3** changed from the previous one(s); different: *a new job, teacher, home* ○ *make new friends.* **4** (usu with *the*) modern; of the latest type: *the new poor/rich*, ie those recently made poor/rich by social changes, etc ○ *the new conformism among the young.* **5** [usu attrib] **(a)** just beginning: *a new day* ○ *a new era in the history of our country.* **(b)** beginning again; renewed: *start a new life* ○ *This government offers new hope to the people.* **(c)** refreshed in mind or body: *I feel (like) a new man.* **6** (idm) **brave new world** ⇨ BRAVE. **break fresh/new ground** ⇨ GROUND[1]. **clean as a new pin** ⇨ CLEAN[1]. **fresh/new blood** ⇨ BLOOD[1]. **(as) good as ˈnew** in as good a condition as when new: *I'll just sew up that tear, and the coat will be as good as new.* **a new ˈbroom (sweeps clean)** (*saying*) a person newly appointed to a responsible position (starts to change and improve things energetically, in a way that is sometimes resented by others). **a new deal** programme of political, social and economic reform. **a ˌnew lease of ˈlife**; *US* **a ˌnew lease on ˈlife** chance to live longer or with greater vigour, satisfaction, etc: *Since recovering from her operation, she's had a new lease of life.* ○ (*fig*) *A bit of oil and some paint could give that old bike a new lease of life.* **a new one on ˈsb** (*infml*) thing that sb is not familiar with: *'Hadn't you heard he's been promoted?' 'No, that's a new one on me.'* **ring out the old year and ring in the new** ⇨ RING[2]. **teach an old dog new tricks** ⇨ TEACH. **turn over a new ˈleaf** change one's way of life to become a better, more responsible person: *The thief was determined to turn over a new leaf once he left prison.*

▷ **new-** (forming compound *adjs*) recently: *a new-born baby* ○ *new-laid eggs* ○ *new-mown hay* ○ *new-found faith.*

newly *adv* (usu before a past participle) **1** recently: *a newly married couple* ○ *a newly formed group.* **2** in a new different way: *newly arranged furniture.* **ˈnewly-wed** *n* (usu *pl*) person who has recently married: *the young newly-weds.*

newness *n* [U].

□ **ˈnewcomer** *n* person who has recently arrived in a place.

the ˌNew ˈDeal economic measures introduced in the USA by President Franklin *Roosevelt during the *Depression in 1933 (eg employing people on large publicly funded projects), which reduced unemployment by over 7 million.

ˌnewˈfangled *adj* [usu attrib] (*usu derog*) (of ideas or things) modern or fashionable in a way that many dislike or refuse to accept: *I don't like all these ˌnewfangled ˈgadgets.* ○ *You and your newfangled notions!*

the ˌNew Jeˈrusalem 1 Heaven as it is described in Revelation, the last book of the Bible. **2** an ideal form of society: *parties naive enough to promise a New Jerusalem.*

the ˌNew ˈLeft movement of radical left-wing thinkers, esp in the USA in the 1960s.

ˈnew-look *adj* [attrib] (*infml*) that has been changed, esp to give a modern appearance: *The new-look party has dropped its more controversial policies.*

the ˌNew Model ˈArmy army organized by Oliver *Cromwell to fight the supporters of *Charles I in the English Civil War.

new ˈmoon (a) the moon when it is seen as a thin crescent. **(b)** time when this is so: *after the next new moon.* Cf FULL MOON (FULL).

ˈNew Style (of a date) calculated according to the *Gregorian calendar used today, but not adopted in Britain until 1752.

the ˌNew ˈTestament second part of the Bible, concerned with the teachings of Jesus and his earliest followers. ⇨ App 5.

ˈnew town (*Brit*) town planned and built all at once with the help of government funds.

the New ˈWorld North and South America. Cf THE OLD WORLD (OLD).

new ˈyear the first few days of January: *I'll see you in the new year.* ○ *Happy New Year!* **New Year's ˈDay** (*US* **New Year's**) 1 January. **New Year's ˈEve** 31 December.

NOTE ON USAGE: Compare **recent**, **current**, **contemporary**, **modern** and **new**. **1** Recent and **current** have the most restricted and neutral meanings. **Recent** describes events that occurred a short time ago, but which may now have finished, or things which no longer exist: *Recent problems have been solved.* ○ *She's spent all her recent pay rise.* **Current** suggests a situation that exists today but which may be temporary: *The factory cannot maintain current levels of production.* ○ *How long will she keep her current job?* **2** Modern, **contemporary** and **new** often indicate a positive quality of being up-to-date, especially in style: *contemporary/modern dance, music, art, etc.* **Modern** can refer to a longer period up to the present: *Modern English*, ie since 1500. **Contemporary** need not relate to the present: *Shakespeare's plays tell us a lot about contemporary life,* ie the life of the 16th century. **New** can also mean 'original': *a completely new type of computer.* Note that **actual** cannot be used to mean **contemporary** or **current.** It means 'real': *I need the actual figures, not an estimate.* ○ *His actual age was 45, not 40 as he had stated on his form.*

newel /ˈnjʊəl; *US* ˈnuːəl/ *n* **1** central pillar of a winding staircase. **2** (also **ˈnewel post**) post supporting the handrail of a stair at the top or bottom of a staircase.

New England /ˌnjuː ˈɪŋglənd/ the north-eastern US states of Maine, New Hampshire, Vermont, Massachusetts, Rhode Island and Connecticut. The area was colonized by Puritan emigrants from England in the 17th century, and it was there that the American independence movement started.

□ **ˌNew ˈEnglander**.

New Forest /ˌnjuː ˈfɒrɪst; *US* ˌnuː ˈfɔːrəst/ **the New Forest** area of heath and woodland in southern Hampshire, England, which has been the property of the Crown since 1079. **New Forest ponies** live there in almost wild conditions and are popular children's pets when tamed.

Newfoundland /ˈnjuːfəndlənd; *US* ˈnuː-/ large island at the mouth of the Saint Lawrence river in Canada. It forms part of the province of Newfoundland and Labrador. Formerly a separate state, Newfoundland became part of Canada in 1949.

▷ **Newfoundland** *n* breed of large dog, usu with black hair.

Newgate /ˈnjuːgeɪt; *US* ˈnuː-/ prison built in London in the Middle Ages. In the 18th century it became famous for the dreadful conditions in which prisoners were kept. *The Newgate Calendar* was a series of books telling the stories of some of the notorious criminals of the time.

New Guinea /ˌnjuː ˈgɪnɪ; *US* ˌnuː-/ large island to the north of Australia. The eastern half is the independent state of Papua New Guinea, while the western half is part of Indonesia. ⇨ maps at INDONESIA, MELANESIA.

New Hampshire /ˌnjuː ˈhæmpʃə(r); *US* ˌnuː-/ state in the north-eastern USA on the Atlantic coast. The *Appalachian mountains cross the north of the state, while the south is an industrial centre. It was one of the 13 original American states. ⇨ map at App 1.

New Jersey /ˌnjuː ˈdʒɜːzɪ; *US* ˌnuː-/ state in the north-eastern USA. It lies close to New York and its small area is densely populated and heavily industrialized. It was one of the 13 original American states. ⇨ map at App 1.

Newman[1] /ˈnjuːmən; *US* ˈnuː-/ John Henry (1801-91), English priest and poet. As vicar of the Anglican University Church in Oxford he caused a scandal by his near-Catholic opinions. He became a Roman Catholic priest and was made a cardinal in 1879. His writings, esp the *Apologia*, had a wide influence.

Newman[2] /ˈnjuːmən; *US* ˈnuː-/ Paul (1925-), American film actor and director. Often cast as the heroic outsider, as in *The Hustler* or *Hud*, he is famous for the physical and emotional appeal of his acting. He has also directed films, eg *Rachel, Rachel.*

New Mexico /ˌnjuː ˈmeksɪkəʊ; *US* ˌnuː-/ state in the south-western USA. The impressive landscape of mountains and canyons attracts many tourists. It has important mineral reserves. ⇨ map at App 1.

news /njuːz; *US* nuːz/ *n* **1 (a)** [U] new or fresh information; report(s) of recent events: *What's the latest news?* ○ *Have you heard the news? Mary has got a job!* ○ *I want to hear all your news.* ○ *items/pieces/bits of news* ○ *It's news to me*, ie I haven't heard about it before. ○ *She is always in the news*, ie Her doings are regularly reported in the newspapers, on TV, etc. ○ *The news that the enemy were near alarmed everybody.* ○ *Have you any news of* (ie Have you heard anything about) *where she is staying?* ○ [attrib] *a news item, report, broadcast, bulletin, etc* ○ *the news media*, ie newspapers, TV, radio, etc. **(b) the news** [sing *v*] regular broadcast of the latest news on the radio and TV: *Here is the news*, eg said by a newsreader at the start of a broadcast. ○ *The news lasts half an hour.* **2** [U] person, thing, event, etc that is (interesting enough to be) reported as news: *When a man bites a dog, that's news!* ○ *Pop stars are always news.* **3** (idm) **break the ˈnews (to sb)** be the first to tell sb about sth, esp sth exciting or unwelcome. **no news is ˈgood news** (*saying*) if there were bad news we would hear it, so since we have heard nothing we can assume that all is well.

▷ **newsy** *adj* (**-ier, -iest**) (*infml*) full of (usu not very serious) news: *a newsy letter* ○ *a bright, newsy magazine.*

□ **ˈnewsagent** *n* (*Brit*) (*US* **ˈnewsdealer**) shopkeeper who sells newspapers, magazines, etc.

ˈnews agency agency that gathers news and sells it to newspapers, TV, radio, etc.

ˈnewscast *n* broadcast news report. **ˈnewscaster** (also **ˈnews-reader**) *n* person who reads the news on TV, radio, etc.

ˈnews conference = PRESS CONFERENCE (PRESS[1]).

ˈnewsdealer *n* (*US*) = NEWSAGENT.

ˈnews flash (also **flash**) short item of important news broadcast on radio or television, sometimes interrupting another programme.

ˈnews-letter *n* informal printed report giving information and regularly sent to members of a club, society, etc.

ˈnewsmonger *n* (*usu derog*) person who gossips.

newspaper /ˈnjuːspeɪpə(r); *US* ˈnuːz-/ *n* **1** [C] printed publication, issued usu daily or weekly with news, advertisements, articles on various subjects, etc. **2** [U] paper on which newspapers are printed: *a parcel wrapped in newspaper.*

ˈnewsprint *n* [U] paper used for printing newspapers on.

Newspapers

Almost every adult in Britain reads or sees a daily newspaper, and many people remain loyal to a particular paper for life. There are daily papers, published from Monday to Saturday, and Sunday papers. In some cities, evening papers are also published. Newspapers are broadly divided into the quality press and the popular press. The 'qualities', also sometimes known as the 'heavies', are the serious and more expensive papers, with detailed and extensive coverage of home and overseas news, and with a range of additional features such as sports sections, financial reports, book reviews, women's pages, arts summaries, travel news and usually a daily topical feature, such as a profile of someone in the news. All 'qualities' are broadsheet in format, that is with a large page size.

The 'populars', also known as the 'tabloids' (because of their smaller page size) or, disparagingly, as the 'gutter press', cater for the less demanding reader, who is not interested in detailed news reports. They are cheaper in price, and are easily distinguishable by their large, bold headlines, colloquial use of English, and abundant photographs, often in colour. Their many short items and features usually concentrate on the personal aspects of the news, with reports of the latest scandals, sensations and sexual liaisons, especially of celebrities, not excluding the royal family. However, some of the 'populars' also offer their readers news coverage of a more conventional kind, and some of their 'scoops' are newsworthy and important.

The oldest of the daily 'qualities' is *The Times*, founded in 1785. It has a long-standing reputation as one of the most influential papers in the country, and has become well-known for its extensive news coverage, its sober and generally unbiased editorials, its letters to the editor, its financial and sporting pages, its personal column and its daily crossword. It claims to be politically independent, but is inclined to be right-wing and has an 'establishment' image. It is in close competition with two rivals: *The Guardian*, founded in 1825 (as *The Manchester Guardian*), and *The Independent*, founded in 1986. *The Guardian* is noted for its lively reporting, its original features, and generally for its campaigning support for 'worthy causes', such as educational reform, the protection and conservation of the environment, and animal rights. Politically it is left of centre, and it formerly supported the Liberal Party. *The Independent* has rapidly acquired a reputation for its excellent news coverage, intelligent reporting, informed comment, and the care it takes not to patronize its readers.

Each of these three papers has a circulation of just under half a million. *The Daily Telegraph*, founded in 1855, has a circulation roughly twice as big. It is noted for its detailed reporting and good international news coverage, as well as its exceptionally wide and thorough coverage of sport. It is right of centre, supports the Conservative Party, and has a generally middle-aged to elderly but very loyal readership. The *Financial Times*, founded in 1888, specializes in City news but also carries some general news items, features and reviews. It is printed on distinctive pink paper, so that it is sometimes nicknamed 'The Pink 'Un'.

Although newspapers are normally associated with a particular political viewpoint, either of the right or the left, most have no formal links with political parties. (The one exception is the *Morning Star*.) The views expressed are those of the editor, who is appointed by the proprietor of the newspaper. The largest newspaper company in Britain is News International, owned by Rupert Murdoch, the publisher of *The Times*, *The Sun*, *Today*, the *News of the World* and *The Sunday Times*.

The Sun, founded in 1964, has a circulation of around 4 million and currently outsells all other daily 'populars'. Its most famous feature is its 'Page Three' photograph of a nude or nearly nude young woman. The *Daily Mirror*, with a circulation of about 3 million, was founded in 1903, and has traditionally supported the Labour party. Both the *Daily Express* and *Daily Mail* have circulations of about 1.5 million, and were founded in 1900 and 1896 respectively. The *Express* has established a reputation for its lively writing and 'no nonsense' reporting, while the *Mail* is the most sophisticated of the 'populars', with well-written 'crusading' articles and serialized fiction. Both papers have weekly book reviews, women's pages and other regular features. The *Daily Star*, founded in 1978, is similar to the *Mirror*. It has a greater number of young women readers than the *Mirror*, but a lower overall circulation of under 1 million. *Today*, founded in 1986, has maintained a high standard of original journalism. Its circulation is about half a million.

Despite the general classification of 'quality' and 'popular', the *Express*, *Mail* and *Today* are distinctive enough from the *Sun*, *Star* and *Mirror* to be more accurately defined as 'middle market'. In a class of its own is the *Morning Star*, founded in 1930 by the Communist Party as the *Daily Worker*. It is now struggling to survive, with a circulation of less than 18 000.

Of the Sunday 'qualities', the *Sunday Times* leads the field with a circulation of over a million. It has built a reputation for the range and excellence of its writing and reporting, and is produced in eight separate sections: a main news section and others devoted to sport, news reviews, business, the arts, job advertisements (mainly in industry and business), fashion and travel, and book reviews. It was founded in 1822 and is politically right of centre. *The Observer* is the oldest Sunday paper, founded in 1791. It has a circulation of around half a million and politically it is 'middle of the road'. The *Sunday Telegraph*, founded in 1961, is more right-wing, like its sister daily. Its circulation, now about half a million, has been steadily declining. *The Independent on Sunday* was first published in 1990.

The best-selling Sunday 'popular' is the *News of the World*, with a circulation of around 5 million. The paper, founded in 1843, has a reputation for its detailed reports of crime and sex stories but also for its sports reports and its political comment. The *Sunday Mirror* has a circulation of about 3 million, and like its sister daily paper contains mainly popular items on celebrities in the news, with much gossip and many photographs. Its rival is *The People*, a paper with a circulation of about 2.5 million and an emphasis on 'true life' stories and features. Both the *Sunday Express* and *Mail on Sunday* have circulations of just under 2 million, and likewise resemble their daily equivalents in style and content. The *Sunday Sport*, founded in 1986, contains many colour photographs of people, especially nudes, in unconventional poses, as well as generally titillating stories. It has a circulation of about half a million. Almost all Sunday papers have accompanying colour magazines.

As well as the national press, there are many regional daily papers such as the *Yorkshire Post*, the *Northern Echo*, the *Western Mail* and the *Scotsman*. Evening papers include the *Evening Standard* in London, the *Manchester Evening News* and the *Liverpool Echo*. There are also local weekly papers, and many local papers delivered free and paid for entirely from advertising.

Because of the size of the USA, there are few national newspapers. Apart from the popular paper *USA Today*, only the *New York Times*, the *Chicago Tribune* and the *Wall Street Journal* have anything like a nationwide readership, mainly thanks to satellite technology. The *Times* is generally regarded as America's most prestigious paper. The *Journal* is the leading financial and business newspaper, and currently has a circulation of about 2 million, the highest in the country. But there are influential regional papers, among them the *Washington Post*, the *New York Daily News*, the *Philadelphia Enquirer*, the *Los Angeles Times*, the *Boston Globe*, the *San Francisco Examiner*, and the *Christian Science Monitor* (not a religious paper, despite its title). *USA Today*, founded in 1982, is the leading popular daily paper, with short news reports, lively feature stories, and items of practical advice. The tabloid weekly newspapers, such as the *National Enquirer* and the *Star*, with circulations of around 4.5 and 3.5 million respectively, are sold in supermarkets throughout the country.

There are no separate Sunday papers, as there are in Britain, but most dailies have special Sunday editions, with the notable exception of the *Wall Street Journal* and *USA Today*. Some of them are remarkable for their size, particularly the *New York Times*, which can run to 150 pages.

ˈnews-reader *n* = NEWSCASTER.

ˈnewsreel *n* short film of recent events, with a commentary.

ˈnews-room *n* room at a newspaper office or radio or TV station where news is received and prepared for printing or broadcasting.

ˈnews-sheet *n* simple type of newspaper, with few pages.

ˈnews-stand *n* = BOOKSTALL (BOOK[1]).

ˈnews-vendor *n* person selling newspapers.

ˈnewsworthy *adj* interesting or important enough to be reported as news: *a newsworthy story, scandal, etc.*

New South Wales /ˌnju: saʊθ ˈweɪlz/ (*abbr* **NSW**) state in south-eastern Australia. It is the most densely populated Australian state and industry is concentrated around its capital, Sydney. The western plains produce wheat and sheep. ⇨ map at App 1.

newspeak /ˈnjuːspiːk; *US* ˈnuː-/ *n* [U] (*derog*) type of language, used esp by officials and politicians, which uses euphemisms and technical words to hide the truth. The term was originally applied to the official language used in George *Orwell's novel *1984*.

newt /njuːt; *US* nuːt/ *n* **1** small lizard-like animal that can live in water or on land. **2** (idm) **pissed as a newt** ⇨ PISSED (PISS).

Newton /ˈnjuːtn; *US* ˈnuː-/ Sir Isaac (1642-1727), English mathematician and physicist. His description of the laws of mechanics and gravitation, with its concepts of force and mass, was the greatest contribution to physics until the work of *Einstein. It is supposed to have been first suggested by the sight of an apple falling in a garden. He also discovered differential calculus at the same time as *Leibniz, and made other important discoveries in astronomy and optics. ▷ **Newtonian** /njuːˈtəʊnɪən; *US* nuː-/ *adj* [attrib] of Newton or his theories: *Newtonian physics*.

newton /ˈnjuːtn; *US* ˈnuː-/ *n* SI unit of force, equal to the force that accelerates one kilogram at one metre per second per second.

New York /ˌnjuː ˈjɔːk; *US* ˌnuː-/ **1** state in the north-eastern USA. It is the country's most economically important state. Besides the financial and industrial activities in New York City, there are several major industrial towns, eg Buffalo and Syracuse, as well as much agricultural land. It was one of the 13 original American states. ⇨ map at App 1. **2** (also ˌ**New York ˈCity**) largest city in the USA, on the the NE Atlantic coast. Most of the city is on two islands, Manhattan and Long Island. It is the richest, most densely populated city in the USA, and its largest port. It contains *Wall Street, the financial centre, industries of every kind, two universities, world-famous art galleries, the theatres on *Broadway, cultural complexes like the *Lincoln Center and the headquarters of the *United Nations. ▷ ˌ**New ˈYorker** *n*.

New Zealand /ˌnjuː ˈziːlənd; *US* ˌnuː-/ country in the southern Pacific, a member of the Commonwealth; pop approx 3 292 000; official language English; capital Wellington; unit of currency dollar (= 100 cents). The country is made up of two large and several smaller islands. The North Island, with its warmer climate, fertile soils and volcanic mountains, is more densely populated than the rugged South Island with its fjord coastline. Agriculture, esp sheep and dairy farming, is the main economic activity. The mountains provide a source of hydroelectric energy. The original Maori population (about 10% of the total) has begun an active campaign to reclaim its land and fishing rights. ⇨ map at POLYNESIA. ▷ **New Zealander** *n*.

next¹ /nekst/ *adj* [attrib] ~ **(to sb/sth)**; ~ **(to do sth/that...)** **1** (usu with *the*) coming immediately after (sb/sth) in order, space or time: *the next name on the list* ○ *How far is it to the next* (ie nearest) *petrol station?* ○ *The next train to Manchester is at 10.00.* ○ *The very next time I saw her she was working in London.* ○ *The next person to speak* (ie who speaks) *will be punished.* ○ *The next six months will be the hardest.* ○ *I felt a sharp pain in my head and the next thing I knew was waking up in hospital.* **2** (used without *the* before eg *Monday, week, winter, year* to indicate the one immediately following): *Next Thursday is 12 April.* ○ *I'm going skiing next winter.* ⇨ Usage at LAST¹. **3** (idm) **better luck next time** ⇨ BETTER¹. **first/last/next but one, two, three, etc** ⇨ FIRST¹. **as good, well, far, much, etc as the ˈnext man** as good, well, etc as the average person: *I can enjoy a joke as well as the next man, but this is going too far.* **the next world** state that one is believed to pass into after death.

▷ **the next** *n* [sing] person or thing that is next: *The first episode was good — now we have to wait a week for the next.*

□ ˌ**next ˈdoor** in or into the next house or room: *She lives next door.* ○ *The manager's office is just next door.* ○ [attrib] *our ˌnext-door ˈneighbours.* **next door to** in the house or flat next to (sb/sth): *Next door to us there's a couple from the USA.* ○ (*fig*) *Such ideas are next door to* (ie close to) *madness.* ˌ**next of ˈkin** (*fml*) (with *sing* or *pl v*) closest living relative(s): *Her next of kin have been informed.* ○ *Who is your next of kin?*

next to *prep* **1** in or into a position immediately to one side of (sb/sth); beside: *Peter sat next to Paul on the sofa.* **2** in the position after (sb/sth); following: *Next to skiing her favourite sport was ice-hockey.* ○ *Birmingham is the largest city in Britain next to London.* **3** almost: *Papering the ceiling proved next to impossible without a ladder.* ○ *I got it for next to nothing in a jumble sale.* ○ *My horse came next to last* (ie last but one) *in the race.*

NOTE ON USAGE: Compare **nearest** and **next**. **(The) next** indicates 'the following' in a sequence of events or places: *When is your next appointment?* ○ *Turn left at the next traffic lights.* **(The) nearest** means 'the closest' (of several) in time or place: *'When can I have my birthday party?' 'On the Saturday nearest to it.'* ○ *Where's the nearest supermarket?* Notice the difference between the prepositions **nearest (to)** and **next (to)**: *Janet's sitting nearest (to) the window (of all the children).* ○ *Sarah's sitting next to the window (beside it).*

next² /nekst/ *adv* **1** after this or that; then: *Who's next on the list?* ○ *What did you do next?* ○ *Next we visited Tokyo.* ○ *What comes next* (ie follows)? **2** taking the following place in order: *The next oldest building is the church.* **3** (used after question words to express surprise): *You're learning to be a parachutist! Whatever next!*

□ ˌ**next-ˈbest** *adj* to be preferred if one's first choice is not available: *The next-best solution is to abandon the project altogether.* ○ *Borrowing tapes from the library would be the next-best thing.*

nexus /ˈneksəs/ *n* (*pl* ~**es** /-səsɪz/) (*fml*) connected group or series; bond or connection: *Shared ambition is the vital nexus between them.*

NF /ˌen ˈef/ *abbr* National Front.

NFU /ˌen ef ˈjuː/ *abbr* (*Brit*) National Farmers' Union.

NGA /ˌen dʒiː ˈeɪ/ *abbr* (*Brit*) National Graphical Association (a trade union of printers, merged with SOGAT in 1991 to become GPMU). ⇨ article at TRADE UNION.

NHS /ˌen eɪtʃ ˈes/ *abbr* (*Brit*) National Health Service: *I got my hearing-aid on the NHS.*

NI *abbr* **1** (*Brit*) National Insurance: *NI deductions*, eg on a pay slip. **2** Northern Ireland.

Ni *symb* nickel.

niacin /ˈnaɪəsɪn/ *n* [U] vitamin found in meat, yeast and some cereals.

Niagara /naɪˈægrə/ (also **Niˌagara ˈFalls**) **1** waterfall on the US-Canadian border, over 45 m (150 ft high), a major source of hydroelectric power. **2** (idm) **a Niagara of sth** (*infml*) a continuous flow of sth: *We were submerged by a Niagara of applications.*

nib /nɪb/ *n* metal point of a pen.

nibble /ˈnɪbl/ *v* **1** (**a**) [I, Ipr, Tn, Tn·p] ~ **(at sth)** take tiny bites of sth: *fish nibbling (at) the bait* ○ *She nibbled his ears playfully.* ○ *Mice have nibbled all the cheese away.* (**b**) [I] eat small amounts: *No nibbling between meals!* **2** (phr v) **nibble at sth** show cautious interest in (an offer, etc): *He nibbled at my idea, but would not make a definite decision.*

▷ **nibble** *n* (**a**) act of nibbling: *I felt a nibble on the end of my line.* (**b**) small amount of food: *Drinks and nibbles will be served.*

nibs /nɪbz/ *n* (idm) **his nibs** (*Brit infml joc*) (used as a mock title by others when talking about a man (esp one in authority) who thinks he is more important than he really is): *Please tell his nibs that we'd like his help with the washing-up!*

Nicaragua /ˌnɪkəˈrægjʊə; *US* ˌnɪkəˈrɑːgwə/ country in Central America; pop approx 3 990 000; official language Spanish; capital Managua; unit of currency córdoba (= 100 centavos). The country is largely mountainous and densely covered in forest. Agriculture is virtually the only economic activity, the main crops being coffee and cotton. In 1979 the dictatorship of the Somoza family was ended by the Sandinista Revolution; the Sandinistas were defeated in elections in 1990 after a severe economic crisis, made worse by US sanctions and attacks by rebels from Honduras, but amid confused alliances and fighting that now involved rebels on their own left wing they resumed a parliamentary majority in 1993. ⇨ map at CENTRAL AMERICA. ▷ **Nicaraguan** *adj, n*.

nice /naɪs/ *adj* (**-r**, **-st**) **1** (**a**) pleasant; agreeable: *a nice person, smile, taste, remark* ○ *a nice day* ○ *nice weather* ○ *a nice little girl* ○ *That tastes nice!* ○ *We had a nice time at the beach.* ○ *It's not nice to pick your nose.* (**b**) ~ **(to sb)** kind; friendly: *Try to be nice to my father when he visits.* Cf NASTY. **2** (*ironic*) bad; unpleasant: *This is a nice mess you've got us into!* ○ *That's a nice thing to say!* **3** needing precision and care; fine; subtle: *a nice distinction* ○ *a nice point of law*, ie one that may be difficult to decide ○ *nice* (ie very slight) *shades of meaning*. **4** (**a**) hard to please; having refined tastes: *too nice in one's dress.* (**b**) (usu in negative expressions) respectable; scrupulous: *She's not too nice in her business methods.* **5** (idm) **nice and** (used before *adjs*) (*infml approv*) agreeably: *nice and warm by the fire* ○ *nice and cool in the woods.* **good/nice work** ⇨ WORK¹. **nice work if you can get it** (*saying*) (used to express envy of what sb has been lucky or clever enough to get or do).

▷ **nicely** *adv* **1** in a pleasant manner: *nicely dressed, done, said.* **2** (*infml*) very well; all right: *That will suit me nicely.* ○ *The patient is doing nicely*, ie is making good progress.

niceness *n* [U].

nicety /ˈnaɪsətɪ/ *n* **1** [U] accuracy; precision: *nicety of judgement* ○ *a point of great nicety*, ie one that requires very careful and detailed thought. **2** [C usu *pl*] subtle distinction or detail: *I can't go into all the niceties of meaning.* ○ *observe the social niceties*, ie of polite behaviour, etc. **3** (idm) **to a nicety** exactly right: *You judged the distance to a nicety.*

niche

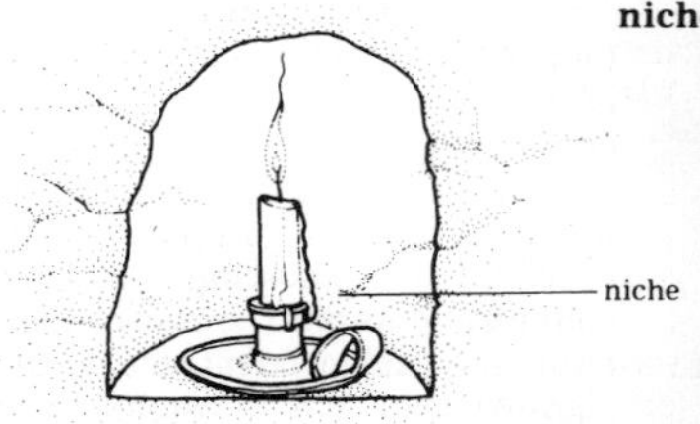

niche /nɪtʃ, niːʃ/ *n* **1** shallow recess, esp in a wall: *a niche with a shelf.* ⇨ illus. **2** (*fig*) suitable or comfortable position, place, job, etc: *I don't think he's yet found his niche in life*, ie the occupation that gives him most satisfaction and happiness. ○ *an ecological niche*, ie the conditions in which an organism exists and survives, eg the food and temperature it needs.

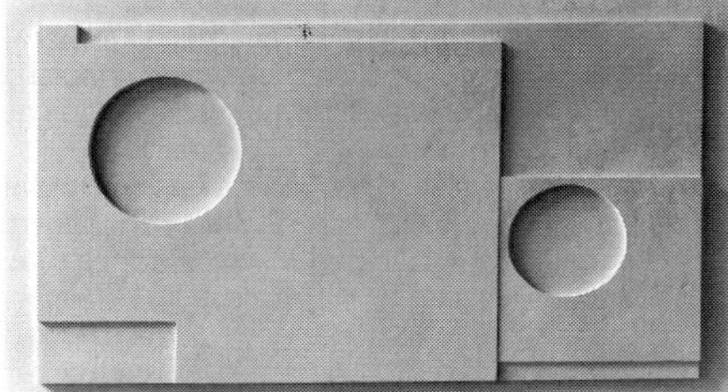

Ben Nicholson: White Relief

Nicholson /ˈnɪkəlsn/ Ben (1894-1982), British painter. One of the most distinguished pioneers of abstract art in Britain, he is known chiefly for his geometric abstractions in relief. During the 1940s and 1950s he and his second wife Barbara *Hepworth were among the group of avant-garde artists who made their centre at St Ives, Cornwall

⇨ illus.

nick[1] /nɪk/ *n* **1** small cut or notch: *Make a nick in the cloth with the scissors.* **2** (idm) **in good, bad, etc ˈnick** (*Brit sl*) in good, etc condition or health: *She's in pretty good nick for a 70-year-old.* ○ *The car's in poor nick.* **in the ˌnick of ˈtime** only just in time; at the last moment: *You got here in the nick of time — the train's just leaving.*

▷ **nick** *v* **1** [Tn] make a nick in (sth): *nick one's chin when shaving.* **2** [I] (of a mating or mated animals) produce young of high quality.

nick[2] /nɪk/ *n* **the nick** [sing] (*Brit sl*) prison or police station: *She spent a year in the nick.* ○ *The burglar was taken to the local nick.*

▷ **nick** *v* [Tn, Tn·p] (*Brit sl*) **1** ~ **sb (for sth)** arrest sb: *He was nicked for stealing.* **2** ~ **sth (from sb/sth)** steal sth: *He nicked £5 (from his friend).*

nickel /ˈnɪkl/ *n* **1** [U] (*symb* **Ni**) chemical element, a hard silver-white metal often used in alloys: *nickel-plated.* ⇨ App 11. **2** [C] coin of the US or Canada, worth 5 cents. ⇨ App 9.

▷ **nickel** *v* (**-ll-**; *US* **-l-**) [Tn] coat (sth) with nickel.

□ **ˌnickel-and-ˈdime** *adj* [attrib] (*US sl derog*) on a very small and unimportant scale: *They run some nickel-and-dime outfit.*

ˌnickel ˈsilver alloy of nickel, zinc and copper.

nickelodeon /ˌnɪkəˈləʊdɪən/ *n* (*US infml*) **1** juke-box. **2** early cinema, entrance to which cost five cents.

nicker /ˈnɪkə(r)/ *n* (*pl* unchanged) (*Brit dated sl*) pound sterling: *He got fifty nicker to keep quiet.*

nick-nack = KNICK-KNACK.

nickname /ˈnɪkneɪm/ *n* familiar or humorous name given to a person instead of or as well as his real name, often a short form of the real name, or a reference to the person's character, etc. Some nicknames are traditional, eg those for people from particular countries: any male Scot can be called *Jock*, any Welshman *Taffy* (now rather dated), and an Irishman *Paddy, Pat* or *Mick*. The English are known as *Limeys* by Americans and as *Poms* or *Pommies* by Australians. The English call Americans *Yanks* or *Yankies* and the Australians *Aussies*. Such nationality nicknames can give offence: *Harold's nickname was Harry.* ○ *He got the nickname 'Smiler' because he always looked so miserable.*

▷ **nickname** *v* [Tn, Cn·n esp passive] give a nickname to (sb): *He was nicknamed Shorty because he was so tall!*

nicotine /ˈnɪkəti:n/ *n* [U] poisonous oily substance found in tobacco: *nicotine-stained fingers* ○ [attrib] *cigarettes with a low nicotine content.*

niece /ni:s/ *n* daughter of one's brother or sister, or daughter of one's brother-in-law or sister-in-law. ⇨ App 8. Cf NEPHEW.

Nietzsche /ˈni:tʃə/ Friedrich (1844-1900), German philosopher. His concept of the 'superman', superior to the rest of humanity and to Christian morality, influenced the ideas of Nazism.

niff /nɪf/ *n* (*Brit sl*) smell; stink: *What a niff!*

▷ **niffy** *adj* (*Brit sl*) having an unpleasant smell; smelly: *That meat's a bit niffy.*

nifty /ˈnɪftɪ/ *adj* (**-ier, -iest**) (*infml*) **1** (**a**) clever; skilful: *a footballer's nifty footwork.* (**b**) efficient; useful; handy: *a nifty little gadget for peeling potatoes.* **2** smart; stylish: *wearing a nifty new outfit.*

Niger /ni:ˈʒeə(r)/ country in central W Africa; pop approx 6 688 000; official language French; capital Niamey; unit of currency franc. Much of the country is desert, with agriculture, mainly livestock, concentrated around the River Niger in the south-west. Its main resources and exports are uranium and tin. ⇨ map at NIGERIA.

Nigeria /naɪˈdʒɪərɪə/ country on the west coast of Africa, a member of the Commonwealth; pop approx 105 472 000; official language English; capital Abuja; unit of currency naira (= 100 kobo). It is the most heavily populated country in Africa, but most of the population and the economic activity is concentrated in the south. The discovery of oil and the development of the petrochemical industries has had a harmful effect on agriculture; the country is no longer

West Africa

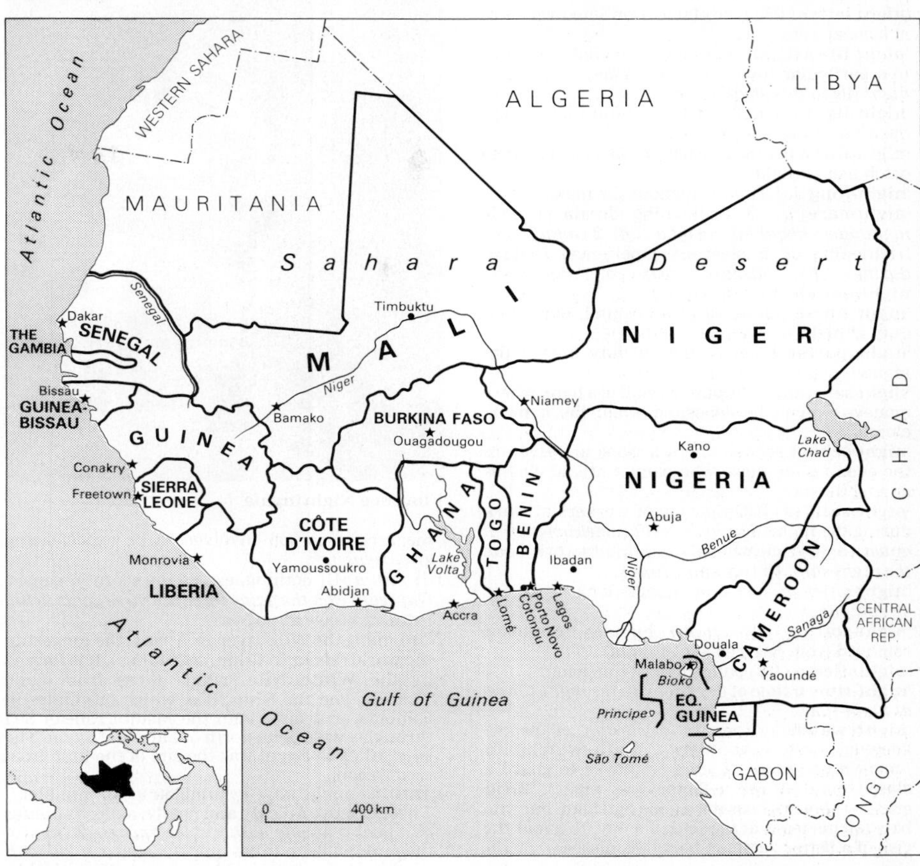

self-sufficient in food, and the economy is vulnerable to changes in the price of oil. ⇨ map (WEST AFRICA). ▷ **Nigerian** *adj, n.*

niggard /ˈnɪgəd/ *n* mean stingy person.

▷ **niggardly** *adj* **1** mean; stingy: *a niggardly old miser.* **2** (of a gift, etc) having little value: *a niggardly contribution to the fund.* **niggardliness** *n* [U].

nigger /ˈnɪgə(r)/ *n* **1** (⚠ *derog offensive*) black person; negro. **2** (idm) **a ˌnigger in the ˈwoodpile** (*often considered offensive*) thing or person that causes or is likely to cause unexpected problems.

niggle /ˈnɪgl/ *v* **1** [I, Ipr] ~ **(about/over sth)** give too much time and attention to unimportant details; criticize in a petty way: *Stop niggling about every penny we spend.* **2** [Tn] irritate (sb) in a minor way; annoy: *His untidiness constantly niggled her.*

▷ **niggling** /ˈnɪglɪŋ/ *adj* **1** too unimportant to give time or attention to; trifling: *Don't waste time on niggling details.* **2** annoying in a minor but persistent way: *a niggling pain* ○ *niggling criticism.*

nigh /naɪ/ *adv, prep* (**-er, -est**) (*arch*) near (to): *The end of the world is nigh!* Cf WELLNIGH.

night /naɪt/ *n* [C, U] **1** time of darkness between sunset and sunrise: *in/during the night* ○ *on Sunday night* ○ *on the night of Friday 13 June* ○ *a late-night show at the cinema*, ie one given much later than the other shows ○ *Nightfell*, ie It became dark. ○ *He stayed three nights at the hotel*, ie slept there for three nights. ○ *Can you stay the night/stay over night* (ie spend the night here)? **2** evening on which a specified activity takes place: *the first night of a play* ○ *the last night of the Proms.* **3** (idm) **all night (long)** throughout the whole night. **all right on the night** ⇨ RIGHT[1]. **at night** when night comes; during the night: *These animals only come out at night.* ○ *10 o'clock at night*, ie 10 pm. **by day/night** ⇨ DAY: *travelling by night.* **an early/a late ˈnight** night when one goes to bed earlier/later than usual: *You've been having too many late nights recently.* **have a good/bad ˈnight** sleep well/badly during the night. **in the/at dead of night** ⇨ DEAD. **like a thief in the night** ⇨ THIEF. **the livelong day/night** ⇨ LIVELONG. **make a ˈnight of it** spend much of the night in celebrating, eg at a party. **ˌnight after ˈnight** for many nights in succession. **ˌnight and ˈday/ˌday and ˈnight** continuously; all the time: *machines kept running night and day.* **a night ˈout** evening spent enjoying oneself away from home: *I enjoy an occasional night out at the theatre.* **ships that pass in the night** ⇨ SHIP[1]. **spend the night with sb** ⇨ SPEND. **the still of the night** ⇨ STILL[1] *n.* **things that go bump in the night** ⇨ THING. **turn ˌnight into ˈday** do at night what is usually done during the day.

▷ **nightie** (also **nighty**) *n* (*infml*) = NIGHT-DRESS.

nightly *adj, adv* (happening, done, etc) at night or every night: *nightly performances* ○ *a film show twice nightly* ○ *appearing nightly at the local theatre.*

nights *adv* (*esp US*) in the night-time repeatedly: *I can't sleep nights.* ○ *He works nights.*

□ **ˈnight-bird** *n* **1** bird (eg an owl) that is active at night. **2** (*fig infml*) person who is most active at night.

ˌnight-ˈblindness *n* [U] inability to see properly in the dark or in dim light.

ˈnightcap *n* **1** (formerly) soft cap worn in bed. **2** (usu alcoholic) drink taken before going to bed. ⇨ article at DRINK.

ˈnight clothes clothes, eg pyjamas or a night-dress, that are worn in bed.

ˈnight-club *n* club open until late at night for drinking, dancing, entertainment, etc.

ˈnight-dress (also *infml* **nightie, nighty**) *n* long loose garment worn by a woman or child in bed.

ˈnightfall *n* [U] time when darkness comes; dusk: *We hope to be back by nightfall.*

ˈnight-gown *n* = NIGHT-DRESS.

ˈnightjar *n* night-bird with a long tail, like a

swift's, and with a harsh cry.
ˈ**night letter** (*US*) type of telegram sent overnight at a cheap rate.
ˈ**night-life** *n* [U] entertainments available at night in a particular town, area, etc: *There's not much night-life in this small town.*
ˈ**night-light** *n* small candle or bulb that is kept burning in a bedroom at night.
ˈ**night-line** *n* fishing line left in a lake, river, etc to catch fish at night.
ˈ**night-long** *adj, adv* throughout the night.
ˈ**nightmare** *n* **1** frightening dream: *I have nightmares about falling off a cliff.* **2** (*infml*) very frightening or unpleasant experience: *Driving during the blizzard was a nightmare.* **nightmarish** /ˈnaɪtmeərɪʃ/ *adj.*
ˈ**night nurse** nurse, eg in a hospital, who is on duty at night.
ˈ**night porter** hotel porter on duty during the night.
ˈ**night safe** safe in the outside wall of a bank where money, etc can be deposited when the bank is closed.
ˈ**night-school** school where lessons are given in the evening for those who cannot attend classes during the day.
ˈ**night shift** (**a**) [CGp] group of workers at work during the night: *The night shift come/comes off at dawn.* (**b**) [C] time when these workers work: *be on the night shift.* Cf DAY SHIFT (DAY).
ˈ**night-shirt** *n* boy's or man's long shirt for sleeping in.
ˈ**night-soil** *n* [U] (*euph*) human excrement removed from latrines, etc at night.
ˈ**nightstick** *n* (*US*) policeman's truncheon.
ˈ**night-time** *n* time of darkness: *in the night-time* ○ *at night-time.*
ˌ**night-ˈwatch** *n* (person or group of people keeping) watch at night. ˌ**night-ˈwatchman** /-mən/ *n* (*pl* **-men**) **1** man employed to guard a closed building (eg a factory) at night. **2** (in cricket) player who is not a good batsman, but who bats for his team at the end of a day, to avoid the risk of a better batsman being dismissed.

NOTE ON USAGE: Compare **at night**, **by night**, **in the night**, **during the night**, **on a (...) night (...)**. **At night** is used of something habitually happening during the hours of darkness: *Nocturnal animals such as bats and owls only come out at night.* ○ *I don't like driving at night.* **By night** can cover the meanings of **at night.** It is used especially when the conditions or circumstances of an action are being empahsized: *The enemy attacked by night,* ie under cover of darkness. **In the night** usually refers to the night immediately past: *I'm exhausted. The baby woke up three times in the night.* **During the night** can also be used in this sense: *Everything was quiet during the night.* **On** is used when the night in question is further defined: *on a night in May* ○ *on a cold winter's night.* For further information on prepositions of time, see the note on usage at TIME[1].

Nightingale /ˈnaɪtɪŋgeɪl; *US* -tng-/ Florence (1820-1910), British nurse. She became famous for her service as a nurse in the *Crimean War, improving conditions of hygiene in military hospitals and earning the nickname 'the Lady of the Lamp' for walking round the wards at night, comforting the patients. She later campaigned for the reform of the British hospital system and for the improved training of nurses. ➪ illus.

Florence Nightingale

nightingale /ˈnaɪtɪŋgeɪl; *US* -tng-/ *n* small reddish-brown bird of the thrush family, the male of which sings tunefully by night as well as by day.
nightshade /ˈnaɪt-ʃeɪd/ *n* [U, C] any of several types of wild plant with poisonous berries: *deadly nightshade.*
nihilism /ˈnaɪɪlɪzəm, ˈnɪhɪl-/ *n* [U] **1** total rejection of all religious and moral beliefs. **2** belief that nothing really exists.
▷ **nihilist** /-ɪst/ *n* believer in nihilism.
nihilistic /ˌnaɪɪˈlɪstɪk, ˌnɪhɪˈl-/ *adj* of nihilism.
-nik *suff* (*joc sometimes derog*) (forming *ns* meaning a person involved in or experiencing sth): *refusenik.*
nil /nɪl/ *n* [U] nothing, esp as the score in games: *Our team won the game three nil/three goals to nil,* ie 3-0. ➪ Usage at NOUGHT.
Nile /naɪl/ **the Nile** river in Africa, the longest in the world (about 6 740 km, 4 180 miles). It is formed by the **White Nile**, which flows from Lake Victoria, and the **Blue Nile**, which originates in Ethiopia, and flows into the Mediterranean Sea through a wide delta north of Cairo in *Egypt. The Nile valley in Egypt was the site of the first great civilization.
nimble /ˈnɪmbl/ *adj* (**-r** /ˈnɪmblə(r)/, **-st** /ˈnɪmblɪst/) **1** able to move quickly and neatly; agile: *as nimble as a goat* ○ *sewing with nimble fingers.* **2** (*fig*) (of the mind) able to think quickly; sharp: *a lad with nimble wits.* ▷ **nimbleness** *n* [U]. **nimbly** /ˈnɪmblɪ/ *adv.*
nimbus /ˈnɪmbəs/ *n* (*pl* ~**es** /-bəsɪz/ or **-bi** /-baɪ/) **1** (in paintings, etc) bright circle shown round or over the head of a saint; halo. **2** rain cloud.
nimby /ˈnɪmbɪ/ *n* (*joc derog*) person who claims to be in favour of sth, but objects if it causes any personal inconvenience (from the phrase *not in my backyard*): *the nimbies stopping the redevelopment programme* ○ [attrib] *a nimby attitude.* Cf BACKYARD (BACK[2]).
nincompoop /ˈnɪŋkəmpu:p/ *n* (*infml*) foolish person.
nine /naɪn/ *pron, det* **1** 9; one more than eight. ➪ App 9. **2** (idm) ˌ**nine to ˈfive** normal working hours in an office, etc: *I work nine to five.* ○ [attrib] *a nine-to-five job.*
▷ **nine** *n* **1** the number 9. **2** (*US*) baseball team. **3** (idm) **dressed up to the nines** ➪ DRESS[2].
nine- (in compounds) having nine of the thing specified: *a nine-hole golf-course.*
ninth /naɪnθ/ *pron, det* 9th; next after eighth. — *n* one of nine equal parts of sth. **ninthly** *adv*
For the uses of *nine* and *ninth* see the examples at *five* and *fifth.*
ninepin /ˈnaɪnpɪn/ *n* **1 ninepins** [sing *v*] game in which a ball is rolled along the floor at nine bottle-shaped blocks of wood in order to knock them down. Cf SKITTLE, TENPIN BOWLING. **2** [C] any of these blocks of wood. **3** (idm) ˌ**go down like ˈninepins** fall or be knocked over, etc in great numbers: *There's a lot of flu about — people are going down* (ie catching the disease) *like ninepins.*
nineteen /ˌnaɪnˈti:n/ *pron, det* 19; one more than eighteen. ➪ App 9.
▷ **nineteen** *n* the number 19.
nineteenth /ˌnaɪnˈti:nθ/ *pron, det* 19th; next after eighteenth. — *n* one of nineteen equal parts of sth. ˌ**nineteenth ˈhole** (*joc*) bar[1](9) at a golf club.
For the uses of *nineteen* and *nineteenth* see the examples at *five* and *fifth.*
ninety /ˈnaɪntɪ/ *pron, det* 90; one more than eighty-nine. ➪ App 9.
▷ **ninetieth** /ˈnaɪntɪəθ/ *pron, det* 90th; next after eighty-ninth. — *n* one of ninety equal parts of sth.
ninety *n* **1** the number 90. **2 the nineties** [pl] numbers, years or temperature from 90 to 99. **3** (idm) **in one's nineties** between the ages of 90 and 100. **ninety-nine times out of a hundred** almost always.
For the uses of *ninety* and *ninetieth* see the examples at *five* and *fifth.*
Nineveh /ˈnɪnɪvə/ capital city of ancient *Assyria on the bank of the River Tigris.
ninny /ˈnɪnɪ/ *n* (*infml*) foolish person: *Don't be such a ninny!*
niobium /naɪˈəʊbɪəm/ *n* [U] (*symb* **Nb**) soft grey-blue metallic element, used in steel alloys and superconductors.
nip /nɪp/ *v* (**-pp-**) **1** (**a**) [Tn] press (sth) hard (eg between the finger and thumb, or the teeth, or with the claws as a crab does); pinch: *A crab nipped my toe while I was paddling.* ○ *She nipped her finger in the door,* ie between the door and the doorpost. ○ *The dog nipped me in the leg.* (**b**) [I, Ipr] ~ (**at sth**) take small bites with the front teeth: *That dog nips!* ○ *The dog was nipping at her ankles.* **2** [Tn] (of frost, cold wind, etc) stop the growth of (plants); damage: *The icy breeze nipped the young blooms.* **3** [Ipr, Ip] (*infml*) move quickly; hurry: *Where did she nip off to?* ○ *He nipped in* (ie got in quickly) *just in front of me.* ○ *I'll nip on ahead and open the door.* ○ *She has nipped out to the bank.* ➪ Usage at WHIZ. **4** (idm) ˌ**nip and ˈtuck** a situation in which sth is narrowly avoided, or where there is close competition: *The two runners contested the race closely — it was nip and tuck all the way.* **nip sth in the bud** stop or destroy sth at an early stage in its development: *She wanted to be an actress, but her father soon nipped that idea in the bud.* **5** (phr v) **nip sth in** (in sewing) reduce the width of sth: *nip the waist in* ○ *nip in the sides of a dress,* eg by altering the seams. **nip sth off (sth)** remove sth by nipping: *nip the shoots off (a plant).*
▷ **nip** *n* **1** sharp pinch or bite: *The dog gave me a nasty nip on the leg.* ○ *a cold nip in the air,* ie a feeling of frost. **2** (*infml*) small drink, esp of spirits: *a nip of brandy.*
nipper /ˈnɪpə(r)/ *n* **1** [C usu *pl*] claw of a crab, lobster, etc. **2 nippers** [pl] (*infml*) any tool for gripping or cutting, eg pincers: *a pair of nippers.* **3** [C] (*Brit infml*) small child: *a mother with two young nippers* ○ *He's a cheeky little nipper.*
nipple /ˈnɪpl/ *n* **1** (**a**) small projection on the breast through which a baby sucks its mother's milk. (**b**) similar projection on the chest of a human male. Cf TEAT. ➪ illus at HUMAN. **2** = TEAT. **3** thing shaped like a nipple: ˈ*grease nipples,* ie for squirting grease into machinery. **4** (*US*) short section of pipe with a screw thread at each end, used for connecting two longer sections of pipe.
nippy /ˈnɪpɪ/ *adj* (**-ier**, **-iest**) (*infml*) **1** nimble; quick: *a nippy little car.* **2** cold; chilly: *It's jolly nippy today, isn't it?*
nirvana /nɪəˈvɑ:nə/ *n* [U] (in Buddhism and Hinduism) state of perfect bliss in which the individual becomes absorbed into the supreme spirit.
Nissen hut /ˈnɪsn hʌt/ tunnel-shaped hut made of curved sheets of corrugated iron covering a concrete floor.
nit /nɪt/ *n* **1** (egg of a) louse or other parasitic insect. **2** (*infml esp Brit*) = NITWIT.
□ ˈ**nit-picking** *adj, n* [U] (*derog*) finding fault in a petty way: *nit-picking criticism.*
nitrate /ˈnaɪtreɪt/ *n* [U, C] salt formed by the chemical reaction of nitric acid with an alkali, esp *potassium nitrate* or *sodium nitrate,* used as fertilizers: *soil enriched with nitrates* ○ [attrib]: *nitrate pollution of streams.*
▷ **nitrate** /naɪˈtreɪt/ *v* [Tn] treat (a substance) with nitric acid, esp so as to produce a nitrate.
nitre (*US* **niter**) /ˈnaɪtə(r)/ *n* [U] potassium or sodium nitrate; saltpetre.
nitric /ˈnaɪtrɪk/ *adj* of or containing nitrogen.
□ ˌ**nitric ˈacid** clear colourless powerful acid that

corrodes and destroys most substances.

nitrogen /ˈnaɪtrədʒən/ *n* [U] (*symb* **N**) chemical element, a gas without colour, taste or smell that forms about four-fifths of the atmosphere. It is usu obtained by distilling liquefied air. Nitrogen is essential to life and is found in all protein. Compounds include ammonia, nitric acid and nitrates. ⇨ App 11. ▷ **nitrogenous** /naɪˈtrɒdʒənəs/ *adj*.

□ ˈ**nitrogen cycle** cycle in which nitrogen passes from the air into living beings and from living beings back into the air. A short form of the cycle could be: bacteria absorb nitrogen from the air and turn it into nitrates absorbed by plant roots; the plant is eaten by an animal; the dead body or excreta of the animal decays and returns nitrogen compounds to the soil; they are then either absorbed by other plants or broken down by other bacteria that release nitrogen into the air.

ˌ**nitrogen fixˈation** process by which bacteria convert nitrogen from the air into nitrates which can be absorbed by plants.

nitro-glycerine (also *esp US* **-glycerin**) /ˌnaɪtrəʊ ˈglɪsəri:n; *US* -rɪn/ *n* [U] powerful explosive made by adding glycerine to a mixture of nitric acid and sulphuric acid.

nitrous /ˈnaɪtrəs/ *adj* of or like nitre.

□ ˌ**nitrous** ˈ**oxide** (also **laughing-gas**) gas sometimes used as an anaesthetic, esp by dentists.

nitty-gritty /ˌnɪtɪ ˈgrɪtɪ/ *n* **the nitty-gritty** [sing] (*infml*) the basic facts or realities of a matter: *Let's get down to (discussing) the nitty-gritty.*

nitwit /ˈnɪtwɪt/ (also **nit**) *n* (*infml*) stupid or foolish person: *Why did you do that, you nitwit?*

▷ **nitwitted** /ˌnɪtˈwɪtɪd/ *adj* (*infml*) stupid; foolish.

nix /nɪks/ *n* [U] (*sl*) nothing: *It cost me absolutely nix.*

Nixon /ˈnɪksn/ Richard Milhous (1913-), American politician, vice-president 1953-61, president 1969-74. His presidency was marked by decisive foreign policy, including the ending of the Vietnam war and the improvement of US relations with the Soviet Union and China. However, when his involvement in the *Watergate scandal was revealed, he was forced to resign. ⇨ App 2.

No *abbr* **1** (*US*) North(ern). **2** (also **no**) (*pl* **Nos**, **nos**) (*US symb* **#**) number: *No 10 (Downing Street)*, ie the official residence of the British Prime Minister ○ *room no 145*, eg in a hotel.

No *symb* nobelium.

no /nəʊ/ *neg det* **1** (used with *pl* [C] *ns*, *sing* [C] *ns* or [U] *ns*) not any; not one; not a: *No words can express my grief.* ○ *No student is to leave the room.* ○ *I have no time at all to write to you.* ○ *No two people think alike.* **2** (used to indicate that sth is not allowed): *No smoking.* ○ *No dogs in the restaurant.* **3** (used to express the exact opposite of what is said): *It was no easy part to play*, ie It was very difficult. ○ *She was wearing no ordinary hat*, ie Her hat was very unusual. ○ *She's no fool*, ie She is intelligent.

▷ **no** *interj* (used to give a negative reply): *'Is it raining?' 'No, it isn't.'* ○ *'Haven't you finished?' 'No, not yet.'* ○ *'Are you still a student?' 'No, I've got a job now.'*

no *neg adv* (used before comparative *adjs* and *advs*) not: *It's no worse than the last exercise.* ○ *This book is no more expensive than that one.* ○ *If you're no better by tomorrow I'll call the doctor.*

noes /nəʊz/ *n* [pl] total number of people voting 'no' in a formal debate: *The noes have it*, ie Those voting 'no' are in the majority.

□ ˌ**no-ˈball** *n* unlawfully bowled ball in cricket. — *v* [Tn usu passive] (of an umpire) declare (a bowler) to have bowled such a ball.

ˌ**no-claims** ˈ**bonus** sum deducted from the money paid annually, esp by a motorist, for insurance after a year when no claims are made.

ˌ**no-ˈgo area** area to which entry is forbidden to certain people or groups. Cf NO GO (GO[1]).

ˈ**no man's land** (in war) ground between the fronts of two opposing armies.

ˈ**no-no** *n* (*infml joc*) suggestion, proposal, etc that is not practical or acceptable: *Sorry, another loan is a definite no-no!*

ˈ**no one** = NOBODY.

ˌ**no-ˈshow** *n* (*infml*) person who has a ticket for a journey by air, rail or sea but does not use it.

Noah /ˈnəʊə/ (in the Old Testament) man saved with his family from the flood sent by God to destroy humanity. He was told to build a boat (or *ark*) and to take a pair of every animal on board until the waters went down. When they did his boat came to rest on Mount Ararat.

nob /nɒb/ *n* (*sl derog esp Brit*) upper-class, important or high-ranking person: *He acts as if he's one of the nobs.*

nobble /ˈnɒbl/ *v* (*Brit sl*) [Tn] **1** tamper with (a racehorse) so that it is less likely to win a race. **2** influence or get the favour of (sb), esp by unfair or illegal means: *nobble* (eg bribe) *the judge before a trial.* **3** get (sth) dishonestly or by devious means. **4** catch (a criminal).

nobelium /nəˈbi:lɪəm/ *n* [U] (*symb* **No**) artificial radioactive element.

Nobel prize /nəʊˌbel ˈpraɪz/ each of six international prizes awarded each year (since 1901) for outstanding achievements in the fields of science, literature and the promotion of world peace. The prizes are named after the Swedish chemist and philanthropist Alfred Nobel: *the winner of this year's Nobel prize for chemistry.*

nobility /nəʊˈbɪlətɪ/ *n* **1** [U] quality of being noble in mind, character, birth or rank: *Her nobility of character made her much admired.* **2 the nobility** [Gp] people of noble birth or rank: *a member of the British nobility* ○ *marry into the nobility.* Cf ARISTOCRACY.

noble /ˈnəʊbl/ *adj* (**-r** /ˈnəʊblə(r)/, **-st** /ˈnəʊblɪst/) **1** belonging to the aristocracy by birth or rank: *a family of noble descent.* **2** having or showing an excellent character; not petty or mean: *a noble leader, mind, gesture* ○ *noble sentiments* ○ *It was noble of you to accept a lower salary to help the company.* **3** impressive in size, appearance, etc; splendid: *a noble building, horse* ○ *a woman with a noble bearing.*

▷ **noble** *n* person of noble birth or rank.

nobly /ˈnəʊblɪ/ *adv* in a noble manner; splendidly: *nobly born* ○ *thoughts nobly expressed.*

□ ˌ**noble** ˈ**gas** any of six gas elements (helium, neon, argon, krypton, xenon and radon) formerly thought not to form any chemical compounds.

ˈ**nobleman** /-mən/ (*pl* **-men**), ˈ**noblewoman** (*pl* **-women**) *ns* person of noble birth or rank; peer or peeress. Cf ARISTOCRAT.

ˌ**noble** ˈ**metal** metal, eg gold, that does not rust or corrode.

ˌ**noble** ˈ**savage** primitive human being imagined by some 18th- and 19th-century writers, esp *Rousseau, to be free from the corrupting influence of civilized society.

noblesse oblige /nəʊˌbles əˈbli:ʒ/ (*French saying*) people with high rank, privilege, etc must accept the responsibilities that go with their position.

nobody /ˈnəʊbədɪ/ (also **no one** /ˈnəʊwʌn/) *neg pron* not anybody; no person: *Nobody came to see me.* ○ *When I arrived there was nobody there.* ○ *He found that nobody could speak English.* ○ *Nobody remembered to sign their names.* ⇨ Usage at SOMEBODY.

▷ **nobody** *n* unimportant person: *He was just a nobody before he met her.* ○ *Your friends are all just a bunch of nobodies.*

nock /nɒk/ *n* notch at the end of an arrow or at either end of a bow, into which the bowstring fits.

nocturnal /nɒkˈtɜ:nl/ *adj* **1** of or in the night; done or happening in the night: *a nocturnal visit, trip, etc.* **2** (of creatures) active during the night: *nocturnal birds*, eg owls. ▷ **nocturnally** *adv*.

nocturne /ˈnɒktɜ:n/ *n* **1** soft dreamy piece of music. **2** painting of a night scene.

nod /nɒd/ *v* (**-dd-**) **1** [I, Ipr, Tn] ~ (**to/at sb**) move (the head) down and then up again quickly to show agreement, or as a greeting or command: *The teacher nodded in agreement.* ○ *I asked her if she wanted to come and she nodded.* ○ *She nodded (to me) as she passed.* ○ *Why are you nodding (your head) if you disagree?* **2** [Tn, Dn·n, Dn·pr, Dpr·t] ~ **sth (to sb)** indicate something by nodding: *She nodded her approval.* ○ *He nodded me a welcome/nodded a welcome to me.* ○ *He nodded to me to leave the room.* **3** [I] let one's head fall forward when drowsy or asleep: *The old lady sat nodding by the fire.* **4** [I] (of flowers, etc) bend downwards and sway: *nodding pansies.* **5** [I] make a mistake because of lack of alertness or attention. **6** (idm) **have a nodding acquaintance with sb/sth** know sb/sth slightly: *I have no more than a nodding acquaintance with her novels.* **Homer (sometimes) nods** ⇨ HOMER. **7** (phr v) **nod off** (*infml*) fall asleep: *I often nod off for a little while after lunch.*

▷ **nod** *n* **1** act of nodding the head: *She gave me a nod as she passed.* **2** (idm) **the Land of Nod** ⇨ LAND[1]. **a nod is as good as a wink (to a blind horse)** (*saying*) a hint, suggestion, etc can be understood without being explicitly stated. **on the** ˈ**nod** (*infml*) **(a)** (*Brit*) with formal assent and without discussion: *The proposal went through* (ie was approved) *on the nod.* **(b)** (*esp Brit*) on credit: *buy sth on the nod.*

noddle /ˈnɒdl/ *n* (*infml*) head.

Noddy /ˈnɒdɪ/ popular character in the children's stories of Enid *Blyton. He and his friend Big Ears have adventures which usu lead to trouble with the policeman, PC Plod.

noddy /ˈnɒdɪ/ *n* **1** (*infml derog*) silly or simple person. **2** tropical sea-bird, similar to the tern.

node /nəʊd/ *n* **1** (*botany*) **(a)** knob on a root or branch. **(b)** point on the stem of a plant where a leaf or bud grows out. **2** hard swelling, eg on a joint in the human body. **3** (*physics*) point or line in a vibrating body that remains still. **4** (*mathematics*) point at which a curve crosses itself. ▷ **nodal** /ˈnəʊdl/ *adj*.

nodule /ˈnɒdju:l; *US* ˈnɒdʒu:l/ *n* small rounded lump or swelling.

▷ **nodular** /-lə(r)/, **nodulated** /-leɪtɪd/ *adjs* having nodules.

Noel /nəʊˈel/ *n* (esp in carols) Christmas.

noggin /ˈnɒgɪn/ *n* **1** small measure of alcoholic drink, usu $\frac{1}{4}$ pint. **2** (*infml*) head.

Noh /nəʊ/ *n* [U] form of traditional Japanese drama. In a Noh play the acting is stylized, with the main character wearing a mask. There is a chorus and a band of drummers and a flute player. The five main subjects are the gods, warriors, women, fools and demons.

nohow /ˈnəʊhaʊ/ *adv* (*dialect or infml*) in no way; not at all: *We couldn't fix it nohow.*

noise /nɔɪz/ *n* **1 (a)** [C, U] sound, esp when it is loud, unpleasant, confused or unwanted: *the noise of jet aircraft* ○ *I heard a rattling noise.* ○ *What's that noise?* ○ *Who's making those strange noises?* ○ *Don't make so much noise.* ○ [attrib] ˈ*noise pollution*, ie loud noises from aircraft, traffic, radios, etc, that are considered to spoil the environment. **(b)** [U] electrical interference that prevents eg a radio programme or transmission being heard properly. **2 noises** [pl] conventional remarks (used esp as in the expressions shown): *She made polite noises about my work.* ○ *He made all the right noises.* **3** (idm) **a big noise** ⇨ BIG. **make a noise (about sth)** talk or complain loudly: *She made a lot of noise about the poor food.*

▷ **noise** *v* (phr v) **noise sth abroad** (*dated or fml*) make sth publicly known: *It is being noised abroad that he has been arrested.*

noiseless *adj* making little or no noise: *with noiseless footsteps.* **noiselessly** *adv*. **noiselessness** *n* [U].

□ ˌ**noises** ˈ**off** sounds made behind the scenes in a theatre that are meant to be heard by the audience.

noisome /ˈnɔɪsəm/ *adj* (*fml*) offensive; disgusting; stinking: *a noisome sight, smell, etc.*

noisy /ˈnɔɪzɪ/ *adj* (**-ier**, **-iest**) **1** making or accompanied by a lot of noise: *noisy children* ○ *noisy games* ○ *Don't be so noisy! Jim's asleep.* **2** full of noise: *a noisy classroom, playground, etc* ○ *I can't work in here — it's far too noisy.* ▷ **noisily** /-ɪlɪ/ *adv*. **noisiness** *n* [U].

Nolan /ˈnəʊlən/ Sidney (1917-), Australian painter. He is famous for his sometimes humorous paintings of scenes from his country's history and

Sidney Nolan: Grime's Apprentice

landscape. ⇨ illus.

nomad /ˈnəʊmæd/ *n* **1** member of a tribe that wanders from place to place looking for pasture for its animals and having no fixed home. **2** (*fig*) wanderer.

▷ **nomadic** /nəʊˈmædɪk/ *adj* of nomads; wandering: *a nomadic existence, society.*

nom de plume /ˌnɒm də ˈpluːm/ *n* (*pl* **noms de plume** /ˌnɒm də ˈpluːm/) (*French*) = PSEUDONYM.

nomenclature /nəˈmenklətʃə(r); *US* ˈnəʊmənkleɪtʃər/ *n* (*fml*) **(a)** [C, U] system of naming, esp in a particular branch of science: *botanical nomenclature* ○ *the nomenclature of chemistry.* **(b)** [U] names used in such a system.

nominal /ˈnɒmɪnl/ *adj* **1** existing, etc in name only; not real or actual: *the nominal ruler of the country* ○ *the nominal value of the shares* ○ *She is only the nominal chairman: the real work is done by somebody else.* **2** (of a sum of money, etc) very small, but paid because some payment is necessary: *a nominal rent*, ie one very much below the actual value of the property ○ *She charged only a nominal fee for her work.* **3** (*grammar*) of a noun or nouns. ▷ **nominally** /-nəlɪ/ *adv.*

nominate /ˈnɒmɪneɪt/ *v* **1** [Tn, Tn·pr, Cn·n/a, Cn·t] ~ **sb (for/as sth)** formally propose that sb should be chosen for a position, office, task, etc: *She has been nominated (as candidate) for the Presidency.* ○ (*infml*) *I nominate Tom to make the tea.* **2** [Tn, Tn·pr, Cn·n/a] ~ **sb (to/as sth)** appoint sb to an office: *be nominated to a committee* ○ *The board nominated her as the new director.* **3** [Tn, Cn·n/a] ~ **sth (as sth)** formally decide on (a date or place) for an event, meeting, etc: *1 December has been nominated as the day of the election.*

nomination /ˌnɒmɪˈneɪʃn/ *n* **(a)** [U] nominating or being nominated. **(b)** [C] instance of this: *How many nominations have there been* (ie How many people have been nominated) *so far?*

nominative /ˈnɒmɪnətɪv/ *n* special form of a noun, a pronoun or an adjective used (in some inflected languages) when it is the subject, or is in agreement with the subject, of a verb: *Is this noun in the nominative?*

▷ **nominative** *adj* of or in the nominative: *'I', 'we', 'she' and 'they' are all nominative pronouns.*

nominee /ˌnɒmɪˈniː/ *n* person who is nominated for an office, a position, etc.

non- *pref* (used widely with *ns, adjs* and *advs*) not: *nonsense* ○ *non-fiction* ○ *non-alcoholic* ○ *non-church-going* ○ *non-committally.* ⇨ Usage at UN-.

nonage /ˈnəʊnɪdʒ/ *n* [U] (*fml*) state of being under full legal age; minority(2).

nonagenarian /ˌnɒnədʒɪˈneərɪən/ *n, adj* (person who is) of any age from 90 to 99.

non-aggression /ˌnɒn əˈgreʃn/ *n* [U, esp attrib] not attacking; not starting a war, etc: *a non-aggression pact/treaty.*

non-aligned /ˌnɒn əˈlaɪnd/ *adj* (of a state) not allied to or supporting any major country or group of countries: *the non-aligned movement, nations.*

▷ **non-alignment** /ˌnɒn əˈlaɪnmənt/ *n* [U] principle or practice of being non-aligned.

nonce /nɒns/ *n* (idm) **for the nonce** (*dated or rhet*) **(a)** for this one occasion only. **(b)** for the time being.

□ ˈ**nonce-word** *n* word invented for one particular occasion.

nonchalant /ˈnɒnʃələnt/ *adj* not feeling or showing interest or enthusiasm; calm and casual: *She defeated all her rivals for the job with nonchalant ease.* ▷ **nonchalance** /-ləns/ *n* [U]: *Beneath his apparent nonchalance he is as nervous and excited as the rest of us.* **nonchalantly** *adv.*

non-combatant /ˌnɒn ˈkɒmbətənt/ *n* person (esp in the armed forces, eg a doctor or chaplain) not involved in the fighting in a war.

non-commissioned /ˌnɒn kəˈmɪʃənd/ *adj* not having a commission(5) in the armed services: *non-commissioned officers,* eg sergeants or corporals.

non-committal /ˌnɒn kəˈmɪtl/ *adj* not showing what one thinks, which side one supports, etc; not committing oneself: *a non-committal attitude, reply, letter* ○ *She was very non-committal about my suggestion.* Cf COMMIT 4. ▷ **non-committally** *adv.*

non-compliance /ˌnɒn kəmˈplaɪəns/ *n* [U] refusal to comply (with an order, a rule, etc).

non compos mentis /ˌnɒn ˌkɒmpəs ˈmentɪs/ *adj* [pred] (*Latin*) **1** (*law*) not legally responsible because of insanity. **2** (*infml*) not able to think clearly: *I had had a few beers and was completely non compos mentis.*

non-conductor /ˌnɒn kənˈdʌktə(r)/ *n* substance that does not conduct heat or electricity.

nonconformist /ˌnɒnkənˈfɔːmɪst/ *n, adj* **1** (person) who does not conform to normal social conventions. **2 Nonconformist** (member) of a (usu Protestant) sect that does not conform to the beliefs and practices of the Church of England. Cf DISSENTER (DISSENT[2]).

▷ **nonconformity** *n* [U] **1** (also **nonconformism**) failure to conform to normal social conventions. **2** (also **nonconformism**) beliefs and practices of Nonconformist sects. **3** lack of correspondence between things.

non-contributory /ˌnɒn kənˈtrɪbjʊtrɪ; *US* -tɔːrɪ/ *adj* not involving the payment of contributions: *a non-contributory pension scheme.*

nondescript /ˈnɒndɪskrɪpt/ *n, adj* (person or thing) without a distinctive character and so not easily classified: *He's such a nondescript you'd never notice him in a crowd.* ○ *a nondescript landscape, face, voice* ○ *nondescript clothes.*

none /nʌn/ *indef pron* **1 (a)** ~ **(of sb/sth)** (referring back to a plural *n* or *pron*) not one; not any: *We had three cats once — none (of them) is/are alive now.* **(b)** ~ **of sb/sth** (referring forward to a plural *n* or *pron*) not one; not any: *None of the guests wants/want to stay.* (Cf *They none of them want to stay.*) ○ *None of them has/have come back yet.* **2 (a)** ~ **(of sb/sth)** (referring back to a [U] *n* or *pron*) not any: *I wanted some string but there was none in the house.* ○ *'Is there any bread left?' 'No, none at all.'* **(b)** ~ **of sb/sth** (referring forward to a [U] *n* or *pron*) not any: *None of this money is mine.* ○ *I want none of your cheek!* ie Stop being cheeky! ○ *I'll have none of* (ie I do not wish to take part in) *your wild ideas.* **3** (*fml*) (with comparatives and *than*) nobody: *He is aware, none better than he, that…* ○ *The choir sang sweetly, and none more so than the Welsh boy.* **4** (idm) ˈ**none but** only: *None but the best is good enough for my child.* ○ (*saying*) *None but the brave deserves the fair.* **none** ˈ**other than** (used for emphasis): *The new arrival was none other than the President.*

▷ **none** *adv* **1** (used with *the* and a comparative) not at all: *After hearing her talk on computers I'm none the wiser.* ○ *He's none the worse for falling into the river.* **2** (used with *too* and *adjs* or *advs*) not very: *The salary they pay me is none too high.*

□ ˌ**none the** ˈ**less** nevertheless: *It's not cheap but I think we should buy it none the less.*

nonentity /nɒˈnentətɪ/ *n* **1** (*derog*) person without any special qualities or achievements; unimportant person: *How could such a nonentity become chairman of the company?* **2** thing that does not exist or exists only in the imagination.

nonesuch (also **nonsuch**) /ˈnʌnsʌtʃ/ *n* [sing] (*fml*) person or thing that is better than all others. Cf NONPAREIL.

non-event /ˌnɒnɪˈvent/ *n* (*infml*) event that is expected to be interesting, etc, but is in fact a disappointment: *The party was a non-event; hardly anyone came!*

non-existent /ˌnɒnɪgˈzɪstənt/ *adj* not present or existing in a particular place: *Bread was practically non-existent.* ○ *a non-existent danger, threat, enemy.*

non-fiction /ˌnɒnˈfɪkʃn/ *n* [U] prose writings that deal with facts (as distinct from novels, stories, etc which deal with unreal people and events): *I prefer non-fiction to fiction.* ○ [attrib] *the non-fiction shelves in the library.* Cf FICTION 1.

non-flammable /ˌnɒnˈflæməbl/ *adj* (in official use) (of clothes, materials, etc) not catching fire easily. ⇨ Usage at INVALUABLE.

non-interference /ˌnɒnɪntəˈfɪərəns/ (also **non-intervention** /ˌnɒnɪntəˈvenʃn/) *n* [U] principle or practice of not becoming involved in the disputes of others, esp in international affairs: *a strict policy of non-interference in the internal affairs of other countries.*

non-iron /ˌnɒnˈaɪən; *US* -ˈaɪərn/ *adj* drying without creases after washing, without needing to be ironed: *a non-iron* ˈ*fabric,* ˈ*shirt,* ˈ*blouse, etc.*

non-observance /ˌnɒnəbˈzɜːvəns/ *n* [U] (*fml*) failure to keep or observe (a rule, custom, etc): *accused of non-observance of the test-ban agreement.*

no-nonsense /ˌnəʊˈnɒnsns; *US* -sens/ *adj* [attrib] straightforward, sensible and serious: *Let's have a clear no-nonsense agreement to start work as soon as possible.* ○ *She has a firm, no-nonsense attitude towards her staff.*

nonpareil /ˌnɒnpəˈreɪl; *US* -ˈrel/ *n* [sing], *adj* [attrib] (*fml*) (person or thing) without an equal or rival. Cf NONESUCH.

non-payment /ˌnɒnˈpeɪmənt/ *n* [U] (*fml*) failure to pay (a debt, fine, etc): *He was taken to court for non-payment of rent.*

nonplus /ˌnɒnˈplʌs/ *v* (**-ss-**; *US* **-s-**) [Tn esp passive] surprise or puzzle (sb) greatly: *I was completely nonplussed by his sudden appearance.*

non-profit-making /ˌnɒn ˈprɒfɪt meɪkɪŋ/ *adj* (also *esp US* ˌ**non-ˈprofit**) (of an organization) that does not operate mainly to make a profit.

non-proliferation /ˌnɒnprəlɪfəˈreɪʃn/ *n* [U, esp attrib] limitation of the number and spread (esp of nuclear and chemical weapons): *a non-proliferation treaty aimed at stopping the spread of nuclear weapons.*

non-resident /ˌnɒnˈrezɪdənt/ *adj* (*fml*) **1** not living in a place: *This block of flats has a non-resident caretaker.* **2** (also **non-residential** /ˌnɒnreziˈdenʃl/) (of a job) not requiring the holder to live on the premises: *a non-resident(ial) post.*
▷ **non-resident** *n* person not staying at a hotel, etc: *The bar is open to non-residents.*

nonsense /ˈnɒnsns; *US* -sens/ *n* **1** [U] meaningless words: *jumble up the words in a sentence to produce nonsense* ○ *This so-called translation is pure nonsense.* **2** (**a**) [U, sing] foolish talk, ideas, etc: *You're talking nonsense!* ○ *'I won't go.' 'Nonsense! You must go!'* ○ *This discovery makes (a) nonsense of* (ie clearly disproves) *previous theories.* (**b**) [U] foolish or unacceptable behaviour: *Stop that nonsense, children, and get into bed!* ○ *He won't stand for any nonsense from the staff.* **3** (idm) **stuff and nonsense** ⇨ STUFF[1].
▷ **nonsensical** /nɒnˈsensɪkl/ *adj* not making sense; absurd: *a nonsensical sentence, remark, suggestion, etc.* **nonsensically** /-klɪ/ *adv.*
□ ˈ**nonsense verse** humorous verse which tells absurd stories and often uses language in a ridiculous way. Edward *Lear and Lewis *Carroll are two of the most famous writers of nonsense verse.

non sequitur /ˌnɒn ˈsekwɪtə(r)/ *n* (*Latin*) statement that does not follow logically from the previous statement(s) or argument(s): *This non sequitur invalidates his argument.*

non-skid /ˌnɒnˈskɪd/ *adj* (of tyres) designed to prevent or reduce the risk of skidding.

non-smoker /ˌnɒnˈsməʊkə(r)/ *n* **1** person who does not smoke tobacco. **2** compartment in a train, etc where smoking is forbidden. ▷ ˌ**non-ˈsmoking** *adj*: *a non-smoking section in the cinema.*

non-starter /ˌnɒnˈstɑːtə(r)/ *n* **1** horse that is entered for a race but does not run in it: *Number 18 in the 2.30 at Lingfield is a non-starter.* Cf STARTER 1. **2** (*fig infml*) thing or person that has no chance of success: *Your proposal is absurd; it's an absolute non-starter.*

non-stick /ˌnɒnˈstɪk/ *adj* (of a pan, surface, etc) coated with a substance that prevents food sticking to it during cooking: *It's very difficult to make pancakes without a ˌnon-stick ˈfrying-pan.*

non-stop /ˌnɒnˈstɒp/ *adj, adv* (**a**) (of a train, journey, etc) without any stops: *a non-stop flight to Tokyo* ○ *fly non-stop from New York to Paris.* (**b**) (done) without ceasing: ˌ*non-stop* ˈ*talk,* ˈ*work, etc* ○ *He chattered non-stop all the way.*

nonsuch = NONESUCH.

non-U /ˌnɒnˈjuː/ *adj* (*Brit infml*) (of language, behaviour or dress) not upper-class: *a* ˌ*non-U* ˈ*accent* ○ ˌ*non-U* ˈ*speech, vo*ˈ*cabulary,* ˈ*manners.* Cf U.

non-union /ˌnɒnˈjuːnɪən/ *adj* [usu attrib] **1** not belonging to a trade union: *Non-union labour was used to end the strike.* **2** (of a business, company, etc) not having trade-union members: *a* ˌ*non-union* ˈ*factory,* ˈ*industry, etc.*

non-violence /ˌnɒnˈvaɪələns/ *n* [U] policy of not using force to bring about political or social change. ▷ **non-violent** /-lənt/ *adj*: *a non-violent protest, rally, demonstration, etc.*

non-voting /ˌnɒnˈvəʊtɪŋ/ *adj* (of a share in a company) that entitles the holder to receive dividends but not to vote at meetings.

non-white /ˌnɒnˈwaɪt/ *n, adj* (person) not belonging to the white-skinned races: *These policies will affect non-whites especially.*

noodle[1] /ˈnuːdl/ *n* (usu *pl*) long thin strip made of flour-and-water or flour-and-egg paste and used in soups, with sauces, etc: *Chinese food is often served with rice or noodles.* ○ [attrib] *chicken noodle soup.* Cf PASTA.

noodle[2] /ˈnuːdl/ *n* (*dated infml*) fool.

nook /nʊk/ *n* **1** sheltered quiet place or corner: *a shady nook in the garden.* **2** (idm) **every** ˌ**nook and** ˈ**cranny** (*infml*) every part of a place; everywhere: *I've searched every nook and cranny but I still can't find the keys.*

nooky (also **nookie**) /ˈnʊkɪ/ *n* [U] (*sl esp joc*) sexual intercourse.

noon /nuːn/ *n* [sing] (*fml*) (used without *a* or *the*) 12 o'clock in the middle of the day; midday: *They arrived at noon.* ○ *My lecture's at twelve noon.* ○ *She stayed until noon.* ○ *He has been working since noon.* ○ [attrib] *the noon bell,* ie bell rung at noon.
□ ˈ**noonday** /-deɪ/, ˈ**noontide** /-taɪd/ *ns* [sing] (*dated or rhet*) midday: [attrib] *the noonday sun.*

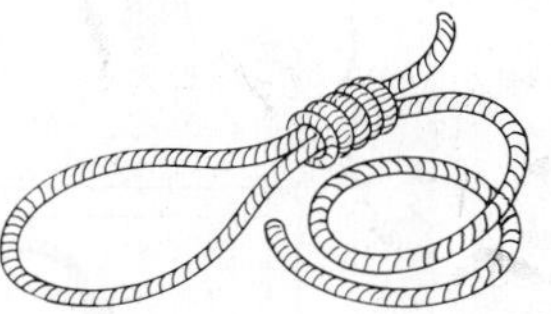

noose

noose /nuːs/ *n* **1** loop in one end of a rope, with a knot that allows the loop to be tightened as the other end of the rope is pulled: *He's facing the hangman's noose,* ie waiting to be hanged. ⇨ illus. **2** (idm) **put one's head in the noose** ⇨ HEAD[1].

nope /nəʊp/ *interj* (*sl*) no!

nor /nɔː(r)/ *conj, adv* **1** (used after *neither* or *not*) and not: *He has neither talent nor the desire to learn.* ○ *Not a leaf nor an insect stirred.* **2** (*fml*) (used with *aux vs* and *modal vs*, with the subject following the *v*) and...not...either: *He can't see, nor could he hear until a month ago.* ○ *She isn't rich; nor do I imagine that she ever will be.* ○ *It won't arrive today. Nor tomorrow.* ○ *Nor am I aware that anyone else knows the secret.* Cf NEITHER.

nor'- ⇨ NORTH.

Nordic /ˈnɔːdɪk/ *adj* **1** of the countries of Scandinavia. **2** of the European racial type that is tall, with blue eyes and blond hair: *Nordic features, peoples.*

Norfolk /ˈnɔːfək/ county in SE England, part of East Anglia. ⇨ map at App 1.

norm /nɔːm/ *n* **1** (usu with *the* when *sing*) standard or pattern that is typical (of a group, etc): *Criminal behaviour seems to be the norm in this neighbourhood.* ○ *You must adapt to the norms of the society you live in.* **2** [C] (in some industries) amount of work expected or required in a working day: *fulfil one's norm* ○ *There's a production norm below which each worker must not fall.*

normal /ˈnɔːml/ *adj* **1** in accordance with what is typical, usual or regular: *the normal time, place, method, position* ○ *normal behaviour, thinking, views* ○ *in the normal course of events* ○ *the normal temperature of the human body* ○ *Weeping is a normal response to pain.* **2** free from mental or emotional disorder: *People who commit crimes like that aren't normal.* Cf ABNORMAL. **3** (*mathematics*) ~ (**to sth**) at right angles or perpendicular (to eg a plane).
▷ **normal** *n* **1** [U] usual state, level, standard, etc: *Her temperature is above/below normal.* ○ *Things have returned to normal.* **2** [C] (*mathematics*) normal(3) line.
normality /nɔːˈmæl ətɪ/ (also esp *US* **normalcy** /ˈnɔːməlsɪ/) *n* [U] state of being normal.
normalize, -ise /ˈnɔːməlaɪz/ *v* **1** [I, Tn] (cause sth to) become normally friendly again after a period of dispute: *Relations between our two countries have normalized.* ○ *Our relationship has been normalized.* **2** [Tn] make (sth) regular in pattern or as expected: *The editors have normalized the author's rather unusual spelling.* **normalization, -isation** /ˌnɔːməlaɪˈzeɪʃn; *US* -lɪˈz-/ *n* [U].
normally /ˈnɔːməlɪ/ *adv.*

Normandy /ˈnɔːməndɪ/ part of northern France on the Channel coast. Vikings settled there in the 10th century. In 1944 it was the scene of the Allied landings that helped to bring the Second World War to an end: *the Normandy beaches.*

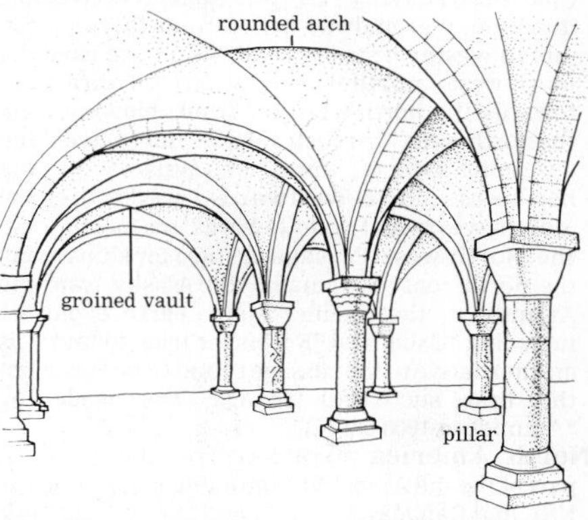

Norman architecture: the crypt at Canterbury Cathedral

▷ **Norman** /ˈnɔːmən/ *adj* **1** (*architecture*) of the style introduced into England in the 11th century by invaders from Normandy (**Normans**). Its main features were rounded arches and heavy pillars: *a Norman arch, cathedral, etc.* ⇨ illus. **2** of the Normans: *the Norman Conquest,* ie the invasion of England by Normans in the 11th century.

normative /ˈnɔːmətɪv/ *adj* (*fml*) describing or setting standards or rules of language, behaviour, etc, which should be followed: *A normative grammar of a language describes how its authors think the language should be spoken or written.*

Norse /nɔːs/ *n* [U] (also **Old Norse**) language of ancient Scandinavia, esp Norway.
▷ **Norse** *adj* [esp attrib] of ancient Scandinavia, esp Norway: *Norse myths and legends.*

north /nɔːθ/ *n* [sing] (*abbr* **N**) **1** (esp with *the*) one of the four main points of the compass, lying to the left of a person facing the sunrise: *cold winds from the north* ○ *He lives to the north of here.* ○ *Do you know which way is north?* Cf EAST, SOUTH, WEST. **2 the north, the North** part of any country, etc that lies further in this direction than other parts: *the North of England* ○ *The north is less expensive to live in than the south.*
▷ **north** *adj* [attrib] (**a**) of, in or towards the north: *the north wall,* ie the one facing north. (**b**) coming from the north: *a north wind,* ie blowing from the north ○ *a north light,* ie from the north.
north *adv* to or towards the north: *sail, drive, walk, etc north.*
northerly /ˈnɔːðəlɪ/ *adj* **1** (of winds) from the north. **2** to, towards or in the north: *travel in a northerly direction.* — *n* northerly wind: *Cold northerlies will bring rain to Scotland this week.*
northwards /ˈnɔːθwədz/ (also **northward**) *adv* towards the north. ⇨ Usage at FORWARD[2].
□ ˈ**northbound** travelling or leading in a northerly direction: *northbound traffic* ○ *the northbound carriageway of the M6.*
the ˈ**North Country** the northern part of England.
ˌ**North-**ˈ**countryman** /-mən/ *n* native of the North of England.
ˌ**north-**ˈ**east** sometimes, esp nautical, **nor'-east** (/ˌnɔːrˈiːst/) *n* [sing], *adj, adv* (*abbr* **NE**) (region, direction, etc) midway between north and east.
ˌ**north**ˈ**easter** *n* strong wind, storm, etc from the north-east. ˌ**north-**ˈ**easterly** *adj* (of direction) towards the north-east; (of wind) blowing from the north-east. — *n* such a wind. ˌ**north-**ˈ**eastern** /-ˈiːstən/ *adj* of, from or situated in the north-east.
ˌ**north-**ˈ**eastwards** /-ˈiːstwədz/ (also ˌ**north-**ˈ**eastward**) *adv* towards the north-east.
the ˌ**North** ˈ**Pole** northernmost point of the earth, at 90° N. It was first reached by the American Robert Peary in 1909. ⇨ illus at GLOBE.
the ˌ**North** ˈ**Sea** part of the Atlantic Ocean between mainland Europe and the east coast of Britain. There are large reserves of oil and natural

gas below its bed. ⇨ articles at ELECTRICITY, OIL.

the ˌNorth ˈStar = POLE STAR (POLE).

ˌnorth-ˈwest sometimes, esp nautical, **nor'-west** (/ˌnɔːˈwest/) *n* [sing], *adj*, *adv* (*abbr* **NW**) (region, direction, etc) midway between north and west. **ˌnorthˈwester** *n* strong wind, storm, etc from the north-west. **ˌnorth-ˈwesterly** *adj* (of direction) towards the north-west; (of wind) blowing from the north-west. — *n* such a wind. **ˌnorth-ˈwestern** /-ˈwestən/ *adj* of, from or situated in the north-west. **ˌnorth-ˈwestwards** /-ˈwestwədz/ (also **ˌnorth-ˈwestward**) *adv* towards the north-west.

the ˌNorth-west ˈPassage passage for ships along the north coast of Canada and Alaska from the Atlantic to the Pacific. Many early explorers including *Cabot and *Frobisher tried to find it as an alternative to the passage round Cape Horn, but the first successful voyage was made by *Amundsen 1903-06.

North America /ˌnɔːθ əˈmerɪkə/ the northern part of the the American continent, containing the USA and Canada.

Northamptonshire /nɔːˈθæmptənʃə(r)/ (*abbr* **Northants**) county in the E Midlands of England. ⇨ map at App 1.

North Carolina /ˌnɔːθ kærəˈlaɪnə/ state on the east coast of the USA, containing America's main tobacco-growing region. It was one of the 13 original states. ⇨ map at App 1.

Northcliffe /ˈnɔːθklɪf/ Alfred Harmsworth, Viscount Northcliffe (1865-1922), British newspaper proprietor. Beginning as a journalist, he started *The Daily Mail* and *The Daily Mirror*, and bought *The Times*. His papers had a strong influence on policy during the First World War and after the war he was made responsible for overseas propaganda.

North Dakota /ˌnɔːθ dəˈkəʊtə/ state in the north central USA, containing plains and prairies used for growing wheat and other crops. ⇨ map at App 1.

northern /ˈnɔːðən/ *adj* [usu attrib] of or in the north: *the northern region, frontier, climate* ○ *the northern hemisphere.*

▷ **northerner** /ˈnɔːðənə(r)/ *n* person born or living in the northern part of a country.

northernmost /-məʊst/ *adj* [usu attrib] lying farthest to the north.

□ **the ˌnorthern ˈlights** ⇨ AURORA 1.

Northern Ireland /ˌnɔːðən ˈaɪələnd/ north-eastern part of Ireland made up of six counties of the historic *Ulster, forming a province of the United Kingdom. Agriculture, esp dairy farming, is important, but the industrial economy remains troubled despite attempts to revive it. Northern Ireland remained part of the United Kingdom rather than joining an independent Ireland because of the wishes of the Protestant majority. The Catholic minority has traditionally been at an economic disadvantage. Since the protests of the late 1960s and the arrival of British troops, the activities of terrorist groups have given the province a reputation as a violent and dangerous place, making economic and social progress difficult. ⇨ map at UNITED KINGDOM. ⇨ article at IRELAND.

Northern Territory /ˌnɔːðən ˈterətrɪ/ (*abbr* **NT**) territory in north central Australia. The region is not yet a full state and is administered by the federal government. Most of it is arid, but there are considerable mineral resources. ⇨ map at App 1.

northing /ˈnɔːθɪŋ/ *n* [U] (*nautical*) distance measured or travelled towards the north. Cf EASTING.

Northumberland /nɔːˈθʌmbələnd/ county in NE England, on the Scottish border. It is mainly rural, and sheep-farming is the chief activity. ⇨ map at App 1. ▷ **Northumbrian** /-brɪən/ *n*, *adj*.

North Yorkshire /ˌnɔːθ ˈjɔːkʃə(r)/ county in NE England, formed in 1974 from the North Riding of (the former county of) Yorkshire. ⇨ map at App 1.

Norway

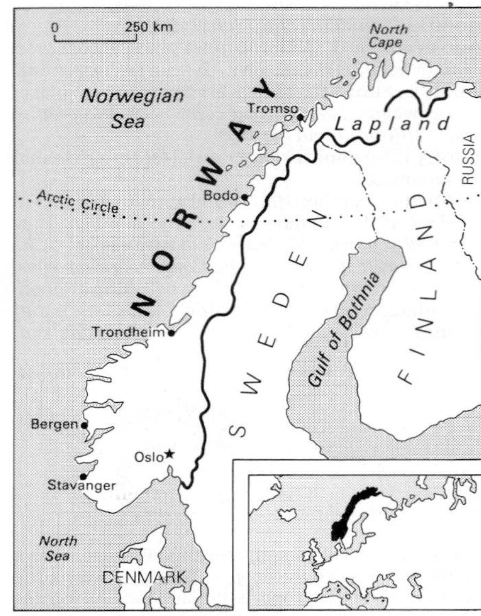

Norway /ˈnɔːweɪ/ country in NW Scandinavia; pop approx 4 196 000; official language Norwegian; capital Oslo; unit of currency krone (= 100 ore). It is a mountainous country, partly within the Arctic Circle, famous for the fiords along its coastline. Agriculture is limited, but forestry and fishing are economically important. It has large oil and gas reserves in the North Sea. ⇨ map.

▷ **Norwegian** /ˌnɔːˈwiːdʒən/ *adj* of Norway. — *n* **1** [C] native or inhabitant of Norway. **2** [U] Scandinavian language of Norway.

Nos (also **nos**) *abbr* numbers.

nose[1] /nəʊz/ *n* **1** [C] part of the face above the mouth, used for breathing and smelling: *give sb a punch on the nose.* ⇨ illus. ⇨ illus at HEAD. ⇨ Usage at BODY. **2** [C] thing like a nose in shape or position, eg the front of an aircraft body, the front of a car, etc: *He brought the aircraft's nose up and made a perfect landing.* ⇨ illus at AIRCRAFT. **3** [sing] (**a**) sense of smell: *a dog with a good nose.* (**b**) ~ **for sth** (*infml*) an ability to detect or find sth: *a reporter with a nose for news, scandal, etc.* **4** (idm) **be no skin off one's nose** ⇨ SKIN. **blow one's nose** ⇨ BLOW[1]. **by a nose** by a very small margin: *The horse won by a nose.* ○ *The candidate lost the election by a nose.* **ˌcut off one's ˌnose to ˌspite one's ˈface** (*infml*) hurt oneself in trying to take revenge on sb else: *If you refuse her help because you're angry with her, you're cutting off your nose to spite your face.* **follow one's nose** ⇨ FOLLOW. **get up sb's ˈnose** (*sl*) annoy sb: *Her cheeky remarks really get up my nose!* **have one's nose in sth** (*infml*) read sth very attentively: *Peter's always got his nose in a book.* **keep one's ˈnose clean** (*infml*) avoid doing anything unacceptable, illegal, etc: *If you keep your nose clean, the boss might promote you.* **keep one's/sb's nose to the ˈgrindstone** (*infml*) keep oneself/sb working hard. **lead sb by the nose** ⇨ LEAD[3]. **look down one's ˈnose at sb/sth** (*infml*) treat sb/sth with contempt: *I gave the dog some lovely steak, and he just looked down his nose at it!* **on the ˈnose** (*sl esp US*) precisely; exactly: *You've hit it* (ie described or understood it) *on the nose!* **pay through the nose** ⇨ PAY[2]. **plain as the nose on one's face** ⇨ PLAIN[1]. **poke/stick one's nose into sth** (*infml*) interfere in sth although it is not one's concern: *Don't go poking your nose into other people's business!* **put sb's ˈnose out of joint** (*infml*) embarrass, offend or annoy sb: *He's so conceited that when she refused his invitation, it really put his nose out of joint.* **rub sb's nose in it** ⇨ RUB[2]. **thumb one's nose at sb/sth** ⇨ THUMB *v*. **turn one's ˈnose up at sth** (*infml*) treat sth with contempt: *She turned her nose up at my small donation.* **(right) under sb's (very) ˈnose** (*infml*) (**a**) directly in front of sb: *I put the bill right under his nose so that he couldn't miss it.* (**b**) in sb's presence, usu without him noticing anything: *They were having an affair under my very nose, and I didn't even realize!* **with one's nose in the ˈair** (*infml*) very haughtily; in a very superior way: *She walked past us with her nose in the air.*

▷ **-nosed** (forming compound *adjs*) having a nose of the specified kind: *red-nosed* ○ *long-nosed.*

□ **ˈnosebag** (*US* **ˈfeedbag**) *n* bag containing food for a horse, fastened to its head.

ˈnosebleed *n* bleeding from the nose.

ˈnose-cone *n* cone-shaped front end of a rocket, guided missile, etc.

ˈnosedive *n* **1** sharp vertical descent by an aircraft, etc, with the nose pointing towards the earth: *go into a sudden nosedive.* **2** (*fig*) sudden plunge or drop: *Prices have taken a nosedive.* — *v* [I] **1** (of an aircraft, etc) descend vertically with the nose pointing towards the earth. **2** (*fig*) fall sharply: *Demand for oil has nosedived.*

ˈnose-flute *n* musical instrument blown with the nose, used in parts of Asia.

ˈnosering *n* ring fixed in the nose of a bull, etc, for leading it.

ˈnose-wheel *n* front landing-wheel under the nose of an aircraft.

noses

nose[2] /nəʊz/ *v* **1** [Ipr, Tn·pr] (cause sth to) go forward slowly: *The car nosed carefully round the corner.* ○ *The plane nosed into the hangar.* ○ *He nosed the car into the garage.* ○ *The ship nosed its way slowly through the ice.* **2** (phr v) **nose about/around; nose into sth** (*infml*) pry into or search sth: *a reporter nosing around for news* ○ *Don't nose into/nose about in other people's affairs.* **nose sth out** (*infml*) (**a**) discover sth by smelling: *The dog nosed out a rat.* (**b**) (*fig*) discover sth by searching: *That man can nose out a news story anywhere.*

nosegay /ˈnəʊzgeɪ/ *n* small bunch of (usu sweet-smelling) flowers.

nosey (also **nosy**) /ˈnəʊzɪ/ *adj* (**-ier**, **-iest**) (*infml often derog*) over-curious; rudely inquisitive: *I've always found her unbearably nosey.* ▷ **nosily** *adv.* **nosiness** *n* [U].

□ **Nosey Parker** /ˌnəʊzɪ ˈpɑːkə(r)/ *n* (*Brit infml derog*) over-inquisitive person; busybody: *I caught that Nosey Parker reading my diary.*

nosh /nɒʃ/ *n* (*sl esp Brit or Austral*) **1** [U] food: *There was lots of nosh at the party.* **2** [sing] (quick) meal, snack, etc: *We'll have a (quick) nosh, then start out.*

▷ **nosh** *v* (*sl esp Brit*) [I] eat.

□ **ˈnosh-up** *n* (*sl esp Brit*) meal, esp a large one: *We had a great nosh-up at Bill's wedding.*

nostalgia /nɒˈstældʒə/ *n* [U] sentimental longing for things that are past.

▷ **nostalgic** /nɒˈstældʒɪk/ *adj* of, feeling or causing nostalgia: *I get very nostalgic when I watch these old musicals on TV.* ○ *a nostalgic song, poem, etc.* **nostalgically** /-klɪ/ *adv.*

Nostradamus /ˌnɒstrəˈdɑːməs; *US* ˌnəʊstrəˈdɑːməs/ Latin name of Michel de

Notredame (1503-66), French astrologer. He is famous for his mysterious predictions, some of which are about the end of the world. They can be interpreted in such a way that some of them appear to have come true.

nostril /ˈnɒstrəl/ *n* either of the two external openings in the nose through which the breath passes. ⇨ illus at HEAD.

nostrum /ˈnɒstrəm/ *n* (*fml derog*) **1** medicine falsely recommended as effective; quack remedy. **2** over-simple measure put forward as a solution to political or social problems: *Some nostrum peddled as a cure for unemployment.*

not /nɒt/ *adv* **1** (**a**) (used with *aux vs* and *modal vs* to form the negative; often contracted to *-n't* /nt/ in speech and informal writing): *She did not see him.* ○ *You may not be chosen.* ○ *They aren't here.* ○ *I mustn't forget.* ○ *Wouldn't you like to go home?* (**b**) (used with non-finite *vs* to form the negative): *He warned me not to be late.* ○ *The difficulty was in not laughing out loud.* **2** (**a**) (used after *believe, expect, hope, trust,* etc instead of a clause beginning with *that* and containing a negative *v*): *'Will it rain?' 'I hope not* (ie that it will not rain).*'* ○ *'Does he know?' 'I believe not.'* ○ *'Can I come in?' 'I'm afraid not.'* (**b**) (used to indicate the negative alternative after questions with *Are you, Can he, Shall we,* etc): *Is she ready or not?* ○ *Can you mend it or not?* ○ *I don't know if/whether he's telling the truth or not.* **3** (**a**) (used to reply in the negative to part or all of a question): *'Are you hungry?' 'Not hungry, just very tired.'* ○ *'Would you like some more?' 'Not for me, thank you.'* ○ *'Do you go in the sea every day?' 'Not in the winter.'* (**b**) (used to deny the significance of the following word or phrase): *It was not greed but ambition that drove him to crime.* ○ *Not all the students have read the book.* ○ *'Who will do the washing-up?' 'Not me.'* (**c**) (used to show that the opposite of the following word or phrase is intended): *a town that is not a million miles from here,* ie very close ○ *She argued, and not without reason* (ie reasonably), *that no one could afford to pay.* ○ *We plan to meet again in the not too distant future,* ie quite soon. **4** (idm) **not only...(but) also** (used to emphasize the addition of sb/sth): *Not only the grandparents were there but also the aunts, uncles and cousins.* ○ *He not only writes his own plays, he also acts in them.* ˈ**not that** though one is not suggesting that: *She hasn't written to me yet — not that she ever said she would.*

notable /ˈnəʊtəbl/ *adj* deserving to be noticed; remarkable: *a notable success, event, discovery* ○ *a notable artist, writer, etc.*

▷ **notable** *n* famous or important person.

notability /ˌnəʊtəˈbɪlətɪ/ *n* [C] famous or important person.

notably /ˈnəʊtəblɪ/ *adv* noticeably; remarkably: *notably successful.*

notary /ˈnəʊtərɪ/ *n* (also ˌ**notary** ˈ**public**) person with official authority to witness the signing of legal documents and perform certain other legal functions.

notation /nəʊˈteɪʃn/ *n* **1** [C] system of signs, symbols, etc used to represent numbers, amounts, musical notes, etc: *develop a new and simpler notation.* **2** [U] representing of numbers, etc by such signs, symbols, etc: *musical notation* ○ *scientific notation.*

notch /nɒtʃ/ *n* **1** ~ (**in/on sth**) V-shaped cut in an edge or surface: *cut/make a notch in a stick.* ⇨ illus at GROOVE. **2** level or grade of excellence: *Acting and direction are several notches up on the standards we are used to.* **3** (*US*) narrow mountain pass.

▷ **notch** *v* [Tn] **1** make a notch or notches in (sth). **2** (phr v) **notch sth up** (*infml*) score sth; achieve sth: *notch up a win, record, etc* ○ *With this performance, she has notched up her third championship title.*

note[1] /nəʊt/ *n* **1** [C] short written record (of facts, etc) to aid the memory: *make a note (of sth)* ○ *She lectured without notes.* ○ *He sat taking notes of everything that was said.* **2** [C] (**a**) short letter: *a note of thanks* ○ *He wrote me a note asking if I would come.* (**b**) official diplomatic letter: *an exchange of notes between governments.* **3** [C] short comment on or explanation of a word or passage in a book, etc: *a new edition of 'Hamlet', with copious notes* ○ *See the editor's comments, page 259, note 3.* Cf FOOTNOTE (FOOT[1]). **4** [C] (also ˈ**banknote**, *US* usu **bill**) piece of paper money issued by a bank: *a £5 note* ○ *Do you want the money in notes or coins?* **5** [C] (**a**) single sound of a certain pitch and duration, made by a musical instrument, voice, etc: *the first few notes of a tune* ○ (*arch*) *the blackbird's merry note,* ie song. (**b**) sign used to represent such a sound in a manuscript or in printed music: *Quavers, crotchets and minims are three of the different lengths of note in written music.* ⇨ illus at MUSIC. (**c**) any one of the keys of a piano, organ, etc: *the black notes and the white notes.* **6** [sing] ~ (**of sth**) quality (of sth); a hint or suggestion (of sth): *There was a note of self-satisfaction in his speech.* ○ *The book ended on an optimistic note.* **7** [U] notice; attention: *worthy of note* ○ *Take note of what he says,* ie pay attention to it. **8** (idm) **compare notes** ⇨ COMPARE. **of** ˈ**note** that is important, distinguished, well-known, etc: *a singer, writer, etc of some note* ○ *Nothing of particular note happened.* **make a mental note (of sth/to do sth)** ⇨ MENTAL. **hit/strike the right/wrong note** do, say or write sth that is fitting/not fitting for a particular occassion, etc. **strike/sound a** ˈ**note (of sth)** express feelings, views, etc of the stated kind: *She sounded a note of warning in her speech.* ○ *The article struck a pessimistic note; it suggested there would be no improvement.* **strike/sound a false note** ⇨ FALSE.

▷ **notelet** /ˈnəʊtlɪt/ *n* sheet of paper, often decorated, for writing short letters on.

□ ˈ**notebook** *n* small book for writing notes (NOTE 1) in.

ˈ**notecase** *n* wallet for banknotes.

ˈ**notepad** *n* block of sheets of paper for taking notes (NOTE 1) on.

ˈ**notepaper** *n* [U] paper for writing letters on: *headed notepaper,* ie with a printed address on.

note[2] /nəʊt/ *v* **1** [Tn, Tf, Tw] (*esp fml*) notice (sth); observe: *Please note my words.* ○ *She noted (that) his hands were dirty.* ○ *Note how I do it, then copy me.* **2** (phr v) **note sth down** record sth in writing; write sth down: *The policeman noted down every word she said.*

▷ **noted** *adj* ~ (**for/as sth**) well-known; famous: *a noted pianist* ○ *a town noted for its fine buildings, as a health resort.*

□ ˈ**noteworthy** *adj* deserving to be noted; remarkable: *a noteworthy performance by a young soloist.*

nothing /ˈnʌθɪŋ/ *neg pron* **1** not anything; no single thing: *Nothing gives me more pleasure than listening to Mozart.* ○ *There's nothing interesting in the newspaper.* ○ *I've had nothing to eat since lunchtime.* ○ *There's nothing you can do to help.* ○ *We went swimming with nothing* ˈ*on,* ie naked. ○ *He's five foot nothing,* ie exactly five feet tall. ○ *It used to cost nothing to visit a museum.* ○ *What's the matter? Nothing serious, I hope.* ○ *There is nothing as refreshing as lemon tea.* ○ *I had nothing stronger than orange juice to drink.* ⇨ Usage at NOUGHT. **2** (idm) **be nothing to sb** be a person for whom sb has no feelings: *'What is she to you?' 'She's nothing to me.'* **be nothing to sb/sth** be far less good, remarkable, etc than sb/sth else: *They're a good team, but nothing to ours.* ○ *That's nothing to what'll happen if your father finds out!* ie he will be even more angry. **for** ˈ**nothing** (**a**) without payment; free: *Children under 5 can travel for nothing.* ○ *We could have got in for nothing — nobody was collecting tickets.* (**b**) with no reward or result; to no purpose: *All that preparation was for nothing because the visit was cancelled.* **have nothing on sb** (*infml*) (**a**) not be as clever, capable, etc as sb: *Sherlock Holmes has nothing on you — you're a real detective.* (**b**) (of the police) have no information that could lead to sb's arrest: *They've got nothing on me — I've got an alibi.* **have nothing to** ˈ**do with sb/sth** not concern oneself with sb/sth; avoid sb/sth: *He's a thief and a liar; I'd have nothing to do with him, if I were you.* **make nothing of sth** (*fml*) manage or deal with sth easily: *We expected her to make nothing of the translation, but she seemed to find it difficult.* **nothing but** only: *Nothing but a miracle can save her now.* ○ *I want nothing but the best for my children.* **nothing if not** (*infml*) extremely; very: *The holiday was nothing if not varied.* **nothing less than** completely; totally: *His negligence was nothing less than criminal.* **nothing like** (*infml*) (**a**) not at all like: *It looks nothing like a horse.* (**b**) absolutely not: *Her cooking is nothing like as good as yours.* **nothing more than** only: *It was nothing more than a shower.* ˌ**nothing** ˈ**much** not a great amount (of sth); nothing of great value or importance: *There's nothing much in the post.* ○ *I got up late and did nothing much all day.* (**there's**) **nothing** ˈ**to it** (it's) very simple: *I did the crossword in half an hour — there was nothing to it.* **there is/was nothing (else)** ˈ**for it (but to do sth)** there is no other action to take (except the one specified): *There was nothing else for it but to resign.*

▷ **nothingness** *n* [U] state of not being; state of being nothing: *pass into nothingness.*

notice /ˈnəʊtɪs/ *n* **1** [C] (sheet of paper, etc giving) written or printed news or information, usu displayed publicly: *put up a notice* ○ *notices of births, deaths and marriages in the newspapers.* **2** [U] (**a**) warning (of what will happen): *receive two months' notice to leave (a house, job, etc)* ○ *at short notice,* ie with little warning, little time for preparation, etc ○ *leave at (only) ten days' notice,* ie with a warning given only ten days beforehand ○ *You must give notice* (ie tell people beforehand) *of changes in the arrangements.* ○ *The bar is closed until further notice.* (**b**) formal letter, etc stating that sb is to leave a job at a specified time: *He handed in his notice* (ie left his job) *last week.* ○ *He gave her a month's notice,* ie told her that she had to leave her job in a month's time. ○ *leave without notice,* ie without giving the agreed amount of warning. **3** [C] short review of a book, play, etc in a newspaper, etc: *The play received good notices.* **4** (idm) **be beneath one's notice** (*fml*) be sth one should ignore: *He regarded all these administrative details as beneath his notice.* **bring sth to sb's** ˈ**notice** (*fml*) tell sb about sth, show sb sth, etc: *It was Susan who brought the problem to our notice.* **come to sb's notice** (*fml*) be seen, heard, etc by sb: *It has come to my notice that you have been stealing.* **escape notice** ⇨ ESCAPE[1]. **sit up and take notice** ⇨ SIT. **take no** ˈ**notice/not take any notice (of sb/sth)** pay no attention (to sb/sth): *Take no notice/Don't take any notice (of what he says)!*

▷ **notice** *v* **1** [I, Tn, Tf, Tw, Tng, Tni] become aware of (sb/sth); observe: *Didn't you notice? He has dyed his hair.* ○ *Sorry, I didn't notice you.* ○ *I noticed (that) he left early.* ○ *I noticed how she did it.* ○ *Did you notice him coming in/come in?* **2** [Tn esp passive] pay attention to (sb): *a young actor trying desperately to be noticed by the critics* ○ *She just wants to be noticed, that's why she dresses so strangely.*

noticeable /-əbl/ *adj* easily seen or noticed: *There's been a noticeable improvement in her handwriting.* **noticeably** /-əblɪ/ *adv.*

□ ˈ**notice-board** *n* (*US* ˈ**bulletin board**) board for notices (NOTICE 1) to be pinned on.

notify /ˈnəʊtɪfaɪ/ *v* (*pt, pp* **-fied**) [Tn, Tn·pr, Dn·pr, Dn·f] ~ **sb (of sth)**; ~ **sth to sb** (*infml*) inform sb (of sth); report sth to sb: *Have the authorities been notified (of this)?* ○ *notify the police (of a loss)/notify a loss to the police* ○ *He notified us that he was going to leave.*

▷ **notifiable** /ˈnəʊtɪfaɪəbl/ *adj* [esp attrib] (of diseases) which must by law be reported to the public health authorities because they are so dangerous: *Typhoid is an example of a notifiable disease.*

notification /ˌnəʊtɪfɪˈkeɪʃn/ *n* [C, U] (*fml*) (act of) notifying (a birth, death, case of infectious disease, etc): *There have been no more notifications of cholera cases in the last week.*

notion /ˈnəʊʃn/ *n* **1** [C] ~ (**that...**) (**a**) idea or belief; concept: *a system based on the notions of* *personal equality and liberty.* (**b**) idea or belief that is odd, vague or possibly incorrect: *I had a notion that she originally came from Poland.* ○ *Your head is full of silly notions.* ○ *He has a notion that I'm cheating him.* **2** [sing] ~ **of** (**sth**) (used esp after *no, any, some*) understanding: *Do you have the slightest notion of what this means?* ○ *She has no notion of the difficulty of this problem.* **3 notions** [pl] (*US*) small items used for sewing, eg pins, buttons, reels of thread, etc.

▷ **notional** /-ʃənl/ *adj* assumed to be actual or real for a particular purpose; based on guesses or estimates: *My calculation is based on notional figures, since the actual figures are not yet available.*

notochord /ˈnəʊtəkɔ:d/ *n* type of simple spinal column in certain animals.

notorious /nəʊˈtɔ:rɪəs/ *adj* ~ (**for**/**as sth**) (*derog*) well-known for some bad quality, deed, etc: *a notorious criminal, area, bend in the road* ○ *She's notorious for her wild behaviour.* ○ *He was notorious as a gambler and rake.*

▷ **notoriety** /ˌnəʊtəˈraɪətɪ/ *n* [U] (*derog*) fame for being bad in some way: *achieve a certain notoriety* ○ *His crimes earned him considerable notoriety.*

notoriously *adv.*

Nottinghamshire /ˈnɒtɪŋəmʃə(r)/ (*abbr* **Notts**) county in the Midlands of England. There are many coal-mines in its western part. ⇨ map at App 1.

notwithstanding /ˌnɒtwɪθˈstændɪŋ/ *prep* (*fml*) (can also follow the *n* to which it refers) without being affected by (sth); in spite of: *Notwithstanding a steady decline in numbers, the school has had a very successful year.* ○ *Language difficulties notwithstanding, he soon grew to love the country and its people.*

▷ **notwithstanding** *adv* (*fml*) in spite of this; however; nevertheless: *Many people told her not to try, but she went ahead notwithstanding.*

nougat /ˈnu:gɑ:, *also* ˈnʌgət; *US* ˈnu:gət/ *n* [U] type of hard sweet made with nuts, sugar or honey, and egg-white.

nought /nɔ:t/ *n* **1** the figure 0: *write three noughts on the blackboard* ○ *nought point one (0.1).* ⇨ App 9. **2** (also **naught**) (*arch*) nothing: *His crime has gained him naught.*

□ ˌ**noughts and** ˈ**crosses** (*US* ˌ**tick-tack-**ˈ**toe**) game played by writing 0s and Xs on a grid of nine squares, attempting to complete a row of three 0s or three Xs.

NOTE ON USAGE: The figure **0** has several different names in British English. **1** In speaking about temperature and in the language of science **zero** is used: *The temperature rarely falls below zero here.* **2 Nought** is commonly used when referring to the figure 0 as part of a number: *A million is 1 followed by six noughts (1 000 000).* **3** When reading a telephone or bank account number (ie when the number does not represent a quantity) we say the letter **'O'** /əʊ/ : *The account number is 0-two-0-four-three-eight-one (0204381).* ○ *Their phone number is four-seven-double 0-five (47005).* **4** In reporting the score in a team game we use **nil** or **nothing**: *The final score was three nil/nothing (3-0).* ○ *Wales won 28-nil.* In US English **zero** is commonly used in all these cases.

noun /naʊn/ *n* (*grammar*) word which can be the subject or object of a verb or the object of a preposition; word marked *n* in this dictionary. Cf COMMON NOUN (COMMON[1]), PROPER NAME (PROPER).

□ ˈ**noun phrase** (*grammar*) phrase whose function in a sentence is equivalent to that of a noun, and which usu contains a noun or pronoun as its main part.

nourish /ˈnʌrɪʃ/ *v* [Tn] **1** keep (a person, an animal, a plant) alive and well with food: *Most plants are nourished by water drawn up through their roots.* ○ *well-nourished children.* **2** (*fml fig*) maintain or increase (a feeling, etc): *nourish feelings of hatred* ○ *nourish hopes of a release from captivity.* Cf UNDERNOURISHED.

▷ **nourishing** *adj*: *nourishing food.*

nourishment *n* [U] food: *obtain nourishment from the soil.*

nous /naʊs/ *n* [U] (*Brit infml approv*) common sense; resourcefulness: *None of them had the nous to shut the door when the fire broke out.*

nouveau riche /ˌnu:vəʊ ˈri:ʃ/ *n* (*pl* **nouveaux riches** /ˌnu:vəʊ ˈri:ʃ/) (usu *pl*) (*derog*) person who has recently, and often suddenly, become rich, esp one who displays his wealth ostentatiously.

nouvelle cuisine /ˌnu:vel kwɪˈzi:n/ (*French*) modern style of French cooking producing light dishes from very fresh ingredients, often using fast methods of cooking such as steaming and quick frying, and combining fruit with savoury foods.

Nov *abbr* November: *21 Nov 1983.*

nova /ˈnəʊvə/ *n* (*pl* ~**s** or **-vae** /-vi:/) (*astronomy*) star that suddenly becomes much brighter for a short period. Cf SUPERNOVA.

Nova Scotia /ˌnəʊvə ˈskəʊʃə/ province of south-eastern Canada. Forestry, paper-making and fishing are economically important. ⇨ map at App 1.

novel[1] /ˈnɒvl/ *adj* (*esp approv*) new and strange; of a kind not known before: *a novel idea, fashion, design, experience.*

novel[2] /ˈnɒvl/ *n* book-length story in prose about either imaginary or historical characters: *the novels of Jane Austen* ○ *historical novels.*

▷ **novelette** /ˌnɒvəˈlet/ *n* short novel, often of inferior quality.

novelist /ˈnɒvəlɪst/ *n* writer of novels.

Novello /nəˈveləʊ/ Ivor (real name David Ivor Davies, 1893-1951), Welsh composer. He wrote many popular songs and musicals, such as *King's Rhapsody,* some of which he also acted in and produced. ⇨ article at MUSIC.

novelty /ˈnɒvltɪ/ *n* **1** [U] quality of being novel; newness; strangeness: *The novelty of his surroundings soon wore off,* ie He grew accustomed to them. ○ [attrib] *There's a certain novelty value in this approach.* **2** [C] previously unknown thing, experience, etc; new or strange thing or person: *A British businessman who can speak a foreign language is still something of a novelty.* **3** [C] small toy, ornament, etc of low value: *a chocolate egg with a plastic novelty inside.*

November /nəʊˈvembə(r)/ *n* [U, C] (*abbr* **Nov**) the eleventh month of the year, next after October.

For the uses of *November* see the examples at *April.*

novena /nəˈvi:nə/ *n* (in the Roman Catholic Church) prayer said over nine successive days to a saint or the Virgin Mary, esp to obtain some favour: *make a novena to St Martin.*

novice /ˈnɒvɪs/ *n* **1** person who is new and inexperienced in a job, situation, etc; beginner: *She's a complete novice as a reporter.* ○ [attrib] *a novice writer, salesman, cook, etc.* **2** person who is to become a monk or a nun but has not yet taken the final vows. Cf POSTULANT.

▷ **noviciate** (also **novitiate**) /nəˈvɪʃɪət/ *n* period or state of being a novice(2).

now /naʊ/ *adv* **1** (**a**) the present time: *Where are you living now?* ○ *It is now possible to put a man on the moon.* ○ *Now* (eg After all these interruptions) *I can get on with my work.* ○ *Now is the best time to visit the gardens.* (**b**) immediately; at once: *Start writing now.* ○ *You've got to ask her. It's now or never.* (**c**) (used after a *prep*) the present time: *I never realized I loved you until now* ○ *He should have arrived by now.* Cf THEN. **2** (used by the speaker, without reference to time, to continue a narrative, request, warning, etc): *Now the next thing he did was to light a cigarette.* ○ *Now be quiet for a few moments and listen to this.* ○ *No cheating, now.* **3** (idm) (**the**) **here and now** ⇨ HERE. (**every**) **now and again**/**then** at irregular intervals; occasionally: *I like to go to the opera now and then.* ○ *Every now and again she went upstairs to see if he was still asleep.* ˌ**now,** ˈ**now**; ˈ**now then** (used before expressing disapproval or admonishment): *Now, now, stop quarrelling.* ○ *Now then, that's enough noise.* ○ *Now, now, cheer up and forget about it.* **now...now/then** at one time...at another time: *Her moods kept changing — now happy, now filled with despair.* ˈ**now then** (**a**) ⇨ NOW, NOW. (**b**) (used to introduce a statement that makes a suggestion or invites a response): *Now then, why don't you volunteer?* ○ *Now then, are there any comments on this report?* (**c**) (used to fill a pause when one is thinking what to do or say next): *I must say I enjoyed that. Now then, what's next?* **now for sb/sth** (used when turning to a fresh task or subject): *Now for a spot of gardening.* ○ *And now for some travel news.*

▷ **now** *conj* ~ (**that**)... because of the fact (that)...: *Now (that) you mention it, I do remember the incident.* ○ *Now you've passed your test you can drive on your own.*

nowadays /ˈnaʊədeɪz/ *adv* at the present time (in contrast with the past): *Nowadays, children often prefer watching TV to reading.*

nowhere /ˈnəʊweə(r); *US* -hweər/ *adv* **1** not anywhere: *'Where are you going at the weekend?' 'Nowhere special* (ie Not to any special place).*'* ○ *He was getting nowhere* (ie making no progress) *with his homework until his sister helped him.* ○ *£20 goes nowhere* (ie does not buy much) *when you're feeding a family these days.* ○ *One of the horses I backed came second; the rest were/came nowhere,* ie were not among the first three to finish the race. **2** (idm) **get nowhere** ⇨ GET. **in the middle of nowhere** ⇨ MIDDLE. **nowhere near** ⇨ NEAR[2]. ˌ**nowhere to be** ˈ**found**/ˈ**seen** impossible for anyone to find or see: *The children were nowhere to be seen.* ○ *The money was nowhere to be found.*

noxious /ˈnɒkʃəs/ *adj* (*fml*) harmful; poisonous: *noxious fumes, gases, etc.* ▷ **noxiously** *adv.* **noxiousness** *n* [U].

nozzle /ˈnɒzl/ *n* spout or end-piece of a pipe, etc through which a stream of air or liquid is directed.

Np *symb* neptunium.

nr *abbr* near, eg in the address of a small village: *Warpsgrove, nr Chalgrove, Oxfordshire.*

NSB /ˌen es ˈbi:/ *abbr* (*Brit*) National Savings Bank (operated by the Post Office).

NSC /ˌen es ˈsi:/ *abbr* (*US*) National Security Council.

NSPCC /ˌen es ˌpi: si: ˈsi:/ *abbr* (*Brit*) National Society for the Prevention of Cruelty to Children. ⇨ article at CHARITY.

NSW *abbr* New South Wales.

NT *abbr* **1** (*Brit*) National Trust (land), eg on a map. **2** New Testament (of the Bible). Cf OT. **3** Northern Territory.

Nth *abbr* North: *Nth Pole,* eg on a map.

nth /enθ/ *adj* (*infml*) **1** [attrib] latest or last in a long series: *You're the nth person to ask me that,* ie Many others have asked me the same thing. ○ *For the nth time, you can't go!* **2** (idm) **to the** ˌ**nth de**ˈ**gree** in a very extreme way: *He's methodical to the nth degree.*

nuance /ˈnju:ɑ:ns; *US* ˈnu:-/ *n* subtle difference in meaning, colour, feeling, etc: *be able to react to nuances of meaning.*

nub /nʌb/ *n* [sing] **the** ~ **of sth** central or essential point of a problem, matter, etc: *The nub of the problem is our poor export performance.*

nubile /ˈnju:baɪl; *US* ˈnu:bl/ *adj* (of girls or young women) **1** old enough to marry. **2** sexually attractive: *a photograph of a nubile young woman.*

nuclear /ˈnju:klɪə(r); *US* ˈnu:-/ *adj* [usu attrib] **1** of a nucleus, esp of an atom: *a nuclear particle* ○ *nuclear physics.* **2** using or producing nuclear energy: *a nuclear missile, power-station, reactor* ○ *nuclear-powered submarines.*

□ ˌ**nuclear dis**ˈ**armament** removal or dismantling of nuclear weapons.

ˌ**nuclear** ˈ**energy** (also ˌ**nuclear** ˈ**power**) extremely powerful form of energy produced by nuclear fission. ⇨ article at ELECTRICITY.

ˌ**nuclear** ˈ**family** (*sociology*) the family considered as mother, father and children only, and not including any less close relations.

ˌ**nuclear** ˈ**fission** splitting of the nucleus of an atom, esp of uranium or plutonium, into smaller nuclei, releasing a considerable quantity of energy. The process is used in producing nuclear energy and in nuclear weapons.

Nuclear Power

By the beginning of the 1990s, Britain's 16 nuclear power stations were generating 20 per cent of the country's electricity supply. They are controlled either by Nuclear Electric, one of the companies formed in 1990 to run the nuclear power stations in England and Wales when the former state-owned Central Electricity Generating Board (CEGB) was privatized, or by Scottish Nuclear Ltd, one of the two companies that succeeded the state-owned South of Scotland Electricity Board (SSEB) in Scotland. (Nuclear Electric and Scottish Nuclear Ltd are still in the public sector but operate as independent commercial companies.) The first nuclear power stations to be built in the country were the Magnox stations at Calder Hall in north-west England, which opened in 1956, and Chapelcross in south-west Scotland, which first operated in 1962. ('Magnox', which stands for 'magnesium no oxidation', is the trade name for the magnesium-based alloy used to make the fuel for the reactors.)

After 1971, when there were nine Magnox stations in operation, seven further stations were then commissioned, based on the advanced gas-cooled reactor, in which carbon dioxide is used as a coolant. The first two opened at Hinckley Point B, in south-west England, and Hunterston B, in western Scotland, in 1976. A pressurized water reactor is also under construction at Sizewell B, on the east coast of England. There are also two prototype stations at Winfrith in Dorset and Dounreay in Scotland which are operated by the Atomic Energy Authority (AEA), the body responsible for research and development in the nuclear industry.

British Nuclear Fuels is a government-owned company that manufactures nuclear fuel at Springfields in Lancashire, enriches uranium to provide the fuel at Capenhurst in Cheshire, and reprocesses used fuel at Sellafield in Cumbria. In 1983 there was considerable public alarm at Sellafield when nuclear waste was shown to have leaked onto the nearby seashore. Subsequent reports claimed that this had caused a marked increase in the incidence of leukaemia among local children. The government denied that the radiation was harmful, however, and ran a campaign to reassure the public that Sellafield was operating safely.

In 1994 the government plans to review the economics and safety of Britain's nuclear power stations, and to decide whether a nuclear option should be kept. Subject to the outcome of the review, formal approval was given in 1990 for a third nuclear power station to be built at Hinckley Point.

In the USA there are 103 nuclear power stations in operation producing, as in Britain, 20 per cent of the country's electricity. In 1979 a major accident occurred at the nuclear reactor on Three Mile Island, Pennsylvania, when radioactive gases leaked through the plant's venting system and a large hydrogen gas bubble formed at the top of the reactor containment vessel. In 1988 a congressional report expressed concern about the number of failures at American power stations, attributing this to ageing equipment, poor management and lax safety standards. There is much public concern both in Britain and the USA about the safety of nuclear installations.

ˌnuclear-ˈfree *adj* [esp attrib] (of an area, etc) not having or allowing any nuclear weapons or materials: *They have declared their country a ˌnuclear-free ˈzone.*

ˌnuclear ˈfusion process in which atomic nuclei come together to form a heavier nucleus. This normally requires a very high temperature and produces even higher temperatures, and attempts to use it as a commercial source of energy have so far failed. It occurs in the explosion of a nuclear weapon and naturally at the centre of the sun.

ˌnuclear ˈwar war waged with weapons using nuclear energy as their explosive force.

ˌnuclear ˈwinter period without light, heat or growth which would follow a nuclear war.

nucleic acid /nju:ˈkli:ɪk ˈæsɪd; *US* nu:-/ either of two acids (DNA and RNA) occuring in all living cells.

nucleus /ˈnju:klɪəs; *US* ˈnu:-/ *n* (*pl* **nuclei** /-klɪaɪ/) **1** central part, around which other parts are grouped or collected: *The fortress was the nucleus of the ancient city.* ○ *These paintings will form the nucleus of a new collection,* ie Others will be added to them. **2** (a) (*physics*) central part of an atom, consisting of protons and neutrons. (b) (*biology*) central part of a living cell.

nude /nju:d; *US* nu:d/ *adj* (esp of a human figure in art) naked: *the nude torso.*

▷ **nude** *n* **1** naked human figure, esp in painting, photography, etc. **2** (idm) **in the ˈnude** having no clothes on; naked: *swimming in the nude.*

nudism /-ɪzəm/ (also **naturism**) *n* [U] practice of not wearing clothes, esp for health reasons.

nudist /-ɪst/ (also **naturist**) *n* person who practises nudism.

nudity /ˈnju:dətɪ; *US* ˈnu:-/ *n* [U] nakedness: *Some people regard nudity as offensive.*

□ **ˈnudist camp** (also **ˈnudist colony**) place where nudists can live and move about naked.

nudge /nʌdʒ/ *v* [Tn] **1** touch or push (sb) with one's elbow to draw his attention to sth: *I nudged her and pointed to the man across the street.* **2** push (sb/sth) gently or gradually: *The horse nudged my pocket with its nose.* ○ *He accidentally nudged the gatepost with the front of the car.*

▷ **nudge** *n* push given in this way: *She gave me a nudge in the ribs.*

NOTE ON USAGE: **Nudge**, **prod**, **poke**, **jab** and **stab** indicate the action of pushing a hard or sharp object (eg a finger or stick) into a person or thing and are shown here in increasing order of force or violence. **Nudge** = push or touch gently, especially with one's elbow, in order to catch somebody's attention: *She nudged him with her elbow.* **Prod (at)** = push, especially with a finger or stick, in order, for example, to make something move: *He prodded at the pig with his walking-stick.* The three remaining verbs can be used in two constructions: **poke/jab/stab** somebody or something with a sharp object OR **poke/jab/stab** a sharp object into somebody or something. **Poke (at)** = push sharply: *He poked (at) the fire with a stick. He poked a stick into the fire.* **Jab (at)** = strike forcefully and roughly with a sharp object: *The vet jabbed (at) the dog with a needle/jabbed a needle into the dog.* **Stab** = strike forcefully into somebody or something with a pointed object, especially a knife, in order to wound: *The killer stabbed him with a knife/stabbed a knife into him.*

Nuffield /ˈnʌfi:ld/ William Richard Morris, 1st Viscount Nuffield (1877-1963), British motor manufacturer. He was the first to mass-produce cars in Britain. He gave much of his fortune to charitable causes, esp to Oxford University and other educational institutions.

nugatory /ˈnju:gətərɪ; *US* ˈnu:gətɔ:rɪ/ *adj* (*fml*) worthless; pointless; not valid: *a nugatory idea, argument, proposal, etc.*

nugget /ˈnʌgɪt/ *n* **1** lump of (esp valuable) metal, eg gold, found in the earth. **2** (*fig*) small thing that is regarded as valuable: *a book full of nuggets of useful information.*

nuisance /ˈnju:sns; *US* ˈnu:-/ *n* thing, person or behaviour that is troublesome or annoying: *You are a confounded nuisance. Stop pestering me.* ○ *The noise was so loud that it was a nuisance to the neighbours.*

NUJ /ˌen ju: ˈdʒeɪ/ *abbr* (*Brit*) National Union of Journalists. ➪ article at TRADE UNION.

nuke /nju:k; *US* nu:k/ *n* (*sl*) nuclear weapon.

▷ **nuke** *v* [Tn] (*sl*) attack or destroy (eg a city) with a nuclear weapon.

null /nʌl/ *adj* (idm) **null and void** (*law*) having no legal force; not valid: *This contract is null and void.*

▷ **nullify** /ˈnʌlɪfaɪ/ *v* (*pt, pp* **-fied**) [Tn] **1** make (an agreement, etc) lose its legal force. **2** make (sth) ineffective; counteract: *How can we nullify the enemy's propaganda?* **nullification** /ˌnʌlɪfɪˈkeɪʃn/ *n* [U].

nullity /ˈnʌlətɪ/ *n* [U] lack of legal force; lack of validity: *the nullity of a marriage* ○ [attrib] *a nullity suit,* ie legal action that asks for a marriage to be declared null and void.

NUM /ˌen ju: ˈem/ *abbr* (*Brit*) Nation Union of Mineworkers. ➪ article at TRADE UNION.

numb /nʌm/ *adj* without the power to feel or move: *fingers numb with cold* ○ (*fig*) *The shock left me numb.* ○ *She was numb with terror.*

▷ **numb** *v* [Tn esp passive] **1** make (sb/sth) numb: *Her fingers were numbed by the cold.* ○ *His leg was numbed by the intense pain.* **2** (*fig*) make (sb) emotionally incapable of thinking or acting: *She was completely numbed by the shock of her father's death.*

numbly *adv.*

numbness *n* [U].

number /ˈnʌmbə(r)/ *n* **1** [C] symbol or word indicating a quantity of units; numeral: *3, 13, 33 and 103 are numbers.* ○ *Three and thirteen are also numbers.* ○ *My telephone number is 622998.* ○ *What's the number of your car?* ➪ App 9, Cf CARDINAL NUMBER (CARDINAL[1]), ORDINAL NUMBER (ORDINAL). **2** (*sing* or *pl* in form; always with *pl v* when the subject is preceded by an *adj*) quantity or amount: *A large number of people have applied.* ○ *Considerable numbers of* (ie Very many) *animals have died.* ○ *The enemy won by force of numbers,* ie because there were so many of them. ○ *A number of* (ie some) *problems have arisen* ○ *A large number of books have been stolen from the library.* ○ *The number of books stolen from the library is large.* ○ *We were fifteen in number,* ie there were fifteen of us. **3** [sing] (*fml*) group; collection: *one of our number,* ie one of us ○ *among their number,* ie among them. **4** [C] (*abbrs* **No, no**; *US symb* #) (used before a figure to indicate the place of sth in a series): *Room number 145 is on the third floor of the hotel.* ○ *He's living at No 4,* ie house number four. **5** [C] issue of a periodical, newspaper, etc: *the current number of 'Punch'* ○ *back numbers* (ie earlier issues) *of 'Nature'* **6** [C] (*music*) song, dance, etc, esp in a theatrical performance: *sing a slow, romantic number.* **7** [U] (*grammar*) variation in the form of nouns and verbs to show whether one or more than one thing or person is being spoken of: *'Men' is plural in number.* ○ *The subject of a sentence and its verb must agree in number.* **8** [sing] (preceded by an *adj* or *adjs*) (*sl*) item (eg a dress, car, etc) that is admired: *She was wearing a snappy little red number.* ○ *That new Fiat is a fast little number.* **9 numbers** [pl] (*infml*) arithmetic: *He's not good at numbers.* **10** (idm) **by ˈnumbers** following a sequence of instructions identified by numbers: *drill movement by numbers*

Nursery Rhymes

Nursery rhymes are passed from one generation to the next as parents recite to their children the verses they remember hearing in their own childhood. Although the rhymes are traditional, many are probably not quite so old in origin as is generally believed, and may date back no earlier than the 18th century.

The rhymes usually tell of an incident or adventure in the life of one or more named characters. Claims have been made that some of the characters are based on real people, and the stories on historic events, but this is now generally regarded as unlikely. Take, for instance, this well-known nursery rhyme:

Little Jack Horner
Sat in the corner
Eating a Christmas pie;
He put in his thumb,
And pulled out a plum,
And said, 'What a good boy am I!'

The rhyme is supposed to explain how the Horner family came to live at Mells Manor. Jack Horner was supposedly steward to the Abbot of Glastonbury at the time of the Dissolution of the Monasteries (by Henry VIII in 1539). He is said to have been taking to the king the title deeds of 12 manors hidden in a pie, which he opened during the journey to extract the 'plum', the deeds of the manor of Mells.

Another rhyme runs:

Little Miss Muffet
Sat on a tuffet
Eating her curds and whey;
There came a big spider
Who sat down beside her
And frightened Miss Muffet away.

Miss Muffet, it is said, was the daughter of a famous entomologist named Dr Thomas Muffet, who lived in the 16th century. In fact the rhyme did not appear in print until 1805.

Many nursery rhymes are used in children's counting games, for example:

One, two, three, four,
Mary at the cottage door,
Five, six, seven, eight,
Eating cherries off a plate.

Other rhymes have animals as characters, like the following well-known example:

Three blind mice, see how they run!
They all ran after the farmer's wife
Who cut off their tails with a carving knife,
Did you ever see such a thing in your life,
As three blind mice?

Some familiar rhymes contain words that are now nonsensical.

Hickory, dickory, dock,
The mouse ran up the clock.
The clock struck one,
The mouse ran down,
Hickory, dickory, dock!

It is claimed by some, perhaps on good grounds, that the three first words are distortions of old words for the numbers 'eight', 'nine' and 'ten' in an early Celtic language. Yet the rhyme itself has not been found in print earlier than the mid 18th century.

Other rhymes serve as riddles, like this one:

Every lady in this land
Has twenty nails upon each hand
Five and twenty on hands and feet
All this is true without deceit.

The meaning becomes clear if commas are placed after 'nails' and 'five'.

Some nursery rhymes are lullabies, and are sung rather than recited. One of the best known of this kind, both in Britain and North America is:

Hush-a-bye, baby, on the tree top,
When the wind blows the cradle will rock;
When the bough breaks the cradle will fall,
Down will come baby, cradle, and all.

This is sung to a traditional tune.

Early collections of nursery rhymes were *Tommy Thumb's Song Book*, published in 1744, and *Mother Goose's Melody*, published in 1780. Because of the popularity of the latter, especially in North America, nursery rhymes are still called Mother Goose rhymes in US English. Today, new editions of the old rhymes are frequently published, usually with modern illustrations.

○ *painting by numbers.* **a cushy number** ⇨ CUSHY. **have got sb's ˈnumber** (*sl*) know what sb is really like, what his intentions really are, etc: *She pretends to be friendly but I've got her number; she just likes to know everything.* **in penny numbers** ⇨ PENNY. **in round figures/numbers** ⇨ ROUND[1]. **sb's ˈnumber is up** (*sl*) the time has come when sb will die, be ruined, etc: *When the wheel came off the car I thought my number was up!* **number ˈone** (*infml*) (**a**) oneself: *You can depend on it that she'll always look after number one.* (**b**) the most important (person or thing): *This company is number one in the oil business.* ○ [attrib] *the number one problem, project, etc.* **sb's opposite number** ⇨ OPPOSITE. **there's safety in numbers** ⇨ SAFETY. **times without number** ⇨ TIME[1]. **weight of numbers** ⇨ WEIGHT[1].

▷ **number** *v* **1** [Tn, Tn·pr] give a number to (sth): *The doors were numbered 2, 4, 6 and 8.* ○ *We'll number them from one to ten.* **2** [In/pr] amount to (sth); add up to: *We numbered 20* (ie There were 20 of us) *in all.* **3** (idm) **sb's/sth's days are numbered** ⇨ DAY. **4** (phr v) **number sb/sth among sth** include sb/sth in a particular group: *I number her among my closest friends.* ○ *I number that crash among the most frightening experiences of my life.* **number off** (*military*) call out one's number in a sequence: *The soldiers numbered off, starting from the right-hand man.*

numberless *adj* (*fml*) too many to be counted; innumerable: *numberless stars, bacteria, grains of sand.* ⇨ Usage at INVALUABLE.

□ **ˈnumber-plate** (also *esp US* **licence plate, license plate**) *n* rectangular piece of plastic or metal on a motor vehicle showing its registration number (REGISTRATION). In Britain, number plates are usu reflective, white at the front and yellow at the rear of the vehicle. The numbers and letters form a code which show where the vehicle was first registered and the year in which it was made. ⇨ illus at CAR.

the ˈnumbers game (*US*) illegal form of gambling in which people bet on a combination of numbers appearing in a newspaper or the numbers of winning horses in certain races.

ˌNumber ˈTen (also **Number 10, No 10**) **1** Number 10 Downing Street, the official residence of the British prime minister in London. **2** (*fig*) the British prime minister or his or her officials: *There has been no comment from Number Ten.*

ˈnumber theory branch of mathematics that deals with the properties and relationships of numbers.

Numbers /ˈnʌmbəz/ fourth book of the Old Testament, telling how *Moses and the Israelites wandered for 40 years in the desert before reaching the promised land (PROMISE[2]). ⇨ App 5.

numeral /ˈnju:mərəl; *US* ˈnu:-/ *n* word or figure representing a number. Cf ARABIC NUMERALS (ARABIC), ROMAN NUMERALS (ROMAN), ⇨ App 9.

numerate /ˈnju:mərət; *US* ˈnu:-/ *adj* having a good basic knowledge of arithmetic or mathematics in general: *the importance of making children numerate.* Cf LITERATE 1. ▷ **numeracy** /ˈnju:mərəsɪ; *US* ˈnu:-/ *n* [U].

numeration /ˌnju:məˈreɪʃn; *US* ˌnu:-/ *n* [U] (*mathematics*) **1** method or process of numbering. **2** expression in words of numbers written in figures.

numerator /ˈnju:məreɪtə(r); *US* ˈnu:-/ *n* number above the line in a vulgar fraction, eg 3 in $\frac{3}{4}$. Cf DENOMINATOR.

numerical /nju:ˈmerɪkl; *US* nu:-/ *adj* of, expressed in or representing numbers: *in numerical order* ○ *numerical symbols.*

▷ **numerically** /-klɪ/ *adv* in terms of numbers: *The enemy were numerically superior*, ie There were more of them.

numerous /ˈnju:mərəs; *US* ˈnu:-/ *adj* (*fml*) very many: *her numerous friends* ○ *on numerous occasions.*

numinous /ˈnju:mɪnəs; *US* ˈnu:-/ *adj* (*religion*) inspiring awe; divine.

numismatics /ˌnju:mɪzˈmætɪks; *US* ˌnu:-/ *n* [sing *v*] study of coins, coinage and medals.

▷ **numismatist** /nju:ˈmɪzmətɪst; *US* nu:-/ *n* expert in numismatics; collector of coins and medals.

numskull (also **numbskull**) /ˈnʌmskʌl/ *n* (*infml derog*) stupid person.

nun /nʌn/ *n* woman living in a convent, usu after taking religious vows. Cf MONK.

▷ **nunnery** /ˈnʌnərɪ/ *n* house where an order of nuns lives; convent. Cf MONASTERY.

nunc dimittis /ˌnʌŋk dɪˈmɪtɪs/ hymn with words taken from St Luke's Gospel, beginning 'Lord now lettest thou thy servant depart in peace', sung or recited at church services, esp evensong.

nuncio /ˈnʌnsɪəʊ/ *n* (*pl* ~**s**) Pope's ambassador or representative in a foreign country.

NUPE /ˈnju:pɪ/ *abbr* (*Brit*) National Union of Public Employees. ⇨ article at TRADE UNION.

nuptial /ˈnʌpʃl/ *adj* [attrib] (*fml or joc*) of marriage or of a wedding: *the nuptial ceremony* ○ *nuptial bliss.*

▷ **nuptials** *n* [pl] (*fml or joc*) wedding: *the day of his nuptials.*

NUR /ˌen ju: ˈɑ:(r)/ *abbr* (*Brit*) National Union of Railwaymen. ⇨ article at TRADE UNION.

nurd = NERD.

Nuremberg /ˈnjʊərəmbɜ:g; *US* ˈnʊə-/ city in *Bavaria, Germany; German name **Nürnberg**. It was a famous cultural centre in the Renaissance. Mass Nazi rallies were held there in the 1930s. The **Nuremberg trials** were held in 1946 to try German war criminals.

Nureyev /ˈnjʊərɪef; *US* nʊˈreɪef/ Rudolf (1939-93), Russian ballet dancer and choreographer, who defected to the West in 1961. He is famous as the partner of Margot *Fonteyn in classical works and has produced several ballets of his own.

nurse[1] /nɜ:s/ *n* **1** person, usu female, trained to help a doctor to look after the sick or injured: *Red Cross nurses* ○ *Male nurses are often employed in hospitals for the mentally ill.* ○ *a psychiatric nurse*, ie one who works in a mental hospital. **2** (also **ˈnursemaid**) woman or girl employed to look after babies or small children. Cf NANNY 1. **3** (also **ˈwet nurse**) woman employed to breast-feed a baby who is not her own.

nurse[2] /nɜːs/ *v* **1** [I, Tn] take care of (the sick or injured); look after (sb): *My mother's been nursing for 40 years.* ○ *She nurses her aged mother.* **2** [I, Tn] be breast-fed; breast-feed (sb): *The baby was nursing/being nursed at its mother's breast.* **3** [Tn] hold (sb/sth) carefully and lovingly: *nurse a child, puppy* ○ *nurse a fragile vase in one's arms.* **4** (**a**) [Tn, Tn·p] give special care to (sth); help to develop: *nurse young plants (along)* ○ *nurse a project* ○ *nurse a constituency*, ie visit it often, etc in order to gain or retain votes ○ *nurse a cold*, ie stay warm, stay in bed, etc in order to cure it quickly. (**b**) [Tn] think a lot about (sth); foster (sth) in the mind: *nurse feelings of revenge, hopes of promotion, etc* ○ *nurse a grievance.*

▷ **nursing** *n* [U] the art or practice of looking after the sick or injured: *train for (a career in) nursing* ○ [attrib] *the nursing profession* ○ *nursing skills.*

□ ˈ**nursing-home** *n* small, usu privately owned, hospital.

ˌ**nursing** ˈ**mother** woman breast-feeding her baby.

nursery /ˈnɜːsərɪ/ *n* **1** place where young children are cared for, usu while their parents are at work, etc: *a day nursery.* Cf CRÊCHE. **2** room in a (usu large) house for the special use of children: *We've turned the smallest bedroom into a nursery for our new baby.* **3** (often *pl* though referring to a single place) place where young plants and trees are grown for transplanting later and usu for sale: *I'm going to the nursery/nurseries in Hampton to buy some plants.*

□ ˈ**nurseryman** /-mən/ *n* (*pl* **-men**) man who works in a plant nursery.

ˈ**nursery nurse** nurse trained to look after small children.

ˈ**nursery rhyme** (usu traditional) poem or song for children.

ˈ**nursery school** school for children aged from 2 or 3 to 5. Cf PLAYGROUP (PLAY[1]).

ˈ**nursery slope** slope suitable for inexperienced skiers, ie not steep.

ˈ**nursery stakes** race for two-year-old horses.

nurture /ˈnɜːtʃə(r)/ *v* [Tn] **1** care for and educate (a child): *children nurtured by loving parents.* **2** (**a**) encourage the growth of (sth); nourish: *nurture delicate plants.* (**b**) (*fig*) help the development of (sth); support: *We want to nurture the new project, not destroy it.*

▷ **nurture** *n* [U] care; encouragement; support: *the nurture of a delicate child, plant* ○ *the nurture of new talent.*

NUS /ˌen juː ˈes/ *abbr* (*Brit*) **1** National Union of Seamen. **2** National Union of Students. ⇨ article at TRADE UNION.

NUT /ˌen juː ˈtiː/ *abbr* (*Brit*) National Union of Teachers. ⇨ article at TRADE UNION.

nut /nʌt/ *n* **1** [C] (often in compounds) fruit consisting of a hard shell with a kernel inside it that can be eaten: *chocolate with fruit and nuts* ○ *a Brazil-nut* ○ *a hazelnut.* ⇨ illus. ⇨ illus at TREE.

nut

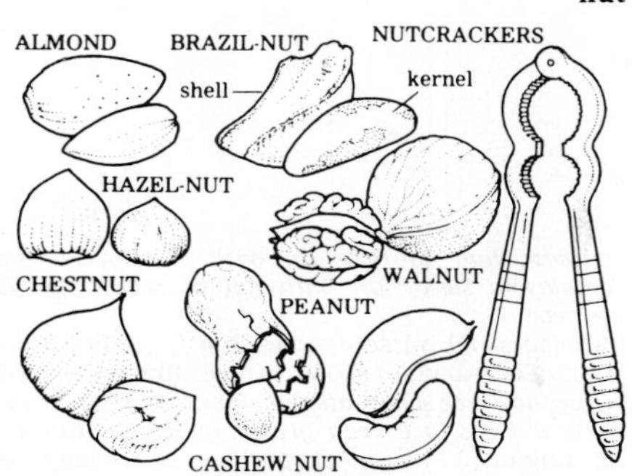

📖 Nuts are especially popular in Britain around Christmas time, and are a basic ingredient in some traditional Christmas foods. At other times of the year, nuts are sometimes served with fruit at the end of a meal, especially a celebratory one. In winter, it is traditional to roast chestnuts over an open fire, and bags of hot roasted chestnuts are sold on some city streets. Almonds are often used for cake decoration.

2 [C] small (usu six-sided) piece of metal with a hole through the centre, used for screwing onto a bolt to secure it. ⇨ illus at BOLT. **3** [C] (*sl*) head (of a person): *He cracked his nut on the ceiling.* **4 nuts** [pl] small lumps of coal. **5 nuts** [pl] (⚠ *sl esp US*) testicles: *kick sb in the nuts.* **6** [C] (*sl derog*) (**a**) (*Brit* also **nutter**) foolish, eccentric or mad person: *He drives like a nut — he'll kill himself one day.* (**b**) (preceded by a *n*) person very interested in sth; fanatic: *a movie, fitness, health, soccer nut.* **7** (idm) **do one's ˈnut** (*Brit sl*) be very angry: *She'll do her nut when she sees the broken window.* **for ˈnuts/ˈpeanuts** (*Brit sl derog*) (used with a negative) at all: *He can't play football for nuts!* **a hard/tough ˈnut (to crack)** (*infml*) (**a**) difficult problem or situation (to deal with): *The final exam was a tough nut.* (**b**) person who is difficult to persuade, influence, etc: *She's a tough nut to crack; I don't think she'll give us permission.* **the ˌnuts and ˈbolts** (*infml*) basic practical details: *dealing with the nuts and bolts of the project.* ˌ**off one's ˈnut** (*sl*) mad: *You must be off your nut!*

▷ **nutty** *adj* (**-ier**, **-iest**) **1** tasting of or containing nuts: *a nutty flavour* ○ *nutty cake, chocolate, etc.* **2** (*sl*) crazy; eccentric: *I love her nutty behaviour!* **3** (idm) (**as**) **nutty as a ˈfruitcake** (*sl*) very crazy or eccentric.

□ ˌ**nut-ˈbrown** *adj* (eg of ale) having the dark rich brown colour of ripe hazelnuts.

ˈ**nut-case** *n* (*sl*) mad or eccentric person.

ˈ**nutcrackers** *n* [pl] pincers for cracking open the shells of nuts. ⇨ illus.

ˈ**nut-house** *n* (*sl offensive*) mental hospital.

ˈ**nutshell** /-ʃel/ *n* **1** hard covering around the kernel of a nut. **2** (idm) (**put sth**) **in a nutshell** (say sth) in very few words: *To put it in a nutshell, we're bankrupt.*

nuthatch /ˈnʌthætʃ/ *n* small tree-climbing bird that feeds on nuts, insects, etc.

nutmeg /ˈnʌtmeg/ *n* **1** [C] hard fragrant seed of an E Indian tree. **2** [U] this seed grated to powder, used as a flavouring in food.

nutrient /ˈnjuːtrɪənt; *US* ˈnuː-/ *n, adj* (*fml*) (substance) serving as or providing nourishment, esp for plants or animals: *Plants draw minerals and other nutrients from the soil.*

nutriment /ˈnjuːtrɪmənt; *US* ˈnuː-/ *n* [C, U] (*fml*) nourishing food: *essential nutriments for a growing child.*

nutrition /njuːˈtrɪʃn; *US* nuː-/ *n* [U] **1** (process of giving and receiving) nourishment; food: *adequate nutrition of the body* ○ *This food provides all the nutrition your dog needs.* **2** the study of human diet: *a number of books on nutrition.*

▷ **nutritional** /-ʃənl/ *adj*: *the nutritional value of a food.* **nutritionally** /-ʃənəlɪ/ *adv.*

nutritionist /-ʃənɪst/ *n* expert in nutrition(2).

nutritious /njuːˈtrɪʃəs; *US* nuː-/ *adj* (*fml*) of (high) value as food; nourishing: *a nutritious meal, snack, etc.*

nutritive /ˈnjuːtrətɪv; *US* ˈnuː-/ *adj* (*fml*) **1** serving as food: *a nutritive substance.* **2** of nutrition(1): *the nutritive process.*

nuts /nʌts/ *adj* [pred] (*sl*) **1** crazy; insane. **2** ~ **about sb**; ~ **about/on sth** very much in love with sb; very enthusiastic about sth: *She's beautiful. I'm nuts about her.* ○ *He's nuts about/on cars.*

nutter /ˈnʌtə(r)/ *n* (*Brit sl*) = NUT 6.

nuzzle /ˈnʌzl/ *v* **1** [Tn] press or rub (sb/sth) gently with the nose: *The horse nuzzled my shoulder.* **2** (phr v) **nuzzle up to sb/sth**; **nuzzle (up) against sb/sth** press close to sb/sth, esp by pushing gently with the head or nose: *The dog nuzzled up to/against me on the sofa.*

NW *abbr* North-West(ern): *NW Australia* ○ *London NW6 2PS*, ie as a postal code.

NY *abbr* New York.

NYC *abbr* New York City.

nylon /ˈnaɪlɒn/ *n* **1** [U] very strong man-made fibre used for hosiery, rope, brushes, etc: *This dress is 80% nylon.* ○ [attrib] *nylon tights, blouses, etc.* **2 nylons** [pl] women's stockings: *a pair of nylons.*

nymph /nɪmf/ *n* **1** (in Greek and Roman mythology) minor goddess living in rivers, trees, hills, etc. **2** (esp in poetry) young woman, esp a beautiful one. Cf SYLPH. **3** young insect (eg a young dragonfly) that has a similar form to the adult.

nymphet /nɪmˈfet/ *n* (*infml or joc*) young girl regarded as sexually desirable.

nympho /ˈnɪmfəʊ/ *n* (*pl* ~**s**) (*infml sexist*) nymphomaniac.

nymphomania /ˌnɪmfəˈmeɪnɪə/ *n* [U] excessive and uncontrollable sexual desire in women.

▷ **nymphomaniac** /-ˈmeɪnɪæk/ *n, adj* (*often derog*) (woman) suffering from nymphomania.

nystagmus /nɪˈstægməs/ *n* [U] (disease causing) continuous very fast movement of the eyeballs.

NZ *abbr* New Zealand.

O, o

O[1], **o** /əʊ/ *n* (*pl* **O's, o's** /əʊz/) **1** the fifteenth letter of the English alphabet: *There are two O's in Oxford.* **2** O-shaped sign or mark: *The child's mouth formed a big O in surprise.* **3** (in saying telephone, etc numbers aloud) zero; nought: *'My number is six o double three'*, ie 6033. ○ *'He's in room one o two'*, ie 102. ⇨ Usage at NOUGHT.

O[2] /əʊ/ *interj* **1** = OH: *O look!* **2** (*arch or rhet*) (used when addressing a person, thing, etc): *O God our help in ages past* ○ *O rose, thou art sick.*

O *symb* oxygen.

o' /ə/ *prep* (used esp in compound phrases) of: *3 o'clock* ○ *man-o'-war.*

oaf /əʊf/ *n* (*pl* ~**s**) stupid, clumsy and awkward person (usu male): *Why did she marry that great oaf?*

▷ **oafish** *adj* like an oaf; roughly behaved: *oafish behaviour.*

oak /əʊk/ *n* **1** (a) (also **ˈoak-tree**) [C] type of tree with tough, hard wood, common in many parts of the world: *a forest of oaks* ○ [attrib] *an oak forest.* ⇨ illus at TREE. ⇨ article at NATIONAL. (b) [U] wood of this tree: *The table is (of) solid oak.* ○ [attrib] *oak panels* ○ *an oak table.* **2 the Oaks** [sing *v*] name of a horse-race run at Epsom, near London, every year. **3** (idm) **big/tall/great/large oaks from little ˈacorns grow** (*saying*) great things may come from small or modest beginnings.

▷ **oaken** /ˈəʊkən/ *adj* [attrib] (*dated fml*) made of oak.

□ **ˈoak-apple** *n* growth on an oak leaf or stem caused by an insect. Cf GALL[3].

OAP /ˌəʊ eɪ ˈpiː/ *abbr* (*Brit infml*) old-age pensioner. ⇨ article at RETIREMENT.

oar /ɔː(r)/ *n* **1** long pole with a flat blade, pulled by hand in order to drive a boat through the water. ⇨ illus at ROW. **2** (idm) **put/shove/stick one's ˈoar in; put/shove/stick in one's ˈoar** (*infml*) give an opinion, some advice, etc without being asked; interfere: *I know how to mend a fuse and I don't need you shoving your oar in!*

□ **ˈoarlock** *n* (*US*) = ROWLOCK.

oarsman /ˈɔːzmən/ *n* (*pl* **-men**), **ˈoarswoman** *n* (*pl* **-women**) person who rows a boat; rower.

OAS /ˌəʊ eɪ ˈes/ *abbr* (*US*) Organization of American States.

oasis /əʊˈeɪsɪs/ *n* (*pl* **oases** /-siːz/) **1** fertile place, with water and trees, in a desert. **2** (*fig*) experience, place, etc which is pleasant in the middle of sth unpleasant, dull, etc: *The study was an oasis of calm in a noisy household.*

oast /əʊst/ *n* kiln for drying hops.

□ **ˈoasthouse** *n* building containing an oast.

Oates /əʊts/ Titus (1649-1705), English Protestant clergyman who, in order to discredit the Roman Catholics, claimed to have discovered a Catholic plot to kill King *Charles II and re-establish Catholicism in Britain. He was imprisoned for perjury but later released.

oath /əʊθ/ *n* (*pl* ~**s** /əʊðz/) **1** (words used in making a) solemn promise to do sth or solemn declaration that sth is true (usu appealing to God, etc as a witness): *There is a standard form of oath used in lawcourts.* **2** casual or improper use of the name of God, etc to express anger, surprise, etc; swear-word: *He hurled a few oaths at his wife and walked out, slamming the door.* **3** (idm) **be on/under ˈoath** (*law*) have sworn to tell the truth in a court of law: *The witness was reminded that she was giving evidence on oath.* **on my ˈoath** (*dated*) (used to emphasize that one is telling the truth): *I didn't tell anyone, on my oath.* **put/place sb on/under ˈoath** (*law*) require sb to swear an oath: *The witnesses were placed under oath.* **swear/take an ˈoath** (*esp law*) promise solemnly to tell the truth, give one's loyalty, etc: *Before giving evidence the witness had to take an oath.* ○ *Government employees swear an oath not to reveal official secrets.*

oats /əʊts/ *n* **1** [pl, sometimes sing *v*] (grain from a) type of cereal plant grown in cool climates as food: *Give the horse some oats.* ○ *fields of ripe barley and oats* ○ *Oats is a crop grown widely in Europe.* **2** [sing or pl *v*] oatmeal porridge: *Is/Are porridge oats on the breakfast menu?* **3** (idm) **feel one's oats** ⇨ FEEL[1]. **be getting one's ˈoats** (*infml*) have sex regularly. **(be) off one's ˈoats** (*infml*) (be) lacking appetite for food: *He's been a bit off his oats since his illness.* **sow one's wild oats** ⇨ SOW[2].

□ **ˈoatcake** *n* [U, C] (esp in Scotland and N England) thin flat cake made of oatmeal: *oatcake served with butter and cheese.*

ˈoatmeal *n* [U] meal made from crushed oats, used in porridge, oatcakes, etc.

OAU /ˌəʊ eɪ ˈjuː/ *abbr* Organization of African Unity.

ob *abbr* died (Latin *obiit*). Cf D 2.

Obadiah /ˌəʊbəˈdaɪə/ **1** Hebrew prophet. **2** shortest book of the Old Testament, named after him. ⇨ App 5.

obbligato /ˌɒblɪˈgɑːtəʊ/ *n* (*pl* ~**s** or **-ti** /-tiː/) (*music*) accompanying part forming an essential part of a composition: *with piano obbligato.*

▷ **obbligato** *adj* to be included in a performance.

obdurate /ˈɒbdjʊərət; *US* -dər-/ *adj* (*fml*) impossible to change; stubborn: *an obdurate refusal* ○ *He remained obdurate, refusing to alter his decision.* ▷ **obduracy** /ˈɒbdjʊərəsɪ; *US* -dər-/ *n* [U]. **obdurately** *adv*: *obdurately refusing to go.*

OBE /ˌəʊ biː ˈiː/ *abbr* (*Brit*) Officer (of the Order) of the British Empire: *be (made) an OBE* ○ *Matthew Silkin OBE.*

obedient /əˈbiːdɪənt/ *adj* **1** doing what one is told to do; willing to obey: *obedient children* ○ *His dog is very obedient.* Cf DISOBEDIENT. **2** (idm) **your obedient ˈservant** (*dated fml*) (used as a very formal ending to an official letter, before the signature).

▷ **obedience** /-əns/ *n* [U] action of obeying; being obedient: *The commanding officer expected unquestioning obedience from his men.* **obediently** *adv*: *He whistled, and the dog came obediently.*

obeisance /əʊˈbeɪsns/ *n* (*dated fml*) **1** deep bow (of respect or obedience). **2** (idm) **do/pay/make obeisance to sb** show respectful obedience or submission to sb: *He made obeisance to the king.*

obelisk /ˈɒbəlɪsk/ *n* tall pointed stone pillar with four sides, set up as a monument or landmark.

obese /əʊˈbiːs/ *adj* (*fml or medical*) (of people) very fat: *Obese patients are advised to change their diet.* ⇨ Usage at FAT[1].

▷ **obesity** /əʊˈbiːsətɪ/ *n* [U] being obese: *Obesity is a problem for many people in western countries.*

obey /əˈbeɪ/ *v* [I, Tn] do what one is told or obliged to do (by sb); carry out (a command): *Soldiers are trained to obey without question.* ○ *obey orders* ○ *obey the law.*

obfuscate /ˈɒbfəskeɪt/ *v* [Tn] (*fml*) (deliberately) make (sth) confused or difficult to understand: *The writer often obfuscates the real issues with petty details.*

obiter dictum /ˌɒbɪtə ˈdɪktəm/ *n* (*pl* **dicta** /ˈdɪktə/) (*Latin law or fml*) incidental remark or statement not essential to the main argument, made by a judge in the course of a judgement.

obituary /əˈbɪtʃʊərɪ; *US* -tʃʊerɪ/ (*infml* **obit**) *n* printed notice (eg in a newspaper) of a person's death, often with a short account of his life and achievements: [attrib] *obituary notices* ○ *He writes obits for the local newspaper.*

object[1] /ˈɒbdʒɪkt/ *n* **1** solid thing that can be seen and touched: *glass, wooden and plastic objects* ○ *There were several objects on the floor of the room.* **2** ~ **of sth** person or thing to which sth is done or some feeling or thought is directed: *an object of attention, pity, admiration, etc* ○ *This church is the main object of his interest.* ○ *The sole object of all the child's affection was a soft toy.* **3** thing aimed at; intention; purpose: *with the object of going into business* ○ *with no object in life* ○ *fail/succeed in one's object* ○ *His one object in life is to earn as much money as possible.* **4** (*infml esp Brit*) person or thing of strange appearance, esp if ridiculous: *What an object you look in that old hat!* **5** (*grammar*) noun, noun phrase or noun clause which refers to a person, thing, etc affected by the action of a verb, or which depends on a preposition, eg in *He took the money* and *He took what he wanted*, *'the money'* and *'what he wanted'* are direct objects; in *I gave him the money*, *'him'* is an indirect object; and in *I received the money from her*, *'her'* is a prepositional object. Cf SUBJECT[1] 4. **6** (idm) **expense, money, etc no ˈobject** expense, etc is not important, not a limiting factor, etc: *He always travels first class — expense is no object.*

□ **ˈobject glass, ˈobject lens** = OBJECTIVE *n* 2.

ˈobject lesson practical illustration of some principle, often given or used as a warning: *Let this accident be an object lesson in the dangers of drinking and driving.*

object[2] /əbˈdʒekt/ *v* **1** [I, Ipr] ~ **(to sb/sth)** say that one is not in favour (of sb/sth); protest: *She wanted to cut down the hedge, but her neighbour objected.* ○ *I object to such treatment/to being treated like this.* ○ *I object to the plan on the grounds that it is too expensive.* **2** [Tn, Tf] give (sth) as a reason for opposing sb/sth: *I objected that he was too young for the job.* ○ *'But he's too young,' I objected.*

▷ **objector** *n* person who objects: *objectors to the plans for a new motorway* ○ *conscientious objectors.*

objectify /əbˈdʒektɪfaɪ/ *v* (*pt, pp* **-fied**) [Tn] (*fml*) **1** represent (an abstract idea, concept, etc) as a real or solid object; embody. **2** present or portay (sb) as an object, ie with no personality.

objection /əbˈdʒekʃn/ *n* **1** [C, U] ~ **(to sth/doing sth)** (expression of a) feeling of dislike, disapproval or opposition: *raise/lodge/voice an objection* ○ *He has a strong objection to getting up so early.* ○ *I'd like to come too, if you've no objection.* ○ *Objections to the plan will be listened to sympathetically.* **2** [C] ~ **(to/against sb/sth)** reason for objecting: *My main objection to the plan is that it would be too expensive.*

▷ **objectionable** /-ʃənəbl/ *adj* causing opposition or disapproval; unpleasant: *an objectionable smell* ○ *objectionable remarks* ○ *His drunken behaviour was extremely objectionable.* ○ *I find him most objectionable.* **objectionably** /-ʃənəblɪ/ *adv.*

objective /əbˈdʒektɪv/ *adj* **1** not influenced by personal feelings or opinions; unbiased; fair: *an objective report, account, assessment, etc* ○ *A jury's decision in a court case must be absolutely objective.* ○ *It's hard for nurses to be objective about their patients, if they become too emotionally involved with them.* ○ *He finds it difficult to remain objective where his son is concerned.* **2** (*philosophy*) having existence outside the mind; real. Cf SUBJECTIVE. **3** (*grammar*) of the object[1](5): *the objective case*, ie (in Latin and other inflected languages) the form of a word used when it is the object of a verb or a preposition.

▷ **objective** *n* **1** (a) thing aimed at or wished for; purpose: *Her principal objective was international fame as a scientist.* ○ *Everest is the climber's next objective.* ○ *Let justice be our objective.* (b) (in war) position that soldiers are aiming to capture: *All our objectives were gained.* **2** (also **ˈobject glass**)

ˈ**object lens**) lens of a microscope or telescope closest to the object being viewed.
objectively *adv* in an objective(1) manner; impartially: *see/view/judge things objectively.*
objectivity /ˌɒbdʒekˈtɪvətɪ/ *n* state of being objective(1); ability to free oneself from personal prejudice; impartiality: *The judge had a reputation for complete objectivity.*

objet d'art /ˌɒbʒeɪ ˈdɑː/ *n* (*pl* **objets d'art** /ˌɒbʒeɪ ˈdɑː/) (*French*) small decorative or artistic object: *a house full of antique furniture and objets d'art.*

oblate /ˈɒbleɪt/ *adj* (*geometry*) (of a sphere) flattened at the top and bottom: *The earth is an oblate sphere.*

obligate /ˈɒblɪgeɪt/ *v* [Cn·t usu passive] (*fml*) compel (sb) legally or morally (to do sth): *He felt obligated to help.* ○ *We were obligated to attend the opening ceremony.*

obligation /ˌɒblɪˈgeɪʃn/ *n* **1** [C] law, moral pressure, promise, etc that forces one to do sth: *the obligations of conscience* ○ *the obligations imposed by parenthood* ○ *repay/fulfil an obligation*, eg by returning hospitality that one has received. **2** [C, U] being forced or required to do sth: *We attended the party more out of a sense of obligation than anything else.* **3** (idm) **be under an/no obligation (to sb/to do sth)** (not) be compelled by law, etc; (not) have a moral duty: *You're under no obligation to pay for goods which you did not order.* ○ *She's under an obligation to him because he lent her money.* **place/put sb under an/no obliˈgation (to sb/to do sth)** (not) compel sb by law, etc (to do sth); (not) make sb indebted or grateful (to sb): *Damaging the goods puts you under an obligation to buy them.* ○ *His kindness places us under an obligation to him.*

obligatory /əˈblɪgətrɪ; *US* -tɔːrɪ/ *adj* (*fml*) required by rule, law or custom; compulsory: *Attendance at school is obligatory.* ○ *It is obligatory to remove your shoes before entering.*

oblige /əˈblaɪdʒ/ *v* **1** [Cn·t usu passive] compel or require (sb) by law, agreement or moral pressure to do sth: *The law obliges parents to send their children to school.* ○ *They were obliged to sell their house in order to pay their debts.* ○ *You are not obliged to answer these questions, but it would make our task easier.* **2** [I, Tn, Tn·pr] ~ **sb (with sth/by doing sth)** (*fml*) do sth for sb as a favour or small service: *We'd be happy to oblige.* ○ *Could you oblige me with* (ie lend or give me) *five pounds until the weekend?* ○ *Could you oblige us with a song* (ie perform a song for us) ? ○ *Please oblige me by closing the door.*
▷ **obliged** *adj* **1** [pred] ~ **(to sb) (for sth/doing sth)** grateful (to sb) for performing some service: *I'm much obliged to you for helping us.* **2** (idm) **much oˈbliged** thank you: *'Much obliged,' he said as I opened the door for him.*
obliging *adj* willing to help: *obliging neighbours* ○ *You'll find him most obliging.* **obligingly** *adv.*

oblique /əˈbliːk/ *adj* **1** not horizontal or vertical; sloping; slanting: *an oblique line.* **2** [usu attrib] (*fig*) not going straight to the point; indirect: *He made oblique references to her lack of experience.*
▷ **oblique** *n* (also **oblique stroke, slash**) mark (/) used in maths or punctuation to separate numbers, words, etc as in *4/5 people, male/female*, 27/7/1949.
obliquely *adv.*
obliquity /əˈblɪkwətɪ/ (also **obliqueness**) [C, U] (instance of the) state of being oblique.
□ **obˌlique ˈangle** any angle that is not a right angle (ie not 90°); acute or obtuse angle.

obliterate /əˈblɪtəreɪt/ *v* [Tn] (*fml*) **1** remove all signs of (sth); rub or blot out: *obliterate all fingerprints* ○ (*fig*) *She tried to obliterate all memory of her father.* ○ *The view was obliterated by the fog.* **2** destroy (sth) completely: *The entire village was obliterated by the tornado.* ▷ **obliteration** /əˌblɪtəˈreɪʃn/ *n* [U].

oblivion /əˈblɪvɪən/ *n* [U] **1** state of forgetting; state of being unaware or unconscious: *Alcoholics often suffer from periods of oblivion.* ○ *The pain made him long for oblivion.* **2** state of being forgotten: *His work fell/sank into oblivion after his death.*

oblivious /əˈblɪvɪəs/ *adj* [usu pred] ~ **of/to sth** unaware of or not noticing sth; having no memory of sth: *oblivious of one's surroundings* ○ *oblivious to what was happening* ○ *oblivious to danger.* ▷ **obliviousness** *n* [U].

oblong /ˈɒblɒŋ; *US* -lɔːŋ/ *n, adj* (figure) with four straight sides and angles of 90°, longer than it is wide: *an oblong table* ○ *an oblong bar of chocolate.*

obloquy /ˈɒbləkwɪ/ *n* [U] (*fml*) public shame or disgrace; abuse; discredit.

obnoxious /əbˈnɒkʃəs/ *adj* very unpleasant; nasty; offensive: *obnoxious behaviour* ○ *He is the most obnoxious man I know.* ▷ **obnoxiously** *adv*: *obnoxiously drunk.* **obnoxiousness** *n* [U].

oboe /ˈəʊbəʊ/ *n* (*music*) woodwind instrument of treble pitch, played through a double reed. ⇨ illus at MUSIC.
▷ **oboist** /-ɪst/ *n* person who plays the oboe.

obscene /əbˈsiːn/ *adj* (of words, thoughts, books, pictures, etc) indecent, esp sexually; disgusting and offensive; likely to corrupt: *obscene phone calls* ○ *obscene suggestions, gestures, etc* ○ *obscene literature, language, etc.*
▷ **obscenely** *adv.*
obscenity *n* /əbˈsenətɪ/ *n* **1** [U] being obscene: *laws against obscenity on the television.* **2** [C] obscene word or act: *He shouted obscenities at the woman.*

obscure /əbˈskjʊə(r)/ *adj* **1** not easily or clearly seen or understood; indistinct; hidden: *an obscure corner of the garden* ○ *Is the meaning still obscure to you?* ○ *His real motive for the crime remains obscure.* **2** not well-known: *an obscure poet* ○ *an obscure village in the country.*
▷ **obscure (1)** *v* [Tn] make (sth) obscure(1); hide (sb/sth) from view: *The moon was obscured by clouds.* ○ *Mist obscured the view.* ○ *The main theme of the book is obscured by frequent digressions.*
obscurely *adv.*
obscurity /əbˈskjʊərətɪ/ *n* **1** [U] state of being obscure: *content to live in obscurity.* **2** [C] (*fml*) thing that is obscure or indistinct: *a philosophical essay full of obscurities.*

obsequies /ˈɒbsɪkwɪz/ *n* [pl] (*fml*) funeral ceremonies.

obsequious /əbˈsiːkwɪəs/ *adj* ~ **(to sb)** (*derog*) too willing to obey or serve; too respectful (esp in the hope of getting a reward or favour from sb): *an obsequious shop owner* ○ *a worker who is obsequious to the boss.* ▷ **obsequiously** *adv*: *obsequiously flattering.* **obsequiousness** *n* [U].

observable /əbˈzɜːvəbl/ *adj* [usu attrib] that can be seen or noticed: *an observable lack of enthusiasm* ○ *an observable improvement.*

observance /əbˈzɜːvəns/ *n* **1** [U] ~ **(of sth)** keeping or observing (OBSERVE 2b) a law, custom, festival, holiday, etc: *the observance of school rules* ○ *the observance of New Year's Day as a public holiday.* **2** [C] (*fml*) act performed as part of a religious or traditional ceremony: *religious observances.*

observant /əbˈzɜːvənt/ *adj* **1** quick at noticing things: *An observant shop assistant had remembered exactly what the man was wearing.* ○ *Journalists are trained to be observant.* **2** (*fml*) careful to observe(2a) laws, customs, traditions, etc: (*fml*) *observant of the rules.* ▷ **observantly** *adv.*

observation /ˌɒbzəˈveɪʃn/ *n* **1** [U] action of observing; (state of) being observed: *observation of an animal's behaviour* ○ *observation of a patient* ○ *We escaped observation*, ie were not seen. **2** [U] ability to observe things: *powers of observation* ○ *A scientist's observation should be very good.* **3** [C] remark or comment: *She made one or two observations about the weather.* **4 observations** [pl] (*fml*) (recording of) collected information: *He's just published his observations on British bird life.* **5** (idm) **be under obserˈvation** be carefully and closely watched: *He was under observation by the police.* **keep sb under obserˈvation** watch sb carefully (esp a suspected criminal or a hospital patient): *The patient is seriously ill and is being kept under continuous observation.* **take an obserˈvation** observe the position of the sun or another heavenly body in order to find one's exact geographical position.
□ **obserˈvation car** special railway carriage in a train, with wide windows for watching the scenery.
obserˈvation post position from which the enemy's movements can be watched: *an observation post in a border fortress.*

observatory /əbˈzɜːvətrɪ; *US* -tɔːrɪ/ *n* building from which the stars, the weather, etc can be observed by scientists.

observe /əbˈzɜːv/ *v* **1** [I, Tn, Tf, Tw, Tnt only passive, Tng, Tni] see and notice (sb/sth); watch carefully: *He observes keenly, but says little.* ○ *observe the behaviour of birds* ○ *She observed that he'd left but made no comment.* ○ *They observed how the tiny wings were fitted to the body.* ○ *The woman was observed to follow him closely.* ○ *The police observed the man entering/enter the bank.* **2** [Tn] (*fml*) **(a)** obey (rules, laws, etc): *observe the speed limit* ○ *observe the laws of the land.* **(b)** celebrate (festivals, birthdays, anniversaries, etc): *Do they observe Christmas Day in that country?* **3** [Tn, Tf] (*fml*) say by way of comment; remark: *He observed that it would probably rain.* ○ *'It may rain,' he observed.*
▷ **observer** *n* **1** person who observes: *an observer of nature* ○ *a poor observer of speed restrictions.* **2** person who attends a conference, lesson, etc to listen and watch but not to take part: *an observer at a summit conference* ○ *send sb along as an observer.*

obsess /əbˈses/ *v* [Tn usu passive] fill the mind of (sb) continually: *The fear of death obsessed her throughout her old age.* ○ *obsessed by/with the fear of unemployment* ○ *She was obsessed with the idea that she was being watched.*
▷ **obsession** /əbˈseʃn/ *n* ~ **(with/about sth/sb) 1** [U] state of being obsessed: *His obsession with computers began six months ago.* **2** [C] thing or person that obsesses; fixed idea that fills the mind: *He has many obsessions.* **obsessional** /əbˈseʃənl/ *adj* (*derog*) of, having or causing obsession(s): *obsessional thoughts* ○ *an obsessional character.*
obsessive /əbˈsesɪv/ *adj* (*derog*) of or having an obsession: *an obsessive concern for neatness* ○ *She's obsessive about punctuality.* — *n* (*medical*) person who has an obsession or obsessions: *hysterics and obsessives* ○ *The psychiatrist has done a lot of work with obsessives.* **obsessively** *adv* in an obsessive manner: *obsessively concerned with her appearance.*

obsolescent /ˌɒbsəˈlesnt/ *adj* becoming out of date; going out of use: *obsolescent technology* ○ *Electronic equipment quickly becomes obsolescent.*
▷ **obsolescence** /-ˈlesns/ *n* [U] being obsolescent: *a product with built-in/planned obsolescence*, ie deliberately designed by the manufacturer not to last long, so that consumers are encouraged to buy again.

obsolete /ˈɒbsəliːt/ *adj* no longer used; out of date: *obsolete words found in old texts* ○ *The horse-drawn plough is now obsolete in most European countries.*

obstacle /ˈɒbstəkl/ *n* (*usu fig*) thing in the way that either stops progress or makes it difficult: *obstacles on the race-course* ○ *obstacles to world peace* ○ *Not being able to pass his mathematics exam proved an obstacle to his career.*
□ ˈ**obstacle course** set of natural or artificial obstacles (eg hedges, ditches, car tyres) which people (eg soldiers doing military training) have to climb over, under, through, etc: (*fig*) *Since the dustbin men went on strike the pavements have become an obstacle course for pedestrians*, ie because of the piles of rubbish left uncollected on them.
ˈ**obstacle race** race over an obstacle course.

obstetrics /əbˈstetrɪks/ *n* [sing *v*] (*medical*) branch of medicine and surgery concerned with childbirth: *gynaecology and obstetrics* ○ *She specializes in obstetrics.*
▷ **obstetric** /əbˈstetrɪk/ (also **obstetrical** /-ɪkl/) of obstetrics: *the obstetric ward* ○ *obstetrical complications.*
obstetrician /ˌɒbstəˈtrɪʃn/ *n* doctor who

specializes in obstetrics: *Her obstetrician could not be present at the birth.*

obstinacy /ˈɒbstənəsɪ/ *n* [U] being obstinate; stubbornness: *His obstinacy was irritating.* ○ *Sheer obstinacy prevented her from apologizing.*

obstinate /ˈɒbstənət/ *adj* **1** refusing to change one's opinion or chosen course of action; stubborn: *The obstinate old man refused to go to hospital.* ○ *There's a very obstinate streak in that child,* ie Some of his behaviour is very obstinate. **2** not easily overcome or removed: *obstinate resistance* ○ *an obstinate rash on his face* ○ *an obstinate stain on the carpet.* **3** (idm) **obstinate/stubborn as a mule** ⇨ MULE[1]. ▷ **obstinately** *adv.*

obstreperous /əbˈstrepərəs/ *adj* (*fml*) noisy and uncontrolled; unruly: *obstreperous behaviour, children* ○ *He becomes obstreperous when he's had a few drinks.* ▷ **obstreperously** *adv*: *obstreperously drunk.* **obstreperousness** *n* [U].

obstruct /əbˈstrʌkt/ *v* **(a)** [Tn, Tn·pr] ~ **sth (with sth)** be or get in the way of (sb/sth); block (a road, passage, etc): *Tall trees obstructed his view of the road.* ○ *He was charged with obstructing the highway.* **(b)** [Tn] deliberately prevent (sb/sth) from making progress; put difficulties in the way of (sb/sth): *obstruct the police in the course of their duty* ○ *obstruct a player on the football field* ○ *obstruct the passage of a bill through Parliament,* ie try to prevent a law being passed.

obstruction /əbˈstrʌkʃn/ *n* **1** [U] action of obstructing; being obstructed: *obstruction of the factory gates* ○ *a policy of obstruction.* **2** [C] thing that obstructs; obstacle: *an operation to remove an obstruction in the throat, intestine, stomach, etc* ○ *obstructions on the road,* eg fallen trees ○ *Your car is causing an obstruction,* ie getting in the way of others. **3** [C, U] (*sport*) (act of) unfairly stopping the movement of a player in the other team: *commit an obstruction* ○ *be found guilty of obstruction.*

▷ **obstructionism** /-ʃənɪzəm/ *n* [U] (*fml*) deliberate and systematic obstruction of plans, legislation, etc: *The government were defeated by the obstructionism of their opponents.*

obstructionist /-ɪst/ *n* (*fml*) person who uses or favours obstructionism: *a political obstructionist* ○ *an obstructionist policy.*

obstructive /əbˈstrʌktɪv/ *adj* obstructing or likely or intended to obstruct: *deliberately obstructive* ○ *a policy obstructive to our plans.* ▷ **obstructively** *adv.*

obtain /əbˈteɪn/ *v* **1** [Tn, Dn·pr] ~ **sth (for sb)** get sth; come to own or possess sth (by buying, borrowing, taking, etc): *Where can I obtain a copy of her latest book?* ○ *He always manages to obtain what he wants.* ○ *I obtained this record for you with difficulty.* **2** [I] (*fml*) (of rules, customs, etc) be in use; exist: *The practice still obtains in some areas of England.*

▷ **obtainable** *adj* that can be obtained: *no longer obtainable* ○ *Are his records still obtainable?*

obtrude /əbˈtruːd/ *v* [I, Tn·pr, Tn, Tn·pr] ~ **(oneself/sth on/upon sb)** (*fml*) force (oneself, one's opinions, ideas, etc) upon sb/sth, esp when unwanted: *I've no wish to obtrude, but...* ○ *obtrude on sb's grief* ○ *He persisted in obtruding himself despite our efforts to get rid of him.*

▷ **obtrusion** /əbˈtruːʒn/ *n* **1** [U] (*fml*) action of obtruding: *the obtrusion of unwelcome guests.* **2** [C] thing that obtrudes: *unwelcome obtrusions.*

obtrusive /əbˈtruːsɪv/ *adj* very noticeable or obvious; inclined to obtrude: *I find the music in the bar very obtrusive.* ○ *Try to wear a colour that is less obtrusive.* **obtrusively** *adv.* **obtrusiveness** *n* [U].

obtuse /əbˈtjuːs; *US* -ˈtuːs/ *adj* (*fml derog*) slow to understand; stupid: *He's being deliberately obtuse.* ○ *She cannot possibly be so obtuse.* ▷ **obtusely** *adv.* **obtuseness** *n* [U].

□ **obˌtuse ˈangle** (*geometry*) angle between 90° and 180°. ⇨ illus at ANGLE.

obverse /ˈɒbvɜːs/ *n* (*fml*) **1** face, side, or part of a thing that is most noticeable or intended to be seen or shown: [attrib] *the obverse side.* **2** side of a coin or medal that has the head or main design on it: *The head of the Queen appears on the obverse of British coins.* Cf REVERSE[2] 2. **3** counterpart; opposite: *The obverse of love is hate.*

obviate /ˈɒbvɪeɪt/ *v* [Tn] (*fml*) remove (sth); get rid of: *obviate dangers, difficulties, etc* ○ *The new road obviates the need to drive through the town.*

obvious /ˈɒbvɪəs/ *adj* easily seen, recognized or understood; clear: *His nervousness was obvious right from the start.* ○ *It was obvious to everyone that the child had been badly treated.* ○ *Spending less money is the obvious answer to his financial problems.*

▷ **obviously** *adv* can be clearly seen; plainly: *Obviously, she needs help.* ○ *He was obviously drunk.* ⇨ Usage at HOPEFUL.

obviousness *n* [U]: *The obviousness of the lie was embarrassing.*

OC /ˌəʊ ˈsiː/ *abbr* Officer Commanding: (*fig infml*) *Who's OC* (ie in charge of) *the team kit?*

ocarina /ˌɒkəˈriːnə/ *n* small high-pitched musical instrument, shaped like an egg, with holes for the fingertips, played by blowing and made of clay, metal or plastic.

O'Casey /əʊˈkeɪsɪ/ Sean (1880-1964), Irish playwright whose best-known works, including *Juno and the Paycock* and *The Plough and the Stars,* portray working-class life in Dublin.

Occam /ˈɒkəm/ ⇨ WILLIAM OF OCCAM.

occasion /əˈkeɪʒn/ *n* **1** [C] particular time (at which an event takes place): *on this/that occasion* ○ *on the present/last occasion* ○ *on one occasion,* ie once ○ *on rare occasions* ○ *I've met him on several occasions.* **2** [sing] ~ **(for sth)** suitable or right time (for sth); opportunity: *This is not an occasion for laughter.* ○ *I'll buy one if the occasion arises,* ie if I get the chance. ○ *He used the occasion to express all his old grievances against the chairman.* **3** [U] (*fml*) reason; need: *I've had no occasion to visit him recently.* ○ *You have no occasion to be angry.* ○ *She's not had much occasion to speak French.* **4** [C] special event or celebration: *The wedding was quite an occasion.* **5** [C] (*fml*) immediate but incidental or subordinate cause (of sth): *The real cause of the riot was unclear, but the occasion was the arrest of two men.* **6** (idm) **on ocˈcasion** (*fml*) now and then; whenever there is need. **on the occasion of sth** (*fml*) at the time of (a certain event): *on the occasion of his daughter's wedding.* **(have) a sense of ocˈcasion** (have a) natural feeling for what is right or fitting for a particular event, etc: *He wore his shabbiest clothes to the party: he has no sense of occasion!*

▷ **occasion** *v* [Tn, Dn·n, Dn·pr] ~ **sth (to sb)** (*fml*) be the cause of sth: *What occasioned such an angry response?* ○ *Stephen's behaviour occasioned his parents much anxiety.*

NOTE ON USAGE: **Occasion**, **opportunity** and **chance** all indicate a time when it is possible to do something. **Occasion** suggests that the time is socially suitable for the activity: *A wedding is an occasion for celebration.* ○ *I'll speak to him if the occasion arises.* **Opportunity** and **chance** suggest that the necessary physical circumstances for doing something are present: *I took the opportunity of visiting my aunt while I was in Birmingham.* ○ *I hope you get a chance to relax.* **Chance** can also indicate a degree of probability: *What are your chances of being promoted?* **Occasion** may refer to the particular time when something happens: *I've met her on several occasions recently.*

occasional /əˈkeɪʒənl/ *adj* [usu attrib] **1** happening, coming, done, etc from time to time; not regular: *He pays me occasional visits.* ○ *There will be occasional showers during the day.* ○ *I drink an occasional cup of coffee; but usually I take tea.* ○ *He reads the occasional book, but mostly just magazines.* **2** (*fml*) used, meant, written, etc for a special event: *occasional verses,* eg written to celebrate an anniversary ○ *occasional music for a royal wedding.*

▷ **occasionally** /-nəlɪ/ *adv* now and then; at times: *He visits me occasionally.*

□ **ocˈcasional table** small table for use as required: *The coffee cups were placed on an antiqu occasional table.*

Occident /ˈɒksɪdənt/ *n* **the Occident** [sing] (*fml*) the countries of the West, ie Europe and America. Cf ORIENT[1].

▷ **Occidental** /ˌɒksɪˈdentl/ *n* (*fml*) person from th Occident.

occidental *adj* of or from the Occident.

occiput /ˈɒksɪpʌt/ *n* (*anatomy*) the back of th head. ▷ **occipital** /ɒkˈsɪpɪtl/ *adj* [esp attrib]: *th occipital artery/muscle/nerve/bone.*

occlude /əˈkluːd/ *v* [Tn] **1** (*fml*) block (an opening an entrance, a passage, etc). **2** (*chemistry*) (of a solid substance) absorb and retain (a gas).

▷ **occlusion** /əˈkluːʒn/ *n* **1** [U] occluding or bein occluded. **2** [C] = OCCLUDED FRONT. **3** [U] norma position of the teeth when the jaws are closed.

□ **ocˌcluded ˈfront** (also **occlusion**) condition c the atmosphere that occurs when a mass of col air overtakes a mass of warm air, lifting it off th earth's surface and producing rain.

occult /ɒˈkʌlt; *US* əˈkʌlt/ *adj* **(a)** only for those wit special knowledge or powers; hidden, secret *occult practices.* **(b)** involving supernatural o magical powers: *occult arts,* eg witchcraft.

▷ **the occult** *n* supernatural practices ceremonies, powers, etc: *He's interested in th occult.*

occultist *n* (*fml*) person involved in or believing i the occult.

occupant /ˈɒkjʊpənt/ *n* person who occupies a house, room or position, or who possesses an occupies land: *The previous occupants had left th house in a terrible mess.* ○ *the next occupant of th post.*

▷ **occupancy** /-pənsɪ/ *n* **1** [U] action or fact o occupying a house, land, etc: *a change of occupanc* ○ *sole occupancy of the house.* **2** [C] period o occupying a house, etc as an owner or a tenant: *a occupancy of six months* ○ *During her occupanc the garden was transformed.*

occupation /ˌɒkjʊˈpeɪʃn/ *n* **1** [U] **(a)** action o occupying; state of being occupied (OCCUPY 1): *th occupation of a house by a family.* **(b)** taking an keeping possession: *a country under enem occupation* ○ *an army of occupation.* **2** [C] period o time during which a house, country, etc i occupied (OCCUPY 1, 2): *their four-year occupatio of the farm, that country.* **3** [C] **(a)** (*fml*) job employment: *'What's your occupation?' 'I'm a dancer.'* ○ *Please state your name, age an occupation.* **(b)** activity that occupies a person' (esp spare) time; pastime: *She has man occupations including gardening an wine-making.* ○ *His favourite occupation i reading.* ⇨ Usage at TRADE[1]. **4** [U, C] action o occupying a building, factory, etc as part of a political or other demonstration.

▷ **occupational** /-ʃənl/ *adj* [usu attrib] of, cause by or connected with a person's job: *a occupational advice service.* **occupationa diˈsease** disease connected with a particular job *Skin disorders are common occupational disease among factory workers.* **occupational ˈhazar** risk or danger connected with a particular job *Explosions, though infrequent, are an occupationa hazard for coal-miners.* **occupational ˈtherap** way of treating people with certain physical o mental illnesses by giving them creative o productive work to do. **occupational ˈtherapis** specialist in this.

occupier /ˈɒkjʊpaɪə(r)/ *n* person who has (es temporary) possession of land or a building occupant: *The letter was addressed to the occupie of the house.*

occupy /ˈɒkjʊpaɪ/ *v* (*pt, pp* **-pied**) **1** [Tn] live in o have possession of (a house, land, etc): *The occupy the house next door.* ○ *The family hav occupied the farm for many years.* **2** [Tn] tak possession of and establish troops in (a country position, etc): *The army occupied the enemy' capital.* **3** [Tn] take up or fill (time, space, sb' mind, etc): *The speeches occupied three hours.* ○ *A bed occupied the corner of the room.* ○ *Her time i fully occupied with her three children.* ○ *Man* *problems occupied his mind.* **4** [Tn, Tn·pr] ~ **oneself (in doing sth/with sth)** fill one's time or keep oneself busy (doing sth/with sth): *How does he occupy himself now he's retired?* ○ *The child occupied himself in playing his flute.* **5** [Tn] hold or fill (an official position): *My sister occupies an important position in the Department of the Environment.* **6** [Tn] place oneself in (a building, etc) as a political or other demonstration: *The terrorists have occupied the Embassy.* ○ *The striking office workers have occupied the whole building.*

▷ **occupied** *adj* [pred] **1** in use; filled: *This table is already occupied.* ⇨ Usage at EMPTY[1]. **2** ~ **(in doing sth/with sth)** involved or busy: *She's occupied at the moment; she cannot speak to you.* ○ *He's fully occupied in looking after/with three small children.*

occur /əˈkɜ:(r)/ *v* (-rr-) **1** (a) [I] come into being as an event or a process; happen: *When did the accident occur?* ○ *Death occurred about midnight, the doctor says.* **(b)** [I, Ipr] *(fml)* exist; be found: *Misprints occur on every page.* ○ *The disease occurs most frequently in rural areas.* ⇨ Usage at HAPPEN. **2** [Ipr] ~ **to sb** come into (a person's mind): *An idea has occurred to me.* ○ *Did it ever occur to you that...?* ie Did you ever think that...? ○ *It never occured to her to ask anyone.*

occurrence /əˈkʌrəns/ *n* **1** [C] event; incident; happening: *Robbery is now an everyday occurrence.* ○ *an unfortunate occurrence.* **2** [U] *(fml)* fact, frequency, etc of sth happening: *He's studying the occurrence of accidents on this piece of road,* ie how often, etc they take place. **3** (idm) **be of frequent, rare, common, etc ocˈcurrence** *(fml)* happen or take place frequently, rarely, etc: *Riots are of frequent occurrence in this province.*

NOTE ON USAGE: Compare **event**, **occurrence** and **incident. Occurrence** is the most neutral and does not indicate a particular type of happening: *Divorce has become an everyday occurrence.* An **event** is often a happening of importance: *Their wedding will be quite an event,* ie a large number of people will attend. ○ *The events of 1968 changed Western society.* An **incident** is usually of less importance, often occurring in a narrative: *You don't have to write down every little incident in your life.* It can also refer to a conflict or disagreement, often involving violence: *The kidnapping caused an international incident.*

ocean /ˈəʊʃn/ *n* **1** [U] mass of salt water that covers most of the earth's surface: [attrib] *an ocean voyage* ○ *the ocean waves.* **2 Ocean** [C] one of the main areas into which this is divided: *the Atlantic/Pacific/Indian/Arctic/Antarctic Ocean.* **3** (idm) **a drop in the bucket/ocean** ⇨ DROP[1]. **oceans of sth** *(infml)* very many or much; lots of sth: *oceans of food and drink* ○ *Don't worry — we've got oceans of time.*

▷ **oceanic** /ˌəʊʃɪˈænɪk/ *adj* [usu attrib] *(fml)* of, like or found in the ocean: *an oceanic survey* ○ *oceanic plant life.*

oceanography /ˌəʊʃəˈnɒgrəfɪ/ *n* [U] scientific study of the oceans. **oceanographer** *n* specialist in this.

□ **ˈocean-going** *adj* (of ships) made for crossing the sea, not for coastal or river journeys.

ocean ˈlane one of the routes regularly used by ships: *The ocean lanes are always busy.*

oceanarium /ˌəʊʃəˈneərɪəm/ *n* (*pl* ~**s** or ~**ia** /-rɪə/) establishment containing a large pool in which sea animals (eg fish or dolphins) are kept, either for scientific study or for public entertainment.

Oceania /ˌəʊʃɪˈɑ:nɪə; *US* ˈ-ænɪə/ the islands of the southern Pacific Ocean (sometimes called the South Seas), including *Micronesia, *Melanesia and *Polynesia.

ocelot /ˈəʊsɪlɒt; *US* ˈɒsələt/ *n* type of Central and S American wild cat, similar to a leopard.

ochre (*US* also **ocher**) /ˈəʊkə(r)/ *n* [U] **1** (any of various types of) light yellow or red earth used for making colourings, eg in paints. **2** light yellowish-brown colour: *He painted the walls ochre.*

o'clock /əˈklɒk/ *adv* (used with the numbers 1 to 12 when stating the time, to specify an hour): *He left between five and six o'clock.* ○ *go to bed at/after/before eleven o'clock.*

Oct *abbr* October: *6 Oct 1931.*

oct (also **8vo**) *abbr* octavo.

octagon /ˈɒktəgən; *US* -gɒn/ *n* *(geometry)* flat figure with eight sides and eight angles.

▷ **octagonal** /ɒkˈtægənl/ *adj* having eight sides: *an octagonal coin, table, building* ○ *The room is octagonal.*

octahedron /ˌɒktəˈhi:drən/ (*pl* ~**s** or **-hedra** /-ˈhi:drə/) *n* solid figure with eight (esp triangular) faces. ⇨ illus at CUBE.

octane /ˈɒkteɪn/ *n* hydrocarbon compound present in petrol and used as a measure of its quality and efficiency.

□ **ˈoctane number** (also **ˈoctane rating**) measure of the efficiency and quality of a petrol in comparison with those of a fuel taken as standard (the highest number indicating the highest quality).

octave /ˈɒktɪv/ *n* **1** *(music)* **(a)** note that is six whole tones above or below a given note. **(b)** space between two such notes: *These notes are an octave apart.* **(c)** note and its octave played together: *The child's hands are too small to stretch to an octave on the piano.* **(d)** note and its octave with the six notes in between. Cf SCALE[2] 6. **2** (also **octet**) (in poetry) first eight lines of a sonnet; verse of eight lines.

Octavian. Cf AUGUSTUS.

octavo /ɒkˈteɪvəʊ/ *n* (*pl* ~**s**) (*abbrs* **oct**, **8vo**) (size of a) book or page produced by folding a piece of paper of standard size three times to give eight sheets.

octet (also **octette**) /ɒkˈtet/ *n* **1** (piece of music for) eight singers or players: *an octet by a modern composer* ○ *a jazz octet.* **2** = OCTAVE 2.

oct(o)- *comb form* having or made up of eight of sth: *octagon* ○ *octogenarian* ○ *octopus.*

October /ɒkˈtəʊbə(r)/ *n* [U, C] (*abbr* **Oct**) the tenth month of the year, next after September.

For the uses of *October* see the examples at *April.*

octogenarian /ˌɒktədʒɪˈneərɪən/ *n* person between 80 and 89 years of age: *She is very active for an octogenarian.*

SQUID

OCTOPUS

tentacles

octopus /ˈɒktəpəs/ *n* (*pl* ~**es**) sea-animal with a soft body and eight long arms with suckers on them: *Have you ever tasted octopus?* Cf SQUID.

ocular /ˈɒkjʊlə(r)/ *adj* [esp attrib] *(fml)* **1** of, for or by the eyes: *ocular defects.* **2** that can be seen; visual: *ocular proof/demonstration.*

oculist /ˈɒkjʊlɪst/ *n* specialist in treating diseases and defects of the eye.

OD /ˌəʊˈdi:/ *n* *(sl esp US)* overdose, esp of a narcotic drug.

▷ **OD** *v* (*3rd pers sing pres t* **OD's**, *pres p* **OD'ing**, *pp* **OD'd**) [I, Ipr] ~ **(on sth)** *(sl)* *(esp US)* take an overdose (of a drug): *OD'd on heroin.*

odd /ɒd/ *adj* (**-er**, **-est**) **1** strange; unusual; peculiar: *What an odd man!* ○ *How odd!* ○ *She wears rather odd clothes.* ○ *She gets odder as she grows older.* **2** (no comparative or superlative) (of numbers) that cannot be divided by two; not even: *1, 3, 5 and 7 are odd numbers.* **3** [usu attrib] (no comparative or superlative) **(a)** of one of a pair, set, series, etc when the other(s) is/are missing: *an odd shoe/sock/glove* ○ *two odd volumes of an encyclopedia* ○ *You're wearing odd socks,* ie two that do not form a pair. **(b)** left over; extra; surplus: *She made a cushion out of odd bits of material.* **4** (no comparative or superlative; usu placed directly after a number) a little more than: *five hundred odd,* ie slightly more than 500 ○ *thirty-odd* (ie between 30 and 40) *years later* ○ *twelve pounds odd,* ie £12 and some pence extra. **5** [attrib] (no comparative or superlative) not regular or fixed; occasional: *weed the garden at odd times/moments,* ie at various irregular moments ○ *I take the odd bit of exercise, but nothing regular.* ○ *The landscape was bare except for the odd cactus.* ○ *Do you have an odd minute* (ie a little spare time) *to help me with this?* **6** (idm) **an odd/a queer fish** ⇨ FISH[1]. **the/an odd man/one ˈout** (a) person or thing left over when the others have been put into pairs or groups: *There's always an odd one out when I sort out my socks.* ○ *That boy is always the odd man out when the children are divided into teams.* **(b)** person or thing that is different from the others: *Banana, grape, apple, daisy — which of these is the odd one out?* **(c)** *(infml)* person who cannot fit easily into the society, community, etc of which he is a member: *At school she always felt the odd one out.* ○ *His formal clothes made him the odd one out in the club.*

▷ **oddly** *adv* in a strange or peculiar manner: *behave oddly* ○ *be oddly dressed* ○ *She looked at him very oddly.* ○ *Oddly enough, we were just talking about the same thing.*

oddness *n* [U] quality of being odd(1); strangeness: *the oddness of her appearance* ○ *His oddness frightened her.*

□ **ˈoddball** *n* *(infml)* strange or eccentric person: *The new boss is a bit of an oddball.*

ˌodd ˈjobs small jobs of various types, usu done for other people: *He did odd jobs around the house during his holiday.* ○ *The man does odd jobs in my father's garden.* **odd ˈjob man** /mæn/ person paid to do such jobs.

ˈodd-looking *adj* of strange or unusual appearance: *an odd-looking house* ○ *She's rather odd-looking.*

oddity /ˈɒdɪtɪ/ *n* **1** [U] (also **oddness**) quality of being odd(1); strangeness: *I was puzzled by the oddity of her behaviour.* **2** [C] unusual act, event, person or thing: *a grammatical oddity* ○ *He's something of an oddity in the neighbourhood,* ie unusual in some ways.

oddment /ˈɒdmənt/ *n* (usu *pl*) piece left over or remaining; remnant: *a chair sold as an oddment at the end of the sale* ○ *a patchwork quilt made out of oddments.* Cf ODDS AND ENDS (ODDS).

odds /ɒdz/ *n* [pl] **1** probability or chance (that a certain thing will or will not happen): *The odds are in your favour* (ie You are likely to succeed) *because you have more experience.* ○ *The odds are against him,* ie He's unlikely to succeed. ○ *The odds are that* (ie It is probable that) *she'll win.* **2** difference in strength, numbers, etc (in favour of one person, team, etc); inequalities: *a victory against overwhelming odds* ○ *They were fighting against heavy odds,* ie a much stronger enemy. **3** (in betting) difference in amount between the money bet on a horse, etc and the money that will be paid if it is successful: *The horse was running at odds of ten to one.* ○ *The odds are five to one on that horse.* ○ *I bet three pounds on a horse running at twenty to one and won sixty pounds!* **4** (idm) **against (all) the ˈodds** despite strong opposition or disadvantages: *Against all the odds she achieved her dream of becoming a ballerina.* **be at odds (with sb) (over/on sth)** be disagreeing or quarrelling (with sb) (about sth): *They're constantly at odds with each other.* ○ *He's always at odds with his father over politics.* **even chances/odds/money** ⇨ EVEN[1]. **give/receive ˈodds** *(sport)* give/receive an advantage at the beginning of a game (eg golf) to make it more difficult for the stronger player to win. **have the cards/odds stacked against one** ⇨ STACK *v.* **it makes no ˈodds** it will not affect matters; it is of no consequence: *It makes no odds to me whether you go or stay.* **lay (sb) odds (of)** offer (sb) odds(3) (of):

I'll lay odds of three to one that he gets the job. ˌ**odds and** ˈ**ends**; *Brit infml* ˌ**odds and** ˈ**sods** small articles; bits and pieces of various sorts, usu without much value: *He's moved most of his stuff; there are just a few odds and ends left.* Cf ODDMENT. **over the** ˈ**odds** (*Brit infml*) more than is expected, necessary, etc: *The firm pays over the odds for working in unpopular areas.* ○ *We offered over the odds for the house to make sure we got it.* **what's the** ˈ**odds?** (*infml*) what does it matter?; it's not important: *He's left her? What's the odds? He was never at home anyhow.*

□ ˌ**odds-**ˈ**on** *adj* better than even (chance); likely (to win): *It's odds-on that he'll be late.* ○ *That horse is the* ˌ*odds-on* ˈ*favourite.*

ode /əʊd/ *n* (usu long) poem expressing noble feeling, often written to a person or thing, or celebrating some special event: *Keats's 'Ode to Autumn'.*

odious /ˈəʊdɪəs/ *adj* (*fml*) **1** disgusting; hateful: *What an odious man!* ○ *I find his flattery odious.* **2** (idm) **comparisons are odious** ⇨ COMPARISON.
▷ **odiousness** *n* [U].

odium /ˈəʊdɪəm/ *n* [U] (*fml*) general or widespread hatred or disgust felt towards a person or his actions: *behaviour that exposed him to odium* ○ *He incurred the odium of everyone by sacking the old caretaker.*

odometer /ɒˈdɒmɪtə(r), əʊˈ-/ *n* (*US*) = MILOMETER.

odorous /ˈəʊdərəs/ *adj* (*dated fml*) having a (pleasant or unpleasant) smell.

odour (*US* **odor**) /ˈəʊdə(r)/ *n* (*fml*) **1** [C] (pleasant or unpleasant) smell: *the delicious odour of freshly-made coffee* ○ *the unpleasant odour of over-ripe cheese* ○ *emit, give off a pungent odour* ○ (*fig*) *An odour of corruption hangs about him.* **2** (idm) **be in good/bad** ˈ**odour (with sb)** be well/badly thought of (by sb); have a good/bad reputation (with sb): *I'm in rather bad odour with my boss at the moment.*

▷ **odourless** *adj* without a smell: *an odourless liquid* ○ *Our new product will keep your bathroom clean and odourless.*

Odysseus /əˈdɪsjuːs; *US* əʊˈdɪʃuːs/ (in Greek legend) king of Ithaca, who was one of the Greek leaders at the siege of *Troy. On their way home he and his companions wandered for many years, having a series of adventures which are described in the *Odyssey*. These included being captured by the one-eyed giant Cyclops, and sailing between *Scylla and *Charybdis. In the end Odysseus returned home to his wife *Penelope. Cf ULYSSES.

Odyssey /ˈɒdɪsɪ/ **the Odyssey** ancient Greek poem in 24 books, which tells of the journeys and adventures of Odysseus. It dates from before 700 BC, and is traditionally said to have been written by *Homer.

odyssey /ˈɒdɪsɪ/ *n* long adventurous journey: (*fig*) *a spiritual odyssey.*

OECD /ˌəʊ iː siː ˈdiː/ *abbr* Organization for Economic Co-operation and Development.

oecumenical = ECUMENICAL.

OED /ˌəʊ iː ˈdiː/ *abbr* Oxford English Dictionary.

oedema (*US* **edema**) /ɪˈdiːmə/ *n* swollen condition of a part of the body, caused by the presence of too much fluid. Cf DROPSY. ▷ **oedematous** (*US* **edematous**) *adj.*

Oedipus /ˈiːdɪpəs; *US* ˈed-/ (in Greek legend) king of Thebes, who, in fulfilment of an oracle, killed his father and then married his mother without realizing who they were. When he found out what he had done he went mad and blinded himself.

▷ **Oedipal** /ˈiːdɪpl; *US* ˈed-/ *adj* (*psychology*) of the Oedipus complex.

□ ˈ**Oedipus complex** (*psychology*) unconscious sexual desire of a child for the parent of the opposite sex (esp of a boy for his mother), and jealousy of the other parent. Cf ELECTRA COMPLEX (ELECTRA).

o'er /ɔː(r)/ *adv, prep* (*arch*) over: *o'er valleys and hills.*

oesophagus (also *esp US* **esophagus**) /ɪˈsɒfəgəs/ *n* (*pl* ~**es** or **-gi** /-dʒaɪ/) (*medical*) tube through which food, etc passes from the mouth to the stomach; gullet: *cancer of the oesophagus.* ⇨ illus at DIGESTIVE, THROAT.

oestrogen /ˈiːstrədʒən/ (also *esp US* **estrogen** /ˈes-/) *n* [U, C] any of a group of female sex hormones, produced by the ovaries, which develop and maintain the characteristic features of the female body, eg large breasts, and prepare the body for pregnancy: *an oestrogen deficiency.* Cf PROGESTERONE.

oeuvre /ˈɜːvr/ *n* (*French fml*) **1** work of art (eg a book or painting). **2** (usu *sing*) all the works of art produced by a particular painter, writer, composer, etc: *Picasso's entire oeuvre.*

of /əv; *strong form* ɒv/ *prep* **1** belonging to (sb/sth). **(a)** (followed by a *possess pron* or by a *n*, usu with *'s*): *a friend of mine* ○ *an acquaintance of my wife's* ○ *that house of yours in the country.* **(b)** (followed by a *n* referring to an inanimate object): *the handle of the umbrella* ○ *the lid of the box.* **(c)** (after a *n* referring to sb's rights or duties): *the role of the teacher* ○ *the rights of man* ○ *the privileges of the élite* ○ *the responsibilities of a nurse.* **2** originating from (a background) or living in (a place): *a woman of royal descent* ○ *a man of humble origin* ○ *the miners of Wales* ○ *the inhabitants of the area.* **3** created by (esp referring to sb's works as a whole): *the works of Shakespeare* (Cf *Shakespeare's comedies*) ○ *the paintings of Picasso* ○ *the poems of John Lennon.* **4 (a)** concerning or depicting (sb/sth): *stories of crime and adventure* ○ *a photograph of my dog* ○ *a picture of the Queen* ○ *a map of Ireland.* **(b)** about (sb/sth): *I've never heard of such places.* ○ *He told us of his travels.* **5** (indicating the material used to make sth): *a dress of silk* ○ *shirts made of cotton* ○ *a house (built) of stone.* Cf FROM 8. **6** (used to show a special grammatical relationship) **(a)** (introducing the object of the action expressed by the preceding *n*): *a lover of* (ie sb who loves) *classical music* ○ *fear of the dark* ○ *any hope of being elected* ○ *the forging of a banknote.* **(b)** (introducing the subject of the action expressed by the preceding *n*): *the support of the voters,* ie the voters supporting sb ○ *the feelings of a rape victim towards her attacker* ○ *the love of a mother for her child* ○ *the beliefs of religious groups.* **7 (a)** (indicating what is measured, counted or contained): *a pint of milk* ○ *2 kilos of potatoes* ○ *a sheet of paper* ○ *a loaf of bread* ○ *a box of matches* ○ *a bottle of lemonade* ○ *a bag of groceries.* **(b)** (showing the relationship between part and the whole of sth): *a member of the football team* ○ *for six months of the year.* **(c)** (used after *some, many, a few,* etc and between a numeral or superlative *adj* and a *pron* or *det*): *some of his friends* ○ *a few of my records* ○ *not much of the food* ○ *six of them* ○ *five of the team* ○ *the last of the girls* ○ *the most expensive of the presents* ○ *the richest of all her friends.* **8 (a)** (used in expressions showing distance in space or time): *a village 5 miles north of Leeds* ○ *within 100 yards of the station* ○ *Within a year of their divorce he had remarried.* ○ (*US*) *a quarter of eleven,* ie 10.45 am or pm. **(b)** (used in dates): *the twenty-second of July* ○ *the first of May.* **9** so that sb no longer has or suffers from (sth): *rob sb of sth* ○ *deprived of his mother's protection* ○ *relieved of responsibility* ○ *cure sb of drug-addiction.* **10** (indicating a cause): *die of pneumonia* ○ *ashamed of one's behaviour* ○ *proud of being captain.* **11** (introducing a phrase in apposition): *the city of Dublin* ○ *the issue of housing* ○ *on the subject of education* ○ *at the age of 16.* **12** (introducing a phrase that describes a preceding *n*): *a coat of many colours* (Cf *a multi-coloured coat*) ○ *a girl of ten* (Cf *a ten-year-old girl*) ○ *a woman of genius* ○ *a child of strange appearance* ○ *an item of value* ○ *products of foreign origin.* **13** (used between *ns,* the first describing the second): *He's got the devil of a temper.* ○ *Where's that fool of a receptionist?* ○ *He's a fine figure of a man.* **14** in relation to (sth); concerning (sth): *the result of the debate* ○ *the time of departure* ○ *the topic of conversation* ○ *a dictionary of English* ○ *the Professor of Mathematics* ○ *his chance of winning* ○ *sure of one's facts.* **15** chosen from (others of a kind); contrasted with: *I'm surprised that you of all people think that.* ○ *A flat tyre today of all days — what bad luck!* **16** (used to show who is being described by *It is/was + adj*): *It was kind of you to offer.* ○ *It's wrong of your boss to suggest it.* **17** (*dated*) frequently happening at (a specified time): *They used to visit me of a Sunday,* ie on Sundays. ○ *Often, of an evening* (ie in the evening) *we'd hear the sirens.*

off[1] /ɒf; *US* ɔːf/ *adj* **1** [attrib] = OFF-SIDE[2]. **2** [pred] ~ **(with sb)** (esp after *rather, very, slightly,* etc) (*infml*) impolite or unfriendly (towards sb): *She sounded rather off on the phone.* ○ *He was a bit off with me this morning.* **3** [pred] (of food) no longer fresh: *This fish has gone/is off,* ie can no longer be eaten. ○ *The milk smells/tastes decidedly off.*

□ ˈ**off chance** slight possibility: *There is still an off chance that the weather will improve.* ○ *He came on the off chance of finding me at home.*

off[2] /ɒf; *US* ɔːf/ *adv part* (For special uses with many *vs,* eg *go off, turn sth off, clear off,* see the *v* entries.) **1 (a)** at or to a point distant in space; away: *The town is still five miles off.* ○ *We are some way off, e[illegible] our destination.* ○ *He ran off with the money.* ○ *B[illegible] off/Off with you!* ie Go away! **(b)** at a point distan[t] in time; away: *The holidays are not so far off.* **2** (indicating removal or separation, esp from the human body): *He's had his beard shaved off.* ○ *What beautiful curls — why do you want to have them (cut) off?* ○ *take one's hat, coat, tie, etc off* (C[f] *have (got) one's hat, coat, tie, etc on*) ○ *Don't leave the toothpaste with the top off.* Cf ON[1] 3. **3** startin[g] a journey or race: *She's off to London tomorrow.* ○ *I must be off soon.* ○ *We're off/Off we go!* ○ *They're off,* ie The race has begun. **4** (*infml*) (of st[h] arranged or planned) not going to happen cancelled: *The wedding/engagement is off.* ○ *The miner's strike is off.* Cf ON[1] 8. **5 (a)** disconnected a[t] the mains; not being supplied: *The water/gas electricity is off.* **(b)** (of appliances) not being used: *The TV, radio, light, etc is off.* ○ *Make sure the central heating is off.* Cf ON[1] 4. **(c)** (of an item on a menu) no longer available or being served: *The steak pie is off today.* ○ *Soup's off — we've only go[t] fruit juice.* **6** away from work or duty: *I think I'l[l] take the afternoon off,* ie not do my usual work, etc ○ *She's off today.* ○ *The manager gave the staff the day off.* ○ *I've got three days off next week.* Cf TIME OFF (TIME[1]). **7** reduced in price; cheaper: *All shirts have 10% off.* ○ *Shoes are on sale with £5 off.* ○ *bu[y] a calendar at 50% off.* **8** (in the theatre) behind or at the sides of the stage; not on the stage: *noises, voices off.* **9** (idm) **be off for sth** (*infml*) have supplies of sth: *How are you off for cash?* ie How much have you got? Cf WELL OFF (WELL[3]), BADLY OFF (BAD[1]). ˌ**off and** ˈ**on**/ˌ**on and** ˈ**off** from time to time; now and again: *It rained on and off all day.*
▷ **off** *n* [sing] **1 the off** start of a race: *They're ready for the off.* **2 the off** (in cricket) that half of the field towards which a batsman is facing when waiting to receive a ball: *play the ball to the off* ○ [attrib] *the off stump,* ie the stump on this side. C[f] LEG.

□ **off of** *prep* (*US*) = OFF[3].

off[3] /ɒf; *US* ɔːf/ *prep* (For special uses with many *vs,* eg *get off sth, take (sth) off sth,* see the *v* entries.) **1** down or away from (a position on sth): *fall off a ladder, tree, horse, wall* ○ *The rain ran off the roof* ○ *The ball rolled off the table.* ○ *Keep off the grass* ○ *Cut another slice off the loaf.* ○ *Take a packet off the shelf.* ○ *They were only 100 metres off the summit when the accident happened.* ○ (*fig*) *We're getting right off the subject.* ○ *Scientists are still a long way off (finding) a cure.* **2** (esp of a road or street) accessible from (sth): *a narrow lane off the main road* ○ *another bathroom off the main bedroom* **3** at some distance from (sth): *a big house off the high street* ○ *an island off the coast of Cornwall* ○ *The ship sank off Cape Horn.* **4** (*infml*) not wishing or needing to take (sth): *I was off* (ie did not enjoy eating) *my food for a week.* ○ *He's finally off* (ie is no longer addicted to) *drugs.*

off(-) /ɒf; *US* ɔːf/ *pref* (used widely to form *ns, adjs, vs* and *advs*) not on; away or at a distance from: *off-print* ○ *off-stage* ○ *off-shore* ○ *off-key* ○ *off-load*

Offa /ˈɒfə/ (died 796 AD), Anglo-Saxon king of *Mercia, in central England, 757-96.

□ ˌ**Offa's ˈDyke** huge bank of earth built by Offa to mark the border between Mercia and Wales (roughly the same as the modern border between England and Wales).

offal /ˈɒfl; *US* ˈɔ:fl/ *n* [U] internal parts of an animal (eg heart, kidneys, liver, brains, etc) used as food; once considered to be less valuable than its flesh: *Offal is now thought to be very nutritious.*

off-beat /ˌɒf ˈbi:t; *US* ˌɔ:f-/ *adj* (*infml*) unusual; unconventional: *ˌoff-beat ˈhumour* ○ *an off-beat TV comedy* ○ *Her style of dress is definitely off-beat.*

off-Broadway /ˌɒf ˈbrɔ:dweɪ/ *adj* of a play, etc that is put on at one of the smaller theatres of New York, not in one of the main *Broadway theatres. Such productions are often experimental and relatively inexpensive. Cf OFF-OFF-BROADWAY.

off-cut /ˈɒfkʌt; *US* ˈɔ:f-/ *n* piece of wood, paper, etc remaining after the main piece has been cut; remnant: *She bought some timber off-cuts to build kitchen shelves.*

off-day /ˈɒfdeɪ; *US* ˈɔ:f-/ *n* (*infml*) day when one does things badly, is unlucky, clumsy, etc: *Monday is always an off-day for me.*

offence (*US* **offense**) /əˈfens/ *n* **1** [C] ~ (**against sth**) breaking of a rule or law; illegal act; crime: *commit an offence* ○ *an offence against society, humanity, the state, etc* ○ *a capital offence*, ie one punishable by death ○ *sexual offences* ○ *be charged with a serious offence* ○ *Because it was his first offence* (ie the first crime of which he had been found guilty), *the punishment wasn't too severe.* **2** [U] ~ (**to sb/sth**) (act or cause of) upsetting or annoying (sb); insult: *I'm sorry; I intended no offence when I said that.* ○ *I'm sure he didn't mean to cause offence (to you).* ○ *The anti-British propaganda gave* (ie caused) *much offence.* **3** [C] ~ (**to sb/sth**) (*fml*) thing that causes displeasure, annoyance or anger: *The new shopping centre is an offence to the eye*, ie unpleasant to look at. **4** [U] (*fml*) attack: *weapons of offence rather than defence.* **5** (idm) **no ofˈfence (to sb)** (used to explain that one does/did not intend to upset or annoy sb): *I'm moving out — no offence to you or the people who live here, but I just don't like the atmosphere.* **take ofˈfence (at sth)** feel hurt, upset or offended (by sth): *She's quick to take offence*, ie easily offended.

offend /əˈfend/ *v* **1** (**a**) [Tn esp passive] cause (sb) to feel upset or angry; hurt the feelings of: *She was offended at/by his sexist remarks.* ○ *She may be offended if you don't reply to her invitation.* (**b**) [Tn] cause displeasure or annoyance to (sb/sth): *sounds that offend the ear* ○ *an ugly building that offends the eye.* **2** [Ipr] ~ **against sb/sth** (*fml*) do wrong to sb/sth; commit an offence against sb/sth: *offend against humanity* ○ *His conduct offended against the rules of decent behaviour.*

▷ **offender** *n* (**a**) person who offends, esp by breaking a law: *an offender against society.* (**b**) person found guilty of a crime: *a persistent offender.* Cf FIRST OFFENDER (FIRST[1]).

offense /əˈfens, *also* ˈɒfens/ *n* (*US*) **1** [Gp, U] (*sport*) attacking team or section; method of attack: *Their team had a poor offense.* ○ *They deserved to lose; their offense was badly planned.* Cf DEFENCE 3. **2** [C, U] = OFFENCE.

offensive /əˈfensɪv/ *adj* **1** upsetting or annoying; insulting: *offensive remarks, language, behaviour* ○ *I find your attitude most offensive.* Cf INOFFENSIVE. **2** disgusting; repulsive: *an offensive smell* ○ *She finds tobacco smoke offensive.* **3** (*fml*) used for, or connected with, attack; aggressive: *offensive weapons* ○ *an offensive style of play in rugby.* Cf DEFENSIVE.

▷ **offensive** *n* **1** aggressive action, campaign or attitude; attack: *The new general immediately launched an offensive against the enemy.* ○ (*fig*) *The company has launched a strong marketing offensive to try to increase sales.* **2** (idm) **be on the offensive** be making an attack; act aggressively: (*fig*) *He's always expecting criticism of his work, so he's always on the offensive.* ○ *It's difficult to make friends with her; she's constantly on the offensive.* **go on/take the ofˈfensive** begin to attack: *In meetings she always takes the offensive before she can be criticized.*

offensively *adv*: *offensively loud music* ○ *offensively ugly buildings.*

offensiveness *n* [U].

offer /ˈɒfə(r); *US* ˈɔ:f-/ *v* **1** [Tn, Tn·pr, Dn·n, Dn·pr] ~ **sth (to sb) (for sth)** put forward sth (to sb) to be considered and accepted or refused; present: *The company has offered a high salary.* ○ *She offered a reward for the return of her lost bracelet.* ○ *I've been offered a job in Japan.* ○ *He offered her a cigarette.* ○ *We offered him the house for £35 000.* ○ *He offered £30 000 for the house.* **2** [I, Tn, Tt, Dn·n, Dn·pr] ~ **sth (to sb)** show or express the willingness or intention to do, give, etc sth: *I don't think they need help, but I think I should offer anyway.* ○ *They offered no resistance.* ○ *We offered to leave.* ○ *We offered him a lift, but he didn't accept.* ○ *The company offered the job to someone else.* **3** [I] (*fml*) occur; arise: *Take the first opportunity that offers*, ie that there is. **4** [Tn] (*fml*) give opportunity for (sth); provide: *The job offers prospects of promotion.* ○ *The trees offered welcome shade from the sun.* **5** [Tn, Tn·p, Dn·n, Dn·pr] ~ **sth/sb (up) (to sb) (for sth)** (*fml*) present or give (sth/sb), usu to God or a god and esp as a sacrifice: *She offered (up) a prayer to God for her husband's safe return.* ○ *A calf was offered up as a sacrifice to the goddess.* **6** (idm) ˈ**offer itself/themselves** (*fml*) be present; happen: *Ask her about it when a suitable moment offers itself.* **offer (sb) one's ˈhand** (*fml*) hold out one's hand (in order to shake hands with sb): *He came towards me, smiled and offered his hand.* **offer one's hand (in ˈmarriage)** (*fml*) propose marriage to a woman.

▷ **offer** *n* **1** [C] ~ (**to sb/to do sth**) statement offering to do or give sth to sb: *an offer of help from the community* ○ *your kind offer to help* ○ *an offer of marriage* (ie proposal) *to the youngest sister.* **2** [C] ~ (**for sth**) amount offered: *a firm offer*, ie one which was genuinely meant and not likely to be withdrawn ○ *I've had an offer of £1 200 for the car.* ○ *They made an offer which I couldn't refuse.* **3** (idm) **be open to (an) offer/offers** ⇨ OPEN[1]. **on ˈoffer** for sale at a reduced price: *Baked beans are on offer this week at the local supermarket.* **or nearest offer** ⇨ NEAR[1]. **under ˈoffer** (*Brit*) (of a building for sale) having a prospective buyer who has made an offer: *The office block is under offer.*

offering /ˈɒfərɪŋ; *US* ˈɔ:f-/ *n* **1** [U] action of presenting sth (to be accepted or refused): *the offering of bribes* ○ *the offering of financial assistance.* **2** [C] (*fml*) thing offered, esp as a gift or contribution: *a church offering* ○ *He gave her a box of chocolates as a peace offering*, ie in the hope of restoring peace after an argument, etc.

offertory /ˈɒfətrɪ; *US* -tɔ:rɪ/ *n* (*fml*) money collected during or at the end of a religious service: [attrib] *Money should be put in the offertory box.*

offhand /ˌɒfˈhænd; *US* ˌɔ:f-/ *adj* (of behaviour, speech, etc) too casual; abrupt: *He was rather offhand with me.* ○ *I don't like his offhand manner.*

▷ **offhand** *adv* without previous thought: *I can't say offhand how much money I earn.* ○ *Offhand I can't quote you an exact price.*

offhanded *adj*: *an ˌoffhanded ˈattitude.* **offhandedly** *adv.*

office /ˈɒfɪs; *US* ˈɔ:f-/ *n* **1** [C] (**a**) room(s) or building used as a place of business esp for clerical or administrative work: *our London offices* ○ *Our office is in the centre of the town.* ○ [attrib] *an ˈoffice job* ○ *ˈoffice equipment*, ie stationery, typewriters, etc ○ *ˈoffice workers.* (**b**) (usu small) room in which a particular person works: *a lawyer's office* ○ *the school secretary's office* ○ *The editors have to share an office.* (**c**) (*US*) doctor's surgery: *the pediatrician's office.* **2** [C] (often in compounds) room or building used for a particular purpose (esp to provide a service): *the lost ˈproperty office* ○ *a ˈticket office at a station* ○ *the local ˈtax office.* **3 Office** [sing] (esp in compounds) (buildings of a) government department, including the staff, their work and duties: *the ˈForeign Office* ○ *the ˈHome Office.* **4** [C, U] (work and duties connected with a) (public) position of trust and authority, esp as (part of) the government: *He has held the office of chairman for many years.* ○ *seek/accept/leave/resign office as a cabinet minister* ○ *the office of mayor* ○ *His political party has been out of office* (ie has not formed a government) *for many years.* ○ *Which political party is in office in your country?* **5 Office** [sing] (*religion*) authorized form of Christian worship: *Divine ˈOffice*, ie daily service in the Roman Catholic Church ○ *the Office for the dead.* **6** (idm) ˌ**lay down ˈoffice** (*fml*) resign a position of authority. **through sb's good ˈoffices** (*fml*) with sb's kind help.

□ ˈ**office-block** *n* (usu large) building containing offices (OFFICE 1b), usu belonging to more than one company: *ugly concrete office-blocks* ○ *The bank and the building society are in the same office-block.*

ˈ**office boy** (*fem* ˈ**office girl**) young person employed to do less important duties in an office: *The office boy will deliver the package.*

ˈ**office holder** (also ˈ**office bearer**) person who holds an office: *All the office bearers have to be elected.*

ˈ**office hours** hours during which business is regularly conducted: *Office hours vary from company to company and country to country.*

officer /ˈɒfɪsə(r); *US* ˈɔ:f-/ *n* **1** person appointed to command others in the army, navy, air force, etc: *All the officers and ratings were invited.* ○ *Both commissioned and non-commissioned officers attended.* **2** (often in compounds) person with a position of authority or trust, eg in the government or a society: *executive and clerical officers*, eg in the Civil Service ○ *a customs officer* ○ *officers of state*, ie ministers in the government ○ *the Medical Officer of Health* ○ *We had to vote to appoint all three officers: President, Secretary and Treasurer.* **3** (**a**) = POLICE OFFICER (POLICE). (**b**) (used as a form of address to a policeman or policewoman): *'Yes, officer, I saw the man approach the girl.'*

official /əˈfɪʃl/ *adj* **1** of or concerning a position of authority or trust: *official responsibilities, powers, records* ○ *in his official capacity as mayor.* **2** said, done, etc with authority; recognized by authority: *an official announcement, statement, decision, etc* ○ *the official biography of the princess* ○ *The news is almost certainly true although it is not official.* **3** for, suitable for or characteristic of persons holding office(4); formal: *an official reception, dinner, etc* ○ *written in an official style.*

▷ **official** *n* person who holds a public office (eg in national or local government): *government officials* ○ *the officials of a political party.*

officialdom /-dəm/ *n* (*fml often derog*) **1** [Gp] officials as a group: *Officialdom will no doubt decide our future.* **2** [U] the ways of doing the business of bureaucracy: *We suffer from too much officialdom.*

officialese /əˌfɪʃəˈli:z/ *n* [U] (*derog*) language characteristic of official documents (and thought to be too formal or complicated): *the incomprehensible officialese of income tax documents.* Cf JOURNALESE (JOURNAL).

officially /əˈfɪʃəlɪ/ *adv* **1** in an official manner; formally: *I've been officially invited to the wedding.* ○ *We already know who's got the job but we haven't yet been informed officially.* **2** as announced publicly (esp by officials) though not necessarily true in fact: *Officially, the director is in a meeting, though actually he's playing golf.*

□ **ofˌficial reˈceiver** = RECEIVER 2.

officiate /əˈfɪʃɪeɪt/ *v* [I, Ipr] ~ (**at sth**) perform the duties of an office(4) or position: *The Reverend Mr Smith will officiate at the wedding*, ie perform the marriage ceremony.

officious /əˈfɪʃəs/ *adj* too ready or willing to give orders, offer advice or help, or use one's authority; bossy and interfering: *We were tired of being pushed around by officious civil servants.* ▷ **officiously** *adv.* **officiousness** *n* [U].

offing /ˈɒfɪŋ; *US* ˈɔ:f-/ *n* (idm) **in the offing** (*infml*) likely to appear or happen soon; not far away: *The smell of cooking told them there was a meal in the offing.*

off-key /ˌɒf ˈki:; *US* ˌɔ:f/ *adj, adv* out of tune: *sing off-key* ○ (*fig*) *Some of his remarks were rather* *off-key*, ie not fitting or suitable.

off-licence /ˈɒf laɪsns/ *n* (*Brit*) (**a**) (*US* ˈ**package store**) shop or part of a public house where alcoholic drinks are sold to be taken away. ⇨ article at SHOP. (**b**) licence for this.

off-limits /ˌɒf ˈlɪmɪts; *US* ˌɔːf-/ *adj* (also **off limits**) (*US esp military*) ~ (**to sb**) = OUT OF BOUNDS (BOUNDS): *The town is off-limits to all personnel.*

off-line /ˌɒf ˈlaɪn; *US* ˌɔːf/ *adj* (*computing*) (using equipment) that is not controlled by a central processor: *an* ˌ*off-line* ˈ*process*. Cf ON-LINE.

off-load /ˌɒf ˈləʊd; *US* ˌɔːf/ *v* **1** [Tn] unload (sth): *off-load sacks of coal from a lorry.* **2** [Tn·pr] ~ **sb/sth on/onto sb** (*infml*) get rid of (sb/sth unpleasant or unwelcome) by passing him/it to sb else: *We'll be able to come if we can off-load the children onto my sister.*

off-off-Broadway /ˌɒf ɒf ˈbrɔːdweɪ/ *adj* of a small-scale, highly experimental or avant-garde theatrical production put on in a small theatre, club, café, etc in New York. Cf OFF-BROADWAY.

off-peak /ˌɒf ˈpiːk; *US* ˌɔːf/ *adj* [attrib] in or used at a time that is less popular or less busy (and therefore usu cheaper): ˌ*off-peak elec*ˈ*tricity* ○ ˌ*off-peak* ˈ*holiday prices.* Cf PEAK[1] 4.

offprint /ˈɒfprɪnt; *US* ˈɔːf-/ *n* separate printed copy of an article that is part of a larger publication.

off-putting /ˌɒf ˈpʊtɪŋ; *US* ˌɔːf/ *adj* (*infml esp Brit*) unpleasant; disturbing; disconcerting: *His rough manners were rather off-putting.*

off-season /ˈɒf siːzn; *US* ˈɔːf/ *n* [sing] (in business and tourism) least active time of the year; period when there are few orders or visitors: *Hotel workers wait until the off-season to take their holidays.*

offset /ˈɒfset; *US* ˈɔːf-/ *v* (**-tt-**; *pt*, *pp* **offset**) [Tn, Tn·pr] ~ **sth** (**by sth/doing sth**) compensate for sth; balance sth: *He put up his prices to offset the increased cost of materials.* ○ *Higher mortgage rates are partly offset by increased tax allowances.*

offset[2] /ˈɒfset; *US* ˈɔːf-/ *n* **1** [U] (also **offset process**) method of printing in which the ink is transferred from a metal plate to a rubber surface and then onto paper. **2** [C] (*botany*) shoot that sprouts from the side of a plant, and that can be grown into a new plant. **3** [C] amount that balances or compensates for another amount: [attrib] *offset payments.* **4** [C] sloping ledge in a wall formed by cutting away the area above it. **5** [C] bend in a pipe which allows it to go round obstacles.

offshoot /ˈɒfʃuːt; *US* ˈɔːf-/ *n* stem or branch growing from a main stem: *remove offshoots from a plant* ○ (*fig*) *the offshoot of a wealthy family.*

offshore /ˌɒfˈʃɔː(r); *US* ˌɔːf-/ *adj* [usu attrib] **1** at sea not far from the land: *an* ˌ*offshore* ˈ*oil rig,* ˈ*island,* ˈ*anchorage* ○ ˌ*offshore* ˈ*fishing.* **2** (of winds) blowing from the land towards the sea: ˌ*offshore* ˈ*breezes.*

offside[1] /ˌɒfˈsaɪd; *US* ˌɔːf-/ *adj, adv* (*sport*) **1** (of a player in football, hockey, etc) in a position where the ball may not be legally played, between the ball and the opponents' goal: *The forwards are all offside.* **2** of or about such a position: *be in an* ˌ*offside po*ˈ*sition* ○ *the* ˌ*offside* ˈ*rule.* Cf ONSIDE.

offside[2] /ˌɒfˈsaɪd; *US* ˌɔːf-/ (also **off**) *adj* [attrib] (*Brit*) (of a vehicle, a road or an animal) on the right-hand side: *the rear* ˌ*offside* ˈ*tyre* ○ *the off front wheel of a car.* Cf NEARSIDE (NEAR[1]).

offspring /ˈɒfsprɪŋ; *US* ˈɔːf-/ *n* (*pl* unchanged) (*fml*) (**a**) child or children of a particular person or couple: *She's the offspring of a scientist and a musician.* ○ *Their offspring are all very clever.* (**b**) young of an animal: *How many offspring does a cat usually have?*

off-stage /ˌɒf ˈsteɪdʒ; *US* ˌɔːf/ *adj, adv* not on the stage; not visible to the audience: *an* ˌ*off-stage* ˈ*scream* ○ *At this point in the play, most of the actors are off-stage.*

off-street /ˈɒf striːt; *US* ˈɔːf/ *adj* [attrib] not on the public road: *off-street parking only.*

off-white /ˌɒf ˈwaɪt; *US* ˌɔːf ˈhwaɪt/ *n, adj* not pure white, but with a very pale grey or yellow tinge: *paint a room off-white* ○ ˌ*off-white* ˈ*paint.*

oft /ɒft; *US* ɔːft/ *adv* (*arch*) (esp in compounds) often: *an oft-told tale* ○ *an oft-repeated warning.*

□ ˈ**oft-times** *adv* (*arch*) often.

often /ˈɒfn, *also* ˈɒftən; *US* ˈɔːfn/ *adv* **1** many times; at short intervals; frequently: *We often go there.* ○ *We have often been there.* ○ *We've been there quite often.* ○ *It very often rains here in April.* ○ *He writes to me often.* ○ *How often* (ie At what intervals) *do the buses run?* **2** in many instances: *These types of dog often have eye problems.* ○ *Old houses are often damp.* **3** (idm) **as often as** each time that; as many times as: *As often as I tried to phone him the line was engaged.* **as** ˌ**often as** ˈ**not; more** ˌ**often than** ˈ**not** very frequently: *When it's foggy the trains are late more often than not.* ˌ**every so** ˈ**often** occasionally; from time to time. **once too often** ⇨ ONCE.

ogee /ˈəʊdʒiː/ *n* line consisting of a double curve, like the letter S.

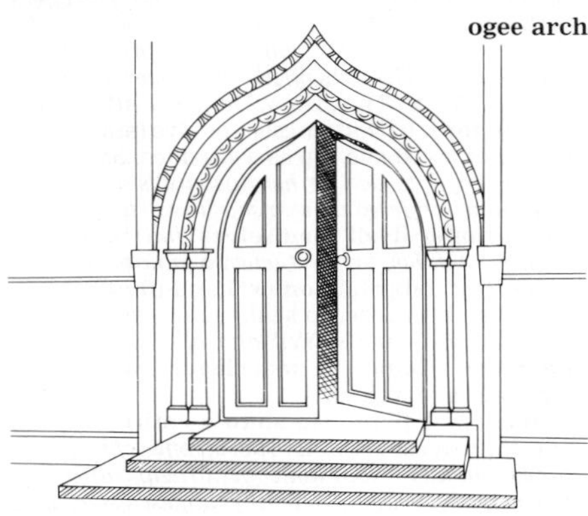
ogee arch

□ ˈ**ogee arch** arch consisting of a pair of ogees which curve outwards at the bottom and then inwards to meet at the top. ⇨ illus.

ogive /ˈəʊdʒaɪv/ *n* **1** band of stone extending diagonally across the underside of the roof of a Gothic building. **2** pointed (or Gothic) arch.

ogle /ˈəʊgl/ *v* [I, Ipr, Tn] ~ **at sb** (*derog*) look or stare at (esp a woman) in a way that suggests sexual interest: *Most women dislike being ogled (at).*

ogre /ˈəʊgə(r)/ *n* (*fem* **ogress** /ˈəʊgres/) **1** (in legends and fairy stories) cruel and frightening giant who eats people. **2** (*fig*) very frightening person: *My boss is a real ogre.*

▷ **ogrish** /ˈəʊgərɪʃ/ *adj* of or like an ogre.

oh (also **O**) /əʊ/ *interj* **1** (expressing surprise, fear, joy, etc): *Oh look!* ○ *Oh, how horrible!* **2** (used for emphasis or to attract sb's attention): *Oh yes I will.* ○ *Oh Pam, can you come over here for a minute?*

Ohio /əʊˈhaɪəʊ/ state of the north-eastern USA, to the south of the *Great Lakes. It produces a lot of coal, wheat and dairy produce, and is also important industrially. ⇨ map at App 1.

ohm /əʊm/ *n* unit of electrical resistance.

OHMS /ˌəʊ eɪtʃ em ˈes/ *abbr* (*Brit*) (esp on official forms, envelopes, etc) On Her/His Majesty's Service.

oho /əʊˈhəʊ/ *interj* (expressing surprise or triumph).

OHP /ˌəʊ eɪtʃ ˈpiː/ *abbr* overhead projector.

-oid *suff* (with *adjs* and *ns*) resembling; similar to: *humanoid* ○ *rhomboid.*

oil /ɔɪl/ *n* **1** [U] any of various thick slippery liquids that do not mix with water and (usu) burn easily, obtained from animals, plants, minerals, etc: ˈ*coconut,* ˈ*sunflower,* ˈ*vegetable, etc oil* ○ ˌ*olive* ˈ*oil* ○ ˈ*cooking oil* ○ ˌ*cod-liver* ˈ*oil* ○ ˈ*salad oil* ○ ˈ*sun-tan oil.* **2** [U] (**a**) petroleum found in rock underground: *drilling for oil in the desert.* ⇨ article. (**b**) (often in compounds) form of petroleum used as fuel, as a lubricant, etc: *an* ˈ*oil-heater/-lamp/-stove* ○ *Put some oil in the car.* **3** [C] (*infml*) picture painted in oil-colours. **4 oils** [pl] paints made by mixing colouring matter in oil: *paint in oils.* **5** (idm) **burn the midnight oil** ⇨ BURN[2]. **pour oil on the flames** ⇨ POUR. **pour oil on troubled waters** ⇨ POUR. **strike lucky/oil/gold** ⇨ STRIKE[2].

▷ **oil** *v* [Tn] **1** put oil on or into (sth) (eg to make part of a machine run smoothly); lubricate: *oil a lock, one's bicycle, a stiff hinge.* **2** (idm) **oil the** ˈ**wheels** make things go smoothly by behaving tactfully or craftily. **oiled** *adj* = WELL-OILED (WELL[3]). **oiler** *n* **1** device for oiling machinery. **2** = OIL-TANKER. **3** (*US*) = OIL WELL.

□ ˈ**oil-bearing** *adj* (of areas of rock underground) containing mineral oil.

ˈ**oilcake** *n* [U] cattle food made from seeds after the oil has been pressed out.

ˈ**oilcan** *n* can (usu with a long nozzle) containing oil, used for oiling machinery.

ˈ**oilcloth** *n* [U] cotton material treated with oil to make it waterproof and used as a covering for shelves, tables, etc.

ˈ**oil-colour** (also ˈ**oil-paint**) *n* [C, U] = OILS (OIL 4).

ˈ**oil drum** cylindrical metal barrel used for transporting oil.

ˈ**oilfield** *n* area where oil is found in the ground or under the sea: *North Sea oilfields.*

ˌ**oil-**ˈ**fired** *adj* (of a boiler, furnace, etc) burning oil as fuel: ˌ*oil-fired central* ˈ*heating.*

ˈ**oil-painting** *n* **1** [U] art of painting using oil-colours: *She enjoys oil-painting.* **2** [C] picture painted in oil-colours. **3** (idm) **be no** ˈ**oil-painting** (*infml joc*) be a plain or ugly person.

ˈ**oil-palm** *n* tropical palm-tree yielding oil.

oil rig

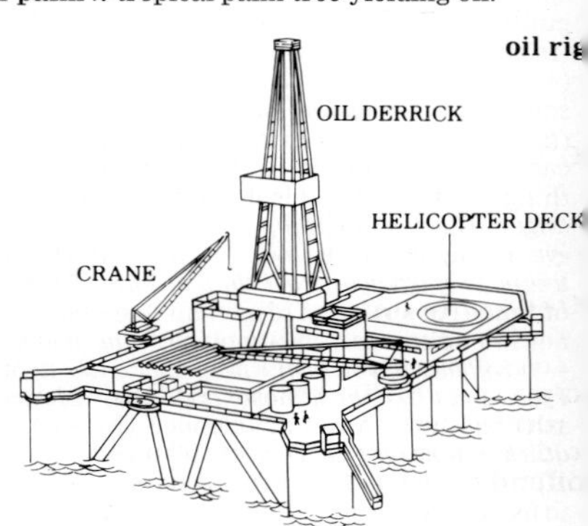

ˈ**oil rig** structure and equipment for drilling for oil (eg in the sea-bed). Cf DERRICK.

ˈ**oilskin** *n* (**a**) [C, U] (coat, etc made of) cloth treated with oil to make it waterproof. (**b**) **oilskins** [pl] suit of clothes made of this material: *Sailors wear oilskins in stormy weather.*

ˈ**oil slick** = SLICK.

ˈ**oil-tanker** *n* large ship with tanks for carrying oil (esp petroleum).

ˈ**oil well** hole drilled into the ground or sea bed to obtain petroleum.

oily /ˈɔɪlɪ/ *adj* (**-ier, -iest**) **1** of or like oil: *an oily liquid.* **2** covered or soaked with oil; containing much oil: *oily fingers* ○ *an oily skin* ○ *an oily old pair of jeans* ○ *oily food.* **3** (*derog*) trying too hard to win favour by flattery; fawning: *I don't like oily shop assistants.* ▷ **oiliness** *n.*

ointment /ˈɔɪntmənt/ *n* [C, U] **1** smooth greasy paste rubbed on the skin to heal injuries or roughness, or as a cosmetic. Cf SALVE 1. **2** (idm) **a/the fly in the ointment** ⇨ FLY[1].

okapi /əʊˈkɑːpɪ/ *n* animal of Central Africa, similar to a giraffe but with a shorter neck and a striped body.

okay (also **OK**) /ˌəʊˈkeɪ/ *adj, adv* (*infml*) all right; satisfactory or satisfactorily: *I hope the children are okay.* ○ *I think I did OK in the exam.* ○ *We'll go to the cinema tomorrow, OK?* ie is that agreed?

▷ **okay** (also **OK**) *interj* (*infml*) all right; yes: *'Will you help me?' 'OK, I will.'* ○ *Okay children, we'll clear up the room now.*

okay (also **OK**) *v* [Tn] (*infml*) agree to (sth); approve of: *He okayed/OK'd my idea.*

okay (also **OK**) *n* (*infml*) agreement; permission: *Have they given you their okay?* ○ *We've got the OK from the council at last.* Cf A-OK (A[1]).

Oil

Until the 1970s, Britain imported most of her oil from Middle Eastern countries. Then in 1969 supplies of oil were discovered in the North Sea, and from the mid 1970s Britain has produced her own crude oil.

By the end of the 1980s, there were 36 North Sea oilfields, and more are planned. One of the most important fields is Brent, off the north-east coast of Scotland. The oil is piped ashore at Sullom Voe, in the Shetland Islands, now one of the country's largest oil terminals. Another large field, further south, is Forties. Oil from there is piped to one terminal in the Orkney Islands and to a second at Cruden Bay, near Aberdeen. Ekofisk, a third and smaller field, lies further south again, with its oil coming ashore at Teesside in north-east England. There are also several land-based oilfields, though their output is not as great as those in the North Sea. The largest, at Wytch Farm in Dorset, produces about 60 per cent of the total from land-based fields. Exploration for oil is carried out in other parts of England, mostly in the south and east Midlands.

Until 1982 Britain's oil industry was run by a state-owned body, the British National Oil Corporation (BNOC). In that year, however, most of its functions were transferred to a private company, Britoil, and two years later a second company, Enterprise Oil, was created from the former state-controlled British Gas Corporation. There are now around 250 other oil companies operating in mainland Britain and the North Sea, British Petroleum (BP) and Shell Transport and Trading being the two largest.

Oil production from most North Sea fields operates from special platforms, called rigs, built to withstand strong winds and heavy seas. There have been several serious accidents in the North Sea, notably in 1980, when the oil rig *Alexander Keilland* overturned with the loss of 123 lives, and in 1988, when the *Piper Alpha* rig exploded, killing 166 men. The latter disaster was the worst in the history of world offshore oil operations, and resulted in loss of production not only from the destroyed rig but from neighbouring rigs as well. The production of oil from the North Sea has also caused considerable pollution in the region, with environmental damage to many coastal areas, especially those of eastern England.

At the beginning of the 1990s, Britain was the eighth largest oil producer in the world. The second largest, after the USSR, was the USA, whose important oil industry dates from the middle of the 19th century, when the first oil well was operated in Pennsylvania. The country's richest oilfields are those in the midwest and south-west of the country, in particular the states of Texas, Oklahoma, Kansas, Louisiana and Arkansas. Until the early 1970s the USA was the world's largest producer of crude oil. Its production has since slowly declined, however, and in 1989 US imports of crude oil exceeded exports for the first time since 1977. At the same time, US oil production, as in Britain and other oil-producing countries, has directly or indirectly resulted in serious environmental damage. The worst oil spillage in American history occured in 1989 when a supertanker ran aground after leaving the port of Valdez, the terminus of the Alaskan pipeline, and millions of tons of crude oil poured out into the sea. The ecological damage done to the Alaskan coastline was considerable.

O'Keeffe /əʊ ˈkiːf/ Georgia (1887-1986), American painter. Her work has had a great influence on modern art. She is best known for her abstract paintings based on enlargements of flower and plant forms.

Oklahoma /ˌəʊkləˈhəʊmə/ south-western state of the USA. It is a major producer of wheat and of oil and gas. ⇨ map at App 1.

okra /ˈəʊkrə/ *n* [U] (tropical plant with) green seed pods eaten as a vegetable.

old /əʊld/ *adj* **(-er, -est)** ⇨ Usage at ELDER[1]. **1** (with a period of time or with *how*) of (a particular) age: *He's forty years old.* ○ *At fifteen years old he left school.* ○ *How old are you?* ○ *A seven-year-old* (ie A child who is seven years of age) *should be able to read.* **2** having lived a long time; advanced in age; no longer young: *Old people cannot be so active as young people.* ○ *He's too old for you to marry.* ○ *What will she do when she is/gets/grows old?* **3 (a)** having been in existence or use for a long time: *old customs, beliefs, habits, etc* ○ *old clothes, cars, houses* ○ *This carpet's getting rather old now.* **(b)** [attrib] belonging to past times; not recent or modern: *old religious practices* ○ *Things were different in the ˈold days.* **4** [attrib] known for a long time; familiar: *an old friend of mine*, ie one I've known for a long time, but not necessarily old in years ○ *We're old rivals*, ie We've been rivals for a long time. **5** former; previous (but not necessarily old in years): *in my old job* ○ *at my old school* ○ *I prefer the chair in its old place.* ○ *We had a larger garden at our old house.* ⇨ Usage. **6** [attrib] (*infml or joc*) (used as a term of affection or intimacy): *Dear old John!* ○ *Good old Angela!* ○ *You're a funny old thing!* **7** [attrib] (*infml*) (used for emphasis): *Any old thing* (ie Anything whatever) *will do.* **8** (*fml*) having much experience or practice: *old in diplomacy* ○ *an old trooper.* **9** (idm) **ˈany old how** (*infml*) carelessly; untidily: *The books were scattered round the room any old how.* **a chip off the old block** ⇨ CHIP[1]. **a dirty old man** ⇨ DIRTY[1]. **for old times' ˈsake** because of tender or sentimental memories of one's past. **the ˈgood/ˈbad old days** an earlier period of time (in one's life or in history) seen as better/worse than the present: *The friends met occasionally to chat about the good old days at school.* **the grand old man** ⇨ GRAND. **have/give sb a high old time** ⇨ HIGH. **money for jam/old rope** ⇨ MONEY. **no fool like an old fool** ⇨ FOOL[1]. **of ˈold** of, in or since former times: *in days of old* ○ *We know him of old*, ie have known him for a long time and so know him well. **(as) old as the ˈhills; (as) old as Meˈthuselah** very old; ancient: *This dress is as old as the hills.* **ˌold beyond one's ˈyears** more mature or wise than is usual or expected for one's age. **old ˈboy, ˈchap, ˈman, etc** (*dated infml*) (used esp by older men of the middle and upper classes as a familiar form of address when talking to another man): *'Excuse me, old man, can I borrow your newspaper?'* **(be) old enough to be sb's ˈfather/ˈmother** (be) significantly older than sb: *You can't marry him! He's old enough to be your father!* **(be) old enough to know ˈbetter** (be) old enough to act in a more sensible way than one did: *Have you been drawing on the walls? I thought you were old enough to know better.* **the old ˈfirm** (*infml*) group of people who know each other well and work well together: *You wash the dishes and I'll dry them up — the old firm's back in business!* **old ˈhat** (*infml derog*) not new or original; old-fashioned: *His ideas are all terribly old hat.* **(have) an ˌold head on young ˈshoulders** (be) a more mature person than is expected for one's age. **an old ˈtrout** (*infml*) bad-tempered or unpleasant old person, esp a woman. **an old ˈwives' tale** old and usu foolish idea or belief. **one of the ˈold school** old-fashioned or conservative person. **pay/settle an old ˈscore** have one's revenge for a wrong done to one in the past. **rake over old ashes** ⇨ RAKE[1]. **ring out the old year and ring in the new** ⇨ RING[2]. **the same old story** ⇨ SAME[1]. **teach an old dog new tricks** ⇨ TEACH. **tough as old boots** ⇨ TOUGH. **young and old** ⇨ YOUNG.

▷ **the old** *n* [pl *v*] old people: *The old feel the cold weather more than the young.*

oldie *n* (*infml*) old person or thing: *This record is a real oldie.*

oldish *adj* rather old.

□ **ˌold ˈage** later part of life; the state of being old: *Old age can bring many problems.* **ˌold-age ˈpension** pension paid by the State to people above a certain age. **ˌold-age ˈpensioner** (*abbr* **OAP**) (also **pensioner, senior citizen**) person who receives such a pension.

the ˌOld ˈBailey famous criminal-law court of London, known officially as the 'Central Criminal Court', where serious cases are tried. Its main building has a dome with a blindfolded figure representing Justice on top, carrying scales and a sword.

ˈold boy (*fem* **ˈold girl**) **1** former pupil of a particular school: *an old boys' reunion.* **2 ˌold ˈboy, ˌold ˈgirl** (*infml*) old person: *the old ˈgirl who lives next door.* **3** (idm) **the old-boy network** the tendency among old boys, esp of British private schools, to help each other in later life.

the ˌOld Conˈtemptibles nickname for the former members of the British army units which went to fight in France at the beginning of the First World War.

the ˈold country one's country of birth (esp when one has left it to live elsewhere).

ˌOld ˈEnglish = ANGLO-SAXON 3.

ˌOld English ˈsheepdog type of large sheepdog with very long thick hair that covers its eyes.

ˌold-esˈtablished *adj* that has been established for a long time: *an ˌold-established traˈdition.*

ˌold-ˈfashioned *adj* (*often derog*) **1** out of date: *ˌold-fashioned ˈclothes, ˈstyles.* **2** believing in old ways, ideas, customs, etc: *My aunt is very old-fashioned.* ○ *She gave me an ˌold-fashioned ˈlook*, ie one expressing disapproval. — *n* (*US*) type of cocktail made with whisky.

old fogey (*US* **old fogy**) /ˌəʊld ˈfəʊgɪ/ person (esp a man) with old-fashioned ideas which he is unwilling to change.

ˌold ˈfolks' home (*infml*) type of hospital in which old people live and are cared for: *His mother is in an old folks' home.*

old girl ⇨ OLD BOY.

ˌOld ˈGlory (*US*) the American flag.

ˌold ˈgold dark yellow colour.

the ˌold ˈguard original or conservative members of a group.

ˌOld ˈHarry (also **ˌOld ˈNick, ˌOld ˈScratch**) (*dated infml joc*) the devil.

ˌold ˈlady (*infml*) one's mother or wife. **the Old Lady of Threadneedle Street** /ðiː ˌəʊld ˌleɪdɪ əv θredˈniːdl striːt/ (*Brit*) nickname for the Bank of England.

ˌold ˈlag (*infml*) person who has been in prison many times.

ˌold ˈmaid 1 [C] (*infml derog*) unmarried woman who is thought to be too old for marriage. **2** [U] children's card-game. **ˌold-ˈmaidish** *adj* (*derog*) fussy; prim.

ˌold ˈman (*infml*) one's father or husband or employer, etc: *How's your old man* (eg your husband) *these days?*

ˌ**old man's ˈbeard** type of wild flowering plant with grey fluffy hairs around the seeds.

ˌ**old ˈmaster** (picture painted by an) important painter of the past (esp the 13th-17th centuries in Europe).

Old Moore's Almanack /ˌəʊld mɔːz ˈɔːlmənæk; *US also* ˈælmənæk/ annual British publication which claims to foretell events of the coming year.

ˌ**old ˈschool** school one attended as a boy or girl.

ˌ**old school ˈtie** (*esp Brit*) **1** tie worn by former pupils of a particular school. **2** (*fig*) symbol of excessive or sentimental loyalty to traditional values, ideas, etc.

ˌ**old ˈstager** (*infml*) person with long experience in a particular activity.

ˈ**old style** (of a date) calculated according to the *Julian calendar (rather than the *Gregorian calendar).

ˌ**old ˈsweat** (*Brit infml*) person (esp a soldier) with many years' experience.

the ˌ**Old ˈTestament** first of the two main divisions of the Bible, telling the history of the Jews and their beliefs. It contains 39 books, most of which were originally written in Hebrew. The first five books (the *Pentateuch) are traditionally said to have been written by *Moses. ⇨ App 5.

ˈ**old-time** *adj* belonging to or typical of former times: *old-time dancing.* **old-ˈtimer** *n* person who has lived in a place or been associated with a club, job, etc for a long time.

ˌ**old ˈwoman** (*infml*) **1** one's wife or mother. **2** (*derog*) fussy or timid man. **old-ˈwomanish** *adj* (*derog*) (esp of a man) fussy or timid.

ˈ**old-world** (also *joc* **olde-worlde**) *adj* belonging to past times; not modern: *a cottage with old-world charm.*

the ˌ**Old ˈWorld** Europe, Asia and Africa. Cf THE NEW WORLD (NEW).

NOTE ON USAGE: Compare **old**, **aged**, **elderly**, **ancient** and **antique. Old** has the widest use and can be applied to people, animals and things. It usually indicates that somebody or something has lived or existed for a long time: *an old woman, dog, church.* It may describe a person who has been known for a long time but is not necessarily old in years: *She's an old friend of ours.* **Old** can also mean 'former' or 'previous': *I was much happier in my old job.* **Aged** is more formal than **old** and is used of very old people who have possibly become physically weak. If one wishes to be polite and respectful, one can describe old people as **elderly. Ancient** and **antique** are usually only applied to things. We call **ancient** something that existed a long time ago: *an ancient civilization* ○ *ancient history, customs, etc.* **Antique** describes an object which has survived from the past and is therefore valuable today: *antique furniture, silver, etc.*

olden /ˈəʊldən/ *adj* [attrib] (*arch*) of a past age: *in olden times/days.*

oldster /ˈəʊldstə(r)/ *n* (*infml joc*) old person.

oleaginous /ˌəʊlɪˈædʒɪnəs/ *adj* (*fml*) like oil or producing oil; oily; fatty: *oleaginous seeds.*

oleander /ˌəʊlɪˈændə(r)/ *n* [C, U] evergreen Mediterranean shrub with red, white or pink flowers and tough leaves.

oleaster /ˌəʊlɪˈæstə(r)/ *n* wild olive tree.

O level /ˈəʊ levl/ (*infml*) = ORDINARY LEVEL (ORDINARY). Cf A LEVEL.

olfactory /ɒlˈfæktərɪ/ *adj* (*fml*) of or concerned with the sense of smell: *the olfactory nerves/organs.*

oligarchy /ˈɒlɪgɑːkɪ/ *n* (*politics*) **1** (**a**) [U] form of government in which a small group of people hold all the power. (**b**) [C] these people as a group. **2** [C] country governed by an oligarchy.
▷ **oligarch** /ˈɒlɪgɑːk/ *n* member of an oligarchy(1).

Oligocene /ˈɒlɪgəʊsiːn, əˈlɪgəsiːn/ *adj* of the period of the earth's history between 38 and 24.6 million years ago, when world temperatures fell and some modern types of animal began to appear. Cf MIOCENE.

olive /ˈɒlɪv/ *n* **1** (**a**) [C] small bitter oval fruit, green when unripe and black when ripe, used for food and for oil: *stuffed olives* ○ *put olives in a salad.* (**b**) (also ˈ**olive-tree**) [C] evergreen tree on which this fruit grows: *a grove of olives.* **2** (also **olive-green**) [U] yellowish-green colour of an unripe olive.
▷ **olive** *adj* **1** yellowish-green: *olive paint.* **2** (of the complexion) yellowish-brown: *an olive skin.*
□ ˈ**olive-branch** *n* **1** emblem of peace. **2** (*fig*) thing said or done to show that one wishes to make peace with sb: *After years of quarrelling we at last sent our cousins a Christmas card as an olive-branch.*
ˌ**olive ˈoil** oil extracted from olives.

Olivier /əˈlɪvɪeɪ/ Laurence Kerr, Baron Olivier (1907-89), English actor. After early success in films (eg *Wuthering Heights*), he established his stage reputation mainly in Shakespeare, and came to be regarded as the greatest English actor of his generation. He performed many Shakespearean roles in films (eg *Henry V, Hamlet, Richard III* and *Othello*, the first three also directed by him). From 1963 to 1973 he was director of the National Theatre.

Olympiad /əˈlɪmpɪæd/ *n* **1** celebration of the modern Olympic Games: *The 21st Olympiad took place in Montreal.* **2** period of four years between celebrations of the Olympic Games.

Olympian /əˈlɪmpɪən/ *adj* (*fml*) (of manners, etc) majestic; superior; god-like: *Even when those around her panic she always maintains an Olympian calm.*

Olympic /əˈlɪmpɪk/ *adj* [attrib] of or connected with the Olympic Games: *an Olympic athlete* ○ *She has broken the Olympic 5 000 metres record.*
□ **the O**ˌ**lympic ˈGames 1** the sports contests held at Olympia in Greece in ancient times. **2** (also **the Olympics**) the international athletic competitions held in modern times every four years in a different country.

OM /ˌəʊ ˈem/ *abbr* (*Brit*) (member of the) Order of Merit: *be awarded the OM* ○ *John Field OM.*

Oman /əʊˈmɑːn/ country at the south-eastern tip of the Arabian peninsula, bordering Saudi Arabia; pop approx 1 378 000; official language Arabic; capital Muscat; unit of currency rial (= 1 000 baiza). Formerly a British protectorate, it has been independent since 1951, ruled by a sultan. It is a major producer of oil. ⇨ map at ARABIAN PENINSULA.
▷ **Omani** /əʊˈmɑːnɪ/ *n, adj* (native or inhabitant) of Oman.

ombudsman /ˈɒmbʊdzmən, *also* -mæn/ *n* (*pl* **ombudsmen** /-mən/) official appointed by a government to investigate and report on complaints made by citizens against public authorities.

omega /ˈəʊmɪgə; *US* əʊˈmegə/ *n* **1** the last letter of the Greek alphabet (Ω, ω). **2** (idm) **Alpha and Omega** ⇨ ALPHA.

omelette (also **omelet**) /ˈɒmlɪt/ *n* **1** eggs beaten together and fried, often with cheese, herbs, vegetables, etc or with a sweet filling: *a cheese and mushroom omelette.* **2** (idm) (**one can't**) **make an omelette without breaking eggs** (*saying*) (one can't) achieve a desired aim without some loss or damage.

omen /ˈəʊmen/ *n* [C, U] ~ (**of sth**) (event regarded as a) sign that sth good or bad will happen in the future: *a good/bad omen* ○ *an omen of victory* ○ *a bird of ill omen.*

ominous /ˈɒmɪnəs/ *adj* suggesting that sth bad is about to happen; threatening: *an ominous silence* ○ *Those black clouds are/look a bit ominous.* ▷ **ominously** *adv.*

omission /əˈmɪʃn/ *n* **1** [U] action of omitting or leaving out sb/sth: *The play was shortened by the omission of two scenes.* ○ *His omission from the team is rather surprising.* ○ (*fml*) *sins of omission*, ie not doing things that should be done. **2** [C] thing that is omitted: *This list of names has a few omissions.*

omit /əˈmɪt/ *v* (**-tt-**) **1** [Tt, Tg] fail or neglect to do sth; leave sth not done: *omit to do/doing a piece of work.* **2** [Tn] not include (sth); leave out: *This chapter may be omitted.*

omni- *comb form* all or everywhere: *omnipotence* ○ *omniscience* ○ *omnivorous.*

omnibus /ˈɒmnɪbəs/ *n* (*pl* ~**es**) **1** (*dated fml*) (esp in names) bus. **2** large book containing a number of books or stories, eg by the same author: *an omnibus volume/edition* ○ *a George Orwell omnibus.* **3** (idm) **the man on the Clapham omnibus** ⇨ MAN[1].

omnipotent /ɒmˈnɪpətənt/ *adj* (*fml*) having unlimited or very great power: *the omnipotent officials, bureaucrats, state police, etc.* ▷ **omnipotence** /-təns/ *n* [U]: *the omnipotence of God.*

omnipresent /ˌɒmnɪˈpreznt/ *adj* (*fml*) present everywhere: *the omnipresent squalor, dread.*

omniscient /ɒmˈnɪsɪənt/ *adj* (*fml*) knowing everything: *Christians believe that God is omniscient.* ▷ **omniscience** /-sɪəns/ *n* [U].

omnivorous /ɒmˈnɪvərəs/ *adj* (*fml*) **1** (of animals) eating both plants and animal flesh: *the omnivorous domestic pig.* **2** (*fig*) reading all types of books, etc; watching all types of TV programmes, etc: *an omnivorous reader.*

on[1] /ɒn/ *adv part* (For special uses with many *vs*, eg *hang on, go on, take sth on*, see the *v* entries.) **1** (indicating continued activity, progress or state): *She talked on for two hours without stopping.* ○ *He can work on without a break.* ○ *If you like a good story, read on.* ○ *They wanted the band to play on.* ○ *The war still went on*, ie didn't end. ○ *He slept on through all the noise.* **2** (indicating movement forward or progress in space or time): *run, walk, hurry, etc on to the bus-stop* ○ *Please send my letter on to my new address.* ○ *from that day on*, ie from then until now ○ *On with the show* (ie Let it begin/continue)*!* **3** (**a**) (of clothes) in position on sb's body; being worn: *Put your coat on.* ○ *Why hasn't she got her glasses on?* ○ *Your hat's not on straight.* (**b**) in the correct position above or forming part of sth: *Make sure the lid is on.* ○ *Leave it with the cover on.* ○ *The skirt is finished — I'm now going to sew a pocket on.* Cf OFF[2] 2. **4** (**a**) (esp of electrical apparatus, etc or power supplies) in action or use; being operated: *The lights were all on.* ○ *The TV is always on in their house.* ○ *Someone has left the tap on*, ie The water is running. ○ *I can smell gas — is the oven on?* ○ *leave the handbrake on.* (**b**) available or connected: *We were without electricity for three hours but it's on again now.* ○ *Is the water on?* Cf OFF[2] 5. **5** (of a performance, play, etc) in progress: *The film was already on when we arrived.* ○ *The strike has been on now for six weeks.* **6** planned to take place in the future: *Is the match on at 2 pm or 3 pm?* ○ *The postal strike is still on*, ie has not been cancelled. Cf OFF[2] 4. **7** (of programmes, films, entertainments, etc) that can be seen; showing; being performed: *Look in the TV guide to see what's on.* ○ *What's on at the cinema tonight?* ○ *There's a good play on at the local theatre.* ○ *What time is the news on?* **8** arranged to take place; happening: *Have we got anything* (ie any engagements, plans, etc) *on for this evening?* **9** (**a**) (of a performer) on the stage; performing: *I'm on in five minutes.* ○ *What time is the group on?* Cf OFF[2] 8. (**b**) (of a worker) on duty; working: *The night nurse is/goes on at 7pm.* Cf OFF[2] 6. **10** in or into a vehicle; inside: *The coach-driver waited until everybody was on.* ○ *Four people got on.* **11** with the specified part in front or at the point of contact: *enter the harbour broadside on* ○ *crash head on with a car* ○ *place it end on with the others.* **12** (idm) **be** ˈ**on** (*infml*) be practical, right or acceptable: *That just isn't on.* ○ *You're on/not on!* ie I accept/don't accept the proposition, bet, etc. **be on** (**for sth**) (*infml*) take part (in sth): *Are you on for this game?* **be/go/keep on about sth** (*infml derog*) talk in a boring, tedious or complaining way about sth: *What's he on about now?* **be/go/keep on at sb** (**to do sth**) (*infml derog*) nag or pester sb (to do sth): *He was on at me again to lend him money.* Cf BE ONTO SB (ONTO). **later on** ⇨ LATE[2]. **on and off** ⇨ OFF[2]. ˌ**on and ˈon** without stopping; continuously: *He kept moaning on and on.*
□ **on to** *prep* = ONTO.

on[2] /ɒn/ *prep* (For special uses in many idioms, eg *have pity on sb*, and phrasal verbs, eg *pin sth on sb*, see the *n* and *v* entries.) **1** (also **upon**) **(a)** (in or into a position) covering, touching or forming part of (a surface): *a picture on the wall* ○ *a drawing on the blackboard* ○ *dirty marks on the ceiling* ○ *Leave the glasses on the table.* ○ *sit on the grass* ○ *leaves floating on the water* ○ *the diagram on Page 5* (Cf *in the next chapter, paragraph*) ○ *stick a stamp on an envelope* ○ *a carpet on the floor* ○ *hit sb on the head* ○ *travel on the continent* (Cf *a country in Europe*). **(b)** supported by or attached to (sb/sth): *a roof on a house* ○ *stand on one foot* ○ *a spot on one's chin* ○ *a blister on one's foot* ○ *a ring on one's finger* ○ *lean on me/my arm* ○ *a flag on a pole* ○ *a coat on a hook* ○ *hanging on a string* ○ *a hat on one's head* ○ *sit on a chair* ○ (*fig*) *have sth on one's mind.* **2** in or into (a large public vehicle): *on the plane from London to New York* ○ *have lunch on the train* ○ *travel on the bus, the tube, the coach, etc* (Cf *travel by bus, etc; sitting in the bus, etc*). **3** (used esp with *pers prons*) being carried by (sb); in the possession of: *Have you got any money on you?* ○ *The burglar was caught with the stolen goods still on him.* **4 (a)** (indicating a time when sth happens; in US English often with *on* omitted): *on Sunday(s)* ○ *on May the first* ○ *on the evening of May the first* (Cf *in the evening*) ○ *on this occasion* ○ *on a sunny day in August* ○ *on your birthday, New Year's day, Christmas day, etc.* Cf IN[2] 3, AT 2. ⇨ Usage at TIME[1]. **(b)** (also **upon**) at or immediately after the time or occasion of: *On my arrival home/On arriving home I discovered the burglary.* ○ *On (my) asking for information I was told I must wait.* ○ *on the death of his parents* ○ *on the unexpected news of his accident.* **5** about; concerning: *speak, write, lecture, etc on Shakespeare* ○ *a lesson on philosophy* ○ *an essay on political economy* ○ *a programme on twentieth-century musicians.* ⇨ Usage at ABOUT[3]. **6** (indicating membership of a group or an organization): *on the committee, staff, jury, panel* ○ *Which/Whose side are you on?* ie Which of two or more opposing views do you support? **7** regularly consuming (sth): *Most cars run on petrol.* ○ *The doctor put me on these tablets.* ○ *live on bread and water* ○ *on* (ie addicted to) *heroin.* **8** (indicating direction) towards: *marching on the capital* ○ *turn one's back on sb* ○ *pull/draw a knife on sb,* ie to attack him ○ *creep up on sb* ○ *On the left you can see the palace.* **9** (also **upon**) near; close to (a place or time): *a town on the coast* ○ *a house on the main road* ○ *a village on the border* ○ *Just on* (ie Almost exactly) *a year ago I moved to London.* ○ *boats moored on both sides of the river* ○ *hedges on either side of the road.* **10** (also **upon**) (indicating a basis, ground or reason for sth) as a result of; because of: *a story based on fact* ○ *have sth on good authority* ○ *On your advice I applied for the job.* ○ *arrested on a charge of theft* ○ *You have it on my word,* ie I promise you it will happen, etc. **11** supported financially by (sb/sth): *live on a pension, one's savings, a student grant, etc* ○ *be on a low wage* ○ *feed a family on £20 a week* ○ *an operation on the National Health Service* ○ (*infml*) *Drinks are on me,* ie I will pay for them. **12** by means of (sth); using: *play a tune on the recorder* ○ *broadcast on the TV/radio* ○ *speak on the telephone.* **13** (also **upon**) (indicating an increase, esp of cost): *a tax on tobacco* ○ *charge interest on the loan* ○ *a strain on our resources.* **14** (indicating an activity, a purpose or a state): *on business/holiday* ○ *go on an errand* ○ *on loan for a week* ○ *on special offer.* **15** in addition to (sth); following: *suffer disaster on disaster* ○ *receive insult on insult.*

onager /ˈɒnəgə(r)/ *n* wild donkey of central Asia.

once /wʌns/ *adv* **1** on one occasion only; (for) one time: *I've only been there once.* ○ *He cleans the car once a week, a fortnight, etc.* ie every week, every fortnight, etc ○ *She goes to see her parents in Wales once every six months.* **2 (a)** at some (indefinite) time in the past: *I once met your mother.* ○ *He once lived in Zambia.* **(b)** formerly: *This book was once famous, but nobody reads it today.* **3** (in negative sentences or questions) ever; at all; even for one time: *He never once offered/He didn't once offer to help.* ○ *Did she once show any sympathy?* **4** (idm) **ˌall at ˈonce** suddenly: *All at once the door opened.* ○ *All at once she lost her temper.* **at ˈonce (a)** immediately; without delay: *Come here at once!* ○ *I'm leaving for Rome almost at once.* **(b)** at the same time: *Don't all speak at once!* ○ *I can't do two things at once.* ○ *The film is at once humorous and moving.* **(just) for ˈonce; just this ˈonce** on this occasion only, as an exception: *Just for once he arrived on time.* ○ *Be pleasant to each other — just this once.* **get/give sb/sth the ˈonce-over** (*infml*) get/give sb/sth a quick inspection or examination: *Before buying the car he gave it the once-over.* ○ *She felt his parents were giving her the once-over.* **once ˈagain; once ˈmore** one more time as before: *I'll tell you how to do it once again.* ○ *Amanda is home from college once again.* **ˌonce and for ˈall** now and for the last (and only) time: *I'm warning you once and for all.* ○ *He's travelled a lot but he's now come back to Britain once and for all.* **ˌonce ˈbitten, ˌtwice ˈshy** (*saying*) after an unpleasant experience one is careful to avoid sth similar: *She certainly won't marry again — once bitten, twice shy.* **ˌonce in a blue ˈmoon** (*infml*) very rarely or never: *I see her once in a blue moon.* **(every) ˌonce in a ˈwhile** occasionally: *Once in a while we go to a restaurant — but usually we eat at home.* **once ˈmore (a)** one more time; again: *Let's sing it once more.* **(b)** = ONCE AGAIN. **ˌonce or ˈtwice** a few times: *I don't know the place well, I've only been there once or twice.* **ˌonce too ˈoften** once more than is sensible or safe: *He had driven home drunk once too often — this time he got stopped by the police.* **ˌonce upon a ˈtime** (used as the beginning of a fairy-tale) at some indefinite time in the past: *Once upon a time there was a beautiful princess....* **you're only young once** ⇨ ONLY[2].

▷ **once** *conj* as soon as; when: *Once you understand this rule, you'll have no further difficulty.* ○ *How would we cope once the money had gone?*

the once *n* [sing] (*infml*) the one time; on one occasion: *She's only done it the once so don't be too angry.*

oncoming /ˈɒnkʌmɪŋ/ *adj* [attrib] advancing; approaching: *oncoming traffic.*

▷ **oncoming** *n* [U] (*fml*) approach: *the oncoming of winter.*

one[1] /wʌn/ *pron, det* **1** 1; one less than two; a single: *I've got two brothers and one sister.* ○ *There's only one piece of cake left.* ○ *Book One, Chapter One,* ie the first chapter of the first book ○ *One of my friends lives in Brighton.* ○ *One of the girls brought her sister.* **2 (a)** (esp of periods of time) a particular but unspecified: *one day/morning/afternoon/evening/night last week* ○ *One day* (ie At an indefinite time in the future) *you'll be glad she left you.* ○ *One morning in June....* **(b)** (used for emphasis and always stressed) a particular (person or thing): *The ˈone way to succeed is to work hard and live a healthy life.* ○ *No ˈone of you could lift that piano,* ie Two or more of you would be needed. **3** (*usu fml*) (used with somebody's name to show that the speaker does not know the person) a certain(5): *One Tim Smith* (Cf *A Mr Smith*) *called to see you but you were out.* ○ *The author of the anonymous article turned out to be one Stanley Carter.* **4** (used with *the other, another* or *other(s)* to show a contrast): *The two girls are so alike that strangers find it difficult to tell (the) one from the other.* ○ *I see you add the egg before the milk. That's ˈone way of doing it,* ie suggesting there are other and possibly better ways. ○ *I'm sorry I can't help you. For one thing* (ie As a first reason) *I'm in a hurry, and for another I have a bad back.* **5** the same: *They all went off in one direction.* ○ *After the union meeting the workers were all of one mind,* ie all had the same opinion. **6** (*infml esp US*) (used instead of *a* or *an* to emphasize the *n* or phrase that follows it): *That's one handsome guy.* ○ *It was one hell of a match,* ie a very good and exciting match. **7** (idm) **be all one to sb** ⇨ ALL[3]. **be at ˈone (with sb/sth)** be in agreement (with sb/sth): *I'm at one with you/We are at one on this subject,* ie Our opinions are the same. **get one over sb/sth** (*infml*) gain an advantage over sb/sth: *They got one over us in the end by deciding to speak in German.* **get sth in ˈone** (*infml*) immediately be able to give an explanation, solve a problem, etc: *'We have to attract younger customers.' 'Exactly, you've got it in one!'* **I, you, etc/sb for ˈone** certainly I, you, etc/sb: *I for one have no doubt that he's lying.* ○ *Lots of people would like to come — your mother for one.* **(ˌall) in ˈone** combined: *He's President, Treasurer and Secretary in one.* ○ [attrib] *the ˌall-in-one first-ˈaid kit for everyday use.* **ˌone after ˈanother/the ˈother** first one person or thing, and then another, and then another up to any number or amount. **ˌone and ˈall** (*dated infml*) everyone: *A Happy New Year to one and all!* **ˌone and ˈonly** (used for emphasis) only; sole: *You have always been my one and only true love.* ○ *Here he is — the one and only Frank Sinatra!* **ˌone and the ˈsame** (used for emphasis) the same: *One and the same idea occurred to each of them.* **ˌone by ˈone** individually in order: *go through the items on a list one by one.* **ˌone or ˈtwo** a few: *One or two people can't come.* **one ˈup (on/over sb)** having an advantage over sb; one step ahead of sb: *Your experience as a sales assistant puts you one up on the other candidates.*

▷ **one** *n* **1** the number 1. **2** (idm) **number one** ⇨ NUMBER.

one- (in compounds) having one of the thing specified: *a one-act play* ○ *a one-piece swimsuit* ○ *a one-parent family.*

For the uses of *one* see the examples at *five.*

□ **ˌone-armed ˈbandit** = FRUIT MACHINE (FRUIT).

ˌone-ˈhorse *adj* [attrib] **1** using a single horse: *a ˌone-horse ˈcart.* **2** (*fig joc*) badly equipped; small and uninteresting: *a ˌone-horse ˈtown,* ie a quiet town without much business, entertainment, etc.

ˌone-ˈliner *n* (*infml*) short joke or remark in a play, comedy programme, etc: *deliver some good one-liners.*

ˌone-man ˈband musician, usu in the street, playing two or three instruments at the same time: (*fig*) *I run the business as a one-man band — just me and no one else.*

ˌone-man ˈshow **1** public performance by one person of dramatic or musical items normally requiring more performers. **2** person doing by himself things that are usually done by several people.

ˌone-night ˈstand **1** single performance in one place of a play, concert, etc as part of a tour of different places. **2** (*infml*) (person involved in a) (usu) sexual relationship that lasts for a very short time, usu a single night: *I was hoping for a lasting affair, not just a one-night stand.*

ˌone-ˈoff *n, adj* (thing) made or happening only once: *Her novel was just a one-off — she never wrote anything as good as that again.*

ˌone ˈp (also **1p**) (*Brit*) (coin worth) one new penny: [attrib] *Two one p stamps, please.*

ˌone-ˈsided *adj* **1** (esp of ideas, opinions, etc) unfair; prejudiced: *a ˌone-sided ˈargument* ○ *His attitude towards the unemployed is very one-sided.* **2** (esp in sport, etc) with opposing players of unequal abilities: *It was a very one-sided game: our team won easily.* **ˌone-ˈsidedly** *adv.* **ˌone-ˈsidedness** *n* [U].

ˈone-time *adj* [attrib] former: *a ˌone-time poliˈtician.*

ˌone-to-ˈone *adj, adv* with one member of one group corresponding to one of another: *a ˌone-to-one ˈratio between teachers and pupils* ○ *teaching one-to-one.*

ˌone-track ˈmind mind that can think only of a single subject, interest, etc: *He's got a one-track mind — all he ever thinks about is sex!*

ˌone-ˈupmanship *n* [U] (*infml*) art of getting (and keeping) the advantage over other people.

ˌone-ˈway *adv, adj* [attrib] (allowing movement) in one direction only: *I'll go by boat one way.* ○ *ˌone-way ˈtraffic* ○ *a ˌone-way ˈstreet* ○ *a ˌone-way* (ie not a return) *ˈticket.*

one[2] /wʌn/ *indef pron* **1** (used as the object of a *v* or *prep* to avoid *a* and the repetition of a *n*): *I forgot to bring a pen. Can you lend me one?* (Cf *I can't find the pen I was given. Have you seen it?*) ○ *I haven't got any stamps. Could you give me one?* ○ *There have* *been a lot of accidents in the fog. I read about one this morning.* **2** ~ **of** (used with a *pl n* preceded by a *det*, eg *the, my, your, these,* etc to indicate a member of a class or group): *Mr Smith is not one of my customers.* ○ *She's knitting a jumper for one of her grandchildren.* ○ *He's staying with one of his friends* (Cf *a friend of his*). ○ *We think of you as one* (ie a member) *of the family.*

▷ **one** *n* (never taking main stress) **1** (used after *this, that, which* or as a 'prop-word' after an *adj* which cannot stand alone): *I prefer ˈthat one.* ○ *Which ones have you ˈread?* ○ *Your plan is a ˈgood one.* ○ *I need a ˈbigger one.* ○ *Those shoes are too small. We must buy some ˈnew ones.* ○ *The chance was too good a one to ˈmiss.* ○ *Her new car goes faster than her ˈold one.* **2** (used with a group of words that identify the person(s) or thing(s) being considered): *Our hotel is the one nearest the beach.* ○ *The boy who threw the stone is the one with curly hair.* ○ *Students who do well in examinations are the ones who ask questions in class.* **3** (idm) **a one** (*infml esp Brit*) (used to show amused surprise at sb's behaviour): *You asked your teacher how old she was? You are a one!* ○ *He is a one, your son. Never out of trouble!* **the one about sb/sth** the joke about sb/sth: *Do you know/Have you heard the one about the bald policeman?*

NOTE ON USAGE: In formal speech or writing the use of the nouns **one/ones** in senses 1 and 2 is avoided in the following cases: **1** After possessive (eg *your, Mary's*), unless it is followed by an adjective: *This is my car and that's my husband's.* ○ (with adjective) *My cheap camera takes better pictures than his expensive one.* **2** When two adjectives indicate a contrast: *compare British and/with American universities* (*compare British universities with American ones* is less formal). **3** After *these* and *those*: *Do you prefer these designs or those* (more formal than *those ones*)? **One/Ones** may be used after *which*, even in formal speech, to distinguish singular from plural: *Here are the designs. Which one(s) do you prefer?* ie You can choose one or several of them.

one[3] /wʌn/ *n* (used, esp *pl*, after an *adj*, to refer to a person or people not previously specified): *It's time the ˈlittle ones were in ˌbed.* ○ *pray to the ˌHoly One* (ie God) *for forˈgiveness.*

▷ **one** *pron* (*fml*) **1** someone: *He worked like one possessed*, ie someone possessed by a spirit. ○ *She was never one to gossip*, ie who would gossip. ○ *He's not one who is easily frightened.* ○ *John is one who must certainly be invited.* **2** (idm) **(be) one for (doing) sth** (be) a person who is good at, spends a lot of time on or enjoys doing sth: *She's a great one for (solving) puzzles.*

□ **ˌone ˈanother** each of two or more reciprocally; each other: *We help one another with the extra work in the summer.* ○ *listening to one another's records.*

one[4] /wʌn/ *pers pron* (*fml*) (used as the subject or object of a *v*, or after a *prep* to refer to people generally, including the speaker or writer): *In these circumstances one prefers to be alone.* ○ *A little delay will give one time to prepare.* ○ *One must be sure of one's facts before making a public accusation.* ○ (*US*) *One does not like to have his word doubted.*

O'Neill /əʊˈniːl/ Eugene Gladstone (1888-1953), American playwright whose powerful naturalistic dramas explore conflicting relationships. His best-known plays include *Mourning Becomes Electra, The Iceman Cometh* and the semi-autobiographical *Long Day's Journey into Night.* He was awarded the Nobel prize for literature in 1936.

oneness /ˈwʌnnɪs/ *n* [U] **1** condition of being one; singleness. **2** ~ **(with sb/sth)** condition of being united with or the same as sb/sth: *Alone in the woods, she felt a oneness with nature.*

onerous /ˈɒnərəs/ *adj* (*fml*) needing effort; burdensome: *onerous duties* ○ *This is the most onerous task I have ever undertaken.*

oneself /wʌnˈself/ *reflex, emph pron* (only taking the main stress in sentences when used emphatically) **1** (*reflex*) (used when people in general cause and are also affected by an action): *one's ability to wash and ˈdress oneself.* **2** (*emph*) (used to emphasize *one*): *One could easily arrange it all oneˈself.* **3** (idm) **(all) by oneˈself** **(a)** alone. **(b)** without help.

ongoing /ˈɒŋgəʊɪŋ/ *adj* [esp attrib] continuing to exist or progress: *an ongoing debate* ○ *an ongoing programme of research.*

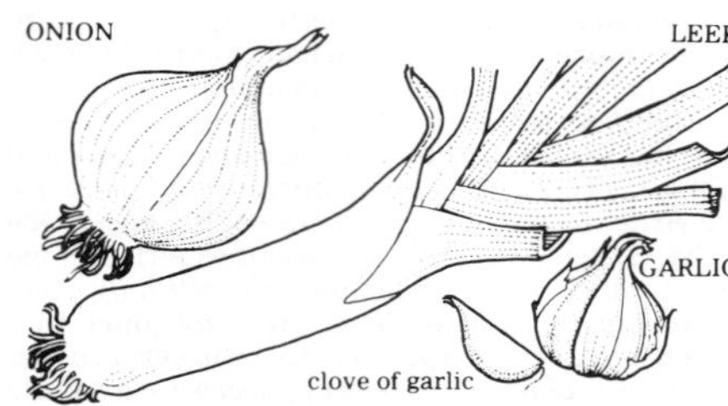

onion /ˈʌnɪən/ *n* **1** **(a)** [C] type of vegetable plant with a round bulb that has a strong smell and flavour, used in cooking: *Spanish onions* ○ *a crop of onions* ○ *spring onions.* **(b)** [C, U] this plant as food: *chop onions to make a sauce* ○ *too much onion in the salad* ○ [attrib] *French onion soup.* **2** (idm) **know one's onions/stuff** ⇨ KNOW.

on-line /ˌɒnˈlaɪn/ *adj* (*computing*) (of a device) connected to and controlled by a computer: *an ˌon-line ˈticket booking system* ○ *We've been on-line* (ie have had on-line equipment) *for about a year now.*

onlooker /ˈɒnlʊkə(r)/ *n* person who watches sth happening (without taking part); spectator: *By the time the ambulance had arrived, a crowd of onlookers had gathered.*

only[1] /ˈəʊnlɪ/ *adj* [attrib] **1** with no other(s) of the same group, style, etc existing or present; sole: *She was the only person able to do it.* ○ *His only answer was a grunt.* ○ *This is the only painting in this style that we have.* ○ *We were the only people there.* **2** (*infml*) most worth considering; best: *She's the only woman for the job.* ○ *She says Italy is the only place to go for a holiday.* **3** (idm) **one and only** ⇨ ONE[1]. **an only ˈchild** child having no brothers or sisters: *My mother was an only child.* ○ *Only children are sometimes spoilt.*

only[2] /ˈəʊnlɪ/ *adv* **1** (modifies a word or phrase and is placed close to it in written or formal spoken style; in informal speech, stress may show which word, etc is modified, so that *only* may have various positions) and no one or nothing else; solely: *I only saw ˈMary*, ie I saw Mary and no one else. ○ (*fml*) *I saw only Mary.* ○ *I only ˈsaw Mary*, ie I saw her but I didn't speak to her. ○ *Only ˈmembers may use the bar.* ○ *Only ˈfive people were hurt in the accident; the rest were uninjured.* ○ *He only lives just round the ˈcorner.* ○ *We only waited a few ˈminutes but it seemed like hours.* ○ *Women only*, eg on a sign or poster. ○ *We can only guess* (ie We cannot be certain about) *what happened.* **2** (idm) **for X's eyes only** ⇨ EYE[1]. **if only** ⇨ IF. **not only ... but also** both ... and: *He not only read the book, but also remembered what he read.* **only have eyes for sb/have eyes only for sb** ⇨ EYE. **only ˈjust** **(a)** not long ago/before: *We've only just arrived.* ○ *I've only just moved to London.* **(b)** almost not; scarcely: *He only just caught the train.* ○ *I've enough milk for the coffee — but only just.* **only to do sth** (used to indicate sth that happens immediately afterwards, esp sth that causes surprise, disappointment, relief, etc): *I arrived at the shop only to find I'd left all my money at home.* **only too** (with an *adj* or *pp*) very: *I shall be only too pleased to get home.* ○ *That's only too true, I'm afraid*, ie really true, and not untrue as the speaker might have hoped or wanted. **you're only young ˈonce** (*saying*) let young people have what enjoyment and freedom they can get, because they will have to work and worry later in their lives: *Enjoy the disco — you're only young once.*

only[3] /ˈəʊnlɪ/ *conj* (*infml*) **(a)** except that; but: *I'd love to come, only I have to work.* ○ *This book's very good, only it's rather expensive.* ○ *He's always making promises, only he never keeps them.* **(b)** were it not for the fact that: *He would probably do well in the examination only he gets very nervous.*

ono /ˌəʊ en ˈəʊ/ *abbr* (*Brit*) (esp in classified advertisements) or near offer: *lady's bike £25 ono*, ie the seller might accept £20.

onomatopoeia /ˌɒnəˌmætəˈpɪə/ *n* [U] combination of sounds in a word that imitates or suggests what the word refers to eg *hiss, cuckoo, thud.* ▷ **onomatopoeic** /-ˈpiːɪk/ *adj*: *'Sizzle' and 'hush' are onomatopoeic words.*

onrush /ˈɒnrʌʃ/ *n* [sing] (*fml*) strong forward rush or flow: *an onrush of water* ○ *the onrush of powerful feelings.*

onset /ˈɒnset/ *n* [sing] vigorous beginning (esp of sth unpleasant): *the onset of winter* ○ *the onset of glandular fever.*

onshore /ˈɒnʃɔː(r)/ *adj* [usu attrib], *adv* **(a)** (of wind) blowing from the sea towards the land: *an onshore breeze.* **(b)** on or near the shore: *an onshore development.*

onside /ˌɒnˈsaɪd/ *adj* [usu pred], *adv* (*sport*) (of a player in football, hockey, etc) in a position where the ball may legally be played (ie behind the ball or with the necessary number of opponents between the player and the goal): *He was definitely onside when he scored that goal.* ○ *The referee declared him onside.* Cf OFFSIDE[1].

onslaught /ˈɒnslɔːt/ *n* ~ **(on sb/sth)** fierce attack: *They survived an onslaught by tribesmen.* ○ (*fig*) *an onslaught on government housing policies.*

on-stage /ˌɒnˈsteɪdʒ/ *adj, adv* on the stage, visible to the audience: *three actors on-stage* ○ *She walked slowly on-stage.*

Ontario /ɒnˈteərɪəʊ/ province of south-east Canada, between *Quebec and *Manitoba. It is Canada's richest and most heavily populated province, and has many important industries. Lake Ontario, the smallest and most easterly of the *Great Lakes, lies between the province and New York State. ⇨ map at App 1.

onto (also **on to**) /ˈɒntə, before vowels and finally ˈɒntuː/ *prep* **1** moving to a position on (a surface): *move the books onto the second shelf* ○ *step out of the train onto the platform* ○ *Water was dripping onto the floor.* ○ *The crowd ran onto the pitch.* ○ *The child climbed up onto his father's shoulders.* Cf OFF[3] 1. **2** (phr v) **be onto sb** **(a)** (*infml*) pursue sb in order to find out about his illegal activities: *The police are onto him about the stolen paintings.* **(b)** be talking to sb in order to inform him of sth or persuade him to do sth: *Have you been onto the solicitor yet?* ○ *My mother's been onto me for ages about the mess in my room.* Cf GET ONTO SB (GET). **be onto sth** have some information or evidence that could lead to an important discovery: *When did you realize you were onto something really big?*

ontology /ɒnˈtɒlədʒɪ/ *n* [U] (*philosophy*) branch of metaphysics that deals with the nature of existence. ▷ **ontological** /ˌɒntəˈlɒdʒɪkl/ *adj*: *ontological speculation.*

onus /ˈəʊnəs/ *n* **the onus** [sing] (*fml*) duty or responsibility (for doing sth); burden: *the onus of bringing up five children* ○ *The onus of proof rests/lies with you*, ie You must prove what you say.

onward /ˈɒnwəd/ *adj* [attrib] (*esp fml*) directed or moving forward: *an onward march, movement, etc* ○ *the onward march of time.* ▷ **onward** (also **onwards** /ˈɒnwədz/) *adv*: *The shop is open from lunchtime onwards.* ○ *move steadily onwards.* ⇨ Usage at FORWARD[2].

onyx /ˈɒnɪks/ *n* [U] stone like marble that has different coloured layers in it, used for ornaments, etc: [attrib] *an onyx paperweight.*

oodles /ˈuːdlz/ *n* [pl] ~ **(of sth)** (*infml*) great amounts (of sth); lots (of sth): *oodles of hot water* ○ *oodles of money.*

oomph /ʊmf/ *n* (*infml*) energy; enthusiasm; sex-appeal: *Marilyn Monroe had lots of oomph.*

oops /ʊps/ *interj* (*infml*) = WHOOPS.

□ **ˈoops-a-daisy** *interj* (*infml*) = UPSIDAISY.

ooze /uːz/ *v* **1** [Ipr, Ip] ~ **from/out of sth**; ~ **out/**

away (of thick liquids) come or flow out slowly: *All the toothpaste had oozed out.* ○ *Black oil was oozing out of the engine.* ○ *Blood was still oozing from the wound.* ○ (*fig*) *Their courage was oozing away.* **2** [Ipr, Tn] ~ **(with sth)** allow (sth) to come out in this way: *toast oozing with butter* ○ *The wound was oozing pus.* ○ (*fig*) *She was simply oozing (with) charm.* ○ *They oozed confidence*, ie showed it freely. ⇨ Usage at DRIP[1].

▷ **ooze** /uːz/ *n* **1** [U] soft liquid mud, esp at the bottom of a river, lake, pond, etc. **2** [sing] (*fml*) slow flow: *the ooze of pus from a wound.*

op /ɒp/ *n* (*infml*) = OPERATION 3.

op (also **Op**) *abbr* opus: *Beethoven's Piano Sonata No 30 in E major, Op 109.*

opacity /əʊˈpæsətɪ/ (also **opaqueness**) *n* [U] quality of being opaque: *the opacity of frosted glass.*

opal /ˈəʊpl/ *n* bluish-white or milky-white semi-precious stone, often used in jewellery, in which changes of colour are seen: *a bracelet made of opals* ○ [attrib] *an opal ring.*

▷ **opalescent** /ˌəʊpəˈlesnt/ *adj* (*fml*) changing colour like an opal; iridescent: *an opalescent silky material.*

opaque /əʊˈpeɪk/ *adj* **1** not allowing light to pass through; not transparent: *opaque glass* ○ *an opaque lens.* **2** (of a statement, piece of writing, etc) not clear; difficult to understand: *I felt his report was deliberately opaque.* ▷ **opaquely** *adv.* **opaqueness** (also **opacity**) *n* [U]: *the opaqueness of her reasoning.*

op art /ˈɒp ɑːt/ (also **optical art**) form of modern abstract art using geometrical patterns that produce optical illusions.

op cit /ˌɒp ˈsɪt/ *abbr* in the work already quoted (Latin *opere citato*). Cf LOC CIT.

OPEC /ˈəʊpek/ *abbr* Organization of Petroleum Exporting Countries.

open[1] /ˈəʊpən/ *adj* **1** allowing things or people to go or be taken in, out or through; not closed: *leave the door open* ○ *The door burst open and the children rushed in.* ○ *sleep in a room with the windows open* ○ *with both eyes open* ○ *The dog escaped through the open gate.* **2** [usu attrib] not enclosed, fenced in or blocked: *He prefers open fires to stoves or radiators.* ○ *open country*, ie without forests, buildings, etc ○ *open fields* ○ *an open stretch of moor* ○ *crack open a nut* ○ *break open a safe.* **3** [usu pred] ready for business; admitting customers or visitors: *The banks aren't open yet.* ○ *The shop isn't open on Sundays.* ○ *Doors open* (eg of a theatre) *at 7.00 pm.* ○ *Is the new school open yet?* ○ *She declared the festival open.* ○ *He kept two bank accounts open.* **4** (**a**) spread out; unfolded: *The flowers are all open now.* ○ *The book lay open on the table.* (**b**) not fastened; undone: *an open shirt* ○ *a blouse open at the neck* ○ *His coat was open.* **5** [attrib] not covered in or over: *an open car*, ie one with no roof or with a roof that is folded back ○ *an open wound*, ie one in which the skin is broken or damaged ○ *He has open sores all over his arms.* ○ *an open drain/sewer.* **6** ~ **(to sb/sth)** that anyone can enter, visit, etc; public: *an open competition, championship, scholarship* ○ *This garden is open to the public.* ○ *She was tried in open court*, ie with the public being freely admitted to hear the trial. **7** (**a**) not kept hidden or secret; known to all: *an open quarrel, scandal, etc* ○ *the lovers' open display of affection.* (**b**) willing to talk; honest; frank: *an open character* ○ *He was quite open about his reasons for leaving.* **8** not finally decided or settled: *Let's leave the matter open.* ○ *Is the job/vacancy/position still open* (ie available, unfilled)*?* **9** [usu attrib] (of cloth, etc) with wide spaces between the threads: *an open texture/weave.* **10** (idm) **be an open ˈsecret** be known to many people, though not publicly or officially acknowledged: *Their love affair is an open secret.* **be/lay oneself (wide) open to sth** behave so that one is likely to receive (esp) criticism, etc: *Don't lay yourself open to attack.* ○ *You're laying yourself wide open to accusations of dishonesty.* **be ˌopen to ˈoffer/ˈoffers** be willing to consider a price to be offered by a buyer: *We haven't decided on a price but we're open to offers.* **have/keep an open ˈmind (about/on sth)** be willing to listen to or accept new ideas, consider other people's suggestions, etc: *I'm not convinced your idea will work, but I'll keep an open mind for the moment.* **in the open ˈair** not inside a house or building; outside: *picnics in the open air* ○ *sleeping in the open air.* **keep one's ˈears/ˈeyes open** be alert and quick to hear or notice things. **keep an eye open/out** ⇨ EYE[1]. **keep one's eyes open/peeled/skinned** ⇨ EYE[1]. **keep open ˈhouse** offer hospitality to visitors at all times. **keep/leave one's options open** ⇨ OPTION. **keep a weather eye open** ⇨ WEATHER[1]. **leave the door open** ⇨ LEAVE[1]. **an open ˈbook** person who is easily understood and very frank: *His mind is an open book.* **open ˈSesame** (magic words used in one of the *Arabian Nights stories to cause a door to open). **an open sesame (to sth)** easier way of gaining sth that is usu difficult to obtain: *Being the boss's daughter is not an open sesame to every well-paid job in the firm.* **open to sb** possible for or available to sb: *It seems to me that there are only two options open to her.* **open to sth** willing to receive sth: *open to suggestions* ○ *open to conviction*, ie willing to be persuaded about sth. **throw sth open (to sb)** make sth available to everybody: *throw the debate open to the audience* ○ *throw one's house open to the public.* **wide open** ⇨ WIDE. **with one's eyes open** ⇨ EYE[1]. **with open ˈarms** with great affection or enthusiasm: *He welcomed us with open arms.*

▷ **open** *n* **1 the open** [sing] open space or country; the open air: *The children love playing out in the open.* Cf IN THE OPEN AIR. **2** (usu **Open**) [C] sporting competition in which both amateurs and professionals may take part: *Jack Nicklaus has won four US Opens*, ie open golf championships. **3** (idm) **bring sth/be/come (out) in(to) the ˈopen** make (esp secret plans, ideas, etc) known publicly; be/become known publicly: *Now the scandal is out in the open, the President will have a lot of questions to answer.*

openly *adv* without secrecy; honestly; publicly: *discuss a subject openly* ○ *go somewhere openly*, ie where one might be expected to go secretly.

openness honesty; frankness: *They were surprised by her openness when talking about her private life.*

□ **ˌopen-ˈair** *adj* [attrib] (taking place) in the open air; outside: *an ˌopen-air ˈswimming-pool* ○ *an ˌopen-air ˈparty.*

ˌopen-and-ˈshut *adj* completely straightforward and obvious: *As far as I can see the whole matter is open-and-shut.* ○ *He's obviously guilty — it's an open-and-shut case.*

ˈopencast *adj* [usu attrib] (of mines or mining) at or from a level near the earth's surface: *opencast coal-mining.* Cf DEEP-MINED (DEEP[2]).

ˌopen ˈcheque one that may be cashed at the bank on which it is drawn; cheque that is not crossed (CROSS[2] 4).

ˈopen day day when the public may visit a place normally closed to them: *an open day at the village school.*

ˌopen-ˈended *adj* without any limits, restrictions or aims set in advance: *an ˌopen-ended ˈcontract* ○ *an ˌopen-ended diˈscussion.*

ˌopen-ˈeyed *adj* (**a**) with open eyes, as in surprise: *open-eyed in terror.* (**b**) watchful; alert.

ˌopen-ˈhanded *adj* giving freely; generous. **ˌopen-ˈhandedly** *adv.* **ˌopen-ˈhandedness** *n* [U].

ˌopen-ˈhearted *adj* sincere; kind.

open-ˈhearth process method of making steel in which iron is heated in a shallow furnace.

ˌopen-heart ˈsurgery (*medical*) surgical operation on the heart while blood is kept flowing by machine.

ˌopen ˈletter letter, usu of protest or comment, addressed to a person or group, but intended to be made public, esp by being printed in a newspaper: *The students wrote an open letter to the Minister of Education.*

ˌopen-ˈminded *adj* willing to consider new ideas; unprejudiced: *He wished his parents were more open-minded on political issues.*

ˌopen-ˈmouthed /-maʊðd/ showing great surprise, etc: *The child stared open-mouthed at the huge cake.*

ˌopen-ˈplan *adj* (of a building) with few interior walls: *complain of the lack of privacy in an ˌopen-plan ˈoffice.*

ˌopen ˈprison prison with fewer restrictions than usual, on prisoners' movements, etc.

ˌopen ˈquestion matter on which different views are possible; question that is not yet decided or answered: *How many people will lose their jobs is an open question.*

ˌopen ˈsandwich slice of bread with meat, cheese, etc on top: *a Danish open sandwich.*

the ˌopen ˈsea area of sea that is not closed in by land: *Sail in and out of the bays — not on the open sea.*

the ˈopen season period of the year when certain fish and animals may be legally killed or hunted for sport: *October to February is the open season for pheasants in Britain.*

the ˌOpen Uniˈversity (*Brit*) university whose students study chiefly from home through correspondence and special TV and radio programmes. ⇨ article at POST-SCHOOL.

ˌopen ˈverdict jury's verdict that does not specify what action or crime caused a person's death.

ˌopen ˈvowel (*phonetics*) vowel made with the tongue lowered considerably from the roof of the mouth, eg. /ɑː, ɒ/.

ˈopen-weave *adj* (of a fabric) having spaces between the threads.

ˈopen-work *n* [U] pattern (in metal, lace, etc) with spaces between threads or strips: [attrib] *open-work lace* ○ *open-work wrought iron.*

open[2] /ˈəʊpən/ *v* **1** (**a**) [I, Ip] become open; be opened: *Does the window open inwards or outwards?* (**b**) [Tn, Tn·pr] cause (sth) to be open; unfasten: *Open your coat.* ○ *open a box, parcel, envelope, etc* ○ *She opened the door for me to come in/to let me in.* ○ *open the window a crack/fraction/bit/little*, ie open it slightly. **2** [Tn, Tn·pr] cut or make a passage through or opening in (sth): *open a mine, well, tunnel, etc* ○ *open a new road through a forest.* **3** [I, Ipr, Tn, Tn·p] ~ **(sth) (out)** (cause sth to) spread out; unfold: *The flowers are opening (out).* ○ *open a book, a newspaper, etc* ○ *open (out) a map on the table* ○ *Open your hand — I know you're hiding something.* **4** (**a**) [Tn] start (sth): *open an account*, eg at a bank ○ *open a meeting, a debate, etc.* (**b**) [I, Tn] (cause sth to) be ready for business, admit users or visitors, etc: *Another supermarket opened last week.* ○ *Banks don't open on Sundays.* ○ *open a business, new shop, hospital, etc.* (**c**) [Tn] ceremonially declare (a building, etc) to be open: *open a garden fête* ○ *The Queen opens Parliament.* **5** (idm) **the heavens opened** ⇨ HEAVEN. **open one's/sb's eyes (to sth)** make one/sb realize sth that surprises one/him: *Foreign travel opened his eyes to poverty for the first time.* **open ˈfire (at/on sb/sth)** start shooting: *He ordered his men to open fire.* **open the floodgates (of sth)** release a great force of emotion, destruction, rebellion, etc previously held under control. **open one's ˈheart/ˈmind to sb** express or discuss one's feelings or ideas freely. **6** (phr v) **open into/onto sth** give access to sth; lead to sth; allow one to reach sth: *This door opens onto the garden.* ○ *The two rooms open into one another.* **open out** (**a**) become wider; become visible: *The road opened out into a dual carriageway.* ○ *The view opened out in front of us as the fog cleared.* (**b**) develop (in personality, etc): *She opened out a lot while she was staying with us.* **open up** (*infml*) talk freely and openly: *After a few drinks he began to open up a bit.* **open (sth) up** (**a**) (cause sth to) open: *Coughing like that might open up your wound.* (**b**) (cause sth to) be available for development, production, etc: *New mines are opening up.* ○ *open up undeveloped land, new territory, etc* ○ *His stories opened up new worlds of the imagination.* (**c**) (cause sth to) begin business: *open up a new restaurant* ○ *He never opens up shop on a Sunday.* **open sth up** unwrap, undo sth; unlock (a room, door, etc): *open up a package* ○ *open up the boot of a car* ○ *open up an unused room* ○ *'Open up!'* (ie 'Unlock the door!') *shouted the police officer.* **open (sth) with sth** start with sth:

The story opens with a murder. ○ *He opened the conference with a speech.*

▷ **opener** /ˈəʊpnə(r)/ *n* (usu in compounds) **1** person or (esp) thing that opens: *a* ˈ*tin-opener* ○ *a* ˈ*bottle-opener.* **2** (idm) **for** ˈ**openers** (*US infml*) for a start; as a beginning: *For openers we'll get rid of this old furniture.*

opening /ˈəʊpnɪŋ/ *n* **1** [C] way in or out; open space; gap: *an opening in a hedge, fence, etc* ○ *an opening in the clouds.* **2** [C esp *sing*] beginning: *the opening of a book, speech, film, etc.* **3** [sing] process of becoming or making open: *the opening of a flower* ○ *the opening of a new library.* **4** [C] ceremony to celebrate (a public building, etc) being ready for use: *Many attended the opening of the new sports centre.* **5** [C] **(a)** position (in a business or firm) which is open or vacant: *an opening in an advertising agency* ○ *There are few openings in publishing for new graduates.* **(b)** good opportunity to do or talk about sth; favourable conditions: *excellent openings for trade* ○ *The last speaker gave me the opening I was waiting for.*

▷ **opening** *adj* [attrib] first: *his opening remarks* ○ *the opening scene of a film.*

□ ˌ**opening** ˈ**night** night on which a new play/film is performed/shown to the public for the first time and to which critics are invited: *The princess attended the opening night of the opera.*

ˈ**opening-time** *n* time at which public houses open and begin to serve drinks.

opera /ˈɒprə/ *n* **1** [C] play in which words are sung to a musical accompaniment: *an opera by Wagner* ○ *Verdi's later operas.* **2** [U] dramatic works of this kind as entertainment, an art form, etc: *We're very fond of opera.* ○ *sing in comic opera* ○ *grand* (ie serious) *opera* ○ *light* (ie not serious) *opera* ○ *tickets for the opera* ○ [attrib] *the opera season.* **3** [C] company performing opera: *The Vienna State Opera.*

▷ **operatic** /ˌɒpəˈrætɪk/ *adj* of or for an opera: *operatic music, singers, scores, arias.* **operatically** /-klɪ/ *adv.*

□ ˈ**opera-glasses** *n* [pl] small binoculars for use in the theatre.

ˈ**opera-house** *n* theatre for performances of operas.

operate /ˈɒpəreɪt/ *v* **1 (a)** [I] (*fml*) work; be in action: *This machine operates night and day.* ○ *The lift was not operating properly.* **(b)** [Tn] cause (a machine, etc) to work; control: *operate machinery* ○ *He operates the lift.* ○ *The kettle is operated by electricity.* **2** [I, Ipr, It] have or produce an effect; be in action: *The system operates in five countries.* ○ *The new law operates to our advantage.* ○ *Several causes operated to bring about the war.* **3** [Ipr, Tn] ~ **(from sth)** do business; manage or direct (sth): *The company operates from offices in London.* ○ *They operate three factories and a huge warehouse.* **4** [I, Ipr] ~ **(on sb) (for sth)** perform a surgical operation: *The doctors decided to operate (on her) immediately.* **5** [I, Ipr] (of soldiers, the police, etc) carry out raids, patrols, etc: *bombers operating from bases in the North* ○ *Police speed traps are operating on this motorway.*

▷ **operable** /ˈɒpərəbl/ *adj* that can be treated by means of an operation: *operable diseases of the chest* ○ *The tumour is operable.*

□ ˈ**operating system** controlling computer program that organizes the running of a number of other programs at the same time.

ˈ**operating-table** *n* table on which surgical operations are performed: *The patient died on the operating table.*

ˈ**operating-theatre** *n* (also ˈ**theatre**, *esp US* ˈ**operating room**) room in a hospital used for surgical operations.

operation /ˌɒpəˈreɪʃn/ *n* **1** [U] way in which sth works; working: *I can use a word processor but I don't understand its operation.* **2** [C] activity, often involving several people and/or spread over a period of time: *mount a rescue operation* ○ *at each stage of the massive police operation* ○ *The entire operation will take about five days.* **3** (also **op**) [C] ~ **(on sb) (for sth)**; ~ **(to do sth)** (*medical*) action performed by a surgeon on any part of the body, to treat or remove by cutting a diseased or injured part: *undergo an operation for appendicitis* ○ *perform an operation to amputate his leg* ○ *a liver transplant operation.* **4** [C] business company: *a huge multinational electronics operation.* **5 (a)** [C usu *pl*] (also **ops**) movement of ships, troops, aircraft, etc in war or during training: *the officer in charge of operations.* **(b) Operation** [sing] (used as part of a code name for military campaigns): *Operation Overlord.* **(c)** [C usu *pl*] planned campaign in industry, business, etc: *involved in building, banking, business operations* ○ *operations research,* ie study of business operations to improve efficiency in industry. **6** [C] (*mathematics*) addition, multiplication, subtraction, division, etc. **7** (idm) **be in operation**; **bring sth/come into operation** (cause sth to) be/become effective: *When does the plan come into operation?* ○ *Is this rule in operation yet?*

▷ **operational** /-ʃənl/ *adj* (*fml*) **1** of, for or used in operations: *early operational problems* ○ *operational costs/expenditure,* ie money needed for operating (machines, etc). **2** ready for use; ready to act: *The telephone is fully operational again.* ○ *The squadron is not yet operational.*

□ **ope**ˈ**rations room** room from which military operations are controlled.

operative /ˈɒpərətɪv; *US* -reɪt-/ *adj* (*fml*) **1** [usu pred] operating; effective; in use: *This law becomes operative on 12 May.* ○ *The station will be operative again in January.* ○ *The oil rig is now fully operative.* **2** (idm) **the operative word** the most significant word (in a phrase, etc that has just been used): *The boss is hopping mad about it — and 'mad' is the operative word.*

▷ **operative** *n* (*fml*) **1** worker, esp a manual one: *factory operatives.* **2** secret agent; spy: *undercover operatives.*

operator /ˈɒpəreɪtə(r)/ *n* **1** person who operates equipment, a machine, etc: *a lift operator* ○ *a computer operator.* **2** person who operates a telephone switchboard at the exchange: *Dial 100 for the operator.* **3** person who operates or owns a business or an industry (esp a private one): *a private operator in civil aviation* ○ *Our holiday was cancelled when the travel operator went bankrupt.* **4** (*infml esp derog*) person acting in the specified (esp cunning) way: *He's a smooth/slick/shrewd/clever operator.*

operculum /əˈpɜːkjʊləm/ *n* (*pl* **-la** /-lə/) (*biology*) flap that covers an opening in animals or plants (eg the gill-cover of fish).

operetta /ˌɒpəˈretə/ *n* short light musical comedy.

ophthalmic /ɒfˈθælmɪk/ *adj* (*medical*) of or for the eye: *ophthalmic surgery.*

□ **oph**ˌ**thalmic op**ˈ**tician** = OPTICIAN 2.

ophthalmology /ˌɒfθælˈmɒlədʒɪ/ *n* [U] (*medical*) scientific study of the eye and its diseases.

▷ **ophthalmologist** /-lədʒɪst/ *n* person specializing in ophthalmology: *the ophthalmologist at our local eye clinic.*

ophthalmoscope /ɒfˈθælməskəʊp/ *n* (*medical*) instrument for examining the eye closely, having a mirror with a hole in the centre.

opiate /ˈəʊpɪət/ *n* (*fml*) drug containing opium, used to relieve pain or to help sb sleep: *become addicted to opiates* ○ (*fig derog*) *the opiate of all-day television.*

opinion /əˈpɪnɪən/ *n* **1** [C] ~ **(of/about sb/sth)** belief or judgement (about sb/sth) not necessarily based on fact or knowledge: *political opinions* ○ *What's your opinion of the new President?* ○ *The chairman's opinion should be sought.* ○ *He was asked to give his honest opinion.* **2** [U] beliefs or views of a group; what people in general feel: *Opinion is shifting in favour of the new scheme.* ○ *The project seems excellent, but local opinion is against it.* **3** [C] professional estimate or advice: *get a lawyer's opinion on the question* ○ *You'd better get a second opinion before you let that man take out all your teeth.* **4** [C] (*law*) **(a)** formal statement made only by a judge sitting in the House of Lords, giving the reasons for a judgement that has been made. **(b)** barrister's written advice. **5** (idm) **be of the opinion that ...** (*fml*) believe or think that ...: *I'm of the opinion that he is right.* **one's considered opinion** ⇨ CONSIDER. **have a good, bad, high, low, etc opinion of sb/sth** think well, badly, etc of sb/sth: *The boss has a very high opinion of her.* ○ *She has a rather poor opinion of your written work.* **in my, your, etc opinion** it is my, your, etc view or feeling that: *In my opinion and in the opinion of most people, it is a very sound investment.* **a matter of opinion** ⇨ MATTER[1].

▷ **opinionated** /-eɪtɪd/ (also ˌ**self-o**ˈ**pinionated**) *adj* (*derog*) holding very strong views which one is not willing to change: *a self-opinionated young fool* ○ *He is the most opinionated man I know.*

□ **o**ˈ**pinion poll** ⇨ POLL[1] 2.

opium /ˈəʊpɪəm/ *n* [U] drug made from poppy seeds, used to relieve pain or to help sb sleep: *opium smuggling.*

□ ˈ**Opium War** either of two wars between Britain and China in the mid 19th century, which resulted from the Chinese refusal to allow the import of opium from British India. China was defeated, and many of its ports were opened to foreign trade.

opossum /əˈpɒsəm/ (*US* also **possum** /ˈpɒsəm/) *n* type of small American or Australian animal that lives in trees and carries its young in a pouch.

opp *abbr* opposite.

Oppenheimer /ˈɒpənhaɪmə(r)/ Julius Robert (1904-67), American physicist who led the team which designed and built the first atomic bomb during the Second World War.

opponent /əˈpəʊnənt/ *n* **(a)** ~ **(at/in sth)** person who is against another person in a fight, a struggle, a game or an argument: *our opponents in Saturday's game* ○ *a political opponent* ○ *Her opponent left the tennis court in tears.* **(b)** ~ **(of sth)** person who is against sth and tries to change or destroy it: *a fierce opponent of nuclear arms* ○ *opponents of abortion.*

opportune /ˈɒpətjuːn; *US* -tuːn/ *adj* (*fml*) **1** (of time) suitable or favourable for a purpose: *arrive at an opportune moment.* **2** (of an action or event) done or coming at the right time: *an opportune remark, statement, intervention, etc* ○ *Your arrival was most opportune.* ▷ **opportunely** *adv.*

opportunism /ˌɒpəˈtjuːnɪzəm; *US* -ˈtuːn-/ *n* [U] (*esp derog*) looking for and using opportunities to gain an advantage for oneself, without considering if this is fair or right: *political opportunism* ○ *a record of shameless opportunism.*

▷ **opportunist** /-ɪst/ *n* (*esp derog*) person who acts like this: *There were many opportunists and few men of principle.*

opportunity /ˌɒpəˈtjuːnətɪ; *US* -ˈtuːn-/ *n* [C, U] **1** ~ **(for/of doing sth)**; ~ **(to do sth)** favourable time, occasion or set of circumstances: *have/get/find/create an opportunity* ○ *have few opportunities of meeting interesting people* ○ *have no/little/not much opportunity for hearing good music* ○ *a great, golden, marvellous, etc opportunity to travel* ○ *I had no opportunity to discuss it with her.* ○ *Don't miss this opportunity: it may never come again.* ⇨ Usage at OCCASION. **2** (idm) **take the opportunity to do sth/of doing sth** recognize and use a good or suitable time to do sth: *Let me take this opportunity to say a few words.* ○ *We took the opportunity of visiting the palace.*

oppose /əˈpəʊz/ *v* **1** [Tn] **(a)** express strong disapproval of or disagreement with (sth/sb), esp with the aim of preventing or changing a course of action: *oppose the building of a motorway* ○ *oppose a scheme* ○ *oppose the Government* ○ *He opposed the proposal to build a new hall.* **(b)** (*fml*) compete against (sb): *Who is opposing you in the match?* **2** [Tn·pr] ~ **sth to/against sth** (*fml*) present sth as a contrast or opposite to sth else: *Do not oppose your will against mine.*

▷ **opposed** *adj* **1** ~ **to sth** strongly against sth: *She seems very much opposed to your going abroad.* **2** (idm) **as opposed to** in contrast to: *I am here on business as opposed to a holiday.*

opposite /ˈɒpəzɪt/ *adj* **1** [usu attrib] ~ **(to sb/sth)** having a position on the other side (of sb/sth); facing: *on the opposite page* ○ *In England you must drive on the opposite side of the road to the rest of*

Europe. ○ *John and Mary sat at opposite ends of the table (to each other).* ○ *This is Number 6, so Number 13 must be on the opposite side of the street.* **2** (used after the *n*) facing the speaker or a specified person or thing: *I asked the man opposite if he would open the door.* ○ *I could see smoke coming out of the windows of the house opposite.* ○ *Can you see where the grammar books are? The dictionaries are on the shelf directly opposite.* **3** [attrib] entirely different; contrary: *travelling in opposite directions* ○ *contact with the opposite sex*, ie of men with women or women with men ○ *The opposite approach is to use a bilingual dictionary.*

▷ **opposite** *adv*: *There's a couple with a dog who live opposite.* ○ *The woman sitting opposite is a detective.*

opposite *prep* ~ **(to sb/sth) 1** on the other side of a specific area from (sb/sth); facing (sb/sth): *I sat opposite to him during the meal.* ○ *The bank is opposite the supermarket.* ○ *Put the wardrobe in the corner opposite the door.* **2** (of actors) taking a part in a play, film, etc as the partner of (sb): *She had always dreamed of appearing opposite Olivier.*

opposite *n* ~ **(of sth)** word or thing that is as different as possible (from sth): *Hot and cold are opposites.* ○ *Light is the opposite of heavy.* ○ *I thought she would be small and pretty but she's completely the opposite.*

□ **one's ˌopposite ˈnumber** person with a similar job or position to one's own in another group or organization: *talks with her opposite number in the White House.*

opposition /ˌɒpəˈzɪʃn/ *n* **1** [U] ~ **(to) sb/sth** state or action of opposing (sb/sth); resistance: *violent opposition to the new committee* ○ *There's not much opposition to the scheme.* ○ *Her proposal met with strong opposition.* ○ *The army came up against fierce opposition in every town.* **2** [Gp] people who oppose (sb); competitors; rivals: *The opposition have a strong defence.* ○ *Before setting up in business, she wanted to get to know the opposition.* **3 the Opposition** [Gp] (*politics esp Brit*) (MPs of the) political party or parties opposing the Government: *We need an effective Opposition.* ○ *the leader of the Opposition* ○ [attrib] *the Opposition benches*, ie seats where MPs of the Opposition sit in Parliament ○ [attrib] *Opposition MPs are few in number.* ⇨ article at POLITICS, PARLIAMENT. **4** (idm) **in opposition (to sb/sth) (a)** opposing: *We found ourselves in opposition to several colleagues on this issue.* **(b)** forming the Opposition: *The Conservative party was in opposition for the first time in years.*

oppress /əˈpres/ *v* [Tn esp passive] **1** rule or treat (sb) with continual injustice or cruelty: *The people are oppressed by the military government.* ○ *Women are often oppressed by men.* **2** make (sb) feel worried, uncomfortable or unhappy: *oppressed with anxiety, worry, poverty, etc* ○ *The heat oppressed him and made him ill.*

▷ **oppressed** *adj* unjustly or cruelly treated: *an oppressed people, group, class, etc.* **the oppressed** *n* [pl *v*] oppressed people: *the oppressed of the world.*

oppression /əˈpreʃn/ *n* [U] oppressing or being oppressed: *a tyrant's oppression of his people* ○ *a history of oppression* ○ *victims of oppression.*

oppressive /əˈpresɪv/ *adj* **1** unjust; cruel: *oppressive laws, rules, measures, etc.* **2** hard to bear; causing distress: *oppressive weather* ○ *The heat in the tropics can be oppressive.* **oppressively** *adv*: *oppresively hot.*

oppressor *n* person or group that oppresses; cruel or unjust ruler: *suffer at the hands of an oppressor.*

opprobrious /əˈprəʊbrɪəs/ *adj* (*fml*) (of words, etc) showing scorn or reproach; abusive: *opprobrious language, remarks, deeds.*

▷ **opprobriously** *adv* (*fml*).

opprobrium /-brɪəm/ *n* [U] (*fml*) public disgrace and shame: *excite/incur opprobrium.*

ops /ɒps/ *n* [pl] (*infml*) = OPERATIONS (OPERATION 5a).

opt /ɒpt/ *v* **1** [Tt] decide to do sth; choose: *He opted to go to Paris rather than London.* **2** (phr v) **opt for sth** decide on sth; choose sth: *Fewer students are opting for science courses nowadays.* ⇨ Usage at CHOOSE. **opt out (of sth)** choose not to take part (in sth): *I think I'll opt out of this game.*

optic /ˈɒptɪk/ *adj* [esp attrib] (*fml*) of or concerned with the eye or the sense of sight: *the optic nerve*, ie from the eye to the brain.

▷ **Optic** *n* (*propr*) valve fitted to a bottle of spirits in a bar, so that a precise amount can be measured out when serving drinks.

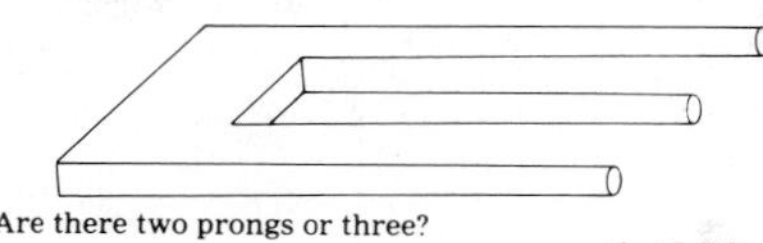

Are there two prongs or three?

optical illusion

optical /ˈɒptɪkl/ *adj* [esp attrib] **1** of the sense of sight: *optical effects and sound effects.* **2** for looking through; to help the eyes: *optical instruments*, eg microscopes and telescopes. ▷ **optically** /-klɪ/ *adv.*

□ **ˌoptical ˈart** = OP ART.

ˌoptical ˈfibre extremely thin glass thread through which information can be transmitted in the form of light signals. Cf FIBRE OPTICS (FIBRE).

ˌoptical ilˈlusion thing by which the eye is deceived: *A mirage is an optical illusion.* ○ *I thought I saw a ghost but it was just an optical illusion.*

optician /ɒpˈtɪʃn/ *n* **1** person who makes and sells optical instruments, esp contact lenses and glasses. **2** (also **ophˌthalmic opˈtician**, *US* **optometrist**) person qualified to examine the eyes and prescribe glasses, etc as well as issue them: *The optician said I needed new glasses.* ○ *I've just been to the optician's*, ie the optician's practice.

optics /ˈɒptɪks/ *n* [sing *v*] scientific study of sight and of light in relation to it.

optimism /ˈɒptɪmɪzəm/ *n* [U] tendency to expect the best in all things; confidence in success; belief that good will triumph over evil in the end: *He was still full of optimism for the future despite his many problems.* ○ *There was a feeling of optimism in the country when the new government was elected.* Cf PESSIMISM.

▷ **optimist** /-mɪst/ *n* person who is always hopeful and expects the best in all things: *He's such an optimist that he's sure he'll soon find a job.* Cf PESSIMIST (PESSIMISM).

optimistic /ˌɒptɪˈmɪstɪk/ *adj* ~ **(about sth)** expecting the best; confident: *an optimistic view of events* ○ *She's not optimistic about the outcome.* **optimistically** /-klɪ/ *adv.*

optimum /ˈɒptɪməm/ (also **optimal** /ˈɒptɪməl/) *adj* [attrib] (*fml*) best or most favourable: *the optimum temperature for the growth of plants* ○ *enjoy optimum economic conditions.*

option /ˈɒpʃn/ *n* **1** [U] power or freedom of choosing; choice: *have little option*, ie not much choice ○ *I haven't much option in the matter*, ie I cannot choose. ○ *I have little option but to go*, ie I have to go. ○ *He did it because he had no other option*, ie no other choice. ○ *He was given one month's imprisonment without the option* (ie alternative) *of a fine.* **2** [C] thing that is or may be chosen; choice: *Make a list of the various options.* ○ *There weren't many options open to him*, ie there was little choice available. **3** [C] ~ **(on sth)** (*commerce*) right to buy or sell sth at a certain price within a certain time: *an option on a package holiday* ○ *have an option on a piece of land* ○ *We have a 12-day option on the house.* **4** (idm) **keep/leave one's ˈoptions open** avoid making a decision now, so that one still has a choice later: *Don't take the job now — keep your options open until you leave university.*

▷ **optional** /-ʃənl/ *adj* that may be chosen or not, as one wishes; not compulsory: *optional subjects at school* ○ *Formal dress is optional.* ○ *The cassette player is an optional with this car*, ie It will cost extra if one chooses to have it. **optionally** *adv.*

optometrist /ɒpˈtɒmətrɪst/ *n* (*esp US*) = OPTICIAN 2.

opulent /ˈɒpjʊlənt/ *adj* (*fml*) **1** having or showing signs of great wealth: *opulent furnishings* ○ *an opulent suburb* ○ *opulent tastes in cars.* **2** abundant: *opulent vegetation.* ▷ **opulence** /-ləns/ *n* [U]. **opulently** *adv*: *opulently furnished rooms.*

opus /ˈəʊpəs/ *n* (*pl* **opera** /ˈɒpərə/) **1** musical composition numbered as one of a composer's works (WORK[1] 5b) (usu in order of publication): *Beethoven's opus 112.* **2** (*fml*) work of art, esp on a large scale.

or /ɔ:(r)/ *conj* **1** (introducing an alternative): *Is it green or blue?* ○ *Are you coming or not?* ○ *Is the baby a boy or a girl?* Cf EITHER...OR (EITHER). **2** (introducing all but the first of a series of alternatives): *I'd like it to be black, (or) white or grey.* **3** if not; otherwise: *Turn the heat down or your cake will burn.* ○ *Please drive faster or we'll be late.* Cf OR ELSE. **4** (after a negative) and neither: *He can't read or write.* ○ *They never dance or sing.* Cf NEITHER...NOR. **5 (a)** (introducing a word or phrase that explains, or means the same as, another): *an increase of 50p, or 10 shillings in old money* ○ *a kilo, or two pounds* ○ *geology, or the science of the earth's crust.* **(b)** (introducing an afterthought): *He was obviously lying — or was he?* ○ *I need a new coat — or do I?* **6** (idm) **either...or** ⇨ EITHER. **or ˈelse (a)** otherwise; because if not; or(3): *Hurry up or ˌelse you'll be ˈlate.* ○ *You must go to work or ˌelse you'll lose your ˈjob.* **(b)** (*infml*) (used as a threat) or something bad will happen: *Pay up or else!* ○ *You'd better give me that book — or else!* **or rather** (used making a statement more accurate or correct): *We stayed at my friend's house, or rather at my friend's parents' house.* ○ *He is my cousin — or rather my ˈfather's cousin.* **or so** (suggesting vagueness or uncertainty about quantity): *There were ˈtwenty or so*, ie about twenty. ○ *We stayed at the party for an ˈhour or so.* **or somebody/something/somewhere; somebody/something/somewhere or other** (*infml*) (expressing uncertainty or vagueness about a person, thing or place): *He's a bank manager or something.* ○ *I put it in the cupboard or somewhere.* ○ *'Who told you?' 'Oh, somebody or other, I've forgotten who.'* ○ *It's somewhere or other in the kitchen.* **or two** (after a singular *n*) or more; about: *After a ˈminute or two we saw him.* ○ *I haven't seen him for a ˈyear or two.* **whether...or; whether or not** ⇨ WHETHER.

-or *suff* (with *vs* forming *ns*) person or thing that does: *actor* ○ *governor* ○ *resistor.* Cf -EE, -ER.

oracle /ˈɒrəkl; *US* ˈɔ:r-/ *n* **1 (a)** (in ancient Greece) holy place where the gods could be asked about the future: *the oracle at Delphi.* **(b)** answer given at such a place (which was often ambiguous or obscure). **(c)** priest(ess) giving the answers: *consult the oracle.* **2** (*fig*) person considered able to give reliable advice: *My sister's the oracle on beauty matters.* **3 Oracle** (*Brit propr*) teletext service provided by the *Independent Broadcasting Authority. Cf CEEFAX. ⇨ article at TELEVISION.

▷ **oracular** /əˈrækjʊlə(r)/ *adj* (*fml or joc*) of or like an oracle; with hidden meaning: *oracular utterances from the headmaster.*

oral /ˈɔ:rəl/ *adj* **1** not written; spoken: *an oral examination* ○ *stories passed on by oral tradition*, ie from one generation to the next without being written down. **2** of, by or for the mouth: *oral hygiene* ○ *oral contraceptives* ○ *oral sex*, ie in which the mouth is used to stimulate the sex organs.

▷ **oral** *n* oral examination: *He failed the oral.*

orally /ˈɔ:rəlɪ/ *adv* **1** through the spoken word: *Tribal lore and custom have been passed down orally.* **2** of, by or for the mouth: *orally administered drugs* ○ *not to be taken orally*, eg of medicines, not to be swallowed.

orange /ˈɒrɪndʒ; *US* ˈɔ:r-/ *n* **1** [C] round thick-skinned juicy edible fruit that is a reddish-yellow colour when ripe: *oranges, lemons and other citrus fruits* ○ [attrib] *orange juice.* ⇨ illus at FRUIT. **2** [C] (usu **ˈorange tree**) evergreen tree on which this fruit grows: *an orange grove.* **3** [U] reddish-yellow colour of this fruit: *a pale shade of orange.* ⇨ illus at SPECTRUM. **4** [U, C] (glass of a) drink made from oranges: *Would you*

like some orange? ○ *A fresh orange, please*, ie real orange juice as opposed to orangeade or orange squash. ○ *I'd like a gin and orange please.*
▷ **orange** *adj* **1** of the colour orange: *an orange hat* ○ *an orange light.* **2 Orange** [attrib] of Orangemen: *the Orange lodges.*
orangeade /ˌɒrɪndʒˈeɪd; *US* ˌɔːr-/ *n* [C, U] (glass of a) fizzy orange-flavoured soft drink.
orangery /ˈɒrɪndʒərɪ/ *n* glass-walled building in which orange trees are grown in cool countries.
□ **ˈorange-blossom** *n* white sweet-scented flower of the orange tree: *Orange-blossom is associated with weddings.*
ˈOrangeman *n* (*pl* **-men**) member of a secret right-wing Protestant organization in N Ireland whose aim is to maintain Protestant political power and oppose Roman Catholic claims. It is named after the Dutch royal house of Orange, to which William III of Britain belonged; he defeated the Catholic James II at the Battle of the Boyne in Ireland in 1690.
the ˌOrange ˈRiver river in South Africa, 1 859 km (1 155 miles) long, which flows westward into the Atlantic Ocean.
ˌorange ˈsquash (*Brit*) still, orange-flavoured soft drink made from juice or syrup diluted with water.

orang-utan /ɔːˌræŋuːˈtæn; *US* əˌræŋəˈtæn/ (also **orang-outang** /-uːˈtæŋ/, **orang-outan**) *n* large ape with long arms found in Borneo and Sumatra. ⇨ illus at APE.

oration /ɔːˈreɪʃn/ *n* (*fml*) formal speech made on a public occasion, esp as part of a ceremony: *a funeral oration.*

orator /ˈɒrətə(r); *US* ˈɔːr-/ *n* (*fml*) (**a**) person who makes formal speeches in public. (**b**) person who is good at public speaking: *a fine political orator.*
▷ **oratorical** /ˌɒrəˈtɒrɪkl; *US* ˌɔːrəˈtɔːr-/ *adj* (*fml sometimes derog*) of speech-making or orators: *oratorical phrases, gestures, etc* ○ *an oratorical contest.*

oratorio /ˌɒrəˈtɔːrɪəʊ; *US* ˌɔːr-/ *n* (*pl* ~**s**) musical composition for solo voices, chorus and orchestra, usu with a Biblical theme: *Handel's oratorios.* Cf CANTATA.

oratory[1] /ˈɒrətrɪ; *US* ˈɔːrətɔːrɪ/ *n* small chapel for private prayer or worship.

oratory[2] /ˈɒrətrɪ; *US* ˈɔːrətɔːrɪ/ *n* [U] (art of) public speaking, esp when used skilfully to affect an audience: *His oratory soon had the crowd booing his opponents.* ○ *Some politicians are famous for their powers of oratory.*

orb /ɔːb/ *n* **1** (*fml or arch*) globe, esp the sun, the moon or one of the planets: *an orb of golden light.* **2** jewelled ball with a cross on top carried by a king or queen as part of ceremonial dress.

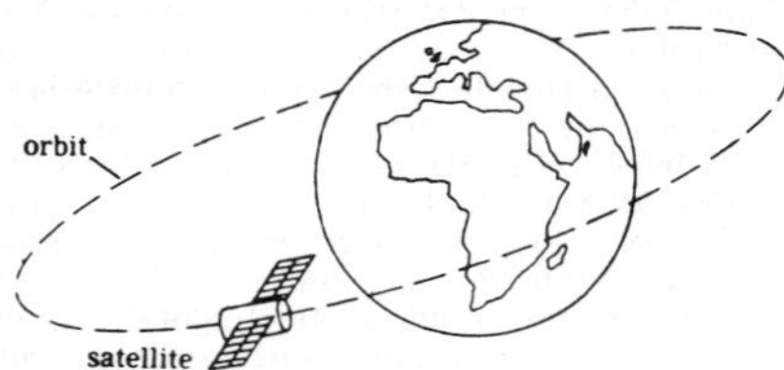

orbit /ˈɔːbɪt/ *n* **1** (**a**) path followed by a planet, star, moon, etc round another body: *the earth's orbit round the sun.* (**b**) path of a man-made object, eg a satellite or space-craft, round a planet, star, etc: *The spacecraft is in orbit* (ie moving in orbit) *round the moon.* ○ *How many satellites have been put into orbit round the earth?* (**c**) (*physics*) path of an electron round an atomic nucleus. **2** area of power or influence; scope: *Marketing does not come within the orbit of his department.* **3** (*anatomy*) either of the two holes in the skull into which the eyes fit.
▷ **orbit** *v* [I, Tn] move in orbit round (sth): *orbit in space* ○ *How many spacecraft have orbited the moon?*
orbital /ˈɔːbɪtl/ *adj* of an orbit: *a spacecraft's orbital distance from the earth* ○ *an orbital motorway*, ie round the outside of a city. — *n* road passing round the outside of a city: *Take the London orbital.*

orchestra: a typical layout

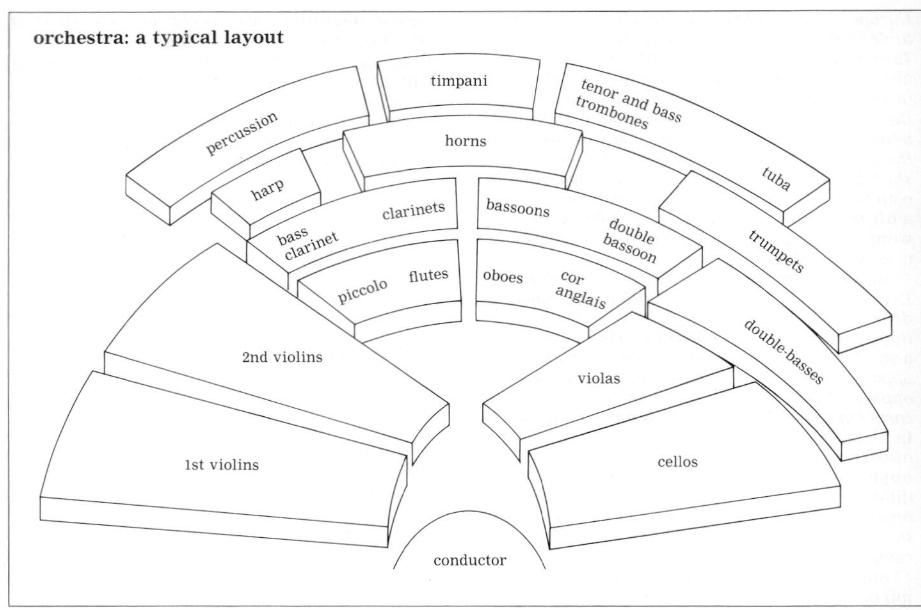

Orcadian /ɔːˈkeɪdɪən/ *n, adj* (native or inhabitant) of the *Orkney Islands.

orch *abbr* orchestra(1); orchestrated (by).

orchard /ˈɔːtʃəd/ *n* (usu enclosed) piece of land in which fruit trees are grown: *apple orchards.*

orchestra /ˈɔːkɪstrə/ *n* [CGp] (usu large) group of people playing various musical instruments together: *a dance, string, symphony orchestra* ○ *She plays the flute in an orchestra.* ○ *He conducts the London Symphony Orchestra.* Cf BAND 3.
▷ **orchestral** /ɔːˈkestrəl/ *adj* [usu attrib] of, for or by an orchestra: *orchestral instruments, music, performances* ○ *an orchestral concert.*
□ **ˈorchestra pit** = PIT[1] 7.
ˈorchestra stalls (*US* **orchestra**) front seats on the floor of a theatre.

orchestrate /ˈɔːkɪstreɪt/ *v* [Tn] **1** arrange (a piece of music) for an orchestra to play: *a set of piano pieces orchestrated by the composer.* **2** carefully (and sometimes unfairly) arrange (sth) in order to bring about a desired result: *The demonstration was carefully orchestrated to attract maximum publicity.* ▷ **orchestration** /ˌɔːkɪˈstreɪʃn/ *n* [C, U].

orchid /ˈɔːkɪd/ (also **orchis** /ˈɔːkɪs/) *n* **1** plant, usu with flowers of unusual shapes and brilliant colours, having one petal larger than the other two: *Many kinds of wild orchid are becoming rare.* **2** one of these flowers (usu expensive to buy): *She wore a single orchid on her evening dress.*

ordain /ɔːˈdeɪn/ *v* **1** [Tn, Cn·n] make (sb) a priest or minister: *He was ordained priest last year.* **2** [Tn, Tf] (*fml*) (of God, law, authority, fate, etc) order or command; decide in advance: *Fate had ordained that he should die in poverty.* ⇨ Usage at DECREE.

ordeal /ɔːˈdiːl, ˈɔːdiːl/ *n* difficult or painful experience (esp one that tests a person's character or powers of endurance): *the ordeal of divorce* ○ *The hostages went through a dreadful ordeal.*

order[1] /ˈɔːdə(r)/ *n* **1** [U] way in which people or things are placed or arranged in relation to one another: *names in alphabetical order* ○ *events in chronological order*, ie according to times, dates, etc ○ *arranged in order of size, merit, importance, etc*, ie according to size, etc. **2** condition in which everything is carefully and neatly arranged: *put/leave/set one's affairs, papers, accounts in order* ○ *Get your ideas into some kind of order before beginning to write.* Cf DISORDER. **3** [U] (condition brought about by) obedience to laws, rules, authority: *Some teachers find it difficult to keep order in their classes/to keep their classes in order.* ○ *The police must try to restore order.* Cf DISORDER. **4** [C] ~ (**for sb to do sth**); ~ (**that...**) command or instruction given by sb in authority: *Soldiers must obey orders.* ○ *He gave orders for the work to be started/that the work should be started immediately.* ○ *My orders prevent me from doing that*, ie I have been instructed not to do it. **5** [C] ~ (**for sth**) (**a**) request to make or supply (goods): *fill an order*, ie supply the goods asked for ○ *He gave his order to the waiter.* ○ *We've received an order for two tons of coal.* (**b**) goods supplied: *A delivery van has brought the grocery order.* ○ *Your order has arrived.* **6** [C] written instruction that allows the holder to be paid money or to do sth: *a ˈbanker's/ˈpostal order*, ie an order to a bank/post office to pay money ○ *obtain a court order to allow a divorced man to visit his children.* **7** [U] system of rules or procedures (at public or committee meetings, or in Parliament, lawcourts, etc): *rules of order* ○ *speak to order*, ie according to rules laid down by the meeting ○ *the order of business* ○ *(on) a point of order*, ie (on) a question of procedure ○ *I wish to raise a point of order.* **8** (**a**) [C] (*fml*) (arrangement of) groups, classes, etc in society (in relation to one another): *The social order of ants is very interesting.* (**b**) [C esp *pl*] (*derog or joc*) members of such a group, class, etc: *the lower orders.* **9** [CGp] (*biology*) group of related animals or plants below a class(7) and above a family(4): *the order of primates* ○ *The rose and the bean families belong to the same order.* Cf PHYLUM, GENUS 1, SPECIES 1. **10** (**a**) [CGp] group of people appointed to a special class as an honour or

orders of architecture

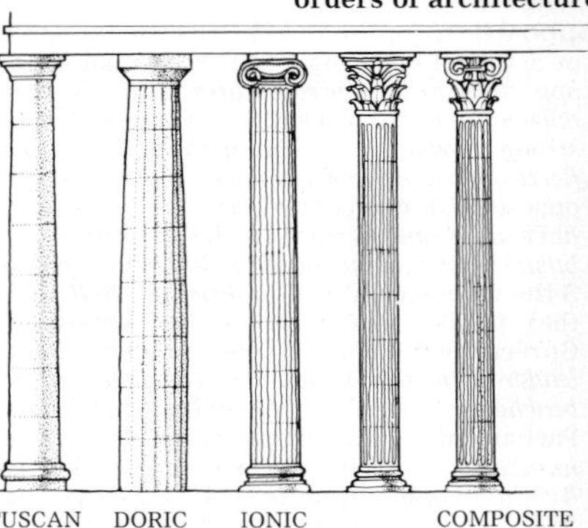

reward: *The Order of the Garter is an ancient order of chivalry.* **(b)** [C] badge, sign, etc worn by members of such a group: *wear all one's orders and medals.* **11** [CGp] group of people who have been ordained as clergymen: *the Order of Priests/Deacons/Bishops.* **12** [CGp] group of people, esp monks, living under religious rules: *the monastic orders* ○ *the Order of Dominican Friars.* **13** [C] style of ancient Greek or Roman architecture characterized by the type of column used: *the five classical orders of architecture* ○ *the Doric order.* ⇨ illus. **14** [U] (*fml*) kind; sort: *skills of the highest order.* **15** [sing] ~ **of sth** exact form of a religious service: *the order of service as laid down in the Prayer Book.* **16** (idm) **be in/take (holy) ˈorders** be/become a priest. **be under orders (to do sth)** have been instructed or commanded (to do sth): *I'm under strict orders not to let any strangers in.* **by order of sb/sth** according to directions given by a person in authority: *by order of the Governor* ○ *by order of the court.* **call sb/sth to order** ⇨ CALL[2]. **get one's/give sb his marching orders** ⇨ MARCH[1]. **in apple-pie order** ⇨ APPLE. **in running/working order** (esp of machines) working well, smoothly, etc: *This lift is hardly ever in working order.* ○ *The engine has been tuned and is now in perfect working order.* **in ˈorder** as it should be; able to be used: *Is your passport in order* (ie still valid)*?* **in order (to do sth)** (*fml*) according to the rules, etc of a meeting, etc: *It is not in order to interrupt.* ○ *Is it in order to speak now?* **in order that** (*fml*) with the intention that; so that: *He left early in order that he should/would/might arrive on time.* **in order to do sth** with the purpose or intention of doing sth: *She arrived early in order to get a good seat.* **in/into reverse order** ⇨ REVERSE. **in short order** ⇨ SHORT 1. **law and order** ⇨ LAW. **of/in the order of sth** (*fml*) about (the same quality, quantity or number as): *Her salary is of the order of £150 a week.* **on ˈorder** requested but not yet received: *I've got two books on order at the bookshop.* **the ˌorder of the ˈday** programme of business to be discussed in Parliament, or at a formal meeting: (*fig joc*) *Good behaviour must be the order of the day when the school inspector comes.* **Order! Order!** (used to call attention to the fact that a person is not observing the usual rules or procedures at a debate, meeting, etc). **an ˌorder to ˈview** written authority from an estate agent to look over a house, etc with the idea of buying it. **ˌout of ˈorder (a)** (of a machine, etc) not working properly: *The phone is out of order.* **(b)** (*fml*) not allowed by the rules of a formal meeting, etc: *His objection was ruled to be out of order.* **the pecking order** ⇨ PECK. **a point of order** ⇨ POINT[1]. **put/set one's (own) house in order** ⇨ HOUSE. **take orders from sb** do as sb instructs: *She said she wouldn't take orders from a junior clerk.* **a tall order** ⇨ TALL. **(made) to order** (made) according to a customer's special requirements: *This company will tailor a suit to order.* **under the orders of sb** commanded or instructed by sb: *serve under the orders of a new general.* **under starter's orders** ⇨ STARTER.

□ **ˈorder-book** *n* book in which a business records orders from customers: *have a full order-book.*

ˈorder-form *n* printed form to be filled in by a customer ordering goods: *It will speed up delivery if you complete the official order-form.*

ˈorder-paper *n* written or printed programme of business for a committee, Parliament, etc on a particular day.

order[2] /ˈɔːdə(r)/ *v* **1** [Tn, Tn·pr, Tf, Dn·t] give an order[1](4) to (sb); command: *The chairman ordered silence.* ○ *The doctor ordered me to (stay in) bed.* ○ *The boy was ordered out of the room.* ○ *The judge ordered that the prisoner should be remanded.* ○ *We ordered him to leave immediately.* **2** [Tn, Tn·pr, Dn·n, Dn·pr] ~ **sth (for sb)** request sb to supply or make (goods, etc): *I've ordered a new carpet (from the shop).* ○ *We don't have the book in stock but we can order it.* ○ *He ordered himself three shirts.* ○ *She ordered a garden chair for her husband.* **3** [I, Tn, Tn·pr, Dn·n, Dn·pr] ~ **sth (for sb)** request sb to bring (food, drink, etc) in a hotel, restaurant, etc: *We haven't ordered yet.* ○ *I've ordered a steak.* ○ *She ordered lunch to be served at 1.30.* ○ *He ordered himself a pint of beer.* ○ *I've ordered you egg and chips/egg and chips for you.* **4** [Tn] (*fml*) put (sth) in order; arrange; direct: *He ordered his life according to strict rules.* ○ *I must have time to order my thoughts.* **5** (idm) **(just) what the doctor ordered** ⇨ DOCTOR. **6** (phr v) **order sb about/around** keep on telling sb to do things: *Even as a boy he was always ordering his friends about.* **order sb off** (*sport*) order sb to leave a sports field, usu for breaking a rule: *The referee ordered Johnson off in the second half for kicking another player.* **order sb out** order (police or troops) to parade, esp to control civil unrest, etc: *The government ordered the police out to restore order in the streets.*

▷ **ordered** /ˈɔːdəd/ *adj* arranged (esp well-arranged): *an ordered life* ○ *a badly ordered existence.*

NOTE ON USAGE: Compare **tell**, **order**, **instruct**, **direct**, **command**. **Tell** is the most generally used verb. It is not very strong and is the word used in everyday situations: *I keep telling him to cut his hair but he takes no notice.* ○ *Do what you're told.* ○ *They've been told to finish the job by tomorrow.* **Order** is stronger and is used of people in authority who expect to be obeyed: *The policeman ordered the motorist to stop.* **Instruct** and **direct** suggest the giving of a precise description of necessary action. They are used in impersonal and official situations: *I have been instructed by the company to offer you a refund.* ○ *The judge directed the defendant to answer.* **Command** is mainly used in military situations: *The officer commanded his men to open fire.*

orderly[1] /ˈɔːdəlɪ/ *adj* **1** well-arranged; in good order; tidy: *an orderly room, desk, etc* ○ (*fig*) *an orderly mind.* **2** well-behaved; peaceful: *an orderly football crowd.* ▷ **orderliness** /ˈɔːdəlɪnɪs/ *n* [U].

orderly[2] /ˈɔːdəlɪ/ *n* **1** (also **medical orderly**) attendant in a hospital, usu without special training, who does unskilled jobs. **2** army officer's attendant.

ordinal /ˈɔːdɪnl; *US* -dənl/ *adj* (of a number) showing order or position in a series. ▷ **ordinal** *n* (also **ˌordinal ˈnumber**): *'First', 'second' and 'third' are ordinals.* ⇨ App 9. Cf CARDINAL[1].

ordinance /ˈɔːdɪnəns/ *n* [C, U] (*fml*) order, rule or law made by a government or an authority: *the ordinances of the City Council* ○ *by ordinance of the mayor.*

ordinary /ˈɔːdənrɪ; *US* ˈɔːrdənerɪ/ *adj* **1** normal; usual: *an ordinary sort of day* ○ *in the ordinary course of events* ○ *ordinary people like you and me* ○ *We were dressed up for the party but she was still in her ordinary clothes.* ○ (*derog*) *a very ordinary meal,* ie nothing special. Cf EXTRAORDINARY. **2** (idm) **in the ˈordinary way** if the circumstances were usual: *In the ordinary way he would have come with us, but he's not feeling well.* **out of the ˈordinary** unusual; exceptional: *Her new house is certainly out of the ordinary.* ○ *His behaviour is nothing out of the ordinary,* ie not unusual.

▷ **ordinarily** /ˈɔːdənrəlɪ; *US* ˌɔːrdnˈerəlɪ/ *adv* **1** in an ordinary way: *behave quite ordinarily.* **2** as a general rule; usually: *Ordinarily, I find this job easy, but today I'm having problems.*

ordinary *n* (in the Roman Catholic Church) rule or book setting out the order of services to be followed in church.

□ **ˈOrdinary level** (also **O level**) (formerly in British education) secondary school examination of basic standard.

the ˌordinary of the ˈMass (in the Roman Catholic Church) the part of the Mass that does not change from day to day.

ˌordinary ˈseaman sailor of the lowest rank on a ship. ⇨ App 4.

ˈordinary shares (*Brit*) (*US* **common stock**) shares in a business company that give the holder a claim on the company's assets (eg to receive a dividend) after holders of preference shares (PREFERENCE) have been paid.

ordinate /ˈɔːdɪnət/ *n* (*mathematics*) straight line from any point drawn parallel to one coordinate axis and meeting the other, usu a coordinate measured parallel to the vertical. Cf ABSCISSA. ⇨ illus at CARTESIAN COORDINATES.

ordination /ˌɔːdɪˈneɪʃn; *US* -dnˈeɪʃn/ *n* **(a)** [U] ceremony of ordaining (a priest or minister). **(b)** [C] example of this.

ordnance /ˈɔːdnəns/ *n* [U] **1** military supplies and materials, esp cannon and similar heavy guns. **2** government service dealing with these.

□ **the ˌOrdnance ˈSurvey** (*Brit*) (government department that prepares) accurate and detailed maps of Great Britain: [attrib] *an Ordnance Survey map.* ⇨ article at COUNTRYSIDE.

Ordovician /ˌɔːdəˈvɪʃən/ *adj* of the period of the earth's history between about 505 and 438 million years ago, when the first animals with backbones appeared. Cf PALAEOZOIC.

ordure /ˈɔːdjʊə(r); *US* -dʒər/ *n* [U] (*fml or euph*) excrement; dung; filth.

ore /ɔː(r)/ *n* [U, C] rock, earth, mineral, etc from which metal can be obtained: *iron ore* ○ *an area rich in ores.*

oregano /ˌɒrɪˈgɑːnəʊ; *US* əˈregənəʊ/ *n* [U] dried leaves of the wild marjoram plant used as a herb.

Oregon /ˈɒrɪgən/ mountainous north-western State of the USA, on the Pacific coast. ⇨ map at App 1.

□ **the ˌOregon ˈTrail** route from *Missouri to Oregon taken by pioneers in the mid 19th century.

Orestes /ɒˈrestiːz/ (in Greek mythology) son of Agamemnon and Clytemnestra who killed his mother and her lover Aegisthus in order to avenge his father's murder.

organ[1] /ˈɔːgən/ *n* **1** part of an animal body or plant serving a particular purpose: *the organs of speech,* ie the tongue, teeth, lips, etc ○ *The eye is the organ of sight.* ○ *the reproductive organs* ○ *The surgeon removed the infected organ.* **2** (*fml*) (official) organization that serves a special purpose; means of getting work done: *Parliament is the chief organ of government.* **3** (*fml*) means for communicating the views of a particular group or party: *organs of public opinion,* ie newspapers, TV, radio, etc ○ *This paper is the official organ of the Communist Party.*

organ[2] /ˈɔːgən/ *n* **1** (*US* also **ˈpipe-organ**) large musical instrument from which sounds are produced by air forced through pipes, played by keys pressed with the fingers and pedals pressed with the feet: *He plays the organ in church.* ○ [attrib] *organ music.* **2** any similar type of instrument without pipes: *an electric organ* ○ *a mouth-organ.* Cf HARMONIUM.

▷ **organist** *n* person who plays an organ: *a church organist.*

□ **ˈorgan-grinder** *n* person who plays a barrel organ.

ˈorgan-loft *n* gallery (in some churches, etc) where the organ is placed.

organdie (*US* also **organdy**) /ɔːˈgændɪ; *US* ˈɔːrgəndɪ/ *n* [U] type of fine, slightly stiff cotton material: *a blouse made of white organdie* ○ [attrib] *an organdie dress.*

organelle /ˌɔːgəˈnel/ *n* (*biology*) any of several structures inside a cell that have particular functions (eg the nucleus).

organic /ɔːˈgænɪk/ *adj* **1** (*fml*) of or affecting an organ or organs of the body: *The illness is organic in origin.* ○ *organic diseases, disorders, etc.* **2** [esp attrib] of, found in, or formed by living things: *organic substances, compounds, matter, etc* ○ *rich organic soil.* Cf INORGANIC. **3** [esp attrib] (of food, farming methods, etc) produced or practised without artificial fertilizers or pesticides: *organic vegetables* ○ *organic horticulture.* **4** (*fml*) made of related parts; arranged as a system: *an organic part of our business.* ▷ **organically** /-klɪ/ *adv*: *The doctor said there was nothing organically wrong with me.* ○ *organically grown tomatoes.*

□ **orˌganic ˈchemistry** chemistry of carbon compounds. Cf INORGANIC CHEMISTRY (INORGANIC).

organism /ˈɔːgənɪzəm/ *n* **1 (a)** (usu small) living

being with parts that work together: *study the minute organisms in water.* (**b**) individual plant or animal. **2** *(fml)* system made up of parts which are dependent on each other: *The business is a large, complicated organism.*

organization, -isation /ˌɔːɡənaɪˈzeɪʃn; *US* -nɪˈz-/ *n* **1** [U] (**a**) activity of organizing: *He's involved in the organization of a new club.* (**b**) condition or state of being organized: *She is brilliant but her work lacks organization.* **2** [C] organized group of people; system: *all the local leisure organizations* ○ *The human body has a very complex organization.*
▷ **organizational, -isational** /-ʃənl/ *adj* [esp attrib]: *excellent organizational skills.*

organize, -ise /ˈɔːɡənaɪz/ *v* **1** [Tn, Tn·pr] ~ **sb/sth (into sth)** put sb/sth into working order; arrange (parts, people) into an efficient system: *organize a political party, a government, a club, an army, etc* ○ *She loves to organize people.* ○ *She organized the class into four groups.* **2** [Tn] make arrangements or preparations for (sth): *organize a picnic* ○ *organize a protest meeting* ○ *They organized an expedition to Everest.* ⇨ Usage at ARRANGE. **3** [Tn, Tn·pr] ~ **sb (into sth)** form (workers) into a trade union, etc: *organize the work force* ○ *organize peasant farmers into a co-operative.*
▷ **organized, -ised** *adj* **1** ordered; orderly; efficient: *a highly organized person* ○ *a well-organized office.* **2** arranged or prepared: *a badly organized event* ○ *organized crime.* **3** (of workers) in a trade union: *organized labour.*
organizer, -iser *n* person who organizes sth: *the organizer of the event, function, party, etc* ○ *She's not a good organizer.*

organza /ɔːˈɡænzə/ *n* [U] thin stiff transparent fabric used in dressmaking.

orgasm /ˈɔːɡæzəm/ *n* climax of sexual excitement: *failure to achieve (an) orgasm.*

orgiastic /ˌɔːdʒɪˈæstɪk/ *adj (fml)* of or like an orgy; frenzied: *orgiastic revels.*

orgy /ˈɔːdʒɪ/ *n* **1** *(often derog)* wild party, usu with a lot of drinking and/or sexual activity: *a drunken orgy.* **2** ~ **(of sth)** *(infml)* great indulgence in one or more activity: *an orgy of killing and destruction* ○ *an orgy of spending before Christmas.*

oriel /ˈɔːrɪəl/ *n* (also ˌ**oriel** ˈ**window**) window projecting from the upper storey of a house, etc.

orient[1] /ˈɔːrɪənt/ *n* **the Orient** [sing] *(fml or rhet)* countries of the (Far) East (eg Japan, China): *perfumes and spices from the Orient.* Cf OCCIDENT.

orient[2] /ˈɔːrɪent/ *v (esp US)* = ORIENTATE.

oriental /ˌɔːrɪˈentl/ *adj* of or from the Orient: *oriental art, pottery, etc* ○ *a department of oriental studies.*
▷ **Oriental** *n (sometimes offensive)* person from the Orient, esp Japan or China.
orientalist /-təlɪst/ *n* person who studies the language, arts, etc of oriental countries.

orientate /ˈɔːrɪənteɪt/ (also *esp US* **orient** /ˈɔːrɪent/) *v* **1** [Tn esp passive, Tn·pr] ~ **sb/sth (towards sb/sth)** (**a**) direct the interest of sb (to sth): *Try to orientate your students towards the science subjects.* ○ *Our firm is orientated towards the export side of the business.* (**b**) direct or aim sth (at sb); specially design sth (for sb): *The course was orientated towards foreign students.* **2** [Tn] ~ **oneself** (**a**) find out how one stands in relation to points of the compass, one's surroundings, etc: *The mountaineers found it difficult to orientate themselves in the fog.* (**b**) make oneself familiar with (a new situation): *It took him some time to orientate himself in his new school.*
▷ **orientation** /ˌɔːrɪənˈteɪʃn/ *n* [U] activity of orientating oneself; state of being orientated: *the orientation of new employees.*
-orientated (forming compound *adjs*) directed towards: *a* ˈ*sports-orientated course.*

orienteering /ˌɔːrɪənˈtɪərɪŋ/ *n* [U] sport of finding one's way across country on foot using a map and compass: *He has taken up orienteering.*

orifice /ˈɒrɪfɪs/ *n (fml)* outer opening in the body, etc: *the nasal orifices,* ie nostrils ○ *at the dark orifice of the cave.*

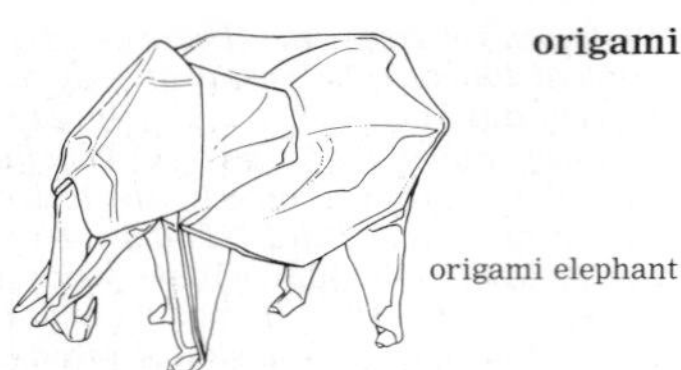
origami
origami elephant

origami /ˌɒrɪˈɡɑːmɪ/ *n* [U] Japanese art of folding paper into ornamental shapes or figures of animals, etc. ⇨ illus.

origin /ˈɒrɪdʒɪn/ *n* **1** [C, U] starting-point; source: *the origins of life on earth* ○ *words of Latin origin* ○ *The origins of the custom are unknown.* **2** [C esp *pl*] person's parentage, background, etc: *He never forgot his humble origins.* **3** [C] *(mathematics)* fixed point from which coordinates are measured. ⇨ illus at CARTESIAN COORDINATES.

original /əˈrɪdʒənl/ *adj* **1** [attrib] existing from the beginning; first or earliest: *The Indians were the original inhabitants of North America.* ○ *I prefer your original plan to this one.* **2** *(usu approv)* (**a**) newly created or formed; fresh: *an original idea* ○ *His designs are highly original.* (**b**) able to produce new ideas; creative: *an original thinker, writer, painter, etc* ○ *an original mind.* **3** painted, written, etc by the artist; not copied: *The original manuscript has been lost; this is a copy.*
▷ **original** *n* **1 the original** [C] the earliest form of sth (from which copies can be made): *This painting is a copy; the original is in Madrid.* ○ *This is a translation; the original is in French.* **2 the original** [sing] language in which sth was first written: *read Homer in the original,* ie in ancient Greek. **3** *(infml esp joc)* person who thinks, behaves, dresses, etc unusually; eccentric person: *Her Aunt Effie is certainly an original.*
originality /əˌrɪdʒəˈnælətɪ/ *n* [U] state or quality of being original(2): *Her designs have great originality.* ○ *The work lacks originality,* ie is copied or imitated.
originally /-nəlɪ/ *adv* **1** in an original(2) way: *speak, think, write, etc originally.* **2** from or in the beginning: *The school was originally quite small.*
□ **o**ˌ**riginal** ˈ**sin** *(religion)* (in Christianity) condition of wickedness thought to be present in everybody since Adam and Eve first sinned in the garden of Eden.

originate /əˈrɪdʒɪneɪt/ *v (fml)* **1** [Ipr] ~ **in sth**; ~ **from/with sb** have sth/sb as a cause or beginning: *The quarrel originated in rivalry between the two families.* ○ *The style of architecture originated from/with the ancient Greeks.* **2** [Tn] be the creator or author of (sth): *originate a new style of dancing* ○ *Who originated the concept of stereo sound?*
▷ **originator** *n* person who originates sth.

oriole /ˈɔːrɪəʊl/ *n* **1** (also ˌ**golden** ˈ**oriole**) type of European bird with black and yellow feathers. **2** similar type of N American bird of which the male has black and yellow feathers.

Orion /əˈraɪən/ large constellation containing several bright stars, named after a legendary ancient Greek hunter. The row of three very bright stars across the middle of the group is called Orion's belt.

Orkney Islands /ˈɔːknɪ aɪləndz/ **the Orkney Islands** (also **the Orkneys**) group of more than 70 islands off the north-eastern tip of Scotland. They belonged to Norway until 1472. Fishing and farming are the main sources of income. Cf ORCADIAN. ⇨ map at UNITED KINGDOM, map at App 1.

ormolu /ˈɔːməluː/ *n* [U, C] (article made of or decorated with) gilded bronze or a gold-coloured alloy of copper, zinc and tin: [attrib] *an ormolu clock.*

ornament /ˈɔːnəmənt/ *n* **1** [U] *(fml)* decoration; adornment: *The palace was rich in ornament.* ○ *The clock is simply for ornament, it doesn't actually work.* **2** [C] thing designed to add beauty to sth, but usu without practical use: *a shelf crowded with ornaments,* ie vases, pieces of china, etc ○ *I've just dropped one of your china ornaments.* **3** *(dated fml)* person, act, quality, etc that adds beauty, charm, etc: *He is an ornament to his profession.*
▷ **ornament** /ˈɔːnəment/ [esp passive: Tn, Tn·pr] ~ **sth (with sth)** add ornament to sth; decorate sth: *a dress ornamented with lace* ○ *a Christmas tree ornamented with tinsel.*
ornamental /ˌɔːnəˈmentl/ *adj* of or for ornament: *Ornamental copper pans hung on the wall.*
ornamentation /ˌɔːnəmenˈteɪʃn/ *n* [U] that which ornaments; decoration: *a church with no ornamentation.*

ornate /ɔːˈneɪt/ *adj (often derog)* (**a**) richly decorated: *ornate carvings in a church* ○ *That style of architecture is too ornate for my taste.* (**b**) (of prose, verse, etc) using complicated language and figures of speech; not simple in style or vocabulary: *ornate descriptions* ○ *an ornate style.*
▷ **ornately** *adv.* **ornateness** *n* [U].

ornithology /ˌɔːnɪˈθɒlədʒɪ/ *n* [U] scientific study of birds.
▷ **ornithological** /ˌɔːnɪθəˈlɒdʒɪkl/ *adj* [esp attrib]: *an ornithological survey.*
ornithologist /ˌɔːnɪˈθɒlədʒɪst/ *n* expert in ornithology.

orotund /ˈɒrəʊtʌnd/ *adj (fml sometimes joc)* **1** (of the voice) dignified; grand: *the orotund tones of the priest.* **2** boastful; pompous.

orphan /ˈɔːfn/ *n* person (esp a child) whose parents are dead: *He has been an orphan since he was five.* ○ [attrib] *an orphan nephew.*
▷ **orphan** *v* [Tn usu passive] make (a child) an orphan: *She was orphaned in the war.*
orphanage /ˈɔːfənɪdʒ/ *n* home for children who are orphans.

Orpheus /ˈɔːfjuːs, ˈɔːfɪəs/ (in Greek legend) poet and musician who went into the underworld to rescue his dead wife Eurydice, but lost her forever by looking back at her as she was coming out.
▷ **Orphean** /ˈɔːfɪən/ *adj* like the music of Orpheus; melodious in an enchanting way.

orrery /ˈɒrərɪ/ *n* mechanical model of the solar system, designed to show how the planets move around the sun.

orris-root /ˈɒrɪsruːt; *US* ˈɔːr-/ *n* sweet-smelling root of certain types of iris plant, dried and used in perfumes and medicines.

orth(o)- *comb form* correct; standard: *orthography* ○ *orthopaedic.*

orthodontics /ˌɔːθəˈdɒntɪks/ *n* [sing *v*] *(medical)* (branch of dentistry that deals with) preventing and correcting irregularities in the position of the teeth and associated facial abnormalities.
▷ **orthodontic** *adj* of orthodontics: *orthodontic surgery.*
orthodontist /-ˈdɒntɪst/ *n* specialist in orthodontics.

orthodox /ˈɔːθədɒks/ *adj* **1** (having beliefs, opinions, etc that are) generally accepted or approved: *orthodox behaviour* ○ *Her ideas are very orthodox.* Cf HETERODOX, UNORTHODOX. **2** *(esp religion)* following the older, more traditional, practices strictly: *orthodox Jews.* ⇨ article at RELIGION.
▷ **orthodoxy** /ˈɔːθədɒksɪ/ *n* **1** [U] state of being orthodox or holding orthodox beliefs. **2** [C esp *pl*] *(fml)* orthodox belief, character, practice, etc: *a firm supporter of Catholic orthodoxies.*
□ **the** ˈ**Orthodox Church** (also **The Eastern** ˈ**Orthodox Church**) branch of the Christian Church, found esp in eastern Europe and Greece, which recognizes the Patriarch of Constantinople (ie Istanbul) as its head bishop.

orthography /ɔːˈθɒɡrəfɪ/ *n* [U] *(fml)* **1** (study or system of) spelling: *In dictionaries, words are listed according to their orthography.* **2** correct or conventional spelling. ▷ **orthographic** (also **orthographical**) /ˌɔːθəˈɡræfɪk/ (/-fɪkl/) *adj.* **orthographically** /-klɪ/ *adv.*

orthopaedics (also **orthopedics**) /ˌɔːθəˈpiːdɪks/ *n* [sing *v*] *(medical)* (branch of surgery that deals with) correction of bone deformities and diseases: [attrib] *the orthopaedics department in the hospital.*
▷ **orthopaedic** (also **orthopedic**) /ˌɔːθəˈpiːdɪk/ *adj* of or concerning orthopaedics: *orthopaedic*

surgery on his spine.
orthopaedist (also **orthopedist**) /-ˈpiːdɪst/ *n* specialist in orthopaedics.

ortolan /ˈɔːtələn/ *n* [U, C] (meat of a) small wild European bird eaten as a delicacy.

Orwell /ˈɔːwel/ George (real name Eric Blair) (1903-50), British novelist, essayist and journalist. Much of his early work describes the conditions in which working people lived (eg *Down and Out in Paris and London* and *The Road to Wigan Pier*). His two best-known novels, *Animal Farm* and *1984*, attack totalitarianism. He warned against the manipulation of people's actions and thoughts by an all-powerful state. ▷ **Orwellian** /ɔːˈwelɪən/ *adj.*

-ory *suff* (with *vs* and *ns* forming *adjs*): *inhibitory* ○ *congratulatory.*

oryx /ˈɒrɪks; *US* ˈɔːr-/ *n* large African antelope with long straight horns.

OS /ˌəʊ ˈes/ *abbr* **1** ordinary seaman. **2** (*Brit*) Ordnance Survey: *an OS map.* **3** (esp on clothing, etc) outsize.

Os *symb* osmium.

Osborne /ˈɒzbɔːn/ John James (1929-), British playwright who achieved fame in the 1950s as a writer of tough realistic drama about working-class life (eg *Look Back in Anger*). He was one of the group of similar writers who were labelled 'angry young men'. ➪ article at PERFORMING ARTS.

Oscar /ˈɒskə(r)/ *n* (statuette presented as an) annual award in the US for excellence in cinema directing, acting, composing, etc: *be nominated for/win an Oscar* ○ *He received an Oscar for his performance.* ○ *This film is the winner of four Oscars.* Cf ACADEMY AWARD (ACADEMY).

oscillate /ˈɒsɪleɪt/ *v* **1** [I, Tn] (cause sth to) move repeatedly and regularly from one position to another and back again: *A pendulum oscillates.* **2** [I, Ipr] ~ (**between sth and sth**) (*fml fig*) keep moving backwards and forwards between extremes of feeling, behaviour, opinion, etc; waver: *He oscillates between political extremes.* ○ *Manic depressives oscillate between depression and elation.* Cf VACILLATE. **3** [I] (*physics*) (of electrical current, radio waves, etc) change in strength or direction at regular intervals.
▷ **oscillation** /ˌɒsɪˈleɪʃn/ *n* (*fml*) **1** [U] action of oscillating or being oscillated: *the oscillation of the compass needle* ○ *the oscillation of radio waves.* **2** [C] single swing or movement of a thing or person that is oscillating: *Her oscillations in mood are maddening.*
oscillator /-tə(r)/ *n* (*physics*) instrument for producing electrical oscillations.

oscillograph /əˈsɪləgrɑːf; *US* -græf/ *n* (*physics*) instrument for recording electrical oscillations.

oscilloscope /əˈsɪləskəʊp/ *n* (*physics*) instrument that shows variations in electrical current as a wavy line on a screen.

-ose *suff* **1** (forming *adjs*) having a particular quality: *grandiose* ○ *verbose.* **2** (forming *ns*) type of carbohydrate: *glucose* ○ *sucrose.*

osier /ˈəʊzɪə(r); *US* ˈəʊʒər/ *n* type of willow tree, the twigs of which are used to make baskets: [attrib] *an osier basket.*

-osis *suff* (with *ns* forming *ns*) abnormal or (esp) diseased bodily condition: *thrombosis* ○ *tuberculosis.*

osmosis /ɒzˈməʊsɪs/ *n* [U] **1** (*biology or chemistry*) gradual passing of a liquid through a porous partition: *Blood can be cleaned by osmosis if the kidneys have failed.* **2** gradual, and often hardly noticeable, acceptance of ideas, etc: *Children seem to learn about computers by osmosis.* ▷ **osmotic** /ɒzˈmɒtɪk/ *adj.*

osprey /ˈɒspreɪ/ *n* large fish-eating bird with a dark back and whitish head.

osseous /ˈɒsɪəs/ *adj* (*fml*) of bone; having bones; bony.

Ossian /ˈɒsɪən; *US* ˈɒʃn/ legendary Irish poet of the 3rd century AD. In the 18th century the Scottish poet James Macpherson published what he claimed were translations of Ossian's poetry, but in fact he wrote them himself.

ossify /ˈɒsɪfaɪ/ *v* (*pt, pp* **-fied**) [I, Tn esp passive] (*fml*) **1** (cause sth to) become hard like bone; change into bone. **2** (*fml derog*) (cause sth to) become rigid and unable to change: *Beliefs have ossified into rigid dogma.*
▷ **ossification** /ˌɒsɪfɪˈkeɪʃn/ *n* [U] (*fml*) process or action of ossifying: *the ossification of traditional practices.*

ostensible /ɒˈstensəbl/ *adj* [attrib] stated (as a reason, etc) though perhaps not true; apparent: *The ostensible reason for his absence was illness, but everyone knew he'd gone to a football match.* ▷ **ostensibly** /-əblɪ/ *adv*: *Ostensibly he was on a business trip, but he spent most of the time on the beach.*

ostentation /ˌɒstenˈteɪʃn/ *n* [U] (*derog*) exaggerated display (of wealth, knowledge, skill, etc) intended to impress people or make them envious: *the vulgar ostentation of the newly rich* ○ *Their daughter's wedding reception was sheer ostentation.*

ostentatious /ˌɒstenˈteɪʃəs/ *adj* (*derog*) showing or liking ostentation: *ostentatious jewellery* ○ *dress in a very ostentatious manner.* ▷ **ostentatiously** *adv*: *ostentatiously dressed.*

oste(o)- *comb form* of or concerning bone or the bones: *osteopath* ○ *osteo-arthritis.*

osteo-arthritis /ˌɒstɪəʊɑːˈθraɪtɪs/ *n* [U] (*medical*) painful disease of the joints of the body that causes inflammation and stiffness.

osteopathy /ˌɒstɪˈɒpəθɪ/ *n* [U] (*medical*) treatment of certain diseases by manipulation of the bones and muscles.
▷ **osteopath** /ˈɒstɪəpæθ/ *n* person who practices osteopathy: *An osteopath has been treating her injured back.*

ostler /ˈɒslə(r)/ *n* (formerly) man looking after horses at an inn; stableman.

Ostpolitik /ˈɒstpɒlɪtiːk/ *n* [U] policy of western European countries towards the (former) Communist countries of eastern Europe.

ostracize, -ise /ˈɒstrəsaɪz/ *v* [Tn] (*fml*) exclude (sb) from a group, club, etc; refuse to meet, talk to, etc: *He was ostracized by his colleagues for refusing to support the strike.*
▷ **ostracism** /-sɪzəm/ *n* [U] (*fml*) action of ostracizing; state of being ostracized: *suffer ostracism.*

ostrich

ostrich /ˈɒstrɪtʃ/ *n* **1** very large African bird with a long neck, unable to fly, but fast-running: [attrib] *Her dress was trimmed with ostrich feathers.* ○ *an ostrich-egg.* **2** (*infml fig*) person who refuses to face unpleasant realities (so called from the mistaken idea that ostriches bury their heads in the sand to avoid danger): *He's such an ostrich — he doesn't want to know about his wife's love affairs.*

OT *abbr* Old Testament. Cf NT 2.

Othello /əˈθeləʊ/ tragedy by *Shakespeare, written in 1604, which tells the story of how Othello, an African who is a commander in the Venetian army, is gradually persuaded by his evil servant Iago that his wife Desdemona is unfaithful to him, and kills her. When he then discovers that she was innocent, he kills himself. The play's theme is how a great man is destroyed by jealousy. ➪ App 6.

other /ˈʌðə(r)/ *indef det* **1** (person or thing) additional to that or those previously mentioned or implied: *Mr Smith and Mrs Jones and three other teachers were there.* ○ *Other people may disagree but I feel the whole thing has gone far enough.* ○ *She's engaged to Peter but she often goes out with other men.* ○ *Did you see any other films?* ○ *Not now, some other time* (ie at an unspecified time in the future), *perhaps.* Cf ANOTHER. **2** (used after *the, my, your, his*, etc with a singular *n*) the second of two: *Hold the bottle and pull the cork out with the other hand.* ○ *Those trousers are dirty — you'd better wear your other pair.* ○ *You may continue on the other side of the paper.* **3** (used after *the* or a possessive with a plural *n*) the remaining (people or things) in a group: *The other students in my class are from Italy.* ○ *Mary is older than me but my other sisters are younger.* ○ *I haven't read 'Cymbeline' but I've read all the other plays by Shakespeare/all Shakespeare's other plays.* **4** (idm) **every other** ➪ EVERY. **none other than** ➪ NONE. **one after the other** ➪ ONE[1]. **somebody/something/somewhere or other** ➪ OR. **the other ˈday, ˈmorning, ˈweek, ˈmonth, etc** recently: *I saw him in town the other day.* **this, that and the other** ➪ THIS.
▷ **other** *adj* [attrib] ~ **...than...** (*fml*) different (people, things, etc) from...: *You will have time to visit other places than those on the itinerary.* ○ *Other women than Sally would have said nothing.*
others *pron* **1** people or things that are additional to or different from those already mentioned or implied: *Some people came by car, others came on foot.* ○ *These shoes don't fit — haven't you got any others?* ○ *We must help others less fortunate than ourselves.* **2** (used after *the* or a *possess det*) the remaining persons or things in a group: *I went swimming while the others played tennis.* ○ *I can't do the fourth and fifth questions but I've done all the others.* ○ *She was the only person who replied to the invitation — none of the others bothered.*
□ **other than** *prep* (esp after a negative) **1** except: *He never speaks to me other than to ask for something.* ○ *She has no close friends other than him.* **2** different(ly) from; not: *I have never known him behave other than selfishly.* ○ *She seldom appears other than happy.*
other-worldly /ˌʌðəˈwɜːldlɪ/ *adj* concerned with or thinking about spiritual (rather than mundane) matters.

otherwise /ˈʌðəwaɪz/ *adv* **1** (*fml*) in another or a different way: *You obviously think otherwise.* ○ *He should have been working, but he was otherwise engaged*, ie doing something else. **2** in other or different respects; apart from that: *The rent is high, (but) otherwise the house is fine.*
▷ **otherwise** *conj* if conditions were different; if not: *Put the cap back on the bottle, otherwise the juice will spill.* ○ *We must run, otherwise we'll be too late.* ○ *Do as you're told, otherwise you'll be in trouble.*
otherwise *adj* [pred] in a different state; not as stated or supposed: *The truth is quite otherwise.* ○ *all employees, whether full-time or otherwise*, ie not full-time.

otiose /ˈəʊtɪəʊs; *US* ˈəʊʃɪəʊs/ *adj* (*fml*) (of language, ideas, etc) serving no useful purpose; unnecessary: *long, otiose passages of description.*

otter /ˈɒtə(r)/ *n* (**a**) [C] small fish-eating river animal with four webbed feet, a flat tail and thick brown fur. ➪ illus at ANIMAL. (**b**) [U] its fur: [attrib] *a jacket made of otter skins.*

ottoman /ˈɒtəmən/ *n* long cushioned seat without a back or arms, often used as a box for storing things (eg sheets and blankets).

Ottoman empire /ˌɒtəmən ˈempaɪə(r)/ **the Ottoman empire** Turkish empire from the 13th to the early 20th century, which at its largest included Asia Minor, the Middle East and much of south-eastern Europe.

OU /ˌəʊ ˈjuː/ *abbr* (*Brit*) Open University: *an OU degree in maths.*

oubliette /ˌuːblɪˈet/ *n* (esp formerly) secret dungeon or underground prison with an entrance only by a trapdoor in the roof.

ouch /aʊtʃ/ *interj* (expressing sudden pain): *Ouch! That hurts!*

ought to /ˈɔːt tə; *before vowels and finally* ˈɔːt tuː/

modal v (*neg* **ought not to**; *contracted form* **oughtn't to** /ˈɔ:tnt/) **1** (**a**) (indicating obligation): *We ought to start at once.* ○ *You ought to say you're sorry.* ○ *Such things ought not to be allowed.* ○ *They oughtn't to let their dog run on the road.* ○ *'Ought I to write to say thank you?' 'Yes, I think you ought (to).'* ○ *She ought to have been more careful.* ⇨ Usage 1 at MUST. (**b**) (indicating advice or recommendation): *You ought to improve your English before going to work in America.* ○ *There ought to be more buses during the rush hour.* ○ *You ought to see her new film.* ○ *She ought to have been a teacher*, ie She would probably have been a good one. ⇨ Usage 2 at MUST. **2** (drawing a tentative conclusion): *If he started at nine, he ought to be here by now.* ○ *That ought to be enough food for all of us.* ○ *Look at the sky — it ought to be a fine afternoon.* ⇨ Usage 3 at MUST[1].

Ouija /ˈwi:dʒə/ (also **ˈOuija-board**) *n* (*propr*) board marked with letters of the alphabet and other signs, used in seances to receive messages said to come from the dead.

ounce[1] /aʊns/ *n* **1** [C] (abbr **oz**) unit of weight, one sixteenth of a pound, equal to 28.35 grams. ⇨ App 10. **2** [sing] ~ **of sth** (*infml*) (used esp with negative *vs*) very small quantity of sth; any: *She hasn't an ounce of common sense.* ○ *There's not an ounce of truth in his story.*

ounce[2] /aʊns/ *n* = SNOW-LEOPARD (SNOW[1]).

our /ɑ:(r), ˈaʊə(r)/ *possess det* **1** of or belonging to us: *Our youngest child is six.* ○ *Our main export is rice.* ○ *Has anybody seen our two dogs?* ○ *They want us to show some of our colour slides.* **2 Our** (used to refer to or address God, etc): *Our Father*, ie God ○ *Our Lady*, ie the Virgin Mary.

▷ **ours** /ɑ:z, ˈaʊəz/ *possess pron* of or belonging to us: *Their house is similar to ours, but ours has a bigger garden.* ○ *Your photos are lovely — do you want to see some of ours?*

ourselves /ɑ:ˈselvz, aʊəˈselvz/ *reflex, emph pron* (only taking the main stress in sentences when used emphatically) **1** (*reflex*) (used when I and another or others, or I and you, cause and are affected by an action): *We try and ˌkeep ourselves ˈinformed about current trends.* ○ *Let's ˈsign ourˈselves 'Your affectionate students'.* ○ *We'd like to see it for ourˈselves.* **2** (*emph*) (used to emphasize *we* or *us*): *We've often thought of going there ourˈselves.* **3** (idm) **by ourˈselves** (**a**) alone. (**b**) without help.

-ous *suff* (with *ns* forming *adjs*) having the qualities or character of: *poisonous* ○ *mountainous* ○ *glorious*. ▷ **-ously** (forming *advs*): *grievously*. **-ousness** (forming uncountable *ns*): *spaciousness*.

oust /aʊst/ *v* [Tn, Tn·pr] ~ **sb** (**from sth**) (*fml*) remove sb (from a position, job, etc) sometimes in order to take his place: *oust a rival from office* ○ *He was ousted from his position as chairman.*

out /aʊt/ *adv part* (For special uses with many *vs*, eg *pick sth out*, *put sb out*, see the *v* entries) **1** away from or not inside a place: *go out for some fresh air* ○ *get up and walk out* ○ *open the door and run out into the garden* ○ *open a bag and take sth out* ○ *find one's way out* ○ *lock sb out* ○ *She shook the bag and some coins fell out.* ○ *Out you go!* ie Go out! Cf IN[1] 1. **2** (**a**) not at home or at a place of work: *I phoned Sally but she was out.* ○ *The manager is out at the moment.* ○ *Let's go out this evening/have an evening out*, eg go to the cinema, a restaurant, the theatre, a disco, etc. (**b**) (of a book, record, etc) not in the library: *The book you wanted is out.* Cf IN[1] 3. **3** (indicating distance away from land, one's country, a town, etc): *The boats are all out at sea.* ○ *She's out in Australia at the moment.* ○ *He lives right out in the country.* ○ *The ship was four days out from Lisbon*, ie had left Lisbon four days earlier. **4** (indicating that sth is no longer hidden): *The secret is out*, ie is revealed or discovered. ○ *The flowers are out*, ie open. ○ *The sun is out*, ie not behind a cloud. ○ *Her new book is out*, ie published. ○ *There's a warrant out* (ie issued) *against him.* ○ *Out with it!* ie Say what you know. **5** (used with superlative *adjs*) in existence; among known examples: *It's the best game out.* **6** not in power, in office or in a position: *The Labour party went out in 1979.* Cf IN[1] 10. **7** not fashionable: *Flared trousers are out this year.* Cf IN[1] 8. **8** unconscious: *He's been out (cold) for ten minutes.* **9** (of a tide) away from the shore; low: *We couldn't swim — the tide was too far out.* Cf IN[1] 6. **10** on strike: *The dockers in Liverpool are out.* **11** (*infml*) not possible or desirable: *Swimming in the sea is out until the weather gets warmer.* **12** (of fire, lights, burning materials, etc) extinguished; not burning: *The fire, gas, candle, etc is out.* ○ *The fire has gone/burnt out.* (Cf *The fire is still in.*) ○ *All the lights were out in the streets.* ○ *Put that cigarette out!* ○ *The wind blew the candles out.* **13** to the end; completely: *hear sb out* ○ *work out a problem* ○ *Supplies are running out*, ie becoming low. ○ *fight it out*, ie settle a dispute by fighting. ○ *I'm tired out*, ie exhausted. ○ *before the week is out*, ie finished. **14** clearly and loudly; without hesitation: *call/cry/shout out* ○ *the need to speak out about sth* ○ *say sth out loud* ○ *tell sb sth right/straight out.* **15** (indicating a mistake) more or less than the correct amount: *be out in one's calculations, reckoning, etc* ○ *We're ten pounds out in our accounts.* ○ *Your guess was a long way out*, ie completely wrong. ○ *My watch is five minutes out*, ie showing a time five minutes earlier or later than the correct time. **16** (*sport*) (**a**) (in cricket, baseball, etc) no longer batting, having been dismissed: *The captain was out for three*, ie after having made only three runs in cricket. ○ *Kent were all out for 137.* (**b**) (in tennis, badminton, etc) (of a ball, etc) having landed outside the line: *He lost the point because the ball was out.* Cf IN[1] 10. **17** (idm) **all out** ⇨ ALL. **be all out for sth** be trying to get or eager to obtain sth: *I'm not out for compliments.* ○ *He's out for your blood*, ie is seeking to attack you. **be out to do sth** be trying, aiming or hoping to do sth: *I'm not out to change the world.* ○ *The company is out to capture the Canadian market.* **ˌout and ˈabout** able to get up, go outdoors, etc after being in bed through illness, injury, etc: *It's good to see old Mr Jenkins out and about again.* **ˌout and aˈway** (with superlatives) by far: *She was out and away the most intelligent student in the class.*

▷ **out** *n* **1** (*US*) (in baseball) act, fact or instant of being OUT(16a). **2** (idm) **the ins and outs** ⇨ IN[3].

□ **ˌout-and-ˈout** *adj* [attrib] thorough; complete: *an out and out crook, professional.*

ˈout-tray *n* tray for holding letters, etc that have been dealt with and are ready to be dispatched.

out- *pref* **1** (with *vs* and *ns* forming transitive *vs*) to a greater extent; surpassing: *outlive* ○ *outgrow* ○ *outnumber* ○ *outwit*. **2** (with *ns*) separate; isolated: *outhouse* ○ *outpost*. **3** (with *vs* forming *ns*, *adjs* and *advs*): *outburst* ○ *outgoing* ○ *outspokenly*.

outback /ˈaʊtbæk/ *n* [sing] (esp in Australia) remote inland area where few people live: *lost in the outback.*

outbid /ˌaʊtˈbɪd/ *v* (**-dd-**; *pt, pp* **outbid**) [Tn] offer more money than (another person at an auction, etc); bid higher than: *She outbid me for the vase.*

outboard motor /ˌaʊtbɔ:d ˈməʊtə(r)/ *n* removable engine that is attached to the outside of the back (stern) of a boat. ⇨ illus at DINGHY.

outbreak /ˈaʊtbreɪk/ (also **outcrop**) *n* sudden appearance or start (esp of disease or violence): *an outbreak of typhoid, hostilities, rioting.*

outbuilding /ˈaʊtbɪldɪŋ/ *n* building, eg a shed or stable, separate from the main building: *a large farmhouse with useful outbuildings.* Cf OUTHOUSE.

outburst /ˈaʊtbɜ:st/ *n* (**a**) bursting out; explosion: *an outburst of steam from the pressure-cooker.* (**b**) sudden violent expression, esp of strong emotion: *an outburst of laughter, anger, etc* ○ *outbursts of vandalism.*

outcast /ˈaʊtkɑ:st; *US* -kæst/ *n, adj* ~ (**from...**) (person) driven away from home, friends, society, etc; homeless and friendless (person): *be treated as an outcast.*

outcaste /ˈaʊtkɑ:st; *US* -kæst/ *n, adj* (esp in India) (person) expelled from or not belonging to a fixed social class or caste.

outclass /ˌaʊtˈklɑ:s; *US* -ˈklæs/ *v* [Tn esp passive] be much better than (sb/sth); surpass: *I was outclassed from the start of the race.* ○ *In design and quality of manufacture they were outclassed by the Italians.*

outcome /ˈaʊtkʌm/ *n* (usu *sing*) effect or result (of an event, circumstances, etc): *What was the outcome of your meeting?*

outcrop /ˈaʊtkrɒp/ *n* **1** (*geology*) part of a layer (of rock, etc) that can be seen above the surface of the ground. **2** = OUTBREAK.

outcry /ˈaʊtkraɪ/ *n* (esp *sing*) ~ (**about/against sth**) strong public protest: *There was a public outcry about the building of a new airport.*

outdated /ˌaʊtˈdeɪtɪd/ *adj* (made) out of date (by the passing of time); old-fashioned: *ˌoutdated ˈclothing* ○ *Her ideas on education are rather outdated now.*

outdistance /aʊtˈdɪstəns/ *v* [Tn] move faster than (another person or animal) and leave him/it behind: *The favourite soon outdistanced the other horses in the race.* ○ *His wife has outdistanced* (ie has been promoted more often than) *him in her career.*

outdo /ˌaʊtˈdu:/ *v* (*3rd pers sing pres t* **-does** /-ˈdʌz/, *pt* **-did** /-ˈdɪd/, *pp* **-done** /-ˈdʌn/) [Tn] do more or better than (sb): *determined to outdo her brother at work and games* ○ *Not to be outdone* (ie Not wanting to let sb else do better) *she tried again.*

outdoor /ˈaʊtdɔ:(r)/ *adj* [attrib] **1** of, used in, done in or existing in the open air (ie outside a building or house): *outdoor activities* ○ *outdoor clothing* ○ *outdoor sports.* Cf INDOOR. **2** fond of activities done in the open air: *He's not really an outdoor type.*

outdoors /ˌaʊtˈdɔ:z/ *adv* in the open air; outside; out of doors: *It's cold outdoors.* ○ *In hot countries you can sleep outdoors.* ○ *Farm workers spend most of their time outdoors.* Cf INDOORS.

▷ **outdoors** *n* (idm) **the ˌgreat outˈdoors** the open air, esp away from towns and cities: *I couldn't live in London, I enjoy the great outdoors too much.*

outer /ˈaʊtə(r)/ *adj* [attrib] (**a**) of or for the outside: *the outer layer of wallpaper* ○ *outer garments* ○ *the outer walls of a house.* (**b**) farther from the inside or centre: *the outer hall* ○ *the outer suburbs of the city.* Cf INNER.

▷ **outermost** /ˈaʊtəməʊst/ *adj* farthest from the inside or centre; most remote: *the outermost planet from the sun* ○ *the outermost districts of the city.*

□ **ˌouter ˈspace** = SPACE 5: *journeys to outer space.*

outface /ˌaʊtˈfeɪs/ *v* [Tn] make (sb) feel uncomfortable or embarrassed by staring at him boldly: *outface one's opponent without flinching.*

outfall /ˈaʊtfɔ:l/ *n* place where water falls or flows out (of a lake, river, etc); outlet.

outfield /ˈaʊtfi:ld/ *n* **1 the outfield** (in cricket and baseball) part of the field furthest from the batsmen or batter. **2** [Gp] players in this part of the field as a group: [attrib] *Their outfield play is weak.* Cf INFIELD.

▷ **outfielder** *n* player in the outfield.

outfight /ˌaʊtˈfaɪt/ *v* (*pt, pp* **outfought** /-ˈfɔ:t/) [Tn] fight better than (an opponent) in battle or in a sports match: *We were outmanoeuvred and outfought throughout the winter campaign.*

outfit /ˈaʊtfɪt/ *n* **1** [C] all the equipment or articles needed for a particular purpose; kit: *a complete car repair outfit.* **2** [C] set of clothes worn together (esp for a particular occasion or purpose): *a white tennis outfit* ○ *She bought a new outfit for her daughter's wedding.* **3** [CGp] (*infml*) group of people working together; organization: *a small publishing outfit.*

▷ **outfitter** *n* supplier of equipment or of men's or children's clothes: *He bought a jacket at the gentleman's outfitters.* ○ *They are the official school outfitters.*

outflank /ˌaʊtˈflæŋk/ *v* [Tn] (*fml*) (**a**) pass round the side of (an enemy force): *an outflanking movement.* (**b**) gain an advantage over (sb) esp by taking an unexpected action: *He was totally outflanked in the debate.*

outflow /ˈaʊtfləʊ/ *n* [c usu *sing*] ~ (**from sth**) flowing out; amount that flows out: *a steady outflow from the tank* ○ *an illegal outflow of currency.*

outfox /ˌaʊtˈfɒks/ *v* [Tn] (*infml*) gain an advantage over (sb) by being more cunning; outwit: *He* *always outfoxes his opponents at chess.*

outgoing /ˈaʊtgəʊɪŋ/ *adj* **1** [attrib] (**a**) going out; leaving: *an outgoing ship, tide* ○ *the outgoing tenant,* ie the one who is leaving the house. (**b**) leaving office, a political post, etc: *the outgoing government* ○ *the outgoing president.* **2** friendly and sociable: *She's very outgoing.* ○ *an outgoing personality* ○ *He's never been an outgoing type.*

outgoings /ˈaʊtgəʊɪŋz/ *n* [pl] amount of money spent; expenditure: *monthly outgoings on rent and food.*

outgrow /ˌaʊtˈgrəʊ/ *v* (*pt* **outgrew** /-ˈgru:/, *pp* **outgrown** /-ˈgrəʊn/) [Tn] **1** grow too big for (esp one's clothes). **2** grow faster or taller than (another person): *He's already outgrown his older brother.* **3** leave (sth) behind or grow weary of (sth) as one grows older; grow out of: *outgrow bad habits, childish interests, etc* ○ *He has outgrown his passion for pop music.* **4** (idm) **outgrow one's ˈstrength** grow too quickly (during childhood) so that one easily becomes weak or ill.

outgrowth /ˈaʊtgrəʊθ/ *n* (*fml*) **1** natural development or result: *The manufacture of this material is an outgrowth of the space industry.* **2** that which grows out of another thing: *an outgrowth on a beech tree* ○ *an outgrowth of hair from the nostrils.*

outhouse /ˈaʊthaʊs/ *n* **1** small building (eg a shed or stable) outside the main building: *She did her washing in one of the outhouses.* Cf OUTBUILDING. **2** (*US*) outside lavatory (enclosed, but separate from the main building).

outing /ˈaʊtɪŋ/ *n* short pleasure trip; excursion: *go on an outing* ○ *an outing to the seaside* ○ *the firm's annual outing to the theatre.*

outlandish /aʊtˈlændɪʃ/ *adj* (*esp derog*) looking or sounding strange: *outlandish clothes, behaviour* ○ *Her views on children are rather outlandish.* ▷ **outlandishly** *adv.* **outlandishness** *n* [U].

outlast /ˌaʊtˈlɑ:st; *US* -ˈlæst/ *v* [Tn] last or live longer than (sth/sb): *This clock has outlasted several owners.* ○ *The political system will outlast most of us.* Cf OUTLIVE.

outlaw /ˈaʊtlɔ:/ *n* (esp formerly) person who has broken the law and is hiding to avoid being caught: *Bands of outlaws lived in the forest.*

▷ **outlaw** *v* [Tn] **1** (formerly) make or declare (sb) an outlaw. **2** declare (sth) to be illegal: *outlaw certain addictive drugs.*

outlay /ˈaʊtleɪ/ *n* ~ (**on sth**) (**a**) [U] spending, esp to help future developments in a business, etc: *There was very little outlay on new machinery.* (**b**) [sing] sum spent in this way: *a considerable outlay on basic research.*

outlet /ˈaʊtlet/ *n* **1** ~ (**for sth**) way out (for water, steam, etc): *an outlet for water* ○ *the outlet of a lake* ○ [attrib] *an outlet valve.* **2** ~ (**for sth**) (*fig*) means of releasing (energy, strong feelings, etc): *Children need an outlet for their energy.* ○ *He needs an outlet for all that pent-up anger.* **3** (*commerce*) shop, etc that sells goods made by a particular company: *This cosmetics firm has 34 outlets in Britain.*

outline /ˈaʊtlaɪn/ *n* **1** line(s) showing the shape or outer edge (of sth): *She could see only the outline(s) of the trees in the dim light.* ○ [attrib] *He drew an outline map of Italy.* **2** statement of the main facts or points: *an outline for an essay, a lecture, etc* ○ *an outline of European history,* eg as the title of a book which summarizes the most important historical events, etc. **3** giving only the main points: *describe a plan in (broad) outline.*

▷ **outline** *v* [Tn] **1** draw or mark the outer edge of (sth): *He outlined the triangle in red.* **2** give a short general description of (sth): *We outlined our main objections to the proposal.*

outlive /ˌaʊtˈlɪv/ *v* [Tn] live longer than (sb): *He outlived his wife by three years.* ○ (*fig*) *When he retired he felt that he had outlived his usefulness,* ie was no longer useful. Cf OUTLAST.

outlook /ˈaʊtlʊk/ *n* **1** ~ (**onto/over sth**) view on which one looks out: *The house has a pleasant outlook over the valley.* **2** ~ (**on sth**) person's way of looking at life, etc; mental attitude: *a narrow outlook on life* ○ *a tolerant, forgiving, pessimistic, etc outlook.* **3** ~ (**for sth**) what seems likely to happen; future prospects: *a bright outlook for trade* ○ *a bleak outlook for the unemployed* ○ *further outlook, dry and sunny,* eg as a weather forecast.

outlying /ˈaʊtlaɪɪŋ/ *adj* [attrib] far from a centre or a city; remote: *outlying regions* ○ *outlying villages, with poor communications.*

outmanoeuvre (*US* **outmaneuver**) /ˌaʊtməˈnu:və(r)/ *v* [Tn] do better than (an opponent, etc) by acting more skilfully and cleverly: *He was completely outmanoeuvred in his campaign to win the support of other ministers.*

outmoded /ˌaʊtˈməʊdɪd/ *adj* (*often derog*) no longer fashionable: *outmoded ideas, styles, views, etc.*

outnumber /ˌaʊtˈnʌmbə(r)/ *v* [Tn esp passive] be more in number than (sb): *The demonstrators were outnumbered by the police.* ○ *We were outnumbered two to one by the enemy,* ie There were twice as many of them.

out of /ˈaʊt əv/ *prep* **1** (situated) at a distance from (a place seen as an enclosed area or volume); not in: *Mr Green is out of town this week.* ○ *Fish can survive for only a short time out of water.* Cf IN[2] 1. **2** (moving) away from (a place seen as an enclosed area or volume): *jump out of bed* ○ *go out of the shop* ○ *fly out of the cage.* **3** (indicating motive or cause): *do sth out of mischief, spite, malice, etc* ○ *help sb out of pity, kindness, generosity, etc* ○ *ask out of curiosity.* **4** from among (a number): *Choose one out of the six.* ○ *To give you only one example out of several....* **5** by using (sth); from: *The hut was made out of pieces of wood.* ○ *She made a skirt out of the pieces of material I gave her.* Cf FROM 8, OF 5. **6** lacking (sth); without: *I'm beginning to feel out of patience.* ○ *He's been out of work for six months.* ○ *be out of* (ie have no) *flour, sugar, tea, etc.* **7** not in the condition specified by the following *n*: *These books are out of order.* ○ *He's still in hospital but out of danger.* (See *n* entries for similar examples.). **8** having (sth) as its origin or source; from: *a scene out of a play by Pinter* ○ *copy a recipe out of a book* ○ *drink beer out of the can* ○ *pay for a new car out of one's savings.* **9** (indicating the loss of sth, esp as a result of dishonesty): *cheat sb out of his money* (See *v* entries for similar examples.). **10** at a specified distance from (sth): *The ship sank 10 miles out of Stockholm.* **11** not concerned with (sth); not involved in: *It's a dishonest scheme and I'm glad to be out of it.* ○ *Brown is out of the England team.* **12** (idm) ˈ**out of it** (*infml*) sad because excluded from a group of people or a community: *We've only just moved here so we still feel a bit out of it.* ○ *She looks rather out of it — perhaps she doesn't speak English.* **out of one's head** ⇨ HEAD[1]. **out of kilter** ⇨ KILTER.

outpace /ˌaʊtˈpeɪs/ *v* [Tn] go faster than (sb): *She soon outpaced the others on the course.*

out-patient /ˈaʊtpeɪʃnt/ *n* person who goes to a hospital for treatment, but does not stay there: *If you do not require surgery you can be treated as an out-patient.* ○ [attrib] *the out-patient department.*

outplay /ˌaʊtˈpleɪ/ *v* [Tn esp passive] play much better than (an opponent): *The English team were totally outplayed by the Brazilians.*

outpoint /ˌaʊtˈpɔɪnt/ *v* [Tn esp passive] (in boxing, etc) defeat (sb) by scoring more points: *He was outpointed by the champion.*

outpost /ˈaʊtpəʊst/ *n* **1** (group of soldiers at an) observation point some distance away from the main army. **2** any distant settlement: *a missionary outpost in the jungle* ○ (*joc*) *You'd better get petrol here — where we're going is the last outpost of civilization.*

outpouring /ˈaʊtpɔ:rɪŋ/ *n* (usu *pl*) uncontrolled expression of strong feeling: *outpourings of the heart* ○ *an outpouring of frenzied grief* ○ *the outpourings of a madman.*

output /ˈaʊtpʊt/ *n* [sing] **1** quantity of goods, etc produced (by a machine, worker, etc): *The average output of the factory is 20 cars a day.* ○ *We must increase our output to meet demand.* ○ *the literary output of the year,* ie all the books, etc published in a year. **2** power, energy, etc produced (by a generator, etc): *an output of 100 watts.* **3** (*computing*) information produced from a computer. Cf INPUT 3.

▷ **output** *v* (-**tt**-; *pt, pp* **output** or **outputted**) [Tn] (*computing*) supply (information, results, etc). Cf INPUT *v*.

□ ˈ**output device** machine by which information is received from a computer.

outrage /ˈaʊtreɪdʒ/ *n* (*derog*) **1** [C, U] (act of) great violence or cruelty: *outrages committed by armed mobs* ○ *never safe from outrage.* **2** [C] act or event that shocks or angers the public: *'The building of the new shopping centre is an outrage,' she protested.* **3** [U] strong resentment or anger: *When he heard the news he reacted with a sense of outrage.* ○ *He leapt up and down in sheer outrage.*

▷ **outrage** *v* [Tn esp passive] shock or offend (sb); upset greatly: *outrage public opinion* ○ *They were outraged by the announcement of massive price increases.*

outrageous /aʊtˈreɪdʒəs/ *adj* **1** very offensive or immoral; shocking: *His treatment of his wife is outrageous.* ○ *The price is outrageous,* ie much too high. **2** very unusual and unconventional: *outrageous hats at Ascot* ○ *outrageous remarks designed to shock listeners.* ▷ **outrageously** *adv*: *outrageously expensive clothes* ○ *outrageously pornographic magazines.*

outrank /ˌaʊtˈræŋk/ *v* [Tn] (*fml*) be of higher rank than (sb): *Colonel Jones outranks everyone here.*

outré /ˈu:treɪ; *US* u:ˈtreɪ/ *adj* (*French derog or joc*) (esp of behaviour, ideas, tastes, etc) not conventional; very unusual or peculiar; eccentric: *an outré style of dress* ○ *She likes to shock people with her outré remarks.*

outrider /ˈaʊtraɪdə(r)/ *n* person on a motor cycle (or, esp formerly, on horseback) escorting the vehicle of an important person: *The President's car was flanked by motor cycle outriders.*

outrigger /ˈaʊtrɪgə(r)/ *n* **1** structure projecting over the side of a boat or ship, eg for the rowlocks in a racing boat or to give stability to a canoe. **2** boat fitted with one of these structures.

outright /ˈaʊtraɪt/ *adv* **1** openly and honestly, with nothing held back: *I told him outright what I thought of his behaviour.* **2** not gradually; instantly: *be killed outright by a single gunshot* ○ *buy a house outright,* ie not by instalments. **3** clearly and completely: *He won outright.*

▷ **outright** *adj* [attrib] **1** without any doubt or reservation: *an outright denial, refusal, etc.* **2** clear; unmistakable: *She was the outright winner.*

outrival /ˌaʊtˈraɪvl/ *v* (-**ll**-; *US also* -**l**-) [Tn] (*fml*) be or do better than (sb) in competition with him: *She outrivals him at all board games.*

outrun /ˌaʊtˈrʌn/ *v* (*pt* **outran** /-ˈræn/, *pp* **outrun**) [Tn] run faster or better than (sb/sth): *The favourite easily outran the other horses in the field.* ○ (*fig*) *His ambition outran his ability,* ie He was ambitious to do more than he was able.

outsell /ˌaʊtˈsel/ *v* (*pt, pp* **outsold** /-ˈsəʊld/) [Tn] **1** sell more (quickly) than (sb): *The Japanese can outsell any competitor in the market.* **2** be sold in greater quantities than (sth): *This model outsells all others on the market.*

outset /ˈaʊtset/ *n* (idm) **at/from the outset (of sth)** at/from the beginning (of sth): *At the outset of her career she was full of optimism but not now.* ○ *From the outset it was clear that he was guilty.*

outshine /ˌaʊtˈʃaɪn/ *v* (*pt, pp* **outshone** /-ˈʃɒn/) [Tn] (*usu fig*) shine more brightly than (sb/sth): *The young girl violinist outshone* (ie was much better than) *all the other competitors.*

outside[1] /ˌaʊtˈsaɪd/ *n* **1** [C usu *sing*] outer side or surface: *The outside of the house needs painting.* ○ *a fruit with a prickly outside* ○ *Lower the window and open the door from the outside.* ○ *Make sure the contents are clearly labelled on the outside.* ○ (*fig*) *She seems calm on the outside but I know how worried she really is.* **2** [sing] area that is close to but not part of the specified building, etc: *walk round the outside of the building* ○ *I only saw it from the outside.* Cf INSIDE[1]. **3** (idm) **at the outside** estimated or calculated as the highest possible figure; at the most: *room for 75 people at the outside*

○ *With tips I can earn £150 a week, at the very outside.* **on the outside** (of motorists, motor vehicles, etc) using the lane that is nearest to the middle of the road or motorway: *overtake sb on the outside.*

▷ **outside** /ˈaʊtsaɪd/ *adj* [attrib] **1** of, on or facing the outer side: *outside repairs, measurements, appearance* ○ *a house with only two outside walls.* **2** (**a**) not in the main building; not internal: *an outside toilet.* (**b**) not included in or connected with a group, an organization, etc: *We'll need outside help before we can finish.* ○ *We may have to use an outside firm of consultants.* ○ *She has a lot of outside interests*, ie not connected with her job or main subject of study. **3** (of choice, possibility, etc) very small: *an outside chance of winning the game.* **4** greatest possible or probable: *My outside price is £100 000.* ○ *150 is an outside estimate.*

□ ˌ**outside** ˈ**broadcast** programme filmed or recorded in a place other than the main studio.

ˌ**outside** ˈ**lane** section of a road or motorway nearest the middle, where traffic moves fastest.

ˌ**outside** ˈ**left**, ˌ**outside** ˈ**right** player (in football, etc) in the forward line who is furthest to the left/right of the centre forward.

ˌ**outside** ˈ**line** connection by telephone to a place that is outside the building or organization.

outside[2] /ˌaʊtˈsaɪd/ (also *esp US* **outside of**) *prep* **1** on or to a place on the outside of (sth): *You can park your car outside our house.* ○ *Don't go outside the school playground.* Cf INSIDE[2]. **2** not within the range or scope of (sth): *The matter is outside my area of responsibility.* ○ *I'm not concerned with what you do outside working hours.* **3** except for (sb); other than: *Outside her brothers and sisters she has no real friends.*

▷ **outside** *adv* **1** on or to the outside: *Please wait outside.* ○ *The house is painted green outside.* ○ *The children are playing outside.* ○ *Don't go outside — it's too cold.* **2** in the open air; not enclosed: *It's warmer outside than in this room.* ○ *The car wouldn't start after standing outside all week.*

outsider /ˌaʊtˈsaɪdə(r)/ *n* **1** person who is not (or is not accepted as) a member of a society, group, etc: *Although she's lived there for ten years, the villagers still treat her as an outsider.* ○ *Women feel like outsiders in that club.* **2** competitor thought to have little chance of winning a race or contest: *That horse is a complete outsider; I wouldn't waste your money on it.* ○ *Amazingly, the job went to a rank outsider.*

outsize /ˈaʊtsaɪz/ *adj* [usu attrib] (*sometimes derog*) (of clothing or people) larger than the standard sizes: *outsize dresses for larger ladies* ○ *She's not really outsize — just well-built.*

outskirts /ˈaʊtskɜːts/ *n* [pl] outlying districts (esp of a city or large town); outer areas: *They live on the outskirts* (ie in an outlying district) *of Paris.*

outsmart /ˌaʊtˈsmɑːt/ *v* [Tn] be cleverer or more cunning than (sb); outwit: *We outsmarted them and got there first by taking a shorter route.*

outspoken /ˌaʊtˈspəʊkən/ *adj* ~ **(in sth/doing sth)** saying openly exactly what one thinks; frank: *an outspoken critic of the government* ○ *be outspoken in one's remarks.* ▷ **outspokenly** *adv*: *outspokenly critical.* **outspokenness** *n* [U].

outspread /ˌaʊtˈspred/ *adj* spread or stretched out: *She ran towards him with* ˌ*outspread* ˈ*arms/with* ˌ*arms* ˈ*outspread.*

outstanding /ˌaʊtˈstændɪŋ/ *adj* **1** exceptionally good; excellent: *an outstanding student, piece of work, performance.* **2** [usu attrib] in a position to be easily noticed; conspicuous: *the outstanding features of the landscape* ○ *an outstanding landmark.* **3** (of payment, work, problems, etc) not yet paid, done, resolved, etc: *outstanding debts* ○ *A good deal of work is still outstanding.*

▷ **outstandingly** *adv* exceptionally: *outstandingly good* ○ *play outstandingly well.*

outstation /ˈaʊtsteɪʃn/ *n* remote station(1); outpost.

outstay /ˌaʊtˈsteɪ/ *v* [Tn] **1** stay longer than (sb): *outstay all the other guests.* **2** (idm) **outstay/overstay one's welcome** ⇨ WELCOME.

outstretched /ˌaʊtˈstretʃt/ *adj* (with limbs) stretched or spread out as far as possible: *He lay outstretched on the grass.* ○ *with* ˌ*arms out*ˈ*stretched/with* ˌ*outstretched* ˈ*arms.*

outstrip /ˌaʊtˈstrɪp/ *v* (**-pp-**) [Tn] **1** run faster than (sb in a race) and leave him behind: *We soon outstripped the slower runners.* **2** become larger, more important, etc than (sb/sth): *Demand is outstripping current production.*

out-take /ˈaʊt teɪk/ *n* part of a film or other recording that is excluded from the final version (eg because it contains a mistake): *a collection of amusing out-takes from her television series.*

outvote /ˌaʊtˈvəʊt/ *v* [Tn esp passive] defeat (sb) by a majority of votes; win more votes than: *Richard and David tried to get the question put on the agenda but they were heavily outvoted.*

outward /ˈaʊtwəd/ *adj* [attrib] **1** (of a journey) going out or away from (a place that one is going to return to): *He got lost on the outward journey.* **2** of or on the outside: *the outward appearance of things* ○ *To (all) outward appearances* (ie As far as one can judge from the outside) *the child seems very happy.* **3** in, or relating to, one's expressions or actions (in contrast to one's mental state or emotions): *She gives no outward sign of the sadness she must feel.* ○ *An outward show of confidence concealed his nervousness.*

▷ **outwardly** *adv* on the surface; apparently: *Though badly frightened, she appeared outwardly calm.*

outwards /-wədz/ (*Brit*) (also *esp US* **outward**) *adv.* ⇨ Usage at FORWARD[2]. **1** towards the outside: *The two ends of the wire must be bent outward(s).* ○ *Her feet turn outwards.* **2** away from home or from the point from which one started: *a train travelling outwards from London.* ˌ**outward** ˈ**bound** going away from home, etc: *The ship is outward bound.* ○ [attrib] *the outward bound train.* ˌ**Outward** ˈ**Bound Movement** scheme designed to provide adventure training outdoors for young people: [attrib] *an Outward Bound (Movement) School.*

outweigh /ˌaʊtˈweɪ/ *v* [Tn] be greater in weight, value or importance than (sth): *This outweighs all other considerations.* ○ *The advantages far outweigh the disadvantages.*

outwit /ˌaʊtˈwɪt/ *v* (**-tt-**) [Tn] win or defeat (sb) by being cleverer or more cunning than him: *Two prisoners outwitted their guards and got away.*

outwork /ˈaʊtwɜːk/ *n* [U] sewing, assembly work, etc supplied by a factory or shop to an individual to be done at home: *do outwork for a clothing factory.*

▷ **outworker** *n* person who does outwork: *Outworkers in the clothing industry are usually badly paid.*

outworn /ˌaʊtˈwɔːn/ *adj* [usu attrib] no longer useful; outdated; old-fashioned: *outworn practices in industry* ○ *outworn scientific theories.*

ouzel /ˈuːzl/ *n* **1** (also **ring ouzel**) small bird of the thrush family. **2** (also **water ouzel, dipper**) type of small diving bird.

ouzo /ˈuːzəʊ/ *n* [U] Greek alcoholic drink flavoured with aniseed, usu drunk with water.

ova *pl* of ovum.

oval /ˈəʊvl/ *n* **1** flat shape or outline that is shaped like an egg: *The playing-field is a large oval.* ○ *an oval-shaped face.* **2 the Oval** cricket ground in S London, where test matches are played.

▷ **oval** *adj* like an egg in shape or outline: *an oval brooch* ○ *The mirror is oval.*

□ **the** ˌ**Oval** ˈ**Office** office of the US President, in the *White House.

ovary /ˈəʊvərɪ/ *n* **1** either of the two organs in female animals that produce egg-cells *(ova)*: *an operation to remove diseased ovaries.* ⇨ illus at FEMALE. Cf OVUM. **2** (*botany*) part of a plant that produces seeds.

▷ **ovarian** /əʊˈveərɪən/ *adj* [attrib] of the ovary: *an ovarian cyst.*

ovation /əʊˈveɪʃn/ *n* great applause or cheering expressing welcome or approval: *She received an enthusiastic ovation from the audience.* ○ *The speaker was given a standing ovation*, ie The audience stood to clap, etc.

oven /ˈʌvn/ *n* **1** enclosed box-like space (usu part of a cooker) in which things are cooked or heated: *Bread is baked in an oven.* ○ *a gas oven* ○ *a microwave oven* ○ [attrib] *You've left the oven door open.* Cf STOVE 1. **2** (idm) **have a bun in the oven** ⇨ BUN. **like an** ˈ**oven** very hot: *Open the window, it's like an oven in here!*

□ ˈ**ovenbird** *n* type of small S American bird that makes its nest out of mud.

ˈ**ovenproof** *adj* (of dishes, etc) suitable for use in an oven.

ˌ**oven-**ˈ**ready** *adj* prepared and ready for cooking: ˌ*oven-ready* ˈ*chickens.*

ovenware /ˈʌvnweə(r)/ *n* [U] heatproof dishes that can be used for cooking food in an oven: [attrib] *ovenware pottery.*

over[1] /ˈəʊvə(r)/ *adv part* (For special uses with many *vs*, eg *give over*, see the relevant *v* entries.) **1** (**a**) outwards and downwards from an upright position: *Don't knock that vase over.* ○ *He fell over on the ice.* ○ *I wobbled uncertainly for a couple of paces, then over I went.* ○ *The wind must have blown it over.* (**b**) from one side to another side: *Turn the patient over onto his front.* ○ *Turn over the page.* ○ *The car skidded off the road and rolled over and over down the slope.* ○ *After ten minutes, turn the meat over*, ie to cook the other side. (**c**) across (a street, an open space, etc): *Take these letters over to the post office.* ○ *Let me row you over to the other side of the lake.* ○ *He has gone over to/is over in France.* ○ *Let's ask some friends over*, ie to our home. ○ *Put the tray over there.* **2** (*esp US*) again: *He repeated it several times over* (ie again and again) *until he could remember it.* ○ *We did the house over* (ie redecorated it) *and bought new furniture.* **3** left unused; remaining: *If there's any food (left) over, put it in the fridge.* ○ *I'll have just £10 over when I've paid all my debts.* ○ *7 into 30 goes 4 with 2 over.* **4** in addition; more: *children of fourteen and over* ○ *10 metres and a bit over.* Cf UNDER 4. **5** ended: *Their relationship is over.* ○ *By the time we arrived the meeting was over.* ○ *'It's all over with him* (ie He is going to die),*' the doctor said gently.* **6** (**a**) (indicating transfer or change from one person, group, place, etc to another): *He's gone over to the enemy*, ie joined them. ○ *Please change the plates over*, ie exchange their positions. (**b**) (used when communicating by radio): *Message received. Over*, ie It is your turn to speak. **7** so as to cover (sb/sth) entirely: *paint sth over* ○ *The lake is completely frozen over.* ○ *Cover her over with a blanket.* **8** (idm) **(all) over a**ˈ**gain** a second time (from the beginning): *He did the work so badly that I had to do it all over again myself.* **over against sth** (*fml*) in contrast with sth: *the benefits of private education over against state education.* ˌ**over and** ˌ**over (a**ˈ**gain)** many times; repeatedly: *I've warned you over and over (again) not to do that.* ○ *Say the words over and over to yourself.*

over[2] /ˈəʊvə(r)/ *prep* (For special uses with many *vs*, eg *argue over sth, get over sth, fall over sth*, see the *v* entries.) **1** (not replaceable by *above* in this sense) resting on the surface of and partly or completely covering (sb/sth): *Spread a cloth over the table.* ○ *She put a rug over the sleeping child.* ○ *He put his hand over her mouth to stop her screaming.* ⇨ Usage at ABOVE[2]. **2** in or to a position higher than but not touching (sb/sth): *They held a large umbrella over her.* ○ *The sky was a clear blue over our heads.* ○ *The balcony juts out over the street.* ○ *There was a lamp (hanging) over the table.* Cf ABOVE[2] 1A, UNDER 1. ⇨ Usage at ABOVE[2]. **3** (**a**) from one side of (sth) to the other; across: *a bridge over the river* ○ *run over the grass* ○ *escape over the frontier* ○ *look over the hedge.* (**b**) on the far side or opposite side of (sth): *He lives over the road.* ○ *Who lives in that house over the way* (ie on the other side of the road or street)? ○ *Over the river is private land.* ○ (*fig*) *We're over* (ie We have completed) *the most difficult stage of the journey.* (**c**) so as to cross (sth) and be on the other side: *climb over a wall* ○ *jump over the stream* ○ *go over the mountain.* **4** (esp with *all*) in or across every part or most parts of (sth/a place): *Snow is falling (all) over the country.* ○ *He's famous all over the world.* ○ *He sprinkled sugar over his cereal.* **5** more than (a specified time, amount, cost, etc): *over 3 million copies sold* ○

She stayed in Lagos (for) over a month. ○ *She's over two metres tall.* ○ *The river is over fifty kilometres long.* ○ *He's over fifty.* Cf UNDER 4. ⇨ Usage at ABOVE². **6** (indicating control, command, authority, superiority, etc): *He ruled over a great empire.* ○ *She has only the director over her.* ○ *He has little control over his emotions.* Cf UNDER 5, BELOW. **7 (a)** (indicating the passing of time) while doing, having, eating, etc (sth); during: *discuss it over lunch* ○ *He went to sleep over his work.* ○ *We had a pleasant chat over a cup of tea.* ○ *Over the next few days they got to know the town well.* **(b)** throughout (a period); during: *stay in Wales over* (ie until after) *Christmas and the New Year.* **8** because of or concerning (sth): *an argument over money* ○ *a disagreement over the best way to proceed.* **9** transmitted by (sth): *We heard it over the radio.* ○ *She wouldn't tell me over* (ie when speaking on) *the phone.* **10** (idm) ˌ**over and aˈbove** besides; in addition to: *The waiters get good tips over and above their wages.*

over³ /ˈəʊvə(r)/ *n* (in cricket) series of six balls bowled in succession from one end of the wicket by the same bowler: *dismiss two batsmen in the same over.*

over- *pref* **1** (with *ns* forming *ns, vs, adjs* and *advs*) above; outside; across: *overcoat* ○ *overhang* ○ *overall* ○ *overhead.* Cf SUPER-. **2** (used widely with *vs, ns, adjs* and *advs*) to excess; too much: *overeat* ○ *overwork* ○ *overtime* ○ *over-rich* ○ *over-aggressively.* Cf HYPER-.

overact /ˌəʊvərˈækt/ *v* [I, Tn] (*derog*) act²(2a) (one's part) in an exaggerated way; overplay: *Amateur actors often overact.* ○ *He overacts the part of the loving husband.* Cf UNDERACT.

overall¹ /ˌəʊvərˈɔːl/ *adj* [attrib] **(a)** including everything; total: *the overall measurements of a room* ○ *the overall cost of the carpet including sales tax and fitting.* **(b)** taking everything into account; general: *There's been an overall improvement recently.*

▷ **overall** *adv* **1** including everything: *How much will it cost overall?* **2** on the whole; generally: *Overall it's been a good match.*

overall² /ˈəʊvərɔːl/ *n* **1** [C] (*Brit*) loose-fitting coat worn over other clothing to protect it from dirt, etc: *The shop assistant was wearing a white overall.* ⇨ illus at APRON. **2 overalls** (*Brit*) (*US* **coveralls** /ˈkʌvərɔːlz/) [pl] loose-fitting one-piece garment made of heavy material and covering the body and legs, usu worn over other clothing by workmen, etc to protect them from dirt, etc: *The carpenter was wearing a pair of blue overalls.* Cf BOILER SUIT (BOILER).

overarm /ˈəʊvərɑːm/ *adj, adv* (of bowling in cricket) with the arm swung over the shoulder: *an overarm bowler* ○ *bowl overarm.* Cf UNDERARM.

overawe /ˌəʊvərˈɔː/ *v* [Tn usu passive] cause (sb) to feel a great deal of fear and respect: *overawed into submission by senior colleagues* ○ *He was overawed by rather grand surroundings.*

overbalance /ˌəʊvəˈbæləns/ *v* [I, Tn] (cause sb/sth to) lose balance and fall over: *He overbalanced and fell into the water.* ○ *If you stand up you'll overbalance the canoe.*

overbearing /ˌəʊvəˈbeərɪŋ/ *adj* (*derog*) forcing others to do what one wants (without caring about their feelings); domineering: *an overbearing manner.* ▷ **overbearingly** *adv*: *overbearingly proud.*

overbid /ˌəʊvəˈbɪd/ *v* (**-tt-**, *pt, pp* **overbid**) **1** [Tn] offer more money than (sb) at an auction; outbid. **2** [I, Tn] (in the game of bridge) make a higher bid than (one's partner) or than one's cards are worth. Cf UNDERBID.

▷ **overbid** /ˈəʊvəbɪd/ *n* act of overbidding.

overblown /ˌəʊvəˈbləʊn/ *adj* **1** (of flowers) past their best; too fully open: ˌ*overblown ˈroses* ○ (*fig*) ˌ*overblown ˈbeauty.* **2** (*fml*) overdone; pretentious: *an overblown style of writing.*

overboard /ˈəʊvəbɔːd/ *adv* **1** over the side of a ship or boat into the water: *fall, jump, be washed overboard.* **2** (idm) **go overboard (about sb/sth)** (*infml often derog*) be very or too enthusiastic (about sth/sb): *He goes overboard about every young woman he meets.* **throw sth/sb overboard** abandon sth; get rid of or stop supporting sb: *After heavily losing the election the party threw their leader overboard.*

overbook /ˌəʊvəˈbʊk/ *v* [Tn esp passive] make reservations for too many passengers or visitors for (an aircraft flight, a hotel, etc): *The flight was overbooked.*

overburden /ˌəʊvəˈbɜːdn/ *v* [usu passive: Tn, Tn·pr] ~ **sb (with sth)** load sb with too much weight, work, worry, etc: *overburdened with committee meetings* ○ *overburdened with guilt, remorse, debt.*

overcapitalize, -ise /ˌəʊvəˈkæpɪtəlaɪz/ *v* [Tn] fix or estimate the money supply of (a company, business, etc) too high. ▷ **overcapitalization, -isation** /ˌəʊvəˌkæpɪtəlaɪˈzeɪʃn; *US* -lɪˈz/ *n* [U].

overcast /ˌəʊvəˈkɑːst; *US* -ˈkæst/ *adj* (of the sky) covered with cloud: *a dark, overcast day* ○ *It's a bit overcast — it might rain.* ○ (*fig*) *a gloomy, overcast* (ie unhappy) *expression on his face.*

▷ **overcast** *v* [Tn] turn over (the edge of cloth) and sew it to prevent loose threads coming out.

overcharge /ˌəʊvəˈtʃɑːdʒ/ *v* **1** [I, Ipr, Tn, Tn·pr, Dn·n] ~ **(sb) (for sth)** charge (sb) too high a price (for sth): *That grocer never overcharges.* ○ *We were overcharged for the eggs.* ○ *They overcharged me (by) £1 for the shopping.* Cf UNDERCHARGE. **2** fill or load (sth) too full or too heavily: *overcharge an electric circuit* ○ (*fig*) *a poem overcharged with emotion.*

overcoat /ˈəʊvəkəʊt/ *n* (also *dated* ˈ**topcoat**) long warm coat worn over other clothes (when going outdoors in cold weather): *He wore a hat, gloves and an overcoat.* ⇨ illus at DRESS.

overcome /ˌəʊvəˈkʌm/ *v* (*pt* **overcame** /-ˈkeɪm/, *pp* **overcome**) **1** [Tn] succeed in a struggle against (sth); defeat: *overcome a bad habit* ○ *He overcame a strong temptation to run away.* **2** [I] (*fml*) be victorious; triumph: *We shall overcome!* **3** [Tn usu passive] make (sb) weak or ill; cause (sb) to become faint or lose control: *be overcome by gas fumes* ○ *be overcome by/with grief, anger, despair, etc.* **4** [Tn] find a way of dealing with or solving (a problem, etc): *We'll overcome that difficulty when we get to it.*

over-compensate /ˌəʊvəˈkɒmpenseɪt/ *v* [I, Ipr] ~ **(for sth)** try to correct (an error, a weakness, etc) but go too far (in the opposite direction): *He had over-compensated for the effect of the wind, and taken the aircraft off course.* ○ *Working mothers often over-compensate for their absences from home by spoiling their children.* ▷ **over-compensation** /ˌəʊvəˌkɒmpenˈseɪʃn/ *n* [U].

overcrop /ˌəʊvəˈkrɒp/ *v* (**-pp-**) [Tn] take too many crops from (farmland) so that it loses fertility.

overcrowded /ˌəʊvəˈkraʊdɪd/ *adj* with too many people in (a place); crowded too much: *Shops are very overcrowded before Christmas.* ○ ˌ*overcrowded ˈbuses, ˈtrains, etc.*

▷ **overcrowding** /ˌəʊvəˈkraʊdɪŋ/ *n* [U] state of having too many people in one place: *the serious overcrowding in the poorer areas of the city.*

overdo /ˌəʊvəˈduː/ *v* (*pt* **overdid** /-ˈdɪd/, *pp* **overdone** /-ˈdʌn/) [Tn] **1** do, perform or express (sth) too fully or for too long; exaggerate: *She rather overdid the sympathy,* ie was so sympathetic that she did not seem sincere. **2** overact (sth): *The comic scenes in the play were overdone.* **3** use too much of (sth): *Don't overdo the garlic in the food — not everyone likes it.* ○ *I think they've rather overdone the red in this room,* ie used too much red paint, wallpaper, etc. **4** cook (sth) for too long: *The fish was overdone and very dry.* **5** (idm) **overˈdo it/things (a)** work, study, exercise, etc too hard: *He's been overdoing things recently.* ○ *You must stop overdoing it — you'll make yourself ill.* **(b)** behave in an exaggerated way (in order to achieve one's aim): *He was trying to be helpful, but he rather overdid it.*

overdose /ˈəʊvədəʊs/ *n* too great an amount (of a drug) taken at one time: *take a massive overdose of sleeping tablets* ○ *die of a heroin overdose* ○ (*fig*) *I've had rather an overdose of TV this week,* ie watched too much.

▷ **overdose** *v* **1** /ˌəʊvəˈdəʊs/ [Tn, Tn·pr] ~ **sb (with sth)** give sb an overdose (of sth): *He's been overdosing himself.* ○ *She overdosed the old woman with pain-killers.* **2** /ˈəʊvədəʊs/ [I, Ipr] ~ **(on sth)** take an overdose (of sth): *He overdosed (on sleeping pills) and died.* Cf OD.

overdraft /ˈəʊvədrɑːft; *US* -dræft/ *n* amount of money by which a bank account is overdrawn: *He has a huge overdraft to pay off.* ○ *I took out an overdraft to pay for my new car.* ○ [attrib] *an overdraft arrangement.*

overdraw /ˌəʊvəˈdrɔː/ *v* (*pt* **overdrew** /-ˈdruː/, *pp* **overdrawn** /-ˈdrɔːn/) **1** [I, Tn] draw more money from (a bank account) than the amount that is in it. **2** [Tn] give an exaggerated account of (sth): *The characters in this novel are overdrawn,* ie not true to life.

▷ **overdrawn** /ˌəʊvəˈdrɔːn/ *adj* **(a)** [pred] (of a person) having an overdraft: *I am overdrawn by £500.* **(b)** (of an account) with more money drawn out than paid or left in: *a heavily overdrawn account.*

overdress /ˌəʊvəˈdres/ *v* [I, Tn usu passive] (*usu derog*) dress (oneself or another person) more formally, richly, etc than is suitable for the occasion: *I feel rather overdressed in this suit — everyone else is wearing jeans!*

overdrive /ˈəʊvədraɪv/ *n* **1** [U] mechanism providing an extra gear above the normal top gear in a vehicle. **2** (idm) **go into ˈoverdrive** use the overdrive mechanism: (*fig*) *She always goes into overdrive* (ie starts working very hard) *before the holidays.*

overdue /ˌəʊvəˈdjuː; *US* -ˈduː/ *adj* [usu pred] not paid, completed, arrived, etc by the due or expected time: *These bills are overdue,* ie should have been paid before now. ○ *The baby is two weeks overdue,* ie still not born two weeks after the expected date of birth. ○ *The train is overdue,* ie late.

overeat /ˌəʊvərˈiːt/ *v* (*pt* **overate** /-ˈet/, *pp* **overeaten** /-ˈiːtn/) [I] eat more than one needs or more than is healthy: *I overate at the party last night and got violent indigestion.* ○ *Obese people find it difficult to stop overeating.*

overestimate /ˌəʊvərˈestɪmeɪt/ *v* [Tn] estimate (sth) to be bigger, higher, better, etc than it is: *I overestimated the amount of milk we'd need for the weekend.* ○ *I overestimated his abilities — he's finding the job very difficult.* Cf UNDERESTIMATE.

overexpose /ˌəʊvərɪkˈspəʊz/ *v* [Tn esp passive] expose (a film, etc) for too long or in too bright a light. Cf UNDEREXPOSE. ▷ **overexposure** *n* [U].

overfish /ˌəʊvəˈfɪʃ/ *v* [Tn esp passive] (of fishermen) remove too many fish from (an area of water), so that stocks become dangerously low: *The North Sea has been badly overfished.*

overflow /ˌəʊvəˈfləʊ/ *v* **1** [I, Tn] flow over the edges or limits of (sth): *Your bath is overflowing.* ○ *The river overflowed (its banks).* ⇨ illus at OVERLAP. **2** [I, Ipr, Tn] ~ **(into sth)** spread beyond the limits of (a room, etc): *The meeting overflowed into the streets.* ○ *The audience easily overflowed the small theatre.* **3** [Ipr] ~ **with sth** be more than filled with sth; be very full of sth: *overflowing with happiness, kindness, gratitude, etc* ○ *a heart overflowing with love.*

▷ **overflow** /ˈəʊvəfləʊ/ *n* **1** [U] **(a)** flowing over of liquid: *stop the overflow from the cistern.* **(b)** that which overflows: *Put a bowl underneath to catch the overflow.* ○ [attrib] *an overflow canal.* **2** [U, sing] something that is too much for the space available: *a large overflow of population from the cities* ○ *find a smaller hall for the overflow from the main meeting.* **3** [C] (also ˈ**overflow pipe**) outlet that allows excess liquid to escape: *The overflow from the bath is blocked.*

overfly /ˌəʊvəˈflaɪ/ *v* (*pt* **overflew** /-ˈfluː/, *pp* **overflown** /-ˈfləʊn/) [Tn] fly over (a city, country, etc): *The journey back took longer than normal, because the plane could not overfly the war zone.*

overgraze /ˌəʊvəˈgreɪz/ *v* [Tn esp passive] keep too many farm animals on (a piece of land), so that all the grass is eaten and the land becomes bare.

overgrown /ˌəʊvəˈgrəʊn/ *adj* **1** [usu attrib]

having grown too large or too fast: *That man behaves like an ˌovergrown ˈchild.* **2** [pred] ~ (**with sth**) covered with (plants, weeds, etc that have grown too thickly in an uncontrolled way): *walls overgrown with ivy* ○ *The garden's completely overgrown (with nettles).*

overgrowth /ˈəʊvəgrəʊθ/ *n* **1** [U, C] plants, weeds, etc growing in an uncontrolled way: *an overgrowth of nettles.* **2** /ˌəʊvəˈgrəʊθ/ [U] growth that is too fast or too much: *Overgrowth is common in adolescents.*

overhang /ˌəʊvəˈhæŋ/ *v* (*pt, pp* **overhung** /-ˈhʌŋ/) [I, Tn] hang over or stand out over (sth) like a shelf: *The ledge overhangs by several feet.* ○ *The cliff overhangs the beach.*

▷ **overhang** /ˈəʊvəhæŋ/ *n* part that overhangs: *a bird's nest under the overhang of the roof.*

overhaul /ˌəʊvəˈhɔːl/ *v* [Tn] **1** examine (sth) carefully and thoroughly and make any necessary repairs: *have the engine of a car overhauled* ○ (*fig*) *The language syllabus needs to be completely overhauled.* **2** catch up with and overtake (sth): *The fast cruiser soon overhauled the old cargo boat.*

▷ **overhaul** /ˈəʊvəhɔːl/ *n* thorough examination followed by any necessary repairs: *I've taken my typewriter in for an overhaul.* ○ *The engine is due for an overhaul.* ○ (*infml joc*) *I'm going to the doctor for my annual overhaul,* ie physical examination.

overhead /ˈəʊvəhed/ *adj* **1** raised above the ground; above one's head: *overhead wires, cables, etc* ○ *an overhead railway,* ie built on a level higher than the street. **2** of or relating to overheads: *overhead expenses, charges, etc.*

▷ **overhead** /ˌəʊvəˈhed/ *adv* above one's head; in the sky: *the stars overhead* ○ *birds flying overhead.*

□ ˌ**overhead proˈjector** (*abbr* **OHP**) device for projecting (PROJECT[2] 2a) the image of a transparency onto a wall or screen behind the user, eg during a lecture.

overheads /ˈəʊvəhedz/ *n* [pl] regular expenses involved in running a business, eg rent, light, heating, salaries: *Heavy overheads reduced his profits.* ○ *If you move to a smaller office you will reduce your overheads.*

overhear /ˌəʊvəˈhɪə(r)/ *v* (*pt, pp* **overheard** /-ˈhɜːd/) [Tn, Tng, Tni] hear (sb, a conversation, etc) without the knowledge of the speaker(s); hear by chance: *I overheard their argument/them.* ○ *I overheard them quarrelling.* ○ *I overheard him say/saying he was going to France.*

overheat /ˌəʊvəˈhiːt/ *v* [I, Tn] (cause sth to) become too hot: *The engine's overheating.* ○ (*fig*) *The economy has become seriously overheated,* ie Demand for goods and services in the economy has grown too fast, causing inflation.

overjoyed /ˌəʊvəˈdʒɔɪd/ *adj* [usu pred] ~ (**at sth/to do sth**) filled with great happiness: *He'll be overjoyed at your news.* ○ *She was overjoyed to hear about the arrival of the baby.*

overkill /ˈəʊvəkɪl/ *n* [U] (*usu fig*) much greater amount than is needed to defeat sb/sth or achieve sth: *It was surely overkill to screen three interviews on the same subject in one evening.*

overland /ˈəʊvəlænd/ *adj* across the land; by land (not by sea or air): *an overland route, journey, etc.*

▷ **overland** *adv*: *travel overland.*

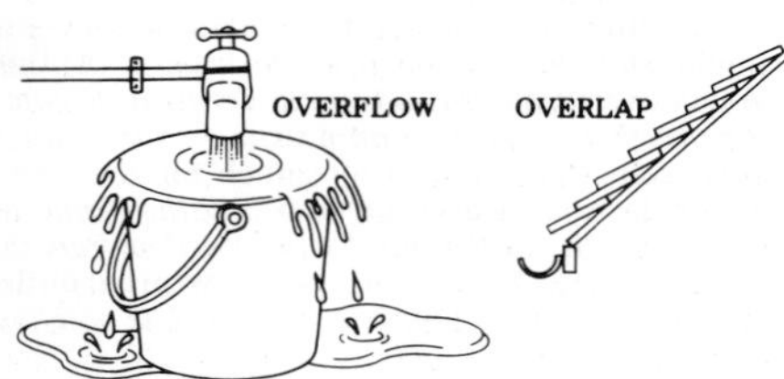

overlap /ˌəʊvəˈlæp/ *v* (**-pp-**) [I, Tn] **1** partly cover (sth) by extending over its edge: *a boat made of overlapping boards* ○ *The tiles on the roof overlap one another.* **2** (*fig*) partly coincide (with sth): *Our visits to the town overlapped.* ○ *His duties and mine overlap,* ie cover part of the same area of interest.

▷ **overlap** /ˈəʊvəlæp/ *n* **1** [C] overlapping part or amount: *an overlap of 50 cm* ○ *a large overlap.* **2** [U] fact or process of overlapping: *There is no question of overlap between the two courses.* ⇨ illus.

overlay /ˌəʊvəˈleɪ/ *v* (*pt, pp* **overlaid** /-ˈleɪd/) [usu passive: Tn, Tn·pr] ~ **sth** (**with sth**) put a thin layer over the surface of (sth): *wood overlaid with gold* ○ *He overlaid the walls with hessian.*

▷ **overlay** /ˈəʊvəleɪ/ *n* thing laid over sth: *a table covered with a copper overlay.*

overleaf /ˌəʊvəˈliːf/ *adv* on the other side of the page (of a book, etc): *see picture overleaf,* ie as an instruction to the reader.

overload /ˌəʊvəˈləʊd/ *v* [esp passive: Tn, Tn·pr] ~ **sth** (**with sth**) **1** put too great a load on or into (sth): *The donkey was so overloaded, it could hardly climb the hill.* **2** put too great an electric charge into (a circuit, etc): *The lights fused because the system was overloaded with electrical appliances.*

overlook /ˌəʊvəˈlʊk/ *v* [Tn] **1** have or give a view of (a place) from above: *My room overlooks the sea.* ○ *We overlook the church from our house.* ○ *Our garden is overlooked by our neighbours' windows,* ie They can see into our garden from their windows. **2** (**a**) fail to see or notice (sth); miss: *He overlooked a spelling error on the first page.* (**b**) take no (official) notice of (sb/sth); ignore: *He was overlooked* (ie He was not considered for the job) *when they set about choosing a new manager.* ○ *We can afford to overlook minor offences.* ○ *She overlooked his rudeness and tried to pretend nothing had happened.*

overlord /ˈəʊvəlɔːd/ *n* (formerly) nobleman on whose land people of lower rank worked: *a feudal overlord* ○ *The peasants owed service and obedience to their overlord.*

overly /ˈəʊvəlɪ/ *adv* (*fml esp Scot or US*) (placed before an *adj* or a *v*) too; excessively: *overly cautious* ○ *I am not overly impressed by his work.* Cf OVER-.

overmanned /ˌəʊvəˈmænd/ *adj* (of a factory, etc) having more workers than are needed to do the work that needs to be done: *Management decided the office was overmanned and sacked three junior typists.* Cf OVERSTAFFED, UNDERMANNED. ▷ **overmanning** /ˌəʊvəˈmænɪŋ/ *n* [U]: *Overmanning can be a serious problem in industry.*

overmastering /ˌəʊvəˈmɑːstərɪŋ; *US* -ˈmæs-/ *adj* [esp attrib] (*fml or rhet*) overpowering; overwhelming: *an overmastering passion,* ie one that is difficult to control.

over-much /ˌəʊvəˈmʌtʃ/ *adj, adv* (*fml*) (esp with a negative *v*) too much; very much: *His book did not display ˌover-much ˈtalent.* ○ *I do not like her over-much.*

overnight /ˌəʊvəˈnaɪt/ *adv* **1** during or for the night: *stay overnight at a friend's house,* ie sleep there for the night. **2** (*infml*) suddenly or very quickly: *She became a celebrity overnight.*

▷ **overnight** /ˈəʊvənaɪt/ *adj* [attrib] **1** during or for the night: *an overnight journey* ○ *an overnight bag* ○ *an overnight stop in Rome.* **2** (*infml*) suddenly; very quickly: *an overnight success.*

overpass /ˈəʊvəpɑːs; *US* -pæs/ *n* (*esp US*) (*Brit* also **flyover** /ˈflaɪəʊvə(r)/) bridge that carries a road over a motorway. Cf UNDERPASS.

overpay /ˌəʊvəˈpeɪ/ *v* (*pt, pp* **overpaid** /-ˈpeɪd/) [Tn, Tn·pr] ~ **sb** (**for sth**) pay sb too much or too highly: *They don't exactly overpay their work-force.* ○ *I think he's overpaid for the little he does.* Cf UNDERPAY.

overplay /ˌəʊvəˈpleɪ/ *v* **1** [Tn] give too much importance to (sth): *overplay certain factors* ○ *You must not overplay his part in the negotiations.* Cf UNDERPLAY. **2** (idm) **overplay one's ˈhand** take too great or too many risks (by overestimating one's own strength): *The union is in danger of overplaying its hand in the current dispute.*

overpower /ˌəʊvəˈpaʊə(r)/ *v* [Tn] be too strong or powerful for (sb); defeat (sb) by greater strength or numbers: *The burglars were easily overpowered by the police.* ○ *He was overpowered by the heat.*

▷ **overpowering** /ˌəʊvəˈpaʊərɪŋ/ *adj* too strong; very powerful: *find the smell overpowering* ○ *overpowering grief.*

overprint /ˌəʊvəˈprɪnt/ *v* (**a**) [Tn, Tn·pr] ~ **sth** (**with sth**) print additional matter on (an already printed surface, eg a postage stamp): *overprint stamps with a new price.* (**b**) [I, Ipr, Tn, Tn·pr] ~ (**sth**) (**on sth**) print (additional matter) in this way: *Additional material is overprinted in red.* ○ *overprint a grid on a map.*

▷ **overprint** /ˈəʊvəprɪnt/ *n* (*fml*) thing overprinted.

overrate /ˌəʊvəˈreɪt/ *v* [Tn esp passive] have too high an opinion of (sb/sth); put too high a value on: *I think I overrated him; he can't handle a senior job.* ○ *He overrated his abilities as a salesman.* Cf UNDERRATE.

▷ **overrated** *adj* (*derog*) having too high a value placed on it: *I think his work is extremely overrated.* ○ *an overrated film.*

overreach /ˌəʊvəˈriːtʃ/ *v* [Tn no passive] ~ **oneself** (*esp derog*) fail by trying to achieve more than is possible: *Don't apply for that job: you're in danger of overreaching yourself.*

over-react /ˌəʊvərɪˈækt/ *v* [I, Ipr] ~ (**to sth**) react too strongly or too intensely to difficulty, danger, etc: *She tends to over-react when things go wrong.* ○ *He over-reacted to the bad news.* ▷ **over-reaction** /-ˈækʃn/ *n* [U, C]: *The stock-market panic was simply over-reaction to the news from Tokyo.*

override /ˌəʊvəˈraɪd/ *v* (*pt* **overrode** /-ˈrəʊd/, *pp* **overridden** /-ˈrɪdn/) [Tn] **1** override or set aside (sb's opinions, etc): *override sb's views, decisions, wishes, etc* ○ *They overrode my protest and continued with the meeting.* **2** be more important than (sth): *Considerations of safety override all other concerns.*

▷ **overriding** /əʊvəˈraɪdɪŋ/ *adj* [usu attrib] more important than any other considerations: *It is of overriding importance to finish the project this week.*

overrule /ˌəʊvəˈruːl/ *v* [Tn] decide against (something already decided, etc) by exercising one's higher authority: *overrule a claim, objection, etc* ○ *The judge overruled the previous decision.* ○ *We were overruled by the majority.*

overrun /ˌəʊvəˈrʌn/ *v* (*pt* **overran** /-ˈræn/, *pp* **overrun**) **1** [Tn esp passive] spread over and occupy (a place) in great numbers: *a country overrun by enemy troops* ○ *a warehouse overrun by rats.* **2** [I, Tn] continue beyond or exceed (a time allowed, etc): *The lecturer overran by ten minutes.* ○ *The news programme overran the allotted time.*

overseas /ˌəʊvəˈsiːz/ *adj* (at, to, from, etc places or countries) across the sea; foreign: *ˌoverseas ˈtrade* ○ *an ˌoverseas ˈbroadcast* ○ *overseas students in Britain.*

▷ **overseas** *adv* across the sea; abroad: *go, live, travel, etc overseas.*

oversee /ˌəʊvəˈsiː/ *v* (*pt* **oversaw** /-ˈsɔː/, *pp* **overseen** /-ˈsiːn/) [Tn] watch over and control (sb/sth); supervise: *You must employ someone to oversee the project.*

▷ **overseer** /ˈəʊvəsɪə(r)/ *n* person whose job is to take charge of work and see that it is properly done: *the production overseer* ○ *The overseer was explaining the job to young trainees.*

over-sexed /ˌəʊvəˈsekst/ *adj* having greater sexual desire than is usual; obsessed by sex. Cf UNDER-SEXED.

overshadow /ˌəʊvəˈʃædəʊ/ *v* [Tn] **1** cause (sth) to be shaded or to have little light: *a village overshadowed by mountains* ○ *Large oak trees overshadow the garden.* **2** (*fig*) cause (sth) to be unhappy or less happy: *His recent death overshadowed the family gathering.* **3** (*fig*) cause (sb) to seem less important or noticeable: *Despite her professional success, she was always overshadowed by her husband.*

overshoe /ˈəʊvəʃuː/ *n* rubber or plastic shoe worn over an ordinary shoe for protection against wet, mud, etc: *a pair of overshoes* ○ *She removed her overshoes at the front door.* Cf GALOSHES.

overshoot /ˌəʊvəˈʃuːt/ *v* (*pt, pp* **overshot** /-ˈʃɒt/) [Tn] **1** go further or beyond (a point aimed at): *The aircraft overshot the runway.* ○ *We overshot the exit for Manchester on the motorway.* **2** (idm) **overshoot the ˈmark** make a mistake as a result of misjudging a person, situation, etc.

oversight /ˈəʊvəsaɪt/ *n* (**a**) [U] unintentional failure to notice sth: *Many errors are caused by oversight.* (**b**) [C] example of this: *Through an unfortunate oversight your letter was left unanswered.*

over-simplify /ˌəʊvəˈsɪmplɪfaɪ/ *v* (*pt, pp* **-fied** /-faɪd/) [I, Tn esp passive] state or explain (a problem, fact, etc) too simply for the truth to be told: *an over-simplified analysis of the problems we face* ○ *an over-simplified interpretation of the reasons for the child's behaviour.*

▷ **over-simplification** /ˌəʊvəˌsɪmplɪfɪˈkeɪʃn/ *n* [C, U] (instance of) over-simplifying.

oversleep /ˌəʊvəˈsliːp/ *v* (*pt, pp* **overslept** /-ˈslept/) [I] sleep longer or later than one intended: *I'm afraid I overslept and missed my usual bus.*

overspill /ˈəʊvəspɪl/ *n* [U] (*esp Brit*) people from the overcrowded parts of a city, etc who are provided with housing, usu of a better standard, in the surrounding areas: *build new houses for London's overspill* ○ [attrib] *an overspill housing development.*

overstaffed /ˌəʊvəˈstɑːft; *US* -stæft/ *adj* (of an office, etc) having more members of staff than are needed for the work to be done: *No wonder the firm makes a loss; the office is terribly overstaffed.* Cf OVERMANNED, UNDERSTAFFED.

overstate /ˌəʊvəˈsteɪt/ *v* [Tn] express or state (sth) too strongly; exaggerate: *Don't overstate your case or no one will believe you.* ○ *The problems have been greatly overstated.*

▷ **overstatement** /ˈəʊvəsteɪtmənt/ *n* **1** [U] action of overstating; exaggeration. **2** [C] exaggerated statement: *a wild overstatement of the facts.*

overstay /ˌəʊvəˈsteɪ/ *v* **1** [Tn] stay longer than (a period of time): *We've already overstayed our visit to Aunt Sophie.* **2** (idm) **outstay/overstay one's welcome** ⇨ WELCOME.

overstep /ˌəʊvəˈstep/ *v* (**-pp-**) [Tn] **1** go beyond (what is normal or permitted): *overstep one's authority* ○ *overstep the bounds of modesty.* **2** (idm) **overstep the ˈmark** do or say more than one should or more than is wise or acceptable; go too far: *It's surely overstepping the mark to behave so rudely to your guests.*

overstock /ˌəʊvəˈstɒk/ *v* [Tn, Tn·pr] ~ **sth (with sth)** supply sth with too large a stock: *a shop overstocked with out-of-date furniture* ○ *overstock a farm with cattle*, ie with more cattle than there is food or space for.

overstrung *adj* **1** /ˌəʊvəˈstrʌŋ/ (of a person) too sensitive and nervous; easily excited: *She was tense and overstrung before the performance.* **2** /ˈəʊvəstrʌŋ/ (of a piano) with strings in sets crossing each other at an oblique angle.

over-subscribe /ˌəʊvəsəbˈskraɪb/ *v* [Tn esp passive] (*esp finance*) apply for more of (an issue of shares, tickets, etc) than are available: *Tickets for this concert have been over-subscribed.* ○ *The flight has been over-subscribed; there are no seats.*

overt /ˈəʊvɜːt; *US* əʊˈvɜːrt/ *adj* [usu attrib] (*fml*) done or shown openly or publicly; not secret or hidden: *overt hostility.* Cf COVERT. ▷ **overtly** *adv* (*fml*): *overtly critical of his work.*

overtake /ˌəʊvəˈteɪk/ *v* (*pt* **overtook** /-ˈtʊk/, *pp* **overtaken** /-ˈteɪkən/) **1** [I, Tn] come level with and pass (esp a moving person or vehicle): *It's dangerous to overtake on a bend.* ○ *overtake other cars on the road* ○ (*fig*) *Supply will soon overtake demand*, ie There will soon be more of sth than is needed. ○ *Italy's economy has overtaken that of its nearest competitors.* **2** [Tn esp passive] (of unpleasant events) come to (sb/sth) suddenly and unexpectedly: *be overtaken by/with fear, surprise, etc* ○ *be overtaken by events*, ie by circumstances changing so rapidly that plans, etc become out of date ○ *Disaster overtook the project.* ○ *On his way home he was overtaken by a storm.*

overtax /ˌəʊvəˈtæks/ *v* [Tn] **1** (*fml*) put too great a strain on (sb/sth): *overtax one's strength* ○ *overtax sb's patience.* **2** make (sb) pay too much tax; tax too heavily: *If you have been overtaxed you will get a tax rebate*, ie money will be paid back to you.

overthrow /ˌəʊvəˈθrəʊ/ *v* (*pt* **overthrew** /-ˈθruː/, *pp* **overthrown** /-ˈθrəʊn/) [Tn] cause the downfall or defeat of (sb/sth); put an end to: *The rebels tried to overthrow the government.*

▷ **overthrow** /ˈəʊvəθrəʊ/ *n* **1** [C usu *sing*] act of overthrowing; defeat: *the overthrow of the monarchy* ○ *the attempted overthrow of the tyrant.* **2** [C] (**a**) (in cricket) throw of the ball by a fielder which goes too far, esp when this results in an extra score for the batsman. (**b**) extra run scored in this way.

overtime /ˈəʊvətaɪm/ *n* [U], *adv* (time spent at work) after the usual working hours: *working overtime* ○ *be paid extra for overtime* ○ [attrib] *overtime payments* ○ *be on overtime*, ie working overtime.

overtone /ˈəʊvətəʊn/ *n* (usu *pl*) something suggested or implied in addition to what is actually stated; hint: *overtones of despair in a letter* ○ *threatening overtones in his comments.* Cf UNDERTONE.

overture /ˈəʊvətjʊə(r)/ *n* **1** [C usu *pl*] ~ **(to sb)** (*fml*) friendly approach, proposal or offer made (to sb) with the aim of starting discussions: *overtures of peace to the enemy* ○ *make overtures of friendship to the new neighbours.* **2** [C] piece of music written as an introduction to an opera, a ballet, a musical play, etc: *The audience must be in their seats before the overture.*

overturn /ˌəʊvəˈtɜːn/ *v* **1** [I, Tn] (cause sb/sth to) turn over or upside-down; upset: *The boat overturned.* ○ *He overturned the boat.* ○ (*fig*) *The Labour candidate overturned the previous Conservative majority of 4000.* ○ (*fig*) *The House of Lords overturned* (ie reversed) *the decision by the House of Commons.* **2** [Tn] cause the downfall of (esp a government); overthrow: *overturn the military regime.*

overview /ˈəʊvəvjuː/ *n* (*fml*) short general description (without unnecessary details); survey: *an overview of the company's plans for the next year.*

overweening /ˌəʊvəˈwiːnɪŋ/ *adj* [attrib] (*fml*) showing too much self-confidence or conceit: *overweening ambition, vanity, pride, etc.*

overweight /ˌəʊvəˈweɪt/ *adj* **1** heavier than is usual or allowed: *If your luggage is overweight you'll have to pay extra.* ○ *Your suitcase is five kilograms overweight.* **2** (of people) too heavy; fat: *an ˌoverweight ˈchild* ○ *I'm overweight by 2kg according to my doctor.* ○ *He's very overweight.* Cf UNDERWEIGHT. ⇨ Usage at FAT[1].

▷ **overweighted** /ˌəʊvəˈweɪtɪd/ *adj* ~ **(with sth)** (*fml*) carrying too much (of sth): *overweighted with packages* ○ (*fig*) *Her lecture was overweighted with quotations.*

overwhelm /ˌəʊvəˈwelm; *US* -ˈhwelm/ *v* [Tn usu passive] (**a**) cover (sth/sb) completely by flowing over or pouring down on it/him; submerge suddenly: *overwhelmed by a flood* ○ *A great mass of water overwhelmed the village.* ○ (*fig*) *be overwhelmed with grief, sorrow, despair, etc* ○ (*fig*) *Overwhelmed with gratitude, he fell to his knees.* (**b**) overpower (sb/sth), esp by force of numbers; defeat: *be overwhelmed by the enemy/by superior forces.*

▷ **overwhelming** *adj* [usu attrib] too great to resist or overcome; very great: *an overwhelming urge to smoke* ○ *an overwhelming victory* ○ *the overwhelming majority of people*, ie the majority by a great number. **overwhelmingly** *adv*: *overwhelmingly successful, generous.*

overwork /ˌəʊvəˈwɜːk/ *v* **1** [I, Tn] (cause a person or an animal to) work too hard or too long: *You'll become ill if you continue to overwork.* ○ *overwork a horse.* **2** [Tn esp passive] use (a word, etc) too much (and so weaken its importance or effectiveness): *an overworked phrase, metaphor, expression, etc* ○ *'Situation' is a word that is greatly overworked.*

▷ **overwork** /ˈəʊvəwɜːk/ *n* [U] working too hard or too long: *ill through overwork* ○ *stress caused by overwork.*

overwrought /ˌəʊvəˈrɔːt/ *adj* in a state of nervous excitement, anxiety, etc; tense and upset: *She was in a very overwrought state after the accident.* ○ *She didn't mean to offend you; she was overwrought.*

Ovid /ˈɒvɪd/ (43 BC-17 AD), Roman poet who wrote the *Metamorphoses*, retelling Greek and Roman myths, and many love poems.

oviduct /ˈəʊvɪdʌkt/ *n* = FALLOPIAN TUBE.

ovine /ˈəʊvaɪn/ *adj* of or like sheep.

oviparous /əʊˈvɪpərəs/ *adj* (*biology*) (of fish, birds, reptiles, etc) producing eggs that hatch outside the body.

ovipositor /ˌəʊvɪˈpɒzɪtə(r)/ *n* long tubular organ through which female insects lay their eggs.

ovoid /ˈəʊvɔɪd/ *adj, n* (*fml*) egg-shaped (object): *large ovoid pebbles.*

ovulate /ˈɒvjʊleɪt/ *v* [I] (*medical or biology*) produce or discharge an ovum from an ovary: *Women who do not ovulate regularly have difficulty in becoming pregnant.* ▷ **ovulation** /ˌɒvjʊˈleɪʃn/ *n* [U]: *She is taking a drug to stimulate ovulation.*

ovum /ˈəʊvəm/ *n* (*pl* **ova** /ˈəʊvə/) (*biology*) female egg-cell capable of developing into a new individual when fertilized by a male sperm. ⇨ illus at FEMALE. Cf OVARY.

owe /əʊ/ *v* **1** (**a**) [Ipr, Tn, Tn·pr, Dn·n, Dn·pr] ~ **(sb) for sth**; ~ **sth (to sb) (for sth)** be in debt to (sb) (for goods, etc): *He still owes (us) for the goods he received last month.* ○ *He owes (his father) £50.* ○ *He owes £50 to his father.* (**b**) [Dn·pr] ~ **sth to sb/sth** recognize sb/sth as the cause or source of sth; be indebted to sb/sth for sth: *He owes his success more to luck than to ability.* ○ *We owe this discovery to Newton.* **2** [Dn·n, Dn·pr] ~ **sth to sb** (**a**) be under an obligation to sb; give sth as a duty to sb: *owe loyalty to a political party, one's union, the company, etc.* (**b**) feel gratitude (to sb) in return for a service, favour, etc: *I owe my teachers and parents a great deal.* ○ *I owe a lot to my wife and children.* **3** (idm) **the world owes one a living** ⇨ WORLD.

Owen /ˈəʊɪn/ Wilfred (1893-1918), English poet who served as a soldier in France in the First World War. His poems (eg 'Strange Meeting' and 'Anthem for Doomed Youth') evoke the horror and futility of war. He was killed fighting only a few hours before the war ended.

Owens /ˈəʊɪnz/ Jesse (1913-80), black American athlete who won four gold medals in track and field events at the 1936 Olympic Games in Berlin. The success of a black man annoyed the Nazi authorities.

owing /ˈəʊɪŋ/ *adj* [pred] (esp of money that has been earned, lent or promised) not yet paid: *£5 is still owing.*

□ **owing to** *prep* because of or on account of (sth): *Owing to the rain, the match was cancelled.* ⇨ Usage at DUE[1].

owl /aʊl/ *n* **1** bird of prey that flies at night and feeds on small animals, eg mice, and is traditionally regarded as a symbol of wisdom. **2** (idm) **wise as an owl** ⇨ WISE.

▷ **owlet** /ˈaʊlɪt/ *n* young owl.

owlish *adj* of or like an owl; (trying to look) solemn and wise: *Her new glasses make her look rather owlish.* **owlishly** *adv*: *owlishly earnest.*

own[1] /əʊn/ *det, pron* **1** (used after possessives to emphasize the idea of personal possession or the individual character of sth) belonging to oneself, itself, ourselves, etc: *I saw it with my own eyes*, ie I didn't hear about it from someone else. ○ *It was her own idea.* ○ *This is my own house/This house is my own*, ie not rented, etc. ○ *Use your own pen; I need mine.* ○ *Our children have grown up and have children of their own.* ○ *I wish I had my (very) own room*, ie didn't have to share one, borrow one, etc. ○ *Your day off is your own*, ie You can spend it as you wish. ○ *For reasons of his own* (ie particular reasons that perhaps only he knew about), *he refused to join the club.* **2** (used to indicate the idea of personal activity); done or produced by and for oneself: *She makes all her own clothes.* ○ *I can cook my own meals.* ○ *It's unwise to try to be your own lawyer.* **3** (idm) **come into one's ˈown** receive the credit, recognition, fame, etc one deserves: *This car really comes into its own on rough ground.* ○ *She really comes into her own when someone is ill.* **hold one's ˈown (against sb/sth) (in sth)** (**a**) maintain one's position against attack, etc; not be defeated: *She can certainly hold her own against anybody in an argument.* (**b**) not lose strength: *The patient is holding her own although she is still very ill.* **of one's ˈown** belonging to oneself and no one else: *He'd like a car of his own.* ○ *Children need toys of their own.* (**all**) **on one's ˈown** (**a**) alone: *I'm all on my own today.* ○ *She lives on her own.* (**b**) without help or supervision; alone: *He can be left to work on his own.* ○ *Although her father is in the firm she got the job on her own.* (**c**) (*infml*) excellent; exceptional: *When it comes to craftsmanship, Sally is on her own*, ie is better than anyone. ⇨ Usage at ALONE. **get/have one's ˈown back** (**on sb**) (*infml*) have one's revenge: *After the fight the defeated boxer swore he'd get his own back (on his rival).*

□ ˌ**own ˈbrand** class of goods in a shop marked with the name of the shop or store instead of that of the manufacturer: [attrib] *Own brand goods are often cheaper.*

ˌ**own ˈgoal** goal scored by a member of a team against his own side.

own² /əʊn/ *v* **1** [Tn] have (sth) as one's property; possess: *This house is mine; I own it.* ○ *She owns a car but rarely drives it.* ○ *Who owns this land?* **2** [Ipr, Tn, Tf, Cn·a, Cn·n] ~ (**to sth/doing sth**) (*dated*) recognize or admit (that sth is true or that one is responsible for sth); confess: *own to having told a lie* ○ *Finally she owned the truth of what he had said.* ○ *They own that the claim is justified.* ○ *He owned himself defeated.* **3** (phr v) **own up** (**to sth**) (*infml*) admit or confess that one is to blame (for sth): *Nobody owned up to the theft.* ○ *Eventually she owned up.*

owner /ˈəʊnə(r)/ *n* person who owns sth: *the owner of a black Mercedes* ○ *the dog's owner* ○ *Who's the owner of this house?*

▷ **ownerless** *adj* having no owner or no known owner: *ownerless dogs* ○ *wrecked ownerless cars.*

ownership *n* [U] state of being an owner; (right of) possession: *The ownership of the land is disputed.* ○ *Ownership of property involves great expense.* ○ *The restaurant is under new ownership.*

□ ˌ**owner-ˈdriver** *n* person who owns the car he drives.

ˌ**owner-ˈoccupied** *adj* (of a house, etc) lived in by the owner (not rented to sb else): *Most of the houses in this street are owner-occupied.* ˌ**owner-ˈoccupier** *n* person who owns the house he lives in. ⇨ article at HOUSE.

ox /ɒks/ *n* (*pl* **oxen** /ˈɒksn/) **1** fully grown bullock used (esp formerly) for pulling carts, farm machinery, etc, or for food. Cf BULL, STEER². **2** (esp *pl*) (*dated*) any domestic cow or bull. Cf CATTLE.

□ ˈ**oxtail** *n* tail of an ox, used for making soup, etc: [attrib] *oxtail soup.*

oxalic acid /ɒkˌsælɪk ˈæsɪd/ poisonous acid, originally obtained from plants, used in various industrial processes (eg cleaning metal).

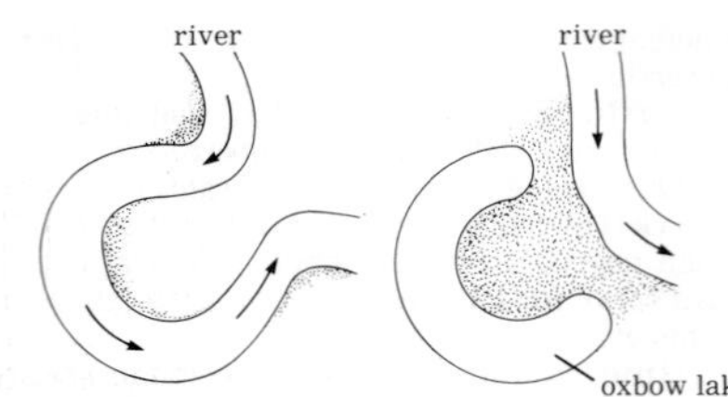

the formation of an oxbow lake

oxbow /ˈɒksbəʊ/ *n* U-shaped bend in a river.

□ ˌ**oxbow ˈlake** lake formed from an oxbow when the river takes a new course across the narrow end of the loop, cutting it off. ⇨ illus.

Oxbridge /ˈɒksbrɪdʒ/ *n* (*sometimes derog*) (invented name for) Oxford and/or Cambridge (contrasted with newer British universities): *You don't have to go to Oxbridge to receive a good university education.* Cf REDBRICK (RED).

ox-eye /ˈɒksaɪ/ *n* (**a**) any of several types of flowering plants. (**b**) flower of one of these: [attrib] *a vase of ox-eye daisies.*

Oxfam /ˈɒksfæm/ *abbr* Oxford Committee for Famine Relief: *a concert in aid of Oxfam.* ⇨ article at CHARITY.

Oxford /ˈɒksfəd/ city in *Oxfordshire, England. It contains Oxford University, founded in 1249, whose college buildings are a major architectural feature of the city. Oxford has been an important car-manufacturing centre. ⇨ article at POST-SCHOOL.

□ ˌ**Oxford ˈblue** dark blue.

the ˌ**Oxford English ˈDictionary** (*abbr* **OED**) very large historical dictionary of the English language published by Oxford University Press. Work on it began in 1858, and the final volume of the first edition appeared in 1928.

the ˈOxford Movement movement in the 1830s and 1840s to restore traditional Catholic teaching and forms of worship in the Church of England. It began in Oxford, and among its leading figures were *Newman and *Keble.

ˈ**Oxford Street** popular shopping street in London, England, containing many large department stores.

Oxfordshire /ˈɒksfədʃə(r)/ county in the south central midlands of England. It contains the city of Oxford, and the River *Thames runs through it. ⇨ map at App 1.

oxidant /ˈɒksɪdənt/ *n* chemical substance that causes another to oxidize.

oxide /ˈɒksaɪd/ *n* [C, U] (*chemistry*) compound of oxygen and one other substance: *iron oxide* ○ *oxide of tin.*

▷ **oxidation** /ˌɒksɪˈdeɪʃən/ (also **oxidization**, **-isation** /ˌɒksɪdaɪˈzeɪʃn; *US* -dɪˈz-/) *n* action or process of oxidizing.

oxidize, **-ise** /ˈɒksɪdaɪz/ *v* [I, Tn] (**a**) (cause sth to) combine with oxygen. Cf REDUCE 6. (**b**) (cause sth to) become rusty.

Oxon /ˈɒksn/ *abbr* **1** (esp in addresses) Oxfordshire (Latin *Oxonia*). **2** (esp in degree titles) of Oxford University (Latin *Oxoniensis*): *Alice Tolley MA (Oxon).* Cf CANTAB.

oxy-acetylene /ˌɒksɪəˈsetəli:n/ *adj, n* (of or using) a mixture of oxygen and acetylene gas (esp for cutting or welding metal): *oxy-acetylene torches, blowpipes, equipment*, ie devices burning oxy-acetylene ○ *oxy-acetylene welding*, ie joining metal by means of a hot flame of oxy-acetylene.

oxygen /ˈɒksɪdʒən/ *n* [U] (*symb* **O**) chemical element, a gas without colour, taste or smell, present in the air and necessary for all forms of life on earth. When animals breathe it in, it is converted into carbon dioxide, which is then breathed out; plants change carbon dioxide back to oxygen by photosynthesis. Water is made up of hydrogen and oxygen: *There was a shortage of oxygen at the top of the mountain.* ○ *She died from lack of oxygen.* ⇨ App 11.

▷ **oxygenate** /-eɪt/ (also **oxygenize**, **-ise** /-aɪz/) *v* [Tn] supply, treat or mix (sth) with oxygen.

□ ˈ**oxygen mask** mask placed over the nose and mouth through which a person can breathe oxygen, eg in an aircraft or hospital: *Oxygen masks are used in aircraft only in emergencies.*

ˈ**oxygen tent** small tent or canopy placed over the head and shoulders of a sick person who needs an extra supply of oxygen: *They placed the child in an oxygen tent when he had difficulty in breathing.*

oxymoron /ˌɒksɪˈmɔ:rɒn/ *n* figure of speech which contains contradictory words (eg *bitter-sweet, precious bane*).

oxytocin /ˌɒksɪˈtəʊsɪn/ *n* [U] hormone that makes the womb contract during childbirth and controls the body's production of milk.

oyez /əʊˈjez/ (also **oyes** /əʊˈjes/) *interj* (cry meaning 'listen' shouted three times (esp formerly) by a town crier or by an official in a lawcourt to demand silence and attention).

oyster /ˈɔɪstə(r)/ *n* **1** shellfish used as food and usu eaten uncooked. Some types produce pearls inside their shells: *fresh oysters* ○ [attrib] *oyster stew.* ⇨ illus at SHELLFISH. **2** (idm) **the world is one's/sb's oyster** ⇨ WORLD.

□ ˈ**oyster bed** place on the bottom of the sea where oysters breed or are bred for food or for producing pearls.

ˈ**oyster-catcher** *n* type of black and white wading sea-bird which catches and eats oysters.

Oz /ɒz/ (*Austral sl*) = AUSTRALIA.

oz *abbr* (*pl* unchanged or **ozs**) ounce (Italian *onza*): *Add 4oz sugar.* Cf LB.

ozone /ˈəʊzəʊn/ *n* [U] (**a**) form of oxygen with a sharp and refreshing smell. (**b**) (*infml*) pure refreshing air as at the seaside: *Just breathe in that ozone!*

□ ˈ**ozone layer** layer of ozone high above the earth's surface that helps to protect the earth from harmful ultraviolet rays from the sun. ⇨ article at ENVIRONMENT.

P, p

P, p /piː/ *n* (*pl* **P's, p's** /piːz/) **1** the sixteenth letter of the English alphabet: *'Philip' begins with (a) P/'P'.* **2** (idm) **mind one's p's and q's** ⇨ MIND².
P *abbr* (on a road sign) parking (area).
P *symb* phosphorus.
p *abbr* **1** (*pl* **pp**) page: *see p 94* ○ *pp 63-97.* **2** /piː/ (*Brit infml*) (decimal) penny or pence: *a 12p stamp.* Cf D 1. **3** (*music*) softly; quietly (Italian *piano*). Cf F 3.
PA /ˌpiː ˈeɪ/ *abbr* **1** (*infml*) personal assistant: *She works as PA to the managing director.* **2** Press Association. **3** public address (system): *I heard it on the PA.*
Pa *symb* proactinium.
pa /pɑː/ *n* (*infml*) father.
pa *abbr* per year (Latin *per annum*): *salary £12 000 pa.*
Pabst /pɑːpst/ George Wilhelm (1885-1967), German film director. In films like *Lulu* (or *Pandora's Box*) he brought a new social realism to the silent cinema and greatly influenced early Hollywood directors.
pace¹ /peɪs/ *n* **1** [C] (length of a) single step in walking or running: *only a few paces away* ○ *She took two paces forward/She advanced two paces.* **2** [sing] **(a)** speed, esp of walking or running: *at a good, fast, slow, walking, etc pace* ○ *quicken one's pace* ○ *She slowed down her pace so I could keep up with her.* ○ (*fig*) *He gave up his job in advertising because he couldn't stand the pace,* ie found the pressure of work too great. **(b)** [U] rate of progress or development, esp of an activity: *the pace of change in the electronics industry* ○ *This novel lacks pace,* ie Its plot develops too slowly. **3** (idm) **at a snail's pace** ⇨ SNAIL. **force the pace** ⇨ FORCE². **keep pace (with sb/sth)** move forward, develop or increase at the same rate (as sb/sth): *He was so unfit he couldn't keep pace (with us).* ○ *It's important for a firm to keep pace with changes in the market.* ○ *Are wages keeping pace with inflation?* **put sb/sth through his/its ˈpaces** test the ability or quality of sb/sth: *The new recruits were put through their paces.* ○ *put a new car through its paces.* **ˌset the ˈpace** run, walk, etc at a (usu fast) speed which others try to follow: (*fig*) *This company is setting the pace* (ie is the most successful) *in the home computer market.*
□ **ˈpacemaker** *n* **(a)** (also **ˈpace-setter**) runner, rider or driver in a race who moves at a (usu fast) speed which others try to follow: (*fig*) *That firm was the pace-setter in car design for many years,* ie introduced new ideas which were copied by others. **(b)** electronic device placed on the heart to make weak or irregular heartbeats stronger or more regular.
pace² /peɪs/ *v* **1 (a)** [Ipr, Ip] walk with slow or regular steps: *He paced up and down (the platform), waiting for the train.* **(b)** [Tn] walk backwards and forwards across (sth) in this way: *The prisoner paced the floor of his cell.* **2** [Tn] set a speed for (a runner, rider, etc in a race). **3** (phr v) **pace sth off/out** measure sth by taking regular steps across it: *She paced out the length of the room.*
pace³ /ˈpeɪsɪ/ *prep* (*Latin*) with respect to (a specified person) who does not or may not agree.
pachyderm /ˈpækɪdɜːm/ *n* any of various types of thick-skinned, four-footed animal, eg an elephant or a rhinoceros.
pacific /pəˈsɪfɪk/ *adj* (*fml*) making or loving peace; peaceful. ▷ **pacifically** /-klɪ/ *adv.*
Pacific Ocean /pəˌsɪfɪk ˈəʊʃn/ **the Pacific Ocean** (also **the Paˈcific**) the world's largest ocean, covering a third of the earth's surface (181 300 000 sq km, 70 000 000 sq miles). It separates Asia and Australia from North and South America, and stretches from the *Bering Strait to *Antarctica.
Pacific Standard Time /pəˌsɪfɪk ˈstændəd taɪm/ (*abbr* **PST**) (also **Paˈcific Time**) standard time used in the time zone of the west coast of the USA and Canada, eight hours behind *Greenwich Mean Time.
pacifism /ˈpæsɪfɪzəm/ *n* [U] belief that all war is morally wrong and that disputes should be settled by peaceful means.
▷ **pacifist** /-ɪst/ *n* person who believes in pacifism (and who therefore refuses to fight in a war). Cf CONSCIENTIOUS OBJECTOR (CONSCIENTIOUS).
pacify /ˈpæsɪfaɪ/ *v* (*pt, pp* **-fied**) [Tn] **1** calm or soothe the anger or distress of (sb): *He tried to pacify his creditors by repaying part of the money.* **2** establish peace in (an area, a country, etc where there is war).
▷ **pacification** /ˌpæsɪfɪˈkeɪʃn/ *n* [U] pacifying or being pacified: *the pacification of the rebel states.*
pacifier *n* (*US*) = DUMMY 3.
pack¹ /pæk/ *n* **1** [C] **(a)** number of things wrapped or tied together for carrying, esp on the back: *The tramp carried his belongings in a pack on his back.* **(b)** bag, usu of canvas or leather, fitted with straps for carrying on the back. Cf BACKPACK, HAVERSACK, RUCKSACK. **2** [C] small paper or cardboard container in which goods are packed for selling; packet: *a six-pack of beer,* ie six cans of beer wrapped and sold together ○ (*esp US*) *a pack of cigarettes.* ⇨ Usage at PACKET. **3** [CGp] **(a)** group of wild animals that hunt together: *Wolves hunt in packs.* **(b)** group of dogs kept for hunting, esp with horses: *a pack of hounds.* **(c)** organized group of Cub Scouts or Brownies: *a ˈBrownie pack.* **(d)** the forwards of a Rugby football team. **4** [CGp] ~ **(of sb/sth)** (*derog*) number of people or things (used esp in the expressions shown): *a pack of fools/thieves* ○ *a pack of lies.* **5** [C] (*US* **deck**) complete set of 52 playing-cards. **6** [C] (only in compounds) thing placed on a part of the body for a period of time, such as a layer of cream or paste for cleansing the skin of the face or a bag of ice for soothing a burn: *a ˈface-pack* ○ *an ˈice-pack.*
□ **ˈpack-animal** *n* animal used for carrying things, eg a horse, mule or camel.
ˈpack-drill *n* [U] **1** drill²(1) in which soldiers carry full marching equipment, used as a punishment in the army. **2** (idm) **no names, no pack-drill** ⇨ NAME¹.
ˈpack-ice *n* [U] large mass of ice floating in the sea, formed from smaller pieces which have frozen together.
ˈpack-saddle *n* saddle with straps for holding packs.
ˈpackthread *n* [U] strong thread for sewing or tying up packs.
pack² /pæk/ *v* **1 (a)** [I, Tn, Tn·pr] ~ **A (in/into B)**; ~ **B (with A)** put sth into a container for transport or storing; fill (a container, esp a suitcase) with sth: *Have you packed (your suitcase) yet?* ○ *Don't forget to pack your toothbrush!* ○ *All these books need to be packed (into boxes).* ○ *pack clothes into a trunk/pack a trunk with clothes* ○ *He takes a packed lunch* (ie sandwiches, etc packed into a box or some other container) *to work every day.* **(b)** [I, Ipr] ~ **(into sth)** be able to be put into a container for transport or storing: *This dress packs easily.* ○ *These clothes won't all pack into one suitcase.* **2** [Tn, Tn·pr] ~ **sth (in sth)** cover or protect sth with (esp soft) material pressed tightly on, in or round it: *pack china in newspaper* ○ *glass packed in straw.* **3** [Tn] prepare and put (meat, fish, etc) in tins in order to preserve it. **4** [esp passive: Tn, Tn·pr] ~ **sth (with sth/sb)** fill, cram or crowd sth (with sth/sb): *Chanting fans packed the stadium/The stadium was packed with chanting fans.* ○ *The show played to packed houses,* ie large audiences. ○ *This book is packed with useful information.* ○ *an action-packed film, novel, etc* ○ *The restaurant was packed,* ie crowded with people. **5** [I, Tn] (of snow, ice, etc) (cause sth to) form a hard compact mass: *The snow had packed against the wall.* ○ *The wind packed the snow against the wall.* **6** [Tn] (*US infml*) carry (sth); be equipped with (sth): *pack a gun.* **7** [Tn] (*derog*) choose (the members of a committee, etc) so that they are likely to decide in one's favour. **8** (idm) **ˌpack one's ˈbags** (prepare to) leave: *After their row she packed her bags and left.* ○ *He was told to pack his bags.* **ˌpack a (hard, etc) ˈpunch** (*infml*) **(a)** (of a boxer) be capable of delivering a powerful blow. **(b)** (*fig*) have a very powerful effect: *Those cocktails pack quite a punch!* **send sb packing** ⇨ SEND. **9** (phr v) **pack sth away** put sth into a box, cupboard, etc because it is not needed: *She packed away the deck-chairs for the winter.*
pack (sb/sth) in; pack (sb/sth) into sth (cause sb/sth to) crowd or press together into a limited space: *All six of us packed into the tiny car.* ○ *That show has been packing them in for months,* ie attracting large audiences. **ˌpack it ˈin** (*infml*) (esp imperative) stop doing or saying sth that angers or annoys sb else: *I'm sick of your complaining — just pack it in, will you?* **pack sth in** (*infml*) give sth up; abandon sth: *She's packed in her job.* ○ *Smoking's bad for you; you ought to pack it in.* **pack sth in; pack sth in/into sth** do (a lot of things) in a limited time: *She managed to pack a lot of sightseeing into three days.*
pack sb off (to...) send sb away, esp quickly and decisively: *She packed the children off to bed.* ○ *We were packed off to stay in the country.*
pack sth out (esp passive) completely fill (a theatre, cinema, etc) with people: *Opera houses were packed out whenever she was singing.*
pack up (*infml*) **(a)** stop doing sth; give up or abandon sth: *Business is terrible — I might as well pack up.* **(b)** (of a machine, engine, etc) stop working or operating; break down: *My car has packed up.* **pack (sth) up** put (one's possessions) into cases, etc before leaving a place: *He packed up his things and left.*
▷ **packer** *n* person, company or machine that packs goods, esp food.
package /ˈpækɪdʒ/ *n* **1 (a)** object or objects wrapped in paper or packed in a box; parcel: *The postman brought me a large package.* **(b)** box, etc in which things are packed. **2** (*US*) = PACKET. ⇨ Usage at PACKET. **3** (also **ˈpackage deal**) set of proposals offered or accepted as a whole: *Ministers are trying to put together a package that will end the dispute.*
▷ **package** *v* [Tn] make (sth) into or put (sth) in a package, eg for selling: *Their products are always attractively packaged.* **packaging** *n* [U] (design and manufacture of) materials for packing goods. ⇨ Usage at PACKET.
□ **ˈpackage holiday, ˈpackage tour** holiday/tour organized by a travel agent, for which one pays a fixed price that includes the cost of transport, accomodation, etc. ⇨ article at HOLIDAY.
ˈpackage store (also **ˌpackage ˈgoods store**) (*US*) = OFF-LICENCE.
packet /ˈpækɪt/ *n* **1** [C] **(a)** (*US* usu **package**) small paper or cardboard container in which goods are packed for selling: *a packet of biscuits, cigarettes, tea, etc.* **(b)** small package or parcel. **2** [sing] (*infml*) large amount of money (used esp in the expressions shown): *make* (ie earn) *a packet* ○ *cost (sb) a packet.* **3** [C] (also **ˈpacket-boat**) boat that carries mail and passengers on a fixed short route. **4** (idm) **cop a packet** ⇨ COP².

NOTE ON USAGE: Some things in shops are sold

in **packets** (*US* **pack**): *a packet of sweets, crisps, cigarettes* ○ *a six-pack of beer.* Note that *a packet/pack of cigarettes* contains some cigarettes but *a cigarette packet/pack* may be empty. A **parcel** (*US* also **package**) is something wrapped, often in brown paper, so that it can be sent by post: *The postman rang the bell because he had a parcel/package to deliver.* A **package** in British English is usually carried and not sent. **Packaging** is the material used to wrap and protect products sold in shops or sent through the post.

packing /ˈpækɪŋ/ *n* [U] **1** process of packing goods. **2** material used for packing (esp fragile objects): *pay extra for postage and packing*, ie when ordering goods by post.
□ ˈ**packing-case** *n* wooden box or case used for storing or transporting goods.

pact /pækt/ *n* agreement (between people, groups, countries, etc); treaty: *They made a pact not to tell anyone.* ○ *a non-aggression pact.*

pad[1] /pæd/ *n* **1** thick piece of soft material used to protect sth from rubbing, jarring or blows, to improve the shape or increase the size of sth, or to absorb liquid: *put a pad of cotton wool and gauze over a wound* ○ ˈ*shoulder pads*, ie to give shape to a jacket or dress. **2** (usu *pl*) piece of flexible padded material worn in certain sports (esp cricket) to protect the legs and ankles: ˈ*shin pads*, ie worn by footballers, etc to protect the shins. ⇨ illus at CRICKET. **3** number of sheets of writing-paper or drawing-paper fastened together at one edge: *a* ˈ*writing pad.* **4** = ˈINK-PAD. **5** soft fleshy under-part of the foot of certain animals, eg dogs, foxes. **6** flat surface from which spacecraft are launched or helicopters take off: *a* ˈ*launching pad.* **7** (*sl*) place where sb lives: *Come back to my pad.* **8** = LILY PAD (LILY).

pad[2] /pæd/ *v* (**-dd-**) **1** [Tn esp passive] fill or cover (sth) with soft material, esp in order to protect it or give it a particular shape or increase its size: *a padded envelope*, ie for sending fragile objects in ○ *a jacket with padded shoulders* ○ *a padded bra*, ie one worn to make the breasts appear larger. **2** (phr v) **pad sth out (a)** put soft material into (a garment) in order to give it a particular shape: *pad out the shoulders of a jacket to make them look square.* **(b)** make (a book, an essay, a speech, etc) longer by adding unnecessary material: *I padded out my answer with plenty of quotations.*
▷ **padding** *n* [U] **1** soft material used to pad things. **2** unnecessary material in a book, an essay, a speech, etc: *There's a lot of padding in this novel.*
□ ˌ**padded** ˈ**cell** room in a mental hospital that has soft walls to prevent violent patients from injuring themselves.

pad[3] /pæd/ *v* (**-dd-**) (phr v) **pad about, along, around, etc** walk in the specified direction with a soft steady sound of steps: *The dog padded along next to its owner.* ○ *pad about the house in one's slippers.*

paddle[1] /ˈpædl/ *n* **1** [C] short oar with a broad blade at one end or both ends, used to move a canoe through the water. ⇨ illus at CANOE. **2** [sing] act or period of paddling (PADDLE[2] 1). **3** [C] instrument shaped like a paddle, esp one used for beating, mixing or stirring food, or for hitting things.
▷ **paddle** *v* **1** [Ipr, Ip, Tn, Tn·pr, Tn·p] **(a)** move (a canoe) through the water using a paddle: *We paddled (the canoe) slowly upstream.* **(b)** row (a boat) with light easy strokes. **2** [Tn] (*US infml*) spank (esp a child). **3** (idm) ˌ**paddle one's** ˌ**own ca**ˈ**noe** (*infml*) depend on oneself and no one else; be independent.
□ ˈ**paddleball** *n* [U] (*US*) game similar to squash played against a wall using a paddle[1](3) as a racket.
ˈ**paddle-boat** *n* boat moved by a paddle-wheel.

paddle-steamer

ˈ**paddle-steamer** *n* steam vessel moved by paddle-wheels.
ˈ**paddle-wheel** *n* wheel with boards round its rim which make a boat move forwards by pressing against the water as the wheel revolves.

paddle[2] /ˈpædl/ *v* **1** [I, Ipr, Ip] walk with bare feet in shallow water: *paddling (about) at the water's edge.* Cf WADE. **2** [Tn] move (one's feet or hands) gently in water: *paddle one's toes in the water.*
▷ **paddle** *n* [sing] act or period of paddling.
□ ˈ**paddling pool** (*US* ˈ**wading pool**) shallow pool in which children may paddle.

paddock /ˈpædək/ *n* **1** small field where horses are kept or exercised. **2** enclosure at a racecourse or race-track where horses or racing-cars are brought together and paraded before a race.

Paddy /ˈpædɪ/ *n* (*infml offensive*) Irish person.

paddy[1] /ˈpædɪ/ *n* **1** (also ˈ**paddy-field**) [C] field where rice is grown. **2** [U] rice that is still growing or in the husk.

paddy[2] /ˈpædɪ/ *n* (*Brit infml*) fit of anger or temper: *There's no need to get into such a paddy.*

padlock /ˈpædlɒk/ *n* detachable lock with a U-shaped bar or chain that fastens through the loop of a staple or ring. ⇨ illus at CHAIN.
▷ **padlock** *v* [Tn, Tn·pr] fasten (sth) with a padlock: *The gate was padlocked.* ○ *She padlocked her bike to the railings.*

padre /ˈpɑːdreɪ/ *n* (*infml*) (used esp as a form of address) **1** clergyman in the armed forces: *Good morning, padre!* Cf CHAPLAIN. **2** (*Brit*) priest or parson.

paean (*US* **pean**) /ˈpiːən/ *n* (*fml*) song of praise or triumph: *a paean of praise.*

paederasty = PEDERASTY.

paediatrics (*US* **pediatrics**) /ˌpiːdɪˈætrɪks/ *n* [sing *v*] branch of medicine concerned with children and their illnesses.
▷ **paediatric** (*US* **pediatric**) *adj* relating to paediatrics: *a paediatric ward*, ie for sick children.
paediatrician (*US* **pedi-**) /ˌpiːdɪəˈtrɪʃn/ *n* doctor who specializes in paediatrics.

paed(o)- (*US* **ped(o)-**) *comb form* child or children: *paediatrics.*

paedophilia (*US* **pedo-**) /ˌpiːdəˈfɪlɪə/ *n* [U] condition of being sexually attracted to children.
▷ **paedophile** (*US* **pedo-**) /ˈpiːdəfaɪl/ *n* person sexually attracted to children.

paella /paɪˈelə/ *n* [U] Spanish dish of rice, chicken, seafood, vegetables, etc cooked and served in a large shallow pan.

pagan /ˈpeɪgən/ *n* **1** (*usu derog or joc*) person who is not a believer in any of the world's chief religions, esp one who is neither a Christian, a Jew nor a Moslem. Cf ATHEIST (ATHEISM). **2** (formerly) person who did not believe in Christianity, esp a heathen who worshipped idols, the sun, etc.
▷ **pagan** *adj* of or relating to pagans: *pagan worship of the sun.*
paganism /-ɪzəm/ *n* [U] beliefs and practices of pagans.

Paganini /ˌpægəˈniːnɪ/ Niccolò (1782-1840), Italian violinist and composer. He was famous for his virtuoso style and the difficulty of the works he wrote for himself. Many composers have written variations on his *Caprice No 24.*

page[1] /peɪdʒ/ *n* **1 (a)** (*abbr* **p**) one side of a sheet of paper in a book, magazine, etc: *read a few pages of a book* ○ *You'll find the quotation on page 35.* **(b)** this sheet of paper itself: *Several pages have been torn out of the book.* **2** episode or period of history that might be written about in a book: *a glorious page of English history.*
▷ **page** *v* [Tn] number the pages of (sth).
□ ˌ**page** ˈ**three** the third page of a British tabloid newspaper, often showing a photograph of a (partially) naked woman: [attrib] *today's page-three girl.* ⇨ article at NEWSPAPER.

page[2] /peɪdʒ/ *n* **(a)** (*US* ˈ**bellboy**) boy or young man, usu in uniform, employed in a hotel or club to carry luggage, open doors for people, etc. **(b)** boy attendant of a person of rank or a bride. ⇨ article at WEDDING.
▷ **page** *v* [Tn] call the name of (sb) over a loudspeaker (eg in an airport) in order to give him a message.
□ ˈ**page-boy** *n* **1** = PAGE[2] b. **2** (also ˌ**page-boy** ˈ**haircut**) woman's hairstyle in which the hair is straight and fairly short, coming down over the forehead in a fringe and rolled slightly inwards at the sides and back.

pageant /ˈpædʒənt/ *n* **1** public entertainment consisting of a procession of people in costume, or an outdoor performance of scenes from history: (*fig*) *the pageant of history*, ie history as a succession of colourful events. **2** brilliant display or spectacle.
▷ **pageantry** /ˈpædʒəntrɪ/ *n* [U] spectacular display: *all the pageantry of a coronation.*

paginate /ˈpædʒɪneɪt/ *v* [Tn] number the pages of (a book, etc).
▷ **pagination** /ˌpædʒɪˈneɪʃn/ *n* [U] (figures used in) numbering the pages of a book, etc.

pagoda

pagoda /pəˈgəʊdə/ *n* religious building in India and E Asia, usu a tall tower with several storeys each of which has its own overhanging roof.

pah /pɑː/ *interj* (*dated*) (used to express disgust, ridicule, etc): *Pah, sir! There's no such thing!*

paid *pt, pp* of PAY[2].

pail /peɪl/ *n* **(a)** bucket: *a pail of water.* **(b)** amount contained in this.
▷ **pailful** /ˈpeɪlfʊl/ *n* amount a pail contains.

paillasse = PALLIASSE.

pain /peɪn/ *n* **1 (a)** [U] physical suffering or discomfort caused by injury or disease: *be in (great) pain* ○ *feel some, no, not much, a lot of, etc pain* ○ *a cry of pain* ○ *scream with pain* ○ *suffer from acute back pain* ○ *Her back causes/gives her a lot of pain.* **(b)** [C] feeling of suffering or discomfort in a particular part of the body: *have a pain in one's back, chest, shoulder, etc* ○ *stomach pains.* **(c)** [U] mental suffering or distress: *His harsh words caused her much pain.* ○ *the pain of separation.* **2** [C] (*infml*) annoying or boring person or thing: *She's been complaining again — she's a real pain!* ○ *We've missed the last bus — what a pain!* **3** (idm) **a pain in the neck** (*infml*) annoying or boring person or thing; pain(2). **on/under pain/penalty of sth** (*fml*) with the risk of incurring a particular punishment: *Prisoners were forbidden to approach the fence under pain of death.*
▷ **pain** *v* [Tn no passive] cause pain to (sb): *My foot is still paining me.* ○ *It pains me to have to tell you that....* **pained** *adj* showing pain or distress: *a pained look, expression, glance, etc.*
painful /-fl/ *adj* **1** causing or suffering pain: *a painful blow on the shoulder* ○ *Her shoulder is still painful.* **2** causing distress or embarrassment: *a painful experience, memory* ○ *His incompetence*

was painful to witness. ○ *It was my painful duty to tell him he was dying.* ○ *Her performance was painful*, ie very bad. **3** difficult or tedious: *the painful process of stripping the paint off the wall.*
painfully /-fəlɪ/ *adv*: *Her thumb is painfully swollen.* ○ *become painfully aware of sth.*
painfulness *n* [U].
painless *adj* not causing pain or distress: *a painless injection.* **painlessly** *adv.* **painlessness** *n* [U].
□ **ˈpain-killer** *n* drug that reduces pain: *She's on* (ie taking) *pain-killers.*

Paine /peɪn/ Thomas (1737-1809), English radical author. In *Common Sense and the Rights of Man* and other works he supported the revolutions in America and France, and in *The Age of Reason* he attacked conventional Christian doctrine.

pains /peɪnz/ *n* [pl] (idm) **be at pains to do sth** take great care or make a particular effort to do sth: *She was at pains to stress the benefits of the scheme.* ○ *He was at great pains to deny the rumour of redundancies.* **be a fool for one's pains** ⇨ FOOL[1]. **for one's pains** as a response to one's efforts or trouble: *She looked after her sick mother for 10 years and all she got for her pains was ingratitude*, ie she received no thanks for her efforts. **spare no pains doing/to do sth** ⇨ SPARE[2]. **take (great) pains (with/over/to do sth)** take great care or make a careful effort to do sth: *She takes great pains with her work.* ○ *Great pains have been taken to ensure the safety of passengers.*
□ **painstaking** /ˈpeɪnzteɪkɪŋ/ *adj* done with, requiring or taking great care or trouble: *a painstaking job, investigation* ○ *painstaking accuracy* ○ *a painstaking student, worker, etc.*
painstakingly *adv.*

paint[1] /peɪnt/ *n* **1 (a)** [U] substance applied to a surface in liquid form to give it colour: *red, green, yellow, etc paint* ○ *give the door two coats of paint*, ie put two layers of paint on it ○ *wet paint*, eg written on a notice to warn people not to touch it ○ [attrib] *paint marks.* **(b)** [U] layer of dried paint on a surface. **2 paints** [pl] (set of) tubes or blocks of paint: *The artist brought his paints with him.* ○ *a set of oil-paints.* **3** [U] (*usu derog*) cosmetics for applying to the face: *She wears far too much paint.*
□ **ˈpaintbox** *n* box containing a set of paints.
ˈpaintbrush *n* brush used for applying paint.
ˈpaintwork *n* [U] painted surface or surfaces: *The paintwork is in good condition.* ○ *A stone hit the car and damaged the paintwork.*

paint[2] /peɪnt/ *v* **1** [I, Tn, Cn·a] put paint onto (sth): *paint a door, wall, room* ○ *paint a house blue.* **2** [I, Ipr, Tn] make (a picture) using paints; portray or represent (sb/sth) in paint: *She paints well.* ○ *paint in oils/water-colours* ○ *paint a picture, a portrait, a still life, etc* ○ *paint flowers, a girl, a landscape* ○ (*fig*) *In her latest novel she paints a vivid picture of life in Victorian England.* **3** [Tn, Cn·a] (*often derog*) put powder, lipstick, etc onto (the face, etc): *She spends hours painting her face.* ○ *paint one's nails red.* **4** (idm) **not as black as it/one is painted** ⇨ BLACK[1]. **paint sth in glowing, etc colours** ⇨ COLOUR[1]. **paint the town ˈred** (*infml*) go out and enjoy a lively, boisterous time in bars, night-clubs, etc. **5** (phr v) **paint sth in** add sth to a picture using paint. **paint sth out** cover (a part of a painting) by putting paint on top of it. **paint over sth** cover sth with paint: *We'll have to paint over the dirty marks on the wall.*
□ **ˌpainted ˈlady** orange-red butterfly with black and white spots.

painter[1] /ˈpeɪntə(r)/ *n* **1** person whose job is painting buildings, walls, etc: *He is a painter and decorator.* **2** artist who paints pictures: *a famous painter.*

painter[2] /ˈpeɪntə(r)/ *n* rope fastened to the front of a boat, used for tying it to a quay, ship, etc.

painting /ˈpeɪntɪŋ/ *n* **1** [U] action or skill of painting sth. **2** [C] picture that has been painted: *a painting by Rembrandt* ○ *famous paintings.*

pair /peə(r)/ *n* **1** [C] two things of the same kind, usu used together: *a pair of gloves, shoes, socks, ear-rings* ○ *a huge pair of eyes.* **2** [C] object consisting of two parts joined together: *a pair of spectacles, tights, scissors, compasses* ○ *My spectacles are broken — I'll need to buy another pair.* ○ *These trousers cost £30 a pair.* **3** [pl v] two people closely connected or doing sth together: *the happy pair*, ie the newly married couple ○ (*infml*) *You've behaved very badly, the pair of you!* **4** [CGp] one male and one female animal of the same species that mate with each other: *a pair of swans nesting by the river.* **5** [C] two horses harnessed together to pull a carriage, etc: *a coach and pair.* **6** [C] (either of) two Members of Parliament of opposing parties who agree that neither will vote in a division, so that neither need attend. **7** (idm) **in ˈpairs** two at a time; in twos: *Cuff-links are only sold in pairs.* **show a clean pair of heels** ⇨ SHOW[2].
▷ **pair** *v* **1** [esp passive: Tn, Tn·pr] ~ **A with B** arrange (people or things) in a pair or pairs: *I've been paired with Bob* (ie Bob and I will play together as partners) *in the next round of the competition.* **2** [I] (of animals) mate. **3** [esp passive: Tn, Tn·pr] ~ **with sb**; ~ **A with B** (in Parliament) (cause sb to) form a pair(6). **4** (phr v) **pair (sb/sth) off (with sb)**: *The students had all paired off by the end of term.* ○ *Her parents tried to pair her off with a rich neighbour.* **pair up (with sb)** form a pair or pairs in order to work, play a game, etc together.

Paisley /ˈpeɪzlɪ/ *adj* having a detailed pattern of curved petal-shaped figures: *a Paisley tie, dressing-gown, etc.*

pajamas (*esp US*) = PYJAMAS.

Paki /ˈpækɪ/ *n, adj* (⚠ *derog offensive sl*) Pakistani.

Pakistan

Pakistan /ˌpækɪˈstɑːn, ˌpɑːk-, -ˈstæn/ country in southern Asia, between India and Afghanistan; pop approx 105 409 000; official language Urdu; capital Islamabad; unit of currency rupee (= 100 paisa). The border with Afghanistan is mountainous, and most of the population lives in the main agricultural region in the valley of the Indus. Agriculture, esp rice and cotton growing, is the main economic activity. Pakistan became independent in 1947, originally as E and W Pakistan, the two main Muslim areas of the Indian subcontinent. In 1971 East Pakistan became Bangladesh. ⇨ map. ▷ **Pakistani** *n, adj.*

pal /pæl/ *n* (*infml*) **1** friend: *We've been pals for years.* **2** (*sometimes ironic*) (used as a form of address) man; fellow: *Now look here, pal, you're asking for trouble!*
▷ **pal** *v* (**-ll-**) (phr v) **pal up (with sb)** (*infml*) become friendly (with sb).

pally /ˈpælɪ/ *adj* ~ **(with sb)** (*infml*) friendly: *She's become very pally with the boss/They've become very pally with each other.*

palace /ˈpælɪs/ *n* **1** official home of a sovereign, an archbishop or a bishop: *Buckingham Palace* ○ *The palace* (ie A spokesman for the king, queen, etc) *has just issued a statement.* ○ [attrib] *a palace spokesman.* **2** any large splendid house: *Compared to ours their house is a palace.*
□ **ˌpalace revoˈlution** overthrow of a monarch, president, etc by people in positions of power working closely with him.

palae(o)- (also *esp US* **pale(o)-**) *comb form* of ancient times; very old: *palaeolithic* ○ *palaeontology.*

Palaeocene /ˈpælɪəsiːn/ *adj* (also *esp US* **Paleo-** /ˈpeɪl-/) of the first epoch of the Tertiary period, lasting from about 65 to 54.9 million years ago, when early types of mammal started to become common.

palaeography /ˌpælɪˈɒgrəfɪ/ (also *esp US* **paleography** /ˌpeɪl-/) *n* [U] study of ancient writing and documents. ▷ **palaeographer** (also *esp US* **paleo-**) /-grəfə(r)/ *n.* **palaeographic** /ˌpælɪəʊˈgræfɪk/ (also *esp US* **paleo-** /ˌpeɪl-/) *adj.*

palaeolithic /ˌpælɪəʊˈlɪθɪk/ (also *esp US* **paleo-** /ˌpeɪl-/) *adj* of the early part of the Stone Age, lasting from about 2.5 million years ago to about 10 000 BC. During this time *Homo sapiens* appeared and stone tools began to be used. Cf MESOLITHIC.

palaeontology /ˌpælɪɒnˈtɒlədʒɪ/ (also *esp US* **paleon-** /ˌpeɪl-/) *n* [U] study of fossils as a guide to the history of life on earth. ▷ **palaeontologist** (also *esp US* **paleon-**) /-ədʒɪst/ *n.*

Palaeozoic /ˌpælɪəˈzəʊɪk/ (also *esp US* **Paleo-** /ˌpeɪl-/) *adj* of the geological era between the Precambrian and the Mesozoic eras, lasting from about 590 to 248 million years ago. During this period reptiles became dominant.

palatable /ˈpælətəbl/ *adj* **(a)** pleasant to taste. **(b)** (*fig*) pleasant or acceptable to the mind: *The truth is not always very palatable.* ▷ **palatably** /-blɪ/ *adv.*

palatal /ˈpælətl *or, rarely,* pəˈlertl/ *adj* **1** of the palate. **2** (*phonetics*) (of a speech sound) made by placing the tongue against or near the palate (usu the hard palate).
▷ **palatal** *n* (*phonetics*) palatal speech sound (eg /j, ʒ, ʃ, dʒ/).

palate /ˈpælət/ *n* **1** roof of the mouth: *the hard/soft palate*, ie its front/back part. ⇨ illus at THROAT. **2** (usu *sing*) sense of taste; ability to distinguish one taste from another: *a refined palate* ○ *Have a good palate for fine wine.*

palatial /pəˈleɪʃl/ *adj* **(a)** like a palace. **(b)** extremely large or splendid: *a palatial dining room, hotel, residence.*

Palatine /ˈpælətaɪn/ *adj* (following *ns*) having some of the privileges of a sovereign: *a Count Palatine.*
▷ **palatinate** /pəˈlætɪnət; *US* -tənət/ *n* area (formerly) ruled over by an Earl Palatine or a Count Palatine.

palaver /pəˈlɑːvə(r); *US* -ˈlæv-/ *n* [U, sing] **1** (*infml derog*) fuss or bother, often with a lot of talking: *What a palaver there was about paying the bill!* **2** (*often joc*) discussion.

pale[1] /peɪl/ *adj* (**-r, -est**) **1** (of a person, his face, etc) having little colour; having less colour than usual: *She has a pale complexion.* ○ *Are you feeling all right? You look rather pale.* ○ *He went/turned deathly pale at the news.* ○ *pale with anger, fear, shock, etc.* **2 (a)** (of colours) not bright or vivid: *pale blue eyes* ○ *a pale sky.* **(b)** (of light) dim; faint: *the pale light of dawn.*
▷ **pale** *v* **1** [I, Ipr] ~ **(with sth) (at sth)** become pale: *She paled with shock at the news.* **2** (phr v) **pale before, beside, etc sth** become less important in comparison with sth: *Her beauty pales beside her mother's.* ○ *Their other problems paled into insignificance beside this latest catastrophe.*
palely /ˈpeɪllɪ/ *adv.*
paleness *n* [U].
□ **ˈpale-face** *n* (*derog*) (said to have been used by N American Indians) white man.

pale[2] /peɪl/ *n* **1** (**a**) pointed piece of wood forming part of a fence; stake. (**b**) fence or boundary. **2** (idm) **beˌyond the ˈpale** considered unacceptable or unreasonable by people in general: *Those remarks he made were quite beyond the pale.*

pale(o)- ⇨ PALAE(O)-.

Palestine /ˈpæləstaɪn/ region in the Middle East formed in biblical times of the kingdoms of Israel and Judah. Throughout history it has been fought over many times. In the time of Jesus it was part of the Roman Empire. In the seventh century AD it was conquered and settled by Arabs; large-scale Jewish immigration began in the late 19th century. Part of the historical Palestine became the state of Israel in 1948, and in 1949 the area on the West Bank of the River Jordan became part of Jordan, but this was occupied by Israel in 1967.
▷ **Palestinian** /ˌpæləˈstɪnɪən/ *n* Arab living in or coming from the area corresponding to historical Palestine. — *adj*.
□ **the ˌPalestine Libeˈration Organization** (*abbr* **PLO**) organization formed in 1964 to fight for the restoration of a homeland for Palestinians by political and military means. It is now recognized by the United Nations.

Palestrina /ˌpæləˈstri:nə/ Giovanni Pierluigi da (1525-94), Italian composer. His unaccompanied church music, including over 100 masses, is remarkable for the beauty of its smooth vocal lines.

palette /ˈpælət/ *n* thin board on which an artist mixes colours when painting, with a hole for the thumb to hold it by.
□ **ˈpalette-knife** *n* (**a**) thin flexible knife used by artists for mixing (and sometimes spreading) oil-paints. (**b**) knife with a long flexible round-ended blade used for spreading and smoothing soft substances in cooking.

palimony /ˈpælɪmənɪ; *US* -məʊnɪ/ *n* [U] (*infml esp US*) amount of money that a court may order one member of an unmarried couple to pay regularly to the other after they have separated.

palimpsest /ˈpælɪmpsest/ *n* (usu old) manuscript from which the original writing has been removed in order to create space for new writing.

palindrome /ˈpælɪndrəʊm/ *n* word or phrase that reads the same backwards as forwards, eg *madam* or *nurses run*.

paling /ˈpeɪlɪŋ/ *n* fence made of pales (PALE[2] 1a).

palisade /ˌpælɪˈseɪd/ *n* **1** [C] strong fence made of pointed wooden stakes or iron poles, esp one used to defend a building. **2 palisades** [pl] (*US*) line of steep high cliffs, esp along a river.
▷ **palisade** *v* [Tn] enclose (sth) with a palisade, esp in order to defend it.

palish /ˈpeɪlɪʃ/ *adj* rather pale.

pall[1] /pɔ:l/ *v* [I, Ipr] ~ (**on sb**) become uninteresting or boring by being experienced too often: *The pleasures of sunbathing began to pall (on us) after a week on the beach.*

pall[2] /pɔ:l/ *n* **1** cloth spread over a coffin. **2** (*fig*) dark or heavy covering (used esp as in the expression shown): *A pall of smoke hung over the town.*
□ **ˈpallbearer** *n* one of a group of people who walk beside or carry the coffin at a funeral.

Palladio /pəˈlɑ:dɪəʊ/ Andrea (1508-80), Italian architect, famous for his writings on architectural theory.
▷ **Palladian** /pəˈleɪdɪən/ *adj* in the architectural style of Palladio, based on that of ancient Greece and Rome. It had a great influence on Inigo *Jones and his followers in Britain in the 18th century, and its main characteristic is a façade with a pediment and columns. ⇨ illus at JONES. ⇨ article at ARCHITECTURE.

palladium /pəˈleɪdɪəm/ *n* [U] (*symb* **Pd**) rare hard white metallic element. It is used as a catalyst, and in electrical contacts, precision instruments and jewellery.

Pallas Athene /ˌpæləs əˈθi:nɪ/ = ATHENE.

pallet[1] /ˈpælɪt/ *n* large wooden or metal tray or platform for carrying goods, esp one that can be raised using a fork-lift truck. ⇨ illus at BOX.

pallet[2] /ˈpælɪt/ *n* **1** mattress filled with straw. **2** hard narrow bed.

palliasse (also **paillasse** /*US* ˌpælɪˈæs/) *n* mattress filled with straw; pallet.

palliate /ˈpælɪeɪt/ *v* [Tn] (*fml*) **1** make (esp a pain or disease) less severe or unpleasant, without removing its cause; alleviate. **2** make (a crime, an offence, etc) seem less serious; excuse or extenuate.
▷ **palliation** /ˌpælɪˈeɪʃn/ *n* [U] palliating or being palliated.

palliative /ˈpælɪətɪv/ *n, adj* **1** (medicine) that reduces pain without removing its cause: *Aspirin is a palliative (drug).* **2** (thing) that reduces the harmful effects of sth without removing its cause: *Security checks are only a palliative (measure) in the fight against terrorism.*

pallid /ˈpælɪd/ *adj* (of a person, his face, etc) pale, esp because of illness: *a pallid complexion* ○ *You look a bit pallid — do you feel all right?* ▷ **pallidly** *adv*. **pallidness** *n* [U].

pallor /ˈpælə(r)/ *n* [U] (esp unhealthy) paleness of the face: *Her cheeks have a sickly pallor.*

pally ⇨ PAL.

palm[1] /pɑ:m/ *n* **1** (**a**) inner surface of the hand between the wrist and the fingers: *sweaty palms* ○ *read sb's palm*, ie tell sb's fortune by looking at the lines on his palm ○ *He held the mouse in the palm of his hand.* ⇨ illus at HAND. (**b**) part of a glove that covers this: *gloves with leather palms.* **2** (idm) **cross sb's palm with silver** ⇨ CROSS[2]. **grease sb's palm** ⇨ GREASE *v*. **have sb in the ˌpalm of one's ˈhand** have complete power or control over sb. **have an itching palm** ⇨ ITCH *v*.
▷ **palm** *v* **1** [Tn] hide (a coin, card, etc) in the hand when performing a conjuring trick. **2** [Tn, Tn·pr] hit (a ball) with the palm of the hand: *The goalkeeper just managed to palm the ball over the crossbar.* **3** (phr v) **palm sb off (with sth)** (*infml*) dishonestly persuade sb to accept sth: *He tried to palm me off with some excuse about the bus being late.* **palm sb/sth off (on sb)** (*infml*) get rid of (an unwanted person or thing) by persuading sb else to accept him/it: *They palmed their unwelcome guests off on the neighbours.*

palm-trees

palm[2] /pɑ:m/ *n* **1** (also **ˈpalm-tree**) any of several types of tree growing in warm or tropical climates, with no branches and a mass of large wide leaves at the top: *a ˈdate palm* ○ *a ˈcoconut palm* ○ [attrib] *palm fronds.* ⇨ illus. **2** leaf of such a tree as a symbol of victory or success: *the victor's palm.*
▷ **palmy** *adj* (**-ier, -iest**) **1** full of palm trees. **2** [esp attrib] flourishing; prosperous: *in my palmy days.*
□ **ˈpalm-oil** *n* [U] oil obtained from the nuts of various types of palm.
ˌPalm ˈSunday the Sunday before Easter.

Palmerston /ˈpɑ:məstən/ Henry, 3rd Viscount Palmerston (1784-1865), British statesman. As foreign secretary and prime minister he vigorously pursued British interests abroad, sometimes causing international controversy with his policies. For example, he nearly involved Britain in the American Civil War, on the side of the South.

palmetto /pælˈmetəʊ/ *n* (*pl* ~**s**) type of small palm-tree with fan-shaped leaves.

palmist /ˈpɑ:mɪst/ *n* person who claims to be able to interpret sb's character or tell sb's future by looking at the lines on the palm of his hand.
▷ **palmistry** /ˈpɑ:mɪstrɪ/ *n* [U] (skill of) doing this.

palomino /ˌpæləˈmi:nəʊ/ *n* (*pl* ~**s**) golden or cream-coloured horse with a light-coloured mane and tail.

palooka /pəˈlu:kə/ *n* (*US sl*) very bad sports player, esp a boxer.

palpable /ˈpælpəbl/ *adj* **1** that can be felt or touched. **2** (*fml*) clear to the mind; obvious: *a palpable lie, error.* ▷ **palpably** /-əblɪ/ *adv*.

palpate /ˈpælpeɪt/ *v* [Tn] (*medical*) examine (sth) by feeling with the hands, esp as part of a medical examination. ▷ **palpation** /pælˈpeɪʃn/ *n* [U].

palpitate /ˈpælpɪteɪt/ *v* **1** [I] (of the heart) beat rapidly. **2** [I, Ipr] ~ (**with sth**) (of a person or a part of his body) tremble or quiver because of fear or excitement, etc: *palpitating with terror.*
▷ **palpitation** /ˌpælpɪˈteɪʃn/ *n* **1** [U] act of palpitation. **2 palpitations** [pl] (period of) rapid beating of the heart: *I get palpitations if I run too fast.* ○ (*fig*) *The thought of flying gives me palpitations*, ie makes me very nervous.

palsy /ˈpɔ:lzɪ/ *n* [U] paralysis, esp with trembling of the limbs: *cerebral palsy.*
▷ **palsied** /ˈpɔ:lzɪd/ *adj* affected with palsy.

palter /ˈpɔ:ltə(r)/ *v* [I, Ipr] ~ (**with sb**) (*dated*) talk (to sb) in an insincere or misleading way.

paltry /ˈpɔ:ltrɪ/ *adj* (**-ier, -iest**) **1** very small; unimportant: *a paltry amount, sum, etc.* **2** worthless; contemptible: *a paltry excuse.*

pampas /ˈpæmpəs; *US* -əz/ *n* **the pampas** [pl] extensive grassy treeless plains in S America. Cf PRAIRIE, SAVANNAH, STEPPE, VELD.
□ **ˈpampas-grass** *n* [U] type of tall ornamental grass with a silver-white feathery flower.

pamper /ˈpæmpə(r)/ *v* [Tn] (*often derog*) treat (a person or an animal) with too much kindness or indulgence; spoil: *the pampered children of the rich* ○ *pamper oneself after a hard day at work.*

pamphlet /ˈpæmflɪt/ *n* small book with a paper cover, usu containing information on a subject of public interest or expressing a political opinion.
▷ **pamphleteer** /ˌpæmfləˈtɪə(r)/ *n* person who writes pamphlets.

Pan /pæn/ (in Greek mythology) god of flocks and herds, represented as a man with the horns, ears and legs of a goat, often playing *pan-pipes*.

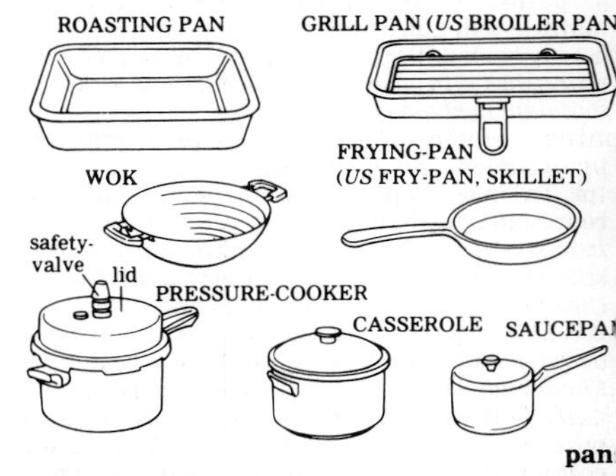

pan

pan[1] /pæn/ *n* (often in compounds) **1** (**a**) wide flat (usu metal) container, with a handle or handles, used for cooking food in: *a ˈfrying-pan* ○ *a saucepan* ○ *pots and pans.* ⇨ illus. (**b**) amount contained in this: *a pan of hot fat.* **2** any of various types of bowl-shaped containers: *a lavatory pan*, ie its porcelain bowl ○ *a ˈbedpan* ○ *a ˈdustpan.* **3** either of the dishes on a pair of scales. ⇨ illus at SCALE. **4** metal dish in which gravel is washed to separate it from gold or other valuable minerals. **5** = SALT-PAN (SALT). **6** small cavity for gunpowder in the lock of an old type of gun. **7** (idm) **a flash in the pan** ⇨ FLASH[1].
▷ **pan** *v* (**-nn-**) **1** [I, Ipr] ~ (**for sth**) wash gravel in a pan in order to find gold or other valuable minerals: *prospectors panning for gold.* **2** [Tn] (*infml*) criticize (sth) severely: *The film was panned by the critics.* **3** (phr v) **pan sth off/out** wash (gravel) in a pan, to separate gold or other valuable minerals from it. **pan out** (**a**) (of gravel, a river, an area, etc) yield gold or other valuable

minerals. (**b**) (*infml*) (of events or circumstances) develop; turn out: *It depends how things pan out.*
□ ˈ**pan-fish** *n* (*pl* unchanged) (*US*) fish, usu caught for one's own use, that can be fried whole in a pan.

pan² /pæn/ *v* (**-nn-**) (*cinema or broadcasting*) (**a**) [Tn, Tn·pr] move (a camera) to the right or left to follow a moving object or to show a wide view. (**b**) [I, Ipr] (of a camera, etc) move in this way: *The shot panned slowly across the room.*

pan- *comb form* of or relating to all or the whole of: *panchromatic* ○ *pan-African* ○ *pantheism.*

panacea /ˌpænəˈsɪə/ *n* ~ (**for sth**) remedy for all diseases or troubles: *There's no single panacea for the country's economic ills.*

panache /pæˈnæʃ; *US* pə-/ *n* [U] confident stylish manner: *She dresses with great panache.*

Panama /ˈpænəmɑː/ country in Central America; pop approx 2 322 000; official language Spanish; capital Panama City; unit of currency balboa (= 100 cents). The country is split in two by the Panama Canal. Most of the population lives on the fertile coastal areas and is involved in agriculture; the main crops are bananas and sugar cane. ⇨ map at CENTRAL AMERICA. ▷ **Panamanian** /ˌpænəˈmeɪnɪən/ *n, adj.*
□ **the ˌPanama Caˈnal** canal about 81 km (51 miles) long, linking the Atlantic and Pacific Oceans across Panama. It was built by the USA in 1904-14, and the zone on either side of the canal is US territory, due to be returned to Panama in 2000.

panama /ˈpænəmɑː/ *n* (also **ˌpanama ˈhat**) hat made of fine woven straw-like material. ⇨ illus at HAT.

panatella /ˌpænəˈtelə/ *n* long thin cigar.

pancake /ˈpæŋkeɪk/ *n* **1** [C] thin cake of batter fried on both sides and (usu) eaten hot, sometimes rolled up with a filling. **2** [U] make-up for the face consisting of powder pressed into a flat solid cake. **3** (idm) **flat as a pancake** ⇨ FLAT².
□ ˈ**Pancake Day** Shrove Tuesday, when pancakes are traditionally eaten.
ˌ**pancake ˈlanding** landing (usu made in an emergency) in which an aircraft descends vertically in a level position.

panchromatic /ˌpænkrəˈmætɪk/ *adj* (of photographic film) sensitive to all colours and able to reproduce them accurately.

pancreas /ˈpæŋkrɪəs/ *n* gland near the stomach that produces substances which help in the digestion of food. ⇨ illus at DIGESTIVE.
▷ **pancreatic** /ˌpæŋkrɪˈætɪk/ *adj* of or relating to the pancreas: ˌ*pancreatic* ˈ*juice.*

panda /ˈpændə/ *n* **1** (also ˌ**giant** ˈ**panda**) large rare bear-like black and white animal living in the mountains of SW China. **2** Indian animal like a raccoon, with brown fur and a long bushy tail.
□ ˈ**panda car** (*Brit*) police patrol car.

pandemic /pænˈdemɪk/ *n, adj* disease occurring over a whole country or the whole world. Cf ENDEMIC, EPIDEMIC.

pandemonium /ˌpændɪˈməʊnɪəm/ *n* [U] wild and noisy disorder or confusion: *There was pandemonium when the news was announced.* ○ *Pandemonium reigned in the classroom until the teacher arrived.*

pander /ˈpændə(r)/ *v* (phr v) **pander to sth/sb** (*derog*) try to satisfy (a vulgar, weak or immoral desire, or sb having this); gratify sth/sb: *newspapers pandering to the public love of scandal.*
▷ **pander** *n* (*arch*) = PIMP.

P and O /ˌpiː ən ˈəʊ/ *abbr* Peninsular and Oriental (Steamship Company): *the P and O line.*

Pandora's box /pænˌdɔːrəz ˈbɒks/ situation, arrangement, etc where interference could produce great difficulties or unhappiness: *If we do that we're opening a whole Pandora's box of problems.*

p and p /ˌpiː ən ˈpiː/ *abbr* (*Brit commerce*) (price of) postage and packing: *price £28.95 including p and p.*

pane /peɪn/ *n* single sheet of glass in a window: *a pane of glass* ○ *a* ˈ*window-pane.* ⇨ illus at HOME.

panegyric /ˌpænɪˈdʒɪrɪk/ *n* (*fml*) speech or piece of writing praising sb/sth.

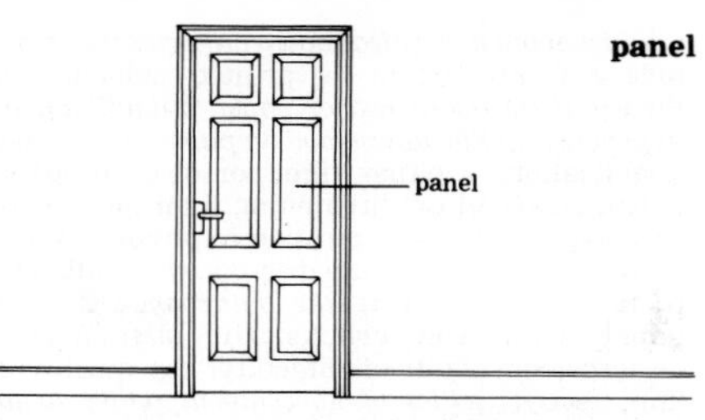

panel /ˈpænl/ *n* **1** [C] separate, usu rectangular, part of the surface of a door, wall, ceiling, etc, usu raised above or sunk below the surrounding area: *a ceiling with carved panels.* ⇨ illus. **2** [C] piece of metal forming a section of the bodywork of a vehicle. **3** [C] strip of material inserted into a garment. **4** [C] vertical board on which the controls and instruments of an aircraft, a car, etc are mounted: *an* ˈ*instrument panel* ○ *a con*ˈ*trol panel.* **5** [CGp] group of people chosen to take part in a quiz, discussion, etc with an audience (esp of listeners to a radio or TV programme): *a panel of experts* ○ [attrib] *a* ˈ*panel game.* **6** (**a**) [C] list of people chosen to serve on a jury. (**b**) [CGp] jury. **7** [C] (*Brit*) list of doctors who treat patients in a certain area as part of the National Health Service.
▷ **panel** *v* (**-ll-**; *US* **-l-**) [Tn esp passive] cover or decorate (sth) with panels: *a panelled room, ceiling, wall, etc.* **panelling** (*US* **paneling**) *n* [U] **1** series of panels, eg on a wall: *a room with fine oak panelling.* **2** wood used for making panels.
panellist (*US* **panelist**) /ˈpænəlɪst/ *n* member of a panel(5).
□ ˈ**panel-beater** *n* person whose job is removing dents from the bodywork of motor vehicles with a hammer.
ˈ**panel heating** form of electric or central heating using pipes or electric elements hidden behind panels in walls or ceilings.
ˈ**panel-pin** *n* very thin nail with a small head, used esp for fixing sheets of hardboard to supports.
ˈ**panel-saw** *n* small saw used for cutting thin sheets of wood.
ˈ**panel truck** (*US*) small enclosed van for delivering goods, etc.

pang /pæŋ/ *n* (usu *pl*) (**a**) sudden sharp feeling of pain: *pangs of hunger/hunger pangs.* (**b**) feeling of painful emotion: *pangs of jealousy, remorse, guilt, conscience, etc.*

Pangaea /ˌpænˈdʒɪə/ huge single continent that geologists believe existed before breaking up to form separate land masses, about 200 million years ago.

pangolin /ˈpæŋgəlɪn/ *n* small ant-eater of tropical Asia and Africa, covered with scales.

panhandle /ˈpænhændl/ *n* (*US*) narrow piece of land projecting from a larger area.
▷ **panhandle** *v* [I, Tn] (*infml*) beg for money from (sb) in the street.

panic /ˈpænɪk/ *n* [C, U] **1** (**a**) sudden irrational feeling of great fear: *be in a (state of) panic (about sth)* ○ *I got into a panic when I found the door was locked.* ○ *The thought of flying fills me with panic.* ○ [attrib] *a panic decision,* ie one resulting from panic. (**b**) fear that spreads quickly through a group of people: *There was (an) immediate panic when the alarm sounded.* ○ *The collapse of the bank caused (a) panic on the Stock Exchange,* ie the value of shares fell quickly. **2** (idm) ˈ**panic stations** (*infml*) state of alarm or panic: *It was panic stations when the police arrived to search the building.*
▷ **panic** *v* (**-ck-**) [I, Tn] **1** (cause a person or an animal to) be affected with panic: *Don't panic!* ○ *The gunfire panicked the horses.* **2** (phr v) **panic sb into doing sth** (often passive) make sb do (sth unwise or hasty) because of panic: *The banks were panicked into selling sterling.*
panicky /ˈpænɪkɪ/ *adj* (*infml*) affected or caused by panic: *Don't get panicky!* ○ *a panicky reaction, feeling, etc.*
□ ˈ**panic-stricken** *adj* in a state of panic; terrified: *You look panic-stricken!*

panjandrum /pænˈdʒændrəm/ *n* (*joc*) pompous self-important person.

Pankhurst /ˈpæŋkhɜːst/ Emmeline (1858-1928), British suffragette leader. She and her daughter Christabel were among the most active campaigners in the struggle to win the right for British women to vote.

pannier /ˈpænɪə(r)/ *n* **1** one of a pair of bags on either side of the back wheel of a bicycle or motor cycle. **2** one of a pair of baskets carried on either side of its back by a horse or donkey.

pannikin /ˈpænɪkɪn/ *n* (*Brit*) (**a**) small metal cup. (**b**) its contents.

panoply /ˈpænəplɪ/ *n* (*fml*) **1** complete or splendid display of sth. **2** (formerly) complete suit of armour.
▷ **panoplied** /ˈpænəplɪd/ *adj* (*fml*) having a panoply.

panorama /ˌpænəˈrɑːmə; *US* -ˈræmə/ *n* **1** (**a**) view of a wide area: *From the summit there is a superb panorama of the Alps.* (**b**) picture or photograph of this. **2** view of a constantly changing scene or series of events: *The book presents a panorama of British history since the Middle Ages.* ▷ **panoramic** /ˌpænəˈræmɪk/ *adj*: *a panoramic view from the top of the tower.*

pan-pipes /ˈpæn paɪps/ *n* [pl] musical instrument made of a series of reeds or pipes fixed together and played by blowing across the open ends.

pansy /ˈpænzɪ/ *n* **1** garden plant with a short stem and broad flat brightly-coloured petals. ⇨ illus at FLOWER. **2** (*infml derog*) effeminate man; homosexual.

pant /pænt/ *v* [I, Ipr] **1** breathe with short quick breaths: *He was panting heavily as he ran.* **2** (phr v) **pant along, down, etc** walk or run in the specified direction while panting: *The dog panted along the road beside me.* **pant for sth** (used only in the continuous tenses) (**a**) show by one's rapid breathing that one needs to drink, catch one's breath, etc: *panting for breath, a cool drink.* (**b**) have or show a strong desire for sth: *panting for revenge* ○ *He was panting with desire for her.* **pant sth out** say sth with difficulty, while panting: *He panted out the message.*
▷ **pant** *n* short quick breath: *breathe in short pants.*
pantingly *adv.*

pantaloon /ˌpæntəˈluːn/ *n* **1 pantaloons** [pl] (*US*; *Brit joc*) trousers. **2** (also **Pantaloon**) (in pantomime) foolish old man on whom the dame plays tricks. ⇨ illus at COMMEDIA DELL'ARTE.

pantechnicon /pænˈteknɪkən/ *n* (*Brit*) large van used for moving furniture from one house to another.

pantheism /ˈpænθɪɪzəm/ *n* [U] **1** belief that God is everything and everything is God. **2** belief in and worship of all gods.
▷ **pantheist** /-θɪɪst/ *n* believer in pantheism.
pantheistic /ˌpænθɪˈɪstɪk/ *adj* of, like or relating to pantheism.

pantheon /ˈpænθɪən; *US* -θɪɒn/ *n* **1** (esp in ancient Greece and Rome) temple dedicated to all the gods. **2** all the gods of a nation or people: *the ancient Egyptian pantheon.* **3** building in which the famous dead of a nation are buried or have memorials.

panther /ˈpænθə(r)/ *n* **1** leopard, esp a black one: *a black panther.* **2** (*US*) puma.

panties /ˈpæntɪz/ *n* [pl] (*infml*) short close-fitting knickers worn by women.

pantihose (also **pantyhose**) /ˈpæntɪhəʊz/ *n* [pl *v*]

(*US*) = TIGHTS.

pantile /ˈpæntaɪl/ *n* curved roof-tile: [attrib] *a pantile roof.*

pant(o)- *comb form* all; universal: *pantograph* ○ *pantomime.*

panto /ˈpæntəʊ/ *n* (*pl* **pantos** /ˈpæntəʊz/) (*infml*) = PANTOMIME 1.

pantograph /ˈpæntəgrɑ:f; *US* -græf/ *n* **1** instrument used to draw an exact copy of a plan, map, etc on any scale. **2** device for carrying an electric current from overhead wires to a train.

pantomime /ˈpæntəmaɪm/ *n* **1** (*Brit*) **(a)** [C] type of play with music, dancing and clowning, based on a traditional story or fairy-tale (eg *Aladdin* and *Babes in the Wood*) and usu performed at Christmas. Standard characters include the principal boy, a young man played by a woman, and the dame, a ridiculous old woman played by a man. Popular songs are put into the dialogue, and there are jokes about well-known people and events: *Let's take the children to the pantomime!* ○ [attrib] *a pantomime horse*, ie played by two actors in a funny costume. **(b)** [U] plays of this type: *She's acted in a lot of pantomime.* **2** [U] expressive movements of the face and body used to tell a story.

pantry /ˈpæntrɪ/ *n* **1** small room in a house where food is kept; larder. **2** (in a hotel, ship, large house, etc) room where glass, silver, table-linen, etc are kept.

pants /pænts/ *n* [pl] **1 (a)** (*Brit*) men's underpants; women's or children's knickers: *a clean pair of pants.* **(b)** (*esp US*) trousers. **2** (idm) **bore, scare, etc the ˈpants off sb** (*infml*) bore, scare sb extremely. **by the seat of one's pants** ➩ SEAT[1]. **catch sb with his pants/trousers down** ➩ CATCH[1]. **have ants in one's pants** ➩ ANT. **in long/short pants** (*US*) grown-up/not grown-up: *I've known him since he was in short pants.* **wear the pants/trousers** ➩ WEAR[2].

pap /pæp/ *n* [U] **1** soft or semi-liquid food suitable for babies or invalids. **2** undemanding, trivial or worthless reading-matter: *How can you bear to read such pap!*

papa /pəˈpɑ:; *US* ˈpɑ:pə/ *n* (*dated infml*) (used esp by children) father. Cf POP[2], POPPA.

papacy /ˈpeɪpəsɪ/ *n* **1 the Papacy** [sing] position or authority of the Pope. **2 (a)** [U] system of government of the Roman Catholic Church by popes. **(b)** [C] period of time when a pope is in office: *during the papacy of John Paul II.*
▷ **papal** /ˈpeɪpl/ *adj* of the Pope or the Papacy: *papal authority.*

paparazzi /pæpəˈrætsɪ/ *n* [pl] (*Italian derog*) newspaper photographers who follow famous people in order to take pictures of them, often without their agreement.

papaw (also **pawpaw**) /pəˈpɔ:; *US* ˈpɔ:pɔ:/ *n* **1 (a)** (also **papaya** /pəˈpaɪə/) [C] tropical American tree similar to a palm tree. **(b)** [C, U] its edible oblong orange-coloured fruit. **2 (a)** [C] small N American evergreen tree. **(b)** [C, U] its small fleshy edible fruit.

paper /ˈpeɪpə(r)/ *n* **1** (often in compounds) [U] substance made in thin sheets from wood pulp or rags and used for writing, printing or drawing on, or for wrapping and packing things: *a piece/sheet of paper* ○ *ˈwriting paper* ○ *ˈtissue paper* ○ [attrib] *a paper bag, handkerchief, towel, etc.* **2** [C] newspaper: *Where's today's paper?* ○ *a daily, an evening, a Sunday paper.* **3** [C, U] wallpaper: *a pretty striped paper for the bedroom.* **4 papers** [pl] **(a)** official documents, esp showing sb's identity, nationality, etc: *Immigration officials will ask to see your papers.* **(b)** pieces of paper which have been written on: *His desk is always covered with papers.* **5** [C] **(a)** set of examination questions on a particular subject: *The geography paper was difficult.* ○ *The French paper was set by our form teacher.* **(b)** written answers to examination questions: *She spent the evening marking examination papers.* **6** article or essay, esp one read to an audience of academics or specialists: *He read a paper at a medical conference on the results of his research.* **7** (idm) **on paper (a)** in writing: *Could you put a few ideas down on paper?* **(b)** when judged from written or printed evidence; in theory: *It's a fine scheme on paper, but will it work in practice?* ○ *She looks good on paper*, ie has good qualifications. **a ˌpaper ˈtiger** person or thing that is less powerful or threatening than he/it really seems or claims to be. **put pen to paper** ➩ PEN.
▷ **paper** *v* **1** put wallpaper on (the walls of a room): *We're papering the bathroom.* **2** (idm) **paper over the cracks (in sth)** hide a disagreement, fault or difficulty, esp quickly or imperfectly: *Critics of government policy argue that the new measures introduced to fight crime are simply papering over the cracks.* **3** (phr v) **paper sth over (a)** cover sth with wall paper: *We papered over the stains on the wall.* **(b)** hide (a disagreement, fault or difficulty), esp quickly or imperfectly.
papery /ˈpeɪpərɪ/ *adj* like paper in texture: *wrinkled, papery skin.*
□ **ˈpaperback** *n* [C, U] book bound in a flexible paper cover: *a cheap paperback* ○ *When is the novel coming out in paperback?* ○ [attrib] *a paperback book, edition.* Cf HARDBACK (HARD[1]). ➩ article at PUBLISHING.
ˈpaper-boy, **ˈpaper-girl** *n* boy/girl who delivers newspapers to people's houses.
ˈpaper-chase *n* cross-country run in which the leader drops a trail of pieces of paper for the other runners to follow.
ˈpaper-clip *n* piece of bent wire or plastic used for holding sheets of paper together.
ˈpaper-knife *n* knife used for cutting the pages of books, opening envelopes, etc.
ˈpaper-mill *n* factory where paper is made.
ˌpaper ˈmoney money in the form of banknotes.
ˈpaperweight *n* small heavy object placed on top of loose papers to keep them in place.
ˈpaperwork *n* [U] written work in an office, such as filling in forms, writing letters and reports, etc: *She's good at paperwork.*

papier mâché /ˌpæpɪeɪ ˈmæʃeɪ; *US* ˌpeɪpər məˈʃeɪ/ (*French*) moulded paper pulp used for making boxes, trays, ornaments, etc.

papist /ˈpeɪpɪst/ *n* (*derog*) (used esp by Protestants) Roman Catholic.

papoose /pəˈpu:s; *US* pæˈpu:s/ *n* **1** type of bag fixed to a frame, used for carrying a young baby on the back. **2** N American Indian baby.

paprika /ˈpæprɪkə; *US* pəˈpri:kə/ *n* **(a)** [C] type of sweet pepper. **(b)** [U] red powder made from this and used as a spice.

Papua New Guinea /ˌpæpjʊə nju: ˈgɪnɪ/ country in the southern Pacific, north of Australia, a member of the Commonwealth; pop approx 3 562 000; official language English; capital Port Moresby; unit of currency kina (= 100 toea). The country occupies the eastern half of the island of New Guinea, with a number of other small islands to the west. Agriculture is the main economic activity; the most important crops are sweet potatoes, cocoa and coffee. ➩ map at MELANESIA.

papyrus /pəˈpaɪərəs/ *n* **1** [U] tall reed-like water-plant with thick fibrous stems used by the Ancient Egyptians to make paper. **2** [U] this paper. **3** [C] (*pl* **papyri** /pəˈpaɪəri:/) manuscript written on this paper.

par /pɑ:(r)/ *n* **1** [sing] (also **par value**) price that is printed on stocks and shares; face value: *sell shares above/at/below par.* **2** [sing] (also **par of exchange**) recognized value of one country's currency in terms of another's. **3** [sing] (in golf) number of strokes considered necessary for a first-class player to complete a hole or course: *Par for the course is 72.* ○ *She went round the course in three below* (ie three strokes less than) *par.* Cf BIRDIE 2, BOGEY 1, EAGLE 2. **4** (idm) **below ˈpar** (*infml*) less well, alert, etc than usual: *I'm feeling a bit below par today.* **be ˌpar for the ˈcourse** (*infml*) be what one would expect to happen or expect sb to do: *She was an hour late, was she? That's about par for the course for her.* **on a par with sb/sth** equal in importance, quality, etc to sb/sth: *As a writer she was on a par with the great novelists.* **up to ˈpar** (*infml*) as good/well as usual: *I didn't think her performance was up to par.*

par (also **para** /ˈpærə/) *abbr* paragraph: *see par 19* ○ *paras 39-42*, eg in a contract.

para-[1] *pref* (forming *ns*) **1** beside; near: *parameter* ○ *paramilitary.* **2** beyond: *parapsychology* ○ *paranormal.*

para-[2] *comb form* protecting from: *parachute* ○ *parasol.*

parable /ˈpærəbl/ *n* (esp in the Bible) story told to illustrate a moral or spiritual truth: *Jesus taught in parables.* ○ *the parable of the prodigal son.*

parabola /pəˈræbələ/ *n* (*geometry*) plane curve formed by cutting a cone on a plane parallel to its side. ➩ illus at HYPERBOLA.

parabolic /ˌpærəˈbɒlɪk/ *adj* **1** of or expressed in a parable. **2** of or like a parabola.

Paracelsus /ˌpærəˈselsəs/ (c1493-1541), Swiss physician and religious reformer. He was the first major critic of classical medicine, advocating a rival system based on chemotherapy.

Paracetamol /ˌpærəˈsi:təmɒl/ *n* (*propr*) [C, U] (tablet of a) medicine used to relieve pain and reduce fever.

parachute /ˈpærəʃu:t/ *n* device for making people or objects fall slowly and safely when dropped from an aeroplane, consisting of an umbrella-shaped canopy attached to a harness: *land by parachute* ○ [attrib] *a parachute jump/drop.*
▷ **parachute** *v* [I, Ipr, Tn, Tn·pr] (cause sb/sth to) drop by parachute from an aircraft: *She enjoys parachuting.* ○ *We parachuted into enemy territory.* ○ *Supplies were parachuted into the earthquake zone.*
parachutist /-ɪst/ *n* person who drops from an aircraft using a parachute.

parade /pəˈreɪd/ *n* [C] **1** formal gathering of troops for inspection, a roll-call, etc: *a drill parade* ○ *ceremonial parades.* **2** = PARADE-GROUND. **3** procession of people or things: *a parade of players before a football match* ○ *a fashion parade*, ie one in which models display new clothes to an audience. **4** (esp in names) public promenade or street of shops: *He lives in North Parade.* **5** (idm) **make a parade of sth** (*esp derog*) display sth in order to impress people: *He's always making a parade of his knowledge.* **on parade** taking part in a parade; being paraded: *The regiment is on parade.* ○ *A number of new hats were on parade at the wedding.*
▷ **parade** *v* **1** [I, Tn] (cause sb to) gather together for inspection, a roll-call, etc: *The colonel paraded his troops.* **2** [I, Ipr, Ip] march or walk in a procession or in order to display sth: *The strikers paraded through the city centre.* ○ *She paraded up and down in her new hat.* **3** [Tn] display (sth); show (sth) off: *She was parading her new fur coat yesterday*, ie wearing it to show it off to others.
□ **paˈrade-ground** *n* place where soldiers gather for inspection, a roll-call, etc.

paradigm /ˈpærədaɪm/ *n* **1** set of all the different forms of a word: *verb paradigms.* **2** type of sth; pattern; model: *a paradigm for others to copy.* ▷ **paradigmatic** /ˌpærədɪgˈmætɪk/ *adj.*

paradise /ˈpærədaɪs/ *n* **1** [sing without *a* or *the*] heaven. **2 (a)** [C] ideal or perfect place: *This island is a paradise for bird-watchers.* **(b)** [U] state of perfect happiness: *Being alone is his idea of paradise.* **3 Paradise** [sing without *a* or *the*] (in the Bible) the Garden of Eden, where Adam and Eve lived in a state of innocence. **4** (idm) **a fool's paradise** ➩ FOOL[1].
▷ **paradisaical** /ˌpærədɪˈzeɪɪkl/ *adj* of or like (a) paradise.

paradox /ˈpærədɒks/ *n* **1 (a)** [C] statement that seems to be absurd or contradictory but is or may be true: *'More haste, less speed' is a well-known paradox.* **(b)** [U] use of this in talking or writing: *Paradox and irony are characteristics of her style.* **2** [C] person, thing or situation displaying contradictory features: *It is a paradox that such a rich country should have so many poor people living in it.* ▷ **paradoxical** /ˌpærəˈdɒksɪkl/ *adj.* **paradoxically** /-klɪ/ *adv.*

paraffin /ˈpærəfɪn/ *n* [U] **1** (also **ˈparaffin oil**)

(*Brit*) (*US* ˈ**coal oil, kerosene**) oil obtained from petroleum, coal, etc and used as a fuel in heaters and lamps and as a solvent: [attrib] *a paraffin lamp, stove.* **2** (also ˈ**paraffin wax**) wax-like substance obtained from petroleum, used esp for making candles.

paragon /ˈpærəgən; *US* -gɒn/ *n* **(a)** ~ **of sth** person who is a perfect example of a quality (used esp in the expression shown): *a paragon of virtue.* **(b)** completely perfect person: *I make no claim to be a paragon.*

paragraph /ˈpærəgrɑːf; *US* -græf/ *n* **1** distinct section of a written or printed text, usu consisting of several sentences dealing with a single theme and starting on a new (usu indented) line: *begin a new paragraph.* **2** (also ˈ**paragraph mark**) sign (¶) used to show where a new paragraph is to begin or as a reference mark. **3** short report in a newspaper: *There's a paragraph on the accident in the local paper.*

▷ **paragraph** *v* [Tn] divide (sth) into paragraphs.

Paraguay

Paraguay /ˌpærəˈgwaɪ/ inland country in South America; pop approx 4 039 000; official language Spanish; capital Asunción; unit of currency guarani (= 100 céntimos). Most of the population is engaged in agriculture; the main crops are soya, maize and cotton. Industry is underdeveloped. ⇨ map. ▷ **Paraguayan** /ˌpærəˈgwaɪən/ *n, adj.*

parakeet /ˈpærəkiːt/ *n* any of various types of small long-tailed parrot.

parallax /ˈpærəlæks/ *n* **(a)** [U] apparent difference in the position or direction of an object caused by seeing it from a different point. **(b)** [C] this difference measured as an angle.

parallel /ˈpærəlel/ *adj* **1 (a)** (of two or more lines) having the same distance between each other at every point: *parallel lines.* ⇨ illus at CONVERGE. **(b)** [pred] ~ **to/with sth** (of a line) having this relationship with another one: *The road runs parallel with the railway.* ○ *The road and the railway are parallel to each other.* **2** exactly corresponding; similar: *a parallel case, career, development.*

▷ **parallel** *n* **1** [C] (also ˌ**parallel** ˈ**line**) line that is parallel to another. **2** (also ˌ**parallel of** ˈ**latitude**) [C] imaginary line on the earth's surface, or a corresponding line on a map, parallel to and passing through all points the same distance north or south of the equator: *the 49th parallel.* **3** [C, U] person, situation, event, etc that is exactly similar to another: *a career without parallel in modern times.* **4** [C] **(a)** comparison (used esp in the expression shown): *draw a parallel between A and B.* **(b)** similarity: *I see parallels between the two cases.* **5** (idm) **in parallel** (of an electric current) having the negative terminals attached to one conductor and the positive ones to another. Cf SERIES 2.

parallel *v* [Tn esp passive] **1** be equal to (sth); match (sth): *His performance has never been paralleled.* **2** be comparable or similar to (sth): *Her experiences parallel mine in many instances.*

parallelism /-ɪzəm/ *n* [U] state of being parallel; similarity: *Don't exaggerate the parallelism between the two cases.*

□ ˌ**parallel** ˈ**bars** pair of bars on posts, used for gymnastic exercises.

parallelogram /ˌpærəˈleləgræm/ *n* (*geometry*) four-sided plane figure with its opposite sides parallel to each other. ⇨ illus at QUADRILATERAL.

paralyse (*US* **paralyze**) /ˈpærəlaɪz/ *v* **1** [Tn] affect (sb) with paralysis: *The accident left her paralyzed from the waist down.* ○ *She is paralysed in both legs.* **2** [Tn·pr esp passive] ~ **sb (with sth)** prevent sb from moving or acting normally: *be paralysed with fear, horror, shock, etc.*

paralysis /pəˈræləsɪs/ *n* (*pl* **-ses** /siːz/) **1** [C, U] loss of feeling in or control of a part of the body, caused by a disease of or an injury to the nerves: *suffer from paralysis of the right leg* ○ *The paralysis affects his right leg and he can only walk with difficulty.* **2** [U] (*fig*) total inability to move, act, operate, etc: *the complete paralysis of industry caused by the electricians' strike.*

paralytic /ˌpærəˈlɪtɪk/ *adj* **1** suffering from paralysis(1). **2** (*Brit infml*) very drunk: *She was/got completely paralytic last night.*

▷ **paralytic** *n* person suffering from paralysis.

paramedical /ˌpærəˈmedɪkl/ *adj* (of services) supporting and supplementing the work of doctors.

▷ **paramedic** /-ˈmedɪk/ *n* person providing paramedical services.

parameter /pəˈræmɪtə(r)/ *n* **1** (*mathematics*) quantity that does not vary in a particular case but does vary in other cases. **2** characteristic or feature, esp one that can be measured or quantified. **3** (usu *pl*) limiting factor or characteristic; limit: *We have to work within the parameters of time and budget.*

paramilitary /ˌpærəˈmɪlɪtrɪ; *US* -terɪ/ *adj* (relating or belonging to a military force that is) organized like but not part of the official armed forces: *a paramilitary force/organization* ○ *paramilitary activity.*

▷ **paramilitary** *n* member of a paramilitary group or organization.

paramount /ˈpærəmaʊnt/ *adj* (*fml*) having the greatest importance or significance; supreme: *This matter is of paramount importance.* ○ *The reduction of unemployment should be paramount in the government's economic policy.*

▷ **paramountcy** /-tsɪ/ *n* [U] (*fml*) (state of) being paramount.

paranoia /ˌpærəˈnɔɪə/ *n* [U] **1** mental illness in which a person is obsessed by mistaken beliefs, esp that he is being badly treated by others or that he is somebody very important. **2** (*infml*) abnormal tendency to suspect and mistrust other people. ▷ **paranoiac** /ˌpærəˈnɔɪæk/ *n, adj* = PARANOID.

paranoid /ˈpærənɔɪd/ (also **paranoiac**) *adj* of, like, suffering from or showing paranoia: *paranoid fears* ○ *paranoid schizophrenia* ○ *She's getting paranoid about what other people think of her.* ○ *I don't think she likes me — or am I just being paranoid?*

▷ **paranoid** *n* paranoid person.

paranormal /ˌpærəˈnɔːml/ *adj* unable to be explained scientifically or rationally: *paranormal phenomena.*

parapet /ˈpærəpɪt, -pet/ *n* **1** low protective wall along the edge of a balcony, bridge, roof, etc. **2** (in war) protective bank of earth, stones, etc along the front edge of a trench.

paraphernalia /ˌpærəfəˈneɪlɪə/ *n* [U] numerous small articles or personal belongings, esp the equipment needed for a hobby or sport: *skiing, climbing, jogging, etc paraphernalia.* ⇨ Usage at DATA.

paraphrase /ˈpærəfreɪz/ *n* re-wording of a piece of writing, statement, etc, esp in order to make it easier to understand: *a paraphrase of the sonnet.*

▷ **paraphrase** *v* [Tn] express the meaning of (a piece of writing, statement, etc) in different words, esp in order to make it easier to understand: *paraphrase a speech in colloquial English.*

paraplegia /ˌpærəˈpliːdʒə/ *n* [U] paralysis of the legs and part or all of the trunk(2).

▷ **paraplegic** /ˌpærəˈpliːdʒɪk/ *n, adj* (person) suffering from paraplegia: *She's (a) paraplegic.* ○ [attrib] *ˌparaplegic ˈsports,* ie of or for paraplegics.

paraquat /ˈpærəkwɒt/ *n* [U] (*propr*) extremely poisonous weed-killer.

parasite /ˈpærəsaɪt/ *n* **1** animal (eg a flea, louse) or plant (eg mistletoe) that lives on or in another and gets its food from it. **2** (*derog*) person who lives off others and gives nothing in return: *live as a parasite on society.*

▷ **parasitic** /ˌpærəˈsɪtɪk/, **parasitical** /ˌpærəˈsɪtɪkl/ *adjs* **(a)** living as a parasite; like a parasite: *a parasitic plant, worm* ○ (*fig*) *He lives a parasitic existence, borrowing money from his friends.* **(b)** caused by a parasite: *a parasitic disease.* **parasitically** /-klɪ/ *adv.*

parasol /ˈpærəsɒl; *US* -sɔːl/ *n* light umbrella used to give shade from the sun. Cf SUNSHADE (SUN). ⇨ illus at DRESS, HOME.

parataxis /ˌpærəˈtæksɪs/ *n* [U] (*grammar*) placing of clauses one after the other without linking them by conjunctions, as in *Tell me, how are you?* ▷ **paratactic** /-ˈtæktɪk/ *adj.*

paratroops /ˈpærətruːps/ *n* [pl] soldiers trained to drop from an aircraft by parachute.

▷ **paratrooper** /ˈpærətruːpə(r)/ *n* one of these soldiers.

paratyphoid /ˌpærəˈtaɪfɔɪd/ *n* [U] type of fever similar to typhoid, but less dangerous.

parboil /ˈpɑːbɔɪl/ *v* [Tn] boil (food) until it is partly cooked: *Potatoes can be parboiled before roasting.*

parcel /ˈpɑːsl/ *n* **1** (*US* also **package**) thing or things wrapped up for carrying or sending by post: *The postman has brought a parcel for you.* ○ *She was carrying a parcel of books under her arm.* ⇨ Usage at PACKET. **2** piece of land, esp on an estate (used esp in the expression shown): *a parcel of land.* **3** (idm) **part and parcel of sth** ⇨ PART[1].

▷ **parcel** *v* (**-ll-**; *US* **-l-**) (phr v) **parcel sth out** divide sth into parts or portions: *He parcelled out the land into small plots.* **parcel sth up** make sth into a parcel; wrap sth up: *She parcelled up the books.*

□ ˈ**parcel bomb** bomb wrapped up to look like a normal parcel and sent by post.

ˈ**parcel post** system of sending parcels by post: *send sth (by) parcel post.*

parch /pɑːtʃ/ *v* [Tn esp passive] **1** make (sth) very dry and hot: *earth parched by the sun* ○ *the parched deserts of N Africa* ○ *parched lips,* eg of a person with a fever. **2** make (sb) very thirsty: *Give me a drink — I'm parched.*

parchment /ˈpɑːtʃmənt/ *n* **1 (a)** [U] heavy paper-like material made from the skin of sheep or goats and used for writing on. **(b)** [C] piece of this material which has been written on. **2** [U] type of paper similar to parchment.

pardon[1] /ˈpɑːdn/ *n* **1** [U] ~ **(for sth)** forgiveness: *ask/seek sb's pardon for sth.* **2** [C] **(a)** cancellation of a punishment incurred for a crime: *He was granted a pardon after new evidence had proved his innocence.* **(b)** document on which this is written. **3** (idm) **beg sb's pardon** ⇨ BEG. **I beg your pardon** ⇨ BEG.

pardon[2] /ˈpɑːdn/ *v* **1** [Tn, Tn·pr, Tsg] ~ **sb (for sth/doing sth)** (*esp fml*) forgive or excuse sb for (sth): *He begged her to pardon him (for his rudeness).* ○ *pardon an offence, a fault, etc* ○ *Pardon me (for) asking/Pardon my asking, but isn't that my hat you're wearing?* **2** (idm) **excuse/pardon my French** ⇨ FRENCH.

▷ **pardon** *interj* (*US* also ˌ**pardon** ˈ**me**) (used to ask sb to repeat sth because one didn't hear it). ⇨ Usage at EXCUSE[2].

pardonable /ˈpɑːdnəbl/ *adj* that can be forgiven or excused: *a pardonable error.* **pardonably** /-əblɪ/ *adv* (*fml*) understandably: *She is pardonably proud of her wonderful cooking.*

pardoner *n* (in the Middle Ages) person who was allowed to sell papal indulgences (INDULGENCE 4a).

pare /peə(r)/ *v* [Tn] **1** trim (sth) by cutting away the edges: *pare one's finger-nails.* **2** cut away the skin or outer covering from (sth); peel: *pare an apple.* **3** (phr v) **pare sth down** reduce sth considerably: *We have pared down our expenses to a bare minimum.* **pare sth off (sth)** remove (skin, peel, etc) from sth in thin strips: *She pared off the thick peel with a sharp knife.* ⇨ Usage at CLIP[2].
▷ **parings** /ˈpeərɪŋz/ *n* [pl] pieces that have been pared off: *ˈnail parings.*

parent /ˈpeərənt/ *n* **1** (usu *pl*) father or mother: *May I introduce you to my parents* (ie my father and mother)*?* ○ *Denise and Martin have recently become parents.* ○ *Do you get on with your parents?* ○ *the duties of a parent.* ⇨ App 8. **2** animal or plant from which others are produced: [attrib] *the parent bird, tree.*
▷ **parentage** /-ɪdʒ/ *n* [U] descent from parents; origin; ancestry: *a person of unknown parentage*, ie having parents whose identity is not known ○ *of humble parentage.*
parental /pəˈrentl/ *adj* [usu attrib] of or relating to a parent or parents: *parental affection, love, support, etc* ○ *children lacking parental care.* **parentally** /pəˈrentəlɪ/ *adv.*
parenthood /ˈpeərənthʊd/ *n* [U] (state of) being a parent: *the responsibilities of parenthood.*
□ ˌ**parent ˈcompany** commercial company that owns or controls one or more other companies.
ˌ**parent-ˈteacher association** (*abbr* **PTA**) organization of teachers and schoolchildren's parents, formed to improve relations and understanding between them.

parenthesis /pəˈrenθəsɪs/ *n* (*pl* **-eses** /-əsi:z/) **1** [C] additional word, phrase or sentence inserted into a passage which would be complete without it, and usu separated from it by brackets, dashes or commas. **2** [C usu *pl*] either of a pair of round brackets (like these) used to enclose an additional word, phrase, etc. ⇨ App 14. **3 in parenthesis** enclosed between parentheses: *The statistics were given in parenthesis.* ○ (*fig*) *Let me add, in parenthesis, ...*, ie as an aside....
▷ **parenthetic** /ˌpærənˈθetɪk/, **parenthetical** /-ɪkl/ *adjs* of, relating to or inserted as a parenthesis: *parenthetical comments, remarks, etc.* **parenthetically** /-klɪ/ *adv.*

par excellence /ˌpɑ:r ˈeksəlɑ:ns; *US* ˌeksəˈlɑ:ns/ *adv* (*French*) (used after a *n*) more than all others of its kind; to the highest degree: *He is the elder statesman par excellence.* ○ *the fashionable quarter par excellence.*

pariah /pəˈraɪə, ˈpærɪə/ *n* **1** social outcast: *be treated as a pariah.* **2** (in India) person of no caste or of very low caste.

parietal /pəˈraɪətl/ *adj* **1** (*anatomy*) of either of the bones (**parietal bones**) forming part of the sides and top of the skull. **2** (*US*) of or relating to residence in a college.

pari-mutuel /ˌpærɪˈmju:tʊəl/ *n* (*US*) system of betting on races in which all the money bet on a race, less a proportion kept by the organizers of the system, is shared amongst the winners.

Paris[1] /ˈpærɪs/ (in Greek legend) Trojan prince appointed by the gods to judge between the beauty of the goddesses Hera, Athene and Aphrodite. He chose Aphrodite, who promised him the most beautiful woman in the world. This was Helen, wife of the Spartan king Menelaus, and by taking her away from her husband he caused the Trojan War.

Paris[2] /ˈpærɪs/ capital of France, situated on the River Seine. It is the country's political and commercial centre; nearly a fifth of the population of France lives in Paris or its surrounding area. It is famous as an international cultural centre, with its many museums and art galleries from the Louvre to the Beaubourg Centre, and for its great architectural heritage, esp in its modern public buildings. ▷ **Parisian** /pəˈrɪzɪən; *US* -ɪʒn/ *n, adj.*

parish /ˈpærɪʃ/ *n* **1** [C] area within a diocese, having its own church and clergyman: *He is vicar of a large rural parish.* ○ [attrib] *a parish church* ○ *a parish priest* ○ *parish boundaries* ○ *the parish magazine*, ie giving news of events in a parish. **2** (also **civil ˈparish**) [C] (in England) area within a county, having its own local government. Cf BOROUGH 1. **3** [CGp] people living in a parish, esp those who attend church regularly: *The parish objected to some of the vicar's reforms.* **4** (idm) ˌ**parish ˈpump** [attrib] of or relating to local affairs: *parish-pump affairs, politics, gossip.*
▷ **parishioner** /pəˈrɪʃənə(r)/ *n* inhabitant of a parish, esp one who attends church regularly.
□ ˌ**parish ˈclerk** official with various duties in connection with a parish church.
ˌ**parish ˈcouncil** administrative body in a parish(1).
ˌ**parish ˈregister** book recording the christenings, marriages and burials that have taken place at the parish church.

parity /ˈpærətɪ/ *n* [U] (*fml*) **1** state of being equal; equality: *parity of status, pay, treatment* ○ *Primary school teachers are demanding parity with* (ie as much pay as) *those in secondary schools.* **2** (*finance*) equivalence of one currency in another; being at par: *The two currencies have now reached parity*, ie are at par.
□ ˌ**parity of exˈchange** official rate of currency exchange agreed by governments.

Park /pɑ:k/ Mungo (1771-1806), Scottish explorer. He made two journeys into W Africa. He became famous with his account of his experiences during the first journey, but he was killed after returning to Africa in 1805.

park[1] /pɑ:k/ *n* **1** public garden or recreation ground in a town: *The children have gone to play in the park.* **2** enclosed area of grassland, usu planted with trees, attached to a large country house. **3** (*US*) sports ground or playing-field. **4** (in compounds) **(a)** (large) area of land used for recreation by the public: *a ˌnational ˈpark* ○ *a saˈfari park* ○ *an aˈmusement park.* **(b)** area adapted for a specific activity: *a techˈnology park*, ie providing facilities for companies involved in modern technology. **5** area used for storing military equipment, vehicles, etc.
□ ˈ**parkland** /-lænd/ *n* [U] open grassland with clumps of trees: *The house stands in 500 acres of rolling parkland.*
ˈ**parkway** *n* (*US*) wide road with trees, shrubs, etc along the sides and/or the central strip.

park[2] /pɑ:k/ *v* **1** [I, Ipr, Tn, Tn·pr] stop and leave (a vehicle) in a place for a time: *Where can we park (the car)?* ○ *You can't park in this street.* ○ *You are/Your car is very badly parked.* **2** [Tn, Tn·pr] (*infml*) **(a)** leave (sb/sth) in a place for a time: *Park your luggage here while you buy a ticket.* **(b)** ~ **oneself** sit down: *Park yourself in that chair while I make you a cup of tea.* **3** [Tn] bring together (esp equipment or vehicles) in a military park[1](5).
□ ˌ**park and ˈride** system designed to reduce traffic problems in cities, in which commuters, shoppers, etc leave their cars in a car-park outside the centre and continue their journey by public transport.

parka /ˈpɑ:kə/ *n* **1** jacket made from skin and with a hood, worn by Eskimos. **2** jacket or coat shaped like this and worn by mountaineers, etc.

Parker[1] /ˈpɑ:kə(r)/ Charlie (1920-55), American jazz saxophone player, known as 'Bird'. He was one of the founders of the bebop style and greatly influenced later jazz musicians.

Parker[2] /ˈpɑ:kə(r)/ Dorothy (1893-1967), American author. She wrote short stories and was also famous as a witty critic of plays and books for the *New Yorker* magazine.

parkin /ˈpɑ:kɪn/ *n* [U] type of cake made with ginger, oatmeal and treacle.

parking /ˈpɑ:kɪŋ/ *n* [U] **(a)** stopping a motor vehicle at a place and leaving it there for a time: *There is no parking between 9 am and 6 pm.* ○ [attrib] *a parking fine*, ie one incurred for parking illegally. **(b)** space or area for leaving vehicles: *Is there any parking near the theatre?*
□ ˈ**parking-lot** *n* (*US*) = CAR-PARK (CAR).
ˈ**parking-meter** *n* meter into which one inserts coins to pay for parking a car beside it for a certain time.
ˈ**parking-ticket** *n* notice of a fine imposed for parking illegally: *I got a parking-ticket today!*

Parkinson's disease /ˈpɑ:kɪnsnz dɪzi:z/ (also **Parkinsonism** /ˈpɑ:kɪnsənɪzəm/) *n* [U] chronic disease of the nervous system causing tremors and weakness of the muscles.

Parkinson's law /ˈpɑ:kɪnsnz lɔ:/ (*joc*) idea that work will always take as long as the time available for it.

parky /ˈpɑ:kɪ/ *adj* [usu pred] (*Brit dialect infml*) (of the air, weather, etc) cold; chilly.

parlance /ˈpɑ:ləns/ *n* [U] (*fml*) particular way of speaking or use of words; phraseology: *in common parlance* ○ *in legal parlance.*

parlay /ˈpɑ:lɪ/ *v* [Tn] (*US*) use (the total money won from a previous bet) for a further bet.
▷ **parlay** *n* bet made by parlaying. Cf ACCUMULATOR.

parley /ˈpɑ:lɪ/ *n* (*pl* ~**s**) (esp formerly) meeting between enemies or opponents to discuss terms for peace, etc: *arrange/hold a parley with sb.*
▷ **parley** *v* [I, Ipr] ~ **(with sb)** have a parley.

parliament /ˈpɑ:ləmənt/ *n* **1** [CGp] assembly that makes the laws of a country: *the French, Dutch German, Spanish, etc parliament.* **2 Parliament (a)** chief law-making assembly of the United Kingdom, consisting of the House of Commons, the House of Lords and the sovereign: *the ˌHouses of ˈParliament* ○ *a ˌMember of ˈParliament* ○ *The issue was debated in Parliament.* ○ *get into* (ie be elected a Member of) *Parliament* ○ *adjourn, dissolve (a) Parliament* ○ *the State Opening of Parliament*, ie the ceremony in which the sovereign opens a new session of Parliament. ⇨ article. **(b)** side that opposed Charles I and the Royalists during the English Civil War, consisting of Members of Parliament and their supporters. **3** (often **Parliament**) [C] Parliament as it exists during the period of time between one General Election and the next: *The government is unlikely to get the bill through within (the lifetime of) this Parliament.* **4** [C] building where a parliament meets.
▷ **parliamentarian** /ˌpɑ:ləmenˈteərɪən/ *n* **1** person who is skilled at debating in parliament: *one of our most eminent parliamentarians.* **2** member of a parliament: *German parliamentarians.* **3 Parliamentarian** supporter of Parliament in the English Civil War: *Royalists and Parliamentarians.*
parliamentary /ˌpɑ:ləˈmentrɪ/ *adj* **1** [usu attrib] of or relating to parliament: *parliamentary debates* ○ *parliamentary procedure* ○ *a parliamentary recess* ○ *the parliamentary party*, ie members of a political party who are MPs rather than its ordinary members ○ *Parliamentary forces*, ie during the English Civil War. **2** (of behaviour, language, etc) polite enough and suitable for parliament.

parlour (*US* **parlor**) /ˈpɑ:lə(r)/ *n* **1** (formerly) sitting-room in a private house, esp one where people may receive visitors or talk privately. **2** (in compounds) (*esp US*) shop providing certain goods or services: *a ˈbeauty/an ice-ˈcream/a ˈfuneral parlor.*
□ ˈ**parlour car** = PULLMAN.
ˈ**parlour game** game played in the home, eg a word-game.

parlous /ˈpɑ:ləs/ *adj* (*fml or rhet*) full of danger or uncertainty; dangerous; very bad: *the parlous state of international relations* ○ *English tennis is in a parlous condition.*

Parmesan /ˈpɑ:mɪzæn; *US* ˌpɑ:rmɪˈzæn/ *n* [U] (also ˌ**Parmesan ˈcheese**) type of hard cheese made in Italy, usu grated and served on pasta dishes.

Parnassus /pɑ:ˈnæsəs/ mountain in central Greece, and the home of *Apollo and the Muses in Greek mythology. The name was used in former times as a symbol of poetry or poetic inspiration.
▷ **Parnassian** *adj.*

Parnell /pɑ:ˈnel/ Charles Stewart (1846-91), Irish nationalist leader. As a British Member of Parliament he led an effective campaign for Irish Home Rule, but a personal scandal ruined his career.

parochial /pəˈrəʊkɪəl/ *adj* **1** [usu attrib] (*fml*) of or

Parliament

The British Parliament makes the laws of the country, and consists of two chambers: the House of Commons, where most of the power lies, and the House of Lords. Its official head is the monarch.

Historically, Parliament developed from the councils which in early times were appointed to advise the king. From the 13th to the 17th century, Parliament was presided over by the king. In the 17th century a struggle developed between the king (Charles I) and Parliament, resulting in the English Civil War. In the 'Glorious Revolution' of 1688 Parliament removed King James II from the throne and replaced him with William of Orange and his wife Mary, who accepted the terms of the Bill of Rights. This guaranteed the rights and liberty of individual citizens and gave Parliament more power than the Crown. Since 1832, the year of the first Reform Act, the House of Commons has become increasingly important, and the House of Lords less so.

The House of Commons has 650 Members of Parliament (MPs), each elected by a majority of votes in a constituency at a general election or by-election. Of the 650 seats, 523 are for England, 38 for Wales, 72 for Scotland and 17 for Northern Ireland. The chief officer of the House of Commons is the Speaker, who is politically neutral and who presides over the House during debates.

The House of Lords has two types of members: Lords Spiritual and Lords Temporal. The Lords Spiritual are the Archbishops of Canterbury and York, the Bishops of London, Durham and Winchester, and the 21 bishops who are next in seniority. The Lords Temporal are all peers, both hereditary and life peers. Certain life peers are appointed to serve as Lords of Appeal or 'Law Lords', their function being to assist the House in its judicial functions. Unlike the MPs in the House of Commons, many members of the House of Lords are not involved in party politics at all. There are just over 1 000 Lords in the House, most of whom are hereditary peers. Some Labour MPs have campaigned for the abolition of the House of Lords, or at least for significant changes in its functions and structure.

The operation of Parliament is closely tied to the country's political system, with the party in power represented by the Prime Minister and the Cabinet, as the Government, and the party with the next highest number of MPs as the Opposition with its Shadow Cabinet. The Conservative and Labour Parties have been the parties of government since the Second World War.

The debating chamber of the House of Commons, in the Palace of Westminster, is actually quite small, and can hold only 346 of the 650 MPs. The Speaker sits at one end, while the seats (called benches) on which members sit in their two opposing parties, run the length of the chamber on both sides of the Speaker's chair. The two sides, Government and Opposition, thus physically face each other in the House. The leading Government members (the Prime Minister and the Cabinet) sit on the front benches to the right of the Speaker, while their equivalents (the Leader of the Opposition and the Shadow Cabinet) sit on the benches on the Speaker's left. MPs representing minority parties sit next to the Opposition. Members of the Cabinet and Shadow Cabinet are known as 'front-benchers', and their respective supporters, who sit behind them, are known as 'back-benchers'. The front bench on the Government's side is known as the 'Treasury bench', because the Prime Minister is also the First Lord of the Treasury. Between the front benches is the 'Table of the House', on which are books and stationery and two dispatch boxes, one on each side of the table. When front-benchers stand up to speak, they often lean on their dispatch box, whereas back-benchers simply stand by their seats. A similar arrangement applies to the House of Lords, but Lords who do not wish to be associated with any party sit on 'cross-benches', seats at the far end of the Chamber at right angles to the rest. In both Houses, there are galleries for the press and members of the public wishing to watch debates.

After a subject is debated, it can either be agreed to without a vote, or decided by voting. A proposal for a new law is called a 'bill'. Its formal introduction is known as the 'first reading', the subsequent debate and vote on it is the 'second reading', and its final review is the 'third reading'. After the third reading, a bill that started in the House of Commons goes to the House of Lords for consideration there, and one that started in the Lords is similarly passed to the Commons. When both Houses are agreed, the bill is passed to the monarch for 'Royal Assent', after which it becomes one of the laws of the land and is known as an Act of Parliament.

Most bills are 'public' bills, relating to the public in general. Some, however, are 'private bills', and are concerned with a particular individual or company or some specific local matter. Public bills can be introduced by any MP, whether a government minister or a 'private' member (the term for an MP who is not a minister). Private bills begin when the individual or body concerned, such as a local authority, presents a petition to Parliament. They then follow the same procedure as for public bills.

The parliamentary day begins at 2.30 pm from Monday to Thursday, and business may well continue until late at night, or even last through the night. On Fridays the House meets between 9.30 am and 2.30 pm. The hours are different then because Friday is the day when most MPs leave London to spend the weekend in their constituencies. The Lords meet in a similar way to the Commons but for fewer days in the year.

Certain parliamentary occasions are particularly important. One is the State Opening of Parliament, which takes place annually, usually at the end of October or after a general election, when the monarch goes from Buckingham Palace to the Palace of Westminster to make the Queen's (or King's) Speech. This is the speech that outlines the Government's programme for the coming session of Parliament. The monarch delivers it in the House of Lords, to which MPs are specially invited. Another occasion is the annual Budget Statement, made by the Chancellor of the Exchequer in the House of Commons, usually on a Tuesday in March or April. In this speech, the Chancellor discusses the economic situation and outlines the measures to be introduced in order to raise the money the Government needs. A third important event in the life of every MP is a 'maiden speech', when a new Member of Parliament stands up to speak for the first time.

When MPs agree with what a particular speaker is saying, they often indicate this by saying 'Hear, hear'. When speeches are controversial, they may be interrupted with jeers and shouted comments. In extreme cases of noise or disorder, the Speaker may have to expel an MP from the Chamber, or suspend a sitting. Maiden speeches, on the other hand, are by tradition never interrupted.

Parliamentary proceedings in the Commons have been broadcast by radio for several years; since 1989 they have also been televised. A written account of each day's speeches and debates in Parliament is printed in the publication *Hansard*, while many newspapers also print edited accounts of speeches and exchanges, particularly important or entertaining ones. (Cf articles at GOVERNMENT and POLITICS.)

---

relating to a church parish: *parochial matters*. **2** (*derog*) showing interest in a limited area only; narrow: *a parochial person, attitude, event* ○ *He is rather too parochial in his outlook.* ▷ **parochialism** /-ɪzəm/ *n* [U]. **parochially** /-kɪəlɪ/ *adv*.

parody /ˈpærədɪ/ *n* **1** [C, U] ~ **(of sth)** (piece of) speech, writing or music that imitates the style of an author, composer, etc in an amusing and often exaggerated way; comic imitation: *a parody of a Shakespearian sonnet, an operatic aria, a well-known politician* ○ *She has a gift for parody.* **2** [C] thing that is done so badly that it seems to be an intentional mockery of what it should be; travesty: *The trial was a parody of justice.*

▷ **parodist** /-ɪst/ *n* person who writes parodies: *a gifted parodist.*

parody *v* (*pt, pp* **-died**) [Tn] make a parody(1) of (sb/sth); imitate comically: *parody an author, a style, a poem.*

parole /pəˈrəʊl/ *n* **1** [C, U] promise made by a prisoner that he will not try to escape if released for a limited time, or commit another crime if released before the end of his sentence (used esp in the expressions shown): *be on parole*, ie have been released after making this promise ○ *let sb out/release sb on parole* ○ *break (one's) parole*, ie commit a crime after being released from prison or fail to return to prison at the specified time. **2** [sing] release of a prisoner after he has made this promise of good behaviour: *He's hoping to get parole.* ⇨ article at PRISON.

▷ **parole** *v* [Tn] release (a prisoner) on parole.

paroxysm /ˈpærəksɪzəm/ *n* sudden attack or outburst (of anger, laughter, pain, etc): *He went into a paroxysm of rage*, ie became very angry. ○ *paroxysms of coughing, giggling, etc.*

parquet /ˈpɑːkeɪ; *US* pɑːrˈkeɪ/ *n* **1** [U] flooring made of wooden blocks arranged in a pattern: [attrib] *a parquet floor.* **2** [sing] (*US*) stalls (STALL 3) in a theatre.

Parr /pɑː(r)/ Catherine (1612-48), sixth and last

wife of King *Henry VIII. She survived him by one year.

parr /pɑ:(r)/ *n* (*pl* unchanged or ~s) young salmon.

parricide /ˈpærɪsaɪd/ *n* **1** [C, U] (act of) killing one's father or a close relative. **2** [C] person guilty of this. Cf PATRICIDE. ▷ **parricidal** /ˌpærɪˈsaɪdl/ *adj*.

parrot

parrot /ˈpærət/ *n* **1** any of various types of esp tropical bird with hooked beaks and brightly-coloured feathers, some of which can be trained to imitate human speech. ⇨ illus.

📖 Parrots are associated with pirates and sailors, who used to return to England with them after voyages abroad. Parrots were often taught to say 'Pretty Polly', in reference to themselves, Polly being the nickname for a parrot. A famous parrot in fiction is Captain Flint, the parrot belonging to the one-legged pirate Long John Silver in *Stevenson's *Treasure Island*. This bird went everywhere with its master, perched on his shoulder, crying 'Pieces of eight!' (ie gold coins, the buried treasure of the book's title).

2 (*esp derog*) person who repeats sb else's words or imitates his actions without thinking. **3** (idm) **sick as a parrot** ⇨ SICK.

▷ **parrot** *v* [Tn] repeat (the words or actions of sb else) without thinking.

□ ˈ**parrot-fashion** *adv* (*derog*) without thinking about or understanding the meaning of sth: *learn/repeat sth parrot-fashion.*

Parry /ˈpærɪ/ Sir Hubert (1848-1914), British composer. With *Stanford he was an important figure in reviving British music and musical life in the late 19th century. His setting of *Blake's *Jerusalem* has become a national patriotic song.

parry /ˈpærɪ/ *v* (*pt, pp* **parried**) [Tn] **1** turn aside or ward off (a blow or an attack) by using one's own weapon or one's hand to block it. ⇨ illus at FENCING. **2** (*fig*) avoid having to answer (sth): *parry an awkward question.*

▷ **parry** *n* act of parrying, esp in fencing and boxing.

parse /pɑ:z; *US* pɑ:rs/ *v* [Tn] (*grammar*) **1** describe the grammatical form and function of (a word), giving its part of speech, case[1](8), etc. **2** divide (a sentence) into parts and describe them grammatically.

parsec /ˈpɑ:sek/ *n* unit of distance used in astronomy, about 3.26 light-years.

Parsee /ˌpɑ:ˈsi:/ *n* member of a religious sect in India whose ancestors originally came from Persia; believer in Zoroastrianism.

parsimony /ˈpɑ:sɪmənɪ; *US* -məʊnɪ/ *n* [U] (*fml*) excessive carefulness in spending money or using resources; meanness.

▷ **parsimonious** /ˌpɑ:sɪˈməʊnɪəs/ *adj* (*fml*) very careful in spending money or using resources; mean: *a parsimonious old man.* **parsimoniously** *adv.* **parsimoniousness** *n* [U] = PARSIMONY.

parsley /ˈpɑ:slɪ/ *n* [U] herb with crinkled green leaves used for flavouring and decorating food: [attrib] *parsley sauce.*

parsnip /ˈpɑ:snɪp/ *n* (**a**) [C] plant with a long, pale yellow, edible root. ⇨ illus at TURNIP. (**b**) [C, U] this root cooked as a vegetable: [attrib] *parsnip soup.*

parson /ˈpɑ:sn/ *n* **1** (in the Church of England) parish priest; vicar or rector. **2** (*infml*) any Protestant clergyman.

▷ **parsonage** /-ɪdʒ/ *n* parson's house; vicarage or rectory.

□ **parson's** ˈ**nose** (*US* **pope's** ˈ**nose**) (*infml*) piece of flesh at the tail end of a cooked bird, esp a chicken.

part[1] /pɑ:t/ *n* (often without *a* when singular) **1** [C] ~ (**of sth**) some but not all of a thing or number of things: *We spent (a) part of our holiday in France.* ○ *The early part of her life was spent in Paris.* ○ *She had a miserable holiday — she was ill for part of the time.* ○ *The film is good in parts.* ○ *Parts of the book are interesting.* ○ *We've done the difficult part of the job.* ○ *The police only recovered part of the stolen money.* ○ *Part of the building was destroyed in the fire.* **2** [C] ~ (**of sth**) (**a**) distinct portion of a human or animal body or of a plant: *the parts of the body* ○ *Which part of your leg hurts?* (**b**) (usu essential) piece or component of a machine or structure: *lose one of the parts of the lawn-mower* ○ *the working parts of a machine* ○ *spare parts.* (**c**) area or region of a country, town, etc: *Which parts of France have you visited?* ○ *Which part of London do you come from?* ○ *Do come and visit us if you're ever in our part of the world.* (**d**) member of sth: *We'd like you to feel you're part of the family.* ○ *work as part of a team.* **3** [C] division of a book, broadcast serial, etc, esp as much as is published or broadcast at one time: *a TV serial in 10 parts*, ie instalments ○ *an encyclopaedia published in 25 weekly parts* ○ *Henry IV, Part II.* **4** [C] each of several equal portions of a whole: *a sixtieth part of a minute* ○ *She divided the cake into three parts.* **5** [C usu *sing*] ~ (**in sth**) person's share in an activity; role: *Everyone must do his part.* ○ *He had no part in the decision.* ○ *I want no part in this sordid business.* **6** [C] (**a**) role played by an actor in a play, film, etc: *He took/played the part of Hamlet.* ○ *He was very good in the part.* ○ (*fig*) *He's always acting/playing a part*, ie pretending to be what he is not. (**b**) words spoken by an actor playing a particular role: *Have you learnt your part yet?* **7** (*music*) melody or other line of music given to a particular voice or instrument: *sing in three parts* ○ *the piano, violin, cello, etc part.* **8 parts** [pl] region or area: *She's not from these parts.* ○ *He's just arrived back from foreign parts.* **9** [C] (*US*) = PARTING 2. **10** (idm) **the best/better part of sth** most of sth (esp a period of time); more than half of sth: *I spent the best part of an hour trying to find my car keys.* ○ *We've lived here for the better part of a year.* ○ *You must have drunk the best part of a bottle of wine last night.* **discretion is the better part of valour** ⇨ DISCRETION. **for the** ˈ**most part** on the whole; usually; mostly: *Japanese TV sets are, for the most part, of excellent quality.* **for** ˈ**my, his, etc part** as far as I am concerned: *For my part, I don't mind where we eat.* **in** ˈ**part** to a certain extent; partly: *His success was due in part to luck.* **look the part** wear clothes or have an appearance suitable for a job, role, position, etc. **a man/woman of (many)** ˈ**parts** person with many skills or talents. **on the part of sb/on sb's part** made or done by sb: *It was an error on my part.* ○ *The agreement has been kept on my part but not on his*, ie by me but not by him. **part and parcel of sth** an essential part of sth: *Keeping the accounts is part and parcel of my job.* (**a**) ˌ**part of the** ˈ**furniture** (*joc*) person or thing that has been in place for a long time and is therefore very familiar: *My aunt has been living with us ever since her husband died so she's become part of the furniture.* **play a part (in sth)** (**a**) be involved in an activity: *She plays an active part in local politics.* (**b**) make a contribution to sth; have a share in sth: *She played a major part in the success of the scheme.* ○ *We all have a part to play in the fight against crime.* ○ *Economic factors have played a significant part in Britain's decline as a world power.* **take sth in good** ˈ**part** react to sth in a good-natured way; not be offended by sth: *He took the teasing in good part.* **take part (in sth)** have a share or role in sth with others; be involved in sth; participate in sth: *take part in a discussion, demonstration, game, fight, celebration* ○ *How many countries will be taking part (in the World Cup)?* **take sb's** ˈ**part** support sb (eg in an argument): *His mother always takes his part.*

▷ **part** *adv* partly: *She is part French, part English.* ○ *The dress is part silk, part wool.* ○ *Her feelings were part anger, part relief.*

partly *adv* to some extent: *She was only partly responsible for the accident.* ○ *It was partly her fault.*

□ ˌ**part-ex**ˈ**change** *n* [U] method of buying sth in which an article (eg a car) is given as part of the payment for a more expensive one: *offer/take sth in part-exchange.*

ˌ**part of** ˈ**speech** (*grammar*) one of the classes into which words are divided in grammar, eg noun, adjective, verb, etc.

ˌ**part-**ˈ**owner** *n* person who shares the ownership of sth with sb else: *Tim is part-owner of the flat.* ˌ**part-**ˈ**ownership** *n* [U].

ˈ**part-singing** *n* [U] singing part-songs.

ˈ**part-song** *n* song with three or more parts (PART[1] 7).

ˌ**part-**ˈ**time** *adj, adv* for only a part of the working day or week: ˌ*part-time* ˈ*work/em*ˈ*ployment* ○ *She's looking for a* ˌ*part-time* ˈ*job.* ○ ˌ*part-time* ˈ*workers* ○ *work part-*ˈ*time.* ˌ**part-**ˈ**timer** *n* part-time worker. Cf FULL-TIME (FULL).

part[2] /pɑ:t/ *v* **1** [I, Ipr, Tn, Tn·pr] ~ (**from sb**); ~ **sb (from sb)** (cause sb to) go away or separate from sb: *I hope we can part (as) friends*, ie leave one another with no feeling of anger or resentment, eg after a quarrel. ○ *They exchanged a final kiss before parting.* ○ *She has parted from her husband/She and her husband have parted*, ie started to live apart. ○ *The children were parted from their father.* **2** [I, Tn] (cause sb/sth to) divide or form separate parts: *Her lips parted in a smile.* ○ *The crowd parted to let them through.* ○ *The clouds parted and the sun shone through.* ○ *The police parted the crowd.* **3** [Tn] separate (the hair of the head) along a line and comb the hair away from it: *He parts his hair in the middle.* **4** (idm) **a fool and his money are soon parted** ⇨ FOOL[1]. **part** ˈ**company (with sb/sth)** (**a**) go different ways or separate after being together: *We parted company at the bus-stop.* ○ *He and his agent have parted company/He has parted company with his agent.* ○ (*joc*) *Her blouse had parted company with her skirt*, ie become untucked. ○ (*fig*) *It is on political questions that their views part company*, ie are different. (**b**) disagree with sb: *I'm afraid I have to part company with you there.* **5** (phr v) **part with sth** give away or relinquish sth: *Despite his poverty, he refused to part with the family jewels.* ○ *He hates parting with* (ie spending) *his money.*

partake /pɑ:ˈteɪk/ *v* (*pt* **partook** /-ˈtʊk/, *pp* **partaken** /-ˈteɪkən/) [I, Ipr] ~ (**of sth**) (*fml or rhet*) eat or drink a part or portion of sth: *They invited us to partake of their simple meal.* ○ *Will you partake of a glass of sherry?*

parterre /pɑ:ˈteə(r)/ *n* level space in a large garden, with ornamental flower beds separated by lawns or paths.

parthenogenesis /ˌpɑ:θɪnəʊˈdʒenəsɪs/ *n* [U] (*biology*) type of reproduction in some insects and plants, in which the ovum develops without being fertilized by the male.

Parthenon /ˈpɑ:θənɒn/ **the Parthenon** temple of *Athene on the *Acropolis in Athens. It was built in 447-432 BC by *Pericles. The *Elgin Marbles were originally carved on the outside of the temple.

Parthian shot /ˌpɑ:θɪən ˈʃɒt/ sharp or telling remark made by sb as he leaves. Cf A PARTING SHOT (PARTING).

partial /ˈpɑ:ʃl/ *adj* **1** of or forming a part; not complete: *a partial recovery*, eg after an illness ○ *Our holiday was only a partial success.* ○ *a partial eclipse of the sun*, ie in which only part of the sun is hidden. **2** [usu pred] ~ (**towards sb/sth**) showing too much favour to one person or side; biased: *The referee was accused of being partial (towards the home team).* Cf IMPARTIAL. **3** [pred] ~ **to sb/sth** having a strong liking for sb/sth: *He's (rather) partial to a glass of brandy after dinner.*

▷ **partiality** /ˌpɑ:ʃɪˈælətɪ/ *n* **1** [U] ~ (**towards sb/sth**) being partial(2); bias; favouritism: *He judged the case without partiality.* **2** [C] ~ **for sb/sth** liking or fondness for sb/sth: *She has a partiality for French cheese.*

partially /ˈpɑːʃəlɪ/ *adv* **1** not completely; partly: *He is partially paralysed.* **2** in a partial(2) manner.

participate /pɑːˈtɪsɪpeɪt/ *v* [I, Ipr] ~ (**in sth**) take part or become involved (in an activity): *participate in a competition, discussion, meeting* ○ *She actively participates in local politics.* ○ *How many countries will be participating (in the Olympic Games)?*

▷ **participant** /pɑːˈtɪsɪpənt/ *n* ~ (**in sth**) person or group of people who participate in sth: *All the participants in the debate had an opportunity to speak.*

participation /pɑːˌtɪsɪˈpeɪʃn/ *n* [U] ~ (**in sth**) (action of) participating in sth: *Union leaders called for the active participation of all members in the day of protest.*

participle /ˈpɑːtɪsɪpl/ *n* (*grammar*) word formed from a verb, ending in *-ing* (*present participle*) or *-ed, -en*, etc (*past participle*) and used in verb phrases (eg *She is going* or *She has gone*) or as an adjective (eg *a fascinating story*): *'Hurrying' and 'hurried' are the present and past participles of 'hurry'.*

▷ **participial** /ˌpɑːtɪˈsɪpɪəl/ *adj* consisting of or being a participle: *'Loving' in 'a loving mother' and 'polished' in 'polished wood' are participial adjectives.*

particle /ˈpɑːtɪkl/ *n* **1** very small bit or piece (of sth): *particles of dust/dust particles* ○ *He choked on a particle of food.* **2** smallest possible amount: *There's not a particle of truth in her story.* **3** (also **adˌverbial ˈparticle**) (*grammar*) word (eg *away, back, down*) used esp after a verb to show position, direction of movement, etc ie In 'breakdown' and 'tell sb off', 'down' and 'off' are adverbial particles.

particoloured (*US* **-colored**) /ˈpɑːtɪkʌləd/ *adj* having different colours in different parts.

particular /pəˈtɪkjʊlə(r)/ *adj* **1** [attrib] relating to one person or thing rather than others; individual: *in this particular case* ○ *his particular problems* ○ *Is there any particular colour you would prefer?* **2** [attrib] more than usual; special; exceptional: *a matter of particular importance* ○ *for no particular reason* ○ *She took particular care not to overcook the meat.* ○ *He is a particular friend of mine.* **3** ~ (**about/over sth**) giving close attention to detail; difficult to please; fussy: *She's very particular about what she wears.* ○ *She's a very particular person.* ○ *particular about cleanliness, money matters, one's appearance.* **4** (idm) **in parˈticular** especially or specifically: *The whole meal was good but the wine in particular was excellent.* ○ *'Is there anything in particular you'd like for dinner?' 'No, nothing in particular.'*

▷ **particular** *n* (often *pl*) piece of information; detail; fact: *Her account is correct in every particular/all particulars.* ○ *He gave full particulars of the stolen property.* ○ *The policewoman wrote down his particulars*, ie his name, address, etc.

particularity /pəˌtɪkjʊˈlærətɪ/ *n* [U] (**a**) quality of being individual or particular(1). (**b**) attention to detail; exactness.

particularize, -ise /pəˈtɪkjʊləraɪz/ *v* [I, Tn] name or state (sth) specially or one by one; specify items.

particularization, -isation /pəˌtɪkjʊləraɪˈzeɪʃn/ *n* [U].

particularly *adv* especially: *I like all her novels, but her latest is particularly good.* ○ *Be particularly careful when driving at night.* ○ *I particularly want to see that film.*

parting /ˈpɑːtɪŋ/ *n* **1** [C, U] (act of) leaving sb; departure: *a tearful parting* ○ [attrib] *a parting kiss.* **2** [C] (*US* **part**) line where the hair is combed away in different directions. ⇨ illus at HAIR. **3** (idm) **a/the ˌparting of the ˈways** (**a**) place where a road, etc divides into two. (**b**) point at which one has to decide between two courses of action. **a ˌparting ˈshot** action or comment, esp an unfriendly or unkind one, made by a person as he departs. Cf PARTHIAN SHOT.

partisan /ˌpɑːtɪˈzæn, ˈpɑːtɪzæn, *US* ˈpɑːrtɪzn/ *n* **1** enthusiastic and often uncritical supporter of a person, group or cause. **2** member of an armed resistance movement in a country occupied by enemy forces: [attrib] *partisan warfare.*

▷ **partisan** *adj* uncritically supporting a person, group or cause; biased: *partisan attitudes, feelings, thinking, etc* ○ *You must listen to both points of view and try not to be partisan.*

partisanship /-ʃɪp/ *n* [U].

partita /pɑːˈtiːtə/ *n* (*music*) suite or set of variations on a theme, usu for a solo instrument.

partition /pɑːˈtɪʃn/ *n* **1** (**a**) [U] action of dividing or state of being divided into parts, esp the division of one country into two or more nations: *the partition of India in 1947.* (**b**) [C] part formed in this way; section. **2** [C] structure that divides a room or space into two parts, esp a thin wall in a house.

▷ **partition** *v* **1** [Tn] divide (sth) into parts: *India was partitioned in 1947.* **2** (phr v) **partition sth off** separate (one area, part of a room, etc) from another with a partition: *We've partitioned off one end of the kitchen to make a breakfast room.*

partitive /ˈpɑːtɪtɪv/ *adj* (*grammar*) (of a word or phrase) referring to or indicating a part or quantity of sth.

▷ **partitive** *n* (*grammar*) partitive word or phrase: *'Some' and 'any' are partitives.*

partner /ˈpɑːtnə(r)/ *n* **1** person who takes part in an activity with another or others, esp one of several owners of a business: *She was made a partner in the firm.* ○ *a senior/junior partner in a firm of solicitors* ○ *They were partners in crime.* **2** either of two people dancing together or playing tennis, cards, etc on the same side: *dancing partners* ○ *Take your partners for the next dance.* ○ *be sb's partner at bridge, badminton, etc.* **3** either of two people who are married to one another or having a sexual relationship with one another: *He doesn't have a regular (sexual) partner at the moment.*

▷ **partner** *v* **1** [Tn] act as or be the partner of (sb): *partner sb at bridge, tennis, etc* ○ *partner sb in a tango.* **2** (phr v) **partner (sb) off (with sb)** (cause two people to) become partners (PARTNER 2): *We (were) partnered off for the next dance.*

partnership /-ʃɪp/ *n* ~ (**with sb**) (**a**) [U] state of being a partner or partners, esp in business: *She worked in partnership with her sister/They worked in partnership.* ○ *He went/entered into partnership with his brother.* ○ *He and his brother went/entered into partnership.* (**b**) [C] two or more people working, playing, etc together as partners: *a successful partnership.*

partook *pt* of PARTAKE.

partridge /ˈpɑːtrɪdʒ/ *n* (**a**) [C] (*pl* unchanged or ~**s**) any of various types of game-bird with brown feathers, plump bodies and short tails. ⇨ illus at BIRD. (**b**) [U] its flesh eaten as food.

parturition /ˌpɑːtjʊˈrɪʃn; *US* -tʃʊ-/ *n* [U] (*medical*) process of giving birth; childbirth.

party /ˈpɑːtɪ/ *n* **1** [C] (esp in compounds) social gathering to which people are invited, esp in order to celebrate sth: *a ˈbirthday party* ○ *a ˈdinner party* ○ *a ˈgarden party* ○ *I'm giving/having/holding a party next Saturday night.* ○ [attrib] *a ˈparty dress.* **2** [CGp] (used esp in compounds or attributively with *ns*) group of people working or travelling together: *a ˈsearch party* ○ *The Government set up a working party to look into the problem.* ○ *a party of schoolchildren, tourists, etc.* **3** [CGp] (used esp in compounds or attributively with *ns*) political organization with stated aims and policies that puts forward candidates in elections: *The main political parties in the United States are the Democrats and the Republicans.* ○ *She's a member of the ˈCommunist Party.* ○ [attrib] *the party ˈleader, ˈpolicy, maniˈfesto* ○ *party ˈinterests, ˈfunds, ˈmembers* ○ *the ˈparty system*, ie government based on political parties. **4** [C] (*law*) person or people forming one side in a legal agreement or dispute: *the guilty party*, ie the person who is to blame for sth ○ *Is this solution acceptable to all parties concerned?* **5** [C] (*dated infml*) person. **6** (idm) **be (a) party to sth** participate in, know about or support (an action, a plan, etc): *be party to an agreement, a crime, a decision* ○ *They refused to be party to any violence.*

□ **ˈparty line** telephone line shared by two or more customers who each have their own number. **ˌparty ˈline** official policies of a political party: *Some MPs refused to follow/toe the party line on defence.*

ˈparty piece song, conjuring trick, etc that a person performs whenever he has to entertain people, eg at a party or dinner: *They made me do my old party piece.* ○ (*fig*) *We've heard the prime minister's party piece* (ie usual arguments) *on the economy before.*

ˌparty ˈpolitics political activity carried out through, by or for parties. **ˌparty poˈlitical** of or relating to a political party or parties: *a party political broadcast by the Labour Party.*

ˌparty ˈspirit **1** strong liking for parties (PARTY 1). **2** loyalty to a political party.

ˌparty-ˈwall *n* wall that divides one property from another and is the joint responsibility of the owners of those properties.

parvenu /ˈpɑːvənjuː; *US* -nuː/ *n* (*derog*) person who has suddenly risen from a low social or economic position to one of wealth or power.

Pascal /pæsˈkæl/ Blaise (1623-62), French philosopher, mathematician and physicist. He did important work in geometry, proved that air has weight and that a vacuum is possible, and invented a calculating machine. He was a *Jansenist, and explained his view of Christianity and the 'hidden God' in his *Pensées*.

pascal /ˈpæskəl/ *n* SI unit of pressure, one newton per square metre.

paschal /ˈpæskl, *also* ˈpɑːskl/ *adj* (*religion*) **1** of the Jewish Passover. **2** of Easter.

pas de deux /ˌpɑː də ˈdɜː/ dance for two people in a ballet.

paso doble /ˌpæsə ˈdəʊbleɪ/ (music for a) Latin American dance in quick time with two beats to the bar.

Pasolini /pæzɒˈliːnɪ/ Pier Paolo (1922-75), Italian film director. His works, including *Theorem* and the naturalistic *Gospel According to St Matthew* have a strong political as well as poetic content.

pass[1] /pɑːs; *US* pæs/ *n* **1** success in an examination: *get a pass in French* ○ *2 passes and 3 fails.* **2** (**a**) paper or card giving sb permission, eg to enter, leave or be absent from a place: *All visitors must show their passes before entering the building.* ○ *There is no admittance without a pass.* (**b**) any of various types of bus ticket or train ticket, esp one allowing sb to travel regularly along a particular route over a specified period of time or to travel at a reduced fare or free of charge: *a monthly bus pass*, ie one that is valid for a month. **3** ~ (**to sb**) (in football, hockey, Rugby, etc) act of kicking, hitting or throwing the ball to a player of one's own side: *a long pass to the striker.* **4** (route through a) gap or low point in a range of mountains. ⇨ illus at ESKER. **5** (in card-games) act of not playing a card or making a bid when it is one's turn. **6** (esp in conjuring) movement of the hand or of sth held in the hand over or in front of sth: *The conjuror made a few passes with his hand over the hat.* **7** = PASSING SHOT (PASSING). **8** (in fencing) thrust or lunge. **9** (idm) **come to such a ˈpass/a pretty ˈpass** reach a sad or critical state: *Things have come to a pretty pass when the children have to prepare their own meals.* **make a pass at sb** (*infml*) try to attract sb sexually. **sell the pass** ⇨ SELL.

□ **ˈpassbook** *n* (**a**) book recording the amounts of money a customer pays into or takes out of an account with a bank or building society. Cf BANK-BOOK (BANK[3]). (**b**) (in S Africa) official document giving details of one's race, residence and employment, which must be carried at all times by non-Whites.

ˈpass degree (in British universities) degree awarded to a student whose work is thought to be acceptable but not of a good enough standard to qualify for honours (HONOUR[1] 6).

ˈpasskey *n* (**a**) key to a door or gate given to people who have a right to enter. (**b**) = MASTER-KEY (MASTER[1]).

ˈpass law (in S Africa) any of a group of laws restricting the movement of non-Whites and requiring them to carry identification at all times.

ˈ**password** (also **watchword**) *n* secret word or phrase used by sb to indicate to sb else (eg a sentry) that he is a friend rather than an enemy: *give the password.*

pass[2] /pɑːs; *US* pæs/ *v* **1** [I, Tn] move forward or to the other side of (sb/sth): *The street was so crowded that cars were unable to pass.* ○ *pass a barrier, sentry, checkpoint, etc* ○ (*fig*) *Not a word passed her lips,* ie She said nothing. **2** [I, Tn] leave (sb/sth) on one side or behind as one goes forward; go past (sb/sth): *Turn right after passing the Post Office.* ○ *She passed me in the street without even saying hello.* ○ *I pass the church on my way to work.* ○ *A car passed* (ie overtook) *me at 90 mph on the motorway.* **3** [Ipr, Ip] go or move in the specified direction: *The procession passed slowly down the hill.* ○ *We passed through Oxford on our way to London.* ○ *He glanced at her and then passed on,* ie continued to walk forward. **4** [Tn·pr] cause sth to move in the specified direction or to be in a certain position: *She passed her hand across her forehead.* ○ *pass a thread through the eye of a needle* ○ *pass a rope round a post.* **5** [Tn, Tn·pr, Tn·p, Dn·n, Dn·pr] ~ **sth (to sb)** give sth to sb by handing it to him: *Pass (me) the salt, please.* ○ *They passed the photograph round,* ie from one person to the next. ○ *Pass me (over) that book.* ○ *She passed the letter to Mary.* **6** [I, Ipr, Tn, Tn·pr] ~ **sth (to sb)** (in football, hockey, Rugby, etc) kick, hit or throw (the ball) to a player of one's own side: *He passed (the ball) to the winger.* **7** [Ipr] ~ **to sb** be transferred from one person to another, esp by inheritance: *On his death, the title passed to his eldest son.* **8** [Ipr] ~ **from sth to/into sth** change from one state or condition to another: *Water passes from a liquid to a solid state when it freezes.* ○ *pass from boyhood to manhood.* **9** (**a**) [I] (of time) go by; be spent: *Six months had passed, and we still had no news of them.* ○ *The holidays passed far too quickly.* (**b**) [Tn] occupy or spend (time): *What did she do to pass the time* (ie to make the period of boredom less tedious) *while she was convalescing?* ○ *How did you pass the evening?* **10** [I] come to an end; be over: *They waited for the storm to pass.* ○ *His anger will soon pass.* **11** (**a**) [I, Tn] achieve the required standard in (an examination, a test, etc): *You'll have to work hard if you want to pass (the exam).* ○ *She hasn't passed her driving test yet.* (**b**) [Tn] examine (sb/sth) and declare to be satisfactory or acceptable: *The examiners passed all the candidates,* ie decided that their work was of the required standard. **12** (**a**) [Tn] approve (a bill, law, proposal, etc) by voting: *Parliament passed the bill.* ○ *The motion was passed by 12 votes to 10.* (**b**) [I, Tn] (esp of a bill, law, proposal, etc) be approved or accepted by (a parliament, an assembly, etc): *The bill passed and became law.* ○ *This film will never pass the censors,* eg because it is too sexually explicit. **13** [I] be allowed or tolerated: *I don't like it, but I'll let it pass,* ie will not make objections. ○ *His rudeness passed without comment,* ie People ignored it. ○ *Such behaviour may pass in some circles but it will not be tolerated here.* **14** [Tn, Tn·pr] ~ **sth (on sb/sth)** pronounce or utter sth (used esp as in the expressions shown): *pass sentence (on sb found guilty of a crime)* ○ *pass judgement on a matter* ○ *pass a remark.* **15** [I, Ipr] ~ **(between A and B)** happen; be said or done: *after all that has passed between them.* **16** [Tn] go beyond the limits of (sth) (used esp in the expressions shown): *pass belief,* ie be unbelievable ○ *pass one's comprehension,* ie be impossible for one to understand. **17** [I] (in card-games) not play a card or make a bid when it is one's turn. **18** [Tn] send (sth) out from the body as or with urine or faeces: *If you're passing blood you ought to see a doctor.* **19** (idm) **bring sth to pass** (*fml*) cause sth to happen. **come to** ˈ**pass** (*fml*) actually happen as predicted, planned or hoped for: *Many people would like the electoral system to be reformed but I don't believe this will ever come to pass.* **make/pass water** ⇨ WATER[1]. ˌ**pass the** ˈ**buck (to sb)** (*infml*) shift the responsibility or blame for sth to sb else. **pass the** ˈ**hat round** (*infml*) collect money, esp for a colleague who is ill or to pay for a celebration. **pass** ˈ**muster** be accepted as adequate or satisfactory. **pass the time of** ˈ**day (with sb)** greet sb and have a short conversation with him. **ships that pass in the night** ⇨ SHIP[1]. **20** (phr v) **pass as sb/sth** = PASS FOR SB/STH.

pass aˈ**way** (*euph*) die: *His mother passed away last year.*

pass by (sb/sth) go past: *I saw the procession pass by.* ○ *The procession passed right by my front door.* **pass sb/sth by (a)** occur without affecting sb/sth: *The whole business passed him by,* ie he was hardly aware that it was happening. ○ *She feels that life is passing her by,* ie that she is not profiting from or enjoying the opportunities and pleasures of life. (**b**) pay no attention to sb/sth; ignore or avoid sb/sth: *We cannot pass this matter by without protest.*

pass sth down (esp passive) pass sth from one generation to the next: *knowledge which has been passed down over the centuries.*

pass for sb/sth be accepted as sb/sth: *He speaks French well enough to pass for a Frenchman.*

pass in (to sth) be admitted (to a school, college, etc) by passing an examination.

pass into sth become a part of sth: *Many foreign words have passed into the English language.* ○ *His deeds have passed into legend,* ie because of their bravery, importance, etc.

pass ˈ**off (a)** (of an event) take place and be completed: *The demonstration passed off without incident.* (**b**) (of pain, the effects of a drug, etc) come to an end gradually; disappear: *The numbness in your foot will soon pass off.* **pass sb/sth off as sb/sth** represent sb/sth falsely as sb/sth: *She passed him off as* (ie pretended that he was) *her husband.* ○ *He escaped by passing himself off as a guard.*

pass ˈ**on** = PASS AWAY. **pass on (to sth)** move from one activity, stage, etc to another: *Let's pass on to the next item on the agenda.* **pass sth on (to sb)** hand or give sth (to sb else), esp after receiving or using it oneself: *Pass the book on to me when you've finished with it.* ○ *I passed her message on to his mother.* ○ *She caught my cold and passed it on to* (ie infected) *her husband.*

pass ˈ**out** lose consciousness; faint. **pass out (of sth)** leave (a military college) after completing a course of training: *a passing-*ˈ*out ceremony/parade,* ie for cadets who have completed their training.

pass sb over not consider sb for promotion (esp when he is or thinks he is eligible): *He was passed over in favour of a younger man.* **pass over sth** ignore or disregard sth; avoid sth: *They chose to pass over her rude remarks.* ○ *Sex is a subject he prefers to pass over,* eg because it embarrasses him.

pass through go through a town, etc, stopping there for a short time but not staying: *We came to say hello as we were passing through.* **pass through sth** experience (a period of time): *She passed through a difficult period after her marriage failed.*

pass sth up (*infml*) refuse to accept (a chance, opportunity, etc): *Imagine passing up an offer like that!*

□ ˌ**passer-**ˈ**by** /ˌpɑːsə ˈbaɪ; *US* ˌpæsər/ *n* (*pl* **passers-by** /ˌpɑːsəz ˈbaɪ/) person who is going past sb/sth, esp by chance: *Police asked passers-by if they had seen the accident happen.*

passable /ˈpɑːsəbl; *US* ˈpæs-/ *adj* **1** [usu pred] (**a**) (of roads) clear of obstructions (esp snow) and therefore able to be driven on: *The mountain roads are not passable until late spring.* (**b**) (of a river) that can be crossed. **2** fairly good but not excellent; adequate: *a passable knowledge of German.*

▷ **passably** /-əblɪ/ *adv* adequately or acceptably.

passage /ˈpæsɪdʒ/ *n* **1** [U] (**a**) process of passing: *the passage of time.* (**b**) action of going past, through or across sth: *The passage of motor vehicles is forbidden.* (**c**) freedom or right to go through or across sth: *They were denied passage through the occupied territory.* **2** [C usu *sing*] way through sth: *force a passage through the crowd.* **3** [C] (cost of a ticket for a) journey from one place to another by ship or plane; voyage: *book one's passage to New York* ○ *He worked his passage to Australia,* eg paid for the journey by doing jobs on the ship he was travelling on. **4** (also ˈ**passageway**) [C] narrow way through sth, esp with walls on both sides; corridor. **5** [C] tube-like structure in the human body, through which air, secretions, etc pass: *the nasal passages* ○ (*infml*) *the back passage,* ie the anus. **6** [C] short section from a book, speech, piece of music, etc quoted or considered on its own: *a passage from the Bible.* **7** [U] passing of a bill[1](4) by a parliament so that it becomes law.

Passchendaele /ˈpæʃəndeɪl/ village in Belgium. In 1917 during the First World War nearly a quarter of a million British troops were killed there in heavy fighting.

passé /ˈpæseɪ; *US* pæˈseɪ/ *adj* [usu pred] (*French*) (**a**) out of date; old-fashioned: *I'm beginning to find her novels rather passé.* (**b**) past his/her/its best: *He was a fine actor but he's a bit passé now.*

passenger /ˈpæsɪndʒə(r)/ *n* **1** person travelling in a car, bus, train, plane, ship, etc, other than the driver, the pilot or a member of the crew: *The driver of the car was killed in the crash but both passengers escaped unhurt.* ○ [attrib] *the passenger seat,* ie the seat next to the driver's seat in a motor vehicle ○ *a passenger train,* ie one carrying passengers rather than goods. **2** (*infml esp Brit*) member of a team, crew, etc who does not do as much work as the others: *This firm can't afford (to carry) passengers.*

passe-partout /ˌpɑːspəˈtuː/ *n* **1** [C] key that can open several locks; master key. **2** [U] adhesive tape used in framing pictures or photographs.

passim /ˈpæsɪm/ *adv* (*Latin*) (of phrases, etc) occurring throughout or at several points in a book, an article, etc.

passing /ˈpɑːsɪŋ; *US* ˈpæs-/ *adj* **1** lasting for a short time; brief; fleeting: *a passing thought, fancy.* **2** casual; cursory: *a passing glance, reference, remark.*

▷ **passing** *n* [U] **1** process of going by: *the passing of time, the years.* **2** (*fml*) (**a**) end: *the passing of the old year,* ie on New Year's Eve. (**b**) (*euph*) death: *They all mourned his passing.* **3** (idm) **in passing** casually; incidentally: *mention sth in passing.*

□ ˈ**passing shot** (also **pass**) (in tennis) shot played so as to make the ball go past one's opponent and out of his reach.

passion /ˈpæʃn/ *n* **1** (**a**) [U, C] strong feeling, eg of hate, love or anger: *She argued with great passion.* ○ *Passions were running high at the meeting,* ie People were in an angry or emotional state. (**b**) [sing] angry state; rage (used esp in the expressions shown): *be in a passion* ○ *get/fly into a passion,* ie become very angry. **2** [U] ~ **(for sb)** intense, esp sexual, love: *His passion for her made him blind to everything else.* **3** [sing] (**a**) ~ **for sth** strong liking or enthusiasm for sth: *a passion for chocolate, detective stories, tennis.* (**b**) thing for which sb has a strong liking or enthusiasm: *Horse-racing is her passion.* ○ *Music is a passion with him.* **4 the Passion** [sing] (*religion*) the suffering and death of Christ.

□ ˈ**passion-flower** *n* any of several types of climbing plant with brightly-coloured flowers.

ˈ**passion-fruit** (also **granadilla**) *n* [C, U] edible fruit of certain types of passion-flower: [attrib] *passion-fruit ice-cream.*

ˈ**passion-play** *n* play in which the Passion of Christ is re-enacted.

ˌ**Passion** ˈ**Sunday** (in the Christian Church) the fifth Sunday in Lent.

ˈ**Passion Week** (in the Christian Church) the week between Passion Sunday and Palm Sunday.

passionate /ˈpæʃənət/ *adj* **1** (**a**) caused by or showing intense sexual love: *a passionate kiss, lover, relationship.* (**b**) caused by or showing strong feelings: *a passionate plea for mercy* ○ *her passionate support for our cause* ○ *a passionate defender of civil liberties.* **2** dominated or easily affected by strong feelings: *a passionate nature, temperament, woman.*

▷ **passionately** *adv* (**a**) in a passionate(1a) way: *He loved her passionately.* (**b**) (used before *adjs*) intensely; very: *She is passionately fond of tennis.* ○

He is passionately opposed to racial discrimination.

passive /ˈpæsɪv/ *adj* **1** not active; submissive: *play a passive role in a marriage* ○ *passive obedience, acceptance* ○ *passive smoking*, ie breathing in fumes from tobacco being smoked by others. **2** showing no interest, initiative or forceful qualities: *a passive audience* ○ *He had a passive expression on his face.* **3** of the form of a verb used when the grammatical subject is affected by the action of the verb, as in *Her leg was broken* and *He was bitten by a dog*: *a passive sentence.* Cf ACTIVE.
▷ **passive** *n* [sing] (also ˌ**passive** ˈ**voice**) (*grammar*) passive(3) form of a verb (phrase) or sentence: *In the sentence 'He was seen there', 'was seen' is in the passive.* Cf ACTIVE VOICE (ACTIVE).
passively *adv.*
passiveness (also **passivity** /pæˈsɪvətɪ/) *n* [U] state or quality of being passive(1, 2).
□ ˌ**passive de**ˈ**vice 1** electronic component, eg a capacitor, that is not able to amplify signals. **2** artificial satellite that reflects signals without amplifying them.
ˌ**passive re**ˈ**sistance** resistance to an enemy who has occupied one's country, or to a government, by refusing to co-operate or obey orders.

Passover /ˈpɑ:səʊvə(r); *US* ˈpæs-/ *n* Jewish religious festival commemorating the freeing of the Jews from their slavery in Egypt.

passport /ˈpɑ:spɔ:t; *US* ˈpæs-/ *n* **1** official document issued by the government of a particular country, identifying the holder as a citizen of that country and entitling him to travel abroad under its protection: *a British passport.* **2** ~ **to sth** thing that enables one to achieve sth: *The only passport to success is hard work.*

past[1] /pɑ:st; *US* pæst/ *adj* **1** gone by in time: *in past years, centuries, ages* ○ *The time for discussion is past.* ○ *in times past.* **2** gone by recently; just finished or ended: *The past month has been a difficult one for him.* ○ *I've seen little of her in the past few weeks.* **3** belonging to an earlier time: *past happiness* ○ *past and present students of the college* ○ *past achievements, failures, generations, presidents.* **4** (*grammar*) (of a verb form) indicating a state or an action in the past: *The past tense of 'take' is 'took'.* ○ *a past participle*, eg *passed, taken, gone.*
▷ **past** *n* **1 the past** [sing] (**a**) time that has gone by: *I've been there many times in the past.* (**b**) things that happened in an earlier time; past events: *memories of the past* ○ *look back on, remember, regret the past* ○ *We cannot change the past.* **2** [C] person's past life or career, esp one that is discreditable: *We know nothing of his past.* ○ *She's a woman with a 'past'.* **3** [sing] (also **past tense**) (form of a) verb used to describe actions in the past: *The past of the verb 'take' is 'took'.* **4** (idm) **a thing of the past** ⇨ THING. **live in the past** ⇨ LIVE[2].
□ ˌ**past** ˈ**master** ~ **(in/of sth)**; ~ **(at sth/doing sth)** person who is very skilled or experienced in a particular activity; expert: *She's a past master at the art of getting what she wants.*

past[2] /pɑ:st; *US* pæst/ *prep* **1** (**a**) (of time) later than (sth); after: *half past two* ○ *ten (minutes) past six* ○ *There's a bus at twenty minutes past the hour*, ie at 1.20, 2.20, 3.20, etc. ○ *It was past midnight when we got home.* (**b**) older than (the specified age): *an old man past seventy* ○ *She's past her thirties*, ie at least 40. **2** on the far side of (sth); from one side to the other of (sth/sb): *You can see the house past the church.* ○ *She walked past the shop.* ○ *He hurried past me without stopping.* **3** (**a**) beyond the limits of (sth/doing sth): *The man is past working*, ie too old, weak, etc to work. ○ *I'm past caring* (ie I no longer care) *what he does.* ○ *It's quite past my comprehension*, ie I can't understand it. (**b**) beyond the age of (sth/doing sth): *She's past playing with dolls.* ○ *She's long past retirement age.* **4** (idm) ˈ**past it** (*infml*) too old to do what one was once capable of; too old to be used for its normal function: *At 93 he's finally realized he's getting past it.* ○ *That overcoat is looking decidedly past it.*
▷ **past** *adv part* from one side to the other of sth: *walk, march, go, rush, etc past.*

pasta /ˈpæstə; *US* ˈpɑ:stə/ *n* [U] dried paste made from flour, eggs and water and cut into various shapes, eg macaroni, spaghetti, ravioli: [attrib] *a pasta dish*, eg lasagne. Cf NOODLE.

paste[1] /peɪst/ *n* **1** [sing] moist soft mixture, esp of a powdery substance and a liquid: *a smooth, thin, thick, etc paste* ○ *She mixed the flour and water to a paste.* **2** [U] mixture of flour and water used to stick things together, esp to stick paper to a wall. **3** [U] (esp in compounds) mixture of ground meat or fish for spreading on bread: *anchovy paste* ○ *liver paste.* **4** [U] hard glass-like substance used to make artificial gems: [attrib] *paste jewellery.*

paste[2] /peɪst/ *v* **1** [I, Tn] put paste[1](2) on (sth). **2** [Tn·pr, Tn·p] ~ **sth (on)to sth**; ~ **sth on (sth)**; ~ **A and B together** stick sth to sth else with paste[1](2): *She pasted posters onto the wall.* ○ *paste pieces of paper together.* **3** [Tn] (*dated infml*) hit or beat (sb). **4** (phr v) **paste sth down** fasten the cover or flap of sth with paste. **paste sth in**; **paste sth into sth** stick (a photo, label, etc) onto a page of a book with paste[1](2): *She pasted the pictures into a scrapbook.* **paste sth up** (**a**) stick sth to an upright surface with paste: *paste up an advertisement, a notice, a poster, etc.* (**b**) fasten (sheets or strips of paper with text and illustrations) onto a larger sheet of paper or board, in order to design a page for a book, magazine, etc.
▷ **pasting** *n* (*infml*) severe beating; defeat: *give sb a pasting* ○ *Our team got/took a real pasting on Saturday.*
□ ˈ**paste-up** *n* sheet of paper or board to which the text and illustrations for a page of a book, magazine, etc have been fastened.

pasteboard /ˈpeɪstbɔ:d/ *n* [U] type of thin board made by pasting thin sheets of paper together.

pastel /ˈpæstl; *US* pæˈstel/ *n* **1** type of crayon made from coloured chalk: *She works in* (ie uses) *pastels.* **2** picture drawn with this. **3** pale delicate colour: [attrib] *pastel shades/colours.*

pastern /ˈpæstən/ *n* part of a horse's foot between the fetlock and the hoof. ⇨ illus at HORSE.

Pasternak /ˈpæstənæk/ Boris (1890-1960), Russian author. His most famous work, the novel *Doctor Zhivago*, was for many years banned in the USSR, where he is better known for his poetry, eg *My Sister, Life.* He was awarded the Nobel prize for literature in 1958 but was forced to decline it.

Pasteur /pæsˈtɜ:(r)/ Louis (1822-95), French bacteriologist. He discovered the role of micro-organisms in fermentation and disease. He was the first to suggest aseptic procedures in surgery to save lives, and pasteurization techniques to prevent the spoiling of wine, beer and milk. He developed the use of vaccination using an attenuated virus, and produced an effective vaccine against rabies.

pasteurize, -ise /ˈpɑ:stʃəraɪz; *US* ˈpæs-/ *v* [Tn] heat (a liquid, esp milk) to a certain temperature and then chill it, in order to kill harmful bacteria.
▷ **pasteurization, -isation** /ˌpɑ:stʃəraɪˈzeɪʃn; *US* ˌpæstʃərɪˈzeɪʃn/ *n* [U] process of pasteurizing sth.

pastiche /pæˈsti:ʃ/ *n* **1** [C] literary, musical or artistic work in the style of another author, composer, etc. **2** [C] musical, literary or artistic work consisting of elements from various sources. **3** [U] art of composing pastiches: *He has a gift for pastiche.*

pastille /ˈpæstəl; *US* pæˈsti:l/ *n* small flavoured sweet for sucking, esp one containing medicine for a sore throat; lozenge: *throat pastilles.*

pastime /ˈpɑ:staɪm; *US* ˈpæs-/ *n* thing done to pass the time pleasantly: *Photography is her favourite pastime.*

pastor /ˈpɑ:stə(r); *US* ˈpæs-/ *n* minister[1] (3), esp of a Nonconformist church.

pastoral /ˈpɑ:stərəl; *US* ˈpæs-/ *adj* **1** relating to or portraying country life, the countryside or shepherds, esp in an idealized way: *a pastoral scene, poem, painting* ○ *pastoral poetry/verse* ○ *Beethoven's 'Pastoral' Symphony.* **2** (of land) used for pasture; grassy: *pastoral farming*, ie of sheep, cows, etc, that feed on grass. **3** of or relating to a clergyman or his work (esp the spiritual guidance he gives to his congregation): *pastoral care, duties, responsibilities, etc.*
▷ **pastoral** *n* **1** pastoral(1) poem, picture, etc. **2** (also **pastoral** ˈ**letter**) letter from a clergyman to his congregation, esp one from a bishop to the members of his diocese.

pastrami /pæˈstrɑ:mɪ/ *n* [U] highly seasoned smoked beef.

pastry /ˈpeɪstrɪ/ *n* **1** [U] mixture of flour, fat and water baked in an oven and used as a base or covering for tarts, pies, etc: *You eat too much pastry*, ie food made with pastry. **2** [C] item of food in which pastry is used, eg a pie or tart: *Danish pastries.*
□ ˈ**pastry-cook** *n* person who makes pastry.

pasture /ˈpɑ:stʃə(r); *US* ˈpæs-/ *n* **1** [C, U] (piece of) land covered with grass and similar plants, suitable for grazing animals: *acres of rich pasture.* **2** [U] grass, etc growing on this land.
▷ **pasture** *v* **1** [Tn, Tn·pr] put (animals) to graze in a pasture: *pasture one's sheep on the village common.* **2** [I, Ipr] (of animals) graze.
pasturage /ˈpɑ:stʃərɪdʒ; *US* ˈpæs-/ *n* [U] **1** land where animals can graze. **2** right to graze animals on this land.

pasty[1] /ˈpeɪstɪ/ *adj* (**-ier, -iest**) **1** of or like paste: *a pasty substance* ○ *mix to a pasty consistency.* **2** pale and unhealthy-looking: *a pasty face, complexion.*
□ ˌ**pasty-**ˈ**faced** *adj* having a pasty complexion: *a* ˌ*pasty-faced* ˈ*youth.*

pasty[2] /ˈpæstɪ/ *n* (*Brit*) piece of pastry folded round a filling of meat, fruit, jam, etc: *a Cornish pasty*, ie one with a filling of meat and potatoes.

Pat *abbr* patent (number): *Pat 1 230 884.*

pat[1] /pæt/ *adv* **1** at once and without hesitation: *Her answer came pat.* **2** (idm) **have/know sth off** ˈ**pat** have memorized or know sth perfectly: *He had all the answers off pat.* ○ *She knows the rules off pat.* **stand pat** (*esp US*) refuse to change a decision one has made, an opinion one holds, etc.
▷ **pat** *adj* **1** exactly right; appropriate. **2** (*derog*) too quick; glib: *It's a complex question and her answer was too pat.*

pat[2] /pæt/ *v* (**-tt-**) **1** [Tn, Tn·pr] tap (sb/sth) gently with the open hand or with a flat object: *pat a dog* ○ *pat sb's hand* ○ *pat a child on the head*, ie as a sign of affection ○ *pat a ball*, ie so that bounces up and down. **2** [Tn·pr, Tn·p, Cn·a] put (sth) in a specified state or position by patting: *She patted her hair into place/shape.* ○ *She patted down a few wisps of hair.* ○ *He patted his face dry (with a towel).* **3** (idm) **pat sb/oneself on the** ˈ**back** congratulate sb/oneself.
▷ **pat** *n* **1** gentle tap with the open hand or with a flat object: *She gave the child a pat on the head.* ○ *He gave her knee an affectionate pat/He gave her an affectionate pat on the knee.* **2** slight sound made by tapping sth gently. **3** ~ **(of sth)** small mass of sth (esp butter) that has been shaped by patting: *a pat of butter.* **4** (idm) **a** ˌ**pat on the** ˈ**back (for sth/doing sth)** gesture of approval or praise: *give sb/get a pat on the back* ○ *She deserves a pat on the back for all the hard work she's done.*
□ ˈ**pat-a-cake** *n* [U] game played by small children in which they clap their hands and pat each other's palms.

Patagonia /ˌpætəˈgəʊnɪə/ most southerly region of South America, formed mainly of a barren plateau in southern Argentina and Chile, between the Andes and the Atlantic. The main activity is sheep farming. ▷ **Patagonian** /-ˈgəʊnɪən/ *n, adj.*

patch[1] /pætʃ/ *n* **1** piece of material placed over a hole or a damaged or worn place to cover or strengthen it: *a jacket with leather patches on the elbows* ○ *She sewed a patch onto the knee of the trousers.* ○ *a patch on the inner tube of a tyre.* **2** pad worn over an injured eye to protect it: *He wears a black patch over his right eye.* **3** part of a surface that is different in colour, texture, etc from the surrounding area: *a black dog with a white patch on its neck* ○ *a worn patch on the elbow of a sweater* ○ *damp patches on a wall.* **4** ~ **(of sth)** small area of sth: *patches of fog, ice, sunlight* ○ *patches of blue in a cloudy sky* ○ *The ground is wet in patches.* **5** small piece of land, esp one used for growing vegetables: *a* ˈ*cabbage, an* ˈ*onion, a* ˈ*potato, etc* *patch.* **6** (*Brit infml*) area in which sb (esp a policeman) works or which he knows well: *He knows every house in his patch.* **7** (idm) (**go through, hit, strike, etc) a bad ˈpatch** (be in, reach, etc) a particularly difficult or unhappy period of time: *Their marriage has been going through a bad patch.* ○ *Our firm has just struck a bad patch.* **not be a patch on sb/sth** (*infml*) not be nearly as good as sb/sth: *Her latest novel isn't a patch on her others.*

□ **ˌpatch-ˈpocket** *n* pocket made by sewing a piece of material onto the outside of a garment.

ˈpatch test test to discover the source of an allergy, using small pieces of allergy-causing substances placed under the skin.

patch[2] /pætʃ/ *v* **1** (**a**) [Tn] cover (a hole or a worn place) with a patch: *patch a hole in a pair of trousers.* (**b**) [Tn, Tn·p] ~ **sth (up)** mend (a garment) by covering a hole or worn place with a patch: *patch up an old pair of jeans* ○ *The elbows of your jersey are worn — I'll need to patch them.* **2** [Tn] (of material) be used as a patch for (sth). **3** (phr v) **patch sth up** (**a**) repair sth, esp quickly or temporarily: *The wrecked car was patched up and resold.* (**b**) settle or resolve (a quarrel, dispute, etc): *They patched up their differences.*

patchouli /ˈpætʃʊlɪ, pəˈtʃu:lɪ/ *n* **1** [C] fragrant plant grown in the Far East. **2** [U] perfume made from this plant.

patchwork /ˈpætʃwɜ:k/ *n* **1** [U] type of needlework in which small pieces of cloth with different designs are sewn together: [attrib] *a patchwork bedcover, cushion, quilt, etc.* **2** [sing] something made of various small pieces or parts: *a patchwork of fields seen from the aeroplane.*

patchy /ˈpætʃɪ/ *adj* (**-ier, -iest**) **1** existing in or having patches: *patchy fog, mist, cloud, etc.* **2** (*fig*) not of the same quality throughout; uneven: *a patchy essay, novel, performance* ○ *His work is rather patchy.* ○ *My knowledge of German is patchy,* ie not complete. ▷ **patchily** *adv.* **patchiness** *n* [U].

pate /peɪt/ *n* (*arch or joc infml*) head or skull: *a shiny bald pate.*

pâté /ˈpæteɪ; *US* pɑ:ˈteɪ/ *n* [U] rich paste made of finely minced meat or fish: *liver, duck, mackerel pâté.*

□ **pâté de foie gras** /ˌpæteɪ də fwɑ: ˈgrɑ:/ pâté made from the liver of a fattened goose.

patella /pəˈtelə/ *n* (*pl* **-lae** /-li:/) (*anatomy*) kneecap. ⇨ illus at SKELETON.

paten /ˈpætən/ *n* plate, usu of gold or silver, on which the blessed bread is placed during the religious service of Communion.

patent[1] /ˈpeɪtnt, *also* ˈpætnt; *US* ˈpætnt/ *adj* ~ (**to sb**) obvious; clear; evident: *a patent lie* ○ *his patent dislike of the plan* ○ *a patent disregard for the truth* ○ *It was patent to anyone that she disliked the idea.* ▷ **patently** *adv* unmistakably; obviously: *It was patently obvious that he was lying.*

patent[2] /ˈpætnt, *also* ˈpeɪtnt; *US* ˈpætnt/ *n* **1** (**a**) official document giving the holder the sole right to make, use or sell an invention and preventing others from imitating it: *take out* (ie obtain) *a patent to protect an invention* ○ *patent applied for,* eg marked on goods not yet protected by a patent. (**b**) right granted by this. **2** invention or process that is protected by a patent: *It's my patent.*

▷ **patent** *adj* **1** [attrib] (of an invention, a product, etc) protected by or having a patent. **2** [attrib] made and sold by a particular firm: *patent drugs, medicines, etc* ○ (*joc*) *his patent* (ie personal) *remedy for hangovers.*

patent *v* [Tn] obtain a patent for (an invention or process).

patentee /ˌpeɪtnˈti:; *US* ˌpætn-/ *n* person who obtains or holds a patent.

□ **patent ˈleather** leather with a hard shiny surface, used for shoes and handbags.

ˈpatent office government department that issues patents.

Pater /ˈpeɪtə(r)/ Walter (1839-94), English author and critic. The main theme of all his writings was 'the desire of beauty, the love of art for art's sake'. They had a great influence on the taste of his period.

paterfamilias /ˌpeɪtəfəˈmɪlɪæs; *US* ˌpæt-/ *n* (*pl* **patresfamilias** /ˌpɑ:treɪzfəˈmɪlɪæs/) (*fml or joc*) head of a family; father.

paternal /pəˈtɜ:nl/ *adj* **1** of a father; fatherly: *paternal affection, authority* ○ *He has a paternal concern for your welfare,* ie like that of a father for his child. **2** related through one's father: *her paternal grandmother,* ie her father's mother. Cf MATERNAL. ▷ **paternally** /-nəlɪ/ *adv.*

paternalism /pəˈtɜ:nəlɪzəm/ *n* [U] policy (of governments or employers) of controlling people in a paternal way by providing them with what they need but giving them no responsibility or freedom of choice. ▷ **paternalistic** /pəˌtɜ:nəˈlɪstɪk/ *adj.* **paternalistically** /-klɪ/ *adv.*

paternity /pəˈtɜ:nətɪ/ *n* [U] **1** state of being a father; fatherhood: *He denied paternity of the child,* ie denied that he was its father. ○ [attrib] *a paternity test,* ie to find out if a man is the father of a child or not. **2** descent from a father: *a child of unknown paternity.*

paternoster /ˌpætəˈnɒstə(r)/ *n* the Lord's Prayer, esp when said in Latin.

path /pɑ:θ; *US* pæθ/ *n* (*pl* ~**s** /pɑ:ðz; *US* pæðz/) **1** (also ˈ**pathway**, ˈ**footpath**) way or track made for or by people walking: *Keep to the path or you'll lose your way.* ○ *The path follows the river and then goes through the woods.* ○ *We took the path across the fields.* ⇨ illus at HOME. **2** line along which sb/sth moves: *the moon's path round the earth* ○ *the path of a tornado* ○ (*fig*) *She threw herself in the path of* (ie in front of) *an oncoming vehicle.* ○ (*fig*) *She has had a difficult path through life.* **3** course of action: *I strongly advised him not to take that path.* **4** (usu *sing*) ~ **to sth** way to reach or achieve sth: *the path to success, victory, riches, power, ruin.* **5** (idm) **cross sb's path** ⇨ CROSS[2]. **lead sb up the garden path** ⇨ LEAD[3]. **the primrose path** ⇨ PRIMROSE. **smooth sb's path** ⇨ SMOOTH[2].

□ **pathfinder** /ˈpɑ:θfaɪndə(r); *US* ˈpæθ-/ *n* **1** person who discovers new places or new ways of doing things. **2** pilot of an aircraft guiding other aircraft to a target which they are going to bomb.

NOTE ON USAGE: A **lane** is a narrow country road. A **path** or **footpath** is a way marked out for people to walk along, between houses in a town or across fields, beside rivers, etc in the country. A **track** is a rough path in the country, often not officially marked, but made by the constant passing of people, animals or vehicles. **Lane** and **track** can also refer to the separate parts of a road (**lane**) or railway (**track**) separating cars or trains passing in opposite directions or overtaking: *a six-lane motorway* ○ *a double-track railway line.* Runners in an athletics stadium run in individual **lanes.** The whole area they run on is called the **track.**

-path ⇨ -PATHY.

pathetic /pəˈθetɪk/ *adj* **1** causing one to feel pity or sadness: *pathetic cries for help* ○ *the pathetic sight of starving children* ○ *His tears were pathetic to witness.* **2** (*infml*) extremely inadequate; contemptible: *a pathetic attempt, performance, excuse* ○ *You're pathetic! Can't you even boil an egg?* ▷ **pathetically** /-klɪ/ *adv*: *pathetically thin* ○ *His answers were pathetically inadequate.*

□ **paˌthetic ˈfallacy** (in literature) describing inanimate objects as if they are living things with feelings.

path(o)- *comb form* disease: *pathology.*

pathogen /ˈpæθədʒən/ *n* (*medical*) bacterium, virus, etc that causes disease. ▷ **pathogenic** /ˌpæθəˈdʒenɪk/ *adj.*

pathological /ˌpæθəˈlɒdʒɪkl/ *adj* **1** of or relating to pathology. **2** of or caused by a physical or mental illness. **3** (*infml*) unreasonable; irrational: *a pathological fear of spiders, obsession with death, hatred of sb* ○ *a pathological* (ie compulsive) *liar.* ▷ **pathologically** /-klɪ/ *adv*: *pathologically jealous, mean, etc.*

pathology /pəˈθɒlədʒɪ/ *n* [U] scientific study of diseases of the body.

▷ **pathologist** /pəˈθɒlədʒɪst/ *n* expert in pathology.

pathos /ˈpeɪθɒs/ *n* [U] quality, esp in speech, writing, acting, etc that causes a feeling of pity or sadness: *the pathos of Hamlet's death.*

-pathy *comb form* (forming *ns*) **1** method of treating disease: *homeopathy* ○ *osteopathy.* **2** feeling: *telepathy.*

▷ **-path** *comb form* (forming *ns*) **1** doctor using a particular method of treating disease: *homeopath* ○ *osteopath.* **2** person suffering from a particular disease: *psychopath.*

-pathic *comb form* (forming *adjs*): *homeopathic* ○ *telepathic.*

patience /ˈpeɪʃns/ *n* [U] **1** ~ (**with sb/sth**) ability to accept delay, annoyance or suffering without complaining: *I warn you, I'm beginning to lose (my) patience (with you),* ie become impatient. ○ *After three hours of waiting for the train, our patience was finally exhausted.* ○ *She has no patience with* (ie cannot tolerate) *people who are always grumbling.* ○ (*saying*) *Patience is a virtue.* **2** ~ (**for sth/to do sth**) ability to persevere with sth; perseverance: *Learning to walk again after his accident required great patience.* ○ *She hasn't the patience to do embroidery.* **3** (*Brit*) (*US* **solitaire**) type of card-game, usu for one player. **4** (idm) **the ˌpatience of ˈJob** very great patience(1): *His behaviour would try* (ie test) *the patience of Job.*

patient[1] /ˈpeɪʃnt/ *adj* ~ (**with sb/sth**) having or showing patience: *You'll have to be patient with my mother — she's going rather deaf.* ○ *patient research, questioning, listening* ○ *She's a patient* (ie persevering) *worker.* ▷ **patiently** *adv*: *wait, sit, listen patiently.*

patient[2] /ˈpeɪʃnt/ *n* (**a**) person who is receiving medical treatment, esp in a hospital. (**b**) person who is registered with a doctor, dentist, etc and is treated by him when necessary: *I have been a patient of Dr Smith for many years.*

patina /ˈpætɪnə/ *n* [sing] **1** green coating that forms on the surface of old bronze or copper. **2** glossy surface on old wood.

patio /ˈpætɪəʊ/ *n* (*pl* ~**s** /-əʊz/) **1** paved area next to a house where people can sit, eat, etc outdoors. Cf VERANDA. **2** roofless courtyard within the walls of a Spanish or Spanish-American house. Cf TERRACE 3.

patisserie /pəˈti:sərɪ/ *n* **1** [C] shop selling French pastries and cakes. **2** [U] pastries and cakes sold in such a shop.

patois /ˈpætwɑ:/ *n* (*pl* unchanged /-twɑ:z/) dialect spoken by the common people of a region and differing from the standard language of the country: *He speaks the local patois.*

patri- *comb form* of a father: *patricide* ○ *patriarch.* Cf MATRI-.

patriarch /ˈpeɪtrɪɑ:k; *US* ˈpæt-/ *n* **1** male head of a family or tribe. Cf MATRIARCH. **2 Patriarch** (in the Eastern Orthodox and Roman Catholic Churches) high-ranking bishop. **3** old man who is greatly respected.

▷ **patriarchal** /ˌpeɪtrɪˈɑ:kl; *US* ˌpæt-/ *adj* **1** of or like a patriarch. **2** ruled or controlled by men: *a patriarchal society.*

patriarchate /-eɪt/ *n* position or period of office of a Patriarch of the Church.

patriarchy /-kɪ/ *n* [C, U] (society, country, etc with a) patriarchal(2) system of control or government.

patrician /pəˈtrɪʃn/ *n* member of the aristocracy (esp in ancient Rome). Cf PLEBEIAN *n.*

▷ **patrician** *adj* of or like a patrician; aristocratic: *patrician arrogance, haughtiness, good looks.*

patricide /ˈpætrɪsaɪd/ *n* (**a**) [C, U] (act of) killing one's own father. (**b**) [C] person who does this. Cf MATRICIDE, PARRICIDE.

Patrick /ˈpætrɪk/ Saint (5th century AD), missionary and patron saint of Ireland. He was probably born in Scotland, and was taken as a slave to Ireland, where he later returned to found the Irish Church. Many legends are told about him. St Patrick's day is 17 March. ⇨ article at NATIONAL.

patrimony /ˈpætrɪmənɪ; *US* -məʊnɪ/ *n* [U]

1 property inherited from one's father or ancestors. 2 income or property that a church receives from endowments.
▷ **patrimonial** /ˌpætrɪˈməʊnɪəl/ *adj* of or relating to a patrimony.

patriot /ˈpætrɪət; *US* ˈpeɪt-/ *n* person who loves his country, esp one who is ready to defend it against an enemy: *a true patriot.*
▷ **patriotic** /ˌpætrɪˈɒtɪk; *US* ˌpeɪt-/ *adj* having or showing love of one's country: *patriotic members of the public* ○ *patriotic support, fervour* ○ *patriotic songs.* **patriotically** /-klɪ/ *adv.*
patriotism /-ɪzəm/ *n* [U] love of one's country and readiness to defend it.

patristics /pəˈtrɪstɪks/ *n* [sing *v*] study of the writings of early Christian authors, esp the Fathers of the Church (FATHER[1]). ▷ **patristic** *adj.*

patrol /pəˈtrəʊl/ *v* (-ll-) [I, Tn] go round (a town, an area, etc) to check that all is secure and orderly or to look for wrongdoers, an enemy or people who need help: *The army regularly patrol (along) the border.* ○ *Police patrol the streets at night.*
▷ **patrol** *n* 1 action of patrolling: *carry out a patrol* ○ *The army make hourly patrols of the area.* ○ *The navy are maintaining a 24-hour air and sea patrol,* eg in order to find survivors from a ship that has sunk. 2 person, group of people, vehicle, ship or aircraft that patrols an area: *a naval, army, police patrol* ○ [attrib] *a police paˈtrol car.* 3 group of (usu) 6 members of a Scout troop or a Girl Guide company. 4 (idm) **on patrol** patrolling a particular area: *Terrorists attacked two soldiers on patrol.*
□ **paˈtrolman** /-mən/ *n* (*pl* **-men** /-mən/) 1 person employed by a motorists' organization to patrol roads and help motorists who are in difficulty. 2 (*US*) policeman who patrols a particular area.
paˈtrol wagon (*US*) = BLACK MARIA (BLACK[1]).

patron /ˈpeɪtrən/ *n* 1 person who gives money or other support to a person, cause, activity, etc: *a wealthy patron of the arts.* 2 (*fml*) (regular) customer of a shop, restaurant, theatre, etc: *Patrons are requested to leave their bags in the cloakroom.*
□ ˌ**patron ˈsaint** saint who is traditionally connected with, and is said to protect, a particular country (eg St David, patron saint of Wales), an activity (eg St Cecilia, patron saint of music), or a person or group of people (eg St Christopher, patron saint of travellers). Each has a special day, called a feast-day, set aside to celebrate him or her (eg 30 November is St Andrew's day).

patronage /ˈpætrənɪdʒ; *US* ˈpeɪt-/ *n* [U] 1 support and encouragement given by a patron: *patronage of the arts* ○ *Without the patronage of several large firms, the festival could not take place.* ○ *The theatre is under the patronage of the Arts Council.* 2 (*fml*) customer's support for a shop, restaurant, etc; custom[1](2): *We thank you for your patronage.* 3 right or power to appoint sb to or recommend sb for an important position. 4 (*dated*) patronizing (PATRONIZE 1) manner.

patronize, -ise /ˈpætrənaɪz; *US* ˈpeɪt-/ *v* [Tn] 1 treat (sb) as an inferior; treat (sb) in a condescending way: *He resented the way she patronized him.* 2 (*fml*) be a regular customer of (a shop, etc): *The restaurant is patronized by politicians and journalists.* 3 act as a patron(1) to (sb/sth); support or encourage (sb/sth).
▷ **patronizing, -ising** *adj* condescending: *a patronizing person, manner, attitude, smile, tone of voice.* **patronizingly, -isingly** *adv.*

patronymic /ˌpætrəˈnɪmɪk/ *n, adj* (name) derived from the name of one's father or some other male ancestor.

patsy /ˈpætsɪ/ *n* (*US infml derog*) person who is easily cheated or fooled.

patter[1] /ˈpætə(r)/ *n* [U] rapid and often glib speech used by a comedian, conjuror or salesman.
▷ **patter** *v* 1 [Tn] say or repeat (prayers, etc) in a rapid mechanical way. 2 [I] talk quickly or glibly.

patter[2] /ˈpætə(r)/ *n* 1 [sing] sound of quick light steps or taps: *the patter of rain on a roof* ○ *the patter of footsteps.* 2 (idm) **the patter of tiny ˈfeet** (*joc*) (used to refer to a baby that sb is going to or might be going to have) the sound of young children in a home: *She can't wait for the patter of tiny feet.*
▷ **patter** *v* 1 [I] make this sound: *rain pattering on the windowpanes.* 2 (phr v) **patter along, down, etc (sth)** walk quickly in the specified direction with light footsteps: *She pattered along (the corridor) in her bare feet.*

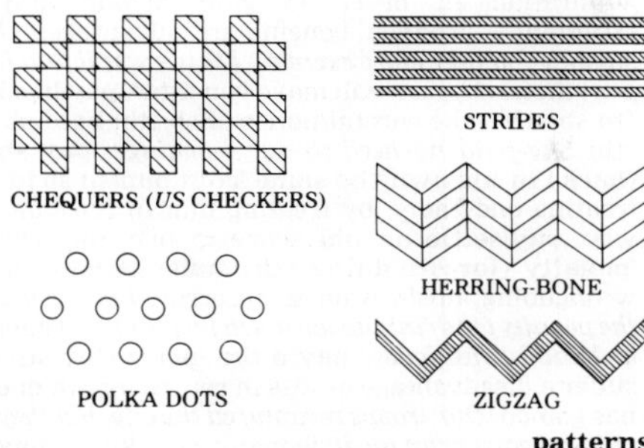

patterns

pattern /ˈpætn/ *n* 1 arrangement of lines, shapes, colours, etc, esp as a decorative design on clothes, carpets, wallpaper, etc: *a checked, flowery, Paisley pattern* ○ *What a pretty pattern!* ○ *She wore a dress with a pattern of roses on it.* ⇨ illus. 2 (a) (often in compounds) model, design or instructions from which sth is to be made: *a knitting/sewing pattern* ○ *a paper pattern,* ie a set of pieces of paper that show the shapes of the various parts of a garment. (b) piece of wood used to make a mould for casting metal. 3 sample of cloth or some other material: *a book of tweed patterns.* 4 way in which sth happens, moves, develops or is arranged: *patterns of behaviour/behaviour patterns* ○ *the pattern of economic decline in Britain* ○ *the pattern of events which led up to the war* ○ *These sentences all have the same grammatical pattern.* ○ *The murders all seem to follow a set pattern,* ie occur in a similar way. 5 excellent example; model: *This company's profit-sharing scheme set a pattern which others followed.*
▷ **pattern** *v* [Tn·pr] ~ **oneself/sth on sb/sth** imitate sb/sth; model sth on sth: *He patterns himself upon his father.* ○ *Her ideas are patterned on Trotsky's.* **patterned** *adj* decorated with a pattern: *patterned china, fabric, wallpaper.*
□ ˈ**pattern-maker** *n* person who makes patterns in an engineering factory.
ˈ**pattern-shop** *n* room in a factory where patterns (PATTERN 2b) are made.

patty /ˈpætɪ/ *n* 1 small savoury pie. 2 (*US*) small flat cake of minced meat (eg used for hamburgers).

paucity /ˈpɔːsətɪ/ *n* [sing] ~ **(of sth)** (*fml*) smallness of number or quantity: *a paucity of evidence.*

Paul /pɔːl/ Saint (1st century AD), Christian missionary known as 'the Apostle of the Gentiles'. His original name was Saul of Tarsus, but he changed it after his conversion on the road to Damascus, as told in the Acts of the Apostles. He travelled widely in the Roman Empire to spread Christianity, and some of the letters he wrote to the early churches are included in the New Testament. ▷ **Pauline** /ˈpɔːlaɪn/ *adj*: *Pauline theology.*

Pauling /ˈpɔːlɪŋ/ Linus (1901-), American scientist. He became famous for his work on molecular structure, esp in living tissue. He received a Nobel prize for chemistry in 1954 and the Nobel Peace prize in 1962 for his campaign against nuclear weapons.

Paul Jones /ˌpɔːl ˈdʒəʊnz/ any of various traditional dances in which the dancers change partners when the music stops.

paunch /pɔːntʃ/ *n* fat stomach, esp a man's: *You're getting quite a paunch,* eg from drinking a lot of beer.
▷ **paunchy** *adj* (-ier, -iest) having a paunch. **paunchiness** *n* [U].

pauper /ˈpɔːpə(r)/ *n* very poor person: *He died a pauper.*
▷ **pauperism** /ˈpɔːpərɪzəm/ *n* [U] state of being a pauper.

pause /pɔːz/ *n* 1 ~ **(in sth)** temporary stop in action or speech: *a moment's pause* ○ *He slipped out during a pause in the conversation.* ○ *After a short pause, they continued walking.* ○ *She spoke for an hour without a pause.* ⇨ Usage at BREAK[2]. 2 (*music*) sign (⌒) over a note(5b) or rest[2](3) to show that it should be longer than usual. 3 (idm) **give pause to sb/give sb pause** make sb hesitate before doing sth: *Weather conditions were bad enough to give pause to even the most experienced climbers.* **a pregnant pause/silence** ⇨ PREGNANT.
▷ **pause** *v* [I, Ipr] ~ **(for sth)** make a pause: *He paused for a moment, and then continued his speech.* ○ *Let's pause for a cup of coffee.* ○ *speak without pausing for breath,* ie very quickly.

pavane /pəˈvæn/ (also **pavan** /ˈpævən/) *n* (music for a) slow stately dance with two beats to the bar.

pave /peɪv/ *v* 1 [esp passive: Tn, Tn·pr] ~ **sth (with sth)** cover (a surface) with flat stones or bricks: *The path is paved with concrete slabs.* 2 (idm) ˌ**pave the ˈway (for sb/sth)** create a situation in which sth specified is possible or can happen: *His economic policies paved the way for industrial expansion.* **the road to hell is paved with good intentions** ⇨ ROAD.
□ ˈ**paving stone** slab of stone used for paving.

pavement /ˈpeɪvmənt/ *n* 1 [C] (*Brit*) (*US* **sidewalk**) path with a paved surface at the side of a road for people to walk on: *Don't ride your bicycle on the pavement.* 2 [U] (*US*) hard surface of a road, street, etc. 3 [C] paved area or surface.
□ ˈ**pavement artist** person who draws on the pavement with coloured chalks, esp in order to be given money by passers-by.

pavilion /pəˈvɪlɪən/ *n* 1 (*Brit*) building next to a sports ground, esp a cricket field, used by players and spectators: *a cricket pavilion.* 2 light building used as a shelter, eg in a park. 3 ornamental building used for concerts, dances, etc: *the Royal Pavilion in Brighton.* 4 temporary building, esp a large tent used to display items at an exhibition.

paving /ˈpeɪvɪŋ/ *n* [U] (a) paved surface. ⇨ illus at HOME. (b) material used for this.

Pavlov /ˈpævlɒf/ Ivan (1849-1936), Russian scientist. He is most famous for his experimental work on conditioned reflexes, using dogs: they salivated when fed at the same time as a bell was rung, and continued to salivate when the bell was rung without any food being produced. The experiments form the basis of much modern work on animal and human conditioning. People are sometimes compared to Pavlov's dogs when their reactions seem automatic rather than deliberate.
▷ **Pavlovian** /pævˈləʊvɪən/ *adj*: *a Pavlovian response.*

Pavlova /ˈpævləvə/ Anna (1881-1931), Russian ballet dancer. She was famous for her grace and lightness in the great roles of classical ballet, and toured all over the world with her own company.

pavlova /ˈpævləvə/ *n* [C, U] (also ˈ**pavlova cake**) dessert consisting of a layer of meringue topped with cream and fruit.

paw /pɔː/ *n* 1 foot of an animal with claws or nails: *a dog's paw.* ⇨ illus at ANIMAL. 2 (*infml joc or derog*) person's hand: *Take your dirty little paws off me!*
▷ **paw** *v* 1 [Ipr, Tn] ~ **(at) sth** (of an animal) feel or scratch (sth) with the paws. 2 [Tn] (of a horse or bull) scrape (the ground) with a hoof. 3 [Tn] touch (sb/sth) with the hands roughly, awkwardly or in a sexually improper manner: *He can't be near a woman without pawing her.*

pawky /ˈpɔːkɪ/ *adj* (-ier, -iest) (*Brit dialect*) drily humorous. ▷ **pawkily** *adv.* **pawkiness** *n* [U].

pawl /pɔːl/ *n* 1 lever with a catch that fits between the teeth (TOOTH 2) of a ratchet to prevent slipping or movement in a particular direction. 2 (*nautical*) short bar used to prevent a capstan or windlass from recoiling.

pawn[1] /pɔːn/ *n* 1 one of the eight chess-men of the smallest size and value. ⇨ illus at CHESS. 2 (*fig*) person or group whose actions are controlled by others: *We are mere pawns in the struggle for power.*

pawn[2] /pɔ:n/ *v* [Tn] **1** leave (an object) with a pawnbroker in exchange for money that can be repaid in order to get the object back: *He pawned his gold watch to pay the rent.* **2** *(fig)* abandon (sth) in order to gain sth: *pawn one's honour.*

▷ **pawn** *n* (idm) **in pawn** in a state of being pawned: *My watch is in pawn.*

□ ˈ**pawnbroker** *n* person licensed to lend money in exchange for articles left with him.

ˈ**pawnshop** *n* place where a pawnbroker works.

ˈ**pawn-ticket** *n* receipt given by a pawnbroker for articles left with him.

pawpaw = PAPAW.

pay[1] /peɪ/ *n* [U] **1** money paid for regular work: *an increase in pay/a pay increase* ○ *He doesn't like the job, but the pay is good.* ○ *(infml) What's the pay like* (ie How much are you paid) *in your job?* ○ [attrib] *pay negotiations.* ⇨ Usage at INCOME. **2** (idm) **in the pay of sb/sth** *(derog)* employed by sb/sth, esp secretly: *a spy in the pay of the enemy.*

□ ˈ**pay-claim** *n* demand for an increase in pay made by a union for its members.

ˈ**pay-day** *n* **1** day of the week or month on which wages or salaries are paid. **2** (in the Stock Exchange) day when stock that has been transferred has to be paid for.

ˈ**pay dirt** *(US)* earth containing enough ore to make mining profitable.

ˈ**payload** *n* **1** part of the load of a ship, an aircraft, etc for which payment is received, eg passengers and cargo, but not fuel. **2** explosive power of a bomb or warhead carried in an aircraft or a missile. **3** equipment carried by a satellite or spacecraft.

ˈ**paymaster** *n* **1** official who pays troops, workers, etc. **2** (usu *pl*) *(derog)* person who pays another person or group to do sth for him and who therefore controls his/their actions: *The paymasters of these petty crooks are the big crime syndicates.* ˌ**Paymaster** ˈ**General** *(Brit)* minister in charge of the department of the Treasury through which payments are made.

ˈ**pay-packet** *n* envelope containing an employee's wages.

ˈ**pay phone** *(US* ˈ**pay station)** coin-operated telephone. ⇨ article at TELEPHONE.

ˈ**payroll** *n* **(a)** list of people employed by a company and the amount of money to be paid to each of them: *a firm with 500 employees on the payroll*, ie one that employs 500 people. **(b)** total amount of wages and salaries to be paid to the employees of a company.

ˈ**pay-slip** *n* piece of paper that gives details of an employee's pay, including deductions for tax, insurance, etc.

pay[2] /peɪ/ *v* (*pt, pp* **paid** /*US* peɪd/) **1 (a)** [I, Ipr, Tn, Tn·pr, Dn·n, Dn·pr] ~ **(sb) (for sth)**; ~ **sth (to sb) (for sth)** give (sb) money (for goods, services, etc): *My firm pays well*, ie pays high wages. ○ *Are you paying in cash or by cheque?* ○ *They tried to leave the restaurant without paying (for their meal).* ○ *Her parents paid for her to go* (ie paid the cost of her travel) *to America.* ○ *Have you paid the milkman this week?* ○ *pay sb by the hour/by the job* ○ *How much did you pay for your house?* ○ *We paid £50 000 for our house.* ○ *You haven't paid me the money you owe me.* ○ *She paid a dealer £2 000 for that car.* ○ *Have you paid that money to the bank yet?* ○ *You're not paid to sit around doing nothing!* **(b)** [Tn, Dn·n, Dn·pr] ~ **sth (to sb)** give (what is owed); hand over the amount of sth: *pay taxes, rates, rent, etc* ○ *pay a bill, debt, fine, subscription, etc* ○ *He paid the terrorist a ransom of £50 000 for his kidnapped son.* ○ *Membership fees should be paid to the club secretary.* **2 (a)** [I] (of a business, etc) be profitable: *The shop closed because it didn't pay.* ○ *It's difficult to make sheep farming pay here.* **(b)** [I, Tn] be advantageous or profitable to (sb): *Crime doesn't pay.* ○ *It would pay (you) to use an accountant.* ○ *It pays to be honest with the taxman.* **3** (idm) **expenses paid** ⇨ EXPENSE. **give/pay lip-service to sth** ⇨ LIP-SERVICE (LIP). **he who** ˌ**pays the** ˌ**piper** ˌ**calls the** ˈ**tune** *(saying)* the person who provides the money for sth should control how it is spent. **pay attention (to sb/sth)** listen carefully to sb/sth; take notice of sb/sth: *Pay attention when I'm talking to you!* ○ *pay attention to one's teacher.* **pay sb a compliment/pay a compliment to sb** praise sb about sth. **pay court to sb** *(becoming dated)* treat (esp a woman) with great respect or admiration in order to gain favour. **pay** ˈ**dividends** produce benefits or advantages: *I suggest you take more exercise; I think you'll find it pays dividends*, ie it will make you fitter. **pay heed (to sb/sth)** take careful notice of sb/sth; heed sb/sth: *She paid no heed to our warnings.* **pay sb (back) in his own/the same** ˈ**coin** punish sb for treating one badly, by treating him in the same way. **pay/settle an old score** ⇨ OLD. **pay the** ˈ**penalty (for sth/doing sth)** suffer because of wrongdoing, misfortune or an error: *I'm paying the penalty for drinking too much last night; I've got a dreadful headache!* **pay a/the** ˈ**price (for sth)** suffer a disadvantage or loss in return for sth one has gained: *Our troops recaptured the city, but they paid a heavy price for it*, ie many were killed. **pay one's re**ˈ**spects (to sb)** *(fml)* visit sb as a sign of respect for him: *Please pay my respects to your mother.* ○ *Hundreds came to pay their last respects to the dead president*, eg by attending his funeral. **pay through the** ˈ**nose (for sth)** *(infml)* pay too much or a lot of money for sth. **pay (a) tribute to sb/sth** express one's admiration or respect for sb/sth: *His colleagues paid generous tributes to the outgoing president.* **pay sb/sth a visit** visit sb/sth. **pay one's/its** ˈ**way** (of a person, business, etc) support oneself/itself with money one/it has earned. **put** ˈ**paid to sth** *(infml)* stop or destroy sth: *Coming to work drunk put paid to her hopes of promotion.* **rob Peter to pay Paul** ⇨ ROB. **there'll be the devil to pay** ⇨ DEVIL[1]. **there will be/was hell to pay** ⇨ HELL. **you** ˌ**pays your** ˌ**money and you** ˌ**takes your** ˈ**choice** *(infml catchphrase)* one should choose whatever alternative course of action, explanation etc one wants, since any one is as good as any other.

4 (phr v) **pay sb back (sth); pay sth back** return (money) to sb that one has borrowed from him: *Have you paid (me) back the money you owe me yet?* ○ *I'll pay you back next week.* **pay sb back (for sth)** punish sb or get one's revenge: *I'll pay him back for the trick he played on me.*

pay for sth suffer or be punished for sth: *The home team paid (dearly) for their defensive errors*, eg by losing the match. ○ *I'll make him pay for his insolence!*

pay sth in; pay sth into sth put (money) into (a bank account): *pay a cheque into one's account.*

pay off *(infml)* (of an esp risky policy, course of action, etc) bring good results; be successful; work: *The gamble paid off.* **pay sb off (a)** pay the wages of sb and dismiss him from a job: *pay off the crew of a ship.* **(b)** *(infml)* give money to sb to prevent him from doing sth; bribe sb. **pay sth off** pay in full (money owed for sth): *pay off one's debts, a loan, a mortgage, etc.*

pay sth out (a) (regularly) make a large payment (of money) for sth: *I had to pay out £200 to get my car repaired!* ○ *We're paying out £300 a month on our mortgage.* **(b)** release or pass (a length or rope, cord, etc) through the hands.

pay up pay in full money that is owed for sth: *I'll take you to court unless you pay up immediately.*

▷ **payable** /ˈpeɪəbl/ *adj* [pred] that must or may be paid: *Instalments are payable on the last day of the month.* ○ *The price of the goods is payable in instalments.*

payee /peɪˈi:/ *n* person to whom sth is (to be) paid.

payer *n* person who pays or who has to pay for sth.

□ ˌ**paid-**ˈ**up** *adj* having paid all money or subscriptions owed to a club, political party, etc: *She's a (fully)* ˌ*paid-up* ˌ*member of the* ˈ*party.*

ˌ**pay-as-you-**ˈ**earn** *n* *(Brit)* (*abbr* **PAYE**) method of collecting income tax by deducting it from an employee's wages or salary.

ˈ**pay-bed** *n* *(Brit)* bed in a National Health hospital for which the user has paid as a private patient.

ˌ**paying** ˈ**guest** person who lives in sb's house and pays for his board and lodging; lodger.

ˈ**pay-off** *n* *(infml)* **1** act or occasion of paying money (esp a bribe) to sb. **2** deserved reward or punishment. **3** climax of a story or of a series of events.

PAYE /ˌpi: eɪ waɪ ˈi:/ *abbr* *(Brit)* (of income tax) pay-as-you-earn. ⇨ article at TAXATION.

payment /ˈpeɪmənt/ *n* ~ **(for sth) 1** [U] paying or being paid: *We would be grateful for prompt payment of your account.* ○ *Payment of subscriptions should be made to the club secretary.* **2** [C] sum of money (to be) paid: *The television can be paid for in ten monthly payments of £50.* ○ *Would you accept £50 as payment (for the work)?* **3** [U, sing] reward for sth: *We'd like you to accept this book in payment for your kindness.* ○ *(ironic) Personal abuse was the only payment he got for his efforts.*

payola /peɪˈəʊlə/ *n* *(esp US)* **1** [C] sum of money offered to sb to use his position or influence to promote the sales of a commercial product. **2** [U] practice of paying money in this way.

Pb *symb* lead.

PBX /ˌpi: bi: ˈeks/ *abbr* private branch exchange (ie private telephone switchboard).

PC /ˌpi: ˈsi:/ *abbr* *(Brit)* **1** personal computer. **2** *(pl* **PCs)** police constable: *PC (Tom) Marsh.* Cf WPC. **3** Privy Councillor.

pc *abbr* **1** *(US* **pct)** *(symb* **%)** per cent: *20 pc.* **2** /ˌpi: ˈsi:/ *(infml)* postcard.

PD /ˌpi: ˈdi:/ *abbr* *(US)* police department.

Pd *symb* palladium.

pd *abbr* paid (eg on a bill).

Pde *abbr* (in street names) parade: *29 North Pde.*

PDSA /ˌpi: di: es ˈeɪ/ *abbr* *(Brit)* People's Dispensary for Sick Animals.

PDT /ˌpi: di: ˈti:/ *abbr* *(US)* Pacific Daylight Time.

PE /ˌpi: ˈi:/ *abbr* physical education: *do PE at school* ○ *a PE lesson.* Cf PT.

pea /pi:/ *n* **1 (a)** climbing plant with long green pods containing edible green seeds that are eaten as a vegetable. **(b)** one of these seeds. **2** (idm) **like as two peas/as peas in a pod** ⇨ LIKE[3].

□ ˌ**pea-**ˈ**green** *adj, n* (having a) bright green colour like that of peas.

ˈ**pea-shooter** *n* small tube from which dried peas are shot by blowing through the tube.

ˌ**pea** ˈ**soup** soup made from dried peas. ˌ**pea-**ˈ**souper** *n* *(dated Brit infml)* very thick yellow fog.

peace /pi:s/ *n* **1 (a)** [U] state of freedom from war or violence: *The two communities live together in peace (with one another).* ○ *After years of fighting the people longed for peace.* ○ [attrib] *a peace treaty* ○ *peace studies, negotiations* ○ *the Peace Movement*, ie the movement campaigning for nuclear disarmament. **(b)** [sing] period of this: *a lasting peace* ○ *After a brief peace, fighting broke out again.* **2** (often **Peace)** [U, sing] treaty ending a war: *Peace/A Peace was signed between the two countries.* ○ *The Peace of Versailles.* **3** [U] (state of) calm or quiet: *break/disturb the peace* ○ *the peace of a summer evening, the countryside* ○ *I would work better if I had a bit of peace and quiet.* ○ *He just wants to be left in peace*, ie not to be disturbed. ○ *peace of mind*, ie freedom from worry ○ *May he rest in peace*, eg carved as an inscription on sb's tombstone. **4** [U] (state of) harmony and friendship. **5** (idm) **(be) at peace (with oneself/sb/sth)** in a state of friendship or harmony (with oneself/sb/sth): *She's never at peace with herself*, ie is always restless. ˌ**hold one's** ˈ**peace/**ˈ**tongue** *(dated)* remain silent or keep quiet although one would like to say sth. ˌ**keep the** ˈ**peace (a)** not create a disturbance in public. **(b)** prevent people from quarrelling, fighting or creating a disturbance in public: *a peace-keeping force*, ie armed troops sent to a country where there is civil war, to prevent more fighting. **make one's peace with sb** end a quarrel with sb, esp by apologizing. **make peace** (of two people, countries, etc) agree to end a war or a quarrel.

□ ˈ**Peace Corps** *(US)* organization that sends young volunteers to work in other countries.

ˈ**peace-loving** *adj* peaceable(1); peaceful(2): *a peace-loving nation, people, tribe, etc.*

ˈ**peacemaker** *n* person who persuades people or countries to make peace.

ˈ**peace offering** present offered to show that one is willing to make peace or in order to apologize for sth: *I bought her some flowers as a peace offering.*

ˈ**peace-pipe** *n* (also ˌ**pipe of** ˈ**peace**) tobacco pipe smoked by N American Indians when they have made peace with an enemy.

ˈ**peacetime** *n* [U] period when a country is not at war.

peaceable /ˈpiːsəbl/ *adj* **1** not quarrelsome; wishing to live in peace with others: *a peaceable temperament, person.* **2** without fighting or disturbance; peaceful: *a peaceable settlement, discussion* ○ *peaceable methods.* ▷ **peaceably** /-əblɪ/ *adv*: *live peaceably with one's neighbours.*

peaceful /ˈpiːsfl/ *adj* **1** not involving war or violence: *a peaceful demonstration, reign, period of history* ○ *peaceful uses of atomic energy* ○ *peaceful co-existence*, eg of countries with opposing political systems. **2** loving or seeking peace: *peaceful nations* ○ *peaceful aims.* **3** quiet; calm; tranquil: *a peaceful evening, scene, death* ○ *peaceful sleep* ○ *It's so peaceful out here in the country.* ▷ **peacefully** /-fəlɪ/ *adv*: *die, sleep peacefully.* **peacefulness** *n* [U].

peach /piːtʃ/ *n* **1** [C] round juicy fruit with downy yellowish-red skin and a rough stone: *tinned peaches* ○ [attrib] *a* ˈ*peach stone.* ⇨ illus at FRUIT. **2** [C] (also ˈ**peach tree**) tree on which this grows. **3** [U] yellowish-red colour of a peach. **4** (*infml*) **(a)** [C] very attractive young woman: *She's a real peach.* **(b)** [sing] ~ **(of a sth)** thing that is exceptionally good or attractive of its kind: *That was a peach of a shot!*

▷ **peachy** *adj* **(-ier, -iest)** **1** like a peach in colour or texture. **2** [usu pred] (*infml often ironic*) (eg of a situation) perfect; fine: *Everything's just peachy!*

□ ˌ**peaches and** ˈ**cream** (*approv*) having an attractive pink colour: *a peaches-and-cream complexion.*

peach Melba /ˌpiːtʃ ˈmelbə/ dessert made with ice-cream, peaches and raspberry sauce (named after Dame Nellie Melba (1859-1931), Australian soprano).

Peacock /ˈpiːkɒk/ Thomas Love (1785-1866), English novelist and poet. In works like *Nightmare Abbey* he satirized political and literary figures of his time, using dialogues between his characters over dinner.

peacock

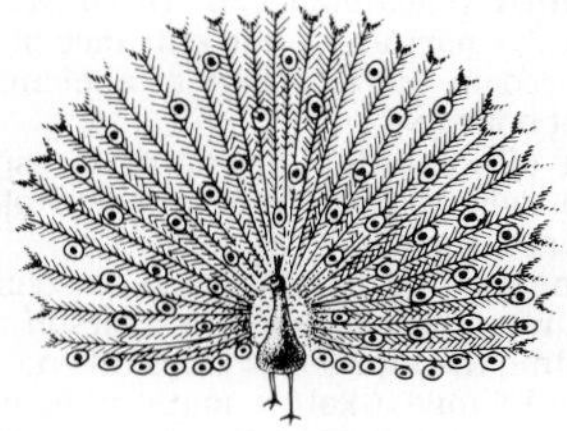

peacock /ˈpiːkɒk/ *n* **1** large male bird with long blue and green tail feathers which can be spread out like a fan: [attrib] *peacock feathers.* **2** (idm) **proud as a peacock** ⇨ PROUD.

□ ˌ**peacock** ˈ**blue** *adj, n* (having a) bright blue-green colour.

ˌ**peacock** ˈ**butterfly** brownish butterfly, with an eye-like spot in the corner of each of its wings.

peahen /ˈpiːhen/ *n* female of a peacock.

pea-jacket /ˈpiːdʒækɪt/ *n* double-breasted overcoat of coarse wool, worn by sailors.

peak[1] /piːk/ *n* **1 (a)** pointed top, esp of a mountain: *The plane flew over the snow-covered peaks.* ⇨ illus at MOUNTAIN. **(b)** the mountain itself: *The climbers made camp half-way up the peak.* **2** any shape, edge or part of sth that narrows to a point: *the peak of a roof* ○ *hair combed into a peak* ○ *widow's peak*, ie hair-style or growth that slopes back on each side from a point in the centre of the forehead. **3** pointed front part of a cap. ⇨ illus at HAT. **4 (a)** point of highest intensity, value, achievement, etc: *Traffic reaches a peak between 8 and 9 in the morning.* ○ *She's at the peak of her career.* **(b)** [attrib] maximum, most busy or intense, etc: *peak periods, production, load* ○ *the peak hour*, ie when the greatest number of people are travelling to or from work ○ *peak hours*, ie when demand for sth, eg electricity, is highest ○ *peak time*, eg when the greatest number of people are watching television ○ *peak rate*, ie highest prices charged at the busiest periods by hotels, airlines, etc. Cf OFF-PEAK (OFF).

▷ **peaked** *adj* having a peak: *a peaked cap, roof.*

□ **the** ˈ**Peak District** area in Derbyshire, England where there are many peaks (PEAK[1] 1). ⇨ map at UNITED KINGDOM.

peak[2] /piːk/ *v* [I] **1** reach the highest point or value: *Toy sales peaked just before Christmas and are now decreasing.* ○ *Demand for electricity peaks in the early evening.* **2** (idm) **peak and pine** become ill because of grief; waste away.

▷ **peaky** **(-ier, -iest)** (also **peaked**) *adj* (*infml*) ill or pale: *look, feel a bit peaky.*

peal /piːl/ *n* **1 (a)** loud ringing of a bell or a set of bells with different notes. **(b)** one of a number of musical patterns that can be rung on a set of bells. **2** set of bells with different notes tuned to each other. **3** loud burst of sound: *a peal of thunder* ○ *break into peals of laughter.*

▷ **peal** *v* **1** [I, Ip] ~ **(out)** sound in a peal: *The bells pealed (out) over the countryside.* **2** [Tn] cause (bells) to ring or sound loudly: *peal the bells to celebrate victory.*

pean (*US*) = PAEAN.

peanut /ˈpiːnʌt/ *n* **1** [C] **(a)** plant of the pea family bearing edible seeds in pods which ripen underground. **(b)** (also ˈ**ground-nut**) one of these seeds. ⇨ illus at NUT. **2 peanuts** [pl] (*sl esp US*) very small amount (esp of money): *He gets paid peanuts for doing that job.*

□ ˌ**peanut** ˈ**butter** paste made from roasted ground peanuts, used as a food.

ˌ**peanut** ˈ**oil** oil made from peanuts, used in cooking.

Peanuts /ˈpiːnʌts/ (*propr*) internationally popular American cartoon series created by C M Schulz (1922-), showing child characters like Charlie Brown and Lucy and the dog Snoopy in situations which gently mock human weaknesses. ⇨ illus.

pear /peə(r)/ *n* **1** sweet juicy yellow or green fruit with a rounded shape that becomes narrower towards the stalk. ⇨ illus at FRUIT. **2** (also ˈ**pear tree**) tree on which this grows.

pearl /pɜːl/ *n* **1 (a)** small hard round silvery-white or bluish-grey lustrous mass that forms inside the shells of some oysters and is of great value as a gem: *a string of pearls* ○ [attrib] *a pearl necklace.* **(b)** man-made imitation of this: *cultivated pearls.* **2** thing resembling a pearl in shape or colour: *pearls of dew on the grass.* **3** very precious or highly valued thing (used esp in the expressions shown): *a pearl among women* ○ *pearls of wisdom.* **4** (idm) **cast pearls before swine** ⇨ CAST[1].

▷ **pearl** *v* [I] form pearl-like drops or beads.

pearl *adj* [attrib] (of a light bulb) coated on the inside to give a soft light.

pearling *n* [U] diving or fishing for pearl-oysters.

pearly *adj* **(-lier, -liest)** of or like a pearl: *a pearly sheen.* **the** ˌ**Pearly** ˈ**Gates** (*joc*) the gates of Heaven.

pearlies *n* [pl] (*Brit*) traditional costume of some London costermongers, decorated with pearl buttons. ˌ**pearly** ˈ**king**, ˌ**pearly** ˈ**queen** (*Brit*) costermonger/costermonger's wife wearing pearlies.

□ ˌ**pearl** ˈ**barley** barley ground into small round grains.

ˌ**pearl** ˈ**button** button made from mother-of-pearl.

ˈ**pearl-diver** (also ˈ**pearl-fisher**, **pearler**) *n* person who dives or fishes for pearl-oysters.

ˌ**pearl** ˈ**onion** small onion used for pickling.

ˈ**pearl-oyster** *n* type of oyster in which pearls are found.

Pearl Harbor harbour on the island of Oahu in Hawaii. In 1941 the US naval base there was attacked by Japanese bombers without any declaration of war. Many US ships were destroyed and many troops killed. As a result, the USA entered the Second World War the following day by declaring war on Japan.

pearmain /ˈpeəmeɪn/ *n* any of several types of apple with a red skin and firm white flesh.

Peary /ˈpɪərɪ/ Robert Edwin (1856-1920), US explorer who was the first person to reach the North Pole, on 6 April 1909.

peasant /ˈpeznt/ *n* **1** (in the rural areas of some countries) farmer owning or renting a (usu small) piece of land which he cultivates himself: [attrib] *peasant farming.* **2** (formerly) poor agricultural worker. **3** (*infml derog*) person with rough unrefined manners: *He's an absolute peasant.*

▷ **peasantry** /ˈpezntrɪ/ *n* [Gp] **(a)** all the peasants (of a country). **(b)** peasants as a social group or class.

□ **the Peasants' Revolt** revolt of peasants from Kent and Essex in 1381, caused by economic hardships and the harsh government of *John of Gaunt. They marched on London, but were persuaded to return home when promises were made to help them. These were never kept. Their leader, Wat *Tyler, was killed while talking to the young King Richard II.

pease-pudding /ˌpiːzˈpʊdɪŋ/ *n* [C, U] (*esp Brit*) (dish of) split peas boiled and made into a thick creamy pudding.

peat /piːt/ *n* [U] plant material partly decomposed by the action of water, esp in marshy places (**peat-bogs**) and used in horticulture or as a fuel: *a bag, bale of peat* ○ [attrib] *a peat fire*, ie one in which cut pieces of peat are burned.
▷ **peaty** *adj* of, like or containing peat: *peaty soil.*

peavey /ˈpiːvɪ/ *n* (*US*) wooden lever with a metal hook and hinge, used by lumberjacks for moving logs.

pebble /ˈpebl/ *n* **1** small stone made smooth and round by the action of water, eg in a stream or on the seashore. **2** (idm) **not the only pebble on the beach** not the only person who matters or who has to be considered.
▷ **pebbly** *adj* covered with pebbles: *a pebbly beach.*
□ ˈ**pebble-dash** *n* [U] (*Brit*) cement mixed with small pebbles used as a coating for the outside walls of a house.

pecan /ˈpiːkən, pɪˈkæn; *US* pɪˈkɑːn/ *n* **1** pinkish-brown smooth nut with an edible kernel. **2** tree on which this grows, a type of hickory from the southern USA.
□ ˌ**pecan** ˈ**pie** traditional US pie made with pecan nuts and covered in a syrup.

peccadillo /ˌpekəˈdɪləʊ/ *n* (*pl* ~**es** or ~**s** /-ləʊz/) small unimportant offence or sin: *guilty of some mild peccadillo.*

peccary /ˈpekərɪ/ *n* (*pl*) type of wild pig-like animal found in Central and S America.

peck[1] /pek/ *v* **1** [I, Ipr, Tn] ~ (**at sth**) (try to) strike (sth) with the beak: *Hens feed by pecking.* ○ *birds pecking at the window* ○ *The lamb had been pecked by crows.* ○ (*fig*) *peck at one's food*, ie (of people) eat very small pieces or eat without appetite. **2** [Tn, Tn·pr] get or make (sth) by striking with the beak: *peck corn* ○ *The birds pecked a hole in the sack.* **3** [Tn, Tn·pr] ~ **sb** (**on sth**) (*infml*) kiss sb lightly and hurriedly: *peck sb on the cheek.* **4** (idm) **a/the** ˈ**pecking order** (*infml*) system of grading that exists in a group of people, so that some are more important, powerful, etc than others: *Newcomers have to accept their position at the bottom of the pecking order.* **5** (phr v) **peck sth out** remove sth by pecking: *Vultures had pecked out the dead sheep's eyes.*
▷ **peck** *n* **1** (**a**) stroke made by pecking. (**b**) mark or wound made by pecking: *The parrot gave me a sharp peck on the finger.* **2** (*infml*) hurried kiss: *She gave her aunt a quick peck on the cheek.*

peck[2] /pek/ *n* (formerly) measure of capacity for dry goods, esp grain, equal to 2 gallons (or approximately 9 litres).

pecker /ˈpekə(r)/ *n* **1** (*US sl*) penis. **2** (idm) ˌ**keep one's** ˈ**pecker up** (*Brit infml*) remain cheerful, esp in spite of difficulties.

peckish /ˈpekɪʃ/ *adj* (*Brit*) (*infml*) hungry: *feel a bit peckish.*

Pecksniff /ˈpeksnɪf/ *n* (*derog*) hypocritical person who likes to talk about his good deeds (from a character of this name in *Dickens's novel *Martin Chuzzlewit*). ▷ **Pecksniffian** /ˌpekˈsnɪfɪən/ *adj.*

pectin /ˈpektɪn/ *n* [U] (*chemistry*) substance similar to sugar that forms in some fruit when ripe and causes jam to set.
▷ **pectic** /ˈpektɪk/ *adj* (**a**) of or from pectin. (**b**) producing pectin.

pectoral /ˈpektərəl/ *adj* **1** of the chest or breast: *pectoral muscles* ○ *a pectoral fin.* **2** worn on the chest or breast: *a pectoral cross*, ie worn by a bishop.
▷ **pectorals** *n* [pl] (*often joc*) chest muscles.

peculate /ˈpekjʊleɪt/ *v* [I, Tn] (*fml*) take (money) dishonestly, esp from public funds; embezzle.
▷ **peculation** /ˌpekjʊˈleɪʃn/ *n* (**a**) [U] peculating. (**b**) [C] instance of this.

peculiar /pɪˈkjuːlɪə(r)/ *adj* **1** (**a**) odd or strange: *a peculiar taste, smell, noise, etc* ○ *a peculiar feeling that one has been here before* ○ *My keys have disappeared — it's most peculiar!* Cf FUNNY PECULIAR (FUNNY). (**b**) (of people) eccentric: *He's a bit peculiar!* ○ *her rather peculiar behaviour.* **2** (*infml*) unwell: *I'm feeling rather peculiar — I think I'll lie down for a while.* **3** [pred] ~ **to sb/sth** (**a**) belonging only to sb/sth: *an accent peculiar to the north of the region* ○ *a flavour peculiar to food cooked on an open fire* ○ *a species of bird peculiar to Asia.* (**b**) used or practised only by sb/sth: *customs peculiar to the 18th century* ○ *slang peculiar to medical students.* **4** [attrib] special or particular: *a matter of peculiar interest* ○ *His own peculiar way of doing things.*
▷ **peculiarity** /pɪˌkjuːlɪˈærətɪ/ *n* **1** [U] quality of being peculiar(1a). **2** [C] distinctive feature; characteristic: *These small spiced cakes are a peculiarity of the region.* **3** [C] odd or eccentric thing, quality, habit, etc: *peculiarities of dress, behaviour, diet, etc.*
peculiarly *adv* (**a**) in a peculiar(1b) manner: *behave peculiarly.* (**b**) more than usually; especially: *a peculiarly annoying noise.*

pecuniary /pɪˈkjuːnɪərɪ; *US* -ɪerɪ/ *adj* (*fml*) of or concerning money: *pecuniary advantage, aid, difficulties* ○ *work without pecuniary reward.*

pedagogue (*US* **-gog**) /ˈpedəgɒg/ *n* **1** (*arch or fml*) teacher. **2** (*derog*) strict or formal teacher.
▷ **pedagogy** /ˈpedəgɒdʒɪ/ *n* [U] study or science of ways and methods of teaching. **pedagogic** /ˌpedəˈgɒdʒɪk/ (also **pedagogical** /-ɪkl/) *adj* of or concerning teaching methods. **pedagogically** /-klɪ/ *adv*: *a pedagogically accepted method of testing students' knowledge.*

pedal[1] /ˈpedl/ *n* **1** lever that drives a machine (eg a bicycle or sewing-machine) when pressed down by the foot or feet: [attrib] *a pedal cyclist* ○ *a pedal boat*, ie one propelled by pedals. ⇨ illus at BICYCLE. **2** lever or key on a musical instrument (eg a piano, a harp or an organ) by the foot: *the loud/soft pedal*, ie on a piano. ⇨ illus at MUSIC, PIANO.
▷ **pedal** *v* (**-ll-**; *US also* **-l-**) **1** [I] use a pedal or pedals: *pedal rapidly to make the machine run smoothly.* **2** [I, Ipr, Ip] move by pedalling; ride: *pedal fast* ○ *pedal down the hill* ○ *pedal along.* **3** [Tn, Tn·pr] move or operate (a machine) by pedalling: *pedal a bicycle across the field.*
□ ˈ**pedal bin** rubbish bin (usu in a kitchen) with a lid that opens when a pedal is pressed.

pedal[2] /ˈpiːdl/ *adj* of or concerning the foot or feet.

pedalo /ˈpedələʊ/ *n* (*pl* ~**s**) (*Brit*) small pleasure-boat driven by pedals.

pedant /ˈpednt/ *n* (*derog*) **1** person who attaches too much importance to detail or to rules, esp when learning or teaching. **2** person who values academic knowledge and likes to display his learning.
▷ **pedantic** /pɪˈdæntɪk/ *adj* of or like a pedant: *a pedantic insistence on the rules.* **pedantically** /-klɪ/ *adv.*
pedantry /ˈpedntrɪ/ *n* (**a**) [U] too much emphasis on formal rules or detail. (**b**) [U] boastful and unnecessary display of learning. (**c**) [C] instance of this.

peddle /ˈpedl/ *v* **1** [I] go from house to house to sell goods; be a pedlar. **2** [Tn, Dn·pr] ~ **sth** (**to sb**) try to sell (goods) by going from house to house or by offering them to individual people: *peddle one's wares* ○ *be arrested for peddling illegal drugs.* ⇨ Usage at SELL. **3** [Tn, Dn·pr] ~ **sth** (**to sb**) offer (ideas, gossip, etc) to individual people: *peddle malicious gossip* ○ *peddling his crazy plan to other party members.*
▷ **peddler** /ˈpedlə(r)/ *n* **1** (*US*) = PEDLAR. **2** person who sells illegal drugs: *dope addicts exploited by peddlers.*

pederasty (also **paederasty**) /ˈpedəræstɪ/ *n* [U] practice of a man having sexual relations with a boy.
▷ **pederast** /ˈpedəræst/ *n* man who practises pederasty.

pedestal

pedestal

pedestal /ˈpedɪstl/ *n* **1** base of a column. **2** base on which a statue or some other piece of sculpture stands. ⇨ illus. **3** (idm) **knock sb off his pedestal/perch** ⇨ KNOCK[2]. **place, etc sb on a** ˈ**pedestal** admire sb greatly, esp without noticing his faults.
□ ˈ**pedestal table** table supported on a central column.

pedestrian /pɪˈdestrɪən/ *n* person walking in the street (contrasted with people in vehicles): *Two pedestrians and a cyclist were injured when the car skidded.* Cf MOTORIST (MOTOR).
▷ **pedestrian** *adj* **1** lacking imagination or inspiration; dull: *a pedestrian description of events that were actually very exciting* ○ *Life in the suburbs can be pretty pedestrian.* **2** [attrib] of or for pedestrians: *a pedestrian walkway.*
□ **pe**ˌ**destrian** ˈ**crossing** (*Brit*) (*US* **crosswalk**) part of a road specially marked with studs, white lines, etc, where vehicles must stop to allow pedestrians to cross. Cf PELICAN CROSSING (PELICAN), ZEBRA CROSSING (ZEBRA).
peˌ**destrian** ˈ**precinct** part of a town, esp a shopping area, where vehicles may not enter.

pedi- *comb form* of the feet: *pedicure.*

pedicel /ˈpedɪsel/ (also **pedicle** /ˈpedɪkl/) *n* (*biology*) small stalk-like structure in a plant or an animal. Cf PEDUNCLE. ⇨ illus at FRUIT.

pedicure /ˈpedɪkjʊə(r)/ *n* [C, U] treatment of the feet, esp corns, bunions, etc, and care of the toe-nails, for medical or cosmetic reasons. Cf MANICURE.

pedigree /ˈpedɪgriː/ *n* **1** (**a**) [C] line of ancestors: *proud of his long pedigree.* (**b**) [U] quality of having this: *people without pedigree.* **2** [C] (**a**) table or list of a person's ancestors; family tree. (**b**) official record of the animals from which an animal has been bred.
▷ **pedigree** *adj* [attrib] (of an animal) descended from a known line of (usu specially chosen) animals of the same breed; pure bred: [attrib] *pedigree cattle, dogs, horses, etc.*

pediment /ˈpedɪmənt/ *n* (*architecture*) (usu) triangular part above the entrance of a building, first used in the buildings of ancient Greece. ⇨ illus at COLUMN.

pedlar (*US* **peddler**) /ˈpedlə(r)/ *n* (esp formerly) person who travels from place to place selling goods at fairs, etc.

pedometer /pɪˈdɒmɪtə(r)/ *n* instrument that measures the distance a person walks by recording the number of steps taken.

peduncle /pɪˈdʌŋkəl/ *n* main stalk of a flower, fruit, etc, esp a main stalk bearing a single flower. Cf PEDICEL.

pee /piː/ *v* [I, Ipr] (*infml*) urinate: *a dog peeing against a fence.*
▷ **pee** *n* (*infml*) (**a**) [U] urine. (**b**) [sing] act of urinating: *go for/have a quick pee.*

peek /piːk/ *v* [I, Ipr] ~ (**at sth**) look quickly and often secretively (at sth): *No peeking!* ○ *peek over the fence* ○ *peek at sb's diary.* Cf PEEP[1] 1, PEER[2].
▷ **peek** *n* [sing] quick (often sly) glance: *take a peek at what was hidden in the cupboard.*

peekaboo /ˌpiːkəˈbuː/ (*Brit* also **peepbo** /ˈpiːpbəʊ/) *interj, n* [U] (exclamation used in) a game played to amuse young children, in which one hides one's face and then uncovers it.

Peel /piːl/ Sir Robert (1788-1850), British statesman. He was one of the most important political figures of the early 19th century and a founder of the modern Conservative Party. He was responsible for the organization of the Metropolitan Police Force, Catholic emancipation and the repeal of the *Corn Laws. British policemen are still informally called 'bobbies' after him, Bob or Bobby being a short form of Robert. ⇨ App 2. ⇨ article at POLICE.

peel /piːl/ *v* **1** (a) [Tn, Dn.n, Dn.pr] ~ **sth (for sb)** take the skin off (fruit, etc): *peel a banana, an apple, a potato, etc* ○ *Would you peel me an orange?* (b) [Ip, Tn·p] ~ **(sth) away/off** (cause skin, etc on a surface to) be removed: *peel away the outer layer* ○ *The label will peel off if you soak it in water.* (c) [I] have a skin or outer layer which comes off: *These oranges peel easily.* **2** (a) [I, Ip] ~ **(off)** (of a covering) come off in strips or flakes: *The wallpaper is peeling (off).* ○ *After sunbathing, my skin began to peel.* ○ *The bark of plane trees peels off regularly.* (b) [I] (of a surface) lose its covering in strips or flakes: *My face is peeling.* ○ *The walls have begun to peel.* **3** (idm) **keep one's eyes peeled/skinned** ⇨ EYE[1]. **4** (phr v) **peel off** (of cars, aircraft, etc) leave a group and turn to one side: *One squadron peeled off to attack enemy bombers.* **peel (sth) off** (*infml*) remove (one's clothes), esp when one is hot or before exercise: *peel off and dive into the sea* ○ *peel off one's jumper.*

▷ **peel** *n* [U] outer covering or skin of fruit, vegetables, etc: *lemon peel* ○ *candied peel,* ie peel of oranges, lemons, etc coated in sugar. Cf RIND, SKIN 4, ZEST 3.

peeler *n* (esp in compounds) device for peeling (fruit, etc): *a po'tato peeler.*

peelings /ˈpiːlɪŋz/ *n* [pl] (esp of fruit and vegetables) parts peeled off.

peep[1] /piːp/ *v* [I, Ipr, Ip] **1** ~ **(at sth)** look quickly and slyly or cautiously (at sth): *peep at a secret document* ○ *be caught peeping through the keyhole.* Cf PEEK, PEER[2]. **2** (of light) appear through a narrow opening: *daylight peeping through the curtains.* **3** appear slowly or partly: *The moon peeped out from behind the clouds.* ○ *green shoots peeping up through the soil.*

▷ **peep** *n* **1** (esp *sing*) short quick look, esp a secret or sly one: *have a peep through the window* ○ *take a peep at the baby asleep in her cot.* **2** (idm) **peep of ˈday** first light of day; dawn.

peeper *n* (usu *pl*) (*sl*) eye.

□ **ˈpeep-hole** *n* small opening in a wall, door, curtain, etc through which one may peep at sth.

ˌPeeping ˈTom (*derog*) person who likes to spy on people when they do not know they are being watched; voyeur.

ˈpeep-show *n* exhibition of small pictures in a box, which are viewed through a magnifying lens placed in a small opening.

ˈpeep-toed *adj* (of shoes) with a small opening at the front.

peep[2] /piːp/ *n* **1** [C] short weak high sound made by mice, young birds, etc; squeak. **2** [C] (also **peep ˈpeep**) [C] (imitation of the) sound of a car's horn. **3** [sing] (*infml*) sound made by sb, esp sth said: *I haven't heard a peep out of the children for an hour.*

▷ **peep** *v* [I] make a peep.

peepul = PIPAL.

peer[1] /pɪə(r)/ *n* **1** (a) [C] person who is equal to another in rank, status or merit: *It will not be easy to find his peer.* ○ *be judged by one's peers.* (b) [C usu *pl*] person who is the same age as another: *He doesn't spend enough time with his peers.* **2** [C] (in Britain) male member of one of the ranks of nobility (eg duke, marquis, earl, viscount, baron): *ˈlife peer.* ⇨ articles at ARISTOCRAT, PARLIAMENT.

▷ **peerage** /ˈpɪərɪdʒ/ *n* **1** [Gp] the whole body of peers: *elevate/raise sb to the peerage,* ie make sb a peer or peeress. **2** [C] rank of a peer: *inherit a peerage.* **3** [C] book containing a list of the peers and details of their ancestry.

peeress /ˈpɪəres/ *n* (a) female peer. (b) wife or widow of a peer.

peerless *adj* superior to all others; without equal.

□ **ˈpeer group** group of people of approximately the same age or status: *mix with one's peer group.*

ˌpeer of the ˈrealm (in Britain) hereditary peer with the right to sit in the House of Lords.

peer[2] /pɪə(r)/ *v* [I, Ipr, Ip] ~ **(at sth/sb)** look closely or carefully, esp as if unable to see well: *peer shortsightedly* ○ *peer at sb over one's spectacles* ○ *peer out of the window/over the wall/through a gap.* ⇨ Usage at LOOK[1]. Cf PEEK, PEEP[1] 1.

peeve /piːv/ *v* [Tn] (*infml*) annoy (sb); put (sb) in a bad temper: *It peeves me to be ordered out of my own house.*

▷ **peeved** *adj* ~ **(about sth)** (*infml*) annoyed: *He looks very peeved about something.*

peevish /ˈpiːvɪʃ/ *adj* easily annoyed (esp by unimportant things); irritable. **peevishly** *adv.* **peevishness** *n* [U].

peewit (also **pewit**) /ˈpiːwɪt/ *n* = LAPWING.

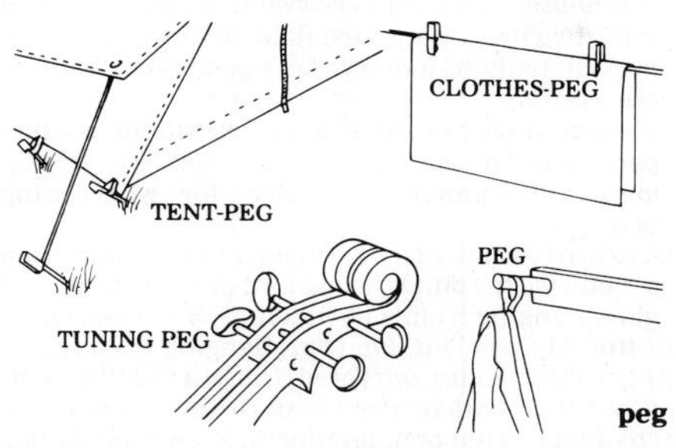

peg[1] /peg/ *n* **1** wooden, metal or plastic pin or bolt, usu narrower at one end than the other, used to hold things together, to hang things on, to mark a position, etc. **2** (a) pin fastened to a wall or door, on which hats and coats may be hung: *a hat/coat peg.* (b) (also **ˈtent-peg**) pin hammered into the ground to hold one of the ropes of a tent in place. ⇨ illus. (c) pin used to mark a position, eg on a piece of land: *a surveyor's peg.* **3** small wooden or metal pin or bolt used to fasten together esp pieces of wood. **4** = CLOTHES-PEG (CLOTHES). **5** (also **ˈtuning peg**) any of several wooden screws for tightening or loosening tension in the strings of a violin, etc. ⇨ illus at MUSIC. **6** piece of wood used to seal the vent in a barrel, etc. **7** (also **peg-leg**) (*infml*) (a) artificial leg, usu wooden. (b) person with an artificial leg. **8** (*dated Brit infml*) small drink of brandy, whisky, etc. **9** (idm) **a peg to hang sth on** reason, excuse or opportunity for (doing) sth: *a minor offence which provided a peg to hang their attack on.* **ˌoff the ˈpeg** (of clothes) not made to measure; ready-made: *buy a suit off the peg* ○ [attrib] *an ˌoff-the-peg ˈsuit.* **a square peg** ⇨ SQUARE[1]. **ˌtake sb ˈdown a peg (or two)** make (a proud or conceited person) more humble.

□ **ˈpeg-board** *n* (a) [C, U] (type of) board with holes in, on which things may be fastened or hung with pegs or hooks for display, etc. (b) [C] board with holes in, into which pegs may be inserted, esp for a game or as a toy.

peg[2] /peg/ *v* (**-gg-**) **1** (esp passive) [Tn, Tn·pr, Tn·p] fasten (sth) with pegs: *peg a tent* ○ *peg the clothes (out) on the line* ○ *peg sth in place.* **2** [Tn, Tn·pr] ~ **sth (at sth)** fix or keep (wages or prices) at a certain level: *Pay increases were pegged at five per cent.* **3** (idm) **level pegging** ⇨ LEVEL[1]. **4** (phr v) **peg away (at sth)** (*infml*) work hard and persistently: *He's been pegging away at his thesis for months.* **peg sb down (to sth)** force or persuade sb to be specific or make a definite promise; pin sb down: *I pegged him down to a price for the work.* **peg sth down** fix sth in place with pegs: *have difficulty pegging the tent down in a storm.* **peg out** (*infml*) die. **peg sth out** (a) mark (an area of land) with pegs: *peg out a claim,* ie mark out the land of which one claims ownership. (b) (esp in the game of cribbage) show (a score) by putting pegs in a board.

Pegasus /ˈpegəsəs/ **1** (in Greek mythology) horse with wings, that sprang from the blood of *Medusa when *Perseus cut off her head. **2** constellation in the northern hemisphere near *Andromeda.

pejorative /pɪˈdʒɒrətɪv; *US* -ˈdʒɔːr- *or, rarely,* ˈpiːdʒərətɪv/ *adj* (*fml*) expressing criticism or scorn; derogatory; disparaging: *pejorative remarks, comments, words, etc.* ▷ **pejoratively** *adv.*

peke /piːk/ *n* (*infml*) Pekinese.

Pekinese (also **Pekingese**) /ˌpiːkɪˈniːz/ *n* (*pl* unchanged or ~**s**) small dog with short legs and long silky hair, originally from China. ⇨ illus at DOG.

Peking /piːˈkɪŋ/ = BEIJING.

pekoe /ˈpiːkəʊ/ *n* [U] type of high-quality tea made from the young buds of the tea plant.

pelagic /pəˈlædʒɪk/ *adj* (*fml*) (a) (of fishing, whaling, etc) carried out on the open sea. (b) (of fish, etc) living near the surface of the open sea.

pelf /pelf/ *n* [U] (*arch or joc*) money.

pelican /ˈpelɪkən/ *n* large water-bird with a pouch under its long bill for storing food.

□ **ˌpelican ˈcrossing** pedestrian crossing with traffic lights that are operated by pedestrians. Cf PEDESTRIAN CROSSING (PEDESTRIAN), ZEBRA CROSSING (ZEBRA).

pelisse /peˈliːs/ *n* **1** long woman's cloak with arm-holes or sleeves. **2** short cape lined with fur, esp one worn as part of a hussar's uniform.

pellagra /pəˈlægrə, -ˈleɪg-/ *n* [U] (*medical*) disease that causes a vitamin B2 deficiency and cracking of the skin. It often leads to insanity.

pellet /ˈpelɪt/ *n* **1** small tightly-packed ball of a soft material such as bread or wet paper, made eg by rolling it between the fingers: *paper pellets.* **2** small pill. **3** small piece of shot[1](5), esp for firing from an airgun.

pell-mell /ˌpelˈmel/ *adv* **1** in a hurrying, disorderly manner; headlong: *The children rushed pell-mell down the stairs.* **2** in disorder; untidily: *The books were scattered pell-mell over the floor.*

pellucid /peˈluːsɪd/ *adj* (*fml*) **1** transparent or translucent; very clear. **2** (*fig*) (of style, meaning, etc) very clear.

Peloponnesian War /peləpəˌniːʃən ˈwɔː(r)/ **the Peloponnesian War** war fought in 431-404 BC between Athens and Sparta and its allies. Athens was defeated and lost its empire, and Sparta became the leading Greek power. Cf THUCYDIDES.

pelota /pəˈləʊtə/ *n* [U] game played in Spain, Latin America and the Philippines, in which the players use a long basket strapped to the wrist to hit a ball against a wall.

pelt[1] /pelt/ *n* skin of an animal, esp with the fur or hair still on it: *beaver pelts.*

pelt[2] /pelt/ *v* **1** [Tn, Tn·pr] ~ **sb (with sth)**; ~ **sth (at sb)** throw sth at sb repeatedly in order to attack him: *pelt sb with snowballs, stones, rotten tomatoes, etc* ○ *The crowd pelted bad eggs at the speaker.* **2** [I, Ipr, Ip] ~ **(down)** (of rain, etc) fall very heavily; beat down: *It was pelting with rain.* ○ *The rain was pelting down.* ○ *hail pelting on the roof.* **3** (idm) **full pelt/tilt/speed** ⇨ FULL. **4** (phr v) **pelt along, down, up, etc (sth)** run very fast in the specified direction: *pelting down the hill.*

pelvis /ˈpelvɪs/ *n* (*pl* ~**es** /ˈpelvɪsɪz/ or **pelves** /ˈpelviːz/) (*anatomy*) basin-shaped framework of bones at the lower end of the body, containing the bladder, rectum, etc. ⇨ illus at SKELETON.

▷ **pelvic** /ˈpelvɪk/ *adj* of or relating to the pelvis.

pemmican /ˈpemɪkən/ *n* [U] dried meat beaten and made into cakes (originally by N American Indians).

Pen *abbr* (esp on a map) Peninsula.

pen[1] /pen/ *n* **1** [C] (often in compounds) instrument for writing with ink, consisting of a pointed piece of split metal, a metal ball, etc, fixed into a metal or plastic holder: *ball-point pen* ○ *felt-tip pen.* **2** [sing] writing, esp as a profession: *He lives by his pen.* **3** (idm) **the ˌpen is ˌmightier than the ˈsword** (*saying*) poets, thinkers, etc, affect human affairs more than soldiers do. **put ˌpen to ˈpaper** (*fml*) (start to) write sth, eg a letter. **a slip of the pen/tongue** ⇨ SLIP[1].

▷ **pen** *v* (**-nn-**) [Tn] (*fml*) write (a letter, etc): *She penned a few words of thanks.*

□ **ˌpen-and-ˈink** *adj* [esp attrib] drawn with a pen: *pen-and-ink drawings, sketches, illustrations, etc.*

ˈpen-friend (also *esp US* **ˈpen-pal**) *n* person with whom one builds a friendship by exchanging letters, esp sb in a foreign country whom one has never met.

ˈpenknife (also **ˈpocket-knife**) *n* (*pl* **-knives**) small knife with one or more blades that fold down into the handle,usu carried in the pocket. ⇨ illus at KNIFE.

ˈ**pen-name** *n* name used by a writer instead of his real name; pseudonym.

ˈ**pen-pusher** *n* (*infml derog*) person (esp a clerk) whose job involves a lot of boring paperwork.

ˈ**pen-pushing** *n* [U] (*infml derog*) boring paperwork.

pen² /pen/ *n* **1** small piece of land surrounded by a fence, esp for keeping cattle, sheep, poultry, etc in: *a* ˈ*sheep-pen*. **2** bomb-proof shelter for submarines.

▷ **pen** *v* (-**nn**-) (phr v) **pen sb/sth in/up** shut sb/sth in, or as if in, a pen: *pen up the chickens for the night* ○ *She feels penned in by her life as a housewife.*

pen³ /pen/ *n* (*US infml*) penitentiary.

pen⁴ /pen/ *n* female swan. Cf COB.

penal /ˈpi:nl/ *adj* [esp attrib] **1** of, relating to or used for punishment, esp by law: *penal laws, reforms* ○ *a* ˈ*penal colony/settlement*, ie a place where criminals are sent as a punishment ○ *penal taxation*, ie taxation which is so heavy that it seems like a punishment. **2** punishable by law: *a penal offence*. ▷ **penally** /ˈpi:nəlɪ/ *adv*.

□ ˈ**penal code** system of laws relating to crime and its punishment.

ˌ**penal** ˈ**servitude** (*Brit law*) (formerly) punishment in which sb is sent to prison and forced to do hard physical work.

penalize, -ise /ˈpi:nəlaɪz/ *v* **1** [Tn, Tn·pr esp passive] ~ **sb** (**for sth**) punish sb for breaking a rule or leavily penalized.: *He was penalized for a foul on the striker*, eg A free kick was awarded to the striker's team. **2** [Tn] put (sb) at a disadvantage; handicap (sb) unfairly: *The new law penalizes the poorest members of society.* **3** [Tn] make (sth) punishable by law. ▷ **penalization** /ˌpi:nəlaɪˈzeɪʃn; *US* -lɪˈz-/ *n* [U].

penalty /ˈpenltɪ/ *n* **1** ~ (**for sth**) (**a**) punishment for breaking a law, rule or contract: *It is part of the contract that there is a penalty for late delivery.* (**b**) thing imposed as a punishment, eg imprisonment or a fine: *the* ˈ*death penalty* ○ *It is an offence to travel without a valid ticket — penalty £100.* ○ *The maximum penalty for this crime is 10 years' imprisonment.* **2** disadvantage, suffering or inconvenience caused by an action or a circumstance: *One of the penalties of fame is loss of privacy.* **3** (**a**) (in sports and games) disadvantage imposed on a player or team as a punishment for breaking a rule, esp (in football) a free shot at goal by the opposing team: *The referee awarded a penalty to the home team.* (**b**) (in football) goal scored with a penalty kick. **4** (idm) **on/under pain/penalty of sth** ⇨ PAIN. **pay the penalty** ⇨ PAY².

□ ˈ**penalty area** (in football) area in front of the goal within which a foul by the defenders is punished by the award of a penalty kick to the attacking team. ⇨ illus at ASSOCIATION FOOTBALL (ASSOCIATION).

ˈ**penalty box** (**a**) (*infml*) = PENALTY AREA. (**b**) (in ice hockey) area at the side of the rink where players who commit a foul are made to sit for part of the game.

ˈ**penalty clause** part of a contract stating that money must be paid if sb breaks the contract.

ˈ**penalty kick** (in football) free kick at the goal awarded to the attacking team for a foul committed in the penalty area.

penance /ˈpenəns/ *n* **1** [C, U] ~ (**for sth**) punishment that one imposes on oneself to show that one is sorry for having done wrong: *an act of penance* ○ *do penance* (ie perform an act that shows one is sorry) *for one's sins* ○ (*joc*) *She made him do the washing-up as (a) penance for forgetting her birthday.* **2** [U] (in the Roman Catholic and Orthodox Churches) sacrament that includes confession, absolution, and an act of penance imposed by the priest.

pence *pl* of PENNY.

penchant /ˈpɑ:nʃɑ:n; *US* ˈpentʃənt/ *n* (*French*) ~ **for sth** liking or taste for sth: *She has a penchant for Indian food.*

pencil /ˈpensl/ *n* **1** (**a**) [C] instrument for drawing or writing with, consisting of a thin stick of graphite or coloured chalk enclosed in a cylinder of wood or fixed in a metal case: [attrib] *a pencil drawing*. (**b**) [U] writing done with a pencil: *Should I sign my name in pencil or ink?* ○ *Pencil rubs out easily.* **2** [C] (usu in compounds) thing used or shaped like a pencil: *an* ˈ*eyebrow pencil*, ie a stick of cosmetic material used by women to darken the eyebrows.

▷ **pencil** *v* (-**ll**-; *US* -**l**-) **1** [Tn] write, draw or mark (sth) with a pencil: *She pencilled the rough outline of a house.* ○ *pencilled eyebrows.* **2** (phr v) **pencil sth in** write (a suggested date, arrangement, etc) provisionally in a diary: *Let's pencil in 3 May for the meeting.*

□ ˈ**pencil-case** *n* small bag, box, etc for holding pencils and pens.

ˈ**pencil-sharpener** *n* device for sharpening pencils.

pendant /ˈpendənt/ *n* **1** ornament that hangs from a chain worn round the neck. **2** piece of decorated glass hanging from a chandelier. **3** = PENNANT.

pendent /ˈpendənt/ *adj* (*fml*) hanging from sth.

pending /ˈpendɪŋ/ *adj* [pred] (*fml*) (**a**) waiting to be decided or settled: *The lawsuit was then pending.* (**b**) about to happen; imminent: *A decision on this matter is pending.*

▷ **pending** *prep* (*fml*) (**a**) while waiting for (sth); until: *She was held in custody pending trial.* (**b**) during (sth): *pending the negotiations.*

pendulous /ˈpendjʊləs; *US* -dʒʊləs/ *adj* (*fml*) hanging down loosely so as to swing from side to side: *pendulous breasts.*

pendulum

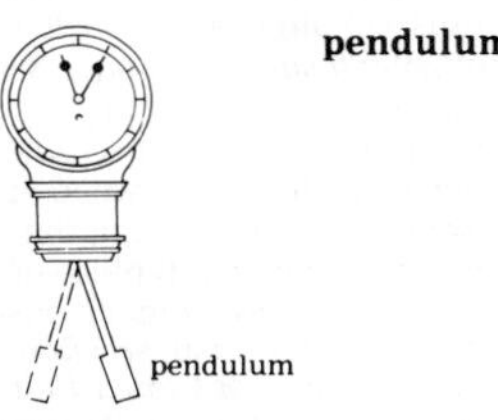

pendulum /ˈpendjʊləm; *US* -dʒʊləm/ *n* **1** weight hung on a cord from a fixed point so that it can swing freely. **2** rod with a weight at the bottom that regulates the mechanism of a clock. ⇨ illus. **3** (idm) **the swing of the pendulum** ⇨ SWING².

penetrable /ˈpenɪtrəbl/ *adj* (*fml*) that can be penetrated. ▷ **penetrability** /ˌpenɪtrəˈbɪlətɪ/ *n* [U].

penetrate /ˈpenɪtreɪt/ *v* **1** [Ipr, Tn] ~ (**into/through**) **sth** make a way into or through sth: *Our troops have penetrated (into) enemy territory.* ○ *The mist penetrated (into) the room.* ○ *The heavy rain had penetrated right through her coat.* ○ (*fig*) *The cat's sharp claws penetrated* (ie pierced) *my skin.* ○ *The party has been penetrated* (ie infiltrated) *by extremists.* ○ *A shrill cry penetrated the silence.* **2** [Tn, Tn·pr esp passive] ~ **sb/sth** (**with sth**) fill or spread through sb/sth: *Cold horror penetrated her whole being.* **3** [Tn] see or show a way into or through (sth): *Our eyes could not penetrate the darkness.* ○ *The headlamps penetrated the fog.* ○ (*fig*) *We soon penetrated his disguise*, ie saw who he really was. **4** [Tn] understand or discover (sth): *It was impossible to penetrate the mystery.* ○ *He penetrated their thoughts.* **5** [I, Tn] be fully understood or realized (by sb): *I explained the problem to him several times but it didn't seem to penetrate.* ○ *Nothing we say penetrates his thick skull!*

▷ **penetrating** *adj* **1** having or showing the ability to think and understand quickly and deeply: *a penetrating mind, question, thinker* ○ *a penetrating look, glance, stare, etc.* **2** (of a voice or sound) loud and carrying; piercing: *a penetrating cry, shriek, yell, etc.* **penetratingly** *adv*.

penetration /ˌpenɪˈtreɪʃn/ *n* [U] **1** (action or process of) penetrating: *our penetration of the enemy's defences.* **2** ability to think and understand quickly and deeply: *the penetration of her mind/her powers of penetration.*

penetrative /ˈpenɪtrətɪv; *US* -treɪtɪv/ *adj* **1** that can penetrate. **2** (of sb's mind, thoughts, etc) astute: *a penetrative analysis.*

penguin

penguin /ˈpeŋgwɪn/ *n* black and white sea-bird living in the Antarctic, with webbed feet and wings like flippers that are used for swimming.

penicillin /ˌpenɪˈsɪlɪn/ *n* [U] substance obtained from mould fungi, used as an antibiotic drug to prevent or treat infections caused by bacteria.

peninsula /pəˈnɪnsjʊlə; *US* -nsələ/ *n* area of land almost surrounded by water or projecting far into the sea: *the Iberian peninsula*, ie Spain and Portugal.

▷ **peninsular** /-lə(r)/ *adj* of or like a peninsula **the Pe**ˌ**ninsular** ˈ**War** one of the Napoleonic Wars, fought in 1808-14 in Spain and Portugal between France and Britain. The British, helped by their Spanish and Portuguese allies, finally forced the French forces to retreat back into France in a campaign led by *Wellington.

penis /ˈpi:nɪs/ *n* organ with which a male animal copulates and (in mammals) urinates. ⇨ illus at MALE.

penitence /ˈpenɪtəns/ *n* [U] ~ (**for sth**) sorrow or regret for having done sth wrong: *show penitence for one's sins.*

penitent /ˈpenɪtənt/ *adj* feeling or showing regret or remorse for having done sth wrong: *a penitent sinner.*

▷ **penitent** *n* (*religion*) penitent person, esp one who is doing penance(2).

penitently *adv*.

penitential /ˌpenɪˈtenʃl/ *adj* of or relating to penitence or penance. ▷ **penitentially** /-ʃəlɪ/ *adv*.

penitentiary /penɪˈtenʃərɪ/ *n* (*US*) federal or state prison for people who have committed serious crimes.

▷ **penitentiary** *adj* (**a**) of or relating to penance (**b**) of or relating to treatment intended to reform offenders.

penmanship /ˈpenmənʃɪp/ *n* [U] skill or style in writing or in handwriting.

Penn /pen/ William (1644-1718), British Quaker and founder of *Pennsylvania. He was put in prison for his religious beliefs, and decided to set up a Quaker colony in America. King *Charles II granted him some territory there, and he drew up the original constitution of the State.

pennant /ˈpenənt/ (also **pendant, pennon**) *n* (**a**) long, narrow flag tapering to a point, used on a ship for signalling or as identification. ⇨ illus FLAG. (**b**) (*US*) flag of this shape used as a school banner or as the symbol of a sports championship.

penniless /ˈpenɪlɪs/ *adj* having no money; very poor; destitute: *a penniless old man.*

Pennines /ˈpenaɪnz/ **the Pennines** chain of hills in northern England, running from the *Peak District to the Scottish border. They are often described as the 'backbone of England'. ⇨ map at UNITED KINGDOM. ▷ **Pennine** *adj*.

□ **the** ˌ**Pennine** ˈ**Way** path used by walkers along the Pennines, about 400 km (250 miles) long.

pennon /ˈpenən/ *n* **1** long narrow triangular or swallow-tailed flag, originally used by a knight on his lance. **2** = PENNANT.

penn'orth /ˈpenəθ/ *n* [sing] (*infml*) = PENNYWORTH (PENNY).

Pennsylvania /ˌpensəlˈveɪnɪə/ state in the north-eastern USA, founded by William *Penn. It is the most important industrial state after New

York, and heavy industry is concentrated in cities like Pittsburgh. It was one of the 13 original states, and the *Declaration of Independence was signed in Philadelphia. ⇨ map at App 1.

penny /ˈpenɪ/ *n* (*pl* **pence** /pens/ or **pennies** /ˈpenɪz/) **1** (*abbr* **p**) (since decimal coinage was introduced in 1971) British bronze coin worth one hundredth of a pound: *Potatoes are 20 pence a pound.* ○ *These pencils cost 40p each.* **2** (*abbr* **d**) former British bronze coin worth one twelfth of a shilling, in use until 1971. **3** (*US infml*) cent. **4** (idm) **be two/ten a ˈpenny (a)** be very cheap. **(b)** be numerous and easy to obtain. **earn/turn an honest penny** ⇨ HONEST. **ˌin for a ˈpenny, ˌin for a ˈpound** (*saying*) having started to do sth, it is worth spending as much time or money as is necessary to complete it. **in ˌpenny ˈnumbers** (*infml*) in small quantities at a time. **ˌpennies from ˈheaven** piece of unexpected good luck. **the ˈpenny drops** (*infml esp Brit*) sb now understands or realizes sth that he had not understood or realized before: *I had to explain the problem to her several times before the penny finally dropped.* **a ˌpenny for your ˈthoughts** (*catchphrase*) (used to ask sb what he is thinking about). **ˌpenny ˈwise (and) ˌpound ˈfoolish** careful about spending small amounts of money but reckless about spending large sums of money. **a pretty penny** ⇨ PRETTY. **spend a penny** ⇨ SPEND. **turn up like a bad ˈpenny** (*infml*) (habitually) appear when one is unwelcome or unwanted.

□ **ˌpenny ˈblack** British penny stamp issued in 1840. It was the first British postage stamp, and the first adhesive stamp to be generally used.

ˌpenny ˈfarthing old type of bicycle with a large front wheel and a small back wheel.

ˈpenny-pincher (*infml*) mean person; miser. **ˈpenny-pinching** *adj* mean; miserly. — *n* [U] miserliness.

the ˌpenny ˈpost British postal system set up in 1840, which allowed a letter to be sent anywhere in the country for a standard charge of one penny.

ˈpennyweight *n* unit of weight equal to 24 grains.

ˌpenny ˈwhistle = TIN WHISTLE (TIN).

ˈpennyworth /ˈpənɪwəθ/ (also **penn'orth** /ˈpenəθ/) *n* [sing] as much as can be bought for a penny.

pennyroyal /ˌpenɪˈrɔɪəl/ *n* [U] type of mint[1](1) that spreads across the ground.

pennywort /ˈpenɪwɜːt/ *n* [U] any of various flowering plants that have rounded disc-like leaves.

penology /piːˈnɒlədʒɪ/ *n* [U] study of crime and its punishment, and the management of prisons.

pension[1] /ˈpenʃn/ *n* [C, U] sum of money paid regularly by the State to people above a certain age and to widowed or disabled people, or by an employer to a retired employee: *an old-age ˈpension* ○ *a retirement pension* ○ *an army pension* ○ *draw one's pension*, eg obtain it regularly from a Post Office ○ *live on a pension.* ⇨ article at RETIREMENT.

▷ **pension** *v* **1** [Tn] pay a pension to (sb). **2** (phr v) **pension sb off** (often passive) allow or force sb to retire, and pay him a pension: *He was pensioned off and replaced with a younger man.* **pension sth off** (often passive); (*infml*) no longer use sth, because it is old and worn: *The old printing press will have to be pensioned off.*

pensionable *adj* giving sb the right to receive a pension: *a pensionable job, position, post, etc* ○ *She is of pensionable age.*

pensioner /ˈpenʃənə(r)/ *n* person who is receiving a pension (esp an old-age pension): *an old-age pensioner.*

pension[2] /ˈpɒnsɪɒn/ *n* (*French*) small private hotel in France and certain other European countries.

pensive /ˈpensɪv/ *adj* thinking deeply about sth, esp in a sad or serious way: *a pensive expression, look, mood* ○ *She looked pensive when she heard the news.* ▷ **pensively** *adv.* **pensiveness** *n* [U].

penstock /ˈpenstɒk/ *n* **1** sluice or floodgate. **2** pipe or conduit for water.

penta- *comb form* having or made up of five of sth: *a pentagon* ○ *the pentathlon.*

pentagon /ˈpentəgən; *US* -gɒn/ *n* **1** [C] geometric figure with five sides and angles. **2 the Pentagon (a)** [sing] the five-sided building near Washington that is the headquarters of the US Department of Defence and the US armed forces. **(b)** [Gp] the leaders of the US armed forces: *a spokesman for the Pentagon.*

▷ **pentagonal** /penˈtægənl/ *adj* having five sides.

pentagram /ˈpentəgræm/ *n* star-like five-sided figure, formerly used as a magic symbol.

pentameter /penˈtæmɪtə(r)/ *n* line of verse with five metrical feet.

Pentateuch /ˈpentətjuːk/ *n* **the Pentateuch** [sing] the first five books of the Bible.

pentathlon /penˈtæθlən, -lɒn/ *n* (also **ˌmodern pentˈathlon**) athletic contest in which each competitor takes part in five events (running, riding, swimming, fencing and shooting). Cf BIATHLON.

Pentecost /ˈpentɪkɒst; *US* -kɔːst/ *n* [sing] **1** Jewish harvest festival that takes place fifty days after the second day of the Passover. **2** (*Brit* also **Whit Sunday**) (in the Christian Church) seventh Sunday after Easter, commemorating the descent of the Holy Ghost on the apostles.

▷ **pentecostal** /ˌpentɪˈkɒstl; *US* -ˈkɔːstl/ *adj* **1** of or relating to Pentecost. **2 Pentecostal** (of a religious group) emphasizing the divine gifts, esp the power to heal the sick. ⇨ article at RELIGION.

penthouse /ˈpenthaʊs/ *n* **1** house or flat built on the roof of a tall building: [attrib] *a luxury penthouse flat/apartment/suite.* **2** sloping roof (esp for a shelter or shed) attached to the wall of a building and supported by it.

pent up /ˌpent ˈʌp/ *adj* (of feelings) not expressed; repressed: *feelings that have been pent up for too long* ○ *ˌpent-up ˈanger, eˈmotion, fruˈstration, etc.*

penultimate /penˈʌltɪmət/ *adj* [attrib] next to and before the last one; last but one: *the penultimate letter of a word* ○ *the penultimate day of the month.*

penumbra /pɪˈnʌmbrə/ *n* (*pl* **-brae** /-briː/ or **-bras** /-brəz/) partly shaded area around the shadow of an opaque object (esp around the total shadow of the moon or earth in an eclipse). Cf UMBRA.

penurious /pɪˈnjʊərɪəs; *US* -ˈnʊr-/ *adj* (*fml*) **1** very poor. **2** mean with money; stingy. ▷ **penuriously** *adv.* **penuriousness** *n* [U] = PENURY.

penury /ˈpenjʊrɪ/ *n* [U] (*fml*) extreme poverty: *living in penury* ○ *reduced to penury.*

peon /ˈpiːən/ *n* **1** (in India, etc) person employed as a messenger. **2** (in Latin America) farm labourer.

peony /ˈpiːənɪ/ *n* garden plant with large round pink, red or white flowers.

people /ˈpiːpl/ *n* **1** [pl *v*] persons: *Were there many people at the party?* ○ *Some people are very inquisitive.* ○ *streets crowded with people* ○ *He meets a lot of famous people in his job.* ○ *Many old people live alone.* ⇨ Usage at MAN[1]. **2 (a)** [C] (all the persons belonging to a) nation, race, tribe or community: *the English-speaking peoples* ○ *The Spartans were a warlike people.* **(b)** [pl *v*] those persons who live in a particular place or have a particular nationality: *the people* (ie inhabitants) *of London* ○ *the British, French, Russian, etc people.* ⇨ Usage. **3 the people** [pl *v*] the citizens of a country, esp those with the right to vote: *The President no longer has the support of the people.* **4 the people** [pl *v*] ordinary persons who do not have a special rank or position in society: *the common people* ○ *a man of the people*, eg a politician who is popular with ordinary people. **5** [pl *v*] subjects (of a king) or supporters (of a leader): *a king loved by his people* ○ *His people worked hard to get him elected.* **6** [pl *v*] (*infml*) person's parents or other relatives: *She's spending Christmas with her people.* **7** (idm) **know, cultivate, etc the right people** ⇨ RIGHT[1]. **people (who live) in glass-houses shouldn't throw stones** (*saying*) one should not criticize others for faults similar to one's own.

▷ **people** *v* [esp passive: Tn, Tn·pr] fill (a place, an area, etc) with people; populate: *He believes the world is peopled with idiots.*

NOTE ON USAGE: Compare **person, persons, people** and **peoples. 1 People** is the most usual plural of **person. Persons** is formal and mostly used in legal language. **2 Person** can also sound formal and is often avoided. In general statements, the sentence can be made plural: *A person has the right to defend himself/People have the right to defend themselves.* When referring to a particular situation, we can say *I saw someone/a man/a woman riding a horse* instead of *I saw a person riding a horse.* **3 People** is also a singular noun (plural **peoples**) meaning 'nation', 'tribe' or 'race': *The Ancient Egyptians were a fascinating people.* ○ *The French-speaking peoples of the world.*

pep /pep/ *n* [U] (*infml*) feeling of liveliness; vigour: *full of pep and running around like a puppy.*

▷ **pep** *v* (**-pp-**) (phr v) **pep sb/sth up** make sb/sth (feel) more lively or energetic; stimulate sb/sth: *A walk in the fresh air will pep me up.* ○ *lively music to pep up the party.*

□ **ˈpep pill** pill containing a drug (usu amphetamine) that stimulates the nervous system.

ˈpep talk talk intended to improve morale, esp by encouraging the listener(s) to work harder, try to win, etc: *The team was given a pep talk on the morning of the big match.*

pepper /ˈpepə(r)/ *n* **1** [U] hot-tasting powder made from the dried berries of certain plants and used for flavouring food: *a dash of pepper.* **2** [C] **(a)** garden plant with large green, yellow or red hollow seed pods; capsicum. **(b)** one of these pods used as a vegetable: *peppers stuffed with meat and rice.*

▷ **pepper** *v* **1** [Tn] put pepper on (food). **2** [Tn·pr] ~ **sb/sth with sth** hit sb/sth repeatedly with small objects: *The wall had been peppered with bullets.* ○ *a batsman peppering the field with shots* ○ (*fig*) *pepper sb with questions.*

peppery /ˈpepərɪ/ *adj* **1** tasting of or like pepper. **2** easily angered; hot-tempered: *a peppery old colonel.*

□ **ˌpepper-and-ˈsalt** *adj* **1** (of cloth) having dark and light wools woven together to show a mixture of dark and light spots. **2** (of hair) white and brown together.

ˈpeppercorn *n* dried berry that is ground to make pepper. **ˌpeppercorn ˈrent** very low rent.

ˈpepper-mill *n* container in which peppercorns are ground to powder for sprinkling on food.

ˈpepper-pot *n* (*US* **ˈpepper box**) small container with holes in the top, used for sprinkling pepper on food. Cf SALT-CELLAR (SALT).

peppermint /ˈpepəmɪnt/ *n* **(a)** [U] type of mint grown for its strong-flavoured oil which is used in sweets and in medicine: *oil of peppermint.* **(b)** (also **mint**) [C] sweet flavoured with oil of peppermint: *suck a peppermint* ○ [attrib] *peppermint creams.* Cf SPEARMINT.

pepsin /ˈpepsɪn/ *n* [U] liquid produced in the stomach which helps food to be digested.

▷ **peptic** /ˈpeptɪk/ *adj* of digestion or the digestive system: *a peptic ulcer*, ie one in the digestive system.

peptide /ˈpeptaɪd/ *n* any of a group of compounds consisting of a chain of amino acids. Some are important as hormones, others as antibiotics.

Pepys /piːps/ Samuel (1633-1703), English diarist. He was an official in the service of *Charles II and *James II, and his diary gives a fascinating account of court and social life of the period.

per /pə(r); *strong form* pɜː(r)/ *prep* (used to express rates, prices, etc) for each (unit of time, length, etc): *£60 per day* ○ *£2 per person* ○ *calculated per square yard* ○ *45 revolutions per minute* ○ *100 miles per hour.*

perambulate /pəˈræmbjʊleɪt/ *v* (*fml or rhet*) **1** [Tn] walk about, through or over (a place): *perambulate the boundaries of his estate.* **2** [I] walk around or up and down: *perambulate after lunch.*

▷ **perambulation** /pəˌræmbjʊˈleɪʃn/ *n* [C, U]: *He saw many strange things during his perambulations in the old city.*

perambulator /pəˈræmbjʊleɪtə(r)/ *n* (*Brit fml*) pram.

per annum /ˌpər ˈænəm/ (*Latin*) for each year; per

year: *an income of £26 000 per annum.*

per capita /ˌpə ˈkæpɪtə/ *adj* [attrib], *adv* (*Latin*) of or for each person in a population, esp expressed as an average: *a per capita income of £12 000 a year.*

perceive /pəˈsiːv/ *v* **1** [Tn, Tf, Tw, Tnt, Tng] (*fml*) become aware of (sb/sth); notice; observe: *I perceived a change in his behaviour/that his behaviour had changed.* ○ *We had already perceived how the temperature fluctuated.* ○ *The patient was perceived to have difficulty in standing and walking.* **2** [Cn·n/a] ~ **sth as sth** interpret sth in a certain way; view: *I perceived his comment as a challenge.* ▷ **perceivable** *adj.*

per cent, *US* **percent** /pə ˈsent/ *adj, adv* in or for every hundred: *a fifty per cent* (ie 50%) *increase in price* ○ *working twenty per cent harder.*

▷ **per cent** (*US* **percent**) *n* [C] one part in every hundred; percentage: *half a per cent* (ie 0.5%) ○ *Over sixty per cent of families own/owns a television.* ○ *What per cent of the population read/reads books?*

percentage /pəˈsentɪdʒ/ *n* **1** [C] rate, number or amount in each hundred: *The figure is expressed as a percentage.* ○ *The salesmen get a percentage* (ie a commission) *on everything they sell.* ○ [attrib] *a percentage increase in ticket prices.* **2** [sing or pl *v*] proportion: *What percentage of his income is taxable?* ○ *An increasing percentage of the population own their own homes.*

percentile /pəˈsentaɪl/ (*US* **centile**) *n* (**a**) (in statistics) any of 99 points at which a range of data is divided to make 100 groups of equal size. (**b**) any of these groups: *an examination score in the 85th percentile,* ie a score higher than 85 per cent of all scores attained in an examination.

perceptible /pəˈseptəbl/ *adj* ~ (**to sb**) (*fml*) **1** that can be observed with the senses: *perceptible movements, sounds, etc.* **2** great enough to be noticed or observed: *perceptible change, deterioration, improvement, increase, loss of colour.* ▷ **perceptibility** /pəˌseptəˈbɪlətɪ/ *n* [U]. **perceptibly** /-əblɪ/ *adv*: *The patient has improved perceptibly.*

perception /pəˈsepʃn/ *n* [U] (*fml*) **1** ability to see, hear or understand: *improve one's powers of perception.* **2** quality of understanding; insight: *His analysis of the problem showed great perception.* **3** ~ (**that...**) way of seeing or understanding sth: *My perception of the matter is that...* ○ *his perception that conditions had not changed.*

perceptive /pəˈseptɪv/ *adj* (*fml*) **1** quick to notice and understand things: *The most perceptive of the three, she was the first to realize the potential danger of their situation.* **2** having or showing understanding or insight; discerning: *a perceptive analysis, comment, judgement, etc.* **3** [attrib] of or concerning perception: *perceptive skills.* ▷ **perceptively** *adv.* **perceptiveness**, **perceptivity** /ˌpɜːsepˈtɪvətɪ/ *ns* [U]: *show rare perceptiveness.*

perch[1] /pɜːtʃ/ *n* **1** (**a**) place where a bird rests, eg a branch. (**b**) bar or rod for this purpose,eg in a bird-cage or hen-roost. **2** (*infml*) high seat or position: *He watched the game from his perch on top of the wall.* **3** (also **pole**, **rod**) measure of length equal to $5\frac{1}{2}$ yds or 5·03 metres, used esp for land. ⇨ App 10. **4** (idm) **knock sb off his pedestal/perch** ⇨ KNOCK.

▷ **perch** *v* **1** [I, Ipr] ~ (**on sth**) (of a bird) come to rest or stay (on a branch, etc): *The birds perched on the television aerial.* **2** [I, Ipr] ~ (**on sth**) (of a person) sit, esp on sth high or narrow: *perch on high stools at the bar* ○ *perch dangerously on a narrow ledge* ○ *perch on the edge of one's seat.* **3** [Tn, Tn·pr] place (sth) esp in a high or dangerous position: *a hut perched at the edge of the cliff* ○ *perch a beret on the side of one's head* ○ *a castle perched above the river.*

perch[2] /pɜːtʃ/ *n* (*pl* **unchanged**) any of several types of freshwater fish with spiny fins, eaten as food.

perchance /pəˈtʃɑːns; *US* -ˈtʃæns/ *adv* (*arch*) **1** perhaps. **2** by chance.

percipient /pəˈsɪpɪənt/ *adj* (*fml*) **1** noticing or understanding things quickly or clearly; perceptive: *a percipient onlooker.* **2** having or showing insight; discerning: *a percipient comment.* ▷ **percipience** /pəˈsɪpɪəns/ *n* [U].

percolate /ˈpɜːkəleɪt/ *v* **1** (also *infml* **perk**) (**a**) [I, Ipr, Ip] ~ (**through sth**)/ ~ (**through**) (of water) pass slowly through (coffee); filter through: *The coffee is percolating,* ie Boiling water is passing through ground coffee beans. (**b**) [Tn, Tn·pr, Tn·p] ~ (**sth through** (**sth**) cause (water) to pass slowly through (coffee): *coffee made by percolating boiling water through ground coffee beans* ○ *I'll percolate some coffee,* ie make it by percolating. **2** (**a**) [Ipr, Ip] ~ **sth** (**through sth/through**) (of liquid) pass slowly through (sth): *water percolating through sand.* (**b**) [Ipr] ~ **through sth** (of an idea, a feeling, information) spread or become known gradually: *The rumour percolated through the firm.*

▷ **percolation** /ˌpɜːkəˈleɪʃn/ *n* [C, U].

percolator *n* (**a**) pot for making and serving coffee, in which boiling water is repeatedly forced up a central tube and filtered down through ground coffee. (**b**) any other apparatus for percolating liquids.

percussion /pəˈkʌʃn/ *n* **1** [U] (**a**) striking of two (usu hard) objects together. (**b**) sound or shock that is the result of this. **2** [U] method of playing a musical instrument by striking it with another object. **3 the percussion** [pl *v*] (also **perˈcussion section**) (players of) percussion instruments in an orchestra. ⇨ illus at MUSIC. **4** [U] (*medical*) gentle tapping of the surface of the body as part of a medical examination.

▷ **percussionist** /-ʃənɪst/ *n* person who plays percussion instruments.

□ **perˈcussion cap** (also **cap**) small metal or paper device containing explosive powder, which explodes when struck.

perˈcussion instrument musical instrument (eg drum, tambourine, xylophone) played by striking it with another object.

perdition /pəˈdɪʃn/ *n* [U] **1** (*fml religion*) everlasting punishment of the wicked after death: *damned to perdition.* **2** (*arch*) total destruction.

peregrination /ˌperɪgrɪˈneɪʃn/ *n* (*fml*) **1** [U] travelling. **2** [C] journey: *his peregrinations in southern Europe.*

peregrine /ˈperɪgrɪn/ *n* (also **peregrine falcon**) large black and white bird of prey that can be trained to hunt and catch small birds and animals.

peremptory /pəˈremptərɪ; *US* ˈperəmptɔːrɪ/ *adj* (*fml*) **1** (*esp derog*) (of a person, his manner, etc) insisting on immediate obedience or submission; domineering: *His peremptory tone of voice irritated everybody.* **2** (of commands) not to be disobeyed or questioned: *a peremptory dismissal, rebuke, shout.* ▷ **peremptorily** /-trəlɪ; *US* -tɔːrəlɪ/ *adv.*

□ **peˌremptory ˈwrit** (*law*) document in which a defendant is ordered to appear in court.

perennial /pəˈrenɪəl/ *adj* **1** lasting for a long time: *a perennial subject of interest.* **2** constantly recurring: *a perennial problem* ○ *perennial complaints.* **3** (of plants) living for more than two years.

▷ **perennial** *n* perennial plant: *hardy perennials,* ie plants that can normally tolerate frost. **perennially** /-nɪəlɪ/ *adv.*

perestroika /ˌpereˈstrɔɪkə/ *n* [U] (*Russian*) restructuring of the Soviet economic and political system.

perfect[1] /ˈpɜːfɪkt/ *adj* **1** (**a**) having everything needed; complete: *in perfect condition* ○ *a perfect set of teeth.* (**b**) without fault; excellent: *a perfect performance of the play* ○ *perfect weather, behaviour* ○ *a perfect score,* ie one in which no points have been lost; 100 per cent ○ *Nobody is perfect.* ○ *speak perfect English.* **2** the best of its kind; ideal: *the perfect meal* ○ *the perfect crime,* ie one in which the criminal is never discovered. **3** exact; precise: *a perfect circle, square* ○ *a perfect copy, match, fit* ○ *perfect accuracy, timing.* **4** ~ **for sb/sth** highly suitable for sb/sth; exactly right for sb/sth: *perfect for each other* ○ *perfect day for a picnic.* **5** (*grammar*) (of verb tenses) composed of *has/have* or *had* + past participle: *the present and past perfect tenses,* eg 'I have eaten'/'I had eaten'. **6** [attrib] (*infml*) total; absolute: *perfect nonsense, rubbish, etc* ○ *a perfect fool, pest, stranger, etc* ○ *She's a perfect angel!* **7** [attrib] (*music*) (of an interval) falling between the tonic and the fourth, fifth or octave in a major or minor scale: *a perfect fifth.* Cf AUGMENTED (AUGMENT). **8** (idm) **practice makes perfect** ⇨ PRACTICE.

▷ **perfect** *n* **the perfect** [sing] perfect tense: *The verb is in the perfect.* ○ *the present/past perfect.*

perfectly *adv* **1** in a perfect way: *The trousers fit perfectly.* **2** completely; quite: *perfectly happy, satisfied, content, etc* ○ *perfectly well* ○ *perfectly able to find her own way.* **3** (*infml*) extremely; absolutely: *a perfectly delicious cake* ○ *perfectly awful weather* ○ *a perfectly foul headache.*

□ **ˌperfect ˈpitch** (also **ˌabsolute ˈpitch**) (*music*) ability to recognize or sing any musical note: *She has perfect/absolute pitch.*

perfect[2] /pəˈfekt/ *v* [Tn] make (sth) perfect or complete: *She needs to perfect her Arabic before going to work in Cairo.* ○ *a violinist who spent years perfecting his technique.*

▷ **perfectible** *adj* that can be perfected. **perfectibility** /pəˌfektəˈbɪlətɪ/ *n* [U].

perfection /pəˈfekʃn/ *n* **1** [U] making perfect: *They are working on the perfection of their new paint formula.* **2** [U] state of being perfect; faultlessness: *Perfection is impossible to achieve in that kind of work.* ○ *aim for perfection* ○ *bring sth to perfection.* **3** [U] highest state or quality; ideal: *Her singing was perfection.* **4** (idm) **a counsel of perfection** ⇨ COUNSEL. **to perˈfection** exactly to the right degree; perfectly: *wine aged to perfection* ○ *a dish cooked to perfection.*

▷ **perfectionist** /-ʃənɪst/ *n* **1** person who is not satisfied with anything less than perfection. **2** (*derog*) person who insists on perfection in every detail even when it is not necessary. **perfectionism** /pəˈfekʃənɪzəm/ *n* [U].

perfidy /ˈpɜːfɪdɪ/ *n* ~ (**to/towards sb**) (*fml*) (**a**) [U] acting in a treacherous or disloyal way. (**b**) [C] instance of this.

▷ **perfidious** /pəˈfɪdɪəs/ *adj* **1** ~ (**to/towards sb**) (*fml*) treacherous, deceitful or disloyal: *betrayed by perfidious allies.* **2** (idm) **perˌfidious ˈAlbion** (*derog*) England considered as being an untrustworthy or treacherous country, esp by the French. **perfidiously** *adv.* **perfidiousness** *n* [U].

perforate /ˈpɜːfəreɪt/ *v* [Tn] **1** make a hole or holes through (sth): *perforate the cover to let air in* ○ [attrib] *a perforated ulcer.* **2** make a row of small holes (esp in paper) so that it will tear easily: [attrib] *a perforated sheet of postage stamps.*

▷ **perforation** /ˌpɜːfəˈreɪʃn/ *n* **1** [U] perforating or being perforated. **2** [C] series of small holes made in paper, etc: *tear the sheet along the perforations.*

perforce /pəˈfɔːs/ *adv* (*arch or fml*) because it is necessary or inevitable.

perform /pəˈfɔːm/ *v* **1** [Tn] do (a piece of work, sth one is ordered to do, sth one has agreed to do): *perform a task, one's duty, a miracle* ○ *perform an operation to save his life.* **2** [I, Ipr, Tn] act (a play), play (a piece of music) or do (tricks) to entertain an audience: *They are performing his play/piano concerto tonight.* ○ *watch sb perform* ○ *perform skilfully on the flute* ○ *perform live on television* ○ *performing seals in a circus.* **3** [I] (of a machine, invention, etc) work or function: *How is the new car performing?* ○ *the new drug has performed well in tests.* **4** [Tn] act in an official way (at sth): *perform a ceremony, rite, ritual, etc.*

▷ **performer** *n* person who performs in front of an audience: *an accomplished performer.*

□ **perˌforming ˈarts** drama, music, dance, etc which are performed in front of an audience. ⇨ article.

performance /pəˈfɔːməns/ *n* **1** [sing] process or manner of performing: *faithful in the performance of his duties.* **2** (**a**) [C] performing of a play at the theatre or some other entertainment: *the evening performance* ○ *give a performance of 'Hamlet'.* (**b**) [U] **in** ~ performing in a concert or other entertainment: *Come and see her in performance with the new band.* **3** (**a**) [C] (esp outstanding) action or achievement: *She won a gold medal for*

The Performing Arts

The performing arts in Britain range from the work of the major national theatre, opera and ballet companies to the smaller touring companies, many of which do experimental work.

Ballet and opera have become increasingly popular in Britain, and are performed by a number of companies. Two of the best-known are the Royal Opera and the Royal Ballet, both based at the Royal Opera House at Covent Garden in London. The English National Opera, with its home at the Coliseum Theatre, London, specializes in performances of opera in English. The Welsh National Opera and the Scottish Opera both tour in the whole of Britain and have become established as major companies.

Britain's leading ballet company is the Birmingham Royal Ballet, based in Birmingham. (Until 1990 it was known as the Sadler's Wells Royal Ballet and was based at the Sadler's Wells Theatre in London.) Other well-known companies specializing in modern ballet are the Rambert Dance Company and the London Contemporary Dance Theatre.

The two leading American opera companies are the Metropolitan Opera and the New York City Opera, both in New York.

British and American ballet are largely of 20th-century origin. Modern dance was developed in the USA, notably in the work of the New York City Ballet. Many of the new forms of American ballet were directly inspired by the work of the teacher and choreographer Martha Graham.

British theatre traces its origins back to medieval mystery and morality plays. In its present form, it has evolved mainly from the theatre of the Elizabethan era, when drama reached a high point in the comedies and tragedies of Shakespeare. The theatre flourished again at the time of the Restoration (1660) after a period when it was banned under Cromwell. It was at this time that women first began to act on the stage. The many comedies of the period had their successors in plays by such well-known 18th-century dramatists as Goldsmith and Sheridan. There was then a general decline in British drama until the end of the 19th century, when there was a revival with the plays of George Bernard Shaw and Oscar Wilde. The 20th century has seen the comedies of Noël Coward and the distinctive 'naturalistic' school of drama of such writers as John Galsworthy, Terence Rattigan and more recently Alan Ayckbourn. Other developments in modern British drama have included the 'absurd' school of Samuel Beckett, the social drama of John Osborne (the original 'Angry Young Man'), Arnold Wesker and John Arden, and the unique blend of realism and the absurd in the plays of Harold Pinter.

In the USA, the leading dramatist of the 20th century was Eugene O'Neill. Other dramatists, such as Tennessee Williams, Arthur Miller and Edward Albee, have written important plays dealing with such themes as isolation and illusion.

London is the centre of theatrical life in Britain. Shakespeare's Globe Theatre was in London and a modern reconstruction of it is being built near the original site. Many of the theatres famous in the past remain in use today, for example the Haymarket, the Theatre Royal in Drury Lane and the Old Vic. In more modern times, the Royal National Theatre has earned a high reputation for the plays staged in its three auditoriums. Almost all London's popular theatres are in the West End, with Shaftesbury Avenue as the focal point. One of Britain's leading theatre companies is the Royal Shakespeare Company, with bases at both the Royal Shakespeare Theatre, Stratford, and the Barbican Theatre, London. The English Stage Company, based at the Royal Court Theatre, London, specializes in modern drama.

Outside London, the large cities and many smaller towns have theatres where visiting companies perform and some cities also have their own repertory companies. Among the best-known are the Glasgow Citizens' Theatre, the Nottingham Playhouse, the Manchester Royal Exchange and the Haymarket in Leicester. There are many annual festivals of theatre, dance and music. One of the most important festivals is the Edinburgh International Festival. The Edinburgh 'fringe' performances are as important a part of the festival as the main productions and offer new and experimental work.

Both the performing and visual arts in Britain receive funding from the Arts Council of Great Britain, which in recent years has had a policy of encouraging the arts in the regions.

The theatrical centre of the USA is New York, and in particular Broadway. The Broadway Theatre was itself modelled on London's Haymarket Theatre. New York also has the so called 'little theatres' staging amateur productions, as well as 'off-Broadway', a term for those professional theatres that lie outside the central Broadway area and that produce mainly experimental and avant-garde plays. A development of the latter in turn is 'off-off-Broadway', a term for the highly experimental productions put on in small halls and cafés. One noted off-Broadway theatre group was Living Theatre, which staged many improvisational and 'revolutionary' plays in the 1950s and 1960s. (Cf article at MUSIC.)

her fine performance in the contest. ○ *His performance in the test was not good enough.* **(b)** [U] ability to move quickly, operate efficiently, etc: *The customer was impressed by the machine's performance.* ○ *Performance is less important than reliability in a car.* 4 [C] (*infml*) **(a)** ridiculous or disgraceful behaviour: *What a performance the child made!* **(b)** (esp unnecessary) fuss or trouble: *He goes through the whole performance of checking the oil and water every time he drives the car.*

perfume /ˈpɜːfjuːm; *US also* pərˈfjuːm/ *n* [C, U] **1** fragrant or pleasant smell: *the perfume of the flowers* ○ *flowery perfumes.* **2** (any of several types of) sweet-smelling liquid, often made from flowers, used esp on the body: *sell perfumes and toilet-waters* ○ *French perfume.*

▷ **perfume** /pəˈfjuːm/ *v* [Tn] **1** (of flowers, etc) give a fragrant smell to (sth): *The roses perfumed the room.* **2** put perfume on (sb/sth): *perfume a handkerchief.*

perfumer /pəˈfjuːmə(r)/ (also **perfumier** /pəˈfjuːmɪeɪ/) *n* person who makes and/or sells perfume.

perfumery /pəˈfjuːmərɪ/ *n* **1** [C] place where perfumes are made or sold. **2** [U] process of making perfume.

perfunctory /pəˈfʌŋktərɪ/ *adj* **(a)** (of an action) done as a duty or routine, without care or interest: *a perfunctory examination, greeting, salute.* **(b)** (of a person) doing things in this way. ▷ **perfunctorily** /-trəlɪ; *US* -tɔːrəlɪ/ *adv*: *check the luggage perfunctorily.* **perfunctoriness** *n* [U].

pergola /ˈpɜːgələ/ *n* structure of posts for climbing plants, forming an arbour or a covered walk in a garden.

perhaps /pəˈhæps, *also* præps/ *adv* it may be (that); possibly: *Perhaps the weather will change this evening.* ○ *Perhaps it will, perhaps it won't.* ○ *It is, perhaps, the best known of his works.* ○ *Perhaps not/so*, ie expressing half-hearted agreement with what a person says. ○ *Perhaps you would be kind enough to...*, ie a polite way of saying 'Would you...?'

peri- *pref* **1** around: *periscope* ○ *periphrasis* ○ *perimeter.* **2** near: *perihelion* ○ *perigee.*

pericardium /ˌperɪˈkɑːdɪəm/ *n* (*pl* **-ia** /-ɪə/) membrane that surrounds the heart.

pericarp /ˈperɪkɑːp/ *n* part of a fruit(2) containing the seed, formed from the wall of the ovary as it hardens. ➪ illus at FRUIT.

Pericles /ˈperɪkliːz/ (c 495-429 BC), Athenian statesman and general. He was one of the greatest figures of the Athenian empire at its height, famous for his *Funeral Oration* in which he described Athenian qualities. He built the *Parthenon, commanded the Athenian army in the early *Peloponnesian War, and was a friend of artists and philosophers. ▷ **Periclean** /ˌperɪˈkliːən/ *adj*: *Periclean Athens.*

perigee /ˈperɪdʒiː/ *n* point in the orbit of the moon, a planet or spacecraft at which it is nearest to the earth.

perihelion /ˌperɪˈhiːlɪən/ *n* (*pl* **-lia** /-lɪə/) point in the orbit of a planet, comet, etc at which it is nearest to the sun.

peril /ˈperəl/ *n* **1** [U] serious danger (esp of death): *in great, mortal, etc peril.* **2** [C usu *pl*] dangerous thing or circumstance: *face the perils of the ocean*, ie storm, shipwreck, etc ○ *These birds are able to survive the perils of the Arctic winter.* **3** (idm) **at one's peril** (used esp when advising sb not to do sth) with a risk of harm to oneself: *The bicycle has no brakes — you ride it at your peril.* ○ *One ignores letters from the bank manager at one's peril.* **in ˌperil of one's ˈlife** in danger of death.

▷ **perilous** /ˈperələs/ *adj* full of risk; dangerous: *a perilous journey across the mountains.* **perilously** *adv*: *perilously hot, fast, steep, etc* ○ *They were perilously close to the edge of the precipice.*

perimeter /pəˈrɪmɪtə(r)/ *n* **1** (length of the) outer edge of a closed geometric shape. **2** boundary of an area: *Guards patrolled the perimeter of the airfield.* ○ [attrib] *the perimeter fence.* Cf CIRCUMFERENCE.

perinatal /ˌperɪˈneɪtl/ *adj* occurring just before or after birth: *perinatal care.*

perineum /ˌperɪˈniːəm/ *n* (*pl* **-nea** /-ˈniːə/) part of the body between the anus and a woman's vulva or a man's scrotum.

period /ˈpɪərɪəd/ *n* **1** length or portion of time: *a period of three years* ○ *He has had several long periods of work abroad.* ○ *a period of peace, recovery, uncertainty* ○ *showers and sunny periods*, eg in a weather forecast ○ *The work must be completed within a two-month period.* ○ *The incubation period* (ie The delay between catching a disease and the symptoms appearing) *is two weeks.* **2 (a)** portion of time in the life of a person, nation or civilization: *a painting belonging to the artist's early period* ○ *the period of the French Revolution* ○ *the post-war period* ○ *The house is 18th century and has furniture of the period*, ie of the same century. ○ *The actors wore costumes of the period*, ie of the time when the events of the play took place. ○ [usu attrib] *period dress, furniture, etc* ○ *a period cottage*, ie not modern. **(b)** (*geology*) portion of time in the development of the earth's surface; part of an era: *the Jurassic period.* Cf ERA, EPOCH. **3** (time allowed for a) lesson in school: *a teaching period of 45 minutes* ○ *a free period* ○ *three periods of geography a week.* **4 (a)** monthly flow of blood from the womb of a woman; menstruation: *have a period* ○ [attrib] *period pains.* **(b)** time of this. **5** (*esp US*) **(a)** = FULL STOP (FULL). **(b)** sign of punctuation (.) marking this in writing and print. ⇨ App 14. **(c)** (*infml*) (added to the end of a statement to stress its completeness): *We can't pay higher wages, period*, ie that is final. **6** (*grammar*) complete sentence, esp one having several clauses. **7** (*astronomy*) time taken to complete one revolution.

□ ˈ**period piece** (*infml*) old-fashioned person or thing: *The play, which once seemed so modern, has become a period piece.*

periodic /ˌpɪərɪˈɒdɪk/ *adj* occurring or appearing at (esp regular) intervals: *periodic attacks of dizziness* ○ *a periodic review of expenditure.*

▷ **periodical** /-kl/ *n, adj* (magazine or other publication) that is published at regular intervals, eg weekly or monthly. **periodically** /-klɪ/ *adv* at (esp regular) intervals.

□ ˌ**periodic** ˈ**table** (*chemistry*) arrangement of chemical elements according to their atomic weights. ⇨ App 11.

peripatetic /ˌperɪpəˈtetɪk/ *adj* **1** going from place to place. **2** (*Brit*) (of teachers) employed at two or more schools and travelling between them: *Peripatetic music teachers visit the school regularly.* ▷ **peripatetically** /-klɪ/ *adv.*

periphery /pəˈrɪfərɪ/ *n* (*fml*) **1 (a)** boundary of a surface or an area. **(b)** area near this on either side: *industrial development on the periphery* (ie outskirts) *of the town.* **2** (*fig*) (esp in social, political or intellectual life) position far away from the centre; the fringe: *The ideas are also expressed by minor poets on the periphery of the movement.*

▷ **peripheral** /-ərəl/ *adj* **1** ~ **(to sth)** of secondary or minor importance (to sth): *topics peripheral to the main theme.* **2** of or on a periphery: *peripheral zones.* — *n* (also **peˌripheral deˈvice**) (*computing*) device attached to a computer that transfers information into or out of the computer: *display units, printers and other peripherals.* **peripherally** /-ərəlɪ/ *adv.*

periphrasis /pəˈrɪfrəsɪs/ *n* (*pl* **-ases** /-əsiːz/) (*fml*) **1 (a)** [U] roundabout way of expressing sth; circumlocution. **(b)** [C] roundabout expression in speaking or writing, eg *'give expression to'* instead of *'express'*. **2** (*grammar*) **(a)** [U] use of an auxiliary word or a syntactic pattern in place of an inflected form, eg '*It does work*' for '*It works*' or '*the word of God*' for '*God's word*'. **(b)** [C] example of this.

▷ **periphrastic** /ˌperɪˈfræstɪk/ *adj* of, expressed in or using periphrasis. **periphrastically** /-klɪ/ *adv.*

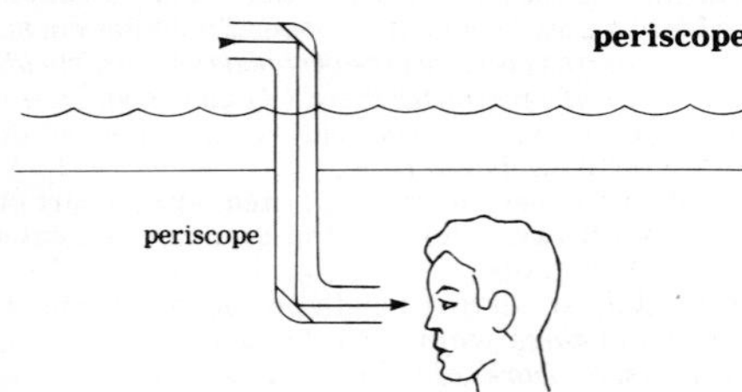

periscope /ˈperɪskəʊp/ *n* apparatus with mirrors and lenses arranged in a tube so that the user has a view of the surrounding area above, eg from a submarine when it is under water.

▷ **periscopic** /ˌperɪˈskɒpɪk/ *adj* of or like a periscope.

perish /ˈperɪʃ/ *v* **1** [I] (*fml*) be destroyed; die: *Thousands of people perished in the earthquake.* ○ *We shall do it or perish in the attempt.* **2** [I, Tn] (*esp Brit*) (cause sth to) rot; (cause rubber to) lose its elasticity: *The seal on the bottle has perished.* ○ *If any oil gets on the car tyres, it will perish them.* **3** (idm) ˌ**perish the** ˈ**thought** (*infml*) may it never happen: *The neighbours' children want to learn to play the trumpet, perish the thought!*

▷ **perishable** *adj* (esp of food) likely to decay or go bad quickly: *Perishable food should be stored in a refrigerator.* **perishables** *n* [pl] goods (esp food) which go bad or decay quickly, such as fish or soft fruit: *Perishables need to be consumed as quickly as possible.*

perished *adj* [pred] (*esp Brit*) in extreme discomfort through cold, etc: *We were perished with cold and hunger.* ○ *The children were perished when they arrived home.*

perisher *n* (*dated Brit sl*) annoying person, esp a child: *Wait till I catch the little perisher!*

perishing *adj* (*esp Brit*) **1** extremely cold: *I'm perishing!* ○ *It's perishing out there.* ○ *a period of perishing cold.* **2** (*dated sl*) (used to express annoyance) damned, etc: *I can't get in — I've lost the perishing key!* **perishing** (also **perishingly**) *adv* (*sl esp Brit*) (used to emphasize sth bad) very: *It's perishing/perishingly cold out there.* ○ *He's too perishing mean to pay his share.*

peristalsis /ˌperɪˈstælsɪs/ *n* [U] involuntary wavelike movement of muscles which sends food, etc through the intestines.

peristyle /ˈperɪstaɪl/ *n* (*architecture*) **(a)** row of columns around a temple, courtyard, etc: *the imposing peristyle of the Parthenon.* **(b)** area enclosed by this.

peritonitis /ˌperɪtəˈnaɪtɪs/ *n* [U] (*medical*) painful inflammation of the membrane that covers the inside wall of the abdomen.

periwinkle[1] /ˈperɪwɪŋkl/ *n* any of several types of evergreen plant with trailing stems and blue or white flowers: [attrib] *periwinkle blue.*

periwinkle[2] /ˈperɪwɪŋkl/ (also **winkle**) *n* any of several types of small edible shellfish shaped like a snail.

perjure /ˈpɜːdʒə(r)/ *v* [Tn] ~ **oneself** (*law*) deliberately tell a lie (esp in a court of law) after one has sworn an oath to tell the truth: *Several witnesses at the trial were clearly prepared to perjure themselves in order to protect the accused.*

▷ **perjurer** /ˈpɜːdʒərə(r)/ *n* (*law*) person who has perjured himself.

perjury /ˈpɜːdʒərɪ/ *n* (*law*) **(a)** [U] action of perjuring oneself: *They tried to persuade her to commit perjury.* **(b)** [C] lie told after swearing to tell the truth, esp in a court of law.

perk[1] /pɜːk/ *v* (phr v) **perk up** (*infml*) become more cheerful, lively or vigorous, esp after illness or depression: *He looked depressed but perked up when his friends arrived.* **perk sb/sth up** (*infml*) **(a)** make sb feel more cheerful or lively: *A holiday would perk you up.* **(b)** make sb look smarter: *He had perked himself up for the occasion.* **(c)** make (an outfit, a room, a garden, etc look smarter, better, more vigorous, etc: *perk up the plants with a good watering* ○ *You need a bright red scarf to perk up that grey suit.* lift up (one's head or ears): *The horse perked up its head when I shouted.*

▷ **perky** *adj* (**-ier, -iest**) (*infml*) **1** full of energy; lively: *He's still in hospital, but he seems quite perky.* **2** (too) full of self-confidence; cheeky: *That child is a bit too perky!* **perkily** /-ɪlɪ/ *adv.* **perkiness** *n* [U].

perk[2] /pɜːk/ *n* (usu *pl*) (*infml*) **(a)** money or goods received as a right in addition to one's pay; perquisite: *His perks include a car provided by the firm.* **(b)** advantage or benefit of a particular job, one's position, etc: *One of the perks is the use of the official car park.*

perk[3] /pɜːk/ *v* = PERCOLATE 1.

perm /pɜːm/ *n* **1** (*infml*) = PERMANENT WAVE (PERMANENT). **2** (*infml*) = PERMUTATION 1.

▷ **perm** *v* [Tn] **1** give (sb's hair) a permanent wave: *Her hair has been permed.* **2** make a permutation of (numbers) in a football pool.

permafrost /ˈpɜːməfrɒst; *US* -frɔːst/ *n* [U] subsoil that is permanently frozen, eg in polar regions.

permanence /ˈpɜːmənəns/ *n* [U] state of continuing or remaining for a long time: *Nothing threatens the permanence of the system.*

▷ **permanency** /-nənsɪ/ *n* (*fml*) **1** [U] = PERMANENCE. **2** [C] permanent thing (esp a job): *Is the new post a permanency?*

permanent /ˈpɜːmənənt/ *adj* **1 (a)** lasting or expected to last for a long time or for ever: *She is looking for permanent employment.* ○ *The injury left him with a permanent limp.* **(b)** not likely to change: *my permanent address.* Cf IMPERMANENT, TEMPORARY. **2** [attrib] (*Brit*) (of a government official) belonging to the Civil Service rather than to the elected government: *the Permanent Secretary at the Foreign Office.* ▷ **permanently** *adv.*

□ ˌ**permanent** ˈ**magnet** magnet that keeps its magnetization after the magnetic field that produced it has been taken away.

ˌ**permanent-**ˈ**press** *adj* (of clothing) chemically treated so that original creases will last, and that other unwanted creases will not appear.

ˈ**permanent tooth** tooth that replaces a milk-tooth (MILK[1]) in mammals, and may last for the rest of life.

ˌ**permanent** ˈ**wave** (*fml*) (*abbr* **perm**) (*US* **permanent**) method of styling the hair in which it is treated with chemicals and set in waves or curls that last for several months.

ˌ**permanent** ˈ**way** (*Brit*) railway track and the foundation on which it is laid.

permanganate /pəˈmæŋgəneɪt/ *n* [U] (also **poˌtassium perˈmanganate**, **perˌmanganate of** ˈ**potash**) dark purple salt of an acid containing manganese, used as a disinfectant and antiseptic when dissolved in water.

permeate /ˈpɜːmɪeɪt/ *v* [Ipr, Tn] ~ **(through) sth** (*fml*) enter sth and spread to every part: *Water has permeated (through) the soil.* ○ *The smell of cooking permeates (through) the flat.* ○ (*fig*) *A mood of defeat permeated the whole army.*

▷ **permeable** /ˈpɜːmɪəbl/ *adj* (*fml*) that can be permeated by fluids or gas; porous. Cf IMPERMEABLE. **permeability** /ˌpɜːmɪəˈbɪlətɪ/ *n* [U]. **permeation** /ˌpɜːmɪˈeɪʃn/ *n* [U] (*fml*) permeating or being permeated.

Permian /ˈpɜːmɪən/ *adj* of the period of the earth's history between about 286 and 248 million years ago, when large numbers of reptiles and amphibians began to appear. Cf PALAEOZOIC.

permissible /pəˈmɪsəbl/ *adj* (*fml*) that is or may be allowed: *Delay is not permissible, even for a single day.* ○ *driving with more than the permissible level of alcohol in the blood.* ▷ **permissibly** /-əblɪ/ *adv.*

permission /pəˈmɪʃn/ *n* [U] ~ **(to do sth)** act of allowing sb to do sth; consent: *You have my permission to leave.* ○ *She refused to give her permission.* ○ *They entered the area without permission.* ○ *with your (kind) permission*, ie if you will allow me.

permissive /pəˈmɪsɪv/ *adj* [usu attrib] (*often derog*) **(a)** allowing great freedom of behaviour, esp to children or in sexual matters: *a permissive upbringing* ○ *permissive parents.* **(b)** showing this freedom: *permissive attitudes, behaviour* ○ *the permissive society*, ie the one resulting from social changes that began in the 1960s, eg with greater freedom of sexual behaviour, lessening of censorship, etc.

▷ **permissively** *adv*: *children who have been brought up permissively.*

permissiveness *n* [U] being permissive in outlook or behaviour.

permit /pəˈmɪt/ *v* (**-tt-**) (*fml*) **1** [Tn, Tg, Dn·n, Dn·t] give permission for (sth); allow: *Dogs are not permitted in the building.* ○ *We do not permit smoking in the office.* ○ *The prisoners were permitted two hours' exercise a day.* ○ *Permit me to explain.* ○ *The council will not permit you to build here.* **2** [I, Tn, Cn·t] make (sth) possible: *I'll come tomorrow, weather permitting*, ie if the weather doesn't prevent me. ○ *The new road system permits the free flow of traffic at all times.* ○ *The windows permit light and air to enter.* **3** [Ipr no passive] (esp in negative sentences) ~ **of sth** admit sth as possible; tolerate: *the situation does not permit of any delay.*

▷ **permit** /ˈpɜːmɪt/ *n* official document that gives sb the right to do sth, esp to go somewhere: *You cannot enter a military base without a permit.*

permittivity /ˌpɜːmɪˈtɪvətɪ/ *n* [U] measure of the ability of a substance to store electrical energy when placed in an electrical field.

permutation /ˌpɜːmjuːˈteɪʃn/ *n (fml)* **1** *(esp mathematics)* **(a)** [U] variation in the order of a set of things. **(b)** [C] any one of these arrangements: *The permutations of x, y and z are xyz, xzy, yxz, yzx, zxy, zyx.* **2** *(infml* **perm)** *(Brit)* (esp in football pools) selection of items from a group, to be arranged in a number of combinations.

permute /pəˈmjuːt/ *v* [Tn] vary the order or arrangement of (sth).

pernicious /pəˈnɪʃəs/ *adj (fml)* ~ **(to sb/sth)** having a very harmful or destructive effect (on sb/sth): *a pernicious influence on society* ○ *a pernicious campaign to blacken his character* ○ *Pollution of the water supply reached a level pernicious to the health of the population.* ▷ **perniciously** *adv.* **perniciousness** *n* [U].

□ **perˌnicious aˈnaemia** *(medical)* severe form of anaemia that is sometimes fatal.

pernickety /pəˈnɪkətɪ/ *adj (infml often derog)* worrying too much about details or unimportant things; fussy.

peroration /ˌperəˈreɪʃn/ *n (fml)* **1** last part of a speech; summing up. **2** *(often derog)* lengthy speech: *We had to listen to a peroration on the evils of drink!*

peroxide /pəˈrɒksaɪd/ *n* [U] **1** any of several compounds of oxygen with another element, containing the maximum proportion of oxygen. **2** (also **ˌhydrogen peˈroxide, peˌroxide of ˈhydrogen**) colourless liquid used as an antiseptic and to bleach hair: [attrib] *a peroxide blonde*, ie a woman with hair that has been bleached with peroxide.

▷ **peroxide** *v* [Tn] bleach (hair) with hydrogen peroxide: *peroxided curls.*

perpendicular /ˌpɜːpənˈdɪkjʊlə(r)/ *adj* **1** ~ **(to sth)** at an angle of 90° (to another line or surface): *a line drawn perpendicular to another.* **2** at a right angle to the horizontal; upright: *the perpendicular marble columns of a Greek temple.* **3** (of a cliff, rock-face, etc) rising very steeply: *The valley ended in a perpendicular rim of granite.* **4** (also **Perpendicular**) *(architecture)* of the style of English Gothic architecture in the 14th and 15th centuries, characterized by the use of vertical lines in its decoration. ➪ article at ARCHITECTURE.

▷ **perpendicular** *n* **1** [C] perpendicular line. **2** (also **the perpendicular**) [U] perpendicular position or direction: *The wall is a little out of (the) perpendicular.*

perpendicularity /ˌpɜːpənˌdɪkjʊˈlærətɪ/ *n* [U].

perpendicularly *adv.*

perpetrate /ˈpɜːpɪtreɪt/ *v* [Tn] *(fml or joc)* **(a)** commit (a crime, etc): *perpetrate a dreadful outrage.* **(b)** be guilty of (a blunder, an error, etc): *Who perpetrated that dreadful extension to the front of the building?*

▷ **perpetration** /ˌpɜːpɪˈtreɪʃn/ *n* [U].

perpetrator *n* person who commits a crime or does sth considered outrageous: *the perpetrator of a hoax.*

perpetual /pəˈpetʃʊəl/ *adj* [usu attrib] **1** continuing indefinitely; permanent: *the perpetual snow of the Arctic.* **2** without interruption; continuous: *the perpetual noise of traffic.* **3** *(infml)* frequently repeated; continual: *He was irritated by their perpetual complaints.* ▷ **perpetually** /-tʃʊəlɪ/ *adv.*

□ **perˌpetual ˈmotion** [U] movement (eg of an imagined machine) that would continue for ever without getting power from an outside source.

perpetuate /pəˈpetʃʊeɪt/ *v* [Tn] cause (sth) to continue: *These measures will perpetuate the hostility between the two groups.* ○ *They decided to perpetuate the memory of their leader by erecting a statue.* ▷ **perpetuation** /pəˌpetʃʊˈeɪʃn/ *n* [U].

perpetuity /ˌpɜːpɪˈtjuːətɪ; *US* -ˈtuː-/ *n* (idm) **in perpetuity** *(fml)* for ever; permanently: *The site of the memorial is granted in perpetuity to Canada.*

perplex /pəˈpleks/ *v* [Tn] make (sb) feel puzzled or confused; bewilder: *The question perplexed me.* ○ *We were perplexed by his failure to answer the letter.* ○ *The whole affair is very perplexing.*

▷ **perplexed** *adj* puzzled or confused: *The audience looked perplexed.* ○ *She had to explain her behaviour to her perplexed supporters.* ○ *He gave her a perplexed look.* **perplexedly** /-ɪdlɪ/ *adv*: *'What is this?' he asked perplexedly.*

perplexity /-ətɪ/ *n* [U] **1** state of being perplexed; bewilderment: *She looked at us in perplexity.* **2** state of being complicated or difficult: *a problem of such perplexity that it was impossible to solve.*

per pro /ˌpɜː ˈprəʊ/ *abbr* = PP 2.

perquisite /ˈpɜːkwɪzɪt/ *n* (esp *pl*) *(fml)* **1** *(infml* **perk)** money or goods given or regarded as a right in addition to one's pay: *Perquisites include the use of the company car.* **2** special advantage or right enjoyed as a result of one's position: *Politics in Britain used to be the perquisite of the property-owning classes.*

Perry /ˈperɪ/ Frederick John (1909-), English tennis player who won the *Wimbledon men's singles championship three years in a row (1934-36).

perry /ˈperɪ/ *n* **(a)** [U] drink made from the fermented juice of pears. **(b)** [C] glass of this. Cf CIDER.

pers *abbr* person; personal.

per se /ˌpɜː ˈseɪ/ *(Latin)* by or of itself; intrinsically: *The drug is not harmful per se, but is dangerous when taken with alcohol.*

persecute /ˈpɜːsɪkjuːt/ *v* **1** [esp passive: Tn, Tn·pr] ~ **sb (for sth)** treat sb cruelly, esp because of his race, his political or religious beliefs, etc: *Throughout history religious minorities have been persecuted (for their beliefs).* **2** [Tn, Tn·pr] ~ **sb (with sth)** allow no peace to sb; hound sb: *Once the affair became public, he was persecuted by the press.*

▷ **persecution** /ˌpɜːsɪˈkjuːʃn/ *n* **(a)** [U] persecuting or being persecuted: *his persecution of his political opponents* ○ *They suffered persecution for their beliefs.* **(b)** [C] instance of this: *He is writing a history of the persecutions endured by his race.* **perseˈcution complex** (also **perseˈcution mania**) *(psychology)* insane belief that one is being persecuted.

persecutor *n* person who persecutes others: *His persecutors were severely punished.*

Perseus /ˈpɜːsjuːs/ (in Greek mythology) son of *Zeus who killed the gorgon *Medusa and rescued *Andromeda from a sea monster.

persevere /ˌpɜːsɪˈvɪə(r)/ *v* [I, Ipr] ~ **(at/in/with sth)**; ~ **(with sb)** *(usu approv)* continue trying to do sth, esp in spite of difficulty: *You'll need to persevere if you want the business to succeed.* ○ *She persevered in her efforts to win the championship.* ○ *It's difficult, but I'm going to persevere with it.* ○ *He was hopeless at French, but his teacher persevered with him.*

▷ **perseverance** /ˌpɜːsɪˈvɪərəns/ *n* [U] continued steady effort to achieve an aim; steadfastness: *After months of disappointment, his perseverance was finally rewarded.* ○ *perseverance in the face of extreme hardship.*

persevering /ˌpɜːsɪˈvɪərɪŋ/ *adj* showing perseverance: [attrib] *persevering efforts* ○ *A few persevering climbers finally reached the top.* **perseveringly** *adv.*

Persia /ˈpɜːʃə; *US* ˈpɜːrʒə/ **1** empire in SW Asia established in the 6th century BC and destroyed by *Alexander the Great in the 4th century BC. At its largest it included parts of India and eastern Europe. **2** former name of *Iran.

Persian /ˈpɜːʃn; *US* ˈpɜːrʒn/ *adj* of Persia, its people or its language. *n* **1** (also **Iranian**) [C] inhabitant of Persia. **2** (also **Farsi**) [U] language of Persia.

□ **ˌPersian ˈcarpet** (also **ˌPersian ˈrug**) carpet of traditional design from the Near East, handmade from silk or wool.

ˌPersian ˈcat (also **Persian**) type of pure-bred cat with long silky hair.

the ˌPersian ˈGulf (also **the ˈGulf**) area of sea that separates the Arabian peninsula from *Iran. It is a busy route for tankers carrying oil from its ports: [attrib] *the Gulf War.* ➪ map at ARABIAN PENINSULA.

ˌPersian ˈlamb silky curled fur, usu black, of a type of Asian lamb, used for coats; astrakhan.

persiflage /ˈpɜːsɪflɑːʒ/ *n* [U] *(fml)* light good-humoured teasing; banter.

persimmon /pəˈsɪmən/ *n* **1** large orange-red plum-like edible fruit. **2** any of several types of tropical tree on which this grows.

persist /pəˈsɪst/ *v* **1** [I, Ipr] ~ **(in sth/in doing sth)** continue to do sth, esp in an obstinate and determined way and in spite of opposition, argument or failure: *If you persist, you will annoy them even more.* ○ *He will persist in riding that dreadful bicycle.* ○ *She persists in the belief/in believing that she is being persecuted.* **2** [Ipr] ~ **with sth** continue doing sth in spite of difficulties: *They persisted with the agricultural reforms, despite opposition from the farmers.* **3** [I] continue to exist: *Fog will persist throughout the night.* ○ *Loyalty to the former king still persists in parts of the country.*

▷ **persistence** /-əns/ *n* [U] **(a)** being persistent: *His persistence was rewarded when they finally agreed to resume discussions.* **(b)** continuing existence: *The doctor couldn't explain the persistence of the high temperature.*

persistent /-ənt/ *adj* **1** refusing to give up: *She eventually married the most persistent of her admirers.* **2 (a)** continuing without interruption: [attrib] *persistent noise, rain, pain* ○ *persistent questioning.* **(b)** occurring frequently: [attrib] *persistent attacks of coughing* ○ *Despite persistent denials, the rumour continued to spread.* **persistently** *adv.*

person /ˈpɜːsn/ *n* (*pl* **people** /ˈpiːpl/ or, in formal or derogatory use, **persons**). ➪ Usage at PEOPLE. **1** human being as an individual with distinct characteristics: *He's just the person we need for the job.* ○ *Here she is — the very person we were talking about!* ○ *I had a letter from the people who used to own the corner shop.* **2** *(fml or derog)* (esp known or unspecified) human being: *A certain person* (ie somebody that I do not wish to name) *told me everything.* ○ *Any person found leaving litter will be prosecuted.* ○ *(law)* accused of *conspiring with person or persons unknown*, eg said when charging sb court. **3** *(grammar)* any of the three classes of personal pronouns, the first person *'I/ we'* referring to the person(s) speaking, the second person *'you'* referring to the person(s) spoken to, and the third person *'he, she, it, they'* referring to the person(s) or thing(s) spoken about. **4** (idm) **about/on one's ˈperson** carried about with one, eg in one's pocket: *A gun was found on his person.* **be no/not be any respecter of persons** ➪ RESPECTER (RESPECT[2]). **in ˈperson** physically present: *The winner will be there in person to collect the prize.* ○ *You may apply for tickets in person or by letter.* **in the person of sb** *(fml)* in the form or shape of sb: *Help arrived in the person of his father.* ○ *The firm has an important asset in the person of the director of research.*

□ **ˌperson-to-ˈperson call** *n (esp US)* telephone call is made via the operator to a particular person and paid for from the time that person answers the phone.

persona /pəˈsəʊnə/ *n* (*pl* **-nae** /- niː/) *(psychology)* character of a person as presented to others or as others perceive it.

□ **perˌsona ˈgrata** /ˈgrɑːtə/ *(Latin)* person who is acceptable to others, esp a diplomat acceptable to a foreign government.

ˌpersona non ˈgrata /nɒn ˈgrɑːtə/ *(Latin)* person who is not acceptable to others, esp to a foreign government: *He was declared persona non grata and forced to leave the country.* ○ *(joc) He forgot to buy more coffee yesterday, so he was persona non grata at breakfast this morning!*

personable /ˈpɜːsənəbl/ *adj* [esp attrib] having a pleasant appearance or manner: *The salesman was a very personable young man.* ▷ **personably** /-əblɪ/ *adv.*

personage /ˈpɜːsənɪdʒ/ *n* person, esp an important or distinguished one: *Political and royal* *personages from many countries attended the funeral.*

personal /ˈpɜːsənl/ *adj* **1** [attrib] of or belonging to a particular person rather than a group or an organization: *one's personal affairs, beliefs* ○ *personal belongings/effects/property* ○ *a car for your personal use only* ○ *She made a personal donation to the fund.* ○ *give sth the personal touch*, ie make it individual or original. **2** not of one's public or professional life; private: *a letter marked 'Personal'* ○ *Please leave us alone — we have something personal to discuss.* ○ *His personal life is a mystery to his colleagues.* **3** [attrib] done or made by a particular person: *The Prime Minister made a personal appearance at the meeting.* ○ *I shall give the matter my personal attention.* **4** [attrib] done or made for a particular person: *We offer a personal service to our customers.* ○ *Will you do it for me as a personal favour?* ○ *a personal account*, ie a bank or building society account in a person's name. **5** critical of a person's faults: *The argument was becoming too personal.* ○ *Try to avoid making personal comments.* **6** [attrib] of the body: *personal cleanliness, freshness, hygiene, etc.*

▷ **personally** /-ənəlɪ/ *adv* **1** not represented by another; in person: *She presented the prizes personally.* ○ *The plans were personally inspected by the minister.* **2** as a person: *I don't know him personally, but I've read his books.* **3** (often at the beginning of a statement, followed by a comma) as far as I am concerned; for myself: *Personally, I don't like him at all.* ○ *Personally speaking/Speaking personally, I'm in favour of the scheme.* ⇨ Usage at HOPEFUL. **4** (idm) **take sth ˈpersonally** be offended by sth: *I'm afraid he took your remarks personally.*

□ ˌ**personal asˈsistant** (*abbr* **PA**) secretary who assists an official or a manager.

ˈ**personal column** column in a newspaper or some other periodical for private messages or short advertisements.

ˌ**personal comˈputer** (*abbr* **PC**) small computer designed for use by a single person, eg in an office.

ˌ**personal ˈpronoun** (*grammar*) any of the pronouns *I, me, she, her, he, him, we, us, you, they, them*, etc.

ˌ**personal ˈproperty** (also ˌ**personal eˈstate**) (*law*) property owned by a person, except land or income from land, that passes to his heir. Cf REAL ESTATE (REAL[1]).

personality /ˌpɜːsəˈnælətɪ/ *n* **1** [C] characteristics and qualities of a person seen as a whole: *a likeable personality* ○ *She has a very strong personality.* ○ *influences which affect the development of a child's personality.* **2** [U, C] distinctive, esp socially attractive, qualities: *We need someone with lots of personality to organize the party.* ○ *His wife was very beautiful, but seemed to have no personality.* **3** [C] famous person, esp in the world of entertainment or sport: *personalities from the film world* ○ *a television personality* ○ *one of the best-known personalities in the world of tennis.* **4 personalities** [pl] critical or impolite remarks about a person: *indulge in personalities*, ie make such remarks ○ *Let's keep personalities out of it*, ie avoid criticizing individual people.

□ **persoˈnality cult** (*often derog*) excessive admiration of a famous person, esp a political leader.

personalize, -ise /ˈpɜːsənəlaɪz/ *v* **1** [Tn esp passive] mark (sth) in order to show that it belongs to a person, esp by putting his address or initials on it: *handkerchiefs personalized with her initials* ○ [attrib] *a personalized number-plate*, ie one on a car, with personally selected letters. **2** [Tn] cause (sth) to become concerned with personal matters or feelings: *We don't want to personalize the issue.*

personify /pəˈsɒnɪfaɪ/ *v* (*pt, pp* **-fied**) [Tn] **1** (**a**) treat (sth) as if it were a human being: *The sun and the moon are often personified in poetry.* (**b**) represent (an idea, a quality, etc) in human form; symbolize: *Justice is often personified as a blindfolded woman holding a pair of scales.* **2** be an example in human form of a quality or characteristic, esp one possessed to an extreme degree: *He personifies the worship of money.* ○ *He is kindness personified.*

▷ **personification** /pəˌsɒnɪfɪˈkeɪʃn/ *n* **1** (**a**) [U] treating sth that is without life as a human being or representing it in human form: *The personification of evil as a devil is a feature of medieval painting.* (**b**) [C usu *sing*] instance of this. **2** [C] ~ **of sth** person who possesses a quality or characteristic to an extreme degree: *He looked the personification of misery.* ○ *She was the personification of elegance.*

personnel /ˌpɜːsəˈnel/ *n* **1** [pl *v*] people employed in one of the armed forces, a firm or a public office; staff: *trained personnel* ○ *Army personnel are not allowed to leave the base.* ○ *Airline personnel can purchase flight tickets at reduced prices.* ○ [attrib] *a personnel carrier*, ie a ship or an aeroplane that carries troops. **2** [Gp] (also **personˈnel department**) department in a firm which deals with employees, esp with their appointment and welfare: *Personnel is/are organizing the training of the new members of staff.* ○ [attrib] *personˈnel manager/officer.*

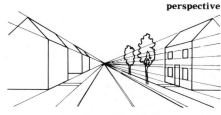

perspective

perspective /pəˈspektɪv/ *n* **1** (**a**) [U] art of drawing solid objects on a flat surface so as to give the right impression of their height, width, depth and position in relation to each other: *She drew a row of trees receding into the distance to demonstrate the laws of perspective.* ○ [attrib] *a perspective drawing.* (**b**) [C] drawing made this way. ⇨ illus. **2** [C] view, esp one stretching into the distance: *get a perspective of the whole valley* ○ (*fig*) *a personal perspective of the nation's history.* **3** (idm) **in/out of perspective** (**a**) showing the correct/incorrect relationship between visible objects: *draw the buildings in perspective* ○ *That tree on the left of the picture is out of perspective.* (**b**) [U] in a way that does not exaggerate any aspect/that exaggerates some aspects: *He sees things in their right perspective.* ○ *view/put/see sth in (its true/its proper) perspective* ○ *see the events in their historical perspective* ○ *get things badly out of perspective.*

Perspex /ˈpɜːspeks/ *n* [U] (*propr*) strong transparent plastic material that is often used instead of glass because it does not splinter.

perspicacious /ˌpɜːspɪˈkeɪʃəs/ *adj* (*fml*) having or showing great insight or judgement; discerning: *a perspicacious analysis of the problem* ○ *It was very perspicacious of you to find the cause of the trouble so quickly.* ▷ **perspicaciously** *adv.* **perspicacity** /ˌpɜːspɪˈkæsətɪ/ *n* [U].

perspicuous /pəˈspɪkjʊəs/ *adj* (*fml*) (**a**) expressed clearly. (**b**) (of a person) expressing things clearly; lucid. ▷ **perspicuously** *adv.* **perspicuousness**, **perspicuity** /-ˈkjuːətɪ/ *ns* [U].

perspire /pəˈspaɪə(r)/ *v* [I] (*fml*) give off moisture through the skin; sweat: *perspiring profusely after a game of squash.*

▷ **perspiration** /ˌpɜːspəˈreɪʃn/ *n* [U] (**a**) moisture given off by the body; sweat: *drops of perspiration rolling down one's forehead.* (**b**) process of giving off moisture through the skin: *Perspiration cools the skin in hot weather.*

persuade /pəˈsweɪd/ *v* **1** [Tn, Tn·pr, Cn·t] ~ **sb** (**into/out of sth**) cause sb to do sth by arguing or reasoning with him: *You try and persuade her (to come out with us).* ○ *He is easily persuaded.* ○ *How can we persuade him into joining us?* ○ *He persuaded his daughter to change her mind.* **2** [Tn esp passive, Tn·pr esp passive, Dn·f] ~ **sb** (**of sth**) (*fml*) cause sb to believe sth; convince sb: *I am not fully persuaded by the evidence.* ○ *We are persuaded of the justice of her case.* ○ *How can I persuade you that I am sincere?*

persuasion /pəˈsweɪʒn/ *n* **1** [U] persuading or being persuaded: *Defeated by her powers of persuasion, I accepted.* ○ *After a lot of persuasion, he agreed to come.* ○ *Gentle persuasion is more effective than force.* **2** [C] (group who hold a) set of (esp religious or political) beliefs: *people of all persuasions* ○ *He is not of their (religious) persuasion.* **3** [sing] (*fml*) something that one believes; conviction: *It is my persuasion that the decision was a mistake.*

persuasive /pəˈsweɪsɪv/ *adj* able to persuade; convincing: *a persuasive manner* ○ *persuasive arguments, reasons, excuses, etc.* ▷ **persuasively** *adv.* **persuasiveness** *n* [U]: *the persuasiveness of his argument.*

pert /pɜːt/ *adj* **1** (esp of a girl or young woman) not showing respect; cheeky: *a pert child, reply* ○ *Don't be so pert!* **2** (*esp US*) amusing; lively: *a pert little red hat.* ▷ **pertly** *adv.* **pertness** *n* [U].

pertain /pəˈteɪn/ *v* [Ipr] ~ **to sth** (*fml*) (used esp in the continuous tenses) (*fml*) **1** be connected with or relevant to sth: *evidence pertaining to the case.* **2** (*law*) belong to sth as a part of it: *the manor and the land pertaining to it.* **3** be appropriate to sth: *the enthusiasm pertaining to youth.*

pertinacious /ˌpɜːtɪˈneɪʃəs; *US* -tnˈeɪʃəs/ *adj* (*fml*) holding firmly to an opinion or a course of action; determined: *His style of argument in meetings is not so much aggressive as pertinacious.* ▷ **pertinaciously** *adv.* **pertinacity** /ˌpɜːtɪˈnæsətɪ; *US* -tnˈæ-/ *n* [U].

pertinent /ˈpɜːtɪnənt; *US* -tənənt/ *adj* ~ (**to sth**) (*fml*) relevant (to sth); to the point: *pertinent comments, points, questions, etc* ○ *remarks not pertinent to the matter we are discussing.* ▷ **pertinently** *adv.* **pertinence** /-əns/ *n* [U].

perturb /pəˈtɜːb/ *v* [Tn esp passive] (*fml*) make (sb) very worried; disturb: *perturbing rumours* ○ *We were perturbed to hear of his disappearance.*

▷ **perturbation** /ˌpɜːtəˈbeɪʃn/ *n* [U] (*fml*) state of being perturbed; anxiety.

Peru

Peru /pəˈruː/ mountainous country in western South America, bordering on Ecuador, Colombia, Brazil and Bolivia; pop approx 21 256 000; official languages Spanish and *Quechua; capital Lima; unit of currency inti (= 1 000 soles). Formerly a Spanish colony, it became independent in 1824. Mining of metals, eg copper, iron, silver and zinc, is an important source of income. ⇨ map. ▷ **Peruvian** /pəˈruːvɪən/ *adj, n.*

peruse /pəˈruːz/ *v* [Tn] **1** (*fml*) read (sth), esp carefully or thoroughly: *peruse a document.* **2** (*joc*) read (sth) quickly and without concentrating: *absent-mindedly perusing the notices on the waiting-room wall.*

▷ **perusal** /pəˈruːzl/ *n* [C, U] (action of) reading

carefully.

pervade /pəˈveɪd/ *v* [Tn] spread to and be perceived in every part of (sth): *The smell of baked apples pervaded the house.* ○ *a pervading sense of disaster* ○ *Her work is pervaded by nostalgia for a past age.*
▷ **pervasion** /pəˈveɪʒn/ *n* [U] (*fml*) pervading or being pervaded.

pervasive /pəˈveɪsɪv/ *adj* present and perceived everywhere; pervading: *pervasive smell, dust, damp, etc* ○ *the pervasive mood of pessimism.* ▷ **pervasively** *adv.* **pervasiveness** *n* [U].

perverse /pəˈvɜːs/ *adj* (*fml*) **1** (of a person) deliberately continuing to behave in a way that is wrong, unreasonable or unacceptable: *a perverse child* ○ *You are being unnecessarily perverse.* **2** [esp attrib] (of behaviour) stubbornly unreasonable: *his perverse refusal to see a doctor* ○ *It would be perverse to take a different view.* ○ *a perverse decision, judgement, etc,* ie one that ignores the facts or evidence. **3** [esp attrib] (of feelings) unreasonable or excessive: *take a perverse pleasure in upsetting one's parents* ○ *a perverse desire to shock.* ▷ **perversely** *adv*: *She continued, perversely, to wear shoes that damaged her feet.* **perverseness**, **perversity** *ns* [U].

perversion /pəˈvɜːʃn; *US* -ʒn/ *n* **1** (**a**) [U] changing sth from right to wrong; perverting: *the perversion of innocence* ○ *the perversion of the evidence to suit powerful interests.* (**b**) [C] perverted form of sth; distortion: *Her account was a perversion of the truth.* **2** [U] (**a**) (esp of sexual feelings) being or becoming unnatural or abnormal: *the perversion of normal desires.* (**b**) [C] (esp sexual) taste or desire which has been perverted: *the treatment of sexual perversion by psychotherapy* ○ *His craving for publicity has become almost a perversion.*

pervert /pəˈvɜːt/ *v* [Tn] **1** turn (sth) away from its proper nature or use: *pervert the truth/the course of justice* ○ *an expression whose meaning has been perverted by constant misuse.* **2** cause (a person, his mind) to turn away from what is right or natural: *pervert (the mind of) a child* ○ *an idealist perverted by the desire for power* ○ *Do pornographic books pervert those who read them?* ○ *a perverted desire to make others suffer.*
▷ **pervert** /ˈpɜːvɜːt/ *n* (*derog*) person whose (esp sexual) behaviour is considered abnormal or unacceptable.

peseta /pəˈseɪtə/ *n* (**a**) unit of currency in Spain; 100 centimos. (**b**) coin of this value.

pesky /ˈpeskɪ/ *adj* (**-ier**, **-iest**) (*US infml*) causing trouble; annoying: *pesky kids, mosquitoes, weeds.*

peso /ˈpeɪsəʊ/ *n* (*pl* ~**s**) unit of currency in many Latin American countries and the Philippines.

pessary /ˈpesərɪ/ *n* (*medical*) **1** small tablet placed in a woman's vagina and left to dissolve (to prevent conception or to cure an infection); vaginal suppository. **2** device placed in a woman's vagina to prevent conception (also **diaphragm pessary**) or to support the womb.

pessimism /ˈpesɪmɪzəm/ *n* [U] **1** tendency to be gloomy and believe that the worst will happen: *His pessimism has the effect of depressing everyone.* **2** (*philosophy*) belief that evil will always triumph over good. Cf OPTIMISM.
▷ **pessimist** /-ɪst/ *n* person who expects the worst to happen: *It's easy to sell insurance to a pessimist.* Cf OPTIMIST (OPTIMISM).
pessimistic /ˌpesɪˈmɪstɪk/ *adj* ~ (**about sth**) influenced by or showing pessimism: *a pessimistic view of the world* ○ *After the pessimistic sales forecasts, production was halved.* **pessimistically** /-klɪ/ *adv.*

pest /pest/ *n* **1** [C] (*infml*) annoying person or thing: *That child is an absolute pest — he keeps ringing the doorbell and then running away!* **2** [C] insect or animal that destroys plants, food, etc: *Stores of grain are frequently attacked by pests, especially rats.* ○ *garden pests*, eg slugs, greenfly, etc. Cf VERMIN 1. **3** [C, U] (*arch*) = PESTILENCE.
□ ˈ**pest control** [U] destruction of pests, eg with poison, traps, etc.

pester /ˈpestə(r)/ *v* [Tn, Tn·pr, Dn·t] ~ **sb** (**for sth**); ~ **sb** (**with sth**) annoy or disturb sb, esp with frequent requests: *He told the photographers to stop pestering him.* ○ *The horses in the meadow were being pestered by flies.* ○ *Beggars pestered him for money.* ○ *He pestered her with requests for help.* ○ *They pestered her to join in the scheme.*

pesticide /ˈpestɪsaɪd/ *n* [C, U] chemical substance used to kill pests, esp insects: *The flea-infested room had to be sprayed with a strong pesticide.* Cf INSECTICIDE (INSECT).

pestilence /ˈpestɪləns/ (also **pest**) *n* [C, U] (*arch*) (any of various types of) deadly infectious disease that spreads quickly through large numbers of people, esp bubonic plague.
▷ **pestilent** /-ənt/ (also **pestilential** /ˌpestɪˈlenʃl/) *adj* of or like a pestilence; 2. [attrib] (*infml*) very irritating: *the pestilential noise of aeroplanes coming in to land* ○ *We must get rid of these pestilential flies.*

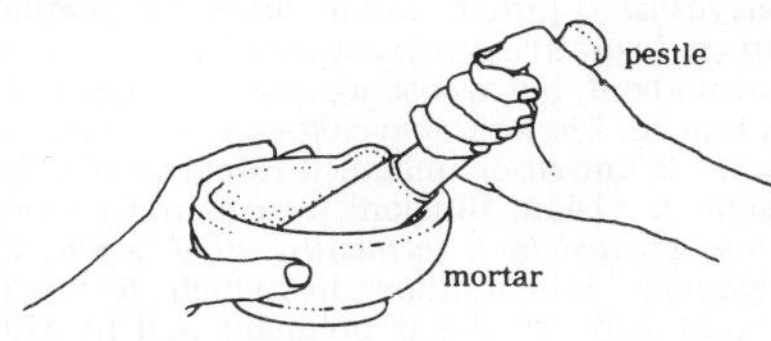

pestle /ˈpesl/ *n* heavy round-ended tool used for crushing and grinding things to powder, esp in a special bowl (*mortar*).

pet[1] /pet/ *n* **1** tame animal or bird kept as a companion and treated with care and affection: *They have many pets, including three cats.* ○ [attrib] *a pet mouse, snake, lamb, etc* ○ *pet food.* **2** (**a**) (*often derog*) (used esp in the expressions shown) person treated as a favourite: *(a/the) teacher's pet* ○ *make a pet of sb.* (**b**) thing that is given special attention by sb: [attrib] *a pet project, theory, cause, etc* ○ *one's pet hate/aversion.* **3** (*infml*) (**a**) kind or lovable person: *Their daughter is a perfect pet.* ○ *Be a pet and post this letter for me.* (**b**) (used as a term of affection, esp for a child or young woman): *That's kind of you, pet.*
▷ **pet** *v* (**-tt-**) **1** [Tn] treat (esp an animal) with affection, esp by stroking it. **2** [I] (*infml*) (of a man and a woman) kiss and caress each other: *heavy* (ie passionate) *petting.*
□ ˈ**pet name** name used affectionately, that is different from, or a short form of, a person's real name. ⇨ App 7.
ˈ**pet shop** shop where animals, birds etc are sold as pets.
pet ˈ**subject** subject that obsesses one; hobby-horse: *Once he starts talking about censorship you can't stop him — it's his pet subject.*

pet[2] /pet/ *n* (idm) **in a** ˈ**pet** in a fit of bad temper, esp about sth trivial: *There's no need to get in a pet about it!*

petal /ˈpetl/ *n* any of the delicate, coloured, leaf-like divisions of a flower: *yellow petals with black markings* ○ ˈ*rose petals.* ⇨ illus at PLANT.
▷ **petalled** (*US* **petaled**) /ˈpetld/ *adj* (esp in compounds) having petals: *a four-petalled flower* ○ *blue-petalled flowers.*

petard /peˈtɑːd/ *n* (idm) **hoist with one's own petard** ⇨ HOIST.

Peter /ˈpiːtə(r)/ **1** Saint (died c 67 AD), one of Christ's apostles, originally a fisherman, named Simon. He is said to have gone to Rome to spread the Christian faith, and he may have been martyred there. He is regarded by Roman Catholics as the first pope. **2** either of two books of the New Testament said to have been written by St Peter. ⇨ App 5.

peter /ˈpiːtə(r)/ *v* (phr v) **peter out** decrease or fade gradually before coming to an end: *The path petered out deep in the forest.* ○ *The story begins dramatically but the plot peters out before the end.*

Peterloo /ˌpiːtəˈluː/ name given to an event in St Peter's Field, Manchester, England on 16 August 1819 when a crowd of peaceful political demonstrators were attacked and shot at by the army. Eleven demonstrators were killed and hundreds injured.

Peter Pan /ˌpiːtə ˈpæn/ **1** young boy who never grew up, in J M *Barrie's play *Peter Pan.* **2** (*fig infml*) person who keeps a youthful appearance despite the passing of time: *Cliff Richard, the Peter Pan of British pop culture.*

petiole /ˈpetɪəʊl, *also, in British use,* ˈpiːtɪəʊl/ *n* thin stalk joining a leaf to a stem.

petit bourgeois /ˌpetɪ ˈbɔːʒwɑː; *US* -bʊərʒ-/ *n* (*pl* unchanged) (*French*) member of the lower middle class: [attrib] *petit bourgeois interests, occupations, prejudices, etc.*

petite /pəˈtiːt/ *adj* (*approv*) (of a girl or a woman) having a small and dainty physique.

petit four /ˌpetɪ ˈfɔː(r)/ (*pl* **petits fours** /ˌpetɪ ˈfɔːz/) small, sweet, often decoratively shaped cake or biscuit, usu served at the end of a meal.

petition /pəˈtɪʃn/ *n* ~ (**to sb**) **1** formal written request, esp one signed by many people appealing to sb in authority: *a petition against closing the swimming-pool signed by hundreds of local residents* ○ *get up a petition about sth.* **2** (*law*) formal application made to a court: *a divorce petition.* **3** (*fml*) earnest request, esp to God; prayer.
▷ **petition** *v* **1** [Dn·pr, Dn·t] ~ **sb** (**for sth**) make a formal request to sb (for sth): *petition the government for a change in the immigration laws* ○ *petition Parliament to allow shops to open on Sunday.* **2** [Ipr] ~ **for sth** ask earnestly or humbly for sth: (*law*) *petition for divorce,* ie ask a court of law to grant a divorce ○ *petition for a retrial in the light of new evidence.* **petitioner** /-ʃənə(r)/ *n* person who petitions, esp in a court of law.

petit mal /ˌpetɪ ˈmæl/ mild form of epilepsy, in which one does not become unconscious (or does so very briefly). Cf GRAND MAL.

petit point /ˌpetɪ ˈpɔɪnt/ embroidery on canvas using small stitches.

petits pois /ˌpetɪ ˈpwɑː/ [pl] small young peas.

Petrarch /ˈpetrɑːk/ Francesco Petrarca (1304-74), Italian poet whose work had a great influence on later Renaissance writers (eg in its choice of themes from classical antiquity). He is best known for his love poems inspired by an idealized woman he called Laura. ▷ **Petrarchan** /peˈtrɑkən/ *adj*: *Petrarchan sonnets.*

petrel /ˈpetrəl/ *n* any of several types of black and white sea-bird that fly far from land. Cf STORMY PETREL (STORM).

Petri dish /ˈpiːtrɪ dɪʃ, ˈpetrɪ/ small shallow transparent dish with a cover, used in laboratories for growing bacteria, etc.

petrify /ˈpetrɪfaɪ/ *v* (*pt, pp* **-fied**) **1** [esp passive: Tn, Tn·pr] ~ **sb** (**with sth**) make sb unable to think, move, act, etc because of fear, surprise, etc: *The idea of making a speech in public petrified him.* ○ *I was absolutely petrified (with fear).* **2** [I, Tn] (cause sth to) change into stone.
▷ **petrifaction** /ˌpetrɪˈfækʃn/ *n* [U] petrifying or being petrified.

petro- *comb form* **1** of petrol: *petrochemical.* **2** of rocks: *petrology.*

petrochemical /ˌpetrəʊˈkemɪkl/ *n* [U, C] any of various chemical substances obtained from petroleum or natural gas: [attrib] *the petrochemical industry.*

petrodollar /ˈpetrəʊdɒlə(r)/ *n* US dollar earned by a country that exports petroleum.

petrol /ˈpetrəl/ (*US* **gasoline**, **gas**) *n* [U] inflammable liquid obtained from petroleum by a refining process and used as a fuel in internal-combustion engines: *fill a car up with petrol* ○ *an increase in the price of petrol.*
□ ˈ**petrol bomb** device (often a bottle) filled with petrol that explodes when it hits something.
ˈ**petrol station** (also ˈ**filling station**, ˈ**service station**) (*US* ˈ**gas station**) place beside a road where petrol and other goods are sold to motorists. Cf GARAGE 2.
ˈ**petrol tank** container for petrol in a motor vehicle. ⇨ illus at CAR.

petroleum /pəˈtrəʊlɪəm/ *n* [U] mineral oil that forms underground and is obtained from wells sunk into the ground, from which petrol, paraffin, diesel oil, etc are obtained by processing.

□ peˌtroleum ˈjelly (*US* **petrolatum** /ˌpetrəˈleɪtəm/) greasy jelly-like substance obtained from petroleum, used in ointments.

petrology /pəˈtrɒlədʒɪ/ *n* [U] scientific study of rocks.

▷ **petrologist** /-dʒɪst/ *n* person who specializes in petrology.

petticoat /ˈpetɪkəʊt/ *n* woman's or girl's lightweight undergarment of dress length, worn hanging from the shoulders or the waist; slip.

pettifogging /ˈpetɪfɒgɪŋ/ *adj* **(a)** (of a person) paying too much attention to unimportant detail, esp in an argument. **(b)** unimportant; trivial: *pettifogging details, objections, etc.*

pettish /ˈpetɪʃ/ *adj* **(a)** (of a person) childishly bad-tempered or impatient, esp about unimportant things. **(b)** (of a remark or act) said or done in a bad-tempered, petulant way. ▷ **pettishly** *adv*. **pettishness** *n* [U].

petty /ˈpetɪ/ *adj* (**-ier**, **-iest**) (*derog*) **1** small or trivial; unimportant: *petty details, queries, regulations, troubles.* **2 (a)** concerned with small and unimportant matters: *petty observance of the regulations.* **(b)** having or showing a small mind; mean: *petty and childish behaviour* ○ *petty spite* ○ *a petty desire to have her revenge* ○ *petty about money.*

▷ **pettily** /ˈpetɪlɪ/ *adv*. **pettiness** *n* [U]: *The pettiness of their criticisms enraged him.*

□ ˌ**petty ˈcash** (usu small) amount of money kept in an office or for small payments.

ˌ**petty ˈlarceny** theft of articles of small value.

ˌ**petty ˈofficer** (*abbr* **PO**) senior non-commissioned officer in the navy. ⇨ App 4.

ˌ**petty ˈsessions** (*dated Brit*) magistrates' court for the trying of minor offences.

petulant /ˈpetjʊlənt; *US* -tʃʊ-/ *adj* unreasonably impatient or irritable: *the petulant demands of spoilt children.* ▷ **petulantly** *adv*. **petulance** /-əns/ *n* [U]: *He tore up the manuscript in a fit of petulance.*

petunia /pəˈtjuːnɪə; *US* -ˈtuː-/ *n* garden plant with funnel-shaped flowers in white, pink, purple or red.

pew /pjuː/ *n* **1** any of the long bench-like seats with a back and (usu) sides, placed in rows in a church for people to sit on. ⇨ illus at CHURCH. **2** (*infml joc*) seat (used esp in the following expressions): *Take/ Grab a pew!* ie Sit down.

pewit = PEEWIT.

pewter /ˈpjuːtə(r)/ *n* [U] **(a)** grey metal made by mixing tin with lead, used (esp formerly) for making mugs, dishes, etc: [attrib] *pewter goblets, bowls, tankards, etc.* **(b)** objects made of this: *a fine collection of old pewter.*

peyote /peɪˈəʊtɪ/ *n* **1** [C] type of Mexican cactus. **2** [U] drug made from this which causes hallucinations; mescaline.

pfennig /ˈfenɪg/ *n* (German coin of the value of) 100th part of a mark.

PG /ˌpiː ˈdʒiː/ *abbr* **1** (*Brit*) (of films) parental guidance, ie containing scenes unsuitable for young children. **2** paying guest.

pH /ˌpiː ˈeɪtʃ/ *n* [sing, U] measure of the acidity or alkalinity of a solution: *Vinegar with a pH of 3.0 is moderately acidic* ○ [attrib] *pH values.*

phaeton /ˈfeɪtn/ *n* **1** light four-wheeled open carriage, usu pulled by two horses. **2** (*US*) early type of motor car with room for several passengers.

phagocyte /ˈfægəsaɪt/ *n* type of white blood cell capable of protecting the body against infection because it absorbs bacteria.

-phagous *comb form* (forming *adjs*) eating: *ichthyophagous* (ie fish-eating) *animals.*

▷ **-phagy** *comb form* (forming *ns*) eating: *ichthyophagy*, ie the eating of fish.

phalanger /fəˈlændʒə(r)/ *n* small marsupial mammal of Australia, New Guinea, etc which lives in trees. One type has a fold of skin between its front and back legs which it uses for gliding.

phalanx /ˈfælæŋks/ *n* (*pl* **phalanges** /fəˈlændʒiːz/ or ~**es**) **1** (in ancient Greece) close formation, esp of infantry ready for battle. **2** number of people standing together to form a compact mass: *a phalanx of riot police.* **3** (*anatomy*) any of the bones in a finger or toe. ⇨ illus at SKELETON.

phallus /ˈfæləs/ *n* (*pl* **-li** /-laɪ/ or ~**es**) (esp in some religions) image of the erect penis as a symbol of the productive power of nature.

▷ **phallic** /ˈfælɪk/ *adj* of or like a phallus: *phallic imagery, symbolism, symbols, etc.*

phantasm /ˈfæntæzəm/ *n* (*fml*) **1** thing seen in the imagination; illusion. **2** = PHANTOM.

▷ **phantasmal** /fænˈtæzməl/ *adj* (*fml*) of or like a phantasm: *phantasmal images, figures.*

phantasmagoria /ˌfæntæzməˈgɒrɪə; *US* -ˈgɔːrɪə/ *n* (*fml*) changing scene of real or imagined figures, etc, eg as seen in a dream or created as an effect in a film. **phantasmagoric** /-ˈgɒrɪk; *US* -ˈgɔːrɪk/ *adj* (*fml*) of or like a phantasmagoria.

phantasy = FANTASY.

phantom /ˈfæntəm/ *n* **1 (a)** (also **phantasm**) ghostly image or figure; ghost: *the phantom of his dead father* ○ [attrib] *the legend of the phantom ship.* **(b)** [esp attrib] (*joc*) person whose actions are known about, but whose identity is (supposedly) not known: *The phantom cake-eater has been here again!* **2** unreal or imagined thing, as seen in a dream or vision; illusion: [attrib] *the phantom visions created by a tormented mind* ○ *phantom pregnancy*, ie condition in which a woman wrongly believes she is pregnant and in which some of the symptoms of pregnancy may appear.

Pharaoh /ˈfeərəʊ/ *n* (title of the) ruler of ancient Egypt: *Pharaoh Rameses II.* ▷ **Pharaonic** /ˌfeəreɪˈɒnɪk/ *adj*.

Pharisee /ˈfærɪsiː/ *n* **1** member of an ancient Jewish sect. According to the New Testament the Pharisees thought themselves very holy, and opposed Christ. Cf SADDUCEE. **2** (*fig derog*) person who claims to be very virtuous.

▷ **Pharisaic** /-ˈseɪɪk/ (also **Pharisaical**) /-ˈseɪɪkl/ *adj* **1** of the ancient Pharisees. **2** (*derog*) claiming to be very virtuous; hypocritical.

pharmaceutical /ˌfɑːməˈsjuːtɪkl; *US* -ˈsuː-/ *adj* of or connected with the making and distribution of drugs and medicines: *the pharmaceutical industry.*

▷ **pharmaceutics** /-ɪks/ *n* [sing *v*] = PHARMACY 1.

pharmacist /ˈfɑːməsɪst/ *n* **(a)** person who has been trained in the preparation of medicines; pharmaceutical chemist. **(b)** person trained in this way, whose job is to sell medicines. Cf CHEMIST.

pharmacology /ˌfɑːməˈkɒlədʒɪ/ *n* [U] scientific study of drugs and their use in medicine.

▷ **pharmacological** /ˌfɑːməkəˈlɒdʒɪkl/ *adj* of or concerning pharmacology: *pharmacological research.*

pharmacologist /-ˈkɒlədʒɪst/ *n* person who specializes in pharmacology.

pharmacopoeia /ˌfɑːməkəˈpiːə/ *n* book containing a list of medicinal drugs and directions for their use, esp one officially published for use in a particular country: *the British Pharmacopoeia.*

pharmacy /ˈfɑːməsɪ/ *n* **1** [U] (study of the) preparation and giving out of medicines and drugs. **2** [C] **(a)** place (eg in a hospital) where medicines are prepared and given out; dispensary. **(b)** (*US* **drugstore**) (part of a) shop where medicines and drugs are sold; chemist's shop.

pharynx /ˈfærɪŋks/ *n* (*pl* **pharynges** /fəˈrɪndʒiːz/ or ~**es**) (*anatomy*) cavity at the back of the mouth and nose, where the passages to the nose and to the mouth connect with the throat. ⇨ illus at THROAT.

▷ **pharyngitis** /ˌfærɪnˈdʒaɪtɪs/ *n* [U] (*medical*) inflammation of the pharynx.

phase /feɪz/ *n* **1** stage in a process of change or development: *a phase of history* ○ *a critical phase of an illness* ○ *the most exciting phase of one's career* ○ *The child is going through a difficult phase.* ○ (*infml*) *It's just a phase (she's going through)*, eg in childhood or adolescence. **2** amount of the bright surface of the moon that is visible at a given time (new moon, full moon, etc): *the phases of the moon.* **3** (*chemistry*) physically distinct form of a particular substance: *Ice and water are different phases of the same substance.* **4** (idm) **in/out of phase** being/not being in the same state at the same time: *The two sets of traffic lights were out of phase* (ie did not show the same change at the same time) *and several accidents occurred.*

▷ **phase** *v* **1** [Tn esp passive] plan or carry out sth in stages: *The modernization of the industry was phased over a 20-year period.* ○ *a phased withdrawal of troops.* **2** (phr v) **phase sth in** introduce sth gradually or in stages: *The use of lead-free petrol is now being phased in.* **phase sth out** withdraw or discontinue sth gradually or in stages: *The old currency will have been phased out by 1992.*

PhD /ˌpiː eɪtʃ ˈdiː/ *abbr* Doctor of Philosophy: *have/ be a PhD in History* ○ *Bill Crofts PhD.* Cf DPHIL, article at POST-SCHOOL.

pheasant /ˈfeznt/ *n* **(a)** [C] (*pl* unchanged or ~**s**) any of several types of long-tailed bird that are often shot for sport and food, the male of which usu has brightly-coloured feathers: *a brace of pheasants.* ⇨ illus at BIRD. **(b)** [U] its flesh prepared as food: *roast pheasant.*

phenobarbitone /ˌfiːnəʊˈbɑːbɪtəʊn/ (*US* **phenobarbital** /ˌfiːnəʊˈbɑːbɪtl/) *n* [U] medicinal drug that calms the nerves and helps one to sleep.

phenol /ˈfiːnɒl/ *n* [U] = CARBOLIC ACID.

phenomenal /fəˈnɒmɪnl/ *adj* **1** very remarkable; extraordinary: *the phenomenal success of the film* ○ *The rocket travels at phenomenal speed.* ○ *The response to the appeal fund has been phenomenal.* **2** (*fml*) of (the nature of) a phenomenon.

▷ **phenomenally** /-nəlɪ/ *adv* (*infml*) to an amazing degree: *Interest in the subject has increased phenomenally.*

phenomenon /fəˈnɒmɪnən; *US* -nɒn/ *n* (*pl* **-ena** /-ɪnə/) **1** fact or occurrence, esp in nature or society, that can be perceived by the senses: *natural, social, historical, etc phenomena* ○ *An eclipse of the moon is a rare phenomenon.* ○ *Bankruptcy is a common phenomenon in an economic recession.* **2** remarkable person, thing or event: *the phenomenon of their rapid rise to power.*

pheromone /ˈferəməʊn/ *n* chemical substance put out by an animal, which acts as a signal to others of the same species (eg to attract animals of the opposite sex).

phew /fjuː/ (also **whew**) *interj* (written representation of a short soft whistling sound made by blowing out or sucking in one's breath, and used to express relief, exhaustion or amazement): *Phew! That was a nasty moment — that car nearly hit us.*

phial /ˈfaɪəl/ (also **vial**) *n* small glass container, esp one for liquid medicine or perfume.

Phi Beta Kappa /ˌfaɪ ˌbiːtə ˈkæpə/ **(a)** national US college society, founded in 1776, to which university students of high academic standard are elected. **(b)** member of this society.

philander /fɪˈlændə(r)/ *v* [I, Ipr] ~ (**with sb**) (*usu derog*) (of a man) amuse oneself by flirting with women: *He spent his time philandering with the girls in the village.* ▷ **philanderer** /-dərə(r)/ *n* (*derog*) man who does this: *He's a bit of a philanderer — don't take him too seriously!*

philanthropy /fɪˈlænθrəpɪ/ *n* [U] **(a)** concern for the welfare of mankind; benevolence. **(b)** charitable actions inspired by this.

▷ **philanthropic** /ˌfɪlənˈθrɒpɪk/ *adj* of or inspired by philanthropy: *philanthropic organizations*, eg to help poor or disabled people ○ *philanthropic motives.*

philanthropically /-klɪ/ *adv*.

philanthropist /fɪˈlænθrəpɪst/ *n* person who helps others, esp through charitable work or donations of money: *The university was founded by a millionaire philanthropist.* Cf MISANTHROPIST.

philately /fɪˈlætəlɪ/ *n* [U] (hobby of) collecting and studying postage stamps.

▷ **philatelic** /ˌfɪləˈtelɪk/ *adj*.

philatelist /fɪˈlætəlɪst/ *n* **(a)** person who collects postage stamps. **(b)** person with expert knowledge of postage stamps.

philharmonic /ˌfɪlɑːˈmɒnɪk/ *adj* (esp in names of orchestras, music societies, etc) devoted to or loving music: *the London Philharmonic Orchestra.*

philhellene /ˌfɪlˈheliːn/ *n, adj* (person) friendly to or admiring the Greeks and Greek civilization. ▷ **philhellenic** /ˌfɪlheˈliːnɪk; *US* -ˈlenɪk/ *adj*.

-philia *comb form* (forming *ns*) **1** (esp abnormal)

love of or fondness for. **2** inclination towards: *haemophilia.* Cf -PHOBIA.

▷ **-phile** (also **-phil**) *comb form* (forming *ns* and *adjs*) (person who is) fond of: *Anglophile* ○ *bibliophile.* Cf -PHOBE (-PHOBIA).

-philiac (forming *adjs*).

Philip /ˈfɪlɪp/ Saint, one of Christ's apostles, who spread Christianity in Asia Minor.

Philip of Macedon /ˌfɪlɪp əv ˈmæsɪdən/ (c 382-336 BC), king of *Macedonia 359-336 BC and father of *Alexander the Great. He defeated the Greek city states and brought them under his control.

Philippians /fɪˈlɪpiənz/ book of the New Testament, consisting of a letter written by St *Paul to the Christians of Philippi in *Macedonia. ⇨ App 5.

philippic /fɪˈlɪpɪk/ *n* (*fml*) speech bitterly attacking sb; invective.

the Philippines

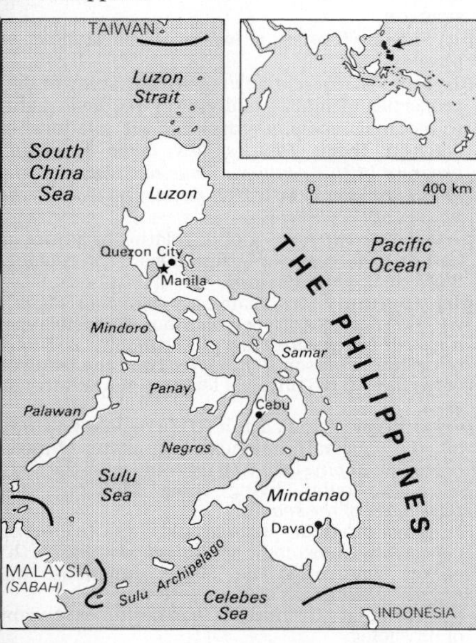

Philippines /ˈfɪlɪpi:nz/ **the Philippines** country in SE Asia, consisting of over 7 000 islands in the Pacific Ocean, to the east of Vietnam; pop approx 58 721 000; official languages *Filipino and English; capital Manila; unit of currency peso (= 100 centavos). For long a Spanish colony (Spanish is still commonly spoken), it was handed over to the USA in 1898. In 1946 it became independent, but US influence remained strong. In 1986 the corrupt rule of Ferdinand Marcos was overthrown by Corazón Aquino. Amongst its main exports are timber, sugar, copra and coconut oil. ⇨ map. Cf FILIPINO.

philistine /ˈfɪlɪstaɪn; *US* -sti:n/ *n* person who has no interest in or understanding of the arts, or is hostile to them; uncultured person: *He accused those who criticized his work of being philistines.*

▷ **philistine** *adj* having no interest in or understanding of the arts, or being hostile to them: *The philistine attitude of the public resulted in the work being abandoned.*

philistinism /-tɪnɪzəm/ *n* [U]: *the philistinism of the popular press.*

Phillips /ˈfɪlɪps/ *adj* [attrib] (*propr*) having or fitting a screw-head with a cross-shaped slot: *a Phillips screwdriver.* ⇨ illus at SCREWDRIVER.

phil(o)- *comb form* liking or fond of: *philanthropy* ○ *philology.*

philology /fɪˈlɒlədʒɪ/ *n* [U] **1** science or study of the development of language or of a particular language. Cf LINGUISTICS (LINGUISTIC). **2** (*US*) study or love of literature.

▷ **philological** /ˌfɪləˈlɒdʒɪkl/ *adj* of or concerning philology.

philologist /fɪˈlɒlədʒɪst/ *n* expert in or student of philology.

philosopher /fɪˈlɒsəfə(r)/ *n* **1** (**a**) person who studies or teaches philosophy. (**b**) person who has developed a particular set of philosophical theories and beliefs: *the Greek philosophers.* **2** (**a**) person whose mind is untroubled by passions and hardships. (**b**) person whose life is governed by reason. (**c**) (*infml*) person who thinks deeply about things: *He's quite a philosopher.*

□ **philosopher's ˈstone** imaginary substance which, it was formerly believed by alchemists, would change any metal into gold; elixir.

philosophy /fɪˈlɒsəfɪ/ *n* **1** (**a**) [U] search for knowledge and understanding of the nature and meaning of the universe and of human life: *moral philosophy*, ie study of the principles on which human behaviour is based; ethics. (**b**) [C] any particular set or system of beliefs resulting from this search for knowledge: *the philosophy of Aristotle* ○ *conflicting philosophies.* **2** [C] set of beliefs or an outlook on life that is a guiding principle for behaviour: *a man without a philosophy of life* ○ *Enjoy yourself today and don't worry about tomorrow — that's my philosophy!* **3** [U] calm quiet attitude towards life even in the face of suffering, danger, etc: *The philosophy of the prisoners during their worst sufferings impressed even their captors.*

▷ **philosophical** /ˌfɪləˈsɒfɪkl/, **philosophic** *adjs* **1** of or according to philosophy: *philosophical principles.* **2** devoted to philosophy: *philosophical works.* **3** ~ (**about sth**) having or showing the calmness and courage of a philosopher(2); resigned: *She seemed fairly philosophical about the loss.* ○ *He heard the news with a philosophical smile.* **philosophically** /-klɪ/ *adv*: *He accepted the verdict philosophically.*

philosophize, -ise /fɪˈlɒsəfaɪz/ *v* **1** [I] think or argue as or like a philosopher. **2** [I, Ipr] ~ (**about/on sth**) discuss or speculate: *They spend their time philosophizing about the mysteries of life.*

phlebitis /flɪˈbaɪtɪs/ *n* [U] inflammation of a vein.

phlegm /flem/ *n* [U] **1** thick semi-liquid substance which forms in the air passages, esp when one has a cold, and which can be removed by coughing. **2** (*dated or fml*) quality of being slow to act or react, or to show feeling; calmness: *show considerable phlegm in facing the crisis.*

▷ **phlegmatic** /flegˈmætɪk/ *adj* calm and even-tempered; showing the quality of phlegm(2): *Commuting in the rush-hour requires a phlegmatic temperament.* **phlegmatically** /-klɪ/ *adv.*

phlox /flɒks/ *n* [U] (*pl* unchanged or ~**es**) any of several types of garden plant with clusters of reddish, purple or white flowers.

phobia /ˈfəʊbɪə/ *n* extreme or abnormal dislike or fear of sth; aversion: *learning to control one's phobia about flying* ○ *Dislike of snakes or spiders is a common phobia.*

-phobia *comb form* (forming *ns*) extreme or abnormal fear of: *claustrophobia* ○ *hydrophobia* ○ *xenophobia.* Cf -PHILIA.

▷ **-phobe** *comb form* (forming *ns*) person who dislikes sth: *Anglophobe* ○ *xenophobe.*

-phobic *comb form* (forming *adjs*) having or showing extreme or abnormal fear of: *claustrophobic* ○ *xenophobic.* Cf -PHILE (-PHILIA).

Phoebus /ˈfi:bəs/ (also ˌ**Phoebus AˈPollo**) (in Greek mythology) *Apollo regarded as the sun god.

phoenix /ˈfi:nɪks/ *n* mythical bird of the Arabian desert, said to live for several hundred years before burning itself and then rising born again from its ashes.

phone[1] /fəʊn/ *n* **1** telephone: *tell sb sth/order sth over the phone*, ie instead of writing ○ *The phone is ringing.* ○ *communicating by phone* ○ [attrib] *make a phone call.* **2** (idm) (**be**) **on the ˈphone** (**a**) (be) talking on the phone: *You can't see her now — she's on the phone.* ○ *They've been on the phone for an hour.* (**b**) (of a person, business, etc) having a telephone: *Are you on the phone yet?*

▷ **phone** *v* **1** [I, Ip, Tn, Tn·p] ~ (**sb**)(**up**) telephone (sb): *Did anybody phone?* ○ *I'll phone them up now.* **2** (phr v) **phone in** telephone (esp one's place of work): *phone in sick*, ie telephone to say one is absent from work because of illness.

□ ˈ**phone book** = TELEPHONE DIRECTORY (TELEPHONE).

ˈ**phone booth** (also ˈ**phone box**) telephone kiosk; call-box.

ˈ**phone-in** (*Brit*) (*US* **call-in**) *n* radio or television programme in which telephoned questions and comments from listeners or viewers are broadcast: [attrib] *a phone-in show.* ⇨ article at TELEPHONE.

phone[2] /fəʊn/ *n* (*linguistics*) single sound (vowel or consonant) in speech.

-phone *comb form* **1** (forming *ns*) instrument using sound: *telephone* ○ *dictaphone* ○ *xylophone.* **2** (forming *adjs*) speaking a particular language: *anglophone* ○ *francophone.*

▷ **-phonic** *comb form* (forming *adjs*) of an instrument using sound: *telephonic.*

phoneme /ˈfəʊni:m/ *n* (*linguistics*) any one of the set of smallest distinctive speech sounds in a language that distinguish one word from another: *English has 24 consonant phonemes.* ○ *In English, the 's' in 'sip' and the 'z' in 'zip' represent two different phonemes.*

▷ **phonemic** /fəˈni:mɪk/ *adj* of or concerning phonemes. **phonemically** /-klɪ/ *adv.*

phonemics *n* [sing *v*] study of the phonemes of a language.

phonetic /fəˈnetɪk/ *adj* (*linguistics*) **1** of or concerning the sounds of human speech. **2** (of a method of writing speech sounds) using a symbol for each distinct sound or sound unit: *phonetic symbols, alphabet, transcription.* **3** (of spelling) corresponding closely to the sounds represented: *Spanish spelling is phonetic.*

▷ **phonetically** /-klɪ/ *adv.*

phonetician /ˌfəʊnɪˈtɪʃn/ *n* expert in or student of phonetics.

phonetics *n* [sing *v*] study of speech sounds and their production.

phoney (also **phony**) /ˈfəʊnɪ/ *adj* (**-ier, -iest**) (*infml derog*) (**a**) (of a person) pretending or claiming to be what one is not: *There's something very phoney about him.* ○ *a phoney doctor*, ie a quack doctor. (**b**) (of a thing) false or faked: *a phoney American accent* ○ *phoney jewels, qualifications, mannerisms* ○ *some phoney excuse for the delay* ○ *the story sounds phoney to me.*

▷ **phoney** (also **phony**) *n* (*pl* ~**s**) phoney person or thing: *The man's a complete phoney.* ○ *This diamond is a phoney.*

phoniness *n* [U].

phonic /ˈfɒnɪk/ *adj* **1** of or concerning sound. **2** of or concerning the sounds of speech.

phon(o)- *comb form* of sound or sounds: *phonetic* ○ *phonograph.*

phonograph /ˈfəʊnəgrɑ:f; *US* -græf/ *n* (*dated*) = RECORD PLAYER (RECORD).

phonology /fəˈnɒlədʒɪ/ *n* [U] (*linguistics*) **1** study of the system of speech sounds, esp in a particular language: *a course in phonology.* **2** system of sounds in a particular language, esp at a particular point in its development: *the phonology of Old English.*

▷ **phonological** /ˌfəʊnəˈlɒdʒɪkl/ *adj.*

phonologist /fəˈnɒlədʒɪst/ *n* expert in or student of phonology.

phooey /ˈfu:ɪ/ *interj* (*infml*) (expressing contempt, disappointment or a refusal to accept the truth of sth).

phosgene /ˈfɒzdʒi:n/ *n* [U] poisonous colourless gas used in chemical warfare, and in industry to make dyes, fertilizers, etc.

phosphate /ˈfɒsfeɪt/ *n* (**a**) [C, U] any salt or compound of phosphoric acid. (**b**) [C often *pl*, U] any artificial fertilizer composed of or containing these.

phosphorescence /ˌfɒsfəˈresns/ *n* [U] (**a**) giving out of light without heat or with so little heat that it cannot be felt. (**b**) giving out of a faint glow in the dark, eg by certain insects or sea creatures. Cf FLUORESCENCE.

▷ **phosphorescent** /-snt/ *adj* (**a**) giving out light

without heat. (**b**) glowing in the dark.

phosphorus /ˈfɒsfərəs/ *n* [U] (*symb* **P**) (*chemistry*) (**a**) pale yellow waxlike poisonous substance that glows in the dark and catches fire easily. (**b**) red allotrope of this, used for the striking surface on boxes of safety matches. ⇨ App 10.

▷ **phosphoric** /fɒsˈfɒrɪk; *US* -ˈfɔːr/ (also **phosphorous** /ˈfɒsfərəs/) *adj* concerning or containing phosphorus.

photic /ˈfəʊtɪk/ *adj* **1** (*physics*) of light. **2** [attrib] (of the layers of the ocean) that are reached by sunlight, allowing underwater plants to grow: *the photic zone.*

photo /ˈfəʊtəʊ/ *n* (*pl* ~**s** /-təʊz/) (*infml*) = PHOTOGRAPH.

□ ˌ**photo** ˈ**finish** (in horse-racing) finish of a race where the leading horses are so close together that only a photograph of them passing the winning-post can show which is the winner.

photo- *comb form* **1** of light: *photoelectric* ○ *photosensitize* ○ *photosynthesis.* **2** of photography: *photocopy* ○ *photogenic.*

photocell /ˈfəʊtəʊsel/ *n* = PHOTOELECTRIC CELL (PHOTOELECTRIC).

photocopy /ˈfəʊtəʊkɒpɪ/ *n* photographic copy of (written, printed or graphic work). Cf XEROX, PHOTOSTAT.

▷ **photocopy** *v* (*pt, pp* **-pied**) (**a**) [Tn] make a photographic copy of (written, printed or graphic work). (**b**) [I] make photographic copies of documents, etc: *do some photocopying.*

photocopier /-pɪə(r)/ *n* machine for photocopying documents.

photoelectric /ˌfəʊtəʊɪˈlektrɪk/ *adj* of or using the electrical effects produced by light.

□ ˌ**photoelectric** ˈ**cell** (also ˈ**photocell** /ˈfəʊtəʊˌsel/, eˌ**lectric** ˈ**eye**) electronic device that uses the effect of light to produce electric current (used eg in photographic light meters and burglar alarms).

photofit /ˈfəʊtəʊfɪt/ *n* picture of a person, esp sb wanted by the police, made by joining together photographs of individual facial features as remembered by a witness: [attrib] *a photofit picture.* Cf IDENTIKIT.

photogenic /ˌfəʊtəʊˈdʒenɪk/ *adj* (**a**) being a good subject for photography: *a photogenic sunset, village, kitten.* (**b**) (of a person) looking attractive in photographs: *I'm not very photogenic.*

photograph /ˈfəʊtəgrɑːf; *US* -græf/ (*infml*) (also *infml* **photo**) *n* **1** picture formed by means of the chemical action of light on a specially prepared surface, eg film or a glass plate, and then transferred to specially prepared paper: *take a photograph (of sb/sth).* **2** (idm) **take a good** ˈ**photograph** look attractive in photographs; be photogenic.

▷ **photograph** *v* **1** [Tn] take a photograph of (sb/sth): *photograph the bride, the wedding, a flower.* **2** [I] (followed by an *adv*) appear in a certain way in photographs: *photograph well/badly.*

photographer /fəˈtɒgrəfə(r)/ *n* person who takes photographs, esp as a job: *The competition is open to both amateur and professional photographers.* ○ *a newspaper photographer* ○ *one of the best photographers in the world.* Cf CAMERAMAN (CAMERA).

photographic /ˌfəʊtəˈgræfɪk/ *adj* [usu attrib] **1** of, used in or produced by photography: *photographic equipment, images, records, reproduction.* **2** (of sb's memory) able to remember things in great detail, exactly as they were seen.

photographically /-klɪ/ *adv.*

photography /fəˈtɒgrəfɪ/ *n* [U] art or process of taking photographs: *black and white/colour/still photography* ○ *Her hobby is photography.* ○ *The photography in the film about arctic wildlife was superb.*

photogravure /ˌfəʊtəgrəˈvjʊə(r)/ *n* **1** [U] process by which an image is transferred from a photographic negative to a metal plate for printing. **2** [C] picture, etc printed from such a plate.

photolithography /ˌfəʊtəʊlɪˈθɒgrəfɪ/ *n* [U] process of transferring an image onto a metal plate by a photographic method, and printing from it.

photon /ˈfəʊtɒn/ *n* (*physics*) indivisible unit of electromagnetic radiation.

photosensitive /ˌfəʊtəʊˈsensətɪv/ *adj* reacting when exposed to light, esp by changing colour: *photosensitive paper.*

▷ **photosensitize**, **-ise** /-taɪz/ *v* [Tn] make (sth) photosensitive.

photosphere /ˈfəʊtəʊsfɪə(r)/ *n* bright surface of a star, esp the sun.

Photostat (also **photostat**) /ˈfəʊtəstæt/ *n* (*propr*) photocopy: [attrib] *a Photostat copy.*

▷ **photostat** *v* [Tn] make a photocopy of (sth).

photosynthesis /ˌfəʊtəʊˈsɪnθəsɪs/ *n* [U] process by which green plants convert carbon dioxide and water into food using the energy in sunlight. Cf CHLOROPHYLL.

▷ **photosynthesize**, **-ise** /-əsaɪz/ *v* [Tn] change (eg carbon dioxide or water) into food by photosynthesis.

photosynthetic /-sɪnˈθetɪk/ *adj.*

phrase /freɪz/ *n* **1** [C] (**a**) (*grammar*) group of words without a verb, esp one that forms part of a sentence: *The 'green car' and 'at half past four' are phrases.* (**b**) group of words forming a short expression, esp an idiom or a clever, striking way of saying sth: *an apt, a memorable, a well-chosen, etc phrase* ○ *That's exactly the phrase I was looking for myself.* **2** [U] way of expressing oneself; style: *the poet's beauty of phrase.* **3** [C] (*music*) short distinct passage forming part of a longer passage. **4** (idm) **to coin a phrase** ⇨ COIN *v.* **turn a** ˈ**phrase** express oneself in an amusing and witty way. **a turn of phrase** ⇨ TURN[2].

▷ **phrasal** /ˈfreɪzl/ *adj* of or concerning a phrase. ˌ**phrasal** ˈ**verb** idiomatic phrase consisting of a verb plus preposition(s) or a verb plus adverbial particle, eg *go in for, fall over, blow up.*

phrase *v* [Tn] **1** express (sth) in words (in the specified way): *phrase one's criticism very carefully* ○ *How shall I phrase it?* ○ *an elegantly phrased compliment.* **2** divide (music) into phrases, esp in performance. **phrasing** *n* [U] **1** (*music*) action or manner of dividing a line into phrases, in composing or performing: *The singer was criticized for poor phrasing.* **2** = PHRASEOLOGY a.

phraseology /ˌfreɪzɪˈɒlədʒɪ/ *n* [U] (**a**) choice or arrangement of words; wording. (**b**) study of fixed phrases and idioms.

□ ˈ**phrase-book** *n* book listing common expressions and their equivalents in another language, esp for use by travellers in a foreign country: *a Spanish phrase-book.*

phrenetic = FRENETIC.

phrenology /frəˈnɒlədʒɪ/ *n* [U] (esp formerly) study of the shape of a person's skull, esp the natural bumps on it, in order to determine his character and abilities.

▷ **phrenological** /ˌfrenəˈlɒdʒɪkl/ *adj.*

phrenologist /frəˈnɒlədʒɪst/ *n* person who practises phrenology.

phut /fʌt/ *adv* (idm) **go** ˈ**phut** (*infml*) (**a**) (esp of electrical or mechanical things) stop functioning; break down: *The washing machine has gone phut.* (**b**) be ruined; collapse: *The business went phut.* ○ *Our holiday plans have gone phut.*

phylactery /fɪˈlæktərɪ/ *n* small leather box containing passages from the Hebrew scriptures, worn on the head and left arm by Jewish men at morning weekday prayer.

phylum /ˈfaɪləm/ *n* (*pl* **-la** /-lə/) (*biology*) major division in the animal or plant kingdom: *The mollusc phylum includes all soft-bodied animals without backbones.* Cf CLASS 7, ORDER[1] 9, FAMILY 4, GENUS 1, SPECIES 1.

physical /ˈfɪzɪkl/ *adj* **1** of or concerning material things (contrasted with moral or spiritual matters): *the physical world, universe, etc.* **2** (**a**) of the body: *physical fitness, well-being, strength, etc* ○ *physical exercise,* eg walking, running, playing sports ○ *physical education,* eg athletics, gymnastics, games, etc ○ (*Brit infml*) *physical jerks,* ie gymnastics. (**b**) bodily: *physical presence.* **3** of or according to the laws of nature: *It is a physical impossibility to be in two places at once.* ○ *physical necessity.* **4** [attrib] of the natural features of the material world: *physical geography,* ie one geography of the earth's structure ○ *a physical map,* ie map showing mountains, rivers, etc. **5** [attrib] of or concerning physics: *physical chemistry,* ie use of physics in the study of chemistry ○ *physical science.* **6** (*infml euph*) using violence; treating roughly: *Are you going to co-operate or do we have to get physical?* ○ *The game was extremely physical — two of the players ended up with broken legs!*

▷ **physical** *n* (*infml*) medical examination to see if one is fit.

physically /-klɪ/ *adv* (**a**) bodily: *physically exhausted, fit, handicapped* ○ *attack sb physically.* (**b**) according to the laws of nature: *physically impossible.*

physician /fɪˈzɪʃn/ *n* doctor, esp one specializing in areas of treatment other than surgery. Cf SURGEON.

physicist /ˈfɪzɪsɪst/ *n* expert in or student of physics.

physics /ˈfɪzɪks/ *n* [sing *v*] (scientific study of the) properties of matter and energy (eg heat, light, sound, magnetism, gravity) and the relationship between them: *Physics has made enormous progress in this century.* ○ *nuclear physics* ○ *the laws of physics* ○ [attrib] *a physics textbook* ○ *the physics of the electron.*

physi(o)- *comb form* **1** of or relating to nature or natural forces or functions: *physiology.* **2** physical: *physiotherapy.*

physiognomy /ˌfɪzɪˈɒnəmɪ; *US* -ˈɒgnəʊmɪ/ *n* (*fml*) **1** [C] (**a**) features of a person's face. (**b**) facial type: *a typical North European physiognomy.* **2** [U] art of judging a person's character from the features of his face. **3** [C] physical features of a country or area.

physiology /ˌfɪzɪˈɒlədʒɪ/ *n* [U] (**a**) scientific study of the normal functions of living things: *reproductive physiology.* (**b**) way in which the body of a particular living thing functions: *the physiology of the snake.*

▷ **physiological** /ˌfɪzɪəˈlɒdʒɪkl/ *adj* (**a**) of or concerning physiology: *physiological research.* (**b**) of or concerning the bodily functions: *the physiological effects of space travel.*

physiologist /ˌfɪzɪˈɒlədʒɪst/ *n* expert in or student of physiology.

physiotherapy /ˌfɪzɪəʊˈθerəpɪ/ *n* [U] treatment of disease, injury or weakness in the joints or muscles by exercises, massage and the use of light, heat, etc.

▷ **physiotherapist** /-pɪst/ *n* (also *infml* **physio**) /ˈfɪzɪəʊ/ person trained to give such treatment.

physique /fɪˈziːk/ *n* [C] general appearance and size of a person's body, esp of the muscles: *a well-developed physique* ○ *build up one's physique* ○ *a fine/poor physique* ○ *He doesn't have the physique for such heavy work.*

pi /paɪ/ *n* **1** the sixteenth letter of the Greek alphabet (Π, π), represented in English spelling by *p.* **2** (*geometry*) symbol (π) representing the ratio of the circumference of a circle to its diameter (ie approximately 3·14159).

Piaget /pɪˈæʒeɪ; *US* pjɑːˈʒeɪ/ Jean (1897-1980), Swiss psychologist who studied the development of reasoning processes in children.

pia mater /ˌpaɪə ˈmeɪtə(r)/ (*anatomy*) innermost membrane that covers the brain and spinal cord. Cf DURA MATER.

piano[1] /ˈpjɑːnəʊ/ *adv, adj* (*music*) (*abbr* **p**) soft(ly). Cf FORTE[2].

▷ **pianissimo** /pɪəˈnɪsɪməʊ/ *adv, adj* (*abbr* **pp**) very soft(ly).

piano[2] /pɪˈænəʊ/ *n* (*pl* ~**s** /-nəʊz/) (also *fml* **pianoforte** /pɪˌænəʊˈfɔːtɪ; *US* pɪˈænəfɔːrt/) large musical instrument played by pressing the black or white keys of a keyboard thus causing small hammers to strike metal strings to produce different notes: *play a tune on the piano* ○ *grand piano,* ie one with horizontal strings, esp used for concerts ○ *upright piano,* ie one with vertical strings ○ [attrib] *piano music* ○ *a piano teacher,*

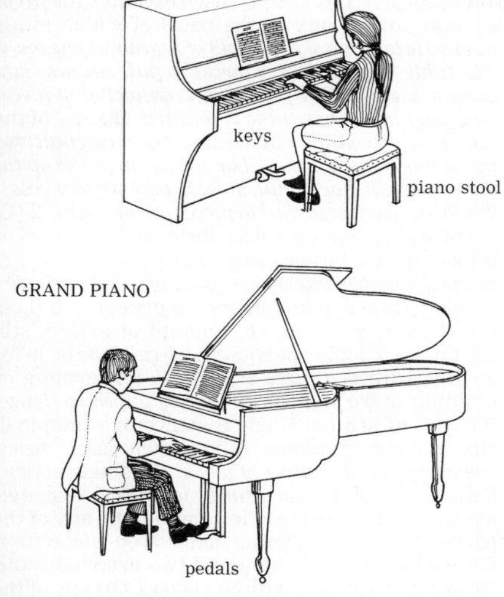

lesson ○ *a piano-player* ○ *a piano-stool.* ⇨ illus.

▷ **pianist** /ˈpɪənɪst/ *n* person who plays the piano: *She's a good pianist.* ○ *a famous concert pianist.*

pianola (also **Pianola**) /pɪəˈnəʊlə/ *n* (*propr*) type of mechanical piano in which the keys are operated by air pressure.

□ **piˌano-acˈcordion** *n* = ACCORDION.

piastre (*US* **piaster**) /pɪˈæstə(r)/ *n* **(a)** 100th part of the unit of money in several Middle Eastern countries. **(b)** coin or banknote of this value.

piazza /pɪˈætsə; *US also* piːˈɑːzə/ *n* public square or marketplace, esp in an Italian town; plaza.

pibroch /ˈpiːbrɒk/ *n* piece of music to be played on the bagpipes, consisting of a theme and variations.

pica /ˈpaɪkə/ *n* **1** one of the sizes of letters used in typewriting (ten letters per inch). **2** (in printing) unit of measurement for type[2](1a).

picador /ˈpɪkədɔː(r)/ *n* (in bullfighting) man mounted on a horse who attacks the bull with a lance in order to make it angry and weaken it.

picaresque /ˌpɪkəˈresk/ *adj* (of a style or type of literature) dealing with the adventures of (often likeable) rogues and vagabonds.

Picasso /pɪˈkæsəʊ/ Pablo (1881-1973), Spanish painter who was one of the most creative and influential of 20th-century artists. Following his early 'Blue Period' (in which his pictures were mainly blue), he settled permanently in France and pioneered cubism. His best-known painting is perhaps *Guernica,* inspired by the bombing of the Basque city of Guernica during the Spanish Civil War.

picayune /ˌpɪkəˈjuːn/ *n* (*US*) **1** small coin, esp one worth five cents. **2** (*infml*) insignificant person or thing.

▷ **picayune** *adj* (*US infml derog*) **(a)** of little value or importance. **(b)** mean; petty.

Piccadilly Circus /ˌpɪkədɪlɪ ˈsɜːkəs/ road junction in central London, England, where several major streets meet, including Piccadilly, Regent Street and Shaftesbury Avenue. It has a statue of *Eros in the middle. A major tourist attraction, it is famous for its brightly lit advertisements. ⇨ article at LONDON.

piccalilli /ˌpɪkəˈlɪlɪ/ *n* [U] yellow hot-tasting pickle made from chopped vegetables, mustard and spices.

piccaninny /ˌpɪkəˈnɪnɪ/ *n* (⚠ *offensive dated*) young Negro or Aboriginal child.

piccolo /ˈpɪkələʊ/ *n* (*pl* ~s) small musical instrument like the flute but producing notes an octave higher than those of the flute. ⇨ illus at MUSIC.

pick[1] /pɪk/ *n* [sing] **1** (right of) selecting; choice: *Of course I'll lend you a pen. Take your pick,* ie whichever one you choose. ○ *The winner has first pick of the prizes.* **2 the ~ of sth** the best (example) of sth: *Only the pick of the crop is good enough for us,* eg in food advertising. ○ *the pick of the new season's fashions* ○ (*infml*) *the pick of the bunch,* ie the best of a number of things or people.

pick[2] /pɪk/ *n* **1** (also **pickaxe**, *US* **pickax** /ˈpɪkæks/) large tool consistiing of a curved iron bar with sharp ends fixed onto a wooden handle, used for breaking up stones, hard ground, etc. ⇨ illus at AXE. **2** (esp in compounds) instrument with a sharp point, used for the purpose specified: *an ˈice-pick* ○ *a ˈtoothpick.* **3** (*infml*) = PLECTRUM.

pick[3] /pɪk/ *v* **1** [Tn] choose or select (sth), eg from a group of things, esp thoughtfully and carefully: *You can pick whichever one you like.* ○ *Only the best players were picked to play in the match.* ○ *pick one's words,* ie express oneself carefully, eg so as not to annoy sb ○ *pick one's way along a muddy path,* ie walk carefully, choosing the best places to put one's feet. ⇨ Usage at CHOOSE. **2** [Tn] pluck, gather or remove (flowers, vegetables, etc) from the place where they grow: *flowers freshly picked from the garden* ○ *pick lettuce, plums, spinach, strawberries, etc.* **3 (a)** [Tn, Cn·a] remove small pieces of matter from (sth), esp in order to clean it: *pick one's nose,* ie remove dried mucus from the nostrils ○ *pick one's teeth,* ie use a small pointed piece of wood, etc to remove particles of food from one's teeth ○ *The dogs picked the bones clean,* ie removed all the meat from the bones. **(b)** [Tn·pr] ~ **sth (from/off sth)** remove sth from a surface, esp with one's fingers or a sharp instrument: *pick the tacking treads (from a garment)* ○ *pick a hair from the collar of one's coat* ○ *pick the toys off the floor* ○ *pick the nuts off the top of the cake.* **(c)** [Tn] open (a lock) without a key, eg by using a piece of bent wire or a pointed tool. **4** [Tn, Tn·pr] ~ **sth (in sth)** make (a hole) in sth by pulling at it or by using one's finger-nails or a sharp instrument: *The child has picked a hole in his new jumper.* ○ *The bird picked a hole in the ice with its beak.* **5 (a)** [Tn] (of birds) take up (grain, etc) in the bill: *chickens picking corn.* **(b)** [Ipr] ~ **at sth** eat (food) in very small amounts or without appetite: *Sparrows picked at the crumbs.* ○ *He never feels hungry and just picks at his food.* **6** [Tn] = PLUCK 4: *pick a banjo.* **7** (idm) **have a bone to pick with sb** ⇨ BONE. **pick and ˈchoose** make a selection from a number of things, esp in a slow, careful or fussy way: *I spent days picking and choosing before deciding on the wallpaper and curtains.* ○ *We had to find a flat in a hurry — there was no time to pick and choose.* **pick sb's ˈbrains** ask sb questions in order to obtain information that one can use oneself: *I need a new French dictionary. Can I pick your brains about the best one to buy?* **pick a ˈfight/ˈquarrel (with sb)** deliberately cause a fight/ quarrel (with sb), eg by behaving aggressively: *He tried to pick a quarrel with me about it but I refused to discuss the matter.* ○ *It was foolish of you to pick a fight with a heavyweight boxing champion!* **pick holes in sth** find fault with sth: *It was easy to pick holes in his argument.* ○ *They pick holes in everything I suggest.* **pick sb's ˈpocket** steal money, etc from sb's pocket. **pick/pull sb/sth to pieces** ⇨ PIECE[1]. **pick up/take up/throw down the gauntlet** ⇨ GAUNTLET[1]. **pick up the ˈpieces/ˈthreads** restore to normality or make better (a situation, one's life, etc) , esp after a setback, shock, disaster, etc: *Their lives were shattered by the tragedy and they are still trying to pick up the pieces.* **pick up ˈspeed** go faster: *We reached the outskirts of town and began to pick up speed.* **pick a ˈwinner (a)** (in horse-racing) choose correctly the horse which will win the race, esp in order to bet on it. **(b)** make a very good choice: (*ironic*) *I really picked a winner with this car — it's always breaking down!*

8 (phr v) **pick sb off** shoot (a person, an animal, a bird, etc, esp one of a group) after aiming carefully: *A sniper hidden on a roof picked off three of the soldiers on patrol.*

pick on sb (a) choose sb (esp repeatedly) for punishment, criticism or blame: *She felt that her parents were picking on her.* **(b)** choose sb for a task, esp an unpleasant one: *I was picked on to announce the bad news.*

pick sb/sth out (a) choose sb/sth from a number of people/things: *She was picked out from thousands of applicants for the job.* ○ *He picked out the ripest peach.* **(b)** distinguish sb/sth from surrounding people or things: *pick out sb/sb's face in a crowd* ○ *It was just possible to pick out the hut on the side of the mountain.* ○ *The window frames are picked out in blue against the white walls.* **pick sth out (a)** play (a piece of music), eg on the piano, esp hesitantly or by trial and error, without having written music to follow. **(b)** discover or recognize sth after careful study: *pick out recurring themes in an author's work* ○ *Can you pick out the operatic arias quoted in this orchestral passage?*

pick sth over look carefully at (vegetables, fruit, clothing, etc) in order to select the best or throw away bad ones: *Pick over the lentils carefully in case there are any stones amongst them.*

pick up (a) become better; improve: *The market always picks up in the spring.* ○ *We're waiting until the weather picks up a bit.* ○ *The performance started badly but picked up towards the end.* ○ *Her health soon picked up after a few days' rest.* **(b)** start again; continue: *We'll pick up where we finished yesterday.* **pick oneself up** get to one's feet, esp after a fall: *Pick yourself up and brush yourself down.* **pick sb up (a)** give sb a lift in a car; collect sb: *I'll pick you up at 7 o'clock.* ○ *He picked up a hitch-hiker.* **(b)** (*infml often derog*) make the acquaintance of sb casually: *He picked up the girl at a college disco.* ○ *She's living with some man she picked up on holiday.* **(c)** rescue sb (eg from the sea): *The lifeboat picked up all the survivors.* **(d)** (of the police, etc) stop and seize sb (eg for questioning): *The police picked him up as he was trying to leave the country.* ○ *He was picked up and taken for questioning.* **(e)** reprimand sb: *She picked him up for using bad language.* **pick sb/sth up (a)** take hold of and lift sb/sth: *He picked up the child and put her on his shoulders.* ○ *I picked up your bag by mistake.* ○ *pick up a stitch,* ie in knitting ○ *He picked up the book from the floor.* ○ *She picked up the telephone and dialled his number.* **(b)** see or hear sb/sth, esp by means of apparatus: *They picked up the yacht on their radar screen.* ○ *I was able to pick you up on the short wave radio.* ○ *The equipment picked up the signal from the satellite.* **pick sth up (a)** learn (a foreign language, a technique, etc) by practising: *She soon picked up French when she went to live in France.* ○ *The children have picked up the local accent.* ○ *pick up bad habits.* **(b)** (an illness) catch: *pick up an infection, a cold, the flu, etc.* **(c)** buy sth, esp cheaply or luckily: *She picked up a valuable first edition at a village book sale.* ○ *They picked up most of the furniture at auctions in country towns.* **(d)** hear or learn (gossip, news, etc): *He picked up an interesting piece of news.* ○ *See if you can pick up anything about their future plans.* **(e)** collect sth: *I've got to pick up my coat from the cleaners.* ○ *I'll pick up* (ie buy) *something for dinner on my way home.* ○ *We can pick up the tickets an hour before the play begins.* **(f)** draw or derive sth: *The trolley bus picks up current from an overhead wire.* **(g)** find sth; locate sth; (re)join: *pick up a trail, a scent* ○ *pick up the track on the other side of the river.* **pick up with sb** (*often derog*): *She's picked up with some peculiar people.*

▷ **picker** *n* (esp in compounds) person or thing that picks (PICK[3] 2): *ˈhop-pickers* ○ *a mechanical ˈapple-picker.*

□ **pick-me-up** /ˈpɪkmɪʌp/ *n* (*infml*) drink taken as a tonic when one feels weak, tired, ill, etc, esp medicine or an alcoholic drink.

pickpocket /ˈpɪkpɒkɪt/ *n* person who steals money, etc from other people's pockets, esp in crowded places.

ˈpick-up *n* **1** (*infml derog*) person one has met casually, esp in a sexual context. **2** part of a record-player that holds the stylus. **3** (also **ˈpick-up truck**) small van or truck, open and with low sides, used by builders, farmers, etc. ⇨ illus at JEEP.

pick-a-back /ˈpɪkəbæk/ (also **piggyback** /ˈpɪgɪbæk/) *adv* on the shoulders or back like a bundle: *carry a child pick-a-back.*
▷ **pick-a-back** (also **piggyback**) *n* ride on a person's back: *Her father gave her a pick-a-back ride for the last bit of the journey.*

picket /ˈpɪkɪt/ *n* **1** worker or group of workers stationed outside the entrance to a place of work during a strike to try to persuade others not to enter: *Five pickets were injured in the scuffle.* ○ [attrib] *a ˈpicket line,* ie a line of pickets, eg outside a factory. **2** small group of people on police duty or of soldiers sent out to watch the enemy. **3** pointed stake set into the ground, eg as part of a fence or to tether a horse to: [attrib] *a picket fence.*
▷ **picket** *v* **1** (**a**) [Tn] place pickets at (a place of work): *picket all the company's offices.* (**b**) [I, Tn] act as a picket at (a place of work): *Some of the union members did not want to picket.* **2** [Tn] place (guards) in position. **3** [Tn] enclose (a place) with stakes or make secure with a stake.

pickings /ˈpɪkɪŋz/ *n* [pl] **1** profits or gains that are easily or dishonestly earned or obtained: *He promised us rich pickings if we bought the shares immediately.* **2** left over scraps of food, etc.

pickle /ˈpɪkl/ *n* **1** (**a**) [U] food (esp vegetables) preserved in vinegar or salt water: *red cabbage pickle.* (**b**) [C usu *pl*] particular vegetable preserved in this way: *The dish was accompanied by a variety of pickles.* ○ *cheese and pickles.* (**c**) [U] liquid used to preserve food in this way: *leave an ox tongue in salt pickle.* Cf RELISH 3, SAUCE 1. **2** [C] (*Brit infml*) mischievous child: *She's a real little pickle!* **3** (idm) (**in**) **a sad, sorry, nice, pretty, etc ˈpickle** (in) a difficult or unpleasant situation; (in) a mess.
▷ **pickle** *v* [Tn] preserve (vegetables, etc) in pickle: *pickled cabbage, onions, walnuts, etc.* **pickled** *adj* (*infml*) drunk: *By this time, he was hopelessly pickled.*

Pickwickian /pɪkˈwɪkɪən/ *adj* **1** of or like Mr Pickwick in *Dickens's *Pickwick Papers*, esp in being good-natured, plump, etc. **2** (of words, phrases, etc) not used with the normal meaning, which might be thought insulting: *I use the term in the Pickwickian sense,* ie You must not think I am being rude even though what I say seems so.

picky /ˈpɪkɪ/ *adj* (**-ier, iest**) (*infml derog esp US*) fussy; choosy.

picnic /ˈpɪknɪk/ *n* **1** (**a**) (*esp Brit*) meal eaten out of doors, esp as part of a pleasure trip: *We'll go to the river and take a picnic with us.* ○ [attrib] *a picnic table, hamper, lunch.* (**b**) pleasure trip that includes a picnic: *It's a nice day — let's go for a picnic.* **2** (idm) **be no ˈpicnic** (*infml*) be difficult or troublesome: *Bringing up a family when you are unemployed is no picnic.*
▷ **picnic** *v* (**-ck-**) [I, Ipr] take part in or have a picnic: *They were picnicking in the woods.* **picnicker** *n* person who picnics: *Picnickers are requested not to leave litter behind,* eg on a notice.

picot /ˈpiːkəʊ/ *n* small loop of thread forming part of a lace edging.

picric acid /ˌpɪkrɪk ˈæsɪd/ *n* [U] bitter yellow substance used in dyeing and in making explosives.

Pict /pɪkt/ *n* member of an ancient people who once lived in northern Britain, and fought against the Roman invaders. ▷ **Pictish** *adj.*

pictograph /ˈpɪktəgrɑːf; *US* -græf/ (also **pictogram** /ˈpɪktəgræm/) *n* **1** written symbol that stands for a word (eg in Chinese). **2** chart on which pictorial symbols represent statistical values.

pictorial /pɪkˈtɔːrɪəl/ *adj* (**a**) represented in a picture or pictures: *a pictorial record of the wedding.* (**b**) having pictures; illustrated: *a pictorial calendar, magazine, etc.*
▷ **pictorial** *n* newspaper or magazine in which pictures are the most important feature.
pictorially *adv* /-əlɪ/.

picture /ˈpɪktʃə(r)/ *n* **1** [C] (**a**) painting, drawing, sketch, etc, esp as a work of art: *His picture of cows won a prize.* ○ *Draw a picture of the house so we know what it looks like.* (**b**) photograph: *They showed us the pictures of their wedding.* ○ *She's taking a picture of the children.* (**c**) portrait (of sb): *Will you paint my picture?* **2** [C usu *sing*] beautiful object, scene, person etc: *The park is a picture when the daffodils are in bloom.* ○ *The children were a picture in their pretty dresses.* **3** [C usu *sing*] (**a**) account or description of sth that enables one to form a mental picture or impression of it: *The book gives a good picture of everyday life in ancient Rome.* (**b**) this mental picture: *Her careful description enabled us to form an accurate picture of what had happened.* **4** [C] (quality of the) image on a television screen: *The picture is much clearer with the new aerial.* **5** (*Brit dated*) (**a**) [C] cinema film: *Have you seen her latest picture?* (**b**) **the pictures** [pl] cinema: *We don't often go to the pictures.* **6** (idm) **be/put sb in the ˈpicture** be/cause sb to be fully informed about sth: *Are you in the picture now?* ○ *Members of Parliament insisted on being put in the picture about the government's plans.* **be the picture of health, happiness, etc** look very healthy, happy, etc. **get the ˈpicture** (*infml*) understand: *I get the picture — you two want to be left alone together.* **pretty as a picture** ⇨ PRETTY.
▷ **picture** *v* **1** [Tn, Tn·pr] ~ **sth** (**to oneself**) form a mental image of sth; imagine sth: *He pictured to himself what it might be like to live in Java.* ○ *I can't picture the village without the old church.* **2** [Tn esp passive] make a picture of (sth/sb): *They were pictured against a background of flowers.*
□ **ˈpicture-book** *n* book with many pictures, esp one for children.
ˈpicture-card *n* (in a pack of playing-cards) card with a picture on it, ie the king, queen or knave; court-card.
ˈpicture-gallery room or building in which paintings are exhibited.
ˌpicture ˈpostcard postcard with a picture on one side.
ˌpicture ˈwindow large window through which a pleasant view can be seen.

picturesque /ˌpɪktʃəˈresk/ *adj* **1** forming a pretty scene; charming or quaint: *a picturesque fishing village in the bay* ○ *a picturesque setting.* **2** (of language) strikingly expressive; vivid. **3** (of a person, his appearance, his manner, etc) strange or unusual; eccentric: *a picturesque figure in her flowery hat and dungarees.* ▷ **picturesquely** *adv.* **picturesqueness** *n* [U].

piddle /ˈpɪdl/ *v* [I] (*infml*) urinate.
▷ **piddle** *n* [U, C] (*infml*) urine: *dog piddle* ○ *The puppy has done a piddle on the carpet.*

piddling /ˈpɪdlɪŋ/ *adj* [esp attrib] (*infml derog*) (**a**) unimportant; trivial: *I don't want to hear all the piddling little details!* (**b**) small: *It's annoying to have to get authorization for spending such piddling amounts of money.*

pidgin /ˈpɪdʒɪn/ *n* any of several languages resulting from contact between European traders and local peoples, eg in W Africa and SE Asia, containing elements of the local language(s) and esp English, French or Dutch, and still used for internal communication: *speak in pidgin* ○ [attrib] *pidgin English,* ie language derived from English and another language. Cf CREOLE.

pie /paɪ/ *n* [C, U] **1** (**a**) (*Brit*) meat or fruit encased in pastry and baked in a (usu deep) dish: *an apple pie* ○ *Have some more pie.* (**b**) (*US*) meat or fruit cooked in a pastry-lined dish, with or without a covering of pastry. Cf FLAN, TART[2]. **2** (idm) **easy as pie** ⇨ EASY[1]. **eat humble pie** ⇨ EAT. **have a finger in every pie** ⇨ FINGER. **ˌpie in the ˈsky** (*infml*) hoped-for or planned event that is very unlikely to happen: *Their ideas about reforming the prison system are just pie in the sky.*
□ **ˈpie chart** diagram consisting of a circle divided into sections that represent specific proportions of the whole, eg in order to show spending in various areas as part of total expenditure. ⇨ illus at CHART.
piecrust /ˈpaɪkrʌst/ *n* [U] baked pastry covering on a pie.
ˌpie-ˈeyed *adj* (*infml*) drunk.

piebald /ˈpaɪbɔːld/ *adj* (of a horse) covered with irregularly-shaped patches of two colours, usu black and white. Cf SKEWBALD.
▷ **piebald** *n* piebald horse or pony.

piece[1] /piːs/ *n* **1** [C usu *pl*] (used esp after the *preps in, into, to*) (**a**) any of the parts of which sth is made: *He lost one of the pieces of his model engine.* ○ *The table is made in five pieces.* ○ *pull sth/take sth/come to pieces* ○ *The furniture is delivered in pieces and you have to assemble it yourself.* (**b**) any of the portions into which sth breaks: *The vase shattered into a thousand pieces.* ○ *The cup lay in pieces on the floor.* ○ *break, hack, pull, smash, tear sth to pieces* ○ *The boat (was) smashed to pieces on the rocks.* **2** [C] ~ (**of sth**) (**a**) amount of a substance (separated or broken from a larger piece): *buy a piece of glass to fit the window frame* ○ *put a piece of wood on the fire* ○ *get a piece of grit in one's eye* ○ *a piece of* (ie a slice) *bread, cake, meat, etc.* (**b**) amount or area of sth, esp for a particular purpose: *a piece of chalk,* ie for writing with ○ *a piece of land,* ie for farming or building on ○ *a piece* (ie a sheet) *of paper.* ⇨ Usage. **3** [C] ~ **of sth** (**a**) single instance or example of sth: *a piece of advice, information, luck, news, treachery* ○ *a fine piece of work.* (**b**) single article; item: *a piece of furniture, jewellery, luggage, porcelain.* **4** [C] (**a**) (esp in compounds) any of the parts of a set: *a jigsaw with 1000 pieces* ○ *a three-piece suite,* ie a sofa and two armchairs ○ *a 50-piece orchestra,* ie with 50 players. (**b**) any of the small objects or figures used in board games, esp in chess. **5** [C] standard length of cloth, wallpaper, etc as an item for sale: *cloth sold by the piece.* **6** [C] ~ (**of sth**) (**a**) (in art, music, etc) single work or composition: *a piece of music, poetry, sculpture.* (**b**) essay or newspaper article: *Did you read her piece in today's paper?* **7** [C] coin: *a ten-pence piece* ○ *a five-cent piece* ○ *a piece of eight,* ie old Spanish silver coin. **8** [C usu *sing*] (*infml becoming dated derog*) woman or girl: *a nice little piece* ○ *Do you know the piece he was with last night?* **9** [C] (*dated*) (esp in compounds) gun: *a ˈfowling-piece,* ie a gun for shooting wildfowl. **10** [sing] (*US infml*) distance: *His house is over there a piece.* **11** (idm) **a bit/piece of tail** ⇨ TAIL. **bits and pieces** ⇨ BIT[1]. **give sb a piece of one's ˈmind** (*infml*) tell sb frankly what one thinks, esp when one disapproves of his behaviour. **go** (**all**) **to ˈpieces** (of a person) have a breakdown; lose control of oneself: *After the car accident, she seemed to go to pieces.* ○ *He went to pieces when they told him the tragic news.* **in one ˈpiece** (of a person) unharmed, esp after a dangerous experience: *They were lucky to get back in one piece.* **a nasty piece of work** ⇨ NASTY. (**all**) **of a piece with sth** (**a**) consistent with sth: *The new measures are all of a piece with the government's policy.* (**b**) of the same substance or character as sth. **pick/pull sb to ˈpieces** criticize sb, esp when they are absent. **pick/pull sth to ˈpieces** argue against sth; find fault with sth. **pick up the pieces/threads** ⇨ PICK[3]. **ˌpiece by ˈpiece** one part at a time: *The bridge was moved piece by piece to a new site.* **a piece/slice of the action** ⇨ ACTION. **a ˌpiece of ˈcake** (*infml*) thing that is very easy: *The exam paper was a piece of cake.* ○ *Persuading him to give us the day off won't be a piece of cake.* **a piece of goods** ⇨ GOODS. **say one's piece** ⇨ SAY. **take a piece out of sb** reprimand sb severely. **the villain of the piece** ⇨ VILLAIN.
□ **ˈpiece-work** *n* [U] work paid for by the amount done and not by the hours worked. **ˈpiece-worker** *n.*

NOTE ON USAGE: The word **piece** can often be replaced by a more specific word: *a slice of bread* ○ *a bar of soap.* Please consult the relevant entry to find the correct word for the item concerned.

piece[2] /piːs/ *v* (phr v) **piece sth together** (**a**) assemble sth from individual pieces: *piece together a jigsaw* ○ *piece together the torn scraps of paper in order to read what was written.* (**b**) discover (a story, facts, etc) from separate pieces of evidence: *We managed to piece together the truth from several sketchy accounts.*

pièce de résistance /ˌpjes də reˈzɪstɑːns; *US* -ˌrezɪˈstɑːns/ *n* (*pl* **pièces de résistance** /ˌpjes də-/) (*French*) (**a**) (esp of creative work) the most important or impressive item: *The architect's pièce de résistance was the City Opera House.* (**b**) (at a meal) the most impressive (usu the main) dish[1](2).

piecemeal /ˈpi:smi:l/ *adv* piece by piece; a part at a time: *work done piecemeal.*

▷ **piecemeal** *adj* arriving, done, etc piecemeal: *I've only had a piecemeal account of what happened.*

pied /paɪd/ *adj* (esp of birds) having mixed colours, esp black and white: *a pied wagtail.*

pied-à-terre /ˌpjeɪd ɑ:ˈteə(r)/ *n* (*pl* **pieds-à-terre** /ˌpjeɪd ɑ:ˈteə(r)/) (*French*) small flat or other accommodation that one keeps for use when necessary: *They own a cottage in Scotland and a house in London as well as a pied-à-terre in Paris.*

Pied Piper /ˌpaɪd ˈpaɪpə(r)/ **the Pied Piper** (in German legend) piper who was employed to get rid of all the rats in the town of Hamelin. Lured by the sound of his music, the rats followed him out of the town. When the townspeople then refused to pay him, he lured away all the children in the same way. The story is the subject of a poem by Robert *Browning.

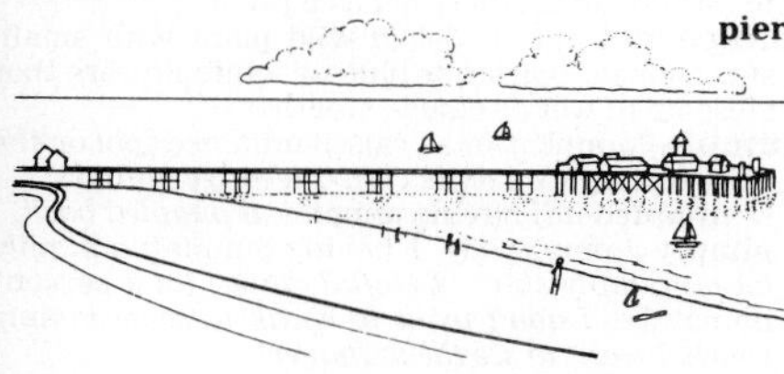

pier /pɪə(r)/ *n* **1** (**a**) structure of wood, iron, etc built out into the sea, a lake, etc so that boats can stop and take on or put down passengers or goods. Cf JETTY. (**b**) similar structure built as a promenade at a seaside resort, often with a restaurant and places of entertainment on it. ⇨ illus. **2** one of the pillars supporting an arch or a span of a bridge. **3** wall between two windows or other openings.

□ ˈ**pier-glass** *n* tall narrow mirror hung on a wall, often between windows.

pierce /pɪəs/ *v* **1** [Tn, Tn·pr] (**a**) (of sharp-pointed instruments) go into or through (sth): *The arrow pierced his shoulder.* ○ (*fig*) *Her suffering pierced their hearts.* ie moved them deeply. (**b**) make a hole in or through (sth), esp with a sharp-pointed instrument: *pierce holes in leather before sewing it* ○ *pierce the skin of cooking sausages with a fork* ○ *She had her ears pierced so that she could wear ear-rings.* **2** [Tn] (of light, sound, etc) penetrate (sth): *Her shrieks pierced the air.* ○ *The beam of the searchlight pierced the darkness.* **3** [Ipr] ~ **through sth** force a way into sth; penetrate sth: *Earth-moving equipment pierced through the jungle.*

▷ **piercing** *adj* (**a**) (of voices, sounds, etc) shrill; penetrating: *a piercing shriek.* (**b**) (of wind, cold, etc) bitter; penetrating: *a piercing chill, wind, breeze.* **piercingly** *adv*: *a piercingly cold wind.*

Piero della Francesca /ˌpɪerəʊ delə frænˈtʃeskə/ (1416-92), Italian painter, now regarded as one of the greatest artists of the 15th century. His best-known work is a series of frescoes, *The Story of the True Cross,* in a church in Arezzo.

pierrot /ˈpɪərəʊ/ *n* (*fem* **pierrette** /pɪəˈret/) **1 Pierrot** character in old French pantomime, with a whitened face and a loose white costume. His role was that of a hopeful but continuously disappointed lover. **2** (esp formerly) member of a group of entertainers performing esp at seaside resorts, with make-up and costume similar to those of the original Pierrot.

Piers Plowman /ˌpɪəz ˈplaʊmən/ long 14th-century English poem by William *Langland, which in a series of 'visions' describes the soul's search for truth and salvation. It contains powerful criticisms of the social and moral evils of medieval England.

pietà /ˌpi:eˈtɑ:/ *n* (*Italian*) painting or sculpture of the Virgin Mary holding the dead body of Christ on her lap.

pietism /ˈpaɪətɪzəm/ *n* [U] **1** (*derog*) pretended or exaggerated piety. **2 Pietism** reforming movement in the German Protestant Church in the 17th and 18th centuries, which emphasized spiritual and devotional Christianity. Pietism influenced similar movements elsewhere, including that of John *Wesley. ▷ **pietistic** /ˌpaɪəˈtɪstɪk/ *adj.*

piety /ˈpaɪətɪ/ *n* (**a**) [U] devotion to God and respect for religious principles; being pious: *filial piety*, ie respect for and obedience to a parent. (**b**) [C] act showing this.

piezo-electric /pi:ˌeɪzəʊɪˈlektrɪk/ *adj* worked by electricity which is produced by exerting pressure on certain crystals.

piffle /ˈpɪfl/ *n* [U] (*infml derog*) meaningless or worthless talk; nonsense: *You're talking piffle!*

▷ **piffling** /ˈpɪflɪŋ/ *adj* (**a**) trivial: *piffling complaints.* (**b**) very small; worthless: *He got paid a piffling sum after weeks of work.*

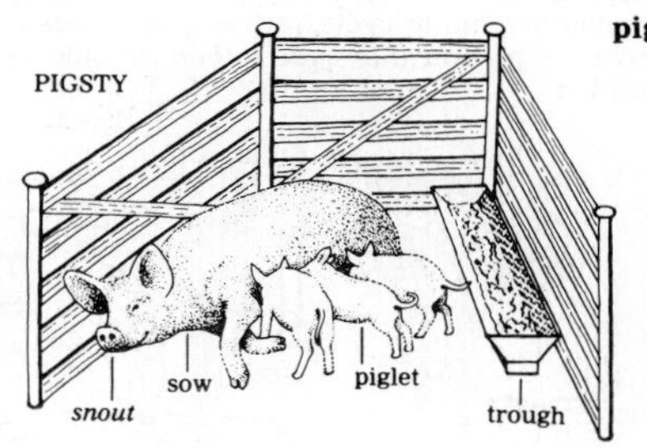

pig /pɪg/ *n* **1** (**a**) [C] domestic or wild animal with short legs, cloven hooves and a broad blunt snout. Cf BOAR, HOG 1, SOW[1], SWINE. (**b**) (also ˈ**pig-meat**) [U] its flesh as meat, ie bacon, ham or pork. **2** [C] (*infml derog*) (**a**) dirty, greedy, inconsiderate or ill-mannered person: *Don't be such a pig!* ○ *You pig!* ○ *Some drivers are real pigs.* (**b**) difficult or unpleasant thing, task, etc: *a pig of a job, day, exam.* **3** (**a**) [C] oblong mass of metal (esp iron or lead) from a smelting furnace. (**b**) [U] = PIG-IRON. **4** [C] (*dated sl*) policeman. **5** (idm) **buy a pig in a poke** ⇨ BUY. **make a** ˈ**pig of oneself** (*infml*) eat or drink too much. **make a** ˈ**pig's ear (out) of sth** (*infml*) do sth badly; make a mess of it. **pig/piggy in the** ˈ**middle** person who is caught eg between two people who are fighting or arguing, and suffers because of it. ˌ**pigs might** ˈ**fly** (*saying*) (used to express disbelief) miracles may happen but they are extremely unlikely: *Tom give up smoking? Yes, and pigs might fly!*

▷ **pig** *v* (**-gg-**) **1** [Tn] ~ **oneself** (*infml*) overeat greedily. **2** (idm) ˈ**pig it/pig to**ˈ**gether** live or behave in a dirty or untidy way.

piggery /ˈpɪgərɪ/ *n* (**a**) place where pigs are bred. (**b**) pig-farm. (**c**) pigsty.

piggish /ˈpɪgɪʃ/ *adj* (**a**) like a pig. (**b**) dirty or greedy. **piggishly** *adv.* **piggishness** *n* [U].

piggy *n* (*infml*) little pig. — *adj* (*infml*) piggish: *He has piggy eyes!* ˈ**piggyback** *adv, n* ⇨ PICK-A-BACK. ˈ**piggy bank** money-box, usu shaped like a pig, with a slot for putting in coins.

□ ˌ**pig**ˈ**headed** *adj* stubborn. ˌ**pig**ˈ**headedly** *adv.* ˌ**pig**ˈ**headedness** *n* [U].

ˈ**pig-iron** *n* [U] impure form of iron from a smelting furnace.

ˈ**pigskin** /-skɪn/ *n* **1** [U] (leather made from a) pig's skin: [attrib] *a* ˌ*pigskin* ˈ*briefcase.* **2** [C] (*US infml*) a football.

ˈ**pigsty** /-staɪ/ (also **sty**) *n* **1** (*US* ˈ**pigpen**) building in which pigs are kept. ⇨ illus. **2** (*infml*) very dirty or untidy place: *He makes a pigsty of the kitchen whenever he does the cooking.*

ˈ**pigswill** /-swɪl/ *n* [U] = SWILL *n* 2.

pigeon /ˈpɪdʒɪn/ *n* **1** (**a**) [C] any of several types of wild or tame bird of the dove family: *a* ˈ*carrier-*/ˈ*homing-pigeon*, ie one trained to carry messages or to race as a sport. ⇨ illus at BIRD. (**b**) [U] flesh of a wild pigeon eaten as food: [attrib] *pigeon pie.* **2** (idm) ˈ**one's pigeon** (*infml*) one's responsibility or business: *I don't care where the money comes from: that's not* ˈ*my pigeon.* **put/set the cat among the pigeons** ⇨ CAT[1].

□ ˈ**pigeon-breasted** *adj* (of a person) having a deformed chest with the breastbone curving outwards.

ˈ**pigeon-hole** *n* any one of a set of small open boxes, esp in a desk, for keeping papers in, or fixed on a wall for messages, letters, etc. — *v* [Tn esp passive] **1** put (papers, etc) in a pigeon-hole (and ignore or forget them): *The scheme was pigeon-holed after a brief discussion.* **2** classify or categorize (sth) esp in a rigid manner: *She felt her son had been pigeon-holed as a problem child.*

ˈ**pigeon-toed** *adj* (of a person) having toes that turn inwards.

piglet /ˈpɪglɪt/ *n* young pig. ⇨ illus at PIG.

pigment /ˈpɪgmənt/ *n* **1** [U, C] colouring matter used for making dyes, paint, etc: *pigment in powder form* ○ *mix pigment with oil* ○ *They used only natural pigments to dye the wool.* **2** [U] colouring matter occurring naturally in the skin, hair, etc of living beings.

▷ **pigmentation** /ˌpɪgmenˈteɪʃn/ *n* [U] colouring of the skin, hair, etc by pigment: *The disease causes patches of pigmentation on the face.*

pigmy *n* = PYGMY.

pigtail /ˈpɪgteɪl/ *n* plait of hair that hangs from the back of the head. ⇨ illus at PLAIT.

pike[1] /paɪk/ *n* type of spear with a long wooden handle, formerly used as a weapon by soldiers on foot.

□ ˈ**pikestaff** /-stɑ:f/ *n* **1** wooden handle of a pike. **2** (idm) **plain as a pikestaff** ⇨ PLAIN[1].

pike[2] /paɪk/ *n* (*pl* unchanged) large freshwater fish with a long narrow snout and very sharp teeth.

pike[3] /paɪk/ *n* (*dialect*) (in N England) pointed or peaked top of a hill: *Langdale Pike in the Lake District.*

pike[4] /paɪk/ *n* = TURNPIKE.

pike[5] /paɪk/ *n* position in diving and gymnastics, with the body first bent double and then straightened; jack-knife(2).

▷ **piked** *adj* with the body in the pike position.

pilaff /pɪˈlæf/ *US* -ˈlɑ:f/ (also **pilaf, pilau** /pɪˈlaʊ/) *n* [U, C] oriental dish of steamed rice, vegetables and spices, often with meat or fish.

pilaster /pɪˈlæstə(r)/ *n* rectangular column, esp an ornamental one set into a wall and partly projecting from it.

Pilate /ˈpaɪlət/ Pontius (1st century AD), Roman governor of Judaea 26-36 AD who ordered Jesus to be executed, after washing his hands as a symbolic gesture to indicate that he did not feel responsible for Jesus's death.

pilchard /ˈpɪltʃəd/ *n* small sea-fish similar to a herring, eaten as food.

pile[1] /paɪl/ *n* heavy column of wood, metal or concrete placed upright in the ground or the sea-bed as a foundation for a building, support for a bridge, etc.

□ ˈ**pile-driver** *n* machine for forcing piles into the ground.

pile[2] /paɪl/ *n* **1** number of things lying one upon another: *a pile of books, laundry, wood* ○ *The rubbish was left in a pile on the floor.* **2** (often *pl*) ~ **of sth** (*infml*) a lot of sth: *a pile of work to do* ○ *The children eat piles of butter on their bread.* ○ *The engine seems to need piles of oil.* **3** (*fml or joc*) large impressive building or group of buildings. **4** (also ˈ**funeral pile**) = PYRE. **5** dry battery for making electric current. **6** (also **atomic** ˈ**pile**) nuclear reactor. **7** (idm) **make a** ˈ**pile** (*infml*) earn a lot of money: *I bet they are making a pile out of the deal.* **make one's** ˈ**pile** (*infml*) make enough money to live on for the rest of one's life; make one's fortune: *He made his pile during the property boom.*

pile[3] /paɪl/ *v* **1** [Tn, Tn·pr, Tn·p] ~ **sth (up)** put (things) one on top of the other; form a pile of (things): *pile the books into a stack* ○ *pile (up) the logs outside the door* ○ *pile the books up* ○ *pile up the old furniture in the shed.* **2** [Tn·pr] ~ **A on(to) B**/ ~ **B with A** put sth on sth in a pile; load sth with sth: *pile papers on the table* ○ *pile the table with* papers ○ *pile plenty of coal onto the fire* ○ *a table piled high with dishes.* **3** (idm) **pile it ˈon** (*infml*) exaggerate: *It's probably not as bad as she says — she does tend to pile it on.* **pile on the ˈagony** (*infml*) treat an unpleasant situation as if it was worse than it really is (and enjoy doing so): *The situation is frightful, but it's just piling on the agony to keep discussing it.* **4** (phr v) **pile into sth/out of sth; pile in/out** enter/leave sth in a disorderly way: *The taxi arrived and we all piled in.* ○ *The children piled noisily into the bus.* ○ *The police were waiting for the hooligans as they piled out of the train.* **pile up** (**a**) increase in quantity; accumulate: *Evidence was piling up against them.* ○ *Her debts are piling up and she has no money to pay them.* (**b**) (of a number of vehicles) crash into each other, esp with each car hitting the one in front.

□ **ˈpile-up** *n* crash involving several vehicles: *The thick fog has caused several bad pile-ups on the motorway.*

pile[4] /paɪl/ *n* [U] soft surface, eg of velvet or of certain carpets formed from cut or uncut loops of fibre: *the thick pile of a luxurious bath towel* ○ [attrib] *a deep pile carpet.* Cf NAP[2].

piles /paɪlz/ *n* [pl] = HAEMORRHOIDS.

pilfer /ˈpɪlfə(r)/ *v* [I, Ipr, Tn] ~ (**sth**) (**from sb/sth**) steal (sth, esp of small value or in small quantities): *He was caught pilfering.* ○ *She had been pilfering from the petty cash for months.*

▷ **pilferer** /ˈpɪlfərə(r)/ *n.*

pilferage /ˈpɪlfərɪdʒ/ *n* [U] (**a**) action of pilfering. (**b**) loss caused by pilfering, esp during transport or storage of goods: *Pilferage in the warehouse reduces profitability by about two per cent.*

pilgrim /ˈpɪlgrɪm/ *n* person who travels to a holy place as an act of religious devotion: *pilgrims on their way to Mecca* ○ *pilgrims visiting the shrine.*

▷ **pilgrimage** /-ɪdʒ/ *n* **1** [C, U] journey made as a pilgrim: *go on/make a pilgrimage to Benares* ○ *Santiago de Compostela was an important place of pilgrimage in the Middle Ages.* **2** [C] journey made to a place associated with sb/sth one respects: *a pilgrimage to Shakespeare's birthplace.*

□ **the Pilgrim ˈFathers** (also **the Pilgrims**) name given to the English Puritans who went to America in 1620 and founded the colony of Plymouth, Massachusetts.

Pilgrim's Progress /ˌpɪlgrɪmz ˈprəʊgres/ book by John *Bunyan, written between 1678 and 1684, which describes allegorically a man's journey through life to heaven. The man, called Christian, meets many symbolic difficulties along the way, becoming stuck in the Slough of Despond and imprisoned by Giant Despair.

pill /pɪl/ *n* **1** [C] small ball or flat round piece of medicine made to be swallowed whole: *a vitamin pill* ○ *He has to take* (ie swallow) *six pills a day until he recovers.* **2 the pill** (also **the Pill**) [sing] (*infml*) artificial hormone in pill form taken regularly to prevent conception; oral contraceptive: *be/go on the pill,* ie be/start taking contraceptive pills regularly ○ *do research on the side-effects of the pill.* **3** (idm) **a bitter pill** ⇨ BITTER. **sugar/sweeten the pill** make sth unpleasant seem less unpleasant.

□ **ˈpillbox** *n* **1** small round box used as a container for pills. **2** small concrete shelter for soldiers, often partly underground, from which a gun may be fired. **3** small round hat.

pillage /ˈpɪlɪdʒ/ *n* [U] (*fml*) (esp formerly) stealing or damaging of property, esp by soldiers in war. Cf LOOT, PLUNDER.

▷ **pillage** *v* [I, Tn] rob (sb/sth of goods, crops, etc) with violence, as in war: *The town was pillaged by the invading army.* **pillager** /-ɪdʒə(r)/ *n* person who pillages.

pillar /ˈpɪlə(r)/ *n* **1** (**a**) upright column of stone, wood, metal, etc used as a support or an ornament, a monument, etc. (**b**) thing in the shape of this: *a pillar of cloud, fire, smoke, etc.* **2** ~ **of sth** strong supporter of sth: *a pillar of the Church, the establishment, the faith* ○ *a scandal involving several pillars* (ie respected members) *of society* ○ *She was a pillar of strength to us* (ie supported us strongly) *when our situation seemed hopeless.* **3** (idm) **go from ˌpillar to ˈpost** (go) from one person or thing to another (esp in an unsatisfactory or upsetting way): *She was driven from pillar to post and each person she spoke to was more unhelpful than the last.*

□ **ˈpillar-box** *n* (*Brit*) public post-box in the shape of a pillar about five feet high and painted bright red: [attrib] *pillar-box red.*

Pillar-boxes were introduced into Britain by Anthony *Trollope during his time at the Post Office. They bear the symbol of the crown and the initials of the king or queen reigning when they were made. The earliest pillar-boxes bear the initials VR for Victoria Regina (Queen Victoria). Collection times are given and the time of the next collection is indicated by a number. In cities, pillar-boxes are sometimes oval in shape, and have one posting slot for 1st class mail and one for 2nd class mail. These were formerly marked 'Town' and 'Country', and separated letters going to local destinations from those going further afield.

pillion /ˈpɪlɪən/ *n* seat for a passenger behind the driver of a motor cycle: [attrib] *pillion passenger/seat.* ▷ **pillion** *adv*: *ride pillion,* ie ride on the pillion.

pillory

pillory /ˈpɪlərɪ/ *n* wooden framework with holes for the head and hands, into which wrongdoers were locked in former times, so that they could be publicly ridiculed. ⇨ illus.

▷ **pillory** *v* (*pt, pp* **-ried** /-lərɪd/) [Tn] attack or ridicule (sb) in public: *She was pilloried in the press for her extravagant parties.*

pillow /ˈpɪləʊ/ *n* (**a**) cushion used to support the head, esp in bed: *sit in bed propped up with pillows.* (**b**) anything on which one rests one's head when sleeping: *He was found asleep on a pillow of leaves and moss.*

▷ **pillow** *v* [Tn] rest or support (sth) on or as if on a pillow: *He pillowed his head on her lap.*

□ **ˈpillowcase** (also **ˈpillowslip**) *n* removable washable cover made of cotton, linen, etc for a pillow.

ˈpillow-fight *n* mock fight between children using pillows as weapons.

ˈpillow talk [U] conversation between lovers in bed.

pilot /ˈpaɪlət/ *n* **1** person who operates the controls of an aircraft. **2** person with special knowledge of a canal, the entrance to a harbour, etc who is licensed to guide ships through them. **3** person or thing acting as a guide.

▷ **pilot** *adj* [attrib] done as an experiment, esp on a small scale, to test sth before it is introduced on a large scale: *a ˈpilot project, study, survey, etc* ○ *a pilot edition of a new language course* ○ *a pilot scheme to vaccinate children against German measles.*

pilot *v* **1** [Tn, Tn·pr] ~ **sb/sth** (**through sth**) (**a**) act as a pilot of sth: *pilot a plane* ○ *pilot a ship through the Panama Canal.* (**b**) guide sb/sth: *pilot sb through a crowd.* (**c**) (in Parliament) make sure that sth (esp a bill) is successful: *pilot a bill through the House.* **2** [Tn] test (sth) by means of a pilot scheme: *Schools in this area are piloting the new maths course.*

□ **ˈpilot-boat** *n* boat that takes a pilot to a ship at sea.

ˈpilot-fish *n* type of small fish that accompanies ships or swims together with sharks, etc.

ˈpilot-light (also **ˈpilot-burner**) *n* small flame that burns continuously, eg on a gas cooker or boiler, and lights a larger burner when the gas is turned on.

ˈPilot Officer (*Brit*) officer in the Royal Air Force below the rank of Flying Officer. ⇨ App 4.

Pilsner (also **Pilsener**) /ˈpɪlznə(r)/ *n* [U, C] pale lager beer of the type made at Pilsen in the Czech Republic.

Piltdown man /ˌpɪltdaʊn ˈmæn/ supposed early type of human being described on the basis of fossil bones found on Piltdown Common, Sussex, England in 1912. These were later proved to have been a hoax, being composed of a human skull and an ape's jaw.

pilule (also **pillule**) /ˈpɪljuːl/ *n* small pill.

pimento /pɪˈmentəʊ/ *n* (*pl* ~**s**) **1** (**a**) (also **allspice**) [U] dried aromatic berries used as a spice. (**b**) [C] West Indian tree on which these grow. **2** (also **pimiento** /pɪˈmjentəʊ/) [C] sweet pepper; capsicum.

pimp /pɪmp/ *n* (**a**) (also **pander**) man who finds customers for a prostitute or a brothel. (**b**) man who controls prostitutes and lives on the money they earn.

▷ **pimp** *v* [I, Ipr] ~ (**for sb**) find customers (for a prostitute or brothel); act as a pimp.

pimpernel /ˈpɪmpənel/ *n* wild plant with small, star-shaped, scarlet or blue or white flowers that close up in wet or cloudy weather.

pimple /ˈpɪmpl/ *n* small raised inflamed spot on the skin: *a pimple on one's chin* ○ *teenage pimples.*

▷ **pimpled** *adj* having pimples: *a pimpled back.*

pimply /ˈpɪmplɪ/ *adj* **1** having pimples: *a pimply face* ○ *pimply skin.* **2** (*infml derog*) (of a person) immature: *I don't want to speak to some pimply youth, I want to see the manager!*

pin[1] /pɪn/ *n* **1** [C] (**a**) short thin piece of stiff wire with a sharp point at one end and a round head at the other, used for fastening together pieces of cloth, paper, etc. (**b**) (esp in compounds) similar piece of wire with a sharp point and a decorated head, used for a special purpose: *a diamond pin* ○ *a ˈtie-pin* ○ *a ˈhat-pin.* **2** [C] (esp in compounds) peg of wood or metal for various special purposes: *a 2-pin plug,* ie a type of electric plug ○ *a ˈdrawing-pin* ○ *a ˈhairpin* ○ *a ˈrolling-pin* ○ *ˈninepins* ○ (*US*) *a ˈclothes-pin,* ie a clothes-peg. **3** [C] (in golf) pole with a flag on top, marking the hole into which the ball is hit. **4** [C] (also **ˈsafety pin**) clip on a hand grenade that stops it from exploding. **5 pins** [pl] (*infml*) legs. **6** (idm) **clean as a new pin** ⇨ CLEAN[1]. **for two pins** with very little persuasion or provocation: *For two pins I'd tell him what I think of him.* **hear a pin drop** ⇨ HEAR. **not care/give a ˈpin/two ˈpins** (**for sth**) attach no importance or value to sth: *He doesn't give two pins for what the critics say about his work.* **on one's pins** (*infml*) when standing or walking: *She's not very steady on her pins.* ○ *be quick on one's pins.*

□ **ˈpin-ball** *n* [U] game in which small metal balls are aimed at numbered pins placed on a sloping board: [attrib] *a pin-ball machine.*

ˈpincushion *n* small pad used (esp by dressmakers) for sticking pins in when they are not being used.

ˈpin-head *n* (*infml*) (**a**) (*derog*) stupid person. (**b**) very small thing or spot. **pin-ˈheaded** *adj* stupid; foolish.

pin-ˈhigh *adv* (of a ball in golf) at the same distance as the pin[1](3).

ˈpin-money *n* [U] (**a**) (esp formerly) small amount of money given to a woman or earned by her for her personal needs, esp clothes. (**b**) money saved or earned for small extra expenses: *She only works for pin-money.*

ˈpinpoint *n* (**a**) sharp end of a pin. (**b**) anything that is very small or sharp: *pinpoint the spot on a map.* (**c**) define (sth) exactly: *pinpoint the causes of the political unrest* ○ *pinpoint the areas in most urgent need of help.*

ˈpinprick *n* **1** prick caused by a pin. **2** (*fig*) thing that is annoying although small or unimportant.

ˌpins and ˈneedles tingling sensation in a part of the body, esp a limb, caused by the blood flowing again after being stopped by pressure.

ˈpin-stripe *n* very narrow stripe in cloth: [attrib] *a pin-stripe suit.*

ˈ**pin-table** *n* table used in pin-ball.

pin[2] /pɪn/ *v* (**-nn-**) **1** [Tn, Tn·pr, Tn·p] ~ **sth to sth**; ~ **sth (together)** attach sth with a pin or pins: *Be careful when you try on the dress — it's only pinned.* ○ *a note pinned to the document* ○ *Pin the bills together so you don't lose them.* ○ (*fig*) *They held him with his arms pinned to his side.* **2** [Tn·pr] ~ **sth on sb** attach or fix sth to sb: *We're pinning all our hopes on you.* ie relying on you completely. **3** (phr v) **pin sb/sth against/under sth** make it impossible for sb to move/sth to be moved: *They pinned him against the wall.* ○ *She was pinned under the wreckage of the car.* ○ *The car was pinned under a fallen tree.* **pin sth back/down/up** fasten sth with pins in the position specified: *pin up a notice on the board*, ie with drawing-pins. **pin sb down (a)** make sb unable to move, esp by holding him firmly: *He was pinned down by his attackers.* **(b)** make sb be specific or declare his intentions clearly: *She's a difficult person to pin down.* **pin sb down (to sth/doing sth)** make sb agree (to sth): *I managed to pin him down to meeting us after work.* ○ *You'll find it difficult to pin him down to (naming) a price.* **pin sth down** define sth exactly: *There's something wrong with this colour scheme but I can't quite pin it down.* **pin sth on sb** make sb seem responsible or take the blame for sth: *The bank manager was really to blame, though he tried to pin it on a clerk.*

□ ˈ**pin-up** *n* (*infml*) **(a)** picture of an attractive or famous person, eg a film star, for pinning on a wall: [attrib] *a pin-up pose.* **(b)** person portrayed in such a picture.

PIN *abbr* (also **PIN number**) personal identification number (issued by a bank, etc to a customer for use with a cash card).

pinafore /ˈpɪnəfɔ:(r)/ *n* loose sleeveless garment worn over clothes to keep them clean; apron. ⇨ illus at APRON.

□ ˈ**pinafore dress** dress without sleeves or a collar, worn over a blouse or sweater.

pince-nez /ˌpænsˈneɪ/ *n* (*pl* unchanged) [sing or pl *v*] pair of spectacles with a spring that clips on the nose, instead of side-pieces which fit over the ears.

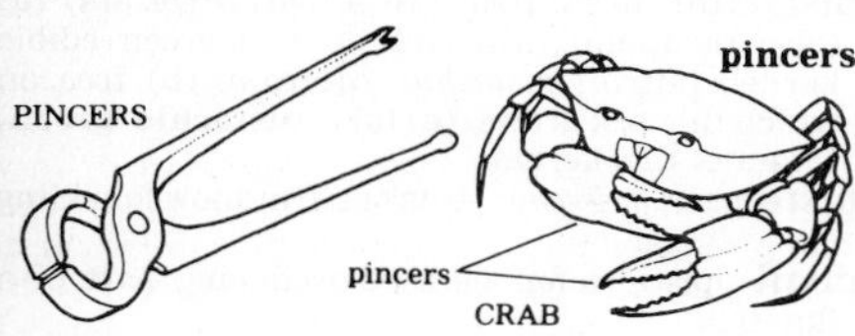

pincer /ˈpɪnsə(r)/ *n* **1** [C] either of the pair of curved claws of certain types of shellfish, eg lobsters, crabs, etc. **2 pincers** [pl] tool made of two crossed pieces of metal and used for pulling nails, etc out of wood: *a pair of pincers.* ⇨ illus.

□ ˈ**pincer movement** military attack on an enemy position by forces advancing from two sides.

pinch /pɪntʃ/ *v* **1** [Tn, Tn·pr] **(a)** take or hold (sth) in a tight grip between the thumb and finger: *He pinched the child's cheek playfully.* **(b)** hurt (sb) by holding his flesh in this way: *The child was crying because somebody had pinched her.* ○ *I was so amazed I had to pinch myself in case it was all a dream.* **(c)** have (sth) in a tight grip between two hard things that are pressed together: *The door pinched my finger as it shut.* **2** [I, Tn] (esp of shoes) hurt (sb) by being too tight: *These new boots pinch (me).* **3** [Tn] ~ **sth (from sb/sth)** (*infml*) take sth without the owner's permission; steal sth: *He's been pinching money from the cashbox.* ○ *Who's pinched my dictionary?* **4** [Tn esp passive] (*sl*) (of the police) catch and arrest (sb): *He was still carrying the stolen goods when he was pinched.* ○ *get pinched for driving while drunk.* **5** (idm) **pinch and** ˈ**save**/ˈ**scrape** live in a very miserly way: *Her parents pinched and scraped so that she could study singing abroad.* Cf SCRIMP AND SAVE (SCRIMP). **6** (phr v) **pinch sth off/out** remove sth by pinching: *pinch out the weak shoots on a plant* ○ *pinch off the dead flowers.*

▷ **pinch** *n* **1** act of pinching; painful squeeze: *She gave him a pinch (on the arm) to wake him up.* **2** as much as can be held between the tips of the thumb and forefinger: *a pinch of chilli powder* ○ *Put another pinch of tea in the pot.* **3** (idm) **at a** ˈ**pinch** just possibly, in a case of necessity: *We can get six people round this table at a pinch.* **feel the pinch** ⇨ FEEL[1]. **if it** ˌ**comes to the** ˈ**pinch** in a case of necessity or in an emergency: *If it comes to the pinch, we shall have to sell the house.* **take sth with a pinch of salt** think that sth is not likely to be true; not wholly believe sth.

pinched *adj* **(a)** ~ **(with sth)** suffering (from sth); wretched: *be pinched with cold/poverty* ○ *look pinched/have a pinched look*, ie drawn or haggard. **(b)** [pred] ~ **for sth** not having enough of sth: *pinched for money, space, time.*

pinchbeck /ˈpɪntʃbek/ *n* [U] alloy of copper and zinc that looks like gold and is used in cheap jewellery, etc.

▷ **pinchbeck** *adj* imitation; sham.

pine[1] /paɪn/ *n* **(a)** [C] (also ˈ**pine tree**) any of several types of evergreen tree that bear cones and have needle-shaped leaves growing in clusters: [attrib] *pine-scented*, ie (esp of a deodorant, disinfectant, soap, etc) smelling of pines. ⇨ illus at TREE. **(b)** [U] its pale soft wood, used in making furniture, floors, window frames, etc: [attrib] *a pine dresser.*

□ ˈ**pine-cone** *n* fruit of the pine.

ˈ**pine-needle** *n* leaf of the pine.

pine[2] /paɪn/ *v* **1** [I] be very unhappy, esp because sb has died or gone away: *She certainly hasn't been pining while you were away!* **2** [Ipr, It] ~ **(for sb/sth)** long for or miss sb/sth: *She was pining for her mother.* ○ *They were pining to return home.* **3** (idm) **peak and pine** ⇨ PEAK[2]. **4** (phr v) **pine away** become ill or waste away (and die) because of grief: *She lost interest in living and just pined away.*

pineal /ˈpaɪnɪəl/ *adj* shaped like a pine-cone.

□ ˌ**pineal** ˈ**gland** cone-shaped gland in the brain. ⇨ illus at BRAIN.

pineapple /ˈpaɪnæpl/ *n* **(a)** [C, U] large juicy tropical fruit with sweet yellow flesh and a prickly skin: *fresh/tinned pineapple* ○ [attrib] ˈ*pineapple juice.* ⇨ illus at FRUIT. **(b)** [C] tropical plant that bears this fruit.

Pinero /pɪˈnɪərəʊ/ Sir Arthur Wing (1855-1934), English dramatist. He wrote many plays, the most famous being *The Second Mrs Tanqueray* and *Trelawny of the 'Wells'*.

ping /pɪŋ/ *n* short sharp ringing sound (as) of a hard object hitting a hard surface: *the ping of a spoon hitting a glass* ○ *the ping of bullets hitting the rocks* ○ *There was a loud ping as the elastic broke.*

▷ **ping** *v* **1** [I, Tn] (cause sth to) make this sound: *bullets pinging overhead* ○ *ping a knife against a glass.* **2** [I] (*US*) = PINK[3]. **pinger** *n* (*infml*) device that makes a ringing sound after a set time, used eg in a kitchen to show that sth is cooked.

ping-pong /ˈpɪŋpɒŋ/ *n* [U] (*infml*) (also ˈ**table tennis**) game played like tennis with bats and a plastic ball on a table with a net across it: *a game of ping-pong* ○ [attrib] *a ping-pong champion.*

pinion[1] /ˈpɪnɪən/ *n* (*fml*) **1 (a)** outer segment of a bird's wing. **(b)** (*dated*) bird's wing. **2** any of the stiff feathers which support a bird when it is flying; flight-feather.

▷ **pinion** *v* **1** [esp passive: Tn, Tn·pr, Tn·p] ~ **sb/sth against/to sth**; ~ **sth together** bind or hold (sb or sb's arms) to prevent him moving: *They were pinioned against the wall by the lorry.* ○ *He was held with his arms pinioned together behind his back.* **2** [Tn] cut off the pinions from (a bird or its wing) to prevent it from flying.

pinion[2] /ˈpɪnɪən/ *n* small cog-wheel with teeth which fit into those of a larger cog-wheel. Cf RACK[1] 3.

pink[1] /pɪŋk/ *adj* **1** of a pale red colour: *rose/salmon pink walls* ○ *go/turn pink with confusion, embarrassment, etc.* **2** (*infml*) having slightly left-wing political views. Cf RED[2]. **3** (idm) **be tickled pink/to death** ⇨ TICKLE.

▷ **pink** *n* **1** [U] (clothes of a) pink colour: *Pink is her favourite colour.* ○ *dressed in pink.* **2** [C] garden plant with sweet-smelling pink, crimson or variegated flowers. **3** [U] (*Brit*) (colour of the) red coat worn by fox-hunters: *dressed in hunting pink.* **4** (idm) **in the pink (of condition/health)** extremely healthy; in perfect condition: *The children all looked in the pink after their holiday.* **pink** ˈ**elephants** (*infml*) strange imaginary things supposedly seen by people when they are drunk. **pinkish** *adj* fairly pink: *a pinkish glow.*

□ ˈ**pink-eye** *n* [U] infectious disease causing inflammation of the surface of the eye; conjunctivitis.

ˌ**pink** ˈ**gin** drink of gin flavoured (and coloured slightly pink) with angostura bitters.

pink[2] /pɪŋk/ *v* [Tn] **1** pierce (sth) slightly. **2** cut a zigzag or scalloped edge on (sth).

□ ˈ**pinking shears** (also ˈ**pinking scissors**) scissors with serrated blades used to make a zigzag edge on fabric and prevent it from fraying. ⇨ illus at SCISSORS.

pink[3] /pɪŋk/ (*US* **ping** /pɪŋ/) *v* [I] (of a car engine) make small explosive sounds when not running properly; knock[2](4).

Pinkerton /ˈpɪŋkətən/ Allan (1819-84), American detective who founded the Pinkerton Detective Agency, a firm of private detectives, in Chicago in 1850.

pinkie (also **pinky**) /ˈpɪŋkɪ/ *n* (*Scot or US*) the smallest finger of the human hand; the little finger.

pinko /ˈpɪŋkəʊ/ *n* (*pl* ~**s**) (*sl derog*) person with left-wing political ideas.

pinnace /ˈpɪnɪs/ *n* small motor boat carried on a ship for taking people ashore, loading goods, etc. Cf LIGHTER[2].

pinnacle /ˈpɪnəkl/ *n* **1** small pointed ornament built on to a roof or buttress. ⇨ illus at CHURCH. **2** high pointed rock or mountain peak. **3** (*fig*) highest point; peak: *the pinnacle of one's career, fame, success, etc.*

pinnate /ˈpɪneɪt/ *adj* (*botany*) (of a leaf) formed of a stem with a row of small leaves on either side.

pinny /ˈpɪnɪ/ *n* (*infml*) pinafore: *Where's my kitchen pinny?*

pinochle /ˈpi:nʌkl/ *n* [U] card-game for two to four people, played esp in the USA with a double pack of 48 cards (nine to ace only).

pint /paɪnt/ *n* **1** (*abbr* **pt**) **(a)** (*Brit*) unit of measure for liquids and some dry goods, $\frac{1}{8}$ of a gallon (equal to 0.568 of a litre): *a pint of beer, milk, shrimps.* **(b)** (*US*) similar measure (equal to 0.473 of a litre). ⇨ App 10. **2** this quantity of (esp) milk or beer: *They stopped at the pub for a pint.* **3** (idm) **put a quart into a pint pot** ⇨ QUART.

□ ˈ**pint-sized** *adj* (*infml*) very small.

pinta /ˈpaɪntə/ *n* (*Brit infml*) pint of milk: *drink a daily pinta.* ⇨ article at DRINK.

Pinter /ˈpɪntə(r)/ Harold (1930-), English dramatist whose plays (eg *The Caretaker*, *The Homecoming* and *No Man's Land)* often have a feeling of unexplained menace. Their naturalistic dialogue illustrates how people often misunderstand each other. ⇨ article at PERFORMING ARTS.

pinto /ˈpɪntəʊ/ *n* (*pl* ~**s**) (*US*) horse with irregular markings of two or more colours; piebald.

▷ **pinto** *adj* mottled: ˈ*pinto beans.*

pioneer /ˌpaɪəˈnɪə(r)/ *n* **1 (a)** person who is among the first to go into an area or country to settle or work there: *land cleared by the pioneers* ○ [attrib] *pioneer wagons.* **(b)** person who goes into previously unknown regions; explorer: *pioneers in space.* **2** person who is the first to study a new area of knowledge: *They were pioneers in the field of microsurgery.* ○ [attrib] *pioneer work.* **3** any one of a group of soldiers who go into an area in advance of an army to clear paths, make roads, etc.

▷ **pioneer** *v* **1** [I] act as a pioneer(1a). **2** [Tn] open up (a way, etc): *pioneer a new route to the coast.* **3** [Tn] be the first person to develop (new methods); help the early development of (sth): *She pioneered the use of the drug.*

pious /ˈpaɪəs/ *adj* **1** having or showing a deep devotion to religion. **2** (*derog*) hypocritically virtuous: *He dismissed his critics as pious do-gooders who were afraid to face the facts.* ▷

piously *adv*. **piousness** *n* [U].

pip[1] /pɪp/ *n* seed, esp of a lemon, an orange, an apple, a pear or a grape.

pip[2] /pɪp/ *n* (idm) **give sb the ˈpip** (*Brit infml*) give sb a feeling of annoyance, bad temper or depression: *She gives me the pip.* ○ *His disgusting jokes gave everybody the pip.*

pip[3] /pɪp/ *n* (usu *pl*) short high-pitched sound used esp as a time-signal on the radio or telephone; bleep: *Wait until you hear the pips and then put in more money*, eg when using a pay phone. ○ *The weather forecast is followed by the pips at 6 o'clock.*

pip[4] /pɪp/ *n* **1** any of the spots on playing-cards, dice and dominoes. **2** (*Brit infml*) star on the shoulder-strap of an army officer's uniform.

pip[5] /pɪp/ *v* (**-pp-**) (*infml*) **1** [Tn] hit (sb) with a shot: *pipped in the shoulder.* **2** (idm) **pip sb at the post** (esp passive) defeat sb narrowly or at the last moment: *We didn't win the contract: we were pipped at the post by a firm whose price was lower.*

pipal (also **peepul**) /ˈpiːpəl/ *n* large Indian fig-tree.

pipe[1] /paɪp/ *n* **1** [C] (esp in compounds) tube through which liquids or gases can flow: *a ˈwater-pipe* ○ *a ˈgas-pipe* ○ *a ˈdrain-pipe* ○ *the ˈwindpipe*, ie air-passage in the body. **2** [C] **(a)** (also **toˈbacco pipe**) narrow tube with a bowl at one end, used for smoking tobacco: *smoke a pipe* ○ [attrib] *ˈpipe tobacco.* **(b)** (also **pipeful** /-fʊl/) amount of tobacco this can hold. **3** [C] (*music*) **(a)** wind instrument consisting of a tube with holes that are covered and uncovered by the fingers to make musical notes: *pipes of Pan*, ie pan-pipes. **(b)** each of the tubes from which sound is produced in an organ. **(c) pipes** [pl] = BAGPIPES. **4** [C] (sound of a) whistle used by a boatswain. **5** [C] song or note of a bird. **6** [C] (contents of a) cask which can hold about 105 gallons of wine. **7** (idm) **put ˈthat in your pipe and smoke it** (*infml*) you have to accept what I have said, whether you like it or not: *I'm not giving up my holiday to suit you, so you can put that in your pipe and smoke it!*

□ **ˈpipeclay** *n* [U] fine white clay used (esp formerly) for making tobacco pipes and for whitening leather, etc.

ˈpipe-cleaner *n* flexible piece of wire covered with soft material, for cleaning inside a tobacco pipe.

ˈpipe-dream *n* hope or plan that is impossible or unworkable.

ˈpipeline *n* **1** series of connected pipes, usu underground, for conveying oil, gas, etc to a distant place. **2** (*fig*) channel of information or supply, esp direct, privileged or confidential: *a pipeline to head office, the Prime Minister, the manufacturer.* **3** (idm) **in the ˈpipeline (a)** (of goods, orders, etc) being dealt with; on the way. **(b)** (of changes, laws, proposals, etc) being prepared or discussed; about to happen: *New laws to deal with this abuse are in the pipeline.*

pipe[2] /paɪp/ *v* **1** [Tn, Tn·pr] convey (water, gas, etc) in pipes: *pipe water into a house/to a farm* ○ *pipe oil across the desert.* **2** [esp passive: Tn, Tn·pr] transmit (esp music) by wire or cable: *Nearly all the shops have piped music*, ie recorded music played continuously. **3** [I, Tn] **(a)** play (a jig) on a pipe or pipes: *He piped (a tune) so that we could dance.* **(b)** (of a bird) whistle or sing (sth). **(c)** (of a person, esp a child) speak (sth) in a high voice. **4** [Tn·pr, Tn·p] (*nautical*) **(a)** summon (sailors) by blowing a boatswain's pipe: *pipe all hands on deck.* **(b)** lead or welcome (sb) by the sound of a boatswain's pipe: *pipe the captain aboard/on board* ○ *pipe the guests in.* **5** [Tn] **(a)** trim or decorate (sth) with piping(2a): *pipe a skirt, cushion, etc with blue silk.* **(b)** put a decoration on (a cake) with icing: *pipe 'Happy Birthday' on a cake.* **6** (phr v) **pipe down** (*infml*) be less noisy; stop talking: *She told the children to pipe down while she was talking on the telephone.* **pipe up** (*infml*) begin to sing or speak, esp suddenly and in a high-pitched voice.

Piper /ˈpaɪpə(r)/ John (1903-), English painter and designer best known for his water-colour pictures of buildings, his stained-glass windows and his stage designs.

piper /ˈpaɪpə(r)/ *n* **1** person who plays on a pipe, esp the bagpipes. **2** (idm) **he who pays the piper calls the tune** ⇨ PAY.

pipette /pɪˈpet/ *n* (esp in chemistry) slender tube, usu filled by sucking, used in a laboratory for transferring or measuring small quantities of liquids.

piping /ˈpaɪpɪŋ/ *n* [U] **1 (a)** (system of) pipes, esp for water or drains: *The piping will need to be renewed.* **(b)** pipe of a certain length: *ten feet of lead piping.* **2 (a)** folded strip of fabric, often enclosing a cord, used to decorate the edges or seams of a garment, cushion, etc. **(b)** cord-like lines of icing or whipped cream used to decorate a cake, etc. **3** (sound made by) playing a pipe[1](3a): *We heard their piping in the distance.*

▷ **piping** *adj* **1** (esp of a person's voice) high-pitched. **2** (idm) **piping ˈhot** (of liquids, food) very hot: *a bowl of soup served piping hot.*

pipistrelle /ˈpɪpɪstrel, ˌpɪpɪˈstrel/ *n* type of small bat[1] that feeds on insects, found in most parts of the world.

pipit /ˈpɪpɪt/ *n* type of small songbird resembling a lark.

pippin /ˈpɪpɪn/ *n* **1** type of apple that can be eaten raw. **2** (*infml*) excellent person or thing: *She's an absolute pippin!*

pip-squeak /ˈpɪpskwiːk/ *n* (*infml or derog*) small, young or unimportant person, esp one who is conceited.

piquant /ˈpiːkənt/ *adj* **1** having a pleasantly sharp taste: *Bland vegetables are often served with a piquant sauce.* **2** pleasantly exciting and stimulating to the mind: *a piquant bit of gossip.*

▷ **piquancy** /-ənsɪ/ *n* [U] quality or state of being piquant: *the delicate piquancy of the soup.*

piquantly *adv*.

pique /piːk/ *v* [Tn esp passive] **1** hurt the pride or self-respect of (sb); offend: *She seemed rather piqued.* ○ *He was piqued to discover that he hadn't been invited.* **2** arouse (a person's interest or curiosity): *Her curiosity was piqued.*

▷ **pique** *n* [U] feeling of annoyance or hurt, usu because one's pride has been offended; resentment: *When he realized nobody was listening to him, he left the room in a fit of pique.* ○ *Out of pique they refused to accept the compromise offered.*

piquet /pɪˈket/ *n* [U] card-game for two players, played with a pack of 32 cards.

Pirandello /ˌpɪrənˈdeləʊ/ Luigi (1867-1936), Italian dramatist and novelist whose plays (eg *Six Characters in Search of an Author* and *Henry IV*) were among the first to challenge the naturalistic conventions of European drama. He was awarded the Nobel prize for literature in 1934.

piranha /pɪˈrɑːnjə/ *n* any of various types of small tropical American freshwater fish which attack and eat live animals.

pirate /ˈpaɪərət/ *n* **1 (a)** (esp formerly) person on a ship who attacks and robs other ships at sea: [attrib] *a pirate crew, ship, flag.* **(b)** (esp formerly) ship used for this purpose. Cf CORSAIR.

📖 The popular image of a pirate is of a jovial sea rover with a patch over one eye, who sailed the seas flying the Jolly Roger (a black flag with a white skull and crossbones on it). Pirates are also imagined urging on their crew with phrases like 'Heave ho, me hearties!', and singing 'Yo ho ho and a bottle of rum'. This fanciful image owes much to pirates like Long John Silver in *Stevenson's *Treasure Island* and Captain Hook in *Barrie's *Peter Pan*, and to the pirates in the comic opera *The Pirates of Penzance* by *Gilbert and *Sullivan.

2 person who copies illegally sth protected by copyright, esp in order to sell it: [attrib] *a pirate edition, video, tape, etc.* **3 (a)** (also **pirate ˈradio**) radio station that broadcasts without a licence (esp from a ship): *interference with radio reception caused by pirates.* **(b)** broadcaster on an illegal radio station.

▷ **piracy** /ˈpaɪərəsɪ/ *n* **(a)** [U] robbery by pirates (PIRATE 1a). **(b)** [U] illegal copying or broadcasting. **(c)** [C] instance of either of these.

pirate *v* [Tn] illegally use or reproduce (printed or recorded material which is protected by copyright), esp for profit: *a pirated edition of the plays.* ⇨ Usage at SMUGGLE.

piratical /ˌpaɪəˈrætɪkl/ *adj* of or in the manner of a pirate. **piratically** /-klɪ/ *adv*.

pirouette /ˌpɪrʊˈet/ *n* rapid turn or spin made by a ballet-dancer while balanced on the point of the toe or the ball of the foot.

▷ **pirouette** *v* [I] perform a pirouette or pirouettes.

pis aller /ˌpiːz ˈæleɪ/ (*French*) course of action which one takes because there is no better alternative.

piscatorial /ˌpɪskəˈtɔːrɪəl/ *adj* **1** of or concerning fishing or fishermen. **2** (of a person) enthusiastic about fishing.

Pisces /ˈpaɪsiːz/ *n* **1** [pl] the twelfth sign of the zodiac, the Fishes. **2** [C] person born under the influence of this sign. ▷ **Piscean** *n*, *adj*. ⇨ Usage at ZODIAC. ⇨ illus at ZODIAC.

piscina /pɪˈsiːnə/ *n* (*pl* **-nae** or **-nas**) **1** stone basin in a church, with a drain for carrying away water used in ceremonial washing. **2** (*arch*) pond or pool, esp for fish.

piss /pɪs/ *v* (⚠ *sl*) **1 (a)** [I] pass urine; urinate. **(b)** [Tn] ~ **oneself** make oneself wet when doing this: (*fig*) *piss oneself laughing*, ie laugh uncontrollably. **(c)** [Tn] pass (blood) with urine: *piss blood.* **2** (phr v) **piss (sb) about/around** act (towards sb) in a foolish, time-wasting or deliberately unhelpful way: *Stop pissing about and get on with your work.* ○ *We were pissed around for hours before they finally gave us the right form.* **piss down** rain heavily. **piss off** (*esp Brit*) (used esp as a command) go away. **piss sb off** (esp passive) annoy or bore sb: *Everybody is pissed off (with all the changes of plan).*

▷ **piss** *n* (⚠ *sl*) **1 (a)** [U] urine. **(b)** [C esp *sing*] (act of) urination: *go for/have a piss.* **2** (idm) **take the ˈpiss (out of sb)** make fun (of sb).

pissed *adj* (⚠ *Brit sl*) **1** drunk. **2** (idm) **(as) pissed as a ˈnewt** very drunk.

Pissarro /pɪˈsɑːrəʊ/ Camille (1830-1903), French impressionist painter, best known for his pictures of rural scenes. He was always interested in new developments in art: among the techniques he used was *Seurat's pointillism.

pistachio /pɪˈstɑːʃɪəʊ; *US* -æʃɪəʊ/ *n* (*pl* ~**s**) **(a)** (also **piˈstachio nut**) nut with a green edible kernel: [attrib] *pistachio ice-cream.* **(b)** tree on which this nut grows. **(c)** (also **pistachio ˈgreen**) colour of this kernel.

piste /piːst/ *n* (*French*) track of firm snow for skiing on.

pistil /ˈpɪstl/ *n* female seed-producing part of a flower.

pistol /ˈpɪstl/ *n* **1** type of small gun, held and fired with one hand: *an automatic pistol.* ⇨ illus at GUN. **2** (idm) **hold a pistol to sb's head** (try to) force sb to do sth he does not want to do by using threats.

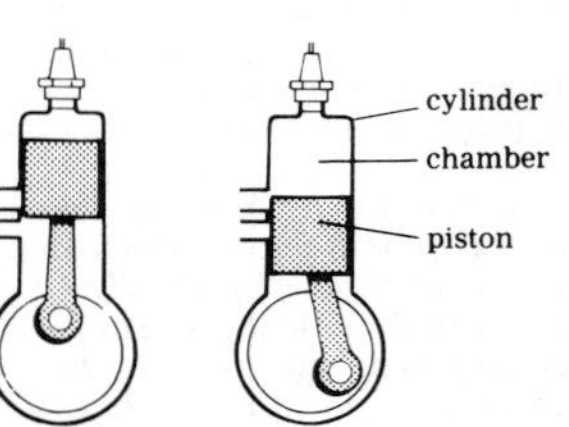

piston /ˈpɪstən/ *n* **1** round plate or short cylinder, usu made of metal or wood, that fits closely inside another cylinder or tube and moves up and down or backwards and forwards inside it. It is used eg in steam or internal combustion engines to cause other parts to move by means of a *connecting rod* (or **ˈpiston-rod**). ⇨ illus. **2** sliding valve in a trumpet or other brass wind instrument.

□ **ˈpiston-engined** *adj* (of an aircraft) having engines with pistons, not jet engines.

ˈpiston ring split metal ring that fits into a groove on the rim of a piston to make a gas-tight seal.

pit[1] /pɪt/ *n* **1** [C] large (usu deep) hollow or opening in the ground. **2** [C] (esp in compounds) **(a)** hole in the ground, usu with steep sides, from which esp minerals are dug out: *a ˈchalk-pit* ○ *a ˈgravel-pit* ○

a ˈlime-pit. **(b)** hole in the ground made for any of various industrial purposes: *a ˈsaw-pit.* **3** [C] = COAL-MINE (COAL): *go down the pit*, ie work as a miner. **4** [C] natural hollow in the surface of a plant or an animal's body: *the pit of the stomach*, ie the hollow between the ribs below the breastbone, thought to be the place where fear is felt ○ *ˈarmpit*, ie hollow underneath the shoulder where the arm joins the body. **5** [C] **(a)** hollow scar left on the skin, esp after smallpox; pock-mark. **(b)** small hollow on a surface, esp of metal or glass. **6 the pit** [sing] *(Brit)* (people sitting in) seats on the ground floor of a theatre behind the stalls. **7** [sing] (also **ˈorchestra pit**) sunken part of the floor of a theatre in front of the stage, for the orchestra. **8 (a)** [C] sunken area in the floor of a garage or workshop where the underneath part of a vehicle can be examined or repaired. **(b) the pits** [pl] (in motor racing) place near the race-track where cars can stop for fuel, new tyres, etc during a race. **9** [sing] *(US)* (esp in compounds) part of the floor of a commodity exchange used for a particular commodity: *the ˈwheat-pit.* **10 the pit** [sing] *(Bible or rhet)* hell. **11** [C] hole dug as a trap for wild animals; pitfall. **12** (idm) **be the pits** *(infml esp US)* be very bad or the worst example of sth: *The comedian's performance was the pits! ○ The food in this restaurant is the pits!*

▷ **pit** *v* (-tt-) **1** [Tn, Tn·pr esp passive] ~ **sth (with sth)** make pits (PIT 5) or hollows in sth: *Acid had pitted the surface of the silver. ○ a face pitted with smallpox ○ The surface of the moon is pitted with craters.* **2** (phr v) **pit sb/sth against sb/sth** test sb/sth in a struggle or competition with sb/sth: *pit one's wits against the bureaucracy of the tax office ○ pit oneself against the reigning champion.*

□ **ˈpit-head** *n* entrance of a coal-mine and the offices, machinery, etc in the area around it: [attrib] *a pit-head ballot*, ie a vote, esp about union matters, taken by miners at the pit-head.

ˈpit pony pony used (esp formerly) underground in a mine to pull heavy loads.

ˈpit-prop *n* prop used to support the roof of a part of a coal-mine from which coal has been removed.

pit² /pɪt/ *n* *(esp US)* = STONE 5.

▷ **pit** *v* [Tn] (-tt-) *(esp US)* remove pits from (fruit): *pitted olives.*

pit-a-pat /ˌpɪtəˈpæt/ (also **pitter-patter** /ˌpɪtəˈpætə(r)/) *adv* with the sound of quick light steps or tapping: *Her heart/feet went pit-a-pat.*

▷ **pit-a-pat** (also **pitter-patter**) *n* this sound: *The pit-a-pat of the rain on the roof.*

Pitcairn Islands /ˈpɪtkeən aɪləndz/ **the Pitcairn Islands** group of islands in the southern Pacific Ocean, of which the largest is Pitcairn Island. It is a British colony. Many of its inhabitants are descended from the sailors of HMS **Bounty* who mutinied in 1789. ⇨ map at POLYNESIA.

pitch¹ /pɪtʃ/ *n* [U] **1** black substance made from coal tar, turpentine or petroleum which is sticky and semi-liquid when hot, and hard when cold, and is used to fill in cracks or spaces, eg between the planks of a floor or of a ship's deck, to make roofs waterproof, etc. **2** (idm) **black as ink/pitch** ⇨ BLACK.

□ **ˌpitch-ˈblack** *adj* completely black.

ˌpitch-ˈdark *adj* **(a)** with no light at all. **(b)** completely black. **the ˌpitch-ˈdark** *n* [U] state of complete darkness: *We couldn't see our way in the pitch-dark.*

ˈpitch-pine *n* [U, C] (wood of a) type of pine-tree which gives off a lot of resin.

pitch² /pɪtʃ/ *v* **1** [Tn] erect and fix in place (a tent or camp), esp for a short time: *They pitched camp on the moor for the night.* Cf STRIKE² 11. **2** [Tn·pr, Cn·a] **(a)** (in music) set in a certain pitch³(3a) or key: *The song is pitched too low for me. ○ pitch sth in a higher key ○ a high-/low-pitched voice ○ (fig) pitch one's hopes high.* **(b)** *(fig)* express (sth) in a particular style or at a particular level: *The programme was pitched at just the right level. ○ an explanation pitched at a simple level so that a child could understand it ○ pitch sth a bit high/strong*, ie exaggerate. **3** [I, Ipr, Ip, Tn, Tn·pr, Tn·p] (cause sb/sth to) fall heavily, esp forwards or outwards: *He pitched (forward) on his head. ○ The car hit the child and she pitched over backwards. ○ The carriage overturned and the passengers (were) pitched out.* **4** [I, Ip] (of a ship or an aircraft) move up and down on the water or in the air: *The ship pitched and rolled and many passengers were sick.* Cf ROLL² 6. **5** [Tn, Tn·pr] throw (sb/sth) in the specified direction; toss: *Let's pitch out the troublemakers. ○ pitch a stone into the river ○ People just pitch their rubbish over the wall.* **6 (a)** [I, Ipr, Ip, Tn·p] (in cricket) (cause the ball to) strike the ground near or around the wicket: *The ball was pitched short. ○ pitch the ball up a bit.* **(b)** [I, Tn] (in baseball) throw (the ball) to the batter. **7** [Tn·pr] (in golf) play (the ball) with a pitch shot (PITCH³3): *She pitched the ball onto the green.* **8** [Tn] *(infml)* tell (a story) or give (an excuse): *They pitched a yarn about finding the jewels.* **9** (phr v) **pitch in; pitch into sth** *(infml)* **(a)** start working energetically: *They all pitched in and soon finished the job. ○ They pitched into the work immediately.* **(b)** eat (sth) with a good appetite: *We had prepared supper for the team and they all pitched in. ○ They pitched into the meal.* **pitch into sb** *(infml)* attack sb violently. **pitch in (with sth)** offer help or support: *They pitched in with contributions of money.*

▷ **pitched** *adj* (of a roof) sloping from a ridge; not flat. **pitched ˈbattle** battle fought with troops arranged in prepared positions and using all available resources: *(fig) Conservationists fought a pitched battle with developers over the future of the site.* Cf SKIRMISH.

□ **ˌpitch-and-ˈtoss** *n* [U] game of skill and chance in which coins are thrown at a particular mark.

pitchfork /ˈpɪtʃfɔːk/ *n* long-handled fork with sharp prongs for lifting and moving hay, etc. — *v* **1** [Tn] lift or move (sth) (as) with a pitchfork. **2** (phr v) **pitchfork sb into sth** force sb into (a position, job, etc), esp suddenly: *young men pitchforked into the army.*

pitch³ /pɪtʃ/ *n* **1** [C] *(sport)* **(a)** (in cricket) part of the ground between the wickets. ⇨ illus at CRICKET. **(b)** (in football, hockey, etc) area of ground marked out for a game; sports ground or field. ⇨ illus at ASSOCIATION FOOTBALL (ASSOCIATION). **2** [C] **(a)** act or process of throwing sth; toss. **(b)** (in cricket) way in which the ball is bowled: *a full pitch*, ie a bowled ball that does not bounce before reaching the batsman. **(c)** (in baseball) act or manner of throwing the ball. **3** (also **ˈpitch shot**) (in golf) shot hit high into the air over a relatively short distance. **4** [U] **(a)** degree of highness or lowness of a musical note or a voice: *give the pitch ○ have absolute/perfect pitch*, ie the ability to recognize or reproduce the pitch of a note. **(b)** quality of a sound in music. **5** [sing] degree or intensity of sth: *Speculation has reached such a pitch that a decision will have to be made immediately.* **6** [U] ~ **of sth** highest point of sth: *the pitch of perfection.* **7** [U] movement of a ship up and down on the water. Cf ROLL¹ 3. **8** [U] degree of slope (esp of a roof). **9** [U, C] distance between the threads on a screw, the teeth of a cog, etc. **10** [C] *(esp Brit)* place where a street trader usu does business or a street entertainer usu performs. **11** [C] (also **ˈsales pitch**) persuasive talk or arguments used by a salesman to sell things: *a clever sales pitch.* **12** (idm) **at concert pitch** ⇨ CONCERT. **at/to fever pitch** ⇨ FEVER. **queer sb's pitch** ⇨ QUEER *v*.

pitchblende /ˈpɪtʃblend/ *n* [U] black shiny mineral ore which is the main source of uranium and radium.

pitcher¹ /ˈpɪtʃə(r)/ *n* **(a)** *(esp Brit)* large (usu earthenware) container for liquids, with one or two handles and a lip for pouring. **(b)** *(US)* jug.

□ **ˈpitcher plant** plant with leaves shaped like long narrow cups, which contain a liquid in which insects are trapped.

pitcher² /ˈpɪtʃə(r)/ *n* (in baseball) player who throws the ball to the batter.

piteous /ˈpɪtɪəs/ *adj* *(fml)* arousing or deserving pity: *a piteous cry, sight, story ○ in a piteous condition.* ▷ **piteously** *adv.* **piteousness** *n* [U].

pitfall /ˈpɪtfɔːl/ *n* **1** unsuspected danger or difficulty: *This text presents many pitfalls for the translator.* **2** = PIT¹ 11.

pith /pɪθ/ *n* **1 (a)** [U] soft spongy substance that fills the stems of certain plants, eg reeds. **(b)** similar substance inside the skin of oranges, etc. **2** [sing] *(fig)* **the ~ of sth** most important or essential part of sth; essence: *That was the pith of his argument.*

▷ **pithy** *adj* **(-ier, -iest) 1** concise and full of meaning; terse: *a pithy description of the event ○ a pithy comment, remark, saying, etc.* **2** of, like or full of pith(1). **pithily** /-ɪlɪ/ *adv* in a pithy(1) manner. **pithiness** *n* [U] state of being pithy(1): *Her work is known for pithiness of style.*

□ **ˈpith hat** (also **ˈpith helmet**) hat made of dried pith(1a) worn (esp formerly) to protect the head from the sun.

pitiable /ˈpɪtɪəbl/ *adj* **1** deserving or arousing pity: *in a pitiable state ○ pitiable misery.* **2** deserving contempt: *a pitiable attempt to save himself from disgrace ○ a pitiable lack of talent.* ▷ **pitiably** /-əblɪ/ *adv.*

pitiful /ˈpɪtɪfl/ *adj* **1** arousing pity: *a pitiful condition, invalid, sight ○ Their suffering was pitiful to see.* **2** deserving contempt: *pitiful efforts, excuses, lies ○ a pitiful coward.*

▷ **pitifully** /-fəlɪ/ *adv* **1** in a pitiful(1) manner: *pitifully injured ○ The child was pitifully thin.* **2** in a pitiful(2) manner: *a pitifully bad performance.*

pitiless /ˈpɪtɪlɪs/ *adj* **1** showing no pity or mercy; cruel: *a pitiless killer, bandit, tyrant, etc ○ pitiless retribution, revenge, etc.* **2** *(fig)* very harsh or severe; unrelenting: *a scorching, pitiless sun ○ the pitiless winds of a Siberian winter.* ▷ **pitilessly** *adv.* **pitilessness** *n* [U].

piton /ˈpiːtɒn/ *n* *(sport)* metal spike or peg, with a ring at one end to hold a rope, that is hammered into a rock or a crack between rocks to support a rope or climber.

Pitot tube /ˈpiːtəʊ tjuːb; *US* -tuːb/ *n* *(propr)* small tube, open at one end, used in instruments that measure fluid pressure or velocity.

Pitt¹ /pɪt/ William, 'the Elder', Earl of Chatham (1708-78), British statesman, prime minister 1756-61 and 1766-68. Having earned a reputation as a brilliant parliamentary orator in opposition, as prime minister he successfully directed British strategy in the *Seven Years War against France and planned the capture of French territory in Canada and India. ⇨ App 2.

Pitt² /pɪt/ William, 'the Younger' (1759-1806), British statesman, prime minister 1783-1801 and 1804-06. Son of Pitt the Elder, he became at 24 the youngest ever British prime minister. In his early years in office he introduced several important financial and parliamentary reforms, and did much to stamp out governmental corruption. Latterly he was a successful war leader against France under Napoleon. ⇨ App 2.

pitta /ˈpɪtə/ *n* [U] (also **pita**, **ˈpitta bread**) type of bread in flat loaves, eaten esp in Greece and the Middle East.

pittance /ˈpɪtns/ *n* (usu *sing*) very small or insufficient amount of money paid or received as wages or an allowance: *work all day for a mere pittance ○ She could barely survive on the pittance she received as a widow's pension.*

pitter-patter = PIT-A-PAT.

pituitary /pɪˈtjuːɪtərɪ; *US* -ˈtuːəterɪ/ *n* (also **piˈtuitary gland**) small gland at the base of the brain which secretes hormones that influence growth and development. ⇨ illus at BRAIN.

pity /ˈpɪtɪ/ *n* **1** [U] ~ **(for sb/sth)** feeling of sorrow caused by the suffering, troubles, etc of others: *be full of/filled with pity for sb ○ be moved to pity by sb's suffering ○ do sth out of pity for sb*, ie because one feels pity for him ○ *feel very little pity for sb.* **2** [sing] ~ **(that...)** cause for mild regret or sorrow (but not a real disaster): *It's a pity the weather isn't better for our outing today. ○ What a pity that you can't come to the theatre with us tonight. ○ The pity (of it) is that...*, ie The regrettable thing is that.... **3** (idm) **have pity on sb** show mercy towards sb. **ˌmore's the ˈpity** *(infml)* unfortunately: *'Did you insure the jewels* *before they were stolen?' 'No, more's the pity!'* **take pity on sb** help sb because one feels pity for him.

▷ **pity** *v* (*pt, pp* **pitied**) [Tn] **1** feel pity for (sb): *Pity the poor sailors at sea in this storm!* ○ *Survivors of the disaster who lost their relatives are much to be pitied.* **2** feel contempt for (sb): *I pity you if you think this is an acceptable way to behave.* ○ *I pity you* (ie I am threatening you) *if you can't pay me the money by tomorrow.* **pitying** *adj* **(a)** expressing pity: *He lay helpless in the street under the pitying gaze of the bystanders.* **(b)** showing pity and some contempt: *The performer received only pitying looks from his audience.* **pityingly** *adv.*

pivot /ˈpɪvət/ *n* **1** central point, pin or shaft on which sth turns. **2** (*fig*) central or most important person or thing: *Because her job had been the pivot of her life, retirement was very difficult.* ○ *That is the pivot of the whole argument.* ⇨ illus at SCALE.

▷ **pivot** *v* **1** (a) [I, Ipr] ~ (**on sth**) turn (as) on a pivot: *The doll pivots at the waist and neck.* ○ *She pivoted on her heels and swept out.* **(b)** [Tn, Tn·pr] provide (sth) with a pivot; mount on a pivot. **2** (phr v) **pivot on sth** (no passive) (of an argument, etc) depend on sth central or essential; hinge on sth: *The whole discussion pivots on this one point.*

pivotal /-tl/ *adj* **1** of or forming a pivot. **2** (*fig*) of great importance because other things depend on it; central: *a pivotal decision.*

pixie (also **pixy**) /ˈpɪksɪ/ *n* small elf or fairy (eg in children's fairy-tales).

Pizarro /pɪˈzɑːrəʊ/ Francisco (c 1478-1541), Spanish conqueror of Peru. In 1531 he led a force of less than 200 men from Panama into Peru, defeated the *Incas and killed their king. He founded the capital Lima, where he was eventually murdered by a rival Spanish faction.

pizza /ˈpiːtsə/ *n* [C, U] Italian dish consisting of a flat (usu round) piece of dough covered with tomatoes, cheese, anchovies, etc and baked in an oven.

pizzazz (also **pizazz, pzazz**) /pəˈzæz/ *n* [U] (*infml*) excitement and energy; liveliness; zest: *a cabaret show with plenty of pizzazz.*

pizzicato /ˌpɪtsɪˈkɑːtəʊ/ *adj, adv* (*music*) (played) by plucking the strings of a violin or similar stringed instrument instead of using the bow.

▷ **pizzicato** *n* (*pl* ~**s**) note or passage (of music) (to be) played in this way.

Pk *abbr* (esp on a map) Park: *St* (ie Saint) *James' Pk.*

pkg *abbr* package.

pkt *abbr* packet: *1 pkt cigarettes.*

Pl *abbr* (esp on a map) Place: *St* (ie Saint) *James' Pl.*

pl *abbr* (*grammar*) plural.

placard /ˈplækɑːd/ *n* written or printed notice (designed to be) publicly displayed, eg by being fixed to a wall or carried on a stick: *The placards condemned the government's action.* ⇨ illus at FLAG.

▷ **placard** *v* [Tn] **1** stick placards on (sth). **2** announce (sth) by using placards.

placate /pləˈkeɪt; *US* ˈpleɪkeɪt/ *v* [Tn] make (sb) less angry; soothe or pacify.

▷ **placatory** /pləˈkeɪtərɪ; *US* ˈpleɪkətɔːrɪ/ *adj* designed to placate or having this effect: *placatory remarks.*

place[1] /pleɪs/ *n* **1** [C] particular area or position in space occupied by sb/sth: *Is this the place where it happened?* ○ *This place seems familiar to me — I think I've been here before.* ○ *I can't be in two places at once.* ○ *He loves to be seen in all the right places,* ie at all the important social events. **2** [C] city, town, village, etc: *We saw so many places on the tour I can't remember them all.* ○ *This town is the coldest place in Britain.* ○ *Australia is a big place.* **3** [C] ~ (**of sth**) (often in compounds) building or area of land used for a particular purpose or where sth occurs: *a ˈmeeting-place, ˈbirthplace, ˈhiding-place, etc* ○ *places of amusement/entertainment,* ie theatres, cinemas, etc ○ *a place of worship,* eg a church ○ *He can usually be contacted at his place of business/work.* ○ *a place of learning,* eg a university ○ *one's place of birth/death.* **4** [C] particular spot or area on a surface: *a sore place on my foot* ○ *The wall was marked with damp in several places.* **5** [C] particular passage or point in a book, play, etc: *The audience laughed in all the right places,* eg in a play. ○ *Put a piece of paper in* (ie in your book) *to mark your place.* **6** [C] seat or position, esp one reserved for or occupied by a person, vehicle, etc: *Come and sit here — I've kept you a place* ○ *There's only one place left in the car park.* ○ *the place of honour at the head of the table* ○ *There will always be a place for you here if you decide to come back.* ○ *Return to your places and get on with your work.* ○ (*fig*) *have an assured place in history* ○ *I went to buy a newspaper and lost my place in the queue.* ⇨ Usage at SPACE. **7** [sing] rank, position or role in society (used esp with the *vs* shown): *keep/know one's place* ○ *forget one's place,* ie not behave according to one's social position ○ *not be one's place* (ie one's proper role) *to give advice.* **8** [C] **(a)** position or office, esp as an employee: *She hopes to get a place in the Civil Service.* **(b)** opportunity to study at a school or university: *She was awarded a place at the Royal College of Music.* ○ *The ballet school offers free places to children who are exceptionally talented.* **(c)** membership of a sports team: *She worked hard for her place in the Olympic team.* **9** [C] **(a)** natural or suitable position (for sth): *Put everything away in its correct place.* ○ (*saying*) *A place for everything and everything in its place.* ○ *The dustbin is the only place for most of these clothes.* **(b)** (usu negative) suitable or proper location (for sb to be): *A railway station is no place for a child to be left alone at night.* ○ *City streets are no place to be if you don't like noise or crowds.* **10** [C] (*mathematics*) position of a figure after a decimal point, etc: *calculated/correct to 5 decimal places/5 places of decimals,* eg 6.57132. **11** [C usu *sing*] **(a)** (in a competition) position among the winning competitors: *He finished in third place.* **(b)** (in horse-racing) position among the first three, esp second or third: *Did you back the horse for a place or to win?* **12** [C] **(a)** house, esp a large one in the country: *They have a flat in town as well as a place in the country.* **(b)** (*infml*) home: *We're having the party at my place.* **13 Place** [sing] (*esp Brit*) **(a)** (as part of a name for a short street, square etc): *Langham Place.* **(b)** (as part of a name for a large country house): *Wakehurst Place.* **14** (idm) **all ˈover the place** (*infml*) **(a)** everywhere: *Firms are going bankrupt all over the place.* **(b)** in an untidy state; disordered: *The contents of the drawers were strewn all over the place.* ○ *Your hair is all over the place.* **another ˈplace** (*Brit*) (used in the House of Commons to refer to the House of Lords and in the House of Lords to refer to the House of Commons). **change/swap ˈplaces (with sb)** **(a)** take sb's position, seat, etc and let him take one's own: *Let's change places — you'll be able to see better from here.* **(b)** be in sb else's situation or circumstances: *I'm perfectly happy — I wouldn't change places with anyone.* **fall, fit, slot, etc into ˈplace** (of a set of facts or series of events) begin to make sense in relationship to each other: *It all begins to fall into place.* **give place to sb/sth** be replaced by sb/sth; give way to sb/sth: *Houses and factories gave place to open fields as the train gathered speed.* **ˈgo places** (*infml*) be increasingly successful, esp in one's career: *two young people who are really going places.* **have one's heart in the right place** ⇨ HEART. **in the ˈfirst, ˈsecond, etc place** (used eg when making points in an argument) firstly, secondly, etc. **in high places** ⇨ HIGH[1]. **in ˈmy, ˈyour, etc place** in my, your, etc situation or circumstances: *In her place I'd sell the lot.* **in ˈplace** **(a)** in the usual or proper position: *She likes everything to be in place before she starts work.* **(b)** suitable or appropriate: *A little gratitude would be in place.* **in place of sb/sth; in sb's/sth's place** instead of sb/sth: *The chairman was ill so his deputy spoke in his place.* **lay/set a ˈplace** put cutlery, dishes, etc for one person in position on the table: *Set a place for him when you lay the table — he may come after all.* **lightning never strikes in the same place twice** ⇨ LIGHTNING. **lose one's place** ⇨ LOSE. **out of ˈplace** **(a)** not in the usual or a correct or suitable place. **(b)** unsuitable; improper: *Her criticisms were quite out of place.* ○ *Modern furniture would be out of place in a Victorian house.* **a place in the ˈsun** situation of equal or shared privilege: *Nations that had been oppressed for centuries were now fighting for a place in the sun.* **pride of place** ⇨ PRIDE. **put oneself in sb else's/sb's ˈplace** imagine oneself in sb else's situation or circumstances. **put sb in his (proper) ˈplace** humiliate sb who has been impertinent or boastful: *He tried to kiss her but she quickly put him in his place.* **take ˈplace** occur; happen: *When does the ceremony take place?* ○ *We have never discovered what took place (between them) that night.* ⇨ Usage at HAPPEN. **take sb's/sth's place; take the place of sb/sth** replace sb/sth: *She couldn't attend the meeting so her assistant took her place.* ○ *Nothing could take the place of the family he had lost.* **there's ˌno place like ˈhome** (*saying*) one's home is the best place to be.

□ **ˈplace-bet** *n* (in horse-racing) bet that a horse will be one of the first three past the winning-post.

ˈplace-kick *n* (in Rugby football) kick made after the ball has been placed on the ground for that purpose.

ˈplace-mat *n* mat on a table on which a person's plates are laid.

ˈplace-name *n* name of a city, town, hill, etc: *an expert on the origin of place-names.*

ˈplace-setting *n* set of cutlery, dishes, etc for one person.

place[2] /pleɪs/ *v* **1** [Tn·pr, Tn·p] **(a)** put (sth) in a particular place: *He placed the money on the counter.* ○ *The notice is placed too high — nobody can read it.* **(b)** put (sth) in its proper place: *Be sure to place them correctly.* ○ *He placed the books in order on the shelf.* **2** [Tn·pr, Tn·p] put (sb) in the situation or circumstances specified (used esp as in the expressions shown): *place sb in charge/command (of sth),* ie make him the leader ○ *place sb under arrest,* ie arrest him ○ *place sb in a dilemma/difficult position/quandary,* ie make matters difficult for sb ○ *place one's faith/trust in sb/sth* ○ *place confidence in sb,* ie be confident that he will help, etc ○ *Responsibility for the negotiations was placed in his hands,* ie He was made responsible for them. **3** [Tn] identify (sb/sth) by using one's memory or past experience: *I've seen his face before but I can't place him.* ○ *She has a foreign accent that I can't quite place.* **4** [Tn, Tn·pr, Tn·p] make a judgement about (sb/sth) in comparison with others; class (sb/sth): *I would place her among the world's greatest sopranos.* **5** [Tn, Tn·pr] ~ **sth (with sb/sth)** give (an order or a bet) to a person or firm: *They have placed an order with us for three new aircraft.* ○ *Place your bets now — the race begins in half an hour!* **6** [Tn, Tn·pr] ~ **sb (in sth)**; ~ **sb (with sb/sth)** find a home, job, etc for sb: *The agency places about 2 000 secretaries per annum.* ○ *They placed the orphans with foster-parents.* **7** [Tn, Tn·pr] invest (money), esp in order to earn interest: *The stockbroker has placed the money in industrial stock.* **8** [esp passive: Tn, Cn·a] state the finishing position of runners (in a race) or contestants (in athletics): *He was responsible for placing the winners.* ○ *She was placed third.* **9** (idm) **be placed** **(a)** (*Brit*) (in horse-racing) finish first, second or third. **(b)** (*US*) (in horse-racing) finish second.

▷ **placement** /ˈpleɪsmənt/ *n* [U] action of placing or state of being placed: *the placement of orphans* ○ [attrib] *a placement agency for secretarial staff.*

placebo /pləˈsiːbəʊ/ *n* (*pl* ~**s**) **1** (*medical*) harmless substance given as if it were medicine to calm a patient who mistakenly believes he is ill: [attrib] *placebo effect,* ie beneficial effect of taking a placebo. **2** thing done or said only to please or humour sb.

placenta /pləˈsentə/ *n* (*pl* **-tae** /-tiː/ or ~**s**) (*anatomy*) organ lining the womb during pregnancy by which the foetus is nourished through the umbilical cord, and which is expelled after birth. ▷ **placental** /-tl/ *adj*: *a placental mammal.*

placid /ˈplæsɪd/ *adj* **(a)** calm and peaceful; undisturbed: *the placid waters of the lake.* **(b)** (of a person, his temperament, etc) not easily excited or irritated: *a placid smile.* ▷ **placidly** *adv*: *cows placidly chewing grass.* **placidity** /plə'sɪdətɪ/ *n* [U]: *the placidity of his temperament.*

placket /'plækɪt/ *n* opening in a woman's skirt to make it easier to put on and take off.

plagiarize, -ise /'pleɪdʒəraɪz/ *v* [Tn, Tn·pr] ~ **sth** (**from sb/sth**) take (sb else's ideas, words, etc) and use them as if they were one's own: *Whole passages of the work are plagiarized.* ○ *He has plagiarized most of the book from earlier studies of the period.*
▷ **plagiarism** /-rɪzəm/ *n* (**a**) [U] action of plagiarizing: *be accused of plagiarism.* (**b**) [C] instance of this.
plagiarist /-rɪst/ *n* person who plagiarizes.

plague /pleɪg/ *n* **1** (**a**) **the plague** [sing] = BUBONIC PLAGUE (BUBONIC). (**b**) [C] any deadly infectious disease that kills many people: [attrib] *The incidence of cholera in the camps has reached plague proportions.* **2** [C] ~ **of sth** large numbers of a pest that invade an area and cause annoyance or damage: *a plague of flies, locusts, rats, etc.* **3** [C usu *sing*] (*infml*) cause of annoyance; nuisance: *What a plague that boy is!* **4** (idm) **avoid sb/sth like the plague** ⇨ AVOID.
▷ **plague** *v* **1** [Tn, Tn·pr] ~ **sb/sth** (**with sth**) (**a**) annoy sb, esp by repeatedly asking questions or making demands: *plague sb with questions, requests for money, etc.* (**b**) cause suffering or discomfort to sb: *She was plagued with arthritis.* **2** [Tn] cause trouble or difficulty to (sb/sth): *a construction schedule plagued by bad weather.*
□ **'plague-ridden** (also **'plague-stricken**) *adj* infected with a/the plague(1, 2).

plaice /pleɪs/ *n* (*pl* unchanged) type of flat-fish with reddish spots, eaten as food.

plaid /plæd/ *n* (**a**) [C] long piece of woollen cloth, worn over the shoulders by Scottish Highlanders. (**b**) [U] cloth (usu with a tartan pattern) used for this, and for kilts, etc: [attrib] *a plaid kilt.* (**c**) [C] tartan pattern for cloth.

Plaid Cymru /ˌplaɪd 'kʌmrɪ/ Welsh political party, founded in 1925, whose aim is to achieve self-government for Wales. ⇨ articles at POLITICS, WALES.

plain[1] /pleɪn/ *adj* (**-er, -est**) **1** easy to see, hear or understand; clear: *The markings along the route are quite plain.* ○ *in plain English* ○ *He made it plain (to us) that he did not wish to continue.* ○ *She made her annoyance plain.* **2** (of people or their actions, thoughts, etc) not trying to deceive; frank and direct: *in plain words*, ie frankly ○ *a plain answer* ○ *the plain truth* ○ *Let me be plain with you*, ie speak openly and frankly. ○ *There will have to be some plain speaking.* **3** (**a**) not decorated or luxurious; ordinary and simple: *a plain but very elegant dress* ○ *plain food/cooking*, ie not spicy or rich ○ *plain cake*, ie without fruit, etc ○ *plain chocolate*, ie made without adding milk. (**b**) without a pattern or marking on it: *plain paper*, ie without lines ○ *plain fabric*, ie without a pattern or design ○ *under plain cover*, ie in an envelope without any special marking. **4** not beautiful or good-looking: *a few rather plain bits of furniture* ○ *From a rather plain child she had grown into a beautiful woman.* **5** (idm) **in plain 'English** bluntly or simply expressed: *If you wanted me to go why didn't you say so in plain English instead of making vague hints?* **make oneself plain** make one's meaning clear: *There is no more money — do I make myself plain?* (**as**) **plain as a pikestaff/the nose on one's face** very obvious or clearly visible. (**all**) **ˌplain 'sailing** course of action that is simple and free from trouble: *Once the design problems were solved, it was all/everything was plain sailing.*
▷ **plain** *adv* (*esp US*) (**a**) clearly: *speak plain.* (**b**) absolutely; simply: *That is just plain stupid.*
plainly *adv* (**a**) clearly: *The mountain tops are plainly visible from the village.* ○ *Try to express yourself more plainly.* (**b**) obviously: *That is plainly wrong.* ○ *You are plainly unwilling to co-operate.* ○ *He was plainly unwelcome.*
plainness *n* [U].
□ **ˌplain 'clothes** (esp of police officers) ordinary clothes, not uniform: *The detectives were in plain clothes.* **'plain-clothes** *adj* wearing plain clothes: *a plain-clothes detective.*
ˌplain 'dealing honesty; straightforwardness.
ˌplain 'flour flour that does not contain baking powder. Cf SELF-RAISING FLOUR.
ˌplain-'spoken *adj* frank in speech, often to the point of rudeness; outspoken.

plain[2] /pleɪn/ *n* large area of flat land; prairie: *a vast, grassy plain* ○ *the great plains of the American Midwest.*
▷ **plainsman** /-zmən/ *n* (*pl* **-men**) person living in a region of plains, esp the great plains of the USA.

plain[3] /pleɪn/ *n* (in knitting) simple basic stitch. Cf PURL.

plainchant /'pleɪntʃɑ:nt; *US* 'pleɪntʃænt/ (also **'plainsong** /-sɒŋ/) *n* [U] medieval type of church music for a number of voices singing together, used in the Anglican and Roman Catholic Churches.

plaint /pleɪnt/ *n* (*law*) charge made against sb in court; accusation.

plaintiff /'pleɪntɪf/ (also **complainant**) *n* person who brings a legal action against sb. Cf DEFENDANT.

plaintive /'pleɪntɪv/ *adj* sounding sad; sorrowful: *a plaintive cry, melody, voice, etc.* ▷ **plaintively** *adv.* **plaintiveness** *n* [U]

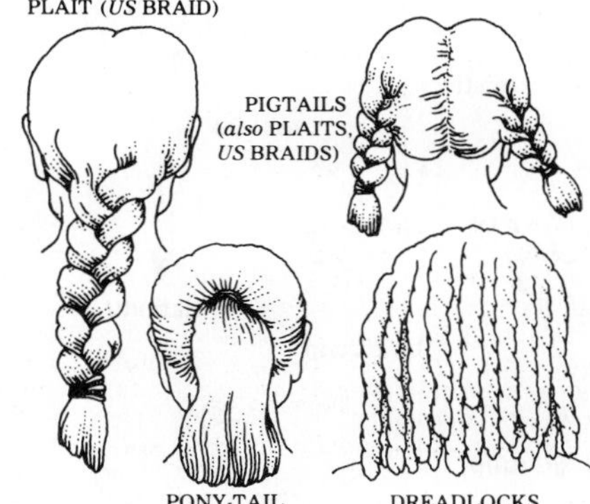

plait /plæt/ (*US* **braid**) *v* [Tn] (**a**) weave or twist (three or more lengths of hair, straw, etc) under and over one another to make one rope-like length: *plait one's hair.* (**b**) make (sth) by doing this: *plait a basket, cord, rope.*
▷ **plait** *n* form made by plaiting: *wear one's hair in plaits/a plait.* ⇨ illus.

plan /plæn/ *n* **1** ~ (**for sth/doing sth**); ~ (**to do sth**) arrangement for doing or using sth, considered or worked out in advance: *make plans (for sth)* ○ *a plan to produce energy from waste material* ○ *What are your plans for the holidays?* ○ *a carefully worked-out plan* ○ *a change of plan*, ie deciding not to do what was planned ○ *a development plan*, eg for an industry, a town or an area ○ *The best plan* (ie The best thing to do) *would be to ignore it completely.* ○ *a plan of attack/campaign*, ie a way of doing sth, esp sth difficult. **2** (**a**) detailed, large-scale diagram of part of a town, district, group of buildings, etc: *a plan of the royal palace and its surroundings* ○ *a plan of the inner city.* (**b**) (esp *pl*) outline drawing (of a building or structure) showing the position and size of the various parts in relation to each other: *draw up plans for an extension* ○ *The architect submitted the plans for approval.* ○ *The plans of the new development are on show at the Town Hall.* (**c**) diagram (of the parts of a machine): *plans of early flying machines.* Cf CHART, MAP. **3** way of arranging sth, esp when shown on a drawing; scheme: *a seating plan*, ie one showing where people are to sit at a table. **4** (idm) **the best-laid schemes/plans of mice and men** ⇨ BEST[2]. **go according to plan** (of events, etc) take place successfully: *If everything goes according to plan, I shall be back before dark.*
▷ **plan** *v* (**-nn-**) **1** [Tn] make a plan of or for (sth): *plan a garden* ○ *a well-planned city* ○ *a planned economy*, ie controlled by the government. **2** [I, Ipr] ~ (**for/on sb/sth**) make preparations: *plan for the future, one's retirement, etc* ○ *I had planned for 20 guests, but only 10 arrived.* ○ *We hadn't planned on twins!* ⇨ Usage at ARRANGE. **3** [Tt] make plans (to do sth); intend: *When do you plan to take your holiday?* ○ *We're planning to visit France this summer.* **4** (phr v) **plan sth out** consider sth in detail and arrange it in advance: *plan out one's annual expenditure* ○ *plan out a traffic system for the town.* **planner** *n* (**a**) person who makes plans. (**b**) (also **ˌtown 'planner**) person who works in or studies town planning. **planning** *n* [U] (**a**) making plans (for sth): *family planning*, ie using birth control to limit the number of children a couple have. (**b**) = TOWN PLANNING (TOWN). **'planning permission** (*esp Brit*) licence to build a new building or change an existing one, granted by a local authority. ⇨ article at ARCHITECTURE.

planchette /plɑ:n'ʃet; *US* plæn-/ *n* small board with wheels and a pencil, which is said to spell out messages from the spirits of the dead when people place their fingers on it.

Planck /plæŋk/ Max Karl Ernst Ludwig (1858-1947), German physicist who developed the quantum theory (QUANTUM). Announced in 1900, it laid the foundation for 20th-century physics, being used by *Einstein in studying photoelectric emissions and by Bohr in analysing the structure of the atom. Planck was awarded the Nobel prize for physics in 1918.

plane[1] /pleɪn/ *n* **1** (**a**) (*geometry*) surface such that a straight line joining any two points in it touches it at all points. (**b**) any flat or level surface. **2** (*fig*) level of thought, existence or development: *They seem to exist on a different spiritual plane.* ○ *This species has reached a higher plane of development.*
▷ **plane** *adj* completely flat; level: *a plane surface.*
plane *v* [I, Ip] (of an aeroplane) move through the air, esp without an engine; glide.
□ **ˌplane ge'ometry** geometry of two-dimensional or plane figures.
ˌplane 'sailing method of calculating a ship's position as though the ship were on a plane surface instead of the curved surface of the earth.
'plane-table *n* instrument used by surveyors for drawing plans in fieldwork, consisting of a circular table with a pivoted sighting-device.

plane

plane[2] /pleɪn/ *n* tool, consisting of a blade set in a flat surface, which makes the surface of wood smooth by shaving very thin layers from it.
▷ **plane** *v* **1** (**a**) [Tn] use a plane on (sth): *plane the edge of the plank.* (**b**) [Cn·a] make (sth) smooth, etc by using a plane: *plane sth smooth.* **2** (phr v) ~ **sth away/down/off** remove sth using a plane: *plane away the irregularities on a surface.*

plane[3] /pleɪn/ (also **'plane-tree**) *n* any of several types of deciduous tree with spreading branches, broad leaves and thin bark that comes off in flakes.

plane[4] /pleɪn/ *n* = AEROPLANE: *travel by plane* ○ *The plane is about to land.* ○ [attrib] *a plane flight.*

planet /'plænɪt/ *n* any of the bodies in space that move around a star (such as the sun) and are illuminated by it: *The planets of our solar system are Mercury, Venus, Earth, Mars, Jupiter, Saturn, Uranus, Neptune and Pluto.*
▷ **planetarium** /ˌplænɪ'teərɪəm/ *n* (*pl* ~**s** or **-ia** /-ɪə/) (building with a) device for representing the positions and movements of the planets and stars by projecting spots of light on a dome which represents the sky.
planetary /'plænɪtrɪ; *US* -terɪ/ *adj* of or like a planet or planets: *planetary movements.*

plangent /'plændʒənt/ *adj* (*fml*) **1** (of sounds) throbbing loudly; reverberating. **2** (of sounds) expressing sadness; mournful. ▷ **plangency**

FLOWERING PLANTS COMMON IN BRITAIN

All the drawings are to scale and represent the average height reached.

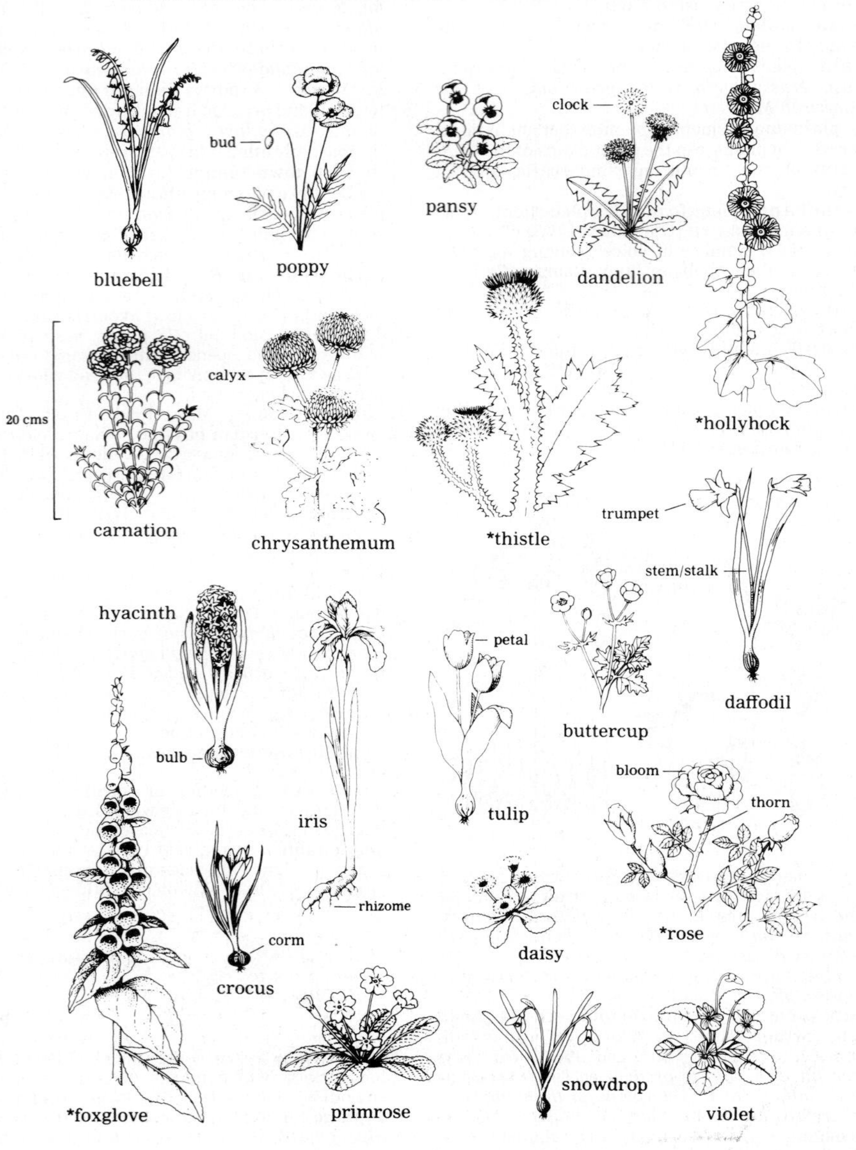

*The illustration shows the top third of the whole plant.

/-dʒənsɪ/ *n* [U]. **plangently** *adv*.

plank /plæŋk/ *n* **1** long flat piece of sawn timber, 50-150mm thick and at least 200mm wide, used for making floors, etc. **2** (*esp politics*) any of the main principles of the policy or programme of a political party: *the main planks of their disarmament platform.* **3** (idm) **thick as two planks** ⇨ THICK. **walk the plank** ⇨ WALK¹.

▷ **plank** *v* (phr v) **plank sth down** (*infml*) **(a)** put (sth) down heavily: *plank down one's luggage.* **(b)** pay (money) at once. Cf PLONK¹ *v*.

planking *n* [U] planks used esp to make a floor; structure made of planks: *Are you going to cover the planking with carpet?*

plankton /ˈplæŋktən/ *n* [U] any of the (mainly microscopic) forms of plant and animal life that drift in or float on the water of seas, rivers, lakes, etc.

plant¹ /plɑːnt; *US* plænt/ *n* **1** [C] **(a)** living organism that is not an animal, which grows in the earth and usu has a stem, leaves and roots: *Plants need light and water.* ○ [attrib] ˈ*plant life.* **(b)** any of the smaller kinds of these as distinct from shrubs or trees: *garden plants* ○ *a* ˈ*strawberry plant* ○ *plants flowering in the window-box.* **2** **(a)** [U] machinery, equipment, etc used in an industrial or manufacturing process: *The firm has made a huge investment in new plant.* ○ [attrib] ˈ*plant hire,* ie renting of machines or equipment. **(b)** [C] piece of machinery or equipment: *The farm has its own* ˈ*power plant.* **3** [C] (*esp US*) place where an industrial or a manufacturing process takes place; factory: *a* ˈ*chemical plant* ○ *a nuclear re*ˈ*processing plant.* ⇨ Usage at FACTORY. **4** [C] (*infml*) **(a)** thing placed deliberately so that its discovery will make an innocent person appear guilty; false or misleading evidence: *He claimed that the stolen jewellery found in his house was a plant.* **(b)** person who joins a group of criminals, conspirators, etc in order to spy on them for others: *They discovered that he was a police plant.*

□ ˈ**plant kingdom** group of living things, characterized by an ability to synthesize food by photosynthesis, comprised of all green plants, including algae, mosses, ferns and flowering plants.

plant² /plɑːnt; *US* plænt/ *v* **1** **(a)** [Tn, Tn·pr] put (plants, seeds, etc) in the ground to grow: *plant flowers around the pool* ○ *We planted beans and peas in the garden.* ○ *Plant in rows two feet apart.* **(b)** [Tn, Tn·pr] ~ **sth (with sth)** put bushes, trees, flowers, etc in (a garden, flower-bed, etc): *plant a garden* ○ *plant the border with spring flowers* ○ *mountain slopes planted with conifers.* Cf sow². **2** [Tn·pr] **(a)** place (sth) in position firmly or forcefully: *He planted his feet firmly on the ground.* ○ *He stood with his feet planted wide apart.* **(b)** (*infml*) position (oneself): *plant oneself in a chair in front of the fire.* **3** [Tn, Tn·pr] (*infml*) **(a)** ~ **sth (on sb)** hide sth where it will be found in order to deceive sb or make an innocent person seem guilty: *plant stolen goods on sb* ○ *He claimed that the weapons had been planted (on him).* **(b)** ~ **sb (in sth)** cause sb to join a group secretly, esp to spy on its members: *The police had planted a spy in the gang.* ○ *The speaker's supporters were planted in the audience and applauded loudly.* **4** [Tn·pr] ~ **sth in sth** fix or establish (an idea, etc) in sb's mind: *Who planted that idea in your head?* ○ *His strange remarks planted doubts in our minds about his sanity.* **5** [Tn·pr] deliver (a blow, etc) with deliberate aim: *plant a kiss on sb's cheek* ○ *plant a blow on the side of sb's head* ○ *plant a knife in sb's back.* **6** (phr v) **plant (sth) out** place (plants) in the ground so that they have enough room to grow: *plant out tomato seedlings.*

▷ **planter** *n* **1** person who grows crops on or manages a plantation: *a* ˈ*sugar-planter,* ˈ*tea-planter,* ˈ*rubber-planter, etc.* **2** machine for planting (PLANT² 1). **3** (*esp US*) container in which plants are grown, esp in a house as an ornament.

Plantagenet /plænˈtædʒənət/ royal family of England between 1154 and 1485, to which all the English kings from *Henry II to *Richard II belonged. It came originally from France, being descended from Geoffrey, Count of Anjou, father of Henry II. ⇨ App 3.

plantain¹ /ˈplæntɪn/ *n* **(a)** [C, U] tropical fruit similar to a banana but usu cooked before being eaten. **(b)** [C] tree-like plant that bears this.

plantain² /ˈplæntɪn/ *n* common wild plant with broad flat leaves and small green flowers, bearing seeds which are used as food for cage-birds.

plantation /plænˈteɪʃn, *also, in British use,* plɑːn-/ *n* **1** large piece of land, esp in a tropical country, where tea, cotton, sugar, tobacco, etc are grown: [attrib] *a plantation manager.* **2** **(a)** area of land planted with trees: *plantations of fir and pine.* **(b)** group of trees or plants planted together.

plaque¹ /plɑːk; *US* plæk/ *n* flat (usu round) piece of stone, metal or porcelain fixed on a wall as an ornament or a memorial: *A simple plaque marks the spot where the martyr died.*

plaque² /plɑːk; *US* plæk/ *n* [U] (*medical*) soft substance that forms on teeth and encourages the growth of harmful bacteria: *It helps to remove plaque by regularly brushing one's teeth.* Cf TARTAR¹ 1.

plasma /ˈplæzmə/ (also **plasm** /ˈplæzəm/) *n* [U] (*anatomy*) **1** **(a)** clear yellowish liquid part of blood, in which the corpuscles float. **(b)** (*medical*) (also ˈ**blood plasma**) this fluid taken from the blood and specially treated for use in blood transfusions. **2** = PROTOPLASM. **3** (*physics*) type of gas containing positively and negatively charged particles in approximately equal numbers, and is present in the sun and most stars.

plaster /ˈplɑːstə(r); *US* ˈplæs-/ *n* **1** [U] soft mixture of lime, sand, water, etc that becomes hard when dry and is used for making a smooth surface on walls and ceilings: *The plaster will have to dry out* *before you can paint the room.* **2** [U] (also ˌ**plaster of** ˈ**Paris**) white paste made from gypsum that becomes very hard when dry, used for making moulds, holding broken bones in place, etc: *She broke her ankle weeks ago and it's still in plaster.* **3** [C, U] = STICKING PLASTER (STICK[2]).

▷ **plaster** *v* **1** (**a**) [Tn] cover (a wall, etc) with plaster(1). (**b**) [Tn·pr] ~ **A with B**/~ **B on(to) A** cover sth with sth thickly, as one puts plaster on a wall: *hair plastered with oil* ○ *an artist who plasters the paint on the canvas* ○ *plaster the town with posters.* **2** [Tn] cover (a wound, etc) with a plaster(2). **3** [Tn] (*infml*) bomb or shell (a target) heavily. **4** (phr v) **plaster sth down** make sth lie flat by putting a wet or sticky substance on it: *plaster one's hair down.* **plastered** *adj* (*sl*) drunk: *be/get plastered.* **plasterer** /ˈplɑːstərə(r)/ *n* person whose job is to put plaster on walls and ceilings.

□ ˈ**plasterboard** *n* [U] board made of sheets of cardboard with plaster(1) between them, used for inside walls and ceilings.

ˈ**plaster cast** (**a**) mould made with gauze and plaster of Paris to hold a broken or dislocated bone in place. (**b**) mould (eg for a small statue) made of plaster of Paris.

plastic /ˈplæstɪk/ *n* **1** (**a**) [C usu *pl*] any of several chemically produced substances that can be formed into shapes when heated or made into thin threads and used in textiles. The first plastics (eg celluloid) were made in the mid 19th century. Today, most are derived from petroleum: *the use of plastics in industry.* (**b**) [U] substance made in this way: *Many items in daily use are made out of plastic.* ○ *Plastic is sometimes used instead of leather.* **2 plastics** [sing *v*] science of making plastics (PLASTIC 1a). **3** [U] (also **plastic money**) (*infml*) credit card(s): *'Have you got any cash or shall we use plastic?' 'Put it on the plastic.'*

▷ **plastic** *adj* **1** (of goods) made of plastic(1b): *a plastic cup, raincoat, spoon, toy, wrist-watch* ○ *fabric with a plastic coating* ○ *a plastic bag*, ie made from very thin soft plastic material. **2** (of materials or substances) easily shaped or moulded: *Clay is a plastic substance.* ○ (*fig*) *The mind of a young child is quite plastic.* **3** of the art of modelling eg clay or wax: *the plastic arts*, ie sculpture, ceramics, etc. **plasticity** /plæˈstɪsətɪ/ *n* [U] state or quality of being able to be moulded or shaped.

□ **the** ˌ**plastic** ˈ**arts** arts concerned with modelling or with representing solid objects (eg pottery and sculpture).

ˌ**plastic** ˈ**bomb** bomb that contains plastic explosive.

ˌ**plastic ex**ˈ**plosive** explosive material that can easily be formed into different shapes or moulded around the object it is used to destroy.

ˌ**plastic** ˈ**surgery** repairing or replacing injured or damaged tissue on the surface of the body, eg after a person has been badly burned.

plasticine (also **Plasticine**) /ˈplæstɪsiːn/ *n* [U] (*propr esp Brit*) substance similar to clay but which does not harden like clay, used for modelling, esp by children.

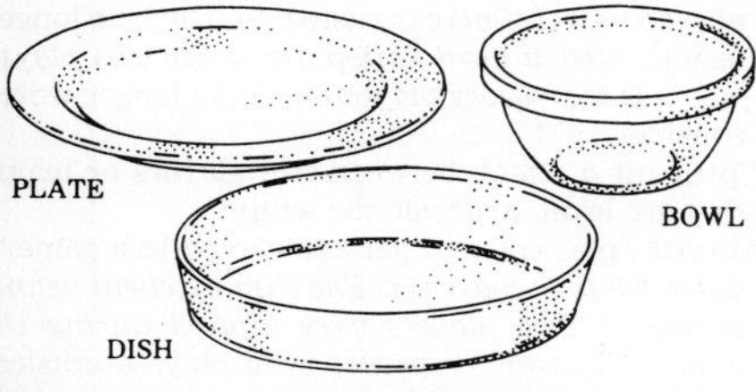

plate[1] /pleɪt/ *n* **1** [C] (**a**) (often in compounds) shallow (usu round) dish made usu of earthenware or china, from which food is served or eaten: *a* ˈ*dinner,* ˈ*meat,* ˈ*soup, etc plate* ○ *paper/plastic* ˈ*plates*, eg at a picnic. ➪ illus. (**b**) contents of this: *a plate of soup, stew, etc.* (**c**) similar dish, usu made of metal or wood, used to collect money from the congregation in church: *pass round the plate* ○ *put £5 in the plate.* **2** [U] (**a**) spoons, forks, dishes, bowls, etc made of gold or silver, esp for use at meals: *a fine piece of plate*, ie one of these articles. (**b**) dishes, bowls, chalices, etc made of gold or silver for use in church: *The plate is kept in a locked cupboard.* **3** [U] (often in compounds) metal other than silver or gold that has been covered with a thin coating of silver or gold: *electroplate*, ie object(s) coated with a thin layer of metal ○ *gold/silver plate* ○ *I thought the teapot was silver, but it's only plate.* **4** [C] (**a**) thin flat sheet of metal, glass, etc: *steel plates*, eg used in shipbuilding. (**b**) (*biology*) thin flat piece of horn, bone, etc: *The armadillo has a protective shell of bony plates.* **5** [C] (*geology*) any of the large rigid sheets of rock that make up the earth's surface: [attrib] *plate tectonics*, ie study of the structure and formation of the earth's surface through the movements of its plates. **6** [C] oblong piece of metal with sth stamped or engraved on it: *a brass* ˈ*plate*, eg on the door of a doctor, solicitor, etc with his name on it ○ *a* ˈ*licence-/*ˈ*number-plate*, eg on a car. **7** [C] (**a**) sheet of metal, plastic, rubber, etc treated so that words or pictures can be printed from it. (**b**) (esp photographic) book illustration esp one that is printed separately from the rest of the text: ˈ*colour plate.* **8** [C, U] (in photography) sheet of (esp) glass coated with a film sensitive to light: ˈ*whole-/*ˈ*half-/*ˈ*quarter-plate*, ie the usual sizes. **9** (also ˈ**dental plate**, **denture**) [C] thin piece of plastic material, moulded to the shape of the gums or roof of the mouth for holding artificial teeth. **10** [C] (**a**) silver or gold cup as a prize for a horse-race. (**b**) the race itself. **11** [C] (*sport*) (in baseball) home base of the batting side. **12** (idm) **hand/give sb sth on a** ˈ**plate** (*infml*) give sb sth or allow sb to obtain sth without any effort on his part: *You can't expect promotion to be handed to you on a plate.* **on one's** ˈ**plate** to occupy one's time or energy: *have enough/a lot/too much on one's plate* ○ *I can't help you at the moment — I've far too much on my plate already.*

▷ ˈ**plateful** /-fʊl/ *n* amount that a plate[1](1a) holds: *The child has eaten three platefuls of porridge!*

□ ˌ**plate** ˈ**glass** very clear glass of fine quality made in thick sheets, used eg for doors, mirrors, shop windows, etc: [attrib] *a plate-glass window.*

ˈ**plate-rack** *n* rack in which food plates are stored or left to drain after being washed. ➪ illus at RACK.

plate[2] /pleɪt/ *v* **1** [Tn, Tn·pr esp passive] ~ **sth** (**with sth**) cover (another metal) with a thin layer esp of gold or silver: *a copper tray plated with silver* ○ *gold-plated dishes* ○ *silver-plated spoons.* **2** [Tn] cover (esp a ship) with metal plates.

plateau /ˈplætəʊ; *US* plæˈtəʊ/ *n* (*pl* ~**s** or **-eaux** /-təʊz/) **1** large area of fairly level land high above sea-level. Cf RIDGE 2. **2** state of little or no change following a period of rapid growth or development: *After a period of rapid inflation, prices have now reached a plateau.*

platelayer /ˈpleɪtleɪə(r)/ *n* (*Brit*) person whose job is to lay and repair railway tracks.

platelet /ˈpleɪtlɪt/ *n* any of the numerous tiny discs in the blood that help it to clot.

platform /ˈplætfɔːm/ *n* **1** level surface raised above the surrounding ground or floor, esp one from which public speakers, performers, etc can be seen by their audience: *the concert platform*, ie place where a pianist performs ○ *Your questions will be answered from the platform.* ○ *appear on the same platform/share a platform with sb*, ie make speeches, etc at the same public meeting. **2** (at a railway station) flat surface built next to and at a higher level than the track, where passengers get on and off trains: *Which platform does the Brighton train leave from?* ○ *Your train is waiting at platform 5.* ○ *He came running along the platform just as the train was leaving.* ○ [attrib] *a* ˈ*platform ticket*, ie allowing sb who is not a passenger to go on to the platform. **3** (*Brit*) floor area at the entrance to a bus where passengers get on and off. **4** (*politics*) main policies and aims of a political party, esp as stated before an election; manifesto: *Fight the election/come to power on a platform of economic reform.*

Plath /plæθ/ Sylvia (1932-63), American poet and novelist, married to the English poet Ted *Hughes. Her best-known poems deal with illness, suffering and death, though in language that is controlled and often witty. Soon after her only novel (*The Bell Jar*) was published she committed suicide.

plating /ˈpleɪtɪŋ/ *n* [U] **1** thin covering of metal, esp silver or gold, on another metal: *The plating is beginning to wear off in places.* **2** layer or covering esp of metal plates: *protected with steel plating.*

platinum /ˈplætɪnəm/ *n* [U] (*symb* **Pt**) (*chemistry*) greyish-white metallic element that does not tarnish, used to make jewellery and, esp in alloys with other metals, in industry: *a sapphire in a platinum setting.* ➪ App 11.

□ ˌ**platinum** ˈ**blonde** (*infml*) (woman) having hair that is very fair or silvery white (but not white with age).

platitude /ˈplætɪtjuːd; *US* -tuːd/ *n* [C] (*fml derog*) commonplace remark or statement, esp when it is said as if it were new or interesting: *We shall have to listen to more platitudes about the dangers of overspending.*

▷ **platitudinous** /ˌplætɪˈtjuːdɪnəs; *US* -ˈtuːdənəs/ *adj* (*fml derog*) commonplace or banal: *platitudinous remarks* ○ *The whole speech was platitudinous nonsense.*

Plato /ˈpleɪtəʊ/ (429-347 BC), Greek philosopher, a pupil of *Socrates. He wrote widely on many aspects of philosophy. In his search for the true nature of knowledge, he proposed the theory that the things we see and touch are merely imperfect copies of perfect entities, called 'forms' or 'ideas', which exist outside the physical world. One aspect of the theory, that the human soul is immortal, formed an important influence on the development of Christianity. His political ideas are set out in his most famous book, the *Republic*; he thought that states should be governed by those best qualified to do so, and was opposed to democracy. He taught *Aristotle.

platonic /pləˈtɒnɪk/ *adj* **1 Platonic** of or concerning the Greek philosopher Plato or his teachings. **2** (of love or a friendship between two people) close and deep but not sexual: *He said that his feelings for her were entirely platonic.* ○ *They'd had a close platonic relationship for more than thirty years.*

platoon /pləˈtuːn/ *n* group of soldiers, a subdivision of a company, acting as a unit under the command of a lieutenant.

platter /ˈplætə(r)/ *n* **1** (**a**) large shallow dish for serving food, esp meat or fish. (**b**) (*arch Brit*) flat dish usu made of wood. **2** (*US infml*) gramophone record.

platypus /ˈplætɪpəs/ *n* (*pl* ~**es**) (also ˌ**duck-billed** ˈ**platypus**) small Australian furred animal with a duck-like beak, webbed feet and a flat tail, that lays eggs but gives milk to its young.

plaudit /ˈplɔːdɪt/ *n* (usu *pl*) (*fml*) applause, praise or some other sign of approval: *She won plaudits for the way she presented her case.*

plausible /ˈplɔːzəbl/ *adj* **1** (of a statement, an excuse, etc) seeming to be right or reasonable; believable: *She could find no plausible explanation for its disappearance.* ○ *His story was/sounded perfectly plausible.* **2** (*derog*) (of a person) skilled in producing convincing arguments, esp in order to deceive: *a plausible trickster, rogue, liar, etc* ○ *She was so plausible — she would have deceived anyone.* Cf IMPLAUSIBLE.

▷ **plausibility** /ˌplɔːzəˈbɪlətɪ/ *n* [U] state of being plausible: *the plausibility of her alibi* ○ *Beware of the plausibility of salesmen!*

plausibly /-əblɪ/ *adv*: *The case was presented very plausibly.* ○ *He argued very plausibly for its acceptance.*

play[1] /pleɪ/ *n* **1** [U] activity done for amusement, esp by children; recreation: *the happy sounds of children at play* ○ *the advantages of learning through play* ○ *His life is all work and no play.* **2** (*sport*) (**a**) [U] playing of a game: *There was no play/Rain stopped play yesterday.* ○ *The tennis players need total concentration during play.* (**b**)

[U] manner of playing a game: *There was some excellent play in yesterday's match.* ○ *They were penalized for too much rough play.* **(c)** [C] (*esp US*) action or manoeuvre in a game: *a good play* ○ *a fine defensive/passing play.* **3** [C] work (written to be) performed by actors; drama: *a radio play* ○ *a fine edition of Shakespeare's plays* ○ *She has just written a new play.* ○ *act/take part in a play* ○ *We are going to see the new play at the Playhouse.* **4** [U] (scope for) free and easy movement: *Give the line more play,* eg in fishing. ○ *a knot with too much play,* ie one that is not tight enough ○ *We need more play on the rope.* **5** [U] activity; operation; interaction: *the play of supernatural forces in human destiny.* **6** [U] light, quick, constantly shifting movement: *the play of sunlight on water.* **7** [U] taking part in card-games, board games, roulette, etc when playing for money; gambling: *lose £500 in one evening's play.* **8** [sing] turn or move in cards, chess, etc: *It's your play,* ie You are the next to make a move. **9** (idm) **bring sth into ˈplay** cause sth to have an influence: *This financial crisis has brought new factors into play.* **call sth into play** ⇨ CALL[2]. **child's play** ⇨ CHILD. **come into ˈplay** (begin to) be active or have an influence: *Personal feelings should not come into play when one has to make business decisions.* **fair play** ⇨ FAIR[1]. **give, etc free play/rein to sb/sth** ⇨ FREE[2]. **give sb/sth full play** ⇨ FULL. **in full play** ⇨ FULL. **in ˈplay** as a joke; not seriously: *The remark was only made in play.* **in/out of ˈplay** (*sport*) (of the ball in football, cricket, etc) in/not in a position where the rules allow it to be played. **make a play for sb/sth** (*esp US*) perform actions that are designed to achieve a desired result: *She was making a big play for the leadership of the party.* ○ *He was making a play for the prettiest girl in the college.* **a play on ˈwords** pun: *The advertising slogan was a play on words.* **the state of play** ⇨ STATE[1].

▷ **playlet** /ˈpleɪlɪt/ *n* short play[1](3).

□ **ˈplay-act** *v* [I] make a show of feelings one does not really have; pretend. **ˈplay-acting** *n* [U] **(a)** performing in a play[1](3). **(b)** pretence, esp of feelings.

ˈplaybill *n* poster announcing the performance of a play[1](3).

ˈplayboy *n* rich (esp young) man who spends his time enjoying himself.

ˌplay-by-ˈplay *n* (*US sport*) detailed commentary on a game, broadcast as it happens.

ˈplayfellow (also **ˈplaymate**) *n* companion with whom (esp) a child plays.

ˈplaygoer /-gəʊə(r)/ *n* person who (often) goes to the theatre.

ˈplayground *n* **(a)** area of land where children play, eg as part of a school. **(b)** (*fig*) area where people like to go on holiday: *The island has become a playground for pop stars and wealthy businessmen.*

ˈplaygroup (also **ˈplayschool**) *n* [CGp] group of children below school age who meet regularly and play together under the supervision of adults. Cf NURSERY SCHOOL (NURSERY).

ˈplayhouse *n* **1** theatre. **2** (also **ˈWendy house**) model of a house large enough for a child to play in.

ˈplay-pen *n* small portable enclosure with wooden bars or netting where a baby or small child can play.

ˈplay-room *n* room in a house for children to play in.

ˈplay-street *n* (*Brit*) street that is reserved for children to play in and in which traffic is forbidden.

ˈplaything *n* **(a)** toy. **(b)** person treated as an unimportant object of amusement by sb else: *She seemed content with her life as a rich man's plaything.*

ˈplaytime *n* [C, U] (period of) time for recreation and relaxation, esp in school: *The children have three playtimes during the day.* ○ *The children are outside during playtime.*

playwright /pleɪraɪt/ *n* person who writes plays; dramatist.

play[2] /pleɪ/ *v*

▶ DOING THINGS FOR AMUSEMENT **1 (a)** [I, Ipr, Ip] ~ **(with sb/sth)** do things for pleasure, as children do; enjoy oneself, rather than work: *There's a time to work and a time to play.* ○ *play with a ball, toy, bicycle* ○ *a little child playing with his friend* ○ *children playing for hours in the garden.* **(b)** [Ipr no passive, Tn no passive, Tg] ~ **(at) sth/** ~ **(at) doing sth** (esp of children) pretend to be sth or do sth for amusement: *Let's play (at) (being) pirates.* ○ *The children were playing at keeping shop.* **2** [Tn, Tn·pr, Dn·n no passive] ~ **sth (on sb)** trick sb for amusement: *play a joke/prank/trick (on sb)* ○ *They played me a rotten trick.*

▶ TAKING PART IN A GAME **3** [I, Ipr, Tn, Tn·pr] ~ **(sth) (with/against sb)**; ~ **sb (at sth)** take part in a game; compete against sb in a game: *play football, cricket, chess, cards, etc* ○ *playing (darts) with one's friends* ○ *She plays (hockey) for England.* ○ *On Saturday France play(s) (Rugby) against Wales.* ○ *Have you played her (at tennis) yet?* **4** [I, Tn] gamble at or on (sth): *play at the roulette table* ○ *play the casinos* ○ *play the stock-market,* ie buy and sell shares, etc to make money. **5 (a)** [Ipr, Tn] take (a particular position) in a team: *Who's playing in goal?* ○ *I've never played (as/at) centre-forward before.* **(b)** [Tn, Tn·pr, Cn·n/a] ~ **sb (as sth)** include sb in a team: *I think we should play Bill on the wing in the next match.* ○ *Who shall we play at/as centre-forward?* **6 (a)** [I, Ipr, Ip, Tn, Tn·pr, Tn·p] (in sport) (try to) strike, kick, throw, etc (the ball, etc), esp in the specified manner or direction: *She played (at the ball) and missed.* ○ *In soccer, only the goal-keeper may play the ball with his hands.* ○ *He played the ball onto his wicket,* ie accidentally struck it so that it hit the wicket. **(b)** [Tn] (in sport) make (a stroke, etc): *play a fast backhand volley.* **7** [I] (of a sports pitch, etc) be in a certain condition for playing: *a pitch that plays well, poorly, etc,* ie allows the ball to move easily, slowly, etc. **8** [I, Tn] **(a)** move (a piece) in chess, etc: *She played her bishop.* **(b)** put (a playing-card) face upwards on the table in a game of cards: *Have you played?* ○ *Don't play out of turn!* ○ *play one's ace, a trump, etc.*

▶ PRODUCING MUSIC OR SOUND **9 (a)** [I, Ipr, Tn, Dn·n, Dn·pr] ~ **(sth) (on sth)**; ~ **sth (to sb)** perform on (a musical instrument); perform (music): *In the distance a band was playing.* ○ *play (the violin, flute, etc) (well)* ○ *play (a sonata) to an audience* ○ *play a tune on a guitar* ○ *play sb a piece by Chopin.* **(b)** [I] (of music) be performed: *I could hear music playing on the radio.* **10 (a)** [Tn, Dn·n, Dn·pr] ~ **sth (for sb)** cause (a record, record-player, etc) to produce sound: *Can you play (me) her latest record?* ○ *Play that jazz tape for me, please.* **(b)** [I] (of a tape, record, etc) produce sound: *There was a record playing in the next room.*

▶ ACTING **11 (a)** [Tn] act in (a drama, etc); act the role of (sb): *They're playing 'Carmen' at the Coliseum.* ○ *play (the part of) Ophelia.* **(b)** [I, Ipr] ~ **(to sb)** (of a drama) be performed: *a production of 'Hamlet' playing to enthusiastic audiences.* **12** [La, Ln, Tn no passive] behave in a specified way; act as if one were (a particular type of person): *play dead,* ie pretend to be dead in order to trick sb ○ *play the politician, diplomat, etc* ○ *play the fool,* ie act foolishly ○ *play the sympathetic friend, the wronged wife, the busy tycoon, etc.*

▶ OTHER MEANINGS **13 (a)** [Ipr] move quickly and lightly, esp often changing direction: *sunlight playing on/over the surface of the lake* ○ (*fig*) *A smile played on/about her lips.* ○ *His mind played on the idea of going away for a holiday.* **(b)** [Tn·pr] direct (esp light or water) in a specified direction: *play the torch beam over the walls* ○ *The firemen played their hoses on the burning building.* ○ *They played the searchlights along the road.* **(c)** [I] (of fountains, etc) produce a steady stream of water. **14** [Tn] allow (a fish) to exhaust itself by pulling against the line. **15** (idm) **what sb is ˈplaying a** (usu expressing anger, irritation, etc) what sb i doing: *I don't know ˈwhat he thinks he's playing at* (For other idioms containing **play**, see entries fo *ns, adjs,* etc, eg **play fair** ⇨ FAIR[2]; **play the gam** ⇨ GAME[1].).

16 (phr v) **play aˈbout/aˈround (with sb/sth)** ac or handle sb/sth in a casual irresponsible way *Stop playing around and get on with the job.* ○ *Yo shouldn't play around with* (ie flirt with) *anothe woman's husband.* ○ *Don't play about with m expensive tools!*

play aˈlong (with sb/sth) pretend to co-operate (*infml*) *She was in charge, so I had to play along with her odd ideas.*

ˈplay at sth/being sth do sth only casually without true interest: *He's only playing at his job i the city: he's much more interested in being a racin driver.*

play sth ˈback (to sb) allow the material recorde on a tape, etc to be heard or seen: *I rewound th cassette and played her voice back to her.*

play sth ˈdown try to make sth appear les important than it is: *The government are trying t play down their involvement in the affair.*

play sb in, out, etc play music as sb enters, leaves etc (a place): *The band played the performers ont the stage.* **play oneself ˈin** play slowly an cautiously at the beginning of a game.

play (sth) ˈoff (of two teams, etc that have th same number of points, have drawn in an earlie match, etc) play the deciding match: *The matc between the joint leaders will be played o tomorrow.* **play A off against B** cause two peopl or groups to oppose each other, esp for one's ow advantage: *She played her two rivals off agains each other and got the job herself.*

play ˈon (*sport*) continue to play; start playin again: *Some of the players claimed a penalty but th referee told them to play on.* **play on sth** rouse (sb' feelings, etc) for one's own purposes: *They playe on his fears of losing his job to get him to do wha they wanted.* ○ *Her speech played heavily on th angry mood of her audience.*

play sth out perform or enact sth, esp in real lif *Their love affair was played out against th background of a country at war.*

play (sb) up (*infml*) cause (sb) problems, pain o difficulties: *My injured shoulder is playing (me) u today.* ○ *schoolchildren playing up their teacher,* e by being noisy. **play sth up** try to make sth appea more important than it is: *She played up her pas achievements just to impress us.* **play up to s** (*infml*) flatter sb in order to win favour.

ˈplay with oneself (*euph*) masturbate. **play wit sb/sth** = PLAY ABOUT/AROUND (WITH SB/STH). **pla with sth** consider (an idea, etc) lightly; toy wit sth: *She's playing with the idea of starting her ow business.*

□ **ˈplay-back** *n* [C, U] (device for) playing bac recorded sound or pictures, eg on a video recorde

played ˈout (*infml*) exhausted; finished; no longe useful: *After a hard gallop, the horse was playe out.* ○ *Is this theory played out*(ie no longer wort considering)*?*

ˈplay-off *n* match between two players or team that are level, to decide the winner.

player /ˈpleɪə(r)/ *n* **1** person who plays a game: *game for four players* ○ *She's an excellent ˈtenni player.* ○ *Two players were injured during th match.* **2** actor. **3** person who plays a musica instrument: *a ˈtrumpet player.* **4** = RECORD-PLAYE (RECORD[1]).

□ **ˈplayer-piano** *n* piano fitted with a mechanis that allows it to be played automatically.

playful /ˈpleɪfl/ *adj* **1** fond of playing; full of fun: *a playful as a kitten* ○ *a playful mood.* **2** done in fu not serious: *a playful smack* ○ *playful remarks.* ▷ **playfully** /-fəlɪ/ *adv.* **playfulness** *n* [U]

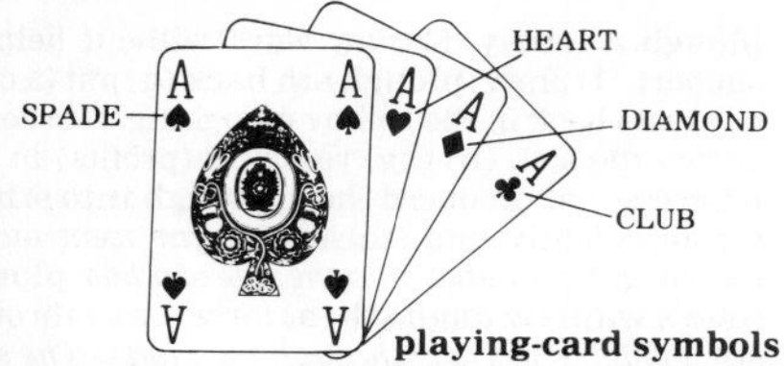

playing-card symbols

playing-card /ˈpleɪɪŋ kɑːd/ (also **card**) *n* any of a set of 52 oblong cards, used for various games (eg bridge, canasta, poker): *a pack of playing-cards.*

playing-field /ˈpleɪɪŋ fiːld/ *n* (*sport*) (**a**) field with special markings, used for cricket, football, hockey, etc. (**b**) = PLAYGROUND (PLAY¹).

plaza /ˈplɑːzə; *US* ˈplæzə/ *n* **1** open square or market-place (esp in a Spanish town). **2** (*esp US*) shopping centre.

PLC (also **plc**) /ˌpiː el ˈsiː/ *abbr* (*Brit*) Public Limited (ie limited liability) Company: *Lloyd's Bank PLC.* Cf INC, LTD. ⇨ article at INDUSTRY.

plea /pliː/ *n* **1** (*fml*) ~ (**for sth**) earnest request; appeal: *a plea for forgiveness, money, more time* ○ *He was deaf to* (ie refused to listen to) *her pleas.* **2** (*law*) statement made by a person charged with an offence in court: *enter a plea of guilty/not guilty.* **3** (idm) **on the plea of sth/that . . .** (*fml*) giving sth as the reason or excuse for not doing sth or for having done sth wrong: *withdraw on the plea of ill health* ○ *He refused to contribute, on the plea that he couldn't afford it.*

□ ˈ**plea bargaining** (*esp US*) arrangement by which a defendant in a legal case pleads guilty to a lesser criminal charge in return for a promise by the prosecution to drop a more serious one.

pleach /pliːtʃ/ *v* [Tn esp passive] make or repair (a hedge) by weaving branches together: *pleached hedges.*

plead /pliːd/ *v* (*pt, pp* **pleaded**; *US* **pled** /pled/) **1** [Ipr, It] ~ (**with sb**) (**for sth**) make repeated urgent requests (to sb) (for sth): *plead for mercy* ○ *He pleaded with his parents for a more understanding attitude.* ○ *She pleaded with him not to leave her alone.* ○ *The boy pleaded to be allowed to ride on the tractor.* **2** [Tn] offer (sth) as an explanation or excuse, esp for failing to do sth or for doing sth wrong: *They asked him to pay for the damage but he pleaded poverty.* ○ *He apologized for not coming to the party, pleading pressure of work.* ○ *Pleading ignorance of the law won't help you if you are caught.* **3** [Ipr] ~ **for/against sb** (*law*) (of a lawyer) speak to a lawcourt (on behalf of the plaintiff/defendant) or draft legal documents in a civil action. **4** [Tn] (*law*) present (a case) to a court of law: *They employed the best lawyer they could get to plead their case.* **5** [Tn] (*law*) put (sth) forward as the basis of a case in a court of law (on behalf of sb): *plead guilty/not guilty*, ie declare that one is guilty/not guilty of the crime one has been accused of. **6** [Ipr, Tn] ~ **for** (**sth**) argue in support of sth; support (a cause) by argument: *plead the cause of political prisoners* ○ *plead for the modernization of the city's public transport.*

▷ **pleadingly** *adv* in a begging or an imploring manner.

pleadings *n* [pl] (*law*) formal (usu written) statements, replies to accusations, etc made by each side in a legal action.

pleasant /ˈpleznt/ *adj* (**-er, -est**) (**a**) ~ (**to sth**) giving pleasure to the mind, feelings or senses; enjoyable: *a pleasant surprise, smell, wine* ○ *a pleasant breeze, temperature, climate* ○ *pleasant to the taste.* (**b**) ~ (**to sb**) polite and friendly: *a pleasant smile, voice, manner* ○ *make oneself pleasant to visitors* ○ *What a pleasant girl!* ○ *Do try to be more pleasant!* ▷ **pleasantly** *adv*: *smile pleasantly* ○ *We were pleasantly surprised at the profit we made.* **pleasantness** *n* [U].

pleasantry /ˈplezntrɪ/ *n* (*fml*) (**a**) humorous remark; joke: *The children smiled politely at the visitor's pleasantries.* (**b**) polite remarks: *After an exchange of pleasantries, the leaders started their negotiations.*

please /pliːz/ *v* **1** [Tn] be agreeable to (sb); make (sb) happy: *It's difficult to please everybody.* ○ *Our main aim is to please the customers.* ○ *He's a very hard/difficult man to please.* ○ *I shall have nothing to do on holiday but please myself*, ie do as I like. **2** [I] (in subordinate clauses beginning with *as* or *what*) (*fml*) (**a**) think desirable or appropriate; choose: *You may stay as long as you please.* ○ *Take as many as you please.* (**b**) want; like: *That child behaves just as he pleases.* ○ *I shall do as I please.* ○ *Do what you please.* **3** (idm) ˌ**if you** ˈ**please** (**a**) (*fml*) (used when making a polite request): *Come this way, if you please.* (**b**) (used to express annoyance or outrage when reporting sth): *And now, if you please, I've been told I'm to get nothing for my work!* ○ *He says the food isn't hot enough, if you please!* ˌ**please** ˈ**God** may God let it happen; if it is pleasing to God: *Please God, things will start to improve soon.* ○ *She'll get better one day, please God.* ˌ**please your**ˈ**self** (*ironic*) do as you like; I don't care what you do: *'I don't want to come with you today.' 'Oh, please yourself then!'*

▷ **please** *interj* **1** (**a**) (used as a polite way of making a request or giving an order): *Please come in.* ○ *Come in, please.* ○ *Two cups of tea, please.* ○ *Tickets, please!* ○ *Would you go now, please!* (**b**) (used to add emphasis or urgency to a request or statement): *Please don't leave me here alone!* ○ *Please, please, don't be late!* ○ *Please, I don't understand what I have to do!* **2** (*infml*) (used when accepting an offer emphatically) yes, please: *'Shall I help you carry that load?' 'Please!'* **3** (idm) **yes, please** (used as a polite way of accepting the offer of sth) I accept and am grateful: *'Would you like some coffee?' 'Yes, please'.* ○ *'Would you like a lift into town?' 'Yes, please'.*

pleased *adj* **1** ~ (**with sb/sth**) feeling or showing satisfaction or pleasure (with sb/sth): *Your mother will be very pleased with you.* ○ *They were all very pleased with the news.* ○ *Are you pleased with the new flat?* ○ *He looks rather pleased with himself*, ie pleased with what he has done. **2** ~ **to do sth** happy to do sth: *I was very pleased to be able to help.* ○ *We were pleased to hear the news.* ○ (*fml*) *The Governor is pleased to accept the invitation.* **3** (idm) (**as**) ˌ**pleased as** ˈ**Punch** very pleased.

pleasing *adj* ~ (**to sb/sth**) giving pleasure (to sb/sth); pleasant: *a pleasing colour scheme, singing voice* ○ *The news was very pleasing to us.* ○ *sounds that are pleasing to the ear.* **pleasingly** *adv*: *everything pleasingly arranged for the guests.*

pleasure /ˈpleʒə(r)/ *n* **1** (**a**) [U] state or feeling of being happy or satisfied: *a work of art that has given pleasure to millions of people* ○ *It gives me great pleasure to welcome our speaker* ○ *Has she gone to Paris on business or for pleasure* (ie for work or for fun)? (**b**) [C] thing that gives happiness or satisfaction: *the pleasures of living in the country* ○ *She has few pleasures left in life.* ○ *It's been a pleasure meeting you.* ○ *'Thank you for doing that!' 'It's a pleasure.'* ○ *Remembering the past was his only pleasure.* **2** [U] sensual enjoyment: *His life is spent in the pursuit of pleasure.* **3** [U] (*fml*) what a person wants; desire: *We await your pleasure.* ○ *You are free to come and go at your pleasure*, ie as you wish. ○ *Is it your pleasure that I cancel the arrangements?* **4** (idm) **have the pleasure of sth/doing sth** (used to make polite requests, issue invitations, etc): *May I have the pleasure of this dance?* ○ (*fml or joc*) *Are we to have the pleasure of seeing you again?* **take** (**no/great**) **pleasure in sth/doing sth** enjoy/not enjoy (doing) sth: *She seemed to take pleasure in our suffering.* ○ *They take great pleasure in reminding us of our poverty.* ○ *She took no pleasure in her work.* **with** ˈ**pleasure** one is pleased to accept, agree, etc: *'Will you join us?' 'Thank you, with pleasure.'* ○ *'May I borrow your car?' 'Yes, with pleasure.'*

▷ **pleasurable** /ˈpleʒərəbl/ *adj* giving pleasure; enjoyable: *a pleasurable sensation* ○ *pleasurable companionship.* **pleasurably** /-əblɪ/ *adv.*

□ ˈ**pleasure-boat** *n* boat used for pleasure only.

ˈ**pleasure-craft** *n* (*pl* unchanged) boat used for pleasure only: *Fishing boats and pleasure-craft followed the great liner into the harbour.*

ˈ**pleasure-ground** *n* area used for public amusement or recreation.

the ˈ**pleasure principle** (*psychology*) theory that people's behaviour is controlled by the need to satisfy their instinctive desires and avoid pain or discomfort.

ˈ**pleasure-seeking** *adj* devoted to pleasure(2).

pleat /pliːt/ *n* pressed or stitched fold made in a piece of cloth: *a shirt with pleats in the front.*

▷ **pleat** *v* [Tn] make pleats in (sth): *pleat a skirt* ○ *pleated curtains.*

pleb /pleb/ *n* (*infml derog*) **1** [C] = PLEBEIAN. **2 the plebs** [pl] the masses.

plebe /pliːb/ *n* (*US infml*) new student at a military training college.

plebeian /plɪˈbiːən/ *adj* **1** (*fml or derog*) of the lower social classes: *of plebeian origins.* **2** (*derog*) lacking refinement; vulgar: *plebeian tastes.* ▷ **plebeian** (also **pleb**) *n* (*derog*) person belonging to the lower social classes (esp in ancient Rome). Cf PATRICIAN.

plebiscite /ˈplebɪsɪt; *US* -saɪt/ *n* (*politics*) (decision made by a) direct vote by all qualified citizens on an important political matter: *A plebiscite was held to decide the fate of the country.* ○ *The question of which state the minority group should belong to was decided by (a) plebiscite.* Cf REFERENDUM.

plectrum /ˈplektrəm/ *n* (*pl* **-tra** /-trə/) (also *infml* **pick**) (*music*) small piece of metal, wood, plastic or bone that is attached to the finger and used for plucking the strings of certain musical instruments, eg the guitar, mandolin, etc.

pled *pt, pp* of PLEAD.

pledge /pledʒ/ *n* **1** solemn promise; vow: *give a pledge never to reveal the secret.* **2** (**a**) thing left with a person to be kept until the giver has done sth promised, eg paid a debt. (**b**) article left with a pawnbroker in exchange for sth, esp money. **3** thing given to sb as a sign of friendship, love, etc: *gifts exchanged as a pledge of friendship.* **4** (idm) **in/out of pledge** left with sb until the giver has paid a debt, etc/no longer left on these conditions: *put/hold sth in pledge* ○ *take sth out of pledge.* **sign/take the** ˈ**pledge** (*esp joc*) make a solemn promise never to drink alcohol. **under pledge of sth** in the state of having agreed to or promised sth: *You are under pledge of secrecy.*

▷ **pledge** *v* **1** (**a**) [Tn, Tn·pr, Dn·n, Dn·t] ~ **sth** (**to sb/sth**) (*fml*) promise solemnly to give (support,etc); give (one's word, honour, etc) as a pledge: *pledge allegiance* (ie loyalty) *to the king* ○ *pledge a donation (to a charity)* ○ *be pledged to secrecy/to keeping a secret.* (**b**) [Tn, Tn·pr, Cn·t] ~ **sb/oneself** (**to sth/to do sth**) promise solemnly that sb/one will do sth or support a cause, etc: *The Government has pledged itself to send aid to the famine victims.* **2** [Tn] leave (sth) with sb as a pledge(1b): *He's pledged* (ie pawned) *his mother's wedding ring.* **3** [Tn] (*fml*) drink to the health of (sb); toast (sb): *pledge the bride and bridegroom.*

Pleiades /ˈplaɪədiːz/ *n* [pl] (also **the Seven Sisters**) group of stars in the constellation *Taurus, of which six or seven can be clearly seen without a telescope.

Pleistocene /ˈplaɪstəsiːn/ *adj* (*geology*) of the epoch in the earth's history that started about a million years ago and lasted for about 800 000 years, when glaciers covered most of the northern hemisphere.

▷ **the Pleistocene** *n* [sing] the Pleistocene epoch.

plenary /ˈpliːnərɪ/ *adj* **1** (of meetings, etc) attended by all who have the right to attend: *a plenary session of the assembly.* **2** (of powers, authority, etc) without limits; absolute: *assume plenary authority.*

plenipotentiary /ˌplenɪpəˈtenʃərɪ/ *n* person (esp an ambassador) with full powers to act on behalf of his government (esp in a foreign country).

▷ **plenipotentiary** *adj* of or like a plenipotentiary: *The minister was given plenipotentiary powers in the trade negotiations.*

plenteous /ˈplentɪəs/ *adj* (*fml*) plentiful. ▷ **plenteously** *adv.*

plentiful /ˈplentɪfl/ *adj* in large quantities or numbers; abundant: *find plentiful supplies of fresh fruit and vegetables* ○ *Eggs are plentiful at the* *moment.* Cf SCARCE. ▷ **plentifully** /-fəlɪ/ *adv*: *The visitors were plentifully supplied with food and drink.*

plenty /ˈplentɪ/ *pron* **1** number or amount that is sufficient for sb or more than sb needs: *plenty of eggs, money, time* ○ *'Do you need more milk?' 'No thanks, there's plenty in the fridge.'* ○ *'Have we got enough plates?' 'Yes, there are plenty in the cupboard.'* ○ *They always gave us plenty to eat.* **2** (idm) **days, years, etc of ˈplenty** (*fml or rhet*) time when very many necessities, esp food and money, are available: *looking back on the years of plenty.* **in ˈplenty** (*fml*) in a large quantity; in abundance: *food and drink in plenty.* ▷ **plenty** *adv* **1** (used with *more* to indicate an excess): *We've got plenty more (of it/them) in the shop.* ○ *There's plenty more paper if you need it.* **2** (*infml*) (used with *big, long, tall,* etc followed by *enough*): *The rope was plenty long enough to reach the ground.*

pleonasm /ˈplɪənæzəm/ *n* **(a)** [U] use of more words than are necessary to express the meaning. **(b)** [C] instance of this: *'Hear with one's ears' and 'divide into four quarters' are pleonasms.* Cf TAUTOLOGY. ▷ **pleonastic** /ˌplɪəˈnæstɪk/ *adj.*

plesiosaurus /ˌpli:zɪəˈsɔ:rəs/ *n* large extinct reptile that lived in the sea, and had a long neck and large flippers.

plethora /ˈpleθərə/ *n* [sing] (*fml*) quantity greater than what is needed; over-abundance: *The report contained a plethora of detail.*

pleurisy /ˈplʊərəsɪ/ *n* [U] (*medical*) serious illness, with inflammation of the delicate membrane of the thorax and the lungs, causing severe pain in the chest or sides.

plexus /ˈpleksəs/ *n* (*pl* unchanged or ~**es**) (*anatomy*) network of fibres or vessels in the body: *the solar plexus,* ie the network of nerves in the abdomen.

pliable /ˈplaɪəbl/ *adj* **1** easily bent, shaped or twisted; flexible: *Cane is pliable when wet.* **2** (of a person or a person's mind) easily influenced: *the pliable minds of children.* ▷ **pliability** /ˌplaɪəˈbɪlətɪ/ *n* [U].

pliant /ˈplaɪənt/ *adj* **1** bending easily; supple: *the pliant branches of young trees.* **2** adapting easily; yielding. ▷ **pliancy** /ˈplaɪənsɪ/ *n* [U]. **pliantly** *adv.*

pliers /ˈplaɪəz/ *n* [pl] tool with long jaws which have flat surfaces that can be brought together for holding, bending, twisting or cutting wire, etc: *a pair of pliers.*

plight[1] /plaɪt/ *n* [sing] serious and difficult situation or condition: *the plight of the homeless* ○ *The crew were in a sorry plight by the time they reached shore.* ○ *I was in a dreadful plight — I had lost my money and missed the last train home.*

plight[2] /plaɪt/ *v* (idm) **plight one's ˈtroth** (*arch*) make a promise to marry sb.

plimsoll /ˈplɪmsəl/ (also **pump**) *n* (*Brit*) (*US* **sneaker**) rubber-soled canvas sports shoe; gym-shoe: *a pair of plimsolls.*

Plimsoll line /ˈplɪmsəl laɪn/ (also **ˈPlimsoll mark** /mɑ:k/) line marked on a ship's side to show how far it may legally go down in the water when loaded.

plinth /plɪnθ/ *n* square block or slab on which a column or statue stands. ⇨ illus at COLUMN.

Pliocene /ˈplaɪəʊsi:n/ *adj* (*geology*) of the last epoch of the Tertiary period in the earth's history, from about 5.1 to 2 million years ago, when many modern mammals appeared and many earlier species became extinct.
▷ **the Pliocene** *n* [sing] the Pliocene epoch.

PLO /ˌpi: el ˈəʊ/ *abbr* Palestine Liberation Organization.

plod /plɒd/ *v* (**-dd-**) **1** [I, Ipr, Ip] ~ (**along/on**) walk with heavy steps or with difficulty; trudge: *Labourers plodded home through the muddy fields.* ○ (*fig*) *We plodded on through the rain for several hours.* ⇨ Usage at STUMP. **2** (phr v) **plod along** move slowly (at some task): *'How's the book?' 'Oh, I'm plodding along.'* **plod away (at sth)** work steadily but slowly (and with difficulty): *He plodded away all night at the accounts but didn't finish them in time.*
▷ **plodder** *n* (*usu derog*) person who works slowly and with determination, but without inspiration. **plodding** *adj.* **ploddingly** *adv.*

plonk[1] /plɒŋk/ (also **plunk** /plʌŋk/) *n* (*usu sing*) (*infml*) sound (as) of sth dropping heavily: *to hear a plonk.*
▷ **plonk** *adv* (*infml*) with a plonk: *The lamp fell plonk on the table.*
plonk *v* (phr v) **plonk sth down; plonk sth (down) on sth** (*infml*) drop sth or put sth down heavily or with a plonking sound: *He plonked the groceries on the kitchen floor.* ○ (*fig*) *We plonked ourselves (down) by the fire.*

plonk[2] /plɒŋk/ *n* [U] (*infml esp Brit*) cheap wine of poor quality.

plop /plɒp/ *n* (*usu sing*) sound (as) of a smooth object dropping into water without making a splash: *He dropped a pebble from the bridge and waited for the plop.*
▷ **plop** *adv* with a plop: *The stone fell plop into the water.*
plop *v* (**-pp-**) **1** [I] make a plop: *Did you hear it plop?* **2** [Ipr, Ip] fall with a plop: *The jelly plopped into the dish.* ○ *The fish plopped back into the river.*

plosive /ˈpləʊsɪv/ *n, adj* (*phonetics*) (consonant sound) made by closing the air passage and then audibly releasing the air, eg /t/ and /p/ in *top.*

plot[1] /plɒt/ *n* small marked or measured piece of land, esp for a special purpose: *a building plot* ○ *a vegetable plot* ○ *a small plot of land.*
▷ **plot** *v* (**-tt-**) **1** [Tn] **(a)** make a plan or map of (sth): *plot an escape route.* **(b)** mark (sth) on a chart or diagram: *plot the ship's course.* **(c)** make (a curve, etc) by connecting points on a graph: *plot a temperature curve.* **2** [Tn, Tn·p] ~ **sth (out)** divide sth into plots.

plot[2] /plɒt/ *n* **1** (plan or outline of the) events in the story of a play or novel: *a neatly worked-out plot* ○ *The plot was too complicated for me — I couldn't follow it.* **2** secret plan made by several people to do sth; conspiracy: *a plot to overthrow the government* ○ *The plot was discovered in time.* **3** (idm) **hatch a plot** ⇨ HATCH. **the plot ˈthickens** (*catchphrase*) a situation in real life, or the plot of a work of fiction, is suddenly more complicated or intriguing.
▷ **plot** *v* (**-tt-**) **(a)** [I, Ipr, Ip, It] ~ (**with sb**) (**against sb**); ~ (**together**) make a secret plan (to do sth); take part in a plot: *plot with others against the State* ○ *plot (together) to do sth.* **(b)** [Tn] plan (sth) with others: *They were plotting the overthrow of the government.* **plotter** *n* person who plots; conspirator.

plough (*US* **plow**)

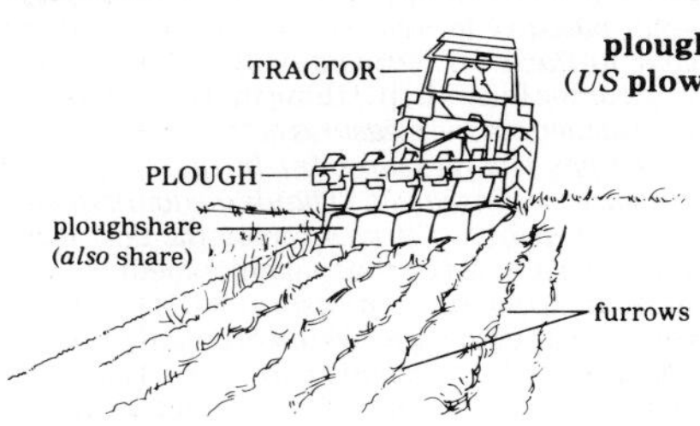

plough (*US* **plow**) /plaʊ/ *n* **1 (a)** [C] implement with a curved blade, used for digging furrows in the soil, esp before seeds are planted, pulled by animals or by a tractor. **(b)** (esp in compounds) implement resembling this: *a ˈsnow-plough,* ie one for clearing snow from roads and railways. **2 the Plough** [sing] (also **Charles's Wain**) (*Brit*) (*US* also **the Big Dipper**) (*astronomy*) group of the seven brightest stars in the constellation of the Great Bear, visible only from the Northern hemisphere. **3** [U] land that has been ploughed: *100 acres of plough.* **4** (idm) **under the ˈplough** (of land) used for growing grain and not for pasture.
▷ **plough** (*US* **plow**) **1** [Tn, Tn·p] ~ **sth (up)** break up the surface of (land) with a plough: *plough a field* ○ *The meadow's been ploughed up.* **2** [I, Tn] (*dated Brit sl*) (cause sb to) fail (an examination): *I ploughed my finals.* ○ *The examiners ploughed half the candidates.* **3** (idm) **plough a lonely ˈfurrow** work without help or support. **4** (phr v) **plough sth back (a)** put (a crop or grass) back in the soil by ploughing in order to enrich the soil. **(b)** (*fig*) re-invest (profits) in the business that produced them. **plough into sth/sb** crash violently into sth/sb: *The car went out of control and ploughed into the side of a bus.* **plough (one's way) through sth (a)** force a way through sth: *plough one's way through the mud* ○ *The ship ploughed through the waves.* **(b)** make progress slowly or with difficulty through sth: *plough through legal text books, a pile of documents, mountains of work, etc.*
□ **ˈploughman** (*US* **plow-**) /-mən/ *n* (**-men** /-mən/) man who guides a plough(1a), esp one pulled by animals. **ˌploughman's ˈlunch** (*Brit*) meal of bread, cheese and pickles, often served with beer in a pub.
ˈploughshare (*US* **plow-**) (also **share**) *n* broad blade of a plough(1a). ⇨ illus.

plover /ˈplʌvə(r)/ *n* any of various types of long-legged short-tailed land bird that live on marshy ground near the sea. ⇨ illus at BIRD.

ploy /plɔɪ/ *n* words or actions, eg in a game, intended to win an advantage over one's opponent: *It was all a ploy to distract attention from his real aims.*

PLP /ˌpi: el ˈpi:/ *abbr* Parliamentary Labour Party.

PLR /ˌpi: el ˈɑ:(r)/ *abbr* public lending right.

pluck /plʌk/ *v* **1** [Tn, Tn·pr, Tn·p] ~ **sth (off/out)** gather or remove sth by pulling; pick sth: *pluck a rose from the garden* ○ *pluck one's eyebrows,* ie use tweezers to remove unwanted hairs ○ *pluck off the dead flowers* ○ *pluck out a grey hair.* **2** [Tn] pull the feathers off (a goose, chicken, etc) in order to prepare it for cooking: *Have the turkeys been plucked?* **3** [Tn, Tn·pr] ~ **(at sth)** take hold of (sth) and pull it; snatch at (sth): *The child was plucking at her mother's skirt.* ○ *A stranger plucked at my sleeve as I was leaving.* **4** (*US* **pick**) [Tn] sound (the strings of a musical instrument) by pulling and releasing them: *pluck the strings of a guitar.* **5** (idm) **pluck up ˈcourage (to do sth)** make an effort to be brave: *I shall have to pluck up courage and speak to her about it.* ○ *He can't pluck up the courage to leave home.*
▷ **pluck** *n* **1** [U] (*infml*) courage, esp in the face of a stronger opponent or of hardship; bravery: *She showed a lot of pluck in dealing with the intruders.* **2** [C usu *sing*] short sharp pull: *feel a pluck at one's sleeve.* **3** [U] heart, liver and lungs of an animal, as food. **plucky** *adj* (**-ier, -iest**) having or showing pluck; brave. **pluckily** *adv.*

plugs

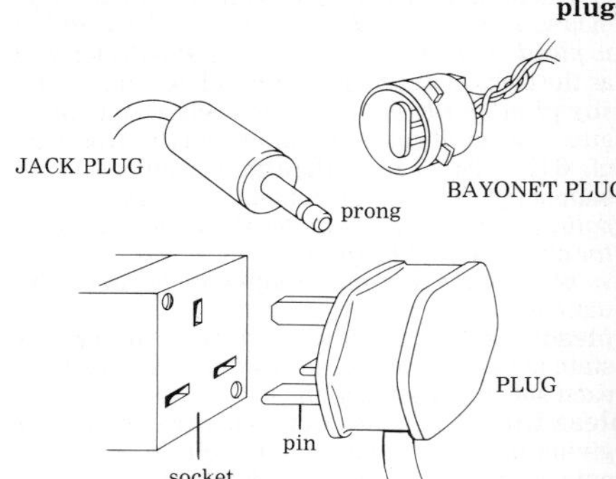

plug /plʌg/ *n* **1 (a)** piece of metal, rubber or plastic that fits tightly into a hole (eg in a barrel, wash-basin, bath, etc): *Pull (out) the plug and let the water drain away.* ○ *He put plugs in his ears because the noise was too loud.* **(b)** (*US*) = STOPPER. **2 (a)** device with metal pins that fit into holes in a socket to make an electrical connection: *a three-/two-pin plug* ○ *Put the plug in the socket.* ○ *I'll have to change the plug on the hair drier.* ⇨ illus. **(b)** (*infml*) electric socket. **3** = SPARKING PLUG (SPARK). **4** (*infml*) piece of favourable publicity in the media for a commercial product, eg a record or book. **5** (a) cake or stick of pressed or twisted tobacco. (b) piece of this cut off for chewing. **6** (idm) **pull the plug on sb/sth** ⇨ PULL[2].

▷ **plug** *v* (-gg-) **1** [Tn, Tn·p] ~ **sth (up)** fill (a hole) or stop up sth with a plug: *plug a leak in the barrel.* **2** [Tn] (*infml*) mention (sth) favourably in the media, esp repeatedly: *They've been plugging his new show on the radio.* **3** [Tn] (*infml esp US*) shoot or hit (sb). **4** (phr v) **plug away (at sth)** work hard and steadily (at sth): *She's been plugging away at her French lessons for months.* **plug sth in** connect (sth) to the electricity supply with a plug(2a): *Plug in the radio, please.* ○ *The recorder wasn't plugged in.*

□ **'plug-hole** *n* (*Brit*) (*US* **drain**) hole into which a plug(1) fits, esp in a basin, sink or wash-basin.

plum /plʌm/ *n* **1** (a) [C] soft round smooth-skinned fruit with sweet flesh and a flattish pointed stone. ⇨ illus at FRUIT. (b) [C] (also **'plum tree**) tree on which this grows. **2** [U] dark reddish-purple colour. **3** (*infml*) thing considered good or worth having, esp a well-paid job: *She's got a plum of a job.* ○ [attrib] *a plum job.*

□ **ˌplum 'duff** (*Brit*) boiled pudding made of flour and suet and containing raisins.

ˌplum 'pudding rich boiled pudding made of flour and suet with dried fruits and spices, traditionally eaten at Christmas.

plumage /ˈpluːmɪdʒ/ *n* **1** [U] feathers covering a bird's body: *the brightly coloured plumage of tropical birds.* **2** (idm) **borrowed plumage** ⇨ BORROW.

plumb /plʌm/ *n* **1** piece of lead that is tied to a cord and used to find the depth of water or test whether a wall, etc is vertical. **2** (idm) **out of 'plumb** not vertical.

▷ **plumb** *adv* **1** exactly: *plumb in the centre.* **2** (*US infml*) quite; absolutely: *He's plumb crazy.*

plumb *v* **1** [Tn] (a) test (sth) by using a plumb-line. (b) (*fig*) (try to) understand (sth) thoroughly: *plumb the mysteries of the universe.* **2** (idm) **plumb the depths of sth** reach the lowest point of sth: *plumb the depths of despair* ○ *a film that really plumbs the depths of bad taste.* **3** (phr v) **plumb sth in** attach (eg a washing-machine) to water-pipes: *We've plumbed in the dishwasher.*

□ **'plumb-line** *n* line with a plumb(1) attached to one end.

plumber /ˈplʌmə(r)/ *n* person whose job is to fit and repair water-pipes, water-tanks, cisterns, etc in buildings.

plumbing /ˈplʌmɪŋ/ *n* [U] **1** system of water-pipes, water-tanks, cisterns, etc in a building: *There is something wrong with the plumbing.* **2** work of a plumber: *We employed a local man to do the plumbing.*

plume /pluːm/ *n* (a) feather, esp a large one used as a decoration. (b) ornament of feathers or similar material, worn in the hair or on a hat or helmet: *a plume of ostrich feathers.* (c) thing that rises into the air in the shape of a feather: *a plume of smoke/steam.*

▷ **plume** *v* **1** [Tn] (of a bird) smooth (sth) with its beak; preen: *a bird pluming itself/its feathers/its wing.* **2** [Tn, Tn·pr] ~ **oneself (on sth)** congratulate or pride oneself (on sth). **plumed** *adj* having or decorated with a plume or plumes: *a plumed hat.*

plummet /ˈplʌmɪt/ *n* **1** (weight attached to a) plumb-line. **2** weight attached to a fishing-line to keep the float upright.

▷ **plummet** *v* [I, Ipr, Ip] fall steeply or rapidly: *House prices have plummeted in this area.* ○ *Pieces of rock plummeted down the mountainside to the ground below.*

plummy /ˈplʌmɪ/ *adj* (**-mier, -miest**) **1** (*infml*) desirable; good: *a plummy job.* **2** (*esp derog*) (of a voice) affectedly upper-class; sounding as if one is speaking with sth (eg a plum) in one's mouth: *a plummy accent/voice.*

plump[1] /plʌmp/ *adj* (a) (esp of an animal, a person, parts of the body) having a full rounded shape; fleshy: *a plump baby, chicken, face* ○ *a baby with plump cheeks.* (b) (*euph*) overweight; fat: *You're getting a bit plump — you need to diet!* ⇨ Usage at FAT[1].

▷ **plump** *v* (phr v) **plump (sth) out/up** (cause sth to) become rounded: *His cheeks are beginning to plump out/up.* ○ *She plumped up the pillows.* **plumpness** *n* [U].

plump[2] /plʌmp/ *v* (phr v) **plump (oneself/sb/sth) down** (cause sb/sth to) fall or drop suddenly and heavily: *plump down the heavy bags* ○ *plump (oneself) down in a chair.* **plump for sb/sth** choose or vote for sb/sth with confidence: *The committee plumped for the most experienced candidate.* ○ *The children plumped for a holiday by the sea.*

▷ **plump** *n* (usu *sing*) (sound made by a) sudden heavy fall: *The book landed with a plump on the floor.*

plump *adv* with a plump: *fall plump into the hole.*

plunder /ˈplʌndə(r)/ *v* **1** [I, Ipr, Tn, Tn·pr] ~ **(sth) (from sth)** steal (goods) from a place, esp during a time of war or civil disorder; pillage: *The conquerors advanced, killing and plundering as they went.* ○ *The invaders plundered food and valuables from coastal towns and villages.* **2** [Tn, Tn·pr] ~ **sth (of sth)** steal goods from (a place), esp during a time of war, etc: *plunder a palace of its treasures* ○ *Tourists have plundered all the archaeological sites.* Cf LOOT, PILLAGE.

▷ **plunder** *n* [U] **1** (action of) plundering: *be guilty of plunder* ○ *goods obtained by plunder.* **2** goods that have been plundered: *They loaded the carts with plunder.*

plunderer /ˈplʌndərə(r)/ *n* person who plunders.

plunge /plʌndʒ/ *v* **1** [Ipr, Ip, Tn·pr, Tn·p] ~ **(sth) into sth**; ~ **(sth) in** (a) (cause sth to) fall into sth suddenly and with force: *plunge (one's hand) into cold water* ○ *They plunged in*, ie dived into the water. ○ *plunge a rod into a blocked drain to clear it.* (b) (cause sth to) enter a specified state or condition: *The country (was) plunged into civil war after the death of the President.* ○ *The news plunged us into despair.* ○ *events which plunged the world into war* ○ *Their extravagant life-style plunged them into debt.* **2** (a) [I, Ipr, Ip, Tn·pr, Tn·p] (cause sb/sth to) move suddenly forwards and/or downwards: *The horse plunged and she fell off.* ○ *Share prices plunged as a result of the gloomy economic forecast.* ○ *a plunging neckline*, ie a very low-cut neck on a woman's dress, blouse, etc ○ *The car plunged over the cliff.* ○ *The sudden jolt plunged her forward.* (b) [I] (of a ship) move with the bows going violently up and down in the water.

▷ **plunge** *n* **1** (a) [C esp *sing*] plunging movement, esp a steep fall: *a plunge into debt, chaos.* (b) [C] act of diving or bathing in water: *a plunge into the sea from the rocks* ○ *a refreshing plunge in the lake.* **2** (idm) **take the 'plunge** take a bold decisive step, esp after thinking about it for some time: *They have finally decided to take the plunge and get married.*

plunger *n* **1** part of a mechanism that moves up and down. **2** (in plumbing) rubber cup fixed on a handle, used for clearing a blocked pipe by means of suction.

plunk = PLONK[1].

pluperfect /ˌpluːˈpɜːfɪkt/ *adj* (also **past perfect**) (*grammar*) (of the form of the verb phrase) expressing an action completed before a particular point in the past: *a pluperfect (form of a) verb phrase.*

▷ **pluperfect** *n* (also **past perfect**) such a form (in English *had* and a past participle, as in 'As he *had* not *received* my letter, he did not come').

plural /ˈplʊərəl/ *n* (*grammar*) form of a noun or verb which refers to more than one person or thing: *The plural of 'child' is 'children'.* ○ *The verb should be in the plural*, eg 'have' in 'they have'. Cf SINGULAR 1.

▷ **plural** *adj* (*grammar*) **1** of or having this form: *Most plural nouns in English end in 's'.* **2** of more than one: *a plural society*, ie one with more than one ethnic group.

pluralism /ˈplʊərəlɪzəm/ *n* [U] **1** (a) existence in one society of a number of groups that belong to different races or have different political or religious beliefs. (b) principle that these different groups can live together peacefully in one society. **2** (*usu derog*) holding of more than one office at one time, esp in the Church.

▷ **pluralist** /ˈplʊərəlɪst/ *n* supporter of pluralism(1b). **pluralist** (also **pluralistic**) /ˌplʊərəˈlɪstɪk/ *adj*: *a pluralist society.*

plurality /plʊəˈrælətɪ/ *n* **1** [U] (*grammar*) state of being plural. **2** [C] large number: *a plurality of influences, interests.* **3** [C] (*US politics*) majority of less than 50%; relative majority. Cf MAJORITY 2. **4** (a) [U] = PLURALISM 2. (b) [C] office held jointly with another.

plus /plʌs/ *prep* (a) with the addition of: *Two plus five is seven.* ○ *The bill was £10, plus £1 for postage.* (b) (*infml*) as well as: *We've got to fit five people plus all their luggage in the car.* Cf MINUS.

▷ **plus** *adj* **1** more than the amount or number indicated: *The work will cost £10 000 plus.* **2** above zero; positive: *5 is a plus quantity.* ○ *The temperature is plus four degrees.*

plus *n* **1** the sign +: *He seems to have mistaken a plus for a minus.* ⇨ App 9. **2** (*infml*) positive quality; advantage: *Her knowledge of French is a plus in her job.* Cf MINUS.

□ **ˌplus-'fours** *n* [pl] wide loose knickerbockers, worn esp by golfers: *a pair of plus-fours.* ⇨ illus at DRESS.

plush /plʌʃ/ *n* [U] type of silk or cotton cloth with a surface like velvet.

▷ **plush** *adj* **1** (also **plushy**) (*infml*) luxuriously smart: *a plush hotel, restaurant, etc.* **2** made of plush: *plush curtains.*

plushy /ˈplʌʃɪ/ *adj* (**-ier, iest**) (*infml*) = PLUSH 1. ▷ **plushiness** *n* [U].

Plutarch /ˈpluːtɑːk/ (c 46-c 120 AD), Greek philosopher and biographer whose best-known work is his *Lives*, a collection of life stories of famous politicians, soldiers, etc of ancient Greece and Rome, which was used by *Shakespeare in writing his plays.

Pluto /ˈpluːtəʊ/ *n* (*astronomy*) the planet ninth in order and furthest from the sun.

plutocracy /pluːˈtɒkrəsɪ/ *n* **1** (a) [U] government by a rich and powerful class. (b) [C] state governed in this way. **2** [CGp] group or class of rich and powerful people; wealthy élite.

▷ **plutocrat** /ˈpluːtəkræt/ *n* (*often derog*) person who is powerful because of his wealth.

plutocratic /ˌpluːtəˈkrætɪk/ *adj* (a) of plutocracy. (b) of or like a plutocrat: *plutocratic control of a media empire.*

plutonium /pluːˈtəʊnɪəm/ *n* [U] (*symb* **Pu**) (*chemistry*) artificially produced radioactive metallic element, derived from uranium and used in nuclear reactors and nuclear weapons. ⇨ App 11.

pluvial /ˈpluːvɪəl/ *adj* **1** (also **pluvious** /ˈpluːvɪəs/) (*fml*) of rain; rainy. **2** (*geology*) caused by rain: *pluvial erosion.*

ply[1] /plaɪ/ *n* [U] (esp in compounds) **1** layer of wood or thickness of cloth: *three-ply wood.* **2** strand of rope or yarn: *three-/four-ply knitting wool.*

□ **plywood** /ˈplaɪwʊd/ *n* [U] board(s) made by gluing thin layers of wood on top of each other: *sheets of plywood* ○ [attrib] *plywood furniture.*

ply[2] /plaɪ/ *v* (*pt, pp* **plied** /plaɪd/) **1** [Tn] (*fml*) use or wield (a tool or weapon): *ply one's needle*, ie work busily at one's sewing ○ *ply the oars*, ie row a boat. **2** [I, Ipr, Tn] (of ships, buses, etc) go regularly to and fro along (a course): *ply the routes between the islands* ○ *ferries that ply between England and France* ○ *ships that ply (across) the South China Sea.* **3** (idm) **ply one's 'trade** work at a (skilled) job. **ply for 'hire** (of taxi drivers, boatmen, etc) wait in a place or move about, looking for passengers: *taxis licensed to ply for hire at the railway station.* **4** (phr v) **ply sb with sth** (a) (repeatedly) give or offer sb (food and drink): *She plied us with cakes.* (b) repeatedly ask sb (questions).

Plymouth Brethren /ˌplɪməθ ˈbreðrɪn/ Christian sect with very strict Protestant beliefs, founded in 1830 in the city of Plymouth, Devon, England. Its members are not allowed to do jobs that do not conform with New Testament teaching.

Plymouth Rock /ˌplɪməθ ˈrɒk/ large rock by the sea at Plymouth, Massachusetts, USA, on which the *Pilgrim Fathers are said to have stepped when they first landed from their ship the *Mayflower*.

PM /ˌpi: ˈem/ *abbr* (*infml esp Brit*) Prime Minister: *an interview with the PM*.

Pm *symb* promethium.

pm /ˌpi: ˈem/ *abbr* (*US* **PM**) after noon (Latin *post meridiem*): *at 3pm*, ie in the afternoon. Cf AM *abbr*.

PMT /ˌpi: em ˈti:/ *abbr* (*infml*) premenstrual tension.

pneumatic /nju:ˈmætɪk; *US* nu:-/ *adj* **1** filled with air: *a pneumatic tyre*. **2** worked by compressed air: *a pneumatic drill*. ▷ **pneumatically** /-klɪ/ *adv*.

pneumoconiosis /ˌnju:məˌkəʊnɪˈəʊsɪs; *US* ˌnu:-/ *n* [U] lung disease caused by breathing in harmful dust. It is suffered esp by miners.

pneumonia /nju:ˈməʊnɪə; *US* nu:-/ *n* [U] serious illness with inflammation of one or both lungs, causing difficulty in breathing.

PO /ˌpi: ˈəʊ/ *abbr* **1** Petty Officer. **2** (also **po**) postal order. **3** Post Office: *PO Box 920*, eg in an address.

Po *symb* polonium.

po /pəʊ/ *n* (*pl* **pos** /pəʊz/) (*dated Brit infml*) chamber-pot (CHAMBER).

poach[1] /pəʊtʃ/ *v* [Tn, Tn·pr] (**a**) cook (fish, fruit, etc) by simmering it gently in a small amount of liquid: *apricots poached in syrup*. (**b**) cook (an egg without its shell) by putting it in (or in a container over) simmering water.

▷ **poacher** *n* pan with one or more cup-shaped containers in which eggs may be poached.

poach[2] /pəʊtʃ/ *v* **1** [I, Ipr, Tn] ~ (**for sth**) catch (game birds, animals or fish) without permission on sb else's property: *go out poaching on a farmer's land* ○ *Fred was caught poaching hares*. **2** (**a**) [Ipr] ~ **on sth** be active in an area that properly belongs to sb else: *Rival salesmen were poaching on his territory*. ○ *By interfering in this matter you are poaching on my preserve*, ie dealing with sth that is my responsibility. (**b**) [Tn] take (staff or ideas) from sb/sth, esp in an underhand way: *A rival firm poached our best computer programmers*. ○ *A new political party usually poaches ideas from its rivals*.

▷ **poacher** *n* person who poaches. Cf POACH[1].

POB /ˌpi: əʊ ˈbi:/ *abbr* Post Office Box (number): *POB 63*.

Pocahontas /ˌpɒkəˈhɒntəs; *US* ˌpəʊk-/ (c 1595-1617), American Indian woman, daughter of a chieftain from Virginia, who rescued an English colonist called John Smith from being killed by her father. She married another colonist, was brought to England, and died on the voyage home.

pock /pɒk/ *n* (**a**) any of the swellings on the skin caused by certain diseases, esp smallpox. (**b**) (also ˈ**pock-mark**) hollow mark left on the skin by this.

▷ **pocked** *adj* ~ (**with sth**) having holes or depressions in the surface: *The moon's surface is pocked with small craters*.

□ ˈ**pock-marked** *adj* having marks left after (esp) smallpox: *The man's face was badly pock-marked*.

pocket /ˈpɒkɪt/ *n* **1** (**a**) small bag sewn into or onto a garment and forming part of it, for carrying things in: *a coat, jacket, trouser, etc pocket* ○ *stand with one's hands in one's pockets* ○ [attrib] *a pocket dictionary, edition, guide, etc*, ie small enough to fit in one's pocket. (**b**) container resembling this, eg on the inside of a car-door, suitcase, cardboard folder, etc; flap[1](1): *You will find information about safety procedures in the pocket in front of you*, eg on an aircraft. **2** (usu *sing*) money that one has available for spending; financial means: *luxury far beyond my pocket* ○ *easy/hard on the pocket*, ie easy/difficult to afford ○ *The resort provides accommodation to suit every pocket*. ○ *The expedition was a drain on her pocket*. **3** small isolated group or area: *Pockets of opposition/resistance to the new regime still remained*. ○ *pockets of unemployment in an otherwise prosperous region*. **4** small cavity in the ground or in rock, containing gold or ore: *pockets of coal*. **5** = AIR POCKET (AIR[1]). **6** (*sport*) any of the six string pouches round a billiard-table into which balls are hit. ⇨ illus at SNOOKER. **7** (idm) **be, etc in sb's** ˈ**pocket** be very close to or intimate with sb: *They live in each other's pockets*. **have sb in one's** ˈ**pocket** have influence or power over sb. ˌ**in**/ˌ**out of** ˈ**pocket** having gained/lost money as a result of sth: *Even after paying all the expenses, we'll still be £100 in pocket*. ○ *His mistake left us all out of pocket*. ○ [attrib] ˌ*out-of-pocket ex*ˈ*penses*, ie money that one has spent (and which will be reimbursed, eg by one's employer). **line one's/sb's pocket** ⇨ LINE[3]. **money burns a hole in sb's pocket** ⇨ MONEY. **pick sb's pocket** ⇨ PICK[3]. **put one's hand in one's pocket** ⇨ HAND[1]. **put one's pride in one's pocket** ⇨ PRIDE.

▷ **pocket** *v* [Tn] **1** put (sth) into one's pocket: *He pocketed the tickets*. ○ *She quickly pocketed the note without reading it*. **2** keep or take (sth) for oneself (esp dishonestly): *She pays £2 for them, sells them for £4 and pockets the difference*. ○ *He was given £20 for expenses, but pocketed most of it*. **3** (eg in billiards) hit (a ball) into a pocket(6). **4** (idm) **swallow/pocket one's** ˈ**pride** ⇨ PRIDE.

pocketful /-fʊl/ *n* amount a pocket holds: *a pocketful of coins*.

□ ˈ**pocket-book** *n* **1** small notebook. **2** (**a**) = WALLET. (**b**) (*US*) purse or small handbag.

ˌ**pocket** ˈ**borough** (in England before 1832) parliamentary constituency controlled by a single person or family, who could ensure that the candidate they nominated would be elected. Cf ROTTEN BOROUGH (ROTTEN).

ˈ**pocket-knife** *n* small knife with one or more blades that fold down into the handle. ⇨ illus at KNIFE.

ˈ**pocket-money** *n* [U] (*Brit*) (**a**) small amount of money given to a child, esp weekly. (**b**) money for small expenses: *We've paid for our travel and accommodation, so we only need to take some pocket-money with us*.

ˌ**pocket** ˈ**veto** (*US*) preventing of a proposed law by the US President's withholding of his official approval until after Congress is adjourned.

pod /pɒd/ *n* **1** long seed-case of various plants, esp peas and beans. **2** (idm) **like as peas in a pod** ⇨ LIKE[1].

▷ **pod** *v* (-**dd**-) [Tn] take (peas, beans, etc) from their pods.

podgy /ˈpɒdʒɪ/ *adj* (-**ier**, -**iest**) (*infml usu derog*) (of people or parts of the body) short and fat: *podgy fingers*. ⇨ Usage at FAT[1]. ▷ **podginess** *n* [U].

podiatry /pəˈdaɪətrɪ/ *n* [U] (*US*) = CHIROPODY. ▷ **podiatrist** /-trɪst/ *n* (*US*) = CHIROPODIST.

podium /ˈpəʊdɪəm/ *n* small platform for the conductor of an orchestra, a lecturer, etc to stand on.

podunk /ˈpəʊdʌŋk/ *n* (*US derog sl offensive*) immigrant from Poland, esp one with rough manners.

Poe /pəʊ/ Edgar Allan (1809-49), American author. His poems and stories (eg *The Fall of the House of Usher*) were among the first to make horror fashionable as a literary subject, and he wrote some of the earliest detective stories.

poem /ˈpəʊɪm/ *n* piece of creative writing in verse, esp one expressing deep feelings or noble thoughts in beautiful language, written with the intention of communicating an experience: *write/compose poems*.

poet /ˈpəʊɪt/ *n* writer of poems.

▷ **poetess** /-es/ *n* woman poet.

□ ˌ**Poet** ˈ**Laureate** (also **Laureate**) poet officially appointed to the Royal Household in Britain, to write poems for state occasions.

ˌ**Poets'** ˈ**Corner** part of *Westminster Abbey where many famous British poets are buried or have monuments that honour them, including *Chaucer, *Shakespeare and *Milton.

poetaster /ˌpəʊɪˈtæstə(r)/ *n* (*derog*) poet who has no talent.

poetic /pəʊˈetɪk/ *adj* **1** (*approv*) like or suggesting poetry, esp in being graceful and aesthetically pleasing: *a poetic rendering of the piano sonata*. **2** [attrib] = POETICAL 1: *his entire poetic output*.

▷ **poetical** /-kl/ *adj* **1** [attrib] of or being poetry: *the poetical works of Keats*. **2** [attrib] = POETIC 1.

poetically /-klɪ/ *adv*.

□ **po**ˌ**etic** ˈ**justice** well-deserved punishment or reward.

poˌ**etic** ˈ**licence** freedom to change the normal rules of language when writing verse (eg by reversing word order, changing meaning, etc): (*ironic*) *his garden shed which, with a certain amount of poetic licence, he calls his summer-house*.

poetry /ˈpəʊɪtrɪ/ *n* [U] **1** poems collectively or in general: *epic, lyric, dramatic, pastoral, symbolist, etc poetry* ○ *Dryden's poetry* ○ [attrib] *a poetry book* ○ *a poetry reading*. Cf PROSE, VERSE. **2** (*approv*) aesthetically pleasing quality: *a ballet dancer with poetry in every movement* ○ *the poetry of motion*, eg in ballet or some forms of athletics.

po-faced /ˈpəʊ feɪst/ *adj* (*Brit infml derog*) with a too solemn or disapproving expression.

pogo /ˈpəʊgəʊ/ *n* (*pl* ~**s**) (also ˈ**pogo stick**) pole, with bars for standing on and a spring at the bottom end, used as a toy for jumping about on.

pogrom /ˈpɒgrəm; *US* pəˈgrɒm/ *n* organized persecution or killing of a particular group or class of people, esp because of their race or religion.

poignant /ˈpɔɪnjənt/ *adj* affecting one's feelings deeply, making one sad, full of pity, etc: *poignant sorrow, regret, memories* ○ *a poignant moment*.

▷ **poignancy** /-jənsɪ/ *n* [U] state or quality of being poignant.

poignantly /-jəntlɪ/ *adv*.

poinsettia /pɔɪnˈsetɪə/ *n* tropical plant with large red leaves that form flower-like clusters, often grown indoors in pots.

point[1] /pɔɪnt/ *n* **1** [C] (often in compounds) sharp or tapered end of sth; tip: *the point of a pin, knife, pencil, etc* ○ *a pin-point, knife-point, pencil point, etc* ○ *The stake had been sharpened to a vicious-looking point*. ○ *the point of the jaw*, eg as the target for a punch in boxing. **2** [C] (often with a capital as part of a name) narrow piece of land sticking out into the sea; headland or promontory: *The ship rounded the point*. ○ *Pagoda Point*. **3** [C] (*geometry*) thing that has position but no size, eg the place where two lines cross: *AB and CD intersect at (the point) P*. **4** [C] (**a**) any dot used in writing or printing, eg as a full-stop, as a marker of decimals, etc: *Two point six (2.6) means the same as* $2\frac{6}{10}$. ○ *The first two figures after the decimal point indicate tenths and hundredths respectively*. ⇨ App 9. (**b**) tiny dot or mark of light or colour: *stars seen as points of light in a dark sky*. **5** [C] (often in compounds) particular place or locality: *Guards had been posted at several points around the perimeter*. ○ *an assembly, rallying, meeting, etc point* ○ *a steamer service calling at Port Said, Aden and all points east*, ie all other ports further east. **6** [C] particular time or instant: *At one point I though she was going to refuse, but in the end she agreed*. ○ *The film started to get very violent, at which point I left*. ○ *at the point of death*, ie about to die at any moment. **7** [C] (often in compounds) stage or degree of progress, increase, temperature, etc: *reach danger point*, ie reach a dangerous level ○ *boiling-/freezing-/melting- point*. **8** [C] any of the 32 marks on the circumference of a compass: *the cardinal points*, ie the four main points: N, E, S and W ○ (*fig*) *Search-parties had been sent out to all points of the compass*, ie in every direction. **9** [C] unit of measurement, value, scoring, etc: *a point on a scale* ○ *The pound fell several points on the Stock Market today*. ○ *We need one more point to win the game*. ○ [attrib] *a points system*. ⇨ App 9. **10** [C] individual idea of sth said, done or planned; single item or detail: *the main points of a story, a discussion, an argument, etc* ○ *points of difference, similarity, agreement, disagreement, etc* ○ *One point in favour of her plan is its cheapness*. ○ *explain a theory point by point*, ie explain each individual idea in it, in order. **11** [C] (**a**) thing said as part of a discussion: *Various committee members made interesting points*. (**b**) effective argument: *'But she might not agree.' 'You've got a point there'*. *That's a point* (ie I had not thought of that.). **12** [C] distinctive feature or characteristic: *sb's good, strong, bad, weak, etc points* ○ *I'm afraid tidiness is not his strong point*, ie he is untidy. **13 the point** [sing] the matter under discussion;

the essential thing: *Let's stop discussing trivial details and come/get to the point.* ○ *The speaker kept wandering off/away from the point.* ○ *The point (at issue) is this....* **14** [U, sing] essential meaning, main feature (of a story, joke, remark, etc); reason; purpose; value: *get, see, miss, understand the point of sth* ○ *a story, remark, etc with a/some/no/little point (to it)* ○ *There's not much point in complaining; they never take any notice.* **15** [U] (*fml*) effectiveness; urgency: *speech, words, remarks, etc that have/lack point.* **16** [C] (often in compounds) electrical socket, into which a plug is put: *a lighting, power, cooker point* ○ *a 13-amp point.* **17 points** [pl] (in ballet) the tips of the toes: *dancing on points.* **18 points** [pl] (*Brit*) (*US* **switch**) set of movable rails at a place where a railway line divides into two tracks, which can be altered to allow a train to use either track: *change/switch the points* ○ [attrib] *a points lever, mechanism, etc.* **19** [sing U] (in cricket) fielder near the batsman on the off side; his position. **20** [U] (as a compound after a number) unit of measurement of type-size in printing: *6-point is small and 18-point is large.* **21** (idm) **at the ˌpoint of a ˈsword, ˈgun, etc** by threatening sb with death or wounding by a sword, gun, etc: *captured at the point of a sword.* **beside the ˈpoint** irrelevant. **carry/gain one's ˈpoint** persuade people to accept one's argument. **a case in point** ⇨ CASE[1]. **the finer points** ⇨ FINE[2]. **give sb points (at sth)** offer sb advantages and still win: *He can give me points at golf,* ie He plays better than I do. **have one's ˈpoints** have certain good qualities: *I suppose wine has its points, but I prefer beer.* **if/when it ˌcomes to the ˈpoint** if or when the moment for action or decision comes: *If it came to the point, would you sacrifice your job for your principles?* **in ˌpoint of ˈfact** in reality; actually: *He said he would pay, but in point of fact he has no money.* **labour the point** ⇨ LABOUR[2]. **make one's ˈpoint** explain fully what one is proposing: *All right, you've made your point; now keep quiet and let the others say what they think.* **make a point of doing sth** do sth because one considers it important or necessary: *I always make a point of checking that all the windows are shut before I go out.* **a moot point/question** ⇨ MOOT. **not to put too fine a point on it** ⇨ FINE[2]. **on the point of doing sth** just about to do sth: *I was on the point of going to bed when you rang.* **on ˈpoints** (of a win in boxing) by the number of points scored without knocking out one's opponent. **a ˌpoint of deˈparture (a)** place or time at which a journey begins. **(b)** (*fig*) starting point for a discussion or enterprise: *Let's take 'Das Kapital' as a point of departure for our survey of Marxism.* **a ˌpoint of ˈhonour/ˈconscience** thing of great importance to one's honour or conscience: *I always pay my debts punctually; it's a point of honour with me.* **the ˌpoint of ˈno ˈreturn (a)** point (on a long voyage, flight, etc) at which fuel supplies, etc will not be sufficient for a return to the starting point, so that one must continue the journey in order to survive. **(b)** (*fig*) point at which one becomes committed to an action or a decision that cannot be reversed. **a ˌpoint of ˈorder** (in formal discussions, eg debates) matter of correct procedure according to the rules: *On a point of order, Mr Chairman, can associate members vote on this matter?* **a/one's ˌpoint of ˈview** attitude; opinion: *This is unacceptable from my point of view.* ○ *What's your point of view on nuclear power?* **possession is nine points of the law** ⇨ POSSESSION. **prove one's/the case/point** ⇨ PROVE. **score a point/points** ⇨ SCORE[2]. **a sore point** ⇨ SORE. **stretch a point** ⇨ STRETCH. **one's/sb's strong point/suit** ⇨ STRONG. **take sb's ˈpoint** understand and accept sb's argument. **to the ˈpoint** (in a way that is) relevant and appropriate: *remarks that were very much to the point* ○ *His speech was short and to the point.* **to the point of sth** to a degree that can be described as sth: *His manner was abrupt to the point of rudeness.* **up to a (certain) ˈpoint** to some extent; in some degree: *I agree with you up to a (certain) point.*

▷ **pointy** *adj* (*infml*) having a sharp point: *a pointy stick.* **ˈpointy-head** *n* (*US sl derog*) person only interested in things of the mind; intellectual.

□ **ˈpoint-duty** *n* [U] (*Brit*) traffic control by a policeman standing typically in the middle of the road.

ˈpointsman *n* (*pl* **-men**) (*Brit*) (*US* **ˈswitchman**) person in charge of railway points.

ˌpoint-to-ˈpoint *n* (*Brit*) race on horses across country from one point to another.

point[2] /pɔɪnt/ *v* **1 (a)** [I, Ipr] ~ **(at/to sb/sth)** direct people's attention at sb/sth by extending one's finger towards him/it, or by using any similar sign or indicator; show the position or direction of sb/sth: *It's rude to point.* ○ *'That's the man who did it,' she said, pointing at me.* ○ *He pointed to a tower on the distant horizon.* ○ *A compass needle points (to the) north.* ○ *The clock hands pointed to twelve,* ie it was noon or midnight. **(b)** [Ipr] ~ **to sth** (*fig*) suggest (the likelihood of) sth; indicate sth: *I can't point to any one particular reason for it.* ○ *All the evidence points to his guilt.* **2** [Tn, Tn·pr] ~ **sth (at/towards sb/sth)** aim or direct sth: *point one's finger (at sb/sth)* ○ *point a gun at sb* ○ *point a telescope at/towards the moon.* **3** [Ipr, Ip] face or be turned in a particular direction: *A hedgehog's spines point backwards.* **4** [Tn] give force to (sth); make more noticeable: *a story that points a moral.* **5** [Tn] fill in the spaces between the bricks of (sth) with mortar or cement: *point a wall, chimney, etc.* **6** [I] (of a hunting dog) take up a position with the body steady and the head indicating the direction of a hunted bird, etc. **7** (idm) **point the ˈfinger (at sb)** (*infml*) accuse sb openly. **point the ˈway (to/towards sth)** show the possibility of future development: *Large electronics companies developed television, but Baird pointed the way with his experiments.* ○ *Tax reforms which point the way to a more prosperous future.* **8** (phr v) **point sth out (to sb)** direct attention to sth: *point out a mistake* ○ *point out to sb the stupidity of his/her behaviour* ○ *I must point out that further delay would be unwise.* **point sth up** give special emphasis to one particular aspect of sth; show sth very clearly: *The recent disagreement points up the differences between the two sides.*

▷ **pointed** *adj* **1** having a sharp tip, end, etc: *a (sharp-)pointed instrument, tool, etc* ○ *a pointed hat.* **2** (*fig*) directed clearly against a particular person or his behaviour: *a pointed remark, rebuke, etc* ○ *She made some pointed references to his careless work.* **3** (*fig*) (of wit) incisive. **pointedly** *adv* in a way that indicates criticism of a particular person or that suggests one's meaning clearly: *She stared pointedly at me.* ○ *He looked pointedly at the door,* eg indicating that I should open it, close it, leave, etc.

pointing *n* [U] cement, mortar, etc put in the spaces between the bricks of a wall, etc.

point-blank /ˌpɔɪnt ˈblæŋk/ *adj* [attrib] **1** (of a shot) aimed or fired at very close range: *He shot her at point-blank range.* **2** (*fig*) (of sth said) direct, complete and immediate, and often rather rude: *a ˌpoint-blank reˈfusal.*

▷ **point-blank** *adv* in a point-blank manner; directly: *fire point-blank at sb* ○ *I asked him point-blank what he was doing there.* ○ *refuse point-blank to do sth.*

pointer /ˈpɔɪntə(r)/ *n* **1** long thin piece of metal, plastic, etc which moves to indicate figures, positions, etc on a dial, scale, etc. **2** rod or stick used to point to things on a map, blackboard, etc. **3** ~ **(on sth)** (*infml*) piece of advice: *Could you give me a few pointers on how to tackle the job?* **4** ~ **(to sth)** thing that shows likely future developments: *journalists studying the minister's speech for pointers to the contents of next month's policy statement.* **5** large short-haired hunting dog trained to stand still with its nose pointing in the direction of hunted birds, etc which it smells. **6 the Pointers** [pl] two stars in the *Great Bear indicating the position of the *Pole Star, or in the *Southern Cross indicating the southern pole of the sky.

pointillism /ˈpɔɪntɪlɪzəm, *also* ˈpwæntiːɪzəm/ *n* [U] technique of painting developed in France in the late 19th century in which the picture is built up from tiny dots of different colours which the eye sees as a blend of colour.

▷ **pointillist** /-lɪst/ *n* person who paints in this way (eg *Seurat).

pointless /ˈpɔɪntlɪs/ *adj* with little or no sense, aim or purpose: *make a pointless remark* ○ *It is pointless to have a car if you cannot drive it!* ▷ **pointlessly** *adv.* **pointlessness** *n* [U]: *the pointlessness of his existence.*

Poirot /ˈpwɑːrəʊ; *US* pwɑːˈrəʊ/ Hercule, fictional Belgian detective created by Agatha *Christie, famous for his brilliant powers of deduction, using his brain's 'little grey cells'.

poise /pɔɪz/ *v* [Ipr, Ip, Tn·pr, Tn·p] be or keep (sth) balanced or suspended: *The eagle poised in mid-air ready to swoop on its prey.* ○ *He poised the javelin in his hand before throwing it.*

▷ **poise** *n* [U] **1** graceful and balanced (control of) bodily position or movement: *poise of the body, head, etc* ○ *moving with the assured poise of a ballet dancer.* **2** quiet dignified self-confidence and self-control: *a woman of great poise.*

poised *adj* **1** [pred] ~ **(in, on, above, etc sth)** in a state of balance, stillness: *poised on tiptoe, in mid-air, etc* ○ *sth poised on the edge of a table,* ie likely to fall off if lightly touched. **2** [pred] ~ **(in/on/above/for sth)**; ~ **(to do sth)** (of people, animals, etc) in a state of physical tension, ready for action: *poised on the edge of the swimming-pool,* ie ready to jump in ○ (*fig*) *The Allies were poised* (ie ready) *for their invasion of Europe.* ○ *Combined Breweries are poised to* (ie about to) *take over the Amalgamated Beer Company.* **3** (*fig*) calmly self-controlled; full of poise(2): *a poised young lady* ○ *a poised manner.*

poison /ˈpɔɪzn/ *n* [C, U] **1** substance causing death or harm if absorbed by a living thing (animal or plant): *rat poison* ○ *poison for killing weeds* ○ *commit suicide by taking poison* ○ [attrib] *poison gas,* ie esp as used to kill people in war. **2** (*infml derog*) extremely unpleasant food: *I'm not eating that poison!* **3** (idm) **what's your poison?** (*Brit joc*) what (alcoholic) drink would you like?

▷ **poison** *v* [Tn, Tn·pr] ~ **sb/sth (with sth) 1 (a)** give poison to (a living thing); kill or harm sb/sth with poison: *His wife poisoned him with arsenic.* ○ *Are our children being poisoned by lead in the atmosphere?* **(b)** put poison in sth: *The chemical companies are poisoning our rivers with effluent.* **2 (a)** injure sth morally; corrupt sth: *poison sb's mind with propaganda.* **(b)** fill sth with suffering, bitterness, etc; spoil or ruin sth: *a quarrel which poisoned our friendship* ○ *an experience that poisons sb's life.* **3** (idm) **poison A's mind against B** (*derog*) make A dislike B by telling A bad and usu untrue things about B. **poisoned** *adj* **1** inflamed because of an infected cut, scratch, etc: *a poisoned hand.* **2** having poison applied to it: *a poisoned arrow.* **poisoner** /ˈpɔɪzənə(r)/ *n* person who murders by means of poison. **poisoning** /ˈpɔɪzənɪŋ/ *n* [C, U] (act or result of) giving or taking poison: *blood poisoning,* ie poisoning of the blood ○ *lead poisoning,* ie poisoning by lead.

poisonous /ˈpɔɪzənəs/ *adj* **1 (a)** using poison as a means of attacking enemies or prey: *poisonous snakes, insects, etc.* **(b)** causing death or illness if taken into the body: *poisonous plants, chemicals.* **2** (*fig derog*) **(a)** morally harmful: *the poisonous doctrine of racial superiority.* **(b)** spiteful; malicious: *sb with a poisonous tongue,* ie who spreads malicious rumours about people. **poisonously** *adv.*

□ **ˌpoison ˈivy** N American climbing plant whose leaves contain a substance that makes the skin sore.

ˌpoison-ˈpen letter malicious letter sent deliberately to upset or offend the receiver.

poke[1] /pəʊk/ *v* **1 (a)** [Tn, Tn·pr] ~ **sb/sth (with sth)** push sb/sth sharply (with a stick, one's finger, etc); jab sb/sth: *poke sb in the ribs,* ie nudge him in a friendly way ○ *poke the fire (with a poker),* ie to make it burn more strongly. **(b)** [Tn·pr] ~ **sth in sth** make (a hole) in sth by pushing one's finger, a sharp instrument, etc through it: *Poke two holes in* *the sack so you can see through it.* (**c**) [Ipr] ~ **at sth** make repeated small pushing movements at sth: *She poked at her meal unenthusiastically.* **2** [Tn·pr, Tn·p] put or move sth in a specified direction, with a sharp push; thrust: *She poked her finger into the hole.* ○ *poke food through the bars of a cage* ○ *poke one's head out of a window* ○ *Mind you don't poke her eye out with that stick!* ○ *He poked his head round the door to see if she was in the room.* ➪ Usage at NUDGE. **3** (idm) **poke ˈfun at sb/sth** (*usu derog*) make fun of sb/sth; mock or ridicule sb/sth: *He enjoys poking fun at others.* **poke/stick one's nose into sth** ➪ NOSE[1]. **4** (phr v) **poke about/ around** (*infml*) search inquisitively: *Why are you poking about among my papers?* **poke out of/through sth**; **poke out/through/up** be visible coming through (a hole, slit, etc); protrude: *a pen poking out (of sb's pocket)* ○ *I see a finger poking through (a hole in your glove).* ○ *A few daffodils were already poking up*, ie starting to grow.

▷ **poke** *n* act of poking; nudge: *give the fire a poke* ○ *give sb a poke in the ribs.*

poke[2] /pəʊk/ *n* (idm) **buy a pig in a poke** ➪ BUY.

poker[1] /ˈpəʊkə(r)/ *n* strong metal rod or bar for moving or breaking up coal in a fire.

□ **ˈpoker-work** *n* [U] (**a**) art of making designs, pictures, etc on wood, leather, etc by burning the surface with a very hot tool. (**b**) such designs.

poker[2] /ˈpəʊkə(r)/ *n* [U] card-game for two or more people in which the players bet on the values of the cards they hold.

□ **ˈpoker dice** dice that have playing-card designs (nine, ten, jack, queen, king, ace) instead of spots. **ˈpoker-face** *n* (*infml*) face that shows no sign of what the person is thinking or feeling. **ˈpoker-faced** *adj.*

pokeweed /ˈpəʊkwi:d/ *n* [U] tall American plant with purple berries.

pokey /ˈpəʊkɪ/ *n* [U] (*US sl*) prison: *in pokey.*

poky /ˈpəʊkɪ/ *adj* (**-ier**, **-iest**) (*infml derog*) (of a place, house, flat, etc) small; limited in space: *a poky little room.* ▷ **pokiness** *n* [U].

polack /ˈpəʊlæk/ *n* (*US derog sl offensive*) person who comes from Poland or whose family comes from Poland.

Poland

Poland /ˈpəʊlənd/ country in eastern central Europe; pop approx 37 862 000; official language Polish; capital Warsaw; unit of currency zloty (= 100 groszy). Its borders have changed often in the course of its history, and the present borders were fixed after the Second World War, when it lost some territory to the USSR but gained some from Germany. Most of the country is flat, with a mountainous region along its southern borders. Its main agricultural products are potatoes and sugar-beet, but it is not agriculturally self-sufficient. Its heavy industry is in decline, but it remains an important producer of coal. Poland's Solidarity trade-union movement was one of the major forces for democratic change in eastern Europe during the 1980s. ➪ map. Cf POLE, POLISH.

polar /ˈpəʊlə(r)/ *adj* [attrib] **1** of or near the North or South Pole: *polar ice* ○ *the polar regions.* **2** of (one of) the poles of a magnet: *polar attraction.* **3** (*fml*) (of opposites) complete; extreme.

▷ **polarity** /pəˈlærətɪ/ *n* **1** [U, C] (**a**) (in a magnet) possession or location of negative and positive poles: *the polarity of a magnet* ○ *reversed polarity/ polarities.* (**b**) positive or negative electrical condition of eg a terminal. **2** [U] ~ (**between A and B**) (*fig*) difference or separation (between people or things) in condition, views, etc: *the growing polarity between the left and right wings of the party.*

□ **ˈpolar bear** white bear living in the north polar regions. ➪ illus at BEAR.

ˌpolar ˈcircle either of the circles lying at latitude 23° 27′ from the N and S Poles.

Polaris /pəˈlɑ:rɪs/ = POLE-STAR (POLE[1]).

polarize, -ise /ˈpəʊləraɪz/ *v* **1** [Tn] (*physics*) cause (light-waves, etc) to vibrate in a single direction or plane. **2** [Tn] give polarity to (a magnet). **3** [I, Ipr, Tn, Tn·pr] ~ (**sth/sb**) (**into sth**) (cause people, views, etc to) form into two groups which conflict with or are completely opposite to each other: *Public opinion has polarized on this issue.* ○ *an issue which has polarized public opinion.*

▷ **polarization, -isation** /ˌpəʊləraɪˈzeɪʃn; *US* -rɪˈz-/ *n* [C, U] act of polarizing; state of being polarized.

Polaroid /ˈpəʊlərɔɪd/ *n* (*propr*) **1** [U] thin transparent film put on sun-glasses, car windows, etc to lessen the brightness of sunlight. **2 Polaroids** [pl] sun-glasses treated with Polaroid.

□ **ˌPolaroid ˈcamera** camera that can produce photographs within seconds after the picture has been taken.

Pole /pəʊl/ *n* native or inhabitant of Poland.

pole[1] /pəʊl/ *n* **1** either of the two points at the exact top and bottom of the Earth, which are the opposite ends of the axis on which it turns: *the North/South Pole.* ➪ illus at GLOBE. **2** (*physics*) either of the two ends of a magnet or the terminal points of an electric battery: *the negative/positive pole.* **3** (*fig*) either of two opposite, conflicting or contrasting extremes: *Our points of view are at opposite poles.* **4** (idm) **be ˈpoles apart** be widely separated; have nothing in common: *The employers and the trade union leaders are still poles apart*, ie are far from reaching an agreement or a compromise.

□ **ˈpole-star** *n* (also **North Star**, **Polaris**) star that is almost exactly overhead at the N Pole, and around which the stars of the northern hemisphere appear to move in a circle.

pole[2] /pəʊl/ *n* **1** long thin rounded piece of wood or metal, used esp as a support for sth or for pushing boats, etc along: *a tent, flag, telegraph, etc pole* ○ *a punt, barge, ski, etc pole.* **2** = PERCH[1] 3. **3** (idm) **up the ˈpole** (*infml esp Brit*) (**a**) in difficulty. (**b**) wrong; mistaken. (**c**) crazy; eccentric.

▷ **pole** *v* [Tn·pr, Tn·p] push (a boat, etc) along by using a pole: *pole a punt up the river.*

□ **ˈpole position** (in motor racing) most favourable position for a car at the start of a race, in front of all the others.

ˈpole-vault *n* (*sport*) jump over a raised bar, using a long pole which is held in the hands. ➪ illus at VAULT. **ˈpole-vault** *v* [I] perform such a jump. **ˈpole-vaulter** *n.* **ˈpole-vaulting** *n* [U].

pole-axe /ˈpəʊl æks/ *n* **1** (formerly) axe for use in war, with a long handle. **2** long-handled axe-like tool used, esp formerly, by butchers for killing cattle by hitting them on the head.

▷ **pole-axe** *v* [Tn] **1** strike (sb/sth) down with a pole-axe: (*fig*) *The punch caught him on the jaw, and he sank down pole-axed*, ie completely knocked out. **2** (usu passive); (*fig*) overwhelm (sb) with surprise and distress: *We were all absolutely pole-axed by the terrible news.*

polecat /ˈpəʊlkæt/ *n* **1** small European animal of the weasel family which has dark brown fur and gives off an unpleasant smell. **2** (*US*), = SKUNK.

polemic /pəˈlemɪk/ *n* (*fml*) **1** (**a**) [C] ~ (**against/in favour of sth/sb**) speech, piece of writing, etc containing very forceful arguments (against or for sth/sb): *He launched into a fierce polemic against the government's policies.* (**b**) [U] such speeches, pieces of writing, etc: *engage in polemic.* **2 polemics** [pl] art or practice of arguing a case formally and usu forcefully.

▷ **polemical** /-ɪkl/ (also **polemic**) *adj* (*fml*) **1** [attrib] of polemics: *polemic(al) skills.* **2** arguing a case very forcefully, often with the intention of being controversial or provocative: *a polemic(al) article, speech, etc.* **polemically** /-klɪ/ *adv.* **polemicist** /pəˈlemɪsɪst/ *n* person skilled in polemics.

police /pəˈli:s/ *n* (**the**) **police** [pl *v*] (members of an) official organization whose job is to keep public order, prevent and solve crime, etc: *the local, state, national, etc police* ○ *There were over 100 police on duty at the demonstration.* ○ *The police have not made any arrests.* ○ [attrib] *a police car, enquiry, raid, report.* ➪ article.

▷ **police** *v* [Tn] keep order in (a place) with or as if with police; control: *The teachers on duty are policing the school buildings during the lunch hour.* ○ (*fig*) *a committee to police the new regulations*, ie make sure they are obeyed.

□ **poˌlice ˈconstable** (*abbr* **PC**) (also **constable**) (in Britain and some other countries) policeman or policewoman of the lowest rank.

poˈlice dog dog trained to track or attack suspected criminals.

poˈlice force body of police officers of a country, district or town.

poˈliceman /-mən/ *n* (*pl* **-men** /-mən/) male member of the police force.

poˈlice-officer (also **officer**) *n* policeman or policewoman.

poˈlice state (*derog*) country controlled by political police, usu a totalitarian state.

poˈlice station office of a local police force: *The suspect was taken to the police station for questioning.*

poˈlicewoman *n* (*pl* **-women**) (*abbr* **PW**) female member of the police force.

policy[1] /ˈpɒləsɪ/ *n* [U, C] ~ (**on sth**) plan of action, statement of ideals, etc proposed or adopted by a government, political party, business, etc: *according to our present policy* ○ *adopt fresh policies* ○ *British foreign policy* ○ *What is the Labour Party's policy on immigration?* ○ (*fig*) *Is honesty the best policy* (ie the best principle for people to live by)*?* ○ [attrib] *a policy maker.*

policy[2] /ˈpɒləsɪ/ *n* (written statement of the) terms of a contract of insurance: *a ˈfire-insurance policy* ○ [attrib] *a ˈpolicy document* ○ *a ˈpolicy holder.*

polio /ˈpəʊlɪəʊ/ (also *fml* **poliomyelitis** /ˌpəʊlɪəʊˌmaɪəˈlaɪtɪs/) *n* [U] infectious disease caused by a virus in which the spinal cord becomes inflamed, often resulting in paralysis: [attrib] *polio vaccine* ○ *ˌanti-ˈpolio injections.*

Polish /ˈpəʊlɪʃ/ *adj* of Poland or the Poles.

▷ **Polish** *n* [U] language of the Poles: *written in Polish.*

polish /ˈpɒlɪʃ/ *v* **1** [I, Ipr, Ip, Tn, Tn·pr, Tn·p] ~ (**sth**) (**up**) (**with sth**) (cause sth to) become smooth and shiny by rubbing: *This table-top polishes up nicely.* ○ *polish (up) wood, furniture, shoes with a cloth.* **2** [Tn] (*fig*) improve (sth) by correcting, making small changes or adding new material: *polish a speech, an article, etc.* **3** (phr v) **polish sth off** (*infml*) finish sth quickly: *polish off a big plateful of stew* ○ *polish off the arrears of correspondence.*

▷ **polish** *n* **1** (**a**) [sing] shiny surface, etc obtained by polishing: *a table-top with a good polish.* (**b**) [sing] action of polishing: *give the floor a thorough polish.* (**c**) [U, C] substance used for polishing: *ˈfurniture, ˈfloor, ˈshoe polish* ○ *a tin of metal polish* ○ *apply polish to sth.* **2** [U] (*fig*) additional quality of fineness or elegance; refinement: *an unsophisticated country fellow who completely lacked polish* ○ *a crude performance of the symphony, quite without polish.* **3** (idm) **spit and polish** ➪ SPIT[1].

Police

Britain had no organized police service until the 19th century, when in 1829 the Home Secretary, Sir Robert Peel, established the Metropolitan Police Force in London. (His name is the origin of the colloquial word 'bobby' for a policeman.) Police forces were then gradually set up in other areas, until eventually all parts of the country had a police force. Today, there is one police officer for approximately every 400 people. Women form about 10 per cent of the police force. Except in Northern Ireland, the police are not normally armed, but carry a truncheon (a short, thick club) as a weapon.

There are 52 police forces in the country, each with its own administrative area, in many cases a county (or a region in Scotland). The main police force in London is still the Metropolitan Police (the 'Met'), with its headquarters at New Scotland Yard. The other London force is that of the City of London.

The head of each police force has the rank of chief constable, with officers under him ranking as deputy chief constable and assistant chief constable. (The heads of the Metropolitan Police and the City of London Police have the rank of commissioner of police.) The other ranks are: chief superintendent, superintendent, chief inspector, inspector, sergeant and constable.

There are several special police branches. The best known is the Criminal Investigation Department (CID) in every police force in the country. The Metropolitan Police CID is often known as 'Scotland Yard' or simply 'the Yard', after the name of its headquarters. The Metropolitan CID in turn has specialized sections. The Flying Squad deals with armed robbery, the Fraud Squad (operating jointly with the City of London Police) investigates banking and company frauds, and the Special Branch deals with state security. The river police of the Thames Division of the Metropolitan Police are also well-known, as are the horses of the mounted branch, used in crowd control and on ceremonial occasions.

The main part of a typical police constable's job is patrol work, often carried out on foot. (Until quite recently, police officers made their patrols by police car, but this was found to distance them from the public, so there was a return to patrols by the 'bobby on the beat'.) Another regular duty is directing traffic. Above all, however, the police constable has the job of preventing and detecting crime, and of arresting anyone suspected of an offence.

The police have a responsibility for developing good relations with the public, and in particular with young people and ethnic minorities. Although they have generally managed to retain their traditional friendly and helpful image, public opinion can often be very critical of police behaviour. Complaints against the police are dealt with by the Police Complaints Authority, which has the power to order an investigation when necessary.

Separate police forces outside the main police service include the British Transport Police, who work on British Rail's trains and stations and the London Underground, the Ministry of Defence Police, who police naval, army and air force establishments, and the United Kingdom Atomic Energy Authority Constabulary, who among other duties escort nuclear material between power stations and other nuclear establishments.

Two important bodies working directly with the main police service are the special constables, who are volunteer police officers carrying out duties in their spare time, and traffic wardens, who are mainly concerned with traffic control and parking offences. They can also patrol pedestrian crossings near schools.

Police constables wear a dark blue uniform with a distinctive tall helmet. Most CID detectives, however, work out of uniform in 'plain clothes'. Traffic wardens also wear a dark blue uniform, but have a peaked cap with a yellow band.

Police forces in the USA are operated by state and city authorities, with state police forces chiefly concerned with traffic control and highway patrols. In major cities like New York, the police are under the control of a police commissioner, who is appointed by the mayor for a specific period of time. County police are usually under the control of a sheriff. Federal bodies such as the Secret Service Division and the Narcotics Bureau operate nationwide, as does the well-known Federal Bureau of Investigation (FBI), the agency of the Justice Department responsible for investigating violations of federal laws. In the USA, the police are armed, which is not usually the case in Britain.

polished *adj* **1** shiny from polishing: *polished wood.* **2** refined; elegant: *polished manners* ○ *a polished style, performance.*

polisher *n* machine for polishing: *a floor polisher.*

politburo /ˈpɒlɪtbjʊərəʊ/ *n* (*pl* ~**s**) chief party decision-making committee in Communist countries.

polite /pəˈlaɪt/ *adj* **1** having or showing that one has good manners and consideration for other people: *a polite child* ○ *It wasn't very polite of you to serve yourself without asking.* ○ *making a few polite remarks to keep the conversation going.* **2** [attrib] (*fml*) (typical) of a superior class in society; refined: *a rude word not mentioned in polite society.*

▷ **politely** *adv.*

politeness *n* (**a**) [U] quality of being polite: *He was noted for his politeness.* (**b**) [C] polite act: *I recall his many politenesses over the years.*

politic /ˈpɒlətɪk/ *adj* (*fml*) (of actions) well judged; prudent: *When the fight began, he thought it politic to leave.*

political /pəˈlɪtɪkl/ *adj* **1** of the State; of government; of public affairs in general: *political rights, liberties, etc* ○ *a political system.* **2** of the conflict or rivalry between two or more parties: *a political party, debate, crisis* ○ *political skill, know-how, opinions* ○ *a party political broadcast,* eg to explain government policy. **3** (of actions) considered to be harmful to the State or government: *a political offence, crime, etc* ○ *imprisoned on political grounds.* **4** (of people) interested in or active in politics: *sb who is very political (in outlook)* ○ *I'm not a political animal,* ie person. **5** (*euph derog*) concerned with power, status, etc within an organization rather than with the true merits of a case: *One suspects he was dismissed for political reasons.* ○ *It must have been a political decision.*

▷ **politically** /-klɪ/ *adv* with regard to politics: *a politically active, astute, naive, etc person* ○ *politically useful, sound, disastrous, etc ideas* ○ *a politically sensitive decision.*

□ **poˌlitical aˈsylum** protection given by a state to sb who has left his own country because he opposes its government: *seek/ask for/be granted political asylum.*

poˌlitical geˈography geography dealing with boundaries, communications, etc between countries.

poˌlitical ˈprisoner person who is imprisoned because he or she opposes the (system of) government.

poˌlitical ˈscience (also **politics**) academic study of government and political institutions.

politician /ˌpɒlɪˈtɪʃn/ *n* **1** person actively (and usu professionally) concerned with politics. **2** (*often derog*) person who is skilled at handling people or situations, or at getting people to do what he wants: *You need to be a bit of a politician to succeed in this company.*

politicize, -ise /pəˈlɪtɪsaɪz/ *v* [I, Tn] (cause sb/sth to) become politically conscious or organized: *The strike has now been politicized.*

politicking /ˈpɒlətɪkɪŋ/ *n* [U, C] (*often derog*) political activity, esp to win votes or support: *A lot of politicking preceded the choice of the new director.*

politico /pəˈlɪtɪkəʊ/ *n* (*pl* ~**s**) (*joc or derog*) politician or political activist: *I wouldn't trust any of these devious politicos.*

politics /ˈpɒlətɪks/ *n* **1** (**a**) [sing or pl *v*] political affairs or life: *party politics* ○ *local politics* ○ *He's thinking of going into politics,* eg trying to become a Member of Parliament. ⇨ article. (**b**) [pl] political views, beliefs: *What are your politics?* (**c**) [sing *v*] (*derog*) rivalry between political parties: *They're not concerned with welfare: it's all politics!* **2** [sing *v*] = POLITICAL SCIENCE (POLITICAL): *She's reading politics at university.* **3** [sing *v*] (*derog*) manoeuvring for power or advantage within a group or organization: *office politics* ○ *church politics.*

polity /ˈpɒlətɪ/ *n* (*fml*) **1** [U] form or process of government. **2** [C] society as an organized state.

polka /ˈpɒlkə; *US* ˈpəʊlkə/ *n* (piece of music for a) lively dance of E European origin.

□ **ˈpolka dots** regular pattern of large dots on cloth: [attrib] *a polka-dot scarf.* ⇨ illus at PATTERN.

poll[1] /pəʊl/ *n* **1** (**a**) [C usu *sing*] voting at an election; counting of votes: *be successful at the poll* ○ *The result of the poll has now been declared.* (**b**) [sing] number of votes cast: *head the poll,* ie have the largest number of votes ○ *a light/heavy poll,* ie voting by a small or large proportion of those entitled to vote. (**c**) **the polls** [pl] place where people vote: *The country is going to the polls* (ie is voting in an election) *tomorrow.* **2** [C] survey of public opinion by putting questions to a representative selection of people: *a public opinion poll* ○ *the Gallup poll* ○ *We're conducting a poll among school leavers.*

□ **ˈpoll-tax** *n* tax levied at the same rate on every (or every adult) person in the community. ⇨ article at TAX.

poll[2] /pəʊl/ *v* [Tn] **1** (of a candidate at an election) receive (a certain number of votes): *Mr Hill polled over 3000 votes.* **2** ask (sb) his or her opinion as part of a public-opinion poll: *Of those polled, seven out of ten said they preferred brown bread.* **3** (**a**) cut off the top of the horns of (cattle). (**b**) = POLLARD *v.*

▷ **polling** *n* [U] (**a**) voting: *heavy polling,* ie in large numbers. (**b**) conducting of public-opinion polls. **ˈpolling-booth, ˈpolling-station** *ns* place where people go to vote in an election. **ˈpolling-day** *n* day appointed for an election.

pollard /ˈpɒləd/ (also **poll**) *v* [Tn esp passive] cut off the top of (a tree) so that many new thin branches will grow, forming a dense head of leaves: *The willows need to be pollarded.*

▷ **pollard** *n* **1** pollarded tree. **2** (**a**) animal whose horns have fallen off or been removed. (**b**) type of

Politics

Both Britain and the USA have political systems based on two opposed parties. In Britain, the two main parties are the Conservative Party (the Tories) and the Labour Party (the Socialists). In the USA the two parties are the Republicans and the Democrats.

The Conservative Party developed in the 1830s out of the Tory Party, which had arisen in the 17th century as a grouping opposed to the exclusion of James, Duke of York, from the royal succession. The name 'Conservative' indicated the party's aim to conserve all that was good in Britain. It is now the leading right-wing party. It advocates a mixed economy, with some industries privately owned and others state-owned, but generally encourages private enterprise and property-owning.

The Labour Party was formed in 1900 as a combination of various trade unions and socialist groups, and is now the main left-wing party. It advocates moderate socialism and favours the nationalization of key industries and general social reform. It introduced the National Health Service (NHS) in 1948.

The Liberal Party formerly played an important role in British politics. It developed in the 1830s from the Whig Party, who were opposed to the Tories, and became the party of reform. Early in the 20th century it lost its place as the main Opposition party to the Labour Party. Even so, until the 1970s it had influence as a third political party and offered a 'moderate' alternative to the two main parties.

The Republican Party in the USA was formed in 1854 by groups opposed to slavery, and had Abraham Lincoln as its first president. It now tends to be more conservative than the Democratic Party, and supports an economy based on free enterprise. It is most strongly supported in the rural and suburban regions of the North, Middle West and West.

The Democratic Party developed in the early 19th century out of the anti-federal party led by Thomas Jefferson, taking its present name in 1840. After the Civil War of 1861-65, it became associated with the South and with slavery, and was out of power for several years. Under Franklin D Roosevelt in the 1930s and 1940s the Democrats came to be regarded as the party of reform, introducing the 'New Deal' of this period and campaigning for civil rights in the 1960s.

Between the end of the Second World War and 1990 there were in Britain seven Conservative and three Labour prime ministers. In the USA there were five Republican and four Democrat presidents in the same period. During the 1980s the Conservative Party under prime minister Margaret Thatcher was in power for three consecutive periods of government. In the USA there was a Republican president, Ronald Reagan.

Other minor parties have emerged in Britain in the present century. One of the best known has been the Social Democratic Party (SDP), which broke away from the Labour Party in 1981. It later merged with the Liberals under the title of the Social and Liberal Democrats (SLD), known simply as Liberal Democrats since 1989. At the time of the merger, a smaller group in turn broke from the alliance and continued under the original name of SDP. They had little support, however, and ceased to exist in 1990.

In Britain, there are also the nationalist parties, campaigning for the separation of their lands from the United Kingdom. The two leading parties are Plaid Cymru ('party of Wales'), founded in 1925 to gain the independence of Wales, and the Scottish National Party (SNP), founded in 1928 to do the same for Scotland. In Ireland, Sinn Fein ('we ourselves') arose before the First World War as a republican movement standing for the political separation of Ireland from Great Britain. Today it is the political wing of the Irish Republican Army (IRA), and campaigns as a political party for Northern Ireland to become part of the Republic of Ireland. Another party supporting the same cause, although not as militantly, is the Social Democratic and Labour Party (SDLP), formed in Northern Ireland in 1970 as a reaction to the 'Troubles'. (Cf article at IRELAND.) Its supporters are mainly Catholics. The SDLP's main opponents are the right-wing Ulster Unionists, whose Protestant supporters wish Northern Ireland to remain part of the United Kingdom.

Increasing popular awareness of environmental issues in recent years has seen some increase in support for the Green Party, founded in 1973 as the Ecology Party and campaigning for a democratic and nuclear-free society.

There are 650 constituencies in Britain, each represented in Parliament by its elected Member of Parliament (MP). Candidates are selected by their local party to stand for election, and the candidate who receives the largest number of votes is elected to Parliament. Most Labour support is in the cities and urban areas, with strong Conservative support traditionally in the south and in rural and agricultural areas. If an MP dies or resigns, there is a by-election in his constituency, which may slightly alter the overall majority of the government in power. The maximum period for which a government can be in office is five years, when another general election must be held.

In the USA, a presidential election is held every four years, at the same time as elections for other federal, state and local offices. Each state has a number of Representatives (in the House of Representatives, the lower house of Congress) according to the size of its population, but there is equal representation for all states in the Senate (the upper house).

Both the British and US electoral systems are favourable to the two main parties at the expense of smaller parties, and in both countries it is possible for one party to win a majority of seats even though the other party wins more votes in a general election. An American president can be elected by a majority in the electoral college even though he has fewer popular votes than his rival. All candidates for election in the USA, except for president, are chosen by their parties at primary (ie preliminary) elections. These can be 'open' primaries, in which any registered candidate can compete, whatever his own party, or 'closed' primaries, in which all candidates are members of the same political party. (Cf articles at GOVERNMENT and PARLIAMENT.)

ox, sheep, etc that has no horns.

pollen /ˈpɒlən/ *n* [U] fine (usu yellow) powder formed in flowers, which fertilizes other flowers when carried to them by the wind, insects, etc.

□ ˈ**pollen count** number indicating the amount of pollen in the atmosphere, used as a guide to possible attacks of hay fever, etc.

pollinate /ˈpɒləneɪt/ *v* [Tn] make (sth) fertile with pollen. ▷ **pollination** /ˌpɒləˈneɪʃn/ *n* [U].

Pollock /ˈpɒlək/ Jackson (1912-56), American painter. He is best known for his technique of 'action painting', in which he produced complex patterns by throwing or dripping paint onto the canvas. ⇨ illus.

pollster /ˈpəʊlstə(r)/ *n* (*infml*) person who conducts public-opinion polls.

pollute /pəˈluːt/ *v* [Tn, Tn·pr] ~ **sth (with sth) 1** make sth dirty or impure, esp by adding harmful or unpleasant substances: *rivers polluted with chemical waste from factories* ○ *polluted water*, ie unfit to drink. **2** (*fig*) destroy the purity or sanctity of sth; corrupt: *pollute the minds of the young with foul propaganda.*

▷ **pollutant** /-ənt/ *n* substance that pollutes, eg exhaust fumes from motor vehicles: *releasing pollutants into the atmosphere.*

pollution /pəˈluːʃn/ *n* [U] (**a**) polluting or being polluted: *the pollution of our beaches with oil.* (**b**) substance that pollutes.

Pollux /ˈpɒləks/ bright star in the constellation Gemini, which also contains its twin star, *Castor.

Pollyanna /ˌpɒlɪˈænə/ *n* (*often derog*) naively optimistic person.

polo /ˈpəʊləʊ/ *n* [U] game in which players on horseback try to hit the ball into a goal using long-handled hammers.

□ ˈ**polo neck** (style of) high round turned-over collar: [attrib] *a* ˌ*polo-neck* ˈ*sweater.* ⇨ illus at NECK.

polonaise /ˌpɒləˈneɪz/ *n* (piece of music for a) slow dance of Polish origin.

poltergeist /ˈpɒltəgaɪst/ *n* type of ghost that makes loud noises, throws objects about, etc.

poly /ˈpɒlɪ/ *n* (*pl* ~**s**) (*infml*) = POLYTECHNIC.

poly- *comb form* many: *polygamy* ○ *polyphony* ○ *polysyllable* ○ *polygamous* ○ *polyphonic* ○ *polysyllabic.*

polyandry /ˈpɒlɪændrɪ/ *n* [U] custom of having more than one husband at the same time.

▷ **polyandrous** /ˌpɒlɪˈændrəs/ *adj* **1** of or practising polyandry. **2** (*botany*) (of plants) having many stamens.

polyanthus /ˌpɒlɪˈænθəs/ *n* [U, C] garden plant of the primrose family, with several (usu multi-coloured) flowers on one stalk.

polychromatic /ˌpɒlɪkrəʊˈmætɪk/ *adj* **1** (*fml*) many-coloured. **2** (*physics*) (of radiation) consisting of more than one wavelength.

polyester /ˌpɒlɪˈestə(r); *US* ˈpɒliːestər/ *n* [U, C] artificial fabric used for making clothes, etc: [attrib] *a polyester shirt.*

polyethylene /ˌpɒlɪˈeθəliːn/ *n* [U] (*US*) = POLYTHENE.

polygamy /pəˈlɪgəmɪ/ *n* [U] custom of having more than one wife at the same time. Cf MONOGAMY.

▷ **polygamist** /-gəmɪst/ man who practices this.

polygamous /pəˈlɪgəməs/ *adj* of or practising polygamy.

polyglot /ˈpɒlɪglɒt/ *adj* (*fml*) knowing, using or written in many languages: *a polyglot edition.*

▷ **polyglot** *n* person who speaks many languages.

polygon /ˈpɒlɪgən; *US* -gɒn/ *n* (*geometry*) plane figure with many (usu five or more) straight sides.

▷ **polygonal** /pəˈlɪgənl/ *adj.*

Jackson Pollock: Yellow Islands

polygraph /ˈpɒlɪɡrɑːf; *US* -ɡræf/ *n* = LIE-DETECTOR (LIE[1]).

polyhedron /ˌpɒlɪˈhiːdrən/ *n* (*pl* ~**s** or **-hedra** /-hiːdrə/) solid figure with many (usu seven or more) faces.

polymath /ˈpɒlɪmæθ/ *n* (*fml approv*) person who knows a great deal about many different subjects.

polymer /ˈpɒlɪmə(r)/ *n* (*chemistry*) natural or artificial compound made up of large molecules which are themselves made from combinations of small simple molecules.

polymorphous /ˌpɒlɪˈmɔːfəs/, **polymorphic** /-fɪk/ *adjs* (*fml*) having or passing through many stages (of development, growth, etc).

Polynesia /ˌpɒlɪˈniːzɪə; *US* -ˈniːʒə/ islands of the central Pacific Ocean, including eg Hawaii, Fiji, Tonga and Samoa. ⇨ map. ▷ **Polynesian** *adj*, *n*.

polynomial /ˌpɒlɪˈnəʊmɪəl/ *n*, *adj* (mathematical expression) consisting of two or more terms added together.

polyp /ˈpɒlɪp/ *n* **1** (*biology*) very simple form of animal (eg a sea anemone) found in water: *Coral is formed by certain types of polyp.* **2** (*medical*) any of several kinds of tumour (eg in the nose). ▷ **polypous** /-pəs/ *adj*.

polyphony /pəˈlɪfənɪ/ *n* [U] combination of several different melodic patterns to form a single piece of music; counterpoint.
▷ **polyphonic** /ˌpɒlɪˈfɒnɪk/ *adj* **1** (*music*) having several (usu vocal) parts in counterpoint. **2** (*fml*) having many voices.

polystyrene /ˌpɒlɪˈstaɪriːn/ *n* [U] type of light firm plastic with good insulating properties, used esp for making containers: [attrib] *a polystyrene box.*

polysyllable /ˈpɒlɪsɪləbl/ *n* word of several (usu more than three) syllables. ▷ **polysyllabic** /ˌpɒlɪsɪˈlæbɪk/ *adj*.

polytechnic /ˌpɒlɪˈteknɪk/ (also *infml* **poly**) *n* (esp in Britain) college for advanced full-time and part-time education, esp in scientific and technical subjects: [attrib] *polytechnic courses, students.* ⇨ article at POST-SCHOOL.

polytheism /ˈpɒlɪθiːɪzəm/ *n* [U] belief in or worship of more than one god. Cf MONOTHEISM. ▷ **polytheistic** /ˌpɒlɪθiːˈɪstɪk/ *adj*.

polythene /ˈpɒlɪθiːn/ *n* [U] type of plastic widely used in the form of flexible, often transparent, sheets for waterproof packaging, insulation, etc: *tins of food wrapped in polythene* ○ [attrib] *a polythene bag, cover.*

polyunsaturated /ˌpɒlɪʌnˈsætʃəreɪtɪd/ *adj* (of many vegetable and some animal fats) having a chemical structure which does not help the harmful formation of cholesterol in the blood: *Polyunsaturated margarine is very popular now.* Cf SATURATED 3.

polyurethane /ˌpɒlɪˈjʊərɪθeɪn/ *n* [U] type of plastic used in making paints: [attrib] *polyurethane gloss*, ie paint that dries with a hard shiny surface.

pom /pɒm/ *n* (*infml*) **1** = POMMY. **2** = POMERANIAN.

pomander /pəˈmændə(r)/ *n* (round container for a) ball of mixed sweet-smelling substances (eg flowers, leaves, spices, etc) used to perfume cupboards, rooms, etc.

Polynesia

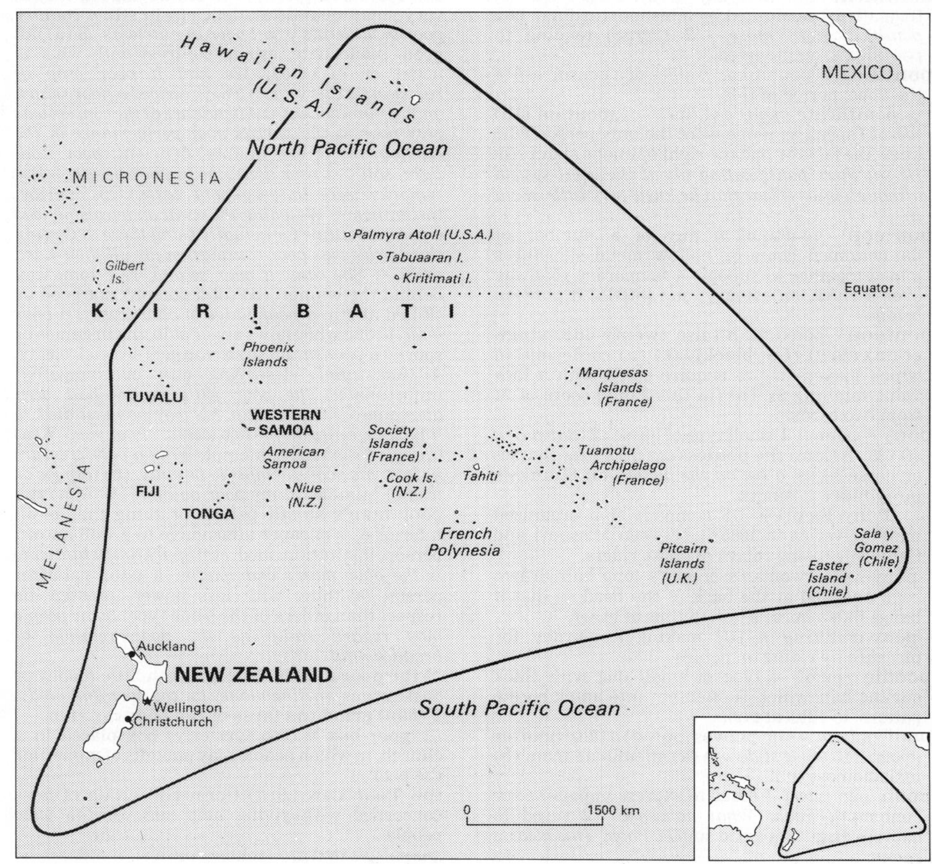

pomegranate /ˈpɒmɪɡrænɪt/ *n* (tree with a) thick-skinned round fruit which, when ripe, has a reddish centre full of large juicy seeds: [attrib] *pomegranate juice, seeds.*

Pomeranian /ˌpɒməˈreɪnɪən/ (also *infml* **pom**) *n* type of small long-haired dog.

pomfret-cake /ˈpʌmfrɪt keɪk/ *n* (also **Pontefract cake**) (*Brit*) round liquorice sweet.

pommel /ˈpɒml/ *n* **1** rounded part of a saddle which sticks up at the front. **2** rounded knob on the handle of a sword.
▷ **pommel** /ˈpʌml/ *v* (**-ll-**; *US* **-l-**) [Tn] = PUMMEL.

pommy /ˈpɒmɪ/ (also **pom**) *n* (*Austral or NZ infml usu derog*) British person.

pomp /pɒmp/ *n* [U] **1** (**a**) splendid display or magnificence, esp at a public event: *the pomp and ceremony of the State Opening of Parliament.* (**b**) (*derog*) such display seen as trivial and meaningless: *forsaking worldly pomp for the life of a monk.* **2** (idm) **pomp and circumstance** magnificent and/or ceremonious display and procedure.

Pompeii /pɒmˈpeiː/ ancient town near Naples, Italy. In 79 AD an eruption of the volcano *Vesuvius buried it under several metres of lava. Excavations by archaeologists have uncovered the town, complete with well-preserved public buildings and private houses which give much information about everyday life in the time of ancient Rome.

pom-pom /ˈpɒmpɒm/ *n* small woollen ball used for decoration, eg on a hat, on the border of a piece of fabric, etc.

pompous /ˈpɒmpəs/ *adj* (*derog*) feeling, or showing that one feels, that one is much more important than other people: *a pompous official* ○ *pompous language*, ie full of high-sounding words.
▷ **pomposity** /pɒmˈpɒsətɪ/ *n* (**a**) [U] being pompous. (**b**) [C] instance of this.

pompously *adv*.

ponce /pɒns/ *n* (*Brit*) **1** man who lives with a prostitute and lives on her earnings. **2** (*infml derog*) man who acts in a showy, esp effeminate, way.

▷ **ponce** *v* (phr v) **ponce about/around** (*Brit infml derog*) (**a**) act in a showy, esp effeminate way. (**b**) act or behave in an ineffective or time-wasting way: *Stop poncing about and get that job finished.*

poncho /ˈpɒntʃəʊ/ *n* (*pl* ~**s**) type of cloak made from a large piece of cloth with a slit in the middle for the head.

pond /pɒnd/ *n* small area of still water, esp one used or made as a drinking place for cattle or as an ornamental garden pool: *a fish pond* ○ [attrib] *pond life*, ie animals living in a pond.

ponder /ˈpɒndə(r)/ *v* [I, Ipr, Tn, Tw] ~ (**on/over sth**) think about (sth) carefully and for a long time, esp in trying to reach a decision; consider: *You have pondered long enough; it is time to decide.* ○ *I pondered (over) the incident, asking myself again and again how it could have happened.* ○ *pondering on the meaning of life* ○ *I am pondering how to respond.*

ponderous /ˈpɒndərəs/ *adj* **1** slow and awkward because of great weight: *a fat man's ponderous movements.* **2** (*derog*) (of speech, written style, etc) without vigour or inspiration; dull; laboured. ▷ **ponderously** *adv*. **ponderousness** *n* [U].

pone /pəʊn/ *n* [U] = CORN PONE (CORN[1]).

pong /pɒŋ/ *n* (*Brit infml often joc*) strong, usu unpleasant, smell: *What a horrible pong!*

▷ **pong** *v* [I] (*Brit infml often joc*) smell strongly and usu unpleasantly.

pongy /ˈpɒŋɪ/ *adj* (**-ier**, **-iest**): *Your feet are rather pongy!*

Pontefract cake /ˈpɒntɪfrækt keɪk/ = POMFRET-CAKE.

pontiff /ˈpɒntɪf/ *n* **1** (*arch*) bishop; chief priest; high priest. **2 the** (**Supreme**) **Pontiff** the Pope.

pontifical /pɒnˈtɪfɪkl/ *adj* **1** (**a**) of the Pope. (**b**) [usu attrib] celebrated by a bishop, cardinal, etc: *pontifical high mass.* **2** (*derog*) tending to pontificate; opinionated.

pontificate /pɒnˈtɪfɪkət/ *n* office of a pontiff, esp of the Pope; period of this.

▷ **pontificate** /-keɪt/ *v* [I, Ipr] ~ (**about/on sth**) (*derog*) speak as if one were the only person who knew the facts or had the right opinions about sth: *He sat there pontificating about the legal system although it was clear that he knew very little about it.*

pontoon[1] /pɒnˈtuːn/ *n* any of a number of flat-bottomed boats or hollow metal structures joined together to support a temporary roadway over a river, an estuary, etc: [attrib] *a pontoon bridge.*

pontoon[2] /pɒnˈtuːn/ *n* (also **twenty-one**, **vingt-et-un**) (*Brit*) (*US* ˈ**blackjack**) (**a**) card-game in which players try to acquire cards with a face value totalling 21. (**b**) (in this game) score of 21 from two cards.

pony /ˈpəʊnɪ/ *n* **1** small type of horse. **2** (*dated Brit sl*) £25. **3** (idm) **the ponies** (*esp US sl*) racehorses or horse-races: *a bet on the ponies.* **on Shanks's pony/mare** ⇨ SHANK.

□ ˌ**Pony Ex**ˈ**press** US company that organized mail deliveries in 1860-61 between Missouri and California, using relays of horse riders.

ˈ**pony-tail** *n* woman's or girl's long hair drawn back and tied at the back of the head so that it hangs like a horse's tail. ⇨ illus at PLAIT.

ˈ**pony-trekking** *n* [U] making a journey for pleasure by riding on ponies.

poodle /ˈpuːdl/ *n* type of small dog with thick curling hair which is often cut into an elaborate pattern. ⇨ illus at DOG.

poof /pʊf/ (*pl* ~**s** or **pooves** /puːvz/) *n* (also **poofter** /ˈpʊftə(r)/) (*Brit sl derog*) (**a**) effeminate man. (**b**) male homosexual.

pooh /puː/ *interj* **1** (used to express impatience or contempt): *Pooh! What nonsense!* **2** (used to express disgust at a bad smell): *Pooh! This meat is rotten.*

pooh-pooh /ˌpuːˈpuː/ *v* [Tn] (*infml*) treat (an idea, a suggestion, etc) with contempt; dismiss scornfully: *They pooh-poohed our scheme for raising money.*

pool[1] /puːl/ *n* **1** small area of still water, esp one that has formed naturally: *After the rainstorm, there were pools on the roads.* **2** shallow patch of water or other liquid lying on a surface: *The body was lying in a pool of blood.* **3** place in a river where the water is deep and there is not much current. **4** = SWIMMING-POOL (SWIM).

pool[2] /puːl/ *n* **1** [C] common fund of money, esp the stakes of all the players in a gambling game. **2** [C] (**a**) common supply of funds, goods or services which are available to a group of people to be used when needed: *a pool of cars used by the firm's salesmen* ○ [attrib] *a pool car.* (**b**) group of people available for work when required: *a pool of doctors available for emergency work* ○ *a* ˈ*typing pool*, ie a pool of typists. **3** [C] arrangement by a number of business firms to agree on prices and share profits, in order to avoid competition. **4** [U] (*esp US*) game played with (usu) 16 coloured balls on a billiard-table, similar to snooker. **5 the pools** [pl] = FOOTBALL POOLS (FOOTBALL): *do the pools every week* ○ *have a win on the pools.* **6** (idm) **shoot pool** ⇨ SHOOT[1].

▷ **pool** *v* [Tn] put (money, resources, etc) into a common fund: *They pooled their savings and bought a house in the country.* ○ (*fig*) *If we pool our ideas, we may find a solution.*

□ ˈ**poolroom** *n* (*US*) place where pool[2](4) is played.

poop /puːp/ *n* (**a**) stern of a ship. (**b**) (also ˈ**poop deck**) raised deck at the stern of a ship.

pooped /puːpt/ *adj* [pred] (also ˌ**pooped** ˈ**out**) (*infml esp US*) very tired; exhausted.

poor /pɔː(r); *US* pʊər/ *adj* (**-er**, **-est**) **1** having very little money with which to buy one's basic needs: *She was too poor to buy clothes for her children.* ○ *He came from a poor family.* ○ *the poorer countries of the world.* **2** [pred] ~ **in sth** having sth only in very small quantities; deficient in sth: *a country poor in minerals* ○ *soil poor in nutrients.* **3** (**a**) not good; inadequate, esp in contrast with what is usual or expected: *We had a poor crop of raspberries this year.* ○ *They received a poor return on their investment.* ○ *Attendance at the concert was very poor.* ○ *the party's poor performance in the election.* (**b**) of low quality; deficient: *poor food, light, soil* ○ *a poor diet* ○ *be in poor health* ○ *Her remarks were in very poor taste.* (**c**) inferior; insignificant: *Watching the event on television was a poor substitute for actually being there.* ○ *Getting third prize was poor consolation for all their hard work.* ○ *She came a poor second*, ie a long way behind the winner. (**d**) (of a person) not good or skilled at sth: *a poor judge of character* ○ *a poor loser*, ie one who shows anger at losing in games or sport ○ *a poor sailor*, ie sb who gets sea-sick easily. **4** (*esp infml*) deserving pity or sympathy; unfortunate: *The poor little puppy had been abandoned.* ○ *Poor chap, his wife has just died.* ○ *'I've been feeling ill for two weeks.' 'Poor you!'* **5** (**a**) (*derog*) deserving contempt: *What a poor creature he is!* ○ *his poor attempts to be witty.* (**b**) (*esp joc or ironic*) humble: *in my poor opinion.* **6** (idm) **the poor man's sb/sth** person or thing that is an inferior or a cheaper alternative to a well-known person, institution, food, etc: *Sparkling white wine is the poor man's champagne.* **a poor relation** person or thing with less power, prestige or respect than others of the same type: *Some people may regard radio as the poor relation of broadcasting.*

▷ **the poor** *n* [pl *v*] **1** people with little money or possessions: *raising money for the poor and needy.* **2** (idm) **grind the faces of the poor** ⇨ GRIND.

□ ˈ**poor-box** *n* (esp formerly) box placed in a church, in which people may put gifts of money for the poor.

the ˈ**Poor Law** (*Brit*) (formerly) group of laws concerned with giving help and care to poor people.

ˌ**poor-**ˈ**spirited** *adj* lacking courage; timid.

ˌ**poor** ˈ**white** (*usu derog or offensive*) (esp in Southern USA) member of a class of poor white-skinned people in a mainly Black community.

poorly /ˈpɔːlɪ; *US* ˈpʊərlɪ/ *adv* **1** in a poor(3) manner; badly: *poorly dressed* ○ *The street is poorly lit.* ○ *She was poorly prepared for the examination.* **2** (idm) **poorly** ˈ**off** (*infml*) having very little money: *The widow and children are very poorly off.*

▷ **poorly** *adj* [esp pred] (*infml*) not well; ill: *The child has been poorly all week.* ○ *You look rather poorly to me.* ⇨ Usage at SICK.

poorness /ˈpɔːnɪs; *US* ˈpʊərnɪs/ *n* [U] lack of a desirable quality or element; state of being poor(2): *the poorness of the soil.* Cf POVERTY.

pop[1] /pɒp/ *n* **1** [C] short sharp explosive sound: *The cork came out of the bottle with a loud pop.* **2** [U] (*infml*) (esp non-alcoholic) fizzy drink: *a bottle of pop.* **3** (idm) **in pop**; *US* **in hock** (*sl*) in pawn.

▷ **pop** *adv* with a pop: *It came out pop.* ○ *go pop*, ie make a pop.

pop[2] /pɒp/ *n* (*infml*) (used esp as a term of address) **1** father. Cf PAPA, POPPA. **2** any older man.

pop[3] /pɒp/ *n* [U, C usu *pl*] (*infml*) modern popular style, esp in music: *pop music, culture* ○ *a pop singer, song, concert* ○ *top of the pops*, ie the most popular current recordings. Cf CLASSICAL 2.

□ ˈ**pop art** style of art developed in the 1960s, based on popular culture and the mass media, using material such as advertisements, comic strips, etc.

ˈ**pop festival** large (usu outdoor) gathering of people to hear performances by pop musicians, sometimes lasting several days.

ˈ**pop group** band and singer(s) who play pop music.

pop[4] /pɒp/ *v* (**-pp-**) **1** [I, Ip] make a short sharp explosive sound (as when a cork comes out of a bottle): *Champagne corks were popping (away) throughout the celebrations.* **2** [Tn] cause (sth) to burst with such a sound: *The children were popping balloons.* **3** [Tn] (*US*) dry (corn) until it bursts open and puffs up: *pop maize.* **4** [Ip] ~ **away/off** (**at sth**) (*infml*) fire a gun (at sth): *They were popping away at the rabbits all afternoon.* **5** [Tn] (*dated Brit infml*) pawn (sth). **6** [Tn] (*sl*) take (drugs, esp amphetamines): *She began popping pills.* **7** (idm) **pop the** ˈ**question** (*infml*) make a proposal of marriage. **8** (phr v) **pop across**, **down**, **out etc** come or go quickly or suddenly in the direction specified: *He's just popped down the road to the shops.* ○ *She's popped over to see her mother.* ○ *He's only popped out for a few minutes.* ○ *Where's Tom popped off to?* **pop sth across**, **in**, **into**, **etc sth** put or take sth somewhere quickly or suddenly: *pop a letter in the post* ○ *She popped the tart into the oven.* ○ *He popped his head round the door to say goodbye.* **pop in** make a brief visit: *She often pops in for coffee.* **pop sth in** deliver sth as one is passing: *I'll pop the books in on my way home.* **pop off** (*infml*) die: *She said she had no intention of popping off for some time yet.* **pop out** (**of sth**) come out suddenly: *The rabbits popped out as soon as we opened the hutch.* ○ (*fig*) *His eyes nearly popped out of his head when he saw what he had won.* **pop up** (*infml*) appear or occur, esp when not expected: *He seems to pop up in the most unlikely places.*

□ ˈ**popcorn** /ˈpɒpkɔːn/ *n* [U] maize that has been heated so that it bursts and forms fluffy balls.

ˈ**pop-eyed** *adj* (**a**) having naturally bulging eyes. (**b**) with eyes wide open with surprise: *She was pop-eyed with amazement.*

ˈ**popgun** /ˈpɒpɡʌn/ *n* child's toy gun that shoots a cork with a popping sound.

ˈ**pop-up** *adj* **1** (of the pages of a book) rising into a 3-dimensional form as the book is opened. **2** [attrib] (of an automatic toaster) that operates by causing the toast to move quickly upwards when it is ready.

pop *abbr* population: *pop 12m*, ie 12 million.

Pope /pəʊp/ Alexander (1688-1744), English poet. His translation of Homer's *Iliad* made him a successful literary figure, but most of his work was satirical, often using the form of the epic for comic effect, as in *The Rape of the Lock* and *The Dunciad*. He was a friend of many of the great writers of his time, including *Swift and *Gay, but his witty attacks made him unpopular with many others.

pope /pəʊp/ *n* head of the Roman Catholic Church who is also the Bishop of Rome: *the election of a new pope* ○ *Pope John Paul*.

▷ **popery** /ˈpəʊpərɪ/ *n* [U] (*derog*) (**a**) Roman Catholicism. (**b**) papal system.

popish /ˈpəʊpɪʃ/ *adj* (*derog*) (**a**) of or relating to Roman Catholicism: *popish forms of worship*. (**b**) of or relating to the papal system. **the ˌPopish ˈPlot** alleged Roman Catholic plot to kill *Charles II in 1678 and make the Duke of York (later *James II) king instead. It was invented by Titus *Oates, a Protestant clergyman. The story was completely untrue, but about 35 Catholics were executed.

□ **pope's ˈnose** (*US infml*) = PARSON'S NOSE (PARSON).

Popeye /ˈpɒpaɪ/ popular American cartoon character, a sailor with a protruding jaw and a pipe clenched between his teeth. He loves a lady called Olive Oyl, and gets the strength needed to fight his opponents (esp Bluto) by eating spinach.

popinjay /ˈpɒpɪndʒeɪ/ *n* (*dated derog*) conceited person, esp a man who is vain about his clothes; fop.

poplar /ˈpɒplə(r)/ *n* (**a**) [C] any of several types of tall straight slender tree. ⇨ illus at TREE. (**b**) [U] its soft wood.

poplin /ˈpɒplɪn/ *n* [U] **1** type of shiny (usu) cotton cloth used esp for making skirts. **2** (formerly) type of cloth with a ribbed surface, made from silk and wool.

popover /ˈpɒpəʊvə(r)/ *n* (*US*) cake in the form of a thin hollow shell made of batter.

poppa /ˈpɒpə/ *n* (*US infml*) (used esp as a term of address) father. Cf PAPA, POP².

poppadom (also **poppadam**) /ˈpɒpədəm/ *n* thin crisp spicy Indian biscuit made from lentil flour.

popper /ˈpɒpə(r)/ *n* (*Brit infml*) = PRESS-STUD (PRESS²).

poppet /ˈpɒpɪt/ *n* (*Brit infml*) (**a**) (used esp as an affectionate name for a child) darling: *How's my little poppet today?* ○ *Don't cry, poppet.* (**b**) small and dainty person: *Isn't she a poppet?*

poppy /ˈpɒpɪ/ *n* any of several types of wild or cultivated plant with showy (esp bright red) flowers, milky juice and small black seeds: *the ˈopium poppy*, ie the type from which opium is obtained ○ [attrib] *poppy fields*. ⇨ illus at FLOWER.

□ **ˈPoppy Day** (in Britain) Remembrance Sunday (REMEMBRANCE), when many people wear paper poppies in memory of those who died in the World Wars. Cf FLANDERS POPPY (FLANDERS).

poppycock /ˈpɒpɪkɒk/ *n* [U] (*infml*) nonsense: *He dismissed the official explanation as complete poppycock.*

Popsicle /ˈpɒpsɪkl/ *n* (*US propr*) = ICE LOLLY (ICE¹).

populace /ˈpɒpjʊləs/ (usu **the populace**) *n* [Gp] (*fml*) the general public; ordinary people: *He had the support of large sections of the populace.* ○ *The populace at large is/are opposed to sudden change.*

popular /ˈpɒpjʊlə(r)/ *adj* **1** (**a**) liked, admired or enjoyed by many people: *a popular politician* ○ *Jeans are popular among the young.* ○ *Jogging is a popular form of exercise.* (**b**) ~ **with sb** liked, admired or enjoyed by sb: *measures popular with the electorate* ○ (*infml*) *I'm not very popular with the boss* (ie He is annoyed with me) *at the moment.* **2** [attrib] (*sometimes derog*) suited to the taste or the education level of the general public: *popular music* ○ *the popular press* ○ *novels with popular appeal* ○ *popular* (ie simplified) *science* ○ *popular* (ie low) *prices*. **3** [attrib] of or by the people: *the popular vote* ○ *issues of popular concern* ○ *by popular demand.* **4** [attrib] (of beliefs, etc) held by a large number of people: *a popular myth, superstition, misconception, etc.*

▷ **popularly** *adv* by many or most people: *a popularly held belief* ○ *It is popularly believed that...* ○ *the European Economic Community, popularly known as the Common Market.*

□ **ˌpopular ˈfront** political party representing left-wing groups.

popularity /ˌpɒpjʊˈlærətɪ/ *n* [U] quality or state of being liked or admired by many people: *win/gain/enjoy/command the popularity of the voters* ○ *His popularity among working people remains as strong as ever.* ○ *Her books have grown in popularity recently.*

popularize, -ise /ˈpɒpjʊləraɪz/ *v* [Tn] **1** make (sth) generally liked. **2** make (sth) known or available to the general public, esp by presenting it in an easily understandable form: *popularize new theories in medicine* ○ *popularize the use of personal computers.* ▷ **popularization, -isation** /ˌpɒpjʊləraɪˈzeɪʃn; *US* -rɪˈz-/ *n* [U].

populate /ˈpɒpjʊleɪt/ *v* [Tn esp passive] (**a**) live in (an area) and form its population: *deserts populated by nomadic tribesmen* ○ *densely/thickly/sparsely/thinly populated regions.* (**b**) move to (an area) and fill it with people: *The islands were gradually populated by settlers from Europe.*

population /ˌpɒpjʊˈleɪʃn/ *n* **1** [CGp] (**a**) people who live in an area, a city, a country, etc: *the populations of Western European countries* ○ *The government did not have the support of the population.* (**b**) particular group or type of people or animals inhabiting an area, etc: *the working population* ○ *the immigrant population.* (**c**) total number of these: *What is the population of Ireland?* ○ *a city with a population of over 10 million.* **2** [U] degree to which an area has been populated: *areas of dense/sparse population.*

□ **popuˌlation exˈplosion** sudden increase in population resulting from an increased birth-rate and/or a reduced death-rate.

populism /ˈpɒpjʊlɪzəm/ *n* [U] type of politics that claims to represent the interests of ordinary people.

▷ **populist** /-ɪst/ *n* supporter or representative of populism. — *adj*: *populist theories.*

populous /ˈpɒpjʊləs/ *adj* having a large population; densely populated: *the populous areas near the coast.*

porcelain /ˈpɔːsəlɪn/ *n* [U] (**a**) hard white translucent material made from china clay, used for making cups, plates, ornaments, etc: [attrib] *a porcelain figure.* (**b**) objects made of this: *a valuable collection of antique porcelain.*

porch /pɔːtʃ/ *n* **1** covered entrance to a building, esp a church or house. ⇨ illus at HOME, CHURCH. **2** (*US*) = VERANDA.

porcine /ˈpɔːsaɪn/ *adj* (*fml*) of or like a pig: *her rather porcine features.*

porcupine /ˈpɔːkjʊpaɪn/ *n* animal related to the squirrel, with a body and tail covered with long spines which it can stick out to protect itself when attacked.

pore¹ /pɔː(r)/ *n* any of the tiny openings in the surface of the skin or of a leaf, through which moisture can pass: *He was sweating at every pore.* ⇨ illus at FRUIT.

pore² /pɔː(r)/ *v* (phr v) **pore over sth** study sth by looking at it or thinking about it very carefully: *She was poring over an old map of the area.* ○ *The child spends hours poring over her books.*

pork /pɔːk/ *n* [U] (usu fresh, not salted or cured) flesh of a pig eaten as food: *roast pork* ○ *a leg of pork* ○ [attrib] *pork sausages.* Cf BACON, GAMMON, HAM 1.

▷ **porker** *n* pig raised for food, esp a young pig fattened for killing.

□ **pork-barrel** *n* (*US sl*) government money spent on local projects in order to win votes.

ˈpork-butcher *n* (*Brit*) butcher who sells pork, ham, bacon and food made from pork, eg sausages, pies, etc.

ˌpork ˈpie pie made of pastry filled with minced pork, often eaten cold. **ˌpork-pie ˈhat** hat with a flat top and a brim turned up all round.

porn /pɔːn/ *n* [U] (*infml*) = PORNOGRAPHY.

porno /ˈpɔːnəʊ/ *adj* (*infml*) = PORNOGRAPHIC (PORNOGRAPHY).

pornography /pɔːˈnɒgrəfɪ/ *n* [U] (**a**) describing or showing sexual acts in order to cause sexual excitement. (**b**) books, films, etc that do this: *the trade in pornography.*

▷ **pornographer** /pɔːˈnɒgrəfə(r)/ *n* person who produces or sells pornography.

pornographic /ˌpɔːnəˈgræfɪk/ *adj* of or relating to pornography: *pornographic films, magazines, subjects.* **pornographically** /-klɪ/ *adv.*

porous /ˈpɔːrəs/ *adj* **1** allowing liquid or air to pass through, esp slowly: *He added sand to the soil to make it more porous.* ○ *In hot weather clothes made of a porous material like cotton are best.* Cf PERMEABLE (PERMEATE). **2** containing pores.

▷ **porousness, porosity** /*US* pɔːˈrɒsətɪ/ *ns* [U] quality or state of being porous.

porphyry /ˈpɔːfɪrɪ/ *n* [U] type of hard red rock which contains red and white crystals, and may be polished and made into ornaments.

porpoise /ˈpɔːpəs/ *n* sea mammal with a blunt rounded snout, similar to a dolphin or small whale.

porridge /ˈpɒrɪdʒ; *US* ˈpɔːr-/ *n* **1** [U] soft food made by boiling a cereal (esp crushed oats) in water or milk: *a bowl of porridge with milk and sugar for breakfast.* **2** (idm) **do porridge** (*Brit sl*) be in prison; serve a prison sentence.

port¹ /pɔːt/ *n* **1** [C, U] place where ships load and unload cargo or shelter from storms; harbour: *a naval/fishing port* ○ *The ship spent four days in port.* ○ *They reached port at last.* **2** [C] town or city with a harbour, esp one where ships load and unload cargo and where customs officers are stationed: *Rotterdam is a major port.* ○ [attrib] *the port authorities.* **3** (esp in compounds) any place where goods or people enter or leave a country: *an airport* ○ *a port of entry.* **4** (idm) **any port in a ˈstorm** (*saying esp ironic*) in times of trouble or difficulty one takes whatever help is available.

□ **ˌport of ˈcall 1** place where a ship stops during a voyage. **2** (*infml*) place where a person goes or stops, esp during a journey: *The visiting politician's first port of call was the new factory.*

port² /pɔːt/ *n* (*nautical*) **1** opening in the side of a ship where people may enter or for loading and unloading cargo. **2** = PORTHOLE.

port³ /pɔːt/ *n* [U] the side of a ship or aircraft that is on the left when one is facing forward: *put the helm to port* ○ *The ship was leaning over to port.* ○ [attrib] *the port side* ○ *a port tack*, ie a course sailed with the wind blowing on the port side. Cf STARBOARD.

port⁴ /pɔːt/ *n* (**a**) [U] strong sweet (usu dark-red) wine made in Portugal. (**b**) [C] glass of this.

📖 Port is traditionally served at the end of a dinner, especially a celebratory one, and at Christmas. In former times, women would leave the table as soon as the port was served, and withdraw to a special 'withdrawing room' (the origin of the modern 'drawing-room'). The men would stay at the table to drink port, to smoke and to converse on 'manly' topics. It was customary to pass the port clockwise round the table.

portable /ˈpɔːtəbl/ *adj* that can be (easily) carried; not fixed permanently in place: *a portable radio, television set, typewriter, etc.*

▷ **portability** /ˌpɔːtəˈbɪlətɪ/ *n* [U]: *I bought it for its portability, not its appearance.*

portable *n* portable version of sth: *The document had been typed on a small portable.*

portage /ˈpɔːtɪdʒ/ *n* **1** [U] (cost of) carrying goods; carriage. **2** (*esp US*) (**a**) [U] carrying boats or goods overland between two rivers, lakes, etc, eg on a canoeing trip. (**b**) [C] place where this is done.

portal /ˈpɔːtl/ *n* (often *pl*); (*fml*) doorway or gateway, esp a grand and imposing one: *temple portals of carved stone.*

□ **portal ˈvein** (*anatomy*) vein carrying blood to the liver or to any organ other than the heart.

portcullis /ˌpɔːtˈkʌlɪs/ *n* (formerly) strong heavy iron grating raised or lowered at the entrance to a castle. ⇨ illus at CASTLE.

portend /pɔːˈtend/ *v* [Tn] (*fml*) be a sign or warning of (sth in the future); foreshadow: *His silence portends trouble.*

portent /ˈpɔːtent/ *n* ~ (**of sth**) (*fml*) sign or warning of a future (often unpleasant) event; omen: *portents of disaster* ○ *I see it as a portent of things to come.*

▷ **portentous** /pɔːˈtentəs/ **1** of or like a portent;

ominous: *portentous events, signs.* **2** (*derog*) pompously solemn. **portentously** *adv*: *'No good will come of this,' she announced portentously.*

Porter /ˈpɔːtə(r)/ Cole (1891-1964), American composer. He wrote the words and music for many witty popular songs (eg 'Let's fall in love'), several of them for his successful Broadway musicals (eg *High Society* and *Kiss Me Kate*).

porter[1] /ˈpɔːtə(r)/ *n* **1** person whose job is carrying people's luggage and other loads, eg in railway stations, airports, hotels, markets, etc: *a hospital porter.* **2** (*US*) attendant in a sleeping-car or parlour-car on a train.
▷ **porterage** /ˈpɔːtərɪdʒ/ *n* [U] (**a**) carrying of luggage or goods by a porter. (**b**) cost of this.

porter[2] /ˈpɔːtə(r)/ *n* (*Brit*) (*US* **doorman**) person whose job is to be on duty at the entrance to a hotel, large building, etc: *The hotel porter will call a taxi for you.*
□ ˌ**porter's ˈlodge** (*Brit*) **1** room at the entrance to a large building, esp a university college. **2** house at the gates of an estate.

porter[3] /ˈpɔːtə(r)/ *n* [U] (esp formerly) type of dark-brown bitter beer.

porterhouse steak /ˌpɔːtəhaʊs ˈsteɪk/ piece of top-quality beefsteak cut for grilling, etc.

portfolio /pɔːtˈfəʊlɪəʊ/ *n* (*pl* ~**s**) **1** flat case (often made of leather) for carrying loose papers, documents, drawings, etc. **2** set of investments (eg stocks and shares) owned by a person, bank, etc: *My stockbroker manages my portfolio for me.* ○ [attrib] *portfolio management.* **3** position and duties of a minister of State: *She resigned her portfolio.* ○ *Minister without portfolio*, ie (in Britain) a Cabinet Minister without responsibility for a particular department.

porthole /ˈpɔːthəʊl/ (also **port**) *n* window-like structure in the side of a ship or an aircraft.

portico /ˈpɔːtɪkəʊ/ *n* (*pl* ~**es** or ~**s**) roof supported by columns, esp one forming an entrance to a large building.

portion /ˈpɔːʃn/ *n* **1** [C] part or share into which sth is divided: *He divided up his property and gave a portion to each of his children.* ○ *You give this portion of the ticket to the inspector and keep the other.* ○ (*dated*) *a marriage portion*, ie a dowry. **2** [C] amount of food suitable for or served to one person: *a generous portion of roast duck* ○ *She cut the pie into six portions.* ○ *Do you serve children's* (ie smaller) *portions?* **3** [sing] (*fml*) person's fate or destiny: *It seemed that suffering was to be his portion in life.*
▷ **portion** *v* (phr v) **portion sth out (among/between sb)** divide sth into shares (SHARE[1] 1) to give to several people: *She portioned out the money equally between both children.* ○ *The work was portioned out fairly.* Cf APPORTION.

Portland cement /ˌpɔːtlənd sɪˈment/ type of cement made from chalk and clay similar in colour to Portland stone.

Portland stone /ˌpɔːtlənd ˈstəʊn/ type of yellowish-white limestone used for building.

portly /ˈpɔːtlɪ/ *adj* (**-ier, -iest**) (esp of an older person) having a stout body; fat: *a portly old gentleman* ○ *portly members of the city council.* ▷ **portliness** *n* [U].

portmanteau /pɔːtˈmæntəʊ/ *n* (*pl* ~**s** or **-teaux** /-təʊz/) (*dated*) large oblong (usu leather) case for clothes that opens on a hinge into two equal parts.
□ **portmanteau ˈword** (also **blend**) invented word that combines parts of two words and their meanings eg *motel* from *motor* and *hotel* or *brunch* from *breakfast* and *lunch*.

portrait /ˈpɔːtreɪt, *also* -trɪt/ *n* **1** painted picture, drawing or photograph of (esp the face of) a person or an animal: *paint sb's portrait* ○ *She had her portrait painted.* ⇨ illus at CARICATURE. Cf LANDSCAPE. **2** description in words: *The book contains a fascinating portrait of life at the court of Henry VIII.*
▷ ˈ**portraitist** /-ɪst/ *n* person who makes portraits: *a skilled portraitist.*
ˈ**portraiture** /-tʃə(r); *US* -tʃʊər/ *n* [U] (art of making) portraits (PORTRAIT 1).
□ ˈ**portrait painter** person who paints portraits; portraitist.

portray /pɔːˈtreɪ/ *v* [Tn, Cn·n/a] ~ **sb (as sb/sth) 1** make a picture of sb: *She is portrayed wearing her coronation robes.* ○ *a picture of the general portraying him as a Greek hero.* **2** describe sb/sth in words: *The diary portrays his family as quarrelsome and malicious.* **3** act the part of sb or represent sth in a play, etc: *She frowned and stamped her feet to portray anger*, eg in a mime.
▷ **portrayal** /pɔːˈtreɪəl/ *n* **1** [U] action of portraying. **2** [C] description or representation: *a skilful portrayal of a lonely and embittered old man.*

Portugal

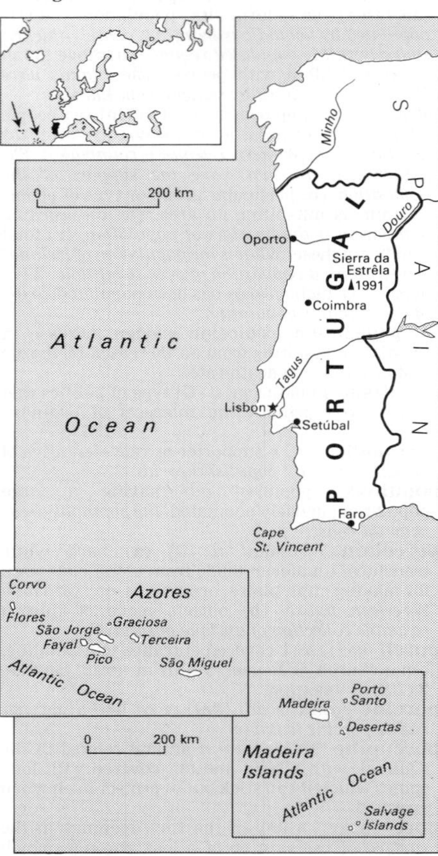

Portugal /ˈpɔːtʃʊgl/ country in western Europe, a member of the European Community since 1986; pop approx 10 408 000; official language Portuguese; capital Lisbon; unit of currency escudo (= 100 centavos). It has a border with Spain to the north and east, and with Spain makes up the Iberian Peninsula. Most of the country is flat, with a mountainous region in the north-east. Portugal is far less industrially developed than the rest of western Europe, and its agriculture, based on sheep, cereals, wine and olives, does not make it self-sufficient. Other important activities are fishing, cork production, shipping and tourism. Portugal and Britain became allies in the 14th century and have remained allies to the present day. ⇨ map.
▷ **Portuguese** /ˌpɔːtʃʊˈgiːz/ *n* (*pl* unchanged) **1** [C] native or inhabitant of Portugal. **2** [U] language of Portugal. — *adj*. **Portuˌguese man-of-ˈwar** (*pl* **Portuguese men-of-war**) type of jellyfish with a sail-shaped crest and a very poisonous sting.

pose /pəʊz/ *v* **1** (**a**) [I, Ipr] ~ (**for sb**) sit or stand in a particular position in order to be painted, drawn or photographed: *He had to pose wearing a laurel wreath.* ○ *The artist asked her to pose for him.* (**b**) [Tn] put (sb) in a particular position in order to paint, draw or photograph him: *The artist posed his model carefully.* ○ *The subjects are well posed in these photographs.* **2** [I] (*derog*) behave in an unnatural or affected way in order to impress people: *Stop posing and tell us what you really think.* **3** [Ipr] ~ **as sb/sth** claim or pretend to be sb/sth: *she poses as an expert in old coins* ○ *The detective posed as a mourner at the victim's funeral.* **4** [Tn] cause (sth) to arise; create or present (followed esp by the *ns* shown): *Winter poses particular difficulties for the elderly.* ○ *Heavy traffic poses a problem in many old towns.* ○ *His resignation poses the question of whether we now need a deputy leader.*
▷ **pose** *n* **1** position in which a person poses or is posed (POSE 1b): *a relaxed pose for the camera* ○ *She adopted an elegant pose.* **2** (*derog*) unnatural or affected way of behaving, intended to impress people: *His concern for the poor is only a pose.* **3** (idm) **strike an attitude/a pose** ⇨ STRIKE[2].
poser *n* **1** (*infml*) awkward or difficult question or problem: *That's quite a poser!* **2** = POSEUR.

Poseidon /pəˈseɪdn/ (in Greek mythology) god of the sea, the equivalent of the Roman god *Neptune.

poseur /pəʊˈzɜː(r)/ (*fem* **poseuse** /pəʊˈzɜːz/) *n* (also **poser**) (*derog*) person who behaves in an unnatural affected way in order to impress others: *Some people admired him greatly while others considered him a poseur.*

posh /pɒʃ/ *adj* (**-er, -est**) (*infml*) (**a**) elegant or luxurious; smart: *a posh car, hotel* ○ *a posh wedding* ○ *You look very posh in your new suit.* (**b**) (*sometimes derog*) upper-class: *a posh accent* ○ *They live in the posh part of town.*

posit /ˈpɒzɪt/ *v* [Tn] (*fml*) suggest or assume (sth) as a fact; postulate.

position /pəˈzɪʃn/ *n* **1** [C] place where sb/sth is: *From his position on the cliff top, he had a good view of the harbour.* ○ *fix a ship's position*, ie by observing the sun or stars ○ *We were sitting in a draughty position near the door.* ○ *The troops stormed the enemy position*, ie where the enemy had placed soldiers and guns. **2** [U] state of being advantageously placed (eg in a competition or a war): *Several candidates had been manoeuvring for position long before the leadership became vacant.* **3** [C, U] way in which sb/sth is placed or arranged; attitude or posture: *sit/lie in a comfortable position* ○ *in an upright, a horizontal, etc position* ○ *They had to stand for hours without changing position.* **4** [C] ~ (**on sth**) view or opinion held by sb: *The candidates had to state their position on unilateral disarmament.* ○ *She has made her position very clear.* **5** [C esp *sing*] situation or circumstances, esp when they affect one's power to act: *Their failure to come to a decision put her in an impossible position.* ○ *He was in the unenviable position of having to choose between imprisonment or exile.* ○ *What would you do in my position?* ○ *I am not in a position* (ie I am unable) *to help you.* ○ *The economic position of the country is disastrous.* **6** (**a**) [C] place or rank in relation to others: *a high/low position in society* ○ *'What is his position in class?' 'He's third from the top.'* (**b**) [U] high rank or status: *people of position* ○ *Wealth and position were not important to her.* **7** [C] (*fml*) paid employment; job: *a position in/with a big company* ○ *He applied for the position of assistant manager.* ○ *She had worked for the firm for twenty years and was in a position of trust.* **8** [C] (*sport*) (in team games) function and/or part of the playing area assigned to a player: *'What position does he play?' 'Centre-forward.'* **9** (idm) **in a false position** ⇨ FALSE. **in/into position** in/into the right or proper place: *The orchestra were all in position, waiting for the conductor.* ○ *The runners got into position on the starting line.* **out of poˈsition** not at the right place: *The chairs are all out of position.*
▷ **position** *v* [Tn] **1** place (sth) in (a certain) position: *position the aerial for the best reception* ○ *She positioned herself near the warm fire.* **2** find or mark the position of (sth); locate: *They were able to position the yacht by means of radar.*

positional /-ʃənl/ *adj*.

positive /ˈpɒzətɪv/ *adj* **1** with no possibility of doubt; clear and definite: *positive instructions, orders, rules, etc* ○ *We have no positive proof of her guilt.* **2** ~ **(about sth/that ...)** (of a person) confidently holding an opinion; convinced: *Are you absolutely positive that it was after midnight?* ○ *She was quite positive about the amount of money involved.* **3 (a)** providing help; constructive: *make positive proposals, suggestions, etc* ○ *Try to be more positive in dealing with the problem.* **(b)** showing confidence and optimism: *a positive attitude, feeling, etc* ○ *positive thinking*, ie a determined mental attitude that helps one achieve success. **4** (*infml*) absolute; complete: *Her behaviour was a positive outrage.* ○ *It was a positive miracle that we arrived on time.* **5** (of the results of a test or an experiment) indicating that a substance is present: *a positive reaction* ○ *The tests proved positive.* ○ *They were hoping for a positive result from the experiment.* **6** (*mathematics*) (of a quantity) greater than zero: *a positive number* ○ *the positive sign*, ie +. **7** tending towards increase or improvement: *Positive progress has been achieved during the negotiations.* ○ *There have been positive developments in international relations.* **8** containing or producing the type of electrical charge produced by rubbing glass with silk: *a positive charge* ○ *the positive terminal of a battery*, ie the one through which electric current leaves the battery. **9** (of a photograph) showing light and shadows as in nature or in the object photographed, not reversed as in a negative: *a positive image.* Cf NEGATIVE. **10** (*grammar*) (of an adjective or adverb) in the simple form, not the comparative or superlative.

▷ **positive** *n* **1** (*grammar*) positive adjective: *'Silly' is the positive and 'sillier' the comparative.* **2** positive quality or quantity. **3** photograph printed from a negative plate or film.

positively *adv* **(a)** (*infml*) extremely; absolutely: *He was positively furious when he saw the mess.* ○ *She was positively bursting to tell us the news.* **(b)** with complete certainty; firmly: *She positively assured me that it was true.* ○ *Are you positively convinced that he is not coming back?*

positiveness *n* [U].

□ **ˌpositive discrimiˈnation** policy of favouring applicants for jobs from certain groups who have traditionally had difficulty obtaining them, eg women and members of ethnic minorities.

ˌpositive ˈpole (a) positive terminal of an electric battery; anode. **(b)** north-seeking pole of a magnet.

ˌpositive ˈvetting close examination of a person's character, background, political views, etc carried out by government officials to see if he is suitable to do work involving national security.

positivism /ˈpɒzɪtɪvɪzəm/ *n* [U] system of philosophy based on things that can be seen or proved rather than on speculation.

▷ **positivist** /-vɪst/ *n* person who studies or teaches positivism.

positron /ˈpɒzɪtrɒn/ *n* (*physics*) minute piece of matter (*elementary particle*) that has a positive electric charge and the same mass as an electron. Cf ELECTRON.

posse /ˈpɒsɪ/ *n* [CGp] (*esp US*) group of people who can be summoned by an officer of the law, eg a sheriff, to find a criminal, maintain order, etc.

possess /pəˈzes/ *v* **1** [Tn] **(a)** have (sth) as one's belongings; own: *He decided to give away everything he possessed and become a monk.* ○ *They possess property all over the world.* ○ *The family possessed documents that proved their right to ownership.* **(b)** have (sth) as a quality: *Does he possess the necessary patience and tact to do the job well?* **2** [Tn esp passive, Cn·t] control or dominate (a person's mind): *She seemed to be possessed (by the devil).* ○ *She was possessed by jealousy.* ○ *He is possessed with the idea that he is being followed.* ○ *What possessed you to do that?* **3** (idm) **be possessed of sth** (*fml*) have (a quality): *She is possessed of a wonderfully calm temperament.* **like one possessed** violently or with great energy, as if taken over by madness or a supernatural spirit: *He fought like a man possessed.*

▷ **possessor** *n* person who possesses sth: *He is at last the proud possessor of a driving-licence.*

possession /pəˈzeʃn/ *n* **1** [U] state of possessing; ownership: *fight for/win/get possession of the ball* ○ *The possession of a passport is essential for foreign travel.* ○ *On her father's death, she came into possession of a vast fortune.* ○ *She has valuable information in her possession.* ○ *The house is for sale with vacant possession*, ie without tenants. **2** [C esp *pl*] thing that is possessed; property: *He lost all his possessions in the fire.* ○ *He came here without friends or possessions and made his fortune.* **3** [C] country controlled or governed by another: *The former colonial possessions are now independent states.* **4** (idm) **in possession (of sth) (a)** having or controlling (sth) so that others are prevented from using it: *Their opponents were in possession of the ball for most of the match.* **(b)** having or living in sth: *He was caught in possession of stolen goods/with stolen goods in his possession.* ○ *While they are in possession we can't sell the house.* **possession is nine points of the ˈlaw** (*saying*) a person who occupies or controls sth is in a better position to keep it than sb else whose claim to it may be greater. **take possession (of sth)** (*fml*) become the owner or occupier (of sth).

possessive /pəˈzesɪv/ *adj* **1** ~ **(with sth/sb) (a)** showing a desire to own things and an unwillingness to share what one owns: *The child was very possessive with his toys.* **(b)** treating sb as if one owns him, demanding total attention or love: *possessive parents* ○ *She found her boyfriend's possessive behaviour intolerable.* **2** (*grammar*) of or showing possession: *the possessive case* ○ *'Anne's', 'the boy's', 'the boys'' are possessive forms.* ○ *'Yours', 'his', etc are possessive pronouns.*

▷ **possessive** *n* (*grammar*) **1** [C] possessive word or form: *'Ours' is a possessive.* **2 the possessive** [sing] the possessive case. Cf GENITIVE.

possessively *adv*.

possessiveness *n* [U].

posset /ˈpɒsɪt/ *n* type of drink made with warm milk and ale or wine with spices, used formerly as a remedy for colds.

possibility /ˌpɒsəˈbɪlətɪ/ *n* **1** [U] ~ **(of sth/doing sth)**; ~ **(that ...)** state of being possible; likelihood: *within/beyond the bounds of possibility* ○ *The possibility of breaking the world record never occurred to him.* ○ *Is there any possibility that we'll see you this weekend?* ○ *What is the possibility of the weather improving?* **2** [C] event that may happen; prospect: *changing jobs is one possibility* ○ *Bankruptcy is a distinct possibility if sales don't improve.* ○ *She prepared for all possibilities by taking a sunhat, a raincoat and a woolly scarf.* **3** [C esp *pl*] capability of being used or improved; potential: *The house is very dilapidated but it has possibilities.* ○ *She saw the possibilities of the scheme from the beginning.*

possible /ˈpɒsəbl/ *adj* **1 (a)** that can be done: *It is not humanly possible* (ie A human is not able) *to lift the weight.* ○ *Come as quickly as possible*, ie as quickly as you can. **(b)** that can exist or happen: *Frost is possible, although unlikely, at this time of year.* ○ *Are you insured against all possible risks?* **2** that is reasonable or acceptable: *a possible solution to the dispute*, ie one that may be accepted, although not necessarily the best ○ *There are several possible explanations.*

▷ **possible** *n* person who is suitable for selection, eg for a job or a sports team: *They interviewed 30 people of whom five were possibles.* ○ *a Rugby trial between 'probables' and 'possibles'.*

possibly /-əblɪ/ *adv* **1** perhaps: *'Will you be leaving next week?' 'Possibly.'* ○ *She was possibly the greatest writer of her generation.* **2** reasonably; conceivably: *I can't possibly lend you so much money.* ○ *I will come as soon as I possibly can.* ○ *You can't possibly take all that luggage with you.*

possum /ˈpɒsəm/ *n* **1** = OPOSSUM. **2** (idm) **play ˈpossum** (*infml*) pretend to be unaware of sth in order to deceive sb (as a possum pretends to be dead when being attacked).

post[1] /pəʊst/ *n* **1** [C] (esp in compounds) piece of metal or wood set upright in the ground to support sth, mark a position, etc: *ˈgate posts* ○ *a ˈgoal post* ○ *a ˈlamp-post*, ie supporting a street light ○ *a ˈsignpost* ○ *ˈboundary posts*, ie marking a boundary ○ *a ˈbedpost*, ie any of the upright supports of a bedstead, esp a four-poster. **2** [sing] place where a race starts or finishes: *the ˈstarting/ˈfinishing/ˈwinning post.* **3** (idm) **be left at the post** ⇨ LEAVE[1]. **deaf as a post** ⇨ DEAF. **first past the post** ⇨ FIRST[2]. **from pillar to post** ⇨ PILLAR. **pip sb at the post** ⇨ PIP[5].

▷ **post** *v* **1 (a)** [Tn, Tn·p] ~ **sth (up)** display (a notice, placard, etc) in a public place: *Post no bills*, eg warning that advertisements, etc must not be posted on a wall. ○ *Advertisements have been posted up everywhere announcing the new show.* **(b)** [esp passive: Tn, Cn·a, Cn·n/a] ~ **sb/sth (as sth)** announce sth about sb/sth by means of a poster, list, etc displayed publicly: *Details of the election will be posted outside the town hall.* ○ *The ship was posted (as) missing*, ie was announced as missing. **2** [Tn, Tn·p] ~ **sth (over)** cover sth with bills, placards, etc: *post a wall (over) with advertisements.*

post[2] /pəʊst/ *n* **1** position of paid employment; job: *He was appointed to the post of general manager.* ○ *She was offered a post in the new government.* ○ *She had been in the same post for 20 years.* ○ *He asked to be relieved of his post*, ie offered his resignation. **2** place where a person is on duty, esp a soldier on watch: *The sentries are all at their posts.* ○ *The guards were ordered not to leave their posts.* **3 (a)** place occupied and defended by soldiers, esp a frontier fort. **(b)** soldiers occupying this. **4** (also **ˈtrading post**) (esp formerly) settlement developed for trading, esp in a region that is undeveloped or sparsely populated.

▷ **post** *v* [Tn, Tn·pr] **1** ~ **sb (to sth)** appoint sb to a job or a responsibility: *post an officer to a unit, the front, overseas* ○ *After several years in London, he was posted to the embassy in Moscow.* **2** ~ **sb (at/on sth)** place (a soldier, etc) at his post[2](2): *We posted sentries (at the gates).* **posting** /-ɪŋ/ *n* (*esp Brit*) appointment to a post[2](1), esp an official one: *The ambassador expects that his next posting will be (to) Paris.*

post[3] /pəʊst/ *n* **1** (also *esp US* **mail**) **(a)** [C, U] letters, parcels, etc; correspondence: *There was a big post/a lot of post this morning.* ○ *He's dealing with his post at the moment.* **(b)** [U] official transport and delivery of these: *send sth by post* ○ *The parcel was damaged in the post.* **(c)** [C] any of the regular collections (esp from a post-box) or deliveries (eg to a house) of letters, etc: *catch/miss* (ie be in time/too late for) *the 2 o'clock post* ○ *The parcel came in this morning's post*, ie by this morning's delivery. **(d) the post** [sing] post-box or post office: *Please take these letters to the post.* **(e) the Post** [sing] = THE POST OFFICE. **2** [C] **(a)** (formerly) any of a number of men placed at stages along a route in order to ride to the next stage with letters, etc. **(b)** (formerly) cart, etc for carrying letters. **3** (idm) **by return post** ⇨ RETURN[2].

□ **ˈpost-bag** *n* **1** (*US* **ˈmail-bag**) bag for carrying post. **2** (*esp Brit infml*) letters received by sb at a particular time: *The newspaper received a huge post-bag of complaints.*

ˈpost-box (*US* **ˈmailbox**) *n* box where letters are placed for collection. Cf PILLAR-BOX (PILLAR).

ˈpostcard *n* card for sending messages by post without an envelope and often with a picture or photograph on one side. People send postcards when they go on holiday. A traditional postcard greeting is 'Wish you were here'. Cf LETTER-CARD (LETTER), PICTURE POSTCARD (PICTURE). ⇨ article at HUMOUR.

ˈpostcode (also **ˈpostal code**, *US* **ˈZip code**) *n* group of numbers (or letters and numbers) used as part of an address so that letters can by sorted by machine.

ˌpost-ˈfree *adv, adj* **(a)** (carried) free of charge by post or with postage already paid: *ˌpost-free deˈlivery* ○ *The book will be delivered post-free.* **(b)** (of a price) including the charge for postage: *a special offer at a post-free price of £5/at £5 post-free.*

Post Office

The British Post Office (formerly called the General Post Office, and still sometimes referred to as the 'GPO') traces its origins back to 1635, and was the first to issue postage stamps (in 1839) for sticking on letters.

The Post Office was a government department until 1969, when it became a public corporation. In principle it has the monopoly of mail deliveries, although the government has the power to license private firms to transport the mail, and a number of private courier agencies are licensed to transport urgent or valuable mail by motorcycle.

The main business of the Post Office is the delivery of letters and parcels and the selling of postage stamps, which it does through its department known officially as the 'Royal Mail'. ('Royal' refers to the origins of the Post Office in the service set up by King Charles I to carry the royal mails, and all post-boxes and post vans are marked with a royal crown and the initials of the sovereign. Thus ER is an abbreviation of the Latin for 'Elizabeth, Queen'.) A traditional type of post-box is the red pillar-box.

Britain has around 21 000 post offices, of which about 1 500 are main post offices in towns and cities, operated by the Post Office. The others, as 'sub-post offices', are run on an agency basis as part of a shop selling other goods. Most of these are in the suburbs of towns or in villages.

Post offices are open from 9.00 am to 5.30 pm daily and usually from 9.00 to 12.30 on Saturday mornings. They also provide a number of other services, including the payment of weekly pensions, the selling of vehicle registration licences ('tax disks'), national insurance stamps and television licences, and the operation of Girobank and National Savings Bank services.

Mail can be sent 'first class', for delivery usually the following working day, or 'second class', for delivery two or more days later. Second-class mail is cheaper than first-class. Money or valuable items can be sent 'registered mail', when they are insured against loss. A simpler form of service for important documents, but not for valuables, is 'recorded delivery', where compensation for loss is less. Both these services involve an extra fee, as does that of 'special delivery', which guarantees delivery on the next working day. An overnight door-to-door delivery service for important documents is 'Datapost'; a similar service that guarantees delivery the same day is called 'Datapost Sameday'.

For businesses, there are usually two deliveries of letters a day, in early and late morning, and one morning delivery of parcels. There is usually one delivery a day to homes. There are no deliveries on Sundays and most bank holidays. A Sunday collection of letters from post-boxes and post offices has been reintroduced, however, after being abolished in 1976.

Stamps are sold singly or in booklets, and can be bought either over the counter in post offices, from machines outside post offices, or from some shops. First-class and second-class stamps are used for postage within Britain, and first-class stamps for mail within the European Community. Postage rates to other countries vary according to distance and there is a choice of surface mail or the more expensive airmail.

All addresses in Britain have a postcode, a combination of letters and numbers that is unique to a street, or part of a street, or even to an individual building. For example, the postcode for the British Museum, London, is WC1B 3DG (with WC standing for the London postal district West Central) and for the Royal Mint in south Wales it is CF7 8YT (with CF standing for Cardiff, the nearest major town).

The US postal service began in Massachusetts in 1639. It was taken over by the government in 1707 and the Post Office Department was formed in 1775. In 1970 this was replaced by the US Postal Service, an independent government agency.

There are about 29 000 post offices in the USA, and mail is sent in one of four classes. First class, the most common, is for standard letters, postcards and other written matter. Second class mail is used for newspapers and magazines sent to regular subscribers. Third class is for printed matter and small parcels. Fourth class is for heavy parcels. There is also a special fourth class for books, films, sound tapes, computer data, etc.

All towns and cities in the USA have a 'Zip code', or distinctive 5-figure number, incorporated in their postal address. For example, the Zip code for part of San Francisco is 94101 (all California Zip codes begin with 9) and 33139 is a Miami Beach code (all Florida Zip codes begin with 32 or 33).

ˈpostman /-mən/ (*US* **ˈmailman**) (*pl* **-men**) *n* person employed to collect and deliver letters, etc. **ˌpostman's ˈknock** traditional children's game, in which one player (the 'postman') has to pretend to deliver a letter to another player who must kiss the postman to obtain it. **ˈpostmark** *n* official mark stamped on letters, parcels, etc giving the place and date of posting and cancelling the postage stamps: [attrib] *postmarked Tokyo* ○ *postmarked Friday*. **ˈpost office 1** building or room where postal business, eg sale of postage stamps, etc takes place. **2 the ˈPost Office** (also **the Post**) public department or corporation responsible for postal services. ⇨ article. **ˈpost-office box** (*abbr* **PˈO box**) numbered place in a post office where letters are kept until the person or company they are for collects them. **ˌpost-ˈpaid** *adj, adv* with postage already paid. **ˈpost-town** *n* town to which the post for a district is delivered.

post[4] /pəʊst/ *v* **1** (also *esp US* **mail**) **(a)** [Tn] put (a letter, etc) into a post-box or take it to a post office: *Could you post this letter for me?* **(b)** [Dn·n, Dn·pr] ~ **sth (to sb)** send (a letter, etc) to sb: *They will post me the tickets/post the tickets to me as soon as they receive my cheque.* **2 (a)** [Tn] (in bookkeeping) enter (an item) in a ledger: *post export sales.* **(b)** [Tn·p] ~ **sth up** (in bookkeeping) bring (a ledger) up to date by transferring items from a day-book: *post up a ledger.* **3** [Ipr] (formerly) travel by stages, using relays of horses: *post from town to town.* **4** (idm) **keep sb posted** keep sb informed of the latest developments, news, etc: *He asked them to keep him posted about the sales of his book.*

□ **ˌpost-ˈhaste** *adv* with great speed: *She went post-haste to the bank and cashed the cheque.*

post- *pref* (with *ns, vs* and *adjs*) after: *postgraduate* ○ *post-date* ○ *Post-Impressionist* ○ *post-school education.* ⇨ article. Cf ANTE-, PRE-.

postage /ˈpəʊstɪdʒ/ *n* [U] amount charged or paid for carrying letters, etc by post: *What is the postage on this parcel?* ○ *How much is the postage for an airmail letter to Canada?*

□ **ˈpostage stamp** small stamp[2](1) for sticking on letters, parcels, etc, showing the amount paid for postage.

postal /ˈpəʊstl/ *adj* **(a)** of the post[3](1b): *postal charges, workers, districts.* **(b)** sent by post[3](1b): *Postal applications must be received by 12 December.* ○ *If you will be on holiday on election day, you may apply for a postal vote.*

□ **ˈpostal code** = POSTCODE (POST[3]). **ˈpostal order** (*Brit*) (*US* **ˈmoney order**) official piece of paper bought from a post office, representing a certain sum of money that can be posted to a specified person who then can exchange it for that sum.

post-date /ˌpəʊstˈdeɪt/ *v* [Tn] **1** put a date on (a document, etc) that is later than the actual date: *a ˌpost-dated ˈcheque*, ie one which cannot be cashed until the date specified. **2** give to (an event) a date later than its actual date or the date previously given to it. **3** be or occur at a later date than (sth). Cf ANTEDATE.

poster /ˈpəʊstə(r)/ *n* **(a)** large placard displayed in a public place: *a poster advertising the circus.* **(b)** large printed picture: *Her bedroom is hung with posters.*

□ **ˈposter paint** (also **ˈposter colour**) type of artist's paint, in strong bright colours.

poste restante /ˌpəʊst ˈrestɑːnt; *US* reˈstænt/ (*US* also **general delivery**) department in a post office where letters for a person may be sent and kept until he collects them.

posterior /pɒˈstɪərɪə(r)/ *adj* (*fml*) **1** ~ **(to sth)** later (than sth) in time or in a series. Cf PRIOR[1]. **2** (in architecture, biology, medicine) placed behind or at the back; from the back: *a posterior view of the skull.* Cf ANTERIOR.

▷ **posterior** *n* (*infml joc*) buttocks: *a large posterior* ○ *a slap on the posterior.*

posterity /pɒˈsterətɪ/ *n* [U] **1** following or future generations: *plant trees for the benefit of posterity.* **2** (*fml*) person's children, grandchildren, etc; descendants: *recorded for posterity* ○ *Posterity will remember him as a truly great man.*

postern /ˈpɒstən/ *n* (*arch*) side or back entrance, esp a concealed entrance to a castle, etc: [attrib] *a postern door/gate.*

postgraduate /ˌpəʊstˈgrædʒʊət/ (*US* **graduate**) *adj* (of studies, etc) done after taking a first degree.

▷ **postgraduate** *n* person doing postgraduate studies. Cf GRADUATE, UNDERGRADUATE.

posthumous /ˈpɒstjʊməs; *US* ˈpɒstʃəməs/ *adj* **(a)** happening or given after death: *posthumous fame, earnings* ○ *the posthumous award of a medal for bravery.* **(b)** (of a literary work) published after its author's death: *Forster's posthumous novel.* **(c)** (of a child) born after its father's death. ▷ **posthumously** *adv*: *The prize was awarded posthumously.*

postilion (also **postillion**) /pɒˈstɪlɪən/ *n* (formerly) person whose job was to ride on one of the horses pulling a carriage.

postmaster /ˈpəʊstmɑːstə(r); *US* -mæst-/ *n* (*fem* **postmistress** /-mɪstrɪs/) person in charge of a post office.

□ **ˌPostmaster ˈGeneral** person in charge of the postal system of a country.

post-mortem /ˌpəʊst ˈmɔːtəm/ *n* **1** medical examination made after death in order to find the cause of death; autopsy: *A post-mortem showed that the victim had been poisoned.* ○ *The doctor carried out a post-mortem on the body.* **2** (*infml*) discussion or review of an event after it has happened: *a post-mortem on the election defeat.*

Post-school Education

In Britain, there are a number of ways to continue one's education after leaving secondary school at 16 or 18. Most post-school education is provided at universities, polytechnics, colleges of further or higher education, adult education centres, or various specialized colleges.

Degree-level courses are offered by universities, polytechnics and other institutions of higher education, with about half the total number of students at this level in universities.

Entrance to such courses normally depends on satisfactory General Certificate of Education (GCSE) and Advanced level (A level) results, and acceptance, usually after an interview, by the university or college concerned. Students do not normally apply to the university they wish to attend, but apply through the Universities' Central Council on Admissions (UCCA). Oxford and Cambridge Universities take part in UCCA but also have a system of entrance examinations and interviews by individual colleges.

All students on a university 'first degree' course are automatically eligible for a grant, awarded by a student's local education authority (LEA). The amount of the grant depends on the level of income of the student's family. Because entrance to higher education is selective, the majority of students successfully complete their course, which usually lasts three years. Most first degrees are for Bachelor of Arts (BA) or Bachelor of Science (BSc). A 'higher degree' is a postgraduate degree taken after a first degree, for example Master of Arts (MA) or Master of Science (MSc) . Students may then proceed to research degrees such as Master of Philosophy (MPhil) and Doctor of Philosophy (DPhil or, at some universities, PhD). For historical reasons, Oxford and Cambridge Universities award MA degrees to all first-degree graduates without requiring them to take a further examination.

There are just under 50 universities in Britain, of which one, Buckingham, is private, and one, the Open University (OU), is open to students of any age including those without formal qualifications. (The OU is not a resident university, but provides tuition by radio and television, in classes at local centres and at summer schools.) It has almost 100 000 students studying on first-degree and postgraduate courses, as well as on shorter courses. Most of them are employed people who study in their leisure time.

There are about 120 polytechnics and other institutions of higher education funded by central government through the Polytechnics and Colleges Funding Council. (Universities are also funded by central government through the Universities Funding Council.) Polytechnics and colleges offer not only first or higher degrees, but also other qualifications, such as a Diploma in Higher Education (DipHE), Higher National Diploma (HND) or Higher National Certificate (HNC). Polytechnics offer a wide range of subjects and many have close links with industry and commerce in their local area. In recent years, many specialist colleges (teacher training colleges, and colleges of art, architecture, music, etc) have been incorporated into polytechnics.

Teachers in Britain either do a first degree and then a one-year course leading to a Postgraduate Certificate of Education (PGCE), or do a four-year course leading to the degree of Bachelor of Education (BEd) at a polytechnic or similar college.

Colleges of further education (CFEs), which are funded, like schools, by local authorities, offer academic and vocational courses for students from the age of 16. It is possible to study for GCSEs and A levels at a CFE. In the private sector, there are many secretarial colleges offering business courses and language schools which specialize in teaching English as a foreign language.

Adult education centres offer a wide range of part-time courses, both academic and practical, including subjects like computer studies, foreign languages, carpentry, cookery and sports skills. They may be funded by local education authorities or by voluntary bodies. Universities also offer part-time courses in their 'extra-mural' or 'continuing education' departments.

In the USA, most post-school education takes place in colleges and universities. Colleges offer a four-year course to students aged between 18 and 22 and award bachelor's degrees in arts and sciences. The first two years (for 'freshmen' and 'sophomores' respectively) cover a broad range of subjects. Students specialize in a major subject area in their third ('junior') and fourth ('senior') years.

Colleges may be independent and privately controlled, or may operate as the undergraduate division of a university. There are also junior colleges, or 'community colleges' as they are increasingly called, offering two-year courses at the end of which they award 'associate in arts' degrees as their highest qualification.

Students do not gain a degree through a 'finals' examination, as they do in British universities, but through the number of 'credits' or hours of study they accumulate. Their work is regularly assessed, with all the credits and grades systematically recorded. At the end of the course, a student's overall record is examined to see if he or she deserves to be awarded a degree. Credits for work done like this can sometimes be transferred between universities, so that a student may gain credits in one university, move to a second, and receive a degree from a third.

American universities are of two kinds, state and private, most being private. Harvard was the first of these to be founded, in 1636, and was originally a college for the education of Puritan ministers. It is now one of the most prestigious in the country. The first state university was that of North Carolina, founded in 1795. Vassar, one of the leading women's colleges, was founded in 1861. Most private universities founded in the 19th century were funded by gifts from rich men. They include the well-known Johns Hopkins, Stanford and Chicago Universities.

Once they have completed high school, students can apply to any college or university they wish. Acceptance depends on high school grades, on the students' performances in a Standard Aptitude Test (SAT) which tests mathematical, verbal and analytical skills, and on the number of places available. All universities, even state ones, are fee-paying. The fees may be paid by a student's parents, but most students have to support themselves by 'working their way through college', that is, by taking part-time jobs and working all through the long summer vacation. The average annual cost of tuition, fees, and college room and board at a private university is about $11 000, although some of the more prestigious universities, such as Johns Hopkins in Baltimore, charge almost twice this. At a state university it is around $4 500 for state residents, and over $7 000 for non-state residents. At a two-year college, tuition and fees are about $4 700.

For much of the present century, the state universities were regarded as inferior to private ones. They have now improved their standards, however, and increased in academic status. Each US state now has one or more state universities. The State University of New York is essentially a 'multiversity', with over 20 individual colleges and about 150 000 students. California State University is similarly diverse, and although it has fewer colleges, it has at least 200 000 students. (Oxford and Cambridge, in Britain, have only about 13 000 students each).

In the USA, as in Britain, some universities are regarded as socially and academically superior to others. Although most colleges are now coeducational, colleges that were once exclusively for male students are known as the 'Ivy League', while those that were at one time solely for female students are called the 'Heavenly Seven'. Ivy League colleges (so called because they belong to a sports league of this name) are Harvard, Yale, Pennsylvania, Princeton, Columbia, Brown, Dartmouth and Cornell. Heavenly Seven colleges (named for their number, and sometimes also known as the 'Seven Sisters') are Barnard (part of Columbia University), Bryn Mawr, Mount Holyoke, Radcliffe (part of Harvard), Smith, Vassar and Wellesley.

American universities differ from British in their 'fraternities' and 'sororities'. These are basically social clubs for men and women students respectively. The name of each is made up of three Greek letters, for example 'Sigma Beta Chi', and the letters are worn on small badges called 'pins'. If a boy gives his 'fraternity pin' to a girl this is regarded as step on the way to an engagement or a proposal of marriage.

Both fraternities and sororities run private halls of residence known as 'fraternity houses' or 'sorority houses', and these are used for entertaining. Both fraternities and sororities exist independently of the university, and are usually organized on a national basis.

▷ **post-mortem** *adj* **(a)** made or occurring after death: *a post-mortem examination.* **(b)** (*infml*) occurring after an event has happened: *post-mortem recriminations.*

postnatal /ˌpəʊstˈneɪtl/ *adj* **(a)** occurring in the period after childbirth: *ˌpostnatal deˈpression.* **(b)** concerning a newborn child: *postnatal care* ○ *a postnatal nurse, unit.* Cf ANTENATAL, PRE-NATAL.

postpone /pəˈspəʊn/ *v* **1** [Tn, Tn·pr, Tg] ~ **sth (to sth)** arrange sth at a later time; defer sth: *The match was postponed to the following Saturday because of bad weather.* ○ *Let's postpone making a* *decision until we have more information.* Cf ADVANCE 6, CANCEL 1. **2** (idm) **postpone the evil ˈhour/ˈday** put off until a later time an unpleasant task, etc that one will eventually have to do.

▷ **postponement** *n* **(a)** [U] act of postponing or delaying: *Rain caused the postponement of several race-meetings.* **(b)** [C] instance of this: *After many difficulties and postponements, the ship was ready for launching.*

postprandial /ˌpəʊstˈprændɪəl/ *adj* (*fml*) happening immediately after a meal: *postprandial speeches* ○ (*joc*) *His postprandial nap was disturbed by the arrival of the boss.*

postscript /ˈpəʊsskrɪpt/ *n* ~ **(to sth)** **1** (*abbr* **PS**) extra message added at the end of a letter after the signature: *She mentioned in a postscript to her letter that the parcel had arrived.* **2** facts or information added to sth after it is completed: *There was an interesting postscript to these events when her private diaries were published.*

postulant /ˈpɒstjʊlənt; *US* -tʃʊ-/ *n* person who lives in a monastery or convent in preparation for entering a religious order. Cf NOVICE 2.

postulate /ˈpɒstjʊleɪt; *US* -tʃʊ-/ *v* [Tn, Tf] (*fml*) put (sth) forward as a fact or accept (sth) as true, esp as a basis for reasoning or argument: *The school building programme postulates an increase in educational investment.* ○ *He postulated that a cure for the disease will have been found by the year 2 000.*

▷ **postulate** /ˈpɒstjʊlət; *US* -tʃʊ-/ *n* thing assumed to be true, or accepted as a basis for reasoning or calculation: *the postulates of Euclidean geometry.* **postulation** /ˌpɒstjʊˈleɪʃn; *US* -tʃʊ-/ *n* [U, C].

posture /ˈpɒstʃə(r)/ *n* **1 (a)** [C] attitude or position of the body: *an awkward posture* ○ *The artist asked his model to take a reclining posture.* **(b)** [U] way in which a person holds himself as he stands, walks or sits: *She has very good posture.* ○ *Poor posture will give you backache.* **2** [C] way of looking at sth; attitude: *The government adopted an uncompromising posture on the issue of independence.* Cf STANCE.

▷ **posture** *v* **1** [I] stand, sit, etc in a self-conscious, exaggerated manner; pose: *Stop posturing in front of that mirror and listen to me!* **2** [Tn] put or arrange (sb) in a certain posture(1a): *posture a model.* **posturing** /ˈpɒstʃərɪŋ/ *n* [U, C esp *pl*] **(a)** standing, sitting, etc in a self-conscious, exaggerated manner. **(b)** behaving in an insincere or artificial manner, esp expressing views one does not really hold: *Her liberal views were soon revealed as mere posturing.* ○ *The electorate is growing tired of his posturings.*

post-war /ˌpəʊst ˈwɔ:(r)/ *adj* [esp attrib] existing or happening (in the period) after a war, esp the Second World War: *the post-war period of economic expansion* ○ *post-war developments in industry.*

posy /ˈpəʊzɪ/ *n* small bunch of flowers; bouquet.

pot¹ /pɒt/ *n* **1** [C] **(a)** round vessel made of earthenware, metal, etc for cooking things in: *pots and pans* ○ *a chicken ready for the pot.* **(b)** (esp in compounds) any of various types of vessel made for a particular purpose: *a ˈteapot* ○ *a ˈcoffee-pot* ○ *a ˈflowerpot* ○ *a ˈchamber-pot* ○ *a ˈlobster-pot.* ⇨ illus. **(c)** amount contained in a pot: *They've eaten a whole pot of jam!* ○ *Bring me another pot of coffee.* ⇨ illus. **2** [C esp *pl*] (*infml*) large sum; a lot of money: *making pots of money.* **3** [C] (*sl*) prize in an athletic contest, esp a silver cup. **4 the pot** [sing] (*esp US*) **(a)** total amount of the bets made on one hand in a card-game. **(b)** all the money pooled by a group of people for a common purpose, esp for buying food; kitty. **5** [C] = POT-BELLY a. **6** [U] (*sl*) marijuana. **7** [C] (*Brit*) (in billiards) stroke that sends the correct ball into one of the pockets. **8** [C] = POT-SHOT. **9** (idm) **go to ˈpot** (*infml*) be spoilt or ruined: *The firm is going to pot under the new management.* **keep the ˈpot boiling (a)** keep sth (eg a children's game) moving at a fast pace. **(b)** keep interest in sth alive. **put a quart into a pint pot** ⇨ QUART. **take ˌpot ˈluck** accept whatever is available, esp food at a meal, without any choice or alternative being offered: *You are welcome to eat with us, but you'll have to take pot luck.* ○ *We seldom book hotels when travelling, we usually just take pot luck.* **the ˌpot calling the ˈkettle black** (*saying*) the accuser having the same fault as the person he is accusing: *She accused us of being extravagant — talk about the pot calling the kettle black!*

□ **ˈpot-belly** *n* **(a)** (also **pot**) large protruding belly. **(b)** person who has this. **ˌpot-ˈbellied** *adj* **(a)** (of a person) having a pot-belly. **(b)** (*fig*) (of a container) curving out below the middle: *a pot-bellied stove*, ie one with a pot-bellied container in which the fuel burns.

ˈpot-boiler *n* book, picture, etc written or painted only to earn money: *She produced regular pot-boilers while also working on her masterpiece.*

ˈpot-bound *adj* (of a plant) having roots that fill its pot¹(1b) completely.

ˈpot-herb *n* any plant whose leaves, stems or roots are used in cooking to add flavour, esp to soups and stews.

ˈpot-hole *n* **1** deep hole worn in rock, eg in limestone caves by water. **2** rough hole in a road surface made by rain and traffic. **ˈpot-holer** *n.* **ˈpot-holing** *n* [U] (*sport*) exploring pot-holes in rocks and caves.

ˈpot-hunter *n* **(a)** (in shooting) person who shoots every bird or animal he sees and thinks only of profit rather than sport. **(b)** person who takes part in a contest only for the sake of the prize.

ˈpot plant plant grown in a flowerpot.

ˈpot-roast *n* piece of meat browned in a pot¹(1a) and cooked slowly with very little water.

ˈpot-shot (also **pot**) *n* **(a)** shot made without taking careful aim. **(b)** (*fig*) random attempt at sth.

pot² /pɒt/ *v* (**-tt-**) **1 (a)** [Tn esp passive] plant (sth) in a flowerpot: *a potted azalea.* **(b)** [Tn, Tn·p] ~ **sth (up)** plant (cuttings or seedlings) in a pot: *pot up chrysanthemum cuttings.* **2** [Tn] (*infml*) put (a baby or young child) on a chamber-pot. **3** [Tn] (in billiards) drive (a ball) into a pocket(6). **4** [Ipr] ~ **at sth** shoot at sth: *pot at a rabbit.* **5** [Tn] kill (sth) with a pot-shot: *They potted dozens of rabbits.* **6** [Tn esp passive] put (cooked meat or fish) in a pot in order to preserve it: *potted beef, ham, shrimps, etc.*

□ **ˈpotting-shed** *n* shed where plants are grown in pots (POT¹ 1b) before being planted outside.

potable /ˈpəʊtəbl/ *adj* (*fml*) fit for drinking; drinkable.

potash /ˈpɒtæʃ/ *n* [U] any of various salts of potassium (esp potassium carbonate) used to make fertilizers, soap and various chemicals.

potassium /pəˈtæsɪəm/ *n* [U] (*symb* **K**) chemical element, a soft shiny silvery-white metal occurring in ores and in the form of mineral salts and essential for all living things. It has few uses in its pure state, but it has many useful compounds, including potash, saltpetre (potassium nitrate) and potassium permanganate, used as a disinfectant. ⇨ App 11.

potation /pəʊˈteɪʃn/ *n* (*fml or joc*) **1** [U] act of drinking. **2** [C] drink, esp an alcoholic one.

potato /pəˈteɪtəʊ/ *n* (*pl* ~**es**) **1 (a)** [C] plant grown for its rounded starchy tubers which are eaten cooked as a vegetable: *The potato is vulnerable to several pests.* **(b)** [C] one of these tubers: *The potatoes are ready to be dug up.* ○ *Would you like another potato?* **(c)** [U] this served as food: *a dish of meat topped with mashed potato* ○ [attrib] *potato soup.* **2** (idm) **a hot potato** ⇨ HOT. **small potatoes** ⇨ SMALL.

□ **potato ˈcrisp** (*Brit*) (*US* **potato ˈchip**) = CRISP *n.*

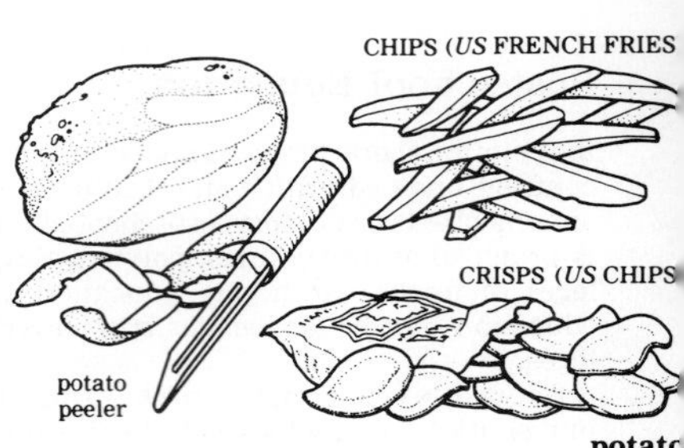

potato

ˈpotato beetle pest that destroys the leaves of potato plants.

poteen /pɒˈti:n/ *n* [U] (in Ireland) whisky made in an illicit still³.

potent /ˈpəʊtnt/ *adj* **1 (a)** (of drugs, etc) having a strong effect: *a potent charm, cure, medicine.* **(b)** having great power: *potent weapons.* **(c)** strongly persuasive; convincing: *potent arguments, reasoning, etc.* **2** (of males) capable of having sexual intercourse; not impotent. ▷ **potency** /-nsɪ/ *n* [U]. **potently** *adv.*

potentate /ˈpəʊtnteɪt/ *n* (esp formerly) ruler with direct power over his people; autocratic monarch: *the splendid court of an Eastern potentate.*

potential /pəˈtenʃl/ *adj* [attrib] **(a)** that can or may come into existence; possible: *a potential source of conflict* ○ *a potential leader* ○ *The book is arguably a potential best seller.* **(b)** in existence and capable of being developed or used: *potential energy, power, resources, etc* ○ *a machine with several potential uses.*

▷ **potential** *n* [U] **1 (a)** ~ **(for sth)** possibility of being developed or used: *She recognized the potential for error in the method being used.* ○ *He studied the German market to find the potential there for profitable investment.* **(b)** qualities that exist and can be developed: *exploit/fulfil/realize one's potential* ○ *She has artistic potential/potential as an artist.* ○ *The product has even more potential in export markets.* **2** energy of an electric charge expressed in volts; voltage: *a current of high potential.*

potentiality /pəˌtenʃɪˈælətɪ/ *n* (esp *pl*) (*fml*) power or quality that exists but has not been developed: *a country with great potentialities.*

potentially /-ʃəlɪ/ *adv*: *a potentially rich country*, ie one with many natural resources that could be developed ○ *a potentially catastrophic situation.*

□ **poˌtential ˈdifference** difference in the values of electric potential at two points in a field or circuit.

poˈtential energy energy that a body or system contains because of its position, state or shape rather than because of its motion. Gravitational energy and nuclear energy are types of potential energy. Cf KINETIC ENERGY (KINETIC).

potion /ˈpəʊʃn/ *n* (formerly) drink of medicine, poison or a liquid used in magic: *a ˈlove potion* ○ *The magician displayed his charms and potions.*

pot-pourri /ˌpəʊˈpʊərɪ; *US* ˌpəʊpəˈri:/ *n* **1** [C, U] mixture of dried petals and spices used to perfume a room, cupboard, etc. **2** [C] musical or literary medley.

potsherd /ˈpɒt-ʃɜ:d/ *n* (esp in archaeology) broken piece of pottery. Cf SHARD.

potted /ˈpɒtɪd/ *adj* **1** grown or preserved in a pot = POT² 1, 6. **2** (*often derog*) (of a book, etc) in a short simplified form: *a potted history of England* ○ *a potted version of 'Hamlet'* ○ (*fig*) *She gave her parents a potted version of the night's events*, ie an account that omitted anything disturbing.

Potter /ˈpɒtə(r)/ Beatrix (1866-1943), English writer of stories for children. She is famous for her tales of Peter Rabbit and his friends. She illustrated them herself, and set some of them in the *Lake District where she lived. ⇨ illus.

illustration from 'The Tale of Peter Rabbit' by Beatrix Potter

potter[1] /ˈpɒtə(r)/ (*US* **putter** /ˈpʌtər/) *v* **1** [I] work or move in a leisurely aimless way: *He loves to potter in the garden.* **2** (phr v) **potter about/around (sth) (a)** move from one place or thing to another in a leisurely way: *potter about the exhibition.* **(b)** work in an unhurried relaxed way, doing small or trivial tasks: *We spent the weekend pottering around (in) the house.*

▷ **potterer** /ˈpɒtərə(r)/ *n* (*often derog*) person who potters, esp one who never finishes a task.

potter[2] /ˈpɒtə(r)/ *n* person who makes earthenware pots by hand.

▷ **pottery** /ˈpɒtərɪ/ *n* **1** [U] earthenware pots, etc made by hand: *a valuable collection of Japanese pottery.* **2** [U] craft of making pots, esp by hand: *She is learning pottery.* ○ [attrib] *a pottery class.* **3** [C] place where pottery is made; potter's workshop. **4 the Potteries** [pl] district in Staffordshire, the centre of the English pottery industry. It is based on Stoke-on-Trent, which in the 19th century was six separate towns: Stoke-on-Trent, Burslem, Hanley, Longton, Fenton and Tunstall.

□ ˌ**potter's ˈwheel** horizontal revolving disc on which wet clay is shaped to make pots.

potty[1] /ˈpɒtɪ/ *adj* (**-ier**, **-iest**) (*Brit infml*) **1 (a)** (of a person or his behaviour) foolish or mad: *Surely you don't expect me to take your potty suggestions seriously?* ○ *He seems to have gone/to be quite potty.* ○ *That noise is driving me potty!* **(b)** ~ **about sb/sth** extremely enthusiastic about sb/sth: *She's potty about jazz.* **2** (*derog*) small or unimportant: *A person with his ambition won't stay long in a potty little firm like this.*

potty[2] /ˈpɒtɪ/ *n* (*infml*) child's chamber-pot.

□ ˈ**potty-trained** *adj* (of a baby or young child) no longer needing to wear a nappy.

pouch /paʊtʃ/ *n* **1** (esp in compounds) small (esp leather) bag carried in the pocket or attached to a belt: *a toˈbacco-pouch* ○ *an* ˌ*ammuˈnition-pouch.* **2** area of baggy loose skin, eg under the eyes of a sick person. **3 (a)** bag-like pocket of skin in which a female marsupial, eg a kangaroo, carries her young. **(b)** bag-like pocket of skin in the cheeks of some rodents, eg hamsters, in which they store and carry food.

▷ **pouch** *v* **1** [I, Tn, Tn·pr] (cause sth to) form a pouch: *wear a dress pouched over a belt.* **2** [Tn] put (sth) into a pouch; pocket: *to pouch a ball*, ie catch it, eg in cricket.

pouffe (also **pouf**) /pu:f/ *n* **1** large thick cushion used as a seat or for resting the feet on. **2** = POOF.

Poulenc /ˈpu:læŋk/ Francis (1899-1963), French composer. He had little formal training and his style is highly individual, often light and witty (eg the ballet music *Les Biches*), but serious and reflective in some of his songs and religious works.

poulterer /ˈpəʊltərə(r)/ *n* (*Brit*) person who sells poultry and game.

poultice /ˈpəʊltɪs/ *n* soft heated mass spread on a cloth and put on a sore place on the body to soothe pain, reduce swelling, etc: *a kaolin, mustard, etc poultice.*

▷ **poultice** *v* [Tn] put a poultice on (sth).

poultry /ˈpəʊltrɪ/ *n* **(a)** [pl *v*] hens, ducks, geese, turkeys, etc kept for eating or for their eggs; domestic fowls: *The poultry have been fed.* ○ [attrib] *poultry farming.* **(b)** [U] meat of these eaten as food: *Poultry is expensive at this time of year.* ○ *There's not much poultry in the shops.*

pounce /paʊns/ *v* [I, Ipr] ~ **(on sb/sth)** make a sudden attack by swooping or springing down: *We saw the tiger about to pounce (on the goat).* ○ *The hawk pounced on its prey and carried it off.* ○ *We hid behind the bushes, ready to pounce on the intruder.* ○ *(fig) pounce on a mistake*, ie spot it very quickly.

▷ **pounce** *n* [sing] sudden attack by pouncing.

Pound /paʊnd/ Ezra (1885-1972), American poet and critic. He had a great influence on 20th-century literature through his *Cantos* and his translations from Chinese and other languages. He championed the work of important writers such as T S *Eliot and James *Joyce. His assocation with Italian fascism during the Second World War greatly harmed his reputation and led to a period in a mental hospital.

pound[1] /paʊnd/ *n* **1** [C] **(a)** (*abbr* **lb**) standard measure of weight, 16 ounces in the avoirdupois system, equal to 0.454 kg: *Apples are sold by the pound.* ○ *The luggage weighs 40 lbs.* ○ *He's eaten a whole pound of plums!* **(b)** standard measure of weight, 12 ounces in the troy system, equal to 0.373 kg. ⇨ App 9, 10. **2** [C] (*symb* **£**) **(a)** (also ˌ**pound ˈsterling**) unit of British money; 100 pence: *The ticket will cost about a pound.* ○ *I've spent £5 on food today.* ○ [attrib] *a five-pound note*, ie a banknote for £5 ○ *a pound coin*, ie a coin worth £1. ⇨ App 9. Cf STERLING *n.* **(b)** unit of money of various other countries, eg Cyprus, Egypt, Ireland, Israel and Malta. **(c) the pound** [sing] value of the British pound on international money markets: *The Government is worried about the weakness of the pound (against other currencies).* **3** (idm) **(have, want, demand, etc) one's pound of ˈflesh** (insist on) receiving the full amount that is legally due to one even when it is morally offensive to do so: *Their distress had no effect on him — he was determined to have his pound of flesh.* **in for a penny, in for a pound** ⇨ PENNY. **penny wise pound foolish** ⇨ PENNY.

pound[2] /paʊnd/ *n* **1** (formerly) enclosed area in a village where cattle, etc that had strayed were kept until their owners claimed them. **2 (a)** place where stray cats and dogs are kept until their owners claim them. **(b)** place where motor vehicles that have been parked illegally are kept until their owners claim them.

pound[3] /paʊnd/ *v* **1** [Tn, Tn·pr] ~ **sth (to sth)** crush or beat sth with repeated heavy strokes: *pound crystals (to powder)* ○ *pound garlic (to a paste) in a mortar* ○ *The ship was pounded to pieces against the rocks.* **2** [Ipr, Ip, Tn] ~ **(away) (at/against/on sth)** hit (sth) with repeated heavy blows or gunfire: *the sound of feet pounding on the stairs* ○ *Someone was pounding at the door.* ○ *The heavy guns pounded (away at) the walls of the fort.* ○ *Who is that pounding (on) the piano?* **3** [I, Ipr] ~ **(with sth)** (of the heart) beat heavily: *a heart pounding (with fear)* ○ *She could feel her heart pounding painfully as she finished the race.* **4** (idm) **pound the ˈbeat** (*infml*) (esp of a policeman) regularly patrol an allotted district on foot. **5** (phr v) **pound along, down, up, etc** move in the direction specified with heavy rapid steps: *The horses came pounding along the track.* ○ *Don't pound up the stairs!*

poundage /ˈpaʊndɪdʒ/ *n* [U] **1** charge of a certain sum (eg 5p) per pound in value (£1). **2 (a)** charge of a certain sum (eg 5p) per pound in weight (1 lb). **(b)** charge of a certain amount (eg 3 oz) per pound in weight (1 lb).

pounder /ˈpaʊndə(r)/ *n* **1** thing that weighs a pound (1 lb). **2** (in compounds) **(a)** thing that weighs a specified number of pounds: *a three-pounder*, eg a fish weighing 3 lb. **(b)** gun that fires a shell of the specified number of pounds: *an eighteen-pounder*, ie a gun that fires shells weighing 18 lb each.

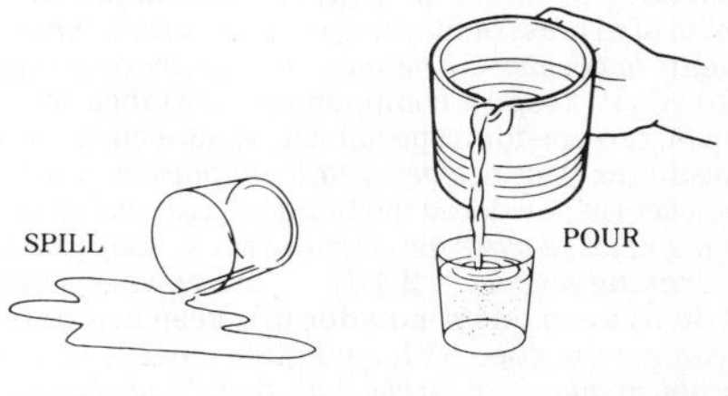

pour /pɔ:(r)/ *v* **1 (a)** [Ipr, Ip] (of a liquid or substance that flows like liquid) flow, esp downwards, in a continuous stream: *Blood was pouring from the wound.* ○ *I knocked over the bucket and the water poured (out) all over the floor.* ○ *Sweat was pouring down his face.* ○ *The ceiling collapsed and rubble poured into the room.* **(b)** [Tn, Tn·pr, Tn·p] cause (a liquid or substance that flows like liquid) to flow in a continuous stream: *Although I poured it carefully, I spilt some of the oil.* ○ *Pour the milk into a jug.* ○ *Pour out the water left in the bucket.* ⇨ illus. **(c)** [I, Ipr, Ip, Tn, Tn·pr, Tn·p, Dn·n, Dn·pr] ~ **sth (for sb)** serve (esp tea or coffee) (to sb) by putting it into a cup: *This teapot doesn't pour well.* ○ *Shall I pour (out) (the tea)?* ○ *I've poured two cups of coffee.* ○ *I've poured coffee into your cup by mistake.* ○ *Shall I pour you some tea?* ○ *Let me pour you a glass of wine.* ○ *I've poured a glass of wine for you.* **2** [I, Ipr, Ip] (of rain) fall heavily: *It's pouring (down).* ○ *She watched the rain pouring down the windows.* ○ (*infml*) *a pouring wet day.* **3** [Ipr, Ip, Tn·pr, Tn·p] (cause people or things to) come or go in a continuous stream: *Commuters were pouring into the station.* ○ *The fans poured out of the stadium cheering wildly.* ○ *The shops and offices pour millions of workers into the street at this time of day.* ○ *Letters of complaint poured in (to head office).* **4** (idm) **it never rains but it pours** ⇨ RAIN[2]. **pour oil on the ˈflames** make a bad situation worse. **pour oil on troubled ˈwaters** (try to) calm a disagreement, violent dispute, etc. **pour scorn on sb/sth** speak of sb/sth with contempt: *She poured scorn on the suggestion that he might never return.* **pour/throw cold water on sth** ⇨ COLD[1]. **5** (phr v) **pour (sth) out** (cause sth to) be expressed freely (and fully): *When he realized we knew the truth, the whole story came pouring out.* ○ *She poured out her troubles to me over a cup of coffee.*

Poussin /ˈpu:sæn/ Nicolas (1594-1665), French painter. He is most famous for his scenes from classical mythology set in idealized landscapes, but he also produced many paintings on subjects from the Bible.

pout /paʊt/ *v* **(a)** [I] push the lips or the lower lip forward, esp as a sign of annoyance or sulking: *Tell that child to stop pouting!* ○ *She pouted to show off her new lipstick.* **(b)** [Tn] push (the lips) forward in this way: *pout one's lips provocatively.*

▷ **pout** *n* (esp *sing*) pouting expression of the face. **poutingly** *adv* with a pout; sulkily.

poverty /ˈpɒvətɪ/ *n* [U] **1** state of being poor: *live in poverty* ○ *She had been worn down by poverty and illness.* **2** existing in too small amounts; scarcity or lack: *His work was criticized for its poverty of imagination.* ○ *They were handicapped by (a) poverty of resources.* **3** state of being inferior; poor quality: *the poverty of the soil* ○ *They were recognizable by the poverty of their dress.* **4** (idm) **grinding poverty** ⇨ GRINDING (GRIND). Cf POORNESS.

□ ˈ**poverty line** minimum level of income needed to buy the basic necessities of life: *There are still too many people living below the poverty line.*

ˈ**poverty-stricken** *adj* affected by poverty(1); extremely poor: *poverty-stricken families, homes, housing.*

ˈ**poverty trap** situation in which one is unable to

improve one's income because one depends on state benefits that are reduced as one's earnings increase.

POW /ˌpi: əʊ ˈdʌblju:/ *abbr* prisoner of war: *a POW camp.*

powder /ˈpaʊdə(r)/ *n* **1 (a)** [U] (substance in the form of a) mass of fine dry particles: *crush lumps of sugar to powder* ○ *The snow was as dry as powder.* **(b)** [C, U] (esp in compounds) substance in this form, esp one for a special use, eg as a cosmetic or medicine: *ˈface-powder* ○ *ˈtalcum powder* ○ *take a powder* (ie powdered medicine) *to cure indigestion* ○ *a special powder for cleaning fur* ○ *ˈsoap powder* ○ *ˈbaking-powder.* **2** [U] = GUNPOWDER (GUN). **3** (idm) **keep one's ˈpowder dry** keep in a state of readiness to cope with a possible emergency: *The problem may not arise, but there's no harm in keeping our powder dry.*

▷ **powder** *v* [Tn] put powder on (sth): *powder one's face/nose* ○ *powder a baby after her bath,* ie with talcum powder ○ *the fashion for powdered hair.* **powdered** *adj* (of a substance that is naturally liquid) dried and made into powder: *The paint is sold in powdered form.* ○ *powdered milk, eggs, etc.*

powdery /ˈpaʊdərɪ/ *adj* **1** like powder: *a light fall of powdery snow.* **2** covered with powder: *a powdery nose.*

□ ˌ**powder ˈblue** (of a) pale blue.

ˈ**powder-keg** *n* **1** small metal barrel for holding gunpowder. **2** (*fig*) potentially dangerous or explosive situation: *Rising tensions have turned the area into a powder-keg and any incident could set off a riot.*

ˈ**powder-magazine** *n* place where gunpowder is stored.

ˈ**powder-puff** (also **puff**) *n* soft fluffy pad used for applying face-powder.

ˈ**powder-room** (*euph*) ladies' lavatory in a department store, hotel, theatre, etc.

Powell[1] /ˈpəʊəl/ Anthony (1905-), English novelist. His most important work is the series of 12 novels, *A Dance to the Music of Time,* an often ironic account of English life and society in the 20th century.

Powell[2] /ˈpaʊəl/ Michael (1905-90), British film director. Films like *Black Narcissus,* made with his partner, Emeric Pressburger, were among the most innovative in the British cinema of the 1940s and 50s, but his career declined after the controversial *Peeping Tom.*

power /ˈpaʊə(r)/ *n* **1** [U] (in people) ability to do or act: *It is beyond/outside/not within my power* (ie I am unable or am not in a position) *to help you.* ○ *I will do everything in my power to help you.* **2 (a)** [U] (also **powers** [pl]) particular faculty of the body or mind: *He has lost the power of speech.* ○ *The drug affects one's power(s) of concentration.* ○ *He had to use all his powers of persuasion.* **(b) powers** [pl] all the faculties of a person's body or mind: *a woman of impressive intellectual powers* ○ *His powers are failing,* ie He is becoming weak. **3** [U] strength or energy behind or contained in sth: *There was a lot of power behind that blow.* ○ *The ship was helpless against the power of the storm.* ○ (*fig*) *They were defeated by the power of her oratory.* ⇨ Usage at STRENGTH. **4** [U] **(a)** control over others: *the power of the law* ○ *have sb in one's power,* ie be able to do what one wishes with sb ○ *have power over sb/sb's fate* ○ *fall into sb's power* ○ *He made the mistake of underestimating the power of the press.* **(b)** political control; rule: *seize power,* ie in a political coup ○ *This government came (in)to power at the last election.* **5** [C esp *pl*] right possessed by or given to a person or group; authority: *The powers of the police need to be clearly defined.* ○ *The President has exceeded his powers,* ie has done more than he is allowed or has the right to do. ○ (*law*) *power of attorney,* ie the authority to act on sb's behalf in business or financial matters. **6** [C] person, group or state with great authority or influence: *world powers,* ie countries with the most influence in international affairs ○ *'Is the press a great power in your country?' 'Yes, it's far more important than the Church.'* ○ *The country was a great naval power in past centuries,* ie had great international influence because it had a large navy. ○ *No power on earth could force me to do it.* **7** [U] **(a)** energy that can be harnessed and used to do work: *wind, nuclear, hydroelectric power* ○ *We need to provide industry with power it can afford.* ○ [attrib] *the power supply.* **(b)** [attrib] operated by mechanical or electrical energy: *power brakes/steering* ○ *power tools.* **(c)** (of an engine, etc) capacity or performance: *a car's power of acceleration* ○ *the terrifying power of the huge machine.* **8** [C esp *sing*] (*mathematics*) result obtained by multiplying a number by itself a certain number of times: *the third power of 2* ($= 2 \times 2 \times 2 = 8$) ○ *the second, third, fourth, etc power of x* ($= x^2, x^3, x^4$, *etc*) ○ *to the power of sth,* ie multiplied by itself a certain number of times ○ 4^5 *represents four to the power of five,* ie $4 \times 4 \times 4 \times 4 \times 4 = 1024$. **9** [U] (of a lens) capacity for magnifying: *the power of a microscope, telescope, etc.* **10** [C] good or evil spirit: *She believed in the existence of a benevolent power.* ○ *the powers of darkness,* ie the forces of evil or of the Devil. **11** (idm) **the corridors of power** ⇨ CORRIDOR. **do sb a ˈpower of good** (*infml*) be very beneficial to sb: *Her holiday has done her a power of good.* ○ *A long cool drink would do us all a power of good!* **in ˈpower** having control or authority: *the party in power* ○ *The Government has been in power for two years.* **more power to sb's ˈelbow** (*infml*) (used to express encouragement to sb doing sth): *She is campaigning for an improved bus service — more power to her elbow!* **the (real) power behind the ˈthrone** the person who really controls an organization, a country, etc, in contrast to the person who is legally in charge: *The President's wife was suspected of being the real power behind the throne.* **the ˌpowers that ˈbe** (*often ironic*) people who control an organization, a country, etc: *He was waiting for the powers that be to decide what his next job would be.*

▷ **powered** *adj* equipped with or operated by mechanical energy: *a new aircraft powered by Rolls Royce engines* ○ *a high-powered car* ○ (*fig*) *rather low-powered political discussions.*

□ ˈ**power-boat** *n* boat with an engine, esp a very powerful one, for racing or towing water-skiers.

ˈ**power cut** interruption in the supply of electricity: *the violent storms caused several power cuts.*

ˈ**power-dive** *n* steep dive made by an aircraft with its engines working. — *v* [I] (of an aircraft) make such a dive.

ˈ**power house 1** = POWER-STATION. **2** (*fig*) **(a)** very powerful group, organization, etc. **(b)** very strong or energetic person.

ˈ**power-point** *n* socket on a wall, etc where electrical appliances can be plugged in to an electric circuit.

ˈ**power politics** political action or diplomacy based on the threat of using force.

ˈ**power-station** (*US* ˈ**power plant**) *n* building where electricity is generated: *a coal-fired power-station* ○ *a nuclear power-station.*

powerful /ˈpaʊəfl/ *adj* **(a)** of or having great power: *a powerful blow* ○ *a powerful machine, motor bike, engine, etc.* **(b)** having a strong effect: *a powerful image, remedy, speech* ○ *a powerful appeal to the public's sense of justice.* **(c)** physically strong: *powerful legs* ○ *a man with a powerful physique.* **(d)** having great control or influence: *a powerful enemy, nation, ruler, trade union.* ▷ **powerfully** /-fəlɪ/ *adv*: *He is very powerfully built,* ie has a large strong physique.

powerless /ˈpaʊəlɪs/ *adj* **1** without power or strength: *render sb powerless.* **2** ~ **to do sth** completely unable to do sth: *I am powerless to intervene in the matter.* ○ *They were powerless to resist.* ▷ **powerlessly** *adv.* **powerlessness** *n* [U].

powwow /ˈpaʊwaʊ/ *n* **1** meeting or conference of N American Indians. **2** (*infml*) meeting to discuss sth: *hold a powwow.*

▷ **powwow** *v* [I, Ipr] ~ **(about sth)** (*infml*) have a discussion (about sth).

Powys /ˈpaʊɪs/ county in central Wales, on the border with England. ⇨ map at App 1.

pox /pɒks/ *n* **1 the pox** [sing] = SYPHILIS. **2** [U] (in compounds) disease that causes pock-marks: *ˈsmallpox* ○ *ˈchicken-pox.*

pp *abbr* **1** pages. **2** /ˌpi: ˈpi:/ (also **per pro** /pɜ: ˈprəʊ/) (before a signature) on behalf of (Latin *per procurationem*): *pp J E Symonds,* eg signed by his secretary in his absence. **3** (*music*) very softly; very quietly (Italian *pianissimo*). Cf FF 2.

PPE /ˌpi: pi: ˈi:/ *abbr* (*Brit*) (esp at Oxford University) philosophy, politics and economics: *a degree in PPE.*

PPS /ˌpi: pi: ˈes/ *abbr* **1** Parliamentary Private Secretary. **2** (also **pps**) (esp at the end of a letter) additional postscript (Latin *post postscriptum*). Cf PS 2.

PR /ˌpi: ˈɑ:(r)/ *abbr* **1** proportional representation. **2** (*infml*) public relations: *a PR exercise,* ie one that aims to create goodwill while not solving problems or achieving results.

Pr *symb* praseodymium.

pr *abbr* **1** (*pl* **prs**) pair. **2** price.

practicable /ˈpræktɪkəbl/ *adj* **1** that can be put into practice; workable: *a practicable scheme, solution, suggestion, etc.* **2** (of roads, etc) fit to be used by traffic; passable: *The mountain route that is practicable only in summer.* Cf IMPRACTICABLE. ▷ **practicability** /ˌpræktɪkəˈbɪlətɪ/ *n* [U]. **practicably** /-əblɪ/ *adv.*

practical /ˈpræktɪkl/ *adj* **1** concerned with practice(1) and action rather than theory: *practical experience, skills* ○ *It's an interesting idea but there are many practical difficulties.* Cf THEORETICAL 1. **2** suitable for the purpose for which it was made; useful: *a practical device with many different uses* ○ *practical clothing for outdoor sports* ○ *Your invention is ingenious, but not very practical.* **3 (a)** (of a person) clever at doing and making things: *She's very practical.* ○ *He has a practical partner who organizes everything for him.* **(b)** sensible and realistic: *We must be practical and work out the cost before we make a decision.* **4** that is so in effect; virtual: *The owner's brother has been in practical control of the firm for years.* **5** (idm) **for (all) ˈpractical purposes** as far as really matters; in reality: *The sale was supposed to last for a week, but for all practical purposes it's over.* Cf IMPRACTICAL.

▷ **practical** *n* (*infml*) practical(1) examination or lesson, eg in a scientific subject: *a physics practical.*

practicality /ˌpræktɪˈkælətɪ/ *n* **1** [U] quality or state of being sensible and realistic: *He questioned the practicality of the proposal.* **2 practicalities** [pl] practical(1) matters rather than ideas: *We need to start discussing practicalities.*

practically /-klɪ/ *adv* **1** almost; virtually: *It rained practically every day.* ○ *His work is practically unknown here.* **2** in a practical manner: *She solved the problem very practically.*

□ ˌ**practical ˈjoke** trick played on sb for amusement, usu involving some physical action: *The children put salt in the sugar bowl as a practical joke.* ˌ**practical ˈjoker** person who plays practical jokes.

practice /ˈpræktɪs/ *n* **1** [U] actual doing of sth; action as contrasted with theory: *put a plan into practice* ○ *The idea would never work in practice,* ie It seems good in theory but would be useless if carried out. **2 (a)** [U] regularly repeated exercise done in order to improve one's skill: *an hour's practice every day* ○ *Playing the piano well requires a lot of practice.* ○ [attrib] *a practice game.* **(b)** [C] period of time spent doing this: *The players will meet for a practice in the morning.* **3 (a)** [U] way of doing sth that is common or habitual: *It is accepted/standard practice to pay a deposit with one's order.* ○ *Paying bills promptly is good financial practice.* ○ *It is the practice in Britain to drive on the left.* **(b)** [C] thing done regularly; habit or custom: *the practice of closing shops on Sundays* ○ *I had coffee after dinner, as is my usual practice.* **4 (a)** [U] work of a doctor or lawyer: *a doctor working in general practice,* ie as a family doctor ○ *She has retired from practice/is no longer in practice.* **(b)** [C] (place of) business of a doctor or lawyer: *a medical/legal* practice ○ *a group practice*, ie a partnership of several doctors ○ *His practice is in the centre of the city.* ○ *She has just bought (into) a very profitable practice.* **5** [U] **(a)** (esp of a doctor or lawyer) practising one's profession: *the practice of law/medicine.* **(b)** exercising one's faith, etc: *the practice of one's religion.* **6** (idm) **ˌin/ˌout of ˈpractice** having/not having spent time doing practice: *It's important to keep in practice* ○ *If you don't play, you'll get out of practice.* **make a habit/practice of sth** ⇨ HABIT. **ˌpractice makes ˈperfect** (*saying*) doing sth (eg a skill or craft) repeatedly is the only way to become very good at it. **sharp practice** ⇨ SHARP.

practician /prækˈtɪʃn/ *n* = PRACTITIONER.

practise (*US* **practice**) /ˈpræktɪs/ *v* **1** [I, Ipr, Tn, Tn·pr, Tg] ~ **(sth) (on sth)** do sth repeatedly or regularly in order to improve one's skill: *I haven't been practising enough.* ○ *She's practising (a new piece) on the piano.* ○ *I need to practise my Italian before my business trip.* ○ *Practise throwing the ball into the net.* **2** [Tn] make (sth) part of one's behaviour by doing it regularly: *practise economy, patience, self-control, etc.* **3** [I, Ipr, Tn] ~ **(as sth)** work as a doctor or lawyer: *Does he still practise?* ○ *She practised as a solicitor for many years.* ○ *practise homoeopathic medicine.* **4** [I, Tn] do (sth) actively: *He was a Catholic but didn't practise (his religion).* ○ *a practising Anglican.* **5** (idm) **ˌpractise what one ˈpreaches** do habitually oneself what one tells others to do.

▷ **practised** (*US* **-ticed**) *adj* ~ **(in sth)** expert, esp as a result of much practice; experienced: *He performed the job with practised skill.* ○ *practised in the art of deception.*

practitioner /prækˈtɪʃənə(r)/ (also **practician**) *n* **1** person who practises a skill or an art. **2** person who practises a profession, esp medicine: *a general practitioner.*

Prado /ˈprɑːdəʊ/ **the Prado** national art gallery of Spain in Madrid. It houses many examples of the great Spanish painters and from the Venetian and Flemish schools, as well as *Picasso's *Guernica*.

praesidium = PRESIDIUM.

Praetorian Guard /prɪˌtɔːrɪən ˈɡɑːd/ **the Praetorian Guard** soldiers who formed the bodyguard of the emperor in ancient Rome.

pragmatic /præɡˈmætɪk/ *adj* **1** treating things in a sensible and realistic way; concerned with practical results: *a politician valued for his pragmatic approach* ○ *a pragmatic solution to the problem.* **2** of or concerning pragmatism(2). ▷ **pragmatically** /-klɪ/ *adv.*

pragmatism /ˈpræɡmətɪzəm/ *n* [U] (*fml*) **1** thinking about or treating things in a practical way. **2** (in philosophy) belief that the truth or value of a theory can only be judged by its practical results.

▷ **pragmatist** /-tɪst/ *n* **1** person who acts in a practical way. **2** believer in pragmatism(2).

prairie /ˈpreərɪ/ *n* wide area of level grassland, esp in N America; plain[2]. Cf PAMPAS, SAVANNAH, STEPPE, VELD.

□ **ˌprairie ˈchicken** type of brown N American grouse.

ˈprairie-dog *n* small N American burrowing animal with a bark like a dog's.

ˌprairie ˈoyster raw egg mixed with Worcester sauce or other spicy flavourings, traditionally swallowed as a cure for a hangover.

ˌprairie ˈschooner (*US*) covered wagon used by pioneers in the American West.

ˌprairie ˈwolf = COYOTE.

praise[1] /preɪz/ *v* **1** [Tn, Tn·pr, Cn·n/a] ~ **sb/sth (for sth)**; ~ **sb/sth as sth** express approval or admiration for sb/sth: *The guests praised the meal.* ○ *He was obviously expecting to be praised.* ○ *He praised her for her courage.* ○ *Critics praised the work as highly original.* **2** [Tn] honour or glorify (God) in prayer; worship. **3** (idm) **praise, etc sb to the skies** ⇨ SKY.

praise[2] /preɪz/ *n* [U] **1** expression of approval or admiration; act of praising (PRAISE[1] 1): *high* (ie great) *praise* ○ *courage beyond* (ie too great for) *praise* ○ *He received praise from his colleagues for winning the prize.* ○ *an achievement worthy of great praise* ○ *The leader spoke in praise of those who had died for their country.* **2** worship (of God); glory: *a hymn of praise* ○ *Praise be (to God)*, ie Thank goodness! **3** (idm) **be loud in one's praise** ⇨ LOUD. **damn sb/sth with faint praise** ⇨ DAMN[1]. **sing sb's/sth's praises** ⇨ SING.

▷ **ˈpraiseworthy** /-wɜːðɪ/ *adj* deserving praise; commendable: *a very praiseworthy achievement.* **praiseworthily** /-ðɪlɪ/ *adv.* **praiseworthiness** *n* [U].

praline /ˈprɑːliːn/ *n* sweet[2](1) made by browning nuts in boiling sugar, used esp as a flavouring or filling for chocolate confectionery.

pram /præm/ *n* (*Brit*) (*US* **ˈbaby buggy**, **baby carriage**, **buggy**) four-wheeled carriage, pushed by hand, for a baby.

prance /prɑːns; *US* præns/ *v* **1** [I] (of a horse) move jerkily by raising the forelegs and springing forward from the hind legs. **2** (phr v) **prance about**, **along**, **around**, **in**, **out**, **etc** move in the specified direction in a high-spirited or arrogant way: *She was prancing along in her new outfit.* ○ *He pranced out of the room in a fury.* ○ *They were prancing about* (ie jumping or dancing happily) *to the music.*

▷ **prance** *n* [sing] prancing movement.

prang /præŋ/ *v* [Tn] (*sl esp Brit*) damage (a vehicle) in a crash: *He's pranged his new bike.*

▷ **prang** *n* (damage caused to a vehicle in a) crash: *He's had a bit of a prang.*

prank /præŋk/ *n* playful or mischievous trick: *a childish prank* ○ *play a prank on sb.*

▷ **prankster** /ˈpræŋkstə(r)/ *n* person who plays pranks.

praseodymium /ˌpreɪzɪəʊˈdɪmɪəm/ *n* [U] (*symb* **Pr**) chemical element, a soft silvery metal. It is used in certain alloys and its compounds are used for colouring glass and ceramics.

prat /præt/ *n* (*Brit sl derog*) foolish or irritating person.

□ **ˈpratfall** *n* (*esp US*) **1** fall on the buttocks, esp in slapstick comedy. **2** (*sl*) stupid mistake.

prate /preɪt/ *v* (*derog*) **(a)** [I, Ip] ~ **(on about sth)** talk or chatter too much (about sth): *Listen to him prating on about nothing.* **(b)** [I] talk (foolishly): *a prating idiot.*

prattle /ˈprætl/ *v* [I, Ip] **1** ~ **(away)** (of a child) talk in a simple way; babble: *The baby is prattling (away) happily in her cot.* **2** (*often derog*) ~ **(on about sth)** (of an adult) talk at length, esp about unimportant things: *prattle on about the village gossip.*

▷ **prattle** *n* [U] unimportant chatter; gossip. **prattler** /ˈprætlə(r)/ *n* (*often derog*) person who prattles (PRATTLE b).

prawn /prɔːn/ *n* type of edible shellfish like a large shrimp: [attrib] *a ˌprawn ˈcocktail*, ie a dish of prawns served with mayonnaise.

pray /preɪ/ *v* **1** [I, Ipr, Tn·pr, Tf, Tt] ~ **(to sb) (for sb/sth)**; ~ **sb (for sth)** offer thanks, make requests known, etc (to God): *The priest prayed for the dying man.* ○ *They prayed (to God) for an end to their sufferings/for their sufferings to end.* ○ *They prayed that she would recover.* ○ *She prayed to be forgiven/(to) God for forgiveness.* **2** [Tn·pr, Dn·t] ~ **sb (for sth)** (*dated fml*) ask sb (for sth/to do sth) as a favour; beg: *We pray you for mercy/to show mercy.* ○ *We pray you to set the prisoner free.* **3** (idm) **hope and pray** ⇨ HOPE.

prayer /preə(r)/ *n* **1 (a)** [C] ~ **(for sth)** solemn request to God or to an object of worship: *say one's prayers* ○ *a prayer for forgiveness, rain, success* ○ *He arrived, as if in answer to her prayers.* **(b)** fixed form of words used for this: *the Lord's Prayer* ○ *prayers he had learnt as a child.* **2** [U] action of praying: *spend time in prayer* ○ *Let us kneel in prayer.* ○ *She believed in the power of prayer.* **3 (a)** [sing] form of religious service consisting mainly of prayers: *Evening/Morning Prayer.* **(b) prayers** [pl] informal meeting in order to pray: *family/morning/evening/daily prayers.* **4** (idm) **not have a ˈprayer** (*infml*) have no chance of sth: *I've applied for the job but I know I haven't got a prayer*, ie I won't get it.

In Britain, the saying of prayers is not confined to places of worship. For example, the House of Commons starts each day of parliamentary business with prayers, and prayers are sometimes said when a new building is opened or when a ship is launched. Pupils in schools and colleges sometimes say a short prayer (called 'grace') before and after meals. Children are sometimes brought up to say their prayers before getting into bed at the end of the day.

□ **ˈprayer-book** *n* **(a)** book containing prayers, for use in church, etc. **(b) the ˈPrayer Book** (also **the ˌBook of ˌCommon ˈPrayer**) prayer-book used in Anglican services.

ˈprayer-mat (also **ˈprayer-rug**) *n* small carpet on which Muslims kneel when praying.

ˈprayer-meeting *n* (esp in Protestant churches) meeting where people say personal prayers aloud to God.

ˈprayer-wheel *n* revolving drum-shaped box inscribed with or containing prayers, used esp by Tibetan Buddhists.

pre- *pref* (used fairly widely with *vs*, *ns*, *adjs* and *advs*) before: *pre-cook* ○ *prefabricate* ○ *pre-medication* ○ *pre-Christian* ○ *prematurely.* Cf ANTE-, POST-.

preach /priːtʃ/ *v* **1 (a)** [I, Ipr] ~ **(to sb) (about/against/on sth)** give a sermon, esp in church: *The vicar preached to the congregation for half an hour.* ○ *He preaches well.* ○ *What did he preach about/on?* ○ *He preached against violence.* **(b)** [Tn, Dn·pr] ~ **sth (to sb)** give (a sermon): *He preaches the same sermon every Christmas.* **(c)** [Tn, Dn·pr] ~ **sth (to sb)** make (a religion or teaching) known by talking about it publicly; teach (sth): *preach the Gospel/the word of God* ○ *They preached the new doctrines throughout Europe.* **2** [Tn] try to persuade people to accept or support (sth); advocate: *She preached economy as the best means of solving the crisis.* ○ *He was always preaching the virtues of capitalism.* **3** [I, Ipr] ~ **(at/to sb)** (*often derog*) give unwanted advice on morals, behaviour, etc, esp in a persistent, annoying manner: *I am tired of listening to you preach (at me).* ○ *You are in no position to preach to me about efficiency!* **4** (idm) **practise what one preaches** ⇨ PRACTISE. **preach to the conˈverted** speak to people in support of views that they already hold: *Telling conservationists that we need to preserve the natural heritage really is preaching to the converted!*

▷ **preacher** *n* person who preaches, esp a clergyman who preaches sermons: *a good preacher* ○ *a preacher famous for his inspiring sermons.*

preamble /priːˈæmbl/ *n* [C, U] ~ **(to sth)** opening statement explaining the purpose of the book, document, lecture, etc that follows: *He launched into his statement without any preamble.*

pre-arrange /ˌpriːəˈreɪndʒ/ *v* [Tn] arrange (sth) in advance: *Run to your positions when you hear the prearranged signal.* ▷ **pre-arrangement** *n* [U].

prebend /ˈprebənd/ *n* (*religion*) income paid to a priest from the revenue of a church, esp a cathedral.

▷ **prebendary** /ˈprebəndrɪ; *US* -derɪ/ *n* priest who receives a prebend.

Precambrian /ˌpriːˈkæmbrɪən/ *adj* of the geological period that lasted from the time of the origin of the earth about 4600 million years ago until the beginning of the *Cambrian period and the *Palaeozoic era about 590 million years ago. During this period micro-organisms are the only living things known to have existed.

▷ **the Precambrian** *n* this period.

precarious /prɪˈkeərɪəs/ *adj* **1** depending on chance; uncertain: *She makes a rather precarious living as a novelist.* **2** unsteady; unsafe: *He was unable to get down from his precarious position on the rocks.* ▷ **precariously** *adv*: *to perch precariously* ○ *They lived precariously on the income from a few small investments.* **precariousness** *n* [U].

pre-cast /ˌpriːˈkɑːst; *US* -ˈkæst/ *adj* (of concrete) made into blocks ready for use in building.

precaution /prɪˈkɔːʃn/ *n* ~ **(against sth)** thing done in advance to avoid danger, prevent problems, etc: *take an umbrella just as a precaution* ○ *fire precautions/precautions against fire* ○ *I took the precaution of locking everything in the safe.*

▷ **precautionary** /prɪˈkɔːʃənərɪ; *US* -nerɪ/ *adj* done as a precaution; preventive: *precautionary measures.*

precede /prɪˈsiːd/ *v* **1** [I, Tn] come or go before (sth) in time, order, rank, etc: *The Mayor entered, preceded by members of the council.* ○ *This point has been dealt with in the preceding paragraph.* ○ *the days that preceded the final catastrophe.* **2** [Tn·pr] ~ **sth with sth** say sth before sth: *She preceded her speech with a vote of thanks to the committee.*

precedence /ˈpresɪdəns/ *n* [U] ~ **(over sb/sth)** right to come before sb/sth in time, order, rank, etc: *The longest-serving officer always takes precedence.* ○ *The elder son has precedence over the younger one.* ○ *The needs of the community must take precedence over* (ie must be met before) *individual requirements.* ○ *a list of the English aristocracy in order of precedence,* ie in order of social rank.

precedent /ˈpresɪdənt/ *n* **(a)** [C] earlier decision, case, event, etc that is regarded as an example or rule for what comes later: *create/establish/set a precedent (for sth)* ○ *serve as a precedent for sth* ○ *There is no precedent for such an action.* **(b)** [U] existing precedents (used esp in the expressions shown): *without precedent* ○ *break with precedent,* ie not act according to precedents.

▷ **precedented** *adj* having or supported by a precedent: *a decision not precedented in English law.*

precentor /prɪˈsentə(r)/ *n* clergyman who is in charge of the music in a cathedral and (often) leads the singers.

precept /ˈpriːsept/ *n* **1** [C] rule or guide, esp for behaviour: *follow the precepts of one's religion* ○ *He lived by the precept 'practise what you preach'.* **2** [U] moral instruction: *Example is better than precept.*

▷ **preceptor** /prɪˈseptə(r)/ *n (fml)* teacher.

precession /prɪˈseʃn/ *n* [U] (also **preˌcession of the ˈequinoxes**) gradual change in the angle at which the earth revolves daily, causing the equinoxes to occur slightly earlier in each successive year.

precinct /ˈpriːsɪŋkt/ *n* **1** [C] area enclosed by definite boundaries, esp the walls of a cathedral, church or college: *a sacred precinct* ○ *these hallowed precincts.* **2** [C] *(Brit)* area in a town for specific or restricted use, esp one where vehicles may not enter: *a shopping precinct* ○ *a pedestrian precinct.* **3** [C] *(US)* subdivision of a county, city, etc: *an election precinct* ○ *a police precinct.* **4 precincts** [pl] **(a)** boundaries; limits: *No parking within the hospital precincts.* **(b)** area around a place; environs: *the old city and its precincts* ○ *the airport and precincts.*

preciosity /ˌpreʃɪˈɒsətɪ/ *n (fml)* **(a)** [U] over-refinement in language and art; being precious(3). **(b)** [C often *pl*] instance of this.

precious /ˈpreʃəs/ *adj* **1** of great value (and beauty): *the precious metals,* ie gold, silver and platinum ○ *precious gems/stones,* ie diamonds, rubies, emeralds, etc. **2** ~ **(to sb)** highly valued; dearly loved: *precious moments together* ○ *each life is precious* ○ *a precious memento of happier times* ○ *She is very precious to him.* ○ *(infml ironic) She talks about nothing except her precious car!* **3** *(derog)* (of language, style, etc) over-refined; unnatural: *poetry full of precious images* ○ *a rather precious young man.* **4** *(infml often ironic)* considerable: *A precious lot of good that will do!*

▷ **precious** *adv* (used before *little, few*) *(infml)* very: *Precious few people can afford prices like that.* ○ *She has precious little to be cheerful about.*

precious *n (infml)* (used as an affectionate name when speaking to sb) dear: *What did you say, (my) precious?*

preciously *adv* in a precious(3) manner.

preciousness *n* [U] quality of being precious(1,2).

precipice /ˈpresɪpɪs/ *n* very steep or vertical face of a cliff, mountain or rock: *(fig) The country's economy was on the edge of the precipice,* ie in danger of collapsing.

precipitate /prɪˈsɪpɪteɪt/ *v* **1** [Tn] *(fml)* cause (sth) to happen suddenly or soon(er); hasten: *events that precipitated his ruin* ○ *One small error precipitated the disaster.* **2** [Tn, Tn·pr] *(fml)* **(a)** throw (sb/sth) with force (as if) from a great height. **(b)** ~ **sb/sth into sth** *(fig)* throw sb/sth suddenly (into a state or condition): *The assassination of the ambassador precipitated the country into war.* **3** *(chemistry)* **(a)** [I] (of a substance) separate into solid form from the liquid in which it is held. **(b)** [Tn] cause (a substance) to do this. **4** [I, Ipr, Tn, Tn·pr esp passive] ~ **(sth)** **(as sth)** (cause vapour to) condense and form rain, snow etc: *The clouds precipitate/are precipitated as snow in winter.*

▷ **precipitate** *n* [C, U] **(a)** solid matter that has been precipitated (PRECIPITATE 3b) from a solution. **(b)** moisture condensed from vapour and deposited (as rain, dew, etc).

precipitate /prɪˈsɪpɪtət/ *adj* **(a)** violently hurried: *a precipitate dash.* **(b)** (of an action) done without care or thought; rash[2]: *his precipitate action in selling the property.* **(c)** (of a person) acting without care or thought; impulsive. **precipitately** *adv.*

precipitation /prɪˌsɪpɪˈteɪʃn/ *n* **1** [U] *(fml)* violent haste: *to act with precipitation.* **2** [U] separation of a solid substance from the liquid in which it is held. **3** **(a)** [C] fall of rain, sleet, snow or hail: *a heavy precipitation.* **(b)** [U] amount of rain, etc that falls in an area: *the annual precipitation of the region.*

precipitous /prɪˈsɪpɪtəs/ *adj (fml)* dangerously high or steep: *From a precipitous height we looked at the town spread out below.* ○ *a precipitous path down the mountainside* ○ *a precipitous climb to the peak.* ▷ **precipitously** *adv*: *perched precipitously on the edge of the cliff.*

précis /ˈpreɪsiː; *US* preɪˈsiː/ *n* [U, C] (*pl* unchanged /-iːz/) restatement in shortened form of the main points or ideas of a speech or written text; summary.

▷ **précis** *v* [Tn] make a précis of (sth): *précising a scientific report.*

precise /prɪˈsaɪs/ *adj* **1** stated clearly and accurately: *precise details, instructions, measurements* ○ *a precise record of events.* **2** [attrib] exact; particular: *at that precise moment* ○ *It was found at the precise spot where she had left it.* **3** (of a person, his mind, etc) taking care to be exact and accurate, esp about minor details: *a precise mind, worker* ○ *100, or 99.8 to be precise* ○ *(often derog) a man with a very prim and precise* (ie too careful or fussy) *manner.*

▷ **precisely** *adv* **1** **(a)** exactly; just: *at 2 o'clock precisely* ○ *I can't remember precisely what happened.* ○ *That is precisely what I mean.* ○ *The two accounts are precisely the same.* **(b)** in a precise(2) manner; carefully: *He enunciated the words very precisely.* **2** (used to express agreement with a statement and often to suggest that it states the obvious) you are right; quite so: *'But if the delivery is late, we will lose the order!' 'Precisely.'*

preciseness *n* [U] **1** quality of being precise(1). **2** = PRECISION 1.

precision /prɪˈsɪʒn/ *n* [U] **1** (also **preciseness**) exactness and clarity; quality of being precise(1): *Your report lacks precision.* ○ *Aim for more precision in your style.* **2** accuracy: *clockwork precision* ○ *The diagram had been copied with great precision.* ○ [attrib] *precision timing* ○ *precision instruments/tools,* ie those designed for very accurate work, measurements, etc.

preclude /prɪˈkluːd/ *v* [Tn, Tn·pr, Tsg] ~ **sb from doing sth** *(fml)* prevent (sth, or sb doing sth); make (sth) impossible: *That sale precludes further development on this site.* ○ *Their move does not preclude others from investing.* ○ *These conditions preclude our taking part in the negotiations.* ▷ **preclusion** /prɪˈkluːʒn/ *n* [U].

precocious /prɪˈkəʊʃəs/ *adj* **(a)** (of a child) having developed certain abilities at an earlier age than usual: *a precocious child who could play the piano at the age of three.* **(b)** (of behaviour, ability, etc) showing this development: *a precocious talent for mimicry* ○ *He shows a precocious interest in the opposite sex.* **(c)** *(derog)* (of a child) behaving in a manner more suited to an older person: *That child is far too precocious!*

▷ **precociously** *adv.*

precociousness, **precocity** /prɪˈkɒsətɪ/ *ns* [U] being precocious.

precognition /ˌpriːkɒgˈnɪʃn/ *n* [U] *(fml or psychology)* knowledge of sth before it occurs.

preconceived /ˌpriːkənˈsiːvd/ *adj* [attrib] (of an idea, opinion, etc) formed in advance and not based on knowledge or experience: *Tourists forget their preconceived ideas as soon as they visit our country.*

preconception /ˌpriːkənˈsepʃn/ *n* ~ **(about sb/sth)** opinion or idea formed in advance and not based on experience or knowledge: *Common preconceptions about life in the Soviet Union are increasingly being challenged.* Cf MISCONCEPTION (MISCONCEIVE).

pre-condition /ˌpriːkənˈdɪʃn/ *n* = PREREQUISITE: *demanded as a pre-condition of their agreeing to the contract.*

precursor /ˌpriːˈkɜːsə(r)/ *n (fml)* ~ **(of sth)** **1** person or thing that comes before sth; forerunner: *small disturbances that were precursors of the revolution to come.* **2** machine or invention that is later developed further: *The first telephone was the precursor of modern communications networks.*

predator /ˈpredətə(r)/ *n* **1** animal that kills and eats other animals: *predators of the African grasslands.* **2** *(derog or joc)* person who exploits others, esp financially or sexually: *He denounced all landlords and money-lenders as evil predators.*

predatory /ˈpredətrɪ; *US* -tɔːrɪ/ *adj* **1** (of animals) (living by) killing other animals for food: *predatory birds* ○ *The domesticated cat retains its predatory instincts.* **2** **(a)** (for the purpose of) plundering: *predatory groups of bandits* ○ *a predatory attack.* **(b)** *(derog or joc)* (of a person) wishing to exploit others for financial or sexual reasons: *predatory advances, attentions, etc* ○ *We were pestered by predatory salesmen.*

predecease /ˌpriːdɪˈsiːs/ *v* [Tn] *(law)* die before (sb): *He left all his money to his wife without thinking that she might predecease him.*

predecessor /ˈpriːdɪsesə(r); *US* ˈpredə-/ *n* **1** person who held an office or position before sb else: *The decision was made by my predecessor.* **2** thing that has been followed or replaced by sth else: *Will the new plan be any more acceptable than its predecessors?* Cf SUCCESSOR.

predestination /ˌpriːdestɪˈneɪʃn/ *n* [U] **1** **(a)** theory or belief that everything that happens has been predetermined by God and that man cannot change it. **(b)** destiny that cannot be changed; fate. **2** doctrine or belief that God has decreed in advance that certain souls will be saved and others will not.

predestine /ˌpriːˈdestɪn/ *v* [esp passive: Tn, Cn·t] *(fml)* decide or determine sth (as if) by fate: *It seemed that his failure was predestined.* ○ *She was obviously predestined to succeed.* ○ *They both felt that they were predestined to spend their lives together.*

predetermine /ˌpriːdɪˈtɜːmɪn/ *v (fml)* [Tn esp passive] decide or fix (sth) in advance; prearrange: *predetermined behaviour, strategies, responses* ○ *A person's health is often genetically predetermined.*

▷ **predetermination** /ˌpriːdɪˌtɜːmɪˈneɪʃn/ *n* [U].

predicament /prɪˈdɪkəmənt/ *n* difficult or unpleasant situation, esp one in which sb is uncertain what to do: *Your refusal puts me in an awkward predicament.* ○ *A loan of money would help me out of my predicament.*

predicate[1] /ˈpredɪkət/ *n (grammar)* part of a statement that says sth about the subject, eg 'is short' in 'Life is short.' Cf SUBJECT[1] 4.

predicate[2] /ˈpredɪkeɪt/ *v (fml)* **1** [Tn, Tf, Tnt] declare or assert that (sth) is the case: *predicate a* *motive to be good* ○ *predicate that the market collapse was caused by weakness of the dollar.* **2** [Tn·pr esp passive] ~ **sth on sth** base sth on sth; make sth necessary as a consequence of sth: *The project was predicated on the assumption that the economy was expanding.*

predicative /prɪˈdɪkətɪv; US ˈpredɪkeɪtɪv/ *adj* (*grammar*) (of an adjective or a noun) coming after a verb such as *be, become, get, seem, look.* Cf ATTRIBUTIVE. ▷ **predicatively** *adv.*

□ **predicative ˈadjective** adjective used only after *be*, etc, eg 'asleep' as in 'She is asleep.'

predict /prɪˈdɪkt/ *v* [Tn, Tf, Tw] say in advance that (sth) will happen; forecast: *The earthquake had been predicted several months before.* ○ *She predicted that the improvement would continue.* ○ *It is impossible to predict who will win.*

▷ **predictable** /-əbl/ *adj* (**a**) that can be predicted: *predictable behaviour, results, weather.* (**b**) (*often derog*) (of a person) behaving in a way that can be predicted: *I knew you'd say that — you're so predictable!* ○ *Opposition to the proposal came from all the predictable quarters.* **predictability** /prɪˌdɪktəˈbɪlətɪ/ *n* [U]. **predictably** *adv.*

prediction /prɪˈdɪkʃn/ *n* **1** [U] (action of) predicting. **2** [C] forecast or prophecy: *Do you take seriously his prediction of a government defeat?*

predictor *n* person, instrument, etc that predicts.

predigest /ˌpriːdaɪˈdʒest/ *v* [Tn esp passive] treat (food) so that it is easy to digest: *special predigested food for babies* ○ (*fig*) *predigested reading matter.*

predilection /ˌpriːdɪˈlekʃn; US ˌpredlˈek-/ *n* (*fml*) ~ **(for sth)** special liking (for sth); preference: *a predilection for Japanese food.*

predispose /ˌpriːdɪˈspəʊz/ *v* (*fml*) **1** [Tn·pr esp passive, Tnt] ~ **sb to/towards sth** influence sb (in a specified way) in advance: *His early training predisposed him to a life of adventure.* ○ *be predisposed in sb's favour*, ie be inclined to favour him. **2** [Tn·pr esp passive] ~ **sb to sth** cause sb to be liable to sth: *The inhabitants are predisposed to rheumatism by the damp climate.*

predisposition /ˌpriːdɪspəˈzɪʃn/ *n* [U, C] ~ **(to/towards sth)**; ~ **(to do sth)** state of mind or body that makes sb liable to act in a certain way or to suffer from a certain disease: *a predisposition towards melancholia* ○ *a predisposition to rheumatism* ○ *a predisposition to criticize others.*

predominant /prɪˈdɒmɪnənt/ *adj* **1** having more power or influence than others: *Which country is the predominant member of the alliance?* ○ *The Socialists were predominant in the last Parliament.* **2** most noticeable; prevailing: *Her predominant characteristic is honesty.*

▷ **predominance** /-əns/ *n* **1** [U, sing] ~ **(of sth)** state of being greater in strength, numbers, etc: *the predominance of blue in the colour scheme* ○ *There is a predominance of men in the club.* **2** [U] ~ **(over sb/sth)** state of being more powerful or influential (than sb/sth): *The policy is designed to prevent the predominance of one group over another.*

predominantly *adv* for the most part; mainly: *a predominantly English-speaking population.*

predominate /prɪˈdɒmɪneɪt/ *v* **1** [I, Ipr] ~ **(over sb/sth)** have control, power or influence (over sb/sth): *A small group has begun to predominate in policy-making.* **2** [I] be superior in numbers, strength, etc: *a colour scheme in which red predominates* ○ *Oak-trees predominate in this forest.*

pre-eminent /ˌpriːˈemɪnənt/ *adj* superior to all others; outstanding: *a scientist pre-eminent in his field.* ▷ **pre-eminence** /-əns/ *n* [U]: *awards for those who achieve pre-eminence in public life.* **pre-eminently** *adv.*

pre-empt /ˌpriːˈempt/ *v* **1** [Tn] obtain (sth) by acting in advance of others. **2** [Tn] (*US*) occupy (public land) in order to have the right to buy it before others. **3** [Tn] prevent (sth) by taking action in advance; forestall: *The workers took control of the factory in order to pre-empt its sale by the owners.* **4** [I] (in bridge) make a high opening bid despite having poor cards, in order to prevent further bidding.

▷ **pre-emption** /ˌpriːˈempʃn/ *n* [U] **1** (*fml*) (**a**) purchase by one person, group, etc before others have the chance to buy. (**b**) right to do this. **2** obtaining or preventing (sth) by acting in advance.

pre-emptive /-tɪv/ *adj* of or concerning pre-emption: *a pre-emptive right to buy* ○ *pre-emptive purchase* ○ *a pre-emptive attack/strike*, ie one designed to forestall a likely enemy attack ○ *a pre-emptive bid*, ie (in bridge) one made to prevent further bidding.

preen /priːn/ *v* [Tn] **1** (of a bird) clean or smooth (its feathers or itself) with its beak. **2** ~ **oneself** (*often derog*) (**a**) (of a person) make oneself look tidy by combing one's hair, etc: *preen oneself in front of the mirror.* (**b**) congratulate oneself; be pleased with oneself.

pre-exist /ˌpriːɪɡˈzɪst/ *v* [I] (**a**) exist beforehand. (**b**) live a life before this life.

▷ **pre-existence** /-əns/ *n* [U] earlier form of existence, esp that of the soul before it enters the body.

pre-existent /-ənt/ *adj* existing previously, esp in an earlier life.

prefab /ˈpriːfæb; US ˌpriːˈfæb/ *n* (*infml*) prefabricated house.

prefabricate /ˌpriːˈfæbrɪkeɪt/ *v* [Tn] manufacture (a building, ship, etc) in sections that can be assembled later on a building site, in a shipyard, etc: *prefabricated kitchens, houses, schools, etc.* ▷ **prefabrication** /ˌpriːfæbrɪˈkeɪʃn/ *n* [U].

preface /ˈprefɪs/ *n* **1** introductory statement at the beginning of a book, esp one that explains the author's aims. Cf FOREWORD, INTRODUCTION 2. **2** preliminary part of a speech.

▷ **preface** *v* [Tn·pr] **1** ~ **sth with sth** provide sth with a preface(1): *He prefaced the diaries with a short account of how they were discovered.* **2** ~ **sth with sth/by doing sth** begin or introduce (a speech, etc): *She prefaced her talk with an apology/by apologizing for being late.*

prefatory /ˈprefətrɪ; US -tɔːrɪ/ *adj* acting as a preface; introductory: *after a few prefatory remarks, comments, etc.*

prefect /ˈpriːfekt/ *n* **1** (*esp Brit*) any of a group of older pupils in a school who have authority over younger pupils and certain responsibilities for discipline, etc. **2** (also **Prefect**) (**a**) (title of the) chief administrative officer of an area in certain countries, eg France and Japan. (**b**) head of the Paris police.

▷ **prefecture** /ˈpriːfektjʊə(r); US -tʃər/ *n* **1** area administrated by a prefect(2) in certain countries, eg France and Japan. **2** (in France) prefect's official place of work or residence. **3** position or period of office of a prefect. **prefectural** /priːˈfektʃərəl/ *adj* of a prefect(2): *the prefectural offices.*

prefer /prɪˈfɜː(r)/ *v* (**-rr-**) **1** [Tn, Tn·pr, Tf, Tt, Tnt] (no passive) [Tg, Cn·a] ~ **sth (to sth)** choose sth rather than sth else; like sth better: *There's coffee or tea. Which would you prefer?* ○ *I prefer walking to cycling.* ○ (*fml*) *I should prefer that/prefer it if you did not go there alone.* ○ *She prefers to be alone.* ○ *Their father prefers them to be home early.* ○ *I prefer walking alone.* ○ *I prefer my coffee black.* **2** (idm) **prefer a ˈcharge/ˈcharges (against sb)** (*law*) make an accusation of an offence (against sb) for hearing in a lawcourt: *prefer a charge against a motorist* ○ *We haven't enough evidence to prefer charges.*

▷ **preferable** /ˈprefrəbl/ *adj* (not used with *more*) ~ **(to sth/doing sth)** to be preferred (to sth); more desirable or suitable: *Cold food would be preferable in this heat.* ○ *He finds country life preferable to living in the city.* ○ *Anything was preferable to that dreadful din in the house.* **preferably** /ˈprefrəblɪ/ *adv* rather than anything, anywhere, etc else: *She wanted a cake, preferably one with chocolate icing.* ○ *They want to buy a new house, near the sea preferably.*

preference /ˈprefrəns/ *n* **1** (**a**) [U, sing] ~ **(for sth)** liking for sth (more than sth else): *There is milk and cream — do you have a preference?* ○ *It's entirely a matter of preference.* ○ *She has a preference for blue.* (**b**) [C] thing that is liked better or best: *What are your preferences?* **2** [U] ~ **(to/towards sb)** favour shown to one person, group, etc rather than another: *Employees who have worked here for many years will be given preference over newcomers.* ○ *She tried not to show preference in her treatment of the children in her care.* **3** (idm) **in preference to sb/sth** rather than sb/sth: *She chose to learn the violin in preference to the piano.*

□ **ˈpreference shares**, **ˈpreference stock** (*US* **ˈpreferred shares/stock**) (*finance*) shares/stock on which a firm must pay the dividend before distributing profits to holders of ordinary shares.

preferential /ˌprefəˈrenʃl/ *adj* **1** of, giving, receiving or showing preference(2): *preferential import duties, tariffs, etc*, ie favouring a particular group, country, etc. **2** (idm) **give sb/get preferential ˈtreatment** treat sb/be treated more favourably than sb else: *Nobody gets preferential treatment in this office!* ▷ **preferentially** /-ʃəlɪ/ *adv*: *be treated preferentially.*

preferment /prɪˈfɜːmənt/ *n* [C, U] (*fml*) promotion to a higher position or rank: *His preferment pleased his many admirers.* ○ *He was hoping for preferment.*

prefigure /ˌpriːˈfɪɡə(r); US -ɡjər/ *v* (*fml*) **1** [Tn] represent beforehand (sth that will happen in the future); foreshadow: *worrying events that may prefigure a period of economic recession.* **2** [Tn, Tf, Tw] picture (sth) to oneself beforehand; imagine.

prefix /ˈpriːfɪks/ *n* **1** (abbreviated as *pref* in this dictionary) word or syllable (eg *co-, ex-, non-, pre-, re-*) placed in front of a word to add to or change the meaning of that word, eg *un-* in *unhappy*. **2** word (eg *Dr, Mrs*, etc) placed before a person's name as a title. Cf SUFFIX.

▷ **prefix** /ˌpriːˈfɪks/ *v* [Tn, Tn·pr] ~ **sth (to sth)** **1** add sth at the beginning or as an introduction: *He prefixed an explanatory note to the list of statistics.* **2** add sth as a prefix (to a word, name, etc).

pregnant /ˈpreɡnənt/ *adj* **1** (of a woman or female animal) having a baby or young animal developing in the womb: *She was six months pregnant*, ie had been pregnant for six months. ○ *She is/got pregnant by another man.* **2** ~ **with sth** (**a**) full of sth: *pregnant with joy, meaning, possibilities.* (**b**) likely to cause sth: *pregnant with consequences, danger.* **3** (idm) **a pregnant ˈpause/ˈsilence** pause/silence full of unexpressed meaning or significance: *There was a pregnant pause before she answered my question.* ○ *His only reaction was a pregnant silence.*

▷ **pregnancy** /-nənsɪ/ *n* (**a**) [U] state or period of being pregnant(1): *discomfort caused by pregnancy* ○ *These drugs should not be taken during pregnancy.* ○ [attrib] *a pregnancy test.* (**b**) [C] instance of being pregnant(1): *She's had three pregnancies in four years.*

pre-heat /ˌpriːˈhiːt/ *v* [Tn esp passive] heat (sth) beforehand (esp an oven to a specified temperature before putting food in it to cook): *Cook the pie for 20 minutes in a pre-heated oven.*

prehensile /ˌpriːˈhensaɪl; US -sl/ *adj* (of an animal's foot or tail) able to grasp and hold things: *the monkey's prehensile tail* ○ *the prehensile claws of an eagle.*

prehistoric /ˌpriːhɪˈstɒrɪk; US -ˈstɔːrɪk/ *adj* of or concerning the time before recorded history: *prehistoric man, monuments, cave paintings* ○ (*joc or derog*) *His ideas on the education of girls are positively prehistoric*, ie extremely old-fashioned.

prehistory /ˌpriːˈhɪstrɪ/ *n* **1** [U] (study of the) period before recorded history: *European, Mexican, Aboriginal prehistory.* **2** [sing] earliest stages of the development of sth: *the prehistory of Western art.*

prejudge /ˌpriːˈdʒʌdʒ/ *v* [Tn] **1** make a judgement about (a person or case) before a proper inquiry has been held: *prejudge a matter, issue, client.* **2** form an opinion about (sb/sth) without having the necessary information: *He felt he had been prejudged by his colleagues.* ▷ **prejudgement** *n* [U, C].

prejudice /ˈpredʒʊdɪs/ *n* **1** (**a**) [U] opinion, or like or dislike of sb/sth, that is not founded on experience or reason: *colour/racial prejudice*, ie prejudice felt or shown against members of other races ○ *Her friendliness soon overcame the prejudice of her stepchildren.* ○ *The selectors were accused of showing prejudice in failing to include him in the team.* **(b)** [C] ~ **(against/in favour of sb/sth)** instance of this: *In order to succeed here you will need to overcome your prejudices.* ○ *She has a prejudice against modern music.* ○ *The anthology reveals a prejudice in favour of lyric poets.* **2** (idm) **to the prejudice of sth** (*esp law*) with the result that sb's interests are harmed: *to the prejudice of sb's rights* ○ *The newspaper reported his remarks, to the prejudice of his chances of being elected.* **without ˈprejudice (to sth)** (*law*) without having an effect on an existing right or claim: *The firm agreed to pay compensation without prejudice*, ie without admitting liability. ○ *The offer was accepted without prejudice to the current pay negotiations.*

▷ **prejudice** *v* **1** [Tn, Tn·pr] ~ **sb (against/in favour of sb/sth)** cause sb to have a prejudice; influence sb: *The judge told the jury that they must not allow their feelings to prejudice them.* ○ *Newspaper gossip had prejudiced her against him.* ○ *Her charm prejudiced the judges in her favour.* **2** [Tn] cause harm to (a case, claim, etc); weaken: *He prejudiced his claim by demanding too much compensation.* ○ *Lack of self-discipline prejudiced her chances of success.*

prejudiced *adj* (*usu derog*) having or showing prejudice: *Try not to be prejudiced in your judgements.* ○ *She regarded her critics as ignorant and prejudiced.* ○ *Since I am his mother, my opinion of him is naturally a prejudiced one.*

prejudicial /ˌpredʒʊˈdɪʃl/ *adj* ~ **(to sth)** (*fml*) causing harm (to a person's rights, interests, etc): *developments prejudicial to the company's future.*

prelacy /ˈpreləsɪ/ *n* **1** [C] office, rank or see of a prelate. **2 the prelacy** [Gp] the whole body of prelates.

prelate /ˈprelət/ *n* high-ranking clergyman, eg a bishop or an archbishop.

prelim /ˈpriːlɪm/ *n* (*infml*) **1** [C usu *pl*] preliminary examination. **2 prelims** [pl] pages of a book (with the title, contents, etc) that come before the text.

preliminary /prɪˈlɪmɪnərɪ; *US* -nerɪ/ *adj* ~ **(to sth)** coming before a more important action or event; preparatory: *after a few preliminary remarks* ○ *preliminary inquiries, experiments, negotiations* ○ (*sport*) *a preliminary contest, heat, round, etc*, ie held before a main contest in order to eliminate weaker players or teams ○ *All this is preliminary to the main election struggle.*

▷ **preliminary** *n* (usu *pl*) preliminary action, event, measure, etc: *the necessary preliminaries to a peace conference*, eg the discussions about agenda and procedures.

prelude /ˈpreljuːd/ *n* **1** ~ **(to sth) (a)** action or event that happens before another larger or more important one and forms an introduction to it: *His frequent depressions were the prelude to a complete mental breakdown.* ○ *The bankruptcy of several small firms was the prelude to general economic collapse.* ○ *I'm afraid that these troubles are just a prelude*, ie to worse ones. **(b)** introductory part of a poem, etc: *The lines form a prelude to his long narrative poem.* **2** (*music*) **(a)** introductory movement coming before a fugue or forming the first part of a suite. **(b)** short piece of music of a similar type.

premarital /ˌpriːˈmærɪtl/ *adj* happening before marriage: *premarital sex, affairs, etc.*

premature /ˈpremətjʊə(r); *US* ˌpriːməˈtʊər/ *adj* **1 (a)** happening before the proper or expected time: *premature baldness, senility* ○ *A fire in the gallery caused the premature closing of the exhibition.* **(b)** (of a baby, its birth, etc) born or occurring at least three weeks before the expected time: *the special care of premature babies* ○ *The baby was five weeks premature.* **2** ~ **(in doing sth)** (*derog*) acting or done too soon; hasty: *a premature conclusion, decision, judgement, etc* ○ *Let's not be premature in closing this case*, eg in a police investigation. ▷ **prematurely** *adv*: *born prematurely* ○ *prematurely bald, grey, wrinkled, etc.*

premeditate /ˌpriːˈmedɪteɪt/ *v* [Tn esp passive] plan (sth) in advance: *a premeditated attack, murder, insult, etc* ○ *We needed to know whether the crime had been premeditated.* ▷ **premeditation** /ˌpriːmedɪˈteɪʃn/ *n* [U].

premenstrual tension /ˌpriːˌmenstrʊəl ˈtenʃn/ (*abbr* **PMT**) mental and physiological upset caused by hormonal changes occurring before menstruation.

premier /ˈpremɪə(r); *US* ˈpriːmɪər/ *adj* [attrib] first in importance, position, etc: *Britain's premier exporter of drilling equipment.* ○ *The company has achieved a premier position in the electronics field.*

▷ **premier** *n* head of a government; prime minister. **premiership** [U] position or period of office of a premier: *during her premiership* ○ *He was offered the premiership.*

première /ˈpremɪeə(r); *US* prɪˈmɪər/ *n* first public performance of (a production of) a play or showing of a film; first night.

▷ **première** *v* [Tn esp passive] perform (a play) or show (a film) to the public for the first time: *The film was premièred at the Cannes festival.*

premise (also **premiss**) /ˈpremɪs/ *n* **1** statement or idea on which reasoning is based; hypothesis: *Advice to investors was based on the premise that interest rates would continue to fall.* **2** (in logic) each of the first two parts (*major premise* and *minor premise*) of a formal argument: *If the major premise is 'Boys like fruit' and the minor premise is 'You are a boy', then the conclusion is 'Therefore you like fruit'.* Cf SYLLOGISM.

premises /ˈpremɪsɪz/ *n* [pl] **1** house or other buildings with its outbuildings, land, etc: *business premises*, ie building(s), esp offices, where a business is carried on ○ *The firm is looking for larger premises.* ○ *He was asked to leave the premises immediately.* **2** (*law*) details of property, names of people, etc specified in the first part of a legal agreement. **3** (idm) **off the ˈpremises** outside the boundary of the premises(1): *see sb off the premises*, ie take a visitor, etc to the exit. **on the ˈpremises** in the building(s), etc: *There is always a manager on the premises.* ○ *Alcohol may not be consumed on the premises.*

premium /ˈpriːmɪəm/ *n* **1** amount or instalment (to be) regularly paid for an insurance policy: *Your first premium is now due.* **2** additional payment, eg one added to wages or interest payments; bonus: *A premium of 2 per cent is paid on long-term investments.* ○ *You have to pay a premium for express delivery.* ○ [attrib] *Premium rents are charged in the city centre.* **3** (idm) **at a ˈpremium (a)** (*finance*) (of stocks and shares) above the normal or usual value: *Shares are selling at a premium.* **(b)** rare or difficult to obtain, and therefore more expensive or more highly valued than usual: *Space is at a premium in this building.* ○ *Honesty is at a premium in this profession, I'm afraid!* **put a premium on sb/sth (a)** make (sb/sth) seem important: *The high risk of infection puts a premium on the use of sterile needles.* **(b)** attach special value or importance to sb/sth: *The examiners put a premium on rational argument.*

□ **ˈPremium Bond** (*Brit*) government savings bond that pays no interest[1](7) but offers instead the chance of winning money as a prize in regular draws (DRAW[1] 1b).

premolar /ˌpriːˈməʊlə(r)/ *n* any of the teeth between the canines and the molars.

premonition /ˌpriːməˈnɪʃn, ˌprem-/ *n* ~ **(of sth/that...)** feeling that sth unpleasant is going to happen: *a premonition of disaster* ○ *My premonition was right.* ○ *As we approached the house, I had a premonition that something terrible had happened.*

▷ **premonitory** /prɪˈmɒnɪtərɪ; *US* -tɔːrɪ/ *adj* (*fml*) giving a warning: *premonitory signs.*

pre-natal /ˌpriːˈneɪtl/ *adj* (*esp US*) of or occurring in the period before (giving) birth; antenatal: *ˌpre-natal ˈcheck-ups, ˈclasses, ˈexercises.* Cf POSTNATAL.

preoccupation /ˌpriːɒkjʊˈpeɪʃn/ *n* **1** [U] **(a)** state of being preoccupied; absent-mindedness. **(b)** ~ **(with sth)** state of constantly thinking or worrying about sth; obsession: *She found his preoccupation with money irritating.* **2** [C] thing that a person thinks about all the time: *His main preoccupation at that time was getting enough to eat.* ○ *A pension is not usually one of the preoccupations of an eighteen year-old!*

preoccupy /priːˈɒkjʊpaɪ/ *v* (*pt, pp* **-pied**) [Tn] engage (sb, his mind, thoughts, etc) so that he cannot think of other things; obsess: *Something seems to be preoccupying her at the moment.* ○ *Health worries preoccupied him for the whole holiday.*

▷ **preoccupied** *adj* inattentive because one is thinking of or worrying about sth else: *She seemed preoccupied all the time I was talking to her.* ○ *He answered me in a rather preoccupied manner.*

pre-ordain /ˌpriːɔːˈdeɪn/ *v* [esp passive: Tn, Tf] decide or determine (sth) beforehand: *Fate had pre-ordained their meeting/that they should meet.* ○ *Her success in life seemed pre-ordained.*

prep /prep/ *n* (*infml*) **1** [C, U] (*Brit*) (esp in private boarding schools) **(a)** school work (to be) done after lessons; homework. **(b)** time when this is (to be) done: *He felt ill during prep.* **2** (*US*) student in a preparatory school.

□ **ˈprep school** = PREPARATORY SCHOOL (PREPARATORY). ⇨ article at SCHOOL.

pre-package /ˌpriːˈpækɪdʒ/ (also **pre-pack** /ˌpriːˈpæk/) *v* [Tn esp passive] put (goods) into packs ready for sale before distribution to shops: *pre-packaged fruit.*

preparation /ˌprepəˈreɪʃn/ *n* **1** [U] preparing or being prepared: *You can't pass an exam without preparation.* ○ *The preparation of the meals is your job.* ○ [attrib] *Food preparation areas must be kept clean.* **2** [C usu *pl*] ~ **(for sth/to do sth)** thing done to prepare for sth: *The country is making preparations for war/to go to war.* ○ *Was your education a good preparation for your career?* **3** [C] substance that has been specially prepared for use as a cosmetic, medicine, etc: *a pharmaceutical preparation* ○ *a preparation for hiding/to hide skin blemishes.* **4** [C, U] (*Brit*) = PREP 1. **5** (idm) **in preparation (for sth)** being prepared (for sth): *The advertising campaign is still in preparation.* ○ *They've sold their house and car in preparation for leaving the country.*

preparatory /prɪˈpærətrɪ; *US* -tɔːrɪ/ *adj* preparing for sth; introductory: *preparatory investigations, measures, training.*

□ **preˈparatory school** (also *infml* **ˈprep school**) **1** (*Brit*) private school for pupils aged between 7 and 13 whose parents pay fees for their education. Cf PUBLIC SCHOOL (PUBLIC). **2** (*US*) (usu private) school that prepares students for college.

prepare /prɪˈpeə(r)/ *v* **1** [I, Ipr, Tn, Tn·pr, Cn·t] ~ **(sb/sth) (for sb/sth)** get or make (sb/sth) ready: *I had no time in which to prepare.* ○ *prepare for trouble* ○ *prepare a meal*, ie get food ready to be eaten ○ *have everything prepared beforehand* ○ *prepare children for an examination* ○ *The troops were being prepared for battle/to go into battle.* **2** (idm) **be prepared for sth** be ready for sth (esp sth unpleasant): *I knew there were problems, but I was not prepared for this!* ○ *She was prepared for anything to happen.* **be prepared to do sth** be able and willing to do sth: *I am prepared to lend you the money if you promise to pay it back.* ○ *I am not prepared to stay and listen to these outrageous insults.* **prepare the ground (for sth)** make it possible or easier to develop sth: *Early experiments with military rockets prepared the ground for space travel.* **3** (phr v) **prepare sb for sth** cause sb to expect sth (esp sth unpleasant): *Prepare yourself for a nasty shock!*

▷ **preparedness** /prɪˈpeərɪdnɪs/ *n* [U] being prepared: *a state of preparedness.*

prepay /ˌpriːˈpeɪ/ *v* (*pt, pp* **prepaid** /-ˈpeɪd/) [Tn esp passive] pay (sth) in advance: *a prepaid envelope*, ie one on which the postage has already been paid ○ *The telegram was sent reply prepaid.* ▷ **prepayment** *n* [C, U].

preponderant /prɪˈpɒndərənt/ *adj* (*fml*) greater in influence, importance, quantity, etc

Melancholy is the preponderant mood of the poem. ▷ **preponderance** /-əns/ *n* [sing]: *a preponderance of blue-eyed people in the population.* **preponderantly** *adv*: *preponderantly optimistic.*

preponderate /prɪˈpɒndəreɪt/ *v* [I, Ipr] ~ **(over sth)** *(fml)* be greater in influence, importance, quantity, etc (than sth else): *Christians preponderate in the population of that part of the country.*

preposition /ˌprepəˈzɪʃn/ *n* *(grammar)* (abbreviated as *prep* in this dictionary) word or group of words (eg *in, from, to, out of, on behalf of*) used esp before a noun or pronoun to show place, position, time, method, etc.

▷ **prepositional** /-ʃənl/ *adj* of or containing a preposition.

□ ˌ**prepositional** ˈ**phrase** preposition and the noun or noun phrase that follows it, eg *in the night, after breakfast.*

prepossessing /ˌpriːpəˈzesɪŋ/ *adj* making a good impression; attractive: *a prepossessing smile, manner, child* ○ *He/His appearance is not at all prepossessing.*

preposterous /prɪˈpɒstərəs/ *adj* completely contrary to reason or common sense; absurd or outrageous: *That is a preposterous accusation!* ○ *They are asking a preposterous price for the work.*

▷ **preposterously** *adv*: *That is a preposterously high price!*

preppy /ˈprepɪ/ *adj* *(US infml usu derog)* like or typical of a student at a US preparatory school, esp one who comes from a wealthy and conservative social background and dresses in an informal but neat way: *preppy clothes.*

▷ **preppy** (also **preppie**) *n* *(US infml usu derog)* preppy person.

prepuce /ˈpriːpjuːs/ *n* *(anatomy)* **1** foreskin. ⇨ illus at MALE. **2** similar fold of skin at the tip of the clitoris.

Pre-Raphaelite /ˌpriːˈræfəlaɪt/ *n* *(art)* member of a group of British late 19th-century artists (the **Pre-Raphaelite Brotherhood**) who painted in a style influenced by that of Italian painting before the time of Raphael. The group included *Millais, *Rossetti and Holman *Hunt, and was admired by *Ruskin and William *Morris. ⇨ illus at HUNT, MILLAIS, ROSSETTI.

▷ **Pre-Raphaelite** *adj* of, concerning or in the style of the Pre-Raphaelites: *a* ˌ*Pre-Raphaelite* ˈ*portrait* ○ *(fig) a* ˌ*Pre-Raphaelite* ˈ*beauty*, ie a young woman who is tall and thin, with a pale complexion and long, typically yellowish hair.

pre-record /ˌpriːrɪˈkɔːd/ *v* [Tn esp passive] *(esp broadcasting)* record (film, sound, a television programme, etc) in advance, for use later: *The sound effects had been pre-recorded and were added to the dialogue.* ○ *The interview was pre-recorded.* Cf LIVE[1] 7.

▷ **pre-recorded** *adj* (of tape) with film or sound already recorded on it.

prerequisite /ˌpriːˈrekwɪzɪt/ *adj* ~ **(for/to sth)** *(fml)* required as a condition (for sth): *A degree is prerequisite for employment at this level.* ○ *A sense of humour is prerequisite to understanding her work.*

▷ **prerequisite** (also **pre-condition**) *n* ~ **(for/of sth)** *(fml)* thing required as a condition for sth to happen or exist: *Careful study of the market is a prerequisite for success.* ○ *Good muscles are one of the prerequisites of physical fitness.*

prerogative /prɪˈrɒgətɪv/ *n* right or privilege, esp one belonging to a particular person or group: *It is the Prime Minister's prerogative to decide when to call an election.* ○ *A monarch has the prerogative of pardoning criminals.* ○ *the* ˌ*royal pre*ˈ*rogative*, ie (in Britain), the (theoretical) right of the sovereign to act without the approval of Parliament.

Pres *abbr* President: *Pres (George) Bush.*

presage /ˈpresɪdʒ/ *n* *(fml)* **(a)** sign that sth (esp sth unpleasant) will happen; omen. **(b)** feeling that sth unpleasant will happen; presentiment.

▷ **presage** /ˈpresɪdʒ, *rarely* prɪˈseɪdʒ/ *v* [Tn] be a sign of (sth that will happen); foretell: *Those clouds presage a storm.*

Presbyterian /ˌprezbɪˈtɪərɪən/ *adj* (of a Church, esp of the national Church of Scotland) governed by elders (ˈ**presbyters**) who are all equal in rank. Cf EPISCOPAL. ⇨ article at SCOTLAND.

▷ **Presbyterian** *n* person who is a member of the Presbyterian Church.

Presbyterianism /-ɪzəm/ *n* [U] **1** beliefs of Presbyterians. **2** Presbyterian system of church government.

presbytery /ˈprezbɪtrɪ; *US* -terɪ/ *n* **1** (regional) administrative court of the Presbyterian Church. **2** house where a Roman Catholic parish priest lives. **3** (in a church) eastern part of the chancel beyond the choir; sanctuary.

pre-school /ˌpriːˈskuːl/ *adj* of the time or age before a child is old enough to go to school: *a* ˌ*pre-school* ˈ*child/a child of pre-school age* ○ ˌ*pre-school* ˈ*learning.*

prescient /ˈpresɪənt/ *adj* *(fml)* knowing about things before they take place; able to see into the future. ▷ **prescience** /-əns/ *n* [U].

prescribe /prɪˈskraɪb/ *v* *(fml)* **1** [Tn, Tn·pr] ~ **sth (for sth)** advise or order the use of (esp a medicine, remedy, etc): *She prescribed some pills to help me to sleep.* ○ *Do not exceed the prescribed dose*, ie quantity of medicine to be taken at one time. ○ *Ask the doctor to prescribe something for that cough.* ○ *(fig) The doctor prescribed a holiday as the best cure for his depression.* ○ *a prescribed text*, ie one that has to be studied, eg for an examination. **2** [Tn, Tn·pr, Tf, Tw] declare with authority that (sth) should be done or is a rule to be followed: *The law prescribes heavy penalties for this offence.* ○ *Police regulations prescribe that an officer's number must be clearly visible.* ○ *Army regulations prescribe how rifles must be carried.* ⇨ Usage at DECREE.

prescript /ˈpriːskrɪpt/ *n* *(fml)* law, rule or command.

prescription /prɪˈskrɪpʃn/ *n* **1** [C] **(a)** doctor's written instruction for the composition and use of a medicine: *The doctor gave me a prescription for pain-killers.* ○ *(fig) His prescription for economic recovery was not well received.* **(b)** medicine prescribed in this way: *The chemist made a mistake when making up the prescription.* ○ [attrib] *prescription charges*, ie (in Britain) money to be paid by the patient for drugs supplied on the National Health Service. **2** [U] action of prescribing: *The prescription of drugs is a doctor's responsibility.*

prescriptive /prɪˈskrɪptɪv/ *adj* *(fml)* **1** **(a)** making rules or giving orders or directions: *prescriptive teaching methods.* **(b)** *(grammar)* telling people how they ought to use a language: *a prescriptive grammar of the English language.* Cf DESCRIPTIVE 2. **2** made legal or acceptable by long-standing custom: *prescriptive rights.* ▷ **prescriptively** *adv.*

presence /ˈprezns/ *n* **1** [U] being present in a place: *The dogs were trained to detect the presence of explosives.* ○ *Your presence is requested at the shareholders' meeting.* ○ *Her presence during the crisis had a calming effect.* Cf ABSENCE. **2** [U, sing] *(approv)* person's way of standing, moving, etc, esp as it affects other people: *a man of great presence* ○ *The power of his stage presence could never be forgotten.* **3** [C] person or thing that is or seems to be present in a place: *There seemed to be a ghostly presence in the room.* **4** [sing] number of eg soldiers or policemen in a place for a special purpose: *a massive police presence at the meeting* ○ *The United Nations maintains a military presence in the area.* **5** (idm) **be admitted to sb's presence** ⇨ ADMIT. **in the presence of sb/in sb's presence** in the place where sb is; with sb there: *He made the accusation in the presence of witnesses.* ○ *She asked them not to discuss the matter in her presence.* **make one's** ˈ**presence felt** make others aware of one's presence or existence by the strength of one's personality, one's superior ability, etc: *The new chairman is certainly making his presence felt!* ˌ**presence of** ˈ**mind** ability to remain calm and act quickly and sensibly in a crisis: *The child showed great presence of mind by grabbing the falling baby.*

present[1] /ˈpreznt/ *adj* **1** [pred] ~ **(at sth)** **(a)** (of a person) being in the place in question: *Were you present when the news was announced?* ○ *The mistake was obvious to all (those) present.* ○ *Everybody present welcomed the decision.* ○ *There were 200 people present at the meeting.* **(b)** ~ **(in sth)** being in a place, substance, etc: *He suspected that a leak was present somewhere along the pipe.* ○ *Analysis showed that cocaine was present in the mixture.* Cf ABSENT[1]. **2** [attrib] existing or happening now: *the present difficulties, problems, uncertainties, etc* ○ *the present administration, government, council, etc* ○ *the present climate of opinion* ○ *You can't use it in its present condition.* **3** [attrib] now being considered, dealt with or discussed: *the present proposal for increasing taxation.* **4** (idm) **present company ex**ˈ**cepted/excepting present** ˈ**company** (used as a polite comment when making a critical remark) what I am saying does not apply to you: *People seem to have drunk far too much tonight, present company excepted of course.* **the** ˌ**present** ˈ**day** the present age; modern times: *After being taken back 200 years, we were suddenly returned to the present day.* ○ [attrib] ˌ*present-day* ˈ*attitudes, con*ˈ*ditions,* ˈ*fashions.* **on** ˈ**present form** (of a judgement) based on sb/sth's previous and/or current actions, behaviour, progress, etc: *He would not be elected on present form.*

▷ **present** *n* **1 the present** [sing] **(a)** the time now passing; the present time: *the past, the present and the future* ○ *Historical romances offer an escape from the present.* **(b)** *(grammar)* = PRESENT TENSE. **2** (idm) **at** ˈ**present** at this time; now: *I'm afraid I can't help you just at present — I'm too busy.* ˌ**by these** ˈ**presents** *(law)* by this document. **for the moment/present** ⇨ MOMENT. **no time like the present** ⇨ TIME[1].

□ ˌ**present** ˈ**participle** *(grammar)* form of the verb that ends in *-ing*, eg *going, having, swimming.* ˌ**present** ˈ**tense** *(grammar)* one of the verb tenses (eg *present, present continuous, present perfect*) that express an action or state in the present at the time of speaking: *The verb is in the present tense.* Cf PAST[1] 4.

present[2] /ˈpreznt/ *n* **1** thing given or received as a gift: *wedding, Christmas, birthday, etc presents* ○ *This book was a present from my brother.* **2** (idm) **make sb a present of sth** give sth to sb as a gift: *He admired my old typewriter so much, I made him a present of it.* ○ *(ironic) Let's not make our opponents a present of any goals*, ie allow them to score easily.

present[3] /prɪˈzent/ *v* **1** [Tn, Tn·pr, Dn·pr] ~ **sb with sth**; ~ **sth (to sb)** give or hand over sth to sb, esp formally at a ceremony: *Colleagues presented the retiring chairman with a cheque/presented a cheque to the retiring chairman.* ○ *They presented a sum of money to the college in memory of their son.* **2** [Tn, Dn·pr] ~ **sb (to sb)** introduce (sb) formally, esp to sb of higher rank, status, etc: *May I present my new assistant (to you).* ○ *The custom of young ladies being presented at court* (ie formally introduced to the monarch) *has disappeared.* **3** [Tn, Tn·pr, Dn·pr] ~ **sth (for sth)**; ~ **sth (to sb)** offer sth for consideration: *a well-presented analysis* ○ *present one's designs for approval/consideration* ○ *They presented a petition to the governor.* ○ *She presented* (ie argued) *her case to the committee.* **4** [Tn, Dn·pr] ~ **sth (to sb)** *(fml)* offer sth: *present one's apologies, compliments, greetings, etc (to sb).* **5** **(a)** [Tn, Tn·pr] ~ **oneself (for sth)** (of a person) appear or attend: *You will be asked to present yourself for interview.* ○ *I have to present myself in court on 20 May.* **(b)** [Tn, Dn·pr] ~ **itself (to sb)** (of an opportunity, a solution, etc) show itself (to sb); occur: *A wonderful opportunity suddenly presented itself.* ○ *The answer presented itself to him when he looked at the problem again.* **6** [Tn, Tn·pr, Dn·pr] ~ **sb with sth**; ~ **sth (to sth)** show or reveal sth to sb: *This job presents many difficulties to the new recruit.* ○ *Falling interest rates present the firm with a new problem.* **7** [Tn, Tn·pr] ~ **sth (for sth)** offer (a bill or cheque) in order to be paid: *Has the builder presented his bill yet?* ○ *The cheque was presented for payment on 21 March.* **8** [Tn] **(a)** show (eg a play) to the public:

The National Theatre presents 'Hamlet' in a new production. (**b**) cause (eg an actor) to perform in public: *Starlight Productions present the Chinese Children's Choir in concert.* (**c**) introduce (a performance) to an audience in the theatre or (a programme) on radio or television: *Who will present his show* (eg on television) *while he's away?* ○ *Our review of this week's papers is presented by the editor of 'The Times'* **9** [Tn] hold (a rifle, etc) upright in front of the body as a salute: *Present arms!* ○ *The soldiers were ordered to present arms.* **10** (*medical*) (**a**) [I, Ipr] ~ (**with sth**) come to be medically examined for a particular condition: *'How did the patient present?' 'She presented with severe stomach pains'.* (**b**) [I] (of a baby in the womb, or part of its body) lie in a particular way or direction: *The head is presenting normally*, ie pointing towards the cervix. (**c**) [I, Ipr] ~ (**as sth**) (of a diseased condition of the body) show itself; occur: *The secondary phase may present as a severe rash.*

▷ **present** *n* [sing] upright position of a weapon in a salute: *rifles at the present*, ie with the weapon held in an upright position.

presenter *n* (esp on radio or television) person who presents (PRESENT[3] 8c) a programme.

presentable /prɪˈzentəbl/ *adj* fit to appear or be shown in public: *He's got dozens of suits but not one of them is presentable.* ○ *I must go and make myself presentable before the guests arrive.* ○ (*approv*) *She was seen at the opera with an extremely presentable escort.* ▷ **presentably** /-əblɪ/ *adv*: *He was dressed quite presentably for a change.*

presentation /ˌpreznˈteɪʃn; *US* ˌpri:zen-/ *n* **1** [U] (**a**) presenting or being presented: *They are preparing for the presentation of a new musical.* ○ *The cheque is payable on presentation*, ie at the bank. (**b**) way in which sth is presented: *The presentation of the material was untidy.* ○ *She needs to improve her presentation of the arguments.* **2** [C] (**a**) thing presented: *We went to the première of their new presentation.* (**b**) gift, esp one given at a formal ceremony: *We want to make her a presentation to celebrate her jubilee.* ○ *The Queen will make the presentation* (ie will hand over the gift) *herself.* ○ [attrib] *a presentation ceremony*, ie one at which a presentation is made ○ *a presentation copy*, ie a free book presented by the publisher or by the author. **3** [C, U] position of a baby in the mother's body just before birth.

presentiment /prɪˈzentɪmənt/ *n* (*fml*) vague feeling that sth (esp sth unpleasant) will happen; foreboding: *a presentiment of trouble ahead.*

presently /ˈprezntlɪ/ *adv* **1** after a short time; soon: *I'll be with you presently.* **2** (*esp US*) at the present time; now: *The Secretary of State is presently considering the proposal.*

NOTE ON USAGE: When **presently** means 'soon' it usually comes at the end of the sentence: *She'll be here presently.* When it means 'after a short time' it sometimes comes at the beginning: *Presently I heard her leave the house.* Increasingly in British as well as US English it means 'now' or 'currently' and is placed with the verb: *She's presently working on her PhD.*

preservation /ˌprezəˈveɪʃn/ *n* [U] **1** action of preserving: *the preservation and conservation of wildlife* ○ *the preservation of food, one's health, works of art* ○ *The aim of the policy is the preservation of peace.* ○ [attrib] *a preserˈvation order*, ie (in Britain) one that makes it illegal to destroy a building, etc because of its historical value. **2** degree to which sth has been unaffected by age, weather etc: *The paintings were in an excellent state of preservation.*

preservative /prɪˈzɜ:vətɪv/ *adj* (used for) preserving: *He painted the posts with a preservative liquid.* ○ *Salt has a preservative effect on food.*

▷ **preservative** *n* [C, U] (type of) substance used for preserving: *food free from preservatives* ○ *Alcohol is used as a preservative in certain foods.* ○ *Preservative is usually added to tinned meat.*

preserve /prɪˈzɜ:v/ *v* **1** (**a**) [Tn] keep or maintain (sth) in an unchanged or perfect condition: *preserve one's eyesight* ○ *a very well-preserved man of eighty* ○ *Wax polish preserves wood and leather.* ○ *Efforts to preserve the peace have failed.* (**b**) [Tn, Tn·pr] ~ **sth** (**for sth**) keep sth safe or alive for the future: *Few of the early manuscripts have been preserved.* ○ *His work must be preserved for posterity.* (**c**) [Tn, Tn·pr] ~ **sb** (**from sb/sth**) keep sb safe from harm or danger: *The calm courage of the pilot preserved the lives of the passengers.* ○ *God preserve us!* **2** [Tn] avoid losing (sth); retain: *She managed despite everything to preserve her sense of humour.* ○ *It is difficult to preserve one's self-respect in that job.* **3** [Tn] keep (food) from decay (by bottling, drying, freezing, etc): *Salt and spices help to preserve meat.* ○ *In the summer, large crops of fruit may be preserved by freezing or bottling.* **4** [Tn esp passive] keep (fishing, game, land, part of a river, etc) for private use: *The fishing in this stretch of the river is strictly preserved.* Cf CONSERVE.

▷ **preserve** *n* **1** (**a**) [C usu *pl*] preserved fruit: *apricot preserves.* (**b**) [U] jam: *strawberry preserve.* Cf CONSERVE *n.* **2** [C] area where game or fish are preserved (PRESERVE 4) for private hunting or fishing. **3** [sing] activities, interests, etc regarded as belonging to a particular person: *She regards negotiating prices with customers as her special preserve.*

preserver *n* person or thing that preserves: *a ˈlife-preserver.*

pre-set /ˌpri:ˈset/ *v* (**-tt-**; *pt, pp* **pre-set**) [Tn, Cn·t] set (a clock, timer, etc) beforehand: *She pre-set the cooker to come on at 6.30.* ○ *The video was pre-set to record the match.*

pre-shrunk /ˌpri:ˈʃrʌŋk/ *adj* (of cloth) shrunk before being made into garments, so that they will not shrink when they are washed: *ˌpre-shrunk ˈjeans.*

preside /prɪˈzaɪd/ *v* **1** [I, Ipr] ~ (**at sth**) be chairman (at a conference, meeting, etc): *Whoever presides will need patience and tact.* ○ *The Prime Minister presides at meetings of the Cabinet.* **2** (phr v) **preside over sth** (**a**) be head or director of sth: *The city council is presided over by the mayor.* (**b**) control or be responsible for sth: *The present director has presided over a rapid decline in the firm's profitability.*

□ **preˌsiding ˈofficer** (*Brit*) official responsible for a polling-station during an election.

presidency /ˈprezɪdənsɪ/ *n* (**a**) **the presidency** (also **the Presidency**) [sing] office(4) of a president: *She hopes to win the presidency.* (**b**) [C] term of office as a president: *the last days of his presidency* ○ *He was elected to a second presidency.*

president /ˈprezɪdənt/ *n* **1 President** elected head of state in the USA and many modern republics: *the President of the United States* ○ *President De Gaulle.* **2** (also **President**) head of some colleges, government bodies or departments, societies, etc: *the President of the Board of Trade* ○ *He was made president of the cricket club.* **3** (*US*) head of a bank, business firm, etc.

▷ **presidential** /ˌprezɪˈdenʃl/ *adj* of a president or presidency: *a presidential candidate, election, policy* ○ (*US*) *a presidential year*, ie one in which an election for president is held.

presidium (also **praesidium**) /prɪˈsɪdɪəm/ *n* (*pl* ~**s**) permanent executive committee of the administration, esp in Communist countries: *the presidium of the Supreme Soviet.*

Presley /ˈprezlɪ/ Elvis (1935-77), American singer. He was the leading figure of early rock and roll and caused a public scandal in the 1950s by his suggestive movements when performing in public (which led to his nickname Elvis 'the Pelvis').

press[1] /pres/ *n* **1** [C usu *sing*] act of pushing steadily with (sth held in) the hand: *Flatten the dough with a press of the hand.* ○ *Those trousers need a press*, ie with a hot iron. **2** [C] (esp in compounds) any of various devices or machines used for compressing or shaping things, extracting juice, etc: *a ˈwinepress* ○ *a ˈcider-press* ○ *an ˈolive-press* ○ *keep one's tennis racket in a press* ○ *a hydraulic press.* **3** (**a**) (also **ˈprinting-press**) [C] machine for printing: *He took a copy of the newspaper as it came off the press.* (**b**) [U] printing or being printed (used esp as in the following phrases): *pass sth for press*, ie give final approval for sth before it goes to be printed ○ *go to press*, ie start to be printed ○ *Prices are correct at the time of going to press, but may be changed.* ○ *stop press.* **4** (often **the Press**) [Gp] (journalists who work for) newspapers, periodicals and the news sections of radio and television: *The Press were not allowed to attend the trial.* ○ *The majority of the press support the Government's foreign policy.* ○ *the local/national/provincial press* ○ *the gutter press*, ie newspapers that concentrate on sensational stories about people's personal lives ○ *The freedom of the press* (ie right of journalists to report events, express opinions, etc freely) *must be protected.* ○ [attrib] *press advertising, comment, freedom* ○ *a press campaign*, eg for a product, political party or cause. **5** [sing] treatment given (to a person, a group, an event, etc) in radio, newspaper, etc reports: *be given/have a good/bad press.* **6** [C] business for printing (and publishing) books or periodicals: *Oxford University Press* ○ *a small press specializing in illustrated books.* **7** [sing] (**a**) crowd or crowding of people: *The child got lost in the press of people leaving the match.* (**b**) pressure of affairs; hurry or stress: *the press of modern life.* **8** [C] large cupboard, usu with shelves, for clothes, books, etc: *a linen press.*

□ **ˈpress agent** person employed by a theatre, etc to organize advertising and publicity in the press.

ˈpress agency **1** office or business of a press agent. **2** business firm that gathers news and supplies it to journalists.

the ˈPress Association (*abbr* **PA**) (*Brit*) press agency that gathers home news and supplies it to the British press[1](4).

ˈpress baron (*infml*) powerful newspaper proprietor.

ˈpress-box *n* place reserved for reporters, eg at a football or cricket match.

ˈpress conference interview given to journalists in order to announce a decision, an achievement, etc: *The Minister called a press conference as soon as the results were known.*

ˈpress cutting (also esp *US* **ˈpress clipping**) paragraph, article, etc cut out from a newspaper or periodical.

ˈpress-gallery *n* place reserved for reporters, esp in Parliament or in a lawcourt.

pressman /ˈpresmən, -mæn/ *n* (*pl* **-men** /ˈpresmən, -men/) **1** (*Brit*) journalist. **2** (*US*) person who operates a printing-press.

ˈpress officer person employed by a business firm, political party, etc to provide information to the press and to answer journalists' questions.

ˈpress photographer newspaper photographer.

ˈpress release official announcement or account of sth given to the press by a government department, political party, etc: *The company issued a press release to try to stop speculation in its shares.*

ˈpress secretary person responsible for an important or well-known person's relations with journalists, often making statements and answering questions on his behalf: *The White House Press Secretary denied the rumour.*

press[2] /pres/ *v* **1** (**a**) [Tn, Tn·p] move (sth) by pushing steadily against it: *press the trigger of a gun* ○ *press (down) the accelerator of a car* ○ *press (in) a button* ○ *press a switch (up).* (**b**) [Ipr, Tn·pr] ~ (**sth/sb/oneself**) **against/on sth**; ~ **sth to sth** (cause sth/sb/oneself to) push steadily against sth: *My boot is pressing against a blister on my toe.* ○ *I had to press myself against the wall to let them pass.* ○ *The child pressed her nose against the window.* ○ *He pressed a handkerchief to his nose.* (**c**) [Tn·pr] ~ **sth into sth** put sth in a place by pushing steadily against it: *press money into sb's hand* ○ *press putty into a hole.* **2** [Tn, Cn·a] apply force or weight to (sth) in order to get juice, etc from it: *press apples, olives, oranges, etc* ○ *press grapes to make wine* ○ *press fruit dry*, ie obtain all its juice. **3** [Tn, Cn·a] (**a**) make (sth) flat or smooth (by using force or weight): *press flowers*, eg between pages of a book ○ *press the soil flat with the back of a spade.* (**b**) shape or remove creases from (clothes) by applying pressure with an iron: *That suit ought to be pressed.* ○ *Press the pleats flat.* **4** (**a**) [Tn·pr] ~ **sb/sth to one** hold sb/sth close; embrace sb/sth: *She pressed the child to her.* (**b**) [Tn] squeeze (a person's arm, hand, etc) as a sign of affection: *Overcome with emotion, he pressed her hand and left her.* **5** [Tn, Tn·pr, Cn·t] ~ **sb** (**for sth**) try repeatedly to persuade sb (to do sth): *I don't want to press you, but shouldn't you be leaving?* ○ *The bank is pressing us for repayment of the loan.* ○ *They are pressing us to make a quick decision.* **6** [Tn] make (one's case, etc) urgently or repeatedly (used esp with the *ns* shown): *I don't wish to press the point, but you do owe me £200.* ○ *She is still pressing her claim for compensation.* ○ *They were determined to press their case at the highest level.* **7** [Tn] make a pressing(*n* a) of (a gramophone record). **8** (idm) **be pressed for sth** have barely enough of sth: *Please hurry — we're a bit pressed for time.* ○ *I'm very pressed for cash at the moment — can I pay you next week?* ˌ**press the** ˈ**flesh** (*sl esp US*) (esp of politicians) shake hands with members of the public, esp to win popularity: *Both candidates have been out pressing the flesh in Indiana.* **press sth home** (**a**) push sth into place: *He locked the door and pressed the bolt home.* (**b**) obtain as much advantage as possible from sth by being determined in attacking, arguing, etc: *press home one's advantage* ○ *press home an argument, an attack, a point, etc.* **press sth into** ˈ**shape** flatten, smooth or shape sth by pushing against it. **time presses** ⇨ TIME[1]. **9** (phr v) **press across, against, around, etc** (**sth**) (of people) move in the specified direction by pushing: *The people pressed round the royal visitors.* ○ *The crowds were pressing against the barriers.* ○ *She had to press through the throng to reach the stage.* **press ahead/ forward/on** (**with sth**) continue (doing sth) in a determined way; hurry forward: *The firm is pressing ahead with the modernization plan.* ○ *We must press on with the project without wasting time.* **press for sth** make repeated and urgent requests for sth: *The chairman is pressing for a change in the procedure.* ○ *The unions are pressing for improved working conditions.* **press sth from sth; press sth out of/in sth** make sth by applying force or weight to a surface: *press car bodies out of sheets of steel* ○ *press holes in a piece of leather* ○ *press out shapes from a piece of card.* **press sth from/out of sth; press sth out** remove (juice, etc) from fruit by squeezing: *press the juice from oranges* ○ *press oil from olives* ○ *press the seeds out of a tomato.* **press** (**down**) **on sb** weigh heavily on sb; oppress sb: *His responsibilities press heavily on him.* **press sth on sb** insist that sb accepts sth (against his will): *They pressed gifts on their benefactors.* ○ *I didn't want to take the money but he pressed it on me.* **press sth on/onto sth** attach sth to sth by pressing: *press a label on a parcel* ○ *press a clean pad onto a wound.*

▷ **pressing** *adj* (**a**) urgent: *a pressing engagement.* (**b**) (of a person, request, etc) insistent: *a pressing invitation to dinner* ○ *He was so pressing I couldn't refuse.* **pressingly** *adv.*

pressing *n* (**a**) thing made by pressing, esp a gramophone record: *10 000 pressings of a symphony.* (**b**) number of gramophone records made at one time: *a pressing of several thousand records.*

□ **press-stud** /ˈprestʌd/ *n* (also *infml* **popper**, *esp US* ˈ**snap fastener**) small fastener for clothes made of two parts that can be pressed together.

ˈ**press-up** (*US* ˈ**push-up**) *n* (usu *pl*) exercise in which a person lies facing the floor and, keeping his back straight, raises his shoulders and trunk by pressing down on his hands.

press[3] /pres/ *v* **1** [Tn esp passive] (formerly) force (sb) to serve in the army or navy. **2** (idm) **press sb/sth into** ˈ**service** use sb/ sth because he/it is urgently needed; use sth as a temporary measure: *Her whole family were pressed into service when the shop was busy.* ○ *Old buses were pressed into service as emergency housing for the refugees.*

□ ˈ**press-gang** *n* [CGp] (**a**) (formerly) group of people employed to force men to join the army or navy. (**b**) group who force others to do sth. — *v* [Tn] force (sb) into service: (*joc*) *We were press-ganged into serving the drinks.*

Pressburger /presˈbɜːgə(r)/ Emeric (1902-88), Hungarian film maker. Cf POWELL.

pressure /ˈpreʃə(r)/ *n* **1** [U] (**a**) force or weight of sth pressing continuously on or against sth that it touches: *the pressure of the crowd against the barriers* ○ *The pressure of the water caused the wall of the dam to crack.* (**b**) amount of this: *The tyre is too hard — reduce the pressure a bit.* ○ *Your blood pressure* (ie force of the blood in the veins and arteries) *is too high.* ○ *a pressure of 6 lb to the square inch* ○ [attrib] *a pressure gauge*, ie an instrument for measuring the pressure of liquid, gas, air, etc ○ (*fig*) *work at high pressure.* **2** [U] weight of the air in the atmosphere: *atmospheric pressure* ○ *A band of low pressure is moving across the country.* **3** [U, C] ~ (**of sth**); ~ (**to do sth**) strong or oppressive influence: *She left home to escape the pressure to conform to her family's way of life.* ○ *The pressures of city life forced him to move to the country.* **4** (idm) **bring pressure to bear on sb** (**to do sth**) use force or strong persuasion (to make sb do sth): *The bank will bring pressure to bear on you if you don't pay.* ○ *The council brought pressure to bear on the landlord to improve his property.* **put pressure on sb** (**to do sth**) (try to) force sb (to do sth, esp quickly): *The birth of twins put pressure on them to find a bigger flat.* ○ *I don't want to put pressure on you to make a decision, but we haven't much time left.* **under** ˈ**pressure** (**a**) (of a liquid or gas held in a container) subject to pressure; compressed: *The gas is stored under pressure in the tank.* ○ *The beer comes out of the barrel under pressure.* (**b**) influenced by urgency or compulsion: *work under pressure* ○ *put sb under pressure (to do sth)* ○ *come under pressure (to do sth).* (**c**) suffering stress: *She is constantly under pressure and it is affecting her health.*

▷ **pressure** *v* = PRESSURIZE.

□ ˈ**pressure-cooker** *n* strong tightly-closed pot in which food can be cooked quickly by steam under high pressure. ⇨ illus at PAN[1].

ˈ**pressure group** [CGp] (in politics, business, etc) organized group who try to influence policy, esp by intensive propaganda and campaigning; lobby.

ˈ**pressure point** point at which a blood vessel can be pressed against a bone so as to reduce bleeding.

pressurize, -ise /ˈpreʃəraɪz/ (also **pressure**) *v* **1** [Tn·pr, Cn·t] ~ **sb into sth/doing sth** use force, influence or strong persuasion to make sb do sth: *She was pressurized into agreeing to a merger.* ○ *He felt that he was being pressurized to resign.* **2** [Tn esp passive] keep (the compartment of a submarine, the cabin of an aircraft, etc) at a constant atmospheric pressure: *a pressurized cabin* ○ *The compartments are fully pressurized.* ▷ **pressurization, -isation** /ˌpreʃəraɪˈzeɪʃn; *US* -rɪˈz-/ *n* [U].

□ ˌ**pressurized-**ˈ**water reactor** type of nuclear reactor that uses water under pressure as a coolant.

Prestel /ˈprestel/ (*Brit propr*) system operated by British Telecom that sends information (eg news) via a telephone line so that it can be viewed on a television screen. ⇨ article at TECHNOLOGY.

prestidigitator /ˌprestɪˈdɪdʒɪteɪtə(r)/ *n* (*fml or joc*) conjurer.

▷ **prestidigitation** /ˌprestɪˌdɪdʒɪˈteɪʃn/ *n* [U] (skill in) performing tricks by conjuring; sleight of hand.

prestige /preˈstiːʒ/ *n* [U] **1** respect based on good reputation, past achievements, etc: *lose/regain prestige* ○ *He suffered a loss of prestige when the scandal was publicized.* **2** power to impress others, esp as a result of wealth, distinction, glamour, etc: *have, enjoy, earn prestige in the community* ○ [attrib] *the prestige value of owning a Rolls Royce.*

▷ **prestigious** /preˈstɪdʒəs/ *adj* having or bringing prestige: *one of the world's most prestigious orchestras.*

presto /ˈprestəʊ/ *adj, adv* **1** (*music*) very quick(ly). **2** (idm) **hey presto** ⇨ HEY.

▷ **presto** *n* (*pl* ~**s**) movement or passage of music (to be) played quickly.

pre-stressed /ˌpriːˈstrest/ *adj* (of concrete) strengthened by having stretched cables inside it.

presumable /prɪˈzjuːməbl; *US* -ˈzuː-/ *adj* (*fml*) that may be presumed: *the presumable result is an election defeat.*

▷ **presumably** /-əblɪ/ *adv* it may be presumed: *She is aware of the difficulties, presumably?* ○ *He will presumably resign in view of the complete failure of his policy.*

presume /prɪˈzjuːm; *US* -ˈzuːm/ *v* **1** [Tf, Cn·a, Cn·t] suppose (sth) to be true; take (sth) for granted: *I presume that an agreement will eventually be reached.* ○ *'Are the neighbours away on holiday?' 'I presume so.'* ○ *In English law, an accused man is presumed (to be) innocent until he is proved guilty.* ○ *Twelve passengers are missing, presumed dead.* **2** [It] venture to do sth; be so bold as to do sth: *I won't presume to disturb you.* ○ *May I presume to advise you?* **3** (phr v) **presume on sth** (*fml*) make a wrong use of sth; take unfair advantage of sth: *presume on sb's good nature*, eg by asking for help.

presumption /prɪˈzʌmpʃn/ *n* **1** (**a**) [U] ~ (**of sth**) presuming sth to be true or the case: *presumption of her innocence by the court.* (**b**) [C] thing presumed to be true or very probable: *The article makes too many false presumptions.* ○ *We're having the party in the garden on the presumption that it's not going to rain.* **2** [U] behaviour that is too bold; arrogance: *She was infuriated by his presumption in making the travel arrangements without first consulting her.*

presumptive /prɪˈzʌmptɪv/ *adj* (*fml esp law*) (**a**) based on reasonable belief: *one's presumptive right.* (**b**) probable: *the presumptive heir/the heir presumptive*, ie the person who will inherit the throne unless sb with a stronger claim is born.

presumptuous /prɪˈzʌmptʃʊəs/ *adj* (**a**) (of a person or his behaviour) too bold or self-confident: *Would it be presumptuous of me to ask you to contribute?* (**b**) (of a person) acting without the necessary authority: *He was presumptuous in making the announcement before the decision had been approved.* ▷ **presumptuously** *adv.*

presuppose /ˌpriːsəˈpəʊz/ *v* [Tn, Tf] (not used in the continuous tenses) **1** assume (sth) to be true beforehand: *We cannot presuppose the truth of his statements.* **2** require (sth) as a condition; imply: *Effects presuppose causes.* ○ *Approval of the plan presupposes that the money will be made available.*

▷ **presupposition** /ˌpriːsʌpəˈzɪʃn/ *n* (*fml*) (**a**) [U] action of presupposing (PRESUPPOSE 1). (**b**) [C] thing that is presupposed: *You have made several unjustified presuppositions.* ○ *Bail was refused on the presupposition of his guilt.*

pre-tax /ˌpriːˈtæks/ *adj* before tax has been deducted: ˌ*pre-tax* ˈ*income*, ˈ*profits*, ˈ*surplus, etc.*

pretence (*US* **pretense**) /prɪˈtens/ *n* **1** (**a**) [U] deception; make-believe: *Their friendliness was only pretence.* ○ *Their way of life was all pretence.* (**b**) [sing] ~ **of sth** false show of sth: *a pretence of strength, grief, sleep.* **2** (**a**) [C] ~ **to sth** claim to (merit, honour, etc): *I have no pretence to being an expert on the subject.* (**b**) [U] (*fml*) ostentation; pretentiousness: *an honest, kindly man without pretence.* **3** (idm) **on/under false pretences** ⇨ FALSE.

pretend /prɪˈtend/ *v* **1** [I, Tf, Tt] make oneself appear to be (doing) sth in order to deceive others or in play: *The time has come to stop pretending!* ○ *She pretended (that) she was not at home when we rang the bell.* ○ *The children pretended to eat the mud pies.* **2** [Tn] claim (sth) falsely, esp as an excuse: *She pretended illness as an excuse.* ○ *His pretended friendship was part of the deception.* **3** [Ipr, Tt] ~ **to sth** (*fml*) make a claim to (do) sth: *Surely he doesn't pretend to any understanding of music!* ○ *I don't pretend to know as much as he does about it.*

▷ **pretend** *adj* (*infml*) imaginary: *The children were playing shop with pretend money* ○ *Don't be scared — it's only pretend.*

pretender *n* person whose claim (to a throne, title, etc) is disputed. In British history the **Old Pretender** was James Edward Stuart (1688-1766), the son of *James II, who led two attempts to regain the throne in 1708 and 1715. His son, Charles Edward *Stuart, was the **Young Pretender**, often known as 'Bonny Prince Charlie'. He led the 1745 uprising that was crushed at *Culloden. ⇨ article at SCOTLAND.

pretension /prɪˈtenʃn/ *n* **1** [C usu *pl*] ~ (**to sth/doing sth**) (making of a) claim: *a poet with serious pretensions to literary greatness* ○ *He has/makes no pretensions to being an expert on the subject.* ○ (*derog*) *His social pretensions* (ie behaving as if he was of a higher class) *make him appear ridiculous.* **2** [U] being pretentious: *Readers may find the pretension and arrogance of her style irritating.*

pretentious /prɪˈtenʃəs/ *adj* claiming (esp without justification) merit or importance; pompous or showy: *expressed in pretentious language* ○ *a pretentious writer, book, style.* ▷ **pretentiously** *adv.* **pretentiousness** *n* [U].

preterite (*US* **preterit**) /ˈpretərət/ *adj, n* (*grammar*) (of the) past simple tense (of a verb): *'Ran' is the preterite of 'run'.*

preternatural /ˌpri:təˈnætʃrəl/ *adj* (*fml*) beyond what is natural or normal; unusual: *preternatural power, force, ability, etc* ○ *a preternatural gift for knowing what others are thinking.* ▷ **preternaturally** *adv.*

pretext /ˈpri:tekst/ *n* ~ (**for sth/doing sth**) reason given (for doing sth) that is not the real reason; excuse: *He came to see me on/under the pretext of asking my advice when he really wanted to borrow money.* ○ *We'll have to find a pretext for not going to the party.*

prettify /ˈprɪtɪfaɪ/ *v* (*pt, pp* **-fied**) [Tn] (*usu derog*) make (sth) pretty in a superficial way: *The old farm workers' cottages are being prettified as holiday homes.* Cf BEAUTIFY.

pretty /ˈprɪtɪ/ *adj* (**-ier, -iest**) **1** pleasing and attractive, without being beautiful or magnificent: *a pretty child, pattern, tune* ○ *a pretty* (ie effeminate-looking) *boy* ○ *What a pretty dress!* ○ *She looks very pretty in that hat.* ○ *The bodies of the victims were not a pretty sight.* ⇨ Usage at BEAUTIFUL. **2** (**a**) (*esp dated*) fine; good: *a pretty wit, compliment, turn of phrase.* (**b**) (*ironic*) not pleasing: *You've got yourself into a pretty mess now!* ○ *This a pretty state of affairs!* **3** (idm) **(as) ˌpretty as a ˈpicture** very pretty. **come to such a pass/a pretty pass** ⇨ PASS¹. **not just a pretty ˈface** not just sb who is superficially attractive without having other qualities or abilities: *His good looks won him the election but he has still to prove that he's not just a pretty face.* **a pretty ˈpenny** a lot of money: *Renovating that house will cost you a pretty penny.*

▷ **pretty** *adv* **1** fairly or moderately: *the situation seems pretty hopeless* ○ *She seemed pretty satisfied with the result.* ⇨ Usage at FAIRLY. **2** (idm) **pretty much/nearly/well** almost: *The two are pretty much the same.* ○ *The car is pretty nearly new.* ○ *My patience is pretty well exhausted.* **sitting pretty** ⇨ SIT.

prettily /ˈprɪtɪlɪ/ *adv* in a pretty or charming way: *She decorated the room very prettily.* ○ *She smiled prettily as she accepted the flowers.*

prettiness *n* [U]: *People commented on the prettiness of the cottage.*

□ **ˈpretty-pretty** *adj* (*infml derog*) too pretty: *a pretty-pretty colour scheme of pale pinks and blues* ○ *a frilly, pretty-pretty dress.*

pretzel /ˈpretsl/ *n* crisp salty biscuit made in the shape of a knot or stick.

prevail /prɪˈveɪl/ *v* **1** [I] ~ (**among/in sth/sb**) exist or happen generally; be widespread: *conditions prevailing in the region* ○ *The use of horses for ploughing still prevails among the poorer farmers.* **2** [I, Ipr] ~ (**against/over sb/sth**) (*fml*) fight successfully (against sb/sth); defeat: *Virtue will prevail against evil.* ○ *The invaders prevailed over the native population.* **3** (phr v) **prevail on sb to do sth** (*fml*) persuade sb to do sth: *May I prevail on you to make a speech after dinner?*

▷ **prevailing** *adj* [attrib] (**a**) most usual or widespread: *the prevailing customs, fashions, style, etc.* (**b**) (of a wind) that blows in an area most frequently: *The prevailing wind here is from the south-west.*

prevalent /ˈprevələnt/ *adj* (*fml*) ~ (**among/in sth/sb**) existing or happening generally; widespread: *The prevalent opinion is in favour of reform.* ○ *Is malaria still prevalent among the population here?*

▷ **prevalence** /-əns/ *n* [U] being prevalent: *They were very surprised by the prevalence of anti-government sentiments.*

prevaricate /prɪˈværɪkeɪt/ *v* [I] (*fml*) try to avoid telling the (whole) truth by speaking in an evasive or a misleading way; equivocate: *Tell us exactly what happened and don't prevaricate.*

▷ **prevarication** /prɪˌværɪˈkeɪʃn/ *n* (**a**) [U] prevaricating. (**b**) [C] instance of this: *The report was full of lies and prevarications.*

prevaricator *n* person who prevaricates.

prevent /prɪˈvent/ *v* [Tn, Tn·pr, Tsg] ~ **sb/sth** (**from doing sth**) stop or hinder sb/sth: *prevent the spread of a disease/a disease from spreading* ○ *Nobody can prevent us/our getting married.* ○ *Your prompt action prevented a serious accident.*

▷ **preventable** *adj* that can be prevented: *preventable accidents, deaths, diseases, etc.*

prevention /prɪˈvenʃn/ *n* **1** [U] (action of) preventing: *the prevention of crime* ○ *the prevention of cruelty to animals.* **2** (idm) **preˌvention is ˌbetter than ˈcure** (*saying*) it is easier to prevent sth happening than to undo the damage or cure the disease later.

preventive /prɪˈventɪv/ (also **preventative** /prɪˈventətɪv/) *adj* (**a**) preventing or intended to prevent sth; precautionary: *preventive measures.* (**b**) (of medicine) preventing or intended to prevent disease; prophylactic: *research into preventive medicine*, ie ways of preventing disease.

▷ **preventive** (also **preventative**) *n* thing (esp a medicine) used or designed to prevent sth.

□ **preˌventive deˈtention** (*law*) imprisonment of sb because it is thought likely that he will commit a crime.

preview /ˈpri:vju:/ *n* (**a**) showing of a film, an exhibition, a play, etc before it is shown to the general public: *a press preview*, ie one for journalists only ○ *We attended a sneak preview of the winter fashion collection.* (**b**) report or description of a film, performance of a play, etc before it is shown to the general public: *a preview of next week's viewing/listening.*

▷ **preview** *v* [Tn] have or give a preview of (sth).

previous /ˈpri:vɪəs/ *adj* **1** [attrib] coming before in time or order: *We had met on a previous occasion.* ○ *He was there the previous day.* ○ *Who was the previous owner?* ○ *I am unable to attend because of a previous engagement.* ○ *The criminal had had four previous convictions.* ○ *Applicants for the job must have previous experience.* **2** [pred] (*infml*) done or acting too hastily; presumptuous: *Aren't you rather previous in assuming I am going to pay?*

▷ **previously** *adv*: *She had previously worked in television.*

pre-war /ˌpri:ˈwɔ:(r)/ *adj* [esp attrib] occurring or existing before a war, esp the Second World War: *in the pre-war period* ○ *ˌpre-war ˈcars, ˈhousing, maˈchinery, etc*, ie built or made before the Second World War ○ *ˌpre-war ˈgovernments.*

prey /preɪ/ *n* **1** (**a**) animal, bird, etc hunted and killed by another for food: *a beast/bird of prey*, ie one that kills and eats others, eg a tiger, an eagle ○ *The lion stalked its prey through the long grass.* ○ *Mice and other small creatures are the owl's prey.* (**b**) (*fig*) person who is exploited or harmed by another; victim: *She was easy prey for dishonest salesmen.* **2** (idm) **be/fall prey to sth** (**a**) (of an animal) be hunted and killed for food by another: *The zebra fell prey to the lion.* (**b**) (of a person) be greatly troubled or tormented by sth: *She was prey to irrational fears.*

▷ **prey** *v* **1** (idm) **prey on sb's ˈmind** trouble sb greatly: *Fear of the consequences preyed on her mind.* ○ *The thought that he was responsible for her death preyed on his mind.* **2** (phr v) **prey on sb/sth** (**a**) hunt or catch (an animal, etc) as prey: *hawks preying on small birds.* (**b**) make sb one's victim; exploit or attack: *a confidence trickster preying on rich widows* ○ *The villagers were preyed on by bandits from the hills.*

price /praɪs/ *n* **1** amount of money for which sth is (to be) bought or sold: *What is the price of this table?* ○ *a woollen sweater, price £19.95* ○ *Prices are rising, falling, going up, going down, shooting up, plummeting, etc.* ○ *I can't afford it at that price.* ○ *charge high prices* ○ *He sold the house at/for a good price.* ○ *Ask the builder to give you a price* (ie say how much he will charge) *for the work.* ○ [attrib] *the fixing of price levels.* ⇨ Usage. **2** what must be done, given or experienced to get or keep sth: *Loss of independence was a high price to pay for peace.* ○ *Being recognized wherever you go is the price you pay for being famous.* ○ *No price is too high for winning their support.* **3** the odds in betting: *Six to one is a good price for that horse.* ○ *the starting price*, ie odds offered by a bookmaker on a race just before it starts. **4** (idm) **at a ˈprice** at a (fairly) high price: *Fresh strawberries are now available — at a price!* **at ˈany price** whatever the cost: *The people wanted peace at any price.* **beyond/above/without ˈprice** (*esp rhet*) extremely valuable; so valuable that it cannot be bought. **cheap at the ˈprice** worth more than the price paid or quoted: *'You're surely not asking £40 for this book?' 'Yes — it's cheap at the price!'* ○ (*joc*) *'It'll cost a fortune to go on holiday there!' 'It'll be cheap at the price if it keeps the family happy.'* **everyone has his ˈprice** (*saying*) everyone can be bribed in some way. **not at ˈany price** in no circumstances, however favourable: *I wouldn't have my sister's children to stay again — not at any price!* **of great ˈprice** (*rhet*) extremely valuable. **pay a/the price** ⇨ PAY². **a ˈprice on sb's head** reward offered for sb's capture or for killing him: *The authorities put a price on the outlaw's head.* ○ *He knew it was dangerous to be seen — there was a price on his head.* **put a price on sth** value sth in terms of money: *You can't put a price on that sort of loyalty.* **what price...?** (*Brit infml*) (**a**) (used when sneering at the failure of sth) see how worthless it was: *What price peaceful protest now?* ○ *What price all your promises now?* (**b**) what is the chance of...?: *What price he'll offer to pay the fine for us?*

▷ **price** *v* **1** [Tn, Tn·pr] ~ **sth** (**at sth**) fix the price of sth (at a particular level): *The agent priced the house at the right level for the market.* ○ *These goods are priced too high.* ○ *Even the cheapest was priced at £5.* **2** [Tn] find or estimate the price of (sth): *I don't know enough about porcelain to be able to price these plates.* **3** [Tn] mark (goods) with a price: *The assistant priced the garments before putting them on display.* **4** (idm) **price oneself/sth out of the ˈmarket** charge such a high price for one's goods, services, etc that nobody buys them.

priceless *adj* **1** too valuable to be priced: *priceless jewels, paintings, treasures, etc* ○ (*fig*) *Her one priceless asset is her unflappability.* ⇨ Usage at INVALUABLE. **2** (*infml*) very amusing or absurd: *a priceless joke* ○ *You look absolutely priceless in that hat!*

pricey (also **pricy**) /ˈpraɪsɪ/ *adj* (**-ier, -iest**) [usu pred] (*Brit infml*) expensive: *This restaurant is a bit pricey for me.*

□ **ˈprice control** control of price levels, esp by a government.

ˈprice-fixing *n* [U] (**a**) (*usu derog*) setting prices by agreement among producers, esp so as to keep them artificially high. (**b**) = PRICE CONTROL.

ˈprice-list *n* list of current prices for goods on sale.

ˈprice-tag *n* (**a**) label showing the price of sth. (**b**) ~ (**on sth**) (*fig*) cost of sth: *The price-tag on the new fighter plane was too high for the government.*

ˈprice war situation in which competing sellers repeatedly reduce their prices in order to attract buyers.

NOTE ON USAGE: The **price** and **cost** of something is the amount of money needed to buy it. **Price** is generally used of objects which can be bought or sold; **cost** usually relates to services or processes: *the price of vegetables, houses, land* ○ *the cost of growing vegetables, decorating the house, building on land* ○ *the cost of a holiday in France.* **Charge** is the amount of money asked, usually for a service: *electricity charges* ○ *the charge for parking.* **Price**, **cost** and **charge** can also be verbs: *They've priced their house very high,* ie They're asking a high price. ○ *How much did your holiday cost?* ○ *How much do they charge for advertising?*

prick[1] /prɪk/ *n* **1** (a) act of pricking: *I gave my finger a prick with a needle.* (b) small hole or mark caused by this: *You can see the pricks where the stitches were.* **2** pain caused by pricking: *I can still feel the prick.* ○ (*fig*) *the pricks of conscience,* ie mental uneasiness. **3** (⚠ *sl*) (a) penis. (b) (*derog*) (stupid) man: *What a stupid prick you are!* **4** (idm) **kick against the pricks** ⇨ KICK[1].

prick[2] /prɪk/ *v* **1** (a) [Tn, Tn·pr] ~ **sth (with sth)** pierce sth with a sharp point; make a tiny hole in sth: *The child pricked the balloon and it burst.* ○ *He pricked the blister on his heel with a sterilized needle.* ○ *prick holes in paper with a pin.* (b) [Tn, Tn·pr] ~ **sth (on/with sth)** cause pain in sth by pricking: *She pricked her finger on/with a needle.* ○ *Be careful — the thorns will prick you.* (c) [Tn] (*fig*) cause mental discomfort to (sb): *His conscience is pricking him now that he realizes what he has done.* **2** [I] feel a sharp pain or a sensation of being pricked: *My fingers are beginning to prick after touching that paste.* ○ *The vapour made his eyes prick.* **3** (idm) **prick the bubble (of sth)** destroy sb's illusion about sth: *The latest trade figures will surely prick the bubble of government complacency about the economic situation.* **prick up one's ears** (a) (of an animal, esp a horse or dog) raise the ears. (b) (of a person) suddenly begin to pay attention to what is being said: *The children pricked up their ears when they heard the word 'ice-cream'.* **4** (phr v) **prick sth out/off** plant (young plants) in small holes made in the soil with eg a pointed stick.
▷ **pricking** *n* (usu *sing*) (a) act of pricking. (b) sensation of being pricked: *She felt a pricking on her scalp.*

prickle /ˈprɪkl/ *n* **1** (a) small pointed growth on the stem or leaf of a plant; thorn. (b) small pointed growth on the skin of certain animals, eg a hedgehog; spine. **2** pricking sensation on the skin.
▷ **prickle** *v* [I, Tn] (cause sb/sth to) have a feeling of being pricked: *The woollen cloth prickles (my skin).* ○ *My scalp began to prickle as I realized the horrible truth.*

prickly /ˈprɪklɪ/ *adj* (**-ier**, **-iest**) **1** (a) covered with prickles (PRICKLE 1a): *prickly rose-bushes.* (b) having or causing a sensation of prickling: *My skin feels prickly.* ○ *a prickly feeling, sensation, etc.* **2** (*infml*) (of a person) easily angered; irritable; touchy: *You're a bit prickly today!* **prickliness** *n* [U]. **prickly ˈheat** skin condition common in hot climates, with inflammation of the skin near the sweat glands which causes a prickly sensation. **prickly ˈpear** (a) type of cactus covered with prickles. (b) its pear-shaped edible fruit.

pride /praɪd/ *n* **1** (a) [U] ~ **(in sb/sth)** feeling of pleasure or satisfaction which one gets from doing sth well, from owning sth excellent or widely admired, etc: *She looked with pride at the result of her work.* ○ *Her pride in her achievements is justified.* ○ *He felt a glow of pride as people admired his new car.* ○ *the pride of parenthood.* (b) [sing] **the ~ of sth** person or thing that is an object or source of this: *The new car was the pride of the whole family.* ○ *He was the pride of the village after winning the championship.* **2** [U] (*derog*) unjustifiably high opinion of oneself or one's achievements; arrogance: *the sin of pride* ○ *He was puffed up with pride.* **3** [U] knowledge of one's own worth or character; dignity and self-respect: *Her pride was hurt.* ○ *He has no pride if he lets the children talk to him so rudely.* ○ *Having to accept the money was a blow to her pride.* ○ *He refused to accept help out of a false sense of pride.* **4** [CGp] group of (esp) lions. **5** (idm) **pride comes/goes before a ˈfall** (*saying*) if you behave arrogantly, sth will happen to make you look foolish. **pride of ˈplace** the most prominent or important position, because of being the best or best-liked: *The model has pride of place in his collection.* **sb's pride and ˈjoy** person or thing that sb is very proud of: *Their baby is their pride and joy.* **put one's pride in one's pocket** do sth that would normally make one feel ashamed and humiliated. **swallow/pocket one's pride** hide or surpress one's feelings of anger or shame. **take (a) pride in sb/sth** be proud of sb/sth: *She takes great pride in her children's success.* **take pride in sth** do sth carefully or well because it is important to one: *He takes no pride in his work.* ○ *You should take more pride in your appearance.*
▷ **pride** *v* (phr v) **pride oneself on sth/doing sth** be proud of sth: *She prides herself on her garden/on her skill as a gardener.* ○ *He prides himself on remaining calm in an emergency.*

Pride's Purge /ˌpraɪdz ˈpɜːdʒ/ the removal in 1648 of those Members of Parliament who might have voted against the proposal to try *Charles I. This action was carried out by Colonel Thomas Pride and his Parliamentary troops. Those Members who were left formed the *Rump Parliament.

priest /priːst/ *n* **1** person appointed to perform religious duties and ceremonies in the Christian Church, esp one who is between a deacon and a bishop in the Roman Catholic, Orthodox or Anglican Church (more usu called a *clergyman* in the Anglican Church): *a parish priest* ○ *the ordination of women priests.* Cf MINISTER[1] 3, VICAR. **2** (*fem* **priestess** /ˈpriːstes/) person who performs religious ceremonies in a non-Christian religion.
▷ **the priesthood** /-hʊd/ *n* (a) [sing] office or position of a priest: *enter the priesthood.* (b) [Gp] whole body of priests (esp of a particular Church or country): *the Catholic priesthood* ○ *the Spanish priesthood.*
priestlike *adj* like a priest.
priestly *adj* [usu attrib] of, like or relating to a priest: *his priestly duties.*

Priestley[1] /ˈpriːstlɪ/ J(ohn) B(oynton) (1894-1984), English author. His many popular novels, essays and plays present his personal view of England, good-humoured though at times highly critical.

Priestley[2] /ˈpriːstlɪ/ Joseph (1733-1804), English chemist and radical thinker. His most famous scientific achievement was the discovery of oxygen (which he called 'dephlogisticated air'). He was one of the founders of *Unitarianism; his support for the French Revolution led to protests which made him leave England to settle in America.

prig /prɪg/ *n* (*derog*) person who behaves as if he were morally superior to everyone else, and disapproves of what others do; self-righteous person.
▷ **priggish** *adj* of or (behaving) like a prig. **priggishly** *adv.* **priggishness** *n* [U].

prim /prɪm/ *adj* (**-mmer**, **-mmest**) (*usu derog*) **1** (of a person) disliking anything that is improper, rude or rough; prudish: *You can't tell that joke to her — she's much too prim and proper.* **2** stiffly formal in appearance, behaviour or manner: *a prim little dress with a white collar.* ▷ **primly** *adv*: *He didn't reply, but just smiled primly.* **primness** *n* [U].

prima ballerina /ˌpriːmə ˌbæləˈriːnə/ leading woman dancer in (a) ballet.

primacy /ˈpraɪməsɪ/ *n* **1** [U] (*fml*) leading position; pre-eminence: *the primacy of moral values, the monarchy, the Communist Party.* **2** [C] office or position of an archbishop.

prima donna /ˌpriːmə ˈdɒnə/ **1** leading woman singer in (an) opera. **2** (*derog*) person who easily gets into a bad temper when others do not do as he wants, when his idea of his own importance is challenged, etc.

primaeval = PRIMEVAL.

prima facie /ˌpraɪməˈfeɪʃiː/ *adj* [attrib], *adv* (*esp law*) based on what seems to be so without further or deeper investigation: *prima facie evidence,* ie sufficient to establish sth legally (unless it is disproved later) ○ *Prima facie he would appear to be guilty.*

primal /ˈpraɪml/ *adj* [attrib] (*fml*) **1** first or original; primeval: *the loss of their primal innocence.* **2** chief or most important; fundamental; primary(2): *of primal importance.*

primary /ˈpraɪmərɪ; *US* -merɪ/ *adj* **1** (a) [usu attrib] earliest in time or order of development: *in the primary stage of development* ○ *The disease is still in its primary stage.* ○ *primary causes* ○ *primary industries,* eg mining or forestry, which provide raw materials. (b) (also **Primary**) of the lowest or earliest series of geological strata: *Primary rocks.* **2** [usu attrib] most important; fundamental: *The primary reason for advertising is to sell more goods.* ○ *the primary* (ie basic) *meaning of a word* ○ *This is of primary importance.* ○ *primary stress/accent,* ie the strongest stress given to a syllable in a word or compound (shown in this dictionary by the mark ˈ). Cf PRINCIPAL. **3** [attrib] of or for primary education: *primary teachers.* Cf SECONDARY.
▷ **primarily** /ˈpraɪmərəlɪ; *US* praɪˈmerəlɪ/ *adv* mainly: *The purpose of the programme is primarily educational.*
primary *n* (also **primary eˈlection**) (in the US) election in which voters select party candidates for a coming election: *the presidential primaries.*
□ **primary ˈcolour** any of the colours from which all other colours can be obtained by mixing, ie (of dye or paint) red, yellow and blue and (of light) red, green and violet.
ˌprimary eduˈcation education in the first years of school, for children of (usu) 5-11 years.
ˈprimary school **1** (*Brit*) first school for children of (usu) 5-11 years. **2** (*US* **grade school**, **grammar school**) part of an elementary school, for children of (usu) 6-9 years. ⇨ article at SCHOOL.

primate[1] /ˈpraɪmeɪt/ *n* archbishop: *the Primate of all England,* ie the Archbishop of Canterbury.

primate[2] /ˈpraɪmeɪt/ *n* member of the most highly developed order of mammals that includes human beings, apes, monkeys and lemurs.

prime[1] /praɪm/ *adj* [attrib] **1** most important; chief; fundamental: *Her prime motive was personal ambition.* ○ *Her prime concern is to protect the property.* ○ *It is a matter of prime importance.* ○ *The prime cause of the trouble was bad management.* **2** of the best quality; excellent: *prime (cuts of) beef* ○ *a prime site for development.* **3** having all the expected or typical qualities: *That's a prime* (ie very typical, excellent) *example of what I was talking about.*
□ **ˌprime ˈcost** basic cost of producing or manufacturing sth (ie the cost of materials and labour) not including such additional items as rent and insurance for premises.
ˌprime meˈridian line of longitude which passes through Greenwich near London, numbered zero, from which the other lines of longitude are calculated.
ˌprime ˈminister chief minister in a government. ⇨ article at PARLIAMENT.
ˌprime ˈmover (a) fundamental source of power for providing movement, such as wind or water. (b) person who originates a plan, course of action, etc and has it put into practice: *He was the prime mover in the revolt against the government.*
ˌprime ˈnumber (*mathematics*) number which can be divided exactly only by itself and 1 (eg 7, 17, 41).
ˌprime ˈtime (in broadcasting) time when the highest number of people are watching or listening: [attrib] *ˌprime-time ˈadvertising, ˈshows, ˈslots.*

prime[2] /praɪm/ *n* [sing] **1** (a) state or time of greatest strength, beauty, vigour, etc: *When is a man in his prime?* ○ *She is past her prime.* (b) state of highest perfection; the best part: *be in the prime of life/youth.* **2** (*rhet*) first or earliest part: *the prime of the year,* ie spring.

prime[3] /praɪm/ *v* [Tn, Tn·pr] ~ **sth/sb (with sth)** **1** make sth ready for use or action: *prime a pump,* ie put liquid in it to make it start working ○ *prime an explosive device,* ie set the trigger. **2** prepare (wood, etc) for painting by covering it with a substance that prevents the paint from being absorbed. **3** supply sb with facts or information in advance, sometimes dishonestly, so that he can deal with a situation: *The witness had been primed by a lawyer.* ○ *The party representative had been well primed with the facts by party headquarters.* ○ *The witness seemed to have been primed* (ie instructed) *about what to say.* **4** (*infml*) give sb plenty of food and drink (in preparation for sth): *We were well primed for the journey with a large breakfast.* **5** (idm) **prime the ˈpump** encourage the growth of a new or inactive business or industry by investing money in it.

primer[1] /ˈpraɪmə(r)/ *n* (*dated*) textbook for people just starting to study a subject: *a Latin primer.*

primer[2] /ˈpraɪmə(r)/ *n* **1** [U, C] substance used to prime[3](2) a surface for painting. **2** [C] amount of explosive in a small container used to explode the main charge of gunpowder in a cartridge, bomb, etc.

primeval (also **primaeval**) /praɪˈmi:vl/ *adj* [usu attrib] (**a**) of the earliest period of the history of the world: *primeval rocks.* (**b**) very ancient: *primeval forests,* ie natural forests, where trees have never been cut down. (**c**) based on instinct rather than reason, as if from the earliest period of the human race: *It aroused strange primeval yearnings in him.*

primitive /ˈprɪmɪtɪv/ *adj* **1** [usu attrib] of or at an early stage of social development: *primitive culture, customs, tribes* ○ *primitive man* ○ *primitive weapons,* eg bows and arrows, spears. **2** (*often derog*) simple and unsophisticated, as if from an earlier period of history: *They built a primitive shelter out of tree trunks.* ○ *Living conditions in the camp were pretty primitive.*

▷ **primitive** *n* (**a**) painter or sculptor of the period before the Renaissance. (**b**) artist of the modern period who paints in a simple childlike style (as if) without any formal artistic training. (**c**) example of the work of a primitive.

primitively *adv.*

primitiveness *n* [U].

primogeniture /ˌpraɪməʊˈdʒenɪtʃə(r); *US* -tʃʊər/ *n* [U] **1** fact of being a first-born child. **2** (also **right of primogeniture**) (*law*) system of inheritance by which an eldest son receives his parents' property.

primordial /praɪˈmɔ:dɪəl/ *adj* [attrib] (*fml*) existing at or from the beginning, esp of the world or the universe; primeval: *The universe was created out of a primordial ball of matter.* ▷ **primordially** /-dɪəlɪ/ *adv.*

primp /prɪmp/ *v* (*dated*) **1** [I, Tn] (*derog*) tidy (oneself, one's hair, etc) in a fussy way: *primp and preen in front of a mirror.* **2** (phr v) **primp oneself up** make oneself look smart.

primrose /ˈprɪmrəʊz/ *n* **1** [C] (**a**) wild plant that has pale yellow flowers in spring. ⇨ illus at PLANT. (**b**) one of its flowers. **2** [U] pale yellow colour. **3** (idm) **the primrose ˈpath** (*rhet*) the pursuit of pleasure or an easy life: *the primrose path to ruin.*

▷ **primrose** *adj* of a pale yellow colour.

□ **the ˌPrimrose ˈLeague** British political organization that supports the Conservative party and its principles.

primula /ˈprɪmjʊlə/ *n* any of various types of plant of the primrose family with clusters of flowers of various colours and sizes, commonly grown in gardens.

Primus /ˈpraɪməs/ *n* (*pl* ~**es**) (also **ˈprimus stove**) (*propr*) type of portable oil-burning stove for cooking on, used eg by campers.

primus inter pares /ˌpraɪməs ɪntə ˈpɑ:ri:z/ (*Latin*) first among equals; person acting as a spokesman, chairman, etc for colleagues or associates.

prince /prɪns/ *n* **1** (**a**) male member of a royal family who is not the king, esp (in Britain) a son or grandson of the sovereign: *the Prince of Wales,* ie (in Britain, the title often given to the) heir to the throne. (**b**) hereditary royal ruler, esp of a small state: *Prince Rainier of Monaco.* (**c**) (in some countries) a nobleman. **2** (*fig*) excellent or outstanding man in a particular field: *Bocuse, a prince among chefs.* **3** (idm) **Hamlet without the prince** ⇨ HAMLET.

▷ **princedom** /-dəm/ *n* (**a**) [U] rank of a prince. (**b**) [C] area ruled by a prince(1b); principality.

princely *adj* (**a**) [usu attrib] of, like or ruled by a prince: *princely states.* (**b**) (**-ier**, **-iest**) splendid or generous: *a princely gift, sum* ○ (*ironic*) *They paid me the princely sum of 50p.*

princess /prɪnˈses/ *n* (**a**) female member of a royal family who is not the queen, esp (in Britain) the daughter or granddaughter of the sovereign: *Princess Margaret.* (**b**) wife of a prince. **ˌPrincess ˈRoyal** (in Britain) (title often given to the) eldest daughter of the sovereign.

□ **ˌPrince ˈCharming 1** handsome prince who is the hero of various children's stories, eg *Cinderella.* **2** (*often joc*) ideal man who is handsome, helpful, etc: *I don't expect I'll ever marry Prince Charming.*

ˌPrince ˈConsort (title often given to the) husband of a reigning queen. Prince Albert, husband of Queen Victoria, was known by this title.

the ˌPrinces in the ˈTower the young sons of *Edward IV who went to live in the royal apartments of the Tower of London in 1483 after their father died. They disappeared and historians believe they were murdered either by *Richard III, who had seized the throne, or by *Henry VII.

Prince Edward Island /ˌprɪns ˈedwəd aɪlənd/ smallest province of Canada, an island on the east coast opposite *Nova Scotia. The main economic activities are agriculture and fishing. ⇨ map at App 1.

principal /ˈprɪnsəpl/ *adj* [attrib] first in rank or importance; chief; main: *the principal members of the government* ○ *The Danube is one of the principal rivers of Europe.* ○ *The principal aim of the policy is to bring peace to the area.* ○ *The low salary is her principal reason for leaving the job.* ○ *the principal beneficiaries of a will.* Cf PRIMARY 2.

▷ **principal** *n* **1** (title of the) person with the highest authority in an organization, esp in certain schools and colleges: *the Principal of St James' College.* **2** person who takes a leading part in a play, an opera, etc. **3** (usu *sing*) (*finance*) money lent or invested on which interest is paid; capital sum: *repay principal and interest.* **4** person for whom another acts as his agent, eg in business or law: *I must consult my principals before agreeing to your proposal.* **5** (*law*) person directly responsible for a crime (contrasted with an accessory or abetter).

principally /-plɪ/ *adv* for the most part; chiefly: *The dialect is spoken principally in the rural areas.* ○ *Weymouth is principally a holiday resort.*

□ **ˌprincipal ˈboy** leading male role in a pantomime, traditionally played by a woman.

ˌprincipal ˈparts (in English) those forms of a verb (ie the infinitive, past tense and past participle) from which all other forms can be derived.

NOTE ON USAGE: Note that **principle** is a noun relating to rules of behaviour: *She leads her life according to Christian principles.* **Principal** is a (rather formal) adjective meaning 'main' or 'most important': *My principal concern is my family's welfare.* ○ *the principal objections to the proposal.* As a noun it is used for the director of certain educational institutions (usually in further education): *The principal and the vice-principal of the college both attended the meeting.*

principality /ˌprɪnsɪˈpælətɪ/ *n* **1** country ruled by a prince: *the principality of Monaco.* **2 the Principality** [sing] (*Brit*) Wales.

principle /ˈprɪnsəpl/ *n* **1** [C] basic general truth that underlies sth (eg a subject or a system of morality): *a textbook which teaches the basic principles of geometry* ○ *the principle of equality of opportunity for all* ○ *Discussing all these details will get us nowhere: we must get back to first principles.* **2** (**a**) [C usu *pl*] guiding rule for personal behaviour: *principles of conduct* ○ *live according to/up to one's principles* ○ *She seems to have no principles at all* (ie behaves immorally) *when it is a question of making money.* ○ *It would be against my principles to lie to you.* (**b**) [U] these rules: *a woman of (high) principle* ○ *He is quite without principle,* ie behaves immorally. ○ *It is a matter of principle with her to answer her children's questions honestly.* **3** [sing] general or scientific law shown in the way a thing works, or used as the basis for constructing a machine, etc: *These machines both work on the same principle.* ○ *The system works on the principle that heat rises.* ⇨ Usage at PRINCIPAL. **4** (idm) **in principle** (**a**) as far as basic principles are concerned: *There's no reason in principle why people couldn't travel to Mars,* ie It is possible, though it has not yet been done. (**b**) in general but not in detail: *They have agreed to the proposal in principle but we still have to negotiate the terms.* **on principle** because of one's (moral) principles or a fixed belief: *Many people are opposed to the sale of arms on principle.*

▷ **principled** *adj* (esp in compounds) based on or having (esp good) principles (PRINCIPLE 2) of behaviour: *a (high-)principled man* ○ *low-principled behaviour* ○ *I have no principled objection to it,* ie no objection based on moral scruples.

print[1] /prɪnt/ *n* **1** [U] letters, words, numbers, etc in printed form: *Headlines are written in large print.* ○ *The print is too small for me to read without glasses.* **2** [C] (esp in compounds) mark left on a surface where sth has (been) pressed on it: *ˈfingerprints* ○ *ˈfootprints.* **3** [C] (**a**) picture or design made by printing from an inked surface: *an old Japanese print* ○ *a series of prints of London life.* (**b**) photograph printed from a negative: *colour prints.* **4** [U, C] printed cotton fabric: *She bought a/some flowery print to make a summer dress.* ○ [attrib] *a print dress.* **5** (idm) **in print** (**a**) (of a book) available for sale from the publisher: *Is that volume still in print?* (**b**) (of a person's work) printed in a book, newspaper, etc: *It was the first time he had seen himself/his work in print.* **ˌout of ˈprint** (of a book) no longer available from the publisher: *Her first novel is out of print now but you may find a second-hand copy.* **rush into print** ⇨ RUSH[1]. **the small ˈprint** ⇨ SMALL.

print[2] /prɪnt/ *v* **1** (**a**) [Tn] make letters, pictures, etc on (paper) by pressing an inked surface against it: *The first 64 pages of the book have been printed.* ○ *They bought a new machine to print the posters.* (**b**) [Tn, Tn·pr] ~ **sth** (**in/on sth**) make (letters, pictures, etc) on paper by pressing an inked surface against it: *The poems were printed on a small hand press.* ○ *You surely won't print* (ie publish, esp in a newspaper) *such a scandalous allegation.* ○ (*fig*) *The events printed themselves on her memory,* ie could not be forgotten. (**c**) [Tn] make (books, pictures, etc) in this way: *The publisher has printed 10000 copies of the book.* ○ *The firm specializes in printing advertisements.* **2** [I, Tn] write (with) separated letters like those used in printing (rather than joined together as in handwriting): *Children learn to print when they first go to school.* ○ *The child carefully printed his name in capitals at the bottom of his picture.* **3** [Tn, Tn·pr] ~ **sth** (**in/on sth**) press (a mark or design) on a surface: *print letters in the sand* ○ *print a flower design on cotton fabric.* **4** [Tn] make a design on (a surface or fabric) by pressing a surface against it which has been coloured with ink or dye: *printed cotton, wallpaper.* **5** [Tn, Tn·p] ~ **sth** (**off**) make (a photograph) from a negative film or plate: *How many copies shall I print (off) for you?* **6** [I] (**a**) (of a photograph) be produced from a negative film or plate: *This snapshot hasn't printed very well.* (**b**) (of a plate or film) produce a picture: *This plate has been damaged — it won't print very well.* **7** (idm) **a licence to print money** ⇨ LICENCE. **the ˌprinted ˈword** what is published in books, newspapers, etc: *the power of the printed word to influence people's attitudes.* **8** (phr v) **print** (**sth**) **out** (*computing*) (of a machine) produce (information from a computer) in printed form.

▷ **printable** /-əbl/ *adj* fit to be published or printed: *The article is too badly written to be printable.* ○ *His comment when he heard the news*

was not printable! ie was too rude to be printed.
printer *n* **1** (**a**) person whose job is printing. (**b**) owner of a printing firm. **2** machine for printing, esp one attached to a computer, word processor, etc.
printing *n* (**a**) [U] action or art of printing. Printing was invented in China around the 8th century AD and came to Europe in the 15th century, when Gutenberg invented movable type, made up of separate letters that can be combined and reused. Today's computerized printers use lasers or jets of ink to produce high-quality material at great speed: *They have made a good job of the printing.* ○ *The invention of printing caused important changes in society.* ○ [attrib] *a printing error.* (**b**) [C] number of copies of a book printed at one time; impression: *a printing of 5 000 copies.*
ˈprinting-ink ink used for the printing of books, newspapers, etc. **ˈprinting-press** (also **ˈprinting-machine**) *n* machine for printing books, newspapers, etc.
□ **ˌprinted ˈcircuit** electric circuit with thin strips of conducting material (instead of wires) on a flat sheet.
ˈprinted matter (also **ˌprinted ˈpapers**) printed material (eg newspapers, magazines) which may be sent by post at a reduced rate.
printout /ˈprɪntaʊt/ *n* [C, U] (piece of) material produced in printed form from a computer or teleprinter: *Get me a printout of the statistics.*

prior[1] /ˈpraɪə(r)/ *adj* [attrib] coming before in time, order or importance: *They have a prior claim to the property*, ie one which invalidates any other claim(s), eg because based on an earlier legal agreement. ○ *My children have a prior claim on my time.* ○ *I shall have to refuse your invitation because of a prior engagement.* ○ *You need no prior knowledge to be able to do this test.* Cf POSTERIOR 1.
□ **prior to** *prep* (*fml*) before: *We received no notification prior to today's date* (ie before today).

prior[2] /ˈpraɪə(r)/ *n* (*fem* **prioress** /ˈpraɪərɪs, *also* ˌpraɪəˈres/) (**a**) person who is head of a religious order, or of a monastery or convent. (**b**) (in an abbey) person next in rank below an abbot or abbess.
▷ **priory** /ˈpraɪərɪ/ *n* monastery governed by a prior or convent governed by a prioress.

prioritize, -ise /praɪˈɒrətaɪz; *US* -ˈɔːr-/ *v* [Tn] give priority to (eg a project). ▷ **prioritization, -isation** /praɪˌɒrətaɪˈzeɪʃn; *US* -ˌɔːr-/ *n* [U].

priority /praɪˈɒrətɪ; *US* -ˈɔːr-/ *n* **1** [U] ~ (**over sb/sth**) (**a**) (state of) being more important (in rank): *Japan's priority (over other countries) in the field of microelectronics.* (**b**) right to have or do sth before others: *I have priority over you in my claim.* (**c**) right to proceed ahead of other traffic: *Vehicles coming from the right have priority.* **2** (**a**) [C] thing that is (regarded as) more important than others: *You must decide what your priorities are.* ○ *Housework is low on her list of priorities.* ○ *Rebuilding the area is a (top) priority.* (**b**) [U] ~ (**over sth**) high or top place among various things to be done: *The Government gave (top) priority to reforming the legal system.* ○ *The search for a new vaccine took priority over all other medical research.* ○ [attrib] *Priority cases, such as homeless families, get dealt with first.* **3** (idm) **get one's priorities right, wrong, etc** know/not know what is most important and act accordingly: *Your trouble is you've got your priorities back to front!*

prise (also *esp US* **prize**) /praɪz/ *v* **1** [Tn·p, Cn·a] ~ **sth off/up** use force to open (a box, etc) or remove (a lid, etc): *She used a chisel to prise off the lid.* ○ *The box had been prised open.* **2** (phr v) **prise sth out of sb** force sb to reveal sth: *She'd promised not to talk, and nothing we could do could prise the information out of her.* Cf PRY[2].

prism /ˈprɪzəm/ *n* **1** solid geometric shape with ends that are parallel and of the same size and shape, and with sides that are parallelograms. **2** transparent object of this shape, usu triangular and made of glass, which breaks up ordinary light into the colours of the rainbow. ⇨ illus at SPECTRUM.

prismatic /prɪzˈmætɪk/ *adj* **1** of, like or being a prism. **2** (of colours) bright, clear and varied; rainbow-like. **3** that uses a prism: *a prismatic compass* ○ *prismatic binoculars.*

prison /ˈprɪzn/ *n* **1** [C] (**a**) place where people are kept locked up as a punishment for crimes they have committed or while awaiting trial: *The prisons are overcrowded.* ○ *A modern prison has replaced the Victorian one.* ○ [attrib] *the prison population*, ie the total number of prisoners in a country. (**b**) (*derog*) place from which sb cannot escape: *Now that he was disabled, his house had become a prison to him.* ○ (*fig*) *the prison of one's mind.* **2** [U] being kept in a prison, esp as a punishment for crime; imprisonment: *She's gone to/is in prison.* ○ *escape from, be released from, come out of prison* ○ *He was sent to prison for five years.* ○ *Does prison do anything to prevent crime?* ⇨ Usage at SCHOOL[1].
▷ **prisoner** *n* **1** (**a**) person kept in prison, as a punishment or awaiting trial: *a prison built to hold 500 prisoners* ○ *political prisoners*, ie those put in prison because of their political beliefs ○ *Prisoner at the bar, do you plead guilty or not guilty?* (**b**) person, animal, etc that has been captured and is being kept in confinement; captive: *You are our prisoner now and we won't release you until a ransom is paid.* ○ *He spent two years as the prisoner of rebel soldiers in the mountains.* ○ (*fig*) *The wretched man is the prisoner of* (ie controlled by) *his own greed.* **2** (idm) **hold/take sb captive/prisoner** ⇨ CAPTIVE. **ˌprisoner of ˈconscience** person kept in prison because of an act of social or political protest. **ˌprisoner of ˈwar** (*abbr* **POW**) person (usu a member of the armed forces) captured during a war by the enemy and kept in prison (usu a prison camp) until the end of the war.
□ **ˈprison camp** guarded camp where prisoners, esp prisoners of war or political prisoners, are kept.

prissy /ˈprɪsɪ/ *adj* (**-ier, -iest**) (*derog*) annoyingly precise and fussy, and (claiming to be) easily shocked by improper things. ▷ **prissily** *adv.* **prissiness** *n* [U].

pristine /ˈprɪstiːn, *also* ˈprɪstaɪn/ *adj* **1** (**a**) in its original condition; unspoilt: *a pristine copy of the book's first edition.* (**b**) (*approv*) fresh and clean, as if new: *in pristine condition* ○ *The ground was covered in a pristine layer of snow.* **2** [attrib] (*rhet*) primitive; ancient: *a remnant of some pristine era.*

privacy /ˈprɪvəsɪ, ˈpraɪv-/ *n* [U] **1** state of being alone or undisturbed: *A high wall round the estate protected their privacy.* ○ *He preferred to read the documents in the privacy of his study.* **2** freedom from interference or public attention: *Newspapers often don't respect the individual's right to privacy.* ○ *She complained that the questions were an invasion of (her) privacy.*

private /ˈpraɪvɪt/ *adj* **1** [esp attrib] of, belonging to or for the use of one particular person or group only; personal: *father's own private chair, which no one else is allowed to use* ○ *a private letter*, ie about personal matters ○ *private property* ○ *a private income/private means*, ie money not earned as a salary, etc but coming from personal property, investments, etc ○ *private fishing* ○ *'Is this a hotel?' 'No, it's a private house.'* **2** (**a**) not (to be) revealed to others; secret: *I'm not going to tell you about it; it's private.* ○ *That's my private opinion.* (**b**) not liking to share thoughts and feelings with others: *He's a rather private person.* **3** (of a conversation, meeting, etc) with only a small number of participants, esp two, and kept secret from others: *I'd like a private chat with you.* **4** (**a**) (of a place) quiet and free from intruders: *Let's find some private spot where we can discuss the matter.* (**b**) [usu pred] (of people) undisturbed by others; alone together: *Let's go upstairs where we can be a bit more private.* **5** (**a**) [attrib] having no official job or position: *She is acting as a private individual in this matter.* ○ *a private citizen.* (**b**) not connected with one's work or official position: *The Queen is making a private visit to Canada.* ○ *The public is fascinated by the private lives of public figures.* **6** of, belonging to or carried out by an individual or an independent company rather than the State; not state-controlled: *private industry* ○ *the private sector*, ie of the economy ○ *private education, medicine, medical treatment, etc* ○ *a private patient*, ie (in Britain) not on the National Health Service ○ *a private pension plan.* Cf PUBLIC.
▷ **private** *n* **1** [C] soldier of the lowest rank: *He enlisted as a private.* ○ *Private Smith.* ⇨ App 4. **2 privates** [pl] (*infml*) = PRIVATE PARTS. **3** (idm) **in private** with no one else present: *She asked to see him in private.*
privately *adv*: *The matter was arranged privately.* ○ *He supported the official policy in public, but privately he knew it would fail.* ○ *a privately-owned firm.*
□ **ˈprivate bill** (*Brit*) law proposed in Parliament that affects a private individual or group rather than the whole country.
ˌprivate ˈcompany business firm that does not issue shares to the general public.
ˌprivate deˈtective (also **ˌprivate inˈvestigator**, *infml* **ˌprivate ˈeye**) detective who is not part of an official police force and who is employed by individuals.
ˌprivate ˈenterprise management of business by independent companies or private individuals, as opposed to state control.
ˌprivate ˈmember (*Brit*) member of the House of Commons who is not a minister. **ˌprivate ˈmember's bill** bill presented to Parliament by a private member.
ˌprivate ˈparts (*euph*) genitals.
ˈprivate school school financed mainly by private funds rather than by money from the government. ⇨ article at SCHOOL.
ˌprivate ˈsoldier (*fml*) = PRIVATE *n* 1.

privateer /ˌpraɪvəˈtɪə(r)/ *n* (formerly) (captain of or sailor on a) ship used for attacking and robbing other ships; pirate (ship).

privation /praɪˈveɪʃn/ *n* (*fml*) **1** [C usu *pl*, U] lack of things necessary for life; deprivation: *The survivors suffered many privations before they were rescued.* ○ *a life of privation and misery.* **2** [C] state of being deprived of sth (not necessarily sth essential): *She didn't find the lack of a car any great privation.* ○ *It would be the greatest imaginable privation for her to have to leave London.*

privatize, -ise /ˈpraɪvɪtaɪz/ *v* [Tn] transfer (sth) from state ownership to private ownership; denationalize. Cf NATIONALIZE 1. ▷ **privatization, -isation** /ˌpraɪvɪtaɪˈzeɪʃn; *US* -tɪˈz-/ *n* [U]: *the privatization of the steel industry.*

privet /ˈprɪvɪt/ *n* [U] evergreen bush with small leaves and small white flowers, often used for garden hedges: [attrib] *a privet hedge.*

privilege /ˈprɪvəlɪdʒ/ *n* **1** (**a**) [C] special right or advantage available only to a particular person, class or rank, or to the holder of a certain position: *Parking in this street is the privilege of the residents.* ○ *the privileges of birth*, eg the benefits of belonging to a wealthy family. (**b**) [U] (*derog*) rights and advantages possessed by the rich and powerful people in a society: *They fought against privilege in order to create a fairer society.* ○ *She had led a life of luxury and privilege.* **2** [C] (**a**) special benefit given to sb as a favour: *Older pupils enjoy special privileges.* ○ *'Thank you for showing us your collection of paintings.' 'It's my privilege* (ie I am honoured to do so).*'* ○ *Use of the library is a privilege, not a right.* (**b**) thing that gives one great enjoyment and that most people do not have the opportunity to do: *It was a privilege to hear her sing/hearing her sing.* **3** [C, U] right to do or say things without risking punishment: *an Act which granted the trade unions certain legal privileges* ○ *parliamentary privilege*, ie the right of Members of Parliament to say things in the House of Commons which might result in an accusation of libel if said outside it ○ *a breach of privilege*, ie breaking the rules of parliamentary behaviour.
▷ **privileged** *adj* **1** (**a**) (*sometimes derog*) having privilege(s): *She came from a privileged background.* ○ *a policy of making higher education available to all and not just a privileged few.* (**b**) [pred] honoured: *We are very privileged to have*

Senator Dobbs with us this evening. **2** that need not be revealed; legally secret: *a privileged communication* ○ *This information is privileged.*

privy /ˈprɪvɪ/ *adj* **1** [attrib] (*arch*) private; secret: *a privy matter.* **2** [pred] ~ **to sth** (*fml*) sharing in the secret of sth: *They were accused of being privy to the plot against the king.* ○ *I wasn't privy to the negotiations.*

▷ **privily** *adv* (*arch*) privately; secretly.

privy *n* primitive lavatory, esp out of doors.

□ ˌ**Privy ˈCouncil** body of statesmen, politicians, etc appointed by the sovereign formerly as advisers on affairs of State, but now (in Britain) more as a personal honour for its members. ⇨ article at GOVERNMENT. ˌ**Privy ˈCouncillor** (also ˌ**Privy ˈCounsellor**) member of the Privy Council. ˌ**privy ˈpurse** amount of money given by the British government for the Sovereign's private expenses.

ˌ**privy ˈseal** British national seal formerly fixed to documents of minor importance: *Lord Privy Seal*, ie the senior British government minister without official duties.

prize[1] /praɪz/ *n* **1** award given to the winner of a competition, race, etc: *She won first prize in the 100 metres race.* ○ *Her book gained several literary prizes.* **2** thing (that can be) won in a lottery or a gambling game: *He won the £20 000 prize on the football pools.* ○ *She had the prize-winning lottery ticket.* ○ [attrib] *prize money.* **3** (*fig*) thing of value worth struggling for: *The greatest prize of all — world peace — is now within our grasp.* **4** (esp formerly) ship or its cargo captured at sea during a war.

▷ **prize** *adj* [attrib] **(a)** winning or likely to win a prize; excellent of its kind: *prize cattle* ○ *a prize exhibit in the flower show.* **(b)** (*infml ironic*) outstandingly bad; complete: *a prize ass, fool, idiot, etc.*

prize *v* [Tn] value (sth) highly: *The portrait of her mother was her most prized possession.* ○ *I prize my independence too much to go and work for them.*

□ ˈ**prize day** (also ˈ**prize-giving day**) annual school ceremony at which prizes are given to the best pupils.

📖 Traditionally, prizes were given at many schools as awards for attendance, especially at church schools and Sunday schools. Each prize was an educational book, and inside the front cover there would be a presentation plate with the name of the winner of the prize and the teacher who had authorized it. Nowadays, books are still given as prizes, though they are awarded for good performance in particular subjects, rather than for attendance.

ˈ**prize-fight** *n* boxing match fought for money. ˈ**prize-fighter** *n*.

prize[2] (*esp US*) = PRISE.

PRO *abbr* **1** Public Record Office. **2** /ˌpiː ɑːr ˈəʊ/ (*infml*) public relations officer.

pro[1] /prəʊ/ *n* (idm) **the pros and cons** arguments for and against sth: *Let's add up the pros and cons.*

pro[2] /prəʊ/ *n* (*pl* ~**s**) (*infml*) professional, esp a professional sportsman: *a golf pro* ○ (*approv*) *He's a real pro.* ○ [attrib] *a pro footballer.*

pro- *pref* **1** (with *ns* and *adjs*) in favour of; supporting: *pro-abortion* ○ *pro-American.* Cf ANTI-. **2** (with *ns*) acting as: *pro-vice-chancellor* ○ *pronoun.*

pro-am /ˌprəʊ ˈæm/ *n, adj* (tennis or golf tournament) in which professional and amateur players take part, often for charity.

probability /ˌprɒbəˈbɪlətɪ/ *n* **1** [U] likelihood: *There is little probability of his succeeding/that he will succeed.* ○ *What is the probability of its success?* **2** [C] thing that is (most) probable; probable event or result: *What are the probabilities?* ○ *A fall in interest rates is a probability in the present economic climate.* **3** [C] (*mathematics*) ratio expressing the chances that a particular outcome will occur. **4** (idm) **in** ˌ**all probaˈbility** very probably: *In all probability he's already left.*

probable /ˈprɒbəbl/ *adj* that may be expected to happen or to be so; likely: *With England leading 3-0, the probable result is an England victory/England are the probable winners.* ○ *Rain is possible but not probable this evening.* ○ *It seems probable that he will arrive before dusk.*

▷ **probable** *n* ~ **(for sth)** person or thing most likely to be chosen, eg for a sports team or as the winner; probable candidate, winner, etc: *He is a probable for the national team.* ○ *The book is a probable for the prize.*

probably /-əblɪ/ *adv* almost certainly: *He's late — he's probably stuck in a traffic jam.* ○ *'Will you be coming?' 'Probably.'* ○ *'Can he hear us?' 'Probably not.'*

probate /ˈprəʊbeɪt/ *n* (*law*) **1** [U] official process of proving that a will is correct: *apply for/take out probate* ○ *grant probate* ○ [attrib] *a probate court.* **2** [C] copy of a will with an official certificate that it is correct.

▷ **probate** *v* [Tn] (*US*) = PROVE 2.

probation /prəˈbeɪʃn; *US* prəʊ-/ *n* [U] **1** (*law*) (system of) keeping an official check on the behaviour of (esp young) people found guilty of crime, ie by putting them under supervision for a fixed period as an alternative to sending them to prison, provided that they do not offend again during that period: *sentenced to three years' probation.* **2** testing of a person's abilities or behaviour to find out if he or she is suitable: *There's a three-month period of probation/probation period for new recruits.* **3** (idm) **on probation (a)** (of a law-breaker) undergoing a period of probation(1): *He's been released from prison on probation*, ie If he does not behave satisfactorily he will be sent back. **(b)** being tested before being finally accepted in employment, etc.

▷ **probationary** /prəˈbeɪʃnrɪ; *US* prəʊˈbeɪʃənerɪ/ *adj* of or for probation: *a probationary period.*

probationer /-ʃənə(r)/ *n* **1** hospital nurse being trained and still on probation(2). **2** law-breaker sentenced to a period of probation(1) or released from prison on probation.

□ **proˈbation officer** person whose job is to supervise law-breakers who are on probation. ⇨ article at PUNISHMENT.

probe /prəʊb/ *n* **1** tool for examining a place which cannot be reached otherwise, esp a thin implement with a blunt end used by a doctor for examining a wound. **2** (also ˈ**space probe**) unmanned spacecraft which obtains information about space and transmits it back to earth: *information about Venus obtained by Russian probes.* **3** ~ **(into sth)** (esp in journalism) thorough and careful investigation of sth: *a probe into the disappearance of government funds.* **4** act of probing.

▷ **probe** *v* **1** [Tn] explore or examine (sth) with or as if with a probe(1): *He probed the swelling anxiously with his finger.* ○ *Searchlights probed the night sky.* **2** [I, Ipr, Tn] ~ **(into sth)** investigate or examine (sth) closely: *The journalist was probing into several financial scandals.* ○ *She tried to probe his mind to find out what he was thinking.* **probing** *adj* intended to discover the truth; searching: *He was asking probing questions.* **probingly** *adv.*

probity /ˈprəʊbətɪ/ *n* [U] (*fml*) quality of being honest and trustworthy; integrity.

problem /ˈprɒbləm/ *n* **1** thing that is difficult to deal with or understand: *How do you cope with the problem of poor vision?* ○ *a knotty problem* ○ *get to the root/heart of a problem* ○ *We've got a problem with the car — it won't start!* ○ *You'll have to mend that leak or it will cause problems later.* ○ *the housing problem in the inner cities* ○ (*infml*) *'Will you be able to get me tickets for the match?' 'Of course, no problem* (ie I shall easily be able to).*'* ○ *'I can't come to the party.' 'Why, what's the problem?'* ○ [attrib] *a problem novel, play, etc*, ie one dealing with a social or moral problem ○ *a newspaper's problem page*, ie with readers' letters about their problems, and suggested solutions. **2** question to be answered or solved: *a mathematical problem* ○ *She has found the answer to/solved the problem.*

▷ **problematic** /ˌprɒbləˈmætɪk/ (also **problematical**) *adj* **1** difficult to deal with or understand. **2** (esp of a result) that cannot be foreseen; doubtful or questionable. **problematically** /-klɪ/ *adv.*

□ ˈ**problem child** child who continually behaves badly, does not learn well, etc.

proboscis /prəˈbɒsɪs/ *n* (*pl* ~**es** /-sɪsiːz/) **1 (a)** elephant's trunk. **(b)** long flexible nose of certain animals, eg the tapir. **2** elongated part of the mouth of certain insects, used for sucking things.

procedure /prəˈsiːdʒə(r)/ *n* **1** [C, U] (regular) order or way of doing things, esp in business, law, politics, etc: *(the) agreed/correct/established/normal/usual procedure* ○ *Stop arguing about (questions of) procedure and let's get down to business.* ○ *parliamentary procedure.* **2** [C] ~ **(for sth)** action or series of actions (to be) completed in order to achieve sth: *Registering a birth or death is a straightforward procedure.* ○ *Obtaining a refund from the company is a complicated procedure.* ○ *What's the procedure for opening a bank account?*

▷ **procedural** /prəˈsiːdʒərəl/ *adj* of procedure(s): *The business of the committee was delayed by procedural difficulties.*

proceed /prəˈsiːd, prəʊ-/ *v* **1 (a)** [I, Ipr, It] ~ **(to sth)** go to a further or the next stage; go on: *Work is proceeding slowly.* ○ *What is the best way of proceeding?* ○ *Let us proceed (to the next item on the agenda).* ○ *Having said how much she liked it, she then proceeded to criticize the way I'd done it.* **(b)** [Ipr] (*fml*) make one's way; go: *I was proceeding along the High Street in a northerly direction when....* **(c)** [I, Ipr] ~ **(with sth)** begin or continue (sth): *Please proceed with your report.* ○ *Shall we proceed with the planned investment?* **2** [Ipr] ~ **against sb** (*law*) take legal action against sb; start a lawsuit against sb. **3** [Ipr] ~ **from sth** (*fml*) arise or originate from sth: *the evils that proceed from war.* **4** [Ipr] ~ **to sth** (*fml*) go on to obtain a higher university degree after obtaining a first degree: *He was allowed to proceed to an MA.*

proceedings /prəˈsiːdɪŋz/ *n* [pl] **1** ~ **(against sb/for sth)** lawsuit: *start proceedings (against sb) for divorce* ○ *institute divorce proceedings.* **2** what takes place, esp at a meeting, ceremony, etc: *The proceedings will begin with a speech to welcome the guests.* ○ *The proceedings were interrupted by the fire alarm.* **3** ~ **(of sth)** (published) report or record of a discussion, meeting, conference, etc; minutes: *His paper was published in the proceedings of the Kent Archaeological Society.*

proceeds /ˈprəʊsiːdz/ *n* [pl] ~ **(of/from sth)** money obtained by selling sth, presenting a performance, etc; profits: *They gave a concert and donated the proceeds to charity.*

process[1] /ˈprəʊses; *US* ˈprɒses/ *n* **1** [C] series of actions or operations performed in order to do, make or achieve sth: *Unloading the cargo was a slow process.* ○ *Reforming the education system will be a difficult process.* ○ *Teaching him Greek was a painful* (ie slow and difficult) *process.* **2** [C] method, esp one used in industry to make sth: *the Bessemer process of steel production* ○ *They have developed a new process for rustproofing car bodies.* **3** [C] (series of) changes, esp ones that happen naturally and unconsciously: *the processes of digestion/the digestive processes* ○ *the process of growing old.* **4** [C] (*law*) **(a)** legal action; lawsuit. **(b)** summons; writ. **5** [C] (*biology*) small projecting part of a plant or of the body of an animal. **6** (idm) **in the ˈprocess** while doing sth previously mentioned: *I started moving the china ornaments but dropped a vase in the process.* **in the process of sth/doing sth** performing a particular task: *We're still in the process of moving house.*

▷ **process** *v* [Tn] **1** put (a raw material, food, etc) through an industrial or manufacturing process in order to change it; treat: *process leather to make it softer* ○ *processed cheese*, ie specially treated to preserve it ○ *process* (ie develop) *photographic film.* **2** deal with (a document, etc) officially: *It may take a few weeks for your application to be processed.* **3** perform operations on (sth) in a computer: *How fast does the new micro process the data?* **processor** *n* machine that processes things: *a food processor.* Cf MICROPROCESSOR.

process[2] /prəˈses/ *v* [I, Ipr, Ip] walk or move (as if) in procession: *The bishops, priests and deacons processed into the cathedral.*

procession /prəˈseʃn/ *n* **1** [C] (**a**) number of people, vehicles, etc moving along in an orderly way, esp as part of a ceremony or demonstration: *a ˈfuneral procession* ○ *The procession moved slowly down the hill.* (**b**) (*fig*) large number of people who come one after the other: *A procession of visitors came to the house.* **2** [U] action of moving forward in this way: *The congregation entered the church in procession.*

▷ **processional** /-ʃənl/ *adj* of, for or used in a (religious) procession. — *n* processional hymn.

pro-choice /ˌprəʊ ˈtʃɔɪs/ *adj* (*esp US*) believing that a pregnant woman has the right to decide whether or not to have her baby, and favouring liberal abortion laws. Cf PRO-LIFE.

proclaim /prəˈkleɪm/ *v* **1** [Tn, Tf, Tw, Cn·n] make (sth) known officially or publicly; announce: *proclaim the good news* ○ *proclaim a public holiday* ○ *After its independence India was proclaimed* (ie officially declared to be) *a republic.* **2** [Tf, Cn·n] (*fml*) show (sth) clearly; reveal: *His accent proclaimed him a Scot/that he was a Scot.*

▷ **proclamation** /ˌprɒkləˈmeɪʃn/ *n* **1** [U] action of proclaiming: *by public proclamation.* **2** [C] thing that is proclaimed: *issue/make a proclamation.*

proclivity /prəˈklɪvətɪ/ *n* ~ (**for/to/towards sth/doing sth**) (*fml*) natural inclination to do sth (esp sth bad); tendency: *a proclivity towards sudden violent outbursts* ○ *his unusual sexual proclivities.*

procrastinate /prəʊˈkræstɪneɪt/ *v* [I] (*fml derog*) delay or postpone action: *He procrastinated until it was too late to do anything at all.*

▷ **procrastination** /prəʊˌkræstɪˈneɪʃn/ *n* **1** [U] (*fml derog*) wasting time; procrastinating. **2** (idm) **procrastination is the thief of ˈtime** (*saying*) procrastinating wastes time.

procreate /ˈprəʊkrɪeɪt/ *v* [I] (*fml*) reproduce offspring sexually. ▷ **procreation** /ˌprəʊkrɪˈeɪʃn/ *n* [U].

proctor /ˈprɒktə(r)/ *n* **1** (*Brit*) (at the universities of Oxford and Cambridge) either of two officials with responsibility for discipline. **2** (*US*) person responsible for supervising students in an examination, esp so that they do not cheat.

procurator fiscal /ˌprɒkjʊreɪtə ˈfɪskl/ (in Scotland) public official whose job is to decide whether sb suspected of crime should be prosecuted.

procurator general /ˌprɒkjʊreɪtə ˈdʒenrəl/ (in Britain) head of the legal department at the *Treasury.

procure /prəˈkjʊə(r)/ *v* **1** [Tn, Dn·n, Dn·pr] ~ **sth** (**for sb**) (*fml*) obtain sth, esp with care or effort; acquire: *The book is out of print and difficult to procure.* ○ *Can you procure some specimens for me/procure me some specimens?* ○ *He was responsible for procuring supplies for the army.* **2** [I, Tn, Dn·pr] ~ **sb** (**for sb**) (*derog*) find (prostitutes) for clients: *He was accused of procuring women for his business associates.*

▷ **procurement** *n* [U] (*fml*) obtaining: *the procurement of goods, raw materials, supplies, weapons.*

procurer /-ˈkjʊərə(r)/ (*fem* **procuress** /-ˈkjʊərɪs/) *n* (*derog*) person who finds prostitutes for clients.

prod /prɒd/ *v* (**-dd-**) **1** [I, Ipr, Tn] ~ (**at sb/sth**) push or poke (sb/sth) with a finger or some other pointed object: *They prodded (at) the animal through the bars of its cage.* ⇨ Usage at NUDGE. **2** [Tn, Tn·pr, Cn·t] ~ **sb** (**into/doing sth**) (*infml*) (try to) make (a slow or unwilling person) do sth; urge: *She is a fairly good worker, but she needs prodding occasionally.* ○ *He needs a crisis to prod him into action.* ○ *I shall have to prod him to pay me what he owes.*

▷ **prod** *n* **1** poke or thrust: *She gave the man a prod with her umbrella.* **2** (*infml*) stimulus to action: *If you don't receive an answer quickly, give them a prod.* **3** instrument for prodding.

prodding *n* [U] action of prodding: *A little gentle prodding may be necessary at this stage.*

prodigal /ˈprɒdɪgl/ *adj* **1** (*fml derog*) spending money or resources too freely; extravagant: *a prodigal administration* ○ *prodigal housekeeping.* **2** ~ (**of sth**) (*fml*) generous or lavish (with sth): *Nature is prodigal of her gifts.* **3** (idm) **the prodigal (son)** person who leaves his home or community to lead a life of pleasure or extravagance, but who later regrets this and returns home: *the return of the prodigal son* ○ *So, the prodigal has returned!*

▷ **prodigality** /ˌprɒdɪˈgælətɪ/ *n* [U] (*fml*) (**a**) (*derog*) wasteful spending; extravagance. (**b**) generosity; lavishness: *the prodigality of the sea,* ie in providing fish.

prodigally /-gəlɪ/ *adv*: *use resources prodigally.*

prodigious /prəˈdɪdʒəs/ *adj* very great in size, amount or degree, so as to cause amazement or admiration; enormous: *a prodigious achievement* ○ *It cost a prodigious amount (of money).* ▷ **prodigiously** *adv*: *The costs are mounting prodigiously.* ○ *She is a prodigiously talented pianist.*

prodigy /ˈprɒdɪdʒɪ/ *n* **1** person with unusual or remarkable qualities or abilities: *a child/infant prodigy,* ie one who is unusually talented for his age, eg in music or mathematics. **2** (*rhet*) (**a**) amazing or wonderful thing, esp a natural phenomenon: *the prodigies of nature.* (**b**) ~ **of sth** outstanding example of sth: *The man is a prodigy of learning,* ie knows a lot.

produce /prəˈdjuːs; *US* -ˈduːs/ *v* **1** [Tn, Tn·pr] ~ **sth** (**from sth**) create sth by making, manufacturing, growing, etc: *America produced more cars this year than last year.* ○ *She has produced very little (work) recently.* ○ *Linen is produced from flax.* ○ *He worked hard to produce good crops from poor soil.* ○ *a well-produced book,* ie one that is printed, bound, etc well. **2** [Tn] cause (sth) to occur; create: *The medicine produced a violent reaction.* ○ *His announcement produced gasps of amazement.* **3** [I, Tn] bear or yield (offspring or crops): *The silkworms are producing well.* ○ *The cow has produced a calf.* ○ *The soil produces good crops.* ○ *The cows are producing a lot of milk.* **4** [Tn, Tn·pr] ~ **sth** (**from/out of sth**) bring out or show sth so that it can be examined or used: *produce a railway ticket for inspection* ○ *The man produced a revolver from his pocket.* ○ *He can produce evidence to support his allegations.* **5** [Tn] arrange the performance of (a play, an opera, etc) or the making of (a film, TV programme, record, etc): *She is producing 'Romeo and Juliet' at the local theatre.* ○ *He hopes to find the money to produce a film about Japan.* **6** [Tn, Tn·pr] ~ **sth** (**to sth**) (*mathematics*) make (a line) longer (so that it reaches a particular point): *produce the line AB to C.*

▷ **produce** /ˈprɒdjuːs; *US* -duːs/ *n* [U] things that have been produced (PRODUCE 1), esp by farming: *fresh produce* ○ *agricultural, farm, garden produce* ○ *It says on the bottle 'Produce of France'.*

producer /prəˈdjuːsə(r); *US* -ˈduː-/ *n* **1** person, company, country, etc that produces (PRODUCE 1) goods or materials: *The firm is Britain's main producer of electronic equipment.* ○ *The producers of the radios could not find a market for them.* ○ *the conflicting interests of producers and consumers.* Cf CONSUMER. **2** (**a**) person in charge of a film or theatrical production, who obtains the money to make the film or put on the play, and arranges the schedules, publicity, etc. Cf DIRECTOR 2. (**b**) person who arranges the making of a TV or radio programme, a record, etc. (**c**) (esp in the amateur theatre) person who arranges the performance of a play, telling the actors what to do; director. (**d**) director of an opera performance.

product /ˈprɒdʌkt/ *n* **1** (**a**) [C, U] thing or substance produced by a natural or manufacturing process: *a firm known for its high-quality products* ○ *the products of manufacturing industry* ○ *pharmaceutical products,* eg drugs, medicines ○ *the finished product,* ie one that has reached the end of the manufacturing process ○ *waste products,* ie waste material produced by eg the body's digestive system. (**b**) [U] (*commerce*) goods produced by a firm, country, etc: *a campaign to increase sales of the firm's product* ○ *gross national product,* ie the annual total value of goods produced and services provided in a country ○ [attrib] *product development.* **2** [C] ~ **of sth** (**a**) state or thing that is the result of sth: *Flower power was a product of the sixties.* ○ *the products of genius,* eg great works of art ○ *Low morale among the work force is the product of bad management.* (**b**) person who has been influenced by sth: *She is the product of a broken home.* ○ *They are the products of post-war affluence.* **3** [C] (**a**) (*mathematics*) quantity obtained by multiplying one number by another: *The product of 4 and 10 is 40.* (**b**) (*chemistry*) chemical element or compound produced by chemical reaction. Cf REACTANT.

production /prəˈdʌkʃn/ *n* **1** [U] action of manufacturing, extracting, etc, esp in large quantities: *oil production* ○ *Production of the new aircraft will start next year.* ○ *Production must become more efficient.* ○ *mass* (ie very large-scale) *production* ○ *Defects in design cannot be put right during production.* ○ *He has moved from acting to film production.* ○ [attrib] *production costs, managers, processes, schedules, difficulties.* **2** [U] quantity produced: *increase production by using more efficient methods* ○ *a fall/increase in production.* **3** [C] thing that has been produced, esp a play, film, etc: *They saw several National Theatre productions.* ○ *'King Lear' in a controversial new production.* **4** (idm) **go ˌinto/ˌout of proˈduction** start/stop being manufactured: *The system will have to be tested before it goes into production.* ○ *That car went out of production five years ago.* **in proˈduction** being manufactured (in large quantities): *The device will be in production by the end of the year.* **on production of sth** by/when showing sth: *On production of your membership card, you will receive a discount on purchases.*

□ **proˈduction line** sequence of groups of machines and workers, in which each group carries out part of the production process: *Cars are checked as they come off the production line.*

productive /prəˈdʌktɪv/ *adj* **1** producing or able to produce goods or crops, esp in large quantities: *They work hard, but their efforts are not very productive.* ○ *productive farming land, manufacturing methods* ○ *a productive worker.* **2** achieving a lot; useful: *It wasn't a very productive meeting.* ○ *I spent a very productive hour in the library.* **3** [pred] ~ **of sth** (*fml*) resulting in sth; causing sth: *The changes were not productive of better labour relations.* ▷ **productively** *adv*: *spend one's time productively.*

productivity /ˌprɒdʌkˈtɪvətɪ/ *n* [U] **1** ability to produce (eg goods or crops); state of being productive: *The size of the crop depends on the productivity of the soil.* **2** efficiency, esp in industry, measured by comparing the amount produced with the time taken or the resources used to produce it: *The management are looking for ways of improving productivity.* ○ [attrib] *a productivity bonus for workers.*

□ **producˈtivity agreement** agreement between management and unions that the cost of higher wages will be paid for by an increase in productivity.

Prof *abbr* Professor (as a title).

prof /prɒf/ *n* (*infml*) = PROFESSOR.

profane /prəˈfeɪn; *US* prəʊ-/ *adj* (*fml*) **1** [attrib] not sacred; secular: *sacred and profane music* ○ *profane* (ie not biblical) *literature.* **2** (**a**) having or showing contempt for God or holy things; blasphemous: *profane behaviour in church* ○ *a profane oath.* (**b**) offensive; obscene: *profane language.*

▷ **profane** *v* [Tn] (*fml*) (**a**) treat (a sacred thing) with irreverence or contempt: *profane the name of God* ○ *Their behaviour profaned the holy place.* (**b**) treat or use (sth worthy of respect) disrespectfully: *His action profaned the honour of his country.* **profanation** /ˌprɒfəˈneɪʃn/ *n* [C, U] (*fml*) (instance of) profaning.

profanely *adv.*

profanity /prəˈfænətɪ; *US* prəʊ-/ *n* (*fml*) **1** [U] profane behaviour, esp the use of profane language. **2** [C esp *pl*] profane word or phrase; obscenity: *He uttered a stream of profanities.*

profess /prəˈfes/ *v (fml)* **1** [Tn, Tf, Tt, Cn·a] claim (sth), often falsely: *I don't profess expert knowledge of/to be an expert in this subject.* ○ *She professed total ignorance of the matter.* ○ *He professed that he knew nothing about the plot.* **2** [Tn, Cn·a] state openly that one has (a belief, feeling, etc): *They professed optimism about the outcome.* ○ *He professed himself satisfied with the progress made.* **3** [Tn] **(a)** publicly declare one's faith in (a religion): *Christians profess their faith when they say the Creed.* **(b)** have or belong to (the specified religion): *profess Islam.*

▷ **professed** *adj* [attrib] **1** (falsely) claimed; alleged: *her professed love of children* ○ *She was betrayed by her professed friends and supporters.* **2** openly acknowledged by oneself; declared: *a professed Christian* ○ *a professed supporter of disarmament.* **3** having made religious vows: *a professed nun.* **professedly** /-ɪdlɪ/ *adv (fml)* according to one's own claim (whether true or false) or admission: *She is professedly a feminist.*

profession /prəˈfeʃn/ *n* **1** **(a)** [C] paid occupation, esp one that requires advanced education and training, eg architecture, law or medicine: *advising college leavers on their choice of profession* ○ *the acting, legal, medical, etc profession.* **(b) the profession** [CGp] body of people working in a particular profession: *The legal profession* (ie lawyers) *has/have always resisted change.* ⇨ Usage at TRADE[1]. **2** [C] ~ **of sth** public statement or claim of sth: *a profession of belief, faith, loyalty, etc* ○ *His professions of concern did not seem sincere.* **3** (idm) **by profession** as one's paid occupation: *She is a lawyer by profession.* ○ *The author of the guidebook is an architect by profession.*

professional /prəˈfeʃənl/ *adj* **1** **(a)** [attrib] of or belonging to a profession: *a professional man, woman, practitioner* ○ *professional associations, codes of practice, conduct* ○ *You will need to seek professional advice about your claim for compensation.* ○ *The doctor was accused of professional misconduct.* **(b)** having or showing the skill or qualities of a professional person: *Many of the performers were of professional standard.* ○ *He was complimented on a very professional piece of work.* ○ *She is extremely professional in her approach to her job.* Cf UNPROFESSIONAL. **2** **(a)** doing as a full-time job sth which others do as a hobby or as a part-time job: *a professional boxer, footballer, golfer, tennis player, etc* ○ *a professional cook, dressmaker, musician, etc* ○ *After he won the amateur championship he turned professional,* ie began to earn money for his sport. **(b)** (of sport, etc) practised as a full-time job: *professional football, golf, tennis, etc* ○ *She had been on the professional stage* (ie a professional actress) *in her youth.* Cf AMATEUR 1. **3** [attrib] *(derog)* repeatedly doing the specified annoying thing: *a professional complainer, gossip, moaner, trouble-maker, etc.*

▷ **professional** *n* **1** person qualified or employed in one of the professions: *studio flats suitable for young professionals* ○ *You need a professional to sort out your finances.* **2** (also *infml* **pro**) professional(2a) player or performer, esp a sportsman employed by a club to teach and advise its members: *a golf professional.* **3** (also *infml* **pro**) *(approv)* highly skilled and experienced person: *She's a true professional!* ○ *This survey is the work of a real professional.*

professionalism /-ʃənəlɪzəm/ *n* [U] **1** *(approv)* **(a)** skill or qualities of a profession or its members: *You can rely on your solicitor's professionalism in dealing with the house purchase.* **(b)** great skill and competence: *They were impressed by the sheer professionalism of the performance.* **2** practice of employing professionals (PROFESSIONAL 2) in sport.

professionally /-ʃənəlɪ/ *adv* **(a)** in a professional way: *A doctor who gives away confidential information about patients is not behaving professionally.* **(b)** by a professional person: *The plans had been drawn professionally.* ○ *Her voice should be professionally trained.* **(c)** as a paid occupation: *He plays cricket professionally.*

□ **proˌfessional ˈfoul** *(euph)* (in sport, esp football) deliberate foul, esp one committed in order to stop the game when a member of the opposing team seems certain to score.

professor /prəˈfesə(r)/ *n (abbr* **Prof***)* **1** (*US* also **full professor**) (title of a) university teacher of the highest grade who holds a chair(3) in a subject: *He is Professor of Moral Philosophy at Oxford.* ○ *She was made professor at the age of 40.* ○ *Professor Smith, may I introduce one of my students to you?* **2** *(US)* teacher at a university or college. **3** *(joc)* title taken by instructors in various subjects: *Professor Pate, the famous phrenologist.*

▷ **professorial** /ˌprɒfɪˈsɔːrɪəl/ *adj* of or like a professor: *a professorial post* ○ *professorial duties.*

professorship *n* position of a university professor; chair(3): *The professorship of zoology is vacant and has been advertised.*

proffer /ˈprɒfə(r)/ *v* [Tn, Dn·n, Dn·pr] ~ **sth (to sb)** *(fml)* offer sth: *He refused the proffered assistance.* ○ *She proffered (him) her resignation.* ○ *May we proffer you our congratulations?*

▷ **proffer** *n (fml)* offer: *a proffer of help.*

proficient /prəˈfɪʃnt/ *adj* ~ **(in/at sth/doing sth)** doing or able to do sth in a skilled or an expert way because of training and practice: *a proficient driver* ○ *proficient in the use of radar equipment* ○ *proficient at operating a computer terminal.*

▷ **proficiency** /-nsɪ/ *n* [U] ~ **(in sth/doing sth)** being proficient (in sth): *a test of proficiency (in English)* ○ *show proficiency in operating a switchboard.*

proficiently *adv.*

profile /ˈprəʊfaɪl/ *n* **1** side view, esp of the human face: *his handsome profile* ○ [attrib] *a profile drawing.* **2** edge or outline of sth seen against a background: *the profile of the tower against the sky.* **3** brief biography of sb or description of sth in a newspaper article, broadcast programme, etc: *The newspaper publishes a profile of a leading sportsman every week.* ○ *The BBC are working on a profile of the British nuclear industry.* **4** cross-section eg of layers of rock or soil showing its structure. **5** (idm) **a ˌhigh/ˌlow ˈprofile** noticeable/inconspicuous way of behaving, so as to attract/avoid public attention: *adopt/keep/maintain a low profile* ○ [attrib] *high-profile politicians.* **in profile** (seen) from the side: *In profile she is very like her mother.* ○ *The Queen's head appears in profile on British stamps.*

▷ **profile** *v* **1** [Tn esp passive] show (sth) in profile against a background: *The huge trees were profiled against the night sky.* **2** [Tn] write or make a profile(3) of (sb/sth).

profit[1] /ˈprɒfɪt/ *n* **1** **(a)** [C, U] financial gain: *do sth for profit* ○ *There's no profit in running a cinema in this town.* ○ *They're only interested in a quick profit.* ○ [attrib] *The capitalist system is based on the profit motive.* **(b)** [C] amount of money gained in business, esp the difference between the amount earned and the amount spent: *They make a profit of ten pence on every copy they sell.* ○ *sell at a profit* ○ *operate at a profit,* ie be profitable ○ *The company has declared an increase in profits/increased profits.* ○ *a clear profit of 20 per cent.* **2** [U] *(fml)* advantage or benefit gained from sth: *You could with profit spend some extra time studying the text.*

▷ **profitless** *adj* without profit[1](2): *Revising the procedure was an entirely profitless exercise.* **profitlessly** *adv*: *I seem to have spent my day quite profitlessly.*

□ **ˌprofit and ˈloss account** (in bookkeeping) account showing income and expenditure for a particular period, with the profit or loss made.

ˈprofit-margin *n* difference between the cost of buying or producing sth and the price for which one sells it: *a gross profit-margin of 25%.*

ˈprofit-sharing *n* [U] system of dividing a portion of a company's profits amongst its employees: [attrib] *a profit-sharing scheme.*

profit[2] /ˈprɒfɪt/ *v* (phr v) **profit by sth** (no passive) learn from (one's experience, mistakes, etc) so that one does not repeat them: *He's getting married again, after two divorces, so he obviously hasn't profited by his experiences.* **profit from sth** benefit from or be helped by sth: *He profited greatly from his year abroad.* ○ *I have profited from your advice.*

profitable /ˈprɒfɪtəbl/ *adj* bringing profit or advantage; beneficial: *profitable investments* ○ *The deal was profitable to all of us.* ○ *It would be more profitable to combine the two factories.* ○ *She spent a profitable afternoon in the library.* ▷ **profitability** /ˌprɒfɪtəˈbɪlətɪ/ *n* [U]. **profitably** /-əblɪ/ *adv*: *They invested the money very profitably.* ○ *She spent the weekend profitably.*

profiteer /ˌprɒfɪˈtɪə(r)/ *v* [I] *(derog)* make too large a profit, esp by exploiting people in difficult times (eg in a war or famine): *Rent controls were introduced to prevent profiteering.*

▷ **profiteer** *n* person who does this.

profiterole /prɒˈfɪtərəʊl/ *n* small hollow bun of light pastry with a sweet or savoury filling.

profligate /ˈprɒflɪgət/ *adj (fml derog)* **1** recklessly extravagant or wasteful: *profligate spending* ○ *a profligate use of scarce resources.* **2** (of a person or his behaviour) shamelessly immoral; dissolute.

▷ **profligacy** /ˈprɒflɪgəsɪ/ *n* [U] *(fml derog)* being profligate.

profligate *n (fml derog)* profligate(2) person.

pro forma /ˌprəʊ ˈfɔːmə/ *adj, adv* as a matter of convention.

▷ **pro forma** (also **pro forma invoice**) invoice that gives details of goods being sent and is sent to the customer in advance of the goods themselves.

profound /prəˈfaʊnd/ *adj* **1** [usu attrib] *(fml)* deep, intense or far-reaching; very great: *a profound sigh, silence, sleep, shock* ○ *take a profound interest in sth* ○ *profound ignorance* ○ *profound changes.* **2** **(a)** [usu attrib] having or showing great knowledge or insight (into a subject): *a profound awareness of the problem* ○ *a profound thinker* ○ *a man of profound learning.* **(b)** needing much study or thought: *profound mysteries.*

▷ **profoundly** *adv* **(a)** deeply; extremely: *profoundly disturbed, grateful, shocked.* **(b)** in a profound(2a) manner.

profundity /prəˈfʌndətɪ/ *n (fml)* **1** [U] depth (esp of knowledge, thought, etc): *He impressed his audience by the profundity of his knowledge.* **2** [C esp *pl*] profound meaning, statement or thought: *a poem full of profundities.*

profuse /prəˈfjuːs/ *adj* **1** in large amounts; abundant: *profuse blossoms, flowers, apologies, gratitude, thanks* ○ *profuse bleeding, sweating, tears.* **2** [pred] ~ **in sth** expressing or giving sth freely or generously; lavish with sth: *profuse in one's apologies, thanks.*

▷ **profusely** *adv*: *bleed, sweat profusely* ○ *thank sb profusely.*

profuseness *n* [U] state of being profuse: *The profuseness of his thanks was embarrassing.*

profusion /prəˈfjuːʒn/ *n* **1** [sing] ~ **of sth** abundant supply of sth: *a profusion of colours, patterns, flowers, good wishes.* **2** (idm) **in profusion** in large quantities or abundance: *Roses were growing in profusion against the old wall.*

progenitor /prəʊˈdʒenɪtə(r)/ *n (fml)* **1** ancestor (of a person, an animal or a plant). **2** *(fig)* originator (of an idea, intellectual or political movement, etc): *Marx was the progenitor of Communism.*

progeny /ˈprɒdʒənɪ/ *n* [pl *v*] *(fml)* **(a)** offspring: *(joc) He appeared, surrounded by his numerous progeny.* **(b)** descendants.

progesterone /prəˈdʒestərəʊn/ *n* [U] one of the sex hormones, that prepares and maintains the uterus for pregnancy and is used in the contraceptive pill because it prevents ovulation. Cf OESTROGEN.

prognosis /prɒgˈnəʊsɪs/ *n* (*pl* **-ses** /-siːz/) **(a)** *(medical)* forecast of the likely course of a disease or an illness: *make one's prognosis* ○ *The prognosis is not good.* Cf DIAGNOSIS. **(b)** *(fig)* forecast of the probable development of sth; outlook: *The prognosis for the future of the electronics industry is encouraging.*

prognosticate /prɒgˈnɒstɪkeɪt/ *v (fml)* **1** [I, Tn, Tf] tell (sth) in advance; predict: *prognosticate disaster.* **2** [Tn, Tf] be a sign of (a future event).

▷ **prognostication** /prɒgˌnɒstɪˈkeɪʃn/ *n (fml)* **(a)** [U] prognosticating. **(b)** [C] thing that is prognosticated: *His gloomy prognostications proved to be false.*

program /ˈprəʊɡræm; *US* -ɡrəm/ *n* **1** (*US*) = PROGRAMME. **2** (*computing*) series of coded instructions to control the operations of a computer: *write a program for producing a balance sheet.*

▷ **program** *v* (**-mm-**; *US* also **-m-**) [Tn, Cn·t] (*computing*) instruct (a computer) (to do sth) by putting a program into it: *The computer has been programmed (to calculate the gross profit margin on all sales).* **programmer** (*US* also **programer**) *n* person who writes programs for a computer.

programme (*US* **program**) /ˈprəʊɡræm; *US* -ɡrəm/ *n* **1** broadcast item (eg a play, discussion or documentary): *There is an interesting programme on television tonight.* ○ *They're putting on a programme about/on wine-making.* **2** plan of what is (intended) to be done: *a political programme* ○ *What's (on) the programme for* (ie What are we going to do) *tomorrow?* ○ *launch a programme to redevelop the inner cities.* **3** (**a**) (notice or list of a) series of items in a concert, on a course of study, etc: *The programme includes two Mozart sonatas.* ○ *plan a programme of lectures for first-year students.* (**b**) (booklet with a) list of the names of the actors in a play, singers in an opera, etc.

▷ **programme** (*US* **program**) *v* (**-mm-**; *US* also **-m-**) **1** [usu passive: Tn, Tn·pr] ~ **sth** (**for sth**) make a programme of or for sth; put sth on a programme; plan or arrange sth: *programme a music festival* ○ *A trip to the museum is programmed for next Tuesday.* **2** [usu passive: Tn, Cn·t] cause (sb/sth) to do sth or behave in a particular way, esp automatically or in an unthinking way: *Their early training programmes them to be obedient and submissive.* ○ *The video is programmed to switch itself on at ten o'clock.* ˌ**programmed** ˈ**course** educational course in which the material to be learnt is presented in small, carefully graded, amounts. ˌ**programmed** ˈ**learning** self-instruction using a programmed course.

□ ˈ**programme music** music intended to suggest a story, picture, etc.

ˈ**programme note** short description or explanation in a programme(3b) of a musical work, a play, an actor's career, etc.

progress /ˈprəʊɡres; *US* ˈprɒɡ-/ *n* **1** [U] forward or onward movement: *The walkers were making slow progress up the rocky path.* ○ *The yacht made good progress with a following wind.* **2** [U] advance or development, esp towards a better state: *the progress of civilization* ○ *There has been very little progress this term.* ○ *The patient is making good progress* (ie is getting better) *after her operation.* ○ *Strike leaders have reported some progress in the talks to settle the dispute.* **3** [C] (*arch*) journey made by a sovereign or ruler: *a royal progress around the country.* **4** (idm) **in progress** being done or made: *work in progress An inquiry is now in progress.* ○ *Please be quiet — recording in progress.*

▷ **progress** /prəˈɡres/ *v* **1** [I] make progress: *The work is progressing steadily.* ○ *She is progressing in her studies.* ○ *In some ways, civilization does not seem to have progressed much in the last century.* **2** [Tn] cause (work, etc) to make regular progress towards completion.

□ ˈ**progress chaser** person whose job is to check the progress of work being done and to investigate delays.

ˈ**progress report** report giving details of the progress of work being done.

progression /prəˈɡreʃn/ *n* **1** [U] ~ (**from sth**) (**to sth**) (process of) moving forward or developing, esp in stages or gradually; progressing: *the team's progression to the first division* ○ *Adolescence is the period of progression from childhood to adulthood.* **2** [C] sequence or series: *a long progression of sunny days.*

progressive /prəˈɡresɪv/ *adj* **1** making a continuous forward movement. **2** increasing steadily or in regular degrees: *a progressive disease,* ie one that gradually increases in its effect ○ *progressive taxation,* ie at rates that increase as the sum taxed increases ○ *Her condition is showing a progressive improvement.* **3** (*approv*) (**a**) advancing in social conditions or efficiency: *a progressive firm, nation.* (**b**) favouring or showing rapid progress or reform: *progressive schools, views* ○ *a progressive education policy* ○ *a progressive political party.*

▷ **progressive** *n* person who supports a progressive(3b) policy or adopts progressive methods.

progressively *adv* increasingly; by degrees: *His eyesight is becoming progressively worse.*

progressiveness *n* [U].

□ **progressive** ˈ**tense** (also **continuous** ˈ**tense**) (*grammar*) any of the verb tenses which express action that continues over a period of time, using the *-ing* form, as in 'I am/was/will be/have been writing': *the present progressive tense.*

prohibit /prəˈhɪbɪt; *US* prəʊ-/ *v* (*fml*) **1** [Tn, Tn·pr] ~ **sth**; ~ **sb** (**from doing sth**) forbid sth or sb from doing sth esp by laws, rules or regulations: *Smoking is prohibited.* ○ *a regulation to prohibit parking in the city centre* ○ *The law prohibits tobacconists from selling cigarettes to children.* **2** [Tn] make (sth) impossible; prevent: *The high cost prohibits the widespread use of the drug.*

prohibition /ˌprəʊhɪˈbɪʃn; *US* ˌprəʊəˈbɪʃn/ *n* **1** [U] forbidding or being forbidden: *They voted in favour of the prohibition of smoking in public areas.* ○ *Use of the drug has not declined since its prohibition.* **2** [C] ~ (**against sth**) edict or order that forbids sth: *a prohibition against the sale of firearms.* **3 Prohibition** [U] period of time (1920-1933) when the making and selling of alcoholic drinks was forbidden by law in the US.

▷ **prohibitionist** /-ʃənɪst/ *n* person who supports the prohibition of sth by law, esp the sale of alcoholic drinks.

prohibitive /prəˈhɪbətɪv; *US* prəʊ-/ *adj* **1** (**a**) intended to or tending to prevent the use or purchase of sth: *a prohibitive tax on imported cars.* (**b**) (of prices, etc) so high that one cannot afford to buy: *The cost of property in the city is prohibitive.* **2** that prohibits: *prohibitive laws, road signs.* ▷ **prohibitively** *adv*: *prohibitively expensive.*

prohibitory /prəˈhɪbɪtərɪ; *US* prəʊˈhɪbətɔːrɪ/ *adj* (*fml*) intended to prohibit sth: *regulations of a prohibitory nature.*

project[1] /ˈprɒdʒekt/ *n* **1** (plan for a) scheme or undertaking: *a housing development project* ○ *a project to establish a new national park* ○ *carry out, fail in, form a project.* **2** task set as an educational exercise which requires students to do their own research and present the results: *The class are doing a project on the Roman occupation of Britain.*

project[2] /prəˈdʒekt/ *v* **1** [Tn esp passive] plan (a scheme, course of action, etc): *a demonstration of the projected road improvement scheme* ○ *Our projected visit had to be cancelled.* **2** (**a**) [Tn, Tn·pr] ~ **sth** (**on/onto sth**) cause (light, shadow, a photographic image, etc) to fall on a surface: *project a slide on a screen* ○ *project a beam of light onto a statue* ○ *project spotlights on a performer.* (**b**) [Tn] show (a film) on a screen using a film projector: *Will you be able to project the film for us?* **3** [I, Tn, Tn·pr] ~ **sth** (**into sth**) send or throw sth outward or forward: *an apparatus to project missiles into space* ○ *An actor must learn to project (his voice).* ○ (*fig*) *project one's thoughts into the future.* **4** [I, Ipr] extend outward beyond a surface; jut out: *a projecting beam* ○ *a balcony that projects over the street.* **5** [Tn·pr] ~ **sth on to sb** (*psychology*) think, esp unconsciously, that sb shares (one's own feelings, usu unpleasant ones): *You mustn't project your guilt on to me,* ie assume that I feel as guilty as you do. **6** [Tn] represent (sth/sb/oneself) to others in a way that creates a strong or favourable impression: *Does the BBC World Service project a favourable view of Great Britain?* ○ *The party is trying to project a new image of itself as caring for the working classes.* **7** [Tn] (**a**) make a systematic drawing of (a solid, esp curved, object) on a flat surface, as maps of the earth are made. (**b**) make (a map) in this way. **8** [Tn, Tn·pr] ~ **sth** (**to sth**) predict (results) based on known data; extrapolate: *project population growth to the year 2000.*

projectile /prəˈdʒektaɪl; *US* -tl/ *n* (**a**) object (to be) shot forward, esp from a gun. (**b**) self-propelling missile, eg a rocket.

▷ **projectile** *adj* that can send objects or be sent forward through air, water, etc: *projectile force* ○ *projectile missiles.*

projection /prəˈdʒekʃn/ *n* **1** (**a**) [U] projecting or being projected: *the projection of images on a screen* ○ *film projection* ○ *the projection of one's feelings onto others* ○ *the projection of a missile through the air.* (**b**) [C] thing that is projected, esp a mental image viewed as reality. **2** [C] thing that juts out from a surface: *a projection of rock on a cliff-face.* **3** [C] representation of the surface of the earth on a plane surface. **4** [C] estimate of future situations or trends, etc based on a study of present ones: *sales projections for the next financial year.*

▷ **projectionist** /-ʃənɪst/ *n* person whose job is to project films onto a screen, esp in a cinema.

□ **pro**ˈ**jection room** room (esp in a cinema) from which films are projected onto a screen.

projector /prəˈdʒektə(r)/ *n* apparatus for projecting photographs or films onto a screen: *a* ˈ*cinema projector* ○ *a* ˈ*slide projector.*

Prokofiev /prəˈkɒfief/ Sergei (1891-1953), Russian composer. The aggressive modernity of his early works mellowed to a more accessible style after his return to Russia in the 1930s, eg in the ballet *Romeo and Juliet*. His gift for deft musical characterization is evident in works like *Peter and the Wolf.*

prolapse /prəʊˈlæps/ *v* [I] (*medical*) (of an organ in the body, eg the bowel or uterus) slip forward or down so that it is out of place.

▷ **prolapse** /ˈprəʊlæps/ *n* (*medical*) (condition caused by) this movement.

prole /prəʊl/ *n* (*infml derog*) member of the proletariat.

proletariat /ˌprəʊlɪˈteərɪət/ *n* **the proletariat** [Gp] **1** (*sometimes derog*) class of (esp industrial and manual) workers who do not own the means of production and earn their living by working for wages: *The dictatorship of the proletariat is one of the aims of Communism.* Cf BOURGEOISIE (BOURGEOIS). **2** (in ancient Rome) lowest class of citizen, owning no property.

pro-life /ˌprəʊ ˈlaɪf/ *adj* (*esp US*) believing that an unborn baby has the right to be born, and favouring strict laws against abortion. Cf PRO-CHOICE.

proliferate /prəˈlɪfəreɪt; *US* prəʊ-/ *v* **1** [I] produce new growth or offspring rapidly; multiply. **2** [Tn] reproduce (cells, etc). **3** [I] increase rapidly in numbers.

▷ **proliferation** /prəˌlɪfəˈreɪʃn; *US* prəʊ-/ *n* **1** [U] proliferating or being proliferated: [attrib] *a nuclear non-proliferation treaty,* ie one aimed at preventing the spread of nuclear weapons to countries that do not already possess them. **2** [C usu *sing*] rapid growth or increase.

prolific /prəˈlɪfɪk/ *adj* **1** (of plants, animals, etc) producing much fruit or many flowers or offspring: *prolific growth.* **2** (of a writer, an artist, etc) producing many works: *a prolific author* ○ *a prolific period in the composer's life.* ▷ **prolifically** /-klɪ/ *adv.*

prolix /ˈprəʊlɪks; *US* prəʊˈlɪks/ *adj* (*fml*) (of a speech, writer, etc) using too many words and so boring to listen to or read: *a prolix speaker* ○ *Her style is tediously prolix.* ▷ **prolixity** /prəʊˈlɪksətɪ/ *n* [U].

prologue (*US* also **prolog**) /ˈprəʊlɒɡ; *US* -lɔːɡ/ *n* ~ (**to sth**) **1** introductory part of a poem or play: *the 'Prologue' to the 'Canterbury Tales'.* Cf EPILOGUE. **2** act or event that is an introduction to sth or leads up to sth; first in a series of events: *The signing of the agreement was a prologue to better relations between the two countries.*

prolong /prəˈlɒŋ; *US* -ˈlɔːŋ/ *v* **1** [Tn] make (sth) longer, esp in time; extend: *drugs that help to prolong life* ○ *They prolonged their visit by a few days.* **2** (idm) **prolong the** ˈ**agony** make an unpleasant experience, a tense situation, etc last longer than necessary: *Don't prolong the agony — just tell us the result!*

▷ **prolongation** /ˌprəʊlɒŋˈgeɪʃn; *US* -lɔːŋ-/ *n* **1** [U] prolonging or being prolonged. **2** [C] addition or extension that prolongs sth.

prolonged *adj* [usu attrib] continuing for a long time: *After prolonged questioning, she finally confessed.* ○ *There will be prolonged delays for rail travellers.*

prom /prɒm/ *n* (*infml*) **1** (*Brit*) = PROMENADE 1a. **2** (*Brit*) = PROMENADE CONCERT (PROMENADE). **3** (*US*) (often formal) dance, esp one held by a class in high school or college.

promenade /ˌprɒməˈnɑːd; *US* -ˈneɪd/ *n* **1** (a) (also *Brit infml* **prom**) public place for walking, esp a paved area along the waterfront at the seaside. (b) (*fml*) walk or ride taken in public for exercise or pleasure. **2** (*US*) formal dance or ball.

▷ **promenade** *v* (*dated or fml*) **1** [I] take a leisurely walk or ride in public (esp along a promenade). **2** [Tn, Tn·pr] (a) take (sb) up and down a promenade for exercise: *She promenaded the children along the sea front after lunch.* (b) walk with (sb) in public, esp in order to show him off: *He proudly promenaded his elegant companion in the park.* **promenader** *n* **1** person who promenades. **2** person who (regularly) attends a promenade concert.

□ **promeˈnade concert** (also *infml* **prom**) (*Brit*) concert at which part of the audience is in an area without seats where they listen to the music standing up.

promeˈnade deck covered upper deck of a passenger ship, where passengers may walk.

prominent /ˈprɒmɪnənt/ *adj* **1** jutting out; projecting: *prominent cheek-bones.* **2** easily seen; conspicuous: *the most prominent feature in the landscape* ○ *The house is in a prominent position on the village green.* **3** distinguished or important: *play a prominent part in public life* ○ *a prominent political figure.*

▷ **prominence** /-əns/ *n* **1** [U] state of being prominent: *a young writer who has recently come to/into prominence* ○ *The newspapers are giving the affair considerable prominence.* **2** [C] (*fml*) prominent thing, esp part of a landscape or building: *a small prominence in the middle of the level plain.*

prominently *adv*: *The notice was prominently displayed.*

promiscuous /prəˈmɪskjʊəs/ *adj* **1** (*derog*) not carefully chosen; indiscriminate or casual: *promiscuous friendships,* ie ones made without careful choice. **2** (*derog*) having (esp casual) sexual relations with many people: *promiscuous behaviour* ○ *a promiscuous lover.* **3** (*dated fml*) mixed and disorderly; unsorted: *piled up in a promiscuous heap.* ▷ **promiscuity** /ˌprɒmɪˈskjuːətɪ/ *n* [U]: *sexual promiscuity.* **promiscuously** *adv.*

promise[1] /ˈprɒmɪs/ *n* **1** [C] ~ **(of sth)** written or spoken declaration that one will give or do or not do sth: *We received many promises of help.* ○ *break/carry out/fulfil/give/keep/make a promise* ○ *I told him the truth under a promise of secrecy.* ○ *I shall keep you/hold you to your promise.* ○ *'I'll come and see you soon.' 'Is that a promise?'* **2** [C, U] ~ **of sth** indication that sth may be expected to come or occur; likelihood or hope of sth: *There is a promise of better weather tomorrow.* ○ *There seems little promise of success for the expedition.* **3** [U] indication of future success or good results: *Her work/She shows great promise.* ○ *a scholarship for young musicians of promise.* **4** (idm) **a lick and a promise** ⇨ LICK *n.*

promise[2] /ˈprɒmɪs/ *v* **1** [I, Tn, Tf, Tt, Dn·n, Dn·pr, Dn·f] ~ **sth (to sb)** make a promise (to sb); assure (sb) that one will give or do or not do sth: *I can't promise, but I'll do my best.* ○ *He has promised a thorough investigation into the affair.* ○ *'Do you promise faithfully to pay me back?' 'Yes, I promise.'* ○ *I have promised myself a quiet weekend.* ○ *She promised me her help.* ○ *The firm promised a wage increase to the workers/promised the workers a wage increase.* ○ *She promised me (that) she would be punctual.* ○ *'Promise (me) you won't forget!' 'I promise.'* **2** [Tn, Tt] make (sth) seem likely: *The clouds promise rain.* ○ *It promises to be warm this afternoon.* **3** (idm) **I (can) ˈpromise you** (*infml*) I assure you: *You won't regret it, I promise you.* **promise (sb) the ˈearth/ˈmoon** (*infml*) make extravagant or rash promises that one is unlikely to be able to keep: *Politicians promise the earth before an election, but things are different once they are in power.* **the promised ˈland (a)** (in the Bible) the fertile country promised to the Israelites by God; Canaan. **(b)** any place or situation in which one expects to find happiness and security. **promise ˈwell** seem likely to give good results: *The new sales policy promises well.*

▷ **promising** *adj* (a) likely to do well; full of promise[1](3): *a promising young pianist.* (b) indicating future success or good results; hopeful: *The results of the first experiments are very promising.* ○ *It's a promising sign.* **promisingly** *adv.*

promissory /ˈprɒmɪsərɪ; *US* -sɔːrɪ/ *adj* (*fml*) conveying a promise.

□ **ˈpromissory note** signed document containing a promise to pay a stated sum of money on demand or on a specified date.

promontory /ˈprɒməntrɪ; *US* -tɔːrɪ/ *n* area of high land jutting out into the sea or a lake; headland. ⇨ illus at COAST.

promote /prəˈməʊt/ *v* **1** (a) [esp passive: Tn, Tn·pr] ~ **sb (to sth)** raise sb to a higher position or rank: *She worked hard and was soon promoted.* ○ *His assistant was promoted over his head,* ie above him. ○ *The football team was promoted to the first division.* (b) [Tn·pr, Cn·n esp passive] ~ **sb (from sth) (to sth)** (*esp Brit*) raise sb to the rank of (sth): *He was promoted to sergeant.* Cf DEMOTE. **2** [Tn] help the progress of (sth); encourage or support: *The organization works to promote friendship between nations.* ○ *promote a bill in Parliament,* ie take the necessary steps for it to be passed. **3** [Tn] publicize (sth) in order to sell it: *a publicity campaign to promote her new book.*

▷ **promoter** *n* (a) person who organizes or finances (esp a business company or a sporting event): *a boxing promoter.* (b) ~ **of sth** supporter of sth: *an enthusiastic promoter of good causes.*

promotion /prəˈməʊʃn/ *n* **1** (a) [U] raising or being raised to a higher rank or position: *gain/win promotion* ○ *If you are successful, you can expect promotion.* ○ [attrib] *promotion prospects.* (b) [C] instance of this: *The new job is a promotion for her.* **2** [U] ~ **of sth** encouragement or aid to the progress of (a cause): *They worked for the promotion of world peace.* **3** (a) [U] advertising or other activity intended to increase the sales of a product: *She is responsible for sales promotion.* ○ *Advertising is often the most effective method of promotion.* (b) [C] advertising or publicity campaign for a particular product: *We are doing a special promotion of our paperback list.*

▷ **promotional** /-ʃənl/ *adj* of or relating to promotion(3b): *a promotional tour by the author.*

prompt[1] /prɒmpt/ *adj* **1** done without delay; punctual: *a prompt reply* ○ *Prompt payment of the invoice would be appreciated.* **2** ~ **(in doing sth/to do sth)** (of a person) acting without delay: *She was very prompt in answering my letter.* ○ *They were prompt to respond to our call for help.*

▷ **prompt** *adv* punctually: *at 6 o'clock prompt.*

promptitude /ˈprɒmptɪtjuːd; *US* -tuːd/ *n* [U] (*fml*) quality of being prompt; readiness to act.

promptly *adv*: *She replied promptly to my letter.*

promptness *n* [U].

prompt[2] /prɒmpt/ *v* **1** [Tn, Dn·t] cause or incite (sb) to do sth: *What prompted him to be so generous?* ○ *The accident prompted her to renew her insurance.* **2** [Tn] inspire or cause (a feeling or an action): *Her question was prompted by worries about her future.* ○ *What prompted that remark?* **3** (a) [Tn] help (a speaker) by suggesting the words that could or should follow: *The speaker was rather hesitant and had to be prompted occasionally by the chairman.* (b) [I, Tn] follow the text of a play and help (an actor) if he forgets hi words, by saying the next line quietly: *Will yo prompt for us at the next performance?* ○ *The acto needed to be prompted frequently.*

▷ **prompt** *n* act of prompting or words spoken t prompt an actor, a speaker, etc: *She needed a occasional prompt.*

prompter *n* person who prompts in a play.

prompting *n* [C, U] (act of) urging or persuading *Despite several promptings from his parents the bo refused to apologize.* ○ *He did it without an prompting from me.*

promulgate /ˈprɒmlgeɪt/ *v* [Tn] (*fml*) **1** mak (sth) widely known; disseminate: *promulgate belief, an idea, a theory, etc.* **2** announce officiall (a decree, new law etc); proclaim. ▷ **promulgation** /ˌprɒmlˈgeɪʃn/ *n* [U]: *th promulgation of a treaty.*

prone /prəʊn/ *adj* **1** (of a person or his position lying flat, esp face downwards: *lying prone* ○ *in prone position.* Cf PROSTRATE 1, SUPINE 1. **2** (a [pred] ~ **to sth/to do sth** liable to sth or likely t do sth; inclined to do sth: *prone to infection after cut scratch* ○ *prone to fall asleep on long ca journeys.* ○ *He is prone to lose his temper whe people disagree with him.* (b) (in compounds liable or susceptible to sth specified (esp st undesirable): *The child is rather ˈaccident-prone.* *ˈstrike-prone industries.* ▷ **proneness** /ˈprəʊnnɪs *n* [U]: *proneness to injury.*

prong /prɒŋ; *US* prɔːŋ/ *n* each of the two or mor long pointed parts of a fork: *One of the prongs of th garden fork went through his foot.* ⇨ illus at FORK

▷ **-pronged** (forming compound *adjs*) having th number or type of prongs specified: *ˌfour-pronged ˈfork* ○ (*fig*) *a three-pronged atˈtack* ie one made by three separate forces, us advancing from different directions.

pronominal /prəʊˈnɒmɪnl/ *adj* (*grammar*) of o like a pronoun.

▷ **pronominally** /-nəlɪ/ *adv* (*grammar*) as pronoun: *a word used pronominally.*

pronoun /ˈprəʊnaʊn/ *n* (*grammar*) word used i place of a noun or noun phrase, eg *he, it, hers, me them,* etc: *demonstrative/interrogative/persona possessive/relative pronouns.*

pronounce /prəˈnaʊns/ *v* **1** [Tn] make the soun of (a word or letter) (in a particular way): *Peopl pronounce the word differently in this part of th country.* ○ *How do you pronounce p-h-l-e-g-m? Loo up 'phlegm' in the dictionary if you don't know.* *The 'b' in 'debt' is not pronounced.* **2** (a) [Tn, Tn·pr Tf, Cn·a] declare or announce (sth) esp formally solemnly or officially: *pronounce judgement on th issue* ○ *The doctors pronounced him to be/that h was no longer in danger.* (b) [Cn·a esp passive declare (sth) as a considered opinion: *The dinne was pronounced excellent by all the guests.* ○ *Sh pronounced herself satisfied with the results* **3** [Ipr] (a) ~ **for/against sb/sth** (*law*) pas judgement in court in favour of/against sb/sth: *Th judge pronounced the sentence.* ○ *The cour pronounced a decree of divorce for the husband.* (b ~ **on/upon sth** express one's opinion on sth, es formally: *The minister was asked to pronounce o the proposed new legislation.*

▷ **pronounceable** /-əbl/ *adj* (of sounds or words that can be pronounced: *I find some of th place-names barely pronounceable.*

pronounced *adj* **1** very noticeable: *a pronounce limp.* **2** (of opinions, views, etc) strongly fel definite: *She has very pronounced views on th importance of correct spelling.* **pronouncedly** *adv*

pronouncement *n* ~ **(on sth)** formal statemen or declaration: *There has been no officia pronouncement yet on the state of the president' health.*

pronto /ˈprɒntəʊ/ *adv* (*infml*) at once; quickly: *want this rubbish cleared away pronto!*

pronunciation /prəˌnʌnsɪˈeɪʃn/ *n* **1** (a) [U] wa in which a language is spoken: *She had difficult learning English pronunciation.* (b) way a perso speaks (the words of) a language: *Their Englis pronunciation is not good, but it is improving.* **2** [C way in which a word is pronounced: *Which of thes* *three pronunciations is the most usual?*

proof[1] /pru:f/ *n* **1** [C, U] (piece of) evidence that shows, or helps to show, that sth is true or is a fact: *What proofs have you that the statement is correct?* ○ *Have you any proof that you are the owner of the car?* ○ *written proof* ○ *documentary proof of his ownership of the land.* **2** [U] testing of whether sth is true or a fact; demonstration or proving: *Is the claim capable of proof?* **3** [U] standard of strength in distilled alcoholic liquors on a scale in which proof spirit is 100%: *The liquor is 80% proof.* ○ *The rum is 30% below proof.* **4** (**a**) [C esp *pl*] trial copy of printed material produced so that corrections may be made: *check/correct/read the proofs of a book* ○ *pass the proofs for press*, ie approve them, so that printing may begin ○ *galley-/page-proofs* ○ [attrib] *a proof copy.* (**b**) [C] trial print of a photograph: *proofs of the wedding photos.* (**c**) [U] stage in book production when proofs have been made: *I read the book in proof.* **5** [C] (*mathematics*) sequence of steps or statements that shows the truth of a proposition: *the proof of a theorem*, ie in geometry. **6** (idm) **be living proof of sth** ⇨ LIVING. **the proof of the ˈpudding (is in the ˈeating)** (*saying*) the real value of sb/sth can be judged only from practical experience and not from appearance or theory: *The new machine is supposed to be the solution to all our production problems, but the proof of the pudding is in the eating.* **put sb/sth to the ˈproof/ˈtest** test sb/sth; test the truth of sth: *Let's put his theory to the proof.* ○ *The crisis put his courage and skill to the test.*

□ **ˈproof-read** *v* [I, Tn] read and correct (proofs): *It is part of your duties to proof-read.* ○ *proof-read twenty pages.* **ˈproof-reader** *n.*

ˌproof ˈspirit mixture of alcohol and water at standard strength, in Britain 49.28% of alcohol by weight (or 57.1% by volume), 50% by volume in the USA. This standard is used for calculating duty to be paid when alcoholic drinks are bought.

proof[2] /pru:f/ *adj* **1** [pred] ~ **against sth** (**a**) providing protection against sth: *The shelter was proof against the bitter weather.* (**b**) that can resist sth: *proof against temptation.* **2** (in compounds) that can resist sth or protect against sth specified: *ˌleak-proof ˈbatteries* ○ *Are these batteries ˈleak-proof?* ○ *ˌbullet-proof ˈglass* ○ *a ˌsound-proof ˈroom* ○ *ˌwaterproof ˈclothing.*

▷ **proof** *v* [Tn] (*fml*) treat (sth) in order to make it proof against sth (esp fabric in order to make it waterproof).

prop

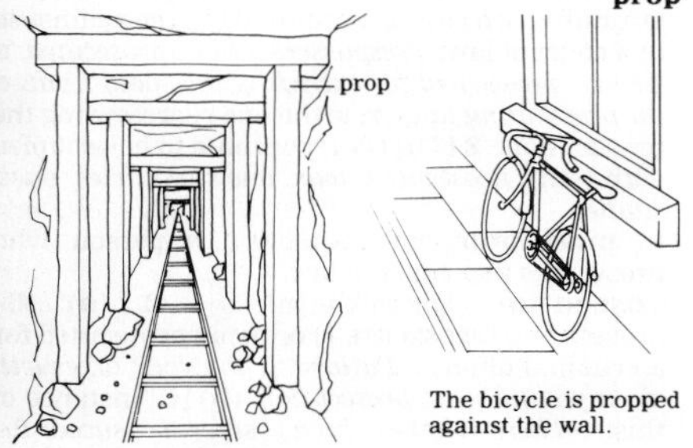

The bicycle is propped against the wall.

prop[1] /prɒp/ *n* **1** (esp in compounds) rigid support, esp a piece of wood, used to prevent sth falling or sagging: *Props were used to prevent the roof collapsing.* ○ *a ˈpit-prop* ○ *a ˈclothes-prop.* **2** (*fig*) person or thing that gives help or (esp moral) support to sb/sth: *a prop and comfort to her parents in their old age* ○ *His encouragement was a great prop to her self-confidence.* **3** (also **ˌprop ˈforward**) (in Rugby) either of the forwards (FORWARD[4]) on the sides of the front line of the scrum.

▷ **prop** *v* (**-pp-**) **1** (**a**) [Tn, Tn·pr, Cn·a] support (sth) or keep (sth) in position with a prop: *The invalid lay propped on the pillows.* ○ *He used a box to prop the door open.* (**b**) [Tn·pr] ~ **sb/sth against sth** lean sb/sth against sth (so that it does not fall down): *She propped her bicycle against the wall.* ○ *He propped himself against the gatepost.* ⇨ illus. **2** (idm) **ˌprop up the ˈbar** (*Brit joc*) spend one's time drinking in a pub or bar: *We found him in the Red Lion, propping up the bar.* **3** (phr v) **prop sth up** (**a**) use a prop or props to raise sth and prevent it from falling: *The roof will have to be propped up while repairs are carried out.* ○ *The baby cannot sit unaided — she has to be propped up on pillows.* (**b**) (*often derog*) support sth that would otherwise fail: *The government refuses to prop up inefficient industries.* ○ *The regime had been propped up by foreign aid.*

□ **ˈprop-word** *n* (*grammar*) the word *one* (or *ones*) when used to stand for a noun, esp a noun that has been mentioned previously, as in *'Which piece would you like?' 'I'd like the bigger one.'*

prop[2] /prɒp/ *n* (*infml*) = PROPELLER (PROPEL).

prop[3] /prɒp/ *n* (*infml*) = PROPERTY 5.

propaganda /ˌprɒpəˈgændə/ *n* [U] (**a**) publicity that is intended to spread ideas or information which will persuade or convince people: *There has been so much propaganda against smoking that many people have given it up.* (**b**) (*derog*) ideas or statements that are intended as publicity for a particular (political) cause but are (often) presented as being unbiased: *The play is sheer political propaganda.* ○ *The people want information from the government, not propaganda.* ○ [attrib] *propaganda films, plays, posters, etc.*

▷ **propagandist** /-dɪst/ *n* (*often derog*) person who creates or spreads propaganda: *anti-smoking propagandists* ○ *political propagandists.*

propagandize, -ise /-daɪz/ *v* (*fml often derog*) (**a**) [I] spread or organize propaganda. (**b**) [Tn] spread (sth) by propaganda: *propagandize political ideology.* (**c**) [Tn] spread propaganda to (a group, class, nation, etc).

propagate /ˈprɒpəgeɪt/ *v* **1** [Tn] increase the number of (plants, animals, etc) by a natural process from the parent stock: *propagate plants from seeds and cuttings* ○ *propagate plants by taking cuttings.* **2** [I, Tn] (of plants) reproduce (themselves): *Plants won't propagate in these conditions.* ○ *Trees propagate themselves by seeds.* **3** [Tn] (*fml*) spread (views, knowledge, beliefs, etc) more widely: *Missionaries went far afield to propagate their faith.* **4** [Tn] (*fml*) cause or allow (sth) to pass through sth; transmit: *propagate vibrations through rock.*

▷ **propagation** /ˌprɒpəˈgeɪʃn/ *n* [U] propagating or being propagated: *the propagation of plants from cuttings.*

propagator person or thing that propagates: *tomato plants growing in a propagator.*

propane /ˈprəʊpeɪn/ *n* [U] (*chemistry*) type of colourless gas, found in natural gas and petroleum and used as a fuel.

propanone /ˈprɒpənəʊn/ *n* [C] = ACETONE.

propel /prəˈpel/ *v* (**-ll-**) [Tn, Tn·pr] move, drive or push (sth) forward: *mechanically propelled vehicles* ○ *a boat propelled by oars* ○ (*fig*) *His addiction to drugs propelled him towards a life of crime.*

▷ **propellant** (also **propellent**) /-ənt/ *n* [C, U] propelling agent, eg an explosive that propels a bullet from a weapon, a fuel that provides thrust for a rocket, or compressed gas that forces out the contents of an aerosol container.

propellent /-ənt/ *adj* that propels: *a propellent agent.*

propeller (also **ˈscrew-propeller**, *infml* **prop**) *n* two or more spiral blades, fixed to a revolving shaft for propelling a ship or an aircraft.

□ **proˌpelling ˈpencil** pencil with a lead that can be moved forwards by turning the outer case.

propensity /prəˈpensətɪ/ *n* ~ **(for/to/towards sth)**; ~ **(for doing/to do sth)** (*fml*) inclination or tendency: *a propensity to exaggerate/towards exaggeration* ○ *a propensity for getting into debt.*

proper /ˈprɒpə(r)/ *adj* **1** (**a**) that fits, belongs or is suitable; fitting or appropriate: *clothes proper for the occasion* ○ *the proper tool for the job* ○ *The teapot has lost its proper lid but this one will do instead.* (**b**) [attrib] according to the rules; right or correct: *the proper way to hold the bat* ○ *The reels of film were not in the proper order.* **2** according to or respecting social conventions; respectable: *After a very proper upbringing he chose to lead the Bohemian life of an artist.* ○ *She's not at all a proper person for you to know.* Cf IMPROPER. **3** (**a**) [attrib] (*infml*) being in fact what it is called; genuine: *She hadn't had a proper holiday for years.* ○ *It was discovered that he was not a proper* (ie qualified) *doctor.* (**b**) (placed after the *n*) strictly so called; itself: *You have to wait in a large entrance hall before being shown into the court proper.* ○ *Students have to do a year's preparation before they start the degree course proper.* **4** [attrib] (*infml*) thorough; complete: *We're in a proper mess now.* ○ *He gave the burglar a proper hiding*, ie beat him thoroughly. **5** (idm) **do the proper/right thing (by sb)** ⇨ THING.

▷ **properly** *adv* **1** in a proper manner: *She will have to learn to behave properly.* ○ *Do it properly or don't do it at all.* ○ *He is not properly* (ie strictly) *speaking a member of the staff.* **2** (*infml*) thoroughly: *He got properly beaten by the world champion.*

□ **ˌproper ˈfraction** (*mathematics*) fraction that has a lower number above the line than below: $\frac{1}{2}$, $\frac{3}{4}$, $\frac{19}{20}$ *are proper fractions.* Cf IMPROPER FRACTION (IMPROPER).

ˈproper name (also **ˈproper noun**) (*grammar*) name of an individual person, place, etc (written with an initial capital letter), eg *Jane, Mr Smith, London, Europe, the Thames.*

property /ˈprɒpətɪ/ *n* **1** [U] thing or things owned; possession(s): *Don't touch those tools — they are not your property.* ○ *The jewels were her personal property.* **2** (**a**) [U] land and buildings; real estate: *a man/woman of property*, ie one who owns property ○ *She invested her money in property.* ○ [attrib] *property development, management, speculation.* (**b**) [C] (*fml*) piece of land and its buildings: *He has a property in the West Country.* ○ *A fence divides the two properties.* **3** [U] (*fml*) owning or being owned; ownership: *Property brings duties and responsibilities.* **4** [C esp *pl*] (*fml*) special quality or characteristic of a substance, etc: *Certain plants have medicinal* (ie healing) *properties.* ○ *the soothing properties of an ointment* ○ *Paraffin has the property of dissolving grease.* **5** [C usu *pl*] (also *infml* **prop**) (on a stage or a film set) movable object, eg a piece of furniture or a costume, used in a performance: *She was responsible for buying the properties for the television series.* **6** (idm) **public property** ⇨ PUBLIC.

▷ **propertied** /ˈprɒpətɪd/ *adj* (*fml*) owning property, esp land: *The tax will affect only the propertied classes.*

prophecy /ˈprɒfəsɪ/ *n* **1** [U] (power of) saying what will happen in the future: *He seemed to have the gift of prophecy.* ○ *All these events had been revealed by prophecy.* **2** [C] statement that tells what will happen in the future: *prophecies of disaster* ○ *Her prophecy was proved to be correct.*

prophesy /ˈprɒfəsaɪ/ *v* (*pt, pp* **-sied**) **1** [I, Ipr] ~ **(of sth)** foretell future events; speak as a prophet; make prophecies. **2** [Tn, Tf, Tw] say (what will happen in the future); foretell: *He prophesied the strange events that were to come.* ○ *They prophesied correctly that the Conservatives would win the election.* ○ *He refused to prophesy when the economy would begin to improve.*

prophet /ˈprɒfɪt/ *n* (*fem* **prophetess** /ˈprɒfɪtes, *also* ˌprɒfɪˈtes/) **1** [C] person who tells, or claims to be able to tell, what will happen in the future: (*joc*) *I'm afraid I'm no weather prophet.* **2** (**a**) (also **Prophet**) [C] (in the Christian, Jewish and Muslim religions) person who teaches religion and is, or claims to be, inspired by God: *the Prophets of the Old Testament.* (**b**) **the Prophet** [sing] the founder of the Muslim religion, Mohammed. (**c**) **the Prophets** [pl] the prophetical books of the Old Testament. **3** [C] ~ **(of sth)** spokesman or advocate of a new belief, cause, theory, etc: *William Morris was one of the early prophets of socialism.* **4** (idm) **a ˌprophet of ˈdoom** person who holds or expresses pessimistic views about sth, esp about the future of the world: *If we* *had listened to the prophets of doom, we would never have started the project.*

prophetic /prəˈfetɪk/ (also **prophetical** /prəˈfetɪkl/) *adj (fml)* **1** of or like a prophet or prophets. **2** ~ (**of sth**) predicting or containing a prediction: *prophetic remarks* ○ *Her early achievements were prophetic of her future greatness.* ▷ **prophetically** /-klɪ/ *adv*: *We were to realize years later how prophetically he spoke on that occasion.*

prophylactic /ˌprɒfɪˈlæktɪk/ *adj (fml)* tending to prevent a disease or misfortune.

▷ **prophylactic** *n (fml)* **1** prophylactic medicine, device or course of action. **2** *(esp US)* = CONDOM.

prophylaxis /-ˈlæksɪs/ *n* [U] *(fml)* preventive treatment against disease, etc.

propinquity /prəˈpɪŋkwətɪ/ *n* [U] *(fml)* (**a**) nearness in space or time: *The neighbours lived in close propinquity to each other.* (**b**) close blood relationship; consanguinity.

propitiate /prəˈpɪʃɪeɪt/ *v* [Tn] *(fml)* win the favour or forgiveness of (sb) (esp when he is angry) by a pleasing act; appease or placate: *They offered sacrifices to propitiate the gods.*

▷ **propitiation** /prəˌpɪʃɪˈeɪʃn/ *n* [U] ~ (**of sb**); ~ (**for sth**): *propitiation of the gods* ○ *in propitiation for their sins.*

propitiatory /prəˈpɪʃɪətrɪ; *US* -tɔ:rɪ/ *adj (fml)* serving or intended to propitiate: *a propitiatory gift, remark, smile.*

propitious /prəˈpɪʃəs/ *adj* ~ (**for sth**) *(fml)* giving or indicating a good chance of success; favourable: *It was not a propitious time to start a new business.* ○ *The circumstances were not propitious for further expansion of the company.* ▷ **propitiously** *adv.*

prop-jet /ˈprɒpdʒet/ *n* = TURBO-PROP.

proponent /prəˈpəʊnənt/ *n* ~ (**of sth**) person who supports a cause, theory, etc: *one of the leading proponents of the Channel Tunnel.*

proportion /prəˈpɔ:ʃn/ *n* **1** [C] comparative part or share of a whole; fraction: *a large proportion of the earth's surface* ○ *The proportion of the population still speaking the dialect is very small.* ○ *A fixed proportion of the fund is invested in British firms.* **2** [U] ~ (**of sth to sth**) relation of one thing to another in quantity, size, etc; ratio: *The proportion of imports to exports* (ie excess of imports over exports) *is worrying the government.* ○ *the proportion of passes to failures in the final examination* ○ *What is the proportion of men to women in the population?* **3** [U, C usu *pl*] correct or ideal relation in size, degree, etc between one thing and another or between the parts of a whole: *the classical proportions of the room* ○ *The two windows are in admirable proportion.* **4 proportions** [pl] measurements or dimensions; size: *a ship of impressive proportions* ○ *a painting of huge proportions.* **5** [U] *(mathematics)* relationship between four numbers in which the ratio of the first two equals the ratio of the second two: *'4 is to 8 as 6 is to 12' is a statement of proportion.* **6** (idm) ˌ**in** ˈ**proportion** (**a**) in the correct relation to other things: *Try to draw the figures in the foreground in proportion.* ○ *Her features are in proportion,* ie are of the correct size relative to each other. ○ *get/see things in proportion* ○ *Try to see the problem in proportion — it could be far worse.* (**b**) *(mathematics)* having equal ratios: $\frac{5}{8}$ *and* $\frac{10}{16}$ *are in proportion.* **in proportion to sth** relative to sth: *The room is wide in proportion to its height.* ○ *Payment will be in proportion to the work done, not to the time spent doing it.* ˌ**out of** ˈ**proportion** (**to sth**) in the wrong relation (to other things): *The figures of the horses in the foreground are out of proportion.* ○ *Her head is out of proportion to the size of her body.* **out of** (**all**) **proportion to sth** too large, serious, etc in relation to sth: *prices out of all proportion to income* ○ *punishment that was out of all proportion to the offence committed.*

▷ **proportioned** *adj* (esp in compounds) having the proportions (PROPORTION 4) specified: *a well-proportioned room.*

proportional /prəˈpɔ:ʃənl/ *adj* ~ (**to sth**) *(fml)* corresponding in size, amount or degree (to sth); in the correct proportion: *Payment will be proportional to the amount of work done.* ▷ **proportionally** /-ʃənəlɪ/ *adv.*

□ **pro**ˌ**portional** ˌ**represen**ˈ**tation** (abbr **PR**) electoral system that gives each party a number of seats in proportion to the number of votes its candidates receive. Cf FIRST PAST THE POST (FIRST[1]).

proportionate /prəˈpɔ:ʃənət/ *adj* ~ (**to sth**) *(fml)* in proportion (to sth); corresponding to sth: *The price increases are proportionate to the increases in the costs of production.* ▷ **proportionately** *adv*: *Costs have risen, and prices will rise proportionately.*

proposal /prəˈpəʊzl/ *n* **1** [U] action of suggesting or putting forward: *the proposal of new terms for a peace treaty.* **2** [C] ~ (**for sth/doing sth**); ~ (**to do sth**) thing that is suggested; plan or scheme: *a proposal for uniting the two companies* ○ *Various proposals were put forward for increasing sales.* ○ *a proposal to offer a discount to regular customers.* **3** [C] suggestion or request, esp from a man to a woman, that the two should marry: *She had had many proposals (of marriage) but preferred to remain single.*

propose /prəˈpəʊz/ *v* **1** [Tn, Tf, Tg] offer or put forward (sth) for consideration; suggest: *The motion* (ie for debate) *was proposed by Mr X and seconded by Mrs Y.* ○ *The committee proposed that new legislation should be drafted.* Cf SECOND[4] 2. **2** [Tn, Tt, Tg] have (sth) as one's plan or intention; intend: *I propose an early start/to make an early start/making an early start tomorrow.* **3** [I, Ipr, Tn, Dn·pr] ~ (**sth**) (**to sb**) suggest or offer marriage (to sb), esp formally: *He was trying to decide whether he should propose (to her).* ○ *He had proposed marriage, unsuccessfully, twice already.* **4** [Tn·pr, Cn·n/a] ~ **sb for sth**; ~ **sb as sth** put forward (sb/sb's name) for an office, membership of a club, etc; nominate sb: *propose him for membership of the society* ○ *I propose Mary Davies as a candidate for the presidency.* **5** (idm) **propose sb's** ˈ**health/a** ˈ**toast** ask people to drink to sb's health and happiness: *I should like to propose a toast to the bride and bridegroom.*

▷ **proposer** *n* person who proposes (esp a motion, a candidate for office, etc). Cf SECONDER (SECOND[4]).

proposition /ˌprɒpəˈzɪʃn/ *n* **1** ~ (**that...**) statement that expresses a judgement or an opinion; assertion: *The proposition is so clear that it needs no explanation.* **2** ~ (**to do sth/that...**) thing that is proposed, esp in business; suggestion: *I made what I hoped was an attractive proposition.* ○ *a proposition to merge the two firms/that the two firms should merge.* **3** *(infml)* matter to be dealt with; problem or task: *It's a tough/not an easy proposition.* ○ *Keeping a shop in this village is not a paying proposition,* ie not profitable. **4** *(geometry)* formal statement of a theorem or problem, usu containing its proof.

▷ **proposition** *v* [Tn] propose sexual intercourse to (a woman), esp in a direct and offensive way: *She was propositioned several times in the course of the evening.*

propound /prəˈpaʊnd/ *v* [Tn] *(fml)* put (sth) forward for consideration or solution: *propound an idea, a problem, a question, a theory, etc.*

proprietary /prəˈpraɪətrɪ; *US* -terɪ/ *adj* [usu attrib] **1** (**a**) (of goods) manufactured and sold by a particular firm, usu under patent: *proprietary medicines* ○ *proprietary brands.* (**b**) (in this dictionary abbreviated as **propr**) (of a brand name) owned and used exclusively by a particular firm: *a proprietary name,* eg Kodak for cameras and films ○ *'Xerox' is a proprietary name and may not be used by other makers of photocopiers.* **2** of or relating to an owner or ownership: *proprietary rights.*

proprietor /prəˈpraɪətə(r)/ *n* (*fem* **proprietress** /prəˈpraɪətrɪs/) owner, esp of a business firm, hotel or patent: *Complaints about standards of service should be addressed to the proprietor.* ○ *a newspaper proprietor.*

▷ **proprietorial** /prəˌpraɪəˈtɔ:rɪəl/ *adj (often derog)* of, like or relating to a proprietor: *She resented the proprietorial way he used her car for trips about town.*

propriety /prəˈpraɪətɪ/ *n (fml)* **1** (**a**) [U] state of being correct in one's social or moral behaviour: *behave with perfect propriety* ○ *The way tourists dress offends local standards of propriety.* (**b**) **the proprieties** [pl] details of the rules of correct behaviour: *Her use of obscene language offends against the proprieties.* ○ *Be careful to observe the proprieties.* **2** [U] ~ (**of sth**) rightness or suitability; fitness: *I am doubtful about the propriety of granting such a request,* ie doubt whether it is right.

propulsion /prəˈpʌlʃn/ *n* [U] driving (sth) forward or being driven forward: *changes in the fuel used for propulsion* ○ *jet propulsion,* ie by means of jet engines.

▷ **propulsive** /prəˈpʌlsɪv/ *adj (fml)* that drives sth (esp a vehicle) forward: *propulsive power, forces, gases.*

pro rata /ˌprəʊ ˈrɑ:tə/ *adj, adv (fml)* proportional(ly): *If production costs go up, there will be a pro rata increase in prices/prices will increase pro rata.*

prorogue /prəˈrəʊg/ *v* [Tn] *(fml)* bring (a session of Parliament) to an end without dissolving Parliament (so that unfinished business may be continued in the next session).

▷ **prorogation** /ˌprəʊrəˈgeɪʃn/ *n* [C, U] *(fml)* (instance of) proroguing.

prosaic /prəˈzeɪɪk/ *adj* (**a**) uninspired, unimaginative: *a prosaic metaphor, style, writer* ○ *a prosaic description of the scene.* (**b**) dull and commonplace; unromantic: *her prosaic life as a housewife.* ▷ **prosaically** /-klɪ/ *adv.*

proscenium /prəˈsi:nɪəm/ *n* (in a theatre) the part of the stage in front of the curtain.

□ **pro**ˌ**scenium** ˈ**arch** arch above this space which forms a frame for the stage when the curtain is opened. ⇨ illus at THEATRE.

proscribe /prəˈskraɪb; *US* prəʊ-/ *v* [Tn] *(fml)* **1** state officially that (sth) is dangerous or forbidden: *The sale of narcotics is proscribed by law.* **2** (formerly) place (sb) outside the protection of the law; outlaw.

▷ **proscription** /prəˈskrɪpʃn; *US* prəʊ-/ *n* [C, U] *(fml)* (instance of) proscribing or being proscribed: *the proscription of newspapers critical of the government.*

prose /prəʊz/ *n* [U] written or spoken language that is not in verse form: *a page of well-written prose* ○ [attrib] *the great prose writers of the 19th century.* Cf POETRY 1, VERSE 1.

prosecute /ˈprɒsɪkju:t/ *v* **1** [Tn, Tn·pr] ~ **sb** (**for sth/doing sth**) bring a criminal charge against sb in a court of law: *Trespassers will be prosecuted.* ○ *He was prosecuted for exceeding the speed limit.* ○ *the prosecuting lawyer,* ie the one representing the prosecution. **2** [Tn] *(fml)* continue to be occupied with (sth): *prosecute a war, one's inquiries, one's studies.*

▷ **prosecutor** /ˈprɒsɪkju:tə(r)/ *n* person who prosecutes in a court of law.

prosecution /ˌprɒsɪˈkju:ʃn/ *n* **1** (**a**) [U] prosecuting (PROSECUTE 1) or being prosecuted for a criminal offence: *Failure to pay your taxes will make you liable to prosecution.* (**b**) [C] instance of this: *There have been several successful prosecutions for drug smuggling recently.* **2 the prosecution** [Gp] person or body that prosecutes in a lawcourt together with lawyers, advisers, etc: *Mr Smith acted as counsel for the prosecution.* ○ *The prosecution based their case on the evidence of two witnesses.* Cf DEFENCE 2. **3** [U] **the** ~ **of sth** *(fml)* carrying out or being occupied with sth: *In the prosecution of his duties he had met with a good deal of resistance.* ⇨ article at LAW.

proselyte /ˈprɒsəlaɪt/ *n (fml)* person who has been converted from one set of religious, political, etc beliefs to another.

▷ **proselytize, -ise** /ˈprɒsəlɪtaɪz/ *v* [I, Tn] *(fml)* (try to) persuade (others) to accept one's own beliefs, religion, etc: *going round the country proselytizing* ○ *attempts to proselytize the younger generation.*

prosody /ˈprɒsədɪ/ *n* [U] **1** science of verse forms

and poetic metres. **2** (study of the) rhythm, pause, tempo, stress and pitch features of a language. ▷ **prosodic** /prəˈsɒdɪk/ *adj*.

prospect[1] /ˈprɒspekt/ *n* **1** [C] **(a)** *(dated)* wide view of a landscape, etc: *a magnificent prospect of mountain peaks and lakes.* **(b)** picture in the mind or imagination, esp of a future event: *She viewed the prospect of a week alone in the house without much enthusiasm.* **2 prospects** [pl] chance of success; outlook: *The prospects for this year's wine harvest are poor.* ○ *The job has no prospects*, ie offers little possibility of promotion. **3** [U] ~ **(of sth/doing sth)** reasonable hope that sth will happen; expectation: *I see little prospect of an improvement in his condition.* ○ *There is no prospect of a settlement of the dispute.* ○ *have little prospect of succeeding* ○ *He is unemployed and has nothing in prospect* (ie no expectation of finding work) *at the moment.* **4** [C] **(a)** candidate or competitor likely to be successful: *She's a good prospect for the British team.* **(b)** possible or likely customer or client: *He was an experienced car salesman and recognized an easy prospect when he saw one!*

prospect[2] /prəˈspekt; *US* ˈprɒspekt/ *v* [I, Ipr] ~ **(for sth)** search for minerals, gold, oil, etc: *a licence to prospect in the northern territory* ○ *The company are prospecting for gold in that area.*
▷ **prospector** *n* person who explores a region looking for gold, ores, etc.

prospective /prəˈspektɪv/ *adj* [esp attrib] expected to be or to occur; future or possible: *prospective changes in the law* ○ *his prospective mother-in-law* ○ *the prospective Labour candidate at the next election* ○ *showing the house to a prospective buyer.*

prospectus /prəˈspektəs/ *n* printed document, leaflet, etc giving details of and advertising sth, eg a private school or a new business: *prospectuses from several universities.*

prosper /ˈprɒspə(r)/ *v* [I] be successful; thrive: *The business is prospering.*

prosperity /prɒˈsperətɪ/ *n* [U] **(a)** state of being successful or rich; good fortune: *He wished the young couple a life of happiness and prosperity.* **(b)** state of being economically successful: *The increase in the country's prosperity was due to the discovery of oil.*

prosperous /ˈprɒspərəs/ *adj* successful or thriving, esp financially: *a prosperous country, businessman, industry* ○ *a prosperous-looking businessman.* ▷ **prosperously** *adv*.

prostate /ˈprɒsteɪt/ *n* (also ˌ**prostate** ˈ**gland**) *(anatomy)* (in male mammals) gland at the neck of the bladder: *in hospital for an operation on his prostate.* ⇨ illus at MALE.

prosthesis /ˈprɒsθɪsɪs, prɒsˈθiːsɪs/ *n* *(pl* **-theses** /ˈprɒsθɪsiːz, prɒsˈθiːsiːz/) *(medical)* **1** [C] artificial substitute for a part of the body, eg a limb, an eye or a tooth: *A prosthesis was fitted after the amputation.* **2** [U] replacement of a missing part of the body, eg after surgery, by an artificial one. ▷ **prosthetic** /prɒsˈθetɪk/ *adj*: *a prosthetic appliance.*

prostitute /ˈprɒstɪtjuːt; *US* -tuːt/ *n* person who offers herself/himself for sexual intercourse for money.
▷ **prostitute** *v* [Tn] *(derog)* **1** ~ **oneself** act as a prostitute: *She prostituted herself in order to support her children.* **2** use (oneself or one's abilities, etc) wrongly or unworthily, esp in order to earn money: *poets prostituting their talent by writing jingles for advertisements.*
prostitution /ˌprɒstɪˈtjuːʃn; *US* -ˈtuːʃn/ *n* **1** [U] (practice of) working as a prostitute: *Prostitution is on the increase in the city.* **2** [C, U] ~ **of sth** unworthy use of sth: *He refused the job, saying it would be (a) prostitution of his talents.*

prostrate /ˈprɒstreɪt/ *adj* **1** (lying) stretched out on the ground face downward, esp because of exhaustion or in order to show submission, respect, etc: *The prisoners were forced to lie prostrate in front of their captors.* ○ *She was found prostrate on the floor of the cell.* Cf PRONE 1, SUPINE 1. **2** ~ **(with sth)** overcome by sth; defeated or helpless: *She was prostrate with grief after his death.* ○ *The country, prostrate after years of war, began slowly to recover.* ○ *The illness left her prostrate for several weeks.*
▷ **prostrate** /prɒˈstreɪt; *US* ˈprɒstreɪt/ *v* **1** [Tn] **(a)** ~ **oneself** throw oneself on the floor and lie face down, esp as a sign of submission or worship: *The slaves prostrated themselves at their master's feet.* ○ *The pilgrims prostrated themselves before the altar.* **(b)** *(fml)* force (sb/sth) to the ground; flatten: *trees prostrated by the gales.* **2** [Tn esp passive] (of illness, weather, etc) make (sb) helpless: *The competitors were prostrated by the heat.*
prostration /prɒˈstreɪʃn/ *n* **1** [C, U] (act of) lying face downwards in submission or worship. **2** [U] state of extreme physical weakness; total exhaustion: *Two of the runners collapsed in a state of prostration.*

prosy /ˈprəʊzɪ/ *adj* (**-ier**, **-iest**) (of a writer, speaker, book, speech, style, etc) dull or commonplace; unimaginative. ▷ **prosily** *adv*. **prosiness** *n* [U].

Prot *abbr* Protestant.

protagonist /prəˈtægənɪst/ *n* **1 (a)** *(fml)* chief character in a drama; hero. **(b)** chief person in a story or chief participant in an actual event, esp a conflict or dispute. **2** ~ **(of sth)** leader or advocate of a cause: *an outspoken protagonist of electoral reform* ○ *a leading protagonist of the women's movement.*

protean /ˈprəʊtɪən, prəʊˈtiːən/ *adj* *(fml)* that can change quickly and easily; variable.

protect /prəˈtekt/ *v* **1** [Tn, Tn·pr] ~ **sb/sth (against/from sth)** keep sb/sth safe from harm, injury, etc; defend sb/sth: *You need warm clothes to protect you against the cold.* ○ *The vaccine was used to protect the whole population against infection.* ○ *The union was formed to protect the rights and interests of miners.* **2** [Tn] guard (one or more industries of a country) against competition by taxing foreign goods: *The country's car industry is so strongly protected that foreign cars are rarely seen there.*

protection /prəˈtekʃn/ *n* **1** ~ **(for sb) (against sth) (a)** [U] protecting or being protected: *appeal for protection from the police* ○ *The shady trees provide protection against the burning rays of the sun.* ○ *Our medical insurance offers protection* (ie payment for medical treatment) *for the whole family in the event of illness.* **(b)** [C] thing that protects: *He wore a thick overcoat as a protection against the bitter cold.* **2** [U] system of protecting (PROTECT 2) home industries by taxing foreign goods: *Textile workers favoured protection because they feared an influx of cheap cloth.* **3** [U] **(a)** (system of) paying money to gangsters so that one's business will not be attacked by them: [attrib] *The gang were running protection rackets in all the big cities.* **(b)** (also **proˈtection money**) money paid to gangsters for this purpose: *He was paying out half his profits as protection.*
▷ **protectionism** /-ʃənɪzəm/ *n* [U] principle or practice of protecting (PROTECT 2) home industries: *accuse rival countries of protectionism.* **protectionist** /-ʃənɪst/ *n* supporter of or believer in protectionism.

protective /prəˈtektɪv/ *adj* **1** [esp attrib] that protects or is intended to protect: *a protective layer of varnish* ○ *Workers who handle asbestos need to wear protective clothing.* ○ *wearing protective headgear on a motor cycle* ○ *proˌtective ˈcolouring*, ie on the bodies of birds, animals and insects, making it difficult for predators to see them ○ *protective duties/tariffs on imported goods.* **2** ~ **(towards sb)** having or showing a wish to protect: *A mother naturally feels protective towards her children.* ○ *He put his arm round her in a protective gesture.*
▷ **protective** *n* *(US)* contraceptive sheath; condom.
protectively *adv*.
□ **proˌtective ˈcustody** keeping a person in prison (supposedly) for his own safety.

protector /prəˈtektə(r)/ *n* **1** person who protects: *their guardian and protector.* **2** thing made or designed to give protection: *The swordsmen wore chest protectors.*

protectorate /prəˈtektərət/ *n* country that is controlled and protected by a more powerful country: *He had been Governor of a British Protectorate.* Cf COLONY 1.

protégé (*fem* **protégée**) /ˈprɒtɪʒeɪ; *US* ˌprəʊtɪˈʒeɪ/ *n* person whose welfare and career are looked after by an influential person, esp over a long period: *a young protégé of a famous violinist* ○ *As the protégé of the most powerful man in the country, his success was guaranteed.*

protein /ˈprəʊtiːn/ *n* [C, U] substance found in meat, eggs, fish, etc that is an important body-building part of the diet of humans and animals: *essential proteins and vitamins* ○ *They were weakened by a diet that was low in protein.* ○ [attrib] *protein deficiency.*

pro tem /ˌprəʊ ˈtem/ *abbr* *(infml)* for the time being; temporarily (Latin *pro tempore*): *This arrangement will have to do pro tem.*

protest[1] /ˈprəʊtest/ *n* **1** [C] statement or action that shows one's strong disapproval or disagreement: *enter/lodge/make/register a protest about/against sth* ○ *Loud protests were heard when the decision was announced.* ○ *stage a protest* (ie organize a demonstration) *against management's handling of the dispute.* **2** [U] strong disapproval or disagreement that is expressed by a statement or an action: *The minister resigned in protest against the decision.* ○ [attrib] *a protest demonstration, march, movement, etc*, ie one organized by people who disagree with official policy ○ *a protest song*, eg about social injustice. ⇨ article. **3** (idm) **under ˈprotest** unwillingly and after making protests: *She paid the fine under protest.*

protest[2] /prəˈtest/ *v* **1** [I, Ipr, Tn] ~ **(about/against/at sth)** express strong disagreement or disapproval about (sth): *She protested strongly at being called a snob.* ○ *Demonstrators protested outside the country's embassies all over Europe.* ○ *They are holding a rally to protest against the government's defence policy.* ○ *(US) A demonstration was planned to protest the mistreatment of prisoners.* **2** [Tn, Tf] declare (sth) solemnly or firmly, esp in reply to an accusation: *He protested his innocence.* ○ *She protested that she had never seen the accused man before.* **3** (idm) **proˈtest too much** affirm or deny sth so strongly that one's sincerity is doubted.
▷ **protester** *n* person who protests: *A group of protesters gathered outside the firm's office.*
protestingly *adv*: *They denied the claim protestingly.*

Protestant /ˈprɒtɪstənt/ *n, adj* (member) of any of the Christian bodies that separated from the Church of Rome in the 16th century, or of their branches formed later: *a Protestant church, minister, service.* Cf ROMAN CATHOLIC (ROMAN). ⇨ article at CHURCH OF ENGLAND.
▷ **Protestantism** /-ɪzəm/ *n* [U] **(a)** system of beliefs, teachings, etc of the Protestants. **(b)** Protestants as a body.

protestation /ˌprɒteˈsteɪʃn/ *n* *(fml)* solemn declaration: *protestations of friendship, innocence, loyalty, etc* ○ *Despite their protestations, they were glad to accept our help.*

prot(o)- *comb form* first, original or primitive: *protozoa* ○ *prototype* ○ *protoplasm.*

protocol /ˈprəʊtəkɒl; *US* -kɔːl/ *n* **1** [U] system of rules governing formal occasions, eg meetings between governments, diplomats, etc; official etiquette: *The organizer was familiar with the protocol of royal visits.* ○ *The delegates have to be seated according to protocol.* ○ *a breach of protocol.* **2** [C] *(fml)* first or original draft of a diplomatic agreement, esp of the agreed terms for a treaty.

proton /ˈprəʊtɒn/ *n* elementary particle with a positive electric charge, which is present in the nuclei of all atoms. Cf ELECTRON, NEUTRON.

protoplasm /ˈprəʊtəplæzəm/ (also **plasma**) *n* [U] *(biology)* colourless jelly-like substance that forms the basis of all animal and plant cells and tissues.

prototype /ˈprəʊtətaɪp/ *n* first or original example of sth that has been or will be copied or developed;

Protest Movements

As well as the many industrial and political protests made by means of strikes and campaigns of various kinds, both Britain and the USA have seen a number of well-defined protest movements. These have largely centred on five main causes: for sexual equality, for racial equality, for abolition of nuclear weapons, for environmental protection, and for the banning of experiments on animals. Campaigners for sexual equality have mainly been women and homosexuals. Women have been fighting for equal rights with men at least since the 18th century, and in the 20th century campaigns have ranged from the suffragette movements of the early years to the 'Women's Lib' movement of the 1960s and 1970s. In the USA, women have campaigned in particular for an equal rights amendment to the Constitution. This was eventually approved in 1972 but subsequently defeated in 1982. A related issue, the controversial question of abortion, has been hotly debated in recent years, and there have been a number of protest rallies by the national Abortion Rights Action League and others against the decision by the US Supreme Court to ban the public funding of abortions.

In the USA, homosexuals have not only campaigned for their right to lead their lives without harassment and repression; in recent years they have actively protested against the US government's reluctance to tackle the growing problem of AIDS, with its constantly increasing annual death toll. In Britain the 'gay rights' cause has been pursued by the Campaign for Homosexual Equality, an organization founded in 1965.

Because of the larger proportion of black people in the USA, the fight for racial equality has been fiercer there than in Britain. There have been several famous (or infamous) racial incidents in the present century. In 1943, 34 blacks lost their lives in a race riot in Detroit. In 1957, nine black students attempted to join an all-white school at Little Rock, but were forced to withdraw for their own safety. Similar protests and 'sit-ins' followed in subsequent years. In Britain, supporters of the Anti-Apartheid Movement, founded in 1959, have campaigned constantly for racial equality in South Africa. A virtually continuous protest meeting was held outside South Africa House in London until Nelson Mandela, the African National Congress leader, was released from prison in 1990.

The anti-nuclear protest movement has been strong since the end of the Second World War. In Britain, the movement has been led by the Campaign for Nuclear Disarmament (CND), which in 1958, the year of its foundation, organized the first of a series of annual protest marches from London to the Atomic Weapons Research Establishment at Aldermaston in Berkshire, as well as holding a number of 'Ban the Bomb' rallies in Trafalgar Square, London, and elsewhere. There have been similar demonstrations in the USA, one of the most notable in recent years being that by hundreds of thousands of people in New York's Central Park in 1982. A continuous anti-nuclear protest was made in Britain in the 1980s by a women's 'peace camp' at Greenham Common in Berkshire, the Royal Air Force base where US cruise missiles were stationed.

Increasing public awareness of the need to conserve the environment has resulted in numerous protests. The leading movement in the campaign against pollution of the environment is Greenpeace, founded in Canada in 1971 but now active worldwide. It strives in particular to halt industrial activities which threaten the environment, and has fought equally hard against the testing of nuclear weapons. In just one action of many, British members of Greenpeace climbed Nelson's Column, London, in 1988 to protest against pollution by acid rain. Another leading anti-pollution organization in Britain is the Friends of the Earth, also founded in 1971, which has campaigned in particular against nuclear hazards and the destruction of the countryside.

Greenpeace also seeks to ban hunting of whales for food and oil, and to prevent the killing of young seals for their fur. In this it is joined by several other 'animal rights' movements. In Britain, there has long been a lobby to ban 'blood sports', that is the hunting of foxes and other wild animals, with the League Against Cruel Sports, founded in 1924, one of the most active in the field. Animal rights campaigners have set fire to stores selling furs, have illegally entered laboratories to destroy equipment used in experiments on animals, and have physically attacked researchers working with animals. In 1990 members of the Animal Liberation Front (ALF), one of the more militant organizations in this area, carried out car bomb attacks on veterinary surgeons. Though supported by some, their violent action was condemned by certain other animal rights groups, especially long-standing bodies such as the British Union for the Abolition of Vivisection, founded in 1898. The ALF originated in the USA, where one of the leading organizations opposed to the killing of young seals is the Fund for Animals.

model or preliminary version: *the prototype for future school buildings* ○ [attrib] *a prototype supersonic aircraft.*

protozoon (also **protozoan**) /ˌprəʊtəˈzəʊən/ *n* (*pl* **-zoa** /-ˈzəʊə/) any of a large group of very small, usu one-celled, living things, that can be seen only under a microscope.

▷ **protozoan** /ˌprəʊtəˈzəʊən/ *adj* of or like a protozoon.

protract /prəˈtrækt; *US* prəʊ-/ *v* [Tn esp passive] (*often derog*) make (sth) last a long time or longer; lengthen or prolong: *Let's not protract the debate any further.* ○ *a protracted lunch break* ○ *protracted delays, discussions, questioning.*

▷ **protraction** /prəˈtrækʃn; *US* prəʊ-/ *n* [C, U] (instance of) making sth last longer; extending: *Further protraction of the discussion will not achieve anything.*

protractor /prəˈtræktə(r); *US* prəʊ-/ *n* instrument, usu in the form of a semi-circle with degrees (0° to 180°) marked on it, used for measuring and drawing angles.

protrude /prəˈtru:d; *US* prəʊ-/ *v* [I, Ipr, Tn, Tn·pr] ~ (**from sth**) (cause sth to) jut or stick out from a surface; (cause sth to) project: *He managed to hang on to a piece of rock protruding from the cliff face.* ○ *protruding eyes, lips, teeth* ○ *a protruding chin.*

▷ **protrusion** /prəˈtru:ʒn; *US* prəʊ-/ *n* (**a**) [U] protruding: *Thumb-sucking can cause protrusion of the teeth.* (**b**) [C] thing that protrudes: *rocky protrusions on the surface of the cliff.*

protrusive /prəˈtru:sɪv; *US* prəʊ-/ *adj* (*fml*) protruding.

protuberant /prəˈtju:bərənt; *US* prəʊˈtu:-/ *adj* (*fml*) bulging, curving or swelling outwards from a surface; prominent: *a protuberant stomach.*

▷ **protuberance** /-əns/ *n* (*fml*) (**a**) [U] being protuberant. (**b**) [C] protuberant thing; bulge or swelling: *The diseased trees are marked by protuberances on their bark.*

proud /praʊd/ *adj* (**-er, -est**) **1** (*approv*) (**a**) ~ (**of sb/sth**); ~ (**to do sth/that . . .**) feeling or showing justifiable pride(1a): *proud of her new car* ○ *His proud parents congratulated him.* ○ *They were proud of their success/of being so successful.* ○ *They were proud to belong/that they belonged to such a fine team.* ○ *She is a remarkable person — I am proud* (ie honoured) *to know her.* ○ (*ironic*) *I hope you feel proud of yourself — you've ruined the game!* ○ *the proud owners of a new house.* (**b**) having or showing self-respect, dignity or independence: *They were poor but proud.* ○ *He had been too proud to ask for help.* ○ *They are a proud and independent people.* (**c**) causing justifiable pride(1a): *It was a proud day for us when we won the trophy.* ○ *The portrait was his proudest possession.* **2** (*derog*) self-important; haughty or arrogant: *He was too proud to join in our fun.* ○ *He is too proud now to be seen with his former friends.* **3** (*fml*) imposing or splendid: *soldiers in proud array.* **4** ~ **of sth** jutting out from or extending above sth: *be, rise, stand proud of sth* ○ *The cement should stand proud of the surface and then be smoothed down later.* **5** (idm) (**as**) ˌ**proud as a** ˈ**peacock** extremely proud.

▷ **proud** *adv* (idm) **do sb** ˈ**proud** (*infml*) treat sb with great honour or hospitality; entertain sb lavishly: *The college did us proud at the centenary dinner.*

proudly *adv* in a proud(1a) manner: *proudly displaying the trophy.*

Proust /pru:st/ Marcel (1871-1922), French novelist. He is most famous for his great series of novels, *À la recherche du temps perdu.* It has no conventional plot, but is a discovery of memory and art as a way for the writer to accept time and death.

Prov *abbr* (esp on a map) Province.

prove /pru:v/ *v* (*pp* **proved**; *US* **proven** /ˈpru:vn/) ⇨ Usage **1** [Tn, Tf, Dn·pr, Dpr·f] ~ **sth** (**to sb**) show that sth is true or certain by means of argument or evidence: *prove sb's guilt/(that) sb is guilty* ○ *Can you prove it to me?* ○ *I shall prove to you that the witness is not speaking the truth.* **2** (*US* **probate**) [Tn] establish that (a will) is genuine: *The will has to be proved before we can inherit.* **3** [La, Ln, Cn·a, Cn·n, Cn·t] ~ (**oneself**) **sth** be seen or found to be sth; turn out to be (sth): *The old methods proved best after all.* ○ *The task proved (to be) more difficult than we'd thought.* ○ *He proved himself (to be) a better driver than the world champion.* **4** [I] (of dough) rise because of the action of yeast: *leave the dough to prove for half an hour.* **5** (idm) **the exception proves the rule** ⇨ EXCEPTION. **prove one's/the** ˈ**case**/ˈ**point** demonstrate that one's/the statement, argument, criticism, etc is true or valid: *He quoted figures to prove his case.* ○ *She claimed that money had been wasted and our financial difficulties seemed to prove her point.*

▷ **provable** /-əbl/ that can be proved: *a provable case of negligence.* **provably** /-əblɪ/ *adv.*

NOTE ON USAGE: **Prove** and **shave** have alternative past participle forms: **proved/proven;**

shaved/shaven. The irregular forms are more common in US than in British English. **Shaven** and **proven** are mostly used adjectivally: *a well-proven method* ○ *a shaven head.*

proven /ˈpruːvn; *Scot* ˈprəʊvn/ *adj* **1** (*approv*) that has been tested or demonstrated: *a man of proven ability.* **2** (idm) **not ˈproven** (verdict in a criminal trial in Scottish law that) there is insufficient evidence to prove that the accused is innocent or guilty, and he must therefore be set free.

provenance /ˈprɒvənəns/ *n* [U] (*fml*) (place of) origin: *the provenance of the word* ○ *antique furniture of doubtful provenance,* eg that may not be genuinely antique.

provender /ˈprɒvɪndə(r)/ *n* [U] **1** food for horses and cattle, eg hay or oats; fodder. **2** (*infml or joc*) food: *enough provender for the party.*

proverb /ˈprɒvɜːb/ *n* short well-known saying that states a general truth or gives advice, eg 'It takes two to make a quarrel' or 'Don't put all your eggs in one basket': *the Book of Proverbs,* ie one of the books of the Old Testament containing the proverbs of Solomon. ⇨ App 5.

▷ **proverbial** /prəˈvɜːbɪəl/ *adj* **1** of, like or expressed in a proverb: *proverbial sayings, wisdom* ○ *He is the proverbial square peg in a round hole.* **2** widely known and talked about: *His stupidity is proverbial.* ○ *I decided not to ask her for a loan in view of her proverbial meanness.* **proverbially** /-bɪəlɪ/ *adv.*

provide /prəˈvaɪd/ *v* **1** [Tn, Tn·pr, Dn·pr] ~ **sb (with sth)**; ~ **sth (for sb)** (**a**) make sth available for sb to use by giving, lending or supplying it: *The management will provide food and drink.* ○ *Please put your litter in the bin provided.* ○ *The firm have provided me with a car.* ○ *Can you provide accommodation for thirty people?* (**b**) (*fig*) offer or present (an answer, example, opportunity, etc): *Let us hope his research will provide the evidence we need.* ○ *The painting provides us with one of the earliest examples of the use of perspective.* **2** [Tf] (*fml*) give as a condition; stipulate: *A clause in the agreement provides that the tenant shall pay for repairs to the building.* **3** (phr v) **provide against sth** (*fml*) make preparations in case sth happens: *The government has to provide against a possible oil shortage in the coming months.* **provide for sb** supply sb with what he needs, esp the basic necessities of life: *They worked hard to provide for their large family.* ○ *He didn't provide for his wife and children in his will,* ie didn't leave them money to live on. **provide for sth** (**a**) make arrangements or decisions which can be carried out if sth occurs: *provide for every eventuality in the budget* ○ *The planners had not provided for a failure of the power system.* (**b**) (of a bill, legal agreement, etc) establish the legal basis or authority for sth to be done later: *The right of individuals to appeal to a higher court is provided for in the constitution.*

▷ **provider** *n* person who provides, esp one who supports a family: *The eldest son is the family's only provider.*

provided /prəˈvaɪdɪd/ (also **provided that, providing** /prəˈvaɪdɪŋ/, **providing that**) *conj* on the condition or understanding that: *I will agree to go provided/providing (that) my expenses are paid.* ○ *Provided we get good weather it will be a successful holiday.*

providence /ˈprɒvɪdəns/ *n* **1** [sing, U] (instance that shows the) way in which God or nature cares for and protects all creatures: *trusting in (a) divine providence.* **2** [U] (*fml*) being provident; foresight. **3** (idm) **tempt fate/providence** ⇨ TEMPT.

provident /ˈprɒvɪdənt/ *adj* (*fml approv*) having or showing wisdom for future needs; thrifty: *Some of the farmers had been provident in the good years but others were ruined by the bad harvests.*

□ **ˈProvident Society** = FRIENDLY SOCIETY (FRIENDLY).

providential /ˌprɒvɪˈdenʃl/ *adj* (*fml*) occurring just at the right time when needed: *Their departure just before the floods was providential.* ▷ **providentially** /-ʃəlɪ/ *adv.*

providing ⇨ PROVIDED.

province /ˈprɒvɪns/ *n* **1** [C] any of the main administrative divisions in certain countries: *Canada has ten provinces.* Cf COUNTY, STATE[1] 3. **2 the provinces** [pl] all the parts of a country except the capital city: *The show will tour the provinces after it closes in London.* ○ (*derog*) *He found life in the provinces boring.* **3 the Province** [sing] (*Brit*) Northern Ireland. **4** [sing] (*fml*) area of learning, activity or responsibility: *The matter is outside my province,* ie I cannot or need not deal with it. ○ *Medieval painting is not his province.* **5** [C] group of dioceses for which an archbishop has overall responsibility.

provincial /prəˈvɪnʃl/ *adj* **1** [attrib] (**a**) of a province(1): *the provincial government* ○ *provincial taxes.* (**b**) of the provinces (PROVINCE 2): *provincial newspapers, theatres, towns.* **2** (*usu derog*) narrow-minded or old-fashioned; not modern or sophisticated: *display provincial attitudes to the theatre.*

▷ **provincial** *n* (*usu derog*) native or inhabitant of the provinces: *Whenever I go to London I feel like a provincial.*

provincialism /-ɪzəm/ *n* (*derog*) **1** [U] provincial(2) attitude or outlook, esp one that indicates an (excessive) attachment to one's own small area: *He wanted to escape from the provincialism of the small university where he taught.* **2** [C] example of provincial(2) behaviour, manners, speech, etc: *embarrassed by his provincialisms.*

provincially /-ʃəlɪ/ *adv.*

provision /prəˈvɪʒn/ *n* **1** ~ **of sth** (**a**) [U] giving, lending, supplying or making sth available; providing sth: *The government is responsible for the provision of medical services.* (**b**) [C usu *sing*] amount of sth that is provided: *The provision of specialist teachers is being increased.* **2** [U] ~ **for/against sth** (**a**) preparation that is made to meet future needs or in case sth happens: *make provision for one's old age* ○ *provision for his wife and children* ○ *provision against possible disaster.* (**b**) ~ **for sth** dealing with sth (in advance): *The present law makes no provision for this.* **3** [C usu *pl*] (supply of) food and drink: *She had a plentiful store of provisions.* ○ [attrib] *a provision merchant.* **4** [C] condition or stipulation in a legal document: *under the provisions of the agreement* ○ *She accepted the contract with the provision that it would be revised after a year.*

▷ **provision** *v* [esp passive: Tn, Tn·pr] ~ **sb/sth (with sth)** (*fml*) supply sb/sth with provisions of food: *provisioned for a long voyage.*

provisional /prəˈvɪʒənl/ *adj* for the present time only, with the possibility of being changed, etc later; temporary: *a provisional appointment, contract, government* ○ *a provisional driving licence,* ie (in Britain) one that has to be obtained before one can start to learn to drive. ▷ **provisionally** /-nəlɪ/ *adv*: *The meeting has been provisionally arranged for 3.00 pm next Friday.*

proviso /prəˈvaɪzəʊ/ *n* (*pl* ~**s**; *US* also ~**es**) clause, etc that is insisted on as a condition of an agreement: *He accepted, with one proviso,* ie on one condition.

provisory /prəˈvaɪzərɪ/ *adj* (*fml*) containing a proviso; conditional: *a provisory clause.*

provocation /ˌprɒvəˈkeɪʃn/ *n* **1** [U] making sb angry by deliberately doing sth annoying or offensive; provoking or being provoked: *the incessant provocation of the hostile crowd* ○ *react with violence only under provocation,* ie when provoked ○ *She loses her temper at/on the slightest provocation.* **2** [C] cause of annoyance; thing that provokes: *He hit her after repeated provocations.*

provocative /prəˈvɒkətɪv/ *adj* **1** tending or intended to arouse anger, annoyance, controversy, etc: *a provocative comment, remark, speech, etc.* **2** tending or intended to arouse sexual desire: *a dress with a provocative slit at the side* ○ *She was sitting in a highly provocative pose.* ▷ **provocatively** *adv.*

provoke /prəˈvəʊk/ *v* **1** (**a**) [Tn] make (sb) angry or annoyed: *I am not easily provoked, but this behaviour is intolerable!* ○ *If you provoke the dog, it will bite you.* (**b**) [Tn·pr, Cn·t] ~ **sb into doing sth/to do sth** cause sb to react to sth esp by making him angry: *His behaviour finally provoked her into leaving him.* ○ *He was provoked by their mockery to say more than he had intended.* **2** [Tn] cause (sth) to occur or arouse (a feeling, etc): *provoke laughter, riots, smiles, violence.*

▷ **provoking** *adj* (*dated or fml*) annoying: *It is very provoking of her to be so late.*

provost /ˈprɒvəst; *US* ˈprəʊ-/ *n* **1** (**a**) (*Brit*) (title of the) head of certain university colleges. (**b**) (*US*) senior administrator in certain universities. **2** (*Scot*) (title of the) head of a town council or burgh. **3** (*Brit*) (title of the) head of the chapter in certain cathedrals.

prow /praʊ/ *n* (*esp fml*) projecting front part of a ship or boat; bow.

prowess /ˈpraʊɪs/ *n* [U] (*fml*) outstanding skill or ability; expertise: *We had to admire his prowess as an oarsman/his rowing prowess.*

prowl /praʊl/ *v* **1** (**a**) [I, Ip] ~ **(about/around)** move quietly and cautiously: *wild animals prowling in the forest* ○ *burglars prowling (around) in the grounds of the house.* (**b**) [Tn] move about, through or in (a place) in this way: *thieves prowling the streets at night.* **2** [I, Ip] ~ **(about/around)** walk or wander restlessly: *I could hear him prowling around in his bedroom all night.*

▷ **prowl** *n* (idm) **(be/go) on the ˈprowl** (be/go) prowling: *There was a fox on the prowl near the chicken coop.* ○ (*joc*) *The soldiers went on the prowl hoping to meet some girls.*

prowler *n* person or animal that prowls.

NOTE ON USAGE: The following verbs indicate the slow, quiet movement of people or animals who do not want to be noticed by others. They suggest a variety of reasons for this secrecy. **Prowl (about, around, etc)** suggests a wild animal or criminal looking for food or for something to steal: *I saw someone prowling around among the trees.* ○ *Wolves prowled the forest in search of prey.* **Skulk (about, around, etc)** refers to someone angrily or guiltily waiting out of sight, possibly intending to do something bad: *He skulked around outside until the police had gone.* **Lurk** is used with similar meaning: *Somebody's lurking in the bushes.* A person **slinks (off, away, etc)** when he or she feels ashamed or frightened. It usually suggests that the head is low: *Don't slink away without apologizing.* ○ *The dog slunk off to lick its wounds.* People **sneak in, out, etc** when they are doing something wrong but not seriously criminal: *She was caught sneaking into the show without paying.* **Sidle** is to move furtively, especially if nervous about one's purpose: *He sidled up/over to her and asked her to dance.* ○ *The boy sidled past the teacher and then ran out of the door.* We **steal, in, out, etc** in great secrecy: *She stole out of the house in the middle of the night.* **Creep** also suggests secrecy and, in animals especially, indicates a crouching position: *The cat crept up on the bird and pounced.* **Tiptoe** is the most neutral verb. The purpose in tiptoeing may be to avoid disturbing other people: *They tiptoed upstairs so as not to wake the baby.*

proximate /ˈprɒksɪmət/ *adj* (*fml*) next before or after (in time, order, etc); nearest.

proximity /prɒkˈsɪmətɪ/ *n* [U] (*fml*) ~ **(to sth)** nearness in space or time; closeness: *in the proximity* (ie neighbourhood) *of the building* ○ *houses built in close proximity to each other* ○ *The restaurant benefits from its proximity to several cinemas.*

proxy /ˈprɒksɪ/ *n* **1** [C] person authorized to act on behalf of another: *act as sb's proxy* ○ *He made his wife his proxy.* **2** (**a**) [U] authority to represent sb else (esp in voting at an election): *vote by proxy* ○ [attrib] *a proxy vote.* (**b**) [C] document that gives such authority.

prude /pruːd/ *n* (*derog*) person who behaves in an extremely or unnaturally proper manner, esp one who is (too) easily shocked by sexual matters: *She was such a prude that she was even embarrassed by* *the sight of naked children.*

▷ **prudery** /ˈpruːdərɪ/ *n* [U] behaviour or attitude of a prude.

prudish /ˈpruːdɪʃ/ *adj* of or like a prude: *a prudish refusal to enjoy rude jokes.* **prudishly** *adv.* **prudishness** *n* [U].

prudent /ˈpruːdnt/ *adj* acting with or showing care and foresight; showing good judgement: *prudent housekeeping* ○ *a prudent saver of money* ○ *It would be prudent to save some of the money.* ○ *That was a prudent decision.*

▷ **prudence** /-dns/ *n* [U] (*fml*) (quality of) being prudent; forethought or wisdom: *One can rely on the prudence of his decisions.*

prune[1] /pruːn/ *n* dried plum: *a dish of stewed prunes.*

prune[2] /pruːn/ *v* **1** (**a**) [Tn, Tn·p] ~ **sth** (**back**) trim the shape of (a tree, bush, etc) by cutting away some of the branches, etc, esp to encourage new growth: *She has been pruning the roses.* (**b**) [Tn, Tn·pr, Tn·p] ~ **sth** (**from/off sth**); ~ **sth** (**away/back/off**) remove (dead wood, branches, etc) by cutting: *These straggly stems should be pruned off the bush.* ○ *Prune back the longer branches.* ⇨ Usage at CLIP[2]. **2** [Tn, Tn·pr, Tn·p] ~ **sth of sth**; ~ **sth down** reduce the extent of sth by cutting unnecessary parts: *Next year's budget will have to be drastically pruned.* ○ *Try to prune your essay of irrelevant detail.* ○ *She's pruning down the novel at the publisher's request.*

▷ **pruning** *n* [U]: *Careful pruning at the right time is the secret of success with roses.* ˈ**pruning-hook** *n* tool with a curved blade used for pruning.

prurient /ˈprʊərɪənt/ *adj* (*fml derog*) having or showing excessive interest in sexual matters: *She showed a prurient interest in the details of the rape case.*

▷ **prurience** /-əns/ *n* [U] (*fml derog*) quality or state of being prurient.

pruriently *adv.*

pruritus /prʊəˈraɪtəs/ *n* [U] (*medical*) severe and persistent itching.

Prussia /ˈprʌʃə/ former kingdom in Germany. It became increasingly powerful from the 17th century onwards, and in the late 19th century it became the centre of the German Empire created by *Bismarck. Its people had the reputation of being disciplined and militaristic. Prussia was formally dissolved in 1947, and much of its historic territory is now part of Poland.

▷ **Prussian** /ˈprʌʃn/ *adj* of or relating to Prussia: *the Prussian army.* — *n* inhabitant or native of Prussia. ˌ**Prussian** ˈ**blue** (of a) deep blue colour.

prussic acid /ˌprʌsɪk ˈæsɪd/ highly dangerous poison.

pry[1] /praɪ/ *v* (*pt, pp* **pried** /praɪd/) [I, Ipr] ~ (**into sth**) inquire too curiously or rudely about other people's private affairs: *safe from prying eyes* ○ *I don't want them prying into my affairs.*

pry[2] /praɪ/ *v* (*pt, pp* **pried** /praɪd/) [Tn·pr, Tn·p, Cn·a] (*esp US*) = PRISE: *pry the lid off a tin* ○ *pry the tin open* ○ (*fig*) *pry information out of sb.*

PS **1** (*Brit*) police sergeant: *PS (Bill) Jones.* Cf WPS. **2** (also **ps**) /ˌpiː ˈes/ *abbr* (esp at the end of a letter) postscript (Latin *postscriptum*): *Love from Tessa. PS I'll bring the car.* Cf PPS.

psalm /sɑːm/ *n* sacred song or hymn, esp one of those in the Book of Psalms in the Old Testament: *The choir sang the 23rd Psalm.*

▷ **psalmist** /-ɪst/ writer of psalms.

psalter /ˈsɔːltə(r)/ *n* book containing a collection of psalms with their music, for use in public worship.

psaltery /ˈsɔːltərɪ/ *n* musical instrument of ancient and medieval times, played by plucking strings that are stretched over a board.

psephology /seˈfɒlədʒɪ; *US* siːˈf-/ *n* [U] study of the way in which people vote in elections, esp by means of opinion polls.

▷ **psephological** /ˌsefəˈlɒdʒɪkl; *US* ˌsiːf-/ *adj* of or relating to psephology.

psephologist /seˈfɒlədʒɪst; *US* siːˈf-/ *n* expert in or student of psephology.

pseud /sjuːd; *US* ˈsuːd/ *n* (*infml derog*) person who tries to appear more knowledgeable, fashionable or cultured than he really is; pretentious and affected person: *She's just a pseud; she knows nothing about art really.*

pseudo /ˈsjuːdəʊ; *US* ˈsuː-/ *adj* (*infml*) not genuine; sham or insincere: *This apparent interest of his in modern music is completely pseudo.*

pseud(o)- *comb form* not authentic; false or pretended: *pseudonym* ○ *pseudo-intellectual* ○ *pseudo-science.*

pseudonym /ˈsjuːdənɪm; *US* ˈsuːdənɪm/ *n* (also ˈ**nom de plume**) person's name that is not his real name, esp one used by an author; pen-name: *George Eliot was the pseudonym of Mary Ann Evans.* ○ *She writes under a pseudonym.*

▷ **pseudonymous** /sjuːˈdɒnɪməs; *US* suː-/ *adj* (*fml*) writing or written under a pseudonym.

psi *abbr* pounds (pressure) per square inch (eg on tyres).

psittacosis /ˌsɪtəˈkəʊsɪs/ *n* [U] serious viral disease causing fever and pneumonia in humans, who can catch it from parrots and other birds.

psoriasis /səˈraɪəsɪs/ *n* [U] skin disease that causes red scaly patches.

psst /pst/ *interj* (used to attract sb's attention secretly or furtively): *'Psst! Let's get out now before they see us!'*

PST /ˌpiː es ˈtiː/ *abbr* (*US*) Pacific Standard Time.

PSV /ˌpiː es ˈviː/ *abbr* (*Brit*) public service vehicle: *have a PSV licence*, ie to drive buses, etc.

psych (also **psyche**) /saɪk/ *v* (*infml*) **1** [Tn, Tn·p] ~ **sb** (**out**) make sb nervous or less confident, etc, esp by psychological means: *Her arrogant behaviour on court psyched her opponent (out) completely.* **2** (phr v) **psych sb/oneself up** prepare sb/oneself mentally for sth: *She had really psyched herself up for the big match.*

psyche /ˈsaɪkɪ/ *n* human soul or mind: *Is aggression an essential part of the human psyche?*

psychedelic /ˌsaɪkɪˈdelɪk/ *adj* **1** (of drugs) producing hallucinations: *Mescalin and LSD are psychedelic drugs.* **2** having intensely vivid colours, sounds, etc like those experienced while hallucinating: *psychedelic music.* ▷ **psychedelically** /-klɪ/ *adv.*

psychiatry /saɪˈkaɪətrɪ; *US* sɪ-/ *n* [U] study and treatment of mental illness. Cf PSYCHOLOGY 1.

▷ **psychiatric** /ˌsaɪkɪˈætrɪk/ *adj* of or concerning psychiatry: *a psychiatric clinic* ○ *psychiatric treatment.*

psychiatrist /-ɪst/ *n* specialist in psychiatry.

psychic /ˈsaɪkɪk/ *adj* **1** (also **psychical** /ˈsaɪkɪkl/) (**a**) concerned with processes and phenomena that seem to be outside physical or natural laws: *psychical research*, ie the study and investigation of psychical phenomena, eg telepathy. (**b**) of the soul or mind. **2** (claiming to be) able to respond to or exercise supernatural or occult powers: *She claims to be psychic and to be able to foretell the future.*

▷ **psychic** *n* person claiming or appearing to be responsive to supernatural powers.

psych(o)- *comb form* of the mind: *psychiatry* ○ *psychology* ○ *psychotherapy.*

psychoanalysis /ˌsaɪkəʊəˈnæləsɪs/ (also **analysis**) *n* [U] (method of treating mental disorders by) repeatedly interviewing a person in order to make him aware of experiences in his early life and trace the connection between them and his present behaviour or feelings. The method was created by *Freud for treating patients for disorders of personality or behaviour. He believed that such disorders had a sexual cause and tried to make them aware of their past through techniques like the free association of ideas and the interpretation of their dreams. Cf GESTALT, JUNG.

▷ **psychoanalyse** /ˌsaɪkəʊˈænəlaɪz/ (also **analyse**, *US* **-lyze**) *v* [Tn] treat or investigate (sb) by means of psychoanalysis.

psychoanalyst /ˌsaɪkəʊˈænəlɪst/ (also **analyst**) *n* person who practises psychoanalysis.

psychoanalytic, **psychoanalytical** /ˌsaɪkəʊˌænəˈlɪtɪk, -ɪkl/ *adjs* relating to psychoanalysis. **psychoanalytically** /-ɪklɪ/ *adv.*

psychology /saɪˈkɒlədʒɪ/ *n* **1** [U] science or study of the mind and how it functions: *child psychology* ○ *industrial psychology.* Cf PSYCHIATRY. **2** [sing] (*infml*) mental characteristics of a person or group: *the psychology of the adolescent.*

▷ **psychological** /ˌsaɪkəˈlɒdʒɪkl/ *adj* **1** of or affecting the mind: *the psychological development of a child.* **2** of or relating to psychology: *psychological methods, research.* **3** (idm) **the** ˌ**psychological** ˈ**moment** the most appropriate time to do sth, in order to achieve success: *We're going to have to ask for more money — it's just a question of finding the (right) psychological moment.* **psychologically** /-klɪ/ *adv.* ˌ**psychological** ˈ**warfare** (waging war by) weakening an enemy's morale or by trying to change his attitudes, beliefs, etc.

psychologist /-ɪst/ *n* student of or expert in psychology.

psychopath /ˈsaɪkəʊpæθ/ *n* person suffering from a severe mental or emotional disorder, esp one who behaves in a violently aggressive or antisocial way.

▷ **psychopathic** /ˌsaɪkəʊˈpæθɪk/ *adj* of or suffering from a severe emotional or mental disorder.

psychosis /saɪˈkəʊsɪs/ *n* (*pl* **-choses** /-ˈkəʊsiːz/) [C, U] severe mental illness that affects the whole personality.

psychosomatic /ˌsaɪkəʊsəˈmætɪk/ *adj* **1** (of disease) caused or made worse by mental stress. **2** dealing with the relationship between the mind and the body: *psychosomatic medicine.* ▷ **psychosomatically** /-klɪ/ *adv.*

psychotherapy /ˌsaɪkəʊˈθerəpɪ/ *n* [U] treatment of mental disorders by psychological methods.

▷ **psychotherapist** /-ɪst/ *n* person who treats people by using psychotherapy.

psychotic /saɪˈkɒtɪk/ *adj* of or suffering from psychosis: *a psychotic disorder.*

▷ **psychotic** *n* person suffering from psychosis.

PT /ˌpiː ˈtiː/ *abbr* physical training: *do PT* ○ *a PT lesson.* Cf PE.

Pt *symb* platinum.

pt *abbr* **1** (also **Pt**) part: *Shakespeare's Henry IV Pt 2.* **2** (*pl* **pts**) pint: *2 pts today please, milkman*, eg on a notice. **3** (*pl* **pts**) point: *The winner scored 10 pts.* **4** (also **Pt**) (esp on a map) port: *Pt Moresby.*

PTA /ˌpiː tiː ˈeɪ/ *abbr* parent-teacher association (eg in schools).

pta (*pl* **ptas**) *abbr* peseta.

ptarmigan /ˈtɑːmɪgən/ *n* bird of the grouse family, with black or grey feathers in summer and white feathers in winter.

Pte *abbr* (*Brit*) (*US* **Pvt**) Private (soldier): *Pte (Jim) Hill.*

pteridophyte /ˈterɪdəfaɪt, təˈrɪdəfaɪt/ *n* (*botany*) fern or similar plant.

pterodactyl /ˌterəˈdæktɪl/ *n* extinct flying reptile.

PTO (also **pto**) /ˌpiː tiː ˈəʊ/ *abbr* (eg at the bottom of a page) please turn over.

Ptolemy /ˈtɒləmɪ/ (2nd century AD), Greek astronomer. His system of astronomy, in which the sun and planets moved around the earth, was accepted up to the time of *Galileo. ▷ **Ptolemaic** /ˌtɒləˈmeɪɪk/ *adj*: *the Ptolemaic system.*

ptomaine /ˈtəʊmeɪn/ *n* [C, U] any of a group of substances formed by decaying animal and vegetable matter.

□ ˈ**ptomaine poisoning** (*dated*) = FOOD POISONING (FOOD).

Pu *symb* plutonium.

pub /pʌb/ *n* (*Brit infml*) public house: *They've gone down/round to the pub for a drink.* ⇨ article at DRINK.

□ ˈ**pub crawl** (*Brit infml*) tour of several pubs or bars with drinking at each of them: *go on a pub crawl.*

puberty /ˈpjuːbətɪ/ *n* [U] stage at which a person's sexual organs are maturing and he or she becomes capable of having children: *reach the age of puberty.*

pubescence /pjuːˈbesəns/ *n* [U] time when puberty begins. ▷ **pubescent** /-ˈbesənt/ *adj*: *pubescent males.*

pubic /ˈpjuːbɪk/ *adj* [usu attrib] of or on the lower part of the abdomen, near the sexual organs: *pubic hair* ○ *the pubic bone.* ⇨ illus at MALE.

public /ˈpʌblɪk/ *adj* **1** (esp attrib) (**a**) of or concerning people in general: *a danger to public health* ○ *The campaign was designed to increase public awareness of the problem.* ○ *public expenditure*, ie money spent by the government on education, defence, etc. (**b**) provided, esp by central or local government, for the use of people in general: *public education, libraries, parks* ○ *the public highway*. (**c**) of or engaged in the affairs, entertainment, service, etc of the people: *He is one of the most admired public figures/figures in public life today.* **2** open or known to people in general: *She decided to make her views public.* ○ *a public admission of guilt* ○ *public speaking*, ie making speeches in public ○ *a public place.* Cf PRIVATE. **3** (idm) **be ˌpublic ˈknowledge** be generally known: *It's public knowledge she's expecting a baby.* **go ˈpublic** (of a company) become a public company by selling shares to the public. **in the public ˈeye** well known to or often seen by the public (in newspapers, on television, etc). **ˌpublic ˈproperty** (thing that is) known to everybody or anybody: *Their financial problems are public property now.*

▷ **public** *n* **1** [Gp] (**a**) **the public** (members of) the community in general: *the British public* ○ *The public is/are not allowed to enter the court room.* (**b**) part of the community having a particular interest in common: *the theatre-going public* ○ *She knows how to keep her public* (eg the readers of her books) *satisfied.* **2** (idm) **in ˈpublic** not in private; openly: *She was appearing in public* (ie in front of people in general) *for the first time since her illness.* **wash one's dirty linen in public** ⇨ WASH².

publicly /-klɪ/ *adv.*

□ **ˌpublic-adˈdress system** (*abbr* **PˈA system**) system of microphones and loudspeakers used at public meetings, sports events, etc.

ˌpublic ˈbar (*Brit*) bar in a public house with simpler or less comfortable furniture than other bars. Cf LOUNGE BAR (LOUNGE).

ˌpublic ˈcompany (also **ˌpublic ˌlimited ˈcompany**) (*abbrs* **ˌPLˈC, plc**) company that sells shares in itself to the public: *The pension fund owns shares in several major public companies.*

ˌpublic conˈvenience (*Brit*) toilet provided for the public to use. ⇨ Usage at TOILET.

ˌpublic deˈfender (*US*) lawyer who is employed to defend people who cannot afford to pay for one. Cf LEGAL AID (LEGAL).

the ˌpublic doˈmain state of not being protected by copyright, and therefore available to everybody without charge: *If the author died over 50 years ago, the book's in the public domain* ○ [attrib] *public-domain software* ○ (*fig*) *The lives of pop stars are in the public domain.*

ˌpublic ˈhouse (*Brit fml*) building (not a club, hotel, etc but often serving meals) where alcoholic drinks are sold and drunk: *Public houses are licensed to sell alcoholic drinks for a certain number of hours per week.* Cf INN, TAVERN.

ˌpublic ˈlending right (*abbr* **ˌPLˈR**) (*Brit*) right of authors to receive payment when their books are borrowed from public libraries. ⇨ article at LIBRARY.

ˌpublic ˈnuisance 1 (*law*) illegal act that is harmful to people in general: *charged with committing a public nuisance.* **2** (*infml*) person who behaves in a way that annoys people in general: *People who park on the pavement are a public nuisance.*

ˌpublic oˈpinion opinions or views of the public in general: *Public opinion was opposed to the war.*

ˌpublic oˈpinion poll ⇨ POLL¹ 2.

ˌpublic ˈownership ownership and management of an industry by the State: *Socialist policy favours public ownership of the coal industry.*

ˌpublic ˈprosecutor (*law*) legal official who conducts prosecutions on behalf of the State or in the public interest.

ˌPublic ˈRecord Office (*Brit*) place where official records are kept and made available to the public. ⇨ article at LIBRARY.

ˌpublic reˈlations (*abbr* **ˌPˈR**) **1** work of presenting a good image of an organization, a commercial firm, etc to the public, esp by distributing information: *She works in public relations.* **2** relationship (esp a friendly one) between an organization, etc and the public: *We support local artistic events; it's good for public relations.* **ˌpublic reˈlations officer** (*abbr* **ˌPRˈO**) person employed in public relations.

ˌpublic ˈschool 1 (in Britain, esp England) private school (usu a boarding-school) for pupils aged between 13 and 18 whose parents pay fees for their education. Cf PREPARATORY SCHOOL (PREPARATORY). **2** (esp in the US) local state school providing free education. ⇨ article at SCHOOL.

ˌpublic ˈspirit readiness to do things that help the community. **ˌpublic-ˈspirited** *adj*: *It's very public-spirited of you to offer to take the old people to the shops each week.*

ˌpublic ˈtransport buses, trains, etc available to the public according to a published timetable: *travel by public transport.*

ˌpublic uˈtility (*fml*) public service such as the supply of water, electricity, gas or a bus or rail network: [attrib] *public utility companies.*

ˌpublic ˈworks work such as building roads or housing, carried out by the state or local government. Public works are sometimes used to create jobs for unemployed people.

publican /ˈpʌblɪkən/ *n* person who owns or manages a public house.

publication /ˌpʌblɪˈkeɪʃn/ *n* **1** (**a**) [U] action of making a book or periodical available to the public: *the date of publication* ○ *It was clear, even before publication, that the book would be a success.* (**b**) [C] book, periodical, etc that is published: *There are many publications on the subject.* **2** [U] action of making sth known to the public: *publication of the exam results* ○ *The government have delayed publication of the trade figures.*

publicist /ˈpʌblɪsɪst/ *n* **1** person whose job is to make sth widely known; press or publicity agent. **2** writer or specialist in current affairs, eg a political journalist.

publicity /pʌbˈlɪsətɪ/ *n* [U] **1** state of being known to, seen by, etc the public: *avoid/shun/seek publicity* ○ *Their marriage took place amid a glare of publicity.* **2** (business of) providing information in order to attract public attention; advertising: *Her new play has attracted a lot of publicity.* ○ *The publicity for the book was poor and sales were low.* ○ [attrib] *a publicity campaign*, ie special effort to publicize and promote sth. **3** (idm) **the glare of publicity** ⇨ GLARE².

□ **pubˈlicity agent** person whose job is to make a performer, book, play, product, etc successful by informing the public about him or it.

publicize, -ise /ˈpʌblɪsaɪz/ *v* [Tn] inform the public about (sth), esp by advertising it: *an advertising campaign to publicize the new train service* ○ *a well-publicized attempt to break the world speed record.*

publish /ˈpʌblɪʃ/ *v* **1** [Tn] (**a**) prepare, have printed and distribute to the public (a book, periodical, etc): *This book is published by Oxford University Press.* ○ *The journal is published monthly.* (**b**) (of an author) have (one's work) printed and distributed: *He publishes articles in various newspapers.* ○ *She is publishing a history of the war period.* **2** [Tn] make (sth) known to the public: *The firm publishes its accounts in August.* ○ *publish the banns of marriage*, ie announce formally (in church) the names of people who are soon to be married. **3** (idm) **ˌpublish and be ˈdamned** (*catchphrase*) (said eg to a blackmailer) make your accusation public if you like; I refuse to be blackmailed.

▷ **publishing** *n* [U] profession or business of publishing books: *She chose publishing as a career.* ⇨ article.

publisher *n* person or firm that publishes (PUBLISH 1a) books, newspapers, etc: *Several publishers are competing in the same market.*

Puccini /puːˈtʃiːnɪ/ Giacomo (1858-1824), Italian composer. He wrote some of the most popular of all tragic grand operas, eg *Tosca* and *La Bohème*, which show his mastery of melody and orchestration.

puce /pjuːs/ *adj, n* [U] (of a) purple-brown colour: *The man's face was puce with rage.*

Puck /pʌk/ (also **Robin Goodfellow**) (in English legend) mischievous spirit who lives in the English countryside. He appears as a character in *Shakespeare's *A Midsummer Night's Dream*.

puck /pʌk/ *n* hard rubber disc struck by players in ice hockey.

pucker /ˈpʌkə(r)/ *v* [I, Ip, Tn, Tn·p] ~ (**sth**) (**up**) (cause sth to) form small folds or wrinkles: *The dress fitted badly and puckered at the waist.* ○ *The child's face puckered (up) and he began to cry.* ○ *pucker one's brows.*

▷ **pucker** *n* small wrinkle, esp an unwanted one, in a garment: *an obvious pucker in the seam of her dress.*

puckish /ˈpʌkɪʃ/ *adj* mischievous, esp in a playful way; impish: *a puckish grin.* ▷ **puckishly** *adv*: *smiling puckishly.*

pudding /ˈpʊdɪŋ/ *n* **1** [C, U] (also *infml* **pud** /pʊd/) (*Brit*) (dish of) sweet food eaten at the end of a meal; dessert: *There isn't a pudding today.* ○ *What's for pudding?* Cf AFTERS. **2** (**a**) [C, U] (also *Brit infml* **pud**) sweet or savoury dish usu made with flour and cooked by baking, boiling or steaming: *bread and butter pudding* ○ *rice pudding* ○ *steak and kidney pudding* ○ *Christmas/plum pudding.* (**b**) [C] thing like this in texture or appearance; (person with a) large, fat face: [attrib] *pudding face.* **3** [C, U] any of various types of sausage: *black pudding*, ie a type of blood sausage made with oatmeal. **4** [C] (also **ˈpudding head**) (*infml*) fat and slow or stupid person. **5** (idm) **the proof of the pudding** ⇨ PROOF¹.

puddle /ˈpʌdl/ *n* [C] small pool of water, esp of rain-water on the road.

▷ **puddle** *v* [Tn] stir (molten iron) in order to expel carbon and produce wrought iron.

pudenda /pjuːˈdendə/ *n* [pl] (*fml*) external genitals, esp of a woman.

pudgy /ˈpʌdʒɪ/ *adj* (**-ier, -iest**) (*infml*) short and fat; podgy: *pudgy fingers* ○ *a pudgy child.* ▷ **pudginess** *n* [U].

puerile /ˈpjʊəraɪl; *US* -rəl/ *adj* (*derog*) showing immaturity; childish and silly: *puerile behaviour, concerns, objections, tasks* ○ *She was tired of answering these puerile questions.*

▷ **puerility** /pjʊəˈrɪlətɪ/ *n* (*fml derog*) (**a**) [U] puerile behaviour; childishness. (**b**) [C esp *pl*] (*fml*) childish and foolish act, idea, statement, etc.

puerperal /pjuːˈɜːpərəl/ *adj* [attrib] (*medical*) of or related to childbirth: *puerperal fever.*

Puerto Rico /ˌpwɜːtəʊ ˈriːkəʊ/ island in the Caribbean; pop approx 3 607 000; official languages Spanish and English; capital San Juan. It is a self-governing Commonwealth, but its inhabitants have American citizenship and it is closely associated with the USA. The island is mountainous, with agricultural land around the coast. The main crops are coffee and sugar-cane, but farming is becoming less important, being replaced by industries like electronics and food processing. The standard of living is much lower than in the USA, which provides large amounts of aid. ⇨ map at CARIBBEAN. ▷ **Puerto Rican** /-ˈriːkən/ *n, adj.*

puff¹ /pʌf/ *n* **1** [C] (**a**) (sound of a) short light blowing of breath or wind: *a puff of wind* ○ *She blew out the candles in one puff.* (**b**) amount of smoke, steam, etc sent out at one time: *There was a puff of steam from the engine before it stopped.* ○ (*fig*) *puffs of cloud in the sky* ○ (*joc*) *vanish in a puff of smoke*, ie disappear quickly. (**c**) (*infml*) short drawing in of breath when smoking a pipe or cigarette: *She stubbed out the cigarette after the first puff.* **2** [C] = POWDER-PUFF (POWDER). **3** [C] (esp in compounds) hollow piece of pastry filled with cream, jam, etc: *a cream puff.* **4** [U] (*infml*) = BREATH¹ 1a: *out of puff*, ie breathless. **5** [C] (*US*) = EIDERDOWN.

▷ **puffy** *adj* (**-ier, -iest**) forming or covered with a soft swelling or swellings: *Beat the mixture until it has a light, puffy texture.* ○ *Her skin is puffy round her eyes.* **puffily** *adv.* **puffiness** *n* [U] state of being

Publishing

Some of the best-known publishers in Britain today trace their origins back to the 18th century. Longman was founded in 1724, and John Murray in 1768. The earliest American publishers also date from this period, such as J B Lippincott, founded in 1792. At that time, publishers undertook the whole process of printing, binding and selling books. The two oldest university presses in Britain were founded even earlier. Cambridge University Press has a continuous history of publishing since 1584, while the first book was printed in Oxford in 1478. By the 19th century publishing (as distinct from printing and bookselling) had become a profession in its own right, and in the USA the rapid growth of membership libraries strengthened the publishing business.

In 1899 the British Publishers' Association, founded three years earlier, negotiated the Net Book Agreement, by which individual publishers agreed the terms on which they would supply certain types of books to booksellers, and the prices at which such books were to be sold. Booksellers undertook in turn not to sell these books at less than the stated price.

The 20th century has seen a number of significant developments in British and American publishing. Paperbacks began to be mass-produced from 1935, when the first Penguin book was published in Britain. In the USA paperbacks were first published by Pocket Books in 1939, and small paperbacks are still often called 'pocket-books' by Americans. Paperbacks were originally cheaper editions of books already published in hard covers but today many books are first published in paperback. Paperback editions of books originally published in hard covers normally appear about a year later than the hard-cover editions.

Book clubs were set up to publish books for their members in cheaper editions. Among the first book clubs in Britain were the Left Book Club, founded in 1936 to publish books on topics of left-wing political interest, and the Readers Union, publishing more general literature, founded in 1937. Two of the best-known book clubs in the USA, the Book of the Month Club and the Literary Guild, were founded earlier, in 1926 and 1927 respectively. A joint British-American book club, Book Club Associates, was founded in 1966 by W H Smith Ltd in Britain and Doubleday in the USA, and this immediately absorbed the Reprint Society, another such club. In Britain, the Folio Society is a book club which specializes in high-quality (often illustrated) editions of established classics.

In 1945, the National Book League (now the Book Trust) was founded in Britain as the successor to the National Book Council, begun in 1925. It aims to promote wider interest in books and also provides advice and information on children's literature. It administers the Booker Prize, one of the most prestigious literary awards, awarded annually for the best novel of the year in the opinion of a panel of judges.

The actual selling of books is promoted by the Booksellers Association, founded in 1895, which protects the interests of booksellers in Britain. It also administers the Whitbread Prize, a literary award made annually for the best book in each of five categories, including the novel, biography and poetry. The book judged the best of the five winners wins the Whitbread Book of the Year award.

Everything that is published is protected by the copyright laws. One of the most important of these gives the publisher or author of a work the exclusive right to control its publication for a given number of years. A published work remains in copyright until 50 years after the author's death.

In recent years a series of take-overs and mergers has created huge publishing groups that have incorporated many independent publishers. The largest in the English-speaking world is News International, owned by the Australian-born Rupert Murdoch. The second largest is Paramount, owner of the American publishers Simon and Schuster and Prentice-Hall. The Pearson Group, owner of Penguin Books, Hamish Hamilton, Longman and Michael Joseph, ranks third. In a contrasting development, many new smaller publishing houses have been created, often by former employees of firms that were taken over. Among the most successful in Britain are Bloomsbury, Granta and Sinclair-Stevenson. Older firms that have remained independent include Weidenfeld, André Deutsch, Duckworth and Faber and Faber. Of the very large publishers, only Macmillan is still privately owned, but the special status of the university presses, for example Oxford University Press and Cambridge University Press, has enabled them to remain independent.

Smaller companies have been also successful in certain specialized areas. For example, Virago Press and the Women's Press have developed a large market for books by women writers, and Bloodaxe Books is the most successful of the smaller publishers of poetry. There are also many smaller presses which specialize in producing high-quality editions of books, including illustrated books, for collectors.

puffy: *Puffiness round the eyes is a sign of poor health.*

□ **ˈpuff-adder** *n* large poisonous African viper that puffs out the upper part of its body when it is excited.

ˈpuff-ball *n* type of fungus with a ball-shaped spore-case that bursts open when it is ripe.

ˌpuff ˈpastry type of light flaky pastry used for pies, cakes, etc.

puff[2] /pʌf/ *v* **1** [Ipr, Tn, Tn·pr] **(a)** (cause sth to) come out in puffs (PUFF[1] 1b): *Smoke puffed from the chimney.* ○ *Don't puff smoke into people's faces.* **(b)** [Ipr, Ip, Tn] ~ **at/on sth** smoke (a pipe, cigarette, etc) in puffs (PUFF[1] 1c): *puff away at/on a cigarette* ○ *He sat puffing his pipe.* **2** [I] *(infml)* breathe loudly or rapidly as after running, etc; pant: *He was puffing hard when he reached the station.* **3** (idm) **huff and puff** ⇨ HUFF[2]. **ˌpuff and ˈblow (a)** (also **ˌpuff and ˈpant**) breathe noisily after physical effort: *puffing and panting at the top of the hill.* **(b)** = HUFF AND PUFF (HUFF[2]). **(be) puffed up with ˈpride, etc** (be) very conceited. **4** (phr v) **puff along, in, out, up, etc** *(infml)* move in the specified direction, sending out small clouds of smoke or breathing heavily: *The train puffed out of the station.* ○ *She puffed up the hill.* **puff sb out** (usu passive) *(infml)* cause sb to be out of breath: *That run has puffed me out.* ○ *He was puffed out after climbing all those stairs.* **puff sth out** extinguish (a candle, etc) by blowing. **puff sth out/up** (cause sth to) swell (as) with air: *The bird puffed out/up its feathers.* ○ *She puffed up the cushions.* ○ *puff out one's cheeks.*

▷ **puffed** *adj* [usu pred] *(infml)* (of a person) breathing with difficulty; out of breath: *He was quite puffed by the time he reached the top.*

puffin /ˈpʌfɪn/ *n* type of N Atlantic sea-bird with a large brightly-coloured bill. ⇨ illus at BIRD.

pug /pʌg/ (also **ˈpug-dog**) *n* small dog with a short flattish nose like that of a bulldog.

□ **ˈpug-nose** *n* short, squat or snub nose. **ˈpug-nosed** *adj* having a pug-nose.

pugilist /ˈpju:dʒɪlɪst/ *n (fml)* professional boxer.

▷ **pugilism** /-lɪzəm/ *n* [U] *(fml)* professional boxing.

pugilistic /ˌpju:dʒɪˈlɪstɪk/ *adj (fml)* **(a)** of or like a pugilist. **(b)** of pugilism.

Pugin /ˈpju:dʒɪn/ Augustus Welby (1812-52), English architect and designer. He was an important figure in the English Gothic revival (GOTHIC), and designed several churches, but he is most famous for the decoration of *Barry's Houses of Parliament.

pugnacious /pʌgˈneɪʃəs/ *adj (fml)* inclined or eager to fight; aggressive: *in a pugnacious mood.* ▷ **pugnaciously** *adj.* **pugnacity** /pʌgˈnæsətɪ/ *n* [U].

puke /pju:k/ *v* [I, Ip, Tn, Tn·p] ~ **(sth) (up)** *(sl)* vomit: *The baby puked (up) all over me.* ○ *It makes me want to puke* (ie It disgusts me)*!*

▷ **puke** *n* [U] vomit.

Pulitzer /ˈpʊlɪtsə(r), ˈpju:l-/ Joseph (1847-1911), American newspaper owner and editor. He was one of the founders of sensational journalism in the USA, and campaigned against social inequalities and injustices.

□ **ˌPulitzer ˈprize** any of a series of prizes awarded each year to American citizens for excellence in journalism and the arts.

pull[1] /pʊl/ *n* **1** [C] ~ **(at/on sth)** act of pulling; tug: *A pull on the rope will make the bell ring.* ○ *I felt a pull at my sleeve and turned round.* **2** [sing] **the ~ of sth (a)** physical force or magnetic attraction found in nature: *The tides depend on the pull of the moon.* ○ *the pull of the current carrying us downstream.* **(b)** *(fig)* force that influences a person's behaviour, career, etc: *the pull of the wandering life* ○ *He felt the pull of the sea again.* **3** [U] *(infml)* influence over other people: *He has a lot of pull with the managing director.* **4** [C] ~ **(at sth) (a)** action of drinking deeply: *take a pull at a bottle.* **(b)** action of inhaling smoke from a cigarette, pipe, etc: *She took a long pull at her cigarette.* **5** [sing] prolonged effort (in walking, rowing etc): *It was a hard pull up to the mountain hut.* ○ *It was a long pull to the shore.* **6** [C] (esp in compounds) handle for pulling sth: *a bell-pull.* **7** [C] (in printing) single impression; proof. **8** [C] (in cricket or golf) type of stroke. Cf PULL[2] 11.

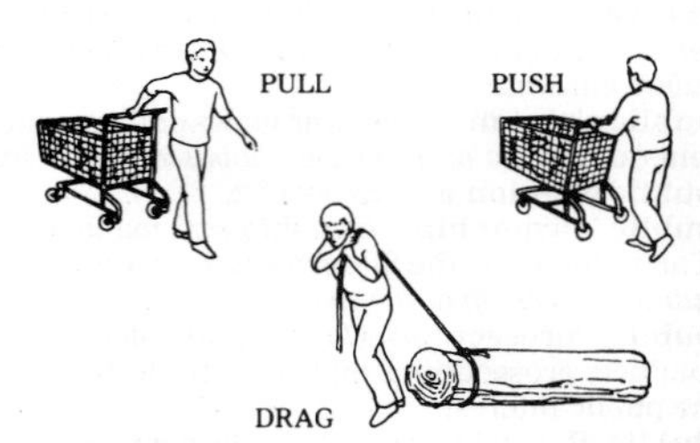

pull[2] /pʊl/ *v* **1 (a)** [I] use force on sth in order to move it towards oneself: *In a tug-of-war, the competitors pull as hard as they can.* ○ *You push and I'll pull.* **(b)** [Tn] use this force on (sth); tug:

Fred pulled his sister's hair and made her cry. ○ *He pulled my ears/me by the ears.* ○ *pull* (ie draw) *the blinds/curtains.* **(c)** [Tn, Tn·pr, Tn·p, Cn·a] cause (sth) to move (in a specified direction) by using this force; draw sth: *How many coaches can that locomotive pull?* ○ *Would you rather push the barrow or pull it?* ○ *The horse was pulling a heavy cart (up a steep slope).* ○ *Pull your chair up to/nearer to the table.* ○ *Pull the plug out.* ○ *The child was pulling the toy along behind her.* ○ *pull the door shut/to* ○ *pull off/on one's shoes, socks, etc.* ⇨ Usage. **2** [Tn] **(a)** remove (sth) by using force; draw sth out: *pull a cork, tooth, stopper* ○ *pull a gun (on sb)*, ie from a pocket, holster, etc ○ *pull (a pint of beer)*, ie draw it out from a barrel ○ *She spent the afternoon pulling weeds in the garden.* ○ *pull a chicken*, ie remove its innards before cooking it. **(b)** damage (sth) by using too much force; strain or tear: *pull a ligament/muscle/tendon.* **3** [I, Ipr, Tn] ~ **(for sth)** (cause a boat to) move through the water by the action of oars: *They pulled hard and reached the shore quickly.* ○ *Pull for shore!* ○ *They pulled (the boat) to the shore.* **4** [Ipr] ~ **at/on sth** **(a)** give a tug on sth: *pull at/on a rope.* **(b)** draw or suck sth: *pull at/on a pipe*, ie draw breath and smoke through a tobacco pipe ○ *pull at* (ie have a drink from) *a bottle.* **5** [Tn] move (a switch, lever, etc) in order to operate a mechanism: *pull the trigger*, ie fire a gun. **6** [Tn] (*sl*) attract (sb) sexually: *He can still pull the girls.* **7** [Tn] (*sl esp US*) succeed in committing (a crime, esp stealing) or in playing a (trick) on sb: *They pulled a bank (job).* ○ *He's pulling some sort of trick.* **8** [I] (of a horse) struggle against the bit, esp habitually. **9** [I, Tn] (cause a vehicle to) move sideways; veer or steer (sth): *The car seems to be pulling to the left.* ○ *She pulled the van to the left to avoid a dog.* **10** [Tn] **(a)** hold back (a horse) in a race in order to avoid winning. **(b)** (in boxing) hold back a blow in order to avoid hurting sb. **11** [Tn] **(a)** (in golf) hit (the ball) wrongly to the left. Cf SLICE 4. **(b)** (in cricket) strike (the ball) forward and to the left of the wicket by striking across the ball's path. **12** (idm) **bring/pull sb up ˈshort/ˈsharply** make sb stop suddenly: *Her remark pulled me up short.* **make/pull ˈfaces/a ˈface** ⇨ FACE[1]. **pick/pull sb/sth to pieces** ⇨ PIECE[1]. **pull the ˌcarpet/ˌrug (out) from under sb's ˈfeet** (*infml*) take the help or support away from sb suddenly: *His mother pulled the carpet from under his feet by announcing that she was selling the house.* **pull a ˈfast one (on sb)** (*infml*) gain an advantage (over sb) by a trick; deceive. **pull sb's ˈleg** (*infml*) make fun of sb, esp by making him believe sth that is untrue; tease sb. **pull the ˈother one (— it's got ˈbells on)** (*infml*) (expression used when one believes that the person one is talking to is pulling one's leg). **pull out all the ˈstops** (*infml*) use all one's power or resources in order to achieve sth: *The airline pulled out all the stops to get him there in time.* **pull the ˈplug on sb/sth** (*sl*) destroy sb/sth. **pull one's ˈpunches** (usu negative) (*infml*) attack (sb) less vigorously than one is able to: *He certainly didn't pull any punches when it came to criticizing the work.* **pull ˈrank (on sb)** make use of one's place or status in society or at work to gain advantages (over sb) to which one is not really entitled. **pull one's ˈsocks up** (*infml*) try harder or improve one's behaviour: *The class were told that there would be no outing unless they pulled their socks up.* **pull ˈstrings/ˈwires (for sb)** (*infml*) use influential friends, indirect pressure, etc in order to obtain an advantage (for sb): *My father pulled a few strings to get me into the Civil Service.* **pull the ˈstrings/ˈwires** control events or the actions of other people. **pull oneself up by one's (own) ˈbootstraps** (*infml*) try to improve one's position by one's own unaided efforts. **pull up one's ˈroots** move from a settled home, job, etc to start a new life elsewhere. **pull one's ˈweight** do one's fair share in a job, project, etc: *We can succeed only if everyone in the team pulls his weight.* **pull the ˈwool over sb's eyes** (*infml*) hide one's real actions or intentions from sb; deceive: *It's no use trying to pull the wool over my eyes — I know exactly what's going on.*

13 (phr v) **pull ahead (of sb/sth)** move in front (of sb/sth): *The car pulled ahead as soon as the road was clear.* ○ *The team has pulled well ahead of the rest in the championship.*

pull (sb) back (cause sb to) retreat; withdraw (sb): *The army pulled back after the battle.*

pull sb down (*infml*) (of an illness) leave sb in a weak condition: *His long illness had pulled him down.* **pull sth down** **(a)** destroy or demolish (eg an old building): *The cinema she used to visit had been pulled down.* **(b)** ⇨ PULL STH IN.

pull sb in **(a)** (*infml*) bring sb to a police station for questioning; detain sb. **(b)** attract (audiences, supporters, etc): *How many voters can he pull in?* ○ *The new show is certainly pulling in the crowds.* **pull sth in** (*US* **pull sth down**) (*infml*) earn (money, a salary, etc): *He's pulling in £50 000 a year.*

pull into sth; pull in (to sth) **(a)** (of a train) enter a station: *The train pulled in right on time.* ○ *Passengers stood and stretched as the train pulled into the station.* **(b)** (of a motor vehicle) move in towards sth: *The bus pulled in to the side of the road.*

pull off (sth) (of a motor vehicle) leave (the road) (and park in a lay-by, etc). **pull sth off** (*infml*) succeed in sth: *pull off a coup, deal, scoop, etc.*

pull out (of a motor vehicle, boat, etc) move out or sideways: *The boat pulled out into the middle of the river.* ○ *A car suddenly pulled out in front of me.* **pull sth out** remove (sth) by pulling; detach: *He pulled out a gun.* **pull out (of sth)** (of a train) leave (a station): *I arrived as the last train was pulling out.* **pull (sb/sth) out (of sth)** (cause sb/sth to) withdraw from sth: *They are pulling their troops out of the battle zone.* ○ *The project became so expensive that we had to pull out.*

pull (sth) over (cause a vehicle, boat, etc to) move or steer to one side (eg in order to let another boat or vehicle pass): *Pull (your car) over and let me pass!*

pull (sb) round/through (*infml*) (help sb to) recover consciousness or from an illness: *She was so ill that it seemed unlikely that she would pull through.* ○ *A sip of brandy helped to pull him round.*

pull together act, work, etc with combined effort in a well-organized way: *After the shock of their electoral defeat, the party really began to pull together.* **pull oneself together** get control of oneself, one's feelings, etc: *You must try to pull yourself together — your family depend on you.*

pull (sth) up (cause a vehicle to) come to a halt: *The driver pulled up at the traffic lights.* **pull sb up** (*infml*) correct or reprimand sb: *He was pulled up by the chairman.* **pull up (to/with sb/sth)** improve one's position (in relation to sb/sth): *At first the new boy was at the bottom of the class but he soon pulled up with the others.*

□ **ˈpull-in** *n* (*Brit infml*) roadside café.

ˈpull-up (*Brit*) (*US* **ˈpull-off**) *n* place where vehicles may leave the road and park.

ˈpull-out *n* part of a magazine, etc that can be pulled out and kept separately: [attrib] *a ˈpull-out supplement.*

NOTE ON USAGE: **Pull**, **drag**, **haul**, **tow**, **trail** and **draw** all indicate the using of strength or force to move something, especially behind oneself. **Pull** has the widest use and its meaning covers that of all the other verbs in this group. A vehicle/animal/person can pull any movable object: *You sometimes see oxen pulling carts in southern Europe.* **Drag** and **haul** suggest that the object is heavy and usually pulled along the ground. It is therefore difficult to move and requires (great) effort. **Drag** suggests greater friction: *He dragged the heavy chest across the floor.* ○ *The police dragged the football fans off the pitch.* **Haul** often indicates the pulling or raising of a heavy object, especially by pulling on a rope: *After a good day's fishing they hauled in the nets and went home.* ○ *Elephants are used in some countries for hauling timber.* **Haul** also has the specific meaning of 'transport goods by lorry/truck': *road haulage.* **Tow** suggests less effort and is used mainly of vehicles. The object being pulled is often damaged and firmly attached to the vehicle by a rope or chain: *My car broke down and had to be towed to a garage.* ○ *The ship needed two tugs to tow it into port.* People **trail** objects behind them, carelessly or for no particular reason. They may also **trail** their arms or hands in the water when travelling in a boat: *The little boy went upstairs trailing his teddy bear behind him.* ○ *She lay back in the boat trailing her fingers in the water.* **Draw** is more formal than **pull**: *Draw/Pull your chair a little closer.* ○ *The men drew/pulled the boat onto the beach.* **Draw** is commonly used to mean 'open/close curtains/blinds'. It is also used in adjectival compounds: *a horse-drawn carriage.*

pullet /ˈpʊlɪt/ *n* young domestic hen, esp at the age when it begins to lay eggs.

pulley /ˈpʊlɪ/ *n* **1** (apparatus consisting of a) wheel or wheels with grooves for ropes or chains, used for lifting things. **2** wheel or drum fixed on a shaft and turned by a belt, used esp to increase speed or power.

□ **ˈpulley-block** wooden block in which a pulley(1) is fixed.

Pullman /ˈpʊlmən/ (also **ˈPullman car**, *US* **ˈparlor car**) *n* (esp formerly) luxurious type of railway carriage without compartments, and with seats grouped at tables.

pullover /ˈpʊləʊvə(r)/ *n* = JERSEY 1.

pulmonary /ˈpʌlmənərɪ; *US* -nerɪ/ *adj* [usu attrib] (*medical*) of, in or affecting the lungs: *pulmonary diseases* ○ *the pulmonary arteries*, ie those that carry blood to the lungs.

pulp /pʌlp/ *n* **1** **(a)** [U] soft fleshy inner part of fruit; flesh: *Scoop out the pulp and serve it with sugar.* ○ *tomato pulp.* **(b)** [U] soft mass of wood fibre, used for making paper: *ˈwood pulp.* **(c)** [U, sing] substance with a soft texture similar to these: *reduce the garlic to a pulp*, ie beat or crush it until it becomes pulp ○ *The beans need to be mashed into (a) pulp.* ○ (*fig*) *The gang threatened to beat him to a pulp* (ie injure him badly) *if he gave any more trouble.* **2** [U] (*derog*) books, magazines that are of poor quality, esp popular sensational literature: *She writes pulp.* ○ [attrib] *pulp fiction, magazines.*

▷ **pulp** *v* [I, Tn] (cause sth to) become pulp: *pulp grapes, olives, raspberries, etc* ○ *pulp* (ie make pulp(1b) from) *old books.*

pulpy *adj* (**-ier**, **-iest**) like or containing a lot of pulp(1c): *a pulpy consistency* ○ *pulpy food.*

pulpit /ˈpʊlpɪt/ *n* **1** [C] (usu small) raised and enclosed platform in a church, where a clergyman stands when he is preaching. ⇨ illus at CHURCH. **2 the pulpit** [sing] (*fml*) (religious teaching of) the clergy: *The policy was condemned* (ie by clergymen) *from the pulpit.*

pulsar /ˈpʌlsɑː(r)/ *n* star that cannot be seen but can be detected by pulsating radio signals.

pulsate /pʌlˈseɪt; *US* ˈpʌlseɪt/ *v* **1** (also **pulse**) [I] expand and contract rhythmically; throb: *blood pulsating in the body.* **2** [I, Tn] (cause sth to) shake with regular movements or sounds; vibrate: *a pulsating rhythm* ○ *The needle pulsates when the engine is running.* **3** [Ipr] ~ **with sth** be moved by (strong emotion); be thrilled: *pulsate with desire, excitement, joy, etc.*

▷ **pulsation** /pʌlˈseɪʃn/ *n* **(a)** [C] single beat or throb; heartbeat: *a rate of 60 pulsations per minute.* **(b)** [U] pulsating; throbbing: *the pulsation of the blood in the body.*

pulse[1] /pʌls/ *n* **1** (usu *sing*) **(a)** regular beating of the arteries as blood is pumped through them by the heart, esp as felt at the wrist: *have a low, irregular, strong, weak, etc pulse* ○ *His pulse raced as he faced the armed intruder.* ○ [attrib] *one's ˈpulse rate*, ie the number of times per minute that one's heart beats, as felt at the wrist. **(b)** regular beat in music: *the throbbing pulse of the drums.* **2** **(a)** single vibration of sound, light, electric current, etc: *The machine emits sound pulses.* **(b)** (usu *sing*) series of these: *The machine is operated by an electronic pulse.* **3** (idm) **feel/take sb's**

ˈpulse find out the speed of the heartbeat by feeling the pulse in the wrist and counting the number of beats per minute. **have/keep one's finger on the pulse** ⇨ FINGER.

▷ **pulse** *v* (**a**) [I, Ipr] ~ (**through sth**) move with strong regular movements; beat or throb: *The news sent the blood pulsing through his veins.* ○ *(fig) the life pulsing through a great city.* (**b**) [I] = PULSATE 1.

pulse[2] /pʌls/ *n* (usu *pl*) seed(s) of various plants (eg beans, lentils, peas) that grow in pods and are dried and used as food: *Pulses are a good source of protein for vegetarians.*

pulverize, -ise /ˈpʌlvəraɪz/ *v* **1** (*fml*) (**a**) [Tn] grind or smash (sth) to powder or dust: *a machine that pulverizes nuts, coffee beans, etc.* (**b**) [I] become powder or dust. **2** [Tn] (*infml or joc*) destroy or defeat (sb/sth) completely: *He pulverized the opposition with the force of his oratory.* ▷ **pulverization, -isation** /ˌpʌlvəraɪˈzeɪʃn; *US* -rɪˈz-/ *n* [U].

puma /ˈpjuːmə/ *n* (also **cougar**, ˌ**mountain** ˈ**lion**) large brown American animal of the cat family.

pumice /ˈpʌmɪs/ (also ˈ**pumice-stone**) *n* [C, U] (piece of) light porous lava used for removing stains or rough patches of skin and (in powder form) for cleaning and polishing.

pummel /ˈpʌml/ *v* (also **pommel**) (**-ll-**; *US* also **-l-**) [Tn] strike (sb/sth) repeatedly, esp with the fist(s); beat: *The child pummelled his mother angrily as she carried him home.*

▷ **pummelling** /ˈpʌməlɪŋ/ *n* [sing] severe beating: *The boxers gave each other a terrific pummelling.* ○ *(fig) The team took a real pummelling in their last match.*

pump[1] /pʌmp/ *n* **1** (esp in compounds) machine or device for forcing liquid, gas or air into, out of or through sth, eg water from a well, petrol from a storage tank, air into a tyre or oil through a pipe-line: *A pump in the boiler sends hot water round the central heating system.* ○ *a petrol pump* ○ *She blew up the flat tyre with a bicycle pump.* ○ *The doctor removed the contents of her stomach with a stomach pump.* ⇨ illus at BICYCLE. **2** pumping (PUMP[1] *v* 1) action: *After several pumps, the water began to flow.* ○ *give sb's hand a pump*, ie shake it energetically up and down. **3** (idm) **all hands to the pump** ⇨ HAND[1]. **parish pump** ⇨ PARISH. **prime the pump** ⇨ PRIME[3].

▷ **pump** *v* **1** [Tn, Tn·pr, Cn·a] cause (air, gas, water, etc) to move in a specified direction by using a pump[1](1): *pump air into a tyre* ○ *The heart pumps blood round the body.* **2** [I] (**a**) use a pump[1](1): *You will need to pump hard for several minutes to fill the tank.* (**b**) (of the heart or blood) beat: *Her heart was pumping very fast.* **3** [Tn, Tn·p] (*infml*) move (sb's hand) up and down like the handle of a pump: *He pumped my hand (up and down) vigorously.* **4** [Tn, Tn·pr] ~ **sb** (**for sth**); ~ **sth out of sb** (*infml*) try to obtain (information) from sb by asking persistent questions: *He tried to pump the secretary for information.* ○ *She succeeded in pumping the name of the winner out of him.* **5** (phr v) **pump sth in; pump sth into sth/sb** (**a**) invest much money (in sth): *The firm pumped money into the development of the new product.* (**b**) (*infml*) persuade or force sb to learn sth: *She tried to pump some facts into his head before the examination.* **pump sth up** inflate (a tyre, etc) by pumping (PUMP[1] *v* 1) air into it.

ˈ**pump-room** *n* (esp formerly) room (at a spa) where mineral water is available for drinking.

pump[2] /pʌmp/ *n* **1** = PLIMSOLL. **2** light soft shoe worn for dancing, etc. **3** (*esp US*) woman's low-heeled shoe without a fastening.

pumpernickel /ˈpʌmpənɪkl/ *n* [U] type of (esp German) wholemeal rye bread.

pumpkin /ˈpʌmpkɪn/ *n* (**a**) [C] (plant that bears a) large round orange-coloured fruit with many seeds: *Some children make lanterns out of pumpkins at Hallowe'en.* (**b**) [U] flesh of this fruit, used as a vegetable and (esp in the USA) as a filling for pies: [attrib] *pumpkin pie.*

pun /pʌn/ *n* ~ (**on sth**) humorous use of a word that has two meanings or of different words that sound the same, eg 'She told the child to *try* not to be so *trying*'; play on words: *The slogan was a pun on the name of the product.* ⇨ article at HUMOUR.

▷ **pun** *v* (**-nn-**) [I, Ipr] ~ (**on sth**) make a pun or puns (on a word): *He's always punning and I don't find it funny.*

a Punch and Judy show

TOBY PUNCH JUDY POLICEMAN

Punch /pʌntʃ/ *n* **1** [sing] (name of a) grotesque humpbacked figure in a traditional **Punch and Judy** puppet show. He is quarrelsome and argues with Judy, his wife, and the other characters (eg the policeman and the doctor), often hitting them with his stick. The characters are glove puppets. The show is presented in a tall booth made of striped canvas, often at the seaside. The name *Punch* was borrowed for a British humorous magazine, founded in 1841. ⇨ illus. **2** (idm) **as pleased as Punch** ⇨ PLEASED (PLEASE).

punch[1] /pʌntʃ/ *n* **1** (**a**) tool or machine for cutting holes in leather, metal, paper, etc. (**b**) tool for forcing nails beneath a surface or bolts out of holes. **2** tool for stamping designs on surfaces.

▷ **punch** *v* **1** [Tn, Tn·pr] ~ **sth** (**in sth**) make (a hole) in sth with a punch[1](1a); perforate sth: *punch a train ticket* ○ *punch holes in a sheet of metal.* **2** (phr v) **punch** (**sb**) **in/out** (*US*) = CLOCK (SB) IN/OUT (CLOCK (2). ˈ**punch card** (also ˈ**punched card**) card on which information is recorded by punching holes in it, used for giving instructions or data to a computer, etc.

punch[2] /pʌntʃ/ *n* [U] drink made of wine or spirits mixed with hot or cold water, sugar, lemons, spice, etc.

□ ˈ**punch-bowl** *n* **1** bowl in which punch is mixed or from which it is served: *a glass punch-bowl.* **2** deep round hollow in a hill.

punch[3] /pʌntʃ/ *v* **1** [Tn, Tn·pr] strike (sb/sth) hard with the fist: *punch a man on the chin* ○ *He has a face I'd like to punch.* **2** [Tn] (*US*) herd (cattle).

▷ **punch** *n* **1** (**a**) [C] blow given with the fist: *give sb a hard punch on the nose.* (**b**) [sing] ability to give such a blow effectively: *a boxer with a strong punch.* **2** [U] (*fig*) effective force or vigour: *a speech with plenty of punch.* **3** (idm) **pack a punch** ⇨ PACK[2]. **pull one's punches** ⇨ PULL[2].

punchy *adj* (**-ier, -iest**) (*infml*) having punch[3](*n* 2); forceful: *a punchy argument, debate, etc.*

□ ˈ**punch-ball** *n* (*US* **punching ball**) inflated or stuffed leather ball held on a stand or hung from above and punched for exercise or training, esp by boxers.

ˌ**punch-**ˈ**drunk** *adj* (**a**) (in boxing) dazed or stupefied by being severely punched. (**b**) (*fig*) dazed or confused, eg after working intensely: *The negotiators seemed punch-drunk after another all-night session.*

ˈ**punch-line** *n* words that form the climax of a joke or story: *He forgot the punch-line of his after-dinner speech.*

ˈ**punch-up** *n* (*Brit infml*) fight with the fists; brawl: *The argument ended in a punch-up.*

punctilio /pʌŋkˈtɪlɪəʊ/ *n* (*pl* ~**s**) [C, U] (*fml*) (instance of) giving careful attention to every small point of ceremony, good conduct, honour, etc.

punctilious /pʌŋkˈtɪlɪəs/ *adj* (*fml*) very careful to carry out one's duties, etc correctly; very attentive to details of behaviour or ceremony: *a punctilious attention to detail* ○ *a punctilious observance of the formalities.* ▷ **punctiliously** *adv.* **punctiliousness** *n* [U].

punctual /ˈpʌŋktʃʊəl/ *adj* happening or doing sth at the agreed or proper time: *a punctual start to the meeting* ○ *be punctual for an appointment* ○ *The tenants are punctual in paying the rent.*

▷ **punctuality** /ˌpʌŋktʃʊˈælətɪ/ *n* [U] being punctual.

punctually /ˈpuŋktʃʊəlɪ/ *adv*: *arrive, depart, etc punctually.*

punctuate /ˈpʌŋktʃʊeɪt/ *v* **1** [I, Tn] put full stops, commas, colons, question marks, etc into (a piece of writing): *The children have not yet learned to punctuate correctly.* ○ *The transcription of his speech must be punctuated.* **2** [Tn, Tn·pr] ~ **sth** (**with sth**) interrupt sth (by/with sth) at intervals: *The announcement was punctuated by cheers from the crowd.* ○ *He punctuated his remarks with thumps on the table.*

▷ **punctuation** /ˌpʌŋktʃʊˈeɪʃn/ *n* [U] (art, practice or system of) punctuating: *The children have never been taught punctuation.*

□ **punctuˈation mark** any of the marks (eg full stop, comma, question mark, etc) used in a written or printed text to separate sentences, etc and to make the meaning clear. ⇨ App 14.

puncture /ˈpʌŋktʃə(r)/ *n* small hole made by a sharp point, esp one made accidentally in a tyre: *I got a puncture on the way and arrived late.*

▷ **puncture** *v* **1** (**a**) [Tn] make a puncture in (sth): *puncture a tyre, an abscess, a balloon* ○ *She was taken to hospital with a punctured lung.* (**b**) [I] (of a tyre, etc) get a puncture: *Two of the tyres punctured on the stony road.* **2** [Tn] reduce (sb's pride, confidence, etc); deflate: *I wish something would happen to puncture her ego*, ie lessen her conceit.

pundit /ˈpʌndɪt/ *n* **1** very learned Hindu. **2** (*often joc*) person who is an authority on a subject; expert: *The pundits disagree on the best way of dealing with the problem.* ○ *a panel of well-known television pundits.*

pungent /ˈpʌndʒənt/ *adj* **1** having a sharp or strong taste or smell: *a pungent odour, sauce, spice, etc.* **2** (of remarks) sharply critical; biting or caustic: *pungent comments, criticism, satire, etc.*

▷ **pungency** /-nsɪ/ *n* [U] quality or state of being pungent.

pungently *adv.*

Punic Wars /ˌpjuːnɪk ˈwɔːz/ **the Punic Wars** three wars between Rome and *Carthage (now in Tunisia) which established the power of Rome over the Mediterranean. In the first (264-241 BC) Rome won control of Sicily; the second (218-201 BC) ended Carthage's position as a sea power; and the third (149-146 BC) ended in the complete destruction of the city of Carthage.

punish /ˈpʌnɪʃ/ *v* **1** [Tn, Tn·pr] (**a**) ~ **sb** (**for sth**) (**by/with sth**) hurt, imprison, fine, etc sb for wrongdoing: *punish those who break the law* ○ *He punished the children for their carelessness by making them pay for the damage.* (**b**) [Tn, Tn·pr] ~ **sth** (**by/with sth**) hurt, imprison, fine, etc sb for (wrongdoing): *Serious crime must be punished by longer terms of imprisonment.* **2** [Tn] (*infml*) treat (sb) roughly, esp by giving hard blows: *He punished his opponent with fierce punches to the body.* ○ *Chapman punished the bowling*, ie (in cricket) scored freely from weak bowling.

▷ **punishable** *adj* ~ (**by sth**) that can be punished (esp by law): *punishable by death* ○ *Giving false information is a punishable offence.*

punishing *adj* [usu attrib] that makes one very tired or weak; severe: *a punishing climb up the hill* ○ *a punishing defeat.* — *n* [sing] (*infml*) severe defeat or damage: *My boots have taken quite a punishing recently — I think I need a new pair.*

punishingly *adv.*

punishment *n* (**a**) [U] punishing or being

Punishment

When people are sent to prison in Britain after being found guilty of a crime, they are given a sentence that specifies the length of their punishment. Most, however, will normally be eligible for a remission of one third of the period stipulated. This means that a person sentenced to a year's imprisonment will normally be released after eight months, and one sentenced to three years will leave prison after two. Moreover, most prisoners sentenced to 12 months or more are also eligible for parole when they have served one third of the stated period, after a minimum of six months in prison. At present about three prisoners out of four obtain parole. However, prisoners sentenced to five or more years for serious offences involving violence, arson or sexual crimes are rarely granted parole. A person on parole is released from prison on condition that he or she remains in touch with a probation officer over the period of time for which the original sentence would have run. If parole conditions are abused, the offender is liable to be recalled to prison.

Although a 'life sentence' for murder rarely means imprisonment for life, it can last for 20 years or more if the crime was the murder of a police officer or prison officer, if it was carried out during a terrorist attack or a robbery, or if it involved the sexual or sadistic killing of a child. The government minister responsible for law and order, the Home Secretary, decides when a prisoner sentenced to life should be released. Such prisoners remain on parole for the rest of their lives, and may be imprisoned again if it seems likely that they will commit a further offence.

On the whole, many courts try to avoid passing prison sentences in the first place, and instead impose some other punishment, such as a fine, or probation, or a community service order. A court may impose a prison sentence 'suspended' for up to two years: the offender will not have to serve the sentence unless he or she commits other offences during the period. Fines are awarded in about eight cases out of 10. 'Probation' involves the offender leading a normal life but under the supervision of a probation officer. Community service involves doing unpaid physical work for between 40 and 240 hours, to be completed within 12 months. Typical examples of community service are painting an elderly person's house or building a playground for children.

Courts also have the power to allow a convicted person to go free, ie to discharge him or her conditionally, especially if imprisonment or other punishment seems inappropriate. If convicted for another offence of the same kind, however, such a person will be brought back to court and be liable for the punishment that could have been imposed in the first place. For a trivial offence, such as a single instance of drunk and disorderly behaviour, the court may 'bind over' the offender, requiring him or her to 'keep the peace' and 'be of good behaviour'. If this condition is not observed, the person may be given a punishment for the original offence, or have to pay a sum of money stipulated when 'bound over'.

There are separate prisons for men and women. Prisons can be 'closed' or 'open'. Open prisons do not have physical barriers such as the locked and barred windows of other prisons. The prisoners are trusted not to escape, and because they are not locked up they can carry out useful work for longer periods than prisoners in closed prisons. There are also special prisons for offenders needing psychiatric treatment.

If a child or young person aged between 10 and 17 commits an offence, he or she is similarly subject to different types of punishment. The sentencing court may place the young person under a 'care order'. In this case the child can remain at home under supervision, or be placed with foster parents, or be sent to a 'community home' run either by the local authority or by a voluntary body. Alternatively, the child may be placed under a 'supervision order', when he or she will continue to live at home but be supervised by a social worker or probation officer.

Courts can fine young offenders, but payment is the responsibility of the parents or guardians. A more serious punishment is to order the offender to spend a period of leisure time at an 'attendance centre'. The centre gives instruction in physical training and practical subjects. The young person can be ordered to spend up to three hours on a Saturday at such a centre, up to a total of 24 hours.

Older children may be sent to a young offender institution, the equivalent of prison for an adult. Boys aged 14 can be sentenced for a period of three weeks to four months, while those of 15 and 16 can be given up to 12 months. Girls of 14 may not be sentenced like this, however, and girls aged 15 and 16 must be sentenced to a period of more than four months. Offenders of either sex aged 16 can also be ordered to carry out up to 120 hours of community service. No child under 10 can be brought to court at all. Sentences for young people aged 17 to 20 are similar but may be for longer periods or on similar conditions as those for adult sentences, eg up to a maximum of 240 hours of community service.

Prison populations have been growing in both Britain and the USA in recent years, with the US prison population increasing by 90 per cent from 1980 to 1988. Many British prisons are seriously overcrowded and, because some date from the 19th century, they have very poor facilities, especially sanitation. Opportunities for exercise and for education and training are restricted in old and overcrowded prisons, and partly as a result of this there have been some serious riots in British prisons. A prison building programme is planned to improve conditions and measures have also been taken to reduce the number of people sent to prison, by using alternative punishments whenever possible. It is still the case, however, that Britain sends a higher proportion of the population to prison than many other European countries.

The death penalty was abolished in Britain in 1965. Until that date, people convicted of murder were hanged. In the USA, capital punishment is still legal in 37 of the states. There were no executions in the USA between 1968 and 1976, but between 1977 and 1987, 93 people were executed. (Cf articles at CRIME and LAW.)

punished: *corporal punishment*, ie punishment by physical beating, etc ○ *capital punishment*, ie punishment by death. (**b**) [C] penalty inflicted on sb who has done sth wrong: *The punishments inflicted on the children were too severe.* ○ *The punishment should fit* (ie be appropriate for) *the crime.* ⇨ article.

punitive /ˈpjuːnətɪv/ *adj* (*fml*) (**a**) intended as punishment: *punitive action, measures, restrictions, etc* ○ *a punitive expedition*, ie a military one intended to punish rebels, etc. (**b**) causing hardship; severe: *punitive taxation* ○ *punitive increases in the cost of living.* ▷ **punitively** *adv.*

Punjab /ˈpʌndʒɑːb/ (also **the Punjab**) state in NW India. It is part of the former region of Punjab which included part of Pakistan. It contains Amritsar, the sacred city of the Sikh religion, and there is a strong independence movement.
▷ **Punjabi** /pʌnˈdʒɑːbɪ/ *adj* of or relating to Punjab. — *n* native or inhabitant of Punjab.

punk /pʌŋk/ *n* **1** (**a**) (also **punk ˈrock**) [U] type of loud violent rock³ music popular since the late 1970s and associated with protest against conventional attitudes: [attrib] *a punk band, concert, fan.* (**b**) [C] (also **punk ˈrocker**) (esp young) person who likes punk music and imitates the appearance of punk musicians, eg by wearing metal chains, clothes with holes in and brightly coloured hair: [attrib] *a punk hairstyle.* **2** (*infml derog*) (**a**) [C] (*esp US*) badly-behaved young man or boy; lout. (**b**) [U] worthless stuff; rubbish: [attrib] *punk material.*

punnet /ˈpʌnɪt/ *n* (*esp Brit*) small basket made of very thin wood, plastic, etc and used as a container for fruit: *Strawberries cost 60p a punnet.*

punster /ˈpʌnstə(r)/ *n* person who habitually makes puns.

punt¹ /pʌnt/ *n* long shallow flat-bottomed boat with square ends that is moved by pushing the end of a long pole against the bottom of a river.
▷ **punt** *v* (**a**) [I, Ipr, Ip] move a punt with a pole (in the specified direction): *She soon learned to punt.* ○ *They punted along the river.* (**b**) [I] (often **go punting**) go along a river in a punt, esp for pleasure.

punt² /pʌnt/ *v* [Tn] kick (a football) after it has dropped from the hands and before it touches the ground.
▷ **punt** *n* kick made in this way.

punt³ /pʌnt/ *v* [I] **1** (in some card-games) lay a stake against the bank. **2** (*infml esp Brit*) speculate in shares, bet money on a horse, etc; gamble.
▷ **punter** *n* (*Brit*) (**a**) person who punts (PUNT³ 1, 2). (**b**) (*infml derog*) foolish or unthinking person who can be persuaded to buy goods or services of poor quality: *You can write what you like, as long as it keeps the punters happy.* ○ *Your average punter* (ie The ordinary uncultured person) *does not go to the opera.*

puny /ˈpjuːnɪ/ *adj* (**-ier**, **-iest**) (*usu derog*) (**a**) small, weak and underdeveloped: *puny limbs, muscles, stature* ○ *What a puny little creature!* (**b**) feeble or pathetic: *They laughed at my puny efforts at rock-climbing.*

pup /pʌp/ *n* **1** (**a**) = PUPPY 1. (**b**) young of various other animals, eg otters, seals: *a mother seal and her pup.* **2** = PUPPY 2. **3** (idm) **in pup** (of a female dog) pregnant. **sell sb a pup** ⇨ SELL.
▷ **pup** *v* (**-pp-**) [I] give birth to a pup or pups.

pupa /ˈpjuːpə/ *n* (*pl* ~ **s** or **pupae** /ˈpjuːpiː/) insect in the stage of development between a larva and an adult insect. ⇨ illus at BUTTERFLY. Cf CHRYSALIS.
▷ **pupal** *adj.*
pupate /pjuːˈpeɪt; *US* ˈpjuːpeɪt/ *v* [I] (*fml*) (of an

insect larva) develop into a pupa.

pupil[1] /ˈpju:pl/ *n* **(a)** person, esp a child, who is taught in school or privately: *There are 30 pupils in the class.* ○ *She takes private pupils as well as teaching in school.* **(b)** person who is taught by an expert; follower: *The painting is the work of a pupil of Rembrandt.* ○ *The tenor was a pupil of Caruso.*

pupil[2] /ˈpju:pl/ *n* circular opening in the centre of the iris of the eye that regulates the amount of light that passing to the retina by becoming larger or smaller. ⇨ illus at EYE.

puppets

GLOVE PUPPET MARIONETTE

puppet /ˈpʌpɪt/ *n* **1** doll or small figure of an animal, etc, either a *marionette* that can be made to move by pulling wires or strings attached to its jointed limbs, or a *glove puppet* that fits one's hand so that one can move the head and arms with one's fingers: [attrib] *a puppet theatre.* ⇨ illus. **2** (*usu derog*) person or group whose actions are controlled by another: *The union representative was accused of being a puppet of the management.* ○ [attrib] *a puppet government/state*, ie one that is controlled by another power.

▷ **puppeteer** /ˌpʌpɪˈtɪə(r)/ *n* person who performs with or controls a puppet(1) or puppets.

puppetry /ˈpʌpɪtrɪ/ *n* art of making and handling puppets (PUPPET 1).

□ ˈ**puppet-play** (also ˈ**puppet-show**) *n* type of entertainment with puppets.

puppy /ˈpʌpɪ/ (also **pup** /pʌp/) *n* **1** young dog. **2** (*infml derog*) conceited or insolent young man: *You insolent young puppy!*

□ ˈ**puppy-fat** *n* [U] (*infml*) fatness, esp of a female child or adolescent, which disappears as the child grows up: *After Jane lost her puppy-fat she became very slim.* ⇨ Usage at FAT[1].

ˈ**puppy-love** (also ˈ**calf-love**) *n* [U] (*infml*) immature infatuation of an adolescent: *He's mad about his biology teacher, but it's only puppy-love.*

purblind /ˈpɜ:blaɪnd/ *adj* (*fml or rhet*) **1** partly blind. **2** (*derog*) lacking understanding; stupid: *You purblind fool!*

Purcell /ˈpɜ:sl, *also* pɜ:ˈsel/ Henry (1659-95), English composer who excelled in all the musical genres of his day. He wrote the first English opera, *Dido and Aeneas*, which shows his gift for setting English words in a musically expressive way. He had a considerable influence on *Handel. ⇨ article at MUSIC.

purchase[1] /ˈpɜ:tʃəs/ *n* **1** (*fml*) **(a)** [U] (action of) buying sth: *the date of purchase* ○ *The receipt is your proof of purchase.* ○ *They began to regret the purchase of such a large house.* ○ *hire-purchase.* **(b)** [C usu *pl*] thing bought: *I have some purchases to make in town.* ○ *It was the most extravagant purchase I have ever made.* **2** [U, sing] (*fml*) firm hold or grip for pulling or raising sth, preventing it from slipping, etc; leverage: *The climbers had difficulty getting a/any purchase on the rock face.*

□ ˈ**purchase price** *n* price (to be) paid for sth: *The purchase price is less if you pay by cash.*

ˈ**purchase tax** tax charged on several types of goods, at varying rates, collected by the retailer (and since 1973 replaced in Britain by VAT). Cf SALES TAX (SALE).

purchase[2] /ˈpɜ:tʃəs/ *v* **1** [Tn, Dn·pr] ~ **sth (with sth)**; ~ **sth (for sb)** (*fml*) buy sth: *houses purchased with loans from building societies* ○ *Employees are encouraged to purchase shares in the firm.* **2** [Tn, Tn·pr] ~ **sth (with sth)** (*rhet*) obtain or achieve sth (at a cost or with sacrifice): *a dearly purchased victory*, ie one for which many lives were lost.

▷ **purchaser** *n* (*fml*) person who buys sth: *The purchaser of the house will pay the deposit next week.* Cf VENDOR (VEND).

□ ˈ**purchasing power** [U] **(a)** wealth and the ability to buy goods with it: *Inflation reduces the purchasing power of people living on fixed incomes.* **(b)** value (of a unit of money) in terms of what it can buy: *a decline in the purchasing power of the dollar.*

purdah /ˈpɜ:də/ *n* [U] (system in Muslim and Hindu societies of) keeping women from public view by means of a veil, curtain, etc: *keep sb/be/live in purdah*, ie concealed in this way ○ (*fig infml*) *I've got a lot of urgent work to do at home and will have to go into purdah for a couple of weeks.*

pure /pjʊə(r)/ *adj* (in senses 1b, 1c, 2 and 4 **-r, -st** /ˈpjʊərə(r), ˈpjʊərɪst/) **1 (a)** not mixed with any other substance: *pure cotton, gold, silk, wool, etc* ○ *The room was painted pure white.* ○ (*fig*) *pure bliss, happiness, etc.* **(b)** without harmful substances; clean or unadulterated: *pure water* ○ *The air is so pure in these mountains.* **(c)** [usu attrib] of unmixed origin or race: *She has pure gypsy blood in her veins.* ○ *He is a pure Red Indian.* **2** without evil or sin, esp sexual sin; virtuous, chaste: (*rhet*) *pure in body and mind* ○ *pure thoughts* ○ *a pure young girl* ○ *keep oneself pure* ○ *His motives were pure.* **3** [attrib] nothing but; mere or sheer: *They met by pure accident.* ○ *pure folly, extravagance, nonsense* ○ *do sth out of pure kindness, malice, mischief, etc* ○ *It was pure chance that I was there.* **4** (of sound) clear and unwavering: *a pure note, voice, etc.* **5** [attrib] (*fml*) dealing with or studied for the sake of theory only; without practical application: *pure mathematics* ○ *pure art*, ie art created for its own sake, and not for decoration, eg painting, sculpture, etc. Cf APPLIED (APPLY). **6** (idm) **(as) pure as the driven snow** extremely pure(2). ˌ**pure and** ˈ**simple** (*infml*) (used after the *n* referred to) and nothing else; sheer: *It's laziness, pure and simple.* ○ *The reason for the change is lack of money, pure and simple.*

▷ **purely** *adv* merely or entirely: *purely by accident* ○ *He bought it purely as an investment.*

pureness *n* [U] = PURITY.

□ ˈ**pure-bred** *adj*, *n* = THOROUGHBRED.

purée /ˈpjʊəreɪ; *US* pjʊəˈreɪ/ *n* [U, C] (often in compounds) thick liquid made by pressing fruit or cooked vegetables through a sieve; pulp: *Make a purée of the vegetables.* ○ *apple, potato, raspberry, etc purée.*

▷ **purée** *v* [Tn] make (fruit or vegetables) into a purée: *She fed the baby on puréed carrots.* ○ *a machine for puréeing vegetables.*

purgation /pɜ:ˈgeɪʃn/ *n* [U] (*fml*) purging or purification.

purgative /ˈpɜ:gətɪv/ *n*, *adj* (substance, esp a medicine) that causes the bowels to empty; strong(ly) laxative: *This oil acts as a purgative/has a purgative effect.* ○ *He was given a purgative before the operation.*

purgatory /ˈpɜ:gətrɪ; *US* -tɔ:rɪ/ *n* [U] **1** (usu **Purgatory**) (in Roman Catholic teaching) place or condition in which the souls of the dead are purified by suffering in preparation for Heaven: *a prayer for the souls in Purgatory.* **2** (*esp infml or joc*) any place or condition of suffering: *He's so impatient that waiting in a queue is sheer purgatory for him!*

▷ **purgatorial** /ˌpɜ:gəˈtɔ:rɪəl/ *adj* (*fml*) of or like purgatory: *purgatorial agony, fires.*

purge /pɜ:dʒ/ *v* **1** [Tn, Tn·pr, Tn·p] ~ **sb (of/from sth)**; ~ **sth (away)** make sb clean or pure by removing (evil, sin, etc): *Catholics go to confession to be purged of sin/purge (away) their sin/purge their souls of sin.* **2** [Tn] (*dated or joc*) empty the bowels (of a person): *A dose of this stuff will purge you!* **3** [Tn, Tn·pr] ~ **sth (of sb)**/~ **sb (from sth)** rid (esp a political party) of (people thought to be undesirable); remove (such people) from (a party): *So-called traitors were purged (from their ranks).* ○ *They promised that the party would be purged of racists/that racists would be purged from the party.* **4** [Tn] (*law*) atone for (an offence, esp contempt of court): *purge one's contempt.*

▷ **purge** *n* **1** action of ridding (a political party, state, etc) of people who are considered undesirable: *a purge of disloyal members* ○ *the political purges that followed the change of government.* **2** (esp formerly) medicine that empties the bowels; purgative.

purify /ˈpjʊərɪfaɪ/ *v* (*pt, pp* **-fied**) [Tn, Tn·pr] **(a)** ~ **sth (of sth)** make sth pure by removing dirty, harmful or foreign substances: *Water is purified by passing through rock.* ○ *purified salts* ○ *The soil has to be purified of all bacteria.* ○ *an air-purifying plant*, eg for providing pure air in a factory. **(b)** ~ **sb (of sth)** make sb pure by removing his sins, esp in a religious ceremony.

▷ **purification** /ˌpjʊərɪfɪˈkeɪʃn/ *n* **1** [U] (action of) purifying: *purification of water* ○ *the purification of souls.* **2 the Purification** [sing] (in the Anglican Church) celebration on 2 February of the presentation of Jesus in the temple in Jerusalem.

purist /ˈpjʊərɪst/ *n* person who pays great attention to correctness, esp in the use of language or in the arts: *Purists were shocked by the changes made to the text of the play.* ▷ **purism** /ˈpjʊərɪzəm/ *n* [U] (*fml*).

puritan /ˈpjʊərɪtən/ *n* **1 Puritan** member of the party of English Protestants in the 16th and 17th centuries who wanted simpler forms of church ceremony: [attrib] *the Puritan settlers in New England.* **2** (*usu derog*) person who is extremely strict in morals and who tends to regard pleasure as sinful: *the puritans who wish to clean up television.*

▷ **puritan** *adj* **1 Puritan** of or relating to a Puritan or Puritanism. **2** = PURITANICAL.

puritanical /ˌpjʊərɪˈtænɪkl/ *adj* (*derog*) very strict and severe in morals: *a puritanical attitude, conscience, upbringing* ○ *pursue vice with puritanical zeal.* **puritanically** /-klɪ/ *adv*: *puritanically opposed to pleasure.*

puritanism /ˈpjʊərɪtənɪzəm/ *n* [U] practices and beliefs of a Puritan or a puritan.

purity /ˈpjʊərətɪ/ (also **pureness**) *n* [U] state or quality of being pure: *test the purity of the water* ○ *question the purity of their motives* ○ *purity of colour, form, sound, etc.*

purl /pɜ:l/ *n* [C, U] (also ˈ**purl stitch**) stitch in knitting that produces ridges on the upper side: *knitted in purl* ○ *Knit two plain, two purl.* Cf PLAIN[3].

▷ **purl** *v* [I, Tn] knit (sth) in this stitch: *Knit one* (ie make one plain stitch), *purl one.*

purler /ˈpɜ:lə(r)/ *n* (*dated Brit sl*) fall in which one's face hits the floor: *He came/took a real purler*, ie fell in this way.

purlieus /ˈpɜ:lju:z/ *n* [pl] (*fml or rhet*) outlying parts; outskirts: *the purlieus of the capital.*

purloin /pɜ:ˈlɔɪn, ˈpɜ:lɔɪn/ *v* [Tn] (*fml or joc*) steal (sth): *food purloined from her employer's kitchen.*

purple /ˈpɜ:pl/ *adj* **1** having the colour of red and blue mixed together: *a purple flower, dress, sunset* ○ *go purple (in the face) with rage.* **2** (*fml*) (of literature) elaborate in style; overwritten: *purple passages/patches/prose.*

▷ **purple** *n* **1** [U] purple colour: *dressed in purple.* **2 the purple** [sing] the purple robes of a Roman emperor or the crimson robes of a cardinal.

purplish /ˈpɜ:pəlɪʃ/ *adj* rather purple in colour: *a purplish complexion.*

□ ˌ**purple** ˈ**heart 1 Purple Heart** (*US*) medal awarded to a soldier who has been wounded in battle. **2** (*infml*) heart-shaped pill containing amphetamine, used as a stimulant.

purport /ˈpɜ:pət/ *n* [sing] ~ **(of sth)** (*fml*) general meaning or intention (of sth): *The purport of the statement is that the firm is bankrupt.*

▷ **purport** /pəˈpɔ:t/ *v* [Tt] (*fml*) be meant to seem (to be); claim or pretend: *The document purports to be an official statement.*

purpose /ˈpɜ:pəs/ *n* **1** [C] thing that one intends to do, get, be, etc; intention: *What is the purpose of the meeting?* ○ *What is your purpose in going to Canada?* ○ *Getting rich seems to be her only purpose in life.* **2** [U] (*fml*) ability to form plans and carry them out; determination: *Her approach to the job lacks purpose.* **3** (idm) **for practical purposes** ⇨ PRACTICAL. **on** ˈ**purpose** not by accident;

intentionally: *'Did he break it accidentally?' 'No, on purpose.'* ○ *She seems to do these things on purpose.* **serve one's/the ˈpurpose** (*fml*) do what is necessary or required: be satisfactory: *We have found a meeting-place that will serve our purpose.* **to little/no/some ˈpurpose** (*fml*) with little/no/ some result or effect: *Money has been invested in the scheme to very little purpose.*

▷ **purpose** *v* [Tt, Tg] (*dated*) intend: *They purpose making/to make a further attempt.*

purposeful /-fl/ *adj* having or showing determination or will-power; resolute: *They dealt with the problem in a purposeful way.* **purposefully** /-fəlɪ/ *adv*: *He strode purposefully into the meeting.*

purposeless *adj* without (a) purpose: *a purposeless existence.* **purposelessly** *adv.*

purposely *adv* on purpose; intentionally: *He was accused of purposely creating difficulties.*

□ **ˌpurpose-ˈbuilt** *adj* (*esp Brit*) made for a particular purpose: *a ˌpurpose-built ˈfactory.*

purr /pɜː(r)/ *v* [I, Ipr] **(a)** (of a cat) make a low continuous vibrating sound: *purring happily.* **(b)** (of machinery) make a similar smooth vibrating sound: *a car engine purring smoothly.*

▷ **purr** *n* purring sound: *the contented purrs of the cat.*

purse[1] /pɜːs/ *n* **1** [C] small bag for money (formerly closed by drawing strings together and now usu with a clasp): *a leather/plastic purse* ○ *Her purse was stolen from her handbag.* Cf WALLET. **2** [sing] money available for spending; funds or resources: *the public purse* ○ *the privy Purse.* **3** [C] sum of money collected and given as a gift or prize: *a purse of £50 000,* eg for the winner of a boxing match. **4** [C] (*US*) handbag. **5** (idm) **hold the ˈpurse-strings** have control of spending: *I can't offer you any more money because I don't hold the purse-strings.* **loosen/tighten the ˈpurse-strings** increase/reduce expenditure.

purse[2] /pɜːs/ *v* [Tn, Tn·p] ~ **sth (up)** draw together or pucker (one's lips) in wrinkles esp as a sign of disapproval or displeasure: *with pursed lips* ○ *purse (up) one's lips.*

purser /ˈpɜːsə(r)/ *n* ship's officer responsible for the accounts, stores, passengers, etc.

pursuance /pəˈsjuːəns; *US* -ˈsuː-/ *n* (idm) **in (the) pursuance of sth** (*fml*) while performing sth; in the course of sth: *injuries suffered in the pursuance of one's duties.*

▷ **pursuant** /-ənt/ *adj* (idm) **pursuant to sth** (*esp law*) in accordance with sth.

pursue /pəˈsjuː; *US* -ˈsuː/ *v* [Tn] (*fml*) **1** follow (sb/ sth), esp in order to catch or kill; chase: *pursue a wild animal, one's prey, a thief* ○ *The police pursued the stolen vehicle along the motorway.* **2** (continue to) be occupied or busy with (sth); go on with: *She decided to pursue her studies after obtaining her first degree.* ○ *I have decided not to pursue* (ie investigate) *the matter any further.*

▷ **pursuer** *n* person who pursues (PURSUE 1): *He managed to avoid his pursuers.*

pursuit /pəˈsjuːt; *US* -ˈsuːt/ *n* (*fml*) **1** [U] ~ **of sth** action of pursuing (PURSUE 2) sth: *The pursuit of profit was the main reason for the changes.* ○ *She devoted her life to the pursuit of pleasure.* **2** [C usu *pl*] thing to which one gives one's time, energy, etc; occupation or activity: *artistic, literary, scientific pursuits* ○ *be engaged in/devote oneself to worthwhile pursuits.* **3** (idm) **in pursuit (of sb/ sth)** with the aim of catching sb/sth: *thirty grown men in pursuit of a single fox.* **in pursuit of sth** with the aim of obtaining sth: *people travelling about the country in pursuit of work.* **in (hot) purˈsuit** pursuing (closely and with determination): *a fox with the hounds in hot pursuit.*

purulent /ˈpjʊərələnt/ *adj* (*medical*) of, containing or discharging pus. ▷ **purulence** /-əns/ *n* [U].

purvey /pəˈveɪ/ *v* [Tn, Dn·pr] ~ **sth (to sb)** (*fml*) provide or supply (esp food, etc) to sb as a trader: *butchers who have purveyed meat to the royal household for generations* ○ *a bureau that purveys information about the stock market to potential investors.*

▷ **purveyance** /-əns/ *n* [U].

purveyor *n* (*fml*) person or firm that supplies goods or services: *Brown and Son, purveyors of fine wines.*

purview /ˈpɜːvjuː/ *n* (*fml*) [U]: *These are questions that lie outside/that do not come within the purview of our inquiry.*

pus /pʌs/ *n* [U] thick yellowish matter formed in and coming out from an infected wound: *The doctor lanced the boil to let the pus out.*

Pusey /ˈpjuːzɪ/ Edward (1800-82), English theologian. He was professor of Hebrew at Oxford University and became the leader of the *Oxford Movement after *Newman.

push[1] /pʊʃ/ *n* **1** [C] act of pushing; shove: *Give the door a hard push.* ○ *He opened the gate with/at one push.* **2** [C] large-scale attack made to break through enemy positions: *The commander decided to postpone the big push until the spring.* **3** [U] (*infml*) determination to succeed; drive: *He hasn't enough push to be a successful salesman.* **4** (idm) **at a ˈpush** (*infml esp Brit*) if one is forced to do so: *We can provide accommodation for six people at a push.* **give sb/get the ˈpush** (*esp Brit infml*) **(a)** dismiss sb/be dismissed from one's job; give sb/get the sack: *He got the push when the new manager came.* **(b)** bring/have brought to an end one's relationship with sb: *He gave his girl-friend the push.* **if/until/when it comes to the ˈpush** if/ until/when a special effort is necessary or a special need arises: *If it comes to the push, we shall have to use our savings.*

□ **ˈpush-start** *v* [Tn] start (a motor vehicle) by pushing it along to make the engine turn. — *n*: *We'll have to give it a push-start, I'm afraid.*

push[2] /pʊʃ/ *v* **1 (a)** [I] use force in order to move sth away from oneself: *You push from the back and I'll pull at the front.* ○ *Push hard and the lever will go down.* **(b)** [Tn, Tn·pr, Cn·a] use force on (sth) in order to move it away from oneself, forward or to a different position: *You can pull a rope, but you can't push it!* ○ *push the pram up the hill* ○ *push the table a bit nearer the wall* ○ *He pushed the door open.* ○ (*fig*) *push a problem to the back of one's mind.* ⇨ illus at PULL. **(c)** [Ipr, Ip, Tn·pr, Tn·p] move forward using force: *The crowd pushed past (us).* ○ *We had to push our way through (the crowd).* **2** [Ipr, Tn] ~ **(on/against) sth** exert pressure on sth; press: *He pushed hard against the door with his shoulder.* ○ *Push the doorbell.* ○ *You can stop the machine by pushing the red button.* **3 (a)** [Tn, Tn·pr, Cn·t] (*infml*) try to make (sb) do sth (that he does not want to do); drive or urge: *One has to push the child or she will do no work at all.* ○ *She was pushed into going to university by her parents.* ○ *We pushed him hard to take up science.* **(b)** [Tn·pr] ~ **sb for sth** try to obtain sth from sb by putting pressure on him: *push sb for payment* ○ *We shall have to push them for a quick decision.* **4** [Tn] (*infml*) persuade people to buy (goods, etc) or accept (an idea, etc): *You will have to push the new product to win sales — there's lots of competition.* ○ *Unless you push your claim, you will not get satisfaction.* **5** [Tn] (*infml*) sell (illegal drugs) to drug-users: *She was arrested for pushing heroin.* ⇨ Usage at SELL. **6** (idm) **be pushed for sth** (*infml*) not have enough of sth: *be pushed for money, time, etc.* **be pushed to do sth** (*infml*) have difficulty doing sth: *We'll be pushed to get there in time.* **push the ˈboat out** (*infml*) celebrate regardless of the expense: *This is the last party we shall give, so let's really push the boat out.* **push one's ˈluck** (*infml*) risk sth in a bold and often foolish way, hoping that one's good fortune will continue: *You didn't get caught last time, but don't push your luck!* **push up (the) ˈdaisies** (*infml joc*) be dead and in one's grave: *I shall be pushing up daisies by the time the project is finished.* **7** (phr v) **push sb about/around** (*infml*) order sb to do things in a bullying way; order sb about/around. **push ahead/forward/on** continue on one's way: *Let's push on — it's nearly nightfall.* **push ahead/ forward/on (with sth)** continue doing sth, in a determined way: *push ahead with one's plans.* **push along** (*infml*) leave: *Goodbye — I'd better be pushing along now.* **push for sth** make repeated and urgent requests for sth; press for sth: *They are pushing for electoral reform.* **push sth forward** force others to consider or notice sth: *He repeatedly pushed forward his own claim.* **push oneself forward** ambitiously draw attention to oneself. **push off** (*infml*) (often as an impolite command) go away: *Push off! We don't want you here.* **push (sth) off/out** push against a bank, etc with an oar or a pole, so that a boat, etc moves away. **push sb/ sth over** cause sb/sth to fall or overturn: *Several children were pushed over in the rush to leave.* **push sth through** get sth accepted or completed quickly: *push a plan through the committee stage.* **push sth up** cause (esp prices) to rise steadily: *A shortage of building land will push property values up.*

▷ **pusher 1** (*infml derog*) person who tries constantly to gain an advantage for himself. **2** (*sl*) person who sells drugs illegally; drug pedlar.

pushing *adj* **1** = PUSHY. **2** [pred] (*infml*) having nearly reached (a certain age): *pushing forty, fifty, sixty, etc.*

□ **ˈpush-bike** *n* (*infml*) bicycle that is operated by pressing the pedals and not by a motor.

ˈpush-button *adj* [attrib] operated automatically by pressing a button: *a radio with push-button tuning.*

ˈpush-cart *n* small cart pushed by hand, eg a barrow for selling fruit, etc.

ˈpush-chair (*Brit*) (also *esp US* **stroller**) *n* small folding chair on wheels for a baby or small child to be pushed around in.

ˈpush-over *n* (*sl*) **(a)** thing that is very easily done, esp a contest that is easily won: *Winning that match was a push-over.* **(b)** client, opponent, etc who is easily convinced or won over: *Getting money from her is easy — she's a push-over.*

ˌpush-ˈpull *adj* (of electrical equipment) containing two valves, etc operated alternately by alternating current: *a push-pull amplifier.*

ˈpush-up *n* (*esp US*) = PRESS-UP (PRESS[2]).

Pushkin /ˈpʊʃkɪn/ Alexander (1799-1837), Russian poet. He is regarded as Russia's greatest author and all later writers have been influenced by him in some way. He is admired for the economy and elegance of his style. He wrote much lyric poetry, several romantic verse narratives including *Eugene Onegin,* and some vivid short stories of Russian life.

pushy /ˈpʊʃɪ/ (**-ier, -iest**) (also **pushing**) *adj* (*infml derog*) trying constantly to draw attention to oneself and gain an advantage; self-assertive: *He made himself unpopular by being so pushy.* ▷ **pushily** /-ɪlɪ/ *adv.* **pushiness** *n* [U].

pusillanimous /ˌpjuːsɪˈlænɪməs/ *adj* (*fml derog*) lacking courage; timid. ▷ **pusillanimity** /ˌpjuːsɪləˈnɪmətɪ/ *n* [U]. **pusillanimously** *adv.*

puss /pʊs/ *n* **1** (word used to call a) cat. **2** (*infml*) playful or coquettish girl: *She's a sly puss.*

▷ **pussy** /ˈpʊsɪ/ *n* **1** (also **ˈpussy-cat**) (used by and to young children) cat. **2** (⚠ *sl*) female genitals; vulva.

□ **ˈpussyfoot** *v* [I, Ip] ~ **(about/around)** (*infml usu derog*) act (too) cautiously or timidly: *Stop pussyfooting around and say what you mean.*

ˈpussy willow willow tree with soft furry catkins.

pustule /ˈpʌstjuːl; *US* -tʃuːl/ *n* (*medical*) pimple or blister, esp one containing pus.

put /pʊt/ *v* (**-tt-**, *pt, pp* **put**) **1 (a)** [Tn·pr, Tn·p] move (sth/sb), esp away from oneself, so that it/he is in the specified place or position: *She put the book on the table.* ○ *'Where did you put the scissors?' 'I put them (back) in the drawer.'* ○ *Did you put sugar in my tea?* ○ *He put his hands in his pockets.* ○ *She put her arm round his shoulders.* ○ *She put her hand to her mouth.* ○ *You've put the picture too high up (on the wall).* ○ *The Americans put a man on the moon in 1969.* ○ *It's time to put the baby to bed.* ○ *Maradona put the ball in the net,* ie scored a goal in a football match. **(b)** [Tn·pr] fit or fix (sth) to sth else: *Will you please put* (ie sew) *a patch on these trousers?* ○ *We must put a new lock on the front door.* **(c)** [Tn·pr] thrust (sth) in a specified direction: *She put a knife between his ribs.* ○ *He put* *his fist through a plate-glass door.* (**d**) [Tn·pr, Tn·p] write or mark (sth) on sth: *put one's signature to a document* ○ *put a cross against sb's name* ○ *Put your name here.* **2** [Tn·pr] cause (sb/sth) to be in the specified state or condition: *The incident put her in a bad mood.* ○ *Your decision puts me in an awkward position.* ○ *The injury to her back will put her out of action for several weeks.* ○ *The Russians plan to put a satellite into orbit round Mars.* **3** [Tn·pr] rate or classify (sb/sth) in the specified way: *I wouldn't put him among the greatest composers.* ○ *I put her in the top rank of modern novelists.* ○ *As a writer I'd put him on a par/level with Joyce.* **4** [Tn, Tn·pr] (used esp with a following *adv* or in questions after *how*) express or state (sth): *She put it very tactfully.* ○ *That's very well put.* ○ *How shall I put it?* ○ *As T S Eliot puts it...* ○ *'The election result was a disaster for the country.' 'I wouldn't put it quite like that.'* **5** [Tn] throw (esp the shot) with an upward movement of the arm, as an athletic exercise. Cf SHOT-PUT (SHOT[1]). **6** (idm) **not put it past sb (to do sth)** (*infml*) (used with *would*) consider sb capable of doing sth malicious, illegal, etc: *I wouldn't put it past him to steal money from his own grandmother!* **put it to sb that...** suggest to sb that it is true that...; invite sb to agree that...: *I put it to you that you are the only person who had a motive for the crime.* **put sb ˈthrough it** (*infml*) force sb to undergo sth demanding or unpleasant: *They really put you through it* (ie ask you difficult questions, etc) *at the interview.* **put toˈgether** (used after a *n* or *ns* referring to a group of people or things) combined: *Your department spent more last year than all the other departments put together.* (For other idioms containing **put**, see entries for *ns, adjs*, etc, eg **put one's foot in it** ⇨ FOOT[1]; **put sth right** ⇨ RIGHT[1].).

7 (phr v) **put (sth) aˈbout** (*nautical*) (cause sth to) change direction: *The ship put slowly about.* ○ *The captain put the ship about.* **put sth about** spread or circulate (false news, rumours, etc): *He's always putting about malicious rumours.* ○ *It's being put about that the Prime Minister may resign.*

put sth above sth ⇨ PUT STH BEFORE/ABOVE STH.

put sth across sb (*infml*) trick sb into accepting a claim, etc that is worthless or untrue: *Are you trying to put one across me?* **put oneself/sth aˈcross/ˈover (to sb)** communicate or convey (one's personality, an idea, etc) to sb: *He doesn't know how to put himself across at interviews.* ○ *She's very good at putting her ideas across.*

put sth aˈside (**a**) place sth to one side: *She put the newspaper aside and picked up a book.* (**b**) save (a sum of money) to use later; reserve (an item) for a customer to collect later: *She's put aside a tidy sum for her retirement.* ○ *We'll put the suit aside for you, Mr Parkinson.* (**c**) disregard, ignore or forget sth: *They decided to put aside their differences.*

put sth at sth calculate or estimate (the size, cost, etc of sth) to be (the specified weight, amount, etc): *I would put his age at about sixty.* ○ *'What would you put the price of this car at?' 'I'd put it at £15 000.'*

put sb aˈway (often passive) (*infml*) confine sb in a prison or mental hospital: *He was put away for ten years for armed robbery* ○ *She went a bit odd and had to be put away.* **put sth aˈway** (**a**) put sth in a box, drawer, etc because one has finished using it: *Put your toys away in the cupboard, when you've finished playing.* ○ *I'm just going to put the car away*, ie in the garage. (**b**) save (money) to use later: *She's got a few thousand pounds put away for her retirement.* (**c**) (*infml*) eat or drink (a large quantity of food or drink): *He must have put away half a bottle of whisky last night.* ○ *I don't know how he manages to put it all away!*

put sth ˈback (**a**) return sth to its proper place; replace sth: *Please put the dictionary back on the shelf when you've finished with it.* (**b**) move (the hands of a clock) back to give the correct time: *My watch is fast; it needs putting back five minutes.* (**c**) move sth to a later time or date; postpone sth: *This afternoon's meeting has been put back to next week.* (**d**) cause sth to be delayed: *The lorry drivers' strike has put back our deliveries by over a month.* (**e**) (*infml*) drink (a large quantity of alcohol): *By midnight he had put back nearly two bottles of wine.*

put sth before/above sth treat or regard sth as more important than sth else: *He puts his children's welfare before all other considerations.*

put sth ˈby save (money) to use in the future: *She has a fair amount of money put by.*

put (sth) ˈdown (of an aeroplane or its pilot) land; land (an aeroplane, etc): *He put (the glider) down in a field.* **put sb down** (**a**) (of a bus, coach, etc) allow sb to get off: *The bus stopped to put down some passengers.* (**b**) (*infml*) humiliate or snub sb: *He's always putting his wife down in public.* **put sth down** (**a**) place sth on a table, shelf, etc; set down sth that is dangerous or a nuisance to others: *Put down that knife before you hurt somebody!* ○ *I can't put this novel down*, ie because I am enjoying it so much. (**b**) place sth in storage; place (wine) in a cellar to mature: *I put down a couple of cases of claret last year.* (**c**) write sth down; make a note of sth: *I'm having a party next Saturday; put it down in your diary so you don't forget.* (**d**) stop, suppress or abolish sth by force or authority: *put down a rebellion, a revolt, an uprising, etc* ○ *The military junta is determined to put down all political opposition.* (**e**) (often passive) kill (an animal) because it is old or sick; destroy sth: *The horse broke a leg in the fall and had to be put down.* ○ *Our cat was getting so old and sick that we had her put down.* (**f**) (esp in Parliament) include sth on the agenda for a meeting or debate: *The Opposition plan to put down a censure motion on the Government's handling of the affair.* **put sb down as sb** consider sb to be (the specified type of person); take sb to be sb: *I put him down as a retired naval officer.* **put sb down for sth** (**a**) write down that sb is willing or wishes to buy or contribute sth: *Put me down for three tickets for Saturday's performance.* (**b**) put (sb's name) on the waiting-list for admission to a private school: *They've put their son down for Eton.* **put sth down to sth** (**a**) charge (an amount or item) to a particular account: *Would you put these shoes down to my account, please?* (**b**) consider that sth is caused by sth; attribute sth to sth: *What do you put her success down to?* ○ *I put it all down to her hard work and initiative.*

put sth forth (*fml*) (of trees and plants) send out or produce (buds, shoots, etc): *Spring has come and the hedges are putting forth new leaves.*

put oneself/sb forward present oneself or propose or recommend sb as a candidate for a job, position, etc: *Two left-wingers have been put forward for the Labour Party's National Executive.* ○ *Can I put you/your name forward for golf club secretary?* **put sth forward** (**a**) move (the hands of a clock) forward to give the correct time: *Put your watch forward; you're five minutes slow.* (**b**) move sth to an earlier time or date: *We've put forward (the date of) our wedding by one week.* (**c**) advance, propose or suggest sth for discussion: *put forward an argument, a plan, a suggestion, etc* ○ *She is putting forward radical proposals for electoral reform.*

put ˈin interrupt another speaker in order to say sth; interject: *'But what about us?' he put in.* **put sb in** (**a**) give duties to sb (eg in an office building): *put in a caretaker, a security man, etc.* (**b**) elect (a political party) to govern a country: *The electorate put the Tories in with an increased majority in 1983.* (**c**) (of the team that wins the toss in cricket) ask (the opposing team) to bat first: *Australia won the toss and put England in (to bat).* **put sth in** (**a**) install or fit sth: *We put new central heating in when we moved here.* ○ *We're having a new shower put in.* (**b**) include or insert sth in a story, narrative, etc: *If you're writing to your mother, don't forget to put in something about her coming to stay.* (**c**) present sth formally; submit sth: *put in a claim for damages, higher wages.* (**d**) manage to strike (a blow) or say sth: *Tyson put in some telling blows to Tucker's chin.* ○ *Could I put in a word* (ie say sth) *at this point?* (**e**) spend (a period of time) working at sth: *She often puts in twelve hours' work a day.* ○ *I must put in an hour's gardening this evening.* **put sth in; put sth into sth/doing sth** devote (time, effort, etc) to sth: *Thank you for al the hard work you've put in.* ○ *We've put a grea deal of time and effort into this project.* ○ *She' putting a lot of work into improving her French*

put in (at...)/put into... (of a ship, its crew, etc enter (a port or harbour): *The boat put in at Lagos put into Lagos for repairs.* **put in for sth** appl formally for sth: *Are you going to put in for tha job?* **put oneself/sb/sth in for sth** enter oneself sb/sth for (a competition): *She's put herself in fo the 100 metres and the long jump.* **put sb in for st** recommend sb for (a job, an award, etc): *Th commanding officer put Sergeant Williams in for medal for bravery.*

put ˈoff (of a boat, its crew, etc) move away from pier, jetty, etc: *We put off from the quay.* **put sb of** (**a**) (of a vehicle, boat, etc) stop in order to allow s to get off: *I asked the bus driver to put me off nea the town centre.* (**b**) postpone or cancel a meeting o an engagement with sb: *We've invited friends t supper and it's too late to put them off now*, ie to te them not to come. ○ *She put him off with the excus that* (ie said that she could not see him because *she had too much work to do.* (**c**) make sb fee dislike; displease, repel or disgust sb: *He's a goo salesman, but his offhand manner does tend to pu people off.* ○ *Don't be put off by his gruff exterio he's really very kind underneath.* **put sb off (sth** disturb sb who is doing sth; distract sb: *Don't pu me off when I'm trying to concentrate.* ○ *The sudde noise put her off her game.* **put sb off sth/doing st** cause sb to lose his interest in or liking or appetit for sth: *The accident put her off driving for life.* *She was put off maths by a bullying an incompetent teacher.* **put sth off** switch sth of *Could you put the lights off before you leave?* **pu sth off; put off doing sth** postpone, delay or defe sth: *We've had to put our wedding off unt September.* ○ *This afternoon's meeting will have t be put off.* ○ *She keeps putting off going to th dentist.*

put it ˈon (esp in the continuous tenses) pretend t be angry, sad, remorseful, etc: *She wasn't angr really; she was only putting it on.* **put sth on (a** clothe oneself with (a garment): *put on one's coa gloves, hat, skirt, trousers, etc* ○ *What dress shall put on for the party?* (**b**) apply sth to one's skin: *pu on lipstick, hand-cream, etc* ○ *She's just putting o her make-up.* (**c**) switch sth on; operate sth: *put o the light, oven, radio, television, etc* ○ *Let's put th kettle on and have a cup of tea.* ○ *She put on th brakes suddenly.* (**d**) make sth begin to play: *put o a record, tape, compact disc, etc* ○ *Do you mind if put some music on?* (**e**) grow fatter or heavier (b the specified amount): *put on a stone in weight How many pounds did you put on over Christmas* (**f**) add (a train, coach, etc) to an existing servic *British Rail are putting on extra trains during th holiday period.* (**g**) produce or present (a play, a exhibition, etc): *The local drama group are puttin on 'Macbeth' at the Playhouse.* (**h**) move (the hand of a clock) forward to show a later time. (**i**) preten to have sth; assume or adopt sth: *put on a silly fac a Liverpool accent, a wounded expression* ○ *Don put on that innocent look; we know you ate all th biscuits.* ○ *He seems very sincere, but it's all put o*

put sth on sth (**a**) add (an amount of money) to th price or cost of sth: *The government has put te pence on the price of a gallon of petrol.* (**b**) impose o place (a tax, etc) on sth: *put a duty on wine.* (**c** place (a bet) on sth: *I've put £10 on 'Black Widow' i the 3.45 at Newmarket.* ○ *I've never put money on horse.* **put sb on to sb/onto sb** (**a**) help sb to fin meet or see sb; put sb in touch with sb: *put sb on a dentist, lawyer, plumber, etc* ○ *Could you put m on to a good accountant?* (**b**) inform (the police, et where sb is, so he can be caught: *Detectives huntin the gang were put on to them by an anonymou telephone call.* **put sb on to sth/onto sth** inform s of the existence of (sth interesting o advantageous); tell sb about sth: *'Who put you on this restaurant? It's superb!' 'Friends put us on t it.'*

put oneself ˈout (*infml*) do sth even though it

inconvenient for oneself: *Please don't put yourself out on our account.* ○ *She's always ready to put herself out to help others.* **put sb out** (**a**) make sb unconscious (by striking him, with an anaesthetic, etc): *He put his opponent out in the fifth round.* (**b**) cause inconvenience to sb: *I hope our arriving late didn't put them out.* (**c**) upset or offend sb: *She was most put out by his rudeness.* ○ *He looked rather put out.* **put sth out** (**a**) take sth out of one's house and leave it, esp for sb to collect: *put out the dustbins, the empty milk bottles, etc* ○ *Have you put the cat out yet?* (**b**) place sth where it will be noticed and used: *put out ashtrays, bowls of peanuts* ○ *put out clean towels for a guest.* (**c**) (of a plant) sprout or display (leaves, buds, etc): *The trees are beginning to put out shoots.* (**d**) produce or generate sth: *The plant puts out 500 new cars a week.* (**e**) issue, publish or broadcast sth (usu for a particular purpose): *Police have put out a description of the man they wish to question.* (**f**) cause sth to stop burning: *Firemen soon put the fire out.* ○ *put out a candle, cigarette, pipe.* (**g**) switch sth off: *put out the lamp, light, gas fire.* (**h**) dislocate (a part of the body): *She fell off her horse and put her shoulder out.* (**i**) cause (a figure, result, calculation, etc) to be wrong: *The devaluation of the pound has put our estimates out by several thousands.* **put sth out** (**to sb**) (**a**) give (a job, task, etc) to a worker or manufacturer who is not one's employee and will do the work in another place: *A lot of proof-reading is put out to freelancers.* ○ *All repairs are done on the premises and not put out.* (**b**) lend (money) to sb in order to get interest on it: *Banks are putting out more and more money to people buying their own homes.* **put ˈout** (**to...**/**from...**) (of a boat or its crew) move out to sea from a harbour, port, etc: *put out to sea* ○ *We put out from Liverpool.*

put oneself/sth over (**to sb**) ⇨ PUT ONESELF/STH ACROSS/OVER (TO SB). **put sth over on sb** (*infml*) persuade sb to accept a claim, story, etc that is untrue or worthless: *He's not the sort of man you can put one over on.*

put sth through complete or conclude (a plan, programme, etc) successfully: *put through a business deal* ○ *The government is putting through some radical social reforms.* **put sb through sth** (**a**) cause sb to undergo (an ordeal, a test, etc): *You have put your family through much suffering.* ○ *Trainee commandos are put through an exhausting assault course.* (**b**) pay for sb to attend (the specified school, college, etc): *He put all his children through boarding-school.* **put sb/sth through** (**to sb/...**) allow sb to speak to sb by making a telephone connection: *Could you put me through to the manager, please.* ○ *I'm trying to put a call through to Paris.*

put sb to sth make sb undergo or suffer (inconvenience, trouble, etc): *I do hope we're not putting you to too much trouble.* ○ *We've already been put to great inconvenience.* **put sth to sb** (**a**) express, communicate or submit sth to sb: *Your proposal will be put to the board of directors.* (**b**) ask sb (a question): *The audience are now invited to put questions to the speaker.* (**c**) ask sb to vote on (an issue, a proposal, etc): *Let's put the resolution to the meeting.* ○ *The question of strike action must be put to union members.*

put sth together construct or repair sth by fitting parts together; assemble sth: *put together a model aeroplane* ○ *He took the machine to pieces and then put it together again.* ○ (*fig*) *put together an essay, a meal, a case for the defence.* Cf PUT TOGETHER (PUT[1] 6).

put sth towards sth give (money) as a contribution to sth: *He puts half of his salary each month towards the skiing holiday he's planning.*

put up sth offer or present (resistance, a struggle, etc) in a battle, game, etc: *They surrendered without putting up much of a fight.* ○ *The team put up a splendid performance*, ie played very well. **put sb up** (**a**) provide food and accommodation for sb: *We can put you up for the night.* (**b**) present sb as a candidate in an election: *The Green Party hopes to put up a number of candidates in the General Election.* **put sth up** (**a**) raise or hoist sth: *put up a flag* ○ *Put your hand up if you want to ask a question.* ○ *She's put her hair up*, ie She is wearing it coiled on top of her head. (**b**) build or erect sth: *put up a fence, memorial, shed, tent* ○ *Many ugly blocks of flats were put up in the 1960s.* (**c**) fix or fasten sth in a place where it will be seen; display sth: *put up Christmas decorations, a notice, a poster* ○ *The team will be put up on the notice-board.* (**d**) raise or increase sth: *My landlord's threatening to put the rent up by £10 a week.* (**e**) provide or lend (money): *A local businessman has put up the £500 000 needed to save the football club.* (**f**) present (an idea, etc) for discussion or consideration: *put up an argument, a case, a proposal, etc.* **put ˈup** (**at...**) obtain food and lodging (at a place); stay: *They put up at an inn for the night.* **put** (**oneself**) **up for sth** offer oneself as a candidate for sth: *She is putting (herself) up for election to the committee.* **put sb up** (**for sth**) propose or nominate sb for a position: *We want to put you up for club treasurer.* ○ *To join the club you have to be put up by an existing member.* **put sb up to sth/doing sth** (*infml*) urge or encourage sb to do sth mischievous or illegal: *I can't believe he'd do a thing like that on his own. He must have been put up to it by some of the older boys.* **put up with sb/sth** tolerate or bear sb/sth: *I don't know how she puts up with him/his cruelty to her.*

□ **ˈput-down** *n* humiliating remark; snub. **ˌput-up ˈjob** (*infml*) scheme to cheat or deceive sb. **ˈput-upon** *adj* (of a person) badly treated; misused or exploited: *a much put-upon person* ○ *I'm beginning to feel just a little put-upon.*

putative /ˈpju:tətɪv/ *adj* [attrib] (*fml*) generally supposed to be; reputed: *his putative father.*

putrefy /ˈpju:trɪfaɪ/ *v* (*pt, pp* **-fied**) [I, Tn] (cause sth to) rot or decay; become or make putrid.
▷ **putrefaction** /ˌpju:trɪˈfækʃn/ *n* [U] **1** (process of) putrefying. **2** rotting matter.

putrescent /pju:ˈtresnt/ *adj* (*fml*) (**a**) in the process of rotting: *a putrescent corpse.* (**b**) of or accompanying this process: *a putrescent smell.* ▷ **putrescence** /-sns/ *n* [U].

putrid /ˈpju:trɪd/ *adj* **1** (**a**) (esp of animal or vegetable matter) that has become rotten; decomposed. (**b**) (rotting and therefore) foul-smelling; noxious: *a pile of rotten, putrid fish* ○ *the putrid smell of rotting fish.* **2** (*infml*) very distasteful or unpleasant or of poor quality: *putrid weather* ○ *Why did you paint the room that putrid colour?*

putsch /pʊtʃ/ *n* attempt to overthrow a government by force; political revolution.

putt /pʌt/ *v* [I, Tn] (in golf) hit (the ball) with a light stroke so that it rolls across the ground into or nearer to the hole, usu from a position on the green[2](5): *You need to practise putting (the ball).*
▷ **putt** *n* putting stroke: *She took three putts* (ie to get the ball into the hole) *from the edge of the green.* **putter** *n* **1** golf club used for putting. **2** person who putts.
□ **ˈputting-green** *n* area of smooth closely-cut grass for putting on, esp one with several holes like a miniature golf course.

puttee /ˈpʌtɪ/ *n* (esp *pl*) long narrow strip of cloth that is wound round the leg from the ankle to the knee for protection and support, esp as part of an army uniform.

putter (*US*) = POTTER[1].

putty /ˈpʌtɪ/ *n* **1** [U] soft paste, a mixture of chalk powder and linseed oil, which is used for fixing glass in window frames, etc and becomes hard when it has set. **2** (idm) (**be**) **putty in sb's ˈhands** (be) easily influenced or controlled by sb: *She was a woman of such beauty and charm that men were putty in her hands.*
▷ **putty** *v* (*pt, pp* **puttied**) **1** [Tn, Tn·p] ~ **sth** (**up**) fill (a hole, gap etc) with putty. **2** (phr v) **putty sth in** fix sth in place with putty: *putty a pane of glass in.*

puzzle /ˈpʌzl/ *n* **1** [C usu *sing*] question that is difficult to understand or answer; mystery: *Their reason for doing it is still a puzzle to me.* **2** [C] (often in compounds) problem or toy that is designed to test a person's knowledge, ingenuity, skill, etc: *crossword puzzles* ○ *a jigsaw puzzle* ○ *find the answer to/solve a puzzle* ○ *set a puzzle for sb/set sb a puzzle.*
▷ **puzzle** *v* **1** [Tn] make (sb) think hard; perplex: *Her reply puzzled me.* ○ *I am puzzled by his failure to reply/that he hasn't replied to my letter.* ○ *He puzzled his brains* (ie thought hard) *to find the answer.* ○ *The sudden fall in the value of the dollar has puzzled financial experts.* ○ *They are puzzled (about) what to do next/how to react.* **2** [Ipr] ~ **over sth** think deeply about sth in order to understand it: *She's been puzzling over his strange letter for weeks.* **3** [Tn·p] ~ **sth out** (try to) find the answer or solution to sth by thinking hard: *The teacher left the children to puzzle out the answer to the problem themselves.* **puzzled** *adj* unable to understand; perplexed or confused: *She listened with a puzzled expression on her face.* **puzzler** /ˈpʌzlə(r)/ *n* (*infml*) person or thing that puzzles: *That question is a real puzzler!* **puzzlement** /ˈpʌzlmənt/ *n* [U] (state of) being puzzled; bewilderment: *He stared at the words in complete puzzlement.* **puzzling** /ˈpʌzlɪŋ/ *adj*: *a puzzling statement, affair, attitude.*

PVC /ˌpi: vi: ˈsi/ *abbr* polyvinyl chloride (a type of plastic): *The seat covers were (made of) PVC.*

Pvt *abbr* (*US*) = PTE.

PW /ˌpi: ˈdʌblju:/ *abbr* (*Brit*) Policewoman: *PW (Christine) Bell.* Cf WPC.

PWR /ˌpi: ˌdʌblju: ˈɑ:(r)/ *abbr* pressurized-water reactor.

PX /ˌpi: ˈeks/ *abbr* (*US*) Post Exchange. Cf NAAFI.

pygmy (also **pigmy**) /ˈpɪgmɪ/ *n* **1 Pygmy** member of a tribal group of very short people living in equatorial Africa. **2** very small person or species of animal; dwarf: [attrib] *the pygmy shrew.*

pyjamas (also *esp US* **pajamas**) /pəˈdʒɑ:məz; *US* -ˈdʒæm-/ *n* [pl] **1** loose-fitting jacket and trousers worn for sleeping in, esp by men: *a pair of pyjamas* ○ *He was wearing striped pyjamas.* **2** loose trousers tied round the waist, worn by Muslims of both sexes in India and Pakistan. **3** (idm) **be the cat's whiskers/pyjamas** ⇨ CAT[1]. ▷ **pyjama** (*US* **pajama**) *adj* [attrib]: *pyjama bottom(s)/top/trousers/jacket.*

pylon /ˈpaɪlən; *US* ˈpaɪlɒn/ *n* **1** tall steel framework used for carrying overhead high-voltage electric cables. **2** tall tower or post that marks a path for aircraft landing.

pyorrhoea (also *esp US* **pyorrhea**) /ˌpaɪəˈrɪə/ *n* [U] diseased condition of the gums that causes them to shrink and the teeth to become loose.

pyracantha /ˌpaɪərəˈkænθə/ *n* [C, U] evergreen thorny shrub with white flowers and red berries.

pyramid /ˈpɪrəmɪd/ *n* **1** structure with a flat square or triangular base and sloping sides that meet in a point at the top, esp one of those built of stone by the ancient Egyptians as tombs. **2** (esp in geometry) solid figure of this shape with a base of three or more sides. ⇨ illus at CUBE. **3** thing or pile of things that has the shape of a pyramid: *a pyramid of tins in a shop window.*
▷ **pyramidal** /pɪˈræmɪdl/ *adj* having the shape of a pyramid.
□ **pyramid ˈselling** (*commerce*) method of selling goods in which a distributor pays a premium for the right to sell a company's goods and then sells part of that right to other distributors.

pyre /ˈpaɪə(r)/ *n* large pile of wood, etc for burning a dead body as part of a funeral ceremony.

Pyrenees /pɪrəˈni:z/ **the Pyrenees** mountain range separating France and Spain, over 3 300 m (11 000 ft) at its highest point.

pyrethrum /paɪˈri:θrəm/ *n* **1** [C] chrysanthemum with finely divided leaves. **2** [U] insecticide made from its dried flowers.

Pyrex /ˈpaɪreks/ *n* [U] (*propr*) type of heat-resistant glass used esp for cooking and serving food in: [attrib] *a Pyrex dish.*

pyrites /paɪˈraɪti:z; *US* pɪˈraɪti:z/ *n* [U] mineral that is a sulphide of iron (*iron pyrites*) or copper and iron (*copper pyrites*).

pyromania /ˌpaɪrəʊˈmeɪnɪə/ *n* [U] illness that causes an uncontrollable desire to start fires.

▷ **pyromaniac** /-nɪæk/ *n* person who suffers from pyromania.

pyrotechnics /ˌpaɪrəˈteknɪks/ *n* **1** [sing *v*] art of making fireworks. **2** [pl] (*fml*) public display of fireworks as an entertainment. **3** [pl] (*fig sometimes derog*) brilliant display of skill, eg by an orator, a musician, etc. ▷ **pyrotechnic** *adj* [usu attrib].

Pyrrhic victory /ˌpɪrɪk ˈvɪktərɪ/ victory that was not worth winning because the winner has lost so much in winning it.

Pythagoras /paɪˈθægərəs/ (late 6th century BC), Greek philosopher and astronomer. He believed that after death souls moved on to inhabit another person or animal. He discovered that the earth rotates on its axis, and may have invented the theorem named after him. ▷ **Pythagorean** /ˌpaɪˌθægəˈriːən/ *adj*.

□ **Pyˈthagoras' theorem** theorem stating that the area of the square on the hypotenuse of a right-angled triangle is equal to the sum of the areas of the squares on the other two sides.

python /ˈpaɪθn; *US* ˈpaɪθɒn/ *n* large snake that crushes and kills its prey by twisting itself round it.

pyx /pɪks/ *n* (in the Christian Church) container in which bread that has been consecrated for Holy Communion is kept.

Q, q

Q, q /kju:/ *n* (*pl* **Q's, q's** /kju:z/) **1** the seventeenth letter of the English alphabet: *'Queen' starts with (a) Q/'Q'.* **2** (idm) **mind one's p's and q's** ⇨ MIND[2].

Q /kju:/ *abbr* question: *Q and A*, ie question and answer ○ *Qs 1-5 are compulsory*, eg in an exam paper. Cf A 2.

Qatar /ˈkætɑ:(r)/ country in the Middle East, a peninsula on the west coast of the Persian Gulf; pop approx 341 000; official language Arabic; capital Doha; unit of currency riyal (= 100 dirhams). The country is mostly desert and agriculture is extremely limited. The economy is based almost entirely on its oil and petrochemical industry. ⇨ map at ARABIAN PENINSULA. ▷ **Qatari** /kæˈtɑ:rɪ/ *adj, n.*

QB /ˌkju: ˈbi:/ *abbr* (*Brit law*) Queen's Bench. Cf KB.

QC /ˌkju: ˈsi:/ *abbr* (*Brit law*) Queen's Counsel: *Mr David Norman QC.* Cf KC.

QED /ˌkju: i: ˈdi/ *abbr* which was to be proved (Latin *quod erat demonstrandum*).

QE2 /ˌkju i: ˈtu:/ *abbr* Queen Elizabeth the Second (a cruise liner): *a holiday on the QE2.*

qr *abbr* quarter(s).

qt *abbr* quart(s).

qto (also **4to**) *abbr* quarto.

qty *abbr* (*commerce*) (esp on order forms) quantity.

qua /kweɪ/ *prep* (*fml*) in the capacity or character of (sb/sth); as: *I don't dislike sport qua sport — I just think it's rather a waste of time.*

quack[1] /kwæk/ *interj, n* harsh sound made by a duck.

▷ **quack** *v* [I] make the sound of a duck.

□ ˈ**quack-quack** *n* (used by and to small children) duck.

quack[2] /kwæk/ *n* (*infml*) person who pretends to have special knowledge and skill, esp in medicine: *Don't be taken in — he's just a quack.* ○ [attrib] *a quack cure for arthritis.*

▷ ˈ**quackery** /-ərɪ/ *n* [U] methods or practices of a quack.

quad /kwɒd/ *n* (*infml*) **1** = QUADRANGLE 2. **2** = QUADRUPLET.

Quadragesima /ˌkwɒdrəˈdʒesɪmə/ *n* the first Sunday in Lent.

quadrangle /ˈkwɒdræŋgl/ *n* **1** plane figure with four sides, esp a square or rectangle. **2** (*fml*) four-sided courtyard surrounded by large buildings, eg in an Oxford college.

▷ **quadrangular** /kwɒˈdræŋgjʊlə(r)/ *adj* having four sides.

quadrant /ˈkwɒdrənt/ *n* **1** quarter of a circle or of its circumference. ⇨ illus at CIRCLE. **2** instrument with an arc of 90° marked off in degrees, for measuring angles.

quadraphonic (also **quadrophonic**) /ˌkwɒdrəˈfɒnɪk/ *adj* (of sound-reproduction) using four transmission channels.

▷ **quadraphony** (also **quadrophony**) /kwɒˈdrɒfənɪ/ *n* [U] system for recording and reproducing sound in this way.

quadratic equation /kwɒˌdrætɪk ɪˈkweɪʒn/ (*algebra*) equation that uses the square (and no higher power) of an unknown quantity, eg $x^2 + 2x - 8 = 0$.

quadrennial /kwɒˈdrenɪəl/ *adj* **1** lasting for four years. **2** happening every fourth year.

quadr(i)- *comb form* **1** having four parts: *quadrilateral* ○ *quadruped.* **2** being one of four parts: *quadrant* ○ *quadruplet.*

quadrilateral /ˌkwɒdrɪˈlætərəl/ *n, adj* (plane figure) with four sides.

quadrille /kwəˈdrɪl/ *n* (music for a) square dance for four couples: *play/dance a quadrille.*

quadrillion /kwɒˈdrɪlɪən/ *pron, det, n* (*pl* unchanged or ~**s**) (after *a* or *one*, a number, or an indication of quantity) **1** (*Brit*) number shown by

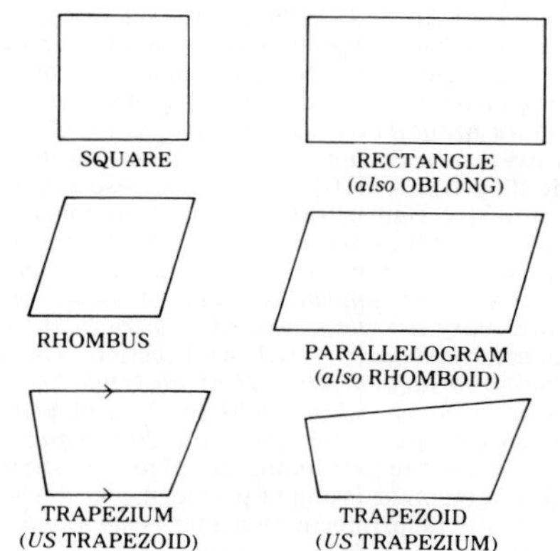

quadrilaterals

1 followed by 24 zeros; one million to the power of 4. **2** (*US*) number shown by 1 followed by 15 zeros; one thousand to the power of 5.

quadrophonic, quadrophony ⇨ QUADRAPHONIC.

quadruped /ˈkwɒdrʊped/ *n* four-footed animal.

quadruple /ˈkwɒdrʊpl; *US* kwɒˈdru:pl/ *adj* consisting of four parts, individuals or groups: *a tune in quadruple time* ○ *a quadruple alliance.*

▷ **quadruple** *n, adv* (number or amount) four times as great as (sth): *20 is the quadruple of 5.* ○ *We need quadruple the number of players we've got for a full orchestra.*

quadruple /kwɒˈdru:pl/ *v* [I, Tn] become multiplied or multiply (sth) by four: *Their profits have quadrupled/They have quadrupled their profits in ten years.*

quadruplet /ˈkwɒdru:plet; *US* kwɒˈdru:p-/ (also *infml* **quad**) *n* (usu *pl*) one of four children born to the same mother at one birth.

quadruplicate /kwɒˈdru:plɪkət/ *n* (idm) **in quadruplicate** in four exactly similar examples or copies: *Please submit your application form in quadruplicate.*

quaff /kwɒf; *US* kwæf/ *v* [Tn] (*dated or rhet*) drink (sth) by swallowing large amounts at a time, not taking small sips: *quaffing his beer by the pint.*

quagmire /ˈkwægmaɪə(r), *also* ˈkwɒg-/ *n* area of soft wet ground; bog or marsh: (*fig*) *The heavy rain had turned the pitch into a quagmire.*

quail[1] /kweɪl/ *n* (*pl* unchanged or ~**s**) **(a)** [C] small bird, similar to a partridge. ⇨ illus at BIRD. **(b)** [U] its meat as food.

quail[2] /kweɪl/ *v* [I, Ipr] ~ **(at/before sb/sth)** feel or show fear; flinch: *His heart quailed.* ○ *She quailed at the prospect of addressing such a large crowd.*

quaint /kweɪnt/ *adj* attractively odd or old-fashioned: *quaint old customs* ○ *quaint little cottages on the village green.* ▷ **quaintly** *adv.* **quaintness** *n* [U].

quake /kweɪk/ *v* [I] **1** (of the earth) shake: *They felt the ground quake as the bomb exploded.* **2** (of persons) tremble: *quaking with fear/cold.* ▷ **quake** *n* (*infml*) = EARTHQUAKE.

Quaker /ˈkweɪkə(r)/ *n* member of the Society of Friends, a religious sect that worships Christ without any formal ceremony or stated creed and is strongly opposed to violence and war.

qualification /ˌkwɒlɪfɪˈkeɪʃn/ *n* **1** [U] qualifying or becoming qualified. **2** [C] **(a)** training, examination or experience that qualifies (QUALIFY 1) sb for work, further training, etc. **(b)** degree, diploma, certificate, etc awarded for this: *What sort of qualifications do you need for the job?* ○ *He's got all the right qualifications but is temperamentally unsuitable.* **3** [C, U] statement that modifies or restricts a previous statement: *She gave her approval to the scheme but not without several qualifications.* ○ *I can recommend him without qualification.*

qualify /ˈkwɒlɪfaɪ/ *v* (*pt, pp* **-fied**) **1** [I, Ipr, Tn, Tn·pr, Cn·n/a, Cn·t] ~ **(sb) (for/as sth)** have or give (sb) the qualities, training, etc that are necessary or suitable (for sth): *I won't qualify until next year.* ○ *Our team has qualified for the semi-final.* ○ *A stroll round the garden hardly qualifies as exercise!* ○ *The training course qualifies you to be/as a driving instructor.* **2** [I, Ipr, It, Tn, Tn·pr, Cn·t] ~ **(sb) (for sth)** have or give (sb) a legal right (to sth/to do sth): *After three years here you'll qualify for a rise.* ○ *Eighteen-year-olds qualify to vote.* ○ *Residence in the area qualifies you for membership.* ○ *Your passport qualifies you to receive free medical treatment.* **3** [Tn] make (a statement, etc) less general or extreme: *I feel I must qualify my earlier remarks in case they are misinterpreted.* **4** [Tn] (*grammar*) name the qualities of (sth); describe in a particular way: *In 'the open door', 'open' is an adjective qualifying 'door'.*

▷ **qualified** *adj* **1** having completed the relevant training or examination: *a qualified doctor* ○ *She's extremely well qualified for the job.* ○ *It takes three years to become qualified.* **2** limited: *give the scheme only qualified approval.*

qualifier /-faɪə(r)/ *n* **1** (*grammar*) word, esp an adjective or adverb, that qualifies another word. **2** person who becomes entitled to compete in the next round of a competition, etc: *The final brings together four qualifiers from each heat.*

qualitative /ˈkwɒlɪtətɪv; *US* -teɪt-/ *adj* of or concerned with quality: *qualitative analysis*, eg to find out what chemical substances a sample is made of ○ *little qualitative improvement in their work.* Cf QUANTITATIVE. ▷ **qualitatively** *adv.*

quality /ˈkwɒlətɪ/ *n* **1 (a)** [U, C] degree of goodness or worth: *goods of the highest quality* ○ *This material is very poor quality.* ○ *There are many different qualities of gold and silver.* **(b)** [U] general excellence: *As an actor she shows real quality.* ○ *This company is more concerned with quality than with quantity.* ○ [attrib] *We specialize in quality furniture.* **2** [C] **(a)** attribute; characteristic: *He possesses the quality of inspiring confidence.* ○ *She had many good qualities despite her apparent rudeness.* **(b)** special or distinguishing feature: *One quality of this plastic is that it is almost unbreakable.* ○ *His voice had a rich melodic quality.* **3** [C] (also ˈ**quality paper**) (*Brit*) newspaper that presents the news in a serious way and is usu bought by well-educated readers: *She's an art critic on one of the Sunday qualities.* Cf TABLOID.

qualm /kwɑ:m/ *n* feeling of doubt, esp about whether what one is doing is right; misgiving: *He had/felt no serious qualms about concealing the information from the police.*

quandary /ˈkwɒndərɪ/ *n* state of not being able to decide what to do; awkward or difficult situation: *I've been offered a better job but at a lower salary — I'm in a quandary about what to do.*

quango /ˈkwæŋgəʊ/ *n* (*pl* ~**s**) administrative organization that operates independently but with support from the government (formed from the initials of 'quasi-autonomous, non-governmental organization').

quantify /ˈkwɒntɪfaɪ/ *v* (*pt, pp* **-fied**) [Tn] express or measure the quantity of (sth): *The cost of the flood damage is impossible to quantify.* ▷ **quantifiable** /-faɪəbl/ *adj.* **quantification** /ˌkwɒntɪfɪˈkeɪʃn/ *n* [U].

quantitative /ˈkwɒntɪtətɪv; *US* -teɪt-/ *adj* of or concerned with quantity: *quantitative analysis.* Cf QUALITATIVE.

quantity /ˈkwɒntətɪ/ *n* **1** [U] that which makes it possible to measure things through having number, size, weight, etc: *His reputation as a writer depends more on quantity than quality*, ie He writes a lot but he doesn't write very well. ○ *Mathematics is the science of pure quantity.* **2** [C, U] number or amount, esp a large one: *What quantity* (ie How many) *do you require?* ○ *a small quantity of cutlery* ○ *It's cheaper to buy goods in quantity/in large quantities.* **3** [U, C] length of vowel sounds or syllables, esp in poetry or phonetics. **4** (idm) **an unknown quantity** ⇨ UNKNOWN.

□ ˈ**quantity surveyor** person who estimates the quantity of materials needed for constructing buildings, etc and how much they will cost.

quantum /ˈkwɒntəm/ *n* (*pl* **quanta** /-tə/) (*fml*) amount that is required or desired.

□ **quantum** ˈ**leap** sudden progress; breakthrough: *This discovery marks a quantum leap forward in the fight against cancer.*

ˌ**quantum me**ˈ**chanics** (*physics*) system of mechanics that is used to explain the properties of atoms and molecules. It studies the movement and interaction of subatomic particles like the electron and neutron, and uses the idea that they can be considered as either separate particles or waves.

ˈ**quantum theory** (*physics*) theory based on the assumption that in radiation energy exists in units that cannot be divided. The theory developed from work by *Planck and others at the beginning of the 20th century to explain certain aspects of electromagnetic radiation from hot bodies. *Einstein later suggested that light itself could be regarded as a series of quanta, which were later called photons. The theory led to the further discoveries of quantum mechanics.

quarantine /ˈkwɒrəntiːn; *US* ˈkwɔːr-/ *n* [C usu *sing*, U] (period of) isolation for people or animals that may carry an infectious disease, until it is known that there is no danger of the disease being passed on to others: *kept in quarantine for a week* ○ *be out of quarantine after five days* ○ [attrib] *quarantine regulations, restrictions, etc.*

▷ **quarantine** *v* [Tn] put (sb/sth) into quarantine: *quarantined because of rabies.*

quark /kwɑːk/ *n* (*physics*) any of several very small parts of which elementary particles (eg protons and neutrons) are thought to consist.

quarrel /ˈkwɒrəl; *US* ˈkwɔːrəl/ *n* **1** ~ (**with sb**) (**about/over sth**) angry argument or disagreement: *pick* (ie provoke or seize the opportunity for) *a quarrel with sb* ○ *I had a quarrel with my flat-mate about who should do the housework.* ○ *Their quarrel wasn't serious.* ⇨ Usage at ARGUMENT. **2** ~ **with/against sb/sth** reason for complaining about sb/sth: *I have no quarrel with him.*

▷ **quarrel** *v* (**-ll-**; *US* **-l-**) **1** [I, Ipr] ~ (**with sb**) (**about/over sth**) break friendly relations; argue angrily: *Stop quarrelling, children!* ○ *She quarrelled with her brother about the terms of their father's will.* **2** [Ipr] ~ **with sth** disagree with sth; find fault with sth: *quarrel with a statement, an account, an estimate, etc* ○ *You can't quarrel with the court's decision — it's very fair.*

quarrelsome /-səm/ *adj* likely to start a quarrel; quick-tempered.

quarry[1] /ˈkwɒrɪ; *US* ˈkwɔːrɪ/ *n* (**a**) animal or bird that is being hunted: *The hunters lost sight of their quarry in the forest.* (**b**) person or thing that is being looked for or pursued eagerly: *It took the police several days to track down their quarry.*

quarry[2] /ˈkwɒrɪ; *US* ˈkwɔːrɪ/ *n* place where stone, slate, etc is extracted from the ground. Cf MINE[2] 1.

▷ **quarry** *v* (*pt, pp* **quarried**) **1** [Tn, Tn·pr, Tn·p] ~ **A for B/B from A**; ~ **sth out** (**of sth**) extract (stone, etc) from (a quarry): *quarrying the hillside for granite* ○ *quarry out a block of marble.* **2** [Ipr] search with great effort for information, etc: *quarrying in old documents for historical evidence.*

quart /kwɔːt/ *n* **1** (*abbr* **qt**) measure of capacity for liquids, equal to 2 pints or approximately 1.14 litres. ⇨ App 5. **2** (idm) **put a quart into a pint** ˈ**pot** (try to) do sth that is impossible, esp to put sth into a space that is too small for it.

quarter /ˈkwɔːtə(r)/ *n* **1** [C] each of four equal or corresponding parts of sth: *a quarter of a mile* ○ *three and a quarter* (ie 3 $\frac{1}{4}$) *inches* ○ *The programme lasted an hour and a quarter.* ○ *Divide the apples into quarters.* ○ *Three quarters of the theatre was full.* ○ (*infml*) *A quarter* (ie of a pound) *of coffee, please.* ⇨ App 9, 10. ⇨ Usage at HALF[1]. **2** [C] point of time fifteen minutes before or after every hour: *It's (a) quarter to* (*US of*) *four now — I'll meet you at quarter past* (*US after*). ○ *The clock strikes the hours, the half-hours and the quarters.* ○ *The buses leave twice every hour on the quarter*, eg at 10.15 and 10.45. ⇨ App 9. **3** [C] three months, esp as a period for which rent or other payment is made, or a firm's earnings are calculated: *The rent is due at the end of each quarter.* ○ *Our gas bill for the last quarter was unusually high.* ○ *Sales of the dictionary are twice what they were in the same quarter last year.* **4** [C] (**a**) direction: *The wind blew from all quarters.* ○ *Her travels had taken her to every quarter of the globe.* (**b**) district; part of a town: *a residential quarter* ○ *the student quarter of the city*, ie the part mainly inhabited by students. **5** [C] person or group of people, esp as a possible source of help, information, etc: *As her mother was now very poor she could expect no help from that quarter.* ○ *The minister's speech is interpreted in some quarters* (ie by some people) *as an admission that the Government was wrong.* **6** [C] (*US*) (coin worth) 25 cents; fourth part of a dollar: *It'll cost you a quarter.* ⇨ App 9. **7** [C] one fourth of a lunar month; position of the moon at the end of the first and third of these: *The moon is in its last quarter.* **8 quarters** [pl] = HINDQUARTERS (HIND[1]). **9** [C usu *sing*] rear part of a ship's side: *on the port/starboard quarter.* **10** [C] fourth part of a hundredweight, ie (in UK) 28 lb or (in US) 25 lb. ⇨ App 9, 10. **11 quarters** [pl] accommodation, esp for soldiers: *take up quarters in the nearest village* ○ *married/single quarters*, ie place where a soldier with/without a family can lodge ○ *ordered to return to their quarters.* **12** [U] (*dated or fml*) mercy shown towards an enemy who has surrendered or to an opponent who is in one's power: *His business rivals knew they could expect no quarter from such a ruthless adversary.* **13** (idm) **at close quarters** ⇨ CLOSE[1].

▷ **quarter** *v* **1** [Tn] divide (sb/sth) into four parts: *quarter an apple* ○ *sentenced to be hung, drawn and quartered*, ie executed by hanging, the body then being opened and cut up. **2** [Tn, Tn·pr] ~ **sb** (**on sb**) provide sb with lodgings: *troops quartered on the local villagers.*

□ ˈ**quarter-back** *n* (in American football) player positioned behind the forward players who directs the team during an attack.

ˈ**quarter-day** *n* first day of a quarter(3) when payments become due.

ˈ**quarterdeck** *n* part of the upper deck of a ship near the stern, usu reserved for officers.

ˌ**quarter-**ˈ**final** *n* (in sport, etc) any of four competitions or matches to choose the players or teams for the semi finals.

ˈ**quarter-light** *n* small triangular section of a window in a car, which can be opened to admit air without opening the main section.

ˈ**quartermaster** *n* **1** (in the army) regimental officer in charge of stores and accommodation for a battalion. **2** (in the navy) petty officer in charge of steering, signals, etc. ˌ**Quartermaster-**ˈ**General** *n* staff officer in charge of supplies for an army.

ˈ**quarter-note** *n* (*US*) = CROTCHET.

ˈ**quarter sessions** (formerly) court of law with limited power to try criminal and civil cases, held every three months.

ˈ**quarterstaff** *n* strong pole, 6 to 8 feet long, formerly used as a weapon.

quarterly /ˈkwɔːtəlɪ/ *adj, adv* produced or occurring once every three months: *I receive quarterly bank statements.* ○ *Subscriptions should be paid quarterly.*

▷ **quarterly** *n* periodical published four times a year.

quartet /kwɔːˈtet/ *n* **1** (piece of music for) four players or singers: *a string quartet*, ie players of or music for two violins, a viola and a cello. **2** set of four people or things: *a quartet of novels with a linking theme.*

quarto /ˈkwɔːtəʊ/ *n* (*pl* ~**s**) (**a**) (*abbrs* **4to, qto**) size of page made by folding a standard sheet of paper twice to form eight pages. (**b**) book made of these folded sheets: *the first quarto of 'Hamlet'* ○ [attrib] *Quarto volumes are too large to fit on this shelf.*

quartz /kwɔːts/ *n* [U] any of various types of hard mineral (esp crystallized silica): [attrib] *a quartz clock/watch*, ie one that is operated, very accurately, by the electric vibrations of a quartz crystal.

quasar /ˈkweɪzɑː(r)/ *n* (*astronomy*) very distant object like a star that is the source of intense electromagnetic radiation.

quash /kwɒʃ/ *v* [Tn] **1** reject (sth) (by legal procedure) as not valid; declare (sth) not to be enforceable by law: *quash a verdict* ○ *They had their sentence quashed by the appeal court judge.* **2** put an end to (sth); suppress or crush: *The rebellion was quickly quashed.*

quasi- /ˈkweɪzaɪ-, ˈkweɪsaɪ-/ *pref* (forming *adjs* and *ns*) **1** to a certain extent: *a quasi-official body.* **2** seemingly but not really: *a quasi-scientific explanation* ○ *a quasi-scholar.*

quatercentenary /ˌkwɒtəsenˈtiːnərɪ; *US* -ˈsentənerɪ/ *n* 400th anniversary: *celebrate the quatercentenary of Shakespeare's birth.*

quaternary /kwəˈtɜːnərɪ/ **1** (*fml*) having four parts. **2 Quaternary** of the second period of the *Cainozoic era. This period began about two million years ago and has lasted up to the present day, comprising the Pleistocene and Holocene epochs.

▷ **the Quaternary** *n* [sing] the Quaternary period.

quatrain /ˈkwɒtreɪn/ *n* poem, or verse of a poem, consisting of four lines.

quatrefoil /ˈkætrəfɔɪl/ *n* **1** figure or design with four pointed curves. **2** flower with four petals or leaf made up of four small leaves.

quattrocento /ˌkwætrəʊˈtʃentəʊ/ **the quattrocento** *n* [sing] the 15th century in Italian art, including the work of artists like *Botticelli, *Brunelleschi, Donatello, Masaccio and Uccello: [attrib] *quattrocento sculpture.*

quaver /ˈkweɪvə(r)/ *v* **1** [I] (of a voice or a musical sound) shake; tremble: *in a quavering voice* ○ *Her top notes quavered a little.* **2** [Tn, Tn·p] ~ **sth** (**out**) say or sing sth in a trembling voice: *The children quavered out their little song.*

▷ **quaver** *n* **1** (usu *sing*) trembling sound: *You could hear the quaver in her voice.* **2** (*US* **eighth note**) note in music that lasts half as long as a crotchet. ⇨ illus at MUSIC.

quavery /ˈkweɪvərɪ/ *adj* (of a voice) shaking; tremulous.

quay /kiː/ *n* landing-place, usu built of stone or iron, for loading and unloading ships.

□ ˈ**quayside** *n* [sing] land situated at the side or edge of a quay: *crowds waiting at the quayside to welcome them.*

queasy /ˈkwiːzɪ/ *adj* (**-ier, -iest**) having a tendency to feel sick; feeling sick: *Travelling on a bus makes me feel queasy.* ○ *She complained of a queasy stomach*, ie a feeling in her stomach that made her want to be sick. ▷ **queasily** *adv.* **queasiness** *n* [U].

Quebec /kwɪˈbek/ province in eastern Canada. Most of the population and the economic activity is concentrated in the fertile valley of the Saint Lawrence river. It is one of Canada's most industrialized provinces and produces nearly half its electricity. Quebec was founded by French settlers and remains French-speaking, with a strong separatist movement. ⇨ map at App 1.

Quechua /ˈketʃwə/ *n* (*pl* unchanged) **1** [C] member of an Indian people of Peru and the surrounding countries. **2** [U] language of this people. Quechua and Spanish are the two official languages of Peru.

queen /kwi:n/ *n* **1** (title of the) female ruler of an independent state, usu inheriting the position by right of birth: *Queen Elizabeth II* ○ *the Queen of the Netherlands* ○ *be made/crowned queen.* Cf KING. **2** wife of a king: *King George VI and Queen Elizabeth.* **3** (**a**) woman, place or thing regarded as best or most important in some way: *Agatha Christie, the queen of detective-story writers* ○ *Marilyn Monroe is the most famous of all American movie queens,* ie leading film actresses. ○ *Venice, the queen of the Adriatic.* (**b**) woman or girl chosen to hold the most important place in a festival or celebration: *Queen of the May,* ie girl chosen to lead a procession, dance, etc to celebrate spring ○ *a carnival queen* ○ *a beauty queen.* **4** fertile female insect (eg ant, bee or wasp) that produces eggs for the whole group: *A hive cannot exist without a queen.* ○ [attrib] *The queen bee never leaves the hive.* **5** (**a**) (in chess) the most powerful piece on the board, used for attack and defence. ⇨ illus at CHESS. (**b**) (in a pack of playing-cards) any of the four cards with the picture of a queen on: *the queen of hearts.* **6** (*sl derog*) effeminate male homosexual. **7** (idm) **the King's/Queen's English** ⇨ ENGLISH. **turn King's/Queen's evidence** ⇨ EVIDENCE. **Queen Anne is dead** (*saying*) everybody already knows that: *'There's a new one-way system down by the station.' 'Yes, and Queen Anne is dead too.'* **the uncrowned king/queen of sth** ⇨ UNCROWNED.

▷ **queen** *v* **1** (**a**) [Tn] (in chess) change (a pawn) into a queen by moving it across the board to the opponent's end. (**b**) [I] (of a pawn) be changed in this way. **2** (idm) **queen it (over sb)** behave as if in a position of power (over sb): *Since her promotion she queens it over everyone else in the office.*

queenly *adj* of, like or suitable for a queen; majestic: *her queenly duties* ○ *give a queenly wave* ○ *dressed in queenly robes.*

Queen Anne table

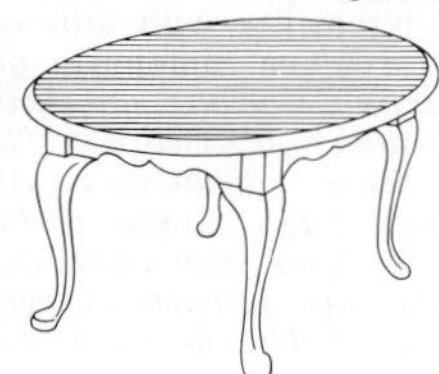

□ ˌ**Queen** ˈ**Anne** (in the) style popular in England at the beginning of the 18th century, during the reign of Queen *Anne. In furniture its main features were simple elegant design, with curved legs and walnut veneers. Queen Anne architecture used red brick and simple classical lines. ⇨ illus. ⇨ illus at DRESS.

queen ˈ**bee 1** ⇨ QUEEN 4. **2** (*fig*) woman who behaves as if she is the most important person in a particular place or group.

queen ˈ**consort** wife of a king.

queen ˈ**dowager** widow of a king.

queen ˈ**mother** widow of a king and mother of a reigning king or queen: *The queen mother waved to the crowd.* ⇨ article at ROYAL FAMILY.

Queen's ˈ**Bench (Division)** ⇨ KING'S BENCH (KING).

Queen's ˈ**Counsel** ⇨ KING'S COUNSEL (KING).

the Queen's ˈ**English** form of written and spoken English generally regarded as the most correct.

the Queen's ˈ**highway** ⇨ THE KING'S HIGHWAY (KING).

Queensberry Rules /ˌkwi:nzbərɪ ˈru:lz/ **the Queensberry Rules** the standard rules for modern boxing, named in honour of the Marquis of Queensberry in 1867. They introduced the use of gloves and short rounds, and forbade wrestling.

Queensland /ˈkwi:nzlənd/ state in NE Australia. The main economic activity is sheep and cattle farming. Industry is concentrated in the towns on the coast. ⇨ map at App 1.

queer /kwɪə(r)/ *adj* **1** (**a**) different from what is expected; strange, esp in an unpleasant way: *The fish had a queer taste.* ○ *His behaviour seemed queer.* ○ *I think she's gone a bit queer in the head,* ie slightly crazy. (**b**) causing doubt or suspicion: *I heard some very queer noises in the garden.* ○ *There's something queer about him.* **2** (*sl derog*) homosexual. **3** (*dated infml*) unwell; faint: *I woke up feeling rather queer.* **4** (idm) **be in** ˈ**Queer Street** (*dated Brit sl*) be in (esp financial) trouble: *He lost all his money gambling and now he's really in Queer Street.* **an odd/a queer fish** ⇨ FISH¹.

▷ **queer** *n* (*sl derog offensive*) homosexual man.

queer *v* (idm) **queer sb's** ˈ**pitch** (*infml*) cause sb's plans to go wrong: *I think I'm likely to get the job, but if Bob applies for it too it/he could queer my pitch.*

queerly *adv.*

queerness *n* [U].

quell /kwel/ *v* [Tn] put an end to (sth); suppress: *quell the rebellion, opposition, uprising, etc* ○ *quell sb's fears, anxieties, etc.*

quench /kwentʃ/ *v* [Tn] **1** extinguish (fire, flames, etc), esp with water: (*fig*) *quench sb's ardent passion.* **2** satisfy (sth) by drinking: *quench one's thirst with cold water.* **3** put an end to (sth): *Nothing could quench her longing to return home again.* **4** cool (a hot substance) rapidly by placing it in water.

querulous /ˈkwerʊləs/ *adj* complaining; irritable: *in a querulous tone.* ▷ **querulously** *adv.* **querulousness** *n* [U].

query /ˈkwɪərɪ/ *n* **1** question: *answer readers' queries* ○ *Your interesting report raises several important queries.* **2** question mark (?): *Put a query against that.*

▷ **query** *v* (*pt, pp* **queried**) **1** [Tn, Tn·pr] ~ **sb (about sth)** ask sb a question or questions: *'Will it be too late?' she queried.* ○ *The minister was queried about his plans for the industry.* **2** [Tn, Tw] express doubt about sth: *query a statement, suggestion, conclusion, etc* ○ *query the amount charged,* ie say that one thinks it is wrong ○ *I query whether he can be trusted.*

quest /kwest/ *n* (*fml or rhet*) **1** ~ **(for sth)** act of seeking sth; search or pursuit: *the quest for gold, knowledge, happiness.* **2** (idm) **in quest of sth** trying to find sth; seeking sth: *She had come in quest of advice.*

▷ **quest** *v* [I, Ipr] ~ **(for sth)** (*fml or rhet*) try to find sth; search: *His questing fingers found the light switch.* ○ *continue to quest for clues.*

question¹ /ˈkwestʃən/ *n* **1** [C] form of expression in speech or writing that requests an answer from sb: *ask a lot of questions* ○ *Question 3 is quite difficult.* ○ *I will be happy to answer questions at the end.* ○ *I'd like to put a question to the speaker.* **2** [C] topic that is being or needs to be discussed; problem that needs to be solved: *What about the question of security?* ○ *We have to consider the question of where to sleep.* ○ *The question of choosing a successor has arisen.* **3** [U] raising of doubt: *There is no/some question about his honesty.* ○ *Her sincerity is beyond question.* ○ *His suitability for the post is open to question.* **4** (idm) **beg the question** ⇨ BEG. **bring sth/come into** ˈ**question** (cause sth to) be discussed or considered as a matter of importance: *My promotion brings into question the status of certain other members of staff.* **call sth in/into** ˈ**question** express doubt about sth: *His moral standards have been called into question.* **a fair question** ⇨ FAIR¹. **in** ˈ**question** being considered or discussed: *The woman in question is sitting over there.* ○ *The job in question is available for three months only.* **it is a question of** what is really involved is: *It isn't a question of whether we can afford a holiday — I'm just too busy at the moment.* ○ *She is so talented that her success can only be a question of time.* **a loaded question** ⇨ LOAD². **a moot point/question** ⇨ MOOT. **out of the** ˈ**question** not worth discussing; impossible: *Missing school to watch the football match is out of the question.* ○ *A new bicycle is out of the question — we can't afford it.* **pop the question** ⇨ POP⁴. **a/the sixty-four thousand dollar question** ⇨ DOLLAR. **there is some/no question of** there is a/no possibility of: *There was some question of selling the business.* ○ *There will be no question of anyone being made redundant.* **a vexed question** ⇨ VEX.

□ ˈ**question mark** the symbol (?) used in writing after a question. ⇨ App 14. Cf QUERY 2.

ˈ**question-master** (also ˈ**quiz-master**) *n* person who asks the questions in a quiz, esp on TV or radio.

ˈ**question time** (*Brit*) (in the House of Commons) period of time during which ministers answer questions from MPs.

question² /ˈkwestʃən/ *v* **1** [Tn] ask (sb) a question or questions: *They questioned her closely about her friendship with the dead man.* ○ *I was questioned by the police for six hours.* ○ *I'd like to question you on your views about the housing problem.* **2** [Tn, Tw] express or feel doubt about (sth): *Her sincerity has never been questioned.* ○ *Do you question my right to read this?* ○ *We must question the value of our link with the university.* ○ *I seriously question whether we ought to continue.*

▷ **questionable** *adj* that can be doubted; not certainly true or advisable or honest: *Such a questionable assertion is sure to provoke criticism.* ○ *an object of questionable value, usefulness, authenticity.* **questionably** /-əblɪ/ *adv.*

questioner *n* person who asks questions, esp in a broadcast programme or a public debate.

questioningly *adv* using a questioning gesture or tone of voice: *She looked at me questioningly.*

questionnaire /ˌkwestʃəˈneə(r)/ *n* written or printed list of questions to be answered by a number of people, esp to collect statistics or as part of a survey: *Please complete and return the enclosed questionnaire.*

queue /kju:/ *n* **1** line of people, vehicles, etc waiting for sth or to do sth: *By 7 o'clock a long queue had formed outside the cinema.* ○ *People had to stand in a queue for hours to buy a ticket.* ○ *Is this the queue for the bus?* ○ *a queue of cars at the traffic-lights.* **2** (idm) **jump the queue** ⇨ JUMP².

▷ **queue** *v* [I, Ipr, Ip] ~ **(up) (for sth)** wait in a queue: *We queued for an hour but didn't get in.* ○ *Queue here for a taxi.* ○ *They're queuing up to see a film.*

📖 Queueing is often thought to be a typically British habit, and foreign visitors to Britain often comment on British people's readiness to queue. People queue in many situations, such as in shops or banks, at bus stops, or in cinemas or theatres, but not on train or underground platforms. 'Jumping the queue' (ie moving to the front of the queue without waiting in one's proper place) causes great annoyance to others in the queue. Many banks, building societies and post offices now have a 'guided' queue, with barriers showing where people should wait in line, and a sign indicating the head of the queue.

quibble /ˈkwɪbl/ *n* **1** objection or criticism, esp a trivial one: *quibbles over the exact amount* ○ *Basically it was a fine performance — I have only minor quibbles to make about her technique.* **2** remark, etc made in order to evade the main point of an argument: *She's only introducing this as a quibble.*

▷ **quibble** *v* [I, Ipr] ~ **(over/about sth)** argue about small differences or disagreements: *Stop quibbling about the use of the comma.* ○ *50p isn't worth quibbling about.*

quiche /ki:ʃ/ *n* [C, U] open pastry tart with a savoury filling, esp of eggs, bacon, cheese, etc.

quick /kwɪk/ *adj* (**-er, -est**) **1** (**a**) (capable of) moving fast or doing sth in a short time: *a quick worker, reader* ○ *quick to respond, react, learn* ○ *Taxis are quicker than buses.* ○ *Go and find the tickets and be quick about it,* ie hurry. ○ *The thief got away — he was too quick for me.* ○ *We must move at a quicker pace or we'll be late.* (**b**) done in a short time: *have a quick meal* ○ *We've just got time for a quick one,* ie a quick (usu alcoholic) drink. ○ *with a quick flick of the wrist* ○ *Are you sure this is the quickest way?* ○ *He fired three shots in quick succession.* **2** (**a**) [attrib] lively; active; alert: *a* *quick ear for music* ○ *a quick eye for imperfections* ○ *Her quick wits saved the boy's life.* (b) easily roused; sensitive: *Be careful not to annoy him — he's got a quick temper*, ie he becomes angry very readily. ○ *She's always very quick to take offence*, ie easily offended. (c) ~ (**at sth**) intelligent; competent: *He's not as quick as his sister.* ○ *His spelling's poor but he's very quick at figures.* **3** (idm) **the ˌquick and the ˈdead** (*arch*) all people alive or dead. **(as) quick as a ˈflash; (as) quick as ˈlightning** very quick(ly): *He got the answer to the riddle as quick as a flash.* ○ *She's as quick as lightning on the tennis court.* **(be) ˌquick off the ˈmark** making a prompt start: *You have to be quick off the mark when you answer a newspaper advertisement.* **quick/slow on the draw** ⇨ DRAW¹. **quick/slow on the uptake** ⇨ UPTAKE.

▷ **quick** *adv* (**-er, -est**) quickly: *Come as quick as you can.* ○ *Everyone is trying to get rich quick nowadays.* ○ *Who ran quickest?* ○ *quick-drying paint.*

quick *n* **1** [sing] soft tender flesh, esp below the finger-nails: *She has bitten her nails (down) to the quick.* **2** (idm) **cut sb to the ˈquick** hurt sb deeply by speaking or acting unkindly: *She was cut to the quick by his insults.*

quickly *adv*: *speak, write, run, learn very quickly.*

quickness *n* [U]: *(saying) The quickness of the hand deceives the eye.*

□ **ˌquick-ˈchange** *adj* [attrib] (of an actor, etc) quickly changing his costume or appearance to play another part: *a quick-change artist.*

ˌquick-ˈfreeze *v* (*pt* **-froze** /-frəʊz/, *pp* **-frozen** /-frəʊzn/) [Tn] freeze (food) very quickly for storing so that it keeps its natural qualities.

ˌquick ˈmarch (used as a military command to march at the usual pace).

ˈquickstep *n* (music for a) ballroom dance with quick steps: *play/dance a quickstep.*

ˌquick-ˈtempered *adj* likely to become angry very quickly.

ˌquick-ˈwitted *adj* able to think quickly; intelligent.

quicken /ˈkwɪkən/ *v* [I, Tn] **1** (cause sth to) become quicker: *His pace quickened* ○ *We quickened our steps.* **2** (*fml*) (cause sth to) become more active: *The child quickened in her womb*, ie She felt the movements of the foetus. ○ *Her pulse quickened.* ○ *His interest was quickened by an article he had read.*

quickie /ˈkwɪkɪ/ *n* (*infml*) thing that is made or done very quickly: *I've just made some coffee — have you time for a quickie?*

quicklime /ˈkwɪklaɪm/ *n* [U] = CALCIUM OXIDE (CALCIUM).

quicksand /ˈkwɪksænd/ *n* [C often *pl*, U] (area of) loose wet deep sand into which people or things will sink.

quicksilver /ˈkwɪksɪlvə(r)/ *n* [U] = MERCURY: *like quicksilver*, ie very quickly.

quid¹ /kwɪd/ *n* (*pl* unchanged) (*Brit infml*) **1** one pound sterling: *Can you lend me five quid?* ○ *It costs a quid* (ie £1) *to get in.* **2** (idm) **quids ˈin** in a position to profit from sth: *Having sold the film and TV rights to his new best seller he's absolutely quids in.*

quid² /kwɪd/ *n* lump of tobacco for chewing.

quiddity /ˈkwɪdɪtɪ/ *n* **1** true nature or character of sth; essence. **2** trivial objection; quibble.

quid pro quo /ˌkwɪd prəʊ ˈkwəʊ/ *n* (*pl* **quid pro quos**) thing given in return for sth else: *Please accept the use of our cottage as a quid pro quo for lending us your car.*

quiescent /kwaɪˈesnt, kwɪˈesnt/ *adj* (*fml*) inactive; passive; quiet: *It is unlikely that such an extremist organization will remain quiescent for long.* ▷ **quiescence** /-sns/ *n* [U].

quiet /ˈkwaɪət/ *adj* (**-er, -est**) **1** with little or no sound; not noisy or loud: *her quiet voice, footsteps* ○ *Be quiet* (ie silent), *please!* ○ *Can't you keep the children quiet? I'm trying to concentrate.* **2** with little or no movement or disturbance: *The roads are usually quiet in the afternoon.* ○ *The sea looks quieter now.* ○ *Business is quiet at this time of the year.* **3** without excitement, activity or interruption: *lead a quiet life* ○ *have a quiet smoke* ○ *have a quiet evening at home* ○ *Their wedding was very quiet.* **4** gentle; not forceful: *a lady of a quiet disposition.* **5** (of colours) not bright; unobtrusive: *a quiet shade of blue.* **6** not expressed loudly; restrained: *have a quiet laugh about sth* ○ *Her manner concealed quiet resentment.* ⇨ Usage. **7** (idm) **keep quiet about sth; keep sth quiet** say nothing about sth: *I've decided to resign but I'd prefer you to keep quiet about it.* **(as) quiet as a ˈmouse** making very little sound.

▷ **quiet** *n* [U] **1** state of being quiet; tranquillity: *the quiet of the countryside* ○ *live in peace and quiet.* **2** (idm) **on the quiet** secretly: *have a drink on the quiet.*

quiet *v* [I, Ip, Tn, Tn·p] ~ (**sb/sth**) (**down**) (*esp US*) become or make (sb/sth) quiet: *quiet a frightened horse.*

quieten /ˈkwaɪətn/ *v* [I, Ip, Tn, Tn·p] ~ (**sb/sth**) (**down**) (*esp Brit*) (cause sb/sth to) become less disturbed, noisy, etc: *Quieten down and get on with your work.* ○ *quieten a screaming baby* ○ *quieten* (ie allay, calm) *sb's fears/suspicions.*

quietly *adv*: *This car engine runs very quietly.* ○ *She died quietly in her bed.*

quietness *n* [U]: *the quietness of the chapel.*

NOTE ON USAGE: **Quiet**, **silent** and **calm** can all be applied to both people and things and generally indicate the absence of a quality rather than the presence of something. A **silent** film has no speech and a **silent** machine makes no noise. The opposite of *reading silently* (or *to oneself*) is *reading aloud*. **Quiet** can mean silent: *Quiet! Don't make any noise!* It can also indicate a lack of disturbance: *a quiet road with few cars.* ○ *Politicians must sometimes long for a quieter life.* The opposite of *quiet music* is *loud music*. **Still** indicates the absence of movement: *Stand still!* It may also suggest a lack of noise: *a still night after a stormy day.* A **calm** person shows no agitation in difficult circumstances. A **calm** sea has no, or only small, waves.

quietism /ˈkwaɪətɪzəm/ *n* [U] form of religious devotion based on a calm and passive acceptance of life and the abandonment of all desires.

▷ **quietist** /-ɪst/ *n* person who practises this.

quietude /ˈkwaɪɪtju:d; *US* -tu:d/ *n* (*fml*) stillness; calm.

quietus /kwaɪˈi:təs/ *n* (usu *sing*); (*fml*) release from life; extinction: *give sb his quietus*, ie put an end to his life ○ *The plan has finally got its quietus*, ie been abandoned.

quiff /kwɪf/ *n* (*Brit*) lock of hair, esp of a man, brushed up above the forehead.

quill /kwɪl/ *n* **1** (a) (also **ˈquill-feather**) large feather from the wing or tail. ⇨ illus at FEATHER. (b) (also **quill-ˈpen**) (formerly) pen made from the hollow stem of this. **2** (usu *pl*) long sharp stiff spine of a porcupine.

quilt /kwɪlt/ *n* thick covering for a bed, made of cloth padded with soft material. Cf DUVET, EIDERDOWN.

▷ **quilt** *v* [Tn] line (a garment or coverlet) with padding held in place by lines of stitches: *a quilted anorak, dressing-gown, etc.*

quin /kwɪn/ (*US* **quint** /kwɪnt/) *n* (*infml*) = QUINTUPLET.

quince /kwɪns/ *n* **1** hard yellowish pear-shaped fruit used for making jam, etc: [attrib] *quince jelly.* **2** tree bearing this fruit.

quincentenary /ˌkwɪnsenˈti:nərɪ; *US* -ˈsentənerɪ/ *n* 500th anniversary: [attrib] *quincentenary celebrations.*

quinine /kwɪˈni:n; *US* ˈkwaɪnaɪn/ *n* [U] bitter liquid made from the bark of a tree and used in drinks or as a medicine against fever.

Quinquagesima /ˌkwɪŋkwəˈdʒesɪmə/ *n* the Sunday before Lent (50 days before Easter).

quinsy /ˈkwɪnzɪ/ *n* [U] inflammation of the throat, esp with an abscess on one of the tonsils.

quintessence /kwɪnˈtesns/ *n* [sing] **the ~ of sth** (*fml*) **1** essential part of (a theory, speech, condition, etc): *Her book captures the quintessence of Renaissance humanism.* **2** perfect example of (a quality): *He is the quintessence of tact and politeness.* ▷ **quintessential** /ˌkwɪntɪˈsenʃl/ *adj.* **quintessentially** /-ʃəlɪ/ *adv*: *a sense of humour that is quintessentially British.*

quintet /kwɪnˈtet/ *n* (piece of music for) five players or singers: *They're playing Schubert's 'Trout' Quintet.*

quintuplet /ˈkwɪntju:plet; *US* kwɪnˈtu:plɪt/ (also **quin**, *US* **quint**) *n* (usu *pl*) any of five children born to the same mother at one birth.

quip /kwɪp/ *n* witty or sarcastic remark: *He ended his speech with a merry quip.*

▷ **quip** *v* (**-pp-**) [I] make a quip or quips: *'Who overslept this morning?' she quipped.*

quire /ˈkwaɪə(r)/ *n* 25 (formerly 24) sheets of paper: *buy/sell paper by the quire/in quires.* Cf REAM¹.

quirk /kwɜ:k/ *n* **1** habit or action that is peculiar to sb/sth: *He had a strange quirk of addressing his wife as Mrs Smith.* **2** accident; coincidence: *one of those odd historical quirks* ○ *By a quirk of fate they had booked into the same hotel.*

quisling /ˈkwɪzlɪŋ/ *n* traitor, esp one who helps an enemy occupying his country.

quit /kwɪt/ *v* (**-tt-**; *pt, pp* **quit** or, in British use, **quitted**) **1** [I, Tn] go away from (a place); leave: *He got his present job when he quitted/quit the army.* ○ *If I don't get a pay rise I'll quit.* ○ *I have received your notice to quit*, ie to leave the accommodation I am renting. **2** [Tn, Tg] (*infml*) stop (doing sth): *quit work for five minutes* ○ *Quit fooling around!* **3** (idm) **be quit of sb/sth** be rid of sb/sth; be released from the company or addition of sb/sth: *I'd like to be quit of the responsibility.* ○ *You're well quit of him*, ie fortunate because he has left.

▷ **quitter** *n* (*often derog*) person who does not finish a task he has started, esp one that is done as a duty: *I've asked you to do this for me because I know you're not a quitter.*

quite /kwaɪt/ *adv* **1** (not used with a negative) (a) (used esp with *adjs* or *advs* that refer to a gradable quality) to some extent; not very; fairly: *quite big, small, good, cold, warm, interesting, etc* ○ *The girl sang quite a long song.* ○ *He plays quite well.* ○ *I quite like some opera music.* ⇨ Usage at FAIRLY. (b) (used as an intensifier with *adjs* or *advs* that express an extreme opinion): *quite awful, delicious, dazzling, amazing, unbelievable, etc* ○ *a quite extraordinary experience* ○ *The view was quite breathtaking.* ○ *That was quite the nicest meal I've ever had.* ○ *She performed quite brilliantly.* **2** (used with absolute measures) completely; entirely: *quite empty, perfect, unique, flawless, enough* ○ *The theatre was not quite* (ie almost) *full.* ○ *Cheer up, it's not quite hopeless yet.* ○ *Are you sure you're quite satisfied?* ○ *He has quite recovered from his illness.* ○ *The answer is 62 — quite right.* ○ *I quite agree/understand.* ○ *talking on the telephone for quite 2 hours* ○ *'I made myself a cup of tea while I was waiting.' 'Oh don't worry, that's quite all right.'* **3** (used as an *interj* to express agreement or understanding): *'It's not something we want to have talked about.' 'Quite (so).'* ○ *'He's bound to feel shaken after his accident' 'Quite.'* **4** (idm) **quite a ˈfew; quite a ˈlot (of)** a considerable number or amount: *Quite a few people came to the lecture.* ○ *We drank quite a lot of wine.* **quite a; quite some** /sʌm/ (*approv esp US*) (used to indicate that a person or thing is unusual): *It must be quite some car.* ○ *We had quite a party.* **ˌquite some** /sʌm/ **ˈtime** a considerable length of time: *It happened quite some time ago.*

▷ **quite** *det* **1** (used before *a/the* + *n* or before a name, as an intensifier): *quite a beauty, hero, swimmer* ○ *We found it quite a change when we moved to London.* ○ *It's not quite the Lake District but the countryside's very pretty.* **2** (idm) **(not) ˌquite the (done) ˈthing** (not) that which is considered socially acceptable: *It wasn't quite the done thing for women to drink in pubs in those days.* **ˌquite the ˈfashion, ˈrage, etc** extremely popular or fashionable: *Black leather trousers seem to be quite the rage these days.*

NOTE ON USAGE: In British English **quite** can

have different meanings partly depending on the intonation of the sentence. **1** If **quite** carries the main stress when used with gradable words (ie those describing qualities which can be of different strengths or degrees) it has a negative meaning such as 'not very': *He's ˈquite handsome.* ○ *She played ˈquite well.* **2** If **quite** receives secondary or no stress the sentence expresses more approval and possibly surprise: *I was quite ˈpleased.* ○ *I think he's quite ˈhandsome.* **3** When **quite** is used with a word expressing an absolute quality, it means 'completely' and does not usually carry the main stress: *It was quite ˈwonderful.* ○ *She played quite ˈbrilliantly.* ○ *I quite aˈgreed with him.* But compare *I ˌquite aˈgree with you* (= I entirely agree with you).

quits /kwɪts/ *adj* (idm) **be quits (with sb)** be on even terms after a debt of money, etc has been repaid: *Are we quits or do you still owe me a pound?* **call it quits** ⇨ CALL[2]. **double or quits** ⇨ DOUBLE[4].

quiver[1] /ˈkwɪvə(r)/ *v* [I, Tn] (cause sth to) tremble slightly or vibrate: *The moth quivered its wings.* ○ *a quivering leaf* ○ *Quivering with rage she slammed the door shut.*

▷ **quiver** *n* quivering sound or movement: *A quiver of expectancy ran through the audience.* ○ *the quiver of an eyelid.*

quiver[2] /ˈkwɪvə(r)/ *n* case used by archers for carrying arrows. ⇨ illus at ARCHERY.

qui vive /ˌki: ˈvi:v/ (idm) **on the qui ˈvive** watching for sth to happen; alert; watchful.

Quixote /ˈkwɪksət/ Don, hero of the book of the same name by *Cervantes. He imagined he was a knight in the days of chivalry and tried to have the sort of adventures described in medieval romances. He was the origin of the idiom *to tilt at windmills* and his name is used to refer to an unrealistic idealist.

quixotic /kwɪkˈsɒtɪk/ *adj* noble, unselfish or gallant in an extravagant or impractical way (like Don Quixote). ▷ **quixotically** /-klɪ/ *adv.*

quiz /kwɪz/ *n* (*pl* **quizzes**) competition, esp on TV or radio, in which people try to answer questions to test their knowledge: *take part in a quiz* ○ *a sports, music, general knowledge, etc quiz* ○ [attrib] *a quiz game/programme/show.*

▷ **quiz** *v* (-zz-) [Tn, Tn·pr] ~ **sb (about sb/sth)** ask sb questions: *She quizzed him all night about the people he'd seen.*

□ ˈ**quiz-master** *n* = QUESTION-MASTER (QUESTION[1]).

quizzical /ˈkwɪzɪkl/ *adj* in a questioning manner, esp when amused: *with a quizzical smile* ○ *He continued in a quizzical tone.* ▷ **quizzically** /-klɪ/ *adv*: *She looked at me quizzically.*

quod /kwɒd/ *n* [U] (*sl esp Brit*) prison (used esp in the expressions shown): *go to quod* ○ *in/out of quod.*

quoin /kɔɪn/ *n* **1** (*architecture*) **(a)** outside corner of a building. **(b)** inside corner of a room. **2** wedge used in traditional printing for keeping type in place.

quoit /kɔɪt; *US* kwɔɪt/ *n* **1** [C] ring, made of eg metal, rubber or rope, that is thrown onto an upright peg. **2 quoits** [sing *v*] game in which this is done, esp when on board a ship: *play deck quoits.*

quondam /ˈkwɒndæm/ *adj* [attrib] (*fml or joc*) former; who used to be: *one of his quondam mistresses.*

Quonset hut /ˈkwɒnsət hʌt/ (*US propr*) = NISSEN HUT.

quorum /ˈkwɔ:rəm/ *n* (usu *sing*) minimum number of people who must be present at a meeting (of a committee, etc) before it can proceed and its decisions, etc can be considered valid: *have/form a quorum.*

quota /ˈkwəʊtə/ *n* **1** fixed share that must be done or contributed or received: *have one's full quota of rations* ○ *I'm going home now — I've done my quota of work for the day.* **2** maximum number or amount of people or things allowed, eg to enter a country: *Grain imports are controlled by strict quotas.*

quotation /kwəʊˈteɪʃn/ *n* **1** [U] quoting or being quoted: *Support your argument by quotation.* **2** (also *infml* **quote**) [C] group of words taken from a book, play, speech, etc and used again, usu by sb other than the original author: *a dictionary of quotations* ○ *She finished her speech with a quotation from Shakespeare.* ⇨ App 14. **3** [C] (statement of the) current price of stocks or commodities: *the latest quotations from the Stock Exchange.* **4** (also **infml quote**) [C] estimate of the likely cost of a piece of work: *The insurance company requires three quotations for repairs to the car.* Cf ESTIMATE[1] 2.

□ **quoˈtation-marks** (also **quotes**) *n* [pl] pair of punctuation marks (' ' or " ") used at the beginning and end of words that are being quoted. ⇨ App 14. Cf INVERTED COMMAS (INVERT).

quote /kwəʊt/ *v* **1** [I, Ipr, Tn, Tn·pr] ~ **(sth) (from sb/sth)** repeat in speech or writing (words previously said or written by another person): *You said (and I quote): 'I have always loved her.'* ○ *He's always quoting verses from the Bible.* ○ *She is quoted as saying she disagrees with the decision.* ○ *I think he's going to resign, but please don't quote me*, ie because I am not sure if it is true. **2** [Tn, Dn·n] mention (sb/sth) in support of a statement: *Can you quote (me) an example of what you mean?* **3** [Tn, Tn·pr, Dn·n] ~ **sth (at sth)** name (an amount) as the price of sth: *The shares are currently being quoted at 54 pence a share.* ○ *This is the best price I can quote you.* Cf ESTIMATE[2] 2.

▷ **quote** *n* (*infml*) **1** [C] = QUOTATION 2. **2 quotes** [pl] = QUOTATION-MARKS (QUOTATION): *His words are in quotes.* **3** (idm) ˈ**quote (...ˈunquote)** (used when speaking to show the beginning (and end) of a passage being quoted, esp when the speaker disagrees with it): *This quote startlingly original novel unquote is both boring and badly written.* **4** (*infml*) = QUOTATION 4.

quotable *adj* that can be or that deserves to be quoted: *full of quotable quotes.*

quoth /kwəʊθ/ *v* [Tn] (1st and 3rd person singular past tense only) (*arch*) said: *quoth I/he/she.*

quotient /ˈkwəʊʃnt/ *n* (*mathematics*) result obtained when one number is divided by another.

qv /ˌkju: ˈvi:/ *abbr* (*fml*) which may be referred to (Latin *quod vide*), eg showing a cross-reference.

qwerty /ˈkwɜ:tɪ/ *adj* [attrib] (esp of a typewriter or computer keyboard) arranged so that the top row of alphabetical keys begins with the letters q, w, e, r, t, y, as on keyboards used in English-speaking countries.

qy *abbr* query.

R, r

R, r /ɑː(r)/ *n* (*pl* **R's, r's** /ɑːz/) **1** the eighteenth letter of the English alphabet: *'Rabbit' begins with (an) R/'R'.* **2** (idm) **roll one's r's** ⇨ ROLL². **the three ˈR's** reading, (w)riting and (a)rithmetic, as the basis of an elementary education.

R *abbr* **1** Queen; King (Latin *Regina*; *Rex*): *Elizabeth R.* **2** (also *symb* ®) (*commerce*) registered (trademark): *Scotch* ®. **3** (*US politics*) Republican (party): *James W Sistino (R).* Cf D. **4** (*US*) (of films) restricted, ie not suitable for people under 17 years of age. **5** River: *R Thames*, eg on a map.

r *abbr* **1** recto. **2** right. Cf L 1.

RA /ˌɑːr ˈeɪ/ *abbr* (*Brit*) **1** Royal Academy; Royal Academician: *George Tophill RA* ○ *be an RA.* **2** Royal Artillery.

Ra *symb* radium.

rabbet /ˈræbɪt/ *n, v* = REBATE².

rabbi /ˈræbaɪ/ *n* (*pl* ~**s**) (title of a) spiritual leader of a Jewish congregation; teacher of the Jewish law: *the Chief Rabbi*, eg of Jewish communities in Britain.

▷ **rabbinical** /rəˈbɪnɪkl/ *adj* of rabbis; of Jewish doctrine or law.

rabbit /ˈræbɪt/ *n* **1** [C] small burrowing animal of the hare family with long ears and a short furry tail. Cf HARE, ⇨ illus ANIMAL. **2** [U] **(a)** its fur: *gloves lined with rabbit.* **(b)** its flesh used as meat: [attrib] *rabbit pie.* **3** [C] (*Brit infml*) poor player of a game, esp tennis. **4** (idm) **breed like rabbits** ⇨ BREED.

▷ **rabbit** *v* **1** [Ipr, Ip] ~ **on (about sb/sth)** (*infml derog*) talk lengthily or in a rambling and pointless way: *What are you rabbiting on about?* **2** [I] (usu **go rabbiting**) hunt rabbits.

rabbity *adj* like a rabbit in appearance, smell or taste.

□ **ˈrabbit-hutch** *n* wooden cage for rabbits.

ˈrabbit punch sharp blow made with the edge of the hand on the back of sb's neck.

ˈrabbit-warren *n* **(a)** area of land full of connected burrows made by wild rabbits. **(b)** (*fig usu derog*) building or district full of narrow winding passages.

rabble /ˈræbl/ *n* **1** [C] disorderly crowd; mob. **2 the rabble** [sing] (*derog*) the common people; the lowest social classes: *speeches, etc appealing to the rabble.*

□ **ˈrabble-rouser** *n* person who tries to rouse the passions of the mob, eg for political aims. **ˈrabble-rousing** *adj, n* [U]: *a rabble-rousing speaker, speech.*

Rabelais /ˈræbəleɪ/ François (c1494-1553), French author. His books on the characters Gargantua and Pantagruel show both his Renaissance mind with its immense learning and curiosity, and also his love of humanity and human pleasures. He was one of the most richly comic and inventive users of the French language. ▷ **Rabelaisian** /-ˈleɪzɪən/ *adj* like Rabelais or his work, esp in humorous treatment of subjects like sex and bodily functions: *Rabelaisian prose.*

rabid /ˈræbɪd; *US also* ˈreɪbɪd/ *adj* **1** suffering from rabies: *a rabid dog, fox, etc.* **2** (*fig*) (of feelings or opinions) violent or extreme; fanatical: *rabid hate, greed, etc* ○ *a rabid racist.*

rabies /ˈreɪbiːz/ *n* [U] fatal virus disease causing madness in dogs, foxes and other animals, transmitted to humans usu by a bite. Cf HYDROPHOBIA.

RAC /ˌɑːr eɪ ˈsiː/ *abbr* (*Brit*) Royal Automobile Club. ⇨ article at EMERGENCY.

raccoon (*esp US*) (*Brit* also **racoon**) /rəˈkuːn; *US* ræ-/ (also *US infml* **coon**) *n* **1** [C] small N American flesh-eating mammal with a pointed snout and a bushy black-ringed tail. **2** [U] (*US*) its fur.

race¹ /reɪs/ *n* **1** ~ **(against/with sb/sth)**; ~ **(between A and B)** **(a)** [C] contest of speed between runners, horses, vehicles, etc to see which reaches a certain place first, or does sth first: *a ˈhorse-race* ○ *a ˈboat-race* ○ *a half-ˈmile race* ○ *run a race with sb* ○ *We had a race* (ie a great hurry) *to repair the house before winter.* **(b) the races** [pl] = RACE-MEETING: *a day at the races.* ⇨ Usage at SPORT. **2** competition or rivalry: *the race for the presidency.* **3** [C] strong, fast current of water in a river, the sea, etc: *a tidal race* ○ *a ˈmill-race*, ie a channel taking water to the wheel of a water-mill. **4** (idm) **a ˌrace against ˈtime** desperate effort to do or finish sth before a certain time: *It was a race against time to stop people dying from starvation.* **the rat race** ⇨ RAT.

□ **ˈracecard** *n* programme of the races, times and runners at a race-meeting.

ˈracecourse *n* (*esp Brit*) (*US* usu **ˈrace-track**) ground where horse-races are run.

ˈracegoer *n* person who regularly attends horse-races.

ˈracehorse *n* horse bred or kept to run in races.

ˈrace-meeting *n* (*Brit*) series of horse-races at one course held at fixed times on one or several days.

ˈrace-track *n* **1** (usu oval track), esp for vehicle races. **2** (*US*) = RACECOURSE.

race² /reɪs/ *v* **1 (a)** [I, Ipr, It] ~ **(against/with sb/sth)** take part in a race: *race for the prize/to win the prize* ○ *The lorries were racing against each other.* ○ *The cars raced round the track.* **(b)** [Tn, Tn·pr] compete with (sb/sth) in speed: *I'll race you to school*, ie try to get there before you do. **2 (a)** [I, Ipr, Ip, It] move very fast: *race along (the road)* ○ *The policeman raced after the thief.* ○ *The days seemed to race by/past.* ○ *We had to race to catch the train.* ⇨ Usage at RUN¹. **(b)** [Tn, Tn·pr] cause (sb/sth) to move very fast: *The patient had to be raced to hospital.* **3** [I, Tn] compete in (esp) horse-racing or cause (eg a horse, vehicle) to compete in races: *She races at all the big meetings.* ○ *race pigeons, dogs, etc* ○ *race saloon cars, bikes, etc in rallies* ○ *The filly has been raced twice this season.* **4** [I, Tn] (cause sth to) operate at high speed: *Don't race your engine*, ie make it run fast when not in gear. ○ *The driver waited for the green light, his engine racing.*

▷ **racer** *n* horse, boat, car, etc used for racing.

racing *n* [U] hobby, sport or profession of competing in horse or vehicle races: [attrib] *a ˈracing man* ○ *a ˈracing car, yacht, etc*, ie designed for racing ○ *keep/run a ˈracing stable*, ie for horses trained to race.

race³ /reɪs/ *n* **1** [C, U] **(a)** any of several large subdivisions of mankind sharing physical characteristics, eg colour of skin, colour and type of hair, shape of eyes and nose: *the Caucasian, Mongolian, Negro, etc race* ○ *people of mixed race.* **(b)** [C] any of the main species, breeds or varieties of animals or plants: *the human race*, ie mankind ○ *breed a race of cattle that can survive drought.* **2** [C] group of people with a common culture, history, language, descent, etc: *the Anglo-Saxon, Germanic, Nordic, etc races* ○ *The British are an island race.* **3** [U] (*fml*) ancestry; descent: *people of ancient and noble race.*

□ **ˈrace relations** relations between two or more races in the same community: *Race relations are good here.* ○ *Race relations is a sensitive issue.*

ˈrace-riot *n* outbreak of violence due to hostility between races in the same community. ⇨ article at ETHNIC.

raceme /ˈræsiːm, *also* rəˈsiːm; *US* ˈreɪ-/ *n* (*botany*) flower cluster having separate flowers on stalks evenly spaced along a central stem, with the lower flowers opening first (as in lupins, hyacinths, etc).

Rachmaninov /rækˈmænɪnɒf/ Sergei (1873-1943), Russian composer. He was also a virtuoso pianist, and his piano concertos are among his most popular music. Like his three symphonies, they are written in a rich romantic style.

racial /ˈreɪʃl/ *adj* characteristic of race³(1a); due to or resulting from race: *a racial feature, type, difference, etc* ○ *racial conflict, harmony, hatred, pride* ○ *racial discrimination.*

▷ **racialism** /-ʃəlɪzəm/ (also **racism**) *n* [U] **1** belief that human abilities, etc depend on race and that some races are superior to others. **2** (aggressive behaviour, speech, etc showing) hostility between races.

racialist /-ʃəlɪst/ (also **racist**) *n, adj* (of or like a) believer in racialism, esp one who is hostile to races thought to be inferior: *a racialist theory, book, speech.*

racially /-ʃəlɪ/ *adv*: *a racially diverse community.*

racily, raciness ⇨ RACY.

Racine /ræˈsiːn/ Jean (1639-99), French playwright. With *Corneille he is one of the great masters of 17th-century tragedy in France. His plays, eg *Andromaque* and *Phèdre*, often take the blind folly of human passion as their subject.

racism /ˈreɪsɪzəm/ *n* [U] = RACIALISM (RACIAL). ▷ **racist** /ˈreɪsɪst/ *n, adj* = RACIALIST (RACIAL). ⇨ article at ETHNIC.

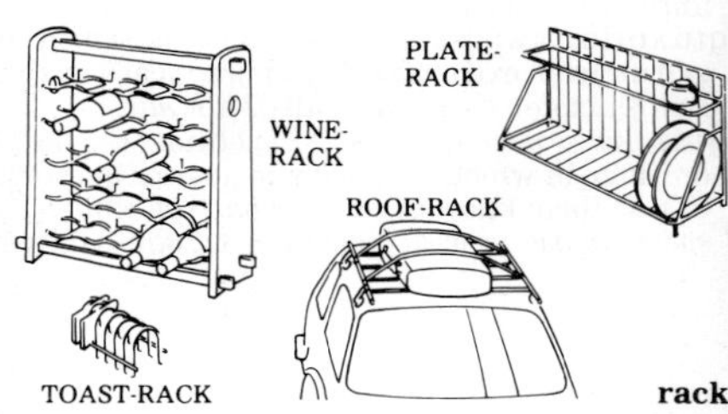

rack

rack¹ /ræk/ *n* **1** (often in compounds) framework, usu with bars or pegs, for holding things or for hanging things on: *a ˈplate-rack* ○ *a ˈwine-rack*, ie for holding wine bottles ○ *a ˈtoast-rack* ○ *a ˈhat-rack.* **2** type of shelf for light luggage, coats, etc over the seats of a bus, train, plane, etc: *a ˈluggage-rack.* **3** rod, bar or rail with teeth or cogs, into which those of a wheel, gear, etc fit: *a ˈsteering rack*, eg on a cable car. Cf PINION². ▷ **rack** *v* (phr v) **rack sth up** (*US infml*) score or gain (eg points in a game): *She racked up nearly 60% of the vote.*

□ **ˈrack-railway** (also *esp US* **cog-railway**) *n* railway that has a cogged central rail with which a cogged wheel on the train engages to drive the train up a steep slope.

rack² /ræk/ *n* **1** (usu **the rack**) (formerly) instrument of torture consisting of a frame with rollers to which a person's wrists and ankles were tied so that his joints were stretched when the rollers were turned: *put sb on the rack.* **2** (idm) **on the ˈrack** in severe pain or mental distress.

▷ **rack** *v* **1** [Tn] torture (sb) on the rack. **2** [Tn esp passive] (of disease, pain or mental distress) cause agony to (sb): *racked with pain, fever, etc* ○ *A coughing fit racked her whole body.* ○ *a voice racked by sobs/weeping* ○ *racked by (feelings of) guilt, remorse, doubt, etc.* **3** (idm) **rack one's ˈbrain(s)** try very hard to think of sth or recall sth: *We racked our brains for an answer.* ○ *I've been racking my brains (trying) to remember his name.*

□ **ˈrack-rent** *n* [C, U] unfairly high rent.

rack³ /ræk/ *n* (idm) **go to ˌrack and ˈruin** fall into a ruined or disorganized state through neglect: *The old empty house soon went to rack and ruin.* ○

This country is going to rack and ruin; we need a change of government.

racket[1] (also **racquet**) /ˈrækɪt/ *n* **1** [C] bat with a round or oval stringed frame, used for hitting the ball in tennis, badminton, etc. ⇨ illus at SQUASH, TENNIS. **2 rackets** (also **racquets**) [sing *v*] ball-game for two or four people played with rackets and a small hard ball in a four-walled court: [attrib] *a rackets court, ball, match.* Cf SQUASH *n* 3.

□ ˈ**racket-press** *n* frame worked by a spring, used for holding a racket tightly when not in use, to prevent warping, etc.

racket[2] /ˈrækɪt/ *n* (*infml*) **1** [sing] loud noise; uproar or noisy disturbance: *What a racket the children are making!* ○ *The students kicked up no end of a racket* (ie were very noisy and boisterous) *in the street.* **2** [C] (**a**) dishonest or illegal way of getting money: *the gambling/protection/drugs racket* ○ *Police investigating the fraud suspected him of being in on* (ie profiting by) *the racket.* (**b**) business or occupation: *What's your racket?* ○ *How did she get into the modelling racket?*

▷ **racket** *v* [I, Ip] ~ (**about/around**) (*infml*) move about noisily; join in wild social activities.

racketeer /ˌrækəˈtɪə(r)/ *n* (*derog*) person involved in or controlling a racket[2](2). **racketeering** *n* [U] (*derog*) activity of racketeers.

rackety *adj* (*infml*) noisy: *a rackety old bicycle.*

Arthur Rackham: illustration from 'English Fairy Tales'

Rackham /ˈrakəm/ Arthur (1867-1939), English artist. He is famous for his illustrations of children's books, drawing a world of goblins and monsters for works like the tales of the Brothers *Grimm. ⇨ illus.

raconteur /ˌrækɒnˈtɜː(r)/ *n* person who tells stories skilfully and wittily: *She's a brilliant raconteur.*

racoon = RACCOON.

racy /ˈreɪsɪ/ *adj* (**-ier, -iest**) **1** (of speech, writing, etc) lively or spirited; vivid: *a racy account of his adventures.* **2** (*infml*) slightly improper or indecent: *Her racy stories can be rather shocking.* **3** strong and distinctive in flavour: *a racy wine.* ▷ **racily** /-ɪlɪ/ *adv.* **raciness** *n* [U].

rad /ræd/ *n* unit of absorbed ionizing radiation.

RADA /ˈrɑːdə/ *abbr* (*Brit*) Royal Academy of Dramatic Art: *a student at RADA.*

radar /ˈreɪdɑː(r)/ *n* [U] (**a**) system for detecting the presence, position or movement of solid objects within its range by sending out short radio waves which they reflect: *locate an aircraft by radar.* (**b**) equipment used for this: *Enemy ships were detected on the radar (screen).* ○ [attrib] *a radar operator, installation, scanner.* Cf SONAR.

□ ˈ**radar trap** (also ˈ**speed trap**) section of road where the police use a radar device to detect vehicles travelling faster than the speed limit.

raddled /ˈrædld/ *adj* (*derog*) (of a person, face, etc) showing the effects of living immorally for a long time: *No amount of make-up could disguise her raddled features*, eg with facial lines, hollow eyes, etc.

radial /ˈreɪdɪəl/ *adj* of or arranged like rays or radii; having bars, lines, etc that radiate from a central point: *radial spokes*, eg in a bicycle wheel ○ *a radial engine*, ie one with cylinders pointing outwards from a central crankshaft.

▷ **radial** *n* (also **radial-ply tyre**) tyre with the cords in its outer casing arranged radially to the hub of the wheel, so making it stronger and able to grip better on wet road surfaces. Cf CROSS-PLY.

radially /-ɪəlɪ/ *adv.*

radian

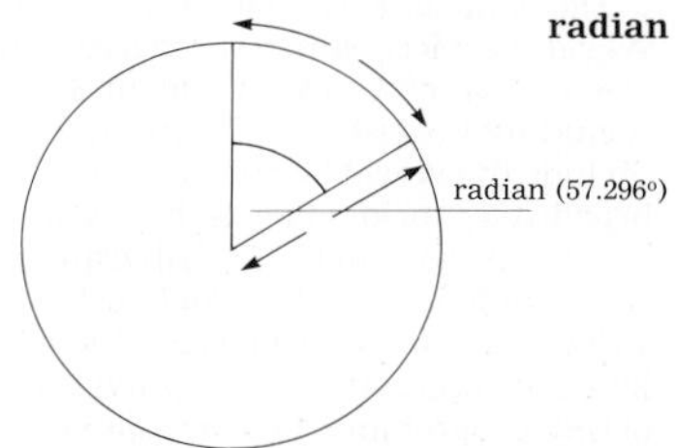

radian /ˈreɪdɪən/ *n* unit used for measuring angles in the SI system, equal to the angle formed at the centre of a circle by two radii separated by an arc which is the same length as the radius, ie approximately 57.296°. ⇨ illus.

radiant /ˈreɪdɪənt/ *adj* **1** [attrib] sending out rays of light; shining brightly: *the radiant sun.* **2** ~ (**with sth**) (of a person, his eyes, look, etc) bright with joy, hope or love: *a radiant face, smile* ○ *radiant beauty* ○ *She was radiant with joy at her wedding.* ○ *You look absolutely radiant!* **3** (*physics*) [attrib] (**a**) transmitting heat or energy by radiation: *a radiant heater.* (**b**) (of heat or energy) transmitted by radiation.

▷ **radiance** /-əns/ *n* [U] quality of being radiant(1, 2).

radiantly *adv*: *smiling radiantly.*

radiate /ˈreɪdɪeɪt/ *v* **1** (**a**) [Tn] send out rays of (light or heat): *a stove that radiates warmth.* (**b**) [Ipr] ~ **from sth** (of light or heat) be sent out from sth by radiation: *warmth radiating from the stove.* **2** (**a**) [Tn] (*fig*) (of a person) give forth a feeling of (sth): *radiating confidence, enthusiasm, health, etc.* (**b**) [Ipr] ~ **from sb/sth** (*fig*) (of a feeling) be given forth by sb/sb's eyes, etc. **3** (of lines, etc) spread out like radii from a central point: *Five roads radiate from this roundabout.*

radiation /ˌreɪdɪˈeɪʃn/ *n* **1** [U] (**a**) (the sending out of) heat, energy, etc in the form of rays: *a combination of radiation and convection*, eg in a gas fire. (**b**) (the sending out of) rays and atomic particles from radioactive substances: *a low/high level of radiation* ○ [attrib] *Some cancers are treated by radiation therapy.* **2** [C] thing that is radiated, esp radioactive particles: *radiations emitted by an X-ray machine.*

□ **radiˈation sickness** illness caused when the body is exposed to high radiation, eg from radioactive material or X-rays.

radiator /ˈreɪdɪeɪtə(r)/ *n* **1** apparatus for radiating heat into rooms, etc, esp a metal casing through which hot water or steam is circulated. **2** device for cooling the engine of a vehicle or an aircraft: *This car has a fan-cooled radiator.* ⇨ illus at CAR.

radical /ˈrædɪkl/ *adj* [usu attrib] **1** of or from the root or base; fundamental: *a radical flaw, error, fault, etc in the system.* **2** thorough or complete; drastic: *radical reforms, changes, etc.* **3** favouring thorough political or social reform; holding extreme views: *a radical politician, thinker, writer, etc* ○ *She is radical in her demands.*

▷ **radical** *n* **1** person with radical(3) opinions. **2** (*mathematics*) quantity forming or expressed as the root of another. **3** (*chemistry*) group of atoms forming part of a compound and not changing during chemical reactions.

radicalism /-kəlɪzəm/ *n* [U] (belief in) radical(3) ideas and principles.

radically /-klɪ/ *adv*: *radically altered, improved, etc.*

radicle /ˈrædɪkl/ *n* part of a plant embryo that develops into the main root.

radii *pl* of RADIUS.

radio /ˈreɪdɪəʊ/ *n* (*pl* ~**s**) **1** [U] process of sending and receiving messages, etc by electromagnetic waves without a connecting wire: *contact a ship at sea by radio* ○ [attrib] *ˈradio waves, communiˈcations* ○ *a radio ˈtelephone.* **2** [C] (**a**) (also ˈ**radio set**) apparatus, eg on ships or planes, for sending and receiving messages in this way: *hear a gale warning on/over a ship's radio* ○ [attrib] *a radio receiver, transmitter.* (**b**) (also *dated* **wireless**) apparatus, eg in the house, for receiving sound broadcasting: *a portable, transistor radio.* **3** (often **the radio**) [U, sing] sound broadcasting by this means: *I heard it on the radio.* ○ *She always listens to the radio.* ○ *a play specially written for radio* ○ *Do you prefer radio or television?* ○ [attrib] *a radio programme, announcer, station.* ⇨ article.

▷ **radio** *v* (*pt, pp* **radioed**) [Ipr, Tn, Tn·pr, Tf, Dn·f, Dpr·f, Dpr·w, Dpr·t no passive] send a message by radio: *radio (to sb) for help* ○ *radio (sb) one's position* ○ *We radioed (to) headquarters that we were in trouble.* ○ *Radio to them to come/where we are.*

□ ˌ**radio asˈtronomy** branch of astronomy in which radio waves from space are received and analysed. In the 1930s astronomers discovered radio waves coming from outside the earth's atmosphere, and in the 1960s they found that there was a uniform background radiation throughout the universe. Many bodies in space send out long-wave radiation. These include pulsars and supernovas, radio galaxies and quasars, where processes involving large amounts of radiation are taking place, about which we know little.

ˈ**radio car**, ˈ**radio cab** car or cab equipped with a radio for communication.

ˌ**radio-conˈtrolled** *adj* controlled from a distance by radio signals: *a ˌradio-controlled ˈtaxi.*

ˌ**radio-ˈfrequency** *n* frequency of electromagnetic waves used in radio and TV transmission, between 10 kilocycles per second and 3 000 000 megacycles per second.

ˈ**radiogram** *n* **1** telegram sent by radio. **2** (*Brit*) (esp formerly) combined radio and record player.

ˌ**radio ˈtelescope** apparatus for finding stars, tracking spacecraft, etc by means of radio waves from outer space.

radio- *comb form* of radiation or radioactivity: *radioactive* ○ *radiologist* ○ *radio-therapy.*

radioactive /ˌreɪdɪəʊˈæktɪv/ *adj* having atoms whose nuclei break up and send out radiation which can penetrate matter and produce harmful effects: *Radium and uranium are radioactive elements.* ○ *ˌradioactive ˈfall-out*, ie dust carried by winds around the earth after a nuclear explosion, etc ○ *radioactive waste*, ie waste material from nuclear power-stations, etc.

▷ **radioactivity** /ˌreɪdɪəʊækˈtɪvətɪ/ *n* [U] property of being radioactive. There are three main types of radioactivity: alpha radiation, which is made up of nuclei of helium atoms; beta radiation, which is made up of fast-moving electrons or positrons; and harmful gamma radiation, which is electromagnetic radiation with very high energy. Such energy may be responsible for the heating processes going on at the earth's core, and is the destructive force used by nuclear weapons. Some parts of the world, eg Cornwall or parts of northern Scotland, have naturally high levels of background radioactivity.

radio-carbon /ˌredɪəʊ ˈkɑːbən/ *n* [U] radioactive

Radio

The British Broadcasting Corporation (BBC) was founded in 1927 as an independent public corporation. There is no advertising on BBC radio. It is not required to make a profit and its income comes almost entirely from the sale of television licences which everyone who owns a television has to buy. Although the chairman and governors of the BBC are appointed by the monarch on the advice of the government, the government has no control over the BBC's broadcasting policy.

The BBC broadcasts radio programmes both at home (within Britain) and abroad (to other countries), its domestic and external services respectively. At home, the BBC currently broadcasts five radio networks, Radios 1, 2, 3, 4 and 5. Radio 1 broadcasts rock and pop music, while Radio 2 transmits mainly popular music, light entertainment and sports programmes. On both these channels the style of presentation is informal. They both broadcast 24 hours a day. Radio 3 broadcasts mainly classical music from 7.00 am to about midnight, but also presents plays, talks, and readings of short stories and poetry. In the early morning, before its regular schedule begins, it transmits programmes for Open University courses. (Cf article at POST-SCHOOL EDUCATION.) Radio 4 is the main speech network. Its programmes include regular news bulletins and reports, as well as plays, documentaries, quiz shows and live broadcasts of important events. It is on the air from 6.00 am to midnight. Radio 5, which began broadcasting in 1990, is aimed at younger listeners and broadcasts mainly educational and sports programmes.

Apart from these national programmes, the BBC also has 36 local radio stations in England and the Channel Islands, and six regional services in Scotland, Wales and Northern Ireland. One of the Welsh stations, Radio Cymru, broadcasts in Welsh. Programmes on local radio concentrate on local news and information, together with music, entertainment and educational broadcasts. The public is able to take part in 'phone-in' programmes, where listeners speak by telephone to a presenter or guest in the studio.

The main external network of the BBC is the World Service, which broadcasts to almost every country of the world in 37 languages, including English. The main English services include the World Service in English, which is broadcast world-wide 24 hours a day, with special programmes for African and South Asian audiences, BBC English by Radio and Television, which teaches English as a foreign language, and a service that provides recordings of BBC programmes for overseas radio stations. Foreign language programmes, such as the African Service, Arabic Service and German Service, are transmitted to audiences in the appropriate countries. The government decides which languages shall be broadcast by the World Service, and the length of time each service is on the air, but the BBC itself is responsible for the content of the programmes.

As well as the BBC's local radio stations, there are 62 independent local radio (ILR) stations, which were originally operated by the Independent Broadcasting Authority (IBA). Their programmes are similar in content to those of the BBC, but include regular breaks for commercial advertising. In 1991 the IBA's responsibility for radio was transferred to a new body, the Radio Authority.

In the USA radio is controlled by private commercial companies, with the exception of National Public Radio, which is supported by grants and donations. By 1928, the USA had three national radio networks, two owned by the National Broadcasting Company (NBC) and one by the Columbia Broadcasting System (CBS). At first, sound broadcasting was almost entirely for entertainment, but schedules are now more varied, and some stations broadcast purely educational programmes. In 1985 there were over 9 000 radio stations in the USA, the largest number in any country in the world.

form of carbon, esp carbon 14, present in organic materials, and used in carbon dating (CARBON). As all living things absorb carbon, it is possible to determine the age of a specimen by finding out how much of the carbon has decayed since its death.

radiograph /ˈreɪdɪəʊɡrɑːf; *US* -ɡræf/ *n* = X-RAY 2.
▷ **radiographer** /ˌreɪdɪˈɒɡrəfə(r)/ *n* person who takes radiographs.
radiography /ˌreɪdɪˈɒɡrəfɪ/ *n* [U] production of X-ray photographs.

radioisotope /ˌreɪdɪəʊˈaɪsətəʊp/ *n* radioactive form of an element, used in medicine, industry, etc to study the path and speed of substances through bodies and objects.

radiology /ˌreɪdɪˈɒlədʒɪ/ *n* [U] scientific study of X-rays and other radiation, esp as used in medicine.
▷ **radiologist** /ˌreɪdɪˈɒlədʒɪst/ *n* expert in radiology.

radio-therapy /ˌreɪdɪəʊ ˈθerəpɪ/ *n* [U] treatment of disease by radiation, esp X-rays.
▷ **ˌradio-ˈtherapist** *n* expert in radio-therapy.

radish /ˈrædɪʃ/ *n* (**a**) plant with a crisp hot-tasting root. (**b**) this root, eaten raw in salads: *bunches of radishes.*

radium /ˈreɪdɪəm/ *n* [U] (*symb* **Ra**) chemical element, a shining white radioactive metal used in the treatment of some diseases, eg cancer: [attrib] *radium therapy.* ⇨ App 11.

radius /ˈreɪdɪəs/ *n* (*pl* **-dii** /-dɪaɪ/) **1** (length of a) straight line from the centre of a circle or sphere to any point on its circumference or surface. ⇨ App 10, ⇨ illus at CIRCLE. **2** circular area measured by its radius: *Police searched all the woods within a six-mile radius/within a radius of six miles.* **3** (*anatomy*) outer shorter bone in the human forearm; corresponding bone in an animal's foreleg or a bird's wing. ⇨ illus at SKELETON. Cf ULNA.

radon /ˈreɪdɒn/ *n* [U] (*symb* **Rn**) chemical element, a radioactive gas produced by the decay of radium. ⇨ App 11.

Sir Henry Raeburn: Colonel Alaistair MacDonnell of Glengarry

Raeburn /ˈreɪbɜːn/ Sir Henry (1756-1823), Scottish painter. He worked in Edinburgh and produced many portraits of important Scottish figures of the time, often in Highland dress and in dramatic settings. ⇨ illus.

RAF /ˌɑːr eɪ ˈef, *or, in infml use,* ræf/ *abbr* (*Brit*) Royal Air Force.

raffia /ˈræfɪə/ *n* [U] soft fibre from the leaves of a type of palm-tree, used for tying up plants, weaving table-mats, etc.

raffish /ˈræfɪʃ/ *adj* (esp of men, their appearance or behaviour) flashy or slightly disreputable; rakish: *He was drinking cheap champagne with a raffish air.* ▷ **raffishly** *adv.* **raffishness** *n* [U].

raffle /ˈræfl/ *n* lottery (esp for charity) with an article as the prize: *win a video in a raffle* ○ [attrib] *a raffle ticket.* Cf DRAW[1] 1. ⇨ article at GAMBLING.
▷ **raffle** *v* [Tn, Tn·p] ~ **sth (off)** offer (goods) as a prize in a raffle.

Raffles[1] /ˈræfəlz/ Sir Thomas Stamford (1781-1826), English colonial administrator. He was responsible for the purchase of *Singapore by the *East India Company and for developing the island as a commercial centre.

Raffles[2] /ˈræfəlz/ hero of a series of novels by the English author E W Hornung (1866-1921). He is a gentleman, educated at a public school, whose hobby is being a burglar. His name is sometimes used to refer to a dishonest man with good manners.

raft[1] /rɑːft; *US* ræft/ *n* (**a**) flat floating structure of logs, barrels, etc tied together, used esp as a substitute for a boat: *shipwrecked sailors on a makeshift raft.* (**b**) number of logs tied together to be floated down a river.
▷ **raft** *v* (**a**) [Tn·pr, Tn·p] carry (people or goods) on a raft: *raft people across/over/up/down (a river).* (**b**) [Ipr, Ip] cross a river, etc on a raft.

raft[2] /rɑːft; *US* ræft/ *n* (usu *sing*) ~ (**of sth**) (*US infml*) large number or amount: *She got a raft of presents.*

rafter /ˈrɑːftə(r); *US* ˈræf-/ *n* any of the parallel sloping beams supporting the tiles, slates, etc of a roof: *hams hanging from the rafters,* eg in an old inn.
▷ **raftered** /ˈrɑːftəd; *US* ˈræf-/ *adj* having rafters, esp ones that are exposed, eg because there is no ceiling.

rag[1] /ræɡ/ *n* **1** [C, U] odd (scrap of) cloth, usu torn, frayed, etc: *I use an oily rag to clean my bike with.* ○ *Instead of a handkerchief he had an old (piece of) rag.* ○ [attrib] *a rag doll,* ie one stuffed with rags.

2 rags [pl] (**a**) old, worn or torn clothes: *a tramp dressed in rags and tatters* ○ *trade in rags and waste paper*. (**b**) pieces of waste cloth used to make good quality paper: [attrib] *ˈrag paper*. **3** [C] (*infml usu derog*) newspaper or journal: *I read it in the local rag*. **4** (idm) **chew the fat/rag** ⇨ CHEW. **from ˌrags to ˈriches** from extreme poverty to wealth: [attrib] *Hers was a rags-to-riches story.* **glad rags** ⇨ GLAD. **like a wet rag** ⇨ WET. **lose one's rag** ⇨ LOSE. **a red rag to a bull** ⇨ RED[1].

□ **rag-and-ˈbone man** (*Brit*) person who goes round buying and selling old clothes, discarded furniture, etc.

ˈrag-bag *n* **1** [C] bag in which scraps of fabric are kept, eg to mend clothes. **2** [sing] (*fig*) confused assortment; hotchpotch: *a rag-bag of strange ideas, theories, etc.*

the ˈrag trade (*infml*) business of designing, making and selling (esp women's) clothes: *go into the rag trade.*

rag[2] /ræg/ *v* (**-gg-**) [Tn, Tn·pr] ~ **sb** (**about/for sth**) (*Brit infml*) play practical jokes on sb; tease sb: *They are always ragging the teacher about his accent.*

▷ **rag** *n* **1** practical joke; prank: *We hid her clothes for a rag.* **2** annual entertainment held by students to collect money for charity: *the college ˈrag* ○ [attrib] *hold a ˈrag week.*

rag[3] /ræg/ *n* piece of ragtime music.

ragamuffin /ˈrægəmʌfɪn/ *n* person, esp a small boy, in dirty untidy clothes.

rage /reɪdʒ/ *n* **1** [U, C] (**a**) (fit of) violent anger: *trembling with rage* ○ *white/livid with rage* ○ *be in/fly into a (towering) rage* ○ *Her rages don't last long.* (**b**) (*fig*) (instance of) violence in nature: *The storm's rage continued.* **2** (idm) **all the fashion/rage** ⇨ FASHION.

▷ **rage** *v* **1** (**a**) [I, Ipr] ~ (**at/against sb/sth**) show violent anger: *He raged against me for disagreeing.* ○ *I raged for hours at the decision.* (**b**) [I] (of storms, fires, battles, etc) continue violently. **2** [I, Ipr] (esp of illnesses) spread rapidly: *A flu epidemic raged through the school for weeks.*

raging *adj* [attrib] extreme or painful: *raging hunger, thirst, passion* ○ *have a raging headache, toothache, etc.*

ragged /ˈrægɪd/ *adj* **1** (**a**) (of clothes) badly worn or in rags; tattered: *a ragged coat, suit, etc* ○ *His sleeves were ragged at the cuffs.* (**b**) (of people) wearing badly worn or torn clothes: *a ragged old man.* **2** (*fig*) having an uneven outline, edge or surface; jagged: *the ragged profile of the cliffs* ○ *ragged clouds driven by the wind.* **3** (*fig*) lacking smoothness or uniformity; imperfect: *The choir gave a ragged performance*, ie The singers were not following the conductor. ○ *A ragged shout went up from the small crowd.* ▷ **raggedly** *adv.* **raggedness** *n* [U].

raglan /ˈræglən/ *n, adj* [attrib] (**a**) (sleeve) that is joined to the body of a garment by sloping seams from the armpit to the neckline. (**b**) (coat, sweater, etc) having sleeves of this kind.

ragout /ˈrægu:; *US* ræˈgu:/ *n* [C, U] (dish of) meat and vegetable stew.

ragtag /ˈrægtæg/ *n* (idm) **ˌragtag and ˈbobtail** disreputable people; riff-raff.

ragtime /ˈrægtaɪm/ *n* [U] type of popular 1920's jazz music first played by Blacks in the US, in which the beat of the melody just precedes the beat of the accompaniment: [attrib] *a ˌragtime ˈband.*

ragweed /ˈrægwi:d/ *n* [U, C] N American weed producing large amounts of pollen which causes hay fever.

ragwort /ˈrægwɜ:t/ *n* [C, U] wild plant with yellow daisy-like flowers and ragged leaves.

raid /reɪd/ *n* ~ (**on sth**) **1** sudden surprise attack and withdrawal by troops, ships or aircraft: *make/launch a bombing raid* (ie by aircraft) *on enemy bases.* **2** sudden surprise attack in order to steal or do harm: *an armed raid* ○ *A security guard was killed in the bank raid.* **3** sudden surprise visit by the police, etc, eg to arrest people or seize illicit goods: *carry out a dawn raid* ○ *a police drugs raid.* **4** (*finance*) attempt by a group of people to lower eg share prices by selling at the same time.

▷ **raid** *v* [Tn] make a raid on (a place): *Customs men raided the house.* ○ (*fig*) *raid the larder*, ie take food from it, usu between meals ○ *boys raiding an orchard*, ie to steal fruit. **raider** *n* person, ship, aircraft, etc that makes a raid.

rail[1] /reɪl/ *n* **1** [C] (**a**) level or sloping bar or connected series of bars of wood or metal, eg forming part of a fence, the top of a banister, a protective barrier, etc: *wooden rails in front of an altar* ○ *the horses on the rails*, ie those on the inside curve of a racecourse ○ *Hold the ˈhandrail for safety*, eg while descending steps. ○ *leaning on the ship's (guard-)rail looking out to sea.* (**b**) level bar fixed to a wall for hanging things on: *a ˈtowel-rail*, eg beside a wash-basin ○ *a ˈcurtain rail.* ⇨ illus at FURNITURE. **2** (**a**) [C esp *pl*] steel bar or continuous line of steel bars fixed to the ground as one side of a track for trains or trams. ⇨ illus at FLANGE. (**b**) [U often attrib] railways as a means of transport: *a rail strike* ○ *rail travel, freight, etc* ○ *send sth by rail* ○ *British Rail.* **3** (idm) **free on board/rail** ⇨ FREE[1]. **go off the ˈrails** (*Brit infml*) (**a**) become disorganized or out of control: *Our schedule went completely off the rails during the strike.* (**b**) become mad or crazy. **jump the rails/track** ⇨ JUMP[2].

▷ **rail** *v* (phr v) **rail sth in/off** surround or separate sth with rails: *rail off a field (from a road)* ○ *The winners' enclosure was railed in.*

□ **ˈrailhead** *n* (**a**) furthest point reached by a railway that is being built. (**b**) point on a railway at which road transport begins or ends.

ˈrailroad *n* (*US*) railway. — *v* (phr v) **railroad sb into (doing) sth** (*infml*) force sb to do sth: *I won't be railroaded into buying a car I don't want!* **railroad sth through (sth)** (*infml*) get sth passed, accepted, etc quickly by applying pressure: *railroad a bill through Congress.*

rail[2] /reɪl/ *v* [I, Ipr] ~ (**at/against sb/sth**) complain, protest or reproach sb/sth strongly: *railing against fate* ○ *She railed at (him for) his laziness.*

rail[3] /reil/ *n* small long-legged bird that lives esp on marshes. Rails have small wings, and seldom fly.

railing /ˈreɪlɪŋ/ *n* (often *pl*) fence or barrier made of rails (RAIL[1] 1a), supported by upright bars.

raillery /ˈreɪlərɪ/ *n* [U] good-humoured mockery or ridicule.

railway /ˈreɪlweɪ/ (*US* **railroad**) *n* **1** track with rails (RAIL[1] 2a) for trains to run on: *railways under construction.* **2** (often *pl*) system of such tracks, together with the trains, etc running on them, and the organization and people needed for their operation. Trains of wagons pulled by horses along rails existed before the steam engine was invented and were used esp in mines. It was the success of George *Stephenson's *Rocket* in 1829 that led to the creation of a railway network, which by the end of the century covered most of Britain. Railways played a key role in opening up new lands, eg the western USA. In the 20th century diesel and electricity replaced steam as the power source of most railways. In many countries railways have suffered a decline in the face of competition from road and air transport, but others (eg France and Japan) are developing new railway technology, with trains that can go at over 250 km (150 miles) per hour: *work on/for the railway(s)* ○ *a network of railways run by the state* ○ [attrib] *a railway station, carriage, engineer.* ⇨ article.

□ **ˈrailwayman** /-mən/ *n* (*pl* **-men** /-mən/) man who works for a railway company.

raiment /ˈreɪmənt/ *n* [U] (*arch*) clothing.

rain[1] /reɪn/ *n* **1** [U] condensed moisture of the atmosphere falling as separate drops; fall of these drops: *heavy/light rain* ○ *Don't go out in the rain.* ○ *Come in out of the rain.* ○ *It looks like* (ie as if there will be a fall of) *rain.* **2 the rains** [pl] season of heavy continuous rain in tropical countries: *The rains come in September.* **3** [C] (preceded by an *adj*) shower of rain of the specified type: *There was a heavy rain during the night.* **4** [sing] ~ **of sth** (*esp fig*) great number of things falling like rain: *a rain of arrows, bullets, etc* ○ *a rain of ashes*, eg from a volcano. **5** (idm) **come ˌrain, come ˈshine; (come) ˌrain or ˈshine** whether there is rain or sunshine; whatever happens: *The fête will take place on Sunday, rain or shine.* **right as rain** ⇨ RIGHT[1]. ▷ **rainless** *adj*: *a rainless day.*

□ **rainbow** /ˈreɪnbəʊ/ *n* arch containing the colours of the spectrum, formed in the sky when the sun shines through rain or spray: *silks dyed in all (the) colours of the rainbow.* **ˈrainbow trout** black-spotted trout with two reddish bands from nose to tail.

ˈrain-check *n* (*US*) **1** ticket for later use when a match, show, etc is cancelled because of rain. **2** (idm) **take a rain-check (on sth)** (*infml*) decline an offer, etc but promise to accept it later: *Thanks for the invitation, but I'll have to take a rain-check on it.*

ˈraincoat *n* light waterproof or water-resistant coat.

ˈraindrop *n* single drop of rain.

ˈrainfall *n* [U] total amount of rain falling within a given area in a given time: *an annual rainfall of 10 cm.* ⇨ App 9.

ˈrain forest thick evergreen forest in tropical regions with heavy rainfall.

ˈrain-gauge *n* instrument for measuring rainfall.

ˈrainproof *adj* that can keep rain out: *a rainproof jacket.*

ˈrain-water *n* soft water that has fallen as rain, eg not taken from wells, etc.

rain[2] /reɪn/ *v* **1** [I] (used with *it*) fall as rain: *It is raining*, ie Rain is falling. ○ *It rained hard all day.* **2** [Ipr] ~ **on sb/sth** (*fig*) fall like rain on sb/sth: *Blows rained on the door.* ○ *The suitcase burst open and its contents rained on the floor.* **3** (idm) **it ˌnever ˌrains but it ˈpours** (*saying*) misfortunes, etc usually come in large numbers: *First my car broke down, then I lost my key: it never rains but it pours!* **rain ˈbuckets; rain cats and ˈdogs** (esp in the continuous tenses) rain very heavily. **4** (phr v) **rain down (sth)** flow or come down in large quantities: *Tears rained down her cheeks.* ○ *Loose rocks rained down (the hillside).* **rain down (on sb/sth)** come down on sb/sth: *Abuse rained down on the noisy students from the open windows.* ○ *Invitations rained down on the visiting writer.* **rain in** (used with *it*): *It is raining in*, ie Rain is coming through the roof, tent, etc. **rain sth off**; *US* **rain sth out** (usu passive) (*infml*) prevent (eg an event) from taking place because of rain: *The match was rained off twice.*

rainy /ˈreɪnɪ/ *adj* (**-ier, -iest**) **1** (of a day, period, etc) on or in which much rain falls; (of sky, weather, etc) bringing much rain: *a rainy afternoon, month, etc* ○ *the ˈrainy season* ○ *a rainy climate, sky.* **2** (idm) **save, keep, etc sth for a ˌrainy ˈday** save (esp money) for a time when one may need it.

raise /reɪz/ *v* **1** [Tn, Tn·pr, Tn·p] (**a**) lift or move (sth) to a higher level; cause to rise: *raise one's hand* ○ *He raised his eyes from his work.* ○ *raise a sunken ship (up) to the surface* ○ *raise one's hat to sb*, ie as a sign of respect. (**b**) move (sth/sb) to an upright position: *raise a man from his knees* ○ *We raised the fence and fixed it in position.* **2** [Tn, Tn·pr] ~ **sth (to sth)** increase the amount or volume or heighten the level of sth: *raise salaries, prices, profits, etc* ○ *He raised his offer to £500.* ○ *raise one's voice*, ie speak more loudly ○ *raise the temperature to 80°* ○ *raise standards of service* ○ *raise sb's hopes*, ie make sb more hopeful. **3** [Tn] cause (sth) to arise or appear: *raise doubts, fears, suspicions, etc in people's minds* ○ *The horses' hooves raised a cloud of dust.* ○ *raise the spirits of the dead* ○ *The dirty joke raised a blush on her cheek.* **4** [Tn] (**a**) cause (sth) to be heard: *raise a commotion, fuss, protest, stink, etc* ○ *raise the alarm/alert* ○ *The retort raised a cheer in support of the speaker.* (**b**) bring (sth) up for discussion or attention; put forward: *The book raises many important issues (for our consideration).* ○ *I'm glad you raised that point.* **5** [Tn] bring or collect (sth) together; manage to obtain: *raise an army* ○ *raise a loan, a subscription, etc* ○ *raise funds for charity*, eg by holding a bazaar ○ *a fund-raising event.* **6** [Tn]

Railways

From the first half of the 19th century, a dense network of railways was built in Britain, and railways were operated by a large number of private companies. Railway lines criss-crossed the countryside, and stations, tunnels, bridges and viaducts were built. Some of these remain today as striking examples of Victorian industrial architecture and engineering.

The many companies were merged in 1923 into four systems which operated on a regional basis: the London, Midland and Scottish Railway (LMS), the London and North Eastern Railway (LNER), the Great Western Railway (GWR) and the Southern Railway (SR). London itself still had several companies, which were merged in 1933 to form the London Passenger Transport Board (LPTB), now called London Regional Transport (LRT).

In 1948 the four main companies were nationalized as British Railways (BR), now usually called British Rail, and were organized in six regions. In 1990 British Rail was again reorganized as five separate businesses providing different types of passenger and freight services.

In the 1960s many unprofitable lines were closed, most of them branch lines, so that the present railway network is far less extensive than formerly. From that time too, steam trains were gradually replaced by diesel and electric locomotives.

There are eight main rail terminals in London, each serving a different part of the country: Paddington for the west and Wales; Euston, St Pancras and King's Cross for the Midlands and the north, including Scotland; Liverpool Street for East Anglia; and Charing Cross, Victoria and Waterloo for the south, including the Channel ports. The construction of a tunnel under the English Channel will provide a direct rail link between London and Paris from the mid 1990s.

The London Underground (also called 'the tube') is a local railway system which operates (not always underground) on 11 different lines: Bakerloo, Central, Circle, District, East London, Jubilee, Metropolitan, Northern, Piccadilly, Victoria, and Docklands Light Railway. Some of these lines are over 100 years old, while the East London and Docklands Light Railway lines were opened only in the 1980s. Two key lines are the Waterloo and City Line (administratively not part of the Underground system although operating within it), taking commuters from British Rail's Waterloo Station to the City and back, and the service on the Piccadilly line to Heathrow Airport. Glasgow is the only other city in Britain to have an underground railway, but in the 1980s a new urban electric railway, the Tyne and Wear Metro, was built between Newcastle and Gateshead in north-east England.

Rail passengers travel in two classes, First and Standard (formerly called Second). First Class is more expensive and usually less crowded, providing more comfort in separate carriages or compartments. On some trains there are special First Class dining cars.

Long-distance express trains are usually called 'InterCity'. The whole of south-eastern England, including London, is operated as 'Network SouthEast', and passengers can travel in this area at two thirds of the normal price by buying a Network SouthEast railcard. Many of the regular travellers are commuters to London, who travel daily from towns as far away as Oxford or Portsmouth. Most such journeys to work also involve further travel on the London Underground (or on buses). The fact that many firms pay for the season ticket of their employees does not really compensate for the frequently uncomfortable and tiring conditions of several hours' travel on crowded trains each day.

The age of the steam train is viewed with nostalgia by many British people. This is reflected in the fact that certain trains are still called by the names of earlier steam expresses like the 'Cornish Riviera' and the 'Flying Scotsman', and explains the number of privately run steam railways that operate as tourist attractions in picturesque areas of the country. One of the best known is the Bluebell Railway in Sussex. The hobby of train-spotting also dates from the age of the steam train. (Cf article at HOBBY.)

Railways (called railroads in US English) were first built in the USA at about the same time as in Britain. The Baltimore and Ohio Railroad was the first to carry freight and passengers, in 1827. The main development, however, occurred after the Civil War of the 1860s, and the first transcontinental railway, the Union Pacific, was completed in 1869.

All US railways are privately run, and there have been many mergers between individual companies. In 1970 the largest company, Penn Central, became bankrupt, and in that year AMTRAK, a body officially known as the National Railroad Passenger Corporation, was organized to run most of America's inter-city passenger services, including those between Boston and Washington. By the end of the 1980s, after a period of financial difficulties, AMTRAK was transporting more passengers more profitably than ever before. Some Amtrak Metroliners, the electric high-speed trains operating in the north-east, have set speed records.

Many large cities in the USA have underground railways, called subways. The New York subway system is the largest in the world.

(**a**) (*esp US*) bring up (a child, etc): *I was raised by my aunt on a farm.* ○ *It's difficult raising a family on a small income.* (**b**) breed (farm animals); grow or produce (crops). Cf REAR². **7** [Tn, Tn·pr] ~ **sth (to sb/sth)** build or erect (a monument, statue, etc): *raise a memorial to those killed in war.* **8** [Tn] end (a siege, etc): *raise a blockade, a ban, an embargo.* **9** [Tn] (*infml*) get in contact with (sb); find (sth): *I can't raise her on the phone.* ○ *I've been trying to raise this spare part everywhere.* **10** [Tn] (in card-games, esp poker) bet more than (another player): *I'll raise you!* **11** (idm) **kick up/raise a dust** ⇨ DUST¹. **lift/raise a finger/hand** ⇨ LIFT. **raise ˈCain/ˈhell/the ˈroof** (*infml*) be very angry; cause an uproar: *He raised Cain when he found he had been cheated.* **raise one's ˈeyebrows (at sth)** (esp passive) show disdain or surprise: *Eyebrows were raised/There were many raised eyebrows when he shaved all his hair off.* **raise one's glass (to sb)** drink a toast to (sb). **raise sb's hackles** ⇨ HACKLES. **raise/start a hare** ⇨ HARE. **raise a ˈlaugh/ˈsmile** amuse people enough to make them laugh/smile. **raise/lower one's sights** ⇨ SIGHT¹. **raise sb's ˈspirits** make sb feel more cheerful or brave: *My win at chess raised my spirits a little.* **raise the ˈtemperature** increase tension, hostility, etc: *This insult raised the temperature of the discussion.* **raise one's voice aˈgainst sb/sth** speak firmly and boldly against sb/sth.

▷ **raise** *n* (*US*) = RISE¹ 3: *get a raise of £200.*

-raiser (forming compound *ns*) person or thing that raises (RAISE 5): *a ˈcurtain-raiser*, ie a short play before the main one ○ *ˈfire-raisers*, ie arsonists ○ *a ˈfund-raiser.*

raisin /ˈreɪzn/ *n* dried sweet grape, used in cakes, puddings, etc. Cf SULTANA 1.

raison d'être /ˌreɪzɒn ˈdetrə/ *n* [sing] (*French*) reason for or justification of sb's/sth's existence: *Work seems to be her raison d'être.*

raj /rɑːdʒ/ *n* [U] **the raj** (also **the British Raj**) (period of) British rule in India: *life under the Raj*, ie before 1947.

rajah (also **raja**) /ˈrɑːdʒə/ *n* (formerly) (title of an) Indian king or prince. Cf RANEE.

rake

rake¹ /reɪk/ *n* **1** (**a**) long-handled tool with a row of prongs at the end for drawing together fallen leaves, smoothing soil, etc. ⇨ illus. (**b**) similar mechanical farm tool on wheels, usu for gathering hay, etc. **2** similar implement, used eg by a croupier for drawing in money at a gambling table.

▷ **rake** *v* **1** [I, Tn, Cn·a] use a rake on (sth); level (sth) with a rake: *I was busy raking.* ○ *rake the soil (smooth)*, eg before planting seeds. **2** [Tn, Tn·p] ~ **sth (out)** remove ashes from (a fire, kiln, etc). **3** [Tn] fire a gun at or point a camera, telescope, etc at (sth) while moving it from one side to the other: *rake the enemy lines with machine-gun fire* ○ *The bird-watcher raked the trees with his binoculars.* **4** (idm) **rake over old ˈashes** revive (usu unpleasant) memories of the past. **5** (phr v) **rake about/around (for sth)** search carefully: *We raked around in the files, but couldn't find the letter.* **rake sth/it in** (*infml*) earn a lot of (money, etc): *raking in the profits* ○ *She gets tips as well as her wages, so she's really raking it in.* **rake sth together, up, etc** move sth together, up, etc with a rake: *rake together dead leaves (into a heap)* ○ *rake hay up* ○ *rake the cut grass off the lawn.* **rake sb/sth together/up** (*infml*) collect (people or things) with difficulty: *We need to rake up two more players to form a team.* ○ *I couldn't rake together enough money for a new bike.* **rake sth up** (*infml*) remind people of (sth that it would be better to forget): *rake up old quarrels, grievances, etc* ○ *Don't rake up the past.*

□ **ˈrake-off** *n* (*infml*) share of profits or commission, esp from dishonest or illegal activity: *She got a rake-off of 5 per cent from the deal.*

rake² /reɪk/ *n* (*dated*) man, esp a rich and fashionable one, who lives a wild immoral life.

▷ **rakish** /ˈreɪkɪʃ/ *adj* **1** of or like a rake: *a rakish appearance, look, etc.* **2** jaunty or dashing: *a hat set at a rakish angle*, eg on the back of the head or sideways. **rakishly** *adv.* **rakishness** *n* [U].

rake[3] /reɪk/ *n* [sing] **(a)** backward slope, eg of a ship's mast or funnel or of a driver's seat; **(b)** downward slope of a stage in a theatre, ie towards the audience.

▷ **rake** *v* [I, Tn] be or place (sth) at a sloping angle: *The stage rakes steeply.* ○ *The seat back is raked for extra comfort.*

Raleigh /ˈrɑːlɪ/ Sir Walter (c 1552-1618), English explorer. He made several voyages to America, bringing back tobacco and the potato. His attempt to found a colony called Virginia failed. He had been supported by *Elizabeth I, but he fell out of favour when *James I came to the throne, and after a last unsuccessful expedition he was executed for treason.

rallentando /ˌrælənˈtændəʊ/ *n* (*pl* **-dos** or **-di** /-dɪː/), *adj, adv* (*music*) (passage performed) with gradually decreasing speed. Cf ACCELERANDO.

rally[1] /ˈrælɪ/ *v* (*pt, pp* **rallied**) **1 (a)** [I, Ipr, Ip] ~ **(round/to sb/sth)**; ~ **(round)** (of people) come together, esp to make new efforts, eg after a defeat or when there is danger, need, etc: *The troops rallied (round their leader/the flag).* ○ *They rallied to their leader's cause.* ○ *When their mother was ill, the children all rallied round.* **(b)** [Tn, Tn·pr, Tn·p] ~ **sb (round sb)**; ~ **sb (together)** bring (people) together in this way: *The leader rallied his men (round him).* **2** [I, Tn] (cause sb/sth to) recover health, strength, etc; revive; rouse: *rally from an illness* ○ *Her spirits rallied on hearing the good news.* ○ *The team rallied after the first half.* **3** [I] (of share prices, etc) increase after a fall.

▷ **rally** *n* **1** [sing] act of rallying: *Bugler, sound the rally!* **2** [C] large gathering of people with a common (usu political) purpose: *a party rally* ○ *hold/stage a ˈpeace rally.* **3** [sing] recovery of health, strength, etc, eg after an illness; revival: *an unexpected rally* (ie increase in the price) *of tin shares on the Stock Market.* **4** [C] (in tennis, squash, etc) series of strokes before a point is scored: *a fifteen-stroke rally.* **5** [C] driving competition for motor vehicles over public roads.

rally[2] /ˈrælɪ/ *v* (*pt, pp* **rallied**) [Tn] (*dated*) mock (sb) in a good-humoured way; tease.

RAM /ˌɑːr eɪ ˈem/ *abbr* **1** (*computing*) random access memory: *A standard RAM now stores a million binary digits.* Cf ROM. **2** (*Brit*) Royal Academy of Music.

ram /ræm/ *n* **1** uncastrated male sheep. ⇨ illus at SHEEP. Cf EWE, TUP. **2 the Ram** [sing] the first sign of the zodiac; Aries. **3** = BATTERING RAM (BATTER[1]). **4** any of several devices in machines for plunging or striking with great force, eg the falling weight of a pile-driver.

▷ **ram** *v* (**-mm-**) **1 (a)** [Ipr, Tn] ~ **(against/into sth)** crash against sth; strike or push sth with great force: *The car rammed against/into the lorry.* ○ *The ice skater rammed into the barrier.* ○ *They rammed the door to smash it down.* **(b)** [Tn] (of a ship) strike or run into (another ship) in an attempt to sink it: *The frigate rammed the submarine.* **2** [Tn·pr] ~ **sth in, into, on, etc sth** drive sth into place by ramming: *ram piles into a river bed* ○ (*infml*) *ram clothes into a suitcase* ○ *He rammed his hat on his head.* **3** (phr v) **ram sth down** flatten (eg a surface) by ramming: *ram down the soil,* eg when building roads. **ram sth home (a)** force sth into place by ramming: *ram a charge* (ie of gunpowder) *home.* **(b)** (*fig*) emphasize (eg a point, an argument) to make it more convincing.

□ **ˈram-jet** *n* (also **ram-jet engine**) type of jet engine that uses air forced in by the speed of flight to burn fuel.

Ramadan /ˌræməˈdæn; *Brit also* -ˈdɑːn/ *n* the ninth month of the Muslim year, during which *Muhammad received the *Koran from *Gabriel, and when Muslims fast between sunrise and sunset. The fast forbids food, drink, tobacco and sexual intercourse, and is meant to make Muslims aware of the needs of the poor and their own need of Allah's mercy.

Ramayana /rɑːˈmaɪənə/ Sanskrit epic poem composed in India about 300 BC. It tells how the hero Rama, the seventh incarnation of *Vishnu, rescues his wife Sita from the evil Ravan, the ten-headed king of Lanka.

Rambert /ˈrɑːmbeə(r)/ Dame Marie (1888-1982), British ballet-dancer and director, born in Poland. The Ballet Rambert, formed by her in 1930, has championed modern ballet and produced many fine new dancers and choreographers.

ramble /ˈræmbl/ *v* **1** [I, Ip] walk for pleasure with no special destination: *I like rambling (around/about) in the country.* Cf HIKE 1. **2** [I, Ipr, Ip] ~ **(on) (about sb/sth)** (*fig*) wander in one's talk or writing by not keeping to the subject: *The old man rambled (on) about the past.* **3** [I] (of plants) grow or climb over other plants, hedges, etc with long trailing shoots.

▷ **ramble** *n* rambling walk: *go for/on a ramble in the country.*

rambler /ˈræmblə(r)/ *n* **1** person who rambles (RAMBLE 1). **2** rambling plant: [attrib] *rambler roses.*

rambling *adj* **1** (esp of buildings, streets, towns, etc) extending in various directions irregularly. **2** (of a plant) growing or climbing with long trailing shoots. **3** (of a speech, essay, etc) not keeping to the subject; disconnected.

Rambo /ˈræmbəʊ/ character played by Sylvester Stallone in a series of US films of the 1980s. His name is used to refer to any very strong man, esp one who is both aggressive and stupid.

rambunctious /ræmˈbʌŋkʃəs/ *adj* (*infml esp US*) = RUMBUSTIOUS.

ramekin /ˈræməkɪn/ *n* **(a)** small mould for baking and serving an individual portion of food: [attrib] *a ˈramekin dish.* **(b)** food served in this: *a cheese ˈramekin.*

Rameses /ˈræməsiːz/ name of 11 Egyptian pharaohs, including Rameses II, 'the Great' (died c 1225 BC), who was responsible for building or restoring many of Egypt's famous monuments, eg the temple of Abu Simbel; and Rameses III (died c 1167 BC), the last of the great pharaohs, whose wars against the Libyans and other invaders kept the kingdom independent until after his death.

ramify /ˈræmɪfaɪ/ *v* (*pt, pp* **-fied**) [I, Tn esp passive] (*fml*) (cause sth to) branch out in many directions; make or become a network: *a ramified system,* eg of railways.

▷ **ramification** /ˌræmɪfɪˈkeɪʃn/ *n* (usu *pl*) part of a complex structure; secondary consequence, esp one that complicates: *widespread ramifications of trade* ○ *I couldn't follow all the ramifications of the plot.*

ramp[1] /ræmp/ *n* **1** slope joining two levels of ground, a floor, a road, etc: *push a wheelchair up/down a ramp* ○ *Beware ramp,* eg seen on a road sign. **2** movable set of steps for entering and leaving an aircraft.

ramp[2] /ræmp/ *n* (*dated Brit sl*) swindle, esp one that involves charging excessively high prices.

rampage /ræmˈpeɪdʒ/ *v* [Ipr, Ip] rush around wildly or violently: *The mob rampaged through the village.*

▷ **rampage** *n* (idm) **be/go on the ˈrampage** go about behaving violently or destructively: *drunken soldiers on the rampage.*

rampant /ˈræmpənt/ *adj* **1** (of disease, crime, etc) flourishing excessively; unrestrained: *Cholera was rampant in the district.* ○ *a city of rampant violence.* **2** (of plants) growing too luxuriantly or thickly: *Rampant ivy had covered the wall.* **3** (usu directly after a *n*) (*heraldry*) (of an animal on a coat of arms) standing on one hind leg with forelegs raised: *lions rampant.* Cf COUCHANT. ▷ **rampantly** *adv.*

rampart /ˈræmpɑːt/ *n* **1** (esp *pl*) defensive wall round a fort, etc consisting of a wide bank of earth with a path for walking along the top. **2** (esp *sing*) defence; protection: *a rampart against infection.*

ramrod /ˈræmrɒd/ *n* **1** iron rod formerly used for ramming the charge into muzzle-loading guns. **2** (idm) **(as) stiff/straight as a ˈramrod** (of a person) very erect: *The soldier stood stiff as a ramrod.*

ramshackle /ˈræmʃækl/ *adj* (of houses, vehicles, etc) almost collapsing: *a ramshackle old bus* ○ (*fig*) *a ramshackle organization.*

ran *pt* of RUN[1].

ranch /rɑːntʃ; *US* ræntʃ/ *n* **(a)** large farm, esp in the USA or Canada, where cattle are bred; similar farm producing crops, fruit, chickens, etc: [attrib] *a ranch house.* **(b)** farm where certain other animals are bred: *a mink ranch.*

▷ **rancher** *n* person who owns, manages or works on a ranch.

rancid /ˈrænsɪd/ *adj* **1** (of fatty foods) tasting or smelling bad because of staleness: *The butter has gone/turned rancid.* **2** (of smells or tastes) like stale fat: *the rancid stench of dirty drains.* ▷ **rancidness** *n* [U].

rancour (*US* **-cor**) /ˈræŋkə(r)/ *n* [U] deep long-lasting bitterness or ill-will; spite: *feel full of rancour against sb.* ▷ **rancorous** /ˈræŋkərəs/ *adj.* **rancorously** *adv.*

rand /rænd/ *n* unit of currency in the Republic of South Africa; 100 cents.

NOTE ON USAGE: The pronunciation of **rand** varies. In South Africa commonly heard variants are /rɑːnd/, /rɑːnt/, /rɒnt/.

R and B (also **R & B**) /ˌɑːr ən ˈbiː/ *abbr* rhythm and blues.

R and D (also **R & D**) /ˌɑːr ən ˈdiː/ *abbr* (*commerce*) research and development.

random /ˈrændəm/ *adj* [usu attrib] done, chosen, etc without method or conscious choice; haphazard: *a random sample, selection, etc* ○ *a few random remarks.*

▷ **random** *n* (idm) **at ˈrandom** without method or conscious choice: *draw the winning numbers at random* ○ *open a book at random,* ie not at any particular page ○ *The terrorists fired into the crowd at random.*

randomly *adv*: *people randomly chosen,* eg to carry out a survey.

□ **random ˈaccess** (also **direct ˈaccess**) (*computing*) process that allows information in a computer to be stored or retrieved without reading through items stored previously. Cf READ ONLY (READ). **ˌrandom access ˈmemory** (*abbr* **RAM**) computer memory used temporarily to store data (usu found by random access) that can be changed or removed. Cf READ ONLY MEMORY (READ).

randy /ˈrændɪ/ *adj* (**-ier, -iest**) (*infml esp Brit*) sexually excited; lustful: *a randy tom-cat* ○ *I feel really randy.* ▷ **randily** *adv.* **randiness** *n* [U].

ranee (also **rani**) /ˈrɑːniː/ *n* (formerly) Hindu queen or princess; rajah's wife or widow.

rang *pt* of RING[2].

range[1] /reɪndʒ/ *n* **1** [C] connected line or row of mountains, hills, etc: *a mountain-range.* **2** [C] group or series of similar things; selection or variety: *sell/stock a whole range of tools, dresses, foods* ○ *The new model comes in an exciting range of colours.* ○ *have a wide/narrow range of interests, hobbies, etc.* **3** [C] limits between which sth varies; extent: *a soprano's range,* ie between her top and bottom notes ○ *What is the salary range for the post?* ○ *The annual range of temperature is from -10°C to 40°C.* ○ *There's a wide range of ability in the class.* ○ *That subject is outside my range,* ie one I have not studied. **4 (a)** [U] distance within which one can see or hear; distance over which sounds will travel: *It came within my range of vision.* ○ *take a long-range shot,* eg with a camera ○ *They live within range of the transmitter.* ○ *She was out of range (of my voice).* **(b)** [U, sing] distance to which a gun will shoot, or over which a missile, shell, etc will travel: *The gun has a range of five miles.* ○ *in/within/out of/beyond (firing) range* ○ *He shot the lion at point-blank range,* ie when it was so near that he could not miss. ○ *fire at close/long range.* **(c)** [C] distance that a vehicle, aircraft, etc will travel before it needs to be refuelled. **5** [C] **(a)** area of ground with targets for soldiers, etc to practise shooting: *an army range* ○ *a ˈrifle-range.* **(b)** area within which rockets and missiles are fired. **6** [C] area within which a particular plant, animal, etc may be found. **7** [sing] (*US*) large open area for hunting or grazing. **8** [C] (esp formerly) cooking stove with ovens and hotplates for pans, etc: *a kitchen range.*

□ **ˈrange-finder** *n* device for finding the distance of sb/sth to be shot at or photographed.

range[2] /reɪndʒ/ *v* **1** (**a**) [esp passive: Tn, Tn·pr] arrange (sb/sth) in a line or in ranks, or in a specified way: *troops ranged facing each other* ○ *The spectators ranged themselves along the route of the procession.* ○ *flowerpots ranged in rows on the window-sill.* (**b**) [Tn·pr] ~ **sb/oneself with sb/sth** place sb/oneself in a certain group: *On this issue, she has ranged herself with the Opposition.* **2** [Ipr] ~ **between A and B/from A to B** vary or extend between specified limits: *Their ages range from 25 to 50.* ○ *Prices range between £7 and £10.* ○ *The frontier ranges from the northern hills to the southern coast.* ○ *His interests ranged from chess to canoeing.* **3** [I, Ipr, Tn] ~ (**over/through sth**) wander freely over/through (an area); roam: *cattle ranging over the plains* ○ (*fig*) *research ranging over a number of fields* ○ *a wide-ranging discussion*, ie covering many topics ○ *range the hills, countryside, etc.* **4** [Ipr] ~ **over sth** (**a**) (of guns) fire bullets, etc over (a distance): *This rifle ranges over a mile.* (**b**) (of bullets, missiles, etc) travel (a distance).

ranger /ˈreɪndʒə(r)/ *n* **1** (**a**) (*Brit*) keeper of a royal park, estate, etc who enforces forest laws. (**b**) (*esp US*) guard who patrols and protects a forest, etc. **2** (*US*) member of a body of armed mounted men acting as police, eg in thinly populated areas: *the Texas Rangers.* **3** (*US*) commando. **4 Ranger** (*Brit*) senior Girl Guide.

rangy /ˈreɪndʒɪ/ *adj* (**-ier, -iest**) very tall, with long arms and legs: *a rangy youth.*

rani = RANEE.

rank[1] /ræŋk/ *n* **1** [C, U] position in a scale of responsibility, quality, social status, etc: *ministers of Cabinet rank* ○ *a painter of the first/top rank*, ie one of the very best ○ *people of (high) rank* ○ *people of all ranks and classes.* **2** [C, U] position or grade in the armed forces: *promoted to the rank of captain* ○ *above/below a major in rank* ○ *officers of high rank* ○ *reach the rank of colonel.* **3** [C] line or row of things: *a ˈcab/ˈtaxi rank* ○ *Take the taxi at the head of the rank*, ie the first in the line. **4** (**a**) [C] line or row of soldiers, policemen, etc standing side by side: *ranks of marching infantry* ○ *keep/break ranks*, ie remain/fail to remain in line. (**b**) **the ranks** [pl] (also **ˈother ranks**) ordinary soldiers, ie privates, corporals, etc, not officers: *join, serve in, etc the ranks* ○ *rise from the ranks*, ie be made an officer after serving as an ordinary soldier ○ *be reduced to the ranks*, ie (of a sergeant, etc) be made an ordinary soldier as a punishment ○ (*fig*) *join the ranks of the unemployed*, ie become unemployed. **5** (idm) **close ranks** ⇨ CLOSE[4]. **pull rank** ⇨ PULL[2].

▷ **rank** *v* (not in the continuous tenses) **1** [Tn, Tn·pr, Cn·n/a] ~ **sb/sth** (**as sth**) place sb/sth in a rank; grade sb/sth according to quality, achievement, etc: *I rank her achievement very highly.* ○ *Where/How do you rank Karpov as a chess player?* ○ *I rank her among the country's best writers.* **2** [Ipr] have a rank or place: *Does he rank among/with the failures?* ○ *A major ranks above a captain.* ○ *a high-ranking official, delegate, etc.* **3** [Tn] (*US*) have a higher rank than (sb).

□ **the ˌrank and ˈfile 1** the ordinary soldiers, not officers. **2** (*fig*) the ordinary members of an organization: *the rank and file of the party* ○ [attrib] *rank-and-file workers.*

ˈranking officer (*US*) officer of the highest rank present.

rank[2] /ræŋk/ *adj* **1** (**a**) (of plants, etc) growing too thickly; over-luxuriant: *rank grass, ivy, etc* ○ *roses that grow rank.* (**b**) ~ (**with sth**) (of land) full of or likely to produce many weeds: *rank soil, earth, etc* ○ *a field rank with nettles and thistles.* **2** smelling or tasting bad; offensive: *rank tobacco* ○ *the rank stench of rotting meat.* **3** [attrib] (*esp derog*) complete and utter; unmistakable: *a rank traitor, lie* ○ *rank insolence, stupidity, injustice, etc* ○ *The winning horse was a rank outsider.* ▷ **rankly** *adv.* **rankness** *n* [U].

rankle /ˈræŋkl/ *v* [I] cause lasting bitterness or resentment: *The insult still rankled in his mind.*

ransack /ˈrænsæk; *US* rænˈsæk/ *v* **1** [Tn, Tn·pr] ~ **sth** (**for sth**) search (a place) thoroughly: *I've ransacked the house for those papers, but I can't find them.* **2** [Tn] plunder (sth); pillage: *Burglars ransacked the stately home.*

ransom /ˈrænsəm/ *n* **1** [U] release of a captive in return for money, etc demanded by his captors: [attrib] *ransom money.* **2** [U, C] money, etc paid for this: *pay ransom to the kidnappers* ○ *The kidnappers demanded a ransom of £10 000 for his release.* **3** (idm) **hold sb to ˈransom** (**a**) keep sb captive and demand ransom for him. (**b**) (*fig*) demand concessions from sb by using threats: *The unions are holding the country to ransom*, eg by a national strike. **a king's ransom** ⇨ KING.

▷ **ransom** *v* [Tn] (**a**) obtain the release of (a captive) in return for payment. (**b**) hold (a captive) and demand ransom for him.

Ransome /ˈrænsəm/ Arthur Michell (1884-1967), English author. He worked as a reporter for the *Manchester Guardian*, but he is most famous for his books for children, esp the *Swallows and Amazons* series.

rant /rænt/ *v* [I, Ipr, Ip, Tn] ~ (**at sb/sth**) (*derog*) **1** speak loudly, violently or theatrically: *He ranted (on) at me about my mistakes.* ○ *This actor rants his lines.* **2** (idm) **ˌrant and ˈrave** (**at sb/sth**) condemn or censure sb/sth loudly and forcefully: *You can rant and rave at the fine, but you'll still have to pay it.* ▷ **ranter** /ˈræntə(r)/ *n.*

RAOC /ˌɑːr eɪ əʊ ˈsiː/ *abbr* (*Brit*) Royal Army Ordnance Corps (part of the British Army dealing with military supplies).

rap[1] /ræp/ *n* **1** [C] (sound of a) quick sharp blow or knock: *a sharp rap on the elbow* ○ *There was a rap at/on the door.* **2** [U] (*US sl*) rapid talk; chatter. **3** (**a**) [U] rhythmical style of speaking a commentary, telling a story, etc, sometimes spontaneously, with a musical accompaniment. Rap originated among American Blacks. (**b**) [C] such a commentary, story, etc. **4** (idm) **beat the rap** ⇨ BEAT[1]. **give sb/get a ˌrap on/over the ˈknuckles** (*infml*) reproach or rebuke sb: *He got a rap over the knuckles from the teacher for not doing enough work.* **take the rap** (**for sth**) (*infml esp US*) be punished, esp for sth one has not done.

▷ **rap** *v* (**-pp-**) **1** (**a**) [Tn] strike (sth) quickly and smartly: *She rapped my knuckles.* (**b**) [Ipr, Tn] knock or tap lightly and quickly: *rap (on) the table* ○ *rap (at) the door.* **2** [Tn] (*infml*) reproach or rebuke (sb): *She rapped the Minister publicly for his indiscreet remarks.* **3** [I] (*US sl*) talk or chatter rapidly. **4** [I] perform a rap(3b). **5** (phr v) **rap sth out** (**a**) say sth abruptly and sharply: *The officer rapped out the orders.* (**b**) express sth by taps: *The prisoner rapped out a message on the cell wall.*

rap[2] /ræp/ *n* (idm) **not care/give a rap** (**about/for sb/sth**) (*infml*) not care at all.

rapacious /rəˈpeɪʃəs/ *adj* (*fml*) **1** greedy, esp for money; grasping: *fall into the clutches of a rapacious landlord* ○ *rapacious business methods.* **2** plundering and robbing others: *rapacious marauders, invaders, etc.*

▷ **rapaciously** *adv.*

rapacity /rəˈpæsətɪ/ *n* [U] greed; desire to rob and plunder.

rape[1] /reɪp/ *v* [Tn] commit the crime of forcing (a woman or girl) to have sexual intercourse against her will.

▷ **rape** *n* [C, U] **1** (act of) raping; being raped: *commit two rapes* ○ *Is rape on the increase?* ○ *Her rape had a profound psychological effect on her.* **2** (*fig*) act of violently interfering with sth: *the rape of the countryside*, eg by removing ancient hedges.

rapist /ˈreɪpɪst/ *n* person who commits rape.

rape[2] /reɪp/ *n* [U] plant grown as food for farm animals and for its seed, from which oil is made: *a field of rape* ○ *ˌrape-seed ˈoil* ○ *ˌoilseed ˈrape.*

Raphael[1] /ˈræfeɪəl/ one of the archangels in the Jewish, Christian and Muslim traditions. He is traditionally associated with healing.

Raphael[2] /ˈræfeɪəl/ (also **Raffaello Sanzio**) (1483-1520), Italian painter. He was regarded as representing the ideal Renaissance artist. He mastered the techniques of earlier artists like *Michelangelo and Leonardo da *Vinci, but never merely imitated them. At the age of 25 he received a commission from Pope Julius II, for whom he painted several of his finest works. He is particularly famous for the expression of classical serenity he gave to his many Madonnas.

rapid /ˈræpɪd/ *adj* **1** (**a**) moving or acting with great speed; fast: *a rapid pulse, heartbeat* ○ *ask several questions in rapid succession* ○ *the rapid to-and-fro movements of a piston.* (**b**) happening in a short time; prompt: *a rapid decline in sales* ○ *Cats have rapid reflexes.* **2** (of a slope) descending steeply. **3** (idm) **make great/rapid strides** ⇨ STRIDE *n.*

▷ **rapidity** /rəˈpɪdətɪ/ *n* [U].

rapidly *adv.*

rapids *n* [pl] swift current in a river caused by a steep downward slope in the river bed: *shoot the rapids*, eg in a canoe.

□ **rapid-fire** *adj* [attrib] (**a**) (of a gun) firing bullets, etc in quick succession. (**b**) (*fig*) (of questions, etc) spoken very quickly, one after the other: *the rapid-fire jokes of a comedian.*

ˌrapid ˈtransit (*US*) (system of) fast urban public transport, eg by underground or overhead railway.

rapier /ˈreɪpɪə(r)/ *n* light thin double-edged sword, used for thrusting: [attrib] (*fig*) *rapier wit.* ⇨ illus at SWORD.

□ **ˈrapier-thrust** *n* (*fig*) witty remark or reply.

rapine /ˈræpaɪn; *US* ˈræpɪn/ *n* [U] (*fml or rhet*) act of seizing property by force; plundering: *land ravaged by pillage and rapine.*

rapport /ræˈpɔː(r); *US* -ˈpɔːrt/ *n* [U, sing] ~ (**with sb/between A and B**) sympathetic and harmonious relationship: *He is in rapport with his pupils.* ○ *The actor developed a close rapport with his audience.* ○ *Father and son have a great rapport.*

rapprochement /ræˈprɒʃmɒŋ, ræˈprəʊʃ-; *US* ˌræprəʊʃˈmɒŋ/ *n* (*French*) ~ (**with sb/between A and B**) renewal of friendly relations, esp between countries: *bring about a rapprochement between warring states, factions, etc.*

rapscallion /ræpˈskæljən/ *n* (*arch or joc*) rascal; rogue.

rapt /ræpt/ *adj* ~ (**in sth**) so intent or absorbed that one is unaware of other things; spellbound: *a rapt expression, look, smile, etc* ○ *rapt in contemplation, thought, devotion, etc* ○ *He listened to the music with rapt attention.* ▷ **raptly** *adv.*

raptorial /ræpˈtɔːrɪəl/ *adj* (*fml*) of or like a bird of prey.

rapture /ˈræptʃə(r)/ *n* **1** [U] intense delight: *gazing in/with rapture at the girl he loved.* **2** (idm) **be in, go into, etc raptures** (**about/over sb/sth**) feel or express great delight or enthusiasm: *I'm in raptures about my new job.*

▷ **rapturous** /ˈræptʃərəs/ *adj* causing or expressing rapture: *rapturous applause* ○ *give sb a rapturous welcome/reception* ○ *a rapturous sigh, look.* **rapturously** *adv.*

rare[1] /reə(r)/ *adj* (**-r, -st**) **1** not often happening or seen, etc; unusual: *a rare occurrence, sight, visitor* ○ *a rare book, plant, butterfly*, ie one of only a few that exist ○ *With rare exceptions, he does not appear in public now.* ○ *It is rare for her to arrive late.* **2** [attrib] (*dated*) unusually good or great: *be shy, tolerant, etc to a rare degree* ○ *We had a rare (old) time at the party.* **3** (of gases, esp the atmosphere) of less than usual density.

▷ **rarely** *adv* not often; seldom: *I rarely eat in restaurants.* ○ (*fml*) *Only rarely do I eat in restaurants.*

rareness *n* [U].

□ **ˌrare ˈearth** any of a group of 17 metallic elements (or their oxides) with similar chemical properties. They are scandium, yttrium and the lanthanides. They are actually quite common, but they tend to occur together in nature and it is difficult to isolate individual elements. They are used in modern alloys and as catalysts in industrial processes, either singly or in combination.

NOTE ON USAGE: A thing or an event may be **rare** when it is found or occurs infrequently. It may once have been common: *The panda is now a rare animal.* ○ *A top hat is a rare sight these days.* It may have a special value: *a painting of rare distinction.* Something, usually a thing in daily use, is **scarce** when it is hard to get because it is in short supply: *Water is scarce in the desert.* ○ *Strawberries are scarce this year.*

rare² /reə(r)/ *adj* (usu of beef) cooked so that the inside is still red and juicy; underdone: *a (medium-)rare steak.*

rarebit /ˈreəbɪt/ *n* = WELSH RAREBIT (WELSH).

rarefy /ˈreərɪfaɪ/ *v* (*pt, pp* **-fied**) [I, Tn esp passive] (cause sth to) become thinner or less dense: *rarefying gases.*

▷ **rarefied** *adj* [usu attrib] **1** (of gases) less dense than is normal; thin: *the rarefied air* (ie with little oxygen) *of the Andes.* **2** (*fig*) (of ideas, etc) subtle and refined; lofty and exclusive: *dons living in a rarefied academic atmosphere.*

raring /ˈreərɪŋ/ *adj* [pred] (*infml*) **1** ~ **to do sth** so eager or willing to do sth that restraint is difficult: *The horses were raring to have a gallop.* ○ *She is raring to try out her new skates.* **2** (idm) **ˌraring to ˈgo** keen to start.

rarity /ˈreərətɪ/ *n* **1** [U] rareness. **2** [C] thing that is uncommon or unusual; thing valued because it is rare: *Rain is a rarity in the desert.* ○ *ancient scrolls and other rarities.*

rascal /ˈrɑːskl; *US* ˈræskl/ *n* **1** dishonest person. **2** (*joc*) mischievous or cheeky person who likes playing tricks, esp a child: *Give me my keys back, you little rascal!*

▷ **rascally** /-kəlɪ/ *adj* of or like a rascal; dishonest: *a rascally person, trick.*

rase = RAZE.

rash¹ /ræʃ/ *n* **1** [C usu *sing*] patch of tiny red spots on the skin: *a ˈnettle-rash* ○ *I break out/come out in a rash* (ie A rash appears on my skin) *if I eat chocolate.* ○ *The heat brought her out in* (ie caused) *a rash.* **2** [sing] ~ **of sth** (*fig*) sudden widespread appearance of sth unpleasant: *a rash of ugly new houses* ○ *a rash of strikes in the steel industry.*

rash² /ræʃ/ *adj* (**-er, -est**) acting or done without careful consideration of the possible consequences; impetuous: *a rash young student* ○ *Don't make rash promises,* ie ones you may regret. ○ *It was rash of you to sign the form without reading it.* ▷ **rashly** *adv.* **rashness** *n* [U]: *I lent him £5 in a moment of rashness.*

rasher /ˈræʃə(r)/ *n* thin slice of bacon or ham: *a fried egg and a couple of rashers of bacon for breakfast.*

rasp /rɑːsp; *US* ræsp/ *n* **1** [C] coarse file with rows of sharp points on its surface(s). **2** [sing] unpleasant grating sound: *the rasp of a saw on wood.*

▷ **rasp** *v* **1** [Tn, Cn·a] scrape (sth) with, or as if with, a rasp: *rasp the surface (smooth).* **2** (a) [Tn, Tn·p] ~ **sth (out)** say sth in an unpleasant grating voice: *rasp (out) orders, insults, etc.* (b) [I, Ip] make an unpleasant grating sound: *a learner rasping (away) on his violin* ○ *a rasping voice.* **3** (phr v) **rasp sth away/off** remove sth with a rasp: *rasp off the rough edges.*

raspberry /ˈrɑːzbrɪ; *US* ˈræzberɪ/ *n* **1** (a) type of bramble: [attrib] *raspberry canes.* (b) its edible sweet red berry: *raspberries and ice-cream* ○ [attrib] *raspberry jam.* **2** (also **razz, Bronx cheer**) (*US infml*) sound made with the tongue and lips to show dislike, contempt, etc: *give/blow sb a raspberry* ○ *The teacher got a raspberry as she turned her back.*

Rasputin /ræsˈpjuːtɪn/ Grigori Efimovich (1871-1916), Russian monk. His alleged powers of healing brought him close to the Russian imperial family, and his supposed influence over Nicholas II increased the Tsar's unpopularity before the revolution. He was murdered by a group of nobles.

Rastafarian /ˌræstəˈfeərɪən/ (also *infml* **Rasta** /ˈræstə/) *n, adj* (member) of a Jamaican sect regarding Blacks as a people chosen by God for salvation. Rastafarians worship the former Emperor Haile Selassie of Ethiopia as God.

rat /ræt/ *n* **1** rodent that looks like, but is larger than, a mouse. ⇨ illus ANIMAL.

Rats are generally regarded as repulsive creatures that live in city sewers and spread disease. These unpleasant associations have been somewhat dispelled in Britain by certain books and television programmes. In *The Wind in the Willows*, by Kenneth *Grahame, Rat is one of the agreeable animal characters; and Roland Rat was a funny and friendly puppet on British television in the 1980s.

2 (*infml fig*) (a) disloyal person, esp one who deserts a cause in times of difficulty: *So you've changed sides, you dirty rat!* (b) unpleasant or despicable man. **3** (idm) **like a drowned rat** ⇨ DROWN. **the rat race** (*infml derog*) fiercely competitive struggle, esp to keep one's position in work or life: *opt out of* (ie withdraw from) *the rat race.* **smell a rat** ⇨ SMELL².

▷ **rat** *v* (**-tt-**) **1** [I] (usu **go ratting**) hunt rats. **2** [I, Ipr] (*infml*) (a) ~ (**on sb/sth**) break an agreement, a promise, etc; fail to do sth one has undertaken to do. (b) ~ (**on sb**) reveal a secret; betray sb: *She's ratted on us — here comes the head teacher!*

rats *interj* (*dated infml*) (used to express annoyance or contempt).

ratter *n* dog or cat that catches rats: *Terriers are good ratters.*

ratty *adj* (**-ier, -iest**) **1** (*Brit infml*) easily made angry; irritable: *be/feel in a ratty mood.* **2** (*US infml*) shabby or dilapidated. **3** of, like or full of rats.

□ **ˈratbag** *n* (*sl esp Austral or NZ*) contemptible person.

ˈratfink *n* (*US sl derog*) **1** unpleasant person. **2** informer.

ratafia /ˌrætəˈfiːə/ *n* **1** [U] liqueur flavoured with almonds or fruit kernels. **2** [C] (*esp Brit*) small biscuit made with or flavoured with almonds.

rat-a-tat, rat-a-tat-tat = RAT-TAT.

ratatouille /ˌrætəˈtuːɪ/ *n* [U] vegetable dish from southern France, made by stewing peppers, aubergines, onions and tomatoes.

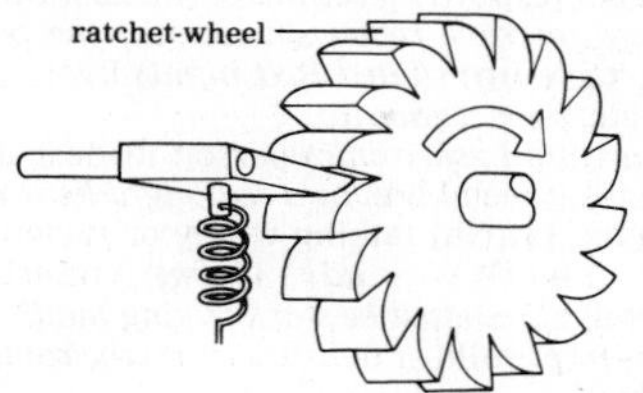

ratchet

ratchet /ˈrætʃɪt/ *n* **1** device consisting of a toothed wheel or bar with a catch that fits between the teeth allowing movement in one direction only. **2** (also **ˈratchet-wheel**) wheel that forms part of this device. ⇨ illus.

rate¹ /reɪt/ *n* **1** standard of reckoning obtained by expressing the quantity or amount of one thing in relation to another: *walk at a/the rate of 3 miles an hour* ○ *produce cars at a rate of 50 a/per week* ○ *the annual ˈbirth/ˈmarriage/ˈdeath rate* ○ *a high ˈpass/ˈfailure rate,* eg in an exam ○ *the exˈchange rate/the rate of exˈchange,* ie the number of units of one currency given in exchange for one unit of another. **2** measure of value, charge or cost: *a first-, ˌsecond-, ˌthird-rate ˈjob* ○ *postal, advertising, insurance, etc rates* ○ *a low/high hourly rate of pay* ○ *special reduced rate for children, students, etc* ○ *Surveys offered at reasonable rates.* ○ *What's the going* (ie current) *rate for baby-sitters?* **3** speed of movement, change, etc; pace: *at a great, dreadful, steady, etc rate* ○ *His pulse-rate dropped suddenly.* ○ *double the rate of production, development, etc* ○ *At the rate you work, you'll never finish.* **4** (usu *pl*) (*Brit*) tax on land and buildings paid to local authorities: *set a rate of 66 pence in the pound,* ie 66p for every pound of a property's value ○ *an extra £5 on/off* (ie added to/deducted from) *the rates.* **5** (idm) **at ˈany rate** whatever may happen; in any case: *That's one part of the job done at any rate.* **at a rate of ˈknots** (*infml*) very rapidly. **at ˈthis/ˈthat rate** (*infml*) if this/that continues; doing things this/that way; if this/that is typical: *At this rate, we shall soon be bankrupt.*

□ **ˈrate-capping** *n* [U] (in Britain) limit on the amount of money a local authority can raise through the rates, imposed by the Government to curb overspending. ⇨ article at TAXATION.

ˈratepayer *n* (*Brit*) person liable to pay rates.

rate² /reɪt/ *v* **1** [Tn, Tn·pr, Cn·n/a] ~ **sth at sth;** ~ **sb/sth as sth** estimate the worth or value of sb/sth: (*infml*) *I don't rate this play* (ie think it is good) *at all.* ○ *What do you rate his income at?* ○ *She is highly rated as a novelist.* **2** [Tn·pr] regard (sb/sth) as; consider: *Do you rate Tom among your friends?* **3** [esp passive: Tn, Tn·pr] ~ **sth (at sth)** (*Brit*) value (property) in order to assess rates (RATE¹ 4): *a house rated at £500 per annum.* **4** [La] rank or be regarded in a specified way: *That task rates low on my priority list.* **5** [Tn] (*US infml*) be worthy of (sth); deserve: *That joke didn't rate a laugh.*

rateable /ˈreɪtəbl/ *adj* (*Brit*) (of property) liable for payment of rates (RATE¹ 4): *the rateable value of a house,* ie the value at which a house is assessed for rates.

rather /ˈrɑːðə(r); *US* ˈræ-/ *adv* **1** (usu indicating criticism, disappointment or surprise) to a certain extent; fairly. (a) (used before *adjs* and *advs*): *We're having rather cold weather for June.* ○ *The book is rather long.* (Cf *This is a rather long book.*) ○ *You've done rather badly in the test.* ○ *For an Englishman he speaks French rather well.* (b) (used before comparatives): *This hotel is rather more expensive than that.* ○ *She drives rather faster than she ought.* (c) (used before *too*): *The exercise was rather too difficult.* ○ *He spoke rather too quickly for me to understand.* **2** to a moderate extent; quite. (a) (used before a *det*): *It seems rather a good idea.* ○ *It's rather a shame that Joyce missed the concert.* (b) (used before a *v*): *I rather suspect we're making a big mistake.* ○ *We were rather hoping you'd be free on Friday.* ○ *The weather rather spoiled our trip to the seaside.* ⇨ Usage at FAIRLY. **3** (idm) **or rather** (used to introduce a more precise expression): *I worked as a secretary, or rather, a typist* ○ *He had to walk — or rather run — to the office.* **would rather...(than)**; *US* also **had rather...(than)** (usu shortened to *'d rather*) prefer to: *I'd rather walk than take a bus.* ○ *She'd rather die than lose the children.* ○ *'Some more wine?' 'Thank you, I'd rather not. I have to drive home.'*

▷ **rather** *interj* (*dated Brit*) (used when replying to a suggestion, etc and always stressed) certainly: *'How about a trip to the coast?' 'Rather!'*

□ **rather than** *prep* in preference to (sb/sth); instead of: *I think I'll have a cold drink rather than coffee.* ○ *It's management that's at fault rather than the work-force.* ○ *Rather than risk breaking up his marriage he told his wife everything.*

ratify /ˈrætɪfaɪ/ *v* (*pt, pp* **-fied**) [Tn] make (an agreement, a treaty, etc) officially valid, usu by signing it.

▷ **ratification** /ˌrætɪfɪˈkeɪʃn/ *n* [U] ratifying or being ratified.

rating /ˈreɪtɪŋ/ *n* **1** (a) [C, U] classification or ranking of sb/sth according to quality, etc: *a high/low popularity, credibility, etc rating* ○ *The critics' rating of the film was low.* ○ *give medical research a high-priority rating.* (b) [C often *pl*] (in the media) popularity of a programme, record, etc, as measured by the number of viewers, buyers, etc: *Our show has gone up in the ratings.* ○ *Blue Funk's new hit has had good ratings in the charts.* **2** [C, U] (*Brit*) (calculation of the) amount payable as a local rate¹(4): *a rating of 60p in the pound.* **3** [C] status of a person or business with regard to financial responsibility and trustworthiness: *have/enjoy a high credit rating.* **4** (*esp Brit*) (in the navy) non-commissioned sailor: *officers and ratings.*

ratio /ˈreɪʃɪəʊ/ *n* (*pl* ~**s**) relation between two

amounts determined by the number of times one contains the other: *The ratios of 1 to 5 and 20 to 100 are the same.* ○ *Men outnumber women here in the ratio of three to one.* Cf PROPORTION.

ratiocination /ˌrætɪˌɒsɪˈneɪʃn; *US* ˌræʃɪ-/ *n* [U] (*fml*) process of logical and methodical reasoning.

ration /ˈræʃn/ *n* **1** [C] fixed quantity, esp an official allowance of food, etc in times of shortage: *the weekly butter, coal, petrol, etc ration*, eg during a war ○ [attrib] *a ration card/book*, ie entitling the holder to a ration. **2 rations** [pl] fixed daily allowance of food in the armed forces, etc: *draw rations.* **3** (idm) **be on short rations** ⇨ SHORT[1].
▷ **ration** *v* **1** [esp passive: Tn, Tn·pr] ~ **sb/sth (to sth)** limit sb/sth to a fixed amount of sth: *People were rationed to one egg a week.* ○ *Bread was rationed to one loaf per family.* **2** (phr v) **ration sth out** distribute (food, etc) in fixed quantities: *ration the remaining water out among the survivors.*
rationing *n* [U] system of limiting and sharing food, clothing, etc in times of shortage: *The Government may have to introduce petrol rationing.*

rational /ˈræʃnəl/ *adj* **1** able to reason: *Man is a rational being.* **2** not foolish or absurd; sensible; reasonable: *rational conduct* ○ *a rational argument, explanation, solution, etc.* **3** lucid or sane: *Despite her recent stroke, she is quite rational.* ○ *No rational person would go to work in his pyjamas.* **4** (*mathematics*) (of a number) that can be expressed as a relation between two whole numbers, eg 0.6 as $\frac{3}{5}$ or $\sqrt{4}$ as $\frac{2}{1}$.
▷ **rationality** /ˌræʃəˈnælətɪ/ *n* [U] quality of being rational; reasonableness.
rationally /-ʃnəlɪ/ *adv*: *think, behave, argue rationally.*

rationale /ˌræʃəˈnɑːl; *US* -ˈnæl/ *n* fundamental reason for or logical basis of sth: *the rationale behind a decision.*

rationalism /ˈræʃnəlɪzəm/ *n* [U] practice of testing all religious belief and knowledge by reason and logic.
▷ **rationalist** /-lɪst/ *adj*, *n* (typical of a) person practising rationalism.
rationalistic /ˌræʃnəˈlɪstɪk/ *adj* of rationalism or rationalists.

rationalize, -ise /ˈræʃnəlaɪz/ *v* **1** [I, Tn] (try to) justify (one's actions, emotions, etc) by giving a rational explanation for them: *He's constantly rationalizing.* ○ *She rationalized her decision to abandon her baby by saying she could not afford to keep it.* **2** [Tn] make (sth) more logical and consistent: *an attempt to rationalize English spelling.* **3** [Tn] reorganize (a process, an industry, etc) in order to increase efficiency and reduce waste: *rationalize production, distribution, etc.* ▷ **rationalization, -isation** /ˌræʃnəlaɪˈzeɪʃn; *US* -lɪˈz-/ *n* [C, U].

ratline (also **ratlin**) /ˈrætlɪn/ *n* (usu *pl*) short rope fixed between the shrouds of a sailing-ship, like a rung of a ladder, and used for climbing up or down.

rattan /ræˈtæn/ *n* **1** [C] (long thin cane-like stem of an) E Indian palm. **2** [C] walking-stick or cane made from a rattan stem. **3** [U] rattan stems used for weaving baskets, furniture, chair seats, etc.

rat-tat /ˌræ ˈtæt/ (also **rat-a-tat** /ˌræt ə ˈtæt/, **rat-a-tat-tat** /ˌræt ə tæt ˈtæt/) *n* [sing] sound of rapping or knocking, esp on a door: *a sharp rat-tat at/on the front door.*

Rattigan /ˈrætɪgən/ Sir Terence (1911-77), English playwright. The dramatic craftsmanship of his plays, including *French Without Tears, The Browning Version* and *The Winslow Boy*, has ensured their lasting popularity.

rattle /ˈrætl/ *v* **1** [I, Tn] (cause sth to) make short sharp sounds quickly, one after the other; (cause sth to) shake while making such sounds: *The windows were rattling in the wind.* ○ *Hailstones rattled on the tin roof.* ○ *The wind rattled the windows.* **2** [Tn esp passive] (*infml*) make (sb) nervous; frighten or alarm: *The policeman's visit really got her rattled.* **3** (phr v) **rattle along, off, past, etc** move with a rattling sound: *The old bus rattled along the stony road.* ○ *A cart rattled past (us).* **rattle away/on** talk idly and at length; chatter: *He rattled on about his job, not noticing how bored she was.* **rattle sth off** say or repeat sth quickly and meaninglessly: *The child rattled off the poem he had learnt.* **rattle through sth** tell (a story), repeat (a list, etc) quickly: *He rattled through the list of names.*
▷ **rattle** *n* **1** [U, C] rattling sound: *the rattle of bottles, chains, etc* ○ *the harsh rattle of machine-gun fire* ○ *The car has several irritating rattles at the back.* **2** [C] toy or device for producing a rattling sound: *a baby's rattle* ○ *Football fans sounded their rattles.* **3** [C] horny rings on a rattlesnake's tail that make a rattling noise when shaken.
rattling /ˈrætlɪŋ/ *adj* [attrib] (*dated infml*) fast or brisk: *set a rattling pace.* — *adv* very: *spin a rattling good yarn*, ie tell a very good story.
□ ˈ**rattlesnake** (also *US infml* **rattler** /ˈrætlə(r)/) *n* poisonous American snake that makes a rattling noise with its tail when alarmed or threatened.
ˈ**rattletrap** *n* (*joc infml*) worn-out old car that rattles a lot.

ratty ⇨ RAT.

raucous /ˈrɔːkəs/ *adj* loud and hoarse; harsh-sounding: *the raucous cries of the crows* ○ *a raucous voice, laugh, etc.* ▷ **raucously** *adv.* **raucousness** *n* [U].

raunchy /rɔːntʃɪ/ *adj* (*infml esp US*) having or showing sexual desire; coarse or obscene: *feel raunchy* ○ *a raunchy joke, story, etc.* ▷ **raunchily** *adv.* **raunchiness** *n* [U].

ravage /ˈrævɪdʒ/ *v* [Tn] **1** damage (sth) badly; destroy: *forests ravaged by fire* ○ (*fig*) *a face ravaged by disease*, eg covered with marks after smallpox. **2** (of armies, etc) rob and plunder (sth) with violence: *Bands of soldiers ravaged the countryside.*
▷ **the ravages** *n* [pl] ~**s of sth** destructive effect of sth; damage done by sth: *the ravages of deforestation on the hills* ○ (*fig*) *The ravages of time had spoilt her looks.*

rave /reɪv/ *v* **1** [I, Ipr] ~ **(at/against/about sb/sth)** talk wildly or furiously as if in a fever or mad: *The patient began to rave incoherently at the nurses.* **2** [Ipr] ~ **about sb/sth** (*infml*) speak or write about sb/sth with enthusiasm or admiration: *She simply raved about French cooking.* **3** (idm) **rant and rave** ⇨ RANT.
▷ **rave** *n* **1** [esp attrib] (*infml*) enthusiastic praise: *The play got rave reviews/notices in the papers.* **2** (also ˈ**rave-up**) (*dated Brit infml*) lively party, dance, etc: *have a rave-up.*
raver *n* (*infml esp ironic*) person leading a wild and exciting social life: *be a real/right little raver.*
raving *adj* [attrib] talking wildly or furiously: *a raving lunatic.* — *adv* (*infml*) utterly or completely: *You must be stark raving mad!*
ravings *n* [pl] wild or delirious talk: *the ravings of a madman.*

Ravel /rəˈvel/ Maurice (1875-1937), French composer. He wrote brilliantly and elegantly for both piano and orchestra, and works like *Schéhérazade*, the suites from the ballet *Daphnis et Chloé* and the *Boléro* are among the most popular pieces of 20th-century music.

ravel /ˈrævl/ *v* (-ll-; *US* also -l-) **1** [I, Ip, Tn, Tn·p] ~ **(sth) (up)** (cause threads or fibres to) tangle and become knotted. **2** [I] (of woven or knitted fabric) separate into threads; become untwisted; fray: *Bind the edge of the rug so that it won't ravel.* Cf UNRAVEL 1.

raven /ˈreɪvn/ *n* large bird like a crow with glossy black feathers and a hoarse cry.
▷ **raven** *adj* [attrib] (of hair) glossy and black: *silky raven hair.*

ravening /ˈrævənɪŋ/ *adj* [attrib] (esp of wolves) hungrily seeking prey or food: *a ravening beast.*

ravenous /ˈrævənəs/ *adj* **1** very hungry: *The ravenous lions tore at the carcass.* ○ (*infml*) *Where's dinner? I'm ravenous!* **2** (of hunger, etc) very great: *a ravenous appetite.*
▷ **ravenously** *adv* very hungrily; as if starving: *eat ravenously.*

ravine /rəˈviːn/ *n* deep narrow steep-sided valley between mountains.

ravioli /ˌrævɪˈəʊlɪ/ *n* [U] (Italian dish of) smal square cases of pasta filled with meat, cheese, et and usu served with a sauce.

ravish /ˈrævɪʃ/ *v* **1** [Tn esp passive] fill (sb) wit delight; enchant: *I was ravished by her beauty* **2** [Tn] (*arch or fml*) rape (a woman or girl).
▷ **ravishing** *adj* (*infml*) delightful or enchanting lovely: *a ravishing view, smile* ○ *Darling, you loo simply ravishing in that dress!* **ravishingly** *adv.*

raw /rɔː/ *adj* **1** uncooked: *raw meat, vegetables, et* ○ *eat oysters raw.* **2** [usu attrib] **(a)** in the natura state; not yet processed or manufactured: *raw silk sewage* ○ *raw* (ie unrefined) *sugar* ○ *raw* (i undiluted) *spirit/alcohol.* **(b)** not yet analysed o corrected: *processing raw data, statistics, etc* ○ *fee raw data into a computer.* **3** [usu attrib] (*fig*) (people) not yet skilled or trained; inexperienced *raw recruits*, eg in the army, etc ○ *a mistake mad by a very raw reporter.* **4 (a)** (of wounds) unhealed bloody: *a raw cut, blister, etc.* **(b)** (of a place on th skin) with the skin rubbed away and therefor sore: *The stirrup leathers rubbed raw patches o his legs.* **5 (a)** artistically crude; lacking finish: *Hi literary style is still rather raw.* **(b)** frank o realistic: *a raw portrayal of working-class life* **6** (of the weather) damp and cold: *raw north-eas winds* ○ *a raw February morning.* **7** (of an edge c cloth) not hemmed or finished to prevent fraying **8** (idm) **a raw/rough deal** ⇨ DEAL[4].
▷ **raw** *n* (idm) **in the** ˈ**raw (a)** not made to seer better, pleasanter, etc than it is; unrefined: *life nature, etc seen in the raw.* **(b)** (*infml*) withou clothes; naked. **touch sb on the raw** ⇨ TOUCH[1].
rawness *n* [U].
□ ˌ**raw-**ˈ**boned** *adj* (*usu derog*) with little flesh o the bones; gaunt: *a* ˌ*raw-boned* ˈ*horse,* ˈ*peasant.*
ˈ**rawhide** *n* **(a)** [U] untanned leather: [attrib *rawhide boots, whips, etc.* **(b)** [C] rawhide whip.
ˌ**raw ma**ˈ**terial** (often *pl*) natural product whic manufacturing processes turn into another: *Coa oil and minerals are the raw materials of industry* ○ (*fig*) *The writer's raw material is life.*

Rawlplug /ˈrɔːlplʌg/ *n* (*propr*) small hollow tube usu made of plastic, that can be placed into a ho to allow a screw to be fixed securely.

Ray /reɪ/ Satyajit (1921-93), Indian film maker. Hi films are noted for their restrained and perceptiv exploration of human drama and contemporar Indian issues, first revealed in the internationall acclaimed *Apu* trilogy.

ray[1] /reɪ/ *n* **1 (a)** narrow beam or line of light o other radiation, eg energy or heat: *the rays of th sun* ○ ˈ*X-rays* ○ ˈ*heat-rays* ○ [attrib] *a* ˈ*ray gun*, eg i science fiction. **(b)** ~ **of sth** (*fig*) slight indicatio of sth good or hoped for: *a ray of comfort (for us) i these troubled times* ○ *a few rays of hope.* **2** any on of a number of lines, bands, etc coming out from centre. **3** (idm) **a ray of** ˈ**sunshine** (*infml ofte ironic*) person or thing that makes sb's lif brighter or more cheerful.

ray[2] /reɪ/ *n* any of various types of large broad fla sea-fish related to the shark, eg the skate: ˈ*sting-ray.*

ray[3] (also **re**) /reɪ/ *n* (*music*) second note in th sol-fa scale.

rayon /ˈreɪɒn/ *n* [U] silk-like fibre or fabric mad from cellulose: [attrib] *rayon shirts.*

raze (also **rase**) /reɪz/ *v* [esp passive: Tn, Tn·pr destroy (a building, town, etc) completely, usu b leaving no walls, etc standing (used esp in th expression shown): *raze sth to the ground.*

razor /ˈreɪzə(r)/ *n* instrument with a sharp blad or with electrically-driven revolving cutters, use for shaving hair from the skin: *a* ˈ*safety razor*, i with guards protecting the blade ○ *Vandals ha slashed the tyres with a razor.* ○ *a* ˈ*razor socket*, e in a bathroom. Cf SHAVER (SHAVE).
□ ˈ**razor-back** *n* (*US*) hog of the southern US with a spinal ridge on its back.
ˈ**razor-bill** *n* large N Atlantic sea-bird, a type c auk, whose beak has sharp edges.
ˈ**razor-blade** *n* blade (esp one that is disposable used in a safety razor.
ˌ**razor-**ˈ**edge** *n* (also ˌ**razor's** ˈ**edge**) (*fig*) **1** shar line of division: *a razor-edge of difference betwee*

genius and madness. **2** (idm) **on a razor-edge/razor's edge** in a dangerous or critical situation: *Since he escaped from gaol, Tom has been living on a razor's edge, terrified of recapture.*
ˌ**razor-ˈsharp** *adj* extremely sharp: (*fig*) *ˌrazor-sharp ˈwit, reparˈtee, ˈcriticism, etc.*
razz /ræz/ (*US infml*) *v* [Tn] make fun of (sb); ridicule: *kids razzing the teacher.*
▷ **razz** *n* (*US infml*) = RASPBERRY 2.
razzle /ˈræzl/ *n* (idm) **be/go (out) on the razzle** (*infml*) be/go out to celebrate and enjoy oneself; be/go on a spree.
razzle-dazzle /ˌræzl ˈdæzl/ *n* [U] (*infml*) **1** excitement and fun. **2** showy and often deceptive advertising or publicity.
razzmatazz /ˌræzməˈtæz/ (also **razzamatazz** /ˌræzəməˈtæz/) *n* [U] (*infml*) glamour and excitement; extravagant publicity: *all the razzamatazz of showbiz.*
Rb *symb* rubidium.
RC /ˌɑː ˈsiː/ *abbr* **1** Red Cross. **2** Roman Catholic: *St Mary's Church (RC)*, eg on a street map.
RCA /ˌɑː siː ˈeɪ/ *abbr* **1** (*US*) Radio Corporation of America. **2** (*Brit*) Royal College of Art.
RCM /ˌɑː siː ˈem/ *abbr* (*Brit*) Royal College of Music.
RCP /ˌɑː siː ˈpiː/ *abbr* (*Brit*) Royal College of Physicians.
RCS /ˌɑː siː ˈes/ *abbr* (*Brit*) **1** Royal College of Science. **2** Royal College of Surgeons. **3** Royal Corps of Signals (part of the British Army that deals with communications).
RD /ˌɑː ˈdiː/ *abbr* (*US*) (in postal addresses) rural delivery: *RD2 West Stockbridge, Massachusetts.*
Rd *abbr* (in street names) road: *12 Ashton Rd.*
RE /ˌɑːr ˈiː/ *abbr* **1** religious education. **2** (*Brit*) Royal Engineers (part of the British Army that builds bridges and other structures and does various sorts of engineering work).
Re *symb* rhenium.
re[1] = RAY[3].
re[2] /riː/ *prep* (*fml*) with reference to (sb/sth); concerning; about: *Re your letter of 1 September....*
re- *pref* (used widely with *vs* and related *ns, adjs* and *advs*) again: *reapply* ○ *redecoration* ○ *re-entered* ○ *reassuringly.*

NOTE ON USAGE: In many verbs beginning with **re-** the prefix is pronounced /rɪ-/ or /re-/ and it may have lost its original meaning of 'again' or 'back': /rɪ-/ *recall, repair*; /re-/ *represent*. Other verbs have had **re-** added to them with the meaning of 'again' and it is pronounced /riː-/: *reopen; recreate*. There are a few verbs which fit into both groups and a hyphen may be used to show the distinction: *recount* /rɪˈkaʊnt/ = 'tell a story', *re-count* /ˌriːˈkaʊnt/ = 'count again'; *recover* /rɪˈkʌvə(r)/ = 'get back' or 'become well again', *re-cover* /ˌriːˈkʌvə(r)/ = 'supply with a new cover'.

reach /riːtʃ/ *v* **1** [Ipr, Ip] ~ **for sth**; ~ **out (to sb/sth)** stretch out (one's hand) in order to touch, grasp or take sth: *He reached for his gun.* ○ *I reached across the table for the jam.* ○ (*fig*) *We must reach out to those in need.* **2** [Tn·p, Dn·n, Dn·pr] ~ **sth down/over**; ~ **sth (down/over) for sb** (*infml*) stretch one's hand out or up and take sth; get and give sth (to sb): *Please reach (me) the atlas down from the bookshelf.* ○ *Can you reach me (over) my slippers? They're under the bed.* **3** [Ipr, Tn] ~ **to (sth)** extend to sth; be able to stretch up, out, etc and touch (sth): *I can just about reach the apples on the top branch.* ○ *My feet can hardly reach the pedals.* ○ *Her hair nearly reached down to her waist.* **4** [Tn] communicate with (sb) esp by telephone: *reach her at home on 0355-694162* ○ *I can't reach him by phone/on the phone.* **5** [Tn] **(a)** go as far as (sb/sth/a place); get to or arrive at: *reach York by one o'clock* ○ *reach the end of the chapter* ○ *reach a speed of 500 mph* ○ *Not a sound reached our ears.* ○ *The rescuers reached him just in time.* **(b)** achieve (sth); attain: *reach a conclusion, decision, verdict, etc* ○ *You'll know better when you reach my age.* ○ *The appeal fund has reached its target of £10 000.* ○ *We can never reach perfection.* **6** (idm) **sth comes to/reaches sb's ears** ⇨ EAR[1]. **hit/make/reach the headlines** ⇨ HEADLINE (HEAD[1]). **reach for the stars** be very ambitious.
▷ **reach** *n* **1** [sing] extent to which a hand, etc can be stretched out: *a boxer with a long reach.* **2** [C usu *pl*] continuous extent of a river between two bends or of a canal between two locks: *the upper/lower reaches of the Thames.* **3** (idm) **beyond/out of/within (one's) ˈreach (a)** outside or inside the distance that a hand, etc can be stretched out: *have a dictionary within (arm's) reach* ○ *The shelf is so high it is well out of/beyond my reach.* ○ *Keep those medicines out of reach of the children/out of the children's reach.* **(b)** (*fig*) beyond or within sb's/sth's capability, authority, effectiveness, etc: *concepts beyond the reach of one's intelligence* ○ *Such highly-paid jobs are out of his reach.* ○ *The gang live abroad, beyond reach of the British police.* **within (easy) ˈreach (of sb/sth)** inside a distance that can be travelled (easily): *The hotel is within easy reach of the beach.*
reachable *adj* that can be reached.
□ ˈ**reach-me-downs** *n* [pl] = HAND-ME-DOWNS (HAND[2]).
react /rɪˈækt/ *v* **1** [I, Ipr] ~ **(to sb/sth)** behave differently or change as a result of sth; respond: *Pinch me and I will react.* ○ *People can react badly to certain food additives.* ○ *react positively/negatively to a suggestion* ○ *She reacted to the insult by turning her back on him.* **2** [I, Ipr] ~ **(against sb/sth)** respond to sb/sth with hostility, resistance, etc: *react strongly against tax increases* ○ *Will the people ever react against this dictator?* **3** (*chemistry*) **(a)** [I, Ipr, Ip] ~ **with sth**; ~ **(together)** (of substances) undergo changes by coming into contact with sth: *Iron reacts with water and air to produce rust.* ○ *Sodium and water react (together).* **(b)** [Ipr] ~ **on sth** have an effect on sth or produce a change in sth: *How do acids react on metals?*
reactant /rɪˈæktənt/ *n* (*chemistry*) substance taking part in a chemical reaction. Cf PRODUCT 3.
reaction /rɪˈækʃn/ *n* **1** [C, U] ~ **(to sb/sth)** response to a situation, an act, an influence, etc: *What was his reaction to the news?* ○ *Her arrest produced an immediate/a sudden reaction from the press.* ○ *the shocked reaction of schools to education cuts* ○ *Reaction to his taunts will only encourage him.* **2** [sing] physical response, usu a bad one, to a drug, chemical substance, etc: *an allergic reaction to animals, birds, etc* ○ *I had a bad reaction after my typhoid injection.* **3** [sing, U] return to a previous state after a period of the opposite condition: *After all the excitement there was (an inevitable) reaction*, eg a time when life seemed dull again. **4** [U] opposition to (esp political) progress or reform: *The forces of reaction made reform difficult.* **5** [C, U] chemical change produced by two or more substances acting upon each other: *nuclear reaction*, ie change within the nucleus of an atom.
▷ **reactionary** /rɪˈækʃənrɪ; *US* -ənerɪ/ *n, adj* (person) opposing (esp political) progress or reform.
reactivate /ˌriːˈæktɪveɪt/ *v* [Tn] bring (sth) back into operation; make active again: *reactivate an old generator* ○ *reactivate a spacecraft's defence system* ○ *reactivate our links/contacts with China.*
reactive /riːˈæktɪv/ *adj* **1** that reacts (readily). **2** (*chemistry*) (of an element) that combines readily in chemical reactions. ▷ **reactivity** /-ækˈtɪvɪtɪ/ *n* [U].
reactor /rɪˈæktə(r)/ *n* **1** (also **nuclear reactor**) apparatus for the controlled production of nuclear energy. **2** substance taking part in or undergoing a chemical reaction.
read /riːd/ *v* (*pt, pp* **read** /red/) **1** [I, Tn] (used in the simple tenses or with *can/be able*) (be able to) understand the meaning of (written or printed words or symbols): *be able to/know how to read and write well* ○ *I can't read your untidy writing.* ○ *read shorthand, Chinese (characters), Braille, music* ○ *A motorist must be able to read traffic signs.* **2** [I, Ipr, Ip, Tn, Tn·p, Tw no passive, Dn·n, Dn·pr] ~ **sth (to sb)** go through (written or printed words, etc) silently or aloud to others: *I haven't enough time to read/for reading.* ○ *He was reading silently/to himself.* ○ *His work is not much read* (ie Few people read it) *nowadays.* ○ *She read (to us) from her book.* ○ *Read (the letter) aloud, please.* ○ *read proofs*, ie read and correct the proofs of a book, etc ○ *He read the article through twice.* ○ *Read this over for mistakes.* ○ *Read what the instructions say.* ○ *She read a story to us/read us a story.* **3** [Ipr, Tn, Tf, Tw no passive] ~ **about/of sb/sth** discover or find out about sb/sth by reading: *I read about/of her in today's paper.* ○ *read the news, the share prices, etc* ○ *I read that he had resigned.* ○ *We read how it was done.* **4** [Ipr, Tn] ~ **(for) sth** study (a subject), esp at a university: *read classics, law, etc at Oxford* ○ *read for a physics degree/a degree in physics* ○ *read for the Bar*, ie study law to become a barrister. **5 (a)** [Tn] learn the significance of (sth); interpret: *read sb's mind/thoughts* ○ *read (sb's fortune in) the cards* ○ *A gypsy read my hand/palm*, ie told me about myself and my future by looking at the lines on the palm of my hand. ○ *Doctors must be able to read symptoms correctly.* ○ *How do you read the present situation?* **(b)** [Cn·n/a esp passive] ~ **sth as sth** (of a statement, action, etc) convey meaning(s) which may not be intended: *Silence must not always be read as consent.* **6** [I] have a certain wording: *The sign reads 'Keep Left.'* ○ *The clause reads thus/as follows....* **7 (a)** [In/pr] (of measuring instruments) indicate a certain weight, pressure, voltage, etc: *What does the scale, dial, gauge, etc read?* ○ *The meter reads 5 500 units.* **(b)** [Tn, Tw] receive information from instruments: *read the gas/electric meter* ○ *I can't read what the thermometer says.* **8** [I] give a certain impression: *The story reads well/badly.* ○ *The poem reads like* (ie sounds as if it is) *a translation.* **9** [Tn] hear and understand (sb speaking on a two-way radio): *'Are you reading me?' 'Reading you loud and clear.'* **10** [Tn·pr, Cn·n/a] ~ **A for B**; ~ **B as A** (of corrections in text) replace (one word, etc) with another: *For 'neat' in line 3 read 'nest'.* **11** [Tn, Tn·pr] (esp of a computer) interpret, copy, transfer or extract (data): *The bar code is read using a scanner.* ○ *read a file from the hard disk.* **12** (idm) ˌ**read between the ˈlines** look for or discover a meaning in sth written or spoken that is not openly stated. ˌ**read sb like a ˈbook** (*infml*) understand clearly sb's motives, thoughts, etc: *I can read you like a book: you're not sorry at all.* ˌ**read (sb) the ˈRiot Act** declare authoritatively (to sb) that sth must stop: *When he came home drunk again, she read him the Riot Act.* ˌ**read oneself/sb to ˈsleep** read until one/sb falls asleep. ˌ**take it/sth as ˈread** assume sth without a need for discussion: *We can take it as read that she will object.* ○ *You can take his agreement as read.* **13** (phr v) **read on** continue reading: *Will Tom and Sue's quarrel mean divorce? Now read on....* **read sth back** read (a message, etc) aloud so that its accuracy can be checked: *Read me back that telephone number.* **read sth into sth** assume that sth means more than it does: *You have read into her letter a sympathy that she cannot possibly feel.* **read sth out** read sth aloud, esp to others: *She read out the letter to all of us.* **read sb/sth up; read up on sb/sth** read extensively about or make a special study of (a subject): *I must read Nelson up/read up on Nelson for the history exam.*
▷ **read** *n* /riːd/ [sing] (*infml esp Brit*) **1** period or act of reading: *have a long, quiet, little, etc read* ○ *Can I have a read of that timetable?* **2** (with an *adj*) writer, book, etc that is interesting to read: *This author/novel is a very good read.*
read /red/ *adj* (preceded by an *adv*) having knowledge gained from reading: *a well-read person* ○ *be widely read in the classics.*
readable /ˈriːdəbl/ *adj* **1** that can be read easily or enjoyably: *a highly readable style, essay, article, etc.* **2** (of handwriting, etc) that can be read. Cf LEGIBLE. **readability** /ˌriːdəˈbɪlətɪ/ *n* [U].
□ ˌ**read ˈonly** (*computing*) (of information) that a person can read but not change: *I have read-only access to my bank files.* Cf RANDOM ACCESS (RANDOM). ˌ**read only ˈmemory** (*abbr* **ROM**) computer memory storing data that cannot be

altered or removed and that can be found by random access: *The most important programs are in the read only memory.* Cf RANDOM ACCESS MEMORY (RANDOM).

ˈ**read-out** *n* [C, U] (*computing*) (act of extracting) information from a memory or storage device.

readdress /ˌri:əˈdres/ (also **redirect**) *v* [Tn, Tn·pr] ~ **sth (to sb/sth)** change the address on (a letter, etc): *readdress the parcel to her new home.*

Reade /ri:d/ Charles (1814-84), English author. His novels and plays often supported social causes, such as prison reform. *The Cloister and the Hearth* is his only novel that has remained popular.

reader /ˈri:də(r)/ *n* **1** person who reads, esp one who is fond of reading: *an avid, slow, etc reader* ○ *Happy Christmas to all our readers!* eg as a notice in a newspaper, magazine, library, etc ○ *He's a great reader of science fiction.* **2** book intended to give students practice in reading: *graded English readers,* eg for foreign learners. **3 Reader** ~ **(in sth)** (*Brit*) senior university teacher of a rank immediately below a professor: *Reader in English Literature.* **4** (also **publisher's reader**) person employed to read and report on the suitability of manuscripts for publication. **5** person employed to read and correct proofs at a printer's. **6** (also **lay reader**) person appointed to read aloud parts of a service in church.

▷ **readership** *n* **1** [C] ~ **(in sth)** (*Brit*) position of a Reader(3): *hold, have a readership in Maths.* **2** [sing] (**a**) number of readers of a newspaper, periodical, etc: *The Daily Echo has a readership of over ten million.* (**b**) number of readers of an author, journalist, etc: *Len Deighton has/commands a large readership.*

readily, readiness ⇨ READY.

reading /ˈri:dɪŋ/ *n* **1** [U] (**a**) action of a person who reads: *be fond of reading* ○ [attrib] *reading matter,* ie books, newspapers, etc ○ *have a reading knowledge of French,* ie understand it when written. (**b**) books, etc intended to be read: *heavy/light reading,* ie for study/entertainment ○ *Her articles make/are interesting reading for travellers.* (**c**) knowledge gained from books: *a pupil of wide reading.* **2** [C] amount indicated or registered by a measuring instrument: *check readings on a thermometer, dial, etc* ○ *The readings we took were well above average.* **3** [C] way in which sth is interpreted or understood: *my reading of this clause in the contract,* ie what I think it means ○ *Give me your reading of the situation.* **4** [C] variant wording of a text, esp when more than one version of it exists: *different readings* (eg by editors) *of a speech in Hamlet.* **5** [C] (**a**) entertainment at which sth is read to an audience; passage read in this way: *a poetry-/play-reading* ○ *readings from Dickens.* (**b**) formal announcement of sth to an audience: *the reading of a will, marriage banns, etc.* (**c**) formal reading aloud of a passage from the Bible: *a reading from St John's gospel.* **6** [C] (in the British parliament) one of the three stages of debate through which a Bill must pass before it is ready for royal assent.

□ ˈ**reading age** one's ability to read, measured by comparing it with the average ability of children of the specified age: *adults with a reading age of eight.*

ˈ**reading-desk** *n* desk for supporting a book that is being read.

ˈ**reading-glasses** *n* [pl] glasses for reading (as contrasted with those for seeing things at a distance).

ˈ**reading-lamp** (also ˈ**reading-light**) *n* lamp designed or placed to give light so that a person can read.

ˈ**reading-room** *n* room in a library, club, etc set aside for reading.

readjust /ˌri:əˈdʒʌst/ *v* **1** [I, Ipr, Tn, Tn·pr no passive] ~ **(oneself) (to sth)** adapt (oneself) again: *It's hard to readjust (oneself) to life in Britain after working abroad.* ○ *You need time to readjust (to living alone).* **2** [Tn] set or adjust (sth) again: *readjust the engine tuning, TV set, lighting.*

▷ **readjustment** *n* **1** [U] readjusting or being readjusted: *go through a period of readjustment.* **2** [C] act of readjusting: *make minor readjustments to the wiring.*

ready /ˈredɪ/ *adj* (**-ier, -iest**) **1** [pred] ~ **(for sth/to do sth)** (**a**) in a fit state for immediate use or action; fully prepared or completed: *get ready for a journey* ○ *I've got my overalls on, so I'm ready to start work.* ○ *Your dinner is ready.* ○ *Ready, steady, go!* ie said at the start of a race. ○ *'Shall we go?' 'I'm ready when you are!'* (**b**) (of a person) resolved to do sth; willing and eager: *He's always ready to help his friends.* ○ *Don't be so ready to find fault.* ○ *The troops were ready for anything.* **2** [pred] ~ **to do sth** on the point of doing sth; about to do sth: *She looked ready to collapse at any minute.* **3** (**a**) [attrib] quick and facile; prompt: *have a ready wit, mind, tongue* ○ *a ready answer to the question* ○ *a ready solution to the problem.* (**b**) [pred] ~ **with sth** (of a person) quick to give sth: *be too ready with excuses, criticisms, etc.* **4** within reach; easily available: *Keep your dictionary ready (to hand) at all times.* ○ *This account provides you with a ready source of income.* ○ *There's a ready market for antiques,* ie Buyers are easily found for them. **5** (idm) **make ready (for sth)** prepare: *make ready for the Queen's visit.* ˌ**ready and** ˈ**waiting** fully prepared and available for a particular task, activity, etc. **rough and ready** ⇨ ROUGH.

▷ **readily** /-ɪlɪ/ *adv* **1** without hesitation; willingly: *answer questions readily.* **2** without difficulty; easily: *The sofa can be readily converted into a bed.*

readiness /ˈredɪnɪs/ *n* [U] **1** state of being ready or prepared: *the troops' readiness for battle* ○ *have everything in readiness for an early start* ○ *hold oneself in readiness to take control.* **2** willingness or eagerness: *her readiness to help.* **3** quickness and facility; promptness: *readiness of wit.*

ready *n* **1 the ready** [sing] (also **readies** [pl]) (*infml*) available money; cash: *not have enough of the ready.* **2** (idm) **at the** ˈ**ready** (**a**) (of a rifle) in the position for aiming and firing. (**b**) ready for immediate action or use: *reserve troops held at the ready* ○ *He had his camera at the ready.*

ready *adv* (used before a past participle) beforehand; already: *ready cooked, mixed, etc.*

ready *v* (*pt, pp* **-died**) [Tn, Tn·pr] ~ **sb/sth (for sth)** make sb/sth ready; prepare sb/sth: *ships readied for battle.*

□ ˌ**ready-**ˈ**made** *adj* **1** (esp of clothes) made in standard sizes, not to any particular customer's measurements: *a* ˌ*ready-made* ˈ*suit.* **2** (**a**) of a standard type: *buy* ˌ*ready-made* ˌ*Christmas deco*ˈ*rations.* (**b**) (*fig derog*) not original: *come to a subject with ready-made ideas.* **3** very appropriate; ideal: *a ready-made answer to the problem.*

ˌ**ready** ˈ**money** (also ˌ**ready** ˈ**cash**) (*infml*) actual coins and notes; immediate payment (instead of credit): *payment in ready money.*

ˌ**ready** ˈ**reckoner** book, table, etc of answers to calculations of the type most commonly needed in business.

reaffirm /ˌri:əˈfɜ:m/ *v* [Tn, Tf] state (sth) positively again; affirm again: *reaffirm one's loyalty* ○ *She reaffirmed that she was prepared to help.*

reafforest /ˌri:əˈfɒrɪst; *US* -ˈfɔ:r-/ (*US* **reforest** /ˌri:ˈfɒrɪst; *US* -ˈfɔ:r-/) *v* [Tn] replant (an area of land) with forest trees. ▷ **reafforestation** /ˌri:əˌfɒrɪˈsteɪʃn; *US* -ˌfɔ:r-/ (*US* **reforestation** /ˌri:ˌfɒr-; *US* -ˌfɔ:r-/) *n* [U].

Reagan /ˈreɪgən/ Ronald Wilson (1911-), American actor and politician, 40th president of the USA 1981-89. After a career in films he entered politics and became governor of California from 1967 to 1975. As a Republican president, he attempted to increase government spending on defence and reduce taxes. Despite his strong opposition to Communism, he agreed with the USSR to reduce nuclear weapons. ⇨ App 2.

reagent /ri:ˈeɪdʒənt/ *n* (*chemistry*) substance used to cause a chemical reaction, esp to detect another substance.

real /rɪəl/ *adj* **1** (**a**) existing as a thing or occurring as a fact; not imagined or supposed: *real and imagined fears, illnesses, achievements* ○ *Was it a real person you saw or a ghost?* ○ *The growth of violent crime is a very real problem.* (**b**) [attrib] not apparent; actual or true: *Real life is sometimes stranger than fiction.* ○ *Who is the real manager of the firm* (ie the person who effectively runs it)*?* ○ *The doctors couldn't bring about a real* (ie permanent) *cure.* ○ *Tell me the real reason.* **2** not imitation; genuine: *real silk, gold, pearls, etc* ○ *Is that real hair or a wig?* **3** [attrib] (of incomes, values, etc) assessed by their purchasing power: *Real incomes have gone up by 10% in the past year.* ○ *This represents a reduction of 5% in real terms,* ie when inflation, etc has been allowed for. **4** (idm) **for** ˈ**real** (*infml*) (**a**) seriously; in earnest: *This isn't a practice game; we're playing for real.* (**b**) genuine: *I don't think her tears were for real.* **the** ˌ**real** ˈ**thing/Mc**ˈ**Coy** /məˈkɔɪ/ (*infml*) (**a**) the ultimate experience, achievement, etc: *Marathons are the real McCoy — these little jogs are no challenge at all.* (**b**) the authentic article: *Bottled lemon juice is no good — you must use the real thing.*

▷ **real** *adv* (*US or Scot infml*) very; really: *have a real fine time, a real good laugh* ○ *I'm real sorry.*

□ ˌ**real** ˈ**ale** (*Brit*) draught ale or beer that is made and stored in the traditional way.

ˈ**real estate 1** (also **realty, real property**) (*law*) immovable property, consisting of land, buildings, etc. Cf PERSONAL PROPERTY (PERSONAL). **2** (*US*) (business of selling) houses, land for building, etc.

ˌ**real** ˈ**number** (*mathematics*) number that has no imaginary part.

ˌ**real** ˈ**tennis** (also ˌ**royal** ˈ**tennis**) ancient form of tennis played in an indoor court.

ˌ**real** ˈ**time** (*computing*) (of a system) that can receive continually changing data from outside sources, process this rapidly, and supply results that influence the sources.

realign /ˌri:əˈlaɪn/ *v* **1** [Tn] bring (sth) into a new or former arrangement; align again: *realign ranks of troops* ○ *The chairs were realigned to face the stage.* **2** [I, Ipr, Tn, Tn·pr no passive] ~ **(oneself) (with sth)** (*esp politics*) form into new groups; reorganize: *The party may realign (itself) with Labour in a new coalition.* ▷ **realignment** *n* [U, C]: *the realignment of car wheels* ○ *various realignments in political parties.*

realism /ˈrɪəlɪzəm/ *n* [U] **1** attitudes and behaviour based on the acceptance of facts and the rejection of sentiment and illusion. **2** (in art and literature) portrayal of familiar things as they really are without idealizing them. Cf CLASSICISM, ROMANTICISM (ROMANTIC). **3** (*philosophy*) theory that matter has real existence independent of our perception of it. Cf IDEALISM.

▷ **realist** *n* **1** writer, painter, etc whose work shows realism(1): [attrib] *a realist writer, novel, style.* **2** person who shows realism(2) in his attitudes and behaviour: *I'm a realist - I know you can't change people's attitudes overnight.*

realistic /ˌrɪəˈlɪstɪk/ *adj* **1** (in art and literature) showing realism(1). **2** based on facts rather than on sentiment or illusion; practical: *a realistic person, attitude* ○ *Be realistic — you can't expect a big salary at eighteen.* **3** (of wages or prices) high enough to pay the worker or seller adequately: *Is this a realistic salary for such a responsible job?* **realistically** /-klɪ/ *adv.*

reality /rɪˈælətɪ/ *n* **1** [U] quality of being real or of resembling an original: *the lifelike reality of his paintings.* **2** [U] all that is real; the real world, as contrasted with ideals and illusions: *bring sb back to reality,* ie make him give up his illusions ○ *escape from the reality of everyday existence* ○ *face (up to)* (ie accept) *reality.* **3** [C often *pl*] thing that is actually experienced or seen; thing that is real: *the harsh realities* (eg poverty, misery, etc) *of unemployment* ○ *He cannot grasp the realities of the situation.* ○ *The plan will soon become a reality,* ie will be carried out. **4** (idm) **in re**ˈ**ality** in actual fact; really: *The house looks very old, but in reality it's quite new.*

realize, -ise /ˈrɪəlaɪz/ *v* **1** [Tn, Tf, Tw no passive] (not used in the continuous tenses) be fully aware of or accept (sth) as a fact; understand: *realize one's mistake* ○ *realize the extent of the damage* ○ *She realized that he had been lying.* ○ *I fully realize* *why you did it.* **2** [Tn esp passive] convert (plans, etc) into reality: *realize one's hopes, ambitions, etc* ○ *Her worst fears were realized,* ie The things she was most afraid would happen did happen. **3** (*fml*) (**a**) [Tn] convert (property, shares, etc) into money by selling: *realize one's assets* ○ *Can these bonds be realized at short notice?* (**b**) [Tn, Tn·pr] ~ **sth (on sth)** (of goods, etc) be sold for (a price); (of a person) sell sth for (a price): *The furniture realized £900 at the sale.* ○ *How much did you realize on those paintings?*

▷ **realizable, -isable** /-əbl/ *adj* that can be realized (REALIZE 2).

realization, -isation /ˌrɪəlaɪˈzeɪʃn; *US* -lɪˈz-/ *n* **1** [U] realizing (facts, hopes, plans, etc): *I was struck by the sudden realization that I would probably never see her again.* **2** [U] converting property into money.

really /ˈrɪəlɪ/ *adv* **1** in reality; truly: *What do you really think about it?* ○ *Your name is on the car's documents, but who really owns it?* ○ *Do you love him — really (and truly)?* **2** thoroughly; very: *a really charming person* ○ *a really cold, fast, long, etc journey.* **3** (used to express interest, surprise, mild protest, doubt, etc): *'We're going to Japan next month.' 'Oh, really?'* ○ *You ˈreally shouldn't smoke.* ○ *'Shut up!' 'Well, really!'* ○ *'She's going to resign.' 'Really? Are you sure?'*

realm /relm/ *n* **1** (*fml or rhet*) kingdom: *the defence of the realm* ○ *coins, peers, laws of the realm.* **2** (*fig*) field of activity or interest; sphere: *in the realm of literature, science, etc* ○ *the realms of the imagination.*

realpolitik /ˌreɪælˈpɒlɪtɪk/ *n* [U] (*German*) approach to politics based on realities and material needs, not on morals or ideals.

realtor /ˈrɪəltə(r)/ *n* (*US*) = ESTATE AGENT (ESTATE).

realty /ˈrɪəltɪ/ *n* = REAL ESTATE (REAL).

ream[1] /riːm/ *n* **1** [C] 500 or 516 (formerly 480) sheets of paper. Cf QUIRE. **2 reams** [pl] (*infml fig*) large quantity (of writing): *write reams (and reams) of bad verse.*

ream[2] /riːm/ *v* [Tn] **1** remove (eg wood) from a hole, esp so as to countersink a screw. **2** (*US*) squeeze the juice from (an orange, lemon, etc).

▷ **reamer** *n* **1** drill-like tool for reaming wood. **2** (*US*) device for squeezing oranges and similar fruits.

reap /riːp/ *v* **1** [I, Tn] cut and gather (a crop, esp grain) as harvest: *reap (a field of) barley.* **2** [Tn] (*fig*) receive (sth) as a result of one's own or others' actions: *reap the reward of years of study* ○ *reap the fruits of one's actions.* **3** (idm) (ˌ**sow the ˈwind and**) ˌ**reap the ˈwhirlwind** (*saying*) (start sth that seems fairly harmless and) have to suffer unforeseen consequences that are serious or disastrous.

▷ **reaper** *n* **1** person who reaps. **2** machine for reaping.

□ ˈ**reaping-hook** *n* sickle.

reappear /ˌriːəˈpɪə(r)/ *v* [I] appear again (after being absent or not visible). ▷ **reappearance** /-rəns/ *n* [U, C].

reappraisal /ˌriːəˈpreɪzl/ *n* [U, C] action of re-examining sth to see whether it or one's attitude to it should be changed; re-evaluation: *a reappraisal of the situation, problem, etc* ○ *a radical reappraisal of our trade with China.*

rear[1] /rɪə(r)/ *n* **1** (usu **the rear**) [sing] the back part: *a kitchen in/at/to the rear of the house* ○ *a view of the house taken from the rear* ○ *attack the enemy's rear* ○ [attrib] *a car's rear doors, lights, wheels, window.* **2** [C] (*infml euph*) buttocks: *a kick in/on the rear.* **3** (idm) ˌ**bring up the ˈrear** be or come last, eg in a procession, race, etc.

▷ **rearmost** /ˈrɪəməʊst/ *adj* furthest back: *the rearmost section of the aircraft.*

rearward /ˈrɪəwəd/ *n* [U] the rear (used esp in the expressions shown): *to rearward of* (ie some distance behind) *sth* ○ *in the rearward,* ie at the back.

rearwards /ˈrɪəwədz/ (also **rearward**) *adv* towards the rear: *move the troops rearwards.*

□ ˌ**rear-ˈadmiral** /ˌrɪər ˈædmərəl/ *n* naval officer holding a rank between those of commodore and vice-admiral: *Rear Admiral (Tom) King.* ⇨ App 4.

ˈ**rearguard** *n* (usu **the rearguard**) [CGp] body of troops sent to guard the rear of an army, esp when it is retreating. Cf VANGUARD. ˈ**rearguard action 1** fight between an army in retreat and the enemy. **2** (*fig*) struggle continued even when it is unlikely to succeed: *The government is fighting a rearguard action against the mass of public opinion.*

ˌ**rear-view ˈmirror** mirror in which a driver can see traffic, etc behind him. ⇨ illus at CAR.

rear[2] /rɪə(r)/ *v* **1** [Tn] (**a**) (*esp Brit*) bring up and educate (children, etc): *rear a family.* (**b**) breed and look after (sheep, poultry, etc); grow or produce (crops). Cf RAISE 6. **2** [I, Ip] ~ (**up**) (of a horse, etc) raise itself on its hind legs: *The horse reared (up) in fright.* **3** [Tn] raise (esp one's head): *The snake reared its head.* ○ (*fig*) *terrorism rearing its ugly head again.*

rearm /ˌriːˈɑːm/ *v* [I, Ipr, Tn, Tn·pr] ~ (**sb/sth**) (**with sth**) supply (an army, etc) with weapons again or with better weapons. ▷ **rearmament** /riːˈɑːməmənt/ *n* [U].

rearrange /ˌriːəˈreɪndʒ/ *v* [Tn] **1** place (sth) in a different way or order: *rearrange the furniture, one's books, etc* ○ *Do you like the way I've rearranged the room?* **2** change (plans, etc) that have already been made: *Let's rearrange the match for next Saturday.* ▷ **rearrangement** *n* [U, C]: *make some rearrangements.*

reason[1] /ˈriːzn/ *n* **1** [C, U] ~ (**for sth/doing sth**); ~ (**to do sth**); ~ (**why.../that...**) (fact put forward as or serving as the) cause of, motive for or justification for sth: *for one/some reason or other* ○ *have adequate/sufficient reason for doing sth* ○ *all the more reason for doing/to do sth* ○ *Give me your reasons for going/the reasons for your going.* ○ *There is/We have (good) reason to believe that he is lying.* ○ *Is there any (particular) reason why you can't come?* ○ *The reason why I'm late is that/because I missed the bus.* ○ *My reason is that the cost will be too high.* ○ *We aren't going, for the simple reason that we can't afford it.* ○ *She complained, with reason* (ie rightly), *that she had been underpaid.* ⇨ Usage. **2** [U] power of the mind to think, understand, form opinions, etc: *Only man has reason.* **3 one's/sb's reason** [sing] one's/sb's sanity: *lose one's reason/senses,* ie go mad ○ *We feared for her reason,* ie were afraid that she might go mad. **4** [U] what is right or practical or possible; common sense or judgement: *see/listen to/hear/be open to* (ie be prepared to accept) *reason* ○ *There's a good deal of reason in what you say.* **5** (idm) **beˌyond/ˌpast all ˈreason** not reasonable or acceptable: *Her outrageous remarks were/went beyond all reason.* ˌ**bring sb to ˈreason**; ˌ**make sb see ˈreason** make sb stop acting foolishly, resisting uselessly, etc. **by reason of sth** (*fml*) because of sth: *He was excused by reason of his age.* **for reasons/some reason best known to oneˈself** (*esp joc*) for reasons that are hard for others to understand or discover: *For reasons best known to himself, he drinks tea from a beer glass.* (**do anything**) **in/within ˈreason** sensible or reasonable: *I'll do anything within reason to earn my living.* **lose all reason** ⇨ LOSE. **rhyme or reason** ⇨ RHYME *n.* **it/that ˌstands to ˈreason** it/that is obvious to everyone: *It stands to reason that nobody will work without pay.*

NOTE ON USAGE: A **cause** (of something) is what makes something happen: *The police are investigating the cause of the explosion.* ○ *The causes of the First World War.* **Reason** (for something) has a wider use. It can be the explanation that people give for why something is done: *What was the reason for his resignation?* ○ *She didn't give any reasons for leaving.* **Reason, justification** and **cause** (for something) can indicate that the explanation is acceptable to people in general, or **reasonable**: *The police had no reason to suspect him/no justification for suspecting him/no cause for suspicion* (ie They didn't suspect him or shouldn't have suspected him). **Ground** is the formal, especially legal, justification for an action. It is commonly used in the plural: *Boredom is not a ground for divorce.* ○ *I left my job on medical grounds.* A **motive** for doing something is a feeling or desire within people which makes them act: *He claimed that his motive for stealing was hunger.* ○ *The crime seemed to have been committed without (a) motive.*

reason[2] /ˈriːzn/ *v* **1** (**a**) [I] use one's power to think, understand, form opinions, etc: *man's ability to reason.* (**b**) [Tf no passive] conclude or state as a step in this process: *He reasoned that if we started at dawn, we would be there by noon.* **2** (idm) **ours, theirs, etc not to reason ˈwhy** (*saying*) (said when one is forced to do sth which seems foolish and illogical): *Making everyone change offices seems an odd decision, but ours is not to reason why!* **3** (phr v) **reason sb into/out of sth** persuade sb by argument to do/not to do sth: *reason sb out of his fears* ○ *She was reasoned into a sensible course of action.* **reason sth out** find an answer to (a problem, etc) by considering various possible solutions: *The detective tried to reason out how the thief had escaped.* **reason with sb** argue in order to convince or persuade sb: *I reasoned with her for hours about the danger, but she would not change her mind.* ○ *There's no reasoning with that woman,* ie She won't listen to arguments.

▷ **reasoned** *adj* [attrib] (of an argument, etc) presented in a logical way: *a reasoned approach to the problem* ○ *She put a (well-)reasoned case for increasing the fees.*

reasoning *n* [U] act or process of using one's reason[1](2); arguments produced when doing this: *great power/strength of reasoning* ○ *Your reasoning on this point is faulty.*

reasonable /ˈriːznəbl/ *adj* **1** (**a**) (of people) ready to use or listen to reason; sensible: *No reasonable person could refuse.* ○ *She's perfectly reasonable in her demands.* (**b**) (of emotions, opinions, etc) in accordance with reason; not absurd; logical: *a reasonable suspicion, fear, belief, etc* ○ *a reasonable attitude, conclusion* ○ *It's not reasonable to expect a child to understand sarcasm.* ○ *Is the accused guilty beyond all reasonable doubt?* **2** (**a**) not unfair or expecting too much; moderate: *a reasonable fee, offer, claim.* (**b**) (of prices, etc) not too expensive; acceptable: *Ten pounds for a good dictionary seems reasonable enough.* **3** [esp attrib] tolerable; average: *reasonable weather, health, food* ○ *There's a reasonable chance that he'll come.* ○ *reasonable expectations of success.*

▷ **reasonableness** *n* [U].

reasonably /-əblɪ/ *adv* **1** in a reasonable way: *discuss the matter calmly and reasonably.* **2** moderately, acceptably or tolerably; fairly or quite: *reasonably good, cheap, intelligent* ○ *a reasonably-priced book* ○ *He seems reasonably satisfied with it.*

reassure /ˌriːəˈʃɔː(r); *US* -ˈʃʊər/ *v* [Tn, Tn·pr, Dn·f] ~ **sb** (**about sth**) remove sb's fears or doubts; make sb confident again: *The police reassured her about her child's safety.* ○ *A glance in the mirror reassured him that his tie wasn't crooked.*

▷ **reassurance** /-rəns/ *n* **1** [U] reassuring or being reassured: *want, need, demand, etc reassurance,* eg from a doctor about one's health. **2** [C] thing that reassures: *numerous reassurances that we were safe.*

reassuring *adj* that reassures: *a reassuring glance, word, pat on the back.* **reassuringly** *adv.*

rebate[1] /ˈriːbeɪt/ *n* amount by which a debt, tax, etc can be reduced; discount or partial refund: *qualify for a rate/rent/tax rebate* ○ *offer a rebate of £1.50 for early settlement,* ie of an account, a bill, etc. Cf DISCOUNT[1].

rebate[2] /ˈriːbeɪt/ (also **rabbet** /ˈræbɪt/) *n* L-shaped cut in a the corner of a piece of wood, eg at the edge of two overlapping doors. ⇨ illus.

▷ **rebate** (also **rabbet**) *v* [Tn] cut a rebate in (eg a door).

rebel /ˈrebl/ *n* (**a**) person who fights against, or refuses to serve, the established government: [attrib] *rebel forces.* (**b**) person who resists

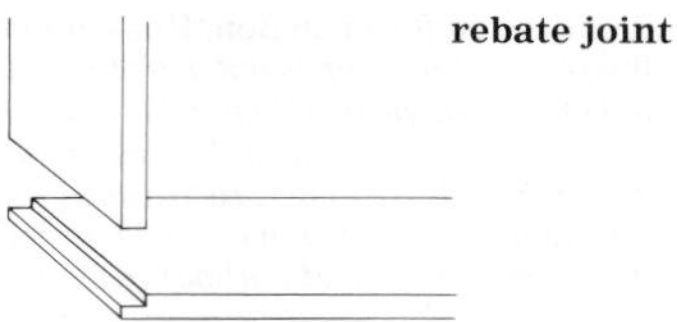
rebate joint

authority or control: *She has always been a bit of a rebel.*

▷ **rebel** /rɪˈbel/ *v* (**-ll-**) [I, Ipr] ~ (**against sb/sth**) **1** fight against or resist the established government. **2** resist authority or control; protest strongly: *Such treatment would make anyone rebel.* ○ *He finally rebelled against his strict upbringing.*

rebellion /rɪˈbelɪən/ *n* ~ (**against sb/sth**) **1** [U] open (esp armed) resistance to the established government; resistance to authority or control: *rise (up) in open rebellion.* **2** [C] act of rebelling: *five rebellions in two years.*

rebellious /rɪˈbelɪəs/ *adj* showing a desire to rebel; not easily controlled: *rebellious tribes* ○ *rebellious acts, activities, behaviour, etc* ○ *a child with a rebellious temperament.* **rebelliously** *adv.* **rebelliousness** *n* [U].

rebind /ˌriːˈbaɪnd/ *v* (*pt, pp* **rebound** /ˌriːˈbaʊnd/) [Tn] put a new binding on (a book, etc).

rebirth /ˌriːˈbɜːθ/ *n* [sing] **1** spiritual renewal or enlightenment caused by religious conversion, etc. **2** revival: *the rebirth of learning*, eg in the Renaissance.

reborn /ˌriːˈbɔːn/ *adj* [pred] **1** spiritually renewed or enlightened. Cf BORN-AGAIN (BORN). **2** brought back to life; revived: *The old man felt reborn in his children.*

rebound[1] /rɪˈbaʊnd/ *v* **1** [I, Ipr] ~ (**against/from/off sth**) spring or bounce back after hitting sth: *The ball rebounded from/off the wall into the pond.* **2** [I, Ipr] ~ (**on sb**) have an adverse effect on (the doer); misfire: *The scheme rebounded on her in a way she had not expected.*

▷ **rebound** /ˈriːbaʊnd/ *n* (idm) **on the ˈrebound (from sth)** (**a**) while bouncing back: *hit a ball on the rebound.* (**b**) (*fig*) while still affected by disappointment, depression, etc: *She quarrelled with Paul and then married Peter on the rebound.*

rebound[2] *pt, pp* of REBIND.

rebuff /rɪˈbʌf/ *n* unkind or contemptuous refusal or rejection (of an offer, request, friendly gesture, etc); snub: *Her kindness to him was met with a cruel rebuff.*

▷ **rebuff** *v* [Tn] give a rebuff to (sb); snub.

rebuild /ˌriːˈbɪld/ *v* (*pt, pp* **rebuilt** /ˌriːˈbɪlt/) [Tn] **1** build or put (sth) together again: *rebuild the city centre after an earthquake* ○ *We rebuilt the engine* (ie took it to pieces and put it together again) *using some new parts.* **2** (*fig*) form (sth) again; restore: *rebuild sb's confidence, hopes, health* ○ *After his divorce, he had to rebuild his life completely.*

rebuke /rɪˈbjuːk/ *v* [Tn, Tn·pr] ~ **sb** (**for sth**) express sharp or severe disapproval to sb, esp officially; reprove sb: *My boss rebuked me for coming to work late.*

▷ **rebuke** *n* act of rebuking sb; reproof: *administer a stern rebuke.*

rebus /ˈriːbəs/ *n* puzzle in which a word or phrase has to be guessed from pictures or diagrams representing the letters or syllables in it.

rebut /rɪˈbʌt/ *v* (**-tt-**) [Tn] prove (a charge, piece of evidence, etc) to be false; refute.

▷ **rebuttal** /-tl/ *n* **1** [U] act of rebutting or being rebutted: *produce evidence in rebuttal of the charge.* **2** [sing] evidence that rebuts a charge, etc.

rec /rek/ *abbr* recreation ground.

recalcitrant /rɪˈkælsɪtrənt/ *adj* (*fml*) resisting authority or discipline; disobedient: *a recalcitrant child, attitude.*

▷ **recalcitrance** /-əns/ *n* [U] (*fml*) quality of being recalcitrant.

recall /rɪˈkɔːl/ *v* **1** (**a**) [Tn, Tn·pr] ~ **sb** (**from...**) (**to...**) order sb to return (from a place): *recall an ambassador (from his post)* ○ *recall (members of) Parliament*, eg for a special debate. (**b**) [Tn] order (sth) to be returned: *recall library books*, eg for stock-taking. **2** [Tn, Tf, Tw, Tg, Tsg] bring (sth/sb) back into the mind; recollect: *I can't recall his name.* ○ *She recalled that he had left early.* ○ *Try to recall (to mind) exactly what happened.* ○ *I recall seeing him.* ○ *I recall her giving me the key.* Cf REMEMBER 1. **3** (phr v) **recall sb to sth** make sb aware or conscious again of sth: *The danger recalled him to a sense of duty.*

▷ **recall** /*also* ˈriːkɔːl/ *n* **1** [sing] order to sb/sth to return: *the temporary recall of embassy staff.* **2** [U] ability to remember; recollection: *a person gifted with total recall* ○ *My powers of recall are not what they were.* **3** [C] signal, esp a bugle-call, to troops, etc to return: *sound the recall.* **4** (idm) **beyond/past reˈcall** that cannot be brought back or cancelled.

recant /rɪˈkænt/ *v* [I, Tn] (*fml*) (**a**) formally reject (a former opinion, belief, etc) as being wrong: *recant one's former beliefs, heresies.* (**b**) take back or withdraw (a statement, an opinion, etc) as being false.

▷ **recantation** /ˌriːkænˈteɪʃn/ *n* (*fml*) **1** [U] recanting. **2** [C] act of recanting; statement that one's former beliefs were wrong.

recap[1] /ˈriːkæp/ *v* (**-pp-**) [I, Tn, Tw] (*infml*) = RECAPITULATE. ▷ **recap** *n* [C, U] (*infml*) = RECAPITULATION 1 (RECAPITULATE).

recap[2] /ˌriːˈkæp/ *v, n* (**-pp-**) = RE-TREAD.

recapitulate /ˌriːkəˈpɪtʃʊleɪt/ (also *infml* **recap**) *v* [I, Tn, Tw] state again or summarize the main points of (a discussion, etc): *Let me just recapitulate (on) what we've agreed so far.*

▷ **recapitulation** /ˌriːkəpɪtʃʊˈleɪʃn/ **1** (also *infml* **recap**) [C, U] (act of) recapitulating: *a brief recapitulation.* **2** [C] (*music*) part of a movement(7) in which the main themes are repeated.

recapture /ˌriːˈkæptʃə(r)/ *v* [Tn] **1** capture again (a person or an animal that has escaped, or sth taken by an enemy): *recapture escaped prisoners, bears* ○ *The town was recaptured from the enemy.* **2** (*fig*) experience again or reproduce (past emotions, etc): *recapture the joys of youth* ○ *recapture a period atmosphere*, eg in a play, film, etc.

▷ **recapture** *n* [U] recapturing; being recaptured: *What led to the prisoner's recapture?*

recast /ˌriːˈkɑːst; *US* -ˈkæst/ *v* (*pt, pp* **recast**) **1** [Tn, Cn·n/a] ~ **sth** (**as sth**) put (sth written or spoken) into a new form: *recast a sentence, chapter, paragraph, etc* ○ *She recast her lecture as a radio talk.* **2** (**a**) [Tn] change the cast of (a play, etc). (**b**) [Tn] change the role of (an actor): *I've been recast as Brutus.*

recce /ˈrekɪ/ *n* [C, U] (*infml*) = RECONNAISSANCE: *make a quick recce of the area.* ▷ **recce** *v* [I, Tn] (*infml*) = RECONNOITRE.

recd *abbr* received: *recd £9.50.*

recede /rɪˈsiːd/ *v* **1** [I, Ipr] ~ (**from sth**) (seem to) move back from a previous position or away from an observer: *As the tide receded (from the shore) we were able to look for shells.* ○ *We reached the open sea and the coast receded into the distance.* ○ (*fig*) *The prospect of bankruptcy has now receded*, ie is less likely. **2** [I] slope backwards: *a receding chin* ○ *Tom has a receding hairline*, ie His hair has stopped growing at the forehead and temples.

receipt /rɪˈsiːt/ *n* **1** [U] ~ (**of sth**) (*fml*) act of receiving or being received: *acknowledge receipt of a letter, an order, etc* ○ *On receipt of the news, he left.* **2** [C] ~ (**for sth**) written statement that sth (esp money or goods) has been received: *get a receipt for your expenses* ○ *sign a receipt* ○ [attrib] *a receipt book.* **3 receipts** [pl] money received by a business: *net/gross receipts.* Cf EXPENDITURE. **4** [C] (*arch*) recipe. **5** (idm) (**be**) **in receipt of sth** (*commerce*) having received sth: *We are in receipt of your letter of the 15th.*

▷ **receipt** *v* [Tn] mark (a bill) as having been paid, eg with a rubber stamp saying 'Paid' or 'Received with thanks'.

receivable /rɪˈsiːvəbl/ *adj* (usu following *ns*) (*commerce*) (of bills, accounts, etc) for which money has not yet been received: *bills receivable.*

▷ **receivables** *n* [pl] assets of a business represented by accounts that still have to be paid.

receive /rɪˈsiːv/ *v* **1** (**a**) [Tn, Tn·pr] ~ **sth** (**from sb/sth**) get, accept or take (sth sent, given, etc): *receive a letter, present, phone call, grant* ○ *receive a good education* ○ *receive severe injuries, blows* ○ *receive insults, thanks, congratulations* ○ *Your comments will receive our close attention.* ○ *You will receive a warm welcome when you come to England.* (**b**) [I, Tn] (*esp Brit*) buy or accept (stolen goods) knowingly. **2** (**a**) [Tn, Tn·pr] ~ **sb** (**into sth**) allow sb to enter, eg as a guest, member, etc; admit sb: *rooms* (eg in a hotel) *ready to receive their new occupants* ○ *He has been received into the Church.* (**b**) [esp passive: Tn, Tn·pr, Cn·n/a] ~ **sb** (**with sth**) (**as sth**) (*fml*) welcome or entertain (guests, etc), esp formally: *The chief was received by the Prime Minister.* ○ *She was received with warm applause.* ○ *He was received as an honoured visitor.* **3** [esp passive: Tn, Tn·pr] ~ **sb/sth** (**with sth**) react in a specified way to sb/sth: *How was the play received?* ○ *My suggestion was received with disdain.* ○ *The reforms have been well received by the public.* **4** [Tn] convert (broadcast signals) into sounds or pictures: *receive a programme via satellite* ○ *Are you receiving me?* ie Can you hear me (said to sb to whom one is speaking on a radio transmitter)? **5** (idm) **be at/on the receiving end** (**of sth**) (*infml*) be the one who suffers sth unpleasant: *The party in power soon learns what it's like to be on the receiving end of political satire.*

▷ **received** *adj* [attrib] widely accepted as correct: *received opinion* ○ *change received ideas about education.* **reˌceived pronunciˈation** (*abbr* **RP**) type of English pronunciation used by most educated speakers of the language in England, varying to some extent throughout the country. It is the British pronunciation shown in this dictionary.

receiver /rɪˈsiːvə(r)/ *n* **1** (**a**) person who receives sth. (**b**) (*esp Brit*) person who buys or accepts stolen goods knowingly. **2** (also **Receiver, Ofˌficial Reˈceiver**) official appointed by law to look after the property and affairs of a minor, bankrupt, etc or to administer disputed property: *call in the receiver* ○ *put the business in the hands of a receiver.* **3** part of an instrument that receives sth, esp the part of a telephone that receives the incoming sound and is held to the ear: *lift, replace, etc the receiver.* **4** radio or TV set that converts broadcast signals into sound or pictures.

▷ **receivership** /-ʃɪp/ *n* [U] (*law*) **1** (period of) office of a Receiver. **2** (idm) **in receivership** (esp of bankrupt companies) under the control of an Official Receiver: *go into/be in receivership.*

recent /ˈriːsnt/ *adj* **1** [usu attrib] (that existed, happened, began, was/were made, etc) not long ago or before: *a recent event, development, occurrence, etc* ○ *In recent years there have been many changes.* ○ *Ours is a recent acquaintance*, ie We only met a short time ago. ⇨ Usage at NEW. **2 Recent** [attrib] (*geology*) of the present geological period, the Holocene.

▷ **recently** *adv* not long ago or before; lately: *until quite recently* ○ *a recently painted house.*

NOTE ON USAGE: **Recently**, **not long ago**, **lately** indicate that the action spoken about took place in the recent past. **1 Recently** has the widest use, in positive and negative statements and questions, with the past tense and the present perfect tense: *Did she have a party recently?* ○ *They've recently bought a new car.* **2 Not long ago** is only used in positive statements with the verb in the past tense: *They arrived in Britain not long ago/recently.* ○ *It's not long ago that they arrived in Britain.* **3 Lately** is used in questions and negative statements. In positive statements it is used generally with **only**, **much** and **a lot.** The verb must be in the present perfect tense: *Have you seen him lately/recently?* ○ *They haven't written lately/recently.* ○ *She's only lately/recently begun working here.* ○ *I've seen a lot of her lately/recently.*

receptacle /rɪˈseptəkl/ *n* (*fml*) container, space, etc for placing or storing sth: *a receptacle for litter,* *washing, waste paper*.

reception /rɪˈsepʃn/ *n* **1** [U] action of receiving or being received: *The bridal suite was prepared for the reception of the honeymooners.* ○ *prepare rooms for the reception of guests* ○ *her reception into the religious order* ○ [attrib] *a reception area, camp, centre, etc*, ie where refugees, immigrants, etc are received and accommodated ○ *a* ˈ*reception committee*. **2** [sing] way in which sb/sth is received (RECEIVE 3): *The play got a favourable reception from the critics.* ○ *His talk met with/was given a warm* (ie enthusiastic) *reception*. **3** [sing] (*Brit*) area in a hotel or an office building where guests or clients are received, registered, etc: *Wait for me at reception.* **4** [C] formal social occasion to welcome sb: *hold a wedding reception* ○ *official receptions for the foreign visitors*. **5** [U] receiving of broadcast signals; efficiency of this: *a radio with excellent reception* ○ *Reception* (eg of TV programmes) *is poor here.* ⇨ article at WEDDING.

▷ **receptionist** /-ʃənɪst/ *n* person employed to make appointments for and receive clients at a hotel, an office building, a doctor's or a dentist's surgery, hairdressing salon, etc.

□ **reˈception desk** (*Brit*) (in a hotel, an office building, etc) counter where guests, clients, etc are received, where they ask for rooms, etc.

reˈception room **1** (used esp when advertising houses for sale) living-room; room other than a kitchen, bathroom or bedroom. **2** room (eg in a hotel) suitable for large social functions.

receptive /rɪˈseptɪv/ *adj* ~ (**to sth**) able or quick to receive new ideas, suggestions, etc: *a receptive person, mind, attitude* ○ *receptive to new developments*. ▷ **receptiveness**, **receptivity** /ˌriːsepˈtɪvətɪ/ *ns* [U].

receptor /rɪˈseptə(r)/ *n* cell or group of cells that can react to sensations like light, heat, sound, etc and send a signal along a sensory nerve.

recess /rɪˈses; *US* ˈriːses/ *n* **1** [C, U] (**a**) (*US* also **vacation**) period of time when work or business is stopped, esp in Parliament, the lawcourts, etc: *the summer recess* ○ *Parliament is in recess.* (**b**) (*US*) break between classes at school. ⇨ Usage at BREAK[2]. **2** [C] space in a room where part of a wall is set back from the main part; alcove: *a door, window, cupboard, etc recess.* **3** [C] hollow space inside sth: *a drawer with a secret recess.* **4** [C usu *pl*] remote or secret place: *the dark recesses of a cave* ○ (*fig*) *in the innermost recesses of the heart/mind*.

▷ **recess** *v* **1** [Tn esp passive] place (sth) in a recess(2): *recessed shelves, windows, etc.* **2** [Tn esp passive] set (a wall) back; provide (a wall) with recesses. **3** [I] (*US*) take a recess(1a).

recession /rɪˈseʃn/ *n* **1** [C] temporary decline in economic activity or prosperity: *an industrial, a trade, etc recession.* Cf SLUMP *n* 1. **2** [U] movement back from a previous position; withdrawal: *the gradual recession of flood waters*.

▷ **recessionary** *adj* **1** [attrib] of a slowing of economic activity: *in the present recessionary period, conditions.* **2** likely to bring about a slowing of economic activity: *a recessionary effect on the economy* ○ *introduce recessionary measures*.

recessional /rɪˈseʃənl/ *n* (also **recessional hymn**) hymn sung while the clergy and choir withdraw after a church service.

recessive /rɪˈsesɪv/ *adj* **1** (*biology*) (of characteristics inherited from a parent, such as the colour of the eyes or of the hair) not appearing in a child but remaining hidden because of the presence of stronger characteristics. Cf DOMINANT. **2** having a tendency to recede or go back.

recharge /ˌriːˈtʃɑːdʒ/ *v* [Tn] **1** charge (a battery, a gun, etc) again. **2** (idm) **recharge one's** ˈ**batteries** (*infml*) have a period of rest and relaxation during which one's energy is built up again. ▷ **rechargeable** *adj*: *rechargeable batteries*.

recherché /rəˈʃeəʃeɪ/ *adj* (*fml*) **1** (*usu derog*) much too studied or refined; affected: *a recherché idea, writing style, image.* **2** chosen or planned with great care; choice: *a recherché menu*, eg for gourmets.

recidivist /rɪˈsɪdɪvɪst/ *n* person who commits crimes repeatedly and seems unable to be cured of criminal tendencies; persistent offender. ▷ **recidivism** /-ɪzəm/ *n* [U].

recipe /ˈresəpɪ/ *n* **1** ~ (**for sth**) set of instructions for preparing a food dish, including the ingredients required: [attrib] *recipe books, cards.* **2** ~ **for sth** (*fig*) method of achieving sth: *What is your recipe for success?* ○ *His plans are a recipe for* (ie are likely to lead to) *disaster*.

recipient /rɪˈsɪpɪənt/ *n* ~ (**of sth**) person who receives sth.

reciprocal /rɪˈsɪprəkl/ *adj* **1** given and received in return; mutual: *reciprocal affection, help, trade* ○ *have a reciprocal agreement to combat terrorism.* **2** corresponding, although opposite in shape, nature, etc: *reciprocal forces*.

▷ **reciprocal** *n* ~ (**of sth**) (*mathematics*) number, fraction, etc that can be multiplied by another fraction, number, etc to give 1. So $\frac{1}{2}$ is the reciprocal of 2 and $\frac{3}{4}$ is the reciprocal of $\frac{4}{3}$.

reciprocally /-klɪ/ *adv*.

□ ˌ**reciprocal** ˈ**pronoun** (*grammar*) pronoun expressing a mutual action or relation, eg *each other, one another*.

reciprocate /rɪˈsɪprəkeɪt/ *v* **1** [I, Tn] (*fml*) (**a**) give and receive (sth) in return; exchange (sth) mutually. (**b**) return (sth done, given or felt): *He reciprocated by wishing her good luck.* ○ *I reciprocate your good wishes.* **2** [I] (of parts of a machine) move alternately backwards and forwards in a straight line: *a reciprocating saw* ○ *reciprocating pistons.* Cf ROTARY 2. ▷ **reciprocation** /rɪˌsɪprəˈkeɪʃn/ *n* [U].

□ **reˈciprocating engine** engine in which pistons move backwards and forwards inside cylinders.

reciprocity /ˌresɪˈprɒsətɪ/ *n* [U] principle or practice of mutual exchange, esp of making concessions or granting privileges, etc in return for concessions or privileges received: *reciprocity in trade (between countries)*.

recital /rɪˈsaɪtl/ *n* **1** [C] public performance of music, dance, etc by a soloist or a small group: *give a piˈano recital* ○ *a* ˈ*song*/ˈ*dance*/ˈ*poetry recital.* Cf CONCERT. **2** [C] detailed account of a series of events, etc: *I had to listen to a long recital of all his complaints.* **3** [U] action of reciting: *his recital of the poem* ○ *music recorded in recital*.

recitation /ˌresɪˈteɪʃn/ *n* **1** [C, U] (instance of) public delivery of passages of prose or poetry learnt by heart: *recitations from Dickens* ○ *the recitation of a ballad, an ode, etc.* **2** [C] piece of prose or poetry (to be) recited. **3** [C] (*US*) student's oral responses to questions on a lesson, etc.

recitative /ˌresɪtəˈtiːv/ *n* [C, U] (passage of) narrative or dialogue in an opera or oratorio sung in the rhythm of ordinary speech with many words on the same note.

recite /rɪˈsaɪt/ *v* **1** [I, Ipr, Tn, Tn·pr] ~ (**sth**) (**to sb**) say (a poem, passage, etc) aloud from memory, esp to an audience: *recite a speech from 'Hamlet' to the class.* **2** [Tn, Tn·pr] ~ **sth** (**to sb**) state (names, facts, etc) one by one; give a list of: *recite one's grievances* ○ *recite the names of all the European capitals*.

reckless /ˈreklɪs/ *adj* ~ (**of sth**) (of people or their actions) not thinking of the consequences or of danger; rash or impulsive: *a reckless spender, gambler, etc* ○ *fined £100 for reckless driving* ○ *He's quite reckless of his own safety.* ▷ **recklessly** *adv*. **recklessness** *n* [U].

reckon /ˈrekən/ *v* **1** [Tn·pr, Tf, Cn·a esp passive, Cn·n esp passive, Cn·n/a esp passive, Cn·t esp passive] ~ **sb/sth among sth**; ~ **sb/sth as sth** (*infml*) (not used in the continuous tenses) be of the opinion or consider that sb/sth is as specified: *We reckon her among our best reporters.* ○ *I reckon (that) he is too old for the job.* ○ *The price was reckoned high.* ○ *She is reckoned (to be) the cleverest pupil in the class.* ○ *One quarter of the country is reckoned as unproductive.* **2** (**a**) [Tf no passive] (*infml*) assume; think: *I reckon we'll go next week.* ○ *The news won't worry her, I reckon.* ○ *What do you reckon our chances are of arriving on time?* (**b**) [Tf, Tt] calculate (time, price, age, etc) approximately; guess: *I reckon it will cost about £100.* ○ *We reckon to arrive in Delhi at noon.* **3** [Tn] find out (the quantity, number, cost, etc) by using numbers; calculate: *reckon the total volume of imports* ○ *Hire charges are reckoned from the date of delivery.* **4** (phr v) **reckon sth in** include sth in a calculation: *When you did your expenses, did you reckon in your taxi fares?* **reckon on sb/sth** base one's plans on sb doing sth or on sth happening; rely on sb/sth: *Can I reckon on you to help?* ○ *We're reckoning on moving house in May.* ○ *You can't always reckon on (having) good weather.* **reckon sth up** find the sum or total of sth; count sth up: *reckon up bills, accounts, costs, etc.* **reckon with sb/sth** take sb/sth into account; consider sb/sth as important: *They had many difficulties to reckon with.* ○ *a force, fact, person to be reckoned with*, ie that cannot be ignored. **reckon without sb/sth** not take sb/sth into account; not consider sb/sth as important: *We wanted a quiet holiday, but we had reckoned without the children*.

▷ **reckoner** /ˈrekənə(r)/ *n* device or table (of figures, etc) used as an aid to reckoning. Cf READY RECKONER (READY).

reckoning /ˈrekənɪŋ/ *n* **1** [U] calculation; estimation: *the reckoning of debts, accounts, etc* ○ *By my reckoning, this short cut will save us five miles.* ○ *You were £5 out* (ie over or under the correct sum) *in your reckoning.* **2** [sing] (*dated*) (settlement of an) account or a bill, eg at a hotel or restaurant: *ask for the reckoning* ○ (*fig*) *There'll be a heavy reckoning to pay!* ie The consequences will be serious. **3** (idm) **a day of reckoning** ⇨ DAY.

reclaim /rɪˈkleɪm/ *v* [Tn, Tn·pr] **1** ~ **sth** (**from sb/sth**) recover possession of sth: *reclaim tax, rent, lost property.* **2** ~ **sth** (**from sth**) make (land) suitable for cultivation, eg by draining or irrigating it: *reclaimed marshland, desert, etc* ○ *reclaim an area from the sea.* **3** ~ **sb** (**from sth**) (*fml*) win sb back or away from sin, error, etc; reform sb: *reclaim young offenders from a life of crime.* **4** ~ **sth** (**from sth**) recover (raw material) from waste products: *reclaim glass from old bottles.* Cf RECYCLE. ▷ **reclamation** /ˌrekləˈmeɪʃn/ *n* [U].

recline /rɪˈklaɪn/ *v* **1** [I, Ipr] lean or lie back in a horizontal or near-horizontal position: *recline on a pillow, a sofa, a grassy bank* ○ *recline in a deck-chair, a punt, a hammock* ○ *a reclining chair*, ie one with a back that tilts ○ *a reclining seat*, eg in a train, plane, etc ○ *a reclining figure*, eg in a painting. **2** [Tn·pr] ~ **sth against/on sb/sth** put or lay (one's head, arms) in a position of rest. **3** [Tn] tilt (a seat, etc) backwards.

recluse /rɪˈkluːs/ *n* person who lives alone and avoids other people: *live/lead the life of a recluse*.

recognition /ˌrekəgˈnɪʃn/ *n* **1** [U] recognizing or being recognized: *an award in recognition of one's services, achievements, etc* ○ *He has won wide recognition in the field of tropical medicine.* ○ (*fml*) *Britain's recognition of* (ie establishment of diplomatic relations with) *the new regime is unlikely.* **2** (idm) **change, etc beyond/out of (all) recogˈnition** change so much that recognition is very difficult: *The town has altered out of all recognition since I was last here*.

recognizance, -nisance /rɪˈkɒgnɪzns/ *n* (*law*) (**a**) formal promise made to a court or magistrate that one will observe certain conditions (eg keep the peace), appear when summoned or pay a debt: *enter into recognizances (for sb)* ○ *bail in one's own recognizance of £500* ○ *be released on one's own recognizance.* (**b**) sum of money pledged as a guarantee that this promise will be kept.

recognize, -ise /ˈrekəgnaɪz/ *v* (not used in the continuous tenses) **1** [Tn, Tn·pr] ~ **sb/sth** (**by sth**) be able to identify (sb/sth that one has seen, heard, etc before); know sb/sth again: *recognize a tune, an old friend, a signal* ○ *I recognized her by her red hat.* **2** [Tn, Cn·n/a, Cn·t] ~ **sb/sth** (**as sth**) be willing to accept sb/sth as valid or genuine; approve: *recognized* (ie qualified or official) *instructors, schools, charities* ○ *recognize sb's claim to ownership* ○ (*fml*) *Britain has recognized* (ie established diplomatic relations with) *the new regime.* ○ *Everyone recognized him to be the lawful* *heir/as the lawful heir.* **3** [Tn, Tf] be prepared to admit or be aware of (sth); realize: *He recognized his lack of qualifications/that he was not qualified for the post.* **4** [Tn] show gratitude or appreciation of (sb's ability, service, etc) by giving him an honour or reward: *The firm recognized Tom's outstanding work by giving him an extra bonus.* ○ *His services to the State were recognized,* eg by a knighthood.

▷ **recognizable, -isable** /ˈrekəgnaɪzəbl, *also* ˌrekəgˈnaɪzəbl/ *adj* that can be recognized: *She was barely recognizable as the girl I had known at school.* **recognizably, -isably** /-əblɪ/ *adv.*

recoil /rɪˈkɔɪl/ *v* **1** [I, Ipr] ~ **(from sb/sth);** ~ **(at sth)** (a) draw oneself back in fear, disgust, etc: *She recoiled from the gunman in terror.* ○ *He recoiled at the sight of the corpse.* **(b)** *(fig)* withdraw mentally: *recoil from murder, violence, etc.* **2** [I] **(a)** (of guns) jerk back when fired. **(b)** (of springs) move or jump back suddenly after impact. **3** (phr v) **recoil on sb** (of harmful actions) return to hurt the person who does them.

▷ **recoil** /ˈri:kɔɪl/ *n* [U, sing] sudden backward movement, esp of a gun when fired.

recollect /ˌrekəˈlekt/ *v* [I, Tn, Tf, Tw, Tg, Tsg no passive] succeed in calling (sth) back to the mind; remember: *As far as I recollect, you came late.* ○ *recollect one's childhood, sb's name* ○ *I recollect that you denied it.* ○ *Can you recollect how it was done?* ○ *She can recollect meeting the king.* ○ *No one can recollect her leaving.*

recollection /ˌrekəˈlekʃn/ *n* **1** **(a)** [U] ability to recollect; action of recollecting: *have amazing powers of recollection* ○ *I have some/no recollection of that day.* ○ *lost in quiet recollection of the past* ○ *to the best of my recollection,* ie if I remember correctly ○ *My recollection of events differs from hers.* **(b)** [C usu *pl*] thing, event, etc recollected: *vague, clear, distant, etc recollections of childhood* ○ *The old letters brought back many happy recollections.* **2** time over which sb's memory goes back: *Such a problem has never arisen within my recollection.*

recommend /ˌrekəˈmend/ *v* **1** [Tn, Cn·n/a, Dn·n, Dn·pr] ~ **sb/sth (to sb) (for sth/as sth)** praise sth as suitable for a purpose; praise sb as suitable for a post, etc; speak favourably of sb/sth: *recommend a car, film, plumber, etc* ○ *What would you recommend for removing ink stains?* ○ *She was strongly recommended for the post.* ○ *I can recommend him as an extremely good accountant.* ○ *Can you recommend me a good novel?* **2** [Tn, Tf, Tw, Tg, Tsg, Dn·t, Dpr·f] suggest (a course of action, treatment, etc); advise: *I'd recommend extreme caution.* ○ *I recommend that you resign.* ○ *I'm not the person to recommend how the job should be done.* ○ *I recommended (your) meeting him first.* ○ *I wouldn't recommend you to go there alone.* **3** [Tn, Dn·pr] ~ **sb/sth (to sb)** (of a quality, etc) make sb/sth seem attractive: *a plan with nothing, little, something, much, etc to recommend it* ○ *His integrity recommended him to his employers.*

▷ **recommendable** /-əbl/ *adj*: *a highly recommendable film, restaurant, camping site.*

recommendation /ˌrekəmenˈdeɪʃn/ *n* **1** [U] action of recommending: *speak in recommendation of sb/sth* ○ *I bought it on your recommendation,* ie because you recommended it. **2** [C] **(a)** statement, letter, etc that recommends sb/sth, esp a person for a job: *write, give sb a recommendation.* **(b)** course of action, etc that is recommended: *The judge made recommendations to the court.* ○ *a recommendation that the offer of 5% be rejected.* **3** quality, etc that makes sb/sth seem attractive: *The cheapness of coach travel is its only recommendation.*

recompense /ˈrekəmpens/ *v* [Tn, Tn·pr] ~ **sb (for sth)** *(fml)* reward sb (for his work, efforts, etc); compensate sb (for his losses, etc): *recompense employees for working overtime* ○ *recompense her for the loss of her job.*

▷ **recompense** *n* [sing, U] ~ **(for sth)** *(fml)* thing that rewards; thing that compensates: *receive adequate recompense for one's services, labours, efforts, etc* ○ *award the victim £500 in recompense for damages.*

reconcile /ˈrekənsaɪl/ *v* **1** **(a)** [esp passive: Tn, Tn·pr] ~ **sb (with sb)** cause (people) to become friends again, eg after quarrelling: *We were finally reconciled when he apologized.* ○ *She refused to be reconciled with her brother.* **(b)** [Tn] bring (a quarrel, disagreement, etc) to an end; settle: *They can't reconcile their differences.* **2** [Tn, Tn·pr] ~ **sth (with sth)** make (aims, statements, ideas, etc) agree when they seem to conflict: *reconcile the evidence with the facts* ○ *Can eating fish be reconciled with vegetarianism?* **3** [Tn·pr] ~ **sb/oneself to sth** (cause sb to) accept reluctantly sth unwelcome, unpleasant, etc: *The high salary reconciled me to living abroad.* ○ *Could you reconcile yourself to a lifetime of unemployment?*

▷ **reconcilable** /-əbl, *also* ˌrekənˈsaɪləbl/ *adj.*

reconciliation /ˌrekənˌsɪlɪˈeɪʃn/ *n* **1** [U] reconciling or being reconciled: *the reconciliation of ideas, opinions, etc.* **2** [sing] end to a quarrel, etc: *bring about a reconciliation between former enemies.*

recondite /ˈrekəndaɪt/ *adj* *(fml)* **1** (of subjects) little known or understood; obscure. **2** (of writers, etc) dealing with subjects that are little known or understood.

recondition /ˌri:kənˈdɪʃn/ *v* [Tn esp passive] repair (sth) and put it into good condition again; overhaul or restore: *a reconditioned engine, cooker* ○ *reconditioned furniture, leather.*

reconnaissance /rɪˈkɒnɪsns/ (also *infml* **recce**) *n* [C, U] (patrol, flight, etc that carries out an) exploration or a survey of an area, esp for military purposes: *make an aerial reconnaissance of an island* ○ *troops engaged in reconnaissance* ○ [attrib] *a reconnaissance plane, party, mission.*

reconnoitre (*US* **-ter**) /ˌrekəˈnɔɪtə(r)/ (also *Brit infml* **recce**) *v* [I, Tn] explore or survey (an enemy area, position, etc): *The platoon was sent to reconnoitre the village before the attack.*

reconsider /ˌri:kənˈsɪdə(r)/ *v* [I, Tn] consider (sth) again, esp to change an earlier opinion, decision, etc: *reconsider one's position, view, decision, etc* ○ *The jury was called upon to reconsider its verdict.* ▷ **reconsideration** /ˌri:kənˌsɪdəˈreɪʃn/ *n* [U].

reconstitute /ˌri:ˈkɒnstɪtju:t; *US* -tu:t/ *v* [Tn esp passive] **1** restore (dried food) to its original state, eg by adding water: *reconstitute dried milk, powdered soup, etc.* **2** *(fml)* reorganize or change the membership of (sth): *a reconstituted board, panel, committee, etc.* ▷ **reconstitution** /ˌri:ˌkɒnstɪˈtju:ʃn; *US* -tu:ʃn/ *n* [U].

reconstruct /ˌri:kənˈstrʌkt/ *v* **1** [Tn] construct or build again, eg after damage. **2** [Tn, Tn·pr, Tw] ~ **sth (from sth)** create again (sth that has existed or happened) by using evidence or imagination: *Police are trying to reconstruct the crime,* eg by using actors at the place where it was committed or by assembling the known facts. ○ *We reconstructed what the dinosaur looked like from a few of its bones.*

▷ **reconstruction** /-ˈstrʌkʃn/ *n* **1** [C, U] (act of) reconstructing or being reconstructed: *plans for the reconstruction of the city centre* ○ *a reconstruction of events by detectives.* **2** **Reconstruction** [sing] *(US)* period of occupation and reform in the Southern states after their defeat in the American Civil War.

record[1] /ˈrekɔ:d; *US* ˈrekərd/ *n* **1** [C] ~ **(of sth)** permanent account, esp in writing, of facts, events, etc: *a record of school attendances, road accidents* ○ *records of births, marriages and deaths* ○ *public, parish, medical, etc records* ○ *make/keep a record of one's expenses.* **2** [sing] ~ **(for sth)** facts, events, etc known (but not always written down) about the past of sb/sth: *He had a good* ˈ*war record,* eg fought bravely. ○ *have a (previous) criminal* ˈ*record,* ie have already been convicted for a crime or crimes ○ *The airline has a bad safety record,* ie Its aircraft often crash. ○ *The school has a poor record for examination passes,* ie Many of its pupils fail. **3** [C] (also ˈ**gramophone record, disc**) ~ **(of sb/sth)** thin circular piece of plastic on which sound has been recorded: *a pop, jazz, hit record* ○ *the band's latest record* ○ *put on/play some records* ○ [attrib] *a record sleeve, album, library.* **4** [C] best performance or highest or lowest level ever reached, esp in sport: *beat/break* (ie surpass) *a record* ○ *an Olympic, world, all-time record* ○ *She holds the world record in/for the 100 metres.* ○ [attrib] *a record performance, score, time* ○ *record profits, sales, crops.* **5** [C] *(computing)* set of related data forming a unit in a computer file. **6** (idm) **(just) for the** ˈ**record** so that it should be noted; for the sake of accuracy: *Just for the record the minister's statement is wrong on two points.* ˌ**of the** ˈ**record** *(infml)* (of statements, opinions, etc) not for publication or not to be officially noted: *The Prime Minister admitted, (strictly) off the record that the talks had failed.* **on** ˈ**record** **(a)** (of facts, events, etc) noted or recorded, esp officially: *Last summer was the wettest on record for 50 years.* **(b)** (of statements, opinions, etc) publicly known or officially noted: *be/go on record as saying that the law should be changed* ○ *put one's views, objections etc on record,* ie publish or broadcast them. **put/set the** ˈ**record straight** give a correct account of facts, events, etc; put right a misunderstanding: *To set the record straight, I must say now that I never supported the idea.*

□ ˈ**record-breaker** *n* person, car, boat, etc that breaks a record[1](4).

ˈ**record-breaking** *adj* [attrib]: *a record-breaking attendance, flight, jump, time.*

ˈ**record-holder** *n* person holding a sports record.

ˈ**record-player** *n* (also *dated* **gramophone**) instrument for reproducing sound from records (RECORD[1] 3).

record[2] /rɪˈkɔ:d/ *v* **1** **(a)** [Tn, Tf, Tw] write down (facts or events) for later use or reference: *record progress, developments, etc* ○ *record the minutes/proceedings of a meeting* ○ *The papers record that inflation has dropped.* ○ *Historians record how Rome fell.* **(b)** [I, Ipr, Tn, Tn·pr, Tng] ~ **(sth) (from sth) (on sth)** preserve (sound or images) on a disc or magnetic tape for later reproduction: *To record press both buttons.* ○ *My voice records quite well.* ○ *record music from the radio* ○ *record a speech, piece of music, TV programme (on tape/video)* ○ *a recorded* (ie not live) *programme, concert, interview, etc* ○ *record sb playing the guitar.* **2** [Tn] (of measuring instruments) mark or indicate (sth); register: *The thermometer recorded a maximum of 40°C.*

□ **re**ˌ**corded de**ˈ**livery** (*US* ˌ**certified** ˈ**mail**) postal service in which delivery is confirmed by the receiver signing a form: *send a letter by recorded delivery.* Cf REGISTERED POST (REGISTER[2]). ⇨ article at POST OFFICE.

recorder /rɪˈkɔ:də(r)/ *n* **1** apparatus for recording sound or pictures, or both: *a* ˈ*tape-recorder* ○ *a* ˈ*video-recorder.* **2** wooden or plastic wind instrument of the flute family, played like a whistle, with eight holes for the fingers. ⇨ illus.

📖 Young children in Britain often learn to play the recorder at primary school. It is regarded as one of the easiest instruments to play, and is also conveniently small and light.

3 *(Brit)* judge in certain lawcourts. ⇨ article at LAW.

recording /rɪˈkɔ:dɪŋ/ *n* **1** [U] action of preserving sound or images on magnetic tape, etc: *during the recording of the show* ○ [attrib] *a re*ˈ*cording studio, session, company.* **2** [C] sound or images that have been preserved in this way: *make a video recording of a wedding* ○ *a good recording of the opera on tape/video.*

recount /rɪˈkaʊnt/ *v* [Tn, Tw, Dn·pr, Dpr·w] ~ **sth (to sb)** give a detailed account of sth; tell about sth: *recount one's adventures, experiences, misfortunes, etc* ○ *He recounted how he had shot the lion.*

re-count /ˌriːˈkaʊnt/ *v* [Tn] count (esp votes) again. ▷ **re-count** /ˈriːkaʊnt/ *n* another count, esp of votes in an election: *The unsuccessful candidate demanded a re-count.*

recoup /rɪˈkuːp/ *v* [Tn, Tn·pr, Tw] ~ **sb/oneself for sth** get back (what one has spent, lost, etc); give sb/oneself back (what has been spent, lost, etc): *We recouped the show's expenses from ticket sales.* ○ *He recouped himself for his losses.* ○ *recoup what the project has cost.*

recourse /rɪˈkɔːs/ *n* [U] **1** possible source of help, eg in an emergency: *They managed without recourse to* (ie without seeking) *outside help.* ○ *Your only recourse is legal action.* **2** (idm) **have recourse to sb/sth** (*fml*) turn to sb/sth for help; get help from sb/sth: *I hope the doctors won't have recourse to surgery.*

recover /rɪˈkʌvə(r)/ *v* **1** [Tn, Tn·pr] ~ **sth (from sb/sth)** find again (sth stolen, lost, etc); regain possession of sth: *recover stolen goods, lost property, etc* ○ *Six bodies were recovered from the wreck.* ○ *recover what was lost.* **2** [Tn] **(a)** get back the use of (one's faculties, health, etc): *recover one's sight, hearing, etc* ○ *recover one's senses/consciousness*, eg after fainting ○ *I'm slowly recovering my strength after a bout of flu.* **(b)** get back the control of (oneself, one's actions, one's emotions, etc): *The skater quickly recovered his balance.* ○ *She recovered herself/her composure and smiled.* ○ *The murderer never recovered his peace of mind.* **3** [Tn, Tn·pr] ~ **sth (from sb/sth)** regain (money, time or position): *They sought to recover damages, costs, expenses, etc from the firm.* ○ *We recovered lost time by setting out early.* ○ *The team recovered its lead in the second half.* **4** [I, Ipr] ~ **(from sb/sth)** return to a normal state, eg of health, mind, prosperity: *He's now fully recovered from his stroke.* ○ *recover from the shock, surprise, strain, etc* ○ *Trade soon recovered from the effects of the war.*

▷ **recoverable** /-rəbl/ *adj* that can be recovered (RECOVER 1): *recoverable deposits, losses, assets.*

re-cover /ˌriːˈkʌvə(r)/ *v* [Tn, Tn·pr] ~ **sth (in/with sth)** put a new cover on sth: *re-cover a cushion (in/with velvet).*

recovery /rɪˈkʌvərɪ/ *n* **1** [U] ~ **(of sth/sb)** recovering (RECOVER 1) or being recovered: *the recovery of the missing diamonds* ○ [attrib] *a recovery vehicle*, ie one for taking broken-down cars, etc to a garage. **2** [sing, U] ~ **(from sth)** return to a normal state, eg of health or prosperity: *make a quick, speedy, good, slow, etc recovery (from illness)* ○ *be well on the way/road to recovery* ○ *the team's recovery from defeat.* **3** [U] (*esp US*) area of a hospital where patients are kept immediately after an operation: *The patient is in recovery.*

□ **reˈcovery room** (*US*) room in a hospital where patients are kept for observation after an operation.

recreant /ˈrekrɪənt/ *n, adj* [usu attrib] (*dated*) (person who is) cowardly, unfaithful or treacherous: *You recreant knave!*

re-create /ˌriːkrɪˈeɪt/ *v* [Tn] create (sth past) again; reproduce: *The play re-creates life before the war.* ▷ **re-creation** /-ˈeɪʃn/ *n* [U, C].

recreation /ˌrekrɪˈeɪʃn/ *n* [C, U] (means of) refreshing or entertaining oneself after work; relaxation: *My favourite recreation is chess.* ○ *walk and climb mountains for recreation* ○ *Gardening is a form of recreation.*

▷ **recreational** /-ʃənl/ *adj* of or for recreation: *take part in recreational activities* ○ *recreational facilities*, eg sports grounds, swimming-pools.

□ **recreˈation ground** (*abbr* **rec**) publicly-owned area of land used for adult sports or games, or having swings, slides, etc for children.

recreˈation room (also **rec room**) (*US*) room in a private house used for games, relaxation, entertainment, etc.

recriminate /rɪˈkrɪmɪneɪt/ *v* [I, Ipr] ~ **(against sb)** (*fml*) accuse or blame (sb by whom one has been accused or blamed).

▷ **recrimination** /rɪˌkrɪmɪˈneɪʃn/ *n* [C usu *pl*, U] (act of making an) accusation in response to an accusation from sb else; countercharge: *bitter, angry, furious, etc recriminations* ○ *Let's not indulge in (mutual) recrimination.*

recriminatory /rɪˈkrɪmɪnətrɪ; *US* -tɔːrɪ/ *adj* of recrimination: *recriminatory remarks, comments, etc.*

recrudesce /ˌriːkruːˈdes/ *v* [I] (*fml*) (of diseases, violence, etc) break out again; recur.

▷ **recrudescence** /-ˈdesns/ *n* [C, U] (*fml*) new outburst; recurrence: *a recrudescence of influenza* ○ *prevent the recrudescence of civil disorder.*

recrudescent /-ˈdesnt/ *adj.*

recruit /rɪˈkruːt/ *n* ~ **(to sth) (from sth) 1** person who has just joined the armed forces or police and is not yet trained: *new, recent, raw* (ie inexperienced) *recruits* ○ *drilling recruits on the parade ground.* **2** new member of a club, society, etc: *gain/seek new recruits* (eg to training schemes) *from among the young unemployed.*

▷ **recruit** *v* [I, Tn, Tn·pr, Cn·n/a] ~ **(sb) (to sth) (from sth)**; ~ **sb (as sth) 1** gain (sb) as a recruit; enlist: *recruit on a regular basis* ○ *a reˈcruiting officer, poster, drive* ○ *recruit new members (to the club)* ○ *recruit sb as a spy.* **2** form (an army, a party, etc) by gaining recruits: *recruit a task force.*

recruitment *n* [U].

rectal /ˈrektəl/ *adj* (*anatomy*) of the rectum.

rectangle /ˈrektæŋgl/ *n* four-sided geometric figure with four right angles, esp one with unequal adjacent sides. ⇨ illus at QUADRILATERAL.

▷ **rectangular** /rekˈtæŋgjʊlə(r)/ *adj* having the shape of a rectangle.

rectify /ˈrektɪfaɪ/ *v* (*pt, pp* **-fied**) **1** [Tn] put (sth) right; correct: *rectify an error, omission, etc* ○ *mistakes that cannot be rectified.* **2** [Tn esp passive] (*chemistry*) purify or refine, esp by repeated distillation: *rectified spirits.* **3** [Tn] convert (alternating current) to direct current.

▷ **rectifiable** /-faɪəbl, *also* ˌrektɪˈfaɪəbl/ *adj* that can be rectified: *an error that is easily rectifiable.*

rectification /ˌrektɪfɪˈkeɪʃn/ *n* **1** [U] rectifying or being rectified: *the rectification of errors, alcohol.* **2** [C] thing that has been rectified; correction.

rectifier *n* device that converts alternating current to direct current.

rectilinear /ˌrektɪˈlɪnɪə(r)/ *adj* **1** in or forming a straight line: *rectilinear motion.* **2** bounded by or having straight lines: *a rectilinear figure.*

rectitude /ˈrektɪtjuːd; *US* -tuːd/ *n* [U] (*fml*) moral correctness or straightforwardness; honesty: *a person of stern (moral) rectitude.*

recto /ˈrektəʊ/ *n* (*pl* ~**s**) right-hand page of an open book: *on the recto page.* Cf VERSO.

rector /ˈrektə(r)/ *n* **1 (a)** (in the Church of England) clergyman in charge of a parish from which he receives his income directly (formerly entitled to receive all the tithes of his parish). Cf VICAR. ⇨ article at CHURCH OF ENGLAND. **(b)** (in the Roman Catholic Church) head of a church or a religious community. **2** (*esp Brit*) head of certain universities, colleges, schools or religious institutions.

▷ **rectory** /ˈrektərɪ/ *n* rector's house.

rectum /ˈrektəm/ *n* (*pl* ~**s** or **recta**) (*anatomy*) lower end of the large intestine, through which solid waste passes to the anus. ⇨ illus at DIGESTIVE.

recumbent /rɪˈkʌmbənt/ *adj* [usu attrib] (*fml*) (esp of a person) lying down; reclining: *a recumbent figure*, eg in a painting or sculpture.

recuperate /rɪˈkuːpəreɪt/ *v* **1** [I, Ipr, Tn] ~ **(from sth)** (*fml*) recover from illness, exhaustion or loss, etc: *He is still recuperating from his operation.* ○ *recuperate one's strength after a climb.* **2** [Tn] get back (money spent or lost): *recuperate costs, expenses, etc.*

▷ **recuperation** /rɪˌkuːpəˈreɪʃn/ *n* [U] recuperating.

recuperative /rɪˈkuːpərətɪv/ *adj* (*fml*) of or aiding recuperation: *the recuperative powers of fresh air.*

recur /rɪˈkɜː(r)/ *v* (**-rr-**) **1** [I] happen again; happen repeatedly: *a recurring problem, error, illness* ○ *The symptoms tend to recur.* ○ *This theme recurs constantly throughout the opera.* **2** (phr v) **recur to sb/sth** (*fml*) (of ideas, events, etc) come back into the mind: *Our first meeting often recurs to me/my mind.*

▷ **recurrence** /rɪˈkʌrəns/ *n* [C, U] (instance of) recurring; repetition: *the recurrence of an illness, error, problem, theme.*

recurrent /-ənt/ *adj* [usu attrib] recurring often or regularly: *recurrent attacks, fits, headaches, etc* ○ *a recurrent problem, theme.*

□ **recurring decimal** decimal fraction in which the same figure(s) are repeated indefinitely, eg 3.999, 4.014014: *The recurring decimal 3.999... is also described as 3.9 recurring.*

recusant /ˈrekjuznt/ *n* (formerly) Roman Catholic who refused to attend Anglican services as required by law.

recycle /ˌriːˈsaɪkl/ *v* [Tn] **(a)** treat (used material) so that it can be used again: *recycle newspaper*, ie by de-inking and pulping it. **(b)** get (natural products) back from used material by treating it: *ˌrecycled ˈglass*, ie from old bottles. Cf RECLAIM 4. ⇨ article at ENVIRONMENT.

red[1] /red/ *adj* (**-dder, -ddest**) **1 (a)** of the colour of fresh blood or a similar colour: *a red sky, door, car* ○ *ruby-red lips* ○ *Maple leaves turn red in the autumn.* ⇨ illus at SPECTRUM. **(b)** (of the eyes) sore and having red veins and rims; bloodshot: *Her eyes were red with weeping.* **(c)** (of the face) flushed with shame, anger, etc: *turn, go, be red in the face.* **2** (of hair or an animal's fur) of a reddish-brown colour; ginger or tawny: *red deer, squirrels.* **3 (a) Red** [attrib] Soviet or Russian: *The Red Army*, ie that of the USSR ○ *Red* (ie Communist) *China.* **(b)** (*infml sometimes derog*) revolutionary; communist. **4** (idm) **neither fish, flesh, nor good red herring** ⇨ FISH[1]. **not (be) worth a red ˈcent; not give a red ˈcent for sth** (*US infml*) (be) worthless; regard sth as being worthless. **paint the town red** ⇨ PAINT[2]. **(as) red as a beetroot** very red in the face, esp because one is embarrassed: *He went as red as a beetroot when I asked about his new girl-friend.* **a red ˈherring** fact, argument, etc that leads attention away from the matter being considered: *Stop chasing red herrings and get back to the point.* **(like) a red rag to a bull** likely to cause strong resentment, anger, violence, etc: *Her remarks were like a red rag to a bull: he was furious with her.* ▷ **redly** *adv*: *The fire glowed redly in the darkened room.* **redness** *n* [U].

□ **ˌred ˈadmiral** European butterfly having black wings with red and white marks.

ˌred aˈlert (esp in the armed services) state of special readiness for an expected attack, disaster, etc: *The base was put on red alert.*

ˌred-ˈblooded *adj* [usu attrib] (*infml*) full of vigour or sexual desire; virile: *ˌred-blooded ˈmales.*

ˈredbreast *n* ⇨ ROBIN.

ˈredbrick *adj* (*Brit sometimes derog*) (of universities) founded near the end of the 19th century or later: *redbrick colleges, campuses, etc.* Cf OXBRIDGE.

ˌred ˈcabbage type of cabbage with red leaves.

ˈredcap *n* (*infml*) **1** (*Brit*) member of the military police. **2** (*US*) railway porter.

ˌred ˈcard (in football, etc) card shown by the referee to a player that he is sending off the field. Cf YELLOW CARD (YELLOW).

ˌred ˈcarpet strip of red carpet laid out for the reception of an important visitor: [attrib] (*fig*) *We must give our guests the red-carpet treatment.*

ˈredcoat *n* (formerly) British soldier.

ˌred ˈcorpuscle (also **ˈred ˈblood cell**) blood cell that carries oxygen to the body tissues and carbon dioxide from them. Cf WHITE CORPUSCLE (WHITE[1]).

ˌRed ˈCrescent (emblem of the) organization in Muslim countries that corresponds to the Red Cross.

ˌRed ˈCross (emblem of the) international organization that works to relieve suffering caused by natural disasters, etc and to help the victims of war. ⇨ article at VOLUNTARY.

ˌ**redˈcurrant** *n* (shrub producing) a small round edible berry: [attrib] *ˌredcurrant ˈjelly.*

ˌ**red ˈensign** red flag of the British merchant navy with a Union Jack in the top left corner. Cf WHITE ENSIGN (WHITE[1]).

ˌ**red ˈflag 1** flag used as a symbol of danger, eg on roads, railways, etc. **2** symbol of revolution or communism. **3 the Red Flag** socialist song, the official song of the British Labour Party.

ˌ**red ˈgiant** large star near the middle of its life that gives out a reddish light. Cf WHITE DWARF (WHITE[1]).

ˌ**red-ˈhanded** *adj* (idm) **catch sb red-handed** ⇨ CATCH[1].

ˌ**red ˈhat** large red round hat with a broad brim, given to a cardinal[3] as a symbol of his office but never actually worn.

ˈ**redhead** *n* person, esp female, with red[1](2) hair.

ˌ**red-ˈhot** *adj* **1** (of a metal) so hot that it glows red. **2** (*fig*) very great: *ˌred-hot ˈanger, enˈthusiasm, etc.* **3** (*fig infml*) (of news) completely new; fresh: *The reporter had a red-hot story.* ˌ**red-hot ˈpoker** garden plant with red or yellow spikes of flowers.

ˌ**Red ˈIndian** (*Brit* ˈ**redskin**) (⚠ *infml offensive*) N American Indian.

ˌ**red ˈlead** red oxide of lead, used in paint.

red-ˈletter day day that is important or memorable because sth good happened on it.

ˌ**red ˈlight** road signal meaning 'stop'; danger signal on railways, etc: *go through, jump a red light,* ie not stop. **red-ˈlight district** part of a town where there are many prostitutes, sex-shops, etc.

ˌ**red ˈmeat** beef, lamb or mutton. Cf DARK MEAT (DARK[2]), WHITE MEAT (WHITE[1]).

ˈ**redneck** *n* (*US often derog*) member of the white working class in the southern USA: [attrib] *redneck* (ie reactionary and bigoted) *views.*

ˌ**red ˈpepper 1** (red fruit of the) capsicum plant. **2** = CAYENNE PEPPER.

redpoll /ˈredpəʊl/ *n* small bird of the finch family with a red patch on its forehead.

ˌ**red ˈrose** (picture of a) red rose used as the symbol of Lancashire, a county in NW England.

ˌ**red ˈsetter** = IRISH SETTER (IRISH).

ˈ**redshank** *n* large type of European sandpiper.

ˈ**red-shift** *n* phenomenon in which lines from the spectrum of the light coming from a galaxy moving away from the earth appear closer to the red end of the spectrum. It is caused by the Doppler effect.

ˈ**redskin** *n* ⇨ RED INDIAN.

ˈ**redstart** *n* small European songbird with a red tail.

ˌ**red ˈtape** (*derog*) excessive bureaucracy, esp in public business: *procedures hedged about with red tape* ○ *It takes weeks to get through the red tape.*

ˌ**red ˈwine** wine made from black grapes and coloured red by contact with their skins. Cf ROSÉ, WHITE WINE (WHITE[1]).

ˈ**redwing** *n* European thrush with red sides.

ˈ**redwood** *n* any type of tree with reddish wood, esp a Californian conifer that sometimes grows to a great height.

red[2] /red/ *n* **1** [U, C] (shade of) red colour: *light, clear, deep, dark, etc red* ○ *There's too much red in the painting.* ○ *the reds and browns of the woods in autumn,* ie of the leaves, undergrowth, etc. **2** [U] red clothes: *dressed in red* ○ *Don't wear red tonight.* **3** [C] (a) **Red** person supporting Socialism or Communism: *the conflict between Reds and Whites,* ie during the Russian Revolution. (b) (*infml or derog*) person supporting revolution or radical policies: *a union infiltrated by reds.* Cf PINK[1]. **4** (idm) **be in the ˈred; get (sb) into the ˈred** (*infml*) have more liabilities than assets; (cause sb to) owe money: *My bank account is £50 in the red.* Cf BE IN THE BLACK (BLACK[2] 4). **be out of the red; get (sb) out of the red** (*infml*) (help sb to) be no longer in debt: *This payment will get me out of the red,* ie into a state of credit. **reds under the ˈbed** supposed secret presence of communists in Western society: *the sort of reactionary who sees reds under the bed,* eg who thinks all trade-unionists are communists. **see ˈred** (*infml*) become very angry: *Her criticisms were enough to make anyone see red.*

redden /ˈredn/ *v* **1** [I, Tn] (cause sth to) become red. **2** [I] (of the face) flush with shame, anger, etc.

reddish /ˈredɪʃ/ *adj* rather red: *reddish fur, hair.*

redeem /rɪˈdiːm/ *v* **1** (a) [Tn, Tn·pr] ~ **sth (from sb/sth)** buy back sth by paying the required sum; recover sth: *I redeemed my watch from the pawn shop.* (b) [Tn] pay off (eg a debt); clear: *redeem a mortgage, loan, etc.* (c) [Tn] convert (bonds, shares, etc) into cash or goods: *This coupon can be redeemed at any of our branches.* **2** [Tn] (*fml*) keep (a promise); fulfil: *redeem one's pledges, obligations.* **3** [Tn, Tn·pr] ~ **sb (from sth)** (a) obtain the freedom of sb, esp by payment; rescue sb: *redeem hostages from captivity.* (b) (*fig*) (of Christ) free or save mankind from sin. **4** [Tn] (a) make up for faults or deficiencies in (sth); compensate for: *The sole redeeming feature of this job is the salary.* ○ *The acting was not good enough to redeem the (awfulness of the) play.* ○ *Jones redeemed his earlier poor performance by scoring two goals.* (b) save (sb/sth/oneself) from blame; vindicate: *redeem one's honour* ○ *The minister redeemed himself in the eyes of the public by resigning.*

▷ **redeemable** /-əbl/ *adj* that can be redeemed.

the Redeemer *n* [sing] Jesus Christ.

redemption /rɪˈdempʃn/ *n* [U] (*fml*) **1** redeeming or being redeemed: *the redemption of one's property, debts, shares, promises.* **2** (idm) **beyond/past reˈdemption** (*esp joc*) in such a poor state that there is no chance of improvement or recovery: *When the third goal was scored against us, we knew the match was past redemption.* ○ *Joan's career with the firm is really beyond redemption.*

▷ **redemptive** *adj* /rɪˈdemptɪv/ *adj* (*fml*) of redemption; serving to redeem.

redeploy /ˌriːdɪˈplɔɪ/ *v* [Tn] give new positions or tasks to (sb): *redeploy troops, workers, scientists, etc* ○ *redeploy teachers into industry.*

▷ **redeployment** *n* [U] redeploying: *the redeployment of staff, labour, manpower, etc.*

redevelop /ˌriːdɪˈveləp/ *v* [Tn] replan or rebuild (an area of land or building(s) in a different way: *redevelop a city centre, housing estate, slum area, etc,* eg modernize them, improve conditions, etc.

▷ **redevelopment** *n* [U] redeveloping or being redeveloped: *an area ripe for development.*

Redford /ˈredfəd/ Robert (1937-), American film actor. Films like *The Sting* and *All the President's Men* showed him as an accomplished screen performer. He won an Oscar for his first film as a director, *Ordinary People.*

rediffusion /ˌriːdɪˈfjuːʒn/ *n* [U] (*esp Brit*) relaying of broadcast radio or TV programmes esp by wire from a central receiver to public places (eg cinemas, etc).

redirect /ˌriːdɪˈrekt/ *v* = READDRESS.

redistribute /ˌriːdɪˈstrɪbjuːt/ *v* [Tn] give (sth) out in a different way: *redistribute jobs, power, land.* ▷ **redistribution** /ˌriːdɪstrɪˈbjuːʃn/ *n* [U]: *the redistribution of wealth, labour, resources, etc.*

redo /ˌriːˈduː/ *v* (*pt* **redid** /-ˈdɪd/, *pp* **redone** /-ˈdʌn/) [Tn] **1** do (sth) again. **2** (*infml*) redecorate (a room, building, etc); repair: *have the kitchen redone,* ie wallpapered, painted, etc ○ *the roof needs redoing,* eg retiling.

redolent /ˈredələnt/ *adj* [pred] ~ **of/with sth** (*fml*) **1** smelling strongly of sth: *have breath redolent of garlic, whisky, tobacco* ○ *a room redolent of roses.* **2** (*fig*) strongly suggestive or reminiscent of sth: *a town redolent of the past.* ▷ **redolence** /-əns/ *n* [U].

redouble /ˌriːˈdʌbl/ *v* [I, Tn] **1** (cause sth to) become greater, stronger, more intense, etc: *Her zeal redoubled.* ○ *We must redouble our efforts.* **2** (in the card-game of bridge) double again (a bid already doubled by an opponent).

redoubt /rɪˈdaʊt/ *n* (a) last defensive position within a system of fortifications. (b) isolated fortified outpost.

redoubtable /rɪˈdaʊtəbl/ *adj* (*fml or joc*) to be feared and respected; formidable: *a redoubtable opponent, fighter.*

redound /rɪˈdaʊnd/ *v* (phr v) **redound on sb/sth** (*fml*) come back on sb/sth; rebound or recoil on sb/sth: *Your practical jokes will redound on you/your own head one day.* **redound to sth** (*fml*) contribute greatly to (one's/sb's reputation, etc); promote sth: *Her hard work redounds to her credit/to the honour of the school.* ○ *This course of action will redound to our advantage.*

redox /ˈriːdɒks/ *n* [U] chemical processes of oxidation and reduction: [attrib] *a redox reaction.* Cf REDUCE 6.

redress /rɪˈdres/ *v* **1** [Tn] (*fml*) put right (a wrong); compensate for (sth): *redress an injustice, an abuse, etc,* ○ *redress a grievance* ○ *redress the damage done.* **2** (idm) **redress the ˈbalance** make things equal again: *The team has more men than women so we must redress the balance,* ie include more women in it.

▷ **redress** *n* [U] ~ **(for sth)** (*fml*) redressing or being redressed; thing that redresses: *seek legal redress for unfair dismissal* ○ *Under the circumstances, you have no redress,* ie You cannot demand compensation.

Red Sea /ˌred ˈsiː/ **the Red Sea** long narrow sea between Africa and Arabia, 438 000 sq km (169 000 sq miles) in area. It is linked to the Mediterranean by the Suez Canal. ⇨ map at ARABIAN PENINSULA.

reduce /rɪˈdjuːs; *US* -ˈduːs/ *v* **1** [Tn, Tn·pr] ~ **sth (from sth) (to/by sb)** make sth smaller in size, number, degree, price, etc: *reduce volume, quantity, pressure, speed* ○ *increase profits by reducing costs* ○ *reduce one's weight from 98 to 92 kilos/by 6 kilos* ○ *Antibiotics will reduce the swelling.* ○ *This shirt was greatly/drastically reduced in the sale.* **2** [I] (*infml esp US*) lose weight intentionally; diet. **3** [Tn·pr] ~ **sb (from sth) to sth** make sb lower in rank or status; demote sb: *reduce a sergeant to the ranks,* ie make him an ordinary soldier ○ *The reform has reduced us to servants of the State.* **4** [Tn·pr] ~ **sb/sth (from sth) to sth** bring sb/sth into a specified (usu worse) state or condition: *be reduced to begging, borrowing* ○ *reduce sb to tears, silence, despair, obedience* ○ *reduce the chaos in one's office to some form of order* ○ *Overwork has reduced him to a physical wreck.* ○ *The fire reduced the house to ashes.* **5** [Tn·pr] ~ **sth to sth** change sth to a more general or basic form: *reduce an equation, argument, issue to its simplest form* ○ *reduce a problem to two main issues.* **6** [Tn, Tn·pr] ~ **sth (to sth)** (*chemistry*) remove oxygen from or add hydrogen or electrons to (a compound): *reduce water* (ie to hydrogen) *by electrolysis* ○ *reduce a compound to its constituent elements.* Cf OXIDIZE (OXIDE).

▷ **reducible** /-əbl/ *adj* ~ **(to sth)** that can be reduced.

reductio ad absurdum /rɪˌdʌktɪəʊ æd əbˈsɜːdəm/ (*Latin*) method of disproving a proposition by showing that, if interpreted literally and precisely, it would lead to an absurd result.

reduction /rɪˈdʌkʃn/ *n* **1** (a) [U] reducing or being reduced: *the reduction of tax* ○ *reduction of an argument to its essentials.* (b) [C] instance of reducing: *a reduction in size, weight, etc* ○ *a price reduction.* (c) [C] amount by which sth is reduced, esp in price: *sell sth at a huge reduction* ○ *make/offer reductions on certain articles.* **2** [C] copy of a map, picture, etc made by reducing the size of the original. Cf ENLARGEMENT (ENLARGE).

redundant /rɪˈdʌndənt/ *adj* **1** (usu of language or art) not needed; superfluous; unnecessary: *a paragraph without a redundant word* ○ *The illustration had too much redundant detail.* **2** (*esp Brit*) (of industrial workers) no longer needed for any available job and therefore dismissed: *become/be made/find oneself redundant* ○ *the plight of redundant miners* ○ *Fifty welders were declared redundant.*

▷ **redundancy** /-ənsɪ/ *n* **1** [U] (a) state of being redundant(2): *a high level of redundancy among unskilled workers* ○ [attrib] *redundancy pay, money, etc,* ie given to sb made redundant. (b) material that is redundant(1): *express oneself without redundancy.* **2** [C] worker made redundant(2): *Two hundred redundancies were*

announced in the shipyards.
redundantly *adv.*

reduplicate /rɪˈdju:plɪkeɪt/ *v* [Tn] (*fml*) repeat (esp a word or syllable), as in *bye-bye*; double. ▷ **reduplication** /rɪˌdju:plɪˈkeɪʃn; *US* -ˌdu:-/ *n* [U].

re-echo /ri:ˈekəʊ/ *v* [I] echo again and again: *Their shouts re-echoed through the valley.*

Reed /ri:d/ Sir Carol (1906-76), British film director. He was one of the most original story-tellers of the British cinema, as shown in *The Third Man* and *Oliver!*, a filmed version of the musical based on *Dickens's *Oliver Twist* for which Reed won an Oscar.

reed /ri:d/ *n* **1** (**a**) [C] (tall hollow stem of) any of various types of grass-like plants growing near water. (**b**) [U] mass of such plants growing together. **2** [C] strip of metal or cane that vibrates to produce sound in eg an oboe, a bassoon, a clarinet: [attrib] *reed instruments.* ⇨ illus at MUSIC. **3** (idm) **a broken reed** ⇨ BROKEN².
▷ **reedy** *adj* (**-ier, iest**) **1** having many reeds (REED 1). **2** (*derog*) (of voices, sounds) high and scratchy instead of full and clear: *a thin, reedy tenor.* **reediness** *n* [U] state of being reedy(2): *an unpleasant reediness of tone.*

re-educate /ri:ˈedʒʊkeɪt/ *v* [Tn, Cn·t] train (sb) to think or behave in a new or different way: *We must re-educate people (to eat more healthily).* ▷ **re-education** /ˌri:edʒʊˈkeɪʃn/ *n* [U].

reef¹ /ri:f/ *n* part of the top or bottom of a sail that can be rolled or folded to reduce the area exposed to the wind.
▷ **reef** *v* [Tn] reduce the area of (a sail) by drawing in a reef or reefs.
□ ˈ**reef-knot** (*US* **square-knot**) *n* type of symmetrical double-knot that will not slip or come undone easily. ⇨ illus at KNOT¹.

reef² /ri:f/ *n* ridge of rock, shingle, sand, etc at or near the surface of the sea: *The ship was wrecked on a coral reef.*

reefer /ˈri:fə(r)/ *n* **1** (also **reefer-jacket**) close-fitting thick double-breasted jacket. **2** (*sl*) hand-rolled cigarette containing marijuana.

reek /ri:k/ *n* [sing] **1** (*derog*) strong bad smell: *the reek of stale tobacco (smoke).* **2** (*Scot*) thick smoke, usu from fires or chimneys.
▷ **reek** *v* **1** [Ipr] ~ (**of sth**) (*derog*) (**a**) smell unpleasantly of sth: *His breath reeked of tobacco.* ○ *The room reeked of cheap perfume.* (**b**) (*fig*) strongly suggest sth unpleasant or suspicious: *Their actions reek of corruption.* **2** [I, Tn] (*Scot*) (usu of fires or chimneys) give out (thick smoke).

reel (*US* **spool**)

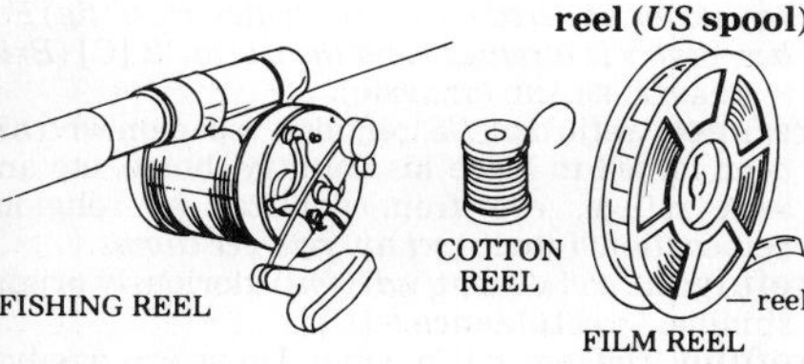

reel¹ /ri:l/ *n* (*US* **spool**) **1** cylinder, roller or similarly shaped object on which thread, wire, fishing line, photographic film, magnetic tape, etc is wound: *a cotton reel* ○ *a cable reel* ○ [attrib] *a reel-to-reel tape-recorder*, ie as opposed to a cassette player. **2** quantity of thread, etc wound on such a cylinder, roller, etc: *a six-reel film.*
▷ **reel** *v* **1** [Tn·p] ~ **sth in/out** wind (sth) on or off a reel; pull (sth) in by using a reel: *reel the line, the hosepipe, etc out* ○ *The angler reeled the trout in slowly.* **2** (phr v) **reel sth off** say or repeat sth rapidly without pause or apparent effort: *reel off a poem, list of names, set of instructions.*

reel² /ri:l/ *v* **1** [I, Ipr, Ip] move unsteadily or sway; stagger: *reel drunkenly down the road* ○ *She reeled (back) from the force of the blow.* ○ *I reeled round in a daze.* **2** [I, Ipr] (*fig*) (of the mind or head) be or become dizzy or confused; be in a whirl: *The very idea sets my head reeling.* ○ *His mind reeled when he heard the news/at the news.* ○ *be reeling from/with/under the shock* ○ (*fig*) *The street reeled* (ie seemed to go round and round) *before her eyes.*

reel³ /ri:l/ *n* (music for a) lively Scottish or Irish dance, usu for two or four couples.

re-elect /ˌri:ɪˈlekt/ *v* [Tn, Tn·pr, Cn·n/a] ~ **sb** (**to sth**); ~ **sb** (**as sth**) elect sb again: *re-elect sb to the Presidency/(as) President.* ▷ **re-election** /-ˈlekʃn/ *n* [C, U].

re-enter /ˌri:ˈentə(r)/ *v* **1** [I, Tn] come in or into (sth) again: *re-enter (the room) by another door.* **2** [I, Ipr] ~ (**for sth**) put one's name forward again, esp for an exam.
▷ **re-entry** /ˌri:ˈentrɪ/ *n* [C, U] **1** (act of) re-entering. **2** return of a spacecraft into the earth's atmosphere: *The capsule gets very hot on re-entry.*

reeve /ri:v/ *n* **1** (*Brit*) (**a**) (formerly) chief magistrate of a town or district. Cf SHERIFF 1. (**b**) (in medieval times) steward of a manor. **2** (in Canada) elected head of a village or town council.

re-examine /ˌri:ɪgˈzæmɪn/ *v* [Tn] (*law*) examine or question (one's own witness) again after he has been cross-examined. ▷ **re-examination** /ˌri:ɪgˌzæmɪˈneɪʃn/ *n* [C, U].

re-export /ˌri:ekˈspɔ:t/ *v* [Tn, Tn·pr] ~ **sth** (**to...**) export (imported goods) again, esp after reprocessing.

ref /ref/ *n* (*infml*) = REFEREE 1.

ref /ref/ *abbr* (*commerce*) reference: *ref no 369* ○ *our ref 14A; your ref 392*, eg at the top of a business letter.

reface /ˌri:ˈfeɪs/ *v* [Tn] put a new surface on (a wall, building, etc).

refectory /rɪˈfektrɪ *or, rarely,* ˈrefɪktrɪ/ *n* dining-hall in a monastery, convent, college, school, etc.

refer /rɪˈfɜ:(r)/ *v* (**-rr-**) **1** [Ipr] ~ **to sb/sth** (**a**) mention or speak of sb/sth; allude to sb/sth: *When I said some people are stupid, I wasn't referring to you.* ○ *Don't refer to this matter again, please.* ○ *This incident in his childhood is never again referred to.* (**b**) be relevant to sb/sth; concern sb/sth: *What I have to say refers to all of you.* **2** [Ipr] ~ **to sth/sb** turn to sth/sb for information, etc: *refer to a dictionary, an expert* ○ *I referred to my watch for the exact time.* ○ *The speaker often referred to his notes.* **3** [Tn·pr esp passive] ~ **sb/sth to sb/sth** send sb/sth to sb/sth for help, advice, action, etc: *refer a patient to a specialist for treatment* ○ *The dispute was referred to the United Nations/to arbitration.* ○ *I was referred to the manager/the enquiry office.* ○ *The reader is referred to page 3.* **4** (phr v) **refer sth back** (**to sb**) return (a document, etc) to the sender for further clarification: *The letter was referred back (to us) with a query.*
▷ **referable** /rɪˈfɜ:rəbl/ *adj* ~ (**to sb/sth**) that can be referred (REFER 3) to sb/sth.
referral /rɪˈfɜ:rəl/ *n* **1** [U] referring (REFER 3) or being referred to sb/sth: *the referral of such cases to a doctor.* **2** [C] person or thing referred (REFER 3) to sb/sth: *several referrals from the clinic.*
□ **re**ˌ**ferred** ˈ**pain** pain felt in a part of the body away from its real cause.

referee /ˌrefəˈri:/ *n* **1** (also *infml* **ref**) (in football, boxing, etc) official who controls matches, prevents rules being broken, etc. ⇨ illus at HOCKEY. Cf UMPIRE. **2** person to whom disputes, eg between employers and employees, are referred for decision. **3** (*Brit*) person willing to make a statement about the character or ability of sb applying for a job: *The head teacher often acts as (a) referee for his pupils.*
▷ **referee** *v* [I, Tn] act as a referee(1) in (sth): *Who refereed (the match)?*

reference /ˈrefərəns/ *n* **1** ~ (**to sb/sth**) (**a**) [U] act of referring (REFER 1a) to sb/sth: *Avoid (making) any reference to his illness.* ○ *The original text is here for ease of reference.* (**b**) [C] statement, etc speaking of or mentioning sb/sth; allusion: *He made pointed* (ie obvious) *references to the recent scandal.* ○ *The book is full of references to places I know.* **2** [C] ~ (**to sb/sth**) note, etc telling a reader in what other book, article, etc information may be found; book, passage, etc referred to in this way or as an authority: *a thesis crowded with references to other sources* ○ *check your references* ○ *cite Green 1986 as a reference.* **3** [C] (*abbr* **ref**) (*commerce*) (on letters, etc) means of identification: *Please quote our reference when replying.* **4** [C] (person willing to make a) statement about a person's character or abilities: *quote sb/sb's name as a reference* ○ *provide a reference for sb* ○ *supply sb with a reference* ○ *She has excellent references from former employers.* ○ *a banker's reference*, ie a note from one's bank saying one's financial position is sound. Cf TESTIMONIAL 1. **5** (idm) **bear/have some/no reference to sth** (not) be connected with sth: *This has no reference to what we were discussing.* **a frame of reference** ⇨ FRAME¹. **in/with reference to sb/sth** (*esp commerce*) about or concerning sb/sth: *I am writing with reference to your job application.* Cf TERMS OF REFERENCE (TERM). **without reference to sb/sth** not taking account of sb/sth: *She issued all these invitations without any reference to her superiors.*
□ ˈ**reference book** book, eg an encyclopedia or a dictionary, which is consulted for information, not read right through.
ˈ**reference library** (also ˈ**reference room**) library or room having books that may be consulted on the premises, but not borrowed.
ˈ**reference marks** marks, eg *, †, ‡, §, used to direct the reader to eg a footnote, where information may be found.

referendum /ˌrefəˈrendəm/ *n* (*pl* ~**s**) [C, U] referring of a political issue to a general vote by all the people of a country for a decision; vote thus taken: *hold a referendum on ending conscription* ○ *settle a national issue by referendum.* Cf PLEBISCITE.

refill /ˌri:ˈfɪl/ *v* [Tn] fill again: *refill a glass, (petrol) tank, (cigarette) lighter, etc.*
▷ **refill** /ˈri:fɪl/ *n* new material used to refill a container; container thus refilled: (*infml*) *Would you like a refill* (ie another glass of beer, wine, etc)? ○ *two refills for a cartridge pen.*

refine /rɪˈfaɪn/ *v* [Tn] **1** remove impurities from (sth); purify: *refine sugar, oil, ore, etc* ○ *refining processes.* **2** ~ (**on/upon**) **sth** improve (sth) by removing defects and attending to detail: *refine one's working methods* ○ *refine earlier systems, designs, theories.* **3** (*fig*) make (sb/sth) more cultured or elegant; remove what is coarse or vulgar from: *refine one's manners, taste, language.*
▷ **refined** *adj* **1** cultured or elegant; free from what is coarse or vulgar: *Her tastes are very refined.* **2** freed from impurities: *refined sugar, oil, etc.*
refiner *n* person, firm or machine that refines (REFINE 1): *sugar refiners.*
refinery /-nərɪ/ *n* factory, etc where sth is refined: *a* ˈ*sugar refinery* ○ *an* ˈ*oil refinery.*

refinement /rɪˈfaɪnmənt/ *n* **1** [U] refining or being refined: *the refinement of oil, sugar, etc* ○ *the gradual refinement of her taste in music.* **2** [U] culture or elegance of manners, taste, language, etc: *a person of great refinement* ○ *lack of refinement.* **3** [C esp *pl*] (**a**) clever development of eg machinery, technique; improvement: *all the refinements of 20th-century technology* ○ *The oven has an automatic timer and other refinements.* ○ *make further refinements to our original model.* (**b**) subtle or ingenious development of eg thought, behaviour: *refinements of meaning, cruelty.*

refit /ˈri:fɪt/ *n* repair or renewal of parts (of a ship, etc): *The liner is in dock for a refit.*
▷ **refit** /ˌri:ˈfɪt/ *v* (**-tt-**) (**a**) [Tn, Cn·n/a] ~ **sth** (**as sth**) give a refit to (a ship, etc): *The ferry was refitted as a troop-ship and joined the fleet.* (**b**) [I] (of a ship, etc) be given a refit: *put into port to refit.*

reflate /ˌri:ˈfleɪt/ *v* [I, Tn] increase the amount of money and credit circulating in (an economy) to restore the system (after a period of deflation) to its previous condition. Cf DEFLATE 2, INFLATE 3.
▷ **reflation** /ri:ˈfleɪʃn/ *n* [U] reflating or being reflated. **reflationary** /ri:ˈfleɪʃnrɪ; *US* -nerɪ/ *adj*: *adopt reflationary policies, measures, etc.*

reflect /rɪˈflekt/ *v* **1** [esp passive: Tn, Tn·pr] (**a**) ~ **sb/sth** (**in sth**) (of a mirror, etc) make a visible image of sb/sth: *trees reflected in a window/lake* ○ *He looked at his face reflected in the mirror.* (**b**) ~

sth (from sth) (of a surface) throw back (light, heat, sound): *The heat reflected from the white sand formed a mirage.* ○ *The moon shines with reflected light.* **2** [Tn] (*fig*) show the nature of or express (sth); correspond to: *Her sad looks reflected the nature of her thoughts.* ○ *The literature of a period reflects its values and tastes.* ○ *Increased sales were reflected in higher profits.* **3** [I, Ipr, Tf, Tw no passive] ~ **(on/upon sth)** think deeply about, or remind oneself of, past events; consider: *I need time to reflect (on your offer/on what you offered).* ○ *She reflected that his argument was probably true.* ○ *How distant those times seemed now, he reflected.* **4** (idm) **reflect (well, badly, etc) on sb/sth** show or suggest that sb/sth is sound, unsound, etc: *This scandal will reflect badly on the Party as a whole.* **reflect credit, discredit, etc on sb/sth** (of actions, results, etc) bring honour, dishonour, etc to sb/sth: *These excellent results reflect great credit on all our staff.* ○ *Stealing reflects dishonour on your family.*

reflection (*Brit* also **reflexion**) /rɪˈflekʃn/ *n* **1** **(a)** [U] reflecting or being reflected: *heat transmitted by reflection.* **(b)** [C] thing reflected, esp an image in a mirror, still water, etc: *see one's reflection in a polished table-top* ○ *the reflection of the trees in the lake* ○ (*fig*) *be a pale reflection of one's former self*, eg after an illness. **2** [C] (*fig*) thing reflecting the nature of eg a person, task, etc: *Your clothes are a reflection of your personality.* **3** **(a)** [U] thought or memory of past events; consideration: *lost in reflection* ○ *act without sufficient reflection* ○ *A moment's reflection will show you are wrong.* **(b)** [C] ~ **(on sth)** (often *pl*) (spoken or written expression of an) idea arising from this: *idle reflections on the past* ○ *publish one's reflections on sexism.* **4** (idm) **be a (bad/poor/adverse) reflection on sb/sth** harm the good reputation of sb/sth; imply blame or criticism of sb/sth: *Your remarks are a reflection on me/my character.* ○ *This mess is a (poor) reflection on her competence.* **on reflection** after reconsidering (sth): *On further reflection, I saw that she might be right, after all.* ○ *She decided, on reflection, to accept the offer.*

reflective /rɪˈflektɪv/ *adj* **1** (of a person, mood, etc) thoughtful: *in a reflective frame of mind.* **2** (of a surface, etc) reflecting (esp light): *reflective number plates*, eg on cars. ▷ **reflectively** *adv*: *answer, comment, etc reflectively.*

reflector /rɪˈflektə(r)/ *n* **1** thing that reflects heat, light or sound. **2** red disc fitted to the back of a vehicle; disc or strip fitted to cycle wheels, etc making them visible in the dark by reflecting the lights of other vehicles. ⇨ illus at BICYCLE. **3** (also **reˌflecting ˈtelescope**) telescope in which the objective is a concave mirror. Cf REFRACTOR.

reflex /ˈri:fleks/ *n* (also ˈ**reflex action**) involuntary action (eg sneezing or shivering) made instinctively in response to a stimulus: *Sorry I hit you; it was a pure reflex.* ○ *have quick, slow, normal, etc reflexes* ○ *test/control one's reflexes* ○ [attrib] *a reflex movement, response, etc*, ie one arising from a reflex.

□ **reflex ˈangle** angle of more than 180°.

ˈ**reflex camera** camera in which the object or scene to be photographed is reflected by a mirror, and focused on a large viewfinder for adjustment up to the moment of exposure.

reflexion (*Brit*) = REFLECTION.

reflexive /rɪˈfleksɪv/ *n, adj* (*grammar*) (word or form) showing that the action of the verb is performed on its subject: *a reflexive verb, pronoun*, eg 'He ˈcut himself'.

NOTE ON USAGE: The reflexive verb is usually stressed. For emphasis, the syllable *-self/-selves* of the reflexive pronoun may be stressed.

refloat /ri:ˈfləʊt/ *v* [I, Tn] (cause a ship, etc to) float again after sinking, running aground, etc.

reflux /ˈri:flʌks/ *n* [C, U] chemical process of boiling a liquid in a special container connected to an apparatus which condenses the vapour produced and returns it to the original container. It is used for carrying out reactions over long periods: *carry out an operation under reflux.*

reforest (*US*) = REAFFOREST.

reform /rɪˈfɔ:m/ *v* [I, Tn] become or make better by removing or putting right faults, errors, etc: *There are signs that he's reforming.* ○ *reform one's ways, habits* ○ *reform an unfair salary structure* ○ *He's given up drink and is now a reformed character.*

▷ **reform** *n* **1** [U] reforming or being reformed: *agitate for, bring about, effect social reform* ○ *the reform of teaching methods* ○ [attrib] *reform laws, bills, measures, etc.* **2** [C] change that removes or puts right faults, errors, etc: *make, carry out reforms in education.*

reformer *n* person who brings about or advocates reform: *a social, political, religious reformer.*

□ **ReˈForm Acts** laws passed by the British Parliament during the 19th century to change the way Members of Parliament were elected and give the vote to more people. The first Reform Act of 1832 abolished the 'rotten boroughs' where a few people could have a Member of Parliament to represent them, and increased the number of seats in Parliament for the counties and growing cities. The number of men able to vote was increased by about 50%. The second Act, in 1867, redistributed seats again and doubled the number of voters to two million; the third in 1884 increased the number again to five million.

re-form /ˌri: ˈfɔ:m/ *v* **1** [I] form again: *Ice re-formed on the plane's wings.* **2** [I, Tn] (make soldiers, etc) get into ranks again.

reformation /ˌrefəˈmeɪʃn/ *n* **1** **(a)** [U] reforming or being reformed: *the reformation of criminals.* **(b)** [C] great change for the better in social, religious or political affairs: *a reformation in state education.* **2 the Reformation** [sing] 16th-century European movement for reform of the Roman Catholic Church, which resulted in the establishment of Reformed or Protestant Churches. Many Christians felt that the Pope had too much political power, that there were many abuses such as the sale of indulgences, and that the spirit of the early Church had been lost. Intellectuals like *Erasmus rediscovered the Bible in the original Greek and wrote about it in a new way. Others went further, and *Luther's protests, followed by those of *Calvin and *Zwingli, led to the creation of separate Churches. In England, *Henry VIII's break with Rome was largely political, but the movement was supported by bishops like *Cranmer and *Latimer, who made Anglicanism more Protestant after Henry's death. In Scotland John *Knox held strongly Calvinist views. The Reformation led to many new Churches; they have widely differing teachings, but they all reject papal authority in favour of that of the Bible. ⇨ article at CHURCH OF ENGLAND.

reformatory /rɪˈfɔ:mətrɪ; *US* -tɔ:rɪ/ *n* (*US*) place where young offenders are sent to be trained and reformed. Cf APPROVED SCHOOL (APPROVE), BORSTAL.

▷ **reformatory** *adj* (*fml*) tending or intended to produce reform.

refract /rɪˈfrækt/ *v* [Tn] bend (a ray of light) where it enters eg water or glass at an oblique angle from a medium of different density: *Light is refracted when passed through a prism.*

▷ **refraction** /rɪˈfrækʃn/ *n* [U] refracting or being refracted. ⇨ illus at SPECTRUM.

refractive /rɪˈfræktɪv/ *adj* of or causing refraction. **reˌfractive ˈindex** ratio of the speed of light travelling through a vacuum and its speed travelling through another medium, or of the speeds at which it travels through two mediums that are in contact with each other, eg air and water. It also indicates the degree of bending of light rays as they pass from one medium to another.

refractor /rɪˈfræktə(r)/ *n* telescope in which the objective is a converging lens. Cf REFLECTOR.

refractory /rɪˈfræktərɪ/ *adj* **1** (*fml*) difficult to control or discipline; wilful or unmanageable: *a very refractory child.* **2** (of a disease, etc) not yielding to treatment. **3** (of substances, metals, etc) difficult to fuse or work; resistant to heat: *refractory brick*, eg in furnace linings.

refrain[1] /rɪˈfreɪn/ *n* **1** lines of a song or poem which are repeated, esp at the end of each verse: *Will you all join in singing the refrain, please?* **2** tune accompanying this: *a haunting refrain* ○ (*fig*) *the familiar refrain of her husband's snoring.*

refrain[2] /rɪˈfreɪn/ *v* [I, Ipr] ~ **(from sth)** (*fml*) keep oneself from doing sth: *refrain from comment, criticism, etc* ○ *refrain from smoking* ○ *Let's hope they will refrain (from hostile action).*

refresh /rɪˈfreʃ/ *v* [Tn] **1** give new strength or vigour to (sb/sth); restore or revive: *refresh oneself with a cup of tea/a hot bath* ○ *She felt refreshed after her sleep.* **2** (idm) **refresh one's/sb's memory (about sb/sth)** remind oneself/sb of facts by referring to notes, etc: *Just refresh my memory, were you born in York?*

▷ **refreshing** *adj* **1** giving new strength or vigour; restoring or reviving: *a refreshing bath, sleep, cup of tea* ○ *This breeze is very refreshing.* **2** (*fig*) welcome and interesting because unusual or novel: *a refreshing sense of humour* ○ *a new and refreshing approach to a problem* ○ *The holiday was a refreshing change for us.* **refreshingly** *adv*: *refreshingly honest, original, different.*

□ **reˈfresher course** course of instruction for eg teachers to learn about new techniques and developments in their field.

refreshment /rɪˈfreʃmənt/ *n* **1** [U] refreshing or being refreshed. **2** **(a)** [U] (*fml or joc*) food and drink: *partake of some refreshment* ○ [attrib] *a refreshment room*, eg at a railway station where food and drink are sold. **(b) refreshments** [pl] snacks: *light refreshments* (eg ice-cream, crisps, chocolate) *are available during the interval.*

refrigerate /rɪˈfrɪdʒəreɪt/ *v* [Tn] make (food, etc) cold in order to freeze or preserve it: *keep meat, milk, etc refrigerated.*

▷ **refrigerant** /-rənt/ *n* substance that refrigerates, eg liquid carbon dioxide.

refrigeration /rɪˌfrɪdʒəˈreɪʃn/ *n* [U] (of food, etc) refrigerating or being refrigerated, in order to freeze or preserve: *Keep perishable foods under refrigeration.* ○ [attrib] *the refrigeration industry.*

refrigerator /rɪˈfrɪdʒəreɪtə(r)/ *n* (also *esp US* **ice-box**, *infml* **fridge** /frɪdʒ/) cabinet or room in which food is kept cold. Cf FREEZER.

refuel /ˌri:ˈfju:əl/ *v* (**-ll-**; *US* **-l-**) [I, Tn] (cause a car, plane, etc to) be filled up with fuel: *stop, land, dock, etc for refuelling.*

refuge /ˈrefju:dʒ/ *n* **1** [C, U] ~ **(from sb/sth)** (place giving) shelter or protection from danger, trouble, pursuit, etc: *a place of refuge* ○ *seek refuge from the storm* ○ *take refuge in the cellar* ○ *a refuge* (eg a safe house) *for battered wives, alcoholics, etc* ○ (*fig*) *For her, poetry is a refuge from the world.* **2** [C] (*Brit*) = TRAFFIC ISLAND (TRAFFIC).

refugee /ˌrefjʊˈdʒi:; *US* ˈrefjʊdʒɪ:/ *n* person who has been forced to leave his country, home, etc and seek refuge, esp from political or religious persecution: [attrib] *set up ˌrefuˈgee camps.*

refulgent /rɪˈfʌldʒənt/ *adj* (*fml*) gloriously bright; shining. ▷ **refulgence** *n* [U].

refund /ri:ˈfʌnd/ *v* [Tn, Dn·n, Dn·pr esp passive] ~**sth (to sb)** pay back (money received); reimburse (expenses incurred): *refund a deposit* ○ *Postage costs will be refunded (to you).* ○ *I'll refund you the full cost of your fare.*

▷ **refund** /ˈri:fʌnd/ *n* [C, U] repayment; reimbursement: *a tax, pension, etc refund* ○ *claim, obtain, pay, etc a refund* ○ *He demanded a refund on the unused tickets.*

refundable *adj* that can be refunded: *a non-refundable deposit.*

refurbish /ˌri:ˈfɜ:bɪʃ/ *v* [Tn] make (sth) clean or bright again; redecorate: *The flat will be refurbished for the new tenants.*

refusal /rɪˈfju:zl/ *n* **1** **(a)** [U] refusing or being refused: *refusal of a request, an invitation, an offer, etc.* **(b)** [C] act of refusing: *a blunt, flat, curt, etc refusal.* **2 the refusal** [sing] right to accept or refuse sth before it is offered to others; option: *have the refusal on a car, house, etc.* Cf FIRST REFUSAL (FIRST[1]).

refuse[1] /ˈrefju:s/ *n* [U] waste or worthless

material; rubbish: *kitchen, garden, household, etc refuse* ○ [attrib] *a refuse bag, dump, bin, etc* ○ *refuse disposal.*

□ ˈ**refuse collector** (*fml*) = DUSTMAN (DUST[1]).

refuse[2] /rɪˈfju:z/ *v* **1** [I, Tn, Tt, Dn·n] say or show that one is unwilling to give, accept, grant or do sth: *refuse one's consent, help, permission* ○ *refuse a gift, an offer, an invitation* ○ *She refused him/his proposal of marriage.* ○ *Our application for visas was refused.* ○ *The car absolutely refused to start.* ○ *I was refused admittance.* Cf AGREE 1. **2** [I] (of a horse in show-jumping or steeplechasing) stop in front of a fence or turn away from it instead of jumping over it.

▷ **refusenik** /rɪˈfju:znɪk/ *n* (*infml*) citizen of the USSR who has been refused permission to emigrate to another country, esp Israel.

refute /rɪˈfju:t/ *v* [Tn] prove (a statement, an opinion, etc or a person) to be wrong: *refute a claim, a theory, an argument* ○ *refute an opponent.*

▷ **refutable** /-əbl, *also* ˈrefjʊtəbl/ *adj* that can be refuted.

refutation /ˌrefju:ˈteɪʃn/ *n* **1** [U] refuting or being refuted. **2** [C] argument that refutes sth; counter-argument.

regain /rɪˈgeɪn/ *v* **1** [Tn] get (sth) back again after losing it; recover: *regain consciousness* ○ *regain one's freedom, health, sight* ○ *Our troops soon regained possession of the town.* **2** [Tn no passive] reach (a place or position) again: *regain the river bank* ○ *regain one's footing/balance*, eg after slipping, stumbling, etc.

regal /ˈri:gl/ *adj* of, like or fit for a king or queen; royal: *regal dignity, splendour, power* ○ (*fig*) *The developers made a regal* (ie generous) *offer for the land.* ▷ **regally** /-gəlɪ/ *adv.*

regale /rɪˈgeɪl/ *v* [Tn·pr] (*fml or joc*) **(a)** ~ **sb with sth** amuse or entertain sb (with stories, jokes, etc): *She regaled us with an account of her school-days.* **(b)** ~ **oneself/sb on/with sth** give (esp choice) food and drink to oneself/sb: *regale an invalid with fruit and other dainty morsels* ○ *We regaled ourselves on caviar and champagne.*

regalia /rɪˈgeɪlɪə/ *n* [U] **1** emblems or robes of royalty used at coronations, eg crown, orb and sceptre: *the king in full regalia.* **2** emblems and costumes of an order (eg the Order of the Garter), or of a certain rank or office: *wearing the mayoral regalia*, ie the mayor's chain of office, etc.

regard[1] /rɪˈgɑ:d/ *v* **1** [Tn] (*fml*) look steadily at (sb/sth) in the specified way: *She regarded him closely, intently, curiously, etc.* **2** [Tn, Tn·pr, Cn·n/a] ~ **sb/sth (with sth)**; ~ **sb/sth as sth** consider or think about sb/sth in the specified way: *How is he regarded locally?* ○ *Your work is highly regarded.* ○ *We regard her behaviour with suspicion.* ○ *regard sb unfavourably/with disfavour* ○ *I regard your suggestion as worth considering/as worthy of consideration.* ○ *We regard your action as a crime/as criminal.* ○ *She's generally regarded as a nuisance.* **3** [Tn] (usu in negative sentences or questions) pay attention to (sth); heed: *He seldom regards my advice.* ○ *He booked the holiday without regarding my wishes.* **4** (idm) **as regards sb/sth** concerning or connected with sb/sth: *I have little information as regards his past.* ○ *As regards the second point in your letter....*

▷ **regarding** *prep* with reference to (sb/sth); concerning: *She said nothing regarding your request.*

regard[2] /rɪˈgɑ:d/ *n* **1** [U] ~ **to/for sb/sth** attention to or concern for sb/sth; care for sb/sth: *drive without regard for/to speed limits* ○ *have, pay, show little regard for the feelings of others.* **2** [U] ~ **(for sb/sth)** esteem or consideration; respect: *hold sb in high/low regard*, ie have a good/bad opinion of sb ○ *have a great regard for sb's judgement, intelligence, achievements.* **3 regards** [pl] (used esp at the end of a letter) kind wishes; greeting: *With kind regards, Yours sincerely...* ○ *Please give/send my regards to your brother.* **4** (idm) **in/with regard to sb/sth; in this/that/one regard** in connection with sb/sth; in this/that connection; concerning sb/sth: *I have nothing to say with regard to your complaints.* ○ *He is very sensitive in this regard*, ie concerning this. ○ *We have succeeded in one crucial regard: making this scandal public.*

▷ **regardless** *adv* (*infml*) paying no attention to sb/sth: *I protested, but she carried on regardless.*

regardless of *prep* paying no attention to (sb/sth); heedless of: *regardless of the consequences, danger, expense* ○ *He continued speaking, regardless of my feelings on the matter.*

regatta /rɪˈgætə/ *n* sporting event at which races are held between rowing-boats or yachts.

regd *abbr* (*commerce*) registered.

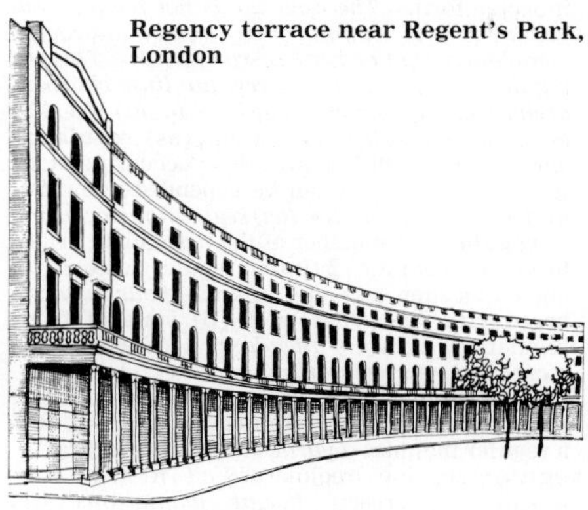

Regency terrace near Regent's Park, London

regency /ˈri:dʒənsɪ/ *n* **1** [C] (period of) office of a regent. **2 the Regency** [sing] (in Britain) the period 1810-20, when George, Prince of Wales (later *George IV) acted as regent. The architecture and design of the period is in a simple elegant style based on ancient classical models. The best-known Regency architect is John *Nash: [attrib] *Regency architecture, furniture.* ⇨ illus. ⇨ illus at DRESS. ⇨ article at ARCHITECTURE.

regenerate /rɪˈdʒenəreɪt/ *v* **1** [Tn] give fresh strength or life to (sb/sth); restore: *After his holiday he felt regenerated.* ○ *Their aim is to regenerate British industry.* **2** [I, Tn] (cause a person or an institution to) reform or improve, esp morally or spiritually: *The party soon regenerated under her leadership.*

▷ **regenerate** /rɪˈdʒenərət/ *adj* [usu attrib] (*fml*) morally or spiritually reformed: *a regenerate society.*

regeneration /rɪˌdʒenəˈreɪʃn/ *n* [U].

regenerative /rɪˈdʒenərətɪv/ *adj*: *enjoy the regenerative powers of sea air.*

regent /ˈri:dʒənt/ (often **Regent**) *n* person appointed to rule a country while the monarch is too young, old, ill, etc, or is absent.

▷ **regent** (often **Regent**) *adj* (following *ns*) performing the duties of a Regent: *the Prince Regent.*

reggae /ˈregeɪ/ *n* [U] type of West Indian popular music and dance with strong rhythms.

regicide /ˈredʒɪsaɪd/ *n* **1** [U] crime of killing a king. **2** [C] person who commits or helps to commit this crime.

regime /reɪˈʒi:m, *also* ˈreʒi:m/ *n* **1 (a)** method or system of government: *a socialist, fascist, etc regime.* **(b)** prevailing method or system of administration (eg in a business): *changes made under the present regime* ○ *the old regime versus the new.* **2** regimen.

regimen /ˈredʒɪmən/ *n* (*medical or fml*) set of rules about diet, exercise, etc aimed at improving sb's health and physical well-being: *follow a strict regimen* ○ *put a patient on a regimen.*

regiment /ˈredʒɪmənt/ *n* **1** [CGp] **(a)** (artillery and armour) unit divided into batteries or squadrons: *an attack by three tank regiments.* **(b)** (British infantry) unit, usu based on a city or county, and represented in the field by battalions: *the 1st battalion of the Lancashire Regiment* ○ *enlist in a crack* (ie outstanding) *infantry regiment.* **2** [CGp] ~ **of sth/sb** (*fig*) large number of things or people: *a whole regiment of volunteers.*

▷ **regiment** /ˈredʒɪment/ *v* [Tn esp passive] (*esp derog*) force strict discipline on (sb/sth); organize rigidly into groups, patterns, etc: *regimented school outings* ○ *tourists regimented into large parties for sightseeing.* **regimentation** /ˌredʒɪmenˈteɪʃn/ *n* [U].

regimental /ˌredʒɪˈmentl/ *adj* [attrib] of a regiment: *a regimental mascot, band, parade, etc* ○ *regimental headquarters, colours, etc.*

▷ **regimentals** *n* [pl] uniform of a regiment: *dressed in full regimentals.*

Regina /rɪˈdʒaɪnə/ *n* (*Latin*) (used esp in signatures on proclamations or in the titles of lawsuits) reigning queen: *Elizabeth Regina* ○ (*law*) *Regina v Hay*, ie the Crown versus Hay. Cf REX.

region /ˈri:dʒən/ *n* **1** part of a surface or body or space with or without definite boundaries or characteristic features: *the Arctic, desert, tropical, etc regions* ○ *the northernmost regions of England* ○ *pains in the abdominal region.* **2** administrative division of a country. **3** (idm) **in the region of sth** approximately (a number, weight, price, etc): *earn (somewhere) in the region of £20 000 a year.*

▷ **regional** /-nl/ *adj* [usu attrib] of a region: *the regional wines of France* ○ *organized, listed, etc on a regional basis.* **regionally** /-nəlɪ/ *adv.*

register[1] /ˈredʒɪstə(r)/ *n* **1** (book containing an) official list or record of names, items, attendances, etc: *a parish register*, ie listing births, marriages and deaths ○ *Lloyd's Register (of Shipping)* ○ *the electoral register/the register of voters*, ie of people entitled to vote ○ *make entries in a register* ○ *The class teacher called the (names on the) register.* **2** mechanical device for indicating or recording speed, force, numbers, etc automatically: *a cash register.* **3** (part of the) range of a human voice or a musical instrument: *notes in the upper/middle register* ○ *the lower register of a clarinet, tenor, etc.* **4** (*linguistics*) range of vocabulary, grammar, etc used by speakers in particular social circumstances or professional contexts: *the informal register of speech* ○ *specialist registers of English*, eg for legal, financial, etc matters. **5** adjustable metal plate for widening or narrowing an opening and regulating draught, esp in a fire-grate.

□ ˈ**register office** ⇨ REGISTRY OFFICE (REGISTRY).

register[2] /ˈredʒɪstə(r)/ *v* **1** [I, Ipr, Tn, Tn·pr, Cn·a only passive, Cn·n/a esp passive] ~ **(at/for/with sth)**; ~ **sth (in sth)**; ~ **sb as sth** formally record (a name, an event, a sale, etc) in a list: *register at a hotel*, ie book in as a guest ○ *You must register with the police, the embassy, etc.* ○ *Where can I register* (ie enrol as a student) *for the Arabic course?* ○ *register one's car, the birth of a child, a patent* ○ *a State Registered Nurse*, ie one who is officially registered ○ *register the house in your name* ○ *She is registered (as) disabled.* **2** [Tn, Tn·pr] ~ **sth (with sb)**; ~ **sth (at sth)** present sth formally in writing for consideration: *register a complaint with the authorities* ○ *register a strong protest at the government's action.* **3 (a)** [I, Tn] (of figures, etc) be indicated or recorded; (of measuring instruments) indicate or record (figures, etc) automatically: *Loss of pressure had not registered on the dials.* ○ *The thermometer registered 32°C.* **(b)** [Tn] (of a person, his face, his actions, etc) show (emotion, etc): *He slammed the door to register his disapproval.* ○ *Her face registered dismay.* **4** [I, Ipr, Tn, Tf] ~ **(with sb)** (*infml*) (of facts, etc) be mentally recorded or fully realized; (of people) remember or notice (sth): *Her name didn't register (with me).* ○ *I registered (the fact) that he was late.* **5 (a)** [Tn] send (letters, etc) by post, paying extra for compensation against loss or damage: *It's wise to register letters containing banknotes.* **(b)** [esp passive: Tn, Tn·pr] ~ **sth (to sth)** send (luggage) by rail or sea, paying extra for compensation against loss or damage: *sea baggage registered to Rio.*

□ ˌ**registered** ˈ**nurse** (*US*) trained nurse licensed by a state authority.

ˌ**registered** ˈ**post** (*US* ˌ**certified** ˈ**mail**) service by which the sender pays extra for compensation against loss or damage. Cf RECORDED DELIVERY (RECORD[2]).

ˌregistered ˈtrade mark (*abbr* **R**; *symb* ®) emblem or name, etc of a manufacturer or trader which is officially recorded as identifying his goods.

registrar /ˌredʒɪˈstrɑː(r), ˈredʒɪstrɑː(r)/ *n* **1** (**a**) official keeper of records or registers, eg of births, marriages and deaths. (**b**) official responsible for admissions, examinations, etc at a university: *an assistant registrar.* **2** (*Brit*) senior hospital doctor being trained as a specialist or consultant(2).

registration /ˌredʒɪˈstreɪʃn/ *n* **1** [U] registering or being registered: *registration of letters, parcels, trunks, etc* ○ *registration of students for a course/examination* ○ [attrib] *registration fees.* **2** [C] entry in a register: *an increase in registrations for ballet classes.*

□ **regiˈstration number** series of letters and numbers displayed at the front and back of a vehicle to identify it. ⇨ illus at CAR.

registry /ˈredʒɪstrɪ/ *n* place, eg in a church or university, where registers are kept.

□ **ˈregistry office** (also **ˈregister office**) place where civil marriages are performed before a registrar, and where records of births, marriages and deaths are made. ⇨ article at WEDDING.

Regius professor /ˌriːdʒɪəs prəˈfesə(r)/ (*Brit*) professor (esp at Oxford or Cambridge) holding a university chair which was founded by a king or queen, or is filled with the monarch's approval.

regnant (often **Regnant**) /ˈregnənt/ *adj* (*fml*) (following *ns*) reigning: *Queen Regnant,* ie one ruling in her own right, not as a consort.

regress /rɪˈgres/ *v* [I, Ipr] ~ (**to sth**) (*fml*) return to an earlier or less advanced form or state.

▷ **regression** /rɪˈgreʃn/ *n* regressing.

regressive *adj* regressing or tending to regress.

regret[1] /rɪˈgret/ *n* **1** [U, C] feeling of sadness at the loss of sb/sth; feeling of disappointment, annoyance or repentance: *express, feel regret at/about a missed opportunity* ○ *I heard of his death with profound/deep/great regret.* ○ *Much to my regret, I am unable to accept your invitation.* ○ *I have no regrets about leaving.* **2 regrets** [pl] (*fml*) (used in polite expressions of refusal, apology, etc): *give/send one's regrets,* eg in answer to a wedding invitation ○ *Please accept my regrets at refusing/that I must refuse.*

▷ **regretful** /-fl/ *adj* feeling or expressing regret: *a regretful smile, look, etc.* **regretfully** /-fəlɪ/ with regret; sadly: *smile regretfully* ○ *Regretfully, I must decline.*

regret[2] /rɪˈgret/ *v* (**-tt-**) **1** [Tn, Tf, Tw, Tt, Tg, Tsg] feel regret about (sth sad, disappointing, annoying, etc): *If you go now, you'll regret it,* ie You will wish you had stayed. ○ *I regret that I cannot help.* ○ *It is to be regretted that...* ○ *I regret what I said.* ○ *I regret to say the job has been filled.* ○ *We regret to inform you...,* ie used in letters when giving bad news. ○ *I regret (his) ever having raised the matter.* **2** [Tn] feel sorrow about (the loss of sb/sth); wish to have (sb/sth) again: *regret lost/missed opportunities* ○ *His death was regretted by all.*

▷ **regrettable** /-əbl/ *adj* that is or should be regretted: *regrettable failures, losses, mistakes, etc* ○ *Her rudeness was most/highly regrettable.* **regrettably** /-əblɪ/ *adv* **1** in a regrettable way: *a regrettably small income.* **2** it is to be regretted that: *Regrettably, the experiment ended in failure.*

regroup /ˌriːˈgruːp/ *v* [I, Ipr, Tn, Tn·pr] ~ (**sth**) (**for sth**) form into groups again; form (sth) into new groups: *The enemy regrouped (their forces) for a new attack.*

Regt *abbr* Regiment.

regular /ˈregjʊlə(r)/ *adj* **1** [esp attrib] happening, coming or done repeatedly at times or places which are the same distance apart: *regular breathing* ○ *a regular pulse, heartbeat, etc* ○ *have regular bowel movements* ○ *have regular habits/be regular in one's habits,* ie do the same things at the same times every day ○ *lampposts placed at regular intervals.* **2** conforming to a principal or standard of procedure; proper: *He applied for the job through the regular channels,* ie in the accepted way. ○ *You should sign a contract to make your job situation regular.* **3** evenly or systematically arranged; symmetrical: (*approv*) *her regular teeth, features* ○ *jets flying in (a) regular formation* ○ *a regular geometrical figure,* eg a polygon, with sides and angles equal. **4** [esp attrib] (**a**) normal or usual: *my regular doctor, dentist, etc* ○ *our regular customers, readers, listeners, etc.* (**b**) continuous or habitual; constant: *have no regular work, employment, etc* ○ *a regular offender,* ie against the law ○ *He was a regular visitor of hers.* **5** [attrib] belonging to the permanent armed forces of a country: *a regular soldier, army, battalion.* **6** (*grammar*) (of verbs, nouns, etc) having normal inflected forms: *The verb 'go' is not regular, but 'walk' is.* **7** (*infml often ironic*) thorough; complete: *a regular hero, rascal, genius* ○ *This is a regular mess.* ○ *You're a regular little charmer, aren't you?* **8** [attrib] (*dated US infml*) likeable; good: *He's a regular guy.* **9** (idm) (**as**) ˌ**regular as ˈclockwork** (*infml*) doing sth or occurring at set times in a way that can be depended upon: *She arrives every day at five, (as) regular as clockwork.*

▷ **regular** *n* **1** member of the permanent armed forces of a country. **2** (*infml*) regular customer or client at a shop, pub, etc: *He's one of our regulars.*

regularity /ˌregjʊˈlærətɪ/ *n* [U] state of being regular: *regularity of attendance at church* ○ *They meet with great regularity.*

regularly *adv* **1** at regular intervals or times: *The post arrives regularly at eight every morning.* **2** in a regular manner: *a garden laid out regularly.*

regularize, -ise /ˈregjʊləraɪz/ *v* [Tn] make (sth) lawful or correct: *Illegal immigrants can regularize their position by obtaining the necessary residence permit.* ▷ **regularization, -isation** /ˌregjʊləraɪˈzeɪʃn; *US* -rɪˈz-/ *n* [U].

regulate /ˈregjʊleɪt/ *v* [Tn] **1** control or direct (sth) by means of rules and restrictions: *regulate one's conduct, expenditure, lifestyle* ○ *regulate the traffic* ○ *The activities of credit companies are regulated by law.* **2** adjust (an apparatus, a mechanism, etc) so that it functions as desired; control (speed, pressure, etc) in this way: *regulate a clock, radiator, etc* ○ *This valve regulates the flow of water.*

▷ **regulator** *n* device that regulates, esp the time: *a pressure, temperature, etc regulator.*

regulation /ˌregjʊˈleɪʃn/ *n* **1** [U] regulating or being regulated; control: *the regulation of share prices.* **2** [C usu *pl*] rule or restriction made by an authority: *regulations laid down for your guidance* ○ *too many rules and regulations* ○ *fire, flood regulations* ○ *ˈsafety regulations,* eg in factories ○ *ˈtraffic regulations,* ie made by the police ○ *contrary to/against (the) regulations.* **3** [attrib] required by the regulations; correct: *in regulation dress, uniform, etc* ○ *drive at the regulation speed,* eg on motorways.

regurgitate /rɪˈgɜːdʒɪteɪt/ *v* (*fml*) **1** [Tn] bring (swallowed food) up into the mouth again. **2** [I] (of liquid, etc) gush back. **3** [Tn] (*fig*) give (opinions, etc gained from others) as if they were one's own: *He's simply regurgitating stuff remembered from lectures.* ▷ **regurgitation** /rɪˌgɜːdʒɪˈteɪʃn/ *n* [U].

rehabilitate /ˌriːəˈbɪlɪteɪt/ *v* [Tn] **1** restore (sb) to a normal life by retraining, medical treatment, etc, esp after imprisonment or illness: *rehabilitate the mentally/physically disabled in the community.* **2** (*fig*) restore (sb who has suffered loss of rank, reputation, etc) to his former position; reinstate: *rehabilitate a disgraced former leader.*

▷ **rehabilitation** /ˌriːəˌbɪlɪˈteɪʃn/ *n* [U] rehabilitating or being rehabilitated: *the patient's slow rehabilitation* ○ [attrib] *a rehabilitation centre,* eg for psychiatric patients.

rehash /ˌriːˈhæʃ/ *v* [Tn, Tn·pr] ~ **sth** (**into sth**) (*infml derog*) put (ideas, material, etc) into a new form with no great change or improvement: *rehash newspaper articles into a book* ○ *His answer was just a rehashed version of my lecture.*

▷ **rehash** /ˈriːhæʃ/ *n* **1** [sing] rehashed material: *a rehash of familiar ideas.* **2** [U] rehashing.

rehear /ˌriːˈhɪə(r)/ *v* (*pt, pp* **reheard** /ˌriːˈhɜːd/) [Tn] hear or consider (a case, etc in a lawcourt) again.

▷ **rehearing** *n* reconsideration (of a case, etc): *get be given, demand a rehearing.*

rehearse /rɪˈhɜːs/ *v* **1** (**a**) [I, Tn] practise (a play piece of music, etc) for public performance *rehearse with a full cast, orchestra, etc* ○ *rehearse an opera.* (**b**) [Tn] supervise or train (sb) by practising in this way: *rehearse the actors for the fight scene.* **2** [Tn] (*fml*) give an account of (sth) esp to oneself; recite: *rehearse one's grievances* ○ *He rehearsed the interview in his mind beforehand*

▷ **rehearsal** /-sl/ *n* **1** [U] rehearsing: *put a play into rehearsal* ○ *have two plays in rehearsal,* ie being rehearsed. **2** [C] practice performance of a play, opera, etc: *have/hold/stage a ˈdress rehearsal* **3** [C] (*fml*) account or recital of sth, esp in the mind: *a rehearsal of what he would say.*

rehouse /ˌriːˈhaʊz/ *v* [Tn] give (sb) a new house flat, etc: *tenants rehoused during building repair* ○ *the need to rehouse people in the inner cities.*

Reich /raɪk/ *n* [sing] the former German state: *th Third Reich,* ie Germany under the Nazi regime (1933-45).

Reichstag /ˈraɪkstɑːg/ **the Reichstag** former parliament of the German Empire and the *Weimar Republic. The Reichstag building in Berlin was burnt down in 1933 when *Hitler came to power, probably as part of a Nazi plot.

reign /reɪn/ *n* (period of) rule of a king or queen: *in during the reign of King Alfred.*

▷ **reign** *v* **1** [I, Ipr] ~ (**over sb/sth**) be king, queen or regent; rule: *reign over the country/over one's subjects.* **2** [I] (*esp fig*) be dominant; prevail *Silence reigned,* ie There was complete silence. ○ *the reigning champion, Miss World, etc* ○ *Chaos reigns supreme in our new house.*

□ ˌ**reign of ˈterror** (**a**) period of violence, eg during a revolution or under a dictator, when many people are unjustly killed or punished. (**b**) **the Reign of Terror** period of the *French Revolution when the Committee of Public Safety and its agents executed about 40 000 people, often without a trial, because they were suspected of opposing the regime.

reimburse /ˌriːɪmˈbɜːs/ *v* [Tn, Tn·pr esp passive Dn·n, Dn·pr] ~ **sth** (**to sb**); ~ **sb** (**for sth**) (*usu fml*) pay back to sb (money that he has spent, lost etc); refund sth: *I was reimbursed in full.* ○ *All expenses will be reimbursed (to you).* ○ *We will reimburse the customer for any loss or damage.*

▷ **reimbursement** *n* [C, U] repayment (of expenses, etc).

rein /reɪn/ *n* **1** (**a**) [C often *pl*] long narrow strap fastened to the bit of a bridle and used to guide and control a horse: *ride on a short/long rein,* ie use more/less control. (**b**) **reins** [pl] similar device for restraining a small child. **2 reins** [pl] (*fml*) means of control: *hold, take up, assume, etc the reins of government,* ie (begin to) govern. **3** (idm) **give, etc free rein to sb/sth** ⇨ FREE[1]. **keep a tight rein on sb/sth** ⇨ TIGHT.

▷ **rein** *v* (phr v) **rein sth in** slow down or stop (a horse) by pulling back the reins.

reincarnate /ˌriːˈɪnkɑːneɪt/ *v* [esp passive: Tn Tn·pr, Cn·n/a] ~ **sb/sth** (**in/as sb/sth**) bring back (a soul after death) in another body: *Some people believe they may be reincarnated in the form of an animal.*

▷ **reincarnate** /ˌriːɪnˈkɑːnət/ *adj* (*dated*) born again in a new body.

reincarnation /ˌriːɪnkɑːˈneɪʃn/ *n* (**a**) [U] belief that the soul enters a new (human or animal) body after death. (**b**) [C] instance of this; new body inhabited in this way.

reindeer /ˈreɪndɪə(r)/ *n* (*pl* unchanged) type of large deer with branched antlers, living in the arctic regions: *a herd of reindeer* ○ [attrib] *reindeer meat.* Cf CARIBOU.

reinforce /ˌriːɪnˈfɔːs/ *v* [Tn] **1** make (sth) stronger by adding material, etc: *reinforce the sleeves of a jumper,* eg with elbow patches ○ *reinforce a wall bridge, dyke, etc.* **2** (*fig*) give more support to (sth) emphasize: *reinforce sb's opinion, argument conviction, etc* ○ *This evidence reinforces my view that he is a spy.* **3** increase the numbers or military strength of (sth): *reinforce a garrison, fleet, etc* ○

Our defences must be reinforced against attack.
▷ **reinforcement** *n* **1** [U] reinforcing or being reinforced. **2 reinforcements** [pl] extra soldiers, ships, tanks, etc sent to reinforce armed forces, etc.
□ ˌ**reinforced** ˈ**concrete** (also **ferroconcrete**) concrete with metal bars or wires embedded in it to give greater strength.

Reinhardt[1] /ˈraɪnhɑːt/ Django (1910-53), jazz guitarist, born in Belgium from a gypsy family. He founded the jazz quintet of the Hot Club de France with Stéphane *Grappelli and was famous for his European melodic style of jazz.

Reinhardt[2] /ˈraɪnhɑːt/ Max (1873-1943), Austrian director and impressario. He was a dominant figure in German drama until 1933, when he went to the USA. He established the importance of the director in theatre and film, and specialized in lavish symbolist productions.

reinstate /ˌriːɪnˈsteɪt/ *v* [Tn, Tn·pr, Cn·n/a] ~ **sb (in/as sth)** restore sb to a previous (esp important) position: *reinstate sb in the post of manager/as manager* ○ *(fig) Sue is now reinstated in his affections*, eg after a quarrel. ▷ **reinstatement** *n* [U].

reissue /ˌriːˈɪʃuː/ *v* **1** [Tn, Tn·pr, Cn·n/a] ~ **sb (with sth)**; ~ **sth (as sth)** issue again (esp sth that has been temporarily unavailable): *reissue a stamp, coin, magazine, etc* ○ *The novel was reissued as a paperback.* **2** [Tn] issue (sth) again, esp after it has been recalled: *reissue library books after stocktaking.*
▷ **reissue** *n* thing reissued, esp a reprint of a book in a new format.

reiterate /riːˈɪtəreɪt/ *v* [Tn, Tf] *(fml)* say or do (sth) again or repeatedly: *reiterate a command, question, offer, etc.* Cf ITERATE.
▷ **reiteration** /riːˌɪtəˈreɪʃn/ *n* [C, U] (instance of) reiterating or being reiterated: *(a) reiteration of past excuses.*

Reith /riːθ/ John, 1st Baron Reith (1889-1971), Scottish industrialist and pioneer of broadcasting. As first Director-General of the BBC (1927-38) he set high standards and helped to keep it free from government control. He believed that radio and television had a responsibility to educate the public and improve their taste. He also founded the **Reith lectures**, a series of talks given each year on BBC radio by a leading figure in a particular field. ▷ **Reithian** *adj.*

reject /rɪˈdʒekt/ *v* **1** [Tn, Cn·n/a] refuse to accept (sb/sth): *reject a gift, a possibility, an opinion, a suggestion* ○ *a rejected candidate, applicant, etc* ○ *She rejected his offer of marriage.* ○ *After the transplant his body rejected* (ie failed to adapt to) *the new heart.* ○ *The army doctors rejected several recruits as unfit.* **2** [Tn] put (sth) aside or throw (sth) away as not to be used, chosen, done, etc; discard: *Imperfect articles are rejected by our quality control.* ○ *reject over-ripe fruit*, eg when making jam. **3** [Tn] not give due affection to (sb/sth); rebuff: *The child was rejected by its parents.*
▷ **reject** /ˈriːdʒekt/ *n* rejected person or thing: *rejects from an officers' training course* ○ *export rejects*, ie damaged or imperfect goods ○ [attrib] *reject china, earthenware, etc.*
rejection /rɪˈdʒekʃn/ *n* **(a)** [U] rejecting or being rejected. **(b)** [C] instance of this: *Her proposal met with continual rejections.* **reˈjection slip** formal note from an editor or a publisher accompanying a rejected article, book, etc.

rejig /ˌriːˈdʒɪg/ *v* (**-gg-**) [Tn] **1** re-equip (a factory, plant, etc) for a new type of work. **2** (*US* **rejigger** /ˌriːˈdʒɪgə(r)/) *(infml)* rearrange (sth): *rejig the kitchen to fit in the new cooker.*

rejoice /rɪˈdʒɔɪs/ *v* **1** [I, Ipr, It] ~ **(at/over sth)** *(fml)* feel or show great joy: *rejoice over a victory* ○ *rejoice at sb's success* ○ *I rejoice to hear that you are well again.* ○ *We rejoiced that the war was over.* **2** (phr v) **rejoice in sth** *(joc)* have or glory in (a title, etc): *She rejoices in the name of Cassandra Postlethwaite.*
▷ **rejoicing** *n* **1** [U] happiness; joy. **2 rejoicings** [pl] expressions of joy; celebrations: *loud rejoicings after the victory.*

rejoin[1] /ˌriːˈdʒɔɪn/ *v* [Tn] **1** join (sb/sth) again; be reunited with: *rejoin one's group, ship, regiment* ○ *She made a detour and rejoined us on the other side of the wood.* ○ *This lane rejoins the main road further on.* **2** join (sth) together again: *rejoin the broken pieces.*

rejoin[2] /rɪˈdʒɔɪn/ *v* [Tf no passive] *(fml)* say in answer or reply; retort: *'You're wrong!' she rejoined.* ○ *He rejoined that this was quite right.*
▷ **rejoinder** /-də(r)/ *n* what is said in reply; retort: *'No!' was his curt rejoinder.*

rejuvenate /rɪˈdʒuːvəneɪt/ *v* [Tn esp passive] restore youthful appearance, strength, etc to (sb): *feel rejuvenated after a holiday.* ▷ **rejuvenation** /rɪˌdʒuːvəˈneɪʃn/ *n* [U, C]: *undergo a total rejuvenation.*

rekindle /ˌriːˈkɪndl/ *v* [I, Tn] (cause sth to) light again: *rekindle the fire by blowing on the ashes* ○ *(fig) rekindle love, enthusiasm, hope, etc.*

re-laid *pt, pp* of RE-LAY.

relapse /rɪˈlæps/ *v* [I, Ipr] ~ **(into sth/doing sth)** fall back into a previous condition or a worse state after making an improvement: *relapse into bad habits* ○ *relapse into unconsciousness, silence, crime* ○ *relapse into smoking twenty cigarettes a day.*
▷ **relapse** *n* act of relapsing, esp after partial recovery from an illness: *have/suffer a relapse.*

relate /rɪˈleɪt/ *v* **1** [Tn, Tw, Dn·pr, Dpr·w] ~ **sth (to sb)** *(fml)* give an account of (facts, experiences, etc); tell (a story, etc): *relate the events of the last week* ○ *She related (to them) how it happened.* **2 (a)** [Tn, Tn·pr] ~ **sth to/with sth** connect (two things) in thought or meaning; associate sth with sth: *It is difficult to relate cause and effect in this case.* ○ *The report relates high wages to/with labour shortages.* **(b)** [Ipr] ~ **to sb/sth** be connected with sb/sth else; refer to sb/sth: *Wealth is seldom related to happiness.* ○ *statements relating to his resignation* ○ *Does the new law relate only to theft?* **3** [Ipr] ~ **to sb/sth** be able to understand and sympathize with sb/sth: *Some adults can't relate to children.* ○ *I just can't relate to* (ie appreciate) *punk music.* **4** (idm) **strange to relate/say** ⇨ STRANGE.
▷ **related** *adj* ~ **(to sb/sth) 1** connected or associated (with sb/sth): *crime related to drug abuse* ○ *chemistry, biology and other related sciences.* **2** [esp pred] in the same family or class, etc: *be closely/distantly related (to sb)* ○ *two related species of ape* ○ *He is related to her by marriage.*
relatedness *n* [U] being related.

relation /rɪˈleɪʃn/ *n* **1** [U] ~ **(between sth and sth)**; ~ **(to sth)** way in which one person or thing is related to another; similarity, contrast or connection between people, things or events: *the relation between rainfall and crop production* ○ *The cost of this project bears/has/shows no relation to the results*, ie It does not justify them. **2 (a)** [C] person who is related to another; relative: *a close/near/distant relation of mine* ○ *a relation by marriage/law.* **(b)** [U] family connection; kinship: *Is he any relation (to you)?* ○ *He's no relation (to me).* ○ *What relation are you (to each other)?* ie How are you related? **3 relations** [pl] ~**s (between sb/sth and sb/sth)**; ~**s (with sb/sth)** links or contacts between people, groups, countries, etc; dealings: *diplomatic, international, business relations* ○ *the friendly relations (existing) between our countries* ○ *Relations are rather strained* (ie difficult or awkward) *at present.* ○ *break off (all) relations with one's family.* **4** (idm) **have (sexual) relations (with sb)** have intercourse (with sb). **in/with relation to sb/sth** *(fml)* concerning sb/sth; with reference to sb/sth. **a poor relation** ⇨ POOR.
▷ **relationship** *n* **1** ~ **(between A and B)**; ~ **(of A to/with B)** state of being connected: *the close relationship between industry and trade/of industry to trade.* **2 (a)** ~ **(between A and B)**; ~ **(of A to B)** state of being related by birth or marriage: *a father-son relationship.* **(b)** ~ **(between A and B)**; ~ **(of A with B)** emotional or sexual liaison: *have a relationship with sb* ○ *Their affair did not develop into a lasting relationship.* **3** ~ **(between A and B)**; ~ **(of A with B)** links or contacts; dealings: *a purely business relationship* ○ *The author had a good working relationship with his editor.*

NOTE ON USAGE: Compare **relation**, **relations** and **relationship**. **Relationship** has the widest use, covering many of the meanings of **relation** and **relations**. **1 Relation** and **relationship** can be used of family connections: *A relation of mine is coming to stay.* ○ *'What's your relationship to her?' 'She's my cousin.'* **2 Relationship** can indicate a strong emotional association: *Their relationship has lasted many years.* **3** When speaking about less personal associations or friendships, **relations** or **relationship** is used: *Relations with the USSR are improving.* ○ *Britain has a unique relationship with the USA.* **4 Relation** and **relationship** can indicate a similarity or correspondence between things: *Some people say that there's no relation/relationship between violence on television and crimes of violence.*

relative /ˈrelətɪv/ *adj* **1** ~ **(to sth)** considered in relation or proportion to sb/sth else; comparative: *the relative merits of the two plans, candidates, cars* ○ *Supply is relative to demand.* ○ *They are living in relative comfort*, ie compared with other people or with themselves at an earlier time. Cf ABSOLUTE 4. **2** ~ **to sth** *(fml)* (following *ns*) having a connection with sth; referring to sth: *the facts relative to the problem* ○ *the papers relative to the case.* **3** [attrib] *(grammar)* referring to an earlier noun, clause or sentence: *a relative pronoun, clause, adverb* ○ *The word 'who' in 'the man who came' is a relative pronoun.*
▷ **relative** *n* person who is related to another; relation: *a close/near/distant relative of hers.*
relatively *adj* **1** in relation or proportion to sb/sth else; comparatively: *Considering the smallness of the car, it is relatively roomy inside.* ○ *Relatively speaking, this matter is unimportant.* **2** *(infml)* quite; moderately: *In spite of her illness, she is relatively cheerful.*
□ ˌ**relative aˌtomic** ˈ**mass** ratio of the average mass of an atom of an element to $\frac{1}{12}$ of the mass of a carbon12 atom.
ˌ**relative moˌlecular** ˈ**mass** ratio of the average mass of a molecule of an element or compound to $\frac{1}{12}$ of the mass of a carbon 12 atom.

relativism /ˈrelətɪvɪzəm/ *n* [U] belief that truth is not always and generally valid, but is limited by the nature of the human mind.

relativity /ˌreləˈtɪvətɪ/ *n* [U] **1** state of being relative(1). **2** *(physics)* *Einstein's theory of the universe, which shows that all motion is relative and treats time as a fourth dimension related to space.
▷ **relativistic** /ˌrelətɪˈvɪstɪk/ *adj (esp physics)* based on relativity.

relax /rɪˈlæks/ *v* **1 (a)** [I, Tn] (make sth) become less tight, stiff, etc: *Let your muscles relax slowly.* ○ *relax one's grip, hold, grasp (on sth).* **(b)** [I, Ipr] ~ **(into sth)** become less anxious, worried or formal in manner; be at ease: *Her features suddenly relaxed.* ○ *I'll only relax when I know you're safe.* ○ *His face relaxed into a smile.* **2** [Tn] let (rules, regulations, etc) become less strict or rigid: *We could relax the procedure slightly in your case.* ○ *Discipline is often relaxed at weekends.* **3** [I, Tn no passive] (make sb) rest after work or effort; calm down: *A holiday will help you relax after your exams.* ○ *These pills will relax you and make you sleep.* **4** [I, Tn] (cause effort, concentration, etc to) become less intense: *His attention never relaxes.* ○ *You cannot afford to relax your vigilance for a moment.*
▷ **relaxation** /ˌriːlækˈseɪʃn/ *n* **1** [U] relaxing or being relaxed: *some relaxation of the rules.* **2** [C, U] (thing done for) recreation or amusement: *Fishing is his favourite relaxation.*
relaxed *adj* not feeling or showing worry, anxiety, tenseness, etc: *look, feel, seem relaxed (about sth)* ○ *a relaxed smile* ○ *a relaxed style of teaching.*
relaxing *adj* helping people to become less tense, anxious, worried, etc: *a relaxing drink, holiday.*

relaxant /rɪˈlæksənt/ *n* medicine that relaxes the muscles.

relay /ˈriːleɪ/ *n* **1** fresh set of people or animals taking the place of others who have finished a period of work: *Rescuers worked in relays to save the trapped miners.* ○ *A new relay of horses was harnessed to the cart.* Cf SHIFT² 2. **2** (also **ˈrelay race**) race between teams in which each member runs, swims, etc part of the total distance, the second, etc member starting when the first, etc finishes: [attrib] *a relay team, runner, etc.* **3** (a) (*radio*) electronic device for receiving signals and transmitting them again with greater strength, thus increasing the distance over which they are carried: [attrib] *a relay station.* (b) broadcast, programme or telegraph message sent out in this way: *a relay from Radio Hamburg.* **4** electrical or electronic device for switching circuits on or off, which operates in response to a change in the current.

▷ **relay** /ˈriːleɪ, *also* rɪˈleɪ/ *v* (*pt, pp* **relayed**) [Tn, Tn·pr] ~ **sth (from...) (to...)** **1** receive and pass on (eg a message): *relay the colonel's orders to the troops.* **2** (*Brit*) broadcast (sth) by passing signals through a transmitting station: *a concert relayed live from the Royal Albert Hall* ○ *The pop festival was relayed all round the world.*

re-lay /ˌriːˈleɪ/ *v* (*pt, pp* **re-laid** /-ˈleɪd/) [Tn] lay (a cable, carpet, lawn, etc) again.

release /rɪˈliːs/ *v* **1** [Tn, Tn·pr] ~ **sb/sth (from sth)** (a) allow (a person or an animal) to go; set free or liberate sb/sth: *release a prisoner, hostage, kidnap victim, etc (from captivity)* ○ *release a rat from a trap* ○ *release the horses into the paddock* ○ *She gently released herself from his arms/embrace.* ○ (*law*) *The robber was released on bail.* ○ (*fig*) *Death released him from his sufferings.* (b) (*fig*) free (sb) from an obligation: *release sb from a promise, duty, undertaking, etc* ○ *release a monk from his vows.* **2** (a) [Tn] remove (sth) from a fixed position; cause (sth) to move freely: *release the clutch, handbrake*, eg of a lorry ○ *release a switch, catch, lever, etc* ○ *release the trigger*, eg of a rifle ○ *use oil to release a rusted lock.* (b) [Tn, Tn·pr] (used esp in the expressions shown) let go (one's hold of sb/sth): *release one's grip (on sth)* ○ *release one's grasp (of sth).* **3** [Tn, Tn·pr] ~ **sth (from sth)** (*fml*) allow sth to fly, fall, etc: *release an arrow, bomb, etc* ○ *The bullet is released from the gun at very high speed.* **4** [Tn, Tn·pr] ~ **sth (to sb/sth)** (a) allow (news, etc) to be made known: *The latest developments have just been released to the media.* ○ *The police have released no further details about the crime.* (b) make sth available to the public: *release a film, book, record, etc* ○ *The new model has now been released for sale (to export markets).* **5** [Tn] (*law*) give up (a right, title, property, etc) to sb else.

▷ **release** *n* **1** [U, C] ~ **(from sth)** releasing or being released: *an order for sb's release from prison/captivity* ○ *a feeling of release*, ie of freedom ○ (*fig*) *Death is often a welcome release from pain.* ○ *the release of a film, record, book, newsflash* ○ *The film is on general release*, ie is being shown widely at local cinemas. **2** [C] thing released (RELEASE 4b): *the latest releases*, ie records, films, etc ○ *a ˈpress release*, ie of news, etc for printing or broadcasting. **3** [C] handle, lever, catch, etc that releases part of a machine: *the ˈcarriage release*, ie on a typewriter ○ [attrib] *a reˈlease gear* ○ *the reˈlease button, knob, etc.*

relegate /ˈrelɪɡeɪt/ *v* [esp passive: Tn, Tn·pr] ~ **sb/sth (to sth)** **1** dismiss sb/sth to a lower or less important rank, task or state: *I have been relegated to the role of a mere assistant.* ○ *relegate old files to the storeroom.* **2** (*esp Brit*) transfer (a sports team) to a lower division: *Will Spurs be relegated to the third division?* ▷ **relegation** /ˌrelɪˈɡeɪʃn/ *n* [U]: *teams threatened with relegation.*

relent /rɪˈlent/ *v* [I] **1** decide to be less strict, determined or harsh: *Afterwards she relented and let the children stay up late to watch TV.* ○ *The police will not relent in their fight against crime.* **2** (of the speed or rate of doing sth, etc) become less intense: *The pressure on us to finish this task will not relent.* **3** (of bad weather) improve: *The rain relented just long enough for me to go shopping.*

▷ **relentless** *adj* **1** not relenting; strict or harsh: *be relentless in punishing offenders.* **2** not ceasing; constant: *driven by a relentless urge, ambition, quest, etc for power* ○ *relentless pursuit, questioning, criticism* ○ *the relentless pressure of her life as a politician.* **relentlessly** *adv.* **relentlessness** *n* [U].

relevant /ˈreləvənt/ *adj* ~ **(to sth/sb)** connected with what is being discussed, what is happening, what is being done, etc: *a highly relevant argument, point, suggestion, etc* ○ *have all the relevant documents ready* ○ *supply the facts (directly) relevant to the case* ○ *Colour and sex are hardly relevant when appointing somebody to a job.*

▷ **relevance** /-əns/ (also **relevancy** /-ənsɪ/) *n* [U]: *have/bear some relevance to the matter in hand.*

reliable /rɪˈlaɪəbl/ *adj* consistently good in quality or performance, and so deserving trust; dependable: *a reliable assistant, witness, report, watch, battery, firm* ○ *be a reliable source of information (about sth)* ○ *My memory's not very reliable these days.*

▷ **reliability** /rɪˌlaɪəˈbɪlətɪ/ *n* [U] state or quality of being reliable.

reliably /-əblɪ/ *adv*: *I am reliably informed that he's about to resign.*

reliance /rɪˈlaɪəns/ *n* [U] ~ **on sb/sth** confidence or trust in sb/sth; dependence on sb/sth: *Don't place too much reliance on his advice.* ○ *his total, absolute, complete reliance on his colleagues.*

▷ **reliant** /-ənt/ *adj* ~ **on sb/sth** [pred] having reliance on sb/sth; dependent on sb/sth: *He's heavily reliant on bank loans.* Cf SELF-RELIANT.

relic /ˈrelɪk/ *n* **1** [C] trace or feature surviving from a past age and serving to remind people of it: *relics of ancient civilizations, rituals, beliefs.* **2** [C] part of the body, clothes, belongings, etc of a holy person kept after his death as sth to be deeply respected. ⇨ Usage at REST³. **3 relics** [pl] (parts of a) dead body surviving destruction or decay; remnants.

relief¹ /rɪˈliːf/ *n* **1** [U, sing] ~ **(from sth)** lessening or removing of pain, distress, anxiety, etc: *bring, seek, find, give, feel relief* ○ *doctors working for the relief of suffering, hardship, etc* ○ *The drug gives some relief from pain.* ○ *I breathed/heaved a sigh of relief when I heard he was safe.* ○ *To my great relief/Much to my relief, I wasn't late.* ○ *It's a great relief to find you here.* ○ *'What a relief!' she said, as she took her tight shoes off.* **2** [U] that which brings relief(1); assistance given to people in need or to a disaster area: *send relief (eg food, tents, money, etc) to those made homeless by floods* ○ *provide relief for refugees* ○ *go/come to the relief of earthquake victims* ○ *committees for famine relief* ○ [attrib] *reˈlief funds, projects, supplies.* **3** [U] ~ **(from sth)** thing that reduces tension, relieves monotony or brings pleasing variety: *His jokes provided some comic relief in what was really a dull speech.* ○ *Two comedians followed (eg in a variety show) by way of light relief.* **4** [C] (a) person taking over or following after another's turn of duty: *stand in as Peter's relief* ○ [attrib] *a reˈlief driver, crew, etc.* (b) bus, train, etc supplementing a regular service: *The coach was full so a relief was put on.* ○ [attrib] *a reˈlief bus, service, etc.* **5** [sing] ~ **(of sth)** ending or raising of the siege (of a town, fort, etc): *the relief of Mafeking.*

□ **reˈlief road** bypass or other road that vehicles can use to avoid an area of heavy traffic.

relief² /rɪˈliːf/ *n* **1** (a) [U] method of carving or moulding in which a design stands out from a flat surface: *in high/low relief*, ie with the background cut out deeply/shallowly. (b) [C] design or carving made in this way. **2** [U] (in drawing, etc) appearance of being done in relief by the use of shading, colour etc: (*fig*) *The hills stood out in sharp relief against the dawn sky.* ○ *The MI5 scandal throws the security issue into stark relief*, ie draws attention to its real nature. **3** [U] differences of height between hills and valleys, etc: *a reˈlief map* ○ *The relief is clearly shown on this plan.*

□ **reˈlief map** map showing hills, valleys, etc either by shading or by their being moulded in relief.

relieve /rɪˈliːv/ *v* [Tn] **1** lessen or remove (pain, distress, anxiety, etc): *relieve suffering, hardship, etc among refugees* ○ *This drug will relieve your discomfort.* **2** ~ **oneself** (*euph*) empty one's bladder or bowels. **3** provide aid or assistance for (people in need, a disaster area, etc): *relieve famine in Africa* ○ *The bypass relieves traffic jams in our city centre.* **4** introduce variety into (sth): *relieve the tedium/boredom/monotony of waiting* ○ *Not a single tree relieved the flatness of the plain.* **5** release (sb) from a duty or task by taking his place (or finding sb else to do so): *relieve the guard/the watch* ○ *relieve a sentry, workmate, driver* ○ *I'm to be relieved at six.* **6** end or raise the siege of (a town, fort, etc). **7** (idm) **relieve one's ˈfeelings** make one's emotions easier to bear by weeping, shouting, behaving violently, etc. **8** (phr v) **relieve sb of sth** (a) (*fml*) take (a burden, responsibility, etc) away from sb: *relieve Mr Brett of his post as manager* ○ *The general was relieved of his command.* (b) (*joc*) carry, take charge, etc of sb's personal effects: *Let me relieve you of your coat and hat.* (c) (*infml joc*) rob sb of sth: *The thief relieved him of his wallet.*

▷ **relieved** *adj* feeling or showing relief(1): *a relieved smile, look, expression, etc* ○ *We were/felt relieved to hear you were safe.*

religion /rɪˈlɪdʒən/ *n* **1** [U] belief in the existence of a god or gods, who has/have created the universe and given man a spiritual nature which continues to exist after the death of the body. **2** [C] particular system of faith and worship based on such a belief: *the Christian, Buddhist and Hindu religions* ○ *practise one's religion.* ⇨ article. **3** [sing] (*fig*) controlling influence on one's life; sth one is devoted or committed to: *Football is like a religion for Bill.* ○ *make a religion of always being punctual.*

religiose /rɪˈlɪdʒɪəʊs/ *adj* (*derog*) pretentiously solemn or pious; too solemn. ▷ **religiosity** /rɪˌlɪdʒɪˈɒsətɪ/ *n* [U].

religious /rɪˈlɪdʒəs/ *adj* **1** [attrib] of religion: *religious worship, belief, faith* ○ *a religious service.* **2** (of a person) believing in and practising a religion; devout. **3** [attrib] of a monastic order: *a religious house*, ie a monastery or convent. **4** (*fig*) scrupulous or conscientious: *pay religious attention to detail* ○ *be religious in one's observance of protocol.*

▷ **religious** *n* (*pl* unchanged) member of one of the Christian orders of monks, friars or nuns.

religiously *adv* **1** in a religious(2) way. **2** (*fig*) scrupulously or conscientiously; regularly: *I followed the instructions religiously.* ○ *She phones him religiously every day.*

religiousness *n* [U].

relinquish /rɪˈlɪŋkwɪʃ/ *v* (*fml*) **1** [Tn] give up or cease to practise, feel, etc (sth); abandon: *relinquish the struggle for power* ○ *relinquish bad habits* ○ *He had relinquished all hope that she was alive.* **2** [Tn, Tn·pr] ~ **sth (to sb)** give up or renounce (a claim, etc); surrender sth: *relinquish a right, privilege* ○ *She relinquished possession of the house to her sister.* ○ *relinquish a post to one's successor.* **3** [Tn, Tn·pr] (used esp in the expressions shown) cease to hold (sb/sth); release: *relinquish one's grip (on sb/sth)* ○ *relinquish one's hold (on sb/sth).*

reliquary /ˈrelɪkwərɪ; *US* -kwerɪ/ *n* container for a relic or relics of a holy person.

relish /ˈrelɪʃ/ *n* **1** [U] ~ **(for sth)** great enjoyment of food, etc; zest: *eat, drink with (great) relish* ○ *She savoured the joke with relish.* **2** [U] (used esp in negative sentences) attractive quality; appeal: *Tennis loses its relish when one gets old.* ○ *Routine office jobs have no relish at all for me.* **3** [C, U] spicy or strongly-flavoured appetizer served with plain food: *cucumber, sweetcorn, etc relish*, ie for hamburgers, etc. Cf PICKLE 1, SAUCE 1.

▷ **relish** *v* [Tn, Tg, Tsg] enjoy or get pleasure out of (sth): *relish a meal, drink, joke* ○ *I don't relish having to get up so early.*

relive /ˌriːˈlɪv/ *v* [Tn] go through (an experience, a period of time, etc) again, esp in one's imagination: *relive the horrors of war* ○ *I relived that fateful day*

Religion

The predominant religion in both Britain and the USA is Christianity, represented chiefly but not exclusively in Britain by the Church of England and in the USA by a number of Protestant Churches and by the Roman Catholic Church. There are two established Churches in Britain, recognized as official Churches of the State. They are the (Anglican) Church of England and the (Presbyterian) Church of Scotland.

At the end of the 1980s, around eight people out of 10 in Britain regarded themselves as Christian, with just over half belonging to the established Churches, one in 10 being Roman Catholics, and the remainder mostly members of one of the 'Free Churches', that is, the Protestant Churches that are not established as Churches of the State. The main Free Churches in Britain are the Methodists, the Baptists and the United Reformed Church. The latter was formed in 1972 through a union between the Presbyterian Church and the Congregational Church. The Salvation Army, although not a 'Church' in the accepted sense, can also be regarded as belonging to this group. Another Protestant body, now growing in number, is that of the Pentecostalists, who have many West Indian members. The Unitarians are also Protestant in origin. A small but notable group of Christians in Britain are the Quakers (officially called the Society of Friends), who number about 18 000. The Quakers, who have no religious hierarchy and who practise silent worship, are active in many charitable causes.

The Roman Catholic Church in Britain, which officially ceased to exist at the time of the Reformation in the 16th century, was restored in 1850. Like the Church of England, it has a hierarchy of archbishops, bishops and priests. It attaches great importance to the education of its children in the Catholic faith, and is responsible for a number of Catholic schools, many of them funded by local authorities. The population of Ireland is predominantly Catholic, and many British Catholics are descended from Irish people who settled in Britain.

A recent development in Christian worship in Britain is the 'house church', with members of different Protestant Churches meeting for worship in the home of one of them. Worship is led by a member nominated on a roster.

Jehovah's Witnesses are not numerous in Britain but are well-known as a result of their door-to-door 'missionary' visiting (which includes the selling of their newspaper, *The Watchtower*). They are opposed to blood transfusions, because they believe it is forbidden in the Bible, and they thus make news when they refuse to allow their children to be given this life-saving treatment.

Over half the population of the USA belongs to one of the Christian Churches. Slightly more than half of these belong to one of the Protestant Churches, and about 40 per cent are Roman Catholics. The main Protestant groups in order of size are the Baptists, the Methodists and the Lutherans, the biggest single denomination being the Southern Baptist Convention with over 14 million members. The Baptist movement in the USA grew from the Baptist Churches to which many of the original English settlers belonged. The Southern Baptist Convention was organized in Georgia in 1845 as an active missionary society. Many black people in the USA are Baptists, the two leading groups being the National Baptist Convention of America and the National Baptist Convention, USA. (The slight difference in name is a result of the rift that occurred in the movement in 1916.) The Presbyterian Church, with over 2 million members, is another Protestant group that originated with the Puritan settlers.

The largest Methodist group, with over 9 million members, is the United Methodist Church, while the Evangelical Lutheran Church in America has more than 5 million members. Many Lutheran Churches evolved from the form of Protestantism practised by the German and Scandinavian immigrants who settled in the Middle West in the 19th century.

The Episcopal Church in the USA, with over 2 million members, developed from the Church of England in the late 18th century, and is still part of the Anglican Communion. In 1989 the Episcopalians appointed the first Anglican woman bishop.

The Pentecostal movement is active in the USA, with over a dozen different denominations. The largest is that of the Assemblies of God, who were formed in 1914 as the result of a union of several smaller groups, and now have more than 2 million members.

Immigrants to the USA have created membership of a million or more for other Christian denominations, such as the Eastern Orthodox Churches, while the large Roman Catholic community, at present numbering over 50 million, owes much of its strength to the Irish immigration to America since the 19th century.

Entirely American in origin are the Mormons, or members of the Church of Jesus Christ of Latter-Day Saints, now numbering about 4 million. Their movement was founded in 1830, and from 1847 their centre has been at Salt Lake City, Utah. They no longer practise polygamy, for which they were formerly noted. Jehovah's Witnesses also originated in the USA, and at present number about 800 000.

In Britain, Muslims form the largest religious group after Christians. There are about one million British Muslims. Most of them are immigrants from Pakistan and Bangladesh, but there are a growing number of British-born Muslims. These are mostly the children of Muslim immigrants, but there are also increasing numbers of Muslim converts. The first Muslim mosque opened in Woking, Surrey, in 1890, but it is the Central Mosque in London that now has the greatest number of worshippers: 60 000 or more during some festivals. Other towns with large Muslim populations and mosques are Liverpool, Manchester, Leicester and Glasgow. In the USA there are an estimated 6 million Muslims.

There are about 350 000 Jews in Britain, forming the second largest community in Europe. Most of them are of German or eastern European origin. The majority are Ashkenazi Orthodox Jews, acknowledging the Chief Rabbi as their head.

Jews began migrating to America in the 17th century, and at first came mostly from Spain and Portugal. From 1820 to about 1870, however, 300 000 Jews arrived from Germany and central Europe, and their numbers were increased by the Yiddish-speaking Jews who left eastern Europe for America towards the end of the 19th century. There are now about 6 million Jews in the USA, around half of these being Conservative (as distinct from Orthodox or Reform) and belonging to the United Synagogue of America.

Indian immigrants to Britain account for the sizeable Sikh and Hindu communities, which number about 500 000 and 300 000 respectively. The largest Sikh temple is in Southall, west London, where congregations of more than 5 000 meet during festivals. The largest Hindu communities are to be found in Leicester, north and north-west London, Birmingham and Bradford, while Sikhs live chiefly in London, Manchester, Birmingham and Nottingham. Buddhists are also found in Britain in a number of urban centres, and there are at least a dozen Buddhist monasteries and several temples. In the USA, there are about 100 000 Buddhists.

On average four out of 10 adult Americans regularly attended church or synagogue in the late 1980s, while about six out of 10 claimed to be members of a church or synagogue. Church membership is declining, but attendance has remained at a fairly constant level since 1969. (Cf article at CHURCH OF ENGLAND.)

over and over in my mind.

relocate /ˌriːləʊˈkeɪt; *US* ˌriːˈləʊkeɪt/ *v* [I, Ipr, Tn, Tn·pr] ~ **(sb/sth) (from ...) (to ...)** move (sb/sth) to, or build (sth) in, another place: *We're relocating just south of Newcastle.* ○ *The company is to relocate its headquarters in the Midlands.* ▷ **relocation** /ˌriːləʊˈkeɪʃn/ *n* [U]: *the relocation of industry* ○ [attrib] *relocation allowances, expenses,* eg for those taking up a new job in a different area.

reluctant /rɪˈlʌktənt/ *adj* ~ **(to do sth)** unwilling and therefore slow to co-operate, agree, etc: *a reluctant helper, recruit, admirer* ○ *She was very reluctant to admit the truth.* ▷ **reluctance** /-əns/ *n* [U]: *She made a great show of reluctance, but finally accepted our offer.* ○ *He left us with (some) reluctance.* **reluctantly** *adv*: *After much thought, we reluctantly agreed.*

rely /rɪˈlaɪ/ *v* (*pt, pp* **relied**) [Ipr] ~ **on/upon sb/sth (to do sth) 1** count or depend on sb/sth: *Nowadays we rely increasingly on computers for help/to help us.* ○ *I relied on you(r) coming early.* ○ *You can rely upon it that it will rain this weekend.* ○ *She cannot be relied on to tell the truth.* **2** have trust or confidence in sb/sth: *You can rely on me to keep your secret.*

rem /rem/ *n* former unit used for measuring the effective dose of radiation absorbed by a person, now replaced by the sievert.

remain /rɪˈmeɪn/ *v* (usu not used in the continuous tenses) **1** [I] be left or still present after other parts have been removed or used or dealt with: *After the fire, very little remained of my house.* ○ *If you take 3 from 8, 5 remains.* ○ *The fact remains that she was lying.* ○ *leave the remaining points for our next meeting.* **2** [It] (*fml*) be left to be seen, done, said, etc: *It remains to be seen* (ie We shall know later) *whether you are right.* ○ *Much remains to be done.* ○ *Nothing remains except for me to say goodbye.* **3** [I, Ipr, Ip] (*esp fml*) stay in the same place; stay behind: *I remain in London until May.* ○ *The aircraft remained on the ground.* ○ *She left, but I remained (behind).* **4** [La, Ln] continue to be; stay in the same condition: *remain standing, seated, etc* ○ *He remained silent.* ○ *Let things remain as they are.* ○ *In spite of their quarrel, they remained the best of friends.*

remainder /rɪˈmeɪndə(r)/ *n* **1** (usu **the remainder**) [Gp] remaining people, things or time; the rest: *Ten people came but the remainder stayed away.* ○ *We spent the remainder of the day sightseeing.* **2** [C usu *sing*] (*mathematics*) quantity left after subtraction or division: *Divide 2 into 7, and the answer is 3, (with) remainder 1.* ⇨ Usage at REST[3]. **3** [C] number of copies of a book left unsold after demand has almost ceased: [attrib] *a remainder merchant.*

▷ **remainder** *v* [Tn esp passive] sell (unsold copies of a book) at a reduced price.

remains /rɪˈmeɪnz/ *n* [pl] **1** what is left after other parts have been removed or used or dealt with: *the remains of a meal, a chicken* ○ *the remains of a defeated army* ○ *I rescued the remains of my slipper from the dog.* **2** ancient buildings, etc that have survived when others were destroyed; ruins: *the remains of an abbey, of ancient Rome.* **3** (*fml*) dead body; corpse: *His mortal remains are buried in the churchyard.* ○ *Investigators found a trench containing human remains.* ⇨ Usage at REST[3].

remake /ˌriːˈmeɪk/ *v* (*pt, pp* **remade** /-meɪd/) make (esp a film) again or differently.

▷ **remake** /ˈriːmeɪk/ *n* thing remade: *produce a remake of the 1932 original.*

remand /rɪˈmɑːnd; *US* -ˈmænd/ *v* [Tn esp passive] send (an accused person) back (from a lawcourt) into custody, esp while further evidence is being gathered: *The accused was remanded in custody for a week.*

▷ **remand** *n* [U] **1** remanding or being remanded: [attrib] *a remand prisoner.* **2** (idm) **on remand** in a state of being remanded: *prisoners on remand* ○ *detention on remand.*

□ **reˈmand centre, reˈmand home** (*Brit*) place where young offenders are sent temporarily. ⇨ article at PUNISHMENT.

remark /rɪˈmɑːk/ *v* **1** [Ipr, Tn, Tf] ~ **on/upon sth/sb** say or write (sth) by way of comment; observe: *I couldn't help remarking on her youth.* ○ *The similarity between them has often been remarked on.* ○ *'I thought it was odd', he remarked.* ○ *Critics remarked that the play was not original.* **2** [Tn] (*dated or fml*) take notice of (sth/sb); perceive: *remark the likeness between father and son.*

▷ **remark** *n* **1** [C] thing said or written as a comment; observation: *pointed, cutting* (ie sarcastic) *remarks* ○ *make a few remarks about sb/on a subject* ○ *In the light of* (ie Considering) *your remarks, we rejected her offer.* **2** [U] (*dated or fml*) notice: *Nothing worthy of remark happened.*

remarkable /-əbl/ *adj* ~ (**for sth**) worth noticing or unusual; exceptional: *a remarkable person, feat, event, book* ○ *a boy who is remarkable for his stupidity.* **remarkably** /-əblɪ/ *adv.*

remarry /ˌriːˈmærɪ/ *v* (*pt, pp* **-ried**) (**a**) [I] marry sb different: *The widower did not remarry.* (**b**) [Tn] marry (sb) again: *She remarried her former husband ten years after their divorce.* ▷ **remarriage** /ˌriːˈmærɪdʒ/ *n.*

Rembrandt /ˈrembrænt/ full name Rembrandt Harmensz van Rijn (1606-69), Dutch painter. He is regarded as one of the greatest portrait painters of all time; he had a remarkable ability to express the inner character of his subjects, most notably himself in his series of over 60 self-portraits. He was also a great etcher, and left a very large collection of drawings.

remedy /ˈremədɪ/ *n* ~ (**for sth**) **1** [C] (*fml*) treatment, medicine, etc that cures or relieves a disease or pain: *a popular remedy for flu, toothache, cramp* ○ *I often use herbal remedies.* ○ *The remedy seems worse than the disease.* **2** [C, U] (*fig*) means of countering or removing sth undesirable: *seek a remedy for injustice* ○ *He found a remedy for his grief in constant hard work.* ○ *The mistake is beyond/past remedy,* ie cannot be put right.

▷ **remedial** /rɪˈmiːdɪəl/ *adj* [attrib] **1** providing, or intended to provide, a remedy or cure: *undergo remedial treatment/therapy,* eg for backache ○ *take remedial measures against unemployment.* **2** (of education) for slow learners or pupils suffering from disadvantages: *remedial classes, lessons, groups* ○ *a remedial French course/a course in remedial French.*

remediable /rɪˈmiːdɪəbl/ *adj* that can be remedied.

remedy *v* (*pt, pp* **-died**) [Tn] provide a remedy for (sth undesirable); rectify: *remedy injustices, mistakes, losses, deficiencies* ○ *The situation could not be remedied,* ie saved.

remember /rɪˈmembə(r)/ *v* (not usu used in the continuous tenses) **1** [I, Tn, Tf, Tw, Tt, Tg, Tsg, Cn·n/a] have or keep (sth) in the memory; recall to one's memory: *If I remember rightly the party starts at 8 pm.* ○ *Have you met my brother? Not as far as I remember.* ○ *I can't/don't remember his name.* ○ *Robert's contribution should also be remembered.* ○ *Remember (that) we're going out tonight.* ○ *Do you remember where you put the key?* ○ *Remember* (ie Don't forget) *to lock the door.* ○ *I remember posting the letters,* ie I have the memory of doing so in my mind. ○ *I remember his objecting to the scheme.* ○ *I remember her* (ie picture her in my mind) *as a slim young girl.* **2** [Tn] give money, etc to (sb/sth): *Please remember* (ie Don't forget to tip) *the waiter.* ○ *remember sb in one's will* ○ *Auntie Jill always remembers my birthday,* eg with a card or present. **3** [Tn] ~ **oneself** (*fml*) stop behaving badly: *Bill, remember yourself! Don't swear in front of the children.* **4** [Tn] mention or commemorate (sb) esp in one's prayers: *remember the sick, the old and the needy* ○ *a church service to remember the war dead.* **5** (phr v) **remember sb to sb** pass greetings from one person to another: *Please remember me to Jenny.* ○ *He asked me to remember him to you.*

remembrance /rɪˈmembrəns/ *n* (*fml*) **1** [U] remembering or being remembered; memory: *have no remembrance of sth* ○ *a service in remembrance of those killed in the war.* **2** [C] thing given or kept in memory of sb/sth; memento: *He sent us a small remembrance of his visit.*

□ **Reˈmembrance Sunday** (*Brit*) (nearest Sunday to) 11 November, on which those killed in the wars of 1914-18 and 1939-45 are commemorated. Cf ARMISTICE DAY (ARMISTICE).

remind /rɪˈmaɪnd/ *v* **1** [Tn, Dn·f, Dn·w, Dn·t] inform (sb) of a fact or tell (sb) to do sth he may have forgotten: *Do I have to remind you yet again?* ○ *That* (eg What you've just said, done, etc) *reminds me. I must feed the cat.* ○ *Travellers are reminded that malaria tablets are advisable.* ○ *I reminded her how much the fare was.* ○ *Remind me to answer that letter.* **2** [Tn·pr] ~ **sb of sb/sth** cause sb to remember or be newly aware of sb/sth: *He reminds me of his brother.* ○ *This song reminds me of France.*

▷ **reminder** *n* **1** thing which reminds sb of a fact or person: *The statue is a lasting reminder of Churchill's greatness.* **2** way of reminding sb to do sth: *send, give sb a gentle reminder,* eg to pay a bill ○ *The waiters were clearing the tables, which served as a reminder that it was time to leave.*

reminisce /ˌremɪˈnɪs/ *v* [I, Ipr] ~ (**about sth/sb**) think or talk about past events and experiences, usu with enjoyment.

reminiscence /ˌremɪˈnɪsns/ *n* **1** [U] recalling of past events and experiences; reminiscing. **2 reminiscences** [pl] spoken or written account of one's remembered experiences: *reminiscences of my youth.*

reminiscent /ˌremɪˈnɪsnt/ *adj* **1** [pred] ~ **of sb/sth** reminding one of or suggesting sb/sth: *His style is reminiscent of Picasso's.* **2** having a tendency to reminisce: *in a reminiscent mood.* ▷ **reminiscently** *adv.*

remiss /rɪˈmɪs/ *adj* [pred] ~ (**in sth**) (*fml*) careless of one's duty; lax: *You have been very remiss in fulfilling your obligations.* ○ *It was remiss of her to forget to pay the bill.* ▷ **remissly** *adv*: *act very remissly.* **remissness** *n* [U].

remission /rɪˈmɪʃn/ *n* **1** [U] pardoning or forgiveness of sins by God. **2** [U, C] (**a**) shortening of a prison sentence because of good behaviour: *get (a) remission of six months/six months' remission.* (**b**) freeing from a debt, payment, penalty, etc; exemption: *gain remission from tax payments* ○ *remission of exam fees.* **3** [U] lessening or weakening (of pain, disease, etc): *slight remission of a fever.*

remit /rɪˈmɪt/ *v* (**-tt-**) (*fml*) **1** [Tn esp passive] (**a**) refrain from inflicting (a punishment, etc): *His prison sentence has been remitted.* (**b**) cancel (a debt, payment, penalty, etc): *The taxes have been remitted.* ○ *Your fees cannot be remitted.* **2** [Tn] make (sth) less intense; relax: *We must not remit our efforts.* **3** [Tn, Dn·n, Dn·pr] ~ **sth (to sb)** send (money, etc) to a person or place, esp by post: *Remit a fee, cheque, payment, etc* ○ *Kindly remit us the balance without delay.* ○ *Remit the interest to her new address.* **4** [Tn·pr] ~ **sth to sb** (*law*) send back a case to a lower court: *The case has been remitted from the High Court to the County Court.*

▷ **remit** /rɪˈmɪt, ˈriːmɪt/ *n* **1** [C] item for consideration, eg by a committee. **2** [sing] subjects that a committee, enquiry, etc is supposed to deal with: *The question is not within the council's remit.*

remittance /-ns/ *n* **1** [U] remitting of money. **2** [C] sum of money remitted: *return the completed form with your remittance.*

remittent /rɪˈmɪtnt/ *adj* (of a fever or disease) becoming less severe at intervals.

remnant /ˈremnənt/ *n* **1** (often *pl*) (**a**) small remaining quantity or part or number of things or people: *remnants of a meal* ○ *the remnants of a shattered army.* (**b**) (*fig*) surviving trace of sth: *remnants of one's former glory.* ⇨ Usage at REST[3]. **2** small piece of cloth or carpet left over from a roll and sold at a reduced price: [attrib] *a remnant sale.*

remold (*US*) ⇨ RETREAD.

remonstrance /rɪˈmɒnstrəns/ *n* [U] (*fml*) remonstrating; protest.

remonstrate /ˈremənstreɪt; *US* rɪˈmɒnstreɪt/ *v* [Ipr] ~ **with sb**; ~ **against sth** (*fml*) make a protest or complaint about sb/sth: *I remonstrated with him about his rudeness.* ○ *remonstrate against cruelty to children.*

remorse /rɪˈmɔːs/ *n* [U] **1** ~ (**for sth**) sense of deep and bitter regret for having done sth wrong: *He was filled with remorse for having refused to visit his dying father.* ○ *In a fit of remorse she burnt all her lover's letters.* ○ *The prisoner shows no remorse for his crimes.* **2** mercy or pity; compunction (used esp with the *prep* shown): *The captives were shot without remorse.*

▷ **remorseful** /-fl/ *adj* filled with remorse(1): *a remorseful confession, mood.* **remorsefully** /-fəlɪ/ *adv.* **remorsefulness** *n* [U].

remorseless *adj* **1** without mercy or pity: *remorseless cruelty.* **2** that does not slacken; relentless: *a remorseless urge, ambition, etc.* **remorselessly** *adv*: *The police pursued the criminal remorselessly.* ○ *Drugs drove him remorselessly to an early death.*

remote /rɪˈməʊt/ *adj* (**-r, -st**) **1** (**a**) ~ (**from sth**) far away from other communities, houses, etc; isolated: *a remote region, village, farmhouse, etc* ○ *in the remotest* (ie most distant) *parts of Asia* ○ *in a house remote from any town or village.* (**b**) [attrib] far away in time: *in the remote past/future.* (**c**) [attrib] distant in relationship or kinship: *a remote ancestor of mine.* (**d**) ~ (**from sth**) separate (in feeling, interest, etc); not connected (with sth): *Your comments are rather remote from the subject we are discussing.* ○ *remote causes, effects, etc.* **2** (of a person or his manner) cold and unfriendly; aloof. **3** small; slight: *a remote possibility/chance* ○ *I haven't the remotest idea who did it.* ○ *The connection between the two events is remote.*

▷ **remotely** *adv* (usu in negative sentences) to a very small or slight degree: *It isn't remotely possible that you will be chosen to go.* ○ *The essay isn't even remotely relevant to the topic.* **remoteness** *n* [U].

□ **reˌmote conˈtrol** control of an apparatus, eg a model aircraft, car, etc, from a distance, usu by radio or electrical signals: *The bomb was exploded by remote control.* ○ *using the remote control to switch TV channels* ○ [attrib] *a remote-conˈtro* device.

re,mote 'sensing gathering of information about the earth's surface by the use of aerial photography, satellites, etc.

remould ⇨ RETREAD.

remount /ˌriːˈmaʊnt/ *v* **1** [I, Tn no passive] get on (a horse, bicycle, etc) again. **2** [Tn no passive] go up (a ladder, hill, etc) again. **3** [Tn] put (a picture, photograph, etc) on a new mount.

▷ **remount** /ˈriːmaʊnt/ *n* fresh horse for a rider.

remove[1] /rɪˈmuːv/ *v* **1** (*esp fml*) **(a)** [Tn, Tn·pr] ~ **sth/sb (from sth)** take sth/sb away from one place to another: *remove the dishes (from the table)* ○ *remove one's hand from sb's shoulder* ○ *The statue was removed to another site.* ○ *They were removed from the English class*, eg to have special lessons. **(b)** [Tn, Tn·pr] ~ **sb (from sth)** dismiss sb from a post, etc: *remove a diplomat from office* ○ *He was removed from his position as chairman.* **(c)** [Tn] take off (clothing, etc) from the body: *remove one's hat, coat, gloves, etc* ○ *remove the bandages/plaster from sb's arm.* **2** [Tn, Tn·pr] ~ **sth (from sth)** **(a)** get rid of sth by cleaning: *remove graffiti from the subway walls* ○ *Washo removes stains!* ○ *She removed her make-up with a tissue.* **(b)** cause sth to disappear; eliminate sth: *remove superfluous hair* ○ *(fig) remove problems, difficulties, objections, etc* ○ *remove doubts, fears, etc from sb's mind* ○ *The threat of redundancy was suddenly removed.* **3** [Ipr] ~ **(from sth)** (*fml*) go to live or work in another place; move: *We are removing from London to the country.* ○ *Our suppliers have removed to Liverpool.* **4** (idm) **once, twice, etc removed** (of cousins) belonging to a different generation: *a first cousin once removed*, ie a first cousin's child.

▷ **removable** /-əbl/ *adj* **(a)** that can be removed or detached: *This coffee-maker has two removable parts.* **(b)** [pred] (of a person) that can be dismissed from office.

removal /-vl/ *n* **1** [U] removing or being removed. **2** [C] transfer of furniture, etc to a different home: [attrib] *a re'moval van, firm, specialist, etc.*

removed *adj* [pred] ~ **(from sth)** (*fig*) distinct or different; remote: *an accent not far removed from Cockney* ○ *an explanation far removed from the truth.*

remover *n* **1** (in compounds) thing that removes sth: *a stain, paint, nail-varnish, etc remover.* **2** (*esp pl*) person or business that moves sb's furniture, etc, to a new house: *a firm of removers.*

remove[2] /rɪˈmuːv/ *n* **1** ~ **(from sth)** (*fml*) stage or degree of difference or distance (from sth): *Your story is several removes from the truth.* ○ *feel a child's suffering at one remove*, ie as a parent. **2** (*Brit*) class or division in some schools, esp for pupils of about 14.

remunerate /rɪˈmjuːnəreɪt/ *v* [Tn, Tn·pr] ~ **sb (for sth)** (*fml*) pay or reward sb for work or services.

▷ **remuneration** /rɪˌmjuːnəˈreɪʃn/ *n* [U] (*fml or rhet*) payment; reward.

remunerative /rɪˈmjuːnərətɪv; *US* -nəreɪtɪv/ *adj* profitable: *a highly remunerative job, post, position, etc.*

renaissance /rɪˈneɪsns; *US* ˈrenəsɑːns/ *n* **1 the Renaissance** [sing] (period of the) revival of art and literature in Europe in the 14th, 15th and 16th centuries, based on classical forms. The Italian city of Florence is usu considered to be the place where the Renaissance started, and people often concentrate on its influence on painting and the visual arts, but its effect on literature and intellectual life was just as great. It was inspired by a rejection of the styles and thought of the Middle Ages and a desire to return to the glories of ancient Greece and Rome. The painter Masaccio and the architect *Brunelleschi rediscovered classical rules of perspective, and Brunelleschi's churches resemble Roman temples rather than Gothic churches. Later 'Renaissance men' like Leonardo da *Vinci, *Michelangelo and *Raphael perfected a realistic style of painting besides using their talents in other fields like sculpture, architecture, poetry or scientific research. Scholars started to learn Greek as well as Latin, and to study new authors. In the religious world, this led to *Erasmus and others presenting a new view of the Bible, esp as a book that should be translated into the ordinary language of the people, and ultimately to the ideas of *Luther and the *Reformation: [attrib] *Renaissance art, literature, etc.* **2** [C] any similar revival: *Folk music is currently enjoying a renaissance.*

renal /ˈriːnl/ *adj* [usu attrib] (*anatomy*) of, in or near the kidneys: *a renal artery* ○ *renal dialysis.*

rename /ˌriːˈneɪm/ *v* [Tn, Cn·n] give a new name to (sb/sth); name again: *rename a street, a country, a racehorse* ○ *The ship was renamed ('Nimrod').*

renascent /rɪˈnæsnt/ *adj* (*fml*) becoming active again; reviving: *a renascent interest in medieval times.*

rend /rend/ *v* (*pt, pp* **rent** /rent/) (*arch or fml*) **1** [Tn, Tn·pr, Tn·p] tear (sth) apart forcibly; split: *rend one's garments*, eg (formerly) to show grief or frustration ○ *The tiger rent its prey to pieces.* ○ *a country rent in two by civil war* ○ *The stone was rent asunder/apart.* ○ *(fig) Loud cries rent the air.* ○ *heart-rending appeals for help.* **2** [Tn·pr] ~ **sb/sth (from sb/sth)** pull or wrench (sb/sth) violently: *Children were rent from their mothers' arms by the brutal soldiers.*

render /ˈrendə(r)/ *v* (*fml*) **1** [Tn, Tn·pr, Dn·n, Dn·pr] ~ **sth (for sth)**; ~ **sth (to sb)** give sth in return or exchange, or as sth which is due: *render homage, obedience, allegiance, etc* ○ *a reward for services rendered* ○ *render good for evil* ○ *render insult for insult* ○ *render sb a service/render a service to sb* ○ *render help to disaster victims* ○ *render thanks to God.* **2** [Tn] present or send in (an account) for payment: *account rendered £50.* **3** [Cn·a] cause (sb/sth) to be in a certain condition: *rendered helpless by an accident* ○ *Your action has rendered our contract invalid.* **4** [Tn esp passive] give a performance of (music, a play, a character, etc); give a portrayal of (sb/sth) in painting, etc: *The piano solo was well rendered.* ○ *'Othello' was rendered rather poorly.* ○ *The artist had rendered her gentle smile perfectly.* **5** [Tn, Tn·pr] ~ **sth (into sth)** express sth in another language; translate sth: *How would you render 'bon voyage' (into English)?* ○ *Rendering poetry into other languages is difficult.* **6** [Tn] cover (stone or brick) with a first layer of plaster: *render walls.* **7** (idm) **render an account of oneself, one's behaviour, etc** (*fml*) explain or justify what one has said, done, etc. **8** (phr v) **render sth down** make (eg fat, lard) liquid by heating it; melt sth down. **render sth up** (*fml*) hand over or surrender sth; yield sth: *render up a fort, town, etc to the enemy* ○ *(fig) He rendered up his soul to God*, ie died.

▷ **rendering** /ˈrendərɪŋ/ *n* **1** [C, U] (instance of) performing a piece of music or a dramatic role: *a moving rendering of a Brahms song* ○ *his rendering of Hamlet.* **2** [C, U] (instance of) translating (sth written): *a Spanish rendering/a rendering in Spanish of the original Arabic.* **3** [C] first layer of plaster (on stone or brick).

rendezvous /ˈrɒndɪvuː/ *n* (*pl* unchanged /-z/) **1** ~ **(with sb)** (place chosen for a) meeting at an agreed time: *arrange/make a rendezvous with Bill at the pub at two o'clock.* **2** place where people often meet: *This café is a rendezvous for writers and artists.*

▷ **rendezvous** *v* [I, Ipr] ~ **(with sb)** meet (sb) at a rendezvous: *The two platoons will rendezvous (with each other) in the woods as planned.*

rendition /renˈdɪʃn/ *n* (*fml*) way in which a dramatic role or piece of music, etc is performed; rendering: *give a spirited rendition of a Bach chorale.*

renegade /ˈrenɪgeɪd/ *n* (*fml derog*) **1** person that deserts a cause, political party, religious group, etc: [attrib] *a renegade priest, spy, soldier.* **2** any outlaw or rebel: *bands of renegades in the mountains.*

renege (also **renegue**) /rɪˈniːg, rɪˈneɪg/ *v* (*fml*) **1** [I, Ipr] ~ **(on sth)** fail to keep a promise, one's word, etc. **2** [I] (in card-games) revoke(2).

renew /rɪˈnjuː; *US* -ˈnuː/ *v* **1** [Tn] replace (sth) with sth new of the same kind: *renew worn tyres, bearings, brake-blocks, etc* ○ *renew the water in the goldfish bowl* ○ *renew* (ie replenish) *one's stock of coal* ○ *The light bulb needs renewing.* **2** [Tn esp passive] (*fig*) put new life and vigour into (sb/sth); restore: *work with renewed enthusiasm* ○ *The brandy renewed his strength/energy.* ○ *After praying, I felt spiritually renewed.* ○ *Her kindness made him regard her with renewed affection.* **3 (a)** [Tn] take up or begin (sth) again, eg after a break or pause; resume: *renew an attack* ○ *We renewed our journey the next day.* ○ *renewed outbreaks of terrorist violence* ○ *renew one's efforts/attempts to break a record.* **(b)** [Tn, Tn·pr] ~ **sth (with sb/sth)** make or form (sth) again; re-establish: *renew a friendship, relationship, acquaintance, etc* ○ *The pilot renewed contact with the control tower.* **(c)** [Tn] say or state sth again; reaffirm sth: *renew a request, complaint, criticism, protest* ○ *We renewed our marriage vows.* ○ *I renewed my offer of help.* **4** [Tn] arrange for (sth) to be valid without a break; extend: *renew a passport, permit, lease, contract* ○ *renew one's subscription to a journal, membership of a club, etc* ○ *renew one's library books* (ie extend the period during which one can borrow them) *for another week.*

▷ **renewable** /-əbl/ *adj* that can be renewed (RENEW 4): *Is the permit renewable?*

renewal /-ˈnjuːəl; *US* -ˈnuːəl/ *n* **1** [U] renewing or being renewed: *Any renewal of negotiations will be welcomed.* ○ *urban renewal*, eg clearing slums to build better housing ○ [attrib] *the renewal date*, eg of a library book, licence, lease, etc. **2** [C] act of renewing: *We've dealt with several renewals this week.*

rennet /ˈrenɪt/ *n* [U] substance used to curdle milk in making cheese and junket.

Renoir[1] /ˈrenwɑː(r), *also* rənˈwɑː(r)/ Jean (1894-1979), French film director. Works like *La Grande Illusion* and *La Règle du Jeu* display great realism and humanity, and his use of light makes him as much a visual artist as his father, the painter Auguste Renoir.

Renoir[2] /ˈrenwɑː(r), *also* rənˈwɑː(r)/ Pierre Auguste (1841-1919), French painter. He belonged to the *Impressionist movement, but had a very personal technique, using pure colours. He is famous for his cheerful subjects, esp his sensual nudes.

renounce /rɪˈnaʊns/ *v* (*fml*) **1** [Tn] **(a)** agree to give up ownership or possession of (sth), esp formally: *renounce a claim, title, right, privilege.* **(b)** give up (esp a habit) voluntarily; abandon: *renounce strong drink, cigarettes, dangerous driving* ○ *They've renounced their old criminal way of life.* ○ *I soon renounced all thought of getting home before dark.* **2** [Tn, Tn·pr] ~ **sb/sth (for sth)** reject or stop following sb/sth; repudiate sb/sth: *renounce Satan and all his works* ○ *renounce terrorism, drugs, etc* ○ *renounce a treaty, an agreement, etc* ○ *renounce one's earlier ideals, principles, convictions, etc* ○ *She renounced Islam for/in favour of Christianity.* **3** [Tn] refuse to associate with or acknowledge (esp sth/sb with a claim to one's care, affection, etc): *renounce a friendship* ○ *He renounced his son (as an unworthy heir).*

▷ **renouncement** *n* [U] = RENUNCIATION 1.

renovate /ˈrenəveɪt/ *v* [Tn] restore (esp old buildings) to good condition.

▷ **renovation** /ˌrenəˈveɪʃn/ *n* **1** [U] renovating or being renovated: *be under renovation* ○ *The college is closed for renovation.* ○ [attrib] *renovation works, plans, schemes.* **2** [C usu pl] act of renovating: *The castle will undergo extensive and costly renovations.*

renovator /-tə(r)/ *n.*

renown /rɪˈnaʊn/ *n* [U] (*fml*) fame or distinction: *win renown (as a singer)* ○ *an artist of great renown.*

▷ **renowned** *adj* ~ **(as/for sth)** famous; celebrated: *renowned as an actress/for her acting.*

rent[1] /rent/ *n* **1** [U, C] regular payment made for the use of land, premises, a telephone, machinery, etc; sum paid in this way: *owe three weeks' rent/be* *three weeks behind with the rent* ○ *live in a house free of rent*, ie without paying rent ○ *Non-payment of rent can mean eviction.* ○ *pay a high/low rent for farming land* ○ *Rents are going up again.* ○ [attrib] *a rent book, agreement, collector.* **2** (idm) **for rent** (*esp US*) available to be rented.

▷ **rent** *v* **1** [Tn, Tn·pr] ~ **sth (from sb)** pay for the occupation or use of (land, premises, a telephone, machinery, etc): *rent a holiday cottage from an agency* ○ *Do you own or rent your video?* **2** [Tn, Tn·pr, Tn·p, Dn·n] ~ **sth (out) (to sb)** allow sb to occupy or use (land, premises, a telephone, machinery, etc) in return for payment: *Mr Hill rents this land (out) to us at £500 a year.* ○ *Will you rent me this television?* ⇨ Usage at LET². **3** [I, Ipr] ~ **(at/for sth)** be let at a specified rent: *The building rents at £3 000 a year.* ○ (*US*) *an apartment renting for 900 a month.* **4** (idm) **rent-a-sth** (*joc derog*) (used to imply that sth is easily available, esp in return for payment, and has no real importance or value): *His speech was attended by the usual rent-a-crowd of hired supporters.* **rentable** *adj* that can be rented or that yields a rent.

rental /ˈrentl/ *n* **1** [C] **(a)** amount of rent paid or received: *pay a telephone rental of £20 a quarter*. **(b)** (*esp US*) thing, eg a house, that is rented. **2** [U] renting: [attrib] *rental charges.* ˈ**rental library** (*US*) library that charges readers for borrowing books.

□ ˈ**rent-boy** *n* (*sl*) young homosexual prostitute.

ˌ**rent-ˈfree** *adj, adv* for which no rent is charged: *a ˌrent-free ˈhouse* ○ *occupy rooms rent-free.*

ˈ**rent rebate** (*Brit*) rebate of rent payable, given by a local authority to low wage-earners, esp council tenants.

rent² /rent/ *n* torn place in cloth, etc; tear; split: (*fig*) *The sun shone through a rent in the clouds.*

rent³ *pt, pp* of REND.

renunciation /rɪˌnʌnsɪˈeɪʃn/ *n* **1** [U] (also **renouncement**) (formal declaration of) giving sth/sb up; renouncing: *the king's renunciation of the throne.* **2** [U] habit of renouncing things; self-denial: *the virtues of renunciation.*

reopen /ˌriːˈəʊpən/ *v* [I, Tn] (cause sth to) open again after closing or being closed for a while: *School/Parliament reopens next week.* ○ *reopen a shop under a new name* ○ *reopen a discussion/debate/dialogue* ○ *The murder inquiry/case/trial was reopened.* ○ (*fig*) *reopen old wounds*, ie cause suffering by referring to painful experiences, disagreements, etc in the past.

reorder /ˌriːˈɔːdə(r)/ *v* **1** [I, Tn] order (sth) again; order fresh supplies of (sth). **2** [Tn] put (sth) in a new order; rearrange: *reorder the furniture.*

▷ **reorder** *n* demand for more or fresh supplies: *put in a reorder for Oxford dictionaries* ○ [attrib] *a reˈorder form.*

reorganize, -ise /ˌriːˈɔːɡənaɪz/ *v* [I, Tn] organize (sth) again or in a new way. ▷ **reorganization, -isation** /ˌriːˌɔːɡənaɪˈzeɪʃn; *US* -nɪˈz-/ *n* [U, C].

rep¹ (also **repp**) /rep/ *n* [U] textile fabric with a corded effect, used in upholstery and curtains.

rep² /rep/ *n* (*infml*) = REPRESENTATIVE *n* 2: *working as a rep for a printing firm.*

rep³ /rep/ *n* (*infml*) = REPERTORY: *act/appear in rep.*

Rep *abbr* (*US*) **1** Representative (in Congress). **2** Republican (party). Cf DEM.

repaid *pt, pp* of REPAY.

repair¹ /rɪˈpeə(r)/ *v* [Tn] **1** restore (sth damaged or badly worn) to good condition: *repair a road, puncture, watch, shirt.* **2** put right or make amends for (sth); remedy: *repair an error, omission, etc* ○ *repair a broken marriage* ○ *Can the damage to international relations be repaired?* Cf FIX¹ 4, MEND 1.

▷ **repair** *n* **1** [U] restoring or being restored to good condition: *a road under repair* ○ *The vase was (damaged) beyond repair*, ie could not be repaired. ○ [attrib] *a bike repair shop.* **2** [C usu *pl*] ~ **(to sth)** act or result of repairing: *The shop is closed for repairs*, ie while repair work is being done. ○ *Heel repairs while you wait*, eg in a shoe shop. **3** (idm) **in good, bad, etc reˈpair; in a good, bad, etc state of reˈpair** in good, bad, etc condition: *keep a car in good repair* ○ *The house is in a shocking state of repair.*

repairable /-rəbl/ *adj* that can be repaired.

repairer *n* person who repairs things: *a watch repairer.*

□ **reˈpair man** (*esp US*) man who repairs things, esp a motor mechanic.

repair² /rɪˈpeə(r)/ *v* [Ipr] ~ **to...** (*fml or rhet*) visit, esp frequently or in large numbers: *repair to seaside resorts in the summer* ○ *Let's repair to the pub.*

reparable /ˈrepərəbl/ *adj* (*fml*) (of a loss, etc) that can be made good. Cf REPAIRABLE (REPAIR¹).

reparation /ˌrepəˈreɪʃn/ *n* (*fml*) **1** [U] ~ **(for sth)** compensating for damage; making amends for loss: *make reparation (to God) for one's sins.* **2 reparations** [pl] compensation for war damages, demanded from a defeated enemy: *exact heavy reparations.*

repartee /ˌrepɑːˈtiː/ *n* [U] **1** (skill in making) sharp clever retorts: *be good at (the art of) repartee.* **2** conversation, dialogue, etc consisting of such retorts: *indulge in brilliant, witty, etc repartee* ○ *The repartee flew back and forth across the dinner table.*

repast /rɪˈpɑːst; *US* rɪˈpæst/ *n* (*fml*) meal: *partake of a light, sumptuous, etc repast.*

repatriate /riːˈpætrɪeɪt; *US* -ˈpeɪt-/ *v* [Tn, Tn·pr] ~ **sb (to sth)** send or bring sb back to his own country: *repatriate refugees, prisoners-of-war, immigrants, etc to their homeland.* ▷ **repatriation** /ˌriːpætrɪˈeɪʃn; *US* riːˌpeɪt-/ *n* [U].

repay /rɪˈpeɪ/ *v* (*pt, pp* **repaid** /rɪˈpeɪd/) **1** **(a)** [Tn, Dn·n, Dn·pr] ~ **sth (to sb)** pay (money) back; refund sth: *repay a debt, mortgage, loan, etc* ○ *If you lend me £2, I'll repay it (to you) tomorrow.* **(b)** [Tn, Dn·n] pay (sb) back; reimburse: *Has she repaid you (the £2)?* **2** [Tn, Tn·pr] ~ **sb (for sth);** ~ **sth (with sth)** give sb sth in return (for a service); reward sb/sth: *How can I ever repay (you for) your kindness?* ○ *The firm repaid her hard work with a bonus.*

▷ **repayable** /-əbl/ *adj* that can or must be repaid.

repayment *n* **1** [U] repaying: *bonds due for repayment* ○ *repayment for your services, efforts.* **2** [C] thing repaid: *make two more repayments to clear the debt* ○ *Repayments can be spread over two years.* ○ *mortgage/loan repayments.*

repeal /rɪˈpiːl/ *v* [Tn] withdraw (a law, etc) officially; revoke. ▷ **repeal** *n* [U].

repeat /rɪˈpiːt/ *v* **1** **(a)** [Tn, Tf, Tw] say or write (sth) again once or more than once; reiterate: *I repeat: the runway is not clear for take-off.* ○ *repeat a comment, promise, demand* ○ *Am I repeating myself?* ie Did I say this before? ○ *She repeated what she had said.* **(b)** [Tn] do or make (sth) again once or more than once: *repeat an action, attempt, attack* ○ *Such bargain offers can't be repeated.* ○ *She repeated the waltz as an encore*, eg at a piano recital. **(c)** [I, Tn] ~ **(itself)** occur again once or more than once: *a repeating decimal* ○ *Does history/the past repeat itself?* ie Do similar events or situations recur? **2** **(a)** [Tn, Tw] say aloud (sth heard or learnt by heart); recite: *Repeat the oath after me.* ○ *He repeated her statement word for word.* **(b)** [Tn, Tw, Dn·pr, Dpr·w] ~ **sth (to sb)** tell sb else (sth one has heard or been told): *His language won't bear repeating*, eg because it's too obscene. ○ *Don't repeat what I said (to anyone) — it's confidential.* **3** [I, Ipr] ~ **(on sb)** (of food) continue to be tasted from time to time after being eaten, esp as a result of belching: *Do you find that onions repeat (on you)?* **4** [Tn] (*commerce*) supply a further consignment of (sth): *repeat an order, a deal.*

▷ **repeat** *n* [C] **1** act of repeating; thing repeated: *a second, etc repeat of a broadcast, TV series, etc* ○ [attrib] *a repeat performance, showing* ○ (*commerce*) *a repeat order*, ie for another consignment of the same goods. **2** (*music*) mark indicating a passage that is to be repeated.

repeatable *adj* [usu pred] that can be repeated: *His comments are not repeatable*, eg because they were rude, obscene, etc.

repeated *adj* [attrib] done, said or occurring again and again: *repeated blows, warnings, accidents.*

repeatedly *adv* again and again: *He begged her repeatedly to stop.*

repeater *n* (*dated*) **1** revolver or rifle that can b fired many times without being reloaded. **2** watc or clock that can strike the last quarter hour o hour again. **3** device that repeats a signal.

repel /rɪˈpel/ *v* (**-ll-**) **1** [Tn] drive (sb/sth) back o away; repulse: *repel an attacker, attack, invasion* (*fig*) *The surface repels moisture*, ie does not allov it to penetrate. **2** [Tn] refuse to accept (sb/sth) spurn: *She repelled him/his advances*, i discouraged him/them. ○ *She repelled all offers o help.* **3** [I, Tn] push (sth) away from itself by a unseen force: *North magnetic poles repel (eac other).* **4** [I, Tn] cause a feeling of distaste o disgust in (sb/sth): *Gratuitous violence repels (mos people).* ○ *His greasy hair repelled her.*

▷ **repellent** /-ənt/ *adj* **1** ~ **(to sb)** arousin distaste or disgust; repulsive: *the repellent smell o rotting meat* ○ *I find his selfishness repellent.* ○ *Th very idea of sniffing glue is repellent to me.* **2** tha cannot be penetrated by a specified substance: *water-repellent fabric.* — *n* [U] **1** chemical tha repels insects: *Rub some of this mosquito-repellen on your legs.* **2** substance used to make fabric leather, etc waterproof.

repent /rɪˈpent/ *v* **1** [I, Ipr, Tn, Tg] ~ **(of sth)** (*fm esp religion*) feel regret or sorrow about (sth on has done or failed to do): *Repent (of your sins) an ask God's forgiveness.* ○ *He bitterly repented hi folly.* ○ *I repent having been so generous to tha scoundrel.* **2** (idm) **marry in haste, repent a leisure** ⇨ MARRY.

▷ **repentance** /-əns/ *n* [U] ~ **(for sth)** regret o sorrow for wrongdoing: *show signs of repentance*

repentant /-ənt/ *adj* ~ **(of sth)** feeling or showin repentance: *a repentant sinner, expression, mood repentant of his folly.*

repercussion /ˌriːpəˈkʌʃn/ *n* **1** [C usu *pl*] indirec effect or result (esp unpleasant) of an event, etc consequence: *His resignation will have seriou repercussions on/for the firm.* ○ *the endles repercussions of living on credit.* **2** **(a)** [U] reco after an impact. **(b)** [C] thing thrown back, esp sound; echo.

repertoire /ˈrepətwɑː(r)/ *n* all the plays, songs pieces, etc which a company, actor, musician, et knows and is prepared to perform: *extend one repertoire*, ie learn sth new ○ *That tune is not in m repertoire.* ○ (*fig*) *He has a wide repertoire of dirt jokes.*

repertory /ˈrepətrɪ; *US* -tɔːrɪ/ (also *infml* **rep**) **1** [U] performance of various plays for shor periods by one company (instead of one play for long time with changes of cast): *act/work i repertory* ○ *play repertory for two years* ○ [attrib] *repertory actor.* ⇨ article at PERFORMING ARTS **2** [C] (*fml*) = REPERTOIRE.

□ ˈ**repertory company** permanent company i which each actor plays a variety of parts in number of plays.

ˈ**repertory theatre** theatre in which repertory i performed.

repetition /ˌrepɪˈtɪʃn/ *n* **1** **(a)** [U] repeating o being repeated: *learn by repetition.* **(b)** [C] act o repeating; recurrence: *after numerous repetition* ○ *Let there be no repetition of this behaviour*, i Don't do it again. **2** [C] copy or replica: *a repetitio of a previous talk.*

▷ **repetitious** /ˌrepɪˈtɪʃəs/, **repetitive** /rɪˈpetətɪv *adjs* (*usu derog*) characterized by repetition: *repetitive job, tune* ○ *repetitive questions complaints, etc.* **repetitiously**, **repetitively** *adj* **repetitiousness, repetitiveness** *ns* [U].

rephrase /ˌriːˈfreɪz/ *v* [Tn] say (sth) again i different words, esp to make the meaning cleare *rephrase a remark, question, point, etc.*

repine /rɪˈpaɪn/ *v* [I, Ipr] ~ **(at/against sth)** (*fm* feel or show discontent; fret: *repine at one misfortune* ○ *repine against Fate.*

replace /rɪˈpleɪs/ *v* **1** [Tn] put (sth) back in it place: *replace the book on the shelf* ○ *replace th receiver*, ie after telephoning. **2** [Tn, Cn·n/a] tak the place of (sb/sth): *Robots are replacing people o assembly lines.* ○ *Can anything replace a mother love?* ○ *His deputy replaced him as leader.* **3** [Tı

Tn·pr] ~ **sb/sth (with sb/sth)** provide a substitute for sb/sth: *He is inefficient and must be replaced.* ○ *replace a broken window (with a new one).*

▷ **replaceable** /-əbl/ *adj* that can be replaced.

replacement *n* **1** [U] replacing or being replaced: *the replacement of worn parts.* **2** [C] ~ **(for sb/sth)** person or thing that replaces another: *find a replacement for Sue* (ie sb to do her work) *while she is ill* ○ [attrib] *replacement staff.*

replant /ˌriːˈplɑːnt; *US* -ˈplænt/ *v* **1** [Tn] plant (eg a crop) again. **2** [I, Ipr, Tn, Tn·pr] ~ **(sth) (with sth)** plant (eg a field) again with a different crop, new trees, etc: *I'm replanting with a more resistant variety.*

replay /ˌriːˈpleɪ/ *v* [Tn] **1** play (eg a football match that was drawn) again. **2** play (sth recorded) again on a tape-recorder, video recorder, etc.

▷ **replay** /ˈriːpleɪ/ *n* **1** replayed match. **2** replaying of a recorded incident or sequence in a game, etc: *an action replay of a penalty kick.*

replenish /rɪˈplenɪʃ/ *v* **1** [Tn, Tn·pr] ~ **sth (with sth)** fill sth again: *Let me replenish your glass*, eg with more wine. ○ *replenish one's wardrobe.* **2** [Tn] get a further supply of (sth): *replenish one's stocks of pet food, timber, notepaper, light bulbs.* ▷ **replenishment** *n* [U].

replete /rɪˈpliːt/ *adj* [pred] ~ **(with sth)** (*fml*) **1** well-fed or full; gorged: *lions replete with their kill* ○ *feel replete after a large meal.* **2** well stocked or supplied: *a house replete with every modern convenience.*

▷ **repletion** /rɪˈpliːʃn/ *n* [U] (*fml*) state of being replete(1): *be full to repletion.*

replica /ˈreplɪkə/ *n* **(a)** exact copy, esp one made by an artist of one of his own pictures, etc. **(b)** model, esp one made on a smaller scale: *make a replica of the Eiffel Tower.*

▷ **replicate** /ˈreplɪkeɪt/ *v* [Tn] (*fml*) be or make a copy of (sth); reproduce: *The chameleon's skin changes to replicate the pattern of its surroundings.*

replication /ˌreplɪˈkeɪʃn/ *n* [U].

reply /rɪˈplaɪ/ *v* (*pt, pp* **replied**) **(a)** [I, Ipr, Tf] ~ **(to sb/sth)**; ~ **(with sth)** say or make an answer, in speech or writing; respond: *fail to reply to a question, letter, accusation* ○ *I replied with a short note.* ○ *'Certainly not,' she replied.* ○ *He replied that he was busy.* **(b)** [I, Ipr] ~ **(to/with sth)** give an answer in the form of an action; respond: *He replied with a nod.* ○ *The enemy replied to our fire*, ie fired back at us.

▷ **reply** *n* **1** [U] act of replying: *She made no reply.* ○ *What did he do in reply to your challenge?* **2** [C] what is replied; response: *get/have/receive several replies to an advertisement* ○ [attrib] *a reply-paid telegram, envelope, etc*, ie paid for by the sender or addressee. Cf ANSWER[1].

report[1] /rɪˈpɔːt/ *v* **1** [I, Ipr, Tn, Tn·pr, Tw, Tg, Tsg, Cn·a] ~ **(on sb/sth) (to sb/sth)**; ~ **sth (to sb)** give a spoken or written account of (sth heard, seen, done, studied, etc); describe: *report on recent developments* ○ *report (on) progress made* ○ *report a debate, strike, kidnapping* ○ *Tom reported his discoveries to the professor.* ○ *I reported how he had reacted.* ○ *She reported (his) having seen the gunman.* ○ *The doctor reported the patient fit and well.* **2 (a)** [Tn, Tf, Tnt, Tg, Tsg, Cn·a] make (sth) known, esp by publishing or broadcasting; announce: *Police reported the closure of the road/that the road was closed.* ○ *The poll reported Labour to be leading.* ○ *They reported sighting the plane.* ○ *The judge reported the case closed.* **(b)** [I, Ipr] ~ **(for sth)** work as a reporter: *report for the Times, the BBC, etc.* **3** [Tn, Tn·pr] ~ **sb (for sth)**; ~ **sb/sth (to sb)** make a formal complaint or accusation about (an offence or offender): *report an official for insolence* ○ *report a burglary, car crash, fraud, etc to the police* ○ *report sb/sb's lateness to the manager.* **4 (a)** [I, Ipr] ~ **(to sb/sth) for sth** present oneself as arrived, returned, ready for work, etc: *report to the receptionist/reception* (eg in a hotel) *for one's room key* ○ *report for duty at 7 am.* **(b)** [La, Cn·n/a] declare or show oneself or sb to be in a certain state or place: *report sick, absent, fit* ○ *The child was reported missing* (ie was said to have disappeared) *on Friday.* ○ *The officer reported his men in position.* **5** [Ipr] ~ **to sb/sth** be responsible to a certain person or department that supervises one's work: *All representatives report (directly) to the sales department.* **6** (phr v) **report back (from sth)** return: *The officer reported back from leave on Sunday night.* **report back (to sb/sth)** give a spoken or written account of sb/sth one has been asked to investigate: *He was requested to report back to the committee about/on the complaint.*

▷ **reportage** /ˌrepɔːˈtɑːʒ, *also* rɪˈpɔːtɪdʒ/ *n* [U] (typical style of) reporting news for the media: *the skilful reportage of sports journalists.*

reportedly *adv* according to reports (REPORT 1): *The star is reportedly very ill.*

reporter *n* person who reports news for the media: *press/TV/radio reporters* ○ *an on-the-spot reporter*, ie one who is at the scene of the event. Cf JOURNALIST (JOURNAL).

□ **reˌported ˈspeech** = INDIRECT SPEECH (INDIRECT).

report[2] /rɪˈpɔːt/ *n* **1** [C] spoken or written account of sth heard, seen, done, studied, etc, esp one that is published or broadcast: *reliable, conflicting, detailed reports* ○ *positive/negative reports* ○ *produce, submit, draw up regular progress reports* ○ *a report on the state of the roads*, eg from an automobile association ○ *a firm's annual, monthly, etc reports*, ie on its profitability ○ *ˈlaw reports*, ie written records of trials, etc in the lawcourts ○ *radio/TV/press reports on the crash.* **2** [C] (*Brit*) periodical written statement about a pupil's or an employee's work and conduct: *a ˈschool report* ○ *get a good report from one's boss.* **3 (a)** [U] (*fml*) common talk or rumour: *Report has it that...*, ie People are saying that.... **(b)** [C] piece of gossip: *I have only reports to go on.* **4** [U] (*fml*) way in which sb/sth is spoken of; repute: *be of good/bad report.* **5** [C] explosive sound, like that of a gun being fired: *the sharp report of a pistol, firework, etc* ○ *The tyre burst with a loud report.*

□ **reˈport card** (*US*) school report.

repose[1] /rɪˈpəʊz/ *v* (*fml*) **1** [I] rest; lie: *repose from toil* ○ *The picture shows a nude reposing on a couch.* ○ *Beneath this stone repose the poet's mortal remains*, ie lies the poet's corpse. **2** [Tn·pr] ~ **sth on sb/sth** lay (an arm, etc) on sb/sth for support: *repose one's head on a cushion.*

▷ **repose** *n* [U] (*fml*) **1** rest; sleep: *disturb sb's repose* ○ *Her face is sad in repose.* **2 (a)** peaceful state; tranquillity: *win repose after months of suffering.* **(b)** ease of manner; composure: *He lacks repose.*

reposeful /-fl/ *adj* calm; quiet.

repose[2] /rɪˈpəʊz/ *v* [Tn·pr] ~ **sth in sth/sb** (*fml*) place (trust, etc) in sb/sth: *He reposed too much confidence in her/her promises.*

repository /rɪˈpɒzɪtrɪ; *US* -tɔːrɪ/ *n* **1** place where things are stored or may be found, esp a warehouse or museum: *a furniture repository.* **2** (*fig*) person or book that receives and stores confidences, secrets, information, etc: *My father is a repository of interesting facts.* ○ *My diary is the repository of all my hopes and plans.*

repossess /ˌriːpəˈzes/ *v* [Tn] regain possession of (esp hire-purchase goods or mortgaged property on which repayments have not been kept up): *repossess furniture* ○ *repossess a flat, site, smallholding, etc.* ▷ **repossession** /ˌriːpəˈzeʃn/ *n* [U].

repp = REP[1].

reprehend /ˌreprɪˈhend/ *v* [Tn] (*fml*) criticize or rebuke (sb or sb's behaviour).

▷ **reprehensible** /ˌreprɪˈhensəbl/ *adj* (*fml*) deserving to be reprehended: *Your conduct/attitude is most reprehensible.* **reprehensibly** /-səblɪ/ *adv.*

represent[1] /ˌreprɪˈzent/ *v* **1** [Tn, Cn·n/a] make an image of or show (sb/sth) in a picture, sculpture or play; depict: *The picture represents a hunting scene.* ○ *The king is represented as a villain in the play.* **2** [Tn, Cn·n/a, Cn·t] describe (sb/sth), often misleadingly, as having a certain character or qualities: *Why do you represent the matter in this way?* ○ *He represented himself as an expert.* ○ *The risks were represented as negligible.* ○ *I am not what you represent me to be.* **3** [Tn, Tf, Dn·pr, Dpr·f] ~ **sth (to sb)** (*fml*) state sth as a protest or appeal: *represent the rashness of a plan, the seriousness of an accusation* ○ *They represented their grievances to the Governor.* ○ *The barrister represented to the court that the defendant was mentally unstable.* **4** [Tn] **(a)** stand for or be a symbol or equivalent of (sb/sth); symbolize: *Phonetic symbols represent sounds.* ○ *What does x represent in this equation?* ○ *The rose represents England.* **(b)** be an example or embodiment of (sth); typify: *This quartet represents a major new trend in modern music.* ○ *Fonteyn represents the best traditions of ballet.* **5** [Tn] be the result of (sth); correspond to: *This new car represents years of research.* ○ *A wage rise of 5% represents an annual increase of £250 for the lowest-paid workers.* **6 (a)** [Tn esp passive] act as a substitute or deputy for (sb): *The Queen was represented at the funeral by the British ambassador.* **(b)** [Tn, Dpr·f] act as a spokesman for (sb): *Members* (ie of Parliament) *representing Welsh constituencies* ○ *Our firm is represented in India by Mr Hall.* ○ *Who is representing you* (ie acting as your lawyer) *in the case?* ○ *He represented to the court that the accused was very remorseful.*

▷ **representation** /ˌreprɪzenˈteɪʃn/ *n* **1** [U] act of representing or state of being represented: *The firm needs more representation in China.* ○ *effective representation* (ie in Parliament) *of voters' interests.* **2** [C] (*fml*) thing, esp a picture, sculpture or play, that represents sb/sth: *stained-glass representations of saints* ○ *an unusual representation of Hamlet.* **3** (idm) **make representations to sb** (*fml*) protest or appeal to sb (about sth): *make representations to the council about the state of the roads* ○ *The ambassador made forceful representations to the White House.*

represent[2] /ˌriːprɪˈzent/ *v* [Tn] submit (a cheque, bill, etc) again for payment.

representative /ˌreprɪˈzentətɪv/ *adj* **1** ~ **(of sb/sth) (a)** serving to show or portray a class or group: *Is a questionnaire answered by 500 people truly representative of national opinion?* **(b)** containing examples of a number of types: *a representative sample, selection, survey, etc* ○ *a representative collection of British insects.* **2** consisting of elected deputies; based on representation by these: *representative elections, governments, institutions.*

▷ **representative** *n* ~ **(of sb/sth)** **1** typical example of a class or group: *Many representatives of the older generation were there.* **2** (also *infml* **rep**) (*commerce*) agent of a firm, esp a travelling salesman: *act as sole representatives of XYZ Oil.* **3 (a)** person chosen or appointed to represent[1](6) another or others; delegate: *the Queen's representative at the ceremony* ○ *send a representative to the negotiations.* **(b)** person elected to represent others in a legislative body: *our representative* (ie MP) *in the House of Commons.*

repress /rɪˈpres/ *v* [Tn] **1 (a)** [Tn] restrain or suppress (an impulse); check: *repress an urge to scream* ○ *repress a sneeze, smile, cough* ○ *He repressed his natural sexual desires as sinful.* **(b)** (usu passive) cause (sb) to restrain or suppress emotion, thoughts, etc: *His childhood was repressed and solitary.* **2 (a)** prevent (a revolt, etc) from breaking out; quell: *All protest is brutally repressed by the regime.* **(b)** prevent (sb) from protesting or rioting; subjugate: *The dictator represses all opposition as illegal.*

▷ **repressed** *adj* suffering from suppression of the emotions.

repression /rɪˈpreʃn/ *n* **1** [U] repressing or being repressed. **2** (*psychology*) **(a)** [U] action of forcing desires and urges, esp those in conflict with accepted standards of conduct, into the unconscious mind, often resulting in abnormal behaviour: *sexual repression.* **(b)** [C] desire or urge repressed in this way.

repressive /rɪˈpresɪv/ *adj* tending to repress; harsh or severe: *a repressive regime, tendency, law*

○ *Parliament condemned the repressive measures taken by the police.* **repressively** *adj.* **repressiveness** *n* [U].

reprieve /rɪˈpriːv/ *v* [Tn] **1** postpone or cancel a punishment for (sb), esp the death sentence: *reprieve a condemned prisoner.* **2** *(fig)* give temporary relief from danger, trouble, etc to (sb/sth): *The tree that was due to be cut down has been reprieved for six months.*

▷ **reprieve** *n* **1 (a)** [U] postponement or cancellation of a punishment, esp the death sentence: *the reprieve of the hostages.* **(b)** [C] order for this to happen: *grant (sb) a reprieve/a reprieve to sb* ○ *The prisoner won a last-minute reprieve.* **2** [U, C] *(fig)* temporary relief from danger, trouble, etc.

reprimand /ˈreprɪmɑːnd; *US* -mænd/ *v* [Tn, Tn·pr] ~ **sb (for sth)** rebuke sb (for a fault, etc), esp officially.

▷ **reprimand** *n* [C, U] rebuke, esp an official one: *receive a stiff, severe, sharp, etc reprimand* ○ *His negligence passed without reprimand.*

reprint /ˌriːˈprɪnt/ *v* **(a)** [Tn] print (a book, etc) again, with few or no changes. **(b)** [I] (of a book, etc) be printed again: *The dictionary is reprinting with minor corrections.*

▷ **reprint** /ˈriːprɪnt/ *n* **(a)** reprinting or new impression of a book with few or no changes: *The work is into its third reprint.* **(b)** such a reprinted book. Cf EDITION.

reprisal /rɪˈpraɪzl/ *n* [C, U] (act of) returning an injury, esp political or military, done to oneself; retaliation: *suffer heavy reprisals* ○ *take reprisals against terrorism* ○ *Civilian targets were bombed in reprisal (for the raid).*

reprise /rɪˈpriːz/ *n (music)* passage that repeats an earlier one.

▷ **reprise** *v (music)* [Tn] play (eg a musical theme) as a reprise.

reproach /rɪˈprəʊtʃ/ *v* [Tn, Tn·pr] **(a)** ~ **sb/oneself (for sth)** criticize sb/oneself, esp for failing to do sth: *She reproached him for forgetting their anniversary.* ○ *I have nothing to reproach myself for,* ie that I need regret. **(b)** ~ **sb/oneself (with sth)** name a fault as a reason for criticizing sb/oneself: *reproach the government with neglect.*

▷ **reproach** *n* **1 (a)** [U] reproaching: *a word, look, sigh of reproach.* **(b)** [C] word, remark, etc that reproaches: *heap reproaches on sb.* **2 (a)** [U] *(fml)* state of disgrace or discredit: *bring reproach upon oneself.* **(b)** [sing] ~ **(to sb/sth)** person or thing that disgraces or discredits sb/sth: *Poverty is/The poor are a constant reproach to our society.* **3** (idm) **above/beyond reproach** perfect; blameless: *Her manners are above reproach.*

reproachful /-fl/ *adj* expressing reproach(1): *a reproachful look, remark, sigh.* **reproachfully** /-fəlɪ/ *adv.*

reprobate /ˈreprəbeɪt/ *adj, n* [attrib] *(fml or joc)* immoral or unprincipled (person): *have reprobate tendencies* ○ *You sinful old reprobate!* ○ *He has always been a bit of a reprobate.*

reproduce /ˌriːprəˈdjuːs; *US* -ˈduːs/ *v* **1** [Tn] make a copy of (a picture, etc): *This copier can reproduce colour photographs.* **2** [Tn·pr] ~ **sth (as sth)** cause sth to be seen or heard again, or to occur again: *a portrait that reproduces every detail of the sitter's face* ○ *Her stereo system reproduces every note perfectly.* ○ *Can this effect by reproduced in a laboratory?* ○ *The computer reproduced the data as a set of diagrams.* **3** [I] have a specified quality when copied: *Some colours reproduce well/badly.* **4** [I, Tn] (of humans, animals, insects, etc) produce (offspring) by natural means: *Ferns reproduce (themselves) by spores.*

▷ **reproducible** /-əbl/ *adj* that can be reproduced.

reproduction /ˌriːprəˈdʌkʃn/ *n* **1** [U] reproducing or being reproduced: *Compact disc recordings give excellent sound reproduction.* **2** [U] process of reproducing (REPRODUCE 4): *study reproduction in shellfish.* **3** [C] thing reproduced, esp a copy of a work of art: *Is that painting an original or a reproduction?* ○ [attrib] *reproduction furniture,* ie made in imitation of an earlier style.

reproductive /ˌriːprəˈdʌktɪv/ *adj* of or for reproduction of offspring: *reproductive organs, systems, urges.*

reproof /rɪˈpruːf/ *n* [C, U] *(fml)* (remark, etc expressing) blame or disapproval: *administer a stern reproof* ○ *conduct deserving a stern reproof* ○ *Tom swept up the broken glass without a word of reproof to his son.*

reprove /rɪˈpruːv/ *v* [Tn, Tn·pr] ~ **sb (for sth)** *(fml)* blame or rebuke sb; censure: *The priest reproved people for not coming to church.*

▷ **reproving** *adj* [usu attrib] expressing reproof: *a reproving glance, remark, etc.* **reprovingly** *adv.*

reptile /ˈreptaɪl; *US* -tl/ *n* any of the class of cold-blooded, egg-laying animals including lizards, tortoises, crocodiles, snakes, etc with relatively short legs or no legs at all.

▷ **reptilian** /repˈtɪlɪən/ *adj, n* (of or like a) reptile.

republic /rɪˈpʌblɪk/ *n* (country with a) system of government in which supreme power is held not by a monarch but by the (elected representatives of the) people, with an elected President: *a constitutional republic,* eg the USA. Cf MONARCHY (MONARCH).

republican /rɪˈpʌblɪkən/ *adj* of or like a republic; supporting the principles of a republic: *a republican movement, party, government* ○ *republican sympathies.*

▷ **republican** *n* **1** person favouring republican government. **2 Republican** member of one of the two main political parties in the US. Cf DEMOCRAT 2.

republicanism /-ɪzəm/ *n* [U] (support for) republican principles.

□ **the Reˈpublican Party** one of the two main political parties in the USA. Cf DEMOCRATIC PARTY (DEMOCRATIC).

repudiate /rɪˈpjuːdɪeɪt/ *v* [Tn] **1** refuse to have any more to do with (sb); disown: *repudiate a son, lover, former friend, etc.* **2 (a)** refuse to accept or acknowledge (sth); reject: *repudiate a charge, view, claim, suggestion* ○ *He utterly repudiated my offer of friendship.* **(b)** refuse to abide by (the ruling of an authority or an agreement): *He repudiated the court's decision to offer bail.* ○ *repudiate a treaty, contract, vow, etc.* **3** refuse to discharge (a debt or an obligation). ▷ **repudiation** /rɪˌpjuːdɪˈeɪʃn/ *n* [U, C].

repugnant /rɪˈpʌgnənt/ *adj* ~ **(to sb) (a)** *(fml)* causing a feeling of strong opposition or dislike; abhorrent: *I find his racist views totally repugnant.* ○ *The idea of accepting a bribe was repugnant to me.* **(b)** causing a feeling of strong disgust; nauseating: *All food was repugnant to me during my illness.*

▷ **repugnance** /-nəns/ *n* [U] ~ **(to sth/doing sth)** strong aversion or disgust: *She has a deep repugnance to the idea of accepting charity.* ○ *I cannot overcome my repugnance to eating snails.*

repulse /rɪˈpʌls/ *v* [Tn] *(fml)* **1** drive back (an attacker or an attack) by fighting; repel. **2** *(fig)* **(a)** refuse to accept (an offer, help, etc); reject: *repulse kindness, sympathy, assistance, etc* ○ *She repulsed his advances.* **(b)** discourage (sb making an offer, wanting to help, etc) by being rude or unfriendly; rebuff. Cf REPEL 1, 2.

▷ **repulse** *n* [sing] **1** defeat of an attack by fighting. **2** *(fig)* rude or unfriendly rejection of an offer, etc; rebuff: *Her request for a donation met with a repulse.*

repulsion /rɪˈpʌlʃn/ *n* [U] **1** ~ **(for sb/sth)** feeling of loathing or aversion; disgust: *feel repulsion for sb.* **2** *(physics)* tendency of bodies (eg magnetic poles) to repel each other. Cf ATTRACTION.

repulsive /rɪˈpʌlsɪv/ *adj* **1** causing a feeling of loathing or aversion; disgusting: *a repulsive sight, smell, person* ○ *Picking your nose is a repulsive habit.* ○ *The sight of him is repulsive to me.* **2** *(physics)* causing repulsion(2); repelling: *repulsive forces.*

▷ **repulsively** *adv* in a repulsive manner: *repulsively ugly.*

repulsiveness *n* [U].

reputable /ˈrepjʊtəbl/ *adj* having a good reputation; respected or trustworthy: *a highly reputable firm, shop, accountant.* ▷ **reputably** /-əblɪ/ *adv.*

reputation /ˌrepjʊˈteɪʃn/ *n* [U, C] ~ **(for sth)** what is generally said or believed about the abilities, qualities, etc of sb/sth: *a school with an excellent, enviable, fine, etc reputation* ○ *a good/bad reputation as a doctor* ○ *have a reputation for laziness/for being lazy* ○ *compromise, ruin sb's reputation* ○ *establish, build up, make a reputation (for oneself)* ○ *live up to one's reputation,* ie behave, perform, etc as one is expected to.

repute /rɪˈpjuːt/ *v* (idm) **be reputed as/to be sb/sth** be generally said or considered to be sb/sth: *He is reputed as/to be the best surgeon in Paris.* ○ *She is reputed to be very wealthy.*

▷ **repute** *n (fml)* **1** [U] reputation: *know sb only by repute* ○ *an inn of good/evil repute* ○ *He has little repute as an academic.* **2** (idm) **of repute** *(fml)* having a good reputation: *wines of repute* ○ *a doctor of repute.*

reputed *adj* [attrib] generally said or considered to be sth/sb (but with some element of doubt): *the reputed father of the child* ○ *her reputed learning.* **reputedly** *adv.*

request /rɪˈkwest/ *n* **1** ~ **(for sth/that...) (a)** act of asking for sth in speech or writing, esp politely: *make repeated requests for help* ○ *your request that I should destroy the letter.* **(b)** thing asked for in this way: *Your requests will be granted.* ○ [attrib] *a request programme, show, etc,* ie in which music is played that has been requested by listeners. **2** (idm) **at sb's request/at the request of sb** because of sb's wish: *I came at your (special) request.* **by request (of sb)** in response to a request (from sb): *By popular request, the chairman was re-elected.* **on reˈquest** when asked for: *Catalogues are available on request.*

▷ **request** *v* [Tn, Tn·pr, Tf, Dn·t] ~ **sth (from/of sb)** *(fml)* ask sb, esp politely, in speech or writing, to do sth: *request compliance with the rules,* eg on a notice. ○ *All I requested of you was that you came early.* ○ *I requested him to help.* ○ *You are (kindly) requested not to smoke.* ⇨ Usage at ASK.

□ **reˈquest stop** *(Brit)* place where buses will only stop if a passenger signals.

requiem /ˈrekwɪəm/ *n* **(a)** (also **requiem ˈmass**) special mass for the repose of the soul of a dead person. **(b)** musical setting for this.

require /rɪˈkwaɪə(r)/ *v* (not used in the continuous tenses) **1** [Tn, Tf, Tnt, Tg] depend on (sb/sth) for success, fulfilment, etc; need: *We require extra help.* ○ *The situation requires that I should be there.* ○ *The manuscript requires an expert to understand it.* ○ *All cars require servicing regularly.* **2** [esp passive: Tn, Tn·pr, Tf, Dn·t] ~ **sth (of sb)** *(fml)* order or command (sth), esp from a position of authority: *I have done all that is required by law.* ○ *It is required (of me) that I give evidence.* ○ *Civil Servants are required to sign the Official Secrets Act.* **3** [esp passive: Tn, Tn·pr] demand (sth) as being obligatory; stipulate: *Hamlet is required reading* (ie must be read) *for the course.* ○ *You must satisfy the required conditions to get your voucher.* ○ *He only did what was required (of him).* **4** [Tn] *(fml)* wish to have: *Will you require tea?* ○ *Is that all that you require, sir?*

▷ **requirement** *n* (esp *pl*) **1** thing depended on or needed: *Our immediate requirement is extra staff.* ○ *stock surplus to requirements,* ie more than is needed ○ *Our latest model should meet your requirements exactly,* ie be just what you want. **2** thing ordered or demanded: *Not all foreign visitors satisfy/fulfil legal entry requirements.*

requisite /ˈrekwɪzɪt/ *adj* [attrib] *(fml)* required by circumstances or necessary for success: *Have you the requisite visa to enter Canada?* ○ *have/lack the requisite capital to start a business.*

▷ **requisite** *n* ~ **(for sth)** thing needed for a purpose: *toilet requisites,* eg soap, perfume, etc ○ *We supply every requisite for travel/all travelling requisites.*

requisition /ˌrekwɪˈzɪʃn/ *n* **1** [C] ~ **(on sb) (for sth)** official, usu written, demand for (esp) the use of property or materials by an army in wartime or by certain people in an emergency: *make a requisition on headquarters for supplies.* **2** [U] action of demanding in this way: *The farm was in/under constant requisition as a base for the rescue team.* ○ [attrib] *a requisition form, order, etc.*

▷ **requisition** *v* **1** [Tn, Tn·pr, Cn·n/a] ~ **sth (from sb)**; ~ **sth as sth** demand (the use of sth) by a requisition: *requisition billets, blankets, horses (from the villagers)* ○ *The town hall was requisitioned as army headquarters.* **2** [Tn·pr, Tnt] ~ **sb (for sth)** command sb officially to do sth: *requisition the villagers for billets/to provide billets.*

requite /rɪˈkwaɪt/ *v* [Tn, Tn·pr] (*fml*) **1** ~ **sth (with sth)** give sth in return for sth else; repay sth: *Will she ever requite my love?* ○ *The Queen requited his services with a knighthood.* **2** ~ **sb (for sth)** take vengeance on sb: *requite sb for wrongs, evils, etc* ○ *requite him for the injury he has done me.*

▷ **requital** /-tl/ *n* [U] (*fml*) **1** repayment: *the requital of her love* ○ *make full requital to sb for his help.* **2** revenge.

reredos /ˈrɪədɒs/ *n* decorative screen, often carved, behind and above the altar in a church.

re-route /ˌriːˈruːt/ *v* [Tn, Tn·pr] send or carry (sb/sth) by a different route: *re-route traffic, shipping, freight, luggage* ○ *My flight was re-routed via Athens.*

rerun /ˌriːˈrʌn/ *v* (**-nn-**; *pt* **reran**, *pp* **rerun**) [Tn] **1** show (a cinema or television film), broadcast (a programme) or play (a tape) again. **2** run (a race) again.

▷ **rerun** /ˈriːrʌn/ *n* film or programme that is shown or broadcast again; repeat: *a rerun of a popular play, series, etc* ○ (*fig*) *We don't want a rerun of Monday's fiasco.*

resale /ˈriːseɪl, riːˈseɪl/ *n* [U] sale to another person of sth that one has bought: *a house up for resale.*

rescind /rɪˈsɪnd/ *v* [Tn] (*law*) cancel or repeal (a law, contract, etc); annul: *rescind an agreement, order, act, etc.*

rescue /ˈreskjuː/ *v* [Tn, Tn·pr] ~ **sb/sth (from sth/sb)** save or bring away sb/sth from danger, captivity, etc: *Police rescued the hostages.* ○ *rescue a man from drowning, attack, bankruptcy* ○ (*fig*) *rescue sb's name from oblivion*, ie prevent him from being forgotten ○ *You rescued me from an embarrassing situation.*

▷ **rescue** *n* **1** [U] rescuing or being rescued: [attrib] *a rescue party, bid, operation.* **2** [C] instance of this: *an attempt at a rescue.* **3** (idm) **come/go to the/sb's ˈrescue** rescue or help sb: *A wealthy sponsor came to our rescue with a generous donation.*

rescuer *n.*

research /rɪˈsɜːtʃ, ˈriːsɜːtʃ/ *n* [U] (also **researches** [pl]) ~ **(into/on sth)**; ~ **(on sb)** careful study or investigation, esp in order to discover new facts or information: *medical, scientific, historical, etc research* ○ *a startling piece of research into the causes of cancer/on cancer* ○ *be engaged in, carry out, do research* ○ (*infml*) *My researches into adventure holidays were very fruitful.* ○ [attrib] *a research worker, grant, degree.*

▷ **research** /rɪˈsɜːtʃ/ *v* [I, Ipr, Tn] ~ **(into/on sth)**; ~ **(on sb)** do research on (sth/sb): *researching into/on the spread of AIDS* ○ *The subject has already been fully researched.* ○ *a well-researched book.* **researcher** *n.*

reseat /ˌriːˈsiːt/ *v* [Tn] **1** supply (sth) with a new seat: *reseat a cane chair.* **2** place (sb/oneself) on a seat again, or on a new seat: *reseat oneself more comfortably.*

resell /ˌriːˈsel/ *v* (**-ll-**; *pt, pp* **resold** /ˌriːˈsəʊld/) [Tn] sell (sth one has bought) to another person: *resell the goods at a profit.*

resemble /rɪˈzembl/ *v* [no passive: Tn, Tn·pr] ~ **sb/sth (in sth)** (not used in the continuous tenses) be like or similar to (another person or thing): *a small object resembling a pin* ○ *She resembles her brother in looks.*

▷ **resemblance** /rɪˈzembləns/ *n* [C, U] ~ **(to sb/sth)**; ~ **(between A and B)** (instance of) likeness or similarity: *a marked, strong, notable, faint resemblance* ○ *There is a degree of resemblance between the two boys.* ○ *Your story bears/has/shows little or no resemblance to the facts.*

resent /rɪˈzent/ *v* [Tn, Tg, Tsg] feel bitter, indignant or angry about (sth hurtful, insulting, etc): *I bitterly resent your criticism.* ○ *Does she resent my being here?*

▷ **resentful** /-fl/ *adj* feeling or showing resentment: *a resentful silence, stare, comment* ○ *He was deeply resentful of/at her interference.* **resentfully** /-fəlɪ/ *adv.* **resentfulness** *n* [U].

resentment *n* [U, sing] (act of) resenting sb/sth: *bear, feel, show, etc no resentment against/towards anyone* ○ *a deep-seated resentment at/of/over the way one has been treated.*

reservation /ˌrezəˈveɪʃn/ *n* **1** [C] reserved seat or accommodation, etc; record of this: *a coach, hotel reservation* ○ *make, hold reservations (in the name of T Hill).* Cf BOOKING (BOOK[2]). **2** [U, C esp *pl*] spoken or unspoken limitation which prevents one's agreement with a plan, acceptance of an idea, etc: *I support this measure without reservation*, ie completely, wholeheartedly. ○ *express certain (mental) reservations about an offer* ○ *I have my reservations* (ie doubts) *about his ability to do the job.* **3** [C] (*Brit*) strip of land between the two carriageways of a road: *the central reservation.* **4** [C] area of land reserved in the USA for occupation by an Indian tribe.

reserve[1] /rɪˈzɜːv/ *v* [Tn, Tn·pr] ~ **sth (for sb/sth)** **1** put aside or keep sth for a later occasion or special use: *Reserve your strength for the climb.* ○ *These seats are reserved for special guests.* **2** have or keep (a specified power); retain: *The management reserves the right to refuse admission.* ○ (*law*) *All rights reserved*, eg for the publisher of the book, record, etc. **3** order or set aside (seats, accommodation, etc) for use by a particular person at a future time; book: *reserve tickets, rooms, couchettes* ○ *reserve a table for two in the name of Hill* ○ *Is your holiday a reserved booking, sir?* **4** (idm) **reserve (one's) ˈjudgement (on sb/sth)** (*fml*) delay giving an opinion, eg until the matter has become clearer.

reserve[2] /rɪˈzɜːv/ *n* **1** [C usu *pl*] thing put aside or kept for later use; extra amount available when needed: *dwindling oil reserves* ○ *have great reserves of capital, energy, stock* ○ *the ˈgold reserve*, ie to support the issue of banknotes ○ [attrib] *a reserve (petrol) tank* ○ *The champion drew on his reserve strength to win in the last 50 yards.* **2** (a) **the Reserve** [sing] forces outside the regular armed services and liable to be called out in an emergency. (b) **reserves** [pl] military forces kept back, for use when needed: *commit one's reserves to the battle.* **3** [C] extra player chosen in case a substitute is needed in a team. **4** [C] (a) area of land reserved esp as a habitat for nature conservation: *a ˈbird, ˈgame, ˈwildlife, etc reserve.* (b) similar area of land reserved for occupation by a native tribe: *ˈIndian reserves*, eg on the Amazon. **5** [U] limitation on one's agreement with a plan, acceptance of an idea, etc: *We accept your statement without reserve*, ie fully. ○ *He spoke without reserve* (ie freely) *of his time in prison.* **6** [C] (also **reserve price**) (*Brit*) (*US* **upset price**) lowest price that will be accepted, esp for an item at an auction: *put a reserve of £95 000 on a house* ○ *The Van Gogh failed to reach its reserve and was withdrawn.* **7** [U] tendency to avoid showing one's feelings and appear unsociable to other people; restraint: *For once, she lost/dropped her customary reserve and became quite lively.* ○ *A few drinks broke through his reserve.* **8** (idm) **in reˈserve** kept back unused, but available if needed: *funds kept/held in reserve.*

▷ **reservist** /rɪˈzɜːvɪst/ *n* member of a country's reserve forces.

□ **reˈserve bank** (*US*) bank holding reserves for others in the Federal Reserve System (FEDERAL).

reserved /rɪˈzɜːvd/ *adj* (of a person or his character) slow to show feelings or express opinions: *a reserved disposition, manner, etc.* Cf COMMUNICATIVE. ▷ **reservedness** /rɪˈzɜːvɪdnɪs/ *n* [U].

reservoir /ˈrezəvwɑː(r)/ *n* **1** natural or artificial lake used as a source or store of water for a town, etc.

Many reservoirs in Britain are used as tourist centres for sport and leisure, and are often equipped with marinas, cafés, car-parks and facilities for boating, sailing, fishing and picnicking. One of the best-known reservoirs of this type is Rutland Water in Leicestershire.

2 container that holds a supply of a liquid, eg oil or ink. **3** ~ **of sth** (*fig*) large supply or collection of sth: *a reservoir of information, facts, knowledge, etc* ○ *The show is a veritable reservoir of new talent.*

reset /ˌriːˈset/ *v* (**-tt-**; *pt, pp* **reset**) [Tn] **1** (a) place (sth) in position again: *reset a diamond in a ring* ○ *reset a broken bone* ○ *reset type*, ie in printing. (b) place (the indicator of a measuring instrument) in a new position: *reset one's watch to local time* ○ *reset a dial, gauge, control, etc at zero.* **2** devise a new set of questions for (an exam, a test, etc).

resettle /ˌriːˈsetl/ *v* (a) [I, Tn] help (esp refugees) to settle again in a new country: *resettle refugees in Canada.* (b) [Tn] cause (land, a country, etc) to be inhabited again: *resettle an island.* ▷ **resettlement** *n* [U]: [attrib] *a government resettlement programme.*

reshuffle /ˌriːˈʃʌfl/ *v* **1** [Tn] interchange the posts or responsibilities of (a group of people). **2** [I, Tn] shuffle (playing-cards) again.

▷ **ˈreshuffle** *n* [C] act of reshuffling (esp a political team): *carry out a Cabinet reshuffle.*

reside /rɪˈzaɪd/ *v* [I, Ipr] (*fml*) **1** ~ **(in/at...)** have one's home (in a certain place); live: *reside abroad* ○ *reside at 10 Elm Terrace* ○ *reside in college.* **2** (phr v) **reside in sb/sth** (of power, rights, etc) be present or vested in sb/sth: *Supreme authority resides in the President/State.*

residence /ˈrezɪdəns/ *n* (*fml*) **1** [C] (a) house, esp a large or impressive one: *10 Downing Street is the British Prime Minister's official residence.* (b) (esp as used by house-agents) house: *a desirable country, family, Georgian, etc residence for sale.* **2** [U] (a) process of residing: *hall of residence*, eg for university students ○ *take up (one's) residence* (ie go and live) *in college.* (b) period of residing: *Foreign visitors are only allowed one month's residence.* **3** (idm) **in ˈresidence** living in a specified place because of one's work or duties: *The royal standard flies when the Queen is in residence.* ○ *Students must remain in residence during term.* ○ *writer, artist, etc in residence*, eg at a college or in a community, etc which pays him to work there for a period of time.

residency /ˈrezɪdənsɪ/ *n* **1** [C] = RESIDENCE 1a, 2. **2** [U] = RESIDENCE 2. **3** (*US*) period of specialized medical training for a doctor.

resident /ˈrezɪdənt/ *n* **1** person who lives or has a home in a place, not a visitor: *a (local) residents' association.* **2** (in a hotel) person staying overnight: *Restaurant open to non-residents.* **3** (*US* also **resident physician**) doctor living at a hospital where he is receiving advanced training.

▷ **resident** *adj* having a home in a place; residing: *the town's resident population*, ie not tourists or visitors ○ *be resident abroad/in the UK* ○ (*joc*) *Stanley is our resident crossword fanatic.*

residential /ˌrezɪˈdenʃl/ *adj* [esp attrib] **1** containing or suitable for private houses: *a residential area, suburb, district, etc*, ie one having no offices, factories, etc. **2** connected with or based on residence: *I often go on residential summer courses.* ○ *residential qualifications for voters*, ie requiring that they should reside in the constituency.

residue /ˈrezɪdjuː; *US* -duː/ *n* (usu *sing*) ~ **(of sth)** **1** what remains after a part or quantity is taken or used. **2** (*law*) part of an estate remaining after all debts, charges, bequests, etc have been settled. ⇨ Usage at REST[3].

▷ **residual** /rɪˈzɪdjʊəl; *US* -dʒʊ-/ *adj* (usu *attrib*) left over as a residue(1); remaining: *residual chalk deposits*, ie left after rocks have been eroded ○ *a few residual faults in the computer program.*

residuary /rɪˈzɪdjʊərɪ; *US* -dʒʊerɪ/ *adj* **1** of a residue(1); residual. **2** (*law*) of the residue (2) of an estate: *a residuary legatee, clause, bequest.*

residuum /rɪˈzɪdjʊəm; *US* -dʒʊ-/ *n* (*pl* **-dua** /-djʊə; *US* -dʒʊə/) (*chemistry*) material left after a process of evaporation or combustion.

resign /rɪˈzaɪn/ *v* **1** [I, Ipr, Tn, Tn·pr] ~ **(from sth)** give up (one's job, position, etc): *The Minister resigned (from office).* ○ *She resigned her directorship and left the firm.* ○ *resign (one's post) as chairman.* Cf RETIRE 1. **2** (phr v) **resign oneself to sth/doing sth** be ready to accept and endure sth as inevitable: *be resigned to one's fate* ○ *The team refused to resign themselves to defeat/to being defeated.*

▷ **resigned** *adj* **1** [attrib] having or showing patient acceptance of sth unwelcome or unpleasant: *a resigned look, smile, gesture.* **2** (idm) **be, etc resigned to sth/doing sth** be ready to endure or tolerate sth: *She seems resigned to not having a holiday this year.* **resignedly** /-nɪdlɪ/ *adv* in a resigned manner.

resignation /ˌrezɪɡˈneɪʃn/ *n* **1** ~ **(from sth)** **(a)** [C, U] (instance of) resigning: *Further resignations are expected.* ○ *He is considering resignation (from the Board).* **(b)** [C] letter, etc to one's employers stating one's wish to resign: *offer, tender, send in, give in, hand in one's resignation* ○ *We haven't yet received his resignation.* **2** [U] patient acceptance or endurance: *accept failure with resignation.*

resilient /rɪˈzɪlɪənt/ *adj* **1** (of an object or material) springing back to its original form after being bent, stretched, crushed, etc; springy. **2** (of a person or character) quickly recovering from shock or depression; buoyant: *physically/mentally resilient* ○ *She is very resilient to change.*

▷ **resilience** /-əns/ (also **resiliency** /-nsɪ/) *n* [U] **1** quality of being springy: *an alloy combining strength and resilience.* **2** (of people) quality of being buoyant: *Her natural resilience helped her overcome the crisis.* **resiliently** *adv.*

resin /ˈrezɪn; *US* ˈrezn/ *n* [C, U] **1** sticky substance that oozes esp from fir and pine trees and is used in making varnish, medicine, etc. **2** similar substance made synthetically, used as a plastic or in making plastics.

▷ **resinous** /ˈrezɪnəs; *US* ˈrezənəs/ *adj* of or like resin.

resist /rɪˈzɪst/ *v* **1** [I, Tn] use force in order to prevent sth happening or being successful; oppose: *He could resist no longer.* ○ *resist an enemy, attack* ○ *He was charged with resisting arrest.* **2** [I, Tn] regard (a plan, an idea, etc) unfavourably: *resist the call for reform.* **3** [Tn] be undamaged or unaffected by (sth): *ovenware, glass, etc that resists heat* ○ *resist corrosion, damp, frost, disease.* **4** [Tn, Tg] succeed in not yielding to (sth/sb): *resist temptation, chocolate* ○ *Jill couldn't resist making jokes about his baldness.*

▷ **resister** *n* person who resists: *passive resisters.* **resistible** *adj* that can be resisted.

resistance /rɪˈzɪstəns/ *n* **1** [U, sing] ~ **(to sth/sb)** (action of) using force to oppose sth/sb: *break down, overcome, put an end to armed resistance* ○ *The demonstrators offered little or no resistance to the police.* ○ *put up (a) passive resistance.* **2** [U, sing] ~ **(to sth)** influence or force that hinders or stops sth: *The firm has to overcome its resistance to new technology.* ○ *a low wind resistance*, eg in the aerodynamic of planes, cars, etc. **3** [U, sing] ~ **(to sth)** power to remain undamaged or unaffected (or only slightly so) by sth: *the body's natural resistance to disease* ○ *build up (a) resistance to infection.* **4** [U] (*physics*) (measure of the) property of not conducting heat or electricity. **5** [U] ~ **(to sth)** desire to oppose sth; antagonism: *make, offer, put up, etc resistance to the proposed changes* ○ *The idea met with some resistance.* ○ (*commerce*) *market resistance*, eg to a new product. **6** (often **the Resistance**) [Gp] secret organization resisting the authorities, esp in a conquered or an enemy-occupied country: [attrib] *a resistance fighter.* **7** (idm) **the line of least resistance** ⇨ LINE[1].

resistant /rɪˈzɪstənt/ *adj* ~ **(to sth)** offering resistance: *insects that have become resistant to DDT* ○ *a resistant strain of virus* ○ *be resistant to change.* ▷ **-resistant** (forming compound *adjs*): *ˈwater-/ˈheat-/ˈrust-resistant.*

resistor /rɪˈzɪstə(r)/ *n* device providing resistance to electric current in a circuit.

resit /ˌriːˈsɪt/ *v* (**-tt-**; *pt, pp* **resat**) [Tn] (*Brit*) sit (an examination or test) again, usu after failing.

▷ **resit** /ˈriːsɪt/ *n* second, etc sitting (of an examination or test): *candidates for the September resit.*

resolute /ˈrezəluːt/ *adj* ~ **(in sth)** having or showing great determination or firmness: *a resolute refusal, approach, measure* ○ *be resolute in one's demands for peace.* ▷ **resolutely** *adv.* **resoluteness** *n* [U].

resolution /ˌrezəˈluːʃn/ *n* **1** [U] quality of being resolute or firm; determination: *show great resolution* ○ *a man lacking in resolution* ○ *His speech ended on a note of resolution.* **2** [C] decision or mental pledge to do or not to do sth; resolve: *make, keep good resolutions* ○ *her resolution never to marry* ○ *New Year resolutions*, eg not to smoke in the new year ahead. **3** [C] formal statement of opinion agreed on by a committee or assembly, esp by means of a vote: *pass, carry, adopt, reject a resolution* ○ *a resolution in favour of/demanding better conditions* ○ *a resolution that conditions should be improved.* **4** [U] (*fml*) solution: *the resolution of a problem, question, difficulty, doubt, etc.* **5** [U] ~ **(into sth)** process of separating sth or being separated into constituent parts: *the resolution of white light into the colours of the spectrum.*

resolve /rɪˈzɒlv/ *v* (*fml*) **1** [Ipr, Tf, Tt] ~ **on/upon/against sth/doing sth** decide firmly; determine: *He resolved on/against (making) an early start.* ○ *She resolved that she would never see him again/never to see him again.* **2** [Tf, Tt] (of a committee or assembly) make a decision by a formal vote: *The senate resolved that….* ○ *The union resolved to strike by 36 votes to 15.* **3** [Tn] solve or settle (problems, doubts, etc): *resolve an argument, a difficulty, a crisis* ○ *Her arrival did little to resolve the situation.* **4** [Tn, Tn·pr] ~ **sth (into sth)** separate (sth) into constituent parts: *resolve a complex argument into its basic elements* ○ *the resolving power of a lens*, ie its ability to magnify things distinctly.

▷ **resolvable** *adj* that can be solved or settled.

resolve *n* (*fml*) **1** [C] thing one has decided to do; resolution(2): *make a resolve to smoke* ○ *show, keep, break one's resolve.* **2** [U] firmness or determination; resolution(1): *be strong/weak in one's resolve* ○ *His opposition served only to strengthen our resolve.*

resolved *adj* [pred] (of a person) resolute or determined: *I was fully/firmly resolved to see him.*

resonant /ˈrezənənt/ *adj* **1** (of sound) continuing to echo; resounding: *deep resonant notes, voices.* **2** (of rooms, bodies, etc) tending to prolong sounds, esp by vibration: *a resonant hall* ○ *the resonant body of a guitar.* **3** ~ **with sth** (of places) resounding or echoing with sth: *Alpine valleys resonant with the sound of church bells.*

▷ **resonance** /-əns/ *n* [U] quality of being resonant.

resonantly *adv.*

resonate /ˈrezəneɪt/ *v* [I] produce or show resonance. **resonator** /-tə(r)/ *n* appliance or system for giving resonance to sound.

resort /rɪˈzɔːt/ *v* [Ipr] **1** ~ **to sth** make use of sth for help; adopt sth as an expedient: *If negotiations fail we shall have to resort to strike action.* ○ *resort to violence, deception, trickery, etc.* **2** [Tn] (*fml*) visit (a place) frequently or habitually; frequent: *The police watched the bars which he was known to resort.*

▷ **resort** *n* **1** [C] person or thing that is turned to for help; expedient: *Our only resort is to inform the police.* **2** [U] ~ **to sth** resorting to sth: *talk calmly, without resort to threats.* **3** [C] **(a)** popular holiday centre: *seaside, skiing, health, etc resorts* ○ *Brighton is a leading south coast resort.* **(b)** (*US*) hotel or guest-house for holiday-makers. **4** (idm) **a/one's last resort** ⇨ LAST[1]. **in the last resort** ⇨ LAST[1].

resound /rɪˈzaʊnd/ *v* **1** [I, Ipr] **(a)** ~ **(through/throughout sth)** (of a sound, voice, etc) fill a place with sound; produce echoes: *The organ resounded (through the church).* **(b)** ~ **(with sth)** (of a place) be filled with sound; echo: *The hall resounded with applause.* **2** [Ipr] ~ **(throughout sth)** (*fig*) (of fame, an event, etc) be much talked of; spread far and wide: *Her name resounded throughout Europe.* Cf REVERBERATE.

▷ **resounding** *adj* [attrib] **1** sounding or echoing loudly: *resounding cheers, shouts, laughs.* **2** (of an event, etc) notable; famous: *win a resounding victory* ○ *The film was/scored a resounding success.* **resoundingly** *adv.*

resource /rɪˈsɔːs, *also* -ˈzɔːs; *US* ˈriːsɔːrs/ *n* **1** [C usu *pl*] supply of raw materials, etc which bring a country, person, etc wealth: *rich in natural, mineral, agricultural, etc resources* ○ *The mortgage is a drain on our financial resources.* ○ *We agreed to pool our resources*, ie available assets. ○ *Is there any resource that we have left untapped?* **2** [C usu *pl*] thing that can be turned to for help, support or consolation when needed: *He has no inner resources and hates being alone.* ○ *An only child is often left to his own resources*, ie left to amuse himself. ○ [attrib] *a resource file, room*, eg containing materials for teachers. **3** [U] (*fml*) ingenuity or quick wit; initiative: *a man of great resource.*

▷ **resourceful** /-fl/ *adj* clever at finding ways of doing things. **resourcefully** /-fəlɪ/ *adv.* **resourcefulness** *n* [U].

respect[1] /rɪˈspekt/ *n* **1** [U] ~ **(for sb/sth)** admiration felt or shown for a person or thing that has good qualities or achievements; regard: *a mark, token, etc of respect* ○ *have a deep, sincere, etc respect for sb* ○ *I have the greatest respect for you/hold you in the greatest respect.* ○ *The new officer soon won/earned the respect of his men.* **2** [U] ~ **(for sb/sth)** politeness or consideration arising from admiration or regard: *Children should show respect for their teachers.* ○ *Out of respect, he took off his hat.* ○ *have some, little, no, etc respect for sb's feelings* ○ *With (all due) respect, sir, I disagree.* **3** [U] ~ **(for sb/sth)** protection or recognition: *very little respect for human rights.* **4** [C] particular aspect or detail: *in this one respect* ○ *in some/all/many/several/few respects* ○ *In what respect do you think the film is biased?* **5** (idm) **in respect of sth** (*fml or commerce*) as regards sth; with special reference to sth: *The book is admirable in respect of style.* ○ *price rises in respect of gas and water costs.* **with respect to sth** (*fml or commerce*) concerning sth: *This is true with respect to English but not to French.* ○ *With respect to your enquiry, I enclose an explanatory leaflet.*

▷ **respects** *n* [pl] (*fml*) **1** polite greetings: *Give/send/offer him my respects.* **2** (idm) **pay one's respects** ⇨ PAY[2].

respect[2] /rɪˈspekt/ *v* **1** [Tn, Tn·pr] ~ **sb/sth (for sth)** admire or have a high opinion of sb/sth (because of sth): *I respect you for your honesty.* **2** [Tn] show consideration for (sb/sth): *respect sb's wishes, opinions, feelings, etc* ○ *respect the environment*, eg by protecting it ○ *People won't respect my (desire for) privacy.* **3** [Tn, Cn·n/a] ~ **sth (as sth)** avoid interfering with or harming sth; agree to recognize: *respect sb's rights, privileges, etc* ○ *respect a treaty, contract, etc* ○ *respect diplomatic immunity* (eg of foreign embassy staff to British law) *as valid.* **4** [Tn] ~ **oneself** have proper respect for one's own character and behaviour: *If you don't respect yourself, how can you expect others to respect you?*

▷ **respecter** *n* (idm) **be no/not be any respecter of ˈpersons** treat everyone in the same way, without being influenced by their importance, wealth, etc: *Death is no respecter of persons.*

respecting *prep* (*fml*) relating to (sth); concerning: *laws respecting property* ○ *information respecting the child's whereabouts.*

respectable /rɪˈspektəbl/ *adj* **1** of acceptable social position; decent and proper in appearance or behaviour: *a respectable married couple* ○ *a respectable middle-class background, upbringing, etc* ○ *She looked perfectly respectable in her bathrobe at breakfast.* ○ (*ironic*) *He's a bit too respectable* (ie staid and conventional) *for my* *tastes.* **2** of a moderately good standard or size, etc; not bringing disgrace or embarrassment: *There was quite a respectable crowd at the match on Saturday.* ○ *£20 000 is a very respectable salary.* ○ *Hunt jumped a respectable round although his horse was unfit.*

▷ **respectability** /rɪˌspektəˈbɪlətɪ/ *n* [U] quality of being socially respectable; decency.

respectably /-əblɪ/ *adv* in a respectable manner: *respectably dressed, behaved, spoken, etc.*

respectful /rɪˈspektfl/ *adj* ~ **(to/towards sb)**; ~ **(of sth)** feeling or showing respect: *listen in respectful silence* ○ *stand at a respectful distance* ○ *respectful of other people's opinions.* ▷ **respectfully** /-fəlɪ/ *adv.* **respectfulness** *n* [U].

respective /rɪˈspektɪv/ *adj* [attrib] of or for or belonging to each as an individual: *They each excel in their respective fields.* ○ *After the party we all went off to our respective rooms.*

▷ **respectively** *adv* separately or in turn, in the order mentioned: *German and Italian courses are held in Munich and Rome respectively.*

Respighi /reˈspiːgɪ/ Ottorino (1879-1936), Italian composer. He is famous mainly for his suites of descriptive music like *The Pines of Rome* and *The Fountains of Rome*, with their brilliant orchestration.

respiration /ˌrespəˈreɪʃn/ *n* **1** [C, U] *(fml)* (single act of) breathing air: [attrib] *respiration rate.* **2** [U] plant's absorption of oxygen and release of carbon dioxide. **3** [U] process in plant and animal cells in which substances containing carbon are converted into simpler substances with a release of energy which can be used by the plant or animal.

respirator /ˈrespəreɪtə(r)/ *n* [C] **1** apparatus for giving artificial respiration over a long period: *put the patient on a respirator.* **2** device worn over the nose and mouth to warm, filter or purify air before it is breathed.

respire /rɪˈspaɪə(r)/ *v* [I] **1** *(fml)* breathe air: *respire deeply.* **2** (of plants) absorb oxygen and release carbon dioxide.

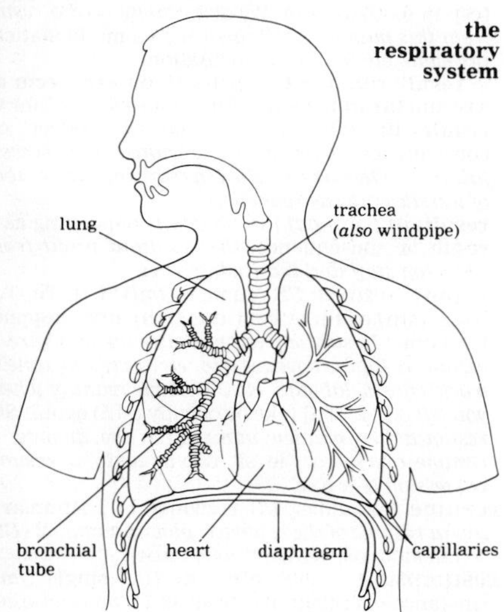

▷ **respiratory** /rɪˈspaɪərətrɪ, ˈrespɪrətrɪ; *US* -tɔːrɪ/ *adj* [esp attrib] *(medical)* of or for breathing air: *respiratory diseases*, eg bronchitis, asthma ○ *respiratory organs, systems.* ⇨ illus.

respite /ˈrespaɪt, ˈrespɪt/ *n* **1** [U, sing] ~ **(from sth)** interval of rest or relief: *longing for a moment of respite* ○ *work without respite* ○ *a brief, welcome respite* ○ *(a) respite from pain, worry, stress, etc.* **2** [C] delay allowed before an obligation must be fulfilled or a penalty suffered; reprieve: *grant sb a respite.*

resplendent /rɪˈsplendənt/ *adj* [usu pred] ~ **(in sth)** *(fml)* brilliant with colour or decorations; splendid: *resplendent in coronation robes* ○ *(ironic) resplendent in her curlers and a face-pack.* ▷ **resplendence** /-əns/ *n* [U]. **resplendently** *adv.*

respond /rɪˈspɒnd/ *v* [I, Ipr] **1** ~ **(to sb/sth) (with sth)** give a verbal or written answer: *She asked where he'd been, but he didn't respond.* ○ *She responded to my letter with a phone call.* **2** ~ **(to sth) (with sth)** act in answer to (sth) or because of the action of another; behave in a similar way: *He responded to my volley with a backhand*, ie in tennis. ○ *I kicked the dog, which responded by growling/with a growl.* **3** ~ **(to sb/sth)** react quickly or favourably (to or because of sb/sth); be easily controlled (by sb/sth): *The car responds well to the controls.* ○ *The patient did not respond to treatment.* ○ *Animals respond to kindness.* **4** ~ **(to sb/sth)** (of people at a church service) make the responses.

respondent /rɪˈspɒndənt/ *n* *(law)* defendant, esp in a divorce case.

response /rɪˈspɒns/ *n* ~ **(to sb/sth) 1** [C, U] answer: *She made no response.* ○ *In response to your inquiry....* ○ *His accusations brought an immediate response.* **2** [C, U] act or feeling produced in answer to a stimulus; reaction: *a poor, generous, united, etc response to the appeal for funds* ○ *Her cries for help met with no, some, little, etc response.* ○ *The tax cuts produced a favourable response from the public.* **3** [C usu *pl*] *(religion)* part of the liturgy said or sung by the people at a church service in answer to the priest. Cf VERSICLE.

responsibility /rɪˌspɒnsəˈbɪlətɪ/ *n* **1** [U] ~ **(for sb/sth)** being responsible or accountable: *a position of real, great, major, etc responsibility* ○ *have, show a sense of responsibility* ○ *take, assume, accept, bear full responsibility for the consequences* ○ *The manufacturers disclaim all responsibility for damage caused by misuse.* **2** [C] ~ **(to sb)** commitment or duty for which a person is responsible: *Our business is a joint/shared responsibility.* ○ *It's my responsibility to lock the doors.* ○ *the various responsibilities of the post.*

responsible /rɪˈspɒnsəbl/ *adj* **1** [pred] ~ **(for sb/sth)**; ~ **(for doing sth)** legally or morally obliged, eg to take care of sb/sth or to carry out a duty, and liable to be blamed if one fails: *All pilots are responsible for their passengers' safety.* ○ *I am wholly/partly responsible for the confusion.* ○ *You must make yourself personally responsible for paying these bills.* **2** [pred] ~ **to sb/sth** having to account for one's actions to an authority or a superior: *be directly/indirectly responsible to the President.* **3** [pred] ~ **(for sth)** answerable for one's behaviour: *A drunk man cannot be held/considered fully responsible for his actions.* **4** (a) (of people) capable of being relied on; trustworthy: *behave like responsible citizens, adults, committee members* ○ *She is very responsible for* (ie considering that she is) *a six-year-old.* Cf IRRESPONSIBLE. (b) [esp attrib] (of jobs, etc) needing sb who can be relied on; involving important duties: *a highly responsible position, appointment, role.* **5** [pred] ~ **(for sth)** being the cause (of sth): *Who's responsible for this mess?* ○ *Smoking is responsible for many cases of lung cancer.*

▷ **responsibly** /-əblɪ/ *adv* in a rational or trustworthy way: *act, behave responsibly.*

responsive /rɪˈspɒnsɪv/ *adj* **1** ~ **(to sb/sth)** (a) responding warmly or favourably; sympathetic: *a responsive class, audience, etc* ○ *be responsive to suggestions, ideas, criticisms, etc.* (b) [usu pred] reacting quickly or favourably; easily controlled: *These brakes should be more responsive.* ○ *a flu virus that is not responsive to treatment* ○ *a horse responsive to the needs of its rider.* **2** [esp attrib] given or made as an answer: *a responsive smile, gesture, wink, etc.* ▷ **responsively** *adv.* **responsiveness** *n* [U].

respray /ˌriːˈspreɪ/ *v* [Tn] paint (eg a car) again, usu in a different colour, using a paint sprayer.

▷ **respray** /ˈriːspreɪ/ *n* act or instance of respraying.

rest[1] /rest/ *v* **1** (a) [I, Ipr] ~ **(from sth)** be still or asleep; stop moving or working, esp in order to regain one's strength: *lie down and rest (for) an hour after lunch* ○ *resting from our exertions, efforts, etc* ○ *(fig) He will never rest* (ie never have peace of mind) *until he knows the truth.* (b) [Tn, Tn·pr] cause or allow (sth/sb) to do this: *You should rest your eyes after a lot of reading.* ○ *Sit down and rest your legs.* ○ *Are you rested enough to go on?* **2** [Ipr, Tn·pr] ~ **(sth) on/against sth** lie or be placed on/against sth for support: *Her elbows rested/She rested her elbows on the table.* ○ *Rest the ladder against the wall.* **3** [Ipr] ~ **on sb/sth** depend or rely on sb/sth: *British hopes of a medal rested on Ovett.* **4** [Ipr] ~ **on sb/sth** (of a look, etc) be directed steadily at sb/sth: *His gaze/eyes rested on her face.* **5** [I] *(fml)* (of a subject under discussion) be left without further investigation or pursuit: *let the matter, topic, affair, etc rest* ○ *The matter cannot rest there — I demand an apology.* **6** [I, Tn] *(esp law)* conclude (one's case); have no more to say about (sth): *(US) The defence rests.* ○ *I rest my case.* **7** [I] *(euph or fig)* be buried: *May he rest* (ie lie in his grave) *in peace.* **8** [I, Tn] (cause land to) be free from disturbance, etc: *Let this field rest/Rest this field for a year.* **9** (idm) **rest assured (that...)** *(fml)* be certain that...: *You may rest assured that everything possible is being done.* **rest on one's ˈlaurels** *(esp derog)* stop trying to achieve further successes; become complacent. **10** (phr v) **rest on sth** (no passive) be based on sth: *His fame rests more on his plays than on his novels.* ○ *an argument, a claim, a theory, etc resting on a false assumption.* **rest with sb (to do sth)** *(fml)* be sb's responsibility (to do sth): *The choice rests entirely with you.* ○ *It rests with the committee to decide.*

□ **ˈresting-place** *n* *(euph)* grave: *His last resting-place is on that hill.*

rest[2] /rest/ *n* **1** [C, U] ~ **(from sth)** (period of) sleep or inactivity as a way of regaining one's strength: *have a good night's rest* ○ *stop for a well-earned/-deserved rest* ○ *have/take a rest from all your hard work* ○ *get some, no, more, etc rest* ○ *Sunday is a day of rest.* ⇨ Usage at BREAK[2]. **2** [C] (often in compounds) support for an object; prop: *a rest for a billiard cue, telescope, telephone receiver* ○ *an ˈarm-, ˈhead-, ˈfoot-rest.* **3** [C] *(music)* (sign making an) interval of silence between notes: *The trumpets have six bars' rest.* ⇨ illus at MUSIC. **4** (idm) **at ˈrest** (a) not moving. (b) free from trouble or anxiety: *(euph) be/lie at rest* (ie be buried) *in a country churchyard.* **come to ˈrest** (of a moving object) stop moving: *The mine finally came to rest on the sea bed.* **give it a ˈrest** *(infml)* stop doing sth that others find annoying, etc: *You've been playing pop music for three hours now — can't you give it a rest?* **lay sb to ˈrest** *(euph)* bury sb: *She was laid to rest beside her late husband.* **put/set sb's mind at ease/rest** ⇨ MIND[1].

▷ **restful** /-fl/ *adj* ~ **(to sb/sth)** giving (a feeling of) rest: *a restful Sunday afternoon* ○ *Pastel colours are restful to the eye.* **restfully** /-fəlɪ/ *adv.* **restfulness** *n* [U].

□ **ˈrest area, ˈrest stop** *(US)* = LAY-BY.

ˈrest-cure *n* long period of rest, usu in bed, as medical treatment for stress, anxiety, etc.

ˈrest-day *n* day spent resting, esp during an international cricket match.

ˈrest-home *n* place where old or convalescent people are cared for.

ˈrest-room *n* *(US euph)* public lavatory in eg a theatre, store. ⇨ Usage at TOILET.

rest[3] /rest/ *n* **the** ~ **(of sth) 1** [sing] the remaining part; the remainder of some amount: *the rest of the world, my life, her money* ○ *watch the rest of a film* ○ *Take what you want and throw the rest away.* **2** [pl *v*] the remaining individuals or number; the others: *While we play tennis what will the rest of you do?* ○ *Her hat was red, like the rest of her clothes.* **3** (idm) **for the ˈrest** *(fml)* as far as other matters are concerned; apart from that: *Ensure that our traditional markets are looked after; for the rest, I am not much concerned.*

NOTE ON USAGE: When speaking about who or what remains from an original total, we use **the rest** or (more formal) **the remainder:** *Some boys* *stay on after school; the rest/remainder (of them) go home.* ○ *The rest/remainder of the time was spent swimming.* If something has been partly used or destroyed, we use **remains** or **remnants.** Of food **left-overs** is often used: *The remains/remnants/left-overs of the meal* (ie the bits of food left uneaten) *were fed to the dog.* **Remains** is also used of old buildings or dead bodies: *the remains of an old castle* ○ *human remains.* A **relic** is a historical object and reminder of the past. A **residue** is what is left after a process, especially a chemical one, has taken place. *There is a green residue in the bottom of the test tube.* In a mathematical calculation the **remainder** (in arithmetic) or the **balance** (in accounting) is the amount left after subtraction or division.

restate /ˌriːˈsteɪt/ *v* [Tn] state (sth) again or in a different way: *restate one's position, case, argument, etc.* ▷ **restatement** *n* [C, U]: *make a restatement of current policy.*

restaurant /ˈrestrɒnt; *US* -tərənt/ *n* public place where meals can be bought and eaten. Cf CAFÉ, ⇨ illus at MOTORWAY.

▷ **restaurateur** /ˌrestərəˈtɜː(r)/ (*US* also **restauranteur** /-tərən-/) *n* (*fml*) manager or owner of a restaurant.

□ ˈ**restaurant car** (*Brit*) = DINING-CAR (DINE).

restitution /ˌrestɪˈtjuːʃn; *US* -ˈtuː-/ *n* [U] ~ (**to sb/sth**) **1** (*fml*) restoration of a thing to its proper owner or original state: *restitution of the deeds to the owner* ○ *the full restitution of property, conjugal rights, diplomatic status.* **2** (*law*) reparation, esp in the form of money, for injury, etc: *make restitution for the damage done.*

restive /ˈrestɪv/ *adj* **1** restless or uneasy: *Another hour passed and the crowd grew/became restive.* **2** (esp of horses) resisting control, esp by refusing to move forwards or by moving sideways or backwards. ▷ **restively** *adv*: *move, shuffle, fiddle about restively.* **restiveness** *n* [U].

restless /ˈrestlɪs/ *adj* **1** constantly moving: *the restless motion of the sea.* **2** unable to be still or quiet, esp because of boredom, impatience, anxiety, etc: *The audience was becoming restless.* ○ *The children grew restless with the long wait.* ○ *After only a month in the job, he felt restless and decided to leave.* **3** without rest or sleep: *spend/pass/have a restless night.* ▷ **restlessly** *adv*: *The wind moved restlessly through the trees.* ○ *The lion paced restlessly up and down in its cage.* **restlessness** *n* [U].

restock /ˌriːˈstɒk/ *v* **1** [Tn, Tn·pr] ~ **sth** (**with sth**) fill sth with new or different things to replace those used, sold, etc: *restock the freezer for Christmas* ○ *restock the library shelves with new books* ○ *restock a lake/river with trout.* **2** [Tn] take (a supply of sth) again, eg after an interval: *restock the dictionary in its new edition.*

restoration /ˌrestəˈreɪʃn/ *n* **1** [U] ~ (**to sb/sth**) return of sth lost, etc to its owner: *the restoration of stolen property, goods, etc.* **2** [U] ~ (**to sth**) restoring or being restored to a former place or condition: *the restoration of the Elgin marbles to Greece* ○ *her restoration to complete health* ○ *the restoration of order after the riots.* **3** [U, C] ~ (**to sb/sth**) reintroduction of sth, eg after it has lapsed or been withdrawn: *the restoration of old customs* ○ *We demand an immediate restoration of our right to vote.* **4** [C, U] (example of the) work of restoring a ruined building, work of art, etc to its original condition: *undergo a lengthy process of restoration* ○ *The palace is closed during restorations/for restoration.* ○ [attrib] *the museum restoration fund* ○ *(a) full/complete restoration of the damaged painting, vase, mosaic, etc.* **5** [C] building formerly ruined and now rebuilt; reconstruction: *The castle is largely a restoration,* ie little of the original is left. **6** [C] model representing the supposed form of an extinct animal, a ruined building, etc: *a restoration of an Iron-Age cave dwelling.* **7 the Restoration** [sing] (period following) the re-establishment of the monarchy and the Church of England in Britain in 1660, when *Charles II became king. Oliver *Cromwell's son Richard was unable to run the country as his father had, and was forced to retire by General George Monck, who had fought with Cromwell in the Civil War. Charles issued the Declaration of Breda promising to pardon almost everyone who had supported Cromwell, and returned to a general welcome. The Restoration had a great effect on artistic life. London's theatres reopened with works by dramatists like *Congreve and *Vanbrugh, and Matthew *Locke produced incidental music for many new plays. ⇨ article at PERFORMING ARTS.

□ ˌ**Restoration** ˈ**comedy** comedy written at the time of the Restoration, often on the subject of the sexual adventures of the upper classes and using bawdy language.

restorative /rɪˈstɔːrətɪv/ *adj* [esp attrib] tending to restore health and strength: *restorative drugs, exercises, tonics* ○ *the restorative powers of sea air.* ▷ **restorative** *n* [C, U] restorative food, medicine or treatment: *The brandy acted as a restorative.*

restore /rɪˈstɔː(r)/ *v* **1** [Tn, Tn·pr] ~ **sth** (**to sb/sth**) (*fml*) give back (sth lost, etc) to its owner: *Police restored the stolen jewels to the showroom.* **2** (**a**) [Tn·pr] ~ **sb/sth to sth** bring sb/sth back to a former place or position: *restore sacked workers to their old jobs* ○ *restore an officer to his command* ○ (*fml*) *He restored the dictionary to the shelf.* (**b**) [Tn, Tn·pr] ~ **sb** (**to sth**); ~ **sth** (**to sb**) bring sb/sth back to a former condition: *restore my health/me to health* ○ *restore sb's beauty, sight, confidence, etc* ○ *The brandy fully/completely restored him.* ○ *Law and order were quickly restored after the riots.* ○ *The deposed chief was restored (to power/to his throne).* **3** [Tn, Tn·pr] ~ **sth** (**to sb**) bring sth back into use, eg after it has lapsed or been withdrawn: *restore ancient traditions, rights, ceremonies, etc* ○ *restore old laws, taxes, charges, etc* ○ *Our Christmas bonus should be restored.* **4** [Tn, Tn·pr] ~ **sth** (**to sth**) rebuild or repair (a ruined building, work of art, etc) so that it is like the original: *restore a Roman fort, a vintage car, an oil painting, a china vase, etc* ○ *The mill was restored to full working order.* Cf RENOVATE.

▷ **restorer** *n* (esp in compounds) (**a**) [C] person who restores (RESTORE 4) things: *picture, furniture restorers.* (**b**) [C, U] substance, etc that restores (RESTORE 2b) things: *hair-restorer,* ie to cure baldness.

restrain /rɪˈstreɪn/ *v* [Tn, Tn·pr] ~ **sb/sth** (**from sth/doing sth**) hold back sb/sth from movement or action; keep sb/sth under control or in check: *restrain one's anger, laughter, tears* ○ *restrain one's natural urges, impulses, etc* ○ *I must learn to restrain myself,* eg not say what I think. ○ *The police had difficulty in restraining the crowd from rushing on to the pitch.*

▷ **restrained** *adj* keeping one's feelings, language or behaviour in check; controlled: *a restrained rebuke, protest, discussion* ○ *He was furious, but his manner was very restrained.*

restraint /rɪˈstreɪnt/ *n* (*fml*) **1** [U] restraining or being restrained: *submit to/break loose from restraint* ○ *The child's affections were kept under/suffered continual restraint.* **2** [C] ~ (**on sb/sth**) thing that checks or controls; restriction: *the restraints on the family budget of a limited income* ○ *throw off the restraints of convention* ○ *impose restraints on wage settlements.* **3** [U] ~ (**in sth**) avoidance of exaggeration or excess; moderation: *He showed/exercised considerable restraint in not suing for a divorce.* **4** (idm) **without reˈstraint** without control; freely: *talk, weep without restraint.*

restrict /rɪˈstrɪkt/ *v* [Tn, Tn·pr] ~ **sb/sth** (**to sth**) put a limit on sb/sth: *Fog restricted visibility.* ○ *measures restricting one's freedom, authority, rights* ○ *Speed is restricted to 30 mph in towns.* ○ *families restricted to (having) one child* ○ *restrict oneself to one meal a day* ○ *You are restricted to eight litres of duty-free wine.*

▷ **restricted** *adj* **1** having certain limitations: *restricted access, development, potential* ○ *The drug has only a restricted commercial use.* ○ (*Brit*) *a restricted area,* ie where speed or parking is strictly controlled. **2** [esp attrib] (**a**) (*Brit*) (of land) not fully open to the public: *enter a restricted zone.* (**b**) (*esp US*) (of land) not fully open to military personnel.

restriction /rɪˈstrɪkʃn/ *n* **1** [U] restricting or being restricted: *restriction of expenditure.* **2** [C esp *pl*] ~ (**on sth**) instance of this; law, etc that restricts: *raise, lift, ban, abolish, etc a restriction* ○ *place, impose, enforce, etc a restriction* ○ *speed, price, import, etc restrictions* ○ *There are currency restrictions on the sums allowed for foreign travel.* ○ *The sale of firearms is subject to many legal restrictions.*

restrictive /rɪˈstrɪktɪv/ *adj* **1** restricting: *restrictive rulings, measures, etc.* **2** (*grammar*) of a relative clause or phrase that limits or defines the noun which it follows: *'My friends who live in London' contains a restrictive clause; 'my parents, who live in Leeds' does not.* ▷ **restrictively** *adv.* **restrictiveness** *n* [U].

□ **re**ˌ**strictive** ˈ**practices** (*Brit*) (in industry) practices that hinder the most effective use of labour, technical resources, etc and hamper efficient production.

restructure /ˌriːˈstrʌktʃə(r)/ *v* [Tn] give a new or different structure or arrangement to (sth): *restructure an organization, a proposal, the plot of a novel.* ▷ **restructuring** *n* [U, C usu *sing*]: *The rating system is undergoing some/a complete restructuring.*

result /rɪˈzʌlt/ *n* **1** (**a**) [C, U] ~ (**of sth**) effect or outcome (of sth): *The flight was delayed as a result of fog.* ○ *His limp is the result of an accident.* ○ (*fml*) *I was late, with the result that* (ie so that) *I missed my train.* ○ *All our hard work produced little or no result.* ○ *My investigations were without result.* (**b**) **results** [pl] significant and pleasing outcome: *That trainer knows how to get results from his horses.* ○ *begin to show, produce, achieve results.* **2** [C] (**a**) (esp *pl*) ~ (**of sth**) statement of the score, marks or name of the winner in a sporting event or a competition or an examination, etc: *ˈfootball, racing, etc results* ○ *have good/bad exam results* ○ *The result of the match was a draw.* ○ *announce the results of an election.* (**b**) (esp *sing*) (*Brit infml*) (esp in football) win: *We desperately need a result from this match.* **3** [C] answer to a mathematical problem, etc found by calculation.

▷ **result** /rɪˈzʌlt/ *v* **1** [I, Ipr] ~ (**from sth**) occur as a result(1a): *injuries resulting from a fall.* **2** (phr v) **result in sth** have a specified effect or consequence: *Our efforts resulted in success/failure.* ○ *The talks resulted in reducing the number of missiles/missile reduction.*

resultant /-ənt/ *adj* [attrib] (*fml*) happening as a result or consequence: *the resultant profit from reducing staff and increasing sales.*

resume /rɪˈzjuːm; *US* -ˈzuːm/ *v* (*fml*) **1** [I, Tn, Tg] begin (sth) again or continue (sth) after stopping for a time: *Hostilities resumed after the cease-fire.* ○ *resume a flight, voyage, trip, etc* ○ *resume (one's) work, efforts, labours, etc* ○ *Resume reading where you left off.* **2** [Tn] take or occupy (sth) again: *She resumed her maiden name after the divorce.* ○ *resume one's seat,* ie sit down again ○ *resume possession of a title.*

résumé /ˈrezjuːmeɪ; *US* ˌrezʊˈmeɪ/ *n* **1** summary: *give a résumé of the evidence, plot, meeting.* **2** (*US*) = CURRICULUM VITAE (CURRICULUM).

resumption /rɪˈzʌmpʃn/ *n* [U, sing] (*fml*) (instance of) resuming (RESUME 1): *no immediate resumption of building work* ○ *a resumption of hostilities, efforts, activities, negotiations.*

resurface /ˌriːˈsɜːfɪs/ *v* **1** [Tn] put a new surface on (a road, etc): *resurfacing work on the motorway.* **2** [I] come to the surface again: *The submarine resurfaced.* ○ (*fig*) *Old prejudices began to resurface.*

resurgent /rɪˈsɜːdʒənt/ *adj* [usu attrib] (*fml*) rising or reviving after destruction, defeat, disappearance, etc: *a resurgent economy* ○ *resurgent hope, nationalism.* ▷ **resurgence** /-əns/ *n* [U, sing]: *a sudden resurgence of interest in Victorian art.*

resurrect /ˌrezəˈrekt/ *v* [Tn] (*usu fig*) **1** bring (sb) back to life again: *That noise is enough to resurrect*

Retirement

The usual age for retirement in Britain is 65 for men and 60 for women. Many people, however, continue to work beyond these ages. Whether they do so or not, they are entitled to a state pension from retirement age, however much they earn, and are officially 'old age pensioners' (OAPs) or 'senior citizens'. Most people receive a pension from their employer as well as the state pension, after contributing to a pension fund during their working life.

People of retirement age are also entitled to a number of other advantages, including reduced charges for some services. For example, they can travel at reduced rates or even free on public transport, do not pay for medical prescriptions, and can buy tickets for concerts, the theatre, etc at reduced prices. Some services such as hairdressing and dry cleaning are offered at reduced prices to pensioners.

Many people move to a smaller house or flat when they retire and some choose to live in the country or by the sea. It is not usual for retired people to live with their children unless they are unable to live independently (for example in a 'granny flat'). When people become too frail to live alone, they are cared for either by relatives or in nursing homes or old people's homes, which are either privately owned or run by local authorities. Many retired people choose to live in 'sheltered housing', ie a block of flats or group of small houses specially built for older people, where there is a resident warden.

Welfare services for old people include the 'meals on wheels' service run by volunteers, which supplies hot meals to people living alone, and domestic cleaning and other services provided by local authority social services departments, including the provision of day centres and pensioners' clubs.

The number of retired people is steadily growing in Britain. It is now about 18 per cent of the population compared with 15 per cent at the beginning of the 1960s. Since people are living longer, they can expect many years of healthy and active retirement. Popular interests for retired people are travel (in Britain and abroad), gardening, local history, and voluntary work for charities or the local community. People who want to learn something new can follow a course at the Open University or attend the classes run by local authorities.

In the USA, people can retire at 62 or 65, when they qualify for social security payments. These are slightly higher if they retire at 65 rather than 62. People who continue to work beyond this age receive a reduced payment, depending on the level of their income, but on reaching the age of 70 they get the full amount. As in Britain, retired people are entitled to certain benefits. One of these is Medicare which provides subsidized medical care for people aged 65 and over. (Cf article at HEALTH).

The proportion of people over retirement age is increasing in the USA as in Britain. In 1990, about 13 per cent of Americans were 65 or over and this figure is likely to rise to almost a quarter of the population by the year 2080.

Many retired Americans belong to the American Association of Retired Persons (AARP). This entitles them to receive the magazine *Modern Maturity* which has one of the highest readerships in the country. Favourite hobbies for retired people include bird-watching, fishing, painting and adult education, and foreign travel is extremely popular. Many Americans enjoy tracing and writing about their family histories. By contrast, many retired British people find an interest in researching local history.

the dead! **2** revive (a practice, etc); bring back into use: *resurrect old customs, habits, traditions, etc* ○ (*joc*) *resurrect an old dress from the sixties.*

▷ **resurrection** /ˌrezəˈrekʃn/ *n* **1 the Resurrection** [sing] (*religion*) **(a)** the rising of Jesus from the tomb. **(b)** the rising of all the dead at the Last Judgement. **2** [U, sing] (*fml fig*) revival after disuse, inactivity, etc: *a resurrection of hope.*

resuscitate /rɪˈsʌsɪteɪt/ *v* [Tn] (*fml*) bring (sb/sth) back to consciousness: *resuscitate a boy rescued from drowning.* ▷ **resuscitation** /rɪˌsʌsɪˈteɪʃn/ *n* [U]: *their efforts/attempts at resuscitation.*

ret (also **retd**) *abbr* **1** retired. **2** returned.

retail /ˈri:teɪl/ *n* [U] selling of goods, which are usu not for resale, in small quantities to the general public: *outlets* (ie shops) *for the retail of leather goods* ○ [attrib] *retail businesses, traders* ○ *manufacturer's recommended retail price £9.99* ○ *the retail price index*, ie the record of average retail prices. Cf WHOLESALE.

▷ **retail** *adv* by retail: *Do you buy wholesale or retail?*

retail *v* **1** [Ipr, Tn·pr] ~ **(sth) at/for sth** be sold or sell (sth) retail at (a price): *These biros retail at/for 70p.* **2** [Tn, Tn·pr] ~ **sth (to sb)** (*fml*) give (details of gossip, scandal, etc) to others, usu repeatedly.

retailer *n* tradesman who sells by retail.

retain /rɪˈteɪn/ *v* [Tn] (*esp fml*) **1** keep (sth) in one's possession or use: *We retained the original fireplace when we decorated the room.* **2** continue to have (sth); not lose: *Despite losing his job he retains his pension.* ○ *These roses retain their scent.* ○ *He is 90 but still retains (the use of) all his faculties.* ○ *The police retained control of the situation.* **3** keep (sth) in one's memory: *be able to retain numbers, dates, facts, etc* ○ *She retains a clear impression/memory of the incident.* **4** keep (sth) in place; hold or contain: *A dyke was built to retain the floods.* ○ *Clay soil retains water.* **5** (*law*) book the services of (esp a barrister) by making a preliminary payment: *a retaining fee.*

▷ **retainer** *n* **1** (*law*) fee paid to sb (esp a barrister) in advance for services as and when one may need them: [attrib] *a retainer agreement.* **2** reduced rent paid to reserve a flat, etc for one's use while one is absent from it. **3** (*arch*) servant, esp one who has been with a family or person for a long time: (*joc*) *an old family retainer.*

□ **reˈtaining wall** wall built to support a mass of earth or to confine water.

retake /ˌri:ˈteɪk/ *v* (*pt* **retook** /-ˈtʊk/, *pp* **retaken** /-ˈteɪkən/) [Tn] **1** capture (sth) again: *retake a fortress, ship, town.* **2** photograph or film (sth) again: *retake a shot, scene, etc.* **3** sit (an examination, etc) again; resit: *retake the physics paper.*

▷ **retake** /ˈri:teɪk/ *n* (*infml*) **1** second, etc filming of a scene: *do several retakes.* **2** (person attending a) second, etc sitting of an examination; resit.

retaliate /rɪˈtælɪeɪt/ *v* [I, Ipr] ~ **(against sb/sth)** repay an injury, insult, etc with a similar one: *He slapped his sister, who retaliated by kicking him.* ○ *If we impose import duties, other countries may retaliate against us.*

▷ **retaliation** /rɪˌtælɪˈeɪʃn/ *n* [U] ~ **(against sb/sth)**; ~ **(for sth)** retaliating: *immediate retaliation against the striking miners* ○ *a terrorist bomb attack in retaliation for recent arrests.*

retaliatory /rɪˈtælɪətrɪ; *US* -tɔ:rɪ/ *adj* done or meant as retaliation: *take retaliatory measures, actions, etc* ○ *The raid was purely retaliatory.*

retard /rɪˈtɑ:d/ *v* [Tn] (*fml*) **1** make (sth) slow or late: *retard the mechanism*, eg of a clock ○ *retard the spark*, eg of an engine. **2** slow the progress or development of (sb/sth); hinder: *Lack of sun retards plant growth.*

▷ **retardation** /ˌri:tɑ:ˈdeɪʃn/ *n* [U]: *mental retardation.*

retarded *adj* backward in physical or (esp) mental development: *be severely (mentally) retarded.*

retch /retʃ/ *v* [I] make the sounds and movements of vomiting, esp involuntarily, but without bringing anything up from the stomach.

retd *abbr* = RET.

retell /ˌri:ˈtel/ *v* (*pt, pp* **retold** /-ˈtəʊld/) [Tn, Tn·pr] ~ **sth (to sb)** tell (a story, etc) again, in a different way or in a different language: *Greek myths retold for children.*

retention /rɪˈtenʃn/ *n* [U, sing] (*fml*) **1** possession or use of sth: *retention of one's rights, privileges, etc* ○ *the full retention of one's (mental) faculties.* **2** ability to remember things: *her limited/extraordinary powers of retention* ○ *show an amazing retention of facts, details, childhood impressions, etc.* **3** action of holding (sth) in position or containing it: *the retention of flood waters, crowds* ○ *suffer from retention of urine*, ie failure to pass it out from the bladder.

retentive /rɪˈtentɪv/ *adj* **1** (of the memory) having the ability to remember facts, impressions, etc. **2** having the ability to hold or contain liquid, etc: *retentive soil*, ie that does not dry out quickly. ▷ **retentively** *adv.* **retentiveness** *n* [U].

rethink /ˌri:ˈθɪŋk/ *v* (*pt, pp* **-thought** /-ˈθɔ:t/) [I, Tn] reconsider or think about (sth) again, esp in order to change it: *rethink a policy, plan, situation, verdict* ○ *A good deal of rethinking is needed on this question.*

▷ **rethink** /ˈri:θɪŋk/ *n* [sing] (*infml*) act of thinking again: *have a quick rethink before deciding.*

reticent /ˈretɪsnt/ *adj* ~ **(about/on sth)** not revealing one's thoughts or feelings easily; reserved: *be reticent about one's plans* ○ *He seemed unduly reticent on the subject of his past.* ▷ **reticence** /-sns/ *n* [U]: *He always displays a certain reticence in discussing personal matters.* **reticently** *adv.*

reticulated /rɪˈtɪkjʊleɪtɪd/ (also **reticulate** /rɪˈtɪkjʊleɪt/) *adj* (*fml*) divided into a network of small squares or intersecting lines: *the reticulated skin of a snake.*

▷ **reticulation** /rɪˌtɪkjʊˈleɪʃn/ *n* [U, C esp *pl*] net-like pattern or structure.

reticule /ˈretɪkju:l/ *n* (*arch or joc*) woman's small bag, usu made of net, etc and shaped like a pouch with a drawstring neck.

reticulum /rɪˈtɪkjʊləm/ *n* (*pl* **-la** /-lə/) **1** second stomach of a cow, sheep, etc. **2** net-like structure, esp a fine network in cytoplasm.

retina /ˈretɪnə; *US* ˈretənə/ *n* (*pl* ~**s** /-nɪ:/ **-inae**) layer of membrane at the back of the eyeball, sensitive to light. ⇨ illus at EYE. ▷ **retinal** /-nəl/ *adj.*

retinue /ˈretɪnju:; *US* ˈretənu:/ *n* [CGp] group of attendants accompanying an important person: *The Queen was flanked by a retinue of bodyguards and policemen.* ○ (*joc*) *the fête organizer and her retinue of helpers.*

retire /rɪˈtaɪə(r)/ *v* **1** **(a)** [I, Ipr] ~ **(from sth)** give up one's regular work, esp because of age: *retire early*, ie before reaching retirement age ○ *retire on a pension at 65* ○ *He will retire from the army/his* *directorship next year.* ○ *the retiring union leader.* (**b**) [Tn esp passive] cause (an employee) to do this: *I was retired on full pay.* Cf RESIGN 1. **2** [I, Ipr] ~ (**from...**) (**to...**) (*fml*) (of an army, etc) withdraw voluntarily, esp in order to reorganize, etc: *Our forces retired to prepared positions.* Cf RETREAT. **3** [I, Ipr] (**a**) ~ (**from...**) (**to...**) (*fml*) retreat or go away, esp to somewhere quiet or private: *The jury retired (from the courtroom) to consider their verdict.* ○ *After lunch he retired to his study.* (**b**) ~ (**to sth**) (*fml or joc*) go to bed: *I decided to retire early with a book.* **4** [La, I, Ipr] ~ (**from sth**) (in sport) withdraw voluntarily from a game, match, etc: *The boxer retired from the contest with eye injuries.* ○ *The batsman retired hurt.*

▷ **retired** *adj* having retired from work: *a retired Civil Servant.* **re'tired list** list of former officers who have retired from any of the armed services.

retiring /rɪ'taɪərɪŋ/ *adj* avoiding society; shy: *Jane had a gentle retiring disposition.*

retirement /rɪ'taɪəmənt/ *n* **1** [C, U] (instance of) retiring or being retired from work: *There have been several retirements in my office recently.* ○ *announce/give notice of one's retirement* ○ *urge older staff to take early retirement,* ie retire before the usual age ○ *be well above/below the age of retirement* ○ [attrib] *retirement benefits* ○ *a retirement pension.* **2** [U, sing] condition of being retired from work: *He lives in retirement in Cornwall.* ○ *a happy and profitable retirement.* ⇨ article. **3** (idm) **go into/come out of retirement** leave/return to one's regular work.

□ **re'tirement age** age at which people normally retire: *reach retirement age* ○ *reduce the retirement age for teachers to 55.*

retort[1] /rɪ'tɔ:t/ *v* [Tn, Tf] make a quick, witty or angry reply, esp to an accusation or challenge: *'Nonsense!' she retorted.* ○ *He retorted that it was my fault as much as his.*

▷ **retort** *n* (**a**) [U] retorting: *He made a rude sign by way of retort.* (**b**) [C] reply of this kind: *make an insolent retort.*

retort[2] /rɪ'tɔ:t/ *n* **1** glass vessel with a long narrow neck turned downwards, used for distilling liquids. **2** receptacle used in making gas or steel.

retouch /ˌri:'tʌtʃ/ *v* [Tn] improve or alter (a photograph, painting, etc) by removing flaws or making minor changes.

retrace /ri:'treɪs/ *v* [Tn] **1** go back over or repeat (a journey, route, etc) exactly: *retrace one's steps,* ie return the way one came. **2** recall a series of (past actions, etc): *Police retraced the movements of the murder victim.*

retract /rɪ'trækt/ *v* [I, Tn] (*fml*) **1** withdraw (a statement, charge, etc): *The accused refused to retract (his statement).* **2** refuse to honour or keep (an agreement, etc): *retract a promise, an offer, etc.* **3** move or pull (sth) back or in: *The undercarriage on light aircraft does not always retract in flight.*

▷ **retractable** /-əbl/ *adj* that can be drawn in: *a retractable undercarriage.*

retractile /rɪ'træktaɪl; US -tl/ *adj* that can be retracted (RETRACT 3): *A cat's claws are retractile.*

retraction /rɪ'trækʃn/ *n* (**a**) [U] retracting. (**b**) [C] instance of this: *publish a retraction of the charge.*

retractor /-tə(r)/ *n* instrument used by surgeons to hold the edges of a wound apart.

retread /ˌri:'tred/ *v* (*pt, pp* **-ed**) (also **remould**, *US* **remold** /ˌri:'məʊld/, *US* also ˌ**re'cap**) [Tn] provide (an old tyre) with a new tread(*n* 3).

▷ **retread** /'ri:tred/ (also **remould**, *US* **remold** /'ri:məʊld/, *US* also **'recap**) *n* tyre made by moulding rubber onto an old foundation.

retreat /rɪ'tri:t/ *v* [I, Ipr, In/pr] **1** (esp of an army, etc) withdraw after being defeated or when faced with danger or difficulty: *force the enemy to retreat (behind their lines)* ○ *crowds retreating before police fire hoses* ○ *We retreated half a mile.* Cf ADVANCE[2] 2. **2** (*fig*) go away to a place of shelter or privacy: *retreat into a world of fantasy* ○ *retreat from the public eye.* Cf RETIRE.

▷ **retreat** *n* **1** [C usu *sing*, U] act or instance of retreating: *The minister made an undignified retreat from his earlier position.* ○ *an orderly retreat from the camp* ○ *The army was in full retreat.* **2 the retreat** [sing] military signal for this: *sound the retreat,* eg on a drum or bugle. **3** (**a**) [U] withdrawal into privacy or seclusion. (**b**) [C] place suitable for this: *spend weekends at my country retreat.* (**c**) [U, C] (*religion*) period of withdrawal from worldly activities for prayer and meditation: *go into/be in retreat* ○ *make an annual retreat.* **4** (idm) **beat a retreat** ⇨ BEAT[1].

retrench /rɪ'trentʃ/ *v* (*fml*) **1** [I] make economies or reduce expenses: *Inflation has forced us to retrench.* **2** [Tn] reduce the amount of (money spent): *retrench one's expenditure.*

▷ **retrenchment** *n* (**a**) [U] retrenching. (**b**) [C] instance of this.

retrial /ˌri:'traɪəl/ *n* action of trying a lawsuit again; new trial: *The judge ordered a retrial because of irregularities.*

retribution /ˌretrɪ'bju:ʃn/ *n* [U] ~ (**for sth**) (*fml*) deserved punishment or compensation for injury, etc: *jailed in retribution for his crimes* ○ *make retribution to God for one's sins* ○ *the day, hour, moment, etc of retribution.*

▷ **retributive** /rɪ'trɪbjʊtɪv/ *adj* [attrib] happening or inflicted as retribution: *reˌtributive 'justice.*

retrieve /rɪ'tri:v/ *v* **1** [Tn, Tn·pr] ~ **sth** (**from sb/sth**) (*esp fml*) get possession of sth again: *retrieve one's suitcase from the left luggage office* ○ (*joc*) *I must retrieve my credit card from the waiter.* **2** [Tn, Tn·pr] (*esp computing*) find again or extract (stored information): *retrieve data from a disk* ○ *retrieve an address from the files.* **3** [Tn] (*fml*) set right (a loss, an error, etc): *He retrieved his losses by betting on a succession of winners.* ○ *We can only retrieve the situation by reducing our expenses.* **4** [I, Tn] (of a trained dog) find and bring back (dead or wounded birds, etc). **5** [Tn, Tn·pr] ~ **sth** (**from sth**) (*fml*) restore sth to a flourishing state; revive sth: *retrieve one's fortunes.*

▷ **retrievable** /-əbl/ *adj* (*esp computing*) that can be retrieved.

retrieval /-vl/ *n* [U] (*fml*) retrieving or being retrieved: *the retrieval of the company's fortunes* ○ *a match lost beyond all hope of retrieval* ○ (*computing*) *information retrieval.*

retriever *n* dog of a breed which is often trained to retrieve game.

retro- *pref* (with *adjs* and *ns*) back or backwards: *retroactive* ○ *retrograde* ○ *retro-rocket.*

retroactive /ˌretrəʊ'æktɪv/ *adj* (*fml*) effective from a past date: *The new law was made retroactive to January,* ie as if it had come into effect then. ▷ **retroactively** *adv.*

retroflex /'retrəfleks/ (also **retroflexed** /-kst/) *adj* [attrib] (*phonetics*) (of a sound) made by bending the tip of the tongue upwards and backwards.

retrograde /'retrəgreɪd/ *adj* (*fml*) **1** going backwards: *retrograde motion.* **2** getting worse; returning to a less good condition: *a retrograde policy, step.*

retrogress /ˌretrə'gres/ *v* [I, Ipr] ~ (**to sth**) (*fml*) **1** go backwards. **2** get worse or deteriorate.

▷ **retrogression** /ˌretrə'greʃn/ *n* [U] return to a less advanced state; decline.

retrogressive *adj.* **retrogressively** *adv.*

retro-rocket /'retrəʊrɒkɪt/ *n* rocket engine providing power in the opposite direction to the path of flight and used to slow down or alter the course of a spacecraft, etc.

retrospect /'retrəspekt/ *n* (idm) **in retrospect** looking back on a past event or situation: *In retrospect, it's easy to see why we were wrong.*

▷ **retrospection** /ˌretrə'spekʃn/ *n* [U] action of looking back on past events, experiences, etc.

retrospective /ˌretrə'spektɪv/ *adj* **1** looking back on the past: *retrospective views, thoughts, etc* ○ *a retrospective exhibition of the painter's work.* **2** (of laws, payments, etc) applying to the past as well as the future; retroactive: *The legislation was made retrospective.* ○ *a retrospective* (ie back-dated) *pay rise.* — *n* exhibition tracing the development of a painter, sculptor, etc. **retrospectively** *adv.*

retroussé /rə'tru:seɪ; *US* ˌretru'seɪ/ *adj* (*French esp approv*) (of the nose) turned up at the end.

retry /ˌri:'traɪ/ *v* (*pt, pp* **retried**) [Tn] try (a lawsuit or a defendant) again: *There are calls for the case to be retried.*

retsina /ret'si:nə; *US* 'retsɪnə/ *n* [U, C] Greek wine flavoured with resin.

return[1] /rɪ'tɜ:n/ *v* **1** [I, Ipr] (**a**) ~ (**to...**) (**from...**) come or go back to a place: *return (home) from a holiday* ○ *return to Paris from London* ○ *She returned to collect her umbrella.* (**b**) ~ (**to sb/sth**) come or go back to an earlier activity or condition: *doubts, symptoms, suspicions that return constantly* ○ *My good humour/spirits soon returned.* ○ *I shall return to this point* (ie discuss it again) *later.* ○ *return to one's old habits* ○ *The bus service has returned to normal after the strike.* **2** (**a**) [Tn, Tn·pr, Cn·a, Dn·n, Dn·pr] ~ **sth** (**to sth/sb**) bring, give, put or send sth back: *Please return all empties,* ie empty milk bottles. ○ (*fml*) *She returned the bird to its cage.* ○ *I returned the letter unopened.* ○ *Please return me my £5/return my £5 to me.* (**b**) [Tn] give (sth) in response; reciprocate: *return an invitation, a visit* ○ *return a greeting, stare, salute, etc* ○ *return a compliment/favour* ○ *I cannot return your love/affection.* ○ *The enemy returned our fire.* ○ *He returned the blow smartly.* (**c**) [Tn] (in cricket, tennis, etc) send (a ball) back: *return a shot, service, volley, etc.* **3** [Tn] (*fml*) state or describe (sth) officially, esp in reply to a formal demand for information: *return the details of one's income,* ie to a tax inspector ○ *The jury returned a verdict of guilty.* **4** [Tn] give (sth) as profit: *Our investment accounts return a high rate of interest.* **5** [esp passive: Tn, Tn·pr, Cn·n/a] ~ **sb** (**to sth**); ~ **sb** (**as sth**) elect sb as a Member of Parliament: *He was returned to Parliament with a decreased majority.* ○ *Smith was returned as MP for Bath.* **6** [Tn] (*dated*) say (sth) in answer; reply: *'Never!' he returned curtly.* **7** (idm) **return to the 'fold** (*fml*) rejoin a group of people, esp a religious or political group with similar beliefs or aims.

▷ **returnable** /-əbl/ *adj* that can or must be returned: *returnable bottles, crates, etc.*

returnee /rɪˌtɜ:r'ni:/ *n* (*US*) person who returns from military service abroad, esp after a war.

□ **re'turning officer** (*Brit*) official who conducts an election in a constituency and announces the result.

return[2] /rɪ'tɜ:n/ *n* **1** [sing] (**a**) ~ (**to...**) (**from...**) coming or going back to a place: *on my return home (from Italy),* ie when I got/get back ○ [attrib] *a return trip, voyage, flight, etc.* (**b**) ~ (**to sth**) coming or going back to an earlier activity or condition: *a return of my doubts, symptoms, suspicions* ○ *the return of spring* ○ *a return to normal working hours, old habits.* **2** [C, U] ~ (**to sb/sth**) bringing, giving, putting or sending back: *the return of library books, milk bottles, faulty goods* ○ *The deposit is refunded on return of the vehicle.* ○ *no deposit, no return,* eg as a notice on a non-returnable bottle, etc ○ *These flowers are a small return* (ie token of thanks) *for your kindness.* ○ *Her return of service* (ie at tennis) *was very fast.* ○ [attrib] *return shots.* **3** [C] official report or statement, esp one made in reply to a formal demand: *make one's '(income-)tax return* ○ *the e'lection returns,* ie figures of the voting at an election. **4** [C esp *pl*] ~ (**on sth**) profit from a transaction, etc: *disappointing returns on capital, investment, etc* ○ *You'll get a good return on these shares.* ○ *small profits and quick returns,* ie the theory behind businesses that rely on large sales and a quick turnover. **5** [C] (*Brit*) (*US* **round trip**) ticket for a journey to a place and back again: *weekend, period, etc returns* ○ *a ˌday-'return to London,* ie valid only for the day of issue. Cf SINGLE 5. **6** [C] theatre ticket bought and then sold back to the box-office: *queuing for returns.* **7** (idm) **by re'turn (of 'post)** (*Brit*) by the next post: *Please reply by return.* ○ *Write now to this address and we will send you a free sample by return.* **in return** (**for sth**) as payment or reward (for sth): *I bought him a drink in return for his help.* **many happy returns** ⇨ HAPPY. **the point of no return** ⇨ POINT[1]. **sale or return** ⇨ SALE.

□ **reˌturn 'fare** (*Brit*) fare needed for a journey to a place and back again.

return 'game, return 'match second game or

match between the same opponents.

return ˈticket (*US* **ˌround-trip ˈticket**) = RETURN 5.

Reuben sandwich /ˌru:bən ˈsænwɪdʒ; *US* -wɪtʃ/ (*US*) sandwich made with hot corned beef, cheese and sauerkraut.

reunion /ˌri:ˈju:nɪən/ *n* **1** [C, U] reuniting or being reunited: *a reunion between the two sisters* ○ *the reunion of the Democrats with the Liberals.* **2** [C] social gathering of people who were formerly friends, colleagues, etc: *emotional, touching, etc reunions* ○ *a family reunion at Christmas* ○ *have/hold an annual reunion of war veterans* ○ [attrib] *a reunion dinner, celebration.*

reunite /ˌri:ju:ˈnaɪt/ *v* [I, Ipr, Tn, Tn·pr] ~ **(sb/sth) (with sb/sth)** (cause sb/sth to) come together again: *her hopes of reuniting with her family* ○ *attempts to reunite the Labour Party* ○ *Parents were reunited with their lost children.*

reuse /ˌri:ˈju:z/ *v* [Tn] use (sth) again: *reuse an old envelope.*

▷ **reuse** /ˌri:ˈju:s/ *n* [U] using or being used again. **reusable** /ˌri:ˈju:zəbl/ *adj* that can be used again: *reusable envelopes* ○ *reusable* (ie rechargeable) *batteries.*

Reuters /ˈrɔɪtəz/ international press agency with journalists in all parts of the world, having a high reputation for objective reporting.

rev /rev/ *n* (usu *pl*) (*infml*) revolution of an engine: *run at maximum revs* ○ *doing a steady 4000 revs (per minute).*

▷ **rev** *v* **(-vv-) 1** [I, Ip] ~ **(up)** (of an engine) revolve; increase the speed of revolution. **2** [Tn, Tn·p] ~ **sth (up)** cause (an engine) to run esp quickly, as when starting a car: *Don't rev the engine so hard.* ○ *Rev it up to warm the engine.*

Rev (also **Revd**) *abbr* Reverend: *Rev George Hill.* Cf RT REV.

revalue /ˌri:ˈvælju:/ *v* **1** [Tn] reassess the value of (sth): *have your house revalued at today's prices.* **2** [I, Tn] increase the exchange value of (a currency): *The franc is to be revalued.* Cf DEVALUE.

▷ **revaluation** /ˌri:vælju:ˈeɪʃn/ *n* [C, U] (instance of) revaluing: *property revaluation* ○ *(a) further revaluation of the yen.*

revamp /ˌri:ˈvæmp/ *v* [Tn] (*infml*) renew (sth), esp superficially; improve the appearance of: *revamp an old comedy routine with some new jokes* ○ *The department was revamped to try to improve its performance.* ○ *revamp a kitchen, study, etc,* ie decorate or modernize it.

reveal /rɪˈvi:l/ *v* **1** [Tn, Tf, Tw, Cn·t, Dn·pr, Dpr·f, Dpr·w] ~ **sth (to sb)** make (facts, etc) known: *reveal secrets, details, methods, faults, feelings* ○ *The survey revealed that the house was damp.* ○ *I can't reveal who told me.* ○ *Her answers revealed her to be innocent.* ○ *The doctor did not reveal the truth to him.* ○ *Teachers revealed to the press that they were going on strike/what action they were taking.* **2** [Tn] cause or allow (sth) to be seen: *The open door revealed an untidy kitchen.* ○ *Close examination revealed a crack in the vase.* ○ (*fig*) *New problems gradually revealed themselves,* ie became apparent.

▷ **revealing** *adj* **1** making (facts, etc) known: *a revealing slip of the tongue, disclosure, comment* ○ *This document is extremely revealing.* **2** (usu preceded by *very, most, rather,* etc) causing or allowing (sth) to be seen: *The X-ray was very revealing.* ○ *a rather revealing* (ie low-cut) *dress.*

□ **reˌvealed reˈligion** religion believed to have been revealed to mankind directly by God.

reveille /rɪˈvælɪ; *US* ˈrevəlɪ/ *n* (also **the reveille**) [sing] military bugle, drum, etc signal to soldiers to get up in the morning: *sound (the) 5.30 reveille.*

revel /ˈrevl/ *v* **(-ll-;** *US* **-l-) 1** [I, Ipr] (*dated or joc*) make merry; celebrate noisily: *revelling until dawn.* **2** (phr v) **revel in sth/doing sth** take great delight in sth: *revelling in her new-found freedom* ○ *revel in wielding power.*

▷ **revel** *n* (usu *pl*) (*dated*) noisy celebrations: *holding midnight revels.*

reveller (*US* **reveler**) /ˈrevələ(r)/ *n* (*dated or joc*) merry-maker: *late-night revellers leaving the pubs.*

revelation /ˌrevəˈleɪʃn/ *n* **1** [U] making known sth that was secret or hidden; revealing: *divine revelation of truth* ○ *the revelation of his identity.* **2** [C] that which is revealed, esp sth surprising: *scandalous revelations in the press* ○ *His Hamlet was a revelation to the critics,* ie They did not expect him to act so well. **3 Revelation** (*Bible*) the last book of the New Testament, also called *The Revelation of St John the Divine,* or (incorrectly) *Revelations.* ⇨ App 5.

revelry /ˈrevlrɪ/ *n* [C usu *pl*, U] noisy celebrations; revels: *The revelries went on all night.* ○ *sounds of drunken revelry.*

revenge /rɪˈvendʒ/ *n* **1** [U] deliberate punishment or injury inflicted in return for what one has suffered: *thirsting for revenge* ○ (*saying*) *Revenge is sweet.* **2** [U] desire to inflict this; vindictiveness: *done in the spirit of revenge.* **3** [U] opportunity given to an opponent in a return game to reverse the result of an earlier one: *give Leeds their revenge.* **4** (idm) **get/have/take one's revenge (on sb) (for sth); take revenge (on sb) (for sth)** return an injury: *They swore to take their revenge on the kidnappers.* **out of/in revenge (for sth)** in order to return an injury: *Terrorists bombed the police station in revenge for the arrests.*

▷ **revenge** *v* **1** [Tn] **(a)** do sth to get satisfaction for (an offence, etc): *revenge an injustice, injury, insult, etc.* **(b)** avenge (sb): *determined to revenge his dead brother.* **2** [Tn·pr] ~ **oneself on sb** get satisfaction by deliberately inflicting injury on sb in return for injury inflicted on oneself. **3** (idm) **be revenged on sb** revenge oneself on sb.

revengeful /-fl/ *adj* feeling or showing a desire for revenge. **revengefully** /-fəlɪ/ *adv.* **revengefulness** *n* [U].

□ **reˈvenge tragedy** dramatic genre popular in England in the 17th century, in which the hero sets out to avenge the murder of a father, mistress, etc, often urged by the ghost of the dead person. The revenge usu takes place on stage and many of the characters die at the end of the play. *Shakespeare's *Hamlet* and *Kyd's *The Spanish Tragedy* are examples of the genre.

revenue /ˈrevənju:; *US* -ənu:/ *n* **1** [U] income, esp the total annual income of the State from taxes, etc: *sources, channels of revenue* ○ *public/private revenue* ○ [attrib] *a ˈrevenue tax,* ie one producing revenue contrasted with one protecting a country's trade. **2 revenues** [pl] separate items of revenue put together: *the revenues of the City Council* ○ *rising/falling oil revenues.*

reverberate /rɪˈvɜ:bəreɪt/ *v* [I, Ipr] ~ **(with sth)** echo or resound repeatedly: *The roar of the train reverberated in the tunnel.* ○ *The room reverberated with the noise of the shot.* ○ (*fig*) *Shock waves reverberated round the department from the manager's resignation.*

▷ **reverberant** /-bərənt/ *adj* (*fml*).

reverberation /rɪˌvɜ:bəˈreɪʃn/ *n* **1** [U] reverberating or being reverberated. **2** [C usu *pl*] repeated echo: *the reverberations of the explosion* ○ (*fig*) *the continuing reverberations* (ie repercussions) *of the scandal.*

Revere /rɪˈvɪə(r)/ Paul (1735-1818), American patriot. He became a folk hero of the *War of American Independence as a result of his ride in the middle of the night from Charlestown to Lexington to warn of the arrival of British troops at Boston.

revere /rɪˈvɪə(r)/ *v* [Tn, Tn·pr] ~ **sb/sth (for sth)** (*fml*) feel deep respect or (esp religious) veneration for sb/sth: *revere virtue, human life, the church's teaching* ○ *The professor was revered for his immense learning.*

reverence /ˈrevərəns/ *n* **1** [U] ~ **(for sb/sth)** feeling of deep respect or (esp religious) veneration: *He removed his hat as a sign of reverence.* ○ *He felt/had/showed great reverence for Leonardo.* **2** [C] (*dated or joc*) title used in speaking to or about a clergyman: *your/his reverence* ○ *Their reverences will have tea.*

▷ **reverence** *v* [Tn] (*fml*) treat (sb/sth) with reverence; revere.

reverend /ˈrevərənd/ *adj* [attrib] **1** deserving to be treated with respect, esp because of age, etc. **2 the Reverend**, (*abbrs* **Rev**, **Revd**) (used as the title of a clergyman): *the Rev John/J/Mr Smith* (but not *the Rev Smith*); *the Very Reverend,* of a dean; *the Right Reverend,* of a bishop; *the Most Reverend,* of an archbishop or Irish Roman Catholic bishop; *the Reverend Father,* of a Roman Catholic priest.

□ **ˌReverend ˈMother** (title of a) Mother Superior of a convent.

reverent /ˈrevərənt/ *adj* feeling or showing reverence: *reverent attitudes, gestures, etc.* ▷ **reverently** *adv*: *wreaths laid reverently on the coffin.*

reverential /ˌrevəˈrenʃl/ *adj* (*fml*) caused by or showing reverence: *ushered in with a reverential bow.* ▷ **reverentially** /-ʃəlɪ/ *adv.*

reverie /ˈrevərɪ/ *n* [U, C] (state of having) idle and pleasant thoughts: *be deep, sunk, lost in reverie* ○ *She fell into a reverie about her childhood.*

revers /rɪˈvɪə(r)/ *n* (*pl* unchanged /-ɪəz/) (usu *pl*) edge of a coat, jacket, etc, turned back to show the reverse side (eg on a lapel or cuff).

reversal /rɪˈvɜ:sl/ *n* [C, U] **1** (instance of) making sth the opposite of what it was; turning around: *a dramatic reversal of her earlier decision* ○ *a reversal of the usual procedures, tendencies, opinions* ○ (*fig*) *His luck suffered a cruel reversal,* ie change for the worse. **2** (instance of) exchanging two positions, functions, etc: *role reversal/reversal of roles,* eg between husband and wife when the husband looks after the house and children while the wife works.

reverse[1] /rɪˈvɜ:s/ *adj* **1** [attrib] ~ **(of/to sth)** contrary or opposite to what is expected: *reverse tendencies, processes* ○ *Statistics showed a reverse trend to that recorded in other countries.* **2** (idm) **in/into reverse ˈorder** from the end towards the start; backwards: *Count down in reverse order — 10, 9, 8...* ○ *Put the letters in 'madam' into reverse order and they still read 'madam'.*

□ **reˌverse ˈgear** = REVERSE[2] 4a.

reˌverse ˈturn = REVERSE[2] 4b.

reverse[2] /rɪˈvɜ:s/ *n* **1 the reverse (of sth)** [sing] thing that is the contrary or opposite to what is expected: *In hot weather, the reverse happens/applies.* ○ *Children's shoes aren't cheap — quite the reverse.* ○ (*fml*) *You were the (very) reverse of polite,* ie You were rude. **2** [sing] **(a)** (design on the) underside or back of a coin, medal, etc: *The 10p coin has a crowned lion on its reverse.* Cf OBVERSE. **(b)** underside or back of sth: *flaws on the reverse of the silk* ○ *a maker's mark on the reverse of a plate.* **3** [C] (*fml*) **(a)** change for the worse; misfortune: *We suffered some serious (financial) reverses.* **(b)** defeat: *a sudden reverse in the guerrilla campaign* ○ *a reverse at the polls,* ie a poor election result. **4 (a)** [U, C usu *sing*] (also **reverse ˈgear**) control used to make a vehicle travel backwards: *Put the car into reverse.* ○ *cars with five forward gears and a reverse.* **(b)** [C] (also **reverse ˈturn**) turn made while driving backwards: *I can't do reverses.* **5** [C] device that reverses sth: *an automatic ribbon reverse,* ie on a typewriter. **6** (idm) **in/into reˈverse** from the end towards the start; backwards: *Ambulances have 'AMBULANCE' printed in reverse on their bonnets* ○ (*fig*) *The superpowers are putting the arms race into reverse.*

reverse[3] /rɪˈvɜ:s/ *v* **1** [Tn] turn (sth) the other way round or up, or inside out: *Writing is reversed in a mirror.* ○ *reverse the collar and cuffs on a shirt,* ie to hide frayed edges. **2 (a)** [I, Ipr, Ip, Tn, Tn·pr, Tn·p] (cause a vehicle to) travel backwards: *reverse round a corner, up a hill, across a side street,etc* ○ *He reversed (the car) into a tree.* ○ *The garage is open, so you can reverse in.* **(b)** [I, Tn] (make an engine, etc) work in the opposite direction: *reverse the thrust of the rocket motors* ○ *brake* (eg a fixed-wheel cycle) *by reversing the pedalling action.* **3** [Tn] **(a)** make (sth) the opposite of what it was; change around completely: *reverse a procedure, process, trend, etc.* **(b)** exchange (two functions, positions, etc): *Husband and wife have reversed roles.* ○ *Their situations are now reversed as employee has become employer.* **4** [Tn] revoke or annul (a decree, etc): *reverse the decision of a lower court* ○ *reverse a decree, judgement, verdict, etc.*

5 (idm) **reverse (the) ˈcharge(s)** (*US* **call ˈcollect**) make a telephone call that will be charged to the person receiving it, not the caller: *reverse the charges on/for a call* ○ *make a reversed-ˈcharge call to New York.*

▷ **reversible** /-əbl/ *adj* that can be reversed: *a reversible coat, scarf, cap, etc,* ie one that can be worn with either side turned out ○ *reversible changes, reactions,* ie after which it is possible to return to the original state. **reversibility** /rɪˌvɜːsəˈbɪlətɪ/ *n* [U].

□ **reˈversing light** white light at the back of a vehicle showing that it is in reverse gear.

revert /rɪˈvɜːt/ *v* [Ipr] **1** ~ **to sth** (**a**) return to (a former state or condition): *fields that have reverted to moorland,* ie are no longer cultivated. (**b**) (*fml*) return to (a former practice or habit): *revert to smoking when under stress* ○ *After her divorce she reverted to (using) her maiden name.* **2** ~ **to sth** (*fml*) return to (a topic in talk or thought): *To revert/Reverting to your earlier question, ...* ○ *The conversation kept reverting to the subject of money.* ○ *Her thoughts often reverted to Italy.* **3** ~ (**to sb/sth**) (*law*) (of property, rights, etc) return or pass to the original owner, the State, etc: *If he dies without an heir, his property reverts to the state.* **4** (idm) **revert to type** return to a natural or an original condition: *Once a socialist, she has now reverted to type and votes Tory like her parents.*

▷ **reversion** /rɪˈvɜːʃn; *US* -ʒn/ *n* **1** [U, sing] reverting: *(a) reversion to swamp, old methods, former habits.* **2** (*law*) (**a**) [C] right to possess property, etc when its present owner dies or gives it up. (**b**) [U] returning of a right or property to the original owner, the State, etc: *succeed to an estate in reversion.* **reversionary** /rɪˈvɜːʃənərɪ; *US* -ʒənerɪ/ *adj* [attrib] (*law*): *reversionary rights.*

revertible /rɪˈvɜːtəbl/ *adj.*

revetment /rɪˈvetmənt/ *n* **1** facing of masonry, concrete, sandbags, etc on a wall or an embankment, esp of a fortification. **2** retaining wall.

review /rɪˈvjuː/ *n* **1** [U, C] (act of) re-examination or reconsideration: *The terms of the contract are subject to review.* ○ *a radical review of manufacturing methods.* **2** [C] survey or report of past events or a subject: *an annual, monthly, etc review of progress* ○ *a review of the year's sport* ○ *a wide-ranging review of recent developments in wildlife conservation.* **3** [C] (**a**) published report that assesses the merits of a book, film, etc: *The play got splendid, excellent, unfavourable, etc reviews.* ○ [attrib] *a review copy,* ie a copy of a book, etc sent by the publishers to a periodical for review. (**b**) (section of a) periodical containing reviews, etc: *a scientific, musical, etc review* ○ *the London Review of Books.* **4** [C] ceremonial display and inspection of troops, a fleet, etc: *hold a review.* **5** (idm) **be/come under reˈview; be/come up for reˈview** be (due to be) re-examined or reconsidered: *Our contracts are currently under review.* ○ *Your case is coming up for review in May.* **keep sth under reˈview** re-examine sth continually: *Salaries are kept under constant review.*

▷ **review** *v* **1** [Tn] (**a**) re-examine or reconsider (sth): *The government is reviewing the situation.* (**b**) go over (esp past events) in one's mind; survey: *review one's successes and failures* ○ *review one's progress.* **2** [I, Ipr, Tn] write a review of (a book, film, etc) for publication: *She reviews for 'The Spectator'.* ○ *The play was well/favourably reviewed.* **3** [Tn] inspect (troops, a fleet, etc) ceremonially. **4** [Tn] (*esp US*) go over (work already learnt) in preparation for an exam; revise. **reviewer** *n* person who writes reviews of books, etc: *a play which reviewers have praised highly.*

revile /rɪˈvaɪl/ *v* [Tn] (*fml*) criticize (sb/sth) in angry and abusive language.

revise /rɪˈvaɪz/ *v* **1** [Tn] re-examine (sth), esp in order to correct or improve it: *revised proposals, estimates, rules, figures* ○ *revise a manuscript before publication* ○ *revise one's opinion of sb.* **2** [I, Ipr, Tn, Tn·pr] ~ (**sth**) (**for sth**) (*Brit*) go over (work already done) in preparation for an examination: *She's revising (her history notes) for the test.*

▷ **revise** *n* (usu *pl*) (in printing) proof-sheet in which errors marked in an earlier proof have been corrected.

revision /rɪˈvɪʒn/ *n* (**a**) [U] ~ (**for sth**) revising or being revised: *Our budget needs drastic revision.* ○ (*Brit*) *do some revision for the exam/some exam revision.* (**b**) [C] instance of this: *undergo a final revision.* (**c**) [C] thing that has been revised: *submit the revision of a novel for publication.*

□ **the Reˌvised ˈStandard Version** (*abbr* **RSV**) British version of the Bible produced in 1946-57, based on an earlier American revision of the Authorized Version.

the Reˌvised ˈVersion (*abbr* **RV**) revision by British scholars in 1870-84 of the Authorized Version of the Bible.

revisionism /rɪˈvɪʒənɪzəm/ *n* [U] (*esp derog*) changes to, or questioning of, orthodox political doctrines or practices, esp Marxism. ▷ **revisionist** /-ʒənɪst/ *n* [attrib]: *revisionist tendencies.*

revitalize, -ise /riːˈvaɪtəlaɪz/ *v* [Tn] put new life into (sth); regenerate: *revitalize industry, the economy, education, etc* ○ *Her appointment as leader revitalized the party.* ▷ **revitalization, -isation** /riːˌvaɪtəlaɪˈzeɪʃn; *US* -lɪˈz-/ *n* [U].

revival /rɪˈvaɪvl/ *n* **1** [U, C] coming or bringing back to health, strength or consciousness; recovery: *the patient's speedy revival after her operation* ○ (*fig*) *the revival of hope, interest, ambition* ○ *Our economy is undergoing a revival.* **2** (**a**) [U] coming or bringing back into use, activity, fashion, etc: *the revival of old customs, values, skills* ○ *the revival of the Welsh language.* (**b**) [C] instance of this: *a religious, commercial, political revival.* **3** [C] new production of a play, etc that has not been performed for some time: *stage a revival of a Restoration comedy.* **4** [U, C] (*religion*) (series of public meetings, etc to promote a) reawakening of (esp Christian faith): *preach (the spirit of) revival* ○ [attrib] *televised revival meetings.*

▷ **revivalism** /-vəlɪzəm/ *n* [U] process of reawakening religious faith.

revivalist /-vəlɪst/ *n* person who organizes or conducts religious revival meetings: [attrib] *revivalist campaigns, missions, etc.*

revive /rɪˈvaɪv/ *v* **1** [I, Tn] come or bring (sb/sth) back to health, strength or consciousness: *The flowers will revive in water.* ○ *She fainted but the brandy soon revived her.* ○ (*fig*) *Our failing hopes/spirits revived.* **2** [I, Tn] come or bring (sth) back into use, activity, fashion, etc: *revive old practices, customs, trends, etc* ○ *efforts to revive the mini-skirt.* **3** [Tn] stage again a play, etc that has not been performed for some time: *revive a 1930's musical.*

revivify /riːˈvɪvɪfaɪ/ *v* (*pt, pp* **-fied**) [Tn] (*fml*) give new life or liveliness to (sth); revitalize.

revocation /ˌrevəˈkeɪʃn/ *n* [C, U] (*fml*) (instance of) revoking or being revoked: *the revocation of laws, contracts, etc.*

revoke /rɪˈvəʊk/ *v* **1** [Tn] (*fml*) withdraw or cancel (a decree, permit, etc): *revoke orders, promises* ○ *His driving licence was revoked after the crash.* **2** [I] (of a player in a card-game) fail to play a card of the same suit as the leading player although able to do so.

revolt /rɪˈvəʊlt/ *v* **1** [I, Ipr] ~ (**against sb/sth**) (**a**) rise in rebellion (against authority): *The people revolted against the military dictator/dictatorship.* (**b**) express protest or defiance: *revolt against parental discipline.* **2** [Ipr, Tn usu passive] ~ **against/at sth** (cause sb to) feel horror or disgust: *Human nature revolts against/at such cruelty.* ○ *I was revolted by his dirty habit of spitting.*

▷ **revolt** *n* **1** (**a**) [C, U] act or state of rebelling or defying authority: *a period of open, armed, political revolt* ○ *stir, incite, etc militant party members to revolt* ○ *quell, put down, etc a revolt.* (**b**) [C] instance of this: *The army has put down/suppressed the revolt.* ○ *a revolt against conformity.* **2** (idm) **in revolt** state of having revolted (REVOLT 1a): *The people broke out/rose in revolt.*

revolting /rɪˈvəʊltɪŋ/ *adj* (**a**) causing disgust or horror: *revolting atrocities.* (**b**) (*infml*) nasty or unpleasant: *His feet smelt revolting.* ○ *a revolting mixture of pasta and curry.* ▷ **revoltingly** *adv*: *revoltingly wet weather.*

revolution /ˌrevəˈluːʃn/ *n* **1** [C, U] (instance of the) overthrow of a system of government, esp by force: *He has lived through two revolutions.* ○ *the French Revolution,* ie in 1789 ○ *foment, stir up revolution* ○ *In politics, evolution is better than revolution.* **2** [C] ~ (**in sth**) (*fig*) complete or drastic change of method, conditions, etc: *a revolution in the treatment of cancer* ○ *a genetic, technological, etc revolution* ○ *Credit cards have brought about a revolution in people's spending habits.* **3** [C, U] ~ (**on/round sth**) (**a**) (act of) revolving or rotating, esp of one planet round another: *make, describe a full revolution* ○ *the revolution of the earth on its axis round the sun.* (**b**) (process of making a) single complete movement or turn round a central point: *a record designed to be played at 45 revolutions per minute.*

▷ **revolutionary** /-ʃənərɪ; *US* -nerɪ/ *adj* **1** [usu attrib] of political revolution: *revolutionary parties, leaders, activities.* **2** involving complete or drastic change: *Genetic engineering will have revolutionary consequences for mankind.* — *n* person who begins or supports a political revolution.

revolutionize, -ise /-ʃənaɪz/ *v* [Tn] cause (sth) to change completely or drastically: *Computers have revolutionized banking.*

revolve /rɪˈvɒlv/ *v* **1** [I, Ipr] ~ (**around/round sth**) (**on sth**) (of a planet, etc) move in a circular orbit: *The earth revolves round the sun (on its axis).* **2** [I, Ipr, Tn] ~ (**around/round/on sth**) (cause sth to) go round in a circle; rotate: *A wheel revolves round/on its axis.* ○ *The mechanism that revolves the turntable is broken.* ○ (*fig fml*) *revolve sth in one's mind*; consider sth carefully. **3** (phr v) **revolve around sb/sth** have sb/sth as its chief concern; centre on sb/sth: *My life revolves around my job.* ○ *He thinks that everything revolves around him.*

▷ **revolving** *adj* [usu attrib] that rotates: *a revolving chair, hat-stand* ○ *This theatre has a revolving stage.*

□ **reˌvolving ˈcredit** (*finance*) credit that is automatically renewed up to a fixed amount, as part of the debt is paid.

revolving ˈdoor door with four or more partitions turning on a central axis to keep out draughts.

revolver /rɪˈvɒlvə(r)/ *n* pistol with a revolving chamber from which bullets are fed into the breech for firing: *draw one's revolver.* ⇨ illus at GUN.

revue /rɪˈvjuː/ *n* [C, U] (type of) theatrical entertainment consisting of a mixture of dialogue, song and dance, esp of a topical and satirical nature: *a political revue* ○ *act, appear, perform, etc in revue* ○ [attrib] *revue artistes.*

revulsion /rɪˈvʌlʃn/ *n* [U, sing] **1** ~ (**against/at/from sth**) feeling of disgust or horror: *feel a sense of revulsion at the bloodshed* ○ *She stared at the snake in revulsion.* **2** (*fml*) sudden violent change of feeling; reaction: *a revulsion of public feeling in favour of the accused.*

reward /rɪˈwɔːd/ *n* **1** [U] recompense for work, merit or services: *work without hope of reward* ○ *He received a medal in reward for his bravery.* **2** [C] something given or received in return for work, merit or services: *reap, receive one's just reward* ○ *emotional, intellectual, financial rewards* ○ *One reward of my job is meeting people.* **3** [C] sum of money offered for the capture of a criminal, return of lost property, etc: *A £1 000 reward has been offered for the return of the stolen painting.* **4** (idm) **virtue is its own reward** ⇨ VIRTUE.

▷ **reward** *v* [esp passive: Tn, Tn·pr] ~ **sb** (**for sth/doing sth**) give a reward to sb: *Is this how you reward me for helping/my help?* ○ *She rewarded him with a smile.* ○ *His persistence was rewarded when the car finally started.* ○ *Anyone providing information which leads to the recovery of the painting will be rewarded.* **rewarding** *adj* (of an activity, etc) worth doing; satisfying: *a rewarding film, study, trip* ○ *Gardening is a very rewarding pastime.* ○ *Teaching is not very rewarding financially.* ie not very well paid.

rewind /ˌriːˈwaɪnd/ *v* (*pp, pt* **rewound** /-ˈwaʊnd/) [Tn] wind (film, tape, etc) back onto the original reel or back to a particular point: *Rewind the video to the point where the fight starts.*

▷ **rewind** /ˈriːwaɪnd/ *n* control or mechanism for rewinding.

rewire /ˌriːˈwaɪə(r)/ *v* [Tn] renew the electrical wiring of (a building, etc): *The house has been completely rewired.*

reword /ˌriːˈwɜːd/ *v* [Tn] change the wording of (sth spoken or written): *reword a telegram to save money.*

rewrite /ˌriːˈraɪt/ *v* (*pt* **rewrote** /-rəʊt/, *pp* **rewritten** /-ˈrɪtn/) [Tn, Tn·pr, Cn·n/a] ~ **sth (for sth)**; ~ **sth (as sth)** write (sth) again in a different form or style: *rewrite the script for radio/as a radio play* ○ *This essay needs to be rewritten.*

▷ **rewrite** /ˈriːraɪt/ *n* thing rewritten: *do a complete rewrite of the original speech.*

Rex /reks/ *n* (*Latin*) (used esp in signatures on proclamations or in the titles of lawsuits) reigning king: *George Rex* ○ (*law*) *Rex v Hill*, ie the Crown versus Hill (when the monarch is a king). Cf REGINA.

Sir Joshua Reynolds: Samuel Johnson

Reynolds /ˈrenəldz/ Sir Joshua (1723-92), English painter. He became the most successful portrait artist of his time, using a formal style known as the 'grand manner'. He painted many important people, including his friend Samuel *Johnson. He became the first president of the *Royal Academy and used his lectures, known as the *Discourses*, to express his views on the value of academic art and the status of the artist. ⇨ illus.

Rf *symb* rutherfordium.

RFC *abbr* (*Brit*) Rugby Football Club.

Rh *symb* rhodium.

rh *abbr* right hand. Cf LH.

rhapsody /ˈræpsədɪ/ *n* **1** (*music*) (often in titles) romantic composition in irregular form: *Liszt's Hungarian Rhapsodies.* **2** (idm) **go into rhapsodies (over sb/sth)** express enthusiasm or delight in speech or writing: *The guests went into rhapsodies over the food.*

▷ **rhapsodic** /ræpˈsɒdɪk/ *adj* (*esp ironic*) expressing enthusiasm or delight: *The rejection of their pay claim was given a less than rhapsodic reception by the miners.*

rhapsodize, -ise /ˈræpsədaɪz/ *v* [I, Ipr] ~ **(about/over sb/sth)** (*esp ironic*) talk or write with great enthusiasm (about sb/sth).

rhea /rɪə/ *n* three-toed ostrich of S America.

rhenium /ˈriːnɪəm/ *n* [U] (*symb* **Re**) rare hard silvery metallic element, never found in isolation and used in some alloys.

rheostat /ˈriːəstæt/ *n* instrument used to control the current in an electrical circuit by varying the resistance in it.

rhesus /ˈriːsəs/ *n* (also **ˈrhesus monkey**) *n* small monkey common in N India, often used in biological experiments.

□ **ˈRhesus factor** (also **Rh factor** /ɑːrˈeɪtʃ fæktə(r)/) (*medical*) substance present in the blood of most people and some animals, causing a blood disorder in a new-born baby whose blood is *Rhesus-positive* (ie containing this substance) while the mother's is *Rhesus-negative* (ie not containing it).

rhetoric /ˈretərɪk/ *n* [U] **1** (art of) using language impressively or persuasively, esp in public speaking: *impassioned rhetoric.* **2** (*derog*) elaborate language which is intended to impress but is often insincere, meaningless or exaggerated: *the empty rhetoric of politicians.*

rhetorical /rɪˈtɒrɪkl; *US* -ˈtɔːr-/ *adj* **1** of the art of rhetoric: *rhetorical figures such as hyperbole.* **2** (*derog*) in or using rhetoric(2): *rhetorical speeches.* ▷ **rhetorically** /-klɪ/ *adv.*

□ **rheˌtorical ˈquestion** question asked only for dramatic effect and not to seek an answer, eg *Who cares?* (ie Nobody cares).

rheumatic /ruːˈmætɪk/ *adj* of, causing or affected by rheumatism: *a rheumatic condition, pain, joint.*

▷ **rheumatic** *n* person who suffers from rheumatism.

rheumaticky *adj* (*infml*) rheumatic.

rheumatics *n* [pl] (*infml*) rheumatism.

□ **rheumatic ˈfever** serious form of rheumatism with fever, chiefly in children.

rheumatism /ˈruːmətɪzəm/ *n* [U] any of several diseases causing pain, stiffness and inflammation in the muscles and joints: *contract, develop rheumatism.* Cf ARTHRITIS, FIBROSITIS.

rheumatoid /ˈruːmətɔɪd/ *adj* of rheumatism.

□ **ˌrheumatoid arˈthritis** chronic progressive form of arthritis causing inflammation, esp in the joints of the hands, wrists, knees and feet.

Rhine /raɪn/ river in western Europe, flowing from the Swiss Alps 1 320 km (820 miles) to the North Sea across Germany and the Netherlands. It is an important commercial waterway and forms part of the border between France and Germany.

□ **the ˈRhineland** /-lænd/ area of Germany crossed by the Rhine, esp on its west bank.

rhinestone /ˈraɪnstəʊn/ *n* imitation diamond.

rhino /ˈraɪnəʊ/ *n* (*pl* unchanged or ~**s** /-nəʊz/) (*infml*) rhinoceros: *black/white rhino* ○ [attrib] *rhino horn.* ⇨ illus.

rhinoceros

rhinoceros /raɪˈnɒsərəs/ *n* (*pl* unchanged or ~**es**) **1** large thick-skinned heavily-built animal of Africa and S Asia, with either one or two horns on its nose. **2** (idm) **have, etc a hide/skin like a rhiˈnoceros** show insensitivity to attack, criticism, insults, etc.

rhizome /ˈraɪzəʊm/ *n* (*botany*) root-like stem of some plants, growing along or under the ground and sending out both roots and shoots. ⇨ illus at FLOWER.

Rhode Island /ˌrəʊd ˈaɪlənd/ state in the north-eastern USA on the Atlantic coast. It is densely populated, with a high level of industrial and commercial activity. It was one of the 13 original states. ⇨ map at App 1.

□ **ˌRhode Island ˈred** type of dark red hen originally bred in Rhode Island for its high production of eggs.

Rhodes[1] /rəʊdz/ Greek island in the south-eastern Aegean, near the Turkish coast. Its natural beauty, warm climate and historic past make it a popular tourist centre. ⇨ map at TURKEY.

Rhodes[2] /rəʊdz/ Cecil John (1853-1902), South African statesman. He made a vast fortune from diamond mining in southern Africa and helped extend British territory throughout South Africa and the area occupied by modern Malawi and Zimbabwe.

□ **ˌRhodes ˈscholar** student from the USA, South Africa, Germany or certain other countries, given a grant to study at Oxford University from funds originally provided by Cecil Rhodes. **ˌRhodes ˈscholarship.**

Rhodesia /rəʊˈdiːʃə; *US* -ˈdiːʒə/ **1** former British colony (later a protectorate) in southern Africa made up of Northern Rhodesia (now Zambia) and Southern Rhodesia (now Zimbabwe). **2** former name of *Zimbabwe.

rhododendron /ˌrəʊdəˈdendrən/ (*US* also **rosebay**) *n* evergreen shrub with large clusters of trumpet-shaped red, purple, pink or white flowers.

rhombus /ˈrɒmbəs/ *n* geometric figure with four equal sides and angles which are not right angles (eg the diamond or lozenge shape on playing cards). ⇨ illus at QUADRILATERAL.

▷ **rhomboid** /ˈrɒmbɔɪd/ *adj* in the shape of a rhombus. — *n* quadrilateral of which only the opposite sides and angles are equal. ⇨ illus at QUADRILATERAL.

Rhône /rəʊn/ river in western Europe, rising in the Swiss Alps and crossing France to the Mediterranean. It is 812 km (505 miles) long.

rhubarb /ˈruːbɑːb/ *n* [U] **1** (garden plant with) fleshy reddish leaf-stalks that are cooked and eaten like fruit: [attrib] *rhubarb pie.* **2** (*infml*) (word that crowd actors repeat to simulate the babble of voices on stage).

rhumb /rʌm/ *n* (*nautical*) **1** any of the 32 main points of the compass. **2** angle formed by the lines indicating two compass points next to each other.

□ **ˈrhumb-line** *n* course of a ship which follows a single compass direction exactly, so that it would cross all the earth's meridians at the same angle.

rhyme /raɪm/ *n* **1** [U] sameness of sound between words or syllables, esp the endings of lines of verse, as in *day, away; visit, is it; puff, rough*: [attrib] *an abba rhyme scheme*, ie in which the first line of a verse rhymes with the fourth, and the second with the third. **2** [C] ~ **(for/to sth)** word that provides a rhyme for another: *Is there a rhyme for/to 'hiccups'?* **3** [C] verse or verses with rhymes: *sing nursery rhymes to the children.* **4** [U] rhyming form: *a story told in rhyme* ○ *Can you put that into rhyme?* **5** (idm) **neither, no, little, etc ˌrhyme or ˈreason** no sense or logic: *a decision without rhyme or reason* ○ *There's neither rhyme nor reason in his behaviour.* ○ *English spelling has little rhyme or reason.*

▷ **rhyme** *v* **1** [Tn, Tn·pr] ~ **sth (with sth)** put (words) together to form a rhyme: *You can rhyme 'hiccups' and/with 'pick-ups'.* ○ *rhymed verse.* **2** [I, Ipr] ~ **(with sth)** (of words or lines of verse) form a rhyme: *'Though' and 'through' don't rhyme, and neither rhymes with 'tough'.* **rhymed** *adj* having rhymes: *rhymed couplets.*

□ **ˈrhyming slang** form of slang which replaces words with rhyming words or phrases, eg *apples and pears* for *stairs: Cockney rhyming slang.*

rhythm /ˈrɪðəm/ *n* **1** (**a**) [U] pattern produced by emphasis and duration of notes in music or by stressed and unstressed syllables in words. (**b**) [C] instance of this: *play the same tune in/with a different rhythm* ○ *Latin-American rhythms.* (**c**) [U, C] movement with a regular succession of strong and weak elements: *the rhythm of her heart/pulse beating.* **2** [U] (*infml*) ability to move, dance, etc in time with a fixed beat: *a natural sense of rhythm.* **3** [U, C] (*fig*) constantly recurring sequence of events or processes: *the rhythm of the tides, seasons* ○ *biological rhythms*, eg of the human body.

▷ **rhythmic** /ˈrɪðmɪk/ (also **rhythmical**) /ˈrɪðmɪkl/ *adj* having rhythm: *rhythmic breathing* ○ *the rhythmic tread of marching feet.* **rhythmically** /-klɪ/ *adv.*

□ **ˌrhythm and ˈblues** (*abbr* **R and B, R & B**) type of popular music based on the blues.

ˈrhythm method method of contraception by avoiding sexual intercourse near the time of ovulation.

RI *abbr* (*Brit*) (on coins) Queen and Empress; King and Emperor (Latin *Regina et Imperatrix*; *Rex et Imperator*).

rib /rɪb/ *n* **1** (**a**) [C] any of the 12 pairs of curved bones extending from the backbone round the chest in humans: *broken, fractured, bruised, etc ribs.* ○ *dig sb/give sb a dig* (ie nudge or poke sb) *in the ribs.* ⇨ illus at SKELETON. (**b**) [C] corresponding bone in animals. **2** [U, C] cut of meat from the ribs of an animal: *barbecued spare-ribs.* **3** [C] curved part of the structure of sth resembling a rib: *the ribs of a leaf, an umbrella, a fan, a boat.* **4** [U, C] (stitch producing a) raised line in knitting: *cuffs knitted in rib.*

▷ **rib** *v* (**-bb-**) [Tn, Tn·pr] ~ **sb (about/for sth)** (*infml*) make fun of sb in a good-natured way; tease: *She was constantly ribbed about her accent.* ○ *rib sb for being shy.* **ribbed** *adj* (esp of fabrics) having raised lines: *ribbed tights/stockings* ○ *ribbed corduroy trousers.* **ribbing** *n* [U] **1** pattern of raised lines in knitting. **2** (*infml*) good-natured teasing: *He takes a good ribbing*, ie can accept being teased.

□ **ˈrib-cage** *n* framework of ribs round the chest.

ˈrib-tickling *adj* (*infml*) funny or amusing.

RIBA /ˌɑ:r aɪ bi: ˈeɪ/ *abbr* Royal Institute of British Architects.

ribald /ˈrɪbld/ *adj* humorous in a vulgar, obscene or disrespectful way: *ribald humour, talk, laughter.*

▷ **ribaldry** /ˈrɪbldrɪ/ *n* [U] ribald language or behaviour.

ribbon /ˈrɪbən/ *n* **1** [C, U] (length of) silk, nylon, etc woven in a narrow strip and used for tying sth or for ornament: *Her hair was tied back with a black ribbon.* ○ *lengths of ribbon hung from the bride's bouquet* ○ [attrib] *ribbon bows/rosettes* ○ (*fig*) *a ribbon of land stretching out into the sea.* **2** [C] ribbon of a special colour, pattern, etc worn to show the award of a medal, an order, etc. **3** [C] long narrow inked strip of material used in a typewriter, etc: *change the typewriter ribbon.* **4** [pl] ragged strips (used esp with the *vs* and *preps* shown): *The wind tore the sail to ribbons.* ○ *Vandals had slashed/cut the train seats to ribbons.* ○ *Her clothes hung in ribbons (about her).*

□ **ˌribbon deˈvelopment** (*Brit esp derog*) (building of) long lines of houses along a main road leading from a town or village (and thought to spoil the countryside).

riboflavin /ˌraɪbəʊˈfleɪvɪn/ *n* [U] vitamin B2, which is found in meat, fish, milk and green vegetables, and also produced synthetically, and which helps growth in man.

ribonucleic acid /ˌraɪbəʊnju:kli:ɪk ˈæsɪd/ (*abbr* **RNA**) complex organic compound found in living cells. One of its functions is to carry instructions from DNA to control the synthesis of proteins.

rice /raɪs/ *n* [U] **1** type of grass grown on wet land in hot countries, esp in E Asia, producing seeds that are cooked and used as food: [attrib] *rice fields/paddies.* **2** these seeds: *a bowl of boiled/fried rice* ○ *long-/short-grain rice* ○ *brown rice*, ie without the husks removed ○ [attrib] *rice pudding*, ie dessert made by cooking rice in milk and sugar.

▷ **rice** *v* [Tn] (*US*) pass (food, eg potatoes) through a special sieve to turn it into long strings. **ricer** *n* (*US*) special sieve used for this.

□ **ˈrice-paper** *n* [U] **1** type of thin paper made from the pith of an oriental plant and used by Chinese artists to paint on. **2** similar type of thin edible paper made from rice straw and used as a base for small cakes, etc.

rich /rɪtʃ/ *adj* (**-er, -est**) (in meanings 1, 3 and 4 the opposite of **poor**) **1** having much money or property; wealthy: *a rich film star* ○ *America is a rich country.* **2** valuable or expensive; splendid or luxurious: *rich clothes, furnishings* ○ *the rich interior of the church.* **3** [pred] ~ **in sth** producing or having a large supply of sth: *Oranges are rich in vitamin C.* ○ *The baroque style is rich in ornament.* ○ *a play rich in humour* ○ *soil rich in minerals.* **4** producing or produced abundantly: *rich soil* ○ *a rich harvest* ○ (*fig*) *a rich supply of ideas* ○ *a rich display of talent.* **5** (of food) containing a large amount of fat, butter, eggs, spices, etc: *a rich fruit cake* ○ *a rich curry, casserole, sauce.* **6** (of colours, sounds or smells) pleasantly deep, full, mellow or strong: *cloth dyed a rich purple* ○ *a rich soothing voice* ○ *the rich bouquet of mature brandy.* **7** (idm) **(as) rich as ˈCroesus** extremely wealthy. **strike it rich** ⇨ STRIKE[2]. **ˌthat's ˈrich** (*Brit infml*) (**a**) that is very amusing. (**b**) (*ironic*) that is ludicrous or preposterous.

▷ **the rich** *n* [pl *v*] rich people: *take from the rich and give to the poor.*

richly *adv* **1** in a splendid or generous manner: *a richly-ornamented design* ○ *I was richly rewarded for my trouble.* **2** (idm) **richly deserve sth** fully or thoroughly deserve sth: *He richly deserved the punishment he received.* ○ *a richly-deserved success* ○ *a novel richly deserving (of) praise.*

richness *n* [U] quality or state of being rich.

Richard I /ˈrɪtʃəd/ (1157-99), king of England 1189-99, often called 'the Lionheart' because of his bravery in battle. He spent most of his reign abroad: he took part in the Third Crusade, was captured by Duke Leopold of Austria and went to war with France. Despite his military successes, he was unable to maintain effective control of his kingdom. ⇨ App 3.

Richard II /ˈrɪtʃəd/ (1367-1400), king of England 1377-99. He is regarded as a weak king, relying for most of his reign on his uncle *John of Gaunt, who was the true ruler of the country. When John died he tried to seize his estate, but John's son returned from exile and imprisoned Richard, taking the throne himself as *Henry IV. ⇨ App 3.

Richard III /ˈrɪtʃəd/ (1452-85), king of England 1483-85. *Shakespeare's play about Richard portrays him as a cruel and ruthless monarch, but not all historians accept this view. He frustrated several plots against him at the beginning of his reign and probably ordered the murder of the *Princes in the Tower (PRINCE). He had some success as a ruler, but was killed at the Battle of Bosworth by Henry Tudor, who became *Henry VII. ⇨ App 3.

Richard Roe /ˌrɪtʃəd ˈrəʊ/ (*US*) name used for sb involved in legal proceedings, whose real name is unknown or kept secret. Cf JOHN DOE 1.

Richardson[1] /ˈrɪtʃədsn/ Sir Ralph David (1902-83), English actor noted esp for his roles in Shakespeare and Ibsen. He also appeared in much contemporary drama, and made many films.

Richardson[2] /ˈrɪtʃədsn/ Samuel (1689-1761), English novelist. His first novel, *Pamela*, written mainly in the form of letters between the characters, tells how the virtuous heroine keeps her virtue and reforms her suitor. The work was parodied by *Fielding, but like his other moral works it had great success and influenced taste and the development of the novel in Europe.

Richelieu /ˈri:ʃljɜ:; *US* ˈri:ʃəlu:/ Armand Jean du Plessis, Duc de Richelieu (1585-1642), French cardinal and statesman. As chief adviser to *Louis XIII he removed all threats to the king's power and made France the strongest nation in Europe.

riches /ˈrɪtʃɪz/ *n* [pl] **1** being rich; wealth: *He claims to despise riches.* ○ *amass great riches* ○ (*fig*) *the riches of Oriental art* ○ *the natural riches of the soil.* **2** (idm) **an embarrassment of riches** ⇨ EMBARRASSMENT (EMBARRASS). **from rags to riches** ⇨ RAG[1].

Richter scale /ˌrɪktə ˈskeɪl/ **the Richter scale** (*geology*) scale from 0 to 9 for measuring the intensity of earthquakes.

rick[1] /rɪk/ *n* [C] (*Brit*) slight sprain or strain.

▷ **rick** *v* [Tn] sprain or strain (a joint, etc) slightly: *rick one's ankle, wrist, back.*

rick[2] /rɪk/ *n* large stack of hay, straw, corn, etc which is built up in the open and covered to protect it from rain.

rickets /ˈrɪkɪts/ *n* [sing or pl *v*] children's disease caused by a lack of vitamin D, resulting in softening and deformity of the bones and enlargement of the liver and spleen.

rickety /ˈrɪkətɪ/ *adj* (*infml*) weak or shaky, esp in the joints; likely to fall or collapse: *rickety wooden stairs* ○ *a rickety stool, table, bed, etc* ○ *a rickety shelter for the bikes.*

rickshaw /ˈrɪkʃɔ:/ *n* **1** light two-wheeled covered vehicle used in India and the Far East, pulled by one or more men: *ride in a rickshaw.* **2** similar three-wheeled vehicle like a bicycle with seats attached behind the driver. Cf PEDICAB.

ricochet /ˈrɪkəʃeɪ; *US* ˌrɪkəˈʃeɪ/ *v* (*pt, pp* **ricocheted, ricochetted** /-ʃeɪd/) [I, Ipr] ~ **(off sth)** (of a bullet, etc) strike a surface and rebound at an angle: *The stone ricocheted off the wall and hit a passer-by.*

▷ **ricochet** *n* [U, C] ~ **(off sth)** (hit made by a) rebound of this kind: *the constant ricochet of bricks and bottles off police riot shields.*

rid /rɪd/ *v* (**-dd-**; *pt, pp* **rid**) **1** [Tn·pr] ~ **sb/sth of sb/sth** make sb/sth free from (sb/sth unpleasant or unwanted): *rid the world of famine* ○ *rid the house of mice.* **2** (idm) **be/get rid of sb/sth** be/become free of: *He was a boring nuisance! I'm glad to be rid of him.* ○ *The shop ordered 20 copies of the book and now it can't get rid of* (ie sell) *them.*

riddance /ˈrɪdns/ *n* (idm) **good riddance (to sb/sth)** (said to express relief, etc at being free of an unwanted or unpleasant person or thing): *He's gone at last, and good riddance (to him)!*

ridden /ˈrɪdn/ **1** *pp* of RIDE[2]. **2** *adj* (usu in compounds) full of or dominated by sth specified: *a ˌflea-ridden ˈbed* ○ *ˈguilt-ridden* ○ (*fml*) *She was ridden by/with guilt.*

riddle[1] /ˈrɪdl/ *n* [C] **1** puzzling question, statement or description, esp one intended to test the cleverness of those wishing to solve it: *ask/tell sb a riddle* ○ *know the answer to/solve a riddle* ○ *She speaks/talks in riddles — it's very difficult to know what she means.* **2** puzzling person, thing, event etc: *She's a complete riddle, even to her parents.* ○ *the riddle of how the universe originated.*

riddle[2] /ˈrɪdl/ *n* [C] coarse sieve for earth, gravel cinders, etc.

▷ **riddle** *v* **1** [Tn] (**a**) pass (gravel, etc) through a riddle. (**b**) shake (a grate, eg in a stove) in order to make ashes, cinders, etc fall through. **2** (**a**) [esp passive: Tn, Tn·pr] ~ **sb/sth (with sth)** make many holes in sb/sth: *The car was riddled from end to end.* ○ *The roof was riddled with bullet holes.* (**b**) [Tn·pr esp passive] ~ **sb/sth with sth** affect sb/sth completely: (*derog*) *They are riddled with disease* ○ *an administration riddled with corruption.*

ride[1] /raɪd/ *n* [C] **1** (**a**) (period of) being carried on or in sth, esp as a passenger: *'Give me a ride on your shoulders, Daddy.'* ○ *We went for a ride in her new car.* ○ *It's a ten-minute ride on the bus.* ○ *Can I hitch a ride with you?* (**b**) (in compounds) journey (in the specified vehicle, etc): *It's only a 5-minute ˈbus-ride to the park.* ○ *go for a ˈdonkey-ride on the beach.* (**c**) (turn on a) roundabout, roller-coaster, big wheel (BIG), etc at a funfair or an amusement park. **2** feel of riding in a car, etc: *The luxury model gives a smoother ride.* **3** track for riding (usu a horse) on, esp through woods. **4** (idm) **go along for the ˈride** (*infml*) join with others in an activity without associating oneself wholeheartedly or sincerely with their aims: *He told the police he only went along for the ride, but they believe he was fully aware of the others' plan from the beginning.* **take sb for a ˈride** (*infml*) deceive or swindle sb.

ride[2] /raɪd/ *v* (*pt* **rode** /rəʊd/, *pp* **ridden** /ˈrɪdn/) **1** [Ipr, Ip] ~ **on sth;** ~ **away, off, etc** sit on a horse etc and be carried along: *children riding on donkeys* ○ *ride off into the distance* ○ *riding on her father's shoulders.* **2** [Tn] sit on and control (sth): *ride a pony, bicycle, etc* ○ *a jockey who has ridden six winners* (ie winning horses) *this season.* **3** [Ipr] ~ **in/on sth** be carried along (in a vehicle) as a passenger: *ride in a bus, on a train, etc* ○ *You ride in the back (of the car) with your brother.* ⇨ Usage a

TRAVEL. **4** [I] go out regularly on horseback (as a pastime, etc): *Do you ride much?* ○ *She hasn't been out riding since the accident.* **5** [Tn, Tn·pr] go through or over (sth) on a horse, bicycle, etc: *ride the prairies* ○ *I've been riding these trails for 40 years.* **6** [I, Ipr, Tn] float or be supported on (water, etc): *surfers riding the waves* ○ *gulls riding (on) the wind* ○ *(fig) The moon was riding* (ie appeared to be floating) *high (in the sky).* **7** [Tn] yield to (a punch, etc) so as to reduce its effect. **8** (idm) **let sth ˈride** (*infml*) take no further (immediate) action on sth: *I'll let things ride for a week and see what happens.* **sb/sth rides aˈgain** (*joc often ironic*) a person or thing reappears, usu after being forgotten or ignored: *Electoral reform rides again*, ie has become an important issue again. **ride at ˈanchor** (of a ship) remain secured by an anchor. **ride for a ˈfall** (used esp in the continuous tenses) act in a risky way which makes disaster likely. **ride ˈherd on sb** (*US infml*) control or discipline sb. **ride ˈherd on sth** (*US infml*) be in charge of or look after sth. **ride ˈhigh** (used esp in the continuous tenses) be successful: *The company is riding high this year.* **ride out/weather the/a storm** ⇨ STORM. **ride roughshod over sb/sth** treat sb/sth harshly, thoughtlessly or with contempt: *He rode roughshod over all opposition to his ideas.* **ride to ˈhounds** (*fml*) go fox-hunting. **9** (phr v) **ride sb down** direct one's horse at sb to knock him down. **ride up** (of an article of clothing) move gradually upwards, out of position: *Your shirt's riding up.*

▷ **rider** *n* **1** person who rides a horse, bicycle, etc: *a poor, an excellent, an average, etc rider* ○ *She's no rider*, ie cannot ride well. **2** ~ **(to sth)** additional remark following a statement, verdict, etc: *We should like to add a rider to the previous remarks.* **riderless** *adj* without a rider: *a riderless horse.*

ridge /rɪdʒ/ *n* **1** raised line where two sloping surfaces meet; narrow raised strip: *the ridge of a roof* ○ *There are ridges on the soles to help the boots grip the surface.* ○ *a series of ridges in a ploughed field.* Cf FURROW. **2** narrow stretch of high land along the top of a line of hills; long mountain range. ⇨ illus at MOUNTAIN. Cf PLATEAU. **3** (in meteorology) elongated region of high pressure. Cf TROUGH 4.

▷ **ridge** *v* [Tn] cover (sth) with or make (sth) into ridges: *a slightly ridged surface.*

□ **ˈridge-pole** *n* horizontal pole at the apex of the roof of a long tent.

ˈridge-tile *n* any of the tiles placed on the apex of the sloping roof of a building.

ˈridgeway *n* (*Brit*) road or track along the ridge of a hill.

ridicule /ˈrɪdɪkju:l/ *n* [U] (process of) making sb/sth appear foolish or absurd; scorn: *incur ridicule* ○ *attempt to escape ridicule* ○ *be held up to ridicule* ○ *He's become an object of ridicule*, ie People say he is foolish/absurd.

▷ **ridicule** *v* [Tn] make fun of (sb/sth); mock: *The opposition ridiculed the government's proposals, saying they offered nothing new.*

ridiculous /rɪˈdɪkjʊləs/ *adj* **1** deserving to be laughed at; absurd: *You look ridiculous in those tight jeans.* ○ *What a ridiculous idea!* **2** (idm) **(go) from the sublime to the ridiculous** ⇨ SUBLIME. ▷ **ridiculously** *adv.* **ridiculousness** *n* [U].

riding[1] /ˈraɪdɪŋ/ *n* [U] **1** sport or pastime of going about on a horse: *enjoy, take up riding.* **2** (in compounds) concerned with or used in riding: *ˈriding-boots.*

□ **ˈriding-crop** *n* = CROP 5.

ˈriding-school *n* school for teaching and practising horse-riding.

riding[2] /ˈraɪdɪŋ/ *n* **1 Riding** (*Brit*) any of the three administrative divisions of Yorkshire until 1974: *East/North/West Riding (of Yorkshire).* **2** (in Canada) electoral constituency.

Ridley /ˈrɪdlɪ/ Nicholas (c1500-55), English bishop. He was a leader of the Reformation in England under *Edward VI. His opposition to *Mary Tudor led to his execution with *Cranmer and *Latimer.

riesling /ˈri:slɪŋ, ˈri:z-/ *n* [U] **(a)** white wine produced esp in Germany and Alsace. **(b)** type of grape from which this is made.

rife /raɪf/ *adj* [pred] (*fml*) **(a)** (esp of bad things) widespread; common: *an area where crime is rife.* **(b)** ~ **with sth** full of (esp sth bad): *the country was rife with rumours of war.*

riff /rɪf/ *n* short repeated pattern of notes in popular music.

riffle /ˈrɪfl/ *v* **1** [Tn] shuffle (playing-cards) by holding part of the pack in each hand and releasing cards alternately so that they form one pack again. **2** (phr v) **riffle through sth** turn the pages of (a book, etc) quickly and casually.

▷ **riffle** *n* (*US*) **1** (stretch of) choppy water in a stream, caused by a rocky shoal or shallow. **2** shoal or shallow.

riff-raff /ˈrɪf ræf/ (esp **the riff-raff**) *n* [U] (*derog*) ill-behaved people of the lowest social class; the rabble: *Don't bring any riff-raff into my house!*

rifle[1] /ˈraɪfl/ *n* type of gun with a long barrel which has spiral grooves inside, usu fired from the shoulder. ⇨ illus at GUN.

▷ **rifle** *v* [Tn] cut spiral grooves in (a gun-barrel). **rifling** /ˈraɪflɪŋ/ *n* [U] these grooves.

□ **ˈrifleman** /-mən/ *n* (*pl* **-men** /-mən/) soldier in a regiment armed with rifles.

ˈrifle-range *n* **1** [C] place for practising shooting with rifles. **2** (also **ˈrifle-shot**) [U] distance that a rifle bullet will travel: *out of/within rifle-range.*

rifle[2] /ˈraɪfl/ *v* [Tn] search and rob (sth): *The safe had been rifled and many documents taken.*

rift /rɪft/ *n* **1** split, crack, break, etc: *a rift in the clouds.* **2** serious disagreement between friends, members of a group, etc: *a growing rift between the two factions.*

□ **ˈrift valley** *n* steep-sided valley caused by subsidence of the earth's crust.

rig[1] /rɪg/ *v* **(-gg-)** **1** [Tn, Tn·pr] ~ **sth (with sth)** fit (a ship or boat) with masts, spars, ropes, sails, etc. **2** (phr v) **rig sb out (in/with sth)** **(a)** provide sb with clothes or equipment: *The sergeant will rig you out (with everything you need).* **(b)** (*infml*) dress sb up: *rigged out in her best clothes.* **rig sth up** set up (a structure, etc) quickly and/or with makeshift materials: *rig up a shelter for the night* ○ *rig up some scaffolding for the workmen.*

▷ **rig** *n* **1** way that a ship's masts, sails, etc are arranged: *the fore-and-aft rig of a schooner.* **2** (esp in compounds) equipment for a special purpose: *an ˈoil rig* ○ *a ˈtest-rig*, ie on which motor-vehicles, electrical appliances, etc are tested. **3** (*infml*) style of dress.

rigging *n* [U] arrangement of ropes, etc that support a ship's masts and sails: *The sailors climbed up into the rigging.* ⇨ illus at YACHT.

□ **ˈrig-out** *n* (*Brit infml*) outfit of clothes: *wearing a bizarre rig-out.*

rig[2] /rɪg/ *v* **(-gg-)** [Tn] manage or control (sth) fraudulently: *He claimed (the result of) the election was rigged.* ○ *rig the market*, ie cause an artificial rise or fall in share prices, etc in order to make (illegal) profits.

Rigel /ˈraɪgl/ seventh brightest star in the sky, part of the constellation *Orion.

right[1] /raɪt/ *adj* **1** [usu pred] (of conduct, actions, etc) morally good; required by law or duty: *Is it ever right to kill?* ○ *You were quite right to refuse/in deciding to refuse/in your decision to refuse.* ○ *It seems only right to warn you that....* Cf WRONG 1. **2** true or correct: *Actually, that's not quite right.* ○ *Did you get the answer right?* ○ *Have you got the right money* (ie exact fare) *for the bus?* ○ *What's the right time?* **3** best in view of the circumstances; most suitable: *Are we on the right road?* ○ *Is this the right way to the zoo?* ○ *He's the right man for the job.* ○ *That coat's just right for you.* ○ *the right side of a fabric*, ie the side meant to be seen or used. **4** (also **all right**) in a good or normal condition: *'Do you feel all right?' 'Yes, I feel quite all right/No, I don't feel (quite) right.'* **5** [attrib] (*Brit infml*) (esp in derogatory phrases) real; complete: *you made a right mess of that!* ○ *She's a right old witch!* **6** (idm) **all ˈright** used to indicate agreement, approval, etc: *'Do you want to join us for dinner?' 'All right!'* **all ˌright on the ˈnight** (*saying*) (of a performance, etc) satisfactory when the time comes for it to be done, etc: *The hall isn't quite ready for the ceremony yet, but it will be all right on the night.* **a bit of all right** ⇨ BIT[1]. **do the right/wrong thing** do sth that is/is not honourable, socially acceptable, etc in the circumstances. **get sth ˈright/ˈstraight** understand sth clearly, without error: *Let's get this right once and for all.* ○ *Let's get one thing straight — I give the orders round here, OK?* **have one's heart in the right place** ⇨ HEART. **hit/strike the right/wrong note** ⇨ NOTE[1]. **(not) in one's right ˈmind** (not) mentally normal; (not) sane. **know, cultivate, etc the right ˈpeople** know, try to make friends with, etc people who are powerful or influential: *Her father-in-law introduced her to all the right people.* **might is right** ⇨ MIGHT[2]. **not (quite) right in the/one's ˈhead** (*infml*) foolish; eccentric; (slightly) mad. **on the right/wrong side of forty, etc** ⇨ SIDE[1]. **on the right/wrong side of sb/sth** ⇨ SIDE[1]. **on the right/wrong track** ⇨ TRACK *n.* **put/set sb/sth right** restore sb/sth to order; correct sb/sth: *put a ˈwatch right*, ie to the correct time ○ *I want to set/put you ˈright on one or two matters.* **right (you are)!** (*Brit* also **right-oh!**) (*infml*) (used to indicate agreement to an order or with a suggestion or (esp *US*) with a request). **(as) right as ˈrain/as a ˈtrivet** (*infml*) in excellent health or working order. **start off on the right/wrong foot** ⇨ START[2]. **touch the right chord** ⇨ TOUCH[1].

▷ **rightly** *adv* justly; correctly; properly; justifiably: *act rightly* ○ *Did I hear rightly?* ○ *She's been sacked, and rightly so.* ○ *He was rightly furious at the decision.*

rightness *n* [U]: *the rightness* (ie justice) *of their cause.*

□ **ˈright angle** angle of 90°: *at right angles/at a right angle (to the wall).* ⇨ illus at ANGLE. ⇨ App 10. **ˈright-angled** *adj* having/consisting of a right angle: *a right-angled triangle* ○ *a right-angled bend in the road.*

ˌright-ˈminded having proper or honest opinions, based on what is right: *All ˌright-minded ˈpeople will surely be shocked by this outrage.* **ˌright-ˈmindedness** *n* [U].

right[2] /raɪt/ *adv* **1** exactly (in position, time, etc); directly: *sitting right beside you* ○ *The wind was right in our faces.* **2** all the way; completely: *Go right to the end of the road.* ○ *I fell right to the bottom of the stairs.* ○ *a fence right around the garden* ○ *The pear was rotten right through.* ○ *turn right round and go in the opposite direction* ○ *The handle came right off in my hand.* **3** correctly; satisfactorily; properly: *Have I guessed right or wrong?* ○ *Nothing seems to be going right for me at the moment*, ie I'm having a lot of problems. **4** immediately: *I must answer that phone, but I'll be right back.* **5** (idm) **ˈright/ˈstraight away/off** without hesitation or delay: *I want it typed right away, please.* ○ *I told her right/straight off what I though of her.* **right ˈnow** immediately; at this moment. **see sb ˈright** ensure that sb has all he needs or wants: *You needn't worry about running out of money — I'll always see you right.* **serve sb right** ⇨ SERVE. **ˌtoo ˈright!** (*infml esp Austral*) (used to indicate enthusiastic agreement).

□ **ˌRight ˈHonourable** title of earls, viscounts, barons, Cabinet Ministers, and certain others: *the Right Honourable James Smith, Foreign Secretary.* Cf HONOURABLE 2.

ˌRight ˈReverend title of a bishop: *the Right Reverend Richard Harries, Bishop of Oxford.*

right[3] /raɪt/ *n* **1** [U] what is good, just, honourable, etc: *know the difference between right and wrong* ○ *You did right to tell me the truth.* **2** **(a)** [U] ~ **to sth/to do sth** proper claim to sth, or authority to do sth: *What right have you to do that?* ○ *What gives you the right to do that?* ○ *have no right/not have any right to do sth.* **(b)** [C] ~ **(to sth)** thing one may do or have by law: *Everyone has a right to a fair trial.* ○ *have no rights as a UK citizen* ○ *Do the police have the right of arrest in this situation?* **3 rights** [pl] legal authority or claim: *the film, translation, foreign rights (of a book)*, ie authority to make a film of it, translate it, sell it abroad, etc ○ *all rights reserved*, ie protected or kept for the owners of the book, film, etc. Cf COPYRIGHT. **4** (idm) **as of ˈright/**

by ˈright (*fml*) justly; correctly; because of having the proper/legal claim: *The property belongs to her as of right.* **be in the ˈright** have justice and truth on one's side. **by right of sth** (*fml*) because of sth: *The Normans ruled England by right of conquest.* **by ˈrights** if justice were done (which, by implication, seems unlikely); in justice: *By rights, half the reward should be mine.* **do right by sb** treat sb fairly. **in one's own ˈright** because of a personal claim, qualification, etc: *She's a peeress in her own right,* ie not merely by marriage to a peer. **put/set sb/sth to ˈrights** correct sb/sth; put (things) in order: *It took me ages to put things to rights after the workmen had finished.* **the rights and ˈwrongs of sth** true facts. **stand on one's ˈrights** insist on being treated in a way that one can properly claim one is entitled to. **two wrongs don't make a right** ⇨ WRONG *n.* **within one's ˈrights (to do sth)** not exceeding one's authority or entitlement: *He's quite within his rights to demand an enquiry.*

□ ˌ**right of ˈway 1** (**a**) right to pass over another person's land: *Is there a right of way across these fields?* (**b**) path subject to such a right: *public rights of way.* **2** (in road traffic) right to proceed while another vehicle must wait: *It's my right of way, so you should have stopped and let me go.*

ˈ**rights issue** (*commerce*) offer of new shares in a company at a reduced price to existing shareholders.

right[4] /raɪt/ *v* [Tn] ~ **itself/sth 1** return itself/sth to a proper, correct or upright position: *I managed to right the car after it skidded.* ○ *The ship righted itself after the big wave had passed.* **2** correct itself/sth: *right a wrong* ○ *The fault will right itself* (ie will correct itself without help) *if you give it time.*

right[5] /raɪt/ *adj* of, on or towards the side of the body which is towards the east when a person faces north: *my right eye* ○ *In Britain we drive on the left side of the road, not the right side.* Cf LEFT[2].

▷ **right** *adv* **1** to the right side: *He looked neither right nor left.* ○ *Turn right at the end of the street.* **2** (idm) **eyes right/left/front** ⇨ EYE[1]. **left, right and centre** ⇨ LEFT[2]. ˌ**right and ˈleft** everywhere: *She owes money right and left.* **would give one's right ˈarm for sth/to do sth** (*infml*) would like very much to have sth/to do sth: *Some people would give their right arm for your education/to have an education like yours.*

right *n* **1** [U] right-hand side or direction: *the first turning to/on the right.* **2** [C] (blow given with the) right hand: *He was hit with a succession of rights.* ○ *Defend yourself with your right.* **3 the Right** [Gp] (*politics*) right wing of a party or group.

rightist *n, adj* (*dated*) (member) of a right-wing political party or group.

□ ˌ**right ˈbank** bank of a river on the right side of a person facing downstream.

ˈ**right field** (in baseball) the part of the field on the side of the first base, which is on the catcher's right.

ˈ**right-hand** *adj* [attrib] of or towards the right side of a person or thing: *a right-hand glove* ○ *make a right-hand turn.* ˌ**right-ˈhanded** *adj* **1** (of a person) using the right hand more, or with more ease, than the left hand. **2** (of a blow) made with the right hand. **3** (of a tool) designed for use with the right hand. **4** (of a screw) designed to be tightened by turning towards the right. — *adv* with the right hand: *play tennis right-handed.* ˌ**right-ˈhandedness** *n* [U]. ˌ**right-ˈhander** *n* right-handed person or blow. ˌ**right-hand ˈman** chief assistant; most reliable helper.

ˌ**right ˈturn** turn to the right into a position at right angles (90°) to the original one.

ˌ**right ˈwing 1** (*politics*) those who support more conservative or traditional policies than others in a group, party, etc: *on the right wing of the Labour Party.* **2** (in football, hockey, etc) the side of a playing field on the right looking towards each of the goals. ˌ**right-ˈwing** *adj*: ˌ*right-wing oˈpinions* ○ *This newspaper's views are very right-wing.* ˌ**right-ˈwinger** *n* **1** person on the right wing of a group, etc. **2** player on the right wing. Cf WING 7, WINGER (WING).

righteous /ˈraɪtʃəs/ *adj* **1** (*fml*) doing what is morally right. **2** morally justifiable: *righteous anger, indignation, wrath* ○ (*derog*) *Don't adopt that righteous tone of voice!* ▷ **righteously** *adv.* **righteousness** *n* [U].

rightful /ˈraɪtfl/ *adj* [attrib] just, proper or legal: *a rightful claim* ○ *his rightful punishment* ○ *the rightful owner, king, father, etc.* ▷ **rightfully** /-fəlɪ/ *adv.*

rigid /ˈrɪdʒɪd/ *adj* **1** stiff; not bending or yielding: *a rigid support for the tent* ○ (*fig*) *Her face was rigid with terror.* **2** strict; firm; unchanging: *a man of very rigid principles* ○ *practise rigid economy,* ie be very frugal. ▷ **rigidity** /rɪˈdʒɪdətɪ/ *n* [U]: *The rigidity of the metal caused it to crack.* ○ *He deplored the rigidity of her views.* **rigidly** *adv*: *rigidly constructed buildings* ○ *rigidly opposed to any change.*

rigmarole /ˈrɪgmərəʊl/ *n* [C usu *sing*] (*derog*) **1** (unnecessarily) complicated procedure: *go through the whole rigmarole of filling out forms.* **2** long wandering story or statement: *I've never heard such a rigmarole.*

rigor mortis /ˌrɪgə ˈmɔːtɪs/ stiffening of the body after death: *Rigor mortis had already set in.*

rigour (*US* **rigor**) /ˈrɪgə(r)/ *n* (*fml*) **1** [U] severity; strictness; (esp mental) discipline: *the utmost rigour of the law* ○ *intellectual rigour.* **2** [C often *pl*] harshness (of weather, conditions, etc): *the rigour(s) of an Arctic winter, of prison life, etc.*

▷ **rigorous** /ˈrɪgərəs/ *adj* (*fml*) **1** severe; strict: *rigorous discipline.* **2** strictly accurate or detailed: *rigorous attention to detail* ○ *a rigorous search, examination, analysis, etc.* **3** (of weather, etc) harsh: *a rigorous climate.* **rigorously** *adv.* **rigorousness** *n* [U].

rile /raɪl/ *v* [Tn] (*infml*) annoy (sb); irritate: *Don't get riled.* ○ *It riles me that he won't agree.*

rim /rɪm/ *n* **1** edge or border of sth that is (approximately) circular: *the rim of a cup, bowl, etc* ○ *a pair of spectacles with gold rims.* **2** outer edge of a wheel, on which the tyre is fitted. ⇨ illus at BICYCLE.

▷ **rim** *v* (**-mm-**) [Tn] provide (sth) with a rim; be a rim for (sth): *Mountains rimmed the valley.*

rimless *adj* (of spectacles) having lenses which have no frames round them.

-rimmed (forming compound *adjs*) having a rim or rims of the type specified: *steel-rimmed glasses* ○ *red-rimmed eyes,* eg from weeping.

Rimbaud /ˈræmbəʊ/ Arthur (1854-91), French poet. A rebel against all authority, he had written all his poetry by the age of 20. The visual imagery of his prose poems (eg *Une saison en enfer*) inspired the Symbolists and Surrealists.

rime /raɪm/ *n* [U] (*esp rhet*) frost.

Rimsky-Korsakov /ˌrɪmskɪ ˈkɔːsəkɒf/ Nicolai (1844-1908), Russian composer. He had intended to be a naval officer, but decided to be a composer, studying mainly by himself. He is famous for his brilliant orchestration and for his use of Russian folk music. His best-known work is the symphonic suite *Sheherazade.* He taught and influenced many famous pupils, including *Stravinsky.

rind /raɪnd/ *n* [C, U] hard outer skin or covering on some fruits (eg oranges, lemons) and some types of cheese, bacon, etc: *cut off the ˈbacon rind.* Cf PEEL *n,* SKIN 4, ZEST 3.

ring[1] /rɪŋ/ *n* **1** small circular band of precious metal, often set with a gem or gems, worn esp on the finger: *a diamond ˈring* ○ *an enˈgagement ring* ○ *a ˈwedding ring* ○ *a ˈnose ring.* **2** (esp in compounds) circular band of any kind of material: *a ˈnapkin ring* ○ *a ˈkey-ring* ○ *inflatable rubber rings,* eg as worn by children on their arms when learning to swim ○ *the rings of Saturn.* **3** circle: *the rings in/of a tree,* ie the concentric circles seen when the trunk is cut straight across, showing the tree's age ○ *puff out ˈsmoke-rings,* ie rings of tobacco smoke ○ *The men were standing in a ring.* ○ *dark rings round her eyes from lack of sleep.* **4** combination of people working together, esp secretly: *a ˈspy ring* ○ *a ring of dealers controlling prices at an antiques auction.* **5** (**a**) (also ˈ**circus ring**) (esp circular) enclosure in which a circus is held. (**b**) (also ˈ**boxing ring**) raised square spa enclosed by ropes for boxing matches: *knock sb o of the ring.* **6** (idm) **run ˈrings round sb** (*infml*) c things much better than sb.

▷ **ring** *v* (*pt, pp* **-ed**) **1** [Tn, Tn·pr esp passive] **sb/sth (with sth)** surround sb/sth: *A high fen ringed the prison camp.* ○ *ringed about wi enemies.* **2** [Tn] make a circular mark round (sth *Ring the correct answer with your pencil.* **3** [T put a metal ring on the leg of (a bird) to identify or in the nose of (a bull, etc).

□ ˈ**ring binder** folder for papers, in which met rings go through holes in the edges of the page holding them in place.

ˈ**ring-dove** *n* = WOOD-PIGEON (WOOD).

ˈ**ring-finger** *n* third finger, usu of the left hand, c which a wedding-ring is traditionally worn. illus at HAND.

ˈ**ringleader** *n* (*esp derog*) person who leads othe in crime or opposition to authority.

ˈ**ring mains** main electrical circuit in a house, et off which branch supplies are taken.

ˈ**ringmaster** *n* person in charge of a circ performance.

ˈ**ring ouzel** = OUZEL 1.

ˈ**ring-pull** *n* small piece of metal with a ri attached which is pulled to open certain types tin can, etc: [attrib] *a ring-pull can.*

ˈ**ring road** (*Brit*) (*US* ˈ**beltway**) road built arou a town to reduce traffic in the centre.

ˈ**ringside** *n* **1** (esp **the ringside**) [U] ar immediately beside a boxing or wrestling rin **2** (idm) **have a ringside ˈseat** be favourab placed for seeing sth.

ˈ**ringworm** *n* [U] skin disease, esp of animals children, producing round red patches.

ring[2] /rɪŋ/ *v* (*pt* **rang** /ræŋ/, *pp* **rung** /rʌŋ/) **1** [make a clear resonant sound, usu like that of a be being struck: *Will you answer the telephone if rings?* ○ *The metal door rang as it slammed shut. The buzzer rang when the meal was ready.* **2** [T Tn·pr] cause (a bell, etc) to sound: *ring the fi alarm* ○ *ring the bell for school assembly.* **3** [L produce a certain effect when heard: *Her wor rang hollow,* ie What she said sounded insincere. *His story may seem incredible, but it rang* (seemed likely to be) *true.* **4** [I, Ipr] ~ (**for sb/st** make a bell sound to call, warn, etc sb: *'Did y ring, sir?' asked the stewardess.* ○ *Someone ringing at the door,* ie ringing the doorbell. ○ *ri for the maid, for room service, etc.* **5** [I, Ipr] ~ (**wi sth**) (*fig*) be filled with (sounds, etc): *T playground rang with children's shouts.* ○ (*rhe The village rang with the joy of Christmas.* **6** [I, Ip (of ears) be filled with a ringing or hummi sound: *The music was so loud it made my ears rin* **7** (*US* **call**) [Tn, Tn·p] ~ **sb/sth (up)** telephone (s sth): *I'll ring you tonight.* ○ *Ring (up) the airpo and find out when the plane leaves.* **8** [Tn] (of chime of bells) mark (the time) by striking: *ri the hours but not the quarters,* ie ring on the ho but not at quarter or half past or quarter **9** (idm) **ring a ˈbell** (*infml*) bring sth vaguely ba to mind; sound familiar: *His name rings a be perhaps we've met somewhere.* **ring the ˈchang** ring church bells in various different orders. **ri the changes (on sth)** vary one's routine, choice actions, etc: *She likes to ring the changes (on ho her office is arranged).* **ring up/down the ˈcurta (on sth)** (**a**) (in a theatre) give the signal for t curtain to be raised/lowered: *ring down the curta on the first act.* (**b**) mark the beginning/end of (enterprise, etc): *ring up the curtain on a ne football season.* ˌ**ring out the ˈold year and** ˌ**ri in the ˈnew** announce and celebrate the end of o year and the beginning of the next. **10** (phr v) **ri off** (*Brit*) end a telephone conversation: *He rang before I could explain.* **ring out** sound loudly a clearly: *A pistol shot rang out.* **ring sth up** reco (an amount, etc) on a cash register: *ring up all t items, the total, £6.99.*

▷ **ring** *n* **1** [C] act of ringing a bell; sound of a be *give two rings of the bell* ○ *There was a ring at t door.* **2** [sing] loud clear sound: *the ring of hap voices.* **3** [sing] ~ **of sth** tone or feeling of

particular kind: *That has a/the ring of truth about it*, ie sounds true. **4** [C] (*Brit infml*) (*US* **call**) telephone call: *I'll give you a ring tomorrow.*
ringer *n* **1** person who rings bells. **2** (*US*) racehorse, etc entered in a race under a false name. **3** (idm) **be a dead ringer for sb** ⇨ DEAD.
ringlet /ˈrɪŋlɪt/ *n* [C esp *pl*] long curl of hair hanging down from sb's head.
rink ⇨ ICE-RINK (ICE[1]), SKATING-RINK (SKATE[1]).
rinse /rɪns/ *v* [Tn] **1** wash (sth) lightly: *He rinsed his hands quickly before eating.* **2** remove dirt, soap, etc from (sth) with water: *Rinse your hair thoroughly after shampooing it.* **3** (phr v) **rinse sth down** (*infml*) have a drink after eating sth: *a sandwich and a glass of beer to rinse it down.* **rinse sth out** remove dirt, etc from sth with water: *He rinsed the teapot out under the tap, to get rid of the tea-leaves.* **rinse sth out of/from sth** remove (dirt, soap, etc) from sth with water: *I rinsed the shampoo out of my hair.*
▷ **rinse** *n* **1** [C] act of rinsing: *Give your hair a good rinse after shampooing it.* **2** [C, U] solution for tinting or conditioning the hair: *a blue rinse.*
Rio Grande /ˌriːəʊ ˈgrænd, *also* -ˈgrændɪ/ **the Rio Grande** N American river which rises in *Colorado and flows 3030 km (1880 miles) to the Gulf of Mexico. Between the sea and El Paso it forms the border between the USA and Mexico.
riot /ˈraɪət/ *n* **1** [C] wild or violent disturbance by a crowd of people: *Riots broke out in several areas.* ○ *The police succeeded in quelling the riot.* ○ (*fig*) *There'll be a riot* (ie People will be very angry) *if the government doesn't invest more in this service.* **2** [sing] ~ **of sth** profuse display (of sth): *The flower-beds were a riot of colour.* ○ *a riot of emotion.* **3 a riot** [sing] (*infml*) very amusing thing or person: *She's an absolute riot!* **4** (idm) **read the Riot Act** ⇨ READ. **run ˈriot** behave in a wild, violent or uncontrolled way: *Football hooligans ran riot through the town.* ○ (*fig*) *weeds running riot in the garden* ○ *Inflation is running riot and prices are out of control.*
▷ **riot** *v* [I, Ipr] take part in a riot: *There's rioting in the streets.* ○ *renewed outbreaks of rioting.* **rioter** *n* person who riots.
riotous /-əs/ *adj* **1** (*fml or law*) disorderly; unruly: *a riotous assembly*, ie of people ○ *charged with riotous behaviour.* **2** [attrib] (*usu derog*) boisterous; unrestrained: *a riotous party* ○ *riotous laughter.* **riotously** *adv* extremely: *riotously funny.* **riotousness** *n* [U] violent disorderly behaviour.
□ **ˈriot police** police trained in dealing with rioters.
ˈriot shield shield for use by police or soldiers dealing with riots.
rip /rɪp/ *v* (**-pp-**) **1** (**a**) [Tn, Tn·pr] divide or make a hole in (sth) by pulling sharply: *I've ripped my trousers.* ○ *rip a piece of cloth (in two).* (**b**) [Cn·a] ~ **sth open** open sth by pulling in this way: *rip open a letter* ○ *My cat had its ear ripped open by a dog.* (**c**) [I] (of material) become torn: *Be careful with that dress; it rips easily.* **2** (idm) **let ˈrip (about/against/at sb/sth)** speak violently or passionately: *let rip against the government.* **let sth ˈrip** (*infml*) (**a**) allow (a car, machine, etc) to go at its top speed: *Let her/it rip!* (**b**) allow (things) to develop naturally, without attempting to control them: *They just let inflation rip.* **3** (phr v) **rip sb off** (*sl*) cheat sb, especially financially: *The shop tried to rip me off.* **rip sth off** (**a**) remove sth by pulling sharply: *rip the cover off (a book).* (**b**) (*sl*) steal sth: *Somebody's ripped off my wallet.*
▷ **rip** *n* **1** uneven or ragged tear or cut: *There's a big rip in my sleeve.* **2** stretch of rough water in a river or the sea. Cf RIP-TIDE.
□ **ˈrip-cord** *n* cord that releases a parachute from its pack: *pull the rip-cord.*
ˈrip-off *n* (usu *sing*); (*sl*) act of defrauding, stealing, overcharging, etc: *£1.50 for a cup of coffee? What a rip-off!*
ˈrip-roaring *adj* [attrib] (*infml*) (**a**) wild and noisy. (**b**) great, huge, etc: *The film was a rip-roaring success.*
ˈrip-saw *n* saw with large coarse teeth, used for cutting wood along the grain.
RIP /ˌɑːr aɪ ˈpiː/ *abbr* (on tombstones, etc) (may he, she, they) rest in peace (Latin *requiescat/requiescant in pace*): *James Dent RIP.*
riparian /raɪˈpeərɪən/ *adj* (*law or fml*) of or inhabiting the banks of a river, lake, etc: *riparian rights*, eg to fish in a river ○ *riparian creatures.*
ripe /raɪp/ *adj* **1** (of fruit, grain, etc) ready to be gathered and used, esp for eating: *Are the apples ripe enough to eat yet?* ○ *harvest the ripe corn* ○ (*fig*) *Her lips were ripe as cherries*, ie full and red like ripe cherries. **2** (of cheese) fully matured or developed: *ripe cheese* ○ (*rare fig*) *ripe judgement, scholarship.* **3** (of a person's age) advanced: *men of riper years* ○ *lived to a ripe old age* ○ (*ironic*) *at the ripe old age of 21.* **4** [pred] ~ **(for sth)** ready; fit; prepared: *land that is ripe for development* ○ *a nation ripe for revolution.* **5** (idm) **the time is ripe** ⇨ TIME[1].
▷ **ripen** /ˈraɪpən/ *v* [I, Tn] (cause sth to) become ripe: *ripening corn* ○ *peaches ripened by the sun.*
ripeness *n* [U].
riposte /rɪˈpɒst/ *n* **1** quick verbal reply or retort, esp to criticism: *a witty riposte.* **2** (in fencing) quick return thrust after parrying.
▷ **riposte** /rɪˈpɒst/ *v* [I, Ipr] ~ **(with sth)** deliver a riposte.
ripple /ˈrɪpl/ *n* [C] **1** small wave or series of waves: *She threw a stone into the pond and watched the ripples spread.* **2** thing like this in appearance or movement: *slight ripples on the surface of the metal.* **3** gentle rising and falling sound: *a ripple of laughter, voices, applause.*
▷ **ripple** *v* [I, Tn] (cause sth to) move in ripples: *corn rippling in the breeze* ○ *rippling muscles* ○ *wind rippling the lake.*
rip-tide /ˈrɪptaɪd/ *n* tide causing strong currents and rough water.
Rip van Winkle /ˌrɪp væn ˈwɪŋkl/ character in a story by Washington *Irving. He runs away from his wife and falls asleep during a walk in the mountains. He does not wake up for 20 years, and finds that the world he knew has completely changed. People often use the name to refer to anyone who spends a long time asleep.
rise[1] /raɪz/ *n* **1** (**a**) upward movement or progress: *His rise to power was very rapid.* ○ *the rise and fall of the British Empire.* (**b**) increase in amount, number or intensity: *a rise in the price of meat, the value of the dollar, the average temperature.* **2** upward slope; small hill: *At the top of the rise they paused for a rest.* ○ *a church situated on a small rise.* **3** (*Brit*) (*US* **raise**) increase (in wages): *demand a rise (in wages) from next October.* **4** (idm) **get/take a rise out of sb** cause sb to show annoyance or make an angry response by teasing, etc. **give rise to sth** (*fml*) cause sth: *Her disappearance gave rise to the wildest rumours.*
▷ **riser** *n* **1** vertical piece between two treads of a staircase. **2** person who habitually gets up early or late in the morning (as specified): *an early/a late riser.*
rise[2] /raɪz/ *v* (*pt* **rose** /rəʊz/, *pp* **risen** /ˈrɪzn/) **1** [I, Ipr, Ip, In/pr] come or go upwards; reach a high or higher level, position, etc: *The cost of living continues to rise.* ○ *The river has risen (by) several metres.* ○ *smoke rising from the chimney* ○ *Her voice rose in anger.* ○ *new tower-blocks rising nearby.* **2** (*fml*) get up from a lying, sitting or kneeling position; get out of bed: *accustomed to rising early* ○ *He rose (in order) to welcome me.* ○ *unable to rise because of his injuries.* **3** [I] (*fml*) (of the people taking part in a meeting or other assembly) disperse: *The House* (ie Members of the House of Commons) *rose at 10 pm.* ○ *Parliament rises* (ie ends its current session) *on Thursday.* **4** become upright or erect: *The hair on the back of my neck rose when I heard the scream.* **5** [I, Ipr, Ip] ~ **(up) (against sb/sth)** (*fml*) rebel: *rise (up) in revolt* ○ *rise (up) against the foreign invaders.* **6** [I] (of the wind) begin to blow (more strongly): *The wind is rising — I think there's a storm coming.* **7** [I] (of the sun, moon, etc) appear above the horizon: *The sun rises in the east and sets in the west.* Cf SET[1] 19. **8** [I] increase in cheerfulness: *Her spirits* (ie her mood, feelings, emotions) *rose at the news.* **9** [I, Ipr] reach a higher rank, status or position (in society, one's career, etc): *He rose from the ranks to become an officer.* ○ *rise from nothing to become a great leader* ○ *a rising young politician.* **10** [I] (of dough, bread, etc) swell under the action of yeast, baking powder, etc: *My cake is a disaster — it hasn't risen.* **11** [I, Ipr] (of a river) begin to flow; have its source: *The Thames rises in the Cotswold Hills.* **12** (idm) **early to bed and early to rise** ⇨ EARLY. **make sb's gorge rise** ⇨ GORGE[1]. **make one's hackles rise** ⇨ HACKLES. **ˌrise above the ˈcrowd** show oneself to be better than most other people, esp by being more generous, tolerant, etc. **ˌrise and ˈshine** (*Brit catchphrase*) (usu imperative) get out of bed and be active. **ˈrise again/from the ˈdead** come to life again after death: *Christians believe that Jesus rose from the dead on Easter Sunday.* **rise to the ˈbait** succumb to a lure or temptation: *As soon as I mentioned money he rose to the bait, and became really interested.* **rise to the ocˈcasion, ˈchallenge, ˈtask, etc** prove oneself able to deal with an unexpected situation, problem, etc. **13** (phr v) **rise above sth** (show oneself to) be superior to sth, capable of dealing with it, etc: *She rose above her difficulties and became a tremendous success.*
▷ **rising** *n* [C] armed rebellion; revolt: *Troops put down a rising in the capital.* — *adv* (idm) **ˌrising ˈfive, twelve, etc** (of a child) nearly five, twelve, etc years old.
□ **ˌrising ˈdamp** dampness rising from the ground into the walls of a building.
ˌrising ˈfives, etc children of nearly five, etc years old: *Mrs Smith teaches the rising fives.*
the ˌrising geneˈration young people who are growing up.
risible /ˈrɪzəbl/ *adj* (*fml or joc*) fit to be laughed at; ridiculous: *The entire proposal is risible: it will never be accepted.*
risk /rɪsk/ *n* **1** [C, U] ~ **(of sth/that ...)** (instance of the) possibility of meeting danger or suffering harm, loss, etc: *Is there any risk of the bomb exploding?* ○ *You shouldn't underestimate the risks of the enterprise.* ○ *There's no risk of her failing/that she'll fail.* ○ *insure a house for all risks*, ie fire, theft, etc ○ [attrib] *an all-risks policy* ○ *an investment involving a high degree of risk.* **2** [C] person or thing insured or representing a source of risk: *He's a good/poor risk.* ○ *All the people who know this secret represent a security risk.* **3** (idm) **at one's own risk** agreeing to make no claims for any loss, injury, etc: *Persons swimming beyond this point do so at their own risk*, ie No one else will take responsibility for whatever happens to them. **at ˈrisk** threatened by the possibility of loss, failure, etc; in danger: *put one's life at risk* ○ *The whole future of the company is at risk.* ○ *My job is at risk*, ie I may be made redundant. **at the risk of (doing sth)** with the possibility of (doing sth): *At the risk of sounding ungrateful, I must refuse your offer.* **at risk to sb/sth** with the possibility of losing or injuring sb/sth: *He saved the child at considerable risk to himself/to his own life.* **a calculated risk** ⇨ CALCULATE. **run the risk (of doing sth); run ˈrisks** do sth that exposes one to a danger, possibility, etc: *We can't run the risk (of losing all that money).* ○ *He runs more risk of being arrested.* ○ *She runs the same risks.* **take a ˈrisk/ˈrisks** do sth that involves the possibility of failure, danger, etc: *You can't get rich without taking risks.* ○ *That's a risk I'm prepared to take.*
▷ **risk** *v* **1** [Tn] expose (sb/oneself) to danger: *risk one's health, fortune, neck* (ie life). **2** [Tn, Tg] accept the possibility of (sth): *risk failure* ○ *risk getting caught in a storm.*
risky *adj* (**-ier, -iest**) full of danger; full of potential for failure, loss, etc: *a risky undertaking.*
riskily /-ɪlɪ/ *adv.* **riskiness** *n* [U].
risotto /rɪˈzɒtəʊ/ *n* (*pl* ~**s**) [C, U] Italian dish of rice cooked in stock, to which vegetables, seafood, etc may be added.
risqué /ˈriːskeɪ; *US* rɪˈskeɪ/ *adj* (of a story, remark, item of clothing, etc) slightly indecent.
rissole /ˈrɪsəʊl/ *n* small flat cake or ball of minced

Rivers and Canals

Britain has a complex network of rivers and canals. Although the longest river, the Severn, is only 290 km (180 miles) long, many British rivers are navigable for much of their length. Numerous canals were constructed, mostly in the 18th and early 19th centuries, to link the major rivers, especially in the Midlands. This opened up the interior of the country to navigation and contributed to the Industrial Revolution.

The first major canal to be built was the Bridgewater Canal, linking Manchester with Worsley. Birmingham later became the centre of the canal network. The canals were used for transporting heavy loads and materials, such as coal and stone, until the development of the railways from about 1830. One of Britain's best known canals, the Manchester Ship Canal, was built in the final years of the 19th century in order to make Manchester accessible as a port to large ocean steamers. In Scotland, the Caledonian Canal, linking Loch Ness with Loch Linnhe and the Moray Firth, allows small vessels to cross Scotland from coast to coast and so avoid the long journey round the northern coast via the Pentland Firth.

The chief rivers of Britain that are navigable to any extent, with the cities that they pass through, are: in England the Thames (London, Reading, Oxford), the Ouse (York), the Humber (Hull), the Mersey (Liverpool, Manchester, via the Manchester Ship Canal), and the Severn (Newport, via the Usk, Bristol, via the Avon, Gloucester), and in Scotland, the firths (estuaries) of the Forth (Edinburgh), the Clyde (Glasgow), the Moray (Inverness), the Solway (Dumfries, via the Nith) and the Tay (Dundee). Northern Ireland's main river is the Foyle (Londonderry).

Most of Britain's navigable rivers and canals, with the notable exception of the Manchester Ship Canal, were nationalized in 1947 and in 1962 placed under the control of the newly formed British Waterways Board (BWB). Many of the once busy canals were no longer being used and a number had fallen into decay. In 1968 an Act of Parliament was passed to renovate and reopen many old canals for pleasure cruising and recreation, and this is how they are used today. People spend holidays in small boats, many of them copies of the narrow canal boats or barges that were formerly used to transport goods. In 1990 the Kennet and Avon Canal, which runs from Reading to Bath and has a spectacular series of 29 locks, was reopened.

Until 1989, the management of rivers as a source of water supply was the responsibility of the ten water and sewage companies. When the companies were privatized in that year, however, management passed to a new body, the National Rivers Authority (NRA).

Although some rivers, especially the larger navigable ones, are still used to transport goods, a large number are used for sport, for example yachting, rowing and water-skiing, while both rivers and canals are used for fishing. Some rowing events have become nationally famous, such as the Royal Regatta at Henley-on-Thames and the University Boat Race on the Thames at London. The Devizes to Westminster Race, a canoe race along the Kennet and Avon Canal and the river Thames, also takes place annually.

Most of the large rivers of the USA are navigable for a considerable distance. The Mississippi, for example, the country's longest river, is navigable as far as Minneapolis, a distance of over 3 000 km (almost 1 900 miles), and with its tributaries the Missouri and the Ohio is a major transport route that gave access to the American heartland in historic times. Other important American rivers are the St Lawrence (for some distance forming the boundary between the USA and Canada), the Columbia and the Yukon.

The development of canals in North America began after 1815. The Erie Canal, linking the river Hudson with Lake Erie, was one of the first to be constructed, and greatly aided the industrial development of the north-east region. The St Lawrence Seaway, opened in 1959 and running from Montreal in Canada to Lake Ontario, enables ships to sail from the Atlantic to Duluth at the western end of Lake Superior, a distance of 3 766 km (2 342 miles). Canals are also important in making agriculture possible in the Central Valley of California and in many parts of Utah.

meat or fish mixed with potato or breadcrumbs and fried.

rite /raɪt/ *n* [C] religious or other solemn ceremony: *marriage/funeral rites* ○ *initiation rites*, eg those performed when a new member joins a secret society.

ritual /ˈrɪtʃʊəl/ *n* **1** (a) [U] series of actions used in a religious or some other ceremony: *the ritual of the Catholic Church* ○ *Some religions employ ritual more than others.* (b) [C] particular form of this: *the ritual of the Japanese tea ceremony.* **2** [C] (*esp joc*) procedure regularly followed in precisely the same way each time: *He went through the ritual of filling and lighting his pipe.*

▷ **ritual** *adj* [attrib] of or done as a ritual: *a ritual dance* ○ *ritual phrases of greeting.* **ritually** /ˈrɪtʃʊəlɪ/ *adv.*

ritualism /-ɪzəm/ *n* [U] (*esp derog*) fondness for or insistence on ritual. **ritualistic** /ˌrɪtʃʊəˈlɪstɪk/ *adj.*

Ritz /rɪts/ **1** any of a number of hotels founded by or named after the Swiss hotelier César Ritz (1850-1918) and famous for their luxury: *The place isn't the Ritz* (ie is very simple) *but at least it's clean.* **2** (idm) **put on the ˈRitz** (*US infml*) behave in an unnatural or affected way in order to impress others.

▷ **ritzy** /ˈrɪtsɪ/ *adj* (**-ier**, **-iest**) (*dated infml*) impressively luxurious.

rival /ˈraɪvl/ *n* ~ (**for/in sth**) person or thing competing with another: *ˈbusiness rivals* ○ *rivals in love* ○ *a new rival for the title of champion* ○ [attrib] *a rival firm* ○ *a violinist without rival*, ie better than any other ○ *She has no rival* (ie no one is as good as she is) *in the field of romantic fiction.*

▷ **rival** *v* (**-ll-**; *US also* **-l-**) [Tn, Tn·pr] ~ **sb/sth** (**for/in sth**) seem or be as good as sb/sth; be comparable to sb/sth: *a view rivalling anything the Alps can offer* ○ *Cricket cannot rival football for/in excitement.*

rivalry /ˈraɪvlrɪ/ *n* [C, U] (instance of) being rivals; competition: *a country paralysed by political rivalries* ○ *the usual rivalry between brother and sister.*

riven /ˈrɪvn/ *adj* [pred] (*fml or rhet*) split; torn violently: *a family riven by ancient feuds.*

river /ˈrɪvə(r)/ *n* [C] **1** large natural stream of water flowing in a channel: *the River Thames* ○ *the Mississippi River* ○ [attrib] *the river mouth* ○ *river traffic.* ⇨ article. Cf CANAL 1. **2** any large flow of similar form: *a river of lava* ○ (*fig rhet*) *rivers of blood*, ie great bloodshed in war, etc. **3** (idm) **sell sb down the river** ⇨ SELL.

□ ˈ**river-bed** *n* ground over which a river usu flows: *It's so long since it rained that the river-bed is dry.*

ˈ**riverside** *n* ground along the bank of a river: *go for a walk along the riverside* ○ [attrib] *a riverside pub.*

rivet /ˈrɪvɪt/ *n* metal pin or bolt for fastening two pieces of metal together, its headless end being hammered or pressed flat to prevent slipping.

▷ **rivet** *v* **1** [Tn, Tn·pr, Tn·p] fasten (sth) with a rivet or rivets: *riveted together/down/in place.* **2** [Tn, Tn·pr usu passive] make (sth) immobile; fix: *We stood riveted (to the spot).* **3** [Tn esp passive] attract and strongly hold the attention of (sb): *I was absolutely riveted by her story.* **riveter** *n.* **riveting** *adj* (*approv*) that holds the attention; enthralling: *an absolutely riveting performance.*

Riviera /ˌrɪvɪˈeərə/ *n* [sing] **1 the Riviera** region along the Mediterranean coast of SE France, Monaco and NW Italy, famous for its climate and beauty and containing many holiday resorts. **2** region thought to resemble this: *the Cornish Riviera.*

rivulet /ˈrɪvjʊlɪt/ *n* small stream: *rivulets running down the mountainside* ○ *rivulets of sweat on his forehead.*

riyal /riːˈɑːl/ *n* **1** unit of money in Dubai and Qatar. **2** (also **rial**) unit of money in Saudi Arabia and the Yemen Republic.

rly *abbr* (eg on a map) railway.

RM /ˌɑːr ˈem/ *abbr* (*Brit*) Royal Marines: *Capt Tom Pullen RM.*

rm *abbr* room: *rm 603*, eg in a hotel.

RN /ˌɑːr ˈen/ *abbr* **1** (*US*) registered nurse. **2** (*Bri* Royal Navy: *Capt L J Grant RN.*

Rn *symb* radon.

RNA /ˌɑːr en ˈeɪ/ *abbr* (*chemistry*) ribonucleic aci

RNIB /ˌɑːr en aɪ ˈbiː/ *abbr* (*Brit*) Royal Nationa Institute for the Blind.

RNLI /ˌɑːr en el ˈaɪ/ *abbr* (*Brit*) Royal Nationa Lifeboat Institution. ⇨ article at CHARITY.

roach[1] /rəʊtʃ/ *n* (*pl* unchanged) small freshwate fish of the carp family.

roach[2] /rəʊtʃ/ *n* (*pl* ~**es**) (*esp US*) **1** (*infml*) COCKROACH. **2** (*sl*) stub of a marijuana cigarette.

road /rəʊd/ *n* **1** (a) way between places, esp or with a prepared surface for the use of moto vehicles: *the road to Bristol/the Bristol road main/major/minor roads* ○ *a quiet suburban roa* ○ [attrib] ˈ*road junctions* ○ ˈ*road signs.* ⇨ articl (b) (in compounds) of or concerning such a way ways: *a ˈroad-map of Scotland* ○ *be considerate other ˈroad-users.* **2 Road** (*abbr* **Rd**) (in names roads, esp in towns): *35 York Rd, London SW16.* Usage. **3** (usu *pl*) stretch of water near the sho where ships may be anchored: *the Southampto Roads.* **4** (idm) **all roads lead to ˈRome** (*sayin* any of the methods, means, etc being considere will bring about the same result in the end. b ˈ**road** in or on a road vehicle: *It's a long way road — the train is more direct.* ○ *It's cheaper to sh goods by road than by rail.* **the end of the lin road** ⇨ END[1]. **get the show on the road** ⇨ SHOW **hit the road** ⇨ HIT[1]. **one for the road** (*infml*) fin drink before leaving for home, on a journey, et **on the ˈroad** travelling, esp as a salesma performer or tramp: *The band has been on the roa for almost a month.* **the road to sth** way towar achieving sth, reaching a goal, etc: *the road success/ruin.* **the road to hell is paved with goo intentions** (*saying*) people may be blamed punished as a result of not putting into practi their original good motives. **rule of the road** RULE. **take to the ˈroad** (*fml*) become a tramp.

Roads

The oldest roads in Britain are the straight roads built by the Romans. Stretches of Roman roads remain today as the basis for modern highways. Examples are the A12 road from London to Colchester and the A33 from Winchester to Basingstoke. Most Roman roads fell into disuse when the Romans left Britain, and bridleways for horses and their riders took their place. Roads remained basic tracks until the mid-18th century, when hard-surface roads began to be built. These in turn were neglected through much of the 19th century, when railways were widely developed, and modern road-making began only in the early 20th century with the coming of the motor car.

Today Britain has roads of three main types: motorways, A-roads (major motor routes) and B-roads (or minor routes). The most important roads radiate from the major cities, especially London, and it is from London that the key motorways run. All roads are numbered, with the lowest numbers designating the most important routes. The A1, for example, is the former Great North Road that ran from London to Edinburgh. The A2 runs from London to Dover, the A3 to Portsmouth, the A4 to Bristol and the A5 to Holyhead in north-west Wales. Other important trunk roads are the A10 from London to Cambridge and King's Lynn, the A30 to Exeter and Penzance, the A40 to Oxford and Fishguard in south-west Wales, and the A41 to Birmingham and Chester. Central government is responsible for A-roads and motorways. B-roads and other roads are built and maintained by local authorities.

The building of motorways began in Britain only in the late 1950s. One of the first was the M1 London-to-Birmingham route, which has now been extended to Leeds. The M2 runs from London to Faversham, and is being extended to Canterbury and Dover, the M3 runs to Winchester, and is being extended to Southampton, the M4 goes to Bristol and South Wales, and is being extended to Carmarthen, the M5 runs south-west from Birmingham to Bristol and Exeter, and the M6 runs north from Birmingham to Carlisle, and is being extended to Scotland. Other important motorways are the M11 London to Cambridge, M40 London to Oxford and Birmingham, and the M8 in Scotland between Glasgow and Edinburgh. One of the most recent motorways to be completed is the M25, which serves as an orbital route or 'ring road' round London.

Traffic on trunk roads (A-roads) and motorways has been growing rapidly, and at present such roads carry not only large numbers of cars but many heavy goods lorries, often called 'juggernauts'. This increase has resulted in frequent hold-ups on motorways, especially the M25, where traffic is often seriously delayed. This is a problem that has yet to be satisfactorily solved, but many by-passes and relief roads have been built to take heavy traffic away from the centre of towns and cities, and most new roads apart from motorways are of this type.

The USA began to build roads later than Britain, but once the states had authorized a construction programme in the 19th century, major road routes began to appear, and today American highways are among the best in the world, even if they have at the same time radically altered the rural landscape. The USA is not called the land of the automobile for nothing: eight out of ten families own a car, and more than a quarter have two or more cars. Moreover, most long journeys are made by car, not by train.

There are three main types of main road in the USA. Expressways are the largest, and are designed to take the heaviest traffic flows. Highways also carry a large volume of traffic, but are also designed to link towns and cities. Other roads are chiefly rural highways and 'feeder' roads, leading to a major highway. There are also parkways, wide roads lined with trees or parkland originally designed to carry heavy traffic flows in urban areas. One of the earliest was the Bronx River Parkway, New York, constructed in 1925. This in turn influenced the Westchester parkway system, built in the extensive residential area just north of New York. Parkways now run in rural areas; one example is the Garden State Parkway, which follows the coast in New Jersey.

America's Interstate Highway System, built in the 1960s and 1970s, is the most extensive of its kind in the world. The system criss-crosses the country, and is designed to carry 20 per cent of all motor traffic. The interstate roads are numbered, with even numbers for those running east to west, and odd numbers for those running north to south.

▷ ˈ**roadie** *n* (*infml*) person who works with a pop group, etc on tour, esp moving and setting up equipment.

□ ˈ**road-bed** *n* **1** base of rubble, stones, etc on which a railway track is built. **2** foundations and surface of a road. **3** (*US*) part of a road used by vehicles; roadway.

ˈ**road-block** *n* barricade across a road, set up by the police or army to stop traffic for search.

ˈ**road-hog** *n* (*infml*) reckless or inconsiderate driver.

ˈ**road-holding** *n* [U] ability of a vehicle or its tyres to move steadily along the road in good or bad weather, without deviating or slipping.

ˈ**road-house** *n* (*dated*) pub, restaurant, etc on a main road in the country.

ˈ**road-metal** (also **metal**) *n* [U] broken stone used for the making and repairing of roads.

ˈ**roadrunner** *n* type of cuckoo of Mexico and southern US.

ˈ**road safety** safety from traffic accidents: *a campaign for road safety*, ie to encourage the prevention of road accidents.

ˈ**road sense** ability to behave safely on roads, esp while driving.

ˈ**road show** play, musical, etc performed by a company on tour.

ˈ**roadside** *n* edge/border of a road: *parked by/at the roadside* ○ [attrib] *a* ˌ*roadside* ˈ*café*.

ˈ**road tax** tax paid by the owner of a motor vehicle to allow him to drive it on public roads. ˈ**road tax disc** (also ˈ**road fund licence**) (*Brit*) certificate of payment of road tax, displayed on the vehicle.

ˈ**road test** test of a vehicle (esp a new model) by using it on a road: *The new sports model achieved 100 miles an hour in road tests.* ˈ**road-test** *v* [Tn] test (a vehicle) in this way.

the ˈ**roadway** *n* part of the road used by vehicles, contrasted with the footpath, pavement, etc.

ˈ**road-works** *n* [pl] work involving the construction or repair of roads: *We were delayed by road-works for two hours.*

ˈ**roadworthy** *adj* (of a vehicle) fit to be driven on a public road. ˈ**roadworthiness** *n* [U]

NOTE ON USAGE: In a town, **street** is the most general word for a road lined with buildings: *a street-map of London.* In British English **street** is not used for roads outside towns but streets in towns may have the word **Road** in their names: *Edgware Road.* An **alley** or **lane** is a narrow street between buildings. An **avenue** is usually a wide street of houses, often in the suburbs and lined with trees. (In US cities **avenues** often run at right angles to **streets.**) **Roads** (*US* **highways**) connect towns and villages: *a road-map of Ireland.* **Motorways** (*US* **freeways/expressways**) are built for long-distance traffic to avoid towns. A **lane** is a narrow country road which winds between fields, connecting villages. **Highway** is seldom used in British English except in certain official phrases: *the Highway Code.* **Road, Street, Lane** and **Avenue** are the most common words used in street names and are often abbreviated in addresses to **Rd, St, La, Ave.**

roam /rəʊm/ *v* **1** [Ipr, Ip, Tn] walk or travel without any definite aim or destination: *roam through the deserted village* ○ *just roaming around* ○ *He used to roam the streets for hours on end.* **2** (phr v) **roam over sth** talk about various things, or various aspects of sth: *The speaker roamed freely over the events of the past week.*

▷ **roam** *n* [sing] walk, etc of this kind.

roamer *n* person or animal who does this: *He's a bit of a roamer*, ie he tends not to stay in one place for very long.

roan /rəʊn/ *n, adj* [attrib] (animal, esp a horse or cow) with a coat of mixed colour, esp brown with white or grey hairs in it: *a roan mare.*

roar /rɔː(r)/ *n* long loud deep sound (like that) made by a lion: *the roar of traffic* ○ *a roar of applause, anger, etc* ○ *roars of laughter.*

▷ **roar** *v* **1** (**a**) [I, Ipr, Ip] make such long loud deep sounds: *tigers roaring in their cages* ○ *roar with laughter, pain, rage, etc* ○ *He just roared* (ie laughed loudly) *when he heard that joke!* ○ *a roaring* (ie large, bright and noisy) *fire.* (**b**) [Tn, Tn·p] ~ **sth (out)** express sth in this way: *The crowd roared its approval.* ○ *roar out an order.* **2** (idm) **roar oneself** ˈ**hoarse, etc** make oneself hoarse, etc by roaring. **3** (phr v) **roar along, down, past, etc** move in the specified direction making a loud, deep sound: *Cars roared past (us).* **roar/shout sb down** silence a speaker by shouting loudly so that he cannot be heard.

roaring /ˈrɔːrɪŋ/ *adj* [attrib] **1** noisy; rough or stormy: *roaring thunder* ○ *a roaring night.* **2** (idm) **do a roaring** ˈ**trade (in sth)** sell (sth) very quickly; do excellent business (in sth). **the roaring** ˈ**forties** part of the Atlantic Ocean, often very stormy, between latitudes of 40° and 50° S. **a roaring suc**ˈ**cess** a very great success. — *adv* extremely and noisily: *roaring mad*, ie very angry ○ *roaring drunk.*

roast /rəʊst/ *v* **1** (**a**) [Tn, Tn·pr] cook (meat, etc) in an oven, or over or in front of a fire: *roast a joint of meat, a chicken, some potatoes.* (**b**) [I, Ipr] be cooked in this way: *the delicious smell of meat roasting in its own juices.* ⇨ Usage at COOK. **2** [Tn] dry (sth) and turn it brown using intense heat: *roast coffee beans, peanuts, chestnuts.* **3** [I, Tn] expose (sb/oneself) to the heat of a fire, the sun, etc: *We're going to lie in the sun and roast for two weeks.* ○ *roast one's toes in front of the fire.* **4** [Tn] (*US infml*) criticize (sb/sth) harshly, esp in jest; ridicule: *The critics roasted her new play.*

▷ **roast** *adj* [attrib] cooked in an oven, etc: *roast beef.*

roast *n* **1** [C] joint of meat that has been roasted or is meant for roasting: *order a roast from the butcher.* **2** [C] (*esp US*) outdoor picnic or barbecue at which food is roasted. **3** [C, U] (*US infml*) (occasion of) harsh criticism or ridicule, esp in jest.

roaster *n* type of chicken, etc suitable for roasting. Cf BROILER (BROIL).

roasting *adj* (*infml*) very hot: *It's roasting today!* ie The weather is very hot. — *n* (idm) **give sb/get a (good, real, etc) ˈroasting** scold sb/be scolded severely.

rob /rɒb/ *v* (-bb-) [Tn, Tn·pr] ~ **sb/sth (of sth)** **1** take property from (a person or place) illegally: *I was robbed (of my cash and cheque-book).* ○ *accused of robbing a bank (of one million pounds).* ⇨ Usage. **2** deprive sb/sth (of what is expected or normal): *Those cats robbed me of my sleep.* ○ (*fig*) *The fact that he had lied before robbed his words of any credibility.* **3** (idm) ˌ**rob** ˌ**Peter to** ˌ**pay** ˈ**Paul** pay one debt, etc with money borrowed from somewhere else, thus creating another debt. **rob sb** ˈ**blind** (*infml*) steal a lot of money from sb in a secret and ruthless way: *Our accountant's been robbing the company blind.*

▷ **robber** *n* person who robs; thief.

robbery /ˈrɒbərɪ/ *n* [C, U] **1** (instance of) stealing; theft: *three robberies in one week* ○ *Armed robbery is on the increase everywhere.* **2** (idm) **daylight robbery** ⇨ DAYLIGHT. **fair exchange is no robbery** ⇨ FAIR[1].

NOTE ON USAGE: Compare **rob**, **steal** and **burgle.** A robber or thief **robs** a place, eg a bank, or a person (of things, especially money) and he **steals** things (from a place or person). A burglar **burgles** a house by forcing a way into it and stealing from it.

Robbia /ˈrɒbɪə/ Luca della (1400-82) and his nephew Andrea della (1435-1525), Italian (Florentine) sculptors. Luca is famous for his figures inspired by ancient Roman friezes, produced in glazed terracotta, a medium invented by him and developed by Andrea.

robe /rəʊb/ *n* **1** (esp in compounds) long loose outer garment: *a beach-robe* ○ *Many Arabs wear long flowing robes.* **2** (esp *pl*) such a garment worn as a sign of rank or office, or for a ceremony: *coroˈnation robes*, ie of a king or queen ○ *cardinals in scarlet robes.* **3** (*US* also ˈ**bathrobe**) dressing-gown.

▷ **robe** *v* [esp passive: Tn, Tn·pr] ~ **sb/oneself (in sth)** (*fml*) dress sb/oneself in a robe, etc: *black-robed judges* ○ *robed in a ceremonial gown.*

Robert the Bruce /ˌrɒbət ðə ˈbru:s/ (1274-1329) king of Scotland 1306-29. He was defeated in his early struggle against *Edward I of England, but rebelled against *Edward II, defeating him at *Bannockburn in 1314 and uniting Scotland as an independent kingdom. ⇨ article at SCOTLAND.

Robeson /ˈrəʊbsn/ Paul (1898-1976), black American singer and actor. His deep bass voice and stage presence made him famous, esp as a performer of negro spirituals.

Robespierre /ˈrəʊbzpjeə(r)/ Maximilien de (1758-94), French revolutionary. At the beginning of the *French Revolution he was a moderate favouring a constitutional monarchy. His belief that the will of the people was supreme and that the Revolution was in danger led him to take part in the *Reign of Terror, at the end of which he himself was executed.

robin /ˈrɒbɪn/ *n* **1** (also ˌ**robin** ˈ**redbreast**) small brown red-breasted bird. ⇨ illus at BIRD. ⇨ article at CHRISTMAS. **2** (*US*) type of N American thrush resembling this.

Robin Goodfellow /ˌrɒbɪn ˈgʊdfeləʊ/ = PUCK.

Robin Hood /ˌrɒbɪn ˈhʊd/ legendary English outlaw and hero who lived in the time of *Richard I. He robbed the rich to give money to the poor and lived in Sherwood Forest near Nottingham, along with his companions (his 'merry men'), who included *Friar Tuck and *Little John.

Robinson /ˈrɒbɪnsən/ Edward G (1893-1973), American actor. He became famous for his roles as gangsters (eg in *Little Caesar*) and investigators (eg in *Double Indemnity*).

Robinson Crusoe /ˌrɒbɪnsn ˈkru:səʊ/ hero of a book of the same name by Daniel *Defoe, published in 1719. Crusoe is shipwrecked alone on a desert island and cleverly uses his few possessions to survive. He is helped by Friday, an islander he saves from death and uses as a servant. The book has been called the first English novel.

robot /ˈrəʊbɒt/ *n* [C] **1** (also **automaton**) machine that (resembles and) can perform the actions of a person, operated automatically or by remote control: *Many production-line tasks in car factories are now performed by robots.* **2** (*esp derog*) person who seems to behave like a machine. Cf AUTOMATON 2. **3** (in Southern Africa) an automatic traffic-light.

▷ **robotic** /rəʊˈbɒtɪk/ *adj* like a robot; stiff and mechanical: *robotic movements.* **robotics** *n* [sing *v*] (study of the) use of robots in manufacturing.

Rob Roy /rɒb ˈrɔɪ/ popular name of Robert MacGregor (1671-1734), Scottish bandit. He led the outlawed clan MacGregor, and was involved in blackmail and stealing cattle. Walter *Scott's novel *Rob Roy* gives a romanticized version of his activities.

robust /rəʊˈbʌst/ *adj* **1** vigorous; healthy and strong: *a robust young man* ○ *a robust appetite.* **2** (*derog*) not delicate or refined: *a rather robust sense of humour.* **3** (of wine) full-bodied. ▷ **robustly** *adv.* **robustness** *n* [U].

roc /rɒk/ *n* (in Arabian legend) type of enormous and powerful bird.

Rochester /ˈrɒtʃɪstə(r)/ John Wilmot, 2nd Earl of Rochester (1647-80), English poet. His adventurous life and the frankly sexual character of many of his poems made him one of the most colourful figures in the court of *Charles II.

rock[1] /rɒk/ *n* **1** (**a**) [U] (usu solid) part of the earth's crust: *They drilled through several layers of rock to reach the oil.* ○ *The volcano poured out molten rock.* (**b**) [C] mass of this standing out from the earth's surface or from the sea: *The ship hit some rocks and sank.* ○ *the Rock of Gibraltar.* **2** [C] (**a**) large detached stone or boulder: *The sign said, 'Danger: falling rocks'.* (**b**) (*US*) small stone or pebble: *That boy threw a rock at me.* **3** [C usu *pl*] (*sl*) diamond or similar jewel. **4** [U] (*Brit*) (*US* **rock candy**) type of hard sugar sweet, usu made in cylindrical sticks and flavoured with peppermint: *a stick of rock.* **5** (idm) **(as) firm/solid as a** ˈ**rock** immovable; dependable. **on the** ˈ**rocks** (**a**) (of a ship) wrecked on rocks. (**b**) (*infml*) (of a marriage, business, etc) in danger of failing; in a severe crisis. (**c**) (*infml*) (of drinks) served with ice cubes but no water: *Scotch* (ie whisky) *on the rocks.*

▷ **rockery** /ˈrɒkərɪ/ (also **rock-garden**) *n* artificial or natural mound or bank containing large stones, planted with rock-plants. ⇨ illus at HOUSE.

rocky *adj* (**-ier, -iest**) **1** of or like rock: *a rocky outcrop.* **2** full of rocks: *rocky soil.* **rockiness** *n* [U].

□ ˌ**rock-**ˈ**bottom** *n* [sing] (used without *a*/*the*) lowest point: *Prices have reached rock-bottom.* ○ [attrib] ˌ*rock-bottom* (ie bargain) ˈ*prices.*

ˈ**rock-cake** *n* small cake or bun with a hard rough surface.

ˌ**rock** ˈ**candy** (*US*) = ROCK[1] 4.

ˈ**rock-climbing** *n* [U] sport of climbing rock surfaces.

ˈ**rock-crystal** *n* [U] pure natural transparent quartz.

ˈ**rock-garden** *n* = ROCKERY.

ˈ**rock-plant** *n* any of various types of plant found growing on or among rocks.

ˌ**rock** ˈ**salmon** (*Brit*) (piece of) dogfish sold as food.

ˈ**rock-salt** *n* [U] common salt as mined in crystal form.

ˌ**rock-**ˈ**steady** *adj* unlikely to fall over, be changed, etc: *a* ˌ*rock-steady* ˈ*chair,* ˈ*friendship* ○ *Prices in the shares market are rock-steady.*

rock[2] /rɒk/ *v* **1** [I, Ipr, Tn, Tn·pr] (cause sb/sth to) move gently (backwards and forwards, or from side to side): *He sat rocking (himself) in his chair.* ○ *rock a baby to sleep* ○ *Our boat was rocked (from side to side) by/on the waves.* **2** [I, Ipr, Tn, Tn·pr] (cause sth to) shake violently: *The whole house rocked (to and fro) when the bomb exploded.* ○ *The town was rocked by an earthquake.* **3** [Tn] (*fig*) disturb or shock (sb/sth) greatly: *The scandal rocked the government.* **4** (idm) **rock the** ˈ**boat** (*infml*) do sth that upsets the balance of a situation, etc: *Things are progressing well — don't (do anything to) rock the boat.*

▷ **rocker** *n* **1** either of the curved pieces of wood on which a rocking-chair, etc rests. ⇨ illus at FURNITURE. **2** = ROCKING-CHAIR. **3** (also ˈ**rocker switch**) switch that changes from 'on' to 'off' by means of a rocking action. **4 Rocker** (*Brit*) member of a 1960s teenage gang or their later followers, wearing leather jackets and riding motor bikes. Cf MOD. **5** (idm) **off one's** ˈ**rocker** (*sl*) out of one's mind; crazy: *You must be off your rocker!*

rocky /ˈrɒkɪ/ *adj* (**-ier, -iest**) shaky; unsteady: *This chair is a trifle rocky.* ○ (*fig*) *Their marriage seems a bit rocky.* **rockiness** *n* [U].

□ ˈ**rocking-chair** (also **rocker**) *n* chair mounted on rockers or with springs so that it can be rocked by the sitter. ⇨ illus at FURNITURE.

ˈ**rocking-horse** *n* wooden horse mounted on rockers or springs so that it can be rocked by a child sitting on it.

rock[3] /rɒk/ *n* [U] (also ˈ**rock music**) type of modern popular music with a strong beat, played on electric guitars, etc: [attrib] *a* ˈ*rock star.*

▷ **rock** *v* [I, Ipr] dance to rock music.

□ ˌ**rock and** ˈ**roll** (also ˌ**rock 'n'** ˈ**roll**) earlier and usu simpler form of rock music: [attrib] *Jerry Lee Lewis was a rock'n'roll singer.* — *v* [I] dance to rock and roll music. ⇨ article at MUSIC.

Rockefeller /ˈrɒkəfelə(r)/ John Davison (1839-1937), American industrialist. He made a vast fortune from his company, Standard Oil. Towards the end of his life he gave much of his money to charitable causes. His name is often used to refer to a very rich person: *as rich as Rockefeller.*

rocke

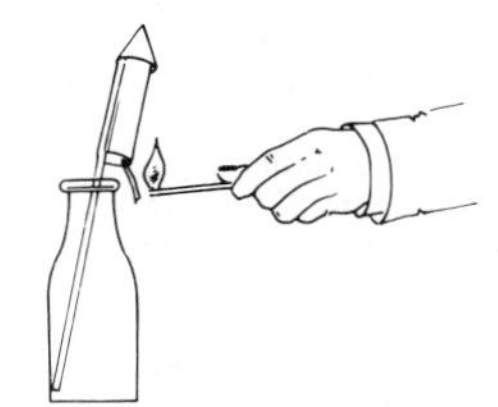

rocket /ˈrɒkɪt/ *n* **1** firework or similar device that shoots into the air when lit and then explodes: *a di*ˈ*stress rocket,* ie used to signal for help. **2** (**a**) cylindrical device that flies by expelling gases produced by combustion, used to propel a warhead or spacecraft. (**b**) bomb or shell together with the rocket propelling it: [attrib] *a* ˈ*rocket attack.* ⇨ illus. **3** (idm) **give sb/get a** ˈ**rocket** (*Brit infml*) reprimand sb/be reprimanded severely.

▷ **rocket** *v* **1** [I, Ipr, Ip] ~ **(up)** increase very rapidly: *Unemployment levels have rocketed (to new heights).* ○ *House prices are rocketing (up).* **2** [Ipr, Ip] move extremely quickly: *He rocketed to stardom* (ie became famous) *overnight.* ○ *rocket along, away, off, past, etc.*

rocketry /ˈrɒkɪtrɪ/ *n* [U] (science or practice of) using rockets for propelling missiles or spacecraft.

rocky ⇨ ROCK[1], ROCK[2].

Rocky Mountains /ˌrɒkɪ ˈmaʊntɪnz; *US* -ntnz/ (also **the Rockies**) chain of mountains in the west of N America, running from the border of the USA and Mexico up to Canada. Several peaks are over 4 000 m (14 000 ft) high.

rococo /rəˈkəʊkəʊ/ *adj* of a style of decoration in furniture, architecture, music, etc with much elaborate decoration, common in Europe in the 18th century.

rod /rɒd/ *n* **1** (often in compounds) thin straight piece of wood or metal: ˈ*curtain-rods* ○ *a* ˈ*measuring rod* ○ ˈ*piston-rods.* **2** stick used for hitting people as a punishment; cane(3a). **3** = FISHING-ROD (FISH[2]). **4** (*US sl*) hand-gun. **5** = PERCH[1] 3. **6** type of cell in the retina of the eye that is sensitive to dim light. Cf CONE 4. **7** (idm) **make a rod for one's own ˈback** do sth likely to cause oneself difficulties later. **a rod/stick to beat sb with** ⇨ BEAT[1]. **rule with a rod of iron** ⇨ RULE *v*. **spare the rod and spoil the child** ⇨ SPARE[2].

rode *pt* of RIDE[2].

rodent /ˈrəʊdnt/ *n* type of small animal that gnaws things with its strong front teeth, eg a rat, squirrel or beaver.

rodeo /rəʊˈdeɪəʊ; *US* ˈrəʊdɪəʊ/ *n* (*pl* ~s) **1** rounding up of cattle on a ranch, for branding, etc. **2** exhibition or contest of cowboys' skill in lassoing and riding cattle, untamed horses, etc.

Rodgers /ˈrɒdʒəz/ Richard (1902-79), American song-writer. He worked with the composers Lorenz Hart and Oscar *Hammerstein to produce some of the most successful American musicals, including *Oklahoma!* and *South Pacific*.

Rodin /ˈrəʊdæn/ Auguste (1840-1917), French sculptor. His earliest work, eg *The Kiss*, is characterized by a striking realism but he later moved towards a rougher and more expressive style. His best-known work is probably *The Thinker*.

rodomontade /ˌrɒdəmɒnˈteɪd, -tɑːd/ *n* [U] (*fml derog*) boastful bragging talk.

roe[1] /rəʊ/ *n* [U, C] (mass of) eggs in a female fish's ovary (*hard roe*) or a male fish's milt (*soft roe*).

roe[2] /rəʊ/ *n* (*pl* unchanged or ~s) (also ˈ**roe deer**) type of small deer.

□ ˈ**roebuck** *n* male roe.

roentgen (also **röntgen**) /ˈrɒntjən; *US* ˈrentgən/ *n* unit of ionizing radiation (eg in X-rays).

rogations /rəʊˈgeɪʃnz/ *n* [pl] special litany sung on the three days (**Roˈgation Days**) before Ascension Day.

□ **Roˌgation ˈSunday** the Sunday before Ascension Day.

roger[1] /ˈrɒdʒə(r)/ *interj* **1** (used in radio communications) your message has been received and understood. **2** (*Brit infml or joc*) okay.

roger[2] /ˈrɒdʒə(r)/ *v* [Tn] (⚠ *Brit sl euph*) (of a male) have sexual intercourse with (sb).

Roget /ˈrɒʒeɪ; *US* rəʊˈʒeɪ/ Peter Mark (1779-1869), English doctor and scholar. He produced the original version of one of the most famous reference works in English, *Roget's Thesaurus* (often called simply 'Roget'), which groups together words and phrases with the same or a similar meaning.

rogue /rəʊg/ *n* **1** (*dated*) dishonest or unprincipled man. **2** (*joc esp approv*) mischievous person: *He's a charming rogue.* **3** wild animal driven or living apart from the herd: [attrib] *a ˌrogue ˈelephant.* **4** individual product, example, etc which is unlike others of the same type, esp in being faulty or incorrect: [attrib] *a ˌrogue ˈcar*, eg one that is always breaking down.

▷ **roguery** /ˈrəʊgərɪ/ *n* [C, U] (instance of) dishonest, unprincipled or mischievous behaviour.

roguish /ˈrəʊgɪʃ/ *adj* mischievous in a playful way: *He gave her a roguish look.* **roguishly** *adv*. **roguishness** *n* [U].

□ ˌ**rogues' ˈgallery** collection of photographs of criminals kept by the police and used for identifying suspects, etc.

roistering /ˈrɔɪstərɪŋ/ *adj* [attrib], *n* [U] (*dated*) noisy merrymaking. ▷ **roisterer** /ˈrɔɪstərə(r)/ *n*.

Roland /ˈrəʊlənd/ **1** (in medieval French legend) nephew of *Charlemagne and one of his bravest knights. In *The Song of Roland* he and his faithful companion Oliver die in battle against the Saracens after being betrayed. **2** (idm) **a ˌRoland for an ˈOliver** (*dated*) case of two well-matched people or things, eg a witty answer to a witty remark.

role (also **rôle**) /rəʊl/ *n* **1** actor's part in a play: *play a variety of roles* ○ *the title-role.* **2** function or importance of sb/sth: *the role of the teacher in the learning process* ○ *the declining role of the railways in the transport system.*

□ ˈ**role-model** *n* person whose behaviour and attitudes are imitated by others, esp children.

ˈ**role-play** *n* [U, C] activity (esp in language teaching or treating mentally ill people) in which a person acts a part. — *v* [I, Tn]: *to role-play a situation.*

ˈ**role reversal** exchange of the roles usu taken by two people in relation to each other: *Unemployment among men can lead to dramatic role reversals in a marriage.*

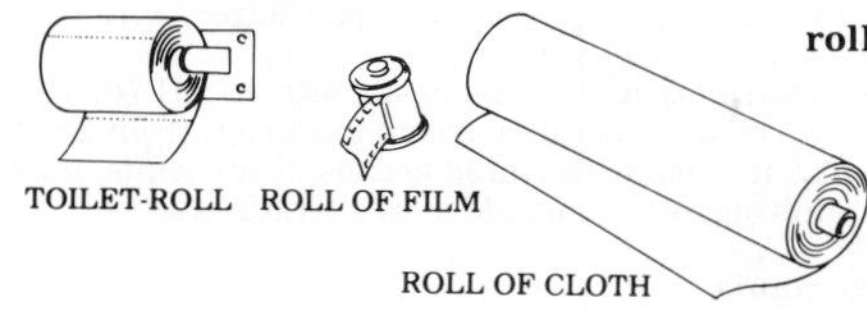

roll[1] /rəʊl/ *n* **1** (**a**) cylinder made by turning flexible material over and over on itself without folding it: *Wallpaper is bought in rolls.* ○ *a roll of carpet, film, cloth.* (**b**) person or thing with this shape: *a man with rolls of fat around his stomach.* **2** (**a**) small individual portion of bread baked in a rounded shape: *Six brown rolls, please.* ⇨ illus at BREAD. Cf BUN 1. (**b**) (with a preceding *n* or *ns*) one of these containing the stated filling: *a ham roll* ○ *a bacon and tomato roll.* **3** swaying movement; action of turning (over) from side to side: *The slow, steady roll of the ship made us feel sick.* ○ *walk with a nautical roll*, ie like a sailor ○ *a horse enjoying a roll in the grass* ○ *The plane went into a roll*, ie turned completely round along its length. Cf PITCH[3] 6. **4** official list or register, esp of names: *the electoral roll*, ie the list of people eligible to vote in an election ○ *call/read the roll in school, class, etc*, ie read aloud a list of names to check whether everyone is present. **5** long steady vibrating sound: *A ˈdrum roll preceded the most dangerous part of the performance.* ○ *the distant roll of thunder.* **6** (*US infml*) (*Brit* ˈ**bankroll**) wad of paper money. **7** (idm) **strike sb off the rolls** ⇨ STRIKE[2].

□ ˈ**roll-bar** *n* bar used to strengthen the roof of a car and protect the occupants if the car rolls over.

ˈ**roll-call** *n* (time of) reading aloud of a list of names to check whether everyone is present: *Roll-call will be at 7 am.*

ˌ**roll of ˈhonour** list of people whose achievements are honoured, esp those who have died in battle.

ˌ**roll-top ˈdesk** desk with a flexible cover that rolls up into a compartment at the top.

roll[2] /rəʊl/ *v* **1** [Ipr, Ip, Tn·pr, Tn·p] (cause sth to) move on wheels or rollers or by turning (over and over): *The ball rolled down the hill.* ○ *The hoop rolled along the pavement.* ○ *The coin fell and rolled away.* ○ *men rolling barrels across a yard* ○ *Roll it over and look at the other side.* **2** [I, Ipr, Ip, Tn, Tn·pr, Tn·p] (cause sth to) turn on an axis or over and over, round and round: *a porpoise rolling in the water* ○ *His eyes rolled strangely*, eg because he was going to faint. ○ *She rolled her eyes in amazement.* ○ *rolling a pencil between his fingers.* **3** [Ipr, Ip, Tn, Tn·pr, Tn·p, Dn·n] ~ (**sth**) (**up**) make (sth) or be made into the shape of a ball or cylinder; fold (sth) over on itself: *The hedgehog rolled up into a spiky ball.* ○ *I always roll my own (cigarettes).* ○ *roll string, wool, etc (up) into a ball.* ○ *roll up a carpet, a map, a towel* ○ *He rolled himself a cigarette.* Cf UNROLL. **4** [Tn, Tn·pr] wrap or cover (sb/sth) in sth: *He rolled himself (up) in his blanket.* ○ *roll the sausages in batter.* **5** [Tn, Tn·pr, Tn·p, Cn·a] flatten (sth) with a roller(1): *roll a lawn* ○ *roll out the dough* ○ *roll the ground flat.* **6** (**a**) [I, Ipr, Ip, Tn, Tn·pr, Tn·p] (cause sb/sth to) sway or rock (from side to side): *The ship was rolling heavily to and fro.* ○ *walk with a rolling gait* ○ *The huge waves rolled the ship from side to side.* Cf PITCH[2] 4. (**b**) [I, Ipr] sway or rock helplessly: *rolling with laughter* ○ *rolling drunk.* **7** [I, Ipr, Ip] (appear to) rise and fall; undulate: *rolling hills* ○ *waves rolling in to the beach.* **8** [I] make a long continuous vibrating sound: *The thunder rolled.* ○ *rolling drums.* **9** [I, Tn] (*infml*) (cause film cameras to) begin working: *Let them roll!*/*Roll 'em!* **10** [Tn] (*US infml*) rob (esp sb drunk or asleep). **11** (idm) **be ˈrolling (in money/it/cash)** (*sl*) have lots (of money): *What do you mean, he can't afford it? He's absolutely rolling (in money)!* **heads will roll** ⇨ HEAD[1]. **keep/start the ball rolling** ⇨ BALL[1]. **rolled into ˈone** combined in one person or thing: *He's an artist, a scientist and a shrewd businessman (all) rolled into one.* ˌ**rolling in the ˈaisles** much amused; helpless with laughter: *The comedian soon had them rolling in the aisles.* **roll one's ˈr's** pronounce the sound of the letter 'r' with vibration of the tongue against the palate. **roll ˈup! roll ˈup!** (used to invite passers-by to join an audience, etc). **roll up one's ˈsleeves** (*fig*) prepare to work or fight. **12** (phr v) **roll sth back** (**a**) turn or force back (eg enemy forces). (**b**) (*esp US*) reduce (prices, etc): *roll back inflation.* **roll in** (*infml*) (**a**) arrive in great numbers or quantities: *Offers of help are still rolling in.* (**b**) arrive casually: *She rolled in for work twenty minutes late.* **roll (sth) on** (**a**) apply, spread, etc (sth) by rolling: *This paint is easy to roll on/rolls on easily.* (**b**) (of time) pass steadily: *The years rolled on.* (**c**) (used in the imperative) come soon: *Roll on the holidays!* **roll up** (*infml*) (of a person or vehicle) arrive: *Bill finally rolled up two hours late.*

□ ˈ**roll-away** *n* (*US*) bed on small wheels that can be folded and stored away.

ˌ**rolled ˈgold** thin coating of gold applied to the surface of another metal.

ˌ**rolled ˈoats** oats that have had the husks removed and have been crushed.

ˈ**rolling-mill** *n* machine or factory in which metal is rolled into sheets, bars, etc.

ˈ**rolling-pin** *n* cylinder of wood, glass, etc used for rolling out dough, pastry, etc. ⇨ illus at KITCHEN.

ˈ**rolling-stock** *n* [U] **1** railway engines, carriages, wagons, etc collectively. **2** (*US*) vehicles used by a road-transport firm.

ˌ**rolling ˈstone** **1** person who does not settle down to live and work in one place. **2** (idm) **a ˌrolling ˌstone ˌgathers no ˈmoss** (*saying*) sb of this type is free of responsibilities, family ties, etc and has no wealth.

ˈ**roll-on** *n* **1** cosmetic applied by means of a ball that rotates in the neck of the container: [attrib] *roll-on deodorants.* **2** (*dated*) woman's elastic corset rolled on over the hips.

ˌ**roll-on roll-ˈoff** *adj* [usu attrib] (*abbr* **roro**) designed to allow vehicles to be driven onto and off it: *a roll-on roll-off ferry.*

ˈ**roll-up** *n* (*infml*) cigarette rolled by hand: *He always smokes roll-ups.*

roller /ˈrəʊlə(r)/ *n* [C] **1** (**a**) cylinder used for flattening or spreading things: *a garden roller*, ie for use on a lawn ○ *a ˈroad-roller*, ie for levelling tarmac on roads, etc. (**b**) cylinder on which sth is placed to enable it to be moved: *The huge machine was moved to its new position on rollers.* (**c**) cylinder on which sth is wound: *a ˈroller-blind*, ie a type of window blind wound on a roller. (**d**) small cylinder of plastic around which hair is wound to make it curl: *put her hair in rollers.* **2** long swelling wave: *rollers crashing on the beach.*

□ ˈ**roller bandage** long surgical bandage which is rolled up before being unrolled onto a limb, etc.

ˈ**roller-coaster** (*Brit* also **switchback**) *n* type of railway with open cars, tight turns and very steep slopes (found in funfairs, amusement parks, etc).

ˈ**roller derby** competition involving two teams of roller-skaters in a race in which team-members can help each other and create difficulties for the other team.

ˈ**roller-skate** (also **skate**) *n* type of shoe with small wheels fitted to the bottom, allowing the wearer to glide over hard surfaces: *a pair of roller-skates.* ⇨ illus at SKATE[1]. — *v* [I, Ipr, Ip] roll about smoothly wearing a pair of these: *She roller-skated across rather unsteadily.* ˈ**roller-skater** *n*. ˈ**roller-skating** *n* [U].

ˌ**roller ˈtowel** continuous loop of towel hung over a roller.

rollicking /ˈrɒlɪkɪŋ/ *adj* [attrib] (*dated*) noisy and jolly: *have a rollicking time.*

Rolling Stones /ˌrəʊlɪŋ ˈstəʊnz/ **the Rolling Stones** British pop group formed in the 1960s. Its original members were Mick Jagger (1943-), Keith Richard (1943-), Brian Jones (1942-69), Bill Wyman (1936-) and Charlie Watts (1941-). The group became famous for the provocative style of their music and appearance.

rollmop /ˈrəʊlmɒp/ *n* (also ˌ**rollmop** ˈ**herring**) herring fillet rolled up and pickled in vinegar.

Rolls-Royce /ˌrəʊlz ˈrɔɪs/ *n* (*propr*) car made by the British company founded by Charles Rolls (1877-1910) and Henry Royce (1863-1933). The cars are famous for their high standard of manufacture and their luxurious comfort. Their name is sometimes used to describe the best product of its type: *They're the Rolls-Royce of golf-clubs.*

roly-poly /ˌrəʊlɪˈpəʊlɪ/ *n* [C, U] **1** (also **roly-poly pudding**) (*Brit*) pudding made from suet pastry spread with jam, rolled up and boiled. **2** (*infml*) short and plump person: *She's a real roly-poly.*

ROM /rɒm/ *abbr* (*computing*) read only memory: *CD ROM discs.* Cf RAM 1.

romaine /rəʊˈmeɪn/ *n* (*US*) = cos¹.

Roman /ˈrəʊmən/ *adj* **1** (**a**) of ancient or modern *Rome. (**b**) of the ancient Roman republic or empire: *ˌRoman reˈmains* ○ *an old Roman road.* **2** of the Roman Catholic Church: *the Roman rite*, eg contrasted with Greek or Russian Orthodox. **3 roman** (of printing type) in ordinary upright form, like that used for this definition: *The words in the definition are roman/are set in roman type.* Cf ITALIC.

▷ **Roman** *n* **1** [C] member of the ancient Roman republic or empire: *after the Romans invaded Britain.* **2** [C] native or inhabitant of the city of *Rome. **3** [C] Roman Catholic. **4 roman** [U] plain upright type (not italic) like that used for the definitions in this dictionary: *The above definition is set in roman; this example is in italics.* **5 Romans** (also **the Eˌpistle to the ˈRomans**) [sing] (*abbr* **Rom**) book of the New Testament, a letter from St *Paul to the early Christians in Rome.

□ **the ˌRoman ˈalphabet** the letters A to Z, used esp in West European languages. Cf CYRILLIC.

ˌ**Roman** ˈ**candle** tubular firework that emits coloured sparks.

the ˌRoman ˌCatholic ˈChurch largest of the Christian Churches, governed by the Pope and the bishops and having an unmarried clergy. This structure developed from that of the early Church during the Middle Ages. It claims to be the authentic continuation of the work of Jesus and the apostles, using tradition and the authority given to it by Jesus to teach and interpret the Bible. The Protestant Churches separated from it at the *Reformation. During the 1960s the second Vatican Council gave the Church a more modern outlook and led to greater dialogue with other Christians. ˌ**Roman** ˈ**Catholic** (also **Catholic**) (member) of the Roman Catholic Church: *He's (a) Roman Catholic.* Cf PROTESTANT. ˌ**Roman Caˈtholicism**.

the ˌRoman ˈEmpire ancient Rome and its outlying provinces during the period when they were ruled by an emperor. Octavian, the adopted son of *Julius Caesar, was proclaimed Emperor *Augustus in 27 BC. The last emperor was deposed in 476 AD. At its greatest the Empire stretched from Armenia in the east to Spain in the west, and from the Danube in the north to N Africa in the south. In 395 AD it was divided into the Eastern and Western empires. The Eastern Empire became the Byzantine Empire, which lasted until 1453. In the west, *Charlemagne set up the new *Holy Roman Empire in 800 AD.

ˌ**Roman** ˈ**nose** nose with a high bridge¹(4a). ⇨ illus at NOSE.

ˌ**Roman** ˈ**numerals** (system of) letters representing numbers. ⇨ App 9. Cf ARABIC NUMERALS (ARABIC).

roman à clef /ˌrəʊmɒn ɑː ˈkleɪ/ (*French*) novel in which some characters are based on real people whose identity can be discovered by the readers.

Romance /rəʊˈmæns/ *adj* [attrib] of those languages (the Romance languages) which are descended from Latin, eg French, Italian, Spanish. Cf LATIN 2.

romance /rəʊˈmæns/ *n* **1** [C, U] imaginative story; literature of this kind: *(a) medieval romance.* **2** [U] romantic atmosphere or feeling: *There was an air of romance about the old castle.* **3** [C] love story; love affair resembling this: *She writes romances about rich men and beautiful women.* ○ *a holiday romance.* **4** [C, U] (instance of) colourful exaggeration or make-believe: *The story he told was complete romance.*

▷ **romance** *v* [I] exaggerate or distort the truth in an imaginative way; romanticize: *given to colourful romancing.*

Romanesque /ˌrəʊməˈnesk/ *adj, n* [U] (of the) style of architecture current in Europe from about 1050 to 1200, with round arches, thick walls, huge vaulting, etc. ⇨ article at ARCHITECTURE.

Romania

Romania (also **Rumania**) /ruːˈmeɪnɪə/ country in SE Europe; pop approx 23 048 000; official language Romanian; capital Bucharest; unit of currency leu (= 100 bani). It has a coastline on the Black Sea, with the delta of the *Danube in the south. Although Romania is fertile and has considerable natural resources, including coal, oil and natural gas, the policies of the Communist regime from 1965-89 left agriculture, industry and society in a state of disarray from which the country is struggling to recover. ⇨ map.

▷ **Romanian** (also **Rumanian**) /-ɪən/ *n* **1** [C] native or inhabitant of Romania. **2** [U] the Romance language spoken in Romania. — *adj.*

Romano- *comb form* Roman; of Rome: *Romano-British settlements.*

Romanov /ˈrəʊmənɒf/ name of the dynasty that ruled Russia from 1613, when Michael Romanov became tsar, until 1917.

romantic /rəʊˈmæntɪk/ *adj* **1** appealing to the emotions by its imaginative, heroic or picturesque quality: *romantic scenes, adventures, tales* ○ *The Lake District is a very romantic area.* **2** [esp attrib] involving a love affair: *a romantic involvement* ○ *romantic complications.* **3** (of people, their characters, etc) enjoying emotional situations: *She has a dreamy romantic nature.* **4** (also **Romantic**) [esp attrib] (of music, literature, etc) marked by the characteristics of Romanticism: *the English Romantic poets*, eg Wordsworth and Keats ○ *a masterpiece of the Romantic school/movement.*

▷ **romantic** *n* **1** person who enjoys romantic situations. **2** (also **Romantic**) romantic artist.

romantically /-klɪ/ *adv.*

romanticism /rəʊˈmæntɪsɪzəm/ *n* [U] **1** romantic feelings, attitudes or behaviour. **2** (also **Romanticism**) movement or tendency in Western literature, art and music marked by a preference for feeling and free expression over intellect and strict forms. It began in the late 18th century and was to some extent inspired by the revolutions in France and America. Its ideals included imagination, liberty, and the love of nature; many romantic artists lived lives which were as emotionally adventurous as their works. In Britain, the movement's greatest achievements were in poetry, esp that of *Wordsworth, *Keats, *Shelley, *Byron and *Blake. In Continental European literature, Jean-Jacques *Rousseau, *Schiller and Victor *Hugo are among its greatest figures. *Beethoven is considered by many as the first great Romantic composer, followed by *Schubert and *Schumann, *Berlioz, *Liszt and *Wagner. The movement is represented by many different styles in art, as in the work of *Delacroix, Goya, and *Turner, showing the vast scope of Romanticism and the many ways in which it could express itself. Cf CLASSICISM, IDEALISM 2, REALISM 2.

romanticist /-tɪsɪst/ *n.*

romanticize, -ise /-tɪsaɪz/ *v* [I, Tn] (*esp derog*) exaggerate or distort (the truth) in an imaginative, falsely heroic, etc way: *Don't romanticize — stick to the facts.* ○ *a novel that refuses to romanticize the grim realities of war.*

Romany /ˈrɒmənɪ/ *n* **1** [C] gipsy. **2** [U] language of the gipsies.

▷ **Romany** *adj* [usu attrib] of gipsies or their language.

Romberg /ˈrɒmbɜːg/ Sigmund (1887-1951), American composer, born in Hungary. He wrote many successful operettas, including *The Student Prince* and *The Desert Song.*

Rome /rəʊm/ **1** capital city of Italy. It is the administrative centre of the country and also contains the *Vatican City, the headquarters of the Roman Catholic Church and an independent state. Its economy is based partly on light industry (including the cinema, with the studios of Cinecittà), but mainly on the service sector. Tourism is particularly important, and millions of visitors come each year to see the historical heritage of ancient and Renaissance Rome, including monuments like the *Colosseum, the Forum and St Peter's Basilica. **2** (idm) ˌ**Rome was not built in a ˈday** (*saying*) time and hard work are necessary for a difficult or important task. **when in ˌRome, do as the ˈRomans do** (*saying*) one should change one's behaviour to suit the customs of the place one is living in or of the people one is living with. Cf ROMAN.

Romeo /ˈrəʊmɪəʊ/ *n* man who is or pretends to be in love with a woman (from the hero of Shakespeare's tragedy *Romeo and Juliet*): (*derog*) *the office Romeo*, ie who tries to attract all the female members of staff.

Rommel /ˈrɒməl/ Erwin (1891-1944), German general. His brilliant campaign during the Second World War in N Africa earned him the nickname 'the Desert Fox'. He was eventually defeated by *Montgomery and *Eisenhower, and later ordered to commit suicide for plotting against *Hitler.

Romney /ˈrɒmnɪ/ George (1734-1802), English painter. He was one of the most fashionable portrait painters of the late 18th century, famous for his use of bright colours. ⇨ illus.

romp /rɒmp/ *v* **1** [I, Ipr, Ip] (esp of children or animals) play about together in a lively way, running, jumping, etc: *puppies romping around in the garden.* **2** (idm) **romp home/in** win, succeed etc easily: *romp home in a race* ○ *The Liberal candidate romped in with thousands of votes to spare.* **3** (phr v) **romp through (sth)** (*infml*) succeed easily (in a test, etc): *She romped through her exams.*

▷ **romp** *n* [sing] instance of romping: *have a romp about.*

rompers /ˈrɒmpəz/ *n* [pl] (also ˈ**romper-suit** [C]) one-piece suit worn by a small child or baby.

rondo /ˈrɒndəʊ/ *n* (*pl* ~**s**) piece of music in which the main theme returns a number of times.

Roneo /ˈrəʊnɪəʊ/ (*propr*) (*pl* ~**s**) *n* machine that makes copies of typewritten pages using stencils.

▷ **roneo** *v* (*pp, pt* ~**ed**) copy (eg a page) using a Roneo machine.

Röntgen /ˈrɒntjən; *US* ˈrentgən/ Wilhelm Conrad von (1845-1923), German physicist. Although most of his work was in other fields, he won fame for the

George Romney: Lady Hamilton as Cassandra

discovery of X-rays and was awarded the Nobel prize for physics in 1901.

röntgen = ROENTGEN.

rood /ru:d/ *n* crucifix, esp one erected on the middle of a rood-screen.

□ ˈ**rood-screen** *n* carved wooden or stone screen separating the nave and choir(2) of a church.

roof /ru:f/ *n* (*pl* ~s) **1** structure covering or forming the top of a building, vehicle, etc: *a flat/sloping roof* ○ *fly above the roofs of the city* ○ *Although divorced, they continued to live under the same roof*, ie in the same house. ○ *a library and concert-hall both under one roof*, ie in the same building ○ *have a/no roof over one's head*, ie have a/no place to live ○ *The roof of the mine passage collapsed.* ○ *a painful sore in the roof of her mouth*, ie the palate ○ (*rhet*) *the roof of the world*, ie the highest part, esp a mountain (range) or plateau. ⇨ illus at HOME, ⇨ illus at CAR. **2** (idm) **go through the roof** (*infml*) become very angry: *She went through the roof when I told her I'd crashed her car.* **hit the ceiling/roof** ⇨ HIT[1]. **raise the roof** ⇨ RAISE.

▷ **roof** *v* (*pt, pp* ~**ed** /ru:ft/) [Tn, Tn·pr, Tn·p] ~ **sth (over/in)**; ~ **sth (with sth)** cover sth with a roof; be a roof for sth: *roof (over) a yard (with sheets of plastic)* ○ *a plan to roof in the stadium* ○ *a hut crudely roofed with strips of bark.*

roofing *n* [U] material used for roofs: [attrib] ˈ*roofing material, tiles, slates, felt, etc.*

□ ˈ**roof-garden** *n* garden on the flat roof of a building.

ˈ**roof-rack** (also ˈ**luggage-rack**) *n* frame for carrying luggage, etc attached to the roof of a vehicle. ⇨ illus at CAR.

ˈ**roof-top** *n* (**a**) outer surface of a roof. (**b**) (*esp rhet*) top of a building: *flying swiftly over the roof-tops.*

ˈ**roof-tree** *n* strong horizontal main beam at the highest point of a roof.

rook[1] /rʊk/ *n* large black crow that nests in colonies.

▷ **rookery** /-ərɪ/ *n* **1** (**a**) colony of rooks. (**b**) group of trees where rooks nest. **2** colony or breeding-place of penguins or seals.

rook[2] /rʊk/ *v* [Tn, Tn·pr] ~ **sb (of sth)** (*infml*) (**a**) overcharge sb: *That hotel really rooked us.* (**b**) cheat or swindle sb at cards, etc: *They rooked him of £100.*

rook[3] /rʊk/ *n* = CASTLE 2.

rookie /ˈrʊkɪ/ *n* (*infml*) inexperienced newcomer to a team, an organization, etc: [attrib] *a rookie half-back.*

room /ru:m, rʊm/ *n* **1** (**a**) [C] part of a building enclosed by walls or partitions, and with a floor and ceiling: *a large airy room on the first floor* ○ *He's in the next room.* (**b**) **rooms** [pl] set of these for living in, usu rented; lodgings: *He's staying in rooms in West Kensington.* **2** [U] ~ **(for sb/sth)**; ~ **(to do sth)** space that is or could be occupied, or is enough for a purpose: *Is there enough room for me in the car?* ○ *This table takes up too much room.* ○ *Can you make room on that shelf for more books?* ○ *There's no room to work here.* ○ *standing room only*, ie no room to sit down, eg in a bus, theatre, etc. ⇨ Usage at SPACE. **3** [U] ~ **(for sth)** opportunity; scope: *There's (plenty of) room for improvement in your work*, ie It is not as good as it could be. ○ *There's no room for doubt*, ie It is quite certain. **4** (idm) **cramped for room/space** ⇨ CRAMP[2]. **leave the room** ⇨ LEAVE[1]. **no room to swing a** ˈ**cat** (*infml saying*) not enough space to live, work, etc in: *There's no room/There isn't (enough) room to swing a cat in here.*

▷ **room** *v* [Ipr] (*US*) occupy a room or rooms in sb else's house; lodge[2](2): *He's rooming with my friend Alan.*

-roomed (forming compound *adjs*) having the stated number of rooms: *a ten-roomed house.*

roomer *n* (*US*) person who rooms; lodger.

roomful /-fʊl/ *n* amount or number a room will hold: *a whole roomful of antiques.*

roomy *adj* (**-ier, -iest**) (*approv*) having plenty of space to contain things or people: *a surprisingly roomy car.* **roominess** *n* [U].

□ ˌ**room and** ˈ**board** accommodation and meals, esp at lodgings.

ˈ**rooming-house** *n* (*US*) building where furnished rooms can be rented.

ˈ**room-mate** *n* person living in the same room or set of rooms as another, eg in a college or lodgings.

ˈ**room service** (those who provide) service of food, etc to a guest in his hotel room: *Call room service and ask for some coffee.*

ˈ**room temperature** temperature inside a comfortably heated room, usu considered to be about 20° C.

Roosevelt[1] /ˈrəʊzəvelt/ Franklin Delano (1882-1945), 32nd president of the USA 1933-45. He was elected four times in succession and is best remembered for the New Deal, a number of government measures designed to counter the effects of the Depression(3b). ⇨ App 2. ⇨ article at POLITICS.

Roosevelt[2] /ˈrəʊzəvelt/ Theodore (1858-1919), 26th president of the USA 1901-08. He is remembered for having the *Panama Canal built under American control and was awarded the Nobel prize for peace after helping to end the war between Russia and Japan. ⇨ App 2.

roost /ru:st/ *n* **1** place where birds perch or settle for sleep: *One of the main starling roosts is on top of the Town Hall.* **2** (idm) **come home to roost** ⇨ HOME[3]. **rule the roost** ⇨ RULE *v.*

▷ **roost** *v* [I, Ipr] (of birds) settle for sleep; perch.

rooster /ˈru:stə(r)/ *n* (*esp US*) = COCK[1] 1.

root[1] /ru:t/ *n* **1** [C] part of a plant that keeps it firmly in the soil and absorbs water and food from the soil: *a plant with very long roots* ○ *pull a plant up by the roots.* **2 roots** [pl] family ties, feelings, etc that attach a person emotionally and culturally to the society or community where he grew up and/or lives or where his ancestors lived: *Many Americans have roots in Europe.* ○ *She has no real roots in this area.* **3** [C] part of a hair, tooth, nail or tongue that attaches it to the rest of the body: *pull hair out by* (ie complete with) *the roots.* **4** [C esp sing] (*fig*) source or basis: *The root of the problem is lack of trust.* ○ *Money is often said to be the root of all evil.* **5** [C] (also **base form**) (*grammar*) form of a word on which its other forms are said to be based: *'Walk' is the root of 'walks', 'walked', 'walking' and 'walker'.* **6** [C] (*mathematics*) quantity which, when multiplied by itself a certain number of times, produces another quantity: *4 is the square root of 16 (4×4=16), the cube root of 64 (4×4×4=64) and the fourth root of 256 (4×4×4×4=256).* ⇨ App 9. **7** (idm) **get at/get to/strike at the** ˈ**root(s) of sth** discover the source of sth (usu problematic or unpleasant) and tackle it there. **pull up one's roots** ⇨ PULL[2]. **put down (new)** ˈ**roots** establish oneself in a place to which one has moved. ˌ**root and** ˈ**branch** thorough(ly); complete(ly): [attrib] *root-and-branch reforms* ○ *destroy an organization root and branch.* **the root cause (of sth)** the fundamental cause: *He argues that one of the root causes of crime is poverty.* **take/strike root** (**a**) (of a plant) send down a root or roots. (**b**) (*fig*) become established: *a country where democracy has never really taken root.*

▷ **rootless** *adj* having no root or roots: *a rootless wandering life.* **rootlessness** *n* [U].

□ ˈ**root beer** (*esp US*) non-alcoholic drink flavoured with the roots of various plants.

ˈ**root-crop** *n* crop grown for its edible roots, eg turnips, carrots, etc.

ˈ**root vegetable** edible root eaten as a vegetable, eg a turnip, carrot, etc.

ˈ**root stock** plant onto which another is grafted.

root[2] /ru:t/ *v* **1** (**a**) [I, Ipr] (of a plant) send down roots and begin to grow: *This type of plant roots easily.* (**b**) [Tn, Tn·pr] plant (sth): *Root the cuttings in peat.* **2** [Tn·pr esp passive] cause (sb) to stand fixed and unmoving: *be/stand rooted to the spot/ground* ○ *Fear rooted him to the spot.* **3** [usu passive: Tn, Tn·pr] establish (sth) deeply and firmly: *a story firmly rooted in reality* ○ *Her affection for him is deeply rooted.* ○ *He has a rooted objection to cold baths.* **4** (phr v) **root sth out** destroy sth completely: *determined to root out corruption.* **root sth up** dig or pull up (a plant, etc) with the roots.

root[3] /ru:t/ *v* (phr v) **root about/around (for sth)** (**a**) (of pigs) turn up the ground with the snout in search of food: *rooting for acorns.* (**b**) (of people) turn things over when searching, esp in an untidy way: *What are you doing rooting around in my desk?* **root for sb/sth** (no passive) (*infml*) cheer for sb/sth; support sb/sth wholeheartedly: *We're rooting for the college baseball team.* ○ *We're all rooting for you — good luck with your job interview!* **root sth out** (*infml*) find sth after hard searching: *I managed to root out a copy of the document.*

rope /rəʊp/ *n* **1** [C, U] (length of) thick cord or wire made by twisting finer cords or wires together: *We tied his feet together with (a) rope.* ○ *The kids tied a (piece of) rope to the tree and used it as a swing.* **2** [C] number of similar things twisted or strung together: *a rope of onions, pearls, etc.* **3 the rope** [sing] (*infml or rhet*) death by hanging: *bring back the rope*, ie the death penalty. **4** (idm) **give sb enough** ˈ**rope (and he'll hang himself)** (*saying*) allow sb enough freedom of action (and he will bring about his own downfall). **give sb plenty of/some** ˈ**rope** allow sb much/some freedom of action. **money for jam/old rope** ⇨ MONEY. **on the** ˈ**ropes** (*infml*) (almost) defeated. **show sb/know/learn the** ˈ**ropes** explain to sb/know/learn the procedures or rules for doing sth: *She's just started — it'll take her a week or two to learn the ropes.*

▷ **rope** *v* **1** [Tn, Tn·pr, Tn·p] fasten or bind (sb/sth) with (a) rope: *rope* (ie lasso and tie up) *cattle* ○ *They roped him to a tree.* ○ *climbers roped together.* **2** (phr v) **rope sb in (to do sth)** (*infml*) (esp passive) persuade sb (to take part in an activity): *All her friends have been roped in to help organize the event.* **rope sth off** enclose sth with rope(s): *rope off the scene of the accident.*

□ ˈ**rope-ladder** *n* ladder made of two long ropes connected by short cross-pieces.

ropy (also **ropey**) /ˈrəʊpɪ/ *adj* (**-ier, -iest**) (*Brit infml*) poor in quality, health, etc: *ropy old furniture* ○ *I'm feeling pretty ropey.* ▷ **ropiness** *n* [U].

Roquefort /ˈrɒkfɔ:(r); *US* ˈrəʊkfərt/ *n* [U] type of blue cheese made from ewes' milk.

roro /ˈrəʊrəʊ/ *abbr* roll-on roll-off.

rorqual /ˈrɔ:kwəl/ *n* any of various types of whale that have a fin on their back and grooves along their throat.

Rorschach test /ˈrɔ:ʃɑ:k test/ psychological test

in which a person's personality is assessed from his reactions to the shape of a blot of ink.

rosaceous /rəʊˈzeɪʃəs/ *adj* of or like the family of plants which includes the rose.

rosary /ˈrəʊzərɪ/ *n* **1 the rosary** [sing] (book containing a) set series of prayers used in the Roman Catholic Church: *say the rosary.* **2** [C] **(a)** string of beads for keeping count of these prayers. **(b)** similar string of beads used in other religions.

rose[1] *pt* of RISE[2].

rose[2] /rəʊz/ *n* **1** [C] (bush or shrub, usu with thorns on its stems, bearing an) ornamental and usu sweet-smelling flower, growing in cultivated and wild varieties: *I found him pruning his roses.* ○ *a bunch of red roses* ○ [attrib] *a* ˈ*rose bush.* ⇨ illus at FLOWER. ⇨ article at NATIONAL. **2** [C] pink colour: *The rose (colour) of clouds at dawn.* **3** [C] perforated nozzle of a watering-can or hose-pipe, used for sprinkling plants, etc. **4** [C] (also ˈ**ceiling rose**) (esp plaster) decoration on a ceiling around the point where the main light is fitted. **5** (idm) **a bed of roses** ⇨ BED[1]. **not all** ˈ**roses** having some discomforts or disadvantages; not perfect: *Being an opera star is not all roses by any means.* **look at/see sth through rose-coloured/rose-tinted** ˈ**spectacles, etc** think of/regard sth (esp life in general) too optimistically.

□ ˈ**rosebay** *n* (*US*) = RHODODENDRON. ˌ**rosebay** ˈ**willow-herb** wild plant of northern regions with deep pink flowers.

ˈ**rose-bud** *n* bud of a rose: [attrib] *a rose-bud mouth,* ie one having this shape.

ˈ**rose-hip** *n* = HIP[2].

ˈ**rose-water** *n* [U] perfume made from roses.

ˌ**rose-**ˈ**window** *n* ornamental circular window, usu in a church.

ˈ**rosewood** *n* [U] type of high-quality hardwood used for making furniture: [attrib] *a rosewood table.*

rosé /ˈrəʊzeɪ; *US* rəʊˈzeɪ/ *n* [U] any of several types of pink wine: *an excellent (bottle of) rosé.* Cf RED WINE (RED[1]), WHITE WINE (WHITE[1]).

roseate /ˈrəʊzɪət/ *adj* [usu attrib] (*rhet*) deep pink: *the roseate hues of dawn.*

rosemary /ˈrəʊzmərɪ; *US* -merɪ/ *n* [U] **(a)** fragrant leaves of a type of evergreen shrub, used for flavouring food. **(b)** this shrub.

Rosetta stone /rəʊˌzetə ˈstəʊn/ **the Rosetta stone** stone found in Egypt in 1799 with an inscription carved in Greek and two forms of ancient Egyptian writing: hieroglyphs and demotic (a simplified sort of hieroglyphs). The French scholar Jean-François Champollion was able to decipher hieroglyphs using the stone, which is now in the *British Museum.

rosette /rəʊˈzet/ *n* **1** rose-shaped badge, usu of silk or ribbon: *The fans are all wearing Arsenal rosettes,* ie showing their support for Arsenal football team. ○ *the Tory candidate with his big blue rosette.* **2** rose-shaped carving on stonework, etc.

Rosh Hashana /ˌrɒʃ hæˈʃɑːnə/ the Jewish New Year, which usu occurs in late September or early October.

Rosicrucian /ˌrəʊzɪˈkruːʃn/ *n, adj* (esp in former times) (member) of any of various real or imaginary secret societies which claimed mystical or alchemical knowledge.

rosin /ˈrɒzɪn; *US* ˈrɒzn/ *n* [U] type of resin(1) used on the strings and bows of stringed musical instruments.

▷ **rosin** *v* [Tn] rub (sth) with rosin.

Rossellini /ˌrɒseˈliːnɪ/ Roberto (1906-77), Italian film director. His realistic documentary techniques in films like *Rome, Open City* were very influential in post-war cinema. He directed his wife, Ingrid *Bergman, in several films, notably *Stromboli.*

Rossetti[1] /rəˈzetɪ/ Christina (1830-94), English poet, sister of Dante Gabriel Rossetti. Her poetry shows her religious faith and a romantic melancholy. She also wrote poems for children.

Dante Gabriel Rossetti: The Daydream

Rossetti[2] /rəˈzetɪ/ Dante Gabriel (1828-82), English poet and painter. He was a founder member of the *Pre-Raphaelite Brotherhood and both his paintings and his poetry were influenced by medieval English and Italian legends. ⇨ illus.

Rossini /rɒˈsiːnɪ/ Gioachino (1792-1868), Italian composer. Although he wrote a number of successful serious operas, he is more famous for comic operas like *The Barber of Seville.* Many of his operas are best known for their overtures (eg *William Tell* and *The Thieving Magpie*).

roster /ˈrɒstə(r)/ *n* (*esp US*) (esp in the army, etc) list of names showing duties to be performed and the times at which those named are to perform them.

▷ **roster** *v* [Tn] (*esp US*) place (sb) on a roster: *proposals for more flexible rostering* ○ *I've been rostered to work all weekend!*

rostrum /ˈrɒstrəm/ *n* (*pl* ~**s** or **-tra** /-trə/) raised platform from which public speeches are made: *mount the rostrum.*

rosy /ˈrəʊzɪ/ *adj* (**-ier, -iest**) **1** of the colour of red roses; deep pink: *rosy cheeks,* ie indicating good health. **2** (*fig*) very encouraging; very hopeful: *The prospects couldn't be rosier.* ○ *She painted a rosy picture of the firm's future.* ▷ **rosiness** *n* [U].

rot /rɒt/ *v* (**-tt-**) **(a)** [I, Ip] decay naturally through the action of bacteria, fungi, etc: *a heap of rotting leaves* ○ *The wood has rotted away completely.* ○ (*fig*) *He was thrown into prison and left to rot.* **(b)** [Tn, Tn·p] cause (sth) to decay or become useless; damage: *Oil and grease will rot the rubber of your tyres.* ○ *Too much sugar will rot your teeth away.*

▷ **rot** *n* **1** [U] rotting; rottenness: *a tree affected by rot* ○ *Rot has set in,* ie started. ○ *There's dry rot in the floor.* **2** [U] (*dated Brit sl*) nonsense; absurd statement(s) or argument(s): *Don't talk such utter rot!* ○ *'They're bound to win.' 'Rot! They haven't a chance!'* **3 the rot** [sing] liver disease of sheep. **4** (idm) **the rot sets** ˈ**in** conditions begin to get worse: *The rot set in when we lost that important customer in Japan.* **stop the rot** ⇨ STOP.

□ ˈ**rot-gut** *n* [U] (*sl*) cheap and unpleasant alcoholic drink, esp inferior spirits that can harm the stomach.

rota /ˈrəʊtə/ *n* (*pl* ~**s**) (*Brit*) (*US* **roster**) list showing duties to be done or names of people to do them in turn.

Rotary /ˈrəʊtərɪ/ (in full ˌ**Rotary Inter**ˈ**national**) international organization of businessmen who meet for social purposes at **Rotary Clubs** and raise money for charity.

▷ **Rotarian** /rəʊˈteərɪən/ *n, adj* (member) of a Rotary Club.

rotary /ˈrəʊtərɪ/ *adj* [esp attrib] **1** (*fml*) (of motion) moving round a central point; circular. **2** (of a machine, an engine, etc) using this type of motion: *a rotary drill, clothes drier, switch, etc* ○ *a rotary printing machine/press,* ie one which prints from metal plates attached to revolving cylinders. Cf RECIPROCATE 2.

▷ **rotary** *n* (*US*) = ROUNDABOUT 2.

rotate /rəʊˈteɪt; *US* ˈrəʊteɪt/ *v* [I, Ipr, Tn, Tn·pr] **1** (cause sth to) move in circles round a central point: *Danger: rotating blades.* ○ *rotate the handle gently.* **2** (cause sb/sth to) take turns or recur in a particular order: *The post of chairman rotates among members of the committee.* ○ *the technique of rotating crops.*

▷ **rotation** /rəʊˈteɪʃn/ *n* **1 (a)** [U] rotating or being rotated: *the rotation of the Earth.* **(b)** [C] one complete movement or this type: *five rotations per hour.* **2** [C, U] regular organized sequence of things or events: *the rotation of crops/crop rotation,* ie varying the crops grown each year on the same land to avoid exhausting the soil. **3** (idm) **in rotation** in turn; in regular succession: *The chairmanship of the committee changes in rotation.* **rotational** /-ʃənl/ *adj.*

rotatory /ˈrəʊtətərɪ, rəʊˈteɪtərɪ; *US* ˈrəʊtətɔːrɪ/ *adj* (*fml*) rotating; of rotation: *rotatory motion.*

ROTC /ˌɑːr əʊ tiː ˈsiː/ *abbr* (*US*) Reserve Officers' Training Corps.

rote /rəʊt/ *n* (idm) **by** ˈ**rote** by heart; from memory, without thinking of the meaning: *do, say, know, learn, etc sth by rote.*

□ ˈ**rote learning** method of study based on learning facts, etc by heart without considering their meaning.

Roth /rɒθ/ Philip (1933-), American novelist. He often draws on his Jewish background, esp in his best-known novel, *Portnoy's Complaint,* which is a satire on American social and sexual habits.

Rothko /ˈrɒθkəʊ/ Mark (1903-70), American painter. His mature style of 'colour field painting' produced large canvases made up of areas of bright colours, or black and grey and other dark colours in his later work.

Rothschild /ˈrɒθstʃaɪld/ name of a family of Jewish bankers, whose financial operations are now found all over the world.

rotisserie /rəʊˈtiːsərɪ/ *n* cooking device for roasting meat, etc on a revolving spit[2](1).

rotor /ˈrəʊtə(r)/ *n* rotating part of a machine, esp on a helicopter. ⇨ illus at HELICOPTER.

rotten /ˈrɒtn/ *adj* **1** decayed; having gone bad: *rotten eggs* ○ *The wood was so rotten you could put your finger through it.* **2** morally corrupt: *an organization, a person, a policy that is rotten to the core,* ie completely rotten. **3** (*infml*) very bad; very unpleasant: *The film was pretty rotten.* ○ *She's a rotten cook.* ○ *What rotten luck!* ○ *rotten weather.*

▷ **rottenly** *adv* (*infml*) very badly: *Her husband treated her rottenly all their married life.*

rottenness *n* [U].

□ ˌ**rotten** ˈ**borough** (in Britain in former times) borough that was allowed to elect a Member of Parliament even though it had very few electors living in it, and was therefore particularly susceptible to bribery. Rotten boroughs were abolished by the *Reform Act of 1832.

rotter /ˈrɒtə(r)/ *n* (*sl joc*) nasty or worthless person: *He's a complete rotter!*

Rottweiler /ˈrɒtvaɪlə(r)/ *n* breed of large guard dog with a black and brown coat, sometimes used for police work and noted for its occasionally aggressive behaviour.

rotund /rəʊˈtʌnd/ *adj* (*euph or joc*) (of a person) rounded; plump; fat.

▷ **rotundity** /-ətɪ/ *n* [U] (*euph or joc*) state of being

rotund.
rotundly *adv.*

rotunda /rəʊˈtʌndə/ *n* type of round building or hall, esp one with a domed roof.

rouble (also **ruble**) /ˈru:bl/ *n* unit of money in the USSR; 100 kopecks.

roué /ˈru:eɪ/ *n* (*dated derog*) dissolute or lecherous man, esp an elderly one.

rouge /ru:ʒ/ *n* [U] **1** reddish cosmetic for colouring the cheeks. **2** fine red powder used for polishing metal: *jewellers' rouge.*
▷ **rouge** *v* [Tn] colour (the cheeks) with rouge.

rough[1] /rʌf/ *adj* (**-er, -est**) **1** having an uneven or irregular surface; not level or smooth: *A jeep is ideal for driving over rough terrain.* ○ *a rough stone wall* ○ *rough hands* ○ *rough woollen cloth.* Cf SMOOTH[1]. **2** not gentle or calm; moving or acting violently: *rough behaviour* ○ *His children are very rough with their toys.* ○ *Rugby is a rough sport.* ○ *That area of the city is quite rough* (ie dangerous) *after dark.* ○ *This suitcase has had some rough handling,* ie has been badly treated. ○ *He has a rough tongue,* ie often speaks rudely or sharply. ○ *rough seas* ○ *have a rough crossing from Dover to Calais.* **3** made or done without (much) attention to detail, esp in haste or as a first attempt; approximate: *a rough sketch, calculation, translation* ○ *a rough draft of his speech* ○ *Give me a rough idea of your plans.* ○ *I'll give you a rough estimate of the costs.* ○ *rough justice,* ie more or less fair, but not necessarily strictly according to law. **4** harsh (in taste, sound, etc): *a rough red wine* ○ *Your engine sounds a bit rough — you'd better have it checked.* ○ *a rough voice.* **5** (*infml*) unwell: *I feel a bit rough — I'm going to bed.* **6** (idm) **be rough (on sb)** (*infml*) be unpleasant or unlucky (for sb): *Losing his job was rough (on him).* **give sb/have a rough ˈtime** (cause sb to) experience hardship, be treated severely, etc: *She had a really rough time when her father died.* **a raw/rough deal** ⇨ DEAL[4]. **ˌrough and ˈready** adequate but unrefined; crude but effective: *The accommodation is rather rough and ready, I'm afraid.* ○ [attrib] *rough and ready methods.* **a rough ˈdiamond** person who is good-natured but lacking polished manners, education, etc.
▷ **roughly** *adv* **1** in a rough manner: *treat sb roughly* ○ *a roughly made table,* ie not finely finished. **2** approximately: *It should cost roughly £10.* ○ *about forty miles, roughly speaking.*
roughness *n* [U] quality or state of being rough: *the roughness of his chin.*
□ **ˌrough-and-ˈtumble** *n, adj* (fight, struggle, etc that is) boisterous and disorganized, but usu not serious: *All the puppies were having a rough-and-tumble in the garden.*
ˈrough house (*infml*) disturbance with violent and noisy behaviour.
ˌrough ˈluck bad luck, worse than is deserved.
ˈroughneck *n* (*US infml*) **1** rowdy person; hooligan. **2** worker on an oil rig.

rough[2] /rʌf/ *adv* **1** in a rough manner: *a team that is notorious for playing rough,* ie in a (physically) somewhat violent way. **2** (idm) **cut up ˈrough** (*infml*) become angry or violent: *I hope he doesn't cut up rough when I tell him what I've done.* **live rough** ⇨ LIVE[2]. **sleep rough** ⇨ SLEEP[2].
□ **ˈroughcast** *n* [U] coarse plaster containing gravel, used for covering the outside walls of buildings.
ˈrough-hewn *adj* (*fml or rhet*) shaped or carved roughly: *a rough-hewn statue.*
ˈroughshod *adv* (idm) **ride roughshod over sb/sth** ⇨ RIDE[2].

rough[3] /rʌf/ *n* **1** (also **the rough**) [U] part of a golf-course where the ground is uneven and the grass uncut. ⇨ illus at GOLF. Cf FAIRWAY 1. **2** [C] rough drawing or design, etc: *Have you seen the (artwork) roughs for the new book?* **3** [C] (*infml*) violent lawless person; (usu male) hooligan: *beaten up by a gang of young roughs.* **4** (idm) **in ˈrough** without great accuracy; approximately: *I've drawn it in rough, to give you some idea of how it looks.* **in (the) ˈrough** in an unfinished state: *We only saw the new painting in the rough.* **take the ˌrough with the ˈsmooth** accept what is unpleasant or difficult as well as what is pleasant or easy.

rough[4] /rʌf/ *v* **1** (idm) **ˈrough it** (*infml*) live without the usual comforts and conveniences of life: *roughing it in the mountains* ○ *You may have to rough it a bit if you come to stay.* **2** (phr v) **rough sth out** shape, plan or sketch sth roughly: *He roughed out some ideas for the new buildings.* **rough sb up** (*infml*) treat sb roughly, with physical violence. **rough sth up** make sth untidy or uneven: *Don't rough up my hair!*

roughage /ˈrʌfɪdʒ/ *n* [U] indigestible material in certain plants used as food (eg bran) that stimulates the action of the intestines, and helps the digestion of other foods.

roughen /ˈrʌfn/ *v* [I, Tn] (cause sth to) become rough: *Roughen the surface before applying the paint.*

roulette /ru:ˈlet/ *n* [U] gambling game in which a small ball falls at random into one of the numbered compartments on a revolving wheel: *play roulette* ○ [attrib] *a roulette wheel.*

round[1] /raʊnd/ *adj* **1** shaped like a circle or a ball: *a round plate, window, table* ○ *round cheeks,* ie plump and curved. **2** full; complete: *a round dozen,* ie not less than twelve ○ *a round* (ie considerable) *sum of money.* **3** (idm) **in round ˈfigures/ˈnumbers** (given) in 10's, 100's, 1 000's etc, without using the other digits: *Add £2.74 to £7.23 and you get £10.00, in round figures.* **a square peg in a round hole** ⇨ SQUARE[1].
▷ **roundish** *adj* approximately round.
roundly *adv* thoroughly; pointedly: *She was roundly rebuked for what she had done.* ○ *We told her roundly that she was unwelcome.*
roundness *n* [U].
□ **round brackets** parentheses.
ˌround-ˈeyed *adj* with the eyes wide open in wonder, etc.
ˈRoundhead *n* supporter of Parliament in the English Civil War. Cf CAVALIER.
ˌround ˈrobin 1 statement, petition, etc signed by a number of people, often with signatures arranged in a circle to conceal who signed first. **2** letter sent in turn to members of a group, each of whom adds sth before sending it on to the next.
ˌround-ˈshouldered *adj* (*derog*) (walking, standing, etc) with the shoulders bent forward. Cf SQUARE-SHOULDERED (SQUARE[1]).
ˌround-ˈtable *adj* [attrib] (of a meeting, etc) in which the participants meet more or less as equals: *a ˌround-table disˈcussion, ˈconference, etc.*
ˌround ˈtrip (a) journey to one or more places and back again, often by a different route. **(b)** (*US*) = RETURN[2] 5: [attrib] *a ˌround-trip ˈticket.*

round[2] /raʊnd/ *adv part* (For special uses with many *vs,* eg *bring round, get round,* see the *v* entries.) **1** so as to be facing in a different (usu the opposite) direction: *turn the car round* ○ *Stop turning (your heads) round to look at people.* **2** making the completion of a full cycle: *How long does it take the minute hand of the clock to go round once?* ○ *Spring will soon come round again.* **3** measuring or marking the circumference of sth: *a young tree measuring only 18 inches round* ○ *They've built a fence all round to stop the children falling in.* **4** to all members of a group in turn: *Hand the biscuits round.* ○ *The news was quickly passed round.* ○ *Have we enough cups to go round?* **5** by a route that is longer than the most direct one: *It's quickest to walk across the field — going round by road takes much longer.* ○ *We decided to come the long way round in order to see the countryside.* **6** (*infml*) to or at a specified place, esp where sb lives: *I'll be round in an hour.* ○ *We've invited the Frasers round this evening.* **7** (idm) **ˌround aˈbout** in the surrounding district: *the countryside round about* ○ *all the villages round about.* Cf AROUND[2].

round[3] /raʊnd/ *n* **1 (a)** complete slice of bread: *a round of toast* ○ *two rounds* (ie sandwiches) *of ham and one of beef.* **(b)** (of food) sth round; a round piece/shape: *Cut the pastry into small rounds, one for each pie.* **2** regular series, succession, route, etc: *the daily round,* ie the ordinary occupations of every day ○ *His life is one long round of meetings.* ○ *the postman's round,* ie the route he takes to deliver letters ○ *a doctor's rounds,* ie his series of daily visits to patients or wards. **3** stage in a game, competition, etc: *a boxing-match of ten rounds* ○ *He was knocked out in the third round/in Round Three.* ○ *have a round of cards* ○ *play a round* (ie 18 holes) *of golf.* **4** (any one of a) set or series: *a round of drinks,* ie one for each person in a group ○ *It's my round,* ie my turn to pay for the next set of drinks. ○ *a new round of pay bargaining.* **5** burst (of applause, cheering, etc): *Let's have a good round of applause for the next performer.* **6** musical composition for two or more voices in which each sings the same melody but starts at a different time. **7** single shot or volley of shots from one or more guns; ammunition for this: *They fired several rounds at us.* ○ *We've only three rounds* (ie shells or bullets) *left.* **8** (idm) **do/go the ˈrounds (of sth)** (*infml*) make a tour; visit places one after another: *We did/went the rounds of all the pubs in town.* **go the round of** circulate in or among: *The news quickly went the round of the village.* **in the ˈround (a)** (of a theatre, play, etc) with the audience (almost) all around the stage. **(b)** (of sculpture) made so that it can be viewed from all sides. **make one's ˈrounds** make one's usual visits, esp of inspection: *the production manager making his rounds.*

round[4] /raʊnd/ *prep* **1** having (sth) as the central point of a circular movement; circling (sth): *The earth moves round the sun.* ○ *Drake sailed round the world.* ○ *goldfish swimming round the bowl.* **2** to or at a point on the other side of (sth): *walk round a corner* ○ *There's a garage round the next bend.* ○ *Go round the roundabout and take the third exit.* **3** covering or at points close to the edge of (sth): *a scarf round his neck* ○ *sitting round the table.* **4** to or at various points in (sth): *look round the room* ○ *show sb round* (ie all the different rooms in) *the house* ○ *There were soldiers positioned all round the town.* **5** ~ **(about) sth** approximately (a time, amount, etc): *We're leaving round about midday.* ○ *A new roof will cost round about £1 000.*

round[5] /raʊnd/ *v* [Tn] **1** make (sth) into the shape of a circle, a ball, an oval, etc: *round the lips,* eg when making the sound /u:/ ○ *stones rounded by the action of water.* **2** go round (sth): *We rounded the corner at high speed.* **3** (phr v) **round sth off (a)** end or complete sth satisfactorily: *round off a sentence, speech, etc* ○ *He rounded off his career by becoming Home Secretary.* **(b)** take the sharp edges off sth: *She rounded off the corners of the table with sandpaper.* **round on/upon sb** attack sb (esp verbally) in sudden anger: *She was amazed when he rounded on her and called her a liar.* **round sth out** supply sth with more explanation, detail, etc: *John will tell you the plan in outline, and then I'll round it out.* **round sb/sth up** cause sb/sth to gather in one place: *The guide rounded up the tourists and led them back to the coach.* ○ *cowboys rounding up cattle* ○ *I spent the morning trying to round up the documents I needed.* **round sth up/down** increase/decrease (a figure, price, etc) to the nearest whole number: *A charge of £1.90 will be rounded up to £2, and one of £3.10 rounded down to £3.*
□ **ˈround-up** *n* **1** act of gathering together people, animals or things into one place: *a round-up of stray cattle.* **2** summary: *Here is a round-up of the latest news.*

roundabout /ˈraʊndəbaʊt/ *adj* [usu attrib] not using the shortest or most direct route, form of words, etc: *take a roundabout route* ○ *I heard the news in a roundabout way.* ○ *a roundabout way of saying sth.*
▷ **roundabout** *n* **1** (*US* also **carousel, merry-go-round, whirligig**) revolving platform with model horses, cars, etc for children to ride on in a playground or at a funfair. **2** (*US* **traffic circle, rotary**) multiple road junction in the form of a circle round which all traffic has to pass in the same direction. ⇨ illus at MOTORWAY, Cf CIRCUS 3. **3** (idm) **swings and roundabouts** ⇨ SWING[2].

roundel /ˈraʊndl/ *n* circular identifying mark

showing nationality, used on military aircraft of some countries.

rounders /ˈraʊndəz/ *n* [sing *v*] (*Brit*) game for two teams, played with a bat and ball, in which players have to run round a circuit of bases. Cf BASEBALL.

Roundhead ⇨ ROUND[1].

roundsman /ˈraʊndzmən/ *n* (*pl* **-men** /-mən/) tradesman's employee delivering goods, etc on a regular route: *Ask your roundsman for extra milk over Christmas.*

rouse /raʊz/ *v* **1** (**a**) [Tn, Tn·pr] ~ **sb** (**from/out of sth**) cause sb to wake: *I was roused by the sound of a bell.* ○ *It's time to rouse the children.* ○ (*fig*) *rouse him from his depression.* (**b**) [I, Ipr] ~ (**from/out of sth**) (*fml*) wake (oneself): *I roused slowly from a deep sleep.* **2** [Tn, Tn·pr] ~ **sb/sth** (**from sth**) (**to sth**) cause sb/sth to become active, interested, etc: *rouse sb/oneself to action* ○ *roused to anger by their insults* ○ *When he's roused, he can get very angry.* Cf AROUSE.

▷ **rousing** *adj* [usu attrib] vigorous; giving encouragement (esp to action): *a rousing speech* ○ *three rousing cheers for the winner.*

Rousseau[1] /ˈruːsəʊ; *US* rʊˈsəʊ/ Henri (1844-1910), French painter known as 'le Douanier Rousseau' (Rousseau the customs official). He was self-taught and painted in a naive, colourful and stylized way.

Rousseau[2] /ˈruːsəʊ; *US* rʊˈsəʊ/ Jean-Jacques (1712-78), Swiss philosopher. He believed that civilization had a bad moral effect and that people should live in the country. In *Du contrat social* he set out the theory that in society people surrender some of their natural rights in return for protection, and that governors are the servants of the people. He was regarded as a hero by the leaders of the *French Revolution.

roustabout /ˈraʊstəbaʊt/ *n* **1** labourer on an oil rig. **2** (*US*) (**a**) = DOCKER (DOCK[1]). (**b**) = DECK-HAND (DECK[1]). **3** (*Austral*) general labourer on a farm.

rout[1] /raʊt/ *n* [C, U] **1** utter defeat (ending in disorder): *After our fifth goal the match became a rout.* **2** (idm) **put sb to ˈrout** (*dated fml*) defeat sb completely.

▷ **rout** *v* [Tn] defeat (sb) completely; make (sb) retreat in confusion: *He resigned after his party was routed in the election.*

rout[2] /raʊt/ *v* (phr v) **rout sb out** (**of sth**) fetch sb out abruptly, forcibly, etc: *We were routed out of our beds at 4 am.*

route /ruːt; *US* raʊt/ *n* **1** way taken or planned to get from one place to another: *We drove home by a roundabout route.* ○ *the main shipping routes across the Atlantic* ○ (*US*) *take Route 66.* **2** (*US*) round[3](2) followed by a policeman, postman, etc.

▷ **route** *v* (*pres p* **routeing**, *pp* **routed**) [Tn·pr esp passive] send (sth) by a specified route: *This flight is routed to Chicago via New York.*

□ **ˈroute march** long march made by soldiers in training.

router /ˈraʊtə(r)/ *n* plane[2] with two handles used for cutting grooves.

routine /ruːˈtiːn/ *n* **1** [C, U] fixed and regular way of doing things: *She found it difficult to establish a new routine after retirement.* ○ *do sth as a matter of routine* ○ [attrib] *routine tasks, chores, duties, etc.* **2** [C] set sequence of movements in a dance or some other performance: *go through a dance routine.* **3** [C] (*computing*) set of instructions that performs a specific task and that can be used several times during a program.

▷ **routine** *adj* usual; habitual; regular: *the routine procedure* ○ *routine maintenance* ○ (*derog*) *give a rather routine* (ie ordinary, undistinguished) *performance.* **routinely** *adv.*

roux /ruː/ *n* (*pl* unchanged) (in cooking) mixture of melted fat and flour blended together and used as the basis for sauces.

rove /rəʊv/ *v* **1** (**a**) [Ipr, Ip, Tn] (*esp rhet*) wander without intending to reach a particular destination; roam: *a roving reporter* ○ *bands of hooligans roving (round) the streets.* (**b**) ~ **about/around** (**sth**) [Ipr, Ip] (of eyes) look in one direction after another. **2** (idm) **have a roving eye** be always looking for a chance to flirt or have love affairs.

▷ **rover** *n* **1** wanderer: *She's always been a rover.* **2** (*arch*) = PIRATE 1a.

□ **ˌroving comˈmission** authority to travel as much as necessary in order to carry out enquiries, duties, etc.

row[1] /rəʊ/ *n* **1** number of people or things arranged in a line: *a row of books, houses, desks* ○ *standing in a row/in rows* ○ *plant a row of cabbages.* **2** line of seats across a theatre, etc: *the front two rows* ○ [attrib] *a ˌfront-row ˈseat.* **3** (idm) **in a row** one after another; in unbroken sequence: *This is the third Sunday in a row that it's rained.*

□ **ˈrow house** (*US*) = TERRACED HOUSE (TERRACE).

row[2] /rəʊ/ *v* **1** [I, Ipr, Ip, Tn, Tn·pr, Tn·p] propel (a boat) by using oars: *Can you row?* ○ *They rowed (the boat) across (the river).* **2** [Tn, Tn·pr, Tn·p] carry (sb/sth) in a rowing-boat: *Row me across (the river).* **3** (**a**) [Tn, Tn·pr] perform in a race, etc against (sb) by rowing: *We're rowing Cambridge in the next race.* (**b**) [I, Ipr] be an oarsman in a racing-boat's crew: *row for Cambridge* ○ *He rows (at) No 5* (ie in this position) *for Oxford.*

▷ **row** *n* (usu *sing*) outing in a boat that one rows; period of rowing: *go for a row* ○ *a long and tiring row.*

rower *n* person who rows a rowing-boat. Cf OARSMAN (OAR).

□ **ˈrowing-boat** (also *esp US* **ˈrow-boat**) *n* small boat propelled by rowing (usu not competitively).

row[3] /raʊ/ *n* (*infml*) **1** [U, sing] loud noise; uproar: *How can I read with all this row going on?* ○ *Could you please make less (of a) row?* ○ *kick up a row.* **2** [C] noisy or violent argument; quarrel: *I think they've had a row.* ○ *the continuing row over the Government's defence policy.* ⇨ Usage at ARGUMENT. **3** [C] instance of being criticized, scolded, etc: *I got/She gave me a row for being late.*

▷ **row** *v* [I, Ipr] ~ (**with sb**) quarrel noisily: *They're always rowing,* ie with each other. ○ *rowing (with his employers) over money.*

rowan /ˈrəʊən, ˈraʊən/ *n* (also **ˈrowan tree**) type of tree that bears hanging clusters of scarlet berries; mountain ash.

rowdy /ˈraʊdɪ/ *adj* (**-ier, -iest**) (*derog*) noisy; disorderly: *a group of rowdy teenagers* ○ *The meeting broke up amid rowdy scenes.*

▷ **rowdily** *adv.*

rowdiness, rowdyism *ns* [U] rowdy behaviour.

rowdy *n* (*dated derog*) rowdy person.

rowel /ˈraʊəl/ *n* revolving pointed disc on a spur.

Thomas Rowlandson: Sunday Morning

Rowlandson /ˈraʊləndsn/ Thomas (1756-1827), English artist. He is famous for his cartoons and caricatures satirizing contemporary society and politics. ⇨ illus.

rowlock /ˈrɒlək; *US* ˈrəʊlɒk/ (*US* also **ˈoarlock**) *n* device on the side of a rowing-boat for keeping an oar in place. ⇨ illus at ROWING-BOAT (ROW[2])

royal /ˈrɔɪəl/ *adj* [usu attrib] **1** of a king or queen: *limitations on royal power* ○ *the royal visit to Canada* ○ *the royal prerogative.* **2** belonging to the family of a king or queen: *the royal princesses.* **3** in the service or under the patronage of a king or queen: *the Royal Society for the Protection of Birds.* **4** suitable for a king, etc; splendid: *a royal welcome.* **5** (idm) **a battle royal** ⇨ BATTLE. **the royal 'we'** monarch's use of the plural pronoun to refer to himself or herself: (*joc*) *'We've never liked Italy.' 'Is that the royal we? I think Italy's great!'*

▷ **royal** *n* (usu *pl*) (*infml*) member of the royal family.

royalist /ˈrɔɪəlɪst/ *n* person who favours monarchy as a form of government.

royally /ˈrɔɪəlɪ/ *adv* in a splendid manner: *We were royally entertained.*

□ **the ˌRoyal Aˌcademy of ˈArts** organization founded in 1768 for the promotion of the fine arts in Britain; its first president was Sir Joshua *Reynolds. Its premises in *Piccadilly, London, contain an art school and extensive galleries, where a famous exhibition of contemporary art is held each summer. ⇨ article at SEASON.

the ˌRoyal ˈAir Force the British air force.

ˌRoyal ˈAscot (also **Ascot**) /ˈæskət/ fashionable British horse-racing event held at *Ascot each year in June. Members of the royal family attend some of the races, but many people go there for social rather than sporting reasons. ⇨ article at SEASON.

ˌroyal asˈsent signing by the king or queen of acts that have been passed by the British Parliament, which makes them offically part of the law.

the ˌRoyal ˈAutomobile Club (abbr **RAC**) British motoring organization, offering various services to motorists who belong to it, esp help when their vehicles break down. Cf THE AUTOMOBILE ASSOCIATION (AUTOMOBILE).

ˌroyal ˈblue (*Brit*) deep bright blue colour.

the ˌRoyal British ˈLegion (also **the British Legion**) charitable organization that helps former members of the British armed forces. It raises money esp by selling paper poppies in the weeks before *Remembrance Sunday. ⇨ article at CLUB.

the ˌRoyal Caˌnadian ˌMounted Poˈlice the Canadian police force. Cf MOUNTIE.

ˌRoyal Comˈmission (*Brit*) group of people officially appointed by the monarch to investigate and report on a particular matter.

ˌroyal ˈfamily the family of a king or queen. ⇨ article.

ˌRoyal ˈHighness (used as the title of a royal person, esp a prince or princess): *Her Royal Highness, the Princess of Wales* ○ *Their Royal Highnesses, the Duke and Duchess of York* ○ *Thank you, Your Royal Highness.*

ˌroyal ˈicing type of hard icing used eg on Christmas and wedding cakes, made from icing sugar and beaten egg whites.

ˌroyal ˈjelly substance secreted by worker bees and fed by them to future queen bees.

the ˌRoyal Maˈrines branch of the British armed forces that can fight on land or at sea.

the ˌRoyal ˈMile the three streets in Edinburgh, Scotland, that connect Edinburgh Castle and *Holyrood House.

the ˌRoyal ˈMint establishment responsible for making the coins used in Britain. Since 1968 it has been in S Wales. It also produces coins for some other countries.

the ˌRoyal ˈNavy the British navy.

the ˌRoyal Soˈciety the oldest and most important scientific society in Britain, founded in 1662. Among the founder members were *Boyle, *Hooke and *Wren and other presidents have included *Newton and *Rutherford.

ˌroyal ˈwarrant (right to use) the royal coat of arms (COAT) displayed on a product, indicating that the firm supplies goods to a member of the British royal family.

royalty /ˈrɔɪəltɪ/ *n* **1** [U] royal person or people: *in the presence of royalty* ○ *a shop patronized by royalty.* **2** [U] being a member of a royal family: *the duties of royalty.* **3** [C] (**a**) sum paid to the owner of

The Royal Family

Britain, one of the few remaining monarchies in the world, has been continuously ruled by a king or queen since the 9th century, except for a brief period from 1649 to 1660, when Oliver Cromwell was Lord Protector of the Commonwealth.

The present sovereign, Queen Elizabeth II, has been on the throne since 1952. Her official royal title is 'Elizabeth the Second, by the Grace of God of the United Kingdom of Great Britain and Northern Ireland and of Her other Realms and Territories Queen, Head of the Commonwealth, Defender of the Faith'. Her husband is Prince Philip, Duke of Edinburgh, and their four children are Prince Charles, who has the title Prince of Wales, Princess Anne, called the Princess Royal, Prince Andrew, who is the Duke of York, and Prince Edward. The Royal Family also includes the Queen's sister, Princess Margaret, and their mother, Queen Elizabeth the Queen Mother, the widow of George VI. The eldest son (or, if there is no son, the eldest daughter) of the monarch is heir to the throne, so Prince Charles is due to succeed his mother on her death or if she abdicates.

Although the Queen personifies the state, and is nominally commander-in-chief of all armed forces as well as 'supreme governor' of the Church of England, it is the government that actually governs in her name. It is said that the Queen 'reigns, not rules' in a constitutional monarchy. The Queen participates in a number of formal acts. As the sovereign she summons or dissolves Parliament, gives royal assent to Bills by Parliament (so that they become Acts), confers peerages and knighthoods, and appoints many important office holders, such as government ministers (including the prime minister), judges, officers in the armed services, diplomats and bishops. The sovereign also grants a royal pardon to a person who is shown to have been wrongly convicted of a crime, but all these acts are performed only at the request of the government in power. The sovereign has no power to act independently.

The Queen and other members of the royal family carry out a number of official duties throughout the year. Some of them, such as the Trooping of the Colour or the State Opening of Parliament, involve considerable ceremony and pageantry. Other typical duties include visiting different parts of the country to open new buildings such as hospitals or schools, awarding prizes, and attending special charity or sporting events. Such royal visits are reported daily in the 'Court Circular' in *The Times* and some other papers.

Trooping the Colour takes place on the Queen's 'Official Birthday' (the second Saturday in June), and this is also when the Birthday Honours are announced. These are the titles and awards conferred by the Queen on the advice of the government to people who are judged to have earned them, and include knighthoods and awards such as Commander of the British Empire (CBE) and Order of the British Empire (OBE). Similar awards are also announced in the New Year Honours list.

The cost of fulfilling these duties is paid from the Civil List, an annual sum granted to members of the royal family by Parliament. Parliament also pays for the cost of maintaining the Royal Yacht, which is used for royal visits abroad, and the Royal Flight (the aircraft similarly used).

The Queen's chief official residence is Buckingham Palace in London, which was originally bought in 1761 by George III. Other royal palaces in Britain, used mostly for holidays, are Windsor Castle, near London, Sandringham House in Norfolk, and Balmoral Castle, near Braemar in Scotland.

The Queen and other members of the royal family, especially the Queen Mother, who celebrated her 90th birthday in 1990, are generally regarded with respect and even affection. Prince Charles is admired by many people for expressing his often controversial views (notably on modern architecture and education) and for his positive aims and ambitions for the future of Britain. (Cf articles at ARISTOCRACY, CHRISTMAS, PARLIAMENT and SEASON.)

a copyright or patent, eg to an author for each copy of his book sold. **(b)** sum paid by a mining or oil company to the owner of the land being mined, etc: *oil royalties.*

RP /ˌɑː ˈpiː/ *abbr* received pronunciation.

RPI /ˌɑː piː ˈaɪ/ *abbr* retail price index.

rpm /ˌɑː piː ˈem/ *abbr* revolutions per minute (esp as a measure of engine speed): *2500 rpm.*

RRP /ˌɑːr ɑː ˈpiː/ *abbr* (*commerce*) recommended retail price: *RRP £35.00, our price £29.95,* eg in a sales catalogue.

RSA /ˌɑːr es ˈeɪ/ *abbr* **1** Republic of South Africa. **2** Royal Society of Arts.

RSC /ˌɑːr es ˈsiː/ *abbr* (*Brit*) Royal Shakespeare Company: *an RSC production.*

RSM /ˌɑːr es ˈem/ *abbr* **1** Regimental Sergeant-Major. **2** Royal School of Music.

RSPB /ˌɑːr es piː ˈbiː/ *abbr* (*Brit*) Royal Society for the Protection of Birds. ⇨ article at ENVIRONMENT.

RSPCA /ˌɑːr es ˌpiː siː ˈeɪ/ *abbr* (*Brit*) Royal Society for the Prevention of Cruelty to Animals. ⇨ articles at ANIMAL, CHARITY.

RSV /ˌɑːr es ˈviː/ *abbr* Revised Standard Version (of the Bible).

RSVP /ˌɑːr es viː ˈpiː/ *abbr* (esp on invitations) please reply (French *répondez s'il vous plaît*).

Rt Hon *abbr* (*Brit*) Right Honourable: *(the) Rt Hon Richard Scott.* Cf HON 2.

Rt Rev (also **Rt Revd**) *abbr* Right Reverend: *(the) Rt Rev George Hill.* Cf REV.

RU *abbr* Rugby Union.

Ru *symb* ruthenium.

rub[1] /rʌb/ *v* (**-bb-**) **1** [I, Tn, Tn·pr, Tn·p] ~ **(sth) (with sth)** (cause sth to) press against (a surface) with a to-and-fro sliding movement: *If you keep rubbing, the paint will come off.* ○ *He rubbed his chin thoughtfully.* ○ *rub the glass (with a cloth)* ○ *rubbing his hands together.* **2 (a)** [Tn·pr, Tn·p] apply (sth) in this way: *Rub the lotion on (to the skin).* **(b)** [Tn·pr] move (one's hand, etc) in this way: *He rubbed his palm across his forehead.* **3 (a)** [Cn·a] cause (sth) to reach the specified condition by rubbing: *rub the surface smooth, clean, dry, etc (with a cloth).* **(b)** [Tn·pr] ~ **sth in sth** make (a hole, etc) in sth by rubbing: *rub a bald patch in one's trousers.* **4** [I, Ipr] ~ **(on/against sth)** be pressed (against sth) and sliding about on it: *The heel of my shoe keeps rubbing,* ie against the heel of my foot. ○ *The wheel's rubbing on the mudguard.* **5** (idm) **rub sb's ˈnose in it** (*infml derog*) remind sb cruelly of their past mistakes, etc. **rub salt into the wound/sb's wounds** make a painful experience even more painful for sb. **rub shoulders with sb** meet sb socially or professionally: *In his job he's rubbing shoulders with film stars all the time.* **rub sb up the wrong ˈway** (*infml*) annoy sb.

6 (phr v) **rub along** (*infml*) (of a person) manage without too much difficulty. **rub along with sb/together** (*infml*) (of two or more people) live together in a reasonably friendly way.

rub (sb/oneself/sth) down rub (sb/oneself/a horse, etc) vigorously with eg a towel to make the skin dry and clean: *The players paused to rub (themselves) down between games.* **rub sth down** make sth smooth or level by rubbing: *Rub the walls down well before painting them.*

rub sth in/into sth force (ointment, etc) into sth by rubbing: *Rub the cream in well.* **rub it in** emphasize or remind sb constantly of an unpleasant fact: *I know I made a mistake but there's no need to rub it in.*

rub (sth) off (sth) (cause sth to) be removed from (a surface) by rubbing: *Rub the mud off your trousers.* ○ *Who's rubbed my figures off the blackboard?* ○ *These stains won't rub off.* **rub off (on/onto sb)** be transferred (to sb) as a result of sb else's example: *Let's hope some of her patience rubs off on her brother.*

rub sb out (*US sl*) murder sb. **rub (sth) out** (cause sth, esp pencil marks, to) be removed by using a rubber[1](2): *rub out a mistake, figure, drawing* ○ *I can't get it to rub out.*

rub sth up polish sth by rubbing. **rub up against sb** (*infml*) meet sb by chance.

▷ **rubbing** *n* impression of sth, eg a brass decoration on a grave, made by rubbing paper laid over it with wax, chalk or charcoal.

rub[2] /rʌb/ *n* **1** [C usu *sing*] act or process of rubbing: *Give the spoons a good rub to get them clean.* **2 the rub** [sing] (*dated*) difficulty or drawback (used esp in the expressions shown): *There's the rub/Therein lies the rub.* **3** (idm) **the ˌrub of the ˈgreen** set-back or piece of bad luck that has to be accepted: *These things happen. I'm afraid it's just the rub of the green.*

rubber[1] /ˈrʌbə(r)/ *n* **1** [U] tough elastic substance made from the milky juice of certain tropical plants, or synthetically: *an electric cable insulated with rubber* ○ [attrib] *a pair of rubber gloves* ○ *rubber car tyres.* **2** [C] (*Brit*) (also *esp US* **eraser**) **(a)** piece of this or some other substance for rubbing out pencil or ink marks: *a pencil with a rubber on the end.* **(b)** piece of material for rubbing out chalk marks on a blackboard. **3** [C] (*infml esp US*) contraceptive sheath; condom. **4 rubbers** [pl] (*esp US*) waterproof rubber coverings worn over the shoes; galoshes.

▷ **rubberize, -ise** /ˈrʌbəraɪz/ *v* [Tn] treat or coat (sth) with rubber: *rubberized material.*

rubbery /ˈrʌbərɪ/ *adj* like rubber in consistency or texture: *chewing a rubbery piece of meat.*

□ **ˌrubber ˈband** (also **elastic band**, *US* **elastic**) loop of rubber used for holding things together: *a pack of cards with a rubber band round them.*

ˈrubber goods (*euph*) contraceptive devices and sexual aids.

ˈrubber plant type of plant with thick shiny green leaves, often grown indoors for decoration.

ˈrubber solution liquid containing rubber used esp as an adhesive for repairing bicycle tyres.

ˌrubber ˈstamp 1 small device for printing dates, signatures, etc on a surface by hand. **2** (*fig*) person or group that automatically gives approval to the actions or decisions of others. **ˌrubber-ˈstamp** *v* [Tn] (*often derog*) approve (sth) automatically and without proper consideration.

rubber[2] /ˈrʌbə(r)/ *n* match of (the best of) three games at bridge, whist, etc: *Let's play another* rubber. ○ *We can win the rubber 2 games to nil or 2-1.*

rubber-neck /ˈrʌbənek/ *v* [I] (*US sl derog*) stare or gape inquisitively.

▷ **rubber-neck** *n* person who does this, esp a tourist or sightseer.

rubbish /ˈrʌbɪʃ/ *n* [U] **1** waste or worthless material: *The dustmen haven't collected the rubbish yet.* ○ [attrib] *a ˈrubbish dump/heap/tip* ○ *a ˈrubbish bin.* **2** (*derog*) (often used as an *interj*) worthless ideas, etc; nonsense: *His book is (a load of) rubbish.* ○ *Don't talk rubbish!* ○ *What he says is all rubbish.*

▷ **rubbish** *v* [Tn] (*Brit or Austral sl*) criticize (sb/sth) contemptuously; treat as worthless: *The film was rubbished by the critics.* ○ *She is often accused of rubbishing her opponents.*

rubbishy *adj* (*infml*) worthless.

rubble /ˈrʌbl/ *n* [U] bits of broken stone, rock or bricks: *a road built on a foundation of rubble* ○ *The explosion reduced the building to (a pile of) rubble*, ie totally demolished it.

Rube Goldberg /ˌruːb ˈɡəʊldbɜːɡ/ (*US joc or derog*) (eg of machinery) complicated and impractical. Cf HEATH ROBINSON.

rubella /ruːˈbelə/ *n* [U] (*medical*) = GERMAN MEASLES (GERMAN).

Rubens /ˈruːbənz/ Sir Peter Paul (1577-1640), Flemish painter, collector and diplomat. As court painter to the Spanish ruler of Flanders he produced a vast number of religious and mythological paintings as well as portraits and landscapes. He was a master of the baroque style and is famous for his plump female nudes. He was knighted by *Charles I after negotiating a peace between Spain and England.

Rubicon /ˈruːbɪkən; *US* -kɒn/ *n* (idm) **cross the Rubicon** ⇨ CROSS².

rubicund /ˈruːbɪkənd/ *adj* (*fml*) (of a person's complexion) red; ruddy: *fat rubicund cheeks.*

Rubinstein /ˈruːbənstaɪn/ Artur (1887-1982), American pianist born in Poland. One of the greatest virtuoso pianists of the 20th century, he was particularly famous for his playing of *Chopin.

ruble = ROUBLE.

rubric /ˈruːbrɪk/ *n* words put as a heading, esp to show or explain how sth should be done, etc.

ruby /ˈruːbɪ/ *n* **1** [C] type of red jewel: [attrib] *ruby red.* **2** [U] colour of a ruby; deep red.

▷ **ruby** *adj* [esp attrib] deep red: *ruby lips.*

□ ˌ**ruby** ˈ**wedding** 40th anniversary of a wedding.

RUC /ˌɑː juː ˈsiː/ *abbr* Royal Ulster Constabulary. ⇨ article at IRELAND.

ruche /ruːʃ/ *n* gathered trimming on a garment, etc.

▷ **ruched** /ruːʃt/ *adj* trimmed with gathered material (eg lace): *a dress with ruched sleeves.*

ruck¹ /rʌk/ *n* **1** [C] (*sport*) (a) (*Brit*) (in Rugby football) loose scrum with the ball on the ground. (b) disorganized group (of players, competitors, etc). **2 the ruck** [sing] ordinary commonplace people or things: *He was eager to get out of the (common) ruck and distinguish himself in some way.*

ruck² /rʌk/ *n* irregular unintentional fold or crease (esp in cloth): *smooth out the rucks in the bedclothes.*

▷ **ruck** *v* (phr v) **ruck up** form rucks: *The sheets on my bed have rucked up.*

rucksack /ˈrʌksæk/ (also **knapsack**, *US* also ˈ**backpack**) *n* bag strapped to the back from the shoulders, used by hikers, climbers, etc. ⇨ illus at LUGGAGE. Cf HAVERSACK.

ruckus /ˈrʌkəs/ *n* (usu *sing*) (*infml esp US*) noisy disturbance; uproar: *cause a ruckus.*

ructions /ˈrʌkʃnz/ *n* [pl] (*infml*) angry protests; noisy argument: *There'll be ructions if you don't do as you're told.*

rudder /ˈrʌdə(r)/ *n* (a) broad flat piece of wood or metal hinged vertically at the stern of a boat or ship, used for steering. ⇨ illus at YACHT. (b) similar piece of metal on the rear of an aircraft, for the same purpose. ⇨ illus at AIRCRAFT.

ruddy¹ /ˈrʌdɪ/ *adj* (**-ier**, **-iest**) **1** (*approv*) (of a person's face) having a fresh healthy colour: *ruddy cheeks.* **2** reddish: *a ruddy glow in the sky.* ▷ **ruddily** *adv.* **ruddiness** *n* [U].

ruddy² /ˈrʌdɪ/ *adj* [attrib], *adv* (*Brit sl euph*) bloody²; damned: *What the ruddy hell are you doing?* ○ *He's a ruddy idiot.* ○ *I work ruddy hard.*

rude /ruːd/ *adj* (**-r**, **-st**) **1** (of a person or his behaviour) showing no respect or consideration; impolite: *He's very rude/a very rude man.* ○ *It's rude to interrupt.* ○ *What a rude reply!* **2** (*euph*) (of a story, etc) slightly indecent; risqué: *a rather rude joke.* **3** [attrib] primitive; simple: *rude stone implements.* **4** [attrib] violent; startling; abrupt: *a rude awakening to the realities of life* ○ *a rude reminder of the danger they were in.* **5** (idm) **in rude** ˈ**health** (*fml or rhet*) vigorously healthy.

▷ **rudely** *adv* **1** impolitely: *behave rudely.* **2** in a primitive manner: *rudely-fashioned weapons.* **3** roughly; abruptly: *rudely awakened by screams and shouts.*

rudeness *n* [U].

rudiment /ˈruːdɪmənt/ *n* **1 rudiments** [pl] ~s (**of sth**) (a) basic or elementary principles (of a subject): *master the rudiments of economics.* (b) imperfect beginning of sth that is not yet fully developed: *working on the rudiments of a new idea.* **2** [C] part or organ that is incompletely developed: *the rudiment(s) of a tail.*

▷ **rudimentary** /ˌruːdɪˈmentrɪ/ *adj* **1** existing in an imperfect or undeveloped form: *Some breeds of dog have only rudimentary tails.* **2** (*derog*) elementary; (not more than) basic: *I have only a rudimentary grasp of physics.*

rue¹ /ruː/ *n* [U] type of evergreen shrub with bitter leaves formerly used in medicine.

rue² /ruː/ *v* (*pres p* **rueing** or **ruing**, *pt, pp* **rued**) [Tn] (*dated or fml*) repent or regret (sth) (used esp in the expressions shown): *You'll live to rue it*, ie You will regret it one day. ○ *He's rueing the day he joined the Army!*

▷ **rueful** /ˈruːfl/ *adj* showing or feeling good-humoured regret: *a rueful smile.* **ruefully** /ˈruːfəlɪ/ *adv.* **ruefulness** *n* [U].

ruff¹ /rʌf/ *n* **1** ring of differently coloured or marked feathers or fur round the neck of a bird or animal. **2** wide stiff frill worn as a collar, esp in the 16th century. ⇨ illus at DRESS. **3** bird of the sandpiper family. The male has a ring of long feathers round its neck.

ruff² /rʌf/ *v* [I, Tn] trump (a card or a player) in a card-game.

ruffian /ˈrʌfɪən/ *n* (*dated derog*) violent lawless man: *a gang of ruffians.*

ruffle /ˈrʌfl/ *v* **1** [Tn, Tn·p] ~ **sth** (**up**) disturb the smoothness or evenness of sth: *a breeze ruffling the surface of the lake* ○ *Don't ruffle my hair, I've just combed it.* ○ *The bird ruffled up its feathers.* **2** [Tn esp passive] upset the calmness or even temper of (sb); disconcert: *Anne is easily ruffled by awkward questions.* **3** (idm) **ruffle sb's** ˈ**feathers** (*infml*) annoy sb. **smooth sb's ruffled feathers** ⇨ SMOOTH².

▷ **ruffle** *n* strip of material gathered into a frill and used to ornament a garment, esp at the wrist or neck.

rug /rʌɡ/ *n* **1** thick floor-mat (usu smaller than a carpet): *a* ˈ*hearth-rug.* **2** piece of thick warm fabric used as a blanket or covering: *a* ˈ*travelling-rug*, ie for covering a passenger's knees in a car, etc. **3** (idm) **pull the carpet/rug from under sb's feet** ⇨ PULL². **snug as a bug in a rug** ⇨ SNUG.

Rugby /ˈrʌɡbɪ/ *n* [U] (also ˌ**Rugby** ˈ**football**) form of football played with an oval ball which may be kicked or carried: [attrib] *a Rugby ball, club, match, player.* ⇨ App 9.

□ ˌ**Rugby** ˈ**League** partly professional form of Rugby, with 13 players in a team.

ˌ**Rugby** ˈ**Union** amateur form of Rugby, with 15 players in a team. ⇨ article at SPORT.

rugged /ˈrʌɡɪd/ *adj* **1** rough; uneven; rocky: *a rugged coastline* ○ *rugged country.* **2** (*esp approv*) sturdy; robust; tough(-looking): *a rugged player* ○ *a car famous for its rugged qualities* ○ *a rugged face* ○ *rugged features.* **3** not refined or gentle: *a rugged individualist* ○ *rugged manners.* ▷ **ruggedly** *adv.* **ruggedness** *n* [U].

Rugby

rugger /ˈrʌɡə(r)/ *n* [U] (*infml esp Brit*) Rugby (esp Rugby Union) football.

ruin /ˈruːɪn/ *n* **1** [U] severe damage or destruction: *a city reduced to a state of ruin by war* ○ *The news meant the ruin of all our hopes.* **2** [U] (a) complete loss of all one's money, resources or prospects: *Ruin was staring her in the face.* ○ *brought to ruin by drugs.* (b) cause of this: *Gambling was his ruin.* **3** [U] state of being decayed, collapsed or destroyed: *The castle has fallen into ruin.* **4** [C] remains of sth that has decayed or collapsed or been destroyed: *The abbey is now a ruin.* ○ *the ruins of Pompeii.* **5** (idm) **go to rack and ruin** ⇨ RACK³. **in** ˈ**ruins** in a severely damaged or decayed condition: *An earthquake left the whole town in ruins.* ○ *His career is/lies in ruins.*

▷ **ruin** *v* [Tn] **1** cause the destruction of (sth/sb): *He ruined his prospects by carelessness.* ○ *The storm ruined the crops.* ○ *He's a ruined man*, ie has lost all his money, prospects, etc. ○ *a ruined building.* **2** (*infml*) spoil (sth/sb): *The island has been ruined by tourism.* ○ *It poured with rain and my dress got/was ruined.* ○ *You're ruining that child*, eg by being too indulgent.

ruination /ˌruːɪˈneɪʃn/ *n* [U] (cause of) being ruined: *Late frosts are ruination for the garden.* ○ *You'll be the ruination of me!*

ruinous /ˈruːɪnəs/ *adj* bringing (esp financial) ruin: *ruinous expenditure* ○ (*joc*) *The prices in that restaurant are absolutely ruinous.* **ruinously** *adv*: *a ruinously expensive meal, restaurant, coat.*

Ruisdael /ˈraɪsdɑːl/ Jacob van (c 1628-82), Dutch painter. He was the greatest of the 17th-century Dutch landscape painters, painting the countryside in sombre colours that create a melancholy effect.

rule /ruːl/ *n* **1** [C] statement of what can, should or must be done in certain circumstances or when playing a game: *The rule is that someone must be on duty at all times.* ○ *the rules of the game* ○ *rules and regulations.* **2** [C usu *sing*] usual practice or habit; normal state of things: *My rule is to get up at seven every day.* ○ *He makes it a rule never to borrow money.* ○ *She made a rule of eating an apple a day.* ○ *Cold winters here are the exception rather than the rule*, ie are comparatively rare. **3** [U] authority; government: *the rule of law* ○ *majority rule* ○ *a country formerly under French rule* ○ *mob rule*, ie the state that exists when a mob takes control. **4** [C] straight measuring device, often jointed, used by carpenters, etc. **5** [C] (usu straight) line drawn by hand or printed. **6** [C] principles on which the life and discipline of a monastic order are based: *the Rule of St Benedict.* **7** (idm) **as a (general)** ˈ**rule** (*fml*) in most cases; usually: *As a rule I'm home by six.* **bend the rules** ⇨ BEND¹. **the exception proves the rule** ⇨ EXCEPTION. **a rule of** ˈ**thumb** rough practical method of assessing or measuring sth, usu based on past experience rather than on exact measurement, etc (and therefore not completely reliable in every case or in every detail): *As a rule of thumb, you should cook a chicken for 20 minutes for each pound that it weighs.* **rule(s) of the** ˈ**road** rules regulating the movement of vehicles, ships, etc when meeting or passing each other. **work to**

ˈrule follow the rules of one's occupation with excessive strictness in order to cause delay, as a form of industrial protest.

▷ **rule** *v* **1** [I, Ipr, Tn] ~ (**over sb/sth**) govern (sb/sth); have authority (over): *She once ruled over a vast empire.* ○ *Charles I ruled (England) for eleven years.* **2** [Tn usu passive] have power or influence over (sb, sb's feelings, etc); dominate: *Don't allow yourself to be ruled by emotion.* ○ *She let her heart rule her head*, ie acted according to her emotions, rather than sensibly. **3** [Ipr, Tf, Cn·a, Cn·t] give a decision as a judge or as some other authority: *rule in favour of the plaintiff* ○ *The chairman ruled that the question was out of order/ruled the speaker out of order.* ○ *The court ruled the action to be illegal.* **4** [Tn] draw (a line) using a ruler, etc; mark parallel lines on (writing-paper, etc): *Do you want ruled paper or plain?* **5** (idm) **rule the ˈroost** be the dominant person in a group. **rule (sb/sth) with a rod of ˈiron/with an iron hand** govern (a group of people, a country, etc) very harshly. **6** (phr v) **rule sth off (from sth)** separate sth from everything else by drawing a line below it, etc: *rule the photographs off from the text.* **rule sb/sth out (as sth)** exclude sb/sth (as irrelevant, ineligible, etc): *That possibility can't be ruled out*, ie It must continue to be considered ○ *He was ruled out as a possible candidate.*

□ ˌ**Rule Briˈtannia** patriotic song composed by Thomas *Arne, now often sung as an unofficial British national anthem.

ruler /ˈruːlə(r)/ *n* **1** person who rules or governs. **2** straight strip of wood, plastic, metal, etc used for measuring or for drawing straight lines.

ruling /ˈruːlɪŋ/ *adj* [attrib] that rules; prevalent; dominant: *the ruling class, party, faction, etc* ○ *His ruling passion was ambition.*

▷ **ruling** *n* decision made by a judge or by some other authority: *When will the committee give/make its ruling?*

rum[1] /rʌm/ *n* [U] **1** strong alcoholic drink distilled from sugar-cane juice.

📖 Rum is the traditional drink of sailors, regarded in the past as one of a sailor's basic pleasures in life. From 1731 to 1970 all sailors were given a small amount (or 'tot') of specially strong naval rum every day. The old naval command for rum to be issued was 'up spirits'. Another strange old naval term is 'splice the mainbrace', which authorized the issue of an extra tot on special occasions.

2 (*US*) any type of alcoholic liquor.

□ ˌ**rum ˈbaba** = BABA.

rum[2] /rʌm/ *adj* (**-mmer, -mmest**) (*dated Brit infml*) peculiar; odd: *He's a rum character.*

Rumania = ROMANIA.

rumba /ˈrʌmbə/ *n* (piece of music for a) type of ballroom dance that originated in Cuba: *dance/do the rumba.*

rumble[1] /ˈrʌmbl/ *v* (**a**) [I] make a deep heavy continuous sound: *thunder rumbling in the distance* ○ *I'm so hungry that my stomach's rumbling.* (**b**) [Ipr, Ip] move (in the specified direction) making such a sound: *trams rumbling through the streets.*

▷ **rumble** *n* **1** [U, C usu *sing*] rumbling sound: *the rumble of drums.* **2** [C] (*US sl*) street fight between gangs.

rumble[2] /ˈrʌmbl/ *v* [Tn] (*Brit sl*) detect the true character of (sb/sth); see through (a deception): *He looks suspicious — do you think he's rumbled us/what we're up to?*

rumbustious /rʌmˈbʌstɪəs/ (also esp *US* **rambunctious**) *adj* (*infml*) cheerful in a noisy, energetic way; boisterous.

ruminant /ˈruːmɪnənt/ *n, adj* (animal) that chews the cud, eg a cow.

ruminate /ˈruːmɪneɪt/ *v* **1** [I, Ipr] ~ (**about/on/over sth**) think deeply; meditate; ponder: *ruminating on recent events.* **2** [I] (of animals) chew the cud.

▷ **rumination** /ˌruːmɪˈneɪʃn/ *n* [U].

ruminative /ˈruːmɪnətɪv; *US* -neɪtɪv/ *adj* inclined to meditate; thoughtful: *in a ruminative mood.* **ruminatively** *adv*: *gazing ruminatively out of the window.*

rummage /ˈrʌmɪdʒ/ *v* [I, Ipr, Ip] ~ (**among/in/through sth**) (**for sth**); ~ (**about/around**) turn things over or disarrange them while searching for sth: *rummaging through (the contents of) a drawer for a pair of socks* ○ *rummage around in the attic.*

▷ **rummage** *n* search of this kind: *have a good rummage around.*

□ ˈ**rummage sale** = JUMBLE SALE (JUMBLE).

rummy /ˈrʌmɪ/ *n* [U] any of various types of simple card-game in which players try to form sets or sequences of cards.

rumour (*US* **rumor**) /ˈruːmə(r)/ *n* [C, U] (instance of) information spread by being talked about but not certainly true: *Rumour has it* (ie says) *that he was fired.* ○ *There are rumours of an impending merger.* ○ *I heard a rumour (that) he was leaving.*

▷ **rumoured** (*US* **rumored**) *adj* reported as a rumour: *They bought the house at a rumoured price of £200 000.* ○ *It's rumoured that she's going to resign/She is rumoured to be on the point of resigning.*

rump /rʌmp/ *n* **1** [C] (**a**) animal's buttocks; tail-end of a bird. (**b**) (*joc*) person's bottom. **2** [C, U] (also ˌ**rump ˈsteak**) (piece of) beef cut from near the rump. **3** [C] (*derog*) small or insignificant remnant (of a larger group): *The election reduced the Party to a rump.*

□ **the ˈRump Parliament** English parliament that sat at the end of the *Long Parliament, after *Pride's Purge. It tried *Charles I and was finally dissolved just before the *Restoration.

rumple /ˈrʌmpl/ *v* [Tn] make (sth) creased or untidy; crumple: *rumple one's clothes, hair.*

rumpus /ˈrʌmpəs/ *n* (usu *sing*) disturbance; noise; uproar: *kick up/make/cause/create a rumpus.*

□ ˈ**rumpus room** (*US dated*) room in a private house (often in the basement) used esp for games, parties, etc; recreation room.

run[1] /rʌn/ *v* (**-nn-**; *pt* **ran** /ræn/, *pp* **run**) **1** [I, Ipr, Ip] move at a speed faster than a walk, never having both or all the feet on the ground at the same time: *He cannot run because he has a weak heart.* ○ *Can you run fast?* ○ *They turned and ran* (ie in order to escape) *when they saw he had a gun.* ○ *She ran/came running to meet us.* ○ *I had to run to catch the bus.* ○ *She ran out (of the house) to see what was happening.* ○ *The boys ran off as soon as we appeared.* ○ *He ran home in tears to his mother.* ⇨ Usage. **2** (**a**) [Tn] cover (the specified distance) by running: *Who was the first man to run a mile in under four minutes?* (**b**) [I, Tn] (in cricket) score (a run or runs) by running between the wickets: *run a quick single* ○ *The batsmen ran two.* **3** (**a**) [I] practise running as a sport: *You're very unfit; you ought to take up running.* ○ *She used to run when she was at college.* (**b**) [I, Ipr, Tn] ~ (**in sth**) take part or compete in (a running race): *Aouita will be running (in the 1 500 metres) tonight.* ○ *run the mile* ○ *Cram ran a fine race to take the gold medal.* (**c**) [Tn] cause (a horse or dog) to take part in a race: *run two horses in the Derby.* (**d**) [Tn esp passive] cause (a race) to take place: *The Grand National will be run in spite of the bad weather.* **4** [Ipr, Ip] go quickly or hurry to the specified place or in the specified direction: *run across to a neighbour's house to borrow some sugar* ○ *I've been running around (town) all morning looking for Christmas presents.* **5** [Ipr] move forward smoothly or easily, esp on wheels: *Trains run on rails.* ○ *Sledges run well over frozen snow.* **6** [Ipr, Ip] (of a ship or its crew) sail or steer in the specified direction: *We ran into port for supplies.* ○ *The ship ran aground.* **7** (**a**) [I, Ipr] (of buses, ferries, trains, etc) travel to and fro on a particular route: *Buses to Oxford run every half hour.* ○ *The trains don't run on Christmas Day.* ○ *There are frequent trains running between London and Brighton.* (**b**) [Tn] cause (buses, trains, etc) to be in service: *London Transport run extra trains during the rush-hour.* **8** [Ipr, Tn·pr, Tn·p] drive (sb) to a place in a car: *It's a lovely sunny day; why don't we run down to the coast?* ○ *Can I run you* (ie give you a lift) *to the station?* **9** (**a**) [Ipr] move, esp quickly, in the specified direction: *The lorry ran down the hill out of control.* ○ *The car ran off the road into a ditch.* ○ *The ball ran* (ie rolled) *to the boundary.* ○ *Her eyes ran critically over her friend's new dress.* ○ *A shiver ran down her spine.* (**b**) [Tn·pr] cause (sth) to move in the specified direction: *She ran her fingers nervously through her hair.* ○ *She ran her fingers lightly over the keys of the piano.* ○ *He ran his eyes over the page.* **10** [Tn, Tn·pr] bring or take (sth) into a country illegally and secretly; smuggle: *He used to run guns across the border.* ○ *run contraband goods/liquor into a country.* ⇨ Usage at SMUGGLE. **11** [I] (of salmon) move up a river in large numbers from the sea: *The salmon are running.* **12** [Ipr] (of plants) grow or spread in the specified direction: *Ivy ran over the walls of the cottage.* **13** [Ipr] extend in the specified direction: *A fence runs round the whole field.* ○ *The road runs parallel to the railway.* ○ *He has a scar running across his left cheek.* **14** [Ipr] ~ (**for...**) continue for the specified period of time without stopping: *The play ran* (ie was performed regularly) *for six months on Broadway.* ○ *Election campaigns in Britain run for three weeks.* **15** [Ipr] operate or be valid for the specified period of time: *The lease on my house has only a year to run.* **16** [I] (of a story, an argument, etc) have the specified wording, content, etc: *The story runs that she poisoned her husband/She poisoned her husband, or so the story runs.* ○ *'Ten shot dead by gunmen,' ran the newspaper headline.* **17** (**a**) [Ipr] (of a liquid) flow: *The River Rhine runs into the North Sea.* ○ *The tears ran down her cheeks.* ○ *Water was running all over the bathroom floor/The bathroom floor was running with water.* (**b**) [Tn, Tn·pr, Dn·n, Dn·pr] ~ **sth (for sb)** cause (a liquid) to flow: *She ran hot water into the bowl.* ○ *run the hot tap* ○ *Could you run me a hot bath/run a hot bath for me?* (**c**) [I] (of a tap, etc) send out a liquid: *Who left the tap running?* ○ *Your nose is running*, ie Mucus is flowing from it. ○ *The smoke makes my eyes run.* ⇨ Usage at DRIP[1]. (**d**) [Ipr] ~ **with sth** (usu in the continuous tenses) be covered with (a flowing liquid): *The streets were running with blood after the massacre.* ○ *His face was running with sweat.* **18** [I] (of dye or colour in a garment) dissolve and spread: *I'm afraid the colour ran when I washed your new skirt.* **19** [I] melt: *It was so hot that the butter ran.* ○ *The wax began to run.* **20** [La, I] (of the sea, the tide, a river, etc) rise higher or flow faster: *The tide was running strong.* **21** [La] pass into or reach the specified state; become: *The water ran cold when I turned the tap on.* ○ *The river ran dry* (ie stopped flowing) *during the drought.* ○ *Supplies are running short/low.* ○ *I have run short of money.* **22** [Tn] be in charge of (sth); manage: *run a hotel, a shop, a language school* ○ *He has no idea of how to run a successful business.* ○ *Stop trying to run* (ie organize) *my life for me!* **23** [Tn] make (a service, course of study, etc) available to people; organize: *The college runs summer courses for foreign learners of English.* **24** [I, Ipr, Tn, Tn·pr] (cause sth to) operate or function: *Your new car seems to run very nicely.* ○ (*fig*) *Her life has run smoothly up to now.* ○ *Could you run the engine for a moment?* ○ *I can run my electric razor off* (ie with power from) *the mains.* **25** [Tn] own and use (esp a vehicle): *I can't afford to run a car on my salary.* ○ *A bicycle is cheap to run.* **26** [I, Ipr] ~ (**for sb/sth**); ~ (**in sth**) (*esp US*) be a candidate in an election (for a political position); stand (for sth): *Reagan ran (for the Presidency) a second time in 1980.* ○ *How many candidates are running in the Presidential election?* **27** [Tn] present or nominate (sb) as a candidate in an election: *How many candidates is the Liberal Party running in the General Election?* **28** [Tn] (of a newspaper or magazine) print and publish (sth) as an item or a story: *The 'Guardian' is running a series of articles on Third World Economics.* **29** [I] (*esp US*) (of a woven or knitted garment) become unwoven or unravelled: *Nylon tights sometimes run*, ie ladder. **30** [La, Ipr] (esp in the continuous tenses) (of an event, a train, etc) happen, arrive, etc at the specified time: *The trains are running an hour late.*

○ *Programmes are running a few minutes behind schedule this evening.* **31** (idm) **come running** be eager to do what sb wants: *If you offer the children rewards for helping they'll all come running.* **ˈrun for it** run in order to escape from sb/sth: *Run for it — he's got a gun!* (For other idioms containing **run**, see entries for *ns, adjs*, etc, eg **run/take its course** ⇨ COURSE[1]; **run riot** ⇨ RIOT.).

32 (phr v) **run across sb/sth** meet sb or find sth by chance: *I ran across my old friend Jean in Paris last week.*

run after sb (no passive) (**a**) run to try to catch sb; chase sb: *The dog was running after a rabbit.* (**b**) (*infml*) (esp of a woman) seek sb's company (in order to have a romantic or sexual relationship with him): *She runs after every good-looking man she meets.*

run aˈlong (*infml*) (used in the imperative to tell sb, esp a child, to go away): *Run along now, children, I'm busy.*

run at sb (no passive) run towards sb (as if) to attack him: *He ran at me with a knife.* **run at sth** (no passive, usu in the continuous tenses) (of a statistic or figure) be at the specified level or rate: *Inflation is running at 25%.* ○ *Interest rates are running at record levels.*

run aˈway (from sb/...) suddenly leave sb/a place; escape from sb/a place: *Don't run away — I want your advice.* ○ *He ran away from home at the age of thirteen.* **run away from sth** try to avoid sth because one is shy, lacking in confidence, etc: *run away from a difficult situation* ○ *Her suicide bid was an attempt to run away from reality.* **run aˈway with one** (of a feeling) gain complete control of one; dominate one: *Don't let your temper run away with you.* ○ *Her imagination tends to run away with her.* **run away with sb; run aˈway (together)** (also *infml* **run off with sb; run ˈoff (together)**) leave home, one's husband etc with sb, in order to have a relationship with him or marry him: *She ran away with her boss/She and her boss ran away (together).* **run away with sth** (**a**) steal sth and carry it away: *A cashier ran away with the day's takings.* (**b**) use up or consume a lot of sth: *My new car really runs away with the petrol.* (**c**) win sth clearly or easily: *The champion ran away with the match.*

run sth back rewind (a film, tape, etc) in order to see or hear it again. **run back over sth** discuss or consider sth again; review sth: *I'll run back over the procedure once again.*

run (sth) down (**a**) (cause sth to) lose power or stop functioning: *My car battery has run down; it needs recharging.* ○ *If you leave your headlights on you'll soon run down the battery.* (**b**) (often in the continuous tenses) (cause sth to) stop functioning gradually or decline in size or number: *British manufacturing industry has been running down for years.* ○ *The local steelworks is being run down and is likely to close within three years.* ○ *The company is running down its sales force.* **run sb/sth down** (**a**) (of a vehicle or its driver) hit sb/sth and knock him/it to the ground; (of a ship) collide with sth: *run down a pedestrian* ○ *The cyclist was run down by a lorry.* ○ *The liner ran down a fishing-boat in thick fog.* (**b**) criticize sb/sth unkindly; disparage sb/sth: *He's always running down his wife's cooking.* ○ *She's always running her children down in public.* (**c**) find sb/sth after looking for him/it for a long time: *I finally ran the book down in the university library.* ○ *The criminal was eventually run down in the woods near his home.*

run sb in (*infml*) arrest sb and take him to a police station: *He was run in for drunk and disorderly behaviour.* **run sth in** prepare (the engine of a new car) for normal use by driving slowly and carefully: *Don't drive your new car too fast until you've run it in.*

run into sb meet sb by chance: *Guess who I ran into today?* ○ *I ran into an old schoolfriend at the supermarket this morning.* **run into sth** (**a**) meet or enter (an area of bad weather) while travelling: *We ran into a patch of thick fog just outside Edinburgh.* (**b**) encounter (difficulties, problems, etc): *The project is running into financial difficulties.* ○ *run into debt, danger, trouble.* (**c**) (no passive) reach (the specified level or amount): *Her income runs into six figures*, ie is more than £100 000. ○ *Her last novel ran into three reprints in its first year of publication.* **run (sth) into sb/sth** (cause a car, etc to) collide with or crash into sb/sth: *The bus went out of control and ran into a shop front.* ○ *She ran* (ie drove) *her car into a tree while reversing.*

run (sth) off (cause liquid to) drain or flow out of a container: *Why don't you ever run the water off after you've had a bath?* **run sth off** (**a**) cause (a race) to be contested: *The heats of the 200 metres will be run off tomorrow.* (**b**) copy, reproduce or duplicate sth, eg on a photocopying machine: *Could you run (me) off twenty copies of the agenda?* **run off with sb; run off (together)** (*infml*) = RUN AWAY WITH SB; RUN AWAY (TOGETHER). **run off with sth** steal sth and carry it away: *The treasurer has run off with the club's funds.*

run ˈon continue without stopping; go on: *The meeting will finish promptly — I don't want it to run on.* ○ *She does run on so!* **run (sth) on** (of a line of type) continue without being indented to show the beginning of a paragraph; continue (a line of type) without indenting it to show the beginning of a paragraph. **run on sth** (no passive) (of thoughts, a discussion, etc) have sth as a subject; be concerned with sth: *Her talk ran on developments in computer software.* ○ *His thoughts kept running on recent events in India.*

run ˈout (of an agreement, a document, etc) become no longer valid; expire: *The lease on our flat runs out in a few months.* ○ *My passport has run out.* **run out (of sth)** (of a supply of sth) be used up, finished or exhausted; (of a person) use up or finish (a supply of sth): *The petrol is running out/We are running out of petrol.* ○ *Our time is running out/We are running out of time.* ○ *Could I have a cigarette? I seem to have run out (of them).* **run (sth) out** (of a rope, etc) be passed out; pass (a rope, etc) out: *The rope ran out smoothly.* ○ *The sailor ran the line out neatly.* **run sb out** (often passive) (in cricket) dismiss (a batsman who is trying to make a run) by striking the wicket with the ball before he has reached his crease: *Border was (brilliantly) run out by Botham for 41.*

run ˈover (of a container or its contents) overflow: *The bath/The bath water is running over.* **run over sb; run sb over** (of a vehicle or its driver) knock sb down and pass over (a part of) his body: *I ran over a cat last night.* ○ *Two children were run over by a lorry and killed.* **run over sth** read through sth quickly; revise or rehearse sth: *I always run over my lines before going on stage.* ○ *She ran over her notes before giving the lecture.* **run over with sth** show a lot of (energy, enthusiasm, etc); overflow with sth: *She's running over with health and vitality.*

run through sth (**a**) (no passive) pass quickly through sth: *An angry murmur ran through the crowd.* ○ *Thoughts of revenge kept running through his mind.* (**b**) (no passive) be present in every part of sth; permeate sth: *A deep melancholy runs through her poetry.* ○ *There is a deep-seated conservatism running through our society.* (**c**) discuss, examine or read sth quickly: *He ran through the names on the list.* (**d**) review or summarize sth: *run through the main points of the news* ○ *Could we run through your proposals once again?* (**e**) perform, act or rehearse sth: *Could we run through Act 3 again, please?* (**f**) use up or spend (money) carelessly or wastefully: *She ran through a lot of money in her first term at university.* **run sth through** play (part of a film or tape) by passing it through a machine: *Could we run that sequence through again?*

run to sth (no passive) (**a**) extend to or reach (the specified amount or size): *The book runs to 800 pages.* ○ *Her latest novel has already run to three impressions.* (**b**) (of a person) have enough money for sth; (of money) be enough for sth: *We can't/Our funds won't run to a holiday abroad this year.*

run ˈup (of a bowler in cricket, a long-jumper, etc) gather speed by running before releasing the ball, jumping, etc: *Hadlee is now running up to bowl.* **run sth up** (**a**) raise or hoist sth: *run up a flag on the mast.* (**b**) make (a garment) quickly, esp by sewing: *run up a blouse, dress, skirt, etc.* (**c**) allow (a bill, debt, etc) to accumulate: *You'll run up a huge gas bill if you leave the heater on.* **run up against sth** meet or encounter (a difficulty, problem, etc): *The government is running up against considerable opposition to its privatization plans.*

□ **ˈrunabout** *n* (*infml*) small light car, esp one for making short journeys in towns.

ˈrun-around *n* (*infml*) (idm) **give sb/get the ˈrun-around** treat sb/be treated in a deceitful or evasive manner: *He's been giving his wife the run-around*, eg sleeping with other women.

ˈrunaway *adj* [attrib] **1** who has run away: *a runaway child.* **2** (of an animal or a vehicle) no longer under the control of its rider or driver: *a runaway horse, lorry, train.* **3** happening very rapidly or easily: *the runaway success of her last play* ○ *a runaway victory, win, etc.* — *n* person who has run away; fugitive.

ˈrun-down *n* (usu *sing*) **1** act of running down an industry, a company, etc; reduction of the size of (an industry, etc): *the government's gradual run-down of the coal industry.* **2** ~ (**of/on sth**) (*infml*) detailed analysis or description (of sth): *give sb/get a run-down on sth* ○ *I want a complete run-down on the situation.*

ˌrun-ˈdown *adj* **1** in bad condition; dilapidated; neglected: *a ˌrun-down ˈarea, ˈtown, ˈindustry, ˈhouse* ○ *The whole district is in a terribly run-down state.* **2** tired and slightly ill, esp from working hard: *be, feel, get run-down* ○ *You look pretty run-down; why don't you take a holiday?*

ˈrun-in *n* **1** ~ (**to sth**) period of time leading to (an event): *during the run-in to the election.* **2** ~ (**with sb**) (*infml esp US*) quarrel or disagreement (with sb): *have a run-in with sb.*

ˈrun-off *n* **1** extra race held to decide the winner when a race has ended in a tie. **2** amount of water that has fallen as rain or snow and that is carried away from the surface of an area by streams and rivers.

ˈrun-through *n* **1** review or summary (of sth): *Could we have a run-through of the main points discussed?* **2** rehearsal or practice: *There will be a run-through of the whole play tonight.*

ˈrun-up *n* **1** (**a**) (of a bowler in cricket, an athlete, etc) running in order to gain speed before releasing the ball, jumping, etc: *a fast, smooth, short, etc run-up.* (**b**) distance run in this way: *Pole vaulters need long run-ups.* **2** ~ (**to sth**) period of time leading to an event: *the run-up to the election.*

NOTE ON USAGE: Compare **run**, **trot**, **jog**, **gallop**, **sprint** and **race.** When describing movement that is faster than walking, **run** is the most general verb. People usually **run** in a race or when they are in a hurry: *I was late for the train so I had to run.* We generally **jog** for physical exercise, running steadily and not very fast. **Trot** and **gallop** are mainly used of horses. When people **trot**, they run quite quickly with short steps: *The girls spent the afternoon trotting up and down the beach.* Informally, **trot** can mean simply to 'go': *I'll just trot round to the shops for some bread.* **Gallop** is to run fast: *He came galloping up the road.* **Race** suggests a need to run very fast, not always in competition: *She raced to the window to stop the child jumping out.* **Sprint** is to run as fast as possible, usually over a short distance: *You'll have to sprint if you want to catch the train.*

run[2] /rʌn/ *n* **1** [C] act or period of running on foot: *go for a run every morning* ○ *Catching sight of her, he broke into a run.* **2** instance or period of travelling by car, train, etc: *take the car out for a run in the country* ○ *Oxford to London is about an hour's run by train.* **3** [C] route taken by vehicles ships, etc: *The boat operates on the Dover-Calais run.* **4** [C] series of performances: *The play had a good run/a run of six months.* ○ *It's just finished its*

West End run, ie in the West End of London. **5** [C] period or succession; spell: *We've enjoyed an exceptional run of fine weather recently.* ○ *a run of bad luck*, ie a series of misfortunes. **6** [C usu *sing*] ~ **on sth** sudden demand for sth by many people: *a run on sterling following its rise in value against the dollar* ○ *a run on the bank*, ie a sudden withdrawal of deposits by many customers. **7** [C] (often in compounds) space for domestic animals, fowl, etc: *a ˈchicken-run* ○ *a ˈsheep-run*, ie an area of pasture for sheep. **8** [C] point scored in cricket or baseball. **9** [sing] **the** ~ **of sth** tendency or trend of sth: *After 40 minutes Spurs scored, against the run of play*, ie although they had been playing poorly. ○ *The run of the cards favoured me*, ie I was dealt good cards. ○ *in accordance with the recent run of events*, ie the way things have been going recently. **10** [C] (*music*) series of notes sung or played quickly up or down the scale. **11** [C] track for some purpose: *a ˈski-run.* **12** [C] = LADDER 2. **13** [C] large number of fish in motion: *a run of salmon*, eg on their way upstream. **14 the runs** [pl] (*sl*) diarrhoea. **15** (idm) **at a ˈrun** running: *He started off at a run but soon tired and slowed to a walk.* **the common, general, ordinary, etc run (of sth)** the average type or class: *the common run of mankind*, ie ordinary average people ○ *a hotel out of the ordinary run*, ie better than average. **give sb/get/have the run of sth** give sb/get/have permission to make full use of sth: *He gave me the run of his library* ○ *He has the run of the house.* **in the long run** ⇨ LONG[1]. **make a bolt/dash/run for it/sth** ⇨ BOLT[2]. **on the ˈrun (a)** fleeing from pursuit or capture: *He's on the run from the police.* ○ *have/keep the enemy on the run.* **(b)** continuously active and moving about: *I've been on the run all day and I'm exhausted.* ○ *on the run from one office to another.* **a (good, etc) run for one's ˈmoney (a)** challenging competition or opposition: *They may win the game, but we'll give them a good run for their money.* **(b)** reward, interest, enjoyment, etc, esp in return for effort: *I feel I've had an excellent run for my money* (ie a rewarding career) *and now I'm happy to retire.*

□ **ˌrun-of-the-ˈmill** *adj* (*often derog*) not special; ordinary: *a ˌrun-of-the-mill deˈtective story.*

Anglo-Saxon runic alphabet

runes

rune /ru:n/ *n* **1** any of the letters in an ancient Germanic alphabet used by the Scandinavians and Anglo-Saxons for carving on wood or in stone. ⇨ illus. **2** similar mark with a mysterious or magic meaning.

▷ **runic** /ˈru:nɪk/ *adj* of runes; written in or inscribed with runes: *a runic calendar, alphabet, sign.*

rung[1] /rʌŋ/ *n* [C] **1** cross-piece forming a step in a ladder. ⇨ illus at LADDER. **2** cross-piece joining the legs of a chair, etc to strengthen it. **3** (*fig*) level or rank in society, one's career, an organization, etc: *start on the lowest/bottom rung of the salary scale* ○ *His promotion has moved him up several rungs on the management ladder.*

rung[2] *pp* of RING[2].

runnel /ˈrʌnl/ *n* (*fml*) small trickle or stream: *The rain ran in shallow runnels alongside the path.*

runner /ˈrʌnə(r)/ *n* **1** person or animal that runs; one taking part in a race: *a long-distance runner* ○ *There are eight runners* (ie horses competing) *in the final race.* **2** messenger, esp for a bank or stockbroker. **3** (esp in compounds) person smuggling the goods stated into or out of an area: *ˈdrug-runners* ○ *ˈgun-runners.* **4** metal or wood strip on which sth slides or moves along: *the runners* (ie blades) *of my ice-skates* ○ *sledge runners.* **5** creeping plant stem that can take root: *strawberry runners.* **6** long narrow strip of embroidered cloth, lace, etc placed on a sideboard, table, etc for ornament or protection.

□ **ˌrunner ˈbean** (also **string bean**) (*Brit*) (*US* **ˈpole bean**) **(a)** type of climbing bean-plant. **(b)** long green pod growing from this.

runner-up /ˌrʌnərˈʌp/ *n* (*pl* **runners-up** /ˌrʌnəzˈʌp/) ~ **(to sb)** person or team finishing second in a race or competition.

running /ˈrʌnɪŋ/ *n* [U] **1** action or sport of running: *take up running* ○ [attrib] *running shoes.* **2** management, maintenance or operation: *the day-to-day running of a shop, business, machine, country* ○ [attrib] *the running costs of a car*, eg of fuel, repairs, insurance. **3** (idm) **in/out of the ˈrunning (for sth)** (*infml*) having some/no chance of succeeding or achieving sth: *be in the running for a management post, a company car.* **make the ˈrunning** (*infml*) set the pace or standard: *Wall Street made Friday's running on the international stock exchange.* ○ *Mike is rather timid with women, so Sue has to make all the running in their relationship.*

▷ **running** *adj* **1** [attrib] performed while running: *a running jump, kick.* **2** [attrib] continuous or uninterrupted: *a running battle for control of the party* ○ *The police kept up a running fire of questions during their interrogation of the suspect.* **3** [pred] (following a number and a *n*) in succession; consecutively: *win three times running* ○ *For the sixth day running, my car wouldn't start.* **4** [attrib] (of water) flowing: *I can hear running water.* ○ *All our rooms have hot and cold running water*, ie from taps. **5** [attrib] (of sores, etc) exuding liquid or pus. **6** (idm) **in running/working order** ⇨ ORDER[1]. **take a running ˈjump (a)** run up to the point where one jumps. **(b)** (*sl*) (used as a command) go away: *I refused to lend him any more money and told him to take a running jump.*

□ **ˈrunning-board** *n* (formerly) foot-board under the doors of a car.

ˌrunning ˈcommentary spoken description of events as they occur, esp by a broadcaster: *From the passenger seat, he kept up a running commentary on her driving.*

ˈrunning dog (*derog*) person, country, etc that willingly serves the interests of another.

ˈrunning knot knot made by tying the end of a rope around another part of itself so that it can slide along, forming an adjustable loop. ⇨ illus at KNOT.

ˈrunning mate 1 (*politics esp US*) candidate for a supporting position in an election, esp for the Vice-Presidency. **2** horse used to set the pace for another in a race.

ˌrunning reˈpairs minor repairs or replacement of parts: *Our photocopier is in continual need of running repairs.*

ˈrunning stitch line of evenly-spaced stitches made by a straight thread passing in and out of the material.

ˌrunning ˈtotal total (eg of costs, expenses) which includes each new item as it occurs.

runny /ˈrʌnɪ/ *adj* (**-ier, -iest**) (*infml*) **1** (*sometimes derog*) more liquid than is usual or expected: *runny jam, sauce, cake-mixture, etc* ○ *Omelettes should be runny* (ie not fully cooked) *in the middle.* **2** (of the nose or eyes) tending to exude mucus: *You've got a runny nose!*

Runnymede /ˈrʌnɪmi:d/ meadow on the bank of the River *Thames near *Windsor, famous as the place near which King *John of England agreed to *Magna Carta.

runt /rʌnt/ *n* **1** undersized animal, esp the smallest and weakest of a litter. **2** (*derog*) insignificant or worthless person.

runway /ˈrʌnweɪ/ *n* prepared surface along which aircraft take off and land.

Runyon /ˈrʌnjən/ Damon (1884-1946), American writer. He was a journalist but is best known for his witty short stories about the New York underworld, written in a highly individual style.

rupee /ru:ˈpi:/ *n* unit of currency in India, Pakistan and certain other countries.

rupture /ˈrʌptʃə(r)/ *n* **1** [C, U] (*fml*) (instance of) breaking apart or bursting: *the rupture of a blood-vessel, seed-pod, membrane.* **2** [C, U] (*fig fml*) (instance of) ending of friendly relations: *deep ruptures within the party.* **3** [C] (*medical*) swelling in the abdomen caused when an organ breaks through the wall of its retaining cavity. Cf HERNIA.

▷ **rupture** *v* **1 (a)** [I, Tn] (cause tissue, an organ, etc to) burst or break: *a ruptured appendix, spleen.* **(b)** [Tn] ~ **oneself** cause such a burst or break to happen to oneself: *He ruptured himself lifting a bookcase.* **2** [I, Tn] (*fml*) (cause a connection, union, etc to) end: *the risk of rupturing East-West relations.*

rural /ˈrʊərəl/ *adj* [esp attrib] of, in or suggesting the countryside: *rural areas, scenes, smells, accents* ○ *rural bus services, MPs, pastimes* ○ *life in rural Britain.* Cf RUSTIC 1, URBAN.

□ **ˌrural ˈdean** = DEAN 2.

ˌrural deˈlivery, ˌrural ˈroute (*US*) delivery of mail in rural areas.

Ruritanian /ˌrʊərɪˈteɪnɪən/ *adj* (of a country or its politics) full of plots and intrigues (as in two melodramatic novels by the English writer Anthony Hope (1863-1933) about an imaginary country in Central Europe called **Ruritania**).

ruse /ru:z/ *n* deceitful way of doing sth or getting sth; trick: *think up a ruse for getting into the cinema without paying* ○ *My ruse failed.*

rush[1] /rʌʃ/ *v* **1** [I, Ipr, Ip, It, Tn·pr, Tn·p, Dn·n, Dn·pr] (cause sb/sth to) go or come with great speed: *Don't rush: take your time.* ○ *Water went rushing through the lock gates.* ○ *The children rushed out of school.* ○ *Don't rush away/off — I haven't finished.* ○ *People rushed to buy the shares.* ○ *Ambulances rushed the injured to hospital.* ○ *Relief supplies were rushed in.* ○ *Please rush me* (ie send me immediately) *your current catalogue.* **2** [I, Ipr, Tn, Tn·pr] ~ **(sb) (into sth/doing sth)** (cause sb to) act hastily: *regret rushed decisions* ○ *rush into marriage* ○ *Don't rush me — this needs thinking about.* ○ *rush sb into signing a contract.* **3** [Tn] attack or capture (sb/sth) by a sudden assault: *rush the enemy's positions, defences, etc* ○ *Fans rushed the stage after the concert.* **4** [Tn, Tn·pr] ~ **sb/sth (for sth)** (*infml*) charge (a customer, etc) a high or exorbitant price: *How much did the garage rush you for those repairs?* **5** (idm) **run/rush sb off his feet** ⇨ FOOT[1]. **rush into ˈprint** publish sth without proper care or consideration. **6** (phr v) **rush sth out** produce sth very quickly: *Editors rushed out a piece on the crash for the late news.* **rush sth through (sth)** cause sth to become official policy, etc very quickly: *rush a bill through Parliament.*

rush[2] /rʌʃ/ *n* **1** [sing] (instance of) rapid headlong movement or swift advance: *The tide comes in with a sudden rush here.* ○ *make a rush for the door* ○ *People were trampled in the headlong rush.* **2** [sing] sudden onset or surge of sth: *a rush of blood to the cheeks* ○ *work in a rush of enthusiasm* ○ *a rush of cold air*, eg as a window is opened. **3** [sing, U] (*infml*) (period of) great activity: *Why all this mad rush?* ○ *the Christmas rush*, ie the period before Christmas when crowds of people go shopping ○ *I'm in a dreadful/tearing rush* (ie hurry) *so I can't stop.* ○ *have a bit of a rush on* ○ [attrib] *a rush job*, ie one done as quickly or as soon as possible. **4** [C] ~ **on/for sth** sudden great demand for goods, etc: *a rush on umbrellas*, eg when there is heavy rain. **5 rushes** [pl] (*infml*) first print of a cinema film before it is cut and edited. **6** (idm) **give sb/get the bum's rush** ⇨ BUM[2].

□ **ˈrush-hour** *n* time each day when traffic is busiest because people are going to or coming from work: *morning/evening rush-hours* ○ [attrib] *I got caught in the rush-hour traffic.*

rush[3] /rʌʃ/ *n* marsh plant with a slender pithy stem which is dried and used for making chair-seats, baskets, etc: [attrib] *rush matting.*

▷ **rushy** *adj* full of rushes.

□ **ˌrush ˈcandle** (also **ˈrush light**) candle made by

dipping the pith of a rush in tallow.

rusk /rʌsk/ *n* type of biscuit or bread baked hard and crisp, esp one used for feeding babies: *ˈteething rusks.*

Ruskin /ˈrʌskɪn/ John (1819-1900), English critic and artist. He championed the work of the *Pre-Raphaelites and *Turner and did much to revive an appreciation of medieval art and architecture. He also gave much of his fortune to social causes and wrote about social justice and education for working people. He was the first Professor of Art at Oxford University; Ruskin College, Oxford, for adult students, is named in his honour.

Russell[1] /ˈrʌsl/ Bertrand, 3rd Earl Russell (1873-1970), British philosopher. He made important contributions to mathematical logic (eg in *Principia Mathematica*, which he wrote with A N *Whitehead) and was one of *Wittgenstein's teachers at Cambridge. He was also a popular writer on matters of social interest and was awarded the Nobel prize for literature in 1950. He was an active campaigner for nuclear disarmament.

Russell[2] /ˈrʌsl/ George William (1867-1935), Irish poet, sometimes writing as 'Æ'. He was a friend of *Yeats and an important figure in the revival of Irish literature, and also wrote on Irish social and cultural matters.

Russell[3] /ˈrʌsl/ Ken (1927-), British film director. He made his name with dramatized television documentaries about the lives of composers and poets (eg Elgar). His later cinema films (eg *Women in Love* and *The Devils*) have often caused controversy because of their sexual frankness and bold visual effects.

russet /ˈrʌsɪt/ *adj* soft reddish-brown: *russet autumn leaves.*

▷ **russet** *n* **1** [U] russet colour. **2** [C] type of rough-skinned apple of this colour.

Russia /ˈrʌʃə/ country in N Asia and E Europe, officially called the Russian Federation; pop approx 148 800 000; official language Russian; capital Moscow; unit of currency rouble (= 100 kopecks). Its name was sometimes used (and may still be understood) to refer to the whole of the former USSR. It is the largest of that group's republics, stretching from the Arctic Circle in the north to the great Asian mountain ranges in the south, and from the Baltic regions in the west to the Pacific in the east. Most of its economic activity and its population is concentrated in the European part west of the Ural Mountains, with the capital and the great cities like St Petersburg (formerly Leningrad). To the east are the plateaus and plains of *Siberia and the mountain ranges of the east coast. Russia is rich in mineral resources including oil, natural gas, iron, gold and other precious metals, but its agricultural system remains inefficient. Boris Yeltsin was elected president of the republic in May 1990. ⇨ map at UNION OF SOVIET SOCIALIST REPUBLICS.

▷ **Russian** /ˈrʌʃn/ *adj* of Russia, its culture, its language or its people: *Russian folklore, dancing.* — *n* **1** [C] person from Russia or, loosely, the former USSR or present CIS. **2** [U] principal language of the former USSR, a Slavonic language related to Czech, Polish, etc. ˌ**Russian rouˈlette** (**a**) act of bravado in which a person holds to his head a revolver of which one (unknown) chamber contains a bullet, and pulls the trigger: *play (at) Russian roulette.* (**b**) (*fig*) any action or situation involving serious and unpredictable risks. ˌ**Russian ˈsalad** salad of vegetables chopped into small pieces and lightly coated with mayonnaise.

Russki /ˈrʌskɪ/ *n, adj* (*dated, derog or joc*) (esp Communist) Russian.

Russo- *comb form* Russian; of Russia or, loosely, the Soviet Union: *the Russo-Japanese war* ○ *Russophiles*, ie people who are friendly to Russia or impressed by Russian achievements.

rust /rʌst/ *n* [U] **1** reddish-brown coating formed on iron or steel by the action of water and air: *badly corroded with rust* ○ [attrib] *rust patches* ○ *rust remover.* **2** reddish-brown: [attrib] *rust colour.* **3** (fungus causing a) plant disease with rust-coloured spots.

▷ **rust** *v* [I, Ip, Tn, Tn·p esp passive] ~ (**sth**) (**away/through**) (cause sth to) be affected with rust: *Brass doesn't rust.* ○ *The hinges had rusted away*, ie been destroyed by rust. ○ *The underneath of the car was badly rusted.*

rusty *adj* (-ier, -iest) **1** affected with rust: *rusty nails.* **2** [esp pred] (*fig*) of a poor quality or standard through lack of practice: *My German is rather rusty.* **3** (of black clothes) having a brownish appearance through age. **rustily** *adv.* **rustiness** *n* [U].

□ ˈ**rust-proof** *adj* (of metal) treated to prevent rusting. — *v* [Tn] treat (metal) this way.

rustic /ˈrʌstɪk/ *adj* [usu attrib] **1** (*approv*) typical of the country or country people: *rustic charm, peace, simplicity* ○ *lead a rustic existence.* Cf RURAL. **2** rough and unrefined: *rustic accents, manners.* **3** made of rough timber or untrimmed branches: *a rustic bench, bridge, fence, etc.*

▷ **rustic** *n* (*esp derog*) peasant or yokel: *country rustics.*

rustically /-klɪ/ *adv.*

rusticity /rʌˈstɪsətɪ/ *n* [U] being typical of the country in appearance or character.

rusticate /ˈrʌstɪkeɪt/ *v* **1** [Tn] (*Brit*) send (a student) away from university temporarily, as a punishment. **2** [I] (*fml*) settle in the country and lead a rural life. ▷ **rustication** /ˌrʌstɪˈkeɪʃn/ *n* [U].

rustle /ˈrʌsl/ *v* **1** [I, Ipr, Tn, Tn·pr] (cause sth to) make a dry light sound, esp by friction or rubbing together: *Her silk dress rustled as she moved.* ○ *Leaves rustled gently in the breeze.* ○ *I wish people wouldn't rustle their programmes during the solos.* **2** [Ipr, Ip] move along making such a sound: *Did you hear something rustling through the bushes?* **3** [Tn] (*US*) steal (cattle or horses that are grazing in the wild). **4** (phr v) **rustle sth/sb up** (*infml*) prepare or provide sth/sb, esp at short notice: *I'll rustle up some eggs and bacon for you.* ○ *I rustled up a few helpers to hand out leaflets.*

▷ **rustle** *n* [sing] rustling sound: *the rustle of banknotes, petticoats.*

rustler /ˈrʌslə(r)/ *n* (*US*) cattle or horse thief.

rustling /ˈrʌslɪŋ/ *n* **1** [C, U] (instance of the) sound made by sth that rustles: *mysterious rustlings at night* ○ *the rustling of dry leaves, sweet-papers* **2** [U] stealing of cattle or horses.

rut[1] /rʌt/ *n* [C] **1** deep track made by a wheel or wheels in soft ground; furrow: *My bike bumped over the ruts.* **2** (idm) **be (stuck) in a ˈrut** have a fixed and boring way of life. **get into/out of a ˈrut** start/stop leading a routine existence: *It's time to get out of the 9 to 5 rut*, ie of the normal working day.

▷ **rut** *v* (-tt-) [Tn esp passive] mark (sth) with ruts: *The lane was rutted with tyre tracks.* ○ *a deeply rutted road.*

rut[2] /rʌt/ *n* (also **the rut**) [U] periodic sexual excitement of a male deer, goat, ram, etc: *stags fight during the rut.*

▷ **rut** *v* (-tt-) [I] be affected by this: *a rutting stag*

rutabaga /ˌru:təˈbeɪgə/ *n* [C, U] (*US*) = SWEDE.

Ruth[1] /ru:θ/ book of the Old Testament, telling the story of Ruth, a widow who remarries and gives birth to the father of *Jesse, an ancestor of *Jesus. ⇨ App 5.

Ruth[2] /ru:θ/ George 'Babe' (1895-1948), American baseball player. He is regarded as one of the greatest batters of all time, and was a popular national figure during his career.

Rutherford /ˈrʌðəfəd/ Sir Ernest, 1st Baron Rutherford of Nelson (1871-1937), British nuclear physicist born in New Zealand. He established the nature of alpha and beta particles, set out the law of radioactive decay, and explained the structure of the atom. He used radiation to turn nitrogen atoms into oxygen and produced the first artificial element. He was awarded the Nobel prize for chemistry in 1908.

ruthless /ˈru:θlɪs/ *adj* **1** having or showing no pity or compassion; cruel: *show ruthless disregard for other people's feelings* ○ *a ruthless dictator* ○ *be utterly ruthless in one's determination to succeed.* **2** never slackening or stopping; unremitting: *set off at a ruthless pace* ○ *ruthless schedules, demands.* ▷ **ruthlessly** *adv*: *be ruthlessly efficient.* **ruthlessness** *n* [U]: *The terrorists' ruthlessness shocked the population.*

RV /ˌɑ: ˈvi:/ *abbr* Revised Version (of the Bible).

Rwanda /rʊˈændə/ country of central Africa; pop approx 6 755 000; official languages Rwanda and French; capital Kigali; unit of currency franc. It lies on a high plateau near the equator. The economy is mainly agricultural, producing sweet potatoes, cassava and beans, and some coffee, tea and bananas for export. ⇨ map at TANZANIA.

▷ **Rwanda** *n* [U] the Bantu language of Rwanda. **Rwandan** /-ən/ *n, adj.*

-ry ⇨ -ERY.

Ryder Cup /ˌraɪdə ˈkʌp/ **the Ryder Cup** professional golf tournament held every two years between teams of American and European players.

rye /raɪ/ *n* **1** [U] (grain of a) type of cereal plant used for making flour or as food for cattle: [attrib] *rye bread.* ⇨ illus at CEREAL. **2** [C, U] (also **rye whisky**) (*esp US*) (glass of) whisky made from rye.

□ ˈ**rye-grass** *n* [U] type of coarse grass used as cattle food and mixed with finer grasses for use in lawns.

S, s

S, s /es/ *n* (*pl* **S's, s's** /ˈesɪz/) the nineteenth letter of the English alphabet: *'Say' begins with (an) 'S'.*
□ **ˈS-bend** *n* bend in a road shaped like an S.
S *abbr* **1** (*pl* **SS**) Saint. Cf ST 1. **2** (esp on clothing) small (size). **3** (*US* also **So**) south(ern): *S Yorkshire.*
S *symb* sulphur.
s *abbr* **1** (in former British currency) shilling(s). **2** (esp on forms) single (status).
SA *abbr* **1** (*religion*) Salvation Army. **2** /ˌes ˈeɪ/ (*infml*) sex appeal. **3** South Africa.
Sabbatarian /ˌsæbəˈteərɪən/ *n* Christian who believes that on the sabbath one should go to church and not work, take part in sports, etc. ▷ **Sabbatarian** *adj* [attrib]: *Sabbatarian beliefs, principles.*
sabbath /ˈsæbəθ/ *n* **the sabbath** day of the week intended for rest and worship of God (Saturday for Jews and Sunday for Christians): *keep/break the sabbath,* ie (not) work or play on the sabbath ○ [attrib] *the sabbath day.*
sabbatical /səˈbætɪkl/ *adj* **1** [attrib] (of leave) given at intervals to academics for travel, study, etc: *a sabbatical term, year, etc.* **2** (*fml*) of or like the sabbath.
▷ **sabbatical** *n* [C, U] (period of) sabbatical leave: *a one-year sabbatical* ○ *be on sabbatical.*
sable /ˈseɪbl/ *n* **1** [C] small Arctic mammal, valued for its dark fur. **2** [U] fur of this mammal: [attrib] *a sable coat, stole, etc.*
▷ **sable** *adj* [usu attrib] (*fml*) black; dark; gloomy.
sabot /ˈsæbəʊ; *US* sæˈbəʊ/ *n* shoe hollowed out of a single piece of wood, or having a wooden sole.
sabotage /ˈsæbətɑːʒ/ *n* [U] damage done secretly to prevent an enemy, a competitor, etc succeeding, esp by destroying his weapons or equipment and spoiling his plans: *Was the fire an accident or (an act of) sabotage?*
▷ **sabotage** *v* [Tn] secretly damage, destroy or spoil (sth): *sabotage a missile, a ship, an engine, etc* ○ *sabotage sb's plans, business* ○ *They tried to sabotage my party by getting drunk.*
saboteur /ˌsæbəˈtɜː(r)/ *n* person who commits sabotage.
sabra /ˈsɑːbrə/ *n* (*esp US*) Israeli Jew born in Israel.
sabre (*US* **saber**) /ˈseɪbə(r)/ *n* **1** heavy cavalry sword with a curved blade. ⇨ illus at SWORD. **2** light sword with a tapering blade, used in fencing (FENCE[2]). Cf ÉPÉE, FOIL[3].
□ **ˈsabre-rattling** *n* [U] attempts to frighten sb by threatening to attack or punish him: *Her speech is mere sabre-rattling,* ie She will not carry out her threats. ○ [attrib] *sabre-rattling tactics.*
ˌsabre-toothed ˈtiger tiger, now extinct, having (usu two) sabre-like teeth.
SAC *abbr* (*US*) Strategic Air Command.
sac /sæk/ *n* bag-like part of an animal or plant.
saccharide /ˈsækəraɪd/ *n* [U] (*chemistry*) any of a group of sweet-tasting carbohydrates found esp in plants, eg glucose.
saccharin /ˈsækərɪn/ *n* [U] very sweet substance used as a substitute for sugar.
▷ **saccharine** /-riːn/ *adj* (*esp derog*) very sweet; too sweet: *a saccharine taste* ○ (*fig*) *a saccharine smile* ○ *I found the film far too saccharine.*
sacerdotal /ˌsæsəˈdəʊtl/ *adj* (*fml*) **1** of a priest or priests. **2** (of a doctrine, etc) claiming supernatural powers for ordained priests. ▷ **sacerdotalism** /-təlɪzəm/ *n* [U].
sachet /ˈsæʃeɪ; *US* sæˈʃeɪ/ *n* **1** sealed plastic or paper pack containing a small amount of a product: *a sachet of sugar, sauce, shampoo, etc.* **2** small bag containing a sweet-smelling substance, placed among clothes, etc to scent them.
sack[1] /sæk/ *n* **1** (contents of) any large bag of strong material used for storing and carrying eg cement, coal, flour, potatoes: *The sack split and the rice poured out.* **2** (*US*) (contents of) any bag: *a sack of candies* ○ *two sacks of groceries.* **3** (also **ˈsack dress**) short loose straight dress. **4** (idm) **hit the hay/sack** ⇨ HIT[1].
▷ **sackful** /-fʊl/ *n* quantity held by a sack: *two sackfuls of flour.*
sacking *n* [U] cloth, eg coarse flax or hemp, used for making sacks.
□ **ˈsackcloth** *n* [U] **1** sacking. **2** (idm) **ˌsackcloth and ˈashes** signs of repentance or mourning.
ˈsack-race *n* race in which competitors put both legs in a sack and move forward by jumping.
sack[2] /sæk/ *v* [Tn] (*infml esp Brit*) dismiss (sb) from a job; fire: *be sacked for incompetence.*
▷ **the sack** *n* [sing] dismissal from a job: *give sb/get the sack* ○ *It's the sack for you!* ie You are going to be dismissed.
sack[3] /sæk/ *v* [Tn] steal or destroy property in (a captured town, etc).
▷ **the sack** *n* [sing] act or process of sacking a town, etc: *the sack of Troy.*
sack[4] /sæk/ *n* [U] (*arch*) dry white wine made in Spain or the Canary Islands.
sackbut /ˈsækbʌt/ *n* early form of trombone.
sacrament /ˈsækrəmənt/ *n* **1** [C] ritual act in the Roman Catholic, Anglican and other Christian Churches through which those who take part believe they receive a special grace from God: *the sacraments of baptism, confirmation, confession, etc.* **2 the ˈsacrament** [sing] (also **the ˌBlessed ˈSacrament, the ˌHoly ˈSacrament**) [sing] the consecrated bread and wine of the Eucharist; Holy Communion: *receive the sacrament.*
▷ **sacramental** /ˌsækrəˈmentl/ *adj* [esp attrib] of or connected with the sacraments: *sacramental wine.*
sacred /ˈseɪkrɪd/ *adj* **1** connected with or dedicated to God or a god; connected with religion: *a sacred rite, place, image* ○ *a sacred building,* eg a church, mosque, synagogue or temple ○ *sacred music,* ie for use in religious services ○ *sacred writings,* eg the Koran, the Bible. **2** ~ **(to sb)** regarded with great respect or reverence: *In India the cow is a sacred animal.* ○ *Her marriage is sacred to her.* ○ (*joc*) *They've changed the time of the news — is nothing sacred?* **3** (*fml*) (of an obligation, etc) regarded as very important; solemn: *a sacred promise, task* ○ *hold a promise sacred* ○ *regard sth as a sacred duty.* **4** ~ **to sb/sth** (phrase seen on tombstones and monuments to the dead) dedicated to sb/sth: *sacred to the memory of....* **5** (idm) **a sacred ˈcow** an idea, institution, etc that many think should not be criticized: *Let's not make a sacred cow of the monarchy.* ▷ **sacredly** *adv.* **sacredness** *n* [U].
□ **the ˌSacred ˈHeart** the heart of *Jesus Christ regarded as a symbol of his love for humanity, and as an object of worship.
sacrifice /ˈsækrɪfaɪs/ *n* **1** ~ **(to sb)** **(a)** [U] offering of sth valuable, often a slaughtered animal, to a god: *the sacrifice of an ox to Jupiter.* **(b)** [C] such an offering; thing offered in this way: *kill a sheep as a sacrifice.* **2** **(a)** [U] giving up of sth, usu in return for sth more important or valuable: *Getting rich isn't worth the sacrifice of your principles.* ○ *He became a top sportsman at some sacrifice to himself,* ie by training very hard, giving up many pleasures, etc. **(b)** [C] thing given up in this way: *Her parents made many sacrifices so that she could go to university.*
▷ **sacrifice** *v* **1** [Ipr, Tn, Tn·pr] ~ **to sb;** ~ **sth (to sb)** make a sacrifice(1) of (sth) to sb: *sacrifice to idols* ○ *sacrifice a lamb to the gods.* **2** [Tn, Tn·pr] ~ **sth (to sb/sth)** give up sth as a sacrifice(2): *She sacrificed her career to marry him.* ○ *The car's designers have sacrificed comfort to economy,* ie have made the car less comfortable in order to sell it at a low price. ○ *I'm not sacrificing my day off just to go shopping with Jane.*
sacrificial /ˌsækrɪˈfɪʃl/ *adj* [usu attrib] of or like a sacrifice. **sacrificially** /-ʃəlɪ/ *adv.*
sacrilege /ˈsækrɪlɪdʒ/ *n* [C usu *sing* U] (act of) treating a sacred thing or place with disrespect: *It is (a) sacrilege to steal a crucifix from an altar.* ○ (*fig*) *She regarded the damage done to the painting as sacrilege.* ▷ **sacrilegious** /ˌsækrɪˈlɪdʒəs/ *adj.* **sacrilegiously** *adv.*
sacristan /ˈsækrɪstən/ *n* person who looks after the contents of a church and prepares the altar for services.
sacristy /ˈsækrɪstɪ/ *n* room in a church where a priest puts on his vestments and where the vestments, candles, etc are kept.
sacrosanct /ˈsækrəʊsæŋkt/ *adj* (*often ironic*) considered too important to be changed, argued about, etc: *You can't cut spending on defence — that's sacrosanct!*
sacrum /ˈseɪkrəm/ *n* (*pl* **sacra** /-krə/ or ~**s**) (*anatomy*) triangular bone that forms the back of the pelvis.
sad /sæd/ *adj* (**-dder, -ddest**) **1** showing or causing sorrow; unhappy: *a sad look, event, story* ○ *John is sad because his dog has died.* ○ *I'm sad you're leaving.* ○ *It was a sad day for us all when the school closed down.* ○ *Why is she looking so sad?* **2** [attrib] worthy of blame or criticism; bad: *a sad state of affairs* ○ *a sad case of cruelty.* **3** making one feel pity or regret: *This once beautiful ship is in a sad condition now.* **4** (of bread, cakes, etc) heavy, having failed to rise[2](10) properly. **5** (idm) **ˌsadder but ˈwiser** having learnt sth important from a disappointing mistake or failure: *The divorce left him a sadder but a wiser man.* **sad to say** (used esp at the beginning of a sentence) unfortunately: *Sad to say, she hasn't given us permission to do it.*
▷ **sadden** /ˈsædn/ *v* [I, Tn] (cause sb to) become sad: *He saddened at the memory of her death.* ○ *The bad news saddened us.*
sadly *adv* **1** in a sad manner: *She looked at him sadly.* **2** regrettably: *a sadly neglected garden.* **3** unfortunately: *Sadly, we have no more money.* ⇨ Usage at HOPEFUL.
sadness *n* **1** [U] being sad. **2** [C usu *pl*] thing that makes one sad: *One of the many sadnesses in his life was that he never had children.*
□ **ˈsad sack** (*US infml*) stupid and incompetent person.
saddle /ˈsædl/ *n* **1** **(a)** seat, often of leather, for a rider on a horse, donkey, etc or on a bicycle or motor cycle. ⇨ illus at BICYCLE. **(b)** part of a horse's back on which this is placed. **2** ridge of high land rising to high points at each end. ⇨ illus at MOUNTAIN. **3** joint of meat from the back of an animal, together with part of the backbone and ribs: *a saddle of lamb, venison, beef, etc.* **4** (idm) **in the ˈsaddle** **(a)** on horseback: *spend hours in the saddle.* **(b)** (*fig*) in a position of control: *The director hopes to remain in the saddle* (ie in his job) *for a few more years.*
▷ **saddle** *v* **1** [Ip, Tn, Tn·p] ~ **up;** ~ **sth (up)** put a saddle on (a horse): *saddle up and ride off* ○ *saddle one's pony (up).* **2** (phr v) **saddle sb with sth** give sb an unwelcome responsibility, task, etc: *I've been saddled with the job of organizing the conference.* ○ *The boss saddled her with all the most difficult customers.*
saddler /ˈsædlə(r)/ *n* maker of saddles and leather goods for horses. **saddlery** /ˈsædlərɪ/ *n* **1** [U] **(a)** goods made or sold by a saddler. **(b)** the art of making these. **2** [C] saddler's business.

□ ˈ**saddleback** *n* **1** roof or hill that has a dipped shape at the top. **2** type of black pig with a white stripe across its back.
ˈ**saddle-bag** *n* **1** either of a pair of bags laid over the back of a horse or donkey. **2** bag attached to the back of a bicycle saddle.
ˈ**saddle-sore** *adj* (of a rider) sore and stiff after riding.
ˈ**saddle stitching** long running-stitch made with thick thread, used decoratively.

Sadducee /ˈsædjʊsiː; *US* ˈsædʒəsiː/ *n* member of a Jewish sect at the time of *Christ that followed the Old Testament law strictly and did not believe in the resurrection of the dead. Cf PHARISEE.

sadhu /ˈsɑːduː/ *n* Hindu holy man who lives an ascetic life.

sadism /ˈseɪdɪzəm/ *n* [U] (**a**) enjoyment of watching or inflicting cruelty: *sadism in the treatment of prisoners.* (**b**) getting sexual pleasure from this. Cf MASOCHISM.
▷ **sadist** /ˈseɪdɪst/ person who practises sadism. **sadistic** /səˈdɪstɪk/ *adj* of or showing sadism: *sadistic laughter* ○ *a sadistic teacher.* **sadistically** /-klɪ/ *adv.*

Sadler's Wells /ˌsædləz ˈwelz/ theatre in NE London, built on the site of a medicinal well discovered by Thomas Sadler in 1683. It specialized in opera and ballet, and in the 1930s under Lilian *Baylis it became famous as the home of the companies that later became the Royal Ballet and the English National Opera. ⇨ article at PERFORMING ARTS.

sado-masochism /ˌseɪdəʊˈmæsəkɪzəm/ *n* [U] combination of sadism and masochism in one person, each type of behaviour being displayed at different times. ▷ **sado-masochist** /ˌseɪdəʊˈmæsəkɪst/ *adj, n.*

sae /ˌes eɪ ˈiː/ *abbr* stamped addressed envelope: *enclose sae for reply.*

safari /səˈfɑːrɪ/ *n* (*pl* **-ris**) [U, C] **1** hunting expedition or overland journey, esp in E or Central Africa: *on safari* ○ *return from (a) safari.* **2** similar expedition organized as a holiday tour.
□ **saˈfari park** park where wild animals are kept in the open for visitors to see from their cars as they drive around.
saˈfari suit casual suit in linen or a similar fabric.

safe[1] /seɪf/ *adj* (**-r, -st**) **1** [pred] ~ (**from sth/sb**) protected from danger and harm; secure: *You'll be safe here.* ○ *safe from attack/attackers.* **2** [pred] not or unlikely to be damaged, hurt, lost, etc: *The missing child was found safe and well.* ○ *She got back safe from her adventure.* ○ *The plane crashed but the crew are safe.* ○ *Will the car be safe outside?* ○ *Your secret is safe with me,* ie I will not tell it to anyone. **3** not likely to cause or lead to damage, injury, loss, etc: *a safe car, speed, road* ○ *safer methods of testing drugs* ○ *Is that ladder safe?* ○ *It's not safe to go out at night.* ○ *Are the toys safe for small children?* ○ *a safe investment,* ie that will not lose money ○ *Put it in a safe place,* ie where it will not be stolen, lost, etc. **4** (**a**) [usu attrib] (of a person) unlikely to do dangerous things; cautious: *a safe driver, worker, goalkeeper.* (**b**) (*often derog*) showing a cautious attitude: *a safe choice* ○ *They appointed a safe person as the new manager,* eg one unlikely to make changes, offend people, etc. **5** (idm) **better safe than sorry** ⇨ BETTER[2]. **for safe ˈkeeping** to be kept safely, protected, etc: *Before the game I gave my watch to my wife for safe keeping.* **in (sb's) safe ˈkeeping** being kept safely, protected, etc (by sb): *Can I leave the children in your safe keeping?* **it is safe to say (that...)** it is almost certainly true: *It is safe to say that the population will continue to grow at the same rate as before.* **on the ˈsafe side** taking no risks: *Although the sun was shining, I took an umbrella (just) to be on the safe side.* **play (it) ˈsafe** carefully avoid risks: *The bus might be early, so we'd better play safe and leave now.* **ˌsafe and ˈsound** unharmed: *The rescuers brought the climbers back safe and sound.* **(as) safe as ˈhouses** very safe: *If you fix the brakes the car will be as safe as houses.* **a safe ˈbet** thing that is certain to be successful: *I'm wearing black for the party — it's always a safe bet.* ▷ **safely** *adv.* **safeness** *n* [U]: *a feeling of safeness.*
□ ˌ**safe ˈconduct** (document granting) freedom from the danger of attack, arrest, etc when passing through an area: *The robbers wanted safe conduct to the airport for themselves and their hostages.*
ˈ**safe deposit** (*US* ˌ**safe deˈposit**) building containing strong-rooms and safes which people may rent separately for storing valuables. **safe-deposit box** small safe in such a building.
ˈ**safe house** house used by criminals, secret agents, etc, where sb can be kept without being discovered or disturbed.
the ˈsafe period time just before and during a woman's period when sexual intercourse is unlikely to make her pregnant.
ˌ**safe ˈseat** (*Brit*) Parliamentary seat which a candidate for a particular party cannot lose.
ˌ**safe ˈsex** sexual intercourse for which precautions have been taken to reduce the risk of spreading sexually transmitted diseases, eg by the use of a condom.

safe[2] /seɪf/ *n* strong lockable box, cabinet, etc for storing valuables.
□ ˈ**safe-breaker** (*Brit*) (also *esp US* ˈ**safe-cracker**) *n* person who breaks into safes to steal valuables.

safeguard /ˈseɪfgɑːd/ *n* ~ (**against sb/sth**) thing that serves as a protection from harm, risk or danger: *We make copies of our computer disks as a safeguard against accidents.* ○ *We will introduce legal safeguards against fraud.*
▷ **safeguard** *v* [Tn, Tn·pr] ~ **sb/sth (against sb/sth)** protect or guard sb/sth: *We have found a way of safeguarding our money.* ○ *a high fence that safeguards (the house) against intruders* ○ *new ways of safeguarding personal data,* ie so that it will remain private.

safety /ˈseɪftɪ/ *n* [U] **1** being safe; not being dangerous or in danger: *I'm worried about the safety of the children,* ie I'm afraid something may happen to them. ○ *I'm worried about the safety of the product,* ie I'm afraid it may be dangerous. ○ *We reached the safety of the river bank,* ie a place where we would be safe. ○ *We're keeping you here for your own safety.* ○ *road safety,* ie stopping accidents on the roads ○ [attrib] *safety precautions* ○ *a safety harness, bolt.* **2** (idm) ˌ**safety ˈfirst** (*saying*) ie safety is the most important thing. **there's ˌsafety in ˈnumbers** (*saying*) being in a group makes one feel more confident: *We decided to go to see the boss together; there's safety in numbers.*
□ ˈ**safety-belt** *n* **1** = SEAT-BELT (SEAT). **2** strap securing a person, eg sb working on a high building.
ˈ**safety-catch** *n* device that prevents the dangerous or accidental operation of a machine, etc, esp one that stops a gun being fired accidentally: *Is the safety-catch on?*
ˈ**safety curtain** fireproof curtain that can be lowered between the stage and the auditorium of a theatre.
ˈ**safety glass** glass that does not shatter or splinter when broken.
ˈ**safety island** (also ˈ**safety zone**) (*US*) = TRAFFIC ISLAND (TRAFFIC).
ˈ**safety lamp** miner's lamp in which the flame is protected so that it will not ignite dangerous gases.
ˈ**safety match** match that will only ignite when rubbed against a special surface, eg on the side of the matchbox.
ˈ**safety net** **1** net placed to catch an acrobat, etc if he should fall. **2** (*fig*) arrangement that helps to prevent disaster if sth goes wrong: *If I lose my job, I've got no safety net.*
ˈ**safety-pin** *n* pin like a brooch, with the point bent back towards the head and covered by a guard when closed.
ˈ**safety razor** razor with a guard to prevent the blade cutting the skin.
ˈ**safety-valve** *n* **1** valve that releases pressure in a steam boiler, etc when it becomes too great. ⇨ illus at PAN. **2** (*fig*) way of releasing feelings of anger, resentment, etc harmlessly: *My hobby is a good safety-valve for the tension that builds up at work.*

saffron /ˈsæfrən/ *n* [U] (colour of the) bright orange strands obtained from the flowers of the autumn crocus, used in cooking. ▷ **saffron** *adj*: *saffron robes.*

sag /sæg/ *v* (**-gg-**) [I] **1** sink or curve down in the middle under weight or pressure: *a sagging roof* ○ *The tent began to sag as the canvas became wet.* **2** hang loosely or unevenly: *old torn curtains sagging at one end* ○ *Your skin starts to sag as you get older.*
▷ **sag** *n* [U, sing] extent to which sth sags; sagging: *too much sag in the mattress* ○ *a sag in the seat of the chair.*

saga /ˈsɑːgə/ *n* **1** long story of heroic deeds, esp of Icelandic or Norwegian heroes. **2** story of a long series of events or adventures, esp one involving several generations of people: *The Forsyte Saga* ○ *His biography is a saga of scientific research.* ○ (*joc*) *the latest episode in her house-hunting saga.*

sagacious /səˈgeɪʃəs/ *adj* (*fml*) showing wisdom and good judgement: *a sagacious person, remark, decision.*
▷ **sagaciously** *adv.*
sagacity /səˈgæsətɪ/ *n* [U] (*fml*) quality of being sagacious; wisdom and good judgement: *Sagacity, unlike cleverness, may increase with age.*

sage[1] /seɪdʒ/ *n* (*fml*) very wise man: *consult the sages of the tribe.*
▷ **sage** *adj* [usu attrib] (*fml often ironic*) wise or wise-looking: *a sage judge, priest, ruler, etc* ○ *in the sage opinion of experienced journalists.*
sagely *adv.*

sage[2] /seɪdʒ/ *n* [U] herb with fragrant greyish-green leaves used to flavour food: *sage and onion stuffing,* ie used to stuff a goose, duck, etc.
□ ˈ**sage-brush** *n* [U] plant with a fragrance like sage growing in the US.

Sagittarius /ˌsædʒɪˈteərɪəs/ *n* **1** [U] the ninth sign of the zodiac, the Archer. **2** [C] person born under the influence of this sign. ⇨ illus at ZODIAC. ▷ **Sagittarian** /-ˈteərɪən/ *n, adj.* ⇨ Usage at ZODIAC.

sago /ˈseɪgəʊ/ *n* [U] starchy food in the form of hard white grains, used in puddings, obtained from the pith of a type of palm-tree (the **sago-palm**).

Sahara /səˈhɑːrə/ desert in North Africa, the largest in the world, covering 9 065 000 sq km (3 500 000 sq miles) from the Atlantic to the Red Sea. In recent years its extent has steadily increased to the south. ⇨ map at ALGERIA. ▷ **Saharan** *adj.*

sahib /sɑːb, ˈsɑːɪb/ *n* (often used in India, formerly to address or refer to a) male European, usu with some social or official status.

said /sed/ **1** *pt, pp* of SAY. **2** *adj* [attrib] (*fml*) = AFOREMENTIONED.

sail[1] /seɪl/ *n* **1** (**a**) [C] (often in compounds) sheet of canvas spread to catch the wind and drive a ship or boat along: *hoist/lower the sails* ○ *the ˈforesail* ○ *the ˈmainsail.* (**b**) [U] sails; propulsion by means of sails: *put on more sail* ○ *take in sail* ○ *the age of sail* ie when ships all used sails. **2** [sing] (**a**) voyage or excursion on water for pleasure: *go for a sail.* (**b**) voyage of a specified length: *a three-day sail to get to Brest* ○ *How many days' sail is it from Hull to Oslo?* **3** [C] (*pl* unchanged) (*nautical*) ship: *a fleet of twenty sail* ○ *There wasn't a sail in sight.* **4** [C] set of slats attached to the arm of a windmill to catch the wind. ⇨ illus at WINDMILL. **5** (idm) **crowd on sail** ⇨ CROWD[2]. **in full sail** ⇨ FULL. **set sail (from/to/for...)** begin a voyage: *We set sail (for France) at high tide.* **take the wind out of sb's sails** ⇨ WIND[1]. **under ˈsail** (moving) with sails spread: *The yacht wasn't under sail because the wind wasn't strong enough.*
□ ˈ**sailboard** (also **windsurfer**) *n* type of large surfboard with a movable sail attached. ˈ**sailboarding** *n* (also **windsurfing**) [U] sport of riding on a sailboard.
ˈ**sailboat** *n* (*US*) boat driven by sails.
ˈ**sailcloth** *n* [U] canvas for sails.
ˈ**sailplane** *n* glider designed to remain in the air for long periods.

sail[2] /seɪl/ *v* **1** (**a**) [Ipr, Ip] travel on water in a ship, yacht, etc using sails or engine power; move forward on ice, a sandy beach, etc in a wheeled vehicle with sails: *sail up/along the coast* ○ *sail into* *the harbour* ○ *an oil tanker sailing by.* (b) [I] (usu **go sailing**) travel on water in a boat with sails, esp as a sport. ⇨ Usage at TRAVEL. **2** [I, Ipr] ~ **(from ...) (for/to ...)** (of a ship or the crew and passengers) begin a voyage: *When does the ship sail?* ○ *He has sailed (from Southampton) for New York.* **3** [Tn] travel by ship across or on (a sea, an ocean, etc): *sail the Aegean in a cruiser.* **4** [I, Tn, Tn·pr, Tn·p] (be able to) control (a ship or boat): *Do you sail?* ○ *She sails her own yacht.* ○ *He sailed the boat between the islands.* **5** (idm) **run/sail before the wind** ⇨ WIND[1]. **sail close/near to the ˈwind** behave in a way that is dangerous or nearly illegal: *He never actually tells lies, but he often sails pretty close to the wind.* **6** (phr v) **sail across, into, past, etc sb/sth** move in a smooth or very confident way in the direction specified: *clouds sailing across the sky* ○ *The manager sailed into the room.* ○ *She sailed past (me), ignoring me completely.* **sail in** enter an argument or dispute energetically: *Ann then sailed in with a furious attack on the chairman.* **sail into sb** attack sb in words: *He sailed into the witness, accusing him of lying.* **sail through (sth)** come through (an examination, a test, etc) without difficulty: *She sailed through her finals.*

▷ **sailing** *n* **1** [U] travelling in a yacht, dinghy, etc, esp as a sport: *I love sailing.* ○ [attrib] *a sailing club, dinghy.* **2** [C] voyage made regularly; departure of a ship on a voyage: *three sailings a day from here to Calais.* **3** (idm) **plain sailing** ⇨ PLAIN[1]. **ˈsailing-boat, ˈsailing-ship** *ns* boat or ship that uses sails. ⇨ illus at DINGHY.

sailor /ˈseɪlə(r)/ *n* **1** member of a ship's crew, esp one below the rank of officer; seaman. **2** (idm) **a good/bad ˈsailor** person who seldom/often becomes seasick in rough weather.

□ **ˈsailor hat** straw hat with a flat top and straight brim.

ˈsailor suit suit for a child made in the style of a sailor's uniform.

sainfoin /ˈsænfɔɪn/ *n* [U] plant with pink flowers, used for feeding cattle, horses, etc.

Sainsbury's /ˈseɪnzbrɪz/ (branch of a) large chain of British supermarkets, originally large traditional grocer's shops, but now also selling a wide range of goods for the home.

saint /seɪnt *or, in British use, before names,* snt/ *n* **1** (a) (*abbr* **St**) person who has been declared by the Christian Church to have deserved veneration through holy living, performing miracles, etc: *the gospel of St John* ○ *St Andrew's Road.* (b) holy person. **2** (usu *pl*) person who has died and is in heaven: *in the company of the saints.* **3** unselfish or patient person: *You must be a saint to be able to stand his temper!*

▷ **sainted** *adj* [usu attrib] (*dated or joc*) declared to be or regarded as a saint: *My sainted aunt!* ie as an exclamation expressing surprise.

sainthood *n* [U].

saintly *adj* (**-ier, -iest**) of or like a saint; very holy or good: *a saintly way of life* ○ *a saintly expression on her face.* **saintliness** *n* [U].

□ **Saint ˈBernard** (often **St Bernard**) breed of large dog with a long coat, originally bred in the Alps to rescue travellers lost in snow.

Saint ˌElmo's ˈfire (often **St Elmo's fire**) electrical discharge sometimes seen around a ship or an aircraft during a storm.

the Saint ˈLeger /ˈledʒə(r)/ (often **the St Leger**) race held every year at Doncaster, S Yorkshire, England, for 3-year-old horses.

ˈsaint's day day of the year when a saint is celebrated, and on which (in some countries) people who are named after that saint also have celebrations.

Saint ˈSwithun's Day (often **St Swithun's Day**) the feast of St Swithun, July 15. According to tradition in Britain, if it rains on this day, rain will continue to fall for forty days.

Saint ˈValentine's Day (often **St Valentine's Day**) February 14, when people traditionally receive anonymous greetings cards from those who are or who pretend to be in love with them. Loving messages are also printed in the personal columns of many newspapers.

Saint Vitus's dance /ˈvaɪtəs/ (often **St Vitus's dance**) disease, esp of children, marked by involuntary jerking movements of the shoulders, hips and face: (*fig*) *The child has St Vitus's dance,* ie fidgets a lot.

Saint Helena (often **St Helena**) /snt hɪˈliːnə/ isolated island in the southern Atlantic, famous as the place where *Napoleon was exiled and died; pop approx 5 000; official language English; capital Jamestown. It is a British dependency and the economy is based on the service sector, esp harbour fees.

Saint James's Palace (often **St James's Palace**) /snt ˌdʒeɪmzɪz ˈpælɪs; *US* ˌseɪnt-/ palace in Pall Mall, London, built by *Henry VIII and the chief residence of the monarch until Queen *Victoria moved into *Buckingham Palace. Foreign ambassadors are still appointed to **the Court of Saint James**.

Saint John Ambulance Brigade (often **St John Ambulance Brigade**) /snt ˌdʒɒn ˈæmbjʊləns brɪˈgeɪd; *US* ˌseɪnt/ British organization made up of volunteers who provide first aid at public events, eg concerts or football matches, and who also run nursing homes and welfare services.

Saint Kitts and Nevis /snt ˌkɪts ən ˈniːvɪs; *US* ˌseɪnt/ (often **St Kitts and Nevis**) state formed by two islands in the Caribbean, a member of the Commonwealth; pop approx 49 000; official language English; capital Basseterre (on St Kitts); unit of currency dollar (= 100 cents). It became independent in 1983, but is associated with Britain, which deals with its defence and foreign policy. The economy is based on the export of sugar cane, tourism and a number of US industries present on the islands. ⇨ map at CARIBBEAN.

Saint Lawrence /snt ˈlɒrəns; *US* ˌseɪnt ˈlɔːrəns/ (often **St Lawrence**) river of North America flowing from Lake Ontario to the Atlantic Ocean. The St Lawrence Seaway includes canalized sections which allow ships to sail along the entire length of the river.

Saint Lucia /snt ˈluːʃə; *US* ˌseɪnt/ (often **St Lucia**) island state in the Caribbean, a member of the Commonwealth; pop approx 133 000; official language English; capital Castries; unit of currency dollar (= 100 cents). The economy is based on tourism and agriculture, the main export crops being bananas and coconuts. ⇨ map at CARIBBEAN.

Saint Paul's Cathedral /snt ˌpɔːlz kəθiːdrəl; *US* ˌseɪnt/ (often **St Paul's**) the Anglican cathedral of London, designed by Christopher *Wren after the *Great Fire of London. It contains the tombs and monuments of many famous British people and is famous for its choir. ⇨ illus at WREN.

Saint Peter's Basilica /snt ˌpiːtəz bəˈzɪlɪkə; *US* ˌseɪnt/ (often **St Peter's**) church in the Vatican City, Rome. Although it is not the cathedral of the city, it is the church where the great ceremonies involving the pope take place. Many great artists, including *Michelangelo, *Raphael and *Bernini, contributed to its design.

Saint-Saëns /ˈsænsɑːns/ Camille (1835-1921), French composer. He produced a vast quantity of music, esp for the organ, but he is now best remembered for only a few works like his third symphony and *The Carnival of the Animals.*

Saint Sophia /snt səˈfiːə; *US* seɪnt səˈfaɪə/ Byzantine building in Istanbul, Turkey. It was originally built as a church to the 'Holy Wisdom' of God, with a remarkable wide shallow dome. It became a mosque in 1453 and is now a museum.

Saint Trinian's /snt ˈtrɪnɪənz; *US* ˌseɪnt/ (often **St Trinians**) private school for girls invented by the British cartoonist Ronald Searle (1920-). The pupils are famous for their very bad behaviour and unattractive appearance.

Saint Vincent and the Grenadines /snt ˈvɪnsnt; *US* ˌseɪnt/ state in the Caribbean, part of the Windward Islands, consisting of the island of St Vincent and the Grenadines; pop approx 108 000; official language English; capital Kingstown; unit of currency dollar (= 100 cents). It is a member of the Commonwealth. The economy is based on tourism and agriculture, the main export crops being bananas and coconuts. ⇨ map at CARIBBEAN.

sake[1] /seɪk/ *n* (idm) **for God's, goodness', Heaven's, pity's, etc sake** (used as an *interj* before or after a command or request, or to express irritation): *For God's sake, stop that whining!* ○ *For goodness' sake! How can you be so stupid?* **for old times' sake** ⇨ OLD. **for the sake of argument** as the basis of a discussion: *Let's assume, for the sake of argument, that inflation will remain at 5% per year for two years.* **for the sake of sb/sth; for sb's/sth's sake** in order to help sb/sth or because one likes sb/sth: *do sth for the sake of one's family* ○ *I'll help you for your sister's sake,* eg because I want to save her trouble. **for the sake of sth/doing sth** in order to get or keep sth: *We made concessions for the sake of peace.* ○ *She argues for the sake of arguing,* ie because she likes arguing. ○ *Let's not spoil the job for the sake of a few pounds.*

sake[2] (also **saki**) /ˈsɑːkɪ/ *n* [U] Japanese alcoholic drink made from fermented rice.

Saki /ˈsɑːkɪ/ pen-name of the English writer H H Munro (1870-1916), best known for his short stories, which display a satirical and sometimes cruel wit.

salaam /səˈlɑːm/ *n, interj* **1** Muslim greeting used in the East. **2** low bow with the right hand touching the forehead.

▷ **salaam** *v* [I, Ipr] make a salaam: *salaam to sb.*

salable (also **saleable**) /ˈseɪləbl/ *adj* fit for sale; that sb will want to buy: *not in a saleable condition* ○ *The houses are highly salable.*

salacious /səˈleɪʃəs/ *adj* (*derog*) (of speech, books, pictures, etc) treating sexual activity, nudity, etc in an obscene way; indecent; lewd. ▷ **salaciously** *adv.* **salaciousness** *n* [U]. **salacity** /səˈlæsətɪ/ *n* [U] (*fml*).

salad

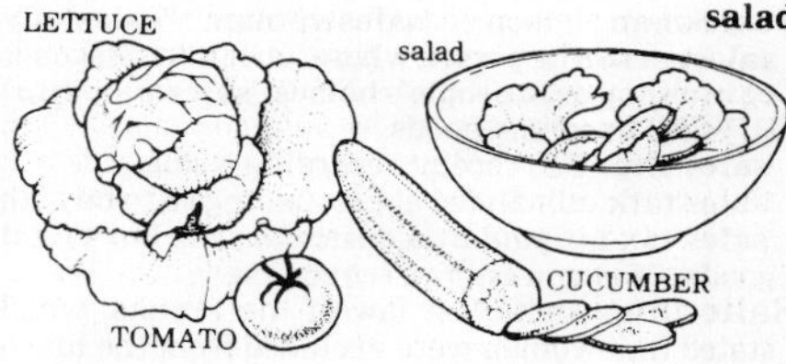

salad /ˈsæləd/ *n* **1** (a) [C, U] (dish of) chopped, usu raw vegetables, such as lettuce, tomatoes, cucumber, often seasoned with oil, vinegar, etc: *prepare/mix a salad* ○ *cold beef and salad* ○ [attrib] *a salad bowl, shaker, etc.* (b) [C, U] (dish of a) specified food served with salad: *a/some chicken, ham, lobster, etc salad.* **2** [U] lettuce, endive or other green vegetable suitable for eating raw. ⇨ illus. **3** [C, U] mixture of other foods, sometimes served with a dressing: *a sweetcorn and pepper salad* ○ *fruit salad.* **4** (idm) **one's ˈsalad days** time when one is young and inexperienced: *I was in my salad days then, and fell in love easily.*

□ **ˈsalad cream** type of mayonnaise, usu sold in jars.

ˈsalad-dressing *n* [U] sauce usu made of oil, vinegar and herbs for putting on salad.

ˈsalad-oil *n* [U] oil used for salad-dressing.

Saladin /ˈsælədɪn/ English name of Salah-ed-Din Yusuf ibn Ayub (1137-93), sultan of Egypt. He reconquered the Holy Land and fought off the threat of the Third Crusade. In legend and tradition he is represented as a brave, noble and generous figure.

salamander /ˈsæləmændə(r)/ *n* lizard-like animal living on land and in water, once thought to be capable of living in fire.

salami /səˈlɑːmɪ/ *n* [U] sausage salted and flavoured with spices, usu eaten cold.

sal ammoniac /ˌsæl əˈməʊnɪæk/ [U] ammonium chloride, used in some types of batteries and the dyeing of cotton.

salary /ˈsælərɪ/ *n* fixed regular (usu monthly) payment to employees doing other than manual or mechanical work: *a salary of £12 000 a year* ○ *Has your salary been paid yet?* ○ *Should doctors' salaries be higher?* ○ [attrib] *a salary agreement, scale, cheque.* ⇨ Usage at INCOME.

▷ **salaried** *adj* receiving a salary; (of employment) paid for by means of a salary: *a salaried employee, post.*

sale /seɪl/ *n* **1** [U] selling or being sold: *the sale of cars, clothes, machinery* ○ *The money was raised by the sale of raffle tickets.* **2** (**a**) [C] act of selling sth: *I haven't made a sale all week.* ○ *She gets £10 commission on each sale.* (**b**) **sales** [pl] amount sold: *vast sales of ice-cream in the hot weather* ○ *Sales are up* (ie More goods have been sold) *this month.* **3** [C] (in a shop, etc) occasion when goods are sold at lower prices than usual: *hold an end-of-season sale* ○ *the January sales*, ie when many shops reduce their prices ○ *buy goods at/in the sales* ○ [attrib] *sale prices, goods, etc.* **4** [U, sing] desire to buy goods; demand: *There's always a ready sale for high-quality furniture.* ○ *They found no sale for their goods*, ie could not sell them. **5** [C] auction. **6** (idm) **for sale** intended to be sold (usu by or on behalf of the owners): *I'm sorry this painting's not for sale.* ○ *She has put her house up for sale.* **on sale** (**a**) (esp of goods in shops, etc) available to be bought: *on sale at your local post office* ○ *The new model is not on sale in the shops.* (**b**) (*US*) being offered at a reduced price. (**on**) ˌ**sale or reˈturn** (of goods) supplied to a retailer, who can send back without paying for them any items that he does not sell. ▷ **saleable** *adj* = SALABLE.

□ ˌ**sale of ˈwork** sale of items, eg cakes or knitting, made by members of a church, club, etc for charity.

ˈ**sale-room** (*US* ˈ**salesroom**) *n* room where goods are sold by public auction.

ˈ**salesclerk** (*US*) = SHOP ASSISTANT (SHOP).

ˈ**sales department** department of a firm concerned with selling its products.

ˈ**salesman** /-mən/, ˈ**saleswoman**, ˈ**saleslady**, **salesperson** *ns* person whose job it is to sell goods, eg in a shop or in people's homes. ˈ**salesmanship** *n* [U] skill in selling goods.

ˈ**sales slip** (*US*) receipt recording a sale.

ˈ**sales talk** talk aimed at persuading sb to buy sth.

ˈ**sales tax** tax paid by a customer who buys retail goods. Cf PURCHASE TAX (PURCHASE[1]).

Salic law /ˌsælɪk ˈlɔː/ law of the Franks, which stated that women were excluded from the line of succession to the throne of France. This law was one of the issues in the claim of the English king Edward III to the French throne and so one of the causes of the *Hundred Years War.

salicylic acid /ˌsælɪsɪlɪk ˈæsɪd/ bitter chemical used as a fungicide and also in the making of aspirin.

salient /ˈseɪlɪənt/ *adj* [attrib] **1** most noticeable or important; main: *the salient points of a speech* ○ *She pointed out all the salient features of the building.* **2** (of an angle) pointing outwards.

▷ **salient** *n* **1** salient angle. **2** (*military*) bulge in a military line of attack or defence.

saline /ˈseɪlaɪn; *US* -liːn/ *adj* [attrib] (*fml*) containing salt; salty: *a saline lake* ○ *saline springs* ○ *saline solution*, eg as used for gargling, storing contact lenses, etc.

▷ **saline** *n* [U] (*medical*) solution of salt and water.

salinity /səˈlɪnətɪ/ *n* [U]: *the high salinity of sea water.*

Salinger /ˈsælɪndʒə(r)/ Jerome David (1919-), American novelist and writer of short stories. His first and best-known book, *The Catcher in the Rye*, is the story of a young boy who runs away to New York and his adventures in the adult world.

saliva /səˈlaɪvə/ (also **slaver**) *n* [U] liquid produced in the mouth that helps one chew and digest food; spittle.

▷ **salivary** /ˈsælɪvərɪ, səˈlaɪvərɪ; *US* ˈsæləverɪ/ *adj* [attrib] of or producing saliva: *the ˈsalivary glands.*

salivate /ˈsælɪveɪt/ *v* [I] (*fml*) produce saliva, esp excessively: *A dog salivates when it sees a bone.* **salivation** /ˌsælɪˈveɪʃn/ *n* [U].

sallow[1] /ˈsæləʊ/ *adj* (**-er, -est**) (of a person's skin or complexion) yellowish. ▷ **sallowness** *n* [U].

sallow[2] /ˈsæləʊ/ *n* type of willow that does not grow to be very tall.

sally /ˈsælɪ/ *n* **1** (**a**) sudden attack, esp by troops surrounded by the enemy: *make a successful sally.* (**b**) (*joc*) quick journey: *a brief sally to the shops.* **2** lively or witty, usu good-humoured, remark.

▷ **sally** *v* (*pt, pp* **sallied**) (phr v) **sally out/forth** (*fml*) (**a**) emerge suddenly, usu from a place where one is surrounded, to attack an enemy: *sally out against the besiegers.* (**b**) (*joc*) set out somewhere or to do sth: *Party workers sallied forth in a drive to find new members.*

salmon /ˈsæmən/ *n* (*pl* unchanged) **1** (**a**) [C] large fish with pinkish flesh, sometimes fished for with rod and line as a sport. (**b**) [U] its flesh as food: *smoked salmon* ○ [attrib] *a salmon salad, mousse, etc.* **2** [U] the colour of its flesh; orange-pink.

□ ˌ**salmon-ˈpink** *adj* orange-pink, the colour of the salmon's flesh.

ˌ**salmon-ˈtrout** *n* trout resembling a salmon.

salmonella /ˌsælməˈnelə/ *n* [U] type of bacteria causing food poisoning: [attrib] *salmonella poisoning.*

Salome /səˈləʊmɪ/ step-daughter of *Herod Antipas. When Herod offered her a reward for her dancing, she was instructed by her mother Herodias to ask for *John the Baptist to be beheaded.

salon /ˈsælɒn; *US* səˈlɒn/ *n* **1** place where customers go to see a hairdresser, beauty consultant, etc: *a ˈbeauty salon* ○ *a ˈhairdressing salon.* **2** (formerly) regular gathering of notable guests at the house of a lady of high society; room used for this: *a literary salon*, ie with writers and critics as guests.

saloon /səˈluːn/ *n* **1** public room on a ship, in a hotel, etc: *the ship's dining-saloon.* **2** public room or building for a specified purpose: *a ˈbilliard/ˈdancing saloon.* **3** (*US*) place where alcoholic drinks may be bought and drunk; bar. **4** (also **saˈloon-car**) (*Brit*) (*US* **sedan**) motor car where the area for the driver and passengers is closed off from the luggage and engine areas. ⇨ illus at CAR.

□ **saˈloon bar** = LOUNGE BAR (LOUNGE).

salsify /ˈsælsɪfɪ/ *n* [U] plant with a long fleshy root cooked as a vegetable.

SALT /sɔːlt/ (also **Salt**) *abbr* Strategic Arms Limitation Talks: *the Salt treaties.*

salt /sɔːlt/ *n* **1** [U] (also **common salt**) common white substance obtained from mines, present in sea water (from which it is obtained by evaporation), used esp for flavouring and preserving food; sodium chloride: *a grain of salt* ○ *too much salt in the soup* ○ ˈ*table salt*, ie powdered so that it can be sprinkled on food ○ ˈ*sea salt.* **2** [C] chemical compound of a metal and an acid. **3 salts** [pl] substance like salt in taste, form, etc, esp such a substance used as a laxative: *a dose of (Epsom) salts* ○ ˈ*bath salts*, ie used to scent bath water. **4** [C] (*dated infml*) experienced sailor: *an old salt.* **5** [U] (*fig*) thing that makes sth more interesting, lively, etc: *Her humour adds salt to her conversation.* Cf SPICE 2. **6** (idm) **like a dose of salts** ⇨ DOSE. **rub salt into the wound/sb's wounds** ⇨ RUB[1]. **the salt of the ˈearth** very decent, honest, etc person or people: *You can trust her: she's the salt of the earth.* **take sth with a pinch of salt** ⇨ PINCH *n.* **worth one's salt** ⇨ WORTH.

▷ **salt** *v* **1** [Tn] put salt on or in (food) to season it. **2** [Tn, Tn·p] ~ **sth** (**down**) preserve (food) with salt: *salt (down) pork* ○ *salted beef.* **3** [Tn] sprinkle salt on (roads, etc) to melt ice or snow. **4** [Tn] make (a mine) seem rich by putting ore into it, usu so as to trick sb who wants to buy it. **5** (phr v) **salt sth away** save (money, etc) secretly and usu dishonestly: *She salted away most of the profit from the business.*

salt *adj* [attrib] containing, tasting of or preserved with salt: *salt beef, pork, etc* ○ *salt water* ○ *salt marshes* ○ *the ˈsalt flats of Utah.*

salty *adj* (**-ier, -iest**) **1** containing or tasting of salt. **2** (*fig*) (of wit, speech, etc) vigorous, vivid, etc: *her salty humour.* **saltiness** *n* [U].

□ ˈ**salt-cellar** (*US* ˈ**salt-shaker**) *n* small container for salt at the table, either open or enclosed with a hole or holes at the top for sprinkling. Cf PEPPER-POT (PEPPER).

ˈ**salt-lick** (also **lick**) *n* place where animals go to lick salty rock or earth.

ˈ**salt-mine** *n* (**a**) mine from which salt is obtained. (**b**) (usu *pl*) (*joc fig*) place where one is sent as a punishment to do hard unpleasant work.

ˈ**salt-pan** (also **pan**) *n* hollow near the sea where salt is obtained by evaporation.

ˈ**salt-water** *adj* [attrib] of the sea: *a salt-water fish.* Cf FRESHWATER (FRESH).

saltire /ˈsɔːltaɪə(r)/ *n* X-shaped cross, eg on a coat of arms.

saltpetre (*US* **-peter**) /sɔːltˈpiːtə(r)/ *n* [U] salty white powder used in making gunpowder, for preserving food and as medicine.

salubrious /səˈluːbrɪəs/ *adj* (*fml*) (esp of the climate) health-giving: *the salubrious mountain air.* ▷ **salubriousness** *n* [U].

saluki /səˈluːkɪ/ *n* breed of tall dog with a long silky coat.

salutary /ˈsæljʊtrɪ; *US* -terɪ/ *adj* having a good effect: *salutary exercise, advice* ○ *The accident is a salutary reminder of the dangers of climbing.*

salutation /ˌsæljuːˈteɪʃn/ *n* (*fml*) **1** (**a**) [U] greeting or respect: *raise one's hat in salutation.* (**b**) [C] sign or expression of this, eg a bow or a kiss: *the polite salutations of the courtier.* **2** [C] (in a letter, etc) words used to address the person being written to, eg *Dear Sir.*

salute /səˈluːt/ *n* **1** (**a**) action performed to show honour, respect or welcome to sb: *fire a salute of ten guns.* (**b**) (esp military) gesture of respect to a senior officer, etc, often a raising of the right hand to the forehead in a certain way: *give a salute* ○ *The officer returned the sergeant's salute*, ie saluted in reply to such a gesture. **2** polite gesture of greeting, eg a bow: *raised his hat as a friendly salute.* **3** (idm) **in saˈlute** as a salute: *They took off their hats by the grave in silent salute.* ○ *They raised their fists in salute to their leader.* **take the saˈlute** acknowledge with a salute the salutes of soldiers marching past.

▷ **salute** *v* (**a**) [I, Tn] give (sb) a salute; greet (sb): *The guard saluted (the general) smartly.* ○ *The royal visitor was saluted by a fanfare of trumpets.* (**b**) [Tn, Cn·n/a] ~ **sb/sth** (**as sth**) (*fml or rhet*) publicly notice (an important person, achievement, etc): *We salute you for your tireless efforts for peace.* ○ *Today should be saluted as the beginning of a new era.*

salvage /ˈsælvɪdʒ/ *n* [U] **1** rescue of a damaged ship or its cargo; rescue of property from damage caused by fire, floods, etc: *Salvage of the wreck was made difficult by bad weather.* ○ [attrib] *a salvage company*, ie one that salvages wrecked ships, recovers valuables from sunken ships, etc ○ *a salvage tug*, ie for towing a disabled ship to port. **2** (money paid for such rescue or the) property rescued in this way. **3** (saving of) waste material that can be used again after being processed: *collect old newspapers and magazines for salvage.*

▷ **salvage** *v* **1** [Tn] save (sth) from loss, fire, wreck, etc. **2** [Tn] save (sth) as salvage(3). **3** [Tn, Tn·pr] ~ **sth** (**from sth**) recover sth (from a wreck, damaged vehicle, etc): *Valuable raw materials were salvaged (from the sunken freighter).* ○ (*fig*) *How can she salvage her reputation after the scandal?*

salvation /sælˈveɪʃn/ *n* [U] **1** (*religion*) saving of a person's soul from sin and its consequences; state of being saved in this way: *pray for the salvation of sinners.* **2** way of avoiding loss, disaster, etc: *I get so depressed about life; work is my salvation*, ie helps me forget my worries.

□ **the Salˌvation ˈArmy** missionary Christian organization whose members wear military-style uniforms, and who work esp to help the poor. ⇨ articles at CHARITY, VOLUNTARY.

salve /sælv; *US* sæv/ *n* **1** [C, U] (esp in compounds) oily substance used on wounds, sores or burns: ˈ*lip-salve.* Cf OINTMENT. **2** [sing] ~ **to sth** action or thought that makes sb feel less guilty, anxious, angry, etc: *She paid the repair bill as a salve to her*

conscience.
▷ **salve** *v* [Tn] make (esp one's conscience) feel better: *It's too late to salve your conscience by apologizing.*

salver /ˈsælvə(r)/ *n* (usu metal) tray on which letters, drinks, etc are placed for handing to people.

salvia /ˈsælvɪə/ *n* any of several garden plants, esp one with red or blue flowers.

salvo /ˈsælvəʊ/ *n* (*pl* ~**s** or ~**es**) **1** firing of several guns at the same time, esp as a salute. Cf VOLLEY 1. **2** outburst of applause.

sal volatile /ˌsæl vəˈlætəlɪ/ *n* [U] sharp-smelling solution of ammonium carbonate given to sb to sniff if he is faint or unconscious; smelling-salts.

Salyut /sælˈjuːt/ any of a series of manned space stations sent into orbit around the earth by the USSR since 1971.

SAM /sæm/ *abbr* surface-to-air missile.

Samaritan /səˈmærɪtən/ *n* **1 the Samaritans** [pl] organization devoted to giving help and friendship to people in despair. ⇨ article at EMERGENCY. **2** (idm) **a** ˌ**good Saˈmaritan** a person who gives sympathy and help to people in trouble (from a character in one of the parables of Jesus in the Bible).

samba /ˈsæmbə/ *n* (music for a) ballroom dance that originated in Brazil: *dance the samba.*

Sambo /ˈsæmbəʊ/ *n* (*pl* ~**s** or ~**es**) (⚠ *sl offensive*) Black person.

Sam Browne /ˌsæm ˈbraʊn/ (also ˌ**Sam Browne** ˈ**belt**) type of leather belt with a strap that passes over the right shoulder, worn by commissioned officers of the British Army, certain police officers, etc.

same[1] /seɪm/ *adj* **1 the** ~ **sb/sth (as sb/sth/ that...)** (also sometimes preceded by *this/that/ these/those*) exactly the one (or ones) referred to or mentioned; not different; identical: *They both said the same thing.* ○ *We have lived in the same house for twenty years.* ○ *He took it off the top shelf and put it back in the same place.* ○ *He is the same age as his wife.* ○ *The cinema is showing the same film as last week.* ○ *I saw the mistake at the (very) same moment that she did.* ○ *I resigned on Friday and left that same day.* **2 the** ~ **sb/sth (as sb/sth/that...)** one that is exactly like the one referred to or mentioned; exactly matching: *I saw the same shoes in a shop last week.* ○ *Men with moustaches all look the same to me.* ○ *I bought the same car as yours/ that you did*, ie another car of that type. ○ *The two recipes are very much the same*, ie only slightly different. ○ (*derog or joc*) *You men are all the same!* eg have the same faults, obsessions, etc. **3** (idm) **amount to/come to/be the same** ˈ**thing** not be different; have the same result, meaning, etc: *You can pay by cash or cheque: it comes to the same thing.* **at the same** ˈ**time (a)** at once; together: *Don't all speak at the same time.* ○ *She was laughing and crying at the same time.* **(b)** (introducing a fact, etc that must be considered) nevertheless; yet: *You've got to be firm, but at the same time you must be sympathetic.* **be in the same boat** be in the same (usu unfortunate) circumstances: *She and I are in the same boat: we both failed the exam.* **be of the same** ˈ**mind (about sb/sth)** (*fml*) having the same opinion: *We're all of the same mind: opposed to the proposal.* **by the same** ˈ**token** in a corresponding way; following from the same argument: *She must be more reasonable, but by the same token you must try to understand her.* **in the same breath** immediately after saying sth else: *He praised my work and in the same breath told me I would have to leave.* **lightning never strikes in the same place twice** ⇨ LIGHTNING[1]. **not in the same street (as sb/sth)** of a much lower standard (than sb/sth). **one and the same** the same person or thing: *It turns out that her aunt and my cousin are one and the same (person).* **on the same wavelength (as sb)** sharing the same way of thinking and the same interests, etc (as sb) and therefore able to understand him: *I find him difficult to talk to — we're on completely different wavelengths.* **pay sb in his own/the same coin** ⇨ PAY[2]. **the** ˌ**same old** ˈ**story** what usually happens: *It's the same old story: everybody wants the house tidy, but nobody wants to tidy it himself.* **speak the same language** ⇨ SPEAK. **tarred with the same brush** ⇨ TAR[1].
▷ **the same** *adv* in the same way; similarly: *I still feel the same about it.* ○ *The two words are spelled differently, but pronounced the same.*
sameness *n* [U] quality of being the same; lack of variety: *the tedious sameness of winter days indoors.*
samey /ˈseɪmɪ/ *adj* (*infml*) not changing enough: *The food we get here is terribly samey.*

same[2] /seɪm/ *pron* **1 (a) the** ~ **(as sb/sth/...)** the same thing: *He and I said the same.* ○ *Their ages are the same.* ○ *I think the same (as you do) about the matter.* ○ *I would do the same again.* ○ (*infml*) *'I'll have a coffee.' 'Same for me, please* (ie I will have one, too).' **(b) the** ~ (*fml or joc*) the same person: *'Was it George who telephoned?' 'The same.'*, ie Yes, it was George. **2** (without *the*; used in bills, etc) (*fml or joc*) the previously mentioned thing: *To dry-cleaning suit, £3; to repairing same, £2.* **3** (idm) ˌ**all/**ˌ**just the** ˈ**same** in spite of this; nevertheless: *All the same, there's some truth in what she says.* ○ *He's not very reliable, but I like him just the same.* ○ *I wasn't able to use your screwdriver, but thanks all the same*, ie for lending it. **(the) same again** (request to sb to serve the same drink as before): *Same again, please!* ˌ**same** ˈ**here** (*infml*) the same thing applies to me; I agree: *'I hate this book.' 'Same here.'* ○ *'I'm not very good at history.' 'Same here.'* **(the)** ˌ**same to** ˈ**you** (used as an answer to an insult, a greeting, etc): *'Stupid!' 'Same to you!'* ○ *'Happy Christmas!' 'And the same to you!'*

samizdat /ˈsæmɪzdæt/ *n* [U] system of secretly publishing forbidden literary work, originally in the USSR, by passing typewritten copies among interested readers.

Samoa /səˈməʊə/ group of Polynesian islands, made up of American Samoa in the east and *Western Samoa, an independent state, in the west. ⇨ map at POLYNESIA. ▷ **Samoan** *n, adj.*

samosa /səˈməʊsə/ *n* spicy snack with a meat or vegetable filling in a triangular case of crisp fried pastry.

samovar /ˈsæməʊvɑː(r)/ *n* container for heating water, used esp in Russia for making tea.

samoyed /səˈmɔɪed/ *n* breed of large white dog originally from the Arctic.

sampan /ˈsæmpæn/ *n* small flat-bottomed boat used along the coasts and rivers of China.

sample /ˈsɑːmpl; *US* ˈsæmpl/ *n* **1** one of a number of things, or part of a whole, that can be looked at to see what the rest is like; specimen: *a sample of his handwriting* ○ *a blood, urine, tissue, etc sample* ○ *The survey covers a representative sample of the population*, ie people of all levels of society. ○ *a sample of the kind of cloth I want to buy.* **2** small amount of a product given away free: *hand out free samples of the perfume* ○ [attrib] *a sample pack, sachet, etc.*
▷ **sample** *v* [Tn] try out or examine (sth) by taking a sample or by experiencing it: *sample a new type of flour for oneself* ○ *sample the delights of Chinese food* ○ *We sampled opinion among the workers about* (ie asked some of them about) *changes in working methods.*

sampler[1] /ˈsɑːmplə(r); *US* ˈsæm-/ *n* piece of cloth embroidered to show skill in needlework and often displayed on a wall.

sampler[2] /ˈsɑːmplə(r); *US* ˈsæm-/ *n* **1** person who collects or examines samples, eg in statistics. **2** (*US*) group of things collected as a representative selection, eg a gramophone record of songs, etc by a particular performer.

Samson /ˈsæmsn/ **1** Israelite leader in the Old Testament, famous for his great strength. His lover *Delilah tricked him into telling her that the secret of his strength was his uncut hair. She betrayed him to the Philistines, who blinded him and cut off his hair. But when it grew again Samson's strength returned, and he pulled down the pillars of a great hall, killing himself and many of his enemies. **2** *n* very strong man.

Samuel /ˈsæmjʊəl/ either of two books of the Old Testament giving a history of Israel from the birth of the prophet Samuel till the death of King *David. ⇨ App 5.

samurai /ˈsæmʊraɪ/ *n* (*pl* unchanged) **1 the samurai** [pl] the military caste in feudal Japan. **2** [C] member of this caste.

sanatorium /ˌsænəˈtɔːrɪəm/ *n* (*US* also **sanitarium** /ˌsænəˈteərɪəm/, **sanitorium** /ˌsænəˈtɔːrɪəm/) (*pl* ~**s** or **-ria** /-rɪə/) clinic where patients suffering or recovering from a long illness are treated.

Sancho Panza /ˌsæntʃəʊ ˈpænzə/ squire and servant of *Don Quixote. He is an ignorant and often cowardly peasant, but helps his master in his adventures by his simple common sense.

sanctify /ˈsæŋktɪfaɪ/ *v* (*pt, pp* **-fied**) **1** [Tn] make (sb/sth) holy: *a life sanctified by prayer.* **2** [Tn esp passive] (*fig*) make (sth) seem right, legal, etc; justify; sanction: *a practice sanctified by tradition.*
▷ **sanctification** /ˌsæŋktɪfɪˈkeɪʃn/ *n* [U].

sanctimonious /ˌsæŋktɪˈməʊnɪəs/ *adj* (*derog*) showing that one feels morally better than other people: *a sanctimonious smile, remark, person, letter of protest.* ▷ **sanctimoniously** *adv.* **sanctimoniousness** *n* [U].

sanction /ˈsæŋkʃn/ *n* **1** [U] permission or approval for an action, a change, etc: *The book was translated without the sanction of the author.* ○ *The government gave its sanction to what the Minister had done.* ○ *These measures have the sanction of tradition*, ie seem justified because they have often been taken before. **2** [C] reason that stops people disobeying laws, rules, etc: *Is prison the best sanction against a crime like this?* ○ *The fear of ridicule is a very effective sanction.* **3** measure taken to force a country to obey international law: *apply economic sanctions against a repressive regime.*
▷ **sanction** *v* [Tn, Tg, Tsg] give one's permission for (sth); authorize or approve: *I can't sanction your methods.* ○ *Who sanctioned bombing the town?* ○ *They won't sanction our spending on this scale.*

sanctity /ˈsæŋktətɪ/ *n* [U] holiness; sacredness: *She gives us a living example of sanctity.* ○ *the sanctity of an oath.*

sanctuary /ˈsæŋktʃʊərɪ; *US* -uerɪ/ *n* **1** [C] **(a)** sacred place, eg a church, temple or mosque. **(b)** holiest part of a temple. **2** [C] **(a)** chancel of a church. **(b)** [C] part of a church containing the main altar. **(c)** (*esp US*) room where general religious services are held. **3 (a)** [C] sacred place where sb is protected from people wishing to arrest or attack him: *The fleeing rebels found a sanctuary in the nearby church.* **(b)** [U] (the right to offer) such protection: *claim/seek/take/be offered sanctuary.* **4** [C] any place where refuge is provided: *Our country is a sanctuary for political refugees from all over the world.* **5** [C] area where birds and wild animals are protected from hunters, etc and are encouraged to breed: *a* ˈ*bird sanctuary.*

sanctum /ˈsæŋktəm/ *n* **1** holy place. **2** (*fig*) room, office, etc where sb may not be disturbed: *I was allowed once into his inner sanctum.*

Sanctus /ˈsæŋktəs/ *n* **(a)** prayer or hymn beginning 'Sanctus, sanctus, sanctus' (meaning 'Holy, holy, holy') which is said or sung during Mass at the end of the first part of the Eucharistic prayer. **(b)** musical setting of this.

Sand /sɑːnd/ George (1804-76), pen-name of Amandine-Aurore Dupin, French novelist. She wrote romantic novels about women's struggles against conventional morality. She was also famous as the mistress of *Chopin.

sand /sænd/ *n* **1** [U] (mass of) very fine fragments of rock that has been worn down, found on beaches, in river-beds, deserts, etc: *mix sand and cement to make concrete.* **2** [U, C usu *pl*] area of sand, eg on a beach: *children playing on the sand(s).* **3 sands** [pl] (used in names) sandbank: *the Goodwin Sands.* **4** (idm) **build on sand** ⇨ BUILD. **bury/hide one's head in the sand** ⇨ HEAD[4]. **the sands are running** ˈ**out** there is not much time left: *The sands are running out: we must have the money by tomorrow.*

▷ **sand** *v* **1** [Tn, Tn·p, Cn·a] ~ **sth** (**down**) smooth or polish sth with sandpaper, etc: *The bare wood must be sanded down.* ○ *The floor has been sanded smooth.* **2** [Tn] sprinkle sand on (sth) or cover (sth) with sand.

sander (also **ˈsanding-machine**) *n* machine for sanding surfaces, eg by means of a rotating pad with sandpaper attached.

sandy *adj* (**-ier**, **-iest**) **1** like sand; covered with sand: *a surface with a sandy texture* ○ *The floor of the beach-hut was sandy.* **2** (of hair, etc) yellowish-red. **sandiness** *n* [U].

□ **ˈsandbag** *n* bag filled with sand, used as a defence (eg in war, against rising flood-water, etc). — *v* (**-gg-**) **1** [Tn] put sandbags in or around (sth): *sandbag the doorway in case of flooding.* **2** [Tn] hit (sb) on the head with a bag filled with sand. **3** [Tn, Tn·pr] ~**sb** (**into sth**/**doing sth**) (*fig infml*) force sb to do sth by violent means or harsh criticism; bully sb.

ˈsandbank *n* bank or shoal of sand in a river or the sea.

ˈsand-bar *n* sandbank at the mouth of a river or harbour.

ˈsand-blast *v* [Tn] clean or decorate (a stone wall, etc) by aiming a jet of sand at it.

ˈsand-box *n* **1** mould made of sand used in casting metals. **2** (*esp US*) box used as a sand-pit for children.

ˈsandboy *n* (idm) **happy as a sandboy** ⇨ HAPPY.

ˈsand-castle *n* pile of sand shaped to look like a castle, usu made by a child on a beach.

ˈsand-dune *n* = DUNE.

ˈsand-fly *n* type of midge common on sea-shores.

ˈsand-glass *n* simple device for measuring short periods of time by letting a quantity of sand held in a glass cup fall through a small opening at the bottom into another cup with an exactly matching shape. Cf HOURGLASS (HOUR).

ˈsandlot *n* (*US*) empty area of usu sandy ground in a city, used for children's games.

the ˈsandman *n* [sing] imaginary person who makes children feel sleepy: *The sandman's coming!* ie It's time for bed!

ˈsand martin bird resembling a swallow that builds its nest in sandy banks.

ˈsand-painting *n* (**a**) [U] art form developed esp by the Navajo and other native American peoples in their religious ceremonies, using sand of different colours to produce pictures of gods, etc. (**b**) [C] picture produced in this way.

ˈsandpaper *n* [U] strong paper coated with sand or a similar substance, used for rubbing surfaces smooth. — *v* [Tn, Tn·p] smooth (sth) with sandpaper.

ˈsandpiper *n* small bird living in wet sandy places near streams.

ˈsand-pit *n* hole in the ground partly filled with sand for children to play in.

ˈsand-shoes *n* [pl] light shoes with rubber or hemp soles for wearing on beaches.

ˈsandstone *n* [U] rock formed of compressed sand.

ˈsandstorm *n* storm in a desert in which sand is blown through the air by the wind.

ˈsand trap (*esp US*) = BUNKER 2.

ˈsand-yacht *n* vehicle with wheels and a sail, driven over sand by the wind.

sandal

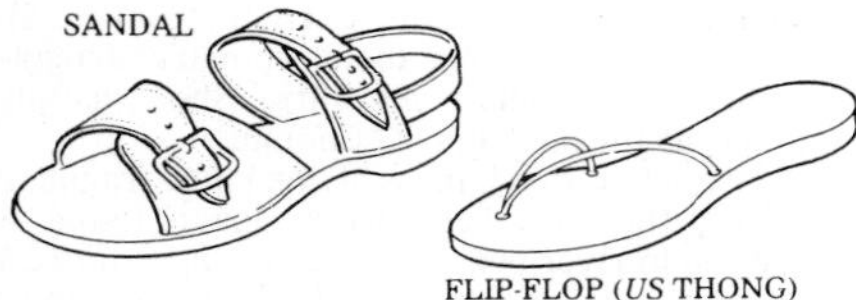

sandal /ˈsændl/ *n* type of open shoe consisting of a sole held on to the foot by straps or cords. Cf BOOT[1] 1, SHOE 1.

▷ **sandalled** *adj* wearing sandals.

sandalwood /ˈsændlwʊd/ *n* [U] hard scented wood used for making fans, caskets, etc: [attrib] *sandalwood soap*, ie smelling like this wood.

Sandhurst /ˈsændhɜːst/ training college for British army officers, officially called 'The Royal Military Academy' now at Camberley in Surrey.

Sandringham House /ˌsændrɪŋəm ˈhaʊs/ one of the official country residences of the British royal family, near King's Lynn in Norfolk. ⇨ article at ROYAL FAMILY.

sandwich /ˈsænwɪdʒ; *US* -wɪtʃ/ *n* two or more slices of bread with meat, cheese, etc between: *ham, chicken, cucumber, etc sandwiches* ○ [attrib] *a sandwich bar, box, filling.*

▷ **sandwich** *v* [Tn, Tn·pr] ~ **sb**/**sth** (**between sb**/**sth**) put sb/sth between two other people or things, esp in a restricted space: *I sandwiched myself between two fat men on the bus.*

□ **ˈsandwich board** either of two connected boards, usu carrying advertisements and hung over the shoulders of a person (a **ˈsandwich man**) who walks about the streets to display them.

ˈsandwich cake (*Brit* also **ˈlayer cake**) cake made from two or more layers of light sponge-cake with a filling of jam and sometimes cream in the middle.

ˈsandwich course course of training in which periods of instruction and practical work alternate.

sane /seɪn/ *adj* (**-r**, **-st**) **1** having a healthy mind; not mad: *It's hard to stay sane under such awful pressure.* **2** (*fig*) showing good judgement; moderate; sensible: *a sane person, decision, policy* ○ *her sane, democratic views.* ▷ **sanely** *adv.*

Sanforized /ˈsænfəraɪzd/ *adj* (*propr*) (of fabric or a garment) treated by a process that prevents further shrinking; pre-shrunk.

San Francisco /ˌsæn frənˈsɪskəʊ/ city on the coast of California in the USA. It is famous for its harbour, entered by a channel called the *Golden Gate, and for the earthquake of 1906 which destroyed much of the city.

sang *pt* of SING.

sang-froid /ˌsɒŋ ˈfrwɑː/ *n* [U] calmness in a situation of danger or in an emergency; composure: *They showed great sang-froid in dealing with the fire.*

sangría /ˈsæŋgrɪə; *US* sæŋˈgriːə/ *n* [U] (*Spanish*) drink made of red wine with fruit, lemonade, etc.

sanguinary /ˈsæŋgwɪnərɪ; *US* -nerɪ/ *adj* (*dated fml*) **1** with much bloodshed; bloody: *a sanguinary battle.* **2** fond of bloodshed; cruel: *a sanguinary ruler.*

sanguine /ˈsæŋgwɪn/ *adj* (*fml*) **1** ~ (**about sth**/**that...**) hopeful; optimistic: *not very sanguine about our chances of success* ○ *sanguine that we shall succeed.* **2** having a red complexion. ▷ **sanguinely** *adv.* **sanguineness** *n* [U].

Sanhedrin /ˈsænɪdrɪn; *US* sænˈhedrən/ supreme council of the Jewish people in New Testament times. In the Bible the members of the Sanhedrin condemned Jesus to death.

sanitarium, sanitorium (*US*) = SANATORIUM.

sanitary /ˈsænɪtrɪ; *US* -terɪ/ *adj* **1** free from dirt or substances that may cause disease; hygienic: *Conditions in the kitchen were not very sanitary.* **2** [attrib] of or concerned with protecting health: *sanitary ware*, ie toilet bowls, etc ○ *a ˈsanitary inspector*, ie an official who checks that the conditions in shops, restaurants, etc are hygienic.

□ **ˈsanitary towel** (also **ˈsanitary pad**) absorbent pad used by a woman during her period.

sanitation /ˌsænɪˈteɪʃn/ *n* [U] systems that protect people's health, esp those that dispose efficiently of sewage.

sanitize, -ise /ˈsænɪtaɪz/ *v* [Tn] **1** make (a place) hygienic. **2** (*fig derog*) make (a story, news, etc) less disturbing, shocking, etc: *They've sanitized my report on army atrocities.*

sanity /ˈsænətɪ/ *n* [U] **1** state of being sane; health of mind: *doubt/question sb's sanity.* **2** soundness of judgement; state of being sensible or moderate: *try to bring some sanity into a difficult situation.*

sank *pt* of SINK[1].

San Marino /ˌsæn məˈriːnəʊ/ very small independent state in northern Italy; pop approx 23 000; official language Italian; capital San Marino; unit of currency lira. It is thought to be the oldest and smallest republic in Europe. The main economic activity is tourism. ⇨ map at ITALY.

sanserif /ˌsænˈserɪf/ *n* [U] (in printing) form of type without serifs. ⇨ illus at SERIF.

Sanskrit /ˈsænskrɪt/ *n* [U] ancient Indo-European language of India, used in Hindu scriptures. Hindi, Bengali and other modern Indian languages have developed from it. ▷ **Sanskrit** (also **Sanskritic**) *adj.*

Santa Claus /ˈsæntə klɔːz/ (also *esp Brit* **Father Christmas**) man with a white beard and dressed in red, who, children are told, comes down chimneys at Christmas to bring presents. Department stores often pay people to dress up as Santa Claus at Christmas-time to entertain the children of customers.

Santayana /ˌsæntəˈjɑːnə/ George (1863-1952), American philosopher and writer, born in Spain, who finally settled in Rome. In addition to his philosophical books, which include *The Life of Reason*, he also wrote poetry, criticism and a successful novel.

São Tomé and Principe /ˌsaʊ təˌmeɪ ən ˈprɪnsɪpeɪ/ country consisting of two islands in the Gulf of Guinea; pop approx 106 000; official language Portuguese; capital São Tomé; unit of currency dobra (= 100 centavos). The main product is cocoa. ⇨ map at NIGERIA.

sap[1] /sæp/ *n* [U] **1** liquid in a plant that carries food to all its parts: *The sap rises in trees in springtime.* **2** (*fig*) vigour or energy: *He's full of sap and ready to start.*

▷ **sappy** *adj* (**-ier**, **-iest**) **1** (of a tree, etc) full of sap. **2** full of youthful vigour.

□ **ˈsapwood** *n* [U] soft outer layers of wood.

sap[2] /sæp/ *n* (*infml*) stupid person: *You poor sap!*

sap[3] /sæp/ *v* (**-pp-**) **1** [esp passive: Tn, Tn·pr] ~ **sb**/**sth** (**of sth**) gradually weaken sb/sth by taking away (strength, vitality, etc): *I was sapped by months of hospital treatment.* ○ *She's been sapped of her optimism.* **2** [Tn] gradually take away (sb's strength, vitality, etc): *Stop sapping her confidence!* ○ *Lack of planning is sapping the company's efficiency.*

sap[4] /sæp/ *n* tunnel or covered trench dug to get nearer to the enemy.

▷ **sapper** *n* soldier carrying out engineering work, eg road and bridge building.

sapient /ˈseɪpɪənt/ *adj* (*fml*) wise. ▷ **sapience** /-əns/ *n* [U]. **sapiently** *adv.*

sapling /ˈsæplɪŋ/ *n* young tree.

Sapphic (also **sapphic**) /ˈsæfɪk/ *n* form of four-line verse typical of the Greek lesbian poetess Sappho.

▷ **Sapphic** *adj* **1** of such verse. **2** (*fml*) lesbian.

sapphire /ˈsæfaɪə(r)/ *n* **1** [C] clear, bright blue jewel. **2** [U] its colour.

▷ **sapphire** *adj* bright blue.

Sappho /ˈsæfəʊ/ (early 7th c BC), Greek poet. The greatest of the early Greek lyric writers, she wrote in various metres, one of which is called the Sapphic. Her poems are characterized by passion, a love of nature and simplicity of style.

saprophyte /ˈsæprəʊfaɪt/ *n* fungus or similar plant living on dead organic matter. ▷ **saprophytic** /ˌsæprəʊˈfɪtɪk/ *adj.*

saraband /ˈsærəbænd/ *n* (**a**) slow Spanish dance. (**b**) piece of music for this dance.

Saracen /ˈsærəsn/ *n* Arab or Muslim at the time of the *Crusades.

Sarajevo /ˌsærəˈjeɪvəʊ/ city in Bosnia-Herzegovina where in 1914 the heir to the Austrian throne, Archduke Franz Ferdinand, was killed by a Slav nationalist. The conflict that followed between supporters of the Austro-Hungarian Empire and of the nationalist cause led to the First World War.

Saratoga /ˌsærəˈtəʊgə/ city in New York State. In 1777, at the beginning of the *War of American Independence, two battles were fought near the city. The British forces were defeated and lost their best chance of ending the rebellion.

sarcasm /ˈsɑːkæzəm/ *n* [U] (use of) bitter, esp ironic, remarks intended to wound sb's feelings: *her constant sarcasm about his poor work.*

▷ **sarcastic** /sɑːˈkæstɪk/ (also *infml* **sarky**) *adj* of or using sarcasm: *a sarcastic person, tone, remark.*

sarcastically /-klɪ/ *adv.*
sarcophagus /sɑːˈkɒfəgəs/ *n* (*pl* **-gi** /-gaɪ/ or **~es** /-gəsɪz/) stone coffin, esp one with carvings, etc, used in ancient times.
sardine /sɑːˈdiːn/ *n* **1** young pilchard or a similar fish, usu tinned in oil or tomato sauce. **2** (idm) **(packed, squashed, etc) like sardines** (*infml*) pressed tightly together: *The ten of us were squashed together like sardines in the lift.*
Sardinia /sɑːˈdɪnɪə/ large Italian island off the country's west coast. Its capital is Cagliari. ▷ **Sardinian** /-ɪən/ *n, adj.*
sardonic /sɑːˈdɒnɪk/ *adj* expressing scorn, usu in a grimly humorous way; mocking: *a sardonic smile, laugh, expression, etc.* ▷ **sardonically** /-klɪ/ *adv.*
Sargasso Sea /sɑːˌgæsəʊ ˈsiː/ **the Sargasso Sea** region of the western Atlantic around latitude 35° N, where large quantities of **sargasso seaweed** float in the water. It is the breeding-place for many European and American eels.
sarge /sɑːdʒ/ *n* (*sl*) (used esp as a form of address) sergeant.

John Singer Sargent: Mrs Fiske Warren and Her Daughter

Sargent /ˈsɑːdʒənt/ John Singer (1856-1925), American painter. For most of his career he produced portraits of figures in French and British society, but later turned to water-colours and landscapes. ⇨ illus.
sari /ˈsɑːrɪ/ *n* length of cotton or silk cloth draped round the body, worn as the main garment by Hindu women.
sarky /ˈsɑːkɪ/ *adj* (*Brit infml*) = SARCASTIC: *She's a sarky little madam.*
sarnie /ˈsɑːnɪ/ *n* (*Brit sl*) sandwich. Cf BUTTY.
sarong /səˈrɒŋ; *US* -ˈrɔːŋ/ *n* long strip of cotton or silk cloth worn as a skirt tucked in at the waist or under the armpits by Malay and Indonesian men and women.
sarsaparilla /ˌsɑːsəpəˈrɪlə/ *n* [U] (soft drink flavoured with a) preparation of the dried roots of various plants, esp smilax.
sarsen /ˈsɑːsn/ *n* sandstone boulder, a remnant of a formerly continuous layer of sandstone that has been eroded away.
sarsenet /ˈsɑːsnɪt/ *n* [U] soft silk fabric used esp as a lining.
sartorial /sɑːˈtɔːrɪəl/ *adj* [attrib] (*fml*) of (usu men's) clothes or a way of dressing: *sartorial elegance.* ▷ **sartorially** /-rɪəlɪ/ *adv.*

Sartre /ˈsɑːtrə/ Jean-Paul (1905-1980), French philosopher and author. In his plays, novels and criticism as much as in his philosophy he developed the ideas of *existentialism. Works like *L'Être et le néant* and *Huis clos* made him one of the most influential thinkers of the 20th century. He was for many years the companion of Simone de *Beauvoir.
Sarum /ˈseərəm/ old name of the English town of Salisbury, Wiltshire, and its diocese.
SAS /ˌes eɪ ˈes/ *abbr* (*Brit*) Special Air Service (of the army).
sash[1] /sæʃ/ *n* long strip of cloth worn around the waist or over one shoulder as an ornament or as part of a uniform.
sash[2] /sæʃ/ *n* either of a pair of window frames, one above the other, opening and closing by sliding up and down in grooves.
□ ˈ**sash-cord** *n* cord with a weight at one end running over a pulley and attached to a sash, allowing the window to be kept open in any position.
ˌ**sash-ˈwindow** *n* window consisting of two sashes. ⇨ illus at HOME.
sashay /ˈsæʃeɪ/ *v* [Ipr, Ip] (*US infml*) walk or move in a casual but showy way: *sashay into the room* ○ *She sashayed past, not condescending to look at us.*
Saskatchewan /səˈskætʃəwən/ province of central Canada; capital Regina. Its main economic activities are agriculture, forestry, fishing and mining. ⇨ map at App 1.
sasquatch /ˈsæskwɒtʃ/ *n* huge hairy man-like monster that is supposed to inhabit the north-western USA and Canada.
sass /sæs/ *n* [U] (*US infml*) disrespectful rudeness; sauce(2): *Just listen to her sass!*
▷ **sass** *v* [Tn] (*US infml*) **1** be disrespectfully rude to (sb): *Don't you dare sass me!* **2** (phr v) **sass sb back** answer sb rudely: *I asked her to go and brush her teeth and she just sassed me back.*
sassy *adj* (**-ier, -iest**) (*US infml*) **1** disrespectfully rude. **2** lively or stylish: *a real sassy dresser.*
sassafras /ˈsæsəfræs/ *n* **1** [C] small tree of N America with a bark that is used in medicines and perfumes. **2** [U] this bark.
Sassenach /ˈsæsənæk/ *n* (*Scot derog or joc*) English person.
Sassoon /səˈsuːn/ Siegfried (1886-1967), English poet and prose writer. The poems he wrote as a soldier in the First World War have a stark realism. He later wrote a three-volume autobiography.
Sat *abbr* Saturday: *Sat 2 May.*
sat *pt, pp of* SIT.
Satan /ˈseɪtn/ *n* the Devil.
▷ **satanic** /səˈtænɪk; *US* seɪ-/ *adj* **1** (often **Satanic**) of or like Satan: *satanic rites*, eg involving the worship of Satan ○ (*joc*) *His Satanic Majesty*, ie Satan. **2** (*esp rhet*) wicked; evil. **satanically** /-klɪ/ *adv.*
Satanism /ˈseɪtənɪzəm/ *n* [U] worship of Satan.
▷ **Satanist** /ˈseɪtənɪst/ *n* worshipper of Satan.
satchel /ˈsætʃəl/ *n* small leather or canvas bag, usu carried over the shoulders and used for carrying school books, etc.
sated /ˈseɪtɪd/ *adj* [usu pred] ~ (**with sth**) (*fml*) having had so much (of sth) that one does not want any more; satiated: *sated with pleasure.*
satellite /ˈsætəlaɪt/ *n* **1** (**a**) natural body in space orbiting round a larger body, esp a planet: *The moon is the Earth's satellite.* (**b**) man-made device, eg a space station, put in orbit round a planet: *a comˌmuniˈcations satellite*, ie one that relays back to the Earth telephone messages or radio and TV signals received from another part of the Earth. ⇨ illus at ORBIT. **2** (also ˈ**satellite state**) (*usu derog*) country dependent on another more powerful country and controlled by it: *the USSR and its satellites.*
satiate /ˈseɪʃɪeɪt/ *v* [Tn usu passive] (*fml*) provide (sb) with so much of sth that he wants no more: *She pushed her chair back from the table, satiated.* ○ *satiated with pleasure.* ▷ **satiation** /ˌseɪʃɪˈeɪʃn/ *n* [U].
Satie /ˈsɑːtɪ/ Erik (1866-1925), French composer. He is famous for the eccentric humour of his titles and his simple, almost naive, style. He was associated with *Cocteau, *Picasso, *Dada and *surrealism, as well as influencing composers such as *Poulenc.
satiety /səˈtaɪətɪ/ *n* [U] (*fml*) condition or feeling of being satiated: *feel full to satiety.*
satin /ˈsætɪn; *US* ˈsætn/ *n* [U] silk material that is shiny and smooth on one side: [attrib] *a satin dress, ribbon, etc.*
▷ **satin** *adj* [usu attrib] smooth like satin: *The paint has a satin finish.*
satiny *adj* having the appearance or texture of satin: *her satiny skin.*
satinwood /ˈsætɪnwʊd; *US* ˈsætn-/ *n* [U] smooth hard wood of a tropical tree, used for making furniture.
satire /ˈsætaɪə(r)/ *n* **1** [U] attacking foolish or wicked behaviour by making fun of it, often by using sarcasm and parody: *a work of bitter satire* ○ *Is there too much satire on TV?* **2** [C] ~ (**on sb/sth**) piece of writing, play, film, etc that makes fun of foolish or wicked behaviour in this way: *Her novel is a satire on social snobbery.*
▷ **satirical** /səˈtɪrɪkl/ (also **satiric** /səˈtɪrɪk/) *adj* containing or using satire: *a satirical play, poem, sketch, etc.* **satirically** /-klɪ/ *adv.*
satirist /ˈsætərɪst/ *n* person who uses or writes satire.
satirize, -ise /ˈsætəraɪz/ *v* [Tn] make fun of (sb/sth) by means of satire: *Politicians are often satirized on TV and radio.*
satisfaction /ˌsætɪsˈfækʃn/ *n* **1** [U] feeling of contentment felt when one has or achieves what one needs or desires: *She can look back on her career with great satisfaction.* ○ *get/obtain/derive satisfaction from one's work* ○ *a look of smug satisfaction* ○ *In old age he finally had the satisfaction of seeing the quality of his work recognized.* ○ *do the work to the satisfaction of the client*, ie so that he is pleased with it ○ *job satisfaction.* **2** [U] fulfilment (of a need, desire, etc): *the satisfaction of one's hunger* ○ *the satisfaction of a hope, desire, ambition, etc.* **3** [C] thing that gives contentment or pleasure: *the satisfactions of doing work that one loves.* **4** [U] (*fml*) (**a**) adequate response (eg compensation or an apology) to a complaint: *When I didn't get any satisfaction from the local people I wrote to the head office.* (**b**) revenge for an insult, etc (esp) by means of duelling: *You have insulted my wife; I demand satisfaction!*
satisfactory /ˌsætɪsˈfæktərɪ/ *adj* good enough for a purpose (but not outstanding): *a satisfactory attempt, meal, book, piece of work* ○ *The result of the experiment was satisfactory.* ○ *Her school report says her French is satisfactory.* ○ *We want a satisfactory explanation of your lateness.*
▷ **satisfactorily** /-tərəlɪ/ *adv* in a satisfactory manner: *The patient is getting on satisfactorily.*
satisfactoriness *n* [U].
satisfy /ˈsætɪsfaɪ/ *v* (*pt, pp* **-fied**) **1** [Tn] give (sb) what he wants, demands or needs; make contented: *Nothing satisfies him: he's always complaining.* ○ *She's not satisfied with anything but the best.* **2** [Tn] fulfil (a need, desire, etc); do enough to meet (a requirement, etc): *satisfy sb's hunger, demands, curiosity* ○ *She has satisfied the conditions for entry into the college.* **3** [Tn, Tn·pr, Dn·f] ~ **sb (as to/of sth)** give sb proof, information, etc; convince sb: *My assurances don't satisfy him: he's still sceptical.* ○ *satisfy the police that one is innocent/as to one's innocence.* (idm) ˌ**satisfy the eˈxaminers** pass an exam.
▷ **satisfied** *adj* feeling satisfaction; contented: *I felt quite satisfied after my big meal.* ○ (*ironic*) *Look! You've broken my watch. Now are you satisfied?*
satisfying *adj* giving satisfaction: *a satisfying meal, result.* **satisfyingly** *adv.*
satsuma /sætˈsuːmə/ *n* small loose-skinned edible fruit like a mandarin orange.
saturate /ˈsætʃəreɪt/ *v* **1** [Tn, Tn·pr] ~ **sth (with/in sth)** make sth very wet; soak sth: *clothes saturated with water* ○ *Saturate the meat in the*

mixture of oil and herbs. **2** [Tn·pr esp passive] ~ **sth/sb with/in sth** cause sth/sb to absorb a lot of sth; fill sth/sb completely with sth: *We lay on the beach, saturated in sunshine.* ○ *The market is saturated with good used cars,* ie There are too many of them for sale.

▷ **saturated** *adj* **1** [usu pred] very wet; soaked: *I went out in the rain and got saturated.* **2** [usu attrib] (*chemistry*) (of a solution) containing the greatest possible amount of the dissolved substance: *a saturated solution of salt.* **3** [usu attrib] (of fats and oils, eg butter) containing chemicals bonded in such a way that eating them is bad for the health. Cf POLYUNSATURATED.

saturation /ˌsætʃəˈreɪʃn/ *n* [U] saturating or being saturated. — *adj* [attrib] (of an attack) carried out in such a way that the whole of an area is affected: *saturation bombing of the town.*

□ ˌ**satuˈration point 1** (*chemistry*) stage at which no more of a substance can be absorbed into a solution. **2** (*fig*) stage at which no more can be absorbed, accepted, etc: *So many refugees have arrived that the camps have reached saturation point.*

Saturday /ˈsætədɪ/ *n* [U, C] (*abbr* **Sat**) the seventh and last day of the week, next after Friday.

For the uses of *Saturday* see the examples at *Monday.*

Saturn /ˈsætən/ *n* (*astronomy*) the planet sixth in order from the sun. It is over 700 times larger than the earth and is surrounded by series of rings, which are in fact icy particles in orbit around it. It has an atmosphere made up largely of hydrogen, and at least fifteen moons.

saturnalia /ˌsætəˈneɪlɪə/ *n* (*pl* unchanged or ~**s**) (*rhet*) wild revelry.

saturnine /ˈsætənaɪn/ *adj* (*fml*) (of a person or his appearance) gloomy: *a saturnine face, frown.*

satyr /ˈsætə(r)/ *n* **1** (in Greek and Roman myths) god of the woods, half man and half goat. **2** (*rhet*) man with very strong sexual desires.

sauce /sɔːs/ *n* **1** [C, U] (type of) liquid or semi-liquid mixture served with food to add flavour: *tomato, soy, cranberry, etc ˈsauce* ○ *fruit pudding and brandy sauce* ○ *What sauces go best with fish?* ○ [attrib] *a ˈsauce bottle.* Cf PICKLE 1, RELISH 3.

📖 Sauces are often used in British cooking to add extra flavour to food. Bottled sauces such as tomato ketchup and brown sauce (a dark brown savoury spicy sauce) are very popular and often found on the tables in cafés. Other popular sauces are mint sauce with lamb, horseradish sauce with beef, bread sauce with turkey or chicken, mornay sauce with fish, chicken, eggs or vegetables, tartar sauce with fish, and apple or cranberry sauce with pork.

2 [U] (*infml*) disrespectful rudeness, often of a harmless kind: *We'll have no more of your sauce, young man!* Cf SASS. **3 the sauce** [sing] (*US infml*) alcoholic drink: *Keep off the sauce!* **4** (idm) **in the ˈsauce** (*US infml*) having had a lot of alcohol; drunk. **what is ˌsauce for the ˈgoose is ˌsauce for the ˈgander** (*saying*) what applies to one person must apply to another in similar circumstances: *If you can arrive late, then so can I: what's sauce for the goose is sauce for the gander.*

▷ **sauce** *v* [Tn] (*infml*) be disrespectfully rude to (sb): *Don't you dare sauce me!*

saucy *adj* (**-ier, -iest**) **1** disrespectfully rude: *You saucy little thing!* **2** (esp of clothes) smart and cheerful; jaunty: *a saucy little hat.* **saucily** /-ɪlɪ/ *adv.* **sauciness** *n* [U].

□ ˈ**sauce-boat** *n* container for serving sauce.

saucepan /ˈsɔːspən; *US* -pæn/ *n* metal cooking pot, usu round and with a lid and a handle, used for cooking things over heat. ⇨ illus at PAN.

saucer /ˈsɔːsə(r)/ *n* **1** small shallow curved dish on which a cup stands: *Where's my cup and saucer?* **2** anything shaped like this, eg the dish of a radio telescope.

Saudi Arabia /ˌsaʊdɪ əˈreɪbɪə/ country in the Middle East occupying most of the Arabian peninsula; pop approx 14 016 000; official language Arabic; capital Riyadh; unit of currency riyal (= 100 halalas). Most of the country is desert but it is rich in oil and oil exports account for 85% of the government's revenue. Saudi Arabia is ruled by its royal family and is one of the most powerful states in the region. ⇨ map at ARABIAN PENINSULA.

▷ **Saudi** *n, adj.* **Saudi Arabian** /əˈreɪbɪən/ *adj.*

sauerkraut /ˈsaʊəkraʊt/ *n* [U] (*German*) chopped pickled cabbage.

sauna /ˈsɔːnə, *also* ˈsaʊnə/ *n* **(a)** period of sitting or lying in a special room heated to a very high temperature, often followed by a quick bath in cold water. **(b)** room for this.

saunter /ˈsɔːntə(r)/ *v* [Ipr, Ip] walk in a leisurely way; stroll: *saunter down the avenue* ○ *He sauntered by with his hands in his pockets.*

▷ **saunter** *n* [sing] leisurely walk or pace: *a casual saunter around the shops.*

saurian /ˈsɔːrɪən/ *n, adj* (animal) of the lizard family including crocodiles, lizards and some extinct species (eg dinosaurs).

sausage

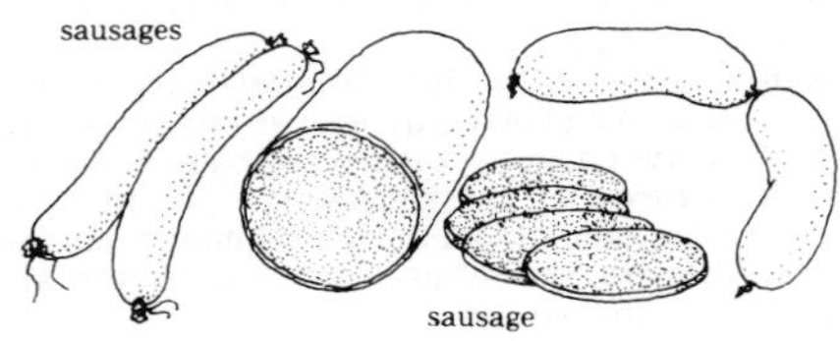

sausage /ˈsɒsɪdʒ; *US* ˈsɔːs-/ *n* **1** [C, U] mixture of minced meat (esp pork or beef) and flavouring, etc in a thin tube-like casing (either cooked and eaten whole or served cold and in slices): *grill some sausages* ○ *a pound of garlic sausage.* **2** (idm) **not a sausage** (*infml*) nothing at all.

□ ˈ**sausage-dog** *n* (*Brit infml*) dachshund.

ˈ**sausage machine** (*infml derog*) institution, organization, etc that is rigidly uniform in its methods and does not encourage the individual development of those passing through it: *The studio had become a sausage machine turning out low-budget movies.*

ˈ**sausage meat** minced meat with cereal, flavourings, etc used for making sausages.

ˌ**sausage ˈroll** sausage meat baked in a tube of pastry.

Saussure /səʊˈsʊə(r)/ Ferdinand de (1857-1913), Swiss scholar, founder of the modern study of linguistics. Although his *Cours de linguistique générale* was only published after his death, his treatment of language as a structured system at a given time changed the way in which the subject was studied. Saussure's approach to language also influenced the later study of the social sciences.

sauté /ˈsəʊteɪ; *US* səʊˈteɪ/ *adj* [attrib] (*French*) (of food) quickly fried in a little fat: *sauté potatoes.*

▷ **sauté** *v* (*pt, pp* ~**ed** or ~**d**, *pres p* ~**ing**) [Tn] fry (food) in this way: *Sauté the onions.* ⇨ Usage at COOK.

savage /ˈsævɪdʒ/ *adj* **1 (a)** wild and fierce: *a savage lion, wolf, etc* ○ *a savage attack by a big dog.* **(b)** cruel, vicious or hostile: *savage criticism, remarks* ○ *The article was a savage attack on her past actions.* ○ *He has a savage temper.* ○ *The savage ruler ordered that the prisoner be executed.* **(c)** extremely severe: *savage cuts in our budget.* **2** (⚠ *offensive*) at an early stage of civilization; primitive: *savage tribes.*

▷ **savage** *n* (⚠ *offensive*) savage(2) person: *an island inhabited by savages* ○ (*derog or joc*) *Those children can be real little savages.*

savage *v* [Tn] **1** attack (sb) savagely; maul: *She was badly savaged by a mad dog.* **2** (*fig*) criticize (sb/sth) severely: *a novel savaged by the reviewers.*

savagely *adv.*

savageness *n* [U] being savage.

savagery /ˈsævɪdʒrɪ/ *n* [U] savage behaviour: *treat prisoners with brutal savagery.*

savannah (also **savanna**) /səˈvænə/ *n* [C, U] (expanse of) treeless grassy plain in tropical and subtropical regions. Cf PAMPAS, PRAIRIE, STEPPE, VELD.

savant /ˈsævənt; *US* sæˈvɑːnt/ *n* (*fml*) person of great learning.

save[1] /seɪv/ *v* **1** [Tn, Tn·pr] ~ **sb/sth (from sth/doing sth)** make or keep sb/sth safe (from harm, loss, etc): *save sb's life* ○ *save sb from drowning* ○ *save a person from himself,* eg from the results of his own foolishness ○ *It was too late to save the sick woman, and she died.* ○ *Can the school be saved from closure?* ○ *She saved the set* (ie at tennis) *by winning the next game.* **2 (a)** [I, Ipr, Ip, Tn, Tn·pr, Tn·p] ~ **(sth) (up) (for sth)**; ~ **(with sth)** keep (money) for future use; not spend: *It's prudent to save.* ○ *save (up) for a new bike/to buy a new bike* ○ *I save with* (ie keep my savings in) *the Brighton Building Society.* ○ *save part of one's salary each month.* **(b)** [Tn, Dn·n, Dn·pr] ~ **sth (for sb/sth)** keep sth for future use; not use up sth completely: *Don't eat all the cake now; save some for tomorrow.* ○ *Save your strength for the hard work you'll have to do later.* ○ *save one's eyes,* ie protect one's eyesight, eg by not reading too much ○ *Don't drink all the wine; save me some/save some for me!* **(c)** [Ipr, Tn] ~ **(on) sth** avoid wasting sth: *save on time and money by shopping at the supermarket* ○ *save fuel by insulating one's house.* **3** [Tn, Tg, Tsg, Dn·n] make (sth) unnecessary; make it unnecessary for sb to use sth, spend sth, etc: *Order the goods by phone and save (yourself) a journey.* ○ *Walking to the office saves (me) spending money on bus fares.* ○ *The gift of money saved our having to borrow from the bank.* ○ *That will save us a lot of trouble.* ○ *We've been saved a lot of expense by doing the work ourselves.* **4** [I, Tn, Tn·pr] ~ **sb (from sth)** set sb free (from the power of sin or its bad consequences): *Jesus saves!* ○ *Jesus Christ came into the world to save us from our sins.* **5** [Tn] (in football, etc) prevent an opponent from making (a scoring shot, etc): *The goalie managed to save a shot struck at close range.* **6** (idm) **be ˌsaved by the ˈbell** be saved from an unpleasant situation by luck at a late stage. **pinch and save/scrape** ⇨ PINCH. **risk/save one's neck** ⇨ NECK. **save sb's ˈbacon** (*infml*) prevent sb from failing, losing, being harmed, etc: *I was nearly bankrupt, but your loan saved my bacon.* ˌ**save one's ˈbreath** not bother to speak when it is useless: *You can save your breath: you'll never persuade her.* ˌ**save the ˈday** manage to prevent a disaster or solve a difficulty: *You saved the day for us by giving us a lift — we'd have been late otherwise.* **save (sb's) ˈface** preserve one's/sb's pride, reputation, etc: *Though she'd lost her job, she saved face by saying she'd left it willingly.* **save one's (own) ˈhide/ˈskin** (*infml usu derog*) escape harm, injury, punishment, loss, etc: *When the rest of the gang were arrested, he saved his own skin by giving evidence against them.* ˌ**save the situˈation** deal successfully with a situation which had seemed hopeless: *Disagreements threatened to wreck the peace talks, but the president's intervention saved the situation.* **scrimp and save** ⇨ SCRIMP. **a stitch in time saves nine** ⇨ STITCH *n.*

▷ **save** *n* (in football, etc) act of preventing a goal from being scored.

saver *n* **1 (a)** person who saves: *Good news for all savers — a rise in interest rates!* ○ *a saver of souls,* eg a priest. **(b)** (esp in compounds) thing that saves: *a boiler that is a good fuel-saver.* **2** (*Brit*) ticket, etc that costs less than the usual price: [attrib] *an off-peak saver ticket.*

saving *adj* (idm) **a saving ˈgrace** thing that makes up for the poor qualities in sb/sth: *He may be stupid and mean, but his one saving grace is his humour.*

-saving (forming compound *adjs*) that saves (SAVE[1] 3) the thing specified: *Modern houses have many labour-saving devices,* eg washing-machines, dishwashers, etc which make housework easier. ○ *energy-saving modifications.*

□ ˌ**save-as-you-ˈearn** *n* (*abbr* **SAYE**) (*dated Brit*) method of saving one's money by having some of it deducted from one's salary each month.

save[2] /seɪv/ (also **saving** /ˈseɪvɪŋ/) *prep, conj* (*fml*) except: *all save him* ○ *We know nothing about her save that her surname is Jones.*

saving /ˈseɪvɪŋ/ *n* **1** amount saved: *a useful saving* *of time and money* ○ *big savings on fuel through greater efficiency.* **2 savings** [pl] money saved up: *keep one's savings in the bank.*

□ **ˈsavings account 1** (*Brit*) any type of bank account that earns more interest than a deposit account. **2** (*US*) any type of account that earns interest. Cf CURRENT ACCOUNT (CURRENT[1]), DEPOSIT ACCOUNT (DEPOSIT[2]).

ˈsavings bank bank that pays interest on money deposited but does not provide other services for its customers.

ˈsavings certificate certificate issued to savers who invest in government funds and entitling them to interest on the money invested.

saviour (*US* **savior**) /ˈseɪvɪə(r)/ *n* **1** person who rescues or saves sb from danger. **2 the Saviour, Our Saviour** Jesus Christ.

savoir-faire /ˌsævwɑːˈfeə(r)/ *n* [U] (*French approv*) ability to behave appropriately in social situations: *possess, display, lack savoir-faire.*

Savonarola /ˌsævənəˈrəʊlə; *US also* səˌvɑːnəˈrəʊlə/ Girolamo (1452-98), Italian preacher. He attacked the immorality of Florence, and virtually ruled the city in 1494-5. He made many enemies, and was finally executed after disobeying the Pope's orders to stop preaching.

savory /ˈseɪvərɪ/ *n* **1** [U] herb of the mint family used in cooking. **2** [C] (*US*) = SAVOURY *n*.

savour (*US* **savor**) /ˈseɪvə(r)/ *n* [C, U] (pleasant) taste or flavour: *soup with a slight savour of garlic* ○ *meat that has lost its savour* ○ (*fig*) *His political views have a savour of fanaticism.* ○ *Life seems to have lost some of its savour,* ie its enjoyable quality.

▷ **savour** *v* **1** [Tn] enjoy the taste or flavour of (sth), esp by eating or drinking it slowly: *savour the finest French dishes* ○ (*fig*) *Now the exams are over, I'm savouring my freedom.* **2** (phr v) **savour of sth** (no passive) have a suggestion or trace of sth (esp sth bad): *Her remarks savour of hypocrisy.*

savoury (*US* **savory**) /ˈseɪvərɪ/ *adj* **1** (of food) having a salty or sharp flavour, not a sweet one: *a savoury pancake.* **2** having an appetizing taste or smell. **3** (usu in negative sentences) morally wholesome or respectable: *I gather his past life was not altogether savoury.* Cf UNSAVOURY.

▷ **savoury** (*US* **savory**) *n* (*Brit*) savoury(1) dish, usu served at the end of a meal.

savoy /səˈvɔɪ/ *n* type of cabbage with wrinkled leaves.

Savoy Operas /səˌvɔɪ ˈɒprəz/ **the Savoy Operas** the operas of *Gilbert and *Sullivan, most of which were first performed at the Savoy Theatre in the *Strand, London, specially built for them by their producer, Richard *D'Oyly Carte.

savvy /ˈsævɪ/ *n* [U] (*sl*) common sense; nous; understanding: *Where's your savvy?*

▷ **savvy** *v* (*pt, pp* **savvied**) [I] (*sl*) (usu in the imperative or present tense) understand; know: *Keep your mouth shut! Savvy?* ○ *No savvy,* ie I do not know/understand.

saw[1] *pt of* SEE[1].

saw[2] /sɔː/ *n* (often in compounds) cutting tool that has a long blade with a sharp-toothed edge, worked by hand (by pushing it backwards and forwards) or mechanically, and used for cutting wood, metal, stone, etc: *cutting logs with a ˈpower saw* ○ *a ˌcircular ˈsaw* ○ *a ˈhandsaw* ○ *a ˈchainsaw.*

▷ **saw** *v* (*pt* **sawed**, *pp* **sawn** /sɔːn/; *US* **sawed**) **1** [I, Ipr, Tn, Tn·pr, Tn·p] use a saw; cut (sth) with a saw; make (logs, etc) by using a saw: *spend half an hour sawing* ○ *saw into the branch* ○ *saw wood* ○ *saw a log into planks/in two* ○ *saw the plank right through.* ⇨ Usage at CUT[1]. **2** [Ipr, Ip, Tn] ~ (**away**) (**at sth**) make to-and-fro movements as if with a saw: *sawing at his fiddle,* ie using the bow as if it were a saw ○ *She was sawing (away at) the bread with a blunt knife.* **3** [I] be capable of being sawn: *This wood saws easily.* **4** (phr v) **saw sth down** bring sth to the ground using a saw: *saw a tree, pole, etc down.* **saw sth off (sth)** cut sth off with a saw: *saw a branch off (a tree)* ○ *a sawn-off shotgun,* ie one with most of the barrel sawn off, used esp by criminals because it is easier to carry and conceal. **saw sth up** saw sth into pieces: *All the trees have been sawn up into logs.*

sawyer /ˈsɔːjə(r)/ *n* person whose job is sawing wood.

□ **ˈsawdust** *n* [U] tiny pieces of wood falling as powder from wood as it is sawn.

ˈsawfish *n* (*pl* unchanged) large sea-fish that has a long saw-like mouth part at the front of its head with sharp teeth along each side.

ˈsaw-horse (*US* also **ˈsawbuck**) *n* wooden frame on which wood is supported while it is being sawn.

ˈsawmill *n* mill with power-operated saws for cutting timber into planks, etc.

ˈsaw-tooth (also **ˈsaw-toothed**) *adj* having a jagged edge.

saw[3] /sɔː/ *n* (*dated*) saying; proverb: *the old saw 'More haste, less speed'.*

sax /sæks/ *n* (*infml*) = SAXOPHONE.

Saxe-Coburg-Gotha /ˌsæksˌkəʊbɜːg ˈgəʊθə/ name of the British Royal Family from the beginning of the reign of Edward VII in 1901 until 1917, when anti-German feeling caused George V to change it to *Windsor. ⇨ App 3.

saxifrage /ˈsæksɪfreɪdʒ/ *n* [U] any of various alpine or rock plants with white, yellow or red flowers.

Saxon /ˈsæksn/ *n* **1** [C] member of a people once living in NW Germany, some of whom conquered and settled in Britain in the 5th and 6th centuries. **2** [U] their language.

▷ **Saxon** *adj* of this people or their language: *Saxon tribes, customs, grammar.*

saxophone /ˈsæksəfəʊn/ (*also infml*) (also **sax**) *n* metal musical instrument played by blowing, made of metal, with keys worked by the player's fingers, typically shaped like a long thin letter S and used mainly for jazz: *a tenor/bass saxophone* ○ [attrib] *a saxophone solo.* ⇨ illus at MUSIC.

▷ **saxophonist** /sækˈsɒfənɪst; *US* ˈsæksəfəʊnɪst/ *n* saxophone player.

say /seɪ/ *v* (*3rd pers sing pres t* **says** /sez/, *pt, pp* **said** /sed/) **1 (a)** [Tn, Tn·pr, Tf, Dn·pr, Dpr·f, Dpr·w] ~ **sth (to sb)** tell sth (to sb), usu in words: *Did you say 'Please'?* ○ *'Hello!' I said.* ○ *She said nothing to me about it.* ○ *He said (that) his friend's name was Sam.* ○ *Everyone said how awful the weather was.* ○ *He finds it hard to say what he feels.* ○ *She said to meet her here.* ○ *I said to myself* (ie thought), *'That can't be right!'* ○ *They say/It's said* (ie People claim) *that he's a genius.* ○ *So you say,* ie I think you may be wrong. ○ *Who said I can't cook?* ie Of course I can! ○ *Be quiet, I've got something to say.* ○ *Having said that* (ie Despite what I have just said), *I agree with your other point.* ○ (*euph*) *If you damage the car, your father will have plenty to say about it,* ie he will be angry. **(b)** [Tn] pronounce (eg words one has learned): *say a short prayer* ○ *Try to say that line with more conviction.* **(c)** [Tn, Tn·pr] ~ **sth (to sb)** make (thoughts, feelings, etc) clear to sb by using words, or else by gestures, behaviour, etc: *This poem doesn't say much to me.* ○ *Just what is the artist trying to say in her work?* ○ *Her angry glance said everything.* **(d)** [no passive: Tn, Tf, Tw, Tt] (of a book, sign, etc) give (information or instructions): *a notice saying 'Keep Out'* ○ *The clock says three o'clock.* ○ *The law says (that) this is quite legitimate.* ○ *The book doesn't say where he was born.* ○ *The guidebook says to turn left.* ⇨ Usage. **2 (a)** [Tn, Tf, Tw] give (an opinion, answer, etc): *I'll say this (for them)* (ie I'll admit that), *they're efficient.* ○ *I can't say I blame her for resigning,* ie I think she was justified. ○ *I would say he's right.* ○ *My wife thinks I'm too fat — what do you say?* ○ *I say* (ie suggest) *we stay here.* ○ *I wouldn't say they were rich,* ie In my opinion they aren't rich. ○ *Say all you want about her* (ie Despite any criticism you can make), *she's still a fine singer.* ○ *It's hard to say who it was.* ○ *There is no saying* (ie Nobody knows) *when the war will end.* ○ *'When will the meal be ready?' 'I couldn't say.'* **(b)** [no passive: Tn, Tf] suppose (sth) as an example or a possibility: *You could learn to play chess in, (let's) say, three months.* ○ *Let's take any writer, say* (ie for example) *Dickens...* ○ *Say you have an accident: who would look after you?* **3** (idm) **before you can/could say Jack Robinson** very quickly or suddenly. **easier said than done** ⇨ EASY[2]. **ˌgo without ˈsaying** be very obvious or natural: *It goes without saying that I'll help you.* **have a good word to say for sb/sth** ⇨ WORD. **have something, nothing, etc to ˈsay for oneself** be ready, unwilling, etc to talk, eg to give one's views or justify oneself: *She hasn't got much to say for herself,* ie doesn't take part in conversation. ○ *You've got too much to say for yourself,* ie You think you are more interesting than you really are. ○ *You've lost your games kit again — what have you got to say for yourself?* **I dare say** ⇨ DARE[1]. **ˈI'll say!** (*infml*) yes indeed: *'Does he come often?' 'I'll say! Nearly every day.'* **I ˈmust say** (used when making a comment): *Well that's daft, I must say!* **I say** (*dated*) (used to express surprise, shock, etc or (unstressed) to start a conversation): *ˌI ˈsay! What a huge cake!* ○ *I say, can you lend me five pounds?* **it is safe to say that** ⇨ SAFE[1]. **it says a ˈlot, very ˈlittle, etc for sb/sth** (used to present a revealing fact about sb/sth): *It says a lot for her that she never lost her temper,* ie It shows how patient she is. ○ *It doesn't say much for our efficiency that* (ie We are not efficient because) *the order arrived a week late.* **I ˌwouldn't say ˈno (to sth)** (*infml*) used to show one wants sth, or to accept sth when it is offered: *'Fancy some coffee?' 'I wouldn't say no.'* ○ *I wouldn't say no to a pizza.* **least said soonest mended** (*saying*) a particular situation will be most quickly remedied if nothing more is said about it. **the less/least said the better** the best thing to do is to say as little as possible (about sth). **let us say** for example. **needless to say** ⇨ NEEDLESS (NEED[3]). **ˌnever say ˈdie** (*saying*) don't give up hope: *Never say die: we might still get there on time.* **no sooner said than done** ⇨ SOON. **not be saying much** (used to point out that sth is not really remarkable): *She's taller than me, but as I'm only five foot, that's not saying much.* **not say boo to a goose** be very or too timid or gentle: *He's such a nervous chap he wouldn't/couldn't say boo to a goose.* **not say a dicky-bird** (*sl*) say nothing. **not to say** (used to suggest that a stronger way of describing sth is justified): *a difficult, not to say impossible, task.* **sad to say** ⇨ SAD. **say/be one's last word** ⇨ LAST[1]. **say ˈcheese** (said by a person taking a photograph of others to make them smile). **say no (to sth)** refuse (an offer, a suggestion, etc): *If you don't invest in these shares, you're saying no to a fortune.* **ˌsay no ˈmore (a)** (used to interrupt sb when one wishes to react to what he is saying): *Say no more! How much do you want to borrow?* **(b)** I understand what you mean: *'He came home with lipstick on his face.' 'Say no more!'* **say one's piece** say what one wants to say. Cf HAVE ONE'S SAY (SAY *n*). **says ˈyou** (*sl*) I do not believe what you say: *'I'll beat him.' 'Says you, you haven't got a chance!'* **say ˈwhen** (used to ask sb to show when one should stop doing sth, esp when one has poured enough to drink). **say the ˈword** give an order; make a request: *Just say the word, and I'll ask him to leave.* **strange to say** ⇨ STRANGE. **suffice it to say** ⇨ SUFFICE. **there is no ˈsaying/ˈtelling** it is impossible to know: *There's no saying what may happen.* ○ *As to her plans, there's simply no telling.* **to ˌsay the ˈleast** without any exaggeration: *I was surprised at what he said, to say the least.* **to say nothing of sth** without even mentioning sth: *He had to go to prison for a month, to say nothing of the fine.* **that is to say** in other words: *three days from now, that's to say Friday.* **what do/would you say (to sth/doing sth)?** would you like sth/to do sth?: *We'll go on holiday together. What do you say?* ○ *What do you say to going to the theatre tonight?* ○ *What would you say to a chocolate?* **what/whatever sb says goes** (*infml*) the specified person has total authority and must be obeyed: *My wife wants the kitchen painted white, and what she says goes.* **you can say ˈthat again** I agree with you: *'She's a violent woman.' 'You can say that again. She's hit me more than once.'* **ˈyou don't ˈsay!** (*infml*) (used to express surprise): *'We're going to get married.' 'You don't say!'* **you ˈsaid it!** (*infml*) that is very true: *'The food was awful!' 'You said it!'* ○ *'I looked a fool.' 'You said it!* (ie I am glad you realized it.)'

▷ **say** *n* **1** [sing, U] ~ **(in sth)** power to decide: *have no, not much, some, any, etc say (in a matter)* ○ *I want a say in the management of the business.* **2** (idm) **have one's 'say** express one's view: *Don't interrupt her: let her have her say.*

say *interj* (*US infml*) (used to express mild surprise or to introduce a remark): *Say! How about a Chinese meal tonight?*

saying /ˈseɪɪŋ/ *n* well-known phrase, proverb, etc; remark often made: *'More haste, less speed,' as the saying goes.*

□ **'say-so** *n* [sing] (*infml*) **1** statement made by sb without proof: *Don't just accept his say-so: find out for yourself.* **2** permission (to do sth); power (to decide sth): *You don't need my say-so to change things.*

NOTE ON USAGE: **1 Say** and **tell** are transitive verbs. The direct object of **say** is usually the words spoken. The direct object of **tell** is usually the information given and the indirect object is the person that it is given to: *He sat in a corner and said nothing all evening,* ie spoke no words. ○ *She told me nothing about herself,* ie she gave me no information. **Say** is commonly used with direct speech: *He said 'Goodnight,' and went to bed.* **Say** and **tell** often report speech. **Tell** must normally be followed by a personal direct object; **say** is used without a personal object: *He hasn't told me/said that he's leaving.* **Tell sb** + infinitive is used for commands: *She told him to hurry up.* **2 Speak** and **talk** are used intransitively and transitively. They are often used with similar meaning, **speak** being more formal: *Can I talk to Susan, please?* ○ *I'd like to speak to Mrs Jones, please.* **Talk** suggests that two or more people are having a conversation with each other, while **speak** is often used of one person addressing a group: *We talked for hours about the meaning of life.* ○ *He spoke to the class about the dangers of smoking.*

SAYE /ˌes eɪ waɪ ˈiː/ *abbr* (*dated Brit*) (of a Post Office savings scheme) save-as-you-earn.

Sayers /ˈseɪəz/ Dorothy Leigh (1893-1957) English writer. She is famous for her detective stories, featuring the aristocratic amateur detective, Lord Peter Wimsey, as well as for her plays on religious themes.

Sb *symb* antimony.

Sc *symb* scandium.

sc *abbr* **1** (also **Sc**) scene: *Act I Sc IV.* **2** namely (Latin *scilicet*).

scab /skæb/ *n* **1** [C, U] dry crust formed over a wound or sore as it heals. **2** [U] disease of skin or plants causing scab-like roughness: *sheep-scab.* **3** [C] (*infml derog*) worker who refuses to join a strike or a trade union, or who takes the place of a striker; blackleg.

▷ **scabby** *adj* (**-ier, -iest**) **(a)** covered with scabs (SCAB 1). **(b)** (*sl derog*) contemptible: *You scabby liar!*

scabbard /ˈskæbəd/ *n* cover for the blade of a sword, dagger or bayonet; sheath. ⇨ illus at SWORD.

scabies /ˈskeɪbiːz/ *n* [U] contagious skin disease causing scabs and itching.

scabious /ˈskeɪbɪəs/ *n* [U] wild or cultivated plant with thick clusters of blue, pink or white flowers.

scabrous /ˈskeɪbrəs; *US* ˈskæb-/ *adj* (*fml*) **1** (of animals, plants, etc) having a rough surface. **2** indecent; obscene: *Her scabrous novels shocked the public.*

scads /skædz/ *n* [pl] ~**s (of sth)** (*US infml*) large numbers or amounts: *scads of money, people.*

scaffold

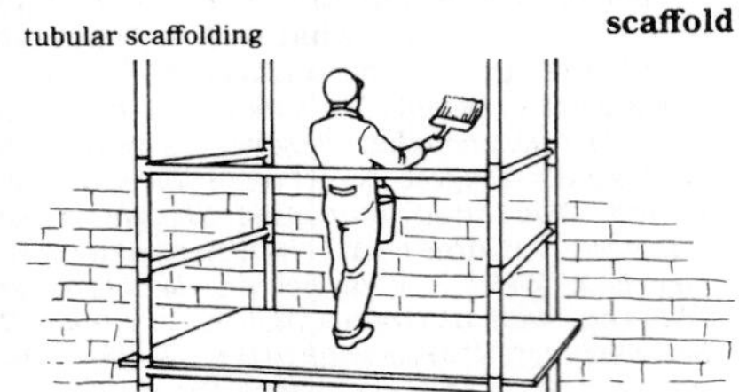

scaffold /ˈskæfəʊld/ *n* **1** frame made of long metal tubes put up next to a building so that builders, painters, etc can work on it, or to support a platform. **2** platform on which criminals are executed: *go to the scaffold,* ie be executed.

▷ **scaffolding** /ˈskæfəldɪŋ/ *n* [U] (materials for a) scaffold(1), eg poles and planks: *tubular scaffolding,* ie metal tubes to be bolted together.

scalar /ˈskeɪlə(r)/ *n, adj* (*mathematics*) (quantity) having size but no direction. Cf VECTOR 1.

scalawag (*US*) = SCALLYWAG.

scald /skɔːld/ *v* **1** [Tn, Tn·pr] burn (oneself or part of one's body) with boiling liquid or steam: *scald one's hand with hot fat* ○ *She was scalded to death when the boiler exploded.* **2** [Tn] heat (esp milk) almost to boiling-point. **3** [Tn] clean (pans, etc) with boiling water. **4** (idm) **like a ˌscalded ˈcat** (*infml*) very fast, usu out of fear: *He took one look at the approaching policeman and ran off like a scalded cat.*

▷ **scald** *n* injury to the skin from boiling liquid or steam: *an ointment for burns and scalds.*

scalding *adj* hot enough to scald: *scalding water, fat, etc.* — *adv* extremely: *scalding hot.*

scale[1] /skeɪl/ *n* **1** [C] any of the thin overlapping plates of hard material covering the skin of many fish and reptiles: *scrape the scales from a herring.* ⇨ illus at FISH. **2** [C] thing resembling this, esp a loose flake of diseased skin. **3** [U] **(a)** (also *esp Brit* **fur**) chalky material deposited by hard water inside boilers, kettles, water-pipes, etc. **(b)** tartar on teeth. **4** (idm) **the scales fall from sb's ˈeyes** someone suddenly realizes the truth after having been deceived: *Then the scales fell from my eyes: he had been lying all the time.*

▷ **scale** *v* **1** [Tn] remove the scales from (fish). **2** (phr v) **scale off (sth)** come off in flakes: *paint/plaster scaling off (a wall).*

scaly *adj* (**-ier, -iest**) covered with scale or scales; coming off in scales: *a scaly skin, surface* ○ *a kettle that's scaly inside.* **scaliness** *n* [U].

scale[2] /skeɪl/ *n* **1** [C] **(a)** series of marks at regular distances for the purpose of measuring (eg on a ruler or thermometer): *This ruler has one scale in centimetres and another in inches.* **(b)** measuring instrument marked in this way. **2** [C] system of units for measuring: *the ˈdecimal scale.* **3** [C] system of grading people or things according to how big, important, rich, etc, they are: *a scale of wages, taxation* ○ *a person who is high on the social scale* ○ *The salary scale goes from £8 000 to £20 000.* **4** [C] relation between the actual size of sth and the map, diagram, etc which represents it: *a scale of ten kilometres to the centimetre, a scale of one to a million* ○ *a large-scale map,* ie one showing a relatively small area in detail ○ *Sheet maps use a much larger scale.* ○ [attrib] *a scale model, drawing, etc.* ⇨ illus at MAP. **5** [U, C] relative size, extent, etc: *entertain on a large scale,* eg hold expensive parties with many guests ○ *The scale of his spending — £50 000 in a year — amazed us all.* ○ *We achieve economies of scale in production,* ie Producing many items reduces the price of each one. **6** [C] (*music*) series of notes arranged at fixed intervals in order of pitch, esp a series of eight starting on a keynote: *the scale of F,* ie with F as the keynote ○ *practise scales on the piano.* Cf OCTAVE 1. **7** (idm) **to scale** in a fixed proportion to the actual size: *draw a map of an area to scale.*

▷ **scale** *v* (phr v) ~ **sth down/up** reduce/increase sth: *We are going to scale down the number of trees being felled.* ○ *We've scaled up production to meet demand.*

scales

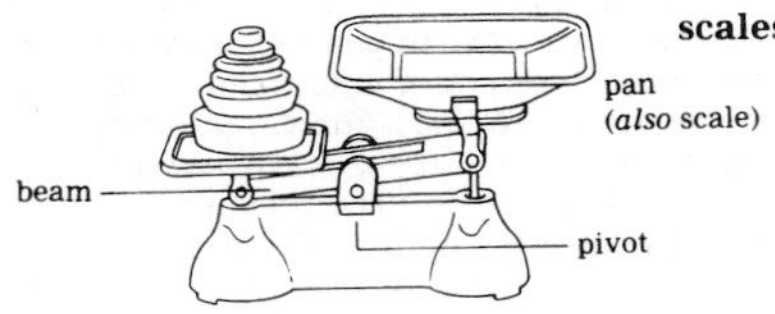

scale[3] /skeɪl/ *n* **1** [C] either of the two pans on a balance. **2 scales** [pl *v*] balance or instrument for weighing: *a pair of scales* ○ *bathroom scales,* ie for weighing oneself. ⇨ illus. **3** (idm) **tip the balance/scale** ⇨ TIP[2]. **tip/turn the scale(s) at sth** (*infml*) weigh (a specified amount): *The jockey turned the scales at 80 lb.*

▷ **scale** *v* [In/pr] weigh (a specified amount): *The boxer scaled 90 kilos.*

scale[4] /skeɪl/ *v* [Tn] climb up (a wall, cliff, etc).

scalene /ˈskeɪliːn/ *adj* (*geometry*) (of a triangle) having no two sides of equal length.

scallion /skælɪən/ *n* **1** = SHALLOT. **2** (*US*) = SPRING ONION (SPRING[2]).

scallop *n* (also **scollop**) /ˈskɒləp/ **1 (a)** shellfish with two fan-shaped shells. **(b)** (also **ˈscallop-shell**) one shell of this used as a container in which food is cooked and served. **2** any one of a series of scallop-shaped curves cut on the edge of fabric, pastry, etc.

▷ **scallop** (also **scollop**) *v* [Tn] **1** decorate (sth) with scallops (SCALLOP 2): *a scalloped hem.* **2** cook (eg oysters) in a scallop-shell.

scallywag /ˈskælɪwæg/ (also *esp US* **scalawag** /ˈskæləwæg/) *n* (used playfully) person, esp a child, who behaves mischievously: *You naughty little scallywag!*

scalp /skælp/ *n* **1** skin of the head excluding the face: *dandruff flaking off one's scalp.* **2** this and the hair rooted in it, formerly cut off a dead enemy as a trophy by some N American Indians: (*fig*) *be out for/after sb's scalp,* ie want to punish, take revenge on sb, etc.

▷ **scalp** *v* [Tn] **1** take the scalp(2) from (an enemy): (*joc*) *You've just about scalped me!* ie cut my hair very short. **2** (*esp US*) buy and resell (eg shares) so as to make a profit quickly.

scalpel /ˈskælpəl/ *n* small light knife used by surgeons.

scam /skæm/ *n* (*US infml*) dishonest scheme: *a betting scam.*

scamp /skæmp/ *n* (often used playfully) mischievous child: *That little scamp Jimmy has hidden my slippers again!*

scamper /ˈskæmpə(r)/ *v* [Ipr, Ip] run quickly and often playfully as children and some small animals do: *scamper up the steps* ○ *The rabbit scampered away in fright.* ⇨ Usage at SCURRY.

▷ **scamper** *n* [sing] scampering movement; act of scampering: *a little scamper round the garden.*

scampi /ˈskæmpɪ/ *n* **1** [pl] large prawns. **2** [U] dish of these as food, usu fried in breadcrumbs: *have some scampi.*

scan /skæn/ *v* (**-nn-**) **1** [Tn] look at every part of (sth) carefully; examine (sth) with great attention: *He scanned the horizon, looking for land.* **2** [Tn] **(a)** (of a searchlight, etc) pass across (an area): *The flashlight's beam scanned every corner of the room.* **(b)** (*medical*) obtain an image of (a body or part of the body) with a scanner. **3** [Tn] glance at (eg a document) quickly but not very thoroughly: *She scanned the newspaper over breakfast.* **4 (a)** [Tn] analyse the metre of (a line of verse) by noting how it is stressed and how many syllables it has, as in *ˈMary /ˈhad a/ˈlittle /ˈlamb.* **(b)** [I] (of verse) have a proper metrical pattern: *a line that does not scan* ○ *The verses scan well.* **5** [Tn] (in television, etc) pass an electronic beam over (sth), esp so as to produce a picture on a screen.

▷ **scan** *n* act of scanning (SCAN 2b): *a ˈbody scan,* ie done by a scanner ○ *a ˈbrain-scan.*

scanner *n* machine for scanning (SCAN 2b), esp one used by doctors, which uses a computer to give a picture of the inside of the body from a series of X-rays or other techniques.

scansion /ˈskænʃn/ *n* [U] scanning of verse; way in which verse scans.

scandal /ˈskændl/ *n* **1 (a)** [C, U] (act, behaviour, etc that causes) public feelings of outrage or indignation: *cause (a) scandal* ○ *A series of corruption scandals led to the fall of the government.* ○ *Her theft from the shop caused (a) scandal in the village.* **(b)** [sing] action, attitude, etc that is disgraceful or shameful: *It is a scandal that the defendant was declared innocent.* ○ *The council's failure to act is a scandal.* **2** [U] talk about the bad things people are thought to have done; gossip: *spread scandal* ○ *Most of us enjoy a bit of*

scandal. ○ *Have you heard the latest scandal?*
▷ **scandalize, -ise** /ˈskændəlaɪz/ *v* [Tn] shock (sb) by sth immoral or outrageous: *scandalize the neighbours by sunbathing naked on the lawn.*
scandalous /ˈskændələs/ *adj* **1** disgraceful; shocking: *scandalous behaviour, talk, books.* **2** [attrib] (of reports or rumours) containing scandal(1a). **scandalously** *adv.*
□ **ˈscandalmonger** /-mʌŋgə(r)/ *n* (*derog*) person who spreads scandal(2). **ˈscandalmongering** /-mʌŋgərɪŋ/ *n* [U].
ˈscandal sheet (*infml derog*) newspaper that regularly prints harmful gossip about public figures.
Scandinavia /ˌskændɪˈneɪvɪə/ group of countries in northern Europe, consisting of Norway and Sweden, with Denmark, Finland and Iceland often included. ▷ **Scandinavian** /-ɪən/ *n, adj.*
scansion ⇨ SCAN.
scant /skænt/ *adj* [attrib] (*fml*) hardly enough; not very much (used esp with the *ns* shown): *pay scant attention to sb's advice* ○ *with scant regard for my feelings.*
▷ **scanty** *adj* (**-ier, -iest**) small in size or amount; hardly large enough: *a scanty supply of soap* ○ *a scanty bikini.* **scantily** *adv*: *scantily dressed.* **scantiness** *n* [U].
-scape *suff* (with *ns* forming *ns*) (picture of a) view of: *landscape* ○ *seascape.*
scapegoat /ˈskeɪpgəʊt/ *n* (also *esp US* **fall guy**) person who is blamed or punished for the wrongdoing of sb else: *I was made the scapegoat, but it was the others who started the fire.*
scapegrace /ˈskeɪpgreɪs/ *n* (*dated*) (usu young) person who is often in trouble because of a wild or thoughtless character.
scapula /ˈskæpjʊlə/ *n* (*anatomy*) shoulder-blade. ⇨ illus at SKELETON.
scapular /ˈskæpjʊlə(r)/ *adj* of the scapula.
▷ **scapular** *n* **1** any of the feathers covering a bird's shoulder. **2** very short cloak-like garment worn over the shoulders by some priests and monks.
scar /skɑː(r)/ *n* **1** mark left on the skin by a wound, sore, etc: *Will the cut leave a scar?* ○ (*fig*) *scars on the cupboard from burning cigarettes.* **2** feelings of great sadness, guilt, etc after an unpleasant experience: *Her years in prison left a scar.*
▷ **scar** *v* (**-rr-**) **1** [Tn] leave a scar or scars on (sb): *a face scarred by smallpox* ○ (*fig*) *scarred by the death of his daughter.* **2** [I, Ip] ~ (**over**) heal by forming a scar; form a scar or scars: *Will the cut scar?* ○ *The wound gradually scarred over.*
scarab /ˈskærəb/ *n* **1** type of beetle regarded as sacred in ancient Egypt. **2** carving of a scarab, worn as an ornament or a charm.
scarce /skeəs/ *adj* **1** not easily obtained and much less than is needed: *scarce resources, supplies, etc* ○ *It was wartime and food was scarce.* Cf PLENTIFUL. **2** [pred] not often found; rare: *This book is now scarce.* ⇨ Usage at RARE[1]. **3** (idm) **make oneself ˈscarce** (*infml*) go away; avoid others: *He's in a bad mood, so I'll make myself scarce.*
▷ **scarcity** /ˈskeəsətɪ/ *n* [C, U] (instance of) shortage: *frequent scarcities of raw materials* ○ *The scarcity of food forced prices up.*
scarcely /ˈskeəslɪ/ *adv* **1** only just; hardly: *There were scarcely a hundred people present.* ○ *I scarcely know him.* ○ *Scarcely had she entered the room when the phone rang.* **2** surely not: *You can scarcely expect me to believe that.* ⇨ Usage at ALMOST.
scare /skeə(r)/ *v* **1** (a) (also *infml* **scarify**) [Tn] frighten (sb): *That noise scared me.* (b) [I] (used esp with an *adv*) become frightened: *He scares easily.* **2** (idm) **frighten/scare the daylights out of sb** ⇨ DAYLIGHTS. **frighten/scare sb to death/out of his wits** ⇨ FRIGHTEN. **scare sb ˈstiff** (*infml*) make sb very nervous; alarm sb: *The thought of my exams next week scares me stiff.* ○ *He's scared stiff of women.* **3** (phr v) **scare sb away/off** make sb leave, stay away, etc by frightening or alarming him: *light a fire to scare off the wolves* ○ *He scares people away by being so brash.* **scare sb into/out of sth/doing sth** make sb do/not do sth by frightening him: *They scared him into handing over the keys.* ○ *We'll scare her out of telling the police.*
▷ **scare** *n* sudden fright; alarm caused by a rumour, etc: *You did give me a scare, creeping up on me like that!* ○ *The explosion at the chemical factory caused a major pollution scare.* ○ [attrib] *a scare story*, eg a newspaper report that spreads panic.
scared *adj* ~ (**of sb/sth**); ~ (**of doing sth/to do sth**) frightened: *I'm scared (of ghosts).* ○ *scared of being attacked, to go out alone* ○ *a very scared man.*
ˈscaredy-cat /ˈskeədɪkæt/ *n* (*infml joc*) (esp as a term of address) timid or cowardly person: *Scaredy-cat! He won't go in the water!*
scary /ˈskeərɪ/ *adj* (**-ier, -iest**) (*infml*) causing fear or alarm: *a scary ghost story.*
□ **ˈscarecrow** *n* figure resembling a person that is dressed in old clothes and set up in a field to frighten away birds.
ˈscaremonger /-mʌŋgə(r)/ *n* (*derog*) person who frightens people by spreading alarming news, rumours, etc.
scarf[1] /skɑːf/ *n* (*pl* **scarfs** /skɑːfs/ or **scarves** /skɑːvz/) piece of material worn for ornament or warmth round the neck or (by women) over the shoulders or hair.
scarf[2] /skɑːf/ *n* joint made by thinning two pieces of wood, etc so that they overlap without an increase in thickness, and fastening them together with bolts, etc.
▷ **scarf** *v* [Tn] join (pieces of wood etc) in this way.
scarify[1] /ˈskærɪfaɪ/ *v* (*pt, pp* **-fied**) [Tn] **1** loosen the surface of (soil, etc) by using a tool or machine with prongs. **2** (*medical*) (in surgery) make small cuts in (skin, etc); cut off skin from (a part of the body).
scarify[2] /ˈskeərɪfaɪ/ *v* (*pt, pp* **-fied**) [Tn] (*infml*) = SCARE 1a.
scarlatina /ˌskɑːləˈtiːnə/ *n* [U] = SCARLET FEVER (SCARLET).
Scarlatti /skɑːˈlætɪ/ Alessandro (1660-1725), and his son Domenico (1685-1757), Italian composers. Alessandro wrote 115 operas (not all of which survive) and played a great part in the development of the genre, as well as much church and keyboard music. Domenico is famous for the virtuosity of his keyboard pieces; he wrote over 500 and they influenced J S *Bach. He too produced many pieces of church music.
scarlet /ˈskɑːlət/ *adj, n* [U] bright red: *dressed all in scarlet* ○ *She blushed scarlet when I swore.*
□ **ˌscarlet ˈfever** (also **scarlatina**) infectious disease causing scarlet marks on the skin.
ˌscarlet ˈpimpernel pimpernel with scarlet flowers which close in cloudy or rainy weather.
ˌscarlet ˈrunner bean plant with scarlet flowers.
ˌscarlet ˈwoman (*dated derog or joc*) immoral woman; prostitute.
Scarlet Pimpernel /ˌskɑːlət ˈpɪmpənel/ **the Scarlet Pimpernel** name taken by the hero of a series of novels by Baroness Orczy. He was a brave and ingenious English aristocrat who rescued many people threatened by the *Reign of Terror during the *French Revolution.
scarp /skɑːp/ *n* steep slope; escarpment.
scarper /ˈskɑːpə(r)/ *v* [I] (*Brit sl*) run away; leave: *Scarper! The cops are coming!*
scary ⇨ SCARE.
scat[1] /skæt/ *v* (**-tt-**) [I] (usu imperative) (*infml*) go away; leave: *I don't want you here, so scat!*
scat[2] /skæt/ *n* [U] style of jazz singing in which the singer makes sounds that imitate musical instruments, instead of real words.
scathing /ˈskeɪðɪŋ/ *adj* **1** (of criticism, ridicule, etc) severe; harsh: *a scathing remark, rebuke, etc* ○ *a scathing review of a new book.* **2** [pred] ~ (**about sb/sth**) very critical (of sb/sth); scornful: *The report was scathing about the lack of safety precautions.*
scatology /skæˈtɒlədʒɪ/ *n* [U] (*derog*) excessive interest in excrement or obscenity. ▷ **scatological** /ˌskætəˈlɒdʒɪkl/ *adj*: *scatological conversation, humour.*
scatter /ˈskætə(r)/ *v* **1** [I, Tn] (cause people or animals to) move, usu quickly, in different directions: *The crowd scattered.* ○ *The police scattered the crowd.* **2** (a) [Tn, Tn·pr, Tn·p] throw (sth) in different directions; put here and there: *scatter seed (over the ground)* ○ *scatter grit on the road* ○ *We scattered plates of food around the room before the party.* ○ (*fig*) *Don't scatter your money around.* (b) [Tn·pr] ~ **sth with sth** cover (a surface, etc) with sth by throwing it in different directions: *scatter the lawn with grass seed.*
▷ **scatter** (also **scattering** /ˈskætərɪŋ/) *n* [sing] amount or number of things scattered; sprinkling: *a scatter of hailstones.*
scattered *adj* lying far apart; not close together: *a few scattered settlements* ○ *a thinly scattered population* ○ *sunshine with scattered showers.*
□ **ˈscatter-brain** *n* (*infml*) person who cannot concentrate on one thing for very long, is forgetful, etc. **ˈscatter-brained** *adj.*
ˈscatter cushion cushion that is one of several placed on armchairs, sofas, etc for decoration rather than comfort.
ˈscatter-gun *n* (*US*) shotgun: [attrib] (*fig*) *using a scatter-gun approach to a problem*, ie tackling it in several different ways in the hope that at least one way will be successful.
ˈscatter-shot *n, adj* firing at random.

NOTE ON USAGE: When we **scatter** something we throw it in different directions. We can also scatter an area (the ground, a field, etc) with something: *scatter seeds on the fields/scatter the fields with seeds.* **Scatter over/about** suggests that the throwing is done carelessly and causes a mess: *Who's scattered my papers all over the floor?* ○ *We came home to find our belongings scattered about the room.* **Strew** is most commonly used in the past participle form **strewn**. It can suggest both intentional and careless throwing: *The streets were strewn with flowers for the royal visit.* ○ *There was litter strewn all over the pavement.* **Sprinkle** is used with water, sand, salt, etc and indicates intentional scattering, usually over a small area: *Sprinkle a little salt on the rice.* ○ *The priest sprinkled holy water on the baby's forehead.* ○ *The grass was sprinkled with dew.*

scatty /ˈskætɪ/ *adj* (**-ier, -iest**) (*Brit infml*) **1** mad; crazy: *The noise would drive anyone scatty.* **2** scatter-brained; absent-minded: *Your scatty son has forgotten his key again.* ▷ **scattily** *adv.* **scattiness** *n* [U].
scavenge /ˈskævɪndʒ/ *v* **1** [I, Ipr] ~ (**for sth**) (of an animal or a bird) search for decaying flesh as food; use decaying flesh for food: *a crow scavenging for carrion.* **2** [I, Ipr, Tn] ~ (**for**) **sth** (of a person) search through waste for items that one can use: *tramps scavenging through dustbins* ○ *a tramp scavenging in dustbins for food* ○ *You can often scavenge nice bits of old furniture from skips.*
▷ **scavenger** *n* animal, bird or person that scavenges.
SCE /ˌes siː ˈiː/ *abbr* Scottish Certificate of Education.
scenario /sɪˈnɑːrɪəʊ; *US* -ˈnær-/ *n* (*pl* ~**s**) **1** written outline of a film, play, etc with details of the scenes and plot. **2** imagined sequence of future events: *a possible scenario for war.*
▷ **scenarist** /sɪˈnɑːrɪst; *US* -ˈnær-/ *n* writer of scenarios.
scene /siːn/ *n* **1** place of an actual or imagined event: *the scene of the accident, crime, etc* ○ *The scene of the novel is set in Scotland.* **2** situation or incident in real life: *the horrific scenes after the earthquake* ○ *There were hilarious scenes when the pig ran into the shop.* **3** (incident where there is an) outburst of emotion or anger: *make a scene* ○ *There was quite a scene when she refused to pay.* ○ *We had a big scene when I fired him.* **4** (a) sequence of continuous action in a play, film, etc: *The scene in the hospital was very moving.* (b) (*abbr* **sc**) part of an act in a play or opera; episode within such a part: *Act 1, Scene 2 of 'Macbeth'* ○ *the duel scene in 'Hamlet'.* **5** place represented on the stage of a theatre; the painted background, woodwork, etc representing such a place; scenery: *The first scene*

of the play is the king's palace. ○ *The scenes are changed during the interval.* **6** view as seen by a spectator: *a delightful rural scene* ○ *The boats in the harbour make a beautiful scene.* ○ *They went abroad for a change of scene,* ie to see and experience new surroundings. **7 the scene** [sing] (modified by a *n*) (*infml*) the current situation in a particular area of activity or way of life: *the ˈdrug scene* ○ *the ˈgay scene* ○ *a newcomer on the ˈfashion scene* ○ *the entertainment scene in the West End of London.* **8** (idm) **behind the ˈscenes** (**a**) out of sight of the audience; behind the stage. (**b**) in secret; without being known to the public: *political deals done behind the scenes.* **come on the ˈscene** arrive: *By the time I came on the scene, it was all over.* **not one's scene** (*infml*) not sth one knows about, is interested in, etc: *I'm not going to the disco: it's just not my scene.* **on the ˈscene** present: *Reporters were soon on the scene after the accident.* **set the ˈscene (for sth)** (**a**) describe a place or a situation in which sth is about to happen: *Radio reporters were in the church to set the scene.* (**b**) prepare for sth; help to cause sth: *His arrival set the scene for another argument.* **steal the scene/show** ⇨ STEAL.

□ **ˈscene-shifter** *n* person who changes the scenery in a theatre.

scenery /ˈsiːnərɪ/ *n* [U] **1** general natural features of an area, eg mountains, valleys, rivers, forests: *mountain scenery* ○ *stop to admire the scenery.* **2** furniture, woodwork, canvas, etc used on a theatre stage to represent the place of action.

scenic /ˈsiːnɪk/ *adj* [usu attrib] **1** having or showing beautiful natural scenery: *the scenic splendours of the Rocky Mountains* ○ *a scenic route across the Alps* ○ *a scenic railway,* eg going through mountains or along rivers. **2** of stage scenery. ▷ **scenically** /-klɪ/ *adv.*

scent /sent/ *n* **1** (**a**) [U] characteristic smell of sth, esp a pleasant one: *the scent of new-mown hay* ○ *Modern roses have no scent.* (**b**) [C] particular type of smell: *scents of lavender and rosemary.* **2** [U] (*esp Brit*) sweet-smelling (usu liquid) substance obtained from flowers, plants, etc; perfume: *a bottle of scent* ○ *put some scent on before going out* ○ [attrib] *a ˈscent bottle.* **3** (**a**) [C usu *sing*] smell left behind by an animal, that allows dogs, etc to track it: *follow, lose, recover the scent* ○ *a strong/hot scent,* ie one that is easy for dogs to follow ○ *a poor/cold scent,* ie one that is difficult for dogs to follow ○ *a false* (ie misleading) *scent.* (**b**) [U] sense of smell, esp in dogs: *hunt by scent.* **4** [sing] ~ **of sth** feeling of the presence of sth: *a scent of danger, fear, trouble.* **5** (idm) **on the scent (of sb/sth)** likely to find sb/sth soon: *The police are now on the scent of the culprit.* **put/throw sb off the ˈscent** mislead sb, esp by giving him false information: *The false alibi threw the police off the scent.*

▷ **scent** *v* **1** [Tn] (**a**) discover (sth) by the sense of smell: *The dog scented a rat.* (**b**) (*fig*) begin to suspect the presence or existence of (sth): *scent a crime* ○ *scent treachery, trouble, etc.* **2** [esp passive: Tn, Tn·pr] ~ **sth (with sth)** give sth a certain scent: *scented notepaper, soap* ○ *a handkerchief scented with lavender* ○ *roses that scent the air.*

scepter (*US*) = SCEPTRE.

sceptic (*US* **skeptic**) /ˈskeptɪk/ *n* **1** person who doubts that a claim, statement, etc is true: *The government must still convince the sceptics that its policy will work.* **2** person who does not think religious teachings are true.

▷ **sceptical** (*US* **skep-**) /-kl/ *adj* ~ **(of/about sth)** unwilling to believe sth; often doubting that claims, statements, etc are true: *I'm rather sceptical about their professed sympathy for the poor.* **sceptically** (*US* **skep-**) /-klɪ/ *adv.*

scepticism (*US* **skep-**) /ˈskeptɪsɪzəm/ *n* [U] sceptical attitude: *her healthy scepticism towards authority* ○ *reports treated wtih scepticism.*

sceptre (*US* **scepter**) /ˈseptə(r)/ *n* staff or rod carried by a ruler as a sign of royal power, eg at a coronation ceremony.

sch *abbr* school.

schadenfreude /ˈʃɑːdnfrɔɪdə/ *n* [U] (*German*) unkind enjoyment of the misfortunes of others.

schedule /ˈʃedjuːl; *US* ˈskedʒʊl/ *n* **1** [C, U] (**a**) programme of work to be done or of planned events: *a factory production schedule* ○ *have a full schedule,* ie have many things to do ○ *a project that is ahead of/on/behind schedule* ○ *Everything is going according to schedule.* (**b**) = TIMETABLE (TIME[1]): *The fog disrupted airline schedules.* **2** list of items, etc: *a spare parts schedule* ○ *The attached schedule gives details of the shipment.*

▷ **schedule** *v* **1** [esp passive: Tn, Tn·pr, Cn·t] ~ **sth (for sth)** include sth in a schedule; arrange sth for a certain time: *One of the scheduled events is a talk on flower arranging.* ○ *The sale is scheduled for tomorrow.* ○ *She is scheduled to give a speech tonight.* ○ *a scheduled flight, service, etc,* ie one that an airline, etc organizes and carries out regularly. **2** [Tn] include (a building) in an official list of those that should be preserved, eg because it is old or architecturally important.

Scheherezade /ʃəˌherəˈzɑːdə/ fictional wife of a Persian king, who to avoid execution entertained her husband for a thousand and one nights by telling him the stories known as the *Arabian Nights.*

schema /ˈskiːmə/ *n* (*pl* **-mata** /-mətə/) (*fml*) diagram or representation of sth.

schematic /skiːˈmætɪk/ *adj* in the form of a diagram or chart: *a schematic representation of the structure of the organization.* ▷ **schematically** /-klɪ/ *adv.*

scheme /skiːm/ *n* **1** ~ **(for sth/to do sth)** (**a**) plan for doing or organizing sth: *a scheme for manufacturing paper from straw* ○ *an imaginative scheme to raise money* ○ *a pension scheme.* (**b**) secret or devious plan: *a scheme for not paying tax.* **2** ordered system; arrangement: *a ˈcolour scheme,* eg for a room, so that the colours in its décor match. **3** (idm) **the best-laid schemes/plans of mice and men** ⇨ BEST[2]. **the ˈscheme of things** the way things are or are planned: *In the scheme of things it is hard for small businesses to succeed.*

▷ **scheme** *v* **1** [I, Ipr, It] ~ **(for sth/against sb)** make (esp secret or devious) plans: *rebels scheming for the overthrow of the leadership* ○ *They are scheming to get her elected as leader.* **2** [Tn] plan (sth) in a devious way: *Her enemies are scheming her downfall.* **schemer** *n* person who schemes in a devious way. **scheming** *adj* often making devious schemes: *scheming rivals.*

scherzo /ˈskeətsəʊ/ *n* (*pl* ~**s**) lively vigorous piece of music; such a passage in a larger work.

Schiller /ˈʃɪlə(r)/ Johann Christoph Friedrich von (1759-1805), German dramatist, poet and essayist. A leading figure of German Romanticism, he was influenced by *Shakespeare and *Rousseau. His 'Ode to Joy' was set to music by *Beethoven in his 9th Symphony.

schism /ˈsɪzəm/ *n* [U, C] strong disagreement, esp in a religious organization over doctrine, in which one group stops recognizing the authority of the other.

▷ **schismatic** /sɪzˈmætɪk/ *adj* of or causing schism. — *n* person who takes part in a schism.

schist /ʃɪst/ *n* [U] (*geology*) metamorphic rock which splits easily into thin plates.

schizo /ˈskɪtsəʊ/ *n* (*pl* ~**s**) (*infml often derog*) = SCHIZOPHRENIC *n*.

schizoid /ˈskɪtsɔɪd/ *adj* resembling or suffering from schizophrenia.

▷ **schizoid** *n* schizoid person.

schizophrenia /ˌskɪtsəʊˈfriːnɪə/ *n* [U] (*medical*) mental illness that causes the sufferer to act irrationally, have delusions, withdraw from social relationships, etc.

▷ **schizophrenic** /ˌskɪtsəʊˈfrenɪk/ *adj* **1** of or suffering from schizophrenia. **2** (*infml*) behaving in an odd way, esp when circumstances keep changing: *Living half the time in Oxford and half in Paris makes me feel quite schizophrenic.* — *n* (also *infml often derog* **schizo**) person suffering from schizophrenia or behaving in a schizophrenic way. **schizophrenically** /-klɪ/ *adv.*

schlemiel /ʃləˈmiːl/ *n* (*US infml*) stupid or unlucky person.

schlep (also **schlepp**) /ʃlep/ *v* (**-pp-**) (*US sl*) **1** [Tn] carry or drag (sth) with effort: *I've got to schlepp these bags up to the fifth floor.* **2** [I, Ipr, Ip] go or work wearily or with effort: *We schlepped back to the station.*

Schlesinger /ˈslezɪndʒə(r)/ John (1926-), British film director. His early films such as *Billy Liar* examined British working-class life, but his great success, *Midnight Cowboy,* was made in Hollywood.

Schliemann /ˈʃliːmən/ Heinrich (1822-90), German archaeologist. Despite having no formal training, he carried out excavations in Turkey and in Crete, and discovered the remains of the Mycenaean civilization.

schlock /ʃlɒk/ *n* [U] (*US infml*) material of poor quality.

schmaltz (also **schmalz**) /ʃmɔːlts/ *n* [U] (*infml*) excessive sentimentality, esp in literature or music. ▷ **schmaltzy** (also **schmalzy**) *adj* (**-ier, -iest**).

schmuck /ʃmʌk/ *n* (*sl esp US*) foolish or contemptible person.

schnapps /ʃnæps/ *n* [U] strong alcoholic drink distilled from grain.

schnauzer /ˈʃnaʊtsə(r)/ *n* German breed of house dog with a short wiry coat.

schnitzel /ˈʃnɪtsl/ *n* [C, U] (*US*) veal cutlet covered with breadcrumbs and fried in butter.

Schoenberg /ˈʃɜːnbɜːg/ Arnold (1874-1951), Austrian composer. He was one of the most influential of 20th-century composers, whose search for order within atonality led to the formation of serialism, a technique in which each of the 12 notes of the octave is placed in a 'series' which governs the total development of the composition. His most famous pupils were Alban *Berg and Anton *Webern.

scholar /ˈskɒlə(r)/ *n* **1** student who has been awarded money after a competitive exam, etc, to be used to finance his education: *a British Council scholar.* **2** person who studies an academic subject deeply: *a Greek, classical, history scholar.*

▷ **scholarly** *adj* **1** showing the learning, care and attention typical of a scholar: *be more scholarly in one's approach to a problem* ○ *a scholarly young woman.* **2** involving or connected with academic study: *a scholarly journal* ○ *scholarly pursuits.*

scholarship /ˈskɒləʃɪp/ *n* **1** [C] (award of a) grant of money to a scholar(1): *win a scholarship to the university.* **2** [U] great learning; care and attention in carrying out scholarly work: *a teacher of great scholarship* ○ *The book shows great scholarship.*

scholastic /skəˈlæstɪk/ *adj* **1** [usu attrib] (*fml*) of schools and education: *my scholastic achievements,* eg examination passes, prizes. **2** of scholasticism.

▷ **scholasticism** /skəˈlæstɪsɪzəm/ *n* [U] system of philosophy and theology taught in the universities in the Middle Ages, which aimed at a better understanding of Christianity, esp by defining and reasoning.

school[1] /skuːl/ *n* **1** [C] (**a**) institution for educating children: *ˈprimary and ˈsecondary schools* ○ *ˈSunday schools* ○ *attend a good school* ○ *the use of computers in schools* ○ [attrib] *a school bus, building, report* ○ *the school year,* ie the total time within a year when teaching is done in schools, usu starting in the autumn. ⇨ article. (**b**) institution for teaching a particular subject: *ˈart school* ○ *secreˈtarial school.* **2** [C] (*US*) college or university: *famous schools like Yale and Harvard.* **3** [U] (used without *the*) (**a**) process of being educated in a school[1](1a): *I hate school!* ○ *two more years of school* ○ *old enough for/to go to school* ○ *the school-ˈleaving age,* ie the age until which children must attend school ○ *Are you still at school?* ○ *He left school when he was sixteen.* (**b**) time when teaching is done in a school; lessons: *meet friends before school* ○ *School begins at 9 am.* ○ *There will be no school* (ie no lessons) *tomorrow.* ○ *Will you come for a walk after school?* ⇨ Usage. **4 the school** [sing] all the pupils or all the pupils and teachers in a school: *The head teacher told the school at assembly.* ○ *Soon, the whole school knew about her win.* **5** [C] department of a university concerned with a particular branch of study: *the*

Schools

Schools in Britain are of two types: state (or maintained) schools, which charge no fees, and independent (or private) schools, which are fee-paying. There are far more state schools than independent, but some independent schools, especially the older public schools, have retained considerable academic and social prestige.

The school year usually runs from early September to mid-July and is divided into three terms of about 12 weeks each.

State schools, which are funded by the government through the local education authority (LEA), are primary, for children aged 5 to 11, and secondary, for pupils aged 11 to 16 or 18, although in some areas there are first schools for children of 5 to 9, middle schools for ages 9 to 13, and secondary or upper schools. All children must receive a full-time education from the age of 5 until the age of 16. Below primary schools are nursery schools, for children under 5. Schools in the state system can be county schools, owned as well as funded by the LEA, or voluntary schools, founded by a voluntary body such as the Church of England or the Roman Catholic Church.

In secondary education most schools (over eight out of ten) are comprehensive schools, offering a general education to all children. There are also a small number of secondary modern schools, offering a more practical education, grammar schools, providing a more academic education, and technical schools, offering a combination of academic and technical teaching. Children who go to a secondary modern, grammar or technical school do so as a result of an examination called the 11-plus or after some other selection procedure. There are also special schools for children with a physical or mental disability.

In the independent sector, the main division is into preparatory schools, for pupils aged 7 to 13, and public schools, for pupils aged 13 to 18. (The name 'public school' is historic, and refers to the fact that such schools were originally opened to 'the public', taking pupils from any area, not just locally.) Almost all independent schools are boarding schools, and unlike state schools are usually for one sex only. About half the public schools, especially the oldest and best-known ones, such as Eton, Harrow and Winchester, are for boys only. However, many boys' public schools take girls in the senior classes, and some are now fully co-educational.

The fees in independent schools are usually several thousand pounds per year. It is possible for a child to win an 'assisted place' so that parents who cannot afford the fees receive financial help from the government.

State schools mostly have larger classes than independent schools, but all schools share the same school-leaving examinations. The main exam is the General Certificate of Secondary Education (GCSE), normally taken at the age of 16, in which pupils sit papers in different subjects (usually five or more) and are awarded a grade in each subject on a seven-point scale, A to G. A further examination, normally taken two years after GCSE, is the A level ('A' meaning 'Advanced'). This is usually done in two or three subjects only. There are also S and A/S-levels. S-level ('S' for 'Special' or 'Scholarship') provides additional, harder papers for A-level students. A/S level ('Advanced Supplementary') is an alternative to A level, with subjects studied on a broader, less specialized basis.

GCSE and A level exams are marked by one of the regional examining boards. A level boards are mostly organized by a particular university, such as the Cambridge University Local Examinations Syndicate or the University of Oxford Delegacy of Local Examinations. Schools are free to choose a board in any area.

Subjects taught in state schools are determined by the National Curriculum. The Curriculum prescribes a course of central ('core') subjects, namely English, mathematics and science, and includes seven basic ('foundation') subjects, which are history, geography, technology, music, art, physical education and (in secondary schools) a modern foreign language. There are attainment targets for what children should be capable of doing and knowing at the ages of 7, 11, 14 and 16. The National Curriculum was introduced by the Education Reform Act of 1988, and this same Act enabled secondary schools and the larger primary schools to opt out of the control of the LEA and to manage their own budgets under a new 'local management of schools' (LMS) scheme.

All state schools are required to include religious education in their syllabus, and they must also hold a daily act of worship. Parents have the right, however, to withdraw their children from the latter. In practice most independent schools also include religious education in their timetable, and many public schools begin the day with a short religious service in the school chapel.

Preparatory schools (colloquially, 'prep schools') are so named because they prepare pupils for entrance to public school. The examination which admits them is the Common Entrance (so called because it is shared in common by most public schools). It is taken at the age of 13 by boys but usually rather younger by girls. The exam itself is set by the Common Entrance Examination Board but is marked by the public school that the pupil has applied to enter. Gifted preparatory school pupils can apply for a 'scholarship', or financial grant, from their chosen public school, in which case they usually sit that school's own special exam as well.

Classes in a school are often designated as 'year' (especially in state schools) or 'form' (more in independent schools). The fifth form is the one at which GCSE is taken, while the sixth form is normally the one preparing for A level, and so the senior class. (It is often divided into 'lower sixth' and 'upper sixth' for the two years.)

Public schools are sometimes accused of being snobbish and 'elitist'. They are normally very well equipped, classes are smaller, teachers' salaries are higher, and many have a sustained record of academic excellence. Unlike state schools, they often attach considerable importance to prowess at sport as well as class work.

Scotland has its own educational system, distinct from England and Wales. (Cf article at SCOTLAND.)

In the USA, there are state schools, known as 'public schools', which are free, and private schools, which charge fees. Most children (at least eight out of 10) attend public schools. The majority of private schools are sponsored by a religious organization such as a church, and are often known as 'parochial schools'. One type of private school is the 'preparatory school' or 'prep school', so called as it prepares for university entrance. ('Preppy' is a colloquial term for the fashionable style of dress of students at these schools.)

The school year runs from early September to mid-June, with continuous weekly attendance of five hours a day, five days a week, apart from seasonal holidays. The main types of school are elementary school, for children aged 6–12 or 6–14 and high school for students aged 14 or 15 to 18. There are also junior high schools for 12–15-year olds. There is no fixed school-leaving age, but all states require a child to attend school between prescribed ages, typically from 6 to 16. Classes are organized in 'grades', with grades 1 to 6 for elementary school pupils, 7 to 9 for junior high school students, and 10 to 12 for senior high school students. Pre-school education for children under 6 is in kindergarten classes (often designated as grade K) or nursery schools.

There is no national curriculum, but basic subjects in elementary schools are 'language arts' (reading, grammar, composition and literature), 'penmanship' (writing), science, social studies (incorporating history and geography), music, art, and physical education, while in high school they are English, science and mathematics, social studies and physical education. Religious instruction is part of the curriculum in private schools, but is not given in public schools.

There are no national examinations. As pupils progress upwards from grade to grade, they are assessed on the basis of performance in tests throughout the year, participation in class discussions, and completion of written and oral assignments. Some schools give their own end-of-year examinations, while a few states, such as New York, give state examinations which are set by the State Department of Education.

The criterion for a particular student's high school graduation (leaving school with a diploma to show satisfactory completion of all courses) is the number of 'units' he has amassed. A high school unit equals about 120 hours (three hours a week) of classes in one subject. The average state requirement is 17.5 units, but students planning to go on to college (university) might take over 20 units.

The normal pattern in high school is for a student to amass the required number of units in basic subjects called 'requirements', then move on for the last two years to specialist subjects, called 'electives', which vary from school to school. A typical choice of electives might be European history for the first year and world politics for the second.

Students are given 'report cards' at least twice a year indicating the grades they have been given in each subject. High schools keep a 'transcript' or summary of the courses taken and grades obtained, and then submit this to the college to which the student has applied for admission.

ˈlaw, ˈmedical, ˈhistory school ○ the School of ˈDentistry. **6** [C] course, usu for adults, on a particular subject: *a ˈsummer school for music lovers.* **7** [C usu *sing*] (*infml*) experience or activity that provides discipline or instruction: *the hard school of adversity.* **8** [C] group of writers, thinkers, etc sharing the same principles or methods, or of artists having a similar style: *the Dutch, Venetian, etc school of painting ○ the Hegelian school*, ie of philosophers influenced by Hegel. **9** [C] group of card-players, gamblers, etc: *a ˈpoker school.* **10** (idm) **one of the old school** ⇨ OLD. **a school of ˈthought** group of people with similar views: *I don't belong to the school of thought that favours radical change.* **teach school** ⇨ TEACH.

▷ **school** *v* [Tn, Tn·pr, Cn·t] ~ **sb/sth (in sth)** train, discipline or control sb/oneself/an animal: *school a horse ○ school oneself in patience/to be patient ○ a child who is well-schooled in good manners.* **schooling** *n* [U] education: *He had very little schooling. ○ Who's paying for her schooling?*

□ ˈ**school age** age between starting and finishing school: *a child of school age.*

ˈ**schoolboy** *n* boy at school: [attrib] *a schoolboy joke, prank, etc.*

ˈ**school-days** *n* [pl] time when sb is at school.

ˈ**schoolfellow** (also ˈ**schoolmate**) *n* member of the same school, either now or in the past.

ˈ**schoolgirl** *n* girl at school.

ˈ**schoolhouse** *n* building of a school, esp a small one in a village.

ˌ**school-ˈleaver** *n* person who has recently left school.

ˈ**schoolman** /-mən/ *n* (*pl* **-men**) teacher in a university in the Middle Ages, esp one teaching scholastic philosophy.

ˈ**school-marm** /ˈskuːlmɑːm/ *n* (*infml*) **1** (*esp US*) schoolmistress. **2** (*derog or joc*) woman who is domineering, prim or easily shocked.

ˈ**schoolmaster** *n* (*fem* ˈ**schoolmistress**) teacher in a school (in Britain, esp one in a private school).

ˈ**schoolmate** *n* = SCHOOLFELLOW.

ˈ**schoolteacher** *n* teacher in a school.

NOTE ON USAGE: When a **school**, **hospital**, etc is being referred to as an institution, we do not use the definite article after a preposition: *She went to school/university/college in York. ○ He's coming out of hospital on Friday. ○ She's been sent to prison for a year.* When we are talking about the place as a building, the definite article is used: *We went to the school to discuss our daughter's progress. ○ I saw her coming out of the hospital/the church.*

school[2] /skuːl/ *n* large number of fish, whales, etc swimming together; shoal.

schooner /ˈskuːnə(r)/ *n* **1** type of sailing-ship with two or more masts and sails set lengthways rather than from side to side. **2** (a) (*Brit*) tall glass for sherry. (b) (*US*) tall glass for beer.

Schopenhauer /ˈʃəʊpənhaʊə(r)/ Arthur (1788-1860), German philosopher. His pessimism saw the will to live as the only reality and the source of all evils. He therefore recommended a strict and celibate way of life, and considered art to be a form of relief from the suffering of existence. His views influenced those of *Nietzsche.

schottische /ʃɒˈtiːʃ; *US* ˈʃɒtɪʃ/ *n* (music for a) type of slow polka.

Schubert /ˈʃuːbət/ Franz (1797-1828), Austrian composer. During his short life he produced an immense quantity of music, including nine symphonies, much piano and chamber music, and above all the songs, over 600 of them which are remarkable for their spontaneous response to poetry. His gift for melody and invention makes him one of the greatest of all composers.

Schumann /ˈʃuːmən; *US* -mɑːn/ Robert (1810-56), German composer. Although an injury to his fingers prevented him from becoming a concert pianist, he produced some of the greatest music for the piano, first championed by the playing of his wife, Clara. His most prolific period followed their marriage, when he wrote most of his chamber and orchestral works.

Schütz /ʃuːts/ Heinrich (1585-1672), German composer. He studied in Italy and the Italian style is apparent in much of his church music, which influenced J S *Bach. He is thought to have composed the first German opera (now lost).

schwa /ʃwɑː/ *n* (*phonetics*) **1** sound occurring in unstressed syllables and diphthongs in English, eg the 'a' in 'about'. **2** phonetic symbol for this, /ə/.

Schweitzer /ˈʃwaɪtsə(r)/ Albert (1875-1965), French doctor, theologian and musician. During the first half of his career he wrote an important historical study of the life of Jesus and gave regular organ recitals. He is best remembered however for his humanitarian work in founding a medical centre at Lambaréné, now in Gabon. For this work, based on his principle of 'reverence for life', he was awarded the Nobel Peace Prize in 1952.

sciatic /saɪˈætɪk/ *adj* [usu attrib] (*anatomy*) of the hip or of the **sciatic nerve**, which goes from the pelvis to the thigh.

▷ **sciatica** /saɪˈætɪkə/ *n* [U] pain in or near the sciatic nerve.

science /ˈsaɪəns/ *n* **1** (a) [U] organized knowledge, esp when obtained by observation and testing of facts, about the physical world, natural laws and society; study leading to such knowledge: *an interest in science ○ a man of science ○ Science is an exact discipline.* (b) [C, U] branch of such knowledge: *the natural sciences*, eg biology and geology ○ *the physical sciences*, eg physics, chemistry ○ *the study of social science.* (c) [U] these sciences taken as a whole: *I prefer science to the humanities. ○ more funding for science in the universities*, ie for the work of those studying it ○ [attrib] *a science teacher, textbook, subject.* Cf ART[1] 3. **2** (a) [U] skill of an expert: *In this game, you need more science than strength.* (b) [sing] activity needing this: *Getting these children to do what you want is a science, I can tell you!* **3** (idm) **blind sb with science** ⇨ BLIND[2].

▷ **scientist** /ˈsaɪəntɪst/ *n* expert in or student of one or more of the natural or physical sciences.

□ ˌ**science ˈfiction** (also *infml* **sci-fi**) fiction often based on future or recent scientific discoveries, and dealing with imaginary worlds, space travel, or life on other planets. Jules *Verne is often regarded as one of the founders of the genre, with works like *From the Earth to the Moon* and *A Journey to the Centre of the Earth*. Despite his great imagination, Verne's books are essentially adventure stories. The themes of menace and warfare emerged with the works of H G *Wells, such as *The War of the Worlds* and *The Time Machine*. Space travel and other technological developments in the 20th century led to a huge growth in the science fiction genre, from the comic strip to the cinema, but it has never gained complete literary respectability. Among the best-known modern works are the books of Isaac *Asimov and Ray Bradbury, and Stanley *Kubrick's film *2001: A Space Odyssey*.

scientific /ˌsaɪənˈtɪfɪk/ *adj* **1** (a) [attrib] of, used in or involved in science: *a scientific discovery, instrument, textbook, researcher ○ the scientific method*, ie using observation and systematic experiments to test ideas, etc. (b) using methods based on those of science: *scientific farming ○ They are very scientific in their approach.* **2** having, using or needing skill or expert knowledge: *a scientific player, game.* ▷ **scientifically** /-klɪ/ *adv.*

Scientology /ˌsaɪənˈtɒlədʒɪ/ *n* [U] (*propr*) system of beliefs based on the study of knowledge and claiming to develop the potential of its members to a high level, founded in 1951 by the American author L Ron Hubbard. ▷ **Scientologist** /-dʒɪst/ *n.*

sci-fi /ˈsaɪfaɪ/ *n* [U] (*infml*) = SCIENCE FICTION (SCIENCE).

Scilly Islands /ˈsɪlɪ aɪləndz/ (also **the Scillies**) group of about 40 islands off the western tip of Cornwall; capital Hugh Town (on St Mary's). They have a mild climate and are a popular tourist resort. ⇨ map at UNITED KINGDOM.

scimitar /ˈsɪmɪtə(r)/ *n* short curved sword with one sharp edge, formerly used by Arabs, Persians, Turks, etc. ⇨ illus at SWORD.

scintilla /sɪnˈtɪlə/ *n* (idm) **not a scintilla of sth** (*fml*) not the slightest amount of sth: *not a scintilla of truth in the claim ○ not a scintilla of evidence to prove it.*

scintillate /ˈsɪntɪleɪt; *US* -təleɪt/ *v* **1** [I] give off sparks; sparkle: *diamonds scintillating in the candlelight.* **2** [I, Ipr] (*fig*) be brilliant, witty, etc: *scintillate with wit.*

▷ **scintillating** *adj* brilliant and witty: *scintillating repartee ○ You were scintillating on TV last night.*

scintillation /ˌsɪntɪˈleɪʃn; *US* -tlˈeɪʃn/ *n* [U].

scion /ˈsaɪən/ *n* **1** (*fml*) young member of a family, esp a noble one. **2** shoot of a plant, esp one cut for grafting or planting.

scissors

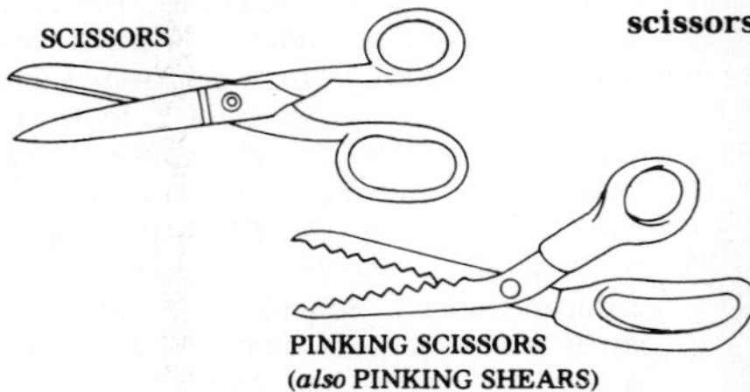

scissors /ˈsɪzəz/ *n* **1** [pl] cutting instrument with two blades, pivoted in the middle, which cut as they come together: *a pair of scissors ○ Scissors won't cut through wire.* **2** (idm) **scissors and ˈpaste** (of articles, books, etc) compiled from parts of others: [attrib] *the programme's a real scissors-and-paste job.*

sclerosis /skləˈrəʊsɪs/ *n* [U] (*medical*) condition in which there is abnormal hardening of soft tissue, eg the walls of the arteries.

▷ **sclerotic** /skləˈrɒtɪk/ *adj* (of tissue) affected by sclerosis. — *n* membrane covering the eyeball.

SCM /ˌes siː ˈem/ *abbr* (*Brit*) State Certified Midwife: *be an SCM ○ Janet Cox SCM.*

scoff[1] /skɒf; *US* skɔːf/ *v* [I, Ipr] ~ **(at sb/sth)** speak contemptuously (about or to sb/sth); jeer or mock: *Don't scoff: he's quite right. ○ scoff at other people's beliefs.*

▷ **scoff** *n* (usu *pl*) scoffing remark; taunt: *She ignored the scoffs of her workmates.*

scoffer *n* person who scoffs.

scoffingly *adv.*

scoff[2] /skɒf; *US* skɔːf/ *v* [Tn] (*sl*) eat (sth) greedily: *Who scoffed all the biscuits?*

▷ **scoff** *n* (*sl*) **1** [sing] act of scoffing: *have a good scoff.* **2** [U] food: *Where's all the scoff gone?*

scold /skəʊld/ *v* [I, Tn, Tn·pr] ~ **sb (for sth/doing sth)** express anger, criticism, etc, esp to a child; rebuke sb: *If I walk in with muddy boots, Dad always scolds (me). ○ Did you scold her for breaking it?*

▷ **scold** *n* (*dated*) person who scolds.

scolding *n*: *give sb/get a scolding for being late.*

scollop = SCALLOP.

sconce /skɒns/ *n* bracket on a wall for holding a light fitting or candlestick.

Scone /skuːn/ village in Tayside, the ancient capital of Scotland. The stone of Scone was a stone on which Scottish kings were crowned. It was brought to England by *Edward I and is now kept under the throne in *Westminster Abbey on which British monarchs are crowned.

scone /skɒn; *US* skəʊn/ *n* soft flat cake of wheat flour or barley meal baked quickly.

scoop /skuːp/ *n* **1** (a) deep shovel-like tool used for picking up and moving grain, flour, sugar, coal, etc. (b) similar small tool with a round bowl, used eg for serving ice-cream. **2** (a) (*infml*) movement made with, or as if with, a scoop: *After three scoops the jar was nearly empty.* (b) (also **scoopful**) amount picked up by a scoop: *two scoops of mashed potato.* **3** (a) piece of news made public by a

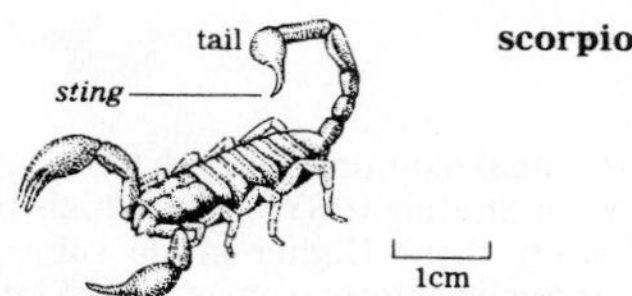

scorpion

newspaper, radio station, etc before its rivals. **(b)** (*commerce*) large profit made by acting before one's competitors do.

▷ **scoop** *v* **1** [Tn, Tn·p] ~ **sth (out)** make (a hole, etc) with, or as if with, a scoop: *scoop a hole in the sand.* **2** [Tn] **(a)** act before (a rival, etc) to get a scoop(3a): *She scooped all the national newspapers to get the story.* **(b)** get (news, a profit, etc) as a scoop(3b): *He scooped £1000 in the lottery.* **3** (phr v) **scoop sth out/up** lift sth with, or as if with, a scoop: *He scooped the coins up in his hands.*

scoot /sku:t/ *v* [I, Ipr, Ip] (esp in commands and in the infinitive) (*infml joc*) run away quickly: *Get out of here! Scoot!* ○ *You'll have to scoot or you'll be late.* ○ *She scooted (off) down the road after them.*

scooter /ˈsku:tə(r)/ *n* **1** (also ˈ**motor-scooter**) light motor cycle, usu with small wheels, a low seat and a metal shield protecting the driver's legs. ⇨ illus at MOTOR.

📖 Scooters were favoured by the *Mods in the 1960s, in contrast to the heavy motor bikes of their rivals, the *Rockers. There are still seasonal rallies of scooter riders, though as a vehicle the scooter has fallen completely out of fashion in Britain.

2 toy vehicle with two wheels, which a child moves forward by pushing against the ground with one foot.

scope /skəʊp/ *n* **1** [U] ~ **(for sth/to do sth)** opportunity to do or achieve sth: *a job with (a lot of) scope for self-fulfilment* ○ *a house with some scope for improvement.* **2** [sing] range of matters being dealt with, studied, etc: *Does feminist writing come within the scope of your book?* ○ *This subject is outside the scope of our inquiry.*

-scope *comb form* (forming *ns*) instrument for looking through or observing with: *microscope* ○ *oscilloscope* ○ *telescope.*

▷ **-scopic(al)** *comb form* (forming *adjs*): *microscopic(al)* ○ *telescopic.*

-scopy *comb form* (forming *ns*) **1** observing: *spectroscopy.* **2** use of an instrument like a microscope, telescope, etc: *microscopy.*

scorbutic /skɔ:ˈbju:tɪk/ *adj* of or suffering from scurvy.

scorch /skɔ:tʃ/ *v* **1 (a)** [Tn] burn or discolour (a surface) by dry heat: *I scorched my shirt when I was ironing it.* **(b)** [I] (of a surface) be burned or discoloured in this way: *The meat will scorch if you don't lower the gas.* **2** [Tn] cause (a plant) to dry up and wither: *The lawn looked scorched after days of sunshine.* **3** (phr v) **scorch off, away, down, etc** (*sl*) go in the direction specified at a very high speed: *motor-cyclists scorching down the road.*

▷ **scorch** (also ˈ**scorch-mark**) *n* mark made on a surface (esp cloth) by scorching.

scorcher *n* (*Brit infml*) **1** very hot day: *Whew! It's a real scorcher today!* **2** remarkable thing, esp a fast ball at cricket, tennis, etc: *The bowler let go a couple of scorchers.*

scorching *adj* very hot: *a scorching day* ○ *It's scorching outside.* — *adv* extremely: *scorching hot.*

□ **scorched** ˈ**earth policy** policy of destroying anything that may be useful to an advancing enemy.

score[1] /skɔ:(r)/ *n* **1** [C] **(a)** number of points, goals, etc made by a player or team in a game, or gained in a competition, etc: *a high/low score* ○ *make a good score of 50 points* ○ *What's my score?* ○ [attrib] *a score-keeper, score-sheet.* ⇨ App 9. **(b)** number of points made by both players or teams in such a game, etc: *keep the score,* ie keep a record of the score as it is made ○ *The final score was 4-3.* **(c)** number of marks gained in a test, examination, etc: *a score of 120 in the IQ test.* **2** [C] cut, scratch or scrape on a surface: *deep scores on the rock,* eg made by a glacier ○ *scores made by a knife on the bark of a tree.* **3** [sing] (*dated infml*) amount of money owed, eg in a restaurant: *pay the score at the hotel.* **4 (a)** [C] (*pl* unchanged) set or group of twenty: *a score of people* ○ *three score and ten,* ie 70. **(b) scores** [pl] very many: *'How many people were there? There were scores (of them).'* **5** [C] **(a)** written or printed version of a piece of music showing what each instrument is to play or what each voice is to sing: *the piano score of the opera,* ie with the orchestra's music arranged for a piano. **(b)** music for a film, play, etc: *a stirring film score by William Walton.* **6** (idm) **know the score** ⇨ KNOW. **on more scores than** ˈ**one** for many good reasons: *I want revenge against her on more scores than one.* **on** ˈ**that score** with regard to that; as far as that is concerned: *You need have no worries on that score.* **pay/settle an old score** ⇨ OLD.

□ ˈ**score-board** *n* board on which a score (eg at cricket) is shown.

ˈ**score-card** *n* card on which a score is recorded.

score[2] /skɔ:(r)/ *v* **1 (a)** [I, Tn] gain (points, goals, etc) in a game or competition, etc: *The home team has yet to score.* ○ *Hughes scored two goals before half-time.* ○ *He scored a century,* ie 100 runs in cricket. **(b)** [I, Tn] gain (marks, etc) in a test or an examination: *score well/high at bridge* ○ *She scored 120 in the IQ test.* **(c)** [I] keep a record of the points, etc gained in a game or competition, etc: *Who's going to score?* **(d)** [Dn·n] give a certain number of marks, points, etc to (a competitor): *The Russian judge scored our skaters 5.8.* **2** [I, Ipr, Tn, Tn·pr] ~ **(sth) (against sb)** achieve (a success, etc); succeed: *He has really scored with his latest book; it's selling very well.* ○ *She scored against him by quoting his earlier statement.* ○ *score an instant success* ○ *The programme scored a real hit with the public.* **3** [I, Ipr] ~ **(with sb)** (*sl*) have sex with a new partner: *Do you think you'll score at the party?* **4** [Tn] make a cut, scratch or scrape on (a surface): *rocks scored by a glacier* ○ *They scored the floor-boards by pushing furniture about.* ○ *score the trees that are due to be felled.* **5** [Tn] (*US*) criticize (sb); scold: *Critics scored him for his foolishness.* **6** [I] (*sl*) succeed in obtaining illegal drugs: *You need a lot of money to score every day.* **7** [esp passive: Tn, Tn·pr] ~ **sth (for sth)** arrange (music) for one or more musical instruments; write sth as a musical score[1](5): *scored for violin, viola and cello.* **8** (idm) **score a point/points (against/off/over sb)** = SCORE OFF SB. **9** (phr v) **score off sb** make sb appear foolish, eg by making a witty remark: *She knows how to score off people who ask difficult questions.* **score sth out/through** draw a line or lines through sth: *Her name had been scored out on the blackboard.*

▷ **scorer** *n* **1** person who keeps a record of points, goals, etc scored in a game. **2** player who scores goals, runs, etc: *a prolific goal-scorer.*

scorn /skɔ:n/ *n* **1** [U] ~ **(for sth)** strong contempt: *be filled with scorn* ○ *dismiss a suggestion with scorn* ○ *He had nothing but scorn for my ideas.* **2** [sing] **the** ~ **of sb** (*fml*) person or thing that is treated with scorn by sb: *She was the scorn of her classmates.* **3** (idm) **laugh sb/sth to scorn** ⇨ LAUGH. **pour scorn on sb/sth** ⇨ POUR.

▷ **scorn** *v* **1** [Tn] feel or show scorn for (sb/sth): *As a professional painter, she scorns the efforts of amateurs.* **2 (a)** [Tn] refuse (sth) proudly: *scorn sb's invitation, advice, offer.* **(b)** [Tt, Tg] (*fml*) reject (sth one is too proud to do): *scorn to ask for help* ○ *He scorns telling lies.*

scornful /-fl/ *adj* showing or feeling scorn: *a scornful remark, smile, look, gesture, etc* ○ *scornful of the greed of others.* **scornfully** /-fəlɪ/ *adv.*

Scorpio /ˈskɔ:pɪəʊ/ *n* **1** [U] the eighth sign of the zodiac, the Scorpion. **2** [C] (*pl* ~s) person born under the influence of this sign. ⇨ illus at ZODIAC.

▷ **Scorpian** *n, adj.* ⇨ Usage at ZODIAC.

scorpion /ˈskɔ:pɪən/ *n* small creature of the spider group with lobster-like claws and a poisonous sting in its long jointed tail.

Scorsese /skɔ:ˈseɪzɪ/ Martin (1942-), American film director. Fascinated by his native New York, he explored its more sordid aspects in *Taxi Driver*, and its eccentrics in *King of Comedy*.

scoop

Scot /skɒt/ *n* native of Scotland: *(The) Scots are an adventurous and inventive people.*

Scotch /skɒtʃ/ *adj* **1** (also **Scots**) of Scottish people. **2** (also **Scottish**) of Scotland. ⇨ Usage at SCOTTISH.

▷ **Scotch** *n* **(a)** [U] Scotch whisky. **(b)** [C] type of this: *only the best Scotches.* **(c)** [C] glass of this: *Have a Scotch!*

□ ˌ**Scotch** ˈ**broth** soup or stew containing pearl barley and vegetables.

ˌ**Scotch** ˈ**cap** man's wide beret, esp as worn with Highland costume.

ˌ**Scotch** ˈ**egg** boiled egg enclosed in sausage meat.

ˌ**Scotch** ˈ**mist** thick mist with fine drizzle, common in the Scottish highlands.

ˌ**Scotch** ˈ**pine** (also ˌ**Scots** ˈ**pine**, ˌ**Scotch** ˈ**fir**) type of European and Asian pine tree having needles and prickly cones.

ˌ**Scotch** ˈ**tape** (*US propr*) transparent adhesive tape made of cellulose or plastic. Cf SELLOTAPE.

ˌ**Scotch** ˈ**terrier** small terrier with rough hair and short legs. ⇨ illus at DOG.

ˌ**Scotch** ˈ**whisky** type of whisky distilled in Scotland.

scotch /skɒtʃ/ *v* [Tn] **(a)** stop (esp a rumour, etc) being believed: *His arrival in the capital scotched reports that he was dead.* **(b)** stop (a plan, etc) being accepted or carried out.

scot-free /ˌskɒt ˈfri:/ *adv* without punishment or harm: *The accused got off/escaped scot-free because of lack of evidence.*

Scotland /ˈskɒtlənd/ northernmost member country of the *United Kingdom; pop approx 5300000; capital Edinburgh; unit of currency pound. Much of the north of the country is covered in lakes (or *loughs*), mountains and forest, and attracts many tourists, while industry is concentrated in the south. Scotland has its own legal system, banknotes and many other institutions, like the clan system, which are distinct from those of the rest of the United Kingdom, but many Scots would prefer a greater degree of self-government. ⇨ article. ⇨ map at UNITED KINGDOM.

Scotland Yard /ˌskɒtlənd ˈjɑ:d/ headquarters of the London police, now officially called New Scotland Yard; its Criminal Investigation Department: *They called in Scotland Yard,* ie asked for the help of this Department. ○ *Scotland Yard is/are investigating the crime.*

Scots /skɒts/ *adj* of Scotland, its people or its dialect of English: *Scots law.* ⇨ Usage at SCOTTISH.

▷ **Scots** *n* dialect of English traditionally spoken in Scotland.

□ ˈ**Scotsman** /-mən/, ˈ**Scotswoman** /-wʊmən/ *ns* native of Scotland.

ˌ**Scots** ˈ**pine** = SCOTCH PINE (SCOTCH).

Scott[1] /skɒt/ Sir George Gilbert (1811-78), English architect. He was one of the leading figures of the *Gothic revival in England, and designed the Albert Memorial and St Pancras station in London, as well as restoring many old churches. ⇨ illus.

Scott[2] /skɒt/ Sir Peter Markham (1909-1989), British naturalist and artist, son of Robert Scott. He did much to preserve wildlife, esp birds, in Britain and elsewhere, and produced many fine paintings of birds.

Scott[3] /skɒt/ Robert Falcon (1868-1912), British explorer. He became a national hero through his two expeditions to Antarctica. He first surveyed the interior of the continent and discovered King Edward VII Land. On his second expedition he reached the South Pole a month after *Amundsen, but died of exposure on the journey back to base camp.

Scotland

England and Wales, as two of the three parts that make up Great Britain, have much in common legally and politically. Scotland, the third, differs in many respects.

It differs first in its separate history. In 1314 the Scottish king Robert I (known as Robert the Bruce) defeated the English at the Battle of Bannockburn. Fourteen years later, in 1328, he achieved his goal of independence for Scotland. In 1371 Robert II, the first king of the Scottish Stuart dynasty, came to the throne. Scotland continued as an independent kingdom until 1603. In 1513 James IV tried to invade England but was defeated at the Battle of Flodden. His great-grandson, the Stuart king James VI, who came to the Scottish throne in 1567, succeeded to the throne of England (as James I) in 1603 on the death of Queen Elizabeth I, who had no children. England, Wales and Scotland, as Great Britain, were ruled by one king, and in 1707 the two parliaments of Scotland and England were united by the Act of Union. When George I came to the throne in 1714 as the first of the Hanover kings, the Scots tried to win back the throne for the Stuarts. There were rebellions in 1714 and 1745, led respectively by James Francis Edward Stuart (the 'Old Pretender') and Charles Edward Stuart (the 'Young Pretender', also known as 'Bonny Prince Charlie'), the son and grandson of James II, but they both failed. The rebellions are called 'Jacobite' after James II.

Against this historical background, which involved much political and religious dispute, most Scots have remained intensely loyal to their country and its traditions, not least its important Celtic element.

Scotland's natural landscape also distinguishes it from much of England. The Highlands, in particular, are regarded as typically 'Scottish', with their mountains, lochs (lakes), moors, rugged coastline and many coastal islands.

The Scots have a popular reputation for being mean with money, which arose as a distorted perception of their native shrewdness and caution, inherent characteristics of people used to long periods of strife and dissent.

The predominant religion in Scotland is that of the Church of Scotland, which became the established Church in 1690. It is a Protestant Church which is Presbyterian in its organization and is governed by elders. All elders are of equal rank, including ministers. The Church of Scotland and its churches are sometimes referred to as 'the kirk', especially by members of the Scottish Episcopal Church, which corresponds to the Church of England (and is officially part of the Anglican Communion). There is also a small but strong representation of the Roman Catholic Church, which became defunct in Scotland in the early 17th century but was restored in 1878. The majority of Roman Catholics are descendants of the Irish people who moved to Scotland to find work in Scottish industries in the Glasgow area during the 19th century.

Politically Scotland has a left-wing tradition, and the majority of Scottish seats in the House of Commons are held by the Labour Party. There is also a strong nationalist movement, represented by the Scottish Nationalist Party (SNP). A referendum on the question of whether Scotland should have its own assembly was held in 1979, but it failed to win the support of the necessary 40 per cent of those entitled to vote, even though the majority of votes actually cast were in favour.

Scotland's legal system differs from that of England and evolved in the 16th century from other European systems. It is based on Roman law while the English legal system is based on common law. Its main civil courts are the Court of Session, which sits only in Edinburgh, and the sheriff court, the sheriff being the chief judge of a town or district.

Equally distinctive is the Scottish educational system. The state schools, especially the secondary schools, are known as 'public schools' (not to be confused with English public schools). Many Scottish schools are named 'Academy', for example Edinburgh Academy and Glasgow Academy.

Under the Scottish school examination system, the main school-leaving exam, taken at the age of 16, is the Standard grade of the Scottish Certificate of Education (SCE). After a further year's study, pupils can take the Higher grade. After one more year, at the age of 18, there is a final examination, the Certificate of Sixth Year Studies (CSYS), for which pupils either study three Higher grade subjects in depth, or aim to improve on existing Standard and Higher grades. A recently introduced alternative to Highers and the CSYS is the National Certificate. The introduction of the National Curriculum in England and Welsh schools did not apply in Scotland.

Many Scots have emigrated to England over the past 200 years or so, mainly in search of work. The rate slowed considerably from the 1970s, however, when the offshore oil and gas industries developed, and many people moved to the north-east of Scotland, where the main on-shore installations are. Scotland's traditional industries such as coal, steel and shipbuilding have all declined in importance since the Second World War, and their place in the economy has partly been taken in recent years by the rapidly growing electronics industry as well as the oil and gas industries. Traditional exports like whisky and woollen goods, especially tweed cloth and knitwear, remain important, however, and tourism is also a major contributor to the Scottish economy. Glasgow remains Scotland's leading commercial and industrial centre. The city was named European City of Culture in 1990. Scotland's traditional cultural centre, though, is Edinburgh, famous for its annual International Festival.

Scotland has a number of popular national foods and dishes. Among the best known are porridge, eaten for breakfast with milk and sugar (or salt), haggis, made from sheep's or calf's offal with oatmeal, suet and seasonings boiled in a skin from the animal's stomach, and shortbread, a sweet biscuit made with butter. Two special Scottish celebrations are Hogmanay (New Year's Eve), when gifts are given and 'first-footing' is marked (by the first person entering a house on New Year's Day), and Burns' Night (25 January), when the birthday of Robert Burns is celebrated with a supper of haggis and 'bashed tatties and neeps' (mashed potatoes and turnips) while a piper wearing Highland dress (with distinctive kilt and sporran) plays the bagpipes, Scotland's national instrument. (Cf article at LANGUAGE.)

St Pancras station, designed by Sir George Gilbert Scott

Scott[4] /skɒt/ Sir Walter (1771-1832), Scottish novelist and poet. Both his early verse and his more famous historical novels were inspired by the traditions, legends and history of Scotland, esp the Border region. Works like *Waverley* and *Rob Roy* show his learning, wit and political attitudes; they were immensely popular and influenced writers both in Britain and Europe, where several of his plots were used for romantic operas.

Scottie /ˈskɒtɪ/ *n (infml)* **1** Scottish person. **2** Scotch terrier.

Scottish /ˈskɒtɪʃ/ *adj* of Scotland, its people or its dialect of English.

□ ˌ**Scottish** ˈ**Nationalist Party** (*abbr* **SNP**) political party formed in 1934 that seeks self-govenment for Scotland. Although a number of its candidates have been elected to the British Parliament, it remains a minority party.

NOTE ON USAGE: Compare **Scottish**, **Scots** and **Scotch.** The adjective **Scottish** is used of the people and things of Scotland, **Scots** only of its people, its law and language. **Scotch** is mainly used of certain products such as whisky and broth. It is sometimes used for **Scottish** or **Scots** but this is generally regarded as offensive or old-fashioned by Scottish people themselves. The noun **Scots** refers to the Scottish dialect of the English language and **Scotch** is whisky. A native of Scotland is a **Scot** (or **Scotsman**/**woman**).

scoundrel /ˈskaʊndrəl/ *n* person who has no moral principles and no conscience; villain.

scour[1] /ˈskaʊə(r)/ *v* **1** [Tn, Tn·p] ~ **sth (out)** make the dirty surface of sth clean or bright by rubbing it with sth rough: *scour the pots and pans* ○ *scour out a saucepan*, ie with a scourer ○ *scour the pipe (out)*. **2** [Tn, Tn·pr, Tn·p] ~ **sth (out)** (of a river etc) clear out or make (a channel, etc) by flowing at high speed: *The torrent scoured a gully down the hillside.* **3** (phr v) **scour sth away/off** remove (dirt) by rubbing with sth rough: *scour the grease off (the floor).*

▷ **scour** *n* [sing] act of scouring: *give the pan a good scour.*

scourer /ˈskaʊərə(r)/ *n* **(a)** [C] pad of stiff nylon or wire used for scouring saucepans, etc. **(b)** [U] powder for this.

scour[2] /ˈskaʊə(r)/ *v* **1** [Tn, Tn·pr] ~ **sth (for sb/sth)** go over (an area) thoroughly searching for sb sth: *Police scoured the woods (looking) for the body.* **2** (phr v) **scour about, through, etc (sth)** move around quickly in search of sb/sth: *hounds scouring about in the copse (after the fox)* ○ *We scoured through the fields, looking for stray sheep.*

scourge /skɜːdʒ/ *n* **1** whip for flogging people. **2** (*fig*) person or thing that causes suffering: *The new boss was the scourge of the inefficient.* ○ *the scourge of war.*

▷ **scourge** *v* [Tn] **1** flog (sb) with a scourge. **2** (*fml*) cause (sb) to suffer: *scourged by guilt.*

scouse /skaʊs/ *n* (*infml*) **1** [U] dialect used by the people of Liverpool. **2** (also **scouser**) [C] native or inhabitant of Liverpool. ▷ **scouse** *adj*: *scouse wit.*

scout /ˈskaʊt/ *n* **1** person, ship or aircraft sent out to get information about the enemy's position, strength, etc. **2 Scout** (also formerly **Boy ˈScout**) member of the **Scout Association**, an organization which aims to teach boys self-reliance, discipline and public service through outdoor activities: [attrib] *a scout troop, hut.* Cf GIRL GUIDE (GIRL). **3** person whose job is to find talented performers (eg footballers, stage artists, etc) and offer them work: *a ˈtalent scout.* **4** servant at an Oxford college.

▷ **scout** *v* [Ipr, Ip] ~ **around/about (for sb/sth) 1** look in various places to find sb/sth: *We'd better start scouting about for a new secretary.* ○ *I've been scouting around town for a better house.* **2** act as a scout(1): *scouting around (looking) for enemy troops.*

Scouter *n* adult member of the Scout Association.

□ **ˈscout car** fast armoured military vehicle used for reconnaissance and liaison.

ˈscoutmaster *n* person who leads a troop of Scouts.

scow /skaʊ/ *n* (*esp US*) small flat-bottomed racing yacht.

scowl /skaʊl/ *n* bad-tempered or angry look on the face.

▷ **scowl** *v* [I, Ipr] ~ **(at sb/sth)** look (at sb/sth) with a scowl: *The receptionist scowled at me.* ⇨ Usage at SMIRK.

Scrabble /ˈskræbl/ *n* [U] (*propr*) game in which words are built up on a board marked with squares, using letters printed on blocks of wood, etc: *be good at Scrabble* ○ [attrib] *a Scrabble board, player, tournament.*

scrabble /ˈskræbl/ *v* (phr v) ~ **about (for sth)** grope about with the fingers, trying to get hold of sth: *scrabble about under the table for the dropped sweets.*

▷ **scrabble** *n* [sing] act of scrabbling: *a noisy scrabble for coins on the floor.*

scrag /skræg/ *n* **1** (also ˌ**scrag-ˈend**) [C, U] bony part of a sheep's neck, used for making soups and stews: *buy a ˌscrag-end of ˈmutton* ○ *a bit of scrag.* **2** [C] skinny person or animal.

▷ **scrag** *v* (**-gg-**) [Tn] **1** strangle or hang (sb). **2** (*infml*) treat (sb) roughly: *Alan's always getting scragged at school.*

scraggly *adj* (**-ier, -iest**) (*infml esp US*) rough, untidy or irregular: *scraggly weeds.*

scraggy *adj* (**-ier, -iest**) (*derog*) thin and bony: *a scraggy neck.* **scragginess** *n* [U].

scram /skræm/ *v* (**-mm-**) [I] (esp in commands and the infinitive) (*sl*) go away quickly: *Scram! I don't want you here!* ○ *Tell those boys to scram.*

scramble /ˈskræmbl/ *v* **1** [Ipr, Ip] climb or crawl quickly, usu over rough ground or with difficulty; clamber: *scramble up the embankment* ○ *The girl scrambled over the wall.* ○ *The children scrambled out of the hollow tree.* **2** [I, Ipr, It] ~ **(for sth)** struggle or compete with others, esp to get sth or a share of sth: *players scrambling for possession of the ball* ○ *The children scrambled for the coins.* ○ *They were all scrambling to get the bargains.* **3** [Tn, Tn·p] ~ **sth (up)** mix (things) together in an untidy way; jumble sth up: *Who has scrambled up my sewing things?* **4** [Tn] mix the whites and yolks of (eggs) together while cooking them in a saucepan with milk and butter. **5** [Tn] change the way (a telephone conversation, etc) sounds by altering the wave frequency, so that only sb with a special receiver can understand it. **6** [I, Tn] (cause a military aircraft to) take off suddenly, eg to repel an enemy raid.

▷ **scramble** *n* **1** [sing] climb or walk done with difficulty or over rough ground: *a scramble over the rocks at the sea-shore.* **2** [sing] ~ **(for sth)** rough struggle (to get sth): *There was a scramble for the best seats.* **3** [C] motor-cycle race over rough ground.

scrambler /ˈskræmblə(r)/ *n* device for scrambling telephone conversations, etc.

scrap[1] /skræp/ *n* **1** (**a**) [C] small, usu unwanted, piece; fragment: *scraps of paper, cloth, wood, etc* ○ (*fig*) *Only a few scraps of news about the disaster have emerged.* (**b**) **scraps** [pl] items of left-over food: *Give the scraps to the dog.* **2** [U] waste or unwanted articles, esp those still of some value for the material they contain: *sell an old car for scrap*, ie so that any good parts can be used again ○ *A man comes round regularly collecting scrap.* ○ [attrib] *scrap iron* ○ *a scrap (metal) merchant* ○ *a scrap car.* **3** [sing] (usu with a negative) small amount of sth: *There's not a scrap of truth in the claim.* ○ *'Does he have evidence to support this?' 'Not a scrap!'*

▷ **scrap** *v* (**-pp-**) [Tn] throw away (sth useless or worn-out): *scrap a car, ship, bicycle, etc* ○ (*fig*) *Lack of cash forced us to scrap plans for a new house.*

scrappy *adj* (**-ier, -iest**) **1** made up of bits and pieces; not well organized; not complete: *a scrappy book consisting of articles published elsewhere* ○ *It was a scrappy, rambling speech.* **2** (*US infml*) liking quarrels; aggressive. **scrappily** /-ɪlɪ/ *adv.* **scrappiness** *n* [U].

□ **ˈscrap-book** *n* book with blank pages in which newspaper cuttings, etc are pasted.

ˈscrap-heap *n* **1** heap of scrap. **2** (idm) **on the ˈscrap-heap** no longer wanted: *Unemployed people often feel they are on the scrap-heap.*

ˈscrap paper (*US* also **ˈscratch paper**) loose bits of paper, often partly used, for writing notes on.

ˈscrap-yard *n* place where scrap[1](2) is collected.

scrap[2] /skræp/ *n* ~ **(with sb)** (*infml*) fight; quarrel: *get into a scrap* ○ *He had a scrap with his sister.*

▷ **scrap** *v* (**-pp-**) [I, Ipr] ~ **(with sb)** fight; quarrel: *He was always scrapping at school.*

scrape[1] /skreɪp/ *v* **1** (**a**) [Tn, Tn·p, Cn·a] ~ **sth (down/out/off)** make (a surface, etc) clean, level or smooth by drawing a sharp tool or sth rough across it: *scrape the floor with a stiff brush* ○ *scrape out a sticky saucepan* ○ *scrape the walls clean* ○ *She is scraping the path clear of snow.* (**b**) [Tn·pr, Tn·p] ~ **sth from/off sth;** ~ **sth away/off** remove (mud, grease, paint, etc) in this way: *scrape the rust off (sth)* ○ *scrape paint from a door.* **2** (**a**) [Tn, Tn·pr] ~ **sth (against/on/along/sth)** injure or damage sth by rubbing with sth rough, sharp, etc: *I fell and scraped my knee.* ○ *I scraped the side of my car against a wall.* (**b**) [Tn·pr, Tn·p] ~ **sth from/off sth;** ~ **sth away/off** remove (skin, paint, etc) accidentally in this way: *She's scraped the skin off her elbow.* ○ *I must have scraped some of the paint off when I was parking the car.* **3** (**a**) [Ipr, Tn·pr] ~ **(sth) against/along/on sth** (cause sth to) rub against sth: *Bushes scraped against the car windows.* ○ *The ship's hull scraped along the side of the dock.* ○ *Don't scrape your feet on the floor.* (**b**) [Ip, Ipr, Tn·p, Tn·pr] ~ **(sth) across, along, over, etc (sth)** (cause sth to) move in the specified direction with a scraping sound. **4** [Tn, Tn·p] ~ **sth (out)** make sth by scraping: *scrape a hole (out) in the soil for planting.* **5** (idm) **bow and scrape** ⇨ BOW[2]. **pinch and save/scrape** ⇨ PINCH. **scrape (up) an acˈquaintance with sb** (*infml*) get to know sb not very well and with difficulty: *I slowly scraped (up) an acquaintance with my neighbours.* **scrape (the bottom of) the ˈbarrel** use the least satisfactory items or people available: *We had to scrape the barrel to get a full team, and then we lost 6-1.* **scrape a ˈliving** earn with difficulty just enough to live on: *I manage to scrape a living by selling my pictures.* **6** (phr v) **scrape along/by (on sth)** manage to live with difficulty: *I can just scrape along on what my parents give me.* **scrape in; scrape into sth** get in/into (eg a job or a school) with difficulty: *She just scraped into university with the minimum qualifications.* **scrape through (sth)** succeed with difficulty in doing sth, esp in passing an exam: *She only just scraped through the test.* **scrape sth together/up** obtain sth with difficulty, or by being careful: *We scraped together an audience of fifty for the play.* ○ *Can you scrape up enough money for a holiday?*

▷ **scraper** *n* tool used for scraping, eg for scraping mud from one's shoes.

scraping *n* (usu *pl*) small bit produced by scraping: *scrapings from the bottom of the pan.*

scrape[2] /skreɪp/ *n* **1** (esp *sing*) act or sound of scraping: *the scrape of sb's pen on paper, of sb's fingernail on a blackboard.* **2** injury or mark made by scraping: *a scrape on the elbow*, eg as a result of a fall ○ *a scrape along the paintwork.* **3** (*infml*) awkward situation caused by foolish behaviour or by not thinking carefully: *She's always getting into scrapes.* ○ *Don't expect me to get you out of your scrapes.*

scrappy ⇨ SCRAP[1].

scratch[1] /skrætʃ/ *v* **1** (**a**) [I, Ipr, Tn] make marks on or in (a surface) with a sharp tool, nails, claws, etc; make a shallow wound in (the skin) in this way: *That cat scratches.* ○ *The dog is scratching at the door.* ○ *The knife has scratched the table.* ○ *She won't scratch you.* (**b**) [Tn, Tn·pr, Tn·p] make (sth) by scratching: *scratch a line on a surface* ○ *scratch (out) a hole in the soil* ○ *He'd scratched his name in the bark of the tree.* **2** [I, Tn] scrape or rub (the skin), esp with the nails to relieve itching: *Stop scratching (yourself).* ○ *Scratching the rash will make it worse.* **3** [Tn, Tn·pr] ~ **sb/sth (on sth)** get (oneself or a part of the body) scratched by accident: *She scratched herself badly while pruning the roses.* ○ *He's scratched his hand on a nail.* **4** [I] make an unpleasant scraping sound: *My pen scratches.* **5** [I, Ipr, Tn, Tn·pr] ~ **(sb/sth) (from sth)** withdraw (sb/sth) from competing in a race, competition, etc: *I had to scratch (from the marathon) because of a bad cold.* ○ *The horse had to be scratched (from its first race).* **6** (idm) **scratch one's ˈhead** think hard in a puzzled way about what to do or say: *We've been scratching our heads for a solution to the problem.* **scratch the ˈsurface (of sth)** treat a subject or deal with a problem without being thorough: *This essay is so short that it can only scratch the surface of the topic.* ○ *The famine is so bad, aid can only scratch the surface.* ˌ**you scratch ˈmy back and ˌI'll scratch ˈyours** (*saying*) you help me and I'll help you, esp in an unfair way: *The contract went to a friend of the chief accountant: it's (a case of) you scratch my back and I'll scratch yours.* **7** (phr v) **scratch about (for sth)** search here and there using sth sharp, one's nails etc: *The monkey scratched about in its mate's fur for fleas.* **scratch sth away, off, etc** remove sth by scratching: *scratch the paint away from the lock.* ○ *scratch the rust off the wheel* ○ *I'll scratch your eyes out!* **scratch sth out (of sth)** erase sth by scratching with sth sharp: *Her name had been scratched out of the list.* **scratch sth together/up** = SCRAPE STH TOGETHER/UP (SCRAPE[1]). **scratch sth up** get sth out of the ground by scratching: *The dog scratched up a bone in the garden.*

□ **ˈscratch pad** (*esp US*) pad of scrap paper.

ˈscratch paper (*US*) = SCRAP PAPER (SCRAP[1]).

scratch[2] /skrætʃ/ *n* **1** [C] mark, cut, injury or sound made by scratching (SCRATCH[1] 1a): *scratches on old records* ○ *Her hands were covered with scratches from the thorns.* ○ *It's only a scratch*, ie a very slight injury. ○ *He escaped without a scratch*, ie completely unhurt. **2** [sing] act or period of scratching (SCRATCH[1] 2): *The dog gave itself a good scratch.* **3** (**a**) [C] line from which competitors start in a race when they receive no handicap. (**b**) [U] status of a player who receives no handicap: *play to scratch*, ie without any handicap ○ [attrib] *a scratch player, golfer, etc.* **4** (idm) **(start sth) from ˈscratch** (begin sth) at the beginning, not using any work that was done before: *There were so many spelling mistakes, I had to write the letter out again from scratch.* **(be/come) up to ˈscratch; (bring sb/sth) up to ˈscratch** as good as sb/sth should be; satisfactory: *Is her schoolwork up to* *scratch?* ○ *We'll have to bring the house up to scratch before we sell it.*

▷ **scratch** *adj* [attrib] made up with whatever people or materials are available: *a scratch meal, team, crew.*

scratchy *adj* (**-ier, -iest**) **1** making the skin feel itchy or irritated: *scratchy clothes, wool, etc.* **2** (of a record) making clicks and hisses when played because of scratches on its surface. **3** (of a pen) making a scratching sound. **4** (of writing or drawings) untidy or carelessly done. **scratchily** *adv.* **scratchiness** *n* [U].

scrawl /skrɔ:l/ *v* [I, Ipr, Tn, Tn·pr] **1** write or draw (sth) in an untidy, careless or unskilful way: *Who's scrawled all over the wall?* ○ *She scrawled a few words on a postcard.* **2** make (meaningless or illegible marks) on sth: *The baby scrawled on the table-top.*

▷ **scrawl** *n* **1** [sing] untidy or unskilful handwriting: *the typical doctor's scrawl* ○ *I could hardly read her childish scrawl.* **2** [C] piece of such writing; scrawled note or letter: *Her signature was an illegible scrawl.*

scrawny /ˈskrɔ:nɪ/ *adj* (**-ier, -iest**) (*derog*) not having much flesh; scraggy: *the scrawny neck of a turkey.* ⇨ Usage at THIN.

scream /skri:m/ *v* **1** [I, Ipr, Ip, Tn, Tn·pr, Tn·p, Tf, Cn·a] ~ **(sth) (out) (at sb)**; ~ **(with sth)** give a long piercing cry of fear, pain or excitement; cry (sth) in this way: *Those cats have been screaming for hours.* ○ *She screamed (out) (at me) in anger.* ○ *The fans screamed with excitement when they saw him.* ○ *We all screamed with laughter*, ie laughed noisily. ○ *'Help!' she screamed.* ○ *He screamed (out) that there was a fire.* ○ *The baby was screaming himself red in the face.* ⇨ Usage at SHOUT. **2** [I] (of the wind, a machine, etc) make a loud piercing sound: *The hurricane screamed outside.* ○ *I pressed the accelerator until the engine screamed.* **3** (phr v) **scream past, through, round, etc** move quickly with a loud piercing sound: *The wind screamed through the trees.* ○ *Racing cars screamed past.*

▷ **scream** *n* **1** [C] loud shrill piercing cry or noise: *the screams of tortured prisoners* ○ *a scream of pain, laughter, excitement, etc.* **2** [sing] (*infml*) person or thing that causes laughter: *He's an absolute scream.* ○ *The play's a scream.*

screamer *n* **1** S American goose-like bird with a shrill cry. **2** (*US*) large headline in a newspaper, esp one describing a sensational news item.

screamingly *adv* enough to cause screams of laughter: *screamingly funny.*

scree /skri:/ *n* [U, C] (area on a mountainside covered by) small loose stones, which slide when trodden on.

screech /skri:tʃ/ *v* **1** [I, Ipr, Ip, Tn, Tn·pr, Tn·p] ~ **(sth) (out) (at sb)** give a harsh high-pitched cry; call out (sth) in such a way: *screech (out) in pain* ○ *monkeys screeching in the trees* ○ *old ladies screeching hymns* ○ *The child screeched insults at us.* **2** [I] make a harsh high-pitched sound: *The brakes screeched as the car stopped.* ○ *The gate screeched as it opened.* **3** (phr v) **screech along, past, through, etc** move with a loud harsh high-pitched sound: *jets screeching over the house-tops* ○ *screech to a halt.*

▷ **screech** *n* [sing] screeching cry or sound: *the screech of tyres*, eg when a car is cornering fast.

□ ˈ**screech-owl** *n* type of owl that makes a screeching cry, rather than a hoot.

screed /skri:d/ *n* **1** [C] long (and usu uninteresting) speech or piece of writing. **2** (**a**) [C, U] layer of cement, mortar, etc spread over a floor to make it smooth. (**b**) [C] flat strip of wood, etc used for levelling the surface of floors made from concrete, etc.

screen /skri:n/ *n* **1** [C] upright, fixed or movable, sometimes folding framework used for dividing a room, concealing sth, protecting sb from excessive heat, light, etc: *a screen in front of the fire* ○ *get undressed behind a screen.* **2** [C] anything that conceals sb or sth or gives protection, eg from the weather: *a screen of trees*, eg hiding a house from a road ○ *use the blanket as a screen to keep the wind off* ○ *a ˈsunscreen*, ie used to protect the skin from

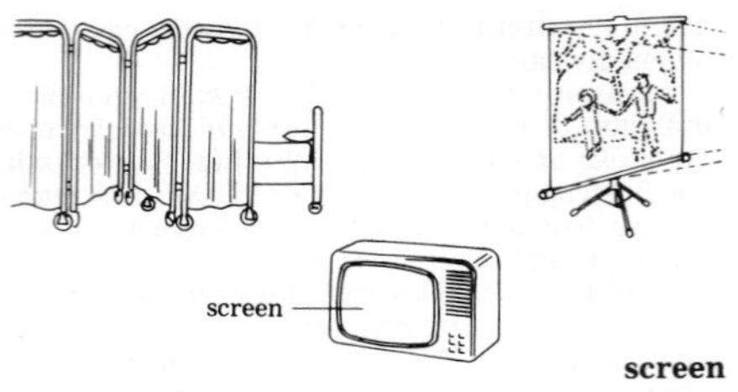

screen

harmful rays from the sun ○ *He was using his business activities as a screen for crime.* **3** [C] (esp in old churches) wood or stone structure that partially separates the main part of a church from the altar, or the nave of a cathedral from the choir. ⇨ illus at CHURCH. **4** (**a**) [C] blank surface onto which still pictures or films are projected. ⇨ illus. (**b**) [C] blank surface, esp on a TV or computer monitor, on which pictures or data are shown. (**c**) (often **the screen**) [sing] the film industry or cinema films: *write for the screen*, ie write the dialogue for films ○ *a star of stage and screen*, ie appearing in plays and films ○ *I work for both the big and the small screen*, ie for both films and TV. ○ [attrib] *a screen actor, performance, writer.* (**d**) [C] cinema, esp one that is part of a complex of cinemas: *Two smaller screens will be opening in May.* **5** [C] frame with fine wire netting to keep out flies, mosquitoes, etc: *a ˈdoor-screen* ○ *a ˈwindow-screen.* **6** [C] large sieve or riddle used for separating coal, gravel, etc into different sizes by passing it through holes of different sizes. **7** [C] = SIGHT-SCREEN (SIGHT[1]). **8** (idm) **the silver screen** ⇨ SILVER.

▷ **screen** *v* **1** [Tn, Tn·pr, Tn·p] ~ **sth/sb (off) (from sth/sb)**; ~ **sth/sb (against sth)** conceal, protect or shelter sth/sb with a screen: *The bushes will screen us while we change.* ○ *The trees screen the house from view.* ○ *The camera lens must be screened from direct sunlight.* ○ *The wall screens us against the wind.* ○ *A bookcase screens off part of the room.* **2** [Tn, Tn·pr] ~ **sb (from sth/sb)** (*fig*) protect sb (from blame, punishment, etc): *Everyone's angry with you, and I can't screen you (from their anger).* ○ *You can't screen your children from real life for ever.* **3** [Tn] pass (coal, gravel, etc) through a screen(6). **4** [Tn, Tn·pr] ~ **sb/sth (for sth)** examine or test sb/sth to find out if there is any disease, defect, etc: *screen women for breast cancer* ○ *The applications were carefully screened in case any of them contained false information.* ○ *Government employees are often screened by the security services*, ie Their past history is checked, to ensure that they are not likely to be disloyal or subversive. **5** [Tn] show (a film, scene, etc) on a screen(4a): *The film has been screened in the cinema and on TV.* **screening** *n* showing of a film, TV programme, etc: *the film's first screening in this country.*

□ ˈ**screenplay** *n* script for a film.

ˈ**screen-printing** printing process used esp by artists, in which ink is forced through a specially prepared fine mesh screen, transferring designs onto paper, cloth, etc.

ˈ**screen test** test to see if sb is suitable to appear in a cinema film.

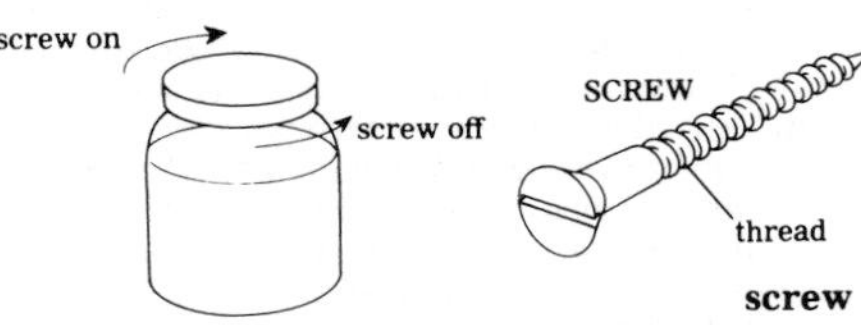

screw

screw /skru:/ *n* **1** [C] metal pin with a slot or cross cut into its head, and a spiral groove around its shaft, that can be turned and forced into wood, metal, etc so as to fasten and hold things together. **2** [C] (often in compounds) thing that is turned like a screw and is used for tightening, gripping, etc: *tighten the screw on a fruit press* ○ *a ˈcorkscrew*, ie for taking corks out of bottles. **3** [C] act of turning; turn: *The nut isn't tight enough yet: give it another screw.* ⇨ illus. **4** [C] propeller, esp of a ship or motor boat: *a twin-screw cruiser.* **5** [C] (*dated esp Brit*) small twisted piece of paper and its contents: *a screw of salt, tea, tobacco, etc.* **6** [sing] (*Brit sl*) salary or wages: *be on/be paid a good screw.* **7** [C] (*Brit sl*) prison warder. **8** [sing] (△ *sl*) (**a**) act of sexual intercourse: *have a screw with sb.* (**b**) partner in sexual intercourse: *be a good screw.* **9** (idm) **have a ˈscrew loose** be slightly mad or eccentric: *She eats nothing but nuts: she must have a screw loose!* **put the ˈscrew(s) on (sb)** force sb to do sth by intimidating him: *The landlord's putting the screws on to get her out of the house.* **a turn of the screw** ⇨ TURN[2].

▷ **screw** *v* **1** [Tn, Tn·pr, Tn·p] fasten or tighten (sth) with a screw or screws: *a tightly screwed joint* ○ *screw a bracket to the wall* ○ *screw a lock on the door* ○ *screw all the parts together.* **2** (**a**) [Tn·pr, Tn·p, Cn·a] twist (sth) round; make tighter by twisting: *screw the lid on/off (the jar)* ○ *screw the joints together* ○ *screw a bulb in* ○ *screw one's head round*, ie in order to look over one's shoulder ○ *screw the nut (up) tight.* (**b**) [Ipr, Ip] be attached by screwing: *This type of bulb screws into the socket.* ○ *Does this lid screw on, or does one press it down?* **3** (*sl*) (**a**) [Tn, Tn·pr] ~ **sb (for sth)** cheat sb: *We got screwed when we bought this house.* ○ *How much did they screw you for?* ie How much did you have to pay? (**b**) [Tn] cause sb/sth to fail, esp maliciously: *They never miss an opportunity of screwing their competitors.* **4** (△ *sl*) (**a**) [I] (of two people) have sexual intercourse: *a couple screwing in the back of a car.* (**b**) [Tn] (esp of a man) have sexual intercourse with: *He accused me of screwing his wife.* **5** (idm) **have one's head screwed on** ⇨ HEAD[1]. **screw him, you, that, etc** (△ *sl*) (used in the imperative to express one's irritation about sb/sth): *Screw you, mate!* **screw up one's ˈcourage** force oneself to be brave: *I screwed up my courage and went to the dentist.* **6** (phr v) **screw sth out of sth** remove sth from sth by twisting: *screw the water out of the sponge.* **screw sth out of sb** force sb to give sth: *They screwed the money out of her by threats.* **screw up** (*sl*) handle a situation very badly: *I was trying to help, but I screwed up again.* **screw sth up** (**a**) fasten sth with screws: *screw up a crate.* (**b**) make (paper, etc) into a tight ball: *I screwed up the note and threw it on the fire.* (**c**) tense the muscles of (the face, the eyes) when the light is too strong, when one feels pain, etc: *The taste of the lemon made her screw up her face.* (**d**) (*sl*) handle (a situation) very badly; make a mess of sth: *Don't ask them to organize the trip, they'll only screw everything up.*

screwy *adj* (**-ier, -iest**) (*infml*) strange, eccentric or crazy: *She's really screwy!* ○ *What a screwy idea!*

□ ˈ**screwball** *n* (*US infml*) eccentric or crazy person: [attrib] *a screwball comedy*

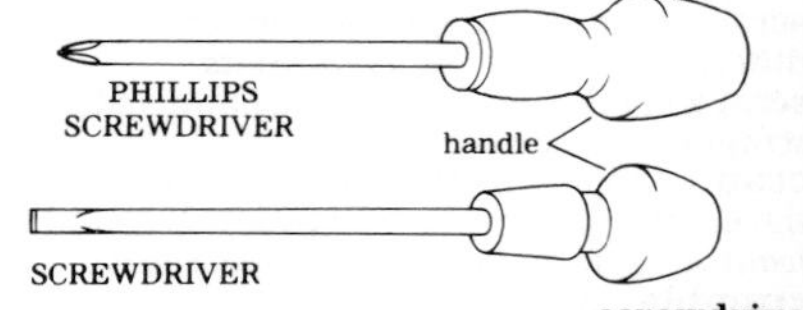

screwdriver

ˈ**screwdriver** *n* tool with a handle and a blade that fits into a slot, etc in the head of a screw to turn it.

ˌ**screwed-ˈup** *adj* (*sl*) upset and not completely able to cope with problems in life: *ˌscrewed-up ˈkids* ○ *I'm still screwed-up about the accident.*

ˈ**screw-topped** (also ˈ**screw-top**) *adj* (of a jar, etc) having a top or lid that screws onto it.

Scriabin /skrɪˈæbɪn; *US* -ˈɑ:bən/ Alexander (1872-1915), Russian composer. His early work experimented with atonal techniques, and he later developed a highly individual style influenced by eastern philosophy. His best-known piece is the orchestral *Poem of Ecstasy*.

scribble /ˈskrɪbl/ *v* [I, Tn, Tn·pr] **1** write (sth) very fast or carelessly: *scribbling (figures) on an envelope.* **2** make (meaningless marks) on sth: *a child scribbling all over a book.*

▷ **scribble** *n* **1** [U, sing] very fast or careless handwriting: *I can't read this scribble.* **2** [C] meaningless marks: *scribbles all over the page.*

scribbler /ˈskrɪblə(r)/ *n* **1** person who scribbles. **2** (*derog*) untalented author, journalist, etc: *the scribblers of Fleet Street.*

□ **ˈscribbling-block** *n* pad of cheap paper for making notes.

scribe /skraɪb/ *n* **1** person who made copies of writings before printing was invented. **2** (in Biblical times) professional religious scholar.

scrim /skrɪm/ *n* [U] strong fabric with an open weave, used esp for lining curtains, etc.

scrimmage /ˈskrɪmɪdʒ/ *n* **1** (also **scrummage**) confused struggle or fight; tussle: *a scrimmage round the bargain counter in the store.* **2** (in US football) period between the moment the ball goes into play and the moment it goes out of play.

▷ **scrimmage** *v* [I] take part in a scrimmage(1).

scrimp /skrɪmp/ *v* (idm) **scrimp and save** manage to live on very little money, esp so as to afford sth: *We had to scrimp and save to pay the bills.*

scrip /skrɪp/ *n* **1** [C] extra share in a business company issued instead of a dividend: [attrib] *a scrip issue.* **2** [U] shares issued in this way.

script /skrɪpt/ *n* **1** [C] text of a play, film, broadcast, talk, etc: *That line isn't in the script.* ○ [attrib] *a script editor.* **2** [U] (**a**) handwriting. (**b**) printed or typewritten cursive characters resembling this. **3** system of writing: *a letter in Cyrillic script.* **4** [C] (*Brit*) candidate's written answer or answers in an examination: *The examiner had to mark 150 scripts.*

▷ **script** *v* [Tn esp passive] write a script for (a film, a TV or radio play, etc): *a film scripted by a famous novelist.* **scripted** *adj* read from a script: *a scripted talk on the radio.*

□ **ˈscript-writer** *n* person who writes scripts for films, TV and radio plays, etc.

scripture /ˈskrɪptʃə(r)/ *n* **1 Scripture** [U] (also **the Scriptures** [pl]) the Bible: [attrib] *a ˈScripture lesson.* **2 scriptures** [pl] holy writings of a religion other than Christianity: *Vedic scriptures.*

▷ **scriptural** /ˈskrɪptʃərəl/ *adj* of or based on the Bible: *wide scriptural knowledge.*

scrofula /ˈskrɒfjʊlə/ *n* [U] disease causing swelling of the glands, probably a form of tuberculosis. ▷ **scrofulous** /ˈskrɒfjʊləs/ *adj.*

scroll /skrəʊl/ *n* **1** (**a**) roll of parchment or paper for writing on. (**b**) ancient book written on such a roll. **2** anything curved like a scroll, esp an ornamental design cut in stone or a flourish in writing.

▷ **scroll** *v* **1** [I, Ipr, Ip] (of text on a computer screen) move gradually up or down. **2** [I, Tn] (of a computer) show (text) moving in this way: *This model scrolls far too slowly.*

Scrooge /skru:dʒ/ *n* (*derog*) person who is miserly and mean-spirited, like the character Scrooge in *Dickens's story *A Christmas Carol.*

scrotum /ˈskrəʊtəm/ *n* (*pl* **scrotums** or **scrota** /ˈskrəʊtə/) pouch of skin enclosing the testicles in most male mammals. ⇨ illus at MALE.

scrounge /ˈskraʊndʒ/ *v* [I, Ipr, Tn, Tn·pr] ~ (**sth**) (**from/off sb**) (*infml often derog*) get (sth) by borrowing or taking it without permission: *She's always scrounging (money) off her brother.* ○ *I managed to scrounge the materials to build a shed.*

▷ **scrounge** *n* (idm) **on the ˈscrounge** (*infml*) trying to borrow or get sth by scrounging: *If you're on the scrounge again, I've no money.*

scrounger *n.*

scrub[1] /skrʌb/ *n* [U] (land covered with) underdeveloped trees or shrubs: *clear the scrub and plough the land* ○ [attrib] *ˈscrub-oak* ○ *ˈscrub-pine*, ie dwarf or underdeveloped types.

▷ **scrubby** /ˈskrʌbɪ/ *adj* (**-ier, -iest**) **1** covered with scrub; (of trees, etc) underdeveloped. **2** small or mean: *a scrubby little shed in a back street.*

scrub[2] /skrʌb/ *v* (**-bb-**) **1** [I, Ip, Tn, Tn·p, Cn·a] ~ **sth (down/out)** clean sth thoroughly by rubbing hard, esp with a brush and soap and water: *He's down on his knees, scrubbing (away).* ○ *scrub the floor* ○ *Scrub the walls down before painting them.* ○ *scrub out a saucepan* ○ *Scrub the table-top clean.* **2** [Tn] (*infml*) cancel (a plan, etc): *We wanted to go for a picnic, but we had to scrub it because of the rain.* ○ *It costs £10 per metre, no, scrub that* (ie ignore what I've just said), *it costs £12 per metre.* **3** [Tn] remove impurities from (esp a gas) using a scrubber. **4** (phr v) **scrub sth away/off** remove sth by scrubbing: *scrub the grease away* ○ *scrub the dirt off the shelf.* **scrub round sth** (*infml*) ignore sth; dispense with sth: *If we haven't time for a game we can easily scrub round it.* **scrub up** (*medical*) (of a surgeon) wash one's hands and arms thoroughly before an operation.

▷ **scrub** *n* [sing] act of scrubbing: *give the floor a good scrub.*

scrubber *n* apparatus that uses chemicals to remove impurities from a gas.

□ **ˈscrubbing-brush** *n* stiff brush for scrubbing floors, etc. ⇨ illus at BRUSH.

scrubber /ˈskrʌbə(r)/ *n* (*Brit infml derog*) prostitute or woman who has sexual intercourse with many partners.

scrudge /skrʌdʒ/ *n* (*Brit*) small bent nail for holding roofing-tiles in place.

scruff /skrʌf/ *n* (idm) **by the scruff of the/one's ˈneck** (grasping or lifting) by the back of an animal's or a person's neck: *The cat picked up the kitten by the scruff of its neck.* ○ *She grabbed me by the scruff of my neck and threw me out.*

scruffy /ˈskrʌfɪ/ *adj* (**-ier, -iest**) (*infml*) dirty and untidy: *You can't go to a job interview looking so scruffy!*

▷ **scruff** *n* (*infml*) dirty and untidy person: *He's a dreadful scruff!*

scruffily *adv.*

scruffiness *n* [U].

scrum /skrʌm/ *n* **1** = SCRUMMAGE 1. **2** (*fig*) confused struggle; tussle: *Shoppers got into a scrum round the bargain counter.*

▷ **scrum** *v* (**-mm-**) (phr v) **scrum down** form a scrummage.

□ **ˌscrum-ˈhalf** *n* half-back who puts the ball into the scrummage.

scrummage /ˈskrʌmɪdʒ/ *n* **1** (also **scrum**) part of a Rugby football game when the forwards of both sides pack together with their heads down to push against the other side, while the ball is thrown between them and they try to kick it back to their own team; all the forwards taking part in this: *...and it's a scrummage just inside the Welsh half.* **2** = SCRIMMAGE 1.

scrumptious /ˈskrʌmpʃəs/ *adj* (*infml*) (esp of food) delicious: *What a scrumptious meal!*

scrumpy /ˈskrʌmpɪ/ *n* [U] (*Brit infml*) rough strong cider, esp as made in the West Country.

scrunch /ˈskrʌntʃ/ *n, v* = CRUNCH.

scruple /ˈskru:pl/ *n* **1** [U, C often *pl*] feeling that prevents one from doing or allowing sth that one thinks may be wrong: *Have you no scruples about buying stolen goods?* ○ *She tells lies without scruple.* **2** [C] weight unit of 20 grains.

▷ **scruple** *v* [It] (usu in negative sentences) hesitate (to do sth) because of scruples: *She wouldn't scruple to tell a lie if she thought it would be useful.*

scrupulous /ˈskru:pjʊləs/ *adj* **1** extremely careful and thorough; paying great attention to details: *a scrupulous examiner* ○ *a scrupulous inspection of the firm's accounts.* **2** ~ (**in sth/doing sth**) careful not to do wrong; absolutely honest: *scrupulous in all her business dealings* ○ *behave with scrupulous honesty.* ▷ **scrupulously** *adv*: *scrupulously exact, careful, honest, clean.*

scrutineer /ˌskru:tɪˈnɪə(r); *US* -tnˈɪər/ *n* (*Brit*) person who checks that an election or other vote is carried out correctly.

scrutinize, -ise /ˈskru:tɪnaɪz; *US* -tənaɪz/ *v* [Tn] look at or examine (sth) carefully or thoroughly: *scrutinize all the documents relating to the trial.*

scrutiny /ˈskru:tɪnɪ; *US* ˈskru:tənɪ/ *n* [C, U] (instance of) careful and thorough examination: *a close scrutiny of the election results* ○ *subject the thesis to careful scrutiny.*

scuba /ˈsku:bə/ *n* underwater breathing apparatus consisting of a cylinder or cylinders of compressed air, attached by a hose to a mouthpiece: [attrib] *ˈscuba diving.*

scud /skʌd/ *v* (**-dd-**) [I, Ipr, Ip] (esp of ships, etc or clouds) move straight, fast and smoothly: *The yacht was scudding along before the wind.* ○ *clouds scudding across the sky.*

scuff /skʌf/ *v* **1** [Tn] (**a**) mark or scrape (a surface etc) with one's shoes: *a badly scuffed door.* (**b**) mark, scrape or wear away (a shoe): *I scuffed the heel of my boot on the step.* **2** [I, Ipr, Ip, Tn no passive] drag (one's feet) while walking; shuffle: *If you scuff (your feet) like that, you'll wear the heels out.* ○ *She scuffed past in her mother's slippers.*

▷ **scuff** (also **ˈscuff-mark**) *n* mark made by scuffing: *scuffs on the skirting-board.*

scuffle /ˈskʌfl/ *n* confused struggle between people who are close together: *Scuffles broke out between police and demonstrators.*

▷ **scuffle** *v* [I, Ipr] ~ (**with sb**) take part in a scuffle: *scuffle with reporters.*

scull /skʌl/ *n* **1** either of a pair of small oars used by a single rower, one in each hand. **2** oar placed over the stern of a boat to drive it with twisting strokes. **3** light racing boat rowed by a single rower with two sculls.

▷ **scull** *v* [I, Ipr, Ip, Tn, Tn·pr, Tn·p] row (a boat) with a scull or sculls: *be able to scull* ○ *scull (the boat) past the boat-house.*

sculler *n* person who sculls.

scullery /ˈskʌlərɪ/ *n* small room (usu in a large house) beside the kitchen, where dishes, etc are washed up.

scullion /ˈskʌlɪən/ *n* (formerly) boy or man who did simple tasks, eg washing-up, in a kitchen.

sculpt = SCULPTURE *v.*

sculptor /ˈskʌlptə(r)/ *n* (*fem* **sculptress** /ˈskʌlptrɪs/) person who makes sculptures.

sculpture /ˈskʌlptʃə(r)/ *n* **1** [U] art of making figures, objects, etc by carving wood or stone, shaping clay, making metal casts, etc: *the techniques of sculpture in stone.* **2** [C, U] a work or works made in this way: *a sculpture of Venus* ○ *a collector of sculpture.*

▷ **sculptural** /ˈskʌlptʃərəl/ *adj* [esp attrib] of, like or connected with sculpture: *a sculptural quality.*

sculpture (also **sculpt** /skʌlpt/) *v* **1** (**a**) [Tn, Tn·pr] represent (sb/sth) in sculpture; make (a sculpture): *saints sculptured in marble* ○ *sculpture a statue out of hard wood.* (**b**) [Tn, Tn·pr] make (sth) into a sculpture: *sculpture the clay into a vase.* (**c**) [Tn] decorate (sth) with sculptures: *sculptured columns.* **2** [I] make sculptures; be a sculptor: *learn to sculpture.*

scum /skʌm/ *n* **1** [U] layer of froth on the surface of a boiling liquid; layer of dirt on a pond or other area of still water. **2** [pl *v*] (*fig derog*) people considered to be bad or contemptible: *You scum!* ○ *She treats smokers like the scum of the earth*, ie as the worst people there are. ○ *I wouldn't have anything to do with those scum.*

▷ **scummy** *adj* (**-ier, -iest**) of, like or containing scum(1).

scupper /ˈskʌpə(r)/ *n* (often *pl*) opening in a ship's side to allow water to run off the deck.

▷ **scupper** *v* (*Brit*) **1** [Tn] sink (one's ship) deliberately. **2** [Tn esp passive] (*infml*) cause (sth) to fail; ruin: *We're scuppered!* ○ *The project was scuppered by lack of money.*

scurf /skɜ:f/ *n* [U] flakes of dead skin, esp on the scalp, that comes off as new skin grows; dandruff: *clean hair that's free of scurf.*

▷ **scurfy** *adj* having or covered with scurf.

scurrilous /ˈskʌrələs/ *adj* abusive and insulting, esp in a crude or obscene way: *a scurrilous rumour, attack, book* ○ *She was often quite scurrilous in her references to me.*

▷ **scurrility** /skəˈrɪlətɪ/ *n* (*fml*) **1** [U] (**a**) quality of being scurrilous: *the scurrility of their journalism.* (**b**) scurrilous language: *a book full of scurrility and slander.* **2** [C often *pl*] scurrilous remark: *I refused to listen to these scurrilities.*

scurrilously *adv.*

scurrilousness *n* [U].

The Sea

The sea has for centuries been a powerful factor in the life of the British, an island race. No place in Britain is more than 120 km (75 miles) from tidal water. In the past the sea was far more important to the country's economy than it is now and its importance is reflected in literature and art as well as in the music of sea shanties, the songs that sailors used to sing as they pulled ropes for the sails. In language, idioms like 'any port in a storm', 'take the wind out of somebody's sails', 'when my ship comes in', 'ships that pass in the night' and 'sail close to the wind' are all evidence of Britain's seafaring past.

Britain is surrounded by four seas: the Irish Sea to the west, the North Sea to the east, the Norwegian Sea to the north and the English Channel to the south. The main ports are London, Dover, Portsmouth, Southampton, Bristol (via Avonmouth), Cardiff, Liverpool, Manchester (via the Manchester Ship Canal), Glasgow, Sullom Voe, Aberdeen, Sunderland, Grimsby and Harwich. The ports vary in their activity. Aberdeen, for example, is primarily a fishing port, Sullom Voe is an oil terminal, and Harwich and Dover are important commercial and passenger ports. The North Sea and Channel ports have become increasingly important as Britain's trade with other European countries has grown, while ports on the west coast, especially Liverpool, have declined. The 20th century has also seen a sharp decrease in Britain's commercial shipping fleet, now only a fraction of what it was in the late 19th century, when over half the world's merchant shipping was British. The fishing industry, too, is now much smaller than in the past.

The sea has always been of strategic and military importance to Britain as a natural defence against invasion. For centuries, Britain was a major naval power, and until the Second World War the Royal Navy was the largest navy in the world. Today, however, like its merchant fleet, Britain's naval force is greatly reduced.

Apart from their economic and military role, Britain's seas and coasts are important for leisure. Sailing is a popular hobby. Many resorts on the coast were developed when seaside holidays became fashionable in the 19th century. Today many of the most popular resorts are on the south coast, where the weather is warmest, and include towns like Brighton, Eastbourne, Bournemouth and Torquay. These southern resorts, where many people go to live when they retire, have a more staid image than the resorts in north-west England such as Blackpool and Morecombe, with their fun-fairs and popular entertainments. Piers were built in many seaside resorts to attract visitors. Some even had several theatres on them. The North Sea coast, because of its colder climate, has fewer resorts, although Scarborough and Skegness attract summer visitors.

Today, the pollution of the sea and beaches is a matter of increasing public concern. Accidents involving oil-tankers have caused serious environmental damage, and the long-established practice of dumping waste at sea has added to the problem of pollution in Britain.

The USA has very extensive seaboards on the Pacific in the west and the Atlantic in the east. The westward drive of the earliest settlers and colonists from the Atlantic to the Pacific was one of the great pioneering endeavours of the country's history. An awareness of this and of the great size of the country is expressed in phrases like 'from coast to coast' and 'from sea to shining sea' (a line from 'America the Beautiful', one of the best known patriotic songs of the USA).

scurry /ˈskʌrɪ/ *v* (*pt, pp* **scurried**) [I, Ipr, Ip] run with short quick steps: *mice scurrying across the floor* ○ *scurry along the road* ○ *They scurried in out of the cold.* ○ *Crowds scurried past.* ○ *The rain sent everyone scurrying for shelter.*

▷ **scurry** *n* **1** (**a**) [sing] act or sound of scurrying: *a/the scurry of feet in the room above.* (**b**) [U] anxious or excited movement; bustle: *the scurry and scramble of town life.* **2** [C] windy shower of rain, snow, etc or cloud of dust; flurry.

NOTE ON USAGE: **Scamper**, **scurry** and **scuttle** indicate people or animals running with short, quick steps. **Scamper** (**around**, **away**, **off**, **etc**) is only used of small animals (puppies, mice, etc) and children. It suggests them playing happily or running away when startled: *The children were scampering around the garden.* ○ *The rabbits scampered away as we approached.* **Scuttle**/**scurry** (**about**, **away**, **off**, **etc**) indicate running in order to escape from danger, bad weather, etc: *The beetle scuttled away when I lifted the stone.* ○ *The spectators scurried for shelter as soon as it began to rain.* **Scurry** can indicate great or hurried activity: *We were scurrying about until the last minute before the party.*

scurvy /ˈskɜːvɪ/ *n* [U] disease of the blood caused by a lack of vitamin C in the diet.

▷ **scurvy** *adj* [attrib] (*dated sl*) contemptible; worthless; mean: *He's a scurvy wretch.* ○ *That was a scurvy trick to play on an old lady.* **scurvily** /-ɪlɪ/ *adv.*

scut /skʌt/ *n* short upright tail, esp of a hare, rabbit or deer.

scuttle[1] /ˈskʌtl/ *v* [I, Ipr, Ip] run with short quick steps: *small animals scuttling about.* ⇨ Usage at SCURRY.

▷ **scuttle** *n* [sing] act of scuttling: *a scuttle down the passage.*

scuttle[2] /ˈskʌtl/ *n* small opening with a lid on a ship's deck or side, or in a roof or wall of a building.

▷ **scuttle** *v* [Tn] sink (a ship) deliberately by opening valves or making holes in its side or bottom.

scuttle[3] /ˈskʌtl/ *n* = COAL-SCUTTLE (COAL).

Scylla /ˈsɪlə/ *n* (idm) **between Scylla and Chaˈrybdis** (*fml*) faced by a problem or danger that one can only avoid by facing another, equally unpleasant problem or danger.

scythe /saɪð/ *n* tool with a slightly curved blade on a long pole, sometimes with two handles, used (esp formerly) for cutting long grass, corn, etc. Cf SICKLE.

▷ **scythe** *v* [I, Tn, Tn·p] cut (grass, etc) with a scythe: *workers scything in the meadow* ○ *scythe the grass (down).*

SDLP /ˌes diː el ˈpiː/ *abbr* (*Brit politics*) (in N Ireland) Social and Democratic Labour Party. ⇨ articles at IRELAND, POLITICS.

SDP /ˌes diː ˈpiː/ *abbr* (*Brit politics*) Social Democratic Party: *the SDP-Liberal alliance.* ⇨ article at POLITICS.

SE *abbr* South-East(ern): *SE Asia* ○ *London SE9 2BX*, ie as a postal code.

Se *symb* selenium.

sea /siː/ *n* **1** (often **the sea**) [U] (*also* **seas** [pl]) the salt water that covers most of the earth's surface and encloses its continents and islands; any part of this, in contrast to areas of fresh water and dry land: *fly over land and sea* ○ *travel by sea* ○ *sail the seas* ○ *the high seas*, ie parts away from the land, where no single country can impose its laws ○ *the cold sea(s) of the Antarctic* ○ *Most of the earth's surface is covered by (the) sea.* ○ *Ships sail on the sea.* ○ *Fish swim in the sea.* ○ *The river flows into the sea near Portsmouth.* ○ [attrib] *a sea animal, fish, voyage.* ⇨ article. **2** (often **Sea**, esp as part of a proper name) (**a**) [C] particular area of the sea, smaller than an ocean: *the Mediterranean Sea* ○ *The Caribbean Sea* ○ *the South China Sea.* (**b**) large inland lake of fresh water or salt water: *the Caspian Sea* ○ *the Sea of Galilee.* **3** [C] (also **seas** [pl]) (state or movement of the) waves of the sea: *a heavy/light sea*, ie with big/small waves ○ *The ship was struck by a heavy sea*, ie a large wave. ○ *The liner foundered in heavy seas.* **4** ~ **of sth** (*fig*) large amount of sth covering a large area: *I stood amid a sea of corn.* ○ *The lecturer looked down at the sea of faces beneath him.* **5** (idm) **at ˈsea** (**a**) on a ship, etc on the sea: *spend three months at sea.* (**b**) not knowing what to do; confused: *I'm all at sea; I've no idea how to repair cars.* ○ *She tried to understand the instructions, but she was completely at sea.* **between the devil and the deep blue sea** ⇨ DEVIL[1]. **beyond/over the ˈsea(s)** (*fml or rhet*) to or in countries on the other side of a sea or seas; overseas; abroad: *our cousins beyond the seas.* **go to ˈsea** be a sailor. **on the ˈsea** at the seaside: *a town on the sea in Devon* ○ *Mudford-on-Sea*, ie as a place-name. **put (out) to ˈsea** leave port or land travelling on a ship, etc. **the seven seas** (*rhet*) all the seas of the world: *He's sailed the seven seas in search of adventure.* **there are more/other fish in the sea** ⇨ FISH.

▷ **ˈseaward** /-wəd/ *adj, adv* towards the sea; in the direction of the sea.

ˈseawards /-wədz/ *adv.*

□ **ˌsea ˈair** air at the seaside, thought to be good for the health: *a breath of sea air.*

ˈsea anemone tube-shaped animal with petal-like tentacles round its mouth.

ˈsea bed floor of the sea.

ˈsea-bird *n* any of several species of bird which live close to the sea, eg on cliffs, islands, etc. ⇨ illus at BIRD.

ˈseaboard *n* coastal region; sea-shore: *on the Atlantic seaboard.*

ˈsea-borne *adj* (esp of trade) carried in ships: *sea-borne commerce, goods, etc* ○ *airborne and sea-borne missiles*, ie carried by aircraft and ships or submarines.

ˈsea-bream *n* = BREAM 2.

ˈsea-breeze *n* breeze blowing from the sea towards the land, esp during the day, followed by a land-breeze at night.

ˈsea change complete (and often unexpected) change in character: *a surprising sea change in the party's fortunes.*

ˈsea-cow *n* type of warm-blooded creature living in the sea and feeding its young with milk.

ˈsea-dog *n* old sailor.

ˈseafarer /-feərə(r)/ *n* sailor.

ˈseafaring /-feərɪŋ/ *adj* [attrib], *n* [U] (of) work or travel on the sea: *a seafaring man* ○ *a life of seafaring.*

ˈsea fog fog along the coast, caused by the difference between the temperatures on land and at sea.

ˈseafood *n* [U] edible fish or shellfish from the sea: [attrib] *a ˈseafood restaurant* ○ *a ˌseafood ˈcocktail.*

ˈsea front part of a town facing the sea: *a hotel on the sea front* ○ [attrib] *a sea-front restaurant.*

ˈseagoing *adj* [attrib] **1** (of ships) built for

crossing the sea, not for coastal voyages only. **2** (of a person) seafaring.

ˌ**sea-ˈgreen** *adj, n* bluish-green, like the colour of the clean sea.

ˈ**seagull** *n* = GULL[1].

ˈ**sea-horse** *n* small fish with a horse-like head.

ˌ**sea-island** ˈ**cotton** long-stapled cotton of high quality.

ˈ**sea-kale** *n* coastal plant whose young white shoots are used as a vegetable.

ˈ**sea-lane** *n* regular route for ships at sea.

ˈ**sea-legs** *n* [pl] ability to walk easily on the deck of a moving ship or to avoid seasickness: *I feel a bit odd; I haven't got my sea-legs yet.*

ˈ**sea-level** *n* level of the sea half-way between high and low tide: *50 metres above/below sea-level.*

ˈ**sea-lion** *n* large seal of the N Pacific Ocean.

ˈ**Sea Lord** (*Brit*) any of the four naval members of the Board of Admiralty.

ˈ**seaman** /-mən/ *n* (*pl* **-men** /-mən/) **1** sailor, esp one in a navy below the rank of an officer. ⇨ App 4. **2** any skilled sailor. ˈ**seamanlike** /-mənlaɪk/ *adj*. ˈ**seamanship** /-mənʃɪp/ *n* [U] skill in managing a boat or ship.

ˈ**sea mile** = NAUTICAL MILE (NAUTICAL).

ˈ**sea-pink** *n* [U] = THRIFT 2.

ˈ**seaplane** *n* aircraft designed so that it can take off from and land on water.

ˈ**seaport** *n* town with a harbour used by seagoing ships.

ˈ**sea power** **1** [U] ability to control the seas with a strong navy. **2** [C] country with a strong navy.

ˈ**sea room** space needed by a ship to turn or manoeuvre at sea.

ˈ**sea salt** salt obtained from sea water by evaporation.

ˈ**seascape** *n* picture of a scene at sea.

ˈ**sea scout** member of the branch of the Scout Association that teaches sailing skills.

ˈ**sea shell** shell of any mollusc living in the sea.

ˈ**sea-shore** *n* [U] **1** land next to the sea: *a walk on/along the sea-shore.* **2** (*law*) area between high- and low-water marks.

ˈ**seasick** *adj* feeling sick or wanting to vomit as the result of the motion of a ship, etc. ˈ**seasickness** *n* [U].

ˈ**seaside** *n* (often **the seaside**) [U] land, place, town, etc by the sea, esp a holiday resort: *two weeks at the seaside* ○ *own a house at the seaside* ○ [attrib] *a seaside town, hotel, holiday.* ⇨ Usage at COAST[1].

ˈ**sea-urchin** (also **urchin**) *n* small sea animal with a prickly shell.

ˌ**sea-ˈwall** *n* wall built to stop the sea flowing onto or eroding the land.

ˈ**sea water** salt water from the sea.

ˈ**sea-way** *n* **1** [C] deep inland waterway along which ocean-going ships can sail. **2** [U] progress by a ship on the sea: *The liner made good sea-way because of the fine weather.*

ˈ**seaweed** *n* [U, C] plant growing in the sea, esp on rocks at the edge of the sea.

ˈ**seaworthy** *adj* (of a ship) in a fit state for a sea voyage: *make a damaged ship seaworthy again.* ˈ**seaworthiness** *n* [U].

seal

seal[1] /siːl/ *n* animal with flippers that lives near and in the sea and eats fish.

▷ **sealer** *n* ship or person that hunts seals.

sealing *n* [U] hunting seals: [attrib] *a sealing expedition.*

□ ˈ**sealskin** *n* [U] skin or fur of a seal used as clothing material: [attrib] *a sealskin jacket.*

seal

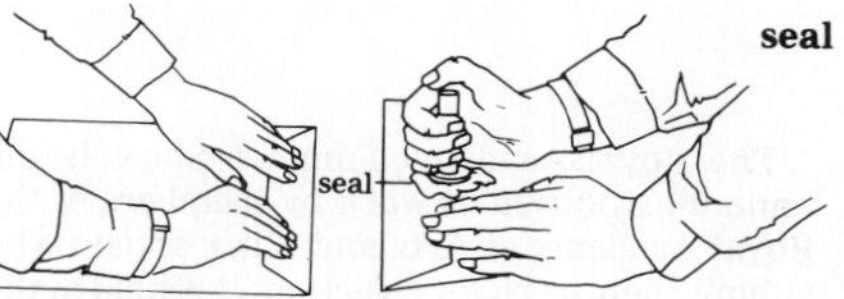

seal[2] /siːl/ *n* **1** (a) piece of wax, lead or other soft material, usu stamped with a design and fixed to a document to show that it is genuine, or to a letter, packet, container, etc to prevent it being opened by the wrong person; design stamped in this way: *The letter bears the seal of the king.* (b) piece of metal, ring, etc with an engraved design used for stamping a seal. ⇨ illus. **2** thing used instead of a seal, eg a paper disc stuck to a document, or an impression stamped on it. **3** (a) substance or device used to fill a gap, crack, etc so that gas or fluid cannot enter or escape: *a rubber seal in the lid of a jar* ○ *I've bought a seal to put around the edge of the bath.* (b) closure made by this: *The putty gives a good seal round the window.* **4** small decorative sticker like a postage stamp, esp one sold in aid of charity. **5** (idm) **a** ˌ**seal of apˈproval** formal approval: *The deal needs the government's seal of approval.* **set the seal on sth** (*fml*) be the high point in sth; complete sth: *This award has set the seal on a successful stage career.*

▷ **seal** *v* **1** [Tn] put a seal[2](1, 2) on (eg a legal document). **2** [Tn, Tn·p] (a) ~ **sth** (**down**) stick down (an envelope, etc). (b) ~ **sth** (**up**) fasten or close sth securely: *sealed orders* ○ *seal the parcel (up) with adhesive tape.* (c) ~ **sth** (**up**) close tightly or put a substance, etc on sth to stop gas or fluid entering or escaping: *The jar must be well sealed.* ○ *Seal (up) the window to prevent draughts.* **3** [Tn] coat or surface (sth) with a protective substance, sealant, etc: *seal the boat's hull with special paint.* **4** [Tn] (*fml*) settle (sth); decide: *seal a bargain* ○ *Her fate is sealed,* ie No one can stop what is going to happen to her. **5** (idm) **one's lips are sealed** ⇨ LIP. **6** (phr v) **seal sth in** keep sth in by sealing: *Our foil packets seal the flavour in.* **seal sth off** prevent anybody or anything entering or leaving (an area, etc): *Police sealed off all the exits from the building.*

sealant /ˈsiːlənt/ *n* [U, C] substance used for waterproofing, stopping leaks, etc: *mend the hole and paint some sealant on.*

□ ˌ**sealed** ˈ**orders** instructions given to an officer in the armed forces in a sealed envelope to be opened at a certain time or place, usu in wartime.

ˈ**sealing-wax** *n* [U] type of wax that melts quickly when heated and hardens quickly when cooled, used for sealing letters, etc.

sealskin ⇨ SEAL[1].

Sealyham /ˈsiːlɪəm/ *n* breed of terrier with short legs and wiry hair.

seam /siːm/ *n* **1** (a) line along which two edges, esp of cloth, are joined or sewn together: *the seams down the side of his trousers.* ⇨ illus at SEW. (b) line where two edges meet, eg of boards forming a ship's deck. **2** layer, eg of coal, between layers of other materials, eg rock, clay. **3** line on a surface, eg a wrinkle or scar on skin. **4** (idm) **be bursting at the seams** ⇨ BURST[1].

▷ **seam** *v* [Tn] join (two pieces of cloth, etc) by means of a seam.

seamed *adj* ~ (**with sth**) having a seam or seams: *seamed stockings* ○ *rock seamed with gold* ○ *a face seamed with wrinkles.*

seamless *adj* without a seam(1a): *seamless stockings.*

□ ˈ**seam bowler** (also **seamer**) (in cricket) bowler who bowls fairly fast and tries to make the ball change direction after bouncing.

seamstress (*Brit* also **sempstress**) /ˈsemstrɪs/ *n* woman who sews, esp as a paid job.

seamy /ˈsiːmɪ/ *adj* (**-ier**, **-iest**) unattractive and sordid: *the seamy side of life,* ie corruption, crime, etc ○ *a seamy bribery scandal.*

Seanad /ˈʃænəd/ **the Seanad** *n* [Gp] upper house of parliament in the Republic of Ireland. Cf DÁIL ÉIREANN.

seance (also **séance**) /ˈseɪɑːns/ *n* meeting, esp of spiritualists, at which people try to talk with the spirits of the dead.

sear /sɪə(r)/ *v* **1** (also **sere**) [Tn] scorch or burn (a surface): *a cloth seared by the heat of the oven* ○ *sear a wound to prevent infection.* **2** [Tn esp passive] (*fig rhet*) affect (sb) with strong emotion: *a soul seared by injustice* ○ *The novel is a searing indictment of poverty.*

search /sɜːtʃ/ *v* **1** [I, Ipr, Ip, Tn, Tn·pr] ~ (**sb/sth**) (**for sb/sth**); ~ **through sth** (**for sth**) empty the pockets, etc of (sb) and examine his body and clothes to see if anything is concealed there; look at, examine or go over (a thing or place) carefully in order to find sb/sth: *We searched (around) for hours, but couldn't find the book.* ○ *search (the woods) for escaped prisoners* ○ *search (through) the drawers for the missing papers* ○ *The police searched her for drugs.* ○ (*fig*) *I searched my memory, but couldn't remember her name.* **2** (idm) **search one's** ˈ**heart**/ˈ**conscience** (*fml*) think carefully about one's motives, actions, feelings, etc: *Search your heart and ask if you're not equally to blame.* ˌ**search** ˈ**me** (*infml*) I don't know: *'Where's the newspaper?' 'Search me, I haven't seen it.'* **3** (phr v) **search sb/sth out** find sb/sth by searching: *We've searched out some of your favourite recipes.* ○ *I want to search out an old school friend.*

▷ **search** *n* **1** act of searching: *a search for a missing aircraft* ○ *make repeated searches for concealed weapons* ○ *Volunteers joined the search for the lost child.* **2** (idm) **in search of sb/sth** searching for sb/sth: *go in search of a cheap hotel* ○ *Scientists are in search of a cure for the disease.*

searching *adj* (of an examination, a question, etc) keen and penetrating; seeking the truth: *She gave me a searching look and asked if I was lying.* ○ *a searching interview technique.* **searchingly** *adv.*

□ ˈ**searchlight** *n* powerful lamp whose beam can be turned in any direction, used esp to discover enemy aircraft at night.

ˈ**search-party** *n* group of people brought together to search for a person or thing.

ˈ**search-warrant** *n* official document allowing a building, etc to be searched, eg for stolen property.

season /ˈsiːzn/ *n* **1** part of the year distinguished according to its particular type of weather, esp one of the four traditional periods into which the year is divided, ie spring, summer, autumn and winter: *the ˈdry/ˈrainy season* ○ *Plants grow fast in the warmest season.* ○ *Spring is my favourite season.* **2** (a) time of the year when sth is easily available or common, or when a certain activity takes place: *the ˈstrawberry, ˈapple, etc season* ○ *the ˈgrowing season* ○ *the ˈfootball, ˈtheatre, ˈopera, etc season* ○ *the ˈnesting season,* ie when birds build nests and lay their eggs ○ *the ˈoff season,* ie (at holiday resorts, etc) the time when there are very few visitors ○ *the ˈholiday/ˈtourist season* ○ *the season of goodwill,* ie Christmas. (b) (usu *sing*) (*fml*) time of the year during which most fashionable social events are held: *The ball was the highlight of the London season.* ⇨ article. (c) series of concerts, plays, etc with a particular theme, eg works by certain artists: *season of silent film classics on Saturday afternoons.* **3** (idm) **in** ˈ**season** (a) (of food) available in large quantities: *Strawberries are cheaper when they're in season.* (b) (of a female animal) ready for mating. (c) at the time when most people take their holidays: *Hotels are often full in season.* (d) at the time of year when certain animals may be legally hunted: *Grouse will soon be in season again.* **in season** (**for sth/to do sth**) (*dated esp US*) at the proper time; in good time. ˌ**out of** ˈ**season** (a) (of food) not in season. (b) at the time when most people do not take their holidays: *Holiday prices are lower out of season.* **the season's** ˈ**greetings** (used as a greeting at Christmas). **the silly season** ⇨ SILLY.

▷ **season** *v* **1** [Tn, Tn·pr] ~ **sth** (**with sth**) flavour (food) with salt, pepper, etc: *highly seasoned sauces* ○ *lamb seasoned with garlic and rosemary* ○ (*fig*)

The Season

'The Season' is the term in Britain for a number of fashionable sporting and cultural events that are held in the summer months and are attended by many of the rich and famous. There are ten main events. They are Glyndebourne, Derby Day, the Royal Academy Summer Show, Royal Ascot, Wimbledon, Henley Royal Regatta, International Polo Day, Goodwood, Cowes Week and Lords. Tickets for these events can be very expensive and difficult to obtain. Increasingly, large firms invite clients to attend as their guests as a form of 'corporate hospitality'. Salmon, strawberries and champagne are served. The fashionably dressed crowds provide abundant material for the gossip columnists, especially when members of the royal family and other famous people attend.

Glyndebourne is a country house in Sussex where since 1934 an opera festival has been held every summer. Guests wear evening dress and many bring picnics to eat on the lawn in front of the house during the long supper interval.

Derby Day is a lively gathering on Epsom Downs south-west of London where one of the most important horse races of the year is run. It is traditionally attended not only by the social élite but by people from all walks of life who like to see the race, place a bet on a possible winner, and enjoy the noisy fun-fair. The royal family watches the race from the Royal Box. There are several enclosures for the public, one of which is entirely filled with open-topped double-decker buses, from which spectators have a good view of the whole event. The race is named after the Earl of Derby, who founded it in 1779.

The Royal Academy Summer Show is the annual exhibition of work by members of the Royal Academy of Arts and other artists who submit their work for selection. It is held at the Academy's London headquarters, Burlington House in Piccadilly.

Royal Ascot is considered to be the main flat-racing event of the season. The course is at the village of Ascot, near Windsor. The Queen and other members of the royal family always attend, and the event opens when they drive along the course in an open carriage to the Royal Enclosure, a special area for spectators where there are strict rules regarding dress: men must wear morning dress, and women's dresses must be long enough to cover the knees. The fashionable climax of Ascot is Ladies' day (usually the third day), when women show off their most extravagant hats.

Wimbledon is the major tennis event of the year, officially known as the All England Championships. It is held on the courts of the All England Lawn Tennis and Croquet Club at Wimbledon, in south London, and attracts nearly 40 000 spectators annually. The most important matches are played on the Centre Court. A Wimbledon tradition is 'afternoon tea', with sandwiches, strawberries and cream. Members of the royal family attend on at least one day.

Henley is the main rowing event of the year, and is officially called Henley Regatta. The contest is held at Henley, a town on the River Thames between London and Oxford. About 2 000 rowers of both sexes attend from many different countries and compete for prizes. The most prestigious award is the Grand Challenge Cup, for eights (crews of eight men). The social aspect of Henley is represented by the colourful boat parties and pleasure launches, and the brightly striped marquees on the river bank.

International Polo Day is held by the Guards Polo Club at Windsor. The event forms the high spot of the polo season, and Prince Charles, a keen player, is one of the participants.

Goodwood is one of the most fashionable horse races of the year, less noisy than Derby day and not as showy as Ascot. The five-day event is nicknamed 'Glorious Goodwood' because of the beautiful setting for the races, which are held on a course in the grounds of Goodwood House, near Chichester in Sussex.

Cowes Week is a major sailing regatta held at Cowes, on the Isle of Wight, where the Royal Yacht Squadron is based. The event attracts about 10 000 yachtsmen and yachtswomen every year. The Queen and the Duke of Edinburgh, who is a senior member of the Royal Yacht Squadron, also attend.

Lord's cricket ground, in north London, is the most important in the country, as it is the headquarters of the Marylebone Cricket Club (MCC), which drew up the rules for the game and which until 1969 was the governing body of world cricket. (The present governing body, also based at Lord's, is the Cricket Council.) The Test Match played every summer at Lord's between the England team and a team from abroad is one of the highlights of the cricket season. The name of the ground has nothing to do with lords but comes from Thomas Lord, who started a cricket club in London (originally on another site) in 1797. The first match was played at Lord's in 1814.

conversation seasoned with wit. **2** (**a**) [I, Tn] (of wood) become fit for use by exposure to the weather; make (wood) fit for use in this way: *well-seasoned oak, birch, etc.* (**b**) [Tn esp passive] (*fig*) make (sb) experienced by practice: *a politician seasoned by six election campaigns* ○ *a seasoned boxer, traveller.*

□ ˈ**season-ticket** (also *Brit infml* **season**) *n* ticket that allows a person to make as many journeys, go to as many concerts, etc as he wishes within a specified period. Cf COMMUTATION TICKET (COMMUTE).

seasonable /ˈsiːznəbl/ *adj* **1** (of the weather) suitable for the time of year: *seasonable snow showers.* **2** (of help, advice, gifts, etc) coming at the right time; opportune. ▷ **seasonably** /-nəblɪ/ *adv.*

seasonal /ˈsiːzənl/ *adj* happening during a particular season; varying with the seasons: *seasonal work*, eg fruit-picking ○ *a seasonal trade*, eg selling Christmas cards ○ *a seasonal increase in unemployment.* ▷ **seasonally** /-nəlɪ/ *adv.*

seasoning /ˈsiːzənɪŋ/ *n* [U, C] herb, spice, etc used to season food: *not enough seasoning in the stew* ○ *adventurous seasonings, like paprika and turmeric.*

seat[1] /siːt/ *n* **1** [C] thing made or used for sitting on, eg a chair, bench or box: *take a seat*, ie sit down ○ *a stone seat in the garden* ○ *The furniture hadn't arrived so we were using crates as seats.* ○ *The back seat of the car is wide enough for three people.* ○ *She rose from her seat to protest.* ⇨ illus at FURNITURE. **2** [C] that part of a chair, bench, stool, etc on which one sits (contrasted with the back, legs, etc): *a chair with a cane seat.* **3** [C] (**a**) (*fml*) the buttocks. (**b**) part of a garment covering these: *a hole in the seat of his trousers.* **4** [C] place where one pays to sit in a vehicle or in a theatre, concert-hall, etc: *There are no seats left on the flight.* ○ *book two seats for the concert* ○ *expensive opera seats.* ⇨ Usage at SPACE. **5** [C] place as a member of a law-making assembly, council, committee, etc: *a seat on the council, in Parliament, etc* ○ *take one's seat*, ie begin one's duties, eg in the House of Commons ○ *win a/lose one's seat*, ie win/lose a place in a parliament, etc in an election ○ *have a majority of 21 seats in the Senate.* **6** [C] (*esp Brit*) parliamentary constituency: *a seat in Devon.* **7** [C] (*fml*) place where sth is based, or where an activity is carried on: *In the USA, Washington is the seat of government and New York City is the chief seat of commerce.* ○ *seats of learning*, ie universities. **8** [C] (also ˌ**country** ˈ**seat**) (*dated*) large house in the country, usu the centre of a large estate: *the family seat in Norfolk.* **9** [sing] way in which sb sits on a horse: *an experienced rider with a good seat.* **10** (idm) **(drive/fly) by the seat of one's** ˈ**pants** (do sth) by instinct rather than careful thought: *None of us had seen an emergency like this and we were all flying by the seat of our pants.* **have a ringside seat** ⇨ RINGSIDE (RING[1]). **the hot seat** ⇨ HOT. **in the driver's seat** ⇨ DRIVER. **(be/keep sb) on the edge of one's seat/chair** ⇨ EDGE[1]. **take a back seat** ⇨ BACK[2].

▷ **-seater** (forming compound *ns* and *adjs*) (vehicle, etc) with the specified number of seats: *a* ˌ*ten-seater* ˈ*minibus* ○ *a fast little* ˌ*two-*ˈ*seater*, ie car.

□ ˈ**seat-belt** (also ˈ**safety-belt**) *n* strap worn as a belt, attached to a seat in an aircraft, car, etc to prevent a passenger being thrown forward if an accident happens: *Fasten your seat-belts!* ⇨ illus at CAR.

seat[2] /siːt/ *v* **1** [Tn esp passive] (*fml*) make (sb/oneself) sit: *Seat the boy next to his brother.* ○ *a statue of a woman seated on a horse* ○ *Please be seated, ladies and gentlemen.* ○ *She seated hersel[f] on the sofa.* **2** [Tn] have seats for (a specifie[d] number of people): *a hall that seats 500.*

▷ **seating** *n* [U] (arrangement of) places to sit seats: *renew the seating in the theatre* ○ [attrib] *seating arrangements* ○ *How much seating room d[o] we have?*

SEATO /ˈsiːtəʊ/ *abbr* (formerly) South-East Asi[a] Treaty Organization. Cf NATO.

sebaceous /sɪˈbeɪʃəs/ *adj* [attrib] producin[g] sebum: *the sebaceous glands in the skin* ○ *[a] sebaceous cyst*, ie formed in a sebaceous gland.

sebum /ˈsiːbəm/ *n* [U] oily substance produced b[y] glands in the skin, which stops the skin and hai[r] becoming too dry.

sec /sek/ *n* (*Brit infml*) = SECOND[3] 2.

sec *abbr* **1** secant. **2** secondary. **3** secretary.

secant /ˈsiːkənt, ˈsek-/ (*mathematics*) **1** straigh[t] line that cuts a curve at two points. **2** in [a] right-angled triangle, the ratio of the length of th[e] hypotenuse to that of the adjacent side.

secateurs /ˈsekətɜːz, ˌsekəˈtɜːz/ *n* [pl] (*Brit*) clippers used for pruning bushes, etc: *a pair o[f] secateurs.* ⇨ illus at CLIPPERS.

secede /sɪˈsiːd/ *v* [I, Ipr] ~ **(from sth)** (*fml*) withdraw (from membership of an organization, [a] state, etc): *the Southern States which seceded fro[m] the Union* (ie from the United States) *in 1860-61.*

▷ **secession** /sɪˈseʃn/ *n* [C, U] ~ **(from sth)** (*fml*) (instance of) seceding. **secessionist** /-ʃənɪst/ *n* person in favour of seceding.

seclude /sɪˈkluːd/ *v* [Tn, Tn·pr] ~ **sb/onesel[f]** **(from sb)** (*fml*) keep sb/oneself apart (fro[m] others): *She secludes herself in her study to work.* ○ *You can't seclude yourself from the world.*

▷ **secluded** *adj* (**a**) (of a place) not visited or see[n] by many people: *a secluded garden behind hig[h]* *walls.* (**b**) away from the company of others: *lead a secluded life.*

seclusion /sɪˈkluːʒn/ *n* [U] (**a**) secluding or being secluded. (**b**) secluded place; privacy: *in the seclusion of one's own home.*

second[1] /ˈsekənd/ *det* **1** 2nd; next after first in time, order, importance, etc: *February is the second month of the year.* ○ *Tom is the second son — he has an elder brother.* ○ *Osaka is the second largest city in Japan.* ○ *Who was second in the race?* ⇨ App 9. Cf TWO. **2** another after the first; additional; extra: *a second helping of soup* ○ *You will need a second pair of shoes.* **3** of an inferior or a less important kind: *We never use second quality ingredients.* ○ (*sport*) *the second eleven*, ie a team of reserves. **4** of the same quality, merit, etc as a previous one: *He thinks he's a second Churchill!* ie believes he has Churchill's abilities. **5** (idm) **ˌsecond ˈonly to sb/sth** having only one person or thing that is better, more important, etc: *He is second only to my own son in my affections.* **ˌsecond to ˈnone** as good as the best: *As a dancer, he is second to none.* (For other idioms containing **second**, see the other major words in each idiom, eg **get one's second wind** ⇨ WIND[1].)

▷ **second** *adv* in second place; second in order or importance: *The English swimmer came second.* ○ *I agreed to speak second.*

secondly *adv* in the second place; furthermore: *First(ly), it's too expensive; and secondly, it's very ugly.* ⇨ Usage at FIRST[2].

□ **ˌsecond-ˈbest** *adj* **1** next after the best: *my ˌsecond-best ˈsuit* ○ *the second-best performance of the tournament.* **2** not as good as one would really like: *I like live music: for me records are definitely second-best.* **3** (idm) **come off ˌsecond-ˈbest** fail to win; fail to do as well as sb else: *When they have to choose between quality and price, quality usually comes off second-best.* — *n* [U] person or thing that is not as good as the best: *I'm used to high quality and won't take second-best.*

ˌsecond ˈchamber upper house in a law-making body.

ˌsecond ˈclass (**a**) standard of accommodation, etc that is of lower quality than first class: [attrib] *a second-class carriage on the train.* (**b**) category of mail that is given less priority than first-class mail: *Second class is cheaper.* ○ [attrib] *ˌsecond-class ˈletters.* ⇨ article at POST OFFICE. **ˌsecond-ˈclass** *adj* **1** of the second-best group or category: *a second-class degree in history.* **2** (*derog*) much less good than the best; second-rate: *a ˌsecond-class hoˈtel* ○ *The old are treated as ˌsecond-class ˈcitizens*, ie not as well as other members of society. — *adv*: *go/travel second class* ○ *It takes longer if you send it second class.*

the ˌsecond ˈcoming the return of Jesus Christ at the Last Judgement.

ˌsecond ˈcousin child of one of one's parents' first cousins. Cf COUSIN. Cf ONCE, TWICE, ETC REMOVED (REMOVE[1]).

ˌsecond-deˈgree *adj* [attrib] (of burns) of the type that is next to the most serious.

ˌSecond ˈEmpire of or in the elaborately decorated style of architecture, furniture, etc developed in France between about 1850 and 1870. The style became very popular in the USA after the American Civil War.

ˌsecond ˈfloor floor above the first (in Britain two floors, in US one floor, above the ground): [attrib] *a ˌsecond-floor aˈpartment.*

ˌsecond-ˈguess *v* [Tn] (*esp US infml*) **1** comment on or criticize (an action, a decision, etc) after its results have become clear: *It's easy to second-guess the casting of the film*, eg say that the wrong actors were chosen. **2** make a better guess than (sb): *The papers have all been trying to second-guess each other about the President's next move.* **3** guess (what is going to happen): *Don't try to second-guess the outcome.*

ˌsecond-ˈhand *adj, adv* **1** previously owned by sb else: *a ˌsecond-hand ˈcar, ˈsuit, ˈcamera* ○ *a ˌsecond-hand ˈbookshop*, ie a shop selling second-hand books ○ *I rarely buy anything second-hand.* **2** (of news, information, etc) obtained from others, not from personal experience, etc: *ˌsecond-hand ˈgossip* ○ *get news second-hand.*

ˌsecond lieuˈtenant army officer next below lieutenant. ⇨ App 4.

ˌsecond-ˈrate *adj* of poor quality; not very good: *a ˌsecond-rate ˈactor, ˈscript, perˈformance* ○ *His novels are very second-rate.*

ˌsecond ˈsight ability to know what is going to happen, or to see events happening far away (as if one were present).

ˌsecond-ˈstring *adj* [attrib] (of a sports player) being a substitute, rather than a regular player.

second[2] /ˈsekənd/ *n, pron* **1 the second** [sing] person or thing that comes next after the first: *the second of May* ○ *George the Second*, ie King George II ○ *I was the first to arrive, and she was the second.* **2** [sing] person or thing additional to one already mentioned: *She published her first book last year, and has now written a second.* ○ *You're the second to ask me that.* **3** [C] ~ (**in sth**) (*Brit*) second-class university degree: *get an upper, a lower second (in economics).* **4** [U] second gear on a car, bicycle, etc: *Are you in first or second?* ○ *Change from second to third.* **5** [C usu *pl*] manufactured article that has a fault and is therefore sold cheaper: *These plates are seconds.* **6 seconds** [pl] second helping of food: *I'm going to ask for seconds.* **7** [C] person who assists a boxer or sb fighting a duel.

□ **ˌsecond in comˈmand** person next below the commanding officer, most senior official, etc in rank: *the sales director and her second in command.*

second[3] /ˈsekənd/ *n* **1** (*symb* ″) 60th part of a minute of time or of angular measurement: *The winning time was 1 minute 5 seconds.* ○ *1°6′10″*, ie one degree, six minutes, and ten seconds. ⇨ App 9, 10, 12. **2** (also *Brit infml* **sec**) short time; moment: *I'll be ready in a sec(ond).* ○ *The food was on the table in seconds.*

□ **ˈsecond hand** hand on some watches and clocks that records seconds. Cf SECOND-HAND (SECOND[1]).

second[4] /ˈsekənd/ *v* [Tn] **1** support or assist (sb), esp in a boxing-match or duel: *I was ably seconded in this research by my son.* **2** formally support (a motion, resolution, etc already proposed by sb else) to show that he is not the only person in favour of it: *Mrs Smith proposed the vote of thanks, and Mr Jones seconded (it).* ○ (*joc*) *'Let's go away this weekend.' 'I'll second that.'* Cf PROPOSE 1.

▷ **seconder** *n* person who seconds a motion, resolution, etc. Cf PROPOSER (PROPOSE).

second[5] /sɪˈkɒnd/ *v* [Tn, Tn·pr] ~ **sb** (**from sth**) (**to sth**) (*esp Brit*) transfer (sb) from his normal duties to other duties: *an officer seconded from the Marines to staff headquarters.* ▷ **secondment** *n* [C, U]: *a two-month secondment* ○ *an officer on secondment* (ie seconded) *overseas.*

secondary /ˈsekəndrɪ; *US* -derɪ/ *adj* **1** ~ (**to sth**) coming after sth that is first or primary; of less importance, value, etc than what is primary: *Such considerations are secondary to our main aim of improving efficiency.* ○ *Her age is of secondary interest.* ○ *secondary stress*, eg on the first syllable of 'ˌsacriˈficial' ○ *secondary picketing*, eg of a company that is thought to be helping the employers of the workers on strike. ⇨ article at TRADE UNION ○ *secondary sexual characteristics*, ie those that distinguish between the sexes but are not related to reproduction, eg men's beards and women's breasts. **2** dependent on, caused by or derived from sth that is original or primary: *secondary literature*, eg criticism or reviews of an author's work ○ *a secondary colour*, ie one produced by mixing two primary colours ○ *a secondary infection*, ie one which occurs as a result of another illness ○ *secondary industries*, ie those that make products by processing raw materials. **3** [attrib] following primary or (in the USA) elementary or junior high schools: *a secondary school* ○ *secondary education.* Cf PRIMARY. ▷ **secondarily** /-drəlɪ; *US* ˌsekənˈderəlɪ/ *adv.*

secrecy /ˈsiːkrəsɪ/ *n* **1** [U] keeping secrets; ability or tendency to keep secrets; state of being secret: *rely on sb's secrecy* ○ *his obsessive secrecy about his work* ○ *The meeting was arranged with the utmost secrecy*, ie very secretly. ○ *the secrecy that still surrounds the accident.* **2** (idm) **swear sb to secrecy** ⇨ SWEAR.

secret /ˈsiːkrɪt/ *adj* **1** ~ (**from sb**) kept or intended to be kept from the knowledge or view of others; not known by others: *a secret marriage, document, meeting* ○ *keep sth secret from one's family* ○ *She escaped through a secret door.* ○ *The party was given secret financial support by some foreign backers.* **2** [attrib] not openly declared or admitted: *I'm a secret fan of soap operas on TV.* **3** [attrib] (of a place) secluded or quiet: *my secret cottage in the country.* **4** [esp pred] (*fml*) fond of keeping secrets, secretive.

▷ **secret** *n* **1** fact, decision, etc that is or must be kept secret: *keep a secret*, ie not tell it to anyone else ○ *The wedding date's a big secret.* ○ *Are you going to let him in on* (ie tell him) *the secret?* ○ *He made no secret of his dislike for me*, ie made it very clear. **2** method of doing or achieving sth that not many people know: *the secret of success* ○ *What's your secret for this wonderful pastry?* **3** anything not properly understood or difficult to understand; mystery: *the secrets of nature.* **4** (idm) **in ˈsecret** without others knowing: *meet in secret* ○ *leave the country in secret.* **in the ˈsecret** (*dated*) among those who know the secret: *Is your brother in the secret?* **an open secret** ⇨ OPEN[1].

secretly *adv.*

□ **ˌsecret ˈagent** (also **agent**) person working secretly for a government and trying to find out secret information, esp the military secrets of another government; spy.

ˌsecret ˈballot voting in which the choice made by each individual voter is kept secret.

ˌsecret poˈlice police force that works in secret to ensure that citizens behave as their government wants.

ˌsecret ˈservice government department dealing with espionage and counter-espionage.

secretariat /ˌsekrəˈteərɪət/ *n* **1** administrative department of a large organization. **2** staff or office of a Secretary-General or of a government Secretary: *the UN secretariat in New York.*

secretary /ˈsekrətrɪ; *US* -rəterɪ/ *n* **1** employee in an office, usu working for another person, dealing with letters, typing, filing, etc and making appointments and arrangements: *I sometimes think my secretary runs the firm.* **2** official of a club, society, etc who deals with its correspondence, records, or business affairs. **3 Secretary** (**a**) = SECRETARY OF STATE. (**b**) (*Brit*) senior Civil Servant. (**c**) (*US*) head of a government department: *Secretary of the Treasury.*

▷ **secretarial** /ˌsekrəˈteərɪəl/ *adj* of (the work of) secretaries: *secretarial staff, duties, training, colleges.*

□ **ˈsecretary bird** large long-legged African bird of prey with a distinctive crest.

ˌSecretary-ˈGeneral *n* (*pl* **Secretaries-General**) chief official in charge of a large organization (eg the UNO).

ˌSecretary of ˈState 1 (also **Secretary, minister**) (*Brit*) head of one of the major government departments: *the Secretary of State for Home Affairs, Defence, etc* ○ *the Home, Defence, etc Secretary.* **2** (*US*) head of the Foreign Affairs department.

secrete /sɪˈkriːt/ *v* (*fml*) **1** [Tn] (of an organ) produce (a substance, usu liquid) either as waste material or for use within the body: *The kidneys secrete urine.* ○ *Saliva is secreted by glands in the mouth.* **2** [Tn, Tn·pr] put or keep (sth) in a secret place; hide: *money secreted in a drawer.*

▷ **secretion** /sɪˈkriːʃn/ *n* (*fml*) **1** [U] secreting (SECRETE 1) or being secreted: *the secretion of bile by the liver.* **2** [C] substance that is secreted, eg saliva, bile, etc. **3** [U] secreting (SECRETE 2) or being secreted.

secretive /ˈsiːkrətɪv/ *adj* liking to keep things secret or to hide one's thoughts, feelings, etc: *a secretive person, nature.* ▷ **secretively** *adv.* **secretiveness** *n* [U].

sect /sekt/ *n* (*sometimes derog*) group of people who share (esp religious) beliefs or opinions which differ from those of most people: *a minor Christian sect.*

sect *abbr* section (esp of a document): *clause 3 sect 2.*

sectarian /sek'teərɪən/ *adj* **1** of a sect or sects: *sectarian violence*, ie between members of different religious sects. **2** (*derog*) showing a lack of tolerance or concern for those outside one's own sect, class, etc: *sectarian views* ○ *Sectarian politics are ruining the country's economy.*

▷ **sectarianism** /-ɪzəm/ *n* [U] (*often derog*) tendency to split up into sects; tendency to be sectarian(2).

section /'sekʃn/ *n* **1** [C] any of the parts into which sth may be or has been divided: *This section of the road is closed.* ○ *White lines divide the playing area into sections.* ○ *the practical sections of the course.* **2** [C] any of a number of parts that can be fitted together to make a structure: *the three sections of a fishing-rod* ○ *The shed comes in sections that you assemble yourself.* **3** [C] separate group within a body of people: *Farm workers make up only a small section of the population.* ○ *a discontented section of the army.* **4** [C] department of an organization, institution, etc: *the library's extensive biology section* ○ *the woodwind section of the orchestra*, ie players of woodwind instruments. **5** [C] separate part of a document, book, etc: *section 4, subsection 2 of the treaty* ○ *the financial section of the newspaper* ○ *The report has a section on accidents at work.* **6** [C] (**a**) (*US*) piece of land one mile square, equal to 640 acres (about 260 hectares). (**b**) (*esp US*) area of a town: *the business, residential, shopping section.* **7** [C] view or representation of sth seen as if cut straight through from top to bottom: *This illustration shows a section through the timber.* **8** (*medical*) (**a**) [U] process of cutting or separating sth surgically: *the section of a diseased organ.* (**b**) [C] piece cut or separated in this way: *put a section of tissue under the microscope.*

▷ **section** *v* **1** [Tn, Tn·pr] divide (sth) into sections: *a library sectioned into subject areas.* **2** [Tn] (*medical*) cut or separate (tissue, etc).

sectional /-ʃənl/ *adj* **1** made or supplied in sections (SECTION 2): *a sectional fishing-rod* ○ *sectional furniture.* **2** [usu attrib] of a group or groups within a community, etc: *sectional interests*, ie the different and often conflicting interests of various parts of the community ○ *sectional jealousies, rivalry, etc.* **sectionalism** /-ʃənəlɪzəm/ *n* [U] (*usu derog*) too much concern for the good of one's own section of the community, rather than that of everybody.

sector /'sektə(r)/ *n* **1** part of a circle lying between two straight lines drawn from the centre to the circumference. ⇨ illus at CIRCLE. **2** part or branch of a particular area of activity, esp of a country's economy: *the manu'facturing sector*, ie all the manufacturing industries of a country ○ *the 'service sector*, eg hotels, restaurants, etc. **3** any of the parts of a battle area, or of an area under military control: *an enemy attack in the southern sector.*

secular /'sekjʊlə(r)/ *adj* **1** not concerned with spiritual or religious affairs; worldly: *secular education, art, music* ○ *the secular power*, ie the State contrasted with the Church. **2** (of priests) not belonging to a community of monks: *the secular clergy*, ie parish priests, etc.

▷ **secularism** /-lərɪzəm/ *n* [U] belief that morality, education, etc should not be based on religion. **secularist** /-lərɪst/ *n* believer in or supporter of secularism.

secularize, -ise /-ləraɪz/ *v* [Tn] (*fml*) make (sth) secular: *secularize church property, courts, education* ○ *Is the country more secularized nowadays?*

secure /sɪ'kjʊə(r)/ *adj* **1** ~ (**about sth**) not feeling worry, doubt, etc: *feel secure about one's future* ○ *a secure faith, belief, etc.* **2** not likely to be lost or to fail; certain; guaranteed: *a secure investment* ○ *have a secure job in the Civil Service* ○ *Her place in the history books is secure.* **3** firmly fixed; not likely to fall, be broken, etc; reliable: *A climber needs secure footholds.* ○ *Is that ladder secure?* **4** ~ (**against/from sth**) (*fml*) safe; protected: *The strong-room is as secure as we can make it.* ○ *Are we secure from attack here?* ○ *When you're insured, you're secure against loss.*

▷ **secure** *v* **1** [Tn] fix (sth) firmly; fasten: *Secure all the doors and windows before leaving.* ○ *secure the ladder with ropes.* **2** [Tn, Tn·pr] ~ **sth** (**against/from sth**) make sth safe; protect: *secure a building (from collapse)* ○ *Can the town be secured against attack?* ○ (*fig*) *The new law will secure the civil rights of the mentally ill.* **3** [Tn, Dn·n, Dn·pr] ~ **sth** (**for sb/sth**) (*fml*) obtain sth, sometimes with difficulty: *We'll need to secure a bank loan.* ○ *They've secured government backing (for the project).*

securely *adv.*

security /sɪ'kjʊərətɪ/ *n* **1** [U] freedom or protection from danger or worry: *children who lack the security of a good home* ○ *have the security of a guaranteed pension.* **2** [U] measures taken to prevent spying, attacks, theft, etc: *There was tight security for the Pope's visit*, eg Many police officers guarded him. ○ *We need greater security in car parks.* ○ *national security*, ie the defence of a country ○ [attrib] *security forces*, eg police, troops, etc fighting terrorism ○ *a security van*, eg for transporting money ○ *a high security prison*, ie for dangerous criminals. **3** [C, U] jewellery, insurance policies, etc that can be used to guarantee that one will pay back borrowed money or keep a promise: *lend money on security*, ie in return for sth given as security ○ *give sth as (a) security.* Cf GUARANTEE[1] 1. **4 securities** [pl] documents or certificates showing who owns stock, bonds, shares, etc: *government securities*, ie for money lent to a government.

□ **se'curity blanket** (*esp US*) small piece of blanket or other familiar object carried around by a child to make it feel safe.

the Se'curity Council the permanent peace-keeping body of the United Nations, with five permanent and ten elected members.

se'curity risk person who, because of his political beliefs, personal habits, etc may endanger the security of the state, eg by revealing secrets to an enemy: *She's a poor/good security risk.*

se'curity guard guard who wears a uniform and provides protection, eg in a public building or when money is being moved between banks.

sedan /sɪ'dæn/ *n* **1** = SALOON 4. **2** (also **se,dan-'chair**) box containing a seat for one person, carried on poles by two people, esp in the 17th and 18th centuries.

sedate[1] /sɪ'deɪt/ *adj* (of a person or his behaviour) calm and dignified; composed. ▷ **sedately** *adv.* **sedateness** *n* [U].

sedate[2] /sɪ'deɪt/ *v* [Tn] (*medical*) give (sb) a drug that calms the nerves or reduces stress.

▷ **sedation** /sɪ'deɪʃn/ *n* [U] sedating or being sedated; condition resulting from being sedated: *the sedation of a hysterical patient* ○ *under (heavy) sedation.*

sedative /'sedətɪv/ *n* drug or medicine that sedates: *give sb a sedative.* Cf TRANQUILLIZER (TRANQUIL). — *adj* [usu attrib]: *a sedative drug, injection, etc.*

sedentary /'sedntrɪ; *US* -terɪ/ *adj* **1** (of work) done sitting down: *a sedentary job, occupation, etc.* **2** (of people) spending a lot of time seated: *a sedentary worker* ○ *lead a sedentary life.*

sedge /sedʒ/ *n* [C, U] grass-like plant growing in marshes or near water.

▷ **sedgy** *adj* covered or bordered with sedge.

sediment /'sedɪmənt/ *n* [U] **1** matter that settles to the bottom of a liquid: *a wine with a gritty sediment.* **2** matter (eg sand, gravel, mud, etc) carried by water or wind and deposited on the surface of the land.

▷ **sedimentary** /,sedɪ'mentrɪ/ *adj* of or like sediment; formed from sediment: *sedimentary rocks*, eg sandstone, limestone, slate.

sedimentation /,sedɪmen'teɪʃn/ *n* [U] (*geology*) process of depositing sediment.

sedition /sɪ'dɪʃn/ *n* [U] words or actions intended to make people rebel against the authority of the State: *speeches advocating open sedition.*

▷ **seditious** /sɪ'dɪʃəs/ *adj* of, causing or spreading sedition: *seditious actions, speeches, writings, etc.* **seditiously** *adv.*

seduce /sɪ'dju:s; *US* -'du:s/ *v* **1** [Tn] tempt (esp sb younger or less experienced) to have sexual intercourse: *He's trying to seduce his secretary.* ○ (*fig*) *Men are seduced* (ie charmed) *by her beauty and wit.* **2** [Tn, Tn·pr] ~ **sb** (**from sth**); ~ **sb** (**into sth/doing sth**) (*fml*) persuade sb to do sth wrong, or sth he would not normally do, esp by offering sth desirable as a reward, etc: *I won't be seduced from my duty.* ○ *Higher salaries are seducing many teachers into industry.* ○ *I let myself be seduced into buying a new car.*

▷ **seducer** *n* person who seduces sb, esp into sexual intercourse.

seduction /sɪ'dʌkʃn/ *n* **1** [C, U] (act of) seducing or being seduced: *the art of seduction* ○ *her seduction by an older man.* **2 seductions** [pl] (*fml*) charming or attractive features: *the seductions of country life.*

seductive /sɪ'dʌktɪv/ *adj* tending to seduce, charm or tempt sb; attractive: *a seductive woman, smile, look* ○ *This offer of a high salary and a free house is very seductive.* ▷ **seductively** *adv.* **seductiveness** *n* [U].

sedulous /'sedjʊləs; *US* 'sedʒʊləs/ *adj* (*fml*) showing much hard work, steady effort or care: *a sedulous researcher, journalist, etc* ○ *sedulous work, study, etc* ○ *pay sedulous attention to details.*

▷ **sedulously** *adv.*

sedum /'si:dəm/ *n* garden plant with fleshy leaves and pink, white or yellow flowers.

see[1] /si:/ *v* (*pt* **saw** /sɔ:/, *pp* **seen** /si:n/)

▶ USING THE EYES **1** [Tn, Tf, Tw, Tng, Tni] (not in the continuous tenses) become aware of (sb/sth) by using the eyes; perceive: *He looked for her but couldn't see her in the crowd.* ○ *I looked out of the window but saw nothing.* ○ *He could see (that) she had been crying.* ○ *If you watch carefully you will see how I do it/how it is done.* ○ *Did you see what happened?* ○ *I hate to see you so unhappy*, ie in such an unhappy state. ○ *She was seen running away from the scene of the crime.* ○ *I saw him put the key in the lock, turn it and open the door.* ○ *She was seen to enter the building about the time the crime was committed.* **2** [I, Ipr, Ip] (not usu in the continuous tenses; often used with *can* and *could*) have or use the power of sight: *If you shut your eyes you can't see.* ○ *On a clear day you can see for miles from the top of the tower.* ○ *It was getting dark and I couldn't see to read.* ○ *She'll never (be able to) see again*, ie She has become blind. ○ *Move out of the way, please: I can't see through you!* ⇨ Usage at FEEL[1].

▶ LOOKING AT **3** [Tn] (not usu in the continuous tenses) look at or watch (sth): *In the evening we went to see a film.* ○ *Have you seen the new production of 'Hamlet' at the Playhouse?* ○ *Fifty thousand people saw the match.* **4** [Tn] (only in the imperative) look at (sth) in order to find information: *See page 158.*

▶ MEETING **5** [Tn] (not usu in the continuous tenses) be near and recognize (sb); meet (sb) by chance: *I saw your mother in town today.* ○ *Guess who I saw at the party yesterday?* **6** (**a**) [Tn] visit: *Come and see us again soon.* (**b**) [Tn, Tn·p] ~ **sb** (**about sth**) have a meeting with sb: *I'm seeing my solicitor tomorrow.* ○ *You ought to see* (ie consult) *a doctor.* ○ *What is it you want to see* (ie talk with) *me about?* **7** [Tn] receive a call or visit from (sb): *The manager can only see you for five minutes.* ○ *She's too ill to see anyone at present.* **8** [Tn] (used esp in the continuous tenses) spend time in the company of (sb): *She doesn't want to see him any more.* ○ *She's seeing* (ie having a relationship with) *a married man.*

▶ GRASPING WITH THE MIND OR IMAGINATION **9** [I, Tn, Tf, Tw] (not usu in continuous tenses) perceive (sth) with the mind; understand (sth): *'The door opens like this.' 'Oh, I see.'* ○ *He didn't see the joke.* ○ *I don't think she saw the point of the story.* ○ *I can see* (ie recognize) *the* *advantages of the scheme.* ○ *Can't you see (that) he's deceiving you?* ○ *Do you see what I mean?* **10** [Tn] (not usu in the continuous tenses) have an opinion of (sth); interpret (sth): *I see things differently now.* ○ *Try to see the matter from her point of view.* **11** [Tng, Cn·n/a] ~ **sb/sth as sth** (not in the continuous tenses) visualize; imagine; envisage: *I can't see her changing her mind.* ○ *Her colleagues see her as a future Prime Minister.*

► DISCOVERING OR CHECKING **12** (not usu in the continuous tenses) **(a)** [I, Tf, Tw no passive] find out or discover (sth) by looking or searching or asking: *'Has the postman been yet?' 'I'll just go and see.'* ○ *Go and see if/whether the postman has been yet.* ○ *I see (that)* (ie I have read in the newspapers that) *there is going to be a general election in France.* ○ *Could you go and see what the children are doing?* ○ *'Is he going to recover?' 'I don't know, we'll just have to wait and see.'* **(b)** [I, Tw] find out or discover by thinking or considering: *'Do you think you'll be able to help us?' 'I don't know; I'll have to see.'* ○ *I'll see what I can do to help.* **13** [Tf] (not usu in the continuous tenses) make sure; ensure; check: *See that all the doors are locked before you leave.* ○ *Could you see (that) the children are in bed by 8 o'clock?* ○ *I'll see that it's done.*

► EXPERIENCING OR WITNESSING **14** [Tn] (not in the continuous tenses) experience or undergo (sth): *This coat of mine has seen hard wear*, ie has been worn a lot. ○ *He has seen a great deal in his long life.* **15** [Tn] (not in the continuous tenses) **(a)** be the time when (an event) happens; witness: *This year sees the tercentenary of Handel's birth.* **(b)** be the scene or setting of (sth): *This stadium has seen many thrilling football matches.*

► OTHER MEANINGS **16** [Tn·pr, Tn·p] accompany or escort: *He saw her to the door.* ○ *I saw the old lady across* (ie helped her to cross) *the road.* ○ *May I see you home* (ie go with you as far as your house)? ○ *My secretary will see you out.* **17** [Tn] (in gambling games) equal (a bet); equal the bet of (another player). **18** (idm) **for all (the world) to ˈsee** clearly visible. **ˌsee for oneˈself** find out or witness sth in order to be convinced or satisfied: *If you don't believe that it's snowing, go and see for yourself!* **seeing that...** in view of the fact that...; since...; because...: *Seeing that he's ill, he's unlikely to come.* **see a lot, nothing, etc of sb** be often, never, etc in the company of sb: *They've seen a lot/nothing/little/more/less of each other recently.* **ˈsee you; (I'll) be ˈseeing you** (*infml*) goodbye: *I'd better be going now. See you!* **see you aˈround** (*infml*) = SEE YOU. (For other idioms containing **see**, see entries for *ns, adjs*, etc, eg **see the light** ⇨ LIGHT[1]; **see red** ⇨ RED[2].)
19 (phr v) **see about sth/doing sth** deal with sth; attend to sth: *I must see about* (ie prepare) *lunch soon.* ○ *I'll have to see about getting the roof mended.* ○ *He says he won't co-operate, does he? Well, we'll soon see about that!* ie I will insist that he does co-operate.
see sth in sb/sth find sb/sth attractive or interesting: *I can't think what she sees in him.*
see sb off (a) go to a railway station, airport, etc to say goodbye to sb who is about to start a journey: *We all went to the airport to see her off.* **(b)** force sb to leave a place, eg by chasing him: *The farmer saw the boys off with a heavy stick.*
see sth out (not in the continuous tenses) last until the end of sth: *We have enough coal to see the winter out.*
see over sth visit and examine or inspect (a place) carefully: *I shall need to see over the house before I can make you an offer.*
see through sb/sth (not in the continuous tenses) not be deceived by sb/sth: *We all saw through him*, ie realized what type of man he really was. ○ *I can see through your little game*, ie am aware of the trick you are trying to play on me. **see sth through** (not usu in the continuous tenses) not abandon a task, undertaking, etc until it is finished: *She's determined to see the job through.*
see sb through (sth) (not in the continuous tenses) satisfy the needs of, help or support sb for a particular (esp difficult) period of time: *Her courage and good humour saw her through the bad times.* ○ *That overcoat should see me through the winter.* ○ *I've only got £10 to see me through until pay-day!*
see to sth attend to or deal with sth: *This machine isn't working; get a mechanic to see to it.* ○ *Will you see to the arrangements for the next committee meeting?* **see to it that...** make sure that...: *See to it that you're ready on time!*

see[2] /siː/ *n* (*fml*) district for which a bishop or archbishop is responsible; office or jurisdiction of a bishop or an archbishop: *the See of Canterbury* ○ *the Holy See/the See of Rome*, ie the Papacy.

seed /siːd/ *n* **1 (a)** [C] part of a plant from which a new plant of the same kind can grow: *a tiny poppy seed* ○ *sow a row of seeds.* ⇨ illus at FRUIT. **(b)** [U] quantity of these for planting, feeding birds, etc: *a handful of grass seed* ○ *Sweet pea seed can be sown in May.* **(c)** [attrib] (to be) used for planting: *seed corn, potatoes, etc.* **2** [U] (*dated fml*) semen: *the fruit of his seed*, ie his child or children. **3** [C] (esp in tennis) seeded (SEED *v* 4) player: *a final between the first and second seeds.* **4** (idm) **go/run to seed (a)** (of a plant) stop flowering as seed is produced. **(b)** (*fig*) begin to look shabby or become less able, efficient, etc: *He started to drink too much and gradually ran to seed.* **(plant/sow) the seeds of sth** the cause or origin of sth: *Are the seeds of criminal behaviour sown early in life?*
▷ **seed** *v* **1** [I] (of a plant) produce seed. **2** [Tn, Tn·pr] ~ **sth (with sth)** sow seed in sth: *a newly-seeded lawn* ○ *seed a field with wheat.* **3** [Tn esp passive] remove the seeds from (sth): *seeded raisins.* **4** [Tn esp passive] (esp in tennis) select (a good player) to play against a poorer player in the early rounds of a knock-out competition, so that all the good players have a chance to reach the later rounds: *The seeded players all won their matches.* **5** [Tn, Tn·pr] ~ **sth (with sth)** place solid particles in (a cloud), esp by dropping them from an aircraft, in order to make the cloud produce rain.
seedless *adj* having no seeds: *seedless raisins.*
seedling /ˈsiːdlɪŋ/ *n* young plant newly grown from a seed.
□ **ˈseed-bed** *n* **1** bed of fine soil for sowing seeds. **2** (*fig*) place or situation in which sth develops: *The tennis club is a seed-bed for young talent.*
ˈseed-cake [C, U] *n* cake containing seeds, eg caraway, as a flavouring.
ˈseed capsule capsule holding a plant's seed.
ˈseed-pearl *n* small pearl.
ˈseedsman /-mən/ *n* (*pl* **-men**) dealer in seeds.

seedy /ˈsiːdɪ/ *adj* (**-ier, -iest**) **1** shabby-looking; disreputable: *a seedy old tramp* ○ *a cheap hotel in a seedy part of town.* **2** [usu pred] (*infml*) unwell: *feeling seedy.* **3** full of seeds: *The grapes are delicious but very seedy.* ▷ **seediness** *n* [U]: *the seediness of his lodgings.*

seeing /ˈsiːɪŋ/ *conj* (also **seeing that**, *infml* **seeing as**) in view of the fact that; because: *Seeing (that) the weather is bad, we'll stay at home.*

seek /siːk/ *v* (*pt, pp* **sought** /sɔːt/) (*fml*) **1 (a)** [I, Ipr esp passive, Tn] ~ **(after/for sth)** look (for sth); try to find or obtain (sth): *We sought long and hard but found no answer.* ○ *seeking (for) solutions to current problems* ○ *the long sought-for cure for the disease* ○ *young graduates seeking (after) success in life* ○ *It's a very/highly/much sought-after* (ie popular) *make of car.* ○ *seek happiness, comfort, wealth, etc* ○ *seek shelter from the rain* ○ *seek safety in flight* ○ *The explanation is not far to seek*, ie is very clear. **(b)** [Tn] try to reach (a place or point); move towards (sth): *Water seeks its own level.* ○ *The flood started and we had to seek higher ground.* **2** [Tn, Tn·pr] ~ **sth (from sb)** ask sb for sth: *seek help, advice, information, etc* ○ *You must seek permission from the manager.* **3** [It] attempt (to do sth); try: *seek to bring the conflict to an end* ○ *They are seeking to mislead us.* **4** (idm) **seek one's ˈfortune** try to find a way to become rich and successful. **5** (phr v) **seek sb/sth out** look for and find sb/sth: *We sought her out to tell her of her success.* ○ *She sought out and acquired all his early paintings.*

seem /siːm/ *v* **1** [La, Ln, Ipr, It] ~ **(to sb) (to be) sth; ~ like sth** (not used in progressive tenses) have or give the impression or appearance of being or doing sth; appear: *She seems happy (to me).* ○ *Do whatever seems best.* ○ *It seems (to me) (to be) the best solution.* ○ *It seemed like a disaster at the time.* ○ *She seems (to me) to be right/It seems (to me) that she's right.* ○ *It would seem that...*, ie a cautious way of saying *'It seems that...'* ○ *'She's leaving.' 'So it seems'*, ie People say so. ○ *They seem to know what they're doing.* ○ *I can't seem to* (ie It seems that I can't) *stop coughing.* ⇨ Usage at APPEAR. **2** (idm) **it seems/seemed as if.../as though...** the impression is/was given that...: *It always seemed as though they would marry in the end.*
▷ **seeming** *adj* [attrib] appearing to be sth, but perhaps not being this in fact; apparent: *seeming intelligence, interest, anger* ○ *Despite his seeming deafness, he could hear every word.* **seemingly** *adv* in appearance; apparently: *They were seemingly unaware of the decision.*

seemly /ˈsiːmlɪ/ *adj* (**-ier, -iest**) (*dated or fml*) proper and suitable by the standards of polite society: *seemly conduct, modesty* ○ *It would be more seemly to tell her after the funeral.* ▷ **seemliness** *n* [U].

seen *pp* of SEE[1].

seep /siːp/ *v* [Ipr, Ip] ~ **through (sth)/into sth/out (of sth)** (of liquids) flow slowly and in small quantities through a substance: *water seeping through the roof of the tunnel* ○ *Oil is seeping out through a crack in the tank.* ⇨ Usage at DRIP[1].
▷ **seepage** /ˈsiːpɪdʒ/ *n* **1** [U, C] process of seeping: *some seepage* ○ *reported seepages from the pipe.* **2** [U] liquid that seeps: *a bowl to catch the seepage.*

seersucker /ˈsɪəsʌkə(r)/ *n* [U] thin striped fabric with a crinkled surface: [attrib] *a seersucker table-cloth.*

see-saw

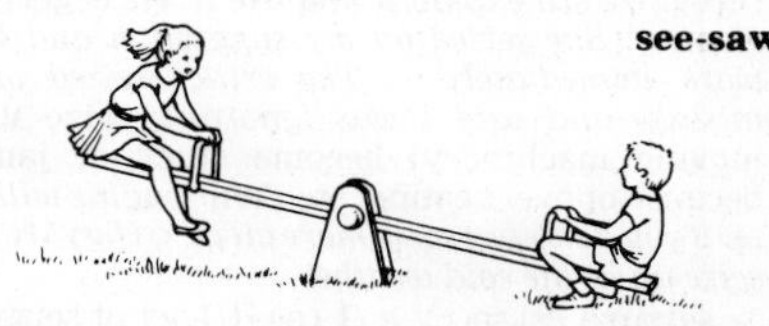

see-saw /ˈsiːsɔː/ *n* **1** [C] long plank, balanced on a centre support, and with a person sitting at each end, which can rise and fall alternately: *have a go on the see-saw.* **2** [sing] **(a)** up-and-down or to-and-fro motion: *the slow see-saw of the branch in the wind.* **(b)** (*fig*) long series of rises and falls: *Changing demand causes a see-saw in prices.*
▷ **see-saw** *v* [I] **1** play on a see-saw. **2 (a)** move up and down or to and fro: *a branch see-sawing in the wind.* **(b)** (*fig*) rise and fall in turn, or move from one position, opinion, etc to another repeatedly: *Prices see-saw according to demand.* ○ *public opinion see-sawing continuously.*

seethe /siːð/ *v* **1** [I] (of liquids) bubble and froth as if boiling: *They fell into the seething waters of the rapids.* **2** [I, Ipr] ~ **(with sth) (a)** be crowded: *streets seething with excited crowds.* **(b)** (usu in the continuous tenses) be very angry, agitated, etc: *She was seething (with rage) at his remarks.*

segment /ˈsegmənt/ *n* **1 (a)** (*geometry*) part of a circle cut off by a line. ⇨ illus at CIRCLE. **(b)** part of sth separated or marked off from the other parts; part of sth that can be separated off in the mind: *She cleaned a small segment of the painting.* ○ *Lines divided the area into segments.* **2** any one of the several sections of which an orange, lemon, etc is made up: *grapefruit segments.*
▷ **segment** /segˈment/ *v* [I, Tn] (cause sth to) separate into segments. **segmentation** /ˌsegmenˈteɪʃn/ *n* [U, C] division into segments.

Segovia /sɪˈgəʊvɪə/ Andrés (1893-1987), Spanish guitarist and composer, mainly responsible for the modern revival of interest in the guitar as a 'classical' instrument.

segregate /ˈsegrɪgeɪt/ *v* [Tn, Tn·pr] ~ **sb/sth (from sb/sth) 1** put sb/sth in a place away from the rest; isolate: *segregate cholera patients* ○ *The two groups of fans must be segregated in the stadium.* **2** separate (esp a racial or religious group) from the rest of the community and treat them unfairly: *Why should the handicapped be segregated from the able-bodied?* ○ *a segregated society*, ie one in which some groups are segregated. Cf INTEGRATE.
▷ **segregation** /ˌsegrɪˈgeɪʃn/ *n* [U] segregating or being segregated; state of being segregated: *a policy of racial segregation* ○ *We oppose segregation on religious grounds.* Cf INTEGRATION (INTEGRATE).

seismic /ˈsaɪzmɪk/ *adj* [usu attrib] of earthquakes: *seismic research, tremors, waves.*
▷ **seismogram** /ˈsaɪzməgræm/ *n* record produced by a seismograph.
seismograph /ˈsaɪzməgrɑ:f; *US* -græf/ *n* instrument for detecting earthquakes and recording how strong they are and how long they last. **seismographer** /saɪzˈmɒgrəfə(r)/ *n* expert in seismography. **seismography** /saɪzˈmɒgrəfɪ/ *n* [U] scientific measurement of earthquakes.
seismology /saɪzˈmɒlədʒɪ/ *n* [U] scienctific study of earthquakes. **seismological** /ˌsaɪzməˈlɒdʒɪkl/ *adj.* **seismologist** /saɪzˈmɒlədʒɪst/ *n.*

seize /si:z/ *v* **1** [Tn, Tn·pr] **(a)** take hold of (sth), suddenly and violently; grab: *an eagle seizing its prey* ○ *seize hold of sth* ○ *She seized me by the wrist.* ○ *He seized the bag and ran off with it.* **(b)** (of the police, customs, etc) take (stolen goods, illegal drugs, etc) away from sb: *20 kilos of heroin were seized yesterday at Heathrow.* **(c)** capture (sth); take: *seize the airport in a surprise attack* ○ *The army has seized power.* **2** [Tn] see (an opportunity, etc) and make use of it eagerly and at once: *seize the chance to make some money* ○ *Seize any opening you can.* **3** [Tn esp passive] (of a strong feeling, desire, etc) affect (sb) suddenly and overwhelmingly: *Panic seized us.* ○ *We were seized by a sudden impulse to run.* **4** (phr v) **seize on/upon sth** recognize sth exploit it and use it, etc eagerly and at once: *She seized on my suggestion and began work immediately.* ○ *The critics seized on my mistake and said I was ignorant.* **seize up** (of moving machinery) become stuck or jammed because of overheating, etc: *Your engine will seize up if you don't put some more oil in.* ○ (*fig*) *My joints seize up in the cold weather.*
▷ **seizure** /ˈsi:ʒə(r)/ *n* **1 (a)** [U] act of seizing by force or legal authority: *the seizure of contraband by Customs officers.* **(b)** [C] instance of this: *impressive seizures of drugs.* **2** [C] sudden attack of apoplexy, etc.

seldom /ˈseldəm/ *adv* not often; rarely: *I have seldom seen such brutality.* ○ *We seldom go out.* ○ *We go out very seldom.* ○ *The island is seldom, if ever, visited by ships.*

select /sɪˈlekt/ *v* [Tn, Tn·pr, Cn·n/a, Cn·t] ~ **sb/sth (as sth)** choose sb/sth, esp as being the best or most suitable: *select a gift, candidate, wine* ○ *select a card from the rack* ○ *selected as the team leader* ○ *Who has been selected to take part in the project?* ⇨ Usage at CHOOSE.
▷ **select** *adj* **1** [usu attrib] carefully chosen, esp as the best out of a larger group: *select passages of Milton's poetry.* **2** (of a society, club, gathering, etc) admitting only certain people; exclusive: *a select group of top scientists* ○ *a film shown to a select audience* ○ *This area is very select*, ie Only the most wealthy, respectable, etc people live here.
selector *n* **1** person who selects (eg members of a national team). **2** device that selects (eg the correct gear).
□ **seˌlect comˈmittee** (in the House of Commons) committee that checks the activities of a particular ministry or that is appointed to conduct a special investigation.

selection /sɪˈlekʃn/ *n* **1** [U] selecting or being selected: *the selection of a football team* ○ *I'm delighted about my selection as leader.* ○ [attrib] *the selection process.* **2** [C] **(a)** number of selected items or people: *selections from 18th century English poetry* ○ *a selection of milk and plain chocolates.* **(b)** number of items from which some can be selected: *a shop with a huge selection of paperbacks.*
□ **seˈlection committee** committee appointed to select eg the members of a sports team.

selective /sɪˈlektɪv/ *adj* **1** using or based on selection: *the selective training of recruits*, ie the training of specially chosen recruits ○ *a selective weed-killer*, ie one that kills weeds but not other plants. **2** ~ **(about sb/sth)** tending to choose carefully: *I'm very selective about the people I associate with.*
▷ **selectively** *adv.*
selectivity /ˌsɪlekˈtɪvətɪ/ *n* [U] **1** quality of being selective. **2** the power of a radio to receive broadcasts from one station without interference from other stations.
□ **seˌlective ˈservice** (*US*) selection of people for compulsory military service.

selenium /sɪˈli:nɪəm/ *n* [U] (*symb* **Se**) (*chemistry*) non-metallic element whose power to conduct electric current increases as the light reaching it becomes more intense. ⇨ App 11.
□ **seˈlenium cell** cell containing a strip of selenium, used in photo-electric devices, eg the exposure meter of a camera.

self /self/ *n* (*pl* **selves** /selvz/) **1 (a)** [U] one's own nature, special qualities, etc; one's personality: *the commitment of the whole self to a relationship* ○ *analysis of the self* ○ *the conscious self.* **(b)** [C] particular part of one's nature: *one's better self*, ie one's generous qualities ○ *By doing that he showed his true self*, ie what he is really like. ○ *She's her old self again*, ie has recovered her usual health, composure, etc. **2** [U] one's own interest, advantage or pleasure: *You always put self first.* ○ *She has no thought of self*, ie is always more concerned for other people. **3** [C] (*commerce or fml or joc*) myself, yourself, himself, etc: *a cheque payable to self*, ie to the person whose signature is on it ○ *Mr Jones, your good self* (ie you) *and I.* **4** (idm) **a shadow of one's/its former self** ⇨ SHADOW.

self- *comb form* of, to or by oneself or itself: *ˌself-conˈtrol* ○ *ˌself-adˈdressed* ○ *ˌself-ˈtaught* ○ *ˌself-closing ˈdoors*, ie ones that close automatically.

self-abnegation /ˌself æbnɪˈgeɪʃn/ *n* [U] (*fml*) = ABNEGATION.

self-absorbed /ˌself əbˈsɔ:bd/ *adj* only concerned about or interested in oneself: *He's too self-absorbed to care about us.* ▷ **self-absorption** /-əbˈsɔ:pʃn/ *n* [U].

self-abuse /ˌself əˈbju:s/ *n* [U] (*euph*) masturbation.

self-addressed /ˌself əˈdrest/ *adj* [usu attrib] (of an envelope that will be used for a reply) addressed to oneself.

self-appointed /ˌself əˈpɔɪntɪd/ *adj* [usu attrib] having decided to be sth, usu without the agreement of others: *a self-appointed judge, expert, critic, etc.*

self-assembly /ˌself əˈsemblɪ/ *adj* [attrib] (esp of furniture) that has to be fitted together by the buyer from a kit.

self-assertive /ˌself əˈsɜ:tɪv/ *adj* expressing one's views, demands, etc confidently. ▷ **self-assertion** /-əˈsɜ:ʃn/, **self-assertiveness** *ns* [U].

self-assured /ˌself əˈʃɔ:d; *US* -ˈʃʊərd/ *adj* = ASSURED (ASSURE). ▷ **self-assurance** /-əˈʃɔ:rəns; *US* -ʃʊər-/ *n* [U] = ASSURANCE 1.

self-catering /ˌselfˈkeɪtərɪŋ/ *adj* [usu attrib] (of a holiday, accommodation, etc) during or in which one has to cook for oneself: *self-catering chalets.*

self-centred (*US* **-centered**) /ˌself ˈsentəd/ *adj* (*derog*) thinking too much about oneself and too little about others: *her self-centred attitude.* ▷ **self-centredness** (*US* **-centered-**) *n* [U].

self-confessed /ˌself kənˈfest/ *adj* [attrib] having confessed that one is (usu sth bad): *a ˌself-confessed alcoˈholic, ˈliar, ˈthief, etc.*

self-confident /ˌself ˈkɒnfɪdənt/ *adj* having confidence in oneself, one's abilities, etc: *a self-confident person, manner, reply* ○ *learn to be more self-confident.* ▷ **self-confidence** /-dəns/ *n* [U].

self-conscious /ˌself ˈkɒnʃəs/ *adj* **1** seeming nervous or unnatural because one is worried about other people's opinions or reactions: *a ˌself-conscious ˈsmile* ○ *be self-conscious about one's appearance.* **2** aware of one's own existence, thoughts and actions. ▷ **self-consciously** *adv.* **self-consciousness** *n* [U].

self-contained /ˌself kənˈteɪnd/ *adj* **1** [usu attrib] (*esp Brit*) (of accommodation) having no shared facilities, and usu having its own private entrance: *a ˌself-contained ˈflat, maisonette, etc.* **2** (of a person) not needing the company of others; reserved.

self-control /ˌself kənˈtrəʊl/ *n* [U] ability to control one's behaviour or not to show one's feelings: *show/exercise great self-control in moments of stress* ○ *lose one's self-control.*
▷ **self-controlled** *adj* showing self-control.

self-deception /ˌself dɪˈsepʃn/ *n* [U] refusal or failure to recognize or accept one's true feelings, motives, etc.

self-defeating /ˌself dɪˈfi:tɪŋ/ *adj* (of a course of action, etc) likely to achieve the opposite of what it should achieve: *Punishing the demonstrators is self-defeating because it only encourages further demonstrations.*

self-defence /ˌself dɪˈfens/ *n* [U] defence of one's body, property, rights, etc: *kill sb in self-defence*, ie while defending oneself against attack ○ *the art of self-defence*, ie boxing, judo, etc.

self-denial /ˌself dɪˈnaɪəl/ *n* [U] choosing not to do or have the things one would like to, esp as a religious practice.

self-destruct /ˌself dɪˈstrʌkt/ *v* [I] (*esp US*) (of a spacecraft, bomb, etc) destroy itself automatically: *The missile is programmed to self-destruct if it malfunctions.* ▷ **self-destruct** *adj* [attrib]: *a ˌself-destruct ˈmechanism, deˈvice, etc.*

self-determination /ˌself dɪtɜ:mɪˈneɪʃn/ *n* [U] right of a nation, people, etc to decide what form of government it will have or whether it will be independent of another country or not.

self-discipline /ˌself ˈdɪsɪplɪn/ *n* [U] (power of) controlling one's own desires, feelings, etc, usu so as to improve oneself: *an athlete's self-discipline* ○ *Dieting demands self-discipline.*

self-drive /ˌself ˈdraɪv/ *adj* [attrib] (*Brit*) (of a hired vehicle) driven by the hirer: *a ˌself-drive ˈcar, ˈvan, etc* ○ *ˌself-drive ˈhire.*

self-educated /ˌself ˈedʒʊkeɪtɪd/ *adj* educated more by one's own efforts than by schools, teachers, etc.

self-effacing /ˌself ɪˈfeɪsɪŋ/ *adj* not trying to impress people; modest: *She's brilliant but self-effacing.* ▷ **self-effacement** /-ɪˈfeɪsmənt/ *n* [U]

self-employed /ˌself ɪmˈplɔɪd/ *adj* working independently for customers or clients and not for an employer. ▷ **self-employment** /-ɪmˈplɔɪmənt/ *n* [U]: *a person in self-employment.*

self-esteem /ˌself ɪˈsti:m/ *n* [U] good opinion of one's own character and abilities: *high/low self-esteem* ○ *injure sb's self-esteem.*

self-evident /ˌself ˈevɪdənt/ *adj* clear without any need for proof, explanation, or further evidence; obvious: *a ˌself-evident ˈtruth, ˈstatement, ˈfact* ○ *Her sincerity is self-evident.*

self-explanatory /ˌself ɪkˈsplænətrɪ; *US* -tɔ:rɪ/ *adj* without any need for (further) explanation; clear: *The diagram is self-explanatory.*

self-expression /ˌself ɪkˈspreʃn/ *n* [U] expressing of one's own personality, individuality, etc: *Modern educational theory emphasizes self-expression.*

self-fertilizing /ˌself ˈfɜ:tɪlaɪzɪŋ/ *adj* (of a plant) fertilizing itself with its own pollen, not with that of other plants. ▷ **self-fertilization** /ˌself ˌfɜ:təlaɪˈzeɪʃn; *US* ˌself ˌfɜ:təlɪz-/ *n* [U].

self-fulfilling /ˌself fʊlˈfɪlɪŋ/ *adj* (of a prophecy, prediction, etc) certain to come true because it has been made and therefore causes other things to happen.

self-fulfilment /ˌself fʊlˈfɪlmənt/ *n* [U] (happiness or satisfaction that comes from the) full development of one's abilities or character.

self-governing /ˌself ˈɡʌvənɪŋ/ *adj* (esp of a country that has formerly been controlled by another) governing itself; independent. ▷ **self-government** /ˌself ˈɡʌvənmənt/ *n* [U].

self-help /ˌself ˈhelp/ *n* [U] use of one's own efforts, resources, etc to achieve things, without the help of others: *Self-help is an important element in therapy for the handicapped.* ○ [attrib] *a self-help group.*

self-image /ˌself ˈɪmɪdʒ/ *n* person's idea of what he is like and how he appears to others.

self-important /ˌself ɪmˈpɔ:tənt/ *adj* (*derog*) thinking that one is much more important than one really is; pompous. ▷ **self-importance** /-təns/ *n* [U].

self-imposed /ˌself ɪmˈpəʊzd/ *adj* (of a duty, task, etc) imposed upon oneself: *a ˌself-imposed ˈdiet, ˈexile.*

self-improvement /ˌself ɪmˈpru:vmənt/ *n* [U] improvement of one's position, education, standard of living, etc by one's own efforts.

self-indulgent /ˌself ɪnˈdʌldʒənt/ *adj* (*derog*) allowing oneself to do or have what one enjoys, instead of controlling one's desires, etc: *The novel is too long and self-indulgent.* ▷ **self-indulgence** /-dʒəns/ *n* [U]: *a life of gross self-indulgence.*

self-interest /ˌself ˈɪntrɪst/ *n* [U] (concern for) one's own interests or personal advantage: *do sth purely from/out of self-interest.*

selfish /ˈselfɪʃ/ *adj* (*derog*) thinking first of one's own interests, needs, etc without concern for others; not sharing what one has with others; (of an action) done from selfish motives: *He's too selfish to think of lending me his car.* ○ *a selfish refusal.* ▷ **selfishly** *adv.* **selfishness** *n* [U].

self-justification /ˌself ˌdʒʌstɪfɪˈkeɪʃn/ *n* [U] action or process of trying to show, to oneself or to others, that what one did was right.

selfless /ˈselflɪs/ *adj* (*fml*) thinking more of others' needs and welfare than of one's own; unselfish: *selfless devotion to one's children.* ▷ **selflessly** *adv.* **selflessness** *n* [U].

self-loading /ˌself ˈləʊdɪŋ/ *adj* (of a gun) reloading itself automatically after firing.

self-locking /ˌself ˈlɒkɪŋ/ *adj* (eg of a door) locking automatically when closed.

self-made /ˌself ˈmeɪd/ *adj* [usu attrib] having become successful, rich, etc by one's own efforts: *a ˌself-made ˈman/ˈwoman.*

self-opinionated /ˌself əˈpɪnjəneɪtɪd/ *adj* (*derog*) always wanting to express one's own strong views without considering that they could be wrong.

self-pity /ˌself ˈpɪtɪ/ *n* [U] (*often derog*) pity for oneself: *a letter full of complaints and self-pity.*

self-portrait /ˌself ˈpɔ:treɪt, *also* -trɪt/ *n* portrait of oneself: *a self-portrait by Van Gogh* ○ (*fig*) *The book's hero is a self-portrait of the author.*

self-possessed /ˌself pəˈzest/ *adj* calm and confident, esp at times of stress or difficulty: *self-possessed in front of the TV cameras.* ▷ **self-possession** /-pəˈzeʃn/ *n* [U] calmness; composure: *keep/lose/regain one's self-possession.*

self-preservation /ˌself prezəˈveɪʃn/ *n* [U] protection of oneself from harm or destruction; natural urge to survive: *the instinct for self-preservation.*

self-propelled /ˌself prəˈpeld/ *adj* driven along by its own motor, ie not pulled or pushed by sb/sth else. ▷ **self-propulsion** /-ˈpʌlʃn/ *n* [U].

self-raising flour /ˌself reɪzɪŋ ˈflaʊə(r)/ (*US* **self-rising flour** /-ˈraɪzɪŋ/) flour containing a substance which makes dough rise during baking without needing baking-powder. Cf PLAIN FLOUR (PLAIN[1]).

self-reliant /ˌself rɪˈlaɪənt/ *adj* relying on one's own abilities and efforts; independent: *too self-reliant to want to borrow from anyone.* ▷ **self-reliance** /-ˈlaɪəns/ *n* [U].

self-respect /ˌself rɪˈspekt/ *n* [U] feeling that one is behaving and thinking in ways that will not make one ashamed of oneself: *lose all self-respect.* ▷ **self-respecting** *adj* [attrib] (usu in negative sentences) having self-respect: *No self-respecting doctor would refuse to treat a sick person.*

self-righteous /ˌself ˈraɪtʃəs/ *adj* (*derog*) showing in a smug way that one believes that what one does, thinks, etc is right: *a self-righteous person, attitude, remark* ○ *self-righteous anger, condemnation.* ▷ **self-righteously** *adv.* **self-righteousness** *n* [U].

self-rule /ˌself ˈru:l/ *n* [U] government of a people by its own representatives.

self-sacrifice /ˌself ˈsækrɪfaɪs/ *n* [U] giving up or willingness to give up things that one wants, in order to help others or for a good purpose: *Her self-sacrifice saved our lives.* ▷ **self-sacrificing** *adj* [usu attrib].

selfsame /ˈselfseɪm/ *adj* [attrib] (used after *the, this, that,* etc) very same; identical: *She said the selfsame thing to me.* ○ *They were both born on that selfsame day.*

self-satisfied /ˌself ˈsætɪsfaɪd/ *adj* (*derog*) too pleased with oneself and one's own achievements; smug: *a self-satisfied person, attitude, grin.*

self-sealing /ˌself ˈsi:lɪŋ/ *adj* [usu attrib] **1** (of an envelope) that can be sealed by pressure only, without wetting. **2** (of a tyre, fuel tank, etc) that seals itself after a puncture.

self-seeking /ˌself ˈsi:kɪŋ/ *adj, n* (*derog*) (having or showing) concern for one's own interests and advantage before those of others.

self-service /ˌself ˈsɜ:vɪs/ *n* [U] system of service in a restaurant, filling-station, etc in which customers take what they want and pay a cashier for it. ▷ **self-service** *adj*: *a ˌself-service canˈteen* ○ *Are these pumps self-service?*

self-starter /ˌself ˈstɑ:tə(r)/ *n* **1** person showing initiative and not needing others to make him work, etc: *The advertisement read 'Young self-starter wanted as salesperson'.* **2** (*dated*) (usu electrical) device for starting an engine.

self-styled /ˌself ˈstaɪld/ *adj* [attrib] (*sometimes derog*) using a name, title, etc which one has given oneself, esp without having any right to do so: *the self-styled leader of the sect, Mr Baker* ○ *The self-styled 'Reverend' Harper is not a real clergyman at all.*

self-sufficient /ˌself səˈfɪʃnt/ *adj* ~ **(in sth)** able to fulfil one's own needs, without help from others: *She's handicapped but very self-sufficient.* ○ *a country self-sufficient in coal,* ie producing all the coal it needs. ▷ **self-sufficiency** /-ʃənsɪ/ *n* [U].

self-supporting /ˌself səˈpɔ:tɪŋ/ *adj* (eg of a person or a business) earning enough to support oneself or itself, without help from others.

self-willed /ˌself ˈwɪld/ *adj* (*derog*) determined to do what one wants; stubborn: *a troublesome ˌself-willed ˈchild.*

self-winding /ˌself ˈwaɪndɪŋ/ *adj* (of a watch) winding itself automatically from the movements of the wearer's wrist.

Selkirk /ˈselkɜ:k/ Alexander (1676-1721), Scottish sailor who was left on an uninhabited island in the southern Pacific Ocean and lived there alone for five years. Daniel *Defoe based the hero of **Robinson Crusoe* on him.

sell /sel/ *v* (*pt, pp* **sold** /səʊld/) **1** [I, Ipr, Tn, Tn·pr, Dn·n, Dn·pr] ~ **(sth) (to sb) (at/for sth)** give (goods, etc) to sb who becomes their owner after paying one money: *Can she be persuaded to sell (the house)?* ○ *I won't sell to a stranger.* ○ *sell (sth) at a high price, a loss, a discount* ○ *sell (one's bike) for £80* ○ *sell sth by auction* ○ *sell sb into slavery,* ie as a slave ○ *I sold my car (to a friend) for £750.* ○ *Will you sell me your camera?* **2** [Tn] **(a)** have a stock of (sth) for sale; be a dealer in (sth): *a shop that sells fruit, clothes, electrical goods* ○ *Do you sell stamps?* **(b)** (of a salesperson) persuade people to buy (sth): *I sell insurance.* **3** [Tn] make people want to buy (sth); cause (sth) to be sold: *It is not price but quality that sells our shoes.* ○ *Her name will help to sell the film.* ⇨ Usage. **4** [I, Ipr, In/pr] ~ **(at/for sth)** be sold; find buyers: *Will such a long novel sell?* ○ *The car is selling well.* ○ *Umbrellas sell best in winter.* ○ *The badges sell at 50p each.* ○ *The group's record has sold millions.* **5** (*infml*) **(a)** [Tn, Dn·n, Dn·pr] ~ **sth/sb (to sb)** make sb believe that sth/sb is good, useful, worth having, etc: *You'll never sell changes like that to the work-force.* ○ *a big poster campaign selling the new party* ○ *You have to sell yourself* (ie show that you are the most suitable applicant) *at a job interview.* **(b)** [Dn·n, Dn·pr] ~ **sth to sb** make sb believe that sth is true: *sell sb an excuse, story, etc* ○ *He tried to sell me a line about losing his wallet.* **6** [Tn, Dn·pr] ~ **oneself (to sb)** accept a bribe, reward, etc (from sb) for doing sth bad: *Are artists who work in advertising selling themselves?* ○ *The police had sold themselves to the gang leaders.* **7** [Tn esp passive] (*dated infml*) cheat (sb): *You've been sold again. That car you bought is a wreck.* **8** (idm) **be sold on sth/sb** (*infml*) be enthusiastic about sth/sb: *I like the house but I'm not sold on the area.* **be sold ˈout (of sth)** have sold all the stock, tickets, etc: *The match was completely sold out.* ○ *We're sold out of Sunday papers, sir.* **sell one's ˈbody** (*rhet*) work as a prostitute. **sell sb down the ˈriver** (*infml*) betray sb, usu for one's own advantage. **sell one's life ˈdearly** (*fml*) kill or wound a number of one's enemies before being killed. **sell like hot cakes** ⇨ HOT. **sell the pass** betray one's cause or one's allies. **sell sb a ˈpup** (*infml*) sell sb sth that is worthless, or worth less than the price paid: *You've been sold a pup — that house is nearly falling down!* **sell sth/sb ˈshort (a)** (*commerce*) sell (shares, etc) that one does not yet own in the hope of being able to buy them soon at a lower price. **(b)** not recognize the true value of sth/sb/oneself: *Don't sell her short: she's very gifted in some areas.* **(c)** cheat sb in value or quantity. **sell one's ˈsoul (to the devil)** do sth dishonourable or unworthy in return for money, fame, etc: *She'd sell her soul to get the job.* **9** (phr v) **sell sth off** sell (esp items which are unwanted or have not sold well) often at very low prices: *sell off old stock.* **sell out** be all sold: *The show has sold out,* ie There are no tickets left. **sell out (of sth)** sell one's whole supply of sth: *We've sold out (of milk) but we'll be getting some more in later.* **sell out (to sb)** betray one's principles: *She's sold out and left the party.* **sell (sth) out (to sb)** sell all or part of (one's share in a business): *She had decided to sell out (her share of the company) and retire.* **sell sb out** betray sb: *They've sold us out by agreeing to work during the strike.* **sell (sth) up** sell (all one's property, one's home, etc) eg when leaving the country or retiring.

▷ **sell** *n* [sing] **1** (*infml*) deception; disappointment: *It's a real sell: the food seems cheap but you pay extra for vegetables.* **2** (idm) **the hard/soft ˈsell** aggressive/persuasive way of selling sth: *They're certainly giving the book the hard sell, with advertisements every night on TV.*

□ **ˈsell-by date** date (esp one marked on food products) by which sth must be sold in shops.

ˈselling-point *n* feature of sth that makes it attractive to buyers: *Double glazing is often a good selling-point for houses.*

ˈselling price price to be paid by the customer. Cf COST PRICE (COST[2]).

ˈsell-out *n* **1** event (eg a concert) for which all the tickets have been sold. **2** (*infml*) betrayal: *The agreement is a compromise, not a sell-out.*

NOTE ON USAGE: Compare **sell, vend, peddle, push** and **flog. 1 Sell** is the most general verb, meaning 'give in exchange for money': *They are selling their house and moving to the country.* ○ *Do you sell magazines here?* **2 Vend** is formal and indicates the selling of small articles. The noun **vendor** is much more common than the verb: *a street vendor, a news-vendor.* It is also a legal term used especially in the selling of a house: *The vendor signs a contract with the purchaser.* **Vending-machine** is also common and is a coin-operated slot machine for the sale of small items. **3 Peddle** indicates the selling of small, inexpensive goods by going from house to house: *He peddled small household articles around the town.* **4 Push** is informal and is used for the selling of illegal drugs: *He was caught pushing heroin to schoolchildren.* **5 Flog** is slang. It often suggests that what is to be sold is of little value, possibly stolen and therefore difficult to sell: *He tried to flog me a broken TV set.*

seller /ˈselə(r)/ *n* **1** (often in compounds) person who sells: *a ˈbookseller ○ the buyer and the seller.* **2** (esp following an *adj*) item that is sold (esp in the manner specified): *This model is a poor seller,* ie Not many have been sold. ○ *This dictionary is a best seller.*

□ ˌ**seller's ˈmarket** situation in which goods are in demand, so that sellers have an advantage: *It's a seller's market for vintage cars,* ie Many people will pay high prices for them.

Sellers /ˈseləz/ Peter (1925-80), British film actor and comedian. His gift for vocal mimicry and absurd comedy became famous through the radio programme, *The Goon Show.* He gained international fame through his portrayal of the incompetent Inspector Clouseau in the *Pink Panther* series of films.

Sellotape /ˈseləʊteɪp/ *n* [U] (*Brit propr*) (also **sticky tape**) (usu transparent) cellulose or plastic sticky tape: *mend a torn map with Sellotape.*

▷ **sellotape** *v* [Tn, Tn·pr, Tn·p] stick Sellotape on (sth); mend or fix (sth) with Sellotape: *sellotape the parcel (up) ○ sellotape torn pieces of paper (together) ○ sellotape a notice to the wall.*

selvage (also **selvedge**) /ˈselvɪdʒ/ *n* edge of cloth woven so that it will not unravel or fray.

selves *pl* of SELF.

semantic /sɪˈmæntɪk/ *adj* [usu attrib] of the meaning of words; of semantics: *the semantic content of a sentence.*

▷ **semantics** *n* [sing *v*] branch of linguistics dealing with the meanings of words and sentences.

semaphore /ˈseməfɔː(r)/ *n* **1** [U] system of sending signals by holding the arms or two flags in certain positions to indicate letters of the alphabet: *send a message by semaphore.* **2** [C] device with red and green lights on mechanically moved arms, used for signalling on railways.

▷ **semaphore** *v* [I, Tn, Tf, Dpr·f, Dpr·w, Dpr·t no passive] send (messages) by semaphore: *semaphore (to sb) that help is needed/to send help.*

semblance /ˈsembləns/ *n* [sing, U] ~ **of sth** appearance of being sth; likeness to sth: *put on a semblance of cheerfulness ○ bring the meeting to some semblance of order.*

semen /ˈsiːmen/ *n* [U] whitish fluid containing sperm produced by male animals.

▷ **seminal** /ˈsemɪnl/ *adj* **1** [usu attrib] of seed or semen: *the seminal fluid ○ a seminal duct.* **2** (*fig often approv*) strongly influencing later developments: *a seminal idea, essay, speech ○ Her theories were seminal for educational reform.*

semester /sɪˈmestə(r)/ *n* (esp in US universities and colleges) either of the two divisions of the academic year: *the summer/winter semester.* Cf TERM 3.

semi /ˈsemɪ/ *n* (*pl* **semis** /ˈsemɪz/) (*Brit infml*) semi-detached house. ⇨ article at HOUSE.

semi- *pref* (used fairly widely with *adjs* and *ns*) half; partially: *semicircular ○ semi-detached ○ semifinal.*

semibreve /ˈsemɪbriːv/ *n* (*US* ˈ**whole note**) the longest written musical note in common use, equal to two minims in length. ⇨ illus at HOME.

semicircle /ˈsemɪsɜːkl/ *n* half of a circle or of its circumference; thing arranged like this: *a semicircle of chairs ○ sitting in a semicircle round the fire.* ⇨ illus at CIRCLE.

▷ **semicircular** /ˌsemɪˈsɜːkjʊlə(r)/ *adj* having the shape of a semicircle.

semicolon /ˌsemɪˈkəʊlən; *US* ˈsemɪk-/ *n* the punctuation mark (;) used in writing and printing, between a comma and a full stop in value. ⇨ App 14. Cf COLON[2].

semiconductor /ˌsemɪkənˈdʌktə(r)/ *n* substance that conducts electricity in certain conditions, but not as well as metals.

semi-conscious /ˌsemɪˈkɒnʃəs/ *adj* partly conscious: *a semi-conscious patient recovering from an anaesthetic.*

semi-detached /ˌsemɪ dɪˈtætʃt/ *adj* (of a house) joined to another house by one shared wall. ⇨ illus at HOME.

semifinal /ˌsemɪˈfaɪnl/ *n* match or round preceding the final, eg in football.

▷ **semifinalist** /-ˈfaɪnəlɪst/ *n* person or team taking part in a semifinal.

seminal ⇨ SEMEN.

seminar /ˈsemɪnɑː(r)/ *n* small group of students at a university, etc meeting to discuss or study a particular topic with a teacher.

seminary /ˈsemɪnərɪ; *US* -nerɪ/ *n* **1** college for training priests or rabbis. **2** (*dated fml*) school for older children or young people: *a seminary for young ladies.*

▷ **seminarist** /ˈsemɪnərɪst/ *n* person studying at a seminary.

semiotics /ˌsemɪˈɒtɪks/ *n* [sing *v*] study of signs and symbols, esp in writing, and of what they mean and how they are used.

semi-permeable /ˌsemɪˈpɜːmɪəbl/ *adj* (of a membrane) allowing small molecules to pass through but not large ones.

semiprecious /ˌsemɪˈpreʃəs/ *adj* [usu attrib] (of a gem) less valuable than a precious stone.

semiquaver /ˈsemɪkweɪvə(r)/ *n* (*US* **sixˈteenth note**) musical note equal to half a quaver. ⇨ illus at MUSIC.

semi-skilled /ˌsemɪ ˈskɪld/ *adj* [usu attrib] (of a worker) having some special training or qualifications, but less than a skilled worker; (of work) for such a worker: *a ˌsemi-skilled maˈchine operator, ˈjob.*

Semite /ˈsiːmaɪt/ *n* member of the group of races including the Jews and Arabs, and formerly the Phoenicians and Assyrians. ▷ **Semitic** /sɪˈmɪtɪk/ *adj*: *Semitic languages, tribes.*

semitone /ˈsemɪtəʊn/ *n* (*US* also ˈ**half step**) half of a tone on the musical scale.

semitropical /ˌsemɪˈtrɒpɪkl/ *adj* [attrib] (of regions) near but not in the tropics: *ˌsemitropical ˈweather, vegeˈtation, ˈcountries.*

semivowel /ˈsemɪvaʊəl/ *n* (letter representing a) sound like a vowel that functions as a consonant, eg /w/, /j/.

semolina /ˌseməˈliːnə/ *n* [U] hard grains of wheat left after it has been ground and sifted, used for making pasta, milk puddings, etc: [attrib] *semolina pudding.*

sempstress /ˈsemstrɪs/ *n* (*Brit*) = SEAMSTRESS.

SEN /ˌes iː ˈen/ *abbr* (*Brit*) State Enrolled Nurse (with 2 years' training): *be an SEN ○ Judy Green SEN.* Cf SRN.

Sen *abbr* **1** Senate. **2** Senator: *Sen John K Nordqvist.* **3** (also **Snr**, **Sr**) Senior: *John F Davis Sen,* ie to distinguish him from his son with the same name. Cf JNR.

senate /ˈsenɪt/ *n* (often **Senate**) **1** [CGp] upper house of the law-making assembly in some countries, eg France, the USA and Australia: [attrib] *a Senate committee, decision.* Cf CONGRESS 2, THE HOUSE OF REPRESENTATIVES (HOUSE[1]). **2** [CGp] governing council of certain universities. **3** [Gp] (in ancient Rome) highest council of state.

▷ **senator** /ˈsenətə(r)/ *n* (often **Senator**, *abbr* **Sen**) member of the senate. **senatorial** /ˌsenəˈtɔːrɪəl/ *adj* [attrib]: *senatorial rank, powers, office.*

send /send/ *v* (*pt, pp* **sent** /sent/) **1** [Tn, Tn·pr, Tn·p, Dn·n, Dn·pr] ~ **sth/sb (to sb/sth)** cause sth/sb to go or be taken without going oneself: *send a letter, telegram, message, etc ○ send goods, documents, information ○ I've sent the children to bed. ○ Send out the invitations to the party. ○ His mother sent him to the shop to get some bread. ○ We sent him a letter/We sent a letter to him.* **2** [Tn, Tn·p] ~ **sth (out)** transmit (a signal, etc) by radio waves: *The radio operator sent (out) an appeal for help to headquarters.* **3** [Tn·pr, Tn·p, Cn·g] cause (sth) to move sharply or quickly, often by force: *Whenever he moved, the wound sent pains all along his arm. ○ Space rockets are being sent up all the time. ○ She bumped against the table and sent the crockery crashing to the ground,* ie knocked it to the ground. ○ *The explosion sent us running in all directions.* ○ (*fig*) *The difficult word sent me to my dictionary,* ie to find its meaning. ○ *The bad weather has sent vegetable prices up. ○ The storm sent the temperature down.* **4** (**a**) [Cn·a] cause (sb) to become: *send sb mad/crazy/insane/berserk.* (**b**) [Tn·pr] ~ **sb to/into sth** make sb enter a specified state: *send sb to sleep ○ send sb into a rage, a frenzy, fits of laughter ○ The news sent the Stock Exchange into a panic.* **5** [It] (*fml*) send a message: *She sent to say that she was safe and well.* **6** [Tn] (*dated infml*) excite (sb); thrill: *That music really sends me.* **7** (idm) **give/send sb one's love** ⇨ LOVE[1]. **send sb about his business** = SEND SB PACKING. **send sb, sth flying** hit or knock sb/sth so that he/it falls over or backwards: *The blow sent him flying.* **send things flying** cause things to be thrown violently in all directions. **send sb ˈpacking** (*infml*) tell sb (roughly or rudely) to go away: *She tried to interfere, but I sent her packing!* **send sb to ˈCoventry** refuse to speak to sb, esp as a punishment by other members of a group: *Men who refused to strike were sent to Coventry by their colleagues.* **8** (phr v) **send away (to sb) (for sth)** = SEND OFF (FOR STH). **send sb down** (*Brit*) (**a**) expel (a student) from a university. (**b**) (*infml*) sentence sb to imprisonment: *He was sent down for ten years for armed robbery.* **send for sth; send for sb (to do sth)** ask or order that sth be brought or delivered, or that sb should come: *send for a fresh supply of paper ○ send for a taxi, an ambulance, a doctor ○ send for sb to repair the TV.* **send sb in** order sb to go to a place in order to deal with a situation: *Soldiers were sent in to quell the riots.* **send sth in** send sth by post to a place where it will be dealt with: *Have you sent in your application for the job?* **send off (for sth)** write to sb to ask for sth to be sent to one by post: *I've sent off for those bulbs I saw advertised in the paper.* **send sb off** (*Brit*) (of a referee, etc) send a footballer, etc off the playing field for breaking the rules of play. **send sth off** send sth by post; dispatch sth: *Have you sent that letter off yet? There's something I want to add to it.* **send sth out** (**a**) give sth out from itself; emit sth: *The sun sends out light and warmth.* (**b**) produce sth: *The trees send out new leaves in spring.* **send sb to...** cause sb to attend a particular place or institution: *They send their daughter to one of the best schools in the country. ○ He was sent to hospital/to prison.* **send sb up** (*US infml*) send sb to prison. **send sb/sth up** (*Brit infml*) make fun of sb/sth, esp by copying in a comical way: *comedians who send up members of the government ○ Bill is constantly being sent up by his children.*

□ ˈ**send-off** *n* act of saying goodbye to sb: *She was given a good send-off at the airport.*

ˈ**send-up** *n* imitation intended to make fun of sth or sb: *Her book is a hilarious send-up of a conventional spy story.*

sender /ˈsendə(r)/ *n* person who sends: *If undelivered, return to sender,* eg on a letter.

Senegal /ˌsenɪˈgɔːl/ country on the west coast of Africa, between *Mauritania and *Guinea-Bissau; pop approx 7 113 000; official language French; capital Dakar; unit of currency franc. Formerly a French colony, it became an independent republic in 1961. Its main export is ground-nuts. ⇨ map at NIGERIA. ▷ **Senegalese** /ˌsenɪgəˈliːz/ *adj.*

senescent /sɪˈnesnt/ *adj* (*fml or medical*) becoming old.

▷ **senescence** /sɪˈnesns/ *n* [U] (*fml or medical*) process of becoming old.

senile /ˈsiːnaɪl/ *adj* suffering from bodily or mental weakness because of old age: *He keeps forgetting things: I think he's getting senile.*

▷ **senility** /sɪˈnɪlətɪ/ *n* [U] state of being senile.

□ **senile dementia** /ˌsiːnaɪl dɪˈmenʃə/ illness of old people resulting in loss of memory, loss of control of bodily functions, etc.

senior /ˈsiːnɪə(r)/ *adj* **1** ~ **(to sb)** (**a**) older: *He is ten years senior to me.* (**b**) higher in rank, authority, etc: *There are separate rooms for senior and junior officers. ○ He is the senior partner in* (ie the head of) *the firm.* (**c**) having been in a job, etc longer: *She is senior to me, since she joined the firm before me.* **2** (*often* **Senior**, *abbr* **Sen**) (placed immediately after sb's name) being the parent of sb with the same name: *John Brown Senior.* **3** [attrib] (of a school) for children over the age of 11. Cf JUNIOR.

▷ **senior** *n* **1** senior person: *She is my senior by*

two years/two years my senior, ie is two years older than me. **2** member of a senior school: *a football match between the juniors and the seniors.* **3** (*US*) student in the year before graduation from a high school or college: [attrib] *her senior year at college.*
seniority /ˌsiːnɪˈɒrətɪ; *US* -ˈɔːr-/ *n* [U] **1** being senior in age, rank, etc: *Should promotion be through merit or seniority?* **2** extent to which sb is senior: *a doctor with five years' seniority over his colleague.*
□ ˌ**senior ˈcitizen** (*euph*) old or retired person. ⇨ article at RETIREMENT.
the ˌsenior ˈservice (*Brit*) the Royal Navy.

senna /ˈsenə/ *n* [U] dried leaves of a tropical plant, used as a laxative.

señor /seˈnjɔː(r)/ *n* (*pl* **señores** /seˈnjɔːreɪz/) (before a name, **Señor**) (title of a) Spanish-speaking man; Mr or sir.
▷ **señora** /seˈnjɔːrə/ *n* (before a name, **Señora**) (title of a) Spanish-speaking woman; Mrs or madam.
señorita /ˌsenjɔːˈriːtə/ *n* (before a name, **Señorita**) (title of an) unmarried Spanish-speaking woman or girl; Miss.

sensation /senˈseɪʃn/ *n* **1** (**a**) [C] feeling in one's body resulting from sth that happens or is done to it: *a sensation of warmth, dizziness, falling* ○ *Massage produces wonderful sensations.* (**b**) [C] general awareness or impression not caused by anything that can be seen or defined: *I had the sensation that I was being watched.* (**c**) [U] ability to feel through the sense of touch: *lose all sensation in one's legs* ○ *Some sensation is coming back to my arm.* **2** [C, U] state of great surprise, excitement, interest, etc among many people: *The news caused a great sensation.* ○ (*derog*) *Sensation-seeking newspapers tried to cash in on her misery.*
▷ **sensational** /-ʃənl/ *adj* **1** (**a**) causing a sensation(2): *a sensational crime, victory, etc.* (**b**) (*derog*) trying to cause a sensation(2): *a sensational newspaper, writer.* **2** (*infml*) extraordinarily good; wonderful: *You look sensational in that dress.* ○ *That music is sensational!* **sensationalism** /-ʃənəlɪzəm/ *n* [U] (*derog*) deliberate use of shocking words, scandalous stories, etc in order to produce a sensation(2): *Avoid sensationalism in reporting crime.* ○ *the sensationalism of the popular press.* **sensationalist** /-ʃənəlɪst/ *n.* **sensationalize, -ise** /-ʃənəlaɪz/ *v* [Tn] (*derog*) treat (sth) in a way that is likely to cause public excitement: *a sensationalized account of a squalid crime.* **sensationally** /-ʃənəlɪ/ *adv*: *Newspapers reported the incident sensationally, making it appear worse than it really was.* ○ *sensationally beautiful.*

sense /sens/ *n* **1** [C] any of the five powers of the body by which a person, an animal, etc receives knowledge of things in the world around, ie sight, hearing, smell, taste and touch: *the five senses* ○ *have a keen sense of hearing.* **2** [U, sing] (**a**) appreciation or understanding of the value or worth of sth: *a sense of the* (ie the ability to know what is) *absurd, ridiculous, etc* ○ *not have much sense of humour*, ie a liking for jokes, funny situations, etc ○ *a person with no sense of direction*, ie who cannot find his way easily. (**b**) consciousness of sth; awareness: *a sense of one's own importance, worth, etc* ○ *have no sense of shame, guilt, etc* ○ *feel a sense of security in her arms.* **3** [U] ability to make reasonable judgements; practical wisdom: *have the sense to come in out of the rain* ○ *There's a lot of sense in what she says.* **4 senses** [pl] normal state of mind; ability to think: *lose/regain one's senses.* **5** [U] reason; purpose: *What's the sense of doing that?* ○ *There's no sense in going alone*, ie It would be better not to. **6** [C] (**a**) meaning of a word, phrase, etc: *a word with several senses* ○ *The sense of the word is not clear.* (**b**) way in which a word, sentence, etc is to be understood: *in the strict/literal/figurative sense of the expression* ○ *I am a worker only in the sense that I work; I don't get paid for what I do.* **7** [sing] **the ~ of sth** (*fml*) general feeling or opinion among a group of people: *The sense of the meeting was* (ie Most people present thought) *that he should resign.* **8** (idm) **beat, knock, drive, etc (some) sense into sb** (*infml*) change sb's behaviour, views, etc by severe or sometimes violent methods: *She's a wild uncontrollable girl, but that new school should knock some sense into her.* **bring sb to his/come to one's ˈsenses** (**a**) (make sb) stop behaving foolishly or irrationally: *He was finally brought to his senses and agreed to let the hostages go.* (**b**) wake (sb) up from unconsciousness: *When I came to my senses, I was lying on the floor.* **in a ˈsense** if the statement, etc is understood in a particular way: *What you say is true in a sense.* **in one's ˈsenses** in one's normal state of mind; sensible: *No one in their right senses would let a small child go out alone.* **make ˈsense** (**a**) have an understandable meaning: *What you say makes no sense.* ○ *These words are jumbled up and don't make sense.* (**b**) be sensible: *It doesn't make sense to buy that expensive coat when these cheaper ones are just as good.* ○ *It would make sense to leave early.* **make sense of sth** understand sth difficult or apparently meaningless: *Can you make sense of this poem?* **out of one's ˈsenses** not in one's normal state of mind; foolish: *You sold it? You must be out of your senses!* **see ˈsense** start to be sensible: *I hope she soon sees sense and stops fighting a battle she cannot win.* **a sense of occasion** special feeling produced in sb by a special event, etc. **a sixth sense** awareness of things one cannot actually see, hear, etc: *A sixth sense told her that he would be waiting for her when she got home.* **take leave of one's senses** ⇨ LEAVE[2]. **talk sense** ⇨ TALK[2].
▷ **sense** *v* **1** [Tn, Tf, Tw] become aware of (sth); feel: *sense sb's sorrow, hostility, etc* ○ *Although she didn't say anything, I sensed (that) she didn't like the idea.* **2** [Tn] (of a machine, etc) detect (sth): *an apparatus that senses the presence of toxic gases.*
□ ˈ**sense-organ** bodily organ, eg the ear or the eye, by which the body becomes aware of what is happening around it.

senseless /ˈsenslɪs/ *adj* **1** pointless; foolish: *a senseless idea, action* ○ *I condemn this senseless violence.* ○ *It would be senseless to continue any further.* **2** [usu pred] unconscious: *fall senseless to the ground.* ▷ **senselessly** *adv.* **senselessness** *n* [U].

sensibility /ˌsensəˈbɪlətɪ/ *n* **1** [C usu *pl*] ability to receive and appreciate delicate impressions; sensitivity: *the sensibility of a poet* ○ *a man of subtle and refined sensibilities.* **2 sensibilities** [pl] capacity for being easily offended or shocked: *wound/offend/outrage readers' sensibilities.*

sensible /ˈsensəbl/ *adj* **1** (**a**) (*approv*) having or showing good sense(3); reasonable: *a sensible person, idea, course of action, suggestion* ○ *It was sensible of you to lock the door.* (**b**) [attrib] (of clothing, etc) practical rather than fashionable: *wear sensible shoes for long walks.* **2** [pred] **~ of sth** (*fml*) aware of sth: *Are you sensible of the dangers of your position?* **3** [attrib] (*dated*) that can be perceived by the senses (SENSE 1); perceptible: *a sensible rise in temperature.*
▷ **sensibly** /-əblɪ/ *adv* in a sensible(1) way: *sensibly dressed for hot weather.*

NOTE ON USAGE: The noun **sense** can mean **1** 'the way the body experiences its surroundings': *the sense of touch, sight, etc*, or **2** 'reason, good judgement': *She talks a lot of good sense.* The adjective **sensitive** usually relates to meaning 1: *She's got very sensitive hearing, skin, etc.* ○ *Don't laugh at him; he's very sensitive.* **Sensible** relates to meaning 2: *She gave me some sensible advice.* ○ *You must try to be more sensible.*

sensitive /ˈsensətɪv/ *adj* **1** (**a**) easily hurt or damaged: *the sensitive skin of a baby* ○ *A sensitive nerve in a tooth can cause great pain.* (**b**) **~ (to sth)** affected greatly or easily by sth: *Photographic paper is highly sensitive to light.* ○ *This material is heat-sensitive*, ie responds quickly to changes in temperature. **2 ~ (about/to sth)** easily offended or emotionally upset: *a frail and sensitive child* ○ *He's very sensitive about being small, so don't mention it.* ○ *A writer mustn't be too sensitive to criticism.* **3** (*approv*) having or showing perceptive feeling or sympathetic understanding: *an actor's sensitive reading of a poem* ○ *When I need advice, he is a helpful and sensitive friend.* **4 ~ (to sth)** (of instruments, etc) able to measure very small changes: *a sensitive thermometer, balance, ammeter, etc* ○ (*fig*) *The Stock Exchange is sensitive to likely political changes.* **5** needing to be treated with great secrecy or tact: *sensitive military information* ○ *a sensitive issue like race relations.* ⇨ Usage at SENSIBLE.
▷ **sensitively** *adv.*
sensitivity /ˌsensəˈtɪvətɪ/ *n* [U] **~ (to sth)** quality or degree of being sensitive: *sensitivity to pain, light, heat* ○ *the sensitivity of a writer.*
sensitize, -ise /ˈsensɪtaɪz/ *v* [esp passive: Tn, Tn·pr] **~ sth/sb (to sth) 1** make sth or sb sensitive: *sensitize students to a poet's use of language.* **2** (in photography) make (film, paper, etc) sensitive to light.
□ ˈ**sensitive plant 1** plant whose leaves curl up when touched, esp mimosa. **2** (*fig esp joc*) sensitive(2) person.

sensor /ˈsensə(r)/ *n* device (eg a photoelectric cell) that detects light, heat, humidity, etc: *Smoke sensors warned us of the fire.*

sensory /ˈsensərɪ/ *adj* [usu attrib] of the senses (SENSE 1) or of sensation: *sensory organs/nerves* ○ *a sensory stimulus* ○ *sensory deprivation.*

sensual /ˈsenʃʊəl/ *adj* (*sometimes derog*) of, suggesting, enjoying or giving physical (often sexual) pleasure: *the sensual feel of a warm bath* ○ *a life devoted entirely to sensual pleasure* ○ *the sensual curves of her body.*
▷ **sensualist** *n* person who enjoys physical pleasures, esp to excess.
sensuality /ˌsenʃʊˈælətɪ/ *n* [U] (excessive) love or enjoyment of physical pleasure.
sensually /-ʃʊəlɪ/ *adv.*

sensuous /ˈsenʃʊəs/ *adj* affecting, noticed by or giving pleasure to the senses: *the sensuous appeal of her painting* ○ *his full sensuous lips.* ▷ **sensuously** *adv*: *She swayed her hips sensuously as she danced.* **sensuousness** *n* [U].

sent *pt, pp* of SEND.

sentence /ˈsentəns/ *n* **1** [C] (*grammar*) largest unit of grammar, usu containing a subject, a verb, an object, etc and expressing a statement, question or command. **2** [C, U] (*law*) (statement of the) punishment given by a lawcourt: *The judge passed/pronounced sentence (on the prisoner)*, ie said what his punishment would be. ○ *She has served her sentence, and will now be released.* ○ *under sentence of death*, ie to be officially killed as a punishment ○ *a sentence of ten years' imprisonment.*
▷ **sentence** *v* [Tn, Tn·pr, Dn·t] **~ sb (to sth)** state that sb is to have a certain punishment: *sentence a thief to six months' imprisonment* ○ *He has been sentenced to pay a fine of £1 000.* ○ (*fig*) *a crippling disease which sentenced him to a lifetime in a wheelchair.*

sententious /senˈtenʃəs/ *adj* (*fml derog*) expressing pompous moral judgements: *a sententious speaker, speech, remark, book.* ▷ **sententiously** *adv*: *'He should have thought of the consequences before he acted,' she concluded sententiously.* **sententiousness** *n* [U].

sentient /ˈsenʃnt/ *adj* [attrib] (*fml*) capable of perceiving or feeling things: *a sentient being.*

sentiment /ˈsentɪmənt/ *n* **1** [U] (*usu derog*) tender feelings of pity, nostalgia, etc, which may be exaggerated or wrongly directed (contrasted esp with reason): *act from rational motives rather than sentiment* ○ *a love story full of cloying sentiment* ○ *There's no room for sentiment in business.* **2** [U, C usu *pl*] (expression of an) attitude or opinion, usu influenced by emotion: *a speech full of lofty sentiments* ○ *Sentiment in the City* (ie the financial centre of London) *is now in favour of a cut in taxes.* **3 sentiments** [pl] (*fml or rhet*) point of view; opinion: *What are your sentiments on this issue?* ○ *My sentiments exactly!* ie I agree!

sentimental /ˌsentɪˈmentl/ *adj* **1** of or concerning the emotions, rather than the reason: *do sth for*

sentimental reasons ○ *have a sentimental attachment to one's birth-place* ○ *a watch with sentimental value*, ie which is precious eg because it was given by sb one loves. **2** (*usu derog*) (**a**) (of things) expressing or arousing tender emotions, such as pity, romantic love or nostalgia, which may be exaggerated or wrongly directed: *sentimental music* ○ *a sloppy, sentimental love story*. (**b**) ~ (**about sb/sth**) (of people) having such emotions: *She's too sentimental about her cat.*
▷ **sentimentalist** /-təlɪst/ *n* (*derog*) person who is sentimental(2b).
sentimentality /ˌsentɪmenˈtælətɪ/ *n* [U] (*derog*) quality of being too sentimental(2a): *the sickly sentimentality of a romantic novel.*
sentimentalize, **-ise** /-təlaɪz/ *v* [I, Tn] (*derog*) speak or write sentimentally; treat (sb/sth) sentimentally: *Don't sentimentalize when you talk about animals.* ○ *This book sentimentalizes the suffering of the disabled.*
sentimentally /-təlɪ/ *adv.*

sentinel /ˈsentɪnl/ *n* (*fml or dated*) sentry: (*fig*) *The Press is a sentinel of* (ie guards or protects) *our liberty.*

sentry /ˈsentrɪ/ *n* soldier posted outside a building, etc in order to watch or guard it: *People approaching the gate were challenged by the sentry.* ○ [attrib] *sentry duty.*
□ ˈ**sentry-box** *n* small hut for a standing sentry.

sepal /ˈsepl/ *n* (*botany*) any of the leaf-like parts which lie under and support the petals of a flower. ⇨ illus at FRUIT.

separable /ˈsepərəbl/ *adj* ~ (**from sth**) that can be separated: *The lower part of the pipe is separable from the upper part.* ▷ **separably** /-əblɪ/ *adv.* **separability** /ˌseprəˈbɪlətɪ/ *n* [U].

separate[1] /ˈseprət/ *adj* **1** ~ (**from sth/sb**) forming a unit by itself; existing apart: *The children sleep in separate beds.* ○ *Violent prisoners are kept separate from the others.* ○ *They lead separate lives*, ie do not live or do things together. ○ *We can't work together any more; I think it's time we went our separate ways*, ie parted. **2** [usu attrib] different or distinct: *It happened on three separate occasions.* ○ *That is a separate issue and irrelevant to our discussion.*
▷ **separately** *adv* as separate people or things; not together: *They are now living separately.* ○ *Can the engine and the gearbox be supplied separately?*
separates *n* [pl] individual items of clothing designed to be worn together in different combinations.
separatism /ˈsepərətɪzəm/ *n* [U] policy of staying or becoming a separate group from other people, esp through political independence.
separatist /ˈsepərətɪst/ *n* [attrib]: *the Basque separatist organization ETA.*

separate[2] /ˈsepəreɪt/ *v* **1** [I, Ipr, Ip, Tn, Tn·pr, Tn·p] (**a**) ~ (**sb/sth**) (**from sb/sth**); ~ **sth** (**up**) (**into sth**) (cause things or people to) come apart; divide: *The two parts of the pipe have separated at the joint.* ○ *The branch has separated from the trunk of the tree.* ○ *This patient should be separated from the others.* ○ *The land has been separated (up) into small plots.* ○ *The children were separated into groups for the game.* (**b**) ~ (**sth**) (**out**) (**from sth**) (cause sth to) stop being combined in a liquid mixture: *Oil and water always separate out.* **2** [Tn, Tn·pr] ~ **sth** (**from sth**) lie or stand between (two countries, areas, etc), keeping them apart: *A deep gorge separates the two halves of the city.* ○ *England is separated from France by the Channel.* ○ (*fig*) *Politics is the only thing which separates us*, ie on which we disagree. **3** [I] (of people) leave each other's company: *We talked until midnight and then separated.* **4** [I] stop living together as a married couple: *After ten years of marriage they decided to separate.* **5** (idm) **separate the sheep from the goats** distinguish good people from bad people. **separate the** ˌ**wheat from the** ˈ**chaff** distinguish valuable people or things from worthless ones: *We have to sift through the application forms very carefully to separate the wheat from the chaff.*
▷ **separated** *adj* [pred] ~ (**from sb**) no longer living together as a married couple (but not necessarily divorced): *I'm separated from my wife.* ○ *We're separated.*
separator *n* device that separates things, esp cream from milk.

separation /ˌsepəˈreɪʃn/ *n* **1** ~ (**from sb/sth**) (**a**) [U] separating; state of being separate: *the separation of infectious patients from other patients* ○ *Separation from his friends made him sad.* (**b**) [C] instance or period of being separated: *after a separation of five years from his parents.* **2** [U, sing] legal arrangement by which a married couple live apart but do not end the marriage: *decide on (a) separation.*

Sephardi /səˈfɑːdɪ/ *n* (*pl* ~**m** /-dɪm/) Jew of Spanish or Portuguese descent. Cf ASHKENAZI. ▷ **Sephardic** /-dɪk/ *adj.*

sepia /ˈsiːpɪə/ *n* [U] **1** brown colouring-matter used in inks and water-colour paints and (esp formerly) for printing photographs. **2** rich reddish-brown colour.
▷ **sepia** *adj* [usu attrib] of sepia colour: *an old sepia photograph.*

sepoy /ˈsiːpɔɪ/ *n* (formerly) Indian soldier serving in the British forces in India during British rule.

sepsis /ˈsepsɪs/ *n* [U] (*medical*) infection of (part of) the body by bacteria. Cf SEPTIC.

Sept *abbr* September: *12 Sept 1969.*

September /sepˈtembə(r)/ *n* [U, C] (*abbr* **Sept**) the ninth month of the year, next after August.
For the uses of *September* see the examples at *April*.

septet /sepˈtet/ *n* (piece of music written for a) group of seven instruments or singers.

sept(i)- *comb form* having or made up of seven of sth: *septuagenarian.*

septic /ˈseptɪk/ *adj* caused by or causing infection with harmful bacteria: *a septic wound* ○ *A dirty cut may become septic*, ie affected by bacteria. Cf SEPSIS.
□ ˌ**septic** ˈ**tank** tank into which sewage flows and where it remains until the action of bacteria makes it liquid enough to drain away.

septicaemia (*US* **-cemia**) /ˌseptɪˈsiːmɪə/ *n* [U] (*medical*) blood-poisoning.

septuagenarian /ˌseptjʊədʒɪˈneərɪən; *US* ˌseptʃʊə-/ *n, adj* [attrib] (*fml*) (person) between the ages of 70 and 79.

Septuagesima /ˌseptjʊəˈdʒesɪmə; *US* ˌseptʃʊə-/ *n* (in the Christian Church) third Sunday before *Lent.

septum /ˈseptəm/ *n* (*pl* **-ta** /-tə/) (*anatomy or biology*) piece of tissue that separates two cavities in a plant or an animal (eg that between the nostrils).

septuple /ˈseptjʊpl/ *adj* [attrib] **1** consisting of seven parts, individuals or groups. **2** seven times as many or as much: *a septuple increase.*

sepulchre (*US* **sepulcher**) /ˈseplkə(r)/ *n* (*arch*) **1** tomb, esp one cut in rock or built of stone: *the Holy Sepulchre*, ie the one in which Jesus Christ was laid. **2** (idm) **a whited sepulchre** ⇨ WHITE[1] *v.*
▷ **sepulchral** /sɪˈpʌlkrəl/ *adj* (*fml*) **1** [usu attrib] of a tomb or of burial. **2** looking or sounding gloomy: *a sepulchral face* ○ *speak in sepulchral tones* ○ *look quite sepulchral.*

sequel /ˈsiːkwəl/ *n* ~ (**to sth**) **1** thing that happens after or as a result of an earlier event: *His speech had an unfortunate sequel, in that it caused a riot.* ○ *Famine is often the sequel to war.* **2** novel, film, etc that continues the story of an earlier one, often using the same characters: *He is writing a sequel to his latest best seller.*

sequence /ˈsiːkwəns/ *n* **1** [U, C] set of events, numbers, actions, etc with each following the one before continuously or in a particular order: *deal with events in historical sequence* ○ *describe the sequence of events*, ie in the order in which they occurred ○ *a sequence of dance movements* ○ *a sequence of playing-cards*, ie three or more next to each other in value, eg 10, 9, 8. **2** [C] part of a cinema film dealing with one scene or topic: *a thrilling sequence that includes a car chase.*
□ ˌ**sequence of** ˈ**tenses** (*grammar*) principles according to which the tenses of subordinate clauses are suited to the tenses of principal clauses.

sequential /sɪˈkwenʃl/ *adj* following in order of time or place; forming a sequence. ▷ **sequentially** /-ʃəlɪ/ *adj*: *files of correspondence arranged sequentially.*

sequester /sɪˈkwestə(r)/ *v* (*fml*) [Tn, Tn·pr] ~ **sb/ oneself** (**from sth**) **1** keep away or apart from other people; seclude: *sequester oneself from the world.* **2** [Tn] (*law*) = SEQUESTRATE.
▷ **sequestered** *adj* [usu attrib] (*fml*) quiet and secluded: *lead a sequestered life* ○ *a sequestered island far from the mainland.*

sequestrate /ˈsiːkwestreɪt/ *v* [Tn] **1** (*law*) take temporary possession of (a debtor's property, funds, etc) until a debt has been paid or other claims met. **2** confiscate. ▷ **sequestration** /ˌsiːkweˈstreɪʃn/ *n* [U].

sequin /ˈsiːkwɪn/ *n* small circular shiny disc sewn onto clothing as an ornament: *Her dress was covered in sequins which twinkled as she moved.*

sequoia /sɪˈkwɔɪə/ *n* either of two types of large evergreen coniferous trees of California, the *redwood* or the *giant sequoia*.

seraglio /seˈrɑːlɪəʊ/ *n* (*pl* ~**s**) part of a Muslim household reserved for women; harem.

seraph /ˈserəf/ *n* (*pl* ~**s** or ~**im** /-fɪm/) (in the Bible) member of the highest order of angels. Cf CHERUB.
▷ **seraphic** /seˈræfɪk/ *adj* (*fml*) **1** like an angel in beauty or purity: *a seraphic child, nature.* **2** feeling or showing great happiness: *a seraphic smile.*

Serbia /ˈsɜːbɪə/ largest of the republics of the former Yugoslavia, and historically an independent kingdom.
▷ **Serb** /sɜːb/ *n* Serbian person.
Serbian /-bɪən/ *n, adj* (person) of or from Serbia.

Serbo-Croat /ˌsɜːbəʊ ˈkrəʊæt/ (also **Serbo-Croatian** /krəʊˈeɪʃn/) *n* [U] *Slavonic language that was the main language of Yugoslavia.

sere = SEAR 1.

serenade /ˌserəˈneɪd/ *n* song or tune (suitable to be) sung or played at night, esp by a lover outside the window of the woman he loves.

serendipity /ˌserənˈdɪpətɪ/ *n* [U] (talent for) making pleasant and unexpected discoveries entirely by chance.

serene /sɪˈriːn/ *adj* calm and peaceful; tranquil: *a serene sky* ○ *a serene look, smile, etc* ○ *In spite of the panic, she remained serene and in control.* ▷ **serenely** *adv*: *He seemed serenely unaware that anything had gone wrong.* **serenity** /sɪˈrenətɪ/ *n* [U].

serf /sɜːf/ *n* **1** (formerly) person forced by a landowner to work on the land in a feudal system. **2** (*fig*) worker treated harshly or like a slave.
▷ **serfdom** /-dəm/ *n* [U] **1** social and economic system under which land was cultivated by serfs: *abolish serfdom.* **2** conditions of a serf's life: *released from his serfdom.*

serge /sɜːdʒ/ *n* [U] strong woollen cloth used for making clothes: [attrib] *a blue serge suit.*

sergeant /ˈsɑːdʒənt/ *n* (often **Sergeant**; *abbrs* **Sergt**, **Sgt**) **1** non-commissioned army officer ranking above a corporal and below a warrant officer. ⇨ App 4. **2** (**a**) (*Brit*) police officer with a rank below that of an inspector. (**b**) (*US*) police officer with a rank below that of a captain or sometimes a lieutenant.
□ ˌ**sergeant-**ˈ**major** *n* (**a**) (*Brit*) warrant officer assisting the adjutant of a regiment or battalion. ⇨ App 4. (**b**) (*US*) highest rank of non-commissioned army officer. ⇨ App 4.

Sergt (also **Sgt**) *abbr* Sergeant: *Sergt (Colin) Hill* ○ *Sgt-Maj*, ie Sergeant-Major.

serial /ˈsɪərɪəl/ *adj* **1** [usu attrib] of, in or forming a series: *number files in serial order* ○ *a serial murderer*, ie one who kills several people one after another. **2** [attrib] (of a story, etc) appearing in parts in a periodical, etc or on TV or radio: *Our new serial thriller begins at 7.30 this evening.*
▷ **serial** *n* serial play, story, etc: *a detective, romantic, thriller, etc serial* ○ [attrib] *serial rights*, ie rights to make a serial out of a novel, story, etc.
serialize, **-ise** /-rɪəlaɪz/ *v* [Tn] publish or broadcast (sth) as a serial: *serialized on radio in twelve parts.*

Services

In Britain many households receive daily deliveries of post, milk and a newspaper, usually in time for breakfast. A milkman does a 'milk round', visiting a number of houses in an area. In towns, electrically operated 'milk floats' are used and other goods such as potatoes, eggs, fruit juice, etc can also be supplied by the milkman. There is a daily postal delivery to every house, however remote. In towns, older schoolchildren can earn pocket money by delivering newspapers (called 'doing a paper round') before they go to school.

Older children and students also earn money by doing baby-sitting. This and other services are often advertised on a display board in the window of a newsagent's or other small shop. Repair men, also called 'odd job men', electricians, gardeners, window cleaners, painters and decorators, plumbers, domestic cleaners (called 'daily helps') and child-minders (women who look after children during the day while the parents are at work) also often advertise their services in this way. Services are also advertised in the 'classified ads' section of local newspapers.

Many services can be ordered by telephone and a special telephone directory, the 'Yellow Pages', lists firms according to the services they provide. You can order a cooked meal to be delivered from a Chinese restaurant or a pizza restaurant. If you want to send a present to someone, you can arrange for chocolates, flowers, etc to be delivered. Many of these delivery services use motor cycles.

Shops and offices in town centres provide services such as dry cleaning, shoe repairs, photocopying and the use of fax machines. In launderettes you can wash and dry clothes in coin-operated machines. There are estate agencies for buying and selling houses, letting agencies for finding rented accommodation and employment agencies for finding a job. Some employment agencies specialize in a particular kind of job, for example secretarial jobs.

serialization, -isation /ˌsɪərɪəlaɪˈzeɪʃn; *US* -lɪˈz-/ *n* [C, U].

serially /-ɪəlɪ/ *adv*.

□ ˈ**serial number** number identifying one item in a series, eg on a banknote or a cheque.

seriatim /ˌsɪərɪˈeɪtɪm/ *adv (fml)* one thing after another; point by point.

series /ˈsɪəri:z/ *n (pl* unchanged) **1** number of things, events, etc of a similar kind, esp placed or occurring one after another: *a series of good harvests* ○ *a series of brilliant leaders* ○ *a series of interconnected caves* ○ *a television/radio series*, ie a number of programmes, each complete in itself, linked to each other by characters, theme, etc ○ *a series of stamps/coins*, eg of different values, but issued all at one time ○ *publish a new series of readers for students of English* ○ *the world series*, eg of important baseball or football games in the US. **2** [C, U] electrical circuit with the supply of current flowing directly through each component: *batteries connected in series* ○ [attrib] *a series circuit, connection, etc.* Cf PARALLEL.

serif /ˈserɪf/ *n* small line at the end of the stroke of a printed letter in certain type-faces: [attrib] *printed in a serif type-face.* Cf SANSERIF.

serio-comic /ˌsɪərɪəʊ ˈkɒmɪk/ *adj* partly serious and partly comic: *a serio-comic remark, style, play.*

serious /ˈsɪərɪəs/ *adj* **1** solemn and thoughtful; not frivolous: *a serious person, mind, appearance* ○ *Her face was serious as she told us the bad news.* ○ *He seems very serious, but in fact he has a delightful sense of humour.* ○ *Please be serious for a minute, this is very important.* **2** [usu attrib] (of books, music, etc) intended to provoke thought; not merely for amusement: *a serious essay about social problems* ○ *Do you ever read serious works?* **3** important because of possible danger or risk; grave: *a serious illness, mistake, accident* ○ *a serious decision about giving up a steady job* ○ *That could cause serious injury.* ○ *The international situation is extremely serious.* **4** ~ **(about sb/sth)** in earnest; sincere: *a serious suggestion* ○ *Are you really serious about him?* ie Do you have sincere affection for him? ○ *Is she serious about learning to be a pilot?*

▷ **seriously** *adv* **1** in a serious way: *speak seriously to her about it* ○ *seriously ill, injured, etc.* **2** *(infml)* (used at the beginning of a sentence when turning to a serious matter): *Seriously though, you could really hurt yourself doing that.* ⇨ Usage at HOPEFUL. **3** (idm) **take sb/sth seriously** regard sb/sth as important and worth treating with respect: *You can't take her promises seriously: she never keeps her word.* ○ *I take this threat very seriously.*

seriousness *n* [U] **1** state of being serious: *the seriousness of his expression* ○ *the seriousness of the crisis.* **2** (idm) **in all** ˈ**seriousness** *(infml)* very seriously: not as a joke: *You can't in all seriousness go out in a hat like that!*

serjeant-at-arms /ˌsɑ:dʒənt ət ˈɑ:mz/ *n* official who performs ceremonial duties for a lawcourt, city council or parliament.

sermon /ˈsɜ:mən/ *n* **1** **(a)** talk on a moral or religious subject, usu given by a clergyman from the pulpit during a religious service. **(b)** such a talk in printed form: *a book of sermons.* **2** *(fig infml)* long talk about moral matters or about sb's faults, etc: *We had to listen to a long sermon about not wasting money.*

▷ **sermonize, -ise** /-aɪz/ *v* [I, Ipr] *(derog)* give (often unwanted) moral advice in a pompous way.

serous /ˈsɪərəs/ *adj* [usu attrib] of or like serum; watery.

serpent /ˈsɜ:pənt/ *n (dated)* **1** snake, esp a large one. **2** person who tempts others to do wrong; sly person: *the old Serpent*, ie the Devil.

▷ **serpentine** /ˈsɜ:pəntaɪn; *US* -ti:n/ *adj (fml)* twisting and curving like a snake: *the serpentine course of the river.*

serrated

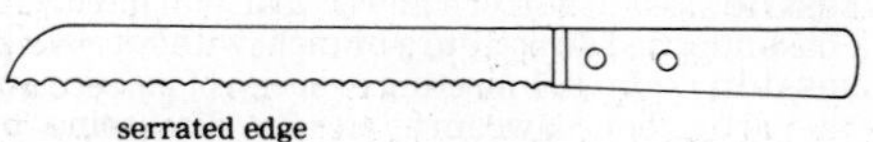
serrated edge

serrated /sɪˈreɪtɪd; *US* ˈsereɪtɪd/ *adj* having notches on the edge like a saw; having a toothed edge: *a knife with a serrated blade* ○ *serrated leaves.*

serration /sɪˈreɪʃn/ *n* **1** [U] being serrated. **2** [C] notch on a serrated edge.

serried /ˈserɪd/ *adj* [usu attrib] *(dated or fml)* (of rows of people or things) arranged close together in order: *serried rows/ranks/lines.*

serum /ˈsɪərəm/ *n (pl* **sera** /ˈsɪərə/ or ~**s**) *(medical)* **1** [U] **(a)** watery liquid in animal bodies. **(b)** thin yellowish liquid that remains from blood after it has clotted. **2** [C, U] (dose of) such liquid taken from an animal that is immune to a disease, used for inoculations. Cf VACCINE.

servant /ˈsɜ:vənt/ *n* **1** person who works in sb else's household for wages, and often for food and lodging: *have/employ a large staff of servants.* **2** ~ **(of sb/sth)** **(a)** employee, esp a faithful and devoted one: *a trusted servant of the company.* **(b)** person devoted to sb/sth: *a servant of Jesus Christ*, eg a Christian priest. **3** (idm) **your obedient servant** ⇨ OBEDIENT.

serve /sɜ:v/ *v* **1** [I, Tn] ~ **(sb)** **(as sth)** work for (sb), esp as a servant: *served as (a) gardener and chauffeur* ○ *He has served his master for many years.* **2** [I, Ipr, Tn] ~ **(in sth/as sth)** perform duties, eg in the armed forces: *serve (a year) in the Army* ○ *served as a naval officer during the war* ○ *serve on* (ie be a member of) *a committee, board, etc* ○ *serve under sb*, ie be under the command of (a superior officer, leader, etc) ○ *She has served her country well*, eg as a civil servant, Member of Parliament, etc. ○ *(fig) This desk has served me well* (ie been very useful to me) *over the years.* **3** **(a)** [I, Ipr, Tn, Tn·pr, Tn·p, Dn·pr] ~ **sb (with sth)**; ~ **sth (up) (to sb)** give food to (sb) at a meal; place (food) on the table at a meal: *learn to serve at table*, ie as a waiter ○ *Who's going to serve?* ○ *Dinner is served*, ie is ready. ○ *We serve coffee in the lounge.* ○ *Have all the guests been served (with) food and drink?* ○ *Four waiters served lunch to us/served us lunch.* **(b)** [I, Tn, Tn·pr, Dn·pr] ~ **sb (with sth)**; ~ **sth (to sb)** attend to (a customer) or supply (sth) in a shop, etc: *He serves in a shoeshop.* ○ *Are you being served?* ○ *He served some sweets to the children.* **(c)** [esp passive: Tn, Tn·pr] ~ **sb/sth (with sth)** provide sb/sth with a facility: *The town is well served with public transport.* **4** [I, Ipr, It, Tn, Tn·pr, Cn·n/a no passive] ~ **(sb) (for/as sth)** *(fml)* satisfy (a need or purpose); be suitable (for): *This room can serve as/for a study.* ○ *This serves to show how foolish you have been.* ○ *It's not exactly what I wanted but it will serve my purpose.* **5** [Tn] (of a portion of food) be enough for: *This packet of soup serves two.* **6** [Tn] *(fml)* treat (sb) in a specified way: *They have served me shamefully*, ie have treated me very badly. **7** [In/pr, Tn] **(a)** spend (a period of time) learning a trade, etc: *serve two years as an apprentice/a two-year apprenticeship.* **(b)** pass (a period of time) in prison: *serve ten years for armed robbery* ○ *(infml) serve time for fraud.* **8** [Tn, Tn·pr] ~ **sth (on sb)**; ~ **sb with sth** *(law)* formally deliver sth to sb: *serve a summons, writ, warrant, etc* ○ *serve a court order on sb/sb with a court order.* **9** [I, Ipr, Tn, Tn·pr] ~ **(sth) (to sb)** (in tennis, etc) put the ball into play by striking it to one's opponent: *It's your turn to serve (to me).* ○ *She's already served two aces this game.* **10** [Tn] (of a male animal) copulate with (a female animal), esp after being hired for this purpose: *His bull will come to serve our cows tomorrow.* **11** [no passive: I, Tn] assist a priest at (a religious service): *Who will serve (at) Mass today?* **12** (idm) **first come, first served** ⇨ FIRST[2]. **if memory serves** ⇨ MEMORY. ˌ**serve one's/its/the** ˈ**purpose** do what is necessary or required; be satisfactory: *It's not ideal, but it'll serve its purpose.* **serve sb** ˈ**right** (of a misfortune, etc) be deserved by sb: *'I got soaked in the rain.' 'It serves you right — I told you to take an umbrella.'* **serve one's/its turn** = SERVE ONE'S PURPOSE. **serve two** ˈ**masters** (usu in negative sentences) follow two conflicting parties, principles, etc. **13** (phr v) **serve sth out** **(a)** give portions of (food) to several people: *Shall I serve out the soup or would you like to help yourselves?* **(b)** serve, work, etc until the end of (a fixed period): *You'll have to serve out your notice before you leave the firm.* **serve sth up** *(infml derog)* offer sth: *She served up the usual excuses for being late.*

▷ **serve** *n* (in tennis, etc) act or manner of serving the ball: *Whose serve is it?* ie Whose turn is it to serve? ○ *a fast serve.*

server *n* **1** person who serves, eg at Mass or in tennis. **2** tray for dishes; salver. **3** (usu *pl*) utensil used for putting a portion of food onto sb's plate: *salad servers.*

serving *n* portion of food for one person: *This recipe will be enough for four servings.*

service /ˈsɜːvɪs/ *n* **1** [U] ~ (**to sth**) performing duties, eg in the armed forces, or working for a government, company, etc: *ten years' service in the navy, police force, etc* ○ *conditions of service* ○ *a life of public service* ○ *many years of faithful service to the company.* **2** [U] (*fig*) work done by a vehicle, machine, etc: *My car has given me excellent service.* ○ *You will get good service from this typewriter.* **3** [C] (**a**) department of people employed by the government or a public organization: *the ˌCivil ˈService* ○ *the ˌDiploˈmatic Service* ○ *the ˌNational ˈHealth Service.* (**b**) branch of the armed forces: *the three services*, ie the Navy, the Army, the Air Force ○ *Which service is she in?* ○ [attrib] *a service rifle, family, house.* **4** [U] (*dated*) being a servant; position as a servant: *be in/go into service*, ie be/become a domestic servant. **5** [C usu *pl*] ~ (**to sb/sth**) work done for another or others; helpful act; favour: *You did me a great service by showing me the truth.* ○ *They need the services of a good lawyer.* ○ *Her services to the state have been immense.* **6** [C] (**a**) system or arrangement that meets public needs, esp for communication: *a ˈbus/ˈtrain service* ○ *the ˈtelephone service* ○ *a good ˈpostal service* ○ *Essential services* (ie the supply of water, electricity, etc.) *will be maintained.* ⇨ article. (**b**) business that does work or supplies goods for customers, but does not make goods; such work or goods: *We get export earnings from goods and services.* ○ *banking and ˈinsurance services* ○ *a new ˈcarpet-cleaning service* ○ [attrib] *a ˈservice industry* ○ *the ˈservice sector.* **7** [U] serving of customers in hotels, restaurants, etc; work done by domestic servants, hotel staff, etc: *The food is good at this hotel, but the service is poor.* ○ *An extra 10% was added to the restaurant bill for service.* ○ [attrib] *a quick-service restaurant* ○ *a service entrance*, ie one for staff, rather than the public. **8** [C] ceremony of religious worship or the prayers, etc used at this: *three services every Sunday* ○ *attend morning/evening ˈservice* ○ *the ˈmarriage, ˈburial, comˈmunion, etc service.* **9** [C, U] maintenance and repair of a vehicle, machine, etc at regular intervals: *take a car in for (a) service every 3 000 miles*, eg to have the oil changed, the brakes checked, etc ○ *a service for a gas boiler* ○ *We offer (an) excellent after-sales service.* ○ [attrib] *a service department, engineer.* **10** [C] set of dishes, etc for serving food at table: *a 30-piece ˈdinner service.* **11** [U] (*law*) delivering of a writ, summons, etc. **12** [C] (**a**) (in tennis, etc) act or manner of serving the ball; person's turn to serve: *a fast service* ○ *Her service has improved.* ○ *Whose service is it?* (**b**) game in which sb serves: *win/hold/lose/drop one's service* ○ *break sb's service*, ie win a game in which one's opponent serves ○ [attrib] *a service game.* **13** [U] serving (SERVE 10) of a female animal by a male animal. **14** (idm) **at sb's ˈservice** ready to help sb: *If you need advice, I am at your service.* (**be**) **of service** (**to sb**) useful or helpful: *Can I be of service to you in organizing the trip?* **press sth into service** ⇨ PRESS[3]. **see service** (**in sth**) (**a**) serve in the armed forces: *He saw service as an infantry officer in the last war.* ○ *He has seen service in many different parts of the world.* (**b**) (*infml*) be very useful, dependable, etc: *These old boots have certainly seen some service.*

▷ **service** *v* [Tn] **1** maintain and repair (a vehicle, machine, etc) at regular intervals: *service a car, boiler, washing-machine* ○ *Has this mower been regularly serviced?* **2** supply a service(6a) or services to (sth): *The power station is serviced* (ie Fuel is delivered to it) *by road transport.* **3** pay interest on (a loan): *The company hasn't enough cash to service its debts.* **4** = SERVE 10. **serviceable** *adj* **1** in usable condition: *The tyres are worn but still serviceable.* **2** suitable for ordinary use or hard wear (and not designed to be ornamental); durable; long-lasting: *serviceable clothes for children.* **serviceably** /-əblɪ/ *adv.*

□ ˈ**service area** area beside a motorway where petrol and refreshments, etc are sold. ⇨ illus at MOTORWAY.

ˈ**service-book** *n* book containing the words used in a church service.

ˈ**service break** = BREAK[2] 6.

ˈ**service charge** sum added to a restaurant bill, eg 10% of the total, to pay for the service given by the waiters, etc: *Does my bill include a service charge?*

ˈ**service court** (in tennis and similar games) part of the court into which the ball must be hit when serving.

ˈ**service flat** (*Brit*) flat in which domestic service and sometimes meals, etc are provided and charged for in the rent.

ˈ**serviceman** /-mən/ *n* (*pl* **-men** /-mən/) man in the armed forces.

ˈ**service road** (*US* also **frontage road**) minor road, off a main road, giving access to houses, etc.

ˈ**service station** = PETROL STATION (PETROL).

ˈ**servicewoman** *n* (*pl* **-women**) woman in the armed forces.

serviette /ˌsɜːvɪˈet/ *n* (*esp Brit*) table napkin: *paper serviettes.*

servile /ˈsɜːvaɪl; *US* -vl/ *adj* **1** (*derog*) too ready to obey others; lacking independence: *servile flattery* ○ *I don't like his servile manner.* **2** of, like or for a servant: *made to do servile tasks.*

▷ **servilely** /-aɪllɪ/ *adv.*

servility /sɜːˈvɪlətɪ/ *n* [U] (*usu derog*) servile behaviour or attitude.

servitude /ˈsɜːvɪtjuːd; *US* -tuːd/ *n* [U] (*fml*) condition of being forced to work for others and having no freedom: *Such ill-paid farm work is a form of servitude.*

servo /ˈsɜːvəʊ/ *n* (*pl* ~**s**) (*infml*) = SERVO-MECHANISM.

servo- *comb form* (of machinery) having a power unit controlling a larger mechanism: *servo-assisted brakes*, eg in a large car.

servo-mechanism /ˌsɜːvəʊ ˈmekənɪzəm/ *n* any mechanism that controls a larger mechanism.

servo-motor /ˈsɜːvəʊ məʊtə(r)/ *n* motor that controls a larger mechanism.

sesame /ˈsesəmɪ/ *n* **1** [U] tropical plant with seeds which are used as food and which give an oil used in salads and in cooking: [attrib] *sesame seeds, oil.* **2** (idm) **open sesame** ⇨ OPEN[1].

sessile /ˈsesaɪl/ *adj* (of a flower, leaf, etc) having its base attached directly to a branch, without a stalk.

session /ˈseʃn/ *n* **1** meeting or series of meetings of a parliament, lawcourt, etc for discussing or deciding sth: *the morning session of the Crown Court* ○ *the next session of arms negotiations* ○ *the autumn session* (ie sitting) *of parliament.* **2** (**a**) school or university year. (**b**) (*US*) school term or period of study. **3** single continuous period spent in one activity: *a reˈcording session*, ie one at which material is recorded on tape or discs, etc ○ *After several sessions at the gym, I feel a lot fitter.* **4** governing body of a Presbyterian church. **5** (idm) **in ˈsession** (**a**) assembled for business: *The court is now in session.* (**b**) not on vacation: *Is Parliament in session during the summer?*

set[1] /set/ *n* **1** [C] ~ (**of sth**) group of similar things that belong together in some way: *a set of cutlery, golf clubs, hand tools* ○ *a set of six dining chairs* ○ *a set of Dickens novels* ○ *a set of false teeth* ○ *a tea set*, ie teapot, cups, saucers, etc ○ *a new set of rules to learn.* **2** [CGp] group of people who spend much time together socially or have similar tastes and interests: *the literary, racing, golfing set* ○ *the smart set*, ie rich fashionable people ○ *the fast set*, eg people who gamble, spend a lot of money, etc. **3** [C] group of pupils with similar ability in a particular subject: *She's in the top set in maths.* **4** [C] (*mathematics*) group of things having a shared quality. **5** [C] device for receiving radio or television signals: *a transistor set* ○ *Do not adjust your (TV) set.* **6** [sing] ~ (**of sth**) way in which sth is placed or arranged; position or angle: *She admired the firm set of his shoulders.* **7** [sing] way in which sth sets (SET[2] 13): *You won't get a good set if you put too much water in the jelly.* **8** [C] (in a tennis match) group of games in which one side must win the greater number of games in order to win that part of the match. **9** (also **sett**) [C] rectangular paving stone. **10** (also **sett**) [C] badger's burrow. **11** [C] (**a**) scenery being used for a play, film, etc: *We need volunteers to help build and paint the set.* (**b**) stage or place where a play or (part of) a film is performed: *The cast must all be on (the) set by 7 pm.* **12** [C] young plant, shoot, etc for planting: *onion sets.* **13** [C] act of setting (SET[2] 15) hair: *A shampoo and set costs £8.* **14** (idm) **the jet set** ⇨ JET[1].

□ ˈ**set theory** (*mathematics*) study or use of sets (SET[1] 4).

set[2] /set/ *v* (**-tt-**, *pt*, *pp* **set**)

► PLACING IN POSITION **1** [Tn·pr, Tn·p] put (sth) in the specified place or position; place: *She set a tray down on the table.* ○ *He set a post in the ground.* ○ (*fml*) *We set food and drink before the travellers.* ○ *The house is set* (ie situated) *in fifty acres of rolling parkland.* ○ *Her eyes are set very close together.* **2** [Tn·pr] ~ **sth to sth** move or place sth so that it is near to or touching sth: *She set the glass to her lips/her lips to the glass.* ○ *He set a match to the dry timber*, ie in order to burn it. ○ *set pen to paper*, ie begin to write. **3** [Tn, Tn·pr] represent the action of (a play, novel, etc) as happening in a specified place or at a specified time: *The novel is set in pre-war London.*

► CAUSING TO BE IN A PARTICULAR STATE OR TO HAPPEN **4** [Tn·pr, Cn·a] cause (sb/sth) to be in or reach the specified state: *The revolution set the country on the road to democracy.* ○ *The firm's accounts need to be set in order.* ○ *She untied the rope and set the boat adrift.* ○ *The hijackers set the hostages free*, ie released them. **5** (**a**) [Cn·g] cause (sb/sth) to begin to do sth: *set a pendulum swinging* ○ *The sudden noise set the dog barking.* ○ *The sight of her set his heart beating faster.* ○ *Her remarks set me thinking.* (**b**) [Cn·t] cause (oneself/sb) to do the specified task: *We set them to chop wood/set them to work chopping wood in the garden.* ○ *I've set myself* (ie resolved) *to finish the job by the end of the month.*

► ADJUSTING OR ARRANGING **6** [Tn, Tn·pr] adjust (sth) so that it is ready for use or in position: *set the controls*, eg of a machine ○ *She set the camera on automatic.* **7** [Tn] (**a**) adjust the hands of (a clock or watch) to show the right time: *I always set my watch by the time-signal on the radio.* (**b**) adjust (an alarm-clock) so that it sounds at a particular time: *She set her alarm for 7 o'clock.* **8** [Tn] arrange knives, forks, etc on (a table) for a meal; lay(1b): *Could you set the table for supper?* ○ *The table is set for six guests.* **9** [Tn·pr esp passive] ~ **A in B**/~ **B with A** fix (sth, esp a precious stone) firmly into (a surface or an object): *She had the sapphire set in a gold ring.* ○ *Her bracelet was set with emeralds.* **10** [Tn, Tn·pr] arrange or fix (sth); decide on (sth): *They haven't set a date for their wedding yet.* ○ *The government plans to set strict limits on public spending this year.*

► CREATING **11** [Tn] (used esp with the *ns* shown) establish (sth): *Imposing a lenient sentence for such a serious crime sets a dangerous precedent.* ○ *She set a new world record for the high jump.* ○ *Rock stars often set fashions in clothes.* ○ *I rely on you to set a good example.* **12** [Tn, Dn·n, Dn·pr] ~ **sth** (**for oneself/sb**) present or impose (a task, piece of work, problem, etc) to be done, dealt with, etc (by oneself/sb): *Who will be setting* (ie writing the questions in) *the French exam?* ○ *What books have been set* (ie are to be studied) *for the Cambridge First Certificate next year?* ○ *She's set herself a difficult task/set a difficult task for herself.* ○ *The sudden drop in share prices has set the government a tricky problem.* ○ *We must set ourselves precise sales targets for the coming year.*

►MAKING OR BECOMING FIRM OR FIXED **13** [I, Tn] (cause sth to) become firm, hard or rigid from a soft or liquid state: *Some kinds of concrete set more quickly than others.* ○ *The jelly hasn't set yet.* **14** [Tn esp passive] fix (one's face or part of the body) into a firm expression: *He set his jaw in a determined fashion.* **15** [Tn] fix (hair) while it is wet so that it will dry in the desired style: *She's having her hair set for the party this evening.* **16** [Tn] put (a broken bone) into a fixed position so that it will mend: *The surgeon set her broken arm.*

►PRESENTING IN THE RIGHT FORM **17** [Tn] choose a specific type² for printing (a book, etc): *This dictionary is set in Nimrod.* **18** [Tn, Tn·pr] ~ **sth (to sth)** provide music for (words, a poem, etc) so that it can be sung: *Schubert set many of Goethe's poems (to music).*

►MOVING OR FLOWING **19** [I] (of the sun, moon or stars) go down below the horizon: *In Britain the sun sets much later in summer than in winter.* ○ *We sat and watched the sun setting.* Cf RISE² 7. **20** [Ipr, Ip] (of the tide, a current, etc) move or flow in the specified direction: *The current sets strongly eastwards.* ○ *The current sets in towards the shore* ○ (*fig*) *The tide of public opinion has set in his favour*, ie He has the support and approval of the public. ○ (*fig*) *Opinion seems to be setting against* (ie People are not in favour of) *the proposal.*
21 (idm) **be all ˈset (for sth/to do sth); be set for sth/to do sth** be ready or prepared for sth/to do sth: *Are we all set?* ○ *We were all set to go when the telephone rang.* ○ *The socialists look set for victory in/set to win the general election.* (For other idioms containing **set**, see entries for *ns, adjs*, etc, eg **set the pace** ⇨ PACE¹; **set fair** ⇨ FAIR¹.)
22 (phr v) **set about sb** (*infml*) attack sb with blows or words: *He set about the intruders with a stick.* **set about sth/doing sth** (no passive) begin (a task); start doing sth: *I must set about my packing.* ○ *I don't know how to set about this job.* ○ *The new government must set about finding solutions to the country's economic problems.*
set sb against sb (no passive) make sb oppose or be hostile to (a friend, relative, etc): *The civil war set brother against brother.* ○ *She accused her husband of setting their children against her.* **set sth (off) against sth** consider (sth good or positive) as balancing or outweighing (sth bad or negative): *You must set the initial cost of a new car against the saving you'll make on repairs.* ○ *Set against her virtues, her faults don't seem nearly so bad.*
set sb/sth apart (from sb/sth) make sb/sth different from or superior to others: *Her clear and elegant prose sets her apart from most other journalists.*
set sth aside (a) place sth to one side: *She set aside her book and lit a cigarette.* **(b)** save or keep (money or time) for a particular purpose: *She sets aside a bit of money every month.* ○ *I try to set aside a few minutes each day to do some exercises.* **(c)** disregard or ignore sth; abandon or reject sth: *Let's set aside my personal feelings.* ○ *Set aside for a moment your instinctive dislike of the man.* **(d)** (*law*) cancel or reject (a verdict, sentence, etc): *The judge's decision was set aside by the Appeal Court.*
set sth back (sth) delay or hinder the progress of sth (by the specified time): *Financial problems have set back our building programme.* ○ *Work on the new theatre has been set back three months.* **set sb back sth** (*infml*) cost sb (the specified amount of money): *The meal is likely to set us back £15 each.* **set sth back (from sth)** (often passive) place or situate sth (esp a building) at a distance from sth: *The house is set well back from the road.*
set sb down (of a vehicle or its driver) stop and allow (a passenger) to get off: *The bus stopped to set down an old lady.* ○ *I'll set you down on the corner of your street.* **set sth down** note or record sth on paper; write sth down: *Why don't you set your ideas down on paper?*
set ˈforth (*fml*) start a journey; set out. **set sth forth** (*fml*) make sth known; declare or present sth: *The Prime Minister set forth the aims of his government in a television broadcast.*
set ˈin (of rain, bad weather, infection, etc) begin and seem likely to continue: *I must get those bulbs planted before the cold weather sets in.* ○ *Those beams will need to be replaced; it looks as though woodworm has set in.*
set ˈoff begin (a journey, race, etc): *What time are you planning to set off tomorrow?* ○ *They've set off on a journey round the world.* ○ *If you want to catch that train we'd better set off for the station immediately.* **set sth off (a)** cause (a bomb, mine, etc) to explode: *Do be careful with those fireworks; the slightest spark could set them off.* **(b)** cause or prompt sth: *Panic on the stock market set off a wave of selling.* **(c)** make sth appear more attractive by contrast: *That jumper sets off the blue of her eyes.* **set sb off (doing sth)** cause sb to start (doing sth): *Don't set him off talking politics or he'll go on all evening.* ○ *Her imitations always set me off (laughing).*
set on sb attack sb: *I was set on by their dog as soon as I opened the gate.* **set sb/sth on sb** cause (a person or an animal) to attack sb: *The farmer threatened to set his dogs on us.*
set ˈout leave a place and begin a journey: *She set out at dawn.* ○ *They set out on the last stage of their journey.* **set sth out (a)** arrange or display (items): *We'll need to set out chairs for the meeting.* ○ *She set out the pieces on the chessboard.* ○ *Her work is always very well set out.* ○ (*fig*) *You haven't set out your ideas very clearly in this essay.* **(b)** state or declare sth: *He set out his objections to the scheme.* ○ *She set out the reasons for her resignation in a long letter.* **set out to do sth** begin a job, task, etc with a particular aim or goal: *She set out to break the world land speed record.* ○ *They succeeded in what they set out to do.*
set ˈto (a) begin doing sth energetically: *The engineers set to on repair work to the bridge.* ○ *If we really set to we can get the whole house cleaned in an afternoon.* **(b)** begin to fight or argue: *The boys set to and had to be separated by a teacher.*
set sb up (*infml*) **(a)** make sb healthier, stronger, more lively, etc: *A hot drink will soon set you up.* ○ *A week in the country will set her up nicely after her operation.* **(b)** provide sb with the money to start a business, buy a house, etc: *Her father set her up in business.* ○ *His father set him up as a bookseller.* ○ *Winning all that money on the pools set her up for life.* **set sth up (a)** place sth in position; erect sth: *set up a memorial, monument, statue, etc* ○ *Police set up road-blocks on routes leading out of the city.* **(b)** make (an apparatus, a machine, etc) ready for use: *How long will it take to set up the projector?* **(c)** establish or create sth: *The government has set up a working party to look into the problem of drug abuse.* ○ *A fund will be set up for the dead men's families.* **(d)** establish (a record speed, time or distance in a sport): *She set up a new world record time in the 100 metres.* **(e)** cause or produce sth: *The slump on Wall Street set up a chain reaction in stock markets around the world.* **(f)** begin to make (the specified loud noise): *set up a commotion, din, row, etc* ○ *The cats set up a frightful yowling when the dog appeared.* **set (oneself) up as sb** establish oneself in business as (a shopkeeper, craftsman, etc): *He moved to Leeds and set up as a printer.* **set oneself up as sb** regard oneself as or claim to be (the specified type of person): *He likes to set himself up as an intellectual.*
□ **ˈset-back** *n* thing that hinders the progress of sth: *Hopes of an early end to the strike received/suffered a severe set-back yesterday.* ○ *Defeat in the by-election is a major set-back to the ruling party.*
ˌset ˈbook (also **ˌset ˈtext**) book on which students must answer questions in an examination: *What are your set books for English A Level?*
setline = TRAWL LINE (TRAWL).
ˌset-ˈto *n* (*pl* **set-tos**) fight or argument: *They had the most frightful set-to.*
ˈset-up *n* (usu *sing*) (*infml*) structure of an organization: *What's the set-up (like) in your company?* ○ *I've only been here for a couple of weeks and don't really know the set-up.*

set³ /set/ *adj* **1** [usu pred] having the specified position: *a house set on a wooded hillside* ○ *She has deep-set eyes.* **2** [usu attrib] (of a person's expression) fixed; stiff: *Her face wore a grim, set look.* ○ *a set* (ie insincere) *smile.* **3** [usu attrib] fixed or arranged in advance: *The meals in this hotel are at set times.* ○ *There is a set procedure for making formal complaints.* ○ *Are there set hours of work in your company?* **4** fixed and unchanging: *He's a man of set opinions.* ○ *She has very set ideas about politics.* ○ *As people get older they become more set in their ways.* **5** [attrib] deliberate; specific: *We've come here for a set purpose.* **6** (idm) **be (dead) ˈset against sth/doing sth** be (firmly) opposed to sth: *The government are set against (the idea of) raising taxes.* **be set on sth/doing sth** be determined to do sth: *He's set on going to university.* ○ *She's absolutely set on publishing as a career.*
□ **ˌset ˈpiece** scene in a novel, film, play, etc arranged in a fixed or typical pattern or style: *The play contains a number of typical Stoppard set pieces.*
ˈset square /ˈset skweə(r)/ triangular piece of plastic, metal or wood with angles of 90°, 60° and 30° (or 90°, 45° and 45°), used for drawing straight lines, esp at these angles.

sett /set/ *n* = SET¹ 9, 10.

settee /seˈti:/ *n* long soft seat with a back and usu with arms, for two or more people. ⇨ illus at FURNITURE.

setter /ˈsetə(r)/ *n* **1** any of several breeds of long-haired dog, trained to stand motionless when it scents animals or birds being hunted. ⇨ illus at DOG. **2** (often in compounds) person or thing that sets sth (in various meanings of SET): *the setter of an examination paper* ○ *a ˈtype-setter* ○ *a trend-setter.*

setting /ˈsetɪŋ/ *n* **1** [C] way or place in which sth is fixed or fastened: *The ring has a ruby in a silver setting.* **2** [C] **(a)** surroundings; environment: *The castle stands in a picturesque setting surrounded by hills.* **(b)** place and time at which an event occurs or a play, novel, etc is set: *The setting of the story is a hotel in Paris during the war.* ○ *a gruesome setting for the murder.* **3** [C] speed, height, temperature, etc at which a device, machine, etc is or can be set to operate: *The cooker has several temperature settings.* **4** [C] music composed for a poem, etc: *Schubert's setting of a poem by Goethe.* **5** [sing] descent (of the sun, moon, etc) below the horizon.

settle¹ /ˈsetl/ *n* wooden seat for two or more people, with a high back and arms, the seat often being the lid of a chest.

settle² /ˈsetl/ *v* **1 (a)** [I, Ipr, Tn esp passive] make one's permanent home in (a country, etc) as a colonist: *The Dutch settled in South Africa.* ○ (*fml*) *This area was settled by immigrants over a century ago.* **(b)** [I, Ipr] make one's home in a place: *After years of travel, we decided to settle here.* ○ *settle in London, in Canada, in the country, near the coast.* **2** [I, Ipr] ~ **(on/over sth)** come to rest on sth; stay for some time on sth: *Will the snow settle?* ie Will it remain on the ground without melting? ○ *The bird settled on a branch.* ○ *Clouds have settled over the mountain tops.* ○ *The dust had settled on everything.* ○ *The cold has settled on my chest*, ie It is making me cough, etc. ○ (*fig*) *A tense silence had settled over the waiting crowd.* **3** [I, Ip, Tn] ~ **(back)** make (sb/oneself) comfortable in a new position: *settle (back) in one's armchair* ○ *The nurse settled her patient for the night*, ie made him comfortable, gave him medicine, etc. ○ *He settled himself on the sofa to watch TV.* **4** [I, Tn] (cause sb/sth to) become calm, composed or relaxed: *Wait until all the excitement has settled.* ○ *Have a drink to settle your stomach.* ○ *The thunderstorm may settle the weather.* ○ *This pill will help to settle your nerves.* ○ *He had been quite anxious, but I managed to settle his mind.* **5 (a)** [Tn, Tn·pr, Tf, Tw] ~ **sth (with sb)** make an agreement about sth; arrange sth finally or satisfactorily; deal with sth: *settle a dispute, an argument, an issue, etc* ○ *That settles the* *matter.* ○ *Nothing is settled yet.* ○ *You should settle your affairs* (eg by making a will) *before you leave.* ○ *It's time you settled your dispute with him.* ○ *We have settled that we will leave next week.* ○ *Have you settled how it will be done?* **(b)** [I, Ipr] ~ **(with sb)** resolve a legal dispute by mutual agreement: *The parties in the lawsuit settled (with each other) out of court*, ie reached an agreement before the case was heard in court. **6 (a)** [I, Ipr, Ip, Tn] ~ **(up) (with sb)** pay (what is owed, a bill, etc): *You owe a lot, and it's now time to settle (with your creditors).* ○ *Have you settled (up) with her for the goods?* ○ *If you pay for both of us now, we can settle up later.* ○ *The insurance company has settled her claim.* ○ *Please settle your bill before leaving the hotel.* **(b)** [Ipr, Tn, Tn·pr] ~ **(sth) (with sb)** (*fig*) punish sb for (an injury, insult, etc that one has suffered): *He thinks he can laugh at me, but I'll settle with him soon.* ○ *settle a score, grievance, etc.* **7 (a)** [I, Tn] (cause sth to) sink to a lower level: *The dregs have settled at the bottom of the bottle.* ○ *Stir the coffee to settle the grounds.* ○ *The shower of rain has settled the dust.* **(b)** [I, Tn] (cause sth to) become clear as solid matter sinks: *Has the beer settled?* ○ *Leave the wine on a shelf for a week to settle it.* **(c)** [I] become more compact; subside: *The wall sagged as the earth beneath it settled.* ○ *The contents of the packet have settled in transit*, ie come closer together, so that there appears to be less. **8** (idm) **pay/settle an old score** ➪ OLD. **settle one's/an acˈcount (with sb)** get revenge for an injury, insult, etc: *She insulted my mother, so I have an account to settle with her.* **settle sb's ˈhash** (*infml*) deal finally with sb who is being awkward, aggressive, etc. **when the dust has settled** ➪ DUST[1].

9 (phr v) **settle down (a)** sit or lie in a comfortable position: *She settled down in an armchair to read her book.* **(b)** adopt a more stable or quiet way of life; get used to a new way of life, job, etc: *When are you going to marry and settle down?* ○ *She is settling down well in her new job.* **settle (sb) down** (cause sb to) become calm, less restless, etc: *Wait until the children settle down before you start the lesson.* ○ *After all the recent excitement things have begun to settle down again.* ○ *The chairman tried to settle the audience down*, ie get them to stop talking, etc. **settle (down) to sth** begin to give one's attention to sth: *The constant interruptions stopped me settling (down) to my work.*

settle for sth accept sth that is seen as not quite satisfactory: *I had hoped to get £1 000 for my old car but had to settle for a lot less.*

settle (sb) in/into sth (help sb to) move into a new home, job, etc and become established there: *We only moved house last week and we haven't settled in yet.* ○ *We settled the children into new schools when we moved to London.*

settle on sth choose sth; decide to take sth: *Have you settled on the wallpaper you prefer?* ○ *We must settle on a place to meet.* **settle sth on sb** (*law*) transfer (property, etc) to sb's ownership: *He settled part of his estate on his son.*

settled /ˈsetld/ *adj* not changing or likely to change; stable: *a settled spell of weather* ○ *lead a more settled life.*

settlement /ˈsetlmənt/ *n* **1 (a)** [U] settling or being settled: *the settlement of a debt, dispute, claim.* **(b)** [C] agreement, etc that settles sth: *a lasting settlement of the troubles* ○ *The strikers have reached a settlement with the employers.* **2** [C] (*law*) (document stating the) terms on which money or property is given to sb; money or property given in this way: *a ˈmarriage settlement*, ie one made by a spouse in favour of his/her spouse when they get married. **3 (a)** [U] process of settling in a colony: *the gradual settlement of the American West.* **(b)** [C] place where colonists have settled: *Dutch and English settlements in North America* ○ *penal settlements in Australia.* **4** (idm) **in settlement (of sth)** as payment (for sth): *I enclose a cheque in settlement of your account.*

□ **ˈsettlement day** day when payment must be made for recent purchases on the Stock Exchange.

settler /ˈsetlə(r)/ *n* person who comes to live permanently in a new, developing country; colonist: *Welsh settlers in Argentina.*

Seurat /ˈsɜːrɑː; *US* səˈrɑː/ Georges (1859-91), French painter. Originally a member of the *Impressionist school, he became the main developer of the technique of pointillism, in which a picture is built up from tiny dots of colour.

seven /ˈsevn/ *pron, det* 7; one more than six. ➪ App 9.

▷ **seven** *n* **1** [C] the number 7. **2 sevens** [pl] Rugby Union match or competition in which each side has seven players (instead of the usual fifteen). **3** (idm) **at sixes and sevens** ➪ SIX.

seven- (in compounds) having seven of the thing specified: *a seven-line poem.*

seventh /ˈsevnθ/ *pron, det* 7th; next after sixth. — *n* one of seven equal parts of sth. **seventhly** *adv*. For the uses of *seven* and *seventh* see the examples at *five* and *fifth*. **the seventh ˈday** the Sabbath (Saturday for Jews, Sunday for Christians). **ˌSeventh-Day ˈAdventist** member of a strict Protestant sect of *Adventists who have their Sabbath on a Saturday and believe that Christ will soon return to earth.

□ **the ˌSeven ˈSisters** = PLEIADES.

the ˌSeven ˌWonders of the ˈWorld the seven most impressive buildings or other structures of ancient times. They were: the pyramids of Egypt; the Hanging Gardens of Babylon; the Mausoleum, a huge marble tomb at Halicarnassus in Asia Minor; the temple of Diana at Ephesus in Asia Minor; the Colossus, a huge statue of the sun-god Helios in *Rhodes harbour; a huge gold and ivory statue of Zeus at Olympia; and the Pharos, a lighthouse at *Alexandria.

the ˌSeven Years ˈWar war (1756-63) between Britain, Prussia and Hanover on one side and Austria, France, Russia, Saxony, Sweden and Spain on the other. Its main causes were the struggle between Britain and France to be the leading imperial power and the struggle between Austria and Prussia for dominance in Central Europe. The British and Prussian side won, with Britain taking over much French territory in Canada and India.

seventeen /ˌsevnˈtiːn/ *pron, det* 17; one more than sixteen. ➪ App 9.

▷ **seventeen** *n* the number 17.

seventeenth /ˌsevnˈtiːnθ/ *pron, det* 17th; next after sixteenth. — *n* one of seventeen equal parts of sth. For the uses of *seventeen* and *seventeenth* see the examples at *five* and *fifth*.

seventy /ˈsevntɪ/ *pron, det* 70; one more than sixty-nine. ➪ App 9.

▷ **seventieth** /ˈsevntɪəθ/ *pron, det* 70th; next after sixty-ninth. — *n* one of seventy equal parts of sth.

seventy *n* **1** [C] the number 70. **2 the seventies** [pl] numbers, years or temperature from 70 to 79. **3** (idm) **in one's ˈseventies** between the ages of 70 and 80.

For the uses of *seventy* and *seventieth* see the examples at *five* and *fifth*.

□ **ˌseventy-ˈeight** *n* old-fashioned type of gramophone record to be played at 78 revolutions per minute.

sever /ˈsevə(r)/ *v* (*fml*) **1 (a)** [Tn, Tn·pr] ~ **sth (from sth)** divide or break or separate sth by cutting: *sever a rope* ○ *a severed limb, artery* ○ *His hand was severed from his arm.* **(b)** [Tn] (*fig*) break off; end: *sever relations with sb* ○ *She has severed her connection with the firm.* **2** [I] break: *The rope severed under the strain.*

▷ **severance** /ˈsevərəns/ *n* (*fml*) [U] cutting or being cut; discontinuation: *the severance of diplomatic relations, of communications, of family ties.*

□ **ˈseverance pay** money paid to an employee whose contract is terminated.

several /ˈsevrəl/ *indef det, indef pron* more than three; some, but fewer than many. **(a)** (*det*): *Several letters arrived this morning.* ○ *He's written several books about India.* ○ *Several more people than usual came to the lunchtime concert.* **(b)** (*pron*): *If you're looking for a photograph of Alice you'll find several in here.* ○ *There was a fire in the art gallery and several of the paintings were destroyed.* ○ *Several of you need to work harder.*

▷ **severally** /ˈsevrəlɪ/ *adv* (*dated or fml*) separately: *They had all severally reached the same conclusion.*

severe /sɪˈvɪə(r)/ *adj* (-r, -st) **1** ~ **(on/with sb/sth)** strict or harsh in attitude or treatment; imposing stern discipline: *a severe look, punishment, measure* ○ *a severe critic of modern drama* ○ *be severe with one's children* ○ *Was the judge too severe on the thief?* **2** very bad, intense, difficult, etc: *a severe storm* ○ *severe pain, injuries, etc* ○ *a severe attack of toothache* ○ *The drought is becoming increasingly severe.* **3** demanding great skill, ability, patience, etc: *a severe test of climbers' stamina* ○ *severe competition for university places* ○ *The pace of the race was too severe to be maintained for long.* **4** (of style, appearance, clothing, etc) unadorned; simple: *Her plain black dress was too severe for such a cheerful occasion.*

▷ **severely** *adv*: *punish sb severely* ○ *severely handicapped* ○ *dress very severely.*

severity /sɪˈverətɪ/ *n* **1** [U] quality of being severe: *punish sb with severity* ○ *the severity* (ie extreme cold) *of the winter.* **2 severities** [pl] (*fml*) severe treatment or conditions: *the harsh severities of life in the desert.*

Seville orange /ˌsevɪl ˈɒrɪndʒ/ *n* type of bitter orange, used esp for making marmalade. It was named after Seville, a city in Spain.

sew

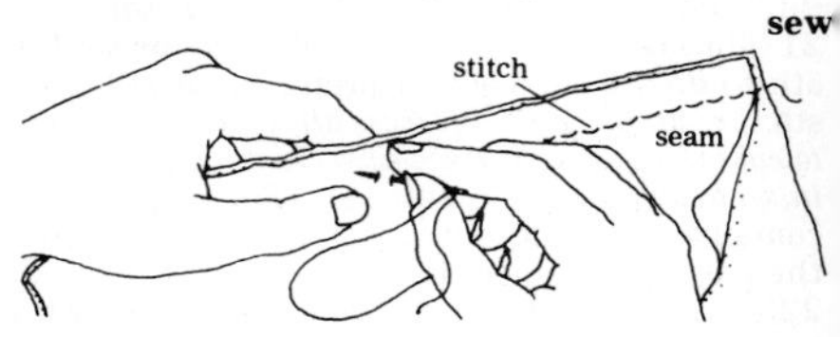

sew /səʊ/ *v* (*pt* **sewed**, *pp* **sewn** /səʊn/ or **sewed**) **1 (a)** [I, Ipr] make stitches in cloth, etc with a needle and thread: *sitting sewing by the fire* ○ *sew by hand/by machine* ○ *sew round the hem* ○ *sew over the seam again.* **(b)** [Tn, Tn·pr, Tn·p] make or attach or fasten (sth) by stitching: *sew a dress, skirt, etc* ○ *a hand-sewn shirt* ○ *sew a button onto the shirt* ○ *sew the parts of the shirt together* ○ *sew the flap of the pocket down.* **2** (phr v) **sew sth in/into sth** enclose sth by sewing: *sew money into the lining of a coat.* **sew sth up (a)** join or mend sth by sewing: *sew up a hole in a sock* ○ *The suit was sewn up along the seams by hand.* **(b)** (esp passive) (*infml*) arrange sth; settle sth: *sew up a deal, project, etc* ○ *By the end of the meeting everything should be nicely sewn up.* **(c)** (*infml esp US*) gain complete control of sth.

▷ **sewer** /ˈsəʊə(r)/ *n*.

sewing *n* [U] **1** activity of sewing. **2** work (clothes, etc) that is being sewn: *Where is my sewing?* ○ *I've got a pile of sewing to do.* ○ *a sewing table, basket, etc.* **ˈsewing-machine** *n* machine for sewing.

sewage /ˈsuːɪdʒ *or, in British use*, ˈsjuː-/ *n* [U] waste matter from human bodies, factories, towns, etc that flows away in sewers (SEWER[1]): *chemical treatment of sewage* ○ [attrib] *sewage disposal.*

□ **ˈsewage farm** place where sewage is treated, esp for use as manure.

ˈsewage works place where sewage is purified so that it can be allowed to flow away safely into a river, etc.

sewer[1] /ˈsuːə(r) *or, in British use*, ˈsjuː-/ *n* underground pipe or passage that carries sewage away to be treated or purified.

▷ **sewerage** /-ɪdʒ/ *n* [U] system of sewers; drainage.

sewer[2] ➪ SEW.

sewn *pp* of SEW.

sex /seks/ *n* **1 (a)** [U] condition of being male or female; gender: *differences of sex* ○ *What sex is your dog?* ○ *Everyone is welcome, regardless of age or sex.* ○ [attrib] *sex discrimination*, ie treating sb differently because of his/her sex. **(b)** [C] either of the two main groups (*male* and *female*) into which living things are placed according to their functions in the process of reproduction (REPRODUCE 4): *Is this behaviour typical of the male sex?* ○ *There has always been some conflict between the sexes.* **2** [U] ~ **(with sb)** sexual intercourse: *have sex (with sb)* ○ *They often had sex together.* ○ [attrib] *sex organs*, ie penis, vagina, etc. **3** [U] activities that lead to and include sexual intercourse; mutual physical attraction between people: *a film with lots of sex in it* ○ *During puberty, young people become more interested in sex.* ○ [attrib] *a sex manual*, ie giving information on sexual behaviour ○ *a sex shop*, ie selling pornography, devices to make sex more enjoyable, etc. **4** (idm) **the weaker sex** ⇨ WEAK.

▷ **sex** *v* [Tn] find out the sex(1) of (a creature): *sexing very young chicks.*

-sexed (forming compound *adjs*) having the specified amount of sexual desire: *a highly-sexed youth* ○ *over-sexed.* ie too interested in sexual matters.

sexless *adj* **1** lacking sexual desire, attractiveness or activity: *a dry, sexless person* ○ *a sexless relationship.* **2** neither male nor female; having neither masculine nor feminine characteristics; neuter.

sexy *adj* (**-ier, -iest**) (*infml*) **1** of or about sex(2, 3): *a sexy book, film, etc* ○ *making sexy suggestions.* **2** (**a**) causing sexual desire: *You look very sexy in that dress.* (**b**) feeling sexual desire: *get/feel sexy.* **sexily** *adv.* **sexiness** *n* [U].

□ **ˈsex act** sexual intercourse.

ˈsex appeal sexual attractiveness: *a man with lots of sex appeal.*

ˈsex change change from being male to being female, or from being female to being male, esp by means of a surgical operation: [attrib] *have a sex-change operation.*

ˈsex chromosome chromosome that determines which sex an individual person or animal will be.

ˈsex life person's sexual activities: *How's your sex life?*

ˈsex linkage condition in which a particular bodily condition (eg colour-blindness) is determined by a gene on a sex chromosome, and so is much commoner in one sex than in the other.

ˈsex-linked *adj* characterized by sex linkage.

ˈsex maniac (*infml often joc*) person who is obsessed with sex and constantly seeks sexual activity.

ˈsex object person regarded only as a source of sexual pleasure.

ˈsex-starved *adj* (*infml*) not having enough opportunities for sexual intercourse.

ˈsex symbol beautiful or glamorous person who is widely regarded as symbolizing sexual attractiveness.

sex- *comb form* six: *sexcentenary*, ie 600th anniversary.

sexagenarian /ˌseksədʒɪˈneərɪən/ *n, adj* [attrib] (*fml*) (person who is) of any age from 60 to 69.

Sexagesima /ˌseksəˈdʒesɪmə/ *n* (in the Christian Church) second Sunday before *Lent.

sexism /ˈseksɪzəm/ *n* [U] (*derog*) prejudice or discrimination against people (esp women) because of their sex: *blatant sexism in the selection of staff.*

▷ **sexist** /ˈseksɪst/ *adj* (*derog*) of or showing sexism: *a sexist person, attitude, remark, book* ○ *It is sexist to say that women are less intelligent than men.* — *n* (*derog*) person who shows sexism or has a sexist attitude.

sexology /sekˈsɒlədʒɪ/ *n* [U] scientific study of human sexual behaviour.

▷ **sexologist** /sekˈsɒlədʒɪst/ *n* expert in sexology.

sext /sekst/ *n* [U] sixth daytime hour of prayer in the Roman Catholic Church, traditionally at 12 noon.

sextant /ˈsekstənt/ *n* instrument used for measuring the altitude of the sun, eg in order to determine the position of one's ship.

sextet (also **sextette**) /seksˈtet/ *n* (piece of music for a) group of six singers or players.

sexton /ˈsekstən/ *n* person who takes care of a church and its churchyard, rings the church bell, etc.

sextuple /ˈsekstjʊpl/ *adj* [attrib] **1** consisting of six parts, individuals or groups. **2** six times as many or as much.

sextuplet /ˈsekstju:plet; *US* sekˈstu:p-/ *n* any of six children born to the same mother at the same time.

sexual /ˈsekʃʊəl/ *adj* **1** (**a**) of sex(2, 3) or the sexes or the physical attraction between them: *sexual feelings, activity, desire* ○ *Her interest in him is primarily sexual.* (**b**) of sex(1) or gender: *sexual differences, characteristics, etc.* **2** [attrib] concerned with the reproduction of offspring: *sexual organs*, ie penis, vagina, etc ○ *sexual reproduction in plants.*

▷ **sexuality** /ˌsekʃʊˈælətɪ/ *n* [U] sexual nature or characteristics.

sexually /-əlɪ/ *adv*: *sexually active* ○ *a sexually transmitted disease.*

□ **sexual ˈintercourse** (also **intercourse**) insertion of a man's penis into a woman's vagina, usu leading to the ejaculation of semen; copulation.

Seychelles /seɪˈʃelz/ **the Seychelles** country in the Indian Ocean consisting of about 115 islands; pop approx 68 000; official languages English and French; capital Victoria; unit of currency rupee (= 100 cents). A British colony since the early 19th century, it became an independent republic in 1976. Tourism is its main source of income, and copra and cinnamon are also exported.

Seymour /ˈsi:mɔ:(r)/ Jane (c 1509-37), third wife of *Henry VIII and mother of *Edward VI. She gave Henry the male heir he wanted, but she died soon afterwards.

SF /ˌes ˈef/ *abbr* (*infml*) science fiction.

sforzando /sfɔ:tˈsændəʊ/ *adj, adv* (*music*) (played) with sudden force.

sgd *abbr* signed (on a form, etc).

Sgt *abbr* = SERGT.

sh /ʃ/ *interj* be quiet!; be silent!: *Sh! You'll wake the baby!*

shabby /ˈʃæbɪ/ *adj* (**-ier, -iest**) **1** (**a**) (of things) in poor condition through much use or being badly cared for: *a shabby dress, chair, room* ○ *a tramp in shabby old clothes.* (**b**) (of people) poorly dressed: *You look rather shabby in those clothes.* **2** (*fig*) (of behaviour) mean and unfair; dishonourable: *a shabby excuse* ○ *play a shabby trick on sb.* ▷ **shabbily** /ˈʃæbɪlɪ/ *adv*: *I think you have been shabbily treated.* **shabbiness** *n* [U].

shack /ʃæk/ *n* roughly built shed, hut or house.

▷ **shack** *v* (phr v) **shack up (with sb/together)** (*Brit sl*) (esp of a couple) live together although not married: *They've decided to shack up together in her flat.*

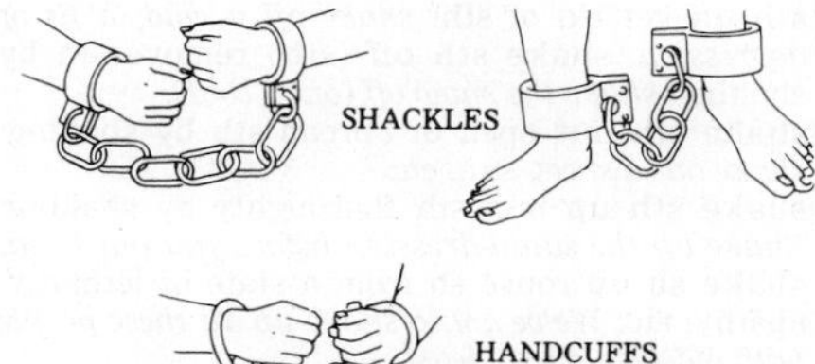

shackle /ˈʃækl/ *n* **1** [C usu *pl*] either of a pair of metal rings linked by a chain, used for fastening a prisoner's wrists or ankles together. **2 shackles** [pl] **the ~s of sth** (*fig*) conditions, circumstances, etc that prevent one from acting or speaking freely: *the shackles of convention.*

▷ **shackle** *v* **1** [Tn] put shackles on (sb). **2** [Tn esp passive] (*fig*) prevent (sb) from acting or speaking freely: *shackled by outdated attitudes.*

Shackleton /ˈʃækltən/ Sir Ernest Henry (1874-1922), Irish polar explorer. He was a member of *Scott's first South Pole expedition 1900-04, and later led expeditions there himself, in 1909, 1914-16 and 1920-22.

shad /ʃæd/ *n* (*pl* unchanged) large edible fish of the N Atlantic coast of N America.

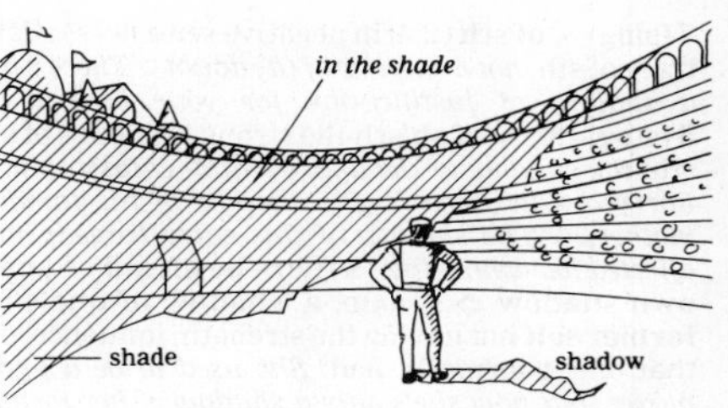

shade /ʃeɪd/ *n* **1** [U] ~ **(from sth)** (place where there is) comparative darkness and often coolness caused by sth blocking direct light or heat, esp of the sun: *a temperature of 35°C in the shade* ○ *sit in the shade of a tree, wall, etc* ○ *Stay in the shade — it's cooler.* ○ *The trees give some welcome shade from the sun.* **2** [C] (often in compounds) thing that shuts out light or makes it less bright: *an ˈeye-shade* ○ *a new shade for the ˈlamp/ˈlampshade.* **3 shades** [pl] **the ~s of sth** (*fml*) the darkness of sth: *the shades of evening/night.* **4 shades** [pl] (*infml esp US*) sun-glasses. **5** [U] darker part(s) of a picture, etc: *There is not enough light and shade in your drawing.* **6** [C] (degree or depth of) colour; hue: *material in several shades of blue* ○ *choose a lighter shade* ○ *Do you like the blouse in this shade?* **7** (**a**) [C] ~ **of sth** slight difference in sth: *a word with many shades of meaning* ○ *people with all shades of opinion.* (**b**) [sing] **a ~ (better, worse, etc)** a small amount: *I think it's a shade warmer today.* ○ *She feels a shade better than yesterday.* **8 shades** [pl] **~s of sb/sth** (*infml*) reminders of sb/sth: *'Shades of Hitler!' I thought, as I listened to the dictator haranguing the crowd.* ○ *In some modern fashions we can see shades of the 1930s.* **9** [C] (*fml*) soul after death; ghost: *the shades of my dead ancestors.* **10** (idm) **put sb/sth in the ˈshade** be very superior to sb/sth: *I thought I was quite a good artist, but your painting puts mine in the shade.*

▷ **shade** *v* **1** [Tn, Tn·pr] ~ **sb/sth (from sth)** block off light from sb/sth; give shade to sb/sth: *She shaded her eyes (from the sun) with her hand.* **2** [Tn] screen (a lamp, light, etc) to reduce its brightness: *shade the bulb with a dark cloth.* **3** [Tn, Tn·p] ~ **sth (in)** darken (a part of a drawing, etc), eg with parallel pencil lines, to give an effect of light and shade: *shade (in) this area to represent the person's shadow* ○ *the shaded areas on the map.* **4** [Ipr, Ip] ~ **from sth into sth**; ~ **(off) into sth** (esp of colours) change gradually into (another colour or variety): *scarlet shading (off) into pink* ○ *a colour that shades from blue into green* ○ (*fig*) *socialism shading into communism.* **5** (*esp finance*) (**a**) [I, Ipr, Ip] ~ **(into sth)**; ~ **(away/off)** (of a price, value, etc) be reduced slightly: *Associated Goldfields stock shaded off in weak trading.* (**b**) [Tn, Tn·pr, Tn·p] ~ **sth (into sth)**; ~ **sth (away/off)** reduce (a price, value, etc) slightly. **shading** *n* [U] (use of) pencil marks, etc that give an effect of darkness in a part of a picture.

shadoof /ʃəˈdu:f/ *n* pivoted pole with a bucket on one end, used in Egypt and other Middle Eastern countries for getting water from a well.

shadow /ˈʃædəʊ/ *n* **1** [C, U] (patch of) shade caused by an object blocking direct rays of light: *The chair casts a shadow on the wall.* ○ *Shadows are longer when the sun is low in the sky.* ○ *Her face was in deep shadow.* ○ (*fig*) *The bad news cast a shadow on/over our meeting*, ie made us sad. ⇨ illus at SHADE. **2** [C] dark patch or area: *have shadows under/round the eyes*, eg because of illness or lack of sleep. **3** [U] shaded part of a picture: *areas of light and shadow* ○ *The light from one side leaves half the subject's face in shadow.* **4 shadows** [pl] partial darkness: *a figure standing in the shadows* ○ *the shadows of evening.* **5** [C] (**a**) person's constant attendant or companion: *The dog is his master's shadow.* (**b**) person who secretly follows and watches sb, eg a criminal: *The police put a shadow on the suspected robber.* **6** [C] thing that is weak or unreal: *catch at shadows*, ie try to obtain sth that does not exist ○ *You can't spend your life chasing after shadows.*

7 [sing] ~ **of sth** (usu in negative sentences) slight trace of sth: *not a shadow of (a) doubt* ○ *There's not a shadow of justification for your behaviour.* **8** [sing] **the** ~ **of sb/sth** the strong influence of sb/sth: *the shadow of the approaching catastrophe* ○ *For years he lived in the shadow of his famous mother.* ○ *The shadow of this early tragedy has affected her whole life.* **9** (idm) **be afraid of one's own shadow** ⇨ AFRAID. **a ˈshadow of one's/its former self** not having the strength, influence, etc that one/it formerly had: *She used to be a great player, but now she's only a shadow of her former self.*

▷ **shadow** *v* [Tn] **1** cast a shadow on (sb/sth): *The wide brim of his hat shadowed his face.* **2** follow and watch (sb) secretly: *A policeman in plain clothes shadowed the criminal all day.*

shadow *adj* [attrib] (*Brit politics*) denoting leading members of the Opposition party who would probably be Cabinet ministers if their party became the Government, and who act as spokesmen on matters for which they would then be responsible: *the Shadow Cabinet* ○ *the Shadow Foreign Secretary.* ⇨ articles at PARLIAMENT, POLITICS.

shadowy *adj* **1** full of shadows or shade: *the shadowy interior of the barn* ○ *cool, shadowy woods.* **2** (*fig*) like a shadow; indistinct: *a shadowy figure glimpsed in the twilight.*

□ **ˈshadow-box** *v* [I] box with an imaginary opponent: *shadow-boxing alone in the ring.* **ˈshadow-boxing** *n* [U].

shady /ˈʃeɪdɪ/ *adj* (**-ier, -iest**) **1** giving shade from sunlight; situated in the shade: *a shady orchard* ○ *a shady corner of the garden.* **2** (*infml derog*) not entirely honest; disreputable: *a shady business, deal, organization* ○ *a shady-looking person.* ▷ **shadily** /-ɪlɪ/ *adv.* **shadiness** *n* [U].

shaft /ʃɑːft; *US* ʃæft/ *n* **1** [C] (**a**) long slender stem of an arrow or a spear. (**b**) [C] (*arch*) arrow; spear. **2** [C] ~ (**of sth**) (*fig*) remark intended to wound or stimulate: *shafts of malice* ○ *her brilliant shafts of wit.* **3** [C] long handle of an axe or other tool, or eg of a golf-club. **4** [C] either of the two bars or poles between which a horse is harnessed to pull a cart, etc. **5** [C] main part of a column, between the base and the capital. ⇨ illus at COLUMN. **6** [C] (often in compounds) bar or rod joining parts of a machine or transmitting power in a machine: *a ˈcrankshaft* ○ *a ˈdrive-shaft.* **7** [C] (often in compounds) long narrow (usu vertical) space, eg for a lift to move up and down in, for entry into a mine, or for ventilation: *a ˈlift-shaft* ○ *a ˈmine-shaft* ○ *sink a shaft.* Cf GALLERY 6. **8 the shaft** [sing] (*US infml*) unfair treatment; trickery: *give sb/get the shaft* ○ *We were given the shaft, and lost a lot of money.* **9** [C] ~ (**of sth**) long thin beam (of light, etc): *a shaft of light/sunlight/moonlight/lightning.*

▷ **shaft** *v* [Tn] (*US infml*) treat (sb) unfairly or harshly; cheat.

Shaftesbury /ˈʃɑːftsbrɪ; *US* -berɪ/ Anthony Ashley Cooper, 7th Earl (1801-85), British politician and social reformer who campaigned to improve the living and working conditions of the large working class created by the *Industrial Revolution. He supported laws limiting working hours, and introduced the law forbidding women and children to work in mines.

shag[1] /ʃæg/ *n* [U] strong coarse type of cut tobacco.

shag[2] /ʃæg/ *v* [I, Tn] (⚠ *Brit sl*) have sexual intercourse with (sb).

shag[3] /ʃæg/ *n* large black sea-bird, a type of cormorant.

shagged /ʃægd/ *adj* [pred] (also **shagged ˈout**) (*Brit sl*) very tired.

shaggy /ˈʃægɪ/ *adj* (**-ier, -iest**) **1** rough, thick and untidy: *shaggy hair, eyebrows* ○ *a shaggy beard.* **2** covered with rough untidy hair or fibres, etc: *a shaggy dog, mat, coat.* ▷ **shaggily** /-ɪlɪ/ *adv.* **shagginess** *n* [U].

□ **ˌshaggy-ˈdog story** long rambling joke, often with a pointless and not very funny ending.

shah /ʃɑː/ *n* (title of a) former ruler of Iran.

shake[1] /ʃeɪk/ *v* (*pt* **shook** /ʃʊk/, *pp* **shaken** /ˈʃeɪkən/) **1** (**a**) [La, I, Tn, Tn·p, Cn·a] ~ **sb/sth** (**about/around**) (cause sb/sth to) move quickly and often jerkily from side to side or up and down: *a bolt shaking loose in an engine* ○ *The earth shook under us*, eg in an earthquake. ○ *The table shook when she banged her fist on it.* ○ *Shake the bottle before taking the medicine.* ○ *He shook the carpet to get rid of the dust.* ○ *He shook her violently as a dog shakes a rat.* ○ *Great sobs shook his whole body.* ○ *The bumpy car ride shook us around a bit.* ○ *Vibrations shook the panel loose.* (**b**) [I, Ipr] ~ (**with sth**) (of a person) tremble; quiver: *laughed until their sides shook* ○ *shaking with laughter, fear, rage, etc* ○ *shaking with cold.* **2** (**a**) [Tn, Tn·p] ~ **sb** (**up**) disturb the calmness of sb; trouble or shock sb: *shaken by the news of her death* ○ *They were badly shaken (up) in the accident.* ○ *This surprising development quite shook me.* (**b**) [Tn] make (sth) less certain; weaken: *shake sb's faith, courage, belief, etc* ○ *Her theory has been shaken by this new evidence.* **3** [I, Ipr] ~ (**with sth**) (of sb's voice) become weak or faltering; tremble: *His voice shook (with emotion) as he announced the news.* **4** [I, Ipr] ~ (**on sth**) (*infml*) shake hands: *We're agreed, so let's shake (on it).* **5** (idm) **shake the dust (of ...) off one's feet** leave a place one does not like, hoping not to return: *After a year of misery here, I'm finally shaking the dust of this town off my feet.* **shake one's ˈfist (at sb)** show that one is angry with sb or threaten sb by shaking one's fist. **shake sb's ˈhand/shake ˈhands (with sb)/shake sb by the ˈhand** grasp sb's hand and move it up and down as a greeting, or to express agreement, etc. **shake one's ˈhead** turn one's head from side to side as a way of indicating 'no', or to express doubt, sorrow, disapproval, etc. **shake in one's ˈshoes** (*infml*) be very frightened: *He was shaking in his shoes at the thought of flying for the first time.* **shake a ˈleg** (*dated Brit sl*) (esp imperative) get moving; start to act; hurry: *Come on, shake a leg, we're late already.* **shake like a leaf** tremble with fear, nervousness, etc.

6 (phr v) **shake down** (**a**) settle down and function properly: *The new office staff are shaking down well.* (**b**) sleep somewhere where there is no proper bed: *You can shake down on the floor.* **shake sb down** (*US infml*) get money from sb by threats, violence, etc. **shake sb/sth down** (*US infml*) search sb/sth thoroughly: *Police shook the club down, looking for narcotics.*

shake sth from, into, onto, out of, etc sth move sth in the specified direction by shaking: *shake scouring powder into the bath* ○ *shake salt from the salt-cellar onto one's food* ○ *shake sand out of one's shoes.*

shake sb off rid oneself of (sb unwanted); escape from sb: *shake off one's pursuers* ○ *She tried to shake him off but he continued to pester her.* **shake sth off** get rid of sth: *shake off a cold, a fit of depression.* **shake sth off (sth)** remove sth by shaking: *shake the snow off (one's coat).*

shake sth out open or spread sth by shaking: *shake out a sheet, sail, etc.*

shake sth up mix sth thoroughly by shaking: *Shake up the salad-dressing before you put it on.* **shake sb up** rouse sb from a state of lethargy, apathy, etc: *We've got to shake up all these people with old-fashioned ideas.*

▷ **shaker** *n* **1** (often in compounds) container in which or from which sth is shaken: *a ˈcocktail-shaker* ○ *a ˈdice-shaker.* **2 Shaker** member of an 18th-century American religious sect, the United Society of Believers in Christ's Second Coming, who lived a simple life in communities in which people did not marry or have sex. Their name comes from the violent movements in their religious dances.

shaking *n* [sing] act of shaking: *give sth a good shaking*, ie shake it well.

□ **ˈshakedown** *n* **1** improvised bed: *a shakedown on the floor.* **2** (*US infml*) act of getting money by violence, threats, etc. **3** (*US infml*) thorough search: *a shakedown of drug dealers.* **4** final test, eg of a ship, aircraft, etc: [attrib] *a shakedown voyage, flight, trial, etc.*

ˈshake-up (also **ˈshake-out**) *n* major reform or reorganization: *The only thing that will save the company is a thorough shake-up of the way it is run.*

shake[2] /ʃeɪk/ *n* **1** [C usu *sing*] act of shaking or being shaken: *a shake of the head*, ie indicating 'no' ○ *I gave my purse a shake, and a coin fell out.* **2 the shakes** [sing *v*] (*infml*) fit of trembling or shivering: *a high temperature and a fit of the shakes.* **3** (idm) **a fair shake** ⇨ FAIR[1]. **in a couple of ˈshakes/in two ˈshakes (of a lamb's tail)** (*infml*) in a moment; very soon: *Hang on! I'll be back in two shakes!* **no great shakes** ⇨ GREAT.

William Shakespeare

Shakespeare /ˈʃeɪkspɪə(r)/ William (1564-1616), English playwright and poet. He was born in Stratford-upon-Avon, the son of a merchant, and was probably educated at the local grammar school. He married Anne *Hathaway, but left her behind in Stratford when he went to London in the mid 1580s to work as an actor and playwright. Not many details are known about his life, but his plays have made him the world's most famous dramatist, both for the beauty of their language and for their insights into the human condition. They include tragedies (eg *Hamlet, King Lear, Macbeth, Othello*), comedies (eg *As You Like It, Love's Labour's Lost, Twelfth Night*) and plays about English history (eg *Henry V, Richard III*). He also wrote many well-known sonnets. ⇨ illus. ⇨ App 6.

▷ **Shakespearian** (also **Shakespearean**) /ʃeɪkˈspɪərɪən/ *adj* (in the style) of Shakespeare: *Shakespearean sonnets* ○ *Shakespearian quotations* ○ *a Shakespearian actor.*

shako /ˈʃækəʊ, ˈʃeɪkəʊ/ *n* (*pl* ~**s**) round military cap with a plume of feathers sticking up from it.

shaky /ˈʃeɪkɪ/ *adj* (**-ier, -iest**) **1** shaking or trembling through weakness, illness, etc: *a shaky walk, voice* ○ *Her hands are shaky because she's nervous.* ○ *He looks a bit shaky on his feet.* **2** not firm and steady; not safe and reliable: *a shaky chair, table, wall* ○ *The tripod is too shaky.* ○ (*fig*) *a shaky argument* ○ *The government is looking very shaky at the moment.* ○ *My French is a bit shaky*, ie I don't speak it very well. ▷ **shakily** /-ɪlɪ/ *adv.* **shakiness** *n* [U].

shale /ʃeɪl/ *n* [U] type of soft rock that splits easily into thin flat pieces. ▷ **shaly** *adj.*

□ **ˈshale-oil** *n* [U] oil extracted from shale.

shall /ʃəl; *strong form* ʃæl/ *modal v* (*esp Brit*) (*neg* **shall not**, *contracted form* **shan't** /ʃɑːnt/; *pt* **should** /ʃʊd/, *neg* **should not**, *contracted form* **shouldn't** /ˈʃʊdnt/) **1** (indicating future predictions): *We shan't know the results until next week.* ○ *Shall we be there in time for tea?* ○ *This time next week I shall be sitting on a beach in Greece.* ○ *I said I should be glad to help.* ⇨ Usage 1. **2** (*fml*) (indicating will or determination): *I shall write to you again at the end of the month.* ○ *You shall have* *a new dress for your birthday.* ○ *He insisted that the papers should be destroyed.* ○ *She was determined that we should finish on time.* **3** (indicating offers or suggestions): *Shall I* (ie Would you like me to) *do the washing-up?* ○ *What shall we do this weekend?* ○ *Let's look at it again, shall we?* ⇨ Usage 3. **4** (*fml*) (indicating orders or instructions): *Candidates shall remain in their seats until all the papers have been collected.* ○ *The lease stated that tenants should maintain the property in good condition.*

NOTE ON USAGE: **1** PREDICTIONS (**shall**, **will**[1]) (**a**) **Shall** is used with *I* or *we* to predict a future event: *I shall be in touch with you again shortly.* **Will** (when speaking usu contracted to **'ll**) is used with *you, he, she, it, they* as well as *I* and *we*, often in more informal contexts than **shall**: *She'll never finish in time.* ○ *It'll be our first holiday for years.* (**b**) In indirect speech, **should** and **would** (when speaking usu contracted to **'d**) are used: *I estimated that I should finish in ten days.* ○ *Bill said he'd soon be back.* **2** VOLITION (**shall, will**[1]) (**a**) Both **shall** and **will** can express determination. **Shall** is more formal, especially when used with pronouns other than **I** or **we**: *He shall be given a fair trial.* ○ *You'll have your radio back on Tuesday.* ○ *We ˈwill get the thing right!* (**b**) **Should** and **would** are used in clauses after *be certain, be determined, insist*, etc: *He insisted that we should make a fresh start.* **3** SUGGESTIONS (**shall, can**[2], **could**[1]) (**a**) **Shall I** and **shall we** are used to make suggestions: *Shall I drive?* ○ *Shall we take our swim-suits?* **Can** (often with *of course* and/or *always*) is also used for this purpose: *We can always come back tomorrow if you prefer.* **Could** is used to make more tentative suggestions: *You could try pushing the car.* ○ *Couldn't we ask a policeman?* (**b**) Any of these verbs can be used to ask for suggestions: *Where shall we go now?* ○ *Can we perhaps try another route?* ○ *How could we make them listen?*

shallot /ʃəˈlɒt/ *n* type of onion that grows as a cluster of small bulbs.

shallow /ˈʃæləʊ/ *adj* (**-er, -est**) **1** not deep: *shallow water* ○ *a shallow saucer, dish, bowl, etc* ○ *the shallow end*, eg of a swimming-pool ○ *shallow breathing.* **2** (*derog*) (of a person) not thinking or capable of thinking seriously; (of ideas, remarks, etc) not showing serious thought: *a shallow writer, argument, conversation, book.* Cf DEEP[1].
▷ **shallow** *v* [I] become shallow.
shallowly *adv.*
shallowness *n* [U].
shallows *n* [pl] shallow place in a river or in the sea.

shalom /ʃəˈlɒm/ *n, interj* (used esp among Jews as a greeting or when saying goodbye).

sham /ʃæm/ *v* (**-mm-**) [I, Tn] pretend (sth); feign: *He's only shamming.* ○ *sham illness, death, sleep* ○ *sham dead*, ie pretend to be dead.
▷ **sham** *n* (*usu derog*) **1** [C] (**a**) person who pretends to be what he is not: *She claims to know all about computers but really she's a sham.* (**b**) (usu *sing*) thing, feeling, etc that is not what sb pretends that it is: *His love was a sham; he only wanted her money.* ○ *Their marriage had become a complete sham.* **2** [U] pretence: *What he says is all sham.*
sham *adj* [attrib] (*usu derog*) pretended; not genuine: *sham piety, sympathy, anger, etc* ○ *sham jewellery.*

shaman /ˈʃæmən, ˈʃɑːmən; *US* ˈʃeɪmən/ *n* (*pl* ~**s**) priest believed to have magic powers (eg for curing illness, seeing into the future, etc).

shamble /ˈʃæmbl/ *v* [I, Ipr, Ip] walk or run awkwardly, without raising one's feet properly: *a shambling gait* ○ *The old tramp shambled up to me.* ○ *The hungry marchers shambled slowly along (the road).* ⇨ Usage at SHUFFLE.
▷ **shamble** *n* [sing] shambling walk.

shambles /ˈʃæmblz/ *n* [sing *v*] (*infml*) scene of complete disorder; muddle; mess: *Your room is (in) a shambles. Tidy it up!*

shambolic /ʃæmˈbɒlɪk/ *adj* (*Brit infml joc*) disorganized; chaotic.

shame /ʃeɪm/ *n* **1** [U] painful feeling caused by wrong, dishonourable, improper or ridiculous behaviour (by oneself, one's family, etc): *feel shame at having told a lie* ○ *hang one's head in shame* ○ *To my shame* (ie I feel shame that) *I never thanked him for his kindness.* **2** [U] ability to feel shame: *How could you do such a thing? Have you no shame?* ○ *She is completely without shame.* **3** [U] dishonour: *bring shame on sb/oneself*, eg by doing sth wrong or unworthy ○ *How can we make people forget the family's shame?* **4 a shame** [sing] (*derog infml*) (**a**) person or thing that causes shame or is unworthy: *It's a shame to take money from those who can't afford it.* (**b**) thing that is regrettable; a pity: *What a shame you didn't win.* ○ *Isn't it a shame that the rain spoiled our picnic?* **5** (idm) **put sb/sth to ˈshame** be greatly superior to sb/sth: *Your beautiful handwriting puts my untidy scrawl to shame.* **ˈshame on you** you should feel shame (about what you have done or said): *How could you treat her so badly? Shame on you!*
▷ **shame** *v* **1** [Tn] (**a**) cause (sb) to feel shame(1): *He was shamed by how much more work the others had done.* (**b**) bring shame(3) upon (sb); dishonour: *You've shamed your family.* ○ *It's quite shaming that our society cares so little for the poor.* **2** (phr v) **shame sb into/out of doing sth** cause sb to do/not to do sth by making him feel shame: *shame sb into apologizing.*
shameful /-fl/ *adj* causing shame; disgraceful: *shameful conduct, deceit, etc.* **shamefully** /-fəlɪ/ *adv.* **shamefulness** *n* [U].
shameless *adj* (*derog*) having or showing no feeling of shame; immodest or impudent: *a shameless hussy* ○ *a shameless cheat, liar, etc* ○ *She's quite shameless about wearing sexy clothes at work.* **shamelessly** *adv.* **shamelessness** *n* [U].
□ **shamefaced** /ˌʃeɪmˈfeɪst/ *adj* showing feelings of shame: *a ˌshame-faced exˈpression, aˈpology, ˈculprit.* **shamefacedly** /-ˈfeɪstlɪ/ *adv.*

shammy /ˈʃæmɪ/ *n* [U, C] (also **shammy leather**) (*infml*) = CHAMOIS-LEATHER (CHAMOIS).

shampoo /ʃæmˈpuː/ *n* (*pl* ~**s**) **1** [C, U] (**a**) (type of) soapy liquid, cream, etc for washing the hair: *a new perfumed shampoo* ○ *Don't use too much shampoo.* ○ *dry shampoo*, ie a powder brushed into the hair to clean it without wetting it. (**b**) (type of) liquid or chemical for cleaning carpets, upholstery, etc or for washing a car. **2** [C] (**a**) act of washing the hair: *give sb a shampoo* ○ *a shampoo and set.* (**b**) act of cleaning a carpet, etc.
▷ **shampoo** *v* (*pt, pp* **-pooed**, *pres p* **-pooing**) [Tn] wash (hair, carpets, upholstery, etc).

shamrock /ˈʃæmrɒk/ *n* [C, U] clover-like plant with three leaves on each stem, the national emblem of Ireland: *wearing some shamrock on his lapel.*

shandy /ˈʃændɪ/ *n* (*Brit*) (**a**) [U] drink made by mixing beer with ginger-beer or lemonade. (**b**) [C] glass of this: *Two lemonade shandies, please.*

shanghai /ʃæŋˈhaɪ/ *v* (*pt, pp* **-haied** /-ˈhaɪd/, *pres p* **-haiing** /-ˈhaɪɪŋ/) **1** [Tn, Tn·pr] ~ **sb (into doing sth)** (*infml*) trick or force sb into doing sth: *tourists shanghaied into buying expensive fakes.* **2** [Tn] (*sl*) (formerly) make (a man) unconscious with drink or drugs and take him away to be a sailor.

Shangri La /ˌʃæŋgrɪ ˈlɑː/ *n* imaginary place where everything is perfect and everyone is happy. The term comes from the name of an imaginary place in Tibet described in James Hilton's novel *Lost Horizon* (1933).

shank /ʃæŋk/ *n* **1** straight slender part of an implement, etc; shaft: *the shank of an anchor, a key, a golf-club.* **2** (usu *pl*) (*often joc or derog*) leg, esp the part between the knee and the ankle: *long thin shanks.* **3** part of an object used for attaching it to another object, eg a solid ring on a button. **4 the** ~ **of sth** [sing] (*US*) remainder or later part of (a period of time): *We spent the shank of the evening together.* **5** (idm) **on Shanks's ˈpony/ˈmare** (*dated infml joc*) on foot (not by car, etc): *If you won't drive me, I'll have to get there on Shanks's pony.*

Shankar /ˈʃæŋkə(r)/ Ravi (1920-), Indian sitar player and composer. He is one of the great modern virtuoso improvisers on the instrument and has done much to make Indian music appreciated in the West.

shan't *contracted form of* SHALL NOT (SHALL).

shantung /ʃænˈtʌŋ/ *n* [U] type of heavy silk material, usu undyed.

shanty[1] /ˈʃæntɪ/ *n* poorly-built hut, shed or cabin; shack.
□ **ˈshanty town** area inside or just outside a town, where poor people live in shanties.

shanty[2] (*US* **chantey, chanty**) /ˈʃæntɪ/ *n* (also **ˈsea-shanty**) song formerly sung by sailors while hauling ropes, etc.

SHAPE (also **Shape**) /ʃeɪp/ *abbr* Supreme Headquarters of Allied Powers in Europe.

shape[1] /ʃeɪp/ *n* **1** [C, U] outer form or appearance; outline of an area, a figure, etc: *clouds of different shapes in the sky* ○ *a garden in the shape of a semicircle* ○ *trees in all shapes and sizes* ○ *the odd shape of his nose* ○ *a dress that hasn't got much shape* ○ *The picture is round in shape.* ○ (*fig*) *He's a devil in human shape.* **2** [C] thing that is difficult to see properly; vague form: *I made out two dim shapes in the gloom.* ○ *A huge shape loomed up out of the fog.* **3** [U] (*infml*) condition; state: *She's in good shape* (ie fit) *after months of training.* ○ *What shape is the team in after its defeat?* ○ *The illness has left him in rather poor shape.* **4** (**a**) [C] mould, etc in which sth, eg jelly, is given a particular form. (**b**) [C, U] jelly, etc shaped in such a mould: *Have some more shape.* **5** (idm) **get (oneself) into ˈshape** take exercise, etc in order to become fit: *I've been jogging a lot to get myself into shape.* **get/knock/lick sth/sb into ˈshape** get sth/sb into an orderly state; arrange sth/sb properly: *We need a new manager to get the business into shape.* ○ *A sergeant soon knocks new recruits into shape.* **give shape to sth** express sth clearly: *I'm having trouble giving shape to my ideas in this essay.* **in ˈany shape (or form)** (*infml*) in whatever form sth appears or is presented: *I don't drink alcohol in any shape or form.* **in ˈshape** fit: *You'll never be in shape until you eat less and take more exercise.* **in the shape/form of sb/sth** (*infml*) appearing specifically as sb/sth: *Help arrived in the shape of our next-door neighbours.* ○ *I received a nasty surprise in the shape of a letter from the taxman.* **out of ˈshape** (**a**) not having the usual shape: *The children have been playing with my hat — they've knocked it out of shape.* (**b**) unfit: *Take exercise if you're out of shape.* **press sth into shape** ⇨ PRESS[2]. **the ˌshape of ˌthings to ˈcome** sign that shows how the future is likely to develop. **take ˈshape** take on a definite form; become more organized: *The plan is beginning to take shape in my mind.* ○ *After months of work, the new book is gradually taking shape.*
▷ **shapeless** *adj* having no definite shape; not elegant in shape: *The book is rather shapeless.* ○ *a shapeless mass, form, dress.* **shapelessly** *adv.* **shapelessness** *n* [U].

shape[2] /ʃeɪp/ *v* **1** [Tn, Tn·pr] ~ **sth (into sth)** give a shape or form to sth: *shape the wet clay on a potter's wheel* ○ *shape the sand into a mound.* **2** [Tn] have a great influence upon (sb/sth); determine the nature of (sth): *These events helped to shape her future career.* ○ *His attitudes were shaped partly by early experiences.* **3** [I, Ip] ~ **(up)** develop in a certain way: *Our plans are shaping (up) well*, ie giving signs that they will be successful. ○ *How is the new team shaping up?* **4** [Tn esp passive] make (a garment) conform to the shape of the body: *The jacket is shaped* (ie becomes narrower) *at the waist.*
▷ **-shaped** (in compounds) having the specified shape: *a ˌkidney-shaped ˈswimming-pool* ○ *His figure is somewhat ˈpear-shaped.* ○ *Rugby is played with an ˌegg-shaped ˈball.*

shapely /ˈʃeɪplɪ/ *adj* (**-ier, -iest**) (*approv*) (esp of a woman's body) having an attractive shape; well formed: *a shapely bosom* ○ *shapely legs.* ▷ **shapeliness** *n* [U].

shard /ʃɑːd/ (also **sherd** /ʃɜːd/) *n* broken piece of pottery, glass, etc. Cf POTSHERD.

share[1] /ʃeə(r)/ *n* **1** [C] ~ **(in/of sth)** part or portion of a larger amount which is divided among several or many people, or to which several or many people contribute: *a fair share of the food* ○ *the robber's share of the stolen money* ○ *Your share of the cost is £10.* ○ *Everyone who helped gets a share in the profits.* **2** [U, sing] ~ **(in/of sth)** person's part in sth done, received, etc by several people: *What share did he have in their success?* ○ *She must take her share of the blame,* ie accept that she was partly responsible. ○ *You're not taking much share in the conversation,* ie You're saying little. **3** [C] any of the equal parts into which the capital of a business company is divided, giving the holder a right to a portion of the profits: *stocks and shares* ○ *buy/hold 500 shares in a shipping company* ○ *£2 shares are now worth £2.75.* ○ [attrib] *share capital, dealing, prices* ○ *a share certificate,* ie showing how many shares an investor holds. **4** (idm) **get, etc a/one's fair share of sth** ⇨ FAIR[1]. **get, etc a slice/share of the cake** ⇨ CAKE. **go 'shares (with sb) (in sth)** (*Brit infml*) share (profits, costs, etc) equally with others: *Let me go shares with you in the taxi fare.* **the lion's share** ⇨ LION.

▷ **share** *v* **1** (a) [Tn·pr, Tn·p] ~ **sth (out) (among/between sb)** give a share of sth to others: *share £100 equally between five people,* ie by giving them £20 each ○ *share the sweets among the children* ○ *The profits are shared (out) equally among the partners.* (b) [I, Ipr, Tn, Tn·pr] ~ **(sth) (with sb)** have a share of (sth) with another or others: *Let's share (the last cake); you have half and I'll have half.* ○ *He would share his last pound with me.* **2** [I, Ipr, Tn, Tn·pr] ~ **(sth) (with sb)** have or use (sth) with others; have (sth) in common: *There's only one bedroom, so we'll have to share.* ○ *share a bed, room, house, etc* ○ *share sb's belief, faith, optimism, etc* ○ *He shares my fears about a possible war.* ○ *We both share the credit for* (ie were both responsible for) *this success.* ○ *Will you share your pen with me?* **3** [Ipr, Tn] ~ **(in) sth** have a share in sth; participate in sth: *I will share (in) the cost with you.* ○ *She shares (in) my troubles as well as my joys.* **4** [Tn, Tn·pr] ~ **sth (with sb)** tell sb about sth: *She won't share her secret (with us).* ○ *I want to share my news with you.* **5** (idm) **share and share a'like** (*saying*) share things equally: *Don't be so selfish — it's share and share alike in this house.*

□ **'share-cropper** *n* (*esp US*) tenant farmer who gives part of his crop as rent to the owner of the land.

'shareholder *n* owner of shares in a business company.

'share index number used to show the current value of shares on the stock market, based on the prices of a selected number of shares: *The Financial Times share index went up five points yesterday.*

'share-out *n* [sing] distribution: *After the robbery the crooks had a share-out (of the stolen money).*

share[2] /ʃeə(r)/ *n* = PLOUGHSHARE (PLOUGH).

shark

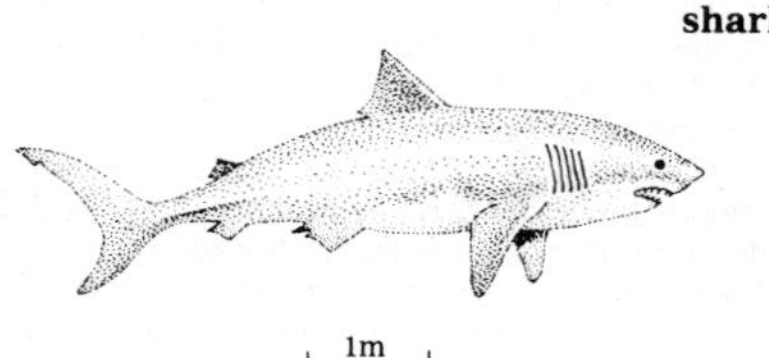

shark /ʃɑːk/ *n* **1** any of various types of sea-fish with a triangular fin on its back, some of which are large and dangerous to bathers. **2** (*infml derog*) person who extorts money from others or lends money at very high interest rates; swindler. **3** (*dated US infml*) person, esp a student, who is very good at his work.

□ **'shark-skin** *n* [U] textile fabric with a smooth, slightly shiny surface, used for outer clothing: [attrib] *a shark-skin jacket, suit, etc.*

Sharp /ʃɑːp/ Cecil (1859-1924), English folk-music specialist. At a time when folk traditions were dying out, he collected many hundreds of songs and dances and led the revival of interest in them.

sharp /ʃɑːp/ *adj* (**-er, -est**) **1** having a fine edge or point; capable of cutting or piercing; not blunt: *a sharp knife, pin, needle, etc* ○ *The shears aren't sharp enough to cut the grass.* **2** (a) (of curves, bends, slopes, etc) changing direction suddenly; abrupt: *a sharp bend in the road* ○ *a sharp turn to the left.* (b) [usu attrib] sudden; abrupt: *a sharp drop in prices* ○ *a sharp rise in crime.* **3** well-defined; distinct; clear: *a sharp outline* ○ *a sharp photographic image,* ie one with clear contrasts between areas of light and shade ○ *in sharp focus* ○ *The TV picture isn't very sharp.* ○ *There is a sharp contrast between the lives of the poorest and the richest members of society.* **4** [usu attrib] (of sounds) shrill; piercing: *a sharp cry of distress* ○ *the sharp raucous cawing of a crow.* **5** (of tastes or smells) producing a smarting sensation; pungent: *the sharp taste of lemon juice* ○ *the sharp smell of the acid* ○ *The cheese is a little too sharp for me,* ie tastes too strong. **6** producing a physical sensation of cutting or piercing; keen: *a sharp frost/wind* ○ *a sharp pain in the back.* **7** quickly aware of things; acute; alert: *sharp eyes, ears, reflexes* ○ *a sharp person, mind, intelligence* ○ *a sharp sense of smell* ○ *keep a sharp look-out* ○ *It was very sharp of you to notice that detail straight away.* **8** ~ **(with sb)** (*derog*) intended or intending to criticize, injure, etc; harsh; severe: *a sharp criticism, rebuke, remark, etc* ○ *She was very sharp with me* (ie rebuked me) *when I forgot my book.* ○ *He has a sharp tongue,* ie often speaks harshly or angrily. **9** [usu attrib] quick; brisk; vigorous: *a sharp struggle, contest, etc* ○ *sharp competition for the job* ○ *That was sharp work,* ie It was done quickly or energetically. **10** (*often derog*) quick to take advantage of sb/sth; unscrupulous: *a sharp lawyer, accountant, etc* ○ *She was too sharp for me,* ie outwitted me. **11** [usu attrib] (*infml*) (too) smart or stylish: *a gambler in a sharp suit* ○ *be a very sharp dresser.* **12** (*music*) (a) (of a sound, an instrument, etc) above the normal or correct pitch: *That note sounded sharp.* (b) (usu following *ns*) (of notes) raised half a tone in pitch: *in the key of C sharp minor.* ⇨ illus at MUSIC. Cf FLAT[2] 10. **13** (idm) **(be) at the 'sharp end (of sth)** (*infml*) (be) involved in the most difficult or dangerous part of an activity: *They don't know what it's like at the sharp end of journalism,* eg reporting from war zones or disaster areas. **look 'sharp** be brisk; hurry: *You'd better look sharp or you'll be late.* **(as) sharp as a needle** very intelligent and quick-witted. **sharp 'practice** business dealings that are not entirely honest.

▷ **sharp** *n* (*symb* ♯) (*music*) (symbol used to indicate a) sharp note: *a difficult piano piece full of sharps and flats.* Cf FLAT[4] 4, NATURAL 6. Cf CARD-SHARP (CARD[1]).

sharp *adv* **1** (*infml*) punctually: *Please be here at seven (o'clock) sharp.* **2** (*infml*) suddenly; abruptly: *stopped sharp* ○ *turn sharp left.* **3** (*music*) above the correct pitch: *sing sharp.*

sharpen /ˈʃɑːpən/ *v* [I, Tn] (cause sth to) become sharp: *The tone of his letters has sharpened* (ie become less friendly) *recently.* ○ *sharpen a pencil* ○ *This knife needs sharpening.* ○ *This incident has sharpened public awareness of the economic crisis.* ○ *sharpen sb's wits,* ie make sb more mentally alert. **sharpener** /ˈʃɑːpnə(r)/ *n* (usu in compounds) device that sharpens: *a 'pencil-sharpener* ○ *a 'knife-sharpener.*

'sharper (also **'card-sharper**) *n* swindler, esp one who makes a living by cheating at cards.

sharpish *adj* rather sharp. — *adv* (*infml*) quickly; briskly.

sharply *adv* **1** in a sharp way: *sharply pointed* ○ *The road bends sharply.* ○ *prices dropping sharply* ○ *sharply contrasted styles* ○ *speak sharply to sb.* **2** (idm) **bring/pull sb up short/sharply** ⇨ SHORT[2].

sharpness *n* [U].

□ **ˌsharp-ˈeyed** *adj* having good eyesight; quick to notice things: *A ˌsharp-eyed poˈlice officer spotted the stolen car.*

'sharpshooter *n* person who is skilled at shooting with a gun, etc.

ˌsharp-ˈsighted *adj* having good eyesight.

ˌsharp-ˈwitted *adj* able to think quickly; alert: *She was sharp-witted enough to dodge her attacker.*

shat *pt, pp* of SHIT.

shatter /ˈʃætə(r)/ *v* **1** [I, Tn] (cause sth to) break suddenly and violently into small pieces: *The pot shattered as it hit the floor.* ○ *The explosion shattered all the windows.* ○ (*fig*) *What an ear-shattering noise!* **2** [Tn] (*infml*) destroy (sth) completely: *shatter sb's hopes* ○ *This event shattered all my previous ideas.* **3** [Tn esp passive] (*infml*) disturb the calmness of (sb); shock: *We were shattered by the news.* **4** [Tn esp passive] (*Brit infml*) exhaust (sb) completely: *We were totally shattered after the long journey.*

▷ **shattering** /ˈʃætərɪŋ/ *adj* very disturbing; shocking: *a shattering experience* ○ *The news was shattering.*

□ **'shatterproof** *adj* designed not to shatter: *shatterproof glass for car windscreens.*

shave /ʃeɪv/ *v* **1** [I, Tn, Tn·pr, Tn·p] ~ **sth (off sth/off)** cut (hair) off the face, etc with a razor; cut hair off the face, etc of (sb) in this way: *I shave every morning.* ○ *The nurse washed and shaved the patient.* ○ *Buddhist priests shave their heads.* ○ *She sometimes shaves the hair off her legs.* ○ *Why don't you shave your beard off?* **2** [Tn] cut or scrape thin slices from the surface of (wood, etc). ⇨ Usage at CLIP[2]. **3** [Tn] (*infml*) pass very close to (sb/sth), or touch (sb/sth) slightly in passing: *The bus just shaved me by an inch.* ○ *The ball narrowly shaved his off stump.* ○ *The lorry shaved the barrier, scraping its side.* **4** (phr v) **shave sth off (sth)** remove (a thin layer) from the surface of sth by cutting or scraping: *shave a millimetre (of wood) off the block* ○ (*fig*) *shave a few seconds off the world record.*

▷ **shave** *n* **1** act of shaving: *A sharp razor gives a close shave.* ○ *Have a shave before you go out.* **2** (idm) **a close shave** ⇨ CLOSE[1].

shaven /ˈʃeɪvn/ *adj* shaved: *ˌclean-ˈshaven* ○ *Their heads were shaven.* ⇨ Usage at PROVE.

shaver *n* **1** (also **electric razor**) razor with an electric motor, operated from the mains or by a battery. **2** (*dated infml*) lad; youngster: *You cheeky young shaver!*

shavings *n* [pl] thin pieces of wood shaved off, esp with a plane: *The floor of the carpenter's shop was covered with shavings.* ⇨ illus at PLANE.

□ **'shaving-brush** *n* brush for spreading lather over the face, etc before shaving.

'shaving-cream, **'shaving-foam** *ns* cream or foam spread over the face, etc before shaving.

'shaving-stick *n* cylindrical piece of soap for making lather to be used for shaving.

Shavian /ˈʃeɪvɪən/ *adj* of or like G B *Shaw and his works, noted esp for wit and socialist opinions.

Shaw /ʃɔː/ George Bernard (1856-1950), Irish author. After writing several unsuccessful novels, he turned to the theatre, producing over 50 plays (eg *Man and Superman, Pygmalion, St Joan*). They often deal with social themes, and show the influence of *Ibsen, but are distinguished by Shaw's own argumentative wit. He campaigned for many causes, esp socialism, feminism and spelling reform. He also wrote important works on music, and was a champion of the work of *Wagner. ⇨ article at PERFORMING ARTS.

shawl /ʃɔːl/ *n* large (usu square or oblong) piece of material worn round the shoulders or head of a woman, or wrapped round a baby.

shawm /ʃɔːm/ *n* early musical instrument similar to the oboe.

Shawnee /ʃɔːˈniː/ *n* **1** [C] (*pl* unchanged or ~**s**) member of a native American people formerly living in the eastern USA and now in Oklahoma. **2** [U] language of this people. ▷ **Shawnee** *adj.*

she /ʃiː/ Detailed Guide 6.2, 3. *pers pron* (used as the subject of a *v*) female person or animal mentioned earlier or being observed now: *My sister's very strong — she can swim 5 miles.* ○ *Doesn't she* (ie the woman we are looking at) *look like her mother?* ○

Do you remember our cat? She had kittens last week. Cf HER[1]. ⇨ Usage at HE.

▷ **she** *n* [sing] female animal: *We didn't know it was a she until it had puppies.*

she- (forming compound *ns*) female: *a ˈshe-goat.*

sheaf /ʃi:f/ *n* (*pl* **sheaves** /ʃi:vz/) **1** bundle of stalks of corn, barley, etc tied together after reaping. **2** bundle of papers, etc laid lengthwise and often tied together.

shear /ʃɪə(r)/ *v* (*pt* **~ed**, *pp* **shorn** /ʃɔ:n/ or **~ed**) **1** [Tn] cut the wool off (a sheep) with shears: *sheep shearing time.* **2** [I, Ip, Tn, Tn·p] ~ **(sth) (off)** (cause sth to) become twisted or break under pressure: *The bolt sheared (off) and the wheel came off.* ○ *The bar fell into the machinery and sheared a connecting-rod.* **3** (phr v) **be shorn of sth** be stripped or deprived of sth: *The room looked bare, shorn of its rich furnishings.* ○ *a deposed king shorn of his former power.* **shear sth off (sb/sth)** remove (fur, hair, etc) by cutting with shears: *All her beautiful tresses have been sheared/shorn off.*

▷ **shearer** *n* person who shears sheep.

shears /ʃɪəz/ *n* [pl] large cutting instrument shaped like scissors, used for shearing sheep, cutting hedges, etc and usu operated with both hands: *a pair of shears* ○ *ˈgardening shears* ○ *ˈpinking shears.* ⇨ illus at CLIPPER.

shearwater /ˈʃɪəwɔ:tə(r)/ *n* long-winged sea-bird that flies close to the surface of the water.

sheath /ʃi:θ/ *n* (*pl* **~s** /ʃi:ðz/) **1** (a) close-fitting cover for the blade of a weapon or tool: *Put the dagger back in its sheath.* ⇨ illus at KNIFE. (b) any similar covering: *the sheath round an electric cable* ○ *the ˈwing-sheath of an insect.* **2** close-fitting (usu rubber) covering for wearing on the penis during intercourse as a contraceptive; condom: *a contraceptive sheath.* **3** woman's close-fitting dress: [attrib] *a sheath gown.*

□ **ˈsheath-knife** *n* (*pl* **-ves**) knife with a fixed blade that fits in a sheath. ⇨ illus at KNIFE.

sheathe /ʃi:ð/ *v* **1** [Tn] (*fml*) put (sth) into a sheath: *He sheathed his sword.* **2** [esp passive: Tn, Tn·pr] ~ **sth (in/with sth)** put a protective covering or casing on sth: *electric wire sheathed with plastic.*

▷ **sheathing** *n* [U, C] protective covering or casing, eg on parts of a building.

sheaves *pl* of SHEAF.

shebang /ʃɪˈbæŋ/ *n* (idm) **the whole shebang** ⇨ WHOLE.

shebeen /ʃɪˈbi:n/ *n* place selling alcoholic liquor illegally, esp in Ireland and Africa.

shed[1] /ʃed/ *n* (often in compounds) one-storey building used for storing things, sheltering animals, vehicles, etc or as a workshop: *a ˈtool-shed* ○ *a ˈwood-shed* ○ *a ˈcoal-shed* ○ *a ˈcattle-shed* ○ *an ˈengine-shed* ○ *a ˈbicycle-shed.* ⇨ illus at HOME. Cf HUT.

shed[2] /ʃed/ *v* (**-dd-**; *pt, pp* **shed**) **1** [Tn] lose (sth) by its falling off; let (sth) fall or come off: *Trees shed their leaves and flowers shed their petals.* ○ *Some kinds of deer shed their horns.* ○ *The snake sheds its skin regularly.* ○ *The lorry has shed its load,* ie Its load has accidentally fallen off onto the road. **2** [Tn] (*fml*) allow (sth) to pour out: *shed tears,* ie weep ○ *shed blood,* ie wound or kill another person or other people ○ *shed one's blood,* ie be wounded or killed. **3** [Tn] take or throw (sth) off; remove: *shedding one's clothes on a hot day* ○ *The duck's feathers shed water immediately.* ○ (*fig*) *You must learn to shed* (ie get rid of) *your inhibitions.* **4** [Tn, Tn·pr] ~ **sth (on sb/sth)** spread or send sth out: *a fire shedding warmth* ○ *The lamp shed soft light on the desk.* ○ (*fig*) *She sheds happiness all around her.* **5** (idm) **cast/shed/throw light on sth** ⇨ LIGHT[1].

she'd /ʃi:d/ *contracted form* **1** she had ⇨ HAVE. **2** she would ⇨ WILL[1], WOULD[1].

sheen /ʃi:n/ *n* [U] gleaming brightness; shiny quality: *the sheen of silk* ○ *hair with a glossy golden sheen.*

sheep /ʃi:p/ *n* (*pl* unchanged) **1** grass-eating animal with a thick fleecy coat, kept in flocks for its flesh as food and for its wool. Cf EWE, LAMB 1, RAM 1, BLACK SHEEP (BLACK[1]). **2** (idm) **count sheep** ⇨ COUNT[1]. **like ˈsheep** too easily influenced or led by others. **make ˈsheep's eyes at sb** (*infml*) look at sb in a loving but foolish way. **one may/might as well be hanged/hung for a sheep as a lamb** ⇨ HANG[1]. **separate the sheep from the goats** ⇨ SEPARATE[2]. **a wolf in sheep's clothing** ⇨ WOLF.

□ **ˈsheep-dip** *n* [U, C] (liquid used in a) bath in which sheep are immersed to kill the insects, etc in their wool.

ˈsheep-dog *n* dog trained to guard and herd sheep; dog of a breed suitable for this: [attrib] *sheep-dog trials,* ie contests for trained sheep-dogs.

ˈsheep-fold *n* enclosure for sheep.

ˈsheepskin *n* **1** [C] (a) rug consisting of a sheep's skin with the wool on it. (b) garment made of two or more such skins. **2** [U] leather or parchment made from the skin of sheep. **3** [C] (*US joc*) diploma.

sheepish /ˈʃi:pɪʃ/ *adj* (feeling) foolish and embarrassed through shame: *a sheepish smile, grin, look, expression, etc.* ▷ **sheepishly** *adv.* **sheepishness** *n* [U].

sheepshank /ˈʃi:pʃæŋk/ *n* knot used to shorten a rope by folding part of it back against itself and putting a loop round each end of the fold. ⇨ illus at KNOT.

sheer[1] /ʃɪə(r)/ *adj* **1** [attrib] complete; thorough; utter: *sheer nonsense* ○ *a sheer waste of time* ○ *by sheer chance.* **2** [usu attrib] (of textiles, etc) thin, light and almost transparent: *sheer nylon.* **3** almost vertical; very steep: *a sheer rock, cliff, etc* ○ *a sheer drop of 50 feet.*

▷ **sheer** *adv* straight up or down: *a cliff that rises sheer from the beach* ○ *The ground dropped away sheer at our feet.*

sheer[2] /ʃɪə(r)/ *v* (phr v) **sheer away (from sth)/ sheer off (sth)** turn suddenly away from a course, topic, etc that one wishes to avoid: *When he saw me coming he sheered off in the opposite direction.* ○ *She tends to sheer away from any discussion of her divorce.*

sheet[1] /ʃi:t/ *n* **1** large rectangular piece of cotton, linen, etc, usu used in pairs between which a person sleeps: *put clean sheets on the bed.* **2** (a) broad thin piece of any material: *a sheet of glass, tin, copper, paper* ○ [attrib] *sheet metal, copper, tin, etc,* ie rolled or hammered into thin sheets. (b) piece of paper for writing or printing on, usu in a standard size: *two sheets of A4* ○ *put a fresh sheet in the typewriter.* **3** wide expanse (of water, ice, snow, flame, etc): (*infml*) *The rain came down in sheets,* ie very heavily. ○ *After the heavy frost the road was a sheet of ice.* **4** (idm) **a clean sheet/slate** ⇨ CLEAN[1]. **white as a sheet** ⇨ WHITE[1].

▷ **sheeting** *n* [U] material used for making sheets (SHEET[1] 1).

□ **ˌsheet ˈlightning** lightning that appears as a broad expanse of light in the sky.

ˈsheet music music published on separate sheets and not bound in a book.

sheet[2] /ʃi:t/ *n* rope or chain fastened to the lower corner of a sail to hold it and control the angle at which it is set.

□ **ˈsheet anchor** person or thing that one depends on in a difficult situation: *I have a small income from shares, which is my sheet anchor if my business should fail.* ○ [attrib] *She played a sheet anchor role for the team when things were going badly.*

ˌsheet ˈbend knot used for tying two ropes that are of different thicknesses. ⇨ illus at KNOT.

sheikh (also **sheik**) /ʃeɪk; *US* ʃi:k/ *n* **1** Arab chief; head of an Arab village, tribe, state, etc. **2** Muslim religious leader.

▷ **sheikhdom** (also **sheikdom**) /-dəm/ *n* area of land ruled by a sheikh.

sheila /ˈʃi:lə/ *n* (*Austral or NZ sl*) girl or young woman.

shekel /ˈʃekl/ *n* **1** [C] (a) ancient silver coin used by the Jews. (b) unit of money in Israel. **2 shekels** [pl] (*infml joc*) money: *She's raking in the shekels* (ie earning a lot of money) *in her new job.*

sheldrake /ˈʃeldreɪk/ *n* (*pl* **shelduck** /ˈʃeldʌk/) type of wild duck with brightly coloured feathers that lives in coastal areas.

shelduck /ˈʃeldʌk/ *n* (*pl* unchanged) female sheldrake.

shelf /ʃelf/ *n* (*pl* **shelves** /ʃelvz/) **1** flat rectangular piece of wood, metal, glass or other material fastened horizontally to a wall or in a cupboard, bookcase, etc for things to be placed on: *put up a shelf* ○ *a shelf full of crockery* ○ *a ˈbookshelf.* ⇨ illus at FURNITURE. **2** thing resembling a shelf, esp a piece of rock projecting from a cliff, etc or from the edge of a mass of land under the sea: *the continental shelf.* **3** (idm) **on the ˈshelf** (*infml*) (a) (of a person) put aside as if no longer useful: *A retired person should not be made to feel he's on the shelf.* (b) (*often sexist*) (of an unmarried woman) regarded as being too old to be likely to be asked to marry sb: *Women used to think they were on the shelf at 30.*

□ **ˈshelf-life** *n* (usu *sing*) time for which a stored item remains usable: *packets of biscuits with a shelf-life of two or three weeks.*

ˈshelf-mark *n* (also **call number**) number marked on a book to show where it should be kept in a library.

shell /ʃel/ *n* **1** [C, U] hard outer covering of eggs, of nut-kernels, of some seeds and fruits, and of animals such as oysters, snails, crabs and tortoises: *collecting sea-shells on the beach* ○ *empty coconut shells* ○ *broken pieces of shell.* ⇨ illus. **2** [C] (a) walls, outer structure, etc of an unfinished or burnt-out building, ship, etc: *Only the shell of the factory was left after the fire had been put out.* (b) any structure that forms a firm framework or covering: *the metal shell of the aircraft engine* ○ *the rigid body shell of a car.* **3** [C] (a) metal case filled with explosive, to be fired from a large gun: *The building was destroyed by an artillery shell.* Cf CARTRIDGE 1, SHOT[1] 4. (b) (*US*) = CARTRIDGE 1. **4** [C] light rowing-boat for racing. **5** [C] group of electrons in orbit around the nucleus of an atom and all having the same energy level. **6** (idm) **come out of one's ˈshell** become less shy, reserved, etc: *She used to be so quiet, but now she's really coming out of her shell and chatting to everyone.* **go, retire, withdraw, etc into one's ˈshell** become more shy, reserved, etc: *Her rejection of him seems to have made him go back into his shell.*

▷ **shell** *v* **1** [Tn] (*US* also **shuck**) remove the shell of (sth): *shell peas, peanuts, almonds, etc* ○ (*saying*) *It's as easy as shelling peas,* ie very easy. **2** [Tn] fire shells (SHELL 3) at (sb/sth): *shell the enemy positions.* **3** (phr v) **shell out (sth) (for sth)** (*infml*) pay out, often reluctantly: *I shall be expected to shell out (the money) for the party.*

□ **ˈshell bean** (*US*) bean of which the seed is eaten and not the pod.

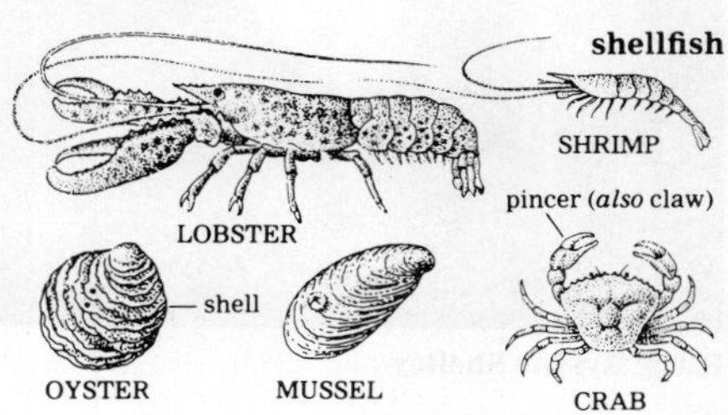

ˈshellfish *n* (*pl* unchanged) (a) [C] type of water animal with a shell, esp one of the edible types, eg oysters, mussels, crabs and shrimps. (b) [U] such animals as food: *I eat lots of shellfish.*

ˈshell-shock *n* [U] nervous illness that can affect

soldiers who have been in battle for a long time. ˈ**shell-shocked** *adj* **1** suffering from shell-shock. **2** (*fig*) shocked; confused; dazed: *I felt totally shell-shocked after coping with five boisterous children all day.*

she'll /ʃi:l/ *contracted form* she will ⇨ WILL[1].

shellac /ʃəˈlæk, *also* ˈʃelæk/ *n* [U] resinous substance in the form of thin sheets or flakes, used in making varnish.

▷ **shellac** *v* (**-ck-**) [Tn] **1** varnish (sth) with shellac. **2** (*US infml*) defeat (sb) soundly or severely. **shellacking** *n* (usu *sing*) (*US infml*) sound or severe defeat: *We gave their team a real shellacking.*

Mary Shelley

Shelley[1] /ˈʃelɪ/ Mary Wollstonecraft (1797-1851), English novelist, daughter of Mary *Wollstonecraft and second wife of P B Shelley. She is most famous as the author of **Frankenstein* and other Gothic stories. ⇨ illus.

Percy Bysshe Shelley

Shelley[2] /ˈʃelɪ/ Percy Bysshe (1792-1822), English poet. By the age of 20 he was a social rebel, both in his way of life and in his writings. Much of his finest work, eg the *Ode to the West Wind*, was written in Italy in the last years of his life, where he died in a storm at sea after visiting *Byron. His works show his remarkable lyrical gift, his originality and his hatred of oppression. ⇨ illus.

Shelta /ˈʃeltə/ *n* [U] type of secret language used by gypsies and others, based on words from Irish or Scots Gaelic.

shelter /ˈʃeltə(r)/ *n* **1** [U] ~ (**from sth**) condition of being protected, kept safe, etc, eg from rain, danger, attack; refuge: *seek/take shelter from the rain*, eg under a tree ○ *get under shelter*, eg when bombs are dropping during an air-raid ○ *They found shelter from the storm in a barn.* ○ *The high fence gives/affords (us) some shelter from the wind.* **2** [C] (often in compounds) (**a**) structure built to give protection, esp from rain, wind or attack: *a* ˈ*bus shelter*, ie one in which people wait for buses ○ *an* ˈ*air-raid shelter*. (**b**) building providing refuge, esp for homeless people.

▷ **shelter** *v* **1** [Tn, Tn·pr] ~ **sb/sth (from sb/sth)** give shelter to sb/sth; protect sb/sth: *trees that shelter a house from the wind* ○ *shelter* (ie hide, protect) *an escaped prisoner* ○ *The wall sheltered the soldiers from gunfire.* ○ *He is trying to shelter his boss from criticism.* ○ *Is our country's industry sheltered from foreign competition?* **2** [I, Ipr] ~ (**from sth**) find a place that gives shelter; take shelter: *shelter under the trees* ○ *shelter from the rain.* **sheltered** *adj* **1** (of a place) not exposed to wind, rain, etc: *find a sheltered spot for a picnic.* **2** kept away from or not exposed to unhappiness or harmful influences: *a sheltered childhood* ○ *He has led a sheltered life in the countryside.* **3** [attrib] (of housing) built or adapted for elderly or handicapped people, with special facilities that allow them to stay in the community rather than in a hospital, etc. ⇨ articles at HOUSE, RETIREMENT.

shelve[1] /ʃelv/ *v* [Tn] **1** put (books, etc) on a shelf or shelves. **2** (*fig*) abandon or postpone consideration of (a plan, project, problem, etc); delay dealing with (sth): *The plans for a new theatre have had to be shelved because of lack of money.*

▷ **shelving** *n* [U] (material for) shelves: *wooden shelving.*

shelve[2] /ʃelv/ *v* [I, Ip] ~ (**away/down/off**) (of land) slope gradually (in the specified direction): *The river-bottom shelves here.* ○ *The shore shelves down to the sea.*

shelves *pl* of SHELF.

shemozzle /ʃɪˈmɒzl/ *n* (usu *sing*); (*infml*) noisy disturbance; rumpus; brawl: *I've never heard such a shemozzle!*

shenanigans /ʃɪˈnænɪgənz/ *n* [pl] (*infml*) **1** mischievous or high-spirited behaviour. **2** trickery; deception.

shepherd /ˈʃepəd/ *n* person who takes care of sheep.

▷ **shepherd** *v* [Tn, Tn·pr, Tn·p] guide or direct (people) as if they were sheep: *A guide shepherded the tourists into the coach.* ○ *The children were shepherded around by two teachers.*

shepherdess /ˌʃepəˈdes; *US* ˈʃepərdɪs/ *n* woman who takes care of sheep.

□ ˌ**shepherd's** ˈ**pie** (also ˌ**cottage** ˈ**pie**) dish of minced meat baked with mashed potatoes on top.

Sheraton /ˈʃerətən/ Thomas (1751-1806), English furniture maker. His work is characterized by delicate and graceful form: [attrib] *Sheraton chairs.*

sherbet /ˈʃɜ:bət/ [C, U] **1** refreshing drink of weak sweet fruit-juice. **2** (*esp Brit*) sweet fizzy drink, or the powder from which it is made. **3** (*US*) = SORBET.

sherd = SHARD.

Sheridan /ˈʃerɪdn/ Richard Brinsley (1751-1816), Anglo-Irish playwright. He wrote a series of popular comedies including *The Rivals* (in which he created the famous Mrs Malaprop) and *The School for Scandal*. His real ambitions, however, were in politics, and he held several important government posts. Despite his public success, however, his debts grew and he died in poverty. ⇨ article at PERFORMING ARTS.

sheriff /ˈʃerɪf/ *n* **1** (often **High** ˈ**Sheriff**) chief officer of the Crown in counties and certain cities of England and Wales, with legal and ceremonial duties. Cf REEVE 1. **2** chief judge of a district in Scotland. **3** (in the US) chief officer responsible for enforcing the law in a county. ⇨ article at LAW.

Sherman /ˈʃɜ:mən/ William Tecumseh (1820-91), American general. He led the Unionist volunteer forces in the Civil War and crushed the forces of the South in his famous march through Georgia, succeeding *Grant as commander of the army in 1869.

Sherpa /ˈʃɜ:pə/ *n* member of a Himalayan people living on the borders of Nepal and Tibet. Their knowledge of the mountains has made them famous as guides, and Sherpa *Tenzing Norgay was the first man to reach the summit of *Everest, with Sir Edmund *Hillary.

sherry /ˈʃerɪ/ *n* (**a**) [U, C] type of yellow or brown fortified wine, originally from S Spain: *Do you like sweet or dry sherry?* ○ *high-quality sherries.* (**b**) [C] glass of this: *have a sherry before dinner.*

she's /ʃi:z/ *contracted form* **1** she is ⇨ BE. **2** she has ⇨ HAVE.

Shetland /ˈʃetlənd/ *n* (also **the Shetlands** [pl]) group of islands off the north coast of Scotland. They lie close to the oilfields of the North Sea and are famous for the wool from their sheep, knitted into sweaters with a distinctive design. ⇨ map at UNITED KINGDOM. ⇨ map at App 1.

□ ˌ**Shetland** ˈ**pony** pony of a small rough-coated breed.

ˌ**Shetland** ˈ**wool** soft fine wool from Shetland sheep.

shew /ʃəʊ/ *v* (*arch*) = SHOW[2].

shibboleth /ˈʃɪbəleθ/ *n* old slogan or principle that is no longer regarded by many as very important: *elderly politicians still clinging to the outmoded shibboleths of party doctrine.*

shied *pt, pp* of SHY[1], SHY[2].

shield /ʃi:ld/ *n* **1** (**a**) piece of (usu metal or leather) armour formerly carried on the arm to protect the body when fighting. (**b**) (in heraldry) drawing or model of a shield displaying a coat of arms (COAT). ⇨ illus at COAT OF ARMS (COAT). (**c**) trophy in the form of a shield: *win the school boxing shield.* **2** ~ (**against sth**) (*fig*) person or thing that protects: *This car polish is an effective shield against rust.* **3** (in machinery, etc) plate or screen that protects the operator or the machine; thing used to keep out wind, dust, etc: *a shield around the grip of a chainsaw* ○ *the* ˈ*heat-shield on a space capsule* ○ *a welder's* ˈ*eye-shield*, ie to stop sparks getting into the eye.

▷ **shield** *v* [Tn, Tn·pr] ~ **sb/sth (against/from sb/sth)** protect sb/sth from harm; defend sb/sth from criticism, attack, etc: *shield one's eyes (from the sun) with one's hand* ○ *The police officer shielded the child with her body.* ○ *You can't shield this criminal from prosecution.* ○ *I tried to shield him against prying journalists.*

shift[1] /ʃɪft/ *v* **1** (**a**) [I, Ipr, Ip, Tn, Tn·pr, Tn·p] ~ (**sth/sb/oneself**) (**from.../to...**); ~ (**sth/sb/oneself**) (**about/around**) (cause sth/sb/oneself to) change or move from one position or direction to another: *The cargo has shifted*, ie has been shaken out of place by the movement of the ship. ○ *The wind shifted from east to north.* ○ *The tools shift around in the car boot every time we turn a corner.* ○ *The audience shifted uneasily in their seats.* ○ (*infml*) *Soap won't shift that stain*, ie wash it off. ○ *Help me to shift the sofa away from the fire.* ○ *You'll have to shift yourselves to another room — I want to clean in here.* ○ *The teacher shifted the chairs around in the classroom.* (**b**) [Tn, Tn·pr] ~ **sth (from A to/onto B)** transfer sth: *Don't try to shift the responsibility onto others: you must do the job yourself.* ○ *He shifted the load from his left to his right shoulder.* **2** [Ipr, Ip, Tn] ~ **out of sth/into sth**; ~ **up/down** (*esp US*) change (gear) in a vehicle: *shift out of first into second* ○ *Shift up when you reach 30 mph.* ○ *You have to shift down to climb steep hills.* ○ *Learn to shift gear at the right moment.* **3** [I] (*Brit infml*) move quickly: *You'll have to shift if you want to get there by nine o'clock.* ○ *That car can really shift!* **4** (idm) **shift one's** ˈ**ground** take a new position or a different way of approaching a subject during an argument. **5** (phr v) **shift for oneself** manage one's life without help from others: *When their parents died, the children had to shift for themselves.*

□ ˈ**shift-key** *n* key on a typewriter, etc that, when pressed, causes the machine to type capital letters.

shift[2] /ʃɪft/ *n* **1** ~ **(in sth)** change of place, nature, form, etc: *a gradual shift of people from the country to the town* ○ *shifts in public opinion* ○ *There has been a shift in fashion from formal to more informal dress.* **2** (period of time worked by a) group of workers which starts work as another group finishes: *the* ˈ*day*/ˈ*night shift* ○ *work an eight-hour shift* ○ *working in shifts* ○ [attrib] *a shift worker* ○ *shift work, pay.* Cf RELAY 1. **3** (*US*) mechanism for changing gears in a motor vehicle. **4** trick or scheme for achieving sth or avoiding a difficulty: *use some dubious shifts to get money* ○ *As a temporary shift, he covered up the leak with a plastic bag.* **5** **(a)** woman's straight narrow dress. **(b)** (*arch*) woman's undergarment like a dress; chemise. **6** mechanism on a typewriter, etc that allows capitals to be typed: *Press 'Shift' and type 'A'.* **7** (idm) **make** ˈ**shift (with sth)** (*becoming dated*) use what is available, though it is seen as barely adequate; manage: *We haven't really got enough food for everyone but we'll have to make shift (with what we've got).*

▷ **shiftless** *adj* (*derog*) lazy and unambitious; lacking the ability to find ways of getting things done: *a shiftless individual who never works and constantly borrows from others.* **shiftlessness** *n* [U].

shifty /ˈʃɪftɪ/ *adj* (**-ier, -iest**) untrustworthy; deceitful; seemingly dishonest: *a shifty-looking person* ○ *shifty behaviour* ○ *shifty eyes, looks.* ▷ **shiftily** /-ɪlɪ/ *adv.* **shiftiness** *n* [U].

Shiite /ˈʃiːaɪt/ *n* member of one of the two main branches of *Islam. Shiites make up about 10% of the Muslim community and live mainly in Iran, Iraq and the Punjab. They were originally a sect that rejected the authority of the first three caliphs, and considered Ali, *Muhammad's adopted son, as his spiritual successor. Cf SUNNI. ▷ **Shiite** *adj.*

shillelagh /ʃɪˈleɪlɪ/ *n* type of club[2](1) used in Ireland.

shilling /ˈʃɪlɪŋ/ *n* **1** (until 1971) British coin worth twelve old pennies; one twentieth of a pound. **2** basic unit of money in Kenya, Uganda and Tanzania; 100 cents.

shilly-shally /ˈʃɪlɪ ʃælɪ/ *v* (*pt, pp* **-shallied**) [I] (*infml derog*) be unable to make up one's mind; be undecided; hesitate: *If you keep shilly-shallying like this we'll be late.*

shim /ʃɪm/ *n* thin wedge pushed between parts that are clamped together, to make them fit properly or tightly.

▷ **shim** *v* (**-mm-**) [Tn] fix a shim or shims between or onto (sth).

shimmer /ˈʃɪmə(r)/ *v* [I] shine with a soft light that seems to waver: *moonlight shimmering on the lake* ○ *The surface of the road shimmered in the heat of the sun.*

▷ **shimmer** *n* [U] shimmering light: *the shimmer of pearls.*

shin /ʃɪn/ *n* front part of the leg below the knee: *get kicked on the shin.* ⇨ illus at HUMAN.

▷ **shin** *v* (**-nn-**) (phr v) **shin up/down (sth)** climb up/down (sth), using the hands and legs to grip: *shin up a tree* ○ *shin down a rope.*

□ ˈ**shin-bone** (also **tibia**) *n* inner and (usu) larger of the two bones from the knee to the ankle.

ˈ**shin-pad** (also ˈ**shin-guard**) *n* pad worn to protect the shin when playing football, etc.

shindig /ˈʃɪndɪg/ *n* (*infml*) **1** lively and noisy party. **2** = SHINDY.

shindy /ˈʃɪndɪ/ (also **shindig**) *n* (usu *sing*) (*infml*) noisy disturbance; brawl: *kick up* (ie cause) *a shindy* ○ *There was a dreadful shindy in the pub last night.*

shine /ʃaɪn/ *v* (*pt, pp* **shone** /ʃɒn; *US* ʃəʊn/ or, in sense 3, **~d**) **1** [I, Ipr, Ip] give out or reflect light; be bright: *Clean the glasses until they shine.* ○ *The moon is shining (through the window).* ○ *The clouds parted and the sun shone (out).* ○ *The hot sun shone down on the scene.* ○ (*fig*) *His face shone with excitement.* **2** [Tn·pr, Tn·p] aim the light of (a torch, etc) in a specified direction: *The police shone a searchlight on the house.* ○ *Shine your torch into the drawer.* ○ *I hate lights being shone in my face.* **3** [Tn] (*infml*) polish (sth): *shine shoes, brassware.* **4** [I, Ipr] ~ **(at/in sth)** excel in some way: *He's a shining* (ie outstanding, excellent) *example of a hard-working pupil.* ○ *She does not shine in conversation,* ie is not a good talker. ○ *I've never shone at tennis.* **5** (idm) **a knight in shining armour** ⇨ KNIGHT. **make hay while the sun shines** ⇨ HAY. **rise and shine** ⇨ RISE[2].

▷ **shine 1** [sing, U] brightness; polished appearance: *Give your shoes a good shine.* ○ *There's too much shine on the seat of these old trousers.* **2** (idm) **come rain, come shine; rain or shine** ⇨ RAIN[1]. **take a shine to sb/sth** (*infml*) suddenly begin to like sb/sth: *I think that dog has taken a shine to me: it follows me everywhere.*

shiner *n* (*dated sl*) black eye: *That's quite a shiner you've got there.*

shiny *adj* (**-ier, -iest**) shining; rubbed until bright: *the shiny head of a bald man* ○ *shiny black leather* ○ *All the cups are clean and shiny.*

shingle[1] /ˈʃɪŋgl/ *n* [U] small rounded pebbles on the sea-shore.

▷ **shingly** /ˈʃɪŋglɪ/ *adj* covered with or consisting of shingle: *I prefer a sandy beach to a shingly one.*

shingle[2] /ˈʃɪŋgl/ *n* **1** small, flat, square or oblong piece of wood used as a covering on roofs and walls. **2** (*US infml*) small wooden signboard put up outside the office of a doctor, dentist, etc.

▷ **shingle** *v* [Tn esp passive] cover (a roof, etc) with shingles: *a shingled church spire.*

shingles /ˈʃɪŋglz/ *n* [sing *v*] (also ˌ**herpes** ˈ**zoster**) disease caused by a virus, with a band of painful spots on the skin, esp around the waist.

Shinto /ˈʃɪntəʊ/ *n* [U] traditional religion of Japan that includes the worship of ancestors and the spirits of nature. Historically Shinto has been closely associated with the state, and until the end of the Second World War the emperor was regarded as a living god descended from the sun goddess: [attrib] *a Shinto priest, temple.* ▷ **Shintoist** /ˈʃɪntəʊɪst/ *n.*

shinty /ˈʃɪntɪ/ *n* **1** [U] traditional game played in Scotland, similar to hockey. **2** [C] stick or ball used in this game.

ship[1] /ʃɪp/ *n* **1** large vessel carrying people or goods by sea: *a* ˈ*sailing-ship* ○ *a* ˈ*merchant ship* ○ *a* ˈ*warship* ○ *the ship's company,* ie the entire crew ○ *board a ship for India.* **2** (*infml*) **(a)** spacecraft: *aboard an alien ship.* **(b)** (*US*) aircraft. **3** (idm) **jump ship** ⇨ JUMP[2]. **(like)** ˌ**ships that** ˌ**pass in the** ˈ**night** people who meet each other briefly and usu only once. **when one's** ˈ**ship comes home/in** when one has become successful: *I'll buy a house in the country when my ship comes in.*

□ **ship** ˈ**biscuit** (also **ship's** ˈ**biscuit**) hard coarse biscuit used formerly as food during long voyages: *a diet of ship biscuit.*

ˈ**shipboard** *adj* [attrib] used or occurring on a ship: *a shipboard romance.* — *n* (idm) **on shipboard** on a ship; on board ship.

ˈ**shipbuilding** *n* [U] building ships: [attrib] *a shipbuilding company, yard.* ˈ**shipbuilder** *n.*

ˈ**ship-canal** *n* canal that is wide and deep enough for seagoing vessels.

ˈ**shipload** *n* as much cargo or as many passengers as a ship can carry: *set sail with a shipload of grain.*

ˈ**shipmate** *n* person travelling or working on the same ship as another: *He and I were shipmates on a trawler once.*

ˈ**shipowner** *n* person who owns a ship or ships, or has shares in a shipping company.

ˌ**ship's** ˈ**chandler** person who deals in supplies and equipment for ships.

ˈ**shipwreck** *n* **(a)** [U] loss or destruction of a ship at sea by storm, collision, etc: *suffer shipwreck.* **(b)** [C] instance of this: *He died in a shipwreck off the south coast.* — *v* [Tn usu passive] cause (sb) to suffer shipwreck: *shipwrecked sailors* ○ *We were shipwrecked on a deserted island.*

ˈ**shipwright** *n* person employed in building or repairing ships.

ˈ**shipyard** *n* place where ships are built or repaired.

ship[2] /ʃɪp/ *v* (**-pp-**) **1** [Tn, Tn·pr, Tn·p] send or transport (sth/sb), esp in a ship: *Are the goods to be flown or shipped?* ○ *We ship grain to the Soviet Union.* ○ *Fresh supplies were shipped (out) by lorry.* **2** [Tn] take (oars) out of the water into the boat: *We shipped (the) oars and moored alongside the bank.* **3** [Tn] (of a boat) take in (water) over the side, eg in a storm: *The waves were very high, and the boat began to ship water.* **4** [I] become a member of a ship's crew: *ship* (ie take a post) *as a steward on an Atlantic liner.* **5** (phr v) **ship sb/sth off** (*infml*) send sb/sth away: *The children had been shipped off to boarding-school at an early age.*

▷ **shipment** /ˈʃɪpmənt/ *n* **1** [U] placing of goods on a ship; transport of goods by any means: *immediate shipment of the cargo* ○ *safe shipment by air.* **2** [C] items shipped; consignment: *a shipment of grain for West Africa.*

shipper *n* person who arranges for goods to be shipped.

shipping *n* [U] **1** ships, esp those of a country or port: *The canal is now open to shipping.* ○ [attrib] *a shipping office* ○ *busy shipping lanes* ○ *the shipping forecast,* ie a report on the weather conditions at sea. **2** transporting goods by ship: *the shipping of oil from the Middle East.* ˈ**shipping-agent** *n* shipowner's representative at a port.

-ship *suff* (with *ns* forming *ns*) **1** state of being; status; office: *friendship* ○ *ownership* ○ *professorship.* **2** proficiency as; skill: *musicianship* ○ *scholarship.* Cf -MANSHIP (MAN[1]).

shipshape /ˈʃɪpʃeɪp/ *adj* [usu pred] in good order; tidy: *get the room all nice and shipshape.*

shire /ˈʃaɪə(r) *or, in compounds,* -ʃə(r)/ *n* **1** [C] (*arch*) county (now chiefly used in the names of certain counties, eg *Hampshire, Yorkshire*). **2 the shires** [pl] certain midland counties of England, esp the parts of these well known for fox-hunting.

□ ˈ**shire-horse** *n* large powerful breed of horse used for pulling carts and wagons.

shirk /ʃɜːk/ *v* [I, Tn, Tg] (*derog*) avoid doing (work, one's duty, etc) through laziness, cowardice, etc: *You're supposed to tidy up, so stop shirking and do it!* ○ *He always shirks the unpleasant tasks.* ○ *She is shirking going to the dentist.* ▷ **shirker** *n.*

shirt /ʃɜːt/ *n* **1** loose-fitting garment (usu worn by men) for the upper part of the body, made of cotton, linen, silk, etc, with long or short sleeves: *a* ˈ*sports shirt,* ie one with short sleeves for casual wear ○ *a* ˈ*dress shirt,* ie a formal one worn with a dinner-jacket, etc. ⇨ illus at JACKET. **2** (idm) **keep one's** ˈ**shirt on** (*infml*) (usu imperative) not lose one's temper: *Keep your shirt on! Nobody meant to offend you.* **lose one's shirt** ⇨ LOSE. **put one's shirt on sth** (*sl*) bet all one's money on (a horse, etc): *He has put his shirt on his team winning the trophy.* **a stuffed shirt** ⇨ STUFF[2].

▷ **shirting** *n* [U] material for making shirts.

□ ˈ**shirt-front** *n* front part of a shirt, esp the stiffened and starched front part of a formal white shirt.

ˈ**shirt-sleeve** *n* sleeve of a shirt: *in one's shirt-sleeves,* ie not wearing a jacket over one's shirt ○ (*fig*) [attrib] *a* ˌ*shirt-sleeve* ˈ*atmosphere,* ie informal and efficient.

ˈ**shirt-tail** *n* part of a shirt that extends below the waist.

ˈ**shirtwaist** *n* (*US*) woman's dress that buttons down the front to the waist.

shirty /ˈʃɜːtɪ/ *adj* (**-ier, -iest**) (*infml*) annoyed; angry; bad-tempered: *Don't get shirty with me!* ▷ **shirtily** *adv.* **shirtiness** *n* [U].

shish kebab /ˌʃɪʃ kɪˈbæb; *US* ˈʃɪʃ kəbæb/ = KEBAB.

shit /ʃɪt/ *n* (⚠ *sl*) **1** [U] waste matter from the bowels; excrement: *a pile of dog shit on the pavement.* **2** [sing] act of emptying the bowels: *have/need a shit.* **3** [U] stupid remarks or writing; nonsense: *You do talk a load of shit!* **4** [C] (*derog*) contemptible person: *That little shit stole my money.* **5** (idm) **in the** ˈ**shit** in trouble. **not give a** ˈ**shit (about sb/sth)** not care at all: *He doesn't give a shit about anybody else.* **scare the shit out of sb** ⇨ SCARE. **the** ˌ**shit hits the** ˈ**fan** trouble starts after

earlier mistakes, crimes, etc: *I don't want to be there when the shit hits the fan.* ○ *If the press gets hold of the story the shit will really hit the fan.* **up shit ˈcreek (without a paddle)** in great trouble.
▷ **shit** *v* (-tt-; *pt, pp* **shitted** or **shat** /ʃæt/) (⚠ *sl*) **1** [I, Tn] empty (solid waste) from the bowels. **2** [Tn] ˈ~ **oneself** **(a)** soil oneself by emptying solid waste from the bowels accidentally. **(b)** be very frightened. **3** (idm) **shit ˈbricks/a ˈbrick** be very frightened: *The engine caught fire and we were all shitting bricks.*
shit *interj* (⚠ *sl*) (used to express annoyance): *Shit! I've missed the train!*

shitty /ˈʃɪtɪ/ *adj* (-ier, -iest) (⚠ *sl esp Brit*) **1** nasty; disgusting: *I'm not going to eat this shitty food.* **2** contemptible; mean; unworthy: *What a shitty way to treat a friend!*

Shiva = SIVA.

shiver[1] /ˈʃɪvə(r)/ *v* [I, Ipr] ~ **(with sth)** tremble, esp from cold or fear: *She shivered at the thought of going into the dark house alone.* ○ *shivering all over with cold.*
▷ **shiver** *n* **1** [C] act of shivering: *The gruesome sight sent a shiver down my spine.* **2 the shivers** [pl] fit of trembling, resulting from fever or fear: *lying in bed with a bout of the shivers* ○ *Having to make a speech always gives me the shivers.*
shivery /ˈʃɪvərɪ/ *adj* tending to shiver; having or causing a feeling of cold, horror, fear, etc: *feel shivery in the damp atmosphere* ○ *a cold, shivery breeze.*

shiver[2] /ˈʃɪvə(r)/ *n* (usu *pl*) any of the many small fragments of sth, esp of glass, that has been broken: *break sth into shivers* ○ *cut one's foot on a small shiver of glass.*
▷ **shiver** *v* [I, Tn] (cause sth to) break into shivers; shatter.

shoal[1] /ʃəʊl/ *n* great number of fish swimming together: *a shoal of herring, cod, etc* ○ *swimming in shoals* ○ *(fig) Shoals of tourists come here in the summer.*
▷ **shoal** *v* [I] (of fish) form a shoal or shoals.

shoal[2] /ʃəʊl/ *n* **1** [C] shallow place in the sea; sandbank, esp one that can be seen when the water level is low: *run aground on a shoal* ○ *steer away from the shoals.* **2 shoals** [pl] *(fig)* hidden dangers or difficulties.
▷ **shoal** *v* [I] become shallow(er).

shock[1] /ʃɒk/ *n* **1** [C] violent blow or shake, caused eg by a collision or an explosion: *earthquake shocks* ○ *The shock of the blast shattered many windows.* ○ *I felt the shock as the aircraft hit the ground.* **2** [C] = ELECTRIC SHOCK (ELECTRIC): *If you touch this live wire, you'll get a shock.* **3** [C] sudden violent disturbance of the mind or emotions caused eg by bad news, a frightening event, etc: *The news of his mother's death was a terrible shock to him.* ○ *The result of the election came as a shock to us all,* ie None of us expected it. ○ *It gave me quite a shock to be told I was seriously ill.* **4** [U] state of extreme weakness caused by physical injury, pain, fright, etc: *be in/go into shock* ○ *suffering from shock* ○ *What is the correct medical treatment for shock?* ○ *She died of shock following an operation on her brain.*
□ ˈ**shock absorber** device fitted to a motor vehicle to absorb vibration caused by the unevenness of the road surface, etc. ⇨ illus at CAR.
ˈ**shock-proof** *adj* (esp of a watch) designed to resist damage when knocked, dropped, etc.
ˈ**shock tactics** sudden, violent or outrageous action taken to achieve a purpose: *The group used shock tactics to get publicity: one of them took his clothes off on TV.*
ˈ**shock therapy** (also ˈ**shock treatment**) way of treating mental illness by giving electric shocks or a drug having a similar effect.
ˈ**shock-troops** *n* [pl] troops specially trained for violent assaults.
ˈ**shock wave** moving region of very high air pressure caused by an explosion or an aircraft moving faster than sound: *(fig) As soon as news of the tragedy was announced, shock waves spread rapidly to all parts of the country.*

shock[2] /ʃɒk/ *n* (usu **shock of hair**) rough untidy mass of hair on the head.
□ ˌ**shock-ˈheaded** *adj* (*dated*) having such hair.

shock[3] /ʃɒk/ *v* [Tn esp passive] cause a shock[1](3) to (sb); cause (sb) to feel disgust, indignation, horror, etc: *I was shocked at the news of her death.* ○ *He was shocked to hear his child swearing.* ○ *I'm not easily shocked, but that book really is obscene.*
▷ **shocker** *n* **1** person who shocks. **2** (*infml*) **(a)** thing that shocks, eg a sensational novel: *Some of these horror stories are real shockers.* **(b)** very bad example of sth: *You've written bad essays before, but this one is a shocker!*
shocking *adj* **1** causing indignation, disgust, etc; very bad or wrong: *shocking behaviour, words, insults* ○ *What she did was so shocking that I can hardly describe it.* **2** causing a shock[1](3): *shocking news,* eg of an accident in which many died. **3** (*infml*) very bad: *shocking luck, weather, handwriting, work* ○ *The food here is shocking.*
shockingly *adv* **1** badly: *You're playing shockingly.* **2** (*infml*) extremely: *a shockingly expensive dress.*

shock[4] /ʃɒk/ *n* group of sheaves of corn that are stacked together in a field.
▷ **shock** *v* [Tn] stack (corn) in shocks.

shod *pt, pp* of SHOE *v*.

shoddy[1] /ˈʃɒdɪ/ *adj* (-ier, -iest) of poor quality or badly made: *shoddy goods, clothes, etc* ○ *shoddy workmanship.* ▷ **shoddily** *adv*: *shoddily made.* **shoddiness** *n* [U].

shoddy[2] /ˈʃɒdɪ/ *n* [U] (poor-quality cloth made from) fibre obtained from old cloth.

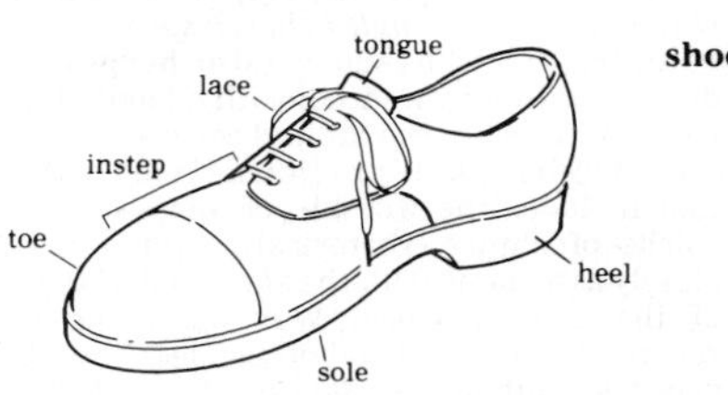

shoe

shoe /ʃu:/ *n* **1** outer covering for a person's foot, usu with a stiff sole and not reaching above the ankle: *a pair of shoes* ○ *walking shoes* ○ *tennis shoes* ○ *put on/take off one's shoes* ○ [attrib] *a shoe brush, shop* ○ *shoe polish, leather.* Cf BOOT[1] 1, SANDAL. **2** = HORSESHOE (HORSE): *cast/throw a shoe,* ie lose one. **3** part of a brake that presses against the wheel or its drum (on a bicycle, in a motor vehicle, etc). **4** any object like a shoe in appearance or use. **5** (idm) **be in/put oneself in sb's shoes** be in/imagine oneself to be in sb else's position: *I wouldn't like to be in your shoes if they find out what you're doing.* **dead men's shoes** ⇨ DEAD. **fill sb's shoes** ⇨ FILL[1]. **shake in one's shoes** ⇨ SHAKE[1]. **step into sb's shoes** ⇨ STEP[1].
▷ **shoe** *v* (*pt, pp* **shod** /ʃɒd/) [Tn] fit (a horse) with a shoe or shoes: *a blacksmith shoeing a pony.*
shod *adj* [attrib] (of a person) wearing shoes of a specified type or quality: *shod in leather* ○ *well shod for wet weather* ○ *(fig) an iron-shod stick,* ie one with an iron tip.
□ ˈ**shoehorn** *n* device with a curved blade used to help the heel slide easily into a shoe. — *v* [Tn·pr] ~ **sth into, past, etc sth** force sth with difficulty into a very small space, short time, etc: *I managed to shoehorn all six of us into the car.*
ˈ**shoe-lace** *n* cord fastened to the edges of a shoe's uppers to hold it tightly on the foot.
ˈ**shoemaker** *n* [C], ˈ**shoemaking** *n* [U] (person whose trade is) making or repairing boots and shoes.
ˈ**shoeshine** *n* (*esp US*) person whose job is polishing other people's shoes: [attrib] *a shoeshine boy.*
ˈ**shoe-string** *n* **1** (*esp US*) shoe-lace. **2** (idm) **on a ˈshoe-string** using very little money: *living on a shoe-string.*
ˈ**shoe-tree** *n* shaped piece of wood, plastic or metal placed inside a shoe so that it keeps its shape.

shofar /ˈʃəʊfɑ:(r)/ *n* trumpet made from a ram's horn, used in some Jewish religious ceremonies.

shogun /ˈʃəʊgən/ *n* commander of the army in feudal Japan. The shogun inherited his command and was often more powerful than the emperor until the feudal system was abolished in 1868.

shone *pt, pp* of SHINE.

shoo /ʃu:/ *interj* (said to make animals or people, esp children, go away): *Shoo, all of you, I'm busy.*
▷ **shoo** *v* (*pt, pp* **shooed**) (phr v) **shoo sb/sth away, off, out, etc** make sb/sth go away, etc, by saying 'shoo': *shooing the chickens away/into the barn* ○ *He shooed the little children out of the shop.*

shoo-in /ˈʃu:ɪn/ *n* (*US infml*) person, team, etc that is thought certain to win.

shook *pt* of SHAKE[1].

shoot[1] /ʃu:t/ *v* (*pt, pp* **shot** /ʃɒt/) **1 (a)** [I, Ipr, Tn, Tn·pr, Tn·p] ~ **(sth) (at sb/sth)**; ~ **sth (from sth)**; ~ **sth (off)** fire (a gun or some other weapon); fire (a bullet, an arrow, etc) at sb/sth: *Aim carefully before shooting.* ○ *Don't shoot — I surrender.* ○ *What are you shooting (your gun) at?* ○ *He shot an arrow from his bow.* ○ *The police only rarely shoot to kill,* ie try to kill the people they shoot at. ○ *The missiles were shot at the aircraft from a ship.* ○ *He shot (off) several bullets before hitting the target.* **(b)** [I] use a gun, etc; hunt with a gun, etc: *Can you shoot (well)?* ○ *learn to shoot straight* ○ *I need more practice at shooting.* ○ *He enjoys riding, fishing and shooting.* ie as sport. **(c)** [Tn, Cn·a] kill or wound (sb/sth) with a bullet, an arrow, etc: *She went out shooting rabbits.* ○ *The soldier was shot* (ie executed by shooting) *for desertion.* ○ *She was shot in the leg.* ○ *The hunter shot the stag dead.* **(d)** [I] (of a gun, bow, etc) fire bullets, arrows, etc: *This is just a toy gun: it doesn't shoot.* ○ *Get a rifle that shoots straight.* **(e)** [Tn·pr] make (sth) by shooting: *The gun/gunman shot a hole in the door.* **2** [Tn] go over (an area) shooting game animals: *shoot a covert, an estate, etc.* ⇨ Usage at HUNT[1]. **3 (a)** [Ipr, Ip, Tn·pr, Tn·p] (cause sth to) move suddenly or quickly in the specified direction: *The sports car shot past us.* ○ *A meteor shot across the sky.* ○ *He shot out of the door after her.* ○ *The runner shot ahead (of the rest).* ○ *Flames were shooting (up) from the burning house.* ○ *The snake's tongue shot out.* ○ *The driver was shot out of the open car as it crashed.* ⇨ Usage at WHIZ. **(b)** [I, Ipr] ~ **(down, up, etc sth)** (of pain) move suddenly and quickly with a stabbing sensation: *a shooting pain in my back* ○ *The pain shot up her arm.* **(c)** (no passive: Tn·pr, Dn·n] ~ **sth at sb** direct sth at sb suddenly or quickly: *journalists shooting questions at the minister* ○ *She shot an angry glance at him/shot him an angry glance.* **4** [I] (of plants and bushes) put forth new twigs or branches from a stem; sprout: *Rose bushes shoot again after being cut back.* **5** [I, Tn, Tng no passive] (*esp cinema*) photograph (an object, a scene, etc): *Cameras ready? OK, shoot!* ○ *We're ready to shoot (the ballroom sequence).* ○ *The film was shot in black and white.* ○ *shoot a woman riding a horse* ○ *a ˈshooting script,* ie the script actually used in the final film. **6** [Tn] (of a boat or a person in a boat) move quickly through, past, etc (sth): *shooting the rapids* ○ *shoot the bridge,* ie pass quickly underneath it. **7** [Tn] push (the bolt of a door) into or out of its slot. **8** [Tn] (*infml*) (in golf) achieve (a specified number of strokes) in a game: *shot a 75 in the first round.* **9** [Tn] (*esp US*) play (certain games): *shoot craps/pool/dice.* **10 (a)** [I, Ipr] ~ **(at sth)** (in football, hockey, etc) try to kick, hit, etc the ball directly into the goal: *She's looking for an opportunity to shoot (at goal).* **(b)** [Tn no passive] score (a goal): *He shot a goal from twenty yards out.* **11** [I] (*US infml*) (only imperative) say what one has to say: *You want to tell me something? Well, shoot!* **12** [Tn no passive] (*sl*) inject (a drug) into one's bloodstream: *shoot heroin.* **13** (idm) **be/get shot of sth/sb** (*infml*) be/get rid of sth/sb. **shoot one's ˈbolt** (*infml*) make one's final effort, so that there is nothing further one can do to achieve one's aim. **shoot the ˈbreeze** (*US infml*) talk casually; gossip: *We sat around in the bar, shooting the breeze.* ˌ**shoot from the ˈhip** (*infml*) speak in a very direct way, often critically and without thinking. ˌ**shoot it ˈout (with sb)** (*infml*) settle a contest, dispute, etc, using guns: *(fig) rival*

Shops

Britain has two main types of shop: those that are part of a chain or a group, and those that are individually owned. Chains such as Woolworths, Marks and Spencer, Boots and W H Smith have branches in most towns and cities. Woolworths sells a wide range of goods, from cheap jewellery to ironmongery and gardening equipment. Marks and Spencer sells clothes (for men, women and children) and food. More people buy their clothes there than at any other shop. Boots, originally a chemist's shop, now sells many other things as well, including electrical goods and kitchenware. W H Smith sells newspapers, magazines, stationery, books and records.

London and other large cities also have large department stores. Harrods in London is one of the largest in the world and boasts that it can supply anything a customer orders. Other famous London department stores are Selfridges, Fortnum and Mason, famous for its luxurious food department, and Liberty, famous for its fabrics, especially its art nouveau prints. New York's most famous ones are Macy's, Saks 5th Avenue and Bloomingdales.

A typical high street in a smallish town in Britain will contain a mixture of chain stores, individual shops, building societies and banks. The individual shops sell goods that are also available in larger stores, but often pride themselves on the quality of their goods and service. Typical examples of such shops are clothes shops, cake shops (many of which also have tea-rooms), butchers, bakers, gift shops, shoe shops, newsagents (which also sell sweets), antique shops, chemists' shops, pet shops, greengrocers, china and glassware shops, delicatessens, jewellers, bookshops, florists, hairdressers, furniture and carpet shops, and shops that provide services such as opticians and estate agents. Most towns also have a gas and an electricity showroom, where bills can be paid.

A special kind of general shop is the 'corner shop', so called because it is often on a street corner in a part of town where there are no other shops. It is similar to a newsagent's, but has a wider variety of goods, including food and drink, cleaning materials, stationery, etc. In rural areas a similar shop is called the 'village shop', often the only shop in a village. Like the corner shop it normally stocks a mixed range of goods and may also be the local post office. In the USA, a similar kind of shop is called a 'variety store'.

In Britain, the usual opening hours for shops are 9.00 am until 5.00 pm. Some places have an 'early closing day' when the smaller shops close at midday on one day of the week. Newsagents open much earlier, and corner shops, too, often open early and close late in the evening. Chain stores usually have the normal opening hours, but supermarkets, which sell mainly food, often stay open until 8.00 or 9.00 pm.

On Sunday almost all shops are closed, with the exception of newsagents which are open in the morning to sell Sunday newspapers. The present laws on Sunday trading are complicated and permit only certain kinds of goods to be sold. (There are many anomalies: newspapers may be sold but not books, medicines but not fruit drinks, motor-cycle accessories but not kitchen equipment.) Chemists are allowed to open (usually for two hours) late on Sunday morning, and wine shops (called 'off-licences') may also open at this time as well as in the evening. Because the laws are so complicated and are considered by many people to be outdated, there is a campaign to get them abolished, but it is opposed by the shopworkers' trade union and the Lord's Day Observance Society, which also campaigns against sporting events taking place on Sunday.

The largest type of shop in Britain is called a hypermarket or superstore, which is a supermarket on a large scale and usually situated outside a town, where there is space for a large car-park. Many supermarkets have cash dispensers, petrol pumps and a café.

Whereas, formerly, the High Street was the main shopping street in a town, larger towns now usually have a shopping centre, which is an area for pedestrians only, with shops grouped together, sometimes enclosed in a large building.

Goods can be bought not only in shops and stores but also in outdoor markets. Almost all towns and cities have a market once or twice a week, often in the original market-place once used for the sale of cattle and sheep. A market today will have a number of stalls, mostly selling cheap or second-hand goods, but also flowers, fresh fruit and vegetables, as well as meat and fish. The stall-holders often come in to the town from the country to sell their goods, or travel round regularly from town to town. The stalls usually start selling early, and may finish by mid-afternoon.

In the USA people do most of their shopping not in individual shops but in department stores, supermarkets and shopping malls. These are mostly far larger than their British counterparts, with supermarkets more like hypermarkets, for example. Rather than go to separate shops such as the baker, butcher, greengrocer, etc, most Americans prefer to do their shopping in a single store. Supermarkets sell not only foods but household goods, and some sell goods as diverse as cameras, guns and ammunition.

Opening hours vary widely, but most suburban department stores are open from 9.00 am to 9.00 pm, while city-centre stores usually close at 6.00 pm. Sunday opening is more widespread than in Britain, although some states, especially in the Midwest, restrict Sunday sales. Often shopping malls outside city centres will open on Sunday afternoons, while city-centre stores do not.

A typically American kind of shop is the 'drugstore', which usually includes a chemist's (called a pharmacy in the USA) but also sells food, alcoholic drink, stationery and even clothes, as well as drinks and snacks. Rural areas often have roadside stalls where local produce is sold, and many cities have 'farmers markets', similar to the weekly markets in British towns.

politicians shooting it out in a television debate. **shoot a ˈline** (*infml*) exaggerate; tell lies: *She said she was an expert skier but I think she was just shooting a line.* **ˌshoot the ˈmoon** (*infml*) secretly leave the place where one is living without paying one's rent, debts, etc. **shoot one's ˈmouth off (about sth)** (*infml*) **(a)** exaggerate; boast: *He's always shooting his mouth off about his success with women.* **(b)** talk indiscreetly: *It's a secret, so don't go shooting your mouth off about it.* **shoot pool** (*US*) play pool²(4). **shoot one's way in/into sth; shoot one's way out/out of sth** get into/out of sth by shooting: *The gangster stole a gun and shot his way out of prison.* **shoot the ˈworks** (*US infml*) gamble or use up all one's money, resources, effort, etc. **14** (phr v) **shoot sb down** kill sb, esp cruelly, by shooting: *His victims were all shot down in cold blood.* **shoot sth/sb down** cause (an aircraft or its pilot) to fall to the ground by shooting eg a missile: *ships shooting down fighter planes* ○ *(fig) His latest theories have been shot down in flames by the experts.* **shoot sth off (a)** sever sth by shooting it with a gun, etc: *His arm was shot off in the war.* **(b)** shoot (a gun, fireworks, etc) into the air: *People were shooting off pistols in the streets to celebrate the victory.* **shoot sth up** terrorize (a place) by going through it firing guns: *The gangsters ran into the bar and started shooting it up.*

□ **ˈshooting-brake** *n* (*Brit dated*) = ESTATE CAR (ESTATE).

ˈshooting-gallery *n* building or room where people practise shooting rifles, etc at targets.

ˈshooting match (idm) **the whole shooting match** ⇨ WHOLE.

ˌshooting ˈstar (also **falling star**) small meteor that burns up as it enters the earth's atmosphere, appearing as a bright streak in the sky.

ˈshooting-stick *n* stick with a spiked end (to be stuck into the ground) and a handle which unfolds to form a small seat.

ˈshoot-out *n* battle fought with guns: *The robbery led to a shoot-out between the robbers and the police.*

shoot² /ʃuːt/ *n* **1** new young growth on a plant or bush, eg a bud: *train the new shoots of a vine.* **2** (*Brit*) **(a)** (expedition made by a) group of people shooting game animals for sport: *members of a grouse shoot.* **(b)** area of land over which game animals are shot in this way. **3** (idm) **the whole (bang) ˈshoot** (*infml*) everything.

-shooter (in compound *ns*) **1** person who shoots: *a ˈsharpshooter.* **2** thing that shoots: *a ˈpea-shooter* ○ *a ˈsix-shooter.*

shop /ʃɒp/ *n* **1** (*US* **store**) building or room where goods or services are sold to the public: *a butcher's, chemist's, etc shop* ○ *a sweet-shop* ○ *a bookshop* ○ *serve in a shop.* ⇨ article. **2** (also **ˈworkshop**) (esp in compounds) place where things are manufactured or repaired: *an engineering shop* ○ *a machine shop* ○ *a paint shop*, eg where cars are painted. **3** (*infml*) place of business; institution; establishment: *I want this shop to run as smoothly as possible.* **4** (idm) **all ˈover the shop** (*sl*) **(a)** in great disorder; scattered everywhere: *His clothes lay all over the shop.* **(b)** everywhere: *I've looked for it all over the shop.* **a bull in a china shop** ⇨ BULL¹. **come/go to the wrong shop** ⇨ WRONG. **keep ˈshop** look after a shop, serve customers, etc: *Will you keep shop while I go out for lunch?* **set up ˈshop** start a business: *She set up shop as a bookseller in the High Street.* **shut up shop** ⇨ SHUT. **talk shop** ⇨ TALK².

▷ **shop** *v* (**-pp-**) **1** [I, Ipr] ~ **(for sth)** (usu **go shopping**) go to a shop or shops to buy things: *go shopping every day* ○ *I'm shopping for Christmas presents.* **2** [Tn] (*US*) visit (a shop) to buy things: *shopping the stores looking for bargains.* **3** [Tn] (*Brit sl*) give information about (sb), esp to the police: *The gang leader was shopped by one of the robbers.* **4** (phr v) **shop around (for sth)** (*infml*) search carefully for goods that are the best value, or for the best services, etc: *Don't buy the first car you see: shop around a bit.* ○ *People must shop around for the best school for their children.* **shopper** *n* person who is shopping: *crowds of Christmas shoppers.* **shopping** *n* [U] **1** activity of shopping: *do one's shopping* ○ [attrib] *a* ˈ*shopping street*, ie one with many shops ○ *a* ˈ*shopping bag, basket, trolley, etc.* **2** goods bought: *Where did I leave my shopping?* ˈ**shopping centre** area where there are many shops. ˈ**shopping list** **(a)** list of things that one wants to buy. **(b)** (*fig*) set of things one wants to be done, conditions one wants to be met, etc: *They have a shopping list of companies they want to take over.* ˈ**shopping mall** (*US*) area, closed to traffic and usu covered, where there are many shops.

□ ˈ**shop-assistant** (*US* **salesclerk**) *n* person who serves customers in a shop.

ˌ**shop-**ˈ**floor** *n* [sing] **1** area in a factory where goods are made: *working on the shop-floor* ○ [attrib] *a shop-floor worker.* **2** workers in a factory (contrasted with the management): *How does the shop-floor feel about these changes?*

ˈ**shopkeeper** (*US* ˈ**storekeeper**) *n* person who owns or manages a shop, usu a small one.

ˈ**shoplift** *v* [I] steal goods from a shop while pretending to be a customer: *started to shoplift as a fifteen-year-old.* ˈ**shoplifter** *n.* ˈ**shoplifting** *n* [U]: *arrested for shoplifting.*

ˈ**shop-soiled** *adj* dirty or faded from being on display in a shop: *a sale of shop-soiled goods at half price.*

ˌ**shop-**ˈ**steward** *n* trade union official elected by his fellow-workers as their spokesman. ⇨ article at TRADE UNION.

ˈ**shopwalker** *n* (*dated Brit*) supervisor in a large shop, department store, etc.

shore[1] /ʃɔː(r)/ *n* [C, U] land along the edge of the sea or of any large body of water: *a house on the shore(s) of Lake Geneva* ○ *swim from the ship to the shore* ○ *go on shore*, eg of sailors from a ship ○ *This island is two miles off shore.* ⇨ illus at COAST. ⇨ Usage at COAST[1].

□ ˈ**shore leave** (period of) leave[2](1) given to a sailor to go ashore.

shore[2] /ʃɔː(r)/ *v* (phr v) **shore sth up** support sth with a wooden beam, etc propped against it: *shore up the side of an old house to stop it falling down* ○ (*fig*) *She used this evidence to shore up her argument.*

▷ **shore** *n* wooden beam, etc used to support sth.

shorn *pp* of SHEAR.

short[1] /ʃɔːt/ *adj* **(-er, -est)** **1** **(a)** measuring little from one end to the other: *a short stick, line, dress, journey* ○ *short grass, fur* ○ *a short distance between the two houses* ○ *You've cut my hair very short.* ○ *She walked with short quick steps.* ○ *The coat is rather short in the sleeves.* Cf LONG[1] 1. **(b)** below the average height: *a short person* ○ *short in stature* ○ *too short to become a police officer.* Cf TALL. **(c)** not lasting long; brief: *a short holiday, speech, film, ceremony* ○ *have a short memory*, ie remember only things that have happened recently ○ *The days get shorter as winter approaches.* Cf LONG[1] 1. **2** ~ **(of sth)** not reaching the usual standard or required weight, length, quantity, etc: *Water is short at this time of year.* ○ *The shopkeeper gave us short weight: we got 7.5 kilos instead of 10 kilos.* ○ *The soldiers complained that they were getting short rations.* ○ *These goods are in short supply*, ie There are not enough to satisfy the demand for them. ○ *This packet is supposed to contain ten screws, but it's two short.* ○ *The missile landed ten miles short (of its target).* ○ *We've only raised £2 000 so far; we're still £500 short (of the amount we need).* **3** [pred] **(a)** ~ **(of sth)** not having much or enough of sth; lacking sth: *short of time, money, ideas* ○ *The hospital is getting short of clean linen.* ○ *We can't lend you any sugar, we're a bit short (of it) ourselves.* ○ (*infml*) *I'm a bit short* (ie of money) *this week.* **(b)** ~ **on sth** (*infml*) lacking (a certain quality): *He's short on tact.* ○ *Her speeches are rather short on wit.* **4** [pred] ~ **for sth** serving as an abbreviation of sth: *'Ben' is usually short for 'Benjamin'.* **5** **(a)** [pred] ~ **(with sb)** (of a person) speaking sharply and briefly; curt; abrupt: *She was rather short with him when he asked for help.* **(b)** (of a remark or sb's manner of speaking) expressed in few words; curt: *He gave her a short answer.* ○ *All his observations were short and to the point.* **6** **(a)** (of a fielder or his position in cricket) relatively near the batsman: *short leg, slip, etc.* **(b)** (of a bowled ball in cricket) bouncing relatively near to the bowler. **7** (of vowels or syllables) pronounced for a relatively brief time: *the short vowel in 'pull' and the long vowel in 'pool'.* **8** (of an alcoholic drink) small and strong, made with spirits: *I rarely have short drinks.* **9** [usu attrib] (*commerce*) (of a bill of exchange, etc) maturing at an early date: *a short bill, bond, etc* ○ *a short date*, ie an early date for the maturing of a bill, bond, etc. **10** [usu attrib] (of cake or pastry) rich and crumbly as a result of containing much fat: *a flan with a short crust.* **11** (idm) **be on short** ˈ**rations** be allowed or able to have less than the usual quantity of food. **by a short** ˈ**head** **(a)** (in horse-racing) by a distance of less than the length of a horse's head: *win/lose by a short head.* **(b)** by only a little: *I got 96 per cent, he got 94, so I beat him by a short head.* **for** ˈ**short** as an abbreviation: *Her name is 'Frances', or 'Fran' for short.* **get/have sb by the short** ˈ**hairs** (*infml*) get/have sb in a difficult position or at one's mercy. **give full/short measure** ⇨ MEASURE[2]. **give sb/sth/get short** ˈ**shrift** /ʃrɪft/ give sb/sth/get curt treatment or attention: *He went to complain to the boss, but got very short shrift: she told him to get out and stay out.* **in long/short pants** ⇨ PANTS. **in the long/short term** ⇨ TERM. **in** ˈ**short** in a few words; briefly: *Things couldn't be worse, financially: in short, we're bankrupt.* **in short** ˈ**order** quickly and without fuss: *When the children are naughty she deals with them in very short order: they're sent straight to bed.* **in short supply** not plentiful; scarce. **little/nothing short of sth** little/nothing less than sth; almost sth: *Our escape was little short of miraculous.* **make short work of sth/sb** deal with, or dispose of sth/sb quickly: *make short work of one's meal* ○ *The team made short work of their opponents.* **on a short** ˈ**fuse** likely to get angry quickly and easily: *Don't irritate her, she's on a short fuse today.* **out of/short of breath** ⇨ BREATH. **(on) short** ˈ**commons** (*dated*) not having enough to eat. **a short** ˈ**cut** **(a)** route that makes a journey, walk, etc shorter: *I took a short cut across the field to get to school.* **(b)** way of doing sth more efficiently, quickly, etc: *Becoming a doctor requires years of training — there are really no short cuts.* ˌ**short and** ˈ**sweet** (*often ironic*) brief but pleasant: *I only needed two minutes with the doctor — the visit was short and sweet.* **thick as two short planks** ⇨ THICK. ▷ **shortness** *n* [U].

□ ˈ**shortbread** *n* [U] crumbly dry cake made with flour, sugar and much butter.

ˈ**shortcake** *n* [U] **(a)** (*Brit*) = SHORTBREAD. **(b)** dessert made from a biscuit dough or sponge mixture with cream and fruit on top: *strawberry shortcake.*

ˌ**short-**ˈ**change** *v* [Tn] cheat (sb), esp by giving him less than the correct change[2](4).

ˌ**short** ˈ**circuit** (also *infml* **short**) (usu faulty) connection in an electric circuit, by which the current flows along a shorter route than the normal one. ˌ**short-**ˈ**circuit** (also *infml* **short**) *v* **1** [I, Tn] (cause sth to) have a short circuit: *The lights short-circuited when I joined up the wires.* ○ *You've short-circuited the washing-machine.* **2** [Tn] (*fig*) avoid (sth); bypass: *short-circuit the normal procedures to get sth done quickly.*

ˈ**shortcoming** *n* (usu *pl*) failure to be of a required standard; fault: *a system/person with many shortcomings.*

ˈ**shortfall** *n* ~ **(in sth)** deficit: *a shortfall in the annual budget.*

ˈ**short game** (in golf) strokes played when one is on the green or approaching it; chips (CHIP[1] 7) and putts.

ˈ**shorthand** *n* (also *esp US* **stenography**) [U] method of writing rapidly, using special quickly-written symbols: [attrib] *a shorthand course, typist, letter.*

ˌ**short-**ˈ**handed** *adj* [usu pred] not having enough workers, helpers, etc: *The shop is short-handed, so we are all having to work harder.*

ˈ**shorthorn** *n* breed of cattle with short curved horns.

ˈ**short list** small number, esp of candidates for a job, selected from a larger number, and from which the final selection is to be made: *draw up a short list* ○ *Are you on the short list?* ˈ**short-list** *v* [Tn, Tn·pr] ~ **sb (for sth)** put sb on a short list: *Have you been short-listed for the post?*

short-lived /ˌʃɔːt ˈlɪvd; *US* ˈlaɪvd/ *adj* lasting for a short time; brief: *a short-lived triumph, relationship* ○ *Her interest in tennis was very short-lived.*

ˌ**short** ˈ**odds** (in betting) nearly even odds, indicating a horse, etc that is likely to win.

ˌ**short** ˈ**order** (*US*) order for food that can be cooked quickly: [attrib] *a* ˌ*short-order* ˈ*chef.*

ˌ**short-**ˈ**range** *adj* [usu attrib] **1** designed for or applying to a limited period of time: *a* ˌ*short-range* ˈ*plan,* ˈ*project, etc* ○ ˌ*short-range* ˈ*weather forecasts*, ie for one or two days ahead. **2** (of missiles, etc) designed to travel over relatively short distances.

ˌ**short** ˈ**sight** ability to see clearly only what is close. ˌ**short-**ˈ**sighted** *adj* **1** suffering from short sight. **2** (*fig*) having or showing an inability to foresee what will happen: *a short-sighted person, attitude, plan.*

ˌ**short-**ˈ**staffed** *adj* [usu pred] not having enough staff; understaffed: *We're very short-staffed in the office this week.*

ˈ**short-stop** *n* (in baseball) fielding position close to the second base.

ˌ**short** ˈ**story** piece of prose fiction that is shorter than a novel, esp one that deals with a single event or theme.

ˌ**short** ˈ**temper** tendency to become angry quickly and easily: *He has a very short temper.* ˌ**short-**ˈ**tempered** *adj*: *Being tired often makes me short-tempered.*

ˌ**short-**ˈ**term** *adj* [usu attrib] of or for a short period: *a* ˌ*short-term* ˈ*plan,* ˈ*loan, a*ˈ*greement, ap*ˈ*pointment.*

ˌ**short** ˈ**time** employment for less than the full working week: *workers on short time* ○ [attrib] ˌ*short-time* ˈ*working.*

ˌ**short** ˈ**wave** (*abbr* **SW**) radio wave with a length between 100 and 10 metres: [attrib] *a* ˌ*short-wave* ˈ*radio,* ˈ*broadcast, etc.*

ˌ**short-**ˈ**winded** *adj* easily getting breathless after exerting oneself, running, etc.

short[2] /ʃɔːt/ *adv* **1** suddenly; abruptly: *He stopped short when he heard his name called.* **2** (idm) **be caught/taken** ˈ**short** (*infml*) suddenly feel the need to go the lavatory urgently. **bring/pull sb up short/sharply** ⇨ PULL[2]. **cut a long story short** ⇨ LONG[1]. **cut sth/sb** ˈ**short** bring sth/sb to an end before the usual or natural time; interrupt sth/sb: *a career tragically cut short by illness* ○ *The interviewer cut short his guest in mid-sentence.* **fall short of sth** not reach sth: *The money collected fell short of the amount required.* ○ *His achievements had fallen short of his hopes.* **go short (of sth)** not have enough (of sth): *If you earn well, you'll never go short.* ○ *The children must not go short of food.* **run short (of sth)** use up most of one's supply (of sth): *Go and get some more oil so we don't run short.* ○ *I'm late for work every day, and I'm running short of excuses.* **sell sth/sb short** ⇨ SELL. **short of sth** without sth; unless sth happens: *Short of a miracle, we're certain to lose now.* **stop short of sth/doing sth** ⇨ STOP[1].

short[3] /ʃɔːt/ *n* (*infml*) **1** = SHORT CIRCUIT (SHORT[1]). **2** short film, esp one shown before the main film at a cinema. **3** (esp *pl*) small strong alcoholic drink, esp of spirits. **4** (idm) **the long and short of it** ⇨ LONG[2]. ▷ **short** *v* [I, Tn] (*infml*) = SHORT-CIRCUIT (SHORT[1]).

shortage /ˈʃɔːtɪdʒ/ *n* [C, U] lack of sth needed; deficiency: *food, fuel, housing shortages* ○ *a shortage of rice, funds, equipment* ○ *owing to (a) shortage of staff* ○ *a shortage of 50 tons* ○ *There was no shortage of helpers.*

shorten /ˈʃɔːtn/ *v* [I, Tn] (cause sth to) become shorter: *The days are beginning to shorten*, eg in autumn. ○ *take two links out of the chain to shorten it* ○ *They want to shorten the time it takes to make the car.* Cf LENGTHEN (LENGTH).

shortening /ˈʃɔːtnɪŋ/ *n* [U] fat used to make pastry light and crumbly.

shortly /ˈʃɔːtlɪ/ *adv* **1** in a short time; not long; soon: *shortly afterwards* ○ *coming shortly* ○ *shortly before noon* ○ *I'll be with you shortly.* **2** in a cross way; curtly: *spoke to me rather shortly.*

shorts /ʃɔːts/ *n* [pl] **1** short trousers that do not reach the knee, eg as worn by children, or by adults playing sports or in hot weather: *a pair of tennis shorts.* **2** (*US*) men's underpants.

shorty /ˈʃɔːtɪ/ *n* (*infml*) **(a)** (*sometimes derog*) (used esp as a term of address) person who is shorter than average. **(b)** garment that is shorter than average: [attrib] *a shorty mackintosh.*

Shoshone /ʃəˈʃəʊnɪ/ *n* **1** [C] (*pl* unchanged or ~**s**) member of a native American people of Wyoming, Idaho, Nevada and neighbouring states. **2** [U] language of this people. ▷ **Shoshone** *adj.*

Shostakovich /ˌʃɒstəˈkəʊvɪtʃ/ Dmitri (1906-75), Russian composer. During *Stalin's period he was often in conflict with the Soviet authorities. His work, which includes 15 symphonies, shows great emotional power and originality.

shot[1] /ʃɒt/ *n* **1** [C] ~ **(at sb/sth)** act of shooting a gun, etc; sound of this: *fire a few shots* ○ *hear shots in the distance* ○ *take a shot at the enemy* ○ *Two of her shots hit the centre of the target.* ○ (*fig*) *His remark was meant as a shot at me.* **2** [C] ~ **(at sth/doing sth)** attempt to do sth; try: *have a shot at (solving) this problem* ○ *After a few shots at guessing who did it, I gave up.* **3** [C] stroke in cricket, tennis, billiards, etc or a kick in football: *a backhand shot* ○ *Good shot!* ○ *The striker had/took a shot at goal*, ie tried to score. **4** [C] **(a)** (*pl* unchanged) (formerly) non-explosive ball of stone or metal shot from a cannon or gun. Cf CARTRIDGE 1, SHELL 3. **(b)** (often **the shot**) [sing] heavy iron ball used in shot-put competitions: *put* (ie throw) *the shot.* **5** [U] (also **lead ˈshot**) large number of tiny balls or pellets of lead packed inside cartridges fired from shotguns. **6** [C] person with regard to his skill in shooting a gun, etc: *a first-class, good, poor, etc shot.* **7** [C] **(a)** photograph or scene photographed: *a long shot*, ie taken with a long distance between the camera and the thing photographed ○ *a shot of the politician making a speech.* **(b)** single continuous film sequence photographed by one camera: *an action shot of a car chase.* **8** [C] launch of a space rocket, missile, etc: *the second space shot this year.* **9** [C] (*infml*) injection of a drug, etc with a hypodermic needle: *Have you had your typhus shots yet?* **10** [C] (*infml*) small amount of whisky, gin, etc: *a shot of vodka.* **11** (idm) **a big noise/shot** ⇨ BIG. **call the shots/tune** ⇨ CALL[2]. **a leap/shot in the dark** ⇨ DARK[1]. **like a ˈshot** (*infml*) **(a)** at once; without hesitation: *If I had the chance to go, I'd take it like a shot.* **(b)** very fast: *The dog was after the rabbit like a shot.* **a long shot** ⇨ LONG[1]. **not by a long chalk/shot** ⇨ LONG[1]. **a parting shot** ⇨ PARTING. **a ˌshot across the/sb's ˈbows** /ˈbaʊz/ thing done or said to warn sb that if he does not act differently, he risks punishment, defeat, etc: *The local election results are a shot across the government's bows.* **a ˌshot in the ˈarm** thing that encourages or gives fresh energy to sb/sth: *The improved trade figures are a much-needed shot in the arm for the economy.*

□ **ˈshotgun** *n* **1** gun for firing cartridges containing shot[1](5), eg at birds, rabbits, etc. ⇨ illus at GUN. **2** (idm) **a shotgun ˈwedding** wedding of two people who are or feel forced to marry, usu because the woman is pregnant.

ˈshot-put *n* [sing] (also **ˌputting the ˈshot**) sports contest in which athletes try to throw a shot[1](4b) as far as possible.

shot[2] /ʃɒt/ *adj* **1** ~ **(with sth)** (of cloth) woven or dyed so as to show different colours when looked at from different angles: *shot silk* ○ *a black curtain shot with silver* ○ (*fig*) *brown hair shot with grey.* **2** [usu pred] (*infml esp US*) worn out; used up; wrecked: *Her patience was completely shot.* **3** (idm) **shot through with sth** containing much of (a quality); suffused with sth: *conversation shot through with humour* ○ *comedy shot through with sadness.*

shot[3] *pt, pp* of SHOOT[1].

should[1] /ʃəd; *strong form* ʃʊd/ *modal v* (*neg* **should not**, *contracted form* **shouldn't** /ˈʃʊdnt/) **1** **(a)** (indicating obligation): *You shouldn't drink and drive.* ○ *Visitors should inform the receptionist of their arrival.* ○ *We should have bought a new lock for the front door.* ⇨ Usage 1 at MUST. **(b)** (indicating advice or recommendation): *He should stop smoking.* ○ *You shouldn't leave a baby alone in the house.* ○ *They should have called the police.* ⇨ Usage 2 at MUST. **2** (drawing a tentative conclusion): *We should arrive before dark.* ○ *The roads should be less crowded today.* ○ *I should have finished reading it by Friday.* ⇨ Usage 3 at MUST. **3** (*fml*) (used to describe the consequence of an imagined event): *If I was asked to work on Sundays I should resign.* ○ *We should move to a larger house if we had the money.* **4** (used in a *that*-clause after the *adjs anxious, sorry, concerned, happy, delighted,* etc): *I'm anxious that he should be well cared for.* ○ *We're sorry that you should feel uncomfortable.* ○ *That he should speak to you like that is quite astonishing.* ○ *I am delighted that he should take that view.* **5** (used after *if* and *in case*, or with subject and *v* reversed, to suggest that an event is unlikely to happen): *If you should change your mind, do let me know.* ○ *If he should have forgotten to go to the airport, nobody will be there to meet her.* ○ *Should anyone phone* (ie If anyone phones), *please tell them I'm busy.* **6** (*fml*) (used after *so that/in order that* to express purpose): *He put the cases in the car so that he should be able to make an early start.* ○ *She repeated the instructions slowly in order that he should understand.* **7** **(a)** (used to make polite requests): *I should like to make a phone call, if possible.* ○ *We should be grateful for your help.* Cf WOULD[1] 2a. **(b)** (used with *imagine, say, think,* etc to give tentative opinions): *I should imagine it will take about three hours.* ○ *I should say she's over forty.* ○ *'Is this long enough?' 'I should think so.'* **8** **(a)** (used with question words to express lack of interest, disbelief, etc): *How should I know?* ○ *Why should he think that?* **(b)** (used with question words to express surprise): *I was thinking of going to see John when who should appear but John himself.* ○ *I turned round on the bus and who should be sitting behind me but my ex-wife.*

should[2] *pt* of SHALL.

shoulder /ˈʃəʊldə(r)/ *n* **1** [C] **(a)** part of the body where an arm, a foreleg or a wing is attached; part of the human body from this point to the neck: *look back over one's shoulder* ○ *shrug one's shoulders* ○ *This coat is too narrow across the shoulders.* ⇨ illus at HUMAN, ⇨ Usage at BODY. **(b)** part of a garment covering this: *a jacket with padded shoulders.* **(c)** [C, U] piece of meat cut from the upper foreleg of an animal: *some shoulder of lamb, beef, etc.* **2** **shoulders** [pl] **(a)** part of the back between the shoulders: *a person with broad shoulders* ○ *a coalman carrying a sack on his shoulders* ○ *give a child a ride on one's shoulders.* **(b)** (*fig*) a person, with regard to the responsibilities, blame, etc he must bear: *shift the blame onto sb else's shoulders* ○ *The burden of guilt has been lifted from my shoulders.* ○ *The duty fell upon her shoulders.* **3** [C] part of a thing resembling a human shoulder in shape or position, eg on a bottle, tool, mountain. ⇨ illus at MOUNTAIN. **4** (idm) **be/stand head and shoulders above sb/sth** ⇨ HEAD[1]. **a chip on one's shoulder** ⇨ CHIP[1]. **give sb/get the cold shoulder** ⇨ COLD[1]. **have a good head on one's shoulders** ⇨ HEAD[1]. **an old head on young shoulders** ⇨ OLD. **put one's shoulder to the ˈwheel** work hard at a task: *Come on, everyone, shoulders to the wheel — we've got a lot to do.* **rub shoulders with sb** ⇨ RUB[1]. **a ˌshoulder to ˈcry on** person who listens to one's troubles in a sympathetic way. **ˌshoulder to ˈshoulder** **(a)** side by side: *soldiers standing shoulder to shoulder.* **(b)** working, fighting, etc together; united: *shoulder to shoulder with one's fellow-workers in the dispute.* **straight from the shoulder** ⇨ STRAIGHT[2].

▷ **shoulder** *v* **1** [Tn] **(a)** put (sth) on one's shoulder(s): *She shouldered her rucksack and set off along the road.* **(b)** (*fig*) take (guilt, responsibility, etc) upon oneself: *shoulder the duties of chairman* ○ *She won't shoulder all the blame for the mistake.* **2** [Tn·pr, Tn·p] push (sb/sth) with one's shoulder: *shoulder sb to one side* ○ *He shouldered off a defender and shot at goal.* **3** (phr v) **shoulder one's way in, through, past, etc** move in the specified direction by pushing with one's shoulder(s): *shoulder one's way into the room* ○ *shoulder one's way through (the crowd).*

□ **ˈshoulder-bag** *n* bag hung over the shoulder by a long strap.

ˈshoulder-blade *n* either of the two large flat bones at the top of the back; scapula. ⇨ illus at SKELETON.

ˈshoulder-strap *n* **(a)** narrow strip of material that goes over the shoulder to support a bra, nightdress, etc. **(b)** narrow strap on the shoulder of a military uniform, a raincoat, an overcoat, etc.

shout /ʃaʊt/ *n* **1** loud call or cry: *shouts of joy, alarm, excitement, etc* ○ *Her warning shout came too late.* ○ *She was greeted with shouts of 'Long live the President!'* **2** (*sl esp Austral or NZ*) person's turn to buy drinks: *What will you have? It's my shout.*

▷ **shout** *v* **1** **(a)** [I, Ipr, Ip, Cn·a, Dpr·f, Dpr·t no passive, Dpr·w] ~ **(at/to sb)**; ~ **(out)** speak or call out in a loud voice: *shout for joy* ○ *shout (out) in pain* ○ *We had to shout because the music was so loud.* ○ *Don't shout at me!* ○ *She shouted to me across the room.* ○ *She shouted herself hoarse cheering on the team.* ○ *He shouted to me that the boat was sinking.* ○ *I shouted to him to shut the gate.* **(b)** [Tn, Tn·pr, Tn·p, Tf no passive] ~ **sth (at/to sb)**; ~ **sth (out)** say sth in a loud voice: *I shouted (out) my name to the teacher.* ○ *'Go back,' she shouted.* ○ *They shouted their disapproval*, ie expressed it by shouting. ○ *She shouted that she couldn't hear properly.* **2** (phr v) **shout sb down** shout to prevent sb from speaking: *The crowd shouted the speaker down.* **shouting** *n* [U] **1** shouts: [attrib] *within shouting distance*, ie near enough to hear sth shouted. **2** (idm) **be all over ˌbar the ˈshouting** (of a performance, contest, etc) be concluded or decided, with only the applause, the official announcement, etc to follow: *Now that most of the election results have been declared, it's all over bar the shouting.*

NOTE ON USAGE: Compare **cry (out)**, **shout**, **yell** and **scream.** These verbs indicate people making different kinds of noise for various reasons. We **cry out** by making a sharp noise as an automatic reaction to pain, surprise, etc: *He cried out in fright as the dark figure approached.* We **shout** in anger or to get attention: *I don't like our teacher; he's always shouting at us.* ○ *I had to shout to make myself heard.* **Yell** is to make a high-pitched shout of pain, fear or excitement: *We heard him yelling for help.* It can also indicate loud shouting: *You don't have to yell; I can hear you.* People **scream** in pain, fear or excitement. It is a very loud, high-pitched noise: *The baby woke up screaming.* These verbs can all be used instead of 'say' to indicate ways of speaking: *'Get out!' she screamed/yelled/shouted.* ○ *'Who's there?' he cried (out).*

shove /ʃʌv/ *v* **1** [I, Tn, Tn·pr, Tn·p] push (sb/sth) roughly: *a crowd pushing and shoving to get in* ○ *Who shoved me?* ○ *He shoved her out of the way.* ○ *The policeman shoved me aside.* **2** [Tn·pr, Tn·p] (*infml*) put (sth) casually (in a place): *shove papers (away) in a drawer* ○ *'Where shall I put the case?' 'Shove it on top of the car.'* **3** (idm) **put/shove/stick one's oar in** ⇨ OAR. **4** (phr v) **shove off** **(a)** push a boat out onto the water away from the shore (eg by pushing the shore with a pole). **(b)** (*infml*) (often imperative) leave; go away: *You* *aren't wanted here, so shove off!* **shove up** (*infml*) move along, esp in order to make more room: *We can get one more in if you shove up.*

▷ **shove** *n* (usu *sing*) rough push: *give sb/sth a good shove.*

□ **shove-halfpenny** /ˌʃʌv ˈheɪpnɪ/ *n* [U] game played in pubs, etc, in which coins are pushed with the hand along a marked board.

shovel /ˈʃʌvl/ *n* **1** tool like a spade with curved edges, used for moving earth, snow, sand, etc. ⇨ illus at SPADE. **2** part of a large earth-moving machine that scoops up earth, etc like a shovel.

▷ **shovel** *v* (**-ll-**; *US* **-l-**) **1** [Tn, Tn·pr, Tn·p] lift or move (sth) with a shovel: *spend hours shovelling snow* ○ *shovel sand into the hole* ○ *shovel up coal into the container* ○ (*fig derog*) *shovelling food into their mouths.* **2** [Tn, Cn·a] make or clear (sth) by shovelling: *shovel a path through the snow* ○ *shovel the pavement clear of snow.*

shovelful /-fʊl/ *n* amount that a shovel can hold: *two shovelfuls of earth.*

shoveller

shoveller (*US* **shoveler**) /ˈʃʌvələ(r)/ *n* type of duck with a shovel-like beak. ⇨ illus.

show[1] /ʃəʊ/ *n* **1** [C] any type of public entertainment, eg a circus, a theatre performance, or a radio or TV programme: *a TV quiz show* ○ *a comedy show on radio* ○ *She has her own chat show.* ○ *The most successful shows in the London theatre are often musicals.* **2** [C] public display or exhibition, eg of things in a competition, new products, etc: *a flower, horse, cattle show* ○ *the motor show*, ie where new models of cars, etc are displayed ○ *the Lord Mayor's Show*, ie a procession through the streets of London when a new Mayor is appointed. ⇨ Usage at DEMONSTRATION. **3** [C, U] (**a**) thing done to give a certain impression, often a false one; outward appearance: *a show of defiance, friendship, sympathy* ○ *a show of force, strength*, ie to frighten one's opponents ○ *His public expressions of grief are nothing but show.* (**b**) splendid or pompous display: *a fine show of blossom on the apple trees* ○ *all the glitter and show of the circus* ○ *They are too fond of show*, ie too ostentatious. **4** [C] flow of blood from the vagina during childbirth, esp when labour is starting. **5** [C usu *sing*] (*Brit infml*) thing done or performed in a specified way: *a poor show*, ie sth done badly ○ *put up a good show*, eg do well in examinations or a contest. **6** [C] (*infml*) anything that is happening; organization, business or undertaking: *She runs the whole show.* ○ *Let's get this show moving*, ie start work. ○ *This is the manager's show: you must ask him about it.* **7** (idm) **for ˈshow** intended to be seen but not used: *She only has those books for show — she never reads them.* **get the ˌshow on the ˈroad** (*infml*) start a piece of work, project, etc in an organized and determined way, esp after delay: *Now the team's found a sponsor we can get the show on the road.* **ˌgood ˈshow!** (*Brit infml*) (used to express approval or congratulation when sth has been done well): *You passed your exams? Good show!* **on ˈshow** being displayed: *All the new products were on show at the exhibition.* **a show of ˈhands** raising of hands by a group of people to vote for or against sth: *The issue was decided by a show of hands.* ○ *Who is in favour of the proposal? Can I have a show of hands, please?* **steal the scene/show** ⇨ STEAL. **stop the show** ⇨ STOP[1].

▷ **showy** *adj* (**-ier, -iest**) (*often derog*) attracting attention through being bright, colourful or exaggerated: *a showy dress, hair-style, manner.* **showily** /-ɪlɪ/ *adv*: *dress very showily.* **showiness** *n* [U].

□ **showbiz** /ˈʃəʊbɪz/ *n* [U] (*infml*) = SHOW BUSINESS.

ˈ**show business** business of professional entertainment, esp in the theatre, in films, in TV, etc: *working in show business* ○ [attrib] *show-business people, news.*

ˈ**show-case** *n* **1** case with a glass top or sides, for displaying articles in a shop, museum, etc. **2** (*fig*) any means of showing sth favourably: *The programme is a show-case for young talent.*

ˈ**show-down** *n* final test, argument or fight to settle a dispute: *The two contenders for the world championship will meet for a show-down next month.* ○ *Management are seeking a show-down with the unions on the issue of illegal strikes.*

ˈ**showgirl** *n* girl (usu one of a group) who sings and dances in a musical show.

ˈ**show house**, ˈ**show flat** etc house, flat, etc that is completed before others in a building development, usu furnished and decorated, and shown to people who might want to buy.

ˈ**show-jumping** *n* [U] sport of riding a horse to jump over barriers, fences, etc: [attrib] *a show-jumping competition.*

ˈ**showman** /-mən/ *n* (*pl* **-men** /-mən/) **1** person who organizes public entertainments, eg musicals, pop concerts, etc. **2** person who is skilled in showmanship: *He's always been a bit of a showman*, ie fond of drawing attention to himself.

ˈ**showmanship** *n* [U] skill in attracting public attention, eg to sth one wishes to sell or to one's own abilities.

ˈ**show-piece** *n* thing that is an excellent example of its type and is therefore used for display.

ˈ**show-place** *n* place that is attractive or interesting, eg for tourists: *old castles, palaces and other show-places.*

ˈ**showroom** *n* place where things, eg goods for sale, are put on display.

ˈ**show-stopper** *n* song, dance, etc that gets great applause during a show. ˈ**show-stopping** *adj*: *fifteen show-stopping hits from Rodgers and Hammerstein.*

ˈ**show trial** (*derog*) trial in which the proceedings are arranged to impress or frighten people rather than in the interests of justice.

show[2] /ʃəʊ/ *v* (*pt* **showed**, *pp* **shown** /ʃəʊn/ or, rarely, **showed**) **1** (**a**) [Tn, Cn·a, Cn·g, Dn·n, Dn·pr] ~ **sb/sth (to sb)** cause sb/sth to be seen; display sb/sth: *You must show your ticket at the barrier.* ○ *The film is being shown at the local cinema.* ○ *Her paintings are being shown* (ie exhibited) *at a gallery in London.* ○ *The photo shows her dressed in black.* ○ *In the portrait he is shown lying on a sofa.* ○ *He showed me his pictures.* ○ *She has shown them to all her friends.* (**b**) [Tn, Tf, Tw] allow (sth) to be seen; reveal: *A dark suit doesn't show the dirt so much.* ○ *My shoes are showing signs of wear.* **2** [I, Ipr, Ip] be visible or noticeable: *Your petticoat is showing, Jane.* ○ *Does the scar still show?* ○ *His fear showed in his eyes.* ○ *Her laziness showed in her exam results.* ○ *His shirt was so thin that his vest showed through (it).* **3** [Tn no passive, Dn·n, Dn·w] point (sth) out; indicate: *The clock shows half past two.* ○ *Show me which picture you drew.* **4** [Tn no passive] (**a**) ~ **itself** be visible: *His annoyance showed itself in his face.* ○ *The sun didn't show itself all day.* (**b**) ~ **oneself** be present; appear: *He showed himself briefly at the party.* ○ *The leader rarely shows herself in public.* **5** [Tn, Dn·n, Dn·pr] treat (sb) with (kindness, respect, cruelty, etc); give; grant: *The king often shows mercy (to prisoners).* ○ *The priest showed me great understanding.* ○ *They showed nothing but contempt for him.* **6** [Tn, Cn·a, Cn·n no passive] give evidence or proof of being or having (sth): *show no signs of intelligence* ○ *a soldier who showed great courage/showed himself to be very brave* ○ *She showed herself unable to deal with money.* ○ *He showed himself (to be) a dishonest rascal.* **7** [Tn, Tf, Tw, Tnt, Dn·n, Dn·pr, Dn·f, Dn·w] ~ **sth (to sb)** make sth clear; demonstrate sth; prove sth: *show the falseness of her claims/that her claims are false* ○ *show (him) how to do it/what to do* ○ *His expression shows how unhappy he is.* ○ *Her new book shows her to be a first-rate novelist.* ○ *They were shown the tragedy of war.* ○ *She showed her methods of analysis to her pupils.* **8** [Tn·pr, Tn·p] lead or conduct (sb) to the specified place or in the specified direction: *We were shown into the waiting-room.* ○ *Please show this lady out (of the building).* ○ *The usherette showed us to our seats.* ○ *Our trained guides will show you round (the museum).* **9** [Tn no passive] (*infml*) prove one's ability or worth to (sb): *They think I can't win, but I'll show them.* **10** (*sl esp US*) appear; show up: *I waited for you all morning but you never showed.* **11** [I] (*US*) win a place (third or better) in a horse race. **12** (idm) **do/show sb a kindness** ⇨ KINDNESS (KIND[1]). **fly/show/wave the flag** ⇨ FLAG[1]. **go to ˈshow** serve to prove or demonstrate: *You've got no money now. It all/only goes to show you shouldn't gamble.* **show (sb) a clean pair of ˈheels** (*infml often joc*) run away. **show sb the ˈdoor** ask sb to leave: *After having insulted his host, he was shown the door.* **show one's ˈface** appear before people: *She daren't show her face in the street.* **show one's ˈhand/ˈcards** reveal one's intentions or plans: *I suspect they're planning something but they haven't shown their hand yet.* **show sb/know/learn the ropes** ⇨ ROPE. **show a ˈleg** (*infml joc*) get out of bed. **show one's teeth** use one's power or authority to intimidate or punish sb. **show (sb) the ˈway** (**a**) tell sb how to get to a certain place: *show him the way to the station.* (**b**) be an example to sb: *Let's hope her bravery will show the way for other young people.* **show the white ˈfeather** act in a cowardly way; show fear. **show ˈwilling** show that one is ready to do sth, eg work hard, help, etc: *I don't think I'm needed as a helper, but I'll go anyway, just to show willing.* **(have) something, nothing, etc to show for sth** (have) something, nothing, etc as a result of sth: *All those years of hard work, and nothing to show for it!* ○ *I've only got £100 to show for all the stuff I sold.* **13** (phr v) **show off** (*infml often derog*) try to impress others with one's abilities, wealth, intelligence, etc: *Do stop showing off — it's embarrassing.* ○ *The child danced around the room, showing off to everybody.* **show sb/sth off** draw people's attention to sb/sth: *a dress that shows off her figure well* ○ *She was showing off her new husband at the party.* ○ *He likes showing off how well he speaks French.* **show up** (*infml*) arrive, often after a delay; appear: *It was ten o'clock when he finally showed up.* ○ *We were hoping for a full team today but only five players showed up.* **show (sth) up** (cause sth to) become visible: *The dust on the shelf shows up in the sunlight.* ○ *Close inspection shows up the cracks in the stonework.* **show sb up** (*infml*) make sb feel embarrassed by behaving badly in his company: *He showed me up by falling asleep at the concert.* **show sb up (as/for sth/to be sth)** show sb to be (dishonest, disreputable, etc): *His diary shows him up as/shows him up to have been a greedy, arrogant man.*

▷ **showing** *n* **1** act of showing: *two showings of the film daily.* **2** (usu *sing*) record or evidence of the success, quality, etc of sb/sth: *the company's poor financial showing in recent years* ○ *On* (ie Judging by) *last week's showing, the team is unlikely to win today.*

□ ˈ**show-off** *n* (*derog*) person who tries to impress others in speech or actions: *Take no notice of him — you know what a show-off he is.*

shower /ˈʃaʊə(r)/ *n* **1** [C] (**a**) brief fall of rain, sleet or hail; sudden sprinkle of water: *be caught in a shower* ○ *a shower of spray.* (**b**) large number of things falling or arriving together: *a shower of stones, arrows, dust, ash* ○ (*fig*) *a shower of insults, blessings.* **2** [C] (**a**) (small room or cabinet containing a) device attached to the water supply, which produces a spray of water for washing: *I'm in the shower.* ○ [attrib] *a shower cap*, ie for keeping the hair dry. (**b**) wash in or under this: *take a shower.* **3** (*US*) party at which presents are given to a person, esp a woman about to get married or have a baby. **4** [Gp] (*Brit infml derog*) group of foolish, incompetent or contemptible people: *Get out of bed, you miserable shower!*

▷ **shower** *v* **1** [Ipr, Ip] ~ **(down) on sb/sth**; ~

down fall in a shower: *Small stones showered (down) on us from above.* ○ *Good wishes showered (down) on the bride and bridegroom.* **2** [Tn·pr] ~ **sb with sth**; ~ **sth on/upon sb** **(a)** cause (a great number of things) to fall on sb: *shower the newly-weds with confetti* ○ *The falling wall showered dust on us.* **(b)** send or give sth to sb in great numbers: *The dancer was showered with praise.* ○ *shower gifts on sb* ○ *Honours were showered upon the hero.* ⇨ Usage at SPRAY².

showery /ˈʃaʊərɪ/ *adj* (of the weather) with frequent showers of rain: *a showery day.*

□ ˈ**shower-proof** *adj* (of clothing) that can keep out light rain.

shown *pp* of SHOW².

shrank *pt* of SHRINK.

shrapnel /ˈʃræpnəl/ *n* [U] small fragments of metal encased in a shell and scattered when the shell explodes: *be hit by (a piece of) shrapnel.*

shred /ʃred/ *n* **1** (esp *pl*) strip or piece torn, cut or scraped from sth: *The jacket was torn to shreds by the barbed wire.* **2** ~ **of sth** (usu *sing*, in questions and negative sentences) (*fig*) small amount of sth: *not a shred of truth in what she says* ○ *Can they find a shred of evidence against me?*

▷ **shred** *v* (**-dd-**) [Tn] tear, cut, etc (sth) into shreds: *shredded cabbage* ○ *shredding top-secret documents.*

shredder *n* device that shreds, esp one that cuts documents into very small pieces so that they cannot be read.

shrew /ʃruː/ *n* **1** small mouse-like animal that feeds on insects. **2** (*dated*) bad-tempered scolding woman.

▷ **shrewish** *adj* bad-tempered; scolding. **shrewishly** *adv*. **shrewishness** *n* [U].

shrewd /ʃruːd/ *adj* (**-er, -est**) having or showing good judgement and common sense; astute: *a shrewd financier, dealer, politician, etc* ○ *a shrewd argument, plan, measure, investment* ○ *make a shrewd guess*, ie one that is likely to be right. ▷ **shrewdly** *adv*. **shrewdness** *n* [U].

shriek /ʃriːk/ *v* **(a)** [Ipr, Ip] ~ **with sth**; ~ **(out)** utter a shrill scream: *shrieking with laughter, excitement* ○ *shriek (out) in fright.* **(b)** [Tn, Tn·p] ~ **sth (out)** utter sth with a shrill scream: *shriek (out) a warning* ○ *'I hate you,' he shrieked.*

▷ **shriek** *n* shrill scream: *shrieks of laughter* ○ *He gave a loud shriek and dropped the pan.*

shrift /ʃrɪft/ *n* (idm) **give sb/sth/get short shrift** ⇨ SHORT¹.

shrike /ʃraɪk/ *n* bird with a strong hooked bill which often impales its prey (small birds and insects) on thorns.

shrill /ʃrɪl/ *adj* **1** (**-er, -est**) (of sounds, voices, etc) high-pitched; piercing; sharp: *a shrill cry, whistle* ○ *the shrill call of the parrot.* **2** (*fig sometimes derog*) making loud, persistent and forceful complaints, demands, etc: *his shrill protests about cruelty* ○ *The Opposition were shrill in their criticism of the Government's action.* ▷ **shrilly** /ˈʃrɪlɪ/ *adv*: *scream shrilly* ○ *complain shrilly in a letter.* **shrillness** *n* [U].

shrimp /ʃrɪmp/ *n* **1** small marine shellfish that is used for food, becoming pink when boiled. ⇨ illus at SHELLFISH. **2** (*joc or derog*) very small person: *a pale, skinny shrimp.*

▷ **shrimp** *v* [I] (usu **go shrimping**) try to catch shrimps.

shrine /ʃraɪn/ *n* **1** any place that is regarded as holy because of its associations with a special person or event: *He built a chapel as a shrine to the memory of his dead wife.* ○ (*fig*) *Wimbledon is a shrine for all lovers of tennis.* **2** tomb or container in which holy relics are kept.

shrink /ʃrɪŋk/ *v* (*pt* **shrank** /ʃræŋk/ or **shrunk** /ʃrʌŋk/, *pp* **shrunk**) **1** [I, Tn] (cause sth to) become smaller, esp because of moisture or heat or cold: *Will this shirt shrink in the wash?* ○ *The dough shrank slowly in the cold air.* ○ *Car sales have been shrinking* (ie Fewer have been sold) *recently.* ○ *The hot water shrank my pullover.* **2** (idm) **a** ˌ**shrinking** ˈ**violet** (*joc*) timid or shy person: *She's no shrinking violet — always ready to speak up for herself.* **3** (phr v) **shrink (away/back) from sth/sb** move back or withdraw from sth/sb, esp through fear or disgust: *As he moved threateningly forward she shrank (back) from him.* **shrink from sth/doing sth** be reluctant to do sth: *He shrinks from hurting animals.*

▷ **shrink** *n* (*sl joc esp US*) psychiatrist.

shrinkage /ˈʃrɪŋkɪdʒ/ *n* [U] **1** process of shrinking; amount by which sth shrinks: *You can expect some shrinkage when the jeans are washed.* ○ *There has been some shrinkage in our export trade.* **2** (*commerce*) loss of profit by a shop, etc caused by thefts or wastage.

shrunken /ˈʃrʌŋkən/ *adj* [usu attrib] having shrunk: *an old, shrunken apple* ○ *the shrunken body of a starving child.*

□ ˌ**shrink-**ˈ**wrap** *v* (**-pp-**) [Tn esp passive] wrap (eg food) in plastic film that shrinks tightly round it: ˌ*shrink-wrapped* ˈ*cheese.*

shrive /ʃraɪv/ *v* (*pt* **shrived** or **shrove** /ʃrəʊv/, *pp* **shrived** or **shriven** /ˈʃrɪvn/) [Tn] (*arch*) (of a priest) hear (sb) confess his sins and tell him that God will forgive him for them.

shrivel /ˈʃrɪvl/ *v* (**-ll-**; *US* **-l-**) [I, Ip, Tn, Tn·p] ~ **(sth) (up)** (cause sth to) shrink and wrinkle from heat, cold or dryness: *The leaves shrivelled (up) in the sun.* ○ *The dry air shrivels the leather.* ○ *He has a shrivelled face*, ie with many wrinkles.

Shropshire /ˈʃrɒpʃə(r)/ county in the W Midlands of England. It lies on the Welsh border and is mainly agricultural. ⇨ map at App 1.

shroud /ʃraʊd/ *n* **1** (also ˈ**winding-sheet**) [C] cloth or sheet in which a dead person is wrapped for burial. **2** [C] ~ **(of sth)** (*fig*) thing that covers and hides: *a shroud of fog, smoke, etc* ○ *cloaked in a shroud of mystery/secrecy.* **3 shrouds** [pl] ropes supporting a ship's masts.

▷ **shroud** *v* [Tn·pr esp passive] ~ **sth in sth** cover or hide sth with sth: *shrouded in darkness, mist, etc* ○ *a crime shrouded in mystery.*

Shrove Tuesday /ˌʃrəʊv ˈtjuːzdɪ, -deɪ; *US* ˈtuːz-/ day before the beginning of Lent, on which people were often shriven. Cf ASH WEDNESDAY (ASH²).

shrub /ʃrʌb/ *n* plant with a woody stem, lower than a tree and often having smaller stems branching off near the ground: [attrib] *shrub roses.* Cf BUSH.

▷ **shrubbery** /ˈʃrʌbərɪ/ *n* [C, U] area planted with shrubs: *plant a shrubbery* ○ *hiding in some shrubbery.*

shrug /ʃrʌɡ/ *v* (**-gg-**) **1** [I, Tn] raise (one's shoulders) slightly to express doubt, indifference, ignorance, etc: *I asked her where Sam was, but she just shrugged (her shoulders)*, ie to show she didn't know or didn't care. **2** (phr v) **shrug sth off** dismiss sth as being unimportant: *I admire the way she is able to shrug off unfair criticism.*

▷ **shrug** *n* (usu *sing*) movement of shrugging the shoulders: *with a shrug of the shoulders* ○ *She gave a shrug and walked away.*

shrunk, shrunken ⇨ SHRINK.

shuck /ʃʌk/ *n* (*US*) **1** [C] outer covering of a nut, etc; shell; husk. **2 shucks** [pl] thing of little value: *not worth shucks.*

▷ **shuck** *v* [Tn] (*US*) remove the shucks from (sth); shell: *shuck peanuts, maize, peas.*

shucks *interj* (*US infml*) (used to express annoyance, regret, embarrassment, etc).

shudder /ˈʃʌdə(r)/ *v* **(a)** [I, Ipr, It] ~ **(with sth)** shiver violently with cold, fear, etc; tremble: *shudder with pleasure in a hot bath* ○ *shudder (with horror) at the sight of blood* ○ *I shudder to think of the problems ahead of us.* **(b)** [I] make a strong shaking movement; vibrate: *The ship shuddered as it hit the rocks.*

▷ **shudder** *n* shuddering movement: *A shudder of fear ran through him.* ○ (*infml*) *It gives me the shudders*, ie terrifies me.

shuffle /ˈʃʌfl/ *v* **1 (a)** [I, Ipr, Ip] walk without lifting the feet completely clear of the ground: *Walk properly — don't shuffle.* ○ *The prisoners shuffled along the corridor and into their cells.* ○ *The queue shuffled forward slowly.* **(b)** [I, Tn] change one's position or move (one's feet) about while standing or sitting, because of nervousness, boredom, etc: *The audience began to shuffle (their feet) impatiently.* ⇨ Usage. **2 (a)** [I, Tn, Tn·p] slide (playing-cards) over one another to change their order: *Who is going to shuffle?* ○ *She shuffled the pack (up).* **(b)** [Tn, Tn·p] move (papers, etc) around to different positions: *He shuffled the papers (around) on the desk, pretending to be busy.* **3** [I] behave as if one is being dishonest, or avoiding responsibility, etc; avoid being definite: *Don't shuffle: give us a clear answer.* **4** (phr v) **shuffle sth off (onto sb)**; **shuffle out of sth** avoid doing (what one ought to do): *He tries to shuffle his work off onto others.* ○ *She shuffled out of the chores by saying she felt ill.*

▷ **shuffle** *n* (usu *sing*) **1** shuffling walk or movement: *walk with an exhausted shuffle.* **2** act of shuffling playing-cards: *give the pack a good shuffle.* **3** rearrangement; reordering: *a shuffle in the Cabinet*, ie reallocating responsibilities among its members, etc.

shuffler /ˈʃʌflə(r)/ *n*.

NOTE ON USAGE: There are a number of verbs which describe abnormal ways of walking. **Shuffle** and **shamble** indicate moving without lifting the feet completely off the ground. **Shuffle** suggests a slow, tired movement; **shamble** may be faster and more careless: *The queue of prisoners shuffled towards the door.* ○ *The beggar shambled past us.* **Stagger** and **stumble** suggest unsteady or uncontrolled movement. A person **staggers** when carrying a heavy load or when drunk. We **stumble** when we hit our feet against unseen objects. **Waddle** is used humorously to describe someone swaying from side to side like a duck because of fatness or while carrying heavy bags. **Hobble** and **limp** describe the uneven movement of someone whose legs are injured. **Limp** is used especially when only one leg is damaged or stiff.

shufty (also **shufti**) /ˈʃʊftɪ/ *n* (idm) **take/have a shufty (at sth/sb)** (*dated Brit sl*) have a look (at sb/sth): *Take a shufty at this box and tell me if it's big enough.*

shun /ʃʌn/ *v* (**-nn-**) [Tn, Tg] keep away from (sth/sb); avoid: *shun temptation, publicity, other people* ○ *She shuns being photographed.*

'shun /ʃʌn/ *interj* (*infml*) = ATTENTION.

shunt /ʃʌnt/ *v* **1 (a)** [Tn, Tn·pr, Tn·p] move (a railway locomotive, wagons, etc) from one track to another: *shunting a train into a siding.* **(b)** [I, Ipr, Ip] (of a train) be shunted. **2** (*fig infml*) **(a)** [Tn·pr, Tn·p] move sb/sth to a different (often less important) place: *She's been shunted off to an office in the annexe.* ○ *The luggage was shunted slowly into the lift.* **(b)** [Tn·pr] change the direction or course of (sth); divert: *shunt the conversation towards more pleasant topics.*

▷ **shunt** *n* **1** (*infml*) collision in which the front of one vehicle hits the rear of another. **2** passage, often created by surgery, through which blood can flow, eg from one part of the heart to another. **3** conductor that joins two points in an electrical circuit, allowing some of the current to be sent in a different direction.

shush /ʃʊʃ/ *interj* be silent!; hush!

▷ **shush** *v* [Tn, Tn·p] ~ **sb (up)** tell sb to be silent.

shut /ʃʌt/ *v* (**-tt-**, *pt, pp* **shut**) **1 (a)** [Tn] move (a door, lid, window, etc) into a position where it blocks an opening: *shut the doors and windows at night* ○ *shut the drawer* ○ *I can't shut the suitcase lid when it's so full.* ○ *He shut the door on her/in her face*, ie wouldn't let her in. **(b)** [I] (of a door, etc) move or be able to be moved into such a position: *The window won't shut.* ○ *The supermarket doors shut automatically.* **2 (a)** [Tn] cause (sth open) to close; close the door, lid, etc of (sth): *shut one's eyes/mouth* ○ *I can't shut my briefcase.* ○ *The cashier shut the till and locked it.* **(b)** [I] (esp of the eyes or mouth) close: *His eyes shut and he fell asleep.* ○ *Her mouth opened and shut, but no sound came out.* **3** [Tn] fold together (sth that opens out): *shut a book, wallet, penknife.* **4** [I, Tn] (cause a business, etc to) stop functioning, esp temporarily: *It's time to shut the shop.* ○ *When do the pubs shut?* ⇨ Usage at CLOSE⁴. **5** (idm) **keep one's mouth shut** ⇨ MOUTH¹. **shut/slam the door in sb's face**

⇨ DOOR. **shut the door on sth** refuse to consider sth: *The union accused the management of shutting the door on further negotiation.* **shut one's ears to sth/sb** refuse to listen to sth/sb: *I begged her for help but she shut her ears to all my appeals.* **shut/close one's eyes to sth** ⇨ EYE[1]. **shut one's ˈmouth/ˈface** (*sl*) (esp imperative) be silent: *Shut your mouth, nobody asked you!* **shut sb's ˈmouth** (*infml*) prevent sb from speaking, revealing secrets, etc. **shut up ˈshop** close one's business, stop trading, etc: *I've lost so much money this year that I'm being forced to shut up shop.* **with one's eyes shut/closed** ⇨ EYE[1].
6 (phr v) **shut sb/sth away** put sb/sth in an enclosed place or away from others: *shut the letters away where no one will find them* ○ *I hate being shut away in the country.*
shut (sth) down (cause a factory, etc to) stop working; close: *The workshop has shut down and the workers are unemployed.* ○ *They've shut down their factory.*
shut sb/oneself in (sth) prevent sb/oneself from getting out of (a place): *She shuts herself in her study for hours.* ○ *We're shut in* (ie surrounded) *by the hills here.* **shut sth in sth** trap or pinch sth by closing sth: *I shut my finger in the car door*, ie between the door and the door-pillar.
shut sth off stop the supply or flow of (eg gas, steam, water): *You must shut the gas supply off if there's a leak.* **shut sb/sth off (from sth)** keep sb/sth away from sth: *His deafness shuts him off from the lives of others.* ○ *The village is shut off from the world by lakes and marshes.*
shut sb out (*infml*) prevent (an opponent) from scoring in a game.
shut sb/sth out (of sth) keep sb/sth out; exclude sb/sth; block sb/sth: *The government wants to shut the refugees out.* ○ *These trees shut out the view.* ○ *He tried to shut all thoughts of her out of his mind.*
shut (sb) up (*infml*) (cause sb to) stop talking: *Oh, shut up, you fool!* ○ *Tell her to shut up.* ○ *Can't you shut him up?* **shut sth up** close all the doors and windows of (a house, etc): *We shut up the house before going on holiday.* **shut sb/sth up (in sth)** confine sb; put sth away: *We shut him up in his room.* ○ *Shut the jewels up in the safe.*
□ ˈ**shut-down** *n* process of closing a factory, etc, either temporarily or permanently: *strikes causing shut-downs in the steel industry.*
ˈ**shut-eye** *n* [U] (*infml*) sleep: *get a bit of shut-eye.*

shutter /ˈʃʌtə(r)/ *n* **1** movable panel or screen that can be closed over a window to keep out light or thieves: *The shop-front is fitted with rolling shutters.* **2** device that opens to allow light to come through the lens of a camera. **3** (idm) **put up the ˈshutters** (*infml*) stop doing business at the end of the day or permanently: *After managing the shop for thirty years she decided it was time to put up the shutters.*
▷ **shutter** *v* [Tn esp passive] close the shutters of (a building); provide with shutters: *The house was empty and shuttered.*

shuttle /ˈʃʌtl/ *n* **1** (**a**) (in a loom) instrument that pulls the thread of weft between the threads of warp. (**b**) (in a sewing-machine) holder that carries the lower thread to meet the upper thread to make a stitch. **2** aircraft, bus, etc that travels regularly between two places: *I'm flying to Boston on the shuttle.* **3** (*infml*) = SHUTTLECOCK.

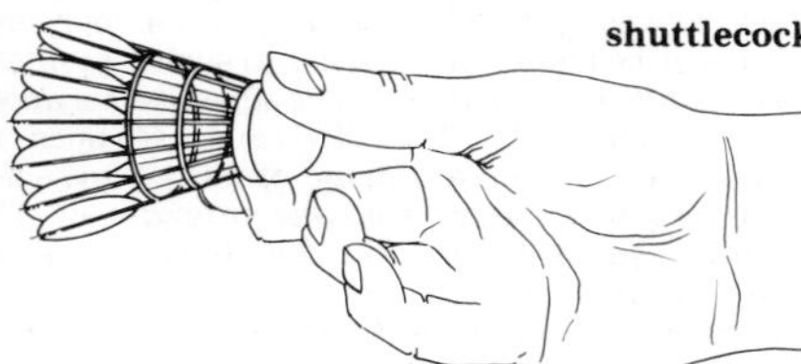

▷ **shuttle** *v* [I, Tn] (cause sth to) move or travel backwards and forwards, or to and fro.
□ ˈ**shuttlecock** *n* round piece of cork, etc with a ring of feathers or of a light synthetic material attached, struck to and fro in badminton.
ˌ**shuttle diˈplomacy** diplomacy that requires the diplomat(s) to travel to and fro between the two groups involved.
ˈ**shuttle service** service of buses, aircraft, etc travelling regularly between two places.

shy[1] /ʃaɪ/ *adj* (**shyer**, **shyest**) **1** (**a**) (of people) timid and nervous in the presence of others; reserved: *He was too shy to speak to her.* ○ *The child isn't at all shy with adults.* (**b**) (of behaviour, etc) showing that one is timid, reserved, etc: *a shy look, smile, etc.* **2** (of animals, birds, etc) unwilling to be seen by or be near to humans; easily frightened. **3** ~ **of sb/doing sth** wary or afraid of (a person or an action): *The dog is shy of strangers.* ○ *I'm shy of buying shares, in case I lose money.* **4** ~ (**on/of sth/sb**) (*US infml*) short of or lacking sth/sb: *We've plenty of wine, but we're shy on beer.* ○ *We are still two men shy (of a full team).* **5** (idm) **fight shy of sb/sth** ⇨ FIGHT[1]. **once bitten, twice shy** ⇨ BITE[1].
▷ **shy** *v* (*pt, pp* **shied** /ʃaɪd/) **1** [I, Ipr] ~ (**at sth**) (of a horse) turn aside or hold back in fear or alarm: *The colt shied at the fence and refused to jump over it.* **2** (phr v) **shy away from sth/doing sth** avoid or move away from (doing) sth because of shyness, fear, etc: *I've always shied away from close friendships.*
-shy (forming compound *adjs*) avoiding or not liking the thing specified: ˈ*camera-shy*, ie reluctant to be photographed ○ *a pubˌlicity-shy poliˈtician* ○ *You've been* ˈ*work-shy all your life.*
shyly *adv.*
shyness *n* [U].

shy[2] /ʃaɪ/ *v* (*pt, pp* **shied** /ʃaɪd/) [Tn, Tn·pr] (*dated infml*) throw (sth): *shy stones (at a bottle, over a wall, etc).*
▷ **shy** *n* (*infml*) act of throwing: *have/take a couple of shies at the tin can in the lake.* Cf COCONUT SHY (COCONUT).

Shylock /ˈʃaɪlɒk/ Jewish money-lender in *Shakespeare's play *The Merchant of Venice.* Although the play shows him as a victim as well as a villain, his name is now used to describe a person who is very mean or greedy for money.

shyster /ˈʃaɪstə(r)/ *n* (*infml esp US*) unscrupulous and dishonest person, esp a lawyer: [attrib] *shyster politicians.*

SI /ˌes ˈaɪ/ *abbr* International System (of units of measurement) (French *Système International*): *SI units.*

Si *symb* silicon.

Siam /saɪˈæm/ former name of *Thailand.
▷ **Siamese** /ˌsaɪəˈmiːz/ *adj* of Siam. — *n* **1** (**a**) [C] (*pl* unchanged) native or inhabitant of Siam. (**b**) [U] = THAI. **2** [C] (*pl* unchanged) = SIAMESE CAT.
ˌ**Siamese ˈcat** cat of an oriental breed having short pale fur with darker face, ears, tail and feet.
ˌ**Siamese ˈtwins** twins born with their bodies joined together.

Sibelius /sɪˈbeɪlɪəs/ Jean (1865-1957), Finnish composer. Much of his work was inspired by Finnish legends. The orchestral sound in his seven symphonies and other works such as *Finlandia* is sometimes rich, sometimes austere, with long atmospheric string passages.

Siberia /saɪˈbɪərɪə/ region east of the *Urals in the Russian Federation. It contains most of the country's mineral resources, esp its oil, coal and gas, but the harsh climate makes it a very hostile environment. Both the tsars and the Communist regime used it as a place of exile for political opponents and criminals. ⇨ map at UNION OF SOVIET SOCIALIST REPUBLICS. ▷ **Siberian** *adj*: *a Siberian climate.*

sibilant /ˈsɪbɪlənt/ *adj* like or produced with a hissing sound: *the sibilant noise of steam escaping.*
▷ **sibilant** *n* sibilant letter or speech-sound, eg /s, z, ʃ, ʒ, tʃ, dʒ/.

sibling /ˈsɪblɪŋ/ *n* (*fml*) any one of two or more people with the same parents; brother or sister: *I have two brothers and a sister: three siblings in all.* ○ [attrib] *sibling rivalry.*

sibyl /ˈsɪbl/ *n* any of a group of women in the ancient world thought to be able to foresee the future.
▷ **sibylline** /ˈsɪbəlaɪn, sɪˈbɪlaɪn *or, rarely US* ˈsɪbəliːn/ *adj* spoken by or characteristic of a sibyl, mysteriously prophetic: *a sibylline utterance.*

sic /sɪk/ *adv* (placed in brackets after a quoted word or phrase that seems to be or is incorrect, in order to show that it is quoted accurately): *The notice read: 'Skool (sic) starts at 9 am.'*

Sicily /ˈsɪsəlɪ/ island in the Mediterranean Sea, off the southern tip of the Italian mainland. It is largely covered in mountains and scrub, limiting its agricultural production, but it specializes in oranges and other citrus fruits. There are some chemical plants but the island is industrially underdeveloped by comparison with the rest of Italy. It is famous as the home of the *Mafia. ▷ **Sicilian** /sɪˈsɪlɪən/ *n, adj.*

sick /sɪk/ *adj* (**-er, -est**) **1** physically or mentally unwell; ill: *a sick person, animal, plant* ○ *She has been sick for weeks.* ○ *He's off (work) sick.* **2** [usu pred] likely to vomit; nauseous: *feeling sick* ○ *a sick feeling in the stomach* ○ *You'll make yourself sick if you eat all those sweets.* ⇨ Usage. **3** [pred] ~ **of sb/sth/doing sth** (*infml*) bored with sb/sth; not liking sb/sth through having had too much of him/it: *I'm sick of waiting around like this.* ○ *She has had the same job for years and is heartily sick of it.* ○ *Get out! I'm sick of the sight of you!* **4** [pred] ~ (**at/about sth/doing sth**) distressed or disgusted: *We were pretty sick about losing the match.* **5** (*infml*) cruel, morbid or perverted; offensive: *a sick joke, mind* ○ *sick humour* ○ *She made a sick remark about dead babies.* **6** (idm) **be ˈsick** throw up food from the stomach; vomit: *The cat's been sick on the carpet.* **eat oneself sick** ⇨ EAT. **fall sick (with sth)**; (*fml*) **take ˈsick** become ill: *He fell sick with malaria on a trip to Africa.* **laugh oneself silly/sick** ⇨ LAUGH. **make sb ˈsick** outrage or disgust sb: *His hypocrisy makes me sick.* ○ *It makes me sick to see her being treated so badly.* **on the ˈsick-list** (*infml*) sick and absent from work, duty, etc: *She's not at her desk today: she's on the sick-list.* **(as) sick as a parrot** (*Brit joc catchphrase*) disgusted. **sick at ˈheart** (*fml*) full of disappointment, fear or grief; unhappy: *She left her home reluctantly and sick at heart.* **sick to death of/sick and tired of sb/sth** (*infml*) wearied, bored or annoyed by sb/sth; fed up with sb/sth: *sick to death of eating boiled cabbage with every meal* ○ *I'm sick and tired of your constant complaints.* **sick to one's ˈstomach** (*US*) outraged or disgusted.
▷ **sick** *n* **1** [U] (*infml*) vomit: *The basin was full of sick.* **2 the sick** [pl *v*] people who are ill: *all the sick and wounded* ○ *visit the sick in hospital.*
sick *v* (phr v) **sick sth up** (*infml*) throw (food) up from the stomach; vomit sth: *The baby sicked up a little milk.*
-sick (forming compound *adjs*) feeling sick(2) as a result of travelling on a ship, plane, etc: ˈ*seasick* ○ ˈ*airsick* ○ ˈ*travel-sick* ○ ˈ*carsick.*
□ ˈ**sick-bay** *n* room or rooms in a ship, boarding-school, etc for people who are ill.
ˈ**sick-bed** *n* bed of a person who is ill: *lying pale on his sick-bed* ○ *The President left his sick-bed to attend the ceremony*, ie attended it although he was ill.
ˌ**sick ˈheadache** (*US*) attack of migraine.
ˈ**sick-leave** *n* [U] permission to be absent from work, duty, etc because of illness; period of such absence: *be granted sick-leave* ○ *two weeks sick-leave.*
ˈ**sick-pay** *n* [U] pay given to an employee who is absent because of illness.
ˈ**sick-room** *n* room that is occupied by or kept ready for sb who is ill: *You should go to the sick-room if you're not feeling well.*

NOTE ON USAGE: **1** (**Be**) **sick** in informal British English means 'bring food up from the stomach' (*US* **vomit**): *Johnny's been sick again — should we call the doctor?* ○ *Do you get seasick/airsick?* ○ *I feel sick — I think it was that fish I ate.* **Sick** in British English is used only before a noun when it means 'ill': *a sick child* ○ *He's looking after his sick mother.* **2 Sick** in US English and **ill** in British English mean 'not well' or 'in bad health', usually as a result of a disease: *I've been too sick/ill to go to work for the last few months.* **3 Poorly** (informal British English) means 'ill'. It is often used of or by children: *My daughter's a bit poorly today, so she didn't go to school.*

sicken /ˈsɪkən/ *v* **1** [Tn] cause (sb) to feel disgusted: *Cruelty sickens most of us.* ○ *Their business methods sicken me.* ○ *I was sickened at/by the sight of the dead body.* **2** [I, Ipr] ~ **(for sth)** (*Brit*) begin to be ill; become ill: *slowly sickened and died* ○ *She looks so pale. Is she sickening for something?* **3** (phr v) **sicken of sth** (*fml*) become weary of or disgusted with sth: *I began to sicken of the endless violence shown on television.*
▷ **sickening** *adj* disgusting: *a sickening sight, smell* ○ *sickening cruelty* ○ *The car hit the tree with a sickening crash.* **sickeningly** *adv.*

Sickert /ˈsɪkət/ Walter (1860-1942), British painter. He was influenced by the *Impressionists in France and *Whistler in England, and is most famous for his scenes of theatrical life.

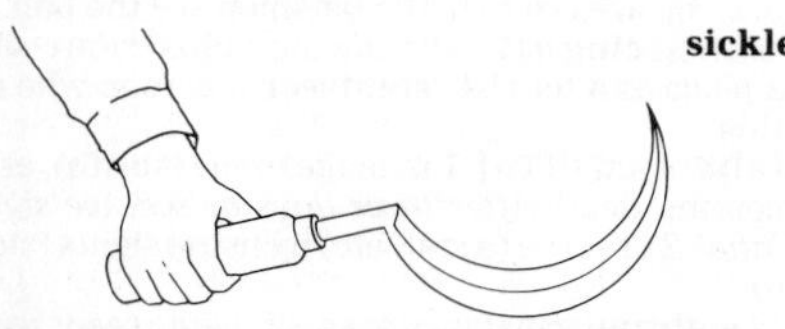
sickle

sickle /ˈsɪkl/ *n* short-handled tool with a curved blade for cutting grass, corn, etc. Cf SCYTHE.
□ ˌ**sickle** ˈ**cell** sickle-shaped red blood-corpuscle found esp in a severe type of hereditary anaemia.

sickly /ˈsɪklɪ/ *adj* (**-ier, -iest**) **1** often ill: *a sickly child.* **2** looking unhealthy: *sickly, dried-out plants* ○ *a pale, sickly complexion* ○ *He looked weak and sickly.* **3** [usu attrib] expressing unhappiness; weak; faint: *a sickly smile, look.* **4** causing or likely to cause a feeling of sickness or distaste: *a sickly smell, taste, etc* ○ *a sickly green colour* ○ (*fig*) *a sickly, sentimental story.*

sickness /ˈsɪknɪs/ *n* [U] **1** illness; ill health: *Is there much sickness in the village now?* ○ *They were absent because of sickness.* **2** [U, C usu *sing*] particular type of illness or disease: *sleeping sickness* ○ *suffering from altitude sickness* ○ *air-/sea-/travel-/car-sickness* ○ *a sickness common in the tropics.* **3** [U] feeling that one is likely to vomit; vomiting: *The sickness passed after I lay down for a while.* ○ *The symptoms of this disease are fever and sickness.*
□ ˈ**sickness benefit** (*Brit*) money paid by the State to sb who is absent from work because of illness: *entitled to sickness benefit.*

Siddons /ˈsɪdnz/ Sarah (1755-1831), English actress. She was the leading tragic actress of her time, famous for roles such as Lady Macbeth. She was painted by both *Gainsborough and *Reynolds.

side[1] /saɪd/ *n* **1** [C] **(a)** any of the flat or nearly flat surfaces of a solid object: *the six sides of a cube.* **(b)** any of the surfaces that is not the top or bottom: *A box has a top, a bottom and four sides.* **(c)** any of the surfaces that is not the top or bottom, front or back: *There is a garage built onto the side of the house.* ○ [attrib] *a side door, entrance, window.* **2** [C] (*mathematics*) any of the lines that form the boundaries of a plane figure, such as a triangle or a rectangle. **3** [C] (area near the) edge or boundary of sth: *a table by one's bedside/by the side of one's bed* ○ *people sitting on both sides of the table,* ie on the two longer sides of a rectangular one ○ *standing at the side of the road* ○ *the south side of the field* ○ *We planted tulips along the side of the lawn.* **4** [C] either of the two surfaces of sth flat and thin, eg paper, cloth, sheet metal: *Write on one side of the paper only.* ○ *Which is the right side of the cloth* (ie the one intended to be seen)? ○ *This side of the glass is filthy.* **5** [C] inner or outer surface of sth more or less upright: *the side of the mountain, tower, haystack* ○ *a steep hillside* ○ *paint the sides of the cylinder* ○ *paintings on the sides* (ie walls) *of the cave* ○ *a puncture in the side of the tyre.* **6** [C] **(a)** either the right or the left part of a person's body, esp from the armpit to the hip: *wounded in the left side* ○ *lying on one's side.* **(b)** region near to this: *sit at/by sb's side* ○ *On my left side stood Fred.* **7** [C] either of the two halves of an animal that has been killed for meat: *a side of beef, bacon, etc.* **8** [C] **(a)** either of the two halves of a surface or an object divided by an imaginary central line: *the left side of the brain* ○ *the left, right, shady, sunny, etc side of the street* ○ *the eastern side of the town* ○ *the debit/credit side of the account* ○ *Go over to the other/far side of the room.* ○ *Which side of the theatre would you like to sit?* **(b)** either of the two areas, etc divided by a line or boundary: *She stood on the other side of the fence.* ○ *He crossed the bridge to this side of the river.* **9** [C] (*Brit dated infml*) television channel: *Switch over to the other side.* **10** [C] **(a)** either or two parties or groups involved in a dispute, contest, etc with each other: *the two sides in the strike,* ie employers and workers ○ *There are faults on both sides.* **(b)** position or opinion held in an argument; attitude or activity of one person or group with respect to another: *She argued her side of the case well.* ○ *You must hear his side of things now.* ○ *Will you keep your side of the bargain?* **11** (*Brit*) sports team: *five-a-side football* ○ *the winning/losing side* ○ *pick sides,* ie choose who will play on each side ○ *Austria has a good side, and should win.* **12** [C] aspect of sth that is different from other aspects; point of view: *study all sides of a question* ○ *the gentle side of her character* ○ *approach the problem from a different side.* **13** [C] line of descent through a father or mother: *a cousin on my father's side,* ie a child of my father's brother or sister. **14** [U] (*dated infml*) behaviour showing that one thinks one is better than others; arrogance: *a person quite without side* ○ *There's absolutely no side to him.* **15** (idm) **a bit on the side** ⇨ BIT[1]. **born on the wrong side of the blanket** ⇨ BORN. **come down on** ˌ**one side of the** ˌ**fence or the** ˈ**other** make a choice between two alternatives: *The jury is considering its verdict and we're waiting to see which side of the fence they'll come down on.* **err on the side of sth** ⇨ ERR. **get on the right/wrong side of sb** please/displease sb. **have got out of bed on the wrong side** ⇨ BED[1]. **know which side one's bread is buttered** ⇨ KNOW. **laugh on the other side of one's face** ⇨ LAUGH. **let the** ˈ**side down** not give one's colleagues, etc the help and support they expect, or behave in a way that disappoints them: *You can always rely on Angela — she'd never let the side down.* **look on the bright side** ⇨ BRIGHT. **on/from all sides; on/from every side** in/from all directions; everywhere: *soldiers attacking on all sides* ○ *There was devastation on every side.* **on the** ˈ**big,** ˈ**small,** ˈ**high, etc side** (*infml*) rather or too big, small, high, etc: *These new trousers are a bit on the large side.* **on the distaff side** ⇨ DISTAFF. **on the** ˌ**right/**ˌ**wrong side of** ˈ**forty,** ˈ**fifty, etc** (*infml often joc*) younger/older than forty, fifty, etc years of age. **on the safe side** ⇨ SAFE[1]. **on the** ˈ**side** (*infml*) **(a)** as a sideline: *a mechanic who buys and sells cars on the side.* **(b)** secretly: *He's married but he has a girl-friend on the side.* **(be) on the side of sb** (be) a supporter of sb; holding the same views as sb: *Whose side are you on anyway?* ie You should be supporting me. ○ *I'm on George's side in this debate.* **on the** ˌ**side of the** ˈ**angels** supporting the side which is believed to be morally right. **on/from the wrong side of the tracks** ⇨ WRONG. **the other side of the** ˈ**coin** the opposite or contrasting aspect of a matter: *Everyone assumes he's to blame but they don't know the other side of the coin.* **put sth on/to one** ˈ**side (a)** put sth aside: *I put the broken glass to one side.* **(b)** leave sth to be dealt with later: *I put his complaint on one side until I had more time.* ˌ**side by** ˈ**side (a)** close together, facing in the same direction: *two children walking side by side.* **(b)** supporting each other: *We stand side by side with you in this dispute.* **split one's sides** ⇨ SPLIT. **take sb on(to) one** ˈ**side** have a private talk with sb: *I took her on one side to ask about her odd behaviour.* **take** ˈ**sides (with sb)** express support for sb in a dispute, etc: *You mustn't take sides in their argument.* ○ *She took sides with me against the teacher.* **a thorn in one's flesh/side** ⇨ THORN. **time is on sb's side** ⇨ TIME[1]. **wrong side out** ⇨ WRONG.
▷ **-sided** (forming compound *adjs*) having a specified number or type of sides: *a six-sided object* ○ *a glass-sided container.*
□ ˈ**sideboard** *n* **1** [C] table, usu with drawers and cupboards, for crockery, etc. **2** ˈ**sideboards** (*US* ˈ**sideburns**) [pl] patches of hair growing on the side of a man's face in front of the ears. ⇨ illus at HAIR.
ˈ**side-car** *n* small vehicle attached to the side of a motor cycle, to seat a passenger.
ˈ**side-dish** *n* extra dish or course at a meal, usu served with another course.
ˈ**side-drum** *n* small double-sided drum. ⇨ illus at MUSIC.
ˈ**side-effect** *n* (often *pl*) secondary, usu unpleasant or unwanted, effect of a drug, etc.
ˈ**side-issue** *n* issue that is less important than the main one: *What I earn is a side-issue. What really matters is that I don't like my work.*
ˈ**sidekick** *n* (*infml esp US*) assistant or close companion: *the gangster and his two sidekicks.*
ˈ**sidelight** *n* **1** either of a pair of small lights at the front of a vehicle. ⇨ illus at CAR. **2** ~ **(on sb/sth)** (*fig*) minor or casual piece of information that helps one to understand a subject, etc: *The article about the theatre gave us a few sidelights on the character of its owner.*
ˈ**sidelong** *adj* [attrib], *adv* (directed) to or from the side; sideways: *a sidelong glance* ○ *look sidelong at sb.*
ˌ**side-**ˈ**on** *adv* with the side of sth towards sth else: *The other car hit us side-on,* ie hit us with its side.
ˈ**side order** (*esp US*) item of food served to a person in addition to the main dish and on a separate plate: *a side order of French fries.*
ˈ**side-road** *n* minor road branching off a main road.
ˈ**side-saddle** *n* saddle for a woman rider made so that both legs can be on the same side of the horse. — *adv* on a side-saddle: *riding side-saddle.*
ˈ**side-show** *n* **1** small show offering a game or some other amusement at a circus, fun-fair, etc. **2** (*fig*) activity of less importance than the main activity.
ˈ**side-slip** *n* **(a)** sideways skid of a motor vehicle. **(b)** sideways movement of an aircraft making a turn. — *v* [I] (**-pp-**) make a side-slip.
ˈ**sidesman** /-mən/ *n* (*pl* **-men** /-mən/) assistant who helps the churchwardens, eg by collecting money from the congregation during church services.
ˈ**side-splitting** *adj* (*infml*) extremely funny: *the clown's side-splitting antics.*
ˈ**side-step** *n* step to one side, eg to dodge sb or to avoid a blow. — *v* (**-pp-**) **1** [Tn] **(a)** avoid (a blow, etc) by stepping to one side: *The footballer side-stepped the tackle.* **(b)** evade (a question, etc): *He side-stepped the issue by saying it was not part of his responsibilities.* **2** [I] make a side-step.
ˈ**side-street** *n* minor street branching off a major street.
ˈ**side-stroke** *n* [U] any of various types of swimming stroke in which the swimmer is on his side: *Can you do side-stroke?*
ˈ**side-swipe** *n* (*US*) **1** indirect blow along the side of sth. **2** (*infml*) critical remark made among remarks of a different kind or on a different subject: *When talking about the performance, she couldn't resist (taking) a side-swipe at the orchestra.*
ˈ**side-track** *v* [Tn esp passive] divert (sb) from the main topic or issue: *The lecturer was discussing politics but got side-tracked by a question from the audience into talking about religion.*
ˈ**side-view** *n* view of sth from the side: *The picture is/shows a side-view of the house.*
ˈ**sidewalk** *n* (*US*) = PAVEMENT 1.
ˈ**sideways** *adv, adj* [attrib] **1** to, towards or from the side: *A crab moves sideways.* ○ *He looked sideways at me.* ○ *a sideways glance.* **2** with one side facing forwards: *carry the sofa sideways*

through the door. **3** (idm) **knock sb sideways** ⇨ KNOCK[2].

ˈ**side-whiskers** *n* [pl] patches of hair growing on the sides of a man's face down to, but not on, the chin.

side-winder /ˈsaɪdwaɪndə(r)/ *n* type of small rattlesnake that moves sideways in a series of loops.

side[2] /saɪd/ *v* (phr v) **side with sb (against sb)** support sb in an argument, dispute, etc: *She sided with her brother against the others in the class.*

sideline /ˈsaɪdlaɪn/ *n* **1** [C] class of goods sold in addition to the main class of goods: *a butcher selling groceries as a sideline.* **2** [C] occupation that is not one's main work: *I'm a teacher really; my writing is just a sideline.* **3 sidelines** [pl] (space immediately outside the) lines forming the boundary of a football pitch, tennis court, etc at the sides: *some spectators on the sidelines.* **4** (idm) **on the** ˈ**sidelines** observing sth but not directly involved in it: *As a journalist, I was on the sidelines during the political crisis.*

▷ **sideline** *v* [Tn] (*esp US*) remove (sb) from a game, team, etc; put out of action: *Our best player has been sidelined by injury.*

sidereal /saɪˈdɪərɪəl/ *adj* (*fml*) of the stars or measured by them: *sidereal time* ○ *the sidereal year*, ie 365 days, 6 hours, 10 minutes.

siding /ˈsaɪdɪŋ/ *n* short track beside a main railway line, into and from which trains can be shunted.

sidle /ˈsaɪdl/ *v* [Ipr, Ip] ~ **up/over (to sb/sth)**; ~ **along, past, away, etc** move (in the specified direction) furtively, or as if shy or nervous: *sidling up to the bar* ○ *She sidled over to me and asked if I recognized her.* ○ *He sidled past, trying to seem casual.* ⇨ Usage at PROWL.

Sidney /ˈsɪdnɪ/ Sir Philip (1554-86), English soldier and poet. He is regarded as one of the great figures of the Elizabethan period, combining literary gifts, as in his *Arcadia*, with the skills of a diplomat and general.

siege /siːdʒ/ *n* **1 (a)** surrounding of a town, fortress, etc by armed forces in order to capture it or force it to surrender: *a siege of 50 days* ○ *be in a state of/under siege* ○ *raise/lift* (ie end) *a siege* ○ *By the time the siege ended, the citizens were nearly starving.* ○ [attrib] *siege guns.* **(b)** surrounding by police, etc of a building in which people are living or hiding. **2** (idm) **lay siege to sth** begin a siege of (a town, fortress, etc).

siemens /ˈsiːmənz/ *n* (*pl* unchanged) the unit of electrical conductance. Cf OHM.

sienna /sɪˈenə/ *n* [U] type of clay used as colouring matter: *burnt sienna*, ie reddish-brown ○ *raw sienna*, ie brownish-yellow.

sierra /sɪˈerə/ *n* long range of mountains with steep slopes and a rugged outline (esp in Spain and Spanish America).

Sierra Leone /sɪˌerə lɪˈəʊn/ country on the coast of W Africa, a member of the Commonwealth; pop approx 3 946 000; official language English; capital Freetown; unit of currency leone (= 100 cents). It is a country of savannah and forests, but it has been badly affected by deforestation. It has a largely agricultural economy, producing rice and other subsistence crops and cacao and coffee for export. It also has considerable diamond reserves. ⇨ map at NIGERIA.

siesta /sɪˈestə/ *n* rest or sleep taken in the early afternoon, esp in hot countries: *have/take a siesta.*

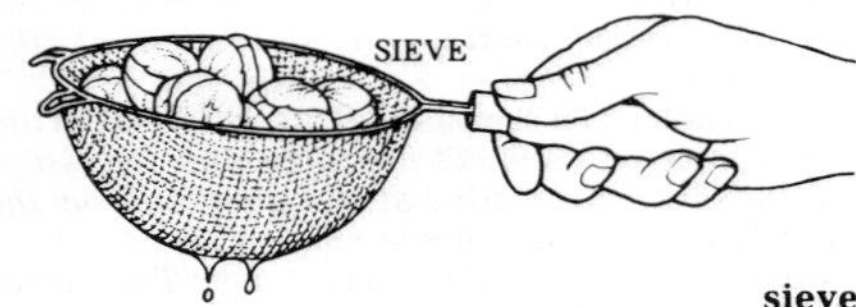

sieve

sieve /sɪv/ *n* **1** utensil consisting of a wire mesh or gauze on a frame, used for separating solids or coarse matter (which do not pass through) from liquids or fine matter (which do pass through). **2** (idm) **have a memory/mind like a sieve** have a very bad memory; forget things easily.

▷ **sieve** *v* [Tn, Tn·pr] put (sth) through a sieve: *sieve the flour into a bowl.*

sievert /ˈsiːvət/ *n* (*symb* **Sv**) SI unit of radiation dose, used to indicate the relative effect of radiation on different parts of the body.

sift /sɪft/ *v* **1 (a)** [Tn] put (sth) through a sieve: *sift the flour, sugar, etc.* **(b)** [Tn·pr, Tn·p] ~ **sth (out) from sth**; ~ **sth out** separate sth from sth by putting it through a sieve: *sift (out) the lumps from the flour, the wheat from the chaff.* **2** [Tn, Tn·pr] shake or sprinkle (sth) through a sieve: *sift flour (into the mixture)* ○ *sift sugar onto a cake.* **3** [Ipr, Tn] ~ **(through) sth** (*fig*) examine sth very carefully: *sift through the piles of correspondence* ○ *sift the evidence, data, etc.*

▷ **sifter** *n* (often in compounds) small utensil like a sieve, used chiefly in cooking: *a flour-sifter.*

sigh /saɪ/ *v* **1** [I, Ipr] ~ **(with sth)** take a long deep breath that can be heard, expressing sadness, tiredness, relief, etc: *She sighed as she lay back on the bed.* ○ *He sighed with pleasure after the excellent meal.* **2** [I] (of the wind) make a sound like sighing. **3** [Tn] express or say (sth) with a sigh: *'I wish I didn't have so much to do,' she sighed.* **4** (phr v) **sigh for sth** (*fml*) feel a deep longing for sth that is lost, far away, etc: *an exile who sighs for home.*

▷ **sigh** *n* act or sound of sighing: *breathe/utter/heave/give a sigh* ○ *with a sigh of relief, sadness, pleasure, etc.*

sight[1] /saɪt/ *n* **1** [U] ability to see; vision: *lose one's sight*, ie become blind ○ *have good, poor, etc sight*, ie eyesight ○ *Some drugs can affect your sight.* **2** [U] ~ **of sb/sth** action of seeing sb/sth: *Their first sight of land came after ten days at sea.* ○ *We laughed at the sight of his strange clothes.* ○ (*fml*) *When can we have sight of your new house?* **3** [U] range within which sb can see or sth can be seen: *in/within (sb's) sight*, ie (of objects, etc) visible ○ *The train is still in sight.* ○ *The ship came into sight out of the fog.* ○ (*fig*) *The end of the project is almost in sight.* **4 (a)** [C] thing (to be) seen, or worth seeing, esp sth remarkable: *The flowers are a lovely sight in spring.* ○ *He saw some amazing sights at the zoo.* ○ *A suffering animal is a distressing sight.* **(b) sights** [pl] interesting buildings, places, features, etc of a place or district: *Come and see the sights of London.* **5 a sight** [sing] (*infml*) person or thing that looks ridiculous, untidy, etc: *What a sight you look in those old clothes!* ○ *This kitchen is a sight. Clean it up at once!* **6** [C usu *pl*] device that one looks through to aim a rifle, etc or to observe sth through a telescope, etc: *the sights of a gun.* **7** (idm) **at first glance/sight** ⇨ GLANCE. **at/on** ˈ**sight** as soon as sb/sth is seen: *play music at sight*, ie when seen in printed form without previous study or practice ○ *They were told to shoot looters on sight.* **catch sight/a glimpse of sb/sth** ⇨ CATCH[1]. **hate, loathe, be sick of, etc the sight of sb/sth** (*infml*) hate, etc sb/sth very much: *I can't stand the sight of you any more.* ○ *She hates the sight of that old car.* **heave in sight** ⇨ HEAVE. **in the sight of sb/in sb's sight** (*fml*) in sb's opinion; in sb's view: *Do what is right in your own sight.* ○ *All men are equal in the sight of God.* **keep sight of sb/sth; keep sb/sth in sight (a)** remain where one can see sb/sth: *Follow that man and keep him in sight all the time.* **(b)** remain aware of sth: *You must keep sight of one fact: your life is in danger.* **know sb by sight** ⇨ KNOW. **lose sight of sb/sth** ⇨ LOSE. **out of** ˈ**sight (a)** in or into a place where people cannot see: *The plane crashed out of our sight.* ○ *The house was out of sight behind a wall.* ○ *We are not yet out of sight of land*, ie can still see it. ○ *You must keep out of sight*, ie stay where you cannot be seen. **(b)** (*sl esp US*) excellent: *The food was out of sight!* ˌ**out of** ˈ**sight,** ˌ**out of** ˈ**mind** (*saying*) we tend to forget people or things that are absent or can no longer be seen. **raise/lower one's** ˈ**sights** be more/less ambitious; expect more/less: *They had to lower their sights and buy a smaller house than they would have liked.* **set one's sights on sth** decide to achieve sth: *I've set my sights on winning the championship.* **a (damn, etc) sight better, etc (than...); a (damn, etc) sight too good, etc** (*infml*) very much better, etc; far too good, etc: *My car goes a (darned) sight faster than yours.* ○ *That child is a damn sight too cheeky.* **a** ˌ**sight for sore** ˈ**eyes** (*infml*) person or thing that one is relieved or pleased to see: *You're a sight for sore eyes — I thought you'd gone for good!* **a sight of sth** (*infml*) a great amount of sth: *It cost him a sight of money/trouble.* **sight un**ˈ**seen** without an opportunity for previous inspection: *You should never buy a car sight unseen.* **take a** ˈ**sight** aim or observe using a sight[1](6) or sights: *take a careful sight before firing* ○ *take a sight with a compass/quadrant.*

▷ **sighted** *adj* able to see; not blind: *the blind and partially sighted* ○ *Those of us who are sighted don't understand the problems of the blind.*

-sighted (in compound *adjs*) having the specified type of eyesight: *short-/long-/far-sighted.*

□ ˈ**sight-read** *v* [I, Tn] (be able to) play or sing (music) without previous study or practice. ˈ**sight-reading** *n* [U].

ˈ**sight-screen** (also **screen**) *n* (in cricket) large movable white structure placed at either end of the playing area to help the batsmen see the ball.

ˈ**sightseeing** *n* [U] visiting the sights (SIGHT[1] 4b) of a place as a tourist. ˈ**sightseer** *n* person who does this.

sight[2] /saɪt/ *v* [Tn] **1** manage to see (sb/sth), esp by coming near: *After three days at sea, we sighted land.* **2** observe (a star, etc) by using sights (SIGHT[1] 6).

▷ **sighting** *n* instance of sb/sth being seen: *several reported sightings of the escaped prisoner* ○ *the first sighting of a new star.*

sightless /ˈsaɪtlɪs/ *adj* unable to see; blind: *a sightless species of bat.*

sign[1] /saɪn/ *n* **1** [C] mark, symbol, etc used to represent sth: *mathematical signs*, eg +, −, ×, ÷. **2** [C] board, notice, etc that directs sb towards sth, gives a warning, advertises a business, etc: *traffic signs*, eg for a speed limit, a bend in the road, etc ○ *a shop-sign, pub-sign, etc* ○ *Look out for a sign to the motorway.* **3** [C] gesture or movement made with the hand, head, etc, used to give information, a command, etc: *the sign of the cross*, ie a movement made with the hand outlining a cross as a blessing, prayer, etc ○ *She gave us a sign to leave the room*, eg by pointing to the door. **4** [C] ~ **(of sth)** thing that shows that sb/sth is present or exists, or that sth may happen: *signs of suffering on his face* ○ *some signs of improvement in her work* ○ *There wasn't a sign of life in the place*, ie It appeared deserted. ○ *She shows no sign of being interested.* ○ *There are some signs of sales increasing.* **5** (also ˌ**sign of the** ˈ**zodiac**) [C] (symbol representing) any of the twelve divisions of the zodiac: *What sign were you born under?* **6** [U] (*US*) tracks or similar marks left by an animal or a human being. **7** (idm) **a** ˌ**sign of the** ˈ**times** (*often derog*) thing that shows the nature of a particular period: *The rising level of crime is a sign of the times.*

□ ˈ**sign language** language, eg for deaf and dumb people, using gestures instead of words.

ˈ**signpost** *n* post at a road junction, etc with arms pointing to places along the roads, and often showing the distances to them. — *v* [Tn usu passive] provide (a road) with signposts; indicate (a route or place) with signposts: *Is the road well signposted?* ○ *Our village is so small it's not even signposted.*

sign[2] /saɪn/ *v* **1** [I, Tn] write (one's name) on (a document, etc), eg to show that one has written it, that it is genuine, or that one agrees with its contents: *sign (your name) here, please.* ○ *sign a letter, cheque, contract, etc* ○ *The painting isn't signed so we don't know who it's by.* **2** [no passive: Dpr·f, Dpr·w, Dpr·t, Dn·t] convey information or a request or an order by making a gesture: *sign to sb that it is time to go/where to go* ○ *The policeman signed (for) them to stop.* ○ *He signed me to be quiet.* **3** [I, Ipr, Tn] (*esp sport*) ~ **(for/with sb)** be engaged or engage (sb), eg as a footballer, by signing a contract: *He signed for Arsenal yesterday.* ○ *Arsenal have just signed a new striker.* **4** (idm) **sign on the dotted** ˈ**line** (*infml*) sign a document, etc that legally binds one, eg to buy sth: *Just sign on the dotted line and the car is yours.* **sign sb's/one's own ˈdeath-warrant** do sth that will result in one's death, defeat, etc: *By informing on the gang, he was signing his own death-warrant.* **5** (phr v) **sign sth away** give up (one's rights, property, etc) by signing a document, etc: *I'll never get married — it's like signing your life away!* **sign for sth** sign a form, etc to show that one has received sth: *The postman asked me to sign for the parcel.* **sign (sb) in/out** write one's/sb's name to show arrival or departure: *You must sign guests in when they enter the club.* ○ *Soldiers sign out when they leave the barracks.* **sign off** (**a**) stop work: *sign off early to go to the dentist.* (**b**) end a letter: *She signed off with 'Yours ever, Janet'.* (**c**) end a broadcast in some way, eg by playing a short piece of music: *This is your resident DJ signing off for another week with our signature tune.* **sign on** (*Brit infml*) register as an unemployed person. **sign (sb) on/up** (cause sb to) sign an agreement to work for sb, become a soldier, etc: *sign on for five years in the army* ○ *sign up more workers to boost production* ○ *The club has just signed up a new goalkeeper.* **sign sth over (to sb)** formally transfer the ownership of sth to sb by signing a document, etc: *She has signed her house over to her daughter.* **sign up (for sth)** join a club, enrol on a course, etc: *sign up for a secretarial course.*

signal[1] /ˈsɪɡnəl/ *n* **1** sign, gesture, sound, etc that conveys a message, command, etc: *a signal made with a red flag* ○ *hand signals*, ie made by the driver of a car, etc to show which way it will turn, etc ○ *She flashed the torch as a signal.* ○ *He raised his arm as a signal for us to stop.* ○ *A red light is usually a signal for/of danger.* **2** any device or object placed to give people a warning, information, etc: *traffic signals*, ie for cars, etc in the streets ○ *The railway signal* (ie light) *was on red, so the train stopped.* **3** (**a**) any event or action that causes some general activity: *The President's arrival was the signal for an outburst of cheering.* (**b**) anything indicating that sth exists or is likely to happen: *Her speech yesterday was a signal that her views have changed.* ○ *Is this announcement the signal of better times ahead?* **4** sequence of electronic impulses or radio waves transmitted or received: *receive a signal from a satellite* ○ *an area with a poor/good TV signal* ○ [attrib] *signal strength.*

▷ **signal** *v* (**-ll-**; *US* **-l-**) [I, Ipr, Tn, Tn·pr, Tf, Tw, Dn·pr, Dn·f, Dpr·f, Dn·w, Dpr·w, Dn·t, Dpr·t no passive] ~ (**to sb/sth**) (**for sth**) make a signal or signals; send or express (sth) in this way; communicate with (sb) in this way: *He seems to be signalling.* ○ *signal wildly with one's arms* ○ *signal a message (to sb)* ○ (*fig*) *signal one's discontent by refusing to vote* ○ (*fig*) *an event signalling a change in public opinion* ○ *signal that one is going to turn/which way one is going to turn* ○ *signal (to) the commanding officer (that...)* ○ *signal to the regiment for the attack to begin* ○ *signal (to) sb which way to go* ○ *signal (to) the waiter to bring the menu.* **signaller** (*US* **signaler**) /ˈsɪɡnələ(r)/ *n* person who signals, esp a soldier specially trained for this purpose.

□ **ˈsignal-box** *n* (*Brit*) building beside a railway, from which railway signals are operated.

ˈsignalman /-mən/ *n* (*pl* **-men** /-mən/) **1** person who operates signals on a railway. **2** person who signals, esp in the army or navy.

signal[2] /ˈsɪɡnəl/ *adj* [attrib] remarkably good or bad; outstanding: *a signal victory, success, failure, etc.*

▷ **signally** /-nəlɪ/ *adv* in a signal way: *You have signally failed to do what was expected of you.*

signatory /ˈsɪɡnətrɪ; *US* -tɔːrɪ/ *n* ~ (**to sth**) person, country, etc that has signed an agreement: *the signatories to the treaty* ○ [attrib] *the signatory powers.*

signature /ˈsɪɡnətʃə(r)/ *n* **1** (**a**) [C] person's name written by himself: *a document with two signatures on it* ○ *Her signature is almost illegible.* (**b**) [U] action of signing sth: *a contract ready for signature.* **2** [C] section of a book made from one sheet of paper folded and cut. **3** [C] (*music*) (**a**) = KEY SIGNATURE (KEY[1]). (**b**) = TIME SIGNATURE (TIME[1]). **4** [C] part of a medical prescription that includes directions for the patient on how to use the medicine.

□ **ˈsignature tune** (also **theme tune**) usu brief tune used to introduce a particular broadcast or performer.

signet /ˈsɪɡnɪt/ *n* person's seal[2](1a) used with or instead of a signature.

□ **ˈsignet ring** finger-ring with a design engraved on it, formerly used as a seal.

significance /sɪɡˈnɪfɪkəns/ *n* [U] **1** meaning: *understand the significance of a remark* ○ *What is the significance of this symbol?* **2** importance: *a speech of great significance* ○ *Few people realized the significance of the discovery.*

significant /sɪɡˈnɪfɪkənt/ *adj* **1** (**a**) having a meaning, esp one that is immediately obvious: *Their change of plan is strange but I don't think it's significant.* (**b**) full of meaning: *a significant remark, look, smile.* **2** important; considerable: *a significant rise in profits.*

▷ **significantly** *adv* **1** in a way that conveys a special meaning: *smile, nod, wink, significantly* ○ *Significantly, he did not deny that there might be an election.* **2** to an important or considerable degree: *Profits have risen significantly.*

□ **sigˌnificant ˈfigures** (number of) digits used in a number to indicate how accurate it is. Results are often expressed to three significant figures, eg 3.56, even though the complete figure may be larger or smaller, eg 3.562 or 3.556.

sigˌnificant ˈform quality that all works of art are supposed to have and that is appreciated regardless of the actual subject-matter.

signification /ˌsɪɡnɪfɪˈkeɪʃn/ *n* (*fml or linguistics*) meaning of a word, etc.

signify /ˈsɪɡnɪfaɪ/ *v* (*pt, pp* **-fied**) **1** [Tn] be a sign of (sth); mean: *What do these marks signify?* ○ *Do dark clouds signify rain?* **2** [Tn, Tf no passive] make (sth) known; indicate: *signify one's agreement/that one agrees by nodding* ○ *She signified her approval with a smile.* **3** [I] (used esp in questions and negative sentences) be of importance; matter: *It doesn't signify, so you needn't worry about it.*

signor /ˈsiːnjɔː(r)/ *n* (*pl* **signori** /siːˈnjɔːrɪ/) (*Italian*) (title used before the name of a man to refer to him, or used alone as a formal and polite term of address) Mr; sir.

signora /siːˈnjɔːrə/ *n* (*pl* **signore** /-ˈnjɔːreɪ/) (*Italian*) (title used before the name of an older or married woman to refer to her, or used alone as a formal and polite term of address) Mrs; madam.

signorina /ˌsiːnjəˈriːnə/ *n* (*pl* **-rine** /-ˈriːneɪ/) (*Italian*) (title used before the name of a young or unmarried woman to refer to her, or used alone as a formal and polite term of address) miss.

Sikh /siːk/ *n, adj* (follower) of Sikhism. Sikhs live mainly in the *Punjab and are trying to gain their own independent state there. Male Sikhs traditionally never cut their beard or hair, which they wear in a turban, and they also wear a comb, short dagger and steel bracelet. ⇨ article at RELIGION.

Sikhism /ˈsiːkɪzəm/ *n* [U] religion founded in the 15th century in India by Guru Nanak. Its followers believe in one god who is beyond human understanding and who can be approached through the repetition of his name and through meditation.

silage /ˈsaɪlɪdʒ/ *n* [U] green fodder stored without drying, esp in a silo, to feed cattle in winter.

silence /ˈsaɪləns/ *n* **1** [U] condition of being quiet or silent; absence of sound: *the silence of the night* ○ *A scream shattered the silence.* ○ *In the library silence reigned*, ie it was totally silent. **2** (**a**) [U] not speaking, answering sth spoken or written, making comments, etc; not mentioning sth or revealing a secret: *All my questions were met with silence from him.* ○ *The teacher's stern look reduced him to silence.* ○ *I can't understand her silence on this matter.* ○ *I assume that your silence implies consent*, ie that by saying nothing you are showing that you do not disagree. ○ *After a year's silence* (ie a year during which she didn't write), *I got a letter from her.* ○ *They tried to buy his silence*, ie to pay him not to reveal a secret. (**b**) [C] period during which sb is silent: *a conversation with many silences* ○ *There was a brief silence, followed by uproar.* **3** (idm) **in silence** without speaking or making a sound; silently: *listen to sb in silence* ○ *The whole ceremony took place in complete silence.* **a pregnant pause/silence** ⇨ PREGNANT. **ˌsilence is ˈgolden** (*saying*) it is often best not to say anything.

▷ **silence** *v* [Tn] cause (sb/sth) to be silent; cause to be quiet(er): *try to silence a noisy crowd, a crying baby* ○ *silence one's critics*, eg by doing sth they cannot criticize ○ *silence the enemy's guns*, eg by destroying them ○ *This insult silenced him completely.* **silencer** *n* (**a**) (*Brit*) (*US* **muffler**) device that reduces the noise made by a vehicle's exhaust. ⇨ illus at CAR. (**b**) device that reduces the noise made by a gun being fired.

silence *interj* be quiet: *'Silence!' shouted the teacher.*

silent /ˈsaɪlənt/ *adj* **1** (**a**) making no or little sound; not accompanied by any sound: *with silent footsteps* ○ *the smooth, silent running of the engine* ○ *The children went out, and the room was silent.* (**b**) not expressed aloud: *a silent prayer, curse, etc.* **2** (**a**) not speaking; making no spoken or written comments: *He was silent for a moment, then began his answer.* ○ *She was silent for months before I got a letter from her.* ○ *On certain important details the report remains strangely silent.* (**b**) saying little: *He is the strong, silent type.* **3** (of a letter) written but not pronounced: *The 'b' in 'doubt' and the 'w' in 'wrong' are silent.* ⇨ Usage at QUIET. **4** (idm) **the ˌsilent maˈjority** the people with moderate views who are unable or unwilling to express them publicly. ▷ **silently** *adv.*

□ **ˌsilent ˈfilm** film without a sound-track, esp one made before the invention of sound-films.

ˈsilent partner (*US*) = SLEEPING PARTNER (SLEEP[2]).

silenus /saɪˈliːnəs/ *n* (*pl* **-eni** /-ˈliːnaɪ/) (in Greek mythology) woodland spirit, usu shown as an old drunken satyr riding on a donkey.

silhouette /ˌsɪluːˈet/ *n* **1** (**a**) dark outline of sb/sth seen against a light background: *the silhouettes of the trees against the evening sky.* (**b**) picture showing sb/sth as a black shape against a light background. **2** (idm) **in silhouette** as a silhouette: *see sth in silhouette* ○ *paint sb in silhouette.*

▷ **silhouette** *v* [usu passive: Tn, Tn·pr] ~ **sth** (**against sth**) cause sth to be seen as a silhouette: *She stood in front of the window, silhouetted against the dawn sky.*

silica /ˈsɪlɪkə/ *n* [U] silicon oxide occurring as quartz or flint, and in sandstone and other rocks.

□ **ˈsilica gel** silica in the form of grains, which attracts water and is used to keep food or objects dry in damp conditions.

silicate /ˈsɪlɪkeɪt/ *n* [C, U] any of the insoluble compounds of silicon commonly occurring in the earth's crust: [attrib] *silicate rocks.*

silicon /ˈsɪlɪkən/ *n* [U] (*symb* **Si**) non-metallic chemical element found combined with oxygen in quartz, sandstone, etc. ⇨ App 11.

□ **ˌsilicon ˈchip** microchip made of silicon, used to make an integrated circuit.

ˌSilicon ˈValley (*infml*) the Santa Clara Valley south-east of *San Francisco, California, where many important micro-electronic companies are based.

silicone /ˈsɪlɪkəʊn/ *n* [U] any of the complex organic compounds of silicon, widely used in paints, varnish and lubricants.

silicosis /ˌsɪlɪˈkəʊsɪs/ *n* [U] disease caused by breathing in dust containing silica, eg in a coal-mine.

silk /sɪlk/ *n* **1** [U] fine soft thread produced by silkworms to make their cocoons, or by certain other insects or spiders. **2** [U] thread or cloth made from this: *dressed all in silk* ○ [attrib] *a silk scarf, dress, etc.* **3 silks** [pl] (**a**) shirt and cap worn by a jockey in a horse-race, whose colours and design identify the owner of the horse. (**b**) (*dated*) clothes made from silk: *dressed in fine silks.* **4** [C] (*Brit infml*) Queen's or King's Counsel, who wears a silk gown in court. **5** (idm) **smooth as silk** ⇨ SMOOTH¹. **take 'silk** become a Queen's or King's Counsel: *After fifteen years as a barrister, she took silk.*

□ ,**silk-screen 'printing** method of printing by forcing ink through a stencil of finely-woven material.

'**silkworm** *n* caterpillar that spins silk to form a cocoon.

silken /'sɪlkən/ *adj* [usu attrib] **1** (*usu approv*) soft and smooth; shiny like silk: *a silken voice* ○ *silken hair.* **2** (*arch*) made of silk: *a silken gown.*

silky /'sɪlkɪ/ *adj* (**-ier, -iest**) (*usu approv*) soft, fine, smooth, etc like silk: *silky hair, skin* ○ (*fig*) *a silky manner, voice.* ▷ **silkiness** *n* [U].

sill /sɪl/ *n* piece of wood or stone, etc forming the base of a window or a door: *a 'window-sill* ○ *a 'door-sill.* ⇨ illus at HOME.

sillabub = SYLLABUB.

silly /'sɪlɪ/ *adj* (**-ier, -iest**) **1** (**a**) not showing thought or understanding; foolish: *a silly little boy* ○ *Don't be silly!* ○ *silly mistakes* ○ *What a silly thing to say!* (**b**) ridiculous in appearance, behaviour, etc: *made us play silly games.* **2** [attrib] (of a fielder in cricket) standing close to the batsman. **3** (idm) **laugh oneself sick/silly** ⇨ LAUGH. **play 'silly buggers** (*Brit sl*) behave in a foolish or irresponsible way: *Stop playing silly buggers and help me lift this.* **the 'silly season** time, usu in the summer, when newspapers are full of trivial stories because there is little news.

▷ **silliness** *n* [U].

silly (also **silly-billy**) *n* (*infml*) (often used to or by children) silly person: *Of course I won't leave you alone, you silly!*

silo /'saɪləʊ/ *n* (*pl* ~**s**) **1** (**a**) tall tower or pit, usu on a farm, in which grass or other food for animals can be kept fresh. (**b**) tower or pit for storing grain, cement or radioactive waste. **2** underground place where missiles are kept ready for firing.

silt /sɪlt/ *n* [U] sand, mud, etc carried by flowing water and left at the mouth of a river, in a harbour, etc.

▷ **silt** *v* (phr v) **silt (sth) up** (cause sth to) become blocked with silt: *The harbour has silted up.* ○ *The sand has silted up the mouth of the river.*

silty *adj* (**-ier, -iest**) covered with, full of or containing silt: *silty rocks* ○ *silty soil.*

Silurian /saɪ'ljʊərɪən; *US* -'lʊə-/ *adj* of the third period of the *Palaeozoic era, following the *Ordovician and before the *Devonian, lasting from about 438 to 408 million years ago.

▷ **Silurian** *n* **the Silurian** [sing] the Silurian period.

silvan (also **sylvan**) /'sɪlvən/ *adj* (*arch or rhet*) (**a**) of the woods: *silvan glades.* (**b**) having woods; rural.

silver /'sɪlvə(r)/ *n* **1** [U] (*symb* **Ag**) chemical element, a shiny white precious metal used for ornaments, jewellery, coins, utensils, etc: *solid silver* ○ [attrib] *a silver mine.* ⇨ App 11. **2** [U] coins made of silver or of an alloy looking like it: *£20 in notes and £5 in silver* ○ *a handful of silver* ○ *Have you any silver on you?* **3** [U] (**a**) dishes, ornaments, etc made of silver: *have all one's silver stolen by burglars* ○ *sell the family silver to pay one's debts.* (**b**) cutlery made of any metal: *We keep the silver in this sideboard.* **4** (idm) **born with a silver spoon in one's mouth** ⇨ BORN. **cross sb's palm with silver** ⇨ CROSS². **every cloud has a silver lining** ⇨ CLOUD¹. **the silver 'screen** a cinema screen or the cinema industry: *stars of the silver screen.* **a ,silver 'tongue** way of speaking that charms or persuades people: *It was his silver tongue that got him the job.*

▷ **silver** *v* **1** [Tn] coat (sth) with silver or sth that looks like silver: *metal silvered to make ornaments* ○ *silver a mirror*, ie coat glass to make it reflect things. **2** [I, Tn] (cause hair, etc to) become bright like silver: *Her hair had silvered.* ○ *The years have silvered her hair.*

silver *adj* made of or looking like silver: *a silver plate, dish, watch* ○ *a silver car, paint, thread* ○ *the silver moon.*

silvery /'sɪlvərɪ/ *adj* **1** shiny or coloured like silver(1): *a silvery surface.* **2** [attrib] (*approv*) (of sounds) high-pitched and clear: *the silvery notes of the little bells.*

□ ,**silver 'birch** common birch tree with a light grey bark.

'**silver-fish** *n* any of various types of small silver-coloured wingless insects feeding on scraps of food, book bindings, etc.

,**silver 'jubilee** (celebration of a) 25th anniversary. Cf DIAMOND JUBILEE (DIAMOND), GOLDEN JUBILEE (GOLDEN).

,**silver 'paper** (*infml*) thin light foil of tin or aluminium, used esp for wrapping cigarettes, chocolates, etc.

,**silver 'plate** metal articles coated with silver. ,**silver-'plated** *adj*: *silver-plated dishes.*

,**silver 'sand** fine white sand used by gardeners for mixing with soil.

'**silverside** *n* [U] (*Brit*) outer side of the top of a leg of beef.

'**silversmith** *n* person who makes or sells silver articles.

,**silver-'tongued** *adj* speaking in a way that charms or persuades people: *a ,silver-tongued 'lawyer.*

'**silverware** *n* [U] articles made of silver.

,**silver 'wedding** 25th anniversary of a wedding. Cf DIAMOND WEDDING (DIAMOND), GOLDEN WEDDING (GOLDEN).

silviculture /'sɪlvɪkʌltʃə(r)/ *n* [U] cultivation of trees in forests; forestry.

Simenon /'si:mənɒn/ Georges (1903-89), Belgian writer. He is best known for his stories involving Maigret, a detective in the Paris police force.

simian /'sɪmɪən/ *adj, n* (*fml*) (of or like a) monkey or ape: *a simian appearance, posture, movement.*

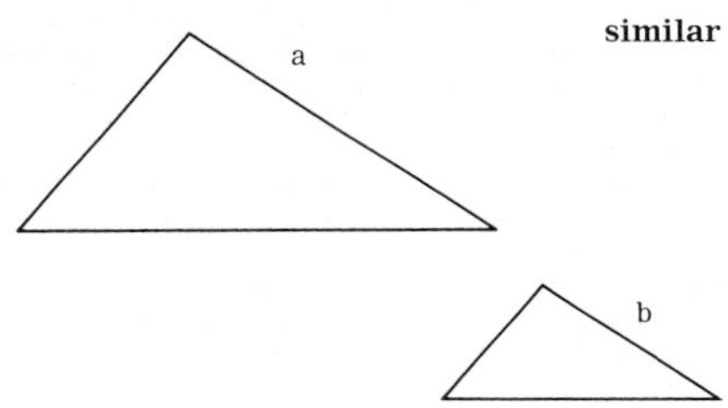

triangles a and b are similar

similar /'sɪmɪlə(r)/ *adj* **1** ~ (**to sb/sth**) resembling sb/sth but not the same; alike: *We have similar tastes in music.* ○ *Gold is similar in colour to brass.* ○ *The brothers look very similar.* **2** (of geometrical figures) that are not the same size, but have the same shape and proportions. ⇨ illus.

▷ **similarity** /,sɪmə'lærətɪ/ *n* **1** [U] being similar; likeness: *points of similarity between the two men.* **2** [C] similar feature or aspect: *similarities in age and background.*

similarly *adv* **1** in a similar way: *The two boys dress similarly.* **2** also; likewise: *She was late and I similarly was delayed.*

simile /'sɪmɪlɪ/ *n* [U, C] (use of) comparison of one thing with another, eg 'as brave as a lion', 'a face like a mask': *use daring similes* ○ *Her style is rich in simile.* Cf METAPHOR.

similitude /sɪ'mɪlɪtju:d; *US* -tu:d/ *n* (*fml*) **1** [U] being similar; similarity. **2** [C] comparison; simile: *talk in similitudes.*

simmer /'sɪmə(r)/ *v* **1** [I, Tn] (cause sth to) remain almost at boiling-point: *Let the soup simmer (for) a few minutes.* ○ *Simmer the stew for an hour.* **2** [I, Ipr] ~ (**with sth**) be filled with (anger, etc) which one can hardly control: *She simmered for a minute or two, then began shouting uncontrollably.* ○ *simmer with rage, annoyance, etc about sth.* **3** [I] (of a quarrel, dispute, etc) continue for a time without any real anger or violence being shown: *This row has been simmering for months.* **4** (phr v) **simmer down** (*infml*) become calm after a period of anger, excitement, violence, etc: *Simmer down, now, and stop shouting.* ○ *Things have simmered down since the riots last week.*

▷ **simmer** *n* **1** [sing] process of simmering: *give the vegetables a five-minute simmer.* **2** (idm) **keep sth at a/on the 'simmer** keep sth simmering: *Keep the potatoes on the simmer for ten minutes.*

Simnel /'sɪmnəl/ Lambert (c1475-1525), Irishman who impersonated the Earl of Warwick in an attempt to overthrow King *Henry VII of England. The plot, organized by the supporters of the House of *York, was defeated. Simnel was pardoned and given a minor position at court.

simnel cake /'sɪmnəl keɪk/ rich fruit-cake with a layer of marzipan inside, traditionally eaten at Easter or on *Mothering Sunday.

simony /'saɪmənɪ/ *n* [U] (formerly) the buying and selling of church appointments, holy relics, etc.

simoom /sɪ'mu:m/ (also **simoon** /sɪ'mu:n/) *n* [sing] hot dry wind that blows in the Sahara and Arabian deserts carrying clouds of dust.

simper /'sɪmpə(r)/ *v* [I] smile in a foolish, affected way: *a simpering waiter.*

▷ **simper** *n* [sing] foolish, affected smile.

simperingly /'sɪmpərɪŋlɪ/ *adv.*

simple /'sɪmpl/ *adj* (**-r, -st**) **1** easily done or understood; not causing difficulty: *a simple task, sum, problem* ○ *written in simple English* ○ *The machine is quite simple to use.* ○ *When speaking to young people, keep it simple*, ie speak in a way they can understand. **2** plain in form, design, etc; without much decoration or ornament: *simple food, furniture* ○ *a simple style of architecture* ○ *the simple life*, ie a way of living without luxury, expensive entertainments, etc ○ *I like my clothes to be simple but elegant.* **3** [usu attrib] (**a**) not made up of many parts or elements: *a simple substance, mixture* ○ *a simple tool, toy* ○ *a simple sentence*, ie one without subordinate clauses. (**b**) not highly developed; basic in structure or function: *simple forms of life, like one-cell organisms* ○ *a fairly simple system of classification.* **4** (**a**) natural and straightforward; not sophisticated: *behave in a simple, open way* ○ *as simple as a child.* (**b**) not having a high position in society; ordinary: *I'm just a simple soldier.* ○ *My father was a simple farm-worker.* **5** (**a**) easily deceived; inexperienced; naive: *Are you simple enough to believe what that liar tells you?* ○ *I'm not so simple as to think it will be easy.* (**b**) (*infml*) not having normal intelligence: *She doesn't understand you. She's a bit simple.* **6** [attrib] nothing more or other than: *It's a simple fact.* ○ *a simple unbiased account of events* ○ *Was it simple greed that made you steal it?* **7** (idm) **pure and simple** ⇨ PURE.

▷ **simple** *n* (*arch*) herb used for treating illness, wounds, etc.

simply /'sɪmplɪ/ *adv* **1** in an easy way: *solved quite simply* ○ *Explain it as simply as you can.* **2** in a plain or unfussy way: *dress simply* ○ *simply dressed* ○ *live simply.* **3** completely; absolutely: *His pronunciation is simply terrible.* ○ *I simply refuse to go!* **4** merely; only: *I bought the house simply because it was large.* ○ *Is success simply a matter of working hard?*

□ ,**simple 'fraction** = VULGAR FRACTION (VULGAR).

,**simple 'fracture** fracture of a bone which does not break out through the skin. Cf COMPOUND FRACTURE (COMPOUND).

,**simple 'interest** interest paid on a capital sum only, not on the interest that is added to it. Cf COMPOUND INTEREST (COMPOUND¹).

,**simple ma'chine** any simple instrument used as (part of) a machine, eg a wheel, lever, pulley.

,**simple-'minded** *adj* (*often derog*) showing very little intelligence: *her more ,simple-minded sup'porters* ○ *a simple-minded approach to the problem.*

simpleton /'sɪmpltən/ *n* person who is foolish, easily deceived or not very intelligent.

simplicity /sɪm'plɪsətɪ/ *n* [U] **1** being easy, plain or straightforward: *the simplicity of the problem* ○ *the simplicity of her style* ○ *a character marked by frankness and simplicity.* **2** (idm) **be sim,plicity it'self** be very easy: *Cleaning the light is simplicity itself; just wipe it with a damp cloth.*

simplify /ˈsɪmplɪfaɪ/ *v* (*pt, pp* **-fied**) [Tn] make (sth) easy to do or understand; make simple(1): *a simplified text*, eg one for learners of the language ○ *simplify the instructions so that children can understand them* ○ *That will simplify my task.*
▷ **simplification** /ˌsɪmplɪfɪˈkeɪʃn/ *n* (a) [U] act or process of simplifying. (b) [C] instance of simplifying; sth simplified: *What she said was a useful simplification of the theory.*

simplistic /sɪmˈplɪstɪk/ *adj* (*derog*) made too simple, so as to ignore the real complexity of sth. ▷ **simplistically** /-klɪ/ *adv.*

simulacrum /ˌsɪmjʊˈleɪkrəm/ *n* (*pl* **-cra** /-krə/) (*fml*) thing resembling or made to resemble sb/sth.

simulate /ˈsɪmjʊleɪt/ *v* [Tn] **1** pretend to have or feel (esp an emotion): *simulate anger, joy, interest, etc* ○ *her carefully simulated disappointment.* **2** reproduce (certain conditions) by means of a model, etc, eg for study or training purposes: *simulate flight using a model plane in a wind tunnel* ○ *The computer simulates conditions on the sea bed.* **3** take on the appearance of (sth/sb): *insects that simulate dead leaves* ○ *change colour to simulate the background.*
▷ **simulated** *adj* [usu attrib] made to look, sound, etc like (sth): *simulated fur, jewels, etc.*
simulation /ˌsɪmjʊˈleɪʃn/ *n* **1** [U] action of simulating: *the simulation of genuine concern* ○ *the simulation of flight conditions.* **2** [C] operation in which a real situation, etc is represented in another form: *a computer simulation of the nuclear reaction.*
simulator *n* any device designed to simulate certain conditions, eg flight, weightlessness, etc.

simultaneous /ˌsɪmlˈteɪnɪəs; *US* ˌsaɪm-/ *adj* ~ **(with sth)** happening or done at the same time (as sth): *simultaneous demonstrations in London and New York* ○ *The explosion was timed to be simultaneous with the plane's take-off.* ▷ **simultaneously** *adv.* **simultaneousness, simultaneity** /ˌsɪmltəˈniːətɪ; *US* ˌsaɪm-/ *ns* [U].

sin /sɪn/ *n* **1** (a) [U] the breaking of a religious or moral law: *a life of sin.* (b) [C] offence against such a law: *commit a sin* ○ *confess one's sins to a priest* ○ *the sin of gluttony.* **2** [C] action regarded as a serious fault or offence: *Being late is an unforgivable sin round here.* ○ (*joc*) *It's a sin to stay indoors on such a fine day.* **3** (idm) **cover/hide a multitude of sins** ⇨ MULTITUDE. **the deadly sins** ⇨ DEADLY. **for my ˈsins** (*joc*) although I regret it or pretend to regret it; as if I were being punished for doing sth wrong: *Every year for my sins I lead the school trip to France.* **live in sin** ⇨ LIVE[2]. **(as) miserable/ugly as ˈsin** (*infml*) very miserable/ugly.
▷ **sin** *v* (**-nn-**) [I, Ipr] ~ **(against sth)** commit a sin or sins; do wrong: *It's human to sin.* ○ (*fig*) *They sinned against the unwritten rules of the school.*
sinful /-fl/ *adj* (*esp fml*) wrong; wicked: *Man is sinful* ○ *sinful deeds* ○ (*infml*) *a sinful waste of good wine.* **sinfully** /-fəlɪ/ *adv.* **sinfulness** *n* [U].
sinless *adj* (*fml*) never sinning; innocent. **sinlessness** *n* [U].
sinner /ˈsɪnə(r)/ *n*: *saints and sinners.*

sin *abbr* (*mathematics*) sine. Cf cos *abbr.*

Sinatra /sɪˈnɑːtrə/ Frank (1915-), American singer and actor. His distinctive style of singing has made him famous as a performer all over the world, and he has also starred in several successful films and musicals, eg *High Society* with Bing *Crosby.

Sinbad (also **Sindbad**) /ˈsɪnbæd/ (in Eastern legend) sailor who has fantastic adventures each time he goes to sea. He is usu known as 'Sinbad the Sailor'. His story is told in the **Arabian Nights.*

since /sɪns/ *prep* (used with the present or past perfect tense) from (a specified time in the past) till a later past time, or till now: *I haven't eaten since breakfast.* ○ *She's been working in a bank since leaving school.* ○ *He had spoken to her only once since the party.*
▷ **since** *conj* **1** (used with the present perfect, past perfect or simple present tense in the main clause) from (a specified event in the past) till a later past event, or till now: *Where have you been since I last saw you?* ○ *It was the first time I'd won since I'd learnt to play chess.* ○ *How long is it since we visited your mother?* **2** because; as: *Since we've no money we can't buy a new car.* **3** (idm) **ever since** ⇨ EVER.
since *adv* (used with the present or past perfect tense) from a specified time in the past till a later past time, or till now: *He left home two weeks ago and we haven't heard from him since.* ○ *She moved to London last May and has since got a job on a newspaper.*

sincere /sɪnˈsɪə(r)/ *adj* **1** (of feelings or behaviour) not pretended; genuine: *sincere friendship, affection, dislike, disagreement, etc* ○ *It is my sincere belief that...* ○ *His was a sincere offer of help.* **2** (of people) only saying things one really means or believes; straightforward: *a sincere Christian* ○ *She wasn't entirely sincere when she said she liked me.*
▷ **sincerely** *adv*: *thank sb sincerely* ○ *yours sincerely.* ⇨ Usage at YOUR.
sincerity /sɪnˈserətɪ/ *n* [U] quality of being sincere; honesty: *the warmth and sincerity of his welcome.*

sine /saɪn/ *n* (*abbr* **sin**) (*mathematics*) (in a right-angled triangle) the ratio of the length of the side opposite one of the acute angles to the length of the hypotenuse. Cf COSINE, TANGENT 2.
□ ˈ**sine wave** (also ˈ**sine curve**) wave[2](6) that has an equation in which one variable is proportional to the sine of the other.

sinecure /ˈsaɪnɪkjʊə(r), ˈsɪn-/ *n* position that requires no work or responsibility, but gives the holder prestige or money.

sine die /ˌsaɪnɪ ˈdaɪiː, ˌsɪnɪ ˈdiːeɪ/ (*fml esp law*) without a date being fixed; indefinitely: *adjourn a meeting sine die.*

sine qua non /ˌsɪneɪ kwɑː ˈnəʊn/ (*fml*) essential condition; thing that is absolutely necessary: *Patience is a sine qua non for a good teacher.*

sinew /ˈsɪnjuː/ *n* **1** [C, U] tough cord of tissue joining a muscle to a bone; tendon. **2 sinews** [pl] (a) muscles: *The athletes waited, with all their sinews tensed.* (b) (*fml fig*) source of strength or energy: *A country's sinews are its roads and railways.*
▷ **sinewy** *adj* **1** having strong sinews; tough; muscular: *sinewy arms, legs, etc.* **2** (*fig*) having or showing strength or vigour: *her sinewy prose style.*

sinfonietta /ˌsɪnfəʊnɪˈetə/ *n* **1** short simple form of symphony. **2** (used esp in proper names) small orchestra: *the Bournemouth Sinfonietta.*

sing /sɪŋ/ *v* (*pt* **sang** /sæŋ/, *pp* **sung** /sʌŋ/) **1** [I, Ipr, Ip, Tn, Tn·pr, Dn·n, Dn·pr] ~ **(sth) (for/to sb)** make musical sounds with the voice; utter (words or notes) with a tune: *She sings well.* ○ *You're not singing in tune.* ○ *Birds sang/were singing away happily outside.* ○ *He sang to a piano accompaniment.* ○ *She was singing a lullaby to her child.* ○ *He sang the baby to sleep.* ○ *Will you sing me a song?* ○ *They sang a song for me.* **2** [I, Ip] make a humming, buzzing or whistling sound: *The kettle was singing (away) on the cooker.* ○ *The explosion made my ears sing*, ie made me hear a singing sound. **3** [I] (*sl esp US*) become an informer: *She'll sing if we put the pressure on.* **4** (idm) **sing a different ˈsong/ˈtune** change one's opinion about or attitude towards sb/sth: *You say you don't believe in marriage, but I bet you sing a different song when you finally fall in love.* **sing sb's/sth's ˈpraises** praise sb/sth greatly: *The critics are singing the praises of her new book.* **5** (phr v) **sing along (with sb)** join in and sing (with sb). **sing out (for sth)** (*infml*) shout (to get sth): *If you need anything, just sing out for it.* **sing sth out** (*infml*) shout (eg an order): *Just sing out what you want.* **sing past, through, etc** move with a humming, buzzing or whistling sound: *A bullet sang past my ear.* **sing up** sing more vigorously or loudly: *Sing up, let's hear you.*
▷ **singer** *n* person who sings, esp in public: *an opera singer.*
singing *n* [U] **1** art of the singer: *teach singing* ○ [attrib] *a singing teacher* ○ *singing lessons.* **2** action or sound of singing: *their beautiful singing of the madrigal* ○ *I heard singing next door.*

Singapore /ˌsɪŋəˈpɔː(r)/ country in SE Asia, a member of the Commonwealth; pop approx 2 647 000; official languages Malay, Chinese, Tamil and English; capital Singapore; unit of currency dollar (= 100 cents). The country is made up of the island of Singapore and 54 smaller islands, and lies off the southern tip of the Malay Peninsula. It was founded by Sir Stamford *Raffles and was previously uninhabited. It has practically no agricultural or mineral resources, but is economically successful though its strong industrial and service sector, including high-technology companies, oil-refining and the activities of the port. ⇨ map at MALAYSIA. ▷ **Singaporean** /-ˈpɔːrɪən/ *n, adj.*

singe /sɪndʒ/ *v* (*pres p* **singeing**) **1** (a) [Tn] blacken (sth) by burning; scorch: *The iron's too hot, you'll singe the dress.* (b) [I] be blackened or scorched in this way: *The rug singed because it was too near the fire.* **2** [Tn] burn off the tips or ends of (hair, feathers, etc).
▷ **singe** *n* slight burn or scorch on cloth, etc.

single /ˈsɪŋgl/ *adj* **1** [attrib] (a) one only; not in a pair, group, etc: *a single apple hanging from the tree* ○ *a single layer of paint* ○ *one double and one single sink-unit.* (b) considered on its own; separate: *the single most important event in the history of the world* ○ *She removed every single thing from the box.* **2** not married: *single men and women* ○ *remain single* ○ *the single state.* **3** [attrib] designed for, or used or done by, one person: *a single bed, sheet* ○ *reserve one single and one double room*, eg at a hotel. **4** [attrib] (*botany*) having only one set of petals: *a single tulip.* **5** [attrib] (*Brit*) (*US* **one-way**) (of a journey) only to a place, not there and back: *a single fare, ticket, etc.* Cf RETURN[2] 5. **6** (idm) **hang by a hair/a single thread** ⇨ HANG[1]. **(in) single ˈfigures** figures less than ten: *Interest rates are in single figures*, ie under 10%. **(in) single file** ⇨ FILE[3]. **two minds with a single thought** ⇨ MIND[1].
▷ **single** *n* **1 singles** [sing *v*] game played with one player rather than a pair of players on each side: *play (a) singles* ○ *the men's/women's singles in the golf tournament* ○ [attrib] *a singles match.* **2** [C] (in cricket) hit for which one run is scored: *get a quick single.* **3** [C] = BASE HIT (BASE[1]). **4** [C] (*infml*) single(5) ticket: *two second-class singles to Leeds.* **5** [C] record with only one short recording on each side: *a hit single.* Cf ALBUM 2, EP, LP. **6 singles** [pl] (*esp US*) unmarried people: *a club for singles* ○ [attrib] *a singles bar, holiday.*
single *v* (phr v) **single sb/sth out (for sth)** select sb/sth from others, eg for special attention: *Which would you single out as the best?* ○ *He was singled out for punishment.*
singleness *n* [U]: *singleness of mind*, ie single-mindedness ○ *singleness of purpose*, ie concentration on one goal, aim, etc.
singly /ˈsɪŋglɪ/ *adv* one by one; on one's own: *Do you teach your students singly or in groups?*
□ ˌ**single ˈcombat** fight, usu with weapons, between two people; duel: *meet in single combat.*
ˌ**single ˈcream** cream that contains relatively little fat.
ˌ**single-ˈdecker** *n* bus with only one deck.
ˌ**single-ˈhanded** *adj, adv* done (by one person) with no help from others: *a* ˌ*single-handed* ˈ*sailing trip* ○ *do sth single-handed.*
ˌ**single-ˈminded** *adj* having or concentrating on one aim, purpose, etc: *too single-minded to be distracted by failures.* **single-mindedly** *adv*: *work single-mindedly at sth.* **single-mindedness** *n* [U].
ˌ**single ˈparent** parent bringing up a child/children on his/her own: [attrib] *a* ˌ*single-parent* ˈ*family.*

singlet /ˈsɪŋglɪt/ *n* (*Brit*) (a) man's sleeveless garment worn under or instead of a shirt; vest. (b) such a garment worn by runners, athletes, etc.

Sing Sing /ˈsɪŋ sɪŋ/ former name of Ossining Correctional Facility, a prison in New York State, USA. It was famous for its strict discipline.

singsong /ˈsɪŋsɒŋ/ *adj* (of a voice or way of speaking) having a rising and falling rhythm: *in a singsong voice, accent, manner.*
▷ **singsong** *n* **1** [sing] singsong manner of

speaking: *the tedious singsong of the preacher's voice* ○ *speak in a singsong.* **2** [C] (*infml*) informal occasion when a group of people sing songs together: *a singsong round the camp-fire.*

singular /ˈsɪŋgjʊlə(r)/ *adj* **1** (*grammar*) of the form used when speaking about one person or thing: *a singular verb, noun, ending.* Cf PLURAL. **2** (*fml*) **(a)** (*dated*) unusual; strange: *a singular occurrence, event, circumstance, etc.* **(b)** outstanding; remarkable: *a person of singular courage and honesty.*

▷ **singular** *n* (*grammar*) (word in a) singular form: *What is the singular of 'children'?* ○ *What is the ending in the singular?*

singularity /ˌsɪŋgjʊˈlærətɪ/ *n* [U] (*fml*) strangeness: *the singularity of the event.*

singularly *adv* (*fml*) **1** (*dated*) unusually; strangely: *rather singularly attired.* **2** very; remarkably: *a singularly gifted pianist.*

Sinhalese /ˌsɪnhəˈliːz/ (also **Singhalese**) /ˌsɪŋgəˈliːz/ *n* **1** [C] (*pl* unchanged) member of a people originally from N India and forming the majority of the population of *Sri Lanka. The Sinhalese are mainly Buddhists and occupy the southern part of the island. **2** [U] language of this people, which belongs to the Indo-European language family.

sinister /ˈsɪnɪstə(r)/ *adj* **1** suggesting evil, or that sth bad may happen: *a sinister motive, action, place.* **2** suggesting an evil nature: *a sinister face* ○ *sinister looks.*

sink[1] /sɪŋk/ *v* (*pt* **sank** /sæŋk/, *pp* **sunk** /sʌŋk/) **1** [I, Ipr, Ip] go down under the surface of a liquid or soft substance: *Wood does not sink in water, it floats.* ○ *The ship sank (to the bottom of the ocean).* ○ *My feet sank (down) into the mud.* ○ *It fell onto the wet sand, then sank (in).* **2** [Tn] **(a)** cause (a ship, etc) to go to the bottom of the sea: *a carrier sunk by a torpedo* ○ *They sank the barge by making a hole in the bottom.* **(b)** (*fig infml*) prevent (sb or sb's plans) from succeeding; ruin: *The press want to sink his bid for the Presidency.* ○ *We'll be sunk if the car breaks down.* **3** **(a)** [I, Ipr, Ip] become lower; fall slowly downwards: *The foundations sank (two feet) after the flood.* ○ *The earthquake made the wall sink and start to crumble.* ○ *The soldier sank to the ground badly wounded.* ○ *I sank (down) into an armchair.* **(b)** [Tn, Tn·pr] cause (sth) to be lower; move (sth) downwards: *sink the cable into position on the sea bed* ○ (*fig*) *sink one's voice to a whisper.* **4** **(a)** [I, Ipr] (of the sun) go down below the horizon: *the sun sinking in the west* ○ *The sun sank slowly behind the hills.* **(b)** [I, Ipr] lose value, strength, etc gradually; decline: *Stocks and shares are sinking.* ○ *The value of our currency has sunk to almost nothing.* ○ *He is sinking fast,* ie will soon die. ○ (*fig*) *sink in the estimation of one's friends* ○ (*fig*) *His voice sank to a whisper.* **5** **(a)** place (sth) in a hole made by digging: *sink two posts (into the ground) here.* **(b)** [Tn, Tn·pr] make (sth) by digging: *sink a well, shaft, etc* ○ *sink a tunnel into the side of the mountain.* **6** [Tn, Tn·pr] send (a ball) into a pocket or hole (in billiards, golf, etc): *sink the red (into the top pocket).* **7** [Tn] (*infml*) drink (esp a large amount of alcohol): *They sank a bottle of gin between them.* **8** (idm) **be sunk in sth** be in a state of (esp despair or deep thought): *She just sat there, sunk in depression.* **one's heart sinks** ⇨ HEART. **sink one's ˈdifferences** agree to forget what one disagrees about: *We must sink our differences and save the firm.* **a/that ˈsinking feeling** (*infml*) feeling that sth bad is about to happen: *When they didn't get back by midnight, I got that sinking feeling.* **sink like a ˈstone** sink straight down immediately. **ˌsink or ˈswim** (*saying*) (used of a situation where one will either fail totally or survive by one's own efforts): *The refugees had lost their homes and their possessions, and it was now (a case of) sink or swim.* **9** (phr v) **sink in/sink into sth** **(a)** (of liquids) go down into another substance; be absorbed: *Rub the cream on your skin and let it sink in.* ○ *The rain sank into the dry ground.* **(b)** (of words, etc) be fully understood: *The scale of the tragedy gradually sank in.* ○ *My warning obviously hasn't sunk into your thick skull.* **sink into sth** (no passive) go into (a less active or happy state): *sink into sleep, a coma, etc* ○ *Don't let yourself sink into despair.* **sink sth into sth** **(a)** make sth go into sth: *sink one's teeth into a bun,* ie bite it ○ *sink a knife into butter.* **(b)** invest (money) in a business, etc: *They sank all their profits into* (ie used them to buy) *property.*

□ **ˈsinking fund** money put aside by a government or company, etc to be used to repay a debt gradually.

sink[2] /sɪŋk/ *n* **1** fixed basin, usu of steel, porcelain, etc, with a water supply and a drain for waste water to flow away, used for washing dishes, cleaning vegetables, etc: [attrib] *a sink unit,* ie a sink with drawers and cupboards underneath. **2** (*US*) wash-basin. **3** cesspool. **4** (idm) **everything but the kitchen sink** ⇨ KITCHEN.

sinker /ˈsɪŋkə(r)/ *n* **1** weight attached to a fishing-line or net to keep it under water. **2** (*US sl*) = DOUGHNUT (DOUGH). **3** (idm) **hook, line and sinker** ⇨ HOOK[1].

Sinn Fein /ˌʃɪn ˈfeɪn/ Irish nationalist movement founded in 1905 to achieve Irish independence. Most members joined the *Fianna Fáil party when it was formed, but part of the movement continued as the political wing of the *IRA. In 1969 it split, like the IRA itself, into Official and Provisional wings. The words *Sinn Fein* mean 'we ourselves'.

Sino- (also **sino-**) *comb form* Chinese; of China: *sinology* ○ *Sino-Japanese.*

sinology /saɪˈnɒlədʒɪ/ *n* [U] knowledge or study of China and its language and culture.

▷ **sinologist** /-dʒɪst/ *n* expert in sinology.

sinter /ˈsɪntə(r)/ *v* [Tn] produce a solid from (a powdered substance, eg glass or an oxide) by heating it at a temperature below melting-point.

▷ **sinter** *n* solid produced by sintering.

sinuous /ˈsɪnjʊəs/ *adj* having many curves and twists; winding: *the sinuous movements of the dancer* ○ *the river's sinuous course.*

▷ **sinuosity** /ˌsɪnjʊˈɒsətɪ/ *n* (*fml*) **1** [U] quality of being sinuous. **2** [C] curve or twist.

sinus /ˈsaɪnəs/ *n* cavity in a bone, esp any of the air-filled spaces in the skull that are connected to the nostrils.

▷ **sinusitis** /ˌsaɪnəˈsaɪtɪs/ *n* [U] inflammation of a sinus membrane.

-sion ⇨ -ION.

Sioux /suː/ *n* **1** [C] (*pl* unchanged) member of a group of native American peoples living in and around the *Great Plains. **2** [U] language of these peoples. ▷ **Sioux** *adj.*

sip /sɪp/ *v* (**-pp-**) [I, Tn] drink (sth), taking very small quantities each time: *drink one's tea, sipping noisily* ○ *sip one's coffee.*

▷ **sip** *n* act of sipping; amount sipped: *a few sips of brandy.*

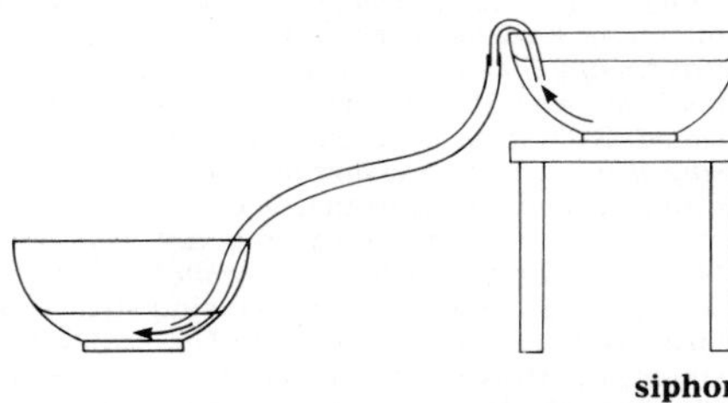

siphon

siphon /ˈsaɪfn/ *n* **1** pipe, tube, etc in the form of an upside-down U, used for making a liquid flow, eg from one container to another, using atmospheric pressure. **2** (also **soda siphon**) bottle from which soda-water can be forced out by the pressure of gas in the bottle. **3** sucking-tube of some insects and animals.

▷ **siphon** *v* (phr v) **siphon sth into/out of sth; siphon sth off/out** draw (a liquid) from one place to another using a siphon: *siphon petrol out of a car into a can* ○ *siphon off all the waste liquid.* **siphon sb/sth off** (*infml often derog*) transfer sb/sth from one place to another, often unfairly or illegally: *The big clubs siphon off all the best players.* ○ *She siphoned off profits from the business into her account.*

sir /sɜː(r)/ *n* **1** **(a)** (used as a polite way of addressing a man): *Yes, sir.* ○ *Are you ready to order, sir?* ○ *Sir, it is my duty to inform you that....* **(b)** (used as a form of address by schoolchildren to a male teacher). Cf MISS[2] 2. **2** **Sir** (used at the beginning of a formal letter): *Dear Sir/Sirs.* **3** **Sir** /sə(r)/ (title used before the first name of a knight or baronet): *Sir ˈEdward* ○ *Sir ˌJohn ˈJackson.* ⇨ article at ARISTOCRAT. **4** (idm) **ˌno ˈsir!** (*US infml*) certainly not: *I never smoke, no sir!*

sire /ˈsaɪə(r)/ *n* male parent of an animal: *the sire of many successful racehorses.*

▷ **sire** *v* [Tn] be the sire of (an animal): *a filly sired by a famous racehorse.*

siren /ˈsaɪərən/ *n* **1** device that makes a long loud sound as a signal or warning: *an air-raid siren* ○ *a police siren* ○ *an ambulance/a fire-engine racing along with its sirens wailing.* **2** (in Greek mythology) one of a number of winged women whose songs lured sailors to their destruction. **3** woman regarded as fascinating and dangerous.

sirenian /saɪˈriːnɪən/ *adj* of or belonging to the group of animals which includes large plant-eating mammals living in water, such as the manatee.

Sirius /ˈsɪrɪəs/ (also **the Dog Star**) brightest star in the northern hemisphere, seen by observers on earth as being near the bottom of the constellation *Orion.

sirloin /ˈsɜːlɔɪn/ *n* [U, C] **1** best part of a loin of beef: *a slice of sirloin* ○ *a top-quality sirloin.* **2** (*US*) = RUMP STEAK (RUMP 2).

sirocco /sɪˈrɒkəʊ/ *n* (*pl* ~s) hot moist wind reaching Italy from Africa.

sirup (*US*) ⇨ SYRUP.

sis /sɪs/ *n* (*dated infml*) (esp as a form of address) sister.

sisal /ˈsaɪsl/ *n* **1** [U] rope-fibre made from the leaves of a tropical plant: [attrib] *sisal grass, fibre, rope, etc.* **2** [C] the plant itself.

Sisley /ˈsɪzlɪ/ Alfred (1839-99), British painter. Although his parents were British he lived in France but never became a French citizen. He belonged to the *Impressionist school and painted subtle landscapes, esp scenes of snow and rain. ⇨ illus.

sissy (also **cissy**) /ˈsɪsɪ/ *n* (*infml derog*) effeminate or cowardly boy or man: *You daren't jump down, you sissy!* ○ [attrib] *sissy games, behaviour.*

sister /ˈsɪstə(r)/ *n* **1** daughter of the same parents as oneself or another person: *my, your, his, etc big sister* ○ *She has been like a sister to me,* ie has behaved as a sister does. **2** (used esp by feminist women) fellow woman: *They supported their sisters in the dispute.* **3** (*US infml*) (used to address a woman): *Come on, sister, hurry along!* **4** (*Brit*) senior hospital nurse. **5** **Sister** member of certain female religious orders; nun: *the Little Sisters of the Poor.* **6** [attrib] (eg of a ship or an organization) of the same design or type: *After the disaster, tests were carried out on the tanker's sister vessels.* ○ *our sister college in Cambridge.*

▷ **sisterhood** *n* **1** [U] relationship of sisters(1,2) (esp as claimed by feminist women). **2** [Gp] society of women with shared interests or aims, esp a religious society.

sisterly *adj* of or like a sister: *sisterly love* ○ *a sisterly kiss.*

□ **ˈsister-in-law** *n* (*pl* **~s-in-law**) sister of one's wife or husband; wife of one's brother.

Sistine Chapel /ˈsɪstiːn/ **the Sistine Chapel** chapel in the *Vatican built for Pope Sixtus IV. It is famous for the ceiling painted by *Michelangelo and his fresco of the Last Judgement. The meeting to elect a new pope is held in the chapel.

Sisyphean /sɪsɪˈfiːən/ *adj* (*fml or rhet*) (of work) involving great effort and seeming to produce little result (like the punishment of Sisyphus in Greek mythology, who was condemned to roll a large stone to the top of a hill, from where it always rolled back down again): *the Sisyphean task of checking inflation.*

sit /sɪt/ *v* (**-tt-**; *pt, pp* **sat** /sæt/) **1** **(a)** [I, Ipr, Ip] be in a position in which the body is upright and resting on the buttocks, either on a seat or on the ground: *Never stand when you can sit.* ○ *Are you sitting comfortably?* ○ *sit on a chair, on the floor, in an armchair, etc* ○ *sit at (a) table to eat* ○ *sit on a horse.* **(b)** [I, Ip, Tn, Tn·p] ~ **(sb) (down)**; ~ **oneself down** (cause sb to) take up such a position; place (sb) in a sitting position: *She sat (down) on the chair and took her shoes off.* ○ *He lifted the child and sat* (ie seated) *her on the wall.* ○ *Sit yourself down and tell us what happened.* ○ *(fig) We must sit down together and settle our differences.* **2** [I, Ipr] ~ **(for sb)** pose for a portrait: *I sat every day for a week until the painting was finished.* ○ *sit for a famous painter.* **3** [I] (of a parliament, lawcourt, committee, etc) hold a meeting: *The House of Commons was still sitting at 3 am.* **4** [I, Ipr] **(a)** (of birds) perch: *a sparrow sitting on a branch.* **(b)** (of certain animals, esp dogs) rest with the hind legs bent and the rear end on the ground: *'Sit!' she told the dog.* **5** [I] (of birds) stay on the nest to hatch eggs: *The hen sits for most of the day.* **6** [I, Ipr] ~ **(on sb)** (usu followed by an *adv*) (of clothes) fit the body well: *a dress that sits well, loosely, etc on sb* ○ *The coat sits badly across the shoulders.* ○ *(fig) His new-found prosperity sits well on him,* ie suits him well. **7** [Ipr] be in a certain position; lie: *The book's still sitting on my shelf,* ie I haven't read it. ○ *The farm sits on top of the hill.* **8** [Ipr, Tn] ~ **(for) sth** be a candidate for (an examination): *sit (for) an exam/a test* ○ *sit for a scholarship.* **9** (idm) **sit at sb's 'feet** be sb's pupil or follower: *She sat at the feet of Freud himself.* **sit in 'judgement (on/over sb)** judge sb, esp when one has no right to do so: *How dare you sit in judgement on me?* **sit on the 'fence** hesitate or fail to decide between two opposite courses of action, sets of beliefs, etc. **sit on one's 'hands** do nothing: *Are you going to sit on your hands while she does all the work?* **ˌsit 'tight** **(a)** remain where one is: *All the others ran away, but I sat tight.* **(b)** refuse to take action, yield, etc: *She threatened us with dismissal if we didn't agree, but we all sat tight.* **a ˌsitting 'duck** person or thing that is an easy target, or is easy to attack: *Without my gun, I'm a sitting duck for any terrorist.* **ˌsitting 'pretty** *(infml)* in a fortunate situation, esp when others are unlucky: *I was properly insured so I'm sitting pretty.* **sit 'up (and take notice)** *(infml)* suddenly start paying attention to what is happening, being said, etc: *I called her a damned hypocrite and that made her sit up.* ○ *This news made us all sit up and take notice.* **10** (phr v) **sit around** spend one's time sitting down, unwilling or unable to do anything: *I've been sitting around waiting for the phone to ring all day.*

sit back **(a)** settle oneself comfortably back, eg in a chair: *I sat back and enjoyed a cup of tea.* **(b)** relax after working; do nothing: *I like to sit back and rest in the evenings.* ○ *Are you going to sit back and let me do everything?*

sit down under sth *(fml)* suffer (insults, etc) without protest or complaint: *He should not sit down under these accusations.*

sit for sth (no passive) *(Brit)* be the Member of Parliament for (a constituency): *I sit for Bristol West.*

sit in occupy (part of) a building as a protest: *The workers are sitting in against the factory closures.* **sit in on sth** attend (a discussion, etc) as an observer, not as a participant: *The teachers allowed a pupil to sit in on their meeting.*

sit on sth **(a)** (no passive) be a member of (a committee, jury, etc): *How many people sit on the commission?* **(b)** *(infml)* fail to deal with sth: *They have been sitting on my application for a month.* **sit on sb** stop sb's bad or awkward behaviour: *I have to sit on the class when they get too rowdy.* ○ *She thinks she knows everything, and needs sitting on.*

sit out sit outdoors: *The garden's so lovely, I think I'll sit out.* **sit sth out** **(a)** stay to the end of (a performance, etc): *sit out a boring play.* **(b)** not take part in (a particular dance): *I think I'll sit out the rumba.*

sit through sth remain in a theatre, etc from the beginning to the end of (a performance, etc): *I can't sit through six hours of Wagner!*

sit up (for sb) not go to bed until later than the usual time, esp because one is waiting for sb: *I shall get back late, so don't sit up (for me).* ○ *The nurse sat up with the patient all night.* ○ *We sat up late watching a film on TV.* **sit (sb) up** (cause sb to) move to an upright position after lying flat, slouching, etc: *The patient is well enough to sit up in bed now.* ○ *We sat the baby up to feed her.* ○ *Sit up straight!* Cf SIT UP (AND TAKE NOTICE).

□ **'sit-down** *n* **1** (also **ˌsit-down 'strike**) strike in which workers occupy a factory, etc until their demands are considered or met. **2** [attrib] (of a meal) served to people sitting down: *a sit-down lunch.*

'sit-in *n* protest made by sitting in: *a sit-in at the city council offices.*

Alfred Sisley: The Boat in the Flood at Port-Marley

ˌsitting 'member *(Brit)* candidate at a general election who holds the seat until the next election is called.

'sitting-room *n (esp Brit)* = LIVING-ROOM (LIVING[2]).

ˌsitting 'tenant tenant who is actually occupying a flat, house, etc: *It's difficult to sell a house with a sitting tenant.*

sitar /sɪ'tɑ:(r), 'sɪtɑ:(r)/ *n* Indian stringed instrument resembling a guitar, with a long neck.

sitcom /'sɪtkɒm/ *n (infml)* = SITUATION COMEDY (SITUATION).

site /saɪt/ *n* **1** place where a building, town, etc was, is, or will be situated: *built on the site of a Roman fort* ○ *a site for a new school* ○ *deliver the materials to a building site* ○ *I picked a sheltered site for the tent.* **2** place where sth has happened or will happen, or for a particular activity: *the site of the battle* ○ *Rescue workers rushed to the site of the plane crash.*

▷ **site** *v* [Tn, Tn·pr] locate (a building, etc); place: *a factory sited next to a railway line* ○ *Is it safe to site the power-station here?*

□ **ˌsite of ˌspecial ˌscientific 'interest** (*abbr* **SSSI**) (in Britain) area in which the wild plants or animals are considered rare or scientifically important, and which is given some protection from damage by farming, building, etc.

sitter /'sɪtə(r)/ *n* **1** person who is being painted or photographed. **2** **(a)** bird or animal that is not flying or moving and is therefore easy to shoot. **(b)** *(sl)* thing that is easy to do, catch, etc: *The purse in her handbag was a sitter for any thief.* **3** (with an *adj*) hen that sits (SIT 5): *a good/poor sitter.* **4** *(infml)* = BABY-SITTER (BABY).

sitting /'sɪtɪŋ/ *n* **1** time during which a lawcourt, parliament, etc sits continuously: *during a long sitting.* **2** period when a group of people eat a meal: *The dining-hall is small, so there are two sittings for lunch.* ○ *About 100 people can be served at one sitting,* ie together, at one time. **3** period spent continuously in one activity: *finish reading a book at one sitting.* **4** period spent by sb being painted or photographed: *The portrait was completed after six sittings.* **5** number of eggs on which a hen sits.

situate /'sɪtjʊeɪt; *US* 'sɪtʃʊeɪt/ *v* [Tn·pr esp passive] *(fml)* place or locate (eg a building or town) in a certain position: *The company wants to situate its headquarters in the north.* ○ *The village is situated in a valley.* ○ *Where will the school be situated?*

▷ **situated** *adj* [pred] (of a person) in circumstances of a specified kind; placed: *Having six children and no income, I was badly situated.* ○ *How are you situated with regard to equipment?* ie Do you have all you need?

situation /ˌsɪtʃʊ'eɪʃn/ *n* **1** set of circumstances or state of affairs, esp at a certain time: *find oneself in an embarrassing situation* ○ *get into/out of a difficult situation* ○ *the worsening diplomatic situation* ○ *The company is in a poor financial situation,* eg is losing money. **2** position of a town, building, etc in relation to its surroundings: *a beautiful situation overlooking the valley.* **3** *(fml)* paid job: *find a new situation* ○ *Situations vacant/Situations wanted,* eg as headings for newspaper advertisements from people offering or looking for jobs. **4** (idm) **save the situation** ⇨ SAVE[1].

□ **ˌsituation 'comedy** (also *infml* **sitcom**) comedy, usu a TV or radio programme, based on a set of characters in a particular situation.

Sitwell /'sɪtwel/ Dame Edith (1887-1964), English poet and critic. Her early work often appeared with that of her brothers Osbert (1892-1969) and Sacheverell (1897-1988). Her most famous work is *Façade*, a set of rhythmic nonsense poems set to music by *Walton, but later more serious poems were inspired by the Second World War.

Siva (also **Shiva**) /'ʃi:və/ one of the most important Hindu gods, seen as both creator and destroyer of the universe, and worshipped in many other aspects, esp in the form of the *linga* or phallus.

six /sɪks/ *pron, det* **1** 6; one more than five. ⇨ App 9. **2** (idm) **at ˌsixes and 'sevens** *(infml)* in confusion: *I haven't had time to arrange everything, so I'm all at sixes and sevens.*

▷ **six** *n* **1** the number 6. **2** (in cricket) shot, scoring six runs, in which the ball crosses the boundary without hitting the ground. **3** (idm) **hit sb for six** ⇨ HIT[1].
sixth /sɪksθ/ *pron, det* 6th; next after fifth. **sixthly** *adv*. — *n* one of six equal parts of sth: *save a sixth of one's income.* ˈ**sixth form** (*Brit*) (in secondary schools) class of pupils preparing for A-level examinations: [attrib] *a sixth-form pupil, lesson.* ˈ**sixth-former** *n* pupil in this form.
For the uses of *six* and *sixth* see the examples at *five* and *fifth*.
□ **sixfold** /ˈsɪksfəʊld/ *adj, adv* **1** six times as much or as many; six times as great: *a sixfold increase* ○ *increase sixfold.* **2** having six parts.
ˌ**six-ˈfooter** *n* (*infml*) **1** person who is six foot tall. **2** thing that is six foot long.
ˈ**six-pack** *n* (*esp US*) case of six bottles or cans, esp of beer.
ˈ**sixpence** /ˈsɪkspəns/ *n* **1** former GB coin having a value of six old pennies (before 1971). **2** sum of six pennies: *It costs sixpence.*
sixpenny /ˈsɪkspənɪ/ *adj* [attrib] costing six pennies.
ˌ**six-ˈshooter** *n* revolver with six bullets when fully loaded.

sixteen /ˌsɪkˈstiːn/ *pron, det* 16; one more than fifteen. ⇨ App 9.
▷ **sixteen** *n* the number 16.
sixteenth /sɪkˈstiːnθ/ *pron, det* 16th; next after fifteenth. — *n* one of sixteen equal parts of sth.
sixˈteenth note (*US*) = SEMIQUAVER.
For the uses of *sixteen* and *sixteenth* see the examples at *five* and *fifth*.

sixty /ˈsɪkstɪ/ *pron, det* 60; one more than fifty-nine. ⇨ App 9.
▷ **sixtieth** /ˈsɪkstɪəθ/ *pron, det* 60th; next after fifty-ninth. — *n* one of sixty equal parts of sth.
sixty *n* **1** the number 60. **2 the sixties** [pl] numbers, years or temperature from 60 to 69. **3** (idm) **in one's ˈsixties** between the ages of 60 and 70.
For the uses of *sixty* and *sixtieth* see the examples at *five* and *fifth*.

size[1] /saɪz/ *n* **1** [U, C] the measurements or amount of sth; degree of largeness or smallness: *a building of vast size* ○ *the car's compact size* ○ *people of all shapes and sizes* ○ *about the size of* (ie about as large as) *a duck's egg* ○ *the size of the cheque* ○ *a house of some size*, ie a fairly large house ○ *They're both of a size*, ie are the same size. **2** [C] any of a number of standard measurements in which items such as clothes are made: *a size fifteen collar* ○ *trousers three sizes too large* ○ *I take size nine shoes.* ○ *You need a smaller size.* ○ *Try this on for size*, ie to see if it fits, whether or not you like it. **3** (idm) **cut sb down to ˈsize** make sb realize he is not as good, important, etc as he thinks: *He's a pretentious bore and needs cutting down to size.* **that's about ˈit/about the ˈsize of it** that is (roughly) how matters stand.
▷ **size** *v* **1** [Tn] sort (sth) according to size. **2** (phr v) **size sb/sth up** (*infml*) form a judgement or opinion of sb/sth: *We sized each other up at our first meeting.*
sizeable (also **sizable**) /-əbl/ *adj* fairly large: *a sizeable field, house, sum of money.*
-sized (forming compound *adjs*) having the specified size: *a medium-sized garden.*

size[2] /saɪz/ *n* [U] sticky substance used to glaze textiles, paper, etc or to seal plaster.
▷ **size** *v* [Tn] glaze or seal (sth) with size.

sizzle /ˈsɪzl/ *v* [I, Ip] (*infml*) make the hissing sound eg of sth frying in fat: *sausages sizzling (away) in the pan* ○ *water sizzling as it falls on a hot rock* ○ (*fig*) *a sizzling hot day.*
▷ **sizzle** *n* [sing] this sound.
sizzler /ˈsɪzlə(r)/ *n* (*infml*) very hot day: *Whew! What a sizzler!*

SJ /ˌes ˈdʒeɪ/ *abbr* Society of Jesus: *Fr Richard Blundon, SJ.*

sjambok /ˈʃæmbɒk/ *n* whip made from rhinoceros skin, used in S Africa, esp by the police.

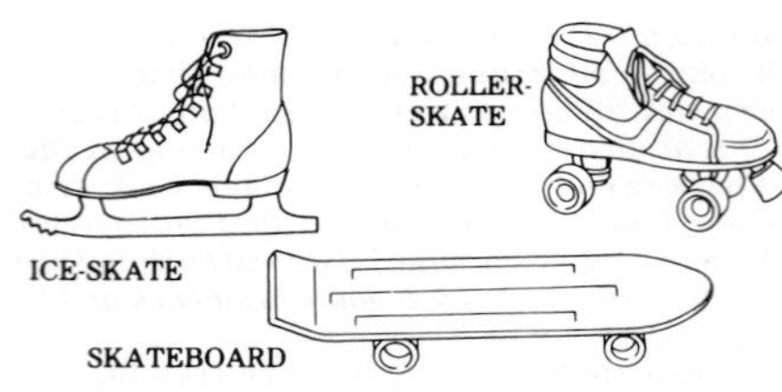

skate[1] /skeɪt/ *n* **1** (**a**) (also ˈ**ice-skate**) either of a pair of boots with steel blades fixed to the soles so that the wearer can glide smoothly over ice. (**b**) one of these blades. **2** = ROLLER-SKATE (ROLLER). **3** (idm) **get/put one's ˈskates on** (*infml*) hurry up: *Get your skates on or you'll miss the bus.*
▷ **skate** *v* [I, Ipr, Ip, Tn] **1** move on skates; perform (sth) while moving in this way: *Can you skate?* ○ *skate along, past, over, etc (sth)* ○ *skate a figure of eight.* **2** (idm) **be skating on thin ˈice** talk about or do sth that can easily cause disagreement, protest or other trouble: *We could ignore him and go direct to the chairman, but we'd be skating on very thin ice.* **3** (phr v) **skate over/round sth** not deal with sth directly: *skate over a difficulty, a delicate issue* ○ *She skated round the likely cost of the plan.* **skater** *n* person who skates. **skating** *n* [U] sport of moving on skates: [attrib] *a skating competition, club.*
□ ˈ**skateboard** *n* narrow board about 50 cm long, with roller-skate wheels fixed to it, which the rider stands on, eg to take part in races, demonstrate skill, etc. ⇨ illus. ˈ**skateboarder** *n* person who uses a skateboard. ˈ**skateboarding** *n* [U] sport of riding a skateboard.
ˈ**skating-rink** *n* area of natural or artificial ice for ice-skating; smooth area used for roller-skating.

skate[2] /skeɪt/ *n* (*pl* unchanged or ~**s**) large flat long-tailed fish that lives in the sea and is eaten as food.

skedaddle /skɪˈdædl/ *v* [I] (*infml*) (usu imperative) go away quickly.

skeet /skiːt/ *n* **1** [U] (also ˈ**skeet shooting**) form of clay-pigeon shooting in which the targets have to be hit from various angles. **2** [C] = CLAY PIGEON (CLAY).

skein /skeɪn/ *n* **1** length of wool, thread, etc wound into a loose coil. **2** group of wild geese, etc in flight.

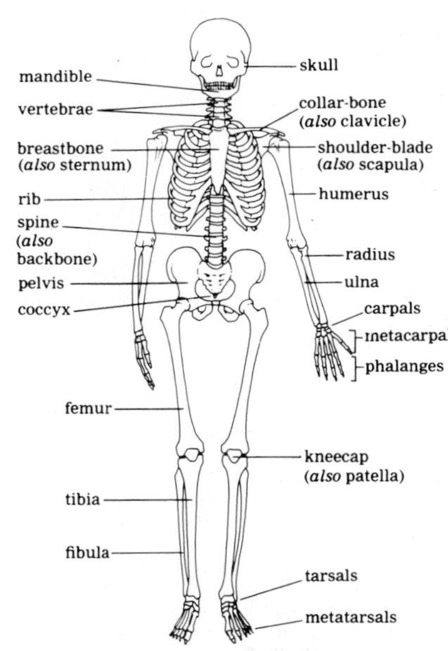

the human skeleton

skeleton /ˈskelɪtn/ *n* **1** (**a**) framework of bones supporting an animal or a human body: *The child was reduced to a skeleton*, ie very thin because of hunger, illness, etc. (**b**) such a framework, or a model of it, fixed in the position it has in the body, used esp for the purposes of study: *ape skeletons in the museum.* **2** (**a**) any supporting structure or framework, eg of a building: *The block is still just a skeleton of girders.* (**b**) outline to which details are to be added: *Her notes give us just the bare skeleton of her theory.* **3** [attrib] having the smallest possible number of people, vehicles, etc needed to run an operation: *a skeleton crew, staff, etc* ○ *We only have a skeleton bus service on public holidays.* **4** (idm) **a skeleton in the ˈcupboard** secret which would embarrass sb if it became known: *bribery of officials and other skeletons in the government's cupboard.*
□ ˈ**skeleton key** key that will open several different locks.

skeptic = SCEPTIC.

skerry /ˈskerɪ/ *n* small reef or rocky island that may be completely covered by the sea, eg at high tide.

sketch /sketʃ/ *n* **1** rough quickly-made drawing, without many details: *make a sketch of a face, place.* **2** short account or description, giving only basic details: *a newspaper sketch of a debate in Parliament* ○ *give a sketch of one's plans.* **3** short funny play or piece of writing: *a sketch set in a doctor's surgery* ○ *She writes satirical sketches for a magazine.*
▷ **sketch** *v* [I, Tn] **1** draw sketches; make a sketch of (sb/sth): *go into the park to sketch (flowers).* **2** (phr v) **sketch sth out** give a general description or account of sth; outline sth: *sketch out proposals for a new road* ○ *Sketch out what you intend to do.*
sketchy *adj* (**-ier, -iest**) (*often derog*) lacking thoroughness and detail; incomplete; rough: *Your essay gives a rather sketchy treatment of the problem.* ○ *I have only a sketchy knowledge of geography.* ○ *Information about the crisis was sketchy and hard to get.* **sketchily** *adv*: *The book treats the problem too sketchily.* **sketchiness** *n* [U].
□ ˈ**sketch-book**, ˈ**sketch-pad** *ns* book of sheets of paper for sketching on.
ˈ**sketch-map** *n* map, usu drawn by hand, that shows only basic details.

skew /skjuː/ *adj* [usu pred] not straight; twisted or slanting: *The picture is a bit skew.* Cf ASKEW.
▷ **skew** *n* (idm) **on the ˈskew** skew.
□ **skew-whiff** /ˌskjuːˈwɪf/ *adj* (*Brit infml*) skew: *You've got your hat on skew-whiff.*

skewbald /ˈskjuːbɔːld/ *n, adj* (animal, esp a horse) having patches of white and another colour (usu not black). Cf PIEBALD.

skewer /ˈskjʊə(r)/ *n* pin of wood or metal with a point, pushed through meat to hold it together while cooking.
▷ **skewer** *v* [Tn] push a skewer or sth similar through (sth): *He skewered his foot on a nail.*

skiing

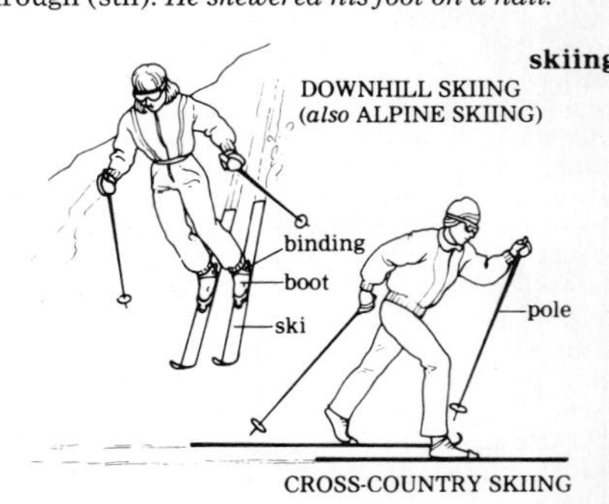

ski /skiː/ *n* either of a pair of long narrow strips of wood, plastic, etc fixed to a person's boots so that he can glide smoothly over snow: *a pair of skis* ○ *bind on one's skis* ○ [attrib] *a ski suit, slope, club.*
▷ **ski** *v* (*pt, pp* **ski'd** or **skied**, *pres p* **skiing**) [I, Ipr, Ip] move over snow on skis, esp as a sport: *go skiing in Switzerland* ○ *ski into a village* ○ *ski past, along, down, etc.* **skier** /ˈskiːə(r)/ *n* person who uses skis. **skiing** *n* [U] activity or sport of moving on skis: [attrib] *a skiing course, instructor, resort* ○

skiing equipment, clothes. ⇨ illus.

□ ˈski-bob *n* vehicle used for races on snow and resembling a low strongly-built bicycle with skis instead of wheels.

ˈski-jump *n* 1 jump made by a skier after sliding down a long ramp. 2 ramp for making such jumps. 3 competition in which such jumps are made.

ˈski-lift *n* device for pulling or carrying skiers up a slope.

ˈski-plane *n* aircraft fitted with skis instead of wheels, enabling it to land on snow.

ˈski-run *n* slope that is suitable or prepared for skiing.

skid /skɪd/ *n* 1 sideways movement made eg by a car slipping on ice or turning a corner too fast: *try to get out of/correct a skid.* 2 log, plank, etc used to make a track over which heavy objects may be dragged or rolled. 3 piece of wood or metal that acts as a brake on the wheel of a cart, etc. 4 (idm) **on the ˈskids** (*sl*) near to disaster or ruin: *The company was on the skids when we took it over.* **put the skids under sb/sth** (*sl*) (a) cause sb/sth to fail: *The government put the skids under the plan by stopping their research grant.* (b) make sb hurry.

▷ **skid** *v* (-dd-) [I, Ipr, Ip] (of a car, etc) move or slip sideways: *The car skidded on the ice.* ○ *The bus skidded (on) into a wall.*

□ ˈskid-pan *n* surface specially prepared for skidding on, so that drivers can practise controlling skids.

skid row /ˌskɪd ˈrəʊ/ (*US sl*) slum area where vagrants live: *He ended up on skid row.*

skiddoo /skɪˈduː/ *interj* (*US sl*) go away!

skies *pl of* SKY.

skiff /skɪf/ *n* small light boat for rowing or sculling, usu by one person.

skiffle /ˈskɪfl/ *n* [U] (*esp Brit*) type of music popular in the 1950s, a mixture of jazz and folk-song often using improvised instruments and a singer with a guitar or a banjo: [attrib] *a skiffle group, song, etc.*

skilful (*US* **skillful**) /ˈskɪlfl/ *adj* ~ (**at sth/doing sth**) having or showing skill: *a skilful painter, driver, performer* ○ *a skilful performance* ○ *skilful at inventing excuses.* ▷ **skilfully** /-fəlɪ/ *adv.*

skill /skɪl/ *n* 1 [U] ~ (**at sth/doing sth**) ability to do sth well: *show great skill at driving, telling stories, playing billiards.* 2 [C] particular type of skill: *the practical skills needed in carpentry.*

▷ **skilled** *adj* 1 ~ (**in/at sth/doing sth**) (a) having skill; skilful: *a skilled negotiator* ○ *skilled at dealing with complaints.* (b) experienced; trained: *a skilled worker, salesperson, etc* ○ *an actor skilled at improvising.* 2 [attrib] (of work) needing skill: *a skilled job.*

skillet /ˈskɪlɪt/ *n* 1 (*esp US*) frying-pan. ⇨ illus at PAN. 2 small metal cooking-pot with a long handle and (usu) feet.

skim /skɪm/ *v* (-mm-) 1 [Tn] remove cream, scum, etc from the surface of (a liquid): *skim milk.* 2 (a) [Ipr, Tn no passive] move or glide lightly over (a surface), not touching it or only occasionally touching it: *swallows skimming (over) the water/along the ground* ○ *aircraft skimming the roof-tops.* (b) [Tn, Tn·pr] cause (a stone, etc) to pass low over water, bouncing several times: *skimming pebbles (over the lake).* 3 [Ipr, Tn] ~ (**through/over**) **sth** read sth quickly, noting only the main points: *skim (through) the report in half an hour* ○ *skim over the list, looking for one's name.* 4 (phr v) **skim sth from/off sth; skim sth off** remove (cream, scum, etc) from the surface of a liquid: *skim the cream from the milk* ○ *skim the fat off (the soup).*

▷ **skimmer** *n* 1 type of spoon with holes in, used for skimming liquids. 2 water bird with long wings.

□ ˌ**skimmed ˈmilk** (also ˌ**skim ˈmilk**) milk from which the cream has been skimmed.

skimp /skɪmp/ *v* [I, Ipr, Tn] ~ (**on sth**) use or provide less than enough of (what is needed): *Use plenty of oil. Don't skimp!* ○ *They have to skimp on fuel in winter.* ○ *skimp material when making a dress.*

▷ **skimpy** *adj* (-ier, -iest) using or having less than enough of what is needed: *a rather skimpy meal* ○ *The dancers wore skimpy dresses*, ie that did not cover much of the body. **skimpily** *adv*: *a skimpily made dress.* **skimpiness** *n* [U].

skin /skɪn/ *n* 1 [U] elastic substance that forms the outer covering of the body of a person or an animal: *a dark, an olive, a fair, etc skin* ○ *She has a beautiful skin*, ie complexion. ○ [attrib] *a skin disease, treatment.* 2 [U, C] (often in compounds) skin of an animal that has been removed from its body, with or without the fur; hide; fur: *ˈpigskin, ˈcalfskin, ˈsheepskin* ○ *a ˈrabbit-skin.* 3 [C] (often in compounds) vessel for storing liquids, made from the whole skin of an animal: *a ˈwineskin.* 4 (a) [C, U] outer covering of a fruit or plant: *slip on a banana skin* ○ *grape skins.* Cf PEEL *n*, RIND, ZEST 3. (b) [C, U] thin covering of a sausage. (c) [C usu *sing*] any outer covering or case: *the metal skin of an aircraft* ○ *a waterproof plastic skin on a metal sheet.* 5 [C, U] thin layer that forms on the surface of certain liquids, eg boiled milk: *the skin on a milk pudding* ○ *a skin forming on the paint in the pot.* 6 (idm) **beauty is only skin deep** ⇨ BEAUTY. **be no skin off one's nose** (*infml*) not concern one; not matter to one: *It's no skin off my nose if I lose this job, I can always get another one.* **by the ˌskin of one's ˈteeth** (*infml*) only just: *He escaped by the skin of his teeth.* **get under sb's ˈskin** (*infml*) (a) annoy or irritate sb: *Don't let him get under your skin!* (b) interest or attract sb greatly: *The charm of the place soon gets under your skin.* **have got sb under one ˈskin** (*infml*) be strongly attracted to sb. **have, etc a hide/skin like a rhinoceros** ⇨ RHINOCEROS. **jump out of one's ˈskin** (*infml*) be startled: *I nearly jumped out of my skin when a hand grabbed me in the dark.* **save one's (own) skin** ⇨ SAVE[1]. **(nothing but/all) skin and ˈbone** (*infml*) very thin: *He was all skin and bone after his illness.* ˌ**soaked/ˌwet to the ˈskin** (of a person) completely soaked: *We were soaked to the skin after the storm.* **(have) a thin/thick ˈskin** (*infml*) (have) a character that makes one easily/not easily hurt by criticism, insults, etc: *You need a thick skin to be a politician.*

▷ **skin** *v* (-nn-) 1 (a) [Tn] take the skin off (eg an animal): *skin a rabbit, fox, etc.* (b) injure by scraping skin off (eg one's knees): *I skinned my elbow against the wall.* 2 (idm) **keep one's eyes open/peeled/skinned** ⇨ EYE[1]. **skin sb alive** (said as a threat) punish sb severely: *Your father'll skin you alive when he sees this!*

-skinned (forming compound *adjs*) having a skin of the specified type: *dark-skinned* ○ *pink-skinned.*

skinny *adj* (-ier, -iest) (*infml usu derog*) very thin: *You're skinny enough without going on a diet!* ⇨ Usage at THIN. **ˈskinny-dipping** *n* [U] (*infml esp US*) swimming naked: *Let's go skinny-dipping in the lake!*

□ ˌ**skin-ˈdeep** *adj* [pred] not deeply felt or lasting: *His political commitment is only skin-deep.*

ˈ**skin-diving** *n* [U] sport of swimming under water with goggles, flippers and an aqualung or a snorkel to breathe with. ˈ**skin-diver** *n.*

ˈ**skin-flick** *n* (*sl*) pornographic film.

skinful /ˈskɪnfʊl/ *n* (*sl*) enough alcohol to make a person drunk: *He'd had a skinful and got into a fight.*

ˈ**skin-graft** *n* surgical operation in which skin taken from one part of sb's body (or from sb else's body) is placed over another part that is burned, wounded, etc.

ˈ**skinhead** *n* (*Brit*) young person with very short hair, esp one who is violent. ⇨ article at YOUTH.

ˌ**skin-ˈtight** *adj* (of a garment) fitting very closely to the body: *a ˌskin-tight ˈdress.*

skinflint /ˈskɪnflɪnt/ *n* (*infml*) miser.

skint /skɪnt/ *adj* [pred] (*Brit*) without any money.

skip[1] /skɪp/ *v* (-pp-) 1 [Ipr, Ip] move lightly and quickly, esp by taking two steps with each foot in turn: *a child skipping along the road, into the house, etc* ○ *skipping along, past, out, etc* ○ *skip out of sb's way*, ie by making a little jump ○ *The lambs were skipping about in the fields.* 2 [I] jump over a rope held in both one's hands or by two other people and passed repeatedly over the head and under the feet: *children skipping in the playground* ○ *skipping games.* ⇨ illus. 3 (a) [Ipr, Ip] (*infml*) go

from one place to another quickly or casually: *skip over/across to Paris for the weekend* ○ (*fig*) *She skipped from one subject to another.* (b) [I, Ipr, Ip, Tn no passive] ~ (**out of ...**); ~ **off** leave (a place) secretly or in a hurry: *skip (out of) the country with the stolen money* ○ *skip off without saying anything to anyone.* 4 [Tn] not attend (a meeting, etc): *skip a lecture, an appointment, a class, etc.* 5 [I, Tn] omit (part of a book when reading, a task, etc): *I read the whole book without skipping (a page).* ○ *Skip the first chapter and start on page 25.* ○ *He managed to skip the washing-up.* 6 (idm) ˈ**skip it!** (*infml*) don't talk about that any more: *I've heard enough about your job, so skip it!*

▷ **skip** *n* skipping movement: *a hop, a skip and a jump.*

□ ˈ**skipping-rope** (*US* ˈ**jump-rope**) *n* length of rope, usu with handles at each end, used esp by a child or a boxer for skipping. ⇨ illus.

skip[2] /skɪp/ *n* large (usu open) metal container for carrying away rubble, rubbish, etc, esp from a building site: [attrib] *skip hire.*

skipper /ˈskɪpə(r)/ *n* 1 captain, esp of a small merchant ship or fishing-boat. 2 (*infml*) captain of a team, eg in football or cricket. 3 (*esp US*) captain of an aircraft.

▷ **skipper** *v* [Tn] act as skipper of (a boat, team, etc).

skirl /skɜːl/ *n* [sing] shrill piercing sound, esp of bagpipes.

skirmish /ˈskɜːmɪʃ/ *n* fight between small groups of soldiers, ships, etc, esp one that is not planned: *a brief skirmish on the frontier* ○ (*fig*) *a skirmish between the two party leaders.* Cf PITCHED BATTLE (PITCH[2]).

▷ **skirmish** *v* [I] take part in a skirmish. **skirmisher** *n.*

skirt /skɜːt/ *n* 1 [C] (a) woman's garment that hangs from the waist. (b) part of a dress or other garment, eg a long coat, that hangs below the waist. 2 [C] any of various types of guard or covering for the base of a vehicle or machine: *the rubber skirt round the bottom of a hovercraft.* 3 **skirts** [pl] = OUTSKIRTS. 4 (*dated sexist sl*) (a) [U] girls or women in general, seen as sexual objects: *a bit of skirt.* (b) [C] girl or woman seen in this way.

▷ **skirt** *v* [Ipr, Tn] 1 be on or move along the edge of (sth): *We skirted (round) the field and crossed the bridge* ○ *The road skirts the forest.* 2 (phr v) **skirt round sth** avoid referring to or treating (a topic, an issue, etc) directly: *She skirted round the problem of the high cost.*

□ ˈ**skirting-board** (*Brit*) (*US* ˈ**baseboard**) *n* board attached to the wall of a room, next to the floor.

skit /skɪt/ *n* ~ (**on sth**) piece of humorous writing or short play that mimics or makes fun of sb/sth serious: *a skit on Wagner/on 'Macbeth'.*

skitter /ˈskɪtə(r)/ *v* [Ip, Ipr] ~ **along, past, etc** (**sth**) move quickly and lightly in the specified direction: *A squirrel skittered across the path in front of us.* ○ *A few loose stones skittered down the slope.*

skittish /ˈskɪtɪʃ/ *adj* 1 (of horses) lively and playful; difficult to control. 2 (of people) fond of flirting; lively and playful: *She gets very skittish when her boy-friend is around.* ▷ **skittishly** *adv.* **skittishness** *n* [U].

skittle /ˈskɪtl/ *n* 1 [C] bottle-shaped wooden pin used in the game of skittles. 2 **skittles** [*sing v*] game in which players try to knock over as many skittles as possible by rolling a ball at them. Cf NINEPIN, TENPIN BOWLING. 3 (idm) **beer and**

skittles ⇨ BEER.

▷ **skittle** *v* (phr v) **skittle sb out** (in cricket) end the turn of (a number of batsmen) quickly: *The whole side was skittled out for 10 runs.*

skive /skaɪv/ *v* [I, Ip] ~ **(off)** (*Brit sl*) avoid work, esp by staying away or going away from where it is being done: *He's usually skiving down at the pub when there's gardening to be done.* ○ *She always skives off early.*

▷ **skiver** *n* (*Brit sl*) person who skives.

skivvy[1] /ˈskɪvɪ/ *n* (*Brit infml derog*) (usu female) servant, esp one who has to do menial jobs like cleaning and washing: *I'm no better than* (ie I'm treated like) *a skivvy in this house.*

▷ **skivvy** *v* (*pt, pp* **skivvied**) [I, Ipr] ~ **(for sb)** (*Brit infml*) work as a skivvy or as if one is a skivvy: *She refused to skivvy for the whole family.*

skivvy[2] /ˈskɪvɪ/ *n* (*US sl*) **1** [C] man's vest or T-shirt. **2 skivvies** [pl] men's underclothes.

skua /ˈskju:ə/ *n* large type of sea-bird that preys on others.

skulduggery (also **skull-**) /skʌlˈdʌɡərɪ/ *n* [U] (*often joc*) deception and planning of evil acts; trickery: *a career ruined by political skulduggery.*

skulk /skʌlk/ *v* [Ipr, Ip] (*derog*) hide or move around as if one is ashamed or trying to hide, esp when one is planning sth bad: *I don't want reporters skulking around (my house).* ⇨ Usage at PROWL.

skull /skʌl/ *n* **1** bony framework of the head under the skin: *The fall fractured his skull.* ⇨ illus at BRAIN, SKELETON. **2** (idm) **a thick skull** ⇨ THICK.

▷ **-skulled** (forming compound *adjs*): *thick-skulled*, ie having a thick skull; stupid.

□ ˌ**skull and** ˈ**cross-bones** picture of a skull above two crossed bones, once used on the flags of pirates' ships and now to warn of danger, eg on bottles of poison.

ˈ**skull-cap** *n* small round cap with no peak that sits on top of the head, nowadays worn esp by male Jews when praying and by Catholic bishops. ⇨ illus at HAT.

skunk

skunk /skʌŋk/ *n* **1** (a) (also **polecat**) [C] small bushy-tailed N American animal that can send out a strong, unpleasant smell as a defence when attacked. (b) [U] its fur. **2** [C] (*infml*) contemptible person: *You cheated me, you skunk!*

▷ **skunk** *v* [Tn] (*US sl*) **1** defeat (sb) completely. **2** not pay (a bill, or a person to whom one owes money).

sky /skaɪ/ *n* **1** (a) [U sing] (usu **the sky** when [sing] and **a sky** or **skies** [pl] when modified by an *adj*) the space seen when one looks upwards from the earth, where clouds and the sun, moon and stars appear: *a patch of blue sky* ○ *birds flying up into the sky* ○ *under the open sky*, ie out of doors ○ *a clear, blue sky* ○ *clouds moving across the sky* ○ *a starry sky/(the) starry skies.* (b) **skies** [pl] climate or weather as shown by this: *a day of rain and cloudy skies* ○ *the sunny skies of Italy.* **2** (idm) **pie in the sky** ⇨ PIE. **praise, etc sb/sth to the** ˈ**skies** praise sb/sth very greatly: *The teacher was extolling her work to the skies.* **the sky's the limit** (*infml saying*) there is no limit: *You could win millions! The sky's the limit!*

▷ **sky** *v* (*pt, pp* **skied** /skaɪd/) [Tn] hit (esp a ball) very high.

□ ˌ**sky-**ˈ**blue** *adj, n* [U] (of the) bright blue colour of the sky on a cloudless day.

ˈ**sky-diver** *n* [C], ˈ**sky-diving** *n* [U] (person who takes part in the) sport of jumping from an aircraft and falling for as long as one safely can before opening one's parachute.

ˌ**sky-**ˈ**high** *adj, adv* very high: *Prices are sky-high at the moment.* ○ *The bomb blew the house sky-high.*

ˈ**Skylab** American spacecraft put into orbit round the earth in 1973. Astronauts on board carried out experiments until 1974 in conditions of zero gravity. It eventually disintegrated in 1979.

ˈ**skylark** *n* type of lark that sings while hovering high in the sky. ⇨ illus at BIRD. — *v* [I, Ip] = LARK[2].

ˈ**skylight** *n* window in a roof or ceiling. ⇨ illus at HOME.

ˈ**skyline** *n* outline of buildings, trees, hills, etc as seen against the sky: *the New York skyline.*

ˈ**sky-rocket** *v* [I] (of prices, etc) rise to a very high level: *sky-rocketing costs.*

ˈ**skyscraper** *n* very tall modern city building. ⇨ article at ARCHITECTURE.

ˈ**skywards** /ˈskaɪwədz/ (also **skyward** /-wəd/) *adj, adv* towards the sky; upwards: *the skywards path of the rocket* ○ *hit the ball skywards.*

ˈ**sky-writing** *n* [U] (forming of) legible words in the sky from the smoke-trails of aircraft, usu to advertise sth.

Skye /skaɪ/ largest island in the Inner *Hebrides. Its mountains and lakes make it a popular tourist centre. After his defeat at *Culloden, Charles Edward *Stuart (Bonny Prince Charlie) escaped to Skye disguised as a maid in a small boat rowed by Flora MacDonald. ⇨ map at UNITED KINGDOM.

□ ˌ**Skye** ˈ**terrier** type of terrier with short legs and a long coat.

slab /slæb/ *n* thick flat, often rectangular or square, piece of stone, wood or other solid substance: *paved with stone slabs* ○ *massive slabs of rock* ○ *a slab of cheese, chocolate.*

slack[1] /slæk/ *adj* (**-er, -est**) **1** not tight or tense; loose: *a slack rope* ○ *The boxer's jaw went slack.* ○ *Your grip on the bar is too slack.* **2** (a) ~ **(at/about sth)** (of a person) giving little care and energy to a task: *He's been getting slack and making silly mistakes.* ○ *Don't get slack about doing your exercises.* (b) not carefully done, planned, etc; lax: *Organization of the conference was rather slack.* **3** (of business) not having many customers, sales, etc; not busy: *Trade is slack in winter.* ○ *Demand is slack over the summer months.* **4** (esp of water) slow-moving; sluggish.

▷ **slack** *v* **1** [I] be lazy; avoid work: *Stop slacking and get on with that digging!* **2** (phr v) **slack off/up** (a) reduce one's level of activity: *After intense work in the summer, we are slacking off now.* (b) reduce speed: *Slack off/up as you approach the junction.* **slack (sth) up** make (a rope, etc) less tight or tense.

slacker *n* (*infml*) person who is lazy or avoids work.

slackly *adv*: *ropes hanging slackly between the boat and the quay* ○ *The firm had been run rather slackly.*

slackness *n* [U].

slack[2] /slæk/ *n* **1** [U] slack part of a rope, etc: *too much slack in the tow-rope.* **2 slacks** [pl] casual trousers for men or women: *a pair of slacks.* **3** [U] coal-dust left over after coal has been screened. **4** (idm) **take up the** ˈ**slack** (a) pull on a rope, etc so that it is no longer slack: *The tractor took up the slack and pulled the trailer out of the mud.* (b) (in industry) make little-used resources more productive.

slacken /ˈslækən/ *v* **1** [I, Tn] (cause sth to) become slack: *The rope slackened.* ○ *slacken the reins* ○ *slacken one's grip.* **2** [I, Tn, Tn·p] ~ **(sth) (off/up)** (cause sth to) become slower, less active, etc: *The ship's speed slackened.* ○ *After hours of digging, we began to slacken up a little.* ○ *Slacken (off) your speed as you approach the village.*

slag /slæɡ/ *n* **1** [U] waste matter that remains after metal has been extracted from ore by smelting. **2** [C] (*Brit derog sl*) woman who does not look respectable and is regarded as sexually immoral.

▷ **slag** *v* (**-gg-**) (phr v) **slag sb/sth off** (*Brit sl*) say offensive and critical things about sb, esp unfairly: *Now he's left, she's always slagging off her old boss.*

□ ˈ**slag-heap** *n* heap of slag from a mine.

slain *pp* of SLAY.

slake /sleɪk/ *v* [Tn] **1** satisfy (one's thirst, or a desire, etc): *slake one's thirst with a cup of tea* ○ (*fml*) *Has this murderer slaked his lust for blood yet?* **2** combine (lime) chemically with water.

slalom /ˈslɑ:ləm/ *n* **1** ski-race along a zigzag course marked out by poles with flags: *win the slalom* ○ [attrib] *a slalom race, champion, course.* **2** any similar race, eg in canoes or on water-skis.

slam[1] /slæm/ *v* (**-mm-**) **1** [I, Ip, Tn, Tn·p, Cn·a] ~ **(sth) (to/shut)** (cause sth to) shut forcefully and loudly: *The door slammed (to).* ○ *Slam the window (shut).* ○ *He slammed the lid down.* **2** [Tn·pr, Tn·p] put, push, throw or knock (sth) with great force: *slam one's brakes on* ○ *She slammed the box down on the table.* ○ *The batsman slammed the ball straight at a fielder.* **3** [Tn] (*infml*) criticize (sb/sth) harshly: *a play slammed by the reviewers* ○ *The minister was slammed by the press for the cuts.* **4** (idm) **shut/slam the door in sb's face** ⇨ DOOR.

▷ **slam** *n* (usu *sing*) noise of sth being slammed: *the slam of a car door.*

slam[2] /slæm/ *n* (in card-games, esp bridge) the winning of all **(grand slam)** or all except one **(little slam)** of the tricks in a hand.

slammer /ˈslæmə(r)/ *n* (*sl esp US*) **the slammer** [sing] prison: *He'd spent three months in the slammer.*

slander /ˈslɑ:ndə(r); *US* ˈslæn-/ *n* [U, C] (offence of making a) false statement intended to damage sb's reputation: *a vicious slander* ○ *a case of slander* ○ *bring an action against sb for slander*, ie sue sb for slander in a lawcourt. Cf LIBEL.

▷ **slander** *v* [Tn] make such a false statement about (sb). **slanderer** /-dərə(r)/ *n*.

slanderous /-dərəs/ *adj*: *a slanderous attack, accusation.* **slanderously** *adv*.

slang /slæŋ/ *n* [U] (*abbr* **sl** in this dictionary) very informal words, phrases, etc commonly used in speech, esp between people from the same social group or who work together, not considered suitable for formal contexts and often not in use for long: *army, prison, railway, etc slang* ○ *'Grass' is criminal slang for 'informer'.* ○ [attrib] *a slang word, expression, etc.* Cf COLLOQUIAL, INFORMAL 3.

▷ **slang** *v* [Tn] (*infml*) **1** attack (sb) using angry uncontrolled language; abuse: *The driver was slanging a pedestrian who had got in his way.* **2** (idm) **a** ˈ**slanging match** quarrel in which each person is angry and uses angry uncontrolled language.

slangy *adj* typical of or containing slang: *a slangy style.* **slanginess** *n* [U].

slant /slɑ:nt; *US* slænt/ *v* **1** [I, Ipr, Tn, Tn·pr esp passive] lean in a particular direction; not be straight: *Her handwriting slants from left to right.* ○ *The picture is slanted to the left.* **2** [Tn] (*usu derog*) present (news, etc) from a particular point of view: *slant the story to protect the minister* ○ *She slanted the report so that I was made to appear incompetent.*

▷ **slant** *n* **1** slope. **2** (*infml*) point of view, sometimes prejudiced, from which sth is seen or presented: *get a new slant on the political situation* ○ *gave the report a right-wing slant.* **3** (idm) **on a/the** ˈ**slant** sloping; not straight.

slanted *adj* showing a prejudiced slant(2): *a rather slanted account of the meeting.*

slantingly, slantwise /-waɪz/ *advs* in a slanting position or direction: *a picture hanging slantwise.*

slap /slæp/ *v* (**-pp-**) **1** [Tn] strike (sb/sth) with the palm of the hand or with sth flat; smack: *slap sb's face/sb on the face* ○ *People slapped me on the back after the fight*, ie to congratulate me. **2** [Tn·pr, Tn·p] put (sth) somewhere with a slapping noise: *slapped the money on the counter* ○ *slap some paint onto a wall* ○ *He slapped the book down (on the table).* **3** (phr v) **slap sb down** (*infml*) stop sb talking, making suggestions, etc in a firm, usu unpleasant, way: *She tried to object, but the chairman slapped her down.* **slap sth on sth** (*infml*) add (an extra amount) to the price of sth: *They've slapped 10p on the price of cigarettes.*

▷ **slap** *n* **1** (sound of a) blow with the palm of the hand or sth flat: *I heard a loud slap behind me.* ○ *give sb a slap on the back.* **2** (idm) **slap and** ˈ**tickle** (*Brit infml joc*) lively cuddling, kissing, etc between lovers: *a bit of slap and tickle on the sofa.* **a slap in the** ˈ**face** snub or insult: *It was a bit of a* *slap in the face when she refused to see me.*

slap *adv* (also ˌ**slap-ˈbang**) *adv* (*infml*) **1** directly; straight: *The car ran slap(-bang) into the wall.* **2** right; exactly: *She stood slap(-bang) in the middle of the path, so I couldn't get past.*

slapdash /ˈslæpdæʃ/ *adj, adv* (done or doing things) in a careless and hasty way: *slapdash work* ○ *a slapdash worker* ○ *do one's work slapdash/in a slapdash way.*

slap-happy /ˌslæp ˈhæpɪ/ *adj* (*infml*) cheerfully irresponsible; carefree: *too slap-happy in his attitude to schoolwork.*

slapstick /ˈslæpstɪk/ *n* [U] comedy based on simple visual jokes, eg hitting people, falling over, etc: [attrib] *slapstick comedy.*

slap-up /ˈslæpʌp/ *adj* [attrib] (*Brit infml*) (of a meal) excellent: *a slap-up dinner at an expensive restaurant.*

slash /slæʃ/ *v* **1** [Ipr, Tn, Cn·a] make a cut or cut (sth) with a sweeping stroke; strike (sb/sth) with a whip: *slash through the rope with a sword* ○ *The blade slashed his leg (open).* ⇨ Usage at CUT[1]. **2** [Tn] cut or reduce (sth) drastically: *slash costs, prices, numbers* ○ *a government promise to slash taxes.* **3** [Tn esp passive] make long narrow cuts in (a garment) for ornament: *slashed sleeves,* ie cut so that the lining or material underneath can be seen. **4** [Tn] criticize (sb/sth) harshly: *a government plan slashed by the press.* **5** (phr v) **slash at sth (with sth)** use a stick, sword, etc to make sweeping strokes at sth: *slashing at the tall weeds with a stick* ○ *slashing wildly at his opponent with a sword.* **slash one's way through, past, etc sth** move through, past, etc with sweeping strokes, eg of a sword, etc: *slashing our way through the jungle with long knives.*

▷ **slash** *n* **1** [C] (**a**) act of slashing: *a wild slash with a sword.* (**b**) long cut or gash. (**c**) slit made in a garment. **2** [C] = OBLIQUE *n.* ⇨ App 14. **3 a slash** [sing] (*Brit sl*) act of urinating: *have a quick slash.*

slat /slæt/ *n* long thin narrow piece of wood, metal or plastic often made to overlap with others, eg in a Venetian blind. ▷ **slatted** *adj*: *a bed with a slatted pine base.*

slate /sleɪt/ *n* **1** (**a**) [U] type of blue-grey rock that splits easily into thin flat layers: *slate-coloured,* ie blue-grey ○ [attrib] *a slate quarry.* (**b**) [C] small thin piece of this, used as a roof tile: [attrib] *a slate roof.* ⇨ illus at HOME. **2** [C] small sheet of slate in a wooden frame, formerly used by schoolchildren for writing on. **3** [C] (*US*) list of candidates for nomination or election: *on the Democratic slate.* **4** (idm) **a clean sheet/slate** ⇨ CLEAN[1]. **(put sth) on the ˈslate** (*infml*) (note sth down) to be paid for later rather than when it is bought: *I've no change, could you put these eggs on the slate?* **wipe the slate clean** ⇨ WIPE.

▷ **slate** *v* **1** [Tn] cover (a roof, etc) with slates. **2** (*US infml*) (**a**) [esp passive: Tn, Tn·pr] ~ **sb (for sth)** propose sb (for an office, appointment, etc): *slated for the Presidency.* (**b**) [esp passive: Tn·pr, Cn·t] ~ **sth (for . . .)** plan that sth will happen at a specified time: *a meeting slated for Thursday/to take place on Thursday.* **3** [Tn, Tn·pr] ~ **sb/sth (for sth)** (*Brit infml*) criticize sb/sth severely, eg in a newspaper review: *slate a play, book, writer* ○ *The idea got slated by the committee.*

slaty *adj* of, like or containing slate(1a): *slaty coal.*

slattern /ˈslætən/ *n* (*fml or derog*) dirty untidy woman.

▷ **slatternly** *adj* (*fml derog*) (of a woman) dirty and untidy. **slatternliness** *n* [U].

slaughter /ˈslɔːtə(r)/ *n* [U] **1** the killing of animals, esp for food. **2** the killing of many people at once; massacre: *the slaughter of innocent civilians* ○ *the slaughter on the roads,* ie the killing of people in road accidents. **3** (*infml*) complete defeat: *the total slaughter of the home team.*

▷ **slaughter** *v* [Tn] **1** (**a**) kill (an animal), usu for food: *slaughter pigs by humane methods.* (**b**) kill (animals or people) in large numbers: *thousands slaughtered by the invading army.* **2** (*fig infml*) defeat (sb/sth) completely, esp in sport: *We slaughtered them at hockey.*

□ ˈ**slaughterhouse** (also **abattoir**) *n* place where animals are killed for food.

Slav /slɑːv/ *n, adj* (member) of a group of peoples from eastern Europe who speak Slavonic languages. They include the Russians, the Poles, the Czechs, etc. Cf SLAVONIC.

slave /sleɪv/ *n* **1** person who is the property of another and is forced to work for him: *sell sb as a slave* ○ [attrib]: *slave labour, owners.* **2** person forced to work very hard, esp in bad conditions: *the slaves who work in the mines* ○ *They're slaves to their children,* ie have to work hard to look after them, please them, etc. **3** ~ **of/to sth** person whose way of life is dominated by (a habit, an interest, etc): *a slave to duty, convention, drink* ○ *a slave of fashion,* ie person who wears only the latest fashions. **4** part of a machine, computer, etc that is controlled by another part: [attrib] *a slave wheel.*

▷ **slave** *v* [I, Ipr, Ip] ~ **(away) (at sth)** work very hard: *slaving (away) in the garden for hours* ○ *I've been slaving at the housework all day.*

slaver *n* **1** person who buys and sells slaves. **2** ship for carrying slaves.

slavery /ˈsleɪvərɪ/ *n* [U] **1** condition of being a slave: *sold into slavery.* **2** practice of having slaves: *people working to abolish slavery.* **3** hard or poorly paid work. Cf WHITE SLAVERY (WHITE[1]).

□ ˈ**slave-driver** *n* **1** person in charge of slaves. **2** (*fig derog*) person who makes those under him work very hard.

ˈ**slave state** any of the 15 states in the south of the USA before the Civil War where slavery was legal.

ˈ**slave-trade** (also ˈ**slave-traffic**) *n* [sing] the capturing, transporting, buying and selling of people as slaves.

slaver /ˈslævə(r)/ *v* [I, Ipr] **1** ~ **(over sth)** let saliva run out of one's mouth; drool: *slavering over a plate of spaghetti.* **2** ~ **(over sb/sth)** (*usu derog*) show great eagerness, desire, etc: *Stop slavering over that baby!* ○ *The dealer was slavering over some precious stones.*

▷ **slaver** *n* [U] = SALIVA.

slavish /ˈsleɪvɪʃ/ *adj* (*derog*) lacking in independence or originality: *slavish devotion to a leader* ○ *His style is a slavish imitation of his teacher's.* ▷ **slavishly** *adv.*

Slavonic /sləˈvɒnɪk/ (also **Slavic** /ˈslɑːvɪk/) *n* [U] group of eastern European languages which includes Russian, Polish, Czech, Bulgarian, etc. The earliest recorded form is Old Church Slavonic, still used in the services of the Russian Orthodox Church.

▷ **Slavonic** (also **Slavic**) *adj* **1** of or belonging to this group of languages. **2** of the Slavs.

slay /sleɪ/ *v* (*pt* **slew** /sluː/, *pp* **slain** /sleɪn/) [Tn] **1** (*fml or US*) kill (esp an enemy) in a violent way: *soldiers slain in battle.* **2** (*fig joc or ironic*) amuse or impress (sb) greatly: *Her sudden enthusiasm for family life really slays me,* ie I find it ridiculous.

sleazy /ˈsliːzɪ/ *adj* (**-ier, -iest**) (*infml*) (esp of a place) dirty and not respectable; sordid: *a sleazy club, hotel, etc* ○ *a rather sleazy appearance.* ▷ **sleazily** /-ɪlɪ/ *adv.* **sleaziness** *n* [U].

sledge (also *esp US* **sled**)

sledge[1] /sledʒ/ (also *esp US* **sled** /sled/) *n* vehicle with long narrow strips of wood, metal, etc instead of wheels, for travelling over ice and snow (larger types being pulled by horses or dogs and smaller ones used in sport for travelling downhill fast). Cf SLEIGH.

▷ **sledge** (also *esp US* **sled**) *v* **1** [I, Ipr, Ip] (often **go sledging**) travel on a sledge, esp downhill for sport: *sledging down the ski slopes.* **2** [Tn] carry (sth/sb) on a sledge: *sledging supplies to remote villages.*

sledge[2] /sledʒ/ (also ˈ**sledge-hammer**) *n* large heavy hammer with a long handle, used eg for driving posts into the ground.

▷ ˈ**sledge-hammer** *adj* [attrib] (*usu derog*) (eg of an argument or criticism) powerful but not subtle: *a sledge-hammer approach to negotiations,* eg forcing sb to accept one's conditions.

sleek /sliːk/ *adj* (**-er, -est**) **1** smooth and glossy: *sleek hair, fur, etc.* **2** (*often derog*) (of a person) looking well-fed and prosperous. **3** well-styled: *a sleek, shiny sports-car.*

▷ **sleek** *v* [Tn] make (one's hair, a cat's fur, etc) sleek.

sleekly *adv.*

sleekness *n* [U].

sleep[1] /sliːp/ *n* **1** [U] condition that occurs regularly in humans and animals, esp at night, in which the eyes are closed and the muscles, nervous system, etc are relaxed: *How many hours' sleep do you need?* ○ *He didn't get much sleep.* ○ *Do you ever talk in your sleep?* ○ *send sb/get to sleep,* ie (make sb) fall asleep ○ *sing/rock a baby to sleep,* ie make the baby fall asleep by singing/rocking. **2** [sing] a period of sleep: *have a short, good, restful, etc sleep.* **3** [U] (*infml*) substance that gathers in the corners of the eyes during sleep: *wash the sleep out of one's eyes.* **4** (idm) **cry/sob oneself to ˈsleep** cry/sob until one falls asleep. ˌ**go to ˈsleep** (**a**) fall asleep: *Go to sleep now, it's late.* (**b**) (*infml*) (eg of a limb) become numb through lack of movement, etc: *I've been sitting on the floor and my foot's gone to sleep.* **not get/have a wink of sleep** ⇨ WINK. **not lose sleep/lose no sleep over sth** ⇨ LOSE. **put sb to ˈsleep** make sb fall asleep, esp by using an anaesthetic. **put (an animal) to ˈsleep** (*euph*) kill (an animal) deliberately, eg because it is ill: *Stray dogs are usually put to sleep if no one claims them.* **read oneself/sb to sleep** ⇨ READ. **sleep the sleep of the just** ⇨ SLEEP[2].

▷ **sleepless** *adj* [usu attrib] without sleep: *pass a sleepless night.* **sleeplessly** *adv.* **sleeplessness** *n* [U].

□ ˈ**sleep-walker** *n* person who walks around while asleep. ˈ**sleep-walking** *n* [U].

sleep[2] /sliːp/ *v* (*pt, pp* **slept** /slept/) **1** [I, Ip, In/pr] be in a state of sleep; be asleep: *Try to sleep in spite of the noise.* ○ *sleep well/badly* ○ *I got up early, but he slept on.* ○ *We slept (for) eight hours.* ○ *I slept at a friend's house last night.* **2** [Tn no passive] have enough beds for (a number of people): *Our caravan sleeps six in comfort.* ○ *The hotel sleeps 300 guests.* **3** (idm) **let sleeping dogs ˈlie** (*saying*) do not try to change a situation that could become a problem if sb interfered: *We decided to let sleeping dogs lie and not take them to court.* **not sleep a wink** ⇨ WINK. **sleep like a ˈlog/ˈtop** (*infml*) sleep soundly. **sleep ˈrough** sleep out of doors wherever one can: *He'd been sleeping rough for a week, in ditches and haystacks.* **sleep the sleep of the ˈjust** not be troubled by any guilty feeling. **sleep ˈtight** (*infml*) (esp imperative) sleep soundly: *Good night, sleep tight!* **4** (phr v) **sleep around** (*infml*) have sex with many partners. **sleep in** (**a**) (*US*) = LIE IN (LIE[2]): *I get a chance to sleep in at the weekend.* (**b**) (esp formerly of servants) sleep at the place where one works: *a housekeeper that sleeps in.* **sleep sth off** recover from sth by sleeping: *sleep off a bad headache, a hangover, etc* ○ *sleep it off,* ie after being drunk. **sleep on sth** (no passive) not decide about sth until the next day: *Don't say now if you'll take the job: sleep on it first.* **sleep out** (**a**) sleep outdoors. (**b**) (esp formerly of servants) not sleep at the place where one works: *a butler who sleeps out.* **sleep through sth** (no passive) not be woken up by (eg a noise or an alarm clock): *You slept right through the thunderstorm.* **sleep together**; **sleep with sb** (*euph*) have sex with sb, esp sb to whom one is not married.

□ ˈ**sleeping-bag** *n* warmly lined bag for sleeping in, esp when camping.

ˌ**Sleeping ˈBeauty** heroine of a fairy-tale who falls asleep for a hundred years because of a bad fairy's spell and is awoken by a kiss from a handsome prince.

ˈ**sleeping-car** *n* railway coach fitted with beds or berths.
ˈ**sleeping partner** (*US* ˈ**silent partner**) partner who has invested capital in a business company but who does not actually work in it.
ˈ**sleeping-pill** *n* pill containing a drug that helps sb to sleep.
ˌ**sleeping po**ˈ**liceman** (*infml*) bump built across a road to make drivers slow down.
ˈ**sleeping sickness** tropical disease carried by the tsetse fly, causing sleepiness and often death.

sleeper /ˈsliːpə(r)/ *n* **1** [C] (with an *adj*) person who sleeps in the specified way: *a good/bad sleeper* ○ *a heavy/light sleeper*, ie one whom it is hard/easy to wake up. **2** [C] (*US* **tie**) beam of wood or other material on which the rails of a railway, etc are fixed. **3** [C] (bed or berth in a) sleeping-car. **4** [C] (*Brit*) small ear-ring used to keep the hole in a pierced ear open. **5** [C] (*US infml*) play, book, person, etc that has an unexpected success, esp after being overlooked or unnoticed. **6** [C] (also **sleepers** [pl]) (*US*) pyjama suit for a baby or young child to sleep in: *a walk-in sleeper*, ie made in one piece.

sleepy /ˈsliːpɪ/ *adj* (**-ier**, **-iest**) **1** needing or ready to go to sleep: *feel, look sleepy* ○ *That beer made me quite sleepy.* **2** (of places) not very busy; without much activity: *a sleepy little village.* ▷ **sleepily** /-ɪlɪ/ *adv*. **sleepiness** *n* [U].
□ ˈ**sleepyhead** *n* (often used as a term of address) sleepy person, esp a child: *It's your bedtime, sleepyhead.*

sleet /sliːt/ *n* [U] falling snow or hail mixed with rain: *showers of sleet.* ▷ **sleet** *v* [I] (used with *it*, usu in the continuous tenses): *It is sleeting*, ie Sleet is falling. **sleety** *adj*: *sleety rain.*

sleeve /sliːv/ *n* **1** part of a garment that covers all or part of the arm: *roll up the sleeves of one's shirt/one's shirt-sleeves* ○ *a dress with short/long sleeves.* ⇨ illus at JACKET. **2** tube that encloses a rod, cable, etc: *a metal cable inside a plastic sleeve.* **3** (*US* **jacket**) stiff envelope for a gramophone record: [attrib] *a sleeve design* ○ *sleeve notes*, ie notes about composers, performers, etc on a sleeve. **4** (idm) **an ace up one's sleeve** ⇨ ACE. **a card up one's sleeve** ⇨ CARD[1]. **laugh up one's sleeve** ⇨ LAUGH. **roll up one's sleeves** ⇨ ROLL[2]. **a trick up one's sleeve** ⇨ TRICK. **(have sth) up one's sleeve** kept secret for use when needed: *Have you any ideas up your sleeve if our money runs out?* **wear one's heart on one's sleeve** ⇨ WEAR[2].
▷ **-sleeved** (forming compound *adjs*) having sleeves of the specified type: *a long-, short-, loose-sleeved shirt.*
sleeveless *adj* without sleeves.

sleigh /sleɪ/ *n* sledge, esp one drawn by a horse: [attrib] *a sleigh ride* ○ *sleigh bells*, ie attached to the horse.
▷ **sleigh** *v* [I, Ipr] travel on a sleigh: *go sleighing* ○ *sleigh over to the village.*

sleight /slaɪt/ *n* (idm) ˌ**sleight of** ˈ**hand** great skill in using the hands in performing conjuring tricks, etc: (*fig*) *The company accounts show a little financial sleight of hand.*

slender /ˈslendə(r)/ *adj* (**-er**, **-est**) **1** (*approv*) (**a**) not very wide but comparatively long or high: *slender fingers* ○ *a slender waist* ○ *a wineglass with a slender stem.* (**b**) (of people) slim: *a slender girl, figure* ○ *a slender, graceful ballet-dancer.* ⇨ Usage at THIN. **2** small in amount or size; inadequate; scanty: *a slender income* ○ *people of slender means*, ie with little money ○ *win by a slender margin.* ▷ **slenderly** *adv*. **slenderness** *n* [U].

slept *pt, pp* of SLEEP[2].

sleuth /sluːθ/ *n* (*infml joc*) detective.
▷ **sleuth** *v* [I] (*infml joc*) do detective work: *I had to go out sleuthing to find your address.*

slew[1] *pt* of SLAY.

slew[2] (*US* also **slue**) /sluː/ *v* [Ipr, Tn·pr] ~ **(sth) round** (cause sth to) turn, esp very fast in a new direction; swing: *The car slewed round on the icy road.* ○ *The driver slewed the crane round.*

slew[3] /sluː/ *n* [sing] ~ **of sth** (*US infml*) great amount of sth: *a whole slew of problems.*

S level /ˈes levl/ (*infml*) special (or scholarship) level: *Are you taking an S level in any exam subject?* ⇨ article at SCHOOLS.

slice /slaɪs/ *n* **1** thin wide flat piece cut off an item of food: *a slice of meat, cake, cheese, etc* ○ *slices of beef between slices of fresh bread.* **2** (*infml*) portion; share: *get a slice of the profit* ○ *She takes a large slice of the credit for our success.* **3** utensil with a broad flat blade for cutting, serving or lifting food, eg cooked fish or fried eggs. **4** (eg in golf) poor stroke that makes the ball spin off in the wrong direction, ie to the right of a right-handed player. Cf PULL[2] 11. **5** (idm) **get, etc a slice/share of the cake** ⇨ CAKE. **a piece/slice of the action** ⇨ ACTION.
▷ **slice** *v* **1** [Tn, Tn·p] ~ **sth (up)** cut sth into slices: *slice the meat, loaf, etc (up)* ○ *a sliced loaf.* **2** [Tn·pr, Tn·p, Dn·n no passive, Dn·pr] ~ **sth off/from sth**; ~ **sth off** cut sth from a larger piece: *slice a piece off (the meat)* ○ *slice a thin wedge from the cake* ○ *Slice me a piece of bread/a piece of bread for me.* **3** [Ipr, Tn] ~ **through/into sth** cut cleanly or easily through sth: *The axe sliced through the wood.* ○ *The falling slate sliced into his arm.* ○ *The bows of the ship sliced the water.* **4** [Tn] (eg in golf) strike (a ball) with a slice(4). **5** (idm) **the best thing since sliced bread** ⇨ BEST[1].

slick /slɪk/ *adj* (**-er**, **-est**) **1** done smoothly and efficiently, apparently without effort: *a slick translation* ○ *a slick take-over* ○ *gave a slick excuse for staying away.* **2** (*often derog*) (of people) doing things in a slick(1) way: *a slick performer, salesperson, negotiator, etc* ○ *She's very slick, but I don't believe a word she says.* **3** smooth and slippery: *The roads were slick with wet mud.*
▷ **slick** *n* (also ˈ**oil slick**) thick patch of oil floating on the sea (esp from an oil-tanker after a collision).
slick *v* (phr v) **slick sth down** flatten (hair) using eg hair-oil: *curls slicked down with grease.*
slicker *n* **1** (*infml esp US*) slick(2) person: *a city slicker*, ie slick by comparison with a person from the country. **2** (*US*) long loose waterproof coat.

slide[1] /slaɪd/ *n* **1** [sing] act of sliding: *have a slide on the ice.* **2** [C] smooth stretch of ice, hard snow, etc used esp by children on sledges. **3** [C] smooth slope, track or chute down which goods can slide or on which children can play at sliding. **4** [C] (**a**) picture, diagram, etc on photographic film, usu held in a small frame and shown on a screen using a projector; transparency. (**b**) (formerly) such a picture on a glass plate. **5** [C] glass plate on which sth is placed so that it can be looked at under a microscope. **6** [C] part of a machine, etc that slides, eg the U-shaped part of a trombone. ⇨ illus at MUSIC. **7** [C] (in compounds) sudden fall of a mass of earth, mud, etc: *a* ˈ*landslide* ○ *a* ˈ*mudslide.* **8** [C] = HAIR-SLIDE (HAIR).

slide[2] /slaɪd/ *v* (*pt, pp* **slid** /slɪd/) **1** [I, Ipr, Ip, Tn·pr, Tn·p, Cn·a] (cause sth to) move smoothly along an even, polished or slippery surface: *I was sliding (about) helplessly (on the ice).* ○ *The ship slid (down) into the water.* ○ *The drawers slide in and out easily.* ○ *We slid down the grassy slope.* ○ *I slid the rug in front of the fire.* ○ *Can the car seat be slid forward a little?* ○ *She slid the door open.* **2** [Ipr, Ip, Tn·pr, Tn·p] (cause sth to) move quietly or so as not to be noticed: *The thief slid out (of the door) while no one was looking.* ○ *She slid a coin into his hand.* ○ *He lifted the mat and slid the key under (it).* **3** [I] (eg of prices) fall gradually: *House values may begin to slide.* **4** (idm) **let sth** ˈ**slide** (*infml*) allow sth to become neglected, less organized, etc: *She got depressed and began to let things slide.* **5** (phr v) **slide into sth** (no passive) gradually pass into (a certain, usu bad, condition): *slide into bad habits, debt* ○ *We mustn't slide into complacency.* **slide over sth** avoid dealing with (a topic, etc) in detail: *She discussed sales, but slid over the problem of how to increase production.*
□ ˈ**slide-rule** *n* ruler with a strip sliding in a groove in the middle, marked with logarithmic scales for making rapid calculations.
ˌ**sliding** ˈ**door** door that slides on runners and is drawn across an opening.
ˌ**sliding** ˈ**scale** scale that relates two things, so that they each increase or decrease together: *Fees are calculated on a sliding scale according to income*, ie Richer people pay more.

slight[1] /slaɪt/ *adj* (**-er**, **-est**) **1** not serious or important; small: *a slight slip, error, change, improvement* ○ *a slight headache* ○ *The differences between the pictures are very slight.* ○ *do sth without the slightest difficulty*, ie with no difficulty at all ○ *She takes offence at the slightest thing*, ie is very easily offended. ○ *Compared to his early work, this is a rather slight novel*, ie not a major one. **2** not thick and strong; frail; slender: *a slight figure, girl* ○ *supported by a slight framework.* **3** (idm) **not in the** ˈ**slightest** not at all: *You didn't embarrass me in the slightest.*
▷ **slightly** *adv* **1** to a slight(1) degree: *a slightly bigger house* ○ *The patient is slightly better today.* ○ *I know her slightly.* **2** slenderly: *a slightly-built child.*
slightness *n* [U].

slight[2] /slaɪt/ *v* [Tn] treat (sb) without proper respect or courtesy; snub: *a slighting remark* ○ *She felt slighted because no one spoke to her.*
▷ **slight** *n* ~ **(to/on sb/sth)** act, remark, etc that offends sb: *My remark was not meant as a slight on you.* ○ *She suffered many slights from colleagues.*
slightingly *adv*.

slim /slɪm/ *adj* (**-mmer**, **-mmest**) **1** (*approv*) not fat or thick; slender: *a slim person, figure, waist* ○ *I'm trying to get slim.* ○ *a slim pocket-book.* ⇨ Usage at THIN. **2** not as big as one would like or expect; small: *slim hopes/chances/prospects of success* ○ *condemned on the slimmest of evidence.*
▷ **slim** *v* (**-mm-**) **1** [I, Ip] ~ **(down)** eat less, take exercise, etc in order to lose weight and become slim: *trying to get fit and slim (down).* **2** (phr v) **slim sth down** reduce sth in size or scale: *slim down the factory's work-force.*
slimly *adv*: *a slimly-built person.*
slimmer *n* person who is slimming: *a slimmers' magazine*, ie one that gives advice on how to slim.
slimness *n* [U].

slime /slaɪm/ *n* [U] **1** thick soft slippery liquid substance, esp mud: *There was a coating of slime on the unwashed sink.* **2** sticky liquid produced by snails, slugs, etc: *a trail of slime.*
▷ **slimy** /ˈslaɪmɪ/ *adj* (**-ier**, **-iest**) **1** of, like or covered with slime: *slip on the slimy steps.* **2** (*infml*) disgustingly dishonest, flattering, hypocritical, etc: *You slimy little creep!* **sliminess** *n* [U].

sling /slɪŋ/ *n* **1** bandage, tied over one shoulder or round the neck, used to support a broken arm, wrist, etc: *have one's arm in a sling.* **2** length of rope, strap, chain, etc looped round an object (eg a barrel) to support or lift it. **3** strap held in a loop used for throwing stones, etc.
▷ **sling** *v* (*pt, pp* **slung** /slʌŋ/) **1** [Tn, Tn·pr, Tn·p] (*infml*) throw (sb/sth) with great force: *slinging stones at birds* ○ *She slung her coat angrily into the car.* ○ *He was slung out (of the club) for fighting.* **2** [Tn, Tn·pr, Tn·p] lift or support (sth) so that it can hang loosely: *sling a hammock between two tree-trunks* ○ *with her bag slung over her shoulder.* **3** (idm) **fling/sling/throw mud** ⇨ MUD. **sling one's** ˈ**hook** (*Brit sl*) go away.
□ ˈ**sling-back** *n* (*Brit*) woman's shoe that has an open back and is held on by a strap across the heel: [attrib] *sling-back sandals.*
ˈ**sling-shot** *n* (*US*) = CATAPULT.

slink /slɪŋk/ *v* (*pt, pp* **slunk** /slʌŋk/) [Ipr, Ip] **1** move as if one feels guilty or ashamed, or does not want to be seen: *The thief slunk down the dark alley.* ○ *The dog slunk out when I shouted at him.* ⇨ Usage at PROWL. **2** move in a seductive way: *slinking around in a tight black dress.*

slinky /ˈslɪŋkɪ/ *adj* (**-ier**, **-iest**) **1** (esp of a woman) moving in a seductive way: *her slinky way of dancing.* **2** (of clothes) clinging to the curves of the body: *a slinky night-dress.* ▷ **slinkiness** *n* [U].

slip[1] /slɪp/ *n* **1** [C usu *sing*] act of slipping; false step: *One slip and you could fall off the cliff.* **2** [C] minor error caused by carelessness or lack of attention: *make a slip* ○ *There were a few trivial slips in the translation.* **3** [C] (**a**) loose sleeveless garment worn under a dress; petticoat. (**b**) = GYM-SLIP (GYM). **4** [C, U] = PILLOWCASE (PILLOW). **5** [C] thin or small piece of paper: *a salary slip*, ie giving details of earnings, tax paid, etc ○ *write o* *phone number on a slip of paper.* **6** [C] cutting[1](2) taken from a plant for grafting or planting. **7 the slips** [pl] = SLIPWAY (SLIP[2]). **8** (a) [C] (in cricket) (position of a) fielder standing close behind and usu to the off (OFF[2] *n* 2) side of the batsman: *first/second/third slip* ○ *Who is (at) first slip?* (b) **the slips** [pl] place where these fielders stand: *fielding in the slips.* **9** [U] almost liquid clay for coating earthenware or making patterns on it. **10** (idm) **give sb the ˈslip** (*infml*) escape from or get away from (sb following or chasing one): *We managed to give our pursuers the slip.* **a ˈslip of a boy, girl, thing, child, etc** a slightly-built boy, etc: *She's just a slip of a thing, but she can run faster than all of us.* **a slip of the ˈpen/ˈtongue** minor error in writing/speech: *A slip of the tongue made me say Robert instead of Richard.* **there's ˌmany a ˌslip ˈtwixt (the) ˌcup and (the) ˈlip** (*saying*) things can easily go wrong before one gets what one wants, expects, hopes for, etc: *They think they'll win the election easily, but there's many a slip 'twixt cup and lip.*

slip[2] /slɪp/ *v* (**-pp-**) **1** (a) [I, Ipr, Ip] ~ **(over) (on sth)** (of a person, an animal, a car, etc) slide accidentally; lose one's balance and fall or nearly fall in this way: *The climber's foot slipped, and she fell.* ○ *She slipped (over) (on the ice) and broke her leg.* ○ *The van slipped (a few feet) down the embankment.* (b) [I, Ipr, Ip] (of an object) slide accidentally out of its proper position: *The lorry turned and its load slipped.* ○ *The razor slipped and cut my cheek.* ○ *The straps keep slipping off (my shoulders).* (c) [Ipr, Ip] move smoothly and easily in a particular direction: *The ship slipped through the water.* ○ *I slipped along the bench next to her.* ○ *This wine slips down easily*, ie is pleasant to drink. **2** (a) [Ipr, Ip] go somewhere quietly or quickly, eg in order not to be noticed, or without being noticed: *The thief slipped out (by the back door).* ○ *We slipped away to Paris for the weekend.* ○ *The ship slipped into the harbour at night.* ○ (*fig*) *Errors have slipped into the book.* ○ (*fig*) *The years slipped by.* ○ (*fig*) *We've slipped behind schedule.* (b) [Tn·pr, Tn·p, Dn·n, Dn·pr] ~ **sth (to sb)** put sth somewhere, often quietly or secretly: *slip an envelope into one's pocket* ○ *I slipped a few jokes into the speech.* ○ *She opened the letter-box and slipped a newspaper through.* ○ *Slip the waiter a tip.* ○ *I tried to slip the note to him while the teacher wasn't looking.* **3** [Ipr, Ip] ~ **from/out of/through sth;** ~ **out/through** fall, get away, escape, etc by being difficult to hold, or by not being held firmly: *The fish slipped out of my hand.* ○ *He caught the ball, then it slipped through his fingers.* ○ *The mouse slipped quickly from the cat's claws.* ○ (*fig*) *I didn't mean to say that; it just slipped out.* **4** [Ipr, Tn·pr, Tn·p] ~ **into/out of sth;** ~ **sth over/round sth;** ~ **sth on/off** put (a coat, one's shoes, etc) on/off, esp quickly and easily: *slip into/out of a dress* ○ *slip a shawl round one's shoulders.* **5** (a) [Tn, Tn·pr] ~ **sth (from/off sth)** detach or release sth: *slip a dog from its leash* ○ *slip the rope off the hook* ○ *slip a stitch*, ie (in knitting) move a stitch from one needle to another without knitting it. (b) [Tn] get free from (sth); escape from: *The ship slipped its moorings.* ○ *The dog slipped its collar.* ○ (*fig*) *That point slipped my attention.* ○ *It had slipped my mind/memory that you were arriving today.* **6** (idm) **be ˈslipping** (*infml*) not be as good, alert, strong, etc as usual: *I've forgotten your name again — I must be slipping.* **let sth slip** (a) miss or not take advantage of (an opportunity, etc): *She let slip a chance to work abroad.* (b) accidentally reveal (a secret, etc); say sth casually: *She let slip that she had not paid her tax.* ○ *I let it slip that I was expecting a baby.* **slip ˈanchor** (of a ship) become detached from the ropes on the anchor. **slip a ˈdisc** suffer from a slipped disc. **slip through sb's ˈfingers** (esp of an opportunity) be missed by sb: *We let the last chance of escape slip through our fingers.* **7** (phr v) **slip up (on sth)** (*infml*) make a careless mistake: *I slipped up and gave you the wrong phone number.* ○ *I slipped up on the date.*

▷ **slippage** /ˈslɪpɪdʒ/ *n* [U] **1** reduction in values, prices, etc. **2** failure to keep to a schedule or target: *production delays due to slippage.*

□ **ˈslip-case** *n* (usu cardboard) case for a book.

ˈslip-cover *n* removable cover for a piece of furniture.

ˈslip-knot *n* **1** knot that can slip easily along the rope on which it is tied, to tighten or loosen the loop. **2** knot that can be undone by pulling one end of a rope. ⇨ illus at KNOT.

ˈslip-on *n*, *adj* [attrib] (garment or shoe) made to be slipped on without fastening buttons, etc.

ˈslip-over *n*, *adj* (garment) made to be slipped easily over the head.

ˌslipped ˈdisc disc between the vertebrae that has moved out of place and causes pain.

ˈslip-road *n* (*US* **ˈaccess road**) road used for driving onto or off a motorway. ⇨ illus at MOTORWAY.

ˈslip stitch sewing stitch used esp for hems, and hidden by not passing the needle completely through the fabric.

ˈslip-stream *n* **1** stream of air behind a moving object, eg a racing-car. **2** stream of air thrust back by an aircraft's engines.

ˈslip-up *n* (*infml*) mistake: *Leaving his name off the list was a bad slip-up.*

ˈslipway [C] (also **the ˈslips** [pl]) *n* sloping track of stone or timber leading down to the water, on which ships are built or pulled up out of the water for repairs.

slipper /ˈslɪpə(r)/ *n* loose-fitting light soft shoe worn in the house: *a pair of slippers.*

▷ **slippered** *adj* wearing slippers.

slippery /ˈslɪpərɪ/ *adj* (**-ier, -iest**) **1** (of a surface) difficult to hold, stand on or move on without slipping because it is smooth, wet, polished, etc: *a slippery road, floor, etc* ○ *Ice made the path slippery underfoot.* **2** (*infml*) (of a person) not to be trusted; unreliable: *a slippery salesman* ○ *She's as slippery as an eel.* **3** (*infml*) (of a situation, topic, problem, etc) difficult to deal with: *the rather slippery subject of race relations* ○ *be on slippery ground*, ie be dealing with a subject that needs tact, care, etc. **4** (idm) **the slippery ˈslope** (*infml*) course of action that can easily lead to disaster, failure, etc: *A one-party state can be the start of the slippery slope towards fascism.* ▷ **slipperiness** *n* [U].

slippy /ˈslɪpɪ/ *adj* (**-ier, -iest**) (*infml*) **1** slippery. **2** (*dated Brit*) quick (used esp in the expressions shown): *Be slippy about it!* ○ *Look slippy!* ie Hurry up!

slipshod /ˈslɪpʃɒd/ *adj* not done or not doing things carefully; careless: *slipshod work* ○ *a slipshod style* ○ *a slipshod worker, writer, etc* ○ *You're too slipshod about your presentation.*

slit /slɪt/ *n* long narrow cut, tear or opening: *the slit of the letter-box*, ie through which letters are put ○ *eyes like slits* ○ *a long slit in her skirt.* Cf SLOT.

▷ **slit** *v* (**-tt-**; *pt*, *pp* **slit**) [Tn, Tn·pr, Cn·a] make a slit in (sth) by cutting; open (sth) by slitting: *slit sb's throat* ○ *a jacket slit up the back* ○ *slit cloth into strips* ○ *slit an envelope open.*

□ **ˈslit trench** narrow trench used esp by soldiers in battle.

slither /ˈslɪðə(r)/ *v* [I, Ipr, Ip] slide or slip unsteadily: *slithering dangerously (on the muddy path)* ○ *slither down an icy slope* ○ *slithering around in the mud* ○ *The snake slithered off (into the grass) as we approached.*

▷ **slithery** *adj* slippery.

sliver /ˈslɪvə(r)/ *n* long thin piece of sth cut or broken off from a larger piece; splinter: *slivers of wood, glass, metal, etc* ○ *Cut me just a small sliver of cheese.*

▷ **sliver** *v* [I, Tn] (cause sth to) break into slivers or break off as a sliver; splinter: *The glass slivered when it fell.*

slob /slɒb/ *n* (*infml derog*) slovenly, untidy, lazy or ill-mannered person: *Get out of bed, you idle slob!*

slobber /ˈslɒbə(r)/ *v* **1** [I] let saliva fall from the mouth; drool: *a slobbering baby.* **2** (phr v) **slobber over sb/sth** (*infml derog*) show one's affection for sb/sth too openly so that it embarrasses other people: *slobbering all over her boy-friend.*

▷ **slobber** *n* [U] (*infml*) saliva.

slobbery /-ərɪ/ *adj*: *slobbery kisses.*

sloe /sləʊ/ *n* **1** small, bluish-back, very bitter wild plum, fruit of the blackthorn bush. **2** the blackthorn bush itself.

□ **sloe-ˈgin** *n* [U] liqueur made from sloes steeped in gin.

slog /slɒg/ (also **slug**) *v* (**-gg-**) **1** [I, Ipr, Tn, Tn·pr] hit (sth/sb) hard: *slog (at) the ball* ○ *slogging one's opponent (all around the ring)*, eg in boxing ○ *slog the ball over the boundary.* **2** (idm) **slog/sweat one's guts out** ⇨ GUT. **slog it out** (*infml*) fight or struggle until a conclusion is reached: *two boxers slogging it out* ○ *The party leaders are slogging it out in a TV debate.* **3** (phr v) **slog (away) at sth** (*infml*) work hard and steadily at sth: *slogging away at my accounts.* **slog down, up, along etc** walk steadily, often with difficulty, in the direction specified: *slog up (the hill) in the dark* ○ *slogging through the snow.* **slog through sth** (*infml*) work hard and steadily to complete sth: *slog through a pile of marking.* ▷ **slog** (also **slug**) *n* (*infml*) **1** hard stroke, eg in cricket. **2** (usu *sing*) period of hard work or walking: *Marking the exam papers was quite a slog.* ○ *It's a long hard slog up the mountain.* **slogger** *n* (*infml*) **1** person who slogs, eg at cricket. **2** hard worker.

slogan /ˈsləʊgən/ *n* word or phrase that is easy to remember, used as a motto eg by a political party, or in advertising: *political slogans* ○ *'Power to the people' is their slogan.*

sloop /slu:p/ *n* small ship with one mast and sails pointing forward and aft.

slop /slɒp/ *v* (**-pp-**) **1** [Ipr, Ip] (of liquids) spill over the edge, esp of a container: *I dropped the bucket, and water slopped out (of it).* ○ *The tea slopped (over) into the saucer.* **2** [Tn, Tn·pr, Tn·p] cause (sth) to spill: *slop the beer, paint, etc carelessly (all over the floor)* ○ *She slopped the dirty water (out) onto the grass.* **3** (phr v) **slop about/around** (of liquids) move around in a small space, esp a container: *Water was slopping around in the bottom of the boat.* **slop about/around (in sth)** (of people) splash around: *Why do some children like slopping around in puddles?* **slop out** empty slops (SLOP *n* 1, 2).

▷ **slop** *n* (usu *pl*) **1** dirty waste water from sinks, baths, etc. **2** urine, excrement and waste water contained in a bucket in prison cells that have no toilet or sink: [attrib] *a ˈslop-bucket.* **3** (a) swill for pigs. (b) liquid food (eg milk, soup), esp for sick people.

slope /sləʊp/ *n* **1** (usu *sing*) slanting line; surface that is at an angle of less than 90° to the earth's surface or a flat surface: *the slope of a roof* ○ *a 40° slope* ○ *a slight/steep slope.* **2** area of rising or falling ground: *mountain slopes* ○ *ski slopes.* **3** (idm) **the slippery slope** ⇨ SLIPPERY.

▷ **slope** *v* **1** [I, Ipr, Ip] have a slope; slant: *a garden sloping gently towards the river* ○ *The field slopes (away) to the east.* ○ *Does your handwriting slope forwards or backwards?* **2** (phr v) **slope off** (*Brit infml*) go away, esp without being noticed, in order to avoid doing work, etc.

sloppy /ˈslɒpɪ/ *adj* (**-ier, -iest**) **1** (*infml*) (a) (of a person) careless and untidy in dress, or in the way he does things: *a sloppy worker, writer, etc* ○ *look sloppy.* (b) done in a careless and untidy way: *sloppy typing* ○ *a sloppy repair.* **2** (*infml*) foolishly sentimental: *sloppy sentiment* ○ *I hate sloppy romantic films.* **3** (*derog*) (a) covered with spilled water, etc: *a sloppy counter, floor.* (b) too liquid: *sloppy porridge.*

▷ **sloppily** /-ɪlɪ/ *adv* (*infml*) in a sloppy(1, 2) way: *sloppily dressed* ○ *talking sloppily about love.*

sloppiness *n* [U].

slosh /slɒʃ/ *v* **1** (*infml*) (a) [I, Ipr, Ip] ~ **(about/around)** (of liquid) move around noisily, eg in a bucket: *water sloshing against the sides of the bath* ○ *Milk sloshed around in the flask.* (b) [Tn·pr, Tn·p] cause (liquid) to move noisily; splash: *slosh the whitewash all over the floor* ○ *sloshing the water around in the pail.* **2** [Tn, Tn·pr] (*Brit sl*) hit (sb): *slosh sb on the chin.* **3** (phr v) **slosh about/around (in sth)** move around noisily in sth liquid: *children sloshing about in puddles.* **slosh sth onto sth** put (paint, etc) on in a careless way: *sloshing whitewash on the wall.* ⇨ Usage at SPRAY[2].

▷ **sloshed** *adj* [pred] (*sl esp Brit*) drunk.

slot /slɒt/ *n* **1** narrow opening into which sth can be put: *put a 10p coin in the slot.* **2** slit, groove or channel into which sth fits or along which sth slides: *a slot on a dashboard for a car radio* ○ *The curtain hooks run along a slot in the curtain rail.* **3** position for sb/sth, eg in a series of broadcasts, a lecture course, etc: *find a slot for a talk on the economy.*

▷ **slot** *v* (**-tt-**) **1** [Tn] make a slot or slots in (sth). **2** (phr v) **slot (sth/sb) in, into, through, etc** (cause sth/sb to) move in, into, through, etc a slot: *The bolt slotted smoothly into place.* ○ *slot the edge of the panel into the groove* ○ *Slot this disk in.* ○ *Can we slot her into a job in the sales department?*

□ ˈ**slot-machine** *n* machine with a slot for coins, used for gambling, or selling cigarettes, bars of chocolate, etc.

sloth[1] /sləʊθ/ *n* [U] (*fml*) laziness; idleness.

▷ **slothful** /-fl/ *adj* (*fml*) lazy; idle. **slothfully** /-fəlɪ/ *adv.* **slothfulness** *n* [U].

sloth[2] /sləʊθ/ *n* S American mammal that lives in trees and moves very slowly.

slouch /slaʊtʃ/ *v* [I, Ipr, Ip] stand, sit or move in a lazy way, often not quite upright: *Don't slouch! Stand up straight!* ○ *She slouched past me with her hands in her pockets.* ○ *slouching about all day doing nothing.*

▷ **slouch** *n* **1** [sing] slouching posture or way of moving: *walk with a slouch.* **2** (idm) **be no slouch at sth** (*infml*) be very good at sth: *She's no slouch at tennis.*

slouchingly *adv.*

□ ˌ**slouch** ˈ**hat** soft hat with a wide turned-down brim.

slough[1] /slaʊ; *US also* sluː/ *n* **1** [C] swamp; marsh. **2** [C] (in western Canada) pond formed by rain or melted snow. **3** [sing] ~ **of sth** (*fml*) bad mental attitude that is hard to change: *a slough of despair, self-pity, etc.*

slough[2] /slʌf/ *n* skin that has fallen away from a snake; any dead tissue that falls away at regular intervals.

▷ **slough** *v* **1** [Tn, Tn·p] ~ **sth (off)** let (skin, dead tissue, etc) fall off; cast sth off: *a snake sloughing (off) its skin.* **2** (phr v) **slough sth off** get rid of sth; abandon sth: *slough off one's bad habits, worries, responsibilities, etc.*

Slovak /ˈsləʊvæk/ *n* **1** [C] native or inhabitant of Slovakia. **2** [U] language of Slovakia. — *adj* of Slovakia, its culture or its people.

Slovakia /sləʊˈvækɪə/ (also **the Slovak Republic**) country in central Europe; pop approx 5 274 000; official language Slovak; capital Bratislava; unit of currency koruna. It was created in 1993 from the eastern area of the former Czechoslovakia. Its industry suffered during the free-market reforms after 1989, and its economy lacks foreign investment. Natural resources include brown coal, natural gas, iron and several other metal ores. ⇨ map at CZECHOSLOVAKIA.

Slovenia /sləʊˈviːnɪə/ country in south-eastern Europe; pop approx 2 020 000; official language Slovene; capital Ljubljana; unit of currency tolar. Until 1991 it was one of the federal republics of the former Yugoslavia. ⇨ map at CZECHOSLOVAKIA.

slovenly /ˈslʌvnlɪ/ *adj* (*derog*) careless, untidy, dirty, etc in appearance, dress or habits: *a slovenly waiter, secretary, cook, etc* ○ *Those terrible overalls would make anyone look slovenly.*

▷ **sloven** /ˈslʌvn/ *n* (*dated derog*) slovenly person. **slovenliness** *n* [U].

slow[1] /sləʊ/ *adj* (**-er, -est**) **1** not moving, acting or done quickly; taking a long time; not fast: *a slow runner, vehicle, journey* ○ *a slow recovery from illness* ○ *We're making slow progress.* ○ *a slow poison* ○ *They played the overture at a fairly slow tempo.* **2** not quick to learn; finding things hard to understand: *a slow child, learner, pupil, etc* ○ *slow at figures*, ie not good at doing calculations, etc. **3** [pred] ~ **to sth/do sth**; ~ **(in/about) doing sth** not doing things immediately; hesitating to act, speak, etc: (*fml*) *slow to anger* ○ *She's not slow to tell us what she thinks.* ○ *They were very slow (about) paying me.* **4** not lively or active enough; sluggish: *The film's too slow*, eg does not have enough exciting scenes, etc. ○ *Business is rather slow today*, eg not many goods are being sold. **5** [pred] (often preceded by *two minutes, one hour*, etc) (of watches and clocks) showing a time earlier than the correct time: *That clock is five minutes slow*, eg It shows 1.55 when it is 2.00. **6** (of a route, etc) not allowing great speed: *the slow road through the mountains.* **7** (of a surface) causing what moves over it (esp a ball) to move at a reduced speed: *a slow billiard table, cricket pitch, etc* ○ *Long grass makes the field slower.* **8** (of photographic film) not very sensitive to light. **9** (idm) **quick/slow on the draw** ⇨ DRAW[1]. **quick/slow on the uptake** ⇨ UPTAKE.

▷ **slowly** *adv* **1** (preceding or following the *v*, as shown) in a slow[1](1) way: *walk, speak, learn, react slowly* ○ *She slowly opened the door.* ○ *Slowly, things began to improve.* **2** (idm) **slowly but surely** making slow but definite progress: *Slowly but surely the great ship glided into the water.* **slowness** *n* [U].

□ ˈ**slowcoach** (*Brit*) (*US* ˈ**slowpoke**) *n* (*infml*) person who moves, acts, works or thinks slowly: *Get on with it, you old slowcoach!*

ˌ**slow** ˈ**handclap** slow rhythmical clapping by an audience to show its impatience or displeasure: *give sb the slow handclap.*

ˈ**slow lane** nearside lane of a motorway, along which slow vehicles move.

ˌ**slow** ˈ**motion** (in cinema photography) method of making action appear slow by filming a scene with a higher number of exposures than usual per second, then showing it at normal speed: *filmed in slow motion* ○ [attrib] *a* ˌ*slow-motion* ˈ*sequence.*

ˌ**slow** ˈ**puncture** puncture with a small hole through which air escapes very gradually.

slow[2] /sləʊ/ *adv* (**-er, -est**) **1** (used after *vs*, after *how* or in compounds with participles) at a slow[1](1) speed; slowly: *Tell the driver to go slower.* ○ *How slow this train goes!* ○ *slow-moving* ○ *slow-cooked food.* **2** (idm) **go** ˈ**slow (a)** (of workers) work slowly, esp as a protest or to make their employer meet their demands. Cf GO-SLOW (GO[1]). **(b)** be less active than usual: *You ought to go slow until you feel really well again.*

slow[3] /sləʊ/ *v* **1** [I, Ipr, Ip, Tn, Tn·pr, Tn·p] ~ **(sth) (up/down)** (cause sth to) go at a slower speed: *The train slowed (down) (to a crawl) as it approached the station.* ○ *Output has slowed (up) a little.* ○ *She slowed the car down and stopped.* ○ *Lack of demand will slow (down) our economic growth.* **2** (phr v) **slow up/down** work less energetically: *Slow up a bit, or you'll make yourself ill.*

□ ˈ**slow-down** *n* reduction of activity, esp a deliberate reduction of industrial production by workers or employers: *a slow-down in the dairy industry.*

slow-worm /ˈsləʊwɜːm/ (also **blindworm**) *n* small non-poisonous European reptile with no limbs.

SLR /ˌes el ˈɑː(r)/ *abbr* (of a type of camera) single lens reflex.

sludge /slʌdʒ/ *n* [U] **1** thick greasy mud or substance resembling this: *some sludge in the bottom of the tank.* **2** sewage.

slue (*US*) = SLEW[2].

slug[1] /slʌg/ *n* small creature like a snail without a shell that moves slowly and leaves a slimy trail. ⇨ illus at SNAIL.

slug[2] /slʌg/ *n* **1** **(a)** bullet, esp of irregular shape. **(b)** (*infml esp US*) any bullet. **2** (in printing) strip of metal with a line of type along one edge. **3** (*US*) piece of metal for use (esp illegally) in a coin-operated machine. **4** (*infml esp US*) small amount of whisky, vodka, etc: *swallow a slug of gin.*

slug[3] /slʌg/ *v* (**-gg-**) (*US*) **1** [I, Ipr, Tn, Tn·pr] = SLOG. **2** (idm) **slug it out** = SLOG IT OUT (SLOG).

▷ **slug** *n* = SLOG.

sluggard /ˈslʌgəd/ *n* (*dated derog*) lazy, slow-moving person.

sluggish /ˈslʌgɪʃ/ *adj* slow-moving; not alert or lively; lethargic: *a sluggish stream, pulse* ○ *sluggish traffic, conversation* ○ *These tablets make me feel rather sluggish.* ▷ **sluggishly** *adv.* **sluggishness** *n* [U].

sluice /sluːs/ *n* **1** (also ˈ**sluice-gate**, ˈ**sluice-valve**) sliding gate or other device for controlling the flow of water out of or into a canal, lake, lock, etc: *open the sluice-gates of a reservoir.* **2** water controlled by this. **3** (also ˈ**sluice-way**) artificial water-channel, esp where gold-miners rinse gold out of sand and dirt.

▷ **sluice** *v* **1** [Tn, Tn·p] ~ **sth (down/out)** wash or rinse sth with a stream of water: *sluice ore*, ie to separate it from gravel, etc ○ *sluice out the stables* ○ *We sluiced the muddy wheels (down) with a hose.* **2** (phr v) **sluice away, out, out of sth, etc** (of water) flow away, out, etc as if from a sluice: *water sluicing out of the hole.*

slum /slʌm/ *n* **1** [C] (house or rooms in a) street, alley, etc of badly-built, overcrowded buildings: *brought up in a slum* ○ [attrib] *a slum area* ○ *slum children* ○ *slum clearance*, ie demolition of slums ○ (*fig*) *I can't stand this slum any longer, tidy it up!* **2 the slums** [pl] area of a town where such buildings are found.

Slums in Britain were one of a series of social and economic problems brought about by the movement of people to the cities during and after the *Industrial Revolution. The slums of London's East End and of Glasgow's Gorbals district were particularly notorious for their overcrowding, lack of air and light, and poor sanitation. The term 'slum' actually came into common usage during the Victorian period, when the condition of slums reached its very worst. Wealthy people would often visit the slum districts, either to perform charitable deeds or simply out of curiosity. The remnants of the slums in the East End were largely destroyed by bombing in the Second World War, and were replaced after the war by high-rise flats. The Gorbals district slums were replaced by high-rise flats during the 1960s.

▷ **slum** *v* (**-mm-**) **1** [I] (usu in the continuous tenses) visit places thought socially inferior to those where one usu works or enjoys oneself, esp out of curiosity: *What are they doing drinking at this end of town? Slumming, I suppose.* **2** (idm) **slum it** (*infml*) choose or be forced to live in poor surroundings: *While he was studying, Nick had to slum it in a tiny room.*

slummy *adj* (**-ier, -iest**) (*derog*) of or like a slum; dirty or untidy: *a slummy district* ○ *It looks terribly slummy in this house.*

slumber /ˈslʌmbə(r)/ *v* [I] (*fml or joc*) sleep, esp peacefully and comfortably: *The baby was slumbering peacefully.*

▷ **slumber** *n* (often *pl*); (*fml or joc esp fig*) sleep: *fall into a deep slumber* ○ *disturb sb's slumber(s).*

slumberer /-bərə(r)/ *n* (*fml*) person who slumbers.

slumberous /-bərəs/ *adj* (*fml*) sleepy.

□ ˈ**slumberwear** *n* [U] (used esp in advertisements) clothes to be worn in bed; pyjamas, night-dresses, etc.

slump /slʌmp/ *v* **1** [I, Ipr, Ip] fall or flop heavily: *Tired from her walk she slumped (down) onto the sofa.* ○ *They found her slumped over the steering wheel.* **2** [I] (of prices, trade, business activity) fall suddenly or greatly: *What caused share values to slump?*

▷ **slump** *n* **1** period when business is bad, sales are few, etc; depression(3). Cf RECESSION 1. **2** (*US*) period when a person, a team, etc has little success, poor results, etc: *a slump in her career.*

slung *pt, pp* of SLING.

slunk *pt, pp* of SLINK.

slur /slɜː(r)/ *v* (**-rr-**) [Tn] **1** run (sounds, words) into each other so that they are indistinct: *the slurred speech of a drunk.* **2** play (musical notes) so that each one runs smoothly into the next. **3** harm (sb's reputation) by making (esp untrue) statements: *slurred by accusations of dishonesty.* **4** (phr v) **slur over sth** avoid dealing with an unpleasant fact, a difficult problem, etc: *She slurred over the high cost of her plan.*

▷ **slur** *n* **1** [C, U] ~ **(on sb/sth)** statement, accusation, etc that may damage sb's reputation, esp when untrue: *cast a slur on sb* ○ *Any suggestion that I accepted bribes would be a monstrous slur.* ○ (*fml*) *She tried to keep her reputation free from slur.* **2** [C] (*music*) the mark (⁀) or (‿), used to show that two or more notes are to be sung to one syllable or played smoothly without a break. **3** [C] slurred sound.

slurp /slɜːp/ *v* [I, Tn, Tn·p] (*infml*) make a loud noise with the lips as one eats or drinks (sth): *Stop slurping!* ○ *He was slurping (down) his soup.*

▷ **slurp** *n* (usu *sing*) sound of slurping.

slurry /ˈslʌrɪ/ *n* [U] thin semi-liquid mixture, esp of cement, clay, mud, etc.

slush /slʌʃ/ *n* [U] **1** soft, usu dirty, melting snow on the ground. **2** (*infml derog*) silly sentimental speech or writing: *a romantic novel full of slush.* ▷ **slushy** *adj* (-ier, -est): *slushy pavements* ○ (*fig*) *slushy sentiment, stories.*

□ ˈ**slush fund** (*derog*) fund created eg by a political party or a business company, for illegal purposes, eg bribing officials.

slut /slʌt/ *n* (*derog*) woman who is slovenly or sexually immoral: *a common slut.* ▷ **sluttish** *adj*: *a sluttish appearance* ○ *sluttish behaviour.*

sly /slaɪ/ *adj* (-er, -est) **1** (*often derog*) acting or done in a secret, often cunning and deceitful, way: *a sly fellow, trick, ruse* ○ (*joc*) *You sly old devil!* ○ *It was sly of you not to tell us you'd already met.* **2** [usu attrib] suggesting that one knows sth secret; knowing: *a sly smile, look, etc* ○ *She cast a sly glance at her bridge partner.* **3** mischievous; playful: *play a sly trick on a friend.* **4** (idm) **on the** ˈ**sly** secretly: *She must have been having lessons on the sly.* ▷ **slyly** *adv.* **slyness** *n* [U].

□ ˈ**sly boots** (*infml*) (often used as an affectionate term of address) sly person: *You old sly boots! When did you get married?*

Sm *symb* samarium.

smack[1] /smæk/ *n* **1** [C] **(a)** (sound of a) blow given with the open hand; slap: *give a child a smack on the bottom.* **(b)** (usu *sing*) loud sound of the lips being parted: *a greedy smack of the lips as he cut into the steak.* **(c)** [C] (*infml*) loud kiss: *a smack on the lips/cheek.* **2** [C usu *sing*] blow; hit: *give the ball a hard smack,* eg with a bat in cricket. **3** [U] (*sl esp Brit*) heroin. **4** (idm) **a smack at sth/doing sth** (*infml*) attempt at doing sth: *have a smack at making an omelette.*

▷ **smack** *v* [Tn] **1** strike (sb) with the open hand; slap: *Don't you dare smack my children!* **2** (idm) **lick/smack one's lips/chops** ⇨ LICK.

smack *adv* **1** in a sudden and violent way: *run smack into a brick wall* ○ *hit sb smack in the eye.* **2** (*US* ˈ**smack-dab**) directly; squarely: *It landed smack(-dab) in the middle of the carpet.*

smacker *n* (*infml*) **1** loud kiss. **2** (*sl*) pound sterling or US dollar: *one hundred smackers.*

smacking *n* [sing] hitting or being hit with the open hand: *The child needs a good smacking.*

smack[2] /smæk/ *n* small sailing-boat for fishing.

smack[3] /smæk/ *v* (phr v) **smack of sth** (no passive) **1** have a slight flavour of sth: *medicine that smacks of sulphur.* **2** suggest that sb has unpleasant attitudes or qualities: *Their comments smack of racism.*

▷ **smack** *n* [sing] ~ **of sth 1** slight flavour of sth: *a smack of garlic.* **2** suggestion; hint: *There was a smack of malice in her reply.*

small /smɔːl/ *adj* **1** not large in size, degree, number, value, etc: *a small house, town, room, audience, sum of money* ○ *This hat is too small for me.* ○ *My influence over her is small, so she won't do as I say.* Cf BIG. ⇨ Usage. **2** young: *Would a small child know that?* ○ *I lived in the country when I was small.* **3** [usu attrib] **(a)** not as big as sth else of the same kind: *the small intestine.* **(b)** (of letters) not written or printed as capitals (CAPITAL[1] 2). **4** [usu attrib] not doing things on a large scale: *a small farmer, trader, shopkeeper, company, etc* ○ *more help for small businesses* ○ *a small eater,* ie a person who does not eat much. **5** unimportant; trivial; slight: *a small matter, change, mistake* ○ *There are only small differences between the two translations.* **6** [attrib] (*derog*) having a mean and petty attitude: *a very small man* ○ *Only somebody with a small mind would have refused to help.* **7** [attrib] (used with uncountable nouns) little or no: *have small cause to be glad* ○ *He failed, and small wonder,* ie it is not surprising. **8** (idm) **(be) grateful/thankful for small** ˈ**mercies** relieved that a bad situation is not worse: *It may be cold but it's not raining — let's be thankful for small mercies.* **great and small** ⇨ GREAT. **in a big/small way** ⇨ WAY[1]. **it's a small** ˈ**world** (*saying*) one is likely to meet, or hear about, sb one knows (however distantly) wherever one goes. **look/feel** ˈ**small** be humiliated: *You made me look so small, correcting me in front of everybody.* **no/little/small wonder** ⇨ WONDER *n.* **small** ˈ**beer** (*US* **small po**ˈ**tatoes**) (*infml*) person or thing of no great importance or value: *That grant was pretty small beer: we shall need a lot more money.* **a small** ˈ**fortune** a lot of money: *The car cost me a small fortune.* ˈ**small fry** (*infml*) people thought to be unimportant. **the** ˈ**small hours** period of time soon after midnight: *working until/into the small hours.* **the small** ˈ**print** the parts of a legal document, contract, etc which are often printed in small type and contain important details that are easy to overlook: *The penalty clause was hidden in the small print.* ○ *Make sure you read all the small print before signing.* **the still small voice** ⇨ STILL[1].

▷ **small** *adv* into small pieces: *chop the wood small.*

small *n* **1 smalls** [pl] (*Brit infml*) small items of clothing, esp underwear. **2** [sing] the slender part of sth (used esp in the phrase shown): *the small of the back.* **3** of a small size: *Don't draw the picture too small.*

smallness *n* [U].

□ ˈ**small ads** /ædz/ (*Brit infml*) = CLASSIFIED ADVERTISEMENTS (CLASSIFY).

ˌ**small** ˈ**arms** weapons light enough to be carried in the hands: [attrib] *small-arms fire.*

ˌ**small** ˈ**change** coins of low value: *I dropped some small change into the collecting tin.* ○ (*fig*) *conversational small change,* eg basic conventional remarks about the weather, people's health, etc.

ˈ**smallholder**, ˈ**smallholding** *ns* (*Brit*) (owner or tenant of a) piece of land, usu more than one acre and less than 50 acres, used for farming.

ˌ**small in**ˈ**testine** part of the digestive system between the stomach and the large intestine (LARGE), made up of the *duodenum, jejunum,* and *ileum.* Food is digested and absorbed there.

ˌ**small-**ˈ**minded** *adj* (*derog*) mean and selfish; petty. ˌ**small-**ˈ**mindedness** *n* [U].

ˈ**smallpox** *n* [U] serious contagious disease causing high fever and leaving permanent scars on the skin: [attrib] *a smallpox injection, epidemic.*

ˌ**small-**ˈ**scale** *adj* **1** (of a map, drawing, etc) drawn to a small scale[2](4) so that few details are shown. **2** not great in size, extent, quantity, etc: ˌ*only a* ˌ*small-scale* ˈ*survey of 20 people.*

ˈ**small talk** conversation about everyday matters, usu at a social event: *I'm afraid I have no small talk,* ie I can't chat about unimportant things.

ˈ**small-time** *adj* (*infml derog*) unimportant; petty: *a small-time criminal.*

NOTE ON USAGE: Compare **small** and **little. Small** is the usual opposite of *big* or *large.* It has comparative and superlative forms and can be modified by adverbs such as 'rather': *Our house is smaller than yours but I think the garden is bigger.* ○ *I have a fairly small income.* The comparative and superlative forms of **little** are rare and it is not usually modified by adverbs. It is generally only used attributively, often following another adjective, to indicate an attitude of affection, dislike, amusement, etc: *He's a horrid little man.* ○ *What a lovely little house!*

smarmy /ˈsmɑːmɪ/ *adj* (-ier, -iest) (*Brit infml derog*) trying to make oneself popular by flattery and charm: *a smarmy salesman* ○ *The waiters' manners are always so smarmy.*

smart[1] /smɑːt/ *adj* (-er, -est) **1** bright and new-looking; well-dressed; neat: *a smart hat, frock, car* ○ *You look very smart in your new suit.* ○ *Make yourself smart before my parents arrive.* **2** (*esp US*) having or showing intelligence; clever; ingenious: *a smart student* ○ *a smart answer, idea* ○ *It was smart of you to bring a map.* **3 (a)** quick; brisk: *go for a smart walk* ○ *set off at a smart pace.* **(b)** (of a blow or of criticism) forceful: *I gave a smart blow on the lid, and it flew open.* ○ *a smart rebuke from the teacher.* **4** fashionable; chic: *the smart set* ○ *a smart restaurant.* **5** (idm) **get** ˈ**smart with sb** (*infml*) behave cheekily towards sb: *Don't try getting smart with me, young man!* **look** ˈ**smart** hurry; not waste time: *Look smart or the shops will be closed.* **the** ˈ**smart money is on sb/sth** (*infml*) people who are well-informed expect sb to win/sth to happen: *The smart money is on an early election.*

▷ **smarten** /ˈsmɑːtn/ *v* (phr v) **smarten (oneself/ sb/sth) up** make oneself/sb/sth neater, tidier, etc: *You'll have to smarten (yourself) up a bit before going out.* ○ *Try to smarten the house up before the visitors arrive.*

smartly *adv*: *smartly dressed* ○ *walk smartly into the room* ○ *hit sth smartly with a hammer.*

smartness *n* [U].

□ ˌ**smart** ˈ**alec** /ˈælɪk/ (*infml usu derog*) person who acts as if he has great ability and knowledge; know-all.

ˈ**smarty-pants** (*infml*) (used esp as an affectionate term of address) person, esp a child, who thinks he is very clever: *OK, smarty-pants, how many questions did you get right?*

smart[2] /smɑːt/ *v* [I, Ipr] ~ **(from sth)** cause or feel a sharp stinging pain (of the body or the mind): *The bee-sting smarted terribly.* ○ *He smarted from the savage attacks on his film.* ○ *They're still smarting from their defeat in the final.*

▷ **smart** *n* [U] (*fml*) sharp physical or mental pain: *the constant smart of the blisters on his feet.*

smash /smæʃ/ *v* **1** [I, Ipr, Tn, Tn·pr, Tn·p, Cn·a] ~ **sth (up)**; ~ **sth open** (cause sth to) be broken violently into pieces: *the sound of a glass smashing (into pieces) on the floor* ○ *smash a window* ○ *smash (up) all the furniture* ○ *smash the furniture to pieces* ○ *The lock was rusty, so we had to smash the door open.* **2 (a)** [Tn, Tn·pr, Tn·p] hit (sth/sb) very hard: *smash the ball (out of the court)* ○ *I'll smash you in the eye!* ○ *The batsman smashed the ball up into the air.* **(b)** [Tn, Tn·pr] (in tennis) hit (a ball) downwards over the net with a hard overhand stroke: *He smashed the lob (straight at his opponent's body).* **3** [Tn, Tn·p] ~ **sth (up)** crash (a vehicle): *She smashed (up) her new car in the fog.* **4** [Tn] (*infml*) defeat or destroy (eg an opponent or his activities); end (esp sth bad): *We are determined to smash terrorism.* ○ *The champions were completely smashed in the final.* ○ *smash a record,* ie (in sport, etc) set a far better record ○ *Police smashed the drug ring.* **5** (phr v) **smash (sth) against, into, through, etc sth** (cause sth to) move with great force into, against etc, sth: *The car smashed into the wall* ○ *The elephant smashed through the trees.* ○ *She smashed the hammer down onto the box.* **smash sth down** make sth fall down by smashing it, eg with a hammer: *The fireman smashed the door down to reach the children.* **smash sth in** make a hole, dent, etc in sth by hitting it with great force: *Vandals smashed the door in.* ○ (*infml*) *I'll smash your head in!* ie said as a threat to hit sb.

▷ **smash** *n* **1** [sing] act or sound of smashing: *the smash of breaking glass* ○ *The plate hit the floor with a smash.* **2** (also ˈ**smash-up**) [C] car crash: *an awful smash(-up) on the motorway.* **3** [C] tennis stroke in which a player smashes the ball: *develop a powerful smash.* **4** [C] (also **smash** ˈ**hit**) (*infml*) play, song, film, etc which is suddenly very successful.

smash *adv* with a smash: *land smash on the floor* ○ *go/run smash into the wall.*

smashed *adj* [pred] (*sl*) drunk.

smasher *n* (*infml esp Brit*) excellent, attractive, etc person or thing: *She's a real smasher!*

smashing *adj* (*infml esp Brit*) excellent: *We had a smashing time on holiday!*

□ ˌ**smash-and-**ˈ**grab** [attrib] (of a robbery) in which the thief smashes a shop window to steal the goods on display: *a* ˌ*smash-and-*ˈ*grab raid.*

smattering /ˈsmætərɪŋ/ *n* [sing] ~ **(of sth)** slight knowledge, esp of a language: *have a smattering of French, German, etc.*

smear /smɪə(r)/ *v* **1** [Tn·pr] ~ **sth on/over sth/sb**; ~ **sth/sb with sth** spread a greasy or sticky substance, eg paint, on sth/sb: *smear oil on the machinery* ○ *smearing mud all over the wall* ○ *We smeared cream on our faces/smeared our faces with* *cream.* **2** [Tn] (**a**) make (sth) dirty or greasy; smudge: *The window was all smeared after the rain.* ○ *Don't smear the lens; I've just polished it.* (**b**) (*fig*) damage (sb or sb's reputation), eg by suggesting they have acted immorally: *In politics you expect to get smeared by your opponents.* **3** [Tn] blur (a drawing, an outline, etc) eg by rubbing it: *smear the print with one's finger.*

▷ **smear** *n* **1** mark made by smearing: *a smear of paint* ○ *smears of blood on the wall.* **2** ~ (**on sb/sth**) suggestion or accusation that damages sb's reputation: *This accusation of bribery is a vile smear on an honourable citizen.* ○ [attrib] *a smear campaign* ○ *smear tactics.* **3** specimen of a substance spread on a slide to be examined under a microscope: *a cervical smear*, ie taken from the cervix ○ [attrib] *a smear test.*

smeary /ˈsmɪərɪ/ *adj* (**-ier**, **-iest**) (*infml*) **1** smeared: *a smeary window.* **2** causing smears: *a smeary paintbrush.*

smell[1] /smel/ *n* **1** [U] ability to smell: *Taste and smell are closely connected.* ○ *The dogs can find drugs by smell.* **2** (**a**) [C, U] thing that is smelled; quality that allows sth to be smelled; odour: *a strong smell of gas* ○ *There's a smell of cooking.* ○ *The smells from the kitchen filled the room.* ○ *The cream has no smell.* (**b**) [sing] unpleasant smell: *There's a bit of a smell in here.* ○ *What a smell!* **3** [C usu *sing*] act of smelling sth: *Have a smell of this egg and tell me if it's bad.* ○ *One smell of the rotten meat was enough!*

▷ **smelly** *adj* (**-ier**, **-iest**) (*infml*) having a bad smell: *a smelly room, car, yard* ○ *smelly feet, breath, fumes.* **smelliness** *n* [U].

smell[2] /smel/ *v* (*pt, pp* **smelt** /smelt/ or **smelled**) ⇨ Usage at DREAM[2]. **1** (**a**) [Tn, Tf, Tng no passive] (not used in the continuous tenses; often with *can* or *could*) notice (sth/sb) by using the nose: *Do you smell anything unusual?* ○ *The dog smelt the rabbit a long way off.* ○ *I could smell (that) he had been smoking.* ○ *I can smell something burning.* (**b**) [Ipr, Tn] ~ (**at**) **sth** sniff sth in order to test its smell: *a dog smelling (at) a lamp-post* ○ *Smell this and tell me what it is.* **2** [I] (not used in the continuous tenses) be able to smell: *Can fish smell?* **3** (**a**) [I] (not used in the continuous tenses) have an unpleasant smell: *Your breath smells.* ○ *The fish has begun to smell.* (**b**) [La, Ipr] ~ (**of sth**) have a smell of the specified type: *The flowers smell sweet.* ○ *The dinner smells good.* ○ *What does the perfume smell like?* ○ *The meat smells of garlic.* ○ *Your breath smells of brandy.* **4** [Tn, Tng no passive] (*fig*) be able to detect (sth) by instinct: *The reporter began to smell a good story.* ○ *I can smell trouble (coming).* **5** (idm) **smell a ˈrat** (*infml*) suspect that sth is wrong: *I smelt a rat when he started being so helpful!* **6** (phr v) **smell sb/sth out** (**a**) detect sb/sth by smelling: *Specially-trained dogs can smell out drugs.* (**b**) discover sth by finding and interpreting clues: *The Secret Service smelled out a plot to kill the President.*

□ **ˈsmelling-salts** *n* [pl] sharp-smelling substances sniffed esp as a cure for faintness.

smelt[1] /smelt/ *v* [Tn] **1** heat and melt (ore) in order to obtain the metal it contains. **2** obtain (metal) in this way: *a copper-smelting works.*

smelt[2] /smelt/ *n* (*pl* unchanged or ~**s**) small fish eaten as food.

smelt[3] *pt, pp* of SMELL[2].

Smetana /ˈsmetənə/ Bedřich (1824-84), Czech composer. A patriot and nationalist, he often used folk tunes, esp in his most famous works, *The Bartered Bride* and *Ma Vlást* (*My Country*).

smew /smju:/ *n* type of small duck with a narrow beak. The male has black and white feathers.

smidgen (also **smidgin**) /ˈsmɪdʒən/ *n* [sing] ~ (**of sth**) (*infml esp US*) small bit or amount: *'Do you want some sugar?' 'Just a smidgen.'*

smilax /ˈsmaɪlæks/ *n* [C, U] **1** climbing plant that often has a prickly stem. The dried roots of some tropical species are used for making a non-alcoholic drink. **2** S African climbing plant of the asparagus family, often used for decoration.

smile /smaɪl/ *n* **1** expression of the face, usu with the corners of the mouth turned up, showing happiness, amusement, pleasure, etc: *with a relieved, amused, cheerful smile on his face* ○ *give sb a happy smile.* **2** (idm) **all ˈsmiles** looking very happy: *She was all smiles at the news of her win.*

▷ **smile** *v* **1** [I, Ipr] ~ (**at sb/sth**) give a smile or smiles: *smile happily, with pleasure, etc* ○ *He never smiles.* ○ *I smiled at the child and said 'Hello'.* **2** [Tn] express (sth) by means of a smile: *She smiled her approval.* ○ *I smiled my thanks.* **3** [Tn] give (the specified type of smile): *She smiled a bitter smile.* **4** (phr v) **smile on sb/sth** (*fml*) approve of or encourage sb/sth: *The council did not smile on our plan*, ie rejected it. ○ *Fortune smiled on us*, ie We were successful. **smilingly** *adv* with a smile or smiles.

smirch /smɜ:tʃ/ *v* [Tn] = BESMIRCH.

smirk /smɜ:k/ *n* silly or self-satisfied smile: *Wipe that smirk off your face!*

▷ **smirk** *v* [I] give a smirk.

NOTE ON USAGE: Compare **smirk**, **sneer**, **frown**, **scowl** and **grimace**. These verbs indicate people twisting their faces to express various, usually negative, attitudes. People **smirk** when they smile in a silly way to show that they are pleased with themselves, usually at the expense of somebody else. When we **sneer**, we curl our upper lip to express a superior or contemptuous attitude to other people: *He's always sneering at my suggestions.* We **frown** by bringing our eyebrows together to indicate displeasure, puzzlement or concentration. When **scowling** we twist the whole face to express anger, bad temper, etc: *He sits alone all day scowling at passers-by.* We also twist the whole face when we **grimace.** We usually **grimace** for a very short time as a reaction to pain or annoyance, or to cause laughter.

smite /smaɪt/ *v* (*pt* **smote** /sməʊt/, *pp* **smitten** /ˈsmɪtn/) [Tn] (*fml or joc*) **1** hit (sb/sth) hard; strike: *He smote the ball into the grandstand.* **2** have a great effect on (sb): *His conscience smote him.*

Smith[1] /smɪθ/ Adam (1723-90), Scottish philosopher and economist. He was a major figure of the Scottish *Enlightenment and a friend of *Hume. His *Inquiry into the Nature and Causes of the Wealth of Nations* is regarded as founding the modern study of economics and sets out the basic principles of the free-enterprise economy, with prices determined by supply and demand.

Smith[2] /smɪθ/ Ian Douglas (1919-), last prime minister of *Rhodesia. He declared the country independent without international recognition and led it until 1979, maintaining rule by the white population.

Smith[3] /smɪθ/ John (1580-1631), English explorer. He joined an expedition to colonize *Virginia in 1606. He claimed that he was taken prisoner by Indians and rescued by *Pocahontas. Later he became the colony's leader.

Smith[4] /smɪθ/ Stevie (1902-71), English poet. She wrote three novels, but is most famous for the biting wit of her poems, often illustrated by her own comic drawings.

Smith[5] /smɪθ/ Sydney (1771-1845), English churchman and author. He campaigned for many important causes, including Catholic emancipation and the abolition of slavery, and was one of the great wits of his day.

smith /smɪθ/ *n* **1** = BLACKSMITH. **2** (in compounds) person who makes metal utensils, ornaments, etc: *a ˈgoldsmith* ○ *a ˈsilversmith.*

▷ **smithy** /ˈsmɪðɪ/ *n* blacksmith's workshop.

smithereens /ˌsmɪðəˈri:nz/ *n* [pl] (used esp with *vs* meaning *break* or *destroy*) small pieces: *smash, blow, hammer, etc sth (in)to smithereens.*

Smithfield /ˈsmɪθfi:ld/ London's central meat market, situated in the *City.

Smith's /smɪθs/ (in full **ˌW H ˈSmith and Son**) (branch of a) large chain of British shops selling books, stationery, newspapers, etc.

Smithsonian Institution /smɪθˌsəʊnɪən ɪnstɪˈtju:ʃn; *US* -ˈtu:ʃn/ **the Smithsonian Institution** museum and research centre in Washington DC. It is the oldest scientific foundation in the USA. ⇨ article at MUSEUM.

smitten[1] *pp* of SMITE.

smitten[2] /ˈsmɪtn/ *adj* [pred] **1** ~ **with sth** deeply affected by (an emotion): *smitten with remorse for one's cruelty.* **2** ~ (**with sb/sth**) (*esp joc*) having taken a sudden, often romantic, liking (to sb): *I met Janet yesterday, and I'm rather smitten with her.*

smock /smɒk/ *n* (**a**) loose garment (often with smocking on it) worn over other clothes to protect them from dirt, etc: *Smocks were formerly worn by farm-workers.* ○ *The artist's smock was covered in paint.* (**b**) loose comfortable shirt-like garment worn esp by pregnant women: *a brightly-coloured smock worn over trousers.*

▷ **smocking** *n* [U] type of decoration on a garment made by gathering the cloth tightly with stitches: *delicate smocking on a baby's dress.*

smog /smɒg/ *n* [U] mixture of fog and smoke: *Smog used to bring London traffic to a standstill.* ⇨ Usage at FOG. ⇨ article at ENVIRONMENT.

smoke[1] /sməʊk/ *n* **1** [U] visible (usu white, grey or black) vapour coming from sth that is burning: *smoke from factory chimneys* ○ *The room was full of cigarette smoke.* **2** [C] (usu *sing*) (**a**) (*infml*) act or period of smoking tobacco: *They stopped work to have a smoke.* ○ *I haven't had a smoke all day.* (**b**) (*dated sl*) thing (esp a cigar or cigarette) to be smoked: *Has anyone got any smokes?* **3** (idm) **ˌgo up in ˈsmoke** (**a**) be completely burnt: *The whole house went up in smoke in less than an hour.* (**b**) (*fig*) result in failure; leave nothing of value behind: *When he crashed his car all his travel plans went up in smoke.* (**there is**) **ˌno ˌsmoke withˌout ˈfire** (*saying*) there is always some reason for a rumour: *He's denied having an affair with his secretary, but of course there's no smoke without fire.*

▷ **smokeless** *adj* [usu attrib] **1** burning with little or no smoke: *smokeless fuel.* **2** free from smoke: *a smokeless zone*, ie an area where smoke is prohibited. ⇨ article at ENVIRONMENT.

□ **ˈsmoke-bomb** (also **ˈsmoke-grenade**) *n* bomb that sends out clouds of smoke (used esp in police or military operations): *Smoke-bombs were thrown during the street riots.*

ˈsmoke detector device that sounds an alarm where there is smoke around, intended to prevent fires and save lives.

ˈsmoke-ring *n* smoke from a cigarette, etc blown out of the mouth in the shape of a ring.

ˈsmoke-screen *n* (**a**) clouds of smoke used to hide military, naval, police, etc operations. (**b**) (*fig*) action, explanation, etc designed to hide one's real intentions, activities, etc: *The export business was just a smoke-screen for his activities as a spy.*

ˈsmoke-stack *n* (**a**) funnel serving as an outlet for steam from a steamship. (**b**) tall chimney. (**c**) (*US*) funnel of a steam train.

smoke[2] /sməʊk/ *v* **1** [I] (**a**) give off smoke or other visible vapour: *a smoking volcano* ○ *smoking factory chimneys.* (**b**) (of a fire or fireplace) give off too much smoke (and send it out into the room instead of up the chimney): *This fireplace smokes (badly).* **2** [I, Tn] draw in smoke from burning tobacco or other substances through the mouth and let it out again; use cigarettes, etc in this way regularly: *Do you smoke?* ○ *She has never smoked.* ○ *He smokes a pipe.* ○ *She smokes 20 (cigarettes) a day.* **3** [Tn esp passive] preserve (meat, fish, etc) with smoke (from wood fires) to give a special taste: *smoked ham, salmon, mackerel, etc.* **4** [Tn esp passive] darken (esp glass) with smoke: *He looked at the sun through a sheet of smoked glass.* ○ *fit smoked plastic lenses in spectacles.* **5** (idm) **put that in your pipe and smoke it** ⇨ PIPE[1]. **a/the ˌsmoking ˈgun** (*esp US*) convincing proof that sb is guilty or that sth is true: *It seems likely she stole it, but there's no smoking gun.* **6** (phr v) **smoke sb/sth out** drive sb/sth out by means of smoke: *smoke out snakes from a hole* ○ (*fig*) *He was determined to smoke out the leaders of the gang*, ie bring them out of hiding. **smoke sth out** fill sth with smoke: *Turn off that pan — you're smoking the place out!*

▷ **smoker** *n* **1** person who smokes tobacco regularly: *a heavy smoker*, ie one who smokes very often ○ *Non-smokers often disapprove of smokers.* **2** carriage on a train where smoking is allowed: *Shall we sit in a smoker or a non-smoker?*

smoking *n* [U] activity or habit of smoking cigarettes, etc: *'No Smoking'*, eg on a notice in a public place ○ *Smoking isn't allowed in this cinema.* ○ *Smoking damages your health.* ○ [attrib] *the smoking section of an aircraft.* ˈ**smoking-jacket** *n* man's comfortable jacket, made of velvet, etc, worn (esp formerly) at home. ˈ**smoking-room** *n* room (in a hotel, etc) where smoking is allowed.

smoky /ˈsməʊkɪ/ *adj* (**-ier, -iest**) **1** giving out or having a lot of smoke; full of smoke: *smoky chimneys, fires, etc* ○ *the smoky atmosphere of an industrial town* ○ *This room is very smoky.* **2** like smoke in smell, taste or appearance: *smoky cheeses* ○ *rather a smoky whisky.* **3** like smoke in colour, appearance, etc: *a pretty smoky glass* ○ *a smoky grey coat.* ▷ **smokiness** *n* [U].

smolder (*US*) = SMOULDER.

Smollett /ˈsmɒlɪt/ Tobias George (1721-71), Scottish novelist. In works such as *Roderick Random* and *Humphry Clinker* he incorporates his own travels and experiences into fast-moving and often humorous stories.

smooch /smu:tʃ/ *v* [I] (*infml*) kiss and cuddle, sometimes when dancing slowly with another person: *hours of smooching in the back seat of the car* ○ *couples smooching on the dance floor.*
▷ **smooch** *n* [sing] (*infml*) activity of smooching: *having a smooch in the back row of the cinema.*

smooth[1] /smu:ð/ *adj* (**-er, -est**) **1** having an even surface without points, lumps, bumps, etc; not rough: *a smooth skin* ○ *a smooth road* ○ *a smooth sheet of ice* ○ *a smooth sea*, ie calm, free from waves ○ *Marble is smooth to the touch*, ie feels smooth when touched. Cf ROUGH[1]. **2** free from difficulties, problems, etc: *as smooth a journey as possible* ○ *The new bill had a smooth passage through Parliament.* ○ *They made things very smooth for me*, ie removed difficulties for me. **3** moving evenly, without bumps, jolts, stops, etc: *a smooth ride in a good car* ○ *a smooth landing in an aircraft* ○ *a smooth crossing by sea* ○ *smooth breathing.* **4** (of a liquid mixture) free from lumps; evenly mixed or beaten: *smooth custard* ○ *Mix the butter and sugar to a smooth paste.* **5** (a) tasting pleasant; not bitter: *a smooth whisky* ○ *a smooth cigar.* (b) (*fig*) flowing easily and evenly: *smooth verse* ○ *a smooth voice.* **6** (*often derog*) (usu used of men) flattering and agreeable (but perhaps insincere); (too) polite: *a smooth manner* ○ *a smooth, plausible individual.* **7** (idm) **in smooth ˈwater(s)** making even and easy progress: *The business seems to be in smooth waters these days.* **(as) smooth as ˈsilk/a baby's ˈbottom/ˈvelvet** very smooth: *Her skin is still as smooth as a baby's bottom.* **a smooth, slick, etc operator** ⇨ OPERATOR. **take the rough with the smooth** ⇨ ROUGH[3].
▷ **smoothie** (also **smoothy**) (*infml derog*) *n* person (usu a man) who behaves in a smooth[1](6) way: *Don't trust him — he's a real smoothie!*
smoothly *adv* in a smooth manner: *The engine is running smoothly now.* ○ *Things are not going very smoothly*, ie There are troubles, interruptions, etc.
smoothness *n* [U]: *the smoothness of her skin* ○ *the smoothness of the sea* ○ *the smoothness of the negotiations.*
□ ˌ**smooth-ˈtongued** (also ˌ**smooth-ˈspoken**) *adj* (*usu derog*) speaking in a smooth[1](6) way; persuasive in speech: ˌ*smooth-tongued* ˈ*salesmen.*

smooth[2] /smu:ð/ *v* **1** [Tn, Tn·pr, Tn·p] ~ **sth (away, back, down, out, etc)** make sth smooth or flat: *smooth down one's dress* ○ *smooth her skirt over her hips* ○ *smooth out a sheet on a bed* ○ *smooth down wood with sandpaper.* **2** (idm) **smooth sb's path** make progress easier for sb: *Speaking the language fluently certainly smoothed our path.* **smooth sb's** ˌ**ruffled** ˈ**feathers** make sb feel less angry or offended. **3** (phr v) **smooth sth away** get rid of (esp problems, difficulties, etc) smoothly and easily, or by smoothing: *smooth away wrinkles with cream* ○ *We'll smooth away any difficulties when we reach them.* ○ *Money helps to smooth away most problems.* **smooth sth over** make (problems, etc) seem less important: *It will be difficult for you to smooth over your differences after so many years.*

smorgasbord /ˈsmɔ:gəsbɔ:d/ *n* [U] (meal with a) variety of hot or cold savoury dishes served from a buffet: *Help yourself from the smorgasbord.*

smote *pt* of SMITE.

smother /ˈsmʌðə(r)/ *v* **1** [I, Tn] (cause sb to) die from lack of air, or from not being able to breathe; suffocate: *He smothered the baby with a pillow.* ○ (*fig*) *She felt smothered with kindness.* **2** [Tn] put out or keep down (a fire) by covering it with ashes, sand, etc: *If you put too much coal on the fire at once you'll smother it.* ○ *Smother the flames from the burning pan with a wet towel.* ○ (*fig*) *smother a yawn, smile, laugh, etc*, ie prevent it from developing ○ (*fig*) *He had to smother a giggle.* **3** [Tn·pr] ~ **sth/sb with/in sth** cover sth/sb thickly or to too great an extent: *a pudding smothered in cream* ○ *smother a child with kisses.*

smoulder (*US* **smolder**) /ˈsməʊldə(r)/ *v* [I] burn slowly without flame: *a cigarette smouldering in the ashtray* ○ (*fig*) *Hate smouldered inside him.* ○ *She smouldered silently with jealousy*, ie did not express it openly.

smudge /smʌdʒ/ *n* dirty or blurred mark, often caused by rubbing: *You've got a smudge of soot on your cheek.* ○ *Wash your hands or you'll make smudges on the writing-paper.*
▷ **smudge** *v* **1** [Tn] make a dirty or blurred mark or marks on (sth): *paper smudged with fingerprints* ○ *You've smudged my picture!* **2** [I] become blurred or smeared: *Wet ink smudges easily.*

smug /smʌg/ *adj* (**-gger, -ggest**) (*usu derog*) too pleased with or proud of oneself, one's achievements, etc; self-satisfied: *a life of smug respectability* ○ *smug optimism.* ▷ **smugly** *adv*: *smile smugly at the failures of others.* **smugness** *n* [U].

smuggle /ˈsmʌgl/ *v* [Tn, Tn·pr, Tn·p] ~ **sth/sb (into/out of/across/through sth)**; ~ **sth/sb in/out/across/through** **1** get (goods) secretly and illegally into or out of a country, esp without paying customs duty: *smuggle Swiss watches into England* ○ *smuggle drugs through customs* ○ *smuggle goods across a frontier* ○ *arrested for smuggling out currency.* **2** send, take or bring (sth/sb) secretly and in defiance of rules and regulations: *smuggle people out of the country* ○ *smuggle a prisoner through the main gates* ○ *smuggle a letter into prison.*
▷ **smuggler** /ˈsmʌglə(r)/ *n* person who smuggles: *This cave was used by smugglers in the eighteenth century.* ○ *drug smugglers.*
smuggling /ˈsmʌglɪŋ/ *n* [U] activity of smuggling: ˈ*drug-smuggling* ○ *There's a lot of smuggling across this frontier.*

NOTE ON USAGE: People **smuggle** goods from one country to another when they illegally take things like watches, drugs, cigarettes, etc across a border. These goods may be banned (eg drugs) or they may be more expensive in the second country because of duty (eg jewellery). Smugglers **run** guns, drugs and other prohibited dangerous items between countries, possibly as a regular activity. Goods (especially alcohol) are **bootlegged** when they are smuggled or manufactured and sold illegally. When records, films, books, etc are illegally copied and sold they are **pirated**.

smut /smʌt/ *n* **1** [C] (mark or spot make by a) bit of soot, dirt, etc: *dozens of smuts on my clean washing.* **2** [U] (*infml derog*) indecent or vulgar words, stories, pictures, etc: *Don't talk smut.* ○ *The tabloid papers are full of smut.*
▷ **smutty** *adj* (**-ier, -iest**) **1** marked with smuts (SMUT 1); dirty: *a child with a smutty face* ○ *smutty marks on the white table-cloth.* **2** (*infml derog*) (of talk, pictures, stories, etc) indecent; vulgar: *smutty books* ○ *smutty humour.* **smuttiness** *n* [U]: *the smuttiness of the comedian's jokes.*

Smuts /smʌts/ Jan Christiaan (1870-1950), S African statesman and general. He led his country's forces against Germany in both World Wars, and was prime minister 1939-48, opposing the policy of apartheid. He also played an important role in the *League of Nations and the *United Nations.

Sn *symb* tin.

snack /snæk/ *n* small meal, usu eaten in a hurry, esp between main meals: *Usually I only have a snack at lunchtime.* ○ *The children have a mid-morning snack of milk and biscuits.* ○ [attrib] *a snack lunch.*
▷ **snack** *v* [I] (*infml*) eat snacks between or instead of main meals: *I prefer to snack when I'm travelling rather than have a full meal.*
□ ˈ**snack-bar** *n* café, counter, etc where snacks may be bought: *We had coffee and sandwiches at the snack-bar.*

snaffle /ˈsnæfl/ *v* [Tn] (*Brit infml*) take (sth) for oneself, usu quickly and greedily or unlawfully: *They snaffled all the food at the party before we got there.* ○ *Thieves snaffled all the goods from the burnt warehouse.*

snafu /snæˈfu:/ *adj* [usu pred] (*sl esp military*) confused and disorganized (from the initial letters of the phrase '*s*ituation *n*ormal; *a*ll *f*ucked *u*p'): *The arrangements were completely snafu.*
▷ **snafu** *n* (*sl*) confused and disorganized situation.

snag /snæg/ *n* **1** small difficulty or obstacle, usu hidden, unknown or unexpected: *come across a snag* ○ *We hit* (ie encountered) *several snags while still at the planning stage.* ○ *There must be a snag in it somewhere.* ○ *The only snag is that I have no money.* **2** rough or sharp projection, which may be dangerous. **3** tear, hole or thread pulled out of place (esp in tights or stockings) in material that has caught on a snag(2): *I have a snag in my best black tights.*
▷ **snag** *v* (**-gg-**) [Tn] catch or tear (sth) on sth rough or sharp: *Her tights were badly snagged.* ○ *He snagged his sweater on the wire fence.*

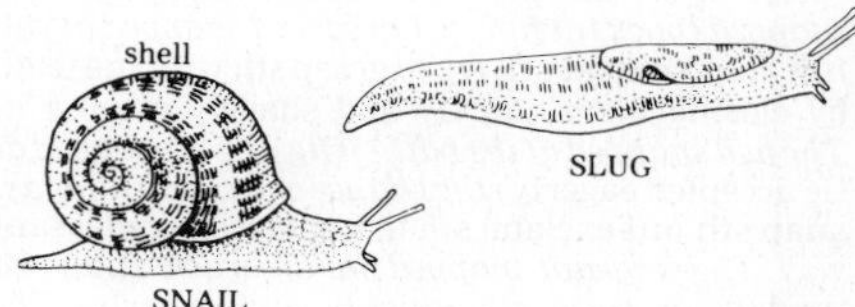

snail /sneɪl/ *n* **1** type of small soft slow-moving animal, usu with a hard spiral shell: *Snails have been eating our lettuces.* ○ *The snail retreated into its shell.* **2** (idm) **at a** ˈ**snail's pace** very slowly: *The old woman crossed the road at a snail's pace.*

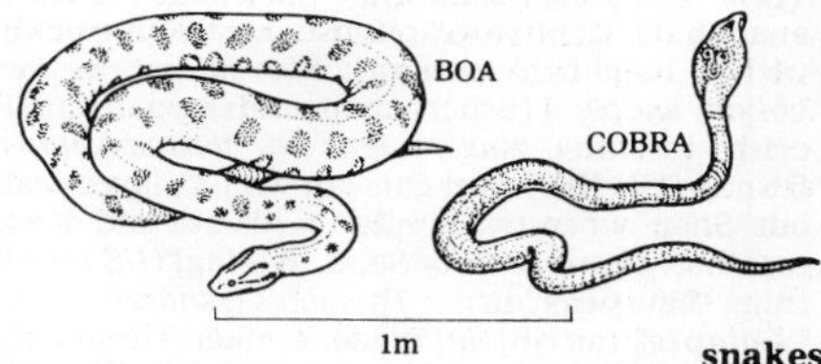

snakes

snake /sneɪk/ *n* **1** any of various types of long, legless crawling reptile, some of which are poisonous: *the scaly skin of the snake* ○ *cobras and other dangerous snakes.* **2** treacherous person. **3** (idm) **a** ˌ**snake in the** ˈ**grass** deceitful or treacherous person who pretends to be a friend: *That snake in the grass reported me to the boss.*
▷ **snake** *v* (phr v) **snake (its way) across, past, through, etc** move in a twisting way like a snake; follow a twisting winding course: *The road snakes (its way) through the mountains.* ○ *The river snaked away into the distance.*
snaky *adj* of or like a snake: *the snaky movements of the young dancers* ○ *narrow snaky roads through the hills.*
□ ˈ**snake-bite** *n* [C, U] wound or condition resulting from being bitten by a poisonous snake: *be ill from a snake-bite* ○ *an antidote for snake-bite*, ie sth that acts against the poison.
ˈ**snake-charmer** *n* entertainer who can control snakes and make them (seem to) move rhythmically to music.

ˌ**snakes and ˈladders** board game played with counters which can move up pictures of ladders (to progress) or down pictures of snakes (to go back).

ˈ**snakeskin** *n* skin of a snake, esp when made into leather (for bags, etc): *shoes made of snakeskin* ○ [attrib] *a snakeskin belt.*

snap[1] /snæp/ *v* (**-pp-**) **1** [I, Ipr, Ip, Tn, Tn·pr, Tn·p] (cause sth to) break suddenly with a sharp noise: *He stretched the rubber band till it snapped.* ○ *Suddenly the branch that he was standing on snapped off.* ○ *The great weight snapped the metal bar (in two).* ○ *(fig) After years of hard work and poverty, he finally snapped*, ie had a nervous breakdown, fell ill, etc. **2** [La, Ip, Tn, Tn·p, Cn·a] open or close (sth) with a sudden sharp noise; (cause sth to) make a sudden sharp noise: *The box snapped open.* ○ *The circus manager snapped his whip.* ○ *He snapped down the lid of the box.* ○ *She snapped her bag shut.* ○ *The shark snapped its jaws shut.* **3** [I, Tn] speak or say (sth) in a sharp (usu angry) voice: *'Come here at once,' she snapped.* ○ *He never speaks calmly — just snaps all the time.* **4** [Tn] (*infml*) take a quick photograph of (sb): *I snapped you sunbathing on the beach.* **5** (idm) **bite/snap sb's head off** ⇨ HEAD[1]. **snap one's ˈfingers** make a clicking noise by moving the second or third finger quickly against the thumb (eg to attract sb's attention, mark the beat of music, etc): *He snapped his fingers to attract the waiter.* ˌ**snap to atˈtention** come quickly and smartly to the position of attention(4). ˌ**snap ˈto it** (*infml*) (usu as a command) start moving, working, etc quickly; hurry up: *'I want those bricks moved; come on, snap to it!'* ˌ**snap ˈout of it** (*infml*) (often as a command) get (quickly) out of a (usu bad, unhappy, etc) mood. **6** (phr v) **snap at sb** speak to sb sharply and rudely: *'Shut up!' she snapped (back) at him.* ○ *I'm sorry I snapped at you just now.* **snap at sth** try to grasp sth with the teeth by closing them quickly and sharply around it: *The fish snapped at the bait.* ○ *(fig) They snapped at* (ie accepted eagerly) *the chance of a cheap holiday.* **snap sth out** exclaim sth in a sharp or unpleasant way: *The sergeant snapped out an order.* **snap sth up** buy or seize sth quickly and eagerly: *The cheapest articles at the sale were quickly snapped up.*

snap[2] /snæp/ *n* **1** [C] act or sound of snapping: *The dog made an unsuccessful snap at the meat.* ○ *The lid shut with a snap.* ○ *The oar broke with a snap.* **2** [C] short spell or period of (usu cold) weather: *There was a cold snap after Christmas.* **3** (also **snapshot**) [C] photograph (usu one taken quickly with a hand-held camera): *She showed us her holiday snaps.* **4** (usu in compounds) type of small crisp biscuit: ˈ*ginger-snaps* ○ ˈ*brandy-snaps.* **5 Snap** [U] (*Brit*) card-game in which players call out 'Snap' when two similar cards are laid down together: *play a game of Snap.* **6** [sing] (*US infml*) thing that is easy to do: *This job's a snap.*

▷ **snap** *adj* [attrib] (*infml*) done, made, etc quickly and with little or no warning: *a snap election* ○ *take a snap vote* ○ *a snap decision.*

snap *interj* (*Brit infml*) **1** (said in the game of Snap[2](5) when one notices that two similar cards have been laid down). **2** (said to draw attention to the similarity of two things): *Snap! You've got the same shoes as me.*

snap *adv* with a snapping sound: *Suddenly the oar went snap*, ie made a snapping sound as it broke.

snappish *adj* inclined to snap[1](3); bad-tempered or irritable: *a snappish small terrier* ○ *a snappish old man.*

snappy *adj* (**-ier**, **-iest**) **1** inclined to snap[1](3); irritable: *a snappy little dog* ○ *She's always snappy early in the morning.* **2** (*infml*) lively; quick: *snappy on her feet* ○ *a snappy dancer.* **3** (*infml*) [usu attrib] smart; trendy: *a snappy outfit* ○ *She's a very snappy dresser*, ie She dresses very smartly and trendily. **4** (idm) ˌ**make it ˈsnappy** (also ˌ**look ˈsnappy**) (*infml*) (often as a command) hurry up; be quick about it: *Look snappy! The bus is coming.* ○ *You'll have to make it snappy if you want to come too.* **snappily** *adv*: *'Go away', she said snappily.* **snappiness** *n* [U].

□ ˈ**snap bean** (*US*) runner bean (RUNNER) or other crisp bean.

ˈ**snap-brimmed** *adj* [attrib] (of a hat) that has a brim that can be turned down at the front and up at the back.

ˈ**snap fastener** (also ˈ**press stud**, *Brit infml* **popper**) device made of two small round metal or plastic parts that are pressed together to fasten dresses, skirts, etc: *the press stud on the collar of his evening shirt* ○ *the poppers on a child's pyjamas.*

ˈ**snapshot** *n* = SNAP[2] 3.

snapdragon /ˈsnæpdrægən/ *n* = ANTIRRHINUM.

snapper /ˈsnæpə(r)/ *n* type of large fish that lives in warm seas and is eaten as food.

snare

snare /sneə(r)/ *n* **1** trap for catching small animals and birds, esp one with a noose made of rope or wire: *The rabbit's foot was caught in a snare.* **2** (*fml*) thing likely to trap or injure sb: *All his promises were snares and delusions.* **3** (*music*) string of gut stretched underneath a side-drum to produce a sharp rattling sound.

▷ **snare** *v* [Tn] catch (sth) in a snare(1) or as if in a snare: *snare a rabbit* ○ *(fig) snare a rich husband.*

snarl[1] /snɑːl/ *v* **1** [I, Ipr] ~ (**at sb/sth**) (of dogs, etc) show the teeth and growl angrily: *The dog snarled at the milkman.* ○ *The tiger snarled frighteningly.* **2** [I, Ipr, Tn, Tn·pr] ~ (**sth**) (**at sb**) (of people) speak in an angry bad-tempered voice: *'Get out of here,' he snarled (at us).* ○ *an unpleasant man who snarled abuse at strangers.*

▷ **snarl** *n* (usu *sing*) act or sound of snarling: *the sudden snarl of the dog* ○ *answer with an angry snarl.*

snarl[2] /snɑːl/ *n* (*infml*) confused state; tangle: *My knitting was in a terrible snarl.*

▷ **snarl** *v* (phr v) **snarl (sth) up** (usu passive) (*infml*) (cause sth to) become confused, jammed, tangled, etc: *The machine snarled the material up.* ○ *Traffic has snarled up the city centre.* ˈ**snarl-up** *n* (*infml*) tangled or jammed state, esp of traffic: *a big snarl-up on the motorway.*

snatch /snætʃ/ *v* **1** [I, Ipr, Tn, Tn·pr, Tn·p] (try to) seize (sth/sb) quickly and sometimes rudely; grab: *It's rude to snatch.* ○ *She snatched the letter from me/out of my hand.* ○ *The baby had been snatched from its pram.* ○ *He snatched up his gun and fired.* **2** [Tn] take or get (sth) quickly, esp when a chance to do so occurs: *snatch an hour's sleep* ○ *snatch a meal between jobs.* **3** (phr v) **snatch at sth** (**a**) try to grasp sth: *He snatched at the ball but did not catch it.* (**b**) (*fig*) grasp sth eagerly and quickly: *snatch at every opportunity.*

▷ **snatch** *n* **1** [sing] sudden attempt to seize (sth) quickly: *make a snatch at sth.* **2** [C esp *pl*] short part or period; brief extract: *work in snatches*, ie not continuously ○ *short snatches of song* ○ *overhear snatches of conversation.*

snatcher *n* (often in compounds) person who snatches (and takes away): *a baby snatcher* ○ *a bag snatcher.*

snazzy /ˈsnæzɪ/ *adj* (**-ier**, **-iest**) (*infml*) (esp of clothes) smart and stylish: *a snazzy little hat* ○ *a very snazzy new car* ○ *She's a very snazzy dresser*, ie She always dresses fashionably. ▷ **snazzily** *adv*: *dress snazzily.* **snazziness** *n* [U].

sneak /sniːk/ *v* **1** [I, Ipr] ~ (**on sb**) (**to sb**) (*Brit infml derog*) (used esp by children) tell an adult about the faults, wrongdoings, etc of another child: *She sneaked on her best friend to the teacher.* **2** [Tn] (*infml*) take (sth) secretly (often without permission): *sneak a chocolate from the box* ○ *sneak a look at the Christmas presents.* **3** (phr v) **sneak into, out of, past, etc sth**; **sneak in, out, away, back, past, etc** go quietly and secretly in the direction specified: *He stole the money and sneaked out of the house.* ○ *The cat ate the food and sneaked off.* **sneak up (on sb/sth)** approach quietly, staying out of sight until the last moment: *James loves sneaking up on his sister to frighten her.* ⇨ Usage at PROWL.

▷ **sneak** *n* (*infml*) cowardly deceitful person (esp one who informs on others).

sneak *adj* [attrib] acting or done without warning; secret and unexpected: *a sneak attack* ○ *a sneak preview* ○ *a sneak look at a letter.*

sneaker *n* (usu *pl*) (*US*; *Brit infml*) = PLIMSOLL: *He wore old jeans and a pair of sneakers.*

sneaking *adj* [attrib] (esp of an unwanted feeling) secret and unexpressed: *have a sneaking respect, sympathy, etc for sb* ○ *I have a sneaking* (ie unproved and vague but possibly right) *suspicion that he stole my wallet.*

sneaky *adj* (**-ier**, **-iest**) (*infml derog*) done or acting in a secret or deceptive way: *sneaky behaviour* ○ *This sneaky girl was disliked by the rest of the class.* **sneakily** *adv.* **sneakiness** *n* [U].

□ ˈ**sneak-thief** *n* person who steals things without using force, eg through open doors and windows.

sneer /snɪə(r)/ *v* [I, Ipr] ~ (**at sb/sth**) smile with the upper lip curled, to show contempt (for sb/sth); laugh scornfully: *sneer at one's supposed inferiors* ○ *I resent the way he sneers at our efforts.* ⇨ Usage at SMIRK.

▷ **sneer** *n* look, smile, word, phrase, etc that shows contempt: *sneers of disbelief* ○ *You can wipe that sneer off your face!*

sneeringly /ˈsnɪərɪŋlɪ/ *adv.*

sneeze /sniːz/ *n* sudden uncontrollable noisy outburst of air through the nose and mouth (usu caused by irritation in the nose from dust, etc or when one has a cold): *coughs and sneezes* ○ *She le[t] out a loud sneeze.*

▷ **sneeze** *v* [I] **1** make a sneeze: *With all that dus[t] about, he couldn't stop sneezing.* ○ *Use a handkerchief when you sneeze.* **2** (idm) **not to be ˈsneezed at** (*infml esp joc*) worth considering or having; not to be despised: *A prize of £50 is not to be sneezed at.*

snick /snɪk/ *v* [Tn] make a small cut or notch in (sth): *I snicked my finger on the sharp knife.*

▷ **snick** *n* small cut or notch: *a tiny snick in the dress material.*

snicker /ˈsnɪkə(r)/ *v* laugh in a suppressed, esp unpleasant, way; snigger: *snickering at obscene pictures.* ⇨ Usage at GIGGLE.

▷ **snicker** *n* suppressed, esp unpleasant, laugh; snigger.

snide /snaɪd/ *adj* (*derog*) **1** critical in an indirect unpleasant way; sneering: *snide remarks about the chairman's wife* ○ *He's always making snide comments about her appearance.* **2** (*US*) (of an action) worthy of contempt: *That was a snide trick*

▷ **snidely** *adv.* **snideness** *n* [U].

sniff /snɪf/ *v* **1** [I] draw air in through the nose so that there is a sound: *sniffing and trying not to weep* ○ *They all had colds and were sniffing and sneezing.* **2** (**a**) [I, Ipr, Tn] ~ (**at**) **sth** draw air in through the nose as one breathes, esp to discover or enjoy the smell of sth: *sniff the sea air* ○ *sniff (at) a rose* ○ *The dog was sniffing (at) the lamp-post.* (**b**) [Tn, Tn·p] ~ **sth** (**up**) draw sth up through the nose: *snif[f] snuff* ○ *He sniffed the vapour up (through his nose)* (**c**) [Tn] (*infml*) take (a dangerous drug) by breathing it in through the nose: *sniff glue.* **3** [Tn] say (sth) in a self-pitying, complaining way: *'Nobody understands me,' he sniffed.* **4** (phr v) **sniff at sth** ignore or show contempt for sth: (*infml*) *His generous offer is not to be sniffed at*, ie should be considered seriously. **sniff sb out** (*infml*) discover sb; find sb out: *sniff out the culprit* ○ *The police were determined to sniff out the ringleaders.*

▷ **sniff** *n* act or sound of sniffing; breath (of air etc): *tearful sniffs* ○ *get a sniff of sea air* ○ *One snif[f] of this is enough to kill you.* ○ *'I'm going,' she said with a sniff.*

sniffle /snɪfl/ *v* [I] sniff slightly or repeatedly (esp because one is crying or has a cold): *I wish you wouldn't keep sniffling.*

▷ **sniffle 1** *n* act or sound of sniffling. **2** (idm) **get** have the ˈ**sniffles** (*infml*) get/have a slight cold.

snifter /ˈsnɪftə(r)/ *n* **1** (*infml*) small amount of an alcoholic drink, esp spirits: *have a quick snifter before the party.* **2** glass shaped like a small bowl that narrows at the top: *a snifter of brandy.*

snigger /ˈsnɪgə(r)/ *n* half-suppressed unpleasant laugh, (esp at sth improper or at another's misfortune): *Her shabby appearance drew sniggers from the guests.*

▷ **snigger** *v* [I, Ipr] ~ **(at sb/sth)** laugh in this way: *superior people who sniggered at her foreign accent.* ⇨ Usage at GIGGLE.

snip /snɪp/ *v* (**-pp-**) **1** [Ipr, Tn] ~ **(at) sth** cut sth sharply (esp with scissors or shears) in short quick strokes: *snip (at) a stray lock of hair.* **2** (phr v) **snip sth off** remove sth with short quick strokes: *snip off a few loose threads* ○ *snip the corner off the carton of milk.*

▷ **snip** *n* **1** cut made by snipping: *There's a snip in this cloth.* **2** small piece cut off by snipping: *snips of material scattered over the floor.* **3** act of snipping: *With a few quick snips of the shears he pruned the bush.* **4** (*Brit infml*) surprisingly cheap article; bargain: *It's a snip at only 50p!*

snipping *n* small piece of material, etc snipped off a larger piece: *a patchwork quilt made of snippings from old clothes.*

snipe[1] /snaɪp/ *n* (*pl* unchanged) water-bird with a long straight bill that lives in marshes. ⇨ illus at BIRD.

snipe[2] /snaɪp/ *v* [I, Ipr] ~ **(at sb/sth) 1** shoot from a hiding place (usu from a distance): *terrorists sniping at soldiers from well-concealed positions.* **2** (*fig*) make unpleasant critical remarks attacking sb/sth: *sniping at political opponents* ○ *Film stars are often sniped at in the newspapers.*

▷ **sniper** *n* person who snipes: *shot by snipers.*

snippet /ˈsnɪpɪt/ *n* **1** small piece cut off. **2** ~ **(of sth)** small piece or item (of information, news, etc); brief extract: *snippets of gossip* ○ *I've got a snippet of information that might interest you.*

snitch /snɪtʃ/ *v* (*Brit sl*) **1** [Tn] steal (sth) by taking it quickly: *'Who's snitched my pen?'* **2** [I, Ipr] ~ **(on sb)** inform on sb; sneak: *Promise you won't snitch (on me)?*

snivel /ˈsnɪvl/ *v* (**-ll-**; *US* also **-l-**) (*derog*) [I] **(a)** cry and sniff in a miserable, usu self-pitying, way: *a tired snivelling baby.* **(b)** complain in a miserable whining way: *She's always snivelling about her unhappy childhood.*

▷ **snivelling** (*US* also **sniveling**) *adj* [attrib] (*derog*) tending to whine and complain; weak: *He's a snivelling idiot!*

sniveller (*US* **sniveler**) *n* (*derog*) person who snivels.

snob /snɒb/ *n* (*derog*) **(a)** person who pays too much respect to social position and wealth, or who despises people of a lower social position: *snobs who despised their working-class son-in-law.* **(b)** person who feels he has superior tastes, knowledge, etc: *an intellectual snob* ○ *a wine snob who will only drink the best wines.*

▷ **snobbery** /ˈsnɒbərɪ/ *n* [U] (*derog*) behaviour, language, etc characteristic of a snob: *They considered her behaviour a shameful piece of snobbery.*

snobbish *adj* (*derog*) of or like a snob: *a snobbish contempt for the poor* ○ *a snobbish attitude to pop music.* **snobbishly** *adv.* **snobbishness** *n* [U].

□ ˈ**snob appeal** (also ˈ**snob value**) qualities that appeal to people's snobbishness: *This part of the town has a lot of snob appeal.* ○ *This car sells well because of its snob value.*

SNOBOL (also **Snobol**) /ˈsnəʊbɒl/ *abbr* (*computing*) string-oriented symbolic language (a programming language, used esp for handling symbols and text).

snog /snɒg/ *v* (**-gg-**) [I, Ipr] ~ **(with sb)** (*Brit infml*) kiss and cuddle: *snog in the back row of the cinema.*

▷ **snog** *n* [sing] (*Brit infml*) act of snogging: *have a bit of a snog.*

snogging *n* [U] (*Brit infml*) action of cuddling and kissing.

snook /snu:k/ *n* (idm) **cock a snook at sb/sth** ⇨ COCK[3].

snooker

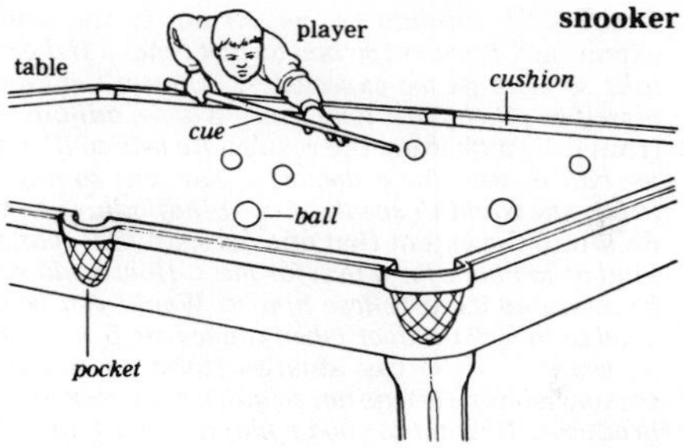

table player cushion cue ball pocket

snooker /ˈsnu:kə(r)/ *n* [U] game played with 15 red balls and 7 balls of other colours on a billiard-table: [attrib] *a snooker match.* ⇨ illus, Cf POOL[2] 4.

▷ **snooker** *v* [Tn esp passive] **1** leave (an opponent) in a difficult position when playing snooker. **2** (*infml fig*) place (sb) in a difficult position; trick or defeat (sb): *You can't win; you've been completely snookered!*

snoop /snu:p/ *v* (*infml usu derog*) **1** [I, Ipr, Ip] ~ **(about/around sth)**; ~ **(about/around)** search or investigate (eg to find mistakes, signs that people are breaking rules, etc) in a persistent and secretive way: *snooping around at night* ○ *snooping about the school entrance looking for late-comers.* **2** [Ipr] ~ **into sth** try to find out things that do not concern oneself; pry into.

▷ **snooper** *n* (*usu derog*) person who snoops: *a government snooper.*

snooty /ˈsnu:tɪ/ *adj* (**-ier**, **-iest**) (*infml derog*) showing disapproval and contempt towards others: *a snooty letter refusing the invitation* ○ *She's so snooty; she never speaks to the neighbours.*

▷ **snootily** /-ɪlɪ/ *adv.* **snootiness** *n* [U].

snooze /snu:z/ *v* [I] (*infml*) take a short sleep (esp during the day); doze: *Dad was snoozing by the fire.*

▷ **snooze** *n* [sing] (*infml*) a short sleep; nap: *I'm going to have a snooze after lunch.*

snore /snɔ:(r)/ *v* [I, Ip] breathe roughly and noisily while sleeping: *snoring noisily with his mouth open* ○ *Does my snoring bother you?*

▷ **snore** *n* act or sound of snoring: *Loud snores from the other room kept her awake.*

snorer /ˈsnɔ:rə(r)/ *n* person who snores habitually.

snorkel /ˈsnɔ:kl/ *n* **1** tube that allows a swimmer to take in air while under water. **2** device that allows a submarine to take in air while under water.

▷ **snorkel** *v* [I] (**-ll-**; *US* **-l-**) swim with a snorkel. **snorkelling** (*US* **-keling**) /ˈsnɔ:kəlɪŋ/ *n* [U] action or sport of swimming with a snorkel.

snort /snɔ:t/ *v* **1** [I] (usu of animals, esp horses) force air out through the nostrils with a loud noise. **2** [I, Ipr] ~ **(at sb/sth)** (of people) do this to show impatience, contempt, disgust, amusement, etc: *snort with rage (at sb/sth)* ○ *snort with mirth at the suggestion.* **3** to sniff (drugs): *snort cocaine.*

▷ **snort** *n* **1** act or sound of snorting: *give a snort of contempt* ○ *She could not conceal a snort of laughter.* **2** (*infml*) small drink of alcohol swallowed in one gulp. **3** (*sl*) small amount of a drug that is sniffed: *a quick snort of cocaine.*

snorter *n* (esp *sing*) (*infml*) thing that is remarkably impressive, violent, difficult, etc: *She sent me a real snorter of a letter.*

snot /snɒt/ *n* [U] (*infml*) mucus of the nose: *snot running down the child's nose.*

▷ **snotty** *adj* (**-ier**, **-iest**) (*infml*) **1** running with or covered with snot: *a child with a snotty nose* ○ *washing his snotty handkerchiefs.* **2** (also ˌ**snotty-**ˈ**nosed**) (*derog*) superior; snooty: *He's such a snotty-nosed little* ˈ*wimp.*

snout /snaʊt/ *n* **1** [C] projecting nose and mouth of an animal (esp a pig): *a sow with her snout in a trough of food.* ⇨ illus at ANIMAL, PIG. **2** [C] projecting front part of sth thought to resemble a snout: *the ugly snout of a revolver.* **3** [C] (*Brit sl derog*) person's nose: *a huge red snout* ○ *She's always poking her snout into everything,* ie interfering. **4** [C] (*Brit sl*) police informer. **5** [U] (*Brit sl*) tobacco: *Got any snout?*

Snow /snəʊ/ C(harles) P(ercy) (1905-80), English author. His works, esp the *Strangers and Brothers* series, draw on his own experiences as a scientist and civil servant and examine the relationship between the arts and the sciences.

snow[1] /snəʊ/ *n* **1** [U] frozen water vapour that falls to the ground from the sky in soft white flakes; mass of such flakes on the ground, etc: *a heavy fall of snow* ○ *roads deep in snow* ○ *Children were playing in the snow.*

British people often associate snow with Christmas. It conjures up images of Christmas-related activities like tobogganing, snowballing and making snowmen, and of being warm and cosy indoors with log fires and roast chestnuts. These romantic associations actually come from North America, where snow at Christmas is much more common than in Britain. One of the most popular songs of all time, for example, is 'I'm dreaming of a white Christmas' by the American composer Irving *Berlin. The image of Father Christmas riding a sledge pulled by reindeer through the snow, often seen on Christmas cards and postage stamps issued around Christmas, also comes from the USA

2 [C usu *pl*] (*fml*) fall of snow: *The snows came early that year.* **3** [U] (*sl*) powdered cocaine. **4** (idm) **pure as the driven snow** ⇨ PURE. **white as snow** ⇨ WHITE[1].

□ ˈ**snowball** *n* mass of snow pressed into a hard ball for throwing in play: *children throwing snowballs at each other.* — *v* [I] **1** throw snowballs: *children snowballing in the park.* **2** (*fig*) grow quickly in size, importance, etc: *Opposition to the war snowballed.*

ˈ**snow-blind** *adj* [usu pred] (temporarily) unable to see because the eyes are dazzled by the glare of the sun on snow. ˈ**snow-blindness** *n* [U]: *skiers suffering from snow-blindness.*

ˈ**snow-blower** *n* (*esp US*) machine for blowing snow from roads, pathways, etc.

ˈ**snow-bound** *adj* unable to travel, go out, etc because of heavy falls of snow: *a snow-bound train* ○ *We were snow-bound in the cottage for two weeks.*

ˈ**snow-capped** *adj* (*rhet*) (of mountains, etc) with the peak covered in snow.

ˈ**snow-covered** (also *rhet* ˈ**snow-clad**) *adj* covered with snow: *snow-covered roofs* ○ *snow-clad fir trees.*

ˈ**snow-drift** *n* deep bank of snow heaped up by the wind: *The train ran into a snow-drift.*

ˈ**snowdrop** *n* type of small white flower growing from a bulb at the end of winter or early spring. ⇨ illus at PLANT.

ˈ**snowfall** *n* **1** [C] fall of snow on one occasion: *There was a heavy snowfall last week.* **2** [U] amount of snow that falls in a period of time (eg one winter or one year) in a certain place: *The average snowfall here is 10 cm a year.*

ˈ**snow-field** *n* permanent wide expanse of snow, eg on high mountains.

ˈ**snowflake** *n* any of the soft small collections of ice crystals that fall as snow: *snowflakes melting as they reached the ground.*

ˈ**snow-goose** *n* large white goose with black wing tips that lives in arctic areas.

ˈ**snow job** (*infml esp US*) attempt at deception or persuasion by elaborate, often insincere, talk: *They're claiming that he's not guilty but that's just a snow job.*

ˈ**snow-leopard** *n* (also **ounce**) type of large wild cat of the mountainous areas of central Asia, with pale brown or grey fur and black markings.

ˈ**snow-line** *n* level (in feet or metres) above which snow lies permanently at any one place: *climb above the snow-line.*

ˈ**snowman** /-mæn/ *n* (*pl* **-men** /-men/) figure of a man made of snow, esp by children for fun.

snowmobile /ˈsnəʊməbi:l/ *n* motor vehicle designed to travel over snow, with runners or special tracks.

ˈ**snow-plough** (*US* **snow-plow**) *n* device or vehicle for clearing snow from roads, railways, etc.

ˈ**snow-shed** *n* (*esp US*) shelter with a long roof over a stretch of road or railway to prevent it being blocked by falling or sliding snow.

ˈ**snow-shoe** *n* device with a frame and leather straps, attached to the bottom of a shoe to allow a person to walk on deep snow without sinking in.

ˈ**snowstorm** *n* heavy fall of snow, esp with a strong wind.

ˌ**snow-**ˈ**white** *adj* pure bright white in colour: *ˌsnow-white ˈshirts.*

snow[2] /snəʊ/ *v* **1** [I] (used only in 3rd pers sing with *it*) come down from the sky as snow: *It snowed all day.* ○ *It was snowing when I woke up.* **2** [Tn] (*US infml*) attempt to deceive or persuade (sb) by elaborate but often insincere talk. **3** (phr v) **snow sb in/up** (usu passive) prevent sb from going out by snowing heavily: *We were snowed in for three days last winter by the blizzards.* **snow sb under** (*US infml*) (esp passive) defeat (eg an opponent) heavily. **snow sb under (with sth)** (usu passive) overwhelm sb: *I was snowed under with work.* ○ *snowed under with applications for the job.*

▷ **snowy** *adj* (**-ier, -iest**) **1** covered with snow: *snowy roofs.* **2** with snow falling: *snowy weather.* **3** as white or fresh as newly fallen snow: *a snowy (white) tablecloth.* ˈ**snowy owl** large white owl of the northern hemisphere.

Snowdon /ˈsnəʊdn/ highest mountain in Wales, 1 085 m (3 560 ft) high. It lies in the Snowdonia National Park, an important tourist centre. A railway goes to the summit.

SNP /ˌes en ˈpiː/ *abbr* Scottish Nationalist Party. ⇨ articles at POLITICS, SCOTLAND.

Snr *abbr* = SEN 3.

snub[1] /snʌb/ *v* (**-bb-**) [Tn esp passive] treat (sb) coldly, rudely or with contempt, esp by paying no attention (to him): *She was repeatedly snubbed by her neighbours.* ○ *She snubbed them by not replying to their invitation.*

▷ **snub** *n* snubbing words or behaviour: *suffer a snub* ○ *hurt by the snubs of the other children.*

snub[2] /snʌb/ *adj* (of a nose) short and turned up at the end.

□ ˈ**snub-nosed** *adj*: *a snub-nosed little dog.*

snuff[1] /snʌf/ *n* **1** [U] powdered tobacco taken into the nose by sniffing: *take a pinch of snuff.* **2** (idm) **up to** ˈ**snuff** (*infml*) (usu with negatives) reaching an acceptable standard: *Your work hasn't been up to snuff lately.*

□ ˈ**snuff-box** *n* small, usu decorative, box for holding snuff: *She collects snuff-boxes.*

snuff[2] /snʌf/ *v* **1** [Tn] cut or pinch off the burnt black end of the wick of (a candle). **2** (idm) ˈ**snuff it** (*Brit sl joc*) die: *His dad snuffed it a couple of years ago.* **3** (phr v) **snuff sth out** (**a**) put out (a candle flame, etc); extinguish sth. (**b**) put an end to sth; finish sth: *His hopes were nearly snuffed out.*

▷ **snuffer** *n* cone-shaped device for putting out candles.

snuffle /ˈsnʌfl/ *v* [I, Ip] (**a**) make sniffing noises: *The dog was snuffling around the roots of a tree.* (**b**) breathe noisily (as when the nose is partly blocked with catarrh): *a child snuffling with a bad cold.*

▷ **snuffle** *n* act or sound of snuffling: *speak in/with a snuffle,* ie with a blocked nose.

snug /snʌg/ *adj* (**-gg-**) **1** sheltered from cold, wind, etc; warm and comfortable; cosy: *a snug little house* ○ *snug in bed* ○ *The children are wrapped up snug by the fire.* **2** (of clothes) fitting (too) tightly or closely: *a snug-fitting coat* ○ *This jacket's a bit snug now.* **3** (*infml*) enough to be comfortable: *a snug little income.* **4** (idm) **(as) snug as a bug in a rug** (*joc infml*) very snug and cosy.

▷ **snug** *n* (*Brit*) small warm room, esp in a pub, with seats for only a few people.

snugly *adv* **1** warmly and comfortably: *They were curled up snugly in bed.* **2** tidily and tightly: *He fitted the map snugly into the bag.*

snugness *n* [U].

snuggle /ˈsnʌgl/ *v* [I, Ip] ~ **(up to sb)**; ~ **(up/down)** lie or get close (to sb) for warmth, comfort or affection: *The child snuggled up to her mother.* ○ *They snuggled up (together) in bed.* ○ *She snuggled down in bed.*

so[1] /səʊ/ *adv* (used before *adjs* and *advs*) **1** to such an extent: *Last time I saw him he was so fat!* ○ *Don't look so angry* (ie as angry as you appear now)! **2 not** ~ + *adj/adv* (+ **as...**) not to the same extent (as): *It wasn't so bad as last time!* ○ *It didn't take so long as we expected.* ○ *I haven't enjoyed myself so much for a long time.* **3** ~ + *adj/adv* + **(that)...** (indicating the result): *He was so ill that we had to send for a doctor.* ○ *She was so angry (that) she couldn't speak.* **4** ~ + *adj/adv* + **as to do sth** to the extent that one does sth: *She was so kind as to phone for a taxi for me.* ○ *How could you be so stupid as to believe him?* ○ *Would you be so good as to lock the door when you leave?* **5** ~ + *adj* + **a/an** + *n* + **(as sb/sth)** (used in making comparisons): *He was not so quick a learner as his brother.* ○ *He's not so good a player as his wife.* ○ *Is this so unusual a case* (ie more unusual than most)? **6** very; extremely: *I'm so glad to see you.* ○ *It was* ˈ*so kind of you to remember my birthday* ○ *We have* ˈ*so much to do.* ○ *She's feeling so much better today.* **7** (idm) **not so much sth as sth** not one thing but rather sth else: *She's not so much poor as careless with money.* **so many/much** an unspecified number or amount: *A recipe tells you that you need so many eggs, so much milk, etc.* ○ *Write on the form that you stayed so many nights at so much per night.* ˌ**so much** ˈ**sth** a great deal of (nonsense, etc): *His promises were just so much meaningless talk.* ˌ**so much for** ˈ**sb/**ˈ**sth** nothing further need be said or done about sb/sth: *So much for our hopes of going abroad — we can forget it.* ˌ**so much** ˈ**so that** /ðæt/ to such an extent that: *We are very busy — so much so that we can't manage to take a holiday this year.* **with not/without so much as sth** with not even sth: *Off he went, without so much as a 'goodbye'.*

so[2] /səʊ/ *adv* **1** in this or that way; thus: *Stand with your arms out, so.* ○ *So it was that he had his first sight of snow.* **2** (used to avoid repetition, esp after *believe, hope, suppose, tell, say, do*): *'Is he coming?' 'I believe so.'* ○ *I'm not sure if I'll succeed, but I certainly hope so.* ○ *'He's got the job?' 'So she said.'* ○ *They think she may try to phone. If so, someone must stay here.* **3** (used to express agreement): *'You were invited to that party, weren't you?' 'So I was, I'd forgotten.'* ○ *'They won the championship five years ago.' 'So they did.'* ○ *'There's a bird nesting in the garage.' 'So there is.'* **4** also: *He is divorced and so am I.* ○ *'I've been to Moscow.' 'So have I.'* **5** (idm) **and** ˈ**so on (and** ˈ**so forth)** (used to show that a list or sequence continues in a similar way): *He talked about how much we owed to our parents, our duty to our country and so on and so forth.* **so as to do sth** with the intention of doing sth: *I left a message so as to be sure of contacting her.* ○ *He disconnected the phone so as not to be disturbed.* **so** ˈ**be it** (indicating an acceptance of events, facts, etc): *If he doesn't want to be involved, then so be it.* **so that; so...that** (**a**) with the aim that; in order that: *She worked hard so that everything would be ready by 6 o'clock.* ○ *He has so organized his life that his wife suspects nothing.* (**b**) with the result that; to the extent that: *Nothing more was heard from him so that we began to wonder if he was dead.* ○ *He so adores his daughters that he keeps buying them expensive toys.*

□ ˈ**so-and-so** *n* (*pl* **so-and-so's**) (*infml*) (**a**) imaginary or unknown person; some person or other: *Let's suppose a Mr So-and-so registers at the hotel.* (**b**) (*derog*) person who is disliked: *Some so-and-so has pinched my towel.* ○ *Our neighbour's a bad-tempered old so-and-so.*

ˌ**so-**ˈ**called** *adj* [usu attrib] (*often derog*) (used to suggest that the words used to describe sb/sth are not appropriate): *Where are your ˌso-called ˈfriends now?* ○ *Our ˌso-called ˈvilla by the sea was a small bungalow two miles from the coast.* ○ *This is the patio, so-called — it's really just the back yard.*

so[3] /səʊ/ *conj* **1** (indicating result) and that is why: *The shops were closed so I didn't get any milk.* ○ *The manager was ill so I went in his place.* ○ *These glasses are very expensive so please be careful with them.* **2** (*infml*) (indicating purpose): *I gave you a map so you wouldn't get lost.* ○ *She whispered to me so no one else would hear.* **3** (used to introduce the next part of the story): *So now it's winter again and I'm still unemployed.* ○ *So after shouting and screaming for an hour she walked out in tears.* **4** (used to introduce a statement on which one wishes to comment in a critical or contrasting way): *So I've been in prison for three years. That doesn't mean I can't do a job.* ○ *So you've come back. What's your story this time?* **5** (idm) **so what?** (*infml*) I admit this may be true but I am not concerned: *He's fifteen years younger than me. So* ˈ*what?* ○ *So ˌwhat if he* ˈ*is?*

so[4] = **soh.**

So *abbr* (*US*) South(ern).

soak /səʊk/ *v* **1** (**a**) [I, Ipr] ~ **(in sth)** become thoroughly wet by being in liquid or by absorbing liquid: *The dirty clothes are soaking in soapy water.* ○ *Leave the dried beans to soak overnight.* (**b**) [Tn, Tn·pr] ~ **sth (in sth)** cause sth to absorb as much liquid as possible: *soak bread in milk* ○ *He soaked his stained shirt in hot water.* ○ (*fig*) *He soaked himself in* (ie allowed himself to absorb) *the atmosphere of the place.* **2** [Ipr, Ip] ~ **into/through sth**; ~ **in** enter (and pass through) sth; penetrate: *The rain had soaked through his coat.* ○ *Clean up that wine before it soaks in(to the carpet).* **3** [Tn] (*infml*) extract money from (sb) by charging or taxing very heavily: *Are you in favour of soaking the rich?* **4** (idm) **soaked/wet to the skin** ⇨ SKIN. **5** (phr v) **soak sth off/out** remove sth by soaking in water: *soak out a stain from a shirt* ○ *Soak a label off a jam jar.* **soak sb through** make a person and his clothes completely wet: *Don't stand out there: you'll get soaked through.* **soak sth up** (**a**) take in (liquid); absorb sth: *Use a paper towel to soak up the cooking oil.* (**b**) receive and absorb sth: *soaking up the sunshine* ○ *soaking up the atmosphere of the Spanish villages* ○ *That child soaks up new facts like a sponge!*

▷ **soak** *n* **1** (also **soaking**) act of soaking: *Give the sheets a good soak.* **2** (*infml*) habitual drinker; alcoholic: *He's a dreadful old soak.*

soaked /səʊkt/ *adj* [pred] **1** completely wet: *You're soaked!* **2** ~ **in sth** (*fig*) full of sth; steeped in sth: *This house is soaked in memories.*

soaking /ˈsəʊkɪŋ/ *adj* (also ˌ**soaking** ˈ**wet**) very wet: *a soaking wet coat.*

the Bank of England, designed by Sir John Soane

Soane /səʊn/ Sir John (1753-1837), English architect. His most famous design was for the *Bank of England in a neo-classical style. His house in London is now a museum housing his personal collection of antiquities. ⇨ illus.

soap /səʊp/ *n* [U] **1** substance used for washing and cleaning, made of fat or oil combined with an alkali: *a bar of soap* ○ *There's no soap in the bathroom!* ○ *Use plenty of soap and water.* **2** [C] (*infml*) = SOAP OPERA: *Do you watch any of the soaps on TV?*

▷ **soap** *v* [Tn, Tn·p] apply soap to (sb/sth); rub with soap: *soap oneself down* ○ *soap the car and then rinse it.*

soapy *adj* (**-ier, -iest**) **1** (**a**) of or like soap: *This* *bread has a soapy taste.* (**b**) full of soap: *soapy water.* **2** (*infml derog*) too anxious to please; ingratiating: *a soapy voice, manner, style.* **soapiness** *n* [U].

□ ˈ**soap-box** *n* **1** improvised stand for a speaker (in a street, park, etc): [attrib] *soap-box oratory* ○ (*fig*) *He gets on his soap-box at the first opportunity*, ie He is always ready to talk at length. **2** child's racing cart made from a wooden crate, usu by the child who rides in it: [attrib] *a* ˌ*soap-box* ˈ*derby*, ie a race between children in soap-boxes.

ˈ**soap-bubble** *n* ball of air surrounded by a film of soap that changes colour and bursts easily: *children blowing soap-bubbles.*

ˈ**soap-flakes** *n* [pl] thin flakes of soap, sold in a packet and used for washing clothes, etc: *use soap-flakes rather than a powder detergent.*

ˈ**soap opera** (also **soap**) (*sometimes derog*) radio or TV serial drama dealing with the events and problems of the characters' daily lives, often in a sentimental way: *a TV diet of soap opera.*

The most popular television programmes in Britain are soap operas. Their huge popularity lies perhaps in the fact that the characters are intended to represent ordinary, 'real' people with joys and problems that are easy to relate to. These characters often seem so real that the viewers discuss them as if they really existed, and sometimes even send letters telling them what to do about their problems. *Coronation Street*, first broadcast in 1964, is one of the best-known British soap operas and has a regular audience of around 15 million people. It is set in a street of an industrial, working-class town near Manchester, in northern England. Other popular 'soaps' include *Neighbours*, set in the residential street of an affluent Australian suburb, and *EastEnders*, set in the working-class East End of London.

ˈ**soap powder** powder made from soap and additives, used for washing clothes.

ˈ**soapstone** (also **steatite**) *n* [U] type of soft stone that feels like soap, used for making ornaments, etc: [attrib] *a soapstone statue.*

ˈ**soapsuds** *n* [pl] frothy lather of soap and water: *He was up to his elbows in soapsuds, washing his shirts.*

soar /sɔ:(r)/ *v* [I, Ipr] **1** (**a**) go up high in the air quickly: *The jet soared into the air.* ○ (*fig*) *Prices are soaring*, ie rising rapidly. ○ (*fig*) *soaring temperatures*, ie rapidly getting very hot. (**b**) be very high or tall: *cliffs soaring above the sea* ○ *Skyscrapers soar above the horizon.* **2** hover in the air without moving the wings or using the engine; glide: *seagulls soaring over the cliffs* ○ *a glider soaring above us.*

sob /sɒb/ *v* (**-bb-**) **1** [I, Ipr] draw in breath noisily and irregularly from sorrow, pain, etc, esp while crying: *We could hear the child sobbing in the other room.* ○ *She sobbed into her handkerchief.* ⇨ Usage at CRY[1]. **2** (idm) **cry/sob oneself to sleep** ⇨ SLEEP[1]. **sob one's** ˈ**heart out** cry bitterly with great emotion. **3** (phr v) **sob sth out** tell sth while sobbing: *She sobbed out the story of her son's violent death.*

▷ **sob** *n* act or sound of sobbing: *The child's sobs gradually died down.*

sobbingly *adv.*

□ ˈ**sob-story** *n* (*infml usu derog*) story intended to arouse sympathy or sadness in the listener or reader: *He told me a real sob-story of how his wife had gone off with his best friend.*

ˈ**sob-stuff** *n* [U] (*infml often derog*) sentimental writing or talking intended to arouse sympathy and sadness: *The idea of all that sob-stuff was to get me to lend her money.*

sober /ˈsəʊbə(r)/ *adj* **1** with one's actions and thoughts not affected by alcohol: *Does he ever go to bed sober?* ○ *He drinks a lot but always seems sober.* **2** serious and thoughtful; solemn: *a very sober and hard-working young man* ○ *make a sober estimate of what is possible* ○ *a sober analysis of the facts* ○ *in sober truth*, ie in fact, contrasted with what is imagined or hoped for. **3** (of colour) not bright; dull: *a sober grey suit.* **4** (idm) (**as**) **sober as a judge** (**a**) not at all drunk. (**b**) very serious and solemn.

▷ **sober** *v* **1** [I, Tn] (cause sb to) become serious and thoughtful: *The bad news had a sobering effect on all of us.* **2** (phr v) **sober (sb) down** (cause sb to) become calm and serious (esp after a period of irresponsible or frivolous behaviour): *Please sober down a bit; I've got some important news for you.* **sober (sb) up** (cause sb to) become sober: *Put him to bed until he sobers up.* ○ *Give her some black coffee — that'll help to sober her up.*

soberly *adv*: *soberly dressed.*

□ ˌ**sober-**ˈ**minded** *adj* serious and thoughtful.

sobriety /səˈbraɪətɪ/ *n* [U] quality or state of being sober(2): *a conscientious man noted for his sobriety.*

sobriquet /ˈsəʊbrɪkeɪ/ (also **soubriquet** /ˈsu:brɪkeɪ/) *n* (*fml or joc*) nickname: *He finds the 'caveman' sobriquet rather irritating.*

Soc *abbr* **1** Socialist. **2** Society: *Amateur Drama Soc.*

soccer /ˈsɒkə(r)/ *n* [U] (in Britain now used mainly in newspapers and on radio and TV; in USA the usual word): = ASSOCIATION FOOTBALL (ASSOCIATION) ○ [attrib] *measures to curb soccer violence* ○ *soccer hooligans*, ie football supporters who cause trouble before, after or during a match.

sociable /ˈsəʊʃəbl/ *adj* fond of the company of other people; friendly: *He has never really been the sociable type.* ○ *I'm not in a sociable mood.* ▷ **sociability** /ˌsəʊʃəˈbɪlətɪ/ *n* [U]. **sociably** /-əblɪ/ *adv.*

social /ˈsəʊʃl/ *adj* **1** [esp attrib] concerning the organization of and relations between people and communities: *social problems* ○ *social customs, welfare, reforms* ○ *the social order*, ie the way society is organized. **2** [attrib] of or in society; of or concerning rank and position within society: *one's social equals*, ie people of the same class as oneself in society ○ *social advancement*, ie improvement of one's position in society ○ (*derog*) *a social climber*, ie sb who constantly strives to improve his social position. **3** [attrib] (of animals, etc) living in groups, not separately: *Most bees and wasps are social insects.* ○ *Man is a social animal.* **4** of or designed for companionship and recreation: *a social club* ○ *a social evening* ○ *a busy social life.* **5** sociable: (*infml*) *He's not a very social person.*

▷ **social** (*US* also **sociable** /ˈsəʊʃəbl/) *n* informal meeting or party organized by a group or club: *a church social.*

socially /-ʃəlɪ/ *adv*: *I know him through work, but not socially.*

□ **the Social Democratic and Labour Party** /ˌsəʊʃl deməˌkrætɪk ən ˈleɪbə pɑ:tɪ/ (*abbr* **SDLP** /ˌes di: el ˈpi:/) socialist party in N Ireland, supported mainly by Catholic voters.

the Social Democratic Party (abbr **SDP**) British political party that merged with the *Liberal Party to form the *Liberal Democrats. ⇨ article at POLITICS.

ˌ**social** ˈ**science** (also ˌ**social** ˈ**studies**) group of subjects concerned with people within society and including economics, sociology, politics and geography: *Social anthropology is one of the social sciences.*

ˌ**social se**ˈ**curity** (*Brit*) (*US* **welfare**) government payments to people who are unemployed, ill, disabled, etc: *Most of the families in our road are on social security*, ie receiving such help. ⇨ article.

ˌ**social** ˈ**services** [pl] organized government service providing help and advice (eg in matters of health, housing, mental illness, child care, the law, etc): *threatened cuts in the social services.*

ˈ**social work** *n* profession of people who work in the social services: *She wants to do social work when she finishes college.* ˈ**social worker** person who works in the social services: *Social workers claimed the children were being ill-treated.* ○ *social workers visiting people just out of hospital.*

socialism /ˈsəʊʃəlɪzəm/ *n* [U] (**a**) political and economic theory advocating that a country's land, transport, natural resources and chief industries should be owned and controlled by the whole community or by the State, and that wealth should be equally distributed. (**b**) policy or practice based on this theory: *the struggle to build socialism* ○ *combine the best features of socialism and capitalism.* Cf CAPITALISM.

▷ **socialist** /ˈsəʊʃəlɪst/ (**a**) supporter of socialism. (**b**) member of a socialist party or movement. — *adj* characterized by, supporting or relating to socialism: *a Socialist Party* ○ *socialist policies.*

socialistic /ˌsəʊʃəˈlɪstɪk/ *adj* characterized by or supporting some of the features of socialism: *Some of her views are rather socialistic.*

socialite /ˈsəʊʃəlaɪt/ *n* (*sometimes derog*) person who is prominent in fashionable society, attending many parties, etc: *rich socialites moving from one fashionable resort to another.*

socialize, -ise /ˈsəʊʃəlaɪz/ *v* **1** [I, Ipr] ~ (**with sb**) mix socially (with others): *an opportunity to socialize with new colleagues.* **2** [Tn] adapt (sb) to society: *recent immigrants to the country who are not fully socialized.* **3** [Tn esp passive] organize (sth) in a socialist way: *socialized medicine*, ie in which health care is paid for by the state. ▷ **socialization, -isation** /ˌsəʊʃəlaɪˈzeɪʃn; *US* -lɪˈz-/ *n* [U].

society /səˈsaɪətɪ/ *n* **1** [U] system whereby people live together in organized communities; social way of living: *a danger to society*, ie a person, an idea, etc that endangers the welfare of members of a community ○ *Society has a right to see law-breakers punished.* **2** [C, U] particular grouping of humanity with shared customs, laws, etc: *modern industrial societies* ○ *working class society* ○ *Islamic society.* **3** [U] (*fml*) company; companionship: *spend an evening in the society of one's friends* ○ *avoid the society of other people.* **4** [U] class of people who are fashionable, wealthy, influential or of high rank in a place; the upper class: *high society*, ie rich and important people ○ *leaders of society* ○ [attrib] *a society wedding* ○ *society news*, ie as printed in some newspaper, etc. **5** [C] organization of people formed for a particular purpose; club; association: *the school debating society* ○ *a co-operative society* ○ *a drama society.* **6** (idm) **the alternative society** ⇨ ALTERNATIVE. **a mutual admiration society** ⇨ MUTUAL.

Society Islands /səˈsaɪətɪ aɪləndz/ **the Society Islands** group of islands in the southern Pacific Ocean, including *Tahiti. They are a French possession. They were named after the *Royal Society, which financed Captain *Cook's voyage to the S Pacific.

Society of Friends /səˌsaɪətɪ əv ˈfrendz/ **the Society of Friends** Christian body, whose members are usu called 'Quakers', founded by George *Fox. Their central belief is in the 'inner light' from God guiding each individual, but they have no set doctrines, sacraments or clergy. Quakers are pacifists and have a tradition of service to society, esp through education and relief work.

Society of Jesus /səˌsaɪətɪ əv ˈdʒi:zəs/ **the Society of Jesus** (*abbr* **SJ**) Catholic religious order founded by Ignatius of Loyola (a 16th-century Spanish priest), whose members are usu called Jesuits. They played an important part in the *Counter-Reformation and as missionaries, esp in S America. Their discipline and supposed tendency to intrigue and deception has sometimes given them a bad reputation.

socio- *comb form* of society; social: *sociology.*

sociology /ˌsəʊsɪˈɒlədʒɪ/ *n* [U] scientific study of the nature and development of society and social behaviour: [attrib] *a sociology course.* Cf ANTHROPOLOGY, ETHNOLOGY.

▷ **sociological** /ˌsəʊsɪəˈlɒdʒɪkl/ *adj* of or concerning sociology: *sociological theories, issues.* **sociologically** /-klɪ/ *adv.*

sociologist /-dʒɪst/ *n* student of or expert in sociology.

sock[1] /sɒk/ *n* **1** short stocking (usu of wool, nylon or cotton) covering the ankle and lower part of the leg, usu well below the knee: *a pair of socks.* **2** (idm) **pull one's 'socks up** (*Brit infml*) (make an effort to) improve one's performance: *His teachers told him to pull his socks up, or he'd undoubtedly fail his exam.* **put a** ˈ**sock in it** (*dated Brit infml*) be

Social Security

In Britain, 'social security' is the term used for all the payments (called 'benefits') made by the government to the retired, sick, disabled and unemployed, as well as to widows, parents and people on very low incomes.

Social security benefits are of two kinds: contributory and non-contributory. Contributory benefits are paid from the National Insurance contributions made regularly by employees, employers and the self-employed. Non-contributory benefits are financed by income from general taxation. The whole system is the responsibility of the Department of Social Security (DSS). National Insurance contributions, like income tax, are normally deducted from an employee's pay by the employer.

The benefits paid to the different categories of people are known by different names. The benefit paid to retired people is the 'state pension' or 'retirement pension', to which women are entitled at the age of 60 and men at 65. Pensioners are able to earn income and still receive their pension in full. In addition to the basic pension, many people receive an earnings-related pension based on their pay during their working life.

Employers can 'contract out' their employees from the state pension scheme for an earnings-related pension and provide their own pension instead. About half the people at work in Britain are now contracted out in this way. The Social Security Act of 1986 also gave people the right to choose their own pension scheme rather than stay in the state earnings-related scheme or their employer's scheme.

Women who leave work to have a baby receive 'maternity pay' from their employer. Women who do not qualify for this, for example the self-employed, receive a 'maternity allowance' from the government.

A woman whose husband dies before he retires, receives a 'widow's pension' if she is aged 45 or over. If she has children, she receives a 'widowed mother's pension'.

There are many different benefits for sick and disabled people, depending on the nature and severity of the illness or disablement. 'Statutory sick pay' (SSP) is paid by an employer for the first 28 weeks of an employee's illness and is related to earnings. Employees who are not entitled to SSP, for example the self-employed, receive the more general 'sickness benefit'. If a person is still unable to work at the end of this period, he or she receives an 'invalidity pension'. Disabled people who find walking difficult or impossible may receive a tax-free 'mobility allowance' to help pay for their transport or to obtain a special vehicle.

'Child benefit' is the main social security payment for children, paid tax free and usually to the mother. It is payable for each child until he or she leaves school (at 16) or longer if the child continues in education (up to the age of 19).

'Unemployment benefit' is payable to a person who is out of work for up to a year in one single spell of unemployment. 'Income support' is paid to people who are unemployed for more than a year or work for less than 24 hours a week, and who have very little money to live on. The amount paid depends on the money a person already has. 'Housing benefit' is paid to people with low incomes to help them pay for the cost of accommodation. 'Family credit' is paid to families with children who have very low incomes. It is paid in addition to child benefit.

Various modifications of these benefits, and additional amounts, are available for special categories of people, for example single parents or war widows (women whose husbands have been killed fighting in a war). There are usually different rates of payment for single people and couples, and a couple will not receive twice the amount that a single person gets.

All benefits are taxable except child benefit. This means that unemployed people are taxed on their benefit, as are pensioners.

In the USA, social security is limited mainly to the provision of pensions and Medicare for the retired and elderly. When an employed person reaches the age of 62, he or she is entitled to a reduced old age pension, and at the age of 65 to the full pension. (The higher pension age is being gradually increased to 67 over a 21-year period, beginning with people aged 62 in the year 2000.) Medicare is the scheme which pays most or all of the fees for hospital or medical treatment for a person of pension age. It is thus roughly equivalent in this respect to the National Health Service (NHS) in Britain, although the NHS provides free treatment for people under pension age as well. Some US states also have a 'state disability insurance' scheme, providing benefit for an employee who cannot work because of illness for seven or more days. Both social security contributions and state disability insurance contributions, where they apply, are compulsory. As in Britain, social security contributions are usually deducted by the employer.

quiet; stop talking or making a noise: *Can't you put a sock in it? I'm trying to work.*

sock[2] /sɒk/ *n* (*infml*) strong blow, esp one given with the fist: *Give him a sock on the jaw!*

▷ **sock** *v* **1** [Tn, Tn·pr] (*infml*) give (sb) such a blow: *Sock him on the jaw!* **2** (idm) **sock it to sb** (*dated infml*) attack sb forcefully; express oneself forcefully: *The speaker really socked it to them!*

socket /ˈsɒkɪt/ *n* natural or artificial hollow into which sth fits or in which sth turns: *the eye socket,* ie the hollow in a human or an animal skull for the eye ○ *a socket for an electric light bulb.* ⇨ illus at PLUG.

sockeye /ˈsɒkaɪ/ *n* (also ˌ**sockeye** ˈ**salmon**) salmon with a blue back, found in the waters around Alaska.

Socrates /ˈsɒkrətiːz/ (469-399 BC), Greek philosopher. Although he is sometimes regarded as the founder of philosophy, he left no written works. We know his ideas through the dialogues written by his disciple *Plato, which show his method of reaching conclusions through questioning. He stressed the importance of self-knowledge, and taught that virtue comes from knowledge. He was unjustly condemned to death on a charge of corrupting the young.

▷ **Socratic** /səˈkrætɪk/ *adj* of or like Socrates: *the Socratic method,* ie of reaching conclusions through a series of questions and answers.

sod[1] /sɒd/ *n* (*fml or rhet*) (**a**) [U] layer of earth with grass growing in it. (**b**) [C] square or piece of this cut off; turf: *sods newly placed on a grave.*

sod[2] /sɒd/ *n* (⚠ *Brit sl*) **1** (**a**) (used as a term of abuse, showing annoyance and sudden anger) person, esp a man: *You stupid sod!* ○ *The new boss is a mean sod!* (**b**) (used as a term of pity or sympathy) person, esp a man: *The poor old sod got the sack yesterday.* **2** thing that is difficult or causes problems: *What a sod this job is proving to be!*

▷ **sod** *v* (**-dd-**) (⚠ *Brit sl*) **1** (idm) **sod (it)!** damn (it)! **2** (phr v) **sod off** (esp imperative) go away.

sodding *adj* [attrib] (⚠ *Brit sl*) (used in anger and annoyance to give emphasis): *What a sodding mess!* ○ *It's all your sodding fault!*

□ ˌ**sod's** ˈ**law** (also **Murphy's law**) (*infml*) ironically humorous rule, eg 'If anything can go wrong, it will', which is supposed to explain accidents and failures: *Just when I finish washing my car, it starts to rain. Ah well, that's sod's law, I suppose.*

soda /ˈsəʊdə/ *n* **1** [U] chemical substance in common use, a compound of sodium: ˈ*washing-soda,* ie sodium carbonate, used for softening water, etc ○ ˈ*baking soda*/*biˌcarbonate of* ˈ*soda,* ie sodium bicarbonate, used in cooking ○ *caustic soda,* ie sodium hydroxide, used in the manufacture of soap. **2** [U, C] = SODA-WATER: *Add some soda to the whisky, please.* ○ *A whisky and soda, please.* **3** [U, C] (also **soda pop**) (*US infml*) fizzy drink made with flavoured soda-water: *a glass of cherry soda* ○ *two lime sodas.* **4** (also ˌ**ice-cream** ˈ**soda**) (*US*) drink made from ice-cream, syrup and soda-water: *three strawberry sodas.*

□ ˈ**soda-fountain** *n* device for supplying soda-water; counter in a shop from which fizzy drinks, ice-cream sodas, etc are served.

ˈ**soda siphon** = SIPHON.

ˈ**soda-water** *n* [U, C] water made fizzy by being filled with carbon dioxide under pressure: *I won't have any wine; I'll just have (a) soda water.*

sodden /ˈsɒdn/ *adj* **1** soaked through; very wet: *My shoes are sodden from walking in the rain.* **2** (in compounds): *drink-sodden,* ie stupid through drinking too much alcohol.

sodium /ˈsəʊdɪəm/ *n* [U] (*symb* **Na**) chemical element, a silver-white metal that comes naturally only in compounds. ⇨ App 11.

□ ˌ**sodium biˈcarbonate** (also **biˌcarbonate of** ˈ**soda**, ˈ**baking soda**) (also *infml* **bicarb** /ˈbaɪkɑːb/) white soluble compound in the form of crystals, used in fizzy drinks, baking-powder and medicines.

ˌ**sodium** ˈ**carbonate** (also ˈ**washing soda**) white soluble compound in the form of crystals, used in making glass, soap and paper, and to soften water.

ˌ**sodium** ˈ**chloride** common table salt.

ˌ**sodium hyˈdroxide** (also ˌ**caustic** ˈ**soda**) white corrosive solid used in making paper, aluminium and soap.

Sodom /ˈsɒdəm/ (in the Bible) city in Palestine destroyed by God along with Gomorrah because of the wickedness of their inhabitants.

sodomy /ˈsɒdəmɪ/ *n* [U] anal sexual intercourse between a man and (esp) another man.

▷ **sodomite** /ˈsɒdəmaɪt/ *n* (*dated fml*) person practising this.

sofa /ˈsəʊfə/ *n* large comfortable padded seat with raised arms and back, wide enough for two or more people: *He was lying on the sofa watching TV.* ○ *The sofa converts into a bed.* ⇨ illus at FURNITURE.

□ ˈ**sofa bed** sofa that can be turned into a bed by folding out the seat. ⇨ illus at FURNITURE.

soft /sɒft; *US* sɔːft/ *adj* (**-er, -est**) **1** changing shape easily when pressed; not hard or firm to the touch: *soft soil, ground, mud, etc* ○ *Warm butter is soft.* ○ *She likes a soft pillow and a hard mattress.* Cf

HARD[1]. **2** (of surfaces) smooth and delicate to the touch: *as soft as velvet* ○ *soft skin* ○ *Our cat has very soft fur.* **3** [usu attrib] (of light, colours, etc) not bright or glaring: *a soft pink rather than a harsh red* ○ *lampshades that give a soft light* ○ *the soft glow of candlelight.* **4** (of outlines) not sharp or clear; indistinct. **5** (of winds, etc) mild and gentle: *soft summer winds* ○ *a soft sea breeze.* **6** (of sounds) quiet and subdued; not loud: *soft music* ○ *in a soft voice* ○ *soft whispers.* **7** (*infml*) (of words, answers, etc) not harsh or angry; gentle; mild: *His reply was soft and calm.* **8** ~ (**on sth/with sb**) sympathetic and kind, sometimes to too great an extent: *have a soft heart* ○ *That teacher is too soft with his class; they're out of his control.* **9** (*infml derog*) weak and childish; lacking in determination, courage, etc: *Don't be so soft — there's nothing to be afraid of.* **10** (*infml derog*) foolish or silly; mad: *He's gone soft in the head.* **11** ~ **on/about sb** (*infml*) feeling attraction for sb; in love with sb. **12** (*infml derog*) not requiring hard work; without problems: *a soft job*, ie an easy, well-paid job ○ *He has a very soft life really.* **13** (of consonants) not hard; not plosive: *C is soft in 'city' and hard in 'cat'.* ○ *G is soft in 'gin' and hard in 'get'.* **14** (of drink) not alcoholic: *Would you like some wine or something soft?* ○ *I'd prefer a soft drink.* **15** (of water) free from mineral salts and therefore good for washing: *Don't use much soap powder — the water here is very soft.* **16** (idm) **an easy/a soft touch** ⇨ TOUCH[2]. **the hard/soft sell** ⇨ SELL *n.* **have a soft ˈspot for sb/sth** (*infml*) be specially fond of sb/sth: *I've always had a real soft spot for him.*

▷ **softish** *adj* rather soft: *softish ice-cream.*
softly *adv* in a soft way: *speak softly* ○ *She pressed his hand softly.* ○ *softly shining lights* ○ *music softly played* ○ *treating the children too softly.*
softness *n* [U].
softy (also **softie**) /ˈsɒftɪ; US ˈsɔːftɪ/ *n* (*infml*) (**a**) (*derog*) physically weak person: *'You're a bunch of softies!' the sergeant shouted to the new recruits.* (**b**) kind-hearted or too sentimental person: *He's a real softie at heart.*

□ **ˈsoftball** (*esp US*) game similar to baseball played on a smaller field with a larger soft ball.
ˌsoft-ˈboiled *adj* (of eggs) boiled for a short time so that the yolk is still soft.
ˌsoft ˈcurrency currency that is not convertible into gold or into certain other currencies which are more in demand.
ˈsoft drug drug not likely to cause addiction (eg marijuana) and less dangerous than a hard drug such as heroin.
ˈsoft fruit small fruits without stones, such as strawberries and currants.
ˌsoft ˈfurnishings (*Brit*) (esp in commercial use) decorative household items made from fabric, eg curtains, rugs, etc.
ˌsoft-ˈhearted *adj* sympathetic and kind, sometimes to too great an extent: *He's always lending her money; he's too soft-hearted.* **ˌsoft-ˈheartedness** *n* [U].
ˌsoft ˈlanding landing of a spacecraft (eg on the moon) that avoids damage or destruction.
ˌsoft ˈoption (*often derog*) alternative which is thought to involve less work, inconvenience, etc: *Language courses are wrongly thought to be soft options.*
ˌsoft ˈpalate back part of the roof of the mouth.
ˌsoft-ˈpedal *v* (-ll-; *US* -l-) [I, Tn] (*infml*) make (an issue, etc) seem less serious or important; play (sth) down: *The government has been soft-pedalling on the question of teachers' pay.*
ˌsoft ˈporn pornography of a less explicit or violent type. ⇨ HARD PORN (HARD[1]).
ˌsoft ˈshoulder (also **verge**) soft edge at the side of a road that is not suitable for vehicles to drive on.
ˌsoft ˈsoap 1 semi-liquid soap. **2** (*fig*) persuasion by flattery: *I'm tired of his soft soap!* **ˌsoft-ˈsoap** *v* [Tn] (*infml*) persuade (sb) by flattery: *Don't try to soft-soap me; I'm not changing my mind.*
ˌsoft-ˈspoken *adj* having a gentle quiet voice: *a ˌsoft-spoken young ˈwoman.*
ˈsoftware *n* [U] (*computing*) data, programmes, etc not forming part of a computer but used when operating it. Cf HARDWARE (HARD[1]).
ˈsoftwood *n* [C, U] wood from coniferous trees such as pine that is cheap to produce and can be cut easily. Cf HARDWOOD (HARD[1]).

soften /ˈsɒfn; US ˈsɔːfn/ *v* [I, Tn] **1** (cause sth to) become soft or softer: *The butter will soften out of the fridge.* ○ *The lampshade will soften the light.* **2** (phr v) **soften sb up** (**a**) weaken (an enemy's position) by shelling or bombing it heavily. (**b**) (*infml*) make sb unable or less able to resist an attack or persuasion to buy sth, etc: *Housewives were softened up with free gifts before the salesmen began the hard talking.*

▷ **softener** *n* [U, C] chemical substance used for softening hard water; device using this.

SOGAT /ˈsəʊgæt/ *abbr* (also **Sogat 82**) (*Brit*) Society of Graphical and Allied Trades (a trade union for employees in the printing and related trades, merged with NGA in 1991 to become GPMU). ⇨ article at TRADE UNION.

soggy /ˈsɒgɪ/ *adj* (**-ier, -iest**) **1** very wet; heavy with water: *The ground was soggy after heavy rain.* **2** (*usu derog*) moist and unpleasantly heavy: *soggy bread.* ▷ **soggily** /-ɪlɪ/ *adv.* **sogginess** *n* [U].

soh /səʊ/ (also **so**, **sol** /sɒl/) *n* the fifth note in the musical octave.

Soho /ˈsəʊhəʊ/ district of London north of *Piccadilly Circus. Many companies in the musical and entertainment industries have offices there, and it is known for its many restaurants. It was once a centre for strip clubs, pornography shops and prostitution, but in the 1980s these were much reduced.

soi-disant /ˌswɑː ˈdiːzɒŋ; US ˌswɑː diːˈzɑːŋ/ *adj* [attrib] (*French derog*) = SO-CALLED (SO[2]): *these soi-disant democrats.*

soigné /ˈswɑːnjeɪ; US swɑːˈnjeɪ/ *adj* (*fem* **soignée**) [usu pred] (*French*) (of a person's way of dressing, etc) carefully and fashionably arranged; elegant.

soil /sɔɪl/ *n* [C, U] **1** upper layer of earth in which plants, trees, etc grow; ground: *good, poor, sandy, etc soil* ○ *heavy soil* ○ *clay soil* ○ (*rhet*) *a man of the soil*, ie one who works on the land. ⇨ Usage at EARTH. **2** (*fml*) country; territory: *one's native soil* ○ *born on British soil.*

▷ **soil** *v* [I, Tn] (*fml*) (cause sth to) become dirty: *This material soils easily.* ○ *a basket for soiled sheets*, ie used ones that are waiting to be washed ○ *He refused to soil his hands*, ie refused to do dirty work.

soirée /ˈswɑːreɪ; US swɑːˈreɪ/ *n* (*fml*) social gathering in the evening, esp for music, conversation, etc and often to help the aims of a club, society, etc.

sojourn /ˈsɒdʒən; US səʊˈdʒɜːrn/ *v* [I] (*fml*) stay (with sb) in a place for a time: *He sojourned with a friend in Wales for two weeks.*

▷ **sojourn** *n* (*fml*) temporary stay (in a place): *a sojourn of two or three weeks in the mountains.*

sol = SOH.

solace /ˈsɒlɪs/ *n* [C, U] (*fml*) (thing that gives) comfort or relief (from pain, trouble, distress, etc): *The sick man found solace in music.* ○ *His work has been a real solace to him.*

▷ **solace** *v* [Tn, Tn·pr] ~ **sb** (**with sth**) (*fml*) give solace to sb: *She was distracted with grief and refused to be solaced.*

solar /ˈsəʊlə(r)/ *adj* [attrib] **1** of, concerning or related to the sun: *solar energy.* **2** using the sun's energy: *solar heating* ○ *solar-powered.*

□ **ˌsolar ˈcell** device (as used in satellites) that converts the energy of sunlight into electric energy.
ˌsolar ˈplexus /ˈpleksəs/ *n* (**a**) system of nerves at the back of the stomach. (**b**) (*infml*) stomach area below the ribs: *a painful punch in the solar plexus.*
the ˈsolar system the sun and the planets which move around it.
ˈsolar time = APPARENT TIME (APPARENT).
the ˌsolar ˈyear the time it takes the earth to go round the sun once, approximately $365\frac{1}{4}$ days.

solarium /səʊˈleərɪəm/ *n* (*pl* ~**s** or, in formal or scientific use, **solaria** /səʊˈleərɪə/) **1** place enclosed with glass, where sunlight can be enjoyed or used in treating patients. **2** bed equipped with special lights used for giving sb an artificial sun-tan or in treating certain medical conditions: *The new sports centre has saunas and solariums.*

sold *pt, pp* of SELL.

solder /ˈsɒldə(r); US ˈsɒdər/ *n* [U] soft mixture of metals used, when melted, for joining harder metals, wires, etc together.

▷ **solder** *v* [Tn, Tn·pr, Tn·p] ~ **sth** (**on/onto sth**); ~ **sth** (**up/on**) join or mend sth with solder: *He soldered the wire back on.* **ˈsoldering-iron** *n* tool used, when heated, to solder things together.

soldier /ˈsəʊldʒə(r)/ *n* **1** member (usu male) of an army, esp one who is not an officer: *two soldiers, a sailor and a civilian* ○ *The children were playing at soldiers.* **2** (idm) **a ˌsoldier of ˈfortune** (*dated*) person who will serve any country or person who will hire him as a soldier; mercenary.

▷ **soldier** *v* (phr v) **soldier ˈon** continue bravely with one's work, etc despite difficulties: *The walkers soldiered on although the weather was terrible.* **soldiering** *n* [U] the life of a soldier: *enjoy soldiering* ○ *peace-time soldiering.*
soldierly (also **soldier-like**) *adj* like a soldier; with the qualities of a soldier: *a tall, soldierly man* ○ *a soldierly bearing.*
soldiery /ˈsəʊldʒərɪ/ *n* [pl *v*] (*dated fml*) soldiers (of a specified, usu bad, type) as a class or group: *the undisciplined soldiery* ○ *brutal soldiery.*

sole[1] /səʊl/ *n* (*pl* unchanged or ~**s**) [C, U] flat sea-fish that is eaten as food: *sole cooked in white sauce* ○ *Would you like some more sole?*

sole[2] /səʊl/ *n* **1** bottom surface of the human foot, the part on which one walks and stands. ⇨ illus at FOOT. **2** part of a sock, shoe, etc covering this (usu not including the heel): *holes in the soles of his socks* ○ *leather soles* ○ *The soles of his boots needed repairing.* ⇨ illus at SHOE.

▷ **sole** *v* [Tn usu passive] put a sole on (a shoe, etc): *have a pair of shoes soled and heeled.*
-soled (forming compound *adjs*) with soles of the specified kind: *rubber-soled boots.*

sole[3] /səʊl/ *adj* [attrib] **1** one and only; single: *the sole cause of the accident* ○ *the sole survivor of the crash.* **2** belonging to or restricted to one person or group; not shared: *have sole responsibility* ○ *We have the sole right to sell this range of goods.*

▷ **solely** /ˈsəʊllɪ/ *adv* alone; only: *solely responsible* ○ *solely because of you.*

solecism /ˈsɒlɪsɪzəm/ *n* (*fml*) **1** mistake in the use of language, esp one that shows sb to be foreign or of low social class. **2** offence against good manners or etiquette.

solemn /ˈsɒləm/ *adj* **1** not happy or smiling; looking very serious: *solemn faces* ○ *look as solemn as a judge.* **2** done, said, etc in a serious and committed way, after deep thought: *a solemn promise, undertaking, pledge, etc.* **3** performed with religious or other ceremony; formal: *a solemn funeral procession.* ▷ **solemnly** *adv.* **solemnness** *n* [U].

solemnity /səˈlemnətɪ/ *n* (*fml*) **1** [U] state or quality of being solemn; seriousness: *the solemnity of the occasion, moment, procession.* **2** [U, C esp *pl*] solemn ceremony: *The Queen was crowned with all solemnity/with all the proper solemnities.*

solemnize, -ise /ˈsɒləmnaɪz/ *v* [Tn] (*fml*) perform (a religious ceremony, esp a wedding): *solemnize a marriage in church.*

▷ **solemnization, -isation** /ˌsɒləmnaɪˈzeɪʃn; US -nɪˈz-/ *n* [U] (*fml*) action of solemnizing.

solenoid /ˈsəʊlənɔɪd/ *n* coil of wire that becomes magnetic when an electrical current is passed through it: [attrib] *a solenoid switch.*

sol-fa /ˌsɒlˈfɑː; US ˌsəʊl-/ *n* (also **ˌtonic sol-ˈfa**) (in teaching sb to sing) method of showing musical notes by syllables (eg do, re, mi, fa, so, la, etc).

solicit /səˈlɪsɪt/ *v* **1** [I, Ipr, Tn, Tn·pr] ~ (**sb**) (**for sth**); ~ (**sth**) (**from sb**) (*fml*) ask (sb) for (eg money, help, votes) earnestly; try to obtain (sth): *solicit (sb) for money/solicit money (from sb)* ○ *solicit information about the new motorway* ○ *Both candidates solicited my opinion.* **2** [I, Tn] (of a prostitute) make a sexual offer (to sb), esp in a public place: *She was fined for soliciting.*

solicitor /səˈlɪsɪtə(r)/ *n* **1** (*Brit*) lawyer who

prepares legal documents (eg for the sale of land or buildings) advises clients on legal matters, and speaks for them in the lower courts. Cf ADVOCATE *n* 2, BARRISTER. ⇨ article at LAW. **2** (*US*) law officer of a city, town, etc. **3** (*US*) person who solicits trade, support, etc, esp by going from door to door; canvasser (eg for votes).

□ **So,licitor-'General** *n* (*pl* **Solicitors-General**) one of the chief law officers in the British Government, advising on legal matters. Cf ATTORNEY-GENERAL (ATTORNEY).

solicitous /səˈlɪsɪtəs/ *adj* ~ **(for/about sth/sb)** (*fml*) very concerned and anxious about (sb's welfare, comfort, etc): *a solicitous husband* ○ *solicitous enquiries about her health* ○ *He was very solicitous for her safe return.*

▷ **solicitously** *adv* (*fml*): *He always enquires most solicitously about your health.*

solicitude /səˈlɪsɪtjuːd; *US* -tuːd/ *n* [U] ~ **(for/about sth/sb)** (*fml*) being solicitous; concern or anxiety: *my deep solicitude for your welfare* ○ *the solicitude of a caring husband for his wife.*

solid /ˈsɒlɪd/ *adj* **1** not in the form of a liquid or gas; keeping its shape; firm: *solid fuels*, eg coal, wood ○ *solid food*, ie not liquid or slightly liquid ○ *When water freezes it becomes solid and we call it ice.* ○ *This horse has good solid muscle on him.* **2** without holes or spaces; not hollow: *a solid sphere* ○ *The word 'teapot' is a solid compound*, ie not hyphenated. ○ *The demonstrators stood in a solid line with linked arms.* **3** (**a**) [attrib] of the same substance throughout; containing only one (specified) material: *solid gold bath taps* ○ *steps cut in the solid rock* ○ *solid silver cutlery.* (**b**) of one (specified) colour only: *the solid blue sky of the painting.* **4** strong and firm in construction; able to support weight or resist pressure; substantial: *solid buildings* ○ *solid furniture* ○ *built on solid foundations* ○ *on solid ground.* **5** that can be depended on; reputable and reliable: *solid arguments* ○ *a solid business firm*, ie one without financial or other problems ○ *a woman of solid character* ○ *a good solid worker.* **6** in complete agreement; unanimous: *The miners were solid on this issue.* ○ *There was a solid vote in favour of the proposal.* **7** [attrib or immediately following a *n*] without a break or pause; continuous: *wait for a solid hour* ○ *sleep ten solid hours/ten hours solid.* **8** (*geometry*) having length, breadth and thickness; three-dimensional: *a solid figure*, eg a cube ○ *solid geometry*, ie study of solid, not flat figures. **9** (idm) **firm/solid as a rock** ⇨ ROCK[1].

▷ **solid** *n* **1** substance or object that is solid, not a liquid or gas: *Cheese is a solid; milk is a liquid.* ○ *The baby is not yet taking solids*, ie solid foods. **2** (*geometry*) figure of three dimensions, having length, breadth and thickness: *A cube is a solid.*

solidity /səˈlɪdətɪ/ (also **solidness**) *n* [U] quality or state of being solid: *the solidity of a building, argument, metal.*

solidly *adv* **1** firmly and substantially: *solidly-built foundations* ○ *These cars are solidly constructed.* **2** continuously: *It rained solidly for three hours.* **3** agreeing completely; unanimously: *We are solidly united on this issue.*

□ **,solid-'state** *adj* [usu attrib] (of electronic devices) using only transistors, ie without valves: *a ,solid-state 'amplifier.*

solidarity /ˌsɒlɪˈdærətɪ/ *n* [U] unity and agreement resulting from shared interests, feelings, actions, sympathies, etc: *national solidarity in the face of danger* ○ *'We must show solidarity with the strikers,' declared the student leaders.*

solidify /səˈlɪdɪfaɪ/ *v* (*pt, pp* **-fied**) [I, Ipr, Tn] ~ **(into sth)** (cause sth to) become solid, hard or firm: *The paint had solidified in the tin.* ○ *The mixture solidifies into toffee.* ○ (*fig*) *Vague objections to the system solidified into firm opposition.* ▷ **solidification** /səˌlɪdɪfɪˈkeɪʃn/ *n* [U].

soliloquy /səˈlɪləkwɪ/ *n* [C, U] (instance of) speaking one's thoughts aloud, esp in a play when a character does this without another character being present on stage: *Hamlet's famous soliloquy.*

▷ **soliloquize, -ise** /səˈlɪləkwaɪz/ *v* [I] (*fml*) talk to oneself; say one's thoughts aloud, esp in a play: (*joc*) *soliloquizing in front of the bathroom mirror.*

solipsism /ˈsɒlɪpsɪzəm/ *n* [U] (*philosophy*) theory that one can have knowledge only of the self.

solitaire /ˌsɒlɪˈteə(r); *US* ˈsɒlɪteə(r)/ *n* **1** [U] game for one person in which marbles, balls, pegs, etc are removed from their places on a special board after other pieces are moved over them, the object being to have only one piece left on the board. **2** = PATIENCE 3. **3** [C] (piece of jewellery such as a ring or an ear-ring having a) single gem or jewel: [attrib] *a solitaire diamond.*

solitary /ˈsɒlɪtrɪ; *US* -terɪ/ *adj* **1** (**a**) [usu attrib] (living) alone; without companions: *a solitary walk* ○ *lead a solitary life* ○ *One solitary tree grew on the mountainside.* (**b**) fond of being alone; used to being alone: *a solitary kind of person.* **2** not often visited; in a lonely remote place: *a solitary valley* ○ *far-flung solitary villages.* ⇨ Usage at ALONE. **3** [usu attrib] (esp in negative sentences and questions) only one; single: *There's not a solitary instance* (ie not even one) *of this having happened before.* ○ *She couldn't answer a solitary question correctly.*

▷ **solitarily** /ˈsɒlɪtrəlɪ; *US* ˌsɒlɪˈterəlɪ/ *adv.*

solitary *n* **1** [U] (*infml*) = SOLITARY CONFINEMENT: *He's in solitary for the weekend.* **2** [C] (*fml*) person who chooses to live completely alone; hermit.

□ **,solitary con'finement** (also *infml* **solitary**) prison punishment in which sb is kept alone in a separate cell: *He has been put in solitary confinement for attacking another prisoner.*

solitude /ˈsɒlɪtjuːd; *US* -tuːd/ *n* [U] (state or quality of) being alone without companions; solitary state: *not fond of solitude* ○ *She enjoys the solitude of her own flat.*

solo /ˈsəʊləʊ/ *n* (*pl* ~**s**) **1** [C] piece of music, dance, entertainment, etc performed by only one person: *a violin, piano, flute, etc solo* ○ *sing a solo.* **2** [C] flight in which the pilot flies alone without an instructor: *The trainee pilot flew his first solo today.* **3** [U] type of whist (a card-game) in which one player opposes others.

▷ **solo** *adj* [attrib], *adv* **1** by oneself, without a companion, etc: *a solo attempt* ○ *his first solo flight* ○ *She wanted to fly solo across the Atlantic.* **2** of, concerning or performed as a solo(1): *a fine solo performance on the flute* ○ *a piece for solo cello* ○ *sing solo.*

soloist *n* person who performs a musical solo.

Solomon /ˈsɒləmən/ (in the Bible) king of Israel, famous for his great wisdom and wealth. He was the son of *David and built the temple at Jerusalem.

Solomon Islands /ˈsɒləmən aɪləndz/ **the Solomon Islands** country made up of a group of islands in the southern Pacific Ocean, a member of the Commonwealth; pop approx 299 000; official language English; capital Honiara; unit of currency dollar (= 100 cents). Most of the islands are covered in dense forest and the main economic activity is agriculture: copra is grown as an export crop and sweet potatoes for subsistence. Fishing is also important. Guadalcanal, the main island, was occupied by the Japanese during the Second World War and was the scene of a fierce battle. ⇨ map at MELANESIA.

solstice /ˈsɒlstɪs/ *n* either of the two times of the year at which the sun is furthest North or South of the equator: *summer solstice*, ie about 21 June in the Northern hemisphere ○ *winter solstice*, ie about 22 December in the Northern hemisphere. Cf EQUINOX.

soluble /ˈsɒljʊbl/ *adj* **1** ~ **(in sth)** that can be dissolved: *soluble aspirin* ○ *tablets soluble in water* ○ *water-soluble vitamins*, ie that can be dissolved in water. **2** (*fml*) that can be solved or explained; solvable: *problems that are not readily soluble.* ▷ **solubility** /ˌsɒljʊˈbɪlətɪ/ *n* [U].

solution /səˈluːʃn/ *n* **1** [U, C] ~ **(to sth)** (action or way of finding an) answer to a problem, question, difficulty, etc: *problems that defy solution*, ie cannot be solved ○ *the solution to a crossword puzzle* ○ *She can find no solution to her financial troubles.* ○ *Resorting to violence is not the best solution to an argument.* **2** [C, U] liquid in whic sth is dissolved; state of being dissolved: *a solutio of salt in water* ○ *salt in solution.* **3** [U] process c dissolving a solid or a gas in liquid: *the solution c sugar in tea.*

solve /sɒlv/ *v* [Tn] **1** find an answer to (a problen etc); explain or make clear (a mystery, etc): *solve crossword puzzle* ○ *solve a mathematical equatio* ○ *solve a crime.* **2** find a way of dealing with (difficulty, etc): *Help me to solve my financia troubles.*

▷ **solvable** *adj* that can be solved or explaine soluble(2): *problems that are not immediatel solvable.*

solver *n* (in compounds) person who finds a answer or a solution: *a crime-solver* ○ *He's a goo problem-solver.*

solvent /ˈsɒlvənt/ *adj* [usu pred] **1** having enoug money to pay one's debts; not in debt: *He's neve solvent.* **2** (*fml*) that can dissolve anothe substance: *the solvent action of water.*

▷ **solvent** *n* [U, C] substance (esp a liquid) able t dissolve another substance: *Petrol is a good greas solvent*, ie dissolves grease well.

solvency /-nsɪ/ *n* [U] being solvent(1).

Solzhenitsyn /ˌsɒlʒəˈnɪtsɪn/ Alexander (1918- Russian novelist. Often in conflict with the Sovi authorities, he examines the theme of people i extreme situations facing basic moral choices. H works include *One Day in the Life of Iva Denisovich* and *The Gulag Archipelago.* He wa awarded the Nobel prize for literature in 1970.

Somalia /səˈmɑːlɪə/ country in NE Africa; pc approx 7 107 000; official language Somali; capit Mogadishu; unit of currency shilling (= 10 cents). The chief economic activity amongst th mainly nomadic population is the rearing c livestock. Some crops are grown along the river in the south of the country. ⇨ map at TANZANI

▷ **Somali** /səˈmɑːlɪ/ *n* **1** [C] native or inhabitant Somalia. **2** [U] language spoken in Somalia.

sombre (*US* **somber**) /ˈsɒmbə(r)/ *adj* **1** dar coloured; dull and dismal: *sombre clothes* ○ *sombre January day.* **2** sad and serious: *a sombr expression on his face* ○ *a sombre picture of th future of the world.* ▷ **sombrely** *adv*: *sombre dressed.* **sombreness** *n* [U].

sombrero /sɒmˈbreərəʊ/ *n* (*pl* ~**s**) man's felt c straw hat with a very wide brim (as worn in Lati American countries, esp Mexico).

some[1] /səm/ *indef det* (used in affirmativ sentences, or in questions expecting a positiv reply; after *if/whether*, when the sentence has positive emphasis; and in invitations an requests) **1** (used with [U] *ns*) an unspecifie amount of: *There's some ice in the fridge.* ○ *Som mail came for you this morning.* ○ *You left som money on the table.* ○ *Would you like some milk i your tea?* ○ *Isn't there some (more) wine in th cellar?* ○ *If you save some money each week, we ca go on holiday.* ○ *Please have some cake.* **2** (use with *pl* [C] *ns*, usu referring to three or more) a unspecified number of: *Some children were playin in the park.* ○ *Why don't you give her some flowers* (Cf *I suggest you give her some flowers.*) ○ *Didn you borrow some records of mine?* (Cf *You borrowe some records of mine, didn't you?*) ○ *If you put som pictures on the wall the room will look brighter.* C ANY[1].

some[2] /sʌm/ *indef det* **1** (used with [C] and [U] *ns* (**a**) a number or amount of sth that is less than th total being considered: *Some people have naturall beautiful voices while others need to be trained. Some modern music sounds harsh and tuneless.* (b a considerable number or amount of: *We wer some* (ie several) *miles out of our way.* ○ *That some help to us*, ie It helps to a certain extent. ○ *shall be gone (for) some time*, ie for quite a lon time. ○ *The headmistress spoke at some* (i considerable) *length.* **2** (used with *sing* [C] *ns* person, place or thing that is unknown c unspecified: *Some man at the door is asking to s you.* ○ *She won a competition in some newspaper c other.* **3** (used with numbers) approximately: *H spent some twelve years of his life in Africa.* ○ *Son* *thirty people attended the funeral.*

some[3] /sʌm/ *indef pron* **1** an unspecified number or amount of people or things. (**a**) (referring back): *Some were at the meeting yesterday.* ○ *You'll find some in the cupboard.* ○ *There's some (more) in the pot.* ○ *I already have some but it's not enough for six.* (**b**) (referring forward): *Some of the chairs are broken.* ○ *Some of the money was stolen.* **2** part of the whole number or amount being considered. (**a**) (referring back): *Thirty people came — some stayed until the end but many left early.* (**b**) (referring forward): *Some of the students had done their homework but most hadn't.* ○ *Some of the letter was illegible.* Cf ANY[2].

-some *suff* **1** (with *ns* and *vs* forming *adjs*) producing; likely to: *fearsome* ○ *quarrelsome* ○ *meddlesome.* **2** (with numbers forming *ns*) group of the specified number: *threesome.*

somebody /ˈsʌmbədɪ/ (also **someone** /ˈsʌmwʌn/) *indef pron* **1** some person: *There's somebody at the door.* ○ *Somebody from your office phoned.* ○ *If you saw somebody drowning what would you do?* **2** an important person: *He thinks he's really somebody.*

NOTE ON USAGE: Indefinite pronouns such as **somebody**, **someone**, **everyone**, **no one**, etc are singular and, grammatically, should be followed by other singular pronouns (**he**, **she**, **his**, **her**, etc). Traditionally, if the sex of the person is unknown, the masculine pronouns **he**, **him**, **his** have been used to refer to both females and males: *Everybody has his own view of what happened.* ○ *Somebody has lost his car keys.* ○ *Did anybody hurt himself?* Many people today consider this shows sexual bias and try to avoid it. The preferred way, especially in speech, is to use **they**, **them** or **their** with a singular neutral meaning: *Everyone said they would help.* ○ *Either John or Jane has to give up their job.* Another way, especially in writing, is to use **(s)he**, **he or she**, **him or her**, **his or her**, though some people find this clumsy: *Somebody has lost his or her car keys.* A third possibility is to rephrase the sentence to make the subject plural, thus avoiding the problem: *Did any of you hurt yourselves?* See also note on usage at HE.

someday /ˈsʌmdeɪ/ *indef adv* (also **some day**) at some time in the future: *Someday we'll be together.* ○ *Some day he will be a king.* Cf SOME[2] 2.

somehow /ˈsʌmhaʊ/ (*US* also **someway** /ˈsʌmweɪ/) *indef adv* **1** in some way; by some means: *We must stop him from seeing her somehow.* ○ *Somehow we must get to Glasgow.* **2** for a reason that is unknown or unspecified: *Somehow, I don't feel I can trust him.* ○ *I always knew I'd get the job, somehow.*

someone /ˈsʌmwʌn/ *indef pron* = SOMEBODY.

someplace /ˈsʌmpleɪs/ *indef adv* (*esp US*) = SOMEWHERE.

somersault /ˈsʌməsɔːlt/ *n* acrobatic rolling movement in which a person turns his feet over his head on the ground or in the air: *A gymnast on the trampoline was turning* (ie performing) *somersaults.*

▷ **somersault** *v* [I, Ipr] perform a somersault or somersaults: *The child somersaulted across the gymnasium.*

Somerset /ˈsʌməset/ county in SW England. It is an agricultural county, producing esp fruit and dairy products. ⇨ map at App 1.

Somerset House /ˌsʌməset ˈhaʊs/ large 18th-century building in the *Strand, London. For many years it was the main office of the General Registry Office (recording births, marriages and deaths) and the *Inland Revenue. It is now an art gallery.

something /ˈsʌmθɪŋ/ *indef pron* **1** some thing: *There's something under the table.* ○ *I want something to eat.* ○ *Have you got something I could read?* ○ *There's something interesting on the front page.* **2** some thing thought to be significant: *There's something* (ie some truth, some fact or opinion worth considering) *in what she says.* ○ *It's something* (ie a thing that one should feel happy about) *to have a job at all these days.* ○ *He's something*/*He does something in* (ie He has a job connected with) *television.* **3** (idm) **or something** (*infml*) or another thing similar to that mentioned: *She's writing a dictionary or something.* ○ *He hit a tree or something.* ○ *She rescued three children from a fire or something.* ˌ**something like a** ˈ**sb/sth** (**a**) partially similar to sb/sth: *A thesaurus is something like a dictionary.* ○ *The ceremony was something like a christening.* ○ *The tune goes something like this.* (**b**) approximately sb/sth: *He earns something like £35 000.* **something** ˈ**like it** roughly what is required or desirable: *That's something like it,* ie That will be satisfactory. **something of a sth** to some degree: *She found herself something of a celebrity.* ○ *I'm something of an expert on antiques.*

sometime /ˈsʌmtaɪm/ *indef adv* (also **some time**) at a particular but unspecified time: *I saw him sometime last summer.* ○ *Phone me some time next week.* Cf SOME[2] 2.

▷ **sometime** *adj* [attrib] (*fml*) former: *Thomas Atkins, sometime vicar of this parish.*

sometimes /ˈsʌmtaɪmz/ *indef adv* at some times but not all the time; occasionally: *He sometimes writes to me.* ○ *Sometimes I go by car.* ○ *Sometimes we went to the beach and at other times we sunbathed on the patio.*

someway /ˈsʌmweɪ/ *indef adv* (*infml esp US*) = SOMEHOW.

somewhat /ˈsʌmwɒt; *US* -hwɒt/ *indef adv* to some degree; rather: *I was somewhat surprised to see him.* ○ *He answered somewhat nervously.*

somewhere /ˈsʌmweə(r); *US* -hweər/ (*US* also **someplace**) *indef adv* in, at or to some place: *He lost it somewhere between here and the station.* ○ *I'm going somewhere else* (ie to a different place) *this evening.*

▷ **somewhere** *indef pron* some place: *I'll think of somewhere to stay.* ○ *I know somewhere (where) you can eat Japanese food.*

Somme /sɒm/ **the Somme** river in NE France, flowing into the English Channel. In 1916 the Battle of the Somme was one of the most disastrous campaigns of the First World War, in which over 1.2 million men died.

somnambulism /sɒmˈnæmbjʊlɪzəm/ *n* [U] (*fml*) activity or habit of walking in one's sleep; sleep-walking.

▷ **somnambulist** /-lɪst/ *n* (*fml*) person who does this; sleep-walker.

somnolent /ˈsɒmnələnt/ *adj* (*fml*) **1** almost asleep; sleepy; drowsy: *feeling rather somnolent after a large lunch.* **2** causing or suggesting sleep: *The noise of the stream had a pleasantly somnolent effect.*

▷ **somnolence** /-əns/ *n* [U] (*fml*) sleepiness; drowsiness.

somnolently *adv.*

son /sʌn/ *n* **1** [C] male child of a parent: *I have a son and two daughters.* **2** [C esp *pl*] (*rhet*) male descendant; male member of a family, country, etc: *one of France's most famous sons* ○ *sons of the tribe going out to hunt* ○ (*fig*) *a son of the soil,* ie sb who follows his father in working on the land. **3** (form of address used by an older man to a young man or boy): *'What's the matter with you, son?' asked the doctor.* ○ *'What is it you want to tell me, my son?' asked the priest.* ○ (*derog*) *Listen, son, don't start giving me orders.* **4 the Son** [sing] Jesus Christ: *the Father, the Son and the Holy Spirit.* **5** (idm) **like father, like son** ⇨ FATHER[1]. **a** ˌ**son of a** ˈ**bitch** (⚠ *sl*) unpleasant person; bastard: *I'll kill that son of a bitch when I get my hands on him!*

□ ˈ**son-in-law** *n* (*pl* ˈ**sons-in-law**) husband of one's daughter.

the ˌ**Son of** ˈ**God, the** ˌ**Son of** ˈ**Man** Jesus Christ.

sonar /ˈsəʊnɑː(r)/ *n* [U] device or system for detecting and locating objects under water by means of reflected sound waves. Cf RADAR.

sonata /səˈnɑːtə/ *n* piece of music composed for one instrument (eg the piano), or two (eg piano and violin), usu with three or four movements: *Bach's cello sonatas.*

Sondheim /ˈsɒndhaɪm/ Stephen (1930-), American composer and lyric-writer. He wrote the lyrics for *Bernstein's *West Side Story* and went on to compose *A Little Night Music* and other successful musicals.

son et lumière /ˌsɒn eɪ luːˈmjeə(r)/ (*French*) night-time entertainment at a famous building or place, where its history is told and acted with special lighting and sound effects: *son et lumière in the grounds of a ruined abbey.*

song /sɒŋ; *US* sɔːŋ/ *n* **1** [C] (usu short) poem set to music and intended to be sung: *a popular song* ○ *a collection of folk-songs* ○ *a beautiful love-song.* **2** [U] music for the voice; (activity of) singing: *burst into song,* ie suddenly begin singing. **3** [U] musical call or sound(s) made by a bird: *the song of the thrush* ○ *the song of the birds* ○ *birdsong.* **4** (idm) **for a** ˈ**song** (*infml*) at a very low price; cheaply: *This table was going for a song at the market.* (**make**) **a song and** ˈ**dance** (**about sth**) (*infml derog*) (make) a great fuss (about sth), usu unnecessarily: *You may be a bit upset, but it's really nothing to make a song and dance about.* **on** ˈ**song** (*infml*) performing well: *When she's on song, she's unbeatable as a tennis-player.* **sing a different song/tune** ⇨ SING. **wine, women and song** ⇨ WINE.

▷ **songster** /-stə(r)/ *n* (*dated or fml*) singer; songbird: *merry songsters singing carols.*

songstress /-strɪs/ *n* (*dated or fml*) female singer.

□ ˈ**songbird** *n* bird noted for its musical cry: *Blackbirds and thrushes are songbirds.*

ˈ**song-book** *n* collection of songs (with both words and music): *a children's song-book.*

ˈ**song thrush** common thrush noted for its beautiful singing.

ˈ**songwriter** *n* person who composes (usu popular) songs as a profession.

sonic /ˈsɒnɪk/ *adj* (usu in compounds) relating to sound, sound-waves or the speed of sound.

□ ˌ**sonic** ˈ**barrier** = SOUND BARRIER (SOUND).

ˌ**sonic** ˈ**boom** noise made when an aircraft exceeds the speed of sound.

sonnet /ˈsɒnɪt/ *n* type of poem containing 14 lines, each of 10 syllables, and with a formal pattern of rhymes: *Shakespeare's sonnets.*

sonny /ˈsʌnɪ/ *n* (*infml*) (familiar, sometimes patronizing, form of address used by an older person to a young boy or young man): *Run along now, sonny; mummy wants to have a rest.* ○ *Don't try to teach me my job, sonny.*

sonorous /ˈsɒnərəs, *also* səˈnɔːrəs/ *adj* (*fml*) **1** having a full deep sound: *a sonorous voice* ○ *the sonorous tones of the priest* ○ *a sonorous bell.* **2** (of language, words, etc) sounding impressive and important: *a sonorous style of writing.* ▷ **sonority** /səˈnɒrətɪ; *US* -ˈnɔːr-/ *n* [U] (*fml*): *the sonority of the bass voices.* **sonorously** *adv.*

soon /suːn/ *adv* **1** (used in mid-position with the *v* or, esp with *too, quite, very,* in end position) not long after the present time or the time mentioned; within a short time: *We shall soon be home.* ○ *We soon got there.* ○ *We shall be home quite soon now.* ○ *He'll be here very soon.* ○ *It will soon be five years since we came to live in Cairo.* **2** (often in the pattern *the sooner...the sooner...*) early; quickly: *How soon can you be ready?* ○ *Must you leave so soon?* ○ *She will be here sooner than you expect.* ○ *The sooner you begin the sooner you'll finish,* ie If you begin earlier you'll finish earlier. ○ *The sooner you leave the sooner you'll be home.* **3** (idm) **as** ˈ**soon as** (used as a *conj*) at the moment that; not later than (the moment when): *He left as soon as he heard the news.* ○ *I'll tell him as soon as I see him.* ○ *He didn't arrive as soon as we'd hoped.* (**just**) **as soon do sth** (**as do sth**) with equal willingness or readiness (as): *I'd (just) as soon stay at home as go for a walk.* **least said soonest mended** ⇨ LEAST. **no** ˌ**sooner** ˌ**said than** ˈ**done** (of a promise, question, request, etc) done, fulfilled, etc immediately. **no sooner...than** immediately when or after: *He had no sooner*/*No sooner had he arrived than he was asked to leave again.* **soon after** (**sb/sth**) a short time after (sb/sth): *He arrived* ˌ*soon after* ˈ*three.* ○ *They left* ˌ*soon after* ˈ*we did.* ○ *I rang for a taxi and it arrived soon* ˈ*after.* **the** ˌ**sooner the** ˈ**better** as quickly as possible: *'When should I ask him?' 'The sooner the better.'* ˌ**sooner**

or ˈlater one day; eventually (whether soon or later on): *You should tell her, because she'll find out sooner or later.* **sooner do sth (than do sth)** (*fml*) rather do sth: *She would sooner resign than take part in such dishonest business deals.* ○ *Go back there? I'd sooner emigrate!* ○ *Will you tell him, or would you sooner* (ie prefer it if) *I did?* **speak too soon** ⇨ SPEAK.

soot /sʊt/ *n* [U] black powder in the smoke of wood, coal, etc: *sweep the soot out of the chimney* ○ *One small fire in the kitchen covered the whole house in soot.*

▷ **soot** *v* (phr v) **soot sth up** (usu passive) cover sth with soot: *The flue has become sooted up.*

sooty 1 covered with soot; black with soot: *the chimney-sweep's sooty face.* 2 the colour of soot; black: *a sooty cat.*

soothe /su:ð/ *v* [Tn] 1 make (a person who is distressed, anxious, etc) quiet or calm; calm or comfort: *soothe a crying baby.* 2 make (pains, aches, etc) less severe or painful; ease: *soothe sb's toothache* ○ *This will help to soothe your sunburn.*

▷ **soothing** *adj*: *soothing music* ○ *a soothing voice* ○ *a soothing lotion.* **soothingly** *adv*: *'There, there,' he said soothingly, 'Don't distress yourself!'*

soothsayer /ˈsu:θseɪə(r)/ *n* (*arch*) fortune-teller; prophet: *the soothsayer in Shakespeare's 'Julius Caesar'.*

sop /sɒp/ *n* 1 [sing] ~ (**to sb/sth**) thing offered to a displeased or troublesome person to calm him or win his favour: *offered as a sop to his anger* ○ *The child was given a prize as a sop to her disappointed parents.* 2 [C] piece of bread, etc dipped in liquid (eg milk, soup) before being eaten or cooked.

▷ **sop** *v* (**-pp-**) (*infml*) 1 [Tn] dip or soak (bread, etc) in liquid: *sop bread in soup.* 2 (phr v) **sop sth up** take up (liquid, etc) with a sponge, cloth, etc: *Sop up the water with a paper towel.*

sopping *adj, adv* very wet; drenched: *Your clothes are sopping (wet)!*

sophist /ˈsɒfɪst/ *n* (*fml*) person who uses clever but false arguments intended to deceive: *Many politicians are cunning sophists.*

▷ **sophism** /ˈsɒfɪzəm/ *n* [C, U] (*fml*) (use of) such arguments.

sophisticated /səˈfɪstɪkeɪtɪd/ *adj* 1 having or showing much worldly experience and knowledge of fashionable life: *a sophisticated woman* ○ *wearing sophisticated clothes* ○ *sophisticated tastes.* 2 complicated and refined; elaborate; subtle: *sophisticated modern weapons* ○ *sophisticated devices used in spacecraft* ○ *a sophisticated discussion, argument, etc.*

▷ **sophisticate** /səˈfɪstɪkeɪt/ *n* (*often ironic*) sophisticated person: *The sophisticates in the office drink lemon tea; we have coffee.*

sophistication /səˌfɪstɪˈkeɪʃn/ *n* [U] quality of being sophisticated: *proud of her newly-acquired sophistication* ○ *the sophistication of modern aircraft.*

sophistry /ˈsɒfɪstrɪ/ *n* (*fml*) (a) [U] use of sophisms: *He won the argument by sophistry.* (b) [C] instance or example of this: *the sophistries of the discussion.*

Sophocles /ˈsɒfəkli:z/ (c 496-406 BC), Greek dramatist. His tragedies, esp *Antigone* and the *Oedipus* trilogy, examine the themes of justice and humanity's ability to control its own destiny. ▷ **Sophoclean** /ˌsɒfəˈkli:ən/ *adj.*

sophomore /ˈsɒfəmɔ:(r)/ *n* (*US*) student in the second year of a course at a high school, college or university. ⇨ article at POST-SCHOOL .

soporific /ˌsɒpəˈrɪfɪk/ *n, adj* (substance, medicine, drink, etc) causing sleep: *a soporific drug* ○ (*fig*) *a soporific speech.* ▷ **soporifically** /-klɪ/ *adv.*

sopping ⇨ SOP.

soppy /ˈsɒpɪ/ *adj* (*Brit infml derog*) foolishly sentimental: *a soppy film* ○ *'She's just a soppy girl,' said her youngest brother.* ▷ **soppily** *adv.* **soppiness** *n* [U].

soprano /səˈprɑ:nəʊ; *US* -ˈpræn-/ *n* (*pl* ~**s** /-nəʊz/) 1 singing voice of the highest range for a woman or boy: [attrib] *a soprano voice.* 2 (a) singer with such a voice: *The sopranos sang beautifully.* (b) musical part written for such a voice: [attrib] *a difficult soprano part.* 3 musical instrument with a range about that of a soprano.

▷ **soprano** *adv* with a soprano voice: *She sings soprano.*

sorbet /ˈsɔ:beɪ, *also* ˈsɔ:bət/ (*US* **sherbet**) *n* type of dessert made from water, sugar and fruit-juice; water-ice: *blackcurrant sorbet.*

Sorbonne /sɔ:ˈbɒn/ **the Sorbonne** educational establishment in Paris, which includes parts of some of the Universities of Paris (III, IV, V), specializing in the arts and humanities. The Sorbonne was originally a college of the University of Paris which became its theology faculty during the Middle Ages. Its name is still sometimes used to refer to the University of Paris as a whole.

sorcerer /ˈsɔ:sərə(r)/ *n* (*fem* **sorceress** /ˈsɔ:sərɪs/) person who is believed to practise magic, esp with the help of evil spirits; magician: *sorcerers in old-fashioned fairy-tales.*

▷ **sorcery** /ˈsɔ:sərɪ/ *n* [U] art, use or practice of magic, esp with evil spirits; witchcraft.

sordid /ˈsɔ:dɪd/ *adj* (*derog*) 1 (of conditions, places, etc) dirty and unpleasant; squalid: *a sordid slum* ○ *living in sordid poverty.* 2 (of people, behaviour, etc) displaying selfishness, meanness, etc: *a sordid affair* ○ *sordid motives.* ▷ **sordidly** *adv.* **sordidness** *n* [U]: *the sordidness of the men's living quarters.*

sore /sɔ:(r)/ *adj* 1 (a) (of a part of the body) hurting when touched or used; tender and painful; aching: *a sore knee, throat, etc* ○ *My leg is still very sore.* (b) [usu pred] feeling pain: *She's still a bit sore after the accident.* 2 [usu pred] ~ (**at sb**) (*infml esp US*) hurt and angry (esp because one has been treated unfairly); irritated: *She feels sore about not being invited to the party.* ○ *Is she still sore at* (ie angry with) *you?* 3 (*fml or dated*) serious; severe: *in sore distress* ○ *in sore need of help* ○ *His mother is a sore trial to him,* ie causes him much distress. 4 (idm) **like a bear with a sore head** ⇨ BEAR[1]. **a sight for sore eyes** ⇨ SIGHT[1]. **a ˌsore ˈpoint** issue or matter that makes sb feel hurt or angry whenever it is mentioned: *I wouldn't ask him about his job interview; it's rather a sore point with him at the moment.* **stand/stick out like a sore ˈthumb** be very obvious or conspicuous, and often unpleasing: *The modern office block sticks out like a sore thumb among the old buildings in the area.*

▷ **sore** *n* painful place on the body (where the skin or flesh is injured): *treat a sore* ○ *Her hands are covered in sores.*

sorely *adv* (*fml*) seriously; very greatly: *be sorely tempted to interrupt* ○ *Your financial help is sorely needed.* ○ *She was sorely missed at the reunion.*

soreness *n* [U]: *the soreness of his skin.*

sorghum /ˈsɔ:gəm/ *n* [U] type of millet grown as food in warm climates.

sorority /səˈrɒrətɪ; *US* -ˈrɔ:r-/ *n* [CGp] (*US*) (members of a) women's social club in a college or university. Cf FRATERNITY 3. ⇨ article at POST-SCHOOL.

sorrel[1] /ˈsɒrəl; *US* ˈsɔ:rəl/ *n* [U] type of herb with sour-tasting leaves used in cooking, in salads, etc: [attrib] *sorrel soup.*

sorrel[2] /ˈsɒrəl; *US* ˈsɔ:rəl/ *n* (a) reddish-brown colour. (b) horse of this colour: *The sorrel easily won the race.*

▷ **sorrel** *adj* of a reddish-brown colour: *a sorrel coat.*

sorrow /ˈsɒrəʊ/ *n* 1 [U] ~ (**at/for/over sth**) feeling of sadness or distress caused esp by loss, disappointment or regret; grief: *express sorrow for having done wrong* ○ *to my great sorrow* ○ *to the sorrow of all those who were present* ○ *sorrow at sb's death* ○ *in sorrow and in joy,* ie when we are sad and also when we are happy. 2 particular cause of this feeling; misfortune: *the sorrow(s) of war* ○ *He has had many sorrows in his life.* ○ *Her death was a great sorrow to everyone.* 3 (idm) **drown one's sorrows** ⇨ DROWN. **more in ˌsorrow than in ˈanger** with more regret than anger for what was done, etc: *It was more in sorrow than in anger that he criticized his former colleague.*

▷ **sorrow** *v* [I, Ipr] ~ (**at/for/over sth**) (*fml*) feel, express or show sorrow; grieve: *sorrowing over his child's death* ○ *sorrowing at his misfortune.*

sorrowful /-fl/ *adj* (*esp fml*) feeling, showing or causing sorrow: *a sorrowful occasion* ○ *Her face was anxious and sorrowful.* **sorrowfully** /-fəlɪ/ *adv*: *weeping sorrowfully.* **sorrowfulness** *n* [U].

sorry /ˈsɒrɪ/ *adj* 1 [pred] ~ (**to do sth/that...**) feeling sadness or regret: *We're sorry to hear of your father's death.* ○ *I'm sorry to say that I won't be able to accept the job.* ○ *I'd be sorry if you were to think that I disliked you.* 2 [pred] ~ (**for/about sth**) full of shame and regret (esp about a past action); apologetic: *Aren't you sorry for/about what you've done?* ○ *If you say you're sorry* (ie if you apologize) *we'll forget the incident.* 3 (used to express mild regret, disagreement or refusal, and in making apologies and excuses): *'Can you lend me a pound?' 'I'm sorry, I can't.'* ○ *I'm sorry, but I don't share your opinion.* ○ *I'm sorry I'm late.* 4 [attrib] (**-ier, -iest**) (*usu derog*) poor and shabby; pitiful: *a sorry sight* ○ *The house was in a sorry state.* ○ (*dated*) *a sorry excuse,* ie a worthless one. 5 (idm) **be/feel sorry for sb** (a) feel sympathy for sb: *I feel sorry for anyone who has to drive in this sort of weather.* (b) feel pity for, or mild disapproval of, sb: *If he doesn't realize the consequences of his actions, I'm sorry for him.* **better safe than sorry** ⇨ BETTER[2]. **cut a sorry, etc figure** ⇨ FIGURE[1]. **ˈsorry for oneself** depressed about a failure, disappointment, illness, etc: *He's got flu and he's feeling rather sorry for himself.*

▷ **sorry** *interj* 1 (used for apologizing, making excuses, etc): *Sorry, did I knock your elbow?* ○ *Sorry, I don't know where she lives.* 2 (*esp Brit*) (used when asking sb to repeat sth one has not heard properly) what did you say?: *'I'm hungry.' 'Sorry?' 'I said I'm hungry.'* ⇨ Usage at EXCUSE[2].

sort[1] /sɔ:t/ *n* 1 [C] group or class of people or things (which are alike in some way); type: *He's the sort of person I really dislike.* ○ *What sort of paint are you using?* ○ *We can't approve of this sort of thing/these sorts of things/things of this sort.* 2 [C usu *sing*] (*infml*) type of character; person: *a good/decent sort* ○ *He's not a bad sort really.* 3 (idm) **it takes all sorts (to make a world)** (*saying*) people vary very much in character and abilities (and this is a good thing). **nothing of the kind/sort** ⇨ KIND[2]. **of a ˈsort/of ˈsorts** (*infml derog*) of a poor or inferior type: *They served coffee of a sort.* ○ *It was a meal of sorts, but nobody enjoyed it.* **a sort of sth** (*infml*) vague, unexplained or unusual type of sth: *I had a sort of feeling he wouldn't come.* **out of ˈsorts** (*infml*) (a) feeling unwell: *She's been out of sorts since the birth of her baby.* (b) in a bad temper; annoyed: *He's always out of sorts early in the morning.* **sort of** (*infml*) to some extent ; in some way or other: *I sort of thought this might happen.* ○ *You sort of twist the ends together.* ○ *I feel sort of queasy.* ⇨ Usage at KIND[2].

sort[2] /sɔ:t/ *v* 1 [Tn, Tn·pr, Tn·p] ~ **sth (out) (into sth)**; ~ **sth (out) from sth** arrange things in groups; separate things of one type, class, etc from things of other types, etc: *He was sorting his foreign stamps (into piles).* ○ *We must sort out the good apples from the bad.* 2 (idm) **sort out the ˌmen from the ˈboys** show or prove which people are truly brave, skilful, competent, etc: *Climbing that mountain will certainly sort out the men from the boys.* 3 (phr v) **sort sth out** (a) separate sth from a larger group: *sort out the smaller plants and throw them away.* (b) (*infml*) put sth in good order: *This room needs sorting out,* ie tidying. **sort sth/oneself out** find a solution to a/one's problems, etc: *I'll leave you to sort this problem out.* ○ *Let's leave them to sort themselves out,* ie clear up their problems, resolve their arguments etc. ○ *I need to sort my life/myself out a bit, before I start looking for a new job.* **sort sb out** (*sl*) deal with sb by punishing or attacking him: *I'll soon sort him out. Just let me get my hands on him!* **sort through sth** go through (a number of things), arranging them in groups: *sort through a pile of old photographs.*

▷ **sorter** *n* person or machine that sorts and arranges letters, postcards, etc: *Many workers in* *the sorting office lost their jobs when an automatic sorter was introduced.*

sortie /ˈsɔ:ti:/ *n* **1** attack made by soldiers coming out from a position of defence on those trying to capture it. **2** flight made by one aircraft during military operations: *The four planes each made two sorties yesterday.* **3** brief trip away from home, esp to an unfamiliar or unfriendly place: *a sortie into the city centre to do some shopping* ○ (*fig*) *His first sortie into* (ie attempt to enter) *politics was unsuccessful.*

SOS /ˌes əʊ ˈes/ *n* [sing] (**a**) urgent message for help (sent by radio, etc, usu in code) from a ship, an aircraft, etc when in danger: *send an SOS to the coastguard* ○ [attrib] *an SOS message.* (**b**) urgent appeal for help or response (eg a radio broadcast to find relatives of a seriously ill person): *We heard the SOS about Bill's father on the car radio.* ○ (*joc*) *Our daughter sent us an SOS for some more money.* Cf MAYDAY.

so-so /ˌsəʊˈsəʊ/ *adj* [pred], *adv* (*infml*) not very good; not very well; reasonably good or well: *'How are you feeling today?' 'Oh, only so-so.'* ○ *'What was the exam like?' 'So-so!'*

sostenuto /ˌsɒstəˈnu:təʊ/ *adj*, *adv* (*music*) in a sustained or even manner.

▷ **sostenuto** *n* (*pl* ~**s**) musical passage (to be) played in this way.

sot /sɒt/ *n* (*dated derog*) person who is in the habit of getting drunk very often, esp sb whose mind has become confused through drinking too much: *her drunken sot of a husband.*

▷ **sottish** /ˈsɒtɪʃ/ *adj* (*dated derog*) in the habit of being drunk and, for this reason, stupid and confused.

sotto voce /ˌsɒtəʊ ˈvəʊtʃɪ/ *adj*, *adv* (*Italian fml or joc*) in a low voice, so as not to be heard by everyone: *a sotto voce remark* ○ *The defendant leant forward and spoke to his barrister, sotto voce.*

sou /su:/ *n* **1** former French coin of low value. **2** (*infml*) very small amount of money: *He hasn't a sou,* ie He's very poor.

soubriquet = SOBRIQUET.

soufflé /ˈsu:fleɪ; *US* su:ˈfleɪ/ *n* [C, U] dish of eggs, milk and flour, flavoured (with cheese, etc), beaten to make it light, and baked: *a spinach soufflé* ○ *Would you like some soufflé?*

sough /sʌf; *US* saʊ/ *v* [I] *n* (*arch or fml*) (make a) murmuring or whispering sound (as of wind in trees): *the sough of the wind in the chimney.*

sought *pt*, *pp* of SEEK.

souk /su:k/ *n* open-air market in Arab countries.

soul /səʊl/ *n* **1** [C] spiritual or non-material part of a person, believed to exist after death: *commend one's soul to God* ○ *Do you believe in the immortality of the soul?* ○ *Christians believe that a person's soul survives the death of his body.* **2** [C, U] decency and honesty of feeling; emotional, moral and intellectual energy, eg as revealed in works of art: *He is a man without a soul.* ○ *a very polished performance, but without soul* ○ *This music has no soul.* **3** [sing] **the** ~ **of sth** perfect example or pattern (of some virtue or quality): *He is the soul of honour/discretion.* **4** [C] spirit of a dead person: *lost souls still walking the earth* ○ *All ˈSouls Day,* ie 2 November. **5** [C] (**a**) person: *There wasn't a soul to be seen,* ie No one was in sight. ○ *Don't tell a soul,* ie Don't tell anybody. (**b**) (with *adjs*, indicating familiarity, pity, etc) person, child, etc: *a dear old soul* ○ *She's a cheery little soul,* ie a cheerful girl, etc. ○ *She's lost all her money, poor soul.* **6** [U] (also **soul music**) type of popular modern Black American music, derived from gospel, blues and jazz, that expresses strong emotion: *the sound of soul* ○ [attrib] *a soul singer.* **7** [U] (*US infml*) Black American culture and racial identity; qualities enabling a person to be in harmony with himself and others. **8** (idm) **bare one's heart/soul** ⇨ BARE[2]. **body and soul** ⇨ BODY. **heart and soul** ⇨ HEART. **keep body and soul together** ⇨ BODY. **the life and soul of sth** ⇨ LIFE. **sell one's soul** ⇨ SELL. **upon my soul!** (*dated*) (used as an exclamation of shock or surprise).

▷ **soulful** /-fl/ *adj* having, affecting or showing deep (usu sad) feeling: *a soulful expression* ○ *soulful music.* **soulfully** /-fəlɪ/ *adv*: *soulfully playing the guitar.* **soulfulness** *n* [U].

soulless /ˈsəʊllɪs/ *adj* **1** (of a person) without higher or deeper feelings. **2** (of life, a job, etc) boring and unimportant: *his soulless work in the factory.* **soullessly** *adv.*

□ **ˈsoul brother** (*fem* **ˈsoul sister**) (*infml esp US*) (used esp by young Black Americans) black person (esp one who thinks and feels in the same way as oneself).

ˈsoul-destroying *adj* (of work, etc) very repetitive and dull: *soul-destroying jobs in the factory.*

ˈsoul food (*US*) food traditionally associated with Black Americans in the southern US.

ˈsoul mate person with whom one has a deep lasting friendship and understanding.

ˈsoul music = SOUL 6.

ˈsoul-searching *n* [U] deep examination of one's conscience and mind: *After days of soul-searching he finally came to the decision to leave home.*

ˈsoul-stirring exciting, moving, etc: *soul-stirring music.*

sound[1] /saʊnd/ *adj* **1** in good condition; not hurt, diseased, injured or damaged: *have sound teeth* ○ *have a sound mind,* ie not mentally ill ○ *a sound constitution* ○ *a house built on sound foundations.* **2** based on reason, sense or judgement; dependable: *a sound argument, policy, etc* ○ *sound advice* ○ *a sound business firm* ○ *Is he sound on state education?* ie Are his views well founded, officially acceptable, etc? **3** [usu attrib] (*esp fml*) full and complete; thorough: *a sound telling-off, thrashing, etc.* **4** careful and accurate; competent: *a sound tennis player* ○ *a sound piece of writing.* **5** [usu attrib] (of sleep or a sleeper) deep, peaceful and uninterrupted: *be a sound sleeper* ○ *a sound night's sleep.* **6** (idm) **safe and sound** ⇨ SAFE[1]. **(as) sound as a bell** in perfect condition: *The doctor said I was as sound as a bell.* **ˌsound in ˌwind and ˈlimb** (*dated or joc*) physically fit: *remarkably sound in wind and limb for his age.*

▷ **sound** *adv* (idm) **be/fall sound aˈsleep** be/become deeply and peacefully asleep.

soundly *adv* in a sound manner; thoroughly and fully: *a soundly based argument* ○ *be soundly beaten at chess* ○ *sleep soundly.*

soundness *n* [U]: *the soundness of her advice* ○ *the soundness of his performance.*

sound[2] /saʊnd/ *n* **1** [U] sensation detected by the ear, caused by the vibration of the air surrounding it: *an experiment to measure the speed at which sound travels* ○ *Sound travels more slowly than light.* **2** [C, U] thing that produces such a sensation; thing that can be heard: *the sound of the wind, sea, a car, voices, breaking glass* ○ *the sound of music* ○ *I heard a strange sound outside.* ○ *He crept upstairs without a sound,* ie noiselessly. ○ *ˈvowel sounds,* eg /u:, ʌ, ə/. **3** [sing] mental impression produced by a piece of news, a description, etc: *I don't like the sound of her husband!* ○ *The news has a sinister sound,* ie seems to be sinister. **4** [U] distance within which sth can be heard: *A true Cockney is born within (the) sound of Bow Bells.* **5** (idm) **like, etc the ˌsound of one's own ˈvoice** (*derog*) talk a lot or too much (usu without wanting to hear what others have to say): *She's much too fond of the sound of her own voice.*

▷ **soundless** *adj* without a sound; silent: *soundless movements.* **soundlessly** *adv.*

□ **ˌsound ˈarchives** (collection of) recordings on record or tape of broadcasts considered important enough to be preserved: *the BBC sound archives.*

ˈsound barrier (also **ˌsonic ˈbarrier**) point at which an aircraft's speed equals that of sound waves, causing sonic booms: *break the sound barrier,* ie move faster than the speed of sound.

ˈsound effect (esp *pl*) sound other than speech or music used in a film, play, etc to produce an atmospheric effect: *The sound effects of the fight were very good in that radio play.*

ˈsound-proof *adj* made or constructed so that sound(s) cannot pass through or in: *sound-proof material* ○ *a sound-proof studio.* — *v* [Tn] make (sth) sound-proof: *I wish we could sound-proof the boys' bedroom!*

ˈsound-recording *n* [C, U] recording in sound only.

ˈsound-track *n* (**a**) (music, etc on a) track or band at the side of a cinema film which has the recorded sound on it. (**b**) recorded music from a film, musical play, etc (on a record, cassette, etc): *I've bought the sound-track of that film.*

ˈsound-wave *n* vibration made in the air or some other medium by which sound is carried.

sound[3] /saʊnd/ *v* **1** (**a**) [La, Ln] give a specific impression when heard: *That music sounds beautiful.* ○ *His voice sounded hoarse.* ○ *His explanation sounds reasonable.* ○ *His excuse sounds unconvincing.* ○ *She sounds just the person we need for the job.* (**b**) (idm) ~ **(to sb) as if.../as though...** (not in the continuous tenses) give the impression that...: *I hope I don't sound as if I'm criticizing you.* ○ *That cough sound's as if it's getting worse.* ○ *It sounds to me as if there's* (ie I think I can hear) *a tap running somewhere.* ⇨ Usage at FEEL[1]. **2** (**a**) [Tn] produce a sound from (sth); make (esp a musical instrument) produce a sound: *sound a trumpet* ○ *The bell is sounded every hour.* (**b**) [I] give out a sound: *The trumpet sounded.* ○ *The A key on this piano won't sound,* ie No sound is produced when the key is struck. **3** [Tn] give (a signal) by making a sound; announce: *sound a note of alarm/danger/warning* ○ *sound the alarm,* eg by ringing a bell ○ *sound the retreat,* eg by blowing a bugle. **4** [Tn esp passive] (*fml*) pronounce (sth): *You don't sound the 'h' in 'hour'.* ○ *The 'b' in 'dumb' isn't sounded.* **5** [Tn] (*fml*) test or examine (sth) by tapping or striking to produce a sound and listening carefully: *sound a person's chest,* ie by tapping it ○ *sound the wheels of a train,* ie by striking them. **6 strike/sound a false note** ⇨ FALSE. **strike/sound a note (of sth)** ⇨ NOTE[1]. **7** (phr v) **sound off (about sth)** (*infml derog*) talk noisily and boastfully (about sth): *He's always sounding off about how he would manage the firm.*

▷ **-sounding** (forming compound *adjs*) having a specified sound or giving a mental impression of a specified kind: *loud-sounding pop music* ○ *a very grand-sounding name.*

□ **ˈsounding-board** *n* (**a**) board or canopy placed over a platform, stage, etc to direct the speaker's voice towards the audience, so enabling him to be heard more clearly. (**b**) means of causing an opinion, a plan, etc to be widely heard: *The magazine became a sounding-board for its editor's political beliefs.*

sound[4] /saʊnd/ *v* **1** [I, Tn] (**a**) test or measure the depth of (the sea, etc) by using a weighted line (called a **sounding line**). (**b**) find the depth of water in a ship's hold (with a **sounding rod**). **2** (phr v) **sound sb out (about/on sth)** try to discover sb's views, opinions, etc (on sth), esp in a cautious or reserved way: *Have you sounded him out* (ie found out his opinions) *yet about taking the job?* ○ *I'll try to sound out the manager on the question of holidays.*

▷ **soundings** *n* [pl] **1** measurements obtained by sounding (sound[4] 1); depth measured: *underwater soundings.* **2** (**a**) [C, U] (action of) finding out sb's views in a cautious way: *take soundings* ○ *What results have your soundings turned up?* (**b**) reactions obtained: *Our soundings are displayed in the form of a graph.*

sound[5] /saʊnd/ (also esp in place names **Sound**) *n* narrow passage of water joining two larger areas of water; strait: *ˌPlymouth ˈSound.*

soup[1] /su:p/ *n* [U, C] **1** liquid food made by cooking vegetables, meat, etc in water: *chicken, tomato, vegetable, etc soup* ○ *a range of tinned soups* ○ *Will you have some soup before the meat course?* **2** (idm) **in the ˈsoup** (*infml*) in trouble or difficulties: *If your Mum finds out what you've done, you'll really be in the soup!*

□ **ˈsoup-kitchen** *n* place where soup and other food is supplied free to people with no money, esp after a disaster such as an earthquake or a flood.

ˈsoup-plate *n* large deep plate with a wide rim, used esp for soup.

soup[2] /su:p/ *v* (phr v) **soup sth up** (esp passive) (*infml*) increase the power of (a car, etc) by modifying the engine: *a souped-up old mini* ○ (*fig*) *The 'new' film is just a souped-up version of the 1948 original.*

soupçon /ˈsu:psɒn; *US* su:pˈsɒn/ *n* [sing] ~ (**of sth**) (*sometimes joc*) very small amount; trace: *a soupçon of garlic in the salad* ○ *a soupçon of malice in his remark.*

sour /ˈsaʊə(r)/ *adj* **1** (**a**) having a sharp taste (like that of vinegar, a lemon or unripe fruit): *sour gooseberries* ○ *This apple is really sour!* (**b**) tasting or smelling sharp and unpleasant from fermentation; not fresh: *The milk's turned sour.* ○ *a sour smell.* **2** having or showing a bad temper; disagreeable in manner: *a sour and disillusioned man* ○ *What a sour face she has!* **3** (idm) **go/turn ˈsour** become unfavourable or unpleasant; turn out badly: *Their relationship soon went sour.* ○ *His original enthusiasm has turned sour.* **sour ˈgrapes** (*saying*) (said when sb pretends that what he cannot have is of little or no value or importance): *He says he didn't want to marry her anyway, but that's just sour grapes.*

▷ **sour** *v* [I, Tn] (cause sth/sb to) become sour: *The hot weather soured the milk.* ○ (*fig*) *His personality has soured.* ○ *The old man has been soured by poverty.*

sourly *adv.*

sourness *n* [U]: *the sourness of the fruit* ○ *the sourness of her expression.*

□ ˌ**sour ˈcream** cream deliberately made sour by the addition of bacteria, used in various savoury dishes.

ˈ**sourdough** *n* (*US*) **1** [U] fermented dough mixture used in bread-making: [attrib] *sourdough bread.* **2** person with long experience in pioneering or gold prospecting (in N Canada or Alaska).

ˈ**sourpuss** *n* (*infml*) bad-tempered person: *She's an old sourpuss.*

source /sɔ:s/ *n* **1** starting-point of a river: *the sources of the Nile* ○ *Where is the source of the Rhine?* **2** place from which sth comes or is obtained: *news from a reliable source* ○ *a limited source of income* ○ *Is that well the source of all the cases of infection?* **3** (esp *pl*) person or thing (esp a book, document, etc) supplying information, esp for study: *He cited many sources for his book.* ○ [attrib] *source material.* **4** (idm) **at ˈsource** at the point of origin or beginning: *money taxed at source,* ie before it is given to the earner ○ *Is the water polluted at source or further downstream?*

Sousa /ˈsu:zə/ John Philip (1854-1932), American composer. After conducting the US Marine Band he formed his own band, performing his own music, esp marches like *Liberty Bell* and *Washington Post.*

sousaphone /ˈsu:zəfəʊn/ *n* very large brass musical instrument that curls round the player's body, used esp in military bands. It is named after the composer J P Sousa.

souse /saʊs/ *v* **1** [Tn] (*infml*) plunge (sb/sth) into or soak in water; throw water on or over. **2** [Tn esp passive] put (fish, etc) into salted water, vinegar, etc to preserve it: *soused herrings.*

▷ **soused** /saʊst/ *adj* [pred] (*sl*) drunk.

south /saʊθ/ *n* **1** [U] (*abbr* **S**, *US* also **So**) one of the four main points of the compass, on the right of a person facing the rising sun: *South is opposite north on a compass.* Cf EAST, NORTH, WEST. **2** [U *sing*] (in) this direction, or any part of the earth lying in this direction: *The window faces south.* ○ *The wind is in* (ie blowing from) *the south today.* ○ *The town is to the south of* (ie situated further south than) *London.* **3 the South** [sing] (**a**) part of a country further south than the rest; southern part or region: *have a holiday in the South of France* ○ *He came to the South to look for a job.* (**b**) south-eastern states of the USA. Until the 1860s, when they were defeated by the North in the *American Civil War, slavery was legal there. Cf DEEP SOUTH (DEEP[1]).

▷ **sou'** /saʊ/ *n* (*esp nautical*) (short form of *south* used in compounds): *sou'-east* ○ *sou'-sou'-west.*

south (also **South**) *adj* [attrib] **1** in, near, towards or at the south: *South Wales* ○ *the South Pacific* ○ *grow roses on a south wall* ○ *on the south coast.* **2** (of a wind) coming from the south: *a south wind.*

south *adv* **1** to or towards the south: *go south out of town* ○ *birds flying south for winter* ○ *The ship was sailing due south.* **2** (idm) **down ˈsouth** (*infml*) to or in the south: *go down south for a few days* ○ *They used to live in Scotland but they moved down south.*

□ **the ˌSouth ˈBank** group of buildings on the south bank of the Thames in central London, which includes the Royal Festival Hall, the National Theatre and the Hayward Gallery.

ˈ**southbound** *adj* travelling towards the south: *a southbound train* ○ *swallows southbound for the winter.*

ˌ**south-ˈeast** *n* [sing], *adj*, *adv* (*abbr* **SE**) (situated in, towards, coming from or in the direction of) the point on the compass midway between south and east: *live in the South-East* ○ *a ˌsouth-east ˈwind* ○ *a house facing south-east.* ˌ**southˈeaster** *n* strong wind blowing from the south-east. ˌ**south-ˈeasterly** *adj* (**a**) (of a wind) from the south-east: *a south-easterly air-flow.* (**b**) (of a direction) towards the south-east. ˌ**south-ˈeastern** /-ˈi:stən/ *adj* of, from or situated in the south-east part (esp of a country): *the south-eastern states of the US.*

ˈ**southpaw** *n* (*infml*) left-handed person (esp in sports such as boxing).

the ˌSouth ˈPole southernmost point of the Earth: *a journey to the South Pole.* ➪ illus at GLOBE.

southward(s) /ˈsaʊθwədz/ *adv*, *adj* (travelling) towards the south: *driving southwards along the motorway.* ➪ Usage at FORWARD[2].

ˌ**south-ˈwest** *n* [sing], *adj*, *adv* (*abbr* **SW**) (situated in, towards, coming from or in the direction of) the point on the compass midway between south and west: *travel south-west* ○ *stand facing south-west* ○ *a south-west wind* ○ *live in the South-West (of a country).* ˌ**southˈwester** *n* = SOU'WESTER 2. ˌ**south-ˈwesterly** *adj* (**a**) (of a wind) from the south-west. (**b**) (of a direction) towards the south-west: *travel in a south-westerly direction for 6 miles.* ˌ**south-ˈwestern** /-ˈwestən/ *adj* of, from or situated in the south-west.

South Africa /ˌsaʊθ ˈæfrɪkə/ (also **Republic of South Africa**) country at the southern tip of Africa; pop approx 33 748 000; official languages English and Afrikaans; capital Pretoria; unit of currency rand (= 100 cents). It is the most economically developed of all African countries. Despite its large desert and mountain regions it uses its relatively small crop-growing areas for intensive production of cereals and fruit. It is one of the world's leading producers of gold, uranium, manganese and diamonds, and several other important minerals. Its policy of apartheid has divided the white, black and coloured populations, keeping power and economic progress largely for the whites. Important political changes are being made, although considerable opposition to them remains. ➪ map at NAMIBIA. ▷ ˌ**South ˈAfrican** *n*, *adj.*

South America /ˌsaʊθ əˈmerɪkə/ large southern half of the American continent, from *Colombia and *Venezuela in the north to *Cape Horn in the south, and with the Pacific Ocean to the west and the Atlantic to the east. The *Andes mountains run parallel to the west coast; much of the north is covered by tropical forest, esp around the *Amazon, and much of the south by the pampas. Most of the states were formerly Spanish possessions that became independent in the 19th century; *Brazil was formerly a Portuguese colony. Political instability has hindered economic progress and there is great poverty in most of the states, but Brazil and Venezuela have developed industrial economies. ▷ ˌ**South Aˈmerican** *n*, *adj.*

South Australia /ˌsaʊθ ɒˈstreɪlɪə; *US* ɔ:ˈst-/ state in south central Australia. It is mostly low-lying, with mountains in the south-east and north-west. Agriculture is important, and it contains much of the country's wine-growing areas. ➪ map at App 1.

South Carolina /ˌsaʊθ ˌkærəˈlaɪnə/ state on the south-east coast of the USA. It is largely a coastal plain with a part of the *Appalachian range in the north-west. Agriculture is important, but the economy is mainly industrial, producing chemicals, textiles and cement. It was one of the 13 original states. ➪ map at App 1.

South Dakota /ˌsaʊθ dəˈkəʊtə/ state of the north central USA. The Missouri river separates the Badlands (BAD[1]) from the *Great Plains. It is a largely agricultural state growing cereals, but also has considerable mineral reserves, esp gold and uranium. ➪ map at App 1.

southerly /ˈsʌðəlɪ/ *adj*, *adv* **1** (of winds) blowing from the south: *southerly breezes.* **2** towards the south: *The plane flew off in a southerly direction.*

▷ **southerly** *n* (esp *pl*) wind blowing from the south: *warm southerlies.*

southern /ˈsʌðən/ (also **Southern**) *adj* in or of the south: *southern Europe* ○ *the Southern states of the USA* ○ *the Southern hemisphere,* ie the southern half of the globe.

▷ **southerner** *n* person from the southern part of a country, eg from the South in the USA: *a southerner now living in the north of England* ○ *You can tell southerners by their accent.*

□ **the ˌSouthern ˈCross** small constellation in the southern hemisphere. It contains the star Alpha Crucis, the 14th-brightest star in the sky.

ˌ**southern ˈlights** = AURORA AUSTRALIS (AURORA 2).

ˈ**southernmost** /-məʊst/ *adj* furthest south: *the southernmost point of an island.*

Southey /ˈsʌðɪ/ Robert (1774-1843), English poet. He was a friend of *Coleridge and *Wordsworth and was one of the *Lake poets. He was made Poet Laureate in 1813. He also wrote history and biographies.

South Glamorgan /ˌsaʊθ gləˈmɔ:gən/ county of S Wales. It is a largely industrial and urban county and contains Cardiff, the capital of Wales. ➪ map at App 1.

South Seas /ˌsaʊθ ˈsi:z/ **the South Seas** (*arch*) the Pacific Ocean.

□ **the ˌSouth Sea ˈBubble** financial scandal in Britain in 1720. The South Sea Company had been formed to trade with Spain's American colonies and the general confidence in the profits to be made led the Company to take responsibility for part of the National Debt. Speculation made the price of shares rise to an absurd level and many investors were ruined when the Company collapsed.

South Yorkshire /ˌsaʊθ ˈjɔ:kʃə(r)/ metropolitan county of NE England, formed in 1974. ➪ map at App 1.

souvenir /ˌsu:vəˈnɪə(r); *US* ˈsu:vənɪər/ *n* thing taken, bought or received as a gift, and kept to remind one of a person, a place or an event: *a souvenir of my holiday* ○ [attrib] *a souvenir shop for tourists.*

sou'wester /ˌsaʊˈwestə(r)/ *n* **1** waterproof hat (usu of oilskin) with a wide flap at the back to protect the neck. **2** (also **southwester** /ˌsaʊθˈw-/) strong wind blowing from the south-west.

sovereign /ˈsɒvrɪn/ *adj* (*fml*) **1** (of power) without limit; highest: *Who holds sovereign power in the state?* **2** [attrib] (of a nation, state, ruler) fully independent and self-governing; having total power: *become a sovereign state.* **3** [attrib] (*fml*) very effective; excellent: *Is there a sovereign remedy for this condition?*

▷ **sovereign** *n* **1** (*fml*) ruler with sovereign power, eg a king, a queen or an emperor. **2** former British gold coin, originally worth one pound.

sovereignty /ˈsɒvrəntɪ/ *n* [U] (*fml*) **1** independent sovereign power. **2** quality of being a country with this power: *respect an island's sovereignty.*

soviet /ˈsəʊvɪət, ˈsɒv-/ *n* **1** [C] any of the councils of workers, etc in any part of the former USSR (the Union of Soviet Socialist Republics): *the Supreme Soviet,* ie the governing council of the whole of the USSR. **2 the Soviets** [pl] (*esp US*) the people of the former USSR; their leaders.

▷ **Soviet** *adj* [usu attrib] of or concerning the former USSR and its people: *Soviet Russia* ○ *the Soviet Union.*

sow[1] /saʊ/ *n* fully grown female pig. ⇨ illus at PIG. Cf BOAR, HOG 1.

sow[2] /səʊ/ *v* (*pt* **sowed**, *pp* **sown** /səʊn/ or **sowed**) **1** [Tn, Tn·pr] ~ **A (in/on B)**/ ~ **B (with A)** put or scatter (seed) in or on the ground; plant (land) with seed: *sow grass* ○ *sow a plot of land with grass* ○ *sow cabbage seed in pots* ○ *sow a field with wheat.* **2** [Tn, Tn·pr] ~ **sth (in sth)** (*fig*) spread or introduce (feelings, ideas, etc): *sow doubt in sb's mind* ○ *sow the seeds of hatred.* **3** (idm) **sow one's wild ˈoats** go through a period of irresponsible pleasure-seeking while young: *He sowed all his wild oats before he married.*

▷ **sower** *n* person who sows: (*fig*) *a sower of discontent among the people.*

soya bean /ˈsɔɪə biːn/ (also *esp US* **soy bean** /ˈsɔɪ biːn/) *n* type of bean (originally from SE Asia) rich in protein, grown for food and used esp as a substitute for meat: *a casserole made with soya beans* ○ [attrib] *soya oil*, ie extracted from soya beans ○ *soya flour* ○ *soya milk*, ie milk substitute made from processed soya beans.

□ **soya ˈsauce** (also **soy ˈsauce**) dark brown sauce made by fermenting soya beans in salty water, used esp in oriental cooking: *adding soy sauce to the stir-fried vegetables.*

Soyinka /ʃɔɪˈɪŋkə/ Wole (1934-), Nigerian author. His plays, novels and poetry explore the relationship of developing modern Africa with its past and with Europe.

Soyuz /sɔɪˈuːz/ any of a series of manned spacecraft launched into orbit round the earth by the USSR after 1967.

sozzled /ˈsɒzld/ *adj* (*infml*) very drunk: *He got absolutely sozzled at the Christmas party.*

sp *abbr* (esp on corrected written work) spelling.

spa /spɑː/ (also in place names **Spa**) *n* (place where there is a) spring of mineral water with medicinal properties: *Cheltenham Spa* ○ [attrib] *spa water.*

space /speɪs/ *n* **1** [C] unused or unfilled gap or area between two or more objects or points: *the spaces between words* ○ *There's a space here for your signature.* ○ *Is there a space for the car in the firm's car park?* ○ *We were separated by a space of ten feet.* **2** [U] unoccupied area or place available for use; room: *There isn't much space left for your luggage.* ○ *Have you enough space to work in?* ○ *There isn't enough space in the classroom for thirty desks.* ⇨ Usage. **3** [C, U] large area (esp of land not built on): *open spaces for children to play on* ○ *a country of wide open spaces* ○ *the freedom and space of the countryside.* **4** [U] continuous expanse in which all things exist and move: *He was staring into space.* **5** [U] (also **outer ˈspace**) (often in compounds) universe beyond the earth's atmosphere in which all other planets and stars exist: *travel through space to other planets* ○ *the exploration of outer space.* **6** [C usu *sing*] interval of time: *(with)in the space of two hours*, ie during a period not longer than two hours ○ *a space of two weeks between appointments.* **7** (idm) **cramped for room/space** ⇨ CRAMP[2]. **watch this ˈspace** (*catchphrase*) (in a newspaper, etc) keep alert because sth interesting or surprising will appear here soon.

▷ **space** *v* [Tn, Tn·p] ~ **sth (out)** set sth out with regular spaces between: *space out the posts three metres apart* ○ *space out* (ie spread) *payments for a house over twenty years* ○ *space the rows 10 inches apart* ○ *the letter was well spaced*, ie typed, etc with a suitable amount of space between each line, etc. **spacing** *n* [U] amount of space left between objects, words, etc in laying or setting sth out: *Be careful with your spacing or you won't get the heading on one line.* ○ *Shall I use single or double spacing* (ie single or double spaces between the lines) *when I type this letter?*

□ **ˈspace-age** *adj* [attrib] very modern and advanced: *space-age technology, equipment.*

ˈspace-bar *n* bar on a typewriter, tapped to make spaces between words.

ˈspacecraft *n* (*pl* unchanged) (also **ˈspaceship**) vehicle manned or unmanned for travelling in space: *spacecraft orbiting the earth.*

ˈspaceman /-mæn/ (*fem* **ˈspacewoman**) *n* (*pl* **-men, -women**) (also **astronaut**) person who travels in outer space.

ˈspace invaders (*propr*) popular computerized game in which players try to prevent creatures from space landing on earth.

ˈspace probe = PROBE 2.

ˈspaceship *n* = SPACECRAFT.

ˈspace shuttle spacecraft designed for repeated use, eg between earth and a space station or the moon.

ˈspace station large manned artificial satellite used as a base for operations in space(5), eg for scientific research, as a launching pad for spacecraft, etc.

ˈspacesuit *n* sealed suit covering the whole body and supplied with air, allowing the wearer to move about in space(5).

ˈspacewalk *n* act or time of moving about in space outside a spacecraft.

NOTE ON USAGE: **Space**, **room**, **place** and **seat** all relate to an area in a room, building, vehicle, etc which can be occupied by a person or thing. **Space** (countable and uncountable) and **room** (uncountable) are the most general and suggest an undefined area, big enough for something or for a purpose: *The wardrobe takes up too much space/room.* **Place** and **seat** (both countable) are used for specific spaces, usually for people to sit: *We'll try to get places/seats at the front of the hall.* ○ *There are only two places/seats left for tonight.*

spacious /ˈspeɪʃəs/ *adj* having or providing much space; roomy: *a very spacious kitchen* ○ *the spacious back seat of a car.* ▷ **spaciously** *adv.* **spaciousness** *n* [U]

spade[1] /speɪd/ *n* **1** tool for digging, with a wooden handle and a broad metal blade: *a garden spade.* **2** (idm) **call a spade a spade** ⇨ CALL[2].

spade and shovel

▷ **spadeful** /ˈspeɪdfʊl/ *n* amount (of earth, etc) carried on a spade: *three spadefuls of sand.*

□ **ˈspadework** *n* [U] (*fig*) hard work done in preparation for sth: *She got the praise for the job but he did all the spadework.*

spade[2] /speɪd/ *n* **1** (a) **spades** [sing or pl *v*] suit of playing-cards marked with black figures shaped like pointed leaves with short stems: *the five of spades* ○ *Spades is/are trumps.* (b) [C] card from this suit: *I've only one spade left.* ⇨ illus at PLAYING-CARD. **2** (idm) **black as the ace of spades** ⇨ BLACK[1].

spaghetti /spəˈɡetɪ/ *n* [U] Italian pasta made in long thin rods, cooked in boiling water until soft and usu served with a sauce.

□ **spaˌghetti ˈwestern** (*usu derog*) western film produced, often cheaply, in the 1960s and 1970s in Italy or by an Italian director.

Spain /speɪn/ country in SW Europe; pop approx 39 054 000; official language Spanish, with Catalan in Catalonia and Basque in the Basque provinces;

Spain

capital Madrid; unit of currency peseta. A large central plateau, the Meseta, occupies much of the country, crossed by a number of mountain ranges. Spain is developing an efficient modern system of agriculture; it is now one of the world's largest orange producers and an important wine-growing country. Although its industry is less developed than that of many other W European countries, Spain is attracting foreign investment, esp in its motor industry, and tourism is very important. Spain became a member of the European Community in 1986. ⇨ map. Cf SPANISH, SPANIARD.

spam /spæm/ *n* [U] (*propr*) type of tinned meat made from spiced and chopped cooked ham, usu eaten cold: *spam and salad.*

span[1] /spæn/ *n* **1** distance or part between the supports of an arch or a bridge: *The arch has a span of 60 metres.* ○ *The bridge crosses the river in a single span.* **2** length of time over which sth lasts or extends from beginning to end: *the span of life* ○ *a short span of time* ○ *over a span of six years* ○ *have a short concentration span,* ie be capable of concentrating for only a short period of time. **3** (dated) distance from the tip of the thumb to the tip of the little finger when the hand is stretched out; about 23 centimetres (9 inches).

▷ **span** (**-nn-**) *v* [Tn] **1** form a bridge or arch over (sth); extend across: *The river Thames is spanned by many bridges.* **2** extend over or across (sth); stretch across: (*fml*) *His knowledge spans many different areas.* ○ *Her life spanned almost the whole of the 19th century.* **3** stretch one's hand across (sth) in one span: *Can you span an octave on the piano?*

span[2] /spæn/ *adj* (idm) **spick and span** ⇨ SPICK[1].

spangle /ˈspæŋgl/ *n* tiny piece of shining metal or plastic used for decoration on a dress, etc, esp in large numbers: *the spangles on the fairy's dress in the pantomime.*

▷ **spangle** *v* [esp passive: Tn, Tn·pr] ~ **sth (with sth)** cover or decorate sth with spangles or small bright objects like spangles: *a dress spangled with tiny silver sequins.*

Spaniard /ˈspænjəd/ *n* native or inhabitant of Spain.

spaniel /ˈspænjəl/ *n* breed of dog with large ears which hang down: *a cocker spaniel.* ⇨ illus at DOG.

Spanish /ˈspænɪʃ/ *adj* of Spain or its people or their language: *a Spanish dance* ○ *Spanish customs.*

▷ **Spanish** *n* **1** [U] the language of Spain: *Do you speak Spanish?* **2 the Spanish** [pl] Spanish people. Cf SPANIARD.

□ **the ˌSpanish Inquiˈsition** ⇨ INQUISITION 1.

the ˌSpanish ˈMain (former name for the) NE coast of S America and the Caribbean Sea near this coast.

ˌSpanish ˈomelette omelette made with various vegetables, including esp onions, which are mixed with the egg during cooking.

spank /spæŋk/ *v* **1** [Tn] slap (esp a child) with a flat hand, esp on the buttocks, as a punishment: *spank a child's bottom.* **2** (phr v) ~ **along** (*dated infml*) (esp of a horse, ship or car) move along quickly: *fairly spanking along.*

▷ **spank** *n* slap with a flat hand, esp on the buttocks: *a spank on the bottom.*

spanking *n* series of spanks; process of spanking: *The boy got a sound spanking.* — *adj* [usu attrib] (*dated infml*) quick and energetic: *go at a spanking pace.* — *adv* (*infml*) (used esp before *adjs* like *fine, new*) outstandingly; very: *a spanking new boat* ○ *spanking white paint.*

spanner
(*US* **wrench**)

FORK SPANNER

ADJUSTABLE SPANNER

RING SPANNER

spanner /ˈspænə(r)/ (*Brit*) (*US* **wrench**) *n* **1** tool for gripping and turning nuts on screws, bolts, etc: *I'll need a spanner to change the back wheel.* **2** (idm) **(throw) a ˈspanner in the works** (*Brit infml*) (cause the) ruin or sabotage of a plan, scheme, etc.

spar[1] /spɑː(r)/ *n* strong wooden or metal pole used as a mast, yard, boom, etc on a ship.

spar[2] /spɑː(r)/ *v* (**-rr-**) [I, Ipr] ~ **(with sb)** **1** box (sb) using light blows, usu for practice only. **2** argue or dispute (with sb), usu in a friendly way: *children sparring with each other.*

□ **ˈsparring-partner** /ˈspɑːrɪŋ/ *n* **1** person with whom a boxer spars as part of training. **2** (*infml*) person with whom one enjoys frequent, usu friendly, arguments: *They've been sparring-partners ever since they were at school together.*

spare[1] /speə(r)/ *adj* **1** in addition to what is usu needed or used; kept in reserve for use when needed: *Do you carry a spare wheel in your car?* ○ *We have no spare room* (ie space) *for a table.* ○ *I wish we had a spare room,* ie an extra bedroom (eg for guests). ○ *I have no spare money this month.* **2** (of time) for leisure; free; unoccupied: *a busy woman with little spare time* ○ *He paints in his spare time.* **3** (*esp fml*) (of people) thin; lean: *a tall spare man* ○ *a spare figure* ○ *spare of build.* **4** [attrib] (*fml*) small in quantity: *a spare meal* ○ *on a spare diet.* **5** (idm) **go ˈspare** (*Brit sl*) become very annoyed or upset: *Your mum will go spare if she finds out what you've done!*

▷ **spare** *n* spare part (for a machine, car, etc), esp an extra wheel for a car: *I've got a puncture and my spare is flat too!* ○ *I'll show you where the spares are kept.*

□ **ˌspare ˈpart** part (for a machine, car, etc) used to replace an identical part if it gets lost, damaged, etc: *It's difficult to get spare parts for old washing-machines.*

ˌspare-ˈrib *n* rib of pork with most of the meat cut off: *barbecued spare-ribs.*

ˌspare ˈtyre **1** extra wheel for a car, etc. **2** (*Brit infml joc*) roll of fat around the waist: *I'll have to exercise to get rid of my spare tyre.*

spare[2] /speə(r)/ *v* **1** [Tn, Dn·n] refrain from hurting, harming or destroying (sb/sth); show mercy to: *Please spare* (ie don't kill) *me!* ○ (*fml*) *spare a person his life,* ie not kill him ○ *if I am spared,* ie if I live ○ *They killed the men but spared the children.* ○ *The woodman spared* (ie did not cut down) *a few trees.* **2** [Tn, Dn·n] refrain from using, giving, etc (sth); use as little as possible: *No trouble was spared to ensure our comfort.* ○ *Try to spare her as much distress as possible when you tell her.* ○ *He does not spare himself,* ie works, etc very hard indeed. ○ *Please spare me* (ie don't tell me) *the gruesome details.* **3** [Tn, Tn·pr, Dn·n, Dn·pr] ~ **sth (for sb/sth)** be able to afford to give (time, money, etc) (to sb for a purpose): *I can't spare the time for a holiday at the moment.* ○ *Can you spare me a few minutes of your time?* ○ *Can you spare me a few litres of petrol?* ○ *Can you spare a cigarette for me?* **4** [Tn, Tn·pr] (*infml*) manage without (sb): *I can't spare him today — we need everybody here.* ○ *I can't spare you for that job; you must finish this one first.* **5** (idm) **no expense spared** ⇨ EXPENSE. **spare sb's ˈblushes** do not embarrass sb by praising him. **spare sb's ˈfeelings** avoid hurting sb's feelings: *He spared her feelings by not criticizing her husband in front of her.* **spare no expense** have no regard for the cost when arranging, designing, etc sth: *They spared no expense in renovating the house.* **spare no pains doing/to do sth** (*fml*) take as much trouble as is necessary to achieve sth: *The hotel staff spared no pains to ensure that our stay was as enjoyable as possible.* **ˌspare the ˌrod and ˌspoil the ˈchild** (*saying*) if you do not punish a child when he does wrong you will spoil his character. **(and) to ˈspare** more than is needed; left over: *We have enough fruit and to spare.* ○ *Do you have any sugar to spare?* ○ *There's no time to spare!* ie You must act, go, etc as quickly as possible.

▷ **sparing** /ˈspeərɪŋ/ *adj* [pred] ~ **with/of/in sth** (*fml*) economical or frugal with sth; not wasteful of sth: *be sparing with the sugar* ○ *sparing of one's energy* ○ *not sparing in his advice to others*

sparingly *adv*: *Use the perfume sparingly!*

Spark /spɑːk/ Muriel (1918-) British author. He novels, such as *The Prime of Miss Jean Brodie* an *The Ballad of Peckham Rye,* are noted for thei ironic humour.

spark /spɑːk/ *n* **1** [C] **(a)** tiny glowing particl thrown off from sth burning or produced whe two hard substances (eg stone, metal, flint) ar struck together: *Sparks from the fire were flying u the chimney.* ○ *The firework exploded in a shower c sparks.* ○ *Rubbing stones together produces spark to start a fire.* **(b)** flash of light produced by th breaking of an electric current: *a faulty ligh switch sending out sparks.* **2** [sing] ~ **of sth** trac (of a particular quality): *He hasn't a spark o generosity in him.* ○ *without a spark of enthusiasm* **3** (idm) **a bright spark** ⇨ BRIGHT. **make the fur sparks fly** ⇨ FLY[2].

▷ **spark** *v* [I] **1** give out sparks (SPARK 1); produc sparks: *The fire is sparking dangerously.* **2** (phr v **spark sth off** (*infml*) be the immediate cause c (usu sth bad); lead to sth: *His comment sparked o a quarrel between them.* ○ *The incident sparked o a whole chain of disasters.*

sparks *n* [sing *v*] (*sl*) electrician or radio operato (esp on a ship).

□ **ˈsparking-plug** (also **ˈspark-plug**) *n* devic producing an electrical spark which fires th petrol mixture in a petrol engine: *The sparking plugs need cleaning.* ⇨ illus at CAR.

sparkle /ˈspɑːkl/ *v* [I, Ipr] ~ **(with sth)** **1** shin brightly with flashes of light: *Her diamond sparkled in the candle-light.* ○ *pavements sparklin with frost* ○ *Her eyes sparkled with excitement.* **2** b full of life and wit: *She was really sparkling (wit happiness) at the wedding.* ○ *She always sparkle at parties.*

▷ **sparkle** *n* [U, C] effect made by sparklin (SPARKLE 1, 2); act of sparkling: *the sparkle c sunlight on snow* ○ *There was a sudden sparkle a the fireworks were lit.* ○ *a performance that lacke sparkle.*

sparkler /ˈspɑːklə(r)/ *n* **1** [C] type of smal hand-held firework that sends off showers o sparks. **2 sparklers** [pl] (*sl*) diamonds.

sparkling /spɑːklɪŋ/ *adj* [attrib] **1** (of wine, etc giving off tiny bubbles of gas: *sparkling white win* ○ *sparkling mineral water.* **2** lively and witty *sparkling conversation* ○ *a brilliant, sparklin young woman.*

sparrow /ˈspærəʊ/ *n* type of small brownish-gre bird common in many parts of the world: *sparrow twittering in the roof-tops.* ⇨ illus at BIRD.

□ **ˈsparrow-hawk** *n* small hawk that eats smalle birds.

sparse /spɑːs/ *adj* not dense, thick or crowded thinly scattered: *a sparse population* ○ *a spars beard* ○ *The television coverage of the event wa rather sparse.* ▷ **sparsely** *adv*: *a sparsel furnished room,* ie one with little furniture *sparsely spread financial resources.* **sparsenes** (also **sparsity** /ˈspɑːsətɪ/) *n* [U]: *the sparseness c trees on the landscape.*

spartan /ˈspɑːtn/ *adj* (*fml*) (of conditions) simpl and harsh; without luxury or comforts (from th harsh life and discipline of the Spartans, a ancient Greek people): *lead a spartan life in th mountains* ○ *a spartan meal,* ie a very simple one

spasm /ˈspæzəm/ *n* [C, U] **1** strong, sudden an uncontrollable tightening of a muscle or muscles *an asthma spasm* ○ *painful muscular spasms* ○ *Th muscles in the athlete's leg went into spasm,* i tightened uncontrollably and painfully. **2** sudde short burst (of activity, emotion, etc): *a spasm o energy, excitement, pain, coughing.*

spasmodic /spæzˈmɒdɪk/ *adj* **1** occurring or don at irregular intervals (usu for short periods at time); not continuous or regular: *spasmodic effort to clean the house* ○ *spasmodic periods of happines followed by misery.* **2** caused by or affected b spasms: *spasmodic asthma.* ▷ **spasmodicall** /-klɪ/ *adv*: *spasmodically energetic.*

spastic /ˈspæstɪk/ *n, adj* (person who is) physicall disabled because of cerebral palsy, a condition i which there are faulty links between the brain and motor nerves causing jerky or uncontrollable movements: *a special school for spastics* ○ *spastic children.*

spat[1] *pt, pp of* SPIT[1].

spat[2] /spæt/ *n* (*US infml*) small or unimportant quarrel: *a spat between brother and sister.*

spat[3] /spæt/ *n* (usu *pl*) cloth or leather covering for the ankle worn formerly by men over the shoe and fastened at the side: *a pair of spats.* ⇨ illus at DRESS.

spate /speɪt/ *n* **1** [sing] sudden fast rush (of business, etc): *a spate of orders* ○ *a spate of new cars on the market* ○ *a spate of (cases of) influenza in the winter.* **2** (idm) **in ˈspate** (of a river, etc) flowing strongly at a much higher level than normal: *After the storm all the rivers were in spate.*

spatial /ˈspeɪʃl/ *adj* (*fml*) of, concerning or existing in space: *the spatial qualities of the new concert hall.* ▷ **spatially** /-ʃəlɪ/ *adv.*

spatter /ˈspætə(r)/ *v* **1** [Tn, Tn·pr] ~ **sth (on/over sb/sth)**; ~ **sb/sth (with sth)** scatter, splash or sprinkle sth in drips (over sb/sth): *spatter oil on one's clothes/spatter one's clothes with oil* ○ *As the bus passed it spattered us with mud.* ⇨ Usage at SPRAY[2]. **2** [I, Ipr, Ip] fall or rain down in drops: *We heard the rain spattering down on the roof of the hut.* ○ *Bullets spattered around us.*

▷ **spatter** *n* [sing] ~ **(of sth) (a)** sprinkling; small shower: *a spatter of rain, bullets, etc.* **(b)** sound of spattering: *the spatter of rain on the tent* ○ *a spatter of applause.*

spatula /ˈspætʃʊlə/ *n* **1** tool with a wide flat blunt blade used for mixing and spreading, esp in cooking and painting: *He scraped the mixture out of the bowl with a plastic spatula.* ○ *She levelled the surface of the cake mixture with a metal spatula.* ⇨ illus at KITCHEN. **2** strip of hard material (usu wood) used by a doctor for pressing the tongue down when examining the throat.

spawn /spɔːn/ *n* [U] (esp in compounds) **1** eggs of fish, shellfish and frogs, toads, etc: *ˈfrog-spawn.* **2** (*biology*) white fibrous matter from which mushrooms and other fungi grow.

▷ **spawn** *v* [I, Tn] **(a)** (of fish, frogs, etc) produce (eggs): *salmon spawning* ○ *Have the frogs spawned yet?* **(b)** (*esp derog*) appear or produce (sth) in great numbers: *departments which spawn committees and sub-committees* ○ *new housing estates spawning everywhere.*

spay /speɪ/ *v* [Tn] remove the ovaries of (a female animal) to prevent it breeding: *Has your cat been spayed yet?*

speak /spiːk/ *v* (*pt* **spoke** /spəʊk/, *pp* **spoken** /spəʊkən/) **1** [I] make use of words in an ordinary voice (not singing); utter words: *He can't speak.* ○ *Please speak more slowly.* ○ *'May I speak to Susan?'*, ie at the beginning of a telephone conversation ○ *'Speaking'*, ie This is Susan speaking (in reply to the previous question). **2** [Tn] (not in the continuous tenses) know and be able to use (a language): *He speaks several languages.* ○ *She speaks a little Urdu.* ○ *Does anyone speak English here?* **3** [Ipr] ~ **(to/with sb) (about/of sb/sth)** have a conversation (with sb); express oneself in words; talk: *I was speaking to him only yesterday.* ○ *Can we speak about plans for the holidays?* ○ *She was speaking about it for hours.* ○ *She didn't speak of her husband at all.* **4** [I, Ipr] ~ **(on/about sth)** make a speech (to an audience): *She spoke for forty minutes at the conference.* ○ *Are you good at speaking in public?* ○ *I told him to speak on any subject he wanted.* **5** [Tn] make (sth) known; say or express: *speak the truth* ○ *He spoke only two words the whole evening.* ⇨ Usage at SAY. **6** [I, Ipr] ~ **(to/with sb)** (usu in negative sentences) (*infml*) be on friendly or polite terms (with sb): *They're not speaking (to each other) after their argument.* **7** (idm) **actions speak louder than words** ⇨ ACTION. **be on ˈspeaking terms (with sb) (a)** know sb well enough to speak to him: *I see him on the train every day but we're not on speaking terms.* **(b)** be on friendly or polite terms; be willing to talk (to sb) (esp after an argument): *At last they're on speaking terms again!* ○ *They're not on speaking terms after their quarrel.* **the facts speak for themselves** ⇨ FACT. **in a manner of speaking** ⇨ MANNER. **nothing to ˈspeak of** nothing worth mentioning; not much: *She has saved a little money, but nothing to speak of.* **not to speak of/no sth to speak of** not worth mentioning/no sth worth mentioning: *We've not had any summer to speak of.* ○ *We've had no food to speak of today.* **roughly, generally, personally, etc speaking** in a rough, general, etc way; from a general, personal, etc point of view: *Generally speaking, I don't like spicy food.* ○ *Personally speaking, I prefer the second candidate.* Cf STRICTLY SPEAKING (STRICT). **ˌso to ˈspeak** one could say; as it were: *The new procedures have been officially christened, so to speak.* **speak for itˈself/themˈselves** need no explaining; be self-evident: *The events of that evening speak for themselves.* **speak for oneˈself** express one's opinion, etc in one's own way: *I'm quite capable of speaking for myself, thank you!* **speak for yourˈself** (*joc or derog catchphrase*) don't think you are speaking on behalf of everyone: *'We all played very badly.' 'Speak for yourself, I think I played quite well.'* **speak ill of sb** (*fml*) speak in an unkind or unfavourable way about sb: *Don't speak ill of the dead.* ○ *I've never spoken ill of him in my life.* **speak one's ˈmind** express one's views directly and frankly. **speak/talk of the devil** ⇨ DEVIL[1]. **speak the same ˈlanguage (as sb)** (*infml*) have similar tastes and ideas (as sb); have a common understanding: *As soon as I met Liz, it was obvious we spoke the same language.* **speak volumes for sb/sth** be strong evidence of sb/sth's merits, qualities, etc: *These facts speak volumes for her honesty.* **speak ˈwell for sb** be evidence in favour of sb: *Her reputation as a good mother speaks well for her.* **ˈspoken for** reserved, etc in advance: *I'm afraid you can't use those chairs — they're already spoken for.* **the spoken/written word** ⇨ WORD. **8** (phr v) **speak for sb** (no passive) **(a)** state the wishes, views, etc, of sb; act as a spokesman for sb: *I'm afraid I can't speak for Geoff, but....* **(b)** give evidence on behalf of sb: *Who is prepared to speak for the accused?* **speak of sth** (*fml*) indicate sth; suggest sth: *Her behaviour speaks of suffering bravely borne.* **speak out (against sth)** say boldly and clearly what one thinks (in opposition to sth): *He was the only one to speak out against the closure of the hospital.* **speak to sb** (*euph*) reprimand; tell off: *Your children are disturbing my wife; can you speak to them, please?* **speak to sth** (*fml*) give information about (a subject), esp at a meeting: *Will you speak to this item, David?* **speak up** speak louder: *Please speak up; we can't hear you at the back.* **speak up (for sb)** state clearly and freely what one thinks (on behalf of sb): *It's time to speak up for those who are suffering injustice.*

▷ **speaker** *n* **1** person who makes speeches; person who speaks or was speaking: *May I introduce our speaker for this evening?* ○ *a good, poor, interesting, etc speaker* ○ *I turned and saw the speaker at the back of the room.* **2** (*infml*) = LOUDSPEAKER (LOUD). **3** person who speaks a language: *French speakers/speakers of French.* **4 the Speaker** person who presides over business in the House of Commons and other legislative assemblies, decides who speaks in a debate and calls for a vote at the end. The Speaker of the Commons has the power to expel or suspend Members of Parliament who break parliamentary rules; he or she is normally chosen from the party in government, but must be impartial: *'Order! Order!' shouted the Speaker.* ○ *MPs trying to attract the attention of the Speaker.* ⇨ article at PARLIAMENT. **ˌSpeakers' ˈCorner** north-east corner of Hyde Park in London, where people are allowed to address the public on subjects they feel strongly about, usu political or religious.

-spoken (forming compound *adjs*) speaking in a specified way: *well-spoken* ○ *a soft-spoken man.*

□ **ˌspeaking ˈclock** (*Brit infml*) telephone service that gives spoken statements of the time. ⇨ article at TELEPHONE.

ˈspeak-easy *n* place where alcohol may be bought illegally (esp formerly in the USA during Prohibition).

-speak *suff* (forming *ns*) (*infml often derog*) language or jargon (esp of a particular group or organization): *computerspeak* ○ *newspeak.*

spear /spɪə(r)/ *n* **1** weapon with a metal point on a long handle, used (esp formerly) for hunting and fighting: *antelopes killed with spears.* **2** long pointed leaf or stem (eg of grass or asparagus) growing directly out of the ground: *spears of the snowdrop plant.*

▷ **spear** *v* [Tn] strike, pierce or wound (sb/sth) with a spear; kill with a spear: *They were standing in the river spearing fish.* ○ *The warriors speared the man to death.*

□ **ˈspearhead** *n* (usu *sing*) person or group that begins or leads an attack: *The new managing director will act as spearhead of the campaign.* — *v* [Tn] act as a spearhead for (sth): *The tanks spearheaded the offensive.*

spearmint /ˈspɪəmɪnt/ *n* [U] common variety of mint used for flavouring (esp chewing-gum): [attrib] *spearmint toffees.* Cf PEPPERMINT.

spec /spek/ *n* (idm) **on ˈspec** (*infml*) as a speculation or gamble, without being sure of obtaining what one wants: *I went to the concert on spec: I hadn't booked a seat.*

special /ˈspeʃl/ *adj* **1** [usu attrib] of a particular or certain type; not common, usual or general: *goods on special offer*, ie cheaper than usual ○ *He did it as a special favour.* ○ *What are your special interests?* ○ *She's a very special friend.* **2** [attrib] designed, reserved or arranged, etc for a particular purpose: *a special train*, eg for a holiday excursion ○ *a special occasion* ○ *You'll need a special tool to do that.* ○ *She has her own special way of doing things.* ○ *Newspapers send special correspondents to places where important events take place.* **3** [attrib] exceptional in amount, degree, quality, etc: *Take special care of it.* ○ *Why should we give you special treatment?* ○ *He takes no special trouble with his work.* Cf ESPECIAL.

▷ **special** *n* **1** person or thing that is not of the usual or regular type, esp a special constable, train or edition (of a newspaper, etc): *an all night television special on the election* ○ *Specials were brought in to help the regular police force.* **2** (*US infml*) reduced price (in a shop) given prominence through advertising, etc: *There's a special on coffee this week.* ○ *Coffee is on special* (ie being sold at a lower price than usual) *this week.*

specialist /-ʃəlɪst/ *n* person who is an expert in a special branch of work or study, esp of medicine: *an ˈeye specialist* ○ *a specialist in plastic surgery.*

specially /-ʃəlɪ/ *adv* **1** for a particular purpose: *I came here specially to see you.* ○ *I made this specially for your birthday.* **2** (also **especially**) exceptionally; particularly: *I enjoyed the evening, but the meal wasn't specially good.*

□ **ˈSpecial Branch** (*Brit*) department of the police force that deals with national security.

ˌspecial ˈconstable person trained to help the police force occasionally, esp in an emergency.

ˈspecial ˈdelivery delivery of mail (a letter, parcel, etc) by a special messenger instead of by the usual postal service: *If you want the letter to arrive tomorrow send it (by) special delivery.*

ˌspecial ˈlicence licence allowing a marriage to take place at a time or place not usu authorized.

ˌspecial ˈpleading (*law*) persuasive but unfair reasoning that favours one side of an argument.

ˈspecial school school for handicapped children.

ˈspecial student (*US*) student at an American university not on a degree course.

speciality /ˌspeʃɪˈælətɪ/ (also *esp US* **specialty** /ˈspeʃəltɪ/) *n* **1** interest, activity, skill, etc to which a person gives particular attention or in which he specializes: *Her speciality is medieval history.* ○ *His speciality is barbecued steaks.* **2** service or product for which a person, place, firm, etc is well-known; particularly good product or service: *Wood-carvings are a speciality of this village.* ○ *Home-made ice-cream is one of our specialities.*

specialize, -ise /ˈspeʃəlaɪz/ *v* [I, Ipr] ~ **(in sth) (a)** be or become a specialist: *He specializes in oriental history.* **(b)** give particular attention to (a subject, product, etc); be well-known for: *This shop specializes in chocolates.*

▷ **specialization, -isation** /ˌspeʃəlaɪˈzeɪʃn; *US* -lɪˈz-/ *n* [U].

specialized, -ised *adj* **1** adapted or designed for a particular purpose: *specialized tools.* **2** of or relating to a specialist: *specialized knowledge* ○ *specialized work.*

specie /ˈspiːʃiː/ *n* [U] (*fml*) money in the form of coins (contrasted with paper): [attrib] *specie payments* ○ *payment in specie.*

species /ˈspiːʃiːz/ *n* (*pl* unchanged) **1** group of animals or plants within a genus(1) differing only in minor details from the others, and able to breed with each other but not with other groups: *a species of antelope* ○ *various animal species* ○ *the human species,* ie mankind. Cf PHYLUM, CLASS 7, ORDER[1] 9, FAMILY 4. **2** (*infml or joc*) sort; type: *an odd species of writer.*

specific /spəˈsɪfɪk/ *adj* **1** detailed, precise and exact: *specific instructions* ○ *What are your specific aims?* **2** relating to one particular thing, etc; not general: *The money is to be used for one specific purpose: the building of the new theatre.*

▷ **specific** *n* **1** (*medical*) drug used to treat a particular disease or condition: *Quinine is a specific for malaria.* **2** particular aspect or precise detail: *moving from the general to the specific* ○ *We all agreed on our basic aims, but when we got down to specifics it became more complicated.*

specifically /-klɪ/ *adv* in a specific manner: *You were specifically warned not to eat fish.* ○ *The houses are specifically designed for old people.*

□ **speˌcific ˈgravity** mass of any substance in relation to an equal volume of water.

specification /ˌspesɪfɪˈkeɪʃn/ *n* **1** [C esp *pl*] details and instructions describing the design, materials, etc of sth to be made or done: *specifications for (building) a garage* ○ *the technical specifications of a new car.* **2** [U] action of specifying: *the specification of details.*

specify /ˈspesɪfaɪ/ *v* (*pt, pp* **-fied**) [Tn, Tf, Tw] (*esp fml*) state or name clearly and definitely (details, materials, etc): *The contract specifies red tiles, not slates, for the roof.* ○ *The regulations specify that you may use a dictionary in the examination.*

specimen /ˈspesɪmən/ *n* **1** thing or part of a thing taken as an example of its group or class (esp for scientific research or for a collection): *There were some fine specimens of rocks and ores in the museum.* ○ [attrib] *a specimen signature* ○ *a publisher's catalogue with specimen pages of a book.* **2** sample (esp of urine) to be tested (usu for medical purposes): *supply specimens for laboratory analysis.* **3** (*infml sometimes derog*) person of a specified sort, esp one who is unusual in some way: *a fine specimen (of humanity)* ○ *That new librarian is an odd specimen, isn't he?*

specious /ˈspiːʃəs/ *adj* (*fml*) seeming right or true but actually wrong or false: *a specious argument.*

▷ **speciously** *adv*: *speciously convincing.* **speciousness** *n* [U].

speck /spek/ *n* very small spot or stain; tiny particle (of dirt, etc): *a speck of soot on his shirt* ○ *Do you ever see specks in front of your eyes?* ○ *The ship was a mere speck on the horizon.*

speckle /ˈspekl/ *n* small mark or spot, esp one of many, often occurring as natural markings on a different coloured background (on the skin, feathers, eggs, etc): *brown speckles on a white egg* ○ *speckles of red in a blue background.*

▷ **speckled** *adj* marked with speckles: *a speckled hen* ○ *speckled eggs.*

specs /speks/ *n* [pl] (*infml*) = GLASSES (GLASS 5).

spectacle /ˈspektəkl/ *n* **1** grand public display, procession, performance, etc: *The ceremonial opening of Parliament was a fine spectacle.* **2** impressive, remarkable or interesting sight: *The sunrise seen from high in the mountains was a tremendous spectacle.* **3** (*usu derog*) object of attention, esp sb/sth unusual or ridiculous: *The poor fellow was a sad spectacle.* **4** (idm) **make a ˈspectacle of oneself** draw attention to oneself by behaving, dressing, etc ridiculously, esp in public: *make a spectacle of oneself by arguing with the waiter.*

spectacles /ˈspektəklz/ *n* [pl] (*usu fml*) = GLASSES (GLASS 5): *I've lost a pair of spectacles.* ○ *Where are my spectacles?*

▷ **spectacled** /-kəld/ *adj* wearing spectacles.

spectacular /spekˈtækjʊlə(r)/ *adj* (**a**) making a very fine display or show: *a spectacular display of fireworks.* (**b**) (attracting attention because) impressive or extraordinary: *a spectacular victory by the French athlete.*

▷ **spectacular** *n* (supposedly) impressive show or performance; spectacle: *a Christmas TV spectacular* ○ *an aerobatic spectacular at the air show.* **spectacularly** *adv*: *a spectacularly daring performance.*

spectator /spekˈteɪtə(r); *US* ˈspekteɪtər/ *n* person who watches (esp a show or game): *noisy spectators at a football match.*

□ **specˈtator sports** sports that attract many spectators, eg football: *Many spectator sports are now televised.*

spectral /ˈspektrəl/ *adj* (*fml*) **1** of or like a spectre(1): *spectral figures.* **2** of the spectrum or spectra: *spectral colours.*

spectre (*US* **specter**) /ˈspektə(r)/ *n* (*fml*) **1** ghost; phantom: *haunted by spectres from the past.* **2** unpleasant and frightening mental image of possible future trouble: *The spectre of unemployment was always on his mind.*

spectro- *comb form* of or concerned with a spectrum: *spectrometer.*

spectrometer /spekˈtrɒmɪtə(r)/ *n* type of instrument that can be used for measuring spectra.

spectroscope /ˈspektrəskəʊp/ *n* instrument for producing and examining the spectra of a ray of light.

▷ **spectroscopic** /ˌspektrəˈskɒpɪk/ *adj* of or by means of a spectroscope: *spectroscopic analysis.*

spectroscopy /spekˈtrɒskəpɪ/ *n* [U] study of methods of producing and analysing spectra. Applications include the analysis of chemical mixtures and molecular structures.

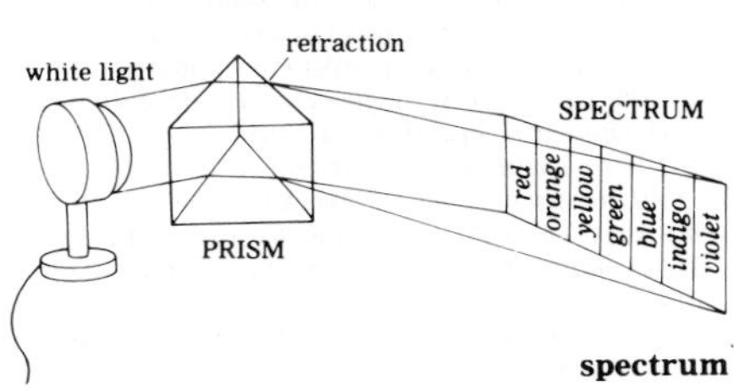

spectrum

spectrum /ˈspektrəm/ *n* (*pl* **spectra** /ˈspektrə/) (*usu sing*) **1** image of a band of colours as seen in a rainbow (and usu described as red, orange, yellow, green, blue, indigo and violet), formed by a ray of light that has passed through a prism. **2** similar series of bands of sound: *the sound spectrum.* **3** (*fig*) full or wide range or sequence: *covering the whole spectrum of ability.* ⇨ Usage at DATA.

speculate /ˈspekjʊleɪt/ *v* **1** [I, Ipr, Tf] ~ (**about/on/upon sth**) form opinions without having definite or complete knowledge or evidence; guess: *speculate about/upon the future* ○ *I wouldn't like to speculate on the reasons for her resignation.* ○ *I can only speculate that he left willingly.* **2** [I, Ipr] ~ (**in sth**) buy and sell goods or stocks and shares in the hope of making a profit through changes in their value, but with the risk of losing money: *speculate in oil shares* ○ *speculating on the stock market.*

▷ **speculator** *n* person who speculates (SPECULATE 2).

speculation /ˌspekjʊˈleɪʃn/ *n* **1** (**a**) [U] ~ (**over/about/upon/on sth**) action of speculating (SPECULATE 1): *much speculation over the cause of the air crash.* (**b**) [C] opinion reached in this way; guess: *My speculations proved totally wrong.* **2** (**a**) [U] ~ (**in sth**) activity of speculating (SPECULATE 2): *speculation in oil* ○ *dishonest speculation in property development.* (**b**) [C] business dea transaction, etc involving this: *make som unprofitable speculations* ○ *buy many shares as speculation.*

speculative /ˈspekjʊlətɪv; *US also* ˈspekjəleɪtɪ *adj* **1** concerned with or formed by speculation(1 *speculative philosophy* ○ *His conclusions are pure speculative.* ie based on reasoning, not facts. **2** as speculation(2): *speculative buying of grain speculative housing.*

sped *pt, pp* of SPEED *v.*

speech /spiːtʃ/ *n* **1** [U] (**a**) power or act of speakin *Man is the only animal that has the faculty speech.* ○ *We can express our thoughts by speech. His illness left him without the power of speech. freedom of speech,* ie freedom to say openly i public what one thinks, eg on social and politic questions. (**b**) manner or way of speaking: *H indistinct speech made it impossible to understan him.* ○ *She's doing a study of children's speech. His speech was slurred: he'd clearly been drinkin* **2** [C] (**a**) ~ (**on/about sth**) formal talk given to a audience: *make/deliver/give a speech* ○ *a speech o about racism* ○ *He made a very boring after-dinn speech.* (**b**) (usu long) group of lines to be spoke by an actor in a play: *I've got some very lon speeches to learn in Act 2.*

▷ **speechless** *adj* (**a**) unable to speak, esp becaus of strong feeling: *speechless with surprise* ○ *Ang left him speechless.* (**b**) that cannot be expressed i words: *speechless rage.* **speechlessly** *ad speechlessly furious.* **speechlessness** *n* [U].

□ **ˈspeech-day** *n* annual school celebration wit speeches and distribution of certificates an prizes.

ˌspeech ˈtherapy the diagnosis, assessment an treatment of language handicaps which may var from an almost total language breakdown in case of severe brain damage (asphasia) to minc pronunciation impediments (eg a lisp). **ˌspeec ˈtherapist** person trained to provide this.

speechify /ˈspiːtʃɪfaɪ/ *v* (*pt, pp* **-fied**) [I] (*infml us derog*) make a speech or speeches pompously; ta as if making speeches: *town councillo speechifying at the opening of a new building.*

speed /spiːd/ *n* **1** [U] quickness of movement swiftness: *He moves with great speed.* ○ *The tenn player's speed is his great asset.* **2** [C, U] rate which sb/sth moves: *at a speed of fifty kilometres a hour* ○ *at (a) very slow speed* ○ *at top speed.* **3** [C (**a**) sensitivity of photographic film to light: *What the speed of the film you're using?* (**b**) time taken b a camera shutter to open and close: *differe shutter speeds* ○ *a photograph taken at a speed of of a second.* **4** [U] (*sl*) amphetamine used as a dru to produce a sense of well-being and excitemen *He's hooked on* (ie addicted to) *speed.* **5** [C] (esp compounds) gear: *a ten-speed bicycle.* **6** (idm) **speed** at high speed; quickly: *It's dangerous to round corners at speed.* **full pelt/tilt/speed** FULL. **full speed/steam ahead** ⇨ FULL. **mo haste, less speed** ⇨ HASTE. **pick up speed** PICK[3]. **a turn of speed** ⇨ TURN[2]. **with all ˈspee ˈhaste** as quickly as possible. **with lightnir speed** ⇨ LIGHTNING[2].

▷ **speed** *v* (*pt, pp* **sped** /sped/; in senses 2 and **speeded**) **1** [Ipr] move along or go quickly: *ca speeding past the school* ○ *He sped down the stre* **2** [Tn, Tn·pr] cause (sth) to move or go quick *This medicine will help speed her recovery.* **3** (usu in the continuous tenses) drive or go fast than the speeds allowed by law: *The police sa he'd been speeding on the motorway.* **4** (phr **speed (sth) up** (cause sth to) increase spee *They've speeded up production of the new car.* ○ *T train soon speeded up.*

speeding *n* [U] traffic offence of travelling at illegal or a dangerous speed: *fined £60 for speedin*

speedometer /spiːˈdɒmɪtə(r)/ *n* instrume showing the speed of a motor vehicle, etc: *T speedometer is faulty.* ⇨ illus at CAR.

speedy *adj* (**-ier, -iest**) **1** (*often infml*) movi quickly; fast: *a speedy business operator.* **2** comin done or carried out, etc without delay: *wish sb a speedy recovery from illness.* **speedily** *adv.* **speediness** *n* [U]: *the speediness of his recovery from the accident.*

□ **ˈspeedboat** *n* motor-boat designed to go at high speeds.

ˈspeed-indicator *n* (*fml*) speedometer.

ˈspeed limit highest speed at which it is legal to travel (on a particular stretch of road): *What's the speed limit on the motorway?* ○ *The speed limit is 40 miles per hour.*

ˈspeed merchant (*sl derog*) person who drives a car or motor bike very fast.

ˈspeed trap system used by the police to catch motorists, etc who are driving faster than the speed limit.

ˈspeedway *n* **(a)** [C] track for fast driving and racing, esp by motor-bikes. **(b)** [U] sport of racing motor bikes on such a track: *Do you like speedway?* **(c)** [C] (*US*) road on which fast driving is allowed.

ˈspeed-up *n* (*infml*) increase in speed; acceleration: *a speed-up in the rate of production.*

speedwell /ˈspi:dwel/ *n* type of small wild plant with bright blue flowers.

speleology (also **spelaeology**) /ˌspi:lɪˈɒlədʒɪ/ *n* [U] **1** scientific study and exploration of caves. **2** sport of walking in and exploring caves.

▷ **speleological** (also **spelae-**) /ˌspi:lɪəˈlɒdʒɪkl/ *adj*: *speleological exploration.*

speleologist (also **spelae-**) /ˌspi:lɪˈɒlədʒɪst/ *n* scientist who studies caves; expert in speleology.

spell[1] /spel/ *n* **1 (a)** [C] words which when spoken are thought to have magical power; charm: *a book of spells* ○ *The wizard recited a spell.* **(b)** [C usu *sing*] state or condition caused by the speaking of such words (used esp in the expressions shown): *be under a spell*, ie be in this state ○ *cast/put a spell on sb.* **2** [sing] great attraction, fascination, etc caused by a person or thing; strong influence: *under the spell of her beauty* ○ *the mysterious spell of music.*

□ **spellbinder** /ˈspelbaɪndə(r)/ *n* person (esp a speaker) who can hold sb's attention completely (as if) by magic. **spellbinding** /-baɪndɪŋ/ *adj* holding the attention in this way; entrancing: *a spellbinding performance.* **spellbound** /-baʊnd/ *adj* [usu pred] with the attention held by, or as if by, a magical spell; entranced: *The magician held* (ie kept) *the children spellbound.*

spell[2] /spel/ *n* **1** period of time during which sth lasts: *a long spell of warm weather* ○ *a cold spell in January* ○ *rest for a short spell.* **2** ~ **(at/on sth)** period of activity or duty (esp one which two or more people share); turn: *a spell at the wheel of the car*, eg when two people are sharing the driving ○ *a spell on the typewriter* ○ *We took spells at carrying the baby.*

▷ **spell** *v* [Tn] let (sb) rest from work, etc by working oneself.

spell[3] /spel/ *v* (*pt, pp* **spelled** /speld/ or **spelt** /spelt/) ⇨ Usage at DREAM[2] **1 (a)** [Tn, Tn·pr, Cn·n] name or write letters of (a word) in their correct order: *How do you spell your name?* ○ *That word is spelt with a PH, not an F.* ○ *You spell his name P-A-U-L.* **(b)** [I, Tn] put the letters (of words) together in the correct or accepted order: *These children can't spell.* ○ *Why don't you learn to spell my name (correctly)?* **2** [Tn] (of letters) form (words) when put together in a particular order: *C-A-T spells cat.* **3** [Tn] have (sth) as a result; mean: *The failure of their crops spelt disaster for the peasant farmers.* **4** (phr v) **spell sth out (a)** say aloud or write the letters of (a word) in their correct order: *Could you spell that word out for me again?* **(b)** make sth clear and easy to understand; explain sth in detail: *My instructions seem simple enough — do I have to spell them out again?* ○ *She's so stupid that you have to spell everything out.*

▷ **speller** *n* person who spells (usu in the way indicated by the *adj*): *She's a good/poor speller.*

spelling *n* **1** [U] **(a)** ability of a person to spell: *His spelling is terrible.* ○ [attrib] *They were given a spelling test.* **(b)** action or process of forming words correctly from letters. **2** [C] way a word is spelt: *Which is the better spelling: Tokio or Tokyo?* ○ *English and American spelling(s).*

spelt ⇨ SPELL[3].

Spencer[1] /ˈspensə(r)/ Herbert (1820-1903), English philosopher. He based his ideas, esp his agnosticism and belief in the freedom of the individual, on the evolutionary theories of *Darwin.

Sir Stanley Spencer: St Francis and the Birds

Spencer[2] /ˈspensə(r)/ Sir Stanley (1891-1959), English painter. He is most famous for his strange and erotic religious scenes, such as his picture of the Resurrection showing people from his home village coming out from their graves. ⇨ illus.

spend /spend/ *v* (*pt, pp* **spent** /spent/) **1** [I, Tn, Tn·pr] ~ **sth (on sth)** give or pay out (money) for goods, services, etc: *He spends as if he were a millionaire.* ○ *She's spent all her money.* ○ *He spends too much (money) on clothes.* **2** [Tn, Tn·pr] ~ **sth (on sth/in doing sth) (a)** use (time, etc) for a purpose: *spend a lot of time on a project/(in) explaining a plan* ○ *spend one's energy cleaning the place up.* **(b)** use sth up; exhaust sth: *The blizzard quickly spent itself*, ie used up all its force. ○ *They went on firing until they had spent all their ammunition.* ○ *I've spent all my energy on this.* **3** [Tn, Tn·pr] pass time: *How do you spend your spare time?* ○ *spend a weekend in Paris* ○ *spend summer holidays by the sea.* **4** (idm) **spend the ˈnight with sb** (*euph*) sleep for a night in the same bed as and have sexual intercourse with sb to whom one is not married. **spend a ˈpenny** (*infml euph*) go to the toilet; urinate: *I'm just going to spend a penny.*

▷ **spender** *n* person who spends money (usu in way indicated by the *adj*): *a big/an extravagant spender* ○ *a miserly spender.*

□ **ˈspendthrift** *n* person who spends money extravagantly and wastefully.

Spender /ˈspendə(r)/ Sir Stephen (1909-), English poet. He was a friend of *Auden and *MacNeice and his work often shows his political and social conscience, although his style can also be tender and personal.

Spenser /ˈspensə(r)/ Edmund (c 1552-99), English poet. His first important work was *The Shepheardes Calendar*, a set of twelve pastoral poems for the months of the year. His masterpiece, *The Faerie Queene*, was written in honour of Queen *Elizabeth I and is an allegorical romance of chivalry. Spenser influenced many later poets, esp *Milton and *Keats.

spent /spent/ *adj* **(a)** [usu attrib] having lost power or strength; used: *a spent match* ○ *a spent cartridge/bullet.* **(b)** (*fml*) exhausted: *He returned home spent, dirty and cold.*

sperm /spɜ:m/ *n* **1** [C] (*pl* unchanged or ~**s**) male reproductive cell able to fertilize a female ovum: *He has a low sperm count*, ie He has few sperm cells and so is not very fertile. **2** [U] fertilizing fluid of a male animal containing these; semen.

▷ **spermicide** /-ɪsaɪd/ *n* substance that kills sperm. **spermicidal** /ˌspɜ:mɪˈsaɪdl/ *adj* [attrib]: *spermicidal jelly.*

□ **ˈsperm whale** (also **cachalot**) large whale from which spermaceti is obtained.

spermaceti /ˌspɜ:məˈsetɪ/ *n* [U] white waxy fatty substance contained in solution in the heads of sperm whales, used (esp formerly) for ointments, candles, etc.

spermatozoon /ˌspɜ:mətəˈzəʊən/ *n* (*pl* **-zoa** /-ˈzəʊə/) (*biology*) sperm.

spew /spju:/ *v* **1** [I, Ip, Tn, Tn·p] ~ **(sth) (out/up)** (*esp infml*) vomit: *spewing up in the basin* ○ *She spewed up the entire meal.* **2** [Ip, Tn, Tn·p] ~ **out**; ~ **sth (out)** (cause sth to) send out in a stream: *Water spewed out of the hole.* ○ *The volcano spewed molten lava.*

sp gr *abbr* specific gravity.

sphagnum /ˈsfægnəm/ *n* (*pl* ~**s** or **sphagna** /ˈsfægnə/) [U, C] type of moss that grows in wet areas, used esp for packing plants.

sphere /sfɪə(r)/ *n* **1 (a)** solid figure that is entirely round (ie with every point on the surface at an equal distance from the centre). ⇨ illus at CUBE. **(b)** any object having approximately this shape (eg a ball, a globe). **2 (a)** range or extent (of sb's interests, activity, influence, etc): *a sphere of influence*, eg area over which a country, etc claims certain rights ○ *Her sphere of interests is very limited.* **(b)** group in society; person's place in society: *It took him completely out of his sphere.* ○ *distinguished in many different spheres*, eg in artistic, literary and political circles.

▷ **spherical** /ˈsferɪkl/ *adj* shaped like a sphere: *a spherical object.*

spheroid /ˈsfɪərɔɪd/ *n* solid object that is almost, but not perfectly, spherical.

-sphere *comb form* (forming *ns*) of or like a sphere: *ionosphere* ○ *atmosphere.* ▷ **-spheric** (also **-spherical**) (forming *adjs*): *atmospheric.*

sphincter /ˈsfɪŋktə(r)/ *n* (*fml*) ring of muscle that surrounds an opening in the body and can contract to close it: *the anal sphincter.*

sphinx /sfɪŋks/ *n* **1** (esp **the Sphinx**) stone statue in Egypt with a lion's body and a man's or an animal's head. **2** person who keeps his thoughts and feelings secret; enigmatic person: *I've always found her rather sphinx-like.*

spic = SPIK.

spice /spaɪs/ *n* **1 (a)** [C] any of various types of substance obtained from plants, with a strong taste and/or smell, used, esp in powder form, for flavouring food: *Ginger, nutmeg, cinnamon, pepper and cloves are common spices.* **(b)** [U] such substances considered as a group: *mixed spice* ○ *too much spice in the cake* ○ [attrib] *a spice jar.* **2** [U] (*fig*) extra interest or excitement: *a story that lacks spice* ○ *add a bit of spice to their marriage.* Cf SALT 5.

▷ **spice** *v* [Tn, Tn·pr] ~ **sth (with sth)** **1** add flavour to sth with spice: *Have you spiced this cake?* ○ *He spiced the biscuits with cinnamon.* **2** (usu passive) add (humour, etc) to give interest, variety, etc: *a boring life spiced with moments of intrigue.* ○ *His stories are spiced with humour.*

spiced *adj* containing spice(1) or spices: *heavily spiced curries* ○ *spiced biscuits.*

spicy *adj* (**-ier, -iest**) **1** flavoured with spice; smelling or tasting of spice: *Do you like spicy food?* **2** exciting or interesting (esp because slightly indecent or scandalous): *spicy details of a film star's love life.* **spiciness** *n* [U]: *the spiciness of Indian food.*

spick[1] /spɪk/ *adj* (idm) **ˌspick and ˈspan** [usu pred] neat, clean and tidy: *They always keep their kitchen spick and span.*

spick[2] = SPIK.

spider /ˈspaɪdə(r)/ *n* any of several types of small creature with eight thin legs, many of which spin webs to trap insects as food.
▷ **spidery** /ˈspaɪdərɪ/ *adj* **1** (esp of handwriting) having thin angular lines like a spider's legs: *written in her spidery scrawl.* **2** full of spiders.
□ ˈ**spider crab** type of crab with long thin legs.
ˈ**spider-man** /-mæn/ *n* (*pl* **-men** /-men/) man who works at a great height in constructing buildings.
ˈ**spider monkey** S American monkey with long limbs and a long tail which can grip branches.
ˈ**spider plant** plant with thin leaves and long stems from which fresh young plants grow.

spied *pt, pp* of SPY.

spiel /ʃpiːl; *US* spiːl/ *n* (*infml usu derog*) long or fast prepared speech (usu intended to persuade sb or as an excuse): *The salesman gave (us) a long spiel about why we should buy his product.*

Spielberg /ˈspiːlbɜːg/ Steven (1947-), American film director and producer. His great successes, like *Jaws, ET* and the *Indiana Jones* trilogy, reveal an instinct for popular taste which resulted in some of the biggest box-office hits of all time.

spigot /ˈspɪgət/ *n* (usu wooden) peg or plug used to stop the hole of a barrel, etc or to control the flow of liquid from a tap.

spik (also **spic**, **spick**) /spɪk/ *n* (*US sl derog offensive*) Spanish-speaking person of the USA or Latin America.

spike /spaɪk/ *n* **1** [C] hard thin pointed piece of metal, wood, etc; sharp point: *sharp spikes on top of the railings in the park.* **2** (**a**) [C] any of a set of metal points attached to the sole of a shoe, etc to prevent the wearer slipping while running in sports, etc. (**b**) **spikes** [pl] running-shoes fitted with these: *a pair of spikes.* **3** [C] long metal nail or pin. **4** [C] ear (of corn, etc): *spikes of barley.* **5** [C] long pointed group of flowers on a single stem: *spikes of lavender.*
▷ **spike** *v* [Tn] **1** (usu passive) put spikes on (shoes, etc): *spiked running shoes.* **2** pierce or injure with a spike. **3** (*esp US*) = LACE *v* 2. **4** (idm) **spike sb's ˈguns** spoil the plans of (an opponent).
spiky *adj* (**-ier, -iest**) **1** having sharp points or spikes: *Your hairbrush is too spiky for me.* **2** (*infml fig*) (of people) easily offended and difficult to please; irritable. **spikiness** *n* [U].

spikenard /ˈspaɪknɑːd/ *n* **1** [C] tall sweet-smelling Indian plant. **2** [U] sweet-smelling ointment formerly made from this plant.

spill[1] /spɪl/ *v* (*pt, pp* **spilt** /spɪlt/ or **spilled**) ⇨ Usage at DREAM[2] **1** [I, Ipr, Ip, Tn, Tn·pr] ~ (**sth**) (**from**, **out of**, **etc sth**); ~ **out** (allow or cause liquid, etc to) run or fall over the edge of a container: *The ink spilt all over the desk.* ○ *He knocked the bucket over and all the water spilt out.* ○ *Who has spilt/spilled the milk?* ⇨ illus at POUR. **2** [Tn] (*infml*) reveal or make sth known: *Who spilt the news?* **3** (idm) **cry over spilt milk** ⇨ CRY[1]. **spill the ˈbeans** (*infml*) reveal (esp secret) information, deliberately or unintentionally. **spill ˈblood** (*fml*) (cause people to) be injured or killed; shed blood: *Much innocent blood is spilt in war.* **4** (phr v) **spill over** overflow from sth that is full: *The meeting spilt over from the hall into the corridor.*
▷ **spill** *n* **1** fall from a horse, bicycle, etc: *have a nasty spill.* **2** (idm) **thrills and spills** ⇨ THRILL *n*.
spillage /ˈspɪlɪdʒ/ *n* (**a**) [U] action of spilling. (**b**) [C] amount spilt: *spillages of drink.*
□ ˈ**spillway** *n* passage for surplus water from a reservoir, river, etc.

spill[2] /spɪl/ *n* thin strip of wood or twisted paper, used for lighting candles, pipes, fires, etc.

spillikins /ˈspɪlɪkɪnz/ *n* [sing *v*] (also **jack straws**) game in which players try to remove thin sticks one at a time from a pile without disturbing the others.

spin /spɪn/ *v* (**-nn-**; *pt* **spun** /spʌn/ or, in archaic use, **span** /spæn/, *pp* **spun**) **1** (**a**) [Tn, Tn·p] ~ **sth** (**round**) make sth turn round and round rapidly: *spin the ball*, eg in cricket or tennis ○ *spin a top* ○ *He spun the wheel of his bicycle.* ○ *They spun a coin to decide who should start*, ie threw it spinning in the air to see which side was uppermost when it landed. (**b**) [I, Ipr, Ip] move round and round rapidly: *The revolving sign was spinning round and round in the wind.* ○ *The collision sent the car spinning across the road.* ○ *The blow sent him spinning back against the wall.* ○ *She spun round to catch the ball.* ○ (*fig*) *My head is spinning*, ie I feel dizzy. **2** (**a**) [I, Tn, Tn·pr] ~ (**A into B**)/(**B from A**) form (thread) from wool, cotton, silk, etc by drawing out and twisting; make (yarn) from wool, etc in this way: *She spins goat's hair into wool/ spins wool from goat's hair.* (**b**) [I] engage in the occupation or pastime of spinning thread: *I enjoy spinning.* **3** [Tn] (of a spider, silkworm, etc) produce (fine silk or silk-like material) from the body in order to make (a web, cocoon, etc): *spiders spinning their webs* ○ *silkworms spinning cocoons.* **4** (idm) **spin (sb) a ˈyarn** tell a (usu long) story, often in order to deceive sb: *The old sailor loves to spin yarns about his life at sea.* ○ *He spun us this unlikely yarn about being trapped for hours in a broken lift.* **5** (phr v) **spin along (sth)** move along rapidly on wheels: *The car was spinning merrily along (the road).* **spin sth out** make sth last as long as possible: *spin out the time by talking* ○ *spin one's money out until the next pay-day.*
▷ **spin** *n* **1** [U, C] turning or spinning movement: [attrib] *spin bowling* ○ *The bowler gave (a) spin to the ball*, eg in cricket, baseball, etc. ○ *He gambled his money on one spin of the wheel*, eg at a game of roulette. **2** [C usu *sing*] fast spinning movement of an aircraft during a diving descent: *go/get into a spin* ○ *come/get out of a spin.* **3** [C] (*infml*) short ride for pleasure (in a car, on a bicycle, etc): *Let's go for a spin in my new car.* **4** (idm) **in a (flat) ˈspin** in a state of panic or confusion: *I've been in a real spin all morning.*
spinner 1 person who makes thread, etc by spinning: *spinners and weavers.* **2** (**a**) = SPIN BOWLER. (**b**) cricket ball bowled with a spinning movement. **3** type of spinning bait used by anglers.
spinning *n* [U] art, occupation or pastime of spinning wool, etc into yarn: *Spinning is one of my hobbies.* ○ [attrib] *spinning wool/thread/yarn.* ˌ**spinning-ˈjenny** *n* early type of machine for spinning more than one thread at a time. ˈ**spinning-wheel** *n* simple household machine for spinning thread continuously on a spindle turned by a large wheel, usu worked by a foot pedal.
□ ˈ**spin bowler** (also **spinner**) (in cricket) bowler who gives the ball a spinning movement.
ˌ**spin-ˈdry** *v* (*pt, pp* **-dried**) [Tn] dry (washed clothes) by spinning them in a rotating drum to remove excess water. ˌ**spin-ˈdrier** *n* machine for doing this.
ˈ**spin-off** *n* benefit or product that is produced incidentally from a larger process, or while it is being developed: *This new material is a spin-off from the space industry.*
ˌ**spun ˈglass** glass made into threads by being spun while heated.
ˌ**spun ˈsilk** cheap material made from short threads and waste pieces of silk, often mixed with cotton.
ˌ**spun ˈsugar** sugar made into fluffy threads by being spun when in a thick liquid form. Cf CANDY-FLOSS (CANDY).

spina bifida /ˌspaɪnə ˈbɪfɪdə/ (*medical*) condition in which certain bones of the spine are not properly developed at birth and allow parts of the spinal cord to protrude (causing severe disability).

spinach /ˈspɪnɪdʒ; *US* -ɪtʃ/ *n* [U] type of common garden plant with wide dark-green leaves that are cooked and eaten as a vegetable: [attrib] *spinach soup.*
■ The health-giving properties of spinach are especially associated with the popular cartoon hero *Popeye, who eats it to develop his extraordinary strength.

spinal /ˈspaɪnl/ *adj* [usu attrib] of or relating to the spine: *a spinal injury.*
□ ˌ**spinal ˈcolumn** backbone; spine.
ˌ**spinal ˈcord** mass of nerve fibres enclosed in the spine. ⇨ illus at BRAIN.

spindle /ˈspɪndl/ *n* **1** thin rod on which thread is twisted or wound by hand in spinning. **2** bar or pin which turns or on which sth (eg an axle or a shaft) turns.
▷ **spindly** /ˈspɪndlɪ/ *adj* (*infml sometimes derog*) very long or tall and thin: *a young foal with spindly legs* ○ *a few spindly plants.*

spine /spaɪn/ *n* **1** row of bones along the back of humans and some animals; backbone: *He sustained an injury to his spine when he fell off his horse.* ⇨ illus at SKELETON. **2** any of the sharp needle-like parts on some plants (eg cactuses) and animals (eg porcupines, hedgehogs). **3** back part of the cover of a book, where the pages are joined together (ie the part that is visible when it is in a row on a shelf, usu with the book's title on it).
▷ **spineless** *adj* **1** (of an animal, etc) having no spine(1); invertebrate. **2** (*fig derog*) (of people) weak, cowardly or easily frightened. **spinelessly** *adv.* **spinelessness** *n* [U].
spiny *adj* (**-ier, -iest**) full of or covered with spines (SPINE 2); prickly: *a spiny fish.*
□ ˈ**spine-chiller** *n* book, film, etc that is frightening in a thrilling way. ˈ**spine-chilling** *adj*: *a spine-chilling horror story.*

spinet /spɪˈnet; *US* ˈspɪnɪt/ *n* old type of musical instrument with a keyboard, similar to a harpsichord.

spinnaker /ˈspɪnəkə(r)/ *n* large triangular extra sail carried on the mainmast of a racing-yacht, used when sailing with the wind coming from behind the boat. ⇨ illus at YACHT.

spinneret /ˌspɪnəˈret/ *n* **1** organ in a spider's body that produces the web. **2** nozzle through which strands of synthetic fibre are forced during manufacture.

spinney /ˈspɪnɪ/ *n* (*Brit*) small wood with thick undergrowth; thicket.

Spinoza /spɪˈnəʊzə/ Baruch de (1632-77), Jewish philosopher, living in Holland. His critical attitude to the Scriptures, influenced by *Descartes, led to his exclusion from the Jewish community. He saw God as within the universe rather than ruling it, the 'intellectual love' of God as the basis of morality, and virtue as the way to happiness.

spinster /ˈspɪnstə(r)/ *n* (**a**) (*law or fml*) unmarried woman. (**b**) (*often derog*) woman who remains single after the usual age for marrying. Cf BACHELOR 1.
▷ **spinsterhood** /-hʊd/ *n* [U] state of being a spinster.

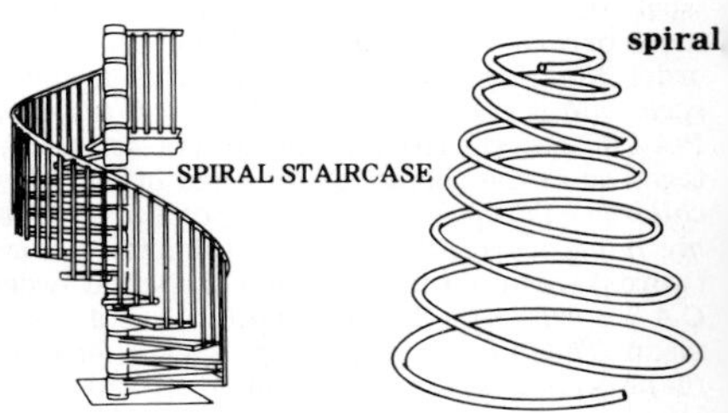

spiral /ˈspaɪərəl/ *adj* advancing or ascending in a continuous curve that winds round a central point: *a spiral staircase* ○ *A snail's shell is spiral in form.*
▷ **spiral** *n* **1** (**a**) spiral line. (**b**) object that has a spiral shape. **2** continuous increase or decrease in two or more quantities alternately because each depends on the other(s): *an inflationary spiral* ○ *the spiral of rising wages and prices.* **3** (idm) **vicious spiral** ⇨ VICIOUS.
spiral *v* (**-ll-**; *US also* **-l-**) **1** [Ipr, Ip] move in a spiral

course: *The falling leaf spiralled to the ground.* ○ *The smoke spiralled upwards.* **2** [I, Ip] increase or decrease continuously: *Prices are still spiralling*, ie increasing rapidly.

spirally *adv*: *a spirally bound book*, ie with its pages held together by wire bent spirally.

spire /ˈspaɪə(r)/ *n* pointed structure in the form of a tall cone or pyramid, esp on a church tower: *a magnificent view of the spires of the city.* ⇨ illus at CHURCH.

The spire of a country church is a typical feature of the rural British landscape, and often appears on Christmas cards and other picturesque images of the countryside. Church spires serve as useful landmarks. In the past, for instance, a distant spire would be used to mark the finishing point of a race on horseback. The word 'steeplechase' derives from this.

spirit /ˈspɪrɪt/ *n* **1** [U, C] person's mind or feelings as distinct from his body; soul: *He is troubled in spirit/His spirit is troubled.* **2** [C] soul thought of as separate from the body; soul without a body; ghost: *the spirits of the dead* ○ *raise spirits*, ie communicate with dead people ○ *It was believed that people could be possessed by evil spirits.* ○ [attrib] *the spirit world.* **3** [C] (*dated*) supernatural creature; elf, fairy, etc. **4** [U, C] life and consciousness not associated with a body: *tribal beliefs that spirit is everywhere and in everything* ○ *God is pure spirit.* ○ *the Holy Spirit.* **5** [C] (always with an *adj*) person (of a specified type, emotion, temper, etc): *a brave, proud, generous, mean, etc spirit* ○ *He was one of the leading spirits of the reform movement.* ○ *She's an independent spirit.* **6** [U] willingness to assert oneself; courage; liveliness: *He answered with spirit.* ○ *break sb's spirit*, ie destroy sb's will, sense of independence, etc ○ *Although they lost, the team played with tremendous spirit.* **7** [sing] state of mind or mood; attitude: *do sth in a spirit of mischief* ○ *approach sth in the wrong/right spirit* ○ *Whether it was unwise or not depends upon the spirit in which it was done.* ○ *The party was successful because everyone entered into the spirit of the thing.* **8** (a) [sing] characteristic quality or mood of sth: *the spirit of the times* ○ *the 16th-century spirit of exploration.* (b) [U] real or intended meaning or purpose: *obey the spirit, not the letter* (ie the apparent meaning of the words) *of the law.* **9** (a) [C usu *pl*] strong distilled alcoholic drink: *I don't drink spirits.* ○ *Whisky, brandy, gin and rum are all spirits.* (b) [U] distilled alcohol for industrial, etc use: *white spirit* ○ *surgical spirit* ○ *methylated spirit(s).* **10 spirits** [pl] person's feelings or state of mind: *in high spirits*, ie cheerful ○ *in low/poor spirits*, ie depressed, gloomy ○ *raise sb's spirits*, ie make sb more cheerful ○ *Have a glass of brandy to keep your spirits up.* **11** (idm) **in spirit** in one's thoughts: *I shall be with you in spirit*, ie thinking about you though not with you physically. **a kindred spirit** ⇨ KINDRED. **the ˌspirit is ˈwilling (but the ˌflesh is ˈweak)** (*saying*) one's intentions and wishes are good but laziness, love of pleasure, etc prevent one from acting according to them.

▷ **spirit** *v* (phr v) **spirit sb/sth away/off** take or carry sb/sth away quickly, secretly or mysteriously (as if by magic): *The pop star was spirited away at the end of the concert before her fans could get near her.*

spirited /ˈspɪrɪtɪd/ *adj* [usu attrib] full of spirit(6); lively; forceful: *a spirited attack, reply, conversation* ○ *a spirited horse.* **spiritedly** *adv*.

-spirited (forming compound *adjs*) having the mood or state of mind specified: *ˌmean-ˈspirited* ○ *ˌhigh-spirited ˈchildren.*

spiritless *adj* **1** without spirit(6); not having or showing liveliness or courage. **2** depressed or unhappy: *The old man seemed dejected and spiritless.*

□ **ˈspirit-lamp** *n* lamp that burns methylated spirit or a similar fuel.

ˈspirit-level *n* glass tube partly filled with water or alcohol, with a bubble of air, used to test whether sth is horizontal by means of the position of the bubble.

spiritual /ˈspɪrɪtʃʊəl/ *adj* [usu attrib] **1** of the human spirit(4) or soul; not of physical things: *concerned about sb's spiritual welfare.* Cf MATERIAL[2]. **2** (a) of the Church or of religion: *The Pope is the spiritual leader of many Christians.* (b) of or from God; divine. Cf TEMPORAL 1. **3** (idm) **one's spiritual ˈhome** place where one is, or thinks one could be, happiest; country to which one feels more strongly attached than to one's own country.

▷ **spiritual** *n* (also **Negro ˈspiritual**) religious folk-song of the type originally sung by black slaves in America.

spirituality /ˌspɪrɪtʃʊˈælətɪ/ *n* [U] state or quality of being concerned with spiritual matters; devotion to spiritual things.

spiritually /-tʃʊlɪ/ *adv*: *a spiritually impoverished culture.*

spiritualism /ˈspɪrɪtʃʊəlɪzəm/ *n* [U] belief in the possibility of receiving messages from the spirits of the dead; practices based on this belief.

▷ **spiritualist** /-ɪst/ *n* person who believes in or practises spiritualism.

spirituous /ˈspɪrɪtʃʊəs/ *adj* (of a drink) containing much alcohol: *spirituous liquors*, ie those that are distilled and not only fermented.

spit[1] /spɪt/ *v* (-tt-; *pt, pp* **spat** /spæt/; also *esp US* **spit**) **1** [Tn, Tn·pr, Tn·p] ~ **sth (out) (at/on/onto sb/sth)** send (liquid, saliva, food, etc) out from the mouth: *He was spitting blood after being hit in the mouth.* ○ *The baby spat its food (out) onto the table.* ○ *He took one sip of the wine and spat it out.* **2** [I, Ipr] (a) send saliva from the mouth: *In many countries it is considered rude to spit in public.* ○ *He's inclined to spit when he talks quickly.* ○ *The boys were spitting out of the train window.* (b) do this as a sign of contempt or anger: *She spat at him/in his face.* **3** (a) [Tn, Tn·p] ~ **sth (out)** utter sth violently or forcefully: *She spat (out) curses at me.* (b) [I, Ipr] make a noise like spitting to show anger: *He walked off spitting with fury.* ○ *The cat spat at the dog.* **4** [I] (of a fire, hot fat, etc) make a spitting noise; throw out sparks, etc violently and noisily: *fried bacon spitting in the pan* ○ *The gun spat twice and he fell dead.* **5** [I] (*infml*) (used with *it*, in the continuous tenses) rain lightly: *It's not raining heavily any more, but it's still spitting a bit.* **6** (idm) **be the (very/spitting) image of sb/sth** ⇨ IMAGE. **spit it ˈout** (*infml*) say what you want to say quickly and concisely: *'What exactly are you trying to tell me? Come on, spit it out!'*

▷ **spit** *n* **1** [U] liquid in the mouth; saliva. **2** [C usu *sing*] act of spitting. **3** [U] white frothy liquid produced by some insects and found on plants, etc. **4** (idm) **be the dead spit of sb** ⇨ DEAD. **spit and ˈpolish** thorough cleaning and polishing of equipment, esp by soldiers.

□ **ˈspitfire** *n* person with a very fiery temper.

spit[2] /spɪt/ *n* **1** long thin metal spike pushed through meat, etc to hold and turn it while it is roasted over a fire or in an oven. **2** small narrow point of land that extends into the sea, a lake, etc.

▷ **spit** *v* (-tt-) [Tn] put a spit through (a piece of meat, a chicken, etc): *a spitted whole lamb.*

spit[3] /spɪt/ *n* depth of earth equal to the length of the blade of a spade: *Dig the whole vegetable plot two spits deep.*

spite /spaɪt/ *n* **1** [U] desire to hurt, annoy or offend another person; ill will: *I'm sure he only said it out of/from spite.* **2** (idm) **in spite of** (used as a *prep*) not being prevented by (sb/sth); regardless of; despite: *They went out in spite of the rain.* ○ *In spite of all his efforts he failed.* ○ *I found myself agreeing in spite of myself*, ie although I did not really want to agree.

▷ **spite** *v* **1** [Tn] (only used in the infinitive with *to*) injure, annoy or offend (sb) because of spite: *The neighbours play their radio loudly every afternoon just to spite us.* **2** (idm) **cut off one's nose to spite one's face** ⇨ NOSE[1].

spiteful /-fl/ *adj* showing or caused by spite; full of spite: *a spiteful comment* ○ *He's just being spiteful.* **spitefully** /-fəlɪ/ *adv*. **spitefulness** *n* [U].

Spitsbergen /ˈspɪtsbɜːgən/ archipelago in the Arctic Ocean, north of Norway and part of Norwegian territory.

spittle /ˈspɪtl/ *n* [U] liquid that forms in the mouth; saliva.

spittoon /spɪˈtuːn/ *n* container for spitting into, eg in a bar.

spiv /spɪv/ *n* (*Brit sl derog*) flashily dressed man who has no regular job but makes money by (usu dishonest) business dealings. ▷ **spivvish, spivvy** *adjs*.

splash /splæʃ/ *v* **1** [Tn, Tn·pr, Tn·p] ~ **sth (about) (on/onto/over sb/sth)**; ~ **sb/sth (with sth)** cause (a liquid) to fly about in drops; make sb/sth wet in this way: *Stop splashing me!* ○ *splash water on/over the floor* ○ *splash paint onto the canvas* ○ *splash the floor with water* ○ *splash water about* ○ *The children love splashing water over each other.* ⇨ Usage at SPRAY[2]. **2** [I, Ipr, Ip] (of a liquid) fly about and fall in drops: *Water splashed into the bucket from the tap.* ○ *The rain splashed down all day.* **3** [usu passive: Tn, Tn·pr] ~ **sth (with sth)** decorate sth with large or irregular patches of colour, paint, etc: *a bath towel splashed with blue and green.* **4** [Tn·pr, Tn·p] ~ **sth (about) (across, on, etc sth)** (a) display (a news story, photograph, etc) prominently: *the story was splashed across the front page of the newspaper.* (b) spend (money) freely and ostentatiously: *He thinks he can win friends by splashing his money about.* **5** (phr v) **splash about (in sth)** sit or stand in water and make it fly about with one's hands or feet: *children happily splashing about in the bath.* **splash across, along, away, through, etc** move across, etc with a splashing noise: *We splashed (our way) across the stream.* ○ *She splashed through the puddles.* **splash down** (esp of a spacecraft) land in water with a splash: *The spacecraft splashed down in the Pacific.* **splash out (on sth)** (*infml*) spend money (on sth) in an impulsive or a carefree way: *She splashed out on a new pair of shoes.*

▷ **splash** *n* **1** (sound or act of) splashing: *He fell into the water with a splash.* **2** mark, spot, etc made by splashing: *There are some splashes of mud on your trousers.* **3** amount of liquid splashed: *splashes of water all over the floor.* **4** bright patch of colour: *Her dog is brown with white splashes.* **5** (*dated Brit infml*) small quantity of a liquid, esp of soda-water, added to a drink. **6** (idm) **make, etc a ˈsplash** (*infml*) do sth or happen in such a way as to attract attention, create a sensation, etc: *She has made quite a splash in literary circles with her first book.* ○ *Their engagement created a terrific splash in the popular press.*

□ **ˈsplash-down** *n* landing of a spacecraft in the sea: *Splash-down is scheduled for 5.30 am.*

splatter /ˈsplætə(r)/ *v* [I, Ipr, Ip, Tn, Tn·pr, Tn·p] (cause sth to) splash, esp with continuous or noisy action: *rain splattering on the roof* ○ *overalls splattered with paint.* ⇨ Usage at SPRAY[2].

▷ **splatter** *n* noisy splash.

splay /spleɪ/ *v* [I, Ip, Tn, Tn·p] ~ **(sth) (out)** (cause sth to) open out and become wider at one end; (cause sth to) slant or slope: *The pipe splays (out) at one end.* ○ *The plumber splayed the end of the pipe before fitting it over the next section.* ○ *splayed feet/fingers/elbows*, ie spread outwards ○ *a splayed window*, eg one in a thick wall with the opening on one side of the wall wider than that on the other.

▷ **splay** *adj* [usu attrib] (esp of feet) broad, flat and turned outwards: *He has splay feet.* **ˌsplay-ˈfooted** *adj* having splay feet.

spleen /spliːn/ *n* **1** [C] organ of the body situated at the left of the stomach, which regulates the quality of the blood. ⇨ illus at DIGESTIVE. **2** [U] (*fml or dated*) bad temper; irritability or grumpiness: *a fit of spleen* ○ *vent one's spleen on sb.*

splendid /ˈsplendɪd/ *adj* **1** magnificent; displaying splendour: *a splendid sunset, house, victory.* **2** (*infml*) very fine; excellent: *a splendid dinner* ○ *a splendid idea, achievement, piece of writing.* ▷ **splendidly** *adv*: *The team played splendidly.*

splendiferous /splenˈdɪfərəs/ *adj* (*infml joc*) splendid.

splendour (*US* **splendor**) /ˈsplendə(r)/ *n* (a) [U] state or quality of being splendid, magnificent, glorious, or grand: *the splendour of the stained* *glass windows* ○ *Can the city recapture its former splendour?* (**b**) **splendours** [pl] splendid, magnificent, etc features or attributes of sth: *the spendours of Rome*, ie its fine monuments, buildings, sights, etc.

splenetic /splɪˈnetɪk/ *adj* (*fml*) habitually grumpy and irritable.

splice /splaɪs/ *v* [Tn] **1** (*nautical*) join (two ends of rope) by weaving the strands of one into the strands of the other. **2** join (two pieces of wood, magnetic tape, film, etc by fastening them at the ends. **3** (idm) **get ˈspliced** (*infml*) get married: *Have you heard? John's just got spliced.* **ˌsplice the ˈmainbrace** (*infml joc*) celebrate (esp the end of a hard day's work) by drinking or distributing strong alcoholic drink.

▷ **splice** *n* join (in a film, tape, rope, etc) made by splicing.

splicer *n* device for joining two pieces of magnetic tape, film, etc.

splint /splɪnt/ *n* piece of wood, metal, etc strapped to an injured arm, leg, etc to keep it in the right position while it heals: *put an arm in splints.*

splinter /ˈsplɪntə(r)/ *n* small thin sharp piece of wood, metal, glass, etc broken off a larger piece: *I've got a splinter in my finger.*

▷ **splinter** *v* **1** [I, Ipr, Ip, Tn, Tn·pr, Tn·p] ~ (**sth**) (**into/to sth**); ~ (**sth**) **off** (cause sth to) break into splinters: *This wood splinters easily.* ○ *The windscreen cracked but did not splinter.* ○ *The waves smashed the boat against the rocks, splintering it to pieces.* **2** [I, Ipr, Ip] ~ (**off**) (**into sth**) (*fig*) separate off from a larger group; form a splinter group.

□ **ˈsplinter group** small group that has broken off from a larger one, esp in politics.

split /splɪt/ *v* (**-tt-**; *pt, pp* **split**) **1** [I, Ipr, Ip, Tn, Tn·pr, Tn·p] ~ (**sth/sb**) (**up**) (**into sth**) (**a**) (cause sth to) break or be broken (into two or more parts), esp from end to end: *Some types of wood split easily.* ○ *She was splitting logs with an axe.* ○ *A skilled person can split slate into layers.* (**b**) (cause people to) separate or divide into (often opposing) groups or parties: *The children split (up) into groups.* ○ *an issue which has split the party (from top to bottom)* ○ *The children split into groups.* **2** [Tn, Tn·pr, Tn·p] ~ **sth** (**up**) (**into sth**) break sth into parts; divide and share sth: *split the cost of the meal* ○ *split the atom*, ie by means of nuclear fission ○ *Would you like to split a bottle with me?* ○ *They split (up) the money between them.* ○ *For the purposes of the survey we've split the town into four areas.* **3** [La, I, Cn·a] ~ (**sth**) (**open**) (cause sth to) break open by bursting: *Suddenly the box split open and a puppy jumped out.* ○ *His coat had split at the seams.* ○ *She split open the coconut.* **4** [I, Tn] (*sl esp US*) leave (a place): *It's boring here — let's split.* ○ *They've split the scene*, ie left the event, place, party, etc. **5** (idm) **split the ˈdifference** (when making a bargain) settle on an amount half-way between two proposed amounts. **split ˈhairs** (*derog*) make very fine but unnecessary distinctions (in an argument, etc). **split an inˈfinitive** (in speaking or writing) place an adverb between *to* and the infinitive (as in 'to quickly read a book'). **split one's ˈsides** (**laughing/with laughter**) laugh uncontrollably. **split the/one's ˈticket** (*US politics*) vote for opposing candidates at an election. **6** (phr v) **split** (**sth**) **away/off** (**from sth**) separate or divide (sth) from a larger body or group: *The group have split away/off from the official union.* ○ *The storm has split the branch off from the main tree trunk.* **split on sb** (**to sb**) (*infml*) give away information about a person (usu an accomplice) that will get him into trouble: *Billy's friend split on him to the teacher.* **split up** (**with sb**) end a friendship, relationship or marriage; separate: *Jenny and Joe have split up.* ○ *John has just split up with his girl-friend.*

▷ **split** *n* **1** [C] act or process of splitting or being split. **2** [C] crack or tear made by splitting: *sew up a split in a seam.* **3** [C] division or separation resulting from splitting: *a split in the Labour Party.* **4** [C] pudding made from fruit (esp a banana) cut in two lengthways with cream, ice-cream, etc on top: *a banana split.* **5 the splits** [pl] acrobatic position in which the legs are stretched across the floor in opposite directions with the rest of the body upright: *do the splits.*

splitting *adj* [attrib] (esp of a headache) very painful: *I've got a splitting headache.*

□ **ˌsplit inˈfinitive** (*grammar*) infinitive with an adverb placed between *to* and the verb.

ˌsplit-ˈlevel *adj* **1** (of a building) having sets of rooms at different levels between storeys in other parts of the building, eg when built on sloping ground. **2** (of a cooker) having the oven placed separately from the burners or hotplates, not below them.

ˌsplit ˈpeas dried peas split into halves.

ˌsplit persoˈnality mental condition in which a person behaves sometimes with one set of emotions, actions, etc, and sometimes with another set; schizophrenia.

ˌsplit ˈpin metal pin with split ends which can be opened out to hold the pin in position.

ˌsplit ˈring ring with its ends not joined but closely overlapping, as used for keeping keys on.

ˌsplit ˈsecond very short moment of time. **ˌsplit-second** *adj* [attrib] very rapid or accurate: *The plan depends on ˌsplit-second ˈtiming.*

ˌsplit ˈshift shift[2](2) in which there are two or more periods of duty.

ˌsplit ˈticket (*US politics*) ballot-paper marked with votes for candidates of more than one party.

splotch /splɒtʃ/ (*Brit* also **splodge** /splɒdʒ/) *n* dirty mark or spot (of ink, paint, etc); irregular patch (of colour, light, etc).

▷ **splotch** (*Brit* also **splodge**) *v* [Tn] mark (sth) with splotches.

splurge /splɜːdʒ/ *n* (*infml*) **1** act of spending money freely: *I had a splurge and bought two new suits.* **2** ostentatious display or effort (intended to attract attention): *make a splurge.*

▷ **splurge** *v* [I, Ipr, Tn, Tn·pr] ~ (**sth**) (**on sth**) spend (money) freely or extravagantly: *She won £100 and then splurged it all on new clothes.*

splutter /ˈsplʌtə(r)/ *v* **1** (also **sputter**) (**a**) [I, Ip] speak quickly and confusedly (from excitement, anger, etc). (**b**) [Tn, Tn·p] ~ **sth** (**out**) say (words) quickly, confusedly or indistinctly: *splutter (out) a few words of apology.* **2** [I] make a series of spitting sounds; sputter: *She dived into the water and came up coughing and spluttering.*

▷ **splutter** *n* spluttering sound: *The candle gave a few faint splutters and then went out.*

Spode /spəʊd/ *n* [U] (*propr*) fine china manufactured at the factory in Stoke-on-Trent, England founded in 1770 by Josiah Spode.

spoil /spɔɪl/ *v* (*pt, pp* **spoilt** /spɔɪlt/ or **spoiled** /spɔɪld/) ⇨ Usage at DREAM[2]. **1** [Tn] make (sth) useless, valueless or unsatisfactory; ruin: *holidays spoilt by bad weather* ○ *spoilt ballot papers*, ie made invalid because the voters have not marked them properly ○ *The new road has completely spoiled the character of the village.* ○ *The bad news has spoilt my day.* ○ *Don't spoil your appetite by eating sweets between meals.* **2** [Tn] (**a**) harm the character of (esp a child) by lack of discipline or too much generosity, attention, praise, etc: *That little girl is terribly spoilt — her parents give her everything she asks for.* (**b**) pay great or too much attention to the comfort and wishes of (sb); pamper: *Everybody enjoys being spoiled from time to time.* **3** [I] (of food, etc) become bad or unfit to be used, eaten, etc: *Some kinds of food soon spoil.* **4** (idm) **be spoiling for sth** be very eager for (a fight, an argument, etc): *He's spoiling for trouble.* **be spoilt for choice** have so many possibilities to choose from that it is difficult to choose. **spare the rod and spoil the child** ⇨ SPARE[2]. **too many cooks spoil the broth** ⇨ COOK *n*.

▷ **spoil** *n* [U] = SPOILS.

spoilage /ˈspɔɪlɪdʒ/ *n* [U] spoiling of food, etc by decay.

spoiler *n* **1** person or thing that spoils. **2** (**a**) device on an aircraft to slow it down by interrupting the flow of air. (**b**) similar device on a vehicle to prevent it being lifted off the road when travelling very fast.

spoils *n* [pl] (also **spoil** [U]) **1** (**a**) stolen goods: *The thieves divided up the spoils.* (**b**) things taken by a victorious army; plunder. **2** profits, benefits, etc gained from political power: *the spoils of office.*

□ **ˈspoil-sport** *n* person who spoils the enjoyment of others: *Don't be such a spoil-sport!*

ˈspoils system (*esp US*) system by which important public positions are given to supporters of the political party that wins power.

spoke[1] /spəʊk/ *n* **1** any of the bars or wire rods that connect the centre (*hub*) of a wheel to its outer edge (*rim*), eg on a bicycle. ⇨ illus at BICYCLE. **2** (idm) **put a ˈspoke in sb's wheel** (*Brit*) prevent sb from carrying out his plans.

spoke[2] *pt* of SPEAK.

spoken *pp* of SPEAK.

spokeshave /ˈspəʊkʃeɪv/ *n* tool used for planing curved surfaces, esp of wood.

spokesman /ˈspəʊksmən/ *n* (*pl* **-men** /-mən/) (*fem* **spokeswoman** /ˈspəʊkswʊmən/, *pl* **-women** /-wɪmɪn/) person who speaks, or is chosen to speak, on behalf of a group. ⇨ Usage at CHAIR.

spoliation /ˌspəʊlɪˈeɪʃn/ *n* [U] (*fml*) activity of spoiling (SPOIL 1) or damaging, esp with force; pillaging or plundering.

spondee /ˈspɒndiː/ *n* metrical foot in poetry consisting of two long or stressed syllables. ▷ **spondaic** /spɒnˈdeɪɪk/ *adj*.

spondulicks /spɒnˈdjuːlɪks; *US* -ˈduː-/ *n* [pl] (*dated sl*) money.

sponge /spʌndʒ/ *n* **1** [C] type of simple sea animal with a light elastic body-structure full of holes that can absorb water easily. **2** [C, U] (part of) one of these, or a substance of similar texture, used for washing, cleaning or padding: *a large bath sponge*, ie for washing one's body in the bath ○ *filled with sponge* ○ [attrib] *sponge rubber.* **3** [C] piece of absorbent material, eg gauze, used in surgery. **4** [C esp *sing*] act of cleaning, wiping, etc with a sponge; sponging: *She gave the floor a vigorous sponge all over.* **5** [C, U] = SPONGE-CAKE: *Would you like some more sponge?* **6** (idm) **throw up the sponge** (*infml*) admit that one is defeated.

▷ **sponge** *v* **1** [Tn, Tn·p] ~ **sb/oneself/sth** (**down**) wipe, wash or clean sb/oneself/sth with a sponge: *sponge a wound* ○ *He sponged down the car to remove the shampoo.* **2** [I, Tn, Tn·pr] (*infml*) get (money, etc) from sb without giving or intending to give anything in return: *sponge a dinner* ○ *sponge a fiver* (ie £5) *from an old friend.* **3** (phr v) **sponge sth off/out** remove sth by sponging: *sponge out a stain in the carpet.* **sponge on/off sb** (*infml usu derog*) live at another person's expense; get money, food, etc from sb without giving or intending to give anything in return: *He always sponges off others.* **sponge sth up** remove (liquid) with a sponge. **sponger** *n* person who sponges (SPONGE *v* 2). **sponging** *n* (usu *sing*) = SPONGE *n* 4; *give a child's face a good sponging.*

spongy *adj* (**-ier**, **-iest**) soft, elastic and able to absorb water like a sponge: *spongy moss.* **sponginess** *n* [U].

□ **ˈsponge-bag** *n* (*Brit*) waterproof bag for holding one's toothpaste, soap, toothbrush, etc, esp when one is travelling.

ˈsponge-cake *n* [C, U] soft light cake made with eggs, sugar and flour.

ˌsponge-ˈpudding *n* [C, U] pudding like a sponge-cake.

sponson /ˈspɒnsn/ *n* **1** part projecting from the side of a tank, ship, etc, on which a gun can be fixed. **2** air-filled container in a canoe that helps to prevent it from sinking.

sponsor /ˈspɒnsə(r)/ *n* **1** person who makes himself responsible for another (eg sb who is training for sth). **2** godparent. **3** person who puts forward or guarantees a proposal (eg for a new law). **4** person or firm that pays for a radio or TV programme, or for a musical, artistic or sporting event, usu in order to use them for advertising. **5** person who pays money to charity in return for a specified activity by another person.

▷ **sponsor** *v* [Tn] act as a sponsor for (sb/sth): *an athlete sponsored by a bank* ○ *a sponsored walk*, ie one over a fixed distance for which the walkers arrange sponsorship beforehand in aid of charity

○ *a government-sponsored cheap textbooks scheme* ○ *I'm doing a sponsored swim on Saturday — will you sponsor me?*
sponsorship *n* [U]: *We're very grateful for his sponsorship.*

spontaneous /spɒnˈteɪnɪəs/ *adj* (a) done, happening, said, etc because of a voluntary impulse from within, not caused or suggested by sth/sb outside: *a spontaneous offer of help* ○ *spontaneous applause.* (b) natural, not forced: *a spontaneous gaiety of manner.*
▷ **spontaneously** *adv.*
spontaneousness (also **spontaneity** /ˌspɒntəˈniːətɪ, -ˈneɪətɪ/) *n* [U] quality of being spontaneous.
□ **sponˌtaneous comˈbustion** burning caused by chemical changes, etc inside the material, not by the application of fire from outside.

spoof /spuːf/ *n* (*infml*) **1** ~ (**of/on sth**) humorous imitation or parody: [attrib] *a spoof horror film.* **2** trick; hoax.
▷ **spoof** *v* [Tn esp passive] (*infml*) trick or swindle (sb): *You've been spoofed.*

spook /spuːk/ *n* (*infml usu joc*) ghost: *Are you afraid of spooks?*
▷ **spook** *v* [Tn] (*infml esp US*) frighten; scare: *Something in the bushes spooked her horse.*
spooky *adj* (**-ier, -iest**) (*infml*) suggesting spooks; frightening: *a spooky old house.* **spookiness** *n* [U].

spool /spuːl/ *n* **1** = REEL[1] 1. **2** amount (of thread, etc) held on one of these: *How many spools of thread did you use?*

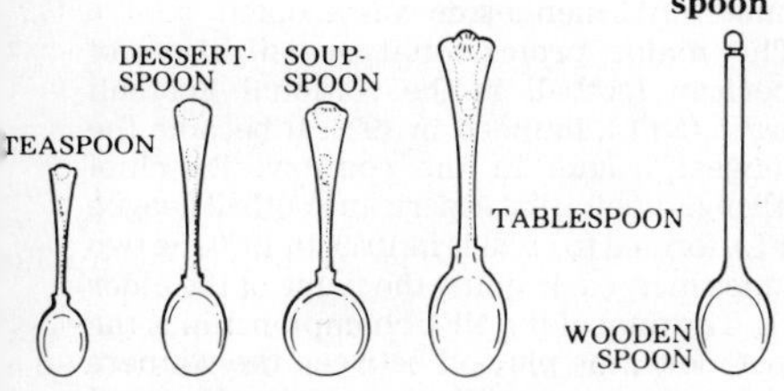

spoon /spuːn/ *n* (often in compounds) **1** utensil with a shallow oval or round bowl on a handle, used for stirring, serving and taking up food (esp puddings and soups) to the mouth: *a large wooden spoon* ○ *a ˈtablespoon* ○ *a ˈsoup-spoon* ○ *a ˈteaspoon.* **2** amount this can hold; spoonful: *two spoons of sugar, please.* **3** (idm) **born with a silver spoon in one's mouth** ➪ BORN.
▷ **spoon** *v* [Tn·pr, Tn·p] **1** lift and move (sth) with a spoon in the specified way or direction: *spoon sugar from the packet into a bowl* ○ *spoon up one's soup* ○ *spoon out the peas.* **2** ~ **sth** (**up**) hit (a ball) feebly upwards.
spoonful /-fʊl/ *n* (*pl* **-fuls**) amount that a spoon can hold: *a heaped spoonful of sugar.*
□ **ˈspoon-feed** *v* (*pt, pp* **-fed**) [Tn] (a) feed (a baby, etc) with a spoon. (b) (*fig esp derog*) give (sb) too much help or teaching in a way that does not allow him to think for himself: *Some teachers spoon-feed their students.*

spoonerism /ˈspuːnərɪzəm/ *n* (often humorous) result of changing round, esp accidentally, the initial sounds of two or more words when speaking, eg *well-boiled icicle* for *well-oiled bicycle* (named after W A Spooner (1844-1930), an English clergyman who made such errors).

spoor /spɔː(r); *US* spʊər/ *n* [C] track or scent left by a wild animal (enabling it to be followed).

sporadic /spəˈrædɪk/ *adj* happening or seen only occasionally or in a few places; occurring irregularly: *sporadic showers* ○ *sporadic raids, gunfire, fighting.* ▷ **sporadically** /-klɪ/ *adv.*

spore /spɔː(r)/ *n* (*botany*) any of the tiny seed-like reproductive cells of some plants such as ferns, mosses and fungi: *mushroom spores.*

sporran /ˈspɒrən/ *n* large pouch, usu made of leather or fur, that is worn by men in front of the kilt as part of the Scottish national dress. ➪ article at SCOTLAND.

sport /spɔːt/ *n* **1** [U] physical activity done, esp outdoors, for exercise and amusement, usu played in a special area and according to fixed rules: *She plays a lot of sport.* ○ *He's very fond of sport.* **2** (a) [C] particular form of such activity; particular game or pastime: *team sports* ○ *Hockey, volleyball, football and tennis are all sports.* ○ *Which sports do you like best?* ○ *athletic sports*, eg running, jumping ○ *country sports*, eg hunting, fishing, shooting, horse-racing ○ [attrib] *sports coverage on TV* ○ *a sports programme* ○ *a ˈsports field.* (b) [U] such activities or pastimes collectively: *the world of sport.* ➪ Usage. **3 sports** [pl] meeting for athletic competitions: *the school sports* ○ *inter-university sports* ○ [attrib] *a ˈsports day.* **4** [U] amusement; fun: *do sth for sport* ○ *say sth in sport*, ie not seriously. **5** [C] (*dated infml*) pleasant, cheerful and generous-minded person: *Come on, be a sport!* ○ *a good/bad sport*, ie sb who behaves well/badly in sporting or similar activities. **6** [C] (*infml esp Austral*) (as a term of address) chap; fellow; friend: *How are you doing, sport!* **7** [C] (*biology*) plant or animal that deviates in some unusual way from the normal type. **8** (idm) **make sport of sb** (*fml*) mock or joke about sb.
▷ **sport** *v* **1** [Tn] have or wear (sth) proudly for others to see: *sport a moustache, a diamond ring, a flower in one's buttonhole.* **2** [I, Ip] (usu in the continuous tenses) play about; amuse oneself; have fun: *seals sporting (about/around) in the water.*
sporty *adj* (*infml*) **1** fond of or good at sport: *She's very sporty.* **2** attractive and dashing: *a sporty new pullover.* **sportily** *adv.* **sportiness** *n* [U].
□ **ˈsports car** low (usu open) car designed for travelling at high speeds.
ˈsportscast *n* (*US*) TV or radio broadcast of sports news or a sports event. **ˈsportscaster** *n* (*US*) person who introduces or commentates on such a programme.
ˈsports-editor *n* newspaper editor responsible for reports of sports and games.
ˈsports jacket (*Brit*) man's jacket for informal wear (not part of a suit). ➪ illus at JACKET.
ˈsportsman /-mən/ *n* (*pl* **-men** /-mən/) (*fem* **ˈsportswoman** /-wʊmən/, *pl* **-women** /-wɪmɪn/) **1** person who takes part in or is fond of sport. **2** person who plays sport fairly, is willing to take risks, and doesn't become upset or bad-tempered if he loses. **ˈsportsmanlike** *adj* behaving fairly and generously: *a sportsmanlike attitude, gesture.* **ˈsportsmanship** *n* [U] sportsmanlike quality or spirit.
ˈsports writer person (esp a journalist) who writes about sport.

NOTE ON USAGE: **Sport** plays a big part in many people's lives. At school children can play football, netball and other **sports** and there are clubs for playing indoor **games** such as chess or snooker. After work, a lot of people enjoy a **game** of tennis or squash. On TV we can watch tennis and football **matches** throughout the year and horse **races** are broadcast almost every day. Events in which people compete against each other, often for prizes, are **competitions** or **contests**: *a dancing competition* ○ *an archery, angling, etc contest.* A **tournament** or **championship** is a series of contests: *a tennis tournament* ○ *the European Football Championship.*

sporting /ˈspɔːtɪŋ/ *adj* **1** [attrib] connected with or interested in sport: *a sporting occasion* ○ *a sporting woman.* **2** showing fairness; generous; sportsmanlike: *It's very sporting of you to give me an initial advantage.* ○ *He made me a sporting offer*, ie one that involved some risk of his losing. **3** (idm) **a sporting ˈchance** a reasonable chance of being successful: *give sb a sporting chance* ○ *We've still got a sporting chance of winning.*

sportive /ˈspɔːtɪv/ *adj* playful. ▷ **sportively** *adv.* **sportiveness** *n* [U].

spot /spɒt/ *n* **1** small (usu round) mark different in colour, texture, etc from the surface it is on: *a white skirt with red spots* ○ *Which has spots, the leopard or the tiger?* **2** roundish mark or stain: *spots of mud on your trousers.* **3** small red mark or blemish on the skin, caused by illness, etc; pimple: *a teenage boy worried about his spots*, ie acne ○ *She had chicken-pox and was covered in spots.* **4** (a) particular place or area: *a nice picnic spot/spot for a picnic* ○ *a well-known beauty spot*, ie a place well-known for its natural beauty ○ *stand rooted to the spot*, ie not moving ○ *This is the (very) spot where he was murdered.* ○ *There are several weak spots in your argument.* (b) (*infml*) place of entertainment: *a popular night spot.* **5** drop: *Did you feel a few spots of rain?* **6** place for an individual item of entertainment, esp a short regular one, in a television, radio or theatre show: *a ten-minute guest spot on a radio programme* ○ *She has a regular cabaret spot at a local night-club.* **7** (usu *sing*) ~ **of sth** (*Brit infml*) small amount of sth: *Are you ready for a spot of lunch?* ○ *What about doing a spot of work?* ○ *You seem to be having a spot of bother with your car — can I help?* **8** (*fig*) flaw in a person's character; moral blemish: *There isn't a spot on her reputation.* **9** (*infml*) = SPOTLIGHT. **10** (*US infml*) playing-card or banknote of a particular (specified) value: *He passed me a ten spot.* **11** (idm) **change one's spots** ➪ CHANGE[1]. **have a soft spot for sb/sth** ➪ SOFT. **a hot spot** ➪ HOT. **in a (tight) ˈspot** (*infml*) in a difficult position or situation: *I'm in a bit of a spot financially.* **knock spots off sb/sth** ➪ KNOCK[2]. **a/the leopard can't change it/his spots** ➪ LEOPARD. **on the ˈspot** (a) immediately; without moving from that place; then and there: *He was hit by a falling tree and killed on the spot.* (b) at the place where an event happened (esp when one is needed): *The police were on the spot within a few minutes of my telephone call.* ○ *Luckily there was a doctor on the spot.* **put sb on the ˈspot** put a person in a difficult position; force sb to take action or justify himself: *You've put me on the spot here — I can't answer your question.*
▷ **spot** *v* (**-tt-**) **1** [I, Tn, Tn·pr usu passive] ~ **sth** (**with sth**) (cause sth to) become marked with a spot or spots: *material that spots easily* ○ *a table spotted with ink.* **2** [Tn, Tw, Tng, Cn·n/a] ~ **sb/sth** (**as sth**) (not in the continuous tenses) pick out (one person or thing from many); catch sight of; recognize; discover: *He finally spotted just the shirt he wanted.* ○ *She spotted her friend in the crowd.* ○ *I can't spot the difference between them.* ○ *Can you spot the flaw in their argument?* ○ *spot the winner of a race*, ie pick out the winner before the race starts ○ *I soon spotted what to do.* ○ *He was spotted by police boarding a plane for Paris.* ○ *She has been spotted as a likely tennis star of the future.* **3** [I, Ipr] (*Brit infml*) (used with *it*) rain slightly; spit: *It's beginning to spot.* ○ *It's spotting with rain.*
spotted *adj* marked or covered with spots: *a spotted dog* ○ *a spotted dress.* **spotted ˈdick** (*Brit*) suet pudding containing currants.
spotter *n* (esp in compounds) person who looks for and writes down details of a specified type of thing or person, as a hobby or job: *an ˈaircraft spotter*, ie one who looks for and identifies different types of aircraft, esp in wartime ○ *a ˈtalent-spotter*, ie an agent who visits clubs, theatres, etc looking for new acts ○ *He's an avid ˈtrain-spotter.* ○ [attrib] *a spotter plane*, ie one used for observing enemy manoeuvres.
spotless *adj* **1** very clean and tidy: *He keeps his house spotless.* **2** (*fig fml*) free from flaws; morally pure: *a spotless reputation.* **spotlessly** *adv.* **spotlessness** *n* [U].
spotty *adj* (**-ier, -iest**) (*infml*) **1** (*esp derog*) (of a person) having spots (SPOT 3), esp on the face: *spotty youths* ○ *a spotty complexion.* **2** marked with spots (SPOT 2); spotted: *a spotty table-cloth.*
□ **ˌspot ˈcash** (*commerce*) money paid immediately for goods when they are bought.
ˌspot ˈcheck check made suddenly and without warning on a person or thing chosen at random: *The campaign against drinking and driving will include spot checks on motorists.*
ˈspot welding welding of small areas of metal that are in contact.
ˌspot-ˈon *adj* [pred] (*infml*) exactly right; accurate:

Sports and Games

Many sports that are popular internationally originated in Britain. Football, known officially as 'association football' and sometimes as 'soccer', is known to have been played as early as the 12th century. The present form of the game was laid down by the Football Association (FA), which was founded in 1863. Rugby football (informally called 'rugger') arose from the game first played at Rugby School, Warwickshire, in 1823, and subsequently developed into two distinct games: Rugby Union, played only by amateurs between teams of 15 players, and Rugby League, played by both amateurs and professionals between teams of 13 players. (Rugby League was first played in 1895 when the Northern Rugby Football Union, later the Rugby Football League, broke away from the Rugby Union, founded in 1841.)

Tennis (still officially called 'lawn tennis' to distinguish it from the older game of 'real tennis', played in an indoor court) traces its origins back to 1874, when it was patented by Major Walter Wingfield. The game was officially adopted by the All England Croquet Club in 1877, and it is the All England Lawn Tennis and Croquet Club that organizes the famous tennis championships at Wimbledon.

Cricket developed in the early 18th century from the 'bat and ball' game played a century earlier, mainly by boys. Its rules were formulated by the Marylebone Cricket Club (MCC), which was founded in 1787 and was for many years the governing body of the game.

Today, football in Britain is governed by the laws of the Football Association, which awarded the first Football Association Cup for a match played in 1872. It is the 'FA Cup' that is now competed for annually at Wembley Stadium, London, in the 'Cup Final', the final match of a knock-out competition between teams of English football clubs. A similar cup is competed for (at Hampden Park in Glasgow) by teams of Scottish football clubs. There are 92 professional clubs in England and Wales and 38 clubs in Scotland, belonging respectively to the Football League (founded by 12 football clubs in 1888) and the Scottish Football League (founded in 1891). The club teams themselves are arranged in four divisions in England and Wales and three in Scotland. Apart from these full-time professional clubs, there are thousands of amateur clubs. Many of the major ones are affiliated to the FA.

The football season lasts from August to May, and the Saturday matches are often attended by large crowds. Important matches are also often televised. In recent years there have been drunken and violent clashes between supporters of opposing teams, and British supporters of teams playing abroad have at times behaved so badly that the image of British football has been seriously damaged.

Many people bet on the results of football matches through the weekly 'football pools' organized by various firms, and 'doing the pools' is a hobby for thousands of people who may not otherwise be interested in the game.

Rugby Union, which is an amateur game, is played at different levels in league, divisional and county championships in England as well as in a series of club knock-out competitions in England and Wales and in the Scottish League Cup Championship. The climax of the Rugby Union year is the 'Five Nations' tournament between England, Scotland, Wales, Ireland and France. Regular overseas tours are made by the British Lions, a team representing Great Britain and Ireland. The Rugby Football Union has its headquarters at Twickenham, in west London, and the ground there is used not only for the home matches of the England team but also for the annual match between Oxford and Cambridge Universities. Rugby League is played mainly in the north of England, where it originated, and is an increasingly popular spectator sport.

Cricket is administered by the Cricket Council, but its laws are still the responsibility of the MCC, which has its headquarters at Lord's cricket ground, London. The most important cricket matches are the annual Test Matches, played in the summer between a team from England and a touring team from Australia, India, New Zealand, Pakistan, Sri Lanka or the West Indies. In the winter, a touring team from England usually plays in one or more of these countries.

Apart from the Tests, a series of cricket league matches is played each summer between teams from 17 English counties. The matches are played in the county grounds and last three or four days. (The names of the counties are the ones used before the county boundary changes of 1974.) Cricket is also widely played as an amateur game. It is played in schools and there are matches in many villages at weekends in the summer. It is mostly still played, as football is, by men and boys, although there are also women's teams.

Most British sports are spectator sports. Football (of both kinds), cricket and tennis attract the biggest crowds, especially for final or championship matches. Many people, however, take part in sports simply for pleasure and to keep fit. Sport is part of the curriculum in schools and matches are played between teams from different schools. Most towns and villages have tennis clubs. The growing number of sports centres has attracted more people to indoor sports such as basketball, squash, judo, table tennis and gymnastics.

In the USA the three main sports are baseball and American football, followed closely by basketball. Baseball developed from the British game of 'rounders' (which is still played by children in Britain) in the early 19th century, and the game is said to have been first played in its modern form in New York in 1839. The Cincinnati Red Stockings were the first professional team, playing 64 games in 1869 without losing once. In 1871 the National Association of Professional Base Ball Players was founded in New York. The association was disbanded in 1876, when the National League of Professional Base Ball Clubs was formed. The game became established professionally, with many cities having teams belonging to the National League. In 1882 the American Association, later called the American League, was formed in cities that were not members of the National League, and the two organizations are traditional rivals. Champions of the National League and the American League have played each other in annual World Series contests since 1903.

The two baseball leagues are each made up of clubs, mostly named after the cities in which they play, such as the Cincinatti Reds in the National League and the Chicago White Sox in the American League. More recently, however, some teams have been named after states, such as the California Angels and the Texas Rangers. New York has two clubs, one in each league, the New York Mets and the New York Yankees, each with its own stadium. For competition purposes, each league is divided into two divisions, East and West, with every team playing a schedule of 162 games in the hope of winning the league championship.

American football developed from the football first played by British colonists in the 17th century. In the early 19th century it was taken up by college students, and at first was simply a rough, tough game with variable rules. After the Civil War of the 1860s it became more sophisticated, however, and in 1869 the first intercollegiate game took place, between Princeton and Rutgers. The rules were still different from those of today: the present form of the game is traditionally dated from 1873, when Columbia, Princeton, Yale and Rutgers adopted a set of rules. In 1880 the standard number of 11 men a side was adopted.

The major professional organization of American football is the National Football League (NFL), founded in 1920. It became the strongest league in the country, its chief challengers being the American Football League (AFL), formed to rival it in 1959. In 1970 the two leagues merged, keeping the name of the older NFL. The final of the NFL championship is the Super Bowl, the play-off between the winners of the two sections of the league, the National Conference and the American Conference, each of these having three divisions, Eastern, Central and Western.

Basketball was invented by Dr James Naismith at Springfield, Massachusetts, in 1891, and is now a major sport in the USA, played by men and women at all levels, from professional level to high schools and clubs. The most famous basketball team is the Harlem Globetrotters, formed in 1927 and internationally renowned for their skilful handling of the ball and humorous antics.

All three sports are extremely popular as spectator events, and many of their games are televised. American football in particular is noted for its fast and furious play, with its many spectacular scrimmages, and for its cheer-leaders, the young women in miniskirts who line the field and spur on their team by dancing and cheering in unison throughout the game. Matches are often attended by huge numbers of spectators, in some cases over 100 000 people.

Many idioms in English derive from sporting terms. For example, 'below the belt', 'pull one's punches' and 'throw in the towel' come from boxing, and 'hit for six' (or 'knock for six'), 'a good innings', 'off one's own bat' and 'a sticky wicket' (and many more) come from cricket. Sometimes the name of a sport itself is used as an idiom, as in 'it's not cricket', which refers to the intricate rules of the game and its 'gentlemanly' code of conduct. Further expressions that refer to the sporting ethic are 'to play ball', 'to play fair' and 'to play the game'.

His assessment of the situation was spot-on. ○ *Your budget figures were spot-on this year.*

spotlight /ˈspɒtlaɪt/ *n* **1** (also **spot**) [C] (lamp used for sending a) strong beam of light directed onto a particular place or person, eg on the stage of a theatre. **2 the spotlight** [sing] *(fig)* full attention or publicity: *a sportsman who likes to be in the spotlight* ○ *This week the spotlight is on the world of fashion.*

▷ **spotlight** *v* (*pt, pp* **spotlit** /-lɪt/ or, esp in sense 2, **spotlighted**) [Tn] **1** direct a spotlight onto (sb/sth): *a spotlit stage.* **2** *(fig)* draw attention to (sth); make conspicuous or obvious: *The report has spotlighted real deprivation in the inner cities.*

spouse /spaʊz; *US* spaʊs/ *n* (*arch or law or joc*) husband or wife.

spout /spaʊt/ *n* [C] **1** projecting pipe or tube through or from which liquid pours, eg for carrying rain-water from a roof or tea from a teapot: *The spout is chipped so it doesn't pour very well.* **2** jet of liquid coming out with great force. **3** (idm) **up the ˈspout** (a) (*infml*) in a hopeless condition; broken, ruined, defeated, etc: *My holiday plans are completely up the spout.* (b) (*sl derog*) pregnant.

▷ **spout** *v* **1** (a) [I, Ipr, Ip] ~ **(out of/from sth)/(out/up)** (of a liquid) come out with great force: *blood spouting from a severed artery* ○ *water spouting (out) from a broken water-pipe.* (b) [Tn, Tn·p] ~ **sth (out/up)** send out (a liquid) with great force: *a broken pipe spouting (out) water* ○ *The wound spouted blood.* (c) [I] (of whales) send a jet of water up through a hole in the head. **2** [I, Ipr, Tn, Tn·pr, Tn·p] (*infml usu derog*) recite (poetry, etc) or speak lengthily and loudly: *Children dislike being spouted at by pompous teachers.* ○ *spouting unwanted advice* ○ *He can spout Shakespeare for hours.*

sprain /spreɪn/ *v* [Tn] injure (a joint in the body, esp a wrist or an ankle) by sudden twisting or wrenching so that there is pain and swelling: *sprain one's wrist* ○ *suffering from a sprained ankle.*

▷ **sprain** *n* injury caused in this way: *a bad sprain.*

sprang *pt* of SPRING[3].

sprat /spræt/ *n* **1** small edible European sea-fish of the herring family. **2** (idm) **a ˌsprat to catch a ˈmackerel** (*saying*) relatively small or unimportant thing that is offered or sacrificed in the hope of getting sth much bigger or better.

sprawl /sprɔːl/ *v* (*esp derog*) **1** (a) [I, Ipr, Ip] ~ **(out/about/around) (across, in, on, etc sth)** sit, lie or fall with the arms and legs spread out loosely: *He was sprawling in an armchair in front of the TV.* ○ *be sent sprawling in the mud* ○ *sprawling about on the sofa.* (b) [usu passive: Tn, Tn·pr, Tn·p] spread (oneself or one's limbs) out loosely in this way: *They were sprawled out in front of the fire.* **2** [I, Ipr, Ip] spread out loosely and irregularly over much space: *sprawling handwriting* ○ *suburbs that sprawl out into the countryside.*

▷ **sprawl** *n* [U, C usu *sing*] **1** sprawling position or movement: *pick one's way through the sprawl of people sunbathing* ○ *He lay in a sprawl over the desk.* **2** widespread untidy area, esp of buildings: *London's suburban sprawl.*

spray[1] /spreɪ/ *n* **1** (a) small branch of a tree or plant, with its leaves and flowers. (b) artificial ornament in a similar form: *a spray of diamonds.* **2** bunch of cut flowers, etc arranged attractively, eg as a decoration on clothes: *He had a spray in his buttonhole.* ○ *She carried a spray of pink roses.*

spray[2] /spreɪ/ *n* **1** [U] liquid sent through the air in tiny drops (by the wind or through an apparatus): *ˈsea spray*, ie blown from waves ○ *the spray of a waterfall.* **2** (a) [C, U] (esp in compounds) liquid (eg perfume, disinfectant, insecticide) applied in the form of spray from a special device (eg an atomizer or aerosol) under pressure: *ˈhair spray* ○ *ˈfly-spray* ○ [attrib] *spray paint.* (b) [C] device (eg an atomizer or aerosol) used for applying such a liquid in this form: *I've lost my throat spray.* ⇨ illus.

spray

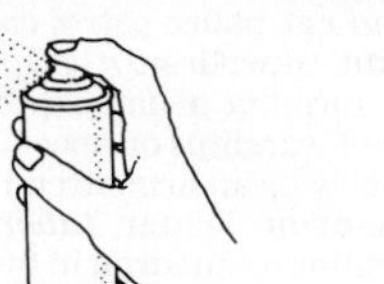

▷ **spray** *v* **1** [Tn, Tn·pr] ~ **sth (on/over sb/sth)**; ~ **sb/sth (with sth)** send out (liquid) onto sb/sth in tiny drops; wet sb/sth with liquid in this way: *spraying paint on her car* ○ *a farmer spraying his crops with pesticide* ○ *(fig) spray the target with bullets.* **2** [Ipr, Ip] ~ **(out) (over, across, etc sb/sth)** (of a liquid) be sent out in tiny drops: *Water sprayed out over the floor.* **sprayer** *n* (a) person who sprays (usu as part of a job): *He's a paint sprayer in the local factory.* (b) apparatus for spraying: *a crop sprayer.*

□ **ˈspray-gun** *n* device using pressure to spray paint, etc over surfaces.

NOTE ON USAGE: Compare **spray**, **shower**, **spatter**, **splatter**, **splash** and **slosh**. These verbs indicate the spreading of liquid or powder in a variety of ways. We **spray** small drops of paint, perfume, chemicals, etc, usually with an aerosol or a spray-gun, in order to cover an area completely: *I had to get my car resprayed after the accident.* **Shower** usually suggests people being covered with drops of water, dust, etc by accident or against their will: *The shoppers were showered with broken glass from the explosion.* **Spatter** suggests larger amounts of paint, mud, blood, etc being thrown at somebody and making him or her dirty: *The bus spattered them with mud as it passed in the rain.* Eggs, etc are **splattered** over the floor when they are dropped or thrown. We **splash** liquids when we spill them accidentally: *Don't let the acid splash on your hand.* We **slosh** large quantities of paint, water, etc by throwing it around carelessly: *He sloshed the paint on without bothering to catch the drips.*

spread /spred/ *v* (*pt, pp* **spread**) **1** (a) [Tn, Tn·pr, Tn·p] ~ **sth (out) (on/over sth)** extend the surface area, width or length of sth by unfolding or unrolling it: *The bird spread (out) its wings.* ○ *spread a cloth on the table* ○ *spread out one's arms*, eg to welcome or embrace sb ○ *spread the map out on the floor.* (b) [Tn·pr] ~ **sth with sth** cover sth with sth by doing this: *spread a table with a cloth.* **2** (a) [Tn·pr] ~ **A on B** put (a substance) on (a surface) and extend its area by flattening, etc; apply sth as a layer on sth: *spread butter on bread* ○ *spread glue on paper.* (b) [Tn·pr] ~ **B with A** cover (a surface) with (a substance) by doing this: *spread bread with butter.* (c) [I] be able to be spread in this way; be applied in a layer: *Butter spreads more easily when it's softer.* ○ *margarine that spreads straight from the fridge*, ie does not go hard when cold. **3** [I, Ipr, Tn, Tn·pr] (a) (cause sth to) become (more) widely known, felt or suffered: *The disease is spreading fast.* ○ *Fear spread quickly through the village.* ○ *The strike has already spread to other factories.* ○ *The water spread over the floor.* ○ *Flies spread disease.* ○ *He spread the news around the town.* (b) (cause sth to) become distributed: *Settlers soon spread inland.* **4** [I, Ipr] extend in size, area, etc: *a desert spreading for hundreds of miles* ○ *The forest spreads as far as the river.* **5** [Tn, Tn·pr] ~ **sth (over sth)** distribute sth over a period of time: *spread the payments over three months* ○ *a course of studies spread over three years.* **6** [usu passive: Tn, Tn·pr] ~ **sth (with sth)** prepare (a table) for a meal: *The table was spread with cakes and sandwiches.* **7** (idm) **spread like ˈwildfire** (esp of rumours, reports, disease) travel, spread, etc very fast: *The news spread like wildfire.* **spread one's ˈnet** prepare to catch sb or get sb in one's power or influence. **ˈspread oneself** (a) occupy much space (eg by lying out with limbs extended): *Since there was no one else in the compartment I was able to spread myself.* (b) talk or write at length (on a subject). (c) spend or provide things generously. **spread one's ˈwings** (have confidence to) extend one's activities and interests: *We hope college life will help him to spread his wings a bit.* **8** (phr v) **spread (sb/oneself) out** move (sb/oneself) away from others in a group so as to cover a wider area: *The search party spread out over the moor.* ○ *Don't all sit together, spread yourselves out.*

▷ **spread** *n* **1** (usu *sing*) (a) extent, width or expanse of sth: *the spread of a bird's wings* ○ *The survey revealed a wide spread of opinion.* (b) extent of space or time; stretch: *a spread of 100 years.* **2** [U] process or activity of spreading (SPREAD 2) or being spread; extension; diffusion: *the spread of disease, knowledge, education* ○ *the spread of crime.* **3** [C] newspaper or magazine article, advertisement, etc, esp one covering more than one printed column: *a double-page spread.* **4** [C] (*infml*) (usu large) meal spread out on a table: *What a spread!* **5** (usu in compounds) (a) [C] thing that is spread(1b), esp a cloth for covering sth: *a ˈbedspread.* (b) [C, U] expansion: (*joc*) *middle-aged spread*, ie increased size around the waist in middle age. **6** [U, C] sweet or savoury paste spread on bread, etc: *chocolate spread* ○ *cheese spreads.*

□ **ˌspread ˈeagle** figure of an eagle with legs and wings extended, as an emblem on coins, etc. **spread-eagle** *v* [Tn] place (sb) in a position with the arms and legs spread out: *Sunbathers lay spread-eagled on the grass.* ○ *The blow spread-eagled him against the wall.* — *adj* [attrib] (*US infml derog*) patriotic in a boastful way.

spreadsheet /ˈspredʃiːt/ *n* (*computing*) program for displaying and manipulating rows of figures, used esp for accounting; display or print-out produced by this.

spree /spriː/ *n* (*infml*) lively and enjoyable outing, usu with much spending of money: *have a spree* ○ *a spending/buying/shopping spree* ○ *go out on a spree*, ie go out to enjoy a spree.

sprig /sprɪg/ *n* **1** ~ **(of sth)** small twig (of a plant or bush) with leaves, etc: *a sprig of holly, parsley, heather, etc* ○ *a sprig of mistletoe for Christmas.* **2** small ornament, esp on fabric or china.

▷ **sprig** *v* (-gg-) [Tn] put a sprig(2) or sprigs on (sth).

sprightly /ˈspraɪtlɪ/ *adj* (-ier, -iest) lively and full of energy: *He's surprisingly sprightly for an old man.* ▷ **sprightliness** *n* [U]

spring

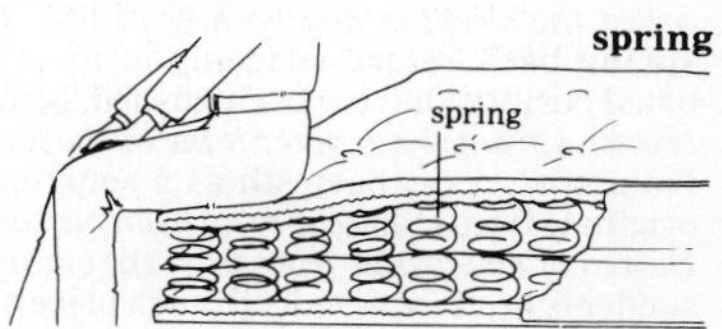

spring[1] /sprɪŋ/ *n* **1** [C] act of springing or jumping up; jump: *With an easy spring the cat reached the branch.* **2** [C] (place where there is) water coming up naturally from the ground; flow of this: *a ˈhot spring* ○ *a ˈmineral spring* ○ [attrib] *spring water.* **3** [C] device of twisted, bent or coiled metal or wire that can be pushed, pulled or pressed but tends to return to its original shape or position when released (used to drive clockwork, make seats more comfortable, etc): *a watch spring* ○ *the springs in an armchair* ○ [attrib] *a spring-ˈmattress*, ie one containing spiral springs in a rigid frame ○ *Don't bounce on the bed — you'll break the springs!* ⇨ illus. **4** [U sing] (a) elastic quality; elasticity: *an old trampoline that has lost some of its spring.* (b) *(fig)* lively, healthy quality: *walk with a spring in one's step/heels.*

▷ **springy** *adj* (-ier, -iest) **1** that can return to its original shape easily after being pushed, pulled, stretched, etc; elastic: *a springy bed* ○ *The turf felt springy under their feet.* **2** having a spring[1](4b): *walk with a youthful springy step.* **springiness** *n* [U].

□ **ˌspring ˈbalance** device that measures weight

by the tension of a spring.
ˈ**springboard** *n* **1** strong flexible board from which a person can jump high before diving or performing a gymnastic feat. **2** ~ **(to/for sth)** (*fig*) starting point that gives impetus to a future activity: *The college debating society was a natural springboard for her career in politics.*
ˌ**spring-ˈtide** *n* tide with the greatest rise or fall, occurring soon after the new and full moon each month. Cf NEAP-TIDE (NEAP).

spring[2] /sprɪŋ/ *n* **1** [U, C] the first season of the year (in which plants begin to grow), coming between winter and summer, ie from March to May in the northern hemisphere: [attrib] *spring flowers, weather* ○ *In (the) spring leaves begin to grow on the trees.* **2** (idm) **full of the joys of spring** ⇨ FULL.
□ ˌ**spring ˈchicken 1** young chicken for eating. **2** (*fig joc*) young person: *She's no spring chicken, is she?*
ˌ**spring-ˈclean** *v* [Tn] clean (a house, room, etc) thoroughly. **spring-clean** (also *esp US* ˌ**spring-ˈcleaning**) *n* (usu *sing*): *give the place a good spring-clean(ing).*
ˌ**spring ˈgreens** (*Brit*) tender young cabbage cooked and eaten as a vegetable.
ˌ**spring ˈonion** (*US* **scallion**) small young onion with a thin white bulb and green stem, usu eaten raw.
ˌ**spring ˈroll** Chinese rolled pancake containing chopped vegetables, esp bean shoots, crisply fried.
ˈ**springtide** *n* [U] (*arch*) = SPRINGTIME.
ˈ**springtime** *n* [U] season of spring: *The blossom on the trees looks lovely in (the) springtime.*

spring[3] /sprɪŋ/ *v* (*pt* **sprang** /spræŋ/, *pp* **sprung** /sprʌŋ/) **1** [Ipr, Ip] jump quickly or suddenly, esp from the ground in a single movement; move suddenly (eg from a hiding-place or a position of relaxation): *spring out of bed, into action, to one's feet* ○ *A cat sprang out of the bushes.* ○ *sprang (up) from his seat* ○ *He sprang forward to help me.* ⇨ Usage at JUMP[2]. **2** [I, Tn] (cause sth to) operate by means of a mechanism: *spring a mine*, ie cause it to explode ○ *spring a trap*, ie cause it to close suddenly ○ *The box sprang open.* **3** [Tn] **(a)** (*infml*) help (a prisoner, etc) to escape: *spring a convict from gaol.* **(b)** cause (an animal) to leave a hiding-place. **4** (idm) **come/spring to mind** ⇨ MIND[1]. **hope springs eternal** ⇨ HOPE. **spring a ˈleak** (of a boat, ship, container, etc) develop a hole so that water enters or leaks out. **spring to ˈlife** suddenly become active: *On hearing his name called the sleeping dog sprang to life.* **5** (phr v) **spring back** return suddenly to its previous or usual position, having been pushed, bent, etc: *The branch sprang back and hit me in the face.* **spring from sth/...** **(a)** have sth as a source or origin; originate from sth: *He sprang from peasant stock.* ○ *Hatred often springs from fear.* **(b)** (*infml*) appear suddenly or unexpectedly from (a place): *Where on earth did you spring from?* **spring sth on sb** (*infml*) present, introduce or propose sth suddenly to sb as a surprise or without warning: *spring bad news on sb* ○ *spring a surprise on sb* ○ *I hate to spring this on you at such short notice.* **spring up** appear, develop, grow, etc quickly or suddenly: *weeds springing up everywhere* ○ *A breeze sprang up as we were returning.* ○ *New houses were springing up all over the town.* ○ *Doubts have begun to spring up in my mind.*

springbok /ˈsprɪŋbɒk/ *n* **1** small S African gazelle that can jump high into the air. **2 the Springboks** [pl] the S African national team in various sports, esp Rugby.

sprinkle /ˈsprɪŋkl/ *v* [Tn, Tn·pr] ~ **A (on/onto/over B)**; ~ **B (with A)** scatter or throw sth in small drops or particles; scatter a shower of small drops, etc on (a surface): *sprinkle water on a dusty path/ sprinkle a dusty path with water* ○ *sprinkle pepper on one's food.* ⇨ Usage at SCATTER.
▷ **sprinkle** *n* (usu *sing*) sprinkling: *a sprinkle of sand.*
sprinkler /ˈsprɪŋklə(r)/ *n* device for sprinkling water (eg on a lawn) or as part of a fire-extinguishing system installed in a building: [attrib] *a* ˈ*sprinkler system*, ie set of sprinklers in a building that operate automatically when there is a rise in temperature caused by a fire. ⇨ illus at HOME.
sprinkling /ˈsprɪŋklɪŋ/ *n* ~ **(of sth/sb)** (usu *sing*) small amount or number: *a sprinkling of rain* ○ *a sprinkling of hooligans in the crowd.*

sprint /sprɪnt/ *v* [I, Ipr, Ip, Tn] run a short distance at full speed: *He had to sprint to catch the bus.* ○ *He sprinted past the other runners just before reaching the tape.* ○ *She sprinted off/away into the distance.* ○ *She sprinted the length of the road.* ⇨ Usage at RUN[1].
▷ **sprint** *n* **1** run of this type: *a 100m sprint.* **2** similar burst of speed in swimming, cycling, etc.
sprinter *n* person who sprints: *I'm a long-distance runner, not a sprinter.*

sprite /spraɪt/ *n* fairy, elf or goblin.

sprocket /ˈsprɒkɪt/ *n* **1** each of several teeth on a wheel that connect with the links of a chain or the holes in a film or in paper or magnetic tape. **2** (also ˈ**sprocket-wheel**) such a wheel, eg on a bicycle. ⇨ illus at BICYCLE.

sprout /spraʊt/ *v* **1** [I, Ipr, Ip] ~ **(out/up) (from sth)** begin to grow or appear; put out leaves, shoots, etc: *We can't use these potatoes; they've all sprouted.* ○ *new buds sprouting on the trees* ○ *The onions are beginning to sprout (up).* ○ *Abundant hair sprouted from his broad chest.* **2** [Tn] develop or produce (sth): *When do deer first sprout horns?* ○ *Tom has sprouted a beard since we saw him last.*
▷ **sprout** *n* **1** new shoot or bud of a plant: *bean sprouts.* **2** = BRUSSELS SPROUT (BRUSSELS).

spruce[1] /spru:s/ *adj* tidy and clean in appearance; smart.
▷ **spruce** *v* (phr v) **spruce (oneself/sb) up** make (oneself/sb) tidy and clean; smarten up: *He spruced (himself) up for the interview.* ○ *They were all spruced up for the party.*
sprucely *adv.*
spruceness *n* [U].

spruce[2] /spru:s/ *n* **(a)** [C] type of fir tree with dense foliage. **(b)** [U] its soft wood, used in paper-making.

sprung[1] /sprʌŋ/ *pp* of SPRING[3].

sprung[2] /sprʌŋ/ *adj* fitted with springs (SPRING[1] 3): *a sprung floor, mattress, seat.*

spry /spraɪ/ *adj* (**-er, -est**) lively and active: *still spry at eighty.* ▷ **spryly** *adv.* **spryness** *n* [U].

spud /spʌd/ *n* (*infml*) potato: *How many spuds do you want?*
□ ˈ**spud-bashing** *n* [U] (*Brit army sl*) peeling potatoes, esp as a punishment.

spume /spju:m/ *n* [U] (*arch*) foam; froth.

spun *pp* of SPIN.

spunk /spʌŋk/ *n* [U] **1** (*dated infml*) courage; spirit. **2** (*Brit sl*) semen.
▷ **spunky** *adj* (**-ier, -iest**) (*dated infml*) having spunk(1); plucky; spirited.

spur /spɜ:(r)/ *n* **1** either of a pair of sharp-toothed wheels or projecting points, worn on the heels of a rider's boots and used to make a horse go faster: *a pair of spurs.* **2** (*fig*) ~ **(to sth)** thing that urges a person on to greater activity; incentive: *the spur of poverty* ○ *a spur to greater efficiency.* **3** thing shaped like a spur, esp the sharp hard projection on the back of a cock's leg. **4** ridge extending from a mountain or hill. **5** road or railway track that branches off the main road or line: [attrib] *a* ˈ*spur road.* **6** (idm) **on the ˌspur of the ˈmoment** on a sudden impulse, without previous planning: *She went to London on the spur of the moment.* ○ [attrib] *a ˌspur-of-the-moment iˈdea.* **win one's ˈspurs** ⇨ WIN.
▷ **spur** *v* (**-rr-**) **1** [Tn, Tn·pr, Tn·p, Tnt] ~ **sb/sth (on to sth/on)** **(a)** make (one's horse) go faster by pricking it with spurs. **(b)** strongly encourage sb/sth to do better, achieve more, etc; incite or stimulate sb/sth: *The magnificent goal spurred the team on to victory.* ○ *He was spurred on by ambition.* **2** [Ip] (*arch*) ride fast or hard: *The rider spurred on/forward to his destination.* **spurred** *adj* [usu pred] having spurs; fitted with spurs: *booted and spurred* ○ *spurred boots.*

spurious /ˈspjʊərɪəs/ *adj* not genuine or authentic; false or fake: *spurious coins, credentials, documents, evidence* ○ *a spurious argument.* ▷ **spuriously** *adv.* **spuriousness** *n* [U].

spurn /spɜ:n/ *v* [Tn] reject or refuse (sb/sth) scornfully or contemptuously: *a spurned lover* ○ *spurn sb's offer of help* ○ *She spurned his advances.*

spurt /spɜ:t/ *v* **1 (a)** [I, Ipr, Ip] ~ **(out) (from sth)** (of liquids, flame, etc) come out in a sudden burst; gush: *water spurting from a broken pipe* ○ *Blood spurted (out) from the wound.* **(b)** [Tn, Tn·p] ~ **sth (out)** send out (liquids, flame, etc) in this way: *The wound was spurting blood.* ○ *The volcano spurted (out) molten lava.* **2** [I] increase one's speed, effort, etc suddenly, esp in a race or other contest: *The runner spurted as he approached the line.*
▷ **spurt** *n* **1** sudden bursting out; gush: *The water came out with a spurt.* **2** sudden burst of speed, effort, activity, etc: *put on* (ie make) *a spurt* ○ *make a spurt for the line* ○ *a sudden spurt of energy, anger* ○ *working in spurts.*

sputnik /ˈspʊtnɪk/ *n* Russian artificial satellite orbiting the earth.

sputter /ˈspʌtə(r)/ *v* [I] **1** make a series of spitting of popping sounds: *sausages sputtering in the frying-pan* ○ *The engine sputtered feebly for a while and then stopped.* **2** = SPLUTTER 1: *sputtering with embarrassment.*
▷ **sputter** *n* sputtering sound or way of speaking.

sputum /ˈspju:təm/ *n* [U] (*fml or medical*) liquid and mucus coughed up from the throat or lungs (esp as used to diagnose some diseases); saliva or spittle.

spy /spaɪ/ *n* **1** person who tries to get secret information about military affairs, etc, esp one employed by a government to do this in another country: *suspected of being a spy* ○ [attrib] *a spy trial.* **2** person who secretly watches and reports on what others do, where they go, etc: *police spies*, ie people employed by the police to watch suspected criminals ○ *industrial spies*, ie those employed to learn the secrets of business rivals, etc. Cf MOLE[2] 2.
▷ **spy** *v* (*pt, pp* **spied**) **1** [I, Ipr] ~ **(on sb)**; ~ **(on/into sth)** **(a)** keep watch secretly: *spy on the enemy's movements* ○ *spy into other people's affairs* ○ *I'm sure my neighbours spy on me.* **(b)** be a spy; collect secret information: *She was accused of spying for the enemy.* **2** [Tn, Tng] (*fml or joc*) (usu not in the continuous tenses) observe (sb/sth); see; notice: *We spied three figures in the distance.* ○ *I spy someone coming up the garden path.* **3** (idm) ˌ**spy out the ˈland** assess the situation by making discreet inquiries, etc. **4** (phr v) **spy sth out** explore and discover (esp an illegal activity) without being observed.
□ ˈ**spyglass** *n* small telescope.

Sq *abbr* (in street names) Square: *6 Hanover Sq.*

sq *abbr* square (measurement): *10 sq cm.*

Sqn Ldr *abbr* Squadron Leader: *Sqn Ldr (Philip) Jones.*

squab /skwɒb/ *n* **1** young pigeon, esp when eaten as food. **2** soft seat or cushion, esp as part of a seat in a car.

squabble /ˈskwɒbl/ *v* [I, Ipr] ~ **(with sb) (about/over sth)** quarrel noisily (as children do), esp over unimportant matters: *birds squabbling over bits of bread* ○ *Tom keeps squabbling with his sister about who is going to use the bicycle.*
▷ **squabble** *n* noisy quarrel about sth unimportant.

squad /skwɒd/ *n* [CGp] **(a)** small group of soldiers working or being trained together. **(b)** group of people, eg athletes or sportsmen, working as a team: *the Olympic squad*, ie the athletes chosen to represent their country at the Olympic Games.
▷ **squaddie** (also **squaddy**) *n* (*Brit sl*) soldier, esp a young private; recruit: *a bunch of squaddies.*
□ ˈ**squad car** police patrol car.

squadron /ˈskwɒdrən/ *n* [CGp] **1** group of military aircraft forming a unit in the Royal Air Force. **2** group of warships on special service. **3** division of a cavalry or an armoured regiment.
□ ˈ**squadron leader** (*abbr* **Sqn Ldr**) officer commanding a squadron in the Royal Air Force. ⇨ App 4.

squalid /ˈskwɒlɪd/ *adj* (*derog*) **1** very dirty and unpleasant (esp because of neglect or poverty): *squalid housing* ○ *living in squalid conditions.* **2** morally degrading; sordid: *a squalid tale of greed and corruption.* ▷ **squalidly** *adv.*

squall /skwɔ:l/ *n* **1** sudden violent wind, often with rain or snow. **2** loud cry or scream of pain or fear (esp from a baby).
▷ **squall** *v* [I] cry noisily: *a squalling baby.*
squally *adj* having squalls (SQUALL 1): *a squally February day* ○ *squally showers of rain or sleet.*

squalor /ˈskwɒlə(r)/ *n* [U] squalid state: *the squalor of the slums* ○ *live in abject squalor.*

squander /ˈskwɒndə(r)/ *v* [Tn, Tn·pr] ~ **sth (on sb/sth)** waste (time, money, etc); use sth wastefully: *He's squandered all his savings on drink.* ○ (*fig*) *Don't squander your affection on him — he'll never love you.* ▷ **squanderer** *n.*

square[1] /skweə(r)/ *adj* **1** having four equal sides and four right angles; having the shape of a square[2](1): *a square room, table, handkerchief.* ⇨ illus at QUADRILATERAL. **2** having or forming (exactly or approximately) a right angle: *square corners* ○ *a square jaw/chin,* ie angular, not curved. **3** of comparatively broad solid shape: *a woman of square frame/build.* **4** [pred] properly arranged; tidy: *We should get everything square before we leave.* **5** [pred] **(a)** ~ **(with sth)** level or parallel: *tables arranged square with the wall.* **(b)** settled; paid for; balanced: *get one's accounts square.* **6** measuring a specified amount on all four sides, as a calculation of area: *one square metre,* ie an area equal to that of a square with sides that are each one metre in length ○ *A carpet six metres square* (ie having all four sides measuring 6 metres) *has an area of 36 square metres.* ⇨ App 10. **7** [pred] straightforward; uncompromising: *a square refusal.* **8** fair; honest: *a square deal* ○ *square dealings,* eg in business ○ *I want you to be square with me.* **9** (*dated infml*) out of touch with new ideas, styles, etc; old-fashioned; conventional. **10** (in cricket) in a position approximately at right angles to the batsman: *a fielder standing square on the off side.* **11** (idm) **be (all) square (with sb) (a)** (in sport) have equal scores: *all square at the ninth hole,* ie in a golf match. **(b)** with neither person in debt to the other: *Let's call it all square, shall we?* **a fair/square deal** ⇨ DEAL[4]. **a square ˈmeal** large and satisfying meal: *He looks as though he hasn't had a square meal for months,* ie looks underfed. **a square ˈpeg (in a round ˈhole)** person whose character or abilities make him unsuitable for or uncomfortable in his job or position.
▷ **square** *adv* **1** squarely; directly: *hit sb square on the jaw.* **2** (idm) **fair and square** ⇨ FAIR[2].
squarely *adv* **1** so as to form a right angle; directly centred: *Her hat was set squarely on her head.* **2** fairly; honestly: *act squarely.* **3** directly opposite: *He faced me squarely across the table.* **4** (idm) **fairly and squarely** ⇨ FAIRLY.
squareness *n* [U].
□ ˌ**square ˈbrackets** the marks [ ]. ⇨ App 14.
ˈ**square dance** (*US*) dance in which sets of four couples dance together, starting by facing inwards from four sides.
ˈ**square knot** (*US*) = REEF KNOT (REEF[1]).
ˌ**square ˈleg** (in cricket) (position of a) fielder at some distance from the batsman's leg-side and nearly in line with the wicket.
ˌ**square ˈmeasure** measurement of an area expressed in square metres, feet, etc.
the ˌ**Square ˈMile** the City of London, esp its financial institutions: *Reactions to the budget in the Square Mile have been rather mixed.*
ˌ**square ˈroot** number greater than 0, which when multiplied by itself gives a particular specified number: *The square root of 16 is 4.* ○ *What is the square root of 9?*
ˌ**square-ˈshouldered** *adj* with the shoulders at right angles to the neck, not sloping. Cf ROUND-SHOULDERED (ROUND[2]).
ˌ**square-ˈtoed** *adj* (of shoes) having a square toe-cap.

square[2] /skweə(r)/ *n* **1** geometric figure with four equal sides and four right angles. ⇨ illus at QUADRILATERAL. **2** object having this shape, or approximately this shape: *the squares on a chess board* ○ *cut the paper into squares* ○ *soldiers drawn up in squares.* **3 (a)** four-sided open area, eg in a town, used as a garden or for recreation, or one enclosed by streets and buildings: *a market square* ○ *listen to the band playing in the square.* **(b) Square** (*abbr* **Sq**) (in addresses) buildings and streets surrounding this: *He lives at No 95 Russell Square/Sq.* **4** result when a number or quantity is multiplied by itself: *The square of 7 is 49.* ○ *49 is a perfect square.* **5** L-shaped or (also **T-square**) T-shaped instrument for drawing or testing right angles. **6** (*dated infml*) person who is out of touch with new ideas, styles, etc; conventional or old-fashioned person: *I'm basically a bit of a square.* **7** (idm) **back to square one** back to the starting-point in an enterprise, a task, etc with no progress made: *That idea hasn't worked, so it's/we're back to square one.* **on the ˈsquare** (*infml*) fair(ly); honest(ly): *Is their business on the square?* **out of square (with sth)** not at right angles (with sth).
□ ˈ**square-bashing** *n* [U] (*sl*) military drill (esp marching, etc).

square[3] /skweə(r)/ *v* **1** [Tn] make (sth) right-angled; give a square shape to; make square: *square timber,* ie give it rectangular edges ○ *squared corners.* **2** [Tn] make (sth) straight or level: *square one's shoulders.* **3** [Tn usu passive] multiply (a number) by itself; get the square[2](4) of (a number): *3 squared is 9* ○ $y^2 = y$ x y, ie y squared. **4** [Tn usu passive] mark (sth) with squares; square off: *squared paper.* **5** [Tn, Cn·t] get the co-operation of (sb) by dishonest means; bribe: *All the officials had to be squared before they would help us.* ○ *He has been squared to say nothing.* **6** [Ipr, Tn·pr] ~ **(sth) with sth** (*infml*) be or make (sth) consistent with sth; (cause sth to) agree with sth: *Your theory doesn't square with the known facts.* ○ *You should square your practice with your principles.* **7** [Tn] cause (a total of points, wins, etc) to be even or level: *This victory has squared the series.* **8** (idm) **square one's acˈcount/square accounts with sb (a)** pay sb or be paid by him what is owed. **(b)** get one's revenge on sb. **square the ˈcircle** (attempt to) do sth that is impossible. **9** (phr v) **square sth off (a)** give sth a square or rectangular shape or outline: *square off a piece of wood.* **(b)** divide (a surface) into squares: *Square the page off with your ruler.* **square up to sb/sth** (*infml*) **(a)** prepare to fight sb (ie by raising the fists like a boxer). **(b)** confront sb or sth (esp a difficult situation) with determination: *He must square up to the reality of being out of work.* **square up (with sb)** pay (sb) the money one owes (esp before leaving a restaurant, etc): *Can I leave you to square up with the waiter?* ○ *It's time we squared up,* ie settled our accounts.

squarish /ˈskweərɪʃ/ *adj* approximately square.

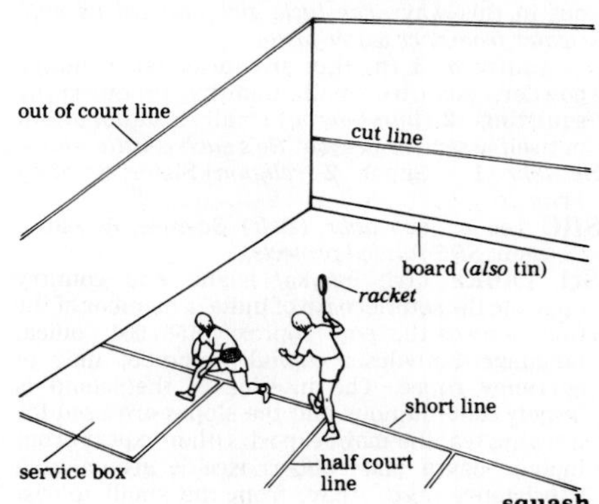

squash

squash[1] /skwɒʃ/ *v* **1 (a)** [Tn, Cn·a] press or squeeze (sb/sth) flat or into a pulp; crush: *squashed tomatoes* ○ *The cat got run over by the lorry and squashed.* ○ *He sat on his hat and squashed it (flat).* **(b)** [I] become squashed or pressed out of shape: *Soft fruit squashes easily.* **2** [Ipr, Ip, Tn·pr, Tn·p] force (sth/sb/oneself) in the specified direction by squeezing; crowd: *Don't all try to squash into the lift together.* ○ *They squashed through the gate into the football ground.* ○ *There's room for one more in the car if you squash in.* ○ *They managed to squash forty people into the bus.* ○ *She squashed her clothes down into the suitcase.* **3** [Tn] (*infml*) silence or subdue (sb) rudely, esp with an unpleasant reply; snub: *I felt completely squashed by her sarcastic comment.* **4** [Tn] **(a)** defeat or subdue (a rebellion, etc); crush. **(b)** (*infml*) reject or dismiss (an idea, a proposal, etc): *My plan was firmly squashed by the committee.* **5** (phr v) **squash (sb) up (against sb/sth)** (cause sb to) press tightly and uncomfortably (against another person or thing): *We had to squash up to make room for the others who wanted to use the lift.* ○ *There were four of us squashed up against each other on the seat.* .
▷ **squash** *n* **1 (a)** [C usu *sing*] crowd of people pressed together in a confined space: *What a squash!* ○ *a violent squash at the gates.* **(b)** state of being pressed together in this way: *It'll be a bit of a squash, but I think I can get you all in the car.* **2** [U, C] (*Brit*) soft drink made from fruit juice, sugar and water, usu sold in bottles and drunk with water added: *some orange squash* ○ *Two squashes, please.* **3** [U] (also *fml* ˈ**squash rackets**) game played with rackets and a small softish hollow rubber ball, in a court enclosed by walls and a roof: [attrib] *a squash racket, ball, court, game* ○ *Do you play squash?* Cf RACKET[1] 2. ⇨ illus.
squashy *adj* easily squashed; soft: *a big squashy sofa* ○ *The fruit is rather squashy.*

squash[2] /skwɒʃ/ *n* (*pl* unchanged or ~**es**) [U, C] any of several types of large gourd common in the US and eaten as a vegetable.

squat[1] /skwɒt/ *v* (**-tt-**) **1** [I, Ipr, Ip] ~ **(down) (a)** (of people) sit on one's heels or on the ground with the knees drawn up under or close to the body; crouch: *The old man squatted (down) by the fire.* ⇨ illus at KNEEL. **(b)** (of animals) crouch with the body close to the ground. **(c)** (*infml esp Brit*) sit: *Can you find somewhere to squat?* **2** [I] occupy an empty building or settle on unoccupied land, etc without permission: *homeless people squatting in a derelict house.*
▷ **squat** *n* **1** [sing] squatting position. **2** [C] building occupied by squatters (SQUATTER 2): *living in a squat.*
squatter *n* **1** person who sits in a squatting position. **2** person who occupies a building or land without permission: *claim squatters' rights.* **3** (*Austral*) sheep-farmer.

squat[2] /skwɒt/ *adj* (**-tter, -ttest**) (*usu derog*) short and thick; dumpy: *a squat man* ○ *a squat teapot.*

squaw /skwɔ:/ *n* N American Indian woman or wife.

squawk /skwɔ:k/ *v* [I] **1** (esp of birds) utter a loud harsh cry (eg when hurt or frightened): *The parrot squawked loudly.* **2** (*infml esp joc*) complain loudly.
▷ **squawk** *n* **1** loud harsh cry. **2** loud complaint.

squeak /skwi:k/ *n* **1** short high-pitched cry or sound: *the squeak of a mouse* ○ *The door opened with a squeak.* **2** (idm) **a narrow squeak** ⇨ NARROW.
▷ **squeak** *v* **1** [I] make a squeak: *Can you hear the mice squeaking?* ○ *These new shoes squeak.* **2** [Tn, Tn·p] ~ **sth (out)** say sth in a squeaking voice: *'Let go of me!' he squeaked nervously.* ○ *squeak out a few frightened words.* **3** [I] (*sl*) give secret information (esp to the police); become an informer: *Somebody's squeaked!* Cf SQUEAL *v.* **squeaker** *n.*
squeaky *adj* (**-ier, -iest**) making a squeaking sound: *a squeaky floor* ○ *in a squeaky voice* ○ *squeaky clean,* ie washed so clean that it squeaks. **squeakily** *adv.* **squeakiness** *n* [U].

squeal /skwi:l/ *n* high-pitched cry or sound, longer and louder than a squeak (often indicating terror or pain): *the squeal of brakes,* eg on lorries ○ *There were squeals of excitement from the children.*
▷ **squeal** *v* **1** [I] make a squeal: *The pigs were squealing.* ○ *He squealed like a pig.* **2** [Tn, Tn·p] ~

sth (**out**) say sth in a squealing voice: *He squealed the words out.* **3** [I, Ipr] ~ (**on sb**) (**to sb**) (*sl*) give secret information (esp to the police about a partner or accomplice in crime); become an informer: *He squealed on his friends.* **squealer** *n* **1** animal that squeals. **2** (*sl*) informer.

squeamish /ˈskwi:mɪʃ/ *adj* **1** (**a**) having a delicate stomach and easily made sick. (**b**) easily disgusted, shocked or offended: *an explicit and violent film, definitely not for the squeamish.* **2** too scrupulous, modest or proper (about principles, morals, etc). ▷ **squeamishly** *adv.* **squeamishness** *n* [U].

squeegee /ˈskwi:dʒi:, ˌskwi:ˈdʒi:/ *n* **1** tool with a rubber edge on a long handle, used for removing water, etc from smooth surfaces: *use a squeegee to clean windows.* **2** similar tool with a small rubber roller on a short handle for pressing water from photographic prints.
▷ **squeegee** *v* (*pt, pp* **-geed**) [Tn] use a squeegee on (sth).

squeeze /skwi:z/ *v* **1** (**a**) [Tn, Tn·p, Cn·a] press on (sth) from opposite sides or all sides: *squeeze a sponge, a tube of toothpaste* ○ *squeeze sb's hand,* eg as a sign of affection, sympathy, etc ○ *a doll that squeaks when you squeeze it* ○ *squeeze the dish-cloth out* ○ *squeeze a lemon dry* ○ (*fig*) *a company squeezed by* (ie under financial pressure because of) *reduced sales.* (**b**) [Tn·pr] ~ **sth into sth** change the shape, size, etc of sth into that specified by doing this: *squeeze paste into a ball.* **2** (**a**) [Tn, Tn·pr, Tn·p] ~ **sth** (**from/out of sth**); ~ **sth** (**out**) get (water, juice, etc) out of sth by pressing it hard: *squeeze the juice out of a lemon* ○ *squeeze the water out (of the cloth)* ○ (*fig*) *squeezed out of the job market by younger men* ○ *She felt as if every drop of emotion had been squeezed out of her.* (**b**) [Tn·pr] cause sth to move from one place to another by squeezing: *squeeze lemon-juice into a glass* ○ *squeeze toothpaste from the tube onto a toothbrush.* **3** [Ipr, Ip, Tn·pr, Tn·p] ~ (**sb/sth**) **into, through, etc sth**; ~ (**sb/sth**) **through, in, past, etc** force (oneself/sb/sth) into, through, etc a narrow gap or restricted space: *squeeze through a gap in the hedge/through a crowd* ○ *squeeze (one's way) onto a crowded bus* ○ *There were already four people in the lift, but he managed to squeeze in.* ○ *Can you squeeze past/by?* ○ *She squeezed as many books onto the shelf as she could.* ○ (*fig*) *I've a busy morning but I could squeeze you in* (ie find time for you) *at 10.15.* **4** (phr v) **squeeze sth out of sb** get sth from sb by applying pressure (eg threats of violence, force, harsh laws): *squeeze more money out of the taxpayer* ○ *squeeze a promise out of sb.* **squeeze** (**sb**) **up** (**against sb/sth**) (cause sb to) press tightly and uncomfortably (against another person or thing); move closer together: *There'll be enough room if we all squeeze up a bit.* ○ *I had to sit squeezed up against the wall.*
▷ **squeeze** *n* **1** [C] (**a**) act of squeezing: *give the tube of toothpaste a squeeze.* (**b**) affectionate hug or clasp: *a hug and a squeeze* ○ *She gave my hand a gentle squeeze.* **2** [C] small amount of sth produced by squeezing: *a squeeze of lemon in your drink.* **3** [sing] state of being squeezed, as when many people or things are pressed tightly together: *It was a tight squeeze but we finally got all the clothes into the case.* **4** [C usu *sing*] difficulty or hardship caused by shortage of money or time, etc: *She's just lost her job, so they're really feeling the squeeze.* **5** [C] (*infml*) restrictions on borrowing, etc during a financial crisis: *a credit squeeze.* **6** (idm) **put the squeeze on sb** (**to do sth**) (*infml*) put pressure on sb to act in a particular way. **a tight squeeze** ⇨ TIGHT.
squeezer *n* (usu in compounds) device for squeezing out juice, etc: *a* ˈ*lemon-squeezer.*

squelch /skweltʃ/ *v* **1** [I] make a sucking sound as when feet are lifted from thick sticky mud: *water squelching in my boots.* **2** [Ipr, Ip] move in the specified direction making this sound: *cows squelching across the field* ○ *squelching along (in the mud).*
▷ **squelch** *n* squelching sound.

squib /skwɪb/ *n* **1** small firework that jumps around on the ground making a hissing sound before exploding. **2** (idm) **a damp squib** ⇨ DAMP[1].

squid /skwɪd/ *n* (*pl* unchanged or ~**s**) [C, U] sea creature related to the cuttle-fish with ten arms round the mouth: *Would you like some squid?* ⇨ illus at OCTOPUS.

squidgy /ˈskwɪdʒɪ/ *adj* (*infml esp Brit*) soft and moist; soggy: *a nice squidgy cream cake.*

squiffy /ˈskwɪfɪ/ *adj* (**-ier, -iest**) (*Brit infml*) slightly drunk.

squiggle /ˈskwɪgl/ *n* short twisting or wavy line, esp in handwriting; scribble: *Is this squiggle supposed to be a signature?* ▷ **squiggly** /ˈskwɪglɪ/ *adj.*

squint /skwɪnt/ *v* **1** [I] have eyes that do not move together but look in different directions at once. **2** [I, Ipr] ~ (**at, through, up, etc sth**) look (at sth) with eyes half shut or turned sideways, or through a narrow opening: *squinting in the bright sunlight* ○ *squinting through the letter-box.*
▷ **squint** *n* **1** (abnormal condition causing the) squinting position of an eyeball or eyeballs: *He was born with a squint.* ○ *They both have squints.* **2** (*Brit infml*) look or glance: *Have/Take a squint at this.*
squint *adv, adj* [usu attrib] (*infml*) not straight; askew: *The bottle-top has been screwed on squint.* **squinty** *adj*: *squinty eyes.*

squire /ˈskwaɪə(r)/ *n* **1** (in titles **Squire**) (formerly) country gentleman, esp the chief landowner in a country district. **2** (formerly) young man who was a knight's attendant until he himself became a knight. **3** (*US*) justice of the peace or local judge. **4** (*Brit infml or joc*) (used as a friendly but respectful form of address by one man to another): *What can I get you, squire?*
▷ **squirearchy** /ˈskwaɪərɑ:kɪ/ *n* [CGp] landowners as a class having political or social influence (esp formerly in England).

squirm /skwɜ:m/ *v* **1** [I, Ipr, Ip] move by twisting the body about; wriggle; writhe: *He was squirming (around) on the floor in agony.* **2** [I] feel embarrassment, discomfort, or shame: *It made him squirm to think how he'd messed up the interview.*

squirrel /ˈskwɪrəl; *US* ˈskwɜ:rəl/ *n* **1** [C] small tree-climbing animal with a bushy tail and red or grey fur: *Red squirrels are now very rare in Britain.* ⇨ illus at ANIMAL. **2** [U] its fur: [attrib] *a squirrel hat.*

squirt /skwɜ:t/ *v* (**a**) [Tn, Tn·pr, Tn·p] ~ **sth** (**out of/from sth**); ~ **sth** (**out**) force (liquid, powder, etc) out in a thin stream or jet: *squirt soda-water into a glass* ○ *squirt oil out (of a can) into a machine* ○ *Stop squirting water at me!* (**b**) [I, Ipr, Ip] ~ (**out of/from sth**); ~ (**out**) (of liquid, powder, etc) be forced out in this way: *Water squirted (from the tap) all over me.* ○ *I squeezed the bottle and the sauce squirted out.* (**c**) [Tn, Tn·pr] ~ **sb/sth** (**with sth**) cover sb/sth with liquid, powder, etc forced out in this way: *The little girl squirted us with (water from) her water-pistol.*
▷ **squirt** *n* **1** (**a**) thin stream or jet of liquid, powder, etc. (**b**) small quantity produced by squirting. **2** (*infml derog*) small or unimportant but self-assertive person: *He's such a little squirt.*

Sr *abbr* **1** = SEN 3. **2** (*religion*) Sister: *Sr Mary Francis.*

SRC /ˌes ɑ: ˈsi:/ *abbr* (*Brit*) Science Research Council: *SRC-funded projects.*

Sri Lanka /ˌʃri: ˈlæŋkə/ island and country opposite the southern tip of India, a member of the Commonwealth; pop approx 16 587 000; offical language Sinhalese; capital Colombo; unit of currency rupee. The interior of the island is largely mountainous and the slopes are used for growing tea, the main export. Other export crops include copra and rubber; rice is grown as a subsistence crop. Apart from the small tourist trade, Sri Lanka's economy is almost entirely agricultural. Its political stability is threatened by tensions between the Tamil and Sinhalese populations. Until 1972 it was called Ceylon. ⇨ map. ▷ **Sri Lankan** *adj, n.*

Sri Lanka

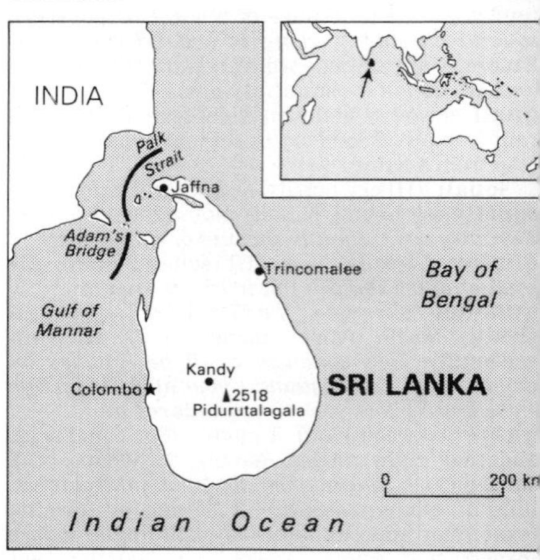

SRN /ˌes ɑ:r ˈen/ *abbr* (*Brit*) State Registered Nurs (with 3 years' training): *be an SRN* ○ *Sally War SRN.* Cf SEN.

SS *abbr* **1** Saints. **2** /ˌes ˈes/ steamship: *SS Warwic Castle.*

SSSI /ˌes es es ˈaɪ/ *abbr* (*Brit*) site of specia scientific interest.

St *abbr* **1** Saint: *St Peter.* Cf S 1. **2** Street: *Fleet S*

st *abbr* (*Brit*) stone (weight): *She weighs 10st.*

Sta *abbr* (esp on a map) Station: *Victoria Sta.*

stab /stæb/ *v* (**-bb-**) **1** [Tn, Tn·pr] pierce (sth) o wound (sb) with a pointed tool or weapon; push (knife, etc) into sb/sth: *He was stabbed to death,* i killed by being stabbed. ○ *She stabbed him in th leg with a kitchen knife.* ○ *He stabbed the meat wit his fork/stabbed his fork into the meat.* **2** (idm) **sta sb in the** ˈ**back** (*infml*) attack sb's positior reputation, etc treacherously; betray sb. **3** (phr v **stab at sb/sth** aim a blow at sb/sth with or as with a pointed weapon: *He stabbed at the earth wit his stick.* ○ *She stabbed at the air with her finger t emphasize what she was saying.* ⇨ Usage at NUDGE
▷ **stab** *n* **1** (**a**) act of stabbing; blow made b stabbing: [attrib] *several stab wounds.* (**b**) woun made by stabbing: *a stab in the arm.* **2** sudde sharp pain caused by, or as if by, stabbing: *a stab c pain in the chest* ○ *a stab of guilt.* **3** (idm) **have a stab at sth/doing sth** (*infml*) attempt (to do) sth *You'll never mend your car like that — let me hav a stab at it.* **a** ˌ**stab in the** ˈ**back** (*infml* treacherous attack, eg on sb's reputation o position; betrayal.
stabber *n* person who stabs sb.
stabbing *adj* [usu attrib] (of pain, etc) very shar and sudden as if caused by a stab: *a stabbing pai in the chest.* — *n* instance of stabbing or bein stabbed with a knife, etc: *The police are worrie about the increase in the number of stabbings in th city.*

stable[1] /ˈsteɪbl/ *adj* (**a**) firmly established or fixed not likely to move or change: *a stable relationship job, government* ○ *a house built on stabl foundations* ○ *The patient's condition is stable.* (**b** (of a person or his character) not easily upset o disturbed; well-balanced; reliable: *Mentally she' very stable.* ○ *He's about the most stable person know.* (**c**) (of a substance) tending to stay in th same chemical or atomic state; not breaking dow easily or naturally: *an element forming stabl compounds.*
▷ **stability** /stəˈbɪlətɪ/ *n* [U] quality or state o being stable.
stabilize, -ise /ˈsteɪbəlaɪz/ *v* [I, Tn] (cause sth/sl to) become stable: *His condition has nou stabilized.* ○ *government measures to stabiliz prices.* **stabilization, -isation** /ˌsteɪbəlaɪˈzeɪʃn; *US* -lɪˈz-/ *n* [U]. **stabilizer -iser** /ˈsteɪbəlaɪzə(r)/ *n* substance or device that stabilizes, esp a devic that prevents an aircraft or ship from rolling, o one that helps to keep a child's bicycle upright: *H*

can now ride his bike without stabilizers.

stably /ˈsteɪblɪ/ *adv* in a stable manner.

stable[2] /ˈsteɪbl/ *n* **1** building in which a horse or horses are kept and fed: [attrib] *a stable door.* **2** (often *pl* with *sing* meaning and sometimes *sing v*) establishment that specializes in keeping horses for a particular purpose; the horses kept in this: *Is there a riding stables near here?* ○ *He owns a racing stable(s),* ie a group of racehorses and the buildings they are kept in. **3** (*fig*) place such as an athletics club, a school, a theatre, etc where a number of people have been trained in the same way: *actors from the same stable.* **4** (idm) **lock, etc the stable door after the horse has bolted** try to prevent or avoid loss, damage, etc when it is already too late.

▷ **stable** *v* [Tn] put or keep (a horse) in a stable: *Where do you stable your pony?*

stabling /ˈsteɪblɪŋ/ *n* [U] accommodation for horses: *The house has stabling for 20 horses.*

□ **ˈstable-boy** (also **ˈstable-lad**) *n* (usu young) person (of either sex) who works in a stable.

staccato /stəˈkɑːtəʊ/ *adj, adv* (*music*) (to be played) with each successive note short, clear and detached; not smooth(ly): *staccato notes* ○ *Play this phrase staccato.* ○ (*fig*) *He shouted a series of staccato orders.*

stack /stæk/ *n* **1** circular or rectangular pile of hay, straw, grain, etc, usu with a sloping top for storage in the open; rick: *a haystack.* **2** pile or heap, usu neatly arranged: *a wood stack* ○ *a stack of newspapers* ○ *They put the rifles into a stack.* **3** (esp *pl*) ~ **of sth** (*infml*) large number or quantity: *stacks of money* ○ *I've got stacks of work to do.* ○ *There's a whole stack of bills waiting to be paid.* **4** (**a**) tall chimney (esp on a factory) or funnel (on a ship) for carrying away smoke. (**b**) group of chimneys standing together. **5** (often *pl*) rack with shelves for books in a library or bookshop. **6** number of aircraft circling at different heights while waiting for instructions to land at an airport. **7** (idm) **blow one's stack** ⇨ BLOW[1].

▷ **stack** *v* **1** [Tn, Tn·pr, Tn·p] ~ **sth (up)** make sth into a stack or stacks; pile sth up: *Please stack your chairs before you leave.* ○ *stack logs (into piles)* ○ *stack (up) the dishes on the draining-board.* **2** [Tn, Tn·pr] ~ **sth (with sth)** put heaps or piles of things on or in (a place): *The whole garden was stacked with bricks.* **3** [Tn, Tn·pr] ~ **sth (against sb)** arrange (playing-cards) unfairly: (*US*) *stack the deck,* ie arrange a whole pack of cards in this way. **4** (**a**) [I, Ip] ~ **(up)** (of an aircraft) fly in a stack(6) while waiting to land. (**b**) [Tn, Tn·p] ~ **sth (up)** make (aircraft) fly in a stack; arrange (aircraft) in a stack. **5** (idm) **have the cards/odds stacked aˈgainst one** be at a disadvantage or in a difficult situation, so that one seems unlikely to succeed. **6** (phr v) **stack up (against sth)** (*US infml*) compare (with sth); measure up (to sth): *How well do you think this washing powder stacks up against your usual brand?*

stadium /ˈsteɪdɪəm/ *n* (*pl* ~**s** or **-dia** /-dɪə/) enclosed area of land for games, athletic contests, etc, usu with seats for spectators: *build a new stadium for the Olympic Games.*

staff /stɑːf; *US* stæf/ *n* **1** [C] strong stick or pole used as a support when walking or climbing, as a weapon, or as a symbol of authority or sign of office: *The old man leant on a long wooden staff.* **2** [C usu *sing*, Gp] group of assistants working together in a business, etc responsible to a manager or person in authority: *the hotel staff* ○ *We need more staff in the office.* ○ *I have a staff of ten.* ○ *The staff in this shop are very helpful.* **3** [pl *v*] people in authority in an organization (contrasted with students, etc); those doing administrative work (as distinct from manual work): *a head teacher and her staff* ○ *a new member of (the) staff* ○ *The school staff are expected to supervise school meals.* ○ [attrib] *a staff party, room, meeting.* **4** [C usu *sing*, Gp] group of senior army officers assisting a commanding officer: *the general's staff* ○ [attrib] *a ˈstaff officer.* **5** (also **stave** /steɪv/) [C] (*music*) set of five horizontal parallel lines on which music is written. ⇨ illus at MUSIC. **6** (idm) **the ˌstaff of ˈlife** (*arch or rhet*) bread.

▷ **staff** *v* [Tn usu passive] provide (sth) with staff(2); act as staff for: *a well-staffed hotel* ○ *The school is staffed entirely by graduates.* ○ *There's nobody to staff the office today.*

□ **ˈstaff nurse** hospital nurse ranking just below a sister(4).

ˈstaff sergeant (**a**) (*Brit*) senior sergeant in a non-infantry (eg cavalry) company. (**b**) (*US*) non-commissioned officer ranking just above a sergeant.

Staffordshire /ˈstæfədʃə(r)/ (*abbr* **Staffs**) county of central England. It is a largely industrial county and contains the *Potteries. ⇨ map at App 1.

stag /stæg/ *n* **1** fully-grown male deer. ⇨ illus at DEER. Cf BUCK[1] 1, DOE, FAWN[1] 1, HART. **2** (*Brit*) person who buys newly issued stocks and shares hoping that the prices will rise and he will be able to make a quick profit.

▷ **stag** *adj* [attrib] for men only: *a stag night at the golf club.*

□ **ˈstag-beetle** *n* large beetle with projecting mouth-parts which resemble a stag's antlers.

ˈstag-party *n* party for men only, esp one for a man just before he gets married. Cf HEN-PARTY (HEN).

stage /steɪdʒ/ *n* **1** [C] platform or area (usu in a theatre) on which plays are performed to an audience: *He was on (the) stage for most of the play.* ⇨ illus at THEATRE. **2 the stage** [sing] the profession of actors and actresses; life and work in the theatre: *She advised her son not to choose the stage as a career.* **3** [sing] (*fig*) scene of action; place where events occur: *Geneva has become the stage for many meetings of world leaders.* **4** [C] point, period or step in the development, growth or progress of sth/sb: *at an early stage in our history* ○ *At this stage it's impossible to know whether our plan will succeed.* ○ *The baby has reached the talking stage,* ie is beginning to talk. **5** [C] (**a**) distance between two stopping-places on a journey; part of a journey: *travel by easy stages,* ie only for a short distance at a time ○ *She did the first stage of the trip by train.* (**b**) (*Brit*) section of a bus route for which there is a fixed fare: *travel two stages for 30p.* (**c**) stopping-place after such a part of a journey or bus-ride. **6** [C] section of a space-rocket with a separate engine, jettisoned when its fuel is used up. **7** [C] (*infml*) = STAGE-COACH: *take the next stage out of town.* **8** (idm) **be/go on the ˈstage** be/become an actor: *She's wanted to go on the stage from an early age.* **set the stage for sth** prepare for sth; make sth possible or easy: *The president's recent death set the stage for a military coup.* **ˌup/ˌdown ˈstage** further from/nearer to the front of the stage when acting in a play, etc.

▷ **stage** *v* [Tn] **1** present (a play, etc) on a stage; put (sth) before the public: *stage a new production of 'King Lear'* **2** arrange for (sth) to take place; carry out: *stage a protest rally* ○ *stage a ˈcome-back,* eg after retiring as a sportsman.

□ **ˈstage-coach** *n* (formerly) public vehicle pulled by horses carrying passengers (and often mail) along a regular route.

ˈstage direction note in the text of a play telling actors where to move, how to perform, etc on stage.

ˌstage ˈdoor entrance at the back of a theatre used by actors, theatre staff, etc.

ˈstage fright nervousness felt by an actor, etc in front of an audience.

ˈstage-hand *n* person employed to help move scenery, etc in a theatre.

ˌstage ˈleft left side of a stage for an actor facing the audience.

ˌstage-ˈmanage *v* [Tn] organize (sth) as or like a stage-manager: *The demonstration had been carefully stage-managed to coincide with the Prime Minister's visit.* **ˌstage-ˈmanager** *n* person in charge of a theatre stage, equipment, scenery, etc during the rehearsals and performances of a play. Cf FLOOR MANAGER (FLOOR[1]).

ˌstage ˈright right side of a stage for an actor facing the audience.

ˈstage-struck *adj* (*often derog*) having a (too) great desire to become an actor: *His ten-year old daughter is completely stage-struck.*

ˌstage ˈwhisper loud whisper (on stage) that is intended to be heard by the audience.

stagflation /ˌstægˈfleɪʃn/ *n* [U] (*finance*) (formed from *stag*nation + in*flation*) state of monetary inflation without a corresponding increase in demand and employment.

stagger /ˈstægə(r)/ *v* **1** [I, Ipr, Ip] walk or move unsteadily as if about to fall (from carrying sth heavy, being weak or drunk, etc): *She staggered and fell.* ○ *stagger to one's feet, across the room, from side to side* ○ *staggering along, around, about, etc.* ⇨ Usage at SHUFFLE. **2** [Tn usu passive] (of news, etc) shock (sb) deeply; cause (sb) astonishment, worry or confusion: *I was staggered to hear/on hearing/when I heard of his death.* **3** [Tn usu passive] place (sth) in a zigzag or alternating arrangement: *a staggered junction,* ie a cross-roads where the side-roads are not directly opposite each other. **4** [Tn] arrange (the times of events) so that they do not occur together: *staggered office hours,* ie arranged so that employees are not all using buses, trains, etc at the same time ○ *stagger the annual holidays.*

▷ **stagger** *n* **1** unsteady staggering movement: *He picked up the heavy suitcase and set off with a stagger.* **2 staggers** [sing *v*] disease in horses and cattle affecting the animal's brain and causing it to stagger when walking.

staggering /ˈstægərɪŋ/ *adj* astonishing; shocking: *a staggering achievement* ○ *I find their decision simply staggering.* **staggeringly** *adv*: *She's staggeringly beautiful.*

staging /ˈsteɪdʒɪŋ/ *n* [C, U] **1** (usu temporary) platform or support for people working, eg on a building site; scaffolding. **2** (way or method of) presenting a play on the stage of a theatre: *an imaginative new staging of 'Macbeth'.*

□ **ˈstaging post** regular stopping-place on a long journey, esp on an air route.

stagnant /ˈstægnənt/ *adj* **1** (of water) not flowing and therefore dirty and smelling unpleasant; still and stale: *water lying stagnant in ponds and ditches.* **2** (*fig*) showing no activity (and therefore not developing or progressing); sluggish: *Business was stagnant last month.* ▷ **stagnancy** /-nənsɪ/ *n* [U].

stagnate /stægˈneɪt; *US* ˈstægneɪt/ *v* [I] **1** be or become stagnant(1). **2** (*fig*) be or become dull or unsuccessful because of lack of activity, development, opportunity, etc: *a stagnating industry* ○ *I feel I'm stagnating in this job.* ○ *His mind has stagnated since his retirement.* ▷ **stagnation** /stægˈneɪʃn/ *n* [U].

stagy /ˈsteɪdʒɪ/ *adj* (**-ier, -iest**) (*usu derog*) (too) theatrical in style, manner or behaviour; exaggerated for effect: *The room was decorated with stagy opulence.* ▷ **stagily** /-ɪlɪ/ *adv.* **staginess** *n* [U].

staid /steɪd/ *adj* (*sometimes derog*) (of people, their appearance, behaviour, tastes, etc) serious, dull and old-fashioned; conservative: *I was surprised to see him at the jazz club; I always thought of him as a rather staid old gentlemen.* ▷ **staidly** *adv.* **staidness** *n* [U].

stain /steɪn/ *v* **1** [esp passive: Tn, Tn·pr, Cn·a] ~ **sth (with sth)** change the colour of sth; leave or make coloured patches or dirty marks on sth, esp ones that are difficult to remove: *fingers stained with nicotine* ○ *blood-stained hands* ○ *a tablecloth stained with gravy* ○ *The blackberry juice stained their fingers (red).* **2** [I] become discoloured or marked in this way: *Our white carpet stains easily.* **3** [Tn, Tn·pr, Cn·a] colour (wood, fabric, etc) with a substance that penetrates the material; dye: *The biologist stained the specimen before looking at it through the microscope.* ○ *He stained the wood dark brown.* **4** [esp passive: Tn, Tn·pr] (*fml fig*) bring disgrace to or damage (sb's reputation, good name, etc); blemish: *The incident stained his career.*

▷ **stain** *n* **1** [U, C] liquid, etc used for staining wood, fabric, etc; dye: *How much stain should I buy*

for the table? ○ *a range of wood stains.* **2** [C] (**a**) dirty mark or patch of colour caused by staining (STAIN *v* 1): *There's an ink stain on your shirt.* ○ *I can't get these coffee stains out of the carpet.* (**b**) thing that causes disgrace (to a person's reputation, etc); moral blemish: *He left the court without a stain on his character.*
stainless *adj* free from stains or blemishes; spotless: *a stainless reputation.* ˌ**stainless** ˈ**steel** type of steel alloy that does not rust or corrode: *knives made of stainless steel* ○ [attrib] *a stainless steel sink.*
□ ˌ**stained** ˈ**glass** glass coloured with transparent colouring while it is being made: [attrib] *a* ˌ*stained glass* ˈ*window*, ie one made of pieces of glass of different colours, as seen in many churches. ⇨ illus at CHURCH.

stair /steə(r)/ *n* **1 stairs** [pl] series of fixed steps from one floor of a building to another, usu inside: *climb a long/short flight of stairs* ○ *She always runs up/down the stairs.* ○ *I passed her on the stairs.* ○ *The stairs need cleaning.* ○ *at the foot/head of the stairs*, ie at the bottom/top of a set of stairs. **2** [C] any one of these steps: *The child was sitting on the bottom stair.* ○ *The top stair is broken.* ⇨ illus. **3** (idm) **below** ˈ**stairs** (*dated*) in the basement of a house (in large houses, formerly the part used by servants): *Their affairs were being discussed below stairs*, ie by the servants.
□ ˈ**stair-carpet** *n* strip of carpet for laying on stairs.

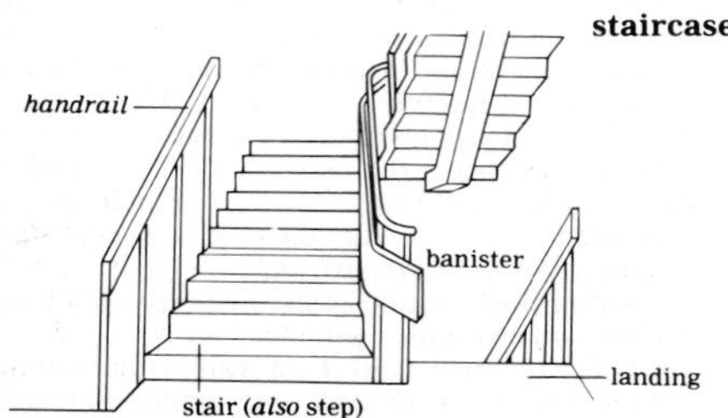

ˈ**staircase** (also ˈ**stairway**) *n* set of stairs (often with banisters) and its supporting structure, inside a building: *a spiral staircase*, ie stairs winding round a central pillar. ⇨ illus.
ˈ**stair-rod** *n* metal or wooden rod fixed in the angle between two stairs to keep a stair-carpet in place.
ˈ**stairway** *n* = STAIRCASE.
ˈ**stairwell** *n* part of a building containing the staircase; space for the stairs.

NOTE ON USAGE: (Flights of) **stairs** are mostly found inside houses or other buildings where people live or work (eg an office block): *He finds it difficult to climb the stairs with his bad leg.* ○ *vacuum the stairs.* A **staircase** is the part of the building including the stairs and banisters and sometimes the walls and ceilings surrounding them: *We must redecorate the staircase.* (Flights of) **steps** are usually made of stone or concrete and found outside or in an uninhabited building. We also talk of individual **steps** which make up a staircase or a flight of steps: *I'll meet you on the steps of the museum.* ○ *There are 150 steps to the top of the tower.* ○ *sitting on the top/bottom step.*

stake /steɪk/ *n* **1** [C] strong wood or metal stick, pointed at one end, that can be driven into the ground, eg to support a young tree, as a post for a fence, etc or as a marker. **2 the stake** [sing] (formerly) post to which a person was tied before being burnt to death as a punishment: *be burnt at the stake* ○ *go to the stake*, ie be killed in this way. **3** [C usu *pl*] money, etc risked or gambled on the unknown result of a future event (eg a race, a card-game): *playing for high stakes.* **4** money, etc invested by sb in an enterprise so that he has an interest or share in it: *have a stake in a company* ○ *She has a stake in the future success of the business.* **5 stakes** (**a**) [pl] prize money, esp in a horse-race. (**b**) (usu **Stakes**) [sing *v*] (esp in names) horse-race in which all the owners of the horses in the race contribute to the prize money: *The Newmarket Stakes is always a popular race.* **6** (idm) **at stake** to be won or lost; being risked, depending on the outcome of an event: *This decision puts our lives at stake.* ○ *Our children's education is at stake.* **go to the stake over sth** maintain (an opinion, a principle, etc) at any cost: *I think I'm right on this issue but I wouldn't go to the stake over it.*
▷ **stake** *v* **1** [Tn] support (sth) with a stake: *stake newly planted trees.* **2** [Tn, Tn·pr] ~ **sth** (**on sth**) gamble or risk (money, one's hopes, one's life, etc) on sth: *stake £5 on the favourite*, eg in a horse-race ○ *I'd stake my life on it*, ie I'm very confident about it. **3** [Tn] (*US infml*) give financial or other support to (sb/sth): *stake a business.* **4** (idm) **stake** (**out**) **a/one's** ˈ**claim** (**to sb/sth**) (**a**) mark out (a piece of land, etc) as one's own (esp formerly when arriving in a new country or area). (**b**) declare a special interest (in sb/sth); claim a right (to sb/sth): *Several clubs have already staked a/their claim to this outstanding young footballer.* **5** (phr v) **stake sth out** (**a**) mark (an area) with stakes (esp formerly to claim ownership). (**b**) declare a special interest in or right to (eg an area of study, a place): *He's staked out this part of the house as his own.* (**c**) (*infml esp US*) (of the police) watch (a place) continuously and secretly: *Detectives have been staking out the house for two days now.*
□ ˈ**stake-out** *n* (*infml esp US*) (**a**) continuous secret watch by the police; surveillance. (**b**) area or house being watched in this way.

Stakhanovite /stəˈkænəvaɪt; *US* -ˈkɑːn-/ *n* (originally in the USSR) person who does far more work than an average worker. ▷ **Stakhanovism** /-vɪzəm/ *n* [U].

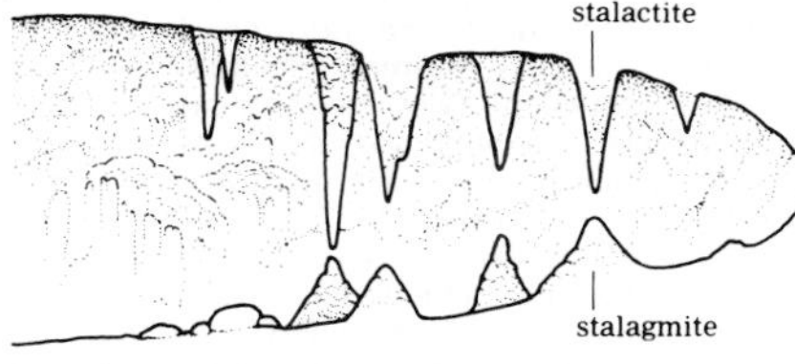

stalactite /ˈstæləktaɪt; *US* stəˈlæktaɪt/ *n* icicle-shaped formation of lime hanging from the roof of a cave, formed by the steady dripping of water containing minerals. ⇨ illus.

stalagmite /ˈstæləgmaɪt; *US* stəˈlægmaɪt/ *n* formation of lime extending upwards like a pillar from the floor of a cave as water from a stalactite drips onto it. ⇨ illus at STALACTITE.

stale /steɪl/ *adj* **1** (esp of food) smelling or tasting unpleasant, mouldy or dry, because no longer fresh: *stale biscuits, bread, cake, beer* ○ *the smell of stale cigarette smoke.* **2** no longer interesting because heard, done, etc too often before; not new: *stale news, jokes, ideas* ○ *Her performance has become stale.* **3** (of athletes, musicians, performers, etc) no longer able to perform well because of too much training, playing, practice, etc.
▷ **stale** *v* [I] become stale: *The pleasure I get from listening to such music never stales.*
staleness *n* [U].

stalemate /ˈsteɪlmeɪt/ *n* [U, C usu *sing*] **1** position of the pieces in the game of chess in which the player whose move it is cannot move without putting his king in check. **2** stage of a dispute, contest, etc at which further action or discussion by either side seems to be impossible; deadlock: *Negotiations have reached (a) stalemate.*
▷ **stalemate** *v* [Tn usu passive] bring (sb/sth) to a position of stalemate.

Stalin /ˈstɑːlɪn/ Joseph (1879-1953), Soviet leader. He was the successor of *Lenin and went on to become the virtual dictator of the USSR. His rule is now regarded as a reign of terror, marked by the persecution of all political opposition, arbitrary purges, the disastrous reorganization of Soviet agriculture, and the subjection of eastern Europe.
▷ **Stalinism** /-ɪzəm/ *n* [U] policy of centralized authoritarian rule (as) practised by Stalin. **Stalinist** *adj.*

stalk[1] /stɔːk/ *n* **1** main stem of a plant (not a tree): *daffodils with long stalks.* ⇨ illus at PLANT. **2** stem that supports a leaf, flower or fruit and joins it to another part of the plant: *Remove the stalks from the cherries before you eat them.* **3** thin structure supporting a part or organ in some animals. **4** (idm) **have one's eyes on stalks** ⇨ EYE[1].

stalk[2] /stɔːk/ *v* **1** (**a**) [Ipr, Ip] walk with slow stiff strides, esp in a proud, self-important or threatening way: *He stalked angrily out of the room.* ○ *stalk along (the road).* (**b**) [Ipr, Tn] (*fml or rhet*) (of an evil force, disease, etc) move silently and threateningly (through a place): *Fear stalked (through) the town at night.* ○ *Ghosts are said to stalk the castle walls.* **2** [Tn] move quietly and slowly towards (wild animals, etc) in order to get near without being seen: *stalking deer* ○ (*fig*) *a rapist stalking his victim.*
▷ **stalker** *n* person who stalks animals.
□ ˈ**stalking horse** person, action, etc that is used by another person or group to disguise plans: *He won't be elected, but he's a stalking horse to show if another challenger might be able to beat her.*

stall /stɔːl/ *n* **1** [C] compartment, usu with three sides, for one animal in a stable or cattle shed. **2** [C] (often in compounds) table, stand or small open-fronted shop from which things are sold in a market, on a street, in a railway station, etc: *a* ˈ*bookstall at the station* ○ *a* ˈ*fruit stall in the market* ○ *run a* ˈ*cake stall at the bazaar.* **3 stalls** [pl] (*Brit*) (set of seats in) the part of a theatre that is nearest to the stage: *two seats in the stalls* ○ *laughter from the stalls.* ⇨ illus at THEATRE. **4** [C] any of several fixed seats, usu with its back and sides enclosed, in the choir or chancel of a church: *the canon's* ˈ*stall* ○ *the* ˈ*choir stalls.* **5** [C] any small room or compartment, usu for one person: *stalls for changing in at the swimming-pool.* **6** [C] (instance of the) stalling of an aircraft or engine; condition resulting from this: *go into/get out of a stall.* **7** [C] = FINGER-STALL (FINGER[1]).
▷ **stall** *v* **1** [Tn] place or keep (an animal) in a stall(1), esp for fattening. **2** (**a**) [I] (of an engine) stop suddenly because of insufficient power or speed: *The car stalled at the roundabout.* (**b**) [I, Tn] (of a driver) cause (an engine) to do this: *Learner drivers often stall (their cars).* **3** (**a**) [I] (of an aircraft) get out of control and start to drop because of loss of speed: *The plane stalled suddenly.* (**b**) [I, Tn] (of a pilot) cause (an aircraft) to do this. **4** (**a**) [I] avoid giving a definite answer or taking action (in order to get more time); delay: *stall for time* ○ *Stop stalling and give me an answer.* (**b**) [Tn] avoid answering (a person, request, etc) in this way: *stall one's creditors.*
□ ˈ**stall-holder** *n* person who rents or owns and runs a stall in a market, etc.

stallion /ˈstælɪən/ *n* fully grown male horse that has not been castrated, esp one used for breeding. Cf COLT 1, GELDING (GELD), MARE[1] 1.

stalwart /ˈstɔːlwət/ *adj* **1** (*dated or fml*) (of a person) strong and sturdy: *a boxer of stalwart build.* **2** [usu attrib] dependable, firm and loyal: *one of the team's most stalwart supporters* ○ *give the team stalwart support.*
▷ **stalwart** *n* loyal supporter (of a political party, etc): *rally the stalwarts of the party.*
stalwartly *adv.*
stalwartness *n* [U].

stamen /ˈsteɪmən/ *n* (*botany*) any of the small thin male parts in the middle of a flower that produce pollen.

stamina /ˈstæmɪnə/ *n* [U] ability to endure much physical or mental strain; long-lasting energy and resilience; staying-power: *Marathon runners need plenty of stamina.* ○ *He doesn't have the stamina to be a teacher.*

stammer /ˈstæmə(r)/ *v* **1** (also **stutter**) [I] speak with sudden pauses and a tendency to repeat rapidly the same sound or syllable (because of a speech defect or from fear, excitement, etc):

'G-g-give me that b-b-book,' said Henry, unable to stop stammering. **2** [Tn, Tn·p] ~ **sth (out)** say sth in this way: *'G-g-goodb-b-bye,' she stammered.* ○ *stammer out a request.*

▷ **stammer** *n* (usu *sing*) **(a)** tendency to stammer: *speak with a stammer* ○ *He's always had a slight stammer.* **(b)** stammering speech.

stammerer /ˈstæmərə(r)/ *n* person who stammers.

stammeringly /ˈstæmərɪŋlɪ/ *adv.*

stamp[1] /stæmp/ *v* **1** [I, Tn, Tn·pr, Tn·p, Cn·a] ~ **sth (down)** put (one's foot) down heavily on (the ground, etc); flatten (sth) by doing this: *He stamped (his foot) in anger.* ○ *stamping the ground to keep warm* ○ *She stamped the soil (flat/down) round the plant.* **2** [I, Ipr, Ip] walk with loud heavy steps: *Don't stamp, you'll wake everyone up.* ○ *stamp about* ○ *stamp out of a room* ○ *stamp upstairs.* **3** [Tn, Tn·pr] ~ **A (on B)**; ~ **B (with A)** print (a design, the date, lettering, etc) on paper, cloth or some other surface; mark (paper, etc) with a design, an official seal, etc: *They didn't stamp my passport.* ○ *The librarian forgot to stamp my library books,* ie with the date on which they should be returned. ○ *stamp one's name and address on an envelope/stamp an envelope with one's name and address* ○ *crates of oranges stamped with the exporter's trade mark.* **4** [Tn esp passive] stick a postage stamp or some other stamp on (a letter, etc): *I enclose a stamped addressed envelope for your reply.* **5** [Tn, Tn·pr, Tn·p] ~ **sth (out) (from sth)** cut and shape (metal, etc) into pieces by striking it with a specially shaped tool or cutter: *a machine for stamping out engine parts.* **6** [Tn, Tn·pr] ~ **sth (on sb/sth)** *(fig)* impress or fix sth permanently: *stamp one's personality/authority on a game,* ie as an outstanding player ○ *The date is stamped on her memory forever.* **7** [Cn·n/a] ~ **sb as sth** give a certain character to sb; mark sb out as sth: *This achievement stamps her as a genius.* **8** (phr v) **stamp sth off (sth)** remove sth by stamping with the foot: *stamped the mud off their shoes.* **stamp on sth (a)** crush sth by bringing one's foot down heavily on it: *stamp on a spider.* **(b)** control or suppress sth, esp by force; quell sth: *The rebellion was soon stamped on by the army.* **stamp sth out (a)** extinguish (a fire, etc) by stamping: *stamp out the embers of the camp fire.* **(b)** eliminate, destroy or suppress sth, esp by force or vigorous action: *stamp out terrorism, a rebellion, an epidemic disease.*

□ **ˈstamping-ground** *n* (*infml*) place where a particular person or animal may usually be found; favourite place or haunt: *one of my old stamping-grounds.*

stamp[2] /stæmp/ *n* **1** small piece of paper (usu rectangular, with perforated edges) with an official design on it, stuck on an envelope or a parcel or a document to show that postage or duty or some other fee has been paid: *an 18p stamp* ○ *a book of (postage) stamps* ○ *I'd like three first-class stamps, please.* ○ *collecting stamps,* ie as a hobby ○ [attrib] *a stamp collection.* **2** (also **ˈtrading stamp**) similar piece of paper given to customers with purchases, exchangeable for various articles or goods. **3** instrument with which a design, mark, etc is stamped on a surface: *a rubber stamp,* ie one on which a design, words, etc are cut, used for printing dates, signatures, addresses, etc. **4** design, word(s), etc made by stamping on a surface: *Have you got any stamps in your passport?* **5** act or sound of stamping with the foot: *give a stamp of impatience.* **6** (usu *sing*) (*fml fig*) characteristic mark or quality: *She bears the stamp of genius.* ○ *His face bears the stamp of suffering.* ○ *Their story has the stamp of truth,* ie seems very likely to be true. **7** (usu *sing*) (*fml fig*) kind; class; sort: *men of a different stamp.*

□ **ˈstamp album** special book in which a stamp-collector keeps his stamps.

ˈstamp-collecting *n* [U] collecting postage stamps as objects of interest or value. **ˈstamp-collector** *n* person who does this.

ˈstamp-duty *n* tax imposed on certain types of legal documents (on which an official stamp is put to show that the tax has been paid).

stampede /stæmˈpiːd/ *n* **1** sudden rush of frightened animals. **2** sudden wild rush or mass movement of people: *There was a stampede towards the stage when the singer appeared.* **3** (in Canada) form of entertainment in which cowboys display their skill at handling animals; rodeo: *the Calgary Stampede.*

▷ **stampede** *v* **1 (a)** [I] (of animals or people) take part in a stampede: *The cattle stampeded towards the farm.* **(b)** [Tn] cause (esp animals) to do this. **2** [Tn·pr] ~ **sb into sth/doing sth** cause sb to rush into rash or unreasonable action: *Don't be stampeded into buying the house.*

stance /stæns *or, in British use,* stɑːns/ *n* (usu *sing*) **1** person's position or way of standing (esp in sports such as cricket, golf, etc when preparing to hit the ball); pose. **2** ~ **(on sth)** moral or intellectual attitude (to sth); standpoint: *He maintains a rigidly right-wing political stance.* ○ *What is your stance on corporal punishment?* Cf POSTURE.

stanch /stɑːntʃ; *US* stæntʃ/ (also **staunch** /stɔːntʃ/) *v* [Tn] **(a)** stop the flow of (esp blood): *stanch the bleeding.* **(b)** stop or control the flow of blood from (a wound): *stanch a cut.*

stanchion /ˈstænʃən; *US* ˈstæntʃən/ *n* upright bar or post forming a support.

stand[1] /stænd/ *n* **1** [sing] stationary condition; halt or standstill: *come to a stand.* **2** [sing] position taken up; act or instance of standing: *He took his stand* (ie stood) *near the window.* **3** [C] (period of time of) resistance to attack: *the rebels' last stand* ○ *a stand of sixty days.* **4** [C] (often in compounds) small piece of furniture (eg a rack, pedestal, frame, etc) on or in which sth may be placed: *a ˈhat/an umˈbrella/ a ˈcoat stand* ○ *a ˈcake stand* ○ *a ˈmusic-stand,* ie for supporting sheet music while it is being played. **5** [C] **(a)** structure (eg a table or kiosk) from which goods are sold; stall: *a ˈnews-stand* ○ *a market stand.* **(b)** area or structure where things are displayed, exhibited, advertised, etc: *one of the stands at a book fair.* **6** [C] place where vehicles may stand in a line in a street, etc while waiting for passengers: *a ˈtaxi-stand* ○ *a stand for six taxis.* **7** [C often *pl*] large, usu sloping, structure at a sports ground, racecourse etc, with rows of seats for spectators: *A cheer rose from the south stand(s).* ⇨ illus at ASSOCIATION FOOTBALL (ASSOCIATION). Cf GRANDSTAND (GRAND). **8** [C] stop made for a performance by a touring theatrical company, pop group, etc: *a series of ˌone-night ˈstands.* **9** [C usu *sing*] (*US*) witness-box (in a lawcourt): *take the stand.* **10** (idm) **make a stand (against/for sth/sb)** be ready to resist, fight, argue, etc: *make a stand against the enemy* ○ *make a stand for one's principles.* **take a/one's stand (on sth)** declare one's position, opinion, etc (on sth): *She took a firm stand on nuclear disarmament.*

stand[2] /stænd/ *v* (*pt, pp* **stood** /stʊd/)

►UPRIGHT POSITION OR EXTENSION **1** [I] have, take or keep an upright position: *She was too weak to stand.* ○ *A chair will not stand on two legs.* ○ *Don't stand there arguing about it.* ○ *Stand still while I take your photograph.* ○ *After the bombing only a few houses were left standing.* **2** [I, Ip] ~ **(up)** rise to one's feet: *Everyone stood (up) when the Queen entered.* ○ *We stood (up) to see better.* ○ *Stand up, please!* **3** [Tn·pr, Tn·p] put (sth/sb) in an upright position; place: *Don't stand cans of petrol near the fire.* ○ *Stand the ladder (up/upright) against the wall.* ○ *I stood the child on a stool so that she could reach the shelf.* **4** [In/pr] have a specified height: *He stands six foot two.* ○ *The tower stands fifty metres.*

►BEING OR REMAINING IN A PLACE OR CONDITION **5** [I] be in a certain place; be situated: *a clock standing on the sideboard* ○ *A tall poplar tree once stood here.* ○ *(fig) Where do you stand* (ie What is your opinion) *on these issues?* **6** [I] (of a vehicle, etc) remain in the same place: *a train standing in the station* ○ *The car stood at the traffic lights for a few moments, then moved off.* **7** [I] remain unchanged; remain valid: *Let the words stand.* ○ *The agreement must stand,* ie it cannot be altered or cancelled. ○ *My offer still stands.* **8 (a)** [La, Ln, I] be in a certain condition or situation: *The house has stood empty for months.* ○ *The emergency services stand* (ie are) *ready to help if necessary.* ○ *She stood convicted of fraud.* ○ *I stand corrected,* ie accept that I was mistaken and that the person who corrected me is right. ○ *She stands high in the esteem of* (ie is greatly respected by) *her colleagues.* ○ *(fig) Will you stand* (ie be) *godmother to the child?* ○ *As things stand, there is little chance of a settlement in the dispute.* **(b)** [Ipr] ~ **at sth** be at a certain level, point of a scale, etc: *The clock stands at ten to four.* ○ *The fund stands at £500,* ie there is £500 in it. **9** [It] be in a situation where one is likely to do sth: *stand to win, lose, gain, etc* ○ *You stand to make a lot of money from this deal.* **10** [I] (of a liquid, mixture, etc) remain still; not flow or be disturbed: *standing pools of rain water* ○ *Mix the batter and let it stand for twenty minutes.*

►OTHER MEANINGS **11** [no passive: Tn, Tt, Tg, Tsg] (esp in negative sentences and in questions, with *can/could*; not in the continuous tenses) endure sth/sb; bear: *He can't stand hot weather.* ○ *My nerves won't stand the strain much longer.* ○ *She says she will stand no nonsense,* ie will not put up with foolish behaviour. ○ *I can't stand* (ie I strongly dislike) *him.* ○ *She couldn't stand to be told what to do.* ○ *He can't stand being kept waiting.* ○ *I can't stand him interrupting all the time.* **12** [Tn no passive, Dn·n] provide (sth) for sb at one's own expense: *stand drinks all round,* ie pay for drinks for everyone ○ *She was kind enough to stand us a meal.* **13** (*esp Brit*) (also *esp US* **run**) [I, Ipr] ~ **(for sth)** be a candidate in an election: *She stood unsuccessfully in the local elections.* ○ *stand for parliament* ○ *stand for President.* **14** [I, Ipr, Ip] (*nautical*) steer a specified course in a ship: *stand westward (for the island).* **15** (idm) **stand well, etc with sb** have a specified type of relationship with sb: *Do you stand well with your boss?* ○ *I don't know how I stand with her.* (For other idioms containing **stand**, see entries for *ns, adjs,* etc, eg **stand trial (for sth)** ⇨ TRIAL; **stand fast** ⇨ FAST[2].)

16 (phr v) **stand aˈside (a)** move to one side: *stand aside to let sb pass.* **(b)** take no part in events; do nothing: *Don't stand aside and let others do all the work.* **(c)** withdraw, eg as a candidate in an election: *stand aside in favour of another applicant.*

stand ˈback (from sth) (a) move back: *The policeman ordered us to stand back.* **(b)** be situated away from sth: *The house stands back a little (from the road).*

stand ˈby (a) be present but not do anything: *How can you stand by and let him treat his dog like that?* **(b)** be ready for action: *The troops are standing by.* **stand by sb** support or help sb: *I'll stand by you whatever happens.* **stand by sth** be faithful to (a promise, etc): *She still stands by every word she said.*

stand ˈdown (a) (of a witness) leave the witness-box in a lawcourt after giving evidence. **(b)** withdraw (eg as a candidate in an election); resign from one's position: *The President has stood down after five years in office.* **stand (sb) ˈdown** (*military*) (order sb to) relax after an alert: *The troops (were) stood down: it was a false alarm.*

ˈstand for sth (a) (no passive) be an abbreviation of sth: *What does 'T. G.' stand for in 'T. G. Smith'?* **(b)** (no passive) represent sth: *I condemn fascism and all it stands for.* **(c)** (no passive) be in favour of sth; support sth: *a party that stands for racial tolerance.* **(d)** (*infml*) tolerate: *I won't stand for this insolence.*

stand ˈin (for sb) take sb's place; deputize: *My assistant will stand in for me while I'm away.* ○ *Another man stands in for the big star in the dangerous scenes.*

stand ˈout (from/against sth) be easily seen; be noticeable: *bright lettering that stands out well from/against a dark background.* **stand ˈout**

the meeting of Stanley and Livingstone in Africa, 1871

(**from sb/sth**) be much better than sb/sth: *Her work stands out from the rest as easily the best.* **stand ˈout (against sth)** continue to resist: *We managed to stand out against all attempts to close the company down.* **stand out for sth** (*infml*) delay reaching an agreement in order to get what one wants: *The nurses have been offered an extra 5%, but they're standing out for a 7% pay rise.*

stand over sb supervise or watch sb closely: *Don't stand over me while I am cooking.* ○ *I hate to have my boss standing over me.*

stand (sb) ˈto (order soldiers to) take up positions against an attack.

stand sb up (*infml*) fail to keep an appointment with sb: *First she agreed to come out with me, then she stood me up.* **stand up for sb/sth** speak, work, etc in favour of sb/sth; support sb/sth: *Always stand up for your friends.* ○ *You must stand up for your rights.* **stand ˈup (to sth)** withstand (a test, etc): *Your argument just won't stand up (to close scrutiny).* **stand up to sb** resist sb: *It was brave of her to stand up to those bullies.* **stand up to sth** (of materials, products, etc) remain in good condition in spite of (hard wear, etc): *Will this car stand up to winter conditions here?* ○ *This cloth is designed to stand up to a lot of wear and tear.*

□ **ˈstand-alone** *adj* [usu attrib] (of a computer system) that works as an independent unit, rather than as part of a network.

ˈstand-by *n* (*pl* **-bys**) **1** person or thing available as a substitute or in an emergency: *Aspirin is a good stand-by for headaches.* ○ [attrib] *a stand-by ticket*, ie a cheaper type of airline ticket available when not all the tickets for a flight have been sold. **2** (idm) **on ˈstand-by** in a state of readiness: *The troops are on 24-hour stand-by*, ie ready to move within 24 hours of receiving the order.

ˈstand-in *n* person who acts as a deputy for or in place of sb else, esp one who takes the part of an actor in dangerous scenes.

ˌstand-off ˈhalf (also **ˈfly-half**) one of the half-backs in Rugby football.

ˌstand-ˈoffish *adj* cold and distant in behaviour; reserved; aloof. **stand-offishly** *adv.* **stand-offishness** *n* [U].

ˈstand-up *adj* [attrib] **1** (of a meal) eaten while standing. **2** (of a comedian) giving a performance which consists of standing in front of an audience and telling a series of jokes: *a stand-up comic.* **3** (of a fight, disagreement, etc) direct and violent: *I had a stand-up row with my boss today.*

standard /ˈstændəd/ *n* **1** thing used as a test or measure for weights, lengths, quality, purity, etc: *the standard of height required for recruits to the police force* ○ *an international standard of weight* ○ *the monetary standard*, ie the proportions of fine metal and alloy in gold and silver coins ○ *People were very poor then, by today's standards*, ie compared with people today. **2** (often *pl*) required, expected or accepted level of quality: *a restaurant with a low standard of hygiene* ○ *a high moral standard* ○ *set low standards of behaviour* ○ *conform to the standards of society*, ie live and behave in a way that is acceptable to others in society. **3** (**a**) average quality: *The standard of her work is high.* (**b**) specified level of proficiency: *His work does not reach the standard required.* **4** (**a**) distinctive ceremonial flag, esp one to which loyalty is given: *the royal standard.* (**b**) carved figure, image, etc fixed to a pole and carried (esp formerly) by an army going into battle: *a Roman standard.* **5** upright pole or stand, esp one used as a support. **6** tree or shrub that has been grafted on an upright stem (contrasted with a bush or climbing plant): [attrib] *standard roses.* **7** song, melody, etc that becomes and remains very popular: *'My Way' and 19 other Sinatra standards on two CDs.* **8** (idm) **be up to/below ˈstandard** be equal to/not so good as what is normal, required, etc: *Their work is not up to standard.*

▷ **standard** *adj* [esp attrib] **1** serving as, used as or conforming to a standard(1): *standard sizes of paper, units of weight, etc.* **2** average, normal or usual; not special or unusual: *the standard model of a car*, ie not the de luxe model, etc ○ *This procedure is standard.* **3** of generally recognized and accepted authority or merit: *This is the standard textbook on the subject.* **4** (of spelling, pronunciation, grammar, etc) widely accepted as the usual form: *standard English.*

□ **ˈstandard-bearer** *n* (**a**) person who carries a standard(4). (**b**) (*fig*) prominent leader in a cause, esp a political one: *a standard-bearer for women's rights.*

ˈstandard lamp (*Brit*) (*US* **ˈfloor-lamp**) household lamp on a tall support, with its base on the floor.

ˌstandard of ˈliving level of material comfort and wealth enjoyed by a person or group: *They have/enjoy a high standard of living.* ○ *The standard of living in our country is lower than in yours.*

ˈstandard time time officially adopted for a country or part of it.

standardize, -ise /ˈstændədaɪz/ *v* [Tn] make (sth) conform to a fixed standard, shape, quality, type, etc: *an attempt to standardize spelling* ○ *Car parts are usually standardized.*

▷ **standardization, -isation** /stændədaɪˈzeɪʃn; *US* -dɪˈz-/ *n* [U] action or process of standardizing; making regular: *the problem of the standardization of the use of hyphens in compounds.*

standing /ˈstændɪŋ/ *n* [U] **1** (esp social) position or reputation; status; rank: *a woman of some standing in the community* ○ *a scientist of good/high standing*, ie respected, eminent. **2** length of time that sth has existed; duration: *a debt, dispute, friendship of long standing.*

▷ **standing** *adj* [attrib] **1** (**a**) remaining in force or use; permanent and established: *a standing army* ○ *a standing committee*, ie a permanent one that meets regularly. (**b**) continuing to be effective or valid: *We have a standing invitation to visit them when we're in the area.* ○ *a standing joke*, ie sth that regularly causes amusement. **2** (*esp sport*) performed without a run; done from a standing position: *a standing start/jump.* **3** upright: *standing corn*, ie not yet cut. **4** (of water, eg in a pond) that is still and does not flow.

□ **ˌstanding ˈorder 1** (**a**) (also **ˌbanker's ˈorder**) customer's instruction to a bank to pay a certain amount at regular intervals (eg rent, mortgage repayments). (**b**) regular order that remains valid and does not have to be repeated: *a standing order for milk, newspapers, etc.* **2 standing orders** rules for organizing debates, meetings, etc, eg in a parliament or council.

ˌstanding oˈvation enthusiastic expression of approval by people standing up from their seats to clap: *The singer got a ten-minute standing ovation.*

ˈstanding-room *n* [U] space for people to stand in, esp in a theatre, sports ground, etc: *There was standing-room only left in the concert hall.*

stand-pipe /ˈstændpaɪp/ *n* vertical pipe connected to a main water supply and used to provide water outside or at a distance from buildings.

standpoint /ˈstændpɔɪnt/ *n* position from which things are seen and opinions are formed; point of view: *from the standpoint of the customer.*

standstill /ˈstændstɪl/ *n* [sing] halt; stop: *be at/come to/bring sth to a standstill* ○ *Work is grinding to a standstill.* ○ *Traffic in the city is at a complete standstill.* ○ [attrib] *a standstill agreement*, ie one that agrees to no change, eg in rates of pay or hours of work.

Stanford /ˈstænfəd/ Sir Charles Villiers (1852-1924), Irish composer. He was a leading figure in British musical life and taught *Vaughan Williams and *Holst. Among his large output his church music is particularly important.

Stanislavsky /ˌstænɪˈslɑːfskɪ/ Konstantin Sergevich (1863-1938), Russian actor and director. He helped to found the Moscow Art Theatre, where he trained actors to develop their roles psychologically. The technique, known as method acting (METHOD), became popular esp in the USA.

stank *pt* of STINK.

Stanley /ˈstænlɪ/ Sir Henry Morton (1841-1904), British explorer and journalist. He became famous as a reporter by discovering the lost *Livingstone. He then continued exploring Africa and became involved in politics. ⇨ illus.

Stannaries /ˈstænərɪz/ **the Stannaries** [pl] the parts of Devon and Cornwall, England, where tin was traditionally mined.

stanza /ˈstænzə/ *n* group of (esp rhyming) lines forming a unit in some types of poem; verse of poetry: *the second stanza.*

staple[1] /ˈsteɪpl/ *n* **1** small thin piece of bent wire that is driven into sheets of paper, etc and flattened to fasten them together. **2** U-shaped piece of metal with pointed ends that is hammered into wood, etc to hold something (eg an electrical wire) in place.

▷ **staple** *v* [Tn] attach or secure (sth) with a staple or staples. **stapler** /ˈsteɪplə(r)/ *n* small hand-operated instrument for fastening papers, etc together with staples.

staple[2] /ˈsteɪpl/ *adj* [attrib] main or principal; standard: *the staple product of a country* ○ *Rice is the staple diet in many Asian countries.* ○ *She seems to be the staple topic of conversation at the moment.*

▷ **staple** *n* (often *pl*) **1** main product that a country or district trades in: *Cotton is one of Egypt's staples.* **2** main or principal item or element (esp of a diet): *Bread, potatoes and other staples continue to rise in price.* ○ *The weather forms the staple of their conversation.*

star /stɑː(r)/ *n* **1** [C] any one of the distant bodies appearing as a point of light in the sky at night: *a fixed star*, ie one which is not a planet ○ *There are no stars out* (ie No stars can be seen) *tonight.* **2** [C] (*astronomy*) any large ball in outer space that is made up of gases and gives out light, such as the sun. **3** [C] **(a)** figure, object, decoration, etc with radiating points, suggesting a star by its shape; an asterisk (*). **(b)** mark of this shape used to indicate a category of excellence: *This restaurant gets three stars in the guidebook.* ○ [attrib] *a five-star hotel.* **(c)** metal badge in the shape of a star, worn on certain uniforms to indicate rank: *a sheriff's star.* **4** [C] famous or brilliant singer, performer, sportsman, etc: *a tennis star* ○ *a film star* ○ *the stars of stage and screen* ○ *I can remember who directed the film but not who the stars* (ie leading performers) *were.* ○ [attrib] *He's got the star role in the new film.* ○ *an all-star cast*, ie one in which the leading players are all stars. **5** [C] (in astrology) planet or heavenly body believed to influence a person's, life, luck, personality, etc: *born under a lucky star*, ie successful and happy. **6 stars** [pl] horoscope: *What do my stars say?* ○ *It's written in the stars.* **7** (idm) **reach for the stars** ⇨ REACH. **see ˈstars** (*infml*) have a feeling of seeing flashes of light, esp as a result of being hit on the head. **thank one's lucky stars** ⇨ THANK.

▷ **star** *v* (-rr-) **1** [Tn usu passive] mark or decorate (sth) with, or as with, a star or stars, eg an asterisk to direct attention to sth on a list, etc: *The starred dishes on the menu are suitable for vegetarians.* **2 (a)** [I, Ipr] ~ **(in sth)** be a star(4) (in a play, film, etc): *taken many starring roles* ○ *She is to star in a new film.* **(b)** [Tn, Tn·pr] ~ **sb (in sth)** present sb as a star(4); feature sb: *My favourite film stars Marilyn Monroe.* ○ *The director wanted to star Michael Caine in his new film.*

stardom /ˈstɑːdəm/ *n* [U] status of being a famous actor, performer, etc: *He is being groomed* (ie prepared and trained) *for stardom.*

starless *adj* with no stars to be seen: *a starless sky/night.*

starlet /ˈstɑːlɪt/ *n* (*sometimes derog*) young actress who hopes to become a film star but is not yet very well known.

starry /ˈstɑːrɪ/ *n* (-ier, -iest) **(a)** lighted by stars: *a starry night.* **(b)** shining like stars: *starry eyes.* **ˌstarry-ˈeyed** *adj* (*infml often derog*) romantically enthusiastic but impractical: *He's completely starry-eyed about his new girl-friend.* ○ *She's got some starry-eyed notion about reforming society.*

□ **the ˌStar ˈChamber** court held in the Palace of *Westminster from the 14th century until 1641, which tried cases affecting the interests of the English Crown. It became very oppressive in its judgements under the *Tudors and *Stuarts, and the term is sometimes now used for a body that makes hasty or unfair decisions.

ˈstar-dust *n* [U] (imaginary twinkling dust-like substance causing a) dreamy, romantic or magic feeling.

ˈstarfish *n* (*pl* unchanged) flattish star-shaped sea animal with five arms.

ˈstar-gazer *n* (*infml often joc*) person who studies the stars as an astronomer or astrologer. **ˈstar-gazing** *n* [U].

ˈstarlight *n* [U] light from the stars: *walk home by starlight.*

ˈstarlit *adj* lighted by the stars: *a starlit scene.*

the ˌStar of ˈDavid star with six points, the symbol of Judaism and the state of *Israel.

the ˌStar-Spangled ˈBanner the US national anthem, originally written to commemorate a battle against British forces in 1812.

the ˌStars and ˈStripes the national flag of the USA. ⇨ article at NATIONAL.

ˈstar sign (*infml*) any one of the 12 signs of the zodiac: *What's your star sign?*

ˈstar-studded *adj* featuring a lot of famous performers: *a star-studded cast.*

ˌstar ˈturn main item in an entertainment or a performance: *The star turn in our show tonight will be a group of Chinese acrobats.*

ˈStar Wars (*infml*) = STRATEGIC DEFENCE INITIATIVE (STRATEGIC).

starboard /ˈstɑːbəd/ *n* [U] side of a ship or aircraft that is on the right when one is facing forward: *alter course to starboard* ○ [attrib] *the starboard side of a ship.* Cf PORT[3].

starch /stɑːtʃ/ *n* **1 (a)** [U] white tasteless carbohydrate food substance found in potatoes, flour, rice, etc. **(b)** [U, C] food containing this: *You eat too much starch.* **2** [U] this substance prepared in powder or other forms and used for stiffening cotton clothes, etc: *Spray starch on the shirt collars before ironing them.*

▷ **starch** *v* [Tn] stiffen (clothes, etc) with starch: *starched white uniforms.*

starchy *adj* (-ier, -iest) **1 (a)** of or like starch. **(b)** containing a lot of starch: *starchy food.* **2** (*infml derog*) (too) formal, stiff or conventional in manner: *He's always been rather starchy.*

stare /steə(r)/ *v* **1** [I, Ipr, Ip] ~ **(at sb/sth)** look (at sb/sth) with the eyes wide open in a fixed gaze (in astonishment, wonder, fear, etc): *It's rude to stare.* ○ *They all stared in/with amazement.* ○ *Do you like being stared at?* ○ *She was staring into the distance/into space.* ○ *He was staring out over the fields.* **2** [I, Ipr, Ip] ~ **(at sb/sth)** (of the eyes) be wide open with a fixed gaze: *He gazed at the scene with staring eyes.* ⇨ Usage at LOOK[1]. **3** [Tn·pr] ~ **sb into sth** bring or force sb into a specified condition by staring: *She stared him into silence.* **4** (idm) **be staring sb in the ˈface** be directly in front of sb; be obvious, easy or clear: *The book I was looking for was staring me in the face.* ○ *Defeat was staring them in the face*, ie seemed certain. ○ *The answer to his problem was staring him in the face.* **make sb ˈstare** surprise or astonish sb. **stark raving/staring mad** ⇨ STARK. **5** (phr v) **stare sb down/out** stare at sb until he feels forced to lower his eyes or turn away: *The two children were having a competition to see who could stare the other out.*

▷ **stare** *n* long fixed gaze; staring look: *give sb a rude stare* ○ *We received a number of curious stares from passers-by.* ○ *with a vacant stare*, ie suggesting an empty mind ○ *with a glassy stare*, ie suggesting indifference.

stark /stɑːk/ *adj* (-er, -est) **1 (a)** desolate and bare; grim; cheerless: *stark prison conditions* ○ *The landscape was grey and stark.* **(b)** [usu attrib] plain and unadorned: *the stark facts.* **2** clearly obvious to the eye or the mind: *in stark contrast.* **3** [attrib] complete; utter; downright: *stark madness.*

▷ **stark** *adv* **1** completely; entirely: *stark naked/crazy/mad.* **2** (idm) **ˌstark raving/staring ˈmad** completely mad.

starkers /ˈstɑːkəz/ *adj* [pred] (*Brit infml esp joc*) completely naked: *We saw him running down the road starkers.*

starkly *adv*: *It soon became starkly evident that....* ○ *The black rocks stood out starkly against the sky.*

starkness *n* [U]: *The starkness of their living conditions shocked him.*

starling /ˈstɑːlɪŋ/ *n* type of small noisy bird with glossy black and brown-spotted feathers. ⇨ illus at BIRD.

starry ⇨ STAR.

start[1] /stɑːt/ *n* **1 (a)** [C] beginning of a journey, an activity, a plan, a race, etc; process or act of starting: *make an early start (on a journey)* ○ *from start to finish* ○ *We won't finish the job today but we'll have made a start.* ○ *I've written one page of my essay: it's not much but it's a start.* ○ *He knew from the start the idea was hopeless.* **(b) the start** [sing] place where a race begins: *runners lined up at the start* ○ (*fig*) *We're only at the start in our house-hunting.* **2** [C] opportunity for, or help in, starting: *give sb a fresh start* ○ *The money gave him just the start he needed.* **3** [U, sing] (amount of) advantage gained or allowed in starting; advantageous position: *The smaller boys were given a start of 10 seconds in the race.* ○ *They didn't give me much/any start.* ○ *He got a good start in business.* **4** [C usu *sing*] sudden quick movement of surprise, fear, etc: *He sat up/woke up with a start.* ○ *The news gave me quite a start*, ie surprised me. **5** (idm) **by/in fits and starts** ⇨ FIT[4]. **a false start** ⇨ FALSE. **for a ˈstart** (used in an argument) as a first point: *I'm not buying it — I can't afford it for a start.* **get off to a good, bad, etc ˈstart** start well, badly, etc: *Their marriage got off to rather a shaky start.*

start[2] /stɑːt/ *v* **1** [I, Ip] ~ **(out)** begin a journey; leave; set off: *We started at six.* ○ *We must start (out) early.* **2** [It, Tn, Tg] begin (sth/to do sth): *It started to rain.* ○ *start work at 9 am* ○ *He's just started a new job.* ○ *start* (ie begin using) *a new tin of paint* ○ *He started laughing.* **3** [Ipr, Tn, Tn·pr] ~ **(on) sth**; ~ **sb on sth** (cause sb to) make a beginning on sth; (cause sb to) begin doing (a job, an activity, a piece of work, etc): *start (on) one's journey home* ○ *Have you started (on)* (ie begun to read or write) *your next book yet?* ○ *It's time to get/time we got started on* (ie began) *the washing up.* ⇨ Usage at BEGIN. **4 (a)** [I] (of an engine, etc) begin running: *The car won't start.* **(b)** [Tn] cause (a machine, etc) to start working: *I can't start the car.* **5** [Tn, Tn·pr, Cn·g] bring into existence; cause or enable to begin or begin happening; establish; originate: *start a fire* ○ *He decided to start a newspaper.* ○ *His uncle started him in business*, ie helped him, eg by supplying money. ○ *The news started me thinking.* ○ *The smoke started her coughing.* **6** [I, Ip] ~ **(up)** (*fml*) **(a)** make a sudden movement or change of position (because of fear, surprise, pain, etc): *She started at the sound of my voice.* **(b)** jump (up) suddenly: *He started (up) from his seat.* **7** [Ipr] (*fml*) move, rise or appear suddenly: *Tears started to* (ie suddenly came into) *her eyes.* ○ *His eyes almost started out of his head*, ie suddenly opened wide (in surprise, etc). **8** [Tn] (*fml*) drive (an animal) from a hiding-place into the open: *start a hare.* **9** (idm) **keep/start the ball rolling** ⇨ BALL[1]. **raise/start a hare** ⇨ HARE. **start a ˈbaby** (*infml esp Brit*) become pregnant. **start a ˈfamily** begin to have children: *They want to start a family but can't afford it at the moment.* **start (sth) from ˈscratch** begin (sth) from the very beginning without advantage or preparation, esp when building or developing sth: *He lost all his money and had to start again completely from scratch.* **start off on the right/wrong ˈfoot (with sb)** (*infml*) begin sth (esp a relationship) in the right/wrong way: *The new student started off on the wrong foot with the teacher by answering back rudely.* **ˈstart something** (*infml*) begin a fight, an argument, trouble, etc: *You shouldn't have spoken to him like that — you've really started something now.* **to ˈstart with (a)** in the first place; as the first point: *To start with we haven't enough money, and secondly we're too busy.* **(b)** at the beginning; initially: *The club had only six members to start with.* **10** (phr v) **start back (a)** begin to return: *Isn't it time we started back? It's getting dark.* **(b)** jump or step back suddenly (in fear, shock, surprise, etc). **start for...** leave one place to go to another: *What time do you start for work?* ○ *Let's start for home.* **start in on sb (for sth)** (*infml*) begin to criticize, scold or shout at sb: *He started in on us again for poor work.* **start in to do sth/on sth/on doing sth** (*infml*) begin to do sth: *We started in to discuss/on a discussion of/on discussing the idea.* **start off** begin to move: *The horse started off at a steady trot.* **start (sb) off (on sth)** (cause sb to) begin working on, doing, saying, etc sth: *It's impossible to stop him talking once he starts off.* ○ *What started him off on this crazy idea?* ○ *Don't start her off on one of her boring stories.* **start out (on sth); start out (to do sth) (a)** begin a journey: *start out on a 20-mile walk* ○ *What time did you start out?* **(b)** (*infml*) take the first steps; intend when starting: *start out in business* ○ *start out on a new career* ○ *start out to write/with the intention of writing a novel.* **start over** (*US*) begin again: *She wasn't satisfied with our work and made us start (all) over.* **start (sth) up** (cause sth to) begin or begin working, running, happening, etc: *The engine started up suddenly.* ○ *start up a new bus company* ○ *What started the argument up?* ○ *We couldn't start the car up.* **start (sb) up (in sth)** (cause sb to) begin a career, working life, etc: *start up in business* ○ *He started his daughter up in the trade.*

□ **ˈstarting-block** *n* either one of two blocks fixed

to the ground against which a runner braces his feet at the start of a race.

ˈstarting-gate *n* barrier that is raised at the start of a horse- or dog-race, allowing the animals to move off.

ˈstarting-point *n* place or point from which sth begins: *We'll take this as the starting-point for our discussion.*

ˈstarting-post *n* place from which competitors start in a race.

ˈstarting-price *n* final odds just before the start of a horse-race, etc.

starter /ˈstɑːtə(r)/ *n* **1** person, horse, etc taking part in a race at the start: *Of the five starters in the race only three finished.* Cf NON-STARTER. **2** person who gives the signal for a race to start: *waiting for the starter's gun to fire.* **3** (usu with an *adj*) person who starts sth (esp in the way specified by the *adj*): *He's a fast starter.* **4** device for starting a machine, esp an engine. **5** (*infml esp Brit*) (*US* also **appetizer**) first course of a meal (esp one with more than two courses): *What would you like as a starter?* **6** (idm) **for ˈstarters** (*infml*) first of all; to start with. **under ˌstarter's ˈorders** (of horses, athletes, etc ready to start a race) waiting for the order or signal to start.

startle /ˈstɑːtl/ *v* [Tn] give a sudden shock or surprise to (a person or an animal); cause to move or jump suddenly (from surprise): *You startled me — I didn't hear you come in.* ○ *I was startled to hear his news/by his news.* ○ *The sudden noise in the bushes startled her horse.* ○ *He had a startled look on his face.*

▷ **startling** /ˈstɑːtlɪŋ/ *adj* very surprising; astonishing; remarkable: *a startling result* ○ *What startling news!* **startlingly** *adv*: *startlingly beautiful.*

starve /stɑːv/ *v* **1** [I, Ipr, Tn, Tn·pr] (cause a person or an animal to) suffer severely or die from hunger: *Thousands of cattle are starving.* ○ *starve to death* ○ (*infml*) *She's starving herself to try to lose weight.* **2** [Ipr, Tn·pr usu passive] ~ **for sth**; ~ **sb of sth** (cause sb to) suffer or long for sth greatly needed or wanted; deprive sb of sth: *children starving for/starved of affection* ○ (*fig*) *Industry is being starved of technical expertise.* **3** [I] (*infml*) (used only in the continuous tenses) feel very hungry: *What's for dinner? I'm starving!* **4** (phr v) **starve sb into sth/doing sth** force sb to do sth by not allowing him to get food: *starved into surrender/surrendering.* **starve sb out (of sth)** force sb out of a hiding-place, etc by stopping supplies of food: *It took 8 days to starve them out (of the building).*

▷ **starvation** /stɑːˈveɪʃn/ *n* [U] suffering or death caused by lack of food: *die of starvation* ○ [attrib] *starvation wages*, ie too low to buy enough food ○ *a starvation diet*, ie barely enough food to keep one alive.

stash /stæʃ/ *v* [Tn, Tn·pr, Tn·p] ~ **sth (away)** (*infml*) store sth safely and secretly; hide sth: *He's got his life savings stashed (away) in an old suitcase.*

▷ **stash** *n* (*infml esp US*) **1** thing that is stored secretly. **2** place where sth is hidden; hiding-place: *a secret stash of stolen jewels.*

state[1] /steɪt/ *n* **1** [C] condition in which a person or thing is (in circumstances, appearance, mind, health, etc); quality of circumstances, characteristics, etc: *The house was in a dirty state.* ○ *These buildings are in a bad state of repair*, ie need to be repaired. ○ *a confused state of mind* ○ *a poor state of health* ○ *in a state of undress*, ie naked ○ *not in a fit state to drive* ○ *a state of emergency*, eg declared by a government because of war, natural disaster, etc ○ *She was in a terrible state* (ie very upset, agitated, etc) *when we arrived.* **2** (also **State**) [C] country considered as an organized political community controlled by one government; territory occupied by this: *the State of Israel* ○ *modern European states.* ⇨ Usage at COUNTRY. **3** (also **State**) [C] organized political community forming part of a country that is a federation or republic: *How many States are there in the United States of America?* ○ *Which state were you born in?* Cf COUNTRY, PROVINCE 1. **4** (esp **the State**) [U] civil government of a country: *matters/affairs of state* ○ *Church and State* ○ *railways run by the state/state-run railways* ○ *Many believe the State should provide schools, homes and hospitals for everyone.* **5** [U] ceremonial formality connected with high levels of government; pomp: *The Queen was in her robes of state.* ○ *The President was driven in state through the streets.* **6 the States** [pl] (*infml*) the United States of America: *I've never been to the States.* **7** (idm) **in/into a ˈstate** (*infml*) **(a)** in/into an excited or agitated state of mind: *She got herself into a state about the exams.* ○ *He was in a real state when I last saw him.* **(b)** dirty, neglected, untidy, etc (according to the context): *What a state this place is in!* **in a state of ˈnature** (*fml or joc*) completely naked. **lie in state** ⇨ LIE[2]. **a state of afˈfairs** circumstances or conditions; situation: *What a shocking state of affairs!* **the state of ˈplay (a)** score (esp in cricket). **(b)** how opposite sides in a dispute stand in relation to one another: *What is the latest state of play in the disarmament talks?*

▷ **state** (also **State**) *adj* [attrib] **1** of, for or concerned with the State(4): *state ˈrailways* ○ *ˈstate schools*, ie free schools run by public authorities ○ *state ˈsecrets* ○ *State Socialism advocates state control of industry.* **2** of, for or involving ceremony; used or done on ceremonial occasions: *a state occasion* ○ *the state apartments* ○ *a state visit*, eg by a monarch to another country ○ *the state opening of Parliament.*

stateless *adj* (of a person) not recognized as a citizen of any country; having no citizenship. **statelessness** *n* [U].

□ **ˈstatecraft** *n* [U] skill in managing State affairs; statesmanship.

the ˈState Department the US government department of foreign affairs.

ˌState Enrolled ˈNurse (*abbr* **SEN**) (*Brit*) (title of a) person who has trained as a nurse and passed examinations that allow her or him to practise most areas of nursing (lower in rank than a State Registered Nurse).

ˈstatehouse *n* building where the law-making body of a US state meets.

ˌstate of the ˈart current state of development of a subject, technique, etc: [attrib] *a state-of-the-art computer program*, ie the most advanced one available.

ˌState of the ˈUnion message speech given each year by the US president to Congress, including a report on the political and economic situation and a summary of proposed new laws.

ˌState Registered ˈNurse (*abbr* **SRN**) (*Brit*) (title of a) person who has trained fully as a nurse and passed examinations that allow her or him to practise all areas of nursing.

ˈstateroom *n* **1** apartment used by royalty, important government members, etc. **2** private cabin or sleeping compartment on a ship.

ˌState's ˈevidence (idm) **ˌturn State's ˈevidence** (*US*) = TURN KING'S/QUEEN'S EVIDENCE (EVIDENCE).

ˈstateside *adj*, *adv* (*US infml*) of, in or towards the USA.

ˌStates' ˈRights rights belonging to individual US states and not to the federal government.

ˈstate university university funded by and managed for a US state.

ˈstatewide *adj* (*US*) throughout a state[1](2, 3).

state[2] /steɪt/ *v* **1** [Tn, Tf, Tw] express (sth) in spoken or written words, esp carefully, fully and clearly: *state one's views* ○ *state the obvious*, ie obvious facts, etc ○ *He stated positively that he had never seen the man.* ○ *The document clearly states what is being planned.* **2** [Tn usu passive] arrange, fix, or announce (sth) in advance; specify: *at stated times/intervals* ○ *You must work the hours stated.*

▷ **statement** *n* **1** [U] (*fml*) stating sth or expressing sth in words: *Clearness of statement is more important than beauty of language.* **2** [C] thing that is stated: *The president made a statement of his aims.* ○ (*fig*) *The artist regards his painting as a political statement.* **3** [C] formal account of facts, views, problems, etc; report: *issue a statement* ○ *The police asked the man to make statement*, ie a written account of facts concernin an alleged crime, used in court if legal actio follows. **4** [C] = BANK STATEMENT (BANK): *My ban sends me monthly statements.*

stately /ˈsteɪtlɪ/ *adj* (**-ier**, **-iest**) dignifie imposing; grand: *a stately old woman* ○ *with state grace.* ▷ **stateliness** *n* [U].

□ **ˌstately ˈhome** (*Brit*) large and grand hous usu of historical interest, esp one that the publi may visit.

statesman /ˈsteɪtsmən/ *n* (*pl* **-men** /-mən/) (*fe* **stateswoman** /-wʊmən/, *pl* **-women** /-wɪmɪn person who plays an important part in th management of State affairs, esp one who is skille and fair; wise political leader.

▷ **statesmanlike** *adj* having or showing th qualities and abilities of a wise statesman.

statesmanship *n* [U] skill and wisdom i managing public affairs.

static /ˈstætɪk/ *adj* **1** not moving or changin stationary: *House prices, which have been static f several months, are now rising again.* ○ *stat water*, eg in a tank, needing to be pumped ○ *rather static performance*, ie one in which there little movement. **2** (*physics*) (of force) acting b weight without motion. Cf DYNAMIC 1.

▷ **static** *n* [U] **1** atmospheric conditions causin poor radio or television reception, marked by lou crackling noises; atmospherics: *There was to much static to hear their message clearly.* **2** (als **ˌstatic elecˈtricity**) electricity that accumulate on or in an object which cannot conduct a curren *Her hair was full of static.*

statics *n* [sing *v*] branch of physics that deals wit bodies remaining at rest or with forces tha balance one another.

station /ˈsteɪʃn/ *n* **1** [C] place, building, etc wher a service is organized and provided, or specialize (esp scientific) work is done: *a ˈbus, poˈlice, ˈfi station* ○ *a ˈradar station* ○ *an agriˌculture reˈsearch station* ○ *a nuclear ˈpower station.* **2** [C company that broadcasts on radio or televisio building from which this is done: *Which TV statio is the programme on?* ○ *a pirate radio station*, one using a frequency illegally. **3** [C] **(a)** plac where trains stop on a railway line; the building (eg ticket office, waiting rooms) connected wit this: *Which station are you going to?* ○ [attrib] *th station platform, staff.* **(b)** similar place wher buses and coaches stop: *The bus leaves the bu station at 9.42 am.* **4** [C] (*dated or fml*) soci position; rank; status: *people in all stations of life He has ideas above his station.* **5** [C] (*Austral*) (us large) sheep or cattle ranch. **6** [C, CGp] (peop living in a) small military or naval base: *He returning to his army station.* **7** [U] position, c relative position, to be taken up or maintained b sb/sth: *One of the warships was out of station*, ie n in its correct position relative to other ship. **8** (idm) **panic stations** ⇨ PANIC.

▷ **station** *v* [esp passive: Tn, Tn·pr] put (s oneself, an army, etc) at or in a certain place: *The regiment is stationed in Cyprus.* ○ *The detecti stationed himself* (ie hid) *among the bushes.*

□ **ˈstation break** (*US*) break between televisio or radio programmes during which th broadcasting company's name is announced, ofte with advertising for its other programmes.

ˈstation house (*US*) = POLICE STATION (POLICE).

ˈstation-master *n* person in charge of a railwa station.

ˌStations of the ˈCross series of fourteen image or pictures telling the story of Christ's suffering and death, at which prayers are said in certai Churches.

ˈstation-wagon *n* (*US*) = ESTATE CAR (ESTATE).

stationary /ˈsteɪʃənrɪ; *US* -nerɪ/ *adj* **1 (a)** n moving: *remain stationary* ○ *collide with stationary van.* **(b)** that cannot be moved or is n intended to be moved: *a stationary crane.* C MOBILE 1. **2** not changing in condition or quantit

stationer /ˈsteɪʃnə(r)/ *n* person who runs a sho that sells stationery: *Is there a good stationer (shop) near here?*

▷ **stationery** /ˈsteɪʃənrɪ; *US* -nerɪ/ *n* [U] writing materials (eg paper, pens, envelopes, etc): [attrib] *a stationery cupboard*, eg in an office. **the ˈStationery Office** (in full **Her/His ˌMajesty's ˈStationery Office**, *abbr* **HMSO**) the body that publishes official books and documents for the British government.

statistics /stəˈtɪstɪks/ *n* **(a)** [pl] collection of information shown in numbers: *Politicians love to use statistics to support their arguments.* ○ *Have you seen the latest statistics on crime?* **(b)** [sing *v*] science of collecting, classifying and analysing such information: *She's studying statistics at university.*

▷ **statistic** *n* item of information expressed in numbers: *unearthed a fascinating statistic.*

statistical /stəˈtɪstɪkl/ *adj* of or shown by statistics: *statistical evidence.* **statistically** /-klɪ/ *adv*: *It has been proved statistically that....*

statistician /ˌstætɪˈstɪʃn/ *n* person who studies or works with statistics.

statuary /ˈstætʃʊərɪ; *US* -ʊerɪ/ *n* [U] **1** statues: *a display of bronze statuary.* **2** art of making statues and sculptures.

the Statue of Liberty

statue /ˈstætʃuː/ *n* figure of a person, an animal, etc in wood, stone, bronze, etc, usu life-size or larger: *erect a statue of the king on a horse.*

▷ **statuesque** /ˌstætʃʊˈesk/ *adj* (*approv*) **(a)** like a statue in size, dignity or stillness. **(b)** (usu of a woman) tall, graceful and dignified: *her statuesque figure.*

statuette /ˌstætʃʊˈet/ *n* small statue: *A china statuette of a shepherdess stood on the table.*

□ **the ˌStatue of ˈLiberty** statue on an island at the entrance to New York harbour, given to the USA by France in 1886 in honour of their alliance in the *War of American Independence. It has become the symbol of the USA, esp as a country dedicated to freedom. ⇨ illus. ⇨ article at NATIONAL.

stature /ˈstætʃə(r)/ *n* [U] **1** natural height of the body: *short of stature.* **2** importance and reputation gained by ability or achievement: *a scientist of international stature.*

status /ˈsteɪtəs/ *n* [U] **1** person's social, legal or professional position or rank in relation to others: *Women have very little status in many countries.* ○ *What's your official status in the company?* **2** high rank or social position: *seek status and security* ○ *He's very aware of his status.*

□ **ˈstatus symbol** possession that is thought to show sb's high social rank, wealth, etc: *He only bought the yacht as a status symbol — he hates sailing.*

status quo /ˌsteɪtəs ˈkwəʊ/ **the status quo** situation or state of affairs as it is now, or as it was before a recent change: *upset/restore/preserve the status quo* ○ *conservatives who defend the status quo.*

statute /ˈstætʃuːt/ *n* [C] **1** law passed by Parliament or a similar law-making body and written down formally: *decreed by statute.* **2** any of the rules of an institution: *under the University's statutes.*

▷ **statutory** /ˈstætʃʊtrɪ; *US* -tɔːrɪ/ *adj* [usu attrib] fixed, done or required by statute: *one's statutory rights* ○ *statutory control of prices and incomes* ○ (*US*) *statutory rape*, ie sexual intercourse with a girl below the legal age of consent. **statutorily** *adv.*

□ **ˈstatute-book** *n* collection of all the laws made by a government; book(s) in which these are recorded: *not on the statute book*, ie not included in statute law.

ˈstatute law all the statutes as a group. Cf CASE-LAW (CASE[1]), COMMON LAW (COMMON[1]).

ˌstatute ˈmile the mile used for measuring distances on land, ie 1760 yards or approximately 1.6 km.

staunch[1] /stɔːntʃ/ *adj* (**-er**, **-est**) firm, loyal and dependable in opinion and attitude: *a staunch Christian, Conservative, Republican, etc* ○ *one of our staunchest allies.*

staunch[2] = STANCH.

stave[1] /steɪv/ *n* **1** any of the curved pieces of wood forming the side of a barrel or tub. **2** (*music*) = STAFF 5.

stave[2] /steɪv/ *v* (*pt, pp* **staved** or **stove** /stəʊv/) (phr v) **stave sth in** break, smash, or make a hole in sth: *The side of the boat was staved in by the collision* ○ *The victim's skull had been stove in by a heavy instrument.* **stave sth off** (*pt, pp* ~**d**) keep sth off or away; delay sth, esp temporarily: *stave off disaster, danger, bankruptcy, the pangs of hunger.*

stay[1] /steɪ/ *v* **1** **(a)** [La, I, Ipr, Ip, It, In/pr] remain or continue in the same place (for a long or short time, permanently or temporarily, as specified by the context); not depart or change: *stay (at) home*, ie not go out or to work ○ *stay late at the office* ○ *I'm afraid I can't stay*, ie I must leave now. ○ *stay in the house, in bed, in one's room, etc* ○ *stay in teaching, journalism, etc*, ie not change one's job ○ *stay away from* (ie not go to) *school* ○ *Stay on this road for two miles then turn left.* ○ *Stay here until I come back.* ○ *We stayed to see what would happen.* ○ *I can only stay a few minutes.* ⇨ Usage at AND. **(b)** [La, Ln] continue in a certain state: *stay awake* ○ *stay single*, ie not marry ○ *He never stays sober for long.* ○ *They stayed friends for years.* **2** [I, Ipr, In/pr] remain or live somewhere temporarily, esp as a visitor or a guest: *It's late — why don't you stay* (ie for the night)? ○ *stay in a hotel* ○ *Why don't you come to stay with us next time you visit Durham?* ○ *Jenny's staying in Dublin for a few days, but she now lives/is now living* (ie has her home) *in Belfast.* ○ *stay the night with sb*, ie sleep at sb's house for the night. **3** [Tn] (*fml*) stop, delay, postpone or check (sth): *stay* (ie delay) *punishment/judgement* ○ *stay the progress of a disease* ○ *a little food to stay* (ie temporarily satisfy) *one's hunger* ○ (*arch*) *stay one's hand*, ie refrain from doing sth. **4** [I] (*arch*) (usu imperative) wait a moment; pause; stop: *Stay! What is this I see?* **5** (idm) **be here to stay/have come to stay** (*infml*) be permanent and generally accepted: *I hope that (the idea of) equality of opportunity for men and women has come to/is here to stay.* **keep/stay/steer clear** ⇨ CLEAR[2]. **stay the ˈcourse** continue going to the end (of sth difficult, eg a race, a struggle): *I don't think he's sufficiently dedicated to stay the course.* **stay ˈput** (*infml*) remain where one/it is or is placed: *The baby wouldn't stay put long enough for the photo to be taken.*

6 (phr v) **stay away (from sb/sth)** keep a distance (from sb/sth); not interfere (with sb/sth): *Tell him to stay away from my sister!*

stay behind remain at a place after others have left (esp to go home): *They stayed behind after the party to help clear up.* ○ *The teacher told him to stay behind after class.* **stay down (a)** (of food) remain in the stomach (rather than be vomited): *She's so ill that nothing will stay down, not even water.* **(b)** remain in a lowered position: *The switch on the kettle won't stay down.*

stay for/to sth remain at a person's house for (a meal): *Won't you stay for/to supper?*

stay in (a) not go outdoors: *The doctor advised me to stay in for a few days.* **(b)** remain at school after others have left, esp as a punishment.

stay on (a) remain in position on top of sth: *My hat won't stay on properly.* **(b)** remain alight, burning, running, etc: *The TV stays on all day at this place.* **stay on (at...)** remain at (a place of study, employment, etc) after others have left: *He stayed on at university to do research.*

stay out (a) remain out of the house or outdoors (esp after dark): *I don't like you staying out so late.* **(b)** remain on strike: *The miners stayed out for a whole year.* **stay out of sth** remain at a point where one cannot be reached or affected by sb/sth: *His father told him to stay out of trouble.*

stay up (a) remain awake; not go to bed: *She promised the children they could stay up for their favourite TV programme.* **(b)** remain in a position where put, built, etc; not fall or sink or be removed: *I'm surprised some of those cheap houses stay up at all.* ○ *My trousers only stay up if I wear a belt.* ○ *The poster only stayed up a few hours, before it was stolen.*

stay with sb (*infml*) continue to listen attentively to sb: *Please stay with me a moment longer — I'm getting to the point of the story.*

▷ **stay** *n* **1** period of staying; visit: *an overnight stay in Karachi* ○ *a fortnight's stay with my uncle.* **2** (idm) **a ˌstay of exeˈcution** (*esp law*) (order permitting a) delay in the carrying out of a court judgement or a postponement of some (usu unpleasant) activity: *They were due to start demolishing the old theatre today but there's been a last-minute stay of execution.*

stayer *n* person or animal with endurance or stamina: *He's not a fast horse but he's certainly a stayer.*

□ **ˈstay-at-home** *n* (*infml usu derog*) person who rarely leaves his home to go anywhere; unadventurous person.

ˈstaying-power *n* [U] ability to keep going; endurance; stamina: *Long-distance runners need staying-power.*

stay[2] /steɪ/ *n* **1** [C] rope or wire supporting a mast, pole, etc. **2** [C] any prop or support: (*fig*) *the prop and stay of* (ie the person who helped him in) *his old age.* **3** **stays** [pl] old-fashioned type of corset, stiffened with strips of bone or plastic.

STD /ˌes tiː ˈdiː/ *abbr* (*Brit*) subscriber trunk dialling (by telephone): *The STD code for Oxford is 0865.*

stead /sted/ *n* (idm) **in sb's/sth's ˈstead** (*fml*) in sb's/sth's place; instead of sb/sth: *I can't attend the meeting but I'll send my assistant in my stead.* **stand sb in good ˈstead** be useful or helpful to sb when needed: *My anorak has stood me in good stead this winter.*

steadfast /ˈstedfɑːst; *US* -fæst/ *adj* ~ (**in sth/to sb/sth**) (*fml usu approv*) firm and not changing or yielding; constant: *a steadfast friend* ○ *a steadfast gaze, refusal* ○ *steadfast in adversity* ○ *be steadfast to one's principles.* ▷ **steadfastly** *adv.* **steadfastness** *n* [U].

steady /ˈstedɪ/ *adj* (**-ier**, **-iest**) **1** firmly fixed, supported or balanced; not shaking, rocking or likely to fall over: *hold the ladder steady* ○ *make a table steady*, eg by repairing a leg ○ *He's not very steady on his legs after his illness.* ○ *Such fine work requires a steady hand and a steady eye.* ○ *She was trembling with excitement but her voice was steady.* **2** done, happening, working, etc in an even and regular way; developing, etc gradually without interruptions: *a steady wind* ○ *a steady speed, flow, rate, pace, etc* ○ *steady progress, improvement, etc.* **3** regular in behaviour, habits, etc; sensible and dependable: *a steady young man* ○ *a steady worker.* **4** constant; unchanging: *a steady faith* ○ *with a steady purpose* ○ *Have you got a steady boy-friend?* ○ *The ship kept to a steady course.* **5** (idm) **steady (ˈon)!** (*infml*) (used as a warning) be careful; control yourself: *I say, steady on! You can't say things like that about someone you've never met.*

▷ **steadily** /ˈstedɪlɪ/ *adv*: *work steadily* ○ *Prices are rising steadily.* ○ *His health is getting steadily worse.*

steady *adv* (idm) **go steady (with sb)** (*dated infml*) (of sb not engaged to marry) go out regularly with sb of the opposite sex; have a serious long-lasting relationship: *Are Tony and Jane going steady?*

steady *n* (*dated infml*) regular boy-friend or girl-friend: *He's my steady.*

steady *v* (*pt, pp* **steadied**) [I, Tn] (cause sth to) become steady; keep steady: *Prices are steadying.* ○ *steady a boat* ○ *He steadied himself by holding on to the rail*, eg on the deck of a rolling ship.

steadiness *n* [U].

□ ˌ**steady** ˈ**state theory** theory about the nature of the universe, claiming that it maintains a constant average density and that more matter is created to fill the void left by galaxies moving away from each other. It is no longer widely accepted. Cf BIG BANG (BIG).

steak /steɪk/ *n* **1** [C, U] (thick slice of) meat (esp beef) or fish, cut for frying or grilling, etc: *fillet/rump steak* ○ *two tuna steaks* ○ [attrib] *a steak knife*, ie for cutting steak, etc when eating it. **2** [U] beef from the front of the animal, cut for stewing or braising.

□ ˈ**steak-house** *n* restaurant that specializes in serving meat steaks.

steal /sti:l/ *v* (*pt* **stole** /stəʊl/, *pp* **stolen** /ˈstəʊlən/) **1** [I, Ipr, Tn, Tn·pr] ~ (**sth**) (**from sb/sth**) take (another person's property) secretly without permission or legal right; take (sth) dishonestly: *It's wrong to steal.* ○ *He stole from the rich to give to the poor.* ○ *Someone has stolen my watch.* ○ *I have had my watch stolen.* ○ *He stole a bun from the shop.* ⇨ Usage at ROB. **2** [Tn, Tn·pr] (*fml*) obtain (sth) quickly or stealthily, esp by a surprise or trick: *steal a few minutes' sleep* ○ *steal a kiss from sb* ○ *steal a glance at sb in the mirror.* **3** [Ipr, Ip] ~ **in, out, away, etc** move in the specified direction secretly and quietly, or without being noticed: *He stole into the room.* ○ *A tear stole down her cheek.* ○ *The morning light was stealing through the shutters.* ⇨ Usage at PROWL. **4** (idm) **steal a** ˈ**march** (**on sb**) gain an advantage over sb by doing sth secretly or slyly, or by acting before he does. **steal the** ˈ**scene**/ˈ**show** attract the most attention and praise (esp unexpectedly): *Despite fine acting by several well-known stars it was a young newcomer who stole the show.* **steal sb's** ˈ**thunder** spoil sb's attempt to impress by anticipating him, detracting from what he is saying, doing, etc.

▷ **steal** *n* **1** (*US sl*) instance of stealing; theft. **2** (*infml esp US*) good bargain; easy task: *'Ladies and gentlemen, it's a steal at only $50.'*

stealth /stelθ/ *n* [U] acting or behaving in a quiet or secret way: *Tracking wild animals requires great stealth.* ○ *The burglars had entered the house by stealth.*

▷ **stealthy** *adj* (**-ier, -iest**) doing things, or done, with stealth: *stealthy footsteps.* **stealthily** /-ɪlɪ/ *adv.* **stealthiness** *n* [U].

steam /sti:m/ *n* [U] **1** (**a**) invisible gas into which water is changed by boiling. (**b**) power obtained using this gas under pressure: *a building heated by steam* ○ [attrib] *a steam brake, whistle, winch, etc*, ie worked by steam ○ *steam cleaning*, ie done by steam. **2** visible mist that forms when steam condenses in the air: *steam coming out of a boiling kettle* ○ *The laundry was full of steam.* **3** (idm) **blow off/let off** ˈ**steam** (*infml*) release surplus energy or emotion from being restrained: *The children were out in the playground letting off steam.* **full speed/steam ahead** ⇨ FULL. **get up** ˈ**steam** (**a**) (of a vehicle or an engine) slowly increase speed. (**b**) (*infml*) (of a person) collect one's energy; gradually become excited or angry. ˌ**run out of** ˈ**steam** (*infml*) become exhausted: *There is a danger of the housing programme running out of steam*, ie losing its impetus. ˌ**under one's own** ˈ**steam** without help from others; unaided.

▷ **steam** *v* **1** [I, Ip] give out steam or vapour: *steaming hot coffee* ○ *The kettle was steaming (away) on the stove.* **2** [Tn, Cn·a] cook, soften or clean (sth), by the use of steam: *steamed pudding* ○ *Steam the fish for 10 minutes.* ○ *steam open an envelope*, ie use steam to soften the glue on the flap. ⇨ Usage at COOK. **3** (idm) **be/get** (**all**) **steamed** ˈ**up** (**about/over sth**) (*infml*) become very enthusiastic, angry, excited, etc: *Calm down — it's nothing to get steamed up about!* **4** (phr v) **steam across, along, away, off, etc** move in the specified direction using the power of steam: *a boat steaming up the Nile* ○ *The train steamed into/out of the station.* ○ *We were steaming along at 50 mph.* **steam sth off** (**sth**) remove (one piece of paper) from another using steam to melt the glue sticking them together: *steam stamps off envelopes.* **steam** (**sth**) **up** (cause sth to) become covered with condensed steam: *The car windows steamed up.*

steamer *n* **1** steamship. **2** metal container with small holes in it, in which food is cooked using steam.

steamy *adj* (**-ier, -iest**) **1** of, like or full of steam: *a steamy jungle.* **2** (*infml*) erotic and passionate: *steamy love scenes.* **steaminess** *n* [U].

□ ˈ**steamboat** *n* boat powered by steam, used (esp formerly) on rivers and along coasts. In the 19th century, the paddle-steamers of the Clyde and Mississippi were popular for passenger transport, besides being an important means of moving goods.

ˈ**steam-engine** *n* locomotive or engine driven by steam. Steam-engines were developed by *Watt, *Stephenson and others in the 19th century and became the main source of power for the *Industrial Revolution, used in factories, mines, and esp in trains and ships.

ˈ**steam-hammer** *n* mechanical hammer, used eg for shaping metal, that is powered by steam.

ˈ**steam iron** electric iron that can send out jets of steam from its flat surface.

ˌ**steam** ˈ**radio** (*infml joc*) radio broadcasting considered as very old-fashioned by comparison with television.

ˈ**steamroller** *n* heavy slow-moving engine with a large roller, used in road-making. — *v* **1** [Tn] crush or defeat (sb/sth) as with a steamroller: *steamrollering all opposition.* **2** (phr v) **steamroller sb into sth/doing sth** force sb into (a situation or course of action).

ˈ**steamship** *n* ship driven by steam. Steamships began to replace sailing ships early in the 19th century, achieving considerably higher speeds, esp on transatlantic routes. The large amounts of fuel they had to carry led in turn to their replacement by vessels with diesel engines.

ˈ**steam-shovel** *n* (*esp US*) machine for excavating, originally worked by steam.

ˈ**steam train** train pulled by a steam-engine: [attrib] *a steam train enthusiast.*

steatite /ˈstɪətaɪt/ *n* [U] = SOAPSTONE (SOAP).

steed /sti:d/ *n* (*arch or joc*) horse: *my trusty steed.*

steel /sti:l/ *n* **1** [U] (**a**) strong hard alloy of iron and carbon, much used for making vehicles, tools, knives, machinery, etc. It is usu produced nowadays by the basic-oxygen process, which purifies the molten steel by introducing oxygen at high pressure: *It's made of steel.* ○ [attrib] *steel knives.* (**b**) industry that produces steel; production of steel: [attrib] *the steel strike* ○ *deserted steel mills* ○ *the steel areas of the north.* **2** [C] thin roughened rod of steel, used for sharpening knives, etc. **3** [C] (*arch*) weapon, esp a sword (contrasted with a gun, etc): *an enemy worthy of one's steel*, ie one who will fight well. **4** (idm) **cold steel** ⇨ COLD[1]. **of** ˈ**steel** of great strength or hardness: *a man of steel* ○ *nerves of steel* ○ *a grip of steel.*

▷ **steel** *v* [Tn, Tn·pr, Cn·t] ~ **oneself/sth** (**for/against sth**) make (oneself, one's heart, etc) hard or strong in preparation for sth: *I'm afraid I have bad news for you, so steel yourself.* ○ *She had to steel her heart against pity.*

steely *adj* (**-ier, -iest**) like steel in colour, hardness, brightness or strength: *a steely look* ○ *with steely determination.* **steeliness** *n* [U].

□ ˌ**steel** ˈ**band** West Indian band of musicians with instruments made from empty oil drums.

ˌ**steel-**ˈ**plated** *adj* covered with steel plates; armoured.

ˌ**steel** ˈ**wool** mass of fine steel shavings used for cleaning, scouring and polishing. Cf WIRE WOOL (WIRE).

ˈ**steel worker** person who works in the steel industry.

ˈ**steelworks** *n* (*pl* unchanged) [sing or pl *v*] factory where steel is made.

Steele /sti:l/ Sir Richard (1672-1729), British author. He wrote a number of unsuccessful comedies, but is most famous for the essays on morals and literature written for *The Tatler* and *The Spectator*, which he produced together with *Addison.

steelyard /ˈsti:ljɑ:d *or, rarely,* ˈstɪljəd/ *n* type of weighing-machine with two arms of unequal lengths, the longer one marked with a scale along which a weight is moved.

steep[1] /sti:p/ *adj* (**-er, -est**) **1** (of a slope, stairs, etc) rising or falling sharply, not gradually: *a steep path, descent, hill, climb, gradient* ○ *a steep roof* ○ *I never cycle up that hill — it's too steep.* **2** (*infml*) (of a price or demand) too much; unreasonable; excessive: *She wants you to feed her cats for four weeks — that's a bit steep!* ○ *I wouldn't pay £300 for his old car — it's too steep.*

▷ **steepen** /ˈsti:pən/ *v* [I, Tn] (cause sth to) become steep[1](1) or steeper: *The path steepens as you climb the hillside.*

steepish *adj* quite steep.

steeply *adv.*

steepness *n* [U].

steep[2] /sti:p/ *v* **1** [esp passive: Tn, Tn·pr] ~ **sth** (**in sth**) soak sth thoroughly in liquid (esp in order to soften, clean or flavour it): *fruit steeped in brandy* ○ *steep onions in vinegar*, ie to pickle them. **2** (phr v) **steep sb/oneself/sth in sth** (esp passive) pervade or fill sth thoroughly with sth; give oneself/sb a thorough knowledge of sth: *steeped in ignorance/prejudice* ○ *a city steeped in history* ○ *He steeped himself in the literature of ancient Greece and Rome.*

steeple /ˈsti:pl/ *n* tall tower with a spire on top, rising above the roof of a church. ⇨ illus at CHURCH.

□ ˈ**steeplejack** *n* person who climbs steeples, tall chimneys, etc to repair or paint them.

steeplechase /ˈsti:pltʃeɪs/ *n* **1** horse-race across country or on a course with various hedges and ditches to be jumped. Cf FLAT RACING (FLAT[2]). **2** race for athletes, across country or on a running track, with obstacles such as fences, hedges and ditches to be jumped.

▷ **steeplechaser** *n* person or horse competing in steeplechases.

steer[1] /stɪə(r)/ *v* **1** (**a**) [I, Ipr, Tn, Tn·pr] direct or control the course of (a boat, car, etc): *You steer and I'll push.* ○ *steer by the stars* ○ *steer a boat into (the) harbour* ○ (*fig*) *He managed to steer the discussion away from the subject of money.* ○ (*fig*) *She steered me towards a table in the corner.* (**b**) [I] (of a boat, car, etc) be able to be steered: *a car that steers well on corners.* **2** [Tn] follow or keep to (a course): *keep steering north/a northerly course.* **3** (idm) **keep/stay/steer clear** ⇨ CLEAR[2].

▷ **steer** *n* (idm) **a bum steer** ⇨ BUM[2].

steerer /ˈstɪərə(r)/ *n* person who steers.

steering /ˈstɪərɪŋ/ *n* [U] equipment or mechanism for steering a car, boat, etc: *power steering* ○ *There is something wrong with the steering.*

steersman /-zmən/ *n* (*pl* **-men** /-mən/) person who steers a boat, ship, etc. Cf HELMSMAN (HELM).

□ ˈ**steering-column** *n* column-shaped part of a car, etc on which the steering-wheel is fitted.

ˈ**steering committee** committee that decides the order of certain business activities and guides their general course.

ˈ**steering lock** mechanism in a vehicle's steering-column that allows the steering-wheel to be locked in a fixed position to prevent anyone stealing the vehicle.

ˈ**steering-wheel** *n* wheel for controlling the steering in a car, ship, etc. ⇨ illus at CAR.

steer[2] /stɪə(r)/ *n* young (usu castrated) male animal of the ox family, raised for its meat. Cf BULL[1] 1, BULLOCK, OX 1.

steerage /ˈstɪərɪdʒ/ *n* [U] **1** action of steering and its effects on a ship, vehicle, etc. **2** section of a ship nearest the rudder, where accommodation was formerly provided for passengers travelling at the lowest fares: *travel steerage* ○ [attrib] *steerage* class.

□ ˈ**steerage-way** *n* [U] (*nautical*) forward movement needed by a ship, boat, etc to allow it to be steered or controlled properly.

Stein /staɪn/ Gertrude (1874-1946), American author. She lived in Paris from 1902, where her friends included *Picasso and *Hemingway. Her many works use a highly individualistic, repetitive prose style.

stein /staɪn/ *n* large pottery mug, often highly decorated, used esp in Germany and Austria for beer.

Steinbeck /ˈstaɪnbek/ John (1902-68), American novelist. Most of his books, eg *The Grapes of Wrath*, examine the lives of poor agricultural workers in California. He was awarded the Nobel prize for literature in 1962.

stellar /ˈstelə(r)/ *adj* [esp attrib] (*fml*) of a star or stars: *stellar light.* Cf INTERSTELLAR.

stem[1] /stem/ *n* **1** (**a**) main central part of a plant, bush or tree coming up from the roots, from which the leaves or flowers grow. ⇨ illus at FUNGUS. (**b**) part of a leaf, flower or fruit that joins it to the main stalk or twig. ⇨ illus at FLOWER. **2** thin stem-shaped part of sth, esp the narrow part of a wineglass between the base and the bowl or the part of a tobacco pipe between the mouthpiece and the bowl. **3** (*grammar*) root or main part of a noun or verb from which other parts or words are made, eg by altering the endings. **4** (*fml*) main line of descent of a family. **5** (idm) **from** ˌ**stem to** ˈ**stern** from the front to the back (esp of a ship): *The liner has been refitted from stem to stern.*

▷ **stem** *v* (**-mm-**) (phr v) **stem from sth** arise from sth; have sth as its origin or cause: *discontent stemming from low pay and poor working conditions.*

-stemmed (forming compound *adjs*) having a stem or stems of the specified type: ˌ*long-*/ˌ*short-*/ˌ*thick-stemmed* ˈ*glasses* ○ *a* ˌ*straight-stemmed* ˈ*flower.*

stem[2] /stem/ *v* (**-mm-**) [Tn] restrain or stop (the flow of liquid, etc): *bandage a cut to stem the bleeding* ○ *stem the flow of water from a burst pipe* ○ (*fig*) *The government are unable to stem the tide of popular indignation.*

Sten /sten/ *n* (also ˈ**Sten gun**) type of small machine-gun, usu fired from the hip.

stench /stentʃ/ *n* (usu *sing*) very unpleasant smell: *the stench of rotting meat.*

stencil /ˈstensl/ *n* [C] **1** thin sheet of metal, cardboard, etc with a design or letters cut out of it, used for putting this design, etc onto a surface when ink or paint is applied to it. **2** design, lettering, etc produced in this way: *decorate a wall with flower stencils.* **3** waxed sheet from which a stencil is made by a typewriter: *cut a stencil.*

▷ **stencil** *v* (**-ll-**; *US* also **-l-**) [I, Tn, Tn·pr] ~ (**A on B**/**B with A**) produce (a design, lettering, etc) by using a stencil; mark (a surface) with a stencil: *Do you know how to stencil?* ○ *stencil a pattern on cloth*/*stencil cloth with a pattern.*

Stendhal /ˈstɒndɑːl; *US* stenˈdɑːl/ pen-name of Henri Beyle (1783-1842), French novelist. In works such as *La Chartreuse de Parme* he presents a psychological portrait of the 'Stendhalian hero', passionately seeking self-fulfilment and contemptuous of society.

steno /ˈstenəʊ/ *n* (*infml esp US*) = STENOGRAPHER (STENOGRAPHY).

stenography /stəˈnɒɡrəfɪ/ *n* [U] (*esp US*) = SHORTHAND (SHORT[1]).

▷ **stenographer** /-fə(r)/ (*esp US*) (*Brit* ˌ**shorthand**-ˈ**typist**) *n* person who can write shorthand or is employed to do this.

stentorian /stenˈtɔːrɪən/ *adj* (*fml*) (of a voice) loud and powerful: *stentorian tones.*

step[1] /step/ *v* (**-pp-**) [Ipr, Ip] **1** lift and put down the foot, or one foot after the other, as in walking: *step on sb's foot* ○ *step in a puddle* ○ *step forwards*/*backwards.* **2** move a short distance in this way in the direction specified: *step across a stream* ○ *step into a boat* ○ *step onto*/*off the platform* ○ *'Kindly step this way* (ie come here, follow me), *please.'* ○ (*fig*) *step into a job,* ie get one without effort. **3** (idm) **step into the** ˈ**breach** help to organize sth by filling the place of sb who is absent. **step into sb's** ˈ**shoes** take control of a responsible task or job from another person. ˈ**step on it** (*US* also **step on the** ˈ**gas**) (*infml*) go faster; increase speed (esp in a vehicle); hurry: *You'll be late if you don't step on it.* ˌ**step out of** ˈ**line** behave or act differently from what is expected: *The teacher warned them that she would punish anyone who stepped out of line.* **4** (phr v) **step aside** allow another person to take one's place, position, job, etc: *He stepped aside to let me pass.* ○ *It's time for me to step aside and let a younger person become chairman.*

step down resign (usu from an important position, job, etc) to allow another person to take one's place.

step forward present oneself (eg to offer help or information); come forward: *The organizing committee is appealing for volunteers to step forward.*

step in intervene (to help or hinder sb/sth): *If the police had not stepped in when they did there would have been serious violence.*

step out walk faster; move more quickly. **step out (with sb)** (*dated infml*) (esp in the continuous tenses) go out (with sb) for pleasure, entertainment, etc: *She's been stepping out with an American.*

step up come forward. **step sth up** increase sth; improve sth: *step up production* ○ *step up* (ie put more effort into) *the campaign for nuclear disarmament.*

□ ˈ**stepping-stone** *n* (**a**) flat stone (usu one of several) providing a place to step on when crossing a stream, river, etc on foot. (**b**) (*fig*) means or stage of progress towards achieving or attaining sth: *a first stepping-stone on the path to success.*

step[2] /step/ *n* **1** [C] act of stepping once (in walking, running, dancing, etc): *walk with slow steps* ○ *The water was deeper at every step.* ○ *He took a step towards the door.* **2** [C] distance covered by this: *retrace one's steps,* ie go back ○ *move a step closer to the fire* ○ *It's only a few steps farther.* ○ *He walked with us every step of the way.* **3** [sing] short distance: *It's only a step to the park from here.* **4** (also ˈ**footstep**) [C] (**a**) sound of sb stepping or walking: *We heard steps outside.* (**b**) way of stepping or walking (as seen or heard): *with a light cheerful step* ○ *That's Lucy — I recognize her step.* **5** [C] particular way of moving the feet in dancing (forming a pattern): *I don't know the steps for this dance.* **6** [C] any one of a series of things done in some process or course of action or development: *a step in the right direction* ○ *This has been a great step forward,* ie Much progress has been made. ○ *What's the next step?* ie What must we do next? **7** [C] level surface on which the foot is placed in going from one level to another: *a flight of steps* ○ *Mind the steps when you go down into the cellar.* ○ *They had to cut steps in the ice as they climbed.* ○ *The child was sitting on the top step.* ⇨ illus at STAIR, ⇨ Usage at STAIR. **8 steps** [pl] = STEP-LADDER: *a pair of steps* ○ *We need the steps to get into the loft.* **9** [C] rank, grade or stage in a series or on a scale; stage of promotion: *Our marketing methods put us several steps ahead of our main rivals.* ○ *When do you get your next step up?* ie When will you be promoted? **10** (idm) **break** ˈ**step** get out of step (when dancing or marching). **change step** ⇨ CHANGE[1]. **a false step** ⇨ FALSE. **in/out of step (with sb/sth)** (**a**) (in marching or dancing) putting/not putting one's correct foot on the ground at the same time as others. (**b**) conforming/not conforming to what others are doing or thinking: *He's out of step with modern ideas.* **keep step (with sb)** walk or (esp) march in step (with sb). **mind/watch one's** ˈ**step** (**a**) walk carefully. (**b**) behave or act cautiously: *You'll be in trouble if you don't watch your step.* ˌ**step by** ˈ**step** proceeding steadily from one stage to the next; gradually: [attrib] *a* ˌ*step-by-step in*ˈ*struction manual.* **take steps to do sth** take action in order to achieve a desired result: *The government is taking steps to control the rising crime rate.*

□ ˈ**step-ladder** *n* portable folding ladder that can stand on its own, with steps rather than rungs and usu a small platform at the top. ⇨ illus at LADDER.

step- *pref* related as a result of one parent's remarrying, not by blood.

□ ˈ**stepbrother**, ˈ**stepsister** *ns* male/female child of one's stepmother or stepfather by an earlier marriage.

ˈ**stepchild** *n* (*pl* **-children**) child of one's husband or wife by an earlier marriage.

ˈ**stepfather**, ˈ**stepmother** *ns* husband of one's mother/wife of one's father by a later marriage.

ˈ**step-parent** *n* later husband of one's mother or wife of one's father.

ˈ**stepson**, ˈ**stepdaughter** *ns* son/daughter of one's husband or wife by an earlier marriage. ⇨ App 8.

stephanotis /ˌstefəˈnəʊtɪs/ *n* [C, U] sweet-smelling tropical climbing plant.

Stephen[1] /ˈstiːvn/ (c 1097-1154), king of England 1135-54. He was the grandson of *William the Conqueror and stole the throne from his cousin *Matilda. He spent much of his reign resisting her attempts to recover the throne, and when he died he left England in a state of deep unrest. ⇨ App 3.

Stephen[2] /ˈstiːvn/ Saint (died c 35AD), the first Christian martyr. He was stoned to death after being charged with blasphemy.

Stephenson /ˈstiːvnsn/ George (1781-1848), English engineer. He designed the *Rocket*, the first steam locomotive, which went from Liverpool to Manchester in 1829. He is considered as the founder of railways.

steppe /step/ *n* (usu *pl*) flat grassy plain with few trees, esp in SE Europe and Siberia. Cf PAMPAS, PRAIRIE, SAVANNAH, VELD.

-ster *suff* (with *ns* and *adjs* forming *ns*) person connected with or having the quality of: *gangster* ○ *prankster* ○ *youngster.*

stereo /ˈsterɪəʊ/ *n* (*pl* **~s**) **1** [U] stereophonic sound or recording: *broadcast in stereo* ○ [attrib] *a stereo recording, record, cassette, system.* **2** stereophonic record-player, radio, etc: *Where's your stereo?* Cf MONO.

stereo- *comb form* having three dimensions; solid: *stereoscope.*

stereophonic /ˌsterɪəˈfɒnɪk/ *adj* **1** (of recorded or broadcast sound) giving the effect of naturally distributed sound, and requiring two loudspeakers placed separately: *a stereophonic recording.* **2** (of apparatus) designed for recording or reproducing sound in this way. Cf MONOPHONIC.

stereoscope /ˈsterɪəskəʊp/ *n* apparatus through which two photographs, taken from slightly different angles, can be seen as if united and with the effect of depth and solidity.

▷ **stereoscopic** /ˌsterɪəˈskɒpɪk/ *adj* giving a three-dimensional effect: *a stereoscopic image, photograph, etc.*

stereotype /ˈsterɪətaɪp/ *n* [C] **1** image, idea, character, etc that has become fixed or standardized in a conventional form without individuality (and is therefore perhaps false): *He doesn't conform to the usual stereotype of the city businessman with a dark suit and rolled umbrella.* ○ [attrib] *a play full of stereotype characters.* **2** printing-plate made from a mould of a set piece of movable printing type.

▷ **stereotyped** *adj* (*often derog*) (of images, ideas, characters, etc) fixed, unchanging or standardized; without individuality: *stereotyped images of women in advertisements.*

stereotyping *n* [U]: *sexual stereotyping.*

sterile /ˈsteraɪl; *US* ˈsterəl/ *adj* **1** (of plants, animals or humans) not producing or not able to produce seeds, young or children: *Medical tests showed that he was sterile.* **2** (of land) that cannot produce crops; barren. **3** (*fig*) (of discussion, communication, etc) producing no useful results; unproductive: *a sterile debate.* **4** free from germs, bacteria, etc: *sterile bandages* ○ *An operating theatre should be completely sterile.* Cf FERTILE.

▷ **sterility** /stəˈrɪlətɪ/ *n* [U] state or quality of being sterile.

sterilize, -ise /ˈsterəlaɪz/ *v* [Tn] **1** make (sth) sterile(4) or free from bacteria: *sterilized milk* ○

sterilized surgical instruments. **2** make (a person or an animal) unable to produce young or children (esp by removal or obstruction of the reproductive organs): *After her fourth child she decided to be have/herself sterilized.* **sterilization, -isation** /ˌsterəlaɪˈzeɪʃn; *US* -lɪˈz-/ *n* [U].

sterling /ˈstɜːlɪŋ/ *adj* [usu attrib] (of a person or his qualities, etc) admirable or excellent in quality: *her sterling qualities as an organizer.*
▷ **sterling** *n* [U] British money: *the pound sterling*, ie the British £ ○ *payable in sterling or American dollars.* Cf POUND[1] 2.
□ **the ˈsterling area** group of countries that formerly kept their reserves in British sterling currency and between which money could easily be transferred.
ˌ**sterling ˈsilver** silver which is 92.5% pure, usu combined with copper.

stern[1] /stɜːn/ *adj* (**-er, -est**) (**a**) serious and grim, not kind or cheerful; expecting to be obeyed: *a stern taskmaster, teacher, parent, etc* ○ *a stern face, expression, look, etc.* (**b**) severe and strict: *stern treatment for offenders* ○ *Police are planning sterner measures to combat crime.* ▷ **sternly** *adv.* **sternness** *n* [U].

stern[2] /stɜːn/ *n* [C] **1** back end of a ship or boat: *standing at/in the stern of the boat* ○ *walk towards the stern of a ship.* ⇨ illus at YACHT. **2** (*infml esp joc*) rear part of anything, esp a person's bottom: *Move your stern, I want to sit down.* **3** (idm) **from stem to stern** ⇨ STEM[1].

Sternberg /ˈstɜːnbɜːg/ Josef von (1894-1969), Austrian-born American film director. He is famous for his early films with Marlene *Dietrich, eg *The Blue Angel* (in German) and *The Scarlet Empress.*

Sterne /ˈstɜːn/ Lawrence (1713-68), British novelist, born in Ireland. He spent most of his life as a clergyman in Yorkshire. He achieved literary success with his *Tristram Shandy*, which parodies the conventions of the novel (then still a new form) and anticipates modern 'stream of consciousness' techniques. He wrote *A Sentimental Journey* after travelling to France and Italy.

sternum /ˈstɜːnəm/ *n* (*pl* ~**s** or **sterna** /ˈstɜːnə/) (*anatomy*) = BREASTBONE (BREAST).

steroid /ˈsterɔɪd, ˈstɪərɔɪd/ *n* (*chemistry*) any of a number of organic compounds naturally produced in the body, including certain hormones and vitamins: *He's being treated with steroids for leukaemia.* ⇨ article at DRUG.

stertorous /ˈstɜːtərəs/ *adj* (*fml*) (of breathing or a person breathing) making a loud snoring noise. ▷ **stertorously** *adv.*

stet /stet/ *v* **1** [I] (used only in the form *stet* as an instruction to a printer, etc when written beside a word that has been crossed out or corrected by mistake) let it stay or remain as written or printed. **2** (-tt-) [Tn] write 'stet' beside (sth); cancel the correction of: *The proof-reader had changed a word but I stetted it.*

stethoscope /ˈsteθəskəʊp/ *n* instrument used by doctors for listening to the beating of the heart, sounds of breathing, etc.

stetson /ˈstetsn/ *n* man's hat with a high crown and wide brim, worn esp by cowboys. ⇨ illus at HAT.

stevedore /ˈstiːvədɔː(r)/ *n* person whose work is loading and unloading ships; docker.

Stevenson /ˈstiːvnsn/ Robert Louis (1850-94), Scottish novelist. Besides his famous adventure stories such as *Treasure Island* and *Kidnapped* and his poetry for children, he wrote more serious psychological works like *The Strange Case of Dr Jekyll and Mr Hyde.* He travelled widely, recording his experiences in works such as *Travels with a Donkey.*

stew /stjuː; *US* stuː/ *v* **1** [I, Tn] (cause sth to) cook slowly in water or juice in a closed dish, pan, etc: *The meat needs to stew for several hours.* ○ *stewing steak*, ie beef suitable for stewing ○ *stewed chicken, fruit* ○ *stewed apple and custard.* **2** [I] (*infml*) be very hot; swelter: *Please open a window — we're stewing in here!* **3** (idm) **let sb ˈstew** (*infml*) leave sb to continue suffering from the unpleasant consequences of his own actions (without offering help, sympathy, etc). **stew in one's own ˈjuice** (*infml*) suffer from the unpleasant consequences of one's own actions: *I don't see why I should help her — she can stew in her own juice for a bit.*
▷ **stew** *n* **1** [C, U] (dish of) stewed meat, vegetables, etc: *make a stew* ○ *have some more stew.* **2** (idm) **get (oneself) into/be in a ˈstew (about sth)** (*infml*) become/be nervous, anxious or agitated (about sth): *He's got himself into a complete stew about his exams.*
stewed *adj* [usu pred] **1** (of tea) tasting unpleasantly strong and bitter from being left in the teapot too long. **2** (*sl*) drunk.

steward /stjʊəd; *US* ˈstuːərd/ *n* **1** person employed to manage another's property, esp a large house or estate. **2** person whose job is to arrange for the supply of food to a college, club, etc. **3** (*fem* **stewardess** /ˌstjʊəˈdes; *US* ˈstuːərdəs/) person who attends to the needs of passengers on a ship, an aircraft or a train: *the baggage/cabin/deck steward* ○ *an ˈair stewardess.* **4** official responsible for organizing a dance, race-meeting, show, public meeting, demonstration, etc: *The stewards will inspect the course to see if racing is possible.*
▷ **stewardship** *n* [U] (*fml*) position and duties of a steward.

Stewart /ˈstjuːət; *US* ˈstuːərt/ James (1908-), American actor. He came to embody the ideal of the average decent American and was a favourite actor of both *Capra (eg *It's a Wonderful Life*) and *Hitchcock (eg *Rear Window*).

Sth *abbr* South: *Sth Pole*, eg on a map.

stick[1] /stɪk/ *n* **1** [C] short thin piece of wood used as a support, as a weapon or as firewood: *collect dry sticks to make a fire* ○ *cut sticks to support peas in the garden.* **2** [C] = WALKING-STICK (WALK[1]): *The old man cannot walk without a stick.* **3** [C] implement used to hit and direct the ball in hockey, polo, etc. **4** [C] (often in compounds) long thin rod-shaped piece of a substance: *sticks of celery, chalk, charcoal, dynamite, rhubarb, wax* ○ *brass candlesticks.* **5** [C] conductor's baton. **6** [C] set of bombs dropped one after the other so that they fall in a row. **7** [C usu *pl*] ~ (**of sth**) (*infml*) piece (of furniture): *These few sticks (of furniture) are all he has left.* **8** [C] (*infml*) person of the specified type, esp a dull or an unsociable one: *He's a rather boring old stick.* **9 the sticks** [pl] (*infml*) rural areas far from cities: *live (out) in the sticks.* **10** (idm) **be in a cleft stick** ⇨ CLEAVE[1]. **the big stick** ⇨ BIG. **the carrot and the stick** ⇨ CARROT. **get the wrong end of the stick** ⇨ WRONG. **get/take stick (from sb)** (*infml*) be punished or treated severely: *The government has taken a lot of stick from the press over the cuts.* **give sb ˈstick** (*infml*) punish or treat sb severely. **a rod/stick to beat sb with** ⇨ BEAT[1]. **up sticks** ⇨ UP *v.*
□ **ˈstick insect** large insect with a body shaped like a twig.
ˈstickpin *n* (*US*) = TIE-PIN (TIE[1]).
ˈstick shift (*US*) way of operating the gears in a car by means of a gear-lever mounted on the floor.

stick[2] /stɪk/ *v* (*pt, pp* **stuck** /stʌk/) **1** (**a**) [Tn·pr, Tn·p] ~ **sth in/into/through sth**; ~ **sth in/through** push or thrust (esp sth pointed) into, through, etc sth: *Stick the fork into the potato.* ○ *The cushion was stuck full of pins.* (**b**) [Ipr, Ip] ~ **in/into/through sth**; ~ **in/through** (of sth pointed) be pushed or thrust into or through sth and remain in position: *The needle stuck in my finger.* ○ *I found a nail sticking in the tyre.* ○ *Your umbrella is sticking into my back.* **2** [I, Ipr, Ip, Tn, Tn·pr, Tn·p] (cause sth to) become fixed, joined or fastened with a sticky substance: *This glue doesn't stick very well.* ○ *The dough stuck to my fingers.* ○ *stick a stamp on a letter* ○ *stick a broken cup (back) together.* **3** [Tn·pr, Tn·p] (*infml*) put or fix (sth) in a position or place, esp quickly or carelessly: *stick up a notice on the notice-board* ○ *He stuck the pen behind his ear.* ○ *Stick the books on the table, will you?* **4** [I, Ipr] ~ (**in sth**) be or become fixed in one place and unable to move: *This drawer sticks badly.* ○ *The key stuck in the lock.* ○ *The bus stuck in the mud.* **5** [Tn] (*infml*) (in negative sentences and questions) tolerate or bear (esp an unpleasant person or situation): *I don't know how you stuck that man for so long.* ○ *I won't stick your rudeness any longer.* **6** [I] (*infml*) be or become established: *They couldn't make the charges stick*, ie prove that they were true. ○ *He got the nickname 'Fatty' on his first day at school — and unfortunately the name has stuck*, ie has been used ever since. **7** (idm) **cling/stick to sb like a leech** ⇨ LEECH. **mud sticks** ⇨ MUD. **poke/stick one's nose into sth** ⇨ NOSE[1]. **put/shove/stick one's oar in** ⇨ OAR. **stand/stick out like a sore thumb** ⇨ SORE. **stand/stick out a mile** ⇨ MILE. **stick/stop at ˈnothing** be willing to do anything to get what one wants, even if it is immoral. ˌ**stick 'em ˈup!** (*infml*) (said by an armed robber telling sb to raise his hands above his head) **stick ˈfast** be or become solidly fixed in one position and unable or unwilling to move: *His head was stuck fast in the railings.* ○ (*fig*) *He stuck fast to his theory*, ie maintained it firmly. **stick in one's craw** ⇨ CRAW. **stick in one's ˈmind** (of a memory, image, etc) be remembered for a long time: *The image of the dead child's face stuck in my mind for ages.* **stick in one's ˈthroat** (*infml*) (**a**) be difficult or impossible to accept: *It sticks in my throat to have to accept charity from them.* (**b**) (of words) be difficult or impossible to say: *I wanted to tell her, but the words stuck in my throat.* **stick one's ˈneck out** (*infml*) do sth risky: *I may be sticking my neck out* (ie in predicting sth uncertain), *but I think he's going to win.* **stick to one's ˈguns** (*infml*) refuse to change one's opinions, actions, etc in spite of criticism. **stick to one's last** not try to do things that one cannot do well.
8 (phr v) **stick around** (*infml*) stay in or near a place (waiting for sth to happen, sb to arrive, etc): *Stick around, we may need you.*
stick at sth work persistently and continuously at sth; persevere: *If we stick at it, we should finish the job today.*
stick by sb (*infml*) continue to support and be loyal to sb (esp through difficult times): *Her husband stuck by her in good times and bad.*
stick sth down (**a**) fasten (the cover, flap, etc of sth) with glue, paste, etc: *stick down (the flap of) an envelope.* (**b**) (*infml*) put or place sth down: *Stick it down anywhere you like.* (**c**) (*infml*) write sth down: *Stick down your names on the list.*
stick sth in/into sth fix, fasten sth into a book, etc with glue, paste, etc: *stick stamps into an album.*
stick sth on (sth) fix, fasten sth (to a surface) with glue, paste, etc: *Stick a label on your suitcase.*
stick (sth) out (cause sth to) project: *His ears stick out.* ○ *a girl sticking her tongue out at her brother* ○ *Don't stick your head out of the car window.* **stick it/sth out** (*infml*) continue with sth to the end, despite difficulty or unpleasantness: *He hates the job — but he's determined to stick it out because he needs the money.* **stick out for sth** (*infml*) refuse to give up until one gets sth one wants: *They're sticking out for higher wages.*
stick to sth (**a**) not abandon or change sth; keep to sth: *'Would you like some wine?' 'No, I'll stick to beer, thanks.'* ○ *We don't want to hear your opinions; stick to the facts!* ○ *That's my story and I'm sticking to it*, ie I shall maintain that it is true. (**b**) continue doing sth (despite difficulties, etc): *stick to a task until it is finished.*
stick together (*infml*) (of people) remain friendly and loyal to one another; be united: *If we keep calm and stick together, we'll be all right.*
stick up project upwards; be upright: *The branch was sticking up out of the water.* **stick sth up** (*infml*) threaten the people in (a place) with a gun in order to rob it: *stick up a bank, post office, etc.*
stick up for sb/oneself/sth support or defend sb/oneself/sth: *Don't allow those big boys to bully you; stick up for yourself!* ○ *stick up for one's rights.*
stick with sb/sth (*infml*) continue to support or retain one's connection with sb/sth: *I'm sticking with my original idea.* ○ *Stick with me and you'll be all right.*
□ **ˈsticking-plaster** (also **plaster**) *n* [C, U] (*Brit*) (*US* **adhesive ˈplaster**) (small strip of) fabric, plastic, etc that can be stuck to the skin to protect

a small wound or cut. Cf BAND-AID.
ˈ**sticking-point** *n* matter on which compromise is impossible: *We reached agreement on everything else, but staff cuts proved to be a sticking-point.*
ˈ**stick-in-the-mud** *n* (*infml derog*) person who resists change: [attrib] *stick-in-the-mud attitudes.*
ˈ**stick-on** *adj* [attrib] having glue, etc on the back; adhesive: *stick-on labels.*
ˈ**stick-up** *n* (*infml*) robbery with a gun; hold-up: *Don't move — this is a stick-up!*

sticker /ˈstɪkə(r)/ *n* **1** sticky label with a picture or message on it: *The child had stickers all over his school books.* **2** (*infml approv*) person who does not give up in spite of difficulties.

stickleback /ˈstɪklbæk/ *n* small freshwater fish with sharp spikes on its back.

stickler /ˈstɪklə(r)/ *n* ~ **for sth** person who thinks that a certain goal is very important and tries to make other people aim at it: *a stickler for accuracy, punctuality, discipline, etc.*

sticky /ˈstɪkɪ/ *adj* (**-ier**, **-iest**) **1** that sticks or tends to stick to anything which touches it: *sticky fingers covered in jam* ○ *The floor's very sticky near the cooker.* **2** (*infml*) (of weather) unpleasantly hot and damp, causing one to sweat: *a sticky August afternoon.* **3** (*infml*) unpleasant; difficult: *His dismissal was rather a sticky business for all concerned.* ○ *Their marriage is going through a sticky patch*, ie an unpleasant period of time. **4** [usu pred] (*infml*) making or likely to make objections, be unhelpful, etc: *The bank manager was a bit sticky about letting me have an overdraft.* **5** (idm) **come to a bad/sticky end** ⇨ END[1]. **sticky** ˈ**fingers** (*euph*) tendency to steal. **a sticky** ˈ**wicket** (*Brit*) (**a**) (in cricket) a wet wicket (playing-surface) which dries quickly in the sun and is difficult to bat on. (**b**) (*fig*) situation that is hard to deal with: *We're on a sticky wicket with these negotiations — they could very well fail.* ▷ **stickily** /-ɪlɪ/ *adv.* **stickiness** *n* [U].
□ **sticky** ˈ**tape** long thin strip of plastic, etc which is sticky on one side, and is used for joining things together.

stiff /stɪf/ *adj* (**-er**, **-est**) **1** not easily bent, folded, moved, changed in shape, etc: *a sheet of stiff cardboard* ○ *a stiff drawer* ○ *a stiff pair of shoes* ○ *have a stiff neck*, ie painful and difficult to move ○ *feel stiff* (ie have stiff muscles and joints) *after a long walk.* **2** thick and hard to stir; not liquid: *Stir the flour and milk to a stiff paste.* **3** (**a**) hard to do; difficult: *a stiff climb* ○ *a stiff exam.* (**b**) severe; tough: *The judge imposed a stiff sentence.* ○ *Competition is stiff.* **4** formal in manner, behaviour, etc; not friendly: *Their manner was rather stiff.* **5** (*infml*) (of a price) (too) high: *pay a stiff membership fee.* **6** (of a breeze) blowing strongly. **7** (of an alcoholic drink) strong and undiluted: *That was a shock — I need a stiff drink!* ○ *a stiff glass of rum.* **8** (idm) **(be) stiff with sth** (*infml*) have a great amount or number of sth: *The whole place was stiff with police.* **stiff/straight as a ramrod** ⇨ RAMROD. **(keep) a** ˌ**stiff upper** ˈ**lip** (show) an ability to appear calm and unworried when in pain, trouble, etc.
▷ **stiff** *adv* (*infml*) to an extreme degree; very much: *worried/scared/frozen stiff* ○ *The opera bored me stiff.*
stiff *n* (*sl*) dead body; corpse.
stiffly *adv*: *He bent down stiffly.*
stiffness *n* [U].
□ ˌ**stiff-**ˈ**necked** *adj* (*fml derog*) obstinate and proud.

stiffen /ˈstɪfn/ *v* [I, Ipr, Ip, Tn, Tn·pr, Tn·p] ~ **(sth) (up) (with sth)** (cause sth to) become stiff or stiffer: *My back has stiffened (up) overnight.* ○ *He stiffened (with terror) at the horrific sight.* ○ *cotton stiffened with starch* ○ (*fig*) *The promise of a reward might stiffen their resolve*, ie make them braver.
▷ **stiffener** /ˈstɪfnə(r)/ *n* thing used to stiffen: *a collar stiffener.*
stiffening /ˈstɪfnɪŋ/ *n* [U] material used to stiffen a piece of cloth or a garment.

stifle /ˈstaɪfl/ *v* **1** [I, Tn] feel or make (sb) unable to breathe (easily) because of lack of fresh air; suffocate: *We were stifling in that hot room with all the windows closed.* ○ *a baby stifled by a pillow* ○ *The smoke filled the room and almost stifled the firemen.* **2** [Tn] extinguish (a fire); put out: *stifle flames with a blanket.* **3** [Tn] suppress (sth); restrain: *stifle a rebellion* ○ *stifle a yawn, laugh, cry, sob, etc* ○ (*derog*) *stifle ideas, initiative.* ▷ **stifling** /ˈstaɪflɪŋ/ *adj*: *It's stifling in here; open a window!* ○ *the stifling atmosphere of the royal court, with all its petty restrictive rules.* **stiflingly** *adv*: *stiflingly hot.*

stigma /ˈstɪgmə/ *n* **1** [C, U] mark of shame or disgrace; shameful feeling or reputation: *There is less stigma attached to illegitimacy now than there used to be.* **2** [C] (*botany*) part that receives the pollen in the centre of a flower.

stigmata /ˈstɪgmətə/ *n* [pl] marks resembling the wounds made by nails on the body of Christ when he was crucified, said to have appeared on the bodies of various saints and considered as a sign of holiness by some Christians.

stigmatize, -ise /ˈstɪgmətaɪz/ *v* [Cn·n/a usu passive] ~ **sb/sth as sth** (*fml*) describe or consider sb/sth as sth disgraceful or shameful: *Society has stigmatized him as a coward and a liar.*

stile /staɪl/ *n* **1** set of steps enabling walkers to get over or through a fence, wall, etc in the country. **2** (idm) **help a lame dog over a stile** ⇨ HELP[1].

stiletto /stɪˈletəʊ/ *n* (*pl* ~**s** /-təʊz/) **1** small dagger or tool with a narrow pointed blade. **2** (usu *pl*) (*Brit infml*) woman's shoe with a stiletto heel.
□ **sti**ˌ**letto** ˈ**heel** (*Brit*) high, very narrow heel on a woman's shoe.

still[1] /stɪl/ *adj* (**-er**, **-est**) **1** (**a**) (almost) without movement or sound; quiet and calm: *still water* ○ *absolutely/completely/perfectly still* ○ *Please keep/stay/hold/sit/stand still while I take your photograph.* (**b**) without wind: *a still day in August.* ⇨ Usage at QUIET. **2** [attrib] (of drinks) not containing bubbles of gas; not sparkling or fizzy: *still cider, orange, mineral water, etc.* **3** (idm) **the still small** ˈ**voice (of conscience)** (*rhet*) a person's sense of right and wrong. **still waters run** ˈ**deep** (*saying*) a quiet or apparently calm person can have strong emotions, much knowledge or wisdom, etc.
▷ **still** *n* **1** single photograph of a scene from a cinema film: *stills from a new film*, eg as used for advertising. **2** (idm) **the still of the** ˈ**night** (*rhet*) the calmness or silence of the night.
still *v* [I, Tn] (*fml*) (cause sth to) become calm or at rest: *The waves stilled.* ○ (*fig*) *She couldn't still her anxiety.*
stillness *n* [U] quality of being still.
□ ˈ**still-birth** (**a**) birth at which the baby is born dead. (**b**) baby born dead. Cf LIVE BIRTH (LIVE[1]).
ˈ**stillborn** *adj* **1** (of a baby) dead when born. **2** (*rhet*) (of an idea or a plan) not developing further.
ˌ**still** ˈ**life** (**a**) [U] representation of non-living objects (eg fruit, flowers, etc) in painting: *I prefer landscape to still life.* (**b**) [C] (*pl* **still lifes**) picture of this type.

still[2] /stɪl/ *adv* **1** (usu in the middle position, but sometimes occuring after a direct object) up to and including the present time or the time mentioned: *She's still busy.* ○ *He still hopes/is still hoping for a letter from her.* ○ *Will you still be here when I get back?* ○ *Do you still live in London?* ○ *I still can't do it.* ○ *We could still change our minds.* ○ *I need you still; don't go yet.* **2** in spite of that; nevertheless; even so: *He's treated you badly: still, he's your brother and you should help him.* ○ *Although she felt ill, she still went to work.* **3** (**a**) (with a comparative) in a greater amount or degree; even: *Tom is tall, but Mary is taller still/still taller.* ○ *That would be nicer still/still nicer.* (**b**) in addition; besides; yet: *He came up with still more stories.* **4** (idm) ˌ**better**/ˌ**worse** ˈ**still** even better/worse.

still[3] /stɪl/ *n* apparatus for making alcoholic liquor (eg brandy, whisky) by distilling.

stillage /ˈstɪlɪdʒ/ *n* bench, frame, etc for keeping things off the floor while they are drying, waiting to be packed, etc.

stilt /stɪlt/ *n* **1** either of a pair of poles, each with a support for the foot, on which a person can walk raised above the ground: *a pair of stilts* ○ *walk on stilts.* **2** any one of a set of posts or poles on which a building, etc is supported above the ground: *a house (up) on stilts.*

stilted /ˈstɪltɪd/ *adj* (*derog*) (of a manner of talking, writing, behaving, etc) stiff and unnatural; artificial: *a rather stilted conversation.* ▷ **stiltedly** *adv.*

Stilton /ˈstɪltən/ *n* [U] white English cheese with green-blue lines of mould running through it and a strong flavour.

stimulant /ˈstɪmjʊlənt/ *n* **1** (drink containing a) drug that increases physical or mental activity and alertness: *Coffee and tea are mild stimulants.* ○ [attrib] *stimulant drugs.* **2** ~ **(to sth)** event, activity, etc that encourages greater or further activity: *It is hoped the tax cuts will act as a stimulant to further economic growth.*

stimulate /ˈstɪmjʊleɪt/ *v* **1** [Tn, Tn·pr, Cn·t] ~ **sb/sth (to sth)** make sb/sth more active or alert; arouse sb/sth: *Praise always stimulates him to further efforts/to make greater efforts.* ○ *The exhibition stimulated interest in the artist's work.* **2** [Tn, Cn·t] cause (sth) to work or function: *a hormone that stimulates ovulation.* **3** [Tn] arouse the interest and excitement of (sb): *a low level of conversation that failed to stimulate me.*
▷ **stimulating** *adj* (**a**) tending to stimulate; arousing: *the stimulating effect of coffee.* (**b**) interesting or exciting: *a stimulating discussion* ○ *I find his work very stimulating.*
stimulation /ˌstɪmjʊˈleɪʃn/ *n* [U]: *a working atmosphere lacking in stimulation.*

stimulus /ˈstɪmjʊləs/ *n* (*pl* **-li** /-laɪ/) ~ **(to sth/to do sth)** **1** thing that produces a reaction in living things: *The nutrient in the soil acts as a stimulus to growth/to make the plants grow.* ○ *Does the child respond to auditory stimuli?* ie Does he react to the sounds around him? **2** (*fml*) thing that encourages or excites sb/sth to activity, greater effort, etc: *the stimulus of fierce competition* ○ *Her words of praise were a stimulus to work harder.*

sting[1] /stɪŋ/ *n* **1** [C] sharp pointed organ of some insects (eg bees, wasps) and other animals, used for wounding and (usu) injecting poison: *The sting of a scorpion is in its tail.* **2** [C] sharp pointed hair on the surface of the leaf of some plants (eg nettles) that causes pain when touched. **3** [C] (**a**) (pain from) wounding by an animal's or a plant's sting: *That bee gave me a nasty sting.* ○ *The sting of a jellyfish is very painful.* (**b**) place of a wound made by a sting: *Her face was covered in wasp stings.* **4** [C, U] any sharp pain of body or mind; wounding effect: *ointment to take the sting out of the burn* ○ *the sting of the wind* ○ *the sting of remorse, jealousy, etc* ○ *His tongue has a nasty sting*, ie He says hurtful things. **5** [C] (*sl*) = CONFIDENCE TRICK (CONFIDENCE): *great stings like the sale of the Eiffel Tower* ○ [attrib] *a sting operation by the police*, ie to catch criminals by trickery. **6** (idm) **a** ˌ**sting in the** ˈ**tail** unpleasant feature which only becomes apparent at the end: *The announcement of the pay rise had a sting in its tail — we would have to work longer hours.*
□ ˈ**sting-ray** *n* large wide flat fish that can cause severe wounds with its stinging tail.

sting[2] /stɪŋ/ *v* (*pt, pp* **stung** /stʌŋ/) **1** [I, Tn] prick or wound (sb) with or as if with a sting; have the ability to do this: *Not all nettles sting.* ○ *a stinging wind* ○ *A bee stung me on the cheek.* ○ *The smoke is stinging my eyes.* ○ *The impact of the tennis ball really stung his leg.* ○ (*fig*) *His words certainly stung (her).* ○ *He was stung* (ie deeply upset) *by their insults.* **2** [I] feel sharp pain: *My eyes are stinging from the smoke.* ○ *His knee stung from the graze.* **3** [Tn, Tn·pr] ~ **sb (to/into sth)** provoke sb by making him angry, upset or offended: *Their taunts stung him to action/into fighting.* ○ *Her insult stung him into making a rude reply.* **4** [Tn, Tn·pr] ~ **sb (for sth)** (*infml*) charge sb too much money (for sth); swindle sb: *He was stung for £5*, ie had to pay this amount. ○ *How much did they sting you for?*
▷ **stinger** *n* (*infml*) thing that stings, esp a painful

blow.

□ ˈ**stinging-nettle** *n* = NETTLE 1.

stingy /ˈstɪndʒɪ/ *adj* (*infml*) spending, using or giving unwillingly; mean: *Don't be so stingy with the sugar!* ○ *He's very stingy about lending money.* ○ *a stingy portion of food.* ▷ **stingily** /-ɪlɪ/ *adv.* **stinginess** *n* [U].

stink /stɪŋk/ *v* (*pt* **stank** /stæŋk/ or **stunk** /stʌŋk/, *pp* **stunk**) (*infml*) **1** [I, Ipr] ~ (**of sth**) have a very unpleasant and offensive smell: *That rotten fish stinks.* ○ *Her breath stank of garlic.* **2** [I, Ipr] ~ (**of sth**) (*fig*) seem very unpleasant, bad or dishonest: *The whole business stinks (of corruption)!* ○ *What do I think of the film? It stinks* (ie is of very low quality)*!* **3** (phr v) **stink sth out** fill a place with a very unpleasant smell: *He stank the whole house out with his tobacco smoke.*

▷ **stink** *n* **1** [C] (*infml*) very unpleasant smell: *What a stink!* **2** [sing] (*sl*) trouble; fuss: *The whole business caused quite a stink.* ○ *kick up/raise/make a ˈstink (about sth).* **3** (idm) **like ˈstink** (*sl*) intensely; very hard: *working like stink.*

stinker *n* (*Brit*) **1** (*dated sl*) very unpleasant person. **2** (*infml*) thing that is very severe or difficult to do: *The biology paper* (ie in an examination) *was a real stinker.*

stinking *adj* [attrib] (*sl*) very bad or unpleasant; horrible: *I don't want your stinking money.* ○ *She'd got a stinking cold.* — *adv* (*sl*) extremely; very: *stinking rich/drunk.*

□ ˈ**stink-bomb** *n* small container which when broken gives off a very unpleasant smell (as a practical joke).

stint /stɪnt/ *v* [I, Ipr, Tn, Tn·pr] ~ **on sth**; ~ **sb/oneself** (**of sth**) (usu in negative sentences) restrict, limit sb/oneself to a small amount of (esp food): *Don't stint (on) the cream!* ○ *She stinted herself of food in order to let the children have enough.* Cf UNSTINTING.

▷ **stint** *n* **1** person's fixed or allotted amount or period of work, etc: *Everybody must do a daily stint in the kitchen.* ○ *Then I had a stint as security officer in Hong Kong.* **2** (idm) **without ˈstint** (*fml*) without holding back; generously and in large amounts: *She praised them without stint.*

stipend /ˈstaɪpend/ *n* official income (esp of a clergyman); salary.

▷ **stipendiary** /staɪˈpendɪərɪ; *US* -dɪerɪ/ *adj* receiving a stipend: *a stipendiary magistrate*, ie a paid professional magistrate. — *n* stipendiary magistrate.

stipple /ˈstɪpl/ *v* [Tn esp passive] **1** paint, draw or engrave (sth) in small dots (not in lines, etc): *a stippled effect.* **2** give a rough surface to (eg cement or plaster) by raising small peaks with a stiff brush while it is wet.

▷ **stipple** *n* [U, C] stippled surface.

stipulate /ˈstɪpjʊleɪt/ *v* [Tn, Tf] (*fml*) state (sth) clearly and firmly as a requirement: *I stipulated red paint, not black.* ○ *It was stipulated that the goods should be delivered within three days.*

▷ **stipulation** /ˌstɪpjʊˈleɪʃn/ *n* (*fml*) (**a**) [U] action of stipulating. (**b**) [C] thing stipulated; condition: *on the stipulation that…* ○ *There are several stipulations.*

stir[1] /stɜː(r)/ *v* (-rr-) **1** (**a**) [Tn, Tn·pr] ~ **sth** (**with sth**) move a spoon, etc round and round in (a liquid or some other substance) in order to mix it thoroughly: *stir one's tea with a spoon* ○ *stir the porridge, cake mixture, sauce, etc.* (**b**) [Tn·pr, Tn·p] ~ **sth into sth**; ~ **sth in** add one substance to another in this way: *stir milk into a cake mixture* ○ *stir the nuts in (well).* **2** [I, Tn] (cause sth to) move slightly: *Not a leaf was stirring*, ie There was no wind to move the leaves. ○ *A gentle breeze stirred the leaves.* ○ *Nobody was stirring in the house*, ie Everybody was resting, sleeping, etc. ○ *She's not stirring/She hasn't stirred yet*, ie She is still in bed. ○ *Stir yourself!* ie Get moving; Get busy! **3** [Tn, Tn·pr] ~ **sb** (**to sth**) excite or arouse (a person or his feelings, etc): *The story stirred the boy's imagination.* ○ *Discontent stirred the men to mutiny.* **4** [I] (esp of a feeling) begin to be felt: *Pity stirred in her heart.* ○ *Old memories stirred as she looked at the photographs.* **5** [I] (*infml derog*) cause trouble between people (esp by telling untrue stories, gossiping, etc): *Who's been stirring?* **6** (idm) **stir one's/the ˈblood** rouse sb to excitement or enthusiasm: *The music really stirred my blood.* **stir one's ˈstumps** (*infml joc*) walk or move faster; hurry. **7** (phr v) **stir sb up** rouse sb to action: *The men are being stirred up by outsiders.* ○ *He needs stirring up.* **stir sth up** cause (trouble, etc): *stir up trouble, unrest, discontent, etc among the workers.*

▷ **stir** *n* **1** [C] action of stirring (STIR[1] 1a): *Give the soup a stir.* **2** [sing] excitement; fuss; disturbance: *The news caused quite a stir in the village.*

stirrer /ˈstɜːrə(r)/ *n* (*infml derog*) person who habitually causes trouble between other people.

stirring /ˈstɜːrɪŋ/ *adj* [usu attrib] very exciting: *stirring adventure stories.* **stirringly** *adv.*

□ ˈ**stir-fry** *v* (*pt, pp* **-fried**) [Tn] cook (vegetables, meat, etc) by frying them for a short time in very hot oil while stirring them. — *n* oriental dish made in this way.

stir[2] /stɜː(r)/ *n* (idm) **in stir** (*sl*) in prison.

stirrup /ˈstɪrəp/ *n* either of a pair of D-shaped metal or leather foot-supports hanging down from a horse's saddle: *a pair of stirrups.*

□ ˈ**stirrup-cup** *n* drink (of wine, etc) given to a rider on horseback before he begins a journey, esp formerly.

ˈ**stirrup-pump** *n* small portable pump used for putting out small fires.

stitch /stɪtʃ/ *n* **1** [C] (**a**) single passing of a needle and thread into and out of cloth, etc in sewing, or into and out of skin tissue, etc in surgery. ⇨ illus at SEW. (**b**) (in knitting or crochet) one complete turn of the wool, etc over the needle. **2** [C] (**a**) loop of thread, wool, etc made in this way: *make long, short, neat, etc stitches* ○ *The cut in my hand needed five stitches.* (**b**) piece of thread used to sew tissue together in surgery: *I'm having my stitches (taken) out today*, ie removed from a wound that has healed. **3** [C, U] (esp in compounds) particular pattern of stitches or way of stitching (in sewing, knitting or crochet): *chain-stitch* ○ *knitting in purl stitch.* **4** [C usu *sing*] sudden sharp pain in the muscles at the side of the body (caused eg by running too hard): *Can we slow down and walk for a bit? I'm getting a stitch.* **5** (idm) **drop a stitch** ⇨ DROP[2]. **have not (got) a ˈstitch on/not be wearing a ˈstitch** (*infml*) be naked. **in ˈstitches** (*infml*) laughing uncontrollably: *The play had us in stitches.* **a ˌstitch in ˌtime saves ˈnine** (*saying*) if one takes action or does a piece of work immediately, it may save a lot of extra work later.

▷ **stitch** *v* **1** (**a**) [I, Tn] put stitches in or on (sth); sew: *stitching (a shirt) by candlelight.* (**b**) [Tn·pr] join or fasten (sth) with stitches: *stitch a button on a dress* ○ *stitch a zip into a skirt.* **2** (phr v) **stitch sth up** join together or close sth by stitching: *stitch up a wound/a hole* ○ *We'll soon have you* (ie your wound) *stitched up!*

stitching *n* [U] (row, group, etc of) stitches: *neat stitching* ○ *The stitching has come undone.*

stoat /stəʊt/ *n* ermine, esp when its fur is brown in the summer. Cf WEASEL.

stock[1] /stɒk/ *n* **1** [C, U] store of goods available for sale, distribution or use, in a shop, warehouse, etc: *a good stock of shoes* ○ *Our new stock of winter clothes will arrive soon.* ○ *Your order can be supplied from stock.* **2** [C, U] ~ (**of sth**) supply or amount of sth available for use, etc: *a good stock of jokes* ○ *get in stocks of coal for the winter* ○ *Stocks of food are running low.* ○ [attrib] *Stationery is kept in the stock cupboard.* **3** (also ˈ**livestock**) [U] farm animals: *buy some more stock for breeding.* **4** [C, U] money lent to a government at a fixed rate of interest: *government stock.* **5** (**a**) [U] capital of a business company. (**b**) [C usu *pl*] portion of this held by an investor (different from *shares* in that it is not issued in fixed amounts): *invest in stocks and shares.* **6** [U] person's line of ancestry; family line (of the type specified by the *adj*): *a woman of Irish stock* ○ *born of farming stock*, ie in a family of farmers. **7** [U] (*fml*) person's standing or reputation in the opinion of others: *His stock is high*, ie He is well thought of. **8** [U] raw material ready to be used in manufacturing sth: ˈ*paper stock*, eg rags, wood, etc to be made into paper **9** [C, U] liquid made by stewing bones, meat, fish vegetables, etc in water, used as a basis for soups gravy, etc: *sauce made with chicken stock.* **10** [C] base, support or handle of an instrument, a tool etc: *the stock of a rifle/plough/whip.* ⇨ illus at GUN **11** [C] lower and thicker part of a tree trunk. **12** [C] growing plant onto which a cutting is grafted. **13 stocks** [pl] framework supporting a ship while it is being built or repaired. **14 stocks** [pl] wooden framework with holes for the feet (and sometimes also the hands) in which wrongdoers were formerly locked, as a punishment: *be put in the stocks.* Cf PILLORY. **15** [C] (**a**) wide band of stiff material formerly worn around the neck by men (**b**) type of cravat worn as part of a formal riding kit. (**c**) piece of black or purple fabric worn hanging from a clergyman's collar over the front of his shirt. **16** [C, U] type of garden plant with single or double brightly coloured and sweet-smelling flowers. **17** (idm) (**be**) **in/out of ˈstock** available/not available (in a shop, etc): *The book is in/out of stock.* ○ *Have you any grey pullovers in stock?* **lock, stock and barrel** ⇨ LOCK[2]. **on the ˈstocks** being constructed or prepared: *Our new model is already on the stocks and will be available in the autumn.* **take stock** (**of sth**) examine and make a list of all the goods (in a shop, warehouse, etc). **take stock** (**of sb/sth**) review, assess and form an opinion (about a situation, sb's abilities, etc): *After a year in the job, she decided it was time to take stock (of her situation).*

▷ **stock** *adj* [attrib] **1** usually kept in stock and regularly available: *stock sizes* ○ *one of our stock items.* **2** commonly used; used too much (and therefore not interesting, effective, etc): *a stock argument* ○ *stock questions/answers* ○ *She's tired of her husband's stock jokes.*

□ ˈ**stock-breeder** *n* farmer who raises or breeds livestock.

ˈ**stockbroker** (also **broker**) *n* person who buys and sells stocks and shares for clients. ˈ**stockbroking** *n* [U]: *He's in stockbroking.* ○ [attrib] *a stockbroking friend of mine.*

ˈ**stock-car** *n* **1** ordinary car that has been specially strengthened for use in racing where deliberate bumping is allowed. **2** (*US*) railway truck for carrying cattle. ˈ**stock-car racing** racing of stock-cars(1).

ˈ**stock certificate** (*US*) certificate for the purchase of shares (SHARE[1] 3).

ˈ**stock company 1** company of actors who have a repertoire of plays which they perform at a particular theatre. **2** (also **joint-ˈstock company**) group of people who carry on a business with money contributed by all.

ˈ**stock-cube** *n* cube of dried stock[1](9) used for making soup, etc: *beef stock-cubes.*

ˈ**stock exchange** place where stocks and shares are publicly bought and sold; (group of professional dealers engaged in) such business. Dealing in shares was at first very informal: the London Stock Exchange grew out of meetings of share traders in coffee-houses in the 18th century; the New York Exchange grew out of an open market in Lower *Wall Street. Nowadays trading is computerized and orders for buying and selling are made over the telephone. Modern telecommunications allow brokers to follow the activity of other markets all over the world: *The London Stock Exchange is in turmoil today.* ○ *lose money on the stock exchange.* ⇨ article at FINANCE.

ˈ**stockholder** *n* (*esp US*) person who owns stocks and shares.

ˌ**stock-in-ˈtrade** *n* [U] **1** everything needed for a particular trade or occupation. **2** (*fig*) words, actions, behaviour, etc commonly used, displayed, etc by a particular person: *Facetious remarks are part of his stock-in-trade.*

ˈ**stockjobber** *n* **1** (in former times) member of a stock exchange who bought and sold stocks and shares so as to take advantage of variations in their prices, dealing with stockbrokers but not with the general public. **2** (*US derog*) = STOCKBROKER.

ˈstockman /-mən/ *n* (*pl* **-men** /-mən/) (*Austral*) man in charge of livestock.

ˈstock-market *n* stock exchange or the business conducted there: *dealings on the stock-market* ○ [attrib] *stock-market prices*.

ˈstockpile *n* large supply of goods, materials, etc collected and kept for future use (esp because they may become difficult to obtain, eg in a war). — *v* [Tn] collect and keep (a supply of goods, etc) in this way: *stockpiling nuclear weapons*.

ˈstock-pot *n* pot in which stock[1](9) is made or kept.

ˈstock-taking *n* [U] **1** making a list of all the stock[1](1) in a shop, etc: *Next week we shall be closed for stock-taking.* **2** review of one's situation, position, resources, etc.

ˈstockyard *n* enclosure where cattle are kept temporarily or sorted, eg at a market, before being killed or sold or moved elsewhere.

stock[2] /stɒk/ *v* **1** [Tn] keep (goods) in stock; keep a supply of: *Do you stock raincoats?* ○ *They stock all sizes.* **2** [Tn, Tn·pr] ~ **sth (with sth)** provide or equip sth with goods, livestock or a supply of sth: *stock a shop with goods* ○ *a shop well stocked with the latest fashions* ○ *a badly stocked library* ○ *(fig) He has a memory well stocked with facts.* **3** (phr v) **stock up (on/with sth) (for sth)** collect and keep supplies (of sth for a particular occasion or purpose): *As soon as they heard about possible food shortages, they began to stock up.* ○ *stock up on fuel for the winter* ○ *stock up with food for Christmas.*

▷ **stockist** /ˈstɒkɪst/ *n* person or business firm that stocks certain goods for sale: *available from all good stockists.*

stockade /stɒˈkeɪd/ *n* line or wall of strong upright (esp wooden) posts, built as a defence.

▷ **stockade** *v* [Tn usu passive] defend (an area) with a stockade.

Stockhausen /ˈʃtɒkhaʊzn/ Karlheinz (1928-), German composer. He is one of the leading composers of modern experimental music, often using electronic instruments and allowing chance and the judgement of the performers to contribute to a piece as it is played.

stockinet (also **stockinette**) /ˌstɒkɪˈnet/ *n* [U] fine elastic machine-knitted material, used for underwear, etc.

stocking /ˈstɒkɪŋ/ *n* **1** either of a pair of tight-fitting coverings for the feet and legs, reaching to or above the knee: *a pair of nylon/silk/woollen/cotton stockings.* Cf TIGHTS. **2** (idm) **in one's stocking(ed) ˈfeet** wearing socks or stockings but not shoes.

□ **ˈstocking filler** small gift, eg a toy or chocolate bar, that can be put into the stocking that a child hangs at the foot of the bed at Christmas.

ˈstocking mask (part of a) nylon stocking or pair of tights worn over the face by a robber, kidnapper, etc to disguise himself.

stock-still /ˌstɒk ˈstɪl/ *adv* motionlessly: *remain standing stock-still.*

stocky /ˈstɒkɪ/ *adj* (**-ier**, **-iest**) (usu of people) short, strong and solid in appearance: *stocky legs* ○ *a stocky little man.* ▷ **stockily** *adv*: *a stockily built man.* **stockiness** *n* [U].

stodge /stɒdʒ/ *n* [U] (*infml usu derog*) food that is heavy, solid and not easy to digest.

▷ **stodgy** /stɒdʒɪ/ *adj* (**-ier**, **-iest**) (*infml derog*) **1** (of food) heavy, solid and difficult to digest: *stodgy school meals.* **2** (of a book, etc) written in a heavy uninteresting way. **3** (of a person) uninteresting; not lively; dull. **stodgily** *adv.* **stodginess** *n* [U].

stoic /ˈstəʊɪk/ *n* **1** (*fml*) person who has great self-control and who endures pain, discomfort or misfortune without complaining or showing signs of feeling it. **2 Stoic** (follower of) any of the ancient Greek philosophers teaching Stoicism.

▷ **stoical** /-kl/ (also **stoic**) *adj* **1** (*fml*) of or like a stoic; enduring pain, etc without complaint: *a very stoical response to hardship.* **2 Stoic** of or like the Stoics. **stoically** /-klɪ/ *adv.*

stoicism /ˈstəʊɪsɪzəm/ *n* [U] **1** (*fml*) stoical behaviour: *She showed great stoicism during her husband's final illness.* ○ *They reacted to the appalling weather with typical British stoicism.* **2 Stoicism** ancient Greek philosophy founded by *Zeno[2] (early 3rd century BC). It taught that virtue is based on knowledge and is the highest good. The virtuous are wise and live in accordance with nature and fate, accepting pleasure and pain as natural elements in life.

stoke /stəʊk/ *v* **1** [Tn, Tn·pr, Tn·p] ~ **sth (up) (with sth)** put (coal or some other fuel) on the fire of a furnace, an engine, etc: *stoke the boiler with coal.* **2** (phr v) **stoke up (with sth)** (**a**) stoke a fire, etc: *The caretaker stokes up twice a day.* (**b**) (*infml*) fill oneself with food; eat a lot: *You should stoke up now — you may not get another meal today.*

▷ **stoker** *n* **1** person who stokes a furnace, etc, esp on a ship. **2** mechanical device for doing this.

□ **ˈstokehole** (also **ˈstokehold**) *n* place where a ship's furnaces are stoked.

Stoker /ˈstəʊkə(r)/ Abraham ('Bram') (1847-1912), Irish novelist. The only work of his which remains popular is *Dracula*, which has undergone many adaptations, esp in the cinema.

STOL /ˌes tiː əʊ ˈel *or, in informal use,* stɒl/ *abbr* (of aircraft) short take-off and landing: *a STOL plane* ○ *flying STOLs.* Cf VTOL.

stole[1] /stəʊl/ *n* **1** women's garment like a wide scarf, worn around the shoulders. **2** strip of silk or other material worn (round the neck with the ends hanging down in front) by some Christian priests during services.

stole[2] *pt* of STEAL.

stolen *pp* of STEAL.

stolid /ˈstɒlɪd/ *adj* (*usu derog*) (of a person) not easily excited; showing little or no emotion or interest: *He conceals his feelings behind a rather stolid manner.* ▷ **stolidly** *adv.* **stolidity** /stəˈlɪdətɪ/ (also **stolidness**) *n* [U].

stomach /ˈstʌmək/ *n* **1** [C] bag-like organ of the body into which food passes when swallowed and in which the first part of digestion occurs: *It's unwise to swim on a full stomach*, ie when one has just eaten a meal. ○ *I don't like going to work on an empty stomach*, ie without having eaten anything. ○ *He felt an aching feeling in (the pit of) his stomach.* ○ [attrib] *a stomach upset, disorder, etc.* ⇨ illus at DIGESTIVE. **2** [C] (*infml*) front part of the body between the chest and thighs; abdomen: *He hit me in the stomach.* **3** [U] (**a**) appetite for food: *have a very small stomach.* (**b**) ~ **for sth** (*fig*) desire or eagerness for sth: *I had no stomach for a fight.* **4** (idm) **sb's eyes are bigger than his stomach** ⇨ EYE[1]. **sick to one's stomach** ⇨ SICK. **a strong stomach** ⇨ STRONG. **turn one's ˈstomach** cause sb to be disgusted or revolted: *The film about eye operations turned my stomach.*

▷ **stomach** *v* [Tn] (esp in negative sentences or questions) **1** eat (sth) without feeling ill: *I can't stomach seafood.* **2** endure (sth); tolerate: *How could you stomach all the violence in the film?*

□ **ˈstomach-ache** *n* [C] pain in the stomach or the bowels.

ˈstomach-pump *n* pump with a flexible tube, inserted into the stomach through the mouth and used to remove (esp poisonous) substances from the stomach or to force liquid into it.

stomp /stɒmp/ *v* [Ipr, Ip] ~ **about, around, off, etc** (*infml*) move, walk, dance, etc with a heavy step (in the specified direction): *stomp about noisily* ○ *She slammed the door and stomped (off) out of the house.* ⇨ Usage at STUMP.

stone /stəʊn/ *n* **1** [U] (often used attributively or in compounds) hard solid mineral substance that is not metallic; (type of) rock: *ˈsandstone* ○ *ˈlimestone* ○ *a house built of grey ˈstone* ○ *stone walls, buildings, floors, statues*, ie made or built of stone ○ *What type of stone is this?* **2** [C] piece of rock of any shape, usu small in size, broken or cut off: *a pile of stones* ○ *a road covered with stones* ○ *Small stones rolled down the hillside as they ran up.* ○ *She picked up the stone and threw it into the river.* **3** [C] (usu in compounds) piece of stone shaped for a particular purpose: *a ˈgravestone* ○ *ˈstepping-stones* ○ *ˈpaving stones* ○ *ˈtombstones* ○ *ˈmillstones.* **4** (also **precious ˈstone**) [C] jewel or gem: *a sapphire ring with six small stones.* **5** (also *esp US* **pit**) [C] (sometimes in compounds) hard shell containing the nut or seed inside some fruits (eg apricots, olives, plums, cherries, peaches): *a damson stone.* ⇨ illus at FRUIT. **6** [C] (esp in compounds) small hard object that has formed in the bladder or kidney and causes pain: *an operation to remove ˈkidney stones.* Cf GALLSTONE (GALL[1]). **7** [C] (*pl* unchanged) (*abbr* **st**) (*Brit*) unit of weight; 14 pounds: *He weighs 10 stone.* ○ *two stone of potatoes.* ⇨ App 10. **8** (idm) **blood out of/from a stone** ⇨ BLOOD[1]. **hard as nails/stone** ⇨ HARD[1]. **a heart of stone** ⇨ HEART. **kill two birds with one stone** ⇨ KILL. **leave no stone unturned** ⇨ LEAVE[1]. **people in glasshouses shouldn't throw stones** ⇨ PEOPLE. **sink like a stone** ⇨ SINK[1]. **a ˈstone's throw** a very short distance: *We live a stone's throw from/within a stone's throw of here.* **a rolling stone gathers no moss** ⇨ ROLL[2].

▷ **stone** *v* [Tn] **1** throw stones at (sb) (esp formerly as a punishment): *stoned to death.* **2** remove the stones (STONE 5) from (fruit): *stoned dates.* **3** (idm) **ˌstone the ˈcrows** (*Brit sl*) (used as an exclamation of surprise, shock, disgust, etc): *Well, stone the crows, he's done it again!* **stoned** *adj* [usu pred] (*sl*) (**a**) very drunk. (**b**) under the influence of (usu soft) drugs.

ˈstoneless *adj* without stones: *stoneless fruit.*

□ **the ˈStone Age** very early period of human history when tools and weapons were made of stone, not metal. Stone was the earliest material to be used for knives, axes and similar tools, along with horn and bone. Tools show an increasing degree of precision and efficiency throughout the Stone Age, which is divided into the palaeolithic, mesolithic and neolithic periods. They are not precise periods of historical time, as progress towards metal tools was faster in some areas than in others: [attrib] *Stone Age settlements.*

ˈstonechat *n* small black-and-white European bird.

ˌstone-ˈcold *adj* completely cold: *The body was stone-cold.* ○ *This soup is stone-cold.* **ˌstone-cold ˈsober** completely sober and not under the influence of alcoholic drinks.

ˌstone-ˈdead *adj* completely dead.

ˌstone-ˈdeaf *adj* completely deaf.

ˈstone-fruit *n* [C, U] fruit of a type that contains stones (STONE 5).

ˈstonemason *n* person who cuts and prepares stone or builds with stone.

ˈstoneware *n* [U] pottery made from clay containing a small amount of flint: [attrib] *stoneware jugs.*

ˈstonework *n* [U] stone parts of a building, etc, esp when decoratively fashioned; masonry: *a church with beautiful stonework.*

Stonehenge

Stonehenge /ˌstəʊnˈhendʒ/ Stone-Age monument on Salisbury Plain, Wiltshire, S England. It consists of a double ring of stones; the inner ring is made up of arches. It was built between about 3000 and 1500 BC, probably for religious festivals. Its main axis is in line with the sunrise on Midsummer's Day. ⇨ illus. ⇨ article at ARCHITECTURE.

stonewall /ˌstəʊnˈwɔːl/ *v* **1** [I, Tn] (*infml esp Brit*) obstruct (a discussion, etc) by non-committal, evasive or very long replies: *a deliberate attempt to stonewall (the debate).* **2** [I] (in cricket) bat without trying to score runs. ▷ **stonewaller** *n.* **stonewalling** *n* [U].

stony /ˈstəʊnɪ/ *adj* (**-ier**, **-iest**) **1** full of, covered in or having stones: *a stony road* ○ *a river with a stony bottom.* **2** hard, cold, and unsympathetic: *a stony stare, glare, look, gaze, etc* ○ *maintaining a stony silence* ○ *ˌstony-ˈhearted.* **3** [pred] (*sl*) completely without money; penniless. **4** (idm) **flat/stony broke** ⇨ BROKE².

▷ **stonily** /-ɪlɪ/ *adv* in a stony(2) manner: *stonily polite* ○ *She stared stonily in front of her.*

stood *pt, pp* of STAND².

stooge /stu:dʒ/ *n* **1** (*theatre sl*) comedian's assistant, used as the object of his jokes. **2** (*infml derog*) (**a**) person used by another to do routine (usu unpleasant) work. (**b**) person whose actions are entirely controlled by another: *She's fed up with being her husband's stooge.*

▷ **stooge** *v* [Ipr] ~ **for sb** act as a stooge for (a comedian on stage).

stool /stu:l/ *n* **1** (often in compounds) seat without a back or arms, usu for one person: *a ˈbar stool* ○ *a ˈpiano stool* ○ *sitting on stools around the table.* ⇨ illus at FURNITURE. **2** = FOOTSTOOL (FOOT¹). **3** (usu *pl*) (*medical or fml*) (piece of) solid waste from the body; faeces. **4** (idm) **fall between two ˈstools** fail to be or take either of two satisfactory alternatives: *The author seems uncertain whether he is writing a comedy or a tragedy, so the play falls between two stools.*

□ **ˈstool-pigeon** *n* (*infml*) person who acts as a decoy, esp to trap a criminal.

stoop¹ /stu:p/ *v* **1** (**a**) [I, Ipr, Ip] ~ (**down**) bend forward and down: *She stooped low to look under the bed.* ○ *He stooped under the low beam.* ○ *stoop (down) to pick sth up.* (**b**) [Tn] bend (a part of the body) forward and down: *stoop one's head to get into the car.* **2** [I] have the head and shoulders habitually bent over: *He's beginning to stoop with age*, ie as he gets older. **3** (idm) **stoop so low (as to do sth)** lower one's moral standards so far (as to do sth): *He tried to make me accept a bribe — I hope I would never stoop so low.* **4** (phr v) **stoop to sth/doing sth** lower one's moral standards to do sth: *He'd stoop to anything*, ie He has no moral standards. ○ *I would never stoop to cheating.*

▷ **stoop** *n* (usu *sing*) stooping position of the body: *walk with a slight stoop.*

stoop² /stu:p/ *n* (*US*) porch or terrace in front of a house.

stop¹ /stɒp/ *v* (**-pp-**) **1** [Tn] put an end to (the movement, progress, operation, etc of a person or thing); cause to halt or pause: *stop a car, train, bicycle, etc* ○ *Rain stopped play*, eg in cricket. ○ *He stopped the machine and left the room.* ○ *The earthquake stopped all the clocks.* ○ (*fig joc*) *He stopped* (ie was hit by) *a bullet in the war.* **2** [Tn, Tg] cease or discontinue (sth); leave off: *stop work* ○ *Stop it!* ie Don't do that! ○ *He never stops talking.* ○ *She's stopped smoking.* ○ *Will you stop making that horrible noise!* ○ *Has it stopped raining yet?* ○ *Supplies have stopped reaching us.* **3** [Tn, Tn·pr, Tsg, Tng] ~ **sb/sth (from) doing sth** prevent sb from doing sth or sth from happening: *I'm sure he'll go, there's nothing to stop him.* ○ *You can't stop our going/us (from) going if we want to.* ○ *Can't you stop your son from getting into trouble?* ○ *I only just managed to stop myself from shouting at him.* ○ *We bandaged his wound but couldn't stop it bleeding/stop the bleeding.* **4** (**a**) [I] refrain from continuing; cease working, moving, etc: *The rain has stopped.* ○ *The clock stopped.* ○ *His heart has stopped.* (**b**) [I, Ipr] come to rest; halt or pause: *They stopped for a while to admire the scenery.* ○ *Do the buses stop here?* ○ *The train stopped at the station.* ⇨ Usage at AND. **5** [Tn, Tn·pr, Tn·p] ~ **sth (up) (with sth)** fill or close (a gap, hole, etc) by plugging or obstructing; block sth: *stop a leak in a pipe, a gap in a hedge* ○ *stop up a mouse hole.* ○ *stop one's ears*, ie cover them with one's hands to avoid hearing sth. **6** [Tn] fill a cavity in (a tooth). **7** [Tn, Tn·pr] ~ **sth (out of/from sth)** refuse to give or allow (sth normally given); keep sth back: *stop a cheque*, ie order a bank not to cash it ○ *The cost was stopped out of* (ie deducted from) *my wages.* **8** [I, Ipr] (*Brit infml*) stay (esp for a short time): *Are you stopping (for supper)?* ○ *I'm stopping (at) home tonight.* ○ *We stopped at a campsite for a week.* **9** [Tn] (*music*) press down (a string or key) or block (a hole on a musical instrument) to produce the note wanted. **10** (idm) **the buck stops here** ⇨ BUCK⁴. **stick/stop at nothing** ⇨ STICK². **stop ˈdead (in one's ˈtracks)** stop very suddenly. **stop the rot** halt or reverse a process of becoming worse: *After the team lost six matches in a row, a new manager was appointed to stop the rot.* **stop short of sth/doing sth** be unwilling to go beyond a certain limit in one's actions: *He can be ruthless in getting what he wants, but I believe he would stop short of blackmail.* **stop the ˈshow** receive so much attention, applause, etc from an audience that the performance, etc cannot continue. **11** (phr v) **stop by** (also **stop round**) (*esp US*) make a short visit to sb's house, etc; call in: *Ask him to stop by for a chat.* **stop off (at/in...)** make a short break in a journey (to do sth): *stop off at the pub on the way home.* **stop over (at/in...)** break one's journey (esp when travelling by air) for a stay: *stop over in Rome for two days en route for the Middle East.* **stop up** not go to bed until later than usual: *stop up (late) to watch a film on TV.*

▷ **stoppage** /ˈstɒpɪdʒ/ *n* [C] **1** interruption of work in a factory, etc, esp because of a strike: *another stoppage at the car plant.* **2 stoppages** [pl] amount of money deducted by an employer from wages and salaries, for tax, national insurance, etc: *There's not much money left after stoppages.* **3** act of cancelling or withholding (payment, holidays, etc): *stoppage of leave*, eg in the army as a punishment. **4** state of being blocked; blockage or obstruction: *a stoppage in a gas pipe.*

stopping *n* filling for a hole in a tooth.

□ **ˈstopcock** *n* valve or tap that can regulate the flow of liquid or gas through a pipe: *If a water-pipe bursts turn off the stopcock immediately.*

ˈstopgap *n* person or thing that acts as a temporary substitute for another: [attrib] *stopgap measures in an emergency.*

ˌstop-ˈgo *n* [esp attrib] (*Brit*) deliberate alternating of periods of inflation and deflation: *a government's ˌstop-go ecoˈnomic policy.*

ˈstop-light *n* (*US*) **1** = TRAFFIC LIGHT (TRAFFIC). **2** = BRAKE LIGHT (BRAKE).

ˈstopover *n* (**a**) break in a journey (esp for one night). (**b**) place where one does this.

ˈstopping train train that stops at many stations between main stations.

ˌstop-ˈpress *n* [U] (*Brit*) late news inserted into a newspaper after printing has begun; space into which this is inserted: *read sth in the stop-press* ○ [attrib] *a ˈstop-press item.*

ˈstop-watch *n* watch with a hand that can be stopped and started by pressing buttons, used to time races, etc very accurately.

stop² /stɒp/ *n* [C] **1** act of stopping or state of being stopped: *make a short stop on a journey* ○ *The train came/was brought to a sudden stop.* ○ *The train goes from London to Leeds with only two stops.* ○ *Production at the factory has come to a complete/full stop.* **2** place where a bus, train, etc stops regularly (eg to allow passengers to get on or off): *Where is the nearest bus-stop?* ○ *Which stop do I get off at?* ○ *Is this a request stop?* **3** punctuation mark, esp a full stop (.). **4** (*music*) (**a**) row of pipes in an organ providing tones of one quality. (**b**) knob or lever controlling these. **5** (*music*) device for covering any of certain holes on a wind instrument (eg a flute) in order to change the pitch. **6** (in a camera) device for regulating the size of the aperture through which light reaches the lens. **7** (*phonetics*) consonant sound produced by the sudden release of air that has been held back (eg /p, b, k, g, t, d/); plosive. **8** (esp in compounds) device or object that regulates or stops the movement of sth: *The door was held open by a doorstop.* **9** (idm) **pull out all the stops** ⇨ PULL². **put an end/a stop to sth** ⇨ END¹.

Stopes /stəʊps/ Marie (1880-1958), Scottish botanist and pioneer of birth control. After the breakdown of her first marriage, she devoted herself to work in family planning and sex education.

Stoppard /ˈstɒpɑ:d/ Tom (1937-), Czech-born British playwright. His plays (eg *Rosencrantz and Guildenstern are Dead* and *Jumpers*) are famous for their intellectual wit and philosophical tone.

stopper /ˈstɒpə(r)/ (*US* **plug**) *n* object that fits into and closes an opening, esp the top of a bottle or pipe: *put the stopper back into a bottle.* ⇨ illus at BOTTLE.

▷ **stopper** *v* [Tn] close (sth) with a stopper.

storage /ˈstɔ:rɪdʒ/ *n* [U] **1** (**a**) storing of goods, etc: [attrib] *storage space* ○ *a loft with large storage capacity.* (**b**) space used or available for this: *fish kept in cold* (ie refrigerated) *storage* ○ *put furniture in storage* ○ [attrib] *storage tanks*, eg for oil. **2** cost of storing things: *have to pay storage.*

□ **ˈstorage battery**, **ˈstorage cell** battery or cell used for storing electricity.

ˈstorage heater electric radiator that stores heat (accumulated during periods when electricity is cheaper).

store /stɔ:(r)/ *n* **1** [C] quantity or supply of sth kept for use as needed: *lay in* (ie buy and keep) *stores of coal for the winter* ○ *have a good store of food in the house.* **2** [C usu *sing*] ~ (**of sth**) large accumulated quantity or amount: *a library with a store of rare books* ○ *She keeps a store of amusing stories in her head.* **3 stores** [pl] (**a**) goods, etc of a particular type, or for a special purpose: *military stores* ○ *government stationery stores.* (**b**) supply of such goods or place where they are kept: *available from stores.* **4** [C] (*computing*) device in a computer for storing and retrieving information. **5** [C] (*esp US*) (often in compounds) shop: *the liquor store* ○ *the drugstore.* **6** [C] (esp large) shop selling many different types of goods: *a big department store* ○ *a general store in the village.* **7** (idm) **in store (for sb/sth)** (**a**) kept ready for (future) use: *He always keeps several cases of wine in store.* (**b**) coming in the future; about to happen: *I can see trouble in store.* ○ *There's a surprise in store for you.* **set (great/little/no/not much) store by sth** consider sth to be of (great/little, etc) importance or value: *I don't set (much) store by weather forecasts.*

▷ **store** *v* **1** [Tn, Tn·pr, Tn·p] ~ **sth (up/away)** collect and keep sth for future use: *a squirrel storing (up) food for the winter* ○ *I've stored my winter clothes (away) in the attic.* **2** [Tn] put (furniture, etc) in a warehouse, etc to be kept safe: *They've stored their furniture while they go abroad.* **3** [esp passive: Tn, Tn·pr] ~ **sth (with sth)** stock sth (with sth useful); supply or fill sth: *a gallery stored with fine paintings* ○ *a mind well stored with facts.* **4** [Tn] hold (sth); contain: *This cupboard can store enough food for a month.* **5** [Tn] (**a**) (of a computer) keep (data) in a memory so that it can be made available to a user when required. (**b**) (of a computer user) put (data) into a computer file.

□ **ˈstorekeeper** *n* (*esp US*) = SHOPKEEPER (SHOP).

ˈstorehouse (**a**) building where things are stored. (**b**) (*fig*) person, place or thing having or containing much information: *This book is a storehouse of useful information.*

ˈstore-room *n* room used for storing things, esp in a house.

storey (*US* **story**) /ˈstɔ:rɪ/ *n* (*pl* **storeys**; *US* **stories**) **1** section of a building with rooms all at the same level; floor: *a house of two storeys* ○ *live on the third storey of a block of flats* ○ *a five-storey building* ○ *a multi-storey car-park.* **2** (idm) **the top storey** ⇨ TOP¹.

▷ **-storeyed** (*US* **-storied**) /-ˈstɔ:rɪd/ (forming compound adjs) having the number of storeys specified: *a six-storeyed building.*

stork /stɔ:k/ *n* large (usu white) water-bird with a long beak, neck and legs, sometimes building its nest on the tops of high buildings.

storm /stɔ:m/ *n* **1** [C] (often in compounds) occasion of violent weather conditions, with strong winds and usu rain or snow or thunder, etc: *a ˈthunder-/ˈwind-/ˈrain-/ˈsnow-/ˈdust-/ˈsand-storm* ○ *A storm is brewing*, ie coming. ○ [attrib] *a storm* *warning* ○ *cross the Channel in a storm* ○ *The forecast says there will be storms.* **2** [C] ~ **(of sth)** sudden violent outburst or display of strong feeling: *a storm of anger, weeping, cheering, abuse, criticism* ○ *His proposal was met by a storm of protest.* **3 storms** [pl] (*US infml*) storm-door or storm-window. **4** (idm) **any port in a storm** ⇨ PORT[1]. **the calm before the storm** ⇨ CALM *n.* **the eye of the storm** ⇨ EYE[1]. **ride out/weather the/a 'storm (a)** (*nautical*) endure and survive a storm (esp at sea). **(b)** survive opposition, criticism, difficult circumstances, etc without being seriously affected. **a storm in a 'teacup** a lot of fuss, excitement, disturbance, etc about sth unimportant. **take sth/sb by 'storm (a)** capture sth by a violent and sudden attack: *take a city by storm.* **(b)** (of a performer or performance) have great and rapid success with (people or a place); captivate sth/sb: *The play took the audience/Paris by storm.*

▷ **storm** *v* **1** [I, Ipr, Tn] ~ **(at sb)** express violent anger; shout angrily and loudly: *'Get out of here!' he stormed.* **2** [Ipr, Ip] ~ **about, around, off, etc** move or walk in a very angry or violent manner in the direction specified: *storming round the house* ○ *storm out of the room* ○ *After the argument she stormed off.* **3** [Ipr, Ip, Tn·pr, Tn·p] ~ **(one's way) across, in, through, etc** attack violently and force a way across, etc (a place): *Three soldiers stormed into the house.* ○ *They stormed (their way) in.* **4** [Tn] capture (sth) by a sudden and violent attack: *storm a castle, fort, building, etc.*

stormy *adj* (**-ier, -iest**) **1** marked by or having strong winds, heavy rain, snow, hail, etc: *stormy weather* ○ *a stormy night* ○ *The day was cold and stormy.* **2** full of strong feeling, violent outbursts, anger, etc: *a stormy discussion, meeting, etc* ○ *stormy scenes during the debate.* **stormily** *adv.* **storminess** *n* [U]. **ˌstormy 'petrel 1** = STORM PETREL. **2** person whose presence seems to attract trouble.

□ **'storm-bound** *adj* prevented by storms from continuing or starting a journey, going out or receiving supplies: *storm-bound ships in harbour* ○ *The island was storm-bound for a week.*

'storm-centre (a) area at the centre of a storm. **(b)** (*fig*) centre of a disturbance or trouble.

'storm-cloud *n* **(a)** large black cloud coming with a storm or indicating that a storm is likely to happen. **(b)** (usu *pl*) (*fig*) sign of sth dangerous or threatening: *storm-clouds of war gathering over Europe.*

'storm-door *n* (*esp US*) door fitted outside another to protect against cold, rain, wind, etc.

'storm-lantern *n* = HURRICANE LAMP (HURRICANE).

ˌstorm 'petrel (also **stormy petrel**) type of small black and white seabird of the N Atlantic and Mediterranean, said to be active before a storm.

'stormproof *adj* that can resist storms: *This house isn't exactly stormproof — the roof leaks!*

'storm-tossed *adj* damaged or blown about by storms.

'storm-trooper *n* soldier specially trained for violent and ruthless attacks.

'storm-window *n* (*esp US*) window fitted outside another to protect against cold, rain, wind, etc.

Stormont /'stɔːmɒnt/ eastern suburb of *Belfast. Stormont Castle is the administrative centre of Northern Ireland and was the seat of its parliament between 1921 and 1972. ⇨ article at IRELAND.

story[1] /'stɔːrɪ/ *n* **1** ~ **(about/of sb/sth) (a)** account of past events, incidents, etc: *the Christmas story* ○ *the story of Martin Luther King* ○ *stories of ancient Greece.* **(b)** account of invented or imagined events, etc: *a 'fairy story* ○ *a 'ghost story* ○ *an adventure story for children* ○ *My father always used to tell us bedtime stories.* ○ *The play is really a love story.* **2** (also **'story-line**) narrative or plot of a book, play, etc: *a spy novel with a strong story(-line).* **3** (*journalism*) **(a)** report of an item of news in a newspaper; article: *a front-page story.* **(b)** event, situation or material suitable for this: *That'll make a good story.* **4** (*infml*) untrue statement, description, etc; lie: *Don't tell stories, Tom.* **5** (idm) **a cock-and-bull story** ⇨ COCK[1]. **cut a long story short** ⇨ LONG[1]. **a hard-luck story** ⇨ HARD[1]. **a likely story** ⇨ LIKELY. **the same old story** ⇨ SAME[1]. **the story goes that.../so the 'story goes** people are saying (that...); so it is said. **a success story** ⇨ SUCCESS. **a tall story** ⇨ TALL. **that's another 'story** (*infml*) that is interesting, but does not concern what we are discussing at the moment. **that's the ˌstory of my 'life** (*infml*) (said by sb who has had an unfortunate experience and regards it as like many similar experiences he has had in the past).

□ **'story-book** *n* book of fictional stories, usu for children: [attrib] *Their love affair had a story-book ending*, ie ended happily, as most children's stories do.

'story-teller *n* **1** person who tells stories. **2** (*infml*) person who makes untrue statements; liar.

story[2] (*US*) = STOREY.

stoup /stuːp/ *n* stone basin for holy water on or in the wall of a church.

stout /staʊt/ *adj* **1** [usu attrib] strong and thick: *stout boots for climbing* ○ *a stout walking-stick.* **2** (*esp euph*) (of a person) rather fat; solidly built: *She's growing rather stout.* ⇨ Usage at FAT[1]. **3** [usu attrib] (*fml*) determined, brave and resolute: *a stout heart* ○ *offer stout resistance.*

▷ **stout** *n* **(a)** [U] type of strong dark beer. **(b)** [C] glass of this: *Three stouts, please.*

stoutly *adv.*

stoutness *n* [U].

□ **ˌstout-'hearted** *adj* (*fml*) brave and resolute.

stove[1] /stəʊv/ *n* [C] **1** apparatus containing one or more ovens, used for cooking: *put a pot on the stove.* Cf COOKER 1. **2** closed apparatus burning wood, coal, gas, oil or other fuel, used for heating rooms: *a wood-burning stove.* Cf FIRE[1] 3, HEATER (HEAT[2]).

□ **'stove-enamel** *n* [U] heat-proof enamel used on stoves, washing-machines, etc. **'stove-enamelled** *adj.*

ˌstove-pipe 'hat (also **'stove-pipe**) type of tall, thin top hat (TOP[1]), worn esp in the 19th century.

stove[2] ⇨ STAVE[2].

stow /stəʊ/ *v* **1** [Tn, Tn·pr, Tn·p] ~ **A with B**; ~ **B (away) in/into A** pack sth, esp carefully, neatly and out of sight: *stow a trunk with clothes* ○ *stow clothes (away) into a trunk* ○ *stow cargo in a ship's hold* ○ *Passengers are requested to stow their hand-baggage in the lockers above the seats.* **2** (idm) **'stow it** (*dated sl*) (used to tell sb to stop doing sth, talking about sth, etc) **3** (phr v) **ˌstow a'way** hide oneself as a stowaway: *stow away on a ship bound for New York.*

▷ **stowage** /'stəʊɪdʒ/ *n* [U] **1** stowing or being stowed. **2** space used or available for this.

□ **'stowaway** *n* person who hides himself in a ship or aircraft before its departure, in order to travel without paying or being seen.

Stowe /stəʊ/ Harriet Beecher (1811-96), American novelist. Her most famous work, *Uncle Tom's Cabin*, roused public opinion against slavery, but created the stereotype of the submissive black slave.

Str *abbr* Strait: *Magellan Str*, eg on a map.

Strachey /'streɪtʃɪ/ Lytton (1880-1932), English author. He was a leading figure in the *Bloomsbury Group and created a new style of irreverent biography in works like *Eminent Victorians* and *Elizabeth and Essex*.

straddle /'strædl/ *v* **1** [I, Tn] sit or stand across (sth) with both legs wide apart: *straddle a fence, ditch, horse.* **2** [Tn] fire shots or drop bombs, etc slightly in front of and behind (a target).

Stradivarius /ˌstrædɪ'veərɪəs/ *n* (also (*infml*) **Strad** /stræd/) violin or other stringed instrument built in Italy by Antonio Stradivari (c 1644-1737) or his family. About 400 such instruments survive and are regarded as the finest ever made.

strafe /strɑːf, streɪf/ *v* [Tn] attack (sth/sb) with gunfire; bombard.

straggle /'strægl/ *v* **1** [I, Ipr] grow or spread in an irregular or untidy manner: *a straggling village* ○ *vines straggling over the fences.* **2** [I, Ipr, Ip] walk, march, etc too slowly to keep up with the rest of the group; drop behind: *a few young children straggling along behind their parents.*

▷ **straggler** /'stræglə(r)/ *n* person who straggles (STRAGGLE 2): *The last stragglers are just finishing the race.*

straggly /'stræglɪ/ *adj* (**-ier, -iest**) straggling: *wet straggly hair.*

straight[1] /streɪt/ *adj* **1** without a bend or curve; extending or moving continuously in one direction only: *a straight road, line, rod* ○ *straight hair*, ie not curly ○ *a straight skirt*, ie not flared. **2** [usu pred] arranged in proper order; tidy; correct: *It took hours to get the house straight.* **3** [pred] properly positioned; parallel to sth else; level or upright: *Put the picture straight.* ○ *Is my tie straight?* ○ *His hat isn't on straight.* **4** (of a person, his behaviour, etc) honest; truthful: *give a straight answer to a straight question* ○ *I don't think you're being straight with me.* ○ *It's time for some straight talking*, ie some frank discussion. **5** [attrib] accurate and without additions; not modified or elaborate: *tell a straight story* ○ *give sb a straight* (ie reliable and accurate) *tip.* **6** [attrib] (of a play or theatrical style) of the ordinary type; serious: *a straight actor* ○ *a straight play*, ie not a musical or variety show. **7** [attrib] in continuous succession: *ten straight wins in a row.* **8** (also **neat**) (of an alcoholic drink) without water, soda-water, etc added; undiluted: *Two straight whiskies, please.* ○ *I like my vodka straight.* **9** (*sl*) **(a)** conventional and conservative. **(b)** heterosexual: *straight men.* **10** (idm) **get sth right/straight** ⇨ RIGHT[1]. **keep a straight 'face** stop oneself from smiling and laughing: *He has such a strange voice that it's difficult to keep a straight face when he's talking.* **put/set the record straight** ⇨ RECORD[1]. **put sb straight (about sth)** correct sb's mistake; make sure that sb knows the correct facts, etc. **put sth straight** make sth tidy: *Please put your desk straight before you leave the office.* **stiff/straight as a ramrod** ⇨ RAMROD. **the ˌstraight and 'narrow** (*infml*) proper, honest and moral way of behaving: *He finds it difficult to stay on/stick to the straight and narrow for long.* **(as) straight as an 'arrow/'die (a)** in a straight line or direction. **(b)** (of a person) honest and straightforward. **(vote) the straight 'ticket** (*US*) (vote for a) political party's complete programme or list of candidates without any changes or modifications to it.

▷ **straight** *n* (*sl*) **(a)** conventional person. **(b)** heterosexual person.

straighten /'streɪtn/ *v* **1** [I, Ip, Tn, Tn·p] ~ **(sth) (up/out)** (cause sth to) become straight: *The road straightens (out) after a series of bends.* ○ *straighten one's tie, skirt* ○ *Straighten your back (up)!* **2** (phr v) **straighten sth out** settle or resolve sth; remove difficulties from sth: *Let's try to straighten out this confusion.* **straighten sb out** (*infml*) remove the doubt or ignorance in sb's mind: *You're clearly rather muddled about office procedures but I'll soon straighten you out.* **straighten (oneself) up** make one's body upright.

straightness *n* [U].

□ **'straight-edge** *n* strip of wood or metal with one edge straight, used for checking or marking straight lines.

ˌstraight 'fight (*esp politics*) competition between only two people or parties.

'straight man member of a comedy act who makes remarks or creates situations for the main performer to make jokes about.

ˌstraight 'razor (*US*) = CUTTHROAT RAZOR (CUTTHROAT).

straight[2] /streɪt/ *adv* **1** not in a curve or at an angle; in a straight line; directly: *sit up straight*, ie without bending one's back ○ *Keep straight on for two miles.* ○ *Look straight ahead.* ○ *The smoke rose straight up.* ○ *He was too drunk to walk straight.* ○ *I can't shoot straight*, ie aim accurately. ○ (*fig*) *I can't think straight*, ie logically. **2** by a direct route; without delay or hesitation: *Come straight home.* ○ *He went straight to Lagos, without stopping in Nairobi.* ○ *She went straight from* *school to university.* ○ *I'll come straight to the point — your work isn't good enough.* **3** honestly and frankly; in a straightforward manner: *I told him straight that I didn't like him.* **4** (idm) **go ˈstraight** live an honest life after leading a life of crime. **play ˈstraight (with sb)** be honest and fair in one's dealings (with sb). **right/straight away/off** ⇨ RIGHT[2]. **ˌstraight from the ˈshoulder** (of criticism, etc) frankly and honestly stated: *She gave it to me straight from the shoulder.* **straight ˈout** without hesitation; frankly: *I told him straight out that I thought he was lying.* ○ *She didn't hesitate for a moment but came straight out with her reply.* **ˌstraight ˈup** (*Brit sl*) (used esp in asking and answering questions) honestly; really.

straight[3] /streɪt/ *n* **1** (usu *sing*) straight part of sth, esp the final part of a track or racecourse: *on the home straight*, ie approaching the finishing line ○ *The two horses were level as they entered the final straight.* **2** (in the card-game of poker) hand with five cards in sequence but from more than one suit.

straightforward /ˌstreɪtˈfɔːwəd/ *adj* **1** (of a person, his manner, etc) honest and frank, without evasion: *straightforward in one's business dealings.* **2** easy to understand or do; without complications or difficulties: *a straightforward examination question* ○ *written in straightforward language* ○ *The procedure is quite straightforward.*
▷ **straightforwardly** *adv*: *behave, speak straightforwardly.* **straightforwardness** *n* [U]: *She admired his straightforwardness.*

straightway /ˌstreɪtˈweɪ/ *adv* (*arch*) at once; immediately.

strain[1] /streɪn/ *v* **1** [Tn, Tn·pr] stretch (sth) tightly by pulling: *strain a rope (to breaking-point/until it breaks).* **2** [I, It, Tn, Tnt] make the greatest possible effort; use all one's power, energy, etc (to do sth): *wrestlers heaving and straining* ○ *strain (one's ears) to hear a conversation* ○ *straining to understand what she meant* ○ *strain one's voice to shout.* **3** [Tn] injure or weaken (esp a part of the body) by stretching too much or trying too hard: *strain a muscle, one's heart* ○ *strain one's eyes*, eg by reading in a bad light ○ *strain one's voice*, ie by speaking or singing too long or too loudly ○ (*ironic*) *I would welcome some help — but don't strain yourself!* **4** [Tn] (*fml fig*) force (sth) beyond a limit of what is acceptable: *strain the credulity of one's listeners* ○ *strain one's authority, rights, power, etc*, ie go beyond what is allowed or reasonable ○ *Her prose strains language* (ie the meaning of words) *to the limits.* **5** [Tn] pass (food, etc) through a sieve, cloth, etc when separating solids from liquids: *strain the soup, vegetables* ○ *The tea hasn't been strained*, ie It is full of tea-leaves. **6** (idm) **strain after efˈfects/an efˈfect** try in a forced or unnatural way to make sth seem impressive. **strain at the ˈleash** (*infml*) be eager to have the freedom to do what one wants: *teenagers straining at the leash to escape parental control.* **strain every ˈnerve (to do sth)** try as hard as one can. **7** (phr v) **strain at sth** make a strenuous effort by pulling at sth: *rowers straining at the oars* ○ *dogs straining at the lead.* **strain sth off (from sth)** remove (eg liquid) from solid matter by using a sieve, etc: *strain off the water from the cabbage when it is cooked.*
▷ **strained** *adj* **1** unnatural, forced and artificial; not easy or relaxed: *a strained laugh* ○ *strained relations*, ie unpleasant tension between people, groups or countries. **2** overtired and anxious: *She looked very strained when I last saw her.*
strainer *n* (esp in compounds) device for straining (STRAIN[1] 5) liquids: *a ˈtea-strainer.*

strain[2] /streɪn/ *n* **1** [C, U] (**a**) condition of being stretched or pulled tightly: *The rope broke under the strain.* (**b**) force causing this: *calculate the strains and stresses of a bridge* ○ *What is the breaking strain of this cable?* ie How much strain would break it? **2** (**a**) [C, U] severe demand on one's mental or physical strength, resources, abilities, etc: *be under severe strain* ○ *beginning to feel the strain* ○ *the strain of modern life* ○ *Paying all the bills is a strain on my resources.* ○ *He finds his new job a real strain.* ○ *How do you stand* (ie cope with) *the strain?* (**b**) [U] state of anxiety, tension or exhaustion caused by this: *suffering from mental/nervous strain.* **3** [C, U] injury to a part of the body caused by twisting a muscle, etc; sprain: *a painful strain* ○ *a groin strain.* **4** [C usu *pl*] (*fml*) part of a tune or piece of music being performed: *hear the strains of the church organ* ○ *the angelic strains of choirboys singing.* **5** [C usu *sing*] tone, style or manner of sth written or spoken: *Her speech continued in the same dismal strain.*

strain[3] /streɪn/ *n* **1** (usu *sing*) ~ (**of sth**) tendency in a person's character: *There's a strain of madness in the family.* **2** breed or type (of animal, insect, plant, etc): *a new strain of wheat* ○ *strains of mosquitoes that are resistant to insecticide.*

strait /streɪt/ *n* **1** [C often *pl* with *sing* meaning, esp in proper names] narrow passage of water connecting two seas or two large areas of water: *the Straits of Gibraltar* ○ *the Magellan Straits.* **2 straits** [pl] trouble; difficulty: *be in (dire/desperate/serious) financial straits.*

straitened /ˈstreɪtnd/ *adj* (idm) **in straitened ˈcircumstances** (*fml esp euph*) having scarcely enough money to live on; in poverty.

strait-jacket /ˈstreɪtdʒækɪt/ *n* **1** strong jacket-like garment put on a violent person (esp one who is mentally ill) to stop him struggling by restricting the arms. **2** (*fig derog*) thing that stops growth or development: *the strait-jacket of repressive taxation.*
▷ **strait-jacket** *v* [Tn] **1** put a strait-jacket on (sb). **2** (*fig*) restrict the growth or development of (sth): *feel strait-jacketed by poverty* ○ *feel strait-jacketed by the lack of government subsidy.*

strait-laced /ˌstreɪt ˈleɪst/ *adj* (*derog*) having or showing a very strict attitude to moral questions; prim and proper: *My old aunts are very strait-laced.*

Strand /strænd/ **the Strand** street in London between Charing Cross and *Fleet Street. It contains a number of famous theatres and hotels, including the Savoy.

strand[1] /strænd/ *n* (*arch or rhet*) sandy shore of a lake, sea or river.
▷ **strand** *v* [Tn esp passive] cause (sth) to be left on the shore and unable to return to the sea; cause to go aground: *a ship stranded on a sandbank* ○ *a whale stranded by the high tide.*
stranded *adj* left in difficulties, eg without money, friends or transport: *stranded tourists* ○ *be left stranded in a foreign country without one's passport.*

strand[2] /strænd/ *n* **1** (**a**) any of the threads, wires, etc twisted together to form a rope or cable. (**b**) single thread of string or fibre: *a strand of cotton hanging from the hem of a skirt.* **2** lock of hair. **3** (*fig*) line of development (in a story, etc): *drawing together the strands of the narrative.*

strange /streɪndʒ/ *adj* (**-r**, **-st**) **1** not previously known, seen, felt, heard of, etc; not familiar or of one's own: *in a strange country, town, neighbourhood, etc* ○ *Never accept lifts from strange men.* **2** unusual; surprising: *What strange clothes you're wearing!* ○ *It's strange we haven't heard from him.* ○ *She says she feels strange*, ie rather unwell, perhaps dizzy. ○ *It feels strange to be visiting the place again after all these years.* **3** [pred] ~ **to sth** fresh or unaccustomed to sth: *He's strange to the work.* ○ *The village boy was strange to city life.* **4** (idm) **ˌstrange to reˈlate/ˈsay...** it is surprising that...: *Strange to say, he won!* ▷ **strangely** *adv*: *The house was strangely quiet.* ○ *It turned out we'd been at school together, strangely enough.* **strangeness** *n* [U].

stranger /ˈstreɪndʒə(r)/ *n* **1** person that one does not know: *I'd met Anna before, but her friend was a complete/total stranger to me.* ○ *Our dog barks at strangers.* **2** person in a new or an unfamiliar place or with people that he does not know: *I'm a stranger in this town*, ie I do not know my way around it. **3** (idm) **be a/no stranger to sth** (*fml*) be unaccustomed/accustomed to a certain feeling, experience, condition, job, etc: *He's no stranger to misfortune*, ie He has experienced it before.

strangle /ˈstræŋɡl/ *v* **1** [Tn] kill (sb) by squeezing or gripping the throat tightly; throttle: *He strangled her with her own scarf.* ○ (*infml*) *I could cheerfully strangle you for getting me into this mess!* ○ (*fig*) *This stiff collar is strangling me*, ie making it difficult for me to breathe. **2** (**a**) [Tn] restrict or prevent the proper growth, operation or development of (sth): *She felt her creativity was being strangled.* (**b**) [Tn usu passive] restrict the utterance of (sth): *a strangled* (ie partly suppressed) *cry.*
▷ **strangler** *n* person who strangles sb.
□ **ˈstranglehold** *n* (**a**) strangling grip. (**b**) (usu *sing*) ~ (**on sth**) (*fig*) firm control, making it impossible for sth to grow or develop properly: *The new tariffs have put a stranglehold on trade.*

strangulate /ˈstræŋɡjʊleɪt/ *v* [Tn esp passive] (*medical*) compress or tightly squeeze (a vein, an intestine, etc) so that nothing can pass through it: *a strangulated hernia*, ie one from which the blood supply has been cut off.
▷ **strangulation** /ˌstræŋɡjʊˈleɪʃn/ *n* [U] **1** strangling or being strangled. **2** strangulating or being strangulated.

strap /stræp/ *n* (esp in compounds) **1** [C] strip of leather, cloth or other flexible material, often with a buckle, used to fasten things together or to keep things in place or to support, hold or hang sth by: *a watch-strap* ○ *My camera strap has broken.* ○ *A rucksack has straps that go over the shoulders.* **2** [C] narrow strip of material worn over the shoulders as part of a dress, etc: *bra-straps* ○ *a summer dress with thin shoulder-straps.* **3 the strap** [sing] (esp formerly) punishment by beating with a leather strap: *I got/was given the strap.*
▷ **strap** *v* **1** [Tn·pr, Tn·p] hold, secure or fasten (sth/sb) with a strap or straps: *strap sth in place* ○ *They strapped their equipment on(to their backs).* ○ *Make sure the passengers are strapped in(to their seats) before driving off.* ○ *The lorry's load had been securely strapped down.* **2** [Tn, Tn·p] ~ **sth (up)** bind (a wound, limb, etc) with bandages: *His injured arm was tightly strapped (up).* **3** [Tn] beat (sb) with a strap.
strapless /ˈstræplɪs/ *adj* (esp of a dress or bra) without straps (STRAP 2).
strapped *adj* [pred] ~ (**for sth**) (*infml*) not having enough (of sth, esp money): *I'm a bit strapped for cash.*
strapping *adj* (*esp joc*) big, tall and strong; robust: *She's a strapping lass.*
□ **straphanger** /ˈstræphæŋə(r)/ *n* (*often derog*) standing passenger in a bus, train, etc who supports himself by holding onto a strap attached to the ceiling; commuter.

strata *pl* of STRATUM.

stratagem /ˈstrætədʒəm/ *n* (*fml*) trick, plan or scheme to deceive sb (esp an enemy): *a cunning stratagem.*

strategic /strəˈtiːdʒɪk/ (also **strategical**) *adj* [usu attrib] **1** of strategy; forming part of a plan or scheme: *strategic(al) decisions.* **2** giving an advantage; right for a particular purpose: *a strategic position, move* ○ *strategic bombing*, eg of industrial areas and communication centres ○ *strategic materials*, ie those that are necessary for war. **3** (of weapons, esp nuclear missiles) directed against an enemy's country rather than used in a battle. Cf TACTICAL (TACTIC). ▷ **strategically** /-klɪ/ *adv*: *a strategically placed microphone.*
□ **Straˌtegic Deˈfence Initiative** (also *infml* **Star Wars**) (*abbr* **SDI**) US defence programme to develop a range of satellites in space capable of identifying and destroying hostile nuclear missiles.

strategy /ˈstrætədʒɪ/ *n* **1** [U] (art of) planning and directing an operation in a war or campaign: *military strategy* ○ *skilled in strategy.* **2** [U] (skill in) planning or managing any affair well: *By careful strategy she negotiated a substantial pay rise.* **3** [C] plan or policy designed for a particular purpose: *economic strategies* ○ *a new police strategy for crowd control.* Cf TACTIC.
▷ **strategist** /-dʒɪst/ *n* person skilled in (esp military) strategy.

Strathclyde /stræθˈklaɪd/ local-government region of SW Scotland. ⇨ map at App 1.

strathspey /stræθˈspeɪ/ *n* (piece of music for a) slow Scottish dance.

stratify /ˈstrætɪfaɪ/ *v* (*pt, pp* **-fied**) [Tn usu passive] arrange (sth) in strata or grades, etc: *stratified rock* ○ *a highly stratified society*, ie having many different levels.

▷ **stratification** /ˌstrætɪfɪˈkeɪʃn/ *n* [U] arrangement in strata, etc; stratifying or being stratified: *social stratification.*

stratocumulus /ˌstrætəʊˈkju:mʊləs; *US* ˌstreɪtəʊˈku:mjələs/ *n* (*pl* **-li** /-laɪ/) [C, U] type of cloud that floats in grey masses low in the sky and covers most of it.

stratosphere /ˈstrætəsfɪə(r)/ *n* [sing] layer of the earth's atmosphere between about 10 and 60 kilometres above the surface of the earth. Cf IONOSPHERE.

stratum /ˈstrɑ:təm; *US* ˈstreɪtəm/ *n* (*pl* **strata** /-tə/) **1** any of a series of horizontal layers, esp of rock in the earth's crust. **2** level or class in society: *a gathering of people from a variety of social strata.*

stratus /ˈstrɑ:təs, ˈstrætəs; *US* ˈstreɪtəs/ *n* (*pl* **-ti** /-taɪ/) [C, U] type of low cloud that forms a long horizontal sheet, often bringing light rain.

Strauss[1] /straʊs/ Johann (1825-99), Austrian composer. Like his father, Johann Strauss the Elder, he led his own orchestra performing the waltzes and other Viennese dance music which he composed. Late in his career he turned to the theatre and wrote operettas such as *Die Fledermaus* and *The Gypsy Baron.*

Strauss[2] /straʊs/ Richard (1864-1949), German composer. He is best known for his symphonic tone poems, eg *Ein Heldenleben* and *Don Juan*, which use a large orchestra to give a vivid sound-picture of characters and events, and for operas such as *Der Rosenkavalier* and *Elektra.*

Stravinsky /strəˈvɪnskɪ/ Igor (1882-1971), Russian composer. He became famous for scores such as *The Firebird, Petrushka* and *The Rite of Spring*, written for Diaghilev's ballet, and they remain his most popular works. His later works explored a wide range of Western musical styles, from the baroque and classical period (eg *Pulcinella*) to the modern avant-garde. In 1945 he became a US citizen.

straw /strɔ:/ *n* **1** [U] cut and dried stalks of grain plants (eg wheat, barley) used as a material for thatching roofs, making hats, mats, etc and as bedding and food for animals: *a stable filled with straw* ○ [attrib] *a straw mattress*, ie one filled with straw. **2** [C] single stalk or piece of this: *There are a few straws in your hair.* **3** [C] thin tube of paper or plastic through which a drink is sucked up: *drinking lemonade through a straw* ○ *A packet of (drinking) straws, please.* **4 a straw** [sing] insignificant thing or amount (used esp in the expressions shown): *not care a straw* ○ *be not worth a straw.* **5** (idm) **clutch at a straw/straws** ⇨ CLUTCH[1]. **the last/final straw (that breaks the camel's back)** additional event, act, task, etc that makes a situation finally intolerable. **make bricks without straw** ⇨ BRICK. **a man of straw** ⇨ MAN[1]. **a straw in the ˈwind** slight indication of how things may develop.

□ ˌ**straw ˈboss** (*US sl*) assistant foreman.

ˈ**straw-coloured** *adj* light yellow.

ˌ**straw ˈpoll** (also ˌ**straw ˈvote**) (*esp US*) unofficial survey of public opinion.

strawberry /ˈstrɔ:brɪ; *US* -berɪ/ *n* **(a)** [C] soft juicy red fruit with tiny yellow seeds on the surface: *fresh strawberries and cream* ○ [attrib] *strawberry jam* ○ *strawberry pink.* **(b)** low-growing plant on which this fruit grows.

□ ˈ**strawberry-mark** *n* reddish birthmark on the skin.

stray /streɪ/ *v* [I, Ipr, Ip] **1** move away from one's group, proper place, etc with no fixed destination or purpose; wander: *Some of the cattle have strayed.* ○ *stray into the path of an oncoming car* ○ *Young children should not be allowed to stray from their parents.* ○ *He had strayed from home while still a boy.* **2** deviate from a direct course or leave a subject: *My mind kept straying from the discussion (to other things).* ○ *Don't stray (away) from the point.*

▷ **stray** *adj* [attrib] **1** having strayed; lost: *a home for stray dogs* ○ (*fig*) *Stray papers littered his desk.* **2** occurring here and there, not as one of a group; isolated: *killed by a stray bullet*, ie by chance, not on purpose ○ *The streets were empty except for a few stray passers-by.*

stray *n* **(a)** person or domestic animal that has strayed: *This dog must be a stray.* Cf WAIF. **(b)** thing that is out of its proper place or separated from others of the same kind.

streak /stri:k/ *n* ~ **(of sth) 1** long thin mark, line or band of a different substance or colour from its surroundings: *streaks of grey in her hair* ○ *a streak* (ie flash) *of lightning* ○ *streaks of fat in the meat.* **2** element or trace (in a person's character): *a streak of jealousy, vanity, cruelty, etc* ○ *have a jealous streak.* **3** (esp in gambling) period of continuous success or failure: *a streak of good luck* ○ *hit* (ie have) *a winning/losing streak.* **4** (idm) **like a streak of lightning** ⇨ LIGHTNING[1]. **a yellow streak** ⇨ YELLOW.

▷ **streak** *v* **1** [esp passive: Tn, Tn-pr] ~ **sth (with sth)** mark sth with streaks: *have one's hair streaked* ○ *white marble streaked with brown.* **2** [Ipr, Ip] (*infml*) move very fast (in the specified direction): *The children streaked off (down the street) as fast as they could.* **3** [I] run through a public place with no clothes on, in order to shock or amuse people. **streaker** *n* person who streaks (STREAK *v* 3).

streaky *adj* (**-ier, -iest**) marked with, having or full of streaks: *streaky bacon*, ie with layers of fat and lean in it.

stream /stri:m/ *n* **1** small river or large brook: *a small stream running through the woods.* **2** ~ **(of sth/sb)** flow (of liquid, people, things, etc): *a stream of blood* ○ *a steady stream of abuse, complaints, etc* ○ *streams of shoppers, traffic.* **3** current or direction of sth flowing or moving: *leaves moving with the stream.* **4** (*esp Brit*) (in some schools) class or division of a class into which children of the same age and level of ability are placed: *the A, B, C, etc stream.* **5** (idm) **go up/down stream** move up/down the river. **go, swim, etc with/against the stream/tide** conform/not conform to accepted behaviour, opinions, etc; be/not be carried along by the course of events: *Teenagers often go against the stream.* **on stream** in active operation or production: *The new plant comes on stream in March.*

▷ **stream** *v* **1** [I, Ipr] flow or move as a stream: *Sweat streamed down his face.* ○ *People were streaming out of the station.* **2 (a)** [Tn] emit a stream of (sth): *The wound streamed blood.* **(b)** [I, Ipr] ~ **(with sth)** run with liquid: *a streaming cold*, ie with much liquid coming from the nose ○ *His face was streaming with sweat.* **3** [I, Ipr, Ip] float or wave at full length (esp in the wind): *Her hair streamed (out) in the wind.* **4** [Tn usu passive] (*esp Brit*) place (schoolchildren) in streams (STREAM 4): *Children are streamed according to ability.* **streamer** *n* **1** long narrow flag. **2** long narrow ribbon of coloured paper: *a room decorated with balloons and streamers.* **3** = BANNER HEADLINE (BANNER). **streaming** *n* [U] (policy of) placing schoolchildren in streams (STREAM 4).

□ ˌ**stream of ˈconsciousness** (writing that seeks to express the) continuous flow of ideas, thoughts and feelings experienced by a person when conscious.

streamline /ˈstri:mlaɪn/ *v* [Tn] **1** give a streamlined form to (sth). **2** make (sth) more efficient and effective, eg by improving or simplifying working methods: *We must streamline our production procedures.*

▷ **streamlined** *adj* having a smooth even shape so as to be able to move quickly and easily through air, water, etc: *modern streamlined cars.*

street /stri:t/ *n* **1** (*abbr* **St**) public road in a city, town or village with houses and buildings on one side or both sides: *cross the street* ○ *meet a friend in the street* ○ *gangs roaming the streets* ○ *His address is 155 Smith Street.* ○ (*Brit*) *We live in Walton Street.* ○ (*US*) *It's on East 88th Street.* ○ [attrib]: *at street level*, ie on the ground floor ○ *a ˈstreet map/plan of York* ○ *street lighting* ○ *street theatre*, ie plays, etc performed in the street, usu with a social or political theme. ⇨ Usage at ROAD. **2** people who live or work in a particular street: *Our street puts on a carnival every year.* **3** (idm) **be in Queer Street** ⇨ QUEER. **be (out) on/walk the streets** (*infml*) **(a)** be homeless. **(b)** (*euph*) work as a prostitute. **go on the streets** (*euph*) earn one's living as a prostitute. **the man in the street** ⇨ MAN[1]. **not in the same street (as sb/sth)** (*infml*) not nearly so good; inferior (to sb/sth). **streets ahead (of sb/sth)** (*infml*) much better, more efficient, cleverer, etc (than sb/sth). **(right) up one's street** (*infml*) within one's area of knowledge, interest, activity, etc: *This job seems right up your street.*

□ ˈ**street arab** (*infml*) child who spends much of his time on the city streets, usu with no proper home.

ˈ**streetcar** *n* (*US*) = TRAM.

ˌ**street crediˈbility** (also ˌ**street ˈcred**) (*infml*) up-to-date image, style, etc, that is acceptable to ordinary (esp young) people.

ˈ**street-girl** (also ˈ**street-walker**) *n* prostitute who looks for customers on the streets.

ˈ**street value** price for which sth illegal or illegally obtained can be sold: *Customs officers have seized drugs with a street value of over £1 million.*

ˈ**street-wise** *adj* (*infml*) knowledgeable about how ordinary people behave, survive, etc, esp in big cities.

strength /streŋθ/ *n* **1** [U] quality of being strong; degree of intensity of this: *a man of great strength* ○ *strength of character, mind, will* ○ *regain one's strength after an illness* ○ *the strength of a rope*, ie its ability to resist strain ○ *put on a show of strength*, ie show how strong one is ○ *For a small woman she has surprising strength.* ○ *The strength of feeling on this issue is considerable.* ○ *How is the strength of alcoholic drinks measured?* ⇨ Usage. **2** [C, U] that which makes sb/sth strong; particular respect in which a person or thing is strong: *the strengths and weaknesses of an argument* ○ *Tolerance is one of her many strengths.* ○ *His strength as a news-reader lies in his training as a journalist.* **3** [U] number of people present or available; full number: *What is the strength of the work-force?* **4** (idm) **be at full/be below strength** have the required/less than the required number of people. **bring sth/be up to (full) strength** make sth reach/be the required number: *We must bring the police force up to (full) strength.* **from strength to strength** with ever-increasing success: *Since her appointment the department has gone from strength to strength.* **in (full, great, etc) strength** in large numbers: *They army paraded in (full) strength.* **on the strength** (*infml*) included as an official member of an organization, armed force, etc. **on the strength of sth** on the basis of sth; relying on (a fact, sb's advice, etc): *I got the job on the strength of your recommendation.* **outgrow one's strength** ⇨ OUTGROW. **a tower of strength** ⇨ TOWER.

▷ **strengthen** /ˈstreŋθn/ *v* [I, Tn] (cause sth/sb to) become stronger: *The current strengthened as we moved down the river.* ○ *a special shampoo to strengthen your hair* ○ *strengthen a garrison with extra troops* ○ *This latest development has further strengthened my determination to leave.*

NOTE ON USAGE: Compare **strength, power, force** and **vigour** (*US* **vigor**). **Strength** and **power** indicate an internal quality of an object or person. The **strength** of a body, bridge or rope is its ability to hold great weight: *I haven't the strength to carry you.* The **power** in a person's body, in a machine or in the wind is the energy within it that can be applied: *We can harness the power of the wind to make electricity.* **Force** and **vigour** relate to the application of energy. The **force** of an explosion, a storm or a blow is the energy released and its impact on objects: *The car was completely wrecked by the force of the collision.* A person's **vigour** is the energy used, especially in work: *She does her work with tremendous vigour.*

strenuous /ˈstrenjʊəs/ *adj* **1** making great efforts; energetic: *strenuous workers* ○ *make a strenuous attempt to reach the top of the mountain.* **2** requiring great effort: *a strenuous itinerary* ○ *strenuous work* ○ *lead a strenuous life.* ▷ **strenuously** *adv*: *She strenuously denies all the charges.*

streptococcus /ˌstreptəˈkɒkəs/ *n* (*pl* **-cocci** /-ˈkɒkaɪ/) (*medical*) any of a group of bacteria that cause serious infections and illnesses. ▷ **streptococcal** /-ˈkɒkl/ *adj*.

streptomycin /ˌstreptəʊˈmaɪsɪn/ *n* [U] (*medical*) antibiotic drug used to treat infections, eg tuberculosis.

stress /stres/ *n* **1** [U, C] (pressure or worry resulting from) mental or physical distress, difficult circumstances, etc: *be under/suffer from stress* ○ *in times of stress*, ie difficulty, trouble, etc ○ *the stresses and strains of modern life.* **2** [U] ~ (**on sth**) special emphasis or significance: *He feels that there is not enough stress on drama at the school.* ○ *She lays great stress on punctuality*, ie regards it as very important. **3** [C, U] (**a**) (result of) extra force used in speaking a particular word or syllable: *In 'strategic' the stress is/falls on the second syllable.* ○ *Stress and rhythm are important in speaking English.* ○ *You must learn where to place the stresses.* Cf INFLECTION 2, INTONATION 2. (**b**) (result of) extra force used when making a sound in music: *Put a stress on the first note in each bar.* **4** [C, U] ~ (**on sth**) (esp in mechanics) force that acts on a thing or between parts of a thing, and tends to pull or twist it out of shape; tension: *High winds put great stress on the structure.* ○ [attrib] *a stress fracture of a bone in the leg.*

▷ **stress** *v* [Tn, Tf] put stress or emphasis on (sth): *You stress the first syllable in 'happiness'.* ○ *He stressed the point that...* ○ *I must stress that what I say is confidential.*

stressful /-fl/ *adj* causing stress(1): *She finds her new teaching job very stressful.*

□ ˈ**stress mark** mark (as used in this dictionary) to indicate the stress(3a) on a syllable in a word: *In the word 'sympathetic' /ˌsɪmpəˈθetɪk/ the primary stress (ˈ) is on the third syllable, and the secondary stress (ˌ) is on the first syllable.*

stretch /stretʃ/ *v* **1** [Tn, Tn·pr, Tn·p, Cn·a] make (sth) longer, wider or tighter by pulling: *stretch a rope across a path* ○ *stretch a pair of gloves/shoes*, eg to make them fit better ○ *stretch a hat to fit one's head* ○ *stretch a rope tight.* **2** [I] be able to become longer, wider, etc without breaking; be elastic; (be liable to) extend beyond the proper limit: *These socks stretch.* ○ *The pullover stretched* (ie out of shape) *after I had worn it a few times.* ○ (*fig*) *I'd love a holiday if our money will stretch that far.* **3** [I, Ipr, Ip, Tn, Tn·pr, Tn·p] extend or thrust out (a limb or part of the body) and tighten the muscles, esp after being relaxed or in order to reach sth: *He woke up, yawned and stretched.* ○ *She stretched across the table for the butter.* ○ *stretch one's arms, legs* ○ *He stretched out his arm to take the book.* ○ *She stretched her neck up*, eg to see over the heads of people in a crowd. **4** [I, Ipr, Ip] spread out over an area or a period of time; extend: *forests stretching for hundreds of miles* ○ *The road stretched (out) across the desert into the distance.* ○ *The ocean stretched as far as they could see on all sides.* ○ *The long summer holiday stretched ahead (of them).* **5** [Tn] make great demands on (sb or sb's ability, strength, etc): *The race really stretched him/his skill as a runner.* ○ *She has not been sufficiently stretched at school this term.* ○ *We can't take on any more work — we're fully stretched* (ie working to the utmost of our powers) *at the moment.* **6** [Tn] strain or exert (sth) as far as possible or beyond a reasonable or an acceptable limit: *stretch the truth*, ie exaggerate or lie ○ *stretch the meaning of a word* ○ *You can't stretch the rules to suit yourself.* **7** (idm) **stretch one's legs** go for a walk as exercise: *She went out to stretch her legs after lunch.* **stretch a point** go beyond what is usually allowed; make a concession: *She doesn't have all the qualifications but I think we should stretch a point in her favour.* **8** (phr v) **stretch (sth) out** (make sth) last or be enough to cover one's needs: *He couldn't stretch out his money to the end of the month.* **stretch (oneself) out** relax by lying at full length: *He stretched (himself) out in front of the fire and fell asleep.*

▷ **stretch** *n* **1** [C usu *sing*] act of stretching or state of being stretched: *With a stretch of his arm, he reached the shelf.* ○ *The dog woke up, had a good stretch and wandered off.* **2** [U] ability to be stretched; elasticity: *This material has a lot of stretch in it.* ○ [attrib] *stretch jeans, seat-covers, underwear.* **3** [C] (**a**) ~ (**of sth**) continuous expanse or extent (of sth): *a beautiful stretch of countryside* ○ *a long stretch of open road.* (**b**) continuous or unbroken period of time: *a four-hour stretch.* **4** [C usu *sing*] (*sl*) period of service or imprisonment: *do a stretch in the army* ○ *He did a long stretch for attempted murder.* **5** [C usu *sing*] straight part of a track or racecourse: *the final/finishing/home stretch*, ie the last part of the course. **6** (idm) **at full stretch** ⇨ FULL. **at a stretch** without stopping; continuously: *She worked for six hours at a stretch.* **not by any/by no stretch of the imagination** however hard one may try to believe or imagine sth: *By no stretch of the imagination could you call him ambitious.*

stretchy /ˈstretʃɪ/ *adj* (**-ier**, **-iest**) (*infml*) that can be stretched; tending to become stretched: *stretchy materials.* **stretchiness** *n* [U].

□ ˈ**stretch marks** creases produced in the skin of the abdomen by stretching during pregnancy.

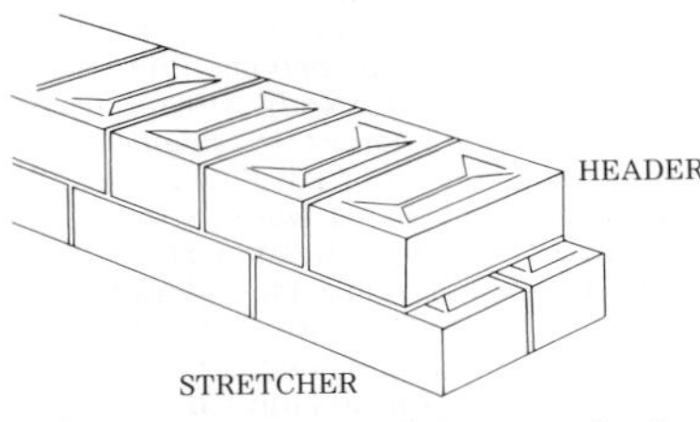

stretcher /ˈstretʃə(r)/ *n* **1** framework of poles, canvas, etc for carrying a sick or injured person in a lying position: *An ambulance officer brought a stretcher for the injured woman.* **2** any of various devices for stretching things or holding things in a stretched position. **3** brick laid with its long edge along the line of the wall. Cf HEADER. ⇨ illus. **4** board that a rower presses his feet against when pulling on an oar.

□ ˈ**stretcher-bearer** *n* person (usu one of two) who helps to carry a stretcher(1).

strew /struː/ *v* (*pt* **strewed**, *pp* **strewed** or **strewn** /struːn/) **1** [Tn, Tn·pr] ~ **A** (**on/over B**); ~ **B with A** scatter sth (over a surface); cover (a surface) with scattered things; sprinkle: *strew papers over the floor/strew the floor with papers.* **2** [Tn] lie scattered on or over (a surface): *a litter-strewn playground* ○ *Papers strewed the floor.* ⇨ Usage at SCATTER.

strewth /struːθ/ *interj* (*Brit sl becoming dated*) (used to express surprise, annoyance, dismay, etc): *Strewth, look at the time! We're late!*

striated /straɪˈeɪtɪd; *US* ˈstraɪeɪtɪd/ *adj* (*fml*) marked with stripes, lines or furrows.

▷ **striation** /straɪˈeɪʃn/ *n* (*fml*) **1** [C] stripe, line or furrow. **2** [U] state of being striated.

stricken /ˈstrɪkən/ *adj* ~ (**by/with sth**) (esp in compounds) affected or overcome (by sth unpleasant, eg illness, grief): *stricken with malaria, cancer, fever, etc* ○ *stricken by poverty/ˈpoverty-stricken* ○ *ˈgrief-/ˈpanic-/ˈterror-stricken* ○ *Rescue teams raced to the stricken ship.*

strict /strɪkt/ *adj* (**-er**, **-est**) **1** demanding total obedience or observance (of rules, ways of behaving, etc); severe; not lenient: *a strict teacher* ○ *a strict upbringing* ○ *a strict rule against smoking* ○ *She's very strict with her children.* **2** (**a**) clearly and exactly defined; precise: *in the strict sense of the word* ○ *the strict truth* ○ *a strict understanding, interpretation.* (**b**) complete; absolute: *give information in strictest confidence/in strict secrecy*, ie expecting complete secrecy.

▷ **strictly** *adv* **1** in a strict manner; completely: *Smoking is strictly prohibited.* **2** (idm) **strictly speaking** if one uses words, applies rules, etc in their exact sense: *Strictly speaking, he's not qualified for the job.*

strictness *n* [U].

stricture /ˈstrɪktʃə(r)/ *n* **1** (usu *pl*) (*fml*) severe criticism or condemnation: *pass strictures on sb.* **2** (*medical*) abnormal constriction or narrowing of a tube-shaped part of the body.

stride /straɪd/ *v* (*pt* **strode**, *pp* rarely **stridden** /ˈstrɪdn/) **1** [Ipr, Ip] walk with long steps (in the specified direction): *stride along the road* ○ *striding across the fields* ○ *She turned and strode off.* ○ *striding out for* (ie walking determinedly towards) *the distant hills.* **2** [Ipr] ~ **across/over sth** cross sth with one step: *stride over a ditch.*

▷ **stride** *n* **1** (distance covered by) one long step: *I was three strides from the door.* **2** person's way of striding; gait. **3** (idm) **get into one's stride** settle into a fast, confident and steady pace (of doing sth): *She found the job difficult at first, but now she's really getting into her stride.* **make great, rapid, etc strides** make good, fast, etc progress; improve quickly: *Tom has made enormous strides in his maths this term.* **take sth in one's stride** accept and deal with sth without special effort: *Some people find retiring difficult, but he has taken it all in his stride.*

strident /ˈstraɪdnt/ *adj* (of a sound, esp a voice) loud and harsh; shrill: *strident protests* ○ *strident in their demands.* ▷ **stridency** /ˈstraɪdənsɪ/ *n* [U]. **stridently** *adv*.

stridulate /ˈstrɪdjʊleɪt; *US* ˈstrɪdʒʊleɪt/ *v* [I] (of insects such as crickets) make high-pitched chirping sounds by rubbing together certain parts of the body. ▷ **stridulation** /ˌstrɪdjʊˈleɪʃn; *US* -dʒ-/ *n* [U].

strife /straɪf/ *n* [U] state of conflict; angry or violent disagreement; quarrelling: *industrial strife*, ie between employers and workers ○ *a nation torn by political strife.*

strike[1] /straɪk/ *n* **1** organized stopping of work by employees because of a disagreement (eg over pay, conditions, etc); act or instance of striking (STRIKE[2] 10): *a miners' strike* ○ *industrial strikes* ○ *a strike by bus drivers* ○ *a general, an unofficial, a wildcat strike* ○ *call a strike* ○ *break a strike* ○ [attrib] *take strike action.* ⇨ article at TRADE UNION. **2** sudden discovery of gold, oil, etc in the earth: (*fig*) *a lucky strike*, ie a fortunate discovery. **3** sudden attack (esp by aircraft or a missile): *an air strike* ○ [attrib] *first strike capacity in a nuclear war*, ie the ability to attack an enemy before they can attack you ○ *The footballer took a strike at the goal.* ○ *the strike of a hawk on its prey.* **4** (in baseball) pitch[3](2c) that counts against the hitter, esp because he fails to hit it: *That's strike three and you're out!* **5** (idm) **be/go on ˈstrike**; **be/come/go out on ˈstrike** be engaged in/start an industrial strike: *We are (going) on strike.* ○ *The ship-builders came/went out on strike for higher pay.*

□ ˈ**strikebound** *adj* unable to function because of an industrial strike: *The docks were strikebound for a week.*

ˈ**strike-breaker** *n* person who continues to work while fellow employees are on strike, or who is employed in place of striking members. Cf BLACKLEG. ˈ**strike-breaking** *n* [U].

ˈ**strike pay** money paid by a trade union to striking members during a strike officially recognized by the union.

strike[2] /straɪk/ *v* (*pt, pp* **struck** /strʌk/) **1** (**a**) [Tn, Tn·pr, Dn·n] subject (sb/sth) to an impact; hit (sb/sth): *The stone struck me on the side of the head.* ○ *He struck the table a heavy blow with his fist.* ⇨ Usage at HIT[1]. (**b**) [I, Tn, Tn·pr] (cause sth to) come sharply into contact with sth: *There was a crash of thunder, then the storm struck.* ○ *People say that* *lightning never strikes twice in the same place.* ○ *The ship struck a rock.* ○ *The tree was struck by lightning.* ○ *He struck his head on/against the beam.* ○ *He struck the beam with his head.* ○ *(fig) The family was struck by yet another tragedy.* **(c)** [Tn] give (a blow): *Who struck the first blow* (ie started the fight)*?* **(d)** [Ipr] ~ **at sb/sth** aim a blow at sb/sth: *He struck at me repeatedly with a stick.* **(e)** [Tn·pr, Tn·p] cause (sb/sth) to move or fall with a blow or stroke: *He struck her to the ground.* ○ *She struck the ball away.* **(f)** [Tn·pr] ~ **sth from sth** remove (sth written) from a document; delete: *The judge ordered the witness's answer to be struck from the record.* **2 (a)** [I] attack, esp suddenly: *Enemy troops struck just before dawn.* ○ *The lioness crouched ready to strike.* **(b)** [I, Tn esp passive] (of disaster, disease, etc) afflict (sb/sth): *It was not long before tragedy struck again.* ○ *The area was struck by an outbreak of cholera.* **3 (a)** [Tn, Tn·pr] produce (a light, spark, etc) by friction: *strike sparks from a flint.* **(b)** [I, Tn] (cause sth to) ignite in this way: *These damp matches won't strike.* ○ *strike a match.* **4 (a)** [Tn, Tn·pr] produce (a musical note, sound, etc): *strike a chord on the piano* ○ *(fig) strike a note of* (ie give an impression of) *gloom, optimism, caution.* **(b)** [I, Tn] (of a clock) indicate (the time) by sounding a bell, etc: *The clock has just struck (three).* ○ *The clock strikes the hours.* **(c)** [I] (of time) be indicated in this way: *Four o'clock had just struck on the church clock.* **5** [Tn] discover or reach (gold, minerals, oil, etc) by digging or drilling: *strike a rich vein of ore.* **6** [Tn] make (a coin, medal, etc) by stamping or punching metal: *The Royal Mint will strike a commemorative gold coin.* **7** [Cn·a esp passive] bring (sb) suddenly into a specified state (as if) by a single stroke: *be struck blind, dumb, silent, etc.* **8** [Tn, Dn·f, Dn·w] (not in the continuous tenses) occur to sb's mind: *An awful thought has just struck me.* ○ *What struck me was/I was struck by* (ie I noticed) *their enthusiasm for the work.* ○ *It strikes me that nobody is in favour of the changes.* ○ *It suddenly struck me how we could improve the situation.* **9** [Tn, Tn·pr] ~ **sb (as sth)** have an effect on sb; impress sb (in the way specified): *How does the idea strike you?* ○ *The plan strikes me as ridiculous.* ○ *The house strikes you as welcoming when you go in.* **10** [I, Ipr] ~ **(for/against sth)** (of workers) stop work in protest about a grievance: *Striking workers picketed the factory.* ○ *The union has voted to strike for a pay increase of 10%.* **11** [Tn] lower or take down (a sail, tent, etc): *strike* (ie dismantle) *the set after the play is over.* Cf PITCH[2] 1. **12** [Tn] arrive at or achieve (an average) by reckoning. **13** [Tn] come upon (a path, etc); find: *It was some time before we struck the track.* **14** [Tn] take (a cutting) from a plant and put it in the soil so that it grows new roots. **15** (idm) **be struck on sb/sth** *(infml)* be favourably impressed by sb/sth; like sb/sth very much: *He's very much struck on his new girl-friend.* **hit/strike home** ⇨ HOME[3]. **hit/strike the right/wrong note** ⇨ NOTE[1]. **lightning never strikes in the same place twice** ⇨ LIGHTNING[1]. **strike an ˈattitude/a ˈpose** hold or put the body in a certain way or use gestures to emphasize what one says or feels; speak or write about one's opinions, intentions or feelings in a dramatic or artificial way: *He struck an attitude of defiance with a typically hard-hitting speech.* **strike at the root of sth** ⇨ ROOT[1]. **strike a ˈbalance (between A and B)** find a sensible middle point between two demands, extremes, etc; compromise: *It was difficult to strike the right balance between justice and expediency.* **strike a ˈbargain (with sb)** come to an agreement (with sb) esp after much discussion and argument: *They struck a bargain with the landlord that they would look after the garden in return for being allowed to use it.* **strike a blow for/against sth** perform an action on behalf of or in support of/against (a belief, cause, principle, etc): *By their action, they struck a blow for democracy.* **strike camp** take down and pack up one's tents, etc. **strike a ˈchord (with sb)** say sth that other people sympathize or identify with: *The speaker had obviously struck a chord with his audience.* **strike/sound a false note** ⇨ FALSE. **strike fear, etc into sb/sb's heart** cause sb to feel fear, etc: *The news of the epidemic struck terror into the population.* **strike ˈgold/ˈoil** discover a rich source of information, wealth, happiness, etc: *She hasn't always been lucky with her boy-friends but she seems to have struck gold this time.* **strike a light!** *(dated Brit sl)* (exclamation expressing astonishment or protest). **strike (it) ˈlucky** *(infml)* have good luck in a particular matter: *We certainly struck (it) lucky with the weather.* **strike/sound a note (of sth)** ⇨ NOTE[1]. **ˌstrike it ˈrich** *(infml)* acquire a lot of money, esp suddenly or unexpectedly. **ˌstrike while the ˌiron is ˈhot** *(saying)* (often imperative) make use of an opportunity immediately; act while conditions are favourable. **take/strike root** ⇨ ROOT[1]. **within ˈstriking-distance** near enough to be reached or attacked easily.

16 (phr v) **strike sb down (a)** *(fml)* hit sb so that he falls to the ground. **(b)** (of a disease, etc) make sb unable to lead an active life; make sb seriously ill or kill sb: *He was struck down by cancer at the age of thirty.*

strike sth off remove sth with a sharp blow; cut sth off: *He struck off the rotten branches with an axe.* **strike sb/sth off (sth)** remove sb/sb's name from sth, esp from membership of a professional body: *Strike her name off the list.* ○ *The doctor was struck off for incompetence.*

strike on sth get or find sth suddenly or unexpectedly: *strike on a brilliant new idea.*

strike out (at sb/sth) aim vigorous blows or attacks: *He lost his temper and struck out wildly.* ○ *(fig) In a recent article she strikes out at her critics.* **strike sth out/through** remove sth by drawing a line through it; cross sth out: *The editor struck out the whole paragraph.* **strike out (for/towards sth)** move in a vigorous and determined way (towards sth): *strike out on foot for the distant hills* ○ *He struck out* (ie started swimming) *strongly for the shore.* ○ *(fig) strike out on one's own,* ie start an independent life, a new career, etc.

strike up (sth) (of a band, an orchestra, etc) begin to play (a piece of music): *The band struck up (a waltz).* **strike up sth (with sb)** begin (a friendship, an acquaintance, a conversation, etc) esp casually: *He would often strike up conversations with complete strangers.*

striker /ˈstraɪkə(r)/ *n* **1** worker who is on strike. **2** *(sport)* **(a)** (in football) attacking player whose most important role is to try to score goals. ⇨ illus at ASSOCIATION FOOTBALL (ASSOCIATION). Cf FORWARD[4]. **(b)** (in cricket) batsman who is facing the bowling.

striking /ˈstraɪkɪŋ/ *adj* **1 (a)** attracting attention or interest: *a striking display, effect* ○ *There is a striking contrast between the two interpretations.* **(b)** attracting attention because of a good appearance; attractive: *his striking good looks* ○ *a very striking young woman.* **2** (of a clock, etc) that strikes. ▷ **strikingly** *adv*: *a strikingly handsome man.*

Strindberg /ˈstrɪndbɜːg/ August (1849-1912), Swedish playwright. His early naturalistic psychological dramas, eg *Miss Julie,* reflected his own troubled life and character. He later wrote several mystical works of symbolism, such as *A Dream Play.*

string[1] /strɪŋ/ *n* **1 (a)** [U] thin cord made of twisted threads; twine: *a ball of string* ○ *tie up a parcel with string* ○ *attach sth with a length/piece of string.* **(b)** [C] length of this or similar material used to fasten or pull sth, or interwoven in a frame to form the head of a racket: *a puppet on strings,* ie made to move by pulling strings attached to its joints ○ *The key is hanging on a string by the door.* ○ *She wore the medal on a string round her neck.* ○ *I have broken several strings in my tennis racket.* **2** [C] tightly stretched piece of catgut or wire, eg in a violin, harp or guitar, which produces a musical note when it vibrates. ⇨ illus at MUSIC. **3 the strings** [pl] (players of) the stringed instruments (eg violins, cellos, etc) in an orchestra. ⇨ illus at MUSIC. **4** [C] **(a)** set or series of things put together on a thread, cord, etc: *a string of beads, pearls, etc* ○ *a string of onions.* **(b)** series or line of people or things: *a string of visitors* ○ *a string of small lakes* ○ *a string of abuse, curses, lies* ○ *a string of wins.* **(c)** group of racehorses that are trained at one stable. **5** [C] tough piece of fibrous substance that connects the two halves of a bean-pod, etc. **6** (idm) **the first/second ˈstring** first/alternative person or thing (to be) relied on for achieving one's purpose. **have/keep sb on a ˈstring** have/keep sb under one's control: *She's had us all on a string for too long.* **have two strings/a second, etc string to one's bow** ⇨ BOW[1]. **one's mother's, etc apron strings** ⇨ APRON. **(with) no ˈstrings attached/without ˈstrings** *(infml)* with no special conditions or restrictions: *a loan of £3 000 and no strings attached.* **pull strings/wires** ⇨ PULL[2]. **pull the strings/wires** ⇨ PULL[2].

▷ **stringy** *adj* **(-ier, -iest) 1** like string: *lank stringy hair.* **2 (a)** (of beans, etc) having a strip of tough fibre. **(b)** (of meat) tough. **stringiness** *n* [U].

□ **ˌstring ˈbag** bag made out of a strong mesh that expands to hold shopping, etc.

ˌstring ˈband, ˌstring ˈorchestra band or orchestra consisting only of stringed instruments.

ˈstring bean = RUNNER BEAN (RUNNER).

ˈstring-course *n* horizontal row of bricks that projects slightly from a wall.

ˌstring quarˈtet (music to be played by) four people playing stringed instruments.

ˌstring ˈvest *(esp Brit)* vest made of material with large meshes.

string[2] /strɪŋ/ *v* (*pt, pp* **strung** /strʌŋ/) **1** [Tn] put a string[1](1b, 2) or strings on (a bow, violin, tennis racket, etc): *loosely/tightly strung.* **2** [Tn] thread (pearls, beads, etc) on a string[1](1b). **3** [Tn·pr, Tn·p] ~ **sth (up)** hang or tie (sth) in place with a string, rope, etc: *Lanterns were strung in the trees around the pool.* ○ *Flags had been strung up across the street.* **4** [Tn] remove the tough fibrous strip from (beans). **5** (phr v) **string sb along** deliberately mislead sb, esp about one's own intentions, beliefs, etc: *She has no intention of marrying him — she's just stringing him along.* **string along (with sb)** stay with or accompany sb casually or as long as it is convenient; tag along: *I don't want them stringing along as well!* ○ *She decided to string along with the others as she had nothing else to do.* **string (sb/sth) out** (cause sb/sth to) be or become spread out at intervals in a line: *The players were told to string out across the field.* ○ *The horses were strung out towards the end of the race.* ○ *Warning notices were strung out along the motorway.* **string sth together** combine (words, phrases, etc) to form meaningful statements: *I can just manage to string a few words of French together.* ○ *He hadn't prepared a speech but he managed to string together a few remarks at the end of the meeting.* **string sb up** *(infml)* kill sb by hanging (esp not legally): *If the crowd catch him, they'll string him up on the nearest tree.*

□ **ˈstringed instrument** musical instrument with strings that are played by touching them with a bow or plectrum: *The viola is a stringed instrument.*

stringent /ˈstrɪndʒənt/ *adj* **1** (of a law, rule, etc) that must be obeyed; strict or severe: *a stringent ban on smoking.* **2** (of financial conditions) difficult because there is not enough money: *a stringent economic climate.* ▷ **stringency** /-nsɪ/ *n* [U]: *in these days of financial stringency.* **stringently** *adv*: *The regulations must be stringently observed.*

stringer /ˈstrɪŋə(r)/ *n* newspaper correspondent who is not on the regular staff.

strip /strɪp/ *v* **(-pp-) 1 (a)** [Tn, Tn·pr, Tn·p, Cn·a] **sth (from/off sth/sb)**; ~ **sth/sb (of sth)**; ~ **sth (off)** take off (clothes, coverings, parts, etc) from sb/sth: *strip* (ie dismantle) *a machine* ○ *strip the bark off a tree/strip a tree of its bark* ○ *The bandits stripped him (naked)/stripped him of his clothes.* ○ *The paint will be difficult to strip off.* ○ *They stripped the house bare,* ie removed everything from it. **(b)** [I, Ipr, Ip] ~ **(down) (to sth)**; ~ **(off)** take off one's clothes: *The doctor asked the patient* *to strip.* ○ *strip to* (ie remove all one's clothes except) *one's underwear* ○ *strip to the waist,* ie remove clothes from the upper part of one's body ○ *They stripped off and ran into the water.* **2** [Tn·pr] ~ **sb of sth** take away (property, honours, etc) from sb: *He was stripped of all his possessions.* ○ *The general was stripped of his rank.* **3** [Tn] damage the thread of (a screw) or the teeth of (a gear), esp by misuse. **4** (idm) **strip to the buff** (*infml*) take all one's clothes off; undress completely. **5** (phr v) **strip sth down** remove all the detachable parts of (esp an engine) in order to clean or repair it.

▷ **strip** *n* **1** act of stripping (STRIP 1b), esp in a striptease show: *do a strip.* **2** long narrow piece (of material, etc) or area (of land, etc): *a strip of paper* ○ *a strip of land suitable for a garden* ○ *a landing-strip in the jungle.* **3** (*infml*) clothes of a particular colour or colours worn by the members of a football team: *England are playing in the blue and white strip.* **4** (idm) **tear sb off a strip/tear a strip off sb** ⇨ TEAR[2].

stripper *n* **1** [C] person who performs in a strip-tease. **2** [C, U] device or solvent for removing paint, etc.

□ ˈ**strip cartoon** (*Brit*) = COMIC STRIP (COMIC).

ˈ**strip club** (*US* also ˈ**strip joint**) club in which strip-tease is performed.

ˈ**strip cropping** (also ˌ**strip culti**ˈ**vation**) system of growing different crops in alternate narrow rows to avoid soil erosion, eg on a hillside.

ˈ**strip lighting**, ˈ**strip light** (method of lighting with a) long tubular fluorescent lamp (instead of a bulb).

ˈ**strip mine** (*esp US*) opencast mine.

ˈ**strip-tease** *n* [C, U] entertainment (eg in a theatre, bar or nightclub) in which a performer slowly undresses in front of an audience.

stripe /straɪp/ *n* **1** long narrow band (usu of the same width throughout its length) on a surface that is usu different from it in colour, material or texture: *a white table-cloth with red stripes* ○ *the tiger's stripes* ○ *The plates have a blue stripe round the edge.* ⇨ illus at PATTERN. **2** badge (often in the shape of a V) that is worn on the uniform of a soldier, policeman, etc as a mark of rank; chevron: *How many stripes are there on a sergeant's sleeve?* ○ *She was awarded another stripe.* **3** (usu *pl*) (*arch*) blow with a whip; stroke.

▷ **striped** /straɪpt/ *adj* marked with or having stripes (STRIPE 1): *striped material* ○ *a striped shirt, suit, tie.*

stripy /ˈstraɪpɪ/ *adj* (**-ier, -iest**) (*infml*) = STRIPED: *bright stripy cloth.*

stripling /ˈstrɪplɪŋ/ *n* (*fml or joc*) male person between boyhood and manhood; youth or lad: *a young man, hardly more than a stripling.*

strive /straɪv/ *v* (*pt* **strove** /strəʊv/, *pp* **striven** /ˈstrɪvn/) (*fml*) **1** [Ipr, It] ~ (**for/after sth**) try very hard (to obtain or achieve sth): *strive for success* ○ *strive to improve one's performance.* **2** [I, Ipr] ~ (**against/with sb/sth**) carry on a conflict; struggle: *strive against oppression, the enemy.*

stroboscope /ˈstrəʊbəskəʊp/ *n* instrument that produces a rapidly flashing bright light. ▷ **stroboscopic** /ˌstrəʊbəˈskɒpɪk/ *adj.*

□ ˈ**strobe light** (also **strobe**) light that flashes rapidly on and off: *disco dancers lit by strobe lights.*

strode *pt* of STRIDE.

stroganoff /ˈstrɒgənɒf/ *n* [C, U] dish prepared from strips of meat, esp beef, cooked in a sauce made from sour cream: *ˌbeef ˈstroganoff.*

Stroheim /ˈstrəʊˌhaɪm/ Erich von (1885-1957), Austrian-born American film director and actor. The extravagance of such films as his silent masterpiece *Greed* limited his opportunities to direct, and he settled for portraying a series of sinister characters.

stroke[1] /strəʊk/ *n* **1** (**a**) act or process of striking; blow: *kill sb with one stroke of a sword* ○ *20 strokes with a whip.* (**b**) (*sport*) (in tennis, golf, etc) act of striking a ball; (in golf) this used as a unit of scoring: *a forehand stroke* ○ *a graceful stroke with the bat* ○ *She won by two strokes.* **2** (**a**) any of a series of repeated movements, esp in swimming or rowing: *long powerful strokes* ○ *a fast/slow stroke,* ie in rowing. (**b**) (esp in compounds) style of stroke in swimming: *do (the) breast-stroke, back-stroke, etc* ○ *Which stroke are you best at?* **3** (in a rowing crew) oarsman who sits nearest the stern of a racing boat, and sets the speed of the strokes. Cf BOW[3] 2. **4** ~ **of sth** single successful or effective action or occurrence (of the specified kind): *Your idea was a stroke of genius!* ○ *It was a stroke of luck that I found you here.* ○ *Various strokes of misfortune led to his ruin.* **5** (mark made by a) single movement of a pen or brush: *thin/thick strokes* ○ *with a stroke of the pen* ○ *put the finishing strokes to a painting.* **6** sound made by a bell or clock striking the hours: *on the stroke of three,* ie at three o'clock exactly. **7** (*medical*) sudden attack of illness in the brain owing to vascular disturbance that is often fatal and also results in loss of power to move, speak clearly, etc in survivors: *The stroke left him paralysed on one side of his body.* Cf APOPLEXY. **8** (idm) **at a/one** ˈ**stroke** with a single immediate action: *They threatened to cancel the whole project at a stroke.* **not do a stroke (of work)** not do any work: *We'll have to get rid of him — he never does a stroke.* **put sb off his** ˈ**stroke** cause sb to falter, hesitate, etc in what he is doing: *My speech went quite well until I was put off my stroke by the interruption.*

▷ **stroke** *v* **1** [Tn] act as a stroke[1](3) to (a boat or crew). **2** [Tn·pr, Tn·p] strike (a ball): *stroked the ball cleverly past her opponent.*

stroke[2] /strəʊk/ *v* [Tn] pass the hand gently over (a surface), usu again and again: *stroke a cat, one's beard, sb's back.*

▷ **stroke** *n* (usu *sing*) act of stroking; stroking movement: *give her hair an affectionate stroke.*

stroll /strəʊl/ *n* slow leisurely walk: *go for/have a stroll.*

▷ **stroll** *v* [I, Ipr, Ip] walk in a slow leisurely way: *strolling (around) in the park* ○ *He strolls in and out as he pleases.* **stroller** *n* **1** person who strolls. **2** (*esp US*) = PUSH-CHAIR (PUSH[2]).

□ ˌ**strolling** ˈ**players** (*often joc*) actors, etc who travel around performing in different places.

Stromboli /ˈstrɒmbəlɪ/ active volcano situated on an island off the south-west coast of Italy. It has given its name to a type of eruption that is intermittent and non-violent.

strong /strɒŋ; *US* strɔːŋ/ *adj* (**-er** /-ŋgə(r)/, **-est** /-ŋgɪst/) **1** (**a**) not easily broken, hurt, injured, captured, etc; solid and sturdy: *a strong stick, fort, structure* ○ *feel quite strong again,* ie in good health after an illness ○ *The chair wasn't strong enough and it broke when he sat on it.* ○ *We need strong defences against the enemy.* ○ *We still have a strong chance of winning.* (**b**) having great power, esp of the body: *strong muscles* ○ *a strong country,* ie one with a large army, etc ○ *an actor with a strong voice* ○ *strong enough to lift a piano alone.* (**c**) done or happening with great power: *a strong push, blow* ○ *play a strong shot,* eg in tennis. **2** (**a**) (of emotions, opinions, etc) that can resist influence: *strong will, belief, determination* ○ *have strong nerves,* ie be not easily frightened, worried, etc. (**b**) that can exert great influence: *a strong conviction, protest* ○ *a strong personality* ○ *strong leadership* ○ *There is strong* (ie convincing) *evidence of her guilt.* (**c**) [attrib] (of a person) convinced; determined: *a strong believer, supporter.* **3** moving quickly: *a strong wind, current, etc.* **4** (**a**) (capable of) having a great effect on the senses; intense or powerful: *a strong light, colour* ○ *a strong feeling of nausea* ○ *Her breath is rather strong,* ie has an unpleasant smell. (**b**) having a lot of flavour: *strong tea, cheese, etc* ○ *a strong taste of garlic.* (**c**) (of a drink) containing much alcohol: *Whisky is stronger than beer.* **5** (of a person) effective; skilful; able: *a strong candidate for a job,* ie one who is likely to get it ○ *a pupil who is strong in physics but weak in English.* **6** (after numbers) having the specified number: *an army 5000 strong/a 5000-strong army.* **7** (*commerce*) (**a**) rising steadily: *strong prices, share values, etc* ○ *The stock market is stronger now,* ie People are more willing to buy shares, etc. (**b**) (of a currency) having a high value in relation to other currencies: *Is the pound strong or weak (against the yen) at the moment?* **8** [usu attrib] (*grammar*) (**a**) (of a verb) forming the past tense by a vowel change (eg *sing, sang*), not by adding *-d, -ed* or *-t.* (**b**) (of the pronunciation of some words) that is the version used when the word is stressed: *The strong form of 'and' is* /ænd/. **9** [pred] (*infml esp Brit*) not to be tolerated, believed, etc: *It was a bit strong of him to call me a liar in front of the whole department.* **10** (idm) **be strong on sth** be good at sth or doing sth: *I'm not very strong on dates.* **one's best/strongest card** ⇨ CARD[1]. **going** ˈ**strong** (*infml*) continuing (a race, an activity, etc) vigorously; continuing to be healthy: *She's 91 years old and still going strong.* ○ *The runner is still going strong on the last lap.* (**as**) **strong as a** ˈ**horse/an** ˈ**ox** having great physical strength; able to do heavy work. **one's/sb's strong** ˈ**point/**ˈ**suit** thing that one/sb does well: *Don't ask me to add up the bill: arithmetic isn't my strong point.* **a strong stomach** ability not to feel nausea: *You have to have a strong stomach to watch animals being slaughtered.* ▷ **strongly** *adv: strongly built* ○ *a light shining strongly* ○ *a strongly-worded protest* ○ *She finished the race strongly.* ○ *I feel strongly that. . .,* ie I firmly believe that. . . .

□ ˈ**strong-arm** *adj* [attrib] using violence: *use strong-arm methods, tactics, etc.*

ˈ**strong-box** *n* sturdy box for keeping valuable things in.

ˈ**stronghold** *n* **1** fort. **2** (*fig*) place where there is much support for a cause, etc: *a stronghold of republicanism.*

ˌ**strong** ˈ**language** (*euph*) language containing curses and swearing.

ˌ**strong-**ˈ**minded** *adj* having a determined mind.

ˈ**strong-room** *n* room, eg in a bank, with thick walls and a sturdy door, where valuables are kept.

strontium /ˈstrɒntɪəm; *US* -nʃɪəm/ *n* [U] (*symb* **Sr**) chemical element, a soft silver-white metal. ⇨ App 11.

□ ˌ**strontium** ˈ**90** radioactive form of strontium found in the fall-out from nuclear explosions and extremely harmful to people and animals when taken into the body.

strop /strɒp/ *n* leather strap on which a razor is sharpened, or a machine used for the same purpose.

▷ **strop** *v* (**-pp-**) [Tn] sharpen (a razor) on a strop.

strophe /ˈstrəʊfɪ/ *n* **1** (in ancient Greek drama) (**a**) movement of the chorus in turning from one side of the stage to the other. (**b**) song that accompanies this movement. Cf ANTISTROPHE, EPODE. **2** (verse or section of a) song or poem.

stroppy /ˈstrɒpɪ/ *adj* (**-ier, -iest**) (*Brit sl*) (of a person) awkward to deal with; bad-tempered: *Don't get stroppy with me — it's not my fault!*

strove *pt* of STRIVE.

struck *pt, pp* of STRIKE.

structuralism /ˈstrʌktʃərəlɪzəm/ *n* [U] method of analysing a subject (eg social sciences, psychology, language, literature), which concentrates on the structure of a system and the relations between its elements, rather than on the function of those elements.

▷ **structuralist** /-rəlɪst/ *adj* [esp attrib]: *a structuralist approach, analysis.* — *n* person who uses structuralist methods.

structure /ˈstrʌktʃə(r)/ *n* **1** [U, C] way in which sth is put together, organized, built, etc: *the structure of the human body* ○ *rules of sentence structure* ○ *the company's management structure* ○ *molecular structure.* **2** [C] anything made of many parts; any complex whole; building: *The model is an odd-looking structure of balls and rods.* ○ *The Parthenon is a magnificent structure.*

▷ **structure** *v* [Tn] give a structure to (sth); plan or organize: *structure one's day, life, career* ○ *an intelligently structured essay.*

structural /ˈstrʌktʃərəl/ *adj* [usu attrib] of a structure or the framework of a structure: *structural alterations to a building,* eg removing internal walls to make rooms bigger. ˌ**structural** ˈ**formula** chemical formula which shows how groups of atoms are arranged within a molecule of a substance. Cf EMPIRICAL FORMULA (EMPIRICAL),

MOLECULAR FORMULA (MOLECULE). **structurally** /-rəlɪ/ *adv*: *The building is structurally sound.*

strudel /ˈstruːdl/ *n* [C, U] type of cake made of sweetened fruit, etc rolled up in thin pastry and baked: *a slice of apple strudel.*

struggle /ˈstrʌgl/ *v* **1 (a)** [I, Ipr, Ip] ~ **(with sb)** fight (with sb): *two boys struggling (together)* ○ *The shopkeeper struggled with the thief.* **(b)** [I, Ipr, Ip, It] ~ **(against/with sb/sth)** move one's body vigorously, eg trying to get free: *The prisoner struggled (against his captors) but couldn't escape.* ○ *She struggled to get away from her attacker.* **2** [I, Ipr, It] ~ **(against/with sb/sth) (for sth)** try to overcome difficulties, etc; make great efforts: *struggle with a problem, one's conscience* ○ *The two leaders are struggling for power.* ○ *a struggling artist*, eg who finds it hard to sell his work ○ *We must struggle against this prejudice for a more tolerant attitude to our beliefs.* ○ *I'm struggling to finish the huge helping you gave me.* **3** [Ipr, Ip] make one's way with difficulty (in the specified direction): *The chick finally broke through the shell and struggled out (of it).* **4** (phr v) **struggle along/on** manage to survive in spite of great difficulties: *We're struggling along on a tiny income.*

▷ **struggle** *n* **1** fight: *a fierce struggle between two wrestlers* ○ *a power struggle* ○ *the class struggle* ○ *We will not surrender without a struggle.* **2** (usu *sing*) great effort: *After a long struggle, she gained control of the business.*

strum /strʌm/ *v* (**-mm-**) [I, Ipr, Ip, Tn] ~ **(on sth)** play (a stringed instrument), esp rather unskilfully or monotonously: *strumming (away) on my guitar* ○ *strum a tune on the banjo.*

strumpet /ˈstrʌmpɪt/ *n* (*arch or joc derog*) female prostitute.

strung *pt, pp* of STRING[2].

□ **strung up** /ˌstrʌŋ ˈʌp/ nervously tense or excited: *I get very strung up before an exam.*

strut[1] /strʌt/ *n* rod or bar placed in a framework to strengthen and brace it.

strut[2] /strʌt/ *v* (**-tt-**) [I, Ipr, Ip] (*often derog*) walk in an upright, proud way: *strutting peacocks* ○ *She strutted past us, ignoring our greeting.*

▷ **strut** *n* (usu *sing*) such a way of walking.

strychnine /ˈstrɪkniːn/ *n* [U] poisonous substance used in very small doses to stimulate the nerves.

Stuart[1] /ˈstjuːət; *US* ˈstuːərt/ name of the family of kings and queens which ruled Scotland 1371-1714 and Britain 1603-1714. ⇨ App 3. ⇨ illus at DRESS.

Stuart[2] /ˈstjuːət; *US* ˈstuːərt/ Charles Edward (1720-88), grandson of *James II, also known as 'the Young Pretender' and 'Bonny Prince Charlie'. He led the *Jacobite uprising of 1745 on behalf of his father James, 'the Old Pretender', capturing Edinburgh and defeating the forces of George II at Prestonpans. He was finally defeated at *Culloden and died in exile in Rome. ⇨ article at SCOTLAND.

stub /stʌb/ *n* **1** short end piece or stump remaining from a pencil, cigarette or similarly-shaped object; butt: *The crayon had been worn down to a stub.* ○ *The dog only has a stub of a tail*, ie a very short one. **2** counterfoil: *fill in a cheque stub.*

▷ **stub** *v* (**-bb-**) **1** [Tn, Tn·pr] ~ **sth (against/on sth)** strike (esp one's toe) accidentally against sth hard: *I've stubbed my toe on a rock.* **2** (phr v) **stub sth out** extinguish (esp a cigarette) by pressing it against sth hard.

stubble /ˈstʌbl/ *n* [U] **1** short ends of grain stalks left in the ground after harvesting. **2** short stiff hairs of a beard: *three days' stubble on his chin.*

▷ **stubbly** /ˈstʌblɪ/ *adj* of or like stubble: *a stubbly beard, chin.*

stubborn /ˈstʌbən/ *adj* **1** (*often derog*) determined not to give way; strong-willed; obstinate: *be too stubborn to apologize* ○ *show stubborn resistance to change.* **2** difficult to move, remove, cure, etc: *You'll have to push hard, that door is a bit stubborn.* ○ *a stubborn cough that has lasted for weeks.* **3** (idm) **obstinate/stubborn as a mule** ⇨ MULE[1]. ▷ **stubbornly** *adv*: *stubbornly refuse to do it.* **stubbornness** *n* [U].

Stubbs /stʌbz/ George (1724-1806), English artist. He is famous for his portraits of horses, which not only show the animal in careful detail, but also convey its spirit and dignity. ⇨ illus.

George Stubbs: Joseph Smyth

stubby /ˈstʌbɪ/ *adj* (**-ier, -iest**) short and thick: *stubby fingers* ○ *a stubby tail.*

stucco /ˈstʌkəʊ/ *n* [U] plaster or cement used for covering or decorating walls or ceilings. ▷ **stuccoed** *adj.*

stuck[1] *pt, pp* of STICK[2].

stuck[2] /stʌk/ *adj* **1** [pred] not able to move or continue doing sth: *Help! I'm stuck in the mud!* ○ *We were stuck in a traffic jam for an hour.* ○ *I'm stuck on* (ie unable to answer) *the second question.* **2** [attrib] (of an animal) that has been stabbed or has had its throat cut: *scream like a stuck pig.* **3** [pred] ~ **on sb** (*infml*) very fond of sb: *He's really stuck on his new girl-friend.* **4** [pred] ~ **with sb/sth** (*infml*) having sb/sth one does not want: *I'm stuck with my sister for the whole day.* ○ *Why am I always stuck with the washing-up?* **5** (idm) **get stuck in(to sth)** (*infml*) start doing sth enthusiastically: *Here's your food. Now get stuck in* (ie start eating it)! ○ *We got stuck into the job immediately.*

stuck-up /ˌstʌk ˈʌp/ *adj* (*infml*) conceited and unwilling to mix with others; snobbish.

stud[1] /stʌd/ *n* **1 (a)** small two-headed button-like device put through buttonholes to fasten a collar, shirt-front, etc. **(b)** piece of jewellery (esp an ear-ring) consisting of a precious stone, etc attached to a small bar: *diamond studs in her ears.* **2 (a)** large-headed nail or knob (usu one of many) on the surface of sth (eg a gate or a shield) as an ornament. **(b)** small round knob on the sole of a shoe or boot, to allow it to grip better: *the studs on a football boot.*

▷ **stud** *v* (**-dd-**) [Tn, Tn·pr usu passive] ~ **sth (with sth)** decorate (a surface) with many studs, precious stones, etc: *millions of stars studding the night sky* ○ *a crown studded with jewels* ○ *a sea studded with small islands.*

stud[2] /stʌd/ *n* **1 (a)** number of horses kept esp for breeding: [attrib] *a stud mare.* **(b)** (also **ˈstud-farm**) place where such horses are kept. **2** (⚠ *infml*) young man, esp one who is thought to be very active sexually and is regarded as a good sexual partner. **3** (idm) **at ˈstud** (of a stallion) available for breeding on payment of a fee. **put sth out to ˈstud** keep (a horse) for breeding.

□ **ˈstud-book** *n* book containing the pedigrees of (esp) racehorses.

ˌstud ˈpoker poker[2] in which bets are made after the cards have been dealt face up.

student /ˈstjuːdnt; *US* ˈstuː-/ *n* **1 (a)** person who is studying for a degree, diploma, etc at a university or some other place of higher education or technical training: *a BA student* ○ *a medical student* ○ [attrib] *a student nurse, teacher, etc* ○ *student politics* ○ *the student body*, ie all the students at a university, etc. **(b)** (*esp US*) boy or girl at school. **2** ~ **of sth** (*fml*) person who is studying or has a particular interest in sth: *a student of politics, human nature, theology.*

studied /ˈstʌdɪd/ *adj* carefully considered; intentional; deliberate: *reply with studied indifference* ○ *the studied slowness of his movements.*

studio /ˈstjuːdɪəʊ; *US* ˈstuː-/ *n* (*pl* ~**s**) **1** work-room of a painter, sculptor, photographer, etc. **2** room from which radio or television programmes are regularly broadcast or in which recordings are made: [attrib] *a studio audience*, ie an audience in a studio, to provide applause, laughter, etc. **3 (a)** place where cinema films are acted and photographed. **(b)** (usu *pl*) cinema company, including all its buildings, offices, etc: [attrib] *a studio executive.*

□ **ˌstudio ˈcouch** couch that can be converted into a bed.

ˈstudio flat (*Brit*) (also *esp US* **ˌstudio aˈpartment**) small flat, usu having a main room for living and sleeping in, with a small kitchen and a bathroom.

studious /ˈstjuːdɪəs; *US* ˈstuː-/ *adj* **1** spending a lot of time studying: *a studious pupil.* **2** [esp attrib] (*fml*) showing great carefulness; deliberate: *the studious checking of details* ○ *with studious politeness.* ▷ **studiously** *adv.* **studiousness** *n* [U].

study[1] /ˈstʌdɪ/ *n* **1** [U] (also **studies** [pl]) process of gaining knowledge of a subject, esp from books: *fond of study* ○ *give all one's spare time to study* ○ *My studies show that...* ○ [attrib] *study time.* **2** [C] **(a)** (book, etc that is the result of an) investigation of a subject: *make a study of the country's export trade* ○ *publish a study of Locke's philosophy.* **(b)** (usu *pl*) subject that is (to be) investigated: *scientific, legal studies.* **3** [C] room, esp in sb's home, used for reading and writing. **4** [C] **(a)** drawing, etc done for practice, esp before doing a larger picture. **(b)** (*music*) composition designed to give a player exercise in technical skills. **5 a study** [sing] thing worth observing; unusual sight: *His* *face was a study as he listened to their amazing news.* **6** (idm) **in a brown study** ⇨ BROWN.

study[2] /ˈstʌdɪ/ *v* (*pt, pp* **studied**) **1** [I, Ipr, It, Tn, Tw] give one's time and attention to learning about (sth), esp by reading, attending a university, etc: *studying (for a degree in) medicine* ○ *studying to be a doctor* ○ *It's hard finding time to study (the subject).* ○ *I'm studying how children learn to speak.* **2** [Tn, Tn·pr] examine (sth) very carefully: *study the map, menu, programme* ○ *Scientists are studying the photographs of Mars for signs of life.*

stuff[1] /stʌf/ *n* [U] **1** material of which sth is made: *What stuff is this jacket made of?* ○ *A kind of plastic stuff is used to make the plates.* ○ *(fig) Real life is the stuff* (ie subject-matter) *of all good novels.* ○ *(fig) We must find out what stuff he is made of,* ie what sort of man he is, what his character is. **2** (*sl*) unnamed things, belongings, activities, subject-matter, etc: *Leave your stuff in the hall.* ○ *This book is really boring stuff.* ○ *Do you call this stuff beer?* ○ *There has been some really good stuff on TV lately.* **3** (*arch*) woollen fabric, as distinct from silk, cotton or linen. **4** (idm) **a bit of stuff** ⇨ BIT[1]. **do one's ˈstuff** (*infml*) show what one can do, etc: *It's your turn to sing now, so do your stuff.* **hot stuff** ⇨ HOT. **kid's stuff** ⇨ KID[1]. **know one's onions/stuff** ⇨ KNOW. **ˌstuff and ˈnonsense** *interj* (*dated infml*) (used to dismiss sth that has been said): *Stuff and nonsense! You don't know what you're talking about.* **ˌthat's the ˈstuff!** (*infml*) that is good or what is needed.

stuff[2] /stʌf/ *v* **1** (**a**) [Tn, Tn·pr, Tn·p] ~ **sth** (**up**) (**with sth**) fill sth tightly (with sth); cram sth (with sth): *stuff a pillow (with feathers)* ○ *stuff up a hole (with newspapers)* ○ *My nose is stuffed up,* ie full of mucus. ○ *(fig) Don't stuff him with silly ideas.* (**b**) [Tn·pr, Tn·p] ~ **sth into sth/in** cram sth tightly into sth: *stuff feathers into a pillow* ○ *She stuffed her clothes in and then tried to close the lid.* **2** [Tn·pr, Tn·p] push (sth) quickly and carelessly (in the specified place or direction): *She stuffed the coins into her pocket.* ○ *He stuffed the letter through (the door) and hurried away.* **3** [I, Tn, Tn·pr] ~ (**sb/oneself**) (**with sth**) fill (sb/oneself) with food; eat greedily: *I'm stuffed* (ie full of food)*!* ○ *She sat stuffing herself with biscuits.* **4** [Tn, Tn·pr] ~ **sth** (**with sth**) put chopped and flavoured food into (a bird, etc) before cooking it: *stuffed veal* ○ *a turkey stuffed with parsley, thyme, chestnuts, etc.* **5** [Tn esp passive] fill the empty carcass of (a bird, an animal, etc) with enough material to restore it to its original shape, eg for exhibition in a museum: *a stuffed tiger, owl, etc.* **6** [Tn] (*sl*) (used to express rejection of sth) dispose of (sth) as unwanted; do as one likes with (sth): *You can stuff the job, I don't want it.* **7** [Tn] (⚠ *dated sl*) have sexual intercourse with (a woman). **8** (idm) **get ˈstuffed** (*Brit sl*) (used to express contempt, rejection, etc): *He wanted to borrow some money from me but I told him to get stuffed.* **a stuffed ˈshirt** (*infml*) pompous or pretentious person.

▷ **stuffing** *n* [U] **1** (*US* **dressing**) chopped and flavoured food used for stuffing (STUFF[2] 4) a bird, etc before it is cooked. **2** padding used to stuff cushions, etc. **3** (idm) **knock the stuffing out of sb** ⇨ KNOCK[2].

stuffy /ˈstʌfɪ/ *adj* (**-ier, -iest**) **1** (of a room, etc) not having much fresh air: *a smoky, stuffy pub.* **2** (*infml*) (of a person or thing) formal and dull; prim; staid: *a stuffy newspaper, club, legal practice* ○ *Only the stuffier members were shocked by her jokes.* **3** (*infml*) (of the nose) blocked so that breathing is difficult; stuffed up. ▷ **stuffily** /-ɪlɪ/ *adv.* **stuffiness** *n* [U].

stultify /ˈstʌltɪfaɪ/ *v* (*pt, pp* **-fied**) [Tn] (*fml*) **1** cause (sth) to be ineffective or seem absurd; negate: *Their unhelpfulness has stultified our efforts to improve things.* **2** cause (sb) to feel dull, bored, etc: *the stultifying effect of work that never varies.* ▷ **stultification** /ˌstʌltɪfɪˈkeɪʃn/ *n* [U].

stumble /ˈstʌmbl/ *v* [I, Ipr] **1** ~ (**over sth**) strike one's foot against sth and almost fall: *stumble and fall* ○ *I stumbled over a tree root.* **2** ~ (**over sth**); ~ **through sth** make a mistake or mistakes as one speaks, plays music, etc: *She stumbled briefly (over the unfamiliar word) but then continued.* ○ *The child stumbled through a piece by Chopin.* **3** (phr v) **stumble about, along, around, etc** move or walk unsteadily (in the specified direction): *A drunk stumbled past us.* ○ *stumbling around in the dark.* ⇨ Usage at SHUFFLE. **stumble across/on sb/sth** find sb/sth unexpectedly or by chance: *Police investigating tax fraud stumbled across a drugs ring.*

▷ **stumble** *n* act of stumbling.

□ **ˈstumblebum** *n* (*US infml derog*) clumsy or incompetent person, esp a drunk or a tramp.

ˈstumbling-block *n* thing that causes difficulty or hesitation; obstacle: *The failure to agree on manning levels is a major stumbling-block to progress in the talks.*

stump /stʌmp/ *n* **1** part of a tree left in the ground after the rest has fallen or been cut down. **2** (**a**) anything similar that remains after the main part has been cut or broken off, or worn down: *the stump of a pencil, cigar, tooth.* (**b**) remaining part of an amputated limb. **3** (in cricket) any of the three short upright poles at which the ball is bowled: *the leg/middle/off stump.* ⇨ illus at CRICKET. **4** (idm) **draw stumps** ⇨ DRAW[2]. **stir one's stumps** ⇨ STIR.

▷ **stump** *v* **1** [Ipr, Ip] walk stiffly or noisily: *They stumped up the hill.* ○ *He stumped out in fury.* ⇨ Usage. **2** [Tn esp passive] (*infml*) be too difficult for (sb); puzzle: *I'm stumped: I just don't know what to do.* ○ *Everybody was stumped by the problem.* **3** [Tn] (*esp US*) go around (a region) making political speeches, eg before an election. **4** [Tn] (of a wicket-keeper in cricket) end the innings of (a batsman) by touching the stumps with the ball while he is out of his crease(3). **5** (phr v) **stump up** (**sth**) (**for sth**) (*infml*) pay (a sum of money): *I'm always being asked to stump up (extra cash) for school outings.*

NOTE ON USAGE: **Stump**, **stomp**, **plod**, **trudge** and **tramp** all indicate styles of walking with heavy steps. **Stump** and **stomp** can both suggest making a noise while walking in order to show anger: *He slammed the door and stumped/stomped upstairs.* Additionally, **stump** can indicate walking with stiff legs: *stumping up the garden path.* **Stomp** can suggest clumsy and noisy walking or dancing: *He looked funny stomping round the dance floor.* **Plod** and **trudge** indicate a slow, weary walk towards a particular destination. **Plod** suggests a steady pace and **trudge** suggests greater effort: *They had to plod wearily on up the hill.* ○ *We trudged home through deep snow.* **Tramp** indicates walking over long distances, possibly with no specified destination: *They tramped the streets, looking for somewhere to stay the night.*

stumpy /ˈstʌmpɪ/ *adj* (**-ier, -iest**) short and thick: *a stumpy little man* ○ *stumpy legs.* ▷ **stumpiness** *n* [U].

stun /stʌn/ *v* (**-nn-**) **1** [Tn] make (a person or an animal) unconscious by a blow, esp to the head: *The punch stunned me for a moment.* ○ *She sat stunned for a while, until she recovered.* **2** (*fig*) (**a**) [Tn] daze or shock (sb), eg with sth unexpected: *I was stunned by the news of his death.* (**b**) [Tn esp passive] impress (sb) greatly: *stunned by her beauty, cleverness, etc.*

▷ **stunner** *n* (*infml*) person, esp a woman, who is very attractive.

stunning *adj* (*infml*) (**a**) impressive; splendid: *You look stunning in your new suit.* ○ *What a stunning idea!* (**b**) surprising or shocking: *a stunning revelation.* **stunningly** *adv.*

stung *pt, pp* of STING[2].

stunk *pp* of STINK.

stunt[1] /stʌnt/ *n* (*infml*) (**a**) thing done to attract attention: *a publicity stunt* ○ *pull* (ie perform) *a stunt.* (**b**) thing dangerous or difficult done as entertainment: *Her latest stunt is riding a motor cycle through a ring of flames.* ○ [attrib] *stunt flying,* ie aerobatics.

□ **ˈstunt man** (*fem* **ˈstunt woman**) person who does dangerous stunts in place of an actor in a film, etc.

stunt[2] /stʌnt/ *v* [Tn esp passive] prevent (sth/sb) from growing or developing properly: *stunted trees* ○ *Inadequate food can stunt a child's development.*

stupefy /ˈstju:pɪfaɪ; *US* ˈstu:-/ *v* (*pt, pp* **-fied**) [esp passive: Tn, Tn·pr] ~ **sb** (**with sth**) **1** dull the mind or senses of (sb): *stupefied with drink* ○ *(fig) the stupefying boredom of this repetitive work.* **2** overcome (sb) with astonishment; amaze: *I was stupefied by what I read.*

▷ **stupefaction** /ˌstju:pɪˈfækʃn; *US* ˌstu:-/ *n* [U] (*fml*) state of being stupefied.

stupendous /stju:ˈpendəs; *US* stu:-/ *adj* amazingly large, impressive, good, etc: *a stupendous mistake, achievement* ○ *The opera was quite stupendous!* ▷ **stupendously** *adv.*

stupid /ˈstju:pɪd; *US* ˈstu:/ *adj* (**-er, -est**) **1** (**a**) slow to learn or understand things; not intelligent or clever: *a stupid person, dog.* (**b**) showing lack of good judgement; foolish: *a stupid plan, idea, remark* ○ *What a stupid thing to do!* (**c**) [attrib] (*infml*) (used dismissively or to show irritation): *I don't want to hear your stupid secret anyway!* ○ *This stupid car won't start.* **2** [usu pred] ~ (**with sth**) (*fml*) in a stupor: *stupid with sleep.*

▷ **stupidity** /stju:ˈpɪdətɪ; *US* stu:-/ *n* **1** [U] state of being stupid. **2** [C usu *pl*] stupid act, remark, etc: *the stupidities of schoolboy humour.*

stupidly *adv.*

stupor /ˈstju:pə(r); *US* ˈstu:-/ *n* [U, C usu *sing*] condition of being dazed or nearly unconscious caused by shock, drugs, alcohol, etc: *in a drunken stupor.*

sturdy /ˈstɜ:dɪ/ *adj* (**-ier, -iest**) **1** (**a**) strong and solid: *a sturdy chair, structure, car.* (**b**) fit and healthy: *a sturdy child, constitution.* **2** determined, firm; sound: *sturdy resistance to the plan* ○ *sturdy common sense.* ▷ **sturdily** /-ɪlɪ/ *adv*: *a sturdily built bicycle, man.* **sturdiness** *n* [U].

sturgeon /ˈstɜ:dʒən/ *n* any of various types of large freshwater fish eaten as food, and from which caviare is obtained.

stutter /ˈstʌtə(r)/ *v* [I, Tn, Tn·p] = STAMMER.

▷ **stutterer** /ˈstʌtərə(r)/ *n* person who stutters.

stutteringly /ˈstʌtərɪŋlɪ/ *adv.*

sty[1] /staɪ/ *n* = PIGSTY (PIG).

sty[2] (also **stye**) /staɪ/ *n* (*pl* **sties** or **styes**) inflamed swelling on the edge of the eyelid.

Stygian /ˈstɪdʒɪən/ *adj* [usu attrib] (*fml*) very dark, gloomy (like the river *Styx in the underworld): *the Stygian blackness of the night.*

style /staɪl/ *n* **1** [C, U] (**a**) manner of writing or speaking, esp contrasted with what is actually written or said: *She's a very popular writer but I just don't like her style.* ○ *write in house style,* ie following the manner of spelling and punctuation etc used by a particular publishing company ○ *a style of speech-making that is easy to listen to.* (**b**) manner that is typical of a particular writer, artist etc or of a particular literary, artistic, etc period: *a poem in classical style* ○ *a building in Gothic, Romanesque, Tudor, etc style* ○ *the architectural styles of ancient Greece.* **2** [C, U] manner of doing anything: *a typically British style of living* ○ *a very unusual style of swimming* ○ *American-style hamburgers* ○ *I like your style,* ie the way you do things. **3** [U] superior or fashionable quality of sb or sth; distinctiveness: *She performs the songs with style and flair.* ○ *The piano gives the room a touch of style.* **4** (**a**) [C, U] fashion in dress, etc: *the latest styles in trousers, hats, shoes, etc* ○ *have a good sense of style.* (**b**) [C] way in which sth is made, shaped, etc; design; type: *a very short hair-style* ○ *We have vases in various styles.* **5** [C] (*fml*) correct title for use when addressing sb: *Has he any right to use the style of Colonel?* **6** [C] (*botany*) narrow extension of the seed-bearing part of a plant. **7** (idm) **cramp sb's style** ⇨ CRAMP[2]. **in** (**great, grand, etc**) **style** in a grand or elegant way: *dine in style* ○ *We arrived in fine style in a hired limousine.* (**not/more**) **sb's style** what sb likes: *Big cars are not my style.* ○ *I don't like opera; chamber music is more my style.*

▷ **style** *v* **1** [Tn, Cn·a] design, shape or make (sth) in a particular (esp fashionable) style: *style sb's hair (shorter).* **2** [Tn, Cn·n] (*fml*) give a style(5) to (sb/oneself): *How should we style her?* ○ *Should he be styled 'Mr' or 'Reverend'?*

styling *n* [U] way in which sth is styled: *the car's brand-new styling.*

stylish *adj* having style(3); fashionable: *stylish clothes, furniture* ○ *a stylish skier, dancer, etc.* **stylishly** *adv*: *stylishly dressed.* **stylishness** *n* [U].

stylist /ˈstaɪlɪst/ *n* **1** person, esp a writer, who has or tries to have a good or distinctive style. **2** person who styles (STYLE *v* 1) things, eg clothes, hair: *a hair-stylist.*

▷ **stylistic** /staɪˈlɪstɪk/ *adj* [usu attrib] of or concerning literary or artistic style: *make a stylistic comparison of the two paintings.* **stylistically** /-klɪ/ *adv.* **stylistics** *n* [sing *v*] study of the style of spoken or written language and how it is used to create certain effects.

stylize, -ise /ˈstaɪlaɪz/ *v* [Tn esp passive] treat (sth) in a fixed conventional style.

▷ **stylization, -isation** /ˌstaɪlaɪˈzeɪʃn; *US* -lɪˈz-/ *n* [U].

stylized, -ised *adj* treated in a fixed conventional style: *the highly stylized form of acting in Japanese theatre.*

stylus /ˈstaɪləs/ *n* **1** sharp needle tipped with diamond or sapphire, used to reproduce sound by resting in the groove of a record as it turns on a record-player. **2** (esp in ancient times) pointed tool for drawing or writing.

stymie /ˈstaɪmɪ/ *n* **1** (in golf) situation on the green in which an opponent's ball is between one's own ball and the hole. **2** (*fig infml*) awkward or difficult situation.

▷ **stymie** *v* (*pt, pp* **stymied**, *pres p* **stymieing**) **1** [Tn] (in golf) put (sb, sb's ball or oneself) in a stymie. **2** [Tn esp passive] (*fig infml*) prevent (sb) from doing sth; obstruct: *I was completely stymied by her refusal to help.*

styptic /ˈstɪptɪk/ *n, adj* [usu attrib] (substance) checking the flow of blood: *a styptic pencil*, ie a stick of this, used eg on a cut made while shaving.

styrene /ˈstaɪriːn/ *n* [U] liquid hydrocarbon used in making polystyrene.

Styrofoam /ˈstaɪrəfəʊm/ *n* [U] (*propr esp US*) type of polystyrene used eg as packing or for making drinks containers.

Styx /stɪks/ (in Greek mythology) one of the rivers of the underworld crossed by the dead in *Charon's boat. Cf STYGIAN.

suave /swɑːv/ *adj* (*sometimes derog*) (usu of a man) having self-confidence and smooth sophisticated manners. ▷ **suavely** *adv.* **suaveness, suavity** /-ətɪ/ *ns* [U].

sub[1] /sʌb/ *n* (*infml*) **1** submarine. **2** substitute, esp in football or cricket. **3** (usu *pl*) subscription to a club, etc. **4** sub-editor.

sub[2] /sʌb/ *v* (**-bb-**) (*infml*) **1** [I, Ipr] ~ (**for sb**) act as a substitute: *I had to sub for the referee, who was sick.* **2** [I, Tn] sub-edit (sth): *subbing on a local newspaper.*

sub- *pref* **1** (with *ns* and *adjs*) under; below: *subway* ○ *subsoil* ○ *submarine.* **2** (with *ns*) lower in rank; inferior: *sub-lieutenant* ○ *subspecies.* **3** (with *adjs*) not quite; almost: *subnormal* ○ *subtropical* ○ *substandard.* **4** (with *vs* and *ns*) (form a) smaller or less important part of: *subdivide* ○ *subcommittee* ○ *subset.* Cf UNDER-.

subaltern /ˈsʌbltən; *US* səˈbɔːltərn/ *n* (*Brit*) any officer in the army below the rank of captain.

subarctic /ˌsʌbˈɑːktɪk/ *adj* [usu attrib] of regions near the Arctic Circle: *ˌsubarctic conˈditions, ˈtemperatures.* Cf SUBTROPICAL.

subatomic /ˌsʌbəˈtɒmɪk/ *adj* [usu attrib] of or concerning particles that are smaller than atoms or occur in atoms: *subatomic theory, research.*

subcommittee /ˈsʌbkəmɪtɪ/ *n* committee formed for a special purpose from members of a main committee.

subconscious /ˌsʌbˈkɒnʃəs/ *adj* of or concerning the thoughts, instincts, fears, etc in the mind, of which one is not fully aware but which influence one's actions: *the subconscious self* ○ *subconscious urges.* Cf UNCONSCIOUS.

▷ **the/one's subconscious** *n* [sing] these thoughts, instincts, fears, etc.

subconsciously *adv*: *I suppose that, subconsciously, I was reacting against my unhappy childhood.*

subcontinent /ˌsʌbˈkɒntɪnənt/ *n* large land mass that forms part of a continent: *the Indian subcontinent.*

subcontract /ˈsʌbkɒntrækt/ *n* contract to carry out a part or all of an existing contract.

▷ **subcontract** /ˌsʌbkənˈtrækt; *US* -ˈkɒntrækt/ *v* [Tn, Tn·pr] ~ **sth (to sb)** give (a job of work) to sb as a subcontract: *subcontract the installation of the new shower to a plumber.* **subcontractor** /ˌsʌbkənˈtræktə(r); *US* -ˈkɒntræk-/ *n* person, company, etc that accepts and carries out a subcontract.

subculture /ˈsʌbkʌltʃə(r)/ *n* behaviour, practices, etc associated with a group within a society: *the teenage subculture.*

subcutaneous /ˌsʌbkjuːˈteɪnɪəs/ *adj* [usu attrib] under the skin: *subcutaneous fat* ○ *a subcutaneous injection.* ▷ **subcutaneously** *adv.*

subdivide /ˌsʌbdɪˈvaɪd/ *v* [I, Ipr, Tn, Tn·pr] ~ **(sth) (into sth)** (cause sth to) be divided again into smaller divisions: *Part of the building has been subdivided into offices.*

▷ **subdivision** /ˌsʌbdɪˈvɪʒn/ *n* **1** [U] action or process of subdividing. **2** [C] thing produced by subdividing: *a subdivision of a postal area* ○ *This division of the chapter has several subdivisions.*

subdue /səbˈdjuː; *US* -ˈduː/ *v* [Tn] **1** bring (sb/sth) under control by force; defeat: *subdue the rebels.* **2** calm (esp one's emotions): *He managed to subdue his mounting anger.*

▷ **subdued** /səbˈdjuːd; *US* -ˈduːd/ *adj* **1** not very loud, intense, noticeable, etc: *a subdued conversation* ○ *subdued lighting* ○ *a note of subdued excitement in her voice.* **2** not showing much excitement, interest, etc: *You're very subdued. What's wrong?*

sub-edit /sʌbˈedɪt/ *v* [Tn] **1** check and correct (the text of a book, newspaper, etc) before it is printed. **2** act as an assistant editor of (a newspaper, etc). ▷ **sub-editor** *n.*

subheading /ˈsʌbhedɪŋ/ *n* heading over part of an article, etc, eg in a newspaper.

subject[1] /ˈsʌbdʒɪkt/ *n* **1** (**a**) person or thing that is being discussed or described (in speech or writing), or represented, eg in a painting; topic; theme: *an interesting subject of conversation* ○ *choose a subject for a poem, a picture, an essay, etc* ○ (*fml*) *What did she say on the subject of* (ie about) *money?* (**b**) branch of knowledge studied in a school, etc: *Physics and maths are my favourite subjects.* **2** person or thing being treated in a certain way or being experimented on: *We need some male subjects for a psychology experiment.* **3** ~ **for sth** person or thing that causes a specified feeling or action: *a subject for pity, ridicule, congratulation* ○ *His appearance was the subject for some critical comment.* **4** (*grammar*) (**a**) word(s) in a sentence naming who or what does or undergoes the action stated by the verb, eg *the book* in *The book fell off the table.* Cf OBJECT[1] 5. (**b**) word(s) in a sentence about which sth is stated, eg *the house* in *The house is old.* Cf PREDICATE[1]. **5** any member of a State apart from the supreme ruler: *I am French by birth and a British subject by marriage.* ⇨ Usage at CITIZEN. **6** (*music*) theme on which a piece of music is based. **7** (idm) **change the subject** ⇨ CHANGE[1].

□ **ˈsubject-matter** *n* [U] content of a book, speech, etc, esp as contrasted with the style: *Although the subject-matter (of her talk) was rather dull her witty delivery kept the audience interested.*

subject[2] /səbˈdʒekt/ *v* **1** [Tn, Tn·pr] ~ **sb/sth (to sth)** bring (a country, etc or a person) under one's control: *Ancient Rome subjected most of Europe (to its rule).* **2** [Tn·pr] ~ **sb/sth to sth** cause sb/sth to experience or undergo sth: *subject sb to criticism, ridicule, abuse, etc* ○ *She was repeatedly subjected to torture.* ○ *As a test the metal was subjected to great heat.*

▷ **subjection** /səbˈdʒekʃn/ *n* [U] subjecting or being subjected: *the country's subjection of its neighbour* ○ *The people were kept in subjection.*

subject[3] /ˈsʌbdʒɪkt/ *adj* **1** [attrib] under the control of sb else; not politically independent: *a subject province* ○ *subject peoples.* **2** [pred] ~ **to sth/sb** obliged to obey sth/sb; under the authority of sth/sb: *We are subject to the law of the land.* ○ *Peasants used to be subject to the local landowner.* **3** [pred] ~ **to sth** often having, suffering or undergoing sth; liable to sth: *Are you subject to colds?* ○ *Trains are subject to delay(s) after the heavy snowfalls.* ○ *The timetable is subject to alteration.* **4** [pred] ~ **to sth** depending on sth as a condition: *sold subject to contract*, ie provided that a contract is signed ○ *The plan is subject to the director's approval.*

subjective /səbˈdʒektɪv/ *adj* **1** (of ideas, feelings, etc) existing in the mind and not produced by things outside the mind: *a subjective impression, sensation, etc* ○ *Our perception of things is often influenced by subjective factors, such as tiredness.* **2** (*sometimes derog*) based on personal taste, views, etc: *a very subjective judgement of the play* ○ *A literary critic should not be too subjective in his approach.* Cf OBJECTIVE.

▷ **subjectively** *adv* in a subjective way: *Don't judge her work too subjectively.* **subjectivity** /ˌsʌbdʒekˈtɪvətɪ/ *n* [U].

subjoin /ˌsʌbˈdʒɔɪn/ *v* [Tn, Tn·pr] ~ **sth (to sth)** (*fml*) add sth to the end of sth: *subjoin a postscript to a letter.*

sub judice /ˌsʌb ˈdʒuːdɪsɪ/ (*Latin*) (of a legal case) still being considered by a lawcourt (and therefore, in the UK, not to be commented on in a newspaper, etc).

subjugate /ˈsʌbdʒʊgeɪt/ *v* [Tn] gain control of (a country, etc); subdue; conquer. ▷ **subjugation** /ˌsʌbdʒʊˈgeɪʃn/ *n* [U].

subjunctive /səbˈdʒʌŋktɪv/ *adj* (*grammar*) of the special form of a verb that expresses a wish, possibility, condition, etc: *In the phrase 'if I were you', 'were' is subjunctive.* Cf IMPERATIVE 3, INDICATIVE.

▷ **subjunctive** *n* (*grammar*) **1 the subjunctive** [U] the whole group of subjunctive verb-forms; the subjunctive mood: *In 'I wish you were here', 'were' is in the subjunctive.* **2** [C] subjunctive verb.

sublease /ˌsʌbˈliːs/ *v* [Tn, Tn·pr] ~ **sth (to sb)** lease (a house, land, etc leased to oneself) to another person; sublet sth: *The company subleases flats to students.*

▷ **sublease** *n* lease of this kind.

sublet /ˌsʌbˈlet/ *v* (**-tt-**; *pt, pp* **sublet**) [I, Tn, Tn·pr] ~ **sth (to sb)** rent (a house, flat, etc of which one is the tenant, or part of it) to sb else: *sublet a room to a friend.*

sub-lieutenant /ˌsʌblefˈtenənt; *US* -luːˈt-/ *n* naval officer next in rank below a lieutenant.

sublimate /ˈsʌblɪmeɪt/ *v* [Tn] **1** (*psychology*) express (instinctual urges, esp sexual ones) in more socially acceptable ways: *sublimating one's sex drive by working hard.* **2** (*chemistry*) convert (a substance) directly from the solid state to vapour by heating it, then allowing it to cool and become solid again, in order to purify it.

▷ **sublimate** *n* substance purified by sublimating (SUBLIMATE 2).

sublimation /ˌsʌblɪˈmeɪʃn/ *n* [U].

sublime /səˈblaɪm/ *adj* **1** of the greatest, most admirable kind; causing awe and reverence: *sublime heroism, beauty, scenery* ○ *her sublime devotion to the cause* ○ (*infml*) *The food was absolutely sublime.* **2** [attrib] (*sometimes derog*) extreme; suggesting a person who is not afraid of the consequences of his actions: *sublime conceit, indifference, impudence* ○ *She approached the angry crowd with a sublime lack of concern for her own safety.* **3** (idm) **from the sublime to the ridiculous** from sth great, admirable, etc to sth trivial, absurd, etc: *Interrupting an opera on television for a pet-food commercial is going from the sublime to the ridiculous.* ▷ **sublimely** *adv*: *play the piano sublimely* ○ *She was sublimely unaware of how foolish she looked.* **sublimity** /səˈblɪmətɪ/ *n* [U].

subliminal /ˌsʌbˈlɪmɪnl/ *adj* being perceived or affecting the mind without one being aware of it: *the subliminal message of the text*, ie one not explicitly stated ○ *subliminal advertising*, eg by means of an image flashed onto a screen so briefly that it is noted only by the subconscious mind. ▷ **subliminally** *adv.*

sublunar /ˌsʌbˈluːnə(r)/, **sublunary** /-nərɪ/ *adjs* **1** between the moon and the earth, esp in a line between the centre of the moon and the centre of the earth. **2** (*esp rhet*) influenced by the moon.

sub-machine-gun /sʌbməˈʃiːngʌn/ *n* lightweight machine-gun held in the hand for firing. ⇨ illus at GUN.

submarine /ˌsʌbməˈriːn; *US* ˈsʌbməriːn/ *n* **1** naval vessel that can operate underwater as well as on the surface: [attrib] *a submarine officer, crew.* **2** (also ˌ**submarine** ˈ**sandwich**) (*esp US*) sandwich made from a long bread roll split lengthwise and filled with meat, cheese, salad, etc.

▷ **submarine** *adj* [attrib] (existing or placed) under the surface of the sea: *submarine plants* ○ *submarine exploration* ○ *a submarine cable.*

submariner /sʌbˈmærɪnə(r); *US* ˈsʌbməriːnər/ *n* member of a submarine's crew.

submerge /səbˈmɜːdʒ/ *v* **1** (**a**) [I] go under the surface of a liquid, the sea, etc: *The submarine submerged to avoid enemy ships.* (**b**) [Tn] cause (sth) to go under the surface of a liquid, the sea, etc; cover with a liquid: *a wall submerged by flood water* ○ *The child submerged all her toys in the bath.* **2** [Tn usu passive] (*fig*) completely cover (sb/sth); overwhelm: *be submerged by paperwork* ○ *The main argument was submerged in a mass of tedious detail.*

▷ **submerged** *adj* under the surface of the sea, etc: *a partly-submerged wreck.*

submergence /səbˈmɜːdʒəns/, **submersion** /səbˈmɜːʃn; *US* -mɜːʒn/ *ns* [U].

submersible /səbˈmɜːsəbl/ *n, adj* (ship or craft) that can be submerged: *exploring the sea bed in a submersible.*

submission /səbˈmɪʃn/ *n* ~ (**to sb/sth**) **1** [U] (**a**) acceptance of another's power; submitting: *submission to sb's will* ○ *starve the city into submission*, ie force it to submit by cutting off its food supplies. (**b**) state in which one accepts the superior power of sb else: *During the occupation, we had to live in total submission (to the invader).* ○ *parents who want children to show complete submission to their wishes.* **2** [C, U] (act of) presenting sth for consideration, a decision, etc: *the submission of a claim, a petition, an appeal, etc.* **3** [C, U] (*law*) argument presented to a judge or jury: *In my submission, the witness is lying.* **4** [C] (in wrestling) admission by a wrestler that he cannot free himself from his opponent's hold on him.

submissive /səbˈmɪsɪv/ *adj* willing to yield to the authority of others; obedient: *a humble and submissive servant.* ▷ **submissively** *adv.* **submissiveness** *n* [U].

submit /səbˈmɪt/ *v* (-tt-) **1** [I, Ipr] ~ (**to sb/sth**) accept the control, superior strength, etc (of sb/sth); yield (to sb/sth): *I refuse to submit.* ○ *submit to discipline, superior force, etc* ○ *submit to the enemy, a tyrant, etc.* **2** [Tn, Tn·pr] ~ **sth** (**to sb/sth**) give sth (to sb/sth) so that it may be considered, decided on, etc: *submit an essay to one's tutor* ○ *submit plans to the council for approval* ○ *submit an application, estimate, claim, etc.* **3** [Tf no passive] (*law*) suggest (sth); argue: *Counsel for the defence submitted that his client was clearly innocent.* ○ *The case, I would submit, is not proven.*

subnormal /ˌsʌbˈnɔːml/ *adj* **1** below normal; less than normal: *subnormal temperatures.* **2** below the normal level of intelligence: *a subnormal child* ○ *educationally subnormal.*

▷ **subnormal** *n* (*infml*) subnormal(2) person.

suborbital /ˌsʌbˈɔːbɪtl/ *adj* less than (or lasting less time than) one orbit of the earth, moon, etc: *a suborbital space flight.*

subordinate /səˈbɔːdɪnət; *US* -dənət/ *adj* (**a**) ~ (**to sb**) lower in rank or position: *He was always friendly to his subordinate officers.* (**b**) ~ (**to sth**) of less importance: *All the other issues are subordinate to this one.*

▷ **subordinate** *n* person who is subordinate to sb else: *the commanding officer and his subordinates.*

subordinate /səˈbɔːdɪneɪt; *US* -dəneɪt/ *v* [Tn, Tn·pr] ~ **sth** (**to sth**) treat sth as of lesser importance (than sth else): *In her book, she subordinates this issue to more general problems.*

subordination /səˌbɔːdɪˈneɪʃn; *US* -dənˈeɪʃn/ *n* [U].

□ **su**ˌ**bordinate** ˈ**clause** (also **de**ˌ**pendent** ˈ**clause**) (*grammar*) clause, usu introduced by a conjunction, that functions like a noun, adjective or adverb, eg *when it rang* in *She answered the phone when it rang.* Cf CO-ORDINATE CLAUSE (CO-ORDINATE[1]).

suborn /səˈbɔːn/ *v* [Tn] (*fml*) use bribery or some other means to persuade (sb) to do sth illegal, esp tell lies in a court of law: *suborn a witness.* ▷ **subornation** /ˌsʌbɔːˈneɪʃn/ *n* [U].

sub-plot /ˈsʌbplɒt/ *n* plot of a play, novel, etc that is separate from but linked to the main plot.

subpoena /səˈpiːnə/ *n* (*law*) written order requiring a person to appear in a lawcourt: *serve a subpoena on a witness.*

▷ **subpoena** *v* [Tn, Cn·n/a, Cn·t] summon (sb) with a subpoena: *subpoena a witness* ○ *The court subpoenaed her (to appear) as a witness.*

subroutine /ˈsʌbruːtiːn/ *n* (*computing*) self-contained section of a computer program for performing a specific task.

subscribe /səbˈskraɪb/ *v* **1** [I, Ipr, Tn, Tn·pr] ~ (**sth**) (**to sth**) (agree to) contribute (a sum of money): *subscribe to a charity* ○ *How much did you subscribe (to the disaster fund)?* **2** [I, Ipr] ~ (**to sth**) (agree to) buy (a newspaper, periodical, etc) regularly over a period of time: *The magazine is trying to get more readers to subscribe.* ○ (*finance*) *The share issue was over-/under-subscribed*, ie too many/few people agreed to buy shares. ○ *Which journal(s) do you subscribe to?* **3** [Tn, Tn·pr] ~ **sth** (**to sth**) (*fml*) sign (esp one's name) at the foot of a document: *subscribe one's name to a petition* ○ *subscribe a few remarks at the end of the essay.* **4** (phr v) **subscribe to sth** (*fml*) agree with (an opinion, a theory, etc): *Do you subscribe to her pessimistic view of the state of the economy?*

▷ **subscriber** *n* **1** person who subscribes(1,2). **2** person who rents a telephone.

subscription /səbˈskrɪpʃn/ *n* **1** [U] subscribing or being subscribed: *a monument paid for by public subscription.* **2** [C] (**a**) sum of money subscribed: *a £5 subscription to charity.* (**b**) fee for membership of a club, etc: *renew one's annual subscription.*

□ **sub**ˌ**scriber** ˈ**trunk dialling** (abbr **STD**) system of making long distance calls in which the caller is automatically connected (instead of using an operator).

subˈ**scription concert** concert where all tickets are paid for in advance.

subsection /ˈsʌbsekʃn/ *n* part of a section, esp in legal documents, etc: *Please turn to section 5, subsection b.*

subsequent /ˈsʌbsɪkwənt/ *adj* [attrib] later; following: *Subsequent events proved me wrong.* ○ *The first and all subsequent visits were kept secret.*

▷ **subsequently** *adv* afterwards: *They subsequently heard he had left the country.*

□ **subsequent to** *prep* (*fml*) following (sth); after: *Subsequent to its success as a play, it was made into a film.* ○ *He confessed to other crimes subsequent to the bank robbery.*

subservient /səbˈsɜːvɪənt/ *adj* ~ (**to sb/sth**) **1** (*often derog*) giving too much respect, obedience, etc; submissive: *a subservient manner, attitude* ○ *Are priests too subservient to their bishops?* **2** less important; subordinate: *People should not be regarded as subservient to the economic system.* ▷ **subservience** /-əns/ *n* [U]. **subserviently** *adv.*

subset /ˈsʌbset/ *n* set[1](1, 4) that is part of a larger set.

subside /səbˈsaɪd/ *v* **1** [I] sink to a lower or to the normal level: *The flood waters gradually subsided.* ○ *The boiling soup subsided when the pot was taken off the heat.* **2** [I] (of land) sink, eg because of mining operations underneath. **3** [I] (of buildings, etc) sink lower into the ground: *Weak foundations caused the house to subside.* **4** [I] become less violent, active, intense, etc: *The storm began to subside.* ○ *He waited until the applause had subsided.* ○ *I took an aspirin and the pain gradually subsided.* **5** [Ipr] (*infml joc*) let oneself drop into a chair, etc: *subsiding onto the sofa/into an armchair.*

▷ **subsidence** /səbˈsaɪdns, ˈsʌbsɪdns/ *n* **1** [U] process of subsiding (SUBSIDE 1): *the gradual subsidence of the river.* **2** [U, C] process or instance of subsiding (SUBSIDE 3, 4): *a building damaged by subsidence* ○ *The railway line was closed because of (a) subsidence.*

subsidiary /səbˈsɪdɪərɪ; *US* -dɪerɪ/ *adj* **1** ~ (**to sth**) connected to but smaller, of less importance, etc than sth else; subordinate: *a subsidiary stream flowing into the main river* ○ *The question of finance is subsidiary to the question of whether the project will be approved.* **2** (of a business company) controlled by another.

▷ **subsidiary** *n* subsidiary thing, esp a business company.

subsidy /ˈsʌbsɪdɪ/ *n* [C, U] money paid, esp by a government, to help an industry, to support the arts, to keep prices down, etc: *food subsidies*, eg to reduce the price of basic foods ○ *increase/reduce the level of subsidy*, eg to the arts, farmers, etc.

▷ **subsidize, -ise** /ˈsʌbsɪdaɪz/ *v* [Tn] give a subsidy to (sth/sb): *subsidized industries.* **subsidization, -isation** /ˌsʌbsɪdaɪˈzeɪʃn; *US* -dɪˈz-/ *n* [U].

subsist /səbˈsɪst/ *v* [I, Ipr] ~ (**on sth**) (*fml*) (continue to) stay alive, esp with little food or money; exist: *How do they manage to subsist (on such a low wage)?* ○ *He subsisted mainly on vegetables and fruit.*

▷ **subsistence** /-təns/ *n* [U] (means of) subsisting: *reduced to subsistence on bread and water* ○ [attrib] *subsistence farming*, ie farming that produces only enough crops for the farmer and his family to live on, leaving no surplus which could be sold ○ *a subsistence wage*, ie one that is only just enough to enable a worker to live.

□ **sub**ˈ**sistence crop** crop grown to be eaten by the grower. Cf CASH CROP (CASH).

subˈ**sistence level** standard of living that is only just high enough to support life.

subsoil /ˈsʌbsɔɪl/ *n* [U] layer of soil lying immediately beneath the surface layer. Cf TOPSOIL (TOP[1]).

subsonic /ˌsʌbˈsɒnɪk/ *adj* (flying at a speed) less than the speed of sound: *a subsonic speed, aircraft, flight.* Cf SUPERSONIC.

substance /ˈsʌbstəns/ *n* **1** [C] particular type of matter: *a poisonous substance like cyanide* ○ *a substance that will prevent rust* ○ *Water and ice are the same substance in different forms.* **2** [U] (**a**) real matter (contrasted with sth only seen, heard or imagined): *They maintained that ghosts had no substance.* (**b**) firmness; solidity: *I like a meal that has some substance to it*, ie has nourishing food in it. ○ (*fig*) *an argument of little substance*, eg lacking specific details, etc. **3** [U] most important or essential part of sth; essential meaning: *the substance of the speech* ○ *I agree with the substance of what you say/with what you say in substance, but differ on points of detail.* **4** [U] (*fml*) money; property: *a man/woman of substance*, eg a property owner.

substandard /ˌsʌbˈstændəd/ *adj* below the usual or required standard: *substandard goods* ○ *She has written good essays before, but this one is substandard.*

substantial /səbˈstænʃl/ *adj* **1** large in amount; considerable: *a substantial improvement, decrease* ○ *Her contribution to the discussion was substantial.* ○ *obtain a substantial loan.* **2** [usu attrib] solidly or strongly built or made: *a substantial padlock, chair, wall.* **3** [usu attrib] owning much property; wealthy: *a substantial business, company* ○ *substantial farmers.* **4** [attrib] concerning the most important part of sth; essential: *We are in substantial agreement.* **5** (*fml*) having physical existence, not merely seen

or heard or imagined; real: *Was it something substantial that you saw, or was it a ghost?*
▷ **substantially** /-ʃəlɪ/ *adv* **1** considerably; greatly: *substantially improved* ○ *They contributed substantially to our success.* **2** concerning the substance(3) of sth; essentially: *Your assessment is substantially correct.*

substantiate /səbˈstænʃɪeɪt/ *v* [Tn] give facts to support (a claim, statement, etc); prove: *Can you substantiate your accusations against him?* ▷ **substantiation** /səbˌstænʃɪˈeɪʃn/ *n.*

substantive[1] /ˈsʌbstəntɪv/ *adj* (*fml*) genuine or actual; real: *a discussion of substantive matters* ○ *a guarantee of substantive progress.*
▷ **substantive** *n* (*dated grammar*) noun.

substantive[2] /səbˈstæntɪv/ *adj* [attrib] (of military rank) permanent; not temporary: *a substantive major.*

substation /ˈsʌbsteɪʃn/ *n* place which relays electric current that has been generated elsewhere.

substitute /ˈsʌbstɪtju:t; *US* -tu:t/ *n* ~ **(for sb/sth)** person or thing that replaces, acts for or serves as sb or sth else: *The manager was unable to attend but sent his deputy as a substitute.* ○ *This type of vinyl is a poor substitute for leather.* ○ [attrib] *a substitute player, horse, machine.*
▷ **substitute** *v* **(a)** [Tn, Tn·pr] ~ **sb/sth (for sb/ sth)** put or use sb/sth as a substitute (for sb/sth else): *The understudy was substituted when the leading actor fell ill.* ○ *We must substitute a new chair for the broken one.* **(b)** [Ipr] ~ **for sb/sth** act or serve as a substitute: *Can you substitute for* (ie go instead of) *me at the meeting?* ○ *Honey can substitute for sugar in this recipe.*
substitution /ˌsʌbstɪˈtju:ʃn; *US* -ˈtu:ʃn/ *n* **1** [U] substituting or being substituted. **2** [C] act of substituting: *Two substitutions* (ie of players) *were made during the match.*

substratum /ˌsʌbˈstrɑ:təm; *US* ˈsʌbstreɪtəm/ *n* (*pl* **substrata** /ˌsʌbˈstrɑ:tə; *US* ˈsʌbstreɪtə/) **1** level lying below another: *a substratum of rock.* **2** (*fig*) foundation; basis: *a substratum of truth in her story.*

substructure /ˈsʌbstrʌktʃə(r)/ *n* underlying or supporting structure; base or foundation. Cf SUPERSTRUCTURE 1.

subsume /səbˈsju:m; *US* -ˈsu:m/ *v* [Tn, Tn·pr] ~ **sth (in/under sth)** (*fml*) include sth in a particular group, class, etc or under a rule: *This creature can be subsumed in the class of reptiles.*

subtenant /ˈsʌbtenənt/ *n* person to whom a house, flat, etc (or part of it) is sublet by a tenant. ▷ **subtenancy** /-ənsɪ/ *n* [C, U]

subtend

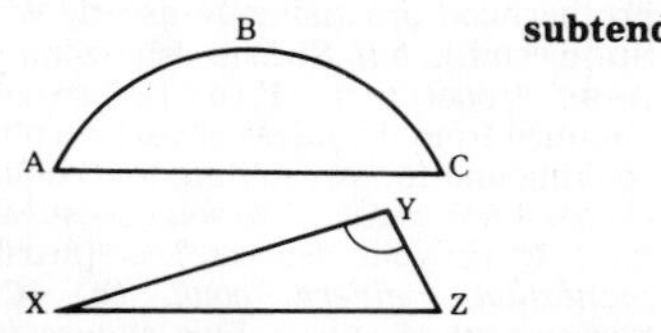

subtend /səbˈtend/ *v* [Tn] (*geometry*) (of a chord[2](1) or the side of a triangle) be opposite to (an arc(1) or angle): *The chord AC subtends the arc ABC.* ○ *The side XZ subtends the angle XYZ.* ⇨ illus.

subterfuge /ˈsʌbtəfju:dʒ/ *n* **(a)** [C] trick or excuse, esp one used to avoid difficulties, blame, failure, etc: *Her claim to be a journalist was simply a subterfuge to get into the theatre without paying.* **(b)** [U] such trickery: *gain sth by subterfuge.*

subterranean /ˌsʌbtəˈreɪnɪən/ *adj* under the earth's surface; underground: *a subterranean passage, river, tunnel* ○ *subterranean digging.*

subtitle /ˈsʌbtaɪtl/ *n* **1** secondary title of a book, etc. **2** (usu *pl*) (*esp cinema*) words printed on a film that translate the dialogue of a foreign film, give those of a silent film or (on television) supply dialogue for deaf viewers.
▷ **subtitle** *v* [Tn usu passive] give a subtitle or subtitles to (sth): *a book subtitled 'A Study of Methodism'.*

subtle /ˈsʌtl/ *adj* (**-r**, **-st**) (*esp approv*) **1** not easy to detect or describe; fine; delicate: *a subtle charm, flavour, style* ○ *subtle humour* ○ *a subtle distinction* ○ *paint in subtle shades of pink.* **2** organized in a clever and complex way; ingenious; cunning: *a subtle argument, design, strategy* ○ *a subtle analysis of the problem.* **3** able to see and describe fine and delicate differences; sensitive: *a subtle observer, critic, analyst, etc* ○ *She has a very subtle mind.*
▷ **subtlety** /ˈsʌtltɪ/ *n* **1** [U] quality of being subtle. **2** [C] subtle distinction, etc.
subtly /ˈsʌtlɪ/ *adv.*

subtopia /ˌsʌbˈtəʊpɪə/ *n* [C, U] unattractive suburbs spreading out into the countryside.

subtotal /ˈsʌbtəʊtl/ *n* total of a set of figures that are part of a larger group of figures.

subtract /səbˈtrækt/ *v* [Tn, Tn·pr] ~ **sth (from sth)** take (a number or quantity) away from (another number, etc): *subtract 6 from 9* ○ *6 subtracted from 9 is 3*, ie 9 − 6 = 3. Cf ADD, DEDUCT.
▷ **subtraction** /səbˈtrækʃn/ *n* **1** [U] process of subtracting. **2** [C] act of subtracting: *Two from five is a simple subtraction.*

subtropical /ˌsʌbˈtrɒpɪkl/ *adj* of regions bordering on the tropics: *ˌsubtropical ˈplants* ○ *a ˌsubtropical ˈclimate.* Cf SUBARCTIC.

suburb /ˈsʌbɜ:b/ *n* (esp residential) district outside the central part of a town or city: *an industrial suburb* ○ *a suburb of Naples* ○ *live in the suburbs*, ie in such a district ○ *the inner/outer suburbs* ○ *a dormitory suburb*, ie one from which people travel elsewhere to work.
📖 Suburbs developed in Britain as cities grew and people started to want to live away from the noise and dirt of the city centre. The word 'suburb' has many connotations in English. It is sometimes used derogatorily to refer to a kind of middle-class way of life, socially respectable but rather dull. Sometimes it alludes to the orderliness of the neatly laid-out, semi-detached houses with front gardens that characterize many suburban areas.
▷ **suburban** /səˈbɜ:bən/ *adj* **1** of or in a suburb: *a suburban street, shop, newspaper.* **2** (*fig derog*) limited in outlook; dull or ordinary: *a rather suburban attitude to life.*
suburbanite /səˈbɜ:bənaɪt/ *n* (*infml often derog*) person who lives in the suburbs.
Suburbia /səˈbɜ:bɪə/ *n* [U] (*usu derog*) (type of life lived by or attitudes held by people who live in the) suburbs.

subvention /səbˈvenʃn/ *n* (*fml*) grant of money to support an industry, a theatre company, etc; subsidy.

subversive /səbˈvɜ:sɪv/ *adj* ~ **(of sth)** trying or likely to weaken or destroy a political system, an accepted belief, etc: *subversive propaganda* ○ *a subversive book, speaker, influence* ○ *Was her speech subversive (of law and order)?*
▷ **subversive** *n* subversive person.
subversively *adv.*
subversiveness *n* [U].

subvert /sʌbˈvɜ:t/ *v* [Tn] **1** destroy the authority of (a political system, religious faith, etc): *subvert the monarchy* ○ *writings that subvert Christianity.* **2** corrupt the morals or loyalty of (sb): *a diplomat subverted by a foreign power.* ▷ **subversion** /səbˈvɜ:ʃn; *US* -ˈvɜ:rʒn/ *n* [U].

subway /ˈsʌbweɪ/ *n* **1** underground pedestrian tunnel, esp one beneath a road or railway: *Use the subway to cross the road.* Cf UNDERPASS. **2** (*US*) underground railway in a city: *travel by subway* ○ [attrib] *a subway train, station.* Cf UNDERGROUND[2] *n*, TUBE 3, METRO.

subzero /ˌsʌbˈzɪərəʊ/ *adj* (of temperatures) below zero: *the ˌsubzero ˈtemperatures of a Siberian winter.*

succeed /səkˈsi:d/ *v* **1** [I, Ipr] ~ **(in sth/doing sth)** do what one is trying to do; achieve the desired end: *The attack succeeded, and the fort was taken.* ○ *She's absolutely determined to succeed (in life).* ○ (*saying*) *If at first you don't succeed, try, try again* ○ (*ironic*) *I tried to clean the watch, but only succeeded in breaking it.* Cf FAIL 1. **2** [Tn] come next after (sb/ sth) and take his/its place: *Who succeeded Churchill (as Prime Minister)?* ○ *The silence was succeeded by the striking of a clock.* **3** [I, Ipr] ~ **(to sth)** gain the right to (a title, property, etc) when sb dies: *When the king died, his eldest son succeeded (to the throne).* **4** (idm) **ˌnothing sucˌceeds like sucˈcess** (*saying*) success often leads to further successes: *I won the essay prize, then was offered a scholarship: nothing succeeds like success!*

success /səkˈses/ *n* **1** [U] achievement of a desired end, or of fame, wealth or social position; succeeding: *achieve great success in life* ○ *make a success of sth* ○ *The race ended in success for* (ie was won by) *the Irish horse.* ○ *I haven't had much success in my applications for jobs.* **2** [C] person or thing that succeeds: *He wasn't a success as a teacher.* ○ *Of her plays, three were successes and one was a failure.* **3** (idm) **ˌnothing sucˌceeds like sucˈcess** ⇨ SUCCEED. **a roaring success** ⇨ ROARING (ROAR). **a sucˈcess story** person or thing that is very successful (esp unexpectedly or in the face of difficulties): *Her rapid rise to the top has been one of the film industry's most remarkable success stories.*
▷ **successful** /-fl/ *adj* having success: *a successful businesswoman, career, plan* ○ *My final attempt to fix it was successful.* **successfully** /-fəlɪ/ *adv.*

succession /səkˈseʃn/ *n* **1** [C] number of things or people coming one after the other in time or order; series: *a succession of wet days, defeats, poor leaders.* **2** [U] the coming of one thing or person after another in time or order: *the succession of the seasons.* **3** [U] (right of) succeeding to a title, the throne, property, etc: *Who is first in succession to the throne?* **4** (idm) **in sucˈcession** one after the other: *three victories in (quick) succession.*

successive /səkˈsesɪv/ *adj* [attrib] coming one after the other in an unbroken series: *successive governments, victories, attempts* ○ *The school has won five successive games.* ▷ **successively** *adv.*

successor /səkˈsesə(r)/ *n* ~ **(to sb/sth)** person or thing that comes after and takes the place of (sb/ sth): *the successor to the throne* ○ *appoint a successor to the headmaster* ○ *This car is the successor to our popular hatchback model.* Cf PREDECESSOR.

succinct /səkˈsɪŋkt/ *adj* (*approv*) expressed briefly and clearly; concise: *a succinct summary of the argument.* ▷ **succinctly** *adv.* **succinctness** *n* [U].

Succoth /ˈsʌkəs, sʊˈkɒt/ *n* Jewish festival of the harvest.

succour (*US* **succor**) /ˈsʌkə(r)/ *n* [U] (*fml*) help given to sb in need or in danger: *bring succour to the sick and wounded.*
▷ **succour** *v* [Tn] (*fml*) give such help to (sb).

succubus /ˈsʌkjʊbəs/ *n* (*pl* **succubi** /ˈsʌkjʊbaɪ/) female demon said to have sexual intercourse with sleeping males. Cf INCUBUS.

succulent /ˈsʌkjʊlənt/ *adj* **1** (*approv*) (of fruit and meat) juicy and delicious: *a succulent steak, pear, etc.* **2** (of plants) having leaves and stems that are thick and contain a lot of water.
▷ **succulence** /-əns/ *n* [U].
succulent *n* succulent plant, eg a cactus.

succumb /səˈkʌm/ *v* [I, Ipr] ~ **(to sth)** (*fml*) stop resisting (temptation, illness, attack, etc); yield: *The city succumbed after only a short siege.* ○ *Several children have measles, and the others are bound to succumb (to it).* ○ *The driver has succumbed to* (ie died of) *his injuries.*

such /sʌtʃ/ *det* **1 (a)** (referring back) of the kind specified earlier: *He noticed her necklace. Such jewels must have cost thousands, he thought.* ○ *He told them about the job he had left. Such information was just what they needed.* ○ *I've been invited to an Asian wedding. What happens on such occasions?* ○ *He said he hadn't got time or made some such excuse.* ○ *This isn't the only story of starving children. Many such cases are reported every day.* **(b)** ~ **sth as/that...** (referring forward) of the specified kind: *Such a disaster as her car being stolen had never happened before.* ○ *Such poets as Keats and Shelley wrote Romantic poetry.* ○ *Such advice as* (ie The little advice that) *he was given proved almost worthless.* ○ *The knot was fastened in such a way that it was impossible to* *undo.* **2** ~ **sth** (**as**/**that ...**) to the specified degree (of importance, worth, etc): *On an occasion such as this* (ie as important as this) *we are privileged to welcome ...* ○ *He showed such concern that people took him to be a relative.* ○ *He's not such a fool as he looks.* ○ *It was such a boring speech (that) I fell asleep.* ○ *I'm afraid I can't remember — it was such a long time ago.* ○ *Such is the influence of TV that it can make a person famous overnight.* **3** (as an intensifier) so great; so very (much): *She's got such talent.* ○ *We're having such a wonderful time.* ○ *Baby giraffes seem to have such long legs.* ○ *I've had such a shock.* ○ *Why are you in such a hurry?*

▷ **such** *pron* **1** person or thing of a specified kind. (**a**) (referring back): *Cricket was boring. Such* (ie That) *was her opinion before meeting Ian.* ○ *She's a competent leader and has always been regarded as such by her colleagues.* (**b**) ~ **as to do sth**; ~ **that ...** (referring forward): *The pain in her foot wasn't such as to stop her walking.* ○ *The damage was such that it would cost too much money to repair.* **2** (idm) **as such** as the word is usually understood; in the strict sense of the word: *The new job is not a promotion as such but it brings good prospects for the future.* ○ *I can't call my book a best seller as such but it's very popular.* **such as** (**a**) like; for example: *Wild flowers such as orchids and primroses are becoming rare.* (**b**) everything that: *Such as remains after tax will be yours when I die.* ˌ**such as it** ˈ**is** (used to apologize for the poor quality of sth): *You're welcome to join us for supper, such as it is — we're only having soup and bread.*

□ ˈ**such-and-such** *pron, det* (thing) of a particular but unspecified type: *Always say at the start of an application that you're applying for such-and-such (a job) because ....*

suchlike /ˈsʌtʃlaɪk/ *pron, det* (things) of the same kind: *You can buy string, glue, paper-clips and suchlike (items) at the corner shop.*

suck /sʌk/ *v* **1** [Tn, Tn·pr, Tn·p] (**a**) draw (liquid or air, etc) into the mouth by using the lip muscles: *suck the juice from an orange* ○ *suck the poison out (of a wound)* ○ *suck milk through a straw.* ⇨ illus at BLOW. (**b**) (of a pump, etc) draw (liquid or air, etc) out of sth: *The pump sucks air out (of the vessel) through this valve.* ○ *plants that suck up moisture from the soil.* **2** [Tn, Cn·a] draw liquid from (sth): *a baby sucking its mother's breast* ○ *suck an orange dry.* **3** [I, Ipr, Ip] ~ (**away**) (**at**/**on sth**) perform the action of sucking sth: *The baby sucked (away) (at its bottle) contentedly.* ○ *The old man was sucking at his pipe.* ○ *Suck on the tube to draw up the water.* **4** [Tn] squeeze or roll (sth) with the tongue while holding it in the mouth: *suck a toffee* ○ *a child that sucks its thumb.* **5** (idm) **milk**/**suck sb**/**sth dry** ⇨ DRY[1]. **teach one's grandmother to suck eggs** ⇨ TEACH. **6** (phr v) **suck sb in**/**into sth** (usu passive) involve sb in (a scandal, an argument, etc), usu unwillingly: *I don't want to get sucked into the row about school reform.* **suck sb**/**sth under, into, etc sth; suck sb**/**sth down, in, etc** pull sb/sth down, under, etc with great force of water or air: *The canoe was sucked (down) into the whirlpool.* ○ *Dangerous currents can suck swimmers under.* **suck up** (**to sb**) (*derog sl*) try to please sb by flattering, helping him, etc: *She sucks up to him by agreeing with everything he says.*

▷ **suck** *n* act of sucking: *have/take a suck (at sth).*

sucks *interj* (*sl*) (used to show contempt for sb, often in the phrase shown): *Sucks to you!*

□ ˈ**sucking-pig** *n* young pig still taking its mother's milk.

sucker /ˈsʌkə(r)/ *n* **1** (**a**) organ of certain animals that enables them to stick to a surface by suction: *An octopus has suckers on its tentacles.* (**b**) concave (usu rubber) disc that sticks to a surface by suction, and is used eg to attach things to a wall. **2** shoot growing from the roots of a tree, shrub, etc. **3** (*infml*) person who is easily deceived: *all the suckers who bought these worthless shares.* **4** ~ **for sb**/**sth** (*infml*) person who cannot resist sb/sth or is very fond of sb/sth: *I've always been a sucker for romantic movies.* **5** (*US*) lollipop.

suckle /ˈsʌkl/ *v* [Tn] feed (a baby or young animal) with milk from the breast or udder. ⇨ illus at COW.

▷ **suckling** /ˈsʌklɪŋ/ *n* (idm) **out of the mouths of babes and sucklings** ⇨ MOUTH[1].

sucrose /ˈsuːkrəʊz, -rəʊs/ *n* [U] sugar obtained from sugar-cane and sugar-beet.

suction /ˈsʌkʃn/ *n* [U] removal of air to create a partial vacuum, used for making two surfaces stick together or for sucking in liquid, dust, etc by means of air pressure: *Some pumps and all vacuum cleaners work by suction.* ○ *Flies' feet stick to surfaces by suction.* ○ [attrib] *a suction pump, pad.*

Sudan /suːˈdɑːn; *US* suːˈdæn/ (also **the Sudan**) country in NE Africa; pop approx 23 798 000; official language Arabic; capital Khartoum; unit of currency pound (=100 piastres). It is the largest country in Africa. Much of the north of the country is desert, and agriculture is concentrated in the south, esp along the Blue Nile and the White Nile, which meet at the capital. The south also contains oil deposits. Although Sudan is fertile and could feed itself and surrounding countries, famine is common, exacerbated by the continuing conflict between the Muslim population in the north and the non-Muslim peoples of the south. ⇨ map at ZAÏRE. ▷ **Sudanese** /ˌsuːdəˈniːz/ *n, adj.*

sudden /ˈsʌdn/ *adj* **1** happening, coming or done quickly and unexpectedly: *a sudden decision, arrival, increase* ○ *a sudden turn in the road* ○ *Your marriage was very sudden. Have you thought things over properly?* **2** (idm) ˌ**all of a** ˈ**sudden** unexpectedly: *All of a sudden, the tyre burst.* ˌ**sudden** ˈ**death** deciding the result of a drawn or tied game by playing one more point or game: [attrib] *a* ˌ*sudden-death* ˈ*play-off.* ▷ **suddenly** *adv*: *The end came quite suddenly.* ○ *Suddenly, everyone started shouting and singing.* **suddenness** *n* [U].

suds /sʌdz/ *n* [pl] **1** mass of tiny bubbles on soapy water. **2** (*US infml*) beer. ▷ **sudsy** *adj*: *sudsy water.*

sue /suː; *also, in British use,* sjuː/ *v* **1** [I, Ipr, Tn, Tn·pr] ~ (**sb**) (**for sth**) make a legal claim (against sb): *If you don't complete the work, I will sue you (for damages)*, ie for money to compensate for my loss. **2** [Ipr] ~ **for sth** (*fml*) formally ask for sth, often in a lawcourt: *sue for peace* ○ *a prisoner suing for mercy* ○ *sue for a divorce.*

suede /sweɪd/ *n* [U] type of soft leather with one side rubbed so that it has a soft roughened surface: [attrib] *a suede coat, dress, etc* ○ *suede shoes.*

suet /ˈsuːɪt; *also, in British use,* ˈsjuːɪt/ *n* [U] hard fat from round the kidneys of cattle and sheep, used in cooking: [attrib] *a suet pudding*, ie one made with flour and suet.

▷ **suety** *adj* like or containing (much) suet.

Suez /ˈsuːɪz; *US* ˌsuːˈez/ port in NE Egypt at the northern end of the **Gulf of Suez**, a part of the *Red Sea. The **Suez Canal** connects the Mediterranean with the Red Sea and provides the shortest route from Europe to Asia.

suffer /ˈsʌfə(r)/ *v* **1** [I, Ipr] ~ (**from**/**with**/**for sth**) feel pain, discomfort, great sorrow, etc: *Do you suffer from* (ie often have) *headaches?* ○ *She's suffering from loss of memory.* ○ *He suffers terribly with* (ie is pained by) *his feet.* ○ *He made a rash decision — now he's suffering for it.* ○ *Think how much the parents of the kidnapped boy must have suffered.* **2** [Tn] experience or undergo (sth unpleasant): *suffer pain, torture, defeat* ○ *We suffered huge losses in the financial crisis.* **3** [I] become worse; lose quality: *Your studies will suffer if you play too much football.* ○ *Her business suffered* (eg made less profit) *when she was ill.* **4** [Tn] (*fml*) tolerate (sth); stand: *How can you suffer such insolence?* **5** (idm) **not**/**never suffer** ˈ**fools gladly** not be patient with people whom one considers to be foolish: *an arrogant, impatient woman who doesn't suffer fools gladly.*

▷ **sufferer** /ˈsʌfərə(r)/ *n* person who suffers: *arthritis sufferers.*

suffering /ˈsʌfərɪŋ/ *n* **1** [U] pain of body or mind: *There is so much suffering in this world.* **2 sufferings** [pl] feelings of pain, unhappiness, etc: *the sufferings of the starving refugees.*

sufferance /ˈsʌfərəns/ *n* [U] (idm) **on** ˈ**sufferance** tolerated but not actually wanted: *He's here on sufferance.*

suffice /səˈfaɪs/ *v* **1** [I, Ipr, It, Tn no passive] ~ (**for sb**/**sth**) (not in the continuous tenses) (*fml*) be enough for (sb/sth); be adequate: *Will £10 suffice for the trip?* ○ *One warning sufficed to stop her doing it.* ○ *A light lunch should suffice me.* **2** (idm) **suffice it to say** (**that**)**...** (used to suggest that even though one could say more, what one does say should be enough to show what one means): *I won't go into all the depressing details; suffice it to say that the whole affair was an utter disaster.*

sufficient /səˈfɪʃnt/ *adj* ~ (**for sth**/**sb**) enough: *sufficient money, time, fuel* ○ *Is £10 sufficient for your expenses?* ○ *Do we have sufficient (food) for ten people?*

▷ **sufficiency** /-nsɪ/ *n* ~ **of sth** [sing] (*fml*) sufficient quantity of sth: *a sufficiency of fuel for the winter.*

sufficiently *adv*: *not sufficiently careful.*

suffix /ˈsʌfɪks/ *n* letter or group of letters added at the end of a word to make another word, eg *-y* added to *rust* to make *rusty*, or as an inflexion, eg *-en* in *oxen*. Cf PREFIX.

suffocate /ˈsʌfəkeɪt/ *v* **1** [I, Tn] (cause sb to) die as a result of not being able to breathe: *Passengers suffocated in the burning aircraft.* ○ *The fireman was suffocated by the fumes.* **2** [I] have difficulty in breathing: *I'm suffocating in here; can't we open a few windows?*

▷ **suffocating** *adj* causing difficulty in breathing: *the suffocating heat of a tropical night* ○ (*fig*) *a suffocating bureaucracy*, ie one which prevents freedom of action.

suffocation /ˌsʌfəˈkeɪʃn/ *n* [U].

Suffolk /ˈsʌfək/ county in eastern England. It is a largely agricultural county growing cereals and sugar beet. ⇨ map at App 1.

suffragan /ˈsʌfrəgən/ *adj* [attrib] (of a bishop) appointed to help another bishop by managing part of his diocese.

▷ **suffragan** *n* suffragan bishop.

suffrage /ˈsʌfrɪdʒ/ *n* [U] right to vote in political elections: *universal suffrage*, ie the right of all adults to vote ○ *Women had to fight for their suffrage.*

▷ **suffragette** /ˌsʌfrəˈdʒet/ *n* member of a group of women who, in the early part of the 20th century, campaigned in Britain for women's suffrage. ⇨ articles at PROTEST, WOMAN.

suffuse /səˈfjuːz/ *v* [Tn, Tn·pr esp passive] ~ **sth** (**with sth**) (esp of colour or moisture) spread all over sth: *A blush suffused his cheeks.* ○ *The evening sky was suffused with crimson.* ▷ **suffusion** /səˈfjuːʒn/ *n* [U].

Sufi /ˈsuːfɪ/ *n* Muslim mystic, often belonging to a brotherhood practising an ascetic way of life. ▷ **Sufic** /ˈsuːfɪk/ *adj.* **Sufism** /ˈsuːfɪzəm/ *n* [U].

sugar /ˈʃʊgə(r)/ *n* **1** (**a**) [U] sweet substance obtained from the juices of various plants, used in cooking and for sweetening tea, coffee, etc: *Don't eat too much sugar.* ○ *Do you take sugar?* ie Do you have it in your tea, etc? ○ [attrib] *a sugar plantation, refinery, bowl.* (**b**) [C] cube or teaspoonful of sugar: *Two sugars in my coffee, please!* **2** (*infml esp US*) (used as a form of address to sb one likes): *Hello, sugar, nice to see you!*

▷ **sugar** *v* [Tn] **1** sweeten or coat (sth) with sugar: *Is this tea sugared?* ○ *sugared almonds.* **2** (idm) ˌ**sugar**/ˌ**sweeten the** ˈ**pill** ⇨ PILL.

sugary /ˈʃʊgərɪ/ *adj* **1** tasting of sugar; sweet: *sugary tea.* **2** (*fig derog*) too sentimental or flattering: *a sugary love scene in a film.* **sugariness** *n* [U].

□ ˈ**sugar-beet** *n* [U] vegetable from whose large round roots sugar is made.

ˈ**sugar-cane** *n* [U] tall tropical grass from which sugar is made.

ˌ**sugar-**ˈ**coated** *adj* **1** coated with sugar. **2** (*fig derog*) made to seem attractive: *a* ˌ*sugar-coated* ˈ*promise.*

ˈ**sugar-daddy** *n* (*infml*) rich man who is generous to a younger woman, usu in return for sexual favours.

ˈ**sugar-lump** *n* small cube of sugar, used to sweeten tea, coffee, etc.

ˈ**sugar-maple** *n* N American maple tree, the sap of which is used to make sugar and syrup.
ˈ**sugar-pea** *n* = MANGE-TOUT.
ˈ**sugar soap** alkaline crystals used esp for cleaning paint.
ˈ**sugar-tongs** *n* [pl] small tongs for picking up lumps of sugar at table: *a pair of sugar-tongs.*

suggest /səˈdʒest; *US* səgˈdʒ-/ *v* **1 (a)** [Tn, Tn·pr, Tf, Tw, Tg, Cn·n/a] ~ **sb (for sth)**; ~ **sb/sth (as sth)** put sth/sb forward for consideration: *I suggest a tour of the museum.* ○ *Whom would you suggest for the job?* ○ *I wrote suggesting that he should come for the weekend.* ○ *Can you suggest how we might tackle the problem?* ○ *He suggested taking the children to the zoo.* ○ *I suggest Paris as a good place for a honeymoon.* **(b)** [Dn·pr, Dpr·f, Dpr·w] ~ **sth to sb** propose sth to sb: *What did you suggest to the manager?* ○ *I suggested to him that we should tackle the problem another way.* **2** [Tn, Tf, Dn·pr, Dpr·f] ~ **sth (to sb)** put (an idea, etc) into sb's mind: *Which illness do these symptoms suggest (to you)?* ○ *His cool response suggested that he didn't like the idea.* **3** [Tn, Tf] state (sth) indirectly; imply: *'Are you suggesting that I'm not telling the truth?' 'I wouldn't suggest such a thing for a moment.'* **4** [Tn, Tn·pr] ~ **itself (to sb)** come into sb's mind; occur to sb: *I tried to think what could have happened, but nothing suggested itself.* ○ *An idea suggests itself to me.*
▷ **suggestible** /-əbl/ *adj* easily influenced: *I did many stupid things when I was young and suggestible.* **suggestibility** /səˌdʒestəˈbɪlətɪ; *US* səgˌdʒ-/ *n* [U].
suggestive /-ɪv/ *adj* **1** ~ **(of sth)** putting particular ideas or associations into sb's mind: *an aroma suggestive of spring flowers* ○ *a complex, suggestive poem.* **2** making sb think of improper (esp sexual) things: *He gave her a suggestive glance, and she blushed.* **suggestively** *adv.*

suggestion /səˈdʒestʃən; *US* səgˈdʒ-/ *n* **1** [U] suggesting (SUGGEST 1) or being suggested: *On/At your suggestion* (ie Because you suggested it) *I bought the more expensive model.* **2** [C] ~ **(that...)** idea, plan, etc or person that is suggested: *I want suggestions about what to do today.* ○ *Janet was my first suggestion as chairperson.* ○ *There's no suggestion that she should resign,* ie That would be completely unthinkable. **3** [C usu *sing*] slight amount of (sth that can be detected): *speak English with the suggestion of a French accent.* **4** [U] putting an idea, etc into sb's mind through linking it to other ideas, pictures, etc: *Most advertisements work through suggestion.*

suicide /ˈsuːɪsaɪd; *also, in British use,* ˈsjuːɪ-/ *n* **1 (a)** [U] killing oneself intentionally: *commit suicide* ○ *four cases of suicide.* **(b)** [C] act of this: *three suicides in one week.* **2** [C] person who commits suicide. **3** [U] (*fig*) any action that may have serious consequences for oneself: *political suicide,* ie action by a politician that will ruin his career ○ *economic suicide,* eg adopting policies that will ruin the economy.
▷ **suicidal** /ˌsuːɪˈsaɪdl; *also, in British use,* ˌsjuːɪ-/ *adj* **1** of suicide; likely to lead to suicide: *suicidal tendencies* ○ *in a suicidal state.* **2** (of a person) likely to commit suicide: *She's feeling suicidal today.* **3** likely to lead to one's ruin: *a suicidal policy.* **suicidally** /-dəlɪ/ *adv*: *suicidally depressed.*

sui generis /ˌsuːiː ˈdʒenərɪs/ (*Latin*) unlike anything else; unique: *a literary style which is entirely sui generis.*

suit[1] /suːt; *also, in British use,* sjuːt/ *n* **1 (a)** set of outer garments of the same material, usu a jacket and trousers for a man and a jacket and skirt for a woman: *a* ˈ*business suit* ○ *a* ˌ*pin-stripe* ˈ*lounge suit* ○ *a* ˌ*two-*/ˌ*three-piece* ˈ*suit,* ie of two/three garments ○ *a* ˈ*dress suit,* ie a man's formal evening suit ○ *a* ˈ*trouser-suit,* ie a woman's suit of jacket and trousers. **(b)** set of clothing for a particular activity: *a* ˈ*spacesuit* ○ *a* ˈ*diving suit* ○ *an as*ˈ*bestos suit,* eg to protect sb from heat ○ *a* ˌ*suit of* ˈ*armour.* **2** any of the four sets (ie *spades, hearts, clubs, diamonds*) forming a pack of playing-cards. ⇨ illus at PLAYING-CARD. **3** (also ˈ**lawsuit**) case in a lawcourt; legal proceedings: *file/bring a suit against sb* ○ *a criminal/civil suit* ○ *a divorce suit.* **4** (*fml*) request made to a person in authority, esp a ruler: *grant sb's suit* ○ *press one's suit,* ie beg persistently. **5** (idm) **follow suit** ⇨ FOLLOW. **in one's birthday suit** ⇨ BIRTHDAY. **one's/sb's strong suit** ⇨ STRONG.
▷ **-suited** (forming compound *adjs*) wearing a suit of the specified kind: *sober-suited city businessmen.*
suiting *n* [U] material for making suits: *serge suiting.*
□ ˈ**suitcase** *n* case with flat sides, used for carrying clothes, etc when travelling. ⇨ illus at LUGGAGE.

suit[2] /suːt; *also, in British use,* sjuːt/ *v* **1** [Tn] (esp of clothes, hairstyles, etc) look attractive on (sb): *Does this skirt suit me?* ○ *It doesn't suit you to have your hair cut short.* ○ *That colour doesn't suit your complexion.* **2 (a)** [I, Tn] be convenient for or acceptable to (sb): *Will Thursday suit (you)?* ○ *The seven o'clock train will suit us very well.* ○ *If you want to go by bus, that suits me fine.* ○ *Would it suit you to come at five?* **(b)** [Tn] (usu in negative sentences) be right or beneficial for (sb/sth): *This climate doesn't suit me.* ○ *Very spicy food doesn't suit my stomach,* ie makes me feel ill. **3** [Tn] ~ **one**ˈ**self** (*infml*) act according to one's own wishes: *You don't want to join the club? Oh well, suit yourself.* **4** [Tn·pr] ~ **sth to sth/sb** make sth appropriate for sth/sb; adapt sth to sth/sb: *suit the punishment to the crime* ○ *suit the play to the audience.* **5** (idm) **suit one's/sb's book** (*infml*) be convenient or acceptable to sb: *It suits my book if I never have to go there again.* **suit sb** ˌ**down to the** ˈ**ground** (*infml*) be very convenient or appropriate for sb: *I've found a job that suits me down to the ground.*
▷ **suited** *adj* [pred] ~ **(for/to sb/sth)** suitable or appropriate (for sb/sth): *He is better suited to a job with older pupils.* ○ *He and his wife are well suited (to each other).*

suitable /ˈsuːtəbl; *also, in British use,* ˈsjuːt-/ *adj* ~ **(for/to sth/sb)** right or appropriate for a purpose or an occasion: *a suitable room, book, proposal, date* ○ *clothes suitable for cold weather* ○ *a place suitable for a picnic* ○ *a suitable case for* (eg surgical, psychiatric, etc) *treatment* ○ *Would now be a suitable moment to show the slides?* ▷ **suitability** /ˌsuːtəˈbɪlətɪ/, **suitableness** *ns* [U]. **suitably** /-əblɪ/ *adv*: *go to a party suitably dressed.*

suite /swiːt/ *n* **1** set of matching pieces of furniture: *a three-piece suite,* eg two armchairs and a sofa ○ *a dining-room suite,* ie a table, chairs, and often a sideboard. **2 (a)** set of rooms, eg (in a hotel) a bedroom, sitting-room and bathroom: *the honeymoon/bridal suite,* ie for a honeymoon couple in a hotel. **(b)** (*US*) apartment; flat. **3** complete set of objects used together: *a suite of programs for a computer.* **4** (*music*) piece of music consisting of three or more related parts. **5** group of people attending an important person, eg a ruler; retinue.

suitor /ˈsuːtə(r); *also, in British use,* ˈsjuː-/ *n* (*dated*) man courting a woman: *She had rejected all her many suitors.*

Sulawesi /ˌsuːləˈweɪsɪ/ large island of *Indonesia, east of Borneo, formerly called Celebes. It is famous esp for the huts of the Torajas people, with their distinctive prow-shaped roofs. ⇨ map at INDONESIA.

sulfate (*US*) = SULPHATE.
sulfide (*US*) = SULPHIDE.
sulfur (*US*) = SULPHUR.

sulk /sʌlk/ *v* [I, Ipr] ~ **(about/over sth)** (*derog*) be silent or unsociable as a result of bad temper or resentment: *He's been sulking for days about being left out of the team.*
▷ **the sulks** *n* [pl] (*infml*) fit of sulking: *have (a fit of) the sulks.*
sulky *adj* **(-ier, -iest)** having or showing a tendency to sulk: *a sulky person, look, mood.* **sulkily** /-ɪlɪ/ *adv.* **sulkiness** *n* [U].

sullen /ˈsʌlən/ *adj* (*derog*) **1** silent, bad-tempered and gloomy: *a sullen person, look* ○ *All my attempts to amuse the children were met with sullen scowls.* **2** (*esp rhet*) dark and gloomy; dismal: *a sullen sky.* ▷ **sullenly** *adv.* **sullenness** *n* [U].

Sullivan /ˈsʌlɪvən/ Sir Arthur (1842-1900), English composer. He is most famous for the light and witty *Savoy Operas, which he wrote with W S Gilbert, though he longed for recognition for his more serious works, now rarely played.

sully /ˈsʌlɪ/ *v* (*pt, pp* **sullied**) [Tn] (*fml or rhet usu fig*) make (sth) dirty; stain; ruin or destroy (sb's reputation, etc): *I wouldn't sully my hands by accepting a bribe.* ○ *sully sb's name, honour, etc.*

sulpha drug (*US* **sulfa drug**) /ˈsʌlfə drʌg/ = SULPHONAMIDE.

sulphate (*US* **sulfate**) /ˈsʌlfeɪt/ *n* [C, U] compound of sulphuric acid and another chemical: *copper sulphate.*

sulphide (*US* **sulfide**) /ˈsʌlfaɪd/ *n* [C, U] compound of sulphur and another element.

sulphonamide (*US* **sulfo-**, **sulpha drug**) /sʌlˈfɒnəmaɪd/ *n* any of a group of chemical compounds which are used to kill bacteria.

sulphur (*US* **sulfur**) /ˈsʌlfə(r)/ *n* [U] (*symb* **S**) chemical element, a light-yellow non-metallic solid that burns with a bright flame and a strong smell, used in medicine and industry. ⇨ App 11.
▷ **sulphuretted** (*US* **sulfur-**) /ˈsʌlfjʊretɪd/ *adj* [attrib] (of a compound) containing sulphur: *sulphuretted hydrogen,* ie hydrogen sulphide.
sulphuric (*US* **sulfu-**) /sʌlˈfjʊərɪk/ *adj* containing a proportion of sulphur. **sulphuric acid** type of very strong corrosive acid.
sulphurous (*US* **sulfu-**) /ˈsʌlfərəs/ *adj* **1** of or like sulphur: *a sulphurous smell coming from the laboratory* ○ *the volcano's sulphurous fumes.* **2** containing a proportion of sulphur. ˌ**sulphurous** ˈ**acid** weak and chemically unstable acid used eg for bleaching.

sultan /ˈsʌltən/ *n* sovereign ruler of certain Muslim countries: *the Sultan of Brunei.*
▷ **sultanate** /ˈsʌltəneɪt/ *n* **1** position or period of rule of a sultan. **2** territory ruled by a sultan: *the Sultanate of Oman.*

sultana /sʌlˈtɑːnə; *US* -ænə/ *n* **1** small seedless raisin used in puddings and cakes. **2** wife, mother, sister or daughter of a sultan.

sultry /ˈsʌltrɪ/ *adj* **(-ier, -iest)** **1** (of the weather, air, etc) oppressively hot and humid: *a sultry summer afternoon.* **2** (of a woman or her looks) darkly and sensually beautiful: *a sultry smile* ○ *a sultry Mexican beauty.* ▷ **sultrily** /-trəlɪ/ *adv.* **sultriness** *n* [U].

sum /sʌm/ *n* **1** [C often *pl*] arithmetical calculation: *do a sum in one's head* ○ *be good at sums.* **2** [C] ~ **(of sth)** amount of money: *He was fined the sum of £200.* ○ *Huge sums have been invested in this project.* **3 (a)** [C usu *sing*] ~ **(of sth)** total obtained by adding together numbers, amounts or items: *The sum of 5 and 3 is 8.* **(b)** [sing] (also ˌ**sum** ˈ**total**) **the** ~ **of sth** all of sth, esp when it is considered as not being enough: *Is that the sum of what you've done in the last two years?* **4** (idm) **in** ˈ**sum** (*dated*) in a few words: *In sum, the plan failed.*
▷ **sum** *v* **(-mm-)** (phr v) **sum (sth) up (a)** give a brief summary (of sth): *Now sum up (your views) in a few words.* **(b)** (of a judge) summarize the evidence or arguments in a legal case. **sum sb/sth up** form an opinion of sb/sth: *I summed her up as a competent manager.* ○ *He summed up the situation at a glance,* ie realized at once what was happening. ˌ**summing-**ˈ**up** *n* (*pl* **summings-up**) speech in which a judge sums up the evidence or arguments in a legal case.
□ ˌ**sum** ˈ**total** **1** final total, esp as formed by adding other totals together. **2** = SUM 3b.

Sumatra /sʊˈmɑːtrə/ largest island of *Indonesia. It is crossed by a chain of volcanos and the interior is covered in dense forest. Crops include rice, coffee and palm-oil and there are coal and oil reserves. ⇨ map at INDONESIA.

Sumer /ˈsuːmə(r)/ southern region of ancient *Mesopotamia around the *Persian Gulf. It was the site of one of the world's earliest developed civilizations. Its achievements included irrigation, metalwork, architecture, and a legal and

administrative system. It also produced the first known form of writing. It reached its height in the 3rd millennium BC.
▷ **Sumerian** /sʊˈmɪərɪən/ *n* **1** [C] member of the early non-Semitic people of Sumer. **2** [U] language of Sumer. — *adj* of the people, language or civilization of Sumer.

summary /ˈsʌmərɪ/ *n* **1** brief statement of the main points of sth: *a two-page summary of a government report* ○ *Here is a summary of the news/a news summary.* **2** (idm) **in ˈsummary** as a brief statement of the main point(s): *And so I would say, in summary, that the campaign has been a great success.*
▷ **summary** *adj* [usu attrib] **1** (*sometimes derog*) done or given immediately, without attention to details or formal procedure: *summary justice, punishment, methods* ○ *Such an offence will lead to a summary fine.* **2** giving the main points only; brief: *a summary account of a long debate.* **summarily** /ˈsʌmərəlɪ; *US* səˈmerəlɪ/ *adv*: *summarily dismissed.*
summarize, -ise /ˈsʌməraɪz/ *v* [I, Tn] be or make a summary of (sth): *a talk summarizing recent trends in philosophy.*

summation /sʌˈmeɪʃn/ *n* (*fml*) **1** summing-up; summary: *begin a summation of the evidence presented.* **2** addition: *do a rapid summation of the figures.* **3** gathering together of different parts to form a representative whole: *The exhibition was a summation of his life's work.*

summer /ˈsʌmə(r)/ *n* [U, C] **1** the second and warmest season of the year outside the tropics, coming between spring and autumn, ie from June to August in the northern hemisphere: *In (the) summer we go on holiday.* ○ *in the summer of 1979* ○ *this/next/last summer* ○ *a cool, hot, wet, etc summer* ○ *a lovely summer's day* ○ (*rhet*) *a girl of ten summers*, ie ten years of age ○ [attrib] *summer weather* ○ *the summer holidays* ○ *a summer cottage*, ie for use during the summer. **2** (idm) **an Indian summer** ⇨ INDIAN. **one swallow does not make a summer** ⇨ SWALLOW[2].
▷ **summery** /ˈsʌmərɪ/ *adj* typical of or suitable for the summer: *a summery day* ○ *a summery dress.*
□ **ˈsummer-house** *n* small hut with seats in a garden, park, etc, providing shade in the summer.
ˌsummer ˈpudding (*Brit*) pudding of fruits such as raspberries and currants pressed into a case of bread and usu served cold.
ˈsummer school course of lectures, etc held in the summer vacation, esp at a university.
ˈsummer-time *n* [U] season of summer: *It's beautiful here in (the) summer-time.*
ˈsummer time (*Brit*) (*US* **ˈfast time**) time kept one hour in advance of the actual time during summer, giving long light evenings. Cf DAYLIGHT SAVING (DAYLIGHT).

summit /ˈsʌmɪt/ *n* **1** highest point; top, esp of a mountain: *climb to the summit* ○ (*fig*) *the summit of her career, ambition, etc.* ⇨ illus at MOUNTAIN. **2** meeting between the heads of two or more governments, esp of the world's most powerful countries: *attend a summit in Washington* ○ [attrib] *a summit/talk/meeting/conference* ○ *the summit powers.*

summon /ˈsʌmən/ *v* **1** (**a**) [Tn, Tn·pr, Tn·p, Dn·t] ~ **sb** (**to sth**); ~ **sb** (**together**) send a message telling sb to come; call (people) together: *I was summoned by my boss (to explain my actions).* ○ *The shareholders were summoned to a general meeting.* ○ *Summon the pupils together in the school hall.* (**b**) [Tn, Dn·t] order (sb) to attend a lawcourt; summons (sb): *The debtor was summoned (to appear before the magistrates).* **2** [Tn] order a group of people to attend (a meeting, etc): *summon a conference* ○ *The Queen has summoned Parliament.* **3** [Tn, Tn·p] ~ **sth** (**up**) force (a particular quality) to come as if from deep inside oneself, in an attempt to do sth: *summon (up) one's courage for the battle* ○ *I had to summon (up) all my nerve to face my boss.* ○ *I can't summon up much enthusiasm for the project.* **4** (phr v) **summon sth up** cause sth to come into the mind; evoke sth: *a smell which summons up memories of my childhood.*

summons /ˈsʌmənz/ *n* (*pl* ~**es**) **1** (**a**) order to attend a lawcourt, esp to answer a charge: *issue a summons.* (**b**) document containing this: *The summons was served by a bailiff.* **2** order to do sth, esp to come to sb: *You must obey the king's summons.*
▷ **summons** *v* [Tn, Tn·pr, Dn·t] ~ **sb** (**for sth**) order sb to attend a lawcourt: *He was summonsed for speeding.*

sumo /ˈsuːməʊ/ *n* (also **ˌsumo ˈwrestling**) [U] Japanese type of wrestling. To win, one fighter must force the other out of a marked circle or cause him to touch the ground with his body. The wrestlers are large, typically very fat men.

sump /sʌmp/ *n* **1** casing under an engine holding the lubricating oil. **2** cavity or hollow area into which waste liquid drains.

sumptuous /ˈsʌmptʃʊəs/ *adj* looking expensive and splendid: *a sumptuous feast* ○ *sumptuous clothes.* ▷ **sumptuously** *adv.* **sumptuousness** *n* [U].

Sun *abbr* Sunday: *Sun 1 June.*

sun /sʌn/ *n* **1** (also **the sun**) [sing] the star around which the earth orbits and from which it receives light and warmth: *the sun's rays* ○ *sending a space probe to the sun* ○ *A watery sun shone through the rain-clouds.* **2** (also **the sun**) [sing, U] light and warmth from the sun; sunshine: *sit in the sun* ○ *have the sun in one's eyes* ○ *draw the curtains to shut out/let in the sun* ○ *I like lots of sun on holiday.* **3** [C] any star, esp one around which planets orbit: *There are many suns larger than ours.* **4** (idm) **catch the sun** ⇨ CATCH[1]. **make hay while the sun shines** ⇨ HAY. **a place in the sun** ⇨ PLACE[1]. **under the ˈsun** (anywhere) in the world: *the best wine under the sun* ○ *every country under the sun.* **with the ˈsun** at dawn or sunset: *get up/go to bed with the sun.*
▷ **sun** *v* (-nn-) [Tn] ˈ~ **oneself** expose oneself to the rays of the sun: *He sat in a deck-chair ˈsunning himself.*
sunless *adj* without sunshine; receiving little or no sunlight: *a sunless day, room.*
sunny *adj* (**-ier, -iest**) **1** bright with sunlight; receiving much sunlight: *a sunny day, room, garden.* **2** (*fig*) cheerful: *a sunny smile, disposition, welcome* ○ *She always looks on the sunny side*, ie is optimistic. **sunnily** /-ɪlɪ/ *adv.* **sunniness** *n* [U]. **ˌsunny-side ˈup** (*US*) (of an egg) fried on one side only.
□ **ˈsun-baked** *adj* (**a**) made hard by the heat of the sun: *sun-baked mud, fields, etc.* (**b**) receiving much sunlight; very sunny: *sun-baked beaches.*
ˈsunbathe *v* [I] expose one's body to the sun, eg to become sun-tanned.
ˈsunbeam *n* ray of sunshine.
ˈsun-blind *n* curtain, awning, etc that stops sunlight coming through a window.
ˈsunburn *n* [U] reddening and blistering of the skin caused by being in the sun too much. Cf SUN-TAN. **sunburned, sunburnt** /ˈsʌnbɜːnt/ *adjs* (**a**) suffering from sunburn: *sunburnt shoulders.* (**b**) sun-tanned.

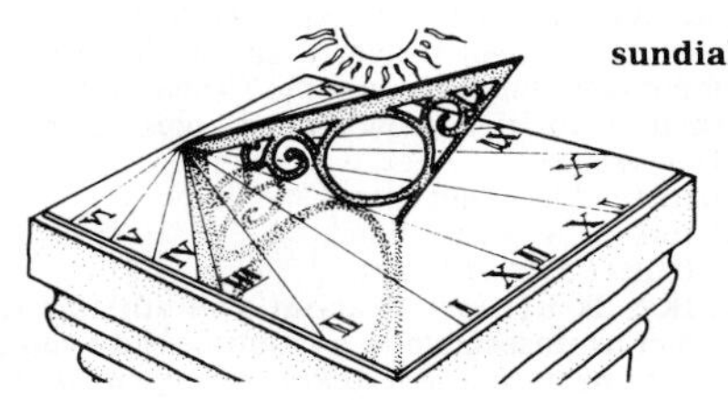

sundial

sundial /ˈsʌndaɪəl/ *n* device showing the time on a clock-like dial by means of a pointer whose shadow moves as the sun moves across the sky.
ˈsundown *n* [U] (*esp US*) sunset. **ˈsundowner** *n* **1** (*Austral*) tramp who usu arrives (at a sheep farm, etc) at sunset, looking for a place to sleep. **2** (*Brit infml*) (usu alcoholic) drink taken at sunset.
ˈsun-drenched *adj* (*approv*) receiving great heat and light from the sun: *sun-drenched beaches along the Riviera.*
ˈsunfish *n* large sea fish that is almost round, like a ball.
ˈsunflower *n* tall garden plant having large flowers with yellow petals round a dark centre: [attrib] *sunflower seeds, oil.*
ˈsun-glasses *n* [pl] glasses with dark lenses to protect the wearer's eyes from bright sunlight: *a pair of sun-glasses.*
ˈsun-god *n* the sun worshipped as a god.
ˈsun-hat *n* hat made to shade the head and neck from sunlight.
ˈsun-lamp *n* lamp producing ultraviolet light, with effects like those of sunlight, used eg for tanning the body.
ˈsunlight *n* [U] light of the sun.
ˈsunlit *adj* [usu attrib] lighted by the sun: *a sunlit garden, scene, landscape.*
ˈsun lounge (*Brit*) (*US* **ˈsun parlor, ˈsun porch**) room, veranda, etc with glass sides, and situated so as to receive much sunlight.
ˈsun-ray *n* ray of ultraviolet light as used on the body for tanning or for medical reasons: [attrib] *a sun-ray lamp* ○ *sun-ray treatment.*
ˈsunrise *n* [U] (time of the) rising of the sun; dawn: *She got up at sunrise.* **ˈsunrise industry** new and expanding industry.
ˈsun-roof *n* (also **ˌsunshine ˈroof**) panel on the roof of a car that can be opened to let in air and sunshine.
ˈsunset *n* **1** [U] (time of the) setting of the sun: *finish work at sunset.* **2** [C] appearance of the sky at sunset: *the beautiful sunsets in the desert.*
ˈsunshade *n* **1** umbrella for protecting sb from hot sunshine. Cf PARASOL. **2** sun-blind.
ˈsunshine *n* [U] **1** light and heat of the sun: *sitting out in the bright/warm sunshine.* **2** (*fig infml*) cheerfulness: *the loss of her closest friend which took the sunshine out of her life.* **3** (*Brit infml*) (used for addressing sb, usu in a cheerful and friendly way): *Hello, sunshine!* **4** (idm) **a ray of sunshine** ⇨ RAY[1]. **ˌsunshine ˈroof** = SUN-ROOF.
ˈsunspot *n* **1** (*astronomy*) any of the dark patches that sometimes appear on the sun's surface, causing electrical disturbances and interfering with radio communications. **2** (*infml*) place that has a sunny climate (eg for holidays).
ˈsunstroke *n* [U] illness caused by being exposed to the heat and light of the sun too much.
ˈsun-tan *n* browning of the skin from exposing it to the sun: *get a good sun-tan* ○ [attrib] *sun-tan oil, lotion, cream, etc.* Cf SUNBURN. **ˈsun-tanned** *adj*: *her sun-tanned legs.*
ˈsun-trap *n* warm sunny place that is sheltered from the wind.
ˈsun-up *n* [U] (*US infml*) sunrise.
ˈsun-worship *n* [U] **1** worship of the sun as a god. **2** (*infml*) extreme fondness for sun-bathing. **ˈsun-worshipper** *n.*

sundae /ˈsʌndeɪ; *US* -diː/ *n* dish of ice-cream with crushed fruit, fruit juice, nuts, etc: *a peach sundae.*

Sunday /ˈsʌndɪ/ *n* (*abbr* **Sun**) **1** [C, U] the first day of the week (coming before Monday), a day of rest and worship for Christians. **2** [C usu *pl*] newspaper published on a Sunday. **3** (idm) **for/in a month of Sundays** ⇨ MONTH. **one's Sunday ˈbest** (*infml joc*) one's best clothes: *Go to the party in your Sunday best.*
□ **ˈSunday school** class held on Sundays at which children receive religious teaching.
For the uses of *Sunday* see the examples at *Monday*.

sunder /ˈsʌndə(r)/ *v* [Tn, Tn·pr] ~ **sth/sb** (**from sth/sb**) (*fml or rhet*) separate sth/sb, esp by force or for ever.

sundry /ˈsʌndrɪ/ *adj* [attrib] **1** various: *on sundry occasions* ○ *rice, flour and sundry other items of food.* **2** (idm) **ˌall and ˈsundry** (*infml*) everyone, without discrimination: *She invited all and sundry to her party.*
▷ **sundry** *n* **1 sundries** [pl] various (esp small) items not separately named: *My expenses claim includes £15 for sundries.* **2** [C] (*Austral*) = EXTRA

n 3.

sung *pp* of SING.

sunk *pt, pp* of SINK[1].

sunken /ˈsʌŋkən/ *adj* **1** [attrib] that has gone to the bottom of the sea: *a sunken ship* ○ *sunken treasure.* **2** (of cheeks, etc) hollow as a result of hunger, illness, etc: *the sunken eyes of the dying man.* **3** [attrib] at a lower level than the surrounding area: *a sunken terrace at the bottom of the garden.*

Sunni /ˈsʊnɪ/, **Sunnite** /ˈsʊnaɪt/ *ns, adjs* (member) of the larger of the two main traditions within Islam. Sunnis form the majority of orthodox Muslims. Historically they accepted the authority of the caliphs and claim to follow the *sunna* or traditions associated with the Prophet *Muhammad. Cf SHIITE.

Sun Yat-Sen /ˌsʊn jæt ˈsen/ (1866-1925), Chinese revolutionary leader. He was involved in attempts to overthrow the Manchu emperors, and became provisional president after their fall in 1911. He is regarded as the 'Father of the Revolution'.

sup /sʌp/ *v* (**-pp-**) **1** [Tn, Tn·p] ~ **sth (up)** (*Brit dialect*) drink sth in small amounts: *They sat supping their beer.* ○ *Come on, sup up your tea.* **2** [I, Ipr] ~ **(on/off sth)** (*arch*) eat supper: *We supped on cold roast beef.*

▷ **sup** *n* (*Brit dialect*) small amount of liquid drunk: *a sup of ale.*

sup *abbr* above; earlier on (in a book, etc) (Latin *supra*). Cf INF.

super[1] /ˈsuːpə(r); *also, in British use,* ˈsjuː-/ *adj* (*infml*) excellent; splendid: *a super meal, book, dress* ○ *You'll like her, she's super.*

super[2] /ˈsuːpə(r); *also, in British use,* ˈsjuː-/ *n* (*Brit infml*) superintendent, esp in the police force: *the chief super.*

super- *pref* **1** (**a**) (with *ns* and *vs*) above; over: *superstructure* ○ *superimpose.* (**b**) (with *adjs* and *advs*) superior to; more than: *superhuman* ○ *supernaturally.* **2** (esp with *adjs*) extremely; very: *super-intelligent* ○ *super-chic.* **3** (esp with *ns*) larger, more efficient, etc than the standard sort: *superglue* ○ *super-lubricant.* Cf OVER-.

superabundant /ˌsuːpərəˈbʌndənt; *also, in British use,* ˌsjuː-/ (*fml*) very abundant; more than enough: *a superabundant harvest.*

▷ **superabundance** /-əns/ *n* [U, sing] ~ **(of sth)** (*fml*) amount that is more than enough: *food in superabundance* ○ *a superabundance of fuel.*

superannuate /ˌsuːpəˈrænjʊeɪt; *also, in British use,* ˌsjuː-/ *v* [Tn] send (an employee) into retirement with a pension.

▷ **superannuated** *adj* [usu attrib] (*infml esp joc*) old and barely fit for work or use: *Are you still riding that superannuated old bike?*

superannuation /ˌsuːpəˌrænjʊˈeɪʃn; *also, in British use,* ˌsjuː-/ *n* [U] **1** superannuating. **2** (money paid towards a) pension that one gets when one retires.

superb /suːˈpɜːb; *also, in British use,* sjuː-/ *adj* excellent; splendid: *a superb player, painting, view* ○ *The sports facilities are superb.* ▷ **superbly** *adv.*

supercharge /ˈsuːpətʃɑːdʒ; *also, in British use,* ˈsjuː-/ *v* [Tn] increase the power of (an engine) by supplying air or fuel above the normal pressure: *a supercharged racing-car (engine).*

▷ **supercharger** *n* device that supercharges an engine.

supercilious /ˌsuːpəˈsɪlɪəs; *also, in British use,* ˌsjuː-/ *adj* (*derog*) thinking or showing that one thinks one is better than other people; arrogant and disdainful: *a supercilious person, smile, attitude* ○ *The shop assistant was very supercilious towards me when I asked for some help.* ▷ **superciliously** *adv.* **superciliousness** *n* [U].

superconductivity /ˌsuːpəˌkɒndʌkˈtɪvətɪ; *also, in British use,* ˌsjuː-/ *n* [U] (*physics*) property of certain metals, at temperatures near absolute zero, of having no electrical resistance, so that once a current is started it flows without a voltage to keep it going.

▷ **superconductor** /ˌsuːpəkənˈdʌktə(r); *also, in British use,* ˌsjuː-/ *n* metal that possesses superconductivity.

supercool /ˈsuːpəkuːl; *also, in British use,* ˈsjuː-/ *v* [Tn] cool (a liquid) to a temperature below its freezing-point without forming a solid or crystal: *supercooled water droplets.*

super-duper /ˌsuːpəˈduːpə(r)/ *adj* (*infml*) excellent; splendid: *I've got a super-duper new radio.*

super-ego /ˈsuːpəregəʊ; *also, in British use,* ˈsjuː-; *US* -iːgəʊ/ *n* (*psychology*) part of a person's mind which contains a set of rules for right and wrong behaviour, acting as a conscience. Cf EGO 1, ID.

supererogation /ˌsuːpərerəˈgeɪʃn; *also, in British use,* ˌsjuː-/ *n* [U] (*fml*) doing or saying more than is needed, expected, or ordered. ▷ **supererogatory** /-ɪˈrɒgətrɪ/ *adj* (*fml*): *supererogatory comments.*

superficial /ˌsuːpəˈfɪʃl; *also, in British use,* ˌsjuː-/ *adj* **1** of or on the surface only: *a superficial wound* ○ *Superficial scratches can be easily removed.* **2** apparent when looked at quickly or carelessly, but perhaps not real: *a superficial similarity.* **3** (**a**) not thorough or profound: *a superficial book, mind* ○ *have only a superficial knowledge of the subject.* (**b**) (*derog*) having no depth of character, feeling or commitment: *You're too superficial to appreciate great literature like this.* ▷ **superficiality** /ˌsuːpəˌfɪʃɪˈælətɪ; *also, in British use,* ˌsjuː-/ *n* [U]. **superficially** /-ʃəlɪ/ *adv*: *only superficially alike.*

superfine /ˈsuːpəfaɪn; *also, in British use,* ˈsjuː-/ *adj* extremely or unusually fine in size, texture or quality: *superfine flour, grains* ○ *a superfine needle* ○ *superfine silk.*

superfluous /suːˈpɜːflʊəs; *also, in British use,* sjuː-/ *adj* more than is needed or wanted: *Repack all the superfluous cups in the box.* ○ *The crowd was so well-behaved that the police presence was superfluous.* ○ *That remark was superfluous,* ie It should not have been made, eg because it contributed nothing or was offensive. ○ *They were only interested in each other, so I felt rather superfluous,* ie felt that I shouldn't be there.

▷ **superfluity** /ˌsuːpəˈflʊətɪ; *also, in British use,* ˌsjuː-/ *n* [U, sing] ~ **(of sth)** (*fml*) superfluous amount: *have food in superfluity/a superfluity of food.*

superfluously: *adv.*

supergrass /ˈsuːpəgrɑːs; *also, in British use,* ˈsjuː-; *US* -græs/ *n* (*sl*) informer who gives evidence against a large number of his former accomplices.

superhighway /ˌsuːpəˈhaɪweɪ/ *n* (*US*) wide road specially built for fast-moving traffic, typically with six or more lanes.

superhuman /ˌsuːpəˈhjuːmən; *also, in British use,* ˌsjuː-/ *adj* exceeding normal human power, size, knowledge, etc: *It required superhuman effort to lift the huge boulder.* ○ *Her intelligence seems almost superhuman.*

superimpose /ˌsuːpərɪmˈpəʊz; *also, in British use,* ˌsjuː-/ *v* [Tn, Tn·pr] ~ **sth (on sth)** put sth on top of sth else, esp so that what is underneath can still be seen, heard, etc: *a map of Great Britain superimposed on a map of Texas,* eg to show comparative size ○ *superimpose an English commentary on the original soundtrack.* ▷ **superimposition** /ˌsuːpəˌrɪmpəˈzɪʃn; *also, in British use,* ˌsjuː-/ *n* [U].

superintend /ˌsuːpərɪnˈtend; *also, in British use,* ˌsjuː-/ *v* [Tn] (*fml*) manage and control (workers, their work, etc); supervise: *appointed to superintend (the staff in) the toy department.*

▷ **superintendence** /-əns/ *n* [U] (*fml*) superintending: *work done under the personal superintendence of the manager.*

superintendent /-ənt/ *n* **1** person who superintends: *the park superintendent.* **2** (in Britain) police officer next in rank above chief inspector.

Superior /suːˈpɪərɪə(r); *also, in British use,* sjuː-/ **Lake Superior** largest of the five *Great Lakes of N America, forming part of the border between the USA and Canada, and lying at the west of the group. It is 82 380 sq km (31 800 sq miles) in area.

superior /suːˈpɪərɪə(r); *also, in British use,* sjuː-/ *adj* **1** (**a**) better than average: *a superior cloth, team, standard* ○ *a girl of superior intelligence* ○ *This candidate is clearly superior.* (**b**) ~ **(to sb/sth)** better, stronger, etc than sb/sth else: *Which of the two methods is superior?* ○ *The match will show who is the superior player.* ○ *This cloth is superior to that.* ○ *The enemy forces were superior in numbers.* ○ *Which side has the superior weapons?* **2** ~ **(to sb)** higher in rank or position: *a superior court* ○ *A soldier must obey his superior officers.* ○ *She works well with those superior to her in the firm.* **3** (*derog*) showing that one thinks one is better than others: *a superior smile, look, air, etc* ○ *Don't be so superior!* **4** [usu attrib] (*fml*) placed higher up; upper: *a superior stratum of rock.* Cf INFERIOR.

▷ **superior** *n* **1** person of higher rank, position, etc: *obey one's superiors.* **2** person or thing that is better: *She is my superior in knowledge,* ie knows more than I do. ○ *He has no superior as a Shakespearian actor.* **3** (in titles) head of a religious community: *the Father Superior,* eg an abbot.

superiority /suːˌpɪərɪˈɒrətɪ; *US* -ˈɔːr-; *also, in British use,* sjuː-/ *n* [U] ~ **(in sth)**; ~ **(to/over sth/sb)** state of being superior: *the superiority of one thing to another* ○ *her superiority in talent* ○ *They won the battle because of their massive superiority in numbers.*

□ **suˌperiˈority complex** (**a**) (*psychology*) state of mind that makes a person act as if he were better or more important than others although he actually feels that they are better, etc than him. (**b**) (*infml*) too great a belief that one is better or more important than others. Cf INFERIORITY COMPLEX (INFERIOR).

superlative /suːˈpɜːlətɪv; *also, in British use,* sjuː-/ *adj* **1** of the highest degree or quality: *a superlative achievement, performance, meal* ○ *This wine is quite superlative.* **2** (*grammar*) of adjectives or adverbs expressing the highest or a very high degree, eg *best, worst, slowest, most difficult.* Cf COMPARATIVE 3.

▷ **superlative** *n* superlative form of an adjective or adverb: *a book review full of superlatives,* ie expressions praising it highly.

superlatively *adv*: *She plays the mandolin superlatively well.*

superman /ˈsuːpəmæn; *also, in British use,* ˈsjuː-/ *n* (*pl* **-men** /-men/) man with greater strength, ability, intelligence, etc than normal humans; superhuman man: *He's a kind of intellectual superman.*

supermarket /ˈsuːpəmɑːkɪt; *also, in British use,* ˈsjuː-/ *n* large shop selling food, household goods, etc which one takes from the shelves oneself and pays for at the exit.

supernatural /ˌsuːpəˈnætʃrəl; *also, in British use,* ˌsjuː-/ *adj* that cannot be explained by natural or physical laws; of the world of spirits, magic, etc: *supernatural beings,* eg angels and devils ○ *witch-doctors believed to have supernatural powers.*

▷ **the supernatural** *n* [sing] supernatural beings, events, etc: *an interest in the supernatural.* **supernaturally** /-ˈnætʃrəlɪ/ *adv.*

supernova /ˌsuːpəˈnəʊvə; *also, in British use,* ˌsjuː-/ *n* (*pl* **-vae** /-viː/ or ~**s**) (*astronomy*) star that suddenly becomes very much brighter as a result of an explosion. Cf NOVA.

supernumerary /ˌsuːpəˈnjuːmərərɪ; *US* -ˈnuːmərerɪ; *also, in British use,* ˌsjuː-/ *adj* (*fml*) in excess of the normal number; extra: *a supernumerary* (ie sixth) *finger.*

▷ **supernumerary** *n* (*fml*) supernumerary person or thing.

superphosphate /ˌsuːpəˈfɒsfeɪt; *also, in British use,* ˌsjuː-/ *n* fertilizer containing soluble phosphates.

superpower /ˈsuːpəpaʊə(r); *also, in British use,* ˈsjuː-/ *n* any of the most powerful nations in the world, esp the USA or USSR: [attrib] *a superpower summit.*

superscript /ˈsuːpəskrɪpt; *also, in British use,* ˈsjuː-/ *adj* [attrib] written or printed just above a word, figure or symbol: *Different words with the same spelling are distinguished in this dictionary by superscript numbers.*

Superstition

The remnants of superstitious beliefs survive in traditional customs that still exist in both Britain and North America, and in the association of certain objects with good or bad luck. Seeing a white horse, a four-leafed clover, two magpies together, a ladybird or a horseshoe, for example, is supposed to bring good luck, whereas it is regarded as bad luck to look at the new moon through glass or see a single magpie. When a black cat crosses one's path, it can mean either good or bad luck. A horseshoe upside down is unlucky, because its luck is 'running out'.

Certain actions are believed to bring bad luck. These include walking under a ladder, breaking a mirror, and killing a spider. If someone spills salt he should immediately throw a pinch of it over his left shoulder. On the other hand, picking up a pin from the ground brings good luck, and it is supposed to be lucky to touch a sailor's collar.

Relics of superstitious actions like these have been preserved in phrases like 'touch wood', for avoiding bad luck, or 'keep your fingers crossed'. Some people accompany such sayings with actions, for example by touching wood when saying 'touch wood'. If a person sneezes, it is common to say 'bless you'.

Actors are traditionally superstitious people, and often observe long-established customs. It is regarded as unlucky for one actor to wish another 'good luck', and some actors say 'break a leg' instead. It is a theatrical superstition that Shakespeare's play *Macbeth* should never be mentioned by name. Actors talk of 'the Scottish play' instead.

Among the strongest superstitious beliefs are those concerning lucky and unlucky numbers. The number 13 is invariably regarded as unlucky. Some hotels even have no room of this number, some buildings have no 13th floor, and aeroplanes often have no 13th row of seats. When the 13th of any month is a Friday it is regarded as particularly unlucky.

Fortune-telling or prophesying the future can range from 'seeing' the future in tea-leaves or in the flames of a fire to having one's palm read by a palmist or one's fortune told by a fortune-teller. Many seaside resorts and funfairs have people who claim special skills in doing this. Almost all popular newspapers and magazines print horoscopes, which foretell the future according to a person's 'stars' or the sign of the zodiac under which he was born.

Schoolchildren and students sometimes take a 'mascot' or lucky charm into an examination room with them. It may be a pet toy, the figure of an animal, or any small object that they feel brings them luck. The mascot may be worn, kept in a pocket, or placed on the desk. Similar lucky objects are often owned by people such as actors and sportsmen, and many car-owners have a mascot (often a toy animal) hanging from the front or back window of their car.

In Britain old houses and inns are sometimes said to be haunted by the ghost of someone who died violently or mysteriously in the house. The ghost may be given a name such as 'the Grey Lady' or 'the Headless Horseman'.

supersede /ˌsu:pəˈsi:d; *also, in British use,* ˌsju:-/ *v* [Tn] take the place of (sth/sb that was present or used before); be introduced so as to be used instead of (sth/sb): *Motorways have largely superseded ordinary roads for long-distance travel.* ○ *Will factory workers be entirely superseded by machines one day?*

supersonic /ˌsu:pəˈsɒnɪk; *also, in British use,* ˌsju:-/ *adj* (that can travel) faster than the speed of sound: *a supersonic aircraft* ○ *supersonic speeds.* Cf SUBSONIC.

superstar /ˈsu:pəstɑ:(r); *also, in British use,* ˈsju:-/ *n* (*infml*) very famous and admired entertainer: *Hollywood superstars* ○ [attrib] *superstar footballers.*

superstition /ˌsu:pəˈstɪʃn; *also, in British use,* ˌsju:-/ *n* [C, U] **1** (idea, practice, etc based on the) belief that certain events cannot be explained by human reason or physical laws; irrational fear of what is unknown or mysterious: *Ignorance and superstition prevent them from benefiting from modern medicine.* **2** idea or belief held by many people for no good or logical reason: *It's just (a) superstition that you shouldn't walk under ladders.* ⇨ article.

▷ **superstitious** /-ˈstɪʃəs/ *adj* **1** of, based on or caused by superstition: *superstitious beliefs, ideas, practices.* **2** believing in superstitions: *I always put my left shoe on first; I'm superstitious (about it).* **superstitiously** *adv.*

superstore /ˈsu:pəstɔ:(r); *also, in British use,* ˈsju:-/ *n* very large shop in which groceries and/or larger types of goods (eg furniture) are sold as in a supermarket: *a DIY superstore.*

superstructure /ˈsu:pəstrʌktʃə(r); *also, in British use,* ˈsju:-/ *n* **1** (**a**) structure built on top of sth else, eg the part of a building above the ground. Cf SUBSTRUCTURE. (**b**) parts of a ship above the main deck. **2** (esp in Marxist theory) institutions and culture that result from the economic system on which a society is based.

supertanker /ˈsu:pətæŋkə(r); *also, in British use,* ˈsju:-/ *n* very large tanker ship.

supertax /ˈsu:pətæks; *also, in British use,* ˈsju:-/ *n* [U] additional tax on income, paid by those who earn a very large amount of money.

supervene /ˌsu:pəˈvi:n; *also, in British use,* ˌsju:-/ *v* [I] (*fml*) occur as an interruption or change: *She was working well until illness supervened.* ▷ **supervention** /-ˈvenʃn/ *n* [U].

supervise /ˈsu:pəvaɪz; *also, in British use,* ˈsju:-/ *v* [I, Tn, Tng] watch or otherwise keep a check on (sb doing sth or sth being done) to make sure it is done properly: *The chief clerk supervises the work of the department.* ○ *I supervised the workers loading the lorry.*

▷ **supervision** /ˌsu:pəˈvɪʒn; *also, in British use,* ˌsju:-/ *n* [U] supervising or being supervised: *Children should not be left to play without supervision.* ○ *This drug should only be taken under the supervision of* (ie as supervised by) *a doctor.*

supervisor *n* person who supervises: *university students showing essays to their supervisor.* **supervisory** /ˈsu:pəvaɪzərɪ; *also, in British use,* ˈsju:-; *US* ˌsu:pəˈvaɪzərɪ/ *adj* supervising: *supervisory duties* ○ *a supervisory committee.*

supine /ˈsu:paɪn; *also, in British use,* ˈsju:-/ *adj* (*fml*) **1** lying flat on the back, face upwards: *a supine figure on the bed.* Cf PRONE, PROSTRATE 1. **2** (*fig derog*) showing a weak or lazy unwillingness to act: *accept unfair treatment in supine submission.* ▷ **supinely** *adv.*

supper /ˈsʌpə(r)/ *n* [C, U] last meal of the day, usu less large and less formal than dinner: *have cold meat for supper* ○ *have a late supper* ○ *eat very little supper.* ⇨ Usage at DINNER.

□ **ˈsupper-time** *n* [U] time at which supper is (usu) eaten.

supplant /səˈplɑ:nt/ *v* [Tn] (*fml*) take the place of (sb/sth); replace: *Oil has supplanted coffee as our main export.* ○ *The party leader has been supplanted by his rival.* ○ *She has been supplanted by another in his affections,* ie He now loves sb else.

supple /ˈsʌpl/ *adj* (**-r**, **-st**) bent or bending easily; not stiff; flexible: *the supple limbs of a child* ○ *Exercise keeps you supple.* ○ *She has a supple mind,* ie is quick to respond to ideas. ▷ **supplely** (also **supply**) /ˈsʌplɪ/ *adv.* **suppleness** *n* [U].

supplement /ˈsʌplɪmənt/ *n* **1** ~ (**to sth**) thing added to sth else to improve or complete it: *The money I get from teaching the piano is a useful supplement to my ordinary income.* **2** (**a**) ~ (**to sth**) book, section of a book, etc that gives further information, treats a special subject, etc: *the supplement to the Oxford English Dictionary.* (**b**) additional section added to a newspaper: *the colour supplements of the Sunday newspapers.* **3** extra amount of money paid for an additional service, item, etc: *a £10 supplement for a single room with a shower.*

▷ **supplement** /ˈsʌplɪment/ *v* [Tn, Tn·pr] ~ **sth** (**with sth**) add to or complete sth with sth else: *I supplement my grant by working in the evenings.* ○ *She supplements her diet with vitamin tablets.*

supplementary /ˌsʌplɪˈmentrɪ; *US* -terɪ/ *adj* ~ (**to sth**) **1** additional; extra: *a supplementary payment, lecture, item.* **2** (*mathematics*) (of an angle) making a total of 180° with another angle.

□ ˌ**supplementary ˈbenefit** (in Britain) money paid regularly by the State to poor people: *a family (living) on supplementary benefit.* Cf WELFARE 3.

suppliant /ˈsʌplɪənt/ *n, adj* (*fml*) (person) asking humbly for sth: *kneel as a suppliant at the altar,* ie praying to God for sth ○ *in a suppliant attitude.*

supplicate /ˈsʌplɪkeɪt/ *v* [Ipr, Tn, Cn·t] ~ (**for**) **sth** (*fml*) ask (sb) humbly or pleadingly for sth: *supplicate for pardon* ○ *supplicate sb's forgiveness,* ie ask sb to forgive one ○ *supplicate sb to help.*

▷ **supplicant** /ˈsʌplɪkənt/ *n* (*fml*) person who supplicates; suppliant.

supplication /ˌsʌplɪˈkeɪʃn/ *n* [C, U] (*fml*) (act of) supplicating: *He was deaf to my supplications.* ○ *kneel in supplication.*

supply /səˈplaɪ/ *v* (*pt, pp* **supplied**) **1** [Tn, Tn·pr] ~ **sth** (**to sb**); ~ **sb** (**with sth**) give sb sth that is needed or useful; provide sb with sth: *a company supplying heating oil (to homes)* ○ *supply consumers with gas, electricity, etc* ○ *He kept me well supplied with cups of coffee while I wrote the report.* **2** [Tn] provide enough (of sth) for (a need); fulfil: *Will the new power-station be able to supply our cheap energy requirements?*

▷ **supply** *n* **1** [U] supplying or being supplied: *a contract for the supply of office stationery* ○ *You promised us fuel, but can you guarantee its supply?* ○ *a reliable source of supply* ○ [attrib] *a supply train.* **2** [C often *pl*] thing that is supplied; stock or store of things provided or available: *the water-supply* ○ *a supply of reading-matter for the journey* ○ *arms, food, fuel supplies* ○ *Have we got enough supplies of coal?* ○ *Helicopters dropped supplies* (ie of food, etc) *for the stranded villagers.* **3** (idm) **in short supply** ⇨ SHORT[1]. **supˌply and deˈmand** (*esp economics*) the amount of goods, etc available and the amount wanted by consumers, the relationship between which is regarded as controlling prices.

supplier /səˈplaɪə(r)/ *n* person or firm supplying goods, etc.

□ **supˈply-side** *adj* (eg of economic policy) promoting measures which will encourage the efficient use of resources by facilitating competition and removing obstacles or disincentives to making an investment.

supˈply teacher teacher employed to do the work of any other teacher who is absent through illness, etc.

support /səˈpɔ:t/ *v* **1** [Tn] bear the weight of (sth/

sb); hold in position; carry: *a beam supporting a roof* ○ *Is this bridge strong enough to support heavy lorries?* ○ *He was weak with hunger, so I had to support him.* **2** (a) [Tn, Tn·pr] ~ **sb/sth (in sth)** help sb/sth by one's approval or sympathy or by giving money: *support a cause, political party, reform* ○ *donate money to support a charity* ○ *The directors were trying to get rid of her, but her staff all supported her.* ○ *The American public stopped supporting the war in Vietnam.* ○ *Will you support me in my campaign for election?* (b) [Tn] be a regular customer of or visitor to (sth); be a fan of (a team, etc): *Support your local theatre: buy tickets regularly!* ○ *Which football team do you support?* **3** [Tn] help to show that (a theory, claim, etc) is true; confirm: *a theory that is not supported by the facts* ○ *This evidence supports my argument that she is guilty.* **4** [Tn] provide (sb) with the necessary money, etc to buy food, accommodation, etc: *I was supported by my parents when I was studying.* **5** [Tn] provide enough food and water to keep (sb/sth) alive: *Such a barren desert can support very few creatures.*

▷ **support** *n* **1** [U] ~ **(for sth)** supporting or being supported: *adequate support for the great weight of the crane* ○ *a proposal that received no, little, not much, etc support* ○ *I need some financial support for this venture.* ○ *Can I rely on your support* (ie Will you vote for me) *in this election?* ○ *She is without any visible means of support*, ie has no work, income, etc. **2** [C] thing that supports or bears the weight of sth: *wearing an athletic support* ○ *supports holding up a collapsing wall.* **3** [C] person who gives help, sympathy, etc: *Jim was a great support to us when father died.* **4** [U] people who support a political party, team, etc: *The theatre has had to close for lack of support.* **5** (idm) **in sup'port** (eg of troops) in reserve; ready to give support: *We have ten people to do the cooking, with several more in support.* **in support of sb/sth** supporting sb/sth; in favour of sb/sth: *speak in support of a ban on arms supplies.*

supportable *adj* (*fml*) **1** that can be supported. **2** (used in negative sentences) that can be tolerated: *Such rudeness is scarcely supportable.*

supporter *n* person who supports a political party, team, etc: *The government's supporters welcomed the new law.*

supporting *adj* [attrib] (in the theatre and cinema) of secondary importance: *a supporting actor/cast/part/role* ○ *a supporting film*, eg one that is shown before the main film.

supportive /sə'pɔːtɪv/ *adj* (*approv*) giving help, encouragement or sympathy: *She has been very supportive during my illness.*

□ **sup'port price** minimum price for eg agricultural produce that is paid as a subsidy if the market price falls below this level.

suppose /sə'pəʊz/ *v* **1** [Tf, Cn·a, Cn·t] accept as true or probable; believe; imagine; assume: *What do you suppose he wanted?* ○ *What makes you suppose (that) I'm against it?* ○ *I don't suppose for a minute that he'll agree*, ie I'm sure that he won't. ○ *She'll be there today, I suppose.* ○ *'Will he come?' 'Yes, I suppose so.'* ○ *I suppose you want to borrow money from me again?* ie showing annoyance ○ *I don't suppose you could help me* (ie Please help me) *with my homework.* ○ *It was generally supposed that it would not happen again.* ○ (*fml*) *Everyone supposes him (to be) poor, but he is really quite wealthy.* ○ *It was widely supposed to have been lost during the war.* **2** [Tn, Tf, Cn·t] pretend that (sth) is true; take (sth) as a fact: *a theory which supposes the existence of other worlds besides our own* ○ *Suppose (that) the news is true: what then?* ○ *Suppose you had a million pounds — how would you spend it?* **3** [Tf] (used in the imperative, to make a suggestion) consider as a proposal: *Suppose we go* (ie Let's go) *for a swim!* **4** [Tn] (*fml*) require (sth) as a condition: *Creation supposes a creator.* **5** (idm) **be supposed to do sth** (a) be expected or required to do sth (by rules, custom, etc): *Am I supposed to* (ie Should I) *clean all the rooms or just this one?* ○ *You're supposed to pay the bill by Friday.* ○ *They were supposed to be here an hour ago.* (b) (*infml*) (used in negative sentences) be allowed to do sth: *You're not supposed to play football in the class-room.*

▷ **supposed** /sə'pəʊzd/ *adj* [attrib] wrongly believed or said to be the specified thing: *His supposed generosity is merely a form of self-interest.* ○ *The supposed beggar was really a police officer in disguise.* **supposedly** /sə'pəʊzɪdlɪ/ *adv* according to what is supposed (but not known for certain): *This picture is supposedly worth more than a million pounds.*

supposing *conj* (also **supposing that**) if we assume the fact or the possibility that; if: *Supposing (that) it rains, can we play the match indoors?*

supposition /ˌsʌpə'zɪʃn/ *n* **1** [U] supposing: *a newspaper article based on supposition*, ie only on what the writer supposes to be true, not on fact ○ *We must not condemn her on pure supposition.* **2** [C] ~ **(that...)** thing supposed; guess: *Our suppositions were fully confirmed.* ○ *I am proceeding on the supposition that...*, ie by assuming it to be true that....

suppository /sə'pɒzɪtrɪ; *US* -tɔːrɪ/ *n* piece of a medicinal substance placed in the rectum or vagina to dissolve.

suppress /sə'pres/ *v* [Tn] **1** put an end to (sth), esp by force; crush: *suppress an uprising, a revolt, etc.* **2** (a) (*usu derog*) prevent (sth) from being known or seen: *suppress the truth about sth* ○ *suppress a newspaper*, ie prevent it from being published ○ *Are the police suppressing some evidence?* ○ *The dictator tried to suppress all criticism of him.* (b) prevent (esp one's feelings) from being expressed: *suppress one's anger, amusement, etc* ○ *He could scarcely suppress a laugh.*

▷ **suppressible** *adj* that can be suppressed: *anger that was barely suppressible.*

suppression /sə'preʃn/ *n* [U] suppressing or being suppressed: *the suppression of a revolt, the facts* ○ *the suppression of one's anger, etc.*

suppressor *n* **1** person or thing that suppresses. **2** device fitted to an electrical apparatus to stop it causing interference on radio or television sets.

suppurate /'sʌpjʊreɪt/ *v* [I] (*fml*) (of a wound, etc) have a thick yellow liquid (*pus*) forming inside it because of infection: *a suppurating sore.* ▷ **suppuration** /ˌsʌpjʊ'reɪʃn/ *n* [U].

supra- /'suːprə/ *pref* above; beyond: *supranational*, ie going beyond national boundaries.

supreme /suː'priːm; *also, in British use*, sjuː-/ *adj* [usu attrib] **1** highest in authority, rank or degree: *the supreme ruler of a vast empire* ○ (*fig*) *After a year without defeat, the team now reigns supreme as the finest in the country.* **2** most important; greatest: *make the supreme sacrifice*, eg die for what one believes in ○ *Winning an Olympic gold medal was, I suppose, the supreme moment of my life.*

▷ **supremacy** /suː'preməsɪ; *also, in British use*, sjuː-/ *n* ~ **(over sb/sth)** [U] being supreme; position of the highest power, authority or status: *achieve military supremacy over neighbouring countries* ○ *challenging Japan's supremacy in the field of electronics* ○ *the dangerous notion of white supremacy*, ie that white races are better than others and should control them. **supremacist** /suː'preməsɪst; *also, in British use*, sjuː-/ *n*: *white supremacists.*

supremely /suː'priːmlɪ; *also, in British use*, sjuː-/ *adv* in a supreme way; extremely: *supremely happy.*

□ **the ˌSupreme 'Being** (*fml*) God.

the Suˌpreme 'Court the highest court in a state of the USA or in the whole of the USA. ⇨ article at LAW.

the Suˌpreme 'Soviet the law-making body of the Soviet Union.

supremo /suː'priːməʊ; *also, in British use*, sjuː-/ *n* (*pl* ~**s**) (*infml*) **1** ruler or commander with complete authority. **2** head of a particular organization, department, etc: *the government's information supremo*, ie who is in charge of press conferences, etc.

Supt *abbr* Superintendent (esp in the police force): *Supt (George) Hill.*

surcharge /'sɜːtʃɑːdʒ/ *n* **1** ~ **(on sth)** payment that is demanded in addition to the usual charge: *a 10% surcharge on the price of a holiday.* **2** mark printed over a postage stamp, changing its value.

▷ **surcharge** /sɜː'tʃɑːdʒ/ *v* [Tn, Tn·pr, Dn·n] ~ **sb (on sth)** demand a surcharge from sb: *They've surcharged us 10% on the price of the holiday because of a rise in air fares.*

surd /sɜːd/ *n* (*mathematics*) mathematical quantity, esp a root, that cannot be expressed as an ordinary number or quantity: *The square root of 5 ($\sqrt{5}$) is a surd.*

sure /ʃɔː(r); *US* ʃʊər/ *adj* (-r, -st) **1** [pred] ~ **(of/about sth)**; ~ **that...**; ~ **what, etc...** not doubting or seeming to doubt what one believes, knows, etc; confident that one is right: *I think he's coming, but I'm not quite sure.* ○ *I'm not sure when I saw her last.* ○ *Are you sure of your facts?* ○ *If you're not sure how to do it, ask me.* ○ *Can we be sure that she's honest?* ○ *I think the answer's right but I'm not absolutely sure about it.* ○ *Jane is reliable, but I'm not so sure about Jim.* ○ *She felt sure that she had done the right thing.* **2** [pred] ~ **of sth** certain to receive, win, etc sth: *You're sure of a warm welcome.* ○ *Can I be sure of a profit if I invest?* ○ *You're sure of passing the exam if you work hard.* **3** ~ **to do sth** definitely going to do sth; certain to do sth: *It's sure to rain.* ○ *You're sure to fail if you do it that way.* **4** undoubtedly true: *in the sure and certain knowledge of her guilt* ○ *One thing is sure: we've won a great victory!* ⇨ Usage at CERTAIN. **5** (usu *attrib*) proven and reliable; trustworthy: *no sure remedy for a cold* ○ *There's only one sure way to do it.* ○ *She has always been a sure friend.* **6** not deviating or wavering; steady and confident: *She drew the outline with a sure hand.* **7** (idm) **be sure to do sth**; **be sure and do sth** don't fail to do sth: *Be sure (to write) and tell me all your news.* **for sure** (*infml*) without doubt: *I think he lives there but I couldn't say for sure.* **make sure (of sth/that...)** (a) find out whether sth is definitely so: *I think the door's locked, but I'd better go and make sure (it is).* (b) do sth to ensure that sth happens: *arrangements to make sure that the visit goes well.* **sure of oneself** (*sometimes derog*) (too) confident of one's own abilities, etc; self-confident: *You seem very sure of yourself, young man!* **ˌsure 'thing** (*infml esp US*) yes; of course: *'Do you want to come too?' 'Sure thing!'* **to be 'sure** (*fml*) I cannot deny (that); admittedly: *He is clever, to be sure, but not very hard-working.*

▷ **sure** *adv* **1** (*infml esp US*) certainly: *It sure was cold!* **2** (idm) **(as) sure as eggs is 'eggs, as 'fate, as I'm standing 'here, etc** (*infml*) very certainly: *He's dead, as sure as eggs is eggs.* **ˌsure e'nough** (used to introduce a statement that confirms a previous prediction, etc): *I said it would happen, and sure enough it did.*

sureness *n* [U] quality of being sure (4, 6): *a picture that shows the artist's sureness of touch.*

□ **'sure-fire** *adj* [attrib] certain to happen, be successful, etc: *a ˌsure-fire suc'cess* ○ *This is a sure-fire way to get publicity.*

ˌsure-'footed *adj* not likely to fall when walking or climbing. **sure-footedly** *adv.* **sure-footedness** *n* [U].

surely /'ʃɔːlɪ; *US* 'ʃʊərlɪ/ *adv* **1** without doubt; certainly: *He will surely fail.* ○ *This will surely cause problems.* **2** (used to show that the speaker is (almost) certain of what he is saying, or to express surprise at sth): *This is surely her best play.* ○ *Surely I've met you before somewhere.* ○ *Surely they won't refuse?* ○ *Surely you're not going to eat that!* ○ *He has refused to help? Surely not!* ○ *'That's his wife.' 'His sister, surely?'* **3** (*infml esp US*) of course; yes: *'Can I borrow your car?' 'Surely.'* **4** (idm) **slowly but surely** ⇨ SLOWLY (SLOW[1]).

surety /'ʃɔːrətɪ; *US* 'ʃʊərtɪ/ *n* [C, U] **1** (money, etc given as a) guarantee that sb will pay his debts, perform a duty, etc: *offer £100 as (a) surety.* **2** person who makes himself responsible for the payment of debts, etc by sb else: *stand* (ie act as a) *surety for sb.*

surfing

surf /sɜ:f/ *n* [U] (white foam on) waves breaking on the seashore: *splashing about in the surf.*

▷ **surf** *v* [I] (usu **go surfing**) stand or lie on a surfboard and allow the surf to carry one towards the shore, as a sport. **surfer** *n.*

□ ˈ**surfboard** *n* long narrow board used for surfing. ⇨ illus.

surface /ˈsɜ:fɪs/ *n* **1** [C] (**a**) outside of an object: *the surface of a sphere, a ball, the earth* ○ [attrib] *the surface area of the brain.* (**b**) any of the sides of an object: *A cube has six surfaces.* (**c**) uppermost area or layer of sth: *the rough surface of the wall* ○ *an asphalt road surface* ○ *The insect's sting penetrates the surface of the skin.* ○ *wipe all the surfaces in the kitchen*, ie the walls, the tops and sides of furniture, etc ○ [attrib] *a surface layer* ○ *a surface wound*, ie not a deep one ○ *surface water*, ie lying on the ground ○ *a surface worker*, ie a miner who works above ground ○ *surface noise*, ie unwanted noise caused by dust, static electricity, etc on a record when it is being played. **2** [C usu *sing*] top of a body of liquid, eg the sea: *The submarine rose to the surface.* ○ *the frozen surface of the lake* ○ [attrib] *a surface vessel*, ie an ordinary ship, not a submarine. **3** [sing] (*fig*) qualities of sb or sth that are easily seen, contrasted with deeper or hidden ones: *Beneath her self-confident surface, she's quite unsure of herself.* ○ *You must not look only at the surface of things.* ○ [attrib] *surface politeness*, ie concealing anger, etc ○ *surface impressions*, ie ones gained too quickly, without proper thought or observation. **4** (idm) **on the ˈsurface** when not observed, thought about, etc deeply or thoroughly; superficially: *The scheme seems on the surface to be quite practical.* ○ *On the surface, she's a charming, helpful person.* **scratch the surface** ⇨ SCRATCH[1].

▷ **surface** *v* **1** [Tn, Tn·pr] ~ **sth (with sth)** put a surface(1c) on sth: *surface a road (with tarmac)* ○ *a wall surfaced with plaster.* **2** [I] (of a submarine, skin-diver, etc) come up to the surface of a body of water. **3** [I] (*infml*) (**a**) appear again after a period of remaining unseen, hidden, away from others, etc: *After living abroad for years, she suddenly surfaced again in London.* ○ *Their old rivalry soon surfaced when they met again.* (**b**) wake from sleep or unconsciousness: *He finally surfaced at midday.*

□ ˈ**surface mail** letters, etc carried by road, rail or sea, not by air.

ˌ**surface ˈtension** property of liquids by which they form a film or layer at their surface and make its area as small as possible.

ˌ**surface-to-ˈair** *adj* [attrib] (of missiles, etc) fired from the ground or from ships, aimed at aircraft.

surfeit /ˈsɜ:fɪt/ *n* (usu *sing*) ~ (**of sth**) too much of sth, esp of food and drink: *A surfeit of rich food is bad for you.* ○ *There has been a surfeit of plays about divorce on the television recently.*

▷ **surfeit** *v* [Tn, Tn·pr] ~ **sb/oneself (with/on sth)** (*fml*) provide sb/oneself with too much of sth, esp food: *surfeit oneself with fruit* ○ *be surfeited with pleasure.*

surge /sɜ:dʒ/ *v* **1** [I, Ipr, Ip] move forward in or like waves: *the surging tide* ○ *The floods surged along the valley.* ○ *The crowd surged (past) into the stadium.* **2** [I, Ip] ~ (**up**) arise suddenly and intensely: *Anger surged (up) within him.*

▷ **surge** *n* (usu *sing*) ~ (**of/in sth**) **1** forward or upward movement: *the surge of the sea.* **2** sudden occurrence or increase: *a surge of anger, pity, etc* ○ *There's a surge in electricity demand at around 7 pm.*

surgeon /ˈsɜ:dʒən/ *n* doctor who performs surgical operations: *a heart surgeon.* Cf PHYSICIAN.

surgery /ˈsɜ:dʒərɪ/ *n* **1** [U] treatment of injuries or diseases by cutting or removing parts of the body. Until the 19th century, surgery was regarded as an inferior branch of medicine; in the Middle Ages it was done by barbers. It was only when anaesthetics and antiseptic conditions were introduced that it began to become safe and respectable. Technological progress allows modern surgeons to perform increasingly delicate operations, such as organ transplants: *qualified in surgery and medicine* ○ *prepare the patient for surgery* ○ *He underwent open-heart surgery.* ○ *cosmetic surgery.* **2** (*Brit*) (**a**) [C] place where a doctor, dentist, etc sees his patients. (**b**) [U] time during which a doctor, etc is available to see patients at his surgery: *Surgery lasts from 9 am to 10 am.* ○ [attrib] ˈ*surgery hours.* **3** [C] (*Brit infml*) time when a Member of Parliament can be consulted by the people he represents: *She holds her surgery on Fridays at 6 pm.*

surgical /ˈsɜ:dʒɪkl/ *adj* [attrib] of, by or for surgery: *surgical instruments, treatment, skills* ○ *a surgical ward*, ie for patients having operations ○ *a surgical stocking*, ie one specially designed to support an injured or diseased leg. ▷ **surgically** /-klɪ/ *adv*: *a tumour removed surgically.*

□ ˌ**surgical ˈspirit** (*Brit*) (*US* ˈ**rubbing alcohol**) clear liquid, consisting mainly of alcohol, used for cleaning wounds, etc.

Suriname /ˌsʊərɪˈnæm/ country on the north-east coast of S America; former name Dutch Guiana; pop approx 392 000; official languages Dutch and English; unit of currency guilder; capital Paramaribo. Most of the country is covered by forest and the population is concentrated around the coast. Rice is the main agricultural crop and there are large reserves of bauxite. ⇨ map at GUYANA. ▷ **Surinamese** /ˌsʊərɪnæˈmi:z/ *n, adj.*

surly /ˈsɜ:lɪ/ *adj* (**-ier, -iest**) bad-tempered and unfriendly: *a surly person, look, refusal* ○ *Don't look so surly!* ▷ **surliness** *n* [U].

surmise /səˈmaɪz/ *v* [Tn, Tf, Tw] (*fml*) suppose (sth) without having evidence that makes it certain; guess: *With no news from the explorers we can only surmise their present position/where they are.* ○ *We surmised that he must have had an accident.*

▷ **surmise** /ˈsɜ:maɪz/ *n* [C, U] (*fml*) guess(ing): *Your first surmise was right.* ○ *This is pure surmise.*

surmount /səˈmaʊnt/ *v* **1** [Tn] deal with (a difficulty, etc); overcome: *We had many problems to surmount before we could start the project.* **2** [usu passive: Tn, Tn·pr] be or be placed on top of (sth tall): *A weather-vane surmounts the spire/The spire is surmounted by a weather-vane.*

▷ **surmountable** *adj* (of difficulties, etc) that can be overcome.

surname /ˈsɜ:neɪm/ *n* name shared by all the members of a family: *Smith is a common English surname.* ⇨ Usage at NAME[1].

▷ **surnamed** *adj* [pred] having a specified surname: *a boy surnamed Harris.*

surpass /səˈpɑ:s; *US* -ˈpæs/ *v* [Tn, Tn·pr] ~ **sb/sth (in sth)** (*fml*) do or be better than sb/sth; exceed sb/sth: *surpass sb in speed, strength, skill* ○ *It will be hard to surpass this very high score.* ○ *The beauty of the scenery surpassed all my expectations.*

▷ **surpassing** *adj* [attrib] (*fml*) of high quality or degree; exceptional: *surpassing beauty.* **surpassingly** *adv.*

surplice /ˈsɜ:plɪs/ *n* loose (usu white) outer garment with wide sleeves worn by priests and singers in the choir during religious services.

surplus /ˈsɜ:pləs/ *n* [C, U] **1** amount left over after one has used all that one needs; amount by which money received is greater than money spent: *Surpluses of food can be sold for cash.* ○ *We have a trade surplus of £400 million.* ○ *a time of great surplus followed by a time of shortage* ○ [attrib] *an army surplus store*, ie one selling clothes, equipment, etc no longer needed by the army. Cf DEFICIT. **2** (idm) **in ˈsurplus** having a surplus: *Our trade is in surplus*, ie We are exporting more than we are importing.

▷ **surplus** *adj* ~ (**to sth**) more than is needed or used: *surplus labour*, ie workers for whom there are no jobs ○ *a sale of surplus stock* ○ *This food is surplus to requirements.*

surprise /səˈpraɪz/ *n* **1** (**a**) [U] feeling caused by sth happening suddenly or unexpectedly: *Their defeat caused little surprise*, ie was expected. ○ *To my surprise, the plan succeeded.* ○ *Imagine our surprise on seeing her there.* ○ *She looked up in surprise when I shouted.* ○ *He expressed surprise that no one had offered to help.* (**b**) [C] event or thing that causes this feeling: *What a surprise!* ○ *We've had some unpleasant surprises.* ○ *The gift came as a complete surprise (to me).* ○ *They sprang quite a surprise on me when they offered me that job.* ○ [attrib] *a surprise visit, attack, party.* **2** (idm) **surˌprise, surˈprise** (*infml ironic*) (used to express acknowledgement or resigned acceptance of expected or predictable news): *The rent's going up, surprise, surprise!* **take sb/sth by surˈprise** attack, capture, etc sb/sth unexpectedly or without warning: *The town was well defended so there was little chance of taking it by surprise.* **take sb by surˈprise** happen unexpectedly, so as to shock sb slightly: *Her sudden resignation took us all by surprise.*

▷ **surprise** *v* **1** [Tn] cause (sb) to feel surprise: *She's over 80? You surprise me!* ○ *She was surprised by the boy's intelligence.* ○ *It wouldn't surprise me/I wouldn't be surprised if they lost*, ie I rather expect them to lose. ○ *Would it surprise you to know that I'm thinking of resigning?* **2** [Tn, Tng] attack, discover, etc (sb) suddenly and unexpectedly: *surprise the opposition*, ie attack them when they are unprepared ○ *We returned early and surprised the burglars searching through the cupboards.* **3** [Tn·pr] ~ **sb into sth/doing sth** cause sb to do sth through sudden unexpected action: *By firing a few shots we can surprise them into revealing their positions.*

surprised *adj* ~ (**at sth/sb**) experiencing or showing a feeling of surprise: *a surprised look, cry* ○ *We were surprised at the news.* ○ *I'm surprised at you, playing with dolls at your age!* ie I disapprove of what you are doing. ○ *I'm very surprised to see you here.* ○ *I'm surprised that he didn't come.* ○ *It's nothing to be surprised about.*

surprising *adj* causing surprise: *a surprising decision, defeat* ○ *It's surprising they lost.* **surprisingly** *adv*: *Surprisingly, no one came.* ○ *She looked surprisingly well.*

surreal /səˈrɪəl/ *adj* unlike reality, esp in having combinations or strange distortions of things, as in a dream; fantastic; bizarre: *Under the influence of the drug my mind was filled with surreal images.* ○ *Meeting you here like this is positively surreal!*

surrealism /səˈrɪəlɪzəm/ *n* [U] 20th-century movement in the arts that tries to express what is in the subconscious mind by showing objects and events as seen in dreams, etc. The earliest surrealists were French poets and authors whose work developed from that of *Dada and the *Symbolists, seeking to express thought without rationalization or traditional artistic values. The movement soon began to influence artists like *Miró and *Dali, film-makers like *Buñuel and even composers like *Satie. It was at its height in the 1920s and 1930s, but many modern artists are still affected by it.

▷ **surrealist** /-lɪst/ *n, adj* [attrib] (artist, writer, etc) of surrealism: *a surrealist painting, exhibition.*

surrealistic /səˌrɪəˈlɪstɪk/ *adj* **1** of surrealism: *a surrealistic style.* **2** surreal.

surrender /səˈrendə(r)/ *v* **1** [I, Ipr, Tn, Tn·pr] ~ (**oneself**) (**to sb**) stop resisting an enemy, etc; yield; give up: *We shall never surrender.* ○ *The hijackers finally surrendered (themselves) to the police.* **2** [Tn, Tn·pr] ~ **sth/sb (to sb)** (*fml*) give up possession of sth/sb when forced by others or by necessity; hand sth/sb over: *We shall never surrender our liberty.* ○ *They surrendered their guns to the police.* ○ *He surrendered his insurance policy*, ie gave up his rights under the policy in return for immediate payment. **3** (phr v) **surrender (oneself) to sth** (*fml or rhet usu derog*) allow (a habit, an emotion, an influence, etc) to control what one does: *He surrendered (himself) to despair and eventually committed suicide.*

▷ **surrender** *n* [U, C] surrendering or being surrendered: *demand the surrender of the town* ○ *She accused the government of a cowardly surrender to big-business interests.* ○ [attrib] *What is the surrender value of these shares?*

surreptitious /ˌsʌrəpˈtɪʃəs/ *adj* (*usu derog*) done or acting secretly or stealthily: *a surreptitious glance* ○ *She carried out a surreptitious search of his belongings.* ○ *I don't mind you smoking occasionally — there's no need to be so surreptitious about it!* ▷ **surreptitiously** *adv*.

Surrey /ˈsʌrɪ/ county of south-eastern England. It is partly agricultural but contains many residential towns dependent on London. ⇨ map at App 1.

surrogate /ˈsʌrəgeɪt/ *n* **1** ~ **(for sb/sth)** (*fml*) person or thing that acts or is used instead of another; substitute: *Fiction is a poor surrogate for real experience.* ○ [attrib] *a surrogate mother*, ie a woman who has a baby on behalf of another who is unable to have babies herself. **2** (*US*) judge responsible for cases involving wills, legal guardians, etc.

surround /səˈraʊnd/ *v* [Tn, Tn·pr] **(a)** ~ **sb/sth (with sb/sth)** (cause sb/sth to) move into position all round sb/sth; encircle sb/sth, esp so as to prevent escape: *Troops have surrounded the town.* ○ *They have surrounded the town with troops.* ○ (*fig*) *He likes to surround himself with beautiful things.* **(b)** ~ **sth/sb (by/with sth)** (esp passive) be all round sth/sb: *Trees surround the pond.* ○ *The house was surrounded by high walls.* ○ (*fig*) *The new plan is surrounded by much speculation*, ie Everyone is wondering about it. ○ *She has always been surrounded with fashionable friends.*

▷ **surround** *n* (usu decorative) border around an object: *a fireplace with a tiled surround.*

surrounding *adj* [attrib] that is around and nearby: *York and the surrounding countryside.*

surroundings *n* [pl] all the objects, conditions, etc that are around (and may affect) sb/sth; environment: *living in pleasant surroundings* ○ *Animals in zoos are not in their natural surroundings.*

surtax /ˈsɜːtæks/ *n* [U] tax charged at a higher rate than the normal on income above a certain level.

Surtees /ˈsɜːtiːz/ R(obert) S(mith) (1805-64), English novelist. He wrote several books describing the world of fox-hunting in 19th-century England, creating the comic characters of Mr Jorrocks and Mr Soapy Sponge.

surveillance /sɜːˈveɪləns/ *n* [U] careful watch kept on sb suspected of doing wrong: *The police are keeping the suspects under round-the-clock surveillance.*

survey /səˈveɪ/ *v* [Tn] **1** look carefully at all of (sth/sb), esp from a distance: *surveying the crowds from a balcony* ○ *survey the countryside from the top of a hill* ○ *She surveyed me haughtily over the top of her glasses.* **2** study (and describe) the general condition of (sth): *a speech in which she surveyed the international situation* ○ *In this book, the author surveys recent developments in linguistics.* **3** find and record the area and features of (a piece of land) by measurement and/or calculation (eg using trigonometry): *survey a plot of land for building.* **4** (*Brit*) examine (a building, etc) to make sure its structure is in good condition: *have a house surveyed before deciding to buy it.* **5** investigate the behaviour, opinions, etc of (a group of people), usu by questioning them: *Of the five hundred householders surveyed, 40% had dishwashers.*

▷ **survey** /ˈsɜːveɪ/ *n* **1** general view, examination or description: *A quick survey of the street showed that no one was about.* ○ *a survey of the situation, subject* ○ *a comprehensive survey of modern music.* **2** act of surveying (SURVEY *v* 3); map or record of this: *an aerial survey*, ie made by taking photographs from an aircraft. **3** (*Brit*) examination of the condition of a house, etc. **4** act of surveying (SURVEY *v* 5); investigation: *a public oˈpinion survey* ○ *Surveys show that 75% of people approve of the new law.*

surveyor /səˈveɪə(r)/ *n* **1** person who surveys (SURVEY *v* 4) and values buildings, etc. **2** person who surveys (SURVEY *v* 3) land, etc. **3** official appointed to check the accuracy, quality, etc of sth: *surveyor of weights and measures* ○ *the surveyor of highways.*

survival /səˈvaɪvl/ *n* **1** [U] state of continuing to live or exist; surviving: *the miraculous survival of some people in the air crash* ○ *the survival of the fittest*, ie the continuing existence of those animals and plants which are best adapted to their surroundings, etc ○ [attrib] *a surˈvival kit*, ie a package of items needed by survivors of a disaster, eg at sea. **2** [C] ~ **(from sth)** person, thing, custom, belief, etc that has survived from an earlier time: *a ceremony which is a survival from pre-Christian times.*

survive /səˈvaɪv/ *v* **1** [I, Ipr] ~ **(from sth)**; ~ **(on sth)** continue to live or exist: *the last surviving member of the family* ○ *Of the six people in the plane that crashed, only one survived.* ○ *Many strange customs have survived from earlier times.* ○ *I can't survive on £30 a week*, ie It is not enough for my basic needs. ○ (*fig*) *Life is hard at the moment, but we're surviving*, ie coping successfully with the difficulties. **2** [Tn] continue to live or exist in spite of nearly being killed or destroyed by (sth): *survive an earthquake, shipwreck, etc* ○ *Few buildings survived the bombing raids intact.* ○ *The plants may not survive the frost.* **3** [Tn] remain alive after (sb): *The old lady has survived all her children.*

▷ **survivor** *n* person who has survived: *send help to the survivors of the earthquake.*

sus (also **suss**) /sʌs/ *v* (-ss-) (*sl*) **1** [Tn, Tn·p, Tf, Tw] ~ **sb/sth (out)** discover sb/sth: *I've got him/it sussed (out)*, ie I now understand him/it. ○ *We've sussed (out) who did it.* **2** (phr v) **sus sth out** investigate sth carefully: *I sent Joe along to sus out the possibility of doing a deal with them.*

▷ **sus** *n* [U] (*Brit sl*) suspicion of having committed a crime: *I was picked up* (ie arrested) *on sus.*

susceptible /səˈseptəbl/ *adj* **1** ~ **to sth** [pred] easily influenced or harmed by sth: *highly susceptible to flattery* ○ *plants that are not susceptible to disease.* **2** easily influenced by feelings; impressionable: *a naive person with a susceptible nature* ○ *He's so susceptible that she easily gained his affection.* **3** ~ **of sth** [pred] (*fml*) that can undergo sth; capable of sth: *Is your statement susceptible of proof?*

▷ **susceptibility** /səˌseptəˈbɪlətɪ/ *n* **1** [U] ~ **(to sth)** state of being susceptible: *take advantage of her susceptibility* ○ *susceptibility to persuasion.* **2** **susceptibilities** [pl] person's feelings, considered as being easily hurt: *Do nothing to offend her susceptibilities.*

suspect /səˈspekt/ *v* **1** [Tn, Tf, Tnt] have an idea of the existence, presence or truth of (sth); believe: *He suspected an ambush.* ○ *I strongly suspect that they're trying to get rid of me.* ○ *Most people don't, I suspect, realize this.* ○ *What she said sounded convincing, but I suspect it to be a lie.* **2** [Tn] feel doubt about (sth); mistrust: *suspect sb's motives* ○ *I suspect the truth of her statement.* **3** [Tn, Tn·pr] ~ **sb (of sth/doing sth)** feel that sb is guilty of sth, without certain proof: *Who do the police suspect (of the crime)?* ○ *What made you suspect her of having taken the money?*

▷ **suspect** /ˈsʌspekt/ *n* person suspected of a crime, etc: *The police are interrogating two suspects.* ○ *He's a prime suspect in the murder case.*

suspect /ˈsʌspekt/ *adj* not to be relied on or trusted; possibly false: *His statements are suspect.* ○ *The car has a suspect tyre*, eg one that is damaged and therefore dangerous.

suspend /səˈspend/ *v* **1** [Tn, Tn·pr] ~ **sth (from sth)** (*fml*) hang sth up: *A lamp was suspended from the ceiling above us.* **2** [Tn·pr usu passive] not allow (sth) to fall or sink in air or liquid, etc: *a balloon suspended above the crowd* ○ *Smoke hung suspended in the still air.* ○ *particles suspended in water.* **3** [Tn] **(a)** prevent (sth) from being in effect for a time; stop (sth) temporarily: *suspend a rule* ○ *Rail services are suspended indefinitely because of the strike.* ○ *During the crisis, the constitution was suspended*, ie people did not have their normal civil rights. **(b)** postpone (sth); delay: *suspend introduction of the new scheme* ○ *suspend judgement*, ie delay forming or expressing an opinion ○ *give a criminal a suspended sentence*, ie not send him to prison unless he commits a further offence. **4** [Tn, Tn·pr] ~ **sb (from sth)** prevent sb officially from holding his usual position, carrying out his usual duties, etc for a time: *The policeman was suspended while the complaint was investigated.* ○ *She was suspended from school for stealing.*

□ **suˌspended aniˈmation** state of being alive but not conscious: (*fig*) *The whole project is in suspended animation while we wait for permission to proceed.*

suspender /səˈspendə(r)/ *n* **1** [C esp *pl*] (*Brit*) short elastic strap for holding up a sock or stocking by its top. **2** **suspenders** [pl] (*US*) = BRACES.

□ **suˈspender belt** (*US* ˈ**garter-belt**) woman's belt-like undergarment, worn round the waist, with straps for holding up stockings.

suspense /səˈspens/ *n* [U] feeling of tenseness, worry, etc about what may happen: *We waited in great suspense for the doctor's opinion.* ○ *Don't keep us in suspense any longer: tell us what happened!*

suspension /səˈspenʃn/ *n* **1** [U] suspending or being suspended: *the suspension of a rule, law, etc* ○ *the suspension of a pupil from school* ○ *She appealed against her suspension.* **2** [U] system of parts (eg springs and shock absorbers) by which a vehicle is supported on its axles: *The poor suspension gives a rather bumpy ride.* ⇨ illus at CAR. **3** [C, U] (state of a) liquid containing tiny particles of solid matter floating in it: *medicine in powder form held in suspension*, ie to be taken by drinking.

□ **suˈspension bridge** bridge suspended from steel cables supported by towers at each end. ⇨ illus at BRIDGE.

suspicion /səˈspɪʃn/ *n* **1** **(a)** [U] suspecting or being suspected: *regard sb with suspicion* ○ *He was arrested on suspicion of having stolen the money.* ○ *Her behaviour aroused no suspicion.* ○ *After a crime, suspicion naturally falls on the person who has a motive for it.* **(b)** [C] ~ **(about sth/sb)**; ~ **(that...)** belief or feeling that sth is wrong, that sb has done wrong, etc: *I have a suspicion that she is not telling me the truth.* ○ *It appears to be genuine, but I have my suspicions (about it).* **2** [sing] ~ **(of sth)** slight taste or amount: *a suspicion of garlic in the stew* ○ *a suspicion of sadness in her voice.* **3** (idm) **aˌbove suˈspicion** too good, honest, etc to be suspected of wrongdoing: *Nobody who was near the scene of the crime is above suspicion.* **under suˈspicion** suspected of wrongdoing.

suspicious /səˈspɪʃəs/ *adj* **1** ~ **(about/of sth/sb)** having or showing suspicion: *a suspicious look, attitude* ○ *I'm very suspicious about her motives.* ○ *He is suspicious of* (ie does not trust) *strangers.* **2** causing suspicion: *a suspicious action, remark* ○ *a suspicious character*, ie sb who may be dishonest ○ *It's very suspicious that she was in the house when the crime happened.* ▷ **suspiciously** *adv*: *acting suspiciously* ○ *Everything was suspiciously quiet.*

suss = SUS.

Sussex /ˈsʌsɪks/ county on the south coast of England, now divided into *East Sussex and *West Sussex. ⇨ map at App 1.

sustain /səˈsteɪn/ *v* [Tn] **1** (*fml*) bear (weight) without breaking or falling: support: *Will this shelf sustain the weight of all these books?* **2** **(a)** keep (sb/sth) alive or in existence: *You should eat good sustaining food*, ie food that gives strength. ○ *not* *enough oxygen to sustain life* ○ *Only the hope that the rescuers were getting nearer sustained the trapped miners*, ie kept them cheerful and enabled them to stay alive. (**b**) keep (a sound, an effort, etc) going; maintain: *The book's weakness is the author's inability to sustain an argument.* ○ *sustain a note*, ie continue to play or sing it without interruption ○ *make a sustained effort to finish off the work* ○ *The clapping was sustained for several minutes.* **3** (*fml*) undergo (sth); suffer: *sustain a defeat, an injury, a loss* ○ *He sustained a severe blow on the head.* **4** (*law*) decide that (a claim, etc) is valid; uphold: *The court sustained his claim that the contract was illegal.* ○ (*US*) *Objection sustained!*

□ **su'staining program** (*US*) radio or television programme paid for by a network rather than an advertiser or sponsor.

sustenance /ˈsʌstɪnəns/ *n* [U] (nourishing quality of) food and drink; nourishment: *There's not much sustenance in a glass of orange squash.* ○ *weak from lack of sustenance.*

Sutherland /ˈsʌðələnd/ Graham (1903-80), English artist. Besides his scenes recording the Second World War, his most famous work includes portraits and the tapestry of Christ in Majesty in Coventry Cathedral.

suture /ˈsu:tʃə(r)/ *n* (*medical*) stitch or stitches made in sewing up a wound, esp following an operation.

▷ **suture** *v* [Tn] (*medical*) sew up (a wound).

suzerain /ˈsu:zəreɪn; *US* -rɪn/ *n* (*fml*) country or ruler that controls the foreign policy of another country but allows it to govern its own internal affairs.

▷ **suzerainty** /ˈsu:zərəntɪ/ *n* [U] (*fml*) authority or rule of a suzerain: *a country under the suzerainty of its powerful neighbour.*

svelte /svelt/ *adj* (*approv*) (of a person) gracefully thin: *a svelte figure.*

Svengali /sveŋˈgɑ:lɪ/ *n* person who is able to control another person in an irresistible and usu evil way.

SW *abbr* **1** (*radio*) short wave. **2** South-West(ern): *SW Australia* ○ *London SW15 6QX*, ie as a postal code.

swab /swɒb/ *n* (**a**) piece of cotton wool, etc used in medicine for cleaning wounds, etc or for taking specimens, eg of mucus, for testing. (**b**) specimen taken in this way: *take swabs from children suspected of having diphtheria.*

▷ **swab** *v* (**-bb-**) **1** [Tn, Tn·pr] clean or wipe (sth) with a swab: *swab the wound with cotton wool* ○ *swab the blood off her face.* **2** [Tn, Tn·p] ~ **sth** (**down**) clean sth with water using a mop, cloth, etc: *swab down the decks.*

swaddle /ˈswɒdl/ *v* [Tn, Tn·pr] ~ **sb** (**in sth**) **1** (*dated*) wrap (a baby) in long narrow strips of cloth to stop it moving about. **2** wrap sb/oneself in warm clothes, etc; swathe sb/oneself: *She sat by the fire, swaddled in a blanket.*

▷ **'swaddling-clothes** /ˈswɒdlɪŋ/ *n* [pl] (*dated*) strips of cloth used for swaddling a baby.

swag /swæg/ *n* **1** [C] carved ornament representing a hanging bunch of fruit and flowers. **2** [U] (*dated sl*) stolen goods. **3** [C] (*Austral*) bundle of belongings carried by a tramp.

□ **'swagman** *n* (*pl* **-men** /-men/) (*Austral*) tramp.

swagger /ˈswægə(r)/ *v* [I, Ipr, Ip] (*usu derog*) walk or behave in a proud or boastful way: *Don't swagger (around) just because you got the job.* ○ *He took his prize and swaggered back to his seat.*

▷ **swagger** *n* [sing] (*sometimes derog*) swaggering movement or way of behaving: *walk with a swagger.*

swaggeringly *adv.*

□ **'swagger-stick** (also **'swagger-cane**) *n* (*Brit*) short stick carried by a military officer.

Swahili /swɑ:ˈhi:lɪ/ *n* (*pl* unchanged or ~**s**) **1** [C] member of a *Bantu people of the island of *Zanzibar and nearby mainland areas of Africa. **2** [U] language of this people, widely spoken as a lingua franca in many other parts of East and Central Africa. It is also the official language of Kenya and Tanzania. ▷ **Swahili** *adj.*

swain /sweɪn/ *n* **1** (*dated or joc*) young male lover; suitor. **2** (*arch*) young man from the country.

swallow[1] /ˈswɒləʊ/ *v* **1** (**a**) [I, Tn] cause or allow (esp food or drink) to go down the throat: *Taking pills is easy; just put them in your mouth and swallow.* ○ *Chew your food properly before swallowing it.* (**b**) [I] use the muscles of the throat as if doing this, eg in fear: *She swallowed hard, and turned to face her accuser.* **2** [Tn] (*infml*) (**a**) accept (an insult, etc) without protest: *She called you a liar. Are you going to swallow that?* ○ *He swallowed all the criticism without saying a thing.* (**b**) believe (sth) too easily: *He flatters her outrageously, and she swallows it whole*, ie believes it entirely. **3** [Tn, Tn·p] ~ **sb/sth** (**up**) (**a**) take sb/sth into itself so that he/it can no longer be seen: *The jungle swallowed up the explorers.* ○ *The aircraft was swallowed (up) in the clouds.* ○ (*fig*) *small firms being swallowed up by giant corporations*, ie taken over so that they disappear. (**b**) use sth up completely: *The cost of the trial swallowed up all their savings.* **4** [Tn] not express (a feeling, etc) openly: *She swallowed her anger and carried on.* ○ *I was forced to swallow my pride and ask for a loan.* **5** (idm) **a bitter pill to swallow** ⇨ BITTER. **swallow the bait** accept sth that has been said, offered, etc to tempt one. **swallow/pocket one's pride** ⇨ PRIDE. **swallow one's words** admit that one has said sth wrong: *He told me I wouldn't pass the test but I'm determined to make him swallow his words*, ie by passing.

▷ **swallow** *n* (**a**) act of swallowing. (**b**) amount swallowed at one time: *take a swallow of beer.*

swallow[2] /ˈswɒləʊ/ *n* **1** any of various types of small quick-flying insect-eating birds with a forked tail that migrate to northern countries (eg Britain) in summer. ⇨ illus at BIRD.

2 (idm) **ˌone swallow ˌdoes not make a ˈsummer** (*saying*) a single fortunate or satisfactory incident, example, etc does not mean that all the others will be as good.

□ **'swallow-dive** (*Brit*) (*US* **swan-dive**) *n* type of dive with the arms spread out until one is close to the water.

swam *pt* of SWIM.

swami /ˈswɑ:mɪ/ *n* Hindu religious teacher.

swamp /swɒmp/ *n* [C, U] (area of) soft wet land; marsh.

▷ **swamp** *v* **1** [Tn] flood or soak (sth) with water: *The sink overflowed and swamped the kitchen.* ○ *A huge wave swamped the boat.* **2** [esp passive: Tn, Tn·pr] ~ **sb/sth** (**with sth**) overwhelm sb/sth with a great quantity of things: *We asked for applications and were swamped (with them).* ○ *I've been swamped with work this year.*

swampy *adj* (**-ier**, **-iest**): *swampy ground.*

Swan /swɒn/ Sir Joseph (1828-1914), British scientist. He is remembered for his invention of an electric light bulb, which he developed with *Edison, and of new photographic materials.

swan /swɒn/ *n* **1** large graceful (usu white) water-bird with a long thin neck. ⇨ illus at BIRD. 📖 Swans are often thought of as 'royal' birds. They used to be eaten at royal banquets, and nowadays the swans on the Thames at *Windsor are the property of the monarch. *Shakespeare's nickname, the 'Swan of Avon', alluded both to the Greek legend that the souls of good poets pass into swans, and to the swans on the river at his birthplace, Stratford-upon-Avon. It was mistakenly believed that swans sing only when they are dying: hence the term 'swan-song'.

2 (idm) **all sb's geese are swans** ⇨ GOOSE. **the ˌSwan of ˈAvon** (*rhet*) *Shakespeare, who was born in Stratford-upon-Avon.

▷ **swan** *v* (**-nn-**) [Ipr, Ip] ~ **off**, **around**, **etc** (*infml derog*) go off, around, etc in a leisurely but irresponsible manner: *swanning around (the town) in her new sports car when she should have been at work* ○ *Are you swanning off on holiday again?*

swannery *n* /ˈswɒnərɪ/ *n* place where swans are kept.

□ **'swan-dive** *n* (*US*) = SWALLOW-DIVE (SWALLOW 2).

'swan-song *n* person's last performance, achievement or composition: *His performance as King Lear was to be his swan-song before retiring.*

'swan-upping *n* [U] (in Britain) ceremony in which young swans on the Thames are collected together and marked on their beaks to show whether they belong to the sovereign or to a livery company (LIVERY).

swank /swæŋk/ *v* [I] (*infml derog*) behave or talk in a boastful way; swagger: *She's swanking just because they said her essay was the best.*

▷ **swank** *n* (*infml derog*) **1** [U] behaviour or talk that is intended to impress people: *wear an expensive watch just for swank.* **2** [C] person who swanks: *Don't be such a swank!*

swanky *adj* (**-ier**, **-iest**) (*infml derog*) **1** fashionable and expensive in a showy way: *He stays in the swankiest hotels.* **2** tending to swank: *Jill and her swanky friends.*

swap (also **swop**) /swɒp/ *v* (**-pp-**) (*infml*) **1** [I, Ipr, Tn, Tn·pr, Tn·p, Dn·n] ~ (**sth**) (**with sb**); ~ (**sb**) **sth for sth**; ~ **sth** (**over/round**) give sth in exchange for sth else; substitute sth for sth else: *Your book looks more interesting than mine: do you want to swap (with me)?* ○ *They swapped* (ie told each other) *stories about their army days.* ○ *I'll swap (you) my Michael Jackson tape for your Bruce Springsteen album.* ○ *She swapped our chairs (round), so I had hers and she had mine.* ○ *I wouldn't swap places with him for anything*, ie would not wish to be in his situation. **2** (idm) **change/swap horses in mid-stream** ⇨ HORSE. **change/swap places** ⇨ PLACE[1].

▷ **swap** *n* **1** (usu *sing*) act of swapping; exchange: *As you like my dress and I like yours, shall we do a swap?* **2** thing swapped or suitable for swapping.

SWAPO /ˈswɑ:pəʊ/ *abbr* South-West Africa People's Organization, a Namibian political and military organization that fought for the country's independence and formed its first government.

sward /swɔ:d/ *n* [U] (*dated or rhet*) turf; grass.

swarm[1] /swɔ:m/ *n* **1** large number of insects, birds, etc moving around together, esp bees following a queen bee: *a swarm of ants, starlings, locusts, etc.* **2** (often *pl*) (unpleasantly) large number of people; crowd: *swarms of children in the park.*

▷ **swarm** *v* **1** [I] (of bees) move around in a swarm, esp following a queen bee. **2** (**a**) [Ipr, Ip] move in large numbers (in the specified direction): *The guests swarmed round the tables where the food was set out.* ○ *The crowd was swarming out through the gates.* (**b**) [I] be present in (unpleasantly) large numbers: *crowds swarming in the streets.* **3** (phr v) **swarm with sb/sth** (of a place) be (unpleasantly) crowded with or full of (people or things): *The beach was swarming with bathers.* ○ *The stables swarmed with flies.*

swarm[2] /swɔ:m/ *v* (phr v) **swarm down/up sth** climb down/up sth by holding on with the hands and feet: *swarm down a rope, up a tree.*

swarthy /ˈswɔ:ðɪ/ *adj* (**-ier**, **-iest**) dark or dark-skinned: *a swarthy skin, face, complexion, person.*

swashbuckling /ˈswɒʃbʌklɪŋ/ *adj* [usu attrib] typical of the exciting adventures and romantic appearance of pirates, soldiers of former times, etc, esp as shown in films: *swashbuckling heroes* ○ *a swashbuckling tale of adventure on the high seas.*

swastika /ˈswɒstɪkə/ *n* symbol in the form of a cross with its ends bent at right angles, formerly used as a Nazi emblem. ⇨ illus at CROSS.

swat /swɒt/ *v* (**-tt-**) [Tn] hit (sth/sb) hard, esp with a flat object: *swat a fly* ○ *She swatted him on the bottom with a rolled-up newspaper.*

▷ **swat** *n* blow of this kind: *Give that fly a swat.*

swatter (also **'fly-swatter**) *n* instrument for swatting flies, etc, usu a flat piece of plastic or metal fixed to a handle.

swathe[1] /sweɪð/ (also **swath** /swɔ:θ/) *n* **1** strip of grass or other plants cut by a mower, scythe, etc: (*fig*) *The storm cut a swathe through* (ie destroyed large areas of) *the forest.* **2** broad strip: *a swathe of daffodils across the lawn.*

swathe[2] /sweɪð/ *v* [Tn, Tn·pr esp passive] ~ **sb/sth**

(**in sth**) wrap sb/sth in several layers of bandages, warm clothes, etc: *thick bandages swathed his head.* ○ *They were swathed in scarves and sweaters.*

sway /sweɪ/ *v* **1** [I, Tn] (cause sth to) move or lean slowly from side to side: *trees swaying in the wind* ○ *He swayed slightly, as if about to fall.* ○ *She swayed her hips seductively as she danced.* **2** [Tn] influence or change the opinions or actions of (sb): *a speech that swayed many voters* ○ *Your arguments won't sway her: she's determined to leave.*
▷ **sway** *n* [U] **1** swaying movement: *The sway of the ferry made him feel sick.* **2** (*rhet*) rule or control: *people under the sway of Rome*, ie ruled by Rome in ancient times. **3** (idm) **hold ˈsway (over sb/sth)** (*dated or rhet*) have the greatest power or influence; be dominant: *Among English playwrights, few would deny that Shakespeare holds sway.*

Swaziland /ˈswɑːzɪlænd/ small country in southern Africa, a member of the Commonwealth; pop approx 737 000; official languages English and Swazi; capital Mbabane; unit of currency emalangeni. Swaziland is entirely surrounded by the territory of other countries and consists largely of high plateaus. It is self-sufficient in agriculture, the main crops being maize, sugar cane and cotton. There are important coal and aluminium reserves. The country's economy is one of the most developed in southern Africa, but is closely linked to that of South Africa. ⇨ map at NAMIBIA.
▷ **Swazi** *n, adj* (native or inhabitant) of Swaziland.

swear /sweə(r)/ *v* (*pt* **swore** /swɔː(r)/, *pp* **sworn** /swɔːn/) **1** [I, Ipr] ~ (**at sb/sth**) use rude or blasphemous words in anger, surprise, etc; curse: *She bumped her head in the doorway and swore loudly.* ○ *The foreman is always swearing at the workers.* **2** [no passive: Tn, Tf, Tt] say or promise (sth) very seriously, definitely or solemnly: *I've never seen him before, I swear it.* ○ *She swore that she'd never seen him.* ○ *I could have sworn* (ie I was certain) *I heard a knock at the door.* ○ *I swore not to tell anybody about it.* **3** [I, Ipr, Tn, Tf, Tt no passive] (cause sb to) make a solemn promise or statement about (sth): *Witnesses have to swear on the bible (to tell the truth).* ○ *They have sworn (an oath of) allegiance to the crown.* ○ *Has the jury been sworn* (ie officially appointed by taking an oath)? ○ *Are you willing to swear in court that you saw him do it?* **4** [Tn, Tn·pr] ~ **sth** (**against sb**) make (a statement) promising officially that it is true: *swear an accusation/a charge against sb.* **5** (idm) **swear ˈblind** (*infml*) say definitely: *She swore blind that she had not taken the money.* **swear like a ˈtrooper** use very obscene or blasphemous language. **swear sb to ˈsecrecy** make sb promise to keep a secret: *I swore her to secrecy about what I had told her.* **6** (phr v) **swear by sb/sth** (**a**) name sb/sth as a guarantee of what one is promising: *I swear by almighty God that I will tell the truth.* (**b**) (*infml*) believe greatly in the usefulness or value of sth (and use it constantly): *Many of my friends are using word processors but I still swear by my old typewriter.* **swear sb in** (esp passive) introduce sb officially or ceremonially to a new position, responsibility, etc by getting him to swear an oath: *The President has to be sworn in publicly.* ○ *Let the witness be sworn in.* **swear off sth** (*infml*) declare that one will stop using sth: *I've decided to swear off smoking.* **swear sth out** (*US*) obtain (a warrant to arrest sb) by making a formal accusation on oath. **swear to sth** (*infml*) say definitely that sth is true: *I think I've met him before, but I wouldn't swear to it*, ie I'm not sure.
▷ **swearer** *n* person who swears (SWEAR 1).
□ ˈ**swear-word** *n* rude or blasphemous word.

sweat /swet/ *n* **1** [U] natural moisture which comes through the skin when one is hot, ill, afraid, working hard, etc: *wipe the sweat from one's forehead* ○ *a vest damp with sweat* ○ (*fig*) *They built it with the sweat of their brow*, ie by working hard. **2 a sweat** [sing] state of sweating or being covered with sweat: *be in/break out in a sweat* ○ *work up a good sweat by running* ○ *They say a good sweat will cure a cold.* **3** [U] moisture that forms on any surface, eg by condensation. **4** (*fig infml*) (**a**) [U] hard work or effort: *Making your own beer? It's not worth the sweat!* (**b**) **a sweat** [sing] task, etc needing much effort: *Climbing all these stairs is a real sweat.* **5** (idm) **all of a ˈsweat** (*infml*) (**a**) wet with sweat. (**b**) anxious or frightened: *I was all of a sweat before the exam.* **no ˈsweat** (*infml*) (used as a way of saying that sth will not be difficult or inconvenient): *'I'm sorry to give you so much extra work.' 'No sweat!'* ie It doesn't bother me.
▷ **sweat** *v* **1** [I] produce sweat, eg when hot, ill, afraid, or working hard: *sweating heavily, profusely, etc* ○ *The long climb made us sweat.* **2** [I] (*fig infml*) be in a state of great anxiety: *They all want to know my decision but I think I'll let them sweat a little*, ie by not telling them yet. **3** [I, Ipr] ~ (**over sth**) work hard: *I really sweated over my last essay.* **4** [Tn] (*Brit*) heat (meat, vegetables, etc) in a pan with fat or water, in order to extract the juices. **5** (idm) **slog/sweat one's guts out** ⇨ GUT. **sweat ˈblood** (*infml*) (**a**) work very hard. (**b**) be very afraid or worried: *I sweated blood for a while thinking I'd broken the TV.* **6** (phr v) **sweat sth off** lose (weight) through strenuous exercise: *I sweated off ten pounds in a week by playing squash every day.* **sweat sth out** cure (a cold, fever, etc) by sweating. **sweat it out** (*infml*) wait uncomfortably for sth to happen or end: *There was nothing more we could do, so we just had to sit and sweat it out until the result was announced.*
sweaty *adj* (**-ier, -iest**) **1** covered or damp with sweat: *sweaty armpits* ○ *a sweaty T-shirt* ○ *I'm all sweaty from running.* **2** causing sb to sweat: *sweaty work* ○ *a hot sweaty day.*
□ ˈ**sweat-band** *n* band of absorbent cloth worn round the head or wrist, for soaking up or wiping away sweat.
ˌ**sweated ˈlabour** (*derog*) (**a**) work done for low wages in bad conditions. (**b**) people forced to do such work.
ˈ**sweat-gland** *n* organ beneath the skin that produces sweat.
ˈ**sweat-shirt** *n* long-sleeved cotton sweater.
ˈ**sweat-shop** *n* (*derog*) place where people are forced to work for low wages in bad conditions.

sweater /ˈswetə(r)/ *n* = JERSEY 1.

swede /swiːd/ (*US* also **rutabaga**) *n* [C, U] type of large yellow turnip. ⇨ illus at TURNIP.

Sweden

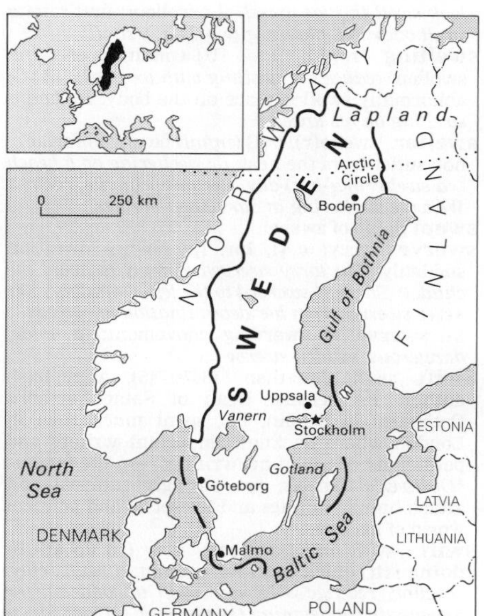

Sweden /ˈswiːdn/ country of northern Europe; pop approx 8 438 000; official language Swedish; capital Stockholm; unit of currency krona (= 100 öre). It lies east of Norway on the Scandinavian peninsula and is covered by many lakes and forests. Although little land can be farmed, it has an agricultural surplus. Sweden has reserves of iron and copper, but no fossil fuels. Its industrial economy is highly developed and several multinational companies are based there, and it has one of the most comprehensive social-security systems in the world. ⇨ map.
▷ **Swede** /swiːd/ *n* native or inhabitant of Sweden.
Swedish *n* [U] Scandinavian language of Sweden. — *adj* of Sweden.

Swedenborg /ˈswiːdnbɔːg/ Emanuel (1688-1772), Swedish scientist and mystic. He had an inventive scientific mind, but became increasingly concerned with spiritual matters. The New Jerusalem Church, to which *Blake belonged, spread his teachings.

sweep[1] /swiːp/ *v* (*pt, pp* **swept** /swept/) **1** (**a**) [I, Tn, Tn·pr, Tn·p] ~ **sth** (**from, off, into, etc sth**); ~ **sth** (**away, up, etc**) remove (dust, dirt, etc) with or as if with a broom or brush: *Have you swept in here?* ○ *sweep the dust from the carpets* ○ *sweep the crumbs under the carpet, off the table, into the dustpan* ○ *sweep away bits of paper* ○ *sweep the dead leaves up.* (**b**) [Tn, Tn·p, Cn·a] ~ **sth** (**out**) clean sth by doing this: *sweep the carpet, floor, yard* ○ *sweep out the porch* ○ *sweep the chimney (free of soot)* ○ *Have the stairs been swept clean?* **2** [Tn·pr, Tn·p] move or remove (sb/sth) powerfully and unstoppably by pushing, flowing, etc: *The current swept the logs down the river.* ○ *We were almost swept off our feet by the waves.* ○ *She got swept along by the crowd.* ○ *Many bridges were swept away by the floods.* ○ (*fig*) *Old laws were swept away by the revolution.* **3** [Ipr, Ip, Tn] move quickly over (an area): *A huge wave swept over the deck.* ○ *The fire swept rapidly across the wooded countryside.* ○ *Rumours swept through the town.* ○ *Cold winds swept the plains.* ○ (*fig*) *The party swept the country*, ie won the election by a large majority. **4** [Ipr, Ip] move in a smooth or dignified way (in the direction specified): *She swept out of the room.* ○ *The big car swept up the drive to the front of the house.* **5** [Ipr, Ip] extend in an unbroken line, curve or slope (in the direction specified): *The road sweeps round the lake.* ○ *The coast sweeps (away) northwards in a wide curve.* **6** [Tn] pass over (sth) in order to examine, search or survey it: *The searchlights swept the sky.* ○ *Her eyes swept the room.* **7** [Tn] move over or along (sth) touching it lightly: *His fingers swept the keys of the piano.* ○ *Her dress swept the ground.* **8** (idm) **sweep sth under the ˈcarpet** hide sth which might cause trouble or a scandal: *sweep embarrassing evidence under the carpet.* **sweep the ˈboard** win all the prizes, money, games, etc: *Switzerland swept the board in the skiing competition.* **sweep sb off his feet** overwhelm sb with emotion, esp with love: *I was swept off my feet by her wit and charm.*
▷ **sweeper** *n* **1** (**a**) person who sweeps: *a pavement sweeper.* (**b**) thing that sweeps: *a carpet sweeper.* **2** (in football) player positioned behind the defenders to tackle anyone who passes them.
sweepings *n* [pl] dust, rubbish, scraps, etc collected by sweeping.
□ ˌ**swept-ˈback** *adj* **1** (of aircraft wings) slanting towards the rear of the aircraft. **2** (of hair) brushed backwards from the face.
ˈ**swept-wing** *adj* [attrib] (of aircraft) having swept-back wings.

sweep[2] /swiːp/ *n* **1** (also ˈ**sweep-out**) [C usu *sing*] act of sweeping: *Give the room a good sweep.* **2** [C] sweeping (SWEEP[1] 2) movement: *the sweep of a pendulum* ○ *with a sweep of his arm, scythe.* **3** [C usu *sing*] long unbroken (often curved) stretch of road, river, coast, etc or of sloping land: *the broad sweep of white cliffs round the bay.* **4** [U] (*fig*) extent covered by sth; range: *the impressive sweep of a historical novel.* **5** [C] (**a**) movement over an area in order to search, attack, etc: *a sweep over the bay by a rescue helicopter* ○ *The police made a thorough sweep of the field where the dead child's body was found.* (**b**) movement of a beam of electrons across a cathode ray tube. **6** [C] = CHIMNEY-SWEEP (CHIMNEY). **7** [C] = SWEEPSTAKE. **8** [C] long oar. **9** (idm) **a clean sweep** ⇨ CLEAN[1].

sweeping /ˈswi:pɪŋ/ *adj* **1** (**a**) having an extremely wide effect; far-reaching: *sweeping reforms, changes, etc* ○ *sweeping reductions in prices.* (**b**) [usu attrib] complete; decisive: *a sweeping victory.* **2** (*derog*) (of statements, etc) without any exceptions; (too) general: *make a sweeping generalization, accusation, etc.*

sweepstake /ˈswi:psteɪk/ (also *infml* **sweep**) *n* (**a**) type of gambling in which all the money bet on the result of a contest is divided among those who by chance have selected or been given tickets corresponding to the eventual winner(s) of the contest. (**b**) horse-race on which money is bet in this way.

sweet[1] /swi:t/ *adj* (**-er, -est**) **1** tasting like sugar or honey; not sour, bitter or salty: *sweet apples, biscuits, drinks, etc* ○ *sweet wine,* ie tasting sweet or fruity, not dry ○ *Do you like your tea sweet?* ○ *This cake is much too sweet.* **2** smelling fragrant or perfumed: *Don't the roses smell sweet!* ○ *gardens sweet with the scent of thyme.* **3** pleasing to hear; melodious: *the sweet song of the blackbird* ○ *The soprano's voice sounded clear and sweet.* **4** fresh and pure; wholesome: *sweet milk* ○ *The spring water was sweet* (ie not salty, polluted, etc) *to the taste.* ○ *the sweet air of the countryside.* **5** giving satisfaction; gratifying: *the sweet feeling of freedom, success, etc.* **6** (**a**) (*infml*) attractive and charming: *a sweet face, smile, gesture* ○ *a sweet little poodle, baby, cottage* ○ *You look so sweet in that hat!* (**b**) having or showing a pleasant nature; lovable: *a sweet child, old lady, etc* ○ *a sweet temper, nature, disposition, etc* ○ *It is sweet of you to have remembered us.* ○ *such a sweet-tempered/sweet-natured girl.* **7** (idm) **at one's ˌown sweet ˈwill; in one's ˌown sweet ˈtime; in one's ˌown sweet ˈway** just as one pleases, or taking as long as one pleases, often in spite of the orders or wishes of others: *It's no good telling him — leave him to find out in his own sweet time.* **be sweet on sb** (*dated infml*) be fond of or in love with sb. **have a sweet ˈtooth** (*infml*) like to eat sweet or sugary things. **keep sb sweet** (*infml*) be specially pleasant with sb in order to win favours: *I have to keep my boss sweet because I need to ask for a rise.* **revenge is sweet** ⇨ REVENGE. **short and sweet** ⇨ SHORT[1]. **sweet ˈnothings** (*infml or joc*) words of affection exchanged by lovers: *She whispered sweet nothings into his ear.*

▷ **sweetish** *adj* rather sweet.

sweetly *adv* in a sweet(2, 6) manner: *sweetly perfumed flowers* ○ *singing, smiling sweetly.*

sweetness *n* **1** [U] quality of being sweet. **2** (idm) **(all) ˌsweetness and ˈlight** (*ironic*) display of mildness and reason: *She's all sweetness and light provided you're doing what she wants.*

□ **ˌsweet-and-ˈsour** *adj* [attrib] (of food) cooked in a sauce containing sugar and either vinegar or lemon: *ˌsweet-and-sour ˈpork,* ie a Chinese dish.

ˌsweet-ˈbriar (also **ˌsweet-ˈbrier**) *n* [U] = EGLANTINE.

ˈsweet corn type of maize with sweet grains.

ˈsweetheart *n* **1** (*dated*) one of a pair of lovers: *They were childhood sweethearts.* ○ *Mary has a sweetheart.* **2** (used esp as a loving form of address, eg to a wife, husband, child, etc).

ˌsweet ˈpea climbing garden plant with brightly-coloured sweet-scented flowers.

ˌsweet poˈtato tropical climbing plant with thick edible roots, cooked as a vegetable. Cf YAM.

ˈsweet talk (*US infml*) flattery. **ˈsweet-talk** *v* [Tn, Tn·pr] ~ **sb (into sth/doing sth)** persuade sb by flattery, etc (to do sth): *You can't sweet-talk me into helping you!*

ˌsweet ˈwilliam *n* garden plant with clustered sweet-scented flowers.

sweet[2] /swi:t/ *n* **1** [C often *pl*] (*Brit*) (*US* **candy** [U, C]) small shaped piece of sweet substance, usu made with sugar and/or chocolate: *a packet of boiled sweets* ○ [attrib] *a sweet shop.* **2** [C, U] (*Brit*) = DESSERT: *What's for sweet?* ○ *have some more sweet.* **3 sweets** [pl] **the ~s of sth** satisfactions or pleasures: *taste the sweets of success, freedom, etc* ○ *enjoy the sweets of life while one is young.* **4** (used as a loving form of address) darling: *Yes, my sweet.*

sweetbread /ˈswi:tbred/ *n* pancreas of a calf or lamb used as food.

sweeten /ˈswi:tn/ *v* **1** [I, Tn] (cause sth to) become sweet or sweeter: *Fruit sweetens as it ripens.* ○ *I never sweeten my tea.* ○ *sweeten (the air in) a room,* eg by opening a window. **2** [Tn, Tn·p] ~ **sb (up)** (*infml*) make sb more agreeable, eg by offering gifts: *I'll sweeten her up a bit by inviting her to the party.* **3** (idm) **sugar/sweeten the pill** ⇨ PILL.

▷ **sweetener** /ˈswi:tnə(r)/ *n* **1** [C, U] (piece of a) substance used to sweeten food or drink, esp as a substitute for sugar. **2** [C] (*infml*) attempt to persuade sb; bribe: *The firm offered her a generous bonus as a sweetener.*

sweetening /ˈswi:tnɪŋ/ *n* [C, U] substance, eg sugar, used to sweeten food or drink: [attrib] *sweetening agents.*

sweetie /ˈswi:tɪ/ *n* (*infml*) **1** (*Brit*) (used esp by and to young children) sweet[2](1). **2** (*esp Brit*) kind or lovable person: *Thanks for helping, you're a sweetie.* **3** (used as a loving form of address) darling.

swell /swel/ *v* (*pt* **swelled** /sweld/, *pp* **swollen** /ˈswəʊlən/ or **swelled**) **1** (**a**) [I, Ipr, Ip, Tn esp passive, Tn·pr esp passive, Tn·p esp passive] ~ **(to sth)**; ~ **(sth) (up) (with sth)** (cause sth to) become larger or bulge outwards, eg because of pressure from inside: *Wood often swells when wet.* ○ *My eyes swelled with tears.* ○ *His face was swollen (up) with toothache.* ○ *limping because of a swollen ankle.* (**b**) [I, Ip, Tn, Tn·p] ~ **(sth) (out)** (cause sth to) curve outwards; billow: *The sails swelled (out) in the wind.* ○ *The wind swelled (out) the sails.* **2** [I, Ipr, Tn, Tn·pr esp passive] ~ **(into/to sth)**; ~ **sth (to sth) (with sth)** (cause sth to) become greater in intensity, number, amount or volume: *The group of onlookers soon swelled (in)to a crowd.* ○ *The murmur swelled into a roar.* ○ *Small extra costs all swell the total.* ○ *The river was swollen with flood water.* **3** [I, Ipr, Tn, Tn·pr] ~ **(sth) (with sth)** (of a person, his heart, etc) feel like bursting with emotion: *His breast/heart swelled with pride at his achievement.* **4** (idm) **have a swelled/swollen ˈhead** (*infml*) be conceited, esp because of a sudden success.

▷ **swell** *n* [U, sing] **1** slow heaving of the sea with waves that do not break: *feel seasick in the heavy swell.* **2** (*music*) gradual increase in the volume of sound.

swell *adj* (*US infml*) **1** fashionable or smart: *You look swell in that dress!* **2** excellent; first-rate: *a swell vacation, player, guy* ○ *That's swell!*

swelling /ˈswelɪŋ/ *n* **1** [U] condition of being swollen: *reduce the swelling with ice-packs.* **2** [C] abnormally swollen place on the body: *He had a swelling on his knee.*

swelter /ˈsweltə(r)/ *v* [I] (*infml*) be uncomfortably hot; suffer from the heat: *lie sweltering on a beach* ○ *a sweltering(-hot) day, summer, climate, room* ○ *We were sweltering in our winter clothes.*

swept *pt, pp* of SWEEP[1].

swerve /swɜ:v/ *v* [I, Ipr, Ip] change direction suddenly: *The lorry swerved sharply to avoid the child.* ○ *The ball swerved to the left.* ○ (*fml fig*) *She never swerves from her determination to succeed.*

▷ **swerve** *n* swerving movement: *a wide, dangerous, sudden swerve.*

Swift /swɪft/ Jonathan (1667-1745), Anglo-Irish author. He became Dean of Saint Patrick's Cathedral in Dublin, but spent much time in London where he knew important writers and politicians. Many of his writings, esp the famous **Gulliver's Travels*, are strongly satirical and attack human failings and the social and political world of his day.

swift[1] /swɪft/ *adj* (**-er, -est**) **1** ~ **(to do sth/in doing sth)** quick or rapid; prompt: *a swift reply, reaction, revenge* ○ *He was swift to condemn the violence/in condemning the violence.* ○ (*fml*) *She is swift to anger,* ie She quickly becomes angry. **2** (often in compounds) that can move fast: *a swift runner, horse* ○ *swift-flowing rivers* ○ *swift-footed greyhounds.* ▷ **swiftly** *adv.* **swiftness** *n* [U].

swift[2] /swɪft/ *n* type of small fast-flying insect-eating bird with long narrow wings.

swig /swɪg/ *v* (**-gg-**) [Ipr, Tn, Tn·pr, Tn·p] ~ **sth (down)** (*infml*) take a drink or drinks of (esp alcohol), usu in large gulps: *swigging beer out of a bottle* ○ *swig down a glass of rum.*

▷ **swig** *n* act of swigging; swallow: *taking long swigs (at a bottle) of beer.*

swill /swɪl/ *v* **1** (**a**) [Tn, Tn·p] ~ **sth (out/down)** (*esp Brit*) rinse or flush sth by pouring large amounts of water, etc into, over or through it: *swill down the front steps* ○ *He swilled his mouth out with antiseptic.* (**b**) [Ipr, Ip] ~ **around, over, through, etc** (of liquid) flow or pour in the specified direction: *Beer swilled around the bottom of the barrel.* ○ *Muddy water swilled over the planks.* **2** [Tn] (*infml derog*) drink (sth) in large quantities; guzzle: *swill beer, tea, etc.*

▷ **swill** *n* **1** [sing] act of swilling; rinse: *give the bucket a swill (out).* **2** (also **ˈpigswill**) [U] left-over vegetable peelings, etc given to pigs as food.

swim /swɪm/ *v* (**-mm-**, *pt*; **swam** /swæm/, *pp* **swum** /swʌm/) **1** (**a**) [I, Ipr, Ip] move the body through water by using arms, legs, fins, tail, etc: *Fish swim.* ○ *Let's go swimming.* ○ *swim on one's back* ○ *When the ship sank we had to swim for it,* ie save ourselves by swimming. ○ *swim underwater, upstream, across, ashore.* (**b**) [Tn] use particular movements to do this: *swim breast-stroke, back-stroke, crawl, etc.* **2** (**a**) [Tn, Tn·pr] cover a distance by swimming: *swim a mile, race, river* ○ *swim two lengths of the pool* ○ *swim the Channel.* (**b**) [no passive: Tn·pr, Tn·p] cause (an animal) to do this: *She swam her horse across (the river).* **3** (usu in the continuous tenses) (**a**) [I, Ipr] ~ **(with sth)** be flooded or overflowing (with liquid): *Her eyes were swimming (with tears).* ○ *The bathroom floor was swimming with water.* (**b**) [Ipr] ~ **in sth** be covered with liquid as if floating in it: *meat swimming in gravy.* **4** (**a**) [I, Ipr] seem to be whirling: *The room swam before his eyes/around him.* (**b**) [I] have a dizzy feeling: *The whiskey made his head swim.* ○ *My head swam at the complexity of the calculations.* **5** (idm) **sink or swim** ⇨ SINK[1].

▷ **swim** *n* **1** action or period of swimming: *go for a swim* ○ *I only had two swims last year.* **2** (idm) **in/out of the ˈswim** (*infml*) aware or involved/not aware or involved in what is going on: *Although I'm retired, voluntary work keeps me in the swim (of things).*

swimmer *n* person who swims (esp in the way specified by the *adj*): *a strong, good, fast, etc swimmer.*

□ **ˈswim-bladder** *n* air-filled structure in a fish's body that regulates the buoyancy of the fish.

ˈswimming-bath *n* (esp *pl*) (*Brit*) indoor swimming-pool.

ˈswimming-costume (also **ˈbathing-costume**) (*esp Brit*) (*US* also **ˈbathing-suit**) *n* one-piece garment worn for swimming.

ˈswimming-pool *n* artificial pool for swimming in.

ˈswimming-trunks *n* [pl] short pants or trousers worn by men and boys for swimming: *a pair of swimming-trunks.*

ˈswim-suit *n* one-piece garment worn by women and girls for swimming.

swimmingly /ˈswɪmɪŋlɪ/ *adv* (*infml*) pleasantly and smoothly: *We're getting along swimmingly.* ○ *Everything went swimmingly,* ie proceded without difficulties.

Swinburne /ˈswɪnbɜ:n/ Algernon Charles (1837-1909), English poet. He had great technical skill, but many found his anti-religious outlook and the masochistic sexual content of his work scandalous. As a critic he stimulated interest in *Blake and the *Brontës.

swindle /ˈswɪndl/ *v* (*infml*) [Tn, Tn·pr] (**a**) ~ **sb/sth (out of sth)** cheat sb/sth, esp in a business transaction: *swindle an insurance company* ○ *You're easily swindled!* ○ *I've been swindled out of £5.* (**b**) ~ **sth (out of sb/sth)** get (money, etc) by fraud: *She swindled £1 000 out of the Social Security.*

▷ **swindle** *n* **1** act of swindling: *victims of a tax,* *mortgage, etc swindle.* **2** person or thing that is presented wrongly in order to deceive people: *That newspaper story's a complete swindle.*

swindler /ˈswɪndlə(r)/ *n* person who swindles.

swine /swaɪn/ *n* **1** [pl] (*arch or fml*) pigs. **2** [C] (*infml derog*) obnoxious person or thing: *Take your hands off me, you filthy swine!* ○ *Those nails were real swines to get out.* **3** (idm) **cast pearls before swine** ⇨ CAST[1].

□ ˌ**swine-ˈfever** *n* [U] (*Brit*) virus disease affecting pigs.

swing[1] /swɪŋ/ *v* (*pt, pp* **swung** /swʌŋ/) **1** [I, Ipr, Ip, Tn, Tn·pr] (cause sb/sth to) move to and fro while hanging or supported: *His arms swung/He swung his arms as he walked.* ○ *The bucket swung from the end of a rope.* ○ *The gymnast swung on the parallel bars.* **2** [Ipr, Ip, Tn·pr, Tn·p] move (sb/oneself) from one place to another by gripping sth and leaping, etc: *The ape swung (along) from branch to branch.* ○ *He swung himself (up) into the saddle/into the driver's seat.* **3** [Ipr, Ip] walk or run with an easy rhythmical movement: *The band swung lightly down the street.* ○ *A company of guardsmen swung past.* **4** [Ipr, Ip, Tn, Tn·pr, Tn·p, Cn·a] (cause sth to) move in a curve: *A car swung sharply round the corner.* ○ *The boom swung over (the deck).* ○ *She swung the rucksack (up) onto her back.* ○ *swing a telescope through 180°* ○ *The gate (was) swung slowly to/shut.* **5** [Ipr, Ip] ~ **around/round** turn suddenly to face the opposite way: *She swung round (on him) angrily.* ○ *He swung round to confront his accusers.* **6** [Ipr, Ip, Tn·pr, Tn·p] ~ **(sb) (from sth) to sth** (cause sb to) change suddenly from one opinion or mood, etc to another: *Voters have/Voting has swung to the left.* ○ *He swings from wild optimism to total despair.* ○ *Can you swing them round to my point of view?* **7** [I] have a rhythmic feeling or drive: *He can write music that really swings.* **8** [Tn] (*infml*) succeed in obtaining or achieving (sth), esp by devious means: *Can you swing it for me so that I get the job?* ○ *She managed to swing an interview with the Prince.* **9** (idm) **room to swing a cat** ⇨ ROOM. ˌ**swing into ˈaction** act swiftly: *The police swung into action against the gunmen.* **swing the ˈlead** (*dated Brit infml*) (try to) avoid work or a duty, usu by pretending to be ill. **10** (phr v) **swing for sb** (*sl or joc*) be executed by hanging for having killed sb: *That wretched child — I'll swing for him one of these days!*

swing[2] /swɪŋ/ *n* **1** [C] swinging movement or action or rhythm: *The golfer took a swing at the ball.* ○ *the swing of a pendulum, pointer, needle, etc* ○ *the swing of her hips as she walked.* **2** [C] **(a)** seat for swinging on, hung from above on ropes or chains: *children riding on the swings.* **(b)** action of swinging on this: *have a swing* ○ *give the children a swing.* **3** [U] (also ˈ**swing music**) smooth rhythmic type of jazz played esp by big dance bands in the 1930s. **4** [U, sing] rhythmic feeling or drive: *music with a swing (to it).* **5** [C] amount by which sth changes from one opinion, etc to another: *Voting showed a 10% swing to the Opposition.* ○ *He is liable to abrupt swings in mood, eg from happiness to despair.* **6** (idm) **get in the ˈswing (of sth)** (*infml*) adapt to a routine, etc: *I've only been at university for a week, so I haven't got into the swing of things yet.* **go with a ˈswing** (*infml*) **(a)** (of music, poetry, etc) have a strong rhythm. **(b)** (of entertainment, etc) be lively and enjoyable: *The party went with a swing.* **in full swing** ⇨ FULL. ˌ**swings and ˈroundabouts** (*infml esp Brit*) a matter of balancing profits against losses: *Higher earnings mean more tax, so it's all swings and roundabouts.* ○ *What you gain on the swings you'll probably lose on the roundabouts.* **the** ˌ**swing of the ˈpendulum** the movement of public opinion from one extreme to the other.

□ ˈ**swing-boat** *n* boat-shaped swing at fairs, etc.

ˌ**swing ˈbridge** bridge that can be swung aside to let ships pass.

ˌ**swing-ˈdoor** *n* door that opens in either direction and closes itself when released.

ˈ**swing shift** (*US infml*) employees on the evening shift, usu from 4 pm to midnight.

ˌ**swing-ˈwing** *n* (aircraft with a) type of wing that can be moved forward for landing, etc and backward for high-speed flying.

swingeing /ˈswɪndʒɪŋ/ *adj* [attrib] (*esp Brit*) **1** (of a blow) hard or forcible. **2** large in amount or number or range: *swingeing fines, taxes, costs, etc* ○ *swingeing cuts in public services.*

swipe /swaɪp/ *v* (*infml*) **1** [Ipr, Tn, Tn·pr] ~ **(at) sth/sb** (try to) hit sth/sb with a swinging or reckless blow: *He swiped at the dog with his stick, but missed.* ○ *He swiped the ball into the grandstand.* **2** [Tn] (*esp joc*) steal (sth), esp by snatching: *Who's swiped my calculator?*

▷ **swipe** *n* ~ **(at sb/sth)** (attempt at a) swinging or reckless blow: *have/take a swipe at the ball* ○ *make a sudden vicious swipe at sb.*

swirl /swɜːl/ *v* [I, Ipr, Ip, Tn·pr esp passive, Tn·p esp passive] (cause air, water, etc to) move or flow with twists and turns and with varying speed: *dust swirling (around) in the streets* ○ *Smoke swirled up the chimney.* ○ *The log was swirled away downstream by the current.*

▷ **swirl** *n* ~ **(of sth) 1** swirling movement; eddy: *Dancers spun in a swirl of skirts.* **2** swirled shape or twist: *strawberries topped with a swirl of cream.*

swish[1] /swɪʃ/ *v* **1** **(a)** [Ipr, Ip, Tn, Tn·pr, Tn·p] (cause sth to) swing through the air with a hissing sound: *Scythes swished to and fro.* ○ *The horse swished its tail (about).* **(b)** [I, Ipr] move with or make this sound; rustle: *We swished through the long grass.* ○ *She swished across the floor in her long silk dress.* **2** (phr v) **swish sth off** cut sth off by swinging a stick, etc at it: *He swished off the tops of the nettles with his cane.*

▷ **swish** *n* [sing] hissing or rustling sound: *Her skirts gave a swish.*

swish[2] /swɪʃ/ *adj* (*infml esp Brit*) smart, fashionable or expensive: *swish hotels, resorts, cars.*

Swiss /swɪs/ *adj* of Switzerland, its people or its dialects.

▷ **Swiss** *n* (*pl* unchanged) native of Switzerland.

□ ˌ**Swiss ˈGuards** group of Swiss soldiers who provide a ceremonial bodyguard for the Pope in the Vatican City.

ˌ**Swiss ˈroll** thin flat sponge-cake spread with jam, etc and rolled up.

ˌ**Swiss ˈchard** = CHARD.

switch /swɪtʃ/ *n* **1** **(a)** device for completing or breaking an electric circuit: *a light switch* ○ *press the on/off switch* ○ *a two-way switch*, eg at the top and bottom of a staircase. **(b)** device at the junction of railway tracks to allow trains to go from one track to another. **(c)** (*US*) = POINTS (POINT[1] 18). **2** (also ˈ**switch-over**) (*infml*) (esp sudden) shift or change: *Polls showed a switch to Labour.* ○ *a switch from gas to electric* ○ *make a switch from publishing to teaching* ○ *a switch in method, policy, opinion.* **3** thin flexible twig or shoot cut from a tree; tapering rod like this used for urging a horse, etc forward. **4** piece of real or false hair for making a woman's hair appear thicker or longer.

▷ **switch** *v* **1** [I, Ipr, Ip, Tn, Tn·pr, Tn·p] ~ **(sth) (over) (to sth)** (cause sth to) shift or change, esp suddenly: *switch to modern methods* ○ *Many voters switched to Labour.* ○ *Computers are everywhere now — our firm is switching over soon.* ○ *switch the conversation to a different topic* ○ *Could you switch the TV over?* **2** [I, Ipr, Ip, Tn, Tn·pr, Tn·p] ~ **(sth) (with sb/sth)**; ~ **(sth) over/round** (cause sb/sth to) exchange positions; change over: *Our glasses have been switched — this is mine.* ○ *Husband and wife should switch roles (with each other) occasionally.* ○ *You drive first and then we'll switch round/over.* **3** [Tn] whip or flick (a horse, etc) with a switch(3). **4** [Tn·pr] move (a train, etc) onto another track: *switch a train into a siding.* **5** (phr v) **switch (sth) off** disconnect (electricity, etc): *Switch off the gas, power, etc at the mains.* ○ *Don't switch (the TV) off yet.* **switch (sb) off** (*infml*) (cause sb to) become dull, bored, etc: *I switch off when he starts talking about cars.* ○ *Long lectures really switch me off.* **switch (sth) on** connect (electricity, etc or an appliance): *Switch on the light at the wall-socket.* ○ *Don't switch (the radio) on yet.*

□ ˈ**switch-blade** *n* = FLICK-KNIFE (FLICK).

switchboard /ˈswɪtʃbɔːd/ *n* (staff controlling a) central panel with a set of switches for making telephone connections or operating electrical circuits: *on duty at the switchboard* ○ *Protesting viewers jammed the BBC switchboard.* ○ [attrib] *switchboard operators.*

ˌ**switched-ˈon** *adj* (*dated infml*) aware of what is going on; up-to-date.

ˈ**switch-engine** *n* engine(2) used for shunting.

ˈ**switch-man** /-mən/ *n* (*pl* **-men** /-mən/) (*US*) = POINTSMAN (POINT[1]).

ˈ**switch-over** *n* = SWITCH 2.

ˈ**switch-yard** *n* (*US*) area where railway cars are switched between lines to make up trains.

switchback /ˈswɪtʃbæk/ *n* **1** (*esp Brit*) = ROLLER-COASTER (ROLLER). **2** zigzag railway or road for ascending or descending steep slopes.

Swithin /ˈswɪðɪn/ Saint (died 862 AD), English bishop. According to legend there was heavy rain when his body was moved from an outdoor grave to a shrine in Winchester Cathedral, and tradition says that if it rains on his feast(2), July 15, it will rain for forty days.

Switzerland

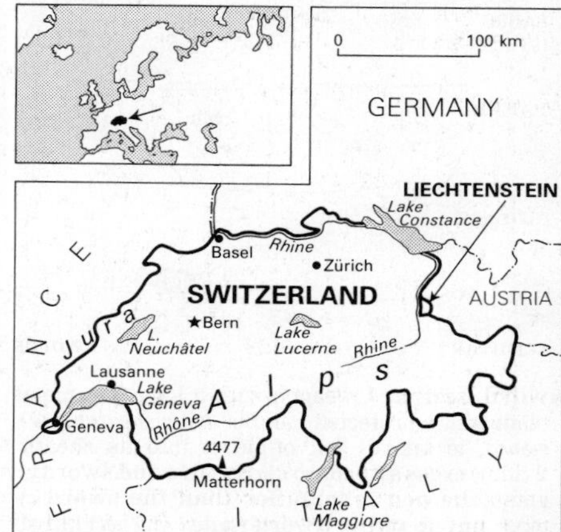

Switzerland /ˈswɪtsələnd/ country in W Europe; pop approx 6 510 000; official languages German, French, Italian and Romansch; capital Bern; unit of currency franc (= 100 centimes). Switzerland is largely mountainous and its agriculture concentrates on dairy farming. It has no mineral resources, but has a thriving industrial economy based on modern industries such as pharmaceuticals and precision instruments. Service industries, esp banking and tourism, are also very important. The country is made up of 26 cantons formed into a federation. It has a long history of neutrality and many international and humanitarian organizations are based there, including the *Red Cross and the *World Health Organization. ⇨ map. Cf SWISS.

swivel /ˈswɪvl/ *n* (esp in compounds) link or pivot between two parts enabling one part to revolve without turning the other: *a swivel-chain, -hook* ○ *a swivel-chair*, ie one that rotates.

▷ **swivel** *v* (**-ll-**; *US* **-l-**) [I, Ip, Tn, Tn·p] ~ **(sth) (round)** (cause sth to) turn on or as if on a swivel: *He swivelled (round) in his chair to face us.* ○ *She swivelled the telescope (round).*

swizz /swɪz/ (also **swizzle**) *n* (usu *sing*) (*Brit infml*) swindle or disappointment: *You didn't get a leaving present? What a swizz!*

swizzle /ˈswɪzl/ *n* **1** any of various types of tall frothy mixed drink, usu made with rum. **2** = SWIZZ.
□ ˈ**swizzle-stick** *n* **(a)** long glass rod for stirring a swizzle(1). **(b)** small stick for stirring or decorating cocktails.

swollen *pp* of SWELL.

swoon /swu:n/ *v* **(a)** [I, Ipr, Ip] (*dated*) lose consciousness; faint: *She swooned into his arms for joy.* ○ *She swooned away.* **(b)** [I, Ipr] ~ **(over sb/sth)** (*fig esp joc*) be emotionally affected (by sb/sth): *All the girls are swooning over the new maths teacher.* ▷ **swoon** *n* (*dated*): *fall into a swoon.*

swoop /swu:p/ *v* **1** [I, Ipr, Ip] ~ **(down) (on sb/sth)** come down suddenly with a rushing movement: *The owl swooped down on the mouse.* ○ *Planes swooped (low) over the ship.* ○ (*fig*) *Detectives swooped (on the house) at dawn.* **2** (phr v) **swoop sth away/up** (*infml*) seize or snatch the whole of sth in one movement: *The robber swooped up the banknotes.*
▷ **swoop** *n* **1** ~ **(on sth/sb) (a)** swooping movement. **(b)** sudden and unexpected attack: *Police made a dawn swoop.* **2** (idm) **at one fell swoop** ⇨ FELL[2].

swop = SWAP.

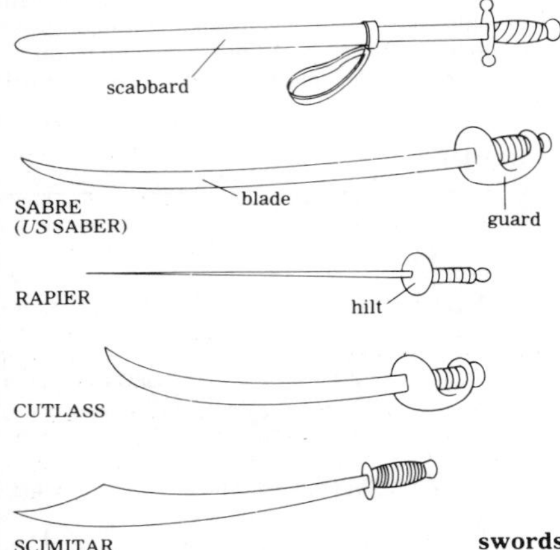

swords

sword /sɔ:d/ *n* **1** weapon with a long thin metal blade and a protected handle: *draw/sheathe one's sword*, ie take it out of/put it into its sheath. **2** (idm) **cross swords** ⇨ CROSS[2]. **fire and sword** ⇨ FIRE[1]. **the pen is mightier than the sword** ⇨ PEN[1]. **put sb to the ˈsword** (*dated or rhet*) kill sb with a sword. **a sword of ˈDamocles** /ˈdæməkli:z/ (*fml*) something unpleasant, dreadful, etc, that seems to be about to happen to sb, and causes a feeling of apprehension and imminent danger: *The possibility of losing her job hung over her like a sword of Damocles all last year.*
□ ˈ**sword-dance** *n* dance between and over swords placed on the ground, or one in which swords are waved or clashed.
ˈ**swordfish** *n* large sea-fish with an extremely long thin pointed upper jaw.
ˈ**sword-play** *n* [U] fighting with swords.
ˈ**swordsman** /-zmən/ *n* (*pl* **-men**) man skilled in the use of a sword: *a good, poor, etc swordsman.*
ˈ**swordsmanship** /-mənʃɪp/ *n* [U].
ˈ**sword-stick** *n* hollow walking-stick concealing a blade that can be used as a sword.

swore *pt* of SWEAR.

sworn[1] *pp* of SWEAR.

sworn[2] /swɔ:n/ *adj* [attrib] **1** made under a solemn promise to tell the truth: *a sworn statement.* **2** extreme in affection or dislike: *sworn friends/enemies.*

swot /swɒt/ *v* (**-tt-**) [I, Ipr, Ip, Tn·p] ~ **(up) (for/on sth)**; ~ **sth up** (*Brit infml often derog*) study sth very hard, esp in preparation for an exam: *swotting for her exams* ○ *I'm swotting up my maths/swotting up on my history.*
▷ **swot** (also **swotter**) *n* person who swots.

swum *pp* of SWIM.

swung *pt, pp* of SWING[1].

sybarite /ˈsɪbəraɪt/ *n* (*fml usu derog*) person who is very fond of luxury and comfort.
▷ **sybaritic** /sɪbəˈrɪtɪk/ *adj* (*fml usu derog*) typical of a sybarite: *sybaritic tastes, pleasures.*

sycamore /ˈsɪkəmɔ:(r)/ *n* **1** [C] **(a)** (*esp Brit*) large tree of the maple family. ⇨ illus at TREE. **(b)** (*esp US*) type of plane tree. **2** [U] valuable hard wood of the sycamore: [attrib] *a sycamore desk, chair, etc.*

sycophant /ˈsɪkəfænt/ *n* (*fml derog*) person who tries to gain people's favour by insincerely flattering them and always agreeing with them. ▷ **sycophancy** /ˈsɪkəfənsɪ/ *n* [U]. **sycophantic** /sɪkəˈfæntɪk/ *adj*: *a sycophantic smile.* **sycophantically** /-klɪ/ *adv.*

syllable /ˈsɪləbl/ *n* **1** any of the units into which a word may be divided, usu consisting of a vowel-sound with a consonant before or after: *'Arithmetic' is a word of four syllables.* **2** (idm) **in words of one syllable** ⇨ WORD.
▷ **syllabary** /ˈsɪləbərɪ; *US* -berɪ/ *n* list of written or printed symbols (eg in Japanese) representing syllables.
syllabic /sɪˈlæbɪk/ *adj* **1** of or in syllables. **2** (of a consonant) making a syllable on its own, without a vowel. **syllabically** /-bɪklɪ/ *adv.*
syllabify /sɪˈlæbɪfaɪ/ *v* (*pt, pp* **-fied**) [Tn] divide (a word or words) into syllables. **syllabification** /sɪlæbɪfɪˈkeɪʃn/ *n* [U] (system of) dividing into syllables.
-syllabled (forming compound *adjs*) having the specified number of syllables: *a two-, three-, four-, etc syllabled word.*

syllabub (also **sillabub**) /ˈsɪləbʌb/ *n* [C, U] dish of sweetened cream mixed vigorously to a froth with wine, etc.

syllabus /ˈsɪləbəs/ *n* (*pl* ~**es**) list of subjects, topics, texts, etc included in a course of study: *'Hamlet' is on this year's English literature syllabus.* Cf CURRICULUM.

syllepsis /sɪˈlepsɪs/ *n* (*pl* **-ses** /-si:z/) figure of speech involving the use of one word in connection with two others, but with a different meaning in each case, as in *She left in a taxi and a great hurry.* Cf ZEUGMA.

syllogism /ˈsɪlədʒɪzəm/ *n* form of reasoning in which a conclusion is drawn from two statements, eg *All men must die; I am a man; therefore I must die.* Cf PREMISE 2.
▷ **syllogistic** /sɪləˈdʒɪstɪk/ *adj* in the form of or being a syllogism.

sylph /sɪlf/ *n* **1** (in ancient myth) one of a type of female nature spirits believed to inhabit the air. **2** (*fml approv*) slender and graceful girl or woman. Cf NYMPH.
▷ ˈ**sylphlike** *adj* (*approv or joc*) slender and graceful: *'You're not exactly sylphlike, are you?' she said to her fat friend.*

sylvan ⇨ SILVAN.

symbiosis /sɪmbɪˈəʊsɪs, -baɪ-/ *n* [U] (*biology*) relationship between two species, organisms, etc that live close together and depend on each other in various ways: *the symbiosis between a plant and the insect that fertilizes it.* ▷ **symbiotic** /-ˈɒtɪk/ *adj.*

symbol /ˈsɪmbl/ *n* **1** ~ **(of sth)** image, object, etc that suggests or refers to sth else; emblem: *The cross is the symbol of Christianity.* ○ *The lion is the symbol of courage.* **2** ~ **(for sth)** mark or sign with a particular meaning, eg plus and minus signs in mathematics, punctuation marks, musical notation, etc: *On maps, a cross is the symbol for a church.* ○ *Au is the chemical symbol for gold.* ○ *algebraic signs and symbols.*
▷ **symbolic** /sɪmˈbɒlɪk/, **symbolical** /-kl/ *adjs* ~ **(of sth)** of, using or used as a symbol: *The cross is symbolic of Christianity.* ○ *The power of the monarchy in Britain today is more symbolical than real.* **symbolically** /-klɪ/ *adv.*
symbolism /ˈsɪmbəlɪzəm/ *n* [U] **1** use of symbols to represent things, esp in art and literature; the symbols thus used: *poetry full of religious symbolism.* **2 Symbolism** movement in late 19th-century French poetry which tried to use words for the power they have to suggest ideas or moods, etc, or for their musical qualities, rather than to give precise descriptions of reality. The most famous members of the movement were Mallarmé, *Verlaine and *Rimbaud. **symbolist** /ˈsɪmbəlɪst/ *n* (often **Symbolist**) artist, writer, etc who habitually uses symbols, esp a poet writing in the style of Symbolism: [attrib] *Symbolist poetry.*
symbolize, -ise /ˈsɪmbəlaɪz/ *v* **1** [Tn] be a symbol of (sth): *a picture of a red disc with rays coming from it, symbolizing the sun.* **2** [Tn, Tn·pr, Cn·n/a] ~ **sth/sb (with/as sth)** represent sth/sb by means of a symbol: *The poet has symbolized his lover with a flower.*

symmetry /ˈsɪmətrɪ/ *n* [U] **1** exact match in size and shape between the two halves of sth: *the perfect symmetry of the building.* **2** pleasingly regular way in which parts are arranged: *the symmetry of her features.*
▷ **symmetric** /sɪˈmetrɪk/, **symmetrical** /-rɪkl/ *adjs* (of a design, etc) having two halves which are the same in size and shape: *The plan of the ground floor is completely symmetrical.* ○ *the symmetrical arrangement of the gardens*, ie one that shows symmetry. Cf ASYMMETRIC. **symmetrically** /-klɪ/ *adv.*

sympathetic /sɪmpəˈθetɪk/ *adj* **1** ~ **(to/towards/with sb)** feeling, showing or resulting from sympathy: *a sympathetic look, smile, remark* ○ *feel sympathetic towards sb who is suffering* ○ *He was enormously sympathetic when my father died.* **2** likeable: *a sympathetic character*, ie person ○ *I don't find her very sympathetic.* **3** [pred] ~ **(to sth/sb)** showing favour or approval: *We asked for her support in the election, but she wasn't sympathetic (to our request).* ▷ **sympathetically** /-klɪ/ *adv.*
□ **sympathetic** ˈ**magic** magic that tries to produce a result by imitating the effect it wishes to achieve, eg by using a doll to represent a person to be cured or harmed.
sympathetic ˈ**string** string on a musical instrument, eg a sitar, which vibrates and makes a sound when another string is played.

sympathy /ˈsɪmpəθɪ/ *n* **1** [U] ~ **(for/towards sb)** (capacity for) sharing the feelings of others; feeling of pity and sorrow (for sb): *feel great sympathy for sb* ○ *She never expressed any sympathy when I was injured.* ○ *Out of sympathy for the homeless children he gave them shelter for the night.* **2 sympathies** [pl] feeling or expression of sorrow, approval, etc: *You have my deepest sympathies on the death of your wife.* ○ *My sympathies are with the workers in this dispute.* **3** [U] ~ **(between sb and sb)** liking for each other produced in people who have similar opinions or tastes: *A bond of sympathy developed between members of the group.* **4** (idm) **in sympathy (with sb/sth)** showing support or approval for a cause etc: *The steel workers came out in sympathy with the miners*, ie went on strike to show support for them. ○ *I'm sure she will be in sympathy with your proposal.* **have no, some, etc sympathy with sb/sth** be unable/able to share sb's views, etc: *He's wrong — I have no sympathy with him.* ○ *I have some sympathy with that point of view.*
▷ **sympathize, -ise** /ˈsɪmpəθaɪz/ *v* [I, Ipr] ~ **(with sb/sth)** feel or express sympathy or support: *I sympathize with you; I've had a similar unhappy experience myself* ○ *We have long sympathized with the aims of the Green Party.*
sympathizer, -iser *n* person who sympathizes, esp one who supports a cause or a political party: *Socialist sympathizers.*

symphony /ˈsɪmfənɪ/ *n* **1** long complex musical composition, usu in three or four parts (*movements*) for a large orchestra: [attrib] *a symphony orchestra*, ie a large orchestra that plays symphonies, etc. **2** (*US*) symphony orchestra: *the symphony's permanent conductor.*

▷ **symphonic** /sɪmˈfɒnɪk/ *adj* of or like a symphony.

symposium /sɪmˈpəʊzɪəm/ *n* (*pl* **-sia** /-zɪə/) **1** small conference for discussion of a particular subject. **2** collection of essays by several people on a particular subject, published as a book: *contribute to a symposium on environmental issues.*

symptom /ˈsɪmptəm/ *n* **1** change in the body that indicates an illness: *the rash that is a symptom of measles.* **2** sign of the existence of sth bad: *This demonstration was a symptom of discontent among the students.*

▷ **symptomatic** /sɪmptəˈmætɪk/ *adj* [pred] ~ (**of sth**) being a symptom: *Chest pains may be symptomatic of heart disease.* ○ *Is inflation symptomatic of economic decline?*

syn- *pref* together or at the same time: *synthesis* ○ *synchronize.*

synagogue /ˈsɪnəgɒg/ *n* building used by Jews for religious worship or teaching.

synapse /ˈsaɪnæps, ˈsɪnæps; *US* səˈnæps/ *n* junction between two nerve-cells where nerve impulses cross a minute gap from one nerve cell to the next.

sync (also **synch**) /sɪŋk/ *n* [U] (*infml*) = SYNCHRONIZATION (SYNCHRONIZE): *The film's sound-track is out of sync/not in sync with the picture.*

synchromesh /sɪŋkrəʊˈmeʃ/ *n* [U] device in a vehicle's gearbox that makes the parts turn at the same speed and thus allows gears to be changed smoothly.

synchronic /sɪŋˈkrɒnɪk/ *adj* **1** (*linguistics*) dealing with words, patterns, etc existing at a particular time (esp the present day), with no reference to their previous forms. Cf DIACHRONIC. **2** = SYNCHRONOUS 1.

synchronize, -ise /ˈsɪŋkrənaɪz/ *v* [I, Ipr, Tn, Tn·pr] ~ (**sth**) (**with sth**) (cause sth to) operate, move, turn, etc at the same time, speed, etc: *The wheels must synchronize as they revolve.* ○ *The sound on a film must synchronize with the action.* ○ *synchronized swimming*, ie in which a team of swimmers performs rehearsed actions in time with music ○ *Let's synchronize our watches*, ie set them to show the same time. ▷ **synchronization, -isation** /sɪŋkrənaɪˈzeɪʃn; *US* -nɪˈz-/ (also *infml* **sync**) *n* [U].

syndicalism /ˈsɪndɪkəlɪzəm/ *n* [U] theory that factories, businesses, etc should be owned and managed by the workers employed in them.

▷ **syndicalist** /-kəlɪst/ *n* supporter of syndicalism.

syndicate /ˈsɪndɪkət/ *n* **1** group of people or business companies combined to undertake a joint project: *a crime syndicate*, ie controlling organized crime. **2** (*US*) (**a**) central distributing agency arranging the publication of material in newspapers. (**b**) group of newspapers owned by a single company.

▷ **syndicate** /ˈsɪndɪkeɪt/ *v* [Tn usu passive] publish (an article, a strip cartoon, etc) in many different newspapers, magazines, etc by means of a central distributing agency: *His column is syndicated throughout the world.* **syndication** /sɪndɪˈkeɪʃn/ *n* [U].

syndrome /ˈsɪndrəʊm/ *n* **1** (*medical*) set of symptoms which together indicate a particular disease or abnormal condition. **2** (*fig*) any set of opinions, events, actions, etc that are characteristic of a particular condition: *Unemployment, inflation and low wages are all part of the same economic syndrome.*

synecdoche /sɪˈnekdəkɪ/ *n* figure of speech in which a reference to a part or aspect of a person, object, etc, is meant to refer to the whole person, object, etc, as in *a village of a hundred souls* where *souls* means 'people'. Cf METONYMY.

Synge /sɪŋ/ J(ohn) M(illington) (1871-1909), Irish playwright. He was encouraged to write by *Yeats. His plays (including his best-known work, *The Playboy of the Western World*) use the language of ordinary Irish country people and workers in a dramatic way. His view of Ireland was poetic but shown with realism. His ironic wit, however, offended many in Ireland.

synod /ˈsɪnəd/ *n* official assembly of church members to discuss and decide on matters of religious teaching, church policy and administration, etc. ⇨ article at CHURCH OF ENGLAND.

synonym /ˈsɪnənɪm/ *n* word or phrase with the same meaning as another in the same language, though perhaps with a different style, grammar or technical use: *'Slay' and 'kill' are synonyms.*

▷ **synonymous** /sɪˈnɒnɪməs/ *adj* ~ (**with sth**) having the same meaning: *'Slay' is synonymous with 'kill' (though it is more forceful and rather dated).* ○ (*fig*) *Wealth is not necessarily synonymous with generosity*, ie Rich people are not always generous. Cf ANTONYM.

synopsis /sɪˈnɒpsɪs/ *n* (*pl* **-opses** /-si:z/) summary or outline of a book, play, etc.

▷ **synoptic** /sɪˈnɒptɪk/ *adj* [attrib] of or forming a synopsis.

□ **the syˌnoptic ˈgospels** (in the Bible) the gospels of Matthew, Mark and Luke, which are very similar (whereas that of John is very different).

synovia /saɪˈnəʊvɪə/ *n* [U] thick fluid that lubricates joints in the body. It is produced by a surrounding membrane. ▷ **synovial** /-vɪəl/ *adj*: *synovial fluid* ○ *synovial membrane.*

syntax /ˈsɪntæks/ *n* [U] (*linguistics*) (rules for the) arrangement of words into phrases and phrases into sentences.

▷ **syntactic** /sɪnˈtæktɪk/ *adj* of syntax: *syntactic differences between English and French.* **syntactically** /-klɪ/ *adv*: *a syntactically complex written style.* Cf GRAMMAR 1, MORPHOLOGY 2.

synthesis /ˈsɪnθəsɪs/ *n* (*pl* **-theses** /-si:z/) **1** (**a**) [U] combining of separate parts, elements, etc to form a complex whole: *develop a new theory by the synthesis of several earlier theories.* (**b**) [C] what is produced in this way: *a new method that is a synthesis of the best features of the old methods* ○ *Her novels are an odd synthesis of English reserve and Welsh emotionalism.* **2** [U] combining of substances into a compound, or the artificial production of a substance that occurs naturally in plants and animals: *produce rubber from petroleum by synthesis* ○ *the synthesis of insulin.*

▷ **synthesize, -ise** /ˈsɪnθəsaɪz/ *v* [Tn] **1** make (sth) by synthesis: *synthesize diamonds, rubber, fuel, etc.* **2** combine (parts) into a whole: *The two elements are synthesized by a chemical process.* **synthesizer, -iser** *n* electronic musical instrument producing a large number of different sounds, including imitations of other instruments. ⇨ illus at MUSIC.

synthetic /sɪnˈθetɪk/ *adj* **1** made by synthesis(2); artificial: *synthetic diamonds, rubber, etc.* **2** [attrib] of synthesis(2): *synthetic chemistry.* **3** (*infml derog*) not genuine or natural; false: *the salesman's synthetic friendliness* ○ *a synthetic blonde*, ie sb whose hair is dyed blonde. — *n* synthetic substance or fibre: *natural fibres and synthetics.* **synthetically** /-klɪ/ *adv.*

syphilis /ˈsɪfɪlɪs/ *n* [U] (also **the pox**) venereal disease that, unless treated, progresses through the lymphatic system to all the tissues of the body. It can be passed by an infected mother to her unborn child and, until the discovery of penicillin, was often fatal.

▷ **syphilitic** /ˌsɪfɪˈlɪtɪk/ *adj* of or suffering from syphilis. — *n* person affected with syphilis.

Syria /ˈsɪrɪə/ country in the Middle East, with a coastline on the Mediterranean; pop approx 10 500 000; official language Arabic; capital Damascus; unit of currency pound (=100 centimes). Much of the country is covered in mountains and desert, with agriculture concentrated along the *Euphrates river; the main

Syria and Lebanon

crops are cereals and cotton. It has considerable oil reserves, but few other mineral resources and little modern industry. Syria has played a major role in the conflicts affecting the Middle East, and military expenditure is a large factor in its economy. ⇨ map. ▷ **Syrian** /-rɪən/ *n, adj.*

Syriac /ˈsɪrɪæk/ *n* [U] language used in the liturgy of the Maronite and other Eastern Churches, descended from ancient Aramaic. ▷ **Syriac** *adj.*

syringa /sɪˈrɪŋgə/ *n* [C, U] **1** shrub with strong-scented white flowers. **2** (*botany*) lilac.

syringe /sɪˈrɪndʒ/ *n* **1** any of various types of device for taking liquid in and forcing it out again in a thin stream, used for spraying plants, washing wounds, etc: *a garden syringe.* **2** = HYPODERMIC SYRINGE (HYPODERMIC). ⇨ illus at INJECTION.

▷ **syringe** *v* [Tn] clean, spray, or inject liquid into (sth) with a syringe: *syringe a wound, plant.*

syrup /ˈsɪrəp/ *n* [U] **1** water in which sugar is dissolved: *tinned peaches in (heavy) syrup* ○ *cough syrup*, ie syrup with medicine in it to cure coughs. **2** any thick sweet liquid, eg treacle.

▷ **syrupy** *adj* **1** of or like syrup: *a drink that is too syrupy.* **2** (*fig derog*) too sentimental; sugary (SUGAR 1): *a rather syrupy love-story.*

system /ˈsɪstəm/ *n* **1** [C] group of things or parts working together as a whole: *the nervous system* ○ *the digestive system* ○ *a railway system* ○ *a stereo system*, eg a record-deck, an amplifier, loud-speakers, etc combined ○ *The lifting device is a system of ropes and pulleys.* **2** [C] person's or animal's body as a whole, including its internal organs and processes: *The poison has passed into his system.* ○ *Alcohol is bad for your system.* **3** [C] set of ideas, theories, principles, etc according to which sth is done: *a system of philosophy* ○ *the democratic system of government* ○ *a good system of teaching languages* ○ *a foolproof new system for winning at roulette.* **4** [U] orderly way of doing things; tidy arrangement: *You'll find little system in his method of work.* ○ *We must introduce some system into our office routine.* **5 the system** [sing] (*infml*) the traditional methods, practices and rules existing in a society, an institution, a business, etc: *You can't beat the system*, ie You must conform to it. **6** (idm) **get sth out of one's ˈsystem** (*infml*) get rid of a strong feeling or desire by expressing it openly or trying to fulfil it: *He desperately wants to be an actor, so you'll have to give him time to get it out of his system.*

▷ **systematic** /sɪstəˈmætɪk/ *adj* **1** done or acting according to a system or plan; methodical: *the* *systematic arrangement of the chairs* ○ *He's very systematic in all he does.* **2** [attrib] (*derog*) planned in advance and done with malicious thoroughness and exactness: *a systematic attempt to ruin sb's reputation.* **systematically** /-klɪ/ *adv*.

systematize, -ise /ˈsɪstəmətaɪz/ *v* [Tn] arrange (sth) according to a well-organized system: *We must try to systematize the way we do the accounts.*

systematization, -isation /sɪstəmətaɪˈzeɪʃn; *US* -tɪˈz-/ *n*.

systemic /sɪˈstemɪk, *also* sɪˈsti:mɪk/ *adj* **1** of or affecting the whole of the body. **2** acting by entering the tissues of a plant and killing insects and other pests which try to feed on it: *systemic fungicides.* **systemically** /-klɪ/ *adv*.

□ ˈ**systems analysis** analysis of all the steps in an operation in order to decide how to perform it most efficiently, esp using a computer. ˈ**systems analyst** expert in systems analysis.

systole /ˈsɪstəlɪ/ *n* [C, U] rhythmical contraction of the heart muscle that forces blood out, followed by expansion (*diastole*). ▷ **systolic** /sɪˈstɒlɪk/ *adj*.

T, t

T, t /tiː/ *n* (*pl* **T's, t's** /tiːz/) **1** the twentieth letter of the English alphabet: *'Committee' is spelt with two t's.* **2** (idm) **dot one's/the i's and cross one's/the t's** ⇨ DOT. **to a ˈT/ˈtee** (*infml*) in every detail; exactly: *This new job suits me to a T.*

□ **ˈT-bone** *n* T-shaped bone, esp one in a piece of beefsteak.

ˈT-junction *n* place where one road or pipe, etc joins another but does not cross it, thus forming the shape of a T.

ˈT-shirt (also **tee-shirt**) *n* shirt with short sleeves that has the shape of a T when spread out flat.

T *symb* tritium.

t (*US* **tn**) *abbr* ton(s); tonne(s): *5t* (ie tonnes) *of wheat per acre.*

Ta *symb* tantalum.

ta /tɑː/ *interj* (*Brit infml*) thank you.

TAB (also **Tab**) /ˌtiː eɪ ˈbiː/ *abbr* typhoid-paratyphoid A and B vaccine: *have a Tab injection.*

tab /tæb/ *n* **1** small projecting flap or strip of cloth, metal, paper, etc, esp one by which sth can be grasped, hung, fastened or identified: *To open, pull tab,* eg on a can of beer. ○ *a ˈname-tab,* ie one sewn into clothes, etc. **2** (*US*) bill[1](1) (used esp as in the expression shown): *pick up* (ie pay) *the tab.* **3** (idm) **keep a tab/tabs on sth/sb** (*infml*) keep account of sth/sb; keep sth/sb under observation: *keep tabs on who's using the phone.*

tabard /ˈtæbɑːd; *US* ˈtæbərd/ *n* **1** sleeveless jacket with a heraldic design on it, worn by royal heralds. **2** jacket without sleeves or with short sleeves worn by women.

Tabasco /təˈbæskəʊ/ *n* [U] (*propr*) spicy sauce made from peppers.

tabby /ˈtæbɪ/ (also **ˈtabby-cat**) *n* cat with grey or brownish fur and dark stripes.

tabernacle /ˈtæbənækl/ *n* **1 the tabernacle** [sing] (*Bible*) the portable shrine used by the Israelites during their wanderings in the wilderness. **2** [C] (in the Roman Catholic Church) receptacle containing consecrated elements of the Eucharist. **3** [C] place of worship used by Nonconformists (eg Baptists) or Mormons.

tabla /ˈtæblə/ *n* Indian musical instrument consisting of two small drums played with the hands.

table /ˈteɪbl/ *n* **1** [C] piece of furniture consisting of a flat top supported on one or more legs: *a ˈdining-table* ○ *a ˈbedside-table* ○ *a ˈbilliard-table* ○ *lay/set the table,* ie prepare it for a meal with plates, cutlery, etc. ⇨ illus at FURNITURE. **2** [sing] people seated at a table for a meal, etc: *His jokes amused the whole table.* ○ *a table of card-players.* **3** [sing] food provided at table: *He keeps a good table,* ie provides good meals. **4** [C] (also **ˈtableland** /-lænd/) large area of high level land; plateau. **5** [C] list of facts or figures systematically arranged, esp in columns: *a table of contents,* ie a summary of what a book contains ○ *learn one's (multiplication) tables* ○ *Do you know your six times table?* ○ *log tables.* **6** (idm) **at ˈtable** (while) having a meal: *Children must learn to behave at table.* ○ (*fml*) *They were at table when we called.* **drink sb under the table** ⇨ DRINK[2]. **lay/put one's cards on the table** ⇨ CARD[1]. **the negotiating table** ⇨ NEGOTIATE. **on the ˈtable** (a) (*Brit*) offered for consideration or discussion: *Management have put several new proposals on the table.* (b) (*esp US*) (of a proposal, etc) left for discussion until some future date. **turn the ˈtables (on sb)** reverse a situation so as to put oneself in a position of superiority. **under the ˈtable** (of money) paid secretly, esp as a bribe. **wait at table** ⇨ WAIT[1].

▷ **table** *v* [Tn] **1** (*Brit*) submit (a motion or report in Parliament, etc) for discussion: *The Opposition have tabled several amendments to the bill.* **2** (*esp US*) leave (a proposal, etc) to be discussed at some future date.

□ **ˈtable-cloth** *n* cloth for covering a table, esp during meals.

ˈtable-knife *n* knife for use while eating. ⇨ illus at KNIFE.

ˈtable licence (*Brit*) licence to serve alcoholic drinks, but only with meals.

ˈtable-linen *n* [U] table-cloths, napkins, etc.

ˈtable manners proper behaviour while eating with others.

ˈtable-mat *n* mat placed under a hot dish, etc to protect the table.

ˈtablespoon *n* **1** large spoon for serving food at table. ⇨ illus at SPOON. **2** (also **ˈtablespoonful** /-fʊl/) amount held by this: *add 2 tablespoons/tablespoonfuls of flour.*

ˈtable-talk *n* [U] conversation during a meal.

ˈtable tennis = PING-PONG.

ˈtable-turning *n* [U] movement of a table at which people are sitting during a seance, thought to be caused by some supernatural force.

ˈtableware *n* [U] plates, bowls, cutlery, etc used for meals.

ˈtable wine ordinary wine suitable for drinking with a meal.

tableau /ˈtæbləʊ/ *n* (*pl* ~**x** /-ləʊz/) **1** (also **tableau vivant** /ˌtæbləʊ ˈviːvɑːn; *US* viːˈvɑːn/, *pl* ~**x vivants** /ˌtæbləʊ ˈviːvɑːn; *US* -viːˈvɑːn/) representation of a picture or scene by a silent and motionless group of people, esp on stage. **2** dramatic or picturesque scene.

table d'hôte /ˌtɑːbl ˈdəʊt/ (of a restaurant meal) consisting of a limited range of dishes served at a fixed inclusive price: *The table d'hôte menu offers good value.* Cf À LA CARTE.

tablet /ˈtæblɪt/ *n* **1** slab or panel with words cut or written on it, esp one fixed to a wall as a memorial. **2** small measured amount of medicine compressed into a solid form; pill: *Take two of the tablets three times daily before meals.* **3** small flattish bar of soap, etc.

tabloid /ˈtæblɔɪd/ *n* popular newspaper with pages that are half the size of those of larger newspapers: [attrib] *the tabloid press* ○ (*often derog*) *tabloid journalism.* Cf BROADSHEET 2.

taboo /təˈbuː; *US* tæˈbuː/ *n* (*pl* ~**s**) **1** [C, U] (in certain cultures) ban or prohibition on sth that is regarded for religious or other reasons as not to be done, touched, used, etc. **2** [C] (*fig*) general agreement not to discuss or to do sth: *There's a taboo on smoking in this office.*

▷ **taboo** *adj* prohibited by a taboo: *Questions and problems that were once taboo are now discussed openly.* ○ *Sex is no longer the taboo subject it used to be.* ○ *Any mention of politics is taboo in his house.*

□ **taˈboo words** words likely to be considered offensive, shocking or indecent by certain people (though not necessarily by everyone), eg those marked ⚠ in this dictionary. ⇨ article.

tabular /ˈtæbjʊlə(r)/ *adj* arranged or displayed in a table(5) or list: *statistics presented in tabular form.*

tabula rasa /ˌtæbjʊlə ˈrɑːzə/ (*pl* **tabulae rasae** /ˌtæbjʊliː ˈrɑːziː/) (*Latin*) the human mind considered as being completely empty (eg at birth), before feelings or ideas come into it.

tabulate /ˈtæbjʊleɪt/ *v* [Tn] arrange (facts or figures) in the form of a table(5) or list.

▷ **tabulation** /ˌtæbjʊˈleɪʃn/ *n* [U, C].

tabulator *n* **1** person or thing that tabulates. **2** device on a typewriter for advancing to a series of set positions in tabular work.

tachograph /ˈtækəɡrɑːf/ *n* device in a motor vehicle which automatically records the speed of the vehicle during a journey and how far it has travelled.

tachometer /tæˈkɒmɪtə(r)/ *n* instrument for measuring the speed of rotation, esp of a vehicle engine.

tacit /ˈtæsɪt/ *adj* [usu attrib] understood without being put into words; implied: *give tacit consent, agreement, etc.* ▷ **tacitly** *adv.*

taciturn /ˈtæsɪtɜːn/ *adj* (in the habit of) saying very little; uncommunicative. ▷ **taciturnity** /ˌtæsɪˈtɜːnətɪ/ *n* [U].

tack /tæk/ *n* **1** [C] small nail with a broad head: *a ˈcarpet tack,* ie one used for securing a carpet to the floor ○ *a ˈtin-tack.* **2** [C] long loose stitch used in fastening pieces of cloth together loosely or temporarily: *tailor's tacks,* ie ones used to mark the place for a seam, etc. **3** [C] (*nautical*) (of sailing vessels) oblique course sailed with the wind blowing towards one side of the ship: *on the right/wrong tack* ○ *on the port/starboard tack,* ie with the wind on the port/starboard side. **4** [U, sing] (*fig*) course of action; policy: *It would be unwise to change tack now.* ○ *try a different tack* ○ *be on the right/wrong tack.* **5** [U] equipment for horse-riding (eg saddles, reins, bridles, etc). **6** (idm) **get down to brass tacks** ⇨ BRASS.

▷ **tack** *v* **1** [Tn, Tn·pr, Tn·p] nail (sth) with a tack(1) or tacks: *tack down the carpet.* **2** [Tn, Tn·pr, Tn·p] stitch (sth) with tacks (TACK 2): *tack a ribbon onto a hat* ○ *tack (up) the hem of a dress* ○ *tack down a fold* ○ *a tacking stitch.* **3** (*nautical*) [I, Ipr, Ip] move from one tack(3) to another; sail a zigzag course in this way: *tack to port/starboard* ○ *tacking about.* **4** (phr v) **tack sth on(to sth)** (*infml*) add sth as an extra item: *a cover charge tacked onto the bill.*

tackle /ˈtækl/ *n* **1** [U] set of ropes and pulleys for working a ship's sails or for lifting weights. **2** [U] equipment for a task or sport: *ˈfishing-tackle.* **3** [C] act of tackling in or as in football, etc: *The policeman brought the thief to the ground with a flying tackle.*

▷ **tackle** *v* **1** [Tn] deal with or overcome (an awkward problem, a difficult piece of work, etc): *It's time to tackle my homework.* ○ *tackle a problem head-on,* ie boldly and vigorously. **2** [Tn·pr] ~ **sb about/over sth** speak to sb about (an awkward matter): *When are you going to tackle your brother about that money he owes me?* **3** [I, Tn] (a) (in football, hockey, etc) try to take the ball from (an opponent) by intercepting it: *no good at tackling* ○ *He was tackled just outside the penalty area.* (b) (in Rugby football) seize and stop (an opponent holding the ball). **tackler** /ˈtæklə(r)/ *n* player who tackles: *renowned as a fearless tackler.*

tacky /ˈtækɪ/ *adj* (**-ier, -iest**) **1** (of paint, glue, etc) slightly sticky; not quite dry: *still tacky to the touch.* **2** (*infml esp US*) in poor taste; shabby or gaudy. ▷ **tackiness** *n* [U].

taco /ˈtækəʊ; *US* ˈtɑːkəʊ/ *n* (*pl* ~**s**) small thin Mexican pancake fried crisp in a curved shape and then filled (eg with minced meat).

tact /tækt/ *n* [U] skill at not offending people or at gaining goodwill by saying or doing the right thing: *She showed great tact in dealing with a tricky situation.* ○ *You need a lot of tact to be an air hostess.*

▷ **tactful** /-fl/ *adj* having or showing tact. **tactfully** /-fəlɪ/ *adv.*

tactless *adj* lacking tact. **tactlessly** *adv.* **tactlessness** *n* [U].

tactic /ˈtæktɪk/ *n* **1** means of achieving sth; expedient: *a brilliant tactic.* **2 tactics** (a) [sing or pl *v*] art of placing or moving fighting forces in a battle. (b) [pl] (*fig*) procedure adopted in order to achieve sth: *use surprise tactics* ○ *These tactics are unlikely to help you.* Cf STRATEGY 1.

▷ **tactical** /-kl/ *adj* [usu attrib] **1** of tactics: *a tactical advantage, error.* **2** planning or planned skilfully: *a tactical move* ○ *tactical voting,* ie voting not for the candidate or party one prefers but for another that is more likely to defeat the candidate,

Taboo Words

As in most languages, there are some words in English that can cause great offence. There are three categories of taboo words in English: words relating to sex, words relating to excretion and blasphemous words. Because blasphemous words used to be the most shocking, using taboo words is often called swearing. Swearing is often a way of displaying membership of a group and the use of taboo words can be acceptable in a group of which one is a member whereas the same words would be extremely shocking if used to a stranger or in an inappropriate context.

Taboo words relating to sex are sometimes called four-letter words, since many of them happen to have four letters. The most commonly used is 'fuck'. When the word appeared in print in an unexpurgated version of D H Lawrence's *Lady Chatterley's Lover* in 1960, the book was banned on the grounds of obscenity. The issue was the subject of a famous court case and publication was subsequently allowed. As a result, attitudes towards the use of taboo words became more relaxed in the years that followed. Many newspapers, however, when reporting speech which contains very strong words, still avoid offending their readers by using such printing devices as f*** or f—. Similarly, in television programmes such as documentaries which contain a lot of swear-words, a bleeper may be used to drown them out when they occur. A decision to do this usually rests on whether the programme's producers consider the taboo words essential to the programme and on whether the programme is being transmitted at a time when children are likely to be watching.

Swear-words relating to sex or excretion are used in various ways. They can replace the more formal (usually medical) word, as in 'have a shit' for defecate, 'balls' for testicles, or 'tits' for breasts. They are often used in exclamations of sudden anger, frustration or surprise, as in 'Shit!', 'Balls!', 'Bollocks!' At their most offensive, they can be used as terms of abuse, as in 'You stupid prick!', 'You little shit!' For some taboo words, there are milder substitutes. For example, 'frigging' or 'effing' are used instead of 'fucking' and 'sugar' instead of 'shit'.

There are relatively few blasphemous words in English, though some frequently used words are in fact derivations of blasphemous expressions, such as 'bloody' ('By Our Lady'), and 'blimey' ('God blind me'). Some blasphemous expressions are more likely to shock than others, for example, saying 'God', 'damn' or 'blast' is not as likely to offend as saying 'Jesus' or 'Christ'.

Derivatives and phrasal verbs related to taboo words are used more frequently than the words themselves and are often considered less shocking. For example, from the word 'piss' there is 'piss off', 'piss around', 'piss down', 'piss somebody off', 'take the piss' and 'get pissed'.

etc one wishes to be defeated. **3** (of weapons, bombing, etc) used or carried out against enemy forces at short range: *tactical missiles.* Cf STRATEGIC. **tactically** /-klɪ/ *adv*: *vote tactically.*
tactician /tækˈtɪʃn/ *n* expert in tactics.

tactile /ˈtæktaɪl; *US* -təl/ *adj* (*fml*) of or using the sense of touch: *a tactile reflex* ○ *tactile organs.*

tad /tæd/ *n* (*US infml*) **1** small child, esp a young boy. **2** small bit: *just a tad more milk.*

tadpole /ˈtædpəʊl/ *n* form of a frog or toad at the stage when it lives under water and has gills and a tail.

taffeta /ˈtæfɪtə/ *n* [U] shiny silk-like dress fabric.

taffrail /ˈtæfreɪl/ *n* rail round the stern of a ship or boat.

Taffy /ˈtæfɪ/ *n* (*infml derog*) Welshman.

taffy (*US*) = TOFFEE.

tag /tæg/ *n* **1** [C] metal or plastic point at the end of a shoe-lace, etc. **2** [C] label fastened to or stuck into sth to identify it, show its price, etc: *put a ˈname-tag on it.* **3** [C] any loose or ragged end or projection. **4** [C] (*linguistics*) word or phrase that is added to a sentence to give emphasis, eg *that is* in *That's nice, that is*: [attrib] *a tag question*, ie a tag in the form of a question, eg *isn't it?, won't you?, aren't they?* **5** [C] phrase, saying or quotation that is often used: *Latin tags.* **6** (also **tig**) [U] game in which one child chases the others and tries to touch one of them.
▷ **tag** *v* (**-gg-**) **1** [Tn] label (sth) with a tag. **2** (phr v) **tag along (after/behind/with sb)** follow closely: *children tagging along behind their mother* ○ *If you're going to the cinema, do you mind if I tag along (with you)?* **tag sth on (to sth)** add sth as an extra item; attach sth: *a postscript tagged on (to her letter) at the end.*
□ ˈ**tag day** (*US*) = FLAG DAY (FLAG[1]).

tagliatelle /ˌtæljəˈtelɪ; *US* ˌtɑːl-/ *n* [U] Italian pasta in the form of long thin flat strips.

Tagore /təˈgɔː(r)/ Sir Rabindranath (1861-1941), Indian poet and philosopher who was awarded the Nobel prize in 1913 for his *Gitanjali: Song-Offering*, a collection of poems modelled on medieval Indian lyrics.

Tahiti /təˈhiːtɪ/ island in the southern Pacific Ocean, one of the *Society Islands; pop approx 116 000. It is a French possession. The sailors of the **Bounty* mutinied near there in 1789. The French painter *Gauguin lived and worked there. ▷ **Tahitian** /təˈhiːʃn/ *n, adj.*

tail[1] /teɪl/ *n* **1** [C] movable part at the end of the body of a bird, an animal, a fish or a reptile: *Dogs wag their tails when they are pleased.* ⇨ illus at ANIMAL. **2** [C] thing like a tail in its shape or position: *the tail of a comet, a kite, an aircraft, a procession.* **3** [C] (*dated infml*) buttocks: *give sb a smack on the tail.* **4** [C] (*infml*) person following or watching sb (usu without being seen by him): *put a tail on sb*, ie tell sb to follow him. **5 tails** [pl] (also ˈ**tailcoat** [C]) man's long coat, divided and tapered at the back, worn as part of formal dress at weddings, etc. Cf MORNING COAT (MORNING) ⇨ illus at DRESS. **6 tails** [sing] *v* side of a coin without the head of a person on it, turned upwards after being tossed. Cf HEADS (HEAD[1] 5). **7** [CGp] (in cricket) the least skilled batsmen in a team, who come in to bat at the end of its innings: *The England tail made some useful runs.* **8** (idm) **have, etc one's tail between one's legs** (*infml*) be humiliated, dejected or defeated. **heads I win, tails you lose** ⇨ HEAD[1]. **heads or tails?** ⇨ HEAD[1]. **make head or tail of sth** ⇨ HEAD[1]. **on sb's ˈtail** following sb closely. **a sting in the tail** ⇨ STING[1]. **the tail wagging the ˈdog** situation in which a minor part of sth is controlling or determining the course of the whole. **turn ˈtail** run away from a fight, etc: *As soon as they saw us coming they turned tail and ran.*
▷ **tail** *v* **1** [Tn, Tn·pr] follow (sb) closely, esp to watch where he goes and what he does: *He tailed the spy to his hotel.* **2** [Tn] remove the stalks of (fruit, etc): *top and tail gooseberries.* **3** (phr v) **tail away; tail off (a)** become smaller, fewer, weaker, etc: *The number of tourists starts to tail off in October.* ○ *The actor's voice tailed away as he forgot his lines.* **(b)** (of remarks, etc) end inconclusively: *His feeble excuses soon tailed off (into silence).* **(c)** fall behind in a straggling line.
-tailed (forming compound *adjs*) having a tail of the specified type: *ˈlong-tailed* ○ *ˈcurly-tailed.*
tailless *adj* having no tail: *a tailless species.*
□ ˈ**tailback** *n* long line of traffic extending back from an obstruction.
ˈ**tail-board** *n* = TAIL-GATE.
ˈ**tailcoat** *n* [C] = TAILS (TAIL[1] 5).
ˌ**tail-ˈend** *n* (usu *sing*) ~ **(of sth)** very last part: *the tail-end of the concert* ○ *I only heard the tail-end of their conversation.*
ˈ**tail-gate** *n* door or flap at the back of a motor vehicle, used for loading or unloading. — *v* [I, Tn] (*US*) drive too closely behind (another vehicle).
ˈ**tail-light** (*US* ˈ**tail-lamp**) *n* red light at the back of a motor vehicle, bicycle, train, etc. ⇨ illus at CAR.
ˈ**tailpiece** *n* **1** (in a book, etc) decoration printed in the blank space at the end of a chapter, etc. **2** part added to the end of sth to lengthen or complete it.
ˈ**tailpipe** *n* exhaust-pipe of a motor vehicle.
ˈ**tailplane** *n* horizontal part or surface of the tail of an aircraft.
ˈ**tail-spin** *n* spiral dive of an aircraft in which the tail makes wider circles than the front.
ˈ**tail wind** wind blowing from behind a travelling vehicle, aircraft, etc. Cf HEAD WIND (HEAD[1]).

tail[2] /teɪl/ *n* [C, U] (*law*) restriction of the inheritance of an estate to a particular person or his descendants: *The estate is in tail*, ie is restricted in this way. Cf ENTAIL.

tailor /ˈteɪlə(r)/ *n* maker of men's clothes, esp one who makes coats, jackets, etc for individual customers: *go to the tailor to be measured for a suit.*
▷ **tailor** *v* **1** [Tn esp passive] make (clothes): *a well-tailored coat.* **2** [Tn·pr esp passive] ~ **sth for/to sb/sth** make or adapt sth for a special purpose: *homes tailored to the needs of the elderly.*
□ ˌ**tailor-ˈmade** *adj* **1** made by a tailor: *a ˌtailor-made ˈsuit.* **2** [esp pred] (*fig*) perfectly suited: *He seems tailor-made for the job.*

taint /teɪnt/ *n* [C, U] trace of some bad quality or decay or infection: *a taint of insanity in the family* ○ *meat free from taint.*
▷ **taint** *v* [esp passive: Tn, Tn·pr] ~ **sth (with sth)** affect sth with a taint: *tainted meat* ○ *His reputation was tainted by the scandal.*
taintless *adj* without taint; pure.

taipan /ˈtaɪpæn/ *n* large poisonous Australian snake.

Taiwan /ˌtaɪˈwɑːn/ island and country off the SE coast of China; pop approx 19 900 000; official language Chinese; capital Taipei; unit of currency dollar (= 100 cents). After the Chinese revolution of 1949, non-Communists formed a separate Chinese republic there. The USA originally regarded it as the official Chinese state, but China never recognized it, and in 1971 its membership of the United Nations was withdrawn. It was formerly known as Formosa. ⇨ map at CHINA. ▷ **Taiwanese** /ˌtaɪwəˈniːz/ *n, adj.*

Tajikistan /tæˌdʒiːkɪˈstɑːn/ country in east central Asia; pop approx 5 093 000; official language Tajik; capital Dushanbe; unit of currency rouble. Part of the Russian empire in the 19th century, it became a member of the USSR and gained independence in 1991. The risk that armed conflict between the government and an Islamic rebel opposition might spread then led central Asian neighbour states in the *CIS to set up border peacekeeping forces. ⇨ map at UNION OF SOVIET SOCIALIST REPUBLICS.

Taj Mahal /ˌtɑːdʒ məˈhɑːl/ temple-like building in Agra, N India, built by the Mogul emperor Shah Jehan in the mid 17th century as a memorial to his dead wife.

take[1] /teɪk/ *v* (*pt* **took** /tʊk/, *pp* **taken** /ˈteɪkən/) **1** [Tn, Tn·pr, Tn·p, Cn·g, Dn·n, Dn·pr] ~ **sb/sth (with one)**; ~ **sth (to sb)** carry sb/sth or accompany sb from one place to another: *Don't forget to take your umbrella (with you) when you go.* ○ *It's your turn to take the dog for a walk.* ○ *She takes her children to school by car.* ○ (*fig*) *Her* *energy and talent took her to the top of her profession.* ○ *The accused was taken away in a police van.* ○ *I'm taking the children swimming/for a swim later.* ○ *She took him some flowers when she went to see him in hospital.* ○ *Take this glass of water (up) to your father/Take your father (up) this glass of water.* **2** [Tn, Tn·pr, Tn·p] get or lay hold of (sb/sth) with the hands, arms, etc or with an instrument: *I passed him the rope and he took it.* ○ *take sb's hand/take sb by the hand* ○ *Would you mind taking* (ie holding) *the baby for a moment?* ○ *Take three eggs and beat them gently.* ○ *She took a cigarette from the packet.* ○ *He took her in his arms and kissed her.* ○ *He took a book (down) from the top shelf.* ○ *She opened the drawer and took out a pair of socks.* **3** (**a**) [Tn] remove (sth) from its proper place without permission or by mistake: *Someone has taken my gloves.* ○ *Who's taken my bicycle?* ○ *Did the burglars take* (ie steal) *anything of value?* (**b**) [Tn·pr] ~ **sth from sth** (not usu in the continuous tenses) remove or obtain sth from (a particular place or source): *Part of her article is taken (straight) from my book on the subject.* ○ *Today's lesson is taken from St Mark's Gospel.* ○ *The machine takes its name from its inventor.* (**c**) [Tn, Tn·pr] ~ **sth (from sth)** (not in the continuous tenses) subtract (a number) from another one: *If you take five from twelve, you're left with seven.* **4** [Tn, Cn·n] (not usu in the continuous tenses) gain possession of (sth); capture or win (sth): *take a fortress, garrison, town, etc*, ie in a war ○ *The army took many prisoners.* ○ *He took my bishop with his queen*, ie in a game of chess. ○ *Our bull took first prize at the agricultural show.* ○ *The enemy took him prisoner/He was taken prisoner by the enemy.* **5** [Tn] (not usu in the continuous tenses) accept or receive (sth): *I'd like you to take this bracelet as a gift.* ○ *He took the blow* (ie The blow hit him) *on the chest.* ○ *Will you take £2 000 for the car* (ie sell it for £2 000)? ○ *The shop took* (ie sold goods worth a total of) *£50 000 last week.* ○ *She was accused of taking bribes.* ○ *Does the hotel take traveller's cheques?* ○ *I'll take the (telephone) call in my office.* ○ *Why should I take the blame for somebody else's mistakes?* ○ *If you take my advice, you'll have nothing more to do with him.* ○ *I take your point* (ie accept the validity of your argument)*, but my views on the matter remain the same.* ○ *The workers would never agree to take a cut in wages.* **6** [Tn] (not usu in the continuous tenses) accept (sb) as a client, patient, tenant, etc: *She takes paying guests.* ○ *Dr Brown takes some private patients.* ○ *The school doesn't take girls*, ie only has boys as pupils. **7** [Tn] (not in the continuous tenses) have enough space for (sb/sth); hold or contain: *This bus takes 60 passengers.* ○ *The tank takes 12 gallons.* ○ *I don't think the shelf will take any more books.* **8** [Tn] (not usu in the continuous tenses) be able to endure (sth); bear: *She can't take criticism/being criticized.* ○ *He can take a joke*, ie does not mind being laughed at. ○ *I don't think I can take much more of your nagging.* ○ *I'm not taking any more of your insults!* ○ *I find his political views a little hard to take.* **9** [Tn] (usu followed by an *adv* or used in questions after *how*) react to (sb/sth) in the specified way: *She knows how to take him/his teasing.* ○ *'How did he take the news of her death?' 'He took it badly'*, ie He was very upset by it. ○ *Police are taking the terrorists' threats of a bombing campaign very seriously indeed.* ○ *You take things too seriously; try to enjoy life a bit more!* **10** [Cn·n/a, Cn·t] ~ **sth as sth** (not in the continuous tenses) understand or interpret sth in a particular way: *She took what he said as a compliment.* ○ *What did you take his comments to mean?* ○ *How am I supposed to take that remark?* **11** [Tn·pr, Cn·t] ~ **sb/sth for sb/sth** (not in the continuous tenses) suppose, assume or consider sb/sth to be sb/sth: *Even the experts took the painting for a genuine Van Gogh.* ○ *Do you take me for a fool?* ○ *I took you to be an honest man.* **12** [Tn] (not in the continuous tenses) understand (sth): *I don't think she took my meaning.* **13** [Tn] rent (a house, etc): *We're taking a cottage in Devon for a month.* ○ *He took lodgings in the East End of London.* **14** [Tn] choose or buy (sth): *I'll take the grey trousers, please.* **15** [Tn] buy (sth, esp a newspaper) regularly: *She takes 'The Guardian'.* **16** [Tn] eat or drink (sth); consume: *Do you take sugar* (ie in tea or coffee)? ○ *The doctor has given her some pills to take for her cough.* ○ *He takes* (ie is addicted to) *drugs.* ○ *Have you ever taken cocaine?* **17** [Tn no passive, Tg, Cn·n] need or require (the specified time, quality, person or action) (often with *it*): *The journey from London to Oxford takes about an hour and a half.* ○ *That cut is taking a long time to heal.* ○ *It'll take time* (ie a long time) *for her to recover from the illness.* ○ *It takes stamina to run a marathon.* ○ *It would take a strong man to lift that weight.* ○ (*infml*) *She didn't take much persuading*, ie She was easily persuaded. ○ *Shifting that wardrobe must have taken some doing!* ○ *It took her three hours to mend her bicycle/It took three hours for her to mend her bicycle.* **18** [Tn no passive] (not in the continuous tenses) wear (a particular size in shoes or clothes): *What size shoes do you take?* ○ *He takes a 42-inch chest.* **19** [Tn] (not in the continuous tenses) (of a verb, etc) have or require (sth) as part of a grammatical construction: *The verb 'eat' takes a direct object.* **20** [Tn] do (an examination, a test, etc) in order to obtain a qualification: *She takes her finals next summer.* ○ *When are you taking your driving test?* **21** [Tn] be awarded or obtain (a degree): *She took a first in English at Leeds.* **22** [Tn] study (an academic subject): *She plans to take a course in applied linguistics.* **23** [Tn, Tn·pr] ~ **sb (for sth)** give sb lessons or instruction (in a particular subject); teach sb: *Mrs Biggs is ill and will be unable to take you today.* ○ *Who takes you for French?* **24** [Tn] find out and record (sth); write down (sth): *The policeman took my name and address.* ○ *Did you take notes at the lecture?* ○ *She hates taking letters.* **25** [Tn] test or measure (sth): *take sb's pulse/temperature/blood pressure* ○ *The tailor took my measurements for a new suit.* **26** [Tn] use (sth) as a means of transport; go by (sth): *take the coach, plane, train, etc* ○ *take a taxi* ○ *'How do you get to work?' 'I take the bus.'* **27** [Tn] use (a road, path, etc) as a route to go to a place: *I usually take the M6 when I go to Scotland.* ○ *Take* (ie Turn into) *the second turning/road on the right after the station.* **28** [Tn] (usu followed by an *adv*; not in the continuous tenses) go over or round (sth): *The horse took the first fence beautifully.* ○ *You took that corner much too fast.* **29** [Tn] (not usu in the continuous tenses) hold or adopt (a view, an attitude, etc): *He takes the view that people should be responsible for their own actions.* ○ *The government is taking a tough line on drug abuse.* **30** [Tn] (usu imperative) consider (sb/sth) as an example: *A lot of women manage to bring up families and go out to work at the same time — take Angela, for example.* **31** [Tn] (not in the continuous tenses) sit down or be seated in (a chair, etc): *take a chair, seat, stool, etc.* **32** [Tn] make (sth) by photography; photograph (sb/sth): *take a photograph/picture/snapshot of sb/sth* ○ *have one's picture taken.* **33** [Tn] officiate at (sth); conduct: *Mr Perkins will take the evening service.* **34** [I] (esp of a drug or dye) have the desired effect: *The inoculation did not take.* ○ *The dye won't take* (ie won't colour things) *in cold water.* **35** [I, Tn] (of fish) bite (the hook on a fisherman's line): *The fish don't seem to be taking today.* ○ (*fig*) *take the bait*, ie be deceived by a trick. **36** [Tn] (of a man) have sexual intercourse with (a woman): *He took her on the sofa.* **37** [Tn] (used with *ns* to show that the specified action is being carried out or performed): *take* (ie have) *a break, a holiday, a rest, etc* ○ *take* (ie have) *a bath, a shower, a wash, etc* ○ *take a look, a walk, a deep breath.* **38** (idm) **take sb/sth as he/it ˈcomes** accept or tolerate sb/sth without wishing him/it to be different: *She takes life as it comes.* **take it (that...)** assume or suppose (that...): *I take it you won't be coming to Sophie's party.* ○ *Are we to take it that you refuse to co-operate?* **take it from ˈme (that...)** (*infml*) you can believe me absolutely (when I say...): *Take it from me — he'll be managing director of this company by the time he's 30.* **take it on/upon oneself to do sth** decide to do sth without asking for permission: *You can't take it upon yourself to make important decisions like that.* **take it/a lot ˈout of sb** make sb physically or mentally tired: *Her job takes a lot out of her.* **take some/a lot of ˈdoing** (*infml*) be very difficult to do: *Did you move all this furniture on your own? That must have taken some doing!* **you can/can't take sb ˈanywhere** the specified person can/cannot be trusted to behave well in any situation: *His manners are appalling — you can't take him anywhere!* (For other idioms containing **take**, see entries for *ns*, *adjs*, etc, eg **take the biscuit** ⇨ BISCUIT; **take sb unawares** ⇨ UNAWARES.)

39 (phr v) **take sb aˈback** (esp passive) shock or surprise sb: *I was taken aback by his rudeness.*

take after sb (no passive) resemble (one's mother or father) in appearance or character: *Your daughter doesn't take after you at all.*

take against sb/sth begin to dislike sb/sth: *Why have you suddenly taken against her?*

take sb/sth apart (*infml*) (**a**) (in sport) defeat sb easily: *Becker took Connors apart in the third set*, ie in tennis. ○ *We were simply taken apart by the opposition.* (**b**) criticize sb/sth severely: *Her second novel was taken apart by the critics.* **take sth apart** separate (esp a machine) into its component parts; dismantle sth: *Let's take the radio apart and see what's wrong with it.*

take sth away (**a**) (*US* **take sth out**) buy (a cooked dish) at a restaurant and carry it away to eat at home: *Two chicken curries and rice to take away, please.* (**b**) cause (a feeling, sensation, etc) to disappear: *The doctor has given her some tablets to take away the pain.* ○ *Nothing can take away the anguish of losing a child.* ○ *Anxiety has taken away his appetite.* **take sb/sth away (from sb/sth)** remove sb/sth (from sb/sth): *What takes you away* (ie Why are you leaving) *so early?* ○ *These books must not be taken away from the library.* ○ *The child was taken away from its parents on the recommendation of social workers.* **take sth away (from sth)** subtract (one number) (from another): *If you take four away from ten, that leaves six/Ten take away four is/leaves six.* **take away from sth** weaken, lessen or diminish the effect or value of sth; detract from sth: *The scandal took away greatly from his public image.*

take sth back (**a**) (of a shop) agree to accept or receive back (goods previously bought there): *We only take goods back if customers can produce the receipt.* (**b**) admit that sth one said was wrong or that one should not have said it; retract or withdraw sth: *I take back what I said (about you being selfish).* **take sb back (to...)** cause sb's thoughts to return to a past time: *The smell of seaweed took him back to his childhood.* ○ *Hearing those old songs takes me back a bit.*

take sb before sth/sb make sb appear in a court, before sb in authority, etc to explain his actions or be punished: *He was taken before the headmaster and made to confess.*

take sth down (**a**) remove sth from a high level: *Will you help me take the curtains down?* (**b**) lower (a garment worn below the waist) without actually removing it: *take down one's skirt, trousers, underpants, etc.* (**c**) remove (a structure) by separating it into pieces; dismantle sth: *take down a tent, gate, fence* ○ *Workmen arrived to take down the scaffolding.* (**d**) write sth down in order to make a record of it: *The reporters took down the speech.* ○ *Anything you say may be taken down and used as evidence against you.*

take sb in (**a**) allow sb to stay in one's home, sometimes for payment: *She takes in lodgers.* ○ *He was homeless, so we took him in.* (**b**) (often passive) deceive, delude or fool sb: *She took me in completely with her story.* ○ *You won't take me in that easily!* ○ *Don't be taken in by his charming manner; he's completely ruthless.* **take sth in** (**a**) absorb sth into the body by breathing or swallowing it: *Fish take in oxygen through their gills.* (**b**) make (a garment) narrower or tighter by altering its seams: *This dress needs to be taken in at the waist.* (**c**) accept (work to do in one's home) for payment: *She supplements her pension by taking in washing.* (**d**) include or cover sth: *The United Kingdom takes in England, Wales, Scotland and Northern Ireland.* ○ *The tour took in six European capitals.* ○ *Her lecture took in all the recent developments in the* *subject.* (**e**) go to see or visit (a film, museum, etc) when one is in a place for a different purpose: *I generally try to take in a show when I'm in New York on business.* (**f**) note sth with the eyes; observe sth: *He took in every detail of her appearance.* ○ *He took in the scene at a glance.* ○ *The children took in the spectacle open-mouthed.* (**g**) understand or absorb sth that one hears or reads: *I hope you're taking in what I'm saying.* ○ *Half-way through the chapter I realized I hadn't taken anything in.*

take ˈoff (**a**) (of an aeroplane, a helicopter, etc) leave the ground and begin to fly: *The plane took off despite the fog.* (**b**) (*infml*) leave hurriedly or suddenly: *He took off for the station at a run.* ○ *When he saw the police coming he took off in the opposite direction.* (**c**) (*infml*) (of an idea, a product, etc) suddenly become successful or popular; (of sales of a product) rise very quickly: *The new dictionary has really taken off.* ○ *Sales of home computers have taken off in recent years.* **take oneself off (to...)** (*infml*) leave a place (in order to reach the specified destination): *It's time I took myself off.* ○ *She's taken herself off to the country for a quiet weekend.* **take sb off** imitate or mimic sb in an amusing or satirical way: *She takes off the Prime Minister to perfection.* **take sth off** (**a**) remove (an item of clothing) from one's body: *take off one's coat, hat, shoes, skirt, trousers, etc* ○ *I wish you'd take* (ie shave) *off that beard!* (**b**) amputate (a part of the body): *His leg had to be taken off above the knee.* (**c**) no longer perform (a play, etc); withdraw sth: *The show had to be taken off because of poor audiences.* (**d**) (often passive) remove or withdraw (a bus, train, etc) from service: *The 7 am express to Bristol will be taken off next month.* (**e**) have (the specified period of time) as a holiday or break from work: *take the day/morning/afternoon off* ○ *I'm taking next week off (work).* **take sb off (sth)** (**a**) rescue sb from (a ship): *The crew were taken off (the wrecked vessel) by helicopter.* (**b**) (often passive) remove sb from (a job, position, etc): *The officer leading the inquiry has been taken off the case.* **take sth off (sth)** (**a**) remove or detach sth from (a surface or an edge): *Would you mind taking your foot off my hand?* ○ *take the lid off a jar* ○ *The heat has taken the paint off the doors.* (**b**) remove (an item) from a menu: *The mixed grill has been taken off (the menu).* **take sth off sth** (**a**) deduct (an amount of money) from sth: *take 10 pence a gallon off the price of petrol.* (**b**) cause (a product) to be no longer on sale: *Doctors recommended that the drug should be taken off the market.*

take ˈon (**a**) (*infml*) become fashionable or popular: *The idea never really took on.* (**b**) (used with an *adv*) (*dated infml*) become upset or agitated: *Don't take on so!* **take on sth** (no passive) begin to have (a particular quality, appearance, etc); assume sth: *He's taken on some irritating mannerisms.* ○ *The chameleon can take on the colours of its background.* ○ *Her eyes took on a hurt expression.* **take sb on** (**a**) employ sb; engage sb: *take on new staff* ○ *She was taken on as a graduate trainee.* (**b**) accept sb as one's opponent in a game, etc; tackle sb: *take sb on at snooker, squash, tennis, etc* ○ *Ajax will take on Juventus in this year's European Cup Final.* **take sb/sth on** (of a bus, plane, ship, etc) allow sb/sth to enter; take sb/sth on board: *The bus stopped to take on more passengers.* ○ *The ship took on more fuel at Freetown.* **take sth on** decide to do sth; undertake sth: *take on extra work* ○ *She took on greater responsibilities when she was promoted.* ○ *Don't take on more than you can cope with.*

take sb out escort or accompany sb to the theatre, a restaurant, etc: *Have you taken her out yet?* ○ *He took his wife out to dinner/for a meal on her birthday.* **take sb/sth out** (*infml*) kill sb or destroy sth; put sb/sth out of action: *Enemy missiles took out two of our fighters.* **take sth out** (**a**) (*US*) = TAKE STH AWAY. (**b**) remove or extract (a part of the body): *She's gone into hospital to have her appendix taken out.* ○ *How many teeth did the dentist take out?* (**c**) obtain (an official document or a service): *take out an insurance policy, a mortgage, a patent.* **take sth out (against sb)** issue (a document that requires sb to appear in court): *The police have taken out a summons against the drivers of both cars involved in the accident.* **take sth out (of sth)** (**a**) remove sth from sth: *Take your hands out of your pockets.* (**b**) withdraw (money) from a bank account: *How much do you need to take out (of the bank)?* (**c**) deduct (an amount of money from sth): *Monthly contributions to the pension scheme will be taken out of your salary.* (**d**) cause sth to disappear from sth: *Cold water should take that stain out of your skirt.* **take it/sth out on sb** behave in an unpleasant way towards sb because one feels angry, disappointed, etc: *I know you've had a bad day — but there's no need to take it out on me!* ○ *He took out his anger on the cat*, eg by kicking it. **take sb ˈout of himself** make sb forget his worries and become less concerned with himself, his thoughts, etc: *A holiday would help to take her out of herself.*

take (sth) ˈover gain control of (a country, political party, etc): *The army is/are threatening to take over if civil unrest continues.* ○ *Has the party been taken over by extremists?* **take sth over** acquire or gain control of (a business company), esp by obtaining the support of a majority of its shareholders: *The firm has been taken over by an American conglomerate.* **take (sth) ˈover (from sb)** take control of or responsibility for sth, esp in place of sb else: *Peter will take over as managing director when Bill retires.* ○ *When she fell ill her daughter took over the business from her.* ○ *George is taking over the running of our American operation.* ○ *Would you like me to take over (the driving) for a while?*

take to... go away to (a place), esp to escape from an enemy; take refuge in (a place): *take to the forest, woods, jungle, etc* ○ *The crew took to the lifeboats when the ship was torpedoed.* **take to sb/sth** develop a liking for sb/sth; develop an ability for sth: *I didn't take to her husband at all.* ○ *I took to her the moment I met her.* ○ *He hasn't taken to his new school.* **take to sth/doing sth** begin to do sth as a habit: *take to smoking a pipe, sleeping late, going on solitary walks* ○ *She's taken to drink*, ie has started to drink a lot of alcoholic drinks. ○ *He took to gardening in his retirement.*

take up continue: *This chapter takes up where the last one left off.* **take up sth** fill or occupy (the specified space or time): *This table takes up too much room.* ○ *Her time is fully taken up with writing.* **take sb up** (**a**) adopt sb as a protégé; help sb: *The young soprano was taken up by a famous conductor.* (**b**) interrupt sb in order to contradict or criticize him: *She took me up sharply when I suggested that the job was only suitable for a man.* **take sth up** (**a**) lift sth up; raise sth: *take up one's pen*, ie in order to write ○ *The carpets had to be taken up when the house was rewired.* (**b**) absorb (a liquid): *Blotting-paper takes up ink.* (**c**) make (a garment, curtains, etc) shorter: *This skirt will need taking up*, ie to be taken up. (**d**) adopt sth as a hobby or pastime: *take up gardening, golf, yoga* ○ *She has taken up* (ie has begun to learn to play) *the oboe.* (**e**) start or begin sth, esp a job: *She has taken up a job as a teacher.* ○ *She takes up her duties/responsibilities next week.* (**f**) add one's voice to sth; join in sth: *The whole crowd took up the cry: 'Long live the King!'* ○ *take up a chorus, refrain, song, etc.* (**g**) continue (a story) that has been interrupted, or left unfinished by sb else: *She took up the narrative where John had left off.* (**h**) adopt or assume (an attitude, a position, etc): *Our troops took up defensive positions on high ground overlooking the river.* (**i**) accept sth: *take up a challenge* ○ *She took up his offer of a drink.* (**j**) mention sth in order that it may be discussed: *I'd like to take up the point you raised earlier.* **take sb up (on sth)** question or challenge sb (about sth); argue with sb (about sth): *I must take you up on that point.* ○ *I'd like to take you up on what you said about unemployment.* **take up with sb** (*infml*) begin to be friendly with or spend a lot of time with sb (esp sb unpleasant or disreputable): *She's taken up with an unemployed actor.* **take sb up on sth** (*infml*) accept (a challenge, a bet, an offer, etc) from sb: *'I bet I can run faster than you.' 'I'll take you up on that.'* ○ *Thanks for the invitation; we may take you up on it some time.* **take sth up with sb** speak or write to sb about sth; raise sth with sb: *I'm thinking of taking the matter up with my MP.* **be taken up with sb/sth** have much of one's time and energies occupied by sb/sth: *She's very taken up with voluntary work at the moment.*

be taken with sb/sth find sb/sth attractive or interesting: *We were all very taken with her.* ○ *I think he's rather taken with the idea.*

□ **ˈtake-away** (*US* **ˈtake-out**) *adj* [attrib] (of food) bought at a restaurant for eating elsewhere: *a take-away hamburger, pizza, curry.* ⇨ article at EAT. — *n* **1** restaurant selling such food: *I'm too tired to cook — let's get something from the Chinese take-away.* **2** meal bought at such a restaurant: *I fancy an Indian take-away.*

ˈtake-home pay amount of one's wages or salary remaining after taxes, etc have been deducted.

ˈtake-off *n* **1** place at which the feet leave the ground in jumping. **2** (of an aeroplane) act of leaving the ground and rising: *a smooth take-off* ○ *The crash occurred only three minutes after take-off.* **3** ~ (**of sb**) humorous imitation of sb: *She does a brilliant take-off of the boss.*

ˈtake-over *n* **1** act of taking control of a company by buying most of its shares (SHARE[1] 3): [attrib] *a take-over bid.* **2** act of taking over a country, etc: *a military take-over.*

ˈtake-up spool (on a cine-projector, tape-recorder, etc) spool onto which film, tape, etc is wound after use.

NOTE ON USAGE: Both **last** and **take** are concerned with duration. **1 Take** indicates that a certain amount of time is needed in order to complete a task, journey, etc. **Take** must be used with an expression of time: *How long will the job take?* ○ *It takes a long time to get there. It took (me) four hours to write the essay.* ○ *I'll clear up - you take too long.* **2 Last** indicates that an event will continue for a period of time or that there is enough of something for the required purpose. The time expression is not obligatory: *His illness has lasted a long time.* ○ *I hope this fine weather lasts.* ○ *Do you think that paint will last (out)?* **3** Notice the difference between : *It takes (me) ten minutes to smoke a cigarette* and *A cigarette lasts (me) ten minutes.* **4** A journey can be seen as either a task or an event: *The journey takes/lasts two hours.*

take[2] /teɪk/ *n* **1** (usu *sing*) (**a**) amount of fish, game[1](6), etc caught. (**b**) amount of money, taken or received, eg in return for tickets sold. **2** (*cinema*) sequence of film photographed at one time without stopping the camera: *shoot the scene in a single take.*

taker /ˈteɪkə(r)/ *n* person who accepts an offer or takes a bet: *There's still some cake left — any takers?* ie Does anyone want some? ○ *The bookies were offering odds of 3 to 1, but there were no takers.*

taking /ˈteɪkɪŋ/ *adj* (*dated*) attractive; charming.
▷ **takings** *n* [pl] amount of money that a shop, theatre, etc gets from selling goods, tickets, etc; receipts: *the day's takings.*

talc /tælk/ (also **talcum** /ˈtælkəm/) *n* [U] **1** smooth soft mineral that is powdered for use as a lubricant. **2** talcum powder.
□ **ˈtalcum powder** talc, powdered and usu perfumed, put on the skin to make it feel smooth and dry.

tale /teɪl/ *n* **1** narrative or story: *ˈfairy tales* ○ *tales of adventure.* **2** report spread by gossip, often false or invented: *I've heard some odd tales about her.* ○ *You hear all sorts of tales.* **3** (idm) **dead men tell no tales** ⇨ DEAD. **live, etc to tell the tale** ⇨ TELL. **an old wives' tale** ⇨ OLD. **tell its own tale** ⇨ TELL. **tell tales** ⇨ TELL. **thereby hangs a tale** ⇨ HANG[1].
□ **ˈtalebearer**, **ˈtaleteller** *ns* person who spreads gossip or reports what is meant to be secret.

talent /ˈtælənt/ *n* **1** [C, U] ~ (**for sth**) (instance of) special or very great ability: *Her talents are well known.* ○ *possess a remarkable talent for music* ○ *a painter of great talent.* **2** [U] people who have this: *We're always looking for new/fresh talent.* ○ *an exhibition of local talent*, eg of works by local amateur artists ○ [attrib] *a television talent show*, ie one featuring talented young performers. **3** [U] (*sl*) sexually attractive people: *eyeing up the local*

talent. **4** [C] unit of money or measure of weight used in ancient times in certain countries.
▷ **talented** *adj* having talent; gifted: *a talented musician.*
talentless *adj* without talent; not talented.
□ ˈ**talent-scout** (also ˈ**talent-spotter**) *n* person whose job is to find talented performers for the entertainment industry, sports teams, etc.

talisman /ˈtælɪzmən, *also* ˈtælɪs-/ *n* (*pl* ~**s**) [C] object that is thought to bring good luck, eg a ring or locket.

talk[1] /tɔ:k/ *n* **1** [C] conversation; discussion: *I had a long talk with the headmaster about my son.* ○ *hold disarmament talks* ○ *The latest round of pay talks has broken down,* ie failed to reach an agreement. **2** [U] (**a**) talking, esp without action or results: *There's too much talk and not enough work being done.* (**b**) rumour or gossip: *There's (some) talk of a general election.* **3** [C] informal lecture or speech: *She gave a talk on her visit to China.* **4** [U] (esp in compounds) way of speaking: *baby-talk.* **5** (idm) **be all** ˈ**talk (and no action)** make empty promises, claims, etc. **fighting talk/words** ⇨ WORD. **the talk of sth** the main subject of conversation in (a place): *Their engagement is the talk of the town.*
□ ˈ**talk show** (*US*) = CHAT SHOW (CHAT).

NOTE ON USAGE: **1 Talk** as an uncountable noun is a general word indicating the activity of speaking: *In politics there is too much talk and not enough action.* ○ *Talk is very important in a child's development.* **Talk** can also be a countable noun referring to a (usually) short informal speech to a small audience, or, when used in the plural, to formal occasions of serious talking, often between politicians: *She gave the society an illustrated talk on her travels in India.* ○ *The two sides in the war have agreed to hold peace talks.* **2 Discussion** indicates (a) talk with a serious purpose. It is often a formal exchange of words in which speakers argue about and examine different aspects of a subject: *The problem was solved only after several lengthy discussions.* ○ *A panel discussion on the radio on the future of the Health Service.* **3 Conversation** is usually social and friendly, often for the exchange of ideas or information: *Television has killed the art of conversation.* ○ *We had an interesting conversation about schools at lunch-time.* **4 Chat** is (a) friendly talk, usually to exchange personal news, etc: *I hadn't seen him for years and we had a long chat about old times.* **5 Gossip** is derogatory and refers to talk about the private lives of other people, often of a critical kind. A **gossip** is a person who gossips: *People always gossip a lot in a small village like this.* ○ *He's a terrible gossip.*

talk[2] /tɔ:k/ *v* **1** [I, Ipr] ~ (**to/with sb**) (**about/of sth/sb**) say things; speak to give information, discuss sth, etc: *We talked* (ie to each other) *for almost an hour.* ○ *He was talking to/with a friend.* ○ *What are they talking about?* ○ *She talked of applying for another job.* ○ *Are they talking in Spanish or Portuguese?* **2** [I] have the power of speech: *The child is learning to talk.* **3** [Tn] (**a**) discuss (sth): *talk business, politics, cricket.* (**b**) express (sth) in words: *talk sense/nonsense* ○ *You're talking rubbish.* **4** [Tn] use (a particular language) when speaking: *talk French.* **5** [Cn·a] bring (oneself) into a certain condition by talking: *talk oneself hoarse.* **6** [I] gossip: *We must stop meeting like this — people are beginning to talk!* **7** [I] give information: *The police persuaded the suspect to talk.* **8** [I] imitate the sounds of speech: *You can teach some parrots to talk.* ⇨ Usage at SAY. **9** (idm) **be/get oneself** ˈ**talked about** be/become the subject of gossip: *Be more discreet or you'll get yourself talked about.* **know what one is talking about** ⇨ KNOW. **look who's** ˈ**talking** (*infml*) you shouldn't say such things about others since you are just as bad yourself. **money talks** ⇨ MONEY. **now you're talking** (*infml*) I welcome that offer or suggestion: *Take the day off? Now you're talking!* **speak/talk of the devil** ⇨ DEVIL[1]. **talk about...** (*infml*) (used for emphasizing the great quantity or extent of sth): *Talk about rain! I thought it'd never stop.* ○ *She hadn't even locked the door. Talk about stupid!* **talk** ˈ**big** boast: *He talks big but doesn't actually do anything.* **talk dirty** use obscene language. **talk one's** ˈ**head off** talk too much. **talk sb's** ˈ**head off** weary sb by talking too much. **talk the hind legs off a donkey** (*infml*) (be able to) talk endlessly. **talk, etc nineteen to the dozen** ⇨ DOZEN. **talk sense** talk sensibly; say sth that is correct, acceptable, etc. **talk** ˈ**shop** (*usu derog*) discuss one's work with colleagues, esp when with other people. **talk through one's** ˈ**hat** talk nonsense. **talk (to sb) like a Dutch** ˈ**uncle** lecture sb severely but kindly. **talk** ˈ**turkey** (*infml esp US*) talk frankly and bluntly. **talk one's way out of sth/doing sth** avoid sth by clever talking: *I'd like to see him talk his way out of this one,* ie this trouble he has got into. **talking of sb/sth** while on the subject of sb/sth: *Talking of Jim, have you heard that he's getting married?* ˈ**you can/can't talk** (*infml*) = LOOK WHO'S TALKING.
10 (phr v) **talk at sb** speak to sb without listening to his replies: *I don't like being talked at.*
talk back (to sb) reply defiantly to a reprimand, etc.
talk sb down stop sb speaking by talking loudly or persistently. **talk sb/sth down** bring (a pilot or an aircraft) to a landing by radio instructions from the ground. **talk down to sb** speak to sb in condescendingly simple language.
talk sb into/out of doing sth persuade sb to do/not to do sth: *He talked his father into lending him the car.* ○ *I tried to talk her out of coming.*
talk sth out (**a**) resolve (a problem, etc) by discussion. (**b**) (*Brit*) prevent (a bill) being approved by Parliament by discussing it for so long that a vote cannot be taken.
talk sb over/round (to sth) persuade sb to accept or agree to sth: *We finally managed to talk them over/round (to our way of thinking).* **talk sth over (with sb)** discuss sth.
talk round sth discuss sth without coming to the point: *waste an hour talking round the real problem.*
talk sb/sth up (*US*) speak in favour of sb/sth; praise sb/sth.
▷ **talkative** /ˈtɔ:kətɪv/ *adj* fond of talking: *a very talkative child.* **talkativeness** *n* [U].
talker *n* **1** (esp with an *adj*) person who talks (in the specified way): *a good/poor talker* ○ *She's a great talker,* ie She talks a lot. ○ *He's a fast talker,* ie able to get out of trouble by talking cleverly. **2** person who talks a lot but does not act: *Don't rely on him to do anything — he's just a talker.*
□ ˌ**talking** ˈ**book** recorded reading of a book, made esp for blind people.
ˌ**talking** ˈ**head** (*infml*) person speaking on television, eg the presenter of a programme, who is seen in close-up looking directly at the camera.
ˈ**talking-point** *n* topic that is likely to be discussed or argued about.
ˈ**talking-shop** *n* (*Brit derog*) place or institution where there is much discussion or argument but little action.
ˈ**talking-to** *n* (*pl* **-tos**) (esp *sing*) reproof; scolding: *That child needs a good talking-to.*

tall /tɔ:l/ *adj* (**-er, -est**) **1** (of people or objects) of more than average height; of objects whose height is greater than their width; higher than surrounding objects: *She's taller than me.* ○ *a tall tree, chimney, spire, mast.* Cf SHORT[1] 1. **2** of a specified height: *Tom is six feet tall.* ⇨ Usage at HEIGHT. **3** (idm) **a tall** ˈ**order** (*infml*) difficult task or unreasonable request. **a tall** ˈ**story** (*infml*) story that is difficult to believe. **ten feet tall** ⇨ FOOT[1]. **walk tall** ⇨ WALK[1]. ▷ **tallness** *n* [U].
□ ˈ**tallboy** (*Brit*) (*US* ˈ**highboy**) *n* tall chest with drawers for clothes, etc.

Tallis /ˈtælɪs/ Thomas (c 1505-85), English composer of church music. His best-known work is a setting of *Spem in alium* for 40 voices. ⇨ article at MUSIC.

tallith /ˈtælɪθ/ *n* (*pl* ~**im** /-ɪm/ or ~**s**) fringed shawl worn by Jewish men at morning prayers.

tallow /ˈtæləʊ/ *n* [U] animal fat used for making candles, soap, lubricants, etc.

tally /ˈtælɪ/ *n* **1** score; reckoning: *Keep a tally of how much you spend.* **2** label or ticket used for identification.
▷ **tally** *v* (*pt, pp* **tallied**) [I, Ipr] ~ (**with sth**) (of stories, amounts, etc) correspond; agree: *His account of the accident tallies with yours.* ○ *The two lists do not tally.*

tally-ho /ˌtælɪ ˈhəʊ/ *n, interj* (*pl* ~**s**) (*esp Brit*) (shout of a huntsman when he has seen a fox, to encourage the hounds to chase it).

Talmud /ˈtælmʊd; *US* ˈtɑ:l-/ *n* collection of ancient writings on Jewish law and tradition.

talon /ˈtælən/ *n* (usu *pl*) claw, esp of a bird of prey.

tamarind /ˈtæmərɪnd/ *n* (edible fruit of a) tropical evergreen tree.

tamarisk /ˈtæmərɪsk/ *n* evergreen shrub with feathery branches and spikes of pink or white flowers.

tambour /ˈtæmbʊə(r)/ *n* **1** rolling top or front for a desk, cabinet, etc, made of narrow strips of wood glued to canvas. **2** small circular frame for holding fabric taut while it is being embroidered.

tambourine /ˌtæmbəˈri:n/ *n* (*music*) percussion instrument that consists of a small shallow drum with jingling metal discs set in the rim, and is played by shaking or hitting with the hand.

tame /teɪm/ *adj* (**-r, -st**) **1** (of animals) gentle and unafraid of human beings; not wild or fierce: *a tame monkey* ○ *The pigeons are so tame they will sit on your shoulder.* **2** [attrib] (*joc*) (of people) available and willing to be told what to do; submissive: *I've got a tame mechanic who keeps my car in order.* **3** dull or unadventurous: *I quite enjoyed the book but found the ending rather tame.* ○ *The scenery around here is a little tame.* ○ *a tame attempt to reform the system.*
▷ **tame** *v* [Tn] make (sth) tame or manageable: *tame wild birds* ○ *man's attempts to tame the elements.* **tameable** *adj* that can be tamed. **tamer** *n* (usu in compounds) person who tames and trains wild animals: *a* ˈ*lion-tamer.*
tamely *adv.*
tameness *n* [U].

Tammany /ˈtæmənɪ/ political organization of the US *Democratic Party founded in New York in 1789 and notorious in the 19th and early 20th century for its corrupt practices, use of bribery, etc.
□ ˌ**Tammany** ˈ**Hall 1** any of the buildings used by Tammany as a headquarters. **2** members of Tammany.

tam-o'-shanter /ˌtæm ə ˈʃæntə(r)/ (also **tammy** /ˈtæmɪ/) *n* round Scottish woollen cap with a soft full top.

tamp /tæmp/ *v* (phr v) **tamp sth down** tap or ram sth down tightly: *tamp down the tobacco in a pipe.*

tamper /ˈtæmpə(r)/ *v* [Ipr] ~ **with sth** meddle or interfere with sth; alter sth without authority: *Someone has been tampering with the lock.* ○ *The records of the meeting had been tampered with.* ○ (*fig*) *tamper with* (ie bribe) *a jury.*

tampon /ˈtæmpɒn/ *n* plug of cotton wool or other absorbent material inserted into a woman's vagina to absorb blood during menstruation.

tan /tæn/ *v* (**-nn-**) **1** [Tn] convert (animal skin) into leather by treating it with tannic acid, etc. **2** [I, Tn] (cause sth to) become brown by exposure to the sun: *My skin tans easily.* ○ *I want to tan my back a bit more.* ○ *You look very tanned — have you been on holiday?* **3** [Tn] (*infml*) beat (sb/sth); thrash. **4** (idm) **tan sb's** ˈ**hide** (*infml*) beat sb hard.
▷ **tan** *n* **1** [U] yellowish-brown colour. **2** [C] brown colour of the skin after exposure to the sun: *get a good tan* ○ *My tan's beginning to fade.*
tan *adj* yellowish-brown: *tan leather gloves.*
tanner *n* person who tans skins to make leather.
tannery /ˈtænərɪ/ *n* place where skins are tanned to make leather.

tan /tæn/ *abbr* (*mathematics*) tangent.

T and AVR (also **TAVR**) *abbr* (*Brit*) Territorial and Army Volunteer Reserve.

tandem /ˈtændəm/ *n* **1** bicycle with seats and pedals for two or more people, one behind another. **2** (idm) **in tandem** one behind another: *drive/ride in tandem* ○ *horses harnessed in tandem* ○ (*fig*) *The two systems are designed to work in tandem,* ie alongside each other, together. ○ *He and his wife run the business in tandem,* ie as partners.

tandoori /tænˈdʊərɪ/ *n* [U] type of Indian food

cooked over charcoal in a clay oven: [attrib] *tandoori chicken.*

tang /tæŋ/ *n* (usu *sing*) sharp taste, flavour or smell, esp one that is characteristic of sth: *with a tang of lemon* ○ *There's a tang of autumn in the air.*
▷ **tangy** /ˈtæŋɪ/ *adj* (**-ier**, **-iest**): *a tangy aroma.*

tangent /ˈtændʒənt/ *n* **1** (*geometry*) straight line that touches the outside of a curve but does not cross it. ⇨ illus at CIRCLE. **2** (*abbr* **tan**) (*mathematics*) (in a right-angled triangle) ratio of the sides opposite and adjacent to a given angle. Cf COSINE, SINE. **3** (idm) **go/fly off at a ˈtangent** change suddenly from one line of thought, action, etc to another.
▷ **tangential** /tænˈdʒenʃl/ *adj* ~ (**to sth**) **1** of or along a tangent. **2** going away from a main or straight path; divergent. **3** not closely connected with the main point; peripheral: *comments tangential to the topic under discussion.*

tangerine /ˌtændʒəˈriːn; *US* ˈtændʒəriːn/ *n* **1** [C] type of small sweet loose-skinned orange. **2** [U] its deep orange-yellow colour.

tangible /ˈtændʒəbl/ *adj* **1** (*fml*) that can be perceived by touch. **2** [usu attrib] clear and definite; real: *tangible advantages* ○ *tangible proof* ○ *the company's tangible assets*, eg its buildings, machinery, etc, but not its reputation, etc. ▷ **tangibility** /ˌtændʒəˈbɪlətɪ/ *n* [U]. **tangibly** /-əblɪ/ *adv.*

tangle /ˈtæŋgl/ *n* [C] **1** confused mass (of string, hair, etc): *brush the tangles out of a dog's fur* ○ *The wool got in a fearful tangle.* **2** confused condition: *His financial affairs are in such a tangle.*
▷ **tangle** *v* **1** [I, Ip, Tn, Tn·p] ~ (**sth**) (**up**) (cause sth to) become twisted into a confused mass: *Her hair got all tangled up in the barbed wire fence.* **2** [Ipr] ~ **with sb/sth** become involved in a quarrel or fight with sb/sth: *I shouldn't tangle with Peter — he's bigger than you.* **tangled** *adj*: *tangled hair, wire, undergrowth.*
tangly *adj* tangled.

tango /ˈtæŋgəʊ/ *n* (*pl* ~**s** /-gəʊz/) (music for a) ballroom dance with gliding steps and a strongly marked rhythm: *dance/do the tango.*
▷ **tango** *v* (*pt, pp* **-goed**, *pres p* **-going**) [I] dance the tango.

tangram /ˈtæŋgræm/ *n* Chinese puzzle consisting of a square cut into seven differently shaped pieces which can be combined into various figures.

tangy ⇨ TANG.

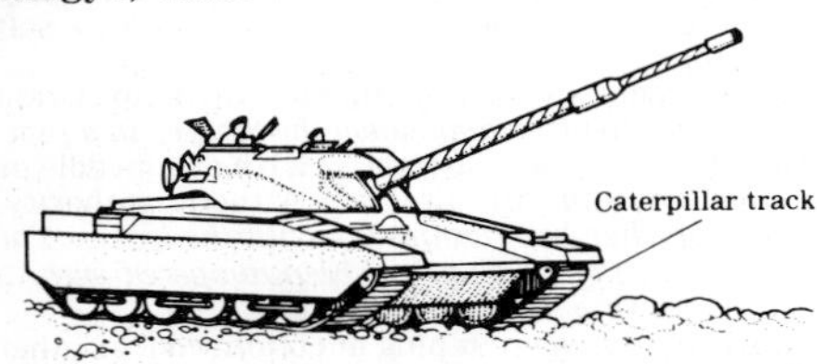

tank

tank /tæŋk/ *n* **1** (**a**) large container, usu for liquid or gas: *the ˈpetrol-tank of a car* ○ *keep tropical fish in a glass tank* ○ *Water is stored in tanks under the roof.* (**b**) (also **tankful** /-fʊl/) contents of this: *We drove there and back on one tank of petrol.* **2** armoured fighting vehicle with guns which moves on Caterpillar tracks: [attrib] *a tank commander.* **3** (in India, Pakistan, etc) large artificial reservoir for storing water.
▷ **tank** *v* (phr v) **tank up** fill the tank of a vehicle, etc. **be/get tanked up** (*sl*) be/become drunk: *We got really tanked up on whisky and beer.*
tanker *n* (**a**) ship or aircraft for carrying petroleum, etc in bulk: *an oil tanker.* (**b**) (*US* also **ˈtank truck**) heavy road vehicle with a large cylindrical tank for carrying oil, milk, etc in bulk.
□ **ˈtank top** sleeveless (usu knitted) garment for the upper body, typically worn over a shirt, etc by men or women.

tankard /ˈtæŋkəd/ *n* large (usu metal) drinking mug with a handle, esp one for beer. ⇨ illus at CUP[1].

tanner, **tannery** ⇨ TAN.

tannic /ˈtænɪk/ *adj* of tannin.
□ **tannic ˈacid** tannin.

tannin /ˈtænɪn/ *n* [U] any of various compounds obtained from the bark of oak and other trees and used in tanning, dyeing, etc.

Tannoy /ˈtænɔɪ/ *n* (*propr*) type of public-address system: *an announcement made over/on the Tannoy.*

tansy /ˈtænzɪ/ *n* [C, U] plant with small yellow flowers and strong-tasting juice that is sometimes used as a medicine or flavouring.

tantalize, -ise /ˈtæntəlaɪz/ *v* [Tn] tease or torment (a person or an animal) by the sight of sth that is desired but cannot be reached: *Give the dog the bone — don't tantalize him.* ○ *He was tantalized by visions of power and wealth.* ▷ **tantalizing, -ising** *adj*: *a tantalizing smell of food.* **tantalizingly, -isingly** *adv*: *tantalizingly near.*

tantalum /ˈtæntələm/ *n* [U] (*symb* **Ta**) (*chemistry*) rare hard white metallic element.

tantalus /ˈtæntələs/ *n* (*esp Brit*) stand or case in which bottles may be locked while still remaining visible.

tantamount /ˈtæntəmaʊnt/ *adj* [pred] ~ **to sth** equal in effect to sth; as good as sth: *The King's request was tantamount to a command.* ○ *Her statement is tantamount to a confession of guilt.*

tantrum /ˈtæntrəm/ *n* outburst of bad temper, esp in a child: *have/throw a tantrum* ○ *be in/get in(to) a tantrum.*

East Africa

Tanzania /ˌtænzəˈniːə/ country in E Africa, bordered by Kenya in the north and Mozambique in the south; pop approx 23 997 000; official languages Swahili and English; capital Dodoma; unit of currency shilling (= 100 cents). It was formed in 1964 from the former British colonies of Tanganyika and Zanzibar. Its main exports are coffee, cotton and sisal. ⇨ map (EAST AFRICA).

Taoiseach /ˈtiːʃək/ *n* prime minister of the Republic of Ireland.

Taoism /ˈtaʊɪzəm, ˈdaʊ-/ *n* [U] Chinese religious and philosophical system which teaches that one should act in harmony with nature. Cf CONFUCIANISM.

tap[1] /tæp/ *n* **1** (*US* **faucet**) device for controlling the flow of liquid or gas out of a pipe or container: *hot and cold taps*, eg on a basin, bath, etc ○ *turn the tap on/off* ○ *Don't leave the taps running*, ie Turn them off. Cf VALVE 1. **2** act of tapping a telephone or connection for doing this: *put a tap on sb's phone.* **3** (idm) **on tap** (**a**) (of beer, etc) in a barrel with a tap; on draught. (**b**) (*fig*) available when needed.
▷ **tap** *v* (**-pp-**) **1** (**a**) [Tn] draw liquid from (sth): *tap a cask of cider.* (**b**) [Tn, Tn·pr, Tn·p] ~ **sth** (**off**) (**from sth**) draw (liquid) through the tap of a barrel: *tap off some cider* ○ *tap cider from a cask.* **2** (**a**) [Tn] cut the bark of (a tree) in order to collect the sap: *tap rubber-trees.* (**b**) [Tn, Tn·pr, Tn·p] ~ **sth** (**off**) collect (sap) in this way. **3** [Tn, Tn·pr] ~ **sth/sb** (**for sth**) extract or obtain (sth) from sth/sb: *vast mineral wealth waiting to be tapped* ○ *new ways of tapping the skills of young people* ○ (*infml*) *tap sb for a loan.* **4** [Tn] fit a listening device to (a telephone line): *I think my phone is being tapped.*
□ **ˈtap-root** *n* chief root of a plant, growing straight downwards.
ˈtap-water *n* [U] water supplied through pipes to taps in a building, esp contrasted with types of bottled water.

tap[2] /tæp/ *n* **1** [C] (sound of a) quick light blow: *They heard a tap at the door.* ○ *He felt a tap on his shoulder.* ○ *She gave the lid a few gentle taps to loosen it.* **2 taps** [sing *v*] (*US*) (in the armed forces) last bugle call of the day, the signal for lights to be put out.
▷ **tap** *v* (**-pp-**) **1** (**a**) [Tn, Tn·pr] ~ **sb/sth** (**with sth**) knock gently on sb/sth: *tab sb on the shoulder* ○ *He tapped the box with a stick.* (**b**) [Tn, Tn·pr] ~ **sth** (**against/on sth**) strike (sth) lightly with sth: *tapping her fingers on the table.* **2** [I, Ipr] ~ (**at/on sth**) give a tap or taps: *Who's that tapping at the window?*
□ **ˈtap-dance** *n* dance in which an elaborate rhythm is tapped with the feet. — *v* [I] perform this dance. **ˈtap-dancer** *n.* **ˈtap-dancing** *n* [U].

tape /teɪp/ *n* **1** [C, U] (piece of a) narrow strip of material used for tying, fastening or labelling things: *three yards of linen tape* ○ *a parcel tied up with tape* ○ *The seat covers are held in place by tapes.* **2** [C] piece of this stretched across a race-track at the finishing-line: *He breasted/broke the tape* (ie finished the race) *half a second ahead of his rival.* **3** [U] strip of paper or other flexible material coated with adhesive for fastening packages, etc: *sticky tape* ○ *insulating tape.* **4** [U] narrow continuous strip of paper on which a teleprinter prints a message. **5** [C, U] (reel of) magnetic tape; recording made on this: *The police seized various books and tapes.* ○ *make a tape of sb's conversation* ○ *listening to a tape of the Beatles* ○ *I've got all the Beethoven symphonies on tape.* **6** [C] = TAPE-MEASURE.
▷ **tape** *v* **1** [Tn, Tn·p] ~ **sth** (**up**) tie or fasten sth with tape. **2** [Tn] record (sb/sth) on magnetic tape: *taped a concert off/from the radio.* **3** (idm) **have** (**got**) **sb/sth taped** (*infml esp Brit*) understand sb/sth fully; be able to manage, influence or control sb/sth: *It took me a while to learn the rules of the game but I think I've got them taped now.*
□ **ˈtape deck** tape recorder as one component in a hi-fi system.
ˈtape-measure *n* (also **tape**, **ˈmeasuring tape**) strip of tape or flexible metal marked in inches or centimetres, etc for measuring length.
ˈtape-recorder *n* apparatus for recording sounds on magnetic tape and playing back the recording.
ˈtape-recording *n* recording made on magnetic tape.
ˈtapeworm *n* tape-like worm that lives as a parasite in the intestines of man and other animals.

taper[1] /ˈteɪpə(r)/ *n* length of wax-covered thread like a very thin candle burned to give light or to light other candles, etc: *put a taper to the fire.*

taper[2] /ˈteɪpə(r)/ *v* **1** [I, Ipr, Ip, Tn, Tn·pr, Tn·p] ~ (**sth**) (**off**) (**to sth**) become or make (sth) gradually narrower: *tapering at the ends* ○ *a blade that tapers off to a fine point* ○ *The trouser legs are slightly* *tapered*. Cf FLARE². **2** [Ip, Tn·p] ~ **(sth) off** (cause sth to) become less in amount, etc or to cease gradually: *The number of applicants for the course has been tapering off recently.* ○ *taper off production.*

▷ **taper** *n* (usu *sing*) gradual narrowing of a long object: *trousers with a slight taper.*

tapestry /ˈtæpəstrɪ/ *n* [C, U] (piece of) cloth into which threads of coloured wool are woven or embroidered by hand to make pictures or designs, used for covering walls and furniture.

▷ **tapestried** *adj* hung or decorated with tapestries: *tapestried walls.*

tapioca /ˌtæpɪˈəʊkə/ *n* [U] starchy food in hard white grains, obtained from the cassava plant.

tapir /ˈteɪpə(r)/ *n* small pig-like animal of tropical America and Malaysia, with a long flexible nose.

tappet /ˈtæpɪt/ *n* projection in a piece of machinery that causes a certain movement by tapping against sth, used eg to open and close a valve.

taps ➪ TAP² 2.

tar¹ /tɑː(r)/ *n* [U] **1** thick black sticky liquid, hard when cold, obtained from coal, etc and used in making roads, to preserve timber, etc. **2** similar substance formed by burning tobacco: [attrib] *low-/middle-/high-tar cigarettes.*

▷ **tar** *v* (**-rr-**) **1** [Tn] cover (sth) with tar: *a tarred road, rope, roof.* Cf TARMAC. **2** (idm) **tar and ˈfeather sb** put tar on sb and then cover him with feathers, as a punishment. **tarred with the same ˈbrush (as sb)** having the same faults (as sb).

tar² /tɑː(r)/ *n* (also **Jack tar**) (*dated infml*) sailor.

taradiddle /ˈtærədɪdl; *US* ˌtærəˈdɪdl/ *n* (*dated infml*) **1** [C] petty lie; fib. **2** [U] nonsense: *That's all taradiddle!*

taramasalata /ˌtærəməsəˈlɑːtə/ *n* [U] edible (usu pink) paste made from the smoked roe of mullet or cod.

tarantella /ˌtærənˈtelə/ *n* (music for a) fast whirling Italian dance.

tarantula /təˈræntjʊlə; *US* -tʃələ/ *n* any of several types of large spider, many of them hairy and some of them poisonous.

tarboosh /tɑːˈbuːʃ/ *n* brimless felt cap like a fez, worn by Muslim men in certain countries.

tardy /ˈtɑːdɪ/ *adj* (**-ier, -iest**) (*fml*) **1** slow to act, move or happen: *tardy in offering help* ○ *tardy progress, repentance, recognition.* **2** (of actions, etc; *US* also of people) late: *a tardy arrival, return, departure, etc* ○ *be tardy for/to school.* ▷ **tardily** /-ɪlɪ/ *adv.* **tardiness** *n* [U].

tare /teə(r)/ *n* **1** weight of the container in which goods are packed, or of the vehicle carrying them. **2** allowance made for this when the goods are weighed together with their container or vehicle.

target /ˈtɑːgɪt/ *n* **1** object or mark that a person tries to hit in shooting, etc; disc marked with concentric circles for this purpose in archery. ➪ illus at ARCHERY. **2** person or thing against which criticism, etc is directed: *become the target of scorn, derision, spite, etc.* **3** result aimed at; objective: *meet one's export targets* ○ *Production so far this year is on/off target.* ○ *The embassy is an obvious target for terrorist attacks.* ○ [attrib] *a target date*, ie one set for completion of a project, etc. **4** (*US*) circular railway signal showing whether points (POINT¹18) are open or closed.

▷ **target** *v* [usu passive: Tn, Tn·pr] ~ **sth (at/on sth/sb)** aim sth: *missiles targeted on Britain* ○ *a sales campaign targeted at the youth market.*

tariff /ˈtærɪf/ *n* **1** list of fixed charges, esp for rooms, meals, etc at a hotel. **2** duty to be paid on imports or (less often) exports: [attrib] *raise tariff barriers against foreign goods.* Cf TAX 1.

Tarmac /ˈtɑːmæk/ *n* [U] (**a**) (*propr*) (also **tar macadam**) material for surfacing roads, etc, consisting of broken stone mixed with tar. (**b**) **tarmac** area surfaced with this, esp on an airfield: *The plane taxied along the tarmac.* Cf MACADAM.

▷ **tarmac** *v* (*pt, pp* **tarmacked**, *pres p* **tarmacking**) [Tn] surface (sth) with Tarmac: *I'm going to tarmac the front drive.*

tarn /tɑːn/ *n* (often in names) small mountain lake.

tarnish /ˈtɑːnɪʃ/ *v* **1** [I, Tn] (cause sth to) lose its brightness by being exposed to air or damp: *mirrors that have tarnished with age* ○ *The brasswork needs polishing — it's badly tarnished.* **2** [Tn] stain or blemish (a reputation, etc): *The firm's good name was badly tarnished by the scandal.*

▷ **tarnish** *n* [C, U] loss of brightness; stain or blemish: *remove the tarnish from silver.*

taro /ˈtɑːrəʊ/ *n* (*pl* ~**s**) tropical plant with a starchy root used as food, esp in the Pacific islands.

tarot /ˈtærəʊ/ *n* (**a**) [C] any one of a special pack of cards used mainly for fortune-telling. (**b**) [sing] game played with these: *playing the tarot* ○ [attrib] *tarot cards.*

tarpaulin /tɑːˈpɔːlɪn/ *n* [C, U] (sheet or covering of) canvas made waterproof, esp by being treated with tar: *goods on a lorry covered by a tarpaulin.*

tarragon /ˈtærəgən; *US* -gɒn/ *n* [U] (herb with) leaves that are used for flavouring salads and vinegar: *add a sprinkling of dried tarragon.*

tarry¹ /ˈtærɪ/ *v* (*pt, pp* **tarried**) [I, Ipr] (*arch or rhet*) delay in coming to or going from a place; linger: *Tarry awhile at this charming country inn.*

tarry² /ˈtɑːrɪ/ *adj* (**-ier, -iest**) of, like or covered with tar.

tarsal /ˈtɑːsl/ *adj* (*anatomy*) of the bones in the ankle.

▷ **tarsal** *n* (*anatomy*) one of the bones in the ankle. ➪ illus at SKELETON.

tarsus /ˈtɑːsəs/ *n* (*pl* **tarsi** /-saɪ/) (*anatomy*) group of seven small bones in the ankle.

tart¹ /tɑːt/ *adj* **1** sharp-tasting; acid: *This fruit tastes rather tart.* **2** [usu attrib] (*fig*) sharp in manner; cutting or sarcastic: *a tart remark, reply, tone* ○ *He can be quite tart.* ▷ **tartly** *adv.* **tartness** *n* [U].

tart² /tɑːt/ *n* **1** (*esp Brit*) pie containing fruit or other sweet filling, often without a covering of pastry. **2** small circle of pastry cooked with jam, etc on it. Cf FLAN.

tart³ /tɑːt/ *n* (*sl*) **1** prostitute. **2** (*derog*) girl or woman, esp one regarded as being sexually immoral.

▷ **tart** *v* (phr v) ~ **sb/sth up** (*infml*) dress or decorate sb/sth in a gaudy way; smarten sb/sth up, esp cheaply or superficially: *tarting herself up for the disco* ○ *They've tarted up the restaurant but the food hasn't improved.*

tartan /ˈtɑːtn/ *n* **1** [C, U] pattern of coloured stripes crossing at right angles, esp one associated with a Scottish clan. **2** [U] woollen fabric woven in such a pattern: [attrib] *a tartan skirt.* ➪ article at SCOTLAND.

tartar¹ /ˈtɑːtə(r)/ *n* [U] **1** hard chalky deposit that forms on the teeth. Cf PLAQUE². **2** reddish deposit that forms on the inside of a cask in which wine is fermented.

▷ **tartaric** /tɑːˈtærɪk/ *adj* of or derived from tartar.

□ **tarˌtaric ˈacid** acid of tartar, found in many plants and the juice of fruit, and used in making baking powder, etc.

tartar² /ˈtɑːtə(r)/ *n* person who has a violent temper or is difficult to deal with.

tartar sauce (also **tartare sauce**) /ˌtɑːtə ˈsɔːs/ cold sauce of mayonnaise with chopped onions, herbs, capers, gherkins, etc, eaten esp with fish.

Tarzan /ˈtɑːzn/ *n* **1** (in stories by the American writer Edgar Rice *Burroughs) son of an English nobleman who is left as a baby in the African jungle, is brought up by apes and grows up to be a strong muscular man with the jungle as his home. **2** (*infml often joc*) any strong muscular agile man.

task /tɑːsk; *US* tæsk/ *n* **1** piece of (esp hard or unpleasant) work that has to be done: *holiday tasks* ○ *I set myself the task of chopping up the firewood.* ○ *perform the gruesome task of identifying the dead bodies* ○ *Becoming fluent in a foreign language is no easy task*, ie is difficult. ➪ Usage at WORK¹. **2** (idm) **take sb to task (about/for/over sth)** rebuke or criticize sb: *I was taken to task for arriving late.* ○ *She took the government to task over its economic record.*

▷ **task** *v* [Tn·pr esp passive] ~ **sb with sth** give sth to sb as a task: *tasked with the design of a new shopping centre.*

□ **ˈtask force** group of people and resources specially organized for a particular (esp military) task.

ˈtaskmaster (*fem* **ˈtaskmistress**) *n* person who is strict in making others work hard: *a hard taskmaster.*

Tasmania /tæzˈmeɪnɪə/ state of Australia consisting of an island off the coast of Victoria. The island was discovered in 1642 by the Dutch explorer Abel Tasman, after whom it is named. Much of it is covered with forests. ➪ map at App 1.

Tasman Sea /ˌtæzmən ˈsiː/ **the Tasman Sea** part of the South Pacific that lies between Australia and New Zealand.

TASS /tæs/ *abbr* USSR news agency which has survived the break-up of the Soviet Union. (Russian *Telegrafnoye Agentstvo Sovietskovo Soyuza*).

tassel

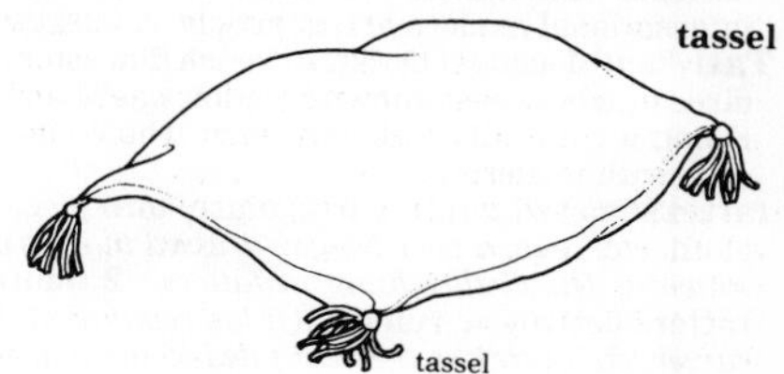

tassel /ˈtæsl/ *n* bunch of threads tied at one end and hanging (from a cushion, table-cloth, hat, etc) as an ornament.

▷ **tasselled** (*US* **tasseled**) *adj* ornamented with a tassel or tassels.

taste¹ /teɪst/ *n* **1** [C, U] sensation caused in the tongue by things placed on it: *Sugar has a sweet taste.* ○ *a strong taste of garlic* ○ *I don't like the taste of this cheese.* ○ *a wine that has no/very little/not much taste.* **2** [U] sense by which flavour is known: *I've got a cold and so I have no taste/have lost my sense of taste.* ○ *bitter to the taste.* **3** [C usu *sing*] ~ **(of sth)** (**a**) small quantity of food or drink taken as a sample: *Just have a taste of this cheese!* (**b**) (*fig*) first/early experience of sth: *her first taste of life in a big city* ○ *Although we didn't know it, this incident was a taste of things to come.* **4** [C, U] ~ **(for sth)** liking or preference: *She has a taste for foreign travel.* ○ *have expensive tastes in clothes* ○ *Modern art is not (to) everyone's taste*, ie Many people dislike it. **5** [U] ability to perceive and enjoy what is beautiful or harmonious, or to behave in an appropriate and a pleasing way: *have excellent taste in clothes, art, music, etc.* ○ *He's got more money than taste*, ie is rich but unrefined. ○ *a room furnished in/with perfect taste* ○ *It would be bad taste to refuse their invitation.* **6** (idm) **an acquired taste** ➪ ACQUIRE. **(be) in good, bad, poor, the best of, the worst of, etc ˈtaste** (of sb's behaviour, etc) appropriate and pleasing/unsuitable and offensive: *She always dresses in the best possible taste.* ○ *I thought his jokes were in very poor taste.* **leave a bad/nasty taste in the mouth** ➪ LEAVE¹. **there's no accounting for taste** ➪ ACCOUNT². **to ˈtaste** (esp in recipes) in the amount preferred: *Add salt to taste.*

▷ **tasteful** /-fl/ *adj* showing good taste¹(5). **tastefully** /-fəlɪ/ *adv*: *tastefully decorated.* **tastefulness** *n* [U].

tasteless *adj* **1** having no flavour. **2** showing poor taste¹(5): *tasteless jokes.* **tastelessly** *adv.* **tastelessness** *n* [U].

tasty *adj* (**-ier, -iest**) having a strong and pleasant flavour; appetizing: *a tasty dish.* **tastily** /-ɪlɪ/ *adv.* **tastiness** *n* [U].

□ **ˈtaste-bud** *n* (usu *pl*) any of the small projections on the tongue by which flavours are perceived.

taste² /teɪst/ *v* **1** [I, Tn] (not used in the continuous tenses; often with *can*) be able to perceive (flavours): *I can't taste, I've got a bad cold.* ○ *Can you taste the garlic in this stew?* **2** [La, Ipr] ~ **(of sth)** have a certain (specified) flavour: *taste sour, bitter, sweet, etc* ○ *It tastes strongly of mint.* **3** [Tn] test the flavour of (sth): *He tasted the soup to see if he had put enough salt in it.* ➪ Usage at FEEL¹. **4** [Tn] eat or drink (food or liquid): *They hadn't tasted hot food for over a week.* ○ *That's the best wine I've ever tasted.* **5** [Tn] (*fig*) experience (sth): *taste power, freedom, failure, defeat, etc.*

▷ **taster** *n* person whose job is to judge the quality of wine, tea, etc by tasting it.

tasting *n* event at which sth is tasted: *go to a wine/cheese tasting.*
-tasting (forming compound *adjs*) having the specified flavour or taste: *sweet-tasting* ○ *fresh-tasting.*

tat[1] /tæt/ *v* (**-tt-**) (**a**) [I] do tatting. (**b**) [Tn] make (sth) by tatting.

tat[2] /tæt/ *n* [U] (*Brit infml*) tatty things; shoddy or shabby goods: *a shop selling dreadful old tat.*

tat[3] /tæt/ *n* (idm) **tit for tat** ⇨ TIT[2].

ta-ta /tə ˈtɑː/ *interj* (*Brit infml*) goodbye.

Tate Gallery /teɪt ˈɡælərɪ/ **the Tate Gallery** art gallery in London which contains the main national collections of British art and of international modern art. ⇨ article at MUSEUM.

Tati /ˈtætɪ/ Jacques (1908-82), French film actor and director whose best-known creation was Monsieur Hulot, a comically awkward man who could not cope with modern life.

tatters /ˈtætəz/ *n* [pl] **1** irregularly torn pieces of cloth, etc; rags: *a poor beggar dressed in rags and tatters* ○ *His clothes hung in tatters.* **2** (idm) **in tatters** destroyed; ruined: *left his reputation, life, career, etc in tatters* ○ *She replied to my points so convincingly that my argument was soon in tatters.*
▷ **tattered** *adj* ragged.

Tattersalls /ˈtætəslz/ English firm of race-horse auctioneers founded in 1776.

tatting /ˈtætɪŋ/ *n* [U] (**a**) type of lace that is made by hand and used for trimming. (**b**) process of making this.

tattle /ˈtætl/ *v* [I] chatter or gossip idly; reveal information by doing this: *Who's been tattling?*
▷ **tattle** *n* [U] idle chatter or gossip.
tattler /ˈtætlə(r)/ (*US* ˈ**tattle-tale**) *n* person who tattles.

tattoo[1] /təˈtuː; *US* tæˈtuː/ *n* (*pl* ~**s**) **1** [sing] evening drum or bugle signal calling soldiers back to their quarters: *beat/sound the tattoo.* **2** [C] elaborate version of this with music and marching, performed as a public entertainment: *a torchlight tattoo.* **3** [C] drumming or tapping: *beating a tattoo on the table with his fingers.*

tattoo[2] /təˈtuː; *US* tæˈtuː/ *v* [Tn, Tn·pr] (**a**) mark (sb's skin) with a permanent picture or pattern by pricking it and inserting a dye. (**b**) put (a picture or pattern) on the skin in this way: *He had a ship tattooed on his arm.*
▷ **tattoo** *n* (*pl* ~**s**) tattooed picture or pattern: *His chest was covered in tattoos.* ○ [attrib] *a tattoo artist.*

tatty /ˈtætɪ/ *adj* (**-ier, -iest**) (*infml*) **1** shabby and untidy; ragged: *tatty old clothes.* **2** cheap and tawdry. ▷ **tattily** /-ɪlɪ/ *adv.* **tattiness** *n* [U].

taught *pt, pp* of TEACH.

taunt /tɔːnt/ *v* [Tn, Tn·pr] ~ **sb** (**with sth**) try to provoke sb with scornful or critical remarks; jeer at sb: *They taunted him with cowardice/with being a coward.*
▷ **taunt** *n* (often *pl*) taunting remark: *ignoring the taunts of the opposition.*
tauntingly *adv.*

Taurus /ˈtɔːrəs/ *n* **1** (**a**) [U] the second sign of the zodiac, the Bull. ⇨ illus at ZODIAC. (**b**) [C] person born under the influence of this sign. **2** constellation containing the star *Aldebaran and the star cluster the *Pleiades. ▷ **Taurean** *n, adj.* ⇨ Usage at ZODIAC.

taut /tɔːt/ *adj* **1** (of rope, wire, cloth, etc) tightly stretched; not slack. **2** (of muscles or nerves) tense. ▷ **tautly** *adv.* **tautness** *n* [U].

tauten /ˈtɔːtn/ *v* [I, Tn] (cause sth to) become taut.

tautology /tɔːˈtɒlədʒɪ/ *n* (**a**) [U] saying the same thing more than once in different ways without making one's meaning clearer or more forceful; needless repetition. (**b**) [C] instance of this. Cf PLEONASM. ▷ **tautological** /ˌtɔːtəˈlɒdʒɪkl/, **tautologous** /tɔːˈtɒləɡəs/ *adjs.*

tavern /ˈtævən/ *n* (*arch or rhet*) inn or public house.

TAVR *abbr* = T AND AVR.

tawdry /ˈtɔːdrɪ/ *adj* (**-ier, -iest**) showy or gaudy but without real value: *tawdry jewellery, furnishings.*
▷ **tawdrily** /-əlɪ/ *adv.* **tawdriness** *n* [U].

Tawney /ˈtɔːnɪ/ Richard Henry (1880-1962), British socialist and economic historian who wrote on capitalism, his best-known book being *Religion and the Rise of Capitalism.* He was influential in the early history of the British Labour Party.

tawny /ˈtɔːnɪ/ *adj* brownish-yellow: *the lion's tawny mane.*

tawse /tɔːz/ *n* leather strap formerly used for whipping pupils as a punishment in Scottish schools.

tax /tæks/ *n* **1** [C, U] (sum of) money to be paid by people or businesses to a government for public purposes: *income/property/sales tax* ○ *value-added tax* ○ *levy a tax on sth* ○ *direct/indirect taxes* ○ *paid over £1 000 in taxes last year* ○ [attrib] *tax evasion.* Cf DUTY 3, TARIFF 2. **2** (idm) **a tax on sth** a burden or strain on sth: *a tax on one's health, patience, strength, etc.*
▷ **tax** *v* [Tn] **1** impose a tax on (sb/sth); require (sb) to pay tax: *tax luxuries* ○ *tax rich and poor alike* ○ *My income is taxed at source,* ie Tax is deducted from it before it is paid to me. **2** make heavy demands on (sth); strain: *His constant requests for help taxed our goodwill.* ○ *All these questions are beginning to tax my patience.* **3** pay tax on (sth): *The car is taxed until July.* **4** (idm) **tax one's/sb's brain(s)** set sb/oneself a difficult mental task: *This crossword will really tax your brain.* **5** (phr v) **tax sb with sth** (*fml*) accuse sb of sth: *She was taxed with negligence/with having been negligent.* **taxable** *adj* that can be or is liable to be taxed: *taxable earnings.* **taxing** *adj* tiring or demanding: *a taxing job.*
taxation /tækˈseɪʃn/ *n* [U] (system of) raising money by taxes; taxes to be paid: *direct/indirect taxation,* ie on incomes/expenditure ○ *reduce/increase taxation.* ⇨ article.
□ ˌ**tax-deˈductible** *adj* (of expenses) that may be deducted from income before the amount of tax to be paid is calculated.
ˈ**tax disc** (*Brit*) = ROAD TAX DISC (ROAD).
ˌ**tax-ˈfree** *adj* on which tax need not be paid: *a* ˌ*tax-free* ˈ*bonus.*
ˈ**tax haven** country where income tax, etc is low.
ˈ**taxman** /-mæn/ *n* (*pl* **-men** /-men/) **1** [C] person whose job is to collect taxes. **2 the taxman** [sing] (*infml*) government department that is responsible for collecting taxes: *He had been cheating the taxman for years.*
ˈ**taxpayer** *n* person who pays taxes (esp income tax).
ˈ**tax return** statement of personal income, etc, used for calculating the amount of tax to be paid.

taxi /ˈtæksɪ/ (also ˈ**taxi-cab**, *esp US* **cab**) *n* car that may be hired for journeys, esp one with a meter that records the fare to be paid: *call/hail/hire/take a taxi.*
▷ **taxi** *v* [I, Ipr, Ip] (of an aircraft) move along on the ground or on water under its own power, esp before or after flying: *The plane taxied/was taxiing along the runway.*
□ ˈ**taxi rank** (ˈ**taxi stand**, *US* ˈ**cabstand**) place where taxis park while waiting to be hired.

taxidermy /ˈtæksɪdɜːmɪ/ *n* [U] art of preparing and stuffing the skins of dead animals, birds and fish so that they look like living ones.
▷ **taxidermist** /-ɪst/ *n* person who practises taxidermy.

taxonomy /tækˈsɒnəmɪ/ *n* (**a**) [U] scientific process of classifying living things. (**b**) [C] instance of this. ▷ **taxonomical** /ˌtæksəˈnɒmɪkl/ *adj.* **taxonomically** /-klɪ/ *adv.* **taxonomist** /tækˈsɒnəmɪst/ *n.*

Taylor /ˈteɪlə(r)/ Elizabeth (1932-), American actress. Her film career began early with *National Velvet* and she later starred in many Hollywood successes, like *Who's Afraid of Virginia Woolf?,* in which she starred with Richard *Burton, to whom she was twice married.

Tayside /ˈteɪsaɪd/ local government region of eastern Scotland, containing the city of Dundee. ⇨ map at App 1.

TB /ˌtiː ˈbiː/ *abbr* tuberculosis: *be vaccinated against TB.*

Tb *symb* terbium.

tbsp (*pl* **tbsps**) *abbr* tablespoonful: *Add 3 tbsps salt.*

Tc *symb* technetium.

Tchaikovsky /tʃaɪˈkɒfskɪ/ Pyotr Ilyich (1840-93), Russian composer. His music, which is characterized by romantic melodies, includes six symphonies, three piano concertos and a violin concerto, the operas *The Queen of Spades* and *Eugene Onegin,* and several ballet scores (eg *Swan Lake, The Sleeping Beauty* and *The Nutcracker*). He was homosexual, and it is believed that he committed suicide to avoid a scandal.

Te *symb* tellurium.

te (also **ti**) /tiː/ *n* (*music*) seventh note in the sol-fa scale.

tea /tiː/ *n* **1** [U] (dried leaves of an) evergreen shrub grown in China, India, etc: *a pound of tea.* **2** (**a**) [U] drink made by pouring boiling water on these leaves: *a cup/mug/pot of tea* ○ *China, lemon, iced tea* ○ *Shall I make (the) tea?* (**b**) [C] cup of this: *Two teas, please.* ⇨ article at DRINK.
Tea is traditionally the most popular drink in Britain, and is usually drunk with milk and sometimes sugar. People may drink tea at any time of day, but especially at breakfast time. Tea is drunk in many different social situations. It may form part of an afternoon tea party, served in elegant china cups and saucers and accompanied by sandwiches and cakes, but it is just as popular drunk from large mugs as a morning or afternoon 'brew' (or 'cuppa') at work. Tea also suggests comfort and warmth, and sitting down with a 'nice cup of tea' is a common response to problems and worries.
3 [U] drink made by pouring boiling water on the leaves of other plants: *camomile, mint, herb tea.* **4** [C, U] (light meal served at an) occasion when tea is drunk, esp in the late afternoon: *The waitress has served twenty teas since 4 o'clock.* ○ *We usually have tea at half-past four.* ○ *When is tea?* ⇨ Usage at DINNER. **5** (idm) **sb's cup of tea** ⇨ CUP[1]. **not for all the tea in** ˈ**China** no matter how great the reward: *I wouldn't marry him for all the tea in China.*
□ ˈ**tea-bag** *n* small paper bag holding enough tea for one person.
ˈ**tea-break** *n* (*Brit*) (in an office, a factory, etc) short period of time when work is stopped and tea, etc may be taken.
ˈ**tea-caddy** (also **caddy**) *n* box in which tea is kept for daily use.
ˈ**teacake** *n* **1** (*Brit*) large flat bun, usu eaten hot with butter at tea: *toasted teacakes.* **2** (*US*) small sweet cake.
ˈ**tea-chest** *n* light wooden box lined with metal, in which tea is exported.
ˈ**tea-cloth** *n* **1** cloth for a tea-table or tea-tray. **2** (*Brit*) = TEA-TOWEL.
ˈ**tea-cosy** *n* cover placed over a teapot to keep the tea inside it warm.
ˈ**teacup** *n* **1** cup in which tea is served. **2** (idm) **a storm in a teacup** ⇨ STORM.
ˈ**tea lady** (*Brit*) woman employed to make tea for workers in an office, etc.
ˈ**tea-leaf** *n* (*pl* **-leaves**) leaf of tea, esp after tea has been made: *throw away the old tea-leaves* ○ *tell sb's fortune from the tea-leaves in his cup.* ⇨ article at SUPERSTITION.
ˈ**tea-party** *n* social occasion at which tea is served esp in the late afternoon.
ˈ**teapot** *n* container with a spout, in which tea is made and from which it is poured into cups, etc. ⇨ illus at POT. (idm) **a tempest in a teapot** ⇨ TEMPEST.
ˈ**tea-room** (also ˈ**tea-shop**) *n* (usu small) restaurant in which tea and light meals are served ⇨ article at EAT.
ˈ**tea rose** rose having pink or yellow flowers with a scent like tea.
ˈ**tea-service** (also ˈ**tea-set**) *n* set of cups, plates, etc for serving tea.
ˈ**teaspoon** *n* **1** small spoon for stirring tea, etc. ⇨ illus at SPOON. **2** amount that this can hold.
ˈ**teaspoonful** /-fʊl/ *n* amount that a teaspoon can hold: *two teaspoonfuls of sugar.*
ˈ**tea-strainer** *n* device for holding back tea-leaves when pouring tea into a cup, etc.
ˈ**tea-table** *n* (usu small) table at which tea is served: [attrib] *tea-table conversation.*
ˈ**tea-things** *n* [pl] (*infml*) = TEA-SERVICE.
ˈ**tea-time** *n* [U] time at or during which tea is taken in the afternoon.
ˈ**tea-towel** *n* (also **tea-cloth**, *US* ˈ**dish towel**

Taxation

In Britain and the USA a variety of taxes are collected in order to pay for government expenditure. The three main kinds of taxation are taxes on income and profits, taxes on capital and taxes on expenditure.

The British financial year runs from April to March and in March each year the Chancellor of the Exchequer presents a budget for the coming year in the House of Commons. Most changes to taxes are made then and new taxes may be introduced.

Income tax is paid on earnings, profits and investment income. Every taxpayer has a personal allowance, an amount of money that is tax-free, and above this allowance all income is taxed. In 1991 there were two bands of income tax, the first taxed at 25 per cent and a higher band taxed at 40 per cent for people with higher than average incomes.

Employees pay tax through the Pay-As-You-Earn (PAYE) system by which tax is deducted by the employer from weekly or monthly earnings and paid to the Inland Revenue (the government body responsible for collecting taxes on income and capital). People who do not pay tax by the PAYE method normally fill in a statement of their earnings (called a tax return) and pay tax directly to the Inland Revenue. Companies pay corporation tax on their profits. In 1991 the rate was 35 per cent, with a lower 25 per cent rate for small companies. There is a special 75 per cent tax on the profits earned from North Sea oil production.

The main taxes on capital are inheritance tax, which is paid on transfers of wealth made on a person's death or in the seven years before it, and capital gains tax (CGT), which is paid at the same rate as income tax on the gains made when assets such as property or shares are sold. A person's home is exempt from capital gains tax.

Taxes on expenditure include Value Added Tax (VAT), customs duties and excise duties. Value Added Tax is a percentage added to the price of goods and services and collected by the Customs and Excise department. In 1991 it was 17.5 per cent. Certain categories of goods are exempt, including food, books, periodicals, children's clothes, public transport and fuel (except petrol). Customs duties are paid on imports except imports from other EC countries. Excise duties are taxes on petrol, alcohol, cigarettes and tobacco, gambling and vehicles.

In addition to the taxes paid to central government, there is a tax payable to the local authority in each area. Formerly a tax on each dwelling, called 'the rates', it was replaced in 1990 by the community charge, a tax on every person on the electoral register (the list of people eligible to vote) in an area. This tax, popularly called the 'poll tax' was extremely unpopular and caused widespread protests. It was in turn replaced in 1991 by a 'council tax', a compromise between the rates as a property-based tax and the community charge. The business rates charged by local authorities were replaced in 1990 by a unified business rate payable to central government.

In the USA, there are two income tax percentage rates, as in Britain, but they are about one third lower. The amount of income that is taxable at one or the other rate varies for single people, married couples, people with children, etc. There is a scheme similar to PAYE, but it is based on a person's estimate of what earnings will be for the coming year, and income tax is deducted on the basis of that. Tax is calculated on the basis of a percentage plus a flat fee which varies according to the level of income. At the end of the tax year (which is the same as the calendar year), the taxpayer has to fill in a complicated form with details of what was actually earned. The difference between what has been deducted and what *should* have been deducted is then paid or refunded, as appropriate.

People who earn less than a specified minimum do not have to complete a tax return. The amount varies, again, according to the person's status. For a couple under pension age (65), for example, it is about $10 000.

In the USA income tax is collected by the Internal Revenue Service (IRS). Some states charge a local income tax in addition to the federal tax. Even where this is the case, however, US income tax levels are still lower than the British.

As well as income tax, other US taxes include gift tax on amounts over $10 000 to a single person in a single year, estate tax (the equivalent of British inheritance tax) on money and property over $40 000, sales tax (the equivalent of British capital gains tax) on the sale of personal property, and property tax (the equivalent of the British council tax) as a local state tax on the value of a person's property.

towel for drying washed crockery, cutlery, etc.

ˈtea-tray *n* small tray suitable for carrying a tea-set, etc.

ˈtea-trolley (also **ˈtea-wagon**) *n* small table on wheels, used for serving tea. ⇨ illus at TROLLEY.

ˈtea-urn *n* container in which water is boiled for making a large quantity of tea, eg in a café. ⇨ illus at URN.

teach /tiːtʃ/ *v* (*pt, pp* **taught** /tɔːt/) **1** (a) [I, Tn, Dn·w, Dn·t] give instruction to (sb); cause (sb) to know or be able to do sth: *She teaches well.* ○ *teach children* ○ *He taught me (how) to drive.* (b) [Tn, Dn·n, Dn·pr] ~ **sth (to sb/sth)** communicate (knowledge, skill, etc): *teach French, history, judo, etc* ○ *She teaches advanced students English/teaches English to advanced students.* ○ *He's taught his dog some clever tricks.* **2** [I, Tn] do this for a living: *She teaches at our local school.* ○ *He taught mathematics for many years.* ⇨ Usage. **3** [Tn, Tf, Dn·n, Dn·f, Dn·t] put (sth) forward as a fact or as a principle; advocate: *Christ taught forgiveness,* ie that we should forgive our enemies, etc. ○ *He taught that the earth revolves around the sun.* ○ *My parents taught me never to tell lies.* **4** [no passive: Tn, Dn·n, Dn·t] (*infml*) persuade (sb) to do or not to do sth by punishment or as a result of experience: *So you lost all your money? That'll teach you (to gamble).* ○ *It taught him a lesson he never forgot.* ○ *I'll teach you to call me a liar!* ie punish you for doing so. **5** (idm) **know/learn/teach sb the ropes** ⇨ ROPE. **teach one's grandmother to suck ˈeggs** tell or show sb how to do sth that he can already do perfectly well, and probably better than oneself. **(you can't) teach an old dog new ˈtricks** (*saying*) (one can't) successfully get old people who are set in their ways to change their ideas, methods of work, etc. **teach ˈschool** (*US*) be a schoolteacher.

▷ **teachable** *adj* **1** (of a subject) that can be taught. **2** (of a person) able to learn by being taught.

teacher *n* person who teaches, esp in a school: *my English teacher.*

teaching *n* **1** [U] work of a teacher; instruction: *Teaching is a demanding profession.* **2** [U, C often *pl*] that which is taught; doctrine: *the teaching(s) of the Church.*

□ **ˈteach-in** *n* (*dated infml*) lecture and discussion, or a series of these, on a subject of topical interest.

ˈteaching hospital hospital where medical students are taught.

NOTE ON USAGE: **1 Educate** refers to the overall development of (especially children's) knowledge and intellect, usually through the formal **education** system of schools and universities: *He was educated at the local comprehensive school.* ○ *The country needs an educated population.* **2 Teach** has the widest use in formal and informal situations and at all levels. It can refer to an academic subject or a practical skill: *She teaches history at a secondary school/to undergraduates.* ○ *My father taught me how to swim.* **3 Coach** is used of non-formal teaching, either of an academic subject (especially for an examination) or of a sport: *I'm coaching their children in A level maths in the evenings.* ○ *She coaches the tennis team at the weekend.* **4 Train** means producing a desired result in behaviour, standard of skill or physical ability. It is sometimes contrasted with **educate**. It can be used of people or animals: *It's hard to train children to behave well at the table.* ○ *He's training the horse for the Grand National.* ○ *The swimming team's in training for the Olympics.* **5 Instruct** means giving practical information or knowledge, especially to groups of trainees (eg soldiers or nurses): *She instructed the trainee nurses in giving injections.*

teak /tiːk/ *n* (a) [U] strong hard wood of a tall evergreen Asian tree, used for making furniture, in shipbuilding, etc: [attrib] *a teak garden seat* ○ *teak oil,* ie for treating the wood. (b) [C] this tree.

teal /tiːl/ *n* (*pl* unchanged) small wild duck living near rivers or lakes.

team /tiːm/ *n* [CGp] **1** group of players forming one side in certain games and sports: *Which team do you play for?* ○ *Leeds was/were the better team.* **2** group of people working together: *a sales team* ○ [attrib] *He's a good team worker,* ie He works well with others. **3** two or more animals pulling a cart, plough, etc together.

▷ **team** *v* [Ipr, Ip] ~ **up (with sb)** work together (with sb), esp for a common purpose: *The two companies have teamed up to develop a new racing car.*

teamster /ˈtiːmstə(r)/ *n* (*US*) lorry driver. ⇨ article at TRADE UNION.

□ **ˈteam-mate** *n* fellow member of a team or group.

ˈteam ministry group of ministers who jointly serve several parishes.

ˌteam ˈspirit (*approv*) willingness to act for the good of one's team rather than one's individual advantage, etc.

ˈteam-work *n* [U] organized co-operation; combined effort: *The success of the project was largely the result of good team-work.*

tear[1] /tɪə(r)/ *n* **1** [C usu *pl*] drop of salty water coming from the eye, esp as the result of grief, irritation by fumes, etc: *A tear rolled down his cheek.* ○ *a tear-stained face* ○ *Her eyes filled with tears.* ○ *a story that moved/reduced us to tears,* ie made us cry ○ *shed/weep bitter tears* ○ *He burst into tears,* ie began to cry. ○ *The memory of his dead mother brought tears to his eyes.* **2** (idm) **bore sb to death/tears** ⇨ BORE[2]. **crocodile tears** ⇨ CROCODILE. **in ˈtears** crying: *She was in tears over the death of her puppy.* **without ˈtears** (*infml*) presented so as to be done or learnt easily: *French* *without tears.*

▷ **tearful** /-fl/ *adj* crying or ready to cry: *her tearful face* ○ *a crowd of tearful mourners.* **tearfully** /-fəlɪ/ *adv.*

□ ˈ**tear-drop** *n* single tear.

ˈ**tear-gas** *n* [U] gas that causes severe irritation and watering of the eyes, used to disperse crowds, etc.

ˈ**tear-jerker** *n* (*infml sometimes derog*) story, film, etc designed to make people cry in sympathy, etc.

tear² /teə(r)/ *v* (*pt* **tore** /tɔ:(r)/, *pp* **torn** /tɔ:n/) **1** (**a**) [Tn, Tn·pr, Tn·p, Cn·a] pull (sth) forcibly apart or away or to pieces: *tear a sheet of paper in two* ○ *a torn handkerchief* ○ *He tore his shirt on a nail.* ○ *tear a parcel open.* (**b**) [Tn·pr] ~ **sth** (**in sth**) make (a hole or split) in sth in this way: *The explosion tore a hole in the wall.* **2** (**a**) [Tn, Tn·pr, Tn·p] cause (sth) to be out of place by pulling sharply: *tear a page out of a book, a notice down from a wall, the leaves off a tree.* (**b**) [Tn·pr] ~ **sb from sb/sth** remove sb from sb/sth by force: *The child was torn from its mother's arms.* ⇨ Usage at CUT¹. **3** [I] become torn: *This cloth tears easily.* ○ *Don't pull the pages so hard or they will tear.* **4** [Tn, Tn·pr esp passive] destroy the peace of (sth): *a country torn by war* ○ *Her heart was torn by grief.* **5** [Ipr, Ip] move (in the specified direction) very quickly or excitedly: *cars tearing past* ○ *She tore downstairs and out of the house shouting 'Fire!'* **6** (idm) **tear sth aˈpart, to ˈshreds, to ˈbits, etc** destroy or defeat sth completely; criticize sth harshly: *tore his hopes to shreds* ○ *The critics tore her new play to pieces.* **tear one's ˈhair** (**out**) (*infml*) show great sorrow, anger, etc: *My boss is tearing his hair out about the delay in the schedule.* (**be in**) **a tearing ˈhurry, ˈrush, etc** (show) extreme or violent haste: *There's no need to be in such a tearing hurry - we've got plenty of time.* **tear sb ˌlimb from ˈlimb** (*often joc*) attack sb very violently. **tear sb ˈoff a strip; tear a ˈstrip off sb** (*infml*) scold sb severely. **ˌthat's ˈtorn it** (*infml*) that has spoilt our plans. **wear and tear** ⇨ WEAR¹. **7** (phr v) **tear at sth** (**with sth**) attack sth violently, esp by cutting or ripping: *tore at the meat with his bare hands.* **tear oneself away** (**from sb/sth**) leave sb/sth reluctantly: *Do tear yourself away from the television and come out for a walk.* **be torn between A and B** have to make a painful choice between two things or people: *torn between love and duty.* **tear sth down** bring sth to the ground by pulling sharply; demolish sth: *They're tearing down these old houses to build a new office block.* **tear into sb/sth** attack sb/sth physically or with words. **tear sth up** destroy (a document, etc) by tearing: *She tore up all the letters he had sent her.* ○ (*fig*) *He accused the government of tearing up* (ie repudiating) *the negotiated agreement.*

▷ **tear** *n* hole or split caused by tearing: *This fabric has a tear in it.*

□ ˈ**tearaway** /ˈteərəweɪ/ *n* (*infml*) impetuous and irresponsible person: *Her son's a bit of a tearaway.*

tease /ti:z/ *v* **1** [I, Tn, Tn·pr] make fun of (sb) in a playful or unkind way; try to provoke (sb) with questions or petty annoyances: *Don't take what she said seriously — she was only teasing.* ○ *The other boys used to tease him because of/about his accent.* ○ *Stop teasing the cat*, eg by pulling its tail. **2** [Tn] arouse the curiosity or sexual desire of (sb) without intending to satisfy it: *She has a reputation for teasing the men.* Cf STRIP-TEASE (STRIP). **3** (**a**) pick (wool) into separate strands. (**b**) brush up the surface of (cloth) to make it fluffy. **4** [Tn] (*esp US*) = BACKCOMB (BACK³).

▷ **tease** *n* person who is fond of teasing others: *What a tease she is!*

teaser *n* (*infml*) problem that is difficult to solve: *This one's a real teaser.*

teasingly *adv* in a teasing manner; in order to tease.

teasel (also **teazel, teazle**) /ˈti:zl/ *n* plant with prickly flowers formerly used (when dried) for teasing cloth, etc.

teat /ti:t/ *n* **1** animal's nipple. ⇨ illus at cow. **2** (also **nipple**) rubber mouthpiece on a child's feeding-bottle, through which the contents are sucked.

tech /tek/ *n* (usu *sing*) (*infml*) technical college or school: *doing an engineering course at the local tech.*

technical /ˈteknɪkl/ *adj* **1** [usu attrib] of or involving the mechanical arts and applied sciences: *a technical school* ○ *a technical education.* **2** [usu attrib] of a particular subject, art or craft, or its techniques: *the technical terms of chemistry* ○ *the technical difficulties of colour printing* ○ *a musician with great technical skill but not much feeling.* **3** (of a book, etc) requiring specialized knowledge; using technical terms: *The article is rather technical in places.* **4** [attrib] in a strict legal sense: *technical assault.*

▷ **technicality** /ˌteknɪˈkælətɪ/ *n* **1** technical term or point: *The book is full of scientific technicalities.* ○ *The lawyer explained the legal technicalities to his client.* **2** detail of no real importanc: *a mere technicality.*

technically /-klɪ/ *adv* **1** with reference to the technique displayed: *Technically the building is a masterpiece, but few people like it.* **2** according to a precise interpretation of the laws, meaning of words, etc; strictly: *Although technically (speaking) you may not have lied, you certainly haven't told us the whole truth.*

□ ˈ**technical college** (*Brit*) college offering students further education in technical and other subjects after they have left school.

ˌ**technical ˈhitch** breakdown caused by a mechanical fault.

ˌ**technical ˈknock-out** (in boxing) victory awarded by the referee to one boxer when the other is too badly hurt, tired, etc to continue.

technician /tekˈnɪʃn/ *n* **1** expert in the techniques of a particular subject, art or craft. **2** skilled mechanic.

Technicolor /ˈteknɪkʌlə(r)/ *n* [U] **1** (*propr*) process of colour photography used for cinema films. **2** (also **technicolour**) (*infml*) vivid or artificially brilliant colour: [attrib] *The fashion show was a technicolour extravaganza.*

technique /tekˈni:k/ *n* (**a**) [C] method of doing or performing sth, esp in the arts or sciences: *applying modern techniques to a traditional craft.* (**b**) [U] skill in this: *displayed (a) flawless technique.*

techno- *comb form* of the applied sciences: *technology* ○ *technocrat.*

technocracy /tekˈnɒkrəsɪ/ *n* (**a**) [U] control or management of a country's industrial resources by technical experts. (**b**) [C] country where this occurs: *Is Britain becoming a technocracy?*

▷ **technocrat** /ˈteknəkræt/ *n* expert in science, engineering, etc, esp one who favours technocracy. **technocratic** /ˌteknəˈkrætɪk/ *adj.*

technology /tekˈnɒlədʒɪ/ *n* [U] **1** scientific study and use of mechanical arts and applied sciences, eg engineering. **2** application of this to practical tasks in industry, etc: *recent advances in medical technology* ○ *the technology of computers.* ⇨ article.

▷ **technological** /ˌteknəˈlɒdʒɪkl/ *adj*: *a major technological breakthrough* ○ *technological changes, problems.* **technologically** /-klɪ/ *adv*: *technologically advanced.*

technologist /tekˈnɒlədʒɪst/ *n* expert in technology.

teddy bear /ˈtedɪ beə(r)/ soft furry toy bear.

📖 Teddy bears are very popular in Britain. Their popularity owes much to *Winnie the Pooh by A A *Milne, and to the Paddington Bear stories for children by Michael Bond, the first of which were published in 1960. Winnie the Pooh was based on the teddy bear belonging to Milne's son, Christopher Robin Milne, who appears in the stories as Christopher Robin. Paddington is a lovable, accident-prone, very 'human' bear. Teddy bears originated in the USA, where they were named after President Theodore (Teddy) *Roosevelt.

Teddy boy /ˈtedɪ bɔɪ/ (also **ted** /ted/) *n* (*Brit infml*) (in the 1950s) young man who expressed rebellion by wearing clothes similar to those of the Edwardian period (1901-10), and sometimes behaved violently.

tedious /ˈti:dɪəs/ *adj* tiresome because of being too long, slow or dull; boring: *The work is tedious.* ○ *We had to sit through several tedious speeches.* ▷ **tediously** *adv*: *tediously long.* **tediousness** *n* [U].

tedium /ˈti:dɪəm/ *n* [U] tediousness; boredom: *two hours of unrelieved tedium.*

tee /ti:/ *n* **1** (**a**) (in golf) flat area from which a player strikes the ball when beginning to play each hole. (**b**) small spiked stand of wood, plastic, etc on which a player places his golf ball before striking it at the start of each hole. **2** mark aimed at in certain games, eg quoits, bowls, curling. **3** (idm) **to a T/tee** ⇨ T.

▷ **tee** *v* (*pt, pp* **teed**) **1** [Tn] place (a golf ball) on a tee. **2** (phr v) **tee off** play the ball from the tee: (*fig*) *If no one else wants to start the discussion, shall I tee off first?* **tee off on sb** (*US sl*) attack sb with words criticize sb severely. **tee sb ˈoff** (*US sl*) make sb angry or annoyed. **tee** (**sth**) **up** prepare to play (a golf ball) by placing it on a tee.

teem¹ /ti:m/ *v* **1** [Ipr] ~ **with sth** have sth in great numbers: *The river was teeming with fish.* ○ (*fig*) *His mind is teeming with bright ideas.* **2** [I] be present in great numbers: *Fish teem in these waters.*

teem² /ti:m/ *v* [I, Ipr, Ip] ~ (**with sth**)/(**down**) (esp in the continuous tenses) (of water, rain, etc) fall heavily; pour: *a teeming wet day* ○ *It was teeming with rain.* ○ *The rain was teeming down.*

teens /ti:nz/ *n* [pl] years of a person's age from 13 to 19: *be in one's teens* ○ *She is not yet out of her teens* ie is under 20.

□ **teenage** /ˈti:neɪdʒ/ *adj* [attrib] of or for teenagers: *teenage fashions, problems, children.* **teenaged** *adj* in one's teens. **teenager** /ˈti:neɪdʒə(r)/ (also *infml esp US* **teen** /ti:n/) *n* person in his or her teens: *a club for teenagers.*

📖 In Britain, it was not until after the Second World War that teenagers began to be recognized as having their own interests and identity. The development of pop music, fashion and youth movements in the 1960s did much to bring this about.

teeny /ˈti:nɪ/ (also **teeny-weeny** /ˌti:nɪ ˈwi:nɪ/, **teensy** /ti:nzɪ/, **teensy-weensy** /ˌti:nzɪ ˈwi:nzɪ/) *adj* (**-ier, -iest**) (*infml*) tiny.

teeny-bopper /ˈti:nɪ bɒpə(r)/ *n* (*infml usu derog*) young teenager, esp a girl, who eagerly follows current fashions in clothes, pop music, etc.

tee-shirt = T-SHIRT (T).

teeter /ˈti:tə(r)/ *v* [I, Ipr, Ip] stand or move unsteadily: *The drunken man teetered on the edge of the pavement.* ○ *She was teetering along/about/around in very high-heeled shoes.* ○ (*fig*) *teetering on the brink/edge of disaster.*

teeth *pl of* TOOTH.

teethe /ti:ð/ *v* [I] (usu in the continuous tenses, or as a gerund or present participle) (of a baby) have its first teeth starting to grow through the gums: *Babies like to chew something when they're teething.*

□ ˈ**teething-ring** *n* ring, esp of plastic, which a baby can chew while it is teething.

ˈ**teething troubles** (*fig*) minor problems occurring in the early stages of an enterprise.

teetotal /ti:ˈtəʊtl; *US* ˈti:təʊtl/ *adj* (in favour of) never drinking alcoholic drinks.

▷ **teetotalism** *n* [U].

teetotaller (*US* also **teetotaler**) /-tlə(r)/ *n* person who is teetotal.

TEFL /ˌti: i: ef ˈel *or, in informal use,* ˈtefl/ *abbr* Teaching English as a Foreign Language. Cf TESL.

tel *abbr* **1** telegraph(ic). **2** telephone (number): *tel 0865-56767.*

tel(e)- *comb form* **1** over a long distance; far: *telepathy* ○ *telescopic.* **2** of television: *teleprompter* ○ *teletext.*

telecommunications /ˌtelɪkəˌmju:nɪˈkeɪʃnz/ *n* [pl] communications by satellite, cable, telegraph, telephone, radio or TV.

telegram /ˈtelɪgræm/ *n* message sent by telegraph and then delivered in written or printed form: *send/receive a telegram (of congratulations, condolence, etc).* Cf CABLE 4.

telegraph /ˈtelɪgrɑ:f; *US* -græf/ *n* (**a**) [U] means of sending messages by the use of electric current along wires. Use of the telegraph began in the

Technology in the Home

Many homes in Britain and the USA now have electrical and electronic aids and instruments that would have been unimaginable a quarter of a century ago.

In 1988 the percentage of British homes with various types of equipment was as follows: television sets 98 per cent, washing-machines 85 per cent, telephones 85 per cent, freezers (including fridge-freezers) 75 per cent, videocassette recorders (VCRs) 50 per cent, microwave ovens 39 per cent and personal computers 17 per cent. Nearly seven homes out of ten also have a car, and the majority have a radio. Kitchen and domestic appliances also found in many homes include electric or electronic clocks, toasters, kettles, blenders, mixers and vacuum cleaners.

In the USA, 98 per cent of households have a television (of which 51 per cent is cable TV), 93 per cent have a telephone, 73 per cent have a washing-machine and 58 per cent have a VCR. Nearly eight homes out of ten also have a car.

In both countries, the amount of money spent on electrical and electronic products has risen significantly in recent years, and many homes contain more specialized equipment such as audio equipment (especially music centres, midi systems and compact disc players) and home computers (including word processors). Computers are used for work (or a hobby or interest) and for recreation, in the latter case mostly in the form of children's computer games. As more and more people are working from home, an increasing number of households now have fax machines, operating over the telephone line, as well as answering machines for the telephone itself.

Since watching television is the most popular leisure activity in both Britain and the USA, and with the increasing sophistication of TV systems themselves, it is not surprising that much recent technology in the home relates specifically to television.

Many televisions in Britain now receive one or more of the three main teletext systems. British Telecom, Britain's largest telecommunications company, provides 'Prestel', a public viewdata system transmitted over the telephone and viewed on a television screen. The two main broadcasting companies also have their own teletext systems. That of the British Broadcasting Corporation (BBC) is called 'Ceefax', and that of the Independent Broadcasting Authority (IBA) is called 'Oracle'. Most modern televisions, too, have remote-control devices, chiefly used for turning on and off, for switching from one channel to another, and for 'zapping' (running a recorded programme 'fast forward'). In addition, an increasing number of televisions can be used with a digital scanner, allowing the viewer to select and store programmes to be watched later. (The scanner, which is usually part of a remote-control system, is run over printed bar codes and then pointed at a VCR linked to the television.)

A number of banks and shops now operate a 'teleshopping' system, enabling people to order goods from shops, book travel tickets, check bank balances and so on by using a small computer terminal plugged into the telephone socket. The text is viewed on a linked screen as part of British Telecom's 'Prestel' system.

There have been similar technological developments in telephones. Many people now have a cordless telephone for home use, which does not need to be plugged into a socket, or a cellphone which can be used in a car or train. A cellphone is a pocket telephone used in a radio system, which operates through a network of transmitters each serving a small, roughly hexagonal geographical area known as a 'cell'. The cellphone switches frequencies automatically as it passes from one cell to another. In Britain there are two competing cellphone systems, Racal-Vodaphone and Cellnet. 'Personal communications networks' (PCNs), a more advanced form of cellphone network, are also being added to the list of facilities available.

1830s, encouraged by the growth of the railway system and the need to communicate between signalmen. The first transatlantic telegraph cable was laid in 1858. **(b)** [C] apparatus for doing this.

▷ **telegraph** *v* **(a)** [I, Ipr, Tn, Tn·pr] send (a message) by telegraph. **(b)** [Dn·t] send instructions to (sb) by telegraph.

telegraphese /ˌtelɪɡrəˈfiːz/ *n* [U] shortened style of language used in telegrams, leaving out all unnecessary words.

telegraphic /ˌtelɪˈɡræfɪk/ *adj* suitable for or sent by telegraphy. **telegraphically** /-klɪ/ *adv.* **telegraphic adˈdress** shortened or registered address for use in telegrams.

telegraphist /tɪˈleɡrəfɪst/ (also **telegrapher** /tɪˈleɡrəfə(r)/) *n* person whose job is to send and receive messages by telegraph.

telegraphy /tɪˈleɡrəfɪ/ *n* [U] process of communication by telegraph: *wireless telegraphy.*

□ **ˈtelegraph-line** (also **ˈtelegraph-wire**) *n* wire along which telegraph or telephone messages travel.

ˈtelegraph-pole (also **ˈtelegraph-post**) *n* pole supporting telegraph-lines.

telekinesis /ˌtelɪkaɪˈniːsɪs/ *n* [U] (ability to cause) movement of an object by the action of the mind, without physical contact. ▷ **telekinetic** /-kaɪˈnetɪk/ *adj.*

Telemann /ˈteləmæn; *US* ˈteɪləmɑːn/ Georg Philipp (1681-1767), German composer who wrote a very large amount of music, including over 40 operas and 600 overtures. In his lifetime, his reputation was greater than that of his contemporary, J S *Bach.

telemetry /tɪˈlemətrɪ/ *n* [U] process of automatically recording the readings of an instrument and transmitting them over a distance, usu by radio.

teleology /ˌtelɪˈɒlədʒɪ, ˌtiːlɪ-/ *n* [U] theory that events and developments are meant to fulfil a purpose and happen because of that.

▷ **teleological** /ˌtelɪəˈlɒdʒɪkl, ˌtiːlɪə-/ *adj.*

teleologist /ˌtelɪˈɒlədʒɪst, ˌtiːlɪ-/ *n* person who believes in teleology.

telepathy /tɪˈlepəθɪ/ *n* [U] **1** communication of thoughts or ideas from one mind to another without the normal use of the senses. **2** (*infml*) ability to be aware of the thoughts and feelings of others.

▷ **telepath** /ˈtelɪpæθ/ *n* telepathic person.

telepathic /ˌtelɪˈpæθɪk/ *adj* **(a)** of or using telepathy. **(b)** (of a person) able to communicate by telepathy: *How did you know what I was thinking? You must be telepathic.* **telepathically** /-klɪ/ *adv.*

telephone /ˈtelɪfəʊn/ (also **phone**) *n* **1** [U] system of transmitting the human voice to a distance by wire or radio: *You can always reach* (ie contact) *me by telephone.* ⇨ article. **2** [C] instrument used for this, with a receiver and mouthpiece: *answer the telephone,* ie pick up the receiver to receive an incoming call. **3** (idm) **on the ˈtelephone (a)** connected to the telephone system: *They've just moved and they're not on the telephone yet.* **(b)** using the telephone: *She's on the telephone at the moment.* ○ *You're wanted* (ie Somebody wants to speak to you) *on the telephone.*

▷ **telephone** (also **phone**) *v* [I, Tn, Tn·pr] send (a message) or speak to (sb) by telephone: *Will you write or telephone?* ○ *We must telephone our congratulations (to the happy couple).* ○ *He telephoned (his wife) to say he'd be late.*

telephonic /ˌtelɪˈfɒnɪk/ *adj.*

telephonist /tɪˈlefənɪst/ *n* = TELEPHONE OPERATOR.

telephony /tɪˈlefənɪ/ *n* [U] process of transmitting sound by telephone.

□ **ˈtelephone box** (also **ˈphone box, ˈtelephone booth, ˈphone booth, ˈcall-box**) small covered or enclosed structure containing a telephone for use by the public.

ˈtelephone directory (also **ˈtelephone book, ˈphone book**) book listing the names, addresses and telephone numbers of people in a particular area who have a telephone.

ˈtelephone exchange (also **exchange**) place where telephone connections are made.

ˈtelephone number (also **ˈphone number**) number assigned to a particular telephone and used in dialling a call to it. ⇨ App 9.

ˈtelephone operator person whose job is to connect calls in a telephone exchange.

telephoto /ˌtelɪˈfəʊtəʊ/ *adj* = TELEPHOTOGRAPHIC.

□ **ˌtelephoto ˈlens** lens that produces a large image of a distant object that is being photographed.

telephotography /ˌtelɪfəˈtɒɡrəfɪ/ *n* [U] process of photographing distant objects using a telephoto lens.

▷ **telephotographic** /ˌtelɪfəʊtəˈɡræfɪk/ *adj* of or for or using telephotography.

teleprinter /ˈtelɪprɪntə(r)/ (*US* **teletypewriter**) *n* device for automatically typing and sending messages by telegraph, and for receiving and typing messages similarly.

teleprompter /ˈtelɪprɒmptə(r)/ *n* device by which a speaker on television can read the text of his script from a screen in front of him that cannot be seen by his audience. Cf AUTOCUE.

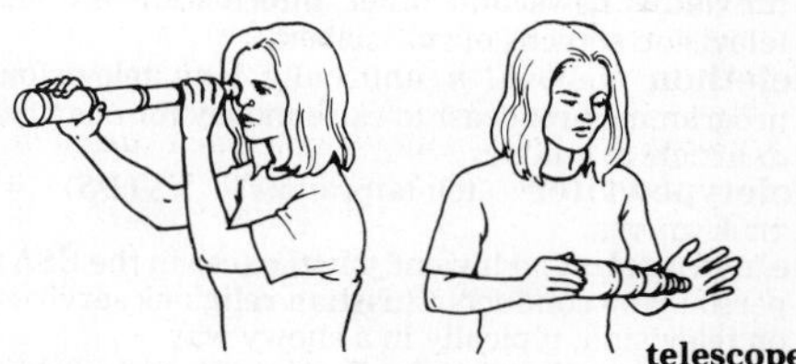

telescope

telescope /ˈtelɪskəʊp/ *n* optical instrument shaped like a tube, with lenses to make distant objects appear larger and nearer.

▷ **telescope** *v* **1** [I, Tn] (cause sth to) become shorter by sliding overlapping sections inside one another. ⇨ illus. **2** [I, Tn] (cause sth to) become compressed forcibly: *The first two carriages of the train (were) telescoped in the crash.* **3** [Tn, Tn·pr] ~ **sth (into sth)** condense sth so that it occupies less space or time: *Three episodes have been telescoped into a single programme.*

telescopic /ˌtelɪˈskɒpɪk/ *adj* **1** of a telescope; magnifying like a telescope: *a telescopic sight,* eg on a rifle, to magnify the target. **2** (that can be) seen through a telescope: *a telescopic view of the moon* ○ *telescopic stars,* ie those that are invisible

Telephone

Until 1981, Britain's telephone service was the responsibility of the Post Office. In that year, however, the Post Office was split into two, one half remaining as the Post Office to run the postal services, and the other formed as British Telecom (BT) to operate the country's telephone system. In 1984 BT was privatized, and it now has a competitor in another telephone company, Mercury Communications. At present, however, BT still operates most of the country's telephones.

Over eight out of ten households in Britain have a telephone, and many people have an extension in other parts of the house. Most people rent their phone from BT on a quarterly basis, and until BT was privatized this was the only way to have a phone. Since 1986, however, people have been able to buy their own telephone, and an increasing number do so. Even so, the telephone line itself must still be rented from BT.

All subscribers get a free copy of two local telephone directories: the general 'Phone Book', which has the names and numbers of all private subscribers in the area (except those who are 'ex-directory' because they have asked for their number not to be included) as well as all commercial numbers, and the 'Yellow Pages', which lists businesses and other organizations alphabetically by category of business, from Abattoirs to Zoos.

Calls are charged at one of five rates. 'Local calls' are the cheapest, and apply in a limited area round a particular telephone exchange. Next is the 'a' rate, for calls up to 56 kilometres (35 miles), followed by 'national calls' at 'b' rate, and the more expensive 'b1' rate for calls on busy lines such as those to and from London. The highest charge is the 'm' rate for calls to mobile telephones. The 'm' rate can be as much as eight times as expensive as a local call. Calls made via the operator are charged for a minimum of three minutes.

The cost of a call also depends on the time when it is made. 'Peak rate', the most expensive, is for calls between 9.00 am and 1.00 pm, Monday to Friday. 'Standard rate', rather cheaper, is for calls between 8.00 and 9.00 am and 1.00 and 6.00 pm on these days. 'Cheap rate', costing the least, applies from 6.00 pm to 8.00 am (8.00 pm to 8.00 am for international calls) and all day (and all night) at the weekends.

Apart from normal calls, BT provides special numbers on which people can find out the right time ('Time line', or 'The Speaking Clock'), the weather forecast, and other information. It also offers a number of extra services to telephone subscribers, such as calling them at a particular time (an 'alarm call'), or telling them the cost of a call after it has been made ('advice of duration and charge', or 'ADC').

Each telephone has its own number, usually consisting of two parts: the exchange number, usually called a 'code', and the individual telephone number. Some numbers can be ten figures or more. For example, the telephone number of the East Midlands Airport is 0332 810621. (The first part of this is the code for Derby.) Large cities have an extra number as a prefix. For London this was 01 until 1990, when it became 071 for Inner London and 081 for Outer London. This means that all London numbers have ten figures, with the three-figure prefix followed by a three-figure code for the local exchange, and then a four-figure number for the individual telephone. For example, the number of Heathrow Airport is 081-759 4321.

Prefixes for other big cities are 021 for Birmingham, 031 for Edinburgh, 041 for Glasgow, 051 for Liverpool, 061 for Manchester and 091 for Newcastle. For an emergency call to the police, fire brigade or ambulance services the number to ring is 999. Some codes give an idea of the cost of a call. For example, all numbers beginning 0800 are 'freefone' numbers: that is, the call is paid for by the company or organization that has the number. Numbers beginning 0860, 0077 and 0898 are charged at 'm' rate.

Almost all calls are now dialled direct between telephones, but calls can also be obtained through the operator, whose number is 100. Other well-known numbers are 192 for 'directory enquiries' (to find out a person's number), 151 to report a fault, 153 for international directory enquiries, 155 for the international operator, and 150 for BT itself. All calls from Britain to a country abroad are prefixed with the number 010.

Until quite recently almost all telephones in Britain had dials. They now usually have 'keypads' with buttons to press. Even so, people still talk of 'dialling' a number.

Public telephones in Britain were for many years housed in distinctive red telephone boxes ('call-boxes' or 'kiosks'). The newer ones are now mostly in ordinary booths or simply inside a cover or shield to reduce external noise.

There are different types of public telephone. The most common is the 'payphone', operated by coins. Another type is the 'cardphone', operated by a 'phonecard', a plastic card resembling a credit card that can be purchased from a newsagent's (or certain other shops) and is valid for calls to a given number of units.

Many people now have portable cordless phones which can be used around the home or while travelling. (Cf article at TECHNOLOGY.)

In the USA the telephone system has always been run by a private company. It is similar to the British one in its technological development and operation. US telephone numbers are prefixed with an area code for a state or a defined region in a state. (The area codes correspond to the prefixes for large cities in Britain, such as Birmingham's 021.) For example, the area code for New Mexico is 505 but for North Carolina it can be 704 or 919, depending on the location of the exchange.

to the naked eye. **3** having sections which slide one within another: *a telescopic aerial, stand, umbrella.* **telescopically** /-klɪ/ *adv.*

teletext /ˈtelɪtekst/ *n* [U] computerized service providing news and other information on the television screens of subscribers.

telethon /ˈtelɪθɒn/ *n* unusually long television programme broadcast to raise money for charity. ⇨ article at CHARITY.

teletypewriter /ˌtelɪˈtaɪpraɪtə(r)/ *n* (*US*) = TELEPRINTER.

televangelist /ˌtelɪˈvændʒəlɪst/ *n* (esp in the USA) person who conducts Christian religious services on television, typically in a showy way.

television /ˈtelɪvɪʒn/ (also *Brit infml* **telly**) *n* (*abbr* **TV**) **1** [U] process of transmitting and reproducing on a screen events, scenes, plays, etc in pictures and sound, using radio signals. ⇨ article. **2** [U] programmes broadcast in this way: *spend the evening watching television* ○ [attrib] *a television documentary.* **3** [C] (also ˈ**television set**) apparatus with a screen and loudspeaker for receiving television broadcasts: *a colour/black-and-white television.* **4** [U] organization producing and transmitting television programmes: *She works in television.* ○ [attrib] *a television announcer.* **5** (idm) **on (the) ˈtelevision** broadcasting or being broadcast by television: *The Prime Minister, speaking on television, denied reports that...* ○ *Is there anything good on (the) television tonight?*

▷ **televise** /ˈtelɪvaɪz/ *v* [Tn] broadcast (sth) by television: *The BBC plans to televise all Shakespeare's plays.* ○ *The Olympic Games are always televised.*

telex /ˈteleks/ *n* **1** [U] system of communication using teleprinters. **2** [C] message sent or received by this system: *Several telexes arrived this morning.* **3** [C] (*infml*) apparatus for sending and receiving messages by telex: *We've installed a new telex in the office.*

▷ **telex** *v* [Tn, Tn·pr, Dn·f] send (a message) or communicate with (sb) by telex.

Telford /ˈtelfəd/ Thomas (1757-1834), Scottish civil engineer who constructed many new roads, canals, bridges, etc throughout Britain. His most famous work is the Menai suspension bridge, connecting Wales and Anglesey.

Tell /tel/ William, legendary 14th-century Swiss hero who helped to free his country from Austrian rule. When he refused to salute the symbol of Austrian authority, he was sentenced to try to shoot an apple off his son's head with a crossbow. This he successfully did.

tell /tel/ *v* (*pt, pp* **told** /təʊld/) **1** [Tn, Dn·n, Dn·pr, Dn·f, Dn·w] ~ **sth (to sb)** make sth known, esp in spoken or written words: *tell jokes/stories* ○ *I could tell you a thing or two about him.* ○ *He told the news to everybody in the village.* ○ *Did she tell you her name?* ○ *They've told us (that) they're not coming.* ○ *Tell me where you live.* ○ *I can't tell you* (ie I can't find words to express) *how happy I am.* ○ *So I've been told,* ie That is what I've been told. **2** [Dn·n, Dn·f, Dn·w, Dn·t] give information to (sb): *a book which will tell you all you need to know about personal taxation* ○ *This gauge tells you the amount of petrol you have left/how much petrol you have left.* **3** [Tn] express (sth) in words; utter: *tell the truth/lies/a lie* ○ (*dated*) *tell* (ie reveal) *one's love.* ⇨ Usage at SAY. **4** [I] reveal a secret: *Promise you won't tell.* ○ (*infml*) *kiss and tell,* ie reveal one's love affairs. **5 (a)** [I, Tf, Tw] decide or determine; know definitely: *It may rain or it may not. It's hard to tell.* ○ *You can tell (that) he's angry when he starts shouting a lot.* ○ *How do you tell when to change gear?* ○ *The only way to tell if you like something is by trying it.* **(b)** [Tn, Tn·pr, Tw] ~ **A from B** (esp with *can/could/be able to*) distinguish A from B: *I can't tell the difference between margarine and butter,* ie can't identify them by their tastes. ○ *Can you tell Tom from his twin brother?* ○ *These kittens look exactly alike — how can you tell which is which?* **6** [I, Ipr] ~ **(on sb)** produce a noticeable effect: *Every blow told.* ○ *The government's policies are beginning to tell.* ○ *All this hard work is telling on him,* ie affecting his health, etc. ○ *Her lack of experience told against her,* ie was a disadvantage to her. **7** [Dn·t, Dn·w] order or direct (sb): *Tell him to wait.* ○ *Do what I tell you.* ○ *Children must do as they're told.* ○ *You won't be told* (ie won't obey orders or listen to advice), *will you?* ⇨ Usage at ORDER². **8** [Tn] (*arch*) count the number of (sth): *tell one's beads,* ie say

Television

Britain's first regular television service opened in 1932, when the British Broadcasting Corporation (BBC) began transmitting four short late-night programmes a week. The development of television was interrupted by the Second World War, but resumed after it, making its first real impact in 1953 when the BBC televised the coronation of Queen Elizabeth II.

In 1955 Independent Television (ITV) began transmitting, at first only in the London area. Unlike the BBC, which funded its broadcasting with the revenue from radio and television licences, ITV derived its main income from its commercial advertising. This arrangement remains today.

In 1964 the BBC began transmitting on two channels, BBC 1 and BBC 2, the latter being mainly for drama, arts and sports programmes. BBC 2 first broadcast in colour in 1967, and BBC 1 and ITV followed suit two years later. A second commercial station, Channel 4, opened in 1982. Like BBC 2, it was intended as a mainly arts and 'cultural' service, but with the specific task of catering for minority interests.

ITV programmes are produced by a number of regional companies. A national company, TV-am, broadcasts news, current affairs and entertainment programmes every morning. The programmes of the regional companies are not restricted to their own area, except for local news coverage. Programmes such as plays and documentaries are seen nationwide. National news programmes on ITV are produced by a separate company, Independent Television News (ITN).

BBC 1 broadcasts a schedule of news, information programmes, documentaries, plays, films and light entertainment (such as comedies and quiz shows) from early morning to late at night. ITV's schedule is similar, but its presentation is generally slicker and more 'glossy'. Its programmes are broadcast round the clock.

Until the end of 1990, ITV's programmes and their schedules were under the supervision of the Independent Broadcasting Authority (IBA), which did not itself produce television programmes, since this was done by the regional companies. The IBA was originally set up by the government in 1954 as the Independent Television Authority (ITA) to provide an additional television service to that of the BBC. It was renamed the IBA in 1972, when its responsibilities were extended to cover independent radio. Its specific functions then came to include the appointing of the ITV companies, the operation of transmitters, and the control of advertising. The IBA ceased to exist in 1991, when its television responsibilities were taken over by a new body, the Independent Television Commission (ITC). Commercial radio services were taken over at the same time by the new Radio Authority. When this change took place, the former ITV channel was renamed Channel 3. A new commercial station, Channel 5, is due to be established by 1993.

Both the BBC and ITV broadcast educational programmes, including broadcasts for schools. The BBC also transmits programmes for Open University students.

In 1989 satellite television was first transmitted on four channels by the privately owned company Sky Television, and it was joined in 1990 by British Satellite Broadcasting (BSB), under contract to the IBA. Because both companies were losing money in their attempts to win viewers, Sky and BSB merged to form a single new company, British Sky Broadcasting, owned equally by News International (the media group that owns *The Times*, among other newspapers) and former BSB shareholders. The new company, trading under the name of Sky Television, offers five satellite channels, including the two main film channels.

Despite the increasing popularity of satellite television, the non-satellite (also called 'terrestrial') channels form the main part of most people's viewing. In 1990, Britain's most watched channel was ITV, with 27 per cent of all regular viewers. Next was BBC 1, with 21 per cent. Sky Movies and Sky One followed in popularity, with Channel 4 a poor fifth (less than 6 per cent) and BBC 2 eighth with only 3 per cent. All viewers must hold an annual television licence. The income from it is used by the government to fund the BBC.

In the USA, television developed rapidly after the Second World War, the first colour transmissions being made in 1954. There are over 1 000 commercial television companies, and at least three households out of ten can receive ten or more of them. Much US television is geared to news, sport and entertainment, the latter often quiz shows and films. Since the early 1970s, one of the most widely watched programmes has been the coverage of the annual Super Bowl American football final.

Most television production is in the hands of 'the Big Three': the Columbia Broadcasting System (CBS), the National Broadcasting Company (NBC) and the American Broadcasting Company (ABC). These three have recently been joined by a fourth: Fox Broadcasting, owned by Rupert Murdoch. There is also non-commercial television, the Public Broadcasting System (PBS), which is financed by grants from companies and individuals. It offers quality drama programmes, children's programmes and national and international news programmes. More than half of all viewers in the USA subscribe to cable television, often referred to as 'public access TV' because members of the public are able to make or contribute to many of its programmes. 'Cable' is available on literally dozens of channels and has become increasingly popular in recent years. Whereas the 'Big Three' are subject to strict regulations concerning the material shown, cable viewers can readily see (and videotape) unexpurgated action films, pornographic films, and coarse comedy shows. In Britain, by contrast, cable was watched in only a minority of homes (only 275 000 by the late 1980s), although over 30 channels were available, including terrestrial, satellite and video broadcasts. The situation altered in 1991, when the Cable Authority, which issued licences, supervised programmes, and promoted cable development, was taken over by the new ITC, giving companies a freer hand.

prayers while counting the beads on a rosary. **9** (idm) **all told** with all people, items, etc counted and included: *There are 23 guests coming, all told.* **dead men tell no tales** ⇨ DEAD. **don't tell me...** (used for expressing dismay or disbelief): *Don't tell me you forgot to bring the tin-opener!* **hear tell of sb/sth** ⇨ HEAR. **I/I'll ˌtell you ˈwhat** (*infml*) (used to introduce a suggestion): *I'll tell you what — let's ask Fred to lend us his car.* **I ˈtold you (so)** (*infml*) I warned you that this would happen: *He loves to say 'I told you so!' when things go wrong.* **ˌlive, etc to ˌtell the ˈtale** survive a difficult or dangerous experience so that one can tell others what really happened. **tell/know A and B apart** ⇨ APART. **tell me aˈnother!** (*infml*) I don't believe you. **tell/see sth a mile off** ⇨ MILE. **tell its own tale** explain itself, without need of further explanation or comment: *The many crashes on the icy roads told their own tale.* **tell ˈtales (about sb)** make known another person's secrets, misdeeds, faults, etc: *Someone's been telling tales about me, haven't they?* **tell ˈthat to the marines!** (*sl*) I don't believe you. **tell the ˈtime** (*US* **tell ˈtime**) read the time from a clock, etc: *She's only five — she can't tell the time yet.* **tell sb ˌwhere to get ˈoff/ˌwhere he gets ˈoff** (*infml*) warn sb that his behaviour is unacceptable and will no longer be tolerated. **ˌtell the ˈworld** announce sth publicly. **that would be ˈtelling** (*infml*) (used when refusing a request for information): *'How much did they pay you?' 'That would be telling, wouldn't it?'* **there is no saying/telling** ⇨ SAY. **to ˌtell (you) the ˈtruth** (used to introduce a confession or an admission): *To tell the truth, I fell asleep in the middle.* **you can ˌnever ˈtell; you ˌnever can ˈtell** you can never be sure, eg because appearances are often deceptive. **you're telling ˈme!** (*infml*) I completely agree with you. **10** (phr v) **tell sb off (for sth/doing sth)** (*infml*) scold or reprimand sb: *You'll get told off if you're caught doing that.* ○ *I told the boys off for making so much noise.* **tell sb off for sth/to do sth** (*fml*) assign (a task or duty) to sb: *Six men were told off to collect fuel.* **tell on sb** (*infml*) reveal sb's activities, esp to a person in authority: *John caught his sister smoking and told on her.*

▷ **telling** *adj* have a noticeable effect; impressive: *a telling argument* ○ *His punches to his opponent's body proved especially telling.* **tellingly** *adv.*

□ **ˌtelling-ˈoff** *n* (usu *sing*) reprimand; scolding: *give sb a telling-off for sth.*

ˈtell-tale *n* **1** person who reports another's secrets, misdeeds, etc: *Don't be such a tell-tale!* **2** mechanical device that serves as an indicator. — *adj* [attrib] revealing or indicating sth: *a tell-tale blush* ○ *the tell-tale smell of cigarette smoke*, ie revealing that sb has been smoking.

teller /ˈtelə(r)/ *n* **1** person who receives and pays out money in a bank. **2** person appointed to count votes, eg in the House of Commons. **3** (esp in compounds) person who tells stories, etc: *a ˈstory-teller* ○ *a marvellous teller of ˈjokes.*

tellurium /teˈljʊərɪəm/ *n* /*US* teˈlʊriəm/ [U] (*symb* **Te**) semi-metallic element that occurs as either a silvery crystalline substance or a powder.

telly /ˈtelɪ/ *n* [U, C] (*Brit infml*) = TELEVISION.

temerity /tɪˈmerətɪ/ *n* [U] (*fml*) audacity; rashness: *He had the temerity to call me a liar.*

temp /temp/ *n* (*infml*) temporary employee, esp a secretary.

▷ **temp** *v* [I] (*infml*) do temporary work: *He's been temping for over a year now and wants a permanent job.*

temp *abbr* temperature: *temp 65°F.*

temper[1] /ˈtempə(r)/ *n* **1 (a)** [C] state of the mind as regards anger or calmness: *in a bad/good temper*, ie angry/amiable. **(b)** [C, U] tendency to become angry easily: *learn to control one's temper* ○ *have a (short/quick/nasty) temper* ○ *fly into a temper* ○ *a fit*

of temper. **2** [U] degree of hardness and elasticity of a tempered metal. **3** (idm) **in a (bad, foul, rotten, etc) ˈtemper** angry. **keep/lose one's ˈtemper** succeed/fail in controlling one's anger.
▷ **-tempered** /-ˈtempəd/ (forming compound *adjs*) having or showing the specified type of temper: *ˌgood-/ˌbad-ˈtempered* ○ *a ˌhot-tempered ˈman* ○ *a ˌsweet-tempered ˈchild.*

temper[2] /ˈtempə(r)/ *v* **1** [Tn] bring (metal) to the required degree of hardness and elasticity by heating and then cooling: *tempered steel.* **2** [Tn, Tn·pr] ~ **sth (with sth)** moderate or soften the effects of sth; mitigate sth: *temper justice with mercy,* ie be merciful when punishing sb justly.

tempera /ˈtempərə/ *n* [U] **1** paint consisting of pigment mixed with yolk or white of egg and water. **2** method of painting on canvas or plaster using this.

temperament /ˈtemprəmənt/ *n* **1** [C, U] person's nature as it affects the way he thinks, feels and behaves: *I've got a very nervous temperament.* ○ *a man with an artistic temperament* ○ *The two brothers have entirely different temperaments.* ○ *To be a champion, skill is not enough — you have to have the right temperament.* ○ *Opera singers often display a lot of temperament,* ie are moody or excitable. **2** [U] (*music*) adjustment of the tuning of a musical instrument, typically so as to provide a consistent set of notes within a key[1](3).
▷ **temperamental** /ˌtemprəˈmentl/ *adj* **1** caused by a person's temperament: *a temperamental aversion to hard work.* **2** (*often derog*) having or showing fits of excitable or moody behaviour; not calm or consistent: *He's a very temperamental player,* ie plays well or badly according to his mood. ○ (*joc*) *My car is a bit temperamental,* ie is likely to break down, fail to start, etc. **temperamentally** /-təlɪ/ *adv*: *temperamentally unsuited for the job.*

temperance /ˈtempərəns/ *n* [U] **1** moderation and self-restraint in one's behaviour or in eating and drinking. **2** drinking no (or almost no) alcoholic drinks: [attrib] *a temperance society,* ie one promoting temperance ○ *a temperance hotel,* ie one that does not serve alcoholic drinks.

temperate /ˈtempərət/ *adj* **1** behaving with temperance(1); showing self-control: *Please be more temperate in your language.* **2** (of climate or climatic regions) having a mild temperature without extremes of heat or cold: *temperate zones,* ie between the tropical and polar regions. ▷ **temperately** *adv.*

temperature /ˈtemprətʃə(r); *US* ˈtempərtʃʊər/ *n* **1** [C, U] degree of heat or cold (in a body, room, country, etc): *keep the house at an even temperature* ○ *heat the oven to a temperature of 200°C* ○ *some places have had temperatures in the 90's,* ie over 90° Fahrenheit ○ *a climate without extremes of temperature.* ⇨ App 9, 10. **2** (idm) **get/have/run a ˈtemperature** get/have an abnormally high temperature of the body. **raise the temperature** ⇨ RAISE. **take sb's ˈtemperature** measure the temperature of sb's body with a thermometer: *The nurse took the temperatures of all the patients.*

tempest /ˈtempɪst/ *n* **1** (*fml or rhet*) violent storm. **2** (idm) **a tempest in a teapot** (*US*) = A STORM IN A TEACUP (STORM).
▷ **tempestuous** /temˈpestʃʊəs/ *adj* stormy; violently agitated; turbulent: *a tempestuous sea* ○ *a tempestuous political debate.* **tempestuously** *adv.* **tempestuousness** *n* [U].

template /ˈtempleɪt/ *n* pattern or gauge, usu of thin board or metal, used as a guide for cutting or drilling metal, stone, wood, etc or for cutting fabric.

temple[1] /ˈtempl/ *n* building used for the worship of a god or gods, esp in non-Christian religions: *a Greek, Roman, Hindu, Buddhist, etc temple.* ⇨ illus.

temple[2] /ˈtempl/ *n* flat part at each side of the forehead. ⇨ illus at HEAD.

tempo /ˈtempəʊ/ *n* (*pl* ~**s** or, in music, **tempi** /ˈtempiː/) **1** speed or rhythm of a piece of music: *Your tempo is too slow.* ○ *in waltz tempo.* **2** (*fig*) pace of any movement or activity: *the exhausting*

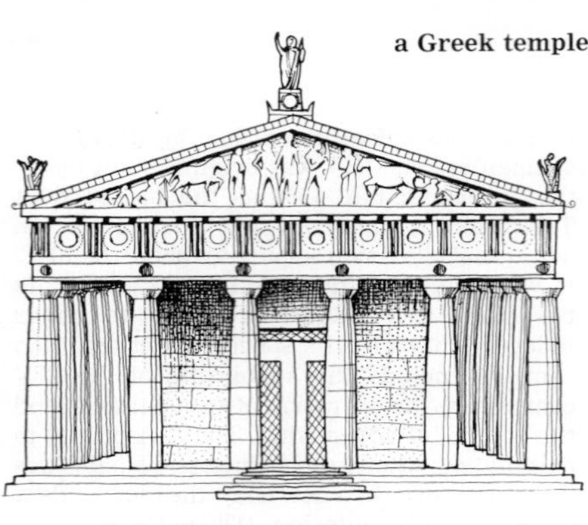

a Greek temple

tempo of city life ○ *upset the even tempo of one's existence.*

temporal /ˈtempərəl/ *adj* **1** of worldly affairs, ie not spiritual; secular: *the temporal power of the Pope,* ie as head of the Vatican State ○ *the lords temporal,* ie British peers of the realm. Cf SPIRITUAL 2. **2** (*grammar*) of or denoting time: *temporal conjunctions,* eg *when, while.* **3** of the temple(s) of the head: *the temporal artery.*

temporary /ˈtemprərɪ; *US* -pərerɪ/ *adj* lasting or meant to last for a limited time only; not permanent: *temporary employment* ○ *a temporary bridge* ○ *This arrangement is only temporary.* Cf IMPERMANENT. ▷ **temporarily** /ˈtemprərəlɪ; *US* ˌtempəˈrerəlɪ/ *adv.* **temporariness** *n* [U].

temporize, -ise /ˈtempəraɪz/ *v* [I] (*fml*) delay making a decision, giving a definite answer or stating one's purpose, in order to gain time: *a temporizing move.*

tempt /tempt/ *v* [Tn, Tn·pr, Cn·t] ~ **sb (into sth/doing sth) 1** persuade or try to persuade sb to do sth, esp sth wrong or unwise: *He was tempted into a life of crime by greed and laziness.* ○ *They tried to tempt her (into staying) with offers of promotion.* ○ *Nothing would tempt me to join the army.* **2** arouse a desire in sb; attract sb: *The warm weather tempted us into going for a swim.* ○ *I am tempted* (ie feel inclined) *to take the day off.* **3** (idm) **tempt ˈfate/ˈprovidence** act rashly; take a risk.
▷ **tempter** *n* **1** [C] person who tempts. **2 the Tempter** [sing] the Devil; Satan.
tempting *adj* attractive; inviting: *a tempting offer* ○ *That cake looks very tempting.* **temptingly** *adv.*
temptress /ˈtemptrɪs/ *n* (*usu joc*) woman who tempts, esp sexually.

temptation /tempˈteɪʃn/ *n* **1** [U] tempting or tempted: *the temptation of easy profits* ○ *yield/give way to temptation* ○ *put temptation in sb's way,* ie tempt him. **2** [C] thing that tempts or attracts: *The bag of sweets on the table was too strong a temptation for the child to resist.* ○ *Clever advertisements are just temptations to spend money.*

ten /ten/ *pron, det* **1** 10; one more than nine. ⇨ App 9. **2** (idm) **ˌten to ˈone** very probably: *Ten to one he'll be late.*
▷ **ten** *n* the number 10.
ten- (in compounds) having ten of the thing specified: *a ten-gallon drum.*
tenth /tenθ/ *pron, det* 10th; next after ninth. — *n* one of ten equal parts of sth. **tenthly** *adv* in the tenth position of place.
For the uses of *ten* and *tenth* see the examples at *five* and *fifth.*
□ **the ˌTen Comˈmandments** (in the Old Testament) laws given by God to *Moses for the *Israelites, forbidding murder, adultery, theft, lying, covetousness, swearing, the making of idols and the worship of other gods, and ordering respect for one's parents and keeping the sabbath holy.
tenfold /ˈtenfəʊld/ *adj, adv* **1** ten times as many or as much. **2** having ten parts.
ˌten ˈpence (also **10p**) /ˌten ˈpiː/ *n* (*Brit*) (coin worth) ten new pence.

tenable /ˈtenəbl/ *adj* **1** that can be defended successfully against opposition or attack: *a tenable position* ○ *The view that the earth is flat is no longer tenable.* **2** [pred] ~ **(for...)** (of an office or position) that can be held (for a certain time): *The lectureship is tenable for a period of three years.* ▷ **tenability** /ˌtenəˈbɪlətɪ/ *n* [U].

tenacious /tɪˈneɪʃəs/ *adj* **1** sticking or clinging firmly together or to an object: *The eagle seized its prey in a tenacious grip.* **2** keeping a firm hold on property, principles, life, etc; resolute: *a tenacious adversary* ○ *She is tenacious in defence of her rights.* **3** (of memory) retentive; not forgetting things. ▷ **tenaciously** *adv*: *Though seriously ill, he still clings tenaciously to life.* **tenacity** /tɪˈnæsətɪ/ *n* [U].

tenant /ˈtenənt/ *n* **1** person who pays rent to a landlord for the use of a room, a building, land, etc: *evict tenants for non-payment of rent* ○ [attrib] *a tenant farmer,* ie one who farms land which he does not own. **2** (*law*) person who occupies or owns a particular building or piece of land.
▷ **tenancy** /-ənsɪ/ **(a)** [U] use of land or buildings as a tenant(1): *during his tenancy of the farm.* **(b)** [C] period of this: *hold a life tenancy of a house.*
tenantry /ˈtenəntrɪ/ *n* [Gp] all the tenants occupying land or buildings on one estate.

NOTE ON USAGE: A **tenant** occupies a flat, a building, a farm, etc but does not own it. He or she pays money **(rent)** regularly for its use to the **landlord**, who is the owner: *Are you an owner-occupier or a tenant?* ○ *He's a tenant farmer. His landlord owns 5000 acres.* A similar relationship exists between a **lessee** and a **lessor**, which are legal terms. They both sign a **lease** (a written legal agreement defining the terms of the **tenancy**): *The lessor can evict the lessee for failure to pay rent.*

tench /tentʃ/ *n* (*pl* unchanged) European freshwater fish of the carp family.

tend[1] /tend/ *v* [Tn] **1** take care of or look after (sb/sth): *nurses tending (the wounds of) the injured* ○ *shepherds tending their sheep.* **2** (*US*) serve customers in (a shop, bar, etc): *tend the store.*

tend[2] /tend/ *v* **1** [It] be likely to behave in a certain way or to have a certain characteristic or influence: *I tend to go to bed earlier during the winter.* ○ *Women tend to live longer than men.* ○ *Recent laws have tended to restrict the freedom of the press.* ○ *It tends to rain here a lot in summer.* **2** [I, Ipr] ~ **to/towards sth** take a certain direction: *The track tends upwards.* ○ (*fig*) *He tends towards extreme views.*
▷ **tendency** /ˈtendənsɪ/ *n* **1** ~ **(to/towards sth)/(to do sth)** way a person or thing tends to be or behave: *a tendency to fat/towards fatness/to get fat* ○ *homicidal tendencies.* **2** direction in which sth moves or changes; trend: *Prices continue to show an upward tendency,* ie to increase.

tendentious /tenˈdenʃəs/ *adj* (*derog*) (of a speech, a piece of writing, etc) aimed at helping a cause; not impartial: *Such tendentious statements are likely to provoke strong opposition.* ▷ **tendentiously** *adv.* **tendentiousness** *n* [U].

tender[1] /ˈtendə(r)/ *adj* **1** easily damaged or hurt; delicate: *tender blossoms, plants, shoots, etc,* eg that can be harmed by frost. **2** painful when touched; sensitive: *My leg is still very tender where it was bruised.* ○ *That's a rather tender subject,* ie one that must be dealt with carefully to avoid hurting people's feelings. **3** easily moved to pity or sympathy; kind: *a tender heart.* **4** loving; gentle: *tender looks* ○ *tender loving care* ○ *be a tender parent* ○ *bid sb a tender farewell.* **5** (of meat) easy to chew; not tough. **6** (idm) **at a tender ˈage/of tender ˈage** young and immature.
▷ **tenderize, -ise** /ˈtendəraɪz/ *v* [Tn] make (meat) more tender (eg by beating it): *tenderized steak.*
tenderly *adv.*
tenderness *n* [U].
□ **ˈtenderfoot** *n* (*pl* **-foots**) newcomer who is unused to hardships; inexperienced person.
ˌtender-ˈhearted *adj* having a kind and gentle nature; tender[1] (4).
ˈtenderloin *n* [U] (also **ˌtenderloin ˈsteak**) (*esp*

US) most tender middle part of a loin of beef or pork. Cf UNDERCUT[1].

ender[2] /ˈtendə(r)/ *n* **1** (esp in compounds) person who looks after or tends sth: *a* ˈ*bartender.* **2** small ship used for carrying freight or passengers to or from a larger ship. **3** truck attached to a steam locomotive, carrying fuel and water.

ender[3] /ˈtendə(r)/ *v* **1** [Tn, Tn·pr] ~ **sth (to sb)** (*fml*) offer or present sth formally: *tender money in payment of a debt* ○ *May I tender my services?* ○ *He tendered his resignation to the Prime Minister.* **2** [I, Ipr] ~ **(for sth)** make an offer (to carry out work, supply goods, etc) at a stated price: *Firms were invited to tender for the construction of the new motorway.*

▷ **tender** (also *esp US* **bid**) *n* formal offer to supply goods or carry out work at a stated price: *put work out to tender*, ie ask for such offers ○ *put in/make/submit a tender for sth* ○ *accept the lowest tender.*

endon /ˈtendən/ *n* strong band or cord of tissue that joins muscle to bone; sinew: *strain a tendon.*

endril /ˈtendrəl/ *n* thread-like part of a climbing plant (eg ivy) by which it clings to a support.

enement /ˈtenəmənt/ *n* **1** apartment or room let for living in. **2** (*US* also ˈ**tenement-house**) large building with apartments or rooms let to a number of families at low rents. **3** (*law*) land or other permanent property held by a tenant.

enet /ˈtenɪt/ *n* principle; belief; doctrine: *one of the basic tenets of the Christian faith.*

enner /ˈtenə(r)/ *n* (*Brit infml*) (note worth) ten pounds sterling; £10: *I'll give you a tenner for your old bike.*

ennessee /ˌtenəˈsi:/ state of the south-eastern central USA, to the east of the Mississippi river. It is mainly agricultural, producing much tobacco and cotton. ⇨ map at App 1.

ir John Tenniel: illustration from 'Alice's dventures in Wonderland'

'enniel /ˈtenjəl/ Sir John (1820-1914), English artist who drew the original illustrations for Lewis *Carroll's *Alice* books. ⇨ illus.

ennis /ˈtenɪs/ *n* [U] (also ˌ**lawn** ˈ**tennis**) game for two or four players, who hit a ball backwards and forwards across a net with rackets. ⇨ App 9. Cf REAL TENNIS (REAL[1]). ⇨ article at SPORT.

□ ˈ**tennis court** marked area on which tennis is played.

ˌ**tennis** ˈ**elbow** painful swelling of the elbow caused by playing tennis, etc.

'ennyson /ˈtenɪsn/ Alfred, 1st Baron Tennyson (1809-92), English poet. Born in Lincolnshire, he spent the later part of his life on the Isle of Wight. His best-known works are verse narratives, mainly on themes from ancient and medieval mythology (eg 'The Lady of Shalott', 'The Lotos-Eaters', 'Morte d'Arthur', *Idylls of the King*), but he also wrote poems on topical themes (eg 'The Charge of the Light Brigade'). All his poetry is characterized by richness and musicality of language. His greatest work, *In Memoriam*, was written after the death of his close friend Arthur Hallam. He was made Poet Laureate in 1850.

tennis

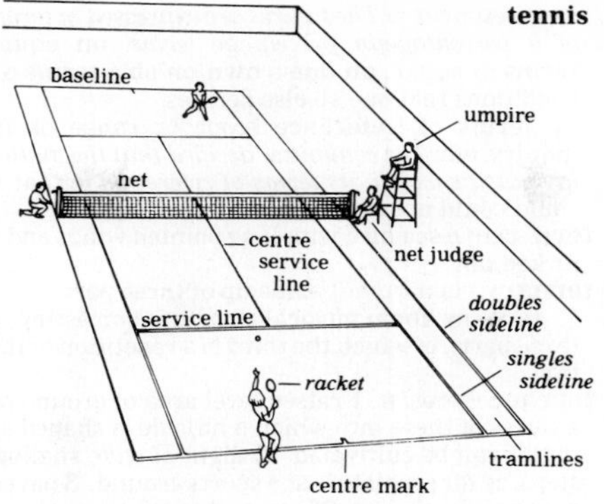

TENNIS COURT

tenon

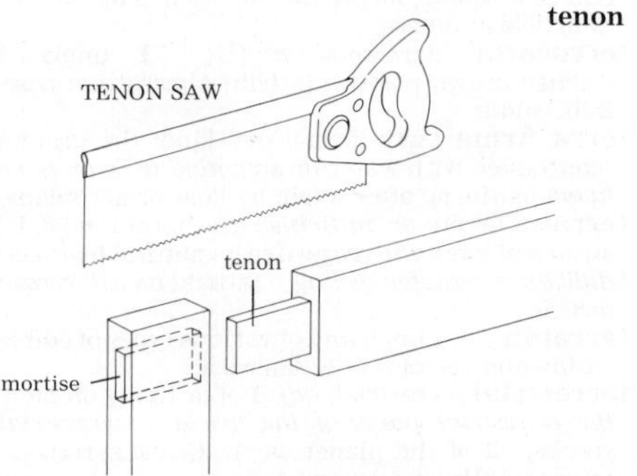

tenon /ˈtenən/ *n* projecting end of a piece of wood shaped to fit into a mortise to make a joint.

□ ˈ**tenon-saw** *n* short saw whose blade has a strengthened top, used esp for fine work. ⇨ illus.

tenor[1] /ˈtenə(r)/ *n* [U] **the** ~ **of sth** **1** general routine or course of sth: *disrupting the even tenor of her life.* **2** general meaning or drift of sth: *know enough of the language to grasp the tenor of what is being said.*

tenor[2] /ˈtenə(r)/ *n* (*music*) **1** (**a**) highest normal adult male voice. (**b**) singer with such a voice. (**c**) part written for such a voice. **2** [esp attrib] instrument with a range about that of a tenor voice: *a tenor saxophone.*

tenpin bowling /ˌtenpɪn ˈbəʊlɪŋ/ (*US* also **tenpins** /ˈtenpɪnz/ [pl]) game like ninepins, but with an extra skittle. Cf SKITTLE.

tense[1] /tens/ *adj* (**-r, -st**) **1** stretched tightly; taut. **2** with muscles tight in anticipation of what may happen: *faces tense with anxiety.* **3** unable to relax; edgy: *He's a very tense person.* **4** causing tenseness: *a tense moment, atmosphere, meeting* ○ *The game is getting tenser all the time.*

▷ **tense** *v* **1** [I, Tn] (cause sb/sth to) become tense[1] (2): *She tensed, hearing the noise again.* ○ *with muscles tensed, waiting for the race to start.* **2** (idm) **be/get tensed** ˈ**up** be/become tense[1] (3): *Players get very tensed up before a match.*

tensely *adv.*

tenseness *n* [U].

tense[2] /tens/ *n* (*grammar*) any of the forms of a verb that may be used to indicate the time of the action or state expressed by the verb: *the present, past, future, etc tense.*

tensile /ˈtensaɪl; *US* ˈtensl/ *adj* **1** [attrib] of tension: *the tensile strength of wire, rope, etc*, ie the load it will support without breaking. **2** that can be stretched.

tension /ˈtenʃn/ *n* **1** [U] state or degree of stretching or being stretched: *adjust the tension of a violin string, a tennis racket, etc* ○ *Massage helps relieve the tension in one's muscles.* **2** [U] mental, emotional or nervous strain; tenseness: *suffer from (nervous) tension* ○ *Tension is a major cause of heart disease.* **3** [U, C usu *pl*] condition when feelings are tense or relations between people, groups, etc are strained: *racial/political/social tension(s)* ○ *The incident has further increased the tension between the two countries.* **4** [U] voltage: *high-tension cables.*

tent /tent/ *n* (usu portable) shelter or dwelling made of canvas, etc supported by poles and ropes attached to pegs driven into the ground: *camping in tents.*

□ ˈ**tent-peg** *n* wooden or metal peg used to fasten a rope supporting a tent, etc to the ground. ⇨ illus at PEG.

tentacle /ˈtentəkl/ *n* slender flexible part extending from the body of certain animals (eg snails, octopuses), used for feeling or grasping things or for moving.

tentative /ˈtentətɪv/ *adj* done, said, etc to test sth; hesitant or exploratory; not definite or decisive: *make a tentative suggestion, proposal, plan, etc* ○ *reach a tentative conclusion.* ▷ **tentatively** *adv*: *played rather too tentatively.* **tentativeness** *n* [U].

tenterhooks /ˈtentəhʊks/ *n* (idm) **(be) on** ˈ**tenterhooks** in a state of anxious suspense or uncertainty: *We were kept on tenterhooks for hours while the judges were deciding the winners.*

tenth ⇨ TEN.

tenuous /ˈtenjʊəs/ *adj* **1** thin; slender: *the tenuous threads of a spider's web.* **2** having little substance or significance; very slight: *tenuous distinctions* ○ *preserve tenuous links with one's former friends* ○ *The difference, if it exists, is extremely tenuous.* ▷ **tenuously** *adv.* **tenuousness** (also *fml* **tenuity** /tɪˈnju:ətɪ; *US* teˈnu:-/) *n* [U].

tenure /ˈtenjʊə(r); *US* -jər/ *n* [U] **1** holding of (eg political) office or land or other property, etc. **2** period or manner of this: *The tenure of the US Presidency is four years.* ○ *freehold/leasehold tenure* ○ *security of tenure*, ie the right to remain as a tenant. **3** (*esp US*) permanent appointment as a teacher, etc in a university or some other institution: *granted tenure after six years.*

Tenzing Norgay /ˌtensɪŋ ˈnɔ:geɪ/ (1914-86), *Sherpa mountaineer who, with Sir Edmund *Hillary, was the first to climb Mount *Everest (1953).

tepee /ˈti:pi:/ *n* cone-shaped tent made of skins or bark on a frame of poles, used (esp formerly) by American Indians. Cf WIGWAM.

tepid /ˈtepɪd/ *adj* lukewarm: *The water was tepid.* ○ (*fig*) *tepid applause.* ▷ **tepidly** *adv.* **tepidness** (also **tepidity** /teˈpɪdətɪ/) *n* [U].

tequila /təˈki:lə/ *n* (**a**) [U] strong alcoholic drink distilled from a tropical plant, chiefly in Mexico. (**b**) [C] glass of this.

terbium /ˈtɜ:bɪəm/ *n* [U] (*symb* **Tb**) (*chemistry*) silver-grey metallic element, used in lasers.

terce /tɜ:s/ *n* [U] (in the Roman Catholic church) set of prayers appointed for the third hour of daytime.

tercel /ˈtɜ:sl/ (also **tiercel** /ˈtɪəsl/) *n* (in falconry) male hawk.

tercentenary /ˌtɜ:senˈti:nərɪ; *US* tɜ:ˈsentənerɪ/ (also **tercentennial** /ˌtɜ:senˈtenɪəl/) *n* 300th anniversary: *the tercentenary of the school's foundation* ○ [attrib] *tercentenary celebrations.* ▷ **tercentennial** *adj* [usu attrib] of a tercentenary.

teredo /təˈri:dəʊ/ *n* (*pl* ~**s**) type of mollusc that bores into wood, eg the underwater parts of wooden boats, etc.

Teresa /təˈri:zə/ Mother (1910-), Roman Catholic nun, born in Yugoslavia, who founded a religious order in India to help the poor and sick. She was awarded the Nobel peace prize in 1979.

Teresa of Avila /təˌri:zə əv ˈævɪlə/ Saint (1515-82), Spanish nun who founded a new, stricter *Carmelite order. She also wrote influentially on meditation and mystic religious experience.

term /tɜ:m/ *n* **1** period of time for which sth lasts; fixed or limited time: *a long term of imprisonment* ○ *during the President's first term of office.* **2** (*fml*) end or completion of such a period of time: *a pregnancy approaching its term* ○ *His life had* *reached its natural term.* **3** any of the three or four periods in the year during which classes are held in schools, universities, etc: *the autumn/spring/summer term* ○ *end-of-term examinations* ○ *during/in term(-time).* Cf SEMESTER. **4** (*law*) period of time during which a lawcourt holds sessions. **5** word or phrase used as the name or symbol of sth: *'The nick' is a slang term for 'prison'.* ○ *technical, legal, scientific, etc terms.* **6** (*mathematics*) each of the quantities or expressions in a series, ratio, etc. **7** (idm) **a contradiction in terms** ⇨ CONTRADICTION (CONTRADICT). **in the ˈlong/ˈshort term** in the distant/near future: *We must aim for world peace in the long term.*

▷ **term** *v* [Cn·a, Cn·n] (*fml*) call (sth/sb) by a certain term(5); name: *term an offer unacceptable* ○ *a type of music that is termed plainsong.*

termagant /ˈtɜːməgənt/ *n* bad-tempered bullying woman.

terminable /ˈtɜːmɪnəbl/ *adj* (*fml*) that can be terminated: *a contract terminable at a month's notice.*

terminal /ˈtɜːmɪnl/ *adj* **1** of the last stage in a fatal disease: *His illness is terminal,* ie cannot be cured. ○ *terminal cancer* ○ *the ˈterminal ward,* ie in a hospital, for patients who are dying ○ *a terminal case,* ie a patient who is terminally ill. **2** of or taking place each term(3): *terminal examinations, inspections, accounts.* **3** of, forming or situated at the end or boundary of sth: *a terminal marker.*

▷ **terminal** *n* **1** (building at the) end of a railway line, bus route, etc. Cf TERMINUS. **2** building at an airport or in a town where air passengers arrive and depart. **3** point of connection in an electric circuit: *the positive/negative terminals,* eg of a battery. **4** (*computing*) apparatus, usu consisting of a keyboard and screen, for communicating with the central processor in a computing system.

terminally /-nəlɪ/ *adv*: *a hospice for the terminally ill.*

□ ˌ**terminal veˈlocity** highest speed reached by sth (eg a falling body pulled by the force of gravity).

terminate /ˈtɜːmɪneɪt/ *v* [I, Tn] (*fml*) come to an end or bring (sth) to an end: *The meeting terminated in disorder.* ○ *terminate sb's contract* ○ *terminate a pregnancy,* eg by means of an abortion.

termination /ˌtɜːmɪˈneɪʃn/ *n* **1** (**a**) [C, U] point at which or way in which sth ends: *the termination of one's contract.* (**b**) [C] (*medical*) ending of a pregnancy with the death of the unborn child; abortion. **2** [C] final part or letter of a word, eg in an inflexion or derivation.

terminology /ˌtɜːmɪˈnɒlədʒɪ/ *n* **1** [U, C] technical terms of a particular subject: *a word not used except in medical terminology* ○ *various scientific terminologies.* **2** [U] proper use of words as names or symbols: *problems, differences of terminology.* ▷ **terminological** /ˌtɜːmɪnəˈlɒdʒɪkl/ *adj.* **terminologically** *adv*: *terminologically incorrect.*

terminus /ˈtɜːmɪnəs/ *n* (*pl* **-ni** /ˈtɜːmɪnaɪ/ or ~**es** /-nəsɪz/) (**a**) station at the end of a railway line. (**b**) last stop on a bus route, etc. Cf TERMINAL *n* 1.

termite /ˈtɜːmaɪt/ *n* small insect, found chiefly in tropical areas, that is very destructive to timber (popularly called a *white ant,* but not of the ant family).

terms /tɜːmz/ *n* [pl] **1** (**a**) conditions offered or accepted: *peace terms* ○ *according to the terms of the contract.* (**b**) payment offered or asked: *hire-purchase on easy terms* ○ *enquire about terms for renting a house.* **2** way of expressing oneself: *protest in the strongest terms* ○ *He referred to your work in terms of high praise/in flattering terms.* **3** (idm) **be on good, friendly, bad, etc ˈterms (with sb)** have a good, etc relationship: *I didn't know you and she were on such intimate terms,* ie were such close friends. **be on speaking terms** ⇨ SPEAK. **come to terms (with sb)** reach an agreement. **come to terms with sth** reconcile oneself to sth; learn to accept sth: *come to terms with her handicap* ○ *You'll just have to come to terms with the fact that....* **in no uncertain terms** ⇨ UNCERTAIN. **in terms of sth; in sth terms** as regards sth; expressed as sth: *Think of it in terms of an investment.* ○ *The figures are expressed in terms of a percentage/in percentage terms.* **on equal terms** ⇨ EQUAL. **on one's own/on sb's terms** on conditions that one/sb else decides.

□ ˌ**terms of ˈreference** scope or range of an inquiry, etc: *The committee decided that the matter lay outside/within its terms of reference,* ie that it could/could not consider lit.

tern /tɜːn/ *n* sea-bird with long pointed wings and a forked tail.

ternary /ˈtɜːnərɪ/ *adj* made up of three parts.

□ ˌ**ternary ˈform** musical structure consisting of three parts, of which the third is a repetition of the first.

terrace /ˈterəs/ *n* **1** raised level area of ground or a series of these into which a hillside is shaped so that it can be cultivated. **2** flight of wide shallow steps, eg for spectators at a sports ground. **3** paved area beside a house. Cf PATIO. **4** continuous row of similarly designed houses in one block: *6 Olympic Terrace,* ie in a postal address. ⇨ illus at HOME.

▷ **terrace** *v* [Tn esp passive] form (sth) into a terrace or terraces: *a terraced hillside.*

□ ˈ**terraced house** (also ˈ**terrace house**) (*Brit*) (*US* **row house**) any of the houses in a terrace(4). ⇨ article at HOUSE.

terracotta /ˌterəˈkɒtə/ *n* [U] **1** unglazed reddish-brown pottery: [attrib] *a terracotta vase.* **2** its colour.

terra firma /ˌterə ˈfɜːmə/ dry land; the ground (contrasted with water or air): *glad to be on terra firma again,* eg after a trip by boat or aeroplane.

terrain /təˈreɪn *or, in British use,* ˈtereɪn/ *n* [C, U] stretch of land, with regard to its natural features: *difficult terrain for cycling* ○ [attrib] *an all-terrain vehicle.*

terrapin /ˈterəpɪn/ *n* any of various types of edible freshwater tortoise of N America.

terrestrial /təˈrestrɪəl/ *adj* **1** of or living on land: *the terrestrial parts of the world* ○ *terrestrial species.* **2** of the planet earth. Cf CELESTIAL. ▷ **terrestrially** /-trɪəlɪ/ *adv.*

terrible /ˈterəbl/ *adj* **1** causing great fear or distress; appalling: *a terrible war, accident, murder.* **2** hard to bear; extreme: *terrible toothache* ○ *The heat was terrible.* **3** (*infml*) very bad: *I'm terrible at tennis.* ○ *What a terrible meal!* ○ *He's a terrible bore.*

▷ **terribly** /-əblɪ/ *adv* **1** very badly: *She suffered terribly when her son was killed.* **2** (*infml*) very: *not a terribly good film* ○ *I'm terribly sorry.*

terrier /ˈterɪə(r)/ *n* any of various types of small active dog: *a fox terrier,* ie one used for hunting foxes.

terrific /təˈrɪfɪk/ *adj* (*infml*) **1** very great; extreme: *a terrific storm* ○ *driving at a terrific speed.* **2** excellent; wonderful: *doing a terrific job* ○ *The view was terrific.*

▷ **terrifically** /-klɪ/ *adv* (*infml*) extremely: *terrifically clever, generous, rich.*

terrify /ˈterɪfaɪ/ *v* (*pt, pp* **-fied**) [Tn] fill (sb) with terror; make very frightened: *terrified his children with ghost stories* ○ *a terrifying experience.*

▷ **terrified** *adj* ~ (**of sb/sth**)/(**at sth**) feeling terror; very afraid: *terrified of spiders, heights, the dark* ○ *I'm terrified at the prospect of being alone in the house.*

terrine /ˈteriːn/ *n* [U, C] paste made of cooked meat; pâté.

territorial /ˌterəˈtɔːrɪəl/ *adj* of a country's territory: *territorial possessions* ○ *have territorial claims against another country,* ie claim part of its territory.

▷ **Territorial** *n* (*Brit*) member of the Territorial Army.

□ **the** ˌ**Territorial ˈArmy** (*Brit*) military force of part-time volunteers trained for the defence of Great Britain. ⇨ article at ARMED FORCES.

ˌ**territorial ˈwaters** the sea near a country's coast and under its control: *fishing illegally in foreign territorial waters.*

territory /ˈterətrɪ; *US* -tɔːrɪ/ *n* **1** [C, U] (area of) land under the control of a ruler, country, city, etc: *Turkish territory in Europe* ○ *occupying enemy territory* ○ *new territories.* **2 Territory** [C] country or area forming part of the USA, Australia or Canada but not ranking as a state or province: *North West Territory.* **3** [C, U] (extent of the) area for which sb has responsibility or over which a salesman, etc operates: *Our representatives travel over a very large territory.* ○ *How much territory does this medical practice cover?* **4** [C, U] (extent of the) area claimed or dominated by one person, group or animal and defended against others: *He seems to regard that end of the office as his territory,* ie He resents anyone else using it. ○ *Mating blackbirds will defend their territory against intruders.* **5** [C] area of knowledge or activity: *Legal problems are very much Andrew's territory,* ie He handles them.

terror /ˈterə(r)/ *n* **1** (**a**) [U] extreme fear: *run away in terror* ○ *scream with terror* ○ *be in terror of one's life,* ie afraid of being killed ○ *strike terror into* (ie terrify) *sb.* (**b**) [C] instance of this: *have a terror of heights* ○ *The terrors of the night were past.* **2** [C] terrifying person or thing: *hooligans who are a terror to/the terror of the entire town* ○ *Death holds no terrors for* (ie does not frighten) *me.* **3** [C] (*infml*) formidable or troublesome person or thing: *My aunt can be a bit of a terror.* ○ *That puppy is an absolute terror,* ie a great nuisance. **4 the Terror** [sing] (also **the** ˌ**Reign of ˈTerror**) period (1793-4) during the French Revolution when the Committee of Public Safety and their agents had many thousands of their enemies executed. **5** (idm) **a holy terror** ⇨ HOLY.

▷ **terrorism** /ˈterərɪzəm/ *n* [U] use of violence and threats of violence, esp for political purposes. **terrorist** /ˈterərɪst/ *n* person who supports or participates in terrorism: *The terrorists are threatening to blow up the hijacked airliner.* ○ [attrib] *terrorist attacks.*

terrorize, -ise /ˈterəraɪz/ *v* (**a**) [Tn] fill (sb/sth) with terror: *local gangs terrorizing the neighbourhood.* (**b**) [Tn·pr] ~ **sb into sth/doing sth** force sb to do sth by threats of violence, etc: *villagers terrorized into leaving their homes.* **terrorization, -isation** /ˌterəraɪˈzeɪʃn; *US* -rɪˈz-/ *n* [U].

□ ˈ**terror-stricken** (also ˈ**terror-struck**) *adj* filled with terror.

Terry /ˈterɪ/ Dame Ellen Alice (1847-1928), English actress famous for her Shakespearian roles. She often acted in partnership with Henry *Irving.

terry /ˈterɪ/ *n* [U] cotton fabric used for towels, etc, with raised loops of thread left uncut.

terse /tɜːs/ *adj* (*sometimes derog*) using few words; concise; curt: *written in a terse style* ○ *a terse reply, comment, remark, etc* ○ *a terse speaker.* ▷ **tersely** *adv.* **terseness** *n* [U].

tertiary /ˈtɜːʃərɪ; *US* -ʃɪerɪ/ *adj* [usu attrib] **1** third in order, rank, importance, etc; next after secondary: *tertiary education,* ie at university or college level ○ *tertiary* (ie very severe) *burns.* **2 Tertiary** of the period in the earth's history between about 65 million and 2 million years ago, when modern types of plant and animal first appeared.

▷ **Tertiary** *n* the Tertiary period.

Terylene /ˈterəliːn/ (*US* **Dacron**) *n* [U] (*propr*) (fabric made from a) type of synthetic fibre.

TESL /ˌtiː iː es ˈel *or, in informal use,* ˈtesl/ *abbr* Teaching English as a Second Language. Cf TEFL.

tessellated /ˈtesəleɪtɪd/ *adj* (of a pavement) made from small flat pieces of stone of various colours arranged in a pattern.

test /test/ *n* **1** (**a**) examination or trial of the qualities, etc of a person or thing: *an enˈdurance test,* eg for a new engine, soldiers in training, etc ○ [attrib] *a ˈtest bore,* ie a hole bored into the ground to discover whether it contains mineral, oil, etc ○ (*fig*) *She left her purse on the table as a test of the child's honesty.* ○ *The long separation was a test of their love.* (**b**) such an examination conducted for medical purposes: *an ˈeye test* ○ *a ˈblood/ˈurine test.* **2** examination of a person's knowledge or ability in a particular area: *give the pupils a test in arithmetic* ○ *an IˈQ/inˈtelligence test* ○ *a ˈdriving-test,* ie to obtain a driving licence. **3** means or procedure for testing: *a ˈlitmus test* ○

[attrib] *a* ˈ*test circuit,* ie one for testing motor vehicles, etc ○ *a test for AIDS, cancer, tetanus, etc* ○ *a* ˈ*pregnancy test.* **4** (*infml*) = TEST MATCH. **5** (idm) **the acid test** ⇨ ACID[1]. **put sb/sth to the proof/test** ⇨ PROOF[1]. **stand the test of** ˈ**time, etc** prove to be durable, reliable or of lasting value over a long period: *fine old buildings that have stood the test of centuries.*

▷ **test** *v* **1** [I, Ipr, Tn, Tn·pr] ~ **(sb/sth) (for sth)**; ~ **sth (on sb/sth)** examine and measure the qualities, etc of (sb/sth): *testing for pollution in the water/testing the water for pollution* ○ *a well-tested remedy* ○ *testing nuclear weapons under the sea* ○ *have one's eyesight/hearing tested* ○ *The long climb tested our powers of endurance.* ○ *Many people are against new drugs being tested on animals.* **2** [Tn, Tn·pr] ~ **sb (on sth)** test sb's knowledge or ability (in a particular area): *She tested the whole class on irregular verbs.*

□ ˈ**test ban** international agreement not to explode nuclear weapons experimentally: [attrib] *a* ˌ*test-ban* ˈ*treaty.*

ˈ**test case** lawsuit or other procedure that provides a decision which is expected to be used in settling similar cases in the future: *The outcome of these wage talks is seen as a test case for future pay negotiations.*

ˈ**test drive** drive taken to judge the performance, etc of a car one is thinking of buying. ˈ**test-drive** *v* (*pt* **-drove**, *pp* **-driven**) [Tn] take a test drive in (a car).

ˈ**test match** (also *infml* **test**) cricket or Rugby match between teams of certain countries, usu one of a series during a tour. ⇨ article at SEASON.

ˈ**test pilot** pilot whose job is to fly newly designed aircraft to test their performance.

test-tube

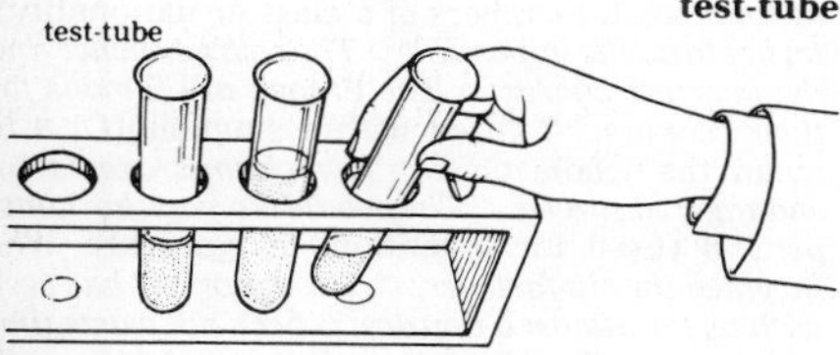

ˈ**test-tube** *n* slender glass tube, closed at one end, used in chemical experiments. ˈ**test-tube baby** baby that is conceived by artificial insemination, or that develops elsewhere than in a mother's body.

testament /ˈtestəmənt/ *n* (*fml*) **1** (usu *sing*) ~ **(to sth)** thing that provides clear proof of sth: *a testament to sb's beliefs* ○ *The new model is a testament to the skill and dedication of the workforce.* Cf THE OLD TESTAMENT (OLD), THE NEW TESTAMENT (NEW). **2** = WILL[4] 4.

▷ **testamentary** /ˌtestəˈmentrɪ/ *adj* (*fml*) of or given in a person's will: *a testamentary bequest.*

testate /ˈtesteɪt/ *adj* (*law*) having left a valid will at one's death.

▷ **testator** /teˈsteɪtə(r); *US* ˈtesteɪtər/ (*fem* **testatrix** /teˈsteɪtrɪks/) *n* person who has made a will[4](4).

testes *pl* of TESTIS.

testicle /ˈtestɪkl/ *n* either of the two glands of the male sex organ in which sperm-bearing fluid is produced. ⇨ illus at MALE.

testify /ˈtestɪfaɪ/ *v* (*pt, pp* **-fied**) **1** [I, Ipr, Tf] ~ **(to sth)**; ~ **(against/in favour of sb)** give evidence; declare as a witness, esp in court: *summoned to testify in court* ○ *The teacher testified to the boy's honesty.* ○ *Two witnesses testified against her and one in her favour.* ○ *He testified under oath that he had not been at the scene of the crime.* **2** [Ipr, Tn] ~ **(to) sth** (*fml*) be evidence of sth: *tears that testified (to) her grief.*

testimonial /ˌtestɪˈməʊnɪəl/ *n* **1** written statement testifying to a person's character, abilities or qualifications: *She sent a testimonial from her former employer when applying for the post.* Cf REFERENCE 4. **2** thing given to sb, eg by his colleagues, to show appreciation of his services or achievements: [attrib] *a testimonial match, game, etc,* ie to honour a distinguished sportsman.

testimony /ˈtestɪmənɪ; *US* -məʊnɪ/ *n* **1** [U, C] written or spoken statement declaring that sth is true, esp one made under oath: *According to the witness's testimony, you were present when the crime was committed.* **2** [U, sing] ~ **(to sth)** evidence in support of sth: *The pyramids are (a) testimony to the Ancient Egyptians' engineering skills.*

testis /ˈtestɪs/ *n* (*pl* **-tes** /-tiːz/) (*anatomy*) testicle.

testosterone /teˈstɒstərəʊn/ *n* [U] male sex hormone which is produced in the testicles and causes male features (eg a deep voice and facial hair).

testy /ˈtestɪ/ *adj* (**-ier, -iest**) easily annoyed; irritable: *a testy person, reply.* ▷ **testily** /-ɪlɪ/ *adv.* **testiness** *n* [U].

tetanus /ˈtetənəs/ *n* [U] disease in which the muscles contract and stiffen, caused by bacteria entering the body. Cf LOCKJAW (LOCK[2]).

tetchy /ˈtetʃɪ/ *adj* (**-ier, -iest**) peevish; irritable: *a tetchy person, mood, remark* ○ *There's no need to be so tetchy (with me)!* ▷ **tetchily** /-ɪlɪ/ *adv.* **tetchiness** *n* [U].

tête-à-tête /ˌteɪt ɑː ˈteɪt/ *n* private conversation between two people: *have regular tête-à-têtes with sb* ○ [attrib] *a tête-à-tête dinner.*

▷ **tête-à-tête** *adv* together in private: *dine tête-à-tête with sb.*

tether /ˈteðə(r)/ *n* **1** rope or chain by which an animal is fastened while it is grazing. **2** (idm) **at the end of one's tether** ⇨ END[1].

▷ **tether** *v* [Tn, Tn·pr] ~ **sth (to sth)** fasten (an animal) with a tether: *He tethered his horse to a tree.*

tetr(a)- *comb form* four: *tetrasyllable,* ie a word with four syllables.

tetrahedron /ˌtetrəˈhiːdrən/ *n* (*geometry*) solid figure with four faces, a pyramid with three triangular faces and a triangular base. ⇨ illus at CUBE.

Teutonic /tjuːˈtɒnɪk; *US* tuː-/ *adj* **1** of the Germanic (ie Anglo-Saxon, Dutch, German and Scandinavian) peoples or their languages. **2** [usu attrib] showing qualities thought to be typical of German people: *Teutonic thoroughness.*

Texas /ˈteksəs/ state of the south-western USA. Originally a Spanish possession, it was an independent country between 1836 and 1845, when it became part of the USA. Amongst its chief products are oil, meat, rice, cotton and fruit. ⇨ map at App 1. ▷ **Texan** /teksən/ *n, adj.*

□ ˌ**Texas** ˈ**Ranger** (formerly) member of a mounted police force in Texas.

text /tekst/ *n* **1** [U] main written or printed part of a book or page (contrasted with notes, diagrams, illustrations, etc): *too much text and not enough pictures* ○ *The index refers the reader to pages in the text.* **2** [C] original words of an author, document, etc (contrasted with later revisions, shortened versions, etc): *the full text of the Prime Minister's speech* ○ *the problems of establishing the text of 'King Lear'* ○ *a corrupt text,* eg one altered by mistakes in copying. **3** [C] sentence or short passage from the Bible, etc used as the subject of a sermon or discussion: *I take as my text….* **4** [C] book, play, etc prescribed for study or as part of a syllabus: *'Hamlet' is a set text for A level this year.*

▷ **textual** /ˈtekstʃʊəl/ *adj* [usu attrib] of or in a text: *textual criticism* ○ *textual errors.* **textually** /-ʊəlɪ/ *adv.*

□ **textbook** /ˈteksbʊk/ *n* book giving instruction in a subject: *an algebra textbook* ○ [attrib] *a textbook example of how the game should be played,* ie worth copying, exemplary.

textile /ˈtekstaɪl/ *n* (esp *pl*) woven or machine-knitted fabric: *factories producing a range of textiles* ○ *get a job in textiles* ○ [attrib] *the textile industry.*

texture /ˈtekstʃə(r)/ *n* **1** [C, U] way a surface, substance or fabric looks or feels to the touch, ie its thickness, firmness, roughness, etc: *the delicate texture of her skin* ○ *cement with a fine/coarse texture* ○ *The cake has a nice light texture.* **2** arrangement of the threads in a fabric: *cloth with a loose/close texture.*

▷ **textured** *adj* (esp in compounds) having a distinct or specified texture: *textured* (ie not smooth) *wallpaper* ○ *The walls have a textured finish.* ○ ˌ*coarse-*ˈ*textured.*

TGWU /ˌtiː ˌdʒiː ˌdʌbljuː ˈjuː/ *abbr* Transport and General Workers' Union (in the UK).

Th *symb* thorium.

-th *suff* **1** (with a few *vs* and *adjs* forming *ns*): *growth* ○ *width.* **2** (with simple numbers except *one, two* and *three* forming ordinal numbers): *sixth* ○ *fifteenth* ○ *hundredth.*

Thackeray /ˈθækərɪ/ William Makepeace (1811-63), English novelist, best known for his first novel, *Vanity Fair,* which satirizes the pretensions of the English upper-middle classes. Other works include *Pendennis, The Newcomes,* the historical novels *Henry Esmond* and *The Virginians,* and the fairy tale *The Rose and the Ring.* He also contributed regularly to magazines such as *Punch,* and was the first editor of the *Cornhill Magazine.*

Thailand

Thailand /ˈtaɪlænd/ country in SE Asia, bordering on Burma, Laos and Cambodia; pop approx 54 536 000; official language Thai; capital Bangkok; unit of currency baht (= 100 satang). It is a monarchy, and until 1939 was known as Siam. It is the world's largest exporter of rice, and also produces rubber, timber, tin and precious stones. ⇨ map.

▷ **Thai** /taɪ/ *adj* of Thailand, its people or its language. — *n* **1** [C] native or inhabitant of Thailand. **2** [U] language of Thailand.

thalamus /ˈθæləməs/ *n* (*pl* **-mi** /-maɪ/) (*anatomy*) inside part of the brain, from which the sensory nerves emanate. ⇨ illus at BRAIN.

thalidomide /θəˈlɪdəmaɪd/ *n* [U] sedative drug formerly given to pregnant women until it was found that some of them gave birth to babies with deformed limbs: [attrib] *a thalidomide child,* ie one born deformed in this way.

Thames /temz/ **the Thames** river in southern England; length 338 km (210 miles). It rises in the *Cotswolds, and flows through London to the *North Sea. In 1982 the Thames barrier was built to protect London from flooding.

than /ðən; *rare strong form* ðæn/ *conj* (used after a comparative *adj* or *adv* to introduce a clause or phrase in which a comparison is expressed): *He's never more annoying than when he's trying to help.* ○ *She's a better player than (she was) last year.* ○ *He loves me more than you do.* ○ *She should know*

better than to poke the animal with her umbrella.
▷ **than** *prep* **1** (used before a *n* or *pron* to express a comparison): *You gave me less than him*, ie less than you gave him or (*infml*) less than he gave me. ○ *I'm older than her.* ○ *Nobody understands the situation better than you.* ○ *There was more whisky in it than soda.* **2** (used after *more* or *less* and before an expression of time, distance, etc to indicate how long sth takes, how far it is, etc): *It cost me more than £100.* ○ *It never takes more than an hour.* ○ *He can't be more than fifteen.* ○ *It's less than a mile to the beach.*

thank /θæŋk/ *v* **1** [Tn, Tn·pr] ~ **sb** (**for sth**/**doing sth**) express gratitude to sb: *There's no need to thank me — I was only doing my job.* ○ *We thanked them for all their help.* ○ (*ironic*) *He won't thank you* (ie He'll be annoyed with you) *for leaving him all the washing-up to do.* **2** (idm) **have oneself**/**sb to thank** (**for sth**) (*ironic*) be responsible/hold sb responsible (for sth): *She only has herself to thank for what happened.* ○ *Who do we have to thank for this fiasco?* **I'll thank you for sth**/**to do sth** (used in making politely formal requests or commands): *I'll thank you for* (ie Please give me) *that book.* ○ *I'll thank you to mind your business.* ˌ**no**, ˈ**thank you** (used to decline an offer, a proposal, etc politely). **thank** ˈ**God**/ˈ**goodness**/ˈ**heaven**(**s**) (used to express relief): *Thank God you're safe!* **thank one's lucky stars** be or feel especially fortunate: *You can thank your lucky stars (that) you don't have to go to this dreary reception.* ˈ**thank you** (used to express gratitude or to accept an offer, a proposal, etc): *Thank you for giving me a lift.* ○ *Thank you very much indeed.*

▷ **thankful** /-fl/ *adj* **1** grateful: *You should be thankful to have escaped*/*that you have escaped with only minor injuries.* **2** (idm) **be grateful**/**thankful for small mercies** ⇨ SMALL. **thankfully** /-fəlɪ/ *adv* **1** in a thankful way. **2** (*infml*) I/we are glad; luckily: *Thankfully, it's at last stopped raining.* ⇨ Usage at HOPEFUL. **thankfulness** *n* [U].

thankless *adj* **1** not feeling or expressing gratitude. **2** (of an action) not likely to win thanks, appreciation or reward for the person performing it: *a thankless role, task.* **thanklessly** *adv.* **thanklessness** *n* [U].

thanks *n* [pl] **1** expressions of gratitude: *Thanks are due to all those who helped.* ○ *My heartfelt thanks to you all.* ○ *give thanks to God.* **2** (idm) **no thanks to sb**/**sth** despite sb/sth: *It's no thanks to you (that) we arrived on time — your short cuts weren't short cuts at all!* **thanks to sb**/**sth** (*sometimes ironic*) because of sb/sth: *The play succeeded thanks to fine acting by all the cast.* ○ *Thanks to the bad weather, the match had been cancelled.* **a vote of thanks** ⇨ VOTE. — *interj* (*infml*) thank you: *'Would you like some more cake?' 'No, thanks.'*

□ ˈ**thanksgiving** *n* [C, U] **1** expression of gratitude, esp to God. **2 Thanksgiving** (**Day**) holiday in the USA (on the fourth Thursday in November) and Canada (on the second Monday in October), originally set apart for giving thanks to God. ⇨ article at HOLIDAY.

ˈ**thank-you** *n* expression of thanks: *Have you said your thank-yous to Mrs Brown for the party?* ○ *She walked away without so much as a thank-you.* ○ [attrib] *thank-you letters.*

that[1] /ðæt/ *det* (*pl* **those** /ðəʊz/) **1** (used to make a person or thing specific, esp when he/it is seen as distant in space or time from the speaker/writer): *Look at that man standing there.* ○ *That box is bigger than this.* ○ *How much are those apples at the back?* ○ *Where did that noise come from?* ○ *Have you read that book about China?* ○ *I was still living with my parents at that time*/*in those days*, ie at that particular time in the past. Cf THIS. **2** (**a**) (used to specify a person or thing that is indicated or mentioned): *Did you see that boy?* ○ *He began by writing a thriller. That book sold a million copies.* (**b**) (used with a *n* followed by a possessive): *Did you meet that friend of his?* ○ *That dress of hers is too short.* **3** (used in front of the antecedent of a relative clause): *Have you forgotten about that money I lent you last week?* ○ *Those students who failed the exam will have to take it again.* ○ *Who was that man you were talking to?*

▷ **that** *adv* to that degree; so: *I can't walk that far*, ie as far as that. ○ *They've spent that much*, ie as much as is indicated. ○ *It's about that long*, ie as long as that. ○ *It isn't all that cold*, ie not as cold as you are suggesting or not extremely cold.

that[2] /ðæt/ *pron* (*pl* **those** /ðəʊz/) **1** (**a**) (used to make a thing specific, esp one more distant in space or time than another): *Those look juicier than these.* ○ *That's a nice hat.* (**b**) (referring to people, only with the verb *be*): *That's Peter at the bus-stop.* ○ *Who's that?* **2** (used to specify a thing, an event, an idea, etc that is indicated or mentioned): *Look at that!* ○ *Do you remember going to Norway? That was a good holiday.* ○ *Send her some flowers — that's the easiest thing to do.* **3** (used as the antecedent of a relative clause): *Is that what you really think?* ○ *That's what he told me.* ○ *Those who expect the worst are less likely to be disappointed.* ○ *Those present were in favour of a change.* ○ *There are those who say* (ie Some people say) *she should never have been appointed.* **4** (idm) ˈ**that is** (**to say**) (**a**) which means: *He's a local government administrator, that is to say a Civil Servant.* (**b**) to be specific: *She's a housewife — when she's not teaching English, that is.* ˌ**that's** ˈ**that** (used to indicate the end of a discussion, search, development, etc): *I take it that's that — we've heard your final offer?* ○ *So that's that. At last we're all agreed.*

that[3] /ðət; *rare strong form* ðæt/ *conj* **1** (used to introduce a clause that is the subject or object of a *v*): *That the attempt to save her had failed soon became widely known.* ○ *She said that the book was based on a true story.* ○ *I thought that 13 May would be the date of the election.* ○ *It's possible that he hasn't received the letter.* **2** (*rhet*) (used to express wishes and regrets): *Oh that I could see him again!* ○ *That I should see a child of mine arrested for selling drugs!*

that[4] /ðət; *rare strong form* ðæt/ *rel pron* **1** (used to introduce a defining clause after a *n*, esp referring to things) (**a**) (as the subject of the *v* in the clause): *The letter that came this morning is from my father.* ○ *The clothes that are on the floor are dirty.* ○ *The woman that spoke to me in the shop used to live next door.* ○ *Who was it that won the World Cup in 1982?* (**b**) (as the object of the *v* in the clause, but usu omitted in this position): *The watch (that) you gave me keeps perfect time.* ○ *Here are the books (that) I borrowed from you a week ago.* ○ *The person (that) I have to phone lives in India.* (**c**) (as the object of a *prep* in the clause, but usu omitted in this position): *The photographs (that) you're looking at were taken by my brother.* ○ *The man (that) I was talking to had just arrived from Canada.* ○ *These are the children (that) I looked after last summer.* **2** (used to introduce a clause following superlatives, *the only*, *all*, etc): *Shakespeare is the greatest English writer that ever lived.* ○ *This is the most expensive watch (that) I've ever owned.* ○ *The only part of the meal (that) I really liked was the dessert.* ○ *All that I have is yours.* **3** (used after an expression of time instead of *when*): *the year that my father died* ○ *the day that war broke out.*

thatch /θætʃ/ *n* **1** [C, U] (roof or roof-covering made of) dried straw, reeds, etc. **2** [sing] (*infml*) thick growth of hair on the head.

▷ **thatch** *v* [Tn] cover (a roof) or roof (a house, etc) with thatch: *a village hut thatched with palm leaves* ○ *a thatched cottage.* **thatcher** *n* person who puts thatch on a house, etc.

Thatcher /ˈθætʃə(r)/ Margaret Hilda (1925-), British politician, elected leader of the Conservative Party in 1975 and prime minister 1979-90 (the first woman to hold this office in Britain). ⇨ App 2.

▷ **Thatcherism** /ˈθætʃərɪzəm/ *n* [U] principles and policies of the Thatcher government, esp the economic policies of the early 1980s designed to reduce inflation.

Thatcherite /-raɪt/ *n*, *adj* (supporter) of Margaret Thatcher or of Thatcherism.

thaw /θɔː/ *v* **1** (**a**) [I, Ip, Tn, Tn·p] ~ (**sth**) (**out** (cause sth to) pass into an unfrozen or a liqui state after being frozen: *All the snow has thawed.* ○ *leave frozen food to thaw before cooking it* ○ *thaw out (the ice in) the pipes.* (**b**) [I] (used only with *it* (of the weather) become warm enough to mel snow and ice: *It's starting to thaw.* ⇨ Usage a WATER[1]. **2** [I, Ip] ~ (**out**) (of people, thei behaviour, etc) become less cool or formal ir manner: *After a few drinks the party atmosphere began to thaw (out).*

▷ **thaw** *n* (usu *sing*) (weather that causes thawing: *go skating before the thaw* ○ *A thaw is setting in.* ○ (*fig*) *a thaw in East-West relations.*

the /ðə, ðɪ; *strong form* ðiː/ ⇨ Guide to Entries 5.2. ⇨ Usage at A[2]. *def art* (used to make the following *n* refer to a specific person, thing, event or group **1** (when it has already been mentioned or implied): *A boy and a girl were sitting on a bench The boy was smiling but the girl looked angry.* ○ *There was an accident here yesterday. A car hit a tree. The driver was killed.* **2** (when a *n* is followed by a phrase that restricts its meaning): *the centre of town* ○ *the topic of conversation* ○ *the man of her dreams* ○ *the house that Jack built.* **3** (**a**) (when i has unique reference): *the sun* ○ *the moon* ○ *the stars.* (**b**) (used with some parts of the natura world without a preceding *adj*): *The sky was blue* (Cf *There was a blue sky.*) ○ *The sea is rough.* (C *There's a rough sea.*) ○ *The atmosphere was stuffy* (Cf *There was a stuffy atmosphere.*). **4** (when the person or thing that is referred to is obvious withir the situation): *The milkman was late this morning* ○ *Have you seen the paper?* ○ *The children are in the garden.* ○ *Would you pass the salt, please?* **5** (usec with superlative *adjs*, *first*, *last*, *next*, etc): *the bes day of your life* ○ *the hottest day of the holiday* ○ *What was the last thing I said?* **6** (used with an *ad* to refer to all members of a class or nationality) *trying to do the impossible* ○ *The rich get richer and the poor get poorer.* ○ *The French are famous fo their cooking.* **7** (used with a singular [C] *n* to mean the whole class): *The chimpanzee is ar endangered species.* ○ *The poodle is a popular house pet.* **8** (used for inventions in general): *Wh invented the zip-fastener?* ○ *The motor car has beer with us for almost a century.* ○ *Let's not waste time re-inventing the wheel*, ie working to develop sth that has already been produced. **9** (used in front o a unit of measure to mean 'every'): *My car does forty miles to the gallon.* ○ *I work free-lance and am paid by the hour.* ○ *The price is 50p the dozen* **10** (used to indicate that the person or thing referred to is well-known or important): *Michae Crawford? Not* ˈ*the Michael Crawford?* ○ *The roya wedding was* ˈ*the social event of the year.* **11** (idm **the more**, **less**, **etc** . . . **the more**, **less**, **etc** . . . (usec to show that the increase/decrease in one amoun or degree of sth continues at the same rate as another): *The more she thought about it, the more depressed she became.* ○ *The more beautiful the hat the more expensive it usually is.* ○ *I want you out o here, and the sooner the better.* ○ *The less said abou the whole affair, the happier I'll be.*

theatre (*US* **theater**) /ˈθɪətə(r); *US* ˈθiːətər/ *n* **1** [C building or outdoor area for the performance o plays and similar entertainments: *West End theatres* ○ *an open-air theatre* ○ *use the schoo gymnasium as a theatre.* ⇨ illus. **2** [C] (**a**) room o hall for lectures, etc with seats in rows rising one behind another. (**b**) (also ˈ**operating-theatre** room in a hospital, etc where surgical operations are performed: *The patient is on her way to (the theatre.* ○ [attrib] *a theatre sister*, ie a nurse assisting during operations. **3** [C] ~ **of sth** (*rhet* scene of important events (esp of war): *the lates theatre of internal conflict.* **4** (**a**) [U] dramatic literature or art; the writing, acting and producing of plays: *a study of Greek theatre* ○ *Do you often go to the theatre* (ie go to see a play)? ○ *The play is wel written but it is not*/*does not make good theatre*, ie is not effective when performed. (**b**) **the theatre** [sing] the theatrical world as a profession or way of life: *She wants to go into the theatre*, eg become an actress.

THEATRE

Shakespearian theatre

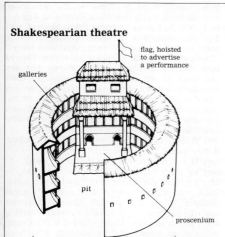

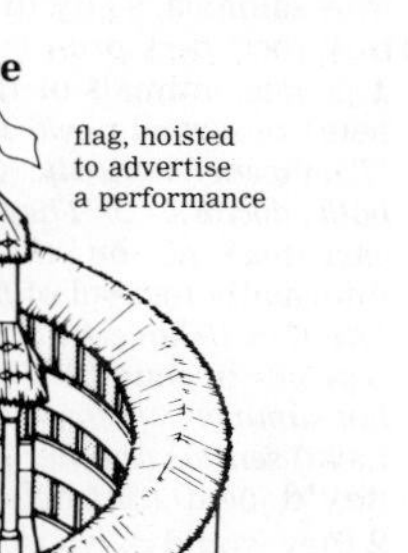

traditional European theatre

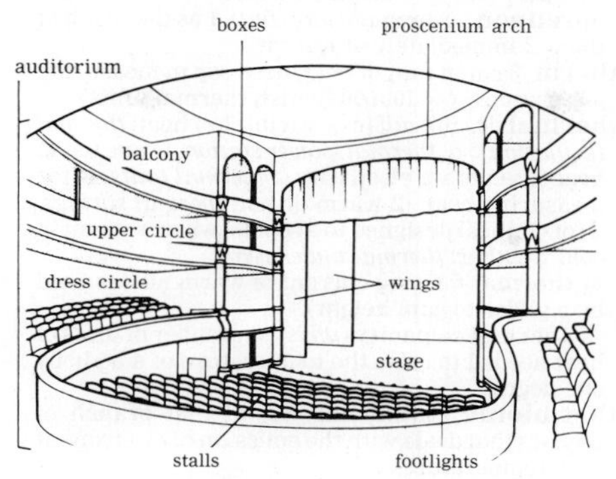

theatre-in-the-round

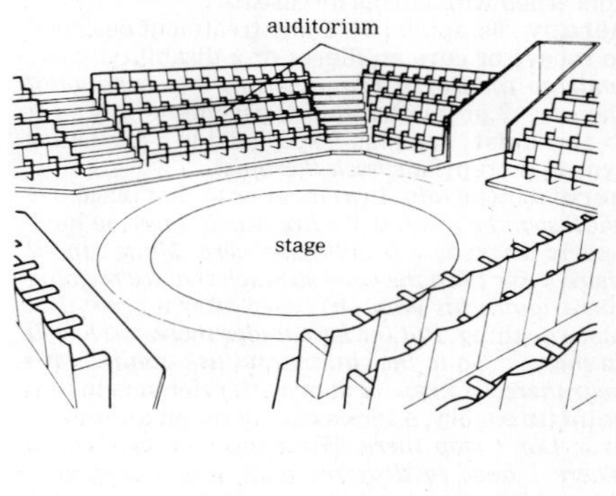

▷ **theatrical** /θɪˈætrɪkl/ *adj* **1** [usu attrib] of or for the theatre: *theatrical scenery, performances, reviews* ○ *a theatrical company.* **2** (of behaviour) exaggerated in order to create an effect; unnaturally showy; histrionic: *theatrical gestures.* **theatrically** /-klɪ/ *adv.*

theatricals *n* [pl] theatrical performances: *amateur theatricals.*

□ ˈ**theatre-goer** *n* person who frequently goes to see plays, etc.

ˌ**theatre-in-the-ˈround** *n* [U] form of dramatic performance with the audience seated around a central stage. ⇨ illus.

the ˌ**Theatre of** ˈ**Cruelty** type of drama, begun by Antonin *Artaud in the 1930s, which aimed to release subconscious feelings by presenting suffering and evil on stage.

the ˌ**Theatre of the Ab**ˈ**surd** type of drama of the second half of the 20th century which expresses human beings' inability to communicate with each other and the futility of human existence. It is characterized by seemingly illogical and meaningless dialogue. Amongst its leading playwrights are *Beckett, *Ionesco and *Pinter.

ˈ**theatre weapons** weapons that are of intermediate range, between tactical and strategic weapons.

Thebes /θi:bz/ **1** city in ancient Egypt, on the Nile. Between about 1600 and 1300 BC it was the capital, and the ruins of many temples, royal tombs, etc survive from that period. **2** city in ancient Greece, which was for a short time in the 4th century BC the most powerful in Greece. ▷ **Theban** /ˈθi:bn/ *adj, n.*

thee /ði:/ *pron* (*arch or dialect*) (object form of *thou*).

theft /θeft/ *n* [C, U] (act or instance of) stealing: *A number of thefts have been reported recently.* ○ *guilty of theft.*

their /ðeə(r)/ *possess det* of or belonging to them: *Their parties are always fun.* ○ *Their own car is being mended — this one is hired.* ○ *Their fame rests entirely on one record.*

▷ **theirs** /ðeəz/ *possess pron* of or belonging to them: *Theirs are the children with very fair hair.* ○ *It's a favourite place of theirs.*

theism /ˈθi:ɪzəm/ *n* [U] belief in the existence of a God or gods, esp a God revealed to man as the creator and ruler of the universe. Cf DEISM.

▷ **theist** /ˈθi:ɪst/ *n* believer in theism.

theistic /θi:ˈɪstɪk/, **theistical** (/-kl/) *adjs.*

them /ðəm; *strong form* ðem/ *pers pron* **1** (used as the object of a *v* or of a *prep*; also used independently or after *be*): *Tell them the news.* ○ *Give them to me.* ○ *Did you eat all of them?* ○ *Oh, them! We needn't worry about them.* **2** (used informally instead of *him* or *her*): *If a customer comes in before I get back ask them to wait.* **3** (idm) ˌ**them and** ˈ**us** rich or powerful people contrasted with ordinary people like the speaker(s): *We should try to get away from a 'them and us' attitude in industrial relations.* Cf THEY.

thematic /θɪˈmætɪk/ *adj* of or related to a theme(1). ▷ **thematically** /-klɪ/ *adv.*

theme /θi:m/ *n* [C] **1** subject of a talk, a piece of writing or a person's thoughts; topic: *The theme of our discussion was 'Europe in the 1990s'.* **2** (*music*) melody that is repeated, developed, etc in a composition, or on which variations are composed. **3** (*US*) (subject set for a) student's essay or exercise.

□ ˈ**theme park** amusement park in which the entertainments are based on a single idea or group of ideas.

ˈ**theme song** (also ˈ**theme tune**) (**a**) melody that is often repeated in a musical play, film, etc. (**b**) = SIGNATURE TUNE (SIGNATURE).

themselves /ðəmˈselvz/ *reflex, emph pron* (only taking the main stress in sentences when used emphatically) **1** (*reflex*) (used when the people or animals performing an action are also affected by it): *The children can look* ˌ*after them*ˈ*selves for a couple of hours.* **2** (*emph*) (used to emphasize *they* or *them*): *They them*ˈ*selves had had a similar experience.* ○ *Denise and Martin paid for it them*ˈ*selves.* ○ *The teachers were them*ˈ*selves too surprised to comment.* **3** (idm) **by them**ˈ**selves** (**a**) alone. (**b**) without help.

then /ðen/ *adv* **1** (referring to past or future time) (**a**) at that time: *We were living in Wales then.* ○ *I was still married to my first husband then.* ○ *See you on Thursday — we'll be able to discuss it then.* ○ *Jackie Kennedy, as she then was, was still only in her twenties.* ○ [attrib] *The then Prime Minister took her husband with her on all her travels.* (**b**) next; after that; afterwards: *I'll have soup first and then the chicken.* ○ *The liquid turned green and then brown.* ○ *We had a week in Rome and then went to Vienna.* (**c**) (used after a *prep*) that time: *From then on he refused to talk about it.* ○ *We'll have to manage without a TV until then.* ○ *She'll have retired by then.* Cf NOW. **2** and also: *There are the vegetables to peel and the soup to heat. Then there's the table to lay and the wine to cool.* ○ *I've sent cards to all my family. Then there's your family and the neighbours.* **3** in that case; therefore: *If it's not on the table then it will be in the drawer.* ○ *Offer to take him out for lunch, then* (ie as a result of this) *he'll feel in a better mood.* ○ *He'll be looking for a new secretary then?* **4** (idm) (**but**) **then a**ˈ**gain** (used to introduce a contrasting piece of information): *He's clumsy and untidy but then again he's always willing to help.* **then and there** ⇨ THERE AND THEN (THERE[1]).

thence /ðens/ *adv* (*arch or fml*) from there: *They travelled by rail to the coast and thence by boat to America.*

the(o)- *comb form* of God or a god: *theology* ○ *theocratic.*

theocracy /θɪˈɒkrəsɪ/ *n* (country with a) system of government by priests or a priestly class in which the laws of the State are believed to be the laws of God. ▷ **theocratic** /ˌθɪəˈkrætɪk/ *adj.*

theodolite /θɪˈɒdəlaɪt/ *n* instrument used by surveyors for measuring horizontal and vertical angles.

theogony /θɪˈɒgənɪ/ *n* (account of the) origins of the gods and their relationship to each other by descent.

theology /θɪˈɒlədʒɪ/ *n* **1** [U] formal study of the nature of God and of the foundations of religious belief: [attrib] *a theology student.* **2** [C] set of religious beliefs; theological system: *rival theologies.*

▷ **theologian** /ˌθɪəˈləʊdʒən/ *n* expert in or student of theology.

theological /ˌθɪəˈlɒdʒɪkl/ *adj*: *theological argument* ○ *a theological college.* **theologically** /-klɪ/ *adv.*

theorem /ˈθɪərəm/ *n* **1** rule in algebra, etc, esp one expressed as a formula. **2** mathematical statement to be proved by a chain of reasoning.

theoretical /ˌθɪəˈretɪkl/ *adj* **1** concerned with the theory of a subject: *a theoretical physicist* ○ *This book is too theoretical; I need a practical guide.* Cf PRACTICAL 1. **2** supposed but not necessarily true: *Lendl's strength on clay gives him a theoretical advantage.* ▷ **theoretically** /-klɪ/ *adv*: *Theoretically we could still win, but it's very unlikely.*

theory /ˈθɪərɪ/ *n* **1** [C] set of reasoned ideas intended to explain facts or events: *Darwin's theory of evolution.* **2** [C] opinion or supposition, not necessarily based on reasoning: *He has a theory that wearing hats makes men go bald.* **3** [U] ideas or suppositions in general (contrasted with *practice*): *It sounds fine in theory, but will it work?* ○ *In theory, three things could happen*, ie there are three possibilities. **4** [C, U] (statement of the) principles on which a subject is based: *studying music theory.*

▷ **theorist** /ˈθɪərɪst/ *n* person who forms theories.

theorize, -ise /ˈθɪəraɪz/ *v* [I, Ipr] ~ (**about sth**) form theories.

theosophy /θi:ˈɒsəfɪ/ *n* [U] (*philosophy*) any of several systems that aim at a direct knowledge of God by means of meditation, prayer, etc.

▷ **theosophical** /ˌθi:əˈsɒfɪkl/ *adj.*

theosophist /θi:ˈɒsəfɪst/ *n* believer in theosophy.

therapeutic /ˌθerəˈpju:tɪk/ *adj* of the art of healing or the curing of disease: *therapeutic exercises*, eg

after a surgical operation ○ *the therapeutic effects of sea air*.
▷ **therapeutically** /-klɪ/ *adv*.
therapeutics *n* [sing *v*] branch of medicine concerned with curing disease.

therapy /ˈθerəpɪ/ *n* [U] **1** any treatment designed to relieve or cure an illness or a disability: *have/undergo therapy* ○ *radio-therapy* ○ *occupational therapy*. **2** physiotherapy. **3** psychotherapy.
▷ **therapist** /ˈθerəpɪst/ *n* specialist in a particular type of therapy: *a speech therapist*.

there[1] /ðeə(r)/ *adv* **1** (**a**) in, at or to that place: *We shall soon be there.* ○ *We are nearly there*, ie have nearly arrived. ○ *If John sits here, Mary can sit there.* ○ *We liked the hotel so much that we're going there again this year.* (**b**) (used after a *prep*) that place or thing: *Put the keys under there.* ○ *They fit in there.* ○ *Go to the church and ask again — it's near there.* Cf HERE. **2** at or with reference to that point (in a story, a series of actions, an argument, etc): *Don't stop there. What did you do then?* ○ *There I have to disagree with you, I'm afraid.* **3** (used for emphasis before some *vs*, eg *go, stand, lie*, to show the location of sb/sth, with the subject following the *v* if it is not a *pron*): *There goes the last bus.* ○ *There it goes.* ○ *There it is: just to the right of the church.* ○ *There you are. I've been waiting for over an hour.* **4** (used to call attention to sth): *There's the school bell — I must run.* ○ (*ironic*) *There's gratitude for you*, ie Look how ungrateful he/she is. **5** (**a**) (used after *that* + a *n* for emphasis): *That woman there is 103.* (**b**) (used to emphasize a call or greeting): *You there! Come back!* ○ *Hello there! Lovely to see you again!* **6** (idm) ˌ**there and** ˈ**back** to and from a place: *Can I go there and back in a day?* ˌ**there and** ˈ**then**; ˌ**then and** ˈ**there** at that time and place: *I took one look at the car and offered to buy it there and then.* ˌ**there you** ˈ**are** (**a**) (used when giving sb a thing he wants or has requested): *There you are. I've brought your newspaper.* (**b**) (used to give reassurance when explaining, demonstrating or commenting on sth): *You switch on, wait until the screen turns green, push in the disk and there you are!* ○ *There you are! I told you it was easy.* ˌ**there you** ˈ**go**/**go a**ˈ**gain** (used to comment, usu critically, on a typical example of sb's behaviour): *There you go again — jumping to conclusions on the slightest evidence.*
▷ **there** *interj* **1** (used to express triumph, dismay, encouragement, etc): *There (now)! What did I tell you?* ie You can see that I was right. ○ *There! You've (gone and) woken the baby!* ○ *There! That didn't hurt too much, did it?* **2** (idm) ˌ**there**, ˈ**there!** (used to comfort a small child): *There, there! Never mind, you'll soon feel better.*

there[2] /ðə(r); *strong form* ðeə(r)/ *adv* **1** (used in place of a subject with *be, seem, appear*, etc, esp when referring to sb/sth for the first time): *There's a man at the bus-stop.* (Cf *The man is at the bus-stop.*) ○ *There's no reason to go.* ○ *There seems (to be) no doubt about it.* ○ *There appeared to be nobody willing to help.* ○ *There can be no going back.* ○ *I don't want there to be any misunderstanding.* ○ *There comes a time* (Cf *The time comes*) *when dying seems preferable to staying alive.* ○ *There once lived a poor farmer who had four sons.* **2** (idm) ˈ**there's a good boy, girl, dog, etc** (used to praise or encourage small children or animals): *Finish your tea, there's a good boy.*

thereabouts /ˈðeərəbaʊts/ (also *US* **thereabout** /ˈðeərəbaʊt/) *adv* (usu after *or*) **1** somewhere near there: *The factory is in Leeds or somewhere thereabouts.* **2** near that number, quantity, time, etc: *I'll be home at 8 o'clock or thereabouts.*

thereafter /ˌðeərˈɑːftə(r); *US* -ˈæf-/ *adv* (*fml*) after that: *You will be accompanied as far as the border; thereafter you must find your own way.*

thereby /ˌðeəˈbaɪ/ *adv* (*fml*) by that means: *They paid cash, thereby avoiding interest charges.*

therefore /ˈðeəfɔː(r)/ *adv* for that reason.

therein /ˌðeərˈɪn/ *adv* (*fml or law*) (**a**) in that place: *the house and all the possessions therein.* (**b**) in that respect: *Therein lies the crux of the matter.*

thereinafter /ˌðeərɪnˈɑːftə(r); *US* -ˈæf-/ *adv* (*law*) in that part (of a document, etc) that follows.

thereof /ˌðeərˈɒv/ *adv* (*fml or law*) of that; of it.

thereto /ˌðeəˈtuː/ *adv* (*fml or law*) to that; to it: *the agreement and the documents appended thereto.*

thereunder /ˌðeərˈʌndə(r)/ *adv* (*fml or law*) under that part (esp of a document, etc).

thereupon /ˌðeərəˈpɒn/ *adv* (*fml*) **1** as the result of that. **2** immediately after that.

therm /θɜːm/ *n* unit of heat, used esp in measuring a gas supply (= 100 000 British thermal units).

thermal /ˈθɜːml/ *adj* [esp attrib] **1** of heat: *thermal insulation* ○ *a* ˌ*thermal* ˈ*power station*, ie one using heat to generate electricity ○ *thermal units*, ie for measuring heat. **2** warm or hot: *thermal springs*. **3** (of clothes) designed to keep the wearer warm in cold weather: *thermal underwear*.
▷ **thermal** *n* rising current of warm air (as used by a glider to gain height).
□ ˌ**thermal ca**ˈ**pacity** (*physics*) number of units of heat needed to raise the temperature of a body by one degree.

thermionic /ˌθɜːmɪˈɒnɪk/ *adj* of that branch of physics that deals with the emission of electrons at high temperatures.
□ ˌ**thermionic** ˈ**valve** (*US* ˌ**thermionic** ˈ**tube**) vacuum tube in which a flow of electrons is emitted by heated electrodes. It can be used for strengthening an electronic signal, and until the development of transistors was widely used in radios, computers, etc.

therm(o)- *comb form* of heat: *thermonuclear* ○ *thermometer*.

thermocouple /ˈθɜːməʊkʌpl/ *n* device for measuring temperature, consisting of a pair of wires of different metals or alloys joined at two junctions, which develop a voltage when the junctions are at different temperatures.

thermodynamics /ˌθɜːməʊdaɪˈnæmɪks/ *n* [sing *v*] branch of physics dealing with the relations between heat and other forms of energy. ⇨ App 12.

thermoelectric /ˌθɜːməʊɪˈlektrɪk/ *adj* producing electricity by difference of temperature.

thermometer /θəˈmɒmɪtə(r)/ *n* instrument for measuring temperature, eg a mercury thermometer which shows change of temperature by the expansion or contraction of mercury in a sealed glass tube. The earliest type was invented by *Galileo. ⇨ illus at BULB.

thermonuclear /ˌθɜːməʊˈnjuːklɪə(r); *US* -ˈnuːklɪər/ *adj* of nuclear reactions that occur only at very high temperatures: *a thermonuclear bomb, missile, warhead, etc*, ie one using such reactions.

thermoplastic /ˌθɜːməʊˈplæstɪk/ *n, adj* (plastic substance) that becomes soft and easy to bend when heated and hardens when cooled.

Thermos /ˈθɜːməs/ *n* (also ˈ**Thermos flask**, *US* ˈ**Thermos bottle**) (*propr*) type of vacuum flask.

thermosetting /ˌθɜːməʊˈsetɪŋ/ *adj* (of plastics) becoming permanently hard when heated.

thermostat /ˈθɜːməstæt/ *n* device for automatically regulating temperature by cutting off or restoring a supply of heat (eg in a centrally-heated building, an oven, etc). ▷ **thermostatic** /ˌθɜːməˈstætɪk/ *adj*: *thermostatic control*. **thermostatically** /-klɪ/ *adv*: *thermostatically controlled*.

thesaurus /θɪˈsɔːrəs/ *n* (*pl* ~**es** /-rəsɪz/ or **thesauri** /θɪˈsɔːraɪ/) **1** book containing lists of words and phrases grouped according to their meanings. **2** dictionary containing words of a certain type: *a thesaurus of slang*.

these ⇨ THIS.

Theseus /ˈθiːsjuːs, ˈθiːsɪəs/ (in Greek mythology) Athenian hero who killed the *Minotaur, with the help of *Ariadne. He was one of the *Argonauts and married Hippolyta, queen of the *Amazons.

thesis /ˈθiːsɪs/ *n* (*pl* **theses** /ˈθiːsiːz/) **1** statement or theory put forward and supported by arguments. **2** long written essay submitted by a candidate for a university degree; dissertation.

Thespian (also **thespian**) /ˈθespɪən/ *adj* (*joc or rhet*) of acting or the theatre.
▷ **Thespian** (also **thespian**) *n* (*joc or rhet*) actor or actress.

Thessalonians /ˌθesəˈləʊnɪənz/ [sing *v*] either of two books of the *New Testament, consisting of letters written by St *Paul to the people of Thessalonica, a city in ancient Greece. ⇨ App 5.

they /ðeɪ/ *pers pron* (used as the subject of a *v*) **1** people, animals or things mentioned earlier or being observed now: *'Where are John and Mary?' 'They went for a walk.'* ○ *I've got two sisters. They're both doctors.* ○ *They* (eg The things you are carrying) *go on the bottom shelf.* **2** (used informally instead of *he or she*): *If anyone arrives late they'll have to wait outside.* ⇨ Usage at HE. **3** people in general: *They say we're going to have a hot summer.* ○ *They've* (ie The people in authority have) *sent us another form to fill in.* Cf THEM.

they'd /ðeɪd/ *contracted form* **1** they had ⇨ HAVE. **2** they would ⇨ WILL[1], WOULD[1, 2].

they'll /ðeɪl/ *contracted form* they will ⇨ WILL[1].

they're /ðeə(r)/ *contracted form* they are ⇨ BE.

they've /ðeɪv/ *contracted form* they have ⇨ HAVE.

thick /θɪk/ *adj* (**-er**, **-est**) **1** of relatively great distance or of a specified distance between opposite surfaces or sides: *a thick slice of bread* ○ *a thick line* ○ *ice three inches thick* ○ *a thick coat, pullover, etc*, ie made of thick material. **2** having a large number of units close together: *a thick forest* ○ *thick hair* ○ *in the thickest part of the crowd.* **3** (of a liquid or paste) relatively stiff in consistency; not flowing easily: *thick soup, paint, glue.* **4** (of a vapour or the atmosphere) not clear; dense: *thick fog, mist, cloud* ○ *thick darkness.* **5** (**a**) (of the voice) unclear, eg because one has a cold; indistinct. (**b**) (of an accent) very noticeable; strong: *speak with/in a thick brogue.* **6** (*infml*) stupid; dull. **7** ~ (**with sb**) (*infml*) intimate: *John is very thick with Anne.* **8** (idm) **a bit thick** ⇨ BIT[1]. **blood is thicker than water** ⇨ BLOOD[1]. **give sb/get a thick** ˈ**ear** (*sl*) punish sb/be punished with a blow, esp on the ear (causing it to swell). **have, etc a thick** ˈ**head** (*infml*) (**a**) be dull or stupid. (**b**) be suffering from a headache, hangover, etc: *I woke up with a very thick head this morning.* **have a thin/thick skin** ⇨ SKIN. (**as**) **thick as** ˈ**thieves** (*infml*) (of two or more people) very friendly. (**as**) **thick as two short** ˈ**planks** (*sl*) very stupid. (**have**) **a thick** ˈ**skull** (*infml*) (show) a lack of intelligence: *How can I get it into your thick skull* (ie make you understand) *that we can't afford a car?* (**be**) **thick with sth/sb** densely covered or filled with things or people: *a garden thick with flowers* ○ *The building was thick with reporters.*
▷ **thick** *adv* thickly: *Don't spread the butter too thick.* ○ *snow lying thick on the ground.* (idm) **lay it on** ˈ**thick/with a** ˈ**trowel** (*infml*) make sth seem bigger, worse, etc than it really is; exaggerate. ˌ**thick and** ˈ**fast** rapidly and in great numbers: *Offers of help are coming in thick and fast.*
thick *n* [U] **1** (idm) **in the thick of sth** in the busiest or most crowded part of sth: *He's always in the thick of it/things.* ○ *We were in the thick of the fight.* **2 through** ˌ**thick and** ˈ**thin** in spite of all the difficulties: *He remained loyal to me through thick and thin.*
thicken /ˈθɪkən/ *v* [I, Tn] **1** (cause sth to) become thicker: *when the sauce thickens* ○ *The fog is thickening.* ○ *Use flour to thicken the gravy.* ○ *Several drinks had thickened his voice.* **2** (idm) **the plot thickens** ⇨ PLOT[2]. **thickening** /ˈθɪkənɪŋ/ *n* [U] material or substance used to thicken sth.
thickly *adv*.
thickness *n* **1** [U] quality or degree of being thick: *4cm in thickness/a thickness of 4cm.* **2** [C] layer: *one thickness of cotton wool and two thicknesses of felt.* **3** [C] part (of sth) that is thick or between two opposite surfaces: *steps cut into the thickness of the wall.*
□ ˌ**thick-**ˈ**headed** *adj* stupid.
ˌ**thick**ˈ**set** *adj* (**a**) having a short stout body; solidly built. (**b**) (of a hedge) with the bushes growing closely together.
ˌ**thick-**ˈ**skinned** *adj* not sensitive to criticism or insults.

thicket /ˈθɪkɪt/ *n* mass of shrubs and small trees, etc growing close together.

thief /θiːf/ *n* (*pl* **thieves** /θiːvz/) **1** person who steals, esp secretly and without violence. Cf

BURGLAR, ROBBER (ROB). **2** (idm) **honour among thieves** ⇨ HONOUR[1]. **like a thief in the night** without being seen or expected; furtively. **procrastination is the thief of time** ⇨ PROCRASTINATION (PROCRASTINATE). **ˌset a ˌthief to ˈcatch a thief** (*saying*) a person who has been a criminal is the best person to catch or prevent another person of the same type. **thick as thieves** ⇨ THICK.

▷ **thieve** /θiːv/ *v* **(a)** [I] be a thief: *a life of thieving* ○ (*joc*) *Take your thieving hands off my radio!* **(b)** [Tn] steal (sth).

thievery /ˈθiːvərɪ/ *n* [U] stealing; theft.

thievish *adj* having the character or habits of a thief. **thievishly** *adv*.

thigh /θaɪ/ *n* **(a)** part of the human leg between the knee and the hip. ⇨ illus at HUMAN. **(b)** corresponding part of the hind legs of other animals.

□ **ˈthigh-bone** *n* bone of this part of the leg; femur.

thimble /ˈθɪmbl/ *n* small cap of metal, plastic, etc worn on the end of the finger to protect it and push the needle in sewing.

□ **thimbleful** /-fʊl/ *n* very small quantity, esp of liquid to drink: *Just a thimbleful of sherry, please.*

thin /θɪn/ *adj* (**-nner** /ˈθɪnə(r)/, **-nnest** /ˈθɪnɪst/) **1** having opposite surfaces relatively close together; of small diameter: *a thin sheet of metal* ○ *That ice is too thin to stand on.* ○ *a thin wire* ○ *a thin layer of glue* ○ *The rope was wearing thin in one place.* ○ *a thin cotton dress*, ie one made out of thin material. **2** not having much flesh; lean: *He's tall and rather thin.* ○ *Her illness had left her looking pale and thin.* Cf FAT[1] 2. ⇨ Usage. **3** lacking density: *a thin mist, haze, etc.* **4** having units that are not closely packed together or numerous: *His hair's/He's getting rather thin on top*, ie He is starting to go bald. ○ *The population is thin in this part of the country.* ○ *a thin audience.* **5** (of a liquid or paste) lacking substance; watery: *thin soup, stew, gravy, etc.* **6** (*fig*) of poor quality or lacking some important ingredient; feeble: *thin humour* ○ *a thin* (ie unconvincing) *excuse* ○ *a thin disguise*, ie one that is easily seen through ○ *The critics found her latest novel rather thin.* **7** (idm) **be skating on thin ice** ⇨ SKATE[1]. **have a thin/thick skin** ⇨ SKIN. **have a thin ˈtime (of it)** (*infml*) be uncomfortable or disappointed: *The team's been having a thin time (of it) recently — not a single win in two months.* **the thin end of the ˈwedge** event, action, demand, etc that seems unimportant but is likely to lead to others that are much more important, serious, etc: *Unions regard the government's intention to ban overtime as the thin end of the wedge.* **(be) thin on the ˈground** not numerous; scarce. **through thick and thin** ⇨ THICK. **vanish, etc into thin ˈair** disappear completely. **wear thin** ⇨ WEAR[2].

▷ **thin** *adv* thinly: *The bread is cut too thin.*

thin *v* (**-nn-**) **1** [I, Ip, Tn, Tn·p] ~ **(sth) (out)** (cause sth to) become less dense or fewer in number: *wait until the fog thins (out)* ○ *The traffic was thinning out.* ○ *War and disease had thinned the population.* ○ *thin out seedlings*, ie remove some to improve the growth of the rest. **2** (phr v) **thin down** become slimmer: *He's thinned down a lot since he went on a diet.* **thin sth down** make sth thinner: *thin down paint with white spirit.*

thinly *adv* in a thin manner: *Spread the butter thinly.* ○ *thinly-sliced ham.*

thinner /ˈθɪnə(r)/ (also **thinners**) *n* [U] substance for diluting paint, etc.

thinness /ˈθɪnnɪs/ *n* [U]

NOTE ON USAGE: Compare **thin**, **skinny**, **underweight**, **slim**, etc. When describing people whose weight is below normal, **thin** is the most general word. It may be negative, suggesting weakness or lack of health: *She's gone terribly thin since her operation.* **Bony** is often applied to parts of the body such as hands or face. **Skinny** and **scrawny** are negative and can suggest lack of strength: *He looks much too skinny/scrawny to be a weight-lifter.* **Underweight** is the most neutral: *The doctor says I'm underweight.* **Emaciated** indicates a serious condition resulting from starvation. It is often thought desirable to be **slim** or **slender**, **slim** being used especially of those who have reduced their weight by diet or exercise: *I wish I was as slim as you.* ○ *You have a beautifully slender figure.*

thine /ðaɪn/ *possess pron* (*arch*) the thing(s) belonging to you.

▷ **thine** *possess det* (*arch*) (form of *thy* before a vowel or an *h*) of or belonging to you; your.

thing /θɪŋ/ *n* **1** [C] any unnamed object: *What's that thing on the table?* ○ *There wasn't a thing* (ie There was nothing) *to eat.* ○ *She's very fond of sweet things*, ie sweet kinds of food. ○ *I haven't a thing to wear*, ie I have no suitable clothes. **2 things** [pl] **(a)** personal belongings, clothing, etc: *Don't forget your swimming things*, ie swim-suit, towel, etc. ○ *Have you packed your things for the journey?* ○ *Put your things* (eg coat, hat) *on and let's go.* **(b)** tools, implements, etc: *my painting things* ○ *wash up the tea-things* (eg, plates, cups, cutlery). **(c)** circumstances or conditions: *Things are going from bad to worse.* ○ *Think things over before you decide.* ○ *You mustn't take things so seriously.* **(d)** (with an *adj* following) all that can be so described: *interested in things Japanese.* **(e)** (*law*) property. **3** [C] **(a)** task, course of action, etc: *a difficult thing to do* ○ *The general, common, usual, established, etc thing is to....* **(b)** fact, subject, etc: *The main thing to remember is...* ○ *There's another thing I want to ask you about.* ○ *I find the whole thing very boring.* **4** [C] (used of a person or an animal, expressing affection, pity, contempt, etc): *What a sweet little thing your daughter is!* ○ *My cat's been very ill, poor old thing.* ○ *You stupid thing!* **5 the thing** [sing] what is appropriate, suitable or most important: *A holiday will be just the thing for you.* ○ *The thing is not to interrupt him while he's talking.* ○ *say the right/wrong thing* ○ *The main thing is to get more orders.* ○ *The thing about her is that she is completely honest.* **6** (idm) **ˌall things conˈsidered** when one considers every aspect of a problem, situation, etc: *All things considered, we're doing quite well.* **as things ˈstand** in the present set of circumstances: *As things stand, we won't finish the job on time.* **be a good thing (that)...** be fortunate that...: *It's a good thing we brought the umbrella.* **be onto a good ˈthing** (*infml*) have found a job or style of life that is pleasant, well paid, etc. **be ˈseeing things** (*infml*) have hallucinations: *Am I seeing things or is that Bill over there? I thought he was dead.* **the best thing since sliced bread** ⇨ BEST. **a close/near ˈthing** a fine balance between success and failure, life and death, doing or not doing sth, etc: *We just managed to win, but it was a close thing.* **do one's own ˈthing** (*infml*) follow one's own interests and inclinations; be independent. **first/last ˈthing** early in the morning/late in the evening: *I always take the dog for a short walk last thing before going to bed.* **first things first** ⇨ FIRST[1]. **for ˈone thing** (used to introduce a reason for sth): *For one thing, I've no money; and for another I'm too busy.* **have a thing about sb/sth** (*infml*) **(a)** be obsessed by sb/sth. **(b)** have a prejudice against sb/sth: *I've got a thing about men with beards.* **know a thing or two** ⇨ KNOW. **make a ˈthing of sth** (*infml*) make a fuss about sth: *I don't want to make a (big) thing of it but you have been late for work three times this week.* **not know the first thing about sth** ⇨ KNOW. **(just) ˌone of those ˈthings** an unfortunate event, experience, etc that one must accept as unavoidable. **one (damned, etc) thing after aˈnother** a succession of unpleasant or unwelcome happenings. **other things being ˈequal** provided that circumstances elsewhere remain the same. **sure thing** ⇨ SURE. **take it/things easy** ⇨ EASY[2]. **taking ˌone thing with aˈnother** considering every aspect of the situation. **the ˌthing ˈis** the question to be considered is: *The thing is, can we afford a holiday?* **a ˌthing of the ˈpast** thing that is old-fashioned or out of date: *The art of writing letters seems to be a thing of the past.* **ˌthings that go ˌbump in the ˈnight** (*joc*) strange or frightening noises, etc. **what with ˌone thing and aˈnother** (*infml*) because of various duties, commitments, happenings, etc: *What with one thing and another, I forgot to tell you we couldn't come.*

thingummy /ˈθɪŋəmɪ/ (also **thingumajig** /ˈθɪŋəmədʒɪg/, **thingumabob** /ˈθɪŋəməbɒb/, **thingy** /ˈθɪŋɪ/) *n* (*infml*) person or thing whose name one does not know or has forgotten or does not wish to mention.

think[1] /θɪŋk/ *v* (*pt, pp* **thought** /θɔːt/) **1** [I, Ipr] ~ **(about sth)** use the mind in an active way to form connected ideas: *Are animals able to think?* ○ *Think before you act*, ie Do not act hastily or rashly. ○ *Let me think a moment*, ie Give me time to think before I answer. ○ *He may not say much but he thinks a lot.* ○ *Do you think in English or translate mentally from your own language?* ○ *You're very quiet — what are you thinking (about)?* **2** [Tf, Tw no passive, Cn·t esp passive, Cn·a, Cn·n] have as an idea or opinion; consider: *'Do you think (that) it's going to rain?' 'Yes, I think so.'* ○ *'It's going to rain, I think.' 'Oh, I don't think so.'* ○ *I think you're very brave.* ○ *I think this is their house but I'm not sure.* ○ *Do you think it likely/that it is likely?* ○ *I thought I heard a scream.* ○ *What do you think she'll do now?* ○ *Who do you think you are?* ie Why are you behaving in this overbearing, etc way? ○ *a species long thought to be extinct* ○ *He's thought to be one of the richest men in Europe.* ○ *You must think me very silly.* ○ *Some people think him a possible future champion.* **3** [Tf] have or form as an intention or plan: *I think I'll go for a swim.* ○ *It is thought that the Prime Minister will visit Moscow next month.* **4** [Tw no passive] (used in negative sentences with *can/could*) form an idea of; imagine: *I can't think what you mean.* ○ *We couldn't think where she'd gone to.* ○ *You can't ˈthink how glad I am to see you!* **5** [Tw no passive] take into consideration; reflect: *Think how nice it would be to see them again.* ○ *I was just thinking (to myself) what a long way it is.* **6** [Tn, Tf, Tt] expect (sth): *Who'd have thought it?* eg of a surprising event ○ *I never thought (that) I'd see her again.* ○ *Who would have thought to find you here?* **7** [I, Tn] (*infml esp US*) direct one's thoughts in a certain manner or to (a subject): *Let's think positive.* ○ *If you want to make money you've got to think money.* **8** (idm) **I ˈthought as much** that is what I expected or suspected. **see/think fit** ⇨ FIT[1]. **ˌthink aˈgain** reconsider the situation and change one's idea or intention: *If you think I'm going to lend you my car you can think again!* **think aˈloud** express one's thoughts as they occur. **think better of (doing) sth** decide against (doing) sth after thinking further about it. **think (all) the better of sb** have a higher opinion of sb. **ˌthink ˈbig** (*infml*) (esp imperative) be ambitious. **think nothing ˈof it** (used as a polite response to apologies, thanks, etc). **think nothing of sth/doing sth** consider (doing) sth to be normal and not particularly unusual: *She thinks nothing of walking thirty miles a day.* **think twice about sth/doing sth** think carefully before deciding to do sth: *You should think twice about employing someone you've never met.* **think the world, highly, a lot, not much, poorly, little, etc of sb/sth** (not used in the continuous tenses) have a good, poor, etc opinion of sb/sth: *His work is highly thought of by the critics.* ○ *I don't think much of my new teacher.*

9 (phr v) **think about sb/sth (a)** reflect upon sb/sth; recall sb/sth: *Do you ever think about your childhood?* **(b)** take sb/sth into account; consider sb/sth: *Don't you ever think about other people?* ○ *All he ever thinks about is money.* **think about sth/doing sth** consider or examine sth to see if it is desirable, practicable, etc: *I'll think about it and let you know tomorrow.* ○ *She's thinking about changing her job.*

think ahead (to sth) cast one's mind forward; anticipate (an event, a situation, etc).

think back (to sth) recall and reconsider sth in the past.

think for oneself form one's opinions, make decisions, etc independently.

think of sth/doing sth (a) take sth into account;

consider sth: *There are so many things to think of before we decide.* ○ *You can't expect me to think of everything!* (**b**) contemplate the possibility of sth (without reaching a decision or taking action): *They're thinking of moving to America.* ○ *I did think of resigning, but I decided not to.* (**c**) imagine sth: *Just think of the expense!* ○ *To think of his not knowing* (ie How surprising that he didn't know) *about it!* (**d**) have the idea of sth (often used with *could, would, should,* and *not* or *never*): *I couldn't think of letting you take the blame.* ○ *She would never think of marrying someone so old.* (**e**) call sth to mind; remember sth: *I can't think of his name at the moment.* (**f**) put sth forward; suggest sth: *Can anybody think of a way to raise money?* ○ *Who first thought of the idea?*
think sth out consider sth carefully; produce (an idea, etc) by thinking: *Think out your answer before you start writing.* ○ *a well-thought-out plan.*
think sth over reflect upon sth (esp before reaching a decision): *Please think over what I've said.* ○ *I'd like more time to think things over.*
think sth through consider (a problem, etc) fully.
think sth up (*infml*) produce sth by thought; invent or devise sth: *There's no telling what he'll think up next.* ○ *Can't you think up a better excuse than that?*
□ ˈ**think-tank** *n* [CGp] organization or group of experts providing advice and ideas on national or commercial problems.

think[2] /θɪŋk/ *n* (*infml*) **1** [sing] act of thinking: *I'd better have a think before I decide.* **2** (idm) **have (got) another think coming** must revise one's opinions, plans, etc; be forced to think again: *If you think I'm going to pay all your bills you've got another think coming.*

thinkable /ˈθɪŋkəbl/ *adj* [pred] (usu with a negative) that can be imagined; conceivable: *Unemployment has reached a level that would not have been thinkable ten years ago.*

thinker /ˈθɪŋkə(r)/ *n* (usu with an *adj*) person who thinks deeply or in a specified way: *a great, an original, an important, etc thinker.*

thinking /ˈθɪŋkɪŋ/ *adj* [attrib] intelligent; rational; thoughtful: *All thinking people must hate violence.*
▷ **thinking** *n* **1** [U] thought; reasoning: *do some hard thinking,* ie think deeply ○ *What's your thinking on* (ie What do you think about) *this question?* **2** (idm) **to ˈmy way of thinking** ➪ WAY[1]; Cf WISHFUL THINKING (WISH).
□ ˈ**thinking-cap** *n* (idm) **put one's ˈthinking-cap on** (*infml*) try to solve a problem by thinking about it.

third /θɜ:d/ *pron, det* 3rd; next after second. ➪ App 9.
▷ **third** *n* **1** one of three equal parts of sth. **2** ~ (**in sth**) (*Brit*) third class of university degree: *get a third in biology at Durham.*
thirdly *adv* in the third position or place. ➪ Usage at FIRST[2].
For the uses of *third* see the examples at *fifth.*
□ ˌ**third deˈgree** long and severe questioning; use of torture to make sb confess or give information.
ˌ**third degree ˈburn** very serious burn on the skin.
the ˌ**third diˈmension** the dimension of height.
ˌ**third ˈparty** another person besides the two main people involved. ˌ**third-party inˈsurance** insurance that gives protection against damage or injury caused by the insured person to other people.
ˌ**third-ˈrate** *adj* of very poor quality: *a* ˌ*third-rate* ˈ*film.*
the ˌ**Third ˈWorld** the developing countries of Africa, Asia and Latin America, earlier used of those not politically aligned with Communist or Western nations: [attrib] ˌ*third-world* ˈ*countries.*

thirst /θɜ:st/ *n* **1** (**a**) [U, sing] feeling caused by a desire or need to drink: *quench* (ie satisfy) *one's thirst with a long drink of water* ○ *Working in the sun soon gave us a (powerful) thirst.* (**b**) [U] suffering caused by this: *They lost their way in the desert and died of thirst.* **2** [sing] ~ (**for sth**) (*fig*) strong desire; craving: *a/the thirst for knowledge, fame, revenge.*
▷ **thirst** *v* **1** [I] (*arch*) feel a need to drink. **2** (phr v) **thirst for sth** be eager for sth: *thirsting for revenge.*
thirsty *adj* (**-ier, -iest**) **1** ~ (**for sth**) feeling thirst: *be/feel thirsty* ○ *Salty food makes you thirsty.* ○ (*fig*) *The team is thirsty for success.* **2** ~ (**for sth**) (of land) in need of water: *fields thirsty for rain.* **3** (*infml*) causing thirst: *thirsty work.* **thirstily** /-ɪlɪ/ *adv*: *They drank thirstily.*

thirteen /ˌθɜ:ˈti:n/ *pron, det, n* 13; one more than twelve. ➪ App 9.
▷ **thirteen** *n* the number 13. ➪ article at SUPERSTITION.
thirteenth /ˌθɜ:ti:nθ/ *pron, det* 13th; next after twelfth. — *n* one of thirteen equal parts of sth.
For the uses of *thirteen* and *thirteenth* see *five* and *fifth.*

thirty /ˈθɜ:tɪ/ *pron, det* 30; one more than twenty-nine. ➪ App 9.
▷ **thirtieth** /ˈθɜ:tɪəθ/ *pron, det* 30th; next after twenty-ninth. — *n* one of thirty equal parts of sth.
thirty *n* **1** [C] the number 30. **2 the thirties** *n* [pl] numbers, years or temperature from 30 to 39. **3** (idm) **in one's thirties** between the ages of 30 and 40.
For the uses of *thirty* and *thirtieth* see the examples at *fifty, five* and *fifth.*
□ ˌ**thirty-ˈnine** *pron, det* 39. **the** ˌ**Thirty-nine ˈArticles** set of religious principles adopted as the official doctrine of the Church of England in 1571.
the ˌ**Thirty Years ˈWar** long war (1618-48) which began as a revolt by some Protestant German states against Catholic Austrian rule but became a general war for control of central Europe, with many European countries being drawn into the conflict. It ended with France as the most powerful European state and much of Germany devastated.

this /ðɪs/ *det, pron* (*pl* **these** /ði:z/) **1** (used to refer to a person, a thing, a place or an event that is close to the speaker/writer, esp when compared with another): *Come here and look at this picture.* ○ *These shoes are more comfortable than those.* ○ *Is this the book you mean?* ○ *Would you give her these?* ○ *What's all this noise about?* ○ *What's this I hear about your getting married?* ○ *This is my husband.* **2** (used to refer to sb/sth previously mentioned): *Jane wrote a letter to a newspaper. This letter contained some startling allegations.* **3** (used to introduce sth): *Listen to this: a boy in London has died of rabies.* ○ *Do it like this,* ie in this way. **4** (used with days or periods of time related to the present): *this* (ie the current) *week, month, year* ○ *this morning,* ie today in the morning ○ *this Tuesday,* ie Tuesday of this week ○ *this minute,* ie now ○ *these days,* ie currently; recently. ➪ Usage at LAST[1]. **5** (*infml*) (used in front of a *n* followed by a possessive): *When are we going to see this car of yours?* ○ *These jeans of mine are dirty.* ○ *This friend of hers is said to be very rich.* **6** (*infml*) (used to refer to people and things in a narrative) a certain: *There was this peculiar man sitting opposite me in the train.* **7** (idm) ˌ**this and ˈthat**; ˌ**this, that and the ˈother** various things, activities, etc: *'What did you talk about?' 'Oh, this and that.'*
▷ **this** *adv* to this degree; so: *It's about this high.* ○ *I didn't think we'd get this far,* ie as far as this. ○ *Can you afford this much* (ie as much as this)*?* Cf THAT[1, 2].

thistle /ˈθɪsl/ *n* any of various types of wild plant with prickly leaves and purple, white or yellow flowers (the national emblem of Scotland). ➪ illus at PLANT.
□ ˈ**thistledown** *n* [U] light fluff that contains thistle seeds and is blown from thistle plants by the wind: *as light as thistledown.*

thither /ˈðɪðə(r)/ *adv* **1** (*arch*) to or towards that place. **2** (idm) **hither and thither** ➪ HITHER.

tho' ➪ THOUGH.

thole /θəʊl/ (also ˈ**thole-pin**) *n* peg set in the gunwale of a boat to keep an oar secure. Cf ROWLOCK.

Thomas[1] /ˈtɒməs/ Dylan Marlais (1914-53), Welsh poet who achieved particular fame with vivid public readings of his works. His poems (eg 'Do not go gentle into that good night') are usu romantic in feeling and rhetorical in style. He also wrote the radio play *Under Milk Wood.*

Thomas[2] /ˈtɒməs/ (Philip) Edward (1878-1917), English poet, most of whose work is on pastoral themes (eg 'Adlestrop'). He was killed in France in the First World War.

Thomas[3] /ˈtɒməs/ Saint, one of Christ's apostles, who refused to believe that Christ had come back to life unless he could see and touch his wounds. Cf DOUBTING THOMAS (DOUBT[2]).

Thomism /ˈtəʊmɪzəm/ *n* [U] philosophical and religious ideas of St Thomas *Aquinas.
▷ **Thomist** /ˈtəʊmɪst/ *n, adj* (follower) of St Thomas Aquinas or his ideas.

Thomson /ˈtɒmsn/ Sir Joseph John (1856-1940), English physicist who discovered the electron and established the electrical theory of the atom. In 1906 he was awarded the Nobel prize for physics.

thong /θɒŋ; *US* θɔ:ŋ/ *n* **1** narrow strip of leather used as a fastening, whip, etc. **2** (*US*) = FLIP-FLOP.

thorax /ˈθɔ:ræks/ *n* (*pl* ~**es** or **thoraces** /θɔ:ˈreɪsi:z/) **1** part of the body between the neck and the abdomen (eg, in man, the chest). **2** middle of the three main sections of an insect (bearing the legs and wings). ➪ illus at INSECT.

Thoreau /ˈθɔ:rəʊ; *US* θəˈrəʊ/ Henry David (1817-62), American writer and naturalist whose works, including *Walden, or Life in the Woods,* describing a two-year period spent in a wooden hut in the forest, were influential in the development of socialist thought.

thorn /θɔ:n/ *n* **1** [C] sharp pointed growth on the stem of a plant: *The thorns on the roses scratched her hands.* ➪ illus at PLANT. **2** [C, U] (usu in compounds) thorny tree or shrub: ˈ*hawthorn* ○ ˈ*blackthorn* ○ [attrib] *a thorn hedge.* **3** (idm) **a thorn in one's flesh/side** person or thing that continually annoys or hinders one: *He's been a thorn in my side ever since he joined this department.*
▷ **thorny** *adj* (**-ier, -iest**) **1** having thorns. **2** (*fig*) causing difficulty or disagreement: *a thorny problem, subject, issue, etc.*

Thorndike /ˈθɔ:ndaɪk/ Dame Sybil (1882-1976), English actress noted for a wide range of Shakespearian roles and also for her portrayal of Joan of Arc in Shaw's *St Joan.*

thorough /ˈθʌrə; *US* ˈθʌrəʊ/ *adj* **1** (**a**) [usu attrib] done completely and with great attention to detail; not superficial: *aim to provide a thorough training in all aspects of the work* ○ *give the room a thorough cleaning.* (**b**) doing things in this way: *He's a slow worker but very thorough.* **2** [attrib] (*derog*) utter; complete: *That woman is a thorough nuisance.* ▷ **thoroughly** *adv*: *The work had not been done very thoroughly.* ○ *He's a thoroughly nice person.* ○ *I'm thoroughly fed up with you.* **thoroughness** *n* [U].
□ ˈ**thoroughgoing** *adj* [attrib] thorough(1a, 2): *a thoroughgoing revision* ○ *It was all a thoroughgoing waste of time.*

thoroughbred /ˈθʌrəbred/ (also ˈ**pure-bred**) *n, adj* (animal, esp a horse) of pure or pedigree stock: *breeding thoroughbred racehorses.*

thoroughfare /ˈθʌrəfeə(r)/ *n* public road or street that is open at both ends, esp for traffic: *The Strand is one of London's busiest thoroughfares.* ○ *No thoroughfare,* ie on a sign, indicating that a road is private or that there is no way through.

those ➪ THAT[1, 2].

thou /ðaʊ/ *pers pron* (*arch*) (used as the second person singular subject of a *v*) you: *Who art thou?*

though (also **tho'**) /ðəʊ/ *conj* **1** (more formal when used at the beginning of the sentence) despite the fact that; although: *She won first prize, though none of us had expected it.* ○ *Strange though it may seem*..., ie Although it seems strange... ○ *Though they lack official support they continue their struggle.* **2** (used to introduce a clause at the end of a sentence) all the same; but: *I'll try to come, though I doubt if I'll be there on time.* ○ *He'll probably say no, though it's worth trying.* ➪ Usage at ALTHOUGH.
▷ **though** *adv* (*infml*) in spite of this; however: *I*

expect you're right — I'll ask him, though. ○ *She promised to phone. I heard nothing, though.*

thought[1] *pt, pp* of THINK[1].

thought[2] /θɔːt/ *n* **1** [U, C] (act, power or process of) thinking: *He spent several minutes in thought before deciding.* ○ *deep/lost in thought,* ie concentrating so much on one's thoughts that one is unaware of one's surroundings ○ *a thought-provoking book,* ie one that makes one think seriously about what is in it ○ *Her thoughts turned/She turned her thoughts to* (ie She started to think about) *what the children were doing.* **2** [U] way of thinking that is characteristic of a particular period, class, nation, etc: *modern, scientific, Greek thought.* **3** [U, C] ~ **(for sb/sth)** consideration; care: *He acted without thought.* ○ *I've read your proposal and given it some serious thought.* ○ *Spare a thought for those less fortunate than you.* ○ *I don't need your help, thank you, but it was a kind thought.* **4** [C often *pl*] idea or opinion produced by thinking: *an article full of striking thoughts* ○ *That boy hasn't a thought in his head,* ie is stupid. ○ *Let me have your thoughts on* (ie Tell what you think about) *the subject.* ○ *He keeps his thoughts to himself,* ie does not reveal what he is thinking. ○ *It's not difficult to read your thoughts,* ie to know what you're thinking. ○ *'How will we find the house if we don't know the address?' 'That's a thought.'* **5** [U] ~ **(of doing sth)** intention: *I had no thought of hurting your feelings.* ○ *You can give up all/any thought of marrying Tom.* ○ *Didn't you have some thought of going to Spain this summer?* ○ *The thought of resigning never crossed my mind,* ie never occurred to me. **6 a thought** [sing] a little; rather: *You might be a thought more considerate of other people.* **7** (idm) **food for thought** ⇨ FOOD. **a penny for your thoughts** ⇨ PENNY. **perish the thought** ⇨ PERISH. **read sb's mind/thoughts** ⇨ READ. **second ˈthoughts** (*US* **second ˈthought**) change of opinion after reconsidering: *We had second thoughts about buying the house when we discovered the price.* ○ *On second thoughts I think I'd better go now.* **a school of thought** ⇨ SCHOOL[1]. **two minds with but a single thought** ⇨ MIND[1]. **the wish is father to the thought** ⇨ WISH *n.*

▷ **thoughtful** /-fl/ *adj* **1** thinking deeply; absorbed in thought: *thoughtful looks.* **2** (of a book, writer, remark, etc) showing signs of careful thought. **3** showing thought[2](3) for the needs of others; considerate: *It was very thoughtful of you to send flowers.* **thoughtfully** /-fəlɪ/ *adv.* **thoughtfulness** *n* [U].

thoughtless *adj* **1** not aware of the possible effects or consequences of one's actions, etc; careless. **2** inconsiderate of others; selfish. **thoughtlessly** *adv.* **thoughtlessness** *n* [U].

□ **ˈthought-reader** *n* person who claims or seems to know what people are thinking without these thoughts being expressed in words.

thousand /ˈθaʊznd/ *pron, det* **1** (after *a* or *one*, an indication of quantity; no *pl* form) 1000; ten hundred: (*infml*) *I've got a thousand and one* (ie many) *things to do.* ⇨ App 9. **2** (idm) **one, etc in a thousand** = ONE, ETC IN A MILLION (MILLION).

▷ **thousand** *n* (*sing* after *a* or *one*, but often *pl*) the number 1000.

thousandfold /-fəʊld/ *adj, adv* one thousand times as much or as many.

thousandth /ˈθaʊznθ/ *pron, det* 1000th; next after nine hundred and ninety-ninth. — *n* one of one thousand equal parts of sth.

For the uses of *thousand* and *thousandth* see the examples at *hundred* and *hundredth.*

□ ˌ**Thousand Island ˈdressing** salad dressing made of mayonnaise with ketchup and chopped pickles, etc.

thrash /θræʃ/ *v* **1** [Tn] beat (a person or an animal) with a stick or whip, esp as a punishment. **2** [Tn] hit (sth) with repeated blows: *The whale thrashed the water with its tail.* **3** [Tn] defeat (sb) thoroughly in a contest: *Chelsea were thrashed 6-1 by Leeds.* **4** [I, Ip] ~ **(about/around)** make violent or convulsive movements: *Swimmers thrashing about in the water.* **5** [Tn] = THRESH. **6** (phr v) **thrash sth out (a)** discuss sth thoroughly and frankly: *call a meeting to thrash out the problem.* **(b)** produce sth by discussion of this kind: *After much argument we thrashed out a plan.*

▷ **thrashing** *n* **1** beating: *give sb/get a good thrashing.* **2** severe defeat: *Leeds celebrated their 6-1 thrashing of Chelsea.*

thread /θred/ *n* **1** [C, U] (length of) spun cotton, wool, silk, etc; thin strand of nylon, etc: *loose threads* ○ *a needle and thread,* ie for sewing ○ *a robe embroidered with gold thread.* **2** [C] ~ **(of sth)** (*fig*) very thin thing resembling a thread: *fine threads of red in the marble* ○ *A thread of light emerged from the keyhole.* **3** [C] (*fig*) line of thought connecting parts of a story, etc: *pick/take up the thread(s),* ie continue after an interruption ○ *The chairman gathered up the threads of the debate,* ie summarized what had been said. **4** [C] spiral ridge of a screw or bolt. ⇨ illus at SCREW. **5 threads** [pl] (*US sl*) clothes. **6** (idm) **hang by a hair/a single thread** ⇨ HANG[1]. **lose the thread** ⇨ LOSE.

▷ **thread** *v* **1** [Tn, Tn·pr] **(a)** pass thread, string, etc through (sth): *thread a needle (with cotton).* **(b)** put (beads, etc) on a thread, etc: *threading pearls (on a string) to make a necklace.* **2** [Tn, Tn·pr, Tn·p] pass (film, tape, string, etc) through sth and into the required position for use: *thread film in(to a projector)* ○ *thread the wire through (the pulley).* **3** (idm) **thread one's way through (sth)** go carefully or with difficulty through (sth): *threading my way through the crowded streets.*

ˈthreadlike *adj* resembling a thread; long and slender: *threadlike strands of glass fibre.*

□ **ˈthreadbare** /-beə(r)/ *adj* **1** (of cloth, clothing, etc) worn thin; shabby: *a threadbare carpet, coat.* **2** (*fig*) too often used or too well known to be effective; hackneyed: *a threadbare argument, joke, plot.*

ˈthreadworm *n* type of small threadlike parasitic worm, esp one that is sometimes found in the rectum of children.

threat /θret/ *n* **1** [C, U] expression of one's intention to punish or harm sb, esp if he does not obey: *make/utter threats (against sb)* ○ *carry out a threat (to do sth)* ○ *an empty threat,* ie one that cannot be put into effect ○ *He is impervious to threat(s).* **2** [C usu *sing*, U] ~ **(to sb/sth) (of sth)** indication or warning of future danger, trouble, etc: *This constitutes a threat to national security.* ○ *a country living under the constant threat of famine* ○ *some threat of rain* ○ *The railway is under threat of closure.* **3** [C usu *sing*] person or thing regarded as likely to cause danger or ruin: *Terrorism is a threat to the whole country.*

threaten /θretn/ *v* **1** [Tn, Tn·pr] ~ **sb (with sth)** make a threat or threats against sb; try to influence sb by threats: *threaten an employee with dismissal* ○ *My attacker threatened me with a gun.* **2** [Tn, Tt] use (sth) as a threat: *He threatened legal action.* ○ *The hijackers threatened to kill all the passengers if their demands were not met.* **3 (a)** [It, Tn] give warning of (sth): *It keeps threatening to snow,* ie Snow seems likely all the time. ○ *The clouds threatened rain.* **(b)** [I, It] seem likely to occur or to do sth undesirable: *under a threatening sky* ○ *If a gale threatens, do not go to sea.* ○ *a mistake that threatens to be costly.* **4** [Tn] be a threat to (sb/sth): *the dangers that threaten us* ○ *a species threatened by/with extinction.* ▷ **threateningly** *adv*: *The dog growled at me threateningly.*

three /θriː/ *pron, det* **1** 3; one more than two. ⇨ App 9. **2** (idm) **by/in twos and threes** ⇨ TWO.

▷ **three** *n* the number 3.

three- (in compounds) having three of the thing specified: *a ˌthree-day eˈvent.*

For the uses of *three* see the examples at *five.*

□ ˌ**three-ˈcornered** *adj* **1** triangular: *a ˌthree-cornered ˈhat.* **2** involving three participants or contestants: *a ˌthree-cornered deˈbate.*

ˌ**three-ˈdecker** *n* **1** (formerly) sailing-ship with three decks. **2** anything with three layers, esp a sandwich or a cake.

ˌ**three-diˈmensional** (also **three-D, 3-D** /ˌθriːˈdiː/) *adj* having the three dimensions of length, breadth and depth: *a ˌthree-dimensional ˈobject.*

ˈthreefold *adj, adv* three times as much or as many.

three-legged race /ˌθriːlegɪd ˈreɪs/ race in which competitors run in pairs, the right leg of one runner being tied to the left leg of the other.

ˌ**three-line ˈwhip** (*Brit*) written notice to Members of Parliament from their party leader insisting that they attend a debate and vote in a particular way.

threepence /ˌθriːˈpens, *formerly* ˈθrepns/ *n* [U] (*Brit*) (esp formerly) sum of three pence.

ˈthreepenny /ˈθrepənɪ, ˈθrʌpənɪ/ [attrib] (*Brit*) costing or worth three pence. **threepenny bit** /ˌθrepnɪ ˈbɪt/ former British coin worth three pence.

ˈthree-piece *adj* consisting of three separate pieces: *a ˌthree-piece ˈsuit,* ie a set of clothes consisting of a skirt or trousers, a blouse and a jacket for a woman, or trousers, a waistcoat and a jacket for a man ○ *a ˌthree-piece ˈsuite,* ie a set of three pieces of furniture (usu a sofa and two armchairs). ⇨ illus at FURNITURE.

ˌ**three-point ˈturn** method of turning a car, etc in a small space by driving forwards, then backwards, then forwards again.

ˈthree-ply *adj* (of wool, wood, etc) having three strands or thicknesses.

ˌ**three-ˈquarter** *adj* [attrib] consisting of three quarters of a whole: *a three-quarter-length coat.* — *n* (in Rugby football) player with a position between the half-backs and the full-back.

ˌ**three-ring ˈcircus** (*US fig*) place full of confused action and entertainment.

the three ˈRs ⇨ R *n.*

ˈthreescore *det* (*arch*) sixty: *threescore years and ten,* ie the age of 70, regarded as being a long life.

threesome /ˈθriːsəm/ *n* **1** group of three people; trio. **2** game played by three people.

thresh /θreʃ/ *v* [I, Tn] beat out or separate (grain) from husks of wheat, etc using a machine or (esp formerly) an implement held in the hand.

▷ **thresher** *n* person or machine that threshes.

threshold /ˈθreʃhəʊld/ *n* **1** piece of wood or stone forming the bottom of a doorway. **2** entrance of a house, etc: *cross the threshold,* ie enter. **3** [usu sing] (*fig*) point of entering or beginning sth: *He was on the threshold of his career.* ○ *at the threshold of a new era in medicine.* **4** (*medical or psychology*) limit below which a person does not react to a stimulus: *above/below the threshold of consciousness* ○ *have a high/low pain threshold,* ie be able to endure much/little pain, eg during illness.

threw *pt* of THROW[1].

thrift /θrɪft/ *n* [U] **1** careful or economical use of money or resources. **2** (also **sea-pink**) seashore or alpine plant with bright pink flowers.

▷ **thrifty** *adj* **(-ier, -iest)** showing thrift; economical. **thriftily** /-ɪlɪ/ *adv.* **thriftiness** *n* [U].

thrill /θrɪl/ *n* **1 (a)** wave of excited feeling; nervous tremor: *a thrill of joy, fear, horror, etc* ○ *He gets his thrills from rock-climbing.* ○ *With a thrill I realized that I had won.* **(b)** experience causing this: *It was a real thrill to meet the Queen.* ○ *the thrill of a lifetime.* **2** (idm) **(the) thrills and spills** excitement caused by taking part in or watching dangerous sports or entertainments.

▷ **thrill** *v* **1** [Tn, Tnt esp passive] cause (sb) to feel a thrill or thrills: *a thrilling experience* ○ *The film thrilled the audience.* ○ *I was thrilled by her beauty.* ○ *We were thrilled to hear your wonderful news.* **2** [I, Ipr] ~ **(with sth)** feel a thrill or thrills: *a film to make you thrill with excitement.* **3** (idm) **(be) thrilled to ˈbits** (*infml*) (be) extremely pleased: *The children were thrilled to bits by their presents.*

thriller *n* novel, play or film with an exciting and gripping plot, esp one involving crime: [attrib] *a thriller writer.*

thrive /θraɪv/ *v* (*pt* **thrived** or **throve** /θrəʊv/, *pp* **thrived** or, in archaic use, **thriven** /ˈθrɪvn/) [I, Ipr] ~ **(on sth)** grow or develop well and vigorously; prosper: *a thriving industry* ○ *A business cannot thrive without investment.* ○ *He thrives on criticism.*

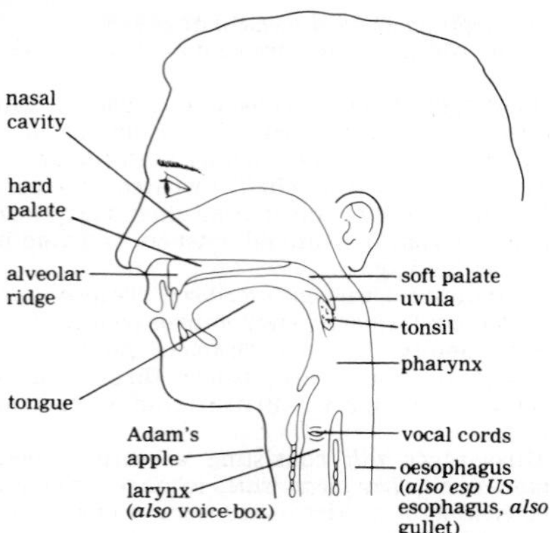

the throat

throat /θrəʊt/ *n* **1** front part of the neck: *grab sb by the throat.* **2** passage in the neck through which food passes to the stomach and air passes to the lungs: *clear one's throat,* ie by coughing, to remove phlegm or hoarseness ○ *A fish bone has stuck in my throat.* ○ *The victim's throat had been cut.* ⇨ illus. **3** (idm) **be at each other's ˈthroats** argue or fight with each other: *I don't think their marriage will last long; they're always at each other's throats.* **cut one's own ˈthroat** (*infml*) act in such a way as to harm oneself or one's interests, by being foolish, stubborn, etc. **force, thrust, ram, etc sth down sb's ˈthroat** (*infml*) try to make sb accept or listen to (one's views, beliefs, etc): *I do dislike having her extremist ideas rammed down my throat.* **have, etc a frog in one's throat** ⇨ FROG. **have, etc a lump in one's/the throat** ⇨ LUMP[1]. **jump down sb's throat** ⇨ JUMP[2]. **lie in/through one's teeth/throat** ⇨ LIE[1]. **stick in one's throat** ⇨ STICK[2].

▷ **-throated** (forming compound *adjs*) having a throat of the specified type or colour: *a deep-throated roar* ○ *a red-throated bird.*

throaty *adj* (**-ier**, **-iest**) (**a**) uttered deep in the throat; guttural: *a throaty laugh.* (**b**) sounding hoarse: *a throaty cough.* **throatily** /-ɪlɪ/ *adv.* **throatiness** *n* [U].

throb /θrɒb/ *v* (**-bb-**) [I, Ipr] ~ (**with sth**) **1** (of the heart, pulse, etc) beat, esp faster or stronger than usual: *His head throbbed,* ie He had a bad headache. ○ *Her heart was throbbing with excitement.* **2** vibrate or sound with a persistent rhythm: *a throbbing wound,* ie one that gives steadily pulsating pain ○ *The ship's engines throbbed quietly.* ○ *a voice throbbing with emotion.*

▷ **throb** *n* steady continuous beat: *throbs of joy, pain, pleasure, etc* ○ *the throb of distant drums.*

throes /θrəʊz/ *n* [pl] **1** severe pains: *the throes of childbirth* ○ *death throes.* **2** (idm) **in the throes of sth/of doing sth** (*infml*) struggling with the task of sth/of doing sth: *in the throes of moving house.*

thrombosis /θrɒmˈbəʊsɪs/ *n* (*pl* **-boses** /-ˈbəʊsi:z/) [C, U] formation of a clot of blood in a blood-vessel or in the heart: *coronary thrombosis.*

throne /θrəʊn/ *n* **1** [C] special chair or seat used by a king, queen, bishop, etc during ceremonies. **2 the throne** [sing] royal authority or power: *Queen Elizabeth* II *succeeded to the throne in 1952.* ○ *Albania lost its throne* (ie ceased to be a monarchy) *after the war.* ○ *come to/ascend/mount the throne,* ie become king or queen ○ *be on the throne,* ie be king or queen. **3** (idm) **the power behind the throne** ⇨ POWER.

throng /θrɒŋ; *US* θrɔ:ŋ/ *n* crowded mass of people or things: *a throng of fans waiting to see the star* ○ *throngs of flies filled the air.*

▷ **throng** *v* **1** [Ipr, Ip, It] move or press in a crowd: *The students thronged forward as the exam results were announced.* ○ *People are thronging to (see) his new play.* **2** [Tn, Tn·pr esp passive] ~ **sth (with sb/sth)** fill (a place) with a crowd: *Crowds thronged the main square of the city.* ○ *The airport was thronged with holiday-makers.*

throttle /ˈθrɒtl/ *v* **1** [Tn] seize (sb) by the throat and stop him breathing; choke; strangle: *throttled the guard before robbing the safe* ○ (*fig*) *accused the government of throttling the freedom of the press.* **2** (phr v) **throttle (sth) back/down** control the supply of fuel, steam, etc in order to reduce the speed of (an engine or a vehicle).

▷ **throttle** *n* valve controlling the supply of fuel, steam, etc to an engine; lever or pedal operating this: *open (out)/close the throttle* ○ *at full/half throttle,* ie with the throttle completely/half open ○ *take one's foot off the throttle,* ie off the accelerator, in a car.

through (*US* also **thru**) /θru:/ *prep* (For special uses with many *vs*, eg *get through sth, see through sb/sth,* see the *v* entries.) **1** (**a**) from one end or side of (a channel, passage, etc) to the other: *The River Thames flows through London.* ○ *The burglar got in through the window.* ○ *Air pressure forces the water through the pipe.* (**b**) from one side of (a surface or screen) to the other: *You can see through glass.* ○ *He could see three people through the mist.* ○ *She drained the water out through a sieve.* ○ *Cars are not allowed to go through the city centre.* ○ *We had to wade through the river to the opposite bank.* (**c**) passing from one side to the other of (sth hard or resistant): *His knees have gone through* (ie made holes in) *his jeans again.* ○ *You need a sharp knife to cut through the knot.* ○ *The bullet went straight through him.* ○ *The blood soaked through his shirt and stained his jacket.* ○ *I can't feel anything through these gloves.* (**d**) (moving) from one side to the other of (sth which has height and may obstruct movement): *He was running through the streets.* ○ *The dog rushed straight through the flower-bed.* ○ *The path led through the trees to the river.* ○ *The doctor pushed through the crowd to get to the injured man.* ○ *She made her way through the traffic to the other side of the road.* Cf ACROSS[2]. **2** from the beginning to the end of (sth): *He will not live through the night,* ie He will die before morning. ○ *The children are too young to sit through a long concert.* ○ *She nursed me through my long illness.* ○ *I'm half-way through (reading) his second novel.* **3** (*US*) up to and including; until: *stay in London Tuesday thru Friday.* **4** (**a**) (indicating the agent or means): *I heard of the job through a newspaper advertisement.* ○ *It was through you* (ie as a result of your help) *that we were able to meet again.* (**b**) (indicating the cause or reason): *We missed the plane through being held up on the motorway.* ○ *The accident happened through no fault of mine.* ○ *The vase was broken through carelessness.* **5** past (a barrier) or avoiding (a control imposed by law): *How did you manage to get all that wine through Customs?* ○ *He drove through a red light* (ie passed it without stopping) *and a policeman saw him.*

▷ **through** (*US* also **thru**) *adv part* (For special uses with many *vs*, eg *go through with sth, pull through,* see the *v* entries.) **1** from one side of sth to the other: *Put the coffee in the filter and let the water run through.* ○ *The tyre's flat — the nail has gone right through.* ○ *We're coming to a farmyard — I suppose we can just walk through.* ○ *It's a bit crowded in here — can you get through?* ○ *The flood was too deep to drive through.* **2** from the beginning to the end of sth: *Don't tell me how it ends — I haven't read all the way through yet.* ○ *We had an awful storm last night but the baby slept right through.* **3** past a barrier or avoiding a control imposed by law: *The light was red but the ambulance drove straight through.* **4** all the way into and out of a place: *This train goes straight through,* ie without stopping. ○ [attrib] *two ˈthrough trains a day* ○ *ˈthrough traffic* ○ *No ˈthrough road,* ie The road is closed at one end. **5** (**a**) (*Brit*) connected by telephone: *Ask to be put through to me personally.* ○ *I tried to ring you but I couldn't get through.* eg because the line was engaged or faulty. ○ *You're through now,* ie You can begin to speak. (**b**) (*US*) ready to end a telephone call: *How soon will you be through?* **6** (idm) **ˌthrough and ˈthrough** completely: *He's an Englishman through and through,* ie He has many typically English characteristics. ○ *We've been friends so long I know you through and through.* **7** (phr v) **be through (with sb/sth)** (indicating that a friendship, practice, etc is ended) have finished: *Keith and I are through.* ○ *She's through with her new boy-friend.* ○ *I'm finally through with* (ie I have stopped taking) *drugs.*

□ **ˈthroughput** *n* [U] amount of material put through a process, esp in a specified period of time.

ˈthroughway *n* (*US*) = EXPRESSWAY (EXPRESS[1]).

throughout /θru:ˈaʊt/ *adv* **1** in every part: *The house was painted green throughout.* ○ *Certain names in the book were underlined throughout.* **2** during the whole duration of sth: *I watched the film and cried throughout.*

▷ **throughout** *prep* **1** in or into every part of (sth): *News spread throughout the country.* ○ *References to pain occur throughout the poem.* **2** during the whole duration of (sth): *Food was scarce throughout the war.* ○ *Throughout his life he had always kept bees.* ○ *Throughout their marriage he had only once seen her cry.*

throve ⇨ THRIVE.

throw[1] /θrəʊ/ *v* (*pt* **threw** /θru:/, *pp* **thrown** /θrəʊn/) **1** [I, In/pr, Tn, Tn·pr, Tn·p, Dn·n] send (sth) through the air with some force, esp by moving the arm: *He throws well.* ○ *How far can you throw?* ○ *Stop throwing stones at that dog!* ○ *Throw the ball to your sister.* ○ *She threw the ball up and caught it again.* ○ *Please throw me that towel.* ○ (*fig*) *She threw me an angry look,* ie glanced angrily at me. **2** [Tn·pr, Tn·p] ~ **sth around/over sb/sth**; ~ **sth on/off** put (clothes, etc) on or off quickly or carelessly: *He threw a blanket over the injured man.* ○ *threw on his uniform* ○ *threw off her coat.* **3** [Tn·pr, Tn·p] turn or move (a part of the body) quickly or violently in the specified direction: *Throw your arms out in front of you as you dive.* ○ *The sergeant threw his shoulders back and his chest out.* ○ *He threw back his head and roared with laughter.* ○ *She threw up her hands in horror at the idea.* **4** [Tn, Tn·pr] hurl (sb) to the ground or the floor: *Two jockeys were thrown in the second race.* ○ *The wrestler succeeded in throwing his opponent (to the canvas).* **5** [Tn] (**a**) cause (dice) to fall to the table after shaking them. (**b**) obtain (a number) by doing this: *He threw three sixes in a row.* **6** [Tn] shape (pottery) on a potter's wheel: *a hand-thrown vase.* **7** [Tn] (*infml*) disturb (sb); disconcert: *The news of her death really threw me.* ○ *The speaker was completely thrown by the interruption.* **8** [Tn·pr esp passive] cause (sb) to be in a certain state: *Hundreds were thrown out of work.* ○ *We were thrown into confusion by the news.* **9** (**a**) [Tn·pr] cause (sth) to extend: *throw a bridge across a river.* (**b**) [Tn, Tn·pr] project or cast (light, shade, etc); cause to be: *The trees threw long shadows across the lawn.* (**c**) [Tn] deliver (a punch): *In the struggle several punches were thrown.* **10** [Tn] move (a switch, lever, etc) so as to operate it. **11** [Tn] (*US infml*) lose (a game or contest) deliberately. **12** [Tn] have or display (a fit, etc): *She regularly throws tantrums.* **13** [Tn] (*infml*) give (a party). **14** (For idioms containing **throw**, see entries for *ns*, *adjs*, etc, eg **throw the book at sb** ⇨ BOOK[1]; **throw cold water on sth** ⇨ COLD[1].) **15** (phr v) **throw sth about/around** scatter sth: *Don't throw litter about like that.*

throw oneself at sth/sb (**a**) rush violently at sth/sb. (**b**) (*infml*) (of a woman) make over-eager advances to (a man): *Everyone can see she's just throwing herself at him.*

throw sth away (**a**) discard sth as useless or unwanted: *That's rubbish — you can throw it away.* (**b**) fail to make use of sth: *throw away an opportunity, advantage, etc* ○ *My advice was thrown away* (ie wasted) *on him.* (**c**) (of actors, etc) speak (words) in a deliberately casual way: *This speech is meant to be thrown away.*

throw sb back on sth (usu passive) force sb to rely on sth (because nothing else is available): *The television broke down so we were thrown back on our own resources,* ie had to entertain ourselves.

throw sth in (**a**) include sth with what one is selling or offering, without increasing the price: *You can have the piano for £60, and I'll throw in the*

stool as well. **(b)** make (a remark, etc) casually. **throw oneself into sth** begin to do sth energetically: *throwing themselves into their work.* **throw sth off** produce or compose sth in a casual way, without apparent effort: *threw off a few lines of verse.* **throw sth/sb off** manage to get rid of sth/sb: *throw off a cold, a troublesome acquaintance, one's pursuers.*
throw oneself on sb/sth *(fml)* rely entirely on sb/sth; entrust oneself to sb/sth: *He was clearly guilty and could only throw himself on the mercy of the court.*
throw sb out (a) force (a trouble-maker, etc) to leave: *The drunk was thrown out (of the pub).* **(b)** distract or confuse sb; cause sb to make a mistake: *Do keep quiet or you'll throw me out in my calculations.* **throw sth out (a)** utter sth in a casual or spontaneous way: *throw out a hint, a suggestion, an idea, etc.* **(b)** reject (a proposal, an idea, etc). **(c)** = THROW STH AWAY (a): *It's time we threw that old chair out — it's completely broken.*
throw sb over desert or abandon sb: *When he became rich he threw over all his old friends.*
throw sb together bring (people) into contact with each other, often casually: *Fate had thrown them together.* ○ *As the only English speakers, we were rather thrown together.* **throw sth together** make or produce sth hastily: *I'll just throw together a quick supper.*
throw sth up (a) vomit (food). **(b)** resign from sth: *throw up one's job* ○ *You've thrown up a very promising career.* **(c)** bring sth to notice: *Her research has thrown up some interesting facts.* **(d)** build sth suddenly or hastily.
□ **ˈthrow-away** *adj* [attrib] **(a)** intended to be discarded after use: *throw-away cups, tissues, razors.* **(b)** spoken in a deliberately casual way; not emphasized: *a throw-away remark.*
ˈthrow-back *n* animal, etc that shows characteristics of an ancestor earlier than its parents. Cf ATAVISM.
ˈthrow-in *n* (in football) throwing in of the ball after it has gone outside the area of play.

throw[2] /θrəʊ/ *n* **1** [C] act of throwing: *a well-aimed throw* ○ *It's your throw,* eg your turn to throw the dice. **2** [C] distance to which sth is or may be thrown: *a throw of 70 metres* ○ *a record throw of the discus.* **3** [C] *(US)* piece of cloth used to cover a chair, sofa, etc. **4** (idm) **a stone's throw** ⇨ STONE. **a throw** [sing] *(infml esp US)* (with an amount of money) as the price of each: *best oranges, 50 cents a throw.*

thru *(US)* = THROUGH.

thrush[1] /θrʌʃ/ *n* any of various types of song bird, esp one with a brownish back and speckled breast (the *song-thrush).* ⇨ illus at BIRD.

thrush[2] /θrʌʃ/ *n* [U] **(a)** infectious disease producing white patches in the mouth and throat, esp in children. **(b)** similar disease affecting the vagina.

thrust /θrʌst/ *v* (*pt, pp* **thrust**) **1** [I, Ipr, Ip, Tn, Tn·pr, Tn·p] push (sth/sb/oneself) suddenly or violently: *a thrusting* (ie aggressive) *young salesman* ○ *He thrust (his way) through the crowd.* ○ *thrust a tip into the waiter's hand* ○ *(fig) My objections were thrust aside,* ie dismissed. ○ *She tends to thrust herself forward too much,* ie to be too self-assertive or ambitious. **2** [Ipr, Tn·pr] ~ **at sb (with sth)**/~ **sth at sb** make a forward stroke at sb with (a sword, etc): *The mugger thrust at his victim with a knife.* ○ *thrust one's bayonet at the enemy.* **3** (phr v) **thrust sth/sb on/upon sb** force sb to accept sth/sb or to undertake sth: *Some men have greatness thrust upon them,* ie become famous without wishing or trying to be. ○ *She is rather annoyed at having three extra guests suddenly thrust on her.*
▷ **thrust** *n* **1** [C] **(a)** act or movement of thrusting: *killed by a bayonet thrust.* **(b)** strong attack in war or in a contest: *a deep thrust into the opponent's territory.* **(c)** *(fig)* hostile remark aimed at sb: *a speech full of thrusts at the government.* **2** [U] forward force produced by a propeller, jet engine, rocket, etc. **3** [U] *(architecture)* stress or pressure between neighbouring parts of a structure (eg an arch). **4** [U] ~ **(of sth)** main point or theme (of remarks, etc); gist: *What was the thrust of his argument?* **5** (idm) **cut and thrust** ⇨ CUT[2].
thruster *n* person who thrusts himself forward (to win an advantage, etc).

Thucydides /θju:ˈsɪdədi:z/ (c 455-c 400 BC), Greek historian, whose *History* records the events of the *Peloponnesian War between Athens and Sparta, in which he himself took part. Despite his obvious admiration for the achievements of *Pericles, his account of the war shows an impartial and analytical approach to the writing of history.

thud /θʌd/ *n* low dull sound like that of a blow on sth soft: *The car hit the child with a sickening thud.*
▷ **thud** *v* (**-dd-**) [Ipr, Ip] move, fall or hit sth with a thud: *The sound of branches thudding against the walls of the hut.* ○ *I could hear him thudding about upstairs in his heavy boots.*

thug /θʌg/ *n* violent criminal or hooligan. ▷ **thuggery** /ˈθʌgərɪ/ *n* [U].

Thule /ˈθju:lɪ/ name used in ancient times for the most northerly land in the world. At various times it was applied to Iceland, the Shetland Islands, and part of Scandinavia.

thulium /ˈθu:lɪəm/ *n* [U] *(symb* **Tm)** silver-coloured metallic element, used in X-ray machines.

thumb /θʌm/ *n* **1** short thick finger set apart from the other four. ⇨ illus at HAND. **2** part of a glove covering this. **3** (idm) **be all (fingers and) ˈthumbs** be very clumsy, esp when handling things. **a rule of thumb** ⇨ RULE. **stand/stick out like a sore thumb** ⇨ SORE. **thumbs ˈup/ˈdown** (phrase or gesture used to indicate success or approval/failure or rejection): *give sb/sth the thumbs up* ○ *I'm afraid it's thumbs down for your new proposal.* **twiddle one's thumbs** ⇨ TWIDDLE. **under sb's ˈthumb** completely under sb's influence or control: *She's got him under her thumb.*
▷ **thumb** *v* **1** [Ipr, Tn] ~ **(through) sth** turn over the pages of (a book); make (a book, pages) worn or dirty by doing this: *thumbing through the dictionary* ○ *a well-thumbed copy.* **2** (idm) **thumb a ˈlift** (try to) get a free ride in a motor vehicle by signalling with one's thumb; hitch-hike. **thumb one's nose at sb/sth** make a rude gesture at sb/sth by putting one's thumb against the end of one's nose.
□ **ˈthumb-index** *n* set of lettered notches cut in the edge of a book, used to identify the position of the various sections in it (eg the words beginning with a certain letter in a dictionary).
ˈthumb-nail *n* nail at the tip of the thumb. — *adj* [attrib] briefly written: *a thumb-nail sketch/portrait/description of sb/sth.*
ˈthumbscrew *n* former instrument of torture that squeezed the thumb.
ˈthumb-stall *n* sheath to cover an injured thumb.
ˈthumb-tack *n (US)* = DRAWING-PIN (DRAWING).

thump /θʌmp/ *v* [I, Ipr, Ip, Tn, Tn·pr, Tn·p, Cn·a] beat or strike or knock heavily, esp with the fist: *My heart was thumping (with excitement).* ○ *Someone thumped (on) the door.* ○ *two boys thumping each other (on the head)* ○ *(fig) He thumped out a tune* (ie played it loudly) *on the piano.* ○ *She thumped the cushion flat.*
▷ **thump** *n* **(a)** heavy blow: *gave him a thump.* **(b)** noise made by this: *The sack of cement hit the ground with a thump.*
thumping (also **thundering**) *adj* [attrib] *(infml)* big: *a thumping lie* ○ *win by a thumping majority.* — *adv (infml)* extremely: *He lives in a thumping great house in the country.*

thunder /ˈθʌndə(r)/ *n* [U] **1** loud noise that follows a flash of lightning: *a crash/peel/roll of thunder* ○ *There's thunder in the air,* ie Thunder is likely. ○ *We haven't had much thunder this summer.* **2** any similar noise: *the thunder of the guns, jets, drums* ○ *a/the thunder of applause.* **3** (idm) **blood and thunder** ⇨ BLOOD[1]. **steal sb's thunder** ⇨ STEAL.
▷ **thunder** *v* **1** [I, In/pr] (used with *it*) sound with thunder: *It thundered all night.* **2 (a)** [Ipr] make a noise like thunder; sound loudly: *A voice thundered in my ear.* ○ *Someone was thundering at the door,* ie beating it. **(b)** [Ipr, Ip] move in the specified direction making a loud noise: *The train thundered through the station.* ○ *heavy lorries thundering along, by, past, etc.* **3 (a)** [Ipr] ~ **against sth/at sb** utter loud threats, etc against sth/sb: *reformers thundering against corruption* ○ *What right have you to thunder at me like that?* **(b)** [Tn] utter (threats, etc) loudly: *'How dare you speak to me like that?' he thundered.* **thunderer** /ˈθʌndərə(r)/ *n.* **thundering** /-dərɪŋ/ *adj, adv* = THUMPING (THUMP): *a thundering (great) nuisance.* **thunderous** /-dərəs/ *adj* like thunder; very loud: *thunderous applause.* **thunderously** *adv.* **thundery** /-dərɪ/ *adj* (of weather) giving signs of thunder: *a thundery day.*
□ **ˈthunderbolt** *n* **1** flash of lightning with a crash of thunder. **2** *(fig)* startling or terrible event or statement: *The unexpected defeat came as a thunderbolt.* ○ *He unleashed a thunderbolt by announcing his resignation.*
ˈthunderclap *n* **1** crash of thunder. **2** sudden terrible event or piece of news; thunderbolt(2).
ˈthunder-cloud *n* large dark cloud that can produce lightning and thunder.
ˈthunderstorm *n* storm with thunder and lightning and usu heavy rain.
ˈthunderstruck *adj* [esp pred] amazed.

Thur (also **Thurs**) *abbr* Thursday: *Thurs 26 June.*

"What have you done with Dr. Millmoss?"

James Thurber: cartoon from 'Men, Women and Dogs'

Thurber /ˈθɜ:bə(r)/ James (Grove) (1894-1961), American humorous writer and cartoonist. Much of his work originally appeared in the *New Yorker* magazine. He invented the character Walter *Mitty. ⇨ illus.

Thursday /ˈθɜ:zdɪ/ *n* [C, U] *(abbrs* **Thur, Thurs)** the fifth day of the week, next after Wednesday. For the uses of *Thursday* see the examples at *Monday.*

thus /ðʌs/ *adv (fml)* **1** in this way; like this: *calculate the area of the triangle thus formed* ○ *Hold the wheel in both hands, thus.* **2** as a result of this; accordingly: *He is the eldest son and thus heir to the title.* **3** to this extent: *Having come thus far do you wish to continue?*

thwack /θwæk/ *v* [Tn] *(infml)* hit (sb/sth) with a heavy blow; whack.
▷ **thwack** *n (infml)* (sound of a) heavy blow.

thwart[1] /θwɔ:t/ *v* [Tn] prevent (sb) doing what he intends; oppose (a plan, etc) successfully: *He was thwarted (in his aims) by bad luck.* ○ *thwarted ambitions.*

thwart[2] /θwɔ:t/ *n* seat across a rowing-boat for an oarsman.

thy /ðaɪ/ *possess det (arch)* of or belonging to thee; your: *hallowed be thy name.*

thyme /taɪm/ *n* [U] **(a)** any of various types of herb with fragrant leaves. **(b)** leaves of this plant used in cookery.

thyroid /ˈθaɪrɔɪd/ *n* (also **thyroid ˈgland**) large gland at the front of the neck, producing a hormone which controls the body's growth and development.

thyself /ðaɪˈself/ *reflex, emph pron (arch)* (used when addressing a single person) yourself.

Ti *symb* titanium.

ti /ti:/ *n (music)* the seventh note in the sol-fa scale.

tiara /tɪˈɑːrə/ *n* **1** woman's crescent-shaped head-dress, usu ornamented with jewels and worn on ceremonial occasions. **2** triple crown worn by the Pope.

Tibet /tɪˈbet/ mountainous region of SW China, to the north of the *Himalaya mountains; pop approx 2 030 000; capital, Lhasa. An independent country since the 5th century AD, it came under Chinese control around 1700. It regained independence in 1912, but in 1951 it was again taken over by China, and in 1959 its spiritual ruler, the *Dalai Lama, was forced to flee.

▷ **Tibetan** *adj* of Tibet, its people or its language. — *n* **1** [C] native or inhabitant of Tibet. **2** [U] Tibetan language, related to Burmese.

tibia /ˈtɪbɪə/ *n* (*pl* ~**e** /-bɪiː/) (*anatomy*) = SHIN-BONE (SHIN). ⇨ illus at SKELETON.

tic /tɪk/ *n* occasional involuntary twitching of the muscles, esp of the face: *have a nervous tic.*

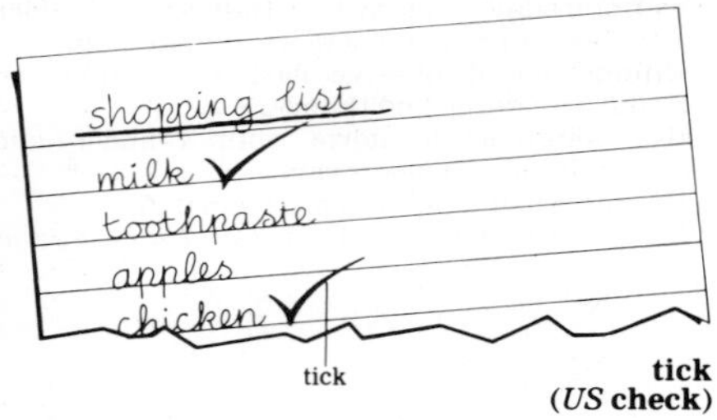

tick

tick
(*US* **check**)

tick[1] /tɪk/ *n* **1** light and regularly repeated sound, esp that of a clock or watch. **2** (*infml*) moment: *Just wait a tick! ○ I'll be down in half a tick/in two ticks.* **3** (*US* **check**) mark put beside an item in a list to show that it has been checked or done or is correct. ⇨ illus.

▷ **tick** *v* **1** [I, Ip] ~ (**away**) (of a clock, etc) make a series of ticks (TICK[1] 1): *My watch doesn't tick because it's electric. ○ listened to the clock ticking/the ticking of the clock ○ While we waited the taxi's meter kept ticking away.* **2** [Tn, Tn·p] ~ **sth** (**off**) put a tick[1](3) beside (an item, etc): *tick (off) the names of those present ○ The jobs that are done have been ticked off.* **3** (idm) **what makes sb ˈtick** (*infml*) what makes sb behave in the way he does: *I've never really understood what makes her tick.* **4** (phr v) **tick away/by** (of time) pass: *Meanwhile the minutes kept ticking away.* **tick sth away** (of a clock, etc) mark the passage of time: *The station clock ticked away the minutes.* **tick sb off** (*infml*) rebuke or scold sb: *get ticked off for careless work.* **tick over** (**a**) (of an engine) idle: *I stopped the car but left the motor ticking over.* (**b**) (of activities) continue in a routine way: *Just try and keep things ticking over while I'm away.*

□ ˌ**ticking-ˈoff** *n* (*pl* **tickings-off**) (*infml*) rebuke or reprimand: *give sb a good ticking-off.*

ˈ**tick-tack** *n* [U] (*Brit*) system of signalling by moving the hands, used by bookmakers on racecourses.

ˌ**tick-tack-ˈtoe** *n* [U] (*US*) = NOUGHTS AND CROSSES (NOUGHT).

ˌ**tick-ˈtock** *n* (usu *sing*) ticking sound of a large clock.

tick[2] /tɪk/ *n* **1** any of various types of small parasitic insect-like animal that suck blood. **2** (*Brit sl*) unpleasant or contemptible person.

tick[3] /tɪk/ *n* **1** [C] case of a mattress or pillow, in which the filling is contained. **2** [U] = TICKING.

tick[4] /tɪk/ *n* [U] (*infml esp Brit*) credit: *get tick ○ buy goods on tick.*

ticker /ˈtɪkə(r)/ *n* (*infml*) **1** heart: *His ticker's not very strong,* ie He has a weak heart. **2** (*dated*) watch.

□ ˈ**ticker-tape** *n* [U] (*esp US*) (**a**) paper tape from a teleprinter, etc: *reading the stock market prices off the ticker-tape.* (**b**) this or similar material thrown from windows to greet a celebrity: [attrib] *a ticker-tape parade ○ get a ticker-tape reception.*

ticket /ˈtɪkɪt/ *n* **1** [C] written or printed piece of card or paper that gives the holder a certain right (eg to travel by plane, train, bus, etc or to a seat in a cinema): *Do you want a single or a return ticket? ○ I've got two tickets for the Cup Final. ○ You must present your library ticket every time you borrow books. ○ Admission by ticket only,* eg as a notice outside a hall, etc. **2** [C] label attached to sth, giving details of its price, size, etc. **3** [C usu *sing*] (*esp US*) list of the candidates put forward by one party in an election: *run for office on the Republican ticket.* **4** [C] official notice of an offence against traffic regulations: *get a parking/speeding ticket.* **5** [C] (*infml*) certificate issued to a qualified ship's master, aircraft pilot, etc. **6 the ticket** [sing] (*dated infml*) the correct or desirable thing: *All packed up and ready to go? That's the ticket.* **7** (idm) **split one's ticket** ⇨ SPLIT. **the straight ticket** ⇨ STRAIGHT[1].

▷ **ticket** *v* [Tn esp passive] put a ticket on (an article for sale, etc).

ticking /ˈtɪkɪŋ/ (also **tick**) *n* [U] strong material for covering mattresses and pillows.

tickle /ˈtɪkl/ *v* **1** [I, Tn, Tn·pr] touch or stroke (sb) lightly, esp at sensitive parts, so as to cause a slight tingling sensation, often with twitching movements and laughter: *This blanket tickles (me). ○ tickle sb in the ribs ○ She tickled my nose with a feather.* **2** [I] feel such a sensation: *My nose tickles.* **3** [Tn] please (sb's vanity, sense of humour, etc); amuse: *The story tickled her fancy/curiosity. ○ I was highly tickled by the idea.* **4** (idm) (**be**) **tickled ˈpink/to ˈdeath** (*infml*) extremely pleased or amused: *I'm tickled pink that my essay won the prize.* **tickle sb's ribs** (*infml*) amuse sb. Cf RIB-TICKLING (RIB).

▷ **tickle** *n* **1** act or sensation of tickling: *I've got this tickle in my throat — I think I may be getting a cold.* **2** (idm) **slap and tickle** ⇨ SLAP *n*.

tickler /ˈtɪklə(r)/ *n* (*dated infml esp Brit*) puzzle; problem: *an awkward little tickler to solve.*

ticklish /ˈtɪklɪʃ/ *adj* **1** (of a person) sensitive to tickling: *I'm terribly ticklish.* **2** (*infml*) (of a problem) requiring careful handling; difficult: *a ticklish question ○ in a ticklish situation.* **ticklishness** *n* [U].

ticky-tacky /ˈtɪkɪ tækɪ/ *adj, n* [U] (*US infml*) (made of) cheap or inferior materials: *suburbs full of ticky-tacky (houses).*

tidal /ˈtaɪdl/ *adj* of or affected by a tide or tides: *a tidal river, estuary, harbour, etc.*

□ **tidal ˈwave 1** great ocean wave, eg one caused by an earthquake. **2** ~ (**of sth**) (*fig*) great wave of popular enthusiasm, indignation, etc: *carried along on a tidal wave of hysteria.*

tidbit (*US*) = TITBIT.

tiddler /ˈtɪdlə(r)/ *n* (*infml*) **1** very small fish, esp a stickleback or minnow. **2** unusually small thing or child.

tiddly /ˈtɪdlɪ/ *adj* (**-ier**, **-iest**) (*infml*) **1** (*esp Brit*) slightly drunk; tipsy: *feeling a bit tiddly.* **2** (*Brit*) very small; negligible: *Two tiddly biscuits with cheese on? You can't call that a proper meal!*

tiddly-winks /ˈtɪdlɪ wɪŋks/ *n* [U] game in which players try to make small plastic discs jump into a cup by pressing them on the edge with a larger disc.

tide /taɪd/ *n* **1** (**a**) [C, U] regular rise and fall in the level of the sea, caused by the attraction of the moon and sun: *spring/neap* (ie maximum/minimum) *tides ○ at high/low tide.* (**b**) [C] water moved by this: *We were cut off by the tide. ○ The tide is (coming) in/(going) out. ○ driftwood washed up by the tide(s) ○ Swimmers should beware of strong tides.* **2** [C usu *sing*] direction in which opinion, events, luck, etc seem to move; trend: *a rising tide of discontent ○ The tide turned in our favour.* **3** [U] (*arch*) (in compounds) season: *ˈyule-tide ○ ˈWhitsuntide.* **4** (idm) **go, swim, etc with/against the stream/tide** ⇨ STREAM[1]. **time and tide wait for no man** ⇨ TIME[1].

▷ **tide** *v* (phr v) **tide sb over** (**sth**) help sb through (a difficult period) by providing what he needs: *Will you lend me some money to tide me over until I get my pay cheque?*

□ ˈ**tide-mark** *n* **1** mark made by the tide water at its highest point on a beach, etc. **2** (*joc*) (**a**) line between washed and unwashed parts of sb's body. (**b**) line left on a bath by the dirty water.

ˈ**tide-table** *n* list showing the times of high tide at a place.

ˈ**tideway** *n* (**a**) channel where a tide runs. (**b**) tidal part of a river.

tidings /ˈtaɪdɪŋz/ *n* [pl] (*arch or joc*) news: *Have you heard the glad tidings?*

tidy /ˈtaɪdɪ/ *adj* (**-ier**, **-iest**) **1** (**a**) arranged neatly and in order: *a tidy room, desk, garden ○ keeps her house very tidy.* (**b**) having the habit of keeping things neat and orderly: *a tidy boy ○ tidy habits ○ have a tidy mind,* ie be able to think clearly and sensibly. **2** [attrib] (*infml*) (esp of a sum of money) fairly large; considerable: *She left a tidy fortune when she died. ○ It must have cost a tidy penny,* ie quite a lot of money.

▷ **tidily** *adv.*

tidiness *n* [U].

tidy *n* receptacle for odds and ends: *a ˈdesk tidy,* ie for pens, paper-clips, etc *○ a ˈsink tidy,* ie for bits of kitchen waste.

tidy *v* (*pt, pp* **tidied**) **1** [I, Ip, Tn, Tn·p] ~ (**sth/sb/oneself**) (**up**) make (sth/sb/oneself) tidy: *Who's been tidying in here? ○ spent all morning tidying up ○ You'd better tidy this room (up) before the guests arrive. ○ I must tidy myself up,* ie make myself look tidy. **2** (phr v) **tidy sth away** put sth in a certain place (esp out of sight) so that a room, etc appears tidy: *Tidy away your toys when you've finished playing.* **tidy sth out** remove unnecessary or unwanted items from sth and arrange the rest neatly: *tidy out one's drawers, a cupboard, etc.*

tie[1] /taɪ/ *n* **1** (also ˈ**necktie**) strip of decorative material worn round the neck under the collar and knotted in front. ⇨ illus at JACKET. **2** piece of cord, wire, etc used for fastening or tying sth: *ties for sealing plastic bags.* **3** (**a**) rod or beam holding parts of a structure together. (**b**) (*US*) = SLEEPER 2. **4** (usu *pl*) (*fig*) thing that unites people; bond: *the ties of friendship ○ family ties ○ The firm has ties with an American corporation.* **5** (*fig*) thing that limits a person's freedom of action: *He doesn't want any ties; that's why he never married. ○ Pets can be a tie when you want to go away on holiday.* **6** equal score in a game or competition: *Each team scored twice and the game ended in a tie.* **7** sports match between two or a group of competing teams or players: *the first leg of the Cup tie between Aberdeen and Barcelona.* **8** (*music*) curved line in a score over two notes of the same pitch that are to be played or sung as one. ⇨ illus at MUSIC.

□ ˈ**tie-beam** *n* horizontal beam connecting rafters.

ˈ**tie-breaker** (also ˈ**tie-break**) *n* means of deciding the winner when competitors have tied (TIE[2] 5): *The first set* (ie of a tennis match) *was won on the tie-break.*

ˈ**tie-pin** (*US* ˈ**stickpin**, ˈ**tie-tack**) *n* ornamental pin for holding a tie[1](1) together or in place.

tie[2] /taɪ/ *v* (*pt, pp* **tied**, *pres p* **tying**) **1** [Tn, Tn·pr, Tn·p] fasten or bind (sth) with rope, string, etc: *Shall I tie the parcel or use sticky tape? ○ The prisoner's hands were securely tied. ○ tie a dog to a lamp-post ○ tie his hands together ○ tie a branch down.* **2** [Tn, Tn·pr, Tn·p] ~ **sth** (**on**) attach sth by means of its strings, etc: *Could you tie this apron round me? ○ tie on a label.* **3** (**a**) [Tn, Tn·pr, Tn·p] arrange (ribbon, string, etc) to form a knot or bow: *tie a ribbon, scarf, tie, cravat, etc ○ She tied her hair in(to) a bun. ○ tie (up) one's shoe-laces.* (**b**) [Tn, Tn·pr] make (a knot or bow) in this way: *tie a knot in a piece of rope.* **4** [I, Ipr, Ip] be fastened: *This rope won't tie properly. ○ Does this sash tie in front or at the back?* **5** [I, Ipr, Tn usu passive, Tn·pr usu passive] ~ (**sb**) (**with sb**) (**for sth**) make the same score as (another competitor): *The two teams tied (with each other). ○ Britain are tied with Italy for second place.* **6** [Tn] (*music*) unite (notes) with a tie[1](8): *tied crotchets.* **7** (idm) **bind/tie sb hand and foot** ⇨ HAND[1]. **have one's hands free/tied** ⇨ HAND[1]. **tie oneself into/(up) in ˈknots** get very confused. **tie the knot** (*infml*) get married. **8** (phr v) **tie sb/oneself down** (**to sth**) restrict sb/oneself (to certain conditions, a fixed occupation or place, etc): *Children do tie you down, don't they?* ○ *refuse to be tied down by petty restrictions.* **tie in (with sth)** (of information, facts, etc) agree or be connected: *This evidence ties in with what we already know.* **tie (sth) up** moor (sth) or be moored: *We tied (the boat) up alongside the quay.* **tie sb up (a)** bind sb with rope, etc so that he cannot move or escape: *The thieves left the night-watchman tied up and gagged.* **(b)** (usu passive) occupy sb so that he has no time for other things: *I'm tied up in a meeting until 3 pm.* **tie sth up (a)** bind sth with cord, rope, etc. **(b)** (often passive) invest (capital) so that it is not easily available for use: *most of his money's tied up in property.* **(c)** make conditions restricting the use or sale of (property, etc). **(d)** bring (work, progress, etc) to a halt; obstruct sth: *The strike tied up production for a week.*

▷ **tied** *adj* [attrib] (of a house) rented to sb on condition that he works for the owners: *a ˌtied ˈcottage* ○ *a job with tied accommodation.* **ˈtied house** (*Brit*) public house that is owned or controlled by a particular brewery. Cf FREE HOUSE (FREE[1]).

□ **ˈtie-dye** *v* [Tn] produce dyed patterns on (fabric) by tying parts of it so that they are protected from the dye. **ˈtie-dyeing** *n* [U].

ˈtie-in *n* **1** product (eg a book or toy) linked with and helping to promote a film, television series, etc: *Batman T-shirts and other tie-ins.* **2** (*US*) (item sold in a) sale in which an additional item must be bought along with the main purchase.

ˈtie-on *adj* [attrib] (of a label, etc) that may be attached by tying.

ˈtie-up *n* **1** ~ **(with sb/sth)** link; merger; partnership. **2** (*esp US*) halt in work, progress, etc; standstill: *a traffic tie-up.*

Tiepolo /ˈtɪeɪpələʊ/ Giovanni Battista (1696-1770), Italian painter, generally regarded as the last of the great Venetian fresco painters. He worked in many parts of Europe, and his paintings are marked by richness of colour and a theatrical splendour.

tier /tɪə(r)/ *n* any of a series of rows (esp of seats) or parts of a structure placed one above the other: *a box in the first tier,* ie in a theatre ○ *a wedding-cake with three tiers/a three-tier wedding-cake.* ⇨ illus at LAYER.

▷ **tiered** *adj* arranged in tiers: *tiered seating.*

-tiered (forming compound *adjs*) having the specified number of tiers: *a three-tiered cake* ○ *a two-tiered system,* ie one with two distinct levels.

Tierra del Fuego /tɪˌerə del ˈfweɪgəʊ/ group of islands at the southern tip of S America, belonging partly to Argentina and partly to Chile.

tiff /tɪf/ *n* slight quarrel between friends or acquaintances: *She's had a tiff with her boy-friend.*

tig /tɪg/ *n* [U] = TAG 6.

tiger /ˈtaɪgə(r)/ *n* **1** large fierce animal of the cat family, with yellowish and black stripes, found in Asia. ⇨ illus at CAT. **2** (idm) **fight like a tiger** ⇨ FIGHT[1]. **a paper tiger** ⇨ PAPER.

▷ **tigerish** /ˈtaɪgərɪʃ/ *adj* like a tiger, esp (of a person) fiercely energetic.

tigress /ˈtaɪgrɪs/ *n* female tiger.

□ **ˈtiger-lily** *n* tall garden lily having orange flowers spotted with black or purple.

ˈtiger-moth *n* moth with wings striped like a tiger's skin.

tight /taɪt/ *adj* (-er, -est) **1** fixed, fastened or drawn together firmly; hard to move or undo: *a tight knot* ○ *I can't get the cork out of the bottle — it's too tight.* ○ *The drawer is so tight I can't open it.* ○ *keep a tight hold on the rope.* **2** (a) fitting closely: *a tight joint* ○ *These shoes are too tight for me.* ○ *a tight ship,* ie one that does not leak ○ *tight* (ie strict) *controls.* **(b)** (in compound *adjs*) made so that a specified thing cannot get in or out: *ˈairtight* ○ *ˈwatertight.* **3 (a)** with things or people arranged closely: *a tight mass of fibres* ○ *a tight schedule,* ie leaving little time to spare. **(b)** (of a game, etc) evenly contested: *a tight race, match, contest, etc.* **4** fully stretched; taut: *a tight rope, belt, rein, etc* ○ *My chest feels rather tight,* eg because of asthma. **5** [usu pred] (*infml*) drunk: *got a bit tight at the party.* **6** (*finance*) **(a)** (of money) not easy to obtain, eg on loan from banks. **(b)** (of the money market) in which credit is severely restricted. **7** (*infml*) stingy; miserly: *She's tight with her money.* **8** (idm) **keep a tight ˈrein on sb/sth** allow little freedom to sb/sth. **a ˌtight ˈsqueeze** cramped or crowded situation: *We managed to get all the luggage into the car but it was a tight squeeze.*

▷ **tight** *adv* **1** tightly (not used before a past participle: *packed tight* but *tightly packed*): *Hold tight!* **2** (idm) **sit tight** ⇨ SIT. **sleep tight** ⇨ SLEEP[2].

tighten /ˈtaɪtn/ *v* **1** [I, Ipr, Ip, Tn, Tn·pr, Tn·p] ~ **(sth) (up) (a)** (cause sth to) become tight or tighter: *This screw needs tightening.* ○ *tighten (up) the ropes* ○ *He tightened his grip on her arm.* **(b)** (cause sth to) become stricter: *Controls have gradually tightened.* ○ *tighten up security.* **2** (idm) **loosen/tighten the purse-strings** ⇨ PURSE. **tighten one's ˈbelt** eat less food, spend less money, etc because there is little available: *The management warned of the need for further belt-tightening,* ie economy. **3** (phr v) **tighten up (on sth)** become more careful, vigilant or strict: *The police are tightening up on drunken driving.*

tightly *adv* in a tight manner: *squeeze sb tightly* ○ *tightly sealed.*

tightness *n* [U].

□ **ˌtight-ˈfisted** *adj* stingy; miserly.

ˌtight-ˈlipped *adj* keeping the lips pressed firmly together, esp to restrain one's emotion or to keep silent; grim-looking.

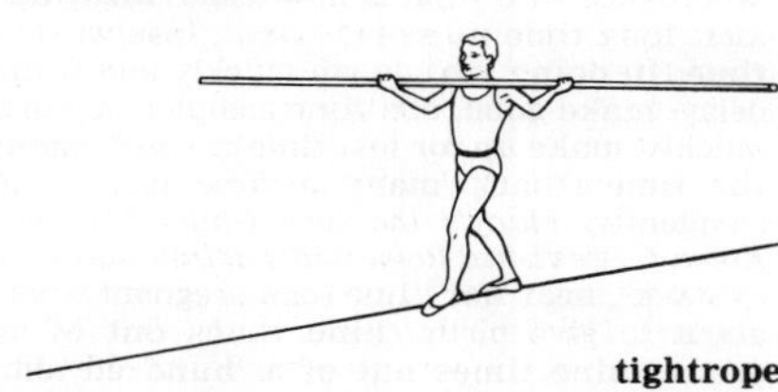

tightrope

tightrope /ˈtaɪtrəʊp/ *n* **1** rope stretched tightly high above the ground, on which acrobats perform: [attrib] *a tightrope walker.* **2** (idm) **tread/walk a ˈtightrope** have to act in a situation which allows little scope for manoeuvre and in which an exact balance must be preserved.

tights /taɪts/ *n* [pl] **1** (also **pantihose, pantyhose**) close-fitting garment covering the hips, legs and feet, worn by girls and women: *a pair of cotton tights.* Cf STOCKING. **2** similar garment covering the legs and body, worn by acrobats, dancers, etc.

tike = TYKE.

tilde /ˈtɪldə, *in sense* 2 tɪld/ *n* **1** mark (˜) placed over the Spanish *n* when it is pronounced *ny* /nj/ (as in *cañon*), or the Portuguese *a* or *o* when it is nasalized (as in *São Paulo*). **2** mark (~) used in this dictionary to replace the headword in certain parts of an entry.

tile /taɪl/ *n* **1** slab of baked clay or other material used in rows for covering roofs, walls, floors, etc: *covered the wall in cork tiles* ○ *insulated the ceiling with expanded polystyrene tiles* ○ *carpet tiles,* ie carpet sold in small squares for laying in rows. ⇨ illus at HOUSE. **2** any of the small flat pieces used in certain board games. **3** (idm) **on the ˈtiles** (*sl*) enjoying oneself away from home in a wild or drunken way.

▷ **tile** *v* [Tn] cover (a surface) with tiles: *a tiled bathroom.*

till[1] ⇨ UNTIL.

till[2] /tɪl/ *n* **1** drawer in which money is kept behind the counter in a shop, bank, etc or in a cash register. **2** (idm) **have, etc one's fingers in the till** ⇨ FINGER[1].

till[3] /tɪl/ *v* [Tn] prepare and use (land) for growing crops.

▷ **tillage** /ˈtɪlɪdʒ/ *n* [U] **1** action or process of tilling. **2** tilled land.

tiller *n* person who tills.

till[4] /tɪl/ *n* [U] = BOULDER CLAY (BOULDER).

tiller /ˈtɪlə(r)/ *n* horizontal bar used to turn the rudder of a small sailing-boat. ⇨ illus at YACHT. Cf HELM.

tilt /tɪlt/ *v* **1** [I, Ipr, Ip, Tn, Tn·pr, Tn·p] (cause sth to) move into a sloping position: *This table tends to tilt (to one side/over).* ○ *Popular opinion has tilted* (ie shifted) *in favour of the Socialists.* ○ *She sat listening, with her head tilted slightly to one side.* ○ *Don't tilt your chair or you'll fall over!* ○ *Tilt the barrel forward to empty it.* **2** [I, Ipr] ~ **(at sb/sth)** run or thrust with a lance in jousting. **3** (idm) **tilt at ˈwindmills** fight imaginary enemies. **4** (phr v) **tilt at sb/sth** attack sb/sth in speech or writing: *a satirical magazine tilting at public figures.*

▷ **tilt** *n* **1** (usu *sing*) tilting; sloping position: *with a tilt of his head* ○ *the table is on/at a slight tilt.* **2** act of tilting with a lance. **3** (idm) **full pelt/speed/tilt** ⇨ FULL. **have a tilt at sb** attack sb in a friendly way during a debate, conversation, etc.

tilth /tɪlθ/ *n* [U] depth of soil affected by cultivation: *rake a seed-bed to a good tilth,* ie until there is a depth of fine crumbly soil.

timber /ˈtɪmbə(r)/ *n* **1** (*US* **lumber**) [U] wood prepared for use in building or carpentry: *dressed timber,* ie sawn, shaped and planed ready for use ○ [attrib] *a ˈtimber-merchant* ○ *a ˈtimber-yard,* ie where timber is stored, bought and sold, etc. **2** [U] trees suitable for this: *standing* (ie growing) *timber* ○ *cut down/fell timber* ○ *put a hundred acres of land under timber,* ie plant it with trees. **3** [C] piece of wood, esp a beam, used in constructing a house or ship: *roof/floor timbers.*

▷ **timber** *interj* (used as a warning that a tree is about to fall after being cut).

timbered /ˈtɪmbəd/ *adj* **1** (of buildings) built of wooden beams or with a framework of these. **2** (of land) planted with trees; wooded.

□ **ˈtimberland** *n* [U] (*US*) land with trees growing on it that are cut down and sold as timber.

ˈtimber-line *n* [sing] = TREE-LINE (TREE).

ˈtimber-wolf *n* large grey wolf of N America.

timbre /ˈtæmbrə, ˈtɪmbə(r)/ *n* characteristic quality of sound produced by a particular voice or instrument.

Timbuktu /ˌtɪmbʌkˈtuː/ **1** town in the African republic of *Mali. **2** (also **Timbuctoo**) (*joc*) any distant or remote place: *Their new house is so far away they might as well be in Timbuctoo.*

time[1] /taɪm/ *n* **1** [U] all the years of the past, present and future: *past/present/future time* ○ *The world exists in space and time.* **2** [U] passing of these taken as a whole: *Time has not been kind to her looks,* ie She is no longer as beautiful as she was. ○ *(old) Father Time,* ie this process personified. **3** [U] indefinite period in the future: *Time heals all wounds.* **4** [U] portion or measure of time: *That will take time,* ie cannot be done quickly. ○ *I don't have (much) time to read these days.* ○ *We have no time to lose,* ie We must hurry. ○ *What a waste of time!* ○ *I spent most of my time (in) sightseeing.* ○ *I'm rather pressed for time,* ie in rather a hurry. ○ *What a (long) time you've been!* ○ *I had a most unpleasant time at the dentist's.* **5** [U] point of time stated in hours and minutes of the day: *What time is it?/What is the time?* ○ *Do you have the time (on you)?* ○ *My youngest daughter has just learnt to tell the time.* ⇨ App 9, App 10. **6** [U, C] period of time measured in units (years, months, hours, etc): *The winner's time was 11.6 seconds.* ○ *He ran the mile in record time,* ie faster than any previous runner. ○ *Although she came second their times were only a tenth of a second apart.* ⇨ App 9, 10, 12. **7** [U] amount of time spent in work, etc: *be on short time,* ie a reduced working week ○ *paid time and a half/double time,* ie paid one and a half times/twice the usual rate. **8** [U] point or period of time used, available or suitable for sth: *at the time you're speaking of* ○ *by the time we reached home* ○ *last time I was there* ○ *every time I see her* ○ *ˈlunch-time* ○ *This is not the time to bring up that subject.* ○ *Now's your time,* ie opportunity. ○ *It's time we were going/time for us to go,* ie We should leave now. ○ *Time is up,* ie The time allowed for sth is ended. ○ *Time, please!* ie warning that a pub is about to close. **9** [C] occasion; instance: *this, that, another, next, last, etc time* ○ *the time before last* ○ *for the first, second, last, etc time* ○ *He failed his* *driving test five times.* ○ *told sb umpteen, a dozen, countless, etc times* (ie repeatedly) *not to do sth.* **10** [C often *pl*] (**a**) period of time associated with certain events, people, etc: *in ˈStuart times/the time(s) of the ˈStuarts*, ie when the Stuart kings ruled ○ *in ˈancient, prehisˈtoric, ˈrecent, etc times* ○ *Mr Curtis was the manager in ˈmy time*, ie when I was working there. ○ *The house is old but it will last ˈmy time*, ie will serve me for the rest of my life. (**b**) period of time associated with certain conditions, experiences, etc: *University was a good time for me.* ○ *Times are hard for the unemployed.* ○ *in time(s) of danger, hardship, prosperity, etc.* **11** [U] (*music*) (**a**) type of rhythm: *ˈcommon time*, ie two or four beats in each bar ○ *three ˈeight time*, ie three quavers to the bar ○ *in ˈwaltz/ˈmarch time* ○ *beating time to the music.* (**b**) rate at which a piece of music is to be played; tempo: *quick time.* **12** (idm) **(and) about ˈtime (ˈtoo)** (*infml*) and this is sth that should have happened some time ago: *I hear old Fred got promoted last week — and about time too, I'd say.* **ahead of ˈtime** earlier than expected. **ahead of one's ˈtime** having ideas that are too advanced or enlightened for the period in which one lives. **all the ˈtime (a)** during the whole of the time in question: *That letter I was searching for was in my pocket all the time*, ie while I was searching for it. (**b**) always: *He's a business man all the time*, ie He has no other interest. **at ˈall times** always: *I'm at your service at all times.* **(even) at the best of times** ⇨ BEST[3]. **at ˈone time** at some period in the past; formerly: *At one time I used to go skiing every winter.* **at ˈother times** on other occasions: *Sometimes he's fun to be with; at other times he can be very moody.* **at the same time** ⇨ SAME. **at a ˈtime** in sequence; separately: *Don't try to do everything at once; take it a bit at a time.* ○ *Take the pills two at a time.* **at the ˈtime** at a certain moment or period in the past: *I agreed at the time but later changed my mind.* ○ *We were living in London at the time.* **at ˈmy, ˈyour, ˈhis, etc time of life** at my, your, his, etc age: *He shouldn't be playing football at his time of life*, ie He is too old for it. **at ˈtimes** sometimes. **before one's ˈtime** before the period one can remember or the point at which one became involved: *The Beatles were a bit before my time.* ○ *The headquarters used to be in Bristol, but that was before my time*, ie before I worked there. **behind ˈtime** late: *The plane was an hour behind time.* ○ *He's always behind time with the rent.* **behind the ˈtimes** no longer fashionable or modern in one's ideas, methods, etc. **better luck next time** ⇨ BETTER[1]. **bide one's time** ⇨ BIDE. **the big time** ⇨ BIG. **born before one's time** ⇨ BORN. **borrowed time** ⇨ BORROW. **buy time** ⇨ BUY. **do ˈtime** (*sl*) serve a prison sentence: *He's done time for armed robbery.* **every time** whenever possible; whenever a choice can be made: *Different people like different sorts of holiday, but give me the seaside every time.* **for old times' sake** ⇨ OLD. **for a ˈtime** for a short period. **for the time ˈbeing** until some other arrangement is made: *You'll have your own office soon but for the time being you'll have to share one.* **from/since ˌtime immeˈmorial** (*saying*) from/since longer ago than anyone can remember. **from ˌtime to ˈtime** now and then; occasionally. **gain time** ⇨ GAIN[2]. **give sb/have a rough, hard, etc ˈtime (of it)** (cause sb to) suffer, esp from harassment, overwork, etc. **(in) half the time (a)** (in) a much shorter time than expected: *If you'd given the job to me I could have done it in half the time.* (**b**) a considerable time; too long a time: *I'm not surprised he didn't complete the exam: he spent half the time looking out of the window.* **have an easy time** ⇨ EASY. **have, etc a good ˈtime** enjoy oneself, generally or on a particular occasion. **have/give sb a high old time** ⇨ HIGH[1]. **have a lot of time for sb/sth** (*infml*) be enthusiastic about sb/sth. **have no time for sb/sth** be unable or unwilling to spend time on sb/sth; dislike sb/sth: *I've no time for lazy people/laziness.* **have a thin time** ⇨ THIN. **have the ˌtime of one's ˈlife** (*infml*) be exceptionally happy or excited: *The children had the time of their lives at the circus.* **have time on one's hands/time to kill** (*infml*) have nothing to do. **have a whale of a time** ⇨ WHALE. **(it is) ˈhigh/aˈbout time** the time is long overdue when sth should happen or be done: *It's high time you stopped fooling around and started looking for a job.* **in course of time** ⇨ COURSE[1]. **in the fullness of time** ⇨ FULLNESS (FULL). **in good time** early: *There wasn't much traffic so we got there in very good time.* **(all) in good ˈtime** after a reasonable or appropriate space of time, but not immediately: *'Can we have lunch now — I'm hungry.' 'All in good time.'* **in the nick of time** ⇨ NICK[1]. **in (less than) ˈno time** very quickly. **in one's own good ˈtime** at the time or rate that one decides oneself: *There's no point getting impatient with her; she'll finish the job in her own good time.* **in one's own time** in one's free time; outside working hours. **in one's own sweet time** ⇨ SWEET[1]. **in one's ˈtime** at a previous period or on a previous occasion in one's life: *I've seen some slow workers in my time but this lot are the slowest by far.* **in ˈtime** sooner or later; eventually: *You'll learn how to do it in time.* **in time (for sth/to do sth)** not late: *Will I be in time for the train/to catch the train?* **in/out of ˈtime** (*music*) in/not in the correct time[1](11): *tapping one's fingers in time to/with the music.* **it's only a matter of time** ⇨ MATTER[1]. **keep ˈtime (a)** (of a clock or watch) show the correct time: *My watch always keeps excellent time.* (**b**) sing or dance in time[1](11). **keep up, move, etc with the ˈtimes** change one's attitudes, behaviour, etc in accordance with what is now usual. **kill time** ⇨ KILL. **long time no see** ⇨ LONG[1]. **lose/waste no time (in doing sth)** do sth quickly and without delay. **make good, etc ˈtime** complete a journey quickly. **make up for lost time** ⇨ LOST[2]. **ˈmany's the time (that)**; **ˈmany a time** many times; frequently: *Many's the time (that) I've visited Rome.* ○ *I've visited Rome many a time.* **mark time** ⇨ MARK[2]. **near her ˈtime** (of a pregnant woman) about to give birth. **ˌnine times out of ˈten**; **ˌninety-nine times out of a ˈhundred** almost always. **(there is) no time like the present** (*saying*) now is the best time to do sth. **once upon a time** ⇨ ONCE. **on ˈtime** neither late nor early; punctually: *The train arrived (right/bang) on time.* **pass the time of day** ⇨ PASS[2]. **play for ˈtime** try to gain time by delaying. **procrastination is the thief of time** ⇨ PROCRASTINATION (PROCRASTINATE). **a race against time** ⇨ RACE[1]. **quite some time** ⇨ QUITE. **a sign of the times** ⇨ SIGN[1]. **a stitch in time saves nine** ⇨ STITCH. **take one's ˈtime (over sth/to do sth/doing sth) (a)** use as much time as one needs; not hurry: *Take your time — there's no rush.* (**b**) (*ironic*) be unreasonably late or slow: *You certainly took your time getting here!* **take time ˈout** (*esp US*) make an opportunity for oneself, in the middle of doing other things: *While you're in New York, take time out to visit the Museum of Modern Art.* **tell the time** ⇨ TELL. **ˌtime after ˈtime**; **ˌtime and (time) aˈgain**; **ˌtimes without ˈnumber** on many occasions; repeatedly. **time and tide wait for ˈno man** (*saying*) no one can delay the passing of time (so one should not put off a favourable opportunity to do sth). **time ˈflies** (*saying*) time passes quickly, esp more quickly than one realizes: *Oh dear — hasn't time flown!* **time hangs/lies heavy on one's ˈhands** time passes too slowly (esp because one has nothing to do). **time is ˈmoney** (*saying*) one should not waste time that could be used to earn money. **time is on sb's ˈside** sb can afford to wait before doing or achieving sth: *Although she failed the exam she has time on her side: she'll still be young enough to take it in her next year.* **the time is ripe for sth/sb to do sth** it is the right moment for (doing) sth. **the time of ˈday** the hour as shown by a clock. **time presses** we must not delay. **time ˈwas (when)...** there has been a time when...: *Time was you could get a good three-course meal for less than a pound.* **time (alone) will ˈtell, etc** it will become obvious with the passing of time: *Time will show which of us is right.* **watch the time** ⇨ WATCH[2]. **work, etc against ˈtime** work, etc as fast as possible so as to finish by a specified time.

PREPOSITIONS OF TIME		
in the	parts of the day (not night)	*in the morning(s), etc*
	months	*in February*
	seasons	*in (the) summer*
	years	*in 1987*
	decades	*in the 1920s*
	centuries	*in the 20th century*
on (the)	days of the week	*on Saturday(s)*
	dates	*on (the) 20th (of) February*
	specific days	*on Good Friday*
		on New Year's Day
		on my birthday
		on the following day
at (the)	clock time	*at 5 o'clock, at 7.45 pm*
	night	*at night*
	holiday periods	*at Christmas*
		at the weekend

□ **ˌtime-and-ˈmotion** *adj* [attrib] concerned with examining the way people work and finding ways to make them work more efficiently: *a time-and-ˈmotion study.*

ˈtime bomb bomb that can be set to explode after a certain period of time.

ˈtime-card (also **ˈtime-sheet**) *n* record of the number of hours sb works.

ˈtime-consuming *adj* taking or needing much time: *Some of the more time-consuming jobs can now be done by machines.*

ˈtime exposure photographic exposure in which the shutter is left open for longer than the briefest time (ie usu more than a second or two).

ˈtime-fuse *n* fuse designed to burn for or explode after a given time.

ˈtime-honoured (*US* **-honored**) *adj* (esp of a custom, etc) respected because of long tradition.

ˈtimekeeper *n* **1** person or device that records time spent at work. **2** (preceded by an *adj*) watch or clock: *a good/bad* (ie accurate/inaccurate) *timekeeper.*

ˈtime-lag *n* interval of time between two connected events: *the time-lag between a flash of lightning and the thunder* ○ *the time-lag between research and development.*

ˈtime-lapse *adj* [attrib] (of photography) involving the taking of individual pictures of a slow process (eg the opening of a flower bud) with an interval of time between them, and then showing them in a continuous sequence, so that the process appears speeded up.

ˈtime-limit *n* limit of time within or by which sth must be done: *set a time-limit for the completion of a job.*

ˌtime ˈoff leisure time, away from one's work or duty: *You don't get much time off in this job.*

ˌtime-ˈout *n* (*esp US*) short stoppage of play in a game (eg of basketball) for the players to rest, discuss tactics, etc. Cf TAKE TIME OUT (TIME).

ˈtimepiece *n* (*fml*) clock or watch.

ˈtime-scale *n* period of time in which a sequence of events takes place; successive stages of a process, an operation, etc.

ˈtime-server *n* (*derog*) person who adopts fashionable opinions or those held by people in power, esp for selfish purposes.

ˈtime-serving *adj* (*esp attrib*) behaving like a time-server: *time-serving politicians.*

ˈtime-sharing *n* [U] **1** use of a computer for different operations by two or more people at the same time. **2** arrangement in which a holiday home is owned jointly by several people who agree to use it each at different times of the year. **ˈtime-share** *n* share in a property on a time-sharing(2) basis: [attrib] *time-share villas.*

ˈtime-sheet *n* = TIME-CARD 4.

ˈtime-signal *n* sound or sounds indicating the exact time of day.

ˈtime signature (*music*) symbol consisting of two numbers placed one above the other, which indicate how many beats there are in each bar of a piece of music (the top number), and how long each beat should be (the bottom number).

ˈtime-switch *n* switch that can be set to operate

automatically at a certain time: *The central heating is on a time-switch.*

ˈ**timetable** (also *esp US* **schedule**) *n* list showing the time at which certain events will take place: *a school timetable*, ie showing the time of each class ○ *a train, bus, ferry, etc timetable* ○ *I've got a very busy timetable this week*, ie a lot of appointments, etc.

ˈ**time warp** (in science fiction) distortion of time so that the past or the future becomes the present.

ˈ**time-worn** *adj* worn or damaged by age: *a time-worn* (ie hackneyed) *expression.*

ˈ**time zone** region (between two parallels of longitude) where a common standard time is used.

ime[2] /taɪm/ *v* **1** [Tn, Tn·pr, Cn·t esp passive] choose the time or moment for (sth); arrange the time of: *You've timed your holiday cleverly — the weather's at its best.* ○ *His remark was well/badly timed*, ie made at a suitable/an unsuitable moment. ○ *Kick-off is timed for 2.30.* ○ *The train is timed to connect with the ferry.* ○ *The bomb was timed to explode during the rush-hour.* **2** [Tn] (*sport*) make (a stroke) or strike (the ball) at a certain moment: *He timed that shot beautifully.* **3** [Tn, Tw] measure the time taken by (a runner, etc) or for (a race, process, etc): *This egg is hard — you didn't time it properly.* ○ *Time me while I do/Time how long it takes me to do a length of the pool.*

▷ **timer** *n* (often in compounds) person or device that times sth: *an* ˈ*egg-timer.*

timing *n* [U] **(a)** determining or regulating the time when an action or event occurs: [attrib] *a* ˈ*timing device* ○ *The timing of the announcement was rather unexpected.* ○ *valve timing*, ie the time at which valves in a motor engine open and close. **(b)** skill in this, as a way of achieving the desired result: *He's not playing his shots well — his timing is faulty.* ○ *A good actor must learn the art of timing*, ie when to deliver a line most effectively.

imeless /ˈtaɪmlɪs/ *adj* (*fml or rhet*) **1** not appearing to be affected by the passing of time: *her timeless beauty* ○ *a landscape with a timeless quality.* **2** unending; permanent: *the timeless laws of nature.* ▷ **timelessly** *adv.* **timelessness** *n* [U].

imely /ˈtaɪmlɪ/ *adj* (**-ier, -iest**) occurring at just the right time; opportune: *thanks to your timely intervention* ○ *This has been a timely reminder of the need for constant care.* ▷ **timeliness** *n* [U].

Times /taɪmz/ **The Times** British daily newspaper, first published in 1785. Originally often critical of government policy (it was nicknamed 'The Thunderer'), it has since the late 19th century represented *Establishment attitudes. ⇨ article at NEWSPAPER.

imes /taɪmz/ *prep* multiplied by: *Five times two is/equals ten*, ie 5 × 2 = 10.

▷ **times** *n* [pl] (used to express multiplication): *This book is three times as long as/three times longer than/three times the length of that one.*

imid /ˈtɪmɪd/ *adj* easily frightened; shy: *as timid as a rabbit.* ▷ **timidity** /tɪˈmɪdətɪ/, **timidness** *ns* [U]. **timidly** *adv.*

Timor /ˈtiːmɔː(r)/ mountainous island that is part of the state of Indonesia.

□ **the** ˌ**Timor** ˈ**Sea** part of the Indian Ocean between Timor and NW Australia.

imorous /ˈtɪmərəs/ *adj* (*fml*) timid. ▷ **timorously** *adv.* **timorousness** *n* [U].

Timothy /ˈtɪməθɪ/ either of two books of the New Testament, written as letters by St *Paul to St Timothy, a Christian leader of the 1st century AD. ⇨ App 5.

impani /ˈtɪmpənɪ/ *n* [sing or pl *v*] set of kettledrums in an orchestra. ⇨ illus at MUSIC.

▷ **timpanist** /ˈtɪmpənɪst/ *n* person who plays the timpani.

in /tɪn/ *n* **1** [U] (*symb* **Sn**) chemical element, a soft white metal used in alloys (eg solder, pewter and bronze) and for coating iron and steel to prevent corrosion. The main producers of tin are Bolivia, Indonesia and Malaysia: [attrib] *tin cans* ○ *a tin whistle.* ⇨ App 11. **2** [C] (also *esp US* **can**) **(a)** container made of tin plate, esp one in which food is sealed to preserve it: *open a tin of beans.* ⇨ illus at CAN. **(b)** contents of this: *He ate a whole tin of stew.* **3** (idm) **a (little) tin** ˈ**god** (*infml*) person or thing that is greatly respected or worshipped for no good reason.

▷ **tin** *v* (**-nn-**) [Tn esp passive] (*US* **can**) seal (food) in a tin(2a) to preserve it: *tinned sardines, peas, peaches.*

tinny *adj* (**-ier, -iest**) (*derog*) **1** (of metal objects) not strong or solid: *a cheap tinny radio.* **2** having a thin metallic sound: *a tinny piano.*

□ **tin** ˈ**foil** very thin sheets of tin or aluminium alloy used for wrapping and packing things: *a roll of tin foil.*

tin ˈ**hat** (*army sl*) soldier's steel helmet.

ˈ**tin-horn** *n* (*US sl*) person, esp a gambler, who pretends to have a lot of ability, experience, money, etc but impresses no one.

ˈ**tin-opener** *n* device or tool for opening tins of food.

ˈ**tin plate** iron or steel sheets coated with tin.

ˈ**tinpot** *adj* [attrib] (*derog*) inferior or worthless: *a tinpot little dictator.*

ˈ**tinsmith** *n* person who makes things out of tin or tin plate.

ˈ**tin-tack** *n* short nail made of iron coated with tin.

tin ˈ**whistle** (also **penny whistle**) simple musical instrument, played by blowing, with six holes for the different notes.

tincture /ˈtɪŋktʃə(r)/ *n* ~ (**of sth**) **1** [C, U] medical substance dissolved in alcohol: *a/some tincture of iodine, quinine, etc.* **2** [sing] (*fml*) slight trace or flavour (of a thing or quality): *a tincture of heresy.*

▷ **tincture** *v* [Tn, Tn·pr esp passive] ~ **sth** (**with sth**) (*fml*) tinge or flavour sth; affect sth slightly (with a quality).

tinder /ˈtɪndə(r)/ *n* [U] any dry substance that catches fire easily.

□ ˈ**tinder-box** *n* box containing tinder with a flint and steel, formerly used for lighting a fire: (*fig*) *There is much racial unrest in the community and the whole place is a tinder-box*, ie violence could easily break out.

tine /taɪn/ *n* **(a)** any of the points or prongs of a fork, harrow, etc. **(b)** branch of a deer's antler.

ting /tɪŋ/ *n* clear ringing sound.

▷ **ting** *v* [I, Tn] (cause sth to) make such a sound.

□ ˌ**ting-a-**ˈ**ling** *n* series of tings, made eg by a small bell. — *adv*: *The bell went ting-a-ling.*

tinge /tɪndʒ/ *v* [Tn, Tn·pr esp passive] ~ **sth** (**with sth**) **1** colour sth slightly: *hair tinged with grey.* **2** affect sth slightly: *admiration tinged with envy.*

▷ **tinge** *n* (esp *sing*) ~ (**of sth**) slight colouring or trace: *There was a tinge of sadness in her voice.* ○ *Do I detect a tinge of irony?*

tingle /ˈtɪŋgl/ *v* **(a)** [I, Ipr] ~ (**with sth**) have a slight pricking, stinging or throbbing feeling in the skin: *The slap she gave him made his cheek tingle.* ○ *fingers tingling with cold.* **(b)** [Ipr] ~ **with sth** (*fig*) be affected by (an emotion): *tingling with excitement, indignation, shock, etc.*

▷ **tingle** *n* (usu *sing*) tingling feeling: *have a tingle in one's fingertips* ○ *feel a tingle of anticipation.*

tinker /ˈtɪŋkə(r)/ *n* **1** [C] person who travels from place to place repairing kettles, pans, etc. **2** [sing] ~ (**at/with sth**) act of tinkering: *I had a tinker at your radio, but I can't mend it.* **3** (*dated Brit infml*) naughty child: *You little tinker!*

▷ **tinker** *v* [I, Ipr, Ip] ~ (**at/with sth**) work in a casual or inexpert way, esp trying to repair or improve sth: *tinker (away) at a broken clock* ○ *He likes tinkering with computers.* ○ *Who's been tinkering (around) with the wiring?*

tinkle /ˈtɪŋkl/ *n* (esp *sing*) **1** series of short light ringing sounds: *the tinkle of a bell, of breaking glass, of ice being stirred in a drink.* **2** (*Brit infml*) telephone call: *Give me a tinkle when you get home.*

▷ **tinkle** *v* [I, Tn] (cause sth to) make a tinkle.

tinny ⇨ TIN.

tin-pan alley /ˌtɪn pæn ˈælɪ/ (*infml sometimes derog*) composers, performers and publishers of popular music and the type of life they live: *He's been in tin-pan alley for twenty years.*

tinsel /ˈtɪnsl/ *n* [U] **1** glittering metallic substance used in strips or threads as a decoration: *decorate a Christmas tree with tinsel* ○ *a dress trimmed with tinsel.* **2** (*derog*) superficial brilliance or glamour.

▷ **tinselled** /-sld/, **tinselly** /-səlɪ/ *adjs* **1** decorated with tinsel. **2** (*derog*) superficially brilliant or glamorous.

tint /tɪnt/ *n* **1** shade or variety of a colour: *tints of green in the sky at dawn* ○ *an artist who excels at flesh tints*, ie painting the colours of the human body ○ *red with a bluish tint.* **2** **(a)** weak dye for colouring the hair. **(b)** act of colouring the hair in this way: *She had a tint.*

▷ **tint** *v* [Tn, Cn·a] apply or give a tint to (sth); tinge: *leaves tinted in autumn colours* ○ *blue-tinted hair* ○ (*fig*) *His comments were tinted with sarcasm.*

Tintoretto /ˌtɪntəˈretəʊ/ born Jacopo Robusti (1518-94), Italian painter who lived and worked in Venice. He is best known for his large-scale dramatic religious pictures. His nickname means literally 'little dyer' (his father was a dyer).

tiny /ˈtaɪnɪ/ *adj* (**-ier, -iest**) **1** very small: *a tiny baby* ○ *living in a tiny cottage* ○ *I feel a tiny bit better today.* **2** (idm) **the patter of tiny feet** ⇨ PATTER[2].

-tion ⇨ -ION.

tip[1] /tɪp/ *n* **1** pointed or thin end of sth: *the tips of one's fingers/one's fingertips* ○ *the tip of one's nose* ○ *walking on the tips of her toes* ○ *the northern tip of the island.* **2** small part or piece fitted to the end of sth: *shoes with metal tips* ○ *a cane with a rubber tip.* **3** (idm) **(have sth) on the tip of one's** ˈ**tongue** just about to be spoken or remembered: *His name's on the tip of my tongue, but I just can't think of it.* **the tip of the** ˈ**iceberg** small but evident part of a much larger concealed situation, problem, etc: *Over 100 burglaries are reported every month, and that's just the tip of the iceberg*, ie many more occur but are not reported.

▷ **tip** *v* (**-pp-**) [Tn, Tn·pr] ~ **sth** (**with sth**) fit a tip to sth; put on the tip of sth: *filter-tipped cigarettes* ○ *The legs of the table were tipped with rubber.* ○ *The native warriors tipped their spears with poison.*

tip[2] /tɪp/ *v* (**-pp-**) **1** [I, Ip, Tn, Tn·p] **(a)** ~ (**sth**) (**up**) (cause sth to) rise, lean or tilt on one side or at one end: *Don't lean on the table or it'll tip up.* ○ *Tip the box up and empty it.* **(b)** ~ (**sth**) (**over**) (cause sth to) turn or fall over: *Careful! You'll tip the boat over.* **2** [Tn, Tn·pr, Tn·p] (*Brit*) cause (the contents of sth) to pour out by tilting: *No rubbish to be tipped here/No tipping*, eg on a notice warning people not to dump rubbish ○ *Tip the dirty water out of the bowl and into the sink.* ○ *My neighbour has been tipping dead leaves over the wall into my garden.* ○ *The train stopped abruptly, nearly tipping me out of my bunk.* **3** (idm) **tip the** ˈ**balance/**ˈ**scale** be the deciding factor for or against sth: *Her greater experience tipped the balance in her favour and she got the job.* **tip/turn the scales at sth** ⇨ SCALE[3].

▷ **tip** *n* **1** place where rubbish may be tipped (TIP[2] 2): *the municipal* ˈ*refuse tip* ○ *take a broken old refrigerator to the tip.* Cf DUMP *n* 1. **2** (*infml*) dirty or untidy place: *Their house is an absolute tip.*

□ ˈ**tipper lorry** (also ˈ**tipper truck**) lorry whose body can be raised at one end to tip out the contents.

ˈ**tip-up** *adj* [attrib] (of seats) that can be raised to allow people to pass easily, eg in a cinema.

tip[3] /tɪp/ *v* (**-pp-**) **1** **(a)** [Tn] touch or strike (sth) lightly: *The ball just tipped the edge of his racket.* **(b)** [Tn·pr, Tn·p] cause (sth) to move in the specified direction by doing this: *She just tipped the ball over the net.* **2** [Tn] give a small sum of money to (a waiter, taxi-driver, etc): *tip the porter 50p.* **3** [Tn, Cn·n/a, Cn·t esp passive] ~ **sb/sth** (**as sth/to do sth**) give advice or an opinion about sb/sth: *tip the winner*, ie name the winner of a race, etc before it takes place ○ *He was widely tipped as the President's successor/to succeed the President.* **4** (idm) **tip sb the** ˈ**wink** (*infml*) give sb private information; warn sb secretly. **5** (phr v) **tip sb off** (*infml*) give sb an advance warning or hint: *Someone tipped off the police about the robbery.*

▷ **tip** *n* **1** small sum of money given to a waiter, taxi-driver, etc as a personal reward for their services: *He left a tip under his plate.* **2** **(a)** small but useful piece of practical advice: *Here's a handy tip for removing stains from clothing.* **(b)** private or special piece of information, esp about horse-races, the stock-market, etc: *a hot* (ie very good) *tip for the Derby* ○ *Take my tip/Take a tip from me and buy these shares now.*

□ ˌ**tip and** ˈ**run** form of cricket in which the batsman must attempt to take a run if he hits the ball.

ˈ**tip-off** *n* hint or warning: *Acting on a tip-off, the police arrested the drug smugglers.*

tippet /ˈtɪpɪt/ *n* **(a)** long piece of fur, etc worn by a woman round the neck and shoulders, with the ends hanging down in front. **(b)** similar article of clothing worn by judges, clergy, etc.

Tippett /ˈtɪpɪt/ Sir Michael (1905-), English composer. His work, which is characterized by a strong rhythmic drive, includes operas (eg *The Midsummer Marriage, The Knot Garden, King Priam, The Ice Break*), oratorios (eg *A Child of Our Time)*, symphonies, concertos, and various orchestral and piano works.

tipple /ˈtɪpl/ *v* [I] be in the habit of drinking alcoholic drinks, esp too often or too much: *He started tippling when his wife left him.*

▷ **tipple** *n* (usu *sing*) (*infml*) alcoholic drink: *What's your tipple?* ie What would you like to drink? ○ *His favourite tipple is whisky.*

tippler /ˈtɪplə(r)/ *n.*

tipster /ˈtɪpstə(r)/ *n* person who gives tips (TIP[3] *n* 2b), usu in return for money.

tipsy /ˈtɪpsɪ/ *adj* (**-ier, -iest**) (*infml*) slightly drunk. ▷ **tipsily** *adv.* **tipsiness** *n* [U].

tiptoe /ˈtɪptəʊ/ *n* (idm) **on** ˈ**tiptoe** on the tips of one's toes; with one's heels not touching the ground: *stand on tiptoe to see over the crowd* ○ *creep around on tiptoe to avoid making a noise.*

▷ **tiptoe** *v* [I, Ipr, Ip] walk quietly and carefully on tiptoe: *She tiptoed (across) to the bed where the child lay asleep.* ⇨ Usage at PROWL.

tiptop /ˌtɪpˈtɒp/ *adj* (*infml*) excellent; first-rate: *tiptop quality* ○ *That meal was tiptop.*

TIR /ˌtiː aɪ ˈɑː(r)/ *abbr* (esp on lorries in Europe) international road transport (French *Transport International Routier*).

tirade /taɪˈreɪd; *US* ˈtaɪreɪd/ *n* long angry speech of criticism or accusation.

tire[1] /ˈtaɪə(r)/ *v* **1** [I, Tn, Tn·p] (cause a person or an animal to) become weary or in need of rest: *She's got so much energy — she never seems to tire.* ○ *Old people tire easily.* ○ *The long walk tired me (out).* **2** [Ipr] ~ **of sth/doing sth** become uninterested in (doing) sth: *After a week I tired of eating fish.* ○ *He never tires of the sound of his own voice,* ie He talks too much.

▷ **tired** /ˈtaɪəd/ *adj* **1** feeling that one would like to sleep or rest: *He was a tired man when he got back from that long climb.* ○ *I'm dead* (ie extremely) *tired.* **2** (*derog*) over-familiar; hackneyed: *The film had a rather tired plot.* ○ *see the same tired old faces at every party.* **3** (idm) **be (sick and) tired of sb/sth/doing sth** have had enough of sb/sth/doing sth; be impatient or bored with sb/sth/doing sth: *I'm tired of (listening to) your criticisms.* ˌ**tired** ˈ**out** completely exhausted. **tiredness** *n* [U].

tireless *adj* not tiring easily; energetic: *a tireless worker* ○ *thanks to your tireless efforts on our behalf.* **tirelessly** *adv.*

tiresome /ˈtaɪəsəm/ *adj* troublesome, tedious or annoying: *Selling your house can be a tiresome business.* ○ *The children were being rather tiresome.* **tiresomely** *adv.*

tiring /ˈtaɪərɪŋ/ *adj*: *a tiring journey* ○ *The work is very tiring.*

tire[2] (*US*) = TYRE.

tiro (also **tyro**) /ˈtaɪərəʊ/ *n* (*pl* ~**s**) (*dated*) person with little or no experience; beginner or novice.

Tirol = TYROL.

tissue /ˈtɪʃuː/ *n* **1** [U, C] mass of cells forming the body of an animal or a plant: *muscular, nervous, connective, etc tissue* ○ *The tissues have been destroyed and a scar has formed.* **2** [C] piece of soft absorbent paper that is thrown away after use (as a handkerchief, etc): *a box of tissues* ○ ˈ*face/*ˈ*facial tissues,* ie for removing make-up, etc. **3** (also ˈ**tissue-paper**) [U] very thin soft paper used for wrapping and packing things. **4** [C, U] (any type of) fine thin woven fabric. **5** [C] ~ **(of sth)** (*fig*) connected or interwoven series: *His story is a tissue of lies.* ○ *the complex tissue of myth and fact.*

tit[1] /tɪt/ *n* any of various types of small bird, often with a dark top to the head: *titmouse* ○ *tomtit* ○ *blue tit.*

tit[2] /tɪt/ *n* (idm) ˌ**tit for** ˈ**tat** blow, injury, insult, etc given in return for one received: *He hit me so I hit him back — it was tit for tat.*

tit[3] /tɪt/ *n* **1** (⚠ *sl*) **(a)** (esp *pl*) woman's breast. **(b)** nipple. **2** (*Brit sl*) (used as a vulgar term of abuse): *He's a stupid little tit!*

Titan /ˈtaɪtn/ *n* **1** **(a)** (in Greek mythology) any of the earliest gods, who were the children of Heaven and Earth. **(b)** (also **titan**) [C] person of great size, strength, intellect, importance, etc. **2** largest of the moons of *Saturn.

▷ **titanic** /taɪˈtænɪk/ *adj* gigantic; immense: *The two of them are locked in a titanic struggle for control of the company.*

Titanic /taɪˈtænɪk/ **the Titanic** large British passenger ship, supposedly unsinkable, that sank on its first voyage in 1912 after hitting an iceberg in the North Atlantic. About 1 500 people were killed.

titanium /taɪˈteɪnɪəm, tɪˈteɪ-/ *n* [U] (*symb* **Ti**) grey metallic element. It is light, strong and resistant to corrosion, and is used in alloys for making aircraft, spacecraft, etc.

titbit /ˈtɪtbɪt/ (*US* **tidbit** /ˈtɪdbɪt/) *n* **(a)** specially attractive bit of food: *She always keeps some titbits to give to her cat.* **(b)** ~ **(of sth)** small but interesting piece of news, gossip, etc: *titbits of scandal.*

tithe /taɪð/ *n* one tenth of the annual produce of a farm, etc formerly paid as a tax to support the clergy and the church.

□ ˈ**tithe barn** barn built to store tithes.

Titian /ˈtɪʃn/ real name Tiziano Vecellio (c 1488-1576), Italian painter, generally considered to be the greatest of the 16th-century Venetian school. His large output of paintings, which are noted for their rich colour, includes religious and mythological scenes (eg *The Entombment of Christ* and *Bacchus and Ariadne*) and portraits.

▷ **Titian** *adj* (also **Titian red**) (of hair) bright auburn in colour, like the colour often used by Titian in his paintings.

titillate /ˈtɪtɪleɪt/ *v* [Tn] stimulate or excite (sb), esp sexually: *The book has no artistic merit — its sole aim is to titillate (the reader).* ▷ **titillating** *adj*: *a mildly titillating film.* **titillation** /ˌtɪtɪˈleɪʃn/ *n* [U].

titivate /ˈtɪtɪveɪt/ *v* [I, Tn] (*infml*) make (esp oneself) smart or attractive: *She spent an hour titivating (herself) before going out.* ▷ **titivation** /ˌtɪtɪˈveɪʃn/ *n* [U].

title /ˈtaɪtl/ *n* **1** [C] name of a book, poem, picture, etc. **2** [C] word used to show a person's rank, occupation, etc (eg *King, mayor, captain*) or used in speaking to or about him (eg *Lord, Doctor, Mrs*): *She has a title,* ie is a member of the nobility. ⇨ article at ARISTOCRAT. **3** [U, C] ~ **(to sth/to do sth)** (*law*) right or claim, esp to the ownership of property: *Has he any title to the land?* ○ *disputing the country's title to the islands.* **4** [C] (*sport*) championship: *win the world heavyweight title* ○ [attrib] *a title fight.*

▷ **titled** /ˈtaɪtld/ *adj* having a title of nobility: *a titled lady,* eg a duchess.

□ ˈ**title-deed** *n* legal document proving sb's title to a property.

ˈ**title-holder** *n* (*sport*) champion: *the British 800-metres title-holder* ○ *Liverpool are the current title-holders.*

ˈ**title-page** *n* page at the front of a book giving the title, author's name, etc.

ˈ**title-role** *n* part in a play, etc that is used as the title: *She has sung the title-role in 'Carmen',* ie sung the role of Carmen in that opera.

titmouse /ˈtɪtmaʊs/ *n* (*pl* **titmice** /-maɪs/) type of tit[1].

Tito /ˈtiːtəʊ/ real name Josip Broz (1892-1980), Yugoslav soldier and politician, leader of Yugoslav resistance to the Germans in the Second World War and president of Yugoslavia 1953-80. He was a Communist but followed a policy independent of the Soviet Union.

titrate /taɪˈtreɪt/ *v* [Tn] (*chemistry*) find out th amount of a particular substance in (a solution) b testing its chemical reaction with a small amoun of a known substance. ▷ **titration** /-ˈtreɪʃn/ *n* [U

titter /ˈtɪtə(r)/ *n* short nervous laugh.

▷ **titter** *v* [I] give a titter: *The audience tittere politely.*

tittle-tattle /ˈtɪtl tætl/ *n* [U] silly or trivial talk petty gossip.

▷ **tittle-tattle** *v* [I] talk about unimportant things gossip.

titular /ˈtɪtjʊlə(r); *US* -tʃʊ-/ *adj* [attrib] (*fml* **1** having a certain title(2) or position but no rea authority: *the titular Head of State* ○ *titula sovereignty.* **2** held as the result of having a title(2 *titular sovereignty.*

Titus /ˈtaɪtəs/ book of the New Testament, writte as a letter by St *Paul to St Titus, his assistant. ⇨ App 5.

tizzy /ˈtɪzɪ/ *n* (usu *sing*) (*infml*) state of nervou excitement or confusion: *be in/get in(to) a tizzy.*

T-junction ⇨ T, T.

Tl *symb* thallium.

TM *abbr* **1** trademark. **2** transcendenta meditation.

Tm *symb* thulium.

tn *abbr* (*US*) ton(s); tonne(s).

TNT /ˌtiː en ˈtiː/ *abbr* trinitrotoluene (a powerfu explosive).

to[1] /*before consonants* tə; *before vowels* tʊ *or* tu *strong form* tuː/ *prep* **1** **(a)** in the direction of (sth towards: *walk to the office* ○ *I'm going to the shops* ○ *fall to the ground* ○ *on the way to the station* *point to sth* ○ *hold it (up) to the light* ○ *turn to th left/right* ○ *travelling from town to town, place t place, etc* ○ *go to Majorca for one's holidays* ○ *H was taken to hospital for treatment.* **(b)** ~ **the st (of sth)** located in a specified direction (from sth) *There are mountains to the north/south/east/west c here.* ○ *Pisa is to the west (of Florence).* ○ *The she is to the side of the house.* **2** towards (a conditior state, quality, etc); reaching the state of (sth): *move to the left,* eg in politics ○ *stir sb to action* *bring/reduce/move sb to tears* ○ *rise to power* ○ *H tore the letter to pieces.* ○ *The mother sang her bab to sleep.* ○ *Wait until the traffic lights change fror red to green.* **3** **(a)** as far as (sth); reaching: *Th garden extends to the river bank.* ○ *Her dres reached down to her ankles.* **(b)** (esp after *from sth* until and including (sth): *from beginning to end* *from first to last* ○ *faithful to the end/last* ○ *we soaked, drenched, etc to the skin* ○ *cooked t perfection* ○ *count (from 1) to 10* ○ *all the colour from red to violet* ○ *from Monday to Friday* ○ *fro morning to night* ○ *How long is it to lunch?* ie Hov much time is there until lunch? **4** (of time) befor (sth): *a quarter to six* ○ *ten (minutes) to two.* C PAST[2] 1. **5** (used to introduce the indirect object c *vs* marked Dn·pr, Dpr·f, Dpr·t, Dpr·w): *He gave it t his sister.* ○ (*fml*) *To whom did she send the book?* (*infml*) *Who did she send the book to?* ○ *She said t us that she was surprised.* ○ *I'll explain to yo where everything goes.* ○ *He shouted to his friend t remember the wine.* **6** belonging to (sb/sth); for: *th key to the door* ○ *be secretary to the managin director* ○ *the words to a tune.* **7** (indicating comparison or ratio): *I prefer walking to climbing* ○ *We won by six goals to three.* ○ *This is inferior superior to that.* ○ *Compared to me, he's rich.* ○ *odd of 100 to 1.* **8** making (sth); adding up to: *There ar 100 pence to the pound,* ie £1 = 100p. ○ *There are 10 centimetres to the metre.* **9** (indicating a rate): *do 3 miles to the gallon* ○ *get 10 francs to the pound.* C PER. **10** (indicating a possible range): *20 to 30 year of age* ○ *3 to 4 centimetres long.* **11** in honour of (sb sth): *drink to sb/to sb's health* ○ *a toast to the coo* ○ *a monument to (the memory of) the soldiers wh died in the war.* **12** close enough to be touchin (sb/sth); facing: *dance cheek to cheek* ○ *with an ea to the door* ○ *sit back to back* ○ *cars queuein bumper to bumper on the motorway.* **13** (used afte *vs* of motion eg *come, go, rush*) with the intention c giving (sth): *come to our aid/help/assistance rescue.* **14** concerning (sth): *a right to the throne* *a solution to a problem* ○ *She's devoted to he* *family.* **15** causing (sth): *To my surprise, delight, annoyance, etc the Labour Party won the election*, ie Their winning caused me surprise, delight, etc. ○ *To my shame, I forgot* (ie I am ashamed that I forgot) *his birthday.* **16** (used after *vs* of perception, eg *seem, appear, feel, look, smell*) in the opinion of (sb); according to: *It feels like velvet to me.* ○ *Does it look to you like gold?* ○ *It sounded like crying to him.* **17** satisfying (sb/sth): *not really to my liking* ○ *quite nice, but not to her taste.*

to[2] /*before consonants* tə, *before vowels* tʊ *or* tu:; *strong form* tu:/ (Used immediately before the simple (root) form of a *v* to form the infinitive. The following are only a few uses of the infinitive; others are given in *n, adj,* and *v* entries.) **1** (used as the object of many *vs*, esp those labelled Tt, Tn·t, Cn·t, Dpr·t, Dn·t): *He wants to go.* ○ *We had hoped to finish by four o'clock.* ○ *She asked me to go.* ○ *She persuaded him to tell the truth.* **2** (expressing purpose or result in an *adv* clause): *They came (in order) to help me.* ○ *She's working hard to earn money.* ○ *We make our goods to last*, ie so that they will last. ○ *They went there to cause trouble.* ○ *She ran to the station only to find that the train had left.* **3** (used alone to avoid repetition of the whole infinitive): *I'd like to do it but I don't know how to.* ○ *I intended to go but forgot to.* ○ *He often does things you wouldn't expect him to.*

to[3] /tu:/ *adv part* (For special uses with *vs* and in compounds, eg *bring sb to, come to, set-to, lean-to,* see the *v* entries.) **1** (usu of a door) in or into a closed position; shut: *Push the door to.* ○ *Leave it to.* **2** (idm) ˌ**to and ˈfro** backwards and forwards: *walking to and fro* ○ *journeys to and fro between London and Paris.*

toad /təʊd/ *n* **1** frog-like animal that lives on land except when breeding. ⇨ illus at FROG. **2** (used esp as a term of abuse) disgusting or disliked person: *You repulsive little toad!*

□ ˌ**toad-in-the-ˈhole** *n* [U] (*Brit*) dish consisting of sausages baked in batter.

toadstool /ˈtəʊdstu:l/ *n* any of various types of umbrella-shaped fungus, esp a poisonous one. ⇨ illus at FUNGUS. Cf MUSHROOM.

toady /ˈtəʊdɪ/ *n* (*derog*) person who flatters another or treats him with excessive respect in the hope of gain or advantage.

▷ **toady** *v* (*pt, pp* **toadied**) [I, Ipr] ~ **(to sb)** (*derog*) behave in this way: *toadying to the boss.*

toast[1] /təʊst/ *n* [U] **1** sliced bread made brown and crisp by heating under a grill, in a toaster, etc: *make some toast for breakfast* ○ *a poached egg on toast* ○ *two slices of buttered toast.* **2** (idm) **have sb on ˈtoast** (*infml*) have sb completely at one's mercy. **warm as toast** ⇨ WARM[1].

▷ **toast** *v* [I, Tn] become or make brown and crisp by heating: *a toasted (cheese) sandwich* ○ (*fig*) *toasting oneself/one's feet in front of the fire.*

toaster *n* electrical device for toasting slices of bread.

□ ˈ**toasting-fork** *n* fork with a long handle used for toasting bread, etc in front of a fire.

ˈ**toast-rack** *n* rack for holding slices of toast at the table. ⇨ illus at RACK.

toast[2] /təʊst/ *v* [Tn] wish happiness, success, etc to (sb/sth) by drinking wine, etc: *toast the bride and groom* ○ *toast the success of a new company.*

▷ **toast** *n* **1** act of toasting: *propose a loyal toast to the Queen* ○ *drink a toast* ○ *reply/respond to the toast*, ie (of the person toasted) make a speech in reply. **2** person, etc toasted: *be the toast of* (ie praised and congratulated by) *the whole neighbourhood.*

□ ˈ**toast-master** *n* person who announces the toasts at a formal banquet.

tobacco /təˈbækəʊ/ *n* (*pl* ~**s**) **1** [C, U] (type of) leaves that are dried, cured and used for smoking (in pipes, cigarettes and cigars) or chewing, or as snuff. **2** [U] plant from which these leaves are obtained.

▷ **tobacconist** /təˈbækənɪst/ *n* shopkeeper who sells cigarettes, cigars and pipe-tobacco.

Tobago ⇨ TRINIDAD AND TOBAGO.

toboggan /təˈbɒgən/ *n* long light narrow sledge, often curved upwards at the front, used for sliding downhill on snow.

▷ **toboggan** *v* [I] use a toboggan: *go tobogganing.*

toby jug /ˈtəʊbɪ dʒʌg/ mug or jug (formerly for beer) in the form of an old man with a three-cornered hat.

toccata /təˈkɑ:tə/ *n* (*music*) composition for a keyboard instrument (esp the organ or harpsichord) in a free style, designed to show the performer's technique or 'touch'.

tocsin /ˈtɒksɪn/ *n* (*dated or fml*) **1** (bell rung as a) signal of alarm. **2** (*fig*) warning of danger.

tod /tɒd/ *n* (idm) **on one's ˈtod** (*Brit infml*) on one's own; alone: *I spent the evening on my tod again.* ○ *You mean you did it all on your tod* (ie without help)*?*

today /təˈdeɪ/ *adv, n* [U] **1** (on) this day: *What are we doing today?* ○ *We're leaving today week/a week (from) today*, ie in a week's time. ○ *Today is my birthday.* ○ *Have you seen today's paper?* **2** (at) the present period or age: *Women today no longer accept such treatment.* ○ *the young people of today.* **3** (idm) ˌ**here toˌday and ˌgone toˈmorrow** (*sometimes derog*) lasting only a short time: *It's one of those ridiculous fashions that are here today and gone tomorrow.*

Todd /tɒd/ Sweeney, legendary 18th-century barber of Fleet Street, London, who murdered his customers. There have been several plays about him.

toddle /ˈtɒdl/ *v* [I, Ipr, Ip] **1** (esp of a young child) walk with short unsteady steps: *Her two-year-old son toddled into the room.* **2** (*infml*) walk: *toddle round to see a friend* ○ *I think we should be toddling along/off*, ie should leave.

▷ **toddler** /ˈtɒdlə(r)/ *n* child who has only recently learnt to walk.

toddy /ˈtɒdɪ/ *n* [C, U] (glass of) alcoholic drink made of spirits, sugar and hot water.

to-do /təˈdu:/ *n* (*pl* ~**s**) (usu *sing*) fuss; commotion: *What's all the to-do about?* ○ *She made a great to-do about his forgetting her birthday.*

toe /təʊ/ *n* **1** (**a**) each of the five divisions of the front part of the human foot. ⇨ illus at FOOT. (**b**) similar part of an animal's foot. **2** part of a sock, shoe, etc that covers the toes. ⇨ illus at SHOE. **3** (idm) **dig one's heels/toes in** ⇨ DIG[1]. **from head to foot/toe** ⇨ HEAD[1]. **from top to toe** ⇨ TOP[1]. **on one's ˈtoes** ready for action; alert: *The constant threat of danger kept us all on our toes.* **tread on sb's corns/toes** ⇨ TREAD.

▷ **toe** *v* (*pt, pp* **toed**, *pres p* **toeing**) (idm) **toe the (party) ˈline**; *US* also **toe the ˈmark** obey the orders of one's group or party; conform.

□ ˈ**toe-cap** *n* outer covering of the toe of a shoe or boot.

ˈ**toe-hold** *n* slight foothold (eg in mountain climbing): (*fig*) *Thanks to this contract the firm gained a toe-hold in the European market.*

ˈ**toe-nail** *n* nail of a human toe. ⇨ illus at FOOT.

toff /tɒf/ *n* (*dated Brit sl*) rich or well-dressed person of high social class.

toffee /ˈtɒfɪ; *US* ˈtɔ:fɪ/ (*US* also **taffy** /ˈtæfɪ/) *n* [C, U] **1** (piece of) hard sticky sweet made by heating sugar, butter, etc. **2** (idm) **can't do sth for ˈtoffee** (*infml*) lack the skill or ability needed to do sth: *She can't sing for toffee!*

□ ˈ**toffee-apple** *n* (*Brit*) apple coated with a thin layer of toffee and fixed on a stick.

ˈ**toffee-nosed** *adj* (*Brit sl*) snobbish; snooty.

tofu /ˈtəʊfu:/ *n* [U] = BEAN CURD (BEAN).

tog /tɒg/ *v* (**-gg-**) (phr v) **tog oneself out/up (in sth)** (*infml*) put on smart clothes; dress up: *children togged out in their Sunday best.*

▷ **tog** *n* **1 togs** [pl] (*infml*) clothes: *games togs* ○ *summer togs.* **2** [C] unit of measurement of the power of duvets, quilted garments, etc to retain warmth.

toga /ˈtəʊgə/ *n* loose outer garment worn by men in ancient Rome.

together /təˈgeðə(r)/ *adv* **1** in or into company; with or towards each other: *Let's go for a walk together.* ○ *I hear they're living together*, ie in the same house. ○ *Get all the ingredients together before you start cooking.* **2** so as to be in contact or united: *glue, nail, tie, etc two boards together* ○ *Mix the sand and cement together, then add water.* ○ (*fig*) *He's got more money than the rest of us (put) together.* **3** in or into agreement or harmony: *negotiations aimed at bringing the two sides in the dispute closer together* ○ *The party is absolutely together on this issue.* **4** at the same time; simultaneously: *All my troubles seem to come together.* ○ *They were all talking together and I couldn't understand a word.* **5** without interruption; in continuous succession: *It rained for three days together.* ○ *She can sit reading for hours together.* **6** (idm) **get sth/it toˈgether** (*sl*) get sth/it organized or under control: *She would be a very good player if only she could get it together.* **together with** as well as; and also: *These new facts, together with the other evidence, prove the prisoner's innocence.*

▷ **together** *adj* (*sl approv esp US*) organized; capable: *He's incredibly together for someone so young.* ○ *a really together organization.*

togetherness *n* [U] feeling of unity, friendship or love.

toggle /ˈtɒgl/ *n* fastening consisting of a short piece of wood, etc that is passed through a loop or hole (eg instead of a button on a coat).

□ ˈ**toggle-switch** *n* electrical switch operated by a short lever which is moved (usu) up and down.

Togo /ˈtəʊgəʊ/ country in W Africa, between *Ghana and *Benin; pop approx 3 247 000; official language French; capital Lomé; unit of currency franc. Formerly a French colony, it became an independent republic in 1960. Its main exports are cocoa, coffee and phosphates. ⇨ map at NIGERIA.

▷ **Togolese** /ˌtəʊgəˈli:z/ *adj, n.*

toil /tɔɪl/ *v* (*fml or rhet*) **1** [I, Ipr, Ip, It] ~ **away (at/over sth)** work long or hard: *students toiling over their homework* ○ *We toiled away all afternoon to get the house ready for our guests.* **2** [Ipr, Ip] move slowly and with difficulty in the specified direction: *The bus toiled up the steep hill.* ○ *The ground was muddy and uneven, but we toiled on.*

▷ **toil** *n* [U] (*fml or rhet*) hard or lengthy work: *after years of toil.* ⇨ Usage at WORK[1].

toiler *n.*

toilet /ˈtɔɪlɪt/ *n* **1** [C] (room containing a) lavatory: *Can you tell me where the toilets are?* ⇨ Usage. **2** [U] (*dated*) process of washing and dressing oneself, arranging one's hair, etc: [attrib] *a ˈtoilet set* ○ ˈ*toilet articles*, ie hair brushes, combs, hand-mirrors, etc.

▷ **toiletries** /ˈtɔɪlɪtrɪz/ *n* [pl] (in shops) articles or products used in washing, dressing, etc.

□ ˈ**toilet-paper** *n* [U] paper for use in a lavatory.

ˈ**toilet-roll** *n* roll of toilet-paper.

ˈ**toilet-train** *v* [Tn, esp passive] train (a child) to control its urination and defecation and to use a lavatory: *She isn't toilet-trained yet.* ˈ**toilet-training** *n* [U].

ˈ**toilet water** scented water for use on the skin, esp after washing.

NOTE ON USAGE: In British English **the toilet** in private houses is called **the lavatory**, **toilet**, **WC** (dated), or **loo** (informal). In public places it is called **the Gents**/**the Ladies** or **public conveniences**. In US English it is called **the lavatory**, **toilet** or **bathroom** in private houses and **the washroom** or **rest-room** in public buildings.

toils /tɔɪlz/ *n* [pl] (*fml usu fig*) nets; traps: *caught in the toils of the law.*

toing /ˈtu:ɪŋ/ *n* (idm) ˌ**toing and ˈfroing** movement backwards and forwards: *After much toing and froing we got all the children back to their homes.*

token /ˈtəʊkən/ *n* **1** sign, symbol or evidence of sth: *A white flag is used as a token of surrender.* ○ *These flowers are a small token of my gratitude.* **2** disc like a coin used to operate certain machines or as a form of payment: *Tokens for the cigarette machine are available at the bar.* ○ *milk tokens*, ie (in Britain) bought from the milkman and left on the doorstep to pay for the milk delivered. **3** (esp in compounds) voucher or coupon, usu attached to a greetings card, which can be exchanged for goods of the value shown: *a £10 ˈbook/ˈrecord/ˈgift token.* **4** (idm) **by the same token** ⇨ SAME[1]. **in token of sth** as evidence of sth: *Please accept this gift in token of our affection for you.*

▷ **token** *adj* [attrib] **1** serving as a sign or pledge of sth: *a token payment*, ie payment of a small part of what is owed, as an acknowledgement of the debt ○ *a token strike*, ie a short strike serving as a warning that a longer one may follow. **2** done, existing, etc on a small scale as a gesture of sth that is not seriously or sincerely meant; superficial or perfunctory: *Our troops encountered only token resistance.* ○ *a token attempt, effort, offer, etc* ○ *the token woman on the committee*, ie included to avoid charges of sexual discrimination.

told *pt, pp* of TELL.

tolerate /ˈtɒləreɪt/ *v* **1** [Tn, Tsg] allow (sth that one dislikes or disagrees with) without interfering: *a government which refuses to tolerate opposition* ○ *I won't tolerate such behaviour/your behaving in this way.* **2** [Tn] endure (sb/sth) without protesting: *How can you tolerate that awful woman?* ○ *tolerate heat, noise, pain, etc well.* **3** [Tn] (*medical*) be able to take (a drug, etc) or undergo (a treatment) without harm: *The body cannot tolerate such large amounts of radiation.*

▷ **tolerable** /ˈtɒlərəbl/ *adj* **1** that can be tolerated; endurable: *The heat was tolerable at night but suffocating during the day.* **2** fairly good; passable: *tolerable weather* ○ *in tolerable health* ○ *We had a very tolerable* (ie excellent) *lunch.* **tolerably** /-əblɪ/ *adv* in a moderate degree; fairly well: *feel tolerably* (ie almost completely) *certain about sth* ○ *He plays the piano tolerably well.*

tolerance /ˈtɒlərəns/ *n* **1** [U] willingness or ability to tolerate sb/sth: *religious/racial tolerance* ○ *As the addict's tolerance increases, he requires ever larger doses of the drug.* **2** [C, U] (*engineering*) amount by which the size, weight, etc of a part can vary without causing problems: *working to a tolerance of 0.0001 of an inch/to very fine tolerances.* **tolerant** /-rənt/ *adj* ~ **(of/towards sb/sth)** having or showing tolerance: *I'm a tolerant man but your behaviour is more than I can bear.* ○ *Her own mistakes made her very tolerant of/towards (the faults of) others.* **tolerantly** *adv.*

toleration /ˌtɒləˈreɪʃn/ *n* [U] action or practice of tolerating (TOLERATE 1, 2).

Tolkien /ˈtɒlkiːn/ John Ronald Reuel (1892-1973), British writer and academic, professor of English at Oxford and author of imaginary legends of ancient times (eg *The Hobbit* and *The Lord of the Rings*) which achieved cult status in the 1960s and 1970s and remain very popular with both young and adult readers.

toll[1] /təʊl/ *n* **1** money paid for the use of a road, bridge, harbour, etc. **2** loss or damage caused by sth: *the death-toll in the earthquake, on the roads, after the massacre*, ie the number of people killed. **3** (idm) **take a heavy toll/take its toll (of sth)** cause loss, damage, etc: *The war took a heavy toll of human life.* ○ *Every year at Christmas drunken driving takes its toll.*

□ ˈ**toll-bridge** *n* bridge at which a toll is charged.

ˈ**toll-gate** *n* gate across a road to prevent anyone passing until the toll has been paid.

ˈ**toll-house** *n* house occupied by the person who collects tolls on a road, etc.

toll[2] /təʊl/ *v* **1** [Tn, Tn·pr] ~ **(for sb/sth)** ring (a bell) with slow regular strokes, esp for a death or funeral. **2** [Ipr] ~ **(for sb/sth)** (of a bell) sound in this way.

▷ **toll** *n* [sing] sound of a tolling bell.

Tolpuddle Martyrs /ˌtɒlpʌdl ˈmɑːtəz/ **the Tolpuddle Martyrs** group of six farm workers from the village of Tolpuddle in Dorset, England, who in the 1830s tried to form a trade union. They were convicted on a legal technicality of taking an oath, and as a punishment they were sent to Australia, though they were later pardoned.

Tolstoy /ˈtɒlstɔɪ/ Count Lev Nikolaevich (1828-1910), Russian writer, whose best-known works are *War and Peace*, a long novel set at the time of *Napoleon's invasion of Russia, and *Anna Karenina*. Around 1880 Tolstoy underwent a spiritual conversion and began to concern himself with matters such as the rejection of private property and of political and religious authority; as a result many of his books were banned in Russia.

toluene /ˈtɒljuiːn/ *n* [U] liquid chemical compound that is poisonous and flammable, used in the making of explosives.

Tom /tɒm/ *n* (idm) **(any/every) ˌTom, Dick and ˈHarry** (*usu derog*) anybody at all; people at random: *We don't want any (old) Tom, Dick and Harry using the club bar.*

tom /tɒm/ *n* = TOM-CAT.

tomahawk /ˈtɒməhɔːk/ *n* light axe used as a tool or weapon by N American Indians.

tomato /təˈmɑːtəʊ; *US* təˈmeɪtəʊ/ *n* (*pl* ~**es**) **(a)** soft juicy red or yellow fruit eaten raw or cooked as a vegetable: [attrib] *tomato juice, sauce, soup, ketchup.* ⇨ illus at SALAD. **(b)** plant on which this fruit grows.

tomb /tuːm/ *n* hole dug in the ground, etc for a dead body, esp one with a stone monument over it.

□ ˈ**tombstone** *n* memorial stone set up over a tomb.

tombola /tɒmˈbəʊlə/ *n* [C, U] (*Brit*) type of lottery with prizes for the holders of tickets picked out of a revolving drum.

tomboy /ˈtɒmbɔɪ/ *n* girl who enjoys rough noisy games. ▷ **tomboyish** *adj.*

tom-cat /ˈtɒm kæt/ (also **tom**) *n* male cat.

tome /təʊm/ *n* large heavy book, esp a scholarly or serious one.

tomfool /ˌtɒmˈfuːl/ *adj* very foolish; stupid: *a tomfool thing to do.*

▷ **tomfoolery** /-ərɪ/ *n* [U, C usu *pl*] foolish behaviour or act.

Tommy /ˈtɒmɪ/ *n* (*dated*) British soldier of the lowest rank, esp in the two World Wars.

tommy-gun /ˈtɒmɪ gʌn/ *n* type of sub-machine-gun.

tommy-rot /ˌtɒmɪ ˈrɒt/ *n* [U] (*infml*) absurd statement; nonsense: *Don't talk such tommy-rot!*

tomorrow /əˈmɒrəʊ/ *n* [U] **1** the day after today: *Today is Tuesday so tomorrow is Wednesday.* ○ *Tomorrow is going to be fine according to the forecast.* ○ *The announcement will appear in tomorrow's newspapers.* ○ [attrib] *tomorrow morning/afternoon/evening/night.* **2** the near future: *Who knows what changes tomorrow may bring?* ○ *tomorrow's world.* **3** (idm) **as ˌif/ˌlike there is/was ˌno toˈmorrow** (*infml*) paying no attention to possible future needs: *spending money like there's no tomorrow.* **the day after tomorrow** ⇨ DAY. **here today, gone tomorrow** ⇨ TODAY. **jam tomorrow** ⇨ JAM[1].

▷ **tomorrow** *adv* on the day after today: *She's getting married tomorrow.* ○ *See you this time tomorrow, then.*

Tom Sawyer /ˌtɒm ˈsɔːjə(r)/ hero of Mark *Twain's novel *The Adventures of Tom Sawyer*, about a lively and mischievous boy living by the Mississippi river. His greatest friend is *Huckleberry Finn.

Tom Thumb /ˌtɒm ˈθʌm/ **1** (in English folklore) tiny person, the hero of various stories. **2 (a)** any very small person. **(b)** small variety of certain types of plant.

tomtit /ˈtɒmtɪt/ *n* type of tit, esp the blue tit.

tom-tom /ˈtɒm tɒm/ *n* **1** long narrow African or Asian drum played with the hands. **2** similar drum used in jazz bands, etc. ⇨ illus at MUSIC.

-tomy *suff* (forming *ns*) surgical cutting: *lobotomy.*

ton /tʌn/ *n* **1** [C] measure of weight, in Britain 2 240 lb (*long ton*) and in the US 2 000 lb (*short ton*) ⇨ App 10. Cf TONNE. **2** [C] measure of capacity for various materials, esp 40 cubic feet of timber. **3** [C] (*nautical*) **(a)** measure of the size of a ship (1 ton = 100 cubic feet). **(b)** measure of the amount of cargo a ship can carry (1 ton = 40 cubic feet). **4 tons** [pl] ~**s (of sth)** (*infml*) a lot: *They've got tons of money.* ○ *I've still got tons (of work) to do.* **5** (idm) **do a/the ˈton** (*sl*) drive at a speed of 100 mph or more: *got caught doing a ton on the motorway.* **(come down on sb) like a ton of ˈbricks** (*infml*) (criticize or punish sb) with great force or violence. **weigh a ton** ⇨ WEIGH.

□ **ton-ˈup** *adj* [attrib] (*dated sl*) (of a driver) driving at a speed of 100 mph or more: *one of the ton-up boys.*

tonal /ˈtəʊnl/ *adj* **1** of (a) tone or tones. **2** (*music*) of tonality.

▷ **tonality** /təʊˈnælətɪ/ *n* [U, C] (*music*) (use of a particular) key, esp as the basis of a melody or composition. Cf ATONALITY.

tone[1] /təʊn/ *n* **1** [C] sound, esp with reference to its pitch, quality, strength, etc: *the ringing tones of an orator's voice* ○ *the alarm bell's harsh tone.* **2** [C] manner of expression in speaking: *speak in an angry, impatient, entreating, etc tone* ○ *a tone of command, reproach, regret, etc* ○ *Don't speak to me in that tone (of voice)*, ie in that unpleasant, insolent, critical, etc way. **3** [C, U] quality or character of sound produced by a musical instrument: *a violin with (an) excellent tone.* **4** [sing] general spirit or character of sth: *Overall, the tone of the book is satirical/the book is satirical in tone.* ○ *set the tone for/of the meeting with a conciliatory speech* ○ *lower/raise the tone of a conversation, an occasion, an organization*, ie make it worse/better. **5** [C] (*music*) interval comprising two semi-tones between one tone and the next. **6** [C] **(a)** tint or shade (of a colour); degree (of light): *a carpet in tones of brown and orange.* **(b)** general effect of colour, light and shade: *a picture in warm, dull, bright, etc tones* ○ *an artist's fine painting of skin tones.* **7** [U] proper firmness of the body: *good muscular tone.* **8** [C] audible signal on a telephone line: *the dialling/ringing tone* ○ *That tone means that the number is engaged.* ○ *Please speak after the tone*, eg as an instruction on an answering machine. **9** [C] (*linguistics*) pitch aspect of a syllable; rise or fall of pitch in speaking: *In 'Are you ill?' there is usually a rising tone on 'ill', while in 'He's ill' there is usually a falling tone on 'ill'.*

▷ **-toned** (forming compound *adjs*) having the specified type of tone[1](3): *silver-toned trumpets.*

toneless *adj* lacking colour, spirit, expression, etc; dull: *answer in a toneless voice.* **tonelessly** *adv.*

□ ˌ**tone-ˈdeaf** *adj* unable to distinguish accurately between different musical notes.

ˈ**tone language** (*linguistics*) language in which the meaning of a word depends on the pitch at which it is uttered (eg Chinese).

ˈ**tone-poem** *n* (*music*) orchestral composition written to illustrate a poetic idea, legend, place, etc musically.

tone[2] /təʊn/ *v* **1** [Tn] give a particular tone of sound or colour to (sth). **2** (phr v) **tone (sth) down** (cause sth to) become less intense: *Their enthusiasm has toned down since they discovered the cost.* ○ *You'd better tone down the more offensive remarks in your article.* **tone in (with sth)** harmonize in colour: *The new curtains tone in beautifully with the carpet.* **tone (sth) up** (cause sth to) become brighter, intenser, or more vigorous: *Exercise tones up the muscles.*

Tonga /ˈtɒŋə, *also* ˈtɒŋgə/ country in the South Pacific Ocean consisting of over 150 small islands; pop approx 116 000; official languages Tongan and English; capital Nukuʻalofa; unit of currency paʻanga (= 100 seniti). In 1900 it became a British protectorate, gaining its independence in 1970. It remains a member of the Commonwealth. Tonga is also called the Friendly Islands. ⇨ map at POLYNESIA.

▷ **Tongan** *adj* of Tonga. — *n* **1** [C] native or inhabitant of Tonga. **2** [U] *Polynesian language of Tonga.

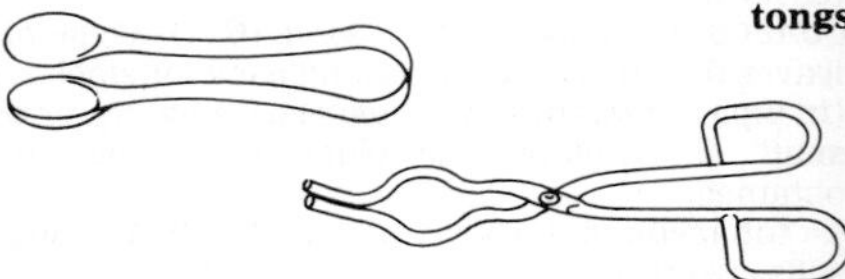

tongs /tɒŋz/ *n* [pl] **1** instrument with two movable arms joined at one end, used for picking up and holding things: *a pair of tongs* ○ ˈ*sugar*/ˈ*coal*/ˈ*ice tongs.* **2** (idm) **be/go at it/each other hammer and tongs** ⇨ HAMMER[1].

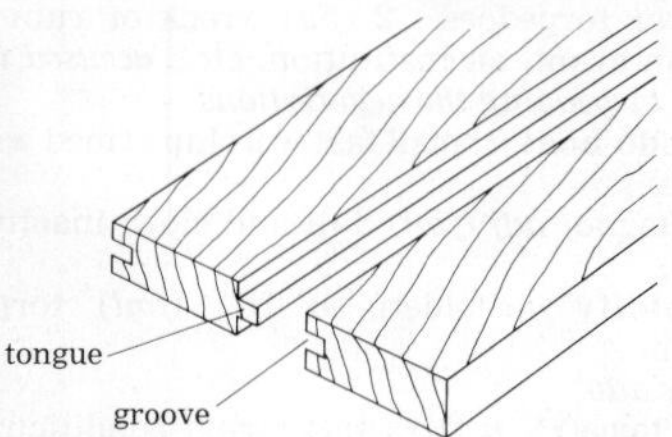

tongue /tʌŋ/ *n* **1** [C] movable organ in the mouth, used in tasting, licking, swallowing and (in man) speaking. ⇨ illus at THROAT, ⇨ Usage at BODY. **2** [C, U] tongue of an ox, etc as food: *ham and tongue sandwiches.* **3** [C] (*fml or rhet*) language: *He speaks English, but his native tongue is German.* Cf MOTHER TONGUE (MOTHER). **4** [C] **(a)** projecting strap or flap: *the tongue of a shoe*, ie the strip of leather under the laces ○ *the tongue* (ie clapper) *of a bell* ○ *a narrow tongue of land* (ie promontory) *jutting out into the sea.* **(b)** tapering jet of flame: *tongues of flame lapping the edges of the bonfire.* **5** (idm) **bite one's tongue** ⇨ BITE[1]. **an evil tongue** ⇨ EVIL. **find/lose one's voice/tongue** ⇨ FIND[1]. **get one's ˈtongue round/around sth** manage to pronounce (a difficult word or name) correctly. **give sb/get the edge of one's/sb's tongue** ⇨ EDGE[1]. **have a loose tongue** ⇨ LOOSE[1]. **hold one's peace/tongue** ⇨ PEACE. **loosen sb's tongue** ⇨ LOOSEN. **on the tip of one's tongue** ⇨ TIP[1]. **put/stick one's ˈtongue out** show one's tongue outside one's lips, eg to a doctor or as a rude gesture: *Don't you dare stick your tongue out at me!* **a silver tongue** ⇨ SILVER. **a slip of the pen/tongue** ⇨ SLIP[1]. **tongues wag** (*infml*) there is gossip or rumour: *Their scandalous affair has really set tongues wagging.* **with (one's) tongue in (one's) ˈcheek** not intending to be taken seriously; with irony or humour: *Don't be fooled by all his complimentary remarks — they were all said with tongue in cheek.* **with one's ˈtongue hanging out (a)** extremely thirsty. **(b)** eagerly expecting sth.

▷ **tongue** *v* [I, Tn] play (notes) on a wind instrument (eg a flute or trumpet) by interrupting the flow of air with the tongue.

-tongued (forming compound *adjs*) having the specified manner of speaking: *sharp-tongued.*

□ ˌ**tongue and ˈgroove** joint made between two pieces of wood by fitting a projecting part on one piece into a groove on the other: [attrib] *tongue-and-groove boarding.* ⇨ illus.

ˌ**tongue-in-ˈcheek** *adj* not intended seriously; ironical or joking: *tongue-in-cheek remarks.*

ˈ**tongue-lashing** *n* severe rebuke or scolding.

ˈ**tongue-tied** *adj* silent because of shyness or embarrassment.

ˈ**tongue-twister** *n* word or phrase that is difficult to pronounce correctly or quickly, eg *She sells sea shells on the sea-shore.*

tonic /ˈtɒnɪk/ *n* **1** [C, U] medicine that gives strength or energy, taken after illness or when tired. **2** [C usu *sing*] (*fig*) anything that makes people feel healthier or happier: *Praise can be a fine tonic.* ○ *The good news acted as a tonic on us all.* ○ [attrib] *the tonic effects of sea air.* **3** [C, U] = TONIC WATER. **4** [C] (*music*) keynote.

□ ˌ**tonic sol-ˈfa** = SOL-FA.

ˈ**tonic water** (also **tonic**) mineral water flavoured with quinine: *a bottle of tonic water* ○ *a gin and tonic* ○ *Two tonic waters/tonics, please.*

tonight /təˈnaɪt/ *n* [U] **(a)** the present evening or night: *Here are tonight's football results.* **(b)** the evening or night of today: *Tonight will be cloudy.*

▷ **tonight** *adv* on the present evening or night or that of today: *See you at nine o'clock tonight, then.* ○ *Are you doing anything tonight?*

tonnage /ˈtʌnɪdʒ/ *n* [U, C] **1** (*nautical*) **(a)** size of a ship, expressed in tons (TON 1). **(b)** amount of cargo a ship can carry, expressed in tons (TON 3b). **(c)** size of a country's merchant fleet, expressed in tons (TON 3a). **2** (*commerce*) charge per ton for carrying cargo or freight.

tonne /tʌn/ *n* metric ton, 1 000 kilograms. ⇨ App 10. Cf TON 1.

tonsil /ˈtɒnsl/ *n* either of two small organs at the sides of the throat near the root of the tongue: *have one's tonsils out*, ie have them removed by a surgeon. ⇨ illus at THROAT.

▷ **tonsillitis** /ˌtɒnsɪˈlaɪtɪs/ *n* [U] inflammation of the tonsils.

tonsure /ˈtɒnʃə(r)/ *n* **1** [U] shaving the top or all of the head of a person about to become a priest or monk. **2** [C] part of the head shaved in this way. ▷ **tonsured** *adj.*

too /tu:/ *adv* **1** (usu placed at the end; in speech, with stress on *too* and the word it modifies) in addition; also: *I've been to Paris ˈtoo*, ie in addition to other people. ○ *I've been to ˈParis, ˈtoo*, ie in addition to other places. ○ *He plays the guitar and ˈsings ˈtoo.* ⇨ Usage at ALSO. **2** (used before *adjs* and *advs*) to a higher degree than is allowed, desirable or possible: *drive too fast*, ie faster than the permitted speed limit or than is sensible ○ *These shoes are much too small for me.* ○ *It's too cold to go in the sea yet.* ○ *This is too difficult a text for them/This text is too difficult for them.* ○ *We can't ski because there's too little snow.* ○ *It's too long a journey to make in one day.* ○ (*fml*) *Her work has been too much ignored for too long.* **3** (indicating surprise and usu displeasure): *I had flu last week. And I was on holiday ˈtoo!* ○ *I've lost an ear-ring. It was an expensive one ˈtoo.* **4** very: *I'm not too sure if this is right.* **5** (idm) **be too much for sb (a)** (require one to) be superior in skill, strength, etc to sb else: *The Cambridge team were too much for the Oxford team in the quiz.* ○ *A cycling holiday would be too much for an unfit person like me.* **(b)** be more than can be tolerated: *All that giggling and whispering was too much for me — I had to leave the room.*

took *pt* of TAKE[1].

tool /tu:l/ *n* **1** instrument held in the hand and used for working on sth: *A screwdriver and a hammer are the only tools you need.* ○ *garden tools*, eg spade, rake, etc. **2** anything used to do or achieve sth: *The computer is now an indispensable tool in many businesses.* ⇨ Usage at MACHINE. **3** person used or exploited by another, esp for selfish or dishonest purposes: *The prime minister was a mere tool in the hands of the country's president.* **4** (⚠ *sl*) penis. **5** (idm) **down tools** ⇨ DOWN[3].

▷ **tool** *v* **1** [Tn esp passive] make a design on (the cover or binding of a book) by pressing with a heated tool(1): *hand-tooled leather* ○ *The spine is tooled in gold.* **2** (phr v) **tool along** (*infml*) drive in a casual and relaxed way. **tool sth up** equip (a factory) with the necessary machine tools.

toot /tu:t/ *n* [C] short sound from a horn, whistle, etc.

▷ **toot** *v* [I, Tn] (cause sth to) make a toot: *The driver tooted his horn as he approached the bend.*

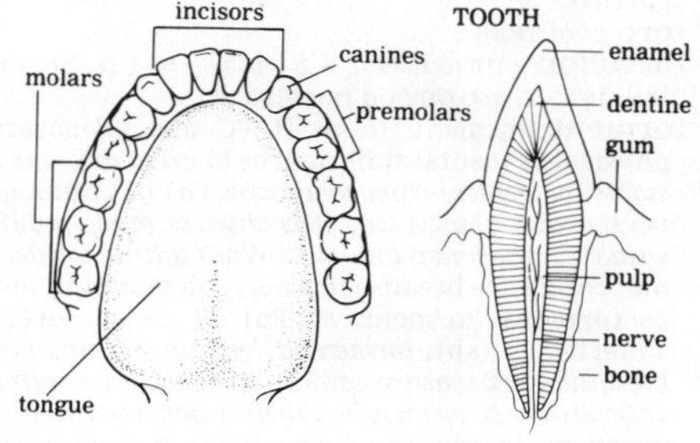

the teeth

tooth /tu:θ/ *n* (*pl* **teeth** /ti:θ/) **1** [C] each of the hard white bony structures rooted in the gums, used for biting and chewing: *The baby's first front teeth are just coming through.* ○ *have a tooth out*, ie extracted by a dentist ○ *She still has all her own teeth*, ie no false ones. **2** [C] tooth-like part, eg on a comb, saw or gear. **3 teeth** [pl] (*infml*) effective force: *The law must be given more teeth if crime is to be properly controlled.* **4** (idm) **armed to the teeth** ⇨ ARM[3]. **bare its teeth** ⇨ BARE[2]. **by the skin of one's teeth** ⇨ SKIN. **cast, fling, throw, etc sth in sb's ˈteeth** reproach sb with sth. **cut one's ˈteeth on sth** gain experience from sth. **cut a ˈtooth** have a tooth that is just pushing out through the gum. **draw sb's/sth's teeth/fangs** ⇨ DRAW[2]. **fight, etc tooth and ˈnail** fight, etc very fiercely or persistently. **get/take the bit between one's/the teeth** ⇨ BIT[2]. **get one's teeth into sth** deal with or concentrate on sth: *Now you know what the job involves here's something to get your teeth into.* **grit one's teeth** ⇨ GRIT *v.* **have a sweet tooth** ⇨ SWEET[1]. **in the teeth of sth (a)** in spite of sth; in opposition to sth: *The new policy was adopted in the teeth of fierce criticism.* **(b)** directly against (the wind, etc). **a kick in the teeth** ⇨ KICK[2]. **lie in/through one's teeth/throat** ⇨ LIE[1]. **long in the tooth** ⇨ LONG[1]. **set sb's ˈteeth on edge** (esp of a sharp sound or taste) annoy or displease sb. **show one's teeth** ⇨ SHOW[2].

▷ **toothed** /tu:θt/ *adj* [attrib] **1** having teeth. **2** (in compounds) having teeth of the specified type: *a saw-toothed wheel.*

toothless *adj* without teeth.

toothy (**-ier, -iest**) *adj* having many, large or noticeable teeth: *a toothy grin.* **toothily** *adv.*

□ ˈ**toothache** *n* [C, U] pain in a tooth or teeth: *I've got (a/the) toothache.*

ˈ**toothbrush** *n* brush for cleaning the teeth. ⇨ illus at BRUSH.

ˈ**toothpaste** *n* [U] paste for cleaning the teeth.

ˈ**toothpick** *n* short pointed piece of wood, etc for removing bits of food from between the teeth.

ˈ**tooth-powder** *n* [U, C] powder for cleaning the teeth.

toothsome /ˈtu:θsəm/ *adj* (*fml*) (of food) tasting pleasant.

tootle /ˈtu:tl/ *v* **1** [I, Ipr] ~ (**on sth**) toot gently or repeatedly. **2** [Ipr, Ip] (*infml*) go in a casual or leisurely way: *tootling into town* ○ *tootle around on one's bike.*

top[1] /tɒp/ *n* **1** [C] highest part or point: *at the top of the hill* ○ *the surrounding hilltops* ○ *five lines from the top of the page* ○ *My office is at the top of the building.* **2** [C] upper surface: *polish the top of the table/the ˈtable-top* ○ *put the luggage on top of the car*, eg on a roof-rack. **3** [sing] ~ (**of sth**) highest or most important rank or position: *come to/rise to/reach the top*, ie achieve fame, success, etc ○ *Liverpool finished the season (at the) top of the football league.* ○ *He's at the top of his profession.* ○ *We've got a lot of things to do, but packing is top of the list.* ○ *the top of the table*, ie the upper end, where eg the most distinguished people sit. **4** [C] **(a)** thing forming or covering the upper part of sth: *the top of the milk*, ie the layer of cream floating on it ○ *Put the top back on that felt-tip pen or it will dry out.* ○ *She took off the top of her bikini.* **(b)** lid or stopper: *Where's the top of this paint can?* ○ *a bottle with a screw-top.* **(c)** (esp woman's) garment covering the upper part of the body: *I need a top to go with these slacks.* **5** [U] = TOP GEAR: *You shouldn't be in top.* **6** [C usu *pl*] leaves of a plant grown chiefly for its root: ˈ*turnip tops.* **7** (idm) **at the top of the ˈtree** in the highest position or rank in a profession, career, etc. **at the top of one's ˈvoice** as loudly as one can: *cheering, shouting, screaming, etc at the top(s) of their voices.* **blow one's top** ⇨ BLOW[1]. **from ˌtop to ˈbottom** completely: *We searched the house from top to bottom.* **from ˌtop to ˈtoe** from head to foot. **in the first/top flight** ⇨ FLIGHT[1]. **off the ˌtop of one's ˈhead** (*infml*) (of sth said) without previous thought or preparation: *I can't tell you the answer off the top of my head.* **on ˈtop (a)** above: *The green book is at the bottom of the pile and the red one is on top.* **(b)** in a superior position; in control: *Lendl was on top throughout the match.* **on top of sth/sb (a)** over or above sth/sb: *Put this record on top of the others.* ○ *Many people were crushed when the* *building collapsed on top of them.* (**b**) in addition to sth: *He gets commission on top of his salary.* ○ *On top of borrowing £50, he asked me to lend him my car.* (**c**) (*infml*) very close to sth: *There is no privacy when houses are built on top of each other like that.* (**d**) in control of sth: *I felt I wasn't on top of the situation; it was getting out of hand.* (**e**) causing worry, unhappiness and stress to sb: *You mustn't let your work get on top of you.* (**be/feel**) **on ˌtop of the ˈworld** very happy or proud, esp because of success or good fortune. **ˌover the ˈtop** (*infml esp Brit*) to an exaggerated or excessive degree: *The film's violent ending is completely over the top.* ○ *an actor who tends to go over the top,* ie to overact. (**the**) **top ˈbrass** (*sl*) senior officers or officials: *Plenty of top brass attended the ceremony.* (**be**) **top ˈdog** (*sl*) person, group, country, etc having superiority or advantages over others. **the top ˈstorey** (*joc*) the brain (of a person): *He's a bit weak in the top storey,* ie not very intelligent.

▷ **top** *adj* [usu attrib] highest in position, rank or degree: *a room on the top floor* ○ *one of Britain's top scientists* ○ *top jobs, people* ○ *travelling at top* (ie maximum) *speed.*

topless *adj* (**a**) (of a woman) having the breasts and upper part of the body bare: *a topless waitress.* (**b**) (of a woman's garment) exposing the breasts: *a topless dress.* — *adv* with the breasts bare: *sunbathe topless.*

□ **ˈtop-boot** *n* boot reaching to just below the knee.

ˈtopcoat *n* **1** last of several coats of paint applied to a surface. Cf UNDERCOAT 1. **2** (*dated*) = OVERCOAT.

ˌtop ˈcopy sheet of paper on which sth is typed (as distinct from copies made of it on carbon paper, by photocopying, etc).

ˌtop ˈdrawer the highest social position: *She's out of the top drawer/She's very top drawer.*

ˌtop-ˈdress *v* [Tn] apply manure, etc to the surface of (soil or land) without ploughing or digging it in.

ˌtop-ˈdressing *n* [C, U] (substance used for) this process.

ˌtop-ˈflight *adv* in the highest rank of achievement: *ˌtop-flight comˈputer scientists.*

ˌtop ˈgear highest gear (usu fourth), allowing the fastest speeds: *If you try to start off in top gear you'll stall.*

ˌtop ˈhat (also **topper**) man's tall black or grey hat, worn with formal dress. ⇨ illus at HAT.

ˌtop-ˈheavy *adj* too heavy at the top and therefore in danger of falling over.

ˈtopknot *n* knot or tuft of hair, usu ornamented with ribbon, feathers, etc, worn or grown on top of the head, esp by women.

ˈtop-level *adj* [attrib] of or involving the highest rank or standard: *ˌtop-level ˈtalks.*

ˌtop-ˈlofty *adj* (*US infml*) arrogant; haughty.

ˈtopmost /-məʊst/ *adj* [attrib] highest: *on the topmost shelf.*

ˌtop-ˈnotch *adj* (*infml*) excellent; first-rate: *a ˌtop-notch ˈlawyer.*

ˌtop-ˈranking *adj* [attrib] of the highest rank or importance; leading.

ˌtop ˈsecret of the highest category of secrecy: *a file of top secret information.*

ˈtopside *n* [U] **1** (*Brit*) joint of beef cut from the upper part of the leg. **2** side of a ship above the water-line.

ˈtopsoil *n* [U] (layer of) soil near the surface. Cf SUBSOIL.

ˌtop ˈten, ˌtop ˈtwenty ten/twenty best-selling pop records: *She's a popular singer, but her records never make* (ie get into) *the top ten.*

top[2] /tɒp/ *v* (**-pp-**) **1** [Tn, Tn·pr esp passive] provide or be a top for (sth): *a church topped by/with a steeple* ○ *ice-cream topped with chocolate sauce.* **2** [Tn] reach the top of (sth): *When we finally topped the hill we had a fine view.* **3** [Tn] (**a**) be higher than (sth); surpass: *Exports have topped the £80 million mark.* (**b**) come first in (a poll, etc): *a chart-topping record.* **4** [Tn] remove the top of (a plant, fruit, etc): *top and tail* (ie remove the ends from) *gooseberries.* **5** [Tn] (esp in golf) mishit (a ball) by striking it above the centre. **6** [Tn] (*sl*) execute (sb) by hanging. **7** (idm) **head/top the bill** ⇨ BILL[1]. **8** (phr v) **top (sth) out** complete (a building) by adding the highest stone, etc. **top (sth) up** fill up (a partly empty container): *top up with petrol/oil* ○ *top up a car battery,* ie by adding distilled water ○ (*infml*) *Let me top you up,* ie refill your glass.

▷ **topping** *n* [C, U] cream, etc on top of a cake, pudding, etc: *a range of fruit-flavoured toppings.*

□ **ˈtop-up** *n* refill: *Who's ready for a top-up* (ie for another drink)*?*

top[3] /tɒp/ *n* **1** toy that spins on a point when it is set in motion by hand or by a string, etc. **2** (idm) **sleep like a log/top** ⇨ SLEEP[2].

topaz /ˈtəʊpæz/ *n* (**a**) [U] transparent yellow mineral. (**b**) [C] semi-precious gem cut from this.

topi /ˈtəʊpɪ; *US* təʊˈpiː/ *n* sun-helmet, esp one worn in tropical countries.

topiary /ˈtəʊpɪərɪ; *US* -ɪerɪ/ *n* [U] art of clipping shrubs, etc into ornamental shapes such as birds and animals: [attrib] *topiary work.*

topic /ˈtɒpɪk/ *n* subject of a discussion, talk, programme, written work, etc: *a topic of conversation* ○ *Is drug abuse a suitable topic for a school debate?*

▷ **topical** /-kl/ *adj* of current interest or relevance: *a play full of topical allusions to well-known people.* **topicality** /ˌtɒpɪˈkælətɪ/ *n* [U]. **topically** /-klɪ/ *adv.*

topography /təˈpɒgrəfɪ/ *n* [U] (description of the) features of a place or district, esp the position of its rivers, mountains, roads, buildings, etc. ▷ **topographical** /ˌtɒpəˈgræfɪkl/ *adj*: *a topographical map.* **topographically** /-klɪ/ *adv.*

topper /ˈtɒpə(r)/ *n* (*infml*) = TOP HAT (TOP[1]).

topping[1] /ˈtɒpɪŋ/ *n* ⇨ TOP[2].

topping[2] /ˈtɒpɪŋ/ *adj* (*dated Brit infml*) excellent.

topple /ˈtɒpl/ *v* **1** (**a**) [I, Ipr, Ip] ~ (**over**) be unsteady and fall: *The pile of books toppled over onto the floor.* (**b**) [Tn, Tn·pr] cause (sth) to do this: *The explosion toppled the old chimney.* **2** [Tn, Tn·pr] (*fig*) cause (sb/sth) to fall from power or authority; overthrow: *a crisis which threatens to topple the government (from power).*

tops /tɒps/ *n* [pl] (usu **the tops**) (*infml*) the very best: *I like most cities, but for me New York is (the) tops.*

topsy-turvy /ˌtɒpsɪ ˈtɜːvɪ/ *adv, adj* **1** in or into a state of disordered confusion: *This sudden development turned all our plans topsy-turvy.* **2** upside-down.

toque /təʊk/ *n* woman's close-fitting soft hat without a brim.

tor /tɔː(r)/ *n* small hill or rocky peak, esp in parts of SW England.

Torah /ˈtɔːrə/ (usu **the Torah**) *n* (in the Jewish religion) first five books of the Old Testament, which are the basis of Jewish religious law; the Pentateuch.

torch /tɔːtʃ/ *n* **1** (*US* **ˈflash·light**) small hand-held electric lamp powered by a battery. **2** (*US*) = BLOWLAMP (BLOW[1]). **3** piece of wood, esp one wrapped in cloth and soaked in oil, etc, which is lit and held in the hand to give light. **4** (idm) **carry a torch for sb** ⇨ CARRY.

□ **ˈtorchlight** *n* [U] light of a torch or torches: *put up the tent by torchlight* ○ [attrib] *a torchlight procession,* ie one in which burning torches are carried.

tore *pt* of TEAR[2].

toreador /ˈtɒrɪədɔː(r); *US* ˈtɔːr-/ *n* (in Spain) bullfighter, esp one on horseback.

torment /ˈtɔːment/ *n* (**a**) [U, C usu *pl*] severe physical or mental suffering: *be in great torment* ○ *suffer torment(s) from toothache.* (**b**) [C] thing or person that causes this: *His shyness made public speaking a torment to him.* ○ *What a little torment that child is!* ie because it is noisy, demanding, etc.

▷ **torment** /tɔːˈment/ *v* [Tn] **1** cause severe suffering to (sb): *tormented by hunger, anxiety, mosquitoes.* **2** tease or annoy (sb): *Stop tormenting your sister.* ○ *tormenting their teacher with silly questions.* **tormentor** /tɔːˈmentə(r)/ *n*: *turn on* (ie fight back against) *one's tormentors.*

torn *pp* of TEAR[2].

tornado /tɔːˈneɪdəʊ/ *n* (*pl* ~**es**) violent and destructive storm over a small area; whirlwind: *The town was hit by a tornado.*

torpedo /tɔːˈpiːdəʊ/ *n* (*pl* ~**es**) tube-shaped explosive underwater missile launched against ships by submarines, aircraft or surface ships.

▷ **torpedo** *v* (*pt, pp* **torpedoed**, *pres p* **torpedoing**) [Tn] **1** attack or sink (a ship) with a torpedo or torpedoes. **2** (*fig*) wreck or ruin (a policy, an event, an institution, etc): *accused the union of torpedoing the negotiations.*

□ **torˈpedo-boat** *n* small fast warship armed with torpedoes.

torpid /ˈtɔːpɪd/ *adj* (*fml*) dull and slow; inactive; sluggish.

▷ **torpidity** /tɔːˈpɪdətɪ/ *n* [U] (*fml*) torpid condition.

torpidly *adv.*

torpor /ˈtɔːpə(r)/ *n* [U] (*fml*) torpid condition: *a state of torpor induced by the tropical heat.*

torque /tɔːk/ *n* [U] twisting force causing rotation in machinery.

torrent /ˈtɒrənt; *US* ˈtɔːr-/ *n* **1** violently rushing stream of water, lava, etc: *mountain torrents* ○ *torrents of rain* ○ *rain falling in torrents.* **2** (*fig*) violent outburst: *a torrent of abuse, insults, questions, etc.*

▷ **torrential** /təˈrenʃl/ *adj* like a torrent: *torrential rain.*

Torricelli /ˌtɒrɪˈtʃelɪ/ Evangelista (1608-47), Italian mathematician and physicist who invented the mercury barometer. He was a pupil of *Galileo.

torrid /ˈtɒrɪd; *US* ˈtɔːr-/ *adj* **1** (of a climate or country) very hot and dry: *the ˈtorrid zone,* ie the part of the earth's surface between the tropics. **2** passionate; erotic: *torrid love-scenes.*

torsion /ˈtɔːʃn/ *n* [U] **1** twisting, esp of one end of sth while the other end is held fixed. **2** state of being twisted in a spiral.

torso /ˈtɔːsəʊ/ *n* (*pl* ~**s**) **1** main part of the human body, not including the head, arms and legs; trunk. **2** statue of this part of the body only.

tort /tɔːt/ *n* (*law*) private or civil wrong (other than breach of contract) for which the wronged person may claim damages.

tortilla /tɔːˈtiːjə/ *n* round thin cake of maize flour, usu eaten hot with a filling of meat, etc, esp in Mexico.

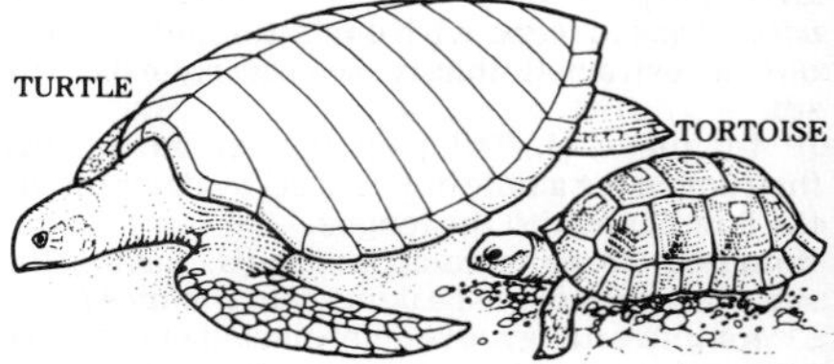

tortoise /ˈtɔːtəs/ *n* slow-moving four-footed reptile with a hard shell.

□ **ˈtortoiseshell** /ˈtɔːtəʃel/ *n* **1** [U] hard shell of certain turtles, esp the type with yellow and brown markings, used to make combs, etc: [attrib] *a hairbrush with a tortoiseshell back.* **2** [C] cat with yellowish-brown markings. **3** [C] type of butterfly with brownish markings.

tortuous /ˈtɔːtʃʊəs/ *adj* **1** full of twists and turns: *followed a tortuous road down the mountainside.* **2** (*fig usu derog*) (of a policy, etc) not straightforward; devious: *a tortuous argument* ○ *tortuous logic.* ▷ **tortuosity** /ˌtɔːtʃʊˈɒsətɪ/ [U]. **tortuously** *adv.*

torture /ˈtɔːtʃə(r)/ *n* [C, U] **1** (method of) deliberately inflicting severe pain, as a punishment or in order to force sb to say or do sth: *barbaric tortures* ○ *the widespread use of torture* ○ *She died under torture.* ○ [attrib] *torture instruments.* **2** (*fig*) (instance of) great physical or mental suffering: *the tortures of suspense, fear, jealousy, etc* ○ *This tooth of mine is sheer torture!*

▷ **torture** *v* [Tn] **1** inflict severe pain on (sb): *accused the regime of torturing its political opponents.* **2** (*fig*) (**a**) cause (sb) great physical or mental suffering: *tortured by anxiety.* (**b**) force (sth) out of its usual or proper form; distort: *a style that tortures English syntax.* **torturer** /ˈtɔːtʃərə(r)/ *n.*

Tory /ˈtɔ:rɪ/ *n, adj* (member) of the British Conservative Party: *the Tory Party conference* ○ *Tory policies.* ⇨ article at POLITICS. ▷ **Toryism** *n* [U].

Toscanini /ˌtɒskəˈni:nɪ/ Arturo (1867-1957), Italian conductor who worked particularly in the USA and at the La Scala opera house, Milan. He was noted for his interpretations of Beethoven and Verdi.

toss /tɒs; *US* tɔ:s/ *v* **1 (a)** [Tn, Tn·pr, Tn·p, Dn·n, Dn·pr] ~ **sth (to sb)** throw sth lightly or carelessly or easily: *He tossed the book down on the table.* ○ *toss sth aside/away/out* ○ *They were tossing a ball about.* ○ *He tossed the beggar a coin/tossed a coin to the beggar.* **(b)** [Tn, Tn·pr, Tn·p] (of a bull, etc) throw (sb) up with the horns. **2** [Tn, Tn·p] jerk (one's head, etc), esp in contempt or indifference. **3** [I, Ipr, Ip, Tn, Tn·pr, Tn·p] (cause sb/sth to) move restlessly from side to side or up and down: *branches tossing in the wind* ○ *I couldn't sleep, but kept tossing and turning/tossing about in bed all night.* ○ *The ship was tossed back and forth by the waves.* **4** [Tn, Tn·pr] coat (food) by shaking or turning it in dressing, etc: *toss the salad in oil and vinegar.* **5** [I, Ipr, Ip, Tn, Tn·pr, Tn·p] ~ **(up) (sth)**; ~ **(sb) for sth** send (a coin) spinning up into the air in order to decide sth by chance, according to which side is uppermost when it falls: *Have the two captains tossed yet* (eg to decide which team will start the match)? ○ *Who's going to cook tonight? Let's toss up.* ○ *There's only one pillow — I'll toss you for it.* **6** (phr v) **toss (oneself) off** (⚠ *Brit sl*) masturbate. **toss sth off (a)** drink sth straight down. **(b)** produce sth quickly and without much thought or effort: *I can toss off my article for the local newspaper in half an hour.*

▷ **toss** *n* **1** tossing action or movement: *The decision depended on the toss of a coin.* ○ *take a toss,* ie be thrown from a horse ○ *a contemptuous, disdainful, scornful, etc toss of the head.* **2** (idm) **argue the toss** ⇨ ARGUE. **not give a ˈtoss (about sb/sth)** (*sl*) not care at all. **win/lose the ˈtoss** guess correctly/incorrectly when a coin is tossed up which way it will fall (esp to decide which team will start a match).

□ **ˈtoss-up** *n* **1** act of tossing a coin. **2** (*infml*) even chance: *Both players are equally good so it's a toss-up* (ie impossible to predict) *who will win.*

tot[1] /tɒt/ *n* **1** small child: *a TV programme for tiny tots.* **2** small glass of alcoholic drink, esp spirits.

tot[2] /tɒt/ *v* (-tt-) (phr v) **tot (sth) up** (*infml*) add up: *It's surprising how the bills tot up.* ○ *Let's tot up our expenses.* **tot up to sth** (*infml*) add up to sth; equal sth: *The bill totted up to almost £40.*

total /ˈtəʊtl/ *adj* [usu attrib] complete; entire: *total silence* ○ *the total number of casualties* ○ *live in total ignorance (of sth)* ○ *That's total nonsense!* ○ *The firm made a total profit of £200 000.* ○ *total war,* ie war waged with the full resources of a country ○ *a total eclipse of the sun/moon,* ie one in which the sun/moon is completely obscured ○ *a total waste of time.*

▷ **total** *n* **1** total number or amount: *What does the total come to?* ○ *England scored a total of 436 runs.* **2** (idm) **in ˈtotal** altogether: *That will cost you £7.50 in total.*

total *v* (-ll-; *US* also -l-) [Tn] **1** count the total of (sb/sth): *The takings haven't been totalled yet.* **2** amount to (sth): *He has debts totalling more than £200.* **3** (*US sl*) wreck (esp a car) completely; destroy.

totality /təʊˈtælətɪ/ *n* **1** [U] state of being total. **2** [C] total number or amount.

totally /ˈtəʊtəlɪ/ *adv* completely; utterly: *totally blind* ○ *I'm afraid I totally forgot about it.*

totalitarian /ˌtəʊtælɪˈteərɪən/ *adj* of a system of government in which there is only one political party and no rival parties or loyalties are allowed, usu demanding that the individual submit totally to the requirements of the State. ▷ **totalitarianism** /-ɪzəm/ *n* [U].

totalizator, -isator /ˈtəʊtəlaɪzeɪtə(r); *US* -lɪz-/ (also *infml* **tote**) *n* (*fml*) device automatically registering the bets staked on horses, etc, so that the total amount can be divided among those who bet on the winner.

tote[1] /təʊt/ *n* (*infml*) = TOTALIZATOR: *betting on the tote.* ⇨ article at GAMBLING.

tote[2] /təʊt/ *v* [Tn, Tn·pr, Tn·p] (*US infml*) carry (sth): *I've been toting this bag round all day.*

□ **ˈtote bag** large open bag for carrying things in (eg parcels, shopping, etc).

totem /ˈtəʊtəm/ *n* (image of a) natural object, esp an animal, considered by N American Indians as the emblem of a clan or family.

□ **ˈtotem-pole** *n* tall wooden pole carved or painted with a series of totems.

totter /ˈtɒtə(r)/ *v* [I, Ipr, Ip] **1** walk or move unsteadily; stagger: *The child tottered across the room.* ○ *She tottered to her feet.* **2** rock or shake as if about to fall: *The tall chimney tottered (to and fro) and then collapsed.* ▷ **tottery** /ˈtɒtərɪ/ *adj*: *feel faint and tottery.*

toucan /ˈtu:kæn, -kən; *US also* tʊˈkɑ:n/ *n* tropical American bird with brightly coloured feathers and a very large beak.

touch[1] /tʌtʃ/ *v* **1** [I, Tn] be or come together with (sth else) so that there is no space between: *The two wires were touching.* ○ *One of the branches was just touching the water.* ○ *The two properties touch (each other),* ie share a boundary. **2** [Tn] press or strike (sth/sb) lightly, esp with the hand: *Don't touch that dish — it's very hot!* ○ *Can you touch the top of the door* (ie reach it with your hand)? ○ *He touched me on the arm,* eg to attract my attention. ○ *Don't let your coat touch the wall — the paint's still wet.* **3** [Tn] move or interfere with (sb/sth); harm: *I told you not to touch my things!* ○ *The valuable paintings were not touched by the fire.* ○ *What he did was perfectly legal — the police can't touch* (ie arrest) *him for it.* **4** [Tn] (usu in negative sentences) eat or drink even a little of (sth): *You've hardly touched your steak.* **5** [Tn, Tn·pr] **(a)** ~ **sb/sth (with sth)** make sb/sb's feelings sympathetic or sad: *Her tragic story touched us all deeply/touched our hearts with sorrow.* ○ *He never seems to have been touched with the slightest remorse for his crimes.* **(b)** [Tn, Tn·pr] ~ **sb/sth (on sth)** cause sb/sb's feelings to be hurt or offended: *Her sarcasm touched his self-esteem.* ○ *You've touched me on a tender spot,* ie mentioned sth I find painful or unpleasant. **6** [Tn] (usu in negative sentences) be associated or connected with (sth): *Your objections do not touch the point at issue.* ○ *I wouldn't touch anything illegal.* ○ *She never touches* (ie drinks) *alcohol.* **7** [Tn] (usu in negative sentences) equal (sb/sth) in excellence; rival: *No one can touch him* (ie He is the best) *as a comedian/in comedy.* ○ *There's nothing to touch mountain air for giving you an appetite.* **8** [Tn] reach (a certain level, etc): *The speedometer was touching 120 mph.* ○ *After touching 143, the price* (ie of shares on the stock-market) *fell back to 108 by the close of trading.* ○ *touch the depths of despair.* **9** (idm) **hit/touch a nerve** ⇨ NERVE. **not touch sb/sth with a ˈbarge-pole** (*Brit infml*) not wish to have or be associated with sb/sth: *I don't know why she's marrying that appalling man; I wouldn't touch him with a barge-pole.* **touch ˈbottom (a)** reach and touch the ground at the bottom of a body of water: *The ship has touched bottom — the estuary must be shallower than we thought.* **(b)** (*fig*) reach the worst possible state or condition: *When he was forced to beg from his friends he felt he had touched bottom and could sink no lower.* **touch sb on the ˈraw** hurt sb's feelings by mentioning sth about which he is sensitive. **touch the right ˈchord** appeal cleverly to sb's feelings. **touch ˈwood** (*catchphrase*) (expression used, often while touching sth made of wood, in the superstitious or humorous hope of avoiding bad luck): *I've been driving for 20 years and never had an accident — touch wood!* **10** (phr v) **touch at sth** (no passive) (of a ship) stop for a period at (a place); call at sth: *Our ship touched at Naples.* **touch down (a)** (of an aircraft) land. **(b)** (in Rugby) score a try by putting the ball on the ground behind the other team's goal line. **touch sb for sth** (*sl*) get sb to give one money (as a loan or by begging): *He tried to touch me for a fiver.* **touch sth off (a)** cause sth to explode or catch fire. **(b)** (*fig*) cause sth to start: *His arrest touched off a riot.* **touch on/upon sth** mention or deal with (a subject) briefly: *The matter was hardly touched on.* **touch sb up** (*sl*) touch sb in a sexually improper or suggestive way. **touch sth up** improve sth by making small changes: *I'm going to touch up those scratches with a bit of paint.*

□ **ˈtouchdown** *n* **1** (of an aircraft) landing. **2** (in American football) score made by taking the ball across the other team's goal line.

touch[2] /tʌtʃ/ *n* **1** [C usu *sing*] act or fact of touching: *I felt a touch on my arm.* ○ *A bubble will burst at the slightest touch.* ○ *He managed to get a touch to the ball.* **2** [U] faculty of perceiving things or their qualities by touching them: *Blind people rely a lot on touch.* ○ *a highly developed sense of touch.* **3** [sing] way sth feels when touched: *soft to the touch* ○ *The material has a warm, velvety touch.* ○ *the cold touch of marble.* **4** [C] small detail: *put the finishing touches to a piece of work* ○ *humorous touches* ○ *That was a clever touch.* **5** [sing] **a** ~ **(of sth)** slight quantity; trace: *This dish needs a touch more garlic.* ○ *'Do you take sugar?' 'Just a touch.'* ○ *There's a touch of frost in the air.* ○ *I've got a touch of flu.* ○ *have a touch of the sun,* ie slight sunstroke. **6** [sing] manner or style of workmanship, performance, etc: *the touch of a master,* ie expert style, eg in painting ○ *play the piano with a light, heavy, firm, delicate, etc touch* ○ *His work lacks that professional touch.* **7** [sing] person's special skill: *I can't do the crossword today — I must be losing my touch.* ○ *Has he regained his old touch?* ○ *another adventure film with that inimitable Steven Spielberg touch.* **8** [U] (in football and Rugby) part of the pitch outside the sidelines: *The ball is out of/in touch.* ○ *kick the ball into touch.* **9** (idm) **at a ˈtouch** if touched, however lightly: *The machine stops and starts at a touch.* **the common touch** ⇨ COMMON[1]. **in/out of ˈtouch (with sb)** in/not in communication: *Let's keep in touch.* ○ *Do get in touch soon,* eg by phone. ○ *Our head office can put you in touch with a branch in your area.* ○ *I'll be in touch again towards the end of the week.* ○ *We've been out of touch with Roger for years now.* **an easy/a soft ˈtouch** (*sl*) person who readily gives or lends money if asked. **in/out of touch with sth** having/not having information about sth: *I try to keep in touch with current events by reading the newspapers.* **lose touch** ⇨ LOSE. **the Midas touch** ⇨ MIDAS. **a touch** (with an *adj* or *adv*) slightly: *It's a touch colder today.* ○ *She hit the ball a touch too hard.*

□ **ˌtouch-and-ˈgo** *adj* [usu pred] (*infml*) uncertain as to the result: *It was touch-and-go whether we would get to the airport in time.* ○ *The patient is out of danger now, but it was touch-and-go* (ie uncertain whether he would survive) *for a while.*

ˈtouch-judge *n* linesman in Rugby football.

ˈtouch-line *n* line marking the side of a football field.

ˈtouch-paper *n* [U] paper treated with a chemical that makes it burn slowly, used for lighting fireworks: *Light the blue touch-paper and retire* (ie move away) *immediately.*

ˈtouch-type *v* [I] type without looking at the keys.

touché /ˈtu:ʃeɪ; *US* tu:ˈʃeɪ/ *interj* (expression used to acknowledge that one's opponent has made a good or effective point in an argument, a discussion, etc).

touched /tʌtʃt/ *adj* [pred] **1** made to feel warm sympathy or gratitude: *I was very touched by/to receive your kind letter.* **2** (*infml*) slightly mad.

touching /ˈtʌtʃɪŋ/ *adj* arousing pity or sympathy: *a touching sight, story, scene* ○ (*ironic*) *She showed a touching* (ie perhaps mistaken) *faith in her own invincibility.*

▷ **touching** *prep* (*fml*) having an effect on (sth); concerning: *measures touching our interests.*

touchingly *adv.*

touchstone /ˈtʌtʃstəʊn/ *n* ~ **(of sth)** test by which one can find the quality of genuineness; criterion: *The answers she gave were a touchstone of her honesty.*

touchy /ˈtʌtʃɪ/ *adj* (-ier, -iest) **1** easily offended:

Don't be so touchy! **2** (of a subject, situation, etc) requiring careful handling because of potential controversy or offence: *Racism remains a touchy issue.* ▷ **touchily** /-ɪlɪ/ *adv.* **touchiness** *n* [U].

tough /tʌf/ *adj* **(-er, -est) 1** not easily cut, broken, or worn out: *as tough as leather* ○ *Tough glass is needed for windscreens.* ○ *a tough pair of walking boots.* **2** able to endure hardship; not easily defeated or injured: *You need to be tough to survive in the jungle.* ○ *Coal-miners are a tough breed.* **3** (*esp US*) rough; violent: *one of the toughest areas of the city* ○ *a tough criminal.* **4** (*derog*) (of meat) hard to cut or chew: *a tough steak.* **5** severe; unyielding: *tough measures to deal with terrorism* ○ *take a tough line with offenders.* **6** difficult: *It's tough finding a job these days.* ○ *a tough game, assignment, problem, journey.* **7** ~ **(on sb)** (*infml*) unfortunate: *That's tough!* ie Bad luck! ○ *It's rather tough on him falling ill just as he's about to go on holiday.* ○ *Oh, tough luck!* **8** (idm) **be/get tough (with sb)** adopt a firm attitude; take severe measures: *It's time to get tough with football hooligans.* ○ [attrib] *a get-tough policy.* **a hard/tough nut** ⇨ NUT. **(as) tough as old ˈboots** (*infml*) (esp of meat) very tough; difficult to chew. **a ˌtough ˈcustomer** (*infml*) person who is difficult to control, overcome, satisfy, etc.

▷ **tough** (also **toughie** /ˈtʌfɪ/) *n* (*infml*) rough and violent person: *a gang of young toughs.*

tough *v* (phr v) **tough sth out** (*infml*) endure (a difficult situation) with determination.

toughen /ˈtʌfn/ *v* [I, Ip, Tn, Tn·p] ~ **(sth/sb) (up)** (cause sth/sb to) become tough or tough(er): *The law needs toughening (up).* ○ *toughened glass.*

toughness *n* [U].

□ ˈ**tough guy** (*infml*) man who is strong and brave and often uses rough or violent methods: [attrib] *his tough-guy image.*

Toulouse-Lautrec /tuːˌluːz ləʊˈtrek/ Henri de (1864-1901), French artist best known for his paintings and posters showing the life of Paris, and particularly its theatres, music-halls, cafés and brothels, at the end of the 19th century. His bold and colourful style often came close to caricature.

toupee /ˈtuːpeɪ; *US* tuːˈpeɪ/ *n* patch of false hair worn to cover a bald spot; small wig.

tour /tʊə(r); *also, in British use,* tɔː(r)/ *n* **1** journey for pleasure during which various places of interest are visited: *a round-the-world tour* ○ *a coach tour of* (ie around) *France* ○ *a cycling/walking tour* ○ [attrib] *tour operators.* **2** brief visit to or through a place: *go on/make/do a tour of the palace, museum, ruins, etc* ○ *a conducted/guided tour,* ie made by a group led by a guide. ⇨ Usage at JOURNEY. **3** official series of visits for the purpose of playing matches, giving performances, etc: *the Australian cricket team's forthcoming tour of England* ○ *The orchestra is currently on tour in Germany.* ○ *The Director leaves tomorrow for a tour of overseas branches,* ie to inspect them. **4** period of duty abroad: *a tour of three years as a lecturer in Nigeria.*

▷ **tour** *v* [I, Ipr, Tn] ~ **(in sth)** make a tour of or in (a place): *They're touring (in) India.* ○ *The play will tour the provinces next month.*

tourer /ˈtʊərə(r); *also, in British use,* ˈtɔːr-/ *n* large car with a roof that can be folded back.

tourism /ˈtʊərɪzəm; *also, in British use,* ˈtɔːr-/ *n* [U] business of providing accommodation and services for tourists: *The country's economy is dependent on tourism.*

tourist /ˈtʊərɪst; *also, in British use,* ˈtɔːr-/ *n* **1** person who is travelling or visiting a place for pleasure: *London is full of tourists in the summer.* ○ [attrib] *a ˈtourist agency.* **2** (*sport*) member of a team on tour(3): *the Australian tourists.* **touristy** *adj* (*infml derog*) full of tourists; designed to attract tourists: *The coast is terribly touristy now.*

ˈ**tourist class** (on aircraft and ships) second class.

ˈ**tourist trap** (*infml*) place that exploits tourists (by overcharging, etc).

□ ˈ**touring-car** *n* (*esp US*) = TOURER.

tour de force /ˌtʊə də ˈfɔːs/ (*pl* **tours de force** /ˌtʊə də ˈfɔːs/) (*French*) outstandingly skilful performance or achievement.

tournament /ˈtɔːnəmənt; *US* ˈtɜːrn-/ *n* **1** series of contests of skill between a number of competitors, often on a knock-out basis: *a tennis, chess, snooker, etc tournament.* ⇨ Usage at SPORT. **2** (formerly) contest between knights on horseback armed with blunted weapons, esp lances.

tourney /ˈtʊənɪ/ *n* (*esp arch or rhet*) = TOURNAMENT: *knights fighting in a tourney* ○ *a tennis tourney.*

▷ **tourney** *v* [I] take part in a tourney.

tourniquet /ˈtʊənɪkeɪ; *US* ˈtɜːrnɪkət/ *n* device for stopping the flow of blood through an artery by twisting sth tightly around a limb: *applying a tourniquet to the wounded man's arm.*

tousle /ˈtaʊzl/ *v* [Tn] make (hair, etc) untidy by pulling or rubbing it about: *a girl with tousled hair.*

tout /taʊt/ *v* **1** [I, Ipr, Tn] ~ **(for sth)** try to get people to buy (one's goods or services), esp in an annoyingly insistent way: *touting for custom* ○ *touting one's wares.* **2** [Tn] (*Brit*) sell (tickets to sports events, concerts, etc) at a price higher than the official one.

▷ **tout** *n* person who touts things: *a ˈticket tout.*

tow[1] /təʊ/ *v* [Tn, Tn·pr, Tn·p] pull (sth) along with a rope, chain, etc: *tow a damaged ship into port* ○ *If you park your car here the police may tow it away.* ⇨ Usage at PULL[2].

▷ **tow** *n* **1** (esp *sing*) act of towing sth: *My car won't start — can you give me a tow?* **2** (idm) **in tow (a)** (*infml*) accompanying or following behind: *He had his family in tow,* ie with him. **(b)** = ON TOW: *The damaged freighter was taken in tow.* **on tow** being towed: *The lorry was on tow.*

□ ˈ**tow-bar** *n* bar fitted to the back of a car for towing a caravan, etc.

ˈ**tow-line**, ˈ**tow-rope** *ns* line or rope used for towing.

ˈ**tow-path** *n* path along the bank of a river or canal, formerly used by horses towing barges, etc.

tow[2] /təʊ/ *n* [U] short coarse fibres of flax or hemp, used for making rope, etc.

towards /təˈwɔːdz; *US* tɔːrdz/ (also **toward** /təˈwɔːd; *US* tɔːrd/) *prep* **1** in the direction of (sb/sth): *walk towards the river* ○ *look out towards the sea* ○ *The child came running towards me.* ○ *She turned her back towards the sun.* **2** moving closer to achieving (sth): *The meeting is seen as the first step towards greater unity between the parties.* ○ *We have made some progress towards reaching an agreement.* **3** in relation to (sb/sth): *The local people are always very friendly towards tourists.* ○ *He behaved very affectionately towards her children.* ○ *As you get older your attitude towards death changes.* **4** with the aim of acquiring or contributing to (sth): *The money will go towards (the cost of) building a new school.* ○ *£30 a month goes towards a pension fund.* **5** near (a point in time): *Food shortages will probably get worse towards the end of the century.* ○ *Now he's getting towards retirement age he's started playing golf.*

towel /ˈtaʊəl/ *n* **1** piece of absorbent cloth or paper for drying oneself or wiping things dry: *a ˈhand-/ˈbath-towel* ○ *a paper ˈtowel.* **2** (idm) **throw in the ˈtowel** (*infml*) admit that one is defeated. Cf THROW UP THE SPONGE (SPONGE).

▷ **towel** *v* (**-ll-**; *US* **-l-**) [Tn, Tn·pr, Tn·p] ~ **oneself/sb (down) (with sth)** dry oneself/sb with a towel.

towelling (*US* **toweling**) *n* [U] thick soft absorbent cloth (of a type) used for making towels.

□ ˈ**towel-rail** *n* rail for hanging towels on.

tower /ˈtaʊə(r)/ *n* **1** tall narrow structure, usu square or circular, either standing alone (eg as a fort) or forming part of a church, or a castle or some other large building: *the church's bell tower.* ⇨ illus at CHURCH. **2 the Tower** = THE TOWER OF LONDON: *Traitors were sent to* (ie imprisoned in) *the Tower.* **3** (idm) **an ivory tower** ⇨ IVORY. **a ˌtower of ˈstrength** person who can be relied upon for protection, strength or comfort in time of trouble.

▷ **tower** *v* (phr v) **tower above/over sb/sth (a)** be of much greater height than others nearby: *the skyscrapers that tower over New York* ○ *At six feet, he towers over his mother.* **(b)** (*fig*) greatly surpass others in ability, quality, fame, etc: *Shakespeare towers above all other Elizabethan dramatists.*

towering /ˈtaʊərɪŋ/ *adj* [attrib] **1** extremely or impressively tall or high: *the towering dome of the cathedral.* **2** (of rage, etc) intense; extreme. **3** (*approv*) outstanding: *Einstein, one of the towering intellects of the age.*

□ ˈ**tower block** (*Brit*) very tall block of flats or offices.

the Tower of Babel /ˌtaʊər əv ˈbeɪbl/ (in the Bible) tower built by the descendants of *Noah to try to reach heaven. To prevent this, God caused them all to speak different languages, so that they could not understand each other. The story was probably inspired by a Babylonian pyramid, and may have been an attempt to explain the existence of different languages. Cf BABEL.

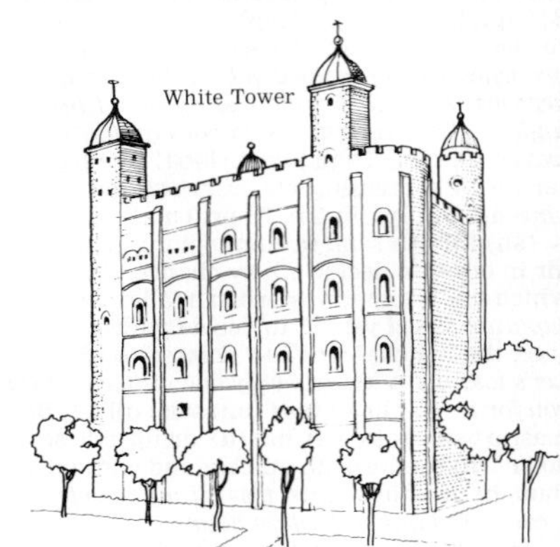

the Tower of London

the Tower of London /ˌtaʊər əv ˈlʌndən/ (also **the Tower**) fortress in London, on the north bank of the River Thames. The oldest part, the White Tower, was begun in 1078. It was later used as a state prison, and the British crown jewels are now kept there. ⇨ illus.

town /taʊn/ *n* **1 (a)** [C] centre of population that is larger than a village but smaller than a city: *drove through several large industrial towns* ○ *the historic town of Cambridge.* **(b)** [CGp] its inhabitants: *The whole town turned out to welcome the team home.* **2** [U] towns or cities, esp as contrasted with the country: *Do you live in town or in the country?* ○ [attrib] *town life.* ⇨ article. **3** [U] (preceded by a *prep* and without *the* or *a*) **(a)** main business and commercial area of a neighbourhood: *I'm going into town this morning — do you want me to get you anything?* **(b)** chief town or city of an area; (in England) London: *Mr Green is not in town/is out of town.* ○ *He went up to town this morning.* ○ *She's spending the weekend in town.* **4** (idm) **go to ˈtown (on sth)** (*infml*) do sth with great vigour or enthusiasm, esp by spending a lot of money: *When they give parties they really go to town.* ○ *The critics really went to town on his latest film,* ie discussed it at length, esp unfavourably. **a man about town** ⇨ MAN. **(out) on the ˈtown** visiting places of entertainment (eg night-clubs, theatres) in a town or city, esp at night: *For a birthday treat they took him out on the town.* **paint the town red** ⇨ PAINT[2].

□ ˌ**town ˈcentre** (*esp Brit*) main business and commercial area of a town. Cf DOWNTOWN.

ˌ**town ˈclerk** official in charge of the records of a town or city.

ˌ**town ˈcouncil** (*Brit*) governing body of a town.

ˌ**town ˈcouncillor** member of this.

ˌ**town ˈcrier** (esp formerly) person employed to make official announcements in public places.

ˈ**town gas** [U] coal gas made for use in homes, factories, etc. ⇨ article at ELECTRICITY.

ˌ**town ˈhall** building containing local government offices and usu a hall for public meetings, concerts, etc.

ˈ**town house 1** house in town owned by sb who also has one in the country. **2** modern house built

Town and Country

Many people in Britain have an idealized picture of rural life. People dream of owning a cottage in the country or retiring to live there, and they try to create the country in town by the way they decorate their houses and plan their gardens. In the past, it was the ambition of everyone who made a fortune to own a country estate and adopt the life-style of the land-owning aristocracy. Today, country sports like shooting and fishing are popular with city businessmen, and many town-dwellers like to escape to the countryside at weekends. 'The Archers', a soap opera about country life, based on the experiences of a farming family, is one of Britain's most popular radio programmes, broadcast five times a week since 1950.

While only about one per cent of the working population are now employed in agriculture, there is a greater tendency for people to live in the country and commute to towns to work, so that the decline in the rural population has been reversed. Many self-employed people now work at home, with facilities like the computer and fax machine, and this may be an increasing trend. There has been a movement away from city centres as the older industries have declined. (Cf article at INDUSTRY.) Urban Development Corporations have been set up by the government to encourage new development in these derelict areas in order to reverse the trend. The most famous example is the area of London's dockland.

The spread of cities has been controlled by the establishment of Green Belt areas, where new building around cities is restricted. About 12 per cent of all land is classified as Green Belt, and this has prevented towns merging into each other and has ensured access to the countryside for city dwellers. There has also been a policy, since the Second World War, of creating new towns in rural areas as an alternative to the growth of existing towns. 32 new towns have been built, with a total population of over two million. Garden cities or suburbs were an earlier development, designed to provide some of the benefits of the countryside for city dwellers.

Life in a rural community is very different from life in a town. The amenities that are taken for granted in town, such as shops, schools, banks and public libraries often do not exist. The nearest secondary school may be miles away. Remote communities have to pay more for goods because of transport costs. People are not protected from the natural environment as town-dwellers are, and snow, high winds and heavy rains cause greater disruption. Public transport is often sparse or non-existent and owning a car may be essential. City-dwellers who move to the country may have an idealized view of life there and find it difficult to adapt. Local people may resent those who have come from cities, especially if they are 'weekenders' who buy a house and only occupy it at weekends.

On the other hand life in the country has many compensations. In a village, the sense of community is much greater than in a large town, the village pub is a friendly meeting place and the proximity of the countryside provides a better quality of life, free from the stresses and strains of city life, with its daily struggle to work and back and its noisy and dirty environment.

as part of a planned group or row of houses.

ˌ**town** ˈ**planning** control of the growth and development of a town, its buildings, roads, etc, esp by a local authority.

ˈ**townsfolk**, ˈ**townspeople** *ns* [pl] people of a town.

ˈ**townsman** /-mən/ *n* (*pl* **-men**) man who lives in a town.

townee /taʊˈniː/ (also **townie**, **towny** /ˈtaʊnɪ/) *n* (*derog*) person who lives in a town or city and is ignorant of country life.

township /ˈtaʊnʃɪp/ *n* **1** (community living in a) small town. **2** (in S Africa) town or suburb designated for use by non-whites. **3** (in the USA and Canada) division of a county; district six miles square.

toxaemia (also **toxemia**) /tɒkˈsiːmɪə/ *n* [U] (*medical*) = BLOOD-POISONING (BLOOD[1]).

toxic /ˈtɒksɪk/ *adj* poisonous: *toxic drugs* ○ *the toxic effects of alcohol.*

▷ **toxicity** /tɒkˈsɪsətɪ/ *n* [U] quality or degree of being toxic: *the comparative toxicity of different insecticides.*

toxicology /ˌtɒksɪˈkɒlədʒɪ/ *n* scientific study of poisons. **toxicologist** /-dʒɪst/ *n* student of or expert in toxicology.

toxin /ˈtɒksɪn/ *n* poisonous substance, esp one formed by bacteria in plants and animals and causing a particular disease.

toy /tɔɪ/ *n* **1** thing to play with, esp for a child. **2** (*usu derog*) thing intended for amusement rather than for serious use: *His latest toy is a personal computer.* ○ *executive toys.*

▷ **toy** *adj* [attrib] **1** made in imitation of the specified thing and used for playing with: *a toy car, gun, telephone* ○ *toy* (ie model) *soldiers.* **2** (of a dog) of a small breed or variety, kept as a pet: *a toy spaniel.*

toy *v* (phr v) **toy with sth 1** consider sth idly or without serious intent: *I've been toying with the idea of moving abroad.* **2** handle or move sth carelessly or absent-mindedly: *toying with a pencil* ○ *She was just toying with her food, as if she wasn't really hungry.*

□ ˈ**toyshop** *n* shop where toys are sold.

Toynbee /ˈtɔɪnbɪ/ Arnold Joseph (1889-1975), English historian who wrote the 12-volume *Study of History*, an attempt to explain the rise and fall of civilizations.

trace[1] /treɪs/ *n* **1** [C, U] mark, track, sign, etc showing what has existed or happened: *traces of prehistoric habitation* ○ *The police have been unable to find any trace of the gang.* ○ *We've lost all trace of him*, ie We no longer know where he is. ○ *The ship had vanished without trace.* **2** [C] very small amount: *The post-mortem revealed traces of poison in his stomach.* ○ *He spoke without a trace of emotion.*

□ ˈ**trace element** substance occurring or needed only in extremely small amounts (esp in the soil, for the proper growth of plants).

trace[2] /treɪs/ *v* **1** (a) [Tn, Tn·pr] ~ **sb/sth (to sth)** follow or discover sb/sth by finding and noticing marks, tracks or other evidence: *I cannot trace the letter to which you refer.* ○ *Archaeologists have traced many Roman roads in Britain.* (b) [Tn] describe the development of (sth): *a book which traces the decline of the Roman empire.* **2** [Tn, Tn·pr, Tn·p] ~ **sth (back) (to sth)** find the origin of sth: *He traces his descent back to an old Norman family.* ○ *Her fear of water can be traced back to a childhood accident.* ○ *The cause of the fire was traced to a faulty fuse-box.* **3** [Tn, Tn·p] ~ **sth (out)** (a) sketch or indicate the outline of sth: *We traced out our route on the map.* ○ (*fig*) *Those who came later followed the policies he had traced out.* (b) form letters, etc slowly and with difficulty: *He traced his signature laboriously.* **4** [Tn] copy (a map, drawing, etc) on transparent paper placed over it.

▷ **tracer** *n* **1** person or thing that traces. **2** bullet or shell whose course is made visible by a line of smoke, etc left behind it: [attrib] *tracer bullets.* **3** radioactive substance whose course through the human body, etc can be traced by the radiation it produces, used for investigating a chemical or biological process.

tracing *n* copy of a map, drawing, etc made by tracing (TRACE[2] 4) it.

□ ˈ**tracing-paper** *n* [U] strong transparent paper for making tracings.

trace[3] /treɪs/ *n* **1** (usu *pl*) either of the two straps, chains or ropes by which a horse is attached to and pulls a wagon, carriage, etc. ⇨ illus at HARNESS. **2** (idm) **kick over the traces** ⇨ KICK[1].

tracery /ˈtreɪsərɪ/ *n* [U, C] **1** ornamental pattern of stonework in a church window, etc. ⇨ illus at CHURCH. **2** decorative pattern resembling this: *the delicate traceries of frost on the window-pane.*

trachea /trəˈkɪə; *US* ˈtreɪkɪə/ *n* (*pl* ~**s** *or, in scientific use,* ~**e** /-kɪiː/) (*anatomy*) windpipe. ⇨ illus at RESPIRE.

tracheotomy /ˌtrækɪˈɒtəmɪ/ *n* (*medical*) operation to cut a hole in the trachea, esp to help breathing.

trachoma /trəˈkəʊmə/ *n* [U] (*medical*) contagious disease of the eye causing inflammation of the inner surface of the eyelids.

track /træk/ *n* **1** (usu *pl*) line or series of marks left by a moving vehicle, person, animal, etc: ˈ*tyre tracks in the mud* ○ *We followed his tracks through the snow.* ○ *fresh* ˈ*bear tracks.* **2** course taken by sth/sb (whether it can be seen or not): *the track of a storm, comet, satellite* ○ *following in the track of earlier explorers.* **3** path or rough road, esp one made by vehicles, people or animals: *a muddy track through the forest* ○ ˈ*sheep tracks across the moor.* **4** (a) set of rails for trains: *a single/double track*, ie one pair/two pairs of rails ○ *The train left the track*, ie was derailed. (b) (*US*) railway platform: *The train for Chicago is on track 9.* **5** prepared course or circuit for racing: *a* ˈ*cycling/*ˈ*running/*ˈ*greyhound/*ˈ*motor-racing track* ○ [attrib] ˈ*track racing.* ⇨ Usage at PATH. **6** (a) section of a gramophone record: *Her new album has two great tracks* (eg songs) *on it.* (b) channel of a recording tape: [attrib] *a sixteen-track tape recorder.* (c) (*computing*) section of a disk, etc in which information is stored. **7** continuous belt round the wheels of a bulldozer, tank, etc, on which it moves. **8** rail along which sth (eg a curtain or a cupboard door) is moved. **9** (idm) **cover one's tracks** ⇨ COVER[1]. **from/on the wrong side of the tracks** ⇨ WRONG. **hot on sb's tracks/trail** ⇨ HOT. **in one's** ˈ**tracks** (*infml*) where one is; suddenly: *He fell dead in his tracks.* ○ *Your question stopped him in his tracks*, ie disconcerted him. **jump the rails/track** ⇨ JUMP[2]. **keep/lose track of sb/sth** keep/fail to keep informed about sb/sth: *It's hard to keep track of* (ie maintain contact with) *all one's old school friends.* ○ *lose track of time*, ie forget what time it is. **make** ˈ**tracks (for ...)** (*infml*) leave (for a place): *It's time we made tracks (for home).* **off the beaten track** ⇨ BEAT[1]. **off the** ˈ**track** away from the subject currently being discussed: *We seem to have got off the track of our discussions.* **on the right/wrong** ˈ**track** thinking or acting in a correct/incorrect way: *We haven't found the solution yet, but I'm sure we're on the right track.* **on sb's track** pursuing sb: *The police are on the track of the gang.*

▷ **track** *v* **1** [Tn, Tn·pr] ~ **sb/sth (to sth)** follow the track of sb/sth: *track a satellite, missile, etc using radar* ○ *The police tracked the terrorists to* *their hide-out.* ○ *track an animal to its lair.* **2** [I, Ipr, Ip] (*cinema*) (of a camera) move along while filming: *a tracking shot.* **3** (phr v) **track sb/sth down** find sb/sth by searching: *track down an animal (to its lair)* ○ *I finally tracked down the reference in a dictionary of quotations.* **tracker** *n* person who tracks wild animals, etc. ˈ**tracker dog** dog used for tracking criminals, etc.

tracked *adj* having tracks (TRACK 7): *tracked vehicles.*

□ ˌ**track and** ˈ**field** (*esp US*) sports performed on a track or on a field, usu one surrounded by a track; athletics.

ˈ**track events** (*sport*) athletic events involving the running of races (eg sprinting, hurdles, steeplechase). Cf FIELD EVENTS (FIELD[1]).

ˈ**tracking station** place from which the movements of satellites, missiles, etc are tracked by radar or radio.

ˈ**track record** past achievements of a person, an organization, etc: *He has an excellent track record* (ie has been very successful) *as a salesman.* ○ *a company with a poor track record.*

ˈ**track suit** warm loose-fitting trousers and jacket worn for athletic practice, as casual clothes, etc.

ˈ**track system** (*US*) system of streaming (STREAM *v* 4) in education.

tract[1] /trækt/ *n* **1** large stretch or area of land: *huge tracts of forest, desert, farmland, etc.* **2** (*anatomy*) system of connected tube-like parts along which sth passes: *the diˈgestive/reˈspiratory/ˈurinary tract.*

tract[2] /trækt/ *n* pamphlet containing a short essay, esp on a religious or political subject.

tractable /ˈtræktəbl/ *adj* (*fml*) easily guided, handled or controlled; docile. ▷ **tractability** /ˌtræktəˈbɪlətɪ/ *n* [U].

traction /ˈtrækʃn/ *n* [U] **1** (power used in) pulling sth along a surface: *electric/steam traction.* **2** (*medical*) treatment involving a continuous pull on a limb, etc: *She's injured her back and is in traction for a month.* **3** ability of a tyre or wheel to grip the ground without sliding: *Winter tyres give increased traction in mud or snow.*

□ ˈ**traction-engine** *n* vehicle, powered by steam or diesel, formerly used for pulling heavy loads.

tractor /ˈtræktə(r)/ *n* **1** powerful motor vehicle used for pulling farm machinery or other heavy equipment. ⇨ illus at PLOUGH. **2** (*US*) part of a tractor-trailer in which the driver sits.

□ ˈ**tractor-trailer** *n* (*US*) = ARTICULATED LORRY (ARTICULATE 2).

Tracy /ˈtreɪsɪ/ Spencer (1900-67), American film actor. He had a great gift for screen acting, equally impressive in serious dramatic roles such as *Bad Day at Black Rock* and comedies, such as those co-starring Katharine *Hepburn.

trad /træd/ *n* [U] (*infml*) traditional jazz (ie in the style of the 1920s, with fixed rhythms and harmonies and much improvisation).

trade[1] /treɪd/ *n* **1** (**a**) [U] ~ (**with sb/sth**) exchange of goods or services for money or other goods; buying and selling: *Since joining the Common Market, Britain's trade with Europe has greatly increased.* ○ *Trade is always good* (ie Many goods are sold) *over the Christmas period.* ○ [attrib] *a trade agreement.* (**b**) [C] ~ (**in sth**) business of a particular kind: *be in the ˈcotton, ˈfurniture, ˈbook trade,* ie sell or make cotton, furniture, etc ○ *The country earns most of its income from the tourist trade.* ○ *The new shop has been doing a brisk trade in cut-price clothes,* ie has been very successful. (**c**) [C] (*esp US*) act or instance of trading, esp exchanging one type of goods for another: *do a trade.* **2** (**a**) [U, C] way of making a living, esp a job that involves making sth; occupation: *be a butcher, carpenter, tailor, etc by trade* ○ *Basket-weaving is a dying* (ie declining) *trade.* ○ *The college offers courses in a variety of trades.* (**b**) **the trade** [Gp] people or firm engaged in a particular business: *We sell cars to the trade, not to the general public* ○ *offer discounts to the trade.* ⇨ Usage. **3 the trades** [pl] (*infml*) trade winds. **4** (idm) **do a roaring trade** ⇨ ROARING (ROAR). **a jack of all trades** ⇨ JACK[1]. **ply one's trade** ⇨ PLY[2]. **the tricks of the trade** ⇨ TRICK.

□ ˈ**trade gap** difference between the value of what a country imports and what it exports.

ˈ**trade mark 1** registered design or name used to identify a manufacturer's goods. **2** (*fig*) distinctive characteristic: *a startling use of line and colour that is this artist's special trade mark.*

ˈ**trade name 1** name given by a manufacturer to a widely available product to identify a particular brand: *Aspirin in various forms is sold under a wide range of trade names.* **2** name taken and used by a person or firm for business purposes.

ˈ**trade price** price charged by a manufacturer or wholesaler to a retailer.

ˌ**trade** ˈ**secret 1** device or technique used by a firm in manufacturing its products, etc and kept secret from other firms or the general public. **2** (*fig infml*) fact, etc that one is not willing to reveal.

ˈ**tradesman** /-zmən/ *n* (*pl* **-men** /-mən/) **1** person who comes to people's homes to deliver goods: *the tradesmen's entrance,* ie the side entrance to a large house. **2** shopkeeper.

ˌ**trade** ˈ**union** (also ˌ**trades** ˈ**union**, **union**, *US* ˈ**labor union**) organized association of employees engaged in a particular type of work, formed to protect their interests, improve conditions of work, etc. ⇨ article. ˌ**trade-**ˈ**unionism** *n* [U] this system of association. ˌ**trade-**ˈ**unionist** *n* member of a trade union. **the** ˌ**Trades** ˌ**Union** ˈ**Congress** (*abbr* **TUC**) association of representatives of British trade unions.

ˈ**trade wind** strong wind continually blowing towards the equator from the SE or the NE.

NOTE ON USAGE: **1 Employment** is formal and official. It indicates the state of having paid work: *The national employment figures are published every month.* ○ *Are you in gainful employment?* ie Do you have a paid job? ○ *Employment agencies help people to find work.* **2 Occupation** and **job** indicate a particular type of paid work. **Occupation** is more formal and is used additionally of work which may not provide a regular income: *'What's his job?' 'He's a lorry driver, teacher, etc.'* ○ *Occupation: Artist,* eg when filling in a form ○ *Do you get any job satisfaction?* **3** A **profession** is an occupation which requires higher education and specific training. A **trade** requires training and skill with the hands: *She's a lawyer by profession.* ○ *He's a carpenter by trade.*

trade[2] /treɪd/ *v* **1** [I, Ipr] ~ (**in sth**) (**with sb**) engage in trade; buy and sell: *The firm is trading* (ie doing business) *at a profit/loss.* ○ *a company which has ceased trading,* ie gone out of business ○ *Britain's trading partners in Europe* ○ *a firm which trades in arms, textiles, grain* ○ *ships trading between London and the Far East* ○ *an increase in the number of firms trading with Japan.* **2** [Ipr] ~ **at sth** (*US*) buy goods at (a particular shop): *Which store do you trade at?* **3** [Tn·pr, Dn·n] ~ (**sb**) **sth for sth** exchange sth for sth else; barter sth for sth: *She traded her roller-skates for Billy's portable radio.* ○ *I'll trade you my stamp collection for your model boat.* ○ *I wouldn't trade my job for anything,* ie because I enjoy it so much. **4** (phr v) **trade sth in** (**for sth**) give (a used article) to a seller as part of the payment for a new article: *He traded in his car for a new model.* ○ *He trades on his father's reputation.* **trade sth off** (**against sth**) give sth up (in exchange for sth else) as a compromise: *The company is prepared to trade off its up-market image against a stronger appeal to teenage buyers.* **trade on sth** (*esp derog*) make use of sth for one's own advantage: *You shouldn't trade on her sympathy.* ○ *He trades on his father's reputation.*

▷ **trader** *n* person who trades; merchant. ⇨ Usage at DEALER.

trading *n* [U] doing business; buying and selling: *Trading was brisk on the Stock Exchange today.*

□ ˈ**trade-in** *n* used article given as part of the payment for a new article: [attrib] *an old cooker's trade-in value.*

ˈ**trade-off** *n* ~ (**between sth and sth**) balancing of various factors in order to achieve the best combination; compromise: *a trade-off between efficiency in use and elegance of design.*

ˈ**trading estate** (*Brit*) area designed to be occupied by a number of industrial and commercial firms. Cf INDUSTRIAL ESTATE (INDUSTRIAL).

ˈ**trading post** = POST[2] 4.

ˈ**trading stamp** stamp that is given by certain shops, etc to their customers and may be exchanged for goods or cash.

tradescantia /ˌtrædɪˈskæntɪə; *US* ˌtrædəˈskæntʃə/ *n* [C, U] plant with large blue, pink or white flowers and striped leaves.

tradition /trəˈdɪʃn/ *n* (**a**) [U] passing of beliefs or customs from one generation to the next, esp without writing: *By tradition, people play practical jokes on 1 April.* ○ *They decided to break with* (ie not observe) *tradition.* (**b**) [C] belief or custom passed on in this way; any long-established method, practice, etc: *It's a tradition to sing 'Auld Lang Syne' on New Year's Eve.* ○ *James Joyce's 'Ulysses' challenged the literary traditions of his day.*

▷ **traditional** /-ʃənl/ *adj* according to or being tradition: *It's traditional in England to eat turkey on Christmas Day.* ○ *country people in their traditional costumes,* ie of a type worn for many centuries. **traditionalism** /-ʃənəlɪzəm/ *n* [U] respect or support for tradition, esp as contrasted with modern or new practices. **traditionalist** /-ʃənəlɪst/ *n* person who follows or supports tradition. **traditionally** /-ʃənəlɪ/ *adv*: *In England, turkey is traditionally eaten on Christmas Day.*

traduce /trəˈdjuːs; *US* -ˈduːs/ *v* [Tn] (*fml*) say damaging untrue things about (sb/sth); slander or defame. ▷ **traducer** *n.*

Trafalgar /trəˈfælgə(r)/ cape on the south coast of Spain, near which a battle was fought on 21 Oct 1805 between the British navy, led by *Nelson, and the combined French and Spanish fleets. The British won, ensuring that *Napoleon would not be able to gain control of the seas, but Nelson was killed.

traffic /ˈtræfɪk/ *n* [U] **1** vehicles moving along a road or street: *heavy/light traffic* ○ *There's usually a lot of traffic at this time of day.* ○ *Traffic was brought to a standstill by the accident.* ○ *London-bound traffic is being diverted via Slough.* ○ [attrib] *a traffic accident.* **2** movement of ships or aircraft along a route: *cross-channel traffic,* ie ships crossing the English Channel ○ [attrib] *a threatened strike by air-traffic controllers.* **3** number of people or amount of goods moved from one place to another by road, rail, sea or air: *an increase in freight/goods/passenger traffic* ○ *the profitable North Atlantic traffic.* **4** ~ (**in sth**) illegal or immoral trading: *the traffic in drugs/arms/stolen goods* ○ *the* ˌ*white* ˈ*slave traffic.*

▷ **traffic** *v* (**-ck-**) [I, Ipr] ~ (**in sth**) trade, esp illegally or immorally: *drug trafficking* ○ *He trafficked in illicit liquor.* **trafficker** *n.*

□ ˈ**traffic circle** (*US*) = ROUNDABOUT.

ˈ**traffic indicator** = TRAFFICATOR.

ˈ**traffic island** (also **island**, **refuge**, **safety island**, *US* **safety zone**) raised area in the middle of a road dividing two streams of traffic, esp for use by pedestrians when crossing the road.

ˈ**traffic jam** situation in which vehicles cannot move freely and traffic comes to a standstill. ⇨ article at ROAD.

ˈ**traffic-light** (also ˈ**stoplight**) *n* (usu *pl*) automatic signal that controls road traffic, esp at junctions, by means of red, yellow and green lights.

ˈ**traffic warden** official whose job is to make sure that people do not park their vehicles illegally, and to report on those who do.

trafficator /ˈtræfɪkeɪtə(r)/ *n* (also ˈ**traffic indicator**) flashing light or other device on a vehicle, used to show the direction in which it is about to turn.

tragedy /ˈtrædʒədɪ/ *n* **1** [C, U] terrible event that causes great sadness: *Investigators are searching the wreckage of the plane to try and find the cause of the tragedy.* ○ *a life blighted by tragedy* ○ (*fig*) *It's a tragedy* (ie extremely regrettable) *for this country*

Trade Unions

Trade unions arose in Britain primarily to enable workers to negotiate wages with employers by collective bargaining, that is negotiating on behalf of all the workers in an industry. Modern trade unionism began in Britain largely as a result of the Industrial Revolution. The first Trades Union Congress (TUC) was held in 1868 and it was the TUC that founded the Labour Party in 1906 and paid the first Labour Members of Parliament, since MPs received no salary at that time. The link between the Labour Party and the TUC is still strong today and many union members pay a 'political levy' to the Labour Party as part of their union membership fee.

The main aim of trade unions in Britain has always been to raise the standard of living for their members and negotiating rates of pay is therefore their most important function. But unions also negotiate on hours of work, pensions, holiday entitlement and working conditions, including health and safety considerations, as well as providing legal advice to members who are in dispute with their employers.

In the past, most agreements on pay were on a national basis but in recent years local pay bargaining has to some extent replaced national agreements. The nationalized industries, however, as well as the Civil Service, teachers, health service employees and other public employees still negotiate national pay levels. There is also a trend towards single union agreements, in which all the employees in a firm belong to the same union, regardless of the kind of work they do.

Organizationally and administratively, most trade unions now consist of a central body, usually known as the 'executive committee', whose members are selected by secret ballot among individual union members. The head of the executive committee usually has the title of 'President'. Each work place, typically a factory or office, normally has its own local or branch union representative, often known as a 'shop steward', especially in industrial work-places. If a dispute arises between employees and employers (workers and management), negotiations for an agreement can be conducted either by the branch representative or by a full-time district union official. In work-places where members belong to two or more different unions, as sometimes happens, the branch representatives may form a joint committee in order to negotiate with the employers.

Membership of the the trade union movement grew rapidly in the 1920s. Increasing industrial unrest coupled with the post-war depression led to the General Strike of 1926, when three million trade union members stopped work for ten days in support of the miners, who had struck in protest against the demands of their employers for lower wages and a longer working week.

At the end of the Second World War, trade union membership was 9.4 million. By the mid-1970s it had risen to around 11.5 million. By 1990, however, it has dropped back to about 8.5 million. The fall in membership has resulted partly from the increase in self-employment, but mainly because of the general move away from manufacturing industries and public services, where membership was traditionally strongest.

There has also been a decline in the actual number of unions, and some long established unions have now merged to form new bodies. In 1973 there were 495 British trade unions, of which over 100 were affiliated to the TUC. In the late 1980s there were 354 unions, with only 78 affiliated to the TUC. In 1988 only six unions had more than half a million members each. The largest was the Transport and General Workers Union (TGWU), whose members are mainly bus and lorry drivers, engineers, dockers and clerical workers. It is the only union with over a million members. The others were the Amalgamated Engineering Union (AEU), the General Municipal, Boilermakers and Allied Trades Union (GMBATU), the National and Local Government Officers Association (NALGO), the National Union of Public Employees (NUPE) and the Manufacturing, Science and Finance Union (MSF). In 1989 the GMBATU merged with the Association of Professional, Executive, Clerical and Computer Staff (APEX) to form a new union, the GMB.

In recent years the trade unions have declined in influence as well as in numbers. In the 1970s, when there was a Labour government, there were close links between the government and the TUC. In 1974, the government set up the Advisory, Conciliation and Arbitration Service (ACAS) to help unions and employers to reach agreements. It was, however, the strikes of the 'winter of discontent' in 1979-80 that led to the defeat of the Labour government in the general election of 1979. Since then, under a Conservative government, the power of the trade unions has been reduced by several pieces of legislation, in particular the banning of the closed shop and of 'secondary picketing', that is picketing by workers who are not themselves involved in a dispute. Unions have become less political in their aims, although their historic ties with the Labour party remain generally as firm as ever.

In the USA trade unions are usually known as 'labour unions'. The equivalent of the TUC is the American Federation of Labor and Congress of Industrial Organizations (AFL-CIO). This was formed in 1955 as the merger of the AFL, founded in 1886 as a unifying body for craft workers, and the CIO, founded in 1935 (as the Committee for Industrial Organization) to organize workers by industries. Union membership has fluctuated over the years, but remains fairly constant at about 17 million. As in Britain union influence and support has declined in recent years, and their bargaining power has been reduced. Their cohesiveness is less clear-cut than in Britain since they have no obvious ideology and are not associated with any political party.

US labour unions with more than one million members each are the International Union of United Automobile, Aerospace and Agricultural Implement Workers of America (UAW), the International Brotherhood of Electrical Workers (IBEW), the United Food and Commercial Workers International Union (UFCW), the American Federation of State, County and Municipal Employees (AFSMCE), and the International Brotherhood of Teamsters, Chauffeurs, Warehousemen and Helpers of America (IBT). The IBT, usually called simply the Teamsters Union, is America's largest labour union, with a membership composed chiefly of truck drivers and workers in related industries, such as aircraft manufacturing. It was expelled from the AFL-CIO in 1957 for corrupt practices. Of all unions, its bargaining power remains the greatest.

---

that he never became prime minister. **2 (a)** [C] serious play with a sad ending: *Shakespeare's tragedies and comedies.* **(b)** [U] branch of drama that consists of such plays: *classical French tragedy.* Cf COMEDY.

▷ **tragedian** /trəˈdʒiːdɪən/ *n* **1** writer of tragedies. **2** actor in tragedy.

tragedienne /trəˌdʒiːdɪˈen/ *n* actress in tragedy.

tragic /ˈtrædʒɪk/ *adj* **1** causing great sadness, esp because extremely unfortunate or having terrible consequences: *a tragic accident, mistake, loss* ○ *Hers is a tragic story.* ○ *The effect of the pollution on the beaches is absolutely tragic.* ○ *It's tragic that he died so young.* **2** [attrib] of or in the style of tragedy: *one of our finest tragic actors.* ▷ **tragically** /-klɪ/ *adv*: *her tragically short life.*

tragicomedy /ˌtrædʒɪˈkɒmədɪ/ *n* [C, U] (type of) play with both tragic and comic elements. ▷ **tragicomic** /-ˈkɒmɪk/ *adj.*

trail /treɪl/ *n* **1** mark or sign in the form of a long line left by sth or sb passing by: *vapour trails,* eg those left in the sky by high-flying aircraft ○ *The hurricane left a trail of destruction behind it.* ○ *tourists who leave a trail of litter everywhere they go.* **2** path, esp through rough country: *a trail through the forest* ○ *a ˈnature trail.* **3** track or scent followed in hunting: *The police are on the escaped convict's trail,* ie are pursuing him. **4** (idm) **blaze a trail** ⇨ BLAZE[3]. **hit the trail** ⇨ HIT[1]. **hot on sb's tracks/trail; hot on the trail** ⇨ HOT.

▷ **trail** *v* **1** [I, Ipr, Ip, Tn, Tn·pr, Tn·p] (cause sth to) be dragged behind: *Her long skirt was trailing along/on the floor.* ○ *a bird trailing a broken wing* ○ *I trailed my hand in the water as the boat drifted along.* ⇨ Usage at PULL[2]. **2** [Ipr, Ip] ~ **along behind (sb/sth), etc** walk or move wearily, esp behind or later than others: *The tired children trailed along behind their parents.* ○ *The horse I had backed trailed in last.* ○ *(fig) This country is still trailing far behind (others) in computer research.* **3** [I, Ipr] ~ **(by/in sth)** (usu in the continuous tenses) be losing a game or other contest: *trailing by two goals to one at half-time* ○ *The party is trailing badly in the opinion polls.* **4** [Ipr] (of plants) grow randomly over a surface, downwards or along the ground with long winding stems: *roses trailing over the walls.* **5** [Tn, Tn·pr] ~ **sb/sth (to sth)** follow the trail of sb/sth; track sb/sth: *trail a criminal, a wild animal.* **6** (phr v) **trail away/off** (of sb's speech) gradually become quieter and then stop, esp because of shyness, confusion, etc.

□ ˈ**trail-blazer** *n* person who does sth new or original; pioneer. ˈ**trail-blazing** *adj* [usu attrib] (*approv*) pioneering: *a trail-blazing scientific discovery.*

ˌ**trailing** ˈ**edge** rear edge of an aircraft wing or propeller blade. Cf LEADING EDGE (LEADING).

trailer /ˈtreɪlə(r)/ *n* **1 (a)** truck or other wheeled container pulled by another vehicle: *They packed the food and camping equipment in the trailer.* **(b)** (*esp US*) = CARAVAN[1]: [attrib] *a trailer park,* ie an area where caravans are parked when taking a holiday. **2** series of short extracts from a film or TV programme, shown in advance to advertise it.

train[1] /treɪn/ *n* **1** railway engine with several

carriages or trucks linked to and pulled by it: *a ˈpassenger/ˈgoods/ˈfreight train* ○ *ˈexpress/ˈstopping trains* ○ *I normally catch/take/get the 7.15 train to London.* ○ *get on/off a train* ○ *You have to change trains at Didcot.* ○ *If you miss the train there's another an hour later.* ○ *Travelling by train is more relaxing than driving.* ○ [attrib] *a ˈtrain driver.* **2** number of people or animals, etc moving in a line: *a ˈcamel train* ○ *the ˈbaggage train*, ie people and animals transporting luggage. **3** group of people who follow sb around; retinue: *The pop star was followed by a train of admirers.* **4** (usu *sing*) ~ **(of sth)** sequence of connected events, thoughts, etc: *His telephone call interrupted my train of thought.* ○ *The military coup brought dire consequences in its train*, ie as a result of it. **5** part of a long dress or robe that trails on the ground behind the wearer. **6** (idm) **in train** (*fml*) being prepared: *Arrangements for the ceremony have been put in train.*

□ **ˈtrain-bearer** *n* attendant who holds up the train[1](5) of sb's dress or robe.

ˈtrainman /-mən/ *n* (*pl* **-men** /-mən/) (*US*) member of the crew operating a railway train.

ˈtrain set toy consisting of a model train which runs on a model track.

ˈtrain-spotter *n* person who collects the numbers of railway locomotives he has seen, as a hobby.

train[2] /treɪn/ *v* **1** **(a)** [Tn, Tn·pr, Cn·n/a, Cn·t] ~ **sb (as sth/in sth)** bring (a person or an animal) to a desired standard of efficiency, behaviour, etc by instruction and practice: *There is a shortage of trained nurses.* ○ *He was trained as an engineer/in engineering.* ○ *I've trained my dog to fetch my slippers.* ⇨ Usage at TEACH. **(b)** [I, Ipr, It] ~ **(as sth/in sth)** undergo such a process: *She trained for a year as a secretary.* ○ *He trained to be a lawyer.* **2** [I, Ipr, Tn, Tn·pr] ~ **(sb/sth) (for sth)** (cause a person or an animal to) become physically fit by exercise and diet: *The challenger has been training hard for the big fight.* ○ *train a horse for a race.* **3** [Tn·pr] ~ **sth on sb/sth** point or aim (a gun, camera, etc) at sb/sth: *He trained his binoculars on the distant figures.* **4** [Tn, Tn·pr] cause (a plant) to grow in a required direction: *train roses against/along/over/up a wall.*

▷ **trainee** /treɪˈniː/ *n* person being trained for a job, etc: [attrib] *a trainee salesman.*

trainer *n* **1** person who trains (esp athletes, sportsmen, racehorses, circus animals, etc). **2** aircraft (or device that behaves like an aircraft) used for training pilots. **3** (usu *pl*) (also **ˈtraining shoe**) soft rubber-soled shoe worn by athletes while exercising, or as casual footwear: *a pair of trainers.*

training *n* [U] process of preparing or being prepared for a sport or job: *He mustn't drink beer; he's in strict training for his next fight.*

ˈtraining-college *n* (*Brit*) college that trains people for a trade or profession.

traipse /treɪps/ *v* [Ipr, Ip] (*infml*) walk wearily; trudge: *We spent the afternoon traipsing from one shop to another.*

trait /treɪt; *also, in British use*, treɪ/ *n* element in sb's personality; distinguishing characteristic: *One of his less attractive traits is criticizing his wife in public.*

traitor /ˈtreɪtə(r)/ *n* ~ **(to sb/sth)** **1** person who betrays a friend, his country, a cause, etc: *He's a traitor to himself*, ie has acted against his own principles. **2** (idm) **ˌturn ˈtraitor** become a traitor.

▷ **traitorous** /ˈtreɪtərəs/ *adj* (*fml*) of or like a traitor; treacherous: *traitorous conduct.*

trajectory /trəˈdʒektərɪ/ *n* curved path of sth that has been fired, hit or thrown into the air, eg a missile: *a bullet's trajectory.*

tram /træm/ (also **tramcar** /ˈtræmkɑː(r)/, *US* **ˈstreetcar, trolley**) *n* public passenger vehicle, usu driven by electricity, running on rails laid along the streets of a town.

□ **ˈtramlines** *n* [pl] **1** rails for a tram. **2** (*infml*) pair of parallel lines on a tennis court marking the additional area used when playing doubles. ⇨ illus at TENNIS.

trammel /træml/ *v* (**-ll-**; *US* **-l-**) [Tn esp passive] (*fml or rhet*) take away the freedom of action of (sb); hamper; impede: *No longer trammelled by his responsibilities as chairman, he could say what he wished.*

▷ **trammels** *n* [pl] (*fml or rhet*) things that limit or impede one's freedom to move, act, etc: *the trammels of routine, convention, superstition.*

tramp /træmp/ *v* **1** [Ipr, Ip] walk with heavy or noisy steps: *We could hear him tramping about upstairs.* ○ *They came tramping through the kitchen leaving dirty footmarks.* **2** [Ipr, Ip, In/pr, Tn] travel across (an area) on foot, esp for a long distance and often wearily: *tramping over the moors* ○ *We tramped (for) miles and miles without finding anywhere to stay.* ○ *tramp the streets looking for work.* ⇨ Usage at STUMP.

▷ **tramp** *n* **1** [C] person with no fixed home or occupation who wanders from place to place; vagrant. **2** [C usu *sing*] long walk: *go for a solitary tramp in the country.* **3** [sing] **the ~ of sb/sth** sound of heavy footsteps: *the tramp of marching soldiers/of soldiers' marching feet.* **4** [C] (also **ˈtramp steamer**) cargo ship that does not travel on a regular route but carries cargo between many different ports. **5** [C] (*dated sl derog*) sexually immoral woman.

trample /ˈtræmpl/ *v* **1** [Tn, Tn·pr, Tn·p] ~ **sth/sb (down)** tread heavily on sth/sb so as to cause damage or destruction: *The campers had trampled the corn (down).* ○ *The crowd panicked and ten people were trampled to death.* **2** [Ipr] ~ **on sth/sb** **(a)** crush or harm sth by treading on it: *trample on sb's toes.* **(b)** (*fig*) disregard sb unfeelingly or contemptuously: *trample on sb's feelings/rights* ○ *I refuse to be trampled on any longer!* **3** [Ipr, Ip] walk with heavy or crushing steps: *I don't want all those people trampling about all over my flower beds.*

trampoline /ˈtræmpəliːn/ *n* sheet of strong fabric attached by springs to a frame, used by gymnasts for jumping high into the air to do somersaults, etc.

▷ **trampoline** *v* [I] use a trampoline: *enjoy trampolining.*

trance /trɑːns; *US* træns/ *n* **1** sleep-like state, caused eg by being hypnotized: *go/fall into a trance* ○ *put/send sb into a trance* ○ *come out of a trance.* **2** dreamy state in which one concentrates on one's thoughts and does not notice what is happening around one: *She's been in a trance all day — I think she's in love.*

tranche /trɑːnʃ/ *n* portion of an amount, esp of shares offered for sale.

tranny /ˈtrænɪ/ *n* (*infml*) = TRANSISTOR 2.

tranquil /ˈtræŋkwɪl/ *adj* calm, quiet and undisturbed: *lead a tranquil life in the country.*

▷ **tranquillity** (*US* also **tranquility**) /træŋˈkwɪlətɪ/ *n* [U] tranquil condition.

tranquillize (*US* also **tranquilize**), **-ise** /-aɪz/ *v* [Tn] make (a person or an animal) calmer or sleepy, esp by means of a drug: *The game wardens tranquillized the rhinoceros with a drugged dart.* ○ *the tranqullizing effect of gentle music.*

tranquillizer (*US* also **tranquilizer**), **-iser** *n* drug for making an anxious person feel calm; sedative: *She's on* (ie is taking) *tranquillizers.*

tranquilly *adv.*

trans *abbr* translated (by).

trans- *pref* **1** (with *adjs*) across; beyond: *transatlantic* ○ *trans-Siberian.* **2** (with *vs*) into another place or state: *transplant* ○ *transform.*

transact /trænˈzækt/ *v* [Tn, Tn·pr] ~ **sth (with sb)** (*fml*) conduct or carry out (business), esp between two people: *This sort of business can only be transacted in private.*

transaction /trænˈzækʃn/ *n* **1** [U] ~ **(of sth)** transacting: *the transaction of business.* **2** [C] piece of business transacted: *Payments by cheque easily outnumber cash transactions.* ○ *transactions on the Stock Exchange.* **3** **transactions** [pl] (record of the) lectures and discussions held at the meetings of an academic society: *the transactions of the Kent Archaeological Society.*

transatlantic /ˌtrænzətˈlæntɪk/ *adj* [esp attrib] **1** on or from the other side of the Atlantic: *The President affirmed America's commitment to its transatlantic* (ie European) *allies.* ○ *Two years in New York have left him with a transatlantic* (ie American) *accent.* **2** crossing the Atlantic: *a transatlantic flight, voyage, telephone call.* **3** concerning countries on both sides of the Atlantic: *a transatlantic trade agreement.*

transcend /trænˈsend/ *v* (*fml*) **1** [Tn] be or go beyond the range of (human experience, belief, powers of description, etc): *Such matters transcend man's knowledge*, ie We cannot know about them. **2** [Tn, Tn·pr] ~ **sb/sth (in sth)** be much better or greater than sb/sth; surpass: *She far transcends the others in beauty and intelligence.*

transcendent /trænˈsendənt/ *adj* (*fml*) **1** [usu attrib] (*approv*) extremely great; supreme: *a writer of transcendent genius.* **2** (of God) existing outside the material universe. ▷ **transcendence** /-dəns/, **transcendency** /-dənsɪ/ *ns* [U].

transcendental /ˌtrænsenˈdentl/ *adj* [usu attrib] going beyond the limits of human knowledge, experience or reason, esp in a mystical or religious way: *Gazing at that majestic painting was for me an almost transcendental experience.* Cf EMPIRICAL.

▷ **transcendentalism** /ˌtræsenˈdentəlɪzəm/ *n* [U] philosophy that stresses belief in transcendental things and the importance of spiritual rather than material existence. **transcendentalist** /-təlɪst/ *n* believer in transcendentalism.

transcendentally /-təlɪ/ *adv.*

□ **ˌTranscenˌdental Mediˈtation** (*US propr*) technique of meditation and relaxation that originates in Hinduism and involves repeating a special phrase to oneself over and over again.

transcontinental /ˌtrænzkɒntɪˈnentl/ *adj* crossing a continent: *a transcontinental highway, flight, journey.*

transcribe /trænˈskraɪb/ *v* **1** [Tn, Tn·pr] ~ **sth (into sth)** copy sth in writing: *She jotted down a few notes, and later transcribed them into an exercise book.* **2** [Tn, Cn·n, Cn·n/a] ~ **sth (as sth)** represent (a sound) by means of a phonetic symbol: *In this dictionary, the last vowel of 'transcendent' is transcribed (as) /ə/.* **3** [Tn, Tn·pr] ~ **sth (for sth)** rewrite (music) so that it can be played on a different instrument, sung by a different voice, etc: *a piano piece transcribed for the guitar.* **4** [Tn, Tn·pr] ~ **sth (on/onto sth)** copy recorded sound using a different recording medium: *a performance now transcribed onto compact disc.*

▷ **transcript** /ˈtrænskrɪpt/ *n* **1** written or recorded copy of what has been said or written: *a transcript of the trial.* **2** (*US*) copy of an official record of a student's work, showing courses taken and grades achieved.

transcription /trænˈskrɪpʃn/ *n* **1** [U] action or process of transcribing: *errors made in transcription.* **2** [C] **(a)** transcript. **(b)** representation of speech sounds in writing: *a phonetic transcription of what they said.* **3** [U] recording of radio or TV programmes for later broadcast: [attrib] *the BBC transcription service.*

transept /ˈtrænsept/ *n* (*architecture*) (either end of the) part of a cross-shaped church which is built at right angles to the main central part (the *nave*): *the north/south transept of the cathedral.* ⇨ illus at CHURCH.

transfer[1] /trænsˈfɜː(r)/ *v* (**-rr-**) **1** [Tn, Tn·pr] ~ **sth/sb (from...) (to...)** move sth/sb from one place to another: *The head office has been transferred from London to Cardiff.* ○ *She's being transferred to our Paris branch.* ○ (*fig*) *transfer one's affections/one's allegiance*, ie become fond of/loyal to sb else. **2** [Tn, Tn·pr] ~ **sth (from sb) (to sb)** hand over the possession of (property, etc): *transfer rights to sb.* **3** [Tn, Tn·pr] ~ **sth (from sth) (to sth)** copy (recorded material) using a different recording or storage medium: *transfer computer data from disk to tape.* **4** [I, Ipr] ~ **(from...) (to...)** **(a)** change to another place, group, occupation, etc: *He has transferred from the warehouse to the accounts office.* **(b)** change to another route, means of transport, etc during a journey: *We had to transfer from Gatwick to Heathrow to catch a plane to Belfast.*

▷ **transferable** /-ˈfɜːrəbl/ *adj* that can be transferred: *This ticket is not transferable*, ie may only be used by the person to whom it is issued. ○ *a transferable vote*, ie one that can be passed on to a candidate who is the voter's second choice if his first choice is defeated. **transferability** /trænsˌfɜːrəˈbɪlətɪ/ *n* [U].

transference /ˈtrænsfərəns; *US* trænsˈfɜːrəns/, **transferral** (*US* also **transferal**) /trænsˈfɜːrəl/ *ns* [U] transferring or being transferred: *the transference of heat from one body to another* ○ *the transferral of power to a civilian government.*

transfer² /ˈtrænsfɜː(r)/ *n* **1** [C, U] (instance of) transferring or being transferred: *The club's goalkeeper isn't happy here, and has asked for a transfer (to another club).* ○ *the transfer of currency from one country to another.* **2** (**a**) [U] changing to a different vehicle, route, etc during a journey: [attrib] *Would all transfer passengers please report to the airport transfer desk.* (**b**) [C] (*esp US*) ticket that allows a passenger to continue his journey on another bus, etc. **3** [C] (*esp Brit*) decorative picture or design that is or can be removed from (usu) a piece of paper and stuck onto another surface by being pressed, heated, etc.

□ ˈ**transfer fee** amount of money paid for a transfer, esp of a professional footballer to another club.

ˈ**transfer list** list of professional footballers who are available for transfer to other clubs.

transfigure /trænsˈfɪgə(r); *US* -gjər/ *v* [Tn] (*fml*) change the appearance of (sb/sth), esp so as to make him/it nobler or more beautiful: *Her face was transfigured by happiness.*

▷ **transfiguration** /ˌtrænsfɪgəˈreɪʃn; *US* -gjəˈr-/ *n* **1** [U, C] (*fml*) change of this sort. **2 the Transfiguration** [sing] Christian festival (6 August) commemorating the moment when Christ appeared before three of his disciples in a mystically changed form.

transfix /trænsˈfɪks/ *v* (*fml*) **1** [esp passive: Tn, Tn·pr] ~ **sth/sb (with/on sth)** stick sth pointed completely through sth/sb: *a fish transfixed with a harpoon.* **2** [usu passive: Tn, Tn·pr] ~ **sb (with sth)** make sb unable to move, think or speak because of fear, astonishment, etc: *He stood staring at the ghost, transfixed with terror.*

transform /trænsˈfɔːm/ *v* [Tn, Tn·pr] ~ **sth/sb (from sth) (into sth)** completely change the appearance or character of sth/sb: *A fresh coat of paint can transform a room.* ○ *She used to be terribly shy, but a year abroad has completely transformed her*, ie so that she is no longer shy. ○ *a complete change of climate which transformed the area from a desert into a swamp* ○ *the process by which caterpillars are transformed into butterflies.*

▷ **transformable** /-əbl/ *adj* that can be transformed.

transformation /ˌtrænsfəˈmeɪʃn/ *n* [C, U] (instance of) transforming or being transformed: *His character seems to have undergone a complete transformation since his marriage.*

transformer *n* apparatus for increasing or reducing the voltage of an electric power supply, to allow a particular piece of electrical equipment to be used.

transfusion /trænsˈfjuːʒn/ *n* [C, U] act or process of putting one person's blood into another person's body: *The injured man had lost a lot of blood and had to be given a transfusion.*

transgress /trænzˈgres/ *v* **1** [Tn] (*fml*) go beyond (the limit of what is morally or legally acceptable): *transgress the bounds of decency.* **2** [I, Ipr] ~ **(against sth)** (*dated*) offend against a moral principle; sin.

▷ **transgression** /trænzˈgreʃn/ *n* (*fml*) (**a**) [U] transgressing. (**b**) [C] instance of this; sin.

transgressor *n* (*fml*) person who transgresses; sinner.

transhumance /ˌtrænsˈhjuːməns/ *n* [U] moving of sheep or other grazing animals to different areas of pasture at various times of the year.

transient /ˈtrænzɪənt; *US* ˈtrænʃnt/ *adj* lasting for only a short time; brief; fleeting: *transient success* ○ *Their happiness was to be sadly transient.* Cf TRANSITORY.

▷ **transience** /-əns/, **transiency** /-nsɪ/ *ns* [U]: *the transience of human life.*

transient *n* person who stays or works in a place for a short time only, before moving on: [attrib] *a transient population.*

transistor /trænˈzɪstə(r), -ˈsɪst-/ *n* **1** small electronic device used in radios, televisions, etc for controlling an electrical signal as it passes along a circuit. **2** (also ˌ**transistor** ˈ**radio**) portable radio with transistors.

▷ **transistorized, -ised** /-təraɪzd/ *adj* equipped with transistors.

transit /ˈtrænzɪt, -sɪt/ *n* **1** [U] process of going or being taken or transported from one place to another: *goods delayed or lost in transit* ○ [attrib] *an urban rapid-transit system.* **2** [C, U] (*astronomy*) movement of one object in space (eg a planet) between another and an observer, so that the first seems to pass across the surface of the second: *observe the transit of Venus*, eg across the sun.

□ ˈ**transit camp** camp providing temporary accommodation for refugees, soldiers, etc.

ˈ**transit lounge** room at an airport in which passengers can sit between leaving one aircraft and getting on another.

ˈ**transit visa** visa allowing a person to pass through a country but not to stay there.

transition /trænˈzɪʃn/ *n* [C, U] ~ **(from sth) (to sth)** (instance of) changing from one state or condition to another: *the transition from childhood to adult life* ○ *a period of transition* ○ *His attitude underwent an abrupt transition*, ie changed suddenly. ▷ **transitional** /-ʃənl/ *adj*: *a transitional stage* ○ *a transitional government*, ie one holding power temporarily during a period of change. **transitionally** /-ʃənəlɪ/ *adv.*

transitive /ˈtrænsətɪv/ *adj* (*grammar*) (of a verb) that is used with a direct object either expressed or understood. Cf INTRANSITIVE. ▷ **transitively** *adv.*

transitory /ˈtrænsɪtrɪ; *US* -tɔːrɪ/ *adj* lasting for only a short time; transient: *a transitory feeling of well-being.* ▷ **transitoriness** *n* [U].

translate /trænzˈleɪt/ *v* **1** [I, Ipr, Tn, Tn·pr] ~ **(sth) (from sth) (into sth)** express (sth spoken or esp written) in another language or in simpler words: *He doesn't understand Greek, so I offered to translate.* ○ *translate an article into Dutch* ○ *'War and Peace', newly translated from the original Russian* ○ *Can someone translate this legal jargon into plain English for me?* **2** [I] be capable of being translated in another language: *Most poetry doesn't translate well.* **3** [Tn·pr] ~ **sth into sth** express (ideas, feelings, etc) in a different (esp a more concrete) form: *It's time to translate our ideas into action.* **4** [Cn·n/a] ~ **sth as sth** judge or guess that sth has the specified meaning or intention; interpret sth as sth: *I translated her silence as assent.* Cf INTERPRET.

▷ **translatable** /-əbl/ *adj* that can be translated.

translation /-ˈleɪʃn/ *n* **1** [U] translating: *errors in translation* ○ *the translation of theories into practice.* **2** [C] thing that is translated: *make/do a translation* ○ *a rough, literal, exact, etc translation* ○ *the available translations of Dante.* **3** (idm) **in translation** translated into another language; not in the original language: *read Cervantes in translation.*

translator *n* person who translates (esp sth written). Cf INTERPRETER (INTERPRET).

transliterate /trænzˈlɪtəreɪt/ *v* [Tn, Tn·pr, Cn·n/a] ~ **sth (into/as sth)** write words or letters in or as the letters of a different alphabet: *transliterate Greek place-names into Roman letters.* ▷ **transliteration** /ˌtrænzlɪtəˈreɪʃn/ *n* [C, U].

translucent /trænzˈluːsnt/ *adj* allowing light to pass through but not transparent: *lavatory windows made of translucent glass.* ▷ **translucence** /-sns/, **translucency** /-snsɪ/ *ns* [U]: *the shimmering translucency of her fine silk gown.*

translunar /trænzˈluːnə(r)/ *adj* **1** lying beyond the moon. Cf CISLUNAR. **2** of or relating to space travel towards the moon.

transmigration /ˌtrænzmaɪˈgreɪʃn/ *n* [U] (**a**) passing of a person's soul after death into another body. (**b**) = MIGRATION (MIGRATE).

transmission /trænzˈmɪʃn/ *n* **1** [U] action or process of transmitting or being transmitted: *the transmission of disease by mosquitoes* ○ *a break in transmission* (ie of a radio or TV broadcast) *due to a technical fault.* **2** [C] radio or TV broadcast: *a live transmission from Washington.* **3** [C, U] connected set of parts (clutch, gears, etc) by which power is passed from the engine to the axle in a motor vehicle: *a car fitted with (a) manual/(an) automatic transmission.* ⇨ illus at CAR.

transmit /trænzˈmɪt/ *v* (**-tt-**) **1** [usu passive: Tn, Tn·pr] ~ **sth (from...) (to...)** send out (a signal, programme, etc) electronically by radio waves, along a telegraph wire, etc: *The World Cup final is being transmitted live to over fifty countries.* **2** [Tn, Tn·pr] ~ **sth/itself (from...) (to...)** send or pass on sth (from one person, place or thing/itself) to another: *sexually transmitted diseases* ○ *transmit knowledge from one generation to another* ○ *The tension soon transmitted itself to all the members of the crowd.* **3** [Tn] allow (sth) to pass through or along: *Iron transmits heat.*

▷ **transmitter** *n* **1** device or equipment for transmitting radio or other electronic signals. **2** person or creature or thing that transmits: *The mosquito is a transmitter of disease.*

transmogrify /trænzˈmɒgrɪfaɪ/ *v* (*pt, pp* **-fied**) [Tn] (*joc*) completely change the appearance or character of (sb/sth), esp in a magical or a surprising way. ▷ **transmogrification** /ˌtrænzmɒgrɪfɪˈkeɪʃn/ *n* [C, U].

transmute /trænzˈmjuːt/ *v* [Tn, Tn·pr] ~ **sth (into sth)** change sth (into sth completely different): *In former times it was thought that ordinary metal could be transmuted into gold.*

▷ **transmutable** /-əbl/ *adj* that can be transmuted.

transmutation /ˌtrænzmjuːˈteɪʃn/ *n* [C, U].

transoceanic /ˌtrænzˌəʊʃɪˈænɪk/ *adj* [esp attrib] beyond or crossing an ocean: *transoceanic colonies* ○ *the transoceanic migration of birds.*

transom /ˈtrænsəm/ *n* **1** horizontal bar of wood, stone, etc across the top of a door or window. ⇨ illus at CHURCH. **2** (*esp US*) window above the transom of a door or of a larger window; fanlight.

transparent /trænsˈpærənt/ *adj* **1** allowing light to pass through so that objects behind can be seen clearly: *a type of plastic that is as transparent as glass but stronger* ○ *a box with a transparent lid.* **2** about which there can be no doubt; unmistakable: *a transparent lie* ○ *a man of transparent sincerity, honesty, etc.* **3** (*approv*) easily understood; clear: *a transparent style of writing.*

▷ **transparency** /-rənsɪ/ *n* **1** [U] state of being transparent. **2** [C] photograph printed on transparent plastic, so that it can be viewed by shining a light through it; slide¹(4a).

transparently *adv*: *transparently honest.*

transpire /trænˈspaɪə(r)/ *v* **1** [I] (used with *it* and a *that*-clause; usu not in the continuous tenses) (of an event, a secret, etc) become known: *This, it later transpired, was untrue.* ○ *It transpired that the gang had had a contact inside the bank.* **2** [I] (*infml*) happen: *You're meeting him tomorrow? Let me know what transpires.* **3** [I, Tn] (of plants) give off (watery vapour) from the surface of leaves, etc.

▷ **transpiration** /ˌtrænspɪˈreɪʃn/ *n* [U] process of transpiring (TRANSPIRE 3).

transplant /trænsˈplɑːnt; *US* -ˈplænt/ *v* **1** [Tn, Tn·pr] ~ **sth (from...) (to...)**; ~ **sth (in/into sth)** remove (a growing plant) with its roots and replant it elsewhere: *Transplant the seedlings into peaty soil.* **2** [Tn, Tn·pr] ~ **sth (from sb/sth) (to sb/sth)** take (tissue or an organ) from one person, animal or part of the body and put it into another: *transplant a kidney from one twin to another.* **3** [Tn, Tn·pr] ~ **sb/sth (from...) (to...)** (*fig*) move (a person, an animal, etc) from one place to another: *He hated being transplanted from his home in the country to the noise and bustle of life in the city.* **4** [I, Ipr] ~ **(from...) (to...)** be able to be transplanted: *an old custom that does not*

transplant easily to the modern world.
▷ **transplant** /ˈtrænsplɑːnt; *US* -plænt/ *n* instance of transplanting (TRANSPLANT 2): *have/perform a bone-marrow transplant* ○ [attrib] *a heart transplant operation.*
transplantation /ˌtrænsplɑːnˈteɪʃn; *US* -plæn-/ *n* [U].

transpolar /trænzˈpəʊlə(r)/ *adj* [esp attrib] across the polar regions: *transpolar flights from London to Tokyo.*

transport[1] /trænˈspɔːt/ *v* [Tn, Tn·pr] ~ **sth/sb (from...) (to...)** **1** take sth/sb from one place to another in a vehicle: *transport goods by lorry.* **2** (esp formerly) send a criminal to a distant place as a punishment: *transported to Australia for life.*
▷ **transportable** /-əbl/ *adj* that can be transported.
transportation /ˌtrænspɔːˈteɪʃn/ *n* [U] **1** (*esp US*) = TRANSPORT: [attrib] *transportation costs.* **2** transporting or being transported: *sentenced to transportation.*
transported *adj* [pred] ~ **(with sth)** (*rhet*) overcome by emotion: *Listening to her recent performance I felt totally transported.* ○ *transported with joy, anger, fear, etc.*
transporter /trænˈspɔːtə(r)/ *n* large vehicle used for carrying cars, etc.

transport[2] /ˈtrænspɔːt/ *n* **1** [U] **(a)** (also *esp US* **transportation**) transporting or being transported: *road and rail transport* ○ *the transport of goods by air* ○ [attrib] *London's transport system* ○ *transport charges.* **(b)** means of transport; vehicle or vehicles: *My car is being repaired so I'm without transport at the moment.* ○ *I normally travel by public transport.* **2** [C] ship or aircraft for carrying troops or supplies. **3** (idm) **in transports of sth** (*rhet*) overcome by emotion: *in transports of rage, delight, terror, etc.*
□ ˈ**transport café** (*Brit*) roadside café, esp for the use of long-distance lorry drivers. ➪ article at EAT.

transpose /trænˈspəʊz/ *v* **1** [Tn] cause (two or more things) to change places: *Two letters were accidentally transposed, and 'hand' got printed as 'hnad'.* **2** [Tn, Tn·pr, Tn·p] ~ **sth (up/down) (from sth) (into/to sth)** (*music*) rewrite or play (a piece of music) in a different key: *transposing the song down to D minor.*
▷ **transposition** /ˌtrænspəˈzɪʃn/ *n* [C, U] (instance of) transposing or being transposed.

transsexual /trænzˈsekʃʊəl/ *n* **1** person who emotionally feels himself or herself to be a member of the opposite sex. **2** person who has had his or her external sexual organs changed surgically in order to resemble the other sex.

transship (also **tranship**) /trænˈʃɪp/ *v* (**-pp-**) [Tn] transfer (cargo) from one ship, carrier, etc to another. ▷ **transshipment** (also **transhipment**) *n* [U].

transubstantiation /ˌtrænsəbˌstænʃɪˈeɪʃn/ *n* [U] (*religion*) doctrine that the bread and wine in the Eucharist are changed by consecration into the body and blood of Christ, though their appearance does not change.

transuranic /ˌtrænzjʊˈrænɪk/ *adj* (*chemistry*) (of an element, eg plutonium) having more protons in its nucleus than uranium, and therefore having a higher atomic number.

Transvaal /ˈtrænzvɑːl; *US* trænsˈvɑːl/ province of the Republic of South Africa, in the north-east of the country.

transverse /ˈtrænzvɜːs/ *adj* [usu attrib] lying or acting in a crosswise direction: *a transverse engine*, ie one placed parallel to the axles of a car, instead of at right angles to them ○ *a transverse flute*, ie one held sideways when played. ▷ **transversely** *adv.*

transvestism /trænzˈvestɪzəm/ *n* [U] dressing in the clothing of the opposite sex, as a sexual tendency.
▷ **transvestite** /trænzˈvestaɪt/ *n* person who does this.

trap /træp/ *n* **1** device for catching animals, etc: *a* ˈ*mouse-trap* ○ *a* ˈ*fly-trap* ○ *lay/set a trap (for rabbits)* ○ *caught in a trap.* **2** (*fig*) **(a)** plan for capturing or detecting sb: *The thieves were caught in a police trap.* **(b)** trick or device to make sb betray himself, reveal a secret, etc: *You fell right into my trap.* ○ *Is this question a trap?* **(c)** unpleasant situation from which it is hard to escape: *For some women marriage is a trap.* **3** U-shaped or S-shaped section of a drain-pipe that holds liquid and so prevents unpleasant gases entering from the drain. **4** light two-wheeled carriage drawn by a horse or pony. **5 (a)** compartment from which a greyhound is released at the start of a race. **(b)** device for sending clay pigeons, balls, etc into the air to be shot at. **6** = TRAPDOOR. **7** (*sl*) mouth: *Shut your trap!*
▷ **trap** *v* (**-pp-**) **1** [Tn, Tn·pr, Tn·p] keep (sb) in a place from which he wants to move but cannot: *Help! I'm trapped — open the door!* ○ *They were trapped in the burning hotel.* ○ *The lift broke down and we were trapped inside (it).* **2** [Tn] keep (sth) in a particular place, usu so that it can be easily removed, used later, etc: *A filter traps dust from the air.* ○ *a special fabric that traps body heat.* **3** [Tn, Tn·pr] ~ **sb (into sth/doing sth)** catch sb by a trick: *trapped into an unhappy marriage* ○ *I was trapped into telling the police all I knew.* **4** [Tn] catch (a creature) in a trap: *It's cruel to trap birds.*
trapper *n* person who traps animals, esp for their fur.
□ ˌ**trap**ˈ**door** (also **trap**) *n* door in a floor, ceiling or roof.
ˈ**trap-shooting** *n* [U] sport of shooting at objects released into the air from a trap(5b).

trapeze /trəˈpiːz; *US* træ-/ *n* horizontal bar hung from ropes, used as a swing by acrobats and gymnasts: *the daring young man on the flying trapeze.*

trapezium /trəˈpiːzɪəm/ *n* (*pl* ~**s**) (*geometry*) **1** (*Brit*) (*US* **trapezoid**) four-sided figure with one pair of opposite sides parallel and the other pair not. ➪ illus at QUADRILATERAL. **2** (*US*) = TRAPEZOID.

trapezoid /ˈtræpɪzɔɪd/ *n* (*geometry*) **1** (*Brit*) (*US* **trapezium**) four-sided figure in which no sides are parallel. ➪ illus at QUADRILATERAL. **2** (*US*) = TRAPEZIUM.

trappings /ˈtræpɪŋz/ *n* [pl] outward signs of prestige, wealth, etc: *a big car, a country house, and all the other trappings of success* ○ *He had the trappings of high office but no real power.*

Trappist /ˈtræpɪst/ *n, adj* (member) of an order of monks who live a very austere life and vow never to speak.

trash /træʃ/ *n* [U] **1** material, writing, etc of poor quality: *He thinks most modern art is trash.* **2** (*US*) household or other waste; refuse: *put out the trash.* **3** (*US infml derog*) people that one does not respect: *white trash*, ie poor or deprived white people.
▷ **trashy** *adj* of poor quality: *trashy novels.*
□ ˈ**trashcan** *n* (*US*) = DUSTBIN (DUST[1]).

trattoria /ˌtrætəˈrɪə/ *n* Italian restaurant.

trauma /ˈtrɔːmə; *US* ˈtraʊmə/ *n* (*pl* ~**s**) [U, C] **1 (a)** (*psychology*) emotional shock producing a lasting harmful effect. **(b)** (*infml*) any distressing or unpleasant experience: *going through the traumas of divorce.* **2** (*medical*) wound or injury.
▷ **traumatic** /trɔːˈmætɪk; *US* traʊ-/ *adj* **1** (*psychology or medical*) of or causing trauma. **2** (*infml*) (of an experience) distressing or unpleasant: *Our journey home was pretty traumatic.* **traumatically** /-klɪ/ *adv.*

travail /ˈtræveɪl; *US* trəˈveɪl/ *n* [U] **1** (*arch or rhet*) painful effort. **2** (*arch*) pains of giving birth to a child.
▷ **travail** *v* [I] (*arch or rhet*) make a painful effort; work long and hard.

travel /ˈtrævl/ *v* (**-ll-**; *US* **-l-**) **1 (a)** [I, Ipr, Ip, In/pr] make a journey: *I love (to go) travelling.* ○ *We travelled all over the country.* ○ *She travels to work by bike.* ○ *We travelled over by car.* ○ *We had been travelling (for) over a week.* **(b)** [Tn, Tn·pr] cover (a distance) in travelling; journey through, around, etc (an area): *He's travelled the whole world.* ○ *travel forty miles to work each day.* ➪ Usage. **2** [I, Ipr, Ip] move; go: *Light travels faster than sound.* ○ *News travels quickly these days.* ○ *The billiard ball travelled gently across the table.* ○ (*fig*) *His mind travelled back to his youth.* **3** [Ipr] ~ **(in sth) (for sb)** go from place to place as a salesman: *He travels in carpets for a big London firm.* **4** [I] (of wine, etc) not be spoilt by long journeys: *Lighter wines often travel badly.* **5** [I] (*infml*) move very fast: *I don't know the car's exact speed, but it was certainly travelling.* **6** (idm) **travel** ˈ**light (a)** travel with as little luggage as possible. **(b)** (*fig*) try to avoid responsibilities, problems, etc.
▷ **travel** *n* **1** [U] travelling, esp abroad: *the cost of travel* ○ *Travel in the mountains can be slow and dangerous.* ○ [attrib] ˈ*travel books.* **2 travels** [pl] journeys, esp abroad: *write an account of one's travels* ○ (*joc*) *If you see John on your travels* (eg about town), *tell him to ring me.* ➪ Usage at JOURNEY. **3** [U] extent, rate or type of movement of a mechanical part: *There's too much travel on the brake, it needs tightening.*
travelled (*US* **traveled**) *adj* (usu in compounds) **1** (of a person) having travelled to many places: *a well-/much-/widely-travelled journalist.* **2** (of a road, etc) used by travellers: *The route was once much travelled but has fallen into disuse.*
traveller (*US* **traveler**) /ˈtrævlə(r)/ *n* **1** person who is travelling or who often travels: *an experienced traveller.* **2** travelling salesman: *a commercial traveller.* **3** (*Brit*) gypsy or other itinerant person. **4** (idm) ˌ**traveller's** ˈ**tales** stories, esp about places and people far away, which are fascinating but hard to believe. ˈ**traveller's cheque** (*US* ˈ**traveler's check**) cheque for a fixed amount, sold by a bank, etc and easily cashed in foreign countries.
travelling (*US* **traveling**) *adj* [attrib]: *a travelling circus* ○ *a travelling clock*, ie one in a case, for use when travelling ○ ˈ*travelling expenses.* ˈ**travelling rug** (*US* **lap-robe**) thick blanket placed over a passenger's lap for warmth. ˌ**travelling** ˈ**salesman** representative of a business firm who visits shops, etc to show products and get orders.
travelogue (*US* also **travelog**) /ˈtrævəlɒg; *US* -lɔːg/ *n* film or lecture about travel.
□ ˈ**travel agent** person whose job is making arrangements for people wishing to travel, eg buying tickets, making hotel reservations, etc: *I booked my holiday through my local travel agent.* ˈ**travel agency** (also ˈ**travel bureau**) firm or office of travel agents.
ˈ**travel-sick** *adj* feeling sick because of the movement of the vehicle in which one is travelling. ˈ**travel-sickness** *n* [U].

NOTE ON USAGE: The person who **drives** a car, bus or train is the person in control of it. Similarly we **ride** a bicycle or horse, **sail** a boat or a ship (whether it sails or has an engine), and **fly** a plane. We **steer** a car, bicycle or ship when we turn it in a particular direction. When travelling as a passenger we **ride in** a car, bus or train, **sail in** a ship, and **fly in** a plane. When talking about means of transport we can use **go by** (car, boat/ship/sea, plane/air, bicycle, etc): *Are you going by sea or by air?* ○ *He always comes to work by bus.*

traverse /trəˈvɜːs/ *v* [Tn] travel, lie or extend across (an area): *searchlights traversing the sky* ○ *skiers traversing the slopes* ○ *The road traverses a wild and mountainous region.*
▷ **traverse** *n* **1** part of a structure that lies across another. **2** sideways movement across sth, esp (in mountaineering) across a rock face, etc; place where this is necessary to continue the ascent or descent.

travesty /ˈtrævəstɪ/ *n* ~ **(of sth)** absurd imitation of or inferior substitute for sth: *The trial was a travesty of justice.*
▷ **travesty** *v* (*pt, pp* **-tied**) [Tn] make or be a travesty of (sth): *travestying sb's style of writing.*

trawl /trɔːl/ *n* **1** (also ˈ**trawl-net**) large net with a wide opening, dragged along the bottom of the sea by a boat. **2** (also ˈ**trawl line**, ˈ**setline**) (*US*) long fishing line, used at sea, to which many short lines with hooks are attached.

▷ **trawl** *v* **1 (a)** [I, Ipr] ~ **(for sth)** fish with a trawl. **(b)** [Tn] fish (an area of water) in this way. **2** [Ipr, Tn] ~ **(through) sth (for sth)** (*fig*) search through (records, etc): *The police are trawling (through) their files for similar cases.* **trawler** *n* boat used in trawling.

tray /treɪ/ *n* **1** flat piece of wood, metal, plastic, etc with raised edges, used for carrying or holding things, esp food: *a ˈtea-tray* ○ *Take her some breakfast on a tray.* ⇨ illus at FURNITURE. **2** shallow open receptacle for holding a person's papers, etc in an office: *Letters were piled high in the tray on his desk.*

treacherous /ˈtretʃərəs/ *adj* **1** behaving with or showing treachery. **2** dangerous, esp when seeming to be safe: *That ice is treacherous*, ie not as strong or thick as it looks. ○ *treacherous currents.*
▷ **treacherously** *adv.*
treachery /ˈtretʃərɪ/ *n* [C, U] (act of) betraying a person or cause, esp secretly: *underhand treachery.*

treacle /ˈtri:kl/ (*US* **molasses**) *n* [U] thick sticky dark liquid produced when sugar is refined. Cf SYRUP.
▷ **treacly** /ˈtri:klɪ/ *adj* **1** like treacle. **2** (*fig derog*) unpleasantly sentimental; cloying: *the treacly clichés of romantic fiction.*

tread /tred/ *v* (*pt* **trod** /trɒd/, *pp* **trodden** /ˈtrɒdn/ or **trod**) **1** [I, Ipr] ~ **(on, etc sth/sb) (a)** set one's foot down; walk or step: *She trod lightly so as not to wake the baby.* ○ *explorers going where no man had trod* (ie been) *before* ○ *tread on sb's toe* ○ *Mind you don't tread in that puddle.* ○ (*fig*) *It is a sensitive issue so we must tread* (ie speak, proceed) *carefully.* **(b)** (of a foot) be set down. **2** [Tn, Tn·pr, Tn·p] ~ **sth (in/down/out)** press or crush sth with the feet: *tread grapes*, ie to make wine ○ *Don't tread your ash into my carpet!* ○ *tread the earth down around the roots* ○ *tread out fire in the grass* ○ (*fig*) *their feelings trodden underfoot* (ie brutally disregarded) *by an uncaring government.* **3** [Tn, Tn·pr] make (a path, etc) by walking: *The cattle had trodden a path to the pond.* **4** [Tn] (of a male bird) copulate with (a female bird). **5** (idm) ˌ**tread the ˈboards** (*rhet or joc*) be an actor. ˌ**tread on ˈair** feel very happy. ˌ**tread on sb's ˈcorns/ˈtoes** (*infml*) offend or annoy sb: *I don't want to tread on anybody's toes so I won't say what I think.* ˌ**tread on sb's ˈheels** follow sb closely. ˌ**tread/ˌwalk a ˈtightrope** ⇨ TIGHTROPE. ˌ**tread ˈwater** keep oneself upright in deep water by making treading movements with the legs.
▷ **tread** *n* **1** [sing] manner or sound of walking: *walk with a heavy tread.* **2** [C] upper surface of a step or stair. **3** [C, U] outer grooved surface of a tyre that is in contact with the road: *Driving with worn tread(s) can be dangerous.*
□ ˈ**treadmill** *n* **1** mill-wheel turned by the weight of people or animals treading on steps round its inside edge (formerly worked by prisoners as a punishment). **2** (*fig*) tiring or monotonous routine work; drudgery: *I can't get off the office treadmill.*

treadle /ˈtredl/ *n* lever worked by the foot to drive a machine, eg a lathe or sewing-machine.

treas *abbr* treasurer.

treason /ˈtri:zn/ *n* [U] treachery to one's country (eg by helping its enemies in wartime) or its ruler (eg by plotting to kill him). ▷ **treasonable** /ˈtri:zənəbl/ *adj*: *a treasonable offence*, ie one that can be punished as treason. **treasonably** /-əblɪ/ *adv.*

treasure /ˈtreʒə(r)/ *n* **1** [C, U] (store of) gold, silver, jewels, etc: *buried treasure.* **2** [C esp *pl*] highly valued object: *ˈart treasures.* **3** [C] person who is much loved or valued: *My dearest treasure!* ○ *Our new secretary is a perfect treasure.*
▷ **treasure** *v* **1** [Tn] value (sth) highly: *treasure sb's friendship* ○ *He treasures your letters.* **2** [Tn, Tn·p] ~ **sth (up)** keep sth as precious or greatly loved: *I shall always treasure the memory of our meetings.* ○ *treasure sth up in one's heart.*
treasurer /ˈtreʒərə(r)/ *n* person responsible for the money, bills, etc of a club or society.
□ ˈ**treasure-house** *n* building where treasure is stored.
ˈ**treasure-hunt** *n* **(a)** search for treasure. **(b)** game in which players try to find a hidden object.
ˈ**treasure trove** /trəʊv/ **1** treasure that is found hidden and whose owner is unknown. **2** (*fig*) place, book, etc containing many useful or beautiful things: *The gallery is a treasure trove of medieval art.*

treasury /ˈtreʒərɪ/ *n* **1 the Treasury** [Gp] (in Britain and some other countries) government department that controls public revenue. **2** [C] place where treasure is stored. **3** [C] (*fig*) book, etc containing items of great value or interest: *a treasury of poetic gems.*
□ ˈ**Treasury bill 1** (*Brit*) bill of exchange issued by the government to raise money for temporary needs. **2** (*US*) investment issued by the government, valid for up to one year and bearing no interest.

treat /tri:t/ *v* **1** [Tn, Tn·pr, Cn·n/a] ~ **sb (as/like sth)** act or behave in a certain way towards sb: *They treat their children very badly.* ○ *You should treat them with more consideration.* ○ *Don't treat me as (if I were) an idiot.* **2** [Cn·n/a] ~ **sth as sth** consider sth in a certain way: *I decided to treat his remark as a joke*, eg instead of being offended by it. **3 (a)** [Tn, Tn·pr] deal with or discuss (a subject): *The problem has been better treated in other books.* ○ *The documentary treated the question in some detail.* **(b)** [Ipr] ~ **of sth** (*dated or fml*) (of a book, lecture, etc) be about sth: *an essay treating of philosophical doubt.* **4** [Tn, Tn·pr] ~ **sb/sth**; ~ **sb (for sth)** give medical or surgical care to (a person or a condition): *a new drug to treat rheumatism* ○ *Last year the hospital treated over forty cases of malaria.* ○ *She was treated for sunstroke.* **5** [Tn, Tn·pr] ~ **sth (with sth)** apply a process or a substance to sth to protect it, preserve it, etc: *wood treated with creosote* ○ *treat crops with insecticide.* **6** [Tn, Tn·pr] ~ **sb/oneself (to sth)** give sb/oneself sth enjoyable, eg special food or entertainment, at one's own expense: *She treated each of the children to an ice-cream.* ○ *I decided to treat myself to a taxi*, eg instead of walking. ○ *We were treated to the unusual sight of the Prime Minister singing on TV.* **7** [Ipr] ~ **with sb** (*dated or fml*) negotiate with sb: *The government refuses to treat with terrorists.* **8** (idm) **treat sb like ˈdirt/a ˈdog** (*infml*) treat sb with no respect at all: *They treat their workers like dirt.*
▷ **treat** *n* **1** thing that gives great pleasure, esp sth unexpected or not always available: *Smoked salmon — what a treat!* ○ *Her son's visits are a great treat for her.* **2** act of treating (TREAT 6) sb to sth: *This is my treat*, ie I'll pay. **3** (idm) **a Dutch treat** ⇨ DUTCH. **a treat** (*infml*) very well; excellently: *This beer goes down a treat!* ie is very good to drink. **trick or treat** ⇨ TRICK *n*.
treatable *adj*: *a treatable cancer.*

treatise /ˈtri:tɪz, -tɪs/ *n* ~ **(on sth)** long written work dealing systematically with one subject.

treatment /ˈtri:tmənt/ *n* **1** [U] process or manner of treating sb or sth: *undergoing medical treatment* ○ *protesting against the brutal treatment of political prisoners* ○ *Shakespeare's treatment of madness in 'King Lear'.* **2** [C] thing done to relieve or cure an illness or a defect, etc: *a new treatment for cancer* ○ *an effective treatment for dry rot.* **3** (idm) **give sb/get preferential treatment** ⇨ PREFERENTIAL.

treaty /ˈtri:tɪ/ *n* **1** [C] formal agreement between two or more countries: *the Treaty of Rome* ○ *make/sign a ˈpeace treaty with a neighbouring country.* **2** [U] formal agreement between people, esp for the purchase of property: *sell a house by private treaty*, ie instead of by public auction, etc.

treble[1] /ˈtrebl/ *adj, n* three times as much or as many: *a treble portion of ice-cream*, ie three times as big as the normal one ○ *He earns treble my salary.*
▷ **treble** *v* [I, Tn] (cause sth to) become three times as much or as many: *He's trebled his earnings in two years.* ○ *The newspaper's circulation has trebled since last year.*
□ ˌ**treble ˈchance** (*Brit*) football pool competition in which people try to predict whether certain matches will be draws or wins for the home team or wins for the away team.

treble[2] /ˈtrebl/ *n* **(a)** highest voice in choral singing, esp the unbroken male voice: *a choir of trebles.* **(b)** child with such a voice. **(c)** part for such a voice: *He sings treble.*
▷ **treble** *adj* [attrib] high-pitched in tone: *a treble voice* ○ *a treble recorder* ○ *the treble clef*, ie the symbol in music showing that the notes following it are high in pitch. Cf BASS.

tree /tri:/ *n* **1** large (usu tall) long-lasting type of plant, having a thick central wooden stem (the *trunk*) from which wooden branches grow, usu bearing leaves: *an oak, ash, elm, etc tree* ○ *We sheltered under the trees.* Cf BUSH, SHRUB. ⇨ illus. **2** (esp in compounds) piece of wood or other material for certain purposes: *a ˈshoe-tree.* **3** (idm) **at the top of the tree** ⇨ TOP[1]. **bark up the wrong tree** ⇨ BARK[2]. **not grow on trees** ⇨ GROW. **not see the wood for the trees** ⇨ WOOD.
▷ **tree** *v* (*pt, pp* **treed**) [Tn usu passive] force (a person or an animal) to climb up a tree for safety.
treeless *adj* without trees: *a treeless plain.*
□ ˈ**tree-creeper** *n* small bird of the northern hemisphere that climbs up the trunks of trees.
ˈ**tree-fern** *n* large fern with an upright woody stem.
ˈ**tree-house** *n* structure built in the branches of a tree, usu for children to play in or on.
ˈ**tree-line** (also ˈ**timber-line**) *n* level of land, eg on a mountain, above which trees will not grow.
ˈ**tree surgeon** person who treats damaged trees, cuts off diseased or dangerous branches, etc.
ˈ**tree-top** *n* (*esp pl*) branches at the very top of a tree: *birds nesting in the tree-tops.*

trefoil /ˈtrefɔɪl/ *n* **1** any of various types of plant with three leaves on each stem (eg clover). **2** ornament or design shaped like such a leaf.

trek /trek/ *n* long hard journey, esp on foot.
▷ **trek** *v* (**-kk-**) [I, Ipr, Ip] make such a journey: *trekking for days across the desert.*

trellis /ˈtrelɪs/ *n* [C, U] light framework of crossing strips of wood, plastic, etc used esp to support climbing plants and often fastened to a wall. ⇨ illus at HOME.

tremble /ˈtrembl/ *v* **1 (a)** [I, Ipr] ~ **(with sth)** shake involuntarily (from fear, cold, weakness, etc); quiver: *trembling hands* ○ *His voice trembled with rage.* ○ *We were trembling with excitement.* **(b)** [I] shake slightly: *leaves trembling in the breeze* ○ *The bridge trembled as the train sped across it.* **2** [I, Ipr, It] be very anxious or agitated: *I tremble at the thought of what may happen.* ○ *She trembled to think what might have happened to him.* **3** (idm) **in fear and trembling** ⇨ FEAR[1].
▷ **tremble** *n* feeling, movement or sound of trembling; tremor: *There was a tremble in his voice.* ○ (*infml*) *She was all of a tremble*, ie trembling all over.
trembler /ˈtremblə(r)/ *n* spring that makes an electrical contact when shaken.
trembly /ˈtremblɪ/ *adj* (*infml*) trembling: *I felt all trembly.*

tremendous /trɪˈmendəs/ *adj* **1** very great; immense: *a tremendous explosion* ○ *travelling at a tremendous speed* ○ *It makes a tremendous difference to me.* ○ *They had the most tremendous row.* **2** (*infml*) very good; extraordinary: *a tremendous film, pianist, experience* ○ *He's a tremendous walker*, ie He walks a lot. ▷ **tremendously** *adv*: *tremendously pleased.*

tremolo /ˈtreməlǝʊ/ *n* (*pl* ~**s**) (*music*) trembling or vibrating sound made by playing a stringed instrument or singing in a special way. Cf VIBRATO.

tremor /ˈtremə(r)/ *n* **1** slight shaking or trembling: *There was a tremor in her voice.* ○ *ˈearth tremors*, eg during an earthquake. **2** thrill: *tremors of fear, delight, anxiety, etc.*

tremulous /ˈtremjʊləs/ *adj* (*fml*) **1** trembling from nervousness or weakness: *in a tremulous voice* ○ *with a tremulous hand.* **2** timid or uncertain: *a tremulous look.* ▷ **tremulously** *adv.*

trench /trentʃ/ *n* ditch dug in the ground, eg for drainage or to give troops shelter from enemy fire: *irrigation trenches* ○ *The workmen dug a trench for*

TREES COMMON IN BRITAIN

All the drawings are to scale and represent the average height reached.

deciduous trees

ash

larch

beech

poplar

25 m

horse-chestnut

branch

conker

10 cms

sycamore

keys

hazel

nut

oak

acorn

birch

twig

willow

evergreen trees

Scots pine

trunk

needle

cone

yew

cypress

the new water-pipe. ○ [attrib] *trench warfare.*
▷ **trench** *v* [Tn] dig a trench or trenches in (the ground).
□ **ˈtrench coat** belted coat or raincoat with pockets and flaps in the style of a military coat. **ˌtrench ˈfoot** [U] disorder of the feet caused by standing too long in cold water. Many soldiers in the trenches in the First World War suffered from it.

trenchant /ˈtrentʃənt/ *adj* (of comments, arguments, etc) strongly and effectively expressed; penetrating: *trenchant wit, criticism.* ▷ **trenchantly** *adv.*

trencher /ˈtrentʃə(r)/ *n* (*arch*) (formerly) large wooden plate on which food was served or carved.
▷ **trencherman** /-mən/ *n* (*pl* **-men** /-mən/) (idm) **a good, etc trencherman** (*joc*) person who usually eats a lot.

trend /trend/ *n* **1** general tendency or direction: *The trend of prices is still upwards.* ○ *a growing trend towards smaller families* ○ *contemporary trends in psychiatry* ○ *following the latest trends in fashion.* **2** (idm) **ˌset a/the ˈtrend** start a style, practice, fashion, etc that others copy.
▷ **trend** *v* [Ipr, Ip] show a particular tendency: *house prices trending upwards.*
trendy *adj* (**-ier**, **-iest**) (*infml*) showing or following the latest trends of fashion: *trendy clothes* ○ (*derog*) *trendy intellectuals*, ie ones who do not examine new ideas carefully. — *n* (*Brit infml esp derog*) trendy person: *middle-aged trendies.* **trendily** *adv.* **trendiness** *n* [U].
□ **ˈtrend-setter** *n* person who leads the way in fashion, etc. **ˈtrend-setting** *adj* [attrib]: *a trend-setting film.*

trepan /trɪˈpæn/ *v* (**-nn-**) [Tn] (*medical*) = TREPHINE.
▷ **trepan** *n* **1** (*medical*) early form of trephine. **2** (*engineering*) bore for drilling a mine shaft.

trephine /trɪˈfiːn; *US* -ˈfaɪn/ *v* [Tn] (*medical*) (also **trepan**) cut a (small hole) in sb's skull or the cornea of the eye.
▷ **trephine** *n* (*medical*) surgeon's cylindrical saw used for this.

trepidation /ˌtrepɪˈdeɪʃn/ *n* [U] great worry or fear about sth unpleasant that may happen: *The threat of an epidemic caused great alarm and trepidation.*

trespass /ˈtrespəs/ *v* **1** [I, Ipr] ~ (**on sth**) enter sb's land or property without his permission or other authority: *He accused me of trespassing on his estate.* ○ *No trespassing*, ie as a warning sign. **2** [Ipr] ~ **on sth** (*fml*) take advantage of sth in a selfish way; use sth unreasonably: *trespass on sb's time/hospitality/privacy.* **3** [I, Ipr] ~ (**against sb**) (*arch or Bible*) do wrong; sin.
▷ **trespass** *n* **1** (**a**) [U] trespassing: *the law of trespass.* (**b**) [C] act or instance of this: *an accidental trespass.* **2** [C] (*arch or Bible*) sin; wrongdoing.
trespasser *n* person who trespasses: *Trespassers will be prosecuted*, eg on a notice.

tress /tres/ *n* (*fml*) **1** [C] lock of a person's hair. **2 tresses** [pl] long hair, esp of a woman: *combing her dark tresses.*

trestle

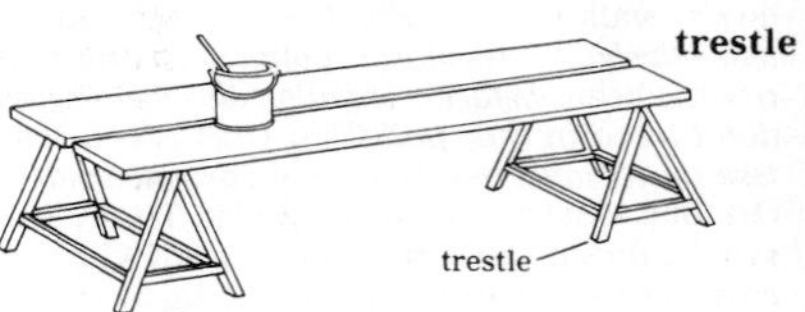

trestle /ˈtresl/ *n* structure of wood, metal, etc with legs, used in pairs to support planks, a table-top, a bench, etc.
□ **ˌtrestle-ˈtable** *n* table supported on trestles.

Trevithick /ˈtrevɪθɪk/ Richard (1771-1833), British engineer who developed the steam-engine so that it could be used in vehicles. His first steam road vehicle appeared in 1801, and the first steam-engine to run on rails was introduced by him in 1804, at a Welsh coal-mine.

trews /truːz/ *n* [pl] close-fitting tartan trousers: *a pair of trews.*

TRH *abbr* Their Royal Highnesses.

tri- *pref* (with *ns* and *adjs*) three; triple: *triangle* ○ *tricolour* ○ *trilingual.* Cf BI-, DI-.

triad /ˈtraɪæd/ *n* **1** group or set of three related people or things. **2** (also **Triad**) Chinese secret organization involved in criminal activities.

trial /ˈtraɪəl/ *n* **1** [C, U] examination of evidence in a lawcourt, by a judge and often a jury, to decide if sb accused of a crime is innocent or guilty: *The trial lasted a week.* ○ *trial by jury* ○ *commit sb for trial*, ie send sb to prison, for later trial ○ *The defendant claimed that he had not had a fair trial.* ○ *The case comes to trial/comes up for trial* (ie will be tried) *next month.* **2** [C, U] (act or process of) testing the ability, quality, performance, etc of sb or sth: *give job applicants a trial* ○ *put a car through safety trials* ○ *a trial of strength*, ie a contest to see who is stronger ○ *The new drug has undergone extensive medical trials.* ○ [attrib] *for trial purposes* ○ *employ sb for a trial period* ○ *a trial separation*, ie of a couple whose marriage is in difficulties. **3** [C] sports match to test the ability of players who may be selected for an important team. **4** [C] ~ (**to sb**) troublesome or irritating person or thing that one must endure: *Her child is a trial to his teachers.* ○ *life's trials.* **5** (idm) **go on ˈtrial/stand ˈtrial (for sth)** be tried in a lawcourt: *She went on/stood trial for murder.* **on ˈtrial** being examined and tested: *Take the machine on trial for a week.* ○ (*fig*) *Democracy itself is on trial as the country prepares for its first free elections.* **put sb/be on ˈtrial (for sth)** (cause sb to) be accused and examined in a lawcourt: *She was put on trial for fraud.* ○ *He's on trial for his life.* **ˌtrial and ˈerror** process of solving a problem by trying various solutions and learning from one's failures: *learn by trial and error* ○ [attrib] *trial-and-error methods.* ˌ**trials and** ˈ**tribulations** irritations and troubles.

□ ˌ**trial** ˈ**run** preliminary test of the quality, effectiveness, ability, etc of sth or sb: *Take the car for a trial run to see if you like it.* ○ *The programme was given a trial run to gauge viewers' reactions.* ○ *She's taking the exam a year early, just as a trial run (for the real thing).*

triangle

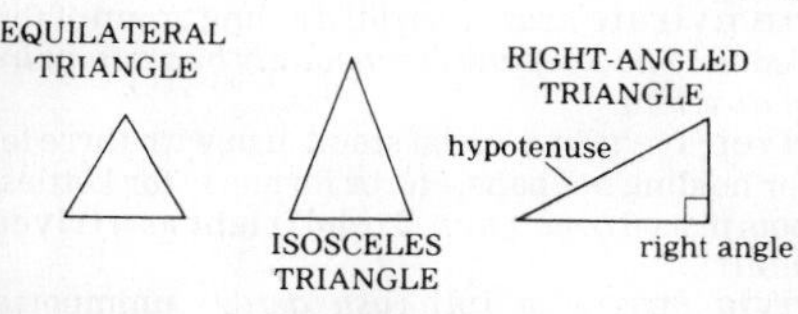

triangle /ˈtraɪæŋgl/ *n* **1** geometric figure with three straight sides and three angles. **2** thing shaped like this: *a scarf made of a triangle of blue silk* ○ *a triangle of grass beside the path* ○ *benches arranged in a triangle.* **3** (*music*) percussion instrument consisting of a steel rod bent in the shape of a triangle and struck with another steel rod. ⇨ illus at MUSIC. **4** situation involving three people, ideas, opinions, etc: *a love triangle.* **5** (idm) **the eternal triangle** ⇨ ETERNAL.

▷ **triangular** /traɪˈæŋgjʊlə(r)/ *adj* **1** shaped like a triangle. **2** involving three people: *a triangular contest in an election*, ie one with three candidates.

triangulation /traɪˌæŋgjʊˈleɪʃn/ *n* [U] (in surveying) division of an area into triangles, so that it can be measured.

Triassic /traɪˈæsɪk/ *adj, n* (of the) period of the earth's history between about 248 and 213 million years ago, when dinosaurs were very common, and the first mammals appeared.

tribal /ˈtraɪbl/ *adj* [usu attrib] of a tribe or tribes: *tribal loyalties, dances, gods, wars.*

▷ **tribalism** /ˈtraɪbəlɪzəm/ *n* [U] **1** state of being organized in a tribe or tribes. **2** behaviour and attitudes that result from belonging to a tribe.

tribe /traɪb/ *n* **1** racial group (esp in a primitive or nomadic culture) united by language, religion, customs, etc and living as a community under one or more chiefs: *Zulu tribes* ○ *the twelve tribes of ancient Israel.* **2** group of related animals or plants. **3** (often *pl*) (*infml esp joc*) large number of people: *tribes of holiday-makers* ○ *What a tribe* (ie large family) *they've got!* **4** (*usu derog*) set or class of people: *I hate the whole tribe of politicians.*

□ ˈ**tribesman** /-zmən/ *n* (*pl* **-men** /-mən/) member of a tribe(1).

tribulation /ˌtrɪbjʊˈleɪʃn/ *n* **1** [C, U] (*rhet*) (sad event, accident, illness, etc that causes) great trouble or suffering: *He bore his tribulations bravely.* ○ *a time of great tribulation.* **2** (idm) **trials and tribulations** ⇨ TRIAL.

tribunal /traɪˈbju:nl/ *n* [C, Gp] group of officials with the authority to settle certain types of dispute: *a rent tribunal*, ie one hearing appeals against high rents ○ (*fig*) *the tribunal of public opinion.*

tribune /ˈtrɪbju:n/ *n* **1** (in ancient Rome) official elected by the common people to protect their rights. **2** (*rhet*) person or organization supporting the rights of ordinary people.

Tribune Group /ˈtrɪbju:n gru:p/ **the Tribune Group** (in Britain) group of left-wing Labour members of parliament, founded in 1966, whose views are published in the weekly journal *Tribune.*

tributary /ˈtrɪbjʊtrɪ; *US* -terɪ/ *n* river or stream that flows into a larger one or into a lake: *The Avon is a tributary of the Severn.*

▷ **tributary** *adj* **1** ~ (**to sth**) (of a river or stream) flowing in this way: *rivers tributary to the Thames.* **2** [attrib] (of a country or ruler) paying tribute(3) to another.

tribute /ˈtrɪbju:t/ *n* **1** [C, U] action, statement or gift that is meant to show one's respect or admiration: *floral tributes*, ie gifts of flowers ○ *Tributes to the dead leader have been received from all around the world.* ○ *The mourners stood in silent tribute as the coffin was laid to rest.* **2** [sing] **a** ~ (**to sth**) indication of the effectiveness of sth: *His recovery is a tribute to the doctors' skill.* **3** [C, U] (esp formerly) payment made by one country or ruler to another, esp to avoid war. **4** (idm) **pay tribute to sb/sth** ⇨ PAY[2].

trice /traɪs/ *n* (idm) **in a trice** very quickly or suddenly: *I'll be with you in a trice.* ○ *In a trice, he was gone.*

triceps /ˈtraɪseps/ *n* (*pl* unchanged) large muscle at the back of the upper arm. Cf BICEPS.

trick /trɪk/ *n* **1** thing done in order to deceive or outwit sb: *play a trick on sb* ○ *We need a trick to get past the guards.* ○ *You can't fool me with that old trick!* ○ (*fig*) *a trick of the light*, ie that makes one see sth that is not there ○ [attrib] *a* ˈ*trick question* ○ ˈ*trick photography.* **2** exact or best way of doing sth; particular technique: *The trick is to hold your breath while you aim.* ○ *I can't open the box — is there a trick to it?* ○ *before artists had mastered the tricks of perspective* ○ *I've never learnt the trick of making friends easily.* **3** skilful act performed for entertainment, esp one involving illusion: *conjuring tricks* ○ *Let me show you some card tricks.* ○ *She had trained her dog to do tricks*, eg to stand on its hind legs. **4** characteristic habit; mannerism: *He has an annoying trick of saying 'You know?' after every sentence.* ○ *My car has developed a trick of stalling on steep hills.* **5** (cards played in) one round of a card-game: *take/win a trick*, ie win a round ○ *How many tricks did we lose?* **6** (idm) **be up to one's (old)** ˈ**tricks** (*infml*) be acting in a characteristic way that sb disapproves of: *Half my money's gone — you've been up to your tricks again, haven't you?* **a dirty trick** ⇨ DIRTY. **dirty tricks** ⇨ DIRTY. **do the job/trick** ⇨ JOB. **every/any trick in the** ˈ**book** every/any trick that can be used to achieve what one wants: *I tried every trick in the book but I still couldn't persuade them.* ○ *He'll use any trick in the book to stop you.* **have a** ˈ**trick up one's sleeve** have an idea, plan, etc that can be used if it becomes necessary. **how's** ˈ**tricks?** (*sl*) how are you? **not/never miss a trick** ⇨ MISS[3]. **teach an old dog new tricks** ⇨ TEACH. ˌ**trick or** ˈ**treat** (*esp US*) (phrase said by children who call at houses on Hallowe'en to receive sweets, etc and threaten mischief if they do not receive any). **the** ˌ**tricks of the** ˈ**trade** (**a**) clever ways of doing things, known to and used by experts. (**b**) ways of attracting customers, gaining advantages over rivals, etc: *She's only been with us a month so she's still learning the tricks of the trade.* **the whole bag of tricks** ⇨ WHOLE.

▷ **trick** *v* **1** [Tn, Tn·pr] deceive (sb): *You've been tricked.* **2** [Tn·pr] (**a**) ~ **sb into sth/doing sth** cause sb to do sth by means of a trick: *She tricked him into marriage/into marrying her.* (**b**) ~ **sb out of sth** cause sb to lose sth by means of a trick; swindle: *Her partner tried to trick her out of her share.* **3** (phr v) **trick sb/sth out/up (in/with sth)** decorate or ornament sb/sth: *tricked herself out in all her finery.*

trickery /-ərɪ/ *n* [U] deception; cheating.

trickster /-stə(r)/ *n* person who tricks or cheats people; swindler.

tricky *adj* (**-ier, -iest**) (**a**) (of work, etc) requiring skill or tact: *a tricky situation, problem, decision.* (**b**) (of people or their actions) crafty; deceptive: *He's a tricky fellow to do business with.* **trickily** *adv.* **trickiness** *n* [U].

□ ˌ**trick** ˈ**cyclist** **1** person who performs tricks while riding a bicycle, esp in a circus. **2** (*infml joc*) psychiatrist.

trickle /ˈtrɪkl/ *v* **1** [I, Ipr, Ip, Tn·pr, Tn·p] (cause sth to) flow in a thin stream: *Blood trickled from the wound.* ○ *tears trickling down her cheeks* ○ *trickle oil into the mixture bit by bit.* **2** [Ipr, Ip] come or go somewhere slowly or gradually: *people trickling into the hall* ○ *The ball trickled into the hole.* ○ *News is starting to trickle out.*

▷ **trickle** *n* **1** thin flow of liquid: *The stream is reduced to a mere trickle in summer.* **2** (usu *sing*) ~ (**of sth**) small amount coming or going slowly: *a trickle of information.*

□ ˈ**trickle charger** device for the slow continuous charging of an accumulator from the mains.

tricolour (*US* **tricolor**) /ˈtrɪkələ(r); *US* ˈtraɪkʌlər/ *n* **1** [C] flag with three colours in stripes. **2 the Tricolour** [sing] the French national flag, with vertical blue, white and red stripes.

tricycle /ˈtraɪsɪkl/ (also *infml* **trike**) *n* vehicle like a bicycle but with one wheel at the front and two at the back.

trident /ˈtraɪdnt/ *n* spear with three points (carried by Neptune and Britannia as a symbol of power over the sea).

Tridentine /traɪˈdentaɪn/ *adj* of or approved by the Council of Trent, a conference held at Trento, N Italy, in the 16th century, which established much Roman Catholic doctrine: *the Tridentine Mass*, ie the traditional Latin mass.

▷ **Tridentine** *n* Roman Catholic who keeps strictly to traditional doctrine.

tried *pt, pp* of TRY[1].

triennial /traɪˈenɪəl/ *adj* lasting for or happening every three years. ▷ **triennially** /-nɪəlɪ/ *adv*: *The games occur triennially.*

trier ⇨ TRY[1].

trifle /ˈtraɪfl/ *n* **1** [C] thing, question or activity that has little value or importance: *I bought a few trifles as souvenirs.* ○ *It's silly to quarrel over trifles.* ○ *He spends all his time on crosswords and other trifles.* **2** [C] small amount of money: *It cost a mere trifle.* **3** [C, U] sweet dish made of sponge-cake and sometimes fruit, usu soaked in wine or jelly, and topped with custard and cream. **4** (idm) **a trifle** slightly; rather: *This dress is a trifle short.* ○ *Isn't the meat a trifle tough?* ○ *Try turning the key a trifle (more).*

▷ **trifle** *v* [Ipr] ~ **with sb/sth** treat sb/sth lightly or casually; toy with sb/sth: *He's not a man to be trifled with*, ie He must be treated with respect. ○ (*fml*) *It's wrong of you to trifle with her affections*, ie make her think you love her when you don't. **trifling** /ˈtraɪflɪŋ/ *adj* unimportant; trivial: *a few trifling errors* ○ *This is no trifling matter*, ie It is serious. **trifler** /ˈtraɪflə(r)/ *n* person who trifles.

trigger /ˈtrɪgə(r)/ *n* lever that releases a spring, esp so as to fire a gun: *squeeze the trigger* ○ *have one's finger on the trigger*, ie be ready to shoot. ⇨ illus at GUN.

▷ **trigger** *v* [Tn, Tn·p] ~ **sth (off)** be the cause of a sudden (often violent) reaction; set an action or a process in motion: *The riots were triggered (off) by a series of police arrests.* ○ *The smoke triggered off the alarm.*

□ ˈ**trigger-happy** *adj* (*infml derog*) ready to react violently, esp by shooting, even when only slightly provoked.

trigonometry /ˌtrɪgəˈnɒmətrɪ/ *n* [U] branch of mathematics dealing with the relationship between the sides and angles of triangles, etc. ▷ **trigonometric, -metrical** /ˌtrɪgənəˈmetrɪk, -kl/ *adjs.* **trigonometrically** /-klɪ/ *adv.*

trike /traɪk/ *n* (*infml*) = TRICYCLE.

trilateral /ˌtraɪˈlætərəl/ *adj* [usu attrib] involving three sides, groups, countries, etc: ˌ*trilateral di*ˈ*scussions* ○ *a* ˌ*trilateral a*ˈ*greement.* ▷ **trilaterally** *adv.*

trilby /ˈtrɪlbɪ/ *n* man's soft felt hat with a narrow brim and the top part hollowed from front to back.

trilingual /ˌtraɪˈlɪŋgwəl/ *adj* speaking or using three languages.

trill /trɪl/ *n* **1** vibrating sound made by the voice or in bird song. **2** (*music*) (sound of) two notes a tone or a semitone apart being played or sung several times one after the other. **3** speech sound made by pronouncing 'r' while vibrating the tongue.

▷ **trill** *v* [I, Ip, Tn] **1** sound or sing (a musical note) with a trill: *The canary was trilling away in its cage.* **2** pronounce (a letter) with a trill.

trillion /ˈtrɪlɪən/ *n, pron, det* **1** (the number) 1 000 000 000 000; one million million ⇨ App 9. **2** (*Brit*) (formerly) (the number) 1 000 000 000 000 000 000; one million million million ⇨ App 9.

trilobite /ˈtraɪləbaɪt/ *n* extinct sea animal found as

a fossil.

trilogy /ˈtrɪlədʒɪ/ *n* group of three related works, esp three novels or operas.

trim[1] /trɪm/ *adj* (**-mmer**, **-mmest**) (*approv*) **1** in a good order; neat and tidy: *a trim ship* ○ *He keeps his garden trim.* **2** slim or elegant: *a trim waistline, figure, etc.* ▷ **trimly** *adv.* **trimness** *n* [U].

trim[2] /trɪm/ *v* (**-mm-**) **1** (**a**) [Tn, Tn·p] make (sth) neat or smooth by cutting away irregular parts: *trim the top of a hedge* ○ *trim one's beard (back).* (**b**) [Tn, Tn·pr, Tn·p] ~ **sth** (**off sth/off**) remove sth or reduce sth by cutting: *The article's too long. Can you trim it (by a quarter)?* ○ *Please trim the excess fat off (the meat).* ○ *I trimmed an inch off the hem of this skirt.* ○ *We had to trim a lot off our travel budget.* ⇨ Usage at CLIP[2]. **2** [Tn, Tn·pr] ~ **sth** (**with sth**) decorate or ornament sth: *trim a dress with lace* ○ *a hat trimmed with flowers.* **3** [Tn] make (a boat, a ship or an aircraft) evenly balanced by arranging the position of the cargo or passengers. **4** [Tn] set (sails) to suit the wind. **5** [Tn] (*dated infml*) (**a**) criticize (sb) sharply; rebuke. (**b**) hit (sb), esp as a punishment; beat; thrash.

▷ **trim** *n* **1** [C, usu sing] trimming of hair, etc: *The lawn needs a trim.* **2** [C, U] decorations or fittings for clothes, furniture, etc: *a yard of gold trim* ○ *The car is available with black or red trim,* ie upholstery, etc. **3** (idm) **be in/get into ˈtrim** be/get ready or fit: *in good, proper, excellent, etc trim* ○ *She's got a month to get into trim for the race.*

trimmer *n* person or thing that trims: *an electric hedge trimmer.*

trimming *n* **1** [U, C] material, eg lace or tinsel, used to decorate sth. **2 trimmings** [pl] (**a**) pieces cut off when sth is trimmed: *pastry trimmings.* (**b**) usual accompaniments of sth; extras: *roast turkey and all the trimmings,* ie vegetables, stuffing, sauces, etc.

trimaran /ˈtraɪməræn/ *n* boat built like a catamaran but with three parallel hulls instead of two.

trimester /traɪˈmestə(r), ˈtraɪmestə(r)/ *n* **1** period of three months. **2** (*US*) university term.

Trinidad and Tobago /ˌtrɪnɪdæd ən təˈbeɪgəʊ/ country in the Caribbean Sea, off the coast of Venezuela, consisting of the islands of Trinidad and Tobago; pop approx 1 243 000; official language English; capital Port of Spain; unit of currency dollar (= 100 cents). Formerly a British colony, it became an independent member of the Commonwealth in 1962. In 1990 there was an attempted coup there. Its main exports are petroleum products. ⇨ map at CARIBBEAN. ▷ **Trinidadian** /-ˈdeɪdɪən/ *adj, n.* **Tobagonian** /-ˈgəʊnɪən/ *adj, n.*

Trinitarian /ˌtrɪnɪˈteərɪən/ *n* person who believes in the doctrine of the Trinity. Cf UNITARIAN.

trinitrotoluene /ˌtraɪˌnaɪtrəʊˈtɒljʊiːn/ *n* [U] ⇨ TNT.

trinity /ˈtrɪnətɪ/ *n* **1** (*fml*) group of three things or people; trio. **2 the Trinity** (in Christianity) the union of Father, Son and Holy Spirit as one God.

□ ˌ**Trinity ˈSunday** Sunday after Whit Sunday.

ˌ**Trinity ˈterm** summer term at some British universities, colleges, etc.

Trinity House /ˌtrɪnətɪ ˈhaʊs/ organization responsible for providing lighthouses and buoys round the English and Welsh coast and licensing ships' pilots in the UK.

trinket /ˈtrɪŋkɪt/ *n* small ornament, piece of jewellery, etc of little value.

trio /ˈtriːəʊ/ *n* (*pl* ~**s**) **1** [CGp] group of three people or things. **2** [C, CGp] (*music*) (composition for a) group of three players or singers: *a piano trio,* eg for piano, violin and cello.

trip /trɪp/ *v* (**-pp-**) **1** (**a**) [I, Ipr, Ip] ~ (**over/up**) catch one's foot on sth and stumble or fall: *She tripped (over the cat) and fell.* ○ *Be careful you don't trip (up) on the mat.* ○ *I tripped over, dropping the tray I was carrying.* (**b**) [Tn, Tn·p] ~ **sb** (**up**) cause sb to do this: *He tried to trip me up.* **2** [I, Ipr, Ip] walk, run or dance with quick light steps: *She came tripping down the garden path.* ○ (*fig*) *a melody with a light tripping rhythm.* **3** [Tn] release (a switch or catch); operate (a mechanism) by doing this: *trip the shutter,* ie of a camera ○ *If anyone tampers with this door it trips the alarm.* **4** [I, Ip] ~ (**out**) (*dated sl*) have a trip(*n* 1). **5** (phr v) **trip** (**sb**) **up** (cause sb to) make a mistake, reveal a secret, etc: *The lawyer was trying to trip the witnesses up,* ie make them contradict themselves. ○ *I tripped up in the interview and said something rather silly.*

▷ **trip** *n* **1** (usu short) journey, esp for pleasure: *a trip to the seaside* ○ *during my last trip to London* ○ *a honeymoon trip to Venice.* ⇨ Usage at JOURNEY. **2** (*sl*) experience, esp one caused by taking a hallucinating drug: *an acid* (ie LSD) *trip* ○ *a good/bad trip.* **3** act of tripping (TRIP *v* 1) or being tripped; fall or stumble. **4** device for tripping (TRIP *v* 3) a mechanism.

tripper *n* person making a short journey for pleasure: *The beach was packed with day trippers.*

tripping *adj* [esp attrib] (of movements, rhythms, etc) quick and light. **trippingly** *adv.*

□ ˈ**trip-hammer** *n* very large hammer that is raised mechanically, used for shaping metal.

ˈ**trip-wire** *n* wire stretched close to the ground, which works a trap or warning device, etc when a person or an animal trips against it.

tripartite /ˌtraɪˈpɑːtaɪt/ *adj* [usu attrib] (*fml*) having three parts or involving three people, groups, etc: *a triˌpartite diˈvision* ○ *triˌpartite disˈcussions* ○ *a triˌpartite aˈgreement.*

tripe /traɪp/ *n* [U] **1** stomach of a cow, etc used as food: *boiled tripe and onions.* **2** (*sl*) (**a**) nonsense: *Don't talk tripe!* (**b**) writing, music, etc of low quality: *I don't read that tripe.*

triple /ˈtrɪpl/ *adj* [usu attrib] **1** having three parts or involving three people, groups, etc: *The plan has a triple purpose,* ie three purposes. ○ *triple time,* ie rhythm with three beats to the bar ○ *a triple alliance,* ie between three countries. **2** three times as much or as many: *travelling at triple the speed* ○ *a triple whisky,* ie a glass containing three times the usual quantity ○ *a triple murderer,* ie one who has killed three people.

▷ **triple** *v* [I, Tn] (cause sth to) become three times as much or as many: *Output has tripled.*

triply *adv.*

□ **the ˌTriple ˈCrown** (in Rugby Union) victory of any one of the home countries (England, Ireland, Scotland and Wales) against all the others in international matches in one season.

the ˈtriple jump athletic contest of jumping as far forward as possible with three leaps, the first two landing on alternate feet, the third on both feet.

triplet /ˈtrɪplɪt/ *n* **1** (usu *pl*) any of three children or animals born at one time: *His wife gave birth to triplets.* **2** set of three things. **3** (*music*) group of three equal notes to be performed in the time usually taken to perform two of the same kind.

triplicate /ˈtrɪplɪkət/ *n* (idm) **in triplicate** consisting of three identical copies, of which one is the original: *submit an application in triplicate.*

▷ **triplicate** /ˈtrɪplɪkeɪt/ *v* [Tn] copy (sth) so that there are three copies including the original.

tripod /ˈtraɪpɒd/ *n* support with three legs for a camera, telescope, etc.

tripos /ˈtraɪpɒs/ *n* (*Brit*) honours examination for the BA degree at Cambridge University.

tripper ⇨ TRIP.

triptych /ˈtrɪptɪk/ *n* picture or carving on three panels fixed side by side, esp one placed over an altar in a church.

trireme /ˈtraɪriːm/ *n* (in ancient Greece, Rome, etc) warship with three sets of rowers on each side.

trisect /traɪˈsekt/ *v* [Tn] divide (a line, an angle, etc) into three equal parts. ▷ **trisection** /traɪˈsekʃn/ *n* [U].

trite /traɪt/ *adj* (of a phrase, an opinion, etc) not new or original, because often used; hackneyed; commonplace.

tritium /ˈtrɪtɪəm/ *n* [U] (*symb* **T**) (*chemistry*) type of hydrogen that is three times heavier than ordinary hydrogen and is radioactive.

triumph /ˈtraɪʌmf/ *n* **1** [U] (joy or satisfaction at) being successful or victorious: *shouts of triumph* ○ *The winning team returned home in triumph.* **2** [C] great achievement or success: *one of the triumphs of modern science* ○ *She scored a resounding triumph over her rival.*

▷ **triumph** *v* [I, Ipr] ~ (**over sb/sth**) be successful or victorious: *Common sense triumphed in the end* ○ *triumph over one's difficulties,* ie overcome them.

triumphal /traɪˈʌmfl/ *adj* [usu attrib] **1** of or for a triumph: *a triumphal arch,* ie one built to honour a victory in war. **2** expressing triumph: *a triumphal chorus.*

triumphant /traɪˈʌmfnt/ *adj* (rejoicing at) having triumphed: *a triumphant cheer.* **triumphantly** *adv.*

triumvirate /traɪˈʌmvɪrət/ *n* ruling group of three people: *The company is run jointly by a triumvirate of directors.*

trivet /ˈtrɪvɪt/ *n* **1** metal stand, usu with three legs, for holding hot pans, etc, or formerly for kettles or pots placed over a fire. **2** (idm) **right as a trivet** ⇨ RIGHT[1].

trivia /ˈtrɪvɪə/ *n* [pl] (*usu derog*) unimportant things, details or pieces of information.

trivial /ˈtrɪvɪəl/ *adj* (*often derog*) that has little importance: *a trivial mistake, loss, offence* ○ *raise trivial objections to sth* ○ (*fml*) *a trivial young man* ie one who is only concerned with trivial things.

▷ **triviality** /ˌtrɪvɪˈælətɪ/ *n* (*derog*) **1** [U] state of being trivial. **2** [C] trivial thing: *waste time on trivialities.*

trivialize, -ise /ˈtrɪvɪəlaɪz/ *v* [Tn] (*derog*) make (a subject, problem, etc) seem trivial: *Too many films trivialize violence.* **trivialization, -isation** /ˌtrɪvɪəlaɪˈzeɪʃn; *US* -lɪˈz-/ *n* [U, C].

trivially /-ɪəlɪ/ *adv.*

trochee /ˈtrəʊkiː/ *n* metrical foot in poetry consisting of one long or stressed syllable followed by one short or unstressed syllable.

▷ **trochaic** /trəʊˈkeɪɪk/ *adj* consisting of trochees: *trochaic metre.*

trod *pt* of TREAD.

trodden *pp* of TREAD.

troglodyte /ˈtrɒglədaɪt/ *n* person living in a cave, esp in prehistoric times.

troika /ˈtrɔɪkə/ *n* **1** small Russian carriage pulled by three horses. **2** group of three people working together, esp as political leaders of a country.

Trojan /ˈtrəʊdʒən/ *n, adj* **1** (inhabitant) of *Troy: *the Trojan war,* ie between the Greeks and the Trojans, as described by *Homer. **2** (idm) **work like a ˈblack/ˈTrojan** ⇨ BLACK[2].

□ ˌ**Trojan ˈhorse 1** (in Greek legend) hollow wooden horse used by the Greeks (who hid warriors inside it) to enter and attack Troy. **2** (*fig*) person or thing used to harm an enemy or opponent, who wrongly believes he is being helped.

troll[1] /trəʊl/ *v* [I, Ipr] ~ (**for sth**) fish with a rod and line by pulling bait through the water behind a boat: *trolling for pike.*

troll[2] /trəʊl/ *n* (in Scandinavian mythology) evil giant or mischievous but friendly dwarf.

trolley

trolley /ˈtrɒlɪ/ *n* (*pl* ~**s**) **1** cart on wheels that can be pushed or pulled along and is used for moving goods: *a ˈluggage trolley* ○ *a ˈshopping trolley,* eg in a supermarket. **2** small table on wheels for transporting or serving food, etc: *a ˈtea-trolley.* ⇨ illus at FURNITURE. **3** small low truck running on rails, used eg by workmen repairing tracks. **4** (also ˈ**trolley-wheel**) small wheel or other device making contact between an electrically powered vehicle and an overhead cable. **5** (*US*) = TRAM.

□ ˈ**trolley bus** *n* bus powered by electricity from an overhead cable.

trollop /ˈtrɒləp/ *n* (*dated derog*) untidy or sexually immoral woman; slut.

Trollope /ˈtrɒləp/ Anthony (1815-82), English novelist, best known for two groups of novels: one set in the imaginary county of Barsetshire and telling of the lives of the local gentry, clergy, etc (eg *The Warden, Barchester Towers, Doctor Thorne*); and the other dealing with the social and political world of London (eg *Phineas Finn, The Eustace Diamonds, The Prime Minister*), often known as the 'Palliser' novels. He was an employee of the Post Office, and invented the pillar-box.

trombone /trɒmˈbəʊn/ *n* large brass musical instrument with a sliding tube used to raise or lower the note. ⇨ illus at MUSIC.

▷ **trombonist** /trɒmˈbəʊnɪst/ *n* person who plays a trombone.

trompe l'oeil /ˌtrɒmp ˈlɔɪ/ *n* (*French*) painting, etc in which objects are represented in such a way that the person looking at them is tricked into thinking that they are real.

troop /tru:p/ *n* **1** [C] large group of people or animals, esp when moving: *a troop of schoolchildren* ○ *troops of deer*. **2 troops** [pl] soldiers: *demand the withdrawal of foreign troops*. **3** [C] unit of armoured vehicles or artillery or cavalry. **4** [C] local group of Scouts.

▷ **troop** *v* **1** [I, Ipr, Ip] (with a *pl* subject) come or go together as a troop or in large numbers: *children trooping out of school*. **2** (idm) ˌ**trooping the** ˈ**colour** (*Brit*) ceremony of carrying a regiment's flag along ranks of soldiers, esp on the birthday of the monarch.

trooper *n* **1** soldier in an armoured unit or a cavalry unit. **2** (*US*) member of a State police force. **3** (idm) **swear like a trooper** ⇨ SWEAR.

□ ˈ**troop carrier** large aircraft, vehicle or ship for transporting soldiers.

ˈ**troop-ship** *n* ship for transporting soldiers.

trope /trəʊp/ *n* (*fml*) figurative use of a word or phrase.

trophic /ˈtrəʊfɪk/ *adj* of nutrition or growth: *trophic levels*, ie different stages of a food-chain.

trophy /ˈtrəʊfɪ/ *n* **1** object awarded as a prize, esp for winning a sports tournament: *the Wimbledon* ˈ*tennis trophy*. **2** object taken or kept as a souvenir of success in hunting, war, etc: *a set of antlers and other trophies*.

tropic /ˈtrɒpɪk/ *n* **1** [C usu *sing*] line of latitude 23° 27′ north (*the tropic of Cancer*) or south (*the tropic of Capricorn*) of the equator. ⇨ illus at GLOBE. **2 the tropics** [pl] region between these two latitudes, with a hot climate.

▷ **tropical** /-kl/ *adj* of, like or found in the tropics: *tropical fruit* ○ *a tropical climate* ○ *He keeps tropical fish in an aquarium*. ○ *August was almost tropical* (ie very hot) *this year*. **tropically** /-klɪ/ *adv*.

tropism /ˈtrəʊpɪzəm/ *n* [U] (*biology*) growth of a plant organ as directed by an external stimulus (eg light or gravity).

troposphere /ˈtrɒpəsfɪə(r); *US* ˈtrəʊp-/ *n* [sing] (usu **the troposphere**) layer of the atmosphere that extends about seven miles upwards from the earth's surface.

Trot /trɒt/ *n* (*sl usu derog*) Trotskyist.

trot /trɒt/ *v* (**-tt-**) **1** (**a**) [I, Ipr, Ip] (of a horse or its rider) move at a pace faster than a walk but slower than a gallop. (**b**) [Tn, Tn·pr, Tn·p] ride (a horse) at such a pace. **2** [I, Ipr, Ip] (**a**) (of a person) run with short steps: *The child was trotting along beside its parents*. (**b**) (*infml*) walk or go (usu at a normal pace): *I'm just trotting round to the pub*. ⇨ Usage at RUN¹. **3** (phr v) **trot sth out** (*infml derog*) produce (esp information, explanations, etc often given before) for sb to hear or see: *He always trots out the same old excuses for being late*.

▷ **trot** *n* **1** [sing] trotting pace: *go at a steady trot*. **2** [C] period of trotting: *go for a trot*. **3 the trots** [pl] (*sl*) diarrhoea: *get the trots*. **4** (idm) **on the** ˈ**trot** (*infml*) (**a**) one after the other: *for eight hours on the trot*. (**b**) continually busy: *I've been on the trot all day*. ○ *Her new job certainly keeps her on the trot*.

trotter *n* **1** horse bred and trained for trotting-races. **2** (usu *pl*) pig's or sheep's foot, esp as food.

trotting *n* [U] sport of racing horses that pull small two-wheeled vehicles.

troth /trəʊθ; *US* trɔ:θ/ *n* (*arch*) (idm) **plight one's troth** ⇨ PLIGHT².

Trotsky /ˈtrɒtskɪ/ Leon, original name Lev Davidovich Bronstein (1879-1940), Russian revolutionary leader, *Lenin's main assistant and commissar of foreign affairs and war 1917-24. He organized the Red Army in the Russian Civil War. After Lenin's death he came into conflict with *Stalin, and in 1929 was forced to leave Russia. He was murdered in Mexico by one of Stalin's agents.

▷ **Trotskyism** /-skɪɪzəm/ *n* [U] political or economic ideas of Leon Trotsky, esp the principle of world-wide socialist revolution. **Trotskyist** /ˈtrɒtskɪɪst/ (also **Trotskyite**) *n, adj* (supporter) of Trotskyism.

troubadour /ˈtru:bədɔ:(r); *US* -dʊər/ *n* French travelling poet and singer in the 11th-13th centuries.

trouble /ˈtrʌbl/ *n* **1** [C, U] (situation causing) worry, pain, difficulty, danger, etc: *We're having trouble with our new car*. ○ *My teeth are giving* (ie causing) *me trouble*. ○ *If we're late, there'll be/it'll mean trouble*, ie unpleasantness, perhaps involving punishment. ○ *family trouble(s)*, eg disagreements between parents and children ○ *Our troubles are not over yet*. ○ *The idea soon ran into trouble*. ○ *The trouble* (ie problem) *(with you) is...* ○ *What's the trouble?* ie What's wrong? **2** (**a**) [U] ~ (**to sb**) inconvenience; bother: *I don't want to be any trouble (to you)*. ○ *Were the children much trouble?* ○ *I can come back tomorrow, it's no trouble*. ○ *Repairing it is more trouble than it's worth*. ○ *I'm sorry to have to put you to so much trouble*. (**b**) [sing] (*fml*) thing that causes inconvenience or difficulty: *This dish is delicious but rather a trouble to prepare*. ○ *I find getting up early a great trouble*. **3** (**a**) [C, U] disputes, fighting, etc; unrest: *the recent trouble(s) in South Africa* ○ *The firm's been hit by a lot of labour trouble*, eg strikes. (**b**) **the Troubles** [pl] political violence in Ireland in the 1920s or in N Ireland from 1968. **4** [U] (**a**) illness: *stomach, heart, liver, etc trouble* ○ *a history of mental trouble*. (**b**) faulty operation, eg of a machine or vehicle: *My car's got engine trouble*. **5** (idm) **ask for trouble/it** ⇨ ASK. ˌ**get into** ˈ**trouble** cause trouble for oneself, eg by making a mistake: *Even an experienced climber can get into trouble*. ○ *He got into trouble with the police*, eg was arrested. **get sb into** ˈ**trouble** (**a**) cause trouble for sb: *Don't mention my name or you'll get me into trouble*. (**b**) (*infml*) make (an unmarried woman) pregnant: *He got his girl-friend into trouble*. **give (sb) (some, no, any, etc)** ˈ**trouble** cause trouble: *The new computer's been giving (us) a lot of trouble*, ie not working properly. **go to a lot of, considerable, etc trouble (to do sth)** do sth even though it involves effort, inconvenience, etc: *Thank you for going to so much trouble to find what I was looking for*. **in trouble** (**a**) in a situation that involves danger, punishment, pain, worry, etc: *If we can't keep to the schedule, we'll be in (a lot of) trouble*. ○ *I'm in trouble with the police over drugs*. (**b**) (*infml*) (of an unmarried woman) pregnant. ˈ**look for trouble** (*infml*) behave in a way that suggests that one is hoping for unpleasantness, a violent reaction, etc: *drunken youths roaming the streets looking for trouble*. **make trouble (for sb)** (eg of an enemy) cause trouble: *If I say no, the boss will only make trouble for me*. **take trouble over sth/with sth/to do sth/doing sth** use much care and effort in doing sth: *They took a lot of trouble to find the right person for the job*. **take the trouble to do sth** do sth even though it involves effort or difficulty: *Decent journalists should take the trouble to check their facts*.

▷ **trouble** *v* **1** [Tn] cause worry, pain or inconvenience to (sb); bother: *be troubled by illness, doubt, bad news* ○ *My back's been troubling me*. ○ *a troubled look* ○ *What troubles me is that...* ○ *I'm sorry to trouble you, but....* **2** [Tn·pr, Cn·t] ~ **sb for sth** (**a**) (*fml*) (used with *may* or *might* in polite requests): *May I trouble you for the salt?* ○ *Might I trouble you to give me a lift to the station?* (**b**) (*dated*) (used with *I'll* or *I must* in ironic or sarcastic requests): *I'll trouble you to watch your manners*. **3** [I, Ipr, It] ~ (**about sth**) (*fml*) (used esp in questions and negative sentences) let oneself be worried or concerned about sth: *'Do you want me to post it for you?' 'No, don't trouble (about it), thank you.'* ○ *Why should I trouble to explain it all?* **4** (idm) **fish in troubled waters** ⇨ FISH². **pour oil on troubled waters** ⇨ POUR.

ˈ**troublesome** /-səm/ *adj* giving trouble; causing annoyance, pain, etc: *a troublesome child, problem, headache* ○ *My cough is rather troublesome today*.

□ ˈ**trouble-maker** *n* person who often causes trouble, esp by upsetting others.

ˈ**trouble-shooter** *n* person who helps to settle disputes (eg in industrial relations), or who traces and corrects faults in machinery, etc.

ˈ**trouble-spot** *n* place where trouble frequently occurs, esp a country where there is a war: *the world's major trouble-spots*.

trough /trɒf; *US* trɔ:f/ *n* **1** long narrow open box for animals to feed or drink from. ⇨ illus at PIG. **2** shallow channel that allows water, etc to drain away. **3** low area between two waves or ridges. ⇨ illus at SURF. **4** (in meteorology) long narrow region of low atmospheric pressure between two regions of higher pressure. Cf RIDGE 3.

trounce /traʊns/ *v* [Tn] **1** defeat (sb) heavily: *Wales were trounced 5-0 by Poland*. **2** (*dated*) punish (sb) severely; thrash.

troupe /tru:p/ *n* [CGp] group of performing artists, esp those of a circus or ballet: *a* ˈ*dance troupe*.

▷ **trouper** *n* **1** (*dated*) member of a theatrical troupe. **2** (*infml approv*) loyal dependable person: *Thanks for helping, you're a real trouper*.

trousers /ˈtraʊzəz/ *n* [pl] **1** outer garment covering both legs and reaching from the waist to the ankles: *a pair of grey trousers*. **2** (idm) **catch sb with his pants/trousers down** ⇨ CATCH¹. **wear the pants/trousers** ⇨ WEAR².

▷ **trouser** *adj* [attrib] of or for trousers: *trouser buttons, legs, pockets* ○ *a trouser press*.

ˈ**trouser-suit** *n* woman's suit of jacket and trousers.

trousseau /ˈtru:səʊ/ *n* (*pl* ~**s** or ~**x** /-səʊz/) (esp formerly) clothes and other possessions, collected by a bride to begin married life with.

trout /traʊt/ *n* (*pl* unchanged) **1** (**a**) [C] any of various types of freshwater fish that are good to eat and fished for by anglers. (**b**) [U] flesh of such fish as food: *a piece of smoked trout*. **2** (idm) **an old trout** ⇨ OLD.

trowel /ˈtraʊəl/ *n* **1** small tool with a flat blade, used for spreading mortar on bricks or stone, plaster on walls, etc. **2** small gardening tool with a curved blade for lifting plants, digging holes, etc. **3** (idm) **lay it on thick/with a trowel** ⇨ THICK *adv*.

Troy /trɔɪ/ ancient city in Asia Minor, near the *Dardanelles. *Homer's **Iliad* tells the story of how the Greeks besieged it for ten years. Finally they defeated it by hiding soldiers in a large wooden horse, which the inhabitants of the city pulled inside its walls. The legend probably reflects real events of the 13th century BC. Cf TROJAN.

troy weight /ˈtrɔɪ weɪt/ British system of weights used for gold, silver and jewels, in which 1 pound = 12 ounces or 5 760 grains.

truant /ˈtru:ənt/ *n* **1** child who stays away from school without permission. **2** person who avoids doing his work or duty; idler. **3** (idm) **play** ˈ**truant** (*US* **play** ˈ**hooky** /ˈhʊkɪ/) stay away from school as a truant.

▷ **truancy** /-ənsɪ/ *n* [C, U] (instance of) playing truant.

truce /tru:s/ *n* (**a**) agreement between enemies or

opponents to stop fighting for a certain time: *declare/negotiate/break a truce.* **(b)** time that such an agreement lasts: *a three-day truce.*

truck[1] /trʌk/ *n* **1** (*Brit*) open railway wagon for carrying goods. **2** (*esp US*) = LORRY. **3** vehicle for carrying goods that is pushed or pulled by hand; handcart or barrow.

▷ **truck** *v* **1** [Tn, Tn·pr] transport (goods, etc) in a truck. **2** [I] (*US*) work as a trucker. **trucker** *n* (*esp US*) person whose job is driving a lorry, esp over long distances. **trucking** *n* [U] (*US*) business or process of carrying goods by road.

truck[2] /trʌk/ *n* [U] **1** (*US*) fresh vegetables, fruit, etc grown for the market. **2** (idm) **have no truck with sb/sth** refuse to deal or associate with sb; refuse to tolerate or consider sth: *I'll have no truck with extremists/extremism.*

□ ˈ**truck farm** (*US*) = MARKET GARDEN (MARKET[1]). ˈ**truck farmer**, ˈ**truck farming**.

truckle /ˈtrʌkl/ *v* (phr v) **truckle to sb** accept sb's orders or authority in a timid or cowardly way: *refusing to truckle to bullies.*

truckle-bed /ˈtrʌkl bed/ (*US* ˈ**trundle-bed**) *n* low bed on wheels that can be pushed under another when not being used.

truculent /ˈtrʌkjʊlənt/ *adj* (*derog*) defiant and aggressive: *truculent behaviour* ○ *He became very truculent and started arguing with me angrily.* ▷ **truculence** /-ləns/ *n* [U]. **truculently** *adv.*

trudge /trʌdʒ/ *v* [I, Ipr, Ip, In/pr] walk slowly or with difficulty because one is tired, on a long journey, etc: *trudging (along) through the deep snow* ○ *He trudged 20 miles.* ⇨ Usage at STUMP.

▷ **trudge** *n* (usu *sing*) long tiring walk.

true /tru:/ *adj* (**-r**, **-st**) **1** corresponding to known facts: *Is it true you're getting married?* ○ *a true story* ○ *The food is good and the same is true of the service,* ie that is good too. ○ *'We've always found somewhere to stay here before.' 'True, but we may not always be so lucky.'* ○ *Unfortunately what you say is only too true.* **2** [esp attrib] **(a)** agreeing with correct principles or accepted standards: *a true judgement, assessment, analysis, etc.* **(b)** rightly called what one/it is called; genuine: *true love* ○ *The frog is not a true reptile.* ○ *claimed to be the true heir.* **3** [esp attrib] exact; accurate: *a true copy of a document* ○ *a true pair of scales.* **4** [esp pred] fitted or placed in its proper (esp upright) position: *Is the wheel true?* ○ *Make sure the post is true before the concrete sets.* **5** ~ (**to sth**) loyal; faithful: *a true patriot* ○ *remain true to one's principles* ○ *be true to one's word/promise,* ie do as one has promised. **6** (idm) **come** ˈ**true** (of a hope, prediction, etc) really happen; become fact: *It's like a dream come* (ie that has come) *true.* **one's true** ˈ**colours** (*often derog*) one's true character; what one is really like: *Once he achieved power he showed (himself in) his true colours.* **true to sth** being or acting as one would expect from sth: *True to form* (ie As usual), *he arrived late.* ○ *The film is very true to life,* ie realistic. ○ *Plants grown from seed are not always true to type,* ie exactly like the plant that gave the seed.

▷ **true** *adv* **1** truly: *She spoke truer than she knew.* **2** accurately: *The arrow flew straight and true to its mark.*

true *n* (idm) ˌ**out of** ˈ**true** not in its proper or accurate position: *The door is out of true.*

□ ˌ**true** ˈ**bill** (*US law*) official statement by a grand jury (GRAND) that an accused person should be tried.

ˌ**true-**ˈ**blue** *n, adj* (person who is) completely faithful and loyal, esp to traditional principles: *a true-blue Tory of the old school.*

ˌ**true-**ˈ**hearted** *adj* loyal.

ˌ**true-**ˈ**life** *adj* [attrib] that really happened: *a* ˌ*true-life ad*ˈ*venture.*

ˈ**true-love** *n* person who loves or is loved genuinely and deeply; sweetheart.

ˌ**true** ˈ**north** north according to the earth's axis, not magnetic north.

Truffaut /ˈtru:fəʊ/ François (1932-84), French film director. Though he was a caustic cinema critic, his own work is full of humanity, literary tributes and humour, as in the series beginning with *les Quatre Cents Coups.* Tragedy is also evident in films like *Jules et Jim.*

truffle /ˈtrʌfl/ *n* **1** type of edible fungus that grows underground and is enjoyed for its rich flavour. **2** soft sweet made of a chocolate mixture.

trug /trʌg/ *n* shallow basket used by gardeners to carry tools, plants, etc.

truism /ˈtru:ɪzəm/ *n* statement that is obviously true, esp one that does not say anything important, eg *Nothing lasts for ever.*

truly /ˈtru:lɪ/ *adv* **1** truthfully: *Tell me truly what you think.* **2** sincerely: *I'm truly grateful.* **3** genuinely; really: *a truly generous act* ○ *Her last novel was truly awful.* **4** (idm) **well and truly** ⇨ WELL[3]. ⇨ Usage at YOUR.

trump[1] /trʌmp/ *n* **1** (in card-games such as whist or bridge) card of a suit that temporarily has a higher value than the other three suits: *Hearts are trumps.* ○ *He took my ace with a low trump.* ○ *We played the game in no trumps,* ie with no suit chosen as trumps. **2** (*infml dated*) person who is generous, loyal, helpful, etc. **3** (idm) ˌ**come**/ˌ**turn up** ˈ**trumps** (*infml*) **(a)** be especially helpful or generous: *Nobody else in the family gave anything for the jumble sale, but my sister came up trumps.* **(b)** do or happen better than expected: *The team turned up trumps on the day.* **declare trumps** ⇨ DECLARE. **draw trumps** ⇨ DRAW[2].

▷ **trump** *v* **1** [Tn, Tn·pr] ~ **sth** (**with sth**) take (a card or trick) with a trump: *trumped my ace (with a six).* **2** (phr v) **trump sth up** (usu passive) invent (a false excuse, accusation, etc) in order to harm sb: *arrested on a trumped-up charge.*

□ ˈ**trump-card** *n* **(a)** card of the suit that is trumps. **(b)** (*fig*) way of gaining what one wants, esp after trying other ways; most valuable resource: *Finally she played her trump-card and threatened to resign.*

trump[2] /trʌmp/ *n* (*arch*) sound made by a trumpet.

trumpery /ˈtrʌmpərɪ/ *adj* [attrib] (*dated derog*) showy but of little value: *trumpery ornaments.*

trumpet /ˈtrʌmpɪt/ *n* **1** brass musical instrument with a bright ringing tone: *hear a distant trumpet,* ie its sound. ⇨ illus at MUSIC. **2** thing shaped like a trumpet, esp the open flower of a daffodil. ⇨ illus at PLANT. **3** (idm) **blow one's own trumpet** ⇨ BLOW[1].

▷ **trumpet** *v* **1** [I, Tn] proclaim (sth) loudly and forcibly: *He's always trumpeting his own opinions.* **2** [I] (of an elephant) make a loud blaring noise like a trumpet. **trumpeter** *n* person who plays a trumpet, esp a cavalry soldier giving signals: *Trumpeter, sound the charge!*

□ ˌ**trumpet-**ˈ**major** *n* chief trumpeter in a cavalry regiment.

truncate /trʌŋˈkeɪt; *US* ˈtrʌŋkeɪt/ *v* [Tn esp passive] shorten (sth) by cutting off the top or end: *a truncated cone, pyramid, etc* ○ *They published her article in truncated form.*

truncheon /ˈtrʌntʃən/ (also **baton**) *n* short thick stick carried as a weapon, esp by police officers.

trundle /ˈtrʌndl/ *v* [I, Ipr, Ip, Tn, Tn·pr, Tn·p] (cause sth to) roll or move heavily: *A goods train trundled past.* ○ *trundling a wheelbarrow down the path.*

□ ˈ**trundle-bed** *n* (*US*) = TRUCKLE-BED (TRUCKLE).

trunk /trʌŋk/ *n* **1** [C] main stem of a tree, from which the branches grow. ⇨ illus at TREE. **2** [C usu *sing*] body apart from the head, arms and legs. ⇨ illus at HUMAN. Cf TORSO. **3** [C] large box with a hinged lid for storing or transporting clothes or other items. ⇨ illus at LUGGAGE. **4** [C] long nose of an elephant. ⇨ illus at ELEPHANT. **5 trunks** [pl] shorts worn by men or boys for swimming, boxing, etc. **6** [C] (*US*) boot of a car. ⇨ illus at CAR.

□ ˈ**trunk-call** *n* (*Brit dated*) (*US* **long-**ˈ**distance call**) telephone call to a distant place in the same country.

ˈ**trunk-road** *n* important main road. ⇨ article at ROAD.

truss /trʌs/ *n* **1** padded belt worn by a person suffering from a hernia. **2** framework supporting a roof, bridge, etc. ⇨ illus at BRIDGE. **3** (*Brit*) bundle of hay or straw.

▷ **truss** *v* **1** [Tn, Tn·pr, Tn·p] ~ **sth/sb** (**up**) (**with sth**) tie or bind sth/sb securely: *truss a chicken,* ie fasten its legs and wings securely before cooking ○ *The thieves had trussed the guard up with rope.* **2** [Tn esp passive] support (a roof, bridge, etc) with trusses (TRUSS 2).

trust[1] /trʌst/ *n* **1** [U] ~ (**in sb/sth**) belief or willingness to believe that one can rely on the goodness, strength, ability, etc of sb/sth: *A good marriage is based on trust.* ○ *I have absolute trust in the (skill of) doctors.* ○ *I put my trust in you.* ○ *You've betrayed my trust,* eg told a secret or not kept a promise. **2** [U] responsibility: *a position of great trust.* **3** (*law*) **(a)** [C] money or property given to a person or people (*trustees*) who must take care of it and use it for another person's benefit or for a specified purpose: *In his will he created trusts for his children.* ○ *The project is financed by a charitable trust.* **(b)** [U] responsibility assumed by trustees; trusteeship. **4** [C] association of business firms formed to reduce competition, control prices, etc: *anti-trust laws.* **5** [C] organization founded to encourage or preserve sth, eg historic buildings or cultural activities: *a wildfowl trust.* **6** (idm) **in trust** kept as a trust[1](3a): *The money is being held in trust for him until he is twenty-one.* **on trust** **(a)** without proof or investigation: *You'll just have to take what I say on trust.* **(b)** on credit: *supply goods on trust.*

▷ **trustful** /-fl/, **trusting** *adjs* showing trust; not suspicious. **trustfully** /-fəlɪ/, **trustingly** *advs.* **trustfulness** *n* [U].

ˈ**trustworthy** *adj* worthy of trust; reliable. ˈ**trustworthiness** *n* [U].

trusty *adj* (**-ier**, **-iest**) (*arch or joc*) trustworthy: *mounted his trusty steed* ○ *my trusty old bicycle.* — *n* prisoner who is given special privileges or responsibilities because of good behaviour.

□ ˈ**trust company** (*esp US*) firm that manages trusts, investments, etc.

ˈ**trust fund** money that is held in trust for sb: *set up a trust fund.*

trust[2] /trʌst/ *v* **1** [Tn] have or place trust[1](1) in (sb/sth); treat (sb/sth) as reliable: *They're not to be trusted/not people I would trust.* ○ *I trust you implicitly.* ○ *You can't trust what the papers say.* **2** [Tn·pr, Cn·t] depend on (sb) to do sth, use sth, look after sth, etc properly or safely: *I can't trust that boy out of my sight.* ○ *I'd trust him with my life.* ○ *Can I trust you to post this letter?* ○ (*ironic*) *Trust you* (ie It is typical of you) *to forget my birthday!* **3** [It, Tf] (*fml*) hope: *We trust to receive a cheque at your earliest convenience.* ○ *I trust (that) she's not seriously ill.* ○ *You've no objection, I trust.* **4** (phr v) **trust in sb/sth** have confidence in sb/sth: *trust in providence* ○ *You must trust in your own judgement.* **trust to sth** leave the result or progress of events to be decided by (chance, etc): *trust to luck, fate, fortune, etc* ○ *At such times you have to trust to instinct.*

trustee /trʌˈsti:/ *n* **1** person who is responsible for managing a trust[1](3a). **2** member of a group of people managing the business affairs of an institution.

▷ **trusteeship** /-ʃɪp/ *n* **1** [U, C] position of a trustee. **2** [U] responsibility for the administration of a territory granted to a country by the United Nations Organization.

truth /tru:θ/ *n* (*pl* ~**s** /tru:ðz/) **1** [U] quality or state of being true: *There's no truth/not a word of truth in what he says.* **2** **(a)** [U] that which is true: *the whole truth* ○ *the search for (the) truth* ○ *tell the truth,* ie speak truthfully, not lie ○ *We found out the truth about him.* ○ *The (plain) truth is, I forgot about it.* **(b)** [C] fact, belief, etc that is accepted as true: *one of the fundamental truths of modern science.* **3** (idm) **a home truth** ⇨ HOME[1]. **in truth** (*fml*) truly; really: *It was in truth a miracle.* **the moment of truth** ⇨ MOMENT. **the naked truth** ⇨ NAKED. **to tell the truth** ⇨ TELL.

▷ **truthful** /-fl/ *adj* **1** (of a person) honest in what he says; never lying. **2** (of statements) true. **truthfully** /-fəlɪ/ *adv.* **truthfulness** *n* [U].

try[1] /traɪ/ *v* (*pt, pp* **tried**) **1** [I, It] (In informal use, *try to* + infinitive is often replaced by *try and* + infinitive, esp in the imperative, and *don't/didn't* *try to* by *don't/didn't try and*.) make an attempt: *I don't know if I can come, but I'll try.* ○ *I tried till I was tired.* ○ *Try to/and be here on time.* ○ *He's trying his best/hardest/utmost*, ie as much as he can. ○ *I tried hard not to laugh.* ○ *You haven't even tried to lift it.* ○ *Don't try to/and swim across the river.* ⇨ Usage at AND. **2** [Tn, Tn·pr, Tg] use, do or test (sth) to see whether it is satisfactory, effective, enjoyable, etc: *I've tried this new detergent with excellent results.* ○ *'Would you like to try some raw fish?' 'Why not, I'll try anything once.'* ○ *Have you ever tried windsurfing?* ○ *Try that door*, ie Try opening it to see if it is locked or to find what is on the other side. ○ *Don't try any funny stuff with me!* ○ *Let's try the table in a different position.* ○ *I think we should try her for the job.* ○ *Try phoning his home number.* **3 (a)** [Tn esp passive] examine and decide (a case) in a lawcourt: *The case was tried before a jury.* **(b)** [Tn, Tn·pr] ~ **sb (for sth)** hold a trial of (sb): *He was tried for murder.* **4** [Tn] be very tiring or difficult to bear for (sb/sth); be a strain on (sb/sth): *Small print tries the eyes.* ○ *Don't try my patience!* ○ *His courage was severely tried by his ordeal.* **5** (idm) **do/try one's damnedest** ⇨ DAMNEDEST (DAMNED). **try one's hand (at sth)** attempt (eg a skill or sport) for the first time: *I'd like to try my hand at computing.* **try one's luck (at sth)** try to do or get sth, hoping to succeed: *I think I'll try my luck at roulette.* **6** (phr v) **try for sth** make an attempt to get or win sth: *try for a scholarship, an Olympic medal, a job in the Civil Service.* **try sth on (a)** put on (clothing, etc) to see if it fits and how it looks: *Try on the shoes before you buy them.* **(b)** (*infml*) do sth (eg ask too high a price for sth or behave badly) that one expects not to be allowed to do, while hoping that sb will not object: *Don't try anything on with me, kid, or you'll be sorry.* **try out (for sth)** (*US*) take a test, a trial, an audition, etc: *You won't make the team if you don't try out.* ○ *She's trying out for the part of Cleopatra.* **try sb/sth out (on sb)** test sb/sth by using him/it: *try out a young quarter-back* ○ *The drug has not been tried out on humans yet.*

▷ **tried** *adj* [attrib] that has been proved to be effective, reliable, etc: *a tried (and tested) remedy* ○ *a tried and true friend.*

trier *n* person who tries hard and always does his best: *He's not very good but he's a real trier.*

trying *adj* that strains one's temper or patience; annoying: *a trying person to deal with* ○ *have a trying day.*

□ ˈ**try-on** *n* (*infml*) doing sth that one does not expect to be allowed to do, while hoping sb will not object.

ˈ**try-out** *n* test of the qualities or performance of a person or thing: *give sb/sth a try-out.*

try[2] /traɪ/ *n* **1** ~ **(at sth/doing sth)** attempt: *I'll give it a try/It's worth a try.* ○ *He had three tries at mending the lock and gave up.* **2** (in Rugby football) action by a player of touching down the ball behind the opponents' goal-line, which also entitles his side to a kick at goal. Cf CONVERT[1] 3.

trypanosome /trɪˈpænəsəʊm/ *n* microscopic parasite that lives in the blood and causes sleeping sickness (SLEEP[2]).

tsar (also **tzar, czar**) /zɑ:(r)/ *n* (title of the) emperor of Russia (before 1917).

▷ **tsarina** (also **tzarina, czarina**) /zɑ:ˈri:nə/ *n* (title of the) empress of Russia or of the wife of the tsar.

tsetse /ˈtsetsɪ/ *n* (also ˈ**tsetse fly**) tropical African fly that carries and transmits disease, esp sleeping sickness, to men and animals by its bite.

T-shirt ⇨ T, T.

tsp (*pl* **tsps**) *abbr* teaspoonful: *Add 2 tsps sugar.*

T-square ⇨ SQUARE[2] 5.

tsunami /tsʊˈnɑ:mɪ/ *n* very large wave caused by an undersea earthquake, volcanic eruption, etc.

TT /ˌti: ˈti:/ *abbr* **1** teetotal(ler). **2** (*Brit*) Tourist Trophy: *the TT motor cycle races on the Isle of Man.* **3** (of milk) tuberculin-tested.

Tuareg /ˈtwɑ:reg/ *n* member of a nomadic people of N Africa.

tub /tʌb/ *n* **1 (a)** (often in compounds) open flat-bottomed (usu round) container used for washing clothes, holding liquids, growing plants, etc: *wash-tubs* ○ *wooden plant-tubs.* ⇨ illus at BUCKET. **(b)** similar small container of plastic, etc used for food, etc: *a tub of ice-cream, cottage cheese, margarine, etc.* **(c)** (also **tub·ful** /-fʊl/) amount held by a tub. **2 (a)** = BATH-TUB (BATH). **(b)** = BATH 1: *have a cold tub before breakfast.* **3** (*infml esp joc*) slow clumsy boat: *a leaky old tub.*

□ ˈ**tub-thumper** *n* (*infml derog*) public speaker with a loud violent or ranting manner. ˈ**tub-thumping** *n, adj.*

tuba /ˈtju:bə; *US* ˈtu:-/ *n* long brass musical instrument of low pitch. ⇨ illus at MUSIC.

tubby /ˈtʌbɪ/ *adj* (**-ier, -iest**) (*infml*) short and fat: *a tubby little man.* ⇨ Usage at FAT[1].

tube /tju:b; *US* tu:b/ *n* **1** [C] long hollow cylinder of metal, glass, rubber, etc for holding or conveying liquids, gases, etc: *laboratory test-tubes* ○ *an inner tube*, eg of a bicycle or car tyre ○ *Blood flowed along the tube into the bottle.* **2** [C] ~ **(of sth)** container made of thin flexible metal or plastic with a screw cap, used for holding pastes, etc ready for use: *tubes of glue, mayonnaise* ○ *squeeze toothpaste from/out of a tube.* **3 the tube** (also **the underground**) [U, sing] (*Brit infml*) the underground railway system in London: *travel to work by tube/on the tube* ○ *take a/the tube to Victoria* ○ [attrib] *tube trains, tickets, etc.* Cf SUBWAY. ⇨ article at RAILWAY. **4 (a)** [C] = CATHODE RAY TUBE (CATHODE). **(b) the tube** [sing] (*infml esp US*) television. **5** [C usu *pl*] hollow tube-shaped organ in the body: *bronchial, Fallopian, Eustachian tubes.* **6** (idm) **(go) down the** ˈ**tube(s)** (*sl esp US*) = (GO) DOWN THE DRAIN (DRAIN[1]). Cf UP THE SPOUT (SPOUT).

▷ **tubeless** *adj* [usu attrib] (of a tyre) having no inner tube.

tubing *n* [U] length of tube; tubes: *two metres of copper, plastic, etc tubing.*

tubular /ˈtju:bjʊlə(r); *US* ˈtu:-/ *adj* **1** tube-shaped: *a tubular container.* **2** having or consisting of tubes; made of tube-shaped pieces: *tubular scaffolding* ○ *tubular furniture.*

tuber /ˈtju:bə(r); *US* ˈtu:-/ *n* short thick rounded part of an underground stem (eg of a potato) or root (eg of a dahlia) which stores food and produces buds from which new plants will grow.

▷ **tuberous** /ˈtju:bərəs; *US* ˈtu:-/ *adj* **1** of or like a tuber. **2** having or producing tubers.

tuberculin /tjʊˈbɜ:kjʊlɪn/ *n* [U] liquid made from tuberculosis bacilli and used for diagnosing tuberculosis.

□ **tu**ˌ**berculin-**ˈ**tested** *adj* (*abbr* **TT**) (of milk) shown to contain no tuberculosis germs.

tuberculosis /tju:ˌbɜ:kjʊˈləʊsɪs; *US* tu:-/ *n* [U] (*abbr* **TB**) infectious wasting disease in which growths appear on body tissue, esp the lungs.

▷ **tubercular** /tju:ˈbɜ:kjʊlə(r); *US* tu:-/ *adj* of, causing or affected with tuberculosis: *a tubercular infection, lung.*

TUC /ˌti: ju: ˈsi:/ *abbr* (*Brit*) Trades Union Congress. ⇨ article at TRADE UNION.

tuck[1] /tʌk/ *n* **1** [C] flat fold stitched into a garment, etc to make it smaller or for ornament: *put in/take out a tuck in a dress.* **2** [U] (*Brit infml esp dated*) food, esp sweets, cakes, pastry, etc that children enjoy: [attrib] *a school tuck-shop.*

tuck[2] /tʌk/ *v* **1** [Tn·pr, Tn·p] **(a)** ~ **sth into sth**; ~ **sth in/up** push or fold or turn the ends or edges (of cloth, paper, etc) so that they are hidden or held in place: *tuck your trousers into your boots* ○ *tuck your shirt in*, ie into your trousers, shorts, etc ○ *He tucked up his shirt-sleeves.* ○ *The sheets were tucked in neatly*, ie under the mattress. ○ *tuck the flap of an envelope in.* **(b)** draw (sth) together into a small space: *The nurse tucked her hair (up) under her cap.* ○ *He sat with his legs tucked (up) under him.* **2** [Tn·pr] put sth round (sb/sth) snugly and comfortably: *tuck a blanket round sb's knees/legs.* **3** [Tn·pr] put (sth) away compactly or tidily: *The hen tucked her head under her wing.* ○ *tucked the map under his arm.* **4** (idm) **nip and tuck** ⇨ NIP. **5** (phr v) **tuck sth away** (*infml esp Brit*) eat (a lot of food). **tuck sth/oneself away** (*infml*) store or hide sth/oneself: *He's got a fortune tucked away in a Swiss bank account.* ○ *The farm was tucked away in the hills.* **tuck into sth/in** (*infml esp Brit*) eat sth heartily: *He tucked into the ham hungrily.* ○ *Come on, tuck in, everybody!* **tuck sb up** cover sb snugly with bedclothes: *tuck the children up in bed.*

□ ˈ**tuck-in** *n* (usu *sing*); (*Brit infml*) large meal: *have a good tuck-in.*

tucker /ˈtʌkə(r)/ *n* (idm) **one's best bib and tucker** ⇨ BEST[1].

▷ **tucker** *v* [usu passive: Tn, Tn·p] ~ **sb (out)** (*US infml*) tire or exhaust (sb): *I'm fair tuckered out.*

Tudor architecture: Little Moreton Hall, Cheshire

Tudor /ˈtju:də(r); *US* ˈtu:dər/ *adj* **1** of the family to which the English monarchs Henry VII, Henry VIII, Edward VI, Mary I and Elizabeth I belonged. It was of Welsh origin. ⇨ App 3. ⇨ illus at DRESS. **2** of the style of English architecture common during the reigns of these monarchs (the 16th and early 17th centuries), characterized by flattened arches and half-timbered buildings. ⇨ illus. ⇨ article at ARCHITECTURE.

▷ **Tudor** *n* member of the Tudor family.

□ ˌ**Tudor** ˈ**rose** picture of a rose used as the symbol of the Tudor kings and queens, a combination of the *Yorkist and *Lancastrian roses.

Tue (also **Tues**) *abbr* Tuesday: *Tues 9 March.*

Tuesday /ˈtju:zdɪ; *US* ˈtu:-/ *n* [U, C] (*abbrs* **Tue, Tues**) the third day of the week, next after Monday.

For the uses of *Tuesday* see the examples at *Monday*.

tuffet /ˈtʌfɪt/ *n* small mound, esp one used as a low seat.

tuft /tʌft/ *n* bunch of hair, feathers, grass, etc, growing or held together at the base.

▷ **tufted** *adj* having, or growing in, a tuft or tufts: *a tufted carpet.*

tug /tʌg/ *v* (**-gg-**) **(a)** [I, Ipr, Tn, Tn·pr] ~ **(at sth)** pull (sth) hard or violently: *We tugged so hard that the rope broke.* ○ *tug at sb's elbow/sleeve*, eg to attract attention. **(b)** [Tn, Tn·p] pull (sth/sb) in a particular direction: *The wind nearly tugged my umbrella out of my hand.* ○ *It is difficult tugging the children round the shops with me*, ie because they resist.

▷ **tug** *n* **1** sudden hard pull: *I felt a tug at my sleeve.* ○ *Tom gave his sister's hair a hard tug.* ○ (*fig*) *She felt a sharp tug at her heart-strings* (ie pang of sorrow) *as he left.* **2** (also ˈ**tugboat**) small powerful boat for towing ships, esp into harbour or up rivers.

□ ˌ**tug of** ˈ**love** (*Brit infml*) dispute over the custody of a child, esp between separated or divorced parents: [attrib] *a tug-of-love drama.*

ˌ**tug of** ˈ**war** contest in which two teams pull at opposite ends of a rope until one drags the other over a central line.

tuition /tju:ˈɪʃn; *US* tu:-/ *n* [U] **(a)** (*esp fml*) teaching or instruction, esp that given to individuals or small groups: *have private tuition in*

French. (**b**) fee paid for this, esp in colleges and universities.

tulip /ˈtju:lɪp; *US* ˈtu:-/ *n* garden plant growing from a bulb in spring, with a large brightly-coloured cup-shaped flower on a tall stem. ⇨ illus at PLANT.

Tull /tʌl/ Jethro (1674-1741), English agriculturist who invented a machine for sowing seeds, enabling agricultural production to be greatly increased, both in England and overseas.

tulle /tju:l; *US* tu:l/ *n* [U] soft fine silky net-like material used esp for veils and dresses.

tumble /ˈtʌmbl/ *v* **1** (**a**) [I, Ipr, Ip, Tn·pr, Tn·p] (cause sb/sth to) fall, esp helplessly or violently, but usu without serious injury: *tumble down the stairs, off a bicycle, out of a tree, over a step, etc* ○ *Toddlers keep tumbling over.* ○ *The children tumbled* (ie pushed) *each other (over) in the snow.* (**b**) [I] fall rapidly in value or amount: *Share prices tumbled on the stock-market.* **2** [I, Ipr, Ip] roll to and fro or over and over or up and down in a restless and disorderly way: *The puppies were tumbling about on the floor.* ○ *The stream tumbled over the rocks.* ○ *The breakers came tumbling onto the shore.* **3** [Ipr, Ip] ~ **into**/**out of sth**; ~ **in**/**out** move or rush in the specified direction in a headlong or blundering way: *I threw off my clothes and tumbled into bed.* ○ *The children tumbled into/out of the car.* ○ *My shopping bag broke and everything tumbled out.* **4** [Tn, Tn·p] rumple or disarrange (sth): *The wind tumbled her hair.* ○ *The bedclothes were tumbled (about) as though the bed had been slept in.* **5** (phr v) **tumble down** fall into ruin; collapse: *The old barn we bought to convert into flats was practically tumbling down.* **tumble to sb/sth** (*infml*) realize the true character of sb or grasp a hidden meaning, etc: *I tumbled to him/to what he was up to when I found some of his letters to Jane.*

▷ **tumble** *n* **1** [C] helpless or violent fall: *have/take a nasty tumble.* **2** [sing] untidy or confused state: *bedclothes in a tumble on the floor.*

□ ˈ**tumbledown** *adj* [attrib] falling or fallen into ruin; dilapidated: *a tumbledown old shack.*

ˈ**tumble-drier** (also ˈ**tumbler-drier**) *n* machine for drying washed clothes in a heated drum that rotates.

ˈ**tumbleweed** *n* [U] bush-like plant of various species growing in desert areas of N America, which withers in autumn, breaks off and is rolled about by the wind.

tumbler /ˈtʌmblə(r)/ *n* **1** (**a**) flat-bottomed straight-sided drinking-glass with no handle or stem. ⇨ illus at GLASS. (**b**) (also **tumblerful** /-fʊl/) amount held by a tumbler: *a tumbler of milk.* **2** part of a lock that holds the bolt until lifted by a key. **3** acrobat who turns somersaults, esp on the ground.

□ **tumbler-drier** *n* = TUMBLE-DRIER (TUMBLE).

tumbrel (also **tumbril**) /ˈtʌmbrəl/ *n* open cart, esp of the kind used to carry condemned people to the guillotine during the French Revolution: *tumbrels rolling through the streets.*

tumescent /tju:ˈmesnt; *US* tu:-/ *adj* (*fml*) (of parts of the body) swelling or swollen, eg in response to sexual stimulation. ▷ **tumescence** /-sns/ *n* [U].

tumid /ˈtju:mɪd; *US* ˈtu:-/ *adj* (*fml*) (of parts of the body) swollen. ▷ **tumidity** /tju:ˈmɪdətɪ; *US* tu:-/ *n* [U].

tummy /ˈtʌmɪ/ *n* (used esp by or to children) stomach: *have a tummy-ache* ○ *one's tummy-button*, ie navel.

tumour (*US* **tumor**) /ˈtju:mə(r); *US* ˈtu:-/ *n* abnormal mass of new tissue growing in or on part of the body: *cancerous tumours* ○ *benign/malignant tumours* ○ *a* ˈ*lung tumour.* Cf GROWTH 4. ▷ **tumorous** *adj.*

tumult /ˈtju:mʌlt; *US* ˈtu:-/ *n* [U, sing] (*fml*) **1** (**a**) disturbance or confusion, esp of a large mass of people: *The demonstration broke up in tumult.* ○ *the tumult of battle.* (**b**) din or uproar produced by this: *One had to shout to be heard above the tumult.* ○ *Her speech threw the House* (ie of Commons) *into a tumult (of protest).* **2** disturbed or agitated state of mind; turmoil: *Her mind was/Her thoughts were in a tumult.* ○ *a tumult of passion, jealousy, excitement, etc* ○ *When the tumult within him subsided....*

▷ **tumultuous** /tju:ˈmʌltʃʊəs; *US* tu:-/ *adj* **1** disorderly or confused; violent: *tumultuous crowds, upheavals, passions.* **2** noisy: *tumultuous applause, support, protest* ○ *give sb a tumultuous welcome.*

tumulus /ˈtju:mjʊləs; *US* ˈtu:-/ *n* (*pl* **-li** /-laɪ/) mound of earth over an ancient burial site. Cf BARROW[2].

tun /tʌn/ *n* **1** large cask for beer, wine, etc. **2** measure of capacity (216 gallons of beer or 252 gallons of wine).

tuna /ˈtju:nə; *US* ˈtu:nə/ *n* (*pl* unchanged or ~**s**) (**a**) (also **tunny**) [C] large sea-fish, eaten as food. (**b**) (also ˈ**tuna-fish**) [U] its flesh as food.

tundra /ˈtʌndrə/ *n* [U, C] vast flat treeless Arctic regions of Europe, Asia and N America where the subsoil is permanently frozen: [attrib] *tundra vegetation.*

tune /tju:n; *US* tu:n/ *n* **1** [C, U] (series of notes with or without harmony forming a) melody, esp a well-marked one: *whistle a catchy tune* ○ *hymn tunes* ○ *He gave us a tune on his fiddle.* ○ *Modern music has no tune to it.* **2** (idm) **call the shots/the tune** ⇨ CALL[2]. **change one's tune** ⇨ CHANGE[1]. **dance to sb's tune** ⇨ DANCE[2]. **the devil has all the best tunes** ⇨ DEVIL[1]. **he who pays the piper calls the tune** ⇨ PAY[2]. ˌ**in/**ˌ**out of** ˈ**tune (with sb/sth)** (**a**) at/not at the correct musical pitch: *The violin is not quite in tune with the piano.* ○ *The choir was (singing) distinctly out of tune in places.* (**b**) (*fig*) in/not in agreement or emotional harmony: *feel out of tune with one's surroundings, companions.* **sing a different song/tune** ⇨ SING. **to the tune of sth** (**a**) using the melody of sth: *We sang these lines to the tune of Yankee Doodle.* (**b**) (*infml*) to the (esp considerable) sum or amount of sth: *He was fined for speeding to the tune of £200.*

▷ **tune** *v* **1** [Tn] adjust (a musical instrument or note) to the correct pitch: *tune a guitar.* **2** [Tn] adjust (an engine, etc) so that it runs smoothly and efficiently. **3** (idm) **(be) tuned (in) to sth** (of a radio, etc) adjusted to receive a certain programme: *Stay tuned to us for the latest sports results.* ○ *You're not properly tuned in.* **4** (phr v) **tune in (to sth)** adjust the controls of a radio, TV, etc so that it receives a certain programme: *tune in to the BBC World Service* ○ *Tune in next week at the same time!* **tune sb in to sth** (usu passive) make sb sympathetically aware of other people's thoughts and feelings, etc: *Voters always elect the candidate most tuned in to their needs.* **tune (sth) up** adjust (musical instruments) so that they can play together in tune: *The orchestra were tuning up as we entered the hall.*

tuneful /-fl/ *adj* having a pleasing tune; melodious. **tunefully** /-fəlɪ/ *adv.* **tunefulness** *n* [U].

tuneless *adj* (*usu derog*) without a tune; not melodious. **tunelessly** *adv.* **tunelessness** *n* [U].

□ ˈ**tune-up** *n* act of tuning (TUNE *v* 2) the engine of a motor-vehicle: *My car needs a tune-up.*

ˈ**tuning-fork** *n* small steel device like a two-pronged fork that produces a note of fixed pitch (usu middle C) when struck.

tuner /ˈtju:nə(r); *US* ˈtu:-/ *n* **1** (esp in compounds) person who tunes musical instruments, esp pianos. **2** part of a radio, TV, etc that selects signals.

tungsten /ˈtʌŋstən/ (also **wolfram**) *n* [U] (*symb* **W**) chemical element, a hard grey metal used in making steel alloys and the filaments of electric light bulbs. ⇨ App 11.

tunic /ˈtju:nɪk; *US* ˈtu:-/ *n* **1** close-fitting jacket worn as part of a uniform by police officers, soldiers, etc. **2** (**a**) loose (usu sleeveless) outer garment reaching to the knees and sometimes gathered at the waist with a belt, as worn by ancient Greeks and Romans. (**b**) similar hip-length garment with open sleeves worn over trousers or a skirt by women or girls.

Tunisia /tju:ˈnɪzɪə; *US* tu:nɪʒə/ country in N Africa, bordered by Algeria and Libya; pop approx 7 809 000; official language Arabic; capital Tunis; unit of currency dinar (= 1 000 millimes). Formerly a French protectorate, it became independent in 1956. The southern part of the country is desert. Its main exports are oil, phosphates and iron ore. ⇨ map at ALGERIA. ▷ **Tunisian** *adj, n.*

tunnel /ˈtʌnl/ *n* **1** (**a**) underground passage, eg for a road or railway through a hill or under a river or the sea: *the Channel Tunnel*, ie between England and France. (**b**) similar underground passage made by a burrowing animal: *Moles dug tunnels under the lawn.* **2** (idm) **light at the end of the tunnel** ⇨ LIGHT[1].

▷ **tunnel** *v* (**-ll-**; *US* **-l-**) **1** [I, Ipr, Ip] ~ **into, through, under, etc** dig a tunnel (in the specified direction): *The prisoners had escaped by tunnelling.* ○ *They tunnelled along under the walls and up into the woods beyond.* **2** [Tn, Tn·pr, Tn·p] ~ **one's way into/through/under sth** make (a way through sth) by digging a tunnel: *The rescuers tunnelled their way (in) to the pot-holers.* ○ *tunnel a hole, shaft, passage, etc.*

□ ˈ**tunnel vision** **1** condition in which sight is poor or lost altogether at the edges of the normal field of vision. **2** (*derog*) inability to grasp the wider implications of a situation, an argument, etc.

tunny /ˈtʌnɪ/ *n* = TUNA.

tup /tʌp/ *n* (*esp Brit*) uncastrated male sheep; ram(1). Cf EWE.

▷ **tup** *v* (**-pp-**) [Tn] (of a male sheep) copulate with (a female sheep).

tuppence /ˈtʌpəns/ *n* (*Brit infml*) **1** = TWOPENCE (TWO). **2** (idm) **not care/give** ˈ**tuppence for sb/sth** consider sb/sth worthless or unimportant. ▷ **tuppenny** /ˈtʌpənɪ/ *adj* [attrib] = TWOPENNY (TWO): *a tuppenny stamp.*

turban /ˈtɜ:bən/ *n* (**a**) men's head-dress (worn esp by Muslims and Sikhs) made by winding a length of cloth tightly round the head. (**b**) woman's close-fitting hat resembling this. ⇨ illus at DRESS.

▷ **turbaned** *adj* wearing a turban: *a turbaned Sikh.*

turbid /ˈtɜ:bɪd/ *adj* (*fml*) **1** (of liquids) opaque or muddy; not clear: *the turbid floodwaters of the river.* **2** (*fig*) disordered or confused: *a turbid imagination* ○ *turbid thoughts.* ▷ **turbidity** /tɜ:ˈbɪdətɪ/, **turbidness** *ns* [U].

turbine /ˈtɜ:baɪn/ *n* machine or motor driven by a wheel which is turned by a current of water, steam, air or gas.

turbofan /ˈtɜ:bəʊfæn/ *n* type of jet engine in which a special fan pulls in air to give extra thrust.

turbo-jet /ˌtɜ:bəʊˈdʒet/ *n* (propellerless aircraft driven by a) turbine engine that delivers its propulsive power in the form of a jet of hot exhaust gases.

turbo-prop /ˌtɜ:bəʊˈprɒp/ (also **prop-jet**) *n* (aircraft driven by a) turbine used as a turbo-jet and also to drive a propeller.

turbot /ˈtɜ:bət/ *n* (*pl* unchanged) (**a**) [C] large European sea-water flat-fish. (**b**) [U] its flesh, highly valued as food.

turbulent /ˈtɜ:bjʊlənt/ *adj* **1** (of air or water) moving violently and unevenly: *turbulent waves* ○ *turbulent weather conditions.* **2** (**a**) in a state of commotion or unrest; disturbed: *turbulent mobs, crowds, factions, etc* ○ *a city with a turbulent past.* (**b**) restless or uncontrolled: *turbulent moods, passions, thoughts.*

▷ **turbulence** /-ləns/ *n* [U] **1** unrest or disturbance: *political, social, religious, etc turbulence* ○ (*fig*) *emotions in a state of turbulence.* **2** violent or uneven movement of air or water: *We experienced some slight turbulence flying over the Atlantic.*

turbulently *adv.*

turd /tɜ:d/ *n* (*sl*) **1** ball or lump of (usu animal) excrement: *dog turds.* **2** (⚠) contemptible or unpleasant person: *You turd!*

tureen /təˈri:n/ *n* deep dish with a lid from which soup, vegetables, etc are served at table.

turf /tɜ:f/ *n* (*pl* **turfs** or **turves** /tɜ:vz/) **1** (**a**) [U] short grass and the surface layer of soil bound together by its roots: *clipped, springy, rolled, etc* *turf* ○ *lay turf*, eg to make a lawn. (**b**) [C] piece of this, usu square or rectangular, cut from the ground. **2** [C, U] (in Ireland) (slab of) peat for fuel. **3 the turf** [sing] the racecourse; horse-racing. **4** [U] (*infml esp US*) one's own neighbourhood or territory: *on my own turf.*

▷ **turf** *v* **1** [Tn] lay (ground) with turf: *a newly-turfed lawn.* **2** (phr v) **turf sb/sth out (of sth)** (*Brit infml*) forcibly remove sb/sth; dispose of sth: *Turf the cat out if you want to sit in the chair.* ○ *You'd have more room in your wardrobe if you turfed out all your old clothes.*

□ ˈ**turf accountant** (*Brit fml*) bookmaker. ⇨ article at GAMBLING.

Turgenev /tɜːˈgeɪnjef/ Ivan Sergeevich (1818-83), Russian novelist and playwright noted for his portrayal of Russian country life and of the Russian gentry. His best-known works are the novel *Fathers and Sons* and the play *A Month in the Country*.

turgid /ˈtɜːdʒɪd/ *adj* **1** (*derog*) (of language, style, etc) pompous and difficult to follow; boring: *a turgid article on medieval law.* **2** swollen; bloated.

▷ **turgidity** /tɜːˈdʒɪdətɪ/ *n* [U]. **turgidly** *adv*.

Turk /tɜːk/ *n* **1** native or inhabitant of Turkey. **2** member of any of a group of Central Asian peoples who speak languages related to Turkish. **3** (idm) **a young Turk** ⇨ YOUNG.

□ ˌ**Turk's** ˈ**head** type of decorative knot shaped like a turban.

Turkey /ˈtɜːkɪ/ country in SW Asia, with the Mediterranean Sea to the south and the Black Sea to the north; pop approx 52 422 000; official language Turkish; capital Ankara; unit of currency lira. From the early 13th century to the early 20th century it was at the centre of the *Ottoman empire. Modern Turkey was created in 1923, under the leadership of *Atatürk. The economy is mainly agricultural, though the land is generally poor. Turkey is a major producer of chrome. ⇨ map.

turkey /ˈtɜːkɪ/ *n* (*pl* ~**s**) **1** (**a**) [C] large bird reared to be eaten, esp at Christmas. ⇨ illus at BIRD. ⇨ article at CHRISTMAS. (**b**) [U] its flesh as food: *a slice of roast turkey.* **2** [C] (*US sl*) failure; flop: *His last movie was a real turkey.* **3** (idm) **cold turkey** ⇨ COLD[1]. **talk turkey** ⇨ TALK[2].

Turkic /ˈtɜːkɪk/ *adj*, *n* (of a) group of languages spoken in Turkey, Iran and the southern part of the USSR.

Turkish /ˈtɜːkɪʃ/ *adj* of Turkey, its people or its language.

▷ **Turkish** *n* [U] language of Turkey.

□ ˌ**Turkish** ˈ**bath** type of bath in which the body is made to sweat in hot air or steam, followed by washing, massage, etc.

ˌ**Turkish** ˈ**coffee** very strong, usu very sweet, black coffee.

ˌ**Turkish de**ˈ**light** sweet consisting of lumps of flavoured gelatine coated with powdered sugar.

Turkmenistan /ˌtɜːkmenɪˈstɑːn/ country in south central Asia; pop approx 3 523 000; official language Turkmenian; capital Ashkhabad; unit of currency rouble. Part of the Russian empire in the 19th century, it became a member of the USSR and gained independence in 1991. The economy is rich in natural gas. ⇨ map at UNION OF SOVIET SOCIALIST REPUBLICS.

Turks and Caicos Islands /ˌtɜːks ən ˈkeɪkəs aɪləndz/ **the Turks and Caicos Islands** British colony consisting of over 30 islands in the West Indies, part of the Bahama Islands; pop approx 9 000; language English; capital Grand Turk.

turmeric /ˈtɜːmərɪk/ *n* [U] (**a**) E Indian plant of the ginger family. (**b**) its root, powdered and used to colour or flavour food, eg in curry powder.

turmoil /ˈtɜːmɔɪl/ *n* [C usu *sing*, U] (instance of) great disturbance, agitation or confusion: *The country was in (a) turmoil during the strike.*

turn[1] /tɜːn/ *v*

► MOVEMENT AROUND A CENTRAL POINT **1** [I, Ipr, Tn, Tn·pr] (cause sth to) move round a point or an axis: *The hands of a clock turn very slowly.* ○ *The earth turns* (ie rotates) *on its axis once every 24 hours.* ○ *The wheels of the car began to turn.* ○ *This tap turns easily*/*It's easy to turn this tap.* ○ *She turned the handle but the door wouldn't open.* ○ *He turned the key in the lock.* ○ *She turned the steering-wheel sharply to the left to avoid a cyclist.* **2** [I, Ip, Tn, Tn·p] ~ **(sb/sth) (over)** (cause sb/sth to) move so that a different side faces outwards or upwards: *If you turn over you might find it easier to get to sleep.* ○ *Brown the meat on one side, then turn it (over) and brown the other side.* ○ *He sat there idly turning the pages of a book.* ○ *She turned the chair on its side to repair it.* ○ *You've turned your jumper inside out.* ○ *Turn the record over and put on* (ie start to play) *the other side.* **3** (**a**) [I, Ipr, Ip, Tn, Tn·pr, Tn·p] (cause sb/sth to) change position or direction so as to face or start moving in the specified direction: *About/Left/Right turn!* ie as military commands ○ *It's time we turned and went back home.* ○ *She turned to look at me.* ○ *He turned towards her.* ○ *We turned off the motorway at Lancaster.* ○ (*fig*) *Her thoughts turned to* (ie She began to think about) *her dead husband.* ○ *He turned his back to the wall.* ○ *She turned (her face) away in embarrassment.* (**b**) [I] (of the tide) start to come in or go out: *The tide is turning; we'd better get back.* **4** [Tn·pr] aim or point (sth) in the specified direction: *Police turned water-cannon on the rioters*, ie to disperse them. ○ *They turned their dogs on us.* ○ *She turned her eyes towards him.* ○ (*fig*) *It's time to turn our attention to the question of money.*

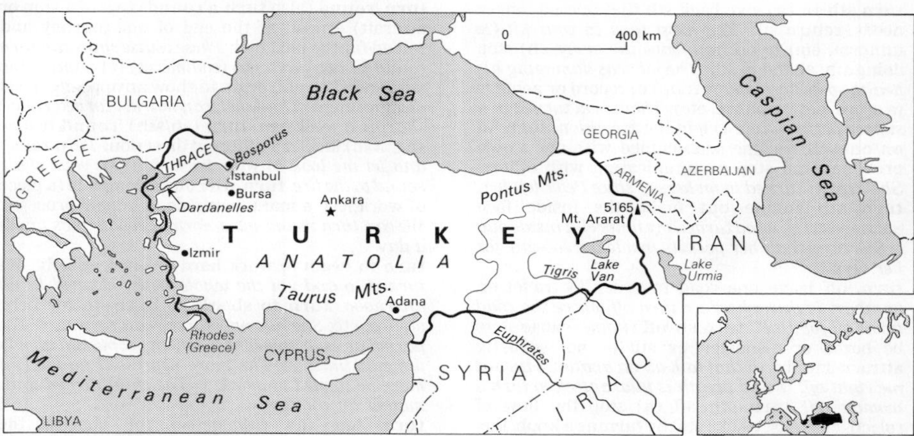

Turkey

► POINTING OR SENDING SOMETHING IN A PARTICULAR DIRECTION **5** [Tn·pr, Tn·p, Cn·a] cause (sb/sth) to go in the specified direction: *turn a horse into a field* ○ *turn a boat adrift* ○ *It would be irresponsible to turn such a man loose on society.* **6** [Tn·p] fold (sth) in the specified way: *She turned down the blankets and climbed into bed.* ○ *He turned up the collar of his coat and hurried out into the rain.*

► CHANGING DIRECTION **7** [Ipr, Tn] ~ **(round) sth** go round sth: *The car turned (round) the corner and disappeared from sight.* ○ *She waved to me as she turned the corner.* **8** [Ln, Ipr] (of a river, road, etc) curve in the specified direction: *The river turns north at this point.* ○ *Just before the trees the path turns sharply right.* ○ *The road turns to the left after the church.* **9** [Tn no passive] perform (the specified movement) by moving one's body in a circle: *turn cartwheels/somersaults* ○ *She turned a pirouette on the ice.*

► CHANGING STATE OR FORM **10** (**a**) [La, Ln, Cn·a] (cause sb/sth to) become: *The milk turned sour in the heat*/*The heat turned the milk sour.* ○ *He turned nasty when we refused to give him the money.* ○ *Leaves turn brown in autumn.* ○ *The weather has turned cold and windy.* ○ *She turned a deathly shade of white when she heard the news.* ○ *He's a clergyman turned politician*, ie He was formerly a clergyman but is now a politician. ⇨ Usage at BECOME. (**b**) [Tn] (not in the continuous tenses) reach or pass (the specified age or time): *She turned forty last June.* ○ *It's turned midnight.* **11** [Ipr, Tn·pr] ~ **(sb/sth) (from A) to/into B** (cause sb/sth to) pass from one condition or state to another one: *Caterpillars turn into butterflies.* ○ *Water turns into ice when it freezes.* ○ *His expression turned from bewilderment to horror as he realized what had happened.* ○ *The experience has turned him into a sad and embittered man.* ○ *The witch turned the prince into a frog.* ○ *The novel was turned into a successful Hollywood film.* **12** [Tn] shape (sth) on a lathe: *turn a chair leg.* **13** [I, Tn] (cause sth to) become sour: *The thundery weather has turned the milk.* **14** [I, Tn] (of the stomach) have a sick feeling; cause (the stomach) to have a sick feeling: *The sight of the greasy stew made his stomach turn*/*turned his stomach.* **15** (idm) **as it/things turned** ˈ**out** as was shown or proved by later events: *I didn't need my umbrella, as it turned out*, ie because it didn't rain. **be well, badly, etc turned** ˈ**out** be well, badly, etc dressed: *Her children are always smartly turned out.* **turn round and do sth** (*infml*) say or do sth that displeases sb: *How could she turn round and say that, after all I've done for her.* (For other idioms containing **turn**, see entries for *ns*, *adjs*, etc, eg **not turn a hair** ⇨ HAIR; **turn a deaf ear** ⇨ DEAF.). **16** (phr v) ˌ**turn a**ˈ**bout** (often used in the form aˌbout ˈturn as a military command) (esp of soldiers) move so as to face in the opposite direction: *The colonel ordered the troops to turn about.* ○ *'About turn!' barked the sergeant-major.*

turn (sb) against sb (cause sb to) become unfriendly or hostile towards sb: *She turned against her old friend.* ○ *After the divorce he tried to turn the children against their mother.*

turn around = TURN ROUND.

turn aˈ**way (from sb/sth)** stop facing or looking at sb/sth: *She turned away in horror at the sight of so much blood.* **turn sb away (from sth)** refuse to allow sb to enter a place; refuse to give help or support to sb: *Hundreds of people had to be turned away from the stadium*, eg because it was full. ○ *turn away a beggar*, ie refuse to give him money ○ *A doctor cannot turn away a dying man.*

turn (sb/sth) ˈ**back** (cause sb/sth to) return the way he/it has come: *The weather became so bad that they had to turn back.* ○ (*fig*) *The project must go ahead; there can be no turning back.* ○ *Our car was turned back at the frontier.*

turn sb/sth ˈ**down** reject or refuse to consider (an offer, a proposal, etc or the person who makes it): *He tried to join the army but was turned down flat because of poor health.* ○ *He asked Jane to marry him but she turned him down*/*turned down his proposal.* **turn sth down** adjust (a cooker, radio, etc) in order to reduce the heat, noise, etc: *Don't forget to turn down the gas after an hour or so.* ○ *Turn that record-player down — I'm trying to get some sleep.*

turn ˈ**in** (**a**) face or curve inwards: *Her feet turn in as she walks.* (**b**) (*infml*) go to bed: *It's late; I think I'll turn in.* **turn sb in** (*infml*) hand sb over to the police to be arrested: *She threatened to turn him in.* **turn sth in** (**a**) give back sth that one no longer needs; return sth: *You must turn in your kit* (ie uniform, etc) *before you leave the army.* (**b**) stop doing sth; abandon sth: *The job was damaging his health so he had to turn it in.* (**c**) record or achieve (a score, performance, etc): *Thompson turned in a superb performance to win the decathlon.* **turn ˈin on oneself** become preoccupied with one's own problems and stop communicating with others: *She's really turned in on herself since Peter left her.* **turn sth inside out** make the inside face outwards: *The wind turned my umbrella inside out.* ○ *She turned all her pockets inside out looking for her keys.*

turn ˈoff leave one road in order to travel on another: *Is this where we turn off/where the road turns off for Hull?* **turn sb ˈoff** (*infml*) cause sb to be bored or disgusted by sth or not sexually attracted to sb: *All that talk about abattoirs turned me right off!* ○ *Bad breath is guaranteed to turn a woman off!* **turn sth off** (**a**) stop the flow of (electricity, gas, water, etc) by turning a knob, tap, etc: *turn off the light, oven, tap* ○ *They've turned off the water while they mend a burst pipe.* (**b**) stop (a radio, television, etc) by pressing a button, moving a switch, etc: *Let's turn the television off, I'd sooner read a book.*

turn on sb attack sb suddenly and unexpectedly: *His normally placid dog turned on him and bit him in the leg.* ○ *Why are you all turning on me* (ie criticizing or blaming me)*?* **turn on sth** have sth as its main topic: *The discussion turned on the need for better public health care.* **turn on sth/doing sth** depend on sth: *The success of a picnic usually turns on the weather.* **turn sb ˈon** (*infml*) excite or stimulate sb, esp sexually: *Jazz has never really turned me on.* ○ *She's often turned on by men with beards.* **turn sth on** cause (an oven, a radio, etc) to start functioning by moving a switch, knob, etc: *turn on the light, television, central heating* ○ *Turn on the gas and light the oven.* ○ *Could you turn on the bath* (ie cause the water to start flowing) *for me while you're upstairs?*

turn ˈout (**a**) be present at an event; appear, assemble or attend: *A vast crowd turned out to watch the match.* ○ *The whole village turned out to welcome the pope.* ○ *Not many men turned out for duty.* (**b**) (used with an *adv* or *adj*, or in questions after *how*) take place or happen in the specified way; prove to be: *If the day turns out wet we may have to change our plans.* ○ *'How did the party turn out?' 'It turned out very well, thanks.'* ○ *I hope all turns out well for you.* **turn (sth) ˈout** (cause sth to) point outwards: *Her toes turn out.* ○ *She turned her toes out.* **turn sb/sth out** produce sb/sth: *The factory turns out 900 cars a week.* ○ *The school has turned out some first-rate scholars.* **turn sth out** (**a**) switch (a light or fire) off; extinguish sth: *Remember to turn out the lights before you go to bed.* (**b**) remove the contents of sth; empty sth: *turn out the attic, one's drawers* ○ *The teacher ordered him to turn out his pockets.* **turn sb out (of/from sth)** force sb to leave a place: *My landlord is turning me out at the end of the month.* ○ *She got pregnant and was turned out of the house by her parents.* **turn out to be sb/sth; turn out that ...** prove to be sb/sth; came to be known that ...: *She turned out to be a friend of my sister/It turned out that she was a friend of my sister.* ○ *The job turned out to be harder than we thought.*

turn over (of a vehicle engine) start running. **turn (sb/sth) over** (cause sb/sth to) face in another direction by rolling: *She turned over and went to sleep.* ○ *The car skidded, turned over and burst into flames.* ○ *The nurse turned the old man over to wash his back.* **turn sth over** (**a**) do business worth (the specified amount): *The company turns over £150 million a year.* (**b**) (of a shop) sell out and replace its stock: *A supermarket turns over its stock very rapidly.* (**c**) consider sth: *I've been turning your suggestion over (in my mind).* (**d**) cause (a vehicle engine) to begin working; start sth. **turn sb over to sb** deliver sb to (the authorities, the police, etc): *Customs officials turned the man over to the police.* **turn sth over to sb** give the control or management of sth to sb: *He turned the business over to his daughter.*

turn ˈround (also **turn aˈround**) (**a**) (of a ship or aircraft) unload at the end of one journey and reload for the next one: *These cruise ships can turn round in two days.* (**b**) (*commerce*) (of shares, the stock-market, etc) begin to show an opposite trend or movement: *The American market turned round sharply a week ago.* **turn (sb/sth) ˈround** (cause sb/sth to) face in a different direction: *Turn round and let me look at your back.* ○ *Turn your chair round to the fire.* **turn sth round** complete (a piece of work, esp a manufacturing or repair process): *We can turn round most normal repair jobs inside a day.*

turn to begin to work hard or energetically: *We turned to and got the whole house cleaned in an afternoon.* **turn to sb/sth** go to sb/sth for help, advice, etc: *She has nobody she can turn to.* ○ *The parish priest is someone to whom people can turn in difficult times.* ○ *The more depressed he got, the more he turned to drink.* ○ *The child turned to its mother for comfort.*

turn ˈup (**a**) (*commerce*) (of shares, the stock-market, etc) rise; increase; improve: *Investment is turning up sharply.* (**b**) make one's appearance; arrive: *We arranged to meet at the cinema at 7.30, but he failed to turn up.* ○ *We invited her to dinner but she didn't even bother to turn up.* (**c**) be found (esp by chance) after being lost: *I'm sure your watch will turn up one of these days.* (**d**) (of an opportunity) present itself; happen: *He's still hoping something* (eg a job or a piece of good luck) *will turn up.* **turn sth up** (**a**) cause sth to face or point upwards: *He turned up his coat collar against the chill wind.* (**b**) shorten (a garment) by folding it up at the bottom: *These trousers are too long; they'll need turning up/to be turned up.* (**c**) discover sth by digging; expose sth: *The farmer turned up a human skull while ploughing the field.* ○ *The soil had been turned up by the plough.* (**d**) increase the loudness of (a radio, television, etc): *I can't hear the radio very well; could you turn it up a bit?*

□ **ˈturn-about** *n* act of turning in a different or the opposite direction: (*fig*) *The government's sudden turn-about* (ie change of policy) *on taxation surprised political commentators.*

ˈturn-around (also **ˈturn-round**) *n* (usu *sing*) complete change, eg from a very bad situation to a very good one: *The change of leader led to a turn-around in the fortunes of the Labour Party.*

ˈturn-off *n* **1** road that leads away from a larger or more important one: *This is the turn-off for Bath.* **2** (usu *sing*) (*infml*) person or thing that bores or disgusts sb, or causes sb not to feel sexually attracted: *Smelly feet are definitely a turn-off as far as I'm concerned.*

ˈturn-on *n* (usu *sing*) (*infml*) person or thing that excites or stimulates sb, esp sexually: *She thinks hairy chests are a turn-on!*

ˈturn-out *n* (usu *sing*) **1** number of people who attend a match, meeting, etc; attendance: *There was a good turn-out at yesterday's meeting.* **2** act of emptying a drawer, a room, etc: *These drawers are full of rubbish; it's time I had a good turn-out.* **3** way in which sb is dressed: *The headmaster praised the boys for their neat turn-out.*

ˈturnover *n* **1** [sing] amount of business done by a company within a certain period of time: *The firm has an annual turnover of £75 million.* ○ *make a profit of £2 000 on a turnover of £20000.* **2** [sing] rate at which goods are sold and replaced in a shop: *We aim for a quick turnover of stock in our stores.* **3** [sing] rate at which workers leave a factory, company, etc and are replaced: *Why does your company have such a rapid turnover of staff?* **4** [C] type of small pie made by folding a piece of pastry round a filling of fruit, jam, etc: *an apple turnover.*

ˈturn-round *n* **1** (also **ˈturn-around**) (usu *sing*) (of a ship or an aircraft) process of being unloaded at the end of one journey and reloaded for the next one. **2** = TURN-AROUND.

ˈturnstile *n* revolving gate that allows one person at a time to enter or leave a stadium or sports ground.

ˈturntable *n* **1** flat round revolving surface on which gramophone records are played. **2** flat round platform onto which a locomotive runs to be turned round.

ˈturn-up *n* **1** (usu *pl*) turned-up end of a trouser leg: *Turn-ups are becoming fashionable again.* **2** (idm) **a ˈturn-up (for the book)** (*infml*) unusual or unexpected happening or event: *The champion beaten in the first round? That's a turn-up for the book!*

turn² /tɜːn/ *n* **1** [C] act of turning sth/sb round; turning movement: *give the handle a few turns.* **2** [C] change of direction; point at which this occurs: *He took a sudden turn to the left.* **3** [C] bend or corner in a road: *a lane full of twists and turns* ○ *Don't take the turn too fast.* **4** [C] development or new tendency in sth: *an alarming turn in international relations* ○ *an unfortunate turn of events* ○ *Matters have taken an unexpected turn.* ○ *Business has taken a turn for the better/worse.* **5** [C usu *sing*] time when each one of a group must or may do sth: *Please wait (until it is/for) your turn to be served.* ○ *Whose turn is it to do the washing-up?* ○ *I'll take a turn at the steering-wheel.* **6** [C] short walk; stroll: *I think I'll take a turn round the garden.* **7** [C] short performance by a comedian, singer, etc: *a comedy, song-and-dance, variety, etc turn* ○ *The star turn* (ie main performance) *was a young rock group.* **8** (*infml*) (**a**) [sing] nervous shock: *You gave me quite a turn, bursting in like that!* (**b**) [C] feeling of illness: *She's had one of her turns.* **9** (idm) **at every ˈturn** everywhere or all the time: *I keep meeting him at every turn.* ○ *She found her plans frustrated at every turn.* **by ˈturns** (of people or their actions) one after the other; in rotation: *We did the work by turns.* ○ *He gets cheerful and depressed by turns.* **do sb a good/bad ˈturn** be helpful/unhelpful to sb. **done, etc to a ˈturn** (of meat, etc) cooked for exactly the right length of time. **have, etc an enquiring, etc turn of ˈmind** have, etc a particular way of thinking about things, tackling a problem, etc: *She's always shown an academic turn of mind.* **in ˈturn** one after the other; in succession: *The girls called out their names in turn.* **not do a hand's turn** ⇨ HAND¹. **on the ˈturn** about to change or go a different way: *His luck is on the turn.* ○ *This milk is on the turn*, ie about to become sour. **ˌone good ˌturn deserves aˈnother** (*saying*) one should help or be kind to others who have been kind to one in the past. **ˌout of ˈturn** (**a**) before or after one's turn²(4). (**b**) not at the correct or permitted time: *speak out of turn*, ie in a tactless or foolish way. **serve one's/sb's turn** ⇨ SERVE. **take ˈturns (at sth)** do sth one after the other: *You can't both use the bike at once — you'll have to take turns.* **(do sth) ˌturn and ˌturn aˈbout** one after another; in succession. **a/the turn of events** change or development in circumstance, often unexpected or beyond one's control. **a ˌturn of ˈphrase** way of expressing or describing sth: *She has an apt turn of phrase for summing up a situation.* **a ˌturn of the ˈscrew** extra amount of pressure, cruelty, etc added to a situation that is already difficult to bear or understand. **a ˌturn of ˈspeed** (ability to achieve) a sudden increase in one's speed or rate of progress: *She put on an impressive turn of speed to overtake the others.* **the ˌturn of the ˈyear/ˈcentury** the time when a new year/century starts.

turncoat /ˈtɜːnkəʊt/ *n* (*derog*) person who changes from one side, party, etc to another.

Turner /ˈtɜːnə(r)/ Joseph Mallord William (1775-1851), English painter. He specialized in landscapes and seascapes (eg *The Fighting Téméraire*), whose most characteristic feature is their treatment of light. In his later paintings (eg *Rain, Steam and Speed* and *Snowstorm*) his hazy swirling representation of light and other atmospheric conditions foreshadowed the work of the *Impressionists and abstract art. ⇨ illus.

turner /ˈtɜːnə(r)/ *n* person who operates a lathe: *a ˈmetal-/ˈwood-turner*, ie person who turns metal/wood on a lathe. Cf TURN¹ 12.

turning /ˈtɜːnɪŋ/ *n* **1** [C] place where one road leads off from another: *take the wrong turning* ○ *Take the second turning on/to the left.* **2** (**a**) [U] use of a lathe. (**b**) **turnings** [pl] small unwanted bits of wood, metal, etc cut from sth being made on a lathe.

□ ˈ**turning-circle** *n* smallest possible circle in which a vehicle can turn.

ˈ**turning-point** *n* time when a decisive change or development takes place: *The meeting proved to be a turning-point in her life.* ○ *The discovery of a vaccine was the turning-point in the fight against smallpox.*

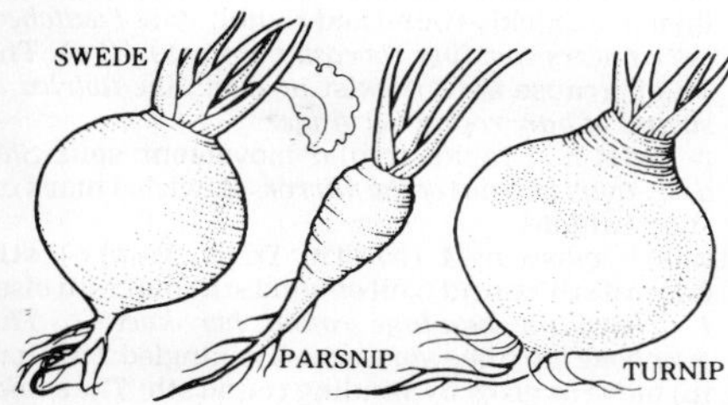

turnip /ˈtɜːnɪp/ *n* **1** [C] (**a**) plant with a round white, or white and purple, root. (**b**) plant with a brownish purple root; swede. **2** [C, U] root of either of these used as a vegetable or as food for cattle: *mashed turnip* ○ [attrib] *turnip soup.*

turnkey /ˈtɜːnkiː/ *adj* [attrib] built and handed over ready for use, occupation, etc: *a turnkey plant, apartment, etc.*

turnpike /ˈtɜːnpaɪk/ *n* **1** (*US*) road for fast-moving traffic which drivers must pay to drive on: *the New Jersey turnpike.* **2** (*Brit* also **pike**) (formerly) gate on a road that was opened when a traveller paid some money.

turpentine /ˈtɜːpəntaɪn/ (also *infml* **turps** /tɜːps/) *n* [U] strong-smelling colourless liquid obtained from the resin of certain trees, used esp for thinning paint and as a solvent.

Turpin /ˈtɜːpɪn/ Dick (1706-39), English highwayman, hanged at York for horse-stealing. Although his crimes were violent and unpleasant, many popular stories soon came to be told about him (eg his supposed ride from London to York on his horse Black Bess to establish an alibi).

turpitude /ˈtɜːpɪtjuːd; *US* -tuːd/ *n* [U] (*fml*) state or quality of being wicked; depravity.

turquoise /ˈtɜːkwɔɪz/ *n* **1** [C, U] type of greenish-blue precious stone: [attrib] *a turquoise brooch.* **2** [U] greenish-blue colour: *pale turquoise.*

□ **turquoise** *adj* of this colour: *a turquoise dress.*

turret /ˈtʌrɪt/ *n* **1** small tower on top of a larger tower or at the corner of a building or defensive wall. **2** (on a ship, an aircraft, a fort or a tank) low flat (often revolving) steel structure where the guns are fixed and which protects the gunners: *a warship armed with twin turrets.*

▷ **turreted** *adj* having a turret(1) or turrets.

turtle /ˈtɜːtl/ *n* **1** large reptile that lives in the sea and has flippers and a large horny shell. **2** (*US*) any of various types of reptile with a large shell, eg a tortoise, terrapin, etc. ⇨ illus at TORTOISE. **3** (idm) **turn** ˈ**turtle** (*infml*) (of a boat) turn upside down; capsize.

□ ˈ**turtle-dove** *n* type of wild dove noted for its soft cooing and its affectionate behaviour towards its mate and young.

ˈ**turtle-neck** *n* (garment, esp a sweater, with a) close-fitting neckband that is higher than a crew neck but does not turn over like a polo-neck. ˈ**turtle-necked** *adj*: *a turtle-necked sweater.* ⇨ illus at NECK.

turves *pl* of TURF.

tusk /tʌsk/ *n* either of a pair of very long pointed teeth that project from the mouth of certain animals, eg the elephant, walrus and wild boar. ⇨ illus at ELEPHANT. Cf IVORY.

Tussaud /ˈtuːsəʊ/ Marie (1760-1850), Swiss waxwork modeller who made likenesses of leading figures in the French Revolution. She came to England in 1802 and opened the waxworks now known as 'Madame Tussaud's' /təˈsɔːdz/, in London.

J M W Turner: The Fighting Téméraire

tussle /ˈtʌsl/ *n* (*infml*) struggle or fight, esp to take sth away from sb: *I had a tussle to get the knife off him.* ○ (*fig*) *We have a tussle every year about where to go on holiday.*

▷ **tussle** *v* [I, Ipr] ~ (**with sb**) (**about**/**for**/**over sth**) struggle or fight to obtain sth; wrestle: *They began to tussle with each other for the coins.* ○ (*fig*) *He tussled all night with the figures, but couldn't balance the account.*

tussock /ˈtʌsək/ *n* tuft or clump of grass that is thicker or higher than the grass growing round it.

tut /tʌt/ (also **tut-tut** /ˌtʌt ˈtʌt/) *interj, n* (way of showing the) sound made by touching the top of one's mouth with the tongue to express disapproval, annoyance, etc: *Tut-tut, the boy's late again!* ○ *a tut of disapproval.*

▷ **tut** (also **tut-tut**) *v* (**-tt-**) [I] express disapproval, impatience, etc in this way: *His wife tut-tutted with annoyance.*

Tutankhamun /ˌtuːtəŋˈkɑːmen, *or, rarely,* ˌtuːtəŋkɑːˈmuːn/ (c 1358-c 1340 BC), Egyptian Pharaoh of the 18th dynasty. His tomb, discovered in 1922 by the English archaeologist Howard Carter, is one of the few such tombs whose contents had not been taken by robbers.

tutelage /ˈtjuːtɪlɪdʒ; *US* ˈtuː-/ *n* [U] (*fml*) **1** (**a**) protection of and authority over a person, country, etc; guardianship: *a child in tutelage* ○ *royal, Papal, princely tutelage.* (**b**) state or period of being under the authority and protection of a guardian. **2** instruction; tuition: *under the tutelage of a master craftsman.*

tutelary /ˈtjuːtɪlərɪ; *US* ˈtuːtəlrɪ/ *adj* (*fml*) (**a**) acting as a guardian or protector. (**b**) of a guardian: *tutelary authority.*

tutor /ˈtjuːtə(r); *US* ˈtuː-/ *n* **1** private teacher, esp one who teaches a single pupil or a very small group: *There is a tutor to teach the children while they're in hospital.* **2** (**a**) (*Brit*) university teacher who supervises the studies of a student: *Her tutor says she is making good progress.* (**b**) (*US*) assistant lecturer in a college. **3** book of instruction in a particular subject, esp music: *a violin tutor.*

▷ **tutor** *v* **1** (**a**) [Tn, Tn·pr] ~ **sb** (**in sth**) act as a tutor(*n* 1, 2) to (sb); teach: *tutor sb for an examination* ○ *tutor sb in mathematics.* (**b**) [I] work as a tutor: *Her work was divided between tutoring and research.* **2** [Tn, Cn·t] (*fml*) control (oneself or one's feelings): *tutor one's passions* ○ *tutor oneself to be patient.*

tutorial /tjuːˈtɔːrɪəl; *US* tuː-/ *adj* of a tutor(*n* 1, 2): *tutorial classes, duties, responsibilities* ○ *in a tutorial capacity.* — *n* period of instruction given, esp to one or two students by a tutor in a university: *attend, give, miss a tutorial.*

tutti-frutti /ˌtuːtɪ ˈfruːtɪ/ *n* (also ˌ**tutti-frutti ice-**ˈ**cream**) [U, C] (portion of) ice-cream that contains various types of fruit and sometimes nuts.

tutu /ˈtuːtuː/ *n* ballet dancer's short skirt made of many layers of stiffened net.

Tuvalu /ˌtuːvɑːˈluː/ country consisting of a group of nine islands in the SW Pacific Ocean; pop approx 9 200; official languages Tuvaluan and English; capital Fongafale; unit of currency dollar (= 100 cents). Formerly part of the British colony of the Gilbert and Ellice Islands, it became independent in 1978. Its main export is phosphates. ⇨ map at POLYNESIA.

▷ **Tuvaluan** /-ˈluːən/ *adj* of Tuvalu. — *n* **1** [C] native or inhabitant of Tuvalu. **2** [U] *Polynesian language of Tuvalu, related to Samoan.

tu-whit, tu-whoo /tʊˌwɪt tʊˈwuː/ *interj* (used to represent the call of an owl).

tuxedo /tʌkˈsiːdəʊ/ *n* (*pl* ~**s** /-dəʊz/) (also *infml* **tux** /tʌks/) (*US*) = DINNER-JACKET (DINNER).

TV /ˌtiː ˈviː/ *abbr* television (set): *What's on TV tonight?* ○ *We're getting a new colour TV.* ○ [attrib] *a TV dinner*, ie a precooked packaged meal that only requires heating.

twaddle /ˈtwɒdl/ *n* [U] nonsense or writing of low quality: *I've never heard such utter twaddle!* ○ *The novel is sentimental twaddle.*

Twain /tweɪn/ Mark, real name Samuel Langhorne Clemens (1835-1910), American humorous writer best known for *The Adventures of Tom Sawyer* and its sequel *The Adventures of Huckleberry Finn*, stories set around the *Mississippi river, not far from where Twain himself was brought up. His other books include *The Prince and the Pauper* and *A Connecticut Yankee at King Arthur's Court.*

twang /twæŋ/ *n* **1** sound made when a tight string is pulled and released, esp when the string or bow of a musical instrument is plucked. **2** nasal quality or tone in speech: *speak with a twang* ○ *a distinctive Texan twang.*

▷ **twang** *v* [I, Tn] (cause sth to) make a twang(1): *The bow twanged and the arrow whistled through* *the air.* ○ *Someone was twanging a guitar in the next room.*

'twas /twɒz/ *contracted form* (*arch or rhet*) it was.

twat /twɒt/ *n* (⚠ *infml*) **1** female genitals. **2** (*derog*) unpleasant or stupid person.

tweak /twi:k/ *v* [Tn] pinch and twist (sth) sharply: *She tweaked his ear playfully.*

▷ **tweak** *n* sharp pinch, twist or pull: *He gave the boy's ear a painful tweak.*

twee /twi:/ *adj* (*Brit infml derog*) attractive to those with sentimental or poor taste: *I can't stand those twee little frills.* ○ *She has a rather twee manner that I find irritating.*

tweed /twi:d/ *n* **1** [U] woollen cloth with a rough surface, often woven with mixed colours: *Scottish tweed* ○ [attrib] *a tweed coat.* **2 tweeds** [pl] clothes made of tweed: *He is usually dressed in tweeds.*

▷ **tweedy** *adj* **(a)** (*infml*) often dressed in tweeds: *The pub was full of tweedy farmers.* **(b)** (*joc often derog*) behaving in a hearty way associated with rich country people in Britain: *a rather tweedy golf partner.*

📖 Tweeds are traditionally worn by the upper-class land-owning gentry in Britain. The image of a person wearing a tweed suit, standing perhaps in the grounds of a large country-house, has been used in advertising, etc to symbolize a prosperous country life-style.

tweet /twi:t/ *n* chirp of a small bird.

▷ **tweet** *v* [I] (of a bird) make this sound.

tweeter /ˈtwi:tə(r)/ *n* small loudspeaker for reproducing high notes. Cf WOOFER.

tweezers /ˈtwi:zəz/ *n* [pl] small pincers for picking up or pulling out very small things, eg hairs from the eyebrows: *a pair of tweezers* ○ *You'll need tweezers to hold up the specimen.*

twelve /twelv/ *pron, det* 12; one more than eleven. ⇨ App 9.

▷ **twelve** *n* **1** [C] the number 12. **2 the Twelve** [pl] the twelve apostles of Jesus.

twelve- (forming compound *adjs*) having twelve of the thing specified: *a twelve-man expedition.*

twelfth /twelfθ/ *pron, det* 12th; next after eleventh. ˌ**twelfth** ˈ**man** (in cricket) reserve player. ˌ**Twelfth** ˈ**Night** night before the feast of the Epiphany, formerly celebrated with festivities. — *n* one of twelve equal parts of sth.

For the uses of *twelve* and *twelfth,* see the examples at *five* and *fifth.*

□ ˈ**twelvemonth** *n* (*dated*) year.

twenty /ˈtwentɪ/ *pron, det* 20; one more than nineteen. ⇨ App 9.

▷ **twentieth** /ˈtwentɪəθ/ *pron, det* 20th; next after nineteen. — one of twenty equal parts of sth.

twenty *n* **1** the number 20. **2 the twenties** [pl] numbers, years or degrees of temperature from 20 to 29.

twenty- (forming compound *adjs*) having twenty of the thing specified: *a twenty-volume dictionary.* For the use of *twenty* and *twentieth,* see the examples at *five* and *fifth.*

□ ˌ**twenty-**ˈ**one** *n* [U] = PONTOON 2.

ˌ**twenty** ˈ**pence** (also ˌ**twenty** ˈ**p**, **20p**) (*Brit*) (coin worth) twenty new pence.

ˌ**twenty-twenty** ˈ**vision** (also **20/20 vision**) good eyesight of the normal standard.

'twere /twɜ:(r)/ *contracted form* (*arch or rhet*) it were (= it would be).

twerp /twɜ:p/ *n* (*infml*) stupid, irritating or contemptible person: *You twerp!* ○ *What a twerp he is!*

twice /twaɪs/ *adv* **1** two times: *I have seen the film twice.* ○ *He has twice lied to us.* **2** double in quantity, rate, etc: *The car's performance is twice as good since the engine's been tuned.* ○ *She did twice as much work as her brother.* **3** (idm) **be** ˈ**twice the man/woman (that sb is)** be much better, stronger, etc: *How dare you criticize him? He's twice the man (that) you are!* **lightning never strikes in the same place twice** ⇨ LIGHTNING[1]. **once bitten, twice shy** ⇨ ONCE. **once or twice** ⇨ ONCE. **think twice about sth/doing sth** ⇨ THINK[1]. ˌ**twice** ˈ**over** not just once but twice: *You've bought enough paint to paint the house twice over!*

twiddle /ˈtwɪdl/ *v* **1** [Ipr, Tn] ~ **with sth** twist or turn (sth), esp idly or aimlessly: *He twiddled with the controls of the radio until he found the station.* ○ *She sat twiddling the ring on her finger.* **2** (idm) **twiddle one's thumbs** move one's thumbs round each other with one's fingers or waste one's time doing nothing: *I sat twiddling my thumbs waiting for him to finish using the phone.* ○ *You're not being paid to twiddle your thumbs all day, you know!*

▷ **twiddle** *n* **(a)** slight twist or turn; twirl. **(b)** twirled mark or sign. **twiddly** /ˈtwɪdlɪ/ *adj* (*infml*) awkward to handle, play, etc: *the twiddly bits at the end of the sonata.*

twig[1] /twɪg/ *n* small thin branch that grows out of a larger branch on a shrub or tree: *They used dry twigs to start the fire.* ⇨ illus at TREE.

▷ **twiggy** *adj* having many twigs: *twiggy sticks.*

twig[2] /twɪg/ *v* (**-gg-**) [I, Tn, Tw] (*Brit infml*) realize or understand (sth): *I gave him another clue, but he still didn't twig (the answer).* ○ *I soon twigged who had told them.*

twilight /ˈtwaɪlaɪt/ *n* [U] **1 (a)** faint light after sunset or before sunrise: *I couldn't see their faces clearly in the twilight.* **(b)** period of this: *farmers walking home at twilight* ○ *Twilight is a dangerous time for drivers.* **2 the** ~ **(of sth)** (*rhet*) period of decreasing importance or strength; decline: *the twilight of his career* ○ [attrib] *his twilight years.*

▷ **twilit** /ˈtwaɪlɪt/ *adj* dimly lit (by the twilight): *in the twilit gloom.*

□ ˈ**twilight zone (a)** inner city area where the buildings are dilapidated. **(b)** uncertain area or condition between others that are more clearly defined: *Wrestling is in a twilight zone between sport and entertainment.*

twill /twɪl/ *n* [U] type of strong woven fabric with diagonal lines across its surface: *cotton/wool twill* ○ [attrib] *a twill skirt.*

'twill /twɪl/ *contracted form* (*arch or rhet*) it will.

twin /twɪn/ *n* **1** [C] either of a pair of children or young animals born of the same mother at the same time: *She is expecting twins.* ○ *One ewe has produced twins.* ○ [attrib] *my twin brother/sister* ○ *twin lambs.* **2** [C] either of a pair of similar, usu matching, things: *The plate was one of a pair, but I broke its twin.* ○ [attrib] *There are twin holes on each side of the instrument.* ○ *a ship with twin* (ie two identical) *propellers.* **3 the Twins** [pl] = GEMINI.

▷ **twin** *v* (**-nn-**) [esp passive: Tn, Tn·pr] ~ **sth (with sth) (a)** join (two people or things) closely together; pair. **(b)** set up a special relationship between (two towns in different countries), eg by organizing social or sporting visits: *Oxford is twinned with Bonn.*

□ ˌ**twin** ˈ**bed** either of a pair of single beds in a room for two people.

ˌ**twin-**ˈ**engined** *adj* (of an aeroplane) having two engines.

ˈ**twin set** (*Brit*) woman's matching jumper and long-sleeved cardigan.

ˌ**twin** ˈ**town** either of a pair of towns, usu in different countries, that have established special links with each other: *Oxford and Bonn are twin towns.* ○ *Oxford's twin town in France is Grenoble.*

twine /twaɪn/ *n* [U] strong thread or string made by twisting two or more strands of hemp, cotton, etc together: *a ball of twine.* ▷ **twine** *v* [Ipr, Tn·pr] ~ **(sth) round sth** (cause sth to) twist, coil or wind round sth: *vines that twine round a tree* ○ *The weed had twined itself round the branches.* ○ *She twined her arms around my neck.*

twinge /twɪndʒ/ *n* **1** short sudden spasm of pain: *an occasional twinge of rheumatism.* **2** short sharp (usu unpleasant) thought or feeling; pang: *a twinge of conscience, fear, guilt, regret, remorse, etc.*

twinkle /ˈtwɪŋkl/ *v* **1 (a)** [I] shine with a light that changes constantly from bright to faint: *stars twinkling in the sky* ○ *the lights of the town twinkling in the distance.* **(b)** [I, Ipr] ~ **(with sth)** (of a person's eyes) look bright or sparkle, esp because one is amused: *Her eyes twinkled with mischief.* **2** [I] (esp of a person's feet) move rapidly to and fro: *The tune set our toes twinkling.*

▷ **twinkle** *n* [sing] **(a)** twinkling light: *We could see the distant twinkle of the harbour lights.* **(b)** sparkle or gleam in the eyes: *She has an amused twinkle in her eye(s).* **(c)** rapid movement: *the twinkle of the dancers' feet.*

twinkling /ˈtwɪŋklɪŋ/ *n* (idm) **in the** ˌ**twinkling of an** ˈ**eye** very quickly; instantaneously: *The mood of the crowd can change in the twinkling of an eye.*

twirl /twɜ:l/ *v* **1** [Tn, Tn·pr] turn (sth) quickly and lightly round and round; spin: *He walked along briskly, twirling his cane in the air.* ○ *She sat twirling the stem of the glass in her fingers.* **2** [I, Ipr, Ip] move quickly round and round; spin: *I watched the dancers twirling (across the floor).* **3** [I, Tn, Tn·pr] (cause sth to) twist or curl: *She twirled a strand of hair round her finger.*

▷ **twirl** *n* **1** rapid circular movement; spin: *She did a twirl in front of the mirror.* **2** twirled mark or sign; twiddle.

twist[1] /twɪst/ *v* **1 (a)** [Tn, Tn·pr, Tn·p] ~ **sth (round sth/round)** coil or wind sth round sth else: *I twisted the bandage round her knee.* ○ *The telephone wire has got twisted,* ie tangled. **(b)** [Ipr, Ip] move or grow by winding round sth: *The snake twisted round my arm.* ○ *The sweet peas are twisting up the canes.* **2 (a)** [Tn, Tn·pr] ~ **sth (into sth)** turn or wind (threads, etc) to make them into a rope, etc: *We twisted the bed sheets into a rope and escaped by climbing down it.* **(b)** [Tn, Tn·pr] ~ **sth (from sth)** make (a rope, etc) by doing this: *twist a cord from/out of silk threads.* **3 (a)** [Tn, Tn·pr] bend or crush (sth) so as to spoil its natural shape: *His face was twisted with pain.* ○ *The car was now just a pile of twisted metal.* ○ (*fig*) *Failure left her bitter and twisted.* **(b)** [I, Ipr] be bent or crushed in this way: *The metal frame tends to twist under pressure.* **4 (a)** [Tn, Tn·pr, Tn·p] turn (sth) round; revolve: *Twist the knob to the right setting.* ○ *I twisted my head round to reverse the car.* **(b)** [I, Ipr, Ip] turn round; revolve: *I twisted round in my seat to speak to her.* ○ *She was still twisting about in pain.* **5** [I, Ipr, Ip] (eg of a road) change its direction often; wind: *Downstream the river twists and turns a lot.* ○ *The path twisted down (the hillside).* **6** [Tn] injure (eg one's wrist) by turning it too far; sprain: *a twisted ankle.* **7** [Tn, Tn·pr] deliberately give a false meaning to (words, etc): *The papers twisted everything I said.* ○ *The police tried to twist his statement into an admission of guilt.* **8** [I, Tn] (in billiards) (cause a ball to) move in a curved path while spinning. **9** (idm) ˌ**twist sb's** ˈ**arm** (*infml*) persuade or force sb to do sth: *She'll let you borrow the car if you twist her arm.* **twist sb round one's little** ˈ**finger** (*infml*) (know how to) get sb to do anything that one wants: *Jane has always been able to twist her parents round her little finger.* **10** (phr v) **twist (sth) off (sth)** (cause sth to) come or break off with a twisting movement: *The cap should twist off easily.* ○ *I can't twist off the lid.*

▷ **twister** *n* (*infml*) **1** dishonest person; liar or cheat: *What a twister!* **2** difficult puzzle or problem: *That's a real twister.* **3** (*US*) tornado; whirlwind.

twist[2] /twɪst/ *n* **1** [C] act of twisting sth (TWIST[1] 2, 4, 6); twisting movement: *He gave my arm a twist.* ○ *With a violent twist, he wrenched off the handle.* ○ *Give the rope a few more twists.* **2** [C] **(a)** thing formed by twisting: *a rope full of twists,* ie kinks or coils ○ *a twist of paper,* ie a small paper packet with screwed-up ends. **(b)** coiled shape: *a twist of smoke* ○ *a shell with a spiral twist.* **(c)** place where a path, etc turns: *a twist in the road* ○ *the twists and turns of the river.* **3** [C] change or development: *the twists and turns in the economy, market, policy* ○ *a strange twist of fate* ○ *The story had an odd twist at the end.* **4** [sing] peculiar tendency in a person's mind and character: *the criminal twist in his personality.* **5** [U, sing] spinning motion given to a ball to make it move in a curved path. **6** (idm) **get one's knickers in a twist** ⇨ KNICKERS. **round the bend/twist** ⇨ BEND[2].

▷ **twisty** *adj* (**-ier, -iest**) full of twists (TWIST[2] 2c): *a twisty path, river, track, etc.*

twit[1] /twɪt/ *n* (*Brit infml often joc*) stupid or annoying person: *He's an arrogant little twit!* ○ *Stop messing around, you silly twit!*

twit[2] /twɪt/ *v* (**-tt-**) [Tn, Tn·pr] ~ **sb** (**about/with sth**) (*dated*) make fun of sb, esp in a friendly way: *His unmarried friends twitted him about his wedding plans.*

twitch /twɪtʃ/ *n* **1** sudden rapid (usu involuntary) movement of a muscle, etc: *I thought the mouse was dead, but then it gave a slight twitch.* **2** sudden pull or jerk: *I felt a twitch at my sleeve.*
▷ **twitch** *v* **1** [I, Tn] (cause sb/sth to) move with a twitch or twitches: *The dog's nose twitched as it smelt the meat.* ○ *Her face twitched with pain.* **2** [Ipr, Tn, Tn·pr] ~ **at sth** pull sth sharply with a light jerk: *He twitched nervously at his tie.* ○ *She twitched the corner of the rug to straighten it.* ○ *The wind twitched the paper out of my hand.*
twitchy *adj* (**-ier, -iest**) (*infml*) worried or frightened; nervous: *People are beginning to get twitchy about all these rumours.* **twitchily** *adv.* **twitchiness** *n* [U].

twitter /ˈtwɪtə(r)/ *v* **1** [I, Ip] (of birds) make a series of light short sounds; chirp. **2** (*infml*) **(a)** [I, Ipr, Ip] ~ (**on**) (**about sth**) talk rapidly in an excited or a nervous way: *Stop twittering!* ○ *What is he twittering (on) about?* **(b)** [Tn] say (sth) in an excited or nervous way: *'It's so marvellous to see you!' she twittered.*
▷ **twitter** *n* [sing] **1** sound of chirping: *the twitter of sparrows.* **2** (*infml*) state of nervous excitement: *a twitter of suspense and anticipation.* **3** (idm) ˌ**all of a** ˈ**twitter** (*infml joc*) nervous and excited: *We were all of a twitter on the wedding day.*
twittery /ˈtwɪtərɪ/ *adj* (*infml*) nervous.

two /tu:/ *pron, det* **1** 2; one more than one. ⇨ App 9, Cf SECOND[1]. **2** (idm) **by/in** ˌ**twos and** ˈ**threes** two or three at a time: *Applications for the job are coming in slowly in twos and threes.* **a** ˈ**day**, ˈ**moment**, ˈ**pound, etc or two** one or a few days, moments, pounds, etc: *May I borrow the book for a day or two?* **in two** in or into two pieces or halves: *The vase fell and broke into two.* ○ *She cut the cake in two and gave me half.* **it takes two to do sth** (*saying*) one person cannot be entirely responsible for (making a happy or an unhappy marriage, a quarrel, a truce, etc). **put** ˌ**two and** ˌ**two** ˈ**together** guess the truth from what one sees, hears, etc: (*joc*) *He is rather inclined to put two and two together and make five*, ie imagine that things are worse, more exciting, etc than they really are. **that makes** ˈ**two of us** (*infml*) I am in the same position or hold the same opinion: *'I'm finding this party extremely dull.' 'That makes two of us!'*
▷ **two** *n* the number 2.
two- (in compounds) having two of the thing specified: *blue and white two-tone shoes* ○ *a two-room flat.*
For the uses of *two* see the examples at *five.*
□ ˌ**two** ˈ**bits** (*US infml*) twenty-five cents. ˈ**two-bit** *adj* (*US infml*) not very good, important, interesting, etc.
ˌ**two-di**ˈ**mensional** *adj* having or appearing to have length and breadth but no depth: *a* ˌ*two-dimensional* ˈ*image* ○ (*fig*) *a* ˌ*two-dimensional* ˈ*character*, ie sb who is not very interesting.
ˌ**two-**ˈ**edged** *adj* **(a)** (of a knife, sword, etc) having two cutting-edges. **(b)** (*fig*) having two possible (and contradictory) meanings or effects at the same time: *a* ˌ*two-edged re*ˈ*mark* ○ *Publicity is a* ˌ*two-edged* ˈ*weapon.*
ˌ**two-**ˈ**faced** *adj* deceitful or insincere.
ˈ**twofold** *adj, adv* **1** twice as much or as many: *a twofold increase* ○ *Her original investment had increased twofold.* **2** consisting of two parts: *a twofold development plan.*
ˌ**two-**ˈ**handed** *adj* **(a)** (of a sword, etc) (to be) held with both hands. **(b)** (of a saw, etc) (to be) used by two people, one at each end.
ˌ**two** ˈ**pence** (also ˌ**two** ˈ**p**, **2p**) (*Brit*) (coin worth) two new pence.
twopence /ˈtʌpəns; *US* ˈtu:pens/ (also **tuppence**) *n* **1** (esp formerly) sum of two pence. **2** even the smallest amount: *I don't give twopence for/care twopence what they think.* ○ *It's not worth twopence.*
twopenny /ˈtʌpənɪ; *US* ˈtu:penɪ/ (also **tuppenny**) *adj* **(a)** costing or worth two pence: *a* ˌ*twopenny* ˈ*stamp.* **(b)** of little or no value; cheap or worthless. **twopenny-halfpenny** /ˌtʌpnɪ ˈheɪpnɪ; *US* ˌtu:penɪ ˈhæfpenɪ/ *adj* (*infml*) insignificant, contemptible or worthless: *some twopenny-halfpenny little reporter.*
ˌ**two-a-**ˈ**penny** *adj* [pred] easily obtained; cheap: *Qualified staff are two-a-penny at the moment.*
ˌ**two-**ˈ**piece** *n* set of two matching garments, eg a skirt and a jacket or trousers and a jacket: [attrib] *a* ˌ*two-piece* ˈ*suit*, ˈ*bathing-costume, etc.*
ˈ**two-ply** *adj* (of wool, wood etc) having two strands or thicknesses.
ˌ**two-**ˈ**seater** *n* car, aircraft, etc with seats for two people.
ˈ**twosome** /-səm/ *n* **1** group of two people; pair; couple. **2** game played by two people.
ˈ**two-step** *n* type of ballroom dance with long sliding steps, in march or polka time.
ˈ**two-stroke** *adj* (of an internal-combustion engine) producing power with a single up-and-down movement of the piston.
ˈ**two-time** *v* [I, Tn] (*infml*) deceive (esp a lover by being unfaithful); double-cross (sb): *a two-timing rogue* ○ *He'd been two-timing me for months!* ˈ**two-timer** *n.*
ˈ**two-tone** *adj* [attrib] having two colours or sounds.
ˌ**two-**ˈ**way** *adj* [usu attrib] **(a)** (of a switch) allowing electric current to be turned on or off from either of two points. **(b)** (of a road or street) in which traffic travels in both directions. **(c)** (of traffic) in lanes travelling in both directions. **(d)** (of radio equipment, etc) for sending and receiving signals. **(e)** (of communication between people, etc) operating in both directions: *a* ˌ*two-way* ˈ*process.*

'twould /twʊd/ *contracted form* (*arch or rhet*) it would.

Tyburn /ˈtaɪbɜ:n/ site in London, near the present-day *Marble Arch, where people were hanged in public between about 1300 and 1783.

tycoon /taɪˈku:n/ *n* (*infml*) wealthy and powerful businessman or industrialist; magnate: *an* ˈ*oil tycoon* ○ *a* ˈ*newspaper tycoon.*

tying ⇨ TIE[2].

tyke (also **tike**) /taɪk/ *n* (*infml*) **1** (used as a term of abuse) worthless person. **2** (*esp US*) small child, esp one who is naughty. **3** dog of mixed breed; cur.

Tyler /ˈtaɪlə(r)/ Wat (died 1381), English leader of the *Peasants' Revolt of 1381. He brought his rebel army from Kent to London and negotiated with Richard II, but was murdered.

tympanum /ˈtɪmpənəm/ *n* (*pl* **-s** or **-na** /-nə/) (*anatomy*) **1** ear-drum. **2** middle ear.

Tyndale /ˈtɪndl/ William (c 1494-1536), English translator of the Bible and a leading figure of the *Reformation in England. His translation of the Bible was produced in Germany, after he had been forced to flee from England. He was burnt at the stake for heresy.

Tyne and Wear /ˌtaɪn ən ˈwɪə(r)/ county of NE England, formed in 1974 from parts of *Durham and *Northumberland. Its administrative centre is Newcastle-upon-Tyne. ⇨ map at App 1.

Tyneside /ˈtaɪnsaɪd/ area of NE England around the River Tyne, including Newcastle-upon-Tyne, Gateshead and South Shields. It was formerly a shipbuilding centre.
▷ **Tynesider** *n* person from Tyneside. Cf GEORDIE.

Tynwald /ˈtɪnwəld/ parliament of the *Isle of Man.

type[1] /taɪp/ *n* **1** ~ (**of sth**) class or group of people or things that have characteristics in common; kind: *different racial types* ○ *Which type of tea do you prefer?* ○ *all types of jobs/jobs of all types* ○ *A bungalow is/Bungalows are a type of house.* ○ *wines of the Burgundy type/Burgundy-type wines.* **2** ~ (**of sth**) person, thing, event, etc considered as a representative example of a class or group: *I don't think she's the artistic type.* ○ *not the type of party I enjoy* ○ *the old-fashioned type of English gentleman* ○ *just the type of situation to avoid* ○ *He's true to type*, ie he behaves as sb of his class, group, etc may be expected to behave. **3** (*infml*) person of a specified character: *a brainy type* ○ *He's not my type (of person)*, ie We have little in common. **4** (idm) **revert to type** ⇨ REVERT.
▷ **type** *v* [Tn] classify (sth/sb) according to its type: *patients typed by age and blood group.*
□ **type-cast** /ˈtaɪpkɑ:st; *US* -kæst/ *v* (*pt, pp* **type-cast**) [esp passive: Tn, Cn·n/a] give (an actor) the kind of role which he has often played successfully before or which seems to fit his personality: *avoid being type-cast as a gangster.*

type[2] /taɪp/ *n* **(a)** [C] small block, esp of metal, with a raised letter or figure, etc on it, for use in printing. **(b)** [U] set, supply, kind or size of these: *set sth in bold, roman, italic, etc type.*
▷ **type** *v* [I, Ip, Tn, Tn·p] ~ **sth** (**out/up**) write sth using a typewriter or word processor: *typing (away) with four fingers* ○ *This will need to be typed (out) again.* **typing** (also ˈ**typewriting**) *n* [U] **1** (skill at) using a typewriter or word processor: *practise typing* ○ [attrib] *a typing pool*, ie a group of typists who share a firm's typing work. **2** writing produced on a typewriter or word processor: *two pages of typing.* **typist** /ˈtaɪpɪst/ *n* person who types, esp one employed to do so: *fast accurate typists required* ○ *copy, shorthand, etc typists.*
□ ˈ**type-face** (also **face**) *n* set of types in a particular design: *headings printed in a different type-face from the text.*
ˈ**typescript** *n* [C, U] typewritten text or document: *We receive several new typescripts a day.* ○ *The poems arrived in (fifty pages of) typescript.*
ˈ**typesetter** *n* person or machine that sets type for printing.
ˈ**typewriter** *n* machine for producing characters similar to those of print by pressing keys which cause raised metal letters, etc to strike the paper, usu through inked ribbon: *an electric typewriter* ○ [attrib] *a typewriter ribbon, keyboard.* Cf WORD PROCESSOR (WORD).
ˈ**typewritten** *adj* written using a typewriter or word processor: *typewritten pages, letters, manuscripts.*

typhoid /ˈtaɪfɔɪd/ *n* [U] (also ˌ**typhoid** ˈ**fever**) serious infectious feverish disease that attacks the intestines, caused by bacteria taken into the body in food or drink: [attrib] *a typhoid epidemic.*

typhoon /taɪˈfu:n/ *n* violent tropical hurricane that occurs in the western Pacific. Cf HURRICANE, CYCLONE.

typhus /ˈtaɪfəs/ *n* [U] infectious disease with fever, great weakness and purple spots on the body.

typical /ˈtɪpɪkl/ *adj* ~ (**of sb/sth**) **1** having the distinctive qualities of a particular type of person or thing; representative: *a typical Scot, teacher, gentleman* ○ *a typical British pub* ○ *a typical cross-section of the population.* **2** characteristic of a particular person or thing: *It was typical of her to forget.* ○ *He answered with typical curtness.* ○ *On a typical* (ie normal, average) *day we receive about fifty letters.* ○ *Such decoration was a typical feature of the baroque period.* ○ (*infml*) *The train's late again — typical!*
▷ **typically** /-klɪ/ *adv* **1** representing a particular type of person or thing: *typically American hospitality.* **2** characteristic of a particular person or thing: *Typically, she had forgotten her keys again.*

typify /ˈtɪpɪfaɪ/ *v* (*pt, pp* **-fied**) [Tn] (usu not in the continuous tenses) be a representative example of (sb/sth): *Now a millionaire, he typifies the self-made man.* ○ *The nurses' strike typifies public concern about our hospitals.*

typist ⇨ TYPE[2].

typo /ˈtaɪpəʊ/ *n* (*pl* ~**s**) (*infml*) mistake (eg a word wrongly spelt) in a printed text.

typography /taɪˈpɒgrəfɪ/ *n* [U] **1** art or practice of printing. **2** style or appearance of printed matter: *set to a high standard of typography.*
▷ **typographer** /taɪˈpɒgrəfə(r)/ *n* person skilled in typography.
typographical /ˌtaɪpəˈgræfɪkl/ *adj.* **typographically** /-klɪ/ *adv.*

tyrannical /tɪˈrænɪkl/ (also *fml* **tyrannous** /ˈtɪrənəs/) *adj* of or like a tyrant; obtaining obedience by force or threats: *a tyrannical regime* ○ *She works for a tyrannical new boss.* ▷ **tyrannically** /-klɪ/ *adv.*

tyrannize, -ise /ˈtɪrənaɪz/ *v* [Ipr, Tn] ~ **(over) sb/sth** rule sb/sth as a tyrant; treat sb cruelly and unjustly: *tyrannize over the weak* ○ *He tyrannizes his family.*

tyrannosaurus /tɪˌrænəˈsɔːrəs/ (also **tyrannosaur** /tɪˈrænəsɔː(r)/) *n* large flesh-eating dinosaur that walked on its hind legs.

tyranny /ˈtɪrənɪ/ *n* **1** (**a**) [U] cruel, unjust or oppressive use of power or authority: *a lifelong hatred of tyranny* ○ *the tyranny of military rule* ○ *(fig) submit to the tyranny of inflexible office hours.* (**b**) [C esp *pl*] instance of this; tyrannical act: *the petty tyrannies of domestic routine.* **2** [C, U] (country under the) rule of a tyrant.

tyrant /ˈtaɪərənt/ *n* cruel, unjust or oppressive ruler, esp one who has obtained complete power by force; despot.

tyre (*US* **tire**) /ˈtaɪə(r)/ *n* covering fitted round the rim of a wheel to absorb shocks, usu of reinforced rubber filled with air or covering a pneumatic inner tube: *a bicycle tyre* ○ *a spare tyre* ○ *a burst/flat/punctured tyre* ○ *Your tyres are badly worn.* ○ [attrib] *tyre pressure.* ⇨ illus at CAR, ⇨ illus at BICYCLE.

tyro = TIRO.

Tyrol (also **Tirol**) /ˈtɪrəl; *US* təˈrəʊl/ mountainous province of western Austria, in the *Alps. It is a popular area for winter sports.

▷ **Tyrolean** (also **Tirolean**) /ˌtɪrəˈliːən/ *adj* (typical) of the Tyrol: *traditional Tyrolean costume.*

Tyrone /tɪˈrəʊn/ county of Northern Ireland.

tzar, tzarina ⇨ TSAR.

U, u

U¹, u /ju:/ *n* (*pl* **U's, u's** /ju:z/) the twenty-first letter of the English alphabet: *'Ursula' begins with (a) U/'U'.*
□ **ˈU-turn** *n* **1** turn of 180° (by a car, etc) so as to face in the opposite direction without reversing: *No U-turns!* ie as a sign on motorways, etc. **2** (idm) **do a ˈU-turn** (*infml*) reverse one's policy: *The government has done a U-turn on its economic policy.*
U² /ju:/ *adj* (*infml approv or joc*) thought to be characteristic of the upper class: *very U behaviour.*
U /ju:/ *abbr* (*Brit*) (of films) universal, ie suitable for anyone, including children: *a U film* ○ *a U certificate.*
U *symb* uranium.
UAE /ˌju: eɪ ˈi:/ *abbr* United Arab Emirates.
UAR /ˌju: eɪ ˈɑ:(r)/ *abbr* United Arab Republic.
ubiquitous /ju:ˈbɪkwɪtəs/ *adj* [esp attrib] (*fml or joc*) (seeming to be) present everywhere or in several places at the same time: *Is there no escape from the ubiquitous cigarette smoke in restaurants?* ○ *ubiquitous traffic wardens.*
▷ **ubiquity** /ju:ˈbɪkwətɪ/ *n* [U] quality of being ubiquitous.
U-boat /ˈju:bəʊt/ *n* (esp in the Second World War) German submarine.
UCCA /ˈʌkə/ *abbr* (*Brit*) Universities Central Council on Admissions: *fill in an UCCA form*, ie with the subjects and universities chosen. ➪ article at POST-SCHOOL.
UDA /ˌju: di: ˈeɪ/ *abbr* Ulster Defence Association.
udder /ˈʌdə(r)/ *n* bag-like organ of a cow, female goat, etc, with two or more teats, which produces milk. ➪ illus at COW.
UDI /ˌju: di: ˈaɪ/ *abbr* unilateral declaration of independence (esp that made by the Rhodesian government in 1965).
UDR /ˌju: di: ˈɑ:(r)/ *abbr* Ulster Defence Regiment. ➪ article at IRELAND.
UEFA /ju:ˈi:fə/ *abbr* Union of European Football Associations: *the UEFA cup.*
Uffizi /u:ˈfɪtsɪ/ **the Uffizi** art gallery in *Florence. It was built by the *Medici family and designed by *Vasari. It contains a remarkable collection of Italian painting dating from the 13th to the 18th century.
UFO (also **ufo**) /ˌju: ef ˈəʊ *or, in informal use,* ˈju:fəʊ/ *abbr* (*pl* ~**s**) unidentified flying object (esp a flying saucer).
Uganda /ju:ˈgændə/ country in E Africa, a member of the Commonwealth; pop approx 17 190 000; official language English; capital Kampala; unit of currency shilling (= 100 cents). The country lies on the equator and much of it is covered by lakes and marshes. The economy is chiefly agricultural, with coffee and cotton as the main export crops. Uganda's economy and stability have suffered for many years from political violence and repression, esp under the regime of Idi Amin in the 1970s. ➪ map at TANZANIA. ▷ **Ugandan** *n, adj.*
ugh (usu suggesting a sound like /ɜ:/ made with the lips either spread or rounded very strongly) *interj* (used to indicate disgust or horror, and usu accompanied by an appropriate facial expression): *Ugh! You're eating snails!*
ugli /ˈʌglɪ/ *n* (*pl* ~**s** or ~**es**) (also **ˈugli fruit**) mottled green and yellow W Indian citrus fruit that is a hybrid of a grapefruit and a tangerine.
ugly /ˈʌglɪ/ *adj* (**-ier, -iest**) **1** unpleasant to look at or to hear: *an ugly face, child, building* ○ *an ugly wound, gash, scar, etc* ○ *the ugly screeching of parrots.* **2** hostile or menacing; ominous: *ugly threats, rumours, insinuations, etc* ○ *an ugly laugh, look, wink, etc* ○ *The situation in the streets was turning/growing ugly.* ○ *The crowd was in an ugly mood.* ○ *An ugly storm is brewing.* **3** (idm) **miserable/ugly as sin** ➪ SIN. **an ˌugly ˈcustomer** (*infml*) person who is difficult, dangerous or unpleasant to deal with. **an ˌugly ˈduckling** person who at first seems unpromising but who later becomes much admired, very able, etc. ▷ **ugliness** *n* [U].
UHF /ˌju: eɪtʃ ˈef/ *abbr* (*radio*) ultra-high frequency. Cf VHF.
UHT /ˌju: eɪtʃ ˈti:/ *abbr* (of dairy products) ultra heat treated (for longer life): *UHT milk.*
UK /ˌju: ˈkeɪ/ *abbr* (esp in addresses) United Kingdom (of Great Britain and Northern Ireland): *a UK citizen.* ➪ Usage at GREAT.
Ukraine /ju:ˈkreɪn/ **the Ukraine** country in the south-western part of the former USSR, with a coast on the Black Sea; pop approx 52 000 000; official language Ukrainian; capital Kiev; unit of currency karbovanets. Once the home of the earliest Russian state, it became part of the Russian empire in the 18th century and subsequently of the USSR until independence in 1991. It is rich in coal and iron, and is also a developed agricultural area. ➪ map at UNION OF SOVIET SOCIALIST REPUBLICS. ▷ **Ukrainian** *n, adj.*
ukulele /ˌju:kəˈleɪlɪ/ *n* small four-stringed Hawaiian guitar similar to a banjo: *strumming tunes on his ukulele.* ➪ illus at BANJO.
ulcer /ˈʌlsə(r)/ *n* open sore containing poisonous matter on the outside of the body or on the surface of an internal organ: *leg ulcers* ○ *gastric ulcers* ○ *My mouth ulcer has burst.*
▷ **ulcerate** /ˈʌlsəreɪt/ *v* [I, Tn] (cause sth to) become affected with an ulcer or ulcers: *Aspirin can ulcerate the stomach lining.* **ulceration** /ˌʌlsəˈreɪʃn/ *n*: *severe ulceration of the legs.*
ulcerous /ˈʌlsərəs/ *adj* affected with or producing ulcers.
ulna /ˈʌlnə/ *n* (*pl* **-nae** /-ni:/) (*anatomy*) inner and thinner of the two bones of the forearm in man; corresponding bone in an animal's foreleg or bird's wing. ➪ illus at SKELETON. Cf RADIUS.
Ulster /ˈʌlstə(r)/ *Northern Ireland. Historically Ulster was a province of Ireland which included the six counties of Northern Ireland along with Cavan, Donegal and Monaghan, which are now in the Irish Republic.
□ **the ˌUlster Democratic ˈUnionist Party** political party in Northern Ireland. It is supported mainly by Protestants and wants Northern Ireland to stay part of the United Kingdom. It was formed in 1971 and is regarded as more militant than the Ulster Unionist Party.
ˈUlsterman /-mən/ (*pl* **-men** /-mən/, *fem* **ˈUlsterwoman**, *pl* **-women**) *n* native or inhabitant of Ulster.
the ˌUlster ˈUnionist Party political party in Northern Ireland. Since 1920 it has been the main party supporting the policy of Northern Ireland staying as part of the United Kingdom. ➪ article at IRELAND.
ulster /ˈʌlstə(r)/ *n* loose overcoat with a belt, made from rough cloth.
ulterior /ʌlˈtɪərɪə(r)/ *adj* [attrib] (*fml*) beyond what is obvious or admitted: *This lever must serve some ulterior purpose.* ○ *Jim had ulterior motives in buying me a drink — he wants to borrow my van.*
ultimate /ˈʌltɪmət/ *adj* [attrib] **1** beyond which no other exists or is possible; last or final: *the ultimate outcome, result, conclusion, etc* ○ *Management must take ultimate responsibility for the strike.* ○ *Nuclear weapons are the ultimate deterrent.* **2** from which everything else is derived; basic or fundamental: *ultimate principles, questions, causes* ○ *the ultimate truths of philosophy and science.* **3** (*infml*) that cannot be surpassed or improved upon; greatest: *The ultimate luxury of the trip was flying by Concorde.*
▷ **ultimate** *n* [sing] ~ **the ultimate (in sth)** (*infml*) the greatest, most advanced, etc of its kind: *These ceramic tiles are the ultimate in modern kitchen design.*
ultimately *adv* **1** in the end; finally: *Ultimately, all the colonies will become independent.* **2** at the most basic level; fundamentally: *All matter ultimately consists of atoms.*
ultimatum /ˌʌltɪˈmeɪtəm/ *n* (*pl* ~**s** or **-ta** /-tə/) final demand or statement of terms to be accepted without discussion, eg one sent to a foreign government and threatening war if the conditions are not accepted: *accept, reject, issue, deliver an ultimatum.*
ultra- *pref* (used fairly freely with *adjs*) **1** extremely; to excess: *ultra-conservative* ○ *ultra-fashionable.* **2** beyond a specified limit, extent, etc: *ultraviolet* ○ *ultra-high.* Cf INFRA-.
ultramarine /ˌʌltrəməˈri:n/ *adj, n* [U] (of a) brilliant pure blue.
ultramontane /ˌʌltrəˈmɒnteɪn/ *adj* (*fml*) **1** situated south of the *Alps. **2** supporting the view that the Pope has supreme spiritual authority.
▷ **ultramontane** *n* person with ultramontane(2) views.
ultrasonic /ˌʌltrəˈsɒnɪk/ *adj* (of sound waves) pitched above the upper limit of human hearing.
▷ **ultrasonics** *n* [sing *v*] study and use of ultrasonic waves, eg in medical diagnosis as an alternative to X-rays and in industrial processes.
ultrasound /ˈʌltrəsaʊnd/ *n* [U] sound with an ultrasonic frequency; ultrasonic waves: [attrib] *an ultrasound scan*, eg to detect abnormality in a foetus.
ultraviolet /ˌʌltrəˈvaɪələt/ *adj* (*abbr* **UV**) [usu attrib] **1** (*physics*) (of radiation) with a wavelength that is just beyond the violet end of the visible spectrum: *ultraviolet rays*, ie causing sun-tanning. **2** of or using such radiation: *an ultraviolet lamp* ○ *ultraviolet treatment*, ie for skin diseases. Cf INFRA-RED (INFRA).
ululate /ˈju:ljʊleɪt/ *v* [I] (*fml*) howl or wail. ▷ **ululation** /-leɪʃn/ *n* [U, C]: *the ululations of the mourning women.*
Ulysses /ju:ˈlɪsɪ:z/ Latin name of *Odysseus.

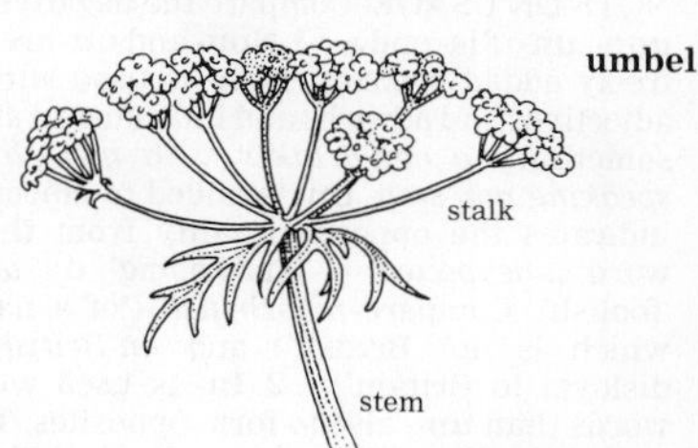

umbel /ˈʌmbl/ *n* cluster of flowers on stalks coming out from a single stem. ➪ illus.
▷ **umbellate** /ˈʌmbəleɪt/ *adj* (of a plant) having umbels.
umbellifer /ʌmˈbelɪfə(r)/ *n* member of an order of plants, including the parsnip and carrot, which have umbels. **umbelliferous** /-bəˈlɪfərəs/ *adj* of or belonging to this order.
umber /ˈʌmbə(r)/ *n* [U] natural colouring-matter similar to ochre but darker and browner: *burnt umber*, ie reddish-brown pigment.
▷ **umber** *adj* yellowish or reddish-brown.
umbilicus /ʌmˈbɪlɪkəs; *also, in medical use,* ˌʌmbɪˈlaɪkəs/ *n* (*anatomy*) navel.
▷ **umbilical** /ʌmˈbɪlɪkl, *also, in medical use* ˌʌmbɪˈlaɪkl/ *adj* of, near or concerning the umbilicus.
□ **umˌbilical ˈcord** flexible tube of tissue connecting the placenta to the navel of the foetus and carrying nourishment to it before birth: (*fig*) *By leaving my parents' home, I cut/broke the*

umbilical cord.

umbra /ˈʌmbrə/ *n* (*pl* **-rae** /-riː/ or ~**s**) (*astronomy*) dark central part of the shadow cast by the earth or the moon in an eclipse, or of a sunspot. Cf PENUMBRA.

umbrage /ˈʌmbrɪdʒ/ *n* (idm) **give ˈumbrage; take ˈumbrage (at sth)** (*fml or joc*) (make sb) feel offended or slighted: *I invited her because I was afraid of giving umbrage.* ○ *He took umbrage at my remarks and left.*

umbrella /ʌmˈbrelə/ *n* **1** folding frame of spokes attached to a stick and handle and covered with fabric, used to shelter a person from rain: *put up/take down an umbrella.* Cf PARASOL, SUNSHADE (SUN). **2** (*fig*) any kind of general protecting force or influence: *sheltering under the American nuclear umbrella* ○ *Police operated under the umbrella of the security forces.* **3** [esp attrib] (*fig*) central controlling agency for a group of related companies: *an umbrella organization, group, project.*

□ **umˈbrella-stand** *n* stand used for holding closed umbrellas, having a base into which wet umbrellas can drain.

umlaut /ˈʊmlaʊt/ *n* (**a**) [U] (in Germanic languages) vowel contrast in related forms of a word, shown by two dots over the vowel in one of them, eg *der Mann/die Männer* in German (= the man/the men). (**b**) [C] sign (consisting of two dots) that shows this. Cf DIAERESIS.

umpire /ˈʌmpaɪə(r)/ *n* (**a**) (in tennis, cricket, etc) person appointed to see that the rules are observed and to settle disputes. ⇨ illus at BASEBALL, CRICKET, TENNIS. (**b**) person chosen to act as a judge between two parties who disagree. Cf REFEREE.

▷ **umpire** *v* [I, Tn] act as umpire in (a game, etc): *umpire a match, competition, dispute.*

umpteen /ˈʌmptiːn/ *pron, det* (*infml*) too many to count; numerous: *Umpteen of them left.* ○ *have umpteen reasons for being late.* ▷ **umpteenth** /ˈʌmptiːnθ/ *pron, det*: *For the umpteenth time, I tell you I don't know!*

'un /ən/ *pron* (*infml*) one: *That's a good 'un!* eg a good photograph, joke, excuse. ○ *He went fishing and caught a big 'un.*

un- *pref* **1** (with *adjs, advs* and *ns*) not: *unable* ○ *unconsciously* ○ *untruth.* **2** (**a**) (with *vs* forming *vs*) reverse or opposite of: *unlock* ○ *undo.* (**b**) (with *ns* forming *vs*) remove from or deprive of: *unearth* ○ *unmask* ○ *unhorse.*

NOTE ON USAGE: Compare the negative prefixes **non-**, **un-**, **dis-** and **a-**. **1 Non-** and **un-** are the most freely added prefixes. **Non-** is used with nouns, adjectives and adverbs and indicates an absence of something: *a non-drinker* ○ *a non-stick pan* ○ *speaking non-stop.* **Un-** is added to adjectives and indicates the opposite quality from the simple word: *unexpected* = 'surprising' ○ *unwise* = 'foolish'. Compare *non-British* ('of a nationality which is not British') and *un-British* ('being disloyal to Britain'). **2 In-** is used with fewer words than **un-**, also to form opposites. There are variant spellings: **il-** before l (*illogical*); **im-** before b, m, p (*imbalance, immaterial, impossible*) and **ir-** before r (*irresponsible*). **3 Dis-** is also used with verbs, adjectives and nouns to form opposites: *dislike* ○ *disobedient* ○ *distrust.* **4 A-** is mostly used in formal or technical words to indicate 'lacking in' or 'lack of': *amorphous* ('lacking in shape') ○ *anarchy* ('lack of rule'). **5** It is not possible to predict whether **un-**, **in-** or **dis-** is used with a particular word and the correct form must be noted and learned.

UN /ˌjuː ˈen/ *abbr* United Nations: *the UN Secretary General.*

unabashed /ˌʌnəˈbæʃt/ *adj* (*fml or joc*) not ashamed, embarrassed or awed, esp when there is reason for being so: *Tim appeared unabashed by all the media attention.*

unabated /ˌʌnəˈbeɪtɪd/ *adj* [usu pred] (of a storm, an argument, a crisis, etc) as strong, violent, serious, etc as before: *The gales continued unabated.* ○ *Our enthusiasm remained unabated.*

unable /ʌnˈeɪbl/ *adj* [pred] ~ **to do sth** (*esp fml*) not having the ability, opportunity or authority to do sth: *She is unable to walk.* ○ *I tried to contact him but was unable to.*

unabridged /ˌʌnəˈbrɪdʒd/ *adj* (of a novel, play, speech, etc) published, performed, etc without being shortened in any way: *unabridged editions/versions of 'War and Peace'.*

unacceptable /ˌʌnəkˈseptəbl/ *adj* that cannot be accepted, approved or forgiven: *unacceptable terms, suggestions, arguments, solutions* ○ *Imprisonment without trial is totally unacceptable in a democracy.* ▷ **unacceptably** /-blɪ/ *adv*: *unacceptably low standards.*

unaccompanied /ˌʌnəˈkʌmpənɪd/ *adj* **1** (*fml*) without a companion; unescorted: *Children unaccompanied by an adult will not be admitted.* ○ *unaccompanied luggage/baggage*, ie travelling separately from its owner. **2** (*music*) performed without an accompaniment: *sing unaccompanied.*

unaccountable /ˌʌnəˈkaʊntəbl/ *adj* **1** that cannot be explained or accounted for: *an unaccountable increase in cot deaths*, ie of babies ○ *For some unaccountable reason, the letter never arrived.* **2** ~ (**to sb/sth**) (*fml*) not answerable for one's actions, etc; not accountable.

▷ **unaccountably** /-əblɪ/ *adv* inexplicably: *unaccountably absent from the meeting.*

unaccounted /ˌʌnəˈkaʊntɪd/ *adj* [pred] ~ **for** (**a**) not included in an account, a tally, etc: *One passenger is still unaccounted for.* (**b**) not explained: *His disappearance is unaccounted for.*

unaccustomed /ˌʌnəˈkʌstəmd/ *adj* **1** ~ **to sth** not in the habit of doing sth; not used to sth: *Unaccustomed as I am to public speaking....* **2** uncharacteristic or unusual: *his unaccustomed silence* ○ *the unaccustomed luxury of cheap foreign travel.*

unacknowledged /ˌʌnəkˈnɒlɪdʒd/ *adj* not fully recognized or appreciated: *an unacknowledged master of his craft* ○ *Her contribution to the research went largely unacknowledged.*

unadopted /ˌʌnəˈdɒptɪd/ *adj* (*Brit*) (of a road) not taken over for maintenance by a local authority.

unadorned /ˌʌnəˈdɔːnd/ *adj* in a basic or natural form, without additions; plain: *the unadorned facts.*

unadulterated /ˌʌnəˈdʌltəreɪtɪd/ *adj* **1** (esp of food) not mixed with other substances; pure. **2** [usu attrib] (*infml*) complete or utter: *talking pure unadulterated nonsense* ○ *unadulterated bliss.*

unaffected /ˌʌnəˈfektɪd/ *adj* **1** ~ (**by sth**) not changed or affected (by sth): *rights unaffected by the new laws* ○ *The children seem unaffected emotionally by their parents' divorce.* **2** free from affectation; sincere: *welcome sb with unaffected pleasure.*

unalloyed /ˌʌnəˈlɔɪd/ *adj* (*fml*) not mixed, eg with negative feelings; pure: *ˌunalloyed ˈjoy, enˈthusiasm, exˈcitement, etc.*

un-American /ˌʌnəˈmerɪkən/ *adj* **1** against what are thought to be normal American customs or values: *State control is a very un-American notion.* **2** against the political interests of the USA: *un-American activities*, eg spying.

unanimous /juːˈnænɪməs/ *adj* (**a**) ~ (**in sth**) all agreeing on a decision or an opinion: *The villagers are unanimous their opposition to lthe building of a bypass.* (**b**) (of a decision, an opinion, etc) given or held by everybody: *He was elected by a unanimous vote.* ○ *The proposal was accepted with unanimous approval.*

▷ **unanimity** /ˌjuːnəˈnɪmətɪ/ *n* [U] complete agreement or unity.

unanimously *adv.*

unannounced /ˌʌnəˈnaʊnst/ *adj* without prior warning or notification; unexpected: *make unannounced safety checks on equipment* ○ *He arrived unannounced.*

unanswerable /ʌnˈɑːnsərəbl; *US* ʌnˈæn-/ *adj* that cannot be answered or refuted by a good argument to the contrary: *His case/defence is unanswerable.*

unapproachable /ˌʌnəˈprəʊtʃəbl/ *adj* (of a person) difficult to talk to (because too stiff, formal, etc).

unarmed /ˌʌnˈɑːmd/ *adj* (**a**) without weapons: *Britain is proud of its unarmed police force*, ie that does not carry guns. ○ *He walked into the camp unarmed.* (**b**) not using weapons: *soldiers trained in unarmed combat.*

unashamed /ˌʌnəˈʃeɪmd/ *adj* feeling or showing no guilt or embarrassment: *They kissed each other with unashamed delight.* ▷ **unashamedly** /ˌʌnəˈʃeɪmɪdlɪ/ *adv*: *unashamedly pursuing her own interests.*

unasked /ˌʌnˈɑːskt; *US* ˌʌnˈæskt/ *adj* without being asked or invited: *The meeting ended and the all-important question remained unasked.* ○ *She came to the party unasked.*

□ **unasked for** without being asked for or requested: [attrib] *unasked-for* (ie voluntary) *contributions to the fund.*

unassailable /ˌʌnəˈseɪləbl/ *adj* (**a**) that cannot be attacked or conquered: *an unassailable stronghold, fortress, etc* ○ *Liverpool have (built up) an unassailable lead at the top of the first division.* (**b**) (*fig*) that cannot be questioned or refuted: *Her position/argument is unassailable.*

unassuming /ˌʌnəˈsjuːmɪŋ; *US* ˌʌnəˈsuː-/ *adj* not drawing attention to oneself or to one's merits or rank; modest: *a gentle, quiet and unassuming manner.* ▷ **unassumingly** *adv.*

unattached /ˌʌnəˈtætʃt/ *adj* **1** not connected with or belonging to a particular body, group, etc: *people unattached to any political organization.* **2** not married or engaged; without a regular companion.

unattended /ˌʌnəˈtendɪd/ *adj* **1** with its owner not present: *unattended vehicles, suitcases, causing suspicion.* **2** ~ (**to**) not supervised or given care or attention: *leave the shop-counter, telephone, etc unattended* ○ *They left the baby at home unattended all evening.* ○ *old correspondence still unattended to.*

unavailing /ˌʌnəˈveɪlɪŋ/ *adj* without effect or success; futile: *unavailing efforts/attempts to stop smoking* ○ *All our protests were unavailing.*

unavoidable /ˌʌnəˈvɔɪdəbl/ *adj* that cannot be avoided: *unavoidable duties.* ▷ **unavoidably** /-əblɪ/ *adv*: *unavoidably absent/delayed.*

unaware /ˌʌnəˈweə(r)/ *adj* [pred] ~ (**of sth/that...**) ignorant or not conscious of sth: *be socially, politically, etc unaware* ○ *He was unaware of my presence/that I was present.* ○ (*fml*) *I am not unaware of the problem.*

▷ **unawares** /-ˈweəz/ *adv* **1** by surprise; unexpectedly: *She came upon him unawares as he was searching her room.* **2** without being aware; unconsciously: *I must have dropped my keys unawares.* **3** (idm) **catch/take sb unaˈwares** surprise or startle sb: *You caught us unawares by coming so early.*

unbalance /ˌʌnˈbæləns/ *v* [I, Tn] upset the balance of (sb/sth): *Her death had an unbalancing effect on Joe*, ie on his mind. ○ *Over-production is seriously unbalancing the EEC economy.*

▷ **unbalanced** *adj* **1** [esp pred] (of a person, his mind, etc) insane, abnormal or eccentric: *mentally unbalanced* ○ *He shot her while temporarily unbalanced.* **2** [esp attrib] (of opinions, etc) giving too much or too little emphasis to a particular idea, etc; biased: *the unbalanced reporting of the popular tabloids.*

unbar /ˌʌnˈbɑː(r)/ *v* (**-rr-**) [Tn] remove bars from (a door, gate, etc) to allow entry: (*fig*) *unbar the way to a nuclear-free world.*

unbearable /ʌnˈbeərəbl/ *adj* that cannot be tolerated or endured: *I find his rudeness unbearable.* ▷ **unbearably** /-əblɪ/ *adv*: *unbearably hot, painful, selfish.*

unbeatable /ˌʌnˈbiːtəbl/ *adj* that cannot be defeated or surpassed: *The Brazilian team is regarded as unbeatable.* ○ *unbeatable prices, discounts, offers, etc* ○ *unbeatable value.*

unbeaten /ˌʌnˈbiːtn/ *adj* not having been beaten, defeated or surpassed: *an unbeaten team* ○ *an unbeaten record for the high jump* ○ *His time of 3 min 2 sec remains unbeaten.*

unbecoming /ˌʌnbɪˈkʌmɪŋ/ *adj* (*fml*) **1** not suited to the wearer: *an unbecoming dress, style, colour*. **2** ~ **(to/for sb)** not appropriate or seemly; improper: *conduct unbecoming to an officer and a gentleman* ○ *It was thought unbecoming for young ladies to smoke.*

unbelief /ˌʌnbɪˈli:f/ *n* [U] (*fml*) lack of belief or state of not believing, esp in God, religion, etc. Cf DISBELIEF (DISBELIEVE).

▷ **unbelievable** /ˌʌnbɪˈli:vəbl/ *adj* that cannot be believed; astonishing: *unbelievable expense, skill, luck*. Cf INCREDIBLE. **unbelievably** /-əblɪ/ *adv*: *unbelievably hot, cheap, stupid*.

unbeliever *n* person who does not believe, esp in God, religion, etc.

unbelieving *adj* not believing; doubting: *She stared at me with unbelieving eyes.* Cf INCREDULOUS.

unbend /ˌʌnˈbend/ *v* (*pt, pp* **unbent** /ˌʌnˈbent/) **1** [I, Tn] (cause sth/sb to) become changed from a bent position; straighten. **2** [I] (*fig*) become relaxed and informal in behaviour: *Most professors unbend outside the lecture theatre.*

▷ **unbending** *adj* (*esp derog*) refusing to alter one's demands, decisions, etc; inflexible: *the government's unbending attitude towards the strikers.*

unbiassed (*US* **unbiased**) /ˌʌnˈbaɪəst/ *adj* not affected by bias or favouritism: *in my unbiassed opinion.*

unbidden /ʌnˈbɪdn/ *adv* (*fml*) **1** not requested, invited or ordered: *walk in/help unbidden.* **2** (*fig*) voluntary or spontaneous: *memories, images, names, etc coming unbidden to one's mind.*

unblock /ˌʌnˈblɒk/ *v* [Tn] remove a blockage in (eg a pipe or drain).

unblushing /ˌʌnˈblʌʃɪŋ/ *adj* (*fml*) shameless: *an unblushing admission of guilt.* ▷ **unblushingly** *adv.*

unborn /ˌʌnˈbɔ:n/ *adj* [esp attrib] not yet born; of the future: *unborn children, calves* ○ *generations as yet unborn.*

unbounded /ˌʌnˈbaʊndɪd/ *adj* without limits; boundless: *unbounded ambition, curiosity, luxury.*

unbowed /ˌʌnˈbaʊd/ *adj* not conquered or subdued: *He remains bloody but unbowed*, ie He has suffered but not submitted.

unbreakable /ˌʌnˈbreɪkəbl/ *adj* that cannot be broken: *unbreakable plastics, toys* ○ (*fig*) *the unbreakable spirit of the resistance.*

unbridled /ˌʌnˈbraɪdld/ *adj* [esp attrib] not controlled or checked: *unbridled passion, enthusiasm, jealousy, etc* ○ (*dated*) *speak with an unbridled tongue*, ie passionately, insolently or indiscreetly. Cf BRIDLE 2.

unbroken /ˌʌnˈbrəʊkən/ *adj* **1** not interrupted or disturbed: *ten hours of unbroken sleep* ○ *the unbroken silence of the woods.* **2** (of records in sport, etc) not beaten or surpassed. **3** (of a horse, etc) not tamed or subdued.

unbuckle /ˌʌnˈbʌkl/ *v* [Tn] loosen or undo the buckle(s) of (a belt, etc).

unburden /ˌʌnˈbɜ:dn/ *v* [Tn, Tn·pr] ~ **oneself/sth (of sth) (to sb)** (*fml fig*) relieve (oneself, one's mind, etc) of worry, etc, eg by talking about one's troubles to a friend: *unburden one's heart, conscience, etc* ○ *unburden oneself of a secret.*

unbusinesslike /ˌʌnˈbɪznɪslaɪk/ *adj* unsystematic or lacking professionalism, esp in business matters: *unbusinesslike methods, transactions, attitudes* ○ *It is unbusinesslike to arrive late for meetings.*

unbutton /ˌʌnˈbʌtn/ *v* [Tn] undo the buttons of (a jacket, etc).

▷ **unbuttoned** *adj* (*fig*) (feeling) free from formality; relaxed: *her unbuttoned style of management.*

uncalled-for /ʌnˈkɔ:ld fɔ:(r)/ *adj* unjustified; unnecessary: *uncalled-for impertinence* ○ *Your comments were quite uncalled-for.*

uncanny /ʌnˈkænɪ/ *adj* (**-ier, -iest**) (**a**) unnatural: *The silence was uncanny.* ○ *I had an uncanny feeling of being watched.* (**b**) beyond what is normal or expected; extraordinary: *an uncanny coincidence, resemblance, etc.* ▷ **uncannily** /-ɪlɪ/ *adv*: *an uncannily accurate prediction.*

uncared-for /ˌʌnˈkeəd fɔ:(r)/ *adj* not looked after; neglected: *uncared-for children, gardens, pets.*

unceasing /ˌʌnˈsi:sɪŋ/ *adj* going on all the time; incessant: *unceasing efforts, protests, campaigns* ○ *nursing him with unceasing devotion.* ▷ **unceasingly** *adv.*

unceremonious /ˌʌnˌserɪˈməʊnɪəs/ *adj* **1** (**a**) without proper formality or dignity: *Their divorce was an unceremonious affair.* (**b**) without ceremony; informal: *The dinner was a relaxed, unceremonious occasion.* **2** lacking in courtesy or politeness; rudely abrupt: *his unceremonious departure, dismissal, removal, etc.* ▷ **unceremoniously** *adv* (*derog*): *I was escorted unceremoniously to the door.*

uncertain /ʌnˈsɜ:tn/ *adj* **1** (**a**) [usu pred] ~ **(about/of sth)** not knowing definitely: *be/feel uncertain (about) what to do* ○ *uncertain about/of one's legal rights.* (**b**) not known definitely: *The outcome is still uncertain.* **2** not to be depended on; unreliable: *His aim is uncertain.* **3** likely to vary; changeable: *uncertain weather* ○ *a man of uncertain temper.* **4** hesitant or tentative: *an uncertain voice, smile* ○ *the baby's first uncertain steps.* **5** (idm) **in ˌno unˌcertain ˈterms** clearly and forcefully: *I told him what I thought of him in no uncertain terms!*

▷ **uncertainly** *adv* hesitantly: *speak, wait uncertainly.*

uncertainty /ʌnˈsɜ:tntɪ/ *n* (**a**) [U] state of being uncertain: *The uncertainty is unbearable!* (**b**) [C esp *pl*] thing which is uncertain: *the uncertainties of life on the dole*, ie as an unemployed person.

uncharitable /ˌʌnˈtʃærɪtəbl/ *adj* severe or harsh, esp in judging (the conduct of) others: *uncharitable remarks, thoughts, etc* ○ *I don't want to be uncharitable, but she's not a terribly good cook.* ▷ **uncharitably** /-əblɪ/ *adv.*

uncharted /ˌʌnˈtʃɑ:tɪd/ *adj* **1** not marked on a map or chart: *an uncharted island.* **2** not explored or mapped: *an uncharted area, zone, etc* ○ (*fig*) *the uncharted depths of human emotions* ○ *Our research is sailing into uncharted waters/seas*, ie investigating fields that have not been researched before.

unchecked /ˌʌnˈtʃekt/ *adj* (*derog*) not resisted or restrained: *the enemy's unchecked advance* ○ *rumours spreading unchecked* ○ *The use of credit continues/grows unchecked.*

unchristian /ˌʌnˈkrɪstʃən/ *adj* contrary to Christian teachings or principles; uncharitable: *unchristian behaviour* ○ *an unchristian attitude.*

uncivil /ˌʌnˈsɪvl/ *adj* ill-mannered; rude: *be uncivil to the neighbours* ○ *It was uncivil of you to say that.* Cf INCIVILITY 1.

uncle /ˈʌŋkl/ *n* **1** (**a**) brother of one's father or mother; husband of one's aunt: *my uncle Jim.* ⇨ App 8. (**b**) man whose brother or sister has a child: *Now you're an uncle.* **2** (*infml*) (used by children, esp in front of a first name) unrelated adult male friend, esp of one's parents. **3** (idm) **bob's your uncle** ⇨ BOB⁴. **talk like a Dutch uncle** ⇨ TALK². □ **ˌUncle ˈSam** (*infml*) (Government of) the United States: *fighting for Uncle Sam.* ⇨ article at NATIONAL.

ˌUncle ˈTom (*US infml derog*) black person who associates with and is eager to please white people.

unclean /ˌʌnˈkli:n/ *adj* (**a**) (of food) that cannot be eaten; forbidden as spiritually impure. (**b**) lacking spiritual purity; unchaste: *ˌunclean ˈminds, ˈhearts, ˈthoughts.*

uncoil /ˌʌnˈkɔɪl/ *v* [I, Tn] (cause sth/oneself to) become straightened from a coiled position; unwind: *The snake uncoiled (itself).* ○ *uncoil electric flex, a hose-pipe.*

uncoloured (*US* **uncolored**) /ˌʌnˈkʌləd/ *adj* ~ **(by sth)** (*fig*) not affected or influenced by sth: *an uncoloured description of events* ○ *His judgement was uncoloured by personal prejudice.*

uncomfortable /ʌnˈkʌmftəbl; *US* -fərt-/ *adj* **1** not comfortable: *uncomfortable chairs, shoes, rooms* ○ *lie in an uncomfortable position.* **2** feeling or causing anxiety or unease: *Children make some people feel uncomfortable.* ○ *The letter was an uncomfortable reminder of my debts.*

▷ **uncomfortably** /-əblɪ/ *adv* **1** not comfortably: *uncomfortably cramped.* **2** in a way that causes disquiet or unease: *The exams are getting uncomfortably close.*

uncommitted /ˌʌnkəˈmɪtɪd/ *adj* ~ **(to sth/sb)** not bound or pledged to (a particular policy, course of action, group, etc): *Some workers remain uncommitted to the project.* ○ *parties appealing to uncommitted voters.* Cf COMMITTED (COMMIT).

uncommon /ʌnˈkɒmən/ *adj* **1** not common; unusual: *an uncommon sight, occurrence, etc* ○ *Hurricanes are uncommon in England.* **2** (*fml*) remarkably close; excessive: *There was an uncommon likeness between the two boys.*

▷ **uncommonly** *adv* (*fml*) remarkably: *uncommonly intelligent, stupid, difficult.*

uncompromising /ʌnˈkɒmprəmaɪzɪŋ/ *adj* not ready to make any compromise; firm or unyielding: *an uncompromising negotiator, attitude, position* ○ *attack the government's uncompromising stand on education cuts.* ▷ **uncompromisingly** *adv.*

unconcern /ˌʌnkənˈsɜ:n/ *n* [U] lack of care or interest: *She heard the news of his death with apparent unconcern.*

unconcerned /ˌʌnkənˈsɜ:nd/ *adj* **1** ~ **(with sth/sb)** not feeling or showing concern; uninterested: *unconcerned with questions of religion or morality.* **2** ~ **(at/by sth)** free from anxiety; untroubled: *Most tourists were unconcerned at the poor weather.* ▷ **unconcernedly** /ˌʌnkənˈsɜ:nɪdlɪ/ *adv.*

unconditional /ˌʌnkənˈdɪʃənl/ *adj* not subject to conditions; absolute: *an ˌunconditional surˈrender, reˈfusal, ˈoffer.* ▷ **unconditionally** /-ʃənəlɪ/ *adv.*

unconditioned /ˌʌnkənˈdɪʃnd/ *adj* (esp of a reflex) not learned; instinctive. Cf CONDITIONED REFLEX (CONDITION²).

unconfirmed /ˌʌnkənˈfɜ:md/ *adj* (of facts, etc) not proved to be true; not confirmed: *ˌunconfirmed reˈports, ˈrumours, etc of a coup.*

unconscionable /ʌnˈkɒnʃənəbl/ *adj* [attrib] (*fml or joc*) unreasonable or excessive: *You take an unconscionable time getting dressed!* ▷ **unconscionably** /-əblɪ/ *adv*: *an unconscionably shy young man.*

unconscious /ʌnˈkɒnʃəs/ *adj* **1** (**a**) not conscious; insensible: *knock sb unconscious.* (**b**) ~ **of sb/sth** not aware: *be unconscious of any change.* **2** done or spoken, etc without conscious intention: *an unconscious slight* ○ *unconscious humour, resentment.*

▷ **the unconscious** *n* (*psychology*) that part of one's mental activity of which one is unaware, but which can be detected and understood through the skilled analysis of dreams, behaviour, etc. Cf SUBCONSCIOUS.

unconsciously *adv*: *He unconsciously imitated his father.*

unconsciousness *n* [U] **1** being unconscious; lack of consciousness; insensibility: *lapse, fall, etc into unconsciousness.* **2** lack of awareness of what one is doing, saying, etc.

unconsidered /ˌʌnkənˈsɪdəd/ *adj* **1** (of words, remarks, etc) spoken or made without proper consideration or thought. **2** disregarded, as if of little value or worth.

uncooperative /ˌʌnkəʊˈɒpərətɪv/ *adj* not willing to co-operate with others: *uncooperative witnesses, patients, pupils, etc.*

uncouple /ˌʌnˈkʌpl/ *v* [Tn, Tn·pr] ~ **sth (from sth)** disconnect (railway carriages, etc).

uncouth /ʌnˈku:θ/ *adj* (of people, their appearance, behaviour, etc) rough, awkward or ill-mannered; not refined. ▷ **uncouthness** *n* [U].

uncover /ʌnˈkʌvə(r)/ *v* [Tn] **1** remove a cover or covering from (sth). **2** (*fig*) make known or disclose (sth); discover: *Agents have uncovered a plot against the President.*

uncritical /ˌʌnˈkrɪtɪkl/ *adj* ~ **(of sth/sb)** (*esp derog*) unwilling or unable to criticize: *an uncritical attitude, view, etc* ○ *uncritical supporters of the government* ○ *The review is uncritical of the violence in the film.* ▷ **uncritically** /-ɪklɪ/ *adv.*

uncrossed /ˌʌnˈkrɒst; *US* -ˈkrɔ:st/ *adj* (*Brit*) (of a cheque) not crossed (CROSS² 4).

uncrowned /ˌʌnˈkraʊnd/ *adj* **1** (of a king, etc) not yet crowned. **2** (idm) **the ˌuncrowned ˈking/ˈqueen (of sth)** person considered to be the most talented or successful in a certain group or field: *the uncrowned king of chess players/chess/the chessboard.*

UNCTAD /ˈʌŋktæd/ *abbr* United Nations Conference on Trade and Development.

unction /ˈʌŋkʃn/ *n* [U] **1** action of anointing with oil as a religious rite. **2** (*fml derog*) = UNCTUOUSNESS.

unctuous /ˈʌŋktjʊəs/ *adj* insincerely earnest or flattering, esp in an oily way: *speak in unctuous tones* ○ *unctuous assurances.* ▷ **unctuously** *adv.* **unctuousness** (also **unction**) *n* [U].

uncurl /ˌʌnˈkɜːl/ *v* [I, Tn] ~ **(sth/oneself)** (cause sth/oneself to) become straightened from a curled position: *The cat uncurled (itself) sensuously.* ○ *She uncurled her legs from under her.*

uncut /ˌʌnˈkʌt/ *adj* **1** (of a book) with the outer folds of the pages not trimmed or cut open. **2** (of a book, film, etc) not abridged or censored: *ˌuncut ˈversions, eˈditions, ˈshowings.* **3** (of a gem) not shaped by cutting: *uncut diamonds.*

undaunted /ˌʌnˈdɔːntɪd/ *adj* [usu pred] (*rhet*) not discouraged or intimidated; fearless: *He continued the climb, undaunted by his fall.*

undeceive /ˌʌndɪˈsiːv/ *v* [Tn] (*fml*) free (sb) from an illusion or a deception: *His behaviour soon undeceived her as to his true intentions.*

undecided /ˌʌndɪˈsaɪdɪd/ *adj* [pred] **1** not settled or certain: *The issue/matter remains undecided.* ○ *The (outcome of the) match is still undecided.* **2** ~ **(about sth/sb)** not having made up one's mind; irresolute: *I'm still undecided (about) who to vote for.*

undeclared /ˌʌndɪˈkleəd/ *adj* (of goods liable to duty) not declared or shown to the Customs officers.

undemonstrative /ˌʌndɪˈmɒnstrətɪv/ *adj* not in the habit of showing strong feelings; reserved.

undeniable /ˌʌndɪˈnaɪəbl/ *adj* that cannot be disputed or denied; undoubtedly true: *undeniable facts* ○ *gems of undeniable worth/value* ○ *His charm is undeniable, but I still mistrust him.* ▷ **undeniably** /-əblɪ/ *adv*: *undeniably difficult* ○ *Undeniably, the final stage is crucial.*

under /ˈʌndə(r)/ *prep* **1** in, to or through a position directly below (sth): *The cat was under the table.* ○ *Have you looked under the bed?* ○ *Let's shelter under the trees.* ○ *He threw himself under a bus.* ○ *The water flows under the bridge.* ○ (*fig*) *What sign of the Zodiac were you born under?* Cf OVER[2] 1, 2. **2** below the surface of (sth); covered by: *Most of the iceberg is under the water.* ○ *Under the mountain there is a network of caves.* ○ *She crept in beside him under the bedclothes.* ○ *She pushed all her hair under a headscarf.* **3** in or to a position next to and lower than (sth): *under the castle wall* ○ *a village under the hill.* **4** (**a**) younger than (a specified age): *Many children under 5 go to nursery school.* ○ *It's forbidden to sell tobacco to children under 16.* ○ *If you are under 26 you can buy cheap rail tickets.* (**b**) less than (a specified amount, distance or time): *Anyone with an annual income of under £5 000 may be eligible to apply.* ○ *It's under a mile from here to the post office.* ○ *It took us under an hour.* Cf OVER[2] 5. **5** (**a**) lower in rank than (sb); responsible to the authority of: *No one under the rank of captain may enter the room.* ○ *She has a staff of 19 working under her.* (**b**) governed or led by (sb): *Britain under Cromwell, Thatcher, the monarchy* ○ *Under its new conductor, the orchestra has established an international reputation.* (**c**) according to the terms of (an agreement, a law or a system): *Six suspects are being held under the Prevention of Terrorism Act.* ○ *Under the terms of the lease you had no right to sublet the property.* **6** carrying (a specified burden): *She was struggling under the weight of three suitcases.* ○ (*fml*) *It was difficult to behave naturally under the burden of knowing the truth.* **7** (**a**) being in a state of (sth): *buildings under repair/construction*, ie being repaired/built ○ *matters under consideration, discussion, etc.* (**b**) being affected by (sb/sth): *He's very much under the influence of the older boys.* ○ *You'll be under (an) anaesthetic, so you won't feel a thing.* **8** (**a**) using (a particular name): *open a bank account under a false name* ○ *write a novel under the pseudonym of Colin Kettle.* (**b**) classified as (sth): *If it's not under sport, try looking under biography.* **9** being planted with (sth): *fields under wheat.*

▷ **under** *adv* **1** under water: *If you take a deep breath you can stay under for more than a minute.* ○ *The ship went under* (ie sank) *on its first voyage.* **2** without consciousness: *She felt herself going under.*

under *adj* [attrib] lower; situated underneath: *the under layer* ○ *under surface.*

under- *pref* **1** (with *ns*) (**a**) below: *undergrowth* ○ *undercurrent.* (**b**) lower in rank; subordinate: *under-secretary* ○ *undergraduate.* **2** (with *adjs, vs* and their related forms) not enough: *underripe* ○ *underestimate* ○ *underdeveloped.* Cf SUB-.

underachieve /ˌʌndərəˈtʃiːv/ *v* [I] (*euph*) do less well than was expected, esp in school work. ▷ **underachiever** *n.*

underact /ˌʌndərˈækt/ *v* [I, Tn] act (a part) with less spirit, force, etc than expected: *He underacted the title-role to considerable effect.* Cf OVERACT.

underarm /ˈʌndərɑːm/ **1** *adj, adv* [attrib] in, of or for the armpit: *underarm hair, perspiration, deodorant.* **2** *adv* (also **underhand**) (in cricket, etc) with the hand kept below the level of the shoulder: *underarm bowling* ○ *bowl, serve, throw, etc underarm.* Cf OVERARM.

underbelly /ˈʌndəbelɪ/ *n* [sing] **1** under surface of an animal's body, eg as a cut of meat, esp pork. **2** (*fig*) area, region, etc that is vulnerable to attack: *The stock-market crisis struck at the soft underbelly of the US economy*, eg its trade deficit.

underbid /ˌʌndəˈbɪd/ *v* (**-dd-**; *pt, pp* **underbid**) **1** [Tn] make a lower bid than (sb else), eg at an auction. **2** [I, Tn] (in bridge, etc) bid less on (a hand of cards) than its strength suggests. Cf OVERBID.

underbrush /ˈʌndəbrʌʃ/ *n* [U] (*US*) = UNDERGROWTH.

undercarriage /ˈʌndəkærɪdʒ/ (also ˈ**landing-gear**) *n* aircraft's landing wheels and their supports: *raise/lower the undercarriage.* ⇨ illus at AIRCRAFT.

undercharge /ˌʌndəˈtʃɑːdʒ/ *v* [I, Ipr, Tn, Tn·pr, Dn·n] ~ **(sb) (for sth)** charge (sb) too low a price (for sth): *He undercharged me £1 for the book/for the book by £1.* Cf OVERCHARGE 1.

undercliff /ˈʌndəklɪf/ *n* bottom part of a cliff where landslides have occurred, usu leaving a set of terraces.

underclothes /ˈʌndəkləʊðz/ *n* [pl] (also *fml* **underclothing** /-kləʊðɪŋ/) [U] = UNDERWEAR.

undercoat /ˈʌndəkəʊt/ *n* **1** [U, C] (paint used for making a) layer of paint under a finishing coat. Cf TOPCOAT (TOP[1]). **2** [C] (*US*) = UNDERSEAL.

undercover /ˌʌndəˈkʌvə(r)/ *adj* [esp attrib] **1** doing things secretly or done secretly; surreptitious: *ˌundercover ˈpayments*, eg bribes. **2** engaged in spying on people while appearing to work normally among them: *ˌundercover ˈagents, acˈtivities, organiˈzations.*

undercurrent /ˈʌndəkʌrənt/ *n* **1** current of water flowing below the surface or below another current: *strong, fierce, fast, dangerous, etc undercurrents.* **2** ~ **(of sth)** (*fig*) underlying feeling or influence or trend, esp one opposite to the apparent one: *There was an undercurrent of resentment in their acceptance of the plan.*

undercut[1] /ˈʌndəkʌt/ *n* **1** [U] (*Brit*) (meat cut from the) underside of sirloin. Cf TENDERLOIN (TENDER[1]). **2** [C] (*US*) notch cut at the bottom of a tree that is going to be cut down, to make it fall in a particular direction.

undercut[2] /ˌʌndəˈkʌt/ *v* (**-tt-**; *pt, pp* **undercut**) [Tn] offer goods or services at a lower price than (one's competitors): *They're undercutting us by 20p a packet.*

underdeveloped /ˌʌndədɪˈveləpt/ *adj* **1** not fully grown or developed: *underdeveloped muscles.* **2** (of a country, etc) not having achieved its potential in economic development.

underdog /ˈʌndədɒg; *US* -dɔːg/ *n* (esp **the underdog**) person or country, thought to be in a weaker position, and therefore unlikely to win a contest, struggle, etc: *crowds supporting the underdog.*

underdone /ˌʌndəˈdʌn/ *adj* not thoroughly done, esp lightly or insufficiently cooked: *nicely underdone vegetables* ○ *The beef was underdone and quite uneatable.*

underestimate /ˌʌndərˈestɪmeɪt/ *v* [Tn] make too low an estimate of (sb/sth): *underestimate the cost, danger, difficulty, etc of the expedition* ○ *I underestimated the time we needed by 30%.* ○ *Never underestimate your opponent*, ie think that you will beat him easily. Cf OVERESTIMATE, UNDERRATE.

▷ **underestimate** /-mət/ *n* estimate that is too low: *a serious underestimate of losses on the Stock Exchange.* Cf OVERESTIMATE.

underexpose /ˌʌndərɪkˈspəʊz/ *v* [Tn esp passive] expose (a film, etc) for too short a time or in too poor a light. Cf OVEREXPOSE. ▷ **underexposure** /-ɪkˈspəʊʒə(r)/ *n* [U].

underfed /ˌʌndəˈfed/ *adj* having had too little food: *underfed cattle, troops, children.*

underfelt /ˈʌndəfelt/ *n* [U, C] felt for laying under a carpet. Cf UNDERLAY.

underfloor /ˌʌndəˈflɔː(r)/ *adj* [attrib] situated beneath the floor: *ˌunderfloor (eˌlectric) ˈwiring* ○ *ˌunderfloor ˈheating*, eg using warm air.

underfoot /ˌʌndəˈfʊt/ *adv* under one's feet; on the ground: *The snow underfoot was soft and deep.* ○ *It's muddy underfoot.* ○ *Fallen riders were trampled underfoot by the charging horses.*

undergarment /ˈʌndəgɑːmənt/ *n* (*dated or fml*) article of underclothing.

undergo /ˌʌndəˈgəʊ/ *v* (*pt* **underwent** /-ˈwent/, *pp* **undergone** /-ˈgɒn; *US* -ˈgɔːn/) [Tn] **1** experience or endure (sth unpleasant or painful): *undergo great hardship, suffering, privation, etc.* **2** be subjected to (a process, etc): *undergo major surgery, reform, repair* ○ *The ship successfully underwent sea trials in coastal waters.* ○ *Our agenda underwent a rapid change after the chairman's resignation.*

undergraduate /ˌʌndəˈgrædʒʊət/ *n* university or college student who has not yet taken his first or bachelor's degree: *Cambridge undergraduates* ○ [attrib] *undergraduate courses, grants, students.* Cf GRADUATE, POSTGRADUATE[1]. ⇨ article at POST-SCHOOL.

underground[1] /ˌʌndəˈgraʊnd/ *adv* **1** under the surface of the ground. **2** (*fig*) in or into secrecy or hiding: *He went underground to avoid the police.*

underground[2] /ˈʌndəgraʊnd/ *adj* [attrib] **1** under the surface of the ground: *underground passages, caves, etc* ○ *an underground car-park.* **2** (*fig*) (**a**) secret, esp of an illegal political organization: *the underground resistance movement*, eg of the French opposing the German occupation of France during the Second World War. (**b**) (esp of art, artists, etc) opposed to established forms and conventions: *an underground magazine.*

▷ **underground** *n* **the underground** **1** [sing] (also *Brit infml* **the tube**, *US* **subway**) underground railway: *travel by underground* ○ *fares on the London Underground* ○ [attrib] *underground stations.* ⇨ articles at LONDON, RAILWAY. **2** [CGp] secret (esp political) organization or activity: *work for, join, contact the underground.*

undergrowth /ˈʌndəgrəʊθ/ (*US* **underbrush**) *n* [U] mass of shrubs, bushes, etc growing closely on the ground, esp under trees: *clear a path through the undergrowth.*

underhand /ˌʌndəˈhænd/ **1** *adj* (also **underhanded** /ˌʌndəˈhændɪd/) done or doing things in a sly or secret way; deceitful: *ˌunderhand ˈtricks, ˈmethods, ˈmeans.* **2** *adj, adv* = UNDERARM 2.

underlay /ˈʌndəleɪ/ *n* [U, C] layer of felt, foam, rubber, etc laid (esp under a carpet) for support and insulation. Cf UNDERFELT.

underlie /ˌʌndəˈlaɪ/ *v* (*pt* **underlay** /ˌʌndəˈleɪ/, *pp* **underlain** /-ˈleɪn/) **1** [I, Tn] lie or exist beneath (sth): *the underlying clay, rock, etc.* **2** [Tn no passive] (*fig*) form the basis of (sb's actions, a theory, etc); account for: *A deep faith underlies her work among refugees.* ○ *the underlying reason for her refusal.*

underline /ˌʌndəˈlaɪn/ (also **underscore**) *v* [Tn] **1** draw a line under (a word, etc). **2** *(fig)* reinforce (an attitude, a situation, etc); emphasize: *Strikes by prison officers underline the need for reform in our gaols.*

underling /ˈʌndəlɪŋ/ *n (derog)* person in a subordinate and inferior position: *hired underlings of a gangster boss.*

undermanned /ˌʌndəˈmænd/ *adj* (of a ship, factory, etc) having too few people to function properly: *complaints that our hospitals are seriously undermanned.* Cf UNDERSTAFFED, OVERMANNED.

undermentioned /ˌʌndəˈmenʃnd/ *adj* [usu attrib] *(Brit fml)* mentioned below or at a later place (in a letter, etc). ▷ **the undermentioned** *n* (*pl* unchanged): *The undermentioned is witness to this contract.* Cf ABOVE-MENTIONED (ABOVE[1]).

undermine /ˌʌndəˈmaɪn/ *v* [Tn] **1** make a hollow or tunnel beneath (sth); weaken at the base: *Badgers had undermined the foundations of the church.* ○ *cliffs undermined by the sea.* **2** *(fig)* weaken (sth/sb) gradually or insidiously: *undermine sb's position, reputation, authority, etc*, eg by spreading scandalous rumours ○ *self-confidence undermined by repeated failures.*

underneath /ˌʌndəˈni:θ/ *prep* beneath (sth); below: *The coin rolled underneath the piano.* ○ *She found a lot of dust underneath the carpet.* ○ *What does a Scotsman wear underneath his kilt?* ○ *Caving means exploring the passages underneath the hills.*

▷ **underneath** *adv* beneath; below: *There's a pile of newspapers in the corner — have you looked underneath?* ○ *When they cleaned up the painting they discovered a Holbein underneath.* ○ *(fig) He seems bad-tempered but he's very soft-hearted underneath.*

underneath *n* [sing] lower surface or part of sth: *the underneath of a car, shelf, sofa.*

undernourished /ˌʌndəˈnʌrɪʃt/ *adj* not provided with sufficient food of the right kind for good health and normal growth: *badly, severely, seriously undernourished.* Cf MALNOURISHED. ▷ **undernourishment** /-ˈnʌrɪʃmənt/ *n* [U].

underpants /ˈʌndəpænts/ (also *infml* **pants**) *n* [pl] short undergarment worn by men and boys covering the lower part of the body: *put on some/a pair of clean underpants* ○ *He stood there in his underpants,* ie not wearing anything else. Cf KNICKERS.

underpass /ˈʌndəpɑ:s; *US* -pæs/ *n* **1** (section of a) road that goes under another road or a railway. Cf OVERPASS. **2** underground passage for pedestrians to cross below a road or railway. Cf SUBWAY 1.

underpay /ˌʌndəˈpeɪ/ *v* (*pt, pp* **underpaid** /-peɪd/) [Tn, Tn·pr] ~ **sb (for sth)** pay (an employee, etc) too little money: *Nurses are overworked and underpaid.* ○ *He underpaid me for the work (by £10).* Cf OVERPAY.

underpin /ˌʌndəˈpɪn/ *v* (**-nn-**) [Tn] **1** support (a wall, etc) from below with masonry, etc. **2** *(fig)* form the basis for (an argument, a claim, etc); strengthen: *The evidence underpinning his case was sound.* ○ *These developments are underpinned by solid progress in heavy industry.*

underplay /ˌʌndəˈpleɪ/ *v* [Tn] give too little importance to (sth): *underplay certain aspects, factors, elements, etc.* Cf OVERPLAY.

underprivileged /ˌʌndəˈprɪvəlɪdʒd/ *adj (euph)* not having the standard of living or rights enjoyed by others in a society; deprived: *socially underprivileged families, groups, etc.* ▷ **the underprivileged** *n* [pl *v*]: *The underprivileged need special support.*

underrate /ˌʌndəˈreɪt/ *v* [Tn] have too low an opinion of (sb/sth): *underrate an opponent, achievement* ○ *an underrated play, actor* ○ *As an actor, he's seriously underrated.* Cf OVERRATE, UNDERESTIMATE.

underscore /ˌʌndəˈskɔ:(r)/ *v* [Tn] = UNDERLINE.

undersea /ˈʌndəsi:/ *adj* [attrib] below the surface of the sea: *undersea exploration.*

underseal /ˈʌndəsi:l/ *(Brit)* (*US* **undercoat**) *n* [U] tar-like or rubber-like substance used to protect the under-side of a motor vehicle against rust, etc. ▷ **underseal** *v* [Tn] coat the under-side of (a motor vehicle, etc) with a protective seal.

under-secretary /ˌʌndəˈsekrətrɪ; *US* -terɪ/ *n* **1** person who is directly subordinate to a government official who has the title of 'secretary' **2** *(Brit)* senior civil servant in charge of a government department: *be Parliamentary under-secretary to the Treasury.*

undersell /ˌʌndəˈsel/ *v* (**-ll-**; *pt, pp* **undersold** /-ˈsəʊld/) [Tn] sell (goods) at a lower price than (one's competitors): *Our goods cannot be undersold,* ie Our prices are the lowest. ○ *They're underselling us.*

under-sexed /ˌʌndəˈsekst/ *adj* having less sexual desire or potency than normal. Cf OVER-SEXED.

undershirt /ˈʌndəʃɜ:t/ *n (US)* = VEST[1] 1.

under-side /ˈʌndəsaɪd/ *n* [sing] side or surface that is underneath; bottom: *His shot hit the under-side of the bar,* ie the one across the goal-posts.

undersigned /ˌʌndəˈsaɪnd/ *adj (fml)* who has or have signed at the bottom of a document. ▷ **the undersigned** *n* (*pl* unchanged): *We, the undersigned* (ie We whose signatures appear below,) *declare that....*

undersized /ˌʌndəˈsaɪzd/ *adj (usu derog)* of less than the usual size: *ˌundersized ˈportions, ˈhelpings,* ie of food ○ *The cubs were sickly and undersized.*

underslung /ˌʌndəˈslʌŋ/ *adj* **1** supported from above. **2** (of a vehicle chassis) hanging lower than the axles.

undersold *pt, pp* of UNDERSELL.

understaffed /ˌʌndəˈstɑ:ft; *US* -ˈstæft/ *adj* (of a school, a hospital, an office, etc) having too few people to function properly: *The school is badly understaffed.* Cf OVERSTAFFED, UNDERMANNED.

understand /ˌʌndəˈstænd/ *v* (*pt, pp* **understood** /-ˈstʊd/) (not used in the continuous tenses) **1 (a)** [I, Tn, Tw] grasp the meaning of (words, a language, a person, etc): *I'm not sure that I fully understand (you).* ○ *understand the instructions, rules, conditions, etc* ○ *I can understand French perfectly.* ○ *I don't understand (a word of) what you're saying,* eg because you're speaking too quickly. **(b)** [Tn, Tw, Tsg] perceive the significance or importance of (sth); perceive the explanation for or cause of: *Do you understand the difficulty of my position?* ○ *I don't understand why he came/what the problem is.* ○ *I just can't understand him/his taking the money.* **2** [I, Tn, Tf, Tw, Tsg] be sympathetically aware of (sb/sth); know how to deal with (sb/sth): *understand children, machinery, modern music* ○ *We thoroughly understand each other/one another, even if we don't always agree.* ○ *I quite understand that you need a change/your needing a change.* ○ *He understands how hard things have been for you.* **3** *(usu fml)* **(a)** [Tf, Cn·t] be aware from information received (that...); gather: *I understand she is in Paris.* ○ *Am I to understand that you refuse?* ○ *The situation, as I understand it, is very dangerous.* ○ *I understood him to say/as saying that he would co-operate.* **(b)** [Tf usu passive] take (sth) for granted: *Your expenses will be paid, that's understood.* **4** [Tn esp passive] supply or insert (an omitted word or phrase) mentally: *In the sentence 'I can't drive', the object 'a car' is understood.* **5** (idm) **give sb to understand (that)...** *(fml)* cause sb to believe or have the idea that...: *We were given to understand that the accommodation was free.* **ˌmake oneself underˈstood** make one's meaning clear: *He doesn't speak much English but he can make himself understood.*

▷ **understandable** /-əbl/ *adj* that can be understood or sympathized with: *The instructions were not readily/easily understandable.* ○ *understandable delays, objections, motives.* **understandably** /-əblɪ/ *adv*: *She was understandably annoyed.*

understanding /ˌʌndəˈstændɪŋ/ *n* **1** [U] power of clear thought; intelligence: *mysteries beyond human understanding.* **2** [U, sing] ~ **(of sth)** knowledge of the meaning, importance or cause (of sth): *I have only a limited understanding of French.* **3** [U, sing] ability to show insight or tolerance; sympathetic awareness: *no real understanding between husband and wife* ○ *our improved understanding of Soviet life* ○ *work for a better understanding between world religions.* **4 (a)** [U] ~ **(of sth)** *(usu fml)* interpretation of information received: *My understanding was that we would meet here.* **(b)** [C usu *sing*] preliminary or informal agreement: *come to/reach an understanding with management about pay* ○ *We have an understanding that/There is an understanding between us that we will not sell to each other's customers.* **5** (idm) **on the understanding that...; on this understanding** on condition that...; on this condition: *I lent him £5 on the understanding that he would repay me today.*

▷ **understanding** *adj* able to show tolerance of or sympathy towards others' feelings and views: *an understanding approach, smile, parent.*

understate /ˌʌndəˈsteɪt/ *v* [Tn] **1** state or express (sth) in a very controlled way: *understate one's views, feelings, reactions, etc* ○ *She gave a beautifully understated performance as Ophelia.* **2** state that (a number, etc) is less than it really is: *understate one's losses,* eg of money, troops.

▷ **understatement** /ˈʌndəsteɪtmənt/ *n* **(a)** [U] (action or practice of) understating: *a clever use of understatement,* eg for effect. **(b)** [C] statement that expresses an idea, etc too weakly: *To say that he was displeased is an understatement,* ie He was furious.

understudy /ˈʌndəstʌdɪ/ *n* ~ **(to sb)** person who learns the part of another in a play, etc in order to be able to take his place at short notice if necessary: *(fig) The Vice-President acts as understudy to the President.*

▷ **understudy** *v* (*pt, pp* **-died**) [Tn] learn (eg a part in a play) as understudy; act as understudy to (sb): *understudy (the role of) Ophelia* ○ *She understudied Judi Dench.*

undertake /ˌʌndəˈteɪk/ *v* (*pt* **undertook** /-ˈtʊk/, *pp* **undertaken** /-ˈteɪkən/) *(fml)* **1** [Tn] (start to) make oneself responsible for (sth): *undertake a mission, task, project, etc* ○ *She undertook the organization of the whole scheme.* **2** [Tf, Tt] agree or promise to do sth: *He undertook to finish the job by Friday.*

▷ **undertaking** /ˌʌndəˈteɪkɪŋ/ *n* **1** [sing] work, etc that one has undertaken; task or enterprise: *a commercial, financial, etc undertaking* ○ *Small businesses are a risky undertaking.* ○ *Getting married is a serious undertaking.* **2** ~ **(that.../to do sth)** *(fml)* promise or guarantee: *an undertaking that the loan would be repaid* ○ *She gave a solemn undertaking to respect their decision.*

undertaker /ˈʌndəteɪkə(r)/ (*US* also **mortician**) *n* person whose business is to prepare the dead for burial or cremation and arrange funerals.

▷ **undertaking** /ˈʌndəteɪkɪŋ/ *n* [U] business of an undertaker.

undertone /ˈʌndətəʊn/ *n* **1** (often *pl*) low, quiet or subdued tone: *speak, murmur, etc in an undertone* ○ *threatening, sympathetic, sibilant undertones.* **2** ~ **(of sth)** underlying feeling, quality, implication, etc; undercurrent: *There were undertones of relief as the visitors left.* Cf OVERTONE. **3** thin or subdued colour: *pink with an undertone of mauve.*

undertow /ˈʌndətəʊ/ *n* [sing] current below the surface of the sea, moving in the opposite direction to the surface current, esp the current caused by the backward flow of a wave breaking on a beach: *caught in an undertow* ○ *The pull of the undertow can drag swimmers out to sea.*

undervalue /ˌʌndəˈvælju:/ *v* [Tn, Cn·n/a] ~ **sb/sth (as sth)** put too low a value on sb/sth: *We had undervalued the flat by £5 000.* ○ *Don't undervalue Jim's contribution to the research.* ○ *We clearly undervalued him as a member of our team.*

underwater /ˌʌndəˈwɔ:tə(r)/ *adj* situated or used

or done below the surface of the water: ˌ*underwater* ˈ*caves*, ˈ*cameras* ○ *underwater archaeology*, eg of wrecks. ▷ **underwater** *adv*: *The duck disappeared underwater.*

underwear /ˈʌndəweə(r)/ *n* [U] (also **underclothes** [pl], *fml* **underclothing** [U]) clothes worn under a shirt, dress, etc next to the skin: *thermal underwear* ○ *She packed one change of underwear*, eg a bra, pants, tights.

underweight /ˌʌndəˈweɪt/ *adj* below the usual, legal or stated weight: *You are only slightly underweight for* (ie in relation to) *your height.* ○ *The coal is six pounds underweight/underweight by six pounds.* ⇨ Usage at THIN. Cf OVERWEIGHT.

underwent /ˌʌndəˈwent/ *pt of* UNDERGO.

underworld /ˈʌndəwɜːld/ *n* **the underworld** [sing] **1** (in mythology) place under the earth inhabited by the departed spirits of the dead. **2** part of society that lives by vice and crime: *police contacts in the London underworld* ○ [attrib] *leading underworld figures*, ie notorious criminals.

underwrite /ˌʌndəˈraɪt/ *v* (*pt* **underwrote** /-ˈrəʊt/, *pp* **underwritten** /-ˈrɪtn/) [Tn] **1** sign and accept liability under (an insurance policy, esp for ships), thus guaranteeing payment in the event of loss or damage. **2** (*finance*) undertake to buy, at an agreed price, all stock in (a company) that is not bought by the public: *The shares were underwritten by the Bank of England.* **3** undertake to finance (an enterprise): *The government underwrote the initial costs of the operation.*

▷ ˈ**underwriter** *n* person or organization that underwrites insurance policies, esp for ships: *an underwriter at Lloyd's.*

undeserved /ˌʌndɪˈzɜːvd/ *adj* not fair or just: *an undeserved punishment, rebuke, reward* ○ *His reputation as a Romeo is quite undeserved.* ▷ **undeservedly** /-dɪˈzɜːvɪdlɪ/ *adv.*

undesirable /ˌʌndɪˈzaɪərəbl/ *adj* **1** likely to cause trouble or inconvenience; unwanted: *The drug has no undesirable side-effects.* ○ *Military intervention is highly undesirable.* **2** (of a person, his habits, etc) of a kind not to be welcomed in society; objectionable: *She's a most undesirable influence.*

▷ **undesirable** *n* undesirable person: *drunks, vagrants and other undesirables* ○ (*joc*) *The club hires a bouncer to keep out undesirables.*

undesirably /-əblɪ/ *adv.*

undeterred /ˌʌndɪˈtɜːd/ *adj* not deterred or discouraged: *undeterred by failure* ○ *It was raining heavily but he set out undeterred.*

undeveloped /ˌʌndɪˈveləpt/ *adj* **1** not fully grown or developed: *undeveloped fruit, muscles, organs.* **2** not yet used for agriculture, industry, building, etc: *undeveloped land* ○ *undeveloped resources, sites.*

undid /ʌnˈdɪd/ *pt of* UNDO.

undies /ˈʌndɪz/ *n* [pl] (*infml*) (esp women's) underclothes: *She appeared in her undies.*

undignified /ʌnˈdɪgnɪfaɪd/ *adj* not showing proper dignity; clumsy: *an undignified retreat, collapse, failure, etc* ○ *His skis crossed and he sat down in a most undignified manner.*

undischarged /ˌʌndɪsˈtʃɑːdʒd/ *adj* (*finance*) **1** (of a debt) not paid. **2** (esp of a bankrupt person or firm) still legally obliged to pay money owing to creditors. Cf DISCHARGE.

undisputed /ˌʌndɪˈspjuːtɪd/ *adj* **1** that cannot be doubted or questioned: *undisputed facts, talents, rights.* **2** accepted without dispute; unchallenged: *the undisputed champion, winner, etc* ○ *the undisputed market leader.*

undistinguished /ˌʌndɪˈstɪŋgwɪʃt/ *adj* lacking any outstanding feature; mediocre or poor: *an undistinguished career, appearance* ○ *be undistinguished as a diplomat.*

undivided /ˌʌndɪˈvaɪdɪd/ *adj* (idm) **give one's undivided attention (to sth/sb); get/have sb's undivided attention** concentrate fully (on sth/sb); be the one thing or person that sb attends to: *You have my (full and) undivided attention.* ○ *Tom seldom got his mother's undivided attention.*

undo /ʌnˈduː/ *v* (*pt* **undid** /ʌnˈdɪd/, *pp* **undone** /ʌnˈdʌn/) [Tn] **1** untie or unfasten (knots, buttons, etc); open (a parcel, an envelope, etc): *My zip has come undone.* ○ *I can't undo my shoelaces.* ○ *undo* (ie unravel) *some knitting.* Cf DO UP (DO[2]), DO STH UP. **2** destroy the effect of (sth); cancel: *He undid most of the good work of his predecessor.* ○ *What is done cannot be undone.*

▷ **undoing** /ʌnˈduːɪŋ/ *n* [sing] (*fml*) cause of sb's ruin or downfall: *Drink was his undoing.* ○ *lead, contribute to sb's undoing.*

undone *adj* [pred] **1** untied, unfastened or opened: *Your buttons are all undone.* **2** not done; unfinished: *The work was left/remained undone.*

undoubted /ʌnˈdaʊtɪd/ *adj* [attrib] not doubted or questioned; indisputable: *her undoubted skill, class, ability, etc as an athlete* ○ *an undoubted improvement in my health* ○ *an undoubted authority on the subject.* ▷ **undoubtedly** *adv*: *The painting is undoubtedly genuine.* ○ *undoubtedly so.*

undreamed-of /ʌnˈdriːmd ɒv/ (also **undreamt-of** /ʌnˈdremt ɒv/) *adj* not thought to be possible; not (even) imagined: *undreamed-of wealth, success* ○ *We now travel round the world in a way previously undreamt-of.*

undress /ˌʌnˈdres/ *v* **1** [I] take off one's clothes: *undress and get into bed.* **2** [Tn] remove the clothes of (sb/sth): *undress a child, doll.*

▷ **undressed** *adj* [usu pred] with one's clothes off; naked: *Are you undressed yet?* ○ *It's time the children got undressed.*

undrinkable /ˌʌnˈdrɪŋkəbl/ *adj* not fit to be drunk, because of impurity or poor quality: *This wine is quite undrinkable.*

undue /ˌʌnˈdjuː; US -ˈduː/ *adj* [attrib] (*fml*) more than is right or proper; excessive: *with* ˌ*undue* ˈ*haste* ○ *show undue concern over sb/sth* ○ *apply undue pressure to make sb change his mind.*

undulate /ˈʌndjʊleɪt; US -dʒʊ-/ *v* [I] have a wave-like movement or appearance: *(a field of) wheat undulating in the breeze* ○ *undulating hills, fields, etc.*

▷ **undulation** /ˌʌndjʊˈleɪʃn; US -dʒʊ-/ *n* (**a**) [U] wave-like movement or appearance. (**b**) [C] one of a number of wave-like curves or slopes: *The downs fell in gentle undulations to the sea.*

unduly /ˌʌnˈdjuːlɪ; US -ˈduːlɪ/ *adv* (*fml*) more than is right or proper; excessively: *without being unduly pessimistic, suspicious, etc* ○ *not unduly influenced/not influenced unduly by the media.*

undying /ˌʌnˈdaɪɪŋ/ *adj* [attrib] everlasting or never-ending: *undying love, hatred, fame.*

unearned /ˌʌnˈɜːnd/ *adj* **1** not gained by working: ˌ*unearned* ˈ*income*, eg from interest on investments. **2** not deserved: ˌ*unearned* ˈ*praise.*

unearth /ʌnˈɜːθ/ *v* [Tn, Tn·pr] ~ **sth (from sth) 1** uncover or obtain sth from the ground by digging: *unearth buried treasure* ○ *The dog has unearthed some bones.* **2** (*fig*) find sth by searching; discover and make known: *I unearthed the portrait from the attic.* ○ *unearth new facts about Shakespeare.*

unearthly /ʌnˈɜːθlɪ/ *adj* **1** supernatural or mysterious or frightening: *unearthly visions, screams* ○ *The silence was unearthly.* **2** [attrib] (*infml*) absurdly early or inconvenient: *Why should I get up at this unearthly hour?* ○ *the unearthly time of 2.30 am.*

uneasy /ʌnˈiːzɪ/ *adj* (**-ier, -iest**) **1** ~ (**about/at sth**) troubled or anxious: *have an uneasy conscience*, ie feel guilty ○ *I'm uneasy in my mind about the future.* **2** fitful or uncomfortable: *an uneasy truce, silence* ○ *pass an uneasy night*, ie sleep badly. **3** disturbing or worrying: *They had an uneasy suspicion that all was not well.*

▷ **unease** /ʌnˈiːz/, **uneasiness** *ns* [U] apprehension: *I waited with growing unease for her return.*

uneasily /ʌnˈiːzɪlɪ/ *adv*: *He moved uneasily in his chair.*

uneatable /ˌʌnˈiːtəbl/ *adj* (of food, etc) not fit to be eaten, esp because of its poor condition. Cf INEDIBLE.

uneconomic /ˌʌnˌiːkəˈnɒmɪk, ˌʌnˌek-/ *adj* not likely to be profitable; not economic: ˌ*uneconomic* ˈ*factories*, ˈ*industries*, ˈ*businesses, etc* ○ *the closure of uneconomic pits*, ie coal-mines.

uneconomical /ˌʌnˌiːkəˈnɒmɪkl, ˌʌnˌek-/ *adj* wasteful or inefficient; not thrifty: *an uneconomical method of housekeeping.* ▷ **uneconomically** /-klɪ/ *adv.*

uneducated /ʌnˈedʒʊkeɪtɪd/ *adj* **1** suggesting lack of the type of education, social background or good manners considered desirable: *uneducated speech, handwriting* ○ *uneducated tastes.* **2** having received little or no formal education at a school etc.

unemployed /ˌʌnɪmˈplɔɪd/ *adj* **1** temporarily without a paid job. **2** not in use: (*finance*) *unemployed capital*, ie capital that is not invested.

▷ **the unemployed** *n* [pl *v*] people who are (temporarily) without work.

unemployment /ˌʌnɪmˈplɔɪmənt/ *n* [U] (**a**) state of being unemployed: *300 workers face unemployment* ○ *throughout the period of your unemployment.* ⇨ articles at EMPLOYMENT, SOCIAL SECURITY. (**b**) amount of unused labour: *reduce unemployment*, eg by creating jobs ○ *the rising level of unemployment* ○ [attrib] *the monthly unemployment figures.*

□ **unemˈployment benefit** (*US* **unemployment compenˈsation**) money paid to a worker who cannot find employment.

unending /ʌnˈendɪŋ/ *adj* **1** everlasting or unceasing: *the unending struggle between good and evil.* **2** (*infml*) frequently repeated: *I'm tired of your unending complaints.*

unequal /ˌʌnˈiːkwəl/ *adj* **1** ~ (**in sth**) different (in size, amount, etc): *The twins are unequal in height.* **2** not at the same level of strength, ability, etc: *an unequal bargain, contest, struggle* ○ *unequal pay and conditions*, eg for women. **3** [pred] ~ **to sth** (*fml*) not strong, clever, etc enough to do sth: *I feel unequal to the task.* ▷ **unequally** /-kwəlɪ/ *adv.*

unequalled /ˌʌnˈiːkwəld/ *adj* superior to all others; unmatched: *His record as a show-jumper is unequalled.* ○ *The husky is unequalled for stamina and endurance.*

unequivocal /ˌʌnɪˈkwɪvəkl/ *adj* (*fml*) having only one possible meaning; clear and unmistakable: *an unequivocal attitude, position, demand.* ▷ **unequivocally** /-kəlɪ/ *adv*: *state one's intentions unequivocally.*

unerring /ˌʌnˈɜːrɪŋ/ *adj* not making mistakes or failing or missing the mark; consistently accurate: *his unerring taste in clothes, instinct for a bargain, sense of direction* ○ *He has an unerring knack of saying the wrong thing.* ○ *His aim was unerring.* ▷ **unerringly** *adv.*

UNESCO (also **Unesco**) /juːˈneskəʊ/ *abbr* United Nations Educational, Scientific and Cultural Organization.

unethical /ˌʌnˈeθɪkl/ *adj* without principles, esp in business or professional conduct: *unethical decisions, practices.* ▷ **unethically** /-klɪ/ *adv.*

uneven /ˌʌnˈiːvn/ *adj* **1** not level or smooth or regular: *an uneven hemline*, ie of a skirt ○ *an uneven pavement, floor.* **2** not uniform or equal; varying: *have an uneven pulse, heartbeat* ○ *Emotion made his voice uneven.* ○ *work of uneven quality.* **3** (of a contest, match, etc) unequal. ▷ **unevenly** *adv.* **unevenness** *n* [U].

unexceptionable /ˌʌnɪkˈsepʃənəbl/ *adj* (*fml*) that cannot be criticized; entirely satisfactory: *her unexceptionable behaviour, conduct, etc.* ▷ **unexceptionably** /-əblɪ/ *adv.*

unexceptional /ˌʌnɪkˈsepʃənl/ *adv* not outstanding or unusual; quite ordinary. ▷ **unexceptionally** /-ʃənəlɪ/ *adv.*

unexpected /ˌʌnɪkˈspektɪd/ *adj* causing surprise because not expected: ˌ*unexpected* ˈ*guests*, ˈ*questions*, ˈ*gifts* ○ ˌ*unexpected* *deˈvelopments*, ˈ*changes*, *reˈsults* ○ *His reaction was quite unexpected.*

▷ **the unexpected** *n* [sing] event, etc that is unexpected: *be prepared for the unexpected (to happen).*

unexpectedly *adv.*

unexpectedness *n* [U].

unfailing /ʌnˈfeɪlɪŋ/ *adj* (*approv*) **1** never coming to an end; constant: *an unfailing source of inspiration* ○ *their unfailing efforts for peace* ○ *his unfailing patience, good humour, devotion, etc.*

2 [usu attrib] that can be relied on; certain: *her unfailing cooperation, support, etc.*
▷ **unfailingly** *adv* at all times: *unfailingly courteous.*

unfair /ˌʌnˈfeə(r)/ *adj* **1** ~ **(on/to sb)** not right or just: *ˌunfair ˈtreatment, compeˈtition* ○ *an ˌunfair deˈcision, comˈparison, adˈvantage* ○ *If some athletes use drugs, it is unfair on/to the others.* ○ *She sued her employer for unfair dismissal.* **2** not following normal rules or principles: *ˌunfair ˈtactics* ○ *ˌunfair ˈplay*, eg at a football match ○ (*commerce*) *ˌunfair ˈtrading.* ▷ **unfairly** *adv.* **unfairness** *n* [U].

unfaithful /ˌʌnˈfeɪθfl/ *adj* ~ **(to sb/sth) 1** having committed adultery: *Her husband is unfaithful (to her).* **2** (*dated*) not loyal; treacherous: *an unfaithful servant, subject, etc.* ▷ **unfaithfully** /-fəlɪ/ *adv.* **unfaithfulness** *n* [U].

unfamiliar /ˌʌnfəˈmɪlɪə(r)/ *adj* **1** ~ **(to sb)** not well known: *His face was unfamiliar to me.* ○ *working in new and unfamiliar surroundings.* **2** [pred] ~ **with sth** (*fml*) not having knowledge of sth; not acquainted with sth: *I'm unfamiliar with this type of computer.* ▷ **unfamiliarity** /ˌʌnfəˌmɪlɪˈærətɪ/ *n* [U].

unfathomable /ʌnˈfæðəməbl/ *adj* (*fml*) **1** so deep that the bottom cannot be reached: *the ocean's unfathomable depths.* **2** (*fig*) too strange or difficult to be understood: *unfathomable motives, mysteries.*

unfeeling /ʌnˈfi:lɪŋ/ *adj* hard-hearted or unsympathetic: *unfeeling behaviour* ○ *an unfeeling person, remark, attitude, reaction.* ▷ **unfeelingly** *adv.*

unfeigned /ʌnˈfeɪnd/ *adj* not pretended; genuine or sincere: *greet sb with unfeigned pleasure, delight, sympathy, etc.* ▷ **unfeignedly** /ˌʌnfeɪnɪdlɪ/ *adv.*

unfit /ˌʌnˈfɪt/ *adj* **1** ~ **(for sth/to do sth) (a)** not of the required standard; unsuitable: *food unfit for human consumption* ○ *houses unfit for people to live in.* **(b)** lacking the ability needed; incapable: *She is unfit for such a senior position.* ○ *He is unfit to drive in his present state*, eg because he is drunk. **2** not perfectly healthy and fit: *The army rejected him as medically unfit.*

unflagging /ˌʌnˈflægɪŋ/ *adj* not showing signs of tiredness; untiring: *unflagging energy, zeal, devotion, etc* ○ *listen with unflagging attention, interest, concentration, etc.* ▷ **unflaggingly** *adv.*

unflappable /ˌʌnˈflæpəbl/ *adj* (*infml esp Brit*) remaining calm in a crisis; imperturbable: *A busy manager needs a completely unflappable secretary.* ▷ **unflappability** /ˌʌnflæpəˈbɪlətɪ/ *n* [U].

unfledged /ˌʌnˈfledʒd/ *adj* **1** (of a young bird) whose feathers have not yet grown. **2** (*fig*) (of a person) inexperienced.

unflinching /ʌnˈflɪntʃɪŋ/ *adj* not showing fear or shrinking in the face of danger, difficulty, etc: *unflinching courage, determination, resoluteness, etc.* ▷ **unflinchingly** *adv*: *He held out his hand unflinchingly for the cane.*

unfold /ʌnˈfəʊld/ *v* **1** [I, Tn] (cause sth to) open or spread out from a folded state: *The garden chair unfolds to make a camp-bed.* ○ *unfold a map, tablecloth, etc* ○ *The eagle unfolded its wings.* **2** [I, Tn, Dn·pr] ~ **sth (to sb)** (*fig*) (cause sth to) be revealed or made known: *The landscape unfolded before us.* ○ *as the story, scene, enquiry unfolds (itself)* ○ *She unfolded her plans to me.*

unforeseen /ˌʌnfɔ:ˈsi:n/ *adj* not known in advance; unexpected: *ˌunforeseen ˈcircumstances, deˈvelopments, ˈdifficulties.*

unforgettable /ˌʌnfəˈgetəbl/ *adj* (*esp approv*) that cannot be easily forgotten; memorable: *an unforgettable experience, moment, scene.*

unformed /ˌʌnˈfɔ:md/ *adj* not (yet) having developed fully; immature: *her ˌunformed ˈhandwriting* ○ *The child's character is as yet unformed.*

unfortunate /ʌnˈfɔ:tʃənɪt/ *adj* **1** having or causing bad luck; unlucky: *I was unfortunate enough to lose my keys.* ○ *an unfortunate expedition* ○ *an unfortunate start to our holiday.* **2** unsuitable or regrettable: *an unfortunate remark, coincidence, mishap* ○ *a most unfortunate choice of words* ○ *It is unfortunate that you missed the meeting.*
▷ **unfortunate** *n* (*esp pl*) unfortunate or wretched person: *Unlike many other poor unfortunates, I do have a job.*
unfortunately *adv* ~ **(for sb)** regrettably; unluckily: *The notice is most unfortunately phrased.* ○ *I can't come, unfortunately.* ○ *Unfortunately for him, he was wrong.*

unfounded /ˌʌnˈfaʊndɪd/ *adj* with no basis in fact; groundless: *unfounded rumours, suspicions, hopes.*

unfreeze /ˌʌnˈfri:z/ *v* (*pt* **unfroze** /-ˈfrəʊz/, *pp* **unfrozen** /-ˈfrəʊzn/) **1** [I, Tn] (cause sth to) thaw: *unfreeze some chops.* Cf DEFROST. **2** [Tn] (*finance*) remove official controls on (the economy, etc): *unfreeze wages, prices, etc* ○ *unfreeze trade restrictions.*

unfriendly /ˌʌnˈfrendlɪ/ *adj* (**-ier, -iest**) ~ **(to/towards sb)** hostile or unsympathetic: *an unfriendly look, gesture, attitude* ○ *He was distinctly unfriendly towards me.*

unfrock /ˌʌnˈfrɒk/ (also **defrock**) *v* [Tn esp passive] dismiss (a priest guilty of bad conduct) from the priesthood.

unfurl /ˌʌnˈfɜ:l/ *v* [I, Tn] unroll, unfold or spread out (sth): *unfurl a flag, banner, sail, etc.*

ungainly /ʌnˈgeɪnlɪ/ *adj* clumsy or awkward; not graceful: *the ungainly movements of ducks out of water* ○ *He walked in long ungainly strides.* ▷ **ungainliness** *n* [U].

unget-at-able /ˌʌngetˈætəbl/ *adj* (*infml*) (in a place that is) not easy to reach; inaccessible.

ungodly /ˌʌnˈgɒdlɪ/ *adj* **1** (*dated or fml*) not giving reverence to God; sinful or wicked: *lead an ungodly life.* **2** [attrib] (*infml*) very inconvenient: *Why are you phoning at this ungodly hour (of the night)?*

ungovernable /ˌʌnˈgʌvənəbl/ *adj* (*fml*) impossible or difficult to control; violent: *fly into an ungovernable rage, temper, etc* ○ *a man of ungovernable passions.*

ungracious /ˌʌnˈgreɪʃəs/ *adj* grudging or resentful; impolite: *her ungracious acceptance of my offer* ○ *It was ungracious of me not to acknowledge your help.* ▷ **ungraciously** *adv.*

ungrammatical /ˌʌngrəˈmætɪkl/ *adj* contrary to the rules of grammar: *ungrammatical sentences, constructions, etc.* ▷ **ungrammatically** /-klɪ/ *adv.*

ungrateful /ʌnˈgreɪtfl/ *adj* ~ **(to sb) (for sth)** not recognizing a kindness, service, etc; not grateful: *You ungrateful wretch!* ▷ **ungratefully** /-fəlɪ/ *adv.*

unguarded /ˌʌnˈgɑ:dɪd/ *adj* **1** not guarded: *The prisoner was left unguarded.* ○ *Never leave your luggage unguarded*, ie unattended. **2** (esp of a person and what he says) careless or indiscreet: *unguarded comments, criticisms, etc* ○ *catch sb in an unguarded moment.*

ungulate /ˈʌŋgjʊleɪt/ *adj* (*zoology*) (of an animal) that has hoofs, like a horse, cow, etc.
▷ **ungulate** *n* animal with hoofs.

unhappy /ʌnˈhæpɪ/ *adj* (**-ier, -iest**) **1 (a)** sad or miserable; not happy: *look, sound, etc unhappy* ○ *an unhappy occasion, atmosphere, face.* **(b)** ~ **(about/at sth)** anxious or dissatisfied: *Investors were unhappy about the risk.* **2** unfortunate or unlucky; regrettable: *an unhappy coincidence, chance, etc* ○ *What has led to this unhappy state of affairs?* **3** [usu attrib] (*fml*) not suitable or appropriate: *an unhappy comment, decision, choice.*
▷ **unhappily** /-ɪlɪ/ *adv* **1** sadly. **2** unfortunately: *Unhappily, she is not here today.*
unhappiness *n* [U].

unhealthy /ʌnˈhelθɪ/ *adj* (**-ier, -iest**) **1** not having or not showing good health: *an unhealthy pallor, complexion, cough* ○ (*fig*) *the unhealthy state of the economy.* **2** harmful to health: *an unhealthy climate, diet, life-style* ○ *living in damp unhealthy conditions.* **3** unwholesome or morbid: *show an unhealthy interest in/curiosity about murder.* **4** (*infml*) dangerous to life: *Terrorist attacks made our position very unhealthy.* ▷ **unhealthily** /-ɪlɪ/ *adv.* **unhealthiness** *n* [U].

unheard /ˌʌnˈhɜ:d/ *adj* [usu pred] having nobody willing to pay attention; unheeded: *Her case was/went unheard by the authorities.*
□ **unheard-of** /ʌnˈhɜ:d ɒv/ *adj* not previously known of or done; unprecedented: *Radiation reached unheard-of levels.* ○ *It was unheard-of for anyone to complain.*

unhinge /ʌnˈhɪndʒ/ *v* [Tn esp passive] cause (sb) to become mentally unbalanced: *The shock unhinged his mind.* ○ *Unhinged by her death, he fell ill.*

unhitch /ˌʌnˈhɪtʃ/ *v* [Tn] release (eg a horse or wagon that was attached by a loop of rope).

unholy /ˌʌnˈhəʊlɪ/ *adj* (**-ier, -iest**) [attrib] **1** wicked or sinful: *an unholy alliance between Communists and Fascists.* **2** (*infml*) (used as an intensifier) outrageous or excessive: *leave things in an unholy muddle/mess* ○ *making an unholy row/din/racket.* ▷ **unholiness** *n* [U].

unhoped-for /ʌnˈhəʊpt fɔ:(r)/ *adj* not hoped for or expected: *an unhoped-for piece of good luck.*

uni- *comb form* having or consisting of one: *unilateral* ○ *unisex.*

Uniat /ˈju:nɪæt/ *adj* (also **Uniate** /-eɪt/) of or belonging to one of the Uniat Churches.
□ **the Uniat Churches** the Churches of eastern Europe and the Middle East which accept the authority of the Pope and are considered as being part of the Roman Catholic Church, but keep their own forms of worship, laws, etc.

unicameral /ˌju:nɪˈkæmərəl/ *adj* (of a law-making assembly) having a single undivided membership; not made up of two or more houses (HOUSE[1] 4).

UNICEF /ˈju:nɪsef/ *abbr* United Nations Children's (formerly International Children's Emergency) Fund.

unicellular /ˌju:nɪˈseljʊlə(r)/ *adj* (*biology*) (of an organism) consisting of a single cell.

unicorn /ˈju:nɪkɔ:n/ *n* mythical animal resembling a horse with a single straight horn projecting from its forehead. ⇨ illus at COAT OF ARMS (COAT).

unidentified /ˌʌnaɪˈdentɪfaɪd/ *adj* that cannot be identified: *an unidentified species, submarine, caller* ○ *information from unidentified sources.*
□ **ˌunidentified ˌflying ˈobject** (*abbr* **UFO**) = FLYING SAUCER (FLYING).

uniform[1] /ˈju:nɪfɔ:m/ *adj* not changing in form or character; unvarying: *of uniform length, size, shape, colour, etc* ○ *The rows of houses were uniform in appearance.* ○ *be kept at a uniform temperature* ○ *uniform distribution of weight.* ▷ **uniformity** /ˌju:nɪˈfɔ:mətɪ/ *n* (*esp derog*) [U]: *a depressing uniformity of taste.* **uniformly** *adv*: *Reaction to the cuts was uniformly negative.*

uniform[2] /ˈju:nɪfɔ:m/ *n* **1** [C, U] distinctive clothing worn by all members of an organization or group, eg the police, the armed forces, nurses: *children wearing school uniform(s).* **2** (idm) **in uniform (a)** wearing such clothing: *officers in full dress uniform.* **(b)** belonging to the armed forces: *How long was he in uniform?*
▷ **uniformed** *adj* wearing uniform: *uniformed staff*, eg at a hotel ○ *the uniformed branch of the police*, ie as contrasted with detectives, who wear plain clothes.

unify /ˈju:nɪfaɪ/ *v* (*pt, pp* **-fied**) [Tn] form (sth) into a single unit or make uniform: *Germany was unified in 1871.* ○ *the unifying effect of the nurses' strike* ○ *England and Scotland do not have a unified legal system.* ▷ **unification** /ˌju:nɪfɪˈkeɪʃn/ *n* [U]: *seeking the unification of Christian churches.*

unilateral /ˌju:nɪˈlætrəl/ *adj* [usu attrib] done by or affecting one person, group, country, etc and not another; one-sided: *unilateral decisions, agreements, declarations, etc* ○ *unilateral (nuclear) disarmament*, ie voluntary removal or dismantling by a country of its (nuclear) weapons. Cf BILATERAL, MULTILATERAL. ▷ **unilaterally** /-rəlɪ/ *adv.*

unimpeachable /ˌʌnɪmˈpi:tʃəbl/ *adj* (*fml approv*) that cannot be doubted or questioned; trustworthy: *unimpeachable honesty, behaviour* ○ *evidence from an unimpeachable source.* ▷ **unimpeachably** /-əblɪ/ *adv.*

unimproved /ˌʌnimˈpru:vd/ *adj* **1** that has not been improved. **2** (of land) that has not been built on or used for farming.

uninformed /ˌʌnɪnˈfɔ:md/ *adj* **1** not having or

Russia and Northern Asia

showing sufficient information: *an uninformed estimate, opinion, criticism* ○ *Her colleagues had deliberately kept her uninformed.* **2** uneducated or ignorant: *the uninformed political discussion you hear in pubs* ○ (*fml or joc*) *Quercus, or, to the uninformed layman, the oak....*

uninhibited /ˌʌnɪnˈhɪbɪtɪd/ *adj* showing no inhibitions or restraint: *After a few drinks their behaviour became remarkably uninhibited.*

uninspired /ˌʌnɪnˈspaɪəd/ *adj* without imagination or inspiration; dull: *an uninspired speech, performance, painting, etc.*

uninspiring /ˌʌnɪnˈspaɪərɪŋ/ *adj* not producing interest or excitement; unpromising: *The book is fascinating, despite its uninspiring title.*

unintelligible /ˌʌnɪnˈtelɪdʒəbl/ *adj* impossible to understand: *unintelligible handwriting, jargon* ○ *speak in an almost unintelligible whisper.* ▷ **unintelligibly** /-əblɪ/ *adv.*

uninterested /ʌnˈɪntrəstɪd/ *adj* ~ (**in sb/sth**) having or showing no interest or concern; indifferent. ➪ Usage at INTEREST[2].

uninviting /ˌʌnɪnˈvaɪtɪŋ/ *adv* not attractive; repellent: *an uninviting meal of cold fish and chips* ○ *The hotel room was bare and uninviting.*

union /ˈjuːnɪən/ *n* **1** [U, sing] ~ (**of A with B/ between A and B**) (act or instance of) uniting or being united: *the union of three towns into one* ○ *support the union between our two parties/the union of our party with yours.* **2** [C] (**a**) (esp political) whole formed by uniting parts, states, etc: *the Union of Soviet Socialist Republics.* (**b**) association or club formed by uniting people or groups: *the National Union of Working Men's Clubs* ○ *members of the Students' Union*, ie a general social and debating society at some universities and colleges ○ *join the Mothers' Union.* (**c**) = TRADE UNION (TRADE[1]). **3** (*fml or joc*) (**a**) [U] state of being in agreement or harmony: *live together in perfect union.* (**b**) [C] instance of this, esp a marriage: *a happy union, blessed with six children.* **4** [C] coupling for rods or pipes. **5 the Union** [sing] (**a**) the joining together of England and Scotland in 1603 under *James I (ie James VI of Scotland) or in 1707 under a single parliament. (**b**) the joining together of Great Britain and Ireland in 1801. (**c**) the United States of America, esp the states of the North that fought against the states wishing to keep slavery during the *American Civil War: [attrib] *the Union army.*

▷ **unionize, -ise** /-aɪz/ *v* [I, Tn] organize (people) into a trade union: *unionize a firm's employees* ○ *a unionized work-force.* **unionization, -isation** /ˌjuːnɪənaɪˈzeɪʃn; *US* -nɪˈz-/ *n* [U].

□ **the ˌUnion ˈJack** (also **the ˌUnion ˈflag**) the national flag of the United Kingdom. ➪ article at NATIONAL.

ˌ**Union ˈTerritory** any of the nine administrative areas of India.

unionist /ˈjuːnɪənɪst/ *n* (**a**) member of a trade union or supporter of trade unions. (**b**) **Unionist** person favouring political union, esp between Britain and Northern Ireland. ➪ article at IRELAND. ▷ **unionism** /ˈjuːnɪənɪzəm/ *n* [U].

Union of Soviet Socialist Republics /ˌjuːnɪən əv ˌsəʊvɪət ˌsəʊʃəlɪst rɪˈpʌblɪks/ **the Union of Soviet Socialist Republics** (also **the Soviet Union**) (*abbr* **USSR**) former country (the first Communist state, 1923-91) extending from eastern Europe across the northern half of Asia. It was the largest country in the world, made up of 15 republics and with over a hundred ethnic groups. *Russia was the largest republic and covered three-quarters of its territory. Although the Soviet Union never achieved self-sufficiency in agriculture, it was one of the world's largest producers of wheat, potatoes and cattle. It had vast mineral resources, including coal, oil, natural gas, gold, silver, iron and diamonds. Its traditionally centralized communist system of planning and large military expenditure handicapped its industry, and living standards for many people were low. That fact, added to demographic changes seen eg in the rising birth-rates of central Asian republics compared with those of the European north-west, led to general discontent by the 1980s. Reforms begun then were accompanied by demands of a nationalist, sometimes religious, kind. Separatist movements increased in many of the republics. The Baltic States of Estonia, Latvia and Lithuania achieved independence in 1991; other republics were by that date also on the path towards recognized independent status, and the USSR declared itself ended in December 1991. Cf COMMONWEALTH OF INDEPENDENT STATES. ➪ map.

unique /juːˈniːk/ *adj* **1** (**a**) being the only one of its type: *a unique work of art.* (**b**) having no like or equal; unparalleled: *a unique opportunity* ○ *a unique ability.* **2** [pred] ~ **to sb/sth** concerning or related to one person or group or thing only: *special difficulties unique to blind people.* **3** (*infml*) unusual; remarkable: *a rather unique little restaurant.* ▷ **uniquely** *adv*: *She is uniquely suited to the job.* **uniqueness** *n* [U].

unisex /ˈjuːnɪseks/ *adj* designed to be suitable for both sexes in style or function: *unisex fashions* ○ *a unisex hairdressing salon.*

unison /ˈjuːnɪsn, ˈjuːnɪzn/ *n* (idm) **in unison** (**with sb/sth**) (**a**) sounding or singing together the same musical note (or the same note in different octaves): *The last verse will be sung in unison.* (**b**) (*fig fml*) acting together in close association or agreement: *The banks have acted in unison with the building societies in lowering interest rates.*

unit /ˈjuːnɪt/ *n* **1** individual thing, person or group regarded for purposes of calculation, etc as single and complete, or as part of a complex whole: *the family as the unit of society* ○ *The course book has twenty units.* **2** quantity chosen as a standard in terms of which other quantities may be expressed, or for which a stated charge is made: *The metre is a unit of length.* ○ *The monetary unit of Great*

Britain is the pound. ○ *SI units* ○ *a bill for fifty units of electricity.* **3** (esp in compounds) **(a)** part with a special function within a large or complex machine: *a ˈfilter unit* ○ *the central ˈprocessing unit in a computer.* **(b)** group with a special function within a large or complex organization: *a unit of highly-trained soldiers* ○ *a bomb-disposal unit.* **4** piece of furniture, equipment, etc designed to fit with others that are similar or complementary: *matching kitchen units* ○ *storage units.* **5 (a)** smallest whole number; the number 1: *The number 34 consists of three tens and four units.* **(b)** any whole number from 0 to 9: *a column for the tens and a column for the units.*

□ **ˌunit ˈprice** price charged for each single item of goods of the same type.

ˌunit ˈtrust (*Brit*) (*US* **ˈmutual fund**) investment company that invests the combined contributions of its members in various securities and pays them a dividend (calculated on the average return from these securities) in proportion to their holdings.

Unitarian /ˌju:nɪˈteərɪən/ *n, adj* (member) of the Christian religious sect which rejects the doctrine of the Trinity and believes that God is one person: *the Unitarian Church.* Cf TRINITARIAN. ▷ **Unitarianism** /-ɪzəm/ *n* [U].

unite /ju:ˈnaɪt/ *v* **1** [I, Ipr, Tn, Tn·pr] ~ **(sb/sth) (with sb/sth)** (cause people or things to) become one; come or bring together; join: *The two parties have united to form a coalition.* ○ *After three years in prison he was again united with his wife and family.* ○ *the common interests that unite our two countries* ○ *The threat of war has united the country behind* (ie in support of) *its leaders.* **2** [I, Ipr] ~ **(in sth/doing sth)** act or work together: *We should unite in fighting/unite to fight poverty and disease.*

▷ **united** *adj* **1** joined together by love or sympathy: *a very united family.* **2** resulting from people joining together for a common purpose: *make a united effort* ○ *present a united front to the enemy.* **3** joined politically: *the campaign for a united Ireland.* **unitedly** *adv.*

United Arab Emirates /ju:ˌnaɪtɪd ˌærəb eˈmɪərəɪts, *also* ˈemɪrəts/ **the United Arab Emirates** country in the Middle East lying on the western side of the *Persian Gulf; pop approx 1 501 000 (of which about two-thirds are citizens of the country); official language Arabic; capital Abu Dhabi; unit of currency dirham (= 100 fils). The country was formed in 1971 from seven sheikhdoms (Abu Dhabi, Ajman, Dubai, Fujairah, Ras al Khaimah, Sharjah, Umm al Qaiwain). The Emirates' economy is based almost entirely on oil and natural gas, with limited agriculture and manufacturing industry. ⇨ map at ARABIAN PENINSULA.

United Kingdom /ju:ˌnaɪtɪd ˈkɪŋdəm/ (in full **the United Kingdom of Great Britain and Northern Ireland** /ðə ju:ˌnaɪtɪd ˌkɪŋdəm əv ˌgreɪt ˌbrɪtn ənd ˌnɔ:ðən ˈaɪələnd/, *abbr* **UK**) country made up of *England, *Wales, *Scotland and *Northern Ireland, a member of the Commonwealth and the European Community; pop approx 57 065 000; official language English; capital London; unit of currency pound (= 100 pence). Despite its small size, the UK has a very varied landscape, from the rugged terrain of *Orkney and *Shetland in the north to the hills and grasslands of the south coast. Its agricultural industry is one of the most efficient in the world and it is the leading mining country of Europe. London is a leading financial and insurance centre. ⇨ map. ⇨ map at App 1.

United Nations /ju:ˌnaɪtɪd ˈneɪʃnz/ (in full **the United Nations Organization** /ðə ju:ˌnaɪtɪd ˈneɪʃnz ɔ:gənaɪzeɪʃn/, *abbrs* **UN, UNO**) international organization, based in New York, whose aims are to maintain peace and security in the world. Most of the world's independent states are members and each has one vote in the General Assembly; the fifteen members of the Security Council form its executive body. Its specialized agencies include the World Health Organization and the International Court of Justice.

United Reformed Church /ju:ˌnaɪtɪd rɪˌfɔ:md ˈtʃɜ:tʃ/ Church formed in Britain in 1972 when the *Congregational Church in England and Wales united with the English *Presbyterian Church.

United States of America /ju:ˌnaɪtɪd ˌsteɪts əv əˈmerɪkə/ **the United States of America** (also **the UˌnitedˈStates**) (*abbrs* **US, USA**) /ˌju: ˈes, ˌju: es ˈeɪ/ country lying in the southern half of N America, with additional territory in *Alaska and *Hawaii; pop approx 246 329 000; official language English; capital Washington DC; unit of currency dollar (= 100 cents). The west of the country is dominated by the chain of the *Rocky Mountains; the Central Plain (including the *Great Plains) extends towards the *Appalachian mountains in the east. It is made up of 50 states and the District of Columbia. It is the world's leading economic power, and has a highly productive agricultural system, with soya, wheat and maize as the main crops as well as intensive pig and cattle farming. The USA has the world's second largest mineral resources (esp fossil fuels and uranium), and its most active manufacturing industry, both traditional and modern. ⇨ map. ⇨ map at App 1.

unity /ˈju:nətɪ/ *n* **1 (a)** [U] state of being one or a unit; oneness: *The figure on the left spoils the unity of the painting.* **(b)** [C] thing consisting of parts that form a whole. **2** [U] (*mathematics*) the number 1. **3** [U] harmony or agreement (in aims, ideas, feelings, etc): *live together in unity* ○ *Christian unity* ○ *political unity* ○ *National unity is essential in wartime.*

Univ *abbr* University: *London Univ* ○ *Univ of Salford.*

universal /ˌju:nɪˈvɜ:sl/ *adj* [esp attrib] of, belonging to, affecting or done by all people or things in the world or in a particular group: *Television provides universal entertainment.* ○ *War causes universal misery.* ○ *universal suffrage,* ie the right of all members of a community to vote ○ *There is universal agreement on this issue.* ○ *Their proposal met with almost universal condemnation.*

▷ **universality** /ˌju:nɪvɜ:ˈsælətɪ/ *n* [U].

universally /-səlɪ/ *adv* by everyone or in every case: *It is universally acknowledged that...* ○ *The rules do not apply universally.*

□ **ˌuniversal ˈjoint** (also **ˌuniversal ˈcoupling**) joint that connects two shafts in such a way that they can be at any angle to each other.

ˌuniversal ˈindicator chemical indicator which

the United Kingdom

the United States of America

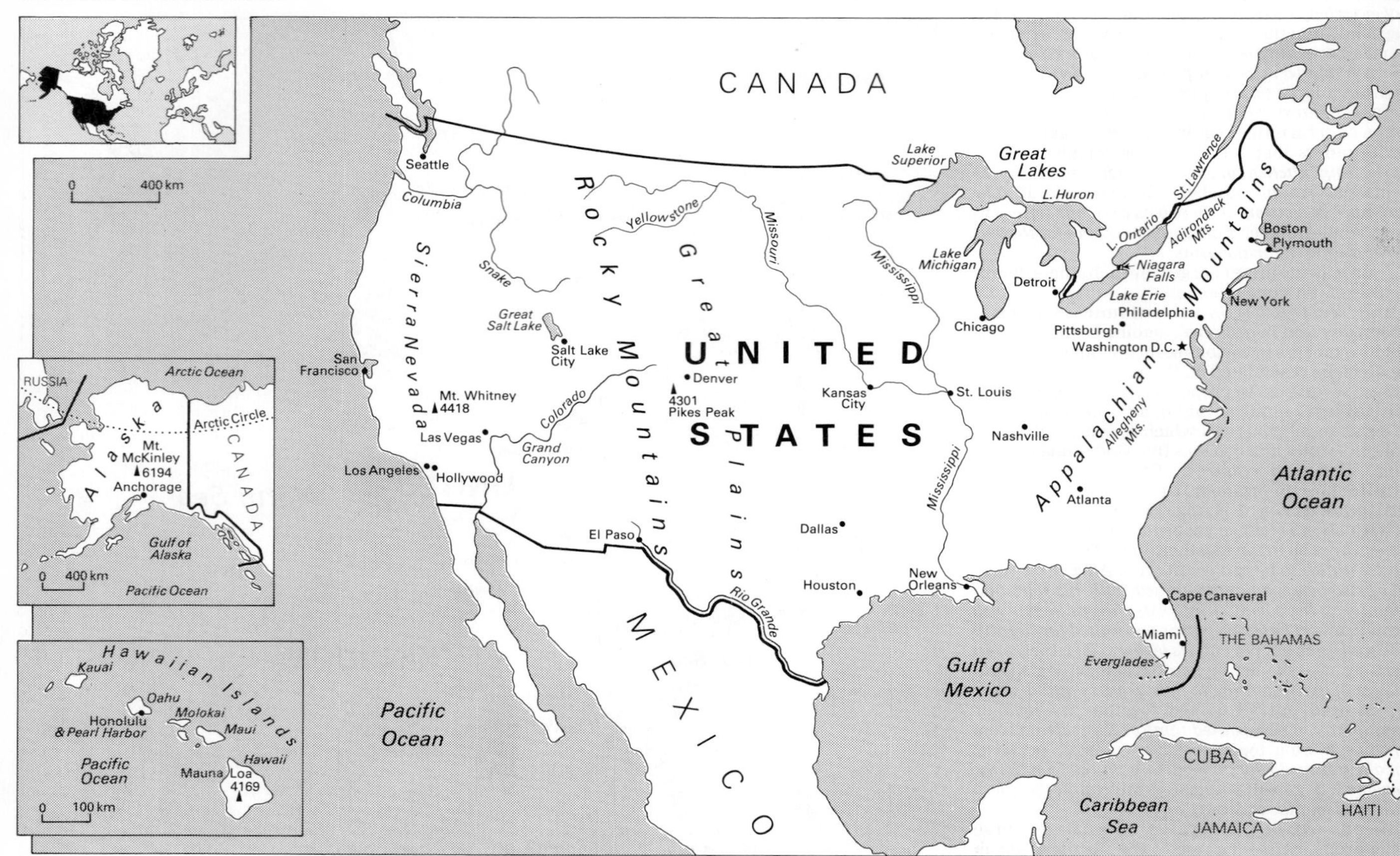

changes colour to show how acidic or alkaline a substance is.

universe /ˈjuːnɪvɜːs/ *n* **1 the universe** [sing] all existing things, including the earth and its creatures and all the stars, planets, etc in space. **2** [C] system of galaxies: *Are there other universes outside our own?*

university /ˌjuːnɪˈvɜːsətɪ/ *n* (**a**) [C] (colleges, buildings, etc of an) institution that teaches and examines students in many branches of advanced learning, awarding degrees and providing facilities for academic research: *She hopes to go to university next year.* ○ [attrib] *a university student, lecturer, professor, etc.* ⇨ article at POST-SCHOOL. (**b**) [CGp] members of such an institution collectively. ⇨ Usage at SCHOOL[1].

unjust /ˌʌnˈdʒʌst/ *adj* not just; not fair or deserved: *an unjust accusation.* ▷ **unjustly** *adv*: *She was unjustly imprisoned without trial.*

unjustifiable /ʌnˈdʒʌstɪfaɪəbl/ *adj* that cannot be justified or excused: *His behaviour was quite unjustifiable.* ▷ **unjustifiably** /-əblɪ/ *adv*.

unkempt /ˌʌnˈkempt/ *adj* not kept tidy; looking dishevelled or neglected: *unkempt hair* ○ *He had an unkempt appearance.* ○ *The garden looks very unkempt.*

unkind /ˌʌnˈkaɪnd/ *adj* not having or showing kindness; cruel or harsh: *an unkind remark* ○ *Don't be so unkind to your brother.*
▷ **unkindly** *adv* in an unkind manner: *Please don't take my remarks unkindly,* ie think I intend to be unkind in saying this.
unkindness *n* [U, C].

unknowing /ʌnˈnəʊɪŋ/ *adj* [usu attrib] not knowing; unaware; unwitting: *He was the unknowing cause of all the misunderstanding.* ▷ **unknowingly** *adv*: *All unknowingly, she had been waiting for hours in the wrong place.*

unknown /ˌʌnˈnəʊn/ *adj* ~ (**to sb**) **1** not known or identified: *The side-effects of the drug are as yet unknown (to scientists).* ○ *Unknown forces were at work to overthrow the government.* **2** not famous or well known; unfamiliar: *The star of the film is a previously unknown actor.* **3** (idm) **an ˌunknown ˈquantity** person or thing that one has no experience of and whose nature, significance, etc one therefore cannot predict: *The new sales director is still a bit of an unknown quantity.* **unknown to sb** without the knowledge of sb: *Quite unknown to me, she'd gone ahead and booked the holiday.*
▷ **unknown** *n* (**a**) (usu **the unknown**) [sing] thing, place, etc that is unknown: *a journey into the unknown* ○ *fear of the unknown.* (**b**) [C] person who is not well known: *The leading role is played by a complete unknown.* (**c**) [C] (*mathematics*) quantity that is not yet determined: *x and y are unknowns.*
□ **the ˌUnknown ˈWarrior** (also **the ˌUnknown ˈSoldier**) member of a country's armed forces who died during a war and whose identity is not known, and whose tomb is kept as a national memorial. Britain's Unknown Warrior died in the First World War and is buried in *Westminster Abbey.

unlace /ʌnˈleɪs/ *v* [Tn] undo the laces of (esp shoes); unfasten or loosen (sth) by slackening its laces.

unladen /ˌʌnˈleɪdn/ *adj* not loaded: *ˌunladen ˈweight,* ie the weight of a vehicle with nothing loaded into or onto it.

unlawful /ˌʌnˈlɔːfl/ *adj* (*fml*) against the law; illegal: *unlawful assembly* ○ *a verdict of unlawful killing.* ▷ **unlawfully** /-fəlɪ/ *adv*.

unlearn /ˌʌnˈlɜːn/ *v* [Tn] cause (sth) to be no longer in one's knowledge or memory: *You must start by unlearning all the bad habits your previous piano teacher taught you!*

unleash /ʌnˈliːʃ/ *v* [Tn, Tn·pr] ~ **sth** (**against/on sb/sth**) (**a**) set sth free from a leash or restraint: *unleash the guard dogs.* (**b**) (*fig*) set sth free from control; release sth in a powerful attack (on sb/sth): *unleash the forces of nuclear power* ○ *He unleashed a torrent of abuse against the unfortunate shop assistant.*

unleavened /ˌʌnˈlevnd/ *adj* (of bread) made without yeast or other raising agent.

unless /ənˈles/ *conj* if...not; except if or except when: *You'll fail in French unless you work harder.* ○ *Unless England improve their game they're going to lose the match.* ○ *I wouldn't be saying this unless I were sure of the facts.* ○ *Come at 8 o'clock unless* *phone,* eg to tell you a different time. ○ *I sleep with the window open unless it's really cold.*

NOTE ON USAGE: **Unless** and **if...not** can often be used in the same way: *Follow the green signs unless you have goods to declare/if you haven't any goods to declare.* **Unless** cannot be used when referring to the result of something not happening and is, therefore, not used in 'imaginary' conditional sentences: *We would have had a lovely holiday if it hadn't rained* (NOT *unless it had rained*) *every day.* ○ *I'll be sorry if she doesn't come* (NOT *unless she comes*) *to the party.* **Unless** (*not* **if ...not**) is often used to introduce an afterthought, ie something added to the main statement: *She hasn't got any hobbies — unless you call watching TV a hobby.* ○ *Have a cup of tea — unless you'd prefer a cold drink.*

unlettered /ˌʌnˈletəd/ *adj* (*fml*) unable to read; uneducated. Cf ILLITERATE.

unlike /ʌnˈlaɪk/ *adj* [pred] dissimilar; different: *They are so unlike nobody would believe they were sisters.*
▷ **unlike** *prep* **1** different from (sth); not like: *Her*

latest novel is quite unlike her earlier work. ○ *The scenery was unlike anything I'd seen before.* ○ *Their celebrations at Christmas are not unlike our own.* **2** uncharacteristic of (sb/sth): *It's very unlike him to be so abrupt.* **3** in contrast to (sb): *Unlike me, my husband likes to stay in bed.* ○ *I was very interested in the lecture, unlike many of the students.* ○ *He managed to finish the race, unlike more than half of the competitors.*

unlikely /ʌnˈlaɪklɪ/ *adj* (**-ier, -iest**) (**a**) not likely or expected to happen: *It is unlikely to rain/that it will rain.* ○ *There is unlikely to be rain.* ○ *His condition is unlikely to improve.* ○ *In the unlikely event of a strike, production would be badly affected.* (**b**) [attrib] not likely to be true; improbable: *an unlikely tale, excuse, explanation, etc.* (**c**) not expected to succeed: *the most unlikely candidate* ○ *an unlikely couple*, ie two people who do not seem to be well suited to each other.

unlimited /ˌʌnˈlɪmɪtɪd/ *adj* not limited; very great in number or quantity: *If only one had an unlimited supply of money!*

unlined /ˌʌnˈlaɪnd/ *adj* **1** without a lining: *a ˌcheap ˌunlined ˈcoat* ○ *The box was rough and unlined.* **2** not marked with lines: *ˌunlined ˈpaper* ○ *a ˌsmooth ˌunlined comˈplexion.*

unlisted /ˌʌnˈlɪstɪd/ *adj* (**a**) not in a published list (esp of Stock Exchange prices): *an unlisted company.* (**b**) (*US*) = EX-DIRECTORY: *He/His number is unlisted.*

unload /ˌʌnˈləʊd/ *v* **1** (**a**) [I, Tn, Tn·pr] ~ **sth (from sth)** remove a load from (sth); remove (a load) from sth: *Dockers started unloading (the ship).* ○ *unload shopping from a car.* (**b**) [Tn] remove the charge from (a gun, etc) or the film from (a camera). **2** [I, Tn] (of vehicles, vessels, etc) have (a load) removed: *Lorries may only park here when loading or unloading.* **3** [Tn, Tn·pr] ~ **sth/sb (on/ onto sb)** (*infml*) pass sb/sth unwanted (to sb else); get rid of sb/sth: *Do you mind if I unload the children onto you this afternoon?* Cf OFFLOAD.

unlock /ˌʌnˈlɒk/ *v* [Tn] **1** unfasten the lock of (a door, etc) using a key: *unlock the gate.* **2** release (sth) by, or as if by, unlocking: *exploration to unlock the secrets of the ocean bed.*

unlooked-for /ʌnˈlʊkt fɔ:(r)/ *adj* (*fml*) not expected; unforeseen: *unlooked-for compliments, difficulties.*

unloose /ˌʌnˈlu:s/ (also **unloosen** /ʌnˈlu:sn/) *v* [Tn] make (sth) loose; untie: *unloose the rope around one's waist* ○ *He unloosened his collar.* ⇨ Usage at LOOSE[1].

unlucky /ʌnˈlʌkɪ/ *adj* not lucky; having or bringing bad luck; unfortunate: *I always seem to be unlucky at cards.* ○ *He was unlucky enough to lose his keys.* ○ *The number thirteen is often considered unlucky.* ○ *an unlucky attempt*, ie one that did not succeed.

▷ **unluckily** *adv* unfortunately: *Unluckily (for Peter) he did not get the job.*

unmade /ˌʌnˈmeɪd/ *adj* (of a bed) with the bedclothes not neatly arranged for sleeping in: *She rushed off to work leaving her bed unmade.*

unman /ˌʌnˈmæn/ *v* (**-nn-**) [Tn] (*arch or rhet*) weaken the self-control or courage of (a man): *Unmanned by grief he broke down and wept.*

unmanageable /ʌnˈmænɪdʒəbl/ *adj* that is hard to control, organize, etc: *It's left my hair totally unmanageable.*

unmanly /ˌʌnˈmænlɪ/ *adj* (of behaviour) uncharacteristic of or inappropriate for men: *It was once thought unmanly not to drink and smoke.*

unmanned[1] *pt, pp* of UNMAN.

unmanned[2] /ˌʌnˈmænd/ *adj* not manned; operated automatically or without a crew: *ˌunmanned ˈrailway signals* ○ *send an unmanned spacecraft to Mars.*

unmannerly /ʌnˈmænəlɪ/ *adj* (*fml derog*) without good manners; ill-mannered: *unmannnerly conduct.*

unmarked /ˌʌnˈmɑ:kt/ *adj* **1** that has no marks that can allow identification: *an unmarked police car* ○ *an unmarked grave.* **2** not noticed: *His comments went quite unmarked.*

unmarried /ˌʌnˈmærɪd/ *adj* not married; single: *an ˌunmarried ˈmother, ˈcouple.*

unmask /ˌʌnˈmɑ:sk; *US* -ˈmæsk/ *v* **1** [I, Tn] remove a mask from (sb): *The revellers unmasked* (ie took off their masks) *at midnight.* **2** [Tn] reveal the true character of (sb/sth); expose: *unmask the culprit* ○ *unmask a plot.*

unmatched /ˌʌnˈmætʃt/ *adj* that cannot be matched; without an equal; matchless: *an achievement that remains unmatched to this day.*

unmentionable /ʌnˈmenʃənəbl/ *adj* [usu attrib] too shocking or embarrassing to be mentioned or spoken about: *an unmentionable disease*, eg venereal disease.

▷ **unmentionables** *n* [pl] (*arch euph or joc*) unmentionable people or things (esp underwear).

unmindful /ʌnˈmaɪndfl/ *adj* [pred] ~ **of sb/sth** (*fml*) not considering sb/sth; forgetting sb/sth: *He worked on, unmindful of the time.*

unmistakable /ˌʌnmɪˈsteɪkəbl/ *adj* clearly recognizable or obvious; impossible to mistake for sb/sth else: *the unmistakable sound of an approaching train.* ▷ **unmistakably** /-əblɪ/ *adv.*

unmitigated /ʌnˈmɪtɪgeɪtɪd/ *adj* [usu attrib] (of sth/sb bad) having no accompanying advantages whatever; complete; absolute: *an unmitigated disaster, scoundrel.*

unmoved /ˌʌnˈmu:vd/ *adj* [pred] not affected by feelings of pity, sympathy, etc: *It's impossible to remain unmoved by the reports of the famine.*

unmusical /ˌʌnˈmju:zɪkl/ *adj* **1** (of music or other sounds) not pleasant to hear, eg because it is too loud, discordant, etc: *an unmusical voice.* **2** not having any musical ability or interest in music.

unnatural /ʌnˈnætʃrəl/ *adj* **1** not natural or normal; differing from what is the usual or expected: *His face turned an unnatural shade of purple.* ○ *It was unnatural for the room to be so tidy.* **2** (*derog*) (**a**) contrary to usual and generally accepted behaviour: *unnatural sexual desires.* (**b**) extremely cruel or wicked: *the unnatural murder of his own father.* **3** not sincere; affected or forced: *an unnatural high-pitched laugh.* ▷ **unnaturally** /-rəlɪ/ *adv*: *Not unnaturally, she was greatly upset by her father's sudden death.* ○ *an unnaturally jovial manner.*

unnecessary /ʌnˈnesəsrɪ; *US* -serɪ/ *adj* (**a**) [usu pred] not necessary or desirable; superfluous: *It's unnecessary to cook a big meal tonight.* (**b**) [usu attrib] more than necessary; excessive: *unnecessary expense.* (**c**) (of remarks, etc) not required in a situation and likely to be offensive; gratuitous: *an unnecessary reference to his criminal past.* ▷ **unnecessarily** /ʌnˈnesəsərəlɪ; *US* ˌʌnˌnesəˈserəlɪ/ *adv.*

unnerve /ˌʌnˈnɜ:v/ *v* [Tn] cause (sb) to lose self-control, confidence or courage: *His encounter with the guard dog had completely unnerved him.*

▷ **unnerving** *adj*: *She found the whole interview rather unnerving.*

unnoticed /ˌʌnˈnəʊtɪst/ *adj* [usu pred] not observed or noticed: *The event passed unnoticed.* ○ *I can't let this act of kindness go unnoticed.*

unnumbered /ˌʌnˈnʌmbəd/ *adj* **1** having no number(s): *unnumbered tickets/seats*, eg at a concert hall or theatre. **2** (*arch or rhet*) more than can be counted; countless: *the unnumbered stars.*

UNO /ˈju:nəʊ/ *abbr* United Nations Organization.

unobtrusive /ˌʌnəbˈtru:sɪv/ *adj* (*usu approv*) not too obvious or easily noticeable; not drawing attention to itself or himself; discreet: *an unobtrusive but pleasing design* ○ *He was so quiet and unobtrusive that you would hardly know he was there!* ▷ **unobtrusively** *adv*: *She slipped away from the party unobtrusively.*

unoccupied /ˌʌnˈɒkjʊpaɪd/ *adj* **1** not occupied; empty; vacant: *find an unoccupied table* ○ *The house had been left unoccupied for several years.* **2** (of a region or country) not under the control of foreign troops: *unoccupied territory.* **3** not busy; idle: *in one of her rare unoccupied moments.*

unofficial /ˌʌnəˈfɪʃl/ *adj* not official: *an ˌunofficial ˈstrike*, ie one not authorized by the union ○ *an ˌunofficial ˈstatement*, ie one not authorized for release to the public ○ *ˌunofficial ˈnews*, ie not confirmed by official sources or authorities. ▷ **unofficially** /-ʃəlɪ/ *adv.*

unorthodox /ˌʌnˈɔ:θədɒks/ *adj* not in accordance with what is orthodox, conventional or traditional: *unorthodox beliefs, opinions, etc* ○ *unorthodox teaching methods* ○ *She has an unorthodox technique, but is an excellent player.* Cf HETERODOX.

unpack /ˌʌnˈpæk/ *v* (**a**) [I, Tn] take packed things out of (sth): *Let's unpack before we go to bed.* ○ *a half-unpacked suitcase.* (**b**) [Tn, Tn·pr] ~ **sth (from sth)** take out (things packed): *unpack the books from the box.*

unpaid /ˌʌnˈpeɪd/ *adj* **1** (**a**) not yet paid: *an ˌunpaid ˈbill/ˈdebt.* (**b**) ~ **for** not paid for: *The car is three years old and still unpaid for.* **2** (**a**) (of people) not receiving payment for work done: *an ˌunpaid ˈbaby-sitter.* (**b**) (of work) done without payment to the worker(s): *ˌunpaid ˈlabour.*

unpalatable /ʌnˈpælətəbl/ *adj* (*fml*) **1** not palatable; unpleasant to taste: *The fish was particularly unpalatable.* **2** (*fig*) unpleasant or unacceptable to the mind: *His views on capital punishment are unpalatable to many.* ▷ **unpalatably** /-əblɪ/ *adv.*

unparalleled /ʌnˈpærəleld/ *adj* having no parallel or equal; unmatched: *an economic crisis unparalleled in modern times.*

unparliamentary /ˌʌnˌpɑ:ləˈmentrɪ/ *adj* (*derog*) contrary to the accepted rules of behaviour in Parliament (because abusive or disorderly): *unparliamentary language, conduct.*

unpick /ˌʌnˈpɪk/ *v* (**a**) [Tn, Tn·pr] ~ **sth (from sth)** take out (the stitches): *unpick the stitches from a curtain.* (**b**) [Tn] take out the stitches from (sth): *unpick a hem, seam, etc.*

unplaced /ˌʌnˈpleɪst/ *adj* not one of the first three to finish in a race or contest.

unplayable /ˌʌnˈpleɪəbl/ *adj* **1** (in games, of a ball) that cannot be played. **2** (of ground) not fit to be played on. **3** (of music) too difficult to be played.

unpleasant /ʌnˈpleznt/ *adj* not pleasant; disagreeable: *unpleasant smells, weather* ○ *an unpleasant surprise* ○ *I found his manner extremely unpleasant.*

▷ **unpleasantly** *adv.*

unpleasantness *n* [C, U] (instance of) bad feeling or quarrelling between people: *I want to avoid any unpleasantness with the neighbours.*

unplug /ˌʌnˈplʌg/ *v* (**-gg-**) [Tn] **1** disconnect (an electrical appliance) by removing its plug from the socket: *Please unplug the TV before you go to bed.* **2** remove an obstruction from (sth): *The drain is blocked and needs unplugging.*

unplumbed /ˌʌnˈplʌmd/ *adj* not properly examined or understood: *the unplumbed depths of the human psyche.*

unpopular /ˌʌnˈpɒpjʊlə(r)/ *adj* ~ **(with sb)** not popular; not liked or enjoyed by a person, a group or people in general: *an unpopular decision* ○ *She's rather unpopular with her boss at the moment.* ▷ **unpopularity** /ˌʌnˌpɒpjʊˈlærətɪ/ *n* [U].

unpractised /ʌnˈpræktɪst/ *adj* having little experience; inexpert; unskilled.

unprecedented /ʌnˈpresɪdentɪd/ *adj* without precedent; never having happened, been done or been known before: *unprecedented levels of unemployment* ○ *a situation unprecedented in the history of the school.*

unpredictable /ˌʌnprɪˈdɪktəbl/ *adj* (**a**) that cannot be predicted: *an unpredictable result.* (**b**) (of a person) whose behaviour cannot be predicted; changeable; unstable: *You never know how she'll react: she's so unpredictable.*

unprejudiced /ʌnˈpredʒʊdɪst/ *adj* free from prejudice; not biased.

unpremeditated /ˌʌnpri:ˈmedɪteɪtɪd/ *adj* not previously and deliberately considered or planned; spontaneous: *an unpremeditated attack.*

unprepared /ˌʌnprɪˈpeəd/ *adj* **1** not prepared in advance: *My speech went well, though it was completely unprepared.* **2** ~ **(for sth)** not ready or equipped for sth: *So many students are really unprepared for university.* ○ *I was quite unprepared for* (ie did not expect) *her reaction.*

unprepossessing /ˌʌnˌpri:pəˈzesɪŋ/ *adj* (*fml*) not

attractive or appealing in appearance: *Though unprepossessing to look at he is highly intelligent.*

unpretentious /ˌʌnprɪˈtenʃəs/ *adj* (*approv*) not showy or pompous; modest: *an unpretentious little book but one that tells a simple story well.*

unprincipled /ʌnˈprɪnsəpld/ *adj* (*fml*) without moral principles; unscrupulous; dishonest: *unprincipled behaviour* ○ *an unprincipled rogue.*

unprintable /ʌnˈprɪntəbl/ *adj* (of words, articles, etc) too offensive or indecent to be printed: *I'm afraid that my views on their private life are unprintable!*

unprofessional /ˌʌnprəˈfeʃənl/ *adj* (*derog*) **1** (esp of conduct) contrary to the standards expected in a particular profession: *The board considers your behaviour highly unprofessional.* **2** (of a piece of work, etc) not done with the skill or care of a trained professional: *He made a very unprofessional job of putting up the garden shed for us.* ▷ **unprofessionally** /-ʃənəlɪ/ *adv.*

unprofitable /ʌnˈprɒfɪtəbl/ *adj* **1** that does not make a profit: *They're closing down the unprofitable parts of the business.* **2** (*fml*) that does not achieve anything useful: *It's quite unprofitable to speculate on what might have happened.*

unpromising /ʌnˈprɒmɪsɪŋ/ *adj* that does not seem likely to succeed or produce good results: *The director has turned an unpromising story into a fascinating film.*

unprompted /ˌʌnˈprɒmptɪd/ *adj* (of an answer or action) not said or done, etc as the result of a hint, suggestion, etc; spontaneous: *an unprompted offer of help.*

unpronounceable /ˌʌnprəˈnaʊnsəbl/ *adj* (of a word, esp a name) too difficult to pronounce.

unprovided /ˌʌnprəˈvaɪdɪd/ *adj* (*fml*) ~ **for** without provision having been made for: *The widow was left unprovided for*, ie No money, etc had been left for her on her husband's death.

unprovoked /ˌʌnprəˈvəʊkt/ *adj* (esp of verbal or physical violence) without provocation; not caused by previous action: *ˌunprovoked agˈgression/atˈtacks.*

unpunished /ˌʌnˈpʌnɪʃt/ *adj* [pred] not punished: *Such a serious crime must not go unpunished.*

unputdownable /ˌʌnpʊtˈdaʊnəbl/ *adj* (*infml*) (of a book, etc) so interesting or absorbing that the reader is reluctant to stop reading until he has finished it.

unqualified /ʌnˈkwɒlɪfaɪd/ *adj* **1** (**a**) ~ (**as sth/for sth/to do sth**) without legal or official qualifications for doing sth: *an unqualified instructor* ○ *unqualified as a teacher/for teaching.* (**b**) [pred] ~ **to do sth** (*infml*) not competent or knowledgeable enough to do sth: *I feel unqualified to speak on the subject.* **2** [usu attrib] not limited or restricted; absolute: *unqualified praise* ○ *an unqualified success.*

unquestionable /ʌnˈkwestʃənəbl/ *adj* beyond doubt; certain; indisputable: *His honesty is unquestionable.* ▷ **unquestionably** /-əblɪ/ *adv.*

unquestioned /ʌnˈkwestʃənd/ *adj* not disputed or doubted: *an unquestioned fact* ○ *Her authority is unquestioned.*

unquestioning /ʌnˈkwestʃənɪŋ/ *adj* done, etc without asking questions, expressing doubt, etc: *He demands unquestioning obedience from his followers.* ▷ **unquestioningly** *adv.*

unquiet /ʌnˈkwaɪət/ *adj* [usu attrib] (*fml*) restless; uneasy; disturbed: *all the signs of an unquiet mind.*

unquote /ʌnˈkwəʊt/ *n* (idm) **quote (... unquote)** ⇨ QUOTE *n.*

unravel /ʌnˈrævl/ *v* (**-ll-**; *US* **-l-**) [I, Tn] **1** (cause sth woven, knotted or tangled to) separate into strands: *My knitting has unravelled.* ○ *unravel a cardigan, a ball of string.* Cf RAVEL. **2** (*fig*) (cause sth to) become clear or solved: *The mystery unravels slowly.* ○ *unravel a plot, puzzle, etc.*

unread /ˌʌnˈred/ *adj* **1** (of a book) that has not been read: *a pile of ˌunread ˈnovels.* **2** (of a person) not having read many books, etc: *She knows so much that she makes me feel very unread.*

unreadable /ˌʌnˈriːdəbl/ *adj* **1** (*derog*) too dull or too difficult to be worth reading. **2** = ILLEGIBLE.

unreal /ˌʌnˈrɪəl/ *adj* (of an experience) not seeming real; imaginary; illusory: *The whole evening seemed strangely unreal.* ▷ **unreality** /ˌʌnrɪˈælətɪ/ *n* [U].

unreasonable /ʌnˈriːznəbl/ *adj* **1** (of people) not reasonable in attitude, etc. **2** going beyond the limits of what is reasonable or just; excessive: *make unreasonable demands on sb.* ▷ **unreasonably** /-əblɪ/ *adv.*

unreasoning /ʌnˈriːzənɪŋ/ *adj* (*fml*) (of a person or of attitudes, beliefs, etc) not using or guided by reason: *an unreasoning fear of foreigners.*

unreel /ˌʌnˈriːl/ *v* [I, Tn] (cause sth to) unwind from a reel: *Unreel the hose fully before use.*

unrelenting /ˌʌnrɪˈlentɪŋ/ *adv* (**a**) not reducing in intensity, etc; continuous; relentless: *unrelenting pressure.* (**b**) (of a person) merciless; unwilling to relent: *a cruel and unrelenting master.* ▷ **unrelentingly** *adv*: *The rain continued unrelentingly.*

unrelieved /ˌʌnrɪˈliːvd/ *adj* having no humour, colour, etc to provide variety; unchanging: *The film was two hours of unrelieved boredom.*

unremitting /ˌʌnrɪˈmɪtɪŋ/ *adj* never relaxing or ceasing; incessant; persistent: *unremitting care, boredom, drudgery.*

unrepeatable /ˌʌnrɪˈpiːtəbl/ *adj* **1** that cannot be repeated or done again: *unrepeatable bargains/offers*, ie at specially low prices. **2** too indecent or offensive to be said again: *His remarks were quite shocking — unrepeatable, in fact.*

unrequited /ˌʌnrɪˈkwaɪtɪd/ *adj* (*fml*) (esp of love) not returned or rewarded: *unrequited passion.*

unreserved /ˌʌnrɪˈzɜːvd/ *adj* **1** (of seats, etc) not reserved for or allocated to a particular person in advance: *We always keep a few unreserved tables.* **2** (*fml*) without any holding back; complete: *Do I have your unreserved attention?*

▷ **unreservedly** /ˌʌnrɪˈzɜːvɪdlɪ/ *adv* without reservation or restriction; openly: *apologize unreservedly.*

unrest /ˌʌnˈrest/ *n* [U] (state of) restlessness or dissatisfaction; disturbance: *civil/industrial/political/social unrest.*

unrestrained /ˌʌnrɪˈstreɪnd/ *adj* not restrained; not held back or controlled; unchecked: *unrestrained anger, temper, violence, etc* ○ *the unrestrained use of military force.*

unripe /ˌʌnˈraɪp/ *adj* not yet ripe: *ˌunripe baˈnanas.*

unrivalled (*US* **unrivaled**) /ʌnˈraɪvld/ *adj* having no rival (in sth); unequalled: *have an unrivalled reputation* ○ *unrivalled in courage.*

unroll /ˌʌnˈrəʊl/ *v* [I, Tn] (cause sth to) open out from a rolled position by rolling: *unroll a carpet, map, sleeping-bag.* Cf ROLL[2] 3.

unruffled /ˌʌnˈrʌfld/ *adj* not upset or agitated; imperturbable: *She spoke with unruffled calm.* ○ *He remained unruffled by the charges.*

unruly /ʌnˈruːlɪ/ *adj* not easy to control or discipline; disorderly: *unruly behaviour* ○ *an unruly mob, crowd, demonstration, etc* ○ (*fig*) *unruly hair*, ie hard to manage. ▷ **unruliness** *n* [U].

UNRWA /ˈʌnrə/ *abbr* United Nations Relief and Works Agency.

unsaid /ˌʌnˈsed/ *adj* (*fml*) **1** [pred] not expressed; unspoken: *Some things are better left unsaid.* **2** *pt, pp* of UNSAY.

unsaturated /ʌnˈsætʃəreɪtɪd/ *adj* **1** not saturated. **2** (*chemistry*) (of an organic compound) that can combine with hydrogen due to the molecule containing double or triple bonds between carbon atoms. Cf POLYUNSATURATED.

unsavoury (*US* **unsavory**) /ˌʌnˈseɪvərɪ/ *adj* **1** unpleasant to the taste or smell; disgusting: *an unsavoury mixture of cold pasta and curry.* **2** (*fml or joc*) morally unpleasant or offensive; disreputable: *unsavoury rumours, details, habits* ○ *an unsavoury character, reputation.* Cf SAVOURY.

unsay /ˌʌnˈseɪ/ *v* (*pt, pp* **unsaid** /-sed/) [Tn esp passive] (*fml*) take back (sth that has been said); retract: *What is said cannot be unsaid.*

unscathed /ˌʌnˈskeɪðd/ *adj* [pred] not injured or hurt; unharmed: *The hostages emerged from their ordeal unscathed.*

unscientific /ˌʌnsaɪənˈtɪfɪk/ *adj* not scientific, eg by being inaccurate or illogical: *unscientific claim made for the drug.*

unscramble /ˌʌnˈskræmbl/ *v* [Tn] **1** restore (a scrambled message) to a form that can be understood. **2** (*infml*) restore (sth) to order from a confused state: *After a few seconds to unscramble my thoughts, I replied ....*

unscrew /ˌʌnˈskruː/ *v* (**a**) [Tn] loosen (a screw, nut etc) by turning it; unfasten (sth) by removing screws: *unscrew the door-handle.* (**b**) [I, Tn] (make sth) come undone by twisting: *The lid of this jam pot won't unscrew.*

unscripted /ˌʌnˈskrɪptɪd/ *adj* (of a speech broadcast, etc) made without a prepared script: *a language course based on natural unscripted dialogues, conversations, etc.*

unscrupulous /ʌnˈskruːpjʊləs/ *adj* without moral principles: *unscrupulous methods, behaviour* ○ *He was utterly unscrupulous in his dealings with rival companies.* ▷ **unscrupulously** *adv* **unscrupulousness** *n* [U].

unseasonable /ʌnˈsiːznəbl/ *adj* **1** (*fml*) not appropriate or reasonable in particular circumstances: *unseasonable demands for money* **2** not appropriate to the season of the year *unseasonable weather.* ▷ **unseasonably** /-əblɪ/ *adv*: *unseasonably hot.*

unseat /ˌʌnˈsiːt/ *v* [Tn] **1** throw (sb) off a horse bicycle, etc. **2** remove (sb) from office, esp from a seat in parliament: *a move to unseat Labour militants.*

unseemly /ʌnˈsiːmlɪ/ *adj* (*fml*) (of behaviour, etc) not proper or seemly; unbecoming: *an unseemly rush to leave work* ○ *make unseemly suggestions* ○ *His language was most unseemly*, ie abusive. ▷ **unseemliness** *n* [U].

unseen /ʌnˈsiːn/ *adj* **1** not seen; invisible: *I slipped from the room unseen*, ie unnoticed. **2** (of a translation) done without previous preparation. **3** (idm) **sight unseen** ⇨ SIGHT[1].

▷ **unseen** *n* (*Brit*) passage for translation from a foreign language into one's own language without previous preparation: *German unseens.*

unserviceable /ˌʌnˈsɜːvɪsəbl/ *adj* (*abbrs* **US**, **u/s**) (*fml or joc*) that cannot be used because worn out broken, etc: *an unserviceable bicycle, telephone, tin-opener, etc.*

unsettle /ˌʌnˈsetl/ *v* [Tn] (**a**) disturb the normal calm state of (sth/sb); upset: *Our move* (ie to another house) *unsettled the children.* ○ *Seafood unsettles my stomach.* (**b**) make (sb) uneasy or anxious; disturb: *Living alone unsettled his nerves*

▷ **unsettled** *adj* (**a**) unstable or upset or disturbed: *Conditions on the stock-market were unsettled.* ○ *an unsettled stomach* ○ *feel unsettled in one's new surroundings.* (**b**) changeable or unpredictable: *unsettled weather* ○ *Our future plans are still unsettled.* (**c**) (of an argument, etc) open to further discussion. (**d**) (of a bill, etc) unpaid.

unshakeable /ʌnˈʃeɪkəbl/ *adj* (of a belief, etc) that cannot be changed; absolutely firm: *an unshakeable conviction, resolve, faith, etc.*

unshrinking /ʌnˈʃrɪŋkɪŋ/ *adj* showing no fear or hesitation: *unshrinking courage.*

unsightly /ʌnˈsaɪtlɪ/ *adj* not pleasant to look at ugly: *unsightly facial hair*, eg on women ○ *London's unsightly suburban sprawl.* ▷ **unsightliness** *n* [U].

unskilled /ˌʌnˈskɪld/ *adj* not having or requiring special skill or training: *ˌunskilled ˈworkers* ○ *ˌunskilled ˈlabour.*

unsociable /ʌnˈsəʊʃəbl/ *adj* disliking the company of others; not sociable. Cf ANTISOCIAL.

unsocial /ʌnˈsəʊʃl/ *adj* **1** unsociable. **2** not conforming to standard working times: *unsocial hours*, eg on night shifts.

unsolicited /ˌʌnsəˈlɪsɪtɪd/ *adj* given or sent voluntarily; not asked for: *ˌunsolicited ˈhelp, adˈvice, etc* ○ *ˌunsolicited ˈcomments, ˈcriticisms, etc* ○ *ˌunsolicited (junk) ˈmail*, ie usu for advertising purposes.

unsophisticated /ˌʌnsəˈfɪstɪkeɪtɪd/ *adj* (*sometimes derog*) **1** simple and natural: *unsophisticated tastes, attitudes, looks* ○ *To the* *unsophisticated* (ie naive) *mind of the average viewer....* **2** not complex or refined; basic: *unsophisticated tools, methods, designs.*

unsound /ˌʌnˈsaʊnd/ *adj* **1** in poor condition; weak: *The house roof was (structurally) unsound.* ○ *His lungs were unsound.* **2** not free from defects or mistakes; flawed: *unsound reasoning, judgement, advice* ○ *The findings of the research seem unsound.* **3** (idm) **of ˌunsound ˈmind** (*law*) insane.

unsparing /ʌnˈspeərɪŋ/ *adj* ~ **(in sth)** **1** giving freely and generously: *be unsparing in one's efforts.* **2** severe or merciless: *Nijinsky was unsparing in his demands for perfection.*

▷ **unsparingly** *adv* **1** generously: *give unsparingly of one's time and money.* **2** mercilessly: *He drove himself unsparingly.*

unspeakable /ʌnˈspi:kəbl/ *adj* (*usu derog*) that cannot be expressed in words; indescribable: *unspeakable cruelty, behaviour, embarrassment* ○ *unspeakable joy, delight, etc.* ▷ **unspeakably** /-əblɪ/ *adv*: *an unspeakably vile habit.*

unstable /ˌʌnˈsteɪbl/ *adj* **1** likely to move or fall; not firm: *an unstable load*, eg on a lorry ○ *an unstable pile of chairs.* **2** likely to change suddenly; unpredictable: *unstable share prices* ○ *The political situation is highly unstable.* **3** mentally or emotionally unbalanced: *His personality is a little unstable.*

unsteady /ˌʌnˈstedɪ/ *adj* (**-ier, -iest**) **1** not firm or secure: *Six whiskies made him unsteady on his feet.* ○ *an unsteady hand, voice* ○ *have an unsteady footing on the ladder.* **2** not uniform or regular: *the candle's unsteady flame* ○ *His heartbeat/pulse was unsteady.* ▷ **unsteadily** /-ɪlɪ/ *adv*: *wobble, tilt, rock, sway, etc unsteadily.* **unsteadiness** *n* [U].

unstinting /ʌnˈstɪntɪŋ/ *adj* ~ **(in sth)** giving freely and generously: *unstinting generosity, support, praise* ○ *She was unstinting in her efforts to help.* ▷ **unstintingly** *adj.*

unstop /ˌʌnˈstɒp/ *v* (**-pp-**) [Tn] remove a blockage from (a waste-pipe): *unstop a sink, toilet, drain, etc.*

unstoppable /ʌnˈstɒpəbl/ *adj* (*esp infml*) that cannot be stopped or prevented: *The Tories in their third term will be unstoppable.*

unstrung /ˌʌnˈstrʌŋ/ *adj* [esp pred] extremely upset and disturbed: *He became completely unstrung when his wife left.*

unstuck /ˌʌnˈstʌk/ *adj* **1** not stuck or glued on or together; detached: *The (flap of the) envelope was unstuck.* **2** (idm) **ˌcome unˈstuck** (*infml*) be unsuccessful; fail: *His plan to escape came badly unstuck.*

unstudied /ˌʌnˈstʌdɪd/ *adj* natural and unaffected: *with ˌunstudied ˈelegance, ˈgrace, ˈcharm, etc.*

unsung /ˌʌnˈsʌŋ/ *adj* (*fml*) not celebrated in poetry or song; unrecognized: *ˌunsung ˈheroes* ○ *His exploits went unsung.*

unsure /ˌʌnˈʃɔ:(r); *US* -ˈʃʊər/ *adj* [pred] **1** ~ **(of oneself)** having little self-confidence: *He's rather unsure of himself.* **2** ~ **(about/of sth)** not having certain knowledge (about sth): *I'm unsure of the facts.* ○ *We were unsure (about) who was to blame.*

unsuspecting /ˌʌnsəˈspektɪŋ/ *adj* feeling no suspicion; trusting: *The murderer crept up on his unsuspecting victim.*

unswerving /ʌnˈswɜ:vɪŋ/ *adj* ~ **(in sth)** steady or constant; unchanging: *unswerving loyalty, devotion, belief, etc* ○ *He is unswerving in pursuit of his aims.*

untangle /ˌʌnˈtæŋgl/ *v* [Tn, Tn·pr] free (sth) from knots, complexities, etc: *untangle knitting wool, electric flex* ○ *She untangled her hair from the hair-drier.* ○ (*fig*) *untangle a plot* ○ *I can't untangle these accounts/figures.*

untapped /ˌʌnˈtæpt/ *adj* not yet used or exploited: *an untapped source of wealth, talent, inspiration* ○ *draw on untapped reserves of strength.*

untenable /ˌʌnˈtenəbl/ *adj* (of a theory, etc) that cannot be defended: *untenable arguments, claims, propositions, etc* ○ *the untenable position of the Flat Earth Society.*

unthinkable /ˌʌnˈθɪŋkəbl/ *adj* too unlikely or undesirable to be considered; inconceivable: *It is unthinkable that we should allow a nuclear holocaust to occur.*

unthinking /ˌʌnˈθɪŋkɪŋ/ *adj* said, done, etc without proper consideration; thoughtless: *unthinking remarks, criticisms* ○ *Unthinking, he threw his lighted match into the waste-paper basket.* ▷ **unthinkingly** *adv.*

untidy /ʌnˈtaɪdɪ/ *adj* (**-ier, -iest**) not neat or orderly: *an untidy desk, kitchen, cupboard, etc* ○ *untidy hair, writing* ○ *He's an untidy worker; he leaves his tools everywhere.* ▷ **untidily** /-ɪlɪ/ *adv.* **untidiness** *n* [U].

until /ənˈtɪl/ (also **till**) (*till* more informal; *until* usu preferred in initial position) *conj* up to the time when: *Wait until the rain stops.* ○ *Don't leave till I arrive.* ○ *Continue in this direction until you see a sign.* ○ *Until she spoke I hadn't realized she was foreign.* ○ *I won't stop shouting until you let me go.* ○ *No names are being released until* (ie before) *the relatives have been told.*

▷ **until** (also **till**) *prep* **(a)** up to (a specified time): *wait until tomorrow* ○ *It may last till Friday.* ○ *Nothing happened until* (ie before) *5 o'clock.* ○ *The street is full of traffic from morning till night.* ○ *Until now I have always lived alone.* ○ *I'd like to stay here up until Christmas.* **(b)** up to the time of (a specified event): *The secret was never told until after the old man's death.* ○ *Don't open it till your birthday.* ○ *She was a bank clerk until the war, when she trained as a nurse.*

untimely /ʌnˈtaɪmlɪ/ *adj* **1** happening at an unsuitable time: *an untimely arrival, remark, intervention.* **2** happening too soon or sooner than normal: *her untimely death at 25.* ▷ **untimeliness** *n* [U].

untiring /ʌnˈtaɪərɪŋ/ *adj* ~ **(in sth)** (*approv*) continuing to work, etc at the same rate without showing tiredness: *untiring campaigners for peace* ○ *She is untiring in her efforts to help the homeless.* ▷ **untiringly** *adv.*

untold /ˌʌnˈtəʊld/ *adj* **1** not told: *Her secret remains untold to this day.* **2** [attrib] (*esp derog*) too many or too much to be counted, measured, etc: *ˌuntold ˈsuffering, ˈdamage, ˈcruelty* ○ *a man of ˌuntold ˈwealth* ○ *ˌuntold ˈthousands, ˈmillions, etc*, ie of pounds.

untouchable /ʌnˈtʌtʃəbl/ *n, adj* (in India) (member) of a Hindu social class (caste) whose touch is regarded as defiling to other higher classes.

untouched /ʌnˈtʌtʃt/ *adj* [usu pred] **1** not touched, moved, etc: *The vase lay untouched in the attic for 50 years.* **2** not dealt with or changed: *The article leaves the central problem quite untouched.* **3** not tasted or eaten: *She ate everything else but left the meat untouched.* **4** ~ **(by sth)** not affected, influenced, etc by sth: *an existence untouched by modern technology.*

untoward /ˌʌntəˈwɔ:d; *US* ʌnˈtɔ:rd/ *adj* (*fml*) inconvenient or unfortunate; awkward: *untoward incidents, developments, discoveries* ○ *I'll come if nothing untoward happens.*

untrammelled (*US also* **-meled**) /ʌnˈtræmld/ *adj* (*fml*) not hampered: *a life untrammelled by responsibilities.*

untried /ˌʌnˈtraɪd/ *adj* not yet tried or tested: *ˌuntried ˈproducts, ˈsystems, ˈmethods.*

untrue /ˌʌnˈtru:/ *adj* **1** not true; contrary to fact. **2** ~ **(to sb/sth)** (*fml*) not loyal: *She was untrue* (ie unfaithful) *to him.*

untruth /ˌʌnˈtru:θ/ *n* **1** [C] (*pl* ~**s** /-ˈtru:ðz/) (*fml euph*) untrue statement; lie: *tell patent* (ie obvious) *untruths.* **2** [U] lack of truth. ▷ **untruthful** /ʌnˈtru:θfl/ *adj.* **untruthfully** /-fəlɪ/ *adv.*

unturned /ˌʌnˈtɜ:nd/ *adj* (idm) **leave no stone unturned** ⇨ LEAVE[1].

untutored /ˌʌnˈtju:təd; *US* -ˈtu:-/ *adj* (*fml or joc*) untaught or untrained; unsophisticated: *To my untutored ear, your voice sounds almost professional.*

unused[1] /ˌʌnˈju:zd/ *adj* never having been used: *an unused envelope, postage stamp.*

unused[2] /ˌʌnˈju:st/ *adj* [pred] ~ **to sth/sb** unaccustomed to or unfamiliar with (sth/sb): *The children are unused to city life/to living in a city.*

unusual /ʌnˈju:ʒl/ *adj* **1** rare or exceptional: *This bird is an unusual winter visitor to Britain.* ○ *It's unusual for him to refuse a drink.* **2** (*esp approv*) remarkable because different; distinctive: *The Lloyds building is nothing if not* (ie is very) *unusual.*

▷ **unusually** /-ʒəlɪ/ *adv* exceptionally or extremely: *an unusually high rainfall for January* ○ *Unusually for him, he wore a tie.*

unutterable /ʌnˈʌtərəbl/ *adj* [attrib] (*fml*) too great, intense, etc to be expressed in words: *unutterable pain, delight, boredom, relief, etc* ○ *He's an unutterable bore.* ▷ **unutterably** /-əblɪ/ *adv*: *unutterably foolish.*

unvarnished /ʌnˈvɑ:nɪʃt/ *adj* [attrib] **1** not varnished. **2** (*fig*) (of a statement, etc) basic or straightforward: *the plain unvarnished truth* ○ *give an unvarnished account of what happened.*

unveil /ˌʌnˈveɪl/ *v* **1** [I, Tn] remove one's veil; remove a veil from (sth/sb). **2** [Tn] **(a)** remove a cloth, etc from (sth), esp as part of a public ceremony: *unveil a statue, monument, plaque, portrait, etc.* **(b)** show or announce (sth) publicly for the first time: *unveil new models at the Motor Show* ○ *She unveiled her plans for reform.*

unversed /ˌʌnˈvɜ:st/ *adj* ~ **in sth** (*fml*) not experienced or skilled in sth: *foreigners unversed in the British way of life* ○ *unversed in social etiquette.*

unvoiced /ˌʌnˈvɔɪst/ *adj* (of thoughts, etc) not expressed or uttered: *an ˌunvoiced ˈprotest, ˈdoubt, suˈspicion.*

unwaged /ˌʌnˈweɪdʒd/ *adj* (*Brit euph*) having no regular paid employment: *Unwaged members pay a lower entrance fee.* ▷ **the unwaged** *n* [pl *v*]: *half-price tickets for the unwaged.*

unwanted /ˌʌnˈwɒntɪd/ *adj* not wanted: *an ˌunwanted ˈpregnancy* ○ *feel unwanted.*

unwarrantable /ʌnˈwɒrəntəbl; *US* -ˈwɔ:r-/ *adj* (*fml*) unjustifiable: *Their intrusion into our private lives is unwarrantable.*

▷ **unwarranted** /ʌnˈwɒrəntɪd; *US* -ˈwɔ:r-/ *adj* unjustified or unauthorized: *unwarranted fears, doubts, misgivings, etc.*

unwary /ʌnˈweərɪ/ *adj* not cautious or aware of possible danger, etc; not vigilant: *Pot-holes can be lethal for the unwary cyclist.* ▷ **the unwary** *n* [pl *v*]: *Small print in documents can contain traps for the unwary.* **unwarily** /-ɪlɪ/ *adv.* **unwariness** *n* [U].

unwholesome /ʌnˈhəʊlsəm/ *adj* **1** harmful to health or to moral well-being: *an unwholesome climate* ○ *unwholesome food* ○ *unwholesome reading for a child.* **2** unhealthy-looking: *an unwholesome complexion.*

unwieldy /ʌnˈwi:ldɪ/ *adj* awkward to move or control because of its shape, size or weight: *long, unwieldy punt poles* ○ (*fig*) *the unwieldy bureaucracy of centralized government.* ▷ **unwieldiness** *n* [U].

unwilling /ʌnˈwɪlɪŋ/ *adj* not willing or inclined to do sth; reluctant: *unwilling volunteers, victims, accomplices* ○ *my unwilling participation in the scheme* ○ *I was unwilling to co-operate without having more information.* ▷ **unwillingly** *adv*: *agree unwillingly to a request.*

unwind /ˌʌnˈwaɪnd/ *v* (*pt, pp* **unwound** /-ˈwaʊnd/) **1** [I, Tn, Tn·pr] ~ **sth (from sth)** (cause sth to) become drawn out from a roll, ball, etc: *unwind a ball of string, a reel of thread, a roll of bandage, etc* ○ *He unwound the scarf from his neck.* **2** [I] (*infml*) relax after a period of work or tension: *Reading is a good way to unwind.* ○ *After a few drinks, he began to unwind*, ie to talk more freely.

unwise /ˌʌnˈwaɪz/ *adj* not wise; foolish: *an ˌunwise deˈcision, ˈmove, ˈstep, etc* ○ *It was unwise (of you) to reject his offer.* ▷ **unwisely** *adv.*

unwitting /ʌnˈwɪtɪŋ/ *adj* [attrib] (*fml*) **1** not knowing or aware: *an unwitting carrier of stolen goods.* **2** not intentional: *my unwitting interruption of their private conversation.* ▷ **unwittingly** *adv*: *If I offended you it was unwittingly.*

unwonted /ʌnˈwəʊntɪd/ *adj* (*fml*) not customary or usual: *an unwonted intrusion, interruption.*

unworkable /ˌʌnˈwɜ:kəbl/ *adj* not practical or

feasible: *an unworkable plan, proposal, scheme, etc.*

unworldly /ˌʌnˈwɜ:ldlɪ/ *adj* spiritually-minded; not worldly: *an unworldly man, outlook, idealism.* ▷ **unworldliness** *n* [U].

unworthy /ʌnˈwɜ:ðɪ/ *adj* **1** lacking worth or merit: *fighting for an unworthy cause.* **2** ~ **(of sth)** not deserving: *trivia unworthy of your attention* ○ *I am unworthy of such an honour.* **3** ~ **(of sb/sth)** not befitting the character of sb/sth: *conduct unworthy of a decent citizen.* ▷ **unworthily** /-ɪlɪ/ *adv.* **unworthiness** *n* [U].

unwound *pt, pp* of UNWIND.

unwritten /ˌʌnˈrɪtn/ *adj* not written down.
□ **an ˌunwritten ˈlaw/ˈrule** law/rule that is based on custom and practice, but is not written down.

unyielding /ʌnˈji:ldɪŋ/ *adj* ~ **(in sth)** not giving way to pressure or influence, etc; firm: *The mattress was hard and unyielding.* ○ *(fig) unyielding in her opposition to the plan.*

up /ʌp/ *adv part* (For special uses with many *vs*, eg *pick sth up, wind sth up, screw sth up,* see the *v* entries.) **1 (a)** to or in an upright position (esp one suggesting readiness for activity): *I stood up to ask a question.* ○ *He jumped up* (ie to a standing position) *from his chair.* Cf DOWN¹ 1. **(b)** not in bed: *Is Peter up* (ie Has he got out of bed) *yet?* ○ *I was up late* (ie didn't go to bed until late) *last night.* ○ *It's time to get up!* ○ *I was up all night with a sick child.* **2** to or in a higher place, position, condition, degree, etc: *Lift your head up.* ○ *Pull your socks up.* ○ *He lives three floors up.* ○ *Prices are still going up,* ie rising. ○ *Put the packet up on the top shelf.* ○ *The sun was coming up* (ie rising) *as we left.* ○ *We were two goals up* (ie ahead of the other team) *at half-time.* Cf DOWN¹ 2. **3** ~ **(to sb/sth)** so as to be close (to a specified person or thing): *He came up (to me) and asked the time.* ○ *She went straight up to the door and knocked loudly.* ○ *A car drove up and he got in.* **4 (a)** to or in an important place (esp a large city): *go up to London for the day* ○ *They're up in London.* ○ [attrib] *The up train* (ie The train to London) *leaves every hour.* **(b)** *(Brit)* to or in a university (esp Oxford or Cambridge): *She is going up to Oxford in October.* ○ *He's up at Cambridge.* **(c)** to or in the north of the country: *We're going up to Edinburgh soon.* ○ *They've moved up north,* ie to the north of England. ○ *She lives up in the Lake District.* Cf DOWN¹ 3. **5** into pieces; apart: *She tore the paper up.* ○ *The road is up,* ie with the surface broken or removed while being repaired. **6** (in phrasal verbs) **(a)** completely: *We ate all the food up.* ○ *The stream has dried up,* ie has become completely dry. **(b)** securely: *lock, fasten, stick, nail, etc sth up.* **7** *(infml)* happening; going on (esp of sth unusual or unpleasant): *I heard a lot of shouting — what's up?* ○ *I could tell something was up by the look on their faces.* **8** (idm) **be on the ˌup-and-ˈup** *(infml)* **(a)** *(Brit)* be steadily improving, becoming more successful, etc: *Business is on the up-and-up.* **(b)** *(US)* be honest. **be up to sb (a)** be required as a duty or obligation from sb: *It's up to us to help those in need.* ○ *It's not up to you to tell me how to do my job.* **(b)** be left to sb to decide: *An Indian or a Chinese meal? It's up to you.* **be up with sb** be a source of discomfort, etc or a cause of illness, etc: *He's very pale. What's up with him?* **not be ˈup to much** not be worth much; not be very good: *His work isn't up to much.* **up against sth (a)** in close contact with sth; close to: *The ladder is leaning up against the wall.* **(b)** *(infml)* faced with (problems, difficulties, etc): *He came up against the local police.* ○ *She's really up against it,* ie in great difficulties. **ˌup and aˈbout; ˌup and ˈdoing** out of bed and active again (esp after illness). **ˌup and ˈdown (a)** backwards and forwards; to and fro: *walking up and down outside our house.* **(b)** so as to rise and fall: *The boat bobbed up and down on/in the water.* **up before sb/sth** appearing in court (in front of a magistrate, etc): *He was/came up before the magistrate for speeding.* ○ *His case was brought up before the court.* **up for sth (a)** being tried (for an offence, etc): *up for speeding.* **(b)** being considered for sth; on offer for sth: *The contract is up for renewal.* ○ *The house is up for auction/sale.* **up to sth (a)** as a maximum number or amount: *I can take up to four people in my car.* ○ *count up to twenty slowly.* **(b)** (also **up until sth**) not further or later than sth; as far as sth: *Read up to page 100.* ○ *Up to now he's been quiet.* ○ *Up until the war she had never lived alone.* **(c)** comparable with sth: *It's not up to his usual standard.* **(d)** capable of sth: *He's not up to the part of Othello.* ○ *I don't feel up to going to work today.* **(e)** *(infml)* occupied or busy with sth: *What's he up to?* ○ *He's up to no good,* ie doing sth bad. ○ *What tricks has she been up to* (ie playing)*?*

▷ **up** *prep* **1** to or in a higher position on (sth): *run up the stairs* ○ *further up the valley* ○ *walk up* (ie along) *the road* ○ *sail up a river,* ie against the current. **2** (idm) **up and down sth** backwards and forwards on sth: *walking up and down the platform.* **ˌup ˈyours!** *(Brit* ⚠ *sl)* (used to express extreme anger, disgust, annoyance, etc towards a person).

up *v* **(-pp-) 1** [I] *(infml or joc)* (followed by *and* and another *v*) get or jump up; rouse oneself: *She upped and left without a word.* **2** [Tn] *(infml)* increase (sth): *up the price* ○ *up an offer.* **3** (idm) **ˌup ˈsticks** move with all one's possessions to live and work in another place.

up *n* **1** [sing] part of a ball's path in which it is still moving upwards after bouncing on the ground: *Try to hit the ball on the up.* **2** (idm) **ˈups and ˌdowns** alternate good and bad luck: *He stuck by her through all life's ups and downs.*

□ **ˌup-and-ˈcoming** *adj (infml)* (of a person) making good progress; likely to succeed (esp in a career): *an ˌup-and-coming young ˈbarrister.*

up- *pref* (with *ns, vs* and their related forms) higher: *upheaval* ○ *upland* ○ *upgrade.*

upbeat /ˈʌpbi:t/ *n (music)* unaccented beat, esp at the end of a bar, shown by the conductor's baton moving upwards. Cf DOWNBEAT.
▷ **upbeat** *adj (fig)* optimistic or cheerful.

upbraid /ˌʌpˈbreɪd/ *v* [Tn, Tn·pr] ~ **sb (for sth)** *(dated or fml)* scold or reproach sb: *upbraid sb for wrongdoing, incompetence, etc.*

upbringing /ˈʌpbrɪŋɪŋ/ *n* (usu *sing*) treatment and education during childhood: *a strict religious upbringing* ○ *The twins had different upbringings.* ○ *Her country upbringing explains her love of nature.*

up-country /ˌʌpˈkʌntrɪ/ *adj, adv* (esp in large thinly-populated countries) in or towards the interior: *ˌup-country ˈdistricts* ○ *travel up-country.*

update /ˌʌpˈdeɪt/ *v* **1** [Tn] bring (sth) up to date; modernize: *update a dictionary, file, law* ○ *update production methods, computer systems.* **2** [Tn, Tn·pr] ~ **sb (on sth)** give sb the latest information (about sth): *I updated the committee on our progress.*
▷ **update** /ˈʌpdeɪt/ *n* act of updating: *Maps need regular updates.* ○ *an update on the political situation.*

Updike /ˈʌpdaɪk/ John (1932-), American novelist. In books such as the *Rabbit* series and *Couples,* written in a markedly elaborate prose style, he explores social and sexual problems in human relationships in modern America.

up-end /ˌʌpˈend/ *v* [I, Tn] rise or set (sth) up on its end: *I up-ended the crate and sat on it.*

upgrade /ˌʌpˈgreɪd/ *v* [Tn, Tn·pr] ~ **sb/sth (to sb/sth)** raise sb/sth to a higher grade or rank: *She was upgraded to (the post of) sales director.* ○ *The consulate was upgraded to embassy status.* Cf DOWNGRADE.
▷ **upgrade** /ˈʌpgreɪd/ *n (US)* upward slope.

upheaval /ʌpˈhi:vl/ *n* **(a)** sudden violent upward movement: *volcanic upheavals.* **(b)** *(fig)* sudden violent change or disturbance: *political, social upheavals* ○ *Moving house causes such an upheaval.*

uphill /ˌʌpˈhɪl/ *adj* **1** sloping upwards; ascending: *an ˌuphill ˈroad, ˈclimb* ○ *The last mile is all uphill.* **2** [attrib] *(fig)* needing effort; difficult: *It's uphill work learning to ride.* ○ *an ˌuphill ˈtask/ˈstruggle.*
▷ **uphill** *adv* up a slope: *walk uphill.*

uphold /ˌʌpˈhəʊld/ *v* (*pt, pp* **upheld** /-ˈheld/) [Tn] **1** support (a decision, etc) against attack: *uphold a verdict, policy, principle.* **2** maintain (a custom, etc): *uphold ancient traditions.*

upholster /ˌʌpˈhəʊlstə(r)/ *v* [Tn, Tn·pr] ~ **sth (in/with sth)** provide (an armchair, etc) with padding, springs, fabric covering, etc: *upholster a sofa in leather* ○ *upholstered in/with velvet.*
▷ **upholsterer** /-stərə(r)/ *n* person whose trade is to upholster furniture.
upholstery /-stərɪ/ *n* [U] **1** trade of an upholsterer. **2** materials used in this trade.

UPI /ˌju: pi: ˈaɪ/ *abbr* United Press International.

upkeep /ˈʌpki:p/ *n* [U] (cost or means of) keeping sth in good condition and repair; maintenance: *I can't afford the upkeep of a large house and garden.*

upland /ˈʌplənd/ *n* (often *pl*) higher or inland parts of a country: *the barren upland(s) of central Spain* ○ [attrib] *an upland region.*

uplift /ˌʌpˈlɪft/ *v* [Tn] *(usu fig)* raise (sb/sth), esp spiritually, morally or emotionally: *with uplifted hands* ○ *an uplifting sermon.*
▷ **uplift** /ˈʌplɪft/ *n* [U] spiritual, moral or emotionally elevating influence: *Her encouragement gave me a great sense of uplift.*

up-market /ˌʌp ˈmɑ:kɪt/ *adj* (of products, services, etc) designed to appeal to or satisfy people in the upper social classes. Cf DOWN-MARKET.

upon /əˈpɒn/ *prep* **1** *(fml)* = ON² 1, 4b, 9, 10, 13. **2** (idm) **once upon a time** ⇨ ONCE. **(almost) uˈpon him, them, us, etc** (of a time in the future) rapidly approaching: *Christmas is almost upon us again.*

upper /ˈʌpə(r)/ *adj* [attrib] **1** higher in place or position; situated above another (esp similar) part: *the upper lip, arm, jaw* ○ *one of the upper rooms, floors, windows* ○ *temperatures in the upper sixties,* ie between 65°F and 70°F. **2** situated on higher ground or to the north or far inland: *Upper Egypt,* ie the part furthest from the Nile delta ○ *the upper (reaches of the) Thames.* **3** higher in rank or wealth: *the upper classes,* ie of society ○ *salaries/people in the upper income bracket.* Cf LOW¹ 3. ⇨ articles at ARISTOCRAT, CLASS. **4** (idm) **gain, get, etc the upper ˈhand (over sb)** get the advantage (over sb); control sb: *Our team gained/had the upper hand in the second half.* ○ *Don't let your feelings get the upper hand over you.* **a stiff upper lip** ⇨ STIFF. **the upper crust** *(infml or joc)* the highest social class: *belong to the upper crust.*
▷ **upper** *n* **1** part of a shoe or boot above the sole. **2** *(infml)* drug that gives an exaggerated feeling of cheerfulness. Cf DOWNER. **3** (idm) **be on one's ˈuppers** *(infml)* have very little money.
□ **ˌupper ˈcase** capital letters, esp in printing-type: *titles set in upper case* ○ [attrib] *ˌupper-case ˈtitles.*
the ˌUpper ˈChamber (also **the ˌUpper ˈHouse**) (in the British Parliament) the House of Lords.
ˈupper-cut *n* (in boxing) punch delivered upwards with the arm bent.

uppermost /ˈʌpəməʊst/ *adj* highest in place or position or importance.
▷ **uppermost** *adv* on or to the highest or most important position: *Store this side uppermost,* eg as a notice on a container. ○ *The children's future is always uppermost in my mind.*

uppish /ˈʌpɪʃ/ *adj (infml esp Brit)* (also *esp US* **uppity** /ˈʌpətɪ/) self-assertive or arrogant: *Don't get uppish with me, young lady!*

upright /ˈʌpraɪt/ *adj* **1** in a vertical position; erect: *his upright bearing/posture/stance.* **2** strictly honest or honourable: *an upright citizen* ○ *be upright in one's business dealings.* **3** (idm) **bolt upright** ⇨ BOLT³.
▷ **upright** *adv* in or into an upright position: *sit, stand, hold oneself upright* ○ *pull the tent-pole upright.*
upright *n* **1** post or rod placed upright, esp as a support: *The ball bounced off the left upright of the goal.* **2** = UPRIGHT PIANO.
uprightness *n* [U] ⇨ illus at PIANO.
□ **ˌupright piˈano** (also **upright**) piano with the strings arranged vertically. ⇨ illus at MUSIC.

uprising /ˈʌpraɪzɪŋ/ *n* revolt against those in power; rebellion: *an armed uprising.*

uproar /ˈʌprɔ:(r)/ *n* [U, sing] (outburst of) noise and excitement or anger; tumult: *The meeting ended in (an) uproar.* ○ *There was (an) uproar over* *the tax increases.*

▷ **uproarious** /ʌpˈrɔːrɪəs/ *adj* [esp attrib] (a) very noisy or high-spirited: *an uproarious welcome, evening, debate* ○ *They burst into uproarious laughter.* (b) very funny: *uproarious jokes, disguises, mistakes.* **uproariously** *adv*: *shout uproariously* ○ *uproariously funny.*

uproot /ˌʌpˈruːt/ *v* 1 [Tn esp passive] pull (a tree, plant, etc) out of the ground together with its roots. 2 [Tn, Tn·pr] ~ **sb/oneself (from sth/...)** (*fig*) force sb/oneself to leave a place where he/one was born or has become settled: *She uprooted herself from the farm and moved to London.*

upset /ˌʌpˈset/ *v* (**-tt-**, *pt, pp* **upset**) 1 [I, Tn] (cause sth to) become overturned or spilt, esp accidentally: *upset one's cup, the milk, a plate of biscuits* ○ *A large wave upset the boat.* 2 [Tn] disrupt (a plan, etc): *upset the balance of trade* ○ *Our arrangements for the weekend were upset by her visit.* ○ *Fog upset the train timetable.* 3 [Tn] (a) distress the mind or feelings of (sb): *be emotionally upset* ○ *Don't upset yourself — no harm has been done.* ○ *The sight of physical suffering always upsets me.* ○ *He was upset at not being invited.* (b) cause (sb) to feel ill by disturbing his digestion: *Cheese often upsets her/her stomach.* 4 (idm) **upset the/sb's ˈapplecart** (a) spoil a plan or disrupt an arrangement: *Her refusal to help quite upset the applecart.* (b) disprove a theory.

▷ **upset** /ˈʌpset/ *n* 1 [U, C] upsetting or being upset: *Last-minute changes caused a great deal of upset.* ○ *She had a major emotional upset.* 2 [C] stomach disorder: (*infml*) *in bed with a tummy upset.* 3 (in sport) unexpected result.

upshot /ˈʌpʃɒt/ *n* [sing] **the ~ (of sth)** the final result or outcome: *The upshot of it all was that he resigned.*

upsidaisy (also **oops-a-daisy**, **upsa-daisy**, **upsy-daisy**, **whoops-a-daisy**) /ˈʊpsədeɪzɪ/ *interj* (*infml*) (said when a child falls, is lifted up, is swung in the air, etc).

upside-down /ˌʌpsaɪd ˈdaʊn/ *adj, adv* 1 with the upper part underneath instead of on top: *That picture is upside-down.* ○ *hold a book upside-down.* 2 (*infml fig*) in or into total disorder or confusion: *He has an upside-down way of doing things*, eg he deals with priorities last. ○ *Burglars had turned the house upside-down.*

upstage /ˌʌpˈsteɪdʒ/ *adj, adv* 1 at or towards the back of a theatre stage: *an ˌupstage ˈdoor* ○ *move upstage.* 2 (*infml*) snobbish(ly): *They're much too upstage for us these days.*

▷ **upstage** *v* [Tn] 1 cause (an actor) to face away from the audience by moving nearer the back of the stage than him. 2 (*fig*) divert attention from (sb) towards oneself; put at a disadvantage: *He upstaged the other speakers by illustrating his talk with slides.*

upstairs /ˌʌpˈsteəz/ *adv* 1 up the stairs; to or on an upper floor: *walk, leap, sleep upstairs* ○ *I was upstairs when it happened.* Cf DOWNSTAIRS. 2 (idm) **kick sb upstairs** ⇨ KICK[1].

▷ **upstairs** *adj* situated on, living on or belonging to an upper floor: *an ˌupstairs ˈroom, ˈwindow* ○ *the families upstairs/the ˌupstairs ˈfamilies.*

upstairs *n* [sing] (*infml*) upper floor of a house, etc: *A bungalow does not have an upstairs.*

upstanding /ˌʌpˈstændɪŋ/ *adj* [attrib] (*fml or rhet*) 1 strong, healthy and vigorous: *a fine upstanding figure of a man.* 2 decent and honest: *upstanding members of the city council.*

upstart /ˈʌpstɑːt/ *n* (*derog*) person who has suddenly risen to wealth or a high position, esp one who behaves arrogantly and causes resentment: *You can't marry that young upstart!* ○ [attrib] *upstart bureaucrats, financiers, officials, etc.*

upstate /ˈʌpsteɪt/ *adj* (*US*) of or in a part of a state distant from the main cities, esp in the north: *upstate New York.* ▷ **upstate** *adv*: *move upstate.*

upstream /ˌʌpˈstriːm/ *adv, adj* in the direction from which a river, etc flows; against the current: *row, swim, walk upstream* ○ *Factories upstream (from us) are polluting the water.* Cf DOWNSTREAM.

upsurge /ˈʌpsɜːdʒ/ *n* (usu *sing*) (a) ~ **(in sth)** sudden increase in sth; rise: *an upsurge in sales, costs, investments.* (b) ~ **(of sth)** sudden rush, esp of feeling: *an upsurge of anger, enthusiasm, violence* ○ *an upsurge of interest in the environment.*

upswing /ˈʌpswɪŋ/ *n* ~ **(in sth)** (esp sudden) upward movement or trend; improvement: *This policy led to an upswing in the party's popularity.* Cf UPTURN.

uptake /ˈʌpteɪk/ *n* (idm) **ˌquick/ˌslow on the ˈuptake** quick/slow to understand what is meant: *You'll have to explain it to me carefully — I'm not very quick on the uptake.*

uptight /ˌʌpˈtaɪt/ *adj* ~ **(about sth)** (*infml*) 1 nervously tense: *get uptight about exams, interviews, etc.* 2 annoyed or hostile: *Offers of help just make him uptight.* 3 (*US*) rigidly conventional.

up-to-date /ˌʌp tə ˈdeɪt/ *adj* [attrib] 1 modern or fashionable: *ˌup-to-date ˈclothes, iˈdeas, ˈbooks.* 2 having or including the most recent information: *an ˌup-to-date ˈdictionary, reˈport.*

up-to-the-minute /ˌʌp tə ðə ˈmɪnɪt/ *adj* [attrib] 1 very modern or fashionable; very up-to-date. 2 having or including the most recent information possible: *an ˌup-to-the-minute acˌcount of the ˈriots.*

uptown /ˌʌpˈtaʊn/ *adj, adv* (*US*) in or to the outer residential districts of a town: *uptown New York* ○ *go, drive, stay uptown.* Cf DOWNTOWN.

upturn /ˈʌptɜːn/ *n* ~ **(in sth)** upward trend in business, fortune, etc; improvement: *an upturn in the sales figures* ○ *Her luck seems to have taken an upturn/to be on the upturn.* Cf UPSWING.

▷ **upturned** /ˌʌpˈtɜːnd/ *adj* turned upwards or upside-down: *a slightly ˌupturned ˈnose* ○ *She felt drops of rain on her ˌupturned ˈface.* ○ *sitting on an ˌupturned ˈcrate.*

upward /ˈʌpwəd/ *adj* [usu attrib] moving, leading or pointing to what is higher, more important, etc: *an upward glance, climb* ○ *the upward trend in prices.*

▷ **upward** (also **upwards** /-wədz/) *adv* towards what is higher: *The missile rose upward into the sky.* ○ *The boat floated bottom upwards*, ie upside-down. ⇨ Usage at FORWARD[2].

upwards of *prep* more than (a number): *Upwards of a hundred people came to the meeting.*

□ **ˌupward moˈbility** movement into a higher and wealthier social class. **ˌupwardly ˈmobile** ready and able to move in this way: *upwardly mobile young executives.*

upwind /ˌʌpˈwɪnd/ *adj, adv* ~ **(of sb/sth)** in the direction from which the wind is blowing: *If we're upwind of the animal it may smell our scent.*

Ural Mountains /ˌjʊərəl ˈmaʊntɪnz; *US* ˈmaʊntnz/ **the Ural Mountains** (also **the ˈUrals**) mountain range in Russia running from the Arctic coast in the north almost to the Caspian Sea in the south. It is 1 600 km (1 000 miles) long and separates the European part of Russia from Asia and Siberia. It contains rich mineral deposits.

uranium /jʊˈreɪnɪəm/ *n* [U] (*symb* **U**) chemical element, a heavy grey radioactive metal used as a source of nuclear energy. ⇨ App 11.

Uranus /ˈjʊərənəs, *also* jʊˈreɪnəs/ the seventh of the planets, discovered by *Herschel in 1781. It is difficult to observe from the earth. Its surface is extremely cold and made up of condensed gases. It has five known satellites.

urban /ˈɜːbən/ *adj* [usu attrib] of, situated in or living in a city or town: *urban areas* ○ *the urban population* ○ *urban renewal*, ie the renovation of old buildings, etc ○ *urban guerrillas*, ie terrorists operating in urban areas by kidnapping, etc. Cf RURAL.

▷ **urbanize**, **-ise** /-aɪz/ [Tn esp passive] change (esp a rural place) into a town-like area. **urbanization**, **-isation** /ˌɜːbənaɪˈzeɪʃn; *US* -nɪˈz-/ *n* [U].

urbane /ɜːˈbeɪn/ *adj* (*fml sometimes derog*) having or showing refined manners, smooth elegance and sophistication: *an urbane man, wit, smile, conversation.* ▷ **urbanely** *adv*. **urbanity** /ɜːˈbænətɪ/ *n* [U, C].

urchin /ˈɜːtʃɪn/ *n* 1 (a) (*esp dated*) mischievous or naughty child, esp a boy: *You little urchin!* (b) (also ˈ**street-urchin**) ragged or dirty child who is homeless and lives in poverty. 2 = SEA-URCHIN (SEA).

Urdu /ˈʊədu:/ *adj, n* [U] (of the) language related to Hindi but having many Persian words. It is the official language of Pakistan and the first language of the Muslim population there, and of about 30 million people in India.

-ure *suff* 1 (with *vs* forming *ns*) action or process of: *closure* ○ *failure* ○ *seizure.* 2 (with *vs* or *ns* forming *ns*) group or thing having a specific function: *legislature* ○ *prefecture.*

urea /jʊəˈrɪə; *US* ˈjʊrɪə/ *n* [U] white soluble crystalline compound contained esp in the urine of mammals.

ureter /jʊəˈriːtə(r)/ *n* either of the two tubes by which urine passes from the kidneys to the bladder.

urethra /jʊəˈriːθrə/ *n* (*pl* ~**s** or, in scientific use, **-rae** /-riː/) (*anatomy*) tube by which urine passes from the bladder out of the body. ⇨ illus at MALE.

urge /ɜːdʒ/ *v* 1 [Tn·pr, Tn·p, Cn·t] drive forcibly or hurry (a horse, etc) in a certain direction: *urge a pony into a canter, up a slope* ○ *urge one's mount on, forward, north* ○ *She urged her mare to jump the fence.* 2 [Tn, Tf, Tg, Tsg, Cn·t] try earnestly or persistently to persuade (sb): *'Don't give in now,' she urged.* ○ *He urged that we should go/urged (our) going/urged us to go.* 3 [Tn, Tn·pr, Cn·t] ~ **sth (on/upon sb/sth)** recommend sth strongly with reasoning or entreaty: *We urged caution.* ○ *The government urged on industry the importance of low pay settlements.* ○ *Motoring organizations are urging drivers not to travel by road if possible.* 4 (phr v) **urge sb on** encourage or stimulate sb to do sth: *The manager urged his staff on (to greater efforts).* ○ *Urged on by his colleagues, he stood for election.* ○ *The need to find a solution urged him on.*

▷ **urge** *n* strong desire or impulse: *sexual urges* ○ *get, have, feel give in to a sudden urge to travel.*

urgent /ˈɜːdʒənt/ *adj* 1 needing immediate attention, action or decision: *an urgent message, case, cry for help* ○ *It is most urgent that we operate.* ○ *My car is in urgent need of repair.* 2 showing that sth is urgent; persistent in one's demands: *speak in an urgent whisper.* ▷ **urgency** /-dʒənsɪ/ *n* [U]: *a matter of great urgency* ○ *I detected a note of urgency in her voice.* **urgently** *adv*: *Ambulance drivers are urgently needed.*

uric /ˈjʊərɪk/ *adj* [attrib] of urine: *uric acid.*

urine /ˈjʊərɪn/ *n* [U] waste liquid that collects in the bladder and is passed from the body.

▷ **urinal** /ˈjʊərɪnl, *or, in British use* jʊəˈraɪnl/ *n* building, place or receptacle for (esp) men and boys to urinate in.

urinary /ˈjʊərɪnərɪ; *US* -nerɪ/ *adj* [usu attrib] of urine or the parts of the body through which it passes: *urinary infections, organs.*

urinate /ˈjʊərɪneɪt/ *v* [I] pass urine from the body.

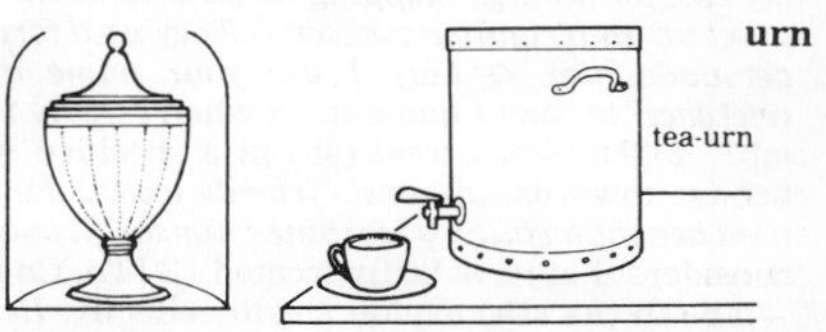

urn /ɜːn/ *n* 1 tall vase, usu with a stem and a base, esp one used for holding the ashes of a cremated person. 2 (esp in compounds) large metal container with a tap, in which tea, coffee, etc is made or from which it is served, eg in cafés or canteens: *a tea urn.* ⇨ illus.

urology /jʊəˈrɒlədʒɪ/ *n* [U] study of the urinary system.

Ursa Major /ˌɜːsə ˈmeɪdʒə(r)/ = THE GREAT BEAR (GREAT).

Ursa Minor /ˌɜːsə ˈmaɪnə(r)/ small constellation which includes the pole-star (POLE[1]).

ursine /ˈɜːsaɪn/ *adj* (*fml*) of or like a bear.

Uruguay

Uruguay /ˈjʊərəgwaɪ; *US* -gweɪ/ country in the east of S America; pop approx 3 060 000; official language Spanish; capital Montevideo; unit of currency peso (= 100 centesimos). It is one of the smallest countries on the continent and made up mostly of pampas-like plains, used largely for cattle-rearing. Uruguay has a relatively developed industrial sector, but goods are mainly for domestic consumption with few exports. ⇨ map.
▷ **Uruguayan** /-ˈgwaɪən; *US* -ˈgweɪən/ *n, adj*.

US /ˌjuː ˈes/ *abbr* **1** United States (of America): *a US citizen.* **2** (also **u/s**) (*infml*) unserviceable (ie useless): *This pen's US. Give me one that writes.*

us /əs; *strong form* ʌs/ *pers pron* (used as the object of a *v* or of a *prep*; also used independently and after *be*) me and another or others; me and you: *She gave us a washing-machine.* ○ *We'll take the dog with us.* ○ *Hello, it's us back again!* Cf WE.

USA /ˌjuː es ˈeɪ/ *abbr* **1** (*US*) United States Army. **2** (esp in addresses) United States of America.

USAF /ˌjuː es eɪ ˈef/ *abbr* United States Air Force.

usage /ˈjuːsɪdʒ, ˈjuːzɪdʒ/ *n* **1** [U] manner of using sth; treatment: *The tractor had been damaged by rough usage.* **2** [U, C] habitual or customary practice, esp in the way words are used: *English grammar and usage* ○ *Languages develop continually through usage.* ○ *It's not a word in common usage.* ○ *A dictionary helps one to distinguish correct and incorrect usages.*

use[1] /juːz/ *v* (*pt, pp* **used** /juːzd/) **1** [Tn, Tn·pr, Tnt, Cn·n/a] ~ **sth (for sth/doing sth)**; ~ **sth (as sth)** employ sth for a purpose; bring sth into service: *Do you know how to use a lathe?* ○ *Use your common sense!* ○ *If you don't use* (ie practise) *your English you'll forget it.* ○ *May I use your phone?* ○ *A hammer is used for driving in nails.* ○ *She uses her unmarried name for professional purposes.* ○ *I use my bike for (going) shopping.* ○ *We used the money to set up an irrigation project.* ○ *They used force to persuade him.* ○ *May I use your name as a reference?* ie May I quote it, eg when I apply for a job? **2** [Tn] (*fml*) treat (sb) in a specified way; behave towards: *use one's friends well* ○ *He has used her shamefully.* ○ *He thinks himself ill used*, ie considers that he is badly treated. **3** [Tn, Cn·n/a] ~ **sb/sth (as sth)** exploit sb/sth selfishly: *He felt used by her.* ○ *She simply used us for her own ends/to get what she wanted.* ○ *He used the bad weather as an excuse for not coming.* **4** [Tn, Tn·pr] consume (sth): *Use the milk sparingly, there's not much left.* ○ *The car used a gallon of petrol for the journey.* **5** [Tn] (*infml*) (**a**) take (drugs). (**b**) (*US*) smoke (cigarettes, etc). **6** (idm) **I, etc could use a ˈdrink, etc** (*infml*) I, etc would very much like a drink, etc: *Boy, could I use a hot bath!* **use one's loaf** (*infml*) think effectively; use one's intelligence. **7** (phr v) **use sth up** (**a**) use (material, etc) until no more is left; find a use for (remaining material or time): *I've used up all the glue.* ○ *She used up the chicken bones to make soup.* (**b**) exhaust or tire sth out: *use up all one's strength, energy, etc.*
▷ **usable** /ˈjuːzəbl/ *adj* [pred] that can be used; that is fit to be used: *This tyre is so worn that it is no longer usable.*

use[2] /juːs/ *n* **1** [U, sing] ~ **(of sth)** using or being used: *the use of electricity for heating* ○ *learn the use of a lathe* ○ *an ingenious use of wind power* ○ *the use of force, terrorism, blackmail, etc* ○ *keep sth for one's own use* ○ *funds for use in emergencies* ○ *The ointment is for external use only*, eg It must not be swallowed. ○ *bought for use, not for ornament* ○ *The lock has broken through constant use.* **2** [C, U] purpose for which sth is used; work that a person or thing is able to do: *a tool with many uses* ○ *find a (new) use for sth.* **3** [U] ~ **(of sth)** (**a**) right to use sth: *allow a tenant the use of the garden* ○ *I have the use of the car this week.* (**b**) power of using sth: *have full use of one's faculties* ○ *lose the use of one's legs*, ie become unable to walk. **4** [U] value or advantage; usefulness: *What's the use of worrying about it?* ○ *It's no use pretending you didn't know.* ○ *You're no use in the choir — you can't sing a note!* ○ *Recycled materials are mostly of limited use.* **5** [U] (*fml*) custom, practice or habit; usage(2): *Long use has accustomed me to it.* **6** (idm) **ˌcome into/ˌgo out of ˈuse** start/stop being used: *When did this word come into common use?* ○ *The present phone boxes will go out of use next year.* **have no use for sb** refuse to tolerate sb; dislike: *I've no use for people who don't try.* **have no use for sth** have no purpose for which sth can be used: *I've no further use for this typewriter, so you can have it.* **in ˈuse** being used. **make the best use of sth** ⇨ BEST[1]. **make use of sth/sb** use or benefit from sth/sb: *Make full use of every chance you have to speak English.* ○ *We will make good use of her talents.* **no earthly use** ⇨ EARTHLY. **of use** serving a purpose; useful: *These maps might be of (some) use to you on your trip.* **put sth to good ˈuse** derive profit from sth: *He'll be able to put his experience to good use in the new job.*

used[1] /juːzd/ *adj* [usu attrib] (of clothes, cars, etc) having been worn, used, etc before; second-hand.

used[2] /juːst/ *adj* ~ **to sth/doing sth** having learned to accept sth; accustomed to sth: *be quite used to hard work/working hard* ○ *After three weeks she had got used to the extreme heat.* ○ *The food in England is strange at first but you'll soon get used to it.*

used to /ˈjuːs tə; *before vowels and finally* ˈjuːs tuː/ *modal v* (*neg* **used not to**, *contracted form* **usedn't to**, **usen't to** /ˈjuːsn tə, *before vowels and finally* ˈjuːsn tuː/) (expressing a frequent or continuous action in the past; in questions and negative sentences usu with *did*): *I used to live in London.* ○ *Life here is much easier than it used to be.* ○ *You used to smoke a pipe, didn't you?*

NOTE ON USAGE: The following negative and question patterns are old-fashioned or very formal: *I usedn't to like her,* ○ *Used you to go there?* ○ *There used to be a cinema here, use(d)n't there?* Most people now use patterns with **did**, especially when speaking or writing informally: *I didn't use to like her.* ○ *Did you use to go there?* ○ *There used to be a cinema here, didn't there?*

useful /ˈjuːsfl/ *adj* **1** that can be used for some practical purpose; serviceable or helpful: *a useful gadget, book, hint, acquaintance* ○ *do sth useful with one's life* ○ *Videos are useful things to have in the classroom.* **2** (*infml*) competent or capable: *He's a useful member of the team.* **3** (idm) **come in handy/useful** ⇨ HANDY. **ˌmake oneself ˈuseful** help by performing useful tasks: *My nephews tried to make themselves useful about the house.* ▷ **usefully** /-fəlɪ/ *adv*: *Is there anything I can usefully do here?* **usefulness** /-fəlnɪs/ *n* [U]: *The old car has outlived its usefulness*, ie is no longer useful or worth keeping.

useless /ˈjuːslɪs/ *adj* **1** not serving a useful purpose; not producing good results: *A car is useless without petrol.* ○ *It's useless arguing/to argue with them.* ○ *All our efforts were useless.* **2** (*infml*) weak or incompetent: *He's a useless player.* ○ *I'm useless at maths.* ▷ **uselessly** *adv.* **uselessness** *n* [U].

user /ˈjuːzə(r)/ *n* (esp in compounds) person or thing that uses: *ˈdrug-users, ˈroad-users* ○ *I'm a great user of public transport.* ○ *The steel industry is one of Britain's greatest users of coal.*
▷ **user-friendly** /ˌjuːzə ˈfrendlɪ/ *adj* (esp of computers, their software, etc) easy for non-experts to use; not difficult or intimidating: *a ˌuser-friendly ˈkeyboard* ○ *Dictionaries should be as user-friendly as possible.*

usher /ˈʌʃə(r)/ *n* **1** person who shows people to their seats in a cinema, church, public hall, etc or into sb's presence. **2** door-keeper in a lawcourt, etc.
▷ **usher** *v* **1** [Tn·pr, Tn·p] lead (sb) in the specified direction; escort as an usher: *The girl ushered me along the aisle to my seat.* ○ *I was ushered in, and stood before the Queen.* **2** (phr v) **usher sth in** (*fig*) mark the start of sth; herald sth: *The new government ushered in a period of prosperity.*
usherette /ˌʌʃəˈret/ *n* girl or woman who ushers people to their seats, esp in a cinema or theatre.

USN /ˌjuː es ˈen/ *abbr* United States Navy.

USS /ˌjuː es ˈes/ *abbr* United States Ship: *USS Oklahoma.* Cf HMS.

USSR /ˌjuː es es ˈɑː(r)/ *abbr* Union of Soviet Socialist Republics.

usual /ˈjuːʒl/ *adj* **1** such as happens or is done or used, etc in many or most instances; customary: *make all the usual excuses* ○ *She arrived later than usual.* ○ *As is usual with children, they soon got tired.* ○ *When the accident happened, the usual crowd gathered.* ○ *He wasn't his usual self.* ○ (*infml*) *I'll have my usual, please*, ie my usual drink, etc. **2** (idm) **as usual** as is usual: *You're late, as usual.* ○ *As usual, there weren't many people at the meeting.* **business as usual** ⇨ BUSINESS.
▷ **usually** /ˈjuːʒəlɪ/ *adv* in the way that is usual; most often: *What do you usually do on Sundays?* ○ *He's usually early.* ○ *The canteen is more than usually busy today.*

usurer /ˈjuːʒərə(r)/ *n* (*dated usu derog*) person who lends money at excessively high interest.

usurp /juːˈzɜːp/ *v* [Tn] (*fml*) take (sb's power, right, position) wrongfully or by force: *usurp the throne* ○ *usurp the role of leader.* ▷ **usurpation** /ˌjuːzɜːˈpeɪʃn/ *n* [U]. **usurper** *n*.

usury /ˈjuːʒərɪ/ *n* [U] (*dated usu derog*) (lending of money at) excessively high interest.

Utah /ˈjuːtɑː; *US* ˈjuːtɔː/ state in the western USA. It lies in the *Rocky Mountain chain and has spectacular canyons in the south-west and the *Great Salt Lake and its surrounding desert in the north-west. It was founded by *Mormons and Utah remains the headquarters of their Church. ⇨ map at App 1.

utensil /juːˈtensl/ *n* implement or container, esp for everyday use in the home: *ˈwriting utensils*, eg pencils, pens, ink ○ *ˈcooking/ˈkitchen utensils*, eg pots, pans.

uterus /ˈjuːtərəs/ *n* (*pl* ~**es** or, in scientific use, **uteri** /-raɪ/) (*anatomy*) womb. ⇨ illus at FEMALE.
▷ **uterine** /ˈjuːtəraɪn/ *adj* of the uterus.

utilitarian /ˌjuːtɪlɪˈteərɪən/ *adj* **1** (*sometimes derog*) designed to be useful rather than luxurious or decorative, etc; severely practical: *The student accommodation is strictly utilitarian.* **2** based on or supporting the ideas of utilitarianism.
▷ **utilitarianism** /-ɪzəm/ *n* [U] the belief, based on the philosophy of *Bentham, that actions are good if they are useful or benefit the greatest number of people.

utility /juːˈtɪlətɪ/ *n* **1** [U] quality of being useful: [attrib] *a utility vehicle*, ie one that can be used for various purposes ○ *the utility value of a dishwasher.* **2** [C] = PUBLIC UTILITY (PUBLIC).
□ **uˈtility room** room, esp in a private house, containing one or more large fixed domestic appliances, eg a washing-machine.

utilize, -ise /ˈjuːtəlaɪz/ *v* [Tn] (*fml*) make use of (sth); find a use for: *utilize the available tools, resources* ○ *utilize solar power as a source of energy.*
▷ **utilization, -isation** /ˌjuːtəlaɪˈzeɪʃn; *US* -lɪˈz-/ *n* [U].

utmost /ˈʌtməʊst/ (also **uttermost** /ˈʌtəməʊst/) *adj* [attrib] greatest; furthest; most extreme: *in the utmost danger* ○ *of the utmost importance* ○ *with the utmost care* ○ *pushed to the utmost limits of endurance.*

▷ **the utmost** (also **the uttermost**) *n* [sing] **1** the greatest, furthest or most extreme degree or point, etc that is possible: *enjoy oneself to the utmost* ○ *Our endurance was tested to the utmost.* **2** (idm) **do/try one's ˈutmost (to do sth)** do or try as much as one can: *I did my utmost to stop them.*

Utopia /ju:ˈtəʊpɪə/ *n* [C, U] imaginary place or state of things in which everything is perfect. The original Utopia was an imaginary island described by Thomas *More in a book of the same name which appeared in 1516. He criticized the political systems of France and England and went on to describe life in Utopia, where there was a system of idealized communism and all its citizens prospered and were happy: *create a political Utopia.*

▷ **Utopian** /-pɪən/ *adj* (*usu derog*) having or aiming for the perfection of Utopia but impossible to achieve; idealistic: *Utopian ideals.*

Utrillo /u:ˈtrɪləʊ/ Maurice (1883-1955), French painter. The illegitimate son of the painter Suzanne Valadon, he was largely self-taught, and won fame for his atmospheric street scenes.

utter[1] /ˈʌtə(r)/ *adj* [attrib] (used to give extra emphasis to a *n*) complete; total; absolute: *utter darkness, bliss, nonsense* ○ *an utter lie, disaster* ○ *to my utter delight, astonishment, etc* ○ *She's an utter stranger to me.* ▷ **utterly** *adv*: *She utterly despises him.* ○ *We failed utterly to convince them.*

utter[2] /ˈʌtə(r)/ *v* [Tn] **(a)** make (a sound or sounds) with the mouth or voice: *utter a sigh, cry of pain, etc.* **(b)** say or speak: *utter threats, slanders, etc* ○ *He never uttered a word of protest.*

▷ **utterance** /ˈʌtərəns/ *n* (*fml*) **1** [U] action of uttering or expressing things in words: *give utterance to one's feelings, thoughts, views, etc* ○ *The speaker had great powers of utterance.* **2** [C] spoken word or words; thing said: *private/public utterances.*

uttermost = UTMOST.

UV /ˌju:ˈvi:/ *abbr* ultraviolet.

uvula /ˈju:vjʊlə/ *n* (*pl* ~**s** or, in scientific use, **-lae** /-li:/) (*anatomy*) small piece of flesh that hangs from the back of the roof of the mouth above the throat. ⇨ illus at THROAT.

uxorious /ʌkˈsɔ:rɪəs/ *adj* (*fml or joc*) excessively fond of one's wife.

Uzbekistan /ˌʊzbekɪˈstɑ:n/ country in south central Asia; pop approx 20 300 000; official language Uzbek; capital Tashkent; unit of currency rouble. Its three Muslim states became part of the Russian empire by the 19th century, and subsequently went into the USSR. Since independence in 1991 its government has kept Islamic religion out of politics, also holding back strong nationalist feelings. ⇨ map at UNION OF SOVIET SOCIALIST REPUBLICS.

V, v

V, v /viː/ *n* (*pl* **V's, v's** /viːz/) **1** the twenty-second letter of the English alphabet: *Vivienne begins with (a) V/'V'.* **2** V-shaped thing: *The geese were flying in a V.* ○ [attrib] *flying in (a) V formation.*

V *abbr* **1** victory: *give/make a V-sign*, ie with the first and second fingers spread to form a V, showing victory (with palm outwards), or vulgar derision (with palm inwards). **2** volt(s): *240V*, eg on a light bulb. Cf W *abbr* 1.

V *symb* vanadium.

V (also **v**) *symb* Roman numeral for 5.

v *abbr* **1** (*pl* **vv**) verse: *St Luke ch 12 vv 4-10.* **2** verso. **3** (also **vs**) (esp in sporting contests) versus (ie against): *England v West Indies.* **4** (*infml*) very: *I was v pleased to get your letter.* **5** see; refer to (Latin *vide*).

vac /væk/ *n* (*Brit infml*) **1** = VACATION. **2** = VACUUM CLEANER (VACUUM).

vacancy /ˈveɪkənsɪ/ *n* **1** [C] unoccupied accommodation: *No vacancies*, eg on a hotel sign. **2** [C] unfilled position or post: *We have vacancies for typists/in the typing pool.* **3** [U] lack of ideas or intelligence; emptiness of mind: *the vacancy of his stare, expression.*

vacant /ˈveɪkənt/ *adj* **1** not filled or occupied; empty: *Is the lavatory vacant?* ○ *a vacant situation, post, hotel room.* ⇨ Usage at EMPTY[1]. **2** (**a**) showing no sign of thought or intelligence; blank: *a vacant stare, look, etc.* (**b**) empty of thought: *a vacant mind.* ▷ **vacantly** *adv*: *stare, look, gaze, etc vacantly into space.*

□ ˌ**vacant pos'session** (used in house advertisements, etc) state of being empty of occupants and available for the buyer to occupy immediately.

vacate /vəˈkeɪt; *US* ˈveɪkeɪt/ *v* [Tn] (*fml*) cease to occupy (a place or position): *vacate a house, hotel room* ○ *vacate one's seat, post* ○ *The squatters were ordered to vacate the premises.*

vacation /vəˈkeɪʃn; *US* veɪ-/ *n* **1** [C] (also **recess**, *Brit infml* **vac**) any of the intervals between terms in universities and lawcourts: *the Christmas, Easter vacation* ○ *the long vacation*, ie in the summer ○ [attrib] *vacation work.* **2** [C] (*esp US*) = HOLIDAY 1b: *take a vacation.* **3** [U] (*fml*) action of vacating: *Immediate vacation of the house is essential.* **4** (idm) **on vacation** (*esp US*) on holiday. ⇨ Usage at HOLIDAY.

▷ **vacation** *v* [I, Ipr] ~ (**at/in** ...) (*US*) have a holiday at/in (a place).

vaccinate /ˈvæksɪneɪt/ *v* [Tn, Tn·pr] ~ **sb/sth** (**against sth**) protect sb/sth (against a disease) by injecting vaccine: *have your dog vaccinated against rabies.* Cf IMMUNIZE (IMMUNE), INOCULATE.

▷ **vaccination** /ˌvæksɪˈneɪʃn/ *n* [C, U] (instance of) vaccinating or being vaccinated.

vaccine /ˈvæksiːn; *US* vækˈsiːn/ *n* [U, C] substance that is injected into the bloodstream and protects the body by making it have a mild form of the disease: *develop a smallpox, polio, rabies, etc vaccine.* Cf SERUM 2.

vacillate /ˈvæsəleɪt/ *v* [I, Ipr] ~ (**between sth and sth**) (*fml usu derog*) keep changing one's mind; move backwards and forwards between two emotions: *She vacillated between hope and fear.* Cf OSCILLATE.

▷ **vacillation** /væsəˈleɪʃn/ *n* [C, U] (*fml usu derog*) (instance of) vacillating: *eternal, continual, constant, etc vacillations.*

vacuity /vəˈkjuːətɪ/ *n* (*fml*) **1** [U] lack of purpose, meaning or intelligence: *the total vacuity of his thoughts, statements.* **2** [C usu *pl*] inane remarks, acts, etc.

vacuole /ˈvækjʊəʊl/ *n* cavity inside the cytoplasm of a living cell that is filled with air, water, sap, etc.

vacuous /ˈvækjʊəs/ *adj* (*fml*) showing or suggesting absence of thought or intelligence; inane: *a vacuous stare, remark, laugh, expression.*

▷ **vacuously** *adv.* **vacuousness** *n* [U].

vacuum /ˈvækjʊəm/ *n* (*pl* ~**s** or, in scientific use, **vacua** /-jʊə/) **1** (**a**) space that is completely empty of all matter or gas(es). (**b**) space in a container from which the air has been completely or partly pumped out: *create a perfect vacuum.* **2** (usu *sing*) (*fig*) situation or environment characterized by emptiness: *There has been a vacuum in his life since his wife died.* **3** (*infml*) = VACUUM CLEANER. **4** (idm) **in a** ˈ**vacuum** isolated from other people, facts, events, etc: *live, work, etc in a vacuum.*

▷ **vacuum** *v* [I, Tn, Tn·p] ~ **sth** (**out**) (*infml*) clean (sth) with a vacuum cleaner: *vacuum the stairs, carpet* ○ *vacuum (out) the car.*

□ ˈ**vacuum brake** brake used in trains, lorries, etc, which operates when a vacuum is created in its cylinder.

ˈ**vacuum cleaner** electrical appliance that takes up dust, dirt, etc by suction.

ˈ**vacuum flask** (also **flask**, *US* ˈ**vacuum bottle**) container with a double wall that encloses a vacuum, used for keeping the contents hot or cold. Cf THERMOS.

ˈ**vacuum-packed** *adj* (esp of perishable foods) sealed in a pack from which most of the air has been removed.

ˈ**vacuum pump** pump that creates a partial vacuum in a vessel.

ˈ**vacuum tube** (*US*) (*Brit* **radio valve**) sealed glass tube with an almost perfect vacuum to enable an electric charge to pass through, formerly used in radios, televisions, etc.

vade-mecum /ˌvɑːdɪˈmeɪkʊm, ˌveɪdɪˈmiːkəm/ *n* handbook or other small useful work of reference: *The spelling dictionary is a vade-mecum for all secretaries.*

vagabond /ˈvægəbɒnd/ *n* wanderer or vagrant, esp an idle or dishonest one: [attrib] *lead a vagabond life.*

vagary /ˈveɪgərɪ/ *n* (usu *pl*) strange, unusual or capricious change; whim: *the vagaries of fashion, the weather, the postal service.*

vagina /vəˈdʒaɪnə/ *n* (*pl* ~**s** or, in scientific use, **-nae** /-niː/) (*anatomy*) passage (in a female mammal) from the external genital organs to the womb. ⇨ illus at FEMALE. ▷ **vaginal** /vəˈdʒaɪnl/ *adj.*

vagrant /ˈveɪgrənt/ *n* (*fml or law*) person without a settled home or regular work; tramp: *vagrant tribes* ○ *lead a vagrant life.*

▷ **vagrancy** /ˈveɪgrənsɪ/ *n* [U] (offence of) being a vagrant: *drunks arrested for vagrancy.*

vague /veɪg/ *adj* (**-r, -st**) **1** not clearly expressed or perceived: *a vague answer, demand, rumour* ○ *vague memories, hopes, fears* ○ *I haven't the vaguest* (ie slightest) *idea/notion what you mean.* **2** not specific or exact; imprecise: *a vague estimate of the cost* ○ *The terms of the agreement were deliberately vague.* ○ *She can only give a vague description of her attacker.* **3** (**a**) (of persons) undecided or uncertain (about needs, intentions, etc): *be vague in/about one's plans* ○ *I'm still vague about what you want.* (**b**) (of a person's looks or behaviour) suggesting unclear thinking or absent-mindedness: *a vague smile, gesture.* **4** not clearly identified; indistinct: *the vague outline of a ship in the fog.*

▷ **vaguely** *adv* **1** in a way one cannot specify: *Her face is vaguely familiar.* **2** roughly; approximately: *He pointed vaguely in my direction.* ○ *The map of Italy vaguely resembles a boot.* **3** absent-mindedly: *smile, gesture vaguely.*

vagueness *n* [U].

vain /veɪn/ *adj* (**-er, -est**) **1** having too high an opinion of one's looks, abilities, etc; conceited. **2** [attrib] (*esp rhet*) having no value or significance: *vain promises, triumphs, pleasures.* **3** [usu attrib] useless or futile: *a vain attempt* ○ *in the vain hope of persuading him.* **4** (idm) **in** ˈ**vain** (**a**) with no result; uselessly: *try in vain to sleep.* (**b**) fruitless or useless: *All our work was in vain.* **take sb's name in vain** ⇨ NAME[1].

▷ **vainly** *adv* **1** in a conceited manner. **2** uselessly or futilely.

vainness *n* [U].

vainglory /ˌveɪnˈglɔːrɪ/ *n* [U] (*dated or fml*) extreme vanity or pride in oneself; boastfulness.

▷ **vainglorious** /-ˈglɔːrɪəs/ *adj* (*dated or fml*) full of vainglory; conceited and boastful.

valance /ˈvæləns/ *n* (**a**) short curtain or frill hung around the frame of a bed. (**b**) (*esp US*) = PELMET.

vale /veɪl/ *n* (*arch except in place names*) valley: *the Vale of the White Horse.*

valediction /ˌvælɪˈdɪkʃn/ *n* (*fml*) [C, U] (words used in) saying farewell, esp on serious occasions: *utter a valediction* ○ *bow in valediction.*

▷ **valedictory** /-tərɪ/ *adj* [usu attrib] (*fml*) serving as or accompanying a farewell: *a valedictory speech, message, gift.* — *n* (*US*) farewell speech given by a top graduating student at a school or college. **valedictorian** /-ˈtɔːrɪən/ *n* (*US*) student giving a valedictory.

valency /ˈveɪlənsɪ/ (*US* **valence**) *n* (*chemistry*) **1** [U] capacity of an atom or ion to combine with, or be replaced by, another or others as compared with that of the hydrogen atom. **2** [C] unit of this.

valentine /ˈvæləntaɪn/ *n* (**a**) (also **valentine card**) sentimental or comic greetings card sent, usu anonymously, on St Valentine's Day (14 February) to a sweetheart. (**b**) sweetheart to whom one sends such a card: *Will you be my valentine?* ⇨ article at GREETING.

Valentino /ˌvælənˈtiːnəʊ/ Rudolph (1895-1926), Italian-born American film star. He was the first 'screen idol', whose sensuality in films like *The Sheikh* had a deep effect on millions of women fans.

valerian /vəˈlɪərɪən/ *n* [U] any of various types of small herb with strong-smelling pink or white flowers. The roots are used in medicine as a stimulant.

valet /ˈvæleɪ, ˈvælɪt/ *n* (**a**) man's personal servant who looks after his clothes, serves his meals, etc. (**b**) hotel employee with similar duties.

▷ **valet** /ˈvælɪt/ *v* **1** [Tn] clean, brush and repair (eg clothes, chair-covers, car fittings): *a valeting service*, eg at a dry-cleaner's or garage. **2** [I, Tn] act as valet to (sb).

valetudinarian /ˌvælɪtjuːdɪˈneərɪən/ *n* (*fml*) person who pays excessive attention to preserving his health. Cf HYPOCHONDRIAC (HYPOCHONDRIA).

Valhalla /vælˈhælə/ (in Scandinavian mythology) hall to which heroes who die in battle are taken. They feast there with Odin.

valiant /ˈvælɪənt/ *adj* (*rhet*) brave or determined: *valiant resistance, efforts* ○ *She made a valiant attempt not to laugh.* ▷ **valiantly** *adv*: *Tom tried valiantly to rescue the drowning man.*

valid /ˈvælɪd/ *adj* **1** (**a**) legally effective because made or done with the correct formalities: *a valid claim, contract* ○ *The marriage was held to be valid.* (**b**) legally usable or acceptable: *a bus pass valid for one week, for ten journeys* ○ *A cheque card is not a valid proof of identity.* **2** (of arguments, reasons, etc) well based or logical; sound: *raise valid objections to a plan* ○ *Her excuse was not valid.*

▷ **validity** /vəˈlɪdətɪ/ *n* [U] **1** state of being legally acceptable: *test the validity of a decision.* **2** state of being logical: *question the validity of an argument, assumption.*

validate /ˈvælɪdeɪt/ *v* [Tn] **1** make (sth) legally valid; ratify: *validate a contract, marriage, passport.* **2** make (sth) logical or justifiable: *validate a theory, an argument, a thesis, etc.* ▷ **validation** /ˌvælɪˈdeɪʃn/ *n* [U].

valise /vəˈliːz; *US* vəˈliːs/ *n* (*dated*) small leather bag for clothes, etc during a journey.

Valium /ˈvælɪəm/ *n* (*propr*) **(a)** [U] drug used to reduce stress and nervous tension. **(b)** [C] (*pl* unchanged or **~s**) tablet of this.

Valkyrie /ˈvælkɪrɪ, vælˈkɪərɪ/ *n* (in Scandinavian mythology) any of a group of twelve women who serve the god Odin and take heroes who die in battle to *Valhalla.

valley /ˈvælɪ/ *n* **1** stretch of land between hills or mountains, often with a river flowing through it. ⇨ illus at MOUNTAIN.
River valleys are generally regarded as rather picturesque and typical features of the British countryside. John *Constable's *Dedham Vale*, showing the wide valley of the river Stour in Essex, is a typical portrayal of this type of scenery. **2** region drained by a river: *the Nile valley.*

Valois /ˈvælwɑː/ Ninette de (1898-), British dancer, teacher and choreographer. The company she founded in 1931 became the Royal Ballet in 1956. Her ballets include *The Rake's Progress*, set to music by *Stravinsky.

valour (*US* **valor**) /ˈvælə(r)/ *n* **1** [U] (*rhet*) bravery, esp in war: *display great valour* ○ *soldiers decorated* (ie given awards) *for valour.* **2** (idm) **discretion is the better part of valour** ⇨ DISCRETION.

valuable /ˈvæljʊəbl/ *adj* **1** worth a lot of money: *a valuable collection of paintings.* **2** very useful or worthwhile or important: *valuable advice, help, information, etc* ○ *wasting valuable time and effort* ○ *The jawbone was our most valuable find/discovery.* ⇨ Usage at INVALUABLE.
▷ **valuables** *n* [pl] valuable things, esp small personal possessions, jewellery, etc: *recover stolen valuables.*

valuation /ˌvæljʊˈeɪʃn/ *n* **1 (a)** [C, U] act of estimating, esp professionally, the financial value of sth: *property, land, stock, etc valuation* ○ *Surveyors carried out a valuation on/of our house.* **(b)** [C] financial value that is estimated in this way: *have a valuation made of one's jewellery* ○ *Experts put/set a high valuation on the painting.* **2** [U] (*fig*) estimation of a person's merit: *take/accept sb at his own valuation*, ie according to his own opinion of himself.

value /ˈvæljuː/ *n* **1 (a)** [C, U] worth of sth in terms of money or other goods for which it can be exchanged: *a decline in the value of the dollar, pound, etc* ○ *pay above/below the market value for sth* ○ *rising share, land, property values* ○ *gain, appreciate, go up, etc in value* ○ *drop, fall, go down, etc in value* ○ *order software to the value of £700.* **(b)** [U] worth of sth compared with the price paid for it: *This tea is good value at 39p a packet.* ○ *Charter flights give/offer the best value for (your) money.* **2** [U] quality of being useful or worthwhile or important: *the value of regular exercise* ○ *be of great, little, some, no, etc value to sb* ○ *have a high novelty, street, entertainment value* ○ *have a high energy, nutritional value* ○ *the news value of a royal romance.* **3 values** [pl] moral or professional standards of behaviour; principles: *artistic, legal, scientific values* ○ *a return to Victorian values* ○ *the values of justice and democracy* ○ *hold, respect, adopt, etc a set of values.* **4 (a)** [C] (*mathematics*) number or quantity represented by a letter: *find the value of x.* **(b)** [C] (*music*) full time indicated by a note: *Give the semibreve its full value.* **(c)** [U] (in language) meaning; effect: *use a word with all its poetic value.* **(d)** [C] (in art) relation of light and shade: *tone values in a painting.* Cf FACE VALUE (FACE[1]).
▷ **value** *v* **1** [Tn, Tn·pr] **~ sth (at sth)** estimate the money value of sth: *He valued the house for me at £80 000.* **2** [Tn, Cn·n/a] **~ sth/sb (as sth)** (not used in the continuous tenses) have a high opinion of sth/sb: *value sb's advice* ○ *value truth above all else* ○ *a valued client, customer, etc* ○ *Do you value her as a friend?* **valuer** *n* person whose job is to estimate the money value of property, land, etc.
valueless *adj* without value or effect; worthless. ⇨ Usage at INVALUABLE.
□ ˌ**value ˈadded tax** (*abbr* **VAT**) tax on the rise in value of a product at each stage of its manufacture.
ˈ**value judgement** (*derog*) estimate of moral, artistic, etc worth based on personal assessment rather than objective fact: *make value judgements.*

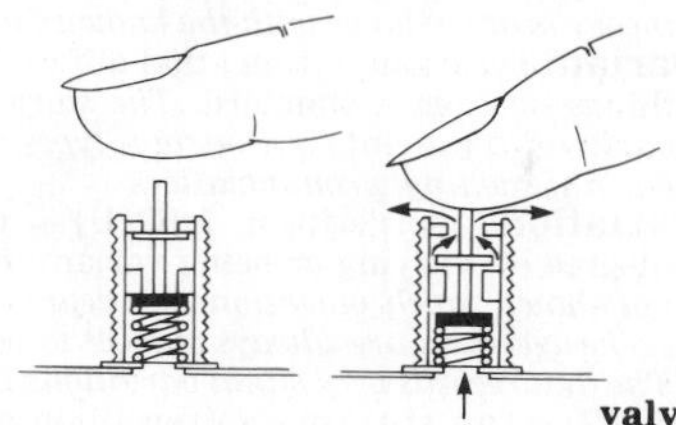
valve

valve /vælv/ *n* **1** mechanical device for controlling the flow of air, liquid or gas in one direction only: *the inlet/outlet valves of a petrol or steam engine* ○ *the valve of a bicycle tyre* ○ *a safety, exhaust valve.* ⇨ illus at BICYCLE. Cf TAP[1] 1. **2** structure in the heart or in a blood-vessel allowing the blood to flow in one direction only. ⇨ illus at HEART. **3** device in certain brass musical instruments, eg cornets, for changing the pitch by changing the length of the column of air. ⇨ illus at MUSIC. **4** (*biology*) each half of the hinged shell of oysters, mussels, etc. Cf BIVALVE. **5** = VACUUM TUBE.
▷ **valvular** /ˈvælvjʊlə(r)/ *adj* of valves, esp those regulating the flow of blood: *a valvular disease of the heart.*

vamoose /vəˈmuːs/ *v* [I] (*dated US infml*) (often imperative) go away quickly.

vamp[1] /væmp/ *n* upper front part of a boot or shoe.

vamp[2] /væmp/ *v* **1** [I, Tn] (*esp derog*) improvise (a basic tune or accompaniment), esp on the piano. **2** (phr v) **vamp sth up** (*infml*) make sth new from old or existing material: *vamp up some lectures out of/from old notes.*

vamp[3] /væmp/ *n* (*dated infml*) (esp in the 1920s and 1930s) seductive woman using her attractions to exploit men.
▷ **vamp** *v* [I, Tn] exploit or flirt with (a man) unscrupulously.

vampire /ˈvæmpaɪə(r)/ *n* **1** reanimated corpse believed by some to leave its grave at night and suck the blood of living people. **2** ruthless person who preys on others. **3** (also ˈ**vampire bat**) any of various types of bloodsucking bat from Central and S America.

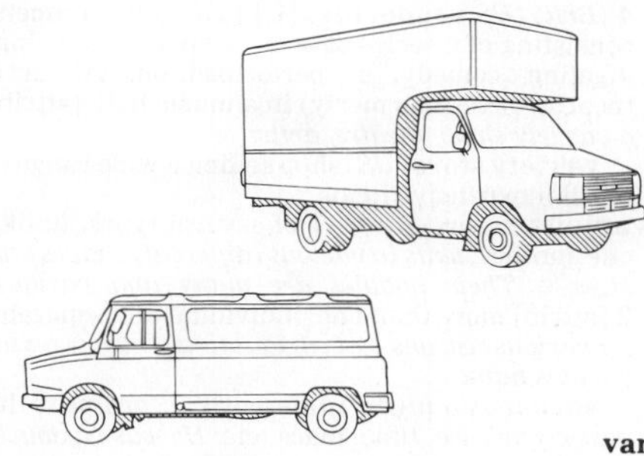
van

van[1] /væn/ *n* **1** covered vehicle, with no side windows, for transporting goods or people: *the* ˈ*baker's van* ○ *a* ˈ*furniture/re*ˈ*moval van* ○ *a po*ˈ*lice van*, ie for transporting police or prisoners ○ [attrib] *a* ˈ*van driver.* **2** (*Brit*) closed railway carriage for luggage, mail or goods, or for the use of the guard: *the* ˈ*luggage van* ○ *the* ˈ*guard's van.*

van[2] /væn/ *n* **the van** [sing] (*dated*) vanguard or forefront of an army or fleet: *positioned in the van.*

vanadium /ˌvəˈneɪdɪəm/ *n* [U] (*symb* **V**) hard whitish metallic element sometimes used in steel alloys. ⇨ App 11.

Van Allen belt /væn ˈælən belt/ either of two regions of intense radiation surrounding the earth, consisting of charged particles trapped within the earth's magnetic field.

Blenheim Palace, designed by Sir John Vanbrugh

Vanbrugh /ˈvænbrə/ Sir John (1664-1726), English architect and playwright. After writing a number of Restoration comedies, including *The Relapse*, he turned to architecture; his masterpiece is *Blenheim Palace. ⇨ illus. ⇨ article at ARCHITECTURE.

V and A /ˌviː ən ˈeɪ/ **the V and A** *abbr* (*Brit infml*) the Victoria and Albert Museum.

Vandal /ˈvændl/ *n* member of a Germanic people who conquered parts of Europe in the 4th-5th centuries AD. They established kingdoms in Gaul and Spain and destroyed Rome in 455.

vandal /ˈvændl/ *n* person who wilfully destroys or damages works of art, public and private property, the beauties of nature, etc: *telephone vandals*, ie vandals who damage public phone boxes.
▷ **vandalism** /-dəlɪzəm/ *n* [U] behaviour characteristic of vandals.
vandalize, -ise /-dəlaɪz/ *v* [Tn esp passive] wilfully destroy or damage (eg public property): *vandalize a train compartment, public convenience, lift* ○ *The ground-floor flats had been badly vandalized.*

Van de Graaff generator /ˌvæn də grɑːf ˈdʒenəreɪt(r)/ machine used to produce a high voltage. An endless belt collects an electric charge from needle points at the bottom end connected to a source of voltage. The belt carries the charge to other needle points at the top which are connected to a metal dome, so increasing the dome's voltage.

Van Dyck /væn ˈdaɪk/ Sir Anthony (1599-1641), Flemish artist. He was a pupil of *Rubens and became court painter to *Charles I, producing portraits showing court figures in elegant but casual poses.
▷ **Vandyke** /ˈvændaɪk/ *adj* [attrib] of or in the style of the figures in Van Dyck's portraits: *a Vandyke beard*, ie pointed and neatly trimmed.

vane /veɪn/ *n* **1** arrow or pointer on the top of a building, turned by the wind so as to show its direction. **2** blade of a propeller, sail of a windmill, or a similar device with a flat surface acted on or moved by wind or water.

Van Eyck /væn ˈaɪk/ Jan (1390-1441), Flemish painter. He was one of the earliest artists to master the techniques of oil painting and perspective. His works include the altar-piece of Ghent cathedral and the portrait *Giovanni Arnolfini and his Wife.*

Van Gogh /væn ˈgɒf/ Vincent (1853-90), Dutch artist. After working in art galleries and as a lay preacher, he became a painter in the last ten years of his life. He was influenced by the *Impressionists and Japanese woodcuts, and worked for a time with *Gauguin, but developed his own unique style with a bold use of colour, often in an expressive rather than a realistic way. He suffered from severe depression which finally led him to suicide.

vanguard /ˈvængɑːd/ *n* **the vanguard** [sing] **1** leading part of an advancing army or fleet. **2** (*fig*) leaders of a movement or fashion: *researchers in the vanguard of scientific progress.*

Cf REARGUARD (REAR[1]).

vanilla /vəˈnɪlə/ *n* **1** [C] tropical orchid with sweet-smelling flowers: [attrib] *a vanilla pod*, ie the fruit of this orchid. **2** [U] flavouring obtained from dried vanilla pods or a synthetic product resembling this: [attrib] *vanilla ice-cream, essence.*

vanish /ˈvænɪʃ/ *v* [I] (**a**) disappear completely and suddenly: *The thief vanished into the crowd.* ○ *vanish into thin air*, ie completely. (**b**) (*fig*) cease to exist or fade away: *My prospects/hopes of success have vanished.*

□ **ˈvanishing cream** cosmetic cream for the skin, esp of the face, which leaves no traces when it is rubbed into the skin.

ˈvanishing-point *n* [sing] (in perspective) point at which all parallel lines in the same plane appear to meet: (*fig*) *Our morale had almost reached vanishing-point*, ie disappeared.

vanity /ˈvænətɪ/ *n* **1** [U] having too high an opinion of one's looks, abilities, etc; conceit: *not a trace of vanity in her behaviour* ○ *tickle sb's vanity*, ie do or say sth that flatters him ○ *injured vanity*, ie resentment caused by some slight or humiliation. **2** (*fml*) (**a**) [U] quality of being unsatisfying or futile; worthlessness: *the vanity of human achievements.* (**b**) **vanities** [pl] vain worthless thing or act.

□ **ˈvanity bag**, **ˈvanity case** woman's small bag or case for carrying cosmetics, toilet articles, etc.

vanquish /ˈvæŋkwɪʃ/ *v* [Tn, Tn·pr] ~ **sb** (**at/in sth**) (*fml*) defeat (an opponent, etc): *vanquish the enemy in battle* ○ (*fig*) *vanquish one's rival at chess, tennis, etc.*

vantage /ˈvɑːntɪdʒ; *US* ˈvæn-/ *n* **1** [U] position, etc that gives sb superiority or advantage: *a point of vantage.* **2** [C] (in tennis) first point scored after deuce. **3** (idm) **a coign of vantage** ⇨ COIGN.

□ **ˈvantage-point** *n* position from which one has a good or advantageous view of sth: *From their vantage-point on the cliff, they could watch the ships coming and going.* ○ (*fig*) *the war, seen from the vantage-point of the 1980s.*

Vanuatu /ˌvænuːˈætuː/ group of islands in the SW Pacific, an independent state and member of the Commonwealth; pop approx 142 000; official languages English and French; capital Vila; unit of currency vatu. The islands are generally mountainous and the main crop is copra. Formerly known as the New Hebrides, they became independent in 1980. ⇨ map at MELANESIA.

vapid /ˈvæpɪd/ *adj* (*fml*) dull or uninteresting: *vapid utterances, remarks, comments, etc* ○ *His conversation was vapid in the extreme.*

▷ **vapidity** /vəˈpɪdətɪ/ *n* (*fml*) (**a**) [U] state of being vapid. (**b**) [C] vapid remark.

vaporize, **-ise** /ˈveɪpəraɪz/ *v* [I, Tn] (cause sth to) become vapour.

▷ **vaporization**, **-isation** /ˌveɪpəraɪˈzeɪʃn; *US* -rɪˈz-/ *n* [U].

vaporizer, **-iser** *n* pressurized container for sending out liquid in the form of a vapour.

vaporous /ˈveɪpərəs/ *adj* (*fml*) full of or like vapour: *vaporous clouds of mist, smoke, steam.*

vapour (*US* **vapor**) /ˈveɪpə(r)/ *n* **1** [C, U] moisture or other substance spread about or hanging in the air: *the steamy vapours of a Turkish bath.* **2** [U] gaseous form into which certain liquid or solid substances can be converted by heating: *ˈwater vapour.* **3 the vapours** [pl] (*arch or joc*) sudden feeling of faintness: *have/get (an attack of) the vapours.*

□ **ˈvapour trail** (also **ˌcondenˈsation trail**) trail of condensed water left in the sky by a high-flying aircraft.

variable /ˈveərɪəbl/ *adj* **1** varying; changeable: *variable pressure, rainfall, weather, speed* ○ *Winds are mainly light and variable.* ○ *His mood/temper is variable.* ○ *The quality of the hotel food is distinctly variable.* **2** (*astronomy*) (of a star) periodically varying in brightness.

▷ **variable** *n* (often *pl*) variable thing or quantity: *With so many variables, the exact cost is difficult to estimate.* ○ *Temperature was a variable in the experiment.* Cf CONSTANT *n*.

variability /ˌveərɪəˈbɪlətɪ/ *n* [U] quality of being variable; tendency to vary.

variably /-əblɪ/ *adv*.

variance /ˈveərɪəns/ *n* **1** (*US*) official permission to do sth which is normally against the law or regulations: *issue a variance.* **2** (idm) **at variance** (**with sb/sth**) (*fml*) disagreeing or having a difference of opinion (with sb); in conflict (with sth): *Jill and Sue are at variance (with each other) over/about their lodger.* ○ *set people at variance (among themselves)*, ie make them quarrel ○ *This theory is at variance with the known facts.*

variant /ˈveərɪənt/ *n* thing that differs from other things or from a standard: *The story has many variants.* ○ [attrib] *forty variant types of pigeon* ○ *variant spelling, pronunciation.*

variation /ˌveərɪˈeɪʃn/ *n* **1** [C, U] ~ (**in/of sth**) (degree of) varying or being variant: *Prices have not shown much variation this year.* ○ *Currency exchange rates are always subject to variation.* ○ *The dial records very slight variations in pressure.* **2** [C] ~ (**on sth**) (*music*) repetition of a simple melody in a different (and usu more complicated) form: *a set of variations on a theme by Mozart* ○ *piano, orchestral, etc variations* ○ (*fig*) *His numerous complaints are all variations on a theme*, ie about the same thing. **3** (**a**) [U] (*biology*) change in structure or form caused by new conditions, environment, etc. (**b**) [U] (*mathematics*) change in a function, etc due to small changes in the values of constants. (**c**) [C] instance of such change.

varicose /ˈværɪkəʊs/ *adj* [esp attrib] (of a vein, esp in the leg) permanently swollen or enlarged and therefore painful: *varicose ulcers*, ie caused by the condition of the veins.

varied /ˈveərɪd/ *adj* **1** of different sorts; diverse: *varied opinions, scenes, menus* ○ *Holiday jobs are many and varied.* **2** showing changes or variety: *lead a full and varied life* ○ *My experience is not sufficiently varied.*

variegated /ˈveərɪgeɪtɪd/ *adj* marked irregularly with differently coloured patches, streaks, spots, etc: *variegated geranium leaves, pansy flowers, etc* ○ *This specimen is richly variegated in colour.*

▷ **variegation** /ˌveərɪˈgeɪʃn/ *n* [U] such irregular colouring or marking.

variety /vəˈraɪətɪ/ *n* **1** [U] quality of not being the same, or not being the same at all times: *offer, show, lack variety* ○ *a life full of change and variety* ○ *We all need variety in our diet.* **2** [sing] ~ (**of sth**) number or range of different things; assortment: *He left for a variety of reasons.* ○ *a large/wide variety of patterns to choose from.* **3** [C] ~ (**of sth**) (**a**) (member of a) class of things that differ from others in the same general group: *collect rare varieties of stamps.* (**b**) (*biology*) subdivision of a species: *several varieties of lettuce, mosquito, deer.* **4** (*Brit*) (*US* **vaudeville**) [U] light entertainment consisting of a series of acts, eg singing, dancing, juggling, comedy, as performed on TV, at a theatre, or (esp formerly) in a music-hall: [attrib] *a vaˈriety show, theatre, artist.*

□ **vaˈriety store** (*US*) shop selling a wide range of small inexpensive items.

various /ˈveərɪəs/ *adj* **1** of several types, unlike one another: *tents in various (different) shapes and sizes* ○ *Their hobbies are many and various.* **2** [attrib] more than one; individual and separate: *for various reasons* ○ *at various times* ○ *write under various names.*

▷ **variously** *adv* (*fml*) differently according to the particular case, time, place, etc: *He was variously described as a hero, a genius and a fool.*

varmint /ˈvɑːmɪnt/ *n* (*US infml*) person, usu a man or boy, considered to be troublesome or untrustworthy: *Clear off, you young/little varmint!*

varnish /ˈvɑːnɪʃ/ *n* [U, C] **1** (**a**) hard shiny transparent coating applied to the surface of esp woodwork or metalwork: *a cover, coat, film, etc of varnish* ○ *scratch, chip, scrape, etc the varnish on a table.* (**b**) (particular type of) liquid used to give such a coating: *a natural, a gloss, an oak, a polyurethane varnish.* Cf LACQUER 1. **2** (*esp Brit*) = NAIL VARNISH (NAIL).

▷ **varnish** *v* [Tn] put varnish on (sth): *a highly varnished table-top* ○ *sand and varnish a chair* ○ *varnish an oil-painting* ○ *Some women varnish their toe-nails.*

varsity /ˈvɑːsətɪ/ *n* **1** (*dated Brit infml*) (not used in names) university, esp Oxford or Cambridge: [attrib] *a varsity tie, match, dinner.* **2** (*US*) team representing a university, college or school, esp in sports competitions. ⇨ article at POST-SCHOOL.

vary /ˈveərɪ/ *v* (*pt, pp* **varied**) **1** [I, Ipr] ~ (**in sth**) be different in size, volume, strength, etc: *These fish vary in weight from 3 lb to 5 lb.* ○ *Opinions vary on this point.* ○ *The results of the experiment varied wildly.* **2** [I, Ipr] ~ (**with sth**); ~ (**from sth to sth**) change, esp according to some factor: *Our routine never varies.* ○ *Prices vary with the seasons.* ○ *Her mood varied from optimism to extreme depression.* ○ *work with varying degrees of enthusiasm.* ⇨ Usage at CHANGE[1]. **3** [Tn] make (sth) different by introducing changes: *vary a programme, route* ○ *varying the pace/speed at which you work.*

Vasari /vəˈsɑːrɪ; *US* vəˈzɑːrɪ/ Giorgio (1511-74), Italian painter, architect and writer. He designed important buildings in Renaissance *Florence, including the *Uffizi, but he is best known for his *Lives of the Painters*, a history of Italian art up till his own time.

vascular /ˈvæskjʊlə(r)/ *adj* of or containing vessels or ducts through which blood or lymph flows in animals or sap in plants: *vascular tissue.*

vas deferens /væs ˈdefərenz/ *n* (*pl* **vasa deferentia** /ˌveɪsə defəˈrentʃə/) tube carrying sperm from the testicles to the penis. ⇨ illus at MALE.

vase /vɑːz; *US* veɪs, *also* veɪz/ *n* vessel without handles, usu made of glass, china, etc and used for holding cut flowers or as an ornament.

vasectomy /vəˈsektəmɪ/ *n* surgical removal of part of each of the ducts through which semen passes from the testicles, esp as a method of birth control.

Vaseline /ˈvæsəliːn/ *n* [U] (*propr*) yellowish petroleum jelly used as an ointment or a lubricant.

vassal /ˈvæsl/ *n* **1** (in the Middle Ages) man promising to fight for and be loyal to a king or lord in return for the right to hold land. **2** (*fig*) person or nation dependent on another: [attrib] *vassal states, kingdoms, etc.* ▷ **vassalage** /ˈvæsəlɪdʒ/ *n* [U]: *reduce a dukedom to vassalage.*

vast /vɑːst; *US* væst/ *adj* [usu attrib] **1** very large in area, size, quantity or degree; immense: *a vast expanse of desert, water, snow, etc* ○ *His business empire was truly vast.* ○ *a vast crowd, throng, gathering, etc.* **2** (*infml*) very great: *a vast fortune, expense, profit, sum of money, etc* ○ *a vast difference.*

▷ **vastly** *adv* (*esp infml*) very greatly: *a vastly superior intellect* ○ *be vastly amused, suspicious.*

vastness *n* [U, C]: *lost in the vastness(es) of space.*

VAT (also **Vat**) /ˌviː eɪ ˈtiː, *also* væt/ *abbr* value added tax: *Prices include 15% VAT.*

vat /væt/ *n* tank or large container for holding liquids, esp in distilling, brewing, dyeing and tanning.

Vatican /ˈvætɪkən/ *n* **the Vatican** (**a**) [sing] the Pope's residence in Rome. (**b**) [Gp] papal government.

Vatican City /ˌvætɪkən ˈsɪtɪ/ **the Vatican City** small independent state contained within the city of *Rome. The government of the Roman Catholic Church is based there and it has its own administrative structure separate from that of Italy.

vaudeville /ˈvɔːdəvɪl/ *n* [U] (*US*) = VARIETY 4. ⇨ article at MUSIC.

Vaughan Williams /ˌvɔːn ˈwɪljəmz/ Ralph (1872-1958), English composer. He led the revival of English music after *Elgar, and was deeply influenced by his country's folk and traditional music. Besides his orchestral works, including nine symphonies, he produced much fine vocal and choral music.

vault[1] /vɔːlt/ *n* **1** arched roof; series of arches forming a roof: *fan vaulting*, ie vaults where the arches have ribs, like a fan. ⇨ illus at CHURCH. **2** (**a**) cellar or underground room used for storing things at a cool temperature: ˈ*wine-vaults*. (**b**) similar room beneath a church or in a cemetery, used for burials: *in the family vault*. **3** similar room, esp in a bank and protected by locks, alarms, thick walls, etc, used for keeping valuables safe. **4** covering like an arched roof: (*rhet*) *the vault of heaven*, ie the sky.

▷ **vaulted** *adj* having a vault or vaults; built in the form of a vault: *a vaulted roof, chamber, etc.*

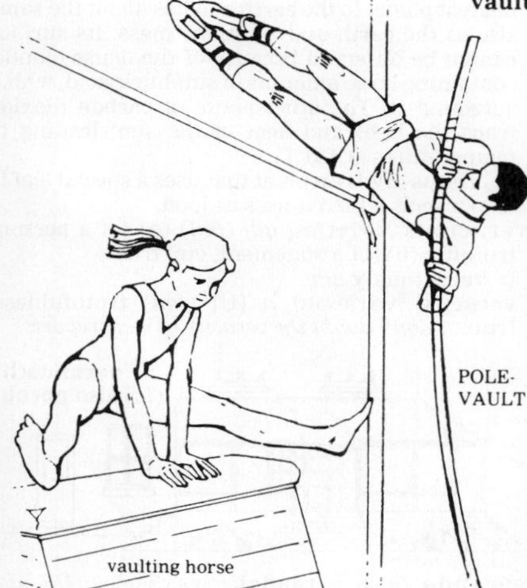

vault[2] /vɔːlt/ *v* [I, Ipr] ~ (**over sth**) jump in a single movement over or onto an object with the hand(s) resting on it or with the help of a pole: *vault (over) a fence* ○ *The jockey vaulted lightly into the saddle.* ○ (*fig fml*) *vaulting* (ie boundless, overreaching) *ambition*.

▷ **vault** *n* jump made in this way.

vaulter *n* (esp in compounds) person who vaults: *a pole-vaulter*.

□ ˈ**vaulting horse** wooden apparatus for practice in vaulting. ⇨ illus.

vaunt /vɔːnt/ *v* [Tn] (*fml derog*) boast about (sth); draw attention to (sth) in a conceited way: *The bank's much-vaunted security system failed completely.* ○ *vaunting her charm, success, wealth for all to see.* ▷ **vauntingly** *adv*.

VC /ˌviː ˈsiː/ *abbr* **1** Vice-Chairman. **2** Vice-Chancellor. **3** Vice-Consul. **4** (*Brit*) Victoria Cross: *be awarded the VC* ○ *Col James Blunt VC.* Cf GC.

VCR /ˌviː siː ˈɑː(r)/ *abbr* video cassette recorder.

VD /ˌviː ˈdiː/ *abbr* venereal disease.

VDU /ˌviː diː ˈjuː/ *abbr* (*computing*) visual display unit: *check a file on the VDU* ○ *a VDU operator.* ⇨ illus at COMPUTER.

veal /viːl/ *n* [U] flesh of a calf used as meat: [attrib] *veal cutlets*.

vector /ˈvektə(r)/ *n* **1** (*mathematics*) quantity that has both magnitude and direction, eg velocity. Cf SCALAR. **2** (*biology*) organism, (esp an insect) that transmits a particular disease or infection. Cf CARRIER 4. **3** compass direction, esp as followed by an aircraft.

Veda /ˈveɪdə/ *n* any of the ancient scriptures of Hinduism, composed in Sanskrit, of which the most famous is the Rig-Veda.

▷ **Vedic** /ˈveɪdɪk/ *adj*: *Vedic religion.* — *n* [U] language of the Vedas.

VE day /ˌviː ˈiː deɪ/ Victory in Europe day, 8 May 1945, when fighting in Europe ended in the Second World War.

veer /vɪə(r)/ *v* **1** (**a**) [I, Ipr, Ip] (esp of a vehicle) change direction or course: *The plane veered wildly.* ○ *The car suddenly veered off the road.* ○ *The wind has veered round.* (**b**) [Ipr] (*fig*) (of a conversation, sb's behaviour or opinion) change suddenly or very noticeably: *The discussion veered away from religion and round to politics.* **2** [I, Ipr, Ip] (of the wind) change gradually in a clockwise direction in the northern hemisphere and an anti-clockwise direction in the southern hemisphere: *The wind veered (round to the) north.* Cf BACK[4] 7.

veg /vedʒ/ *n* [U, C] (*pl* unchanged) (*Brit infml*) vegetable(s): *meat and two veg*.

Vega /ˈviːɡə/ brightest star in the constellation Lyra. The tiny particles around it may eventually form into planets.

vegan /ˈviːɡən/ *n* strict vegetarian who neither eats nor uses any animal products, eg eggs, silk, leather: [attrib] *a vegan diet, restaurant, fruit-cake*.

vegetable /ˈvedʒtəbl/ *n* **1** (part of various types of) plant eaten as food, eg potatoes, beans, onions: *green vegetables*, ie cabbage, lettuce, Brussels sprouts, etc ○ *a salad of raw vegetables* ○ [attrib] *a vegetable curry, garden, knife* ○ *vegetable oils*, eg in margarine. Cf ANIMAL, MINERAL. **2** (*fig*) (**a**) person who is physically alive but mentally inactive because of injury, illness or abnormality: *Severe brain damage turned him into a vegetable.* ○ [attrib] *lead a vegetable existence*. (**b**) person who has a dull monotonous life: *Stuck at home like this, she felt like a vegetable.*

□ ˌ**vegetable** ˈ**marrow** (*fml*) = MARROW[2].

vegetal /ˈvedʒɪtl/ *adj* of or like plants.

vegetarian /ˌvedʒɪˈteərɪən/ *n* person who, for humane, religious or health reasons, eats no meat: [attrib] *a vegetarian meal, diet, restaurant.* Cf VEGAN.

▷ **vegetarianism** /-ɪzəm/ *n* [U] practice or philosophy of being a vegetarian.

vegetate /ˈvedʒɪteɪt/ *v* [I] (*fig*) live a dull life with little activity or interest: *the unemployed vegetating at home*.

vegetation /ˌvedʒɪˈteɪʃn/ *n* [U] plants in general; those found in a particular environment: *There is little vegetation in the desert.* ○ *the luxuriant vegetation of tropical rain forests.*

vegetative /ˈvedʒɪtətɪv; *US* ˈvedʒəteɪtɪv/ *adj* **1** characterized by growth and development rather than sexual reproduction: *vegetative propagation.* **2** (*derog*) (eg of a person's life) having little excitement or interest.

vehement /ˈviːəmənt/ *adj* showing or caused by strong feeling; passionate: *a vehement objection, protest, denial, attack, etc* ○ *a vehement urge, impulse, desire, etc* ○ *He slammed the door with a vehement* (ie furious) *gesture.* ▷ **vehemence** /-məns/ *n* [U]. **vehemently** *adv*: *The charge was vehemently denied.*

vehicle /ˈvɪəkl; *US* ˈviːhɪkl/ *n* **1** (*esp fml*) conveyance such as a car, lorry or cart used for transporting goods or passengers on land: *motor vehicles*, ie cars, buses, motor cycles, etc ○ [attrib] *vehicle licensing laws*, eg for motor vehicles ○ *a space vehicle*, ie for carrying people into space. **2** substance in which another substance is suspended, esp the oil, water, etc in which the pigment is suspended in paint. **3** ~ (**for sth**) (*fig*) means by which thought, feeling, etc can be expressed: *Art may be used as a vehicle for propaganda.* ○ *The play was an excellent vehicle for this actress's talents.*

▷ **vehicular** /vɪˈhɪkjʊlə(r)/ *adj* (*fml*) intended for or consisting of vehicles: *vehicular access* ○ *The road is closed to vehicular traffic.*

veil /veɪl/ *n* **1** [C] (**a**) covering of fine net or other (usu transparent) material worn, esp by women, to protect or hide the face, or as part of a head-dress: *a bridal veil* ○ *She raised/lowered her veil.* (**b**) piece of linen, etc covering the head and sometimes the shoulders, esp of nuns. **2** [sing] (*fig*) thing that hides or disguises: *a veil of mist over the hills* ○ *plot under the veil of secrecy, innocence.* **3** (idm) **draw a curtain/veil over sth** ⇨ DRAW[2]. **take the** ˈ**veil** become a nun.

▷ **veil** *v* [Tn] **1** put a veil over (sb/sth): *a veiled Muslim woman.* **2** (*fig*) hide or disguise (sth): *a thinly veiled threat, insult, hint, etc* ○ *He could hardly veil his contempt at my ignorance.*

vein /veɪn/ *n* **1** [C] any of the tubes carrying blood from all parts of the body to the heart: *Royal blood ran in his veins.* Cf ARTERY. **2** [C] any of the thread-like lines forming the framework of a leaf or of an insect's wing. **3** [C] narrow strip or streak of a different colour in some types of stone, eg marble, or in some cheeses. **4** [C] crack or fissure in rock, filled with mineral or ore; seam: *a vein of gold.* **5** [sing] ~ (**of sth**) (*fig*) distinctive feature or quality; streak: *have a vein of melancholy in one's character* ○ *Her stories struck/revealed a rich vein of humour.* **6** [sing] manner or style; mood: *in a sad, comic, creative, etc vein* ○ *The complaints continued in the same vein.*

▷ **veined** /veɪnd/, **veiny** /ˈveɪnɪ/ *adjs* marked with or having veins: *a veined hand* ○ *veined marble* ○ *blue-veined cheese*, eg Stilton.

velar /ˈviːlə(r)/ *adj* (*phonetics*) (of a speech sound) made by placing the back of the tongue against or near the soft palate.

▷ **velar** *n* velar speech sound (eg /k/, /ɡ/).

Velásquez /vɪˈlæskwɪz; *US* vəˈlɑːzkəs/ Diego Rodríguez de Silva y (1599-1660), Spanish artist. He became court painter to Philip IV of Spain and produced many portraits of the royal family and other court figures, introducing an element of informality characteristic in his work.

velcro (also **Velcro**) /ˈvelkrəʊ/ *n* [U] (*propr*) fastener for clothes, etc consisting of two nylon strips, one rough and one smooth, which stick together when pressed.

veld (also **veldt**) /velt/ *n* [U] flat treeless open grassland of the S African plateau. Cf PAMPAS, PRAIRIE, SAVANNAH, STEPPE.

vellum /ˈveləm/ *n* [U] **1** fine parchment or bookbinding material made from calf, kid or lamb skin. **2** smooth fine-quality writing-paper.

velocity /vɪˈlɒsətɪ/ *n* **1** [U, C] (*esp physics*) (usu of inanimate things) speed, esp in a given direction: *gain/lose velocity* ○ *the velocity of a projectile.* **2** [U] (*fml*) quickness or swiftness: *Gazelles can move with astonishing velocity.*

velour (also **velours**) /vəˈlʊə(r)/ *n* [U] woven fabric like velvet or felt: [attrib] *velour chair-covers, coats, hats*.

velvet /ˈvelvɪt/ *n* [U] **1** woven fabric, esp of silk or nylon, with a thick soft nap on one side: [attrib] *a velvet jacket, curtain.* **2** (idm) **an iron fist/hand in a velvet glove** ⇨ IRON[1]. **smooth as velvet** ⇨ SMOOTH[1].

▷ **velvety** *adj* (*approv*) soft like velvet: *a horse's velvety nose* ○ *her velvety brown eyes.*

velveteen /ˌvelvɪˈtiːn/ *n* [U] cotton fabric with a nap like velvet.

venal /ˈviːnl/ *adj* (*fml*) **1** ready to accept money for doing sth dishonest: *venal judges, politicians, etc.* **2** (of conduct) influenced by or done for bribery: *venal practices.*

▷ **venality** /viːˈnælətɪ/ *n* [U] quality of being venal.

venally /-nəlɪ/ *adv*.

vend /vend/ *v* [Tn] (*esp law*) offer (esp small articles) for sale. ⇨ Usage at SELL.

▷ **vendee** /venˈdiː/ *n* (*law*) person to whom sth is sold.

vendor /-də(r)/ *n* **1** (esp in compounds) person who sells food or other small items from a stall in the open air: ˈ*street vendors* ○ ˈ*news-vendors*, ie newspaper sellers. **2** (*law*) seller of a house or other property. Cf PURCHASER (PURCHASE[2]).

□ ˈ**vending-machine** *n* coin-operated slot machine for the sale of small items, eg cigarettes, drinks, sandwiches.

vendetta /venˈdetə/ *n* **1** hereditary feud between families in which murders are committed in revenge for previous murders. **2** bitter long-standing quarrel: (*joc*) *wage a personal vendetta against the Post Office.*

veneer /vəˈnɪə(r)/ *n* **1** [C, U] (thin layer of) decorative wood or plastic glued to the surface of cheaper wood (for furniture, etc). **2** [sing] ~ **(of sth)** (*fig usu derog*) superficial appearance (of politeness, etc) covering or disguising the true nature of sb/sth: *a thin veneer of Western civilization.* Cf GLOSS[1] 2.

▷ **veneer** *v* [Tn, Tn·pr] ~ **sth (with sth)** put a veneer on (a surface): *veneer a deal desk with walnut.*

venerable /ˈvenərəbl/ *adj* **1** [usu attrib] (*fml*) deserving respect because of age, character, associations, etc: *a venerable scholar* ○ *the venerable ruins of the abbey.* **2** (*religion*) **(a)** (in the Church of England) title of an archdeacon. **(b)** (in the Roman Catholic Church) title of sb thought to be very holy but not yet made a saint. ▷ **venerability** /ˌvenərəˈbɪlətɪ/ *n* [U].

venerate /ˈvenəreɪt/ *v* [Tn] (*fml*) respect (sb/sth) deeply; regard as sacred: *venerate the memory, name, spirit, etc of Mozart.* ▷ **veneration** /ˌvenəˈreɪʃn/ *n* [U]: *The relics were objects of veneration/were held in veneration.*

venereal disease /vəˌnɪərɪəl dɪˈzi:z/ [C, U] (*abbr* **VD**) disease communicated by sexual contact, eg gonorrhea, syphilis.

Venetian /vəˈni:ʃn/ *adj* of Venice.

▷ **Venetian** *n* Venetian person.

□ **veˌnetian ˈblind** window screen made of horizontal wooden or plastic slats that can be adjusted to let in light and air as desired.

Venezuela

Venezuela /ˌvenɪˈzweɪlə/ country on the north coast of S America; pop approx 18 757 000; official language Spanish; capital Caracas; unit of currency bolivar (=100 centimos). The country is divided into the coastal region, the eastern mountains, the central plains and the highlands of the south-east. The main crops are maize, coffee and rice; livestock, fisheries and agriculture are also important. There are rich mineral resources, esp the oil which is Venezuela's main export. ⇨ map. ▷ **Venezuelan** /-n/ *n, adj.*

vengeance /ˈvendʒəns/ *n* **1** [U] ~ **(on/upon sb)** paying back of an injury that one has suffered; revenge: *take/seek/swear vengeance for the bombing.* **2** (idm) **with a ˈvengeance** (*infml*) to a greater degree than is normal, expected or desired: *set to work with a vengeance* ○ *The rain came down with a vengeance.*

vengeful /ˈvendʒfl/ *adj* (*fml*) showing a desire for revenge; vindictive. ▷ **vengefully** /-fəlɪ/ *adv.*

venial /ˈvi:nɪəl/ *adj* [esp attrib] (of a sin or fault) not serious; excusable.

Venice /ˈvenɪs/ city of NE Italy, Italian name **Venezia**. It is built on many islands in a lagoon on the Adriatic coast, with connecting bridges between them. In the Middle Ages, Venice had a powerful empire and was one of the great cultural centres of Italy. Its many artistic treasures and famous buildings like Saint Mark's cathedral attract large numbers of tourists, but it is also an important industrial city, with heavy industries as well as traditional crafts like glass-making. Venice continues to be in danger from pollution and the threat of flooding. Cf VENETIAN.

venison /ˈvenɪzn, ˈvenɪsn/ *n* [U] flesh of a deer used as meat: *roast venison.*

Venn diagram /ˈven daɪəgræm/ diagram used to show mathematical relationships in set theory (SET[1]). Rectangles and circles represent sets which enclose, overlap with or are separate from each other.

venom /ˈvenəm/ *n* [U] **1** poisonous fluid of certain snakes, scorpions, etc, injected by a bite or sting. **2** (*fig*) strong bitter feeling or language; hatred: *'You liar!' he said, with venom in his voice.*

▷ **venomous** /ˈvenəməs/ *adj* **1** (of a snake, etc) secreting venom. **2** (*fig*) full of bitter or spiteful feeling: *a venomous look, remark, insult, etc.* **venomously** *adv.*

venous /ˈvi:nəs/ *adj* **1** (*anatomy*) of or contained in the veins: *venous blood.* **2** (*botany*) having veins: *a venous leaf.*

vent[1] /vent/ *n* **1** opening that allows air, gas, liquid, etc to pass out of or into a confined space. **2** anus of a bird, fish, reptile or small mammal. **3** (idm) **give (full) vent to sth** express sth freely: *He gave vent to his feelings in an impassioned speech.*

▷ **vent** *v* [Tn, Tn·pr] ~ **sth (on sb)** find or provide an outlet for (an emotion): *He vented his anger on his long-suffering wife.*

□ **ˈvent light** small window, usu above a casement window, which opens from hinges at the top edge.

vent[2] /vent/ *n* slit at the bottom of the back or side seam of a coat or jacket.

ventilate /ˈventɪleɪt; *US* -təleɪt/ *v* [Tn] **1** cause air to enter and move freely through (a room, building, etc): *ventilate the galleries of a coal-mine* ○ *My office is well-/poorly-ventilated.* **2** (*fml fig*) make (a question, grievance, etc) widely known and cause it to be discussed: *These issues have been very well ventilated.*

▷ **ventilation** /ˌventɪˈleɪʃn; *US* -təˈleɪʃn/ *n* [U] **1** ventilating or being ventilated: *increase ventilation by opening the top centre part of the carriage window* ○ [attrib] *the ventilation shaft of a coal-mine.* **2** system or method by which a room, building, etc is ventilated: *The ventilation isn't working.*

ventilator /ˈventɪleɪtə(r); *US* -təl-/ *n* **1** device or opening for ventilating a room, etc. **2** machine used in medicine to pump air into and out of the lungs when a patient is unable to breathe normally.

ventral /ˈventrəl/ *adj* (*biology*) of or on the abdomen: *a fish's ventral fins.* ▷ **ventrally** /-trəlɪ/ *adv.* Cf DORSAL.

ventricle /ˈventrɪkl/ *n* (*anatomy*) **1** one of the two hollow chambers in the heart, whose function is to pump blood into the arteries. ⇨ illus at HEART, Cf AURICLE 2. **2** any of various cavities in the body, esp the four in the brain.

ventriloquism /venˈtrɪləkwɪzəm/ *n* [U] art of producing voice-sounds so that they seem to come from a person or place at a distance from the speaker.

▷ **ventriloquist** /-kwɪst/ *n* person skilled in this: *a ventriloquist's dummy.*

venture /ˈventʃə(r)/ *n* **1** project or undertaking, esp a commercial one where there is a risk of failure: *embark on a risky, doubtful, etc venture* ○ *The car-hire firm is their latest (joint) business venture.* ○ [attrib] *venture capital,* ie money invested in a new enterprise, esp a risky one. Cf ENTERPRISE 1. **2** (idm) **at a ˈventure** (*fml*) at random; by chance.

▷ **venture** *v* (*fml*) **1** [Ipr, Ip] dare to go (somewhere dangerous or unpleasant): *venture into the water, over the wall* ○ *venture too near the edge of a cliff* ○ *The mouse never ventured far from its hole.* ○ *I'm not venturing out in this rain.* **2** [Tn, Tt] **(a)** dare to say or utter (sth): *venture an opinion, objection, explanation* ○ *May I venture to suggest a change?* ○ *I venture to disagree.* **(b)** dare to do (sth dangerous or unpleasant): *venture a visit to the doctor/to visit the doctor.* **3** [Tn, Tn·pr] ~ **sth (on sth)** take the risk of losing or failing in sth: *I ventured a small bet on the horse.* **4** (idm) **nothing ˈventure, nothing ˈgain/ˈwin** (*saying*) one cannot expect to achieve anything if one risks nothing. **5** (phr v) **venture on/upon sth** dare to attempt sth: *venture on a trip up the Amazon.*

venturesome /-səm/ *adj* (*fml*) **(a)** (of people) ready to take risks; daring: *be of a venturesome spirit.* **(b)** (of acts or behaviour) involving danger; risky.

venue /ˈvenju:/ *n* place where people agree to meet, esp for a sports contest or match: *a last-minute change of venue.*

Venus /ˈvi:nəs/ *n* **1** (in Roman mythology) goddess of love and mother of *Aeneas, corresponding to the Greek goddess Aphrodite. **2** (*astronomy*) the planet second in order from the sun. It is the nearest planet to the earth and has about the same size as the earth and a similar mass. Its surface cannot be observed because of the dense clouds, containing large amounts of sulphuric acid, which surround it. The atmosphere of carbon dioxide traps the light and heat of the sun, leading to temperatures of 450° C.

□ **ˌVenus ˈfly-trap** plant that uses a special leaf to trap insects which it uses as food.

veracious /vəˈreɪʃəs/ *adj* (*fml*) **(a)** (of a person) truthful. **(b)** (of a statement, etc) true.

▷ **veraciously** *adv.*

veracity /vəˈræsətɪ/ *n* [U] (*fml*) truthfulness; truth: *I don't doubt the veracity of your report.*

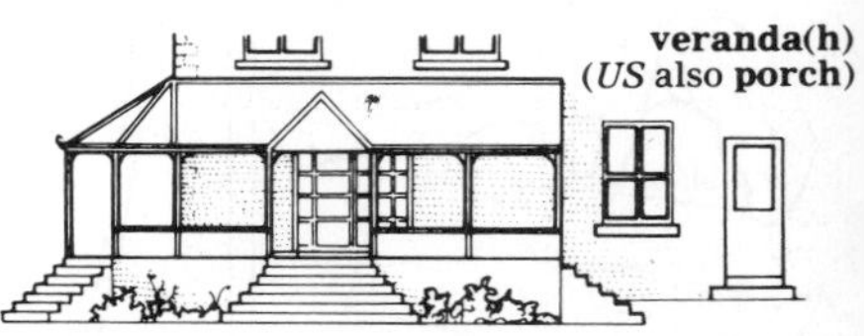

veranda(h) (*US* also **porch**)

veranda (also **verandah**) /vəˈrændə/ (*US* also **porch**) *n* roofed open-fronted terrace or platform which extends from the front, back or side(s) of a house, sports pavilion, etc: *sitting on the veranda.* Cf PATIO 1.

verb /vɜ:b/ *n* word or phrase indicating an action, an event or a state, eg *bring, happen, exist.*

verbal /ˈvɜ:bl/ *adj* **1** of or in words: *verbal skills,* ie reading and writing ○ *non-verbal communication,* ie gestures, facial expressions, etc. **2** spoken, not written: *a verbal explanation, agreement, warning, reminder, etc.* **3** word for word; literal: *a verbal translation.* **4** (*grammar*) of verbs: *a noun performing a verbal function.*

▷ **verbal** *n* (*Brit sl*) statement made to the police, esp by a person suspected of a crime.

verbally /ˈvɜ:bəlɪ/ *adv* in spoken words, not in writing.

□ **verbal ˈnoun** (also **gerund**) noun derived from a verb, eg *swimming* in the sentence *Swimming is a good form of exercise.*

verbalize, -ise /ˈvɜ:bəlaɪz/ *v* [I, Tn] (*fml*) put (ideas or feelings) into words: *find it difficult to verbalize.*

verbatim /vɜ:ˈbeɪtɪm/ *adj, adv* exactly as spoken or written; word for word: *a verbatim report* ○ *report a speech verbatim.*

verbena /vɜ:ˈbi:nə/ *n* type of herbaceous plant whose garden varieties have flowers of many colours.

verbiage /ˈvɜ:bɪɪdʒ/ *n* [U] (*fml derog*) (use of) too many words, or unnecessarily difficult words, to express an idea, etc: *The speaker lost himself in verbiage.* ○ *plough through the verbiage of an official report,* ie read it with difficulty.

verbose /vɜ:ˈbəʊs/ *adj* (*fml*) using or containing more words than are needed: *a verbose speaker, speech, style.*

▷ **verbosely** *adv.*
verbosity /vɜːˈbɒsətɪ/ *n* [U] (*fml*) state or quality of being verbose.

verdant /ˈvɜːdnt/ *adj* (*fml or rhet*) (of grass, vegetation, fields, etc) fresh and green: *verdant lawns* ○ *trees verdant with young leaves.* ▷ **verdancy** /-dnsɪ/ *n* [U].

Verdi /ˈveədɪ/ Giuseppe (1813-1901), Italian composer. His remarkable power of musical expression and characterization made him the great master of grand opera in works like *Rigoletto, Aida, La Traviata* and *Falstaff.* His commitment to the cause of Italian nationalism is apparent in some of his early operas like *Nabucco,* and the powerful *Requiem* was written as a tribute to the author and patriot Manzoni.

verdict /ˈvɜːdɪkt/ *n* **1** decision reached by a jury on a question of fact in a law case: *question/dispute a verdict* ○ *The jury returned/announced/brought in their verdict.* ○ *a verdict of guilty/not guilty* ○ *a majority verdict of 8 to 4.* **2** (*fig*) decision or opinion given after testing, examining or experiencing sth: *the verdict of the electors* ○ (*infml*) *My wife's verdict on my cooking was very favourable.*

verdigris /ˈvɜːdɪgrɪs, -griːs/ *n* [U] greenish-blue substance that forms on copper, brass and bronze surfaces (as rust forms on iron surfaces).

verdure /ˈvɜːdʒə(r)/ *n* [U] (*rhet*) **1** plants, trees, etc. **2** green colour of these.

verge /vɜːdʒ/ *n* **1** (a) = SOFT SHOULDER (SOFT): *Heavy lorries have damaged the grass verge.* (b) grass edging along a path or round a flower-bed, etc. **2** (idm) **on/to the verge of sth** at or close to the point where sth new begins or takes place: *on the verge of war, success, bankruptcy* ○ *Her misery brought her to the verge of tears.*
▷ **verge** *v* (phr v) **verge on sth** be very close or similar to sth; be approaching sth: *a situation verging on the ridiculous, tragic, chaotic, etc* ○ *He's verging on 80 now and needs constant attention.*

verger /ˈvɜːdʒə(r)/ *n* **1** Church of England official who acts as a caretaker and attendant in a church. **2** (*Brit*) official who carries a mace, etc before a bishop or other dignitary.

Vergil = VIRGIL.

verify /ˈverɪfaɪ/ *v* (*pt, pp* **-fied**) **1** [Tn, Tf, Tw] make sure that (sth) is true or accurate; check: *verify statements, allegations, conditions, facts, etc* ○ *verify the figures, details, etc of a report* ○ *The computer verified that/whether the data was loaded correctly.* **2** [Tn, Tf] show that (sb's fears, suspicions, etc) are justified; confirm.
▷ **verifiable** /ˈverɪfaɪəbl/ *adj* that can be verified: *verifiable truths, facts, assets.*
verification /ˌverɪfɪˈkeɪʃn/ *n* [U, C] **1** verifying or being verified: *Verification* (ie Checking that weapons have been removed) *could be an obstacle to an arms agreement.* **2** proof or evidence.

verisimilitude /ˌverɪsɪˈmɪlɪtjuːd; *US* -tuːd/ *n* [U] (*fml*) appearance or semblance of being true or real: *These flower illustrations show the artist's concern for verisimilitude.*

veritable /ˈverɪtəbl/ *adj* [attrib] (*fml or joc*) rightly named or called; real: *a veritable villain* ○ *The rain turned our holiday into a veritable disaster.*

verity /ˈverətɪ/ *n* **1** [U] (*arch*) truth (of a statement, etc). **2** [C usu *pl*] (*fml*) idea, principle, etc generally thought to be true; fundamental fact: *universal, scientific, moral, etc verities.* **3** (idm) **the eternal verities** ⇨ ETERNAL.

Verlaine /vɜːˈlen/ Paul (1844-96), French poet. His work is noted for its simplicity and musicality, and uses the themes of eroticism and religious mysticism. He was influenced by *Rimbaud and was for a time his lover.

Vermeer /vəˈmɪə(r)/ Jan (1632-75), Dutch artist. He left a small number of works, most of them interior scenes of people or street scenes. He is noted for his delicate technique of representing light and materials.

vermicelli /ˌvɜːmɪˈselɪ, -ˈtʃelɪ/ *n* [U] pasta made into long slender threads, like spaghetti but much thinner, and often added to soups.

vermiform /ˈvɜːmɪfɔːm/ *adj* (*anatomy*) worm-like in shape: *the vermiform appendix.* ⇨ illus at DIGESTIVE.

vermilion /vəˈmɪlɪən/ *adj, n* [U] (of a) bright red: *a vermilion sash.*

vermin /ˈvɜːmɪn/ *n* [U, usu pl *v*] **1** certain wild animals and birds (eg rats, foxes, moles) which are harmful to crops and farmyard animals and birds: *put down/exterminate vermin.* Cf PEST 2. **2** insects (eg lice) sometimes found on the bodies of human beings and other animals: *a room alive/crawling with vermin.* **3** human beings who are harmful to society or who prey on others.
▷ **verminous** /-əs/ *adj* **1** infested with fleas, lice, etc: *verminous children.* **2** of the nature of or caused by vermin(1): *verminous diseases.*

Vermont /vɜːˈmɒnt/ state in the north-eastern USA. It is hilly and is one of the least industrialized states of America. The main economic activities are forestry and cattle breeding and tourism is becoming important. ⇨ map at App 1.

vermouth /ˈvɜːməθ; *US* vərˈmuːθ/ *n* (a) [U] strong white wine flavoured with herbs, drunk as an aperitif (often in cocktails). (b) [C] glass or drink of this.

vernacular /vəˈnækjʊlə(r)/ *n* language or dialect spoken in a particular country or region, as compared with a formal or written language: *the Latin Bible translated into the vernacular* ○ *Arabic vernaculars,* ie as compared with classical Arabic.
▷ **vernacular** *adj* [usu attrib] **1** using a vernacular: *a vernacular translation* ○ *a vernacular poet,* ie one writing in a local language. **2** (esp of architectural style) used for ordinary houses, farm buildings, etc in a particular area, rather than for large public buildings.

vernal /ˈvɜːnl/ *adj* [attrib] (*fml or rhet*) of, in or appropriate to the season of spring: *vernal breezes, flowers.*

Verne /vɜːn/ Jules (1828-1905), French novelist. His vivid imagination, humour and interest in science made books like *Around the World in Eighty Days* and *Journey to the Centre of the Earth* among the most popular early works of science fiction.

vernier /ˈvɜːnɪə(r)/ *n* small scale for measuring subdivisions on a graduated scale, eg on a barometer. It is separate from the main scale and is used by putting it next to the point of measurement and noting which of its divisions exactly meets a complete division on the main scale.

Veronal /ˈverənl/ *n* [U] (*propr*) type of sedative drug.

Veronese /ˌverəˈneɪzɪ/ Paolo Caliari (c1528-88), Italian artist. He painted many frescos and religious scenes for the churches of Venice and specialized in large-scale compositions, often marked by his use of light silvery colours.

Veronica /vəˈrɒnɪkə/ Saint, legendary Christian saint who, according to tradition, was one of the women of Jerusalem who wiped the face of Jesus with a cloth as he was going to his crucifixion. An image of his face is supposed to have been left on the cloth.

veronica /vəˈrɒnɪkə/ *n* [U, C] any of various types of herb, often with blue flowers; speedwell.

verruca /vəˈruːkə/ *n* (*pl* ~**s** or, in medical use, **-cae** /-kiː/) small hard infectious growth on the skin (usu on the bottom of the feet); wart.

Versailles /veəˈsaɪ/ town south-west of Paris. It grew up around the palace of Versailles, built by Louis XIII of France. It was considerably enlarged by *Louis XIV for use as his residence and court. The spirit of his reign is expressed by the magnificence of its classical design and the elaborate formal gardens and fountains. The **Treaty of Versailles** signed there with Germany in 1919 formally ended the First World War.

versatile /ˈvɜːsətaɪl; *US* -tl/ *adj* (*approv*) **1** turning easily or readily from one subject, skill or occupation to another: *a versatile cook, writer, athlete* ○ *a versatile mind.* **2** (of a tool, machine, etc) having various uses: *a versatile drill, truck, etc.* ▷ **versatility** /ˌvɜːsəˈtɪlətɪ/ *n* [U].

verse /vɜːs/ *n* **1** [U] (form of) writing arranged in lines, often with a regular rhythm or rhyme scheme; poetry: *Most of the scene is written in verse, but some is in prose.* ○ *blank verse,* ie without rhymes at the end of the lines ○ [attrib] *a verse translation of Homer's 'Iliad'.* Cf PROSE. **2** [C] group of lines forming a unit in a poem or song: *a hymn of/with six verses.* **3 verses** [pl] (*dated*) poetry: *a book of humorous verses.* **4** [C] any one of the short numbered divisions of a chapter in the Bible. **5** (idm) **chapter and verse** ⇨ CHAPTER.

versed /vɜːst/ *adj* ~ **in sth** [pred] knowledgeable about or skilled in sth: *well versed in mathematics, the arts, etc* ○ *well versed in the ways of journalists.*

versicle /ˈvɜːsɪkl/ *n* each of the short sentences in the liturgy said or sung by the clergyman and answered by the congregation. Cf RESPONSE 3.

versify /ˈvɜːsɪfaɪ/ *v* (*pt, pp* **-fied**) (*fml*) **1** [I] compose verse. **2** [Tn] put (prose) into verse: *versify an old legend.*
▷ **versification** /ˌvɜːsɪfɪˈkeɪʃn/ *n* [U] (*fml*) (a) art of composing verse. (b) style in which verse is composed; metre.
versifier *n* (*sometimes derog*) maker of verses: *amateur versifiers.*

version /ˈvɜːʃn; *US* -ʒn/ *n* **1** account of an event, etc from the point of view of one person: *There were contradictory versions of what happened/of what the President said.* **2** (a) special or variant form of sth made: *the standard/de luxe version of this car* ○ *the original/final version of the play.* (b) special adaptation of a book, piece of music, etc: *the radio, film, etc version of 'Jane Eyre'* ○ *an orchestral version of a suite for strings* ○ *a bilingual, an illustrated, etc version of the poems.* **3** translation into another language: *the Authorized/Revised Version of the Bible.*

verso /ˈvɜːsəʊ/ *n* (*pl* ~**s**) any left-hand page of a book having an even number of pages. Cf RECTO.

versus /ˈvɜːsəs/ *prep* (*abbrs* **v, vs**) (*Latin*) against (sb/sth): *the advantage of better job opportunities versus the inconvenience of moving house and leaving one's friends* ○ *Kent v(ersus) Surrey,* eg in cricket ○ (*law*) *Rex v(ersus) Crippen.*

vertebra /ˈvɜːtɪbrə/ *n* (*pl* **-rae** /-riː/) any one of the segments of the backbone. ⇨ illus at SKELETON.
▷ **vertebral** /-rəl/ *adj*: *the vertebral column,* ie the backbone.
vertebrate /ˈvɜːtɪbreɪt/ *n, adj* (animal, bird, etc) having a backbone.

vertex /ˈvɜːteks/ *n* (*pl* **-tices** /-tɪsiːz/) **1** (*fml*) highest point or top; apex: (*anatomy*) *the vertex of the skull.* **2** (*mathematics*) (a) point of a triangle, cone, etc opposite the base. (b) meeting point of lines that form an angle, eg any point of a triangle, polygon, etc.

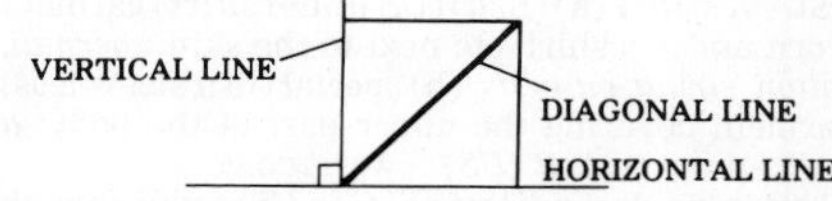

vertical /ˈvɜːtɪkl/ *adj* **1** at a right angle to another line or plane, or to the earth's surface: *the vertical axis of a graph* ○ *The cliff was almost vertical.* ○ *a vertical take-off aircraft,* ie one that rises straight up into the air without needing a runway. **2** in the direction from top to bottom of a picture, etc: *the vertical clues of a crossword.*
▷ **vertical** *n* vertical line, part or position: *out of the vertical,* ie not vertical.
vertically /-klɪ/ *adv.*

vertices *pl* of VERTEX.

vertigo /ˈvɜːtɪgəʊ/ *n* [U] feeling of losing one's balance, caused esp by looking down from a great height; dizziness: *suffer from (an attack of) vertigo.*
▷ **vertiginous** /vɜːˈtɪdʒɪnəs/ *adj* of or causing vertigo: *a vertiginous drop, descent, etc.*

vervain /ˈvɜːveɪn/ *n* [U, C] European plant with small blue, white or purple flowers.

verve /vɜːv/ *n* [U] enthusiasm, spirit or vigour, esp in artistic or literary work: *write, sing, act, etc with verve* ○ *The performance lacked verve.*

very[1] /ˈverɪ/ *adv* **1** (used as an intensifier before adjs, advs and dets) in a high degree; extremely: *very small, hot, useful* ○ *very quickly, soon, far* ○ *very much, few, etc* ○ *'Are you busy?' 'Not very.'*

2 (before a superlative *adj* or *own*) in the fullest sense: *the very best quality* ○ *the very first to arrive* ○ *six o'clock at the very latest* ○ *your very own cheque-book.* 3 exactly: *sitting in the very same seat.*

□ ˌ**very high ˈfrequency** (*abbr* **VHF**) radio frequency of 30 to 300 megahertz.

NOTE ON USAGE: 1 **Very much** is used to modify verbs: *She likes Beethoven very much.* ○ *We have enjoyed staying with you very much.* 2 **Much** or **very much** can modify past participles: *She is (very) much loved by everyone.* ○ 3 **Very** is used to modify adjectives and past participles used as adjectives: *She is very talented.* ○ *I am very tired.* ○ *They were very interested.*

very[2] /ˈverɪ/ *adj* [attrib] 1 itself, himself, etc and no other; actual; truly such: *This is the very book I want!* ○ *At that very moment the phone rang.* ○ *You're the very man I want to see.* ○ *These pills are the very thing for your cold.* 2 extreme: *at the very end/beginning.* 3 (used to emphasize a *n*): *He knows our very thoughts*, ie our thoughts themselves, even our innermost thoughts. ○ *The very idea* (ie The idea alone, quite apart from the reality) *of going abroad delighted him.* ○ *The very idea/thought!* ie That is an impractical or improper suggestion. ○ *Sardine tins can be the very devil* (ie very difficult) *to open.* 4 (idm) **under/before one's very eyes** ⇨ EYE[1].

Very light /ˈverɪ laɪt/ coloured signal flare fired at night, eg as a sign of distress from a ship.

vesicle /ˈvesɪkl/ *n* (*anatomy or biology*) 1 small hollow bladder or cavity in the body of a plant or an animal. 2 blister.

▷ **vesicular** /vəˈsɪkjʊlə(r)/ *adj* [usu attrib] of or characterized by the formation of vesicles: *swine vesicular disease.*

vespers /ˈvespəz/ *n* [pl] church service or prayers in the evening; evensong. Cf MATINS.

Vespucci /veˈspuːtʃɪ/ Amerigo (1451-1512), Italian (Florentine) explorer. He made several voyages to the New World for the king of Portugal and claimed to have been the first to sight the mainland of S America in 1497. It is possible that the name America comes from his first name.

vessel /ˈvesl/ *n* 1 (*fml*) ship or boat, esp a large one: *ocean-going vessels* ○ *cargo vessels.* Cf CRAFT 2. 2 (*fml*) any hollow container, esp one used for holding liquids, eg a cask, bowl, bottle or cup. 3 tube-like structure in the body of an animal or a plant, conveying or holding blood or other fluid: *blood-vessels.*

vest[1] /vest/ *n* 1 (a) (*Brit*) (*US* **undershirt**) garment worn under a shirt, etc next to the skin: *thermal, cotton, string, etc vests.* (b) special (usu sleeveless) garment covering the upper part of the body: *a bullet-proof vest.* 2 (*US*) = WAISTCOAT.

□ ˌ**vest-ˈpocket** *adj* [attrib] (*esp US*) small enough to fit in a waistcoat pocket: *a* ˌ*vest-pocket* ˈ*camera.*

vest[2] /vest/ *v* 1 [Tn·pr usu passive] ~ **sth in sb/sth;** ~ **sb/sth with sth** (*fml*) give sth as a firm or legal right to sb/sth; confer sth on sb/sth: *the powers vested in a priest* ○ *Authority is vested in the people* ○ *vest sb with authority, rights in an estate, etc* ○ *Parliament is vested with the power of making laws.* 2 [Tn] (*arch or religion*) put on (ceremonial garments). 3 (idm) **have a vested interest (in sth)** expect to benefit (from sth): *You have a vested interest in Tim's resignation*, eg because you may get his job.

vestibule /ˈvestɪbjuːl/ *n* 1 (*fml*) lobby or entrance hall, eg where hats and coats may be left: *the vestibule of a theatre, hotel, etc.* 2 (*US*) enclosed space between passenger coaches on a train: [attrib] *vestibule train.*

vestige /ˈvestɪdʒ/ *n* 1 small remaining part of what once existed; trace: *Not a vestige of the abbey remains.* 2 (esp in negative sentences) not even a small amount: *not a vestige of truth/common sense in the report.* 3 (*anatomy*) organ, or part of one, which is a survival of sth that once existed at an earlier stage of evolution: *man's vestige of a tail.*

▷ **vestigial** /veˈstɪdʒɪəl/ *adj* remaining as a vestige.

vestment /ˈvestmənt/ *n* (esp *pl*) ceremonial garment, esp one worn by a priest in church.

vestry /ˈvestrɪ/ *n* room or building attached to a church, where vestments are kept and where clergy and choir can put them on. ⇨ illus at CHURCH.

Vesuvius /vɪˈsuːvɪəs/ active volcano near Naples in Italy, 1 277 m (4 190 ft) high. It erupted in 79AD burying the towns of Herculaneum and *Pompeii.

vet[1] /vet/ *n* (*infml*) = VETERINARY SURGEON (VETERINARY).

vet[2] /vet/ *v* (-tt-) [Tn, Tn·pr] ~ **sth/sb (for sth)** (*Brit*) examine (sb's past record, qualifications, etc) closely and critically: *All staff are vetted for links with extremist groups before being employed.* ○ *be positively vetted for a government post*, ie be found to be trustworthy.

vet[3] /vet/ *n* (*US infml*) = VETERAN 2.

vetch /vetʃ/ *n* plant of the pea family, used as fodder for cattle.

veteran /ˈvetərən/ *n* 1 person with much or long experience, esp as a soldier: *war veterans* ○ *veterans of two World Wars* ○ *veterans of the civil rights campaign* ○ [attrib] *a veteran politician, golfer.* 2 (also *infml* **vet**) (*US*) any ex-serviceman: ˈ*Veterans Day*, ie 11 November, commemorating the armistice (1918) in the First World War.

□ ˌ**veteran** ˈ**car** (*Brit*) car made before 1916, esp before 1905: *a veteran Rolls Royce.* Cf VINTAGE 2.

veterinary /ˈvetrɪnrɪ; *US* ˈvetərɪnerɪ/ *adj* [attrib] of or for the diseases and injuries of (esp farm and domestic) animals: *veterinary medicine, studies.*

□ ˌ**veterinary** ˈ**surgeon** (also *infml* **vet**, *US* **veterinarian** /ˌvetərɪˈneərɪən/) (*fml*) person who is skilled in the treatment of animal diseases and injuries.

veto /ˈviːtəʊ/ *n* (*pl* ~**es**) 1 [C, U] constitutional right to reject or forbid a legislative proposal or action: *the ministerial veto* ○ *exercise the power/right of veto* ○ *Permanent members of the United Nations Security Council have a veto over any proposal.* ○ *Japan used her veto to block the resolution.* 2 [C] statement that rejects or forbids sth.

▷ **veto** *v* (*pres p* **vetoing**) [Tn] reject or forbid (sth) authoritatively: *The President vetoed the tax cuts.* ○ (*joc*) *John's parents vetoed his plan to buy a motor bike.*

vex /veks/ *v* (*dated or fml*) 1 [Tn] anger or annoy (sb), esp with trivial matters: *His silly chatter would vex a saint.* ○ *She was vexed that I was late.* 2 [Tn esp passive] worry or distress (sb): *He was vexed at his failure.* 3 (idm) **a vexed** ˈ**question** difficult problem that causes much discussion: *the vexed question of who pays for the damage.*

▷ **vexation** /vekˈseɪʃn/ *n* 1 [U] state of being annoyed or worried. 2 [C esp *pl*] thing causing annoyance or worry: *life's little vexations.*

vexatious /vekˈseɪʃəs/ *adj* 1 (*dated or fml*) annoying or worrying: *vexatious rules and regulations.* 2 (of legal action or the person taking it) not having good legal grounds and merely causing annoyance to the defendant: *a vexatious litigant.*

vg *abbr* (esp on corrected written work) very good.

VHF /ˌviː eɪtʃ ˈef/ *abbr* (*radio*) very high frequency: *programmes broadcast on VHF* ○ *a VHF radio.* Cf UHF.

via /ˈvaɪə/ *prep* by way of (sth); through: *go from London to Washington via New York* ○ *I can send him a note via the internal mail system.*

viable /ˈvaɪəbl/ *adj* 1 sound and workable; feasible: *a viable plan, proposition, proposal, etc* ○ *scientifically, politically, economically viable.* 2 (*biology*) capable of developing and surviving independently: *viable eggs, seeds, foetuses.* ▷ **viability** /ˌvaɪəˈbɪlətɪ/ *n* [U]: *test the commercial viability of solar power.*

viaduct /ˈvaɪədʌkt/ *n* long bridge, usu with many arches, carrying a road or railway across a valley or dip in the ground.

vial /ˈvaɪəl/ *n* = PHIAL.

viands /ˈvaɪəndz/ *n* [pl] (*arch or rhet*) food.

viaticum /vaɪˈætɪkəm/ *n* (*fml*) Communion (COMMUNION 1) given to a person who is likely to die soon.

vibes /vaɪbz/ *n* 1 [sing or pl *v*] (*infml*) vibraphone: [attrib] *a vibes player*, eg in a jazz band. 2 [pl] (*sl*) = VIBRATIONS (VIBRATION 3): *get good, bad, weird, etc vibes from sth.*

vibrant /ˈvaɪbrənt/ *adj* 1 vibrating strongly; resonant: *the vibrant notes of a cello, contralto, canary.* 2 (*fig*) full of life and energy; exciting: *a vibrant atmosphere, personality, performance* ○ *She was vibrant with health and enthusiasm.* 3 (esp of colours) bright and striking: *vibrant blues and yellows.* ▷ **vibrancy** /-brənsɪ/ *n* [U].

vibraphone /ˈvaɪbrəfəʊn/ *n* musical instrument like a xylophone but with electric resonators under the metal bars giving a vibrating effect.

vibrate /vaɪˈbreɪt; *US* ˈvaɪbreɪt/ *v* [I, Tn] 1 (cause sth to) move rapidly and continuously backwards and forwards; shake: *The whole house vibrates whenever a heavy lorry passes.* 2 (cause sth to) resound or quiver with rapid slight variations of pitch: *The strings of a piano vibrate when the keys are struck.* ○ *His voice vibrated with passion.* ○ *The trilled 'r' is produced by vibrating the tongue against the upper teeth.*

▷ **vibrator** /-tə(r)/ *n* device that vibrates or causes vibrations, esp one used in massage.

vibratory /-tərɪ; *US* -tɔːrɪ/ *adj* [attrib] (*fml*) vibrating or causing vibrations: *a vibratory massage.*

vibration /vaɪˈbreɪʃn/ *n* 1 [U, C] vibrating movement or sensation: *Even at full speed the ship's engines cause very little vibration.* 2 [C] (*physics*) single movement to and fro when equilibrium has been disturbed: *Middle C is equivalent to 256 vibrations per second.* 3 **vibrations** (also *sl* **vibes**) (*infml*) [pl] mood or mental influence produced by a particular person, thing, place, etc.

vibrato /vɪˈbrɑːtəʊ/ *n* [U, C] (*pl* ~**s**) (*music*) throbbing or tremulous effect in singing or on a stringed or wind instrument, consisting of rapid slight variations in pitch. Cf TREMOLO.

viburnum /vaɪˈbɜːnəm/ *n* any of various types of shrub, usu with white flowers.

vicar /ˈvɪkə(r)/ *n* (in the Church of England) clergyman in charge of a parish where tithes formerly belonged to another person or an institution. Cf CURATE, MINISTER[1] 3, PRIEST, RECTOR. ⇨ article at CHURCH OF ENGLAND.

Vicars, especially those in rural parishes, are sometimes presented as well-intentioned but rather scatty, ineffectual people, holding frequent tea-parties on the vicarage lawn and giving useful advice to their parishioners. The stereotypical vicar is also old-fashioned, unworldly and exaggeratedly polite. Although this image has little basis in reality, it is often used in television comedies and in advertising.

▷ **vicarage** /ˈvɪkərɪdʒ/ *n* house of a vicar.

□ ˌ**vicar-ˈgeneral** *n* church official helping a bishop, eg in his administrative duties.

the ˌ**Vicar of** ˈ**Bray** character in an English satirical song, a vicar who changed his religious views according to those of the reigning monarch. The term is sometimes used to describe a person who is prepared to change his convictions to gain some advantage.

ˌ**Vicar of** ˈ**Christ** title sometimes given to the Pope.

vicarious /vɪˈkeərɪəs; *US* vaɪˈk-/ *adj* [esp attrib] 1 felt or experienced indirectly, by sharing imaginatively in the feelings, activities, etc of another person: *vicarious pleasure, satisfaction, etc* ○ *He got a vicarious thrill out of watching his son score the winning goal.* 2 done, felt or experienced by one person on behalf of another: *vicarious punishment, suffering, etc.* ▷ **vicariously** *adv.*

vice[1] /vaɪs/ *n* 1 (a) [U] evil or unprincipled conduct; wickedness: *vice and corruption in the Secret Service.* (b) [C] particular form of this: *Greed is a terrible vice.* Cf VIRTUE 1. 2 [C] (*infml or joc*) fault or bad habit; weakness: *Sherry is one of my little vices!* 3 [U] criminal or immoral behaviour, eg gambling, drug-trafficking, pornography, prostitution: [attrib] ˈ*vice squads*, ie groups of police who try to prevent this ○ *Detectives smash London vice ring*, eg in a newspaper headline. **4** (idm) **a den of iniquity/vice** ⇨ DEN.

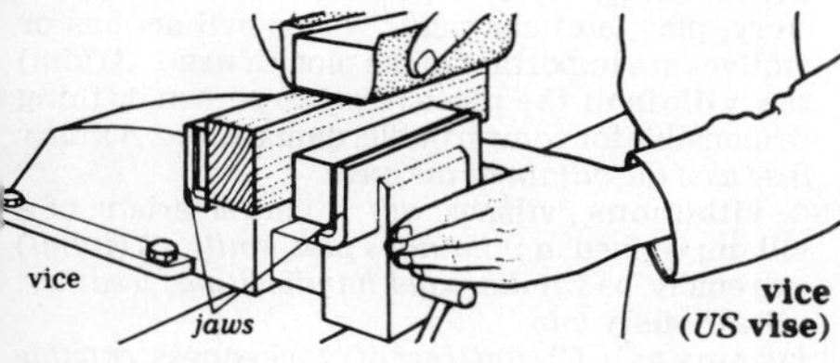

vice (*US* vise)

vice[2] (*US* **vise**) /vaɪs/ *n* metal tool, used in woodwork, etc, with a pair of jaws that hold a thing securely while work is done on it: *(fig) He held my arm in a vice-like* (ie very firm) *grip.*
vice- *comb form* **1** acting as substitute or deputy for: *vice-president.* **2** next in rank to: *vice-admiral.* ⇨ App 4.
vice-chancellor /vaɪsˈtʃɑːnsələ(r); *US* -ˈtʃæn-/ *n* most senior official of a university who is responsible for its administration.
viceroy /ˈvaɪsrɔɪ/ *n* person governing a colony, province, etc as the deputy of a sovereign.
▷ **viceregal** /vaɪsˈriːgl/ *adj* of a viceroy.
vicereine /ˈvaɪsreɪn/ *n* wife of a viceroy; female viceroy.
vice versa /ˌvaɪsɪ ˈvɜːsə/ the other way round; with the terms or conditions reversed: ˌ*We gossip about* ˈ*them and* ˌ*vice* ˈ*versa*, ie they gossip about us.
Vichy /ˈviːʃɪ/ town in central France. During the Second World War it was the headquarters of the French government which collaborated with *Hitler's Germany.
□ ˈ**Vichy water** mineral water produced in Vichy.
vichyssoise /ˌvɪʃɪˈswɑːz/ *n* [U] thick creamy soup made from leeks and potatoes, served cold.
vicinity /vɪˈsɪnətɪ/ *n* (idm) **in the vicinity (of sth)** (*fml*) in the surrounding district; in the neighbourhood: *There isn't a good school in the (immediate) vicinity.* ○ *crowds gathering in the vicinity of Trafalgar Square* ○ *(fig) a population in the vicinity of* (ie of approximately) *100 000.*
vicious /ˈvɪʃəs/ *adj* **1** acting or done with evil intentions; spiteful: *Vicious thugs attacked an elderly man.* ○ *a vicious kick, look, remark.* **2** given up to vice[1](3); depraved: *a vicious life* ○ *vicious practices, habits, etc.* **3** (of animals) savage and dangerous. **4** (*infml*) violent or severe: *a vicious wind, headache, flu virus.* **5** (idm) **a vicious ˈcircle** state of affairs in which a cause produces an effect which itself produces the original cause, so continuing the whole process: *I need experience to get a job but without a job I can't get experience — it's a vicious circle.* **a vicious ˈspiral** continuous rise in one thing (eg prices) caused by a continuous rise in sth else (eg wages). ▷ **viciously** *adv.* **viciousness** *n* [U].
vicissitude /vɪˈsɪsɪtjuːd; *US* -tuːd/ *n* (usu *pl*); (*fml*) change in one's circumstances, esp for the worse: *battling against the vicissitudes of life.*
victim /ˈvɪktɪm/ *n* **1** person, animal or thing that is injured, killed or destroyed as the result of carelessness, crime or misfortune: *Many pets are victims of overfeeding.* ○ *murder, rape victims* ○ *earthquake, accident, strike victims* ○ *(fig) He is the victim of his own success*, eg because overwork has made him ill. **2** (*fig*) person who is tricked or fooled: *the victim of a hoax, practical joke, conspiracy, etc.* **3** living creature killed and offered as a religious sacrifice: *a sacrificial victim.* **4** (idm) **fall victim (to sth)** be overcome (by sth); succumb (to sth): *He soon fell victim to her charms.*
victimize, -ise /ˈvɪktɪmaɪz/ *v* [Tn, Tn·pr] ~ **sb (for sth)** **1** blame or punish sb unfairly for actions that others have carried out: *Union leaders claimed that some members had been victimized* (eg by being dismissed) *for taking part in the strike.* **2** harm sb or make sb suffer unfairly; bully: *The fat boy was victimized by his classmates.* ▷ **victimization, -isation** /ˌvɪktɪmaɪˈzeɪʃn; *US* -mɪˈz-/ *n* [U]: *The strikers agreed to return to work provided there would be no victimization of their leaders.*
victor /ˈvɪktə(r)/ *n* (*fml*) winner of a battle, contest, game, etc: *emerge the victors.*
Victoria[1] /vɪkˈtɔːrɪə/ (1819-1901), queen of the United Kingdom 1837-1901. Her marriage to Prince *Albert in 1840 had a decisive influence on the character of her reign: she became deeply concerned with the affairs of the nation while not favouring any political party. She did however show a confidence in prime ministers Melbourne and *Disraeli that *Palmerston and *Gladstone never enjoyed. After Albert's death she retired from public life, but was encouraged to return by Disraeli, who gained the title of Empress of India for her. She won great love and admiration and was a powerful symbol of Britain at the height of its empire. ⇨ App 3.
▷ **Victorian** *adj* **1** of, living in or dating from the reign of Queen Victoria: *Victorian novels, poets, houses.* ⇨ illus at DRESS. **2** having the qualities and outlook attributed to middle-class people in Britain in the nineteenth century: *Victorian attitudes to sexual morality*, ie ones stressing self-control, family loyalty, etc ○ *Victorian values*, eg thrift, sobriety, hard work. — *n* person living in the reign of Queen Victoria.
Victoriana /vɪktɔːrɪˈɑːnə/ *n* [U] objects of Victorian times, esp when forming a collection.
□ **Vicˌtoria ˈCross** (*abbr* **VC**) highest British military award for bravery: *Private Jones was awarded the Victoria Cross (for his gallantry).*
Victoria[2] /vɪkˈtɔːrɪə/ state in SE Australia. There are plains in the west and the Snowy Mountains run along the south-western coast. Cereals are grown but dairy-farming and sheep-rearing are the main forms of agriculture. ⇨ map at App 1.
Victoria[3] /vɪkˈtɔːrɪə/ **Lake Victoria** lake in East Africa, the largest in the continent and the source of the *Nile. It forms part of the territory of Uganda, Tanzania and Kenya.
victoria /vɪkˈtɔːrɪə/ *n* **1** (also **vicˌtoria ˈplum**) large red sweet-tasting plum. **2** light four-wheeled horse-drawn carriage for two people.
Victoria and Albert Museum /vɪkˌtɔːrɪə ənd ˌælbət mjuːˈziːəm/ **the Victoria and Albert Museum** (*abbr* **V and A**) British national museum of fine art and applied art in South Kensington, London. It has important collections of paintings, ceramics, textiles and furniture.
Victoria Falls /vɪkˌtɔːrɪə ˈfɔːlz/ large waterfall on the *Zambezi river, on the border between Zambia and Zimbabwe. It is 109 m (355 ft) high. ⇨ map at NAMIBIA.
Victory /ˈvɪktərɪ/ **HMS Victory** *Nelson's ship at the battle of *Trafalgar. It is now on display in Portsmouth, a port in S England.
victory /ˈvɪktərɪ/ *n* **(a)** [U] success in a war, contest, game, etc: *lead the troops to victory* ○ [attrib] *victory parades, processions, celebrations, etc.* **(b)** [C] instance or occasion of this: *a narrow, decisive, resounding victory* ○ *gain, win, score, etc a victory over one's rivals* ○ *Labour did not have an easy election victory in East Oxford.* ○ *(fig) The verdict of the court was a victory for common sense.*
▷ **victorious** /vɪkˈtɔːrɪəs/ *adj* ~ **(in sth)**; ~ **(over sb/sth)** having gained a victory; triumphant: *the victorious players, team, etc.* **victoriously** *adv.*
victual /ˈvɪtl/ *v* (**-ll-**; *US* also **-l-**) [Tn] supply (sth) with food and stores: *victual a ship.*
▷ **victualler** (*US* also **victualer**) /ˈvɪtlə(r)/ *n* trader or business supplying food and stores: (*Brit fml*) *a licensed victualler*, ie a public house keeper who sells food, spirits, beer, etc to be consumed on the premises.
victuals *n* [pl] (*dated*) food and drink; provisions.
vicuna /vɪˈkjuːnə; *US* vaɪˈkuːnjə/ *n* **1** [C] S American animal, related to the llama, with fine silky wool. **2** [U] (cloth made from the) wool of this animal: [attrib] *vicuna jackets.*
vide /ˈvɪdeɪ, ˈvaɪdiː/ *v* [Tn] (*Latin fml*) (used only in the imperative) see or refer to (a passage in a book, etc). Cf INFRA.
video /ˈvɪdɪəʊ/ *n* (*pl* ~**s**) **1** [U] recording or broadcasting of moving pictures, as distinct from sound, by using television: *video in schools*, ie as a teaching aid ○ *amateur, commercial video* ○ *The bank robbery was recorded on video.* ○ [attrib] *video frequencies* ○ *The satellite provides a video link between the White House and the Kremlin.* **2** [C] **(a)** (cassette or disc containing a) recording or broadcast made by using video: *watching, making, showing, etc videos* ○ *The firm produced a short promotional video.* ○ [attrib] *video shops, libraries.* **(b)** [C] = VIDEO CASSETTE RECORDER.
▷ **video** *v* (*pres p* **videoing**) [Tn] record (moving pictures) on videotape or videodisc: *I videoed the TV programme you wanted to watch.*
□ ˌ**video caˈssette recorder** (also **video**, ˈ**video recorder**) (*abbr* **VCR**) device which, when linked to a television, can record and show programmes, etc on videotape or videodisc.
ˈ**videodisc** *n* [U, C] plastic disc used, like videotape, to record moving pictures and sound.
ˈ**video game** game played using a home computer, etc in which the player controls images on a TV screen.
ˌ**video ˈnasty** (*infml*) video film showing offensive scenes of sex and violence.
ˈ**videotape** *n* [U, C] magnetic tape used for recording moving pictures and sound — *v* [Tn] = VIDEO *v*.
Vidor /ˈviːdɔː(r)/ King (1894-1982), American film director. His career lasted fifty years, but his greatest achievements were his early silent tributes to the ordinary American, *The Crowd* and *The Big Parade.*
vie /vaɪ/ *v* (*pt, pp* **vied**, *pres p* /vaɪd/, **vying** /ˈvaɪɪŋ/) [Ipr] ~ **with sb (for sth/to do sth)**; ~ **for sth** (*fml*) compete keenly with sb for (sth); rival sb for sth: *old rivals vying (with each other) for first place* ○ *Businesses vied with each other to attract customers.*
Vienna /vɪˈenə/ capital of Austria, German name **Wien**. It lies on the *Danube in the north-east of the country. It is famous as an artistic centre, esp for music in the 18th and 19th centuries, when *Mozart, *Beethoven, *Schubert, *Mahler and others were active in the city. It was also the home of the *Strauss family who perfected the waltz form.
▷ **Viennese** /vɪəˈniːz/ *adj* of Vienna. — *n* (*pl* unchanged) Viennese person.
Vietcong /vjetˈkɒŋ/ *n* **the Vietcong** [pl *v*] the Communist guerilla forces fighting in Vietnam between 1954 and 1976.
Vietminh /vjetˈmɪn/ *n* **the Vietminh** [pl *v*] the Vietnamese independence movement active betweeen 1941 and 1950, or any of various similar movements that existed after 1950.
Vietnam /vjetˈnæm; *US* -ˈnɑːm/ country in SE Asia; pop approx 64 228 000; official language Vietnamese; capital Hanoi; unit of currency dong (= 100 xu). It has two main fertile regions where rice and other crops are grown: the delta of the Red River in the north and of the Mekong in the south. Most of the rest of the country is mountainous. The economy is still suffering from the effects of isolation after the war (1954-75) between Communist North Vietnam and US-supported South Vietnam, but private enterprise is now being encouraged. ⇨ map.
▷ **Vietnamese** /vjetnəˈmiːz/ *adj* of Vietnam. — *n* **1** [C] (*pl* unchanged) native or inhabitant of Vietnam. **2** [U] language spoken in Vietnam, probably related to various other SE Asian languages.
view[1] /vjuː/ *n* **1** [U] state of seeing or being seen from a particular place; field of vision: *The lake came into view/We came in view of the lake as we turned the corner.* ○ *The sun disappeared from view behind a cloud./A cloud hid the sun from view.* ○ *She was soon lost from view among the crowd.* ○ *The man in front was obstructing my view of the pitch.* **2** [C] what can be seen from a particular place, esp fine natural scenery: *enjoying the*

Vietnam and its neighbours

magnificent views from the summit, over the mountains ○ *10 different views of London*, eg on picture postcards ○ [sing] *You'll get a better view of the pianist if you stand up.* **3** (also **viewing**) [C] (opportunity for a) special visual inspection of eg a film or an art exhibition: *We had a private view of the jewels before the public auction.* **4** [C esp *pl*] ~ **(about/on sth)** personal opinion or attitude; thought or observation (on a subject): *have, hold, express, air strong political views* ○ *oppose, support sb's extreme views* ○ *What are your views on her resignation?* ○ *We fell in with* (ie agreed with) *the committee's views.* **5** [sing] way of understanding or interpreting a subject, series of events, etc; mental impression: *The scientific, legal, medical, etc view is that...* ○ *a highly controversial view of modern art* ○ *take a realistic, favourable, pessimistic, etc view of the problem* ○ *This book gives readers an inside view of* (ie an insight into) *MI5.* **6** (idm) **a bird's eye view** ⇨ BIRD. **have, etc sth in ˈview** *(fml)* have, etc sth as a clear idea, intention, plan, etc in the mind: *What the President has in view is a world without nuclear weapons.* ○ *Keep your career aims constantly in view.* **in full view** ⇨ FULL. **in ˈmy, etc view** *(fml)* in my, etc opinion. **in view of sth** taking sth into account; considering sth: *In view of the weather, we will cancel the outing.* **on ˈview** being shown or exhibited: *Our entire range of cars is now on view at your local showroom.* **a point of view** ⇨ POINT[1]. **take a dim, poor, serious, etc ˈview of sb/sth** regard sb/sth unfavourably, seriously, etc: *(infml) He took a dim view of me/my suggestion.* **take the long view** ⇨ LONG[1]. **with a view to doing sth** *(fml)* with the intention or hope of doing sth: *He is decorating the house with a view to selling it.*

□ **ˈviewdata** *n* [U] information, eg news or timetables, displayed on a television screen from a central computer, esp when a telephone line provides a link from the viewer back to the computer. Cf PRESTEL.

ˈviewfinder *n* device on a camera showing the area that will be photographed through the lens. ⇨ illus at CAMERA.

ˈviewpoint *n* = POINT OF VIEW (POINT[1]).

view[2] /vju:/ *v (fml)* **1** [Tn, Tn·pr, Cn·n/a] ~ **sth (as sth)** consider sth in the mind, regard sth (as sth): *How do you view your chances of success?* ○ *Future developments will be viewed with interest.* ○ *Has the matter been viewed from the taxpayers' standpoint?* ○ *Viewed from the outside, the company seemed genuine.* ○ *The attack on the ship was viewed as an act of war.* **2** [Tn] look at or watch (sth) carefully: *view a battle through binoculars from the top of a hill* ○ *The film hasn't been viewed by the censor.* **3** [Tn] inspect (a house, property, etc) with the idea of buying it: *open for viewing between 10.00 and 12.00.* **4** [I] watch television: *the viewing public.* **5** (idm) **an order to view** ⇨ ORDER[1].

▷ **viewer** /ˈvju:ə(r)/ *n* **1** person who views sth: *viewers of the current political scene.* **2** person watching a TV programme: *regular viewers of 'Panorama'.* **3** device for viewing photographic transparencies: *a slide viewer.*

vigil /ˈvɪdʒɪl/ *n* **1** [U, C] (action or period of) staying awake, esp at night, to keep watch or to pray: *tired out by long nightly vigils at her son's bedside* ○ *hold a candle-light vigil for peace.* **2** eve of a religious festival, esp one observed by fasting: *the Easter vigil.*

vigilant /ˈvɪdʒɪlənt/ *adj (fml)* looking out for possible danger, trouble, etc; watchful or alert: *under the vigilant eye of the examiner.* ▷ **vigilance** /-əns/ *n* [U]: *exercise constant, perpetual, etc vigilance* ○ *Police vigilance was eventually rewarded*, eg when an arrest was made. **vigilantly** *adv.*

vigilante /ˌvɪdʒɪˈlæntɪ/ *n (esp derog)* member of a self-appointed group of people who try to prevent crime and disorder in a community.

vignette /vɪˈnjet/ *n* **1 (a)** illustration, esp on the title-page of a book, but not in a definite border. **(b)** photograph or drawing, esp of a person's head and shoulders, with the background gradually shaded off. **2** *(fig)* short written description of sth, a person's character, etc: *charming vignettes of Edwardian life.*

vigour (*US* **vigor**) /ˈvɪgə(r)/ *n* [U] **(a)** physical strength or energy; vitality: *At 40, he was in his prime and full of vigour.* ○ *work with renewed vigour and enthusiasm.* **(b)** forcefulness of thought, language, style, etc: *withstand the vigour of her protest, defence, attack, etc* ○ *music, poetry, etc of tremendous vigour.* ⇨ Usage at STRENGTH.

▷ **vigorous** /ˈvɪgərəs/ *adj* **(a)** strong, active or energetic: *avoid vigorous exercise, exertion, etc* ○ *vigorous supporters of human rights.* **(b)** using forceful language, etc: *vigorous debate, criticism, opposition, etc* ○ *the poem's vigorous rhythms.* **vigorously** *adv*: *shake sb's hand vigorously* ○ *argue vigorously in support of sth.*

Viking /ˈvaɪkɪŋ/ *n* any of the Scandinavian warriors and pirates who settled in parts of N and W Europe, including Britain, in the 8th to 10th centuries AD. Much of E England was occupied by the Vikings and in 1017 *Canute, king of Denmark, became king of England: [attrib] *Viking raiders.*

vile /vaɪl/ *adj* **(-r, -st) 1** extremely disgusting: *a vile smell, taste, etc* ○ *use vile language.* **2** despicable on moral grounds; corrupt: *vile deceits, accusations, slanders, etc* ○ *Bribery is a vile practice.* **3** *(infml)* extremely bad: *vile weather* ○ *be in a vile temper, mood, humour, etc.* ▷ **vilely** /ˈvaɪllɪ/ *adv.* **vileness** *n* [U].

vilify /ˈvɪlɪfaɪ/ *v (pt, pp* **-fied)** [Tn] *(fml)* say evil or insulting things about (sb); slander: *She was vilified by the press for her controversial views.* ▷ **vilification** /ˌvɪlɪfɪˈkeɪʃn/ *n* [U, C].

Villa /ˈvi:ə/ Francisco, known as Pancho Villa (1877-1923), Mexican revolutionary. He took part in several armed uprisings against dictatorships in his country and made an attack on the USA in 1916.

villa /ˈvɪlə/ *n* **1** *(Brit)* (usu as part of an address) large detached or semi-detached house in a suburban or residential district: *No 3 Albert Villas.* **2** house for holiday-makers at the seaside, in the countryside, etc: *rented villas in Spain.* **3** country house with a large garden, esp in S Europe: *the Villa d'Este*, ie in Italy. **4** (in Roman times) country house or farm with an estate attached to it.

village /ˈvɪlɪdʒ/ *n* **1 (a)** [C] group of houses, shops, etc, usu with a church and situated in a country district: [attrib] *the village school, fête, church.* **(b)** [Gp] community of people who live there: *The whole village knew about the scandal.* Cf HAMLET, TOWN. **2** [C] *(US)* smallest unit of local government.

▷ **villager** /ˈvɪlɪdʒə(r)/ *n* person who lives in a village.

villain /ˈvɪlən/ *n* **1 (a)** person guilty or capable of great wickedness. **(b)** *(Brit sl)* (used esp by the police) criminal. **(c)** *(infml)* mischievous rogue or rascal: *Get off my bike, you little villain!* **2** (in a story, play, etc) character whose evil actions or motives are important to the plot. Cf HERO. **3** (idm) **the ˈvillain of the piece** *(esp joc)* person or thing responsible for some trouble, damage, etc: *A faulty fuse was the villain of the piece.*

▷ **villainous** /ˈvɪlənəs/ *adj* **1** characteristic of a villain; wicked: *a villainous plot, smile.* **2** *(infml)* extremely bad: *villainous handwriting, weather.* **villainously** *adv.*

villainy *n* [U, C] *(fml)* (act of) wickedness: *capable of great villainy/villainies.*

villein /ˈvɪleɪn/ *n* (in medieval Europe) feudal tenant of land who was entirely subject to his lord. ▷ **villeinage** /ˈvɪlɪnɪdʒ/ *n* [U] state of being a villein.

vim /vɪm/ *n* [U] *(dated infml)* energy or vigour: *full of vim* ○ *Put more vim into your acting!*

vinaigrette /ˌvɪnɪˈgret/ *n* [U, C] (also ˌ**vinaigrette ˈsauce**) salad dressing made from vinegar and oil, flavoured with herbs.

Vincent de Paul /ˌvɪnsənt də ˈpɔ:l/ Saint (c 1580-1660), French priest. He founded an order of priests and nuns and is famous for his work with the poor and oppressed. A society of Catholic lay people is named after him and continues this work.

vindicate /ˈvɪndɪkeɪt/ *v* [Tn] *(fml)* **1** clear (sb/sth) of blame or suspicion: *The report fully vindicated the unions.* ○ *I consider that I've been completely vindicated.* **2** show or prove the truth, justice, validity, etc (of sth that has been disputed): *Subsequent events vindicated his suspicions.* ○ *Her claim to the title was vindicated by historians.*

▷ **vindication** /ˌvɪndɪˈkeɪʃn/ *n (fml)* **(a)** [U] vindicating or being vindicated: *speak in vindication of one's conduct* ○ *the vindication of her claim.* **(b)** [C] instance of this: *The result was a vindication of all our efforts.*

vindictive /vɪnˈdɪktɪv/ *adj* having or showing a desire for revenge; unforgiving: *vindictive people, acts, urges, comments.* ▷ **vindictively** *adv.* **vindictiveness** *n* [U]: *He withheld the letter out of sheer vindictiveness.*

vine /vaɪn/ *n* **1** climbing or trailing plant with a woody stem whose fruit is the grape: [attrib] *ˈvine-grower* ○ *ˈvine leaves.* **2** any plant with slender stems that trails (eg melons) or climbs (eg peas or hops).

vinegar /ˈvɪnɪgə(r)/ *n* [U] acid liquor made from malt, wine, cider, etc by fermentation and used for flavouring food and for pickling.

▷ **vinegary** /ˈvɪnɪgərɪ/ *adj* **1** of or like vinegar in smell or taste. **2** *(fig)* sour-tempered; peevish.

vineyard /ˈvɪnjəd/ *n* plantation of grape-vines, esp for wine-making.

vingt-et-un /ˌvænteɪˈɜ:n/ *n* [U] *(French)* = PONTOON[2].

vino /ˈvi:nəʊ/ *n* [U] *(infml joc)* wine.

vinous /ˈvaɪnəs/ *adj (fml or joc)* of, like or due to wine: *a vinous flavour* ○ *sunk in a vinous stupor.*

vintage /ˈvɪntɪdʒ/ *n* **1 (a)** [C usu *sing*] (period or season of) gathering grapes for wine-making: *The vintage was later than usual.* **(b)** [C, U] (wine made from the) season's harvest of grapes: *The claret was (of) a rare vintage*, ie (of) a year when the grapes produced a claret of high quality. ○ *1959 was an excellent vintage.* ○ *What vintage* (ie year) *is this wine?* ○ [attrib] *vintage claret, port, etc* ○ *a vintage year for champagne.* **2** [attrib] **(a)** *(fig)* characteristic of a period in the past; classic: *vintage jokes* ○ *vintage science fiction of the 1950s.* **(b)** *(Brit)* (of a car) made between 1917 and 1930: *vintage Fords.* Cf VETERAN CAR (VETERAN). **3** [attrib] *(infml)* (used before proper nouns) representing the best work of (a particular person); typical: *This film is vintage Chaplin.*

vintner /ˈvɪntnə(r)/ *n (dated)* wine-merchant.

vinyl /ˈvaɪnl/ *n* [U, C] (any of various types of)

tough flexible plastic, esp PVC, used for making raincoats, records, book covers, etc.

viol /ˈvaɪəl/ *n* stringed instrument of the Renaissance period, which was played like a cello: *a consort of viols*, ie a set of usu six viols with different pitches.

viola[1] /vɪˈəʊlə/ *n* stringed musical instrument played with a bow, of larger size than a violin. ⇨ illus at MUSIC.

viola[2] /ˈvaɪələ/ *n* any of various types of plant, including pansies and violets.

violate /ˈvaɪəleɪt/ *v* [Tn] **1** break or be contrary to (a rule, principle, treaty, etc): *violate an agreement, oath, etc* ○ *These findings appear to violate the laws of physics.* **2** treat (a sacred place) with irreverence or disrespect: *violate a tomb, shrine, etc.* **3** (*fig*) disturb or interfere with (personal freedom, etc): *violate the peace*, eg by making a noise ○ *violate sb's privacy, right to free speech, etc.* **4** (*fml or euph*) rape (a woman or girl).
▷ **violation** /ˌvaɪəˈleɪʃn/ *n* **(a)** [U] violating or being violated: *act in open/flagrant violation of a treaty.* **(b)** [C] instance of this: *gross violations of human rights.*
violator *n.*

violent /ˈvaɪələnt/ *adj* **1 (a)** using, showing or caused by strong (esp unlawful) physical force: *violent criminals, demonstrators, activists, etc* ○ *a violent attack, protest, struggle, etc* ○ *Students were involved in violent clashes with the police.* ○ *meet with/die a violent death*, eg be murdered. **(b)** using, showing or caused by intense emotion: *violent passions, rages, fits, etc* ○ *violent language, abuse, etc* ○ *in a state of violent shock* ○ *He has a violent dislike of school.* **2** severe or extreme: *violent winds, storms, earthquakes, etc* ○ *violent toothache, pain, etc* ○ *a violent contrast, change, etc.*
▷ **violence** /-əns/ *n* [U] **1 (a)** violent conduct, esp of an unlawful kind: *crimes, acts, outbreaks, etc of violence* ○ *The use of violence against one's attackers.* ○ *TV violence/violence on TV.* **(b)** great emotional intensity; violent feeling: *We expressed our views with some violence.* **2** severity or harshness: *the violence of the gale, collision, outrage.* **3** (idm) **do violence to sth** (*fml*) be contrary to sth; outrage sth: *It would do violence to his principles to eat meat.*
violently *adv*: *attack, disagree, react violently* ○ *The door slammed violently.* ○ *He fell violently in love with her.*

violet /ˈvaɪələt/ *n* **1** [C] small wild or garden plant, usu with sweet-smelling purple or white flowers. ⇨ illus at PLANT. **2** [U] colour of wild violets; bluish-purple. ⇨ illus at SPECTRUM. **3** (idm) **a shrinking violet** ⇨ SHRINK.
▷ **violet** *adj* having the bluish-purple colour of wild violets: *violet eyes.*

violin /ˌvaɪəˈlɪn/ *n* stringed musical instrument held under the chin and played with a bow. ⇨ illus at MUSIC. ▷ **violinist** *n.*

violist *n* **1** /vɪˈəʊlɪst/ person who plays the viola. **2** /ˈvaɪəlɪst/ person who plays the viol.

violoncello /ˌvaɪələnˈtʃeləʊ/ *n* (*pl* ~**s**) (*fml*) = CELLO.

VIP /ˌviː aɪ ˈpiː/ *abbr* (*infml*) very important person: *give sb/get (the) VIP treatment*, ie special favours and privileges ○ *the VIP lounge*, eg at an airport, for interviews with famous people, etc.

viper /ˈvaɪpə(r)/ *n* **1** any of various types of poisonous snake found in Africa, Asia and Europe. **2** (*fig*) spiteful and treacherous person. ▷ **viperish** /ˈvaɪpərɪʃ/ *adj* (*fig*): *have a viperish* (ie malicious) *tongue.*

virago /vɪˈrɑːgəʊ/ *n* (*pl* ~**s**) (*fml*) violent and bad-tempered woman who scolds and shouts.

viral ⇨ VIRUS.

Virgil (also **Vergil**) /ˈvɜːdʒɪl/ (70-19 BC) Roman poet, Latin name Publius Vergilius Maro. His three great works were the *Eclogues*, about the countryside, the *Georgics*, about farming, and the *Aeneid, an epic telling the story of *Aeneas, the founder of Rome, written in honour of the Emperor *Augustus. ▷ **Virgilian** (also **Vergilian**) /vəˈdʒɪlɪən/ *adj.*

virgin /ˈvɜːdʒɪn/ *n* **1** [C] person, esp a girl or woman, who has never had sexual intercourse. **2 the (Blessed) Virgin** [sing] the Virgin Mary, mother of Jesus Christ: [attrib] *the virgin ˈbirth*, ie the doctrine that Jesus was miraculously conceived by the Virgin Mary.
▷ **virgin** *adj* [usu attrib] (*esp approv*) in an original or natural condition; untouched: *virgin snow* ○ *virgin wool*, ie processed and spun for the first time ○ *virgin forest, soil*, ie where cultivation has never been attempted.
virginity /vəˈdʒɪnətɪ/ *n* [U] state of being a virgin; virgin condition: *keep/lose one's virginity.*
□ **the ˌVirgin ˈQueen** *Elizabeth I of England.

virginal /ˈvɜːdʒɪnl/ *adj* (*approv*) of or suitable for a virgin: *virginal innocence.*

virginals /ˈvɜːdʒɪnəlz/ *n* [pl] square keyboard instrument without legs used in the 16th and 17th centuries.

Virginia /vəˈdʒɪnɪə/ state on the Atlantic coast of the USA. It is crossed in the east by the Blue Ridge mountains. Agriculture is important and tobacco is a traditional crop. Industries include chemicals and food processing. ⇨ map at App 1. ▷ **Virginia** *n* [U] type of tobacco originally produced in Virginia: *Golden Virginia* ○ [attrib] *Virginia cigarettes.*
□ **Virˌginia ˈcreeper** (*US* also **woodbine**) ornamental vine often grown on walls, with large leaves which turn scarlet in the autumn.

Virgin Islands /ˈvɜːdʒɪn aɪləndz; *US* ˌvɜːrdʒən ˈaɪləndz/ **the Virgin Islands** group of islands in the Caribbean. The British Virgin Islands (pop approx 14 000; official language English; capital Road Town) comprise 42 islands. The main economic activity is tourism. There are over 50 American Virgin Islands, but only three which are inhabited (pop approx 100 000; official language English; capital Charlotte Amalie). The main economic activities are tourism, oil refining and the processing of bauxite. ⇨ map at CARIBBEAN.

Virgo /ˈvɜːgəʊ/ *n* **1** [U] the sixth sign of the zodiac, the Virgin. ⇨ illus at ZODIAC. **2** [C] (*pl* ~**s**) person born under the influence of this sign. ▷ **Virgoan** *n, adj.* ⇨ Usage at ZODIAC.

virile /ˈvɪraɪl; *US* ˈvɪrəl/ *n* (*usu approv*) **1** (of men) having procreative power; sexually potent: *virile young males.* **2** having or showing typically masculine strength or energy: *virile pursuits such as rowing and mountaineering* ○ *a virile performance of Othello.*
▷ **virility** /vɪˈrɪlətɪ/ *n* [U] **1** (of men) sexual potency: *a need to prove, assert, etc one's virility.* **2** typically masculine strength or energy.

virology /vaɪəˈrɒlədʒɪ/ *n* [U] scientific study of viruses and virus diseases. ▷ **virological** /ˌvaɪərəˈlɒdʒɪkl/ *adj.* **virologist** /vaɪəˈrɒlədʒɪst/ *n.*

virtual /ˈvɜːtʃʊəl/ *adj* [attrib] being or acting as what is described, but not accepted as such in name or officially: *Our deputy manager is the virtual head of the business.* ○ *A virtual state of war exists between the two countries.*
▷ **virtually** /-tʃʊəlɪ/ *adv* in every important respect; almost: *be virtually certain, impossible, fixed, agreed* ○ *He virtually promised me the job*, ie but did not actually do so. ○ *There's virtually none left.*

virtue /ˈvɜːtʃuː/ *n* **1 (a)** [U] moral goodness or excellence: *lead a life of virtue* ○ (*esp joc*) *a paragon of virtue.* **(b)** [C] particular form of this; good habit: (*saying*) *Patience is a virtue.* ○ *extol, praise, etc the virtues of thrift.* Cf VICE[1] 1. **2** [C, U] **the ~ (of sth/being sth/doing sth)** attractive or useful quality; advantage: *This seat has the virtue of being adjustable.* ○ *The great virtue of camping is its cheapness/is that it is cheap.* ○ *learn the virtue(s) of keeping one's mouth shut*, ie of not always saying what one thinks. **3** [U] (*fml or joc*) chastity, esp of a woman: *lose/preserve one's virtue.* **4** (idm) **by virtue of sth** (*fml*) on account of or because of sth: *He was exempt from charges by virtue of his youth/of being so young/of the fact that he was so young.* **make a ˌvirtue of neˈcessity** do sth with a good grace because one has to do it anyway: *Being short of money, I made a virtue of necessity and gave up smoking.* **a woman of easy virtue** ⇨ WOMAN. **virtue is its own reward** (*saying*) behaving virtuously should give one enough satisfaction for one not to expect any further reward.
▷ **virtuous** /ˈvɜːtʃʊəs/ *adj* **1** having or showing moral virtue. **2** (*derog or joc*) claiming to have or show better behaviour or higher moral principles than others; self-righteous: *feel virtuous at/about having done the washing-up.* **virtuously** *adv.* **virtuousness** *n* [U].

virtuoso /ˌvɜːtʃʊˈəʊzəʊ, -ˈəʊsəʊ/ *n* (*pl* ~**s** or **-si** /-ziː, -siː/) **1** person who is exceptionally skilled in the techniques of a fine art, esp playing a musical instrument or singing: *a cello, trumpet, etc virtuoso* ○ *a jazz virtuoso* ○ *great virtuosos of the keyboard* ○ [attrib] *virtuoso players.* **2** [attrib] (*fig*) showing exceptional skill: *His handling of the meeting was quite a virtuoso performance.*
▷ **virtuosity** /ˌvɜːtʃʊˈɒsətɪ/ *n* [U] skill of a virtuoso: *feats, displays, etc of virtuosity.*

virulent /ˈvɪrʊlənt/ *adj* **1** [esp attrib] (of a disease or poison) extremely harmful or deadly: *a virulent strain of flu.* **2** (*fml*) strongly and bitterly hostile: *virulent abuse* ○ *make a virulent attack on the press* ○ *a particularly virulent form of racism.* ▷ **virulence** /-ləns/ *n* [U]. **virulently** *adv.*

virus /ˈvaɪərəs/ *n* (*pl* **viruses**) **1 (a)** simple organism, smaller than bacteria, and causing infectious disease: *the flu, rabies, AIDS, etc virus* ○ [attrib] *attacked by, suffering from, etc a virus infection.* Cf MICROBE. **(b)** (*infml*) disease caused by one of these: *There's a/some virus going round the office*, ie making people ill. **2** (*computing*) hidden code in a computer program, intended to corrupt a system or destroy stored data.
▷ **viral** /ˈvaɪərəl/ *adj* of, like or caused by a virus.

Vis (also **Visc**) *abbr* Viscount(ess).

visa /ˈviːzə/ *n* stamp or mark put on a passport by officials of a foreign country to show that the holder may enter, pass through or leave their country: *entry/transit/exit visas* ○ *get a Polish visa/a visa for Poland* ○ *renew/extend a visa*, ie before it expires.
▷ **visa** *v* (*pt, pp* **visaed** /viːzəd/) [Tn] mark (a passport) with a visa.

visage /ˈvɪzɪdʒ/ *n* (*joc or rhet*) person's face: *the funeral director's gloomy visage.*

vis-à-vis /ˌviːzɑːˈviː/ *prep* (*French*) **1** in relation to (sth): *discuss plans for the company vis-à-vis a possible merger.* **2** in comparison with (sth): *Women's salaries are low vis-à-vis what men earn for the same work.*
▷ **vis-à-vis** *adv* (*French fml*) so that two people or things face each other.

viscera /ˈvɪsərə/ *n* [pl] (usu **the viscera**) (*anatomy*) large internal organs of the body, eg the heart, the liver and the intestines.
▷ **visceral** /ˈvɪsərəl/ *adj* **1** (*anatomy*) of the viscera. **2** (*fig fml*) (of feelings, etc) not rational; instinctive: *a visceral mistrust of their peace moves.*

viscid /ˈvɪsɪd/ *adj* (of a liquid) thick and sticky.

Visconti /vɪsˈkɒntɪ/ Luchino (1906-76), Italian film director, known also for his opera productions. Influenced by Jean *Renoir, he brought a new realism to the Italian cinema in films like *Obsession*. Later works such as *The Leopard* are remarkable for their psychological depth and visual beauty.

viscose /ˈvɪskəʊz, -əʊs/ *n* [U] **(a)** cellulose in a viscous state, used in the manufacture of rayon, etc. **(b)** fabric made of this.

viscount /ˈvaɪkaʊnt/ *n* **1** (in Britain) nobleman ranking higher than a baron but lower than an earl. **2** courtesy title of an earl's eldest son: *Viscount Linley.* ⇨ article at ARISTOCRAT.
▷ **viscountcy** /-tsɪ/ *n* title or rank of a viscount.
viscountess /ˈvaɪkaʊntɪs/ *n* **1** viscount's wife or widow. **2** female viscount.

viscous /ˈvɪskəs/ *adj* (of a liquid) not pouring easily; thick and sticky: *viscous pools of blood, oil, mud.* ▷ **viscosity** /vɪˈskɒsətɪ/ *n* [U].

vise *n* (*US*) = VICE[2].

Vishnu /ˈvɪʃnuː/ one of the three main gods of Hinduism, worshipped as the preserver of the universe. Cf BRAHMA, SIVA.

visible /ˈvɪzəbl/ *adj* ~ **(to sb/sth) 1** that can be seen; in sight: *The hills were barely visible through* *the mist.* ○ *This star is not visible to the naked eye.* **2** (*fig*) that can be noticed or ascertained; apparent: *visible improvements, differences, changes, etc* ○ *speak with visible contempt, dismay, impatience, etc.*

▷ **visibility** /ˌvɪzəˈbɪlətɪ/ *n* [U] **1** fact or state of being visible. **2** condition of the light or weather for seeing things at a distance: *Visibility was down to 100 metres in the fog.* ○ *planes grounded because of poor/low/bad visibility.*

visibly /-əblɪ/ *adv* noticeably: *visibly offended, ill, in love.*

Visigoth /ˈvɪzɪgɒθ/ *n* member of the western branch of the Gothic peoples, who eventually settled in Spain.

vision /ˈvɪʒn/ *n* **1** [U] **(a)** power of seeing; sight: *have perfect, poor, blurred, etc vision* ○ *The blow on the head impaired* (ie damaged) *his vision.* ○ *within/outside my field of vision,* ie that I can/cannot see from a certain point. **(b)** (*fig*) ability to view a subject, problem, etc imaginatively; foresight and wisdom in planning: *a statesman of (great breadth of) vision.* **2** [C] **(a)** dream or similar trance-like state, often associated with a religious experience: *Jesus came to Paul in a vision.* ○ *I had/saw a vision of the end of the world.* **(b)** (esp *pl*) thing seen vividly in the imagination: *the romantic visions of youth* ○ *conjure up visions of married bliss* ○ *I had visions of us going on strike.* **3** [C] ~ **of sth** (*rhet*) person or sight of unusual beauty: *She was a vision of loveliness.* **4** [U] what is seen on a television or cinema screen; picture: *We get good vision but poor sound on this set.*

visionary /ˈvɪʒənrɪ; *US* -ʒənerɪ/ *adj* **1** (*approv*) having or showing foresight or wisdom: *visionary leaders, writers, paintings, ideals.* **2** having or showing too much imagination or fancy to be practical.

▷ **visionary** *n* (*usu approv*) person who has visionary(1) ideas: *True visionaries are often misunderstood by their own generation.*

visit /ˈvɪzɪt/ *v* **1** [I, Tn] **(a)** go or come to see (a person, place, etc) either socially or on business or for some other purpose: *No answer — they must be out visiting.* ○ ˈ*visiting hours* (ie when relatives and friends can see patients) *at a hospital* ○ *visit a friend, dentist, fortune-teller, etc* ○ *Most tourists in London visit the British Museum.* **(b)** go or come to see (a place, an institution, etc) in order to make an official examination or check: *The school inspector is visiting next week.* ○ *The restaurant is visited regularly by public health officers.* **2** [I, Tn] stay temporarily at (a place) or with (a person): *We don't live here, we're just visiting.* ○ *Owls visited the barn to rest.* ○ *I'm going to visit my aunt for a few days.* **3** [Ipr] ~ **with sb** (*US infml*) visit sb, esp for an informal talk or chat: *Please stay and visit with me for a while.* ⇨ Usage. **4** [Tn·pr] ~ **sth on/upon sb/sth** (*arch*) inflict punishment, etc on sb/sth: *visit the sins of the fathers upon the children,* ie make the children suffer for their parents' failings.

▷ **visit** *n* **1** ~ **(to sb/sth) (from sb/sth)** act or period of visiting; temporary stay: *It was his first visit to his wife's parents.* ○ *pay a visit to a friend, a doctor, a prospective customer, etc* ○ *be, come, go on a visit to the seaside* ○ *the Queen's state visit* (ie made for official or political reasons) *to China* ○ *regular visits from the landlord.* **2** (*US infml*) chat or talk: *We had a nice visit on the phone.*

□ ˈ**visiting card** (*US* ˈ**calling card**) small card with one's name, address, company, etc printed on it, which one leaves with clients or social acquaintances.

ˌ**visiting proˈfessor** professor who teaches for a fixed period at another (esp foreign) university or college.

NOTE ON USAGE: We can **visit** (*US* **visit with**) or **go to see** someone at home or at work. **Come/Go and stay** is used in informal English for a longer visit at somebody's house: *Come and stay with us soon.* ○ *I'm hoping to go and stay with my cousin Tom over Christmas.* We **call on** someone for an official purpose: *A representative of the company will call on you to assess the damage.* We **call in on** a friend for a short time, often when we are on our way to somewhere else: *We could call in on Patrick on the way to your mother's.* More informally, we **drop by** at somebody's (house), **drop in on** somebody or (in US English) **visit with** somebody when we make a casual visit to friends or relations: *Let's drop in on Nick when we're in Bristol, shall we?*

visitation /ˌvɪzɪˈteɪʃn/ *n* **1** ~ **(of sb/sth)** (*fml*) official visit, esp of inspection: *a visitation of the sick,* ie made by a clergyman as part of his duties. **2** ~ **(from sb/sth)** (*infml*) visit, esp a prolonged or an unwelcome one: *We had sundry visitations from the Tax Inspector.* **3** ~ **(of sth)** (*fml*) trouble or disaster considered as a punishment from God: *The famine was a visitation of God for their sins.* **4 the Visitation** [sing] **(a)** (*Bible*) the visit made by *Mary to her cousin Elizabeth after the archangel *Gabriel had told her she was going to have a child. **(b)** 2 July, on which this visit is honoured in the Christian Church.

visitor /ˈvɪzɪtə(r)/ *n* ~ **(to sb/sth) (from sb/sth) 1 (a)** person who visits a person or place: *The old lady never has/gets any visitors.* ○ *She was a frequent visitor to the gallery.* ○ *visitors from the insurance company.* **(b)** person who stays temporarily at a place or with a person: *Rome welcomes millions of visitors each year.* **2** migratory bird that lives in an area temporarily or at a certain season: *summer/winter visitors to British shores.*

□ ˈ**visitors' book** book in which visitors write their names, addresses and sometimes comments, eg at a hotel or place of public interest.

visor

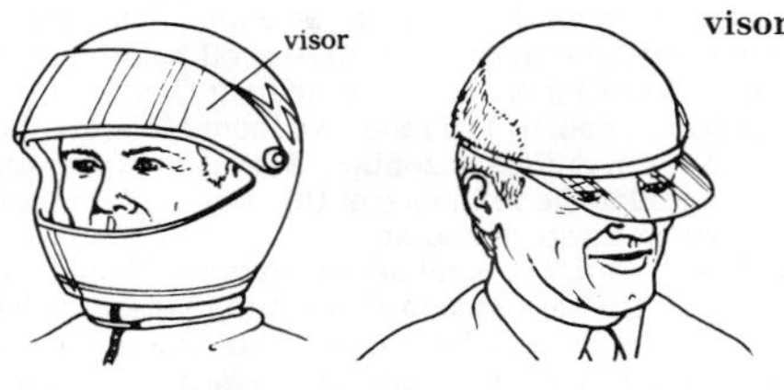

visor /ˈvaɪzə(r)/ *n* **1** moving part of a helmet, used to cover and protect the face: *The motor-cyclist raised/lowered his visor.* **2 (a)** projecting piece of plastic, stiffened cloth, etc worn above the eyes to shield them from the sun. **(b)** similar object forming the projecting front part of a cap; peak.

vista /ˈvɪstə/ *n* (*fml*) **1** view as seen between long rows of trees, buildings, etc: *This street offers a fine vista of the cathedral.* **2** (*fig*) long series of scenes, events, etc that one can look back on or forward to: *This discovery opens up new vistas of research for biologists.*

visual /ˈvɪʒʊəl/ *adj* concerned with or used in seeing: *visual images, effects, etc* ○ *the visual arts,* ie painting, cinema, theatre, etc ○ *visual humour,* ie humour that depends on actions rather than words for its effect ○ *Her designs have a strong visual appeal.* ○ *a good visual memory,* ie ability to remember what one sees.

▷ **visualize, -ise** /-aɪz/ *v* [Tn, Tsg, Cn·n/a] ~ **sb/sth (as sth)** form a mental picture of sb/sth: *I remember meeting him but I just can't visualize him.* ○ *I can't visualize myself ever getting married.* ○ *Tom visualized the house as a romantic ruin.*

visualization, -isation /ˌvɪʒʊəlaɪˈzeɪʃn; *US* -lɪˈz-/ *n* [U]: *powers of visualization.*

visually /ˈvɪʒʊəlɪ/ *adv* **1** in seeing: *visually handicapped,* ie blind or nearly blind. **2** in appearance: *Visually, the decor was very striking.*

□ ˌ**visual** ˈ**aid** (esp *pl*) picture, film, video, etc used as a teaching aid.

ˌ**visual diˈsplay unit** (*abbr* **VDU**) device resembling a TV screen, connected to a computer, etc, on which data can be displayed from the computer or fed in, eg by a keyboard or light pen.

vital /ˈvaɪtl/ *adj* **1** [attrib] connected with or essential to life: *The heart performs a vital bodily function.* ○ *He was wounded in a vital part of his anatomy,* eg the lungs, brain. ○ (*fig*) *The vital spark that would have brought the play to life was missing.* **2** ~ **(to/for sth)** essential to the existence, success, or operation of sth: *vital information, research, legislation* ○ *a vital clue to the killer's identity* ○ *The police perform a vital role in our society.* ○ *It is absolutely vital that the matter is kept secret.* **3** (*approv*) energetic or lively; dynamic: *She's a very vital sort of person.*

▷ **vitally** /ˈvaɪtəlɪ/ *adv* extremely: *vitally important, necessary, etc* ○ *We are vitally concerned to win public support.*

the vitals *n* [pl] (*dated or joc*) important organs of the body: *Fear gripped (at) my vitals.* ○ *She kneed her attacker in the vitals* (ie in the genitals) *and ran away.*

□ ˌ**vital staˈtistics 1** statistics relating to population figures or births, marriages and deaths. **2** (*Brit infml*) measurements of a woman's bust, waist and hips.

vitality /vaɪˈtælətɪ/ *n* [U] **1** persistent energy; liveliness or vigour: *The dog was bouncing with health and vitality.* ○ *The ballet sparkled with vitality.* **2** (*fig*) (of institutions, etc) ability to endure or continue functioning: *The vitality of the movement is threatened.*

vitamin /ˈvɪtəmɪn; *US* ˈvaɪt-/ *n* any of a number of organic substances which are present in certain foods and are essential to the health of humans and other animals: *enriched with vitamins* ○ [attrib] ˈ*vitamin pills* ○ *one's daily vitamin requirements* ○ *Vitamin deficiency can cause illnesses,* eg scurvy, rickets.

▷ **vitaminize, -ise** /ˈvɪtəmɪnaɪz; *US* ˈvaɪt-/ *v* [Tn] add vitamins to (a food).

□ ˌ**vitamin** ˈ**A** vitamin found eg in liver and carrots, needed for the pigments of the eye.

ˌ**vitamin** ˈ**B** any of a group of vitamins (known as B1, B2, etc) needed for the working of various enzymes.

ˌ**vitamin** ˈ**C** (also **ascorbic acid**) vitamin found esp in fresh fruit and vegetables, needed for the growth of healthy cells and tissue.

ˌ**vitamin** ˈ**D** vitamin needed for the growth of healthy bone tissue.

ˌ**vitamin** ˈ**E** vitamin found eg in cereals and green vegetables, needed to prevent the oxidation of certain fatty acids.

ˌ**vitamin** ˈ**K** vitamin found eg in egg yolks and green vegetables, needed for blood clotting.

vitiate /ˈvɪʃɪeɪt/ *v* [Tn] (*fml*) **1** weaken or spoil the quality or efficiency of (sth): *the vitiated atmosphere of our polluted inner cities* ○ *The serum is vitiated by exposure to the air.* **2** weaken the force of (sth); make ineffective: *vitiate a claim, contract, theory.* ▷ **vitiation** /ˌvɪʃɪˈeɪʃn/ *n* [U].

viticulture /ˈvɪtɪkʌltʃə(r), ˈvaɪt-/ *n* [U] (science or practice of the) growing of grapes, esp for use in wine-making.

vitreous /ˈvɪtrɪəs/ *adj* **(a)** having a glass-like texture or finish: *vitreous enamel, china, porcelain, etc.* **(b)** (of rocks) hard and shiny like glass.

□ **the** ˌ**vitreous** ˈ**humour** space in the eyeball between the lens and the retina.

vitrify /ˈvɪtrɪfaɪ/ *v* (*pt, pp* **-fied**) [I, Tn esp passive] (cause sth to) be changed into a glass-like substance, esp by heat: *vitrified glazes,* eg on ceramics. ▷ **vitrifaction** /ˌvɪtrɪˈfækʃn/, **vitrification** /ˌvɪtrɪfɪˈkeɪʃn/ *ns* [U].

vitriol /ˈvɪtrɪəl/ *n* [U] **1** (*dated*) sulphuric acid or any of its salts: *blue vitriol,* ie copper sulphate. **2** (*fig*) savagely hostile comments or criticism: *His attack on the government was pure vitriol.*

▷ **vitriolic** /ˌvɪtrɪˈɒlɪk/ *adj* savagely and bitterly hostile: *vitriolic criticism, attacks, etc* ○ *We deplore the vitriolic nature of his remarks.*

vitro ⇨ IN VITRO.

vituperate /vɪˈtjuːpəreɪt; *US* vaɪˈtuː-/ *v* [I, Tn] ~ **(against sb/sth)** (*fml*) use abusive language or bitter criticism; revile sb/sth: *The prince vituperated against the developers for ruining London's skyline.*

▷ **vituperation** /vɪˌtjuːpəˈreɪʃn; *US* vaɪˌtuː-/ *n* [U] (*fml*) abusive language or bitter criticism.

vituperative /vɪˈtju:pərətɪv; *US* vaɪˈtu:pəreɪtɪv/ *adj*: *vituperative debate, criticism, etc.*
viva[1] /ˈvaɪvə/ *n* (*Brit infml*) = VIVA VOCE.
viva[2] /ˈvi:və/ *interj* (*dated*) long may he or she live (used to applaud sb).
▷ **viva** *n* cry of 'viva'.
vivace /vɪˈvɑ:tʃɪ/ *adv* (*music*) (to be played, sung, etc) in a brisk lively manner.
vivacious /vɪˈveɪʃəs/ *adj* (*approv*) (esp of a woman) lively or high-spirited: *bubbly and vivacious blonde seeks fun-loving gent*, eg as an advertisement in a 'lonely hearts' column ○ *She gave a vivacious laugh.* ▷ **vivaciously** *adv*. **vivacity** /vɪˈvæsətɪ/ (also **vivaciousness**) *n* [U].
Vivaldi /vɪˈvældɪ/ Antonio (1678-1741), Italian composer. He wrote around 500 concertos, many of them for the violin, which he helped to establish as a solo instrument. He had a great influence on *Bach, who transcribed ten of his violin concertos as keyboard concertos. Vivaldi also wrote many operas and liturgical works.
viva voce /ˌvaɪvə ˈvəʊsɪ, ˈvəʊtʃɪ/ (also *Brit infml* **viva**) *n* oral examination, esp in universities: *have, get, take, etc a viva (voce).*
▷ **viva voce** *adj, adv* of a viva voce examination; oral(ly).
vivid /ˈvɪvɪd/ *adj* **1** (of light or colour) strong and bright; intense: *a vivid flash of lightning* ○ *vivid green trousers.* **2** (of a mental faculty) creating ideas, etc in a lively or an active way: *a vivid memory, imagination, etc.* **3** producing strong clear pictures in the mind: *a vivid description, recollection, dream* ○ *The incident left a vivid impression on me.* ▷ **vividly** *adv*. **vividness** *n* [U].
viviparous /vɪˈvɪpərəs; *US* vaɪ-/ *adj* (*biology*) (of most mammals) having offspring that develop within the mother's body, ie that do not hatch from eggs.
vivisection /ˌvɪvɪˈsekʃn/ *n* **(a)** [U] practice of performing surgical experiments on live animals for scientific research: [attrib] *the anti-vivisection lobby.* ⇨ articles at PROTEST, ANIMAL. **(b)** [C] act or instance of this.
▷ **vivisectionist** /-ʃənɪst/ *n* **(a)** person who performs vivisections. **(b)** person who considers vivisection is justifiable.
vixen /ˈvɪksn/ *n* **1** female fox. **2** (*esp dated*) bad-tempered quarrelsome woman: *a real little vixen.* ▷ **vixenish** /ˈvɪksənɪʃ/ *adj*: *her nasty, vixenish ways.*
viz /vɪz/ *abbr* (often read out as *namely*) that is to say; in other words (Latin *videlicet*): *these three persons, viz landlord, lessee and tenant...*

NOTE ON USAGE: The abbreviations **viz**, **ie** and **eg** are mostly used in formal or technical English. In speech and when reading a written text aloud we usually say **namely**, **that is (to say)** and **for example** respectively. **Viz** (or **namely**) is used to expand or specify what has already been said: *There are three major advantages of the design, viz/namely cheapness, simplicity and availability.* ○ *I want to talk today about a major threat facing our society, namely AIDS.* We use **ie** (or **that is**) to explain an unclear statement or word by rephrasing it: *He admitted being 'economical with the truth' (ie lying).* In this dictionary we often use **ie** and **eg** after examples to give further explanation of the meaning of those examples.

vizier /vɪˈzɪə(r)/ *n* (esp formerly) high-ranking officials in some Muslim countries: *the grand vizier*, eg of the old Turkish empire.
vocabulary /vəˈkæbjʊlərɪ; *US* -lerɪ/ *n* **1** [C] total number of words that make up a language. Cf LEXICON. **2** [C, U] (body of) words known to a person or used in a particular book, subject, etc; lexis: *a wide, limited, colourful, etc vocabulary* ○ *Tim has an average (level of) vocabulary for a 3-year-old.* ○ *an active vocabulary*, ie words one recognizes and can use ○ *a passive vocabulary*, ie words one recognizes only ○ *enrich, increase, extend, etc one's vocabulary.* **3** (also *infml* **vocab** /ˈvəʊkæb/) [U, C] list of words with their meanings, esp one which accompanies a textbook in a foreign language. Cf GLOSSARY.
vocal /ˈvəʊkl/ *adj* **1** [usu attrib] of, for or uttered by the voice: *the vocal organs*, ie the tongue, lips, vocal cords, etc ○ *The cantata has a difficult vocal score.* ○ *Callas's vocal range was astonishing.* **2** expressing one's opinions or feelings freely in speech; outspoken: *vocal criticism, support* ○ *We were very vocal about our rights.* ○ *The protesters are a small but vocal minority.*
▷ **vocal** *n* (often *pl*) sung part of a piece of jazz or pop music: *Who was on/sang lead vocal(s) on the group's last record?*
vocalist /ˈvəʊkəlɪst/ *n* singer, esp in a jazz or pop group. Cf INSTRUMENTALIST (INSTRUMENTAL).
vocally /ˈvəʊkəlɪ/ *adv* **1** in a way that uses the voice. **2** freely or outspokenly: *protest vocally.*
□ ˌ**vocal** ˈ**cords** voice-producing part of the larynx. ⇨ illus at THROAT.
vocalize, -ise /ˈvəʊkəlaɪz/ *v* [Tn] (*fml*) say or sing (sounds or words); utter.
vocation /vəʊˈkeɪʃn/ *n* **1** [C] ~ **(for/to sth)** feeling that one is called to (and qualified for) a certain type of work, esp social or religious: *vocations to the priesthood, ministry, etc* ○ *have/follow one's vocation to become a nun* ○ *Nursing is a vocation as well as a profession.* **2** [U] ~ **(for sth)** natural liking or aptitude for a certain type of work: *He has little vocation for teaching.* **3** [C usu *sing*] (*fml*) person's trade or profession: *find one's true vocation (in life)* ○ *You should be an actor — you've missed your vocation*, ie you are following the wrong career.
▷ **vocational** /-ʃənl/ *adj* of or concerning the qualifications, etc needed for a trade or profession: *vocational guidance, training, etc*, eg for students about to leave school.
vocative /ˈvɒkətɪv/ *n* (*grammar*) special form of a noun, a pronoun or an adjective used (in some inflected languages) when addressing or invoking a person or thing.
▷ **vocative** *adj* of or in the vocative.
vociferate /vəˈsɪfəreɪt; *US* vəʊ-/ *v* [I, Tn] (*fml*) say (sth) loudly or noisily; shout.
▷ **vociferous** /vəˈsɪfərəs; *US* vəʊ-/ *adj* loud or noisy; expressing one's views forcibly and insistently: *vociferous complaints, protests, etc* ○ *a vociferous group of demonstrators.* **vociferously** *adv*.
vodka /ˈvɒdkə/ *n* **(a)** [U] strong alcoholic drink distilled from rye and other vegetable products, made esp in Russia. **(b)** [C] glass or drink of this: *a vodka and lime.*
vogue /vəʊg/ *n* [C esp *sing*] **1** ~ **(for sth)** current or prevailing fashion: *a new vogue for low-heeled shoes.* **2** [C, U] popular favour or acceptance: *His novels had a great vogue ten years ago.* **3** (idm) **be** ˌ**all the** ˈ**vogue** (*infml*) be fashionable or popular everywhere. **be in/come into** ˈ**vogue** be/become fashionable or popular: *Short hair came back into vogue about ten years ago.*
□ ˈ**vogue-word** *n* word that is currently fashionable: *'Accountability' is the current vogue-word in politics.* Cf BUZZ-WORD (BUZZ).
voice /vɔɪs/ *n* **1** **(a)** [C] sounds formed in the larynx and uttered through the mouth, esp by a person speaking or singing: *I can hear voices through the wall.* ○ *Keep your voice down*, ie Don't speak loudly. ○ *recognize sb's voice* ○ *speak in a loud, rough, husky, gentle, etc voice* ○ *He has a good singing voice*, ie can sing well. ○ *raise/lower one's voice*, ie speak more loudly/softly ○ *His voice has broken*, ie become deep like a man's. ○ *Her voice shook/trembled with emotion.* **(b)** [U] ability to produce such sounds: *commands given in a firm tone of voice.* **2** (*fig*) **(a)** [U, sing] ~ **(in sth)** (right to express one's) opinion, etc in spoken or written words; influence: *have little, some, no, a voice in the matter* ○ *The workers want a voice in management decisions.* **(b)** [sing] means by which such an opinion, etc is expressed: *listen to the voice of reason, experience, dissent* ○ *Our newspaper represents the voice of the people.* **3** [sing] (*grammar*) contrast between a sentence in which the doer of the action is subject (*active*) and one in which the person or thing affected is subject (*passive*): *in the active/passive voice.* **4** [U] (*phonetics*) sound produced by vibration of the vocal cords and not with breath alone, used in the pronunciation of vowel sounds and certain consonants, eg /b/, /d/, /z/. **5** (idm) **at the** ˌ**top of one's** ˈ**voice** ⇨ TOP[1]. **find/lose one's voice/tongue** ⇨ FIND[1]. **give voice to sth** (*fml*) express (feelings, worries, etc): *give voice to one's indignation, dismay, concern, etc.* **have, etc an edge to one's voice** ⇨ EDGE[1]. **in good, poor, etc** ˈ**voice** singing or speaking as well as usual, worse than usual, etc: *The bass soloist was in excellent voice.* **lift one's voice** ⇨ LIFT. **like, etc the sound of one's own voice** ⇨ SOUND[2]. **make one's** ˈ**voice heard** express one's feelings, opinions, etc in such a way that they are noticed or acted on: *This programme gives ordinary viewers a chance to make their voice(s) heard.* **raise one's voice against sb/sth** ⇨ RAISE. **the still small voice** ⇨ STILL[1]. **with** ˌ**one** ˈ**voice** (*fml*) unanimously: *With one voice, the workers voted to strike.*
▷ **voice** *v* [Tn] **1** express (feelings, etc) in words: *A spokesman voiced the workers' dissatisfaction.* **2** (*phonetics*) utter (a sound) with voice(4): *voiced consonants*, eg /d/, /v/, /z/.
-voiced (forming compound *adjs*) having a voice of the specified kind: *loud-voiced* ○ *gruff-voiced.*
voiceless *adj* (*phonetics*) (of a sound) uttered without voice(4): *The consonants t, f and s are voiceless.*
□ ˈ**voice-box** *n* = LARYNX.
ˈ**voice-over** *n* narration (eg in a film) by a speaker who is not seen.
void /vɔɪd/ *n* (usu *sing*) (*fml or rhet*) empty space; vacuum: *the blue void we call the sky* ○ (*fig*) *an aching void left by the death of her child.*
▷ **void** *adj* (*fml*) **1** empty; vacant. **2** [pred] ~ **of sth** without sth; lacking sth: *Her face was void of all interest.* Cf DEVOID. **3** (idm) **null and void** ⇨ NULL.
void *v* [Tn] **1** (*law*) make (sth) not legally binding. **2** (*fml*) empty the contents of (one's bowels or bladder).
voile /vɔɪl/ *n* [U] thin semi-transparent material of cotton, wool or silk.
vol *abbr* **1** (*pl* **vols**) volume: *an edition in 3 vols* ○ *Complete Works of Byron Vol 2.* **2** volume: *vol 125 ml*, eg on a container.
volatile /ˈvɒlətaɪl; *US* -tl/ *adj* **1** (of a liquid) changing rapidly into vapour. **2** (*esp derog*) (of a person) changing quickly from one mood or interest to another; fickle: *a highly volatile personality, disposition, nature, etc.* **3** (of trading conditions, etc) likely to change suddenly or sharply; unstable: *volatile stock-markets, exchange rates* ○ *a volatile political situation*, eg one that could lead to a change of government. ▷ **volatility** /ˌvɒləˈtɪlətɪ/ *n* [U].
vol-au-vent /ˈvɒləvɑ:ŋ/ *n* small light case of puff pastry filled with meat, fish, etc in a rich sauce.

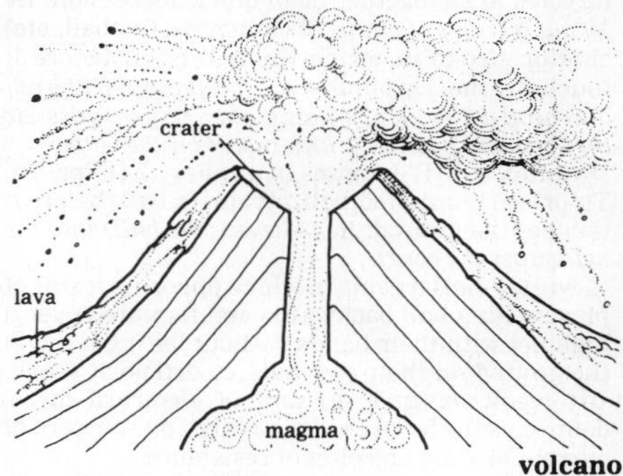

volcano

volcano /vɒlˈkeɪnəʊ/ *n* (*pl* ~**es**) mountain or hill with an opening or openings through which lava, cinders, gases, etc come up from below the earth's surface (*an active volcano*), may come up after an interval (*a dormant volcano*), or have ceased to come up (*an extinct volcano*). ⇨ illus.

Voluntary Organizations

There is a long tradition in Britain of doing voluntary work in the community, and there are thousands of groups, both formal and informal, national and local, that cater for those in need. It is estimated that as many as one adult in three does work of this kind.

Many organizations are registered charities, with fund-raising being an important part of their activity. Others are more concerned with counselling and giving practical help, and many of these are funded by the government or by local authorities, especially when they are working in the field of health or social services. Some voluntary organizations are specifically set up to work in conjunction with government schemes, often as a complement to the National Health Service.

Broadly, the work of voluntary organizations can be divided into three types. The first helps with personal and family problems, especially in areas such as marriage breakdown, cruelty to children, loneliness and poverty. Some of the best known organizations are Relate (formerly the Marriage Guidance Council), the National Society for the Prevention of Cruelty to Children (NSPCC), the Child Poverty Action Group, and the Samaritans, who help people who feel suicidal by providing a sympathetic listener and counsellor by means of a 24-hour telephone service. (They take their name from the parable of the Good Samaritan in the Bible, who helped a stranger in need when no one else would.)

The second kind of voluntary work is concerned with the sick and disabled, and there is a wide range of organizations that do this work. Three of the largest are the British Red Cross Society, the St John Ambulance Brigade (who attend public events to provide first aid) and the Women's Royal Voluntary Service (WRVS). The latter provides a wide range of services, including the 'meals on wheels' service that brings a hot midday meal to people unable to leave their homes. Organizations that provide help with particular disabilities include the Royal National Institute for the Blind (RNIB), which provides a 'talking book' service of recorded readings, the Royal National Institute for the Deaf (RNID), MIND (the official name of the National Association for Mental Health, which works with the mentally ill), MENCAP (the Royal Society for Mentally Handicapped Children and Adults, which works with the mentally handicapped), the Spastics Society, Alcoholics Anonymous (AA), and Age Concern and Help the Aged which both work with old people.

The third type of voluntary work is the community service provided by many organizations, including religious bodies such as the Salvation Army, the Church Army (founded as a missionary society of the Church of England), the Young Men's Christian Association (YMCA), and the Young Women's Christian Association (YWCA). All four organizations are famous for their hostels. The National Association for the Care and Resettlement of Offenders (NACRO) helps ex-prisoners to settle in the community.

There are 1300 Citizens' Advice Bureaus in Britain, staffed mainly by volunteers. They offer advice on people's legal rights and provide information about the help that can be obtained from voluntary bodies and the social services.

There are many 'self-help' groups, often working at a local level, such as those formed by parents to run playgroups for young children, or those that provide practical help for disabled people in a particular community. There are also many groups that provide information and advice to sufferers with a particular illness (for example eczema or multiple sclerosis) and their families. (Cf article at CHARITY.)

▷ **volcanic** /vɒlˈkænɪk/ *adj* [esp attrib] of, from or like a volcano: *volcanic eruptions, gases, etc* ○ *(fig) The French Revolution was a volcanic upheaval in European history.*

vole /vəʊl/ *n* small animal resembling a rat or mouse and living in hedgerows, river-banks, etc: *a ˈwater-vole*, ie a large water-rat. ⇨ illus at ANIMAL.

Volga /ˈvɒlgə/ **the Volga** river in the USSR, rising in the north-west and flowing into the Caspian Sea. It is the longest river in Europe, 3688 km (2292 miles). It is dammed at several points to provide hydroelectric power.

volition /vəˈlɪʃn; *US* vəʊ-/ *n (fml)* **1** [U] act of using one's will in choosing, making a decision, etc. **2** (idm) **of one's own voˈlition** without being forced; voluntarily: *She left entirely of her own volition.* ▷ **volitional** /-ʃənl/ *adj*: *a volitional act.*

volley /ˈvɒlɪ/ *n* **1** (**a**) simultaneous throwing or firing of a number of stones, bullets, etc: *Police fired a volley* (ie of plastic bullets.) *over the heads of the crowd.* (**b**) stones, bullets, etc thrown or fired in this way: *He was hit by a volley of snowballs.* Cf SALVO. **2** *(fig)* number of questions, insults, etc directed at sb together or in quick succession: *He let out a volley of oaths.* **3** (in tennis, football, etc) shot or stroke in which the ball is hit before it touches the ground: *a forehand/backhand/overhead volley*, ie in tennis ○ *play, return, miss, etc an opponent's volley* ○ *kick a ball on the volley.*

▷ **volley** *v* **1** [I] fire guns in a volley. **2** [I, Ipr, Tn, Tn·pr] (in tennis, football, etc) hit (a ball) before it touches the ground: *He volleyed (the ball) into the net/across the court.*

□ **ˈvolley-ball** *n* game in which opposing teams of players hit a ball backwards and forwards over a high net with their hands without letting it touch the ground on their own side. ⇨ article at SPORT.

volt /vəʊlt/ *n (abbr* **v**) unit of electrical force, defined as the force needed to carry one ampere of current against one ohm of resistance.

▷ **voltage** /ˈvəʊltɪdʒ/ *n* [U, C] electrical force measured in volts: *high/low voltage* ○ *check the voltage of an appliance against the supply*, ie before connecting it.

Volta /ˈvɒltə/ Count Alessandro (1745-1827), Italian physicist. He invented several important electrical instruments, esp the first battery capable of producing a continuous electric current.

Voltaire /vɒlˈteə(r); *US* vəʊlˈteər/ (1694-1778), French author, real name François Marie Arouet. He became the most famous figure of the French *Enlightenment. He wrote plays and poetry in the classical tradition, but won both fame and hostility for works like *Zadig* and *Candide*, where he satirizes traditional religious and philosophical views. He regularly challenged authority in his writings and campaigned for many victims of injustice.

volte-face /ˌvɒlt ˈfɑːs/ *n* (usu *sing*) (*esp fml*) complete change or reversal of one's attitude towards sth: *His latest speech represents a complete volte-face in government thinking.*

voluble /ˈvɒljʊbl/ *adj (fml esp derog)* (**a**) (of a person) speaking a lot; talkative. (**b**) (of speech) quick, easy or fluent; glib: *voluble protests, excuses, etc.* ▷ **volubility** /ˌvɒljʊˈbɪlətɪ/ *n* [U]. **volubly** /ˈvɒljʊblɪ/ *adv.*

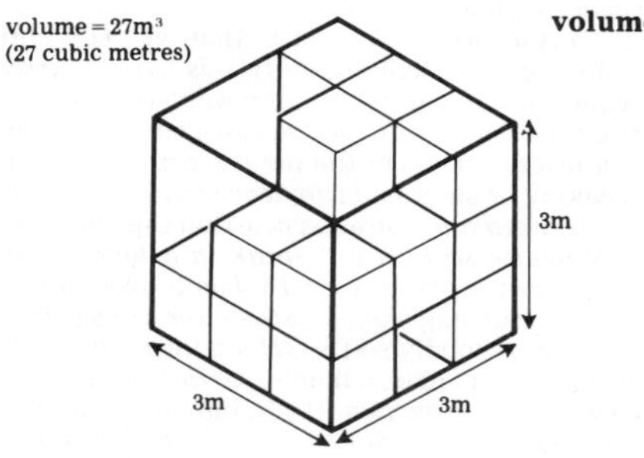

volume /ˈvɒljuːm; *US* -jəm/ *n* **1** [C] book, esp one of a matching set or a series: *an encyclopedia in 20 volumes* ○ *Volume 2 of Shaw's Complete Works is missing.* ○ *(fml) a library of over 12000 volumes.* **2** [U, C] amount of space (often expressed in cubic units) that a substance occupies; cubic capacity of a container: *The liquid was 5 litres in volume.* ○ *The jars hold different volumes of liquid/have different volumes.* ⇨ App 9. ⇨ illus. Cf AREA 1. **3** (**a**) [U] large amount or quantity of sth: *the sheer volume of business, work, mail, etc* ○ *The volume of protest rose/fell.* (**b**) [C usu *pl*] rounded mass of steam, etc: *Volumes of black smoke poured from the chimney.* **4** [U] (**a**) strength or power of sound: *The TV was on at full volume.* ○ *The music doubled in volume.* ○ [attrib] *a volume control.* (**b**) switch on a radio, etc for adjusting this: *turn the volume up/down.* **5** (idm) **speak volumes** ⇨ SPEAK.

voluminous /vəˈluːmɪnəs/ *adj (fml or joc)* **1** (of clothing etc) using much material; loose-fitting or ample: *wrapped in the voluminous folds of a blanket* ○ *voluminous skirts, petticoats, etc*, eg as worn by a Victorian lady. **2** (of writing) great in quantity; abundant: *voluminous correspondence* ○ *the voluminous works of Dickens*, ie filling many books. ▷ **voluminously** *adv*: *He always writes voluminously in his diary.*

voluntary[1] /ˈvɒləntrɪ; *US* -terɪ/ *adj* **1** acting, done or given willingly: *The prisoner made a voluntary statement.* ○ *Attendance is purely voluntary.* ○ *Charities rely on voluntary donations/contributions.* ○ *The firm went into voluntary liquidation.* **2** working, done or maintained without payment: *voluntary helpers*, eg at a fête, bazaar, etc ○ *She does voluntary social work.* ○ *The organization is run on a voluntary basis.* ○ *a voluntary service, institution, centre, etc.* ⇨ article. **3** (of bodily or muscular movements) controlled by the will. Cf INVOLUNTARY.

▷ **voluntarily** /ˈvɒləntrəlɪ; *US* ˌvɒlənˈterəlɪ/ *adv* **1** without compulsion; willingly. **2** without payment; free of charge.

voluntary[2] /ˈvɒləntrɪ; *US* -terɪ/ *n* solo played on a musical instrument before, during or after a church service: *organ, trumpet voluntaries.*

volunteer /ˌvɒlənˈtɪə(r)/ *n* **1** ~ **(for sth/to do sth)** person who offers to do sth without being compelled or paid: *volunteers for the post of treasurer* ○ *volunteers to run the Christmas show* ○ *Few volunteers came forward.* ○ [attrib] *volunteer social workers* ○ *volunteer groups.* **2** person who joins the armed forces voluntarily: [attrib] *volunteer troops, forces, etc.* Cf CONSCRIPT *n.*

▷ **volunteer** *v* **1** [I, Ipr, Tn, Tn·pr, Tt] ~ **(sth) (for sth)** give or offer (one's help, a suggestion, etc) willingly or without being paid: *She volunteered (her services) for relief work.* ○ *'Tim's busy but I'll* *come,' she volunteered.* ○ *volunteer information, advice, financial support* ○ *I volunteered to act as chauffeur.* **2** [I, Ipr, It] ~ (**for sth**) join the forces as a volunteer: *volunteer for military service/to join the army.*

voluptuary /vəˈlʌptʃʊərɪ; *US* -ʊerɪ/ *n* (*fml esp derog*) person who seeks and enjoys luxury and sensual pleasure.

voluptuous /vəˈlʌptʃʊəs/ *adj* **1** (**a**) giving a feeling of luxury or sensual pleasure: *voluptuous thoughts, caresses, smiles* ○ *the voluptuous enjoyment of a hot bath.* (**b**) (*esp derog*) devoted to such pleasure: *voluptuous tastes, indulgences, urges, etc.* **2** (*approv*) (of a woman) having a full and sexually desirable figure: *voluptuous breasts, hips, curves* ○ *Renoir's voluptuous nudes.* ▷ **voluptuously** *adv.* **voluptuousness** *n* [U].

volute /vəˈluːt/ *n* **1** (*architecture*) spiral scroll-shaped ornamentation, esp at the top of Ionic columns. **2** (*biology*) (any of the curves on a) spirally-coiled shell.

▷ **voluted** *adj* decorated with or having volutes: *a voluted sea-shell.*

vomit /ˈvɒmɪt/ *v* **1** [I, Tn, Tn·p] ~ **sth** (**up**) eject (food, etc from the stomach) through the mouth; be sick: *the noise of vomiting* ○ *The mixture of drinks made me vomit.* ○ *vomit blood* ○ *He vomited (up) all he had eaten.* ⇨ Usage at SICK. **2** [Tn, Tn·p] ~ **sth** (**out/forth**) (*fig*) (of a volcano, etc) eject sth violently: *factory chimneys vomiting (forth) smoke.*

▷ **vomit** *n* [U] food, etc from the stomach that has been vomited: *choke to death on one's own vomit.*

voodoo /ˈvuːduː/ (also **voodooism** /-ɪzəm/) *n* [U] form of religion based on belief in witchcraft and magical rites, practised by blacks in the W Indies, esp in Haiti. Its followers believe in a supreme God, but also in the power of spirits, often ancestors or local or African gods. The rites involve trances in which people are said to be possessed by spirits.

voracious /vəˈreɪʃəs/ *adj* **1** very greedy in eating; ravenous: *a voracious eater* ○ *a voracious appetite, hunger.* **2** (*fig*) very eager for knowledge, information, etc: *a voracious reader* ○ *voracious seekers after truth.* ▷ **voraciously** *adv.* **voracity** /vəˈræsətɪ/ *n* [U].

vortex /ˈvɔːteks/ *n* (*pl* ~**es** or, in scientific use, **-tices** /-tɪsiːz/) **1** [C] whirling mass of water, air, etc, as in a whirlpool or whirlwind. **2** [sing] (*fig*) social group, profession, etc seen as sth that swallows those who approach it; whirl of activity: *drawn helplessly into the vortex of society, party politics, etc.*

vorticism /ˈvɔːtɪsɪzəm/ *n* [U] literary and artistic movement in Britain in 1912-15. Its leader was Wyndham *Lewis and it challenged conventional art and adopted the themes of energy, violence and machines. Other artists associated with the movement were Ezra *Pound and Jacob *Epstein.

votary /ˈvəʊtərɪ/ *n* ~ (**of sb/sth**) (*fml*) person who dedicates himself to sth, esp religious work and service: *votaries of peace, disarmament, etc* ○ (*joc*) *votaries of golf.*

vote /vəʊt/ *n* **1** [C] ~ (**for/against sb/sth**); ~ (**on sth**) formal expression of one's opinion or choice, eg by ballot or show of hands: *cast/record one's vote* ○ *take/hold a vote on the motion* ○ *settle, decide, resolve, etc the matter by a vote* ○ *a majority/minority vote* ○ *counting, sorting, checking the votes,* ie papers on which votes are recorded ○ *postal votes* ○ *The Tory candidate received/polled 8 000 votes.* ○ *The measure was passed/defeated by 9 votes to 6.* ○ *The vote went against him/against accepting the plan.* ○ *a vote of confidence/censure,* ie one showing the support/lack of support of the majority of voters. **2 the vote** [sing] votes given by or for a certain group, eg at a political election: *attempts to win the teenage, immigrant, Scottish, etc vote* ○ *increase/decrease the Tory vote by 5%* ○ *split the vote,* eg between rival opposition parties so that the government is re-elected ○ *The Socialists got 35% of the vote.* **3 the vote** [sing] right to vote, esp in political elections; franchise: *UK nationals get the vote at 18.* **4** (idm) **put sth to the ˈvote** decide (an issue, etc) by asking for votes. **a ˌvote of ˈthanks** speech asking an audience to show their appreciation, esp by clapping: *propose a vote of thanks.*

▷ **vote** *v* **1** [I, Ipr, Tn, Tt] ~ (**for/against sb/sth**); ~ (**on sth**) formally express an opinion or choice by vote: *vote by ballot, proxy, post* ○ *20 delegates voted for/against the motion.* ○ *If we cannot agree, let's vote on it.* ○ *Vote (for) Smith/Labour on polling day!* ○ *I voted 'No' in the referendum.* ○ *We voted to continue the strike.* **2** [Cn·n] elect (sb) to a position of authority by a majority of votes: *I was voted chairman.* **3** [Dn·n] grant (a sum of money, etc) by voting: *MPs have just voted themselves a pay rise.* ○ *The hospital was voted £100 000 for research.* **4** [esp passive: Cn·a, Cn·n] (*infml*) declare (sth) to be good, bad, etc by general consent: *The show was voted a success.* **5** [Tf no passive] (*infml*) suggest or propose (sth): *I vote (that) we stay here.* **6** (phr v) **vote sb/sth down** reject or defeat sb/sth by voting. **vote sb in/out/on/off**; **vote sb into/out of/onto/off sth** elect sb to, or reject sb from, a position of authority: *vote the Liberals in* ○ *She was voted out of office/off the board.* **vote sth through** approve or bring into force (a proposal, etc) by voting: *Parliament voted the bill through without a debate.* **voter** *n* person who votes or has the right to vote, esp in a political election: *floating, marginal, tactical, etc voters.*

votive /ˈvəʊtɪv/ *adj* [usu attrib] presented (esp in church) to fulfil a promise made to God: *votive offerings, candles, etc.*

vouch /vaʊtʃ/ *v* [Ipr] **1** ~ **for sb/sth** take responsibility for or express confidence in (a person, his behaviour, etc); guarantee: *I can vouch for him/his honesty.* **2** ~ **for sth** confirm (a claim, etc) by producing evidence or drawing on one's own experience: *Experts vouch for the painting's authenticity.*

voucher /ˈvaʊtʃə(r)/ *n* **1** (*Brit*) document, showing that money has been paid or promised, which can be exchanged for certain goods or services: *ˈgift vouchers,* ie offered as presents and later exchanged at the store for goods ○ *special discount vouchers* ○ *luncheon vouchers,* ie tokens supplied by some employers, exchangeable for food at restaurants which have agreed to accept them. **2** document showing that money has been paid for goods, etc received; receipt.

vouchsafe /vaʊtʃˈseɪf/ *v* [Tn, Dn·n, Dn·pr] ~ **sth** (**to sb**) (*dated or fml*) grant sth (to sb) as a gift or privilege: *be vouchsafed a vision of the future* ○ *vouchsafe to him certain official secrets.*

vow /vaʊ/ *n* solemn promise or undertaking, esp of a religious nature: *recite/pronounce/renew one's ˈmarriage vows* ○ *keep/break a solemn vow* ○ *take a vow of silence, secrecy, etc* ○ *Nuns are under vows of poverty, chastity and obedience.*

▷ **vow** *v* [Tn, Tf, Tt] make a vow about (sth); swear, promise or declare solemnly: *They vowed revenge on their enemies.* ○ *He vowed (that) he would lose weight.* ○ *She vowed never to speak to him again.*

vowel /ˈvaʊəl/ *n* (**a**) speech-sound made without audible stopping of the breath by the tongue, lips, etc: [attrib] *a vowel system.* (**b**) letter or letters used to represent such a sound, eg a, e, i, o, u, ee, oa. Cf CONSONANT[1].

vox populi /ˌvɒks ˈpɒpjʊlaɪ/ (*Latin*) (also *infml* **vox pop** /ˌvɒks ˈpɒp/) public opinion or popular belief, esp as expressed in short media interviews with ordinary people on matters of current interest.

voyage /ˈvɔɪɪdʒ/ *n* long journey, esp by sea or in space: *on the outward/homeward voyage* ○ *make a voyage across the Atlantic* ○ *go on a voyage from Mombasa to Goa* ○ *the voyages of Sinbad the Sailor.* ⇨ Usage at JOURNEY.

▷ **voyage** *v* [I, Ipr] (*fml*) go on a voyage; travel: *voyaging across the Indian Ocean, through space.* **voyager** /ˈvɔɪɪdʒə(r)/ *n* **1** (*dated*) person making a voyage, esp to unknown parts of the world by sea. **2 Voyager** either of two US space vehicles launched in 1977 to explore Jupiter, Saturn, Uranus and Neptune.

voyeur /vɔɪˈɜː(r)/ *n* person who gets pleasure from secretly watching others undressing or engaging in sexual activities.

▷ **voyeurism** /vɔɪˈɜːrɪzəm/ *n* [U] state or practice of being a voyeur. **voyeuristic** /ˌvwɑːjəˈrɪstɪk/ *adj*: *voyeuristic pleasures, pursuits, etc.*

VP (also **V Pres**) *abbr* Vice-President.

vs *abbr* versus.

VS *abbr* Veterinary Surgeon.

VSO /ˌviː es ˈəʊ/ *abbr* (*Brit*) Voluntary Service Overseas (a scheme for people to work in developing countries): *do VSO.*

VSOP /ˌviː es əʊ ˈpiː/ *abbr* very special old pale (type of brandy).

VTOL /ˌviː tiː əʊ ˈel *or, in informal use,* ˈviːtɒl/ *abbr* (of aircraft) vertical take-off and landing: *a VTOL jet* ○ *fly VTOLs.* Cf STOL.

vulcanite /ˈvʌlkənaɪt/ *n* [U] hard black vulcanized rubber.

▷ **vulcanize, -ise** /ˈvʌlkənaɪz/ *v* [Tn] treat (rubber, etc) with sulphur, etc at great heat to make it stronger and more elastic. **vulcanization, -isation** /ˌvʌlkənaɪˈzeɪʃn; *US* -nɪˈz-/ *n* [U].

vulgar /ˈvʌlgə(r)/ *adj* **1** lacking in good taste or refinement: *a vulgar display of wealth* ○ *dressed in cheap and vulgar finery* ○ *a loud and vulgar laugh.* **2** likely to offend many people; rude or obscene: *a vulgar gesture, suggestion, joke.*

▷ **vulgarism** /ˈvʌlgərɪzəm/ *n* rude or obscene word or phrase: *'Arse' is a vulgarism for the buttocks.*

vulgarity /vʌlˈgærətɪ/ *n* (**a**) [C usu *pl*] rude or obscene act or expression. (**b**) [U] state of being vulgar: *the vulgarity of his tastes, clothes, manners.*

vulgarize, -ise /ˈvʌlgəraɪz/ *v* [Tn] **1** cause (a person, his manners, etc) to become vulgar. **2** spoil (sth) by making it too ordinary or well known; popularize. **vulgarization, -isation** /ˌvʌlgəraɪˈzeɪʃn; *US* -rɪˈz-/ *n* [U, C].

vulgarly *adv* **1** in a tasteless, unrefined or offensive manner. **2** (*dated or fml*) commonly or popularly: *The Devil is vulgarly referred to as 'Old Nick'.*

□ ˌ**vulgar** ˈ**fraction** (also **simple fraction**) fraction represented by numbers above and below a line (eg $\frac{3}{4}$, $\frac{5}{8}$). ⇨ App 9. Cf DECIMAL *n.*

ˌ**Vulgar** ˈ**Latin** the form of Latin spoken by the less educated classes, used throughout the Roman Empire. Its later forms developed into the Romance languages.

Vulgate /ˈvʌlgeɪt/ *n* **the Vulgate** [sing] Latin version of the Bible made in the 4th century and preferred by the Roman Catholic Church.

vulnerable /ˈvʌlnərəbl/ *adj* ~ (**to sth/sb**) **1** that can be hurt, wounded or injured: *Young birds are very vulnerable to predators.* ○ *Cyclists are more vulnerable than motorists.* ○ (*fig*) *His wife's death left him feeling vulnerable and depressed.* **2** (*fig*) exposed to danger or attack; unprotected: *vulnerable to abuse, blackmail, criticism* ○ *a vulnerable point in NATO's defences* ○ *The election defeat puts the party leader in a vulnerable position.*

▷ **vulnerability** /ˌvʌlnərəˈbɪlətɪ/ *n* [U]. **vulnerably** /-əblɪ/ *adv.*

vulpine /ˈvʌlpaɪn/ *adj* (*fml*) of or like a fox: *vulpine cunning, stealth, etc* ○ *sharp vulpine features.*

vulture /ˈvʌltʃə(r)/ *n* **1** large bird, usu with head and neck almost bare of feathers, that lives on the flesh of dead animals. **2** (*fig*) greedy person seeking profits from the misfortunes of others: *vultures round the bedside of the dying millionaire.*

vulva /ˈvʌlvə/ *n* (*pl* ~**s** or, in scientific use, **vulvae** /ˈvʌlviː/) (*anatomy*) external opening of the female genitals.

vv *abbr* verses.

vying *pres p* of VIE.

W, w

W, w /ˈdʌblju:/ *n* (*pl* **W's, w's** /ˈdʌblju:z/) the twenty-third letter of the English alphabet.

W *abbr* **1** watt(s): *a 60W light bulb.* Cf V *abbr* 2. **2** west(ern): *W Yorkshire* ○ *London W5 5HY*, ie as a postal code. **3** (esp on clothing) women's (size).

W *symb* tungsten.

WAC (also **Wac**) /ˌdʌblju: eɪ ˈsi: *or, in informal use,* wæk/ *abbr* (*US*) Women's Army Corps: *join the Wacs.*

wacky /ˈwækɪ/ *adj* (**-ier, -iest**) (*infml esp US*) eccentric or crazy; zany: *a wacky comedian.*

wad /wɒd/ *n* **1** lump or bundle of soft material used for keeping things apart or in place, or to block a hole, etc: *The noise was so loud that she put wads of cotton wool in her ears.* **2** quantity of documents or banknotes folded, rolled or held together: *He pulled a wad of £10 notes out of his pocket.* **3** (*Brit sl*) bun or sandwich: *a cup of tea and a wad.*

▷ **wad** *v* (**-dd-**) [Tn] **1** (**a**) fix (sth) in place with a wad, esp to protect it. (**b**) stuff (sth) with a wad. **2** line (a garment, etc) with soft material (esp cotton or wool): *a wadded dressing-gown, jacket, quilt.* **wadding** /ˈwɒdɪŋ/ *n* [U] soft material, usu cotton or wool, used for padding or lining garments, etc or protecting things when packing them.

waddle /ˈwɒdl/ *v* [I, Ipr, Ip] (*often derog*) walk with short steps and a swaying movement, as a duck does: *A short plump woman came waddling along the pavement.* ⇨ Usage at SHUFFLE.

▷ **waddle** *n* [sing] waddling way of walking: *walk with a waddle.*

wade /weɪd/ *v* **1** (**a**) [I, Ipr, Ip] walk with an effort (through water, mud or anything that makes walking difficult): *I can't wade in these boots.* ○ *There's no bridge; we'll have to wade across (the stream).* ○ *The angler waded (out) into the middle of the river.* ○ *They had to wade knee-deep through mud and debris to reach the victims.* Cf PADDLE² 1. (**b**) [Tn] cross (a stream, etc) by wading: *Can we wade the brook?* **2** (phr v) **wade in** (*infml*) start doing sth (esp sth difficult) with energy and determination: *The job has to be done, so let's wade in immediately.* **wade into sb/sth** attack sb/sth vigorously: *She waded straight into her critics with her opening remarks.* **wade through sth** read sth that is long or difficult to read, without interest or enjoyment: *wading through page after page of boring statistics.*

▷ **wader** *n* **1** [C] = WADING BIRD. **2 waders** [pl] angler's high waterproof boots worn when wading: *a pair of waders.*

□ ˈ**wading bird** any of several types of long-legged water-bird that wade (contrasted with web-footed birds that swim).

wadi /ˈwɒdɪ/ *n* (in the Middle East and N Africa) rocky watercourse that is dry except after heavy rain.

WAF (also **Waf**) /ˌdʌblju: eɪ ˈef *or, in informal use,* wæf/ *abbr* (*US*) Women in the Air Force: *join the Wafs.*

wafer /ˈweɪfə(r)/ *n* **1** very thin crisp sweet biscuit: *an ice-cream wafer*, ie for eating with ice-cream. **2** small round piece of unleavened bread used in Holy Communion. **3** small round piece of red paper stuck on the back of a document instead of a seal, to show that it is official.

□ ˌ**wafer-**ˈ**thin** *adj* very thin: *ˌwafer-thin ˈsandwiches* ○ *a ˌwafer-thin maˈjority.*

waffle¹ /ˈwɒfl/ *n* small crisp cake made of cooked batter with a pattern of squares on it, often eaten with syrup.

□ ˈ**waffle-iron** *n* utensil with two shallow metal pans, usu hinged together, in which waffles are cooked.

waffle² /ˈwɒfl/ *v* [I, Ipr, Ip] (*Brit infml derog*) talk or write, esp at great length, without saying anything very important or sensible: *What is she waffling about now?* ○ *He waffled on for hours but no one was listening.*

▷ **waffle** *n* [U] vague, wordy and often meaningless talk or writing: *The report looks impressive but it's really nothing but waffle.*

waft /wɒft; *US* wæft/ *v* [Ipr, Ip, Tn·pr, Tn·p] (cause sth to) be carried lightly and smoothly (as if) through the air: *The sound of their voices wafted across the lake to us.* ○ *Delicious smells wafted up from the kitchen.* ○ *The scent of the flowers was wafted along by the breeze.*

▷ **waft** *n* smell carried through the air; whiff: *a waft of perfume* ○ *wafts of cigar smoke.*

wag¹ /wæg/ *v* (**-gg-**) **1** [I, Ipr, Ip, Tn, Tn·pr, Tn·p] (cause sth to) move quickly from side to side or up and down: *The dog's tail wagged.* ○ *The dog wagged its tail excitedly.* ○ *wag one's finger at sb*, ie as a way of showing one's disapproval of him. Cf WAGGLE, WIGGLE. **2** (idm) **the tail wagging the dog** ⇨ TAIL. **tongues wag** ⇨ TONGUE.

▷ **wag** *n* wagging movement: *The dog gave a wag of its tail.*

wag² /wæg/ *n* (*dated*) person who is fond of making jokes; amusing or facetious person: *He's a bit of a wag.*

▷ **waggish** /ˈwægɪʃ/ *adj* (*dated*) of, like, done or made by a wag: *waggish remarks, tricks, youngsters.* **waggishly** *adv.* **waggishness** *n* [U].

wage¹ /weɪdʒ/ *n* (usu *pl* except in certain phrases and when used attributively) regular (usu weekly) payment made or received for work or services: *wages of £200 a week/a weekly wage of £200* ○ *Wages are paid on Fridays.* ○ *Tax and insurance are deducted from your wages.* ○ *We expect a fair day's wage for a fair day's work.* ○ *The workers are demanding to be paid a living wage*, ie one that enables them to live without hunger or hardship. ○ *a minimum wage*, ie guaranteed basic pay in a particular industry or country ○ [attrib] *a wage increase/rise of £10 a week.* ⇨ Usage at INCOME.

□ ˈ**wage-claim** *n* increase in wages demanded from an employer for workers by their union.

ˈ**wage-earner** *n* (**a**) person who works for wages: *Are you a wage-earner or salaried?* (**b**) member of a family who earns money: *There are two wage-earners in the family.*

ˈ**wage freeze** legal ban on or control of increases in wages.

wage² /weɪdʒ/ *v* [Tn, Tn·pr] ~ **sth (against/on sth)** begin and carry on (a war, campaign, etc): *No country wants to wage a nuclear war.* ○ *The government is waging a campaign against sex discrimination in industry.*

wager /ˈweɪdʒə(r)/ *v* [I, Tn, Tn·pr, Tf, Dn·n, Dn·f] ~ **sth (on sth)** (*dated or fml*) stake (money) on the result of (sth); bet sth: *You won't find better goods anywhere else, I'll wager.* ○ *wager £5 (on a horse)* ○ *I'll wager (you) (any money you like) he won't come.*

▷ **wager** *n* (*dated or fml*) bet: *lay/make a wager* ○ *take up* (ie accept) *a wager.*

waggle /ˈwægl/ *v* [I, Tn] (*infml*) (cause sth to) move with short movements from side to side or up and down: *His bottom waggles in a funny way when he walks.* ○ *She can waggle her ears.* Cf WAG¹, WIGGLE.

▷ **waggle** *n.*

Wagner /ˈvɑ:gnə(r)/ Richard (1813-83), German composer, mainly of operas. Most of these are based on German myths and legends or episodes from German history. They include *Der Fliegende Holländer, Tannhäuser, Tristan und Isolde, Die Meistersinger von Nürnberg, Parsifal* and *Der Ring des Nibelungen*, a four-opera cycle consisting of *Das Rheingold, Die Walküre, Siegfried* and *Götterdämmerung.* Wagner developed his own theories of operatic composition, including the use of leitmotivs, and transformed opera into serious musical drama. He had a theatre built at Bayreuth in southern Germany for the performance of his works.

▷ **Wagnerian** /vɑ:gˈnɪərɪən/ *adj* of or like Wagner, his music or his musical theories: *Wagnerian operas, sopranos.* — *n* person who admires Wagner or his music.

wagon (*Brit* also **waggon**) /ˈwægən/ *n* **1** four-wheeled vehicle for carrying heavy loads, usu pulled by horses or oxen. Cf CART. **2** (*US* **freight car**) open railway truck (eg for carrying coal): *a train with passenger coaches and goods wagons.* **3** trolley used for carrying food, esp tea, etc. **4** (idm) **on the** ˈ**wagon** (*infml*) no longer drinking alcoholic drinks; teetotal: *be/go on the wagon.*

▷ **wagoner** (*Brit* also **waggoner**) *n* person in charge of a wagon(1) and its horses.

□ ˈ**wagon train** (formerly in the USA) line of wagons travelling across country, esp carrying settlers to a new land.

wagon-lit /ˌvægɒn ˈli:/ *n* (*pl* **wagons-lits** /ˌvægɒn ˈli:/) sleeping-car (on Continental railways).

wagtail /ˈwægteɪl/ *n* any of various types of small bird with a long tail that moves constantly up and down when the bird is standing or walking.

waif /weɪf/ *n* **1** homeless person, esp an abandoned child: *a home for waifs and strays*, ie homeless and neglected children ○ *They looked thin, waif-like and half starved.* **2** object or animal with no owner.

wail /weɪl/ *v* **1** (**a**) [I, Ipr] ~ **(about/over sth)** cry or complain (about sth) in a loud (usu shrill) voice: *wail with grief* ○ *The sick child was wailing miserably.* ○ *There's no use wailing about/over mistakes made in the past.* (**b**) [I] (*fig*) make a sound similar to that of a person wailing: *ambulances racing along with sirens wailing* ○ *You can hear the wind wailing in the chimney.* (**c**) [Tn, Tf] say (sth) in a wailing way: *'I've lost all my money!' she wailed.* ○ *The child was wailing loudly that she had hurt her foot.* **2** [Ipr] ~ **for sb** express one's grief at the loss or death of sb; mourn sb: *She was wailing for her lost child.* ⇨ Usage at CRY.

▷ **wail** *n* (**a**) shrill cry, esp of pain or grief: *The child burst into loud wails.* ○ *She uttered a wail of grief.* (**b**) sound similar to this: *the wail of sirens.*

□ **the** ˌ**Wailing** ˈ**Wall** high wall in Jerusalem, originally part of an ancient Jewish temple. It is a sacred place for Jews, who go there to pray and lament the destruction of the temple in 70 AD and pray for its restoration.

wainscot /ˈweɪnskət/ *n* wooden covering, esp panelling on (usu the lower half of) the walls of a room.

▷ **wainscoted** *adj* (of a room) having a wainscot. **wainscoting** *n* [U] (material used for a) wainscot.

waist /weɪst/ *n* **1** part of the body between the ribs and the hips, usu narrower than the rest of the trunk: *She wore a wide belt round her waist.* ○ *She has a 26-inch waist.* ○ *He measures 30 inches round the waist.* ○ *The workmen were stripped to* (ie wearing nothing above) *the waist.* ○ [attrib] *waist measurements.* **2** (**a**) part of a garment that goes round the waist: *If the skirt is too big, we can take in the waist.* ○ *The waist is too tight for me.* ○ *trousers with a 30-inch waist.* (**b**) garment, or part of a garment, that covers the body from the shoulders to the waist. Cf SHIRTWAIST (SHIRT). **3** (**a**) narrow part in the middle of sth: *the waist of an hourglass, a violin, a wasp.* (**b**) part of a ship between the forecastle and the quarterdeck.

▷ **waisted** *adj* (of a garment) becoming narrower at the waist: *a waisted coat.*

-waisted (forming compound *adjs*) having the type of waist specified: ˌ*narrow-ˈwaisted* ○ ˌ*wasp-ˈwaisted* ○ *a* ˌ*high-waisted* ˈ*garment*, ie one with its waist above the waist of the person wearing it.

□ ˈ**waistband** *n* strip of cloth that forms the waist of a garment, esp at the top of trousers or a skirt.

waistcoat /ˈweɪskəʊt; *US* ˈweskət/ (*US* also **vest**) *n* close-fitting sleeveless garment, buttoned down the front, usu worn under a jacket or coat and often forming part of a man's suit ⇨ illus at DRESS.

ˌ**waist-ˈdeep** *adv, adj* up to the waist: *The water was waist-deep.* ○ *They were* ˌ*waist-deep in* ˈ*water.* ○ *wade* ˌ*waist-deep into a* ˈ*stream.*

ˌ**waist-ˈhigh** *adj, adv* high enough to reach the waist: *The grass had grown waist-high.*

ˈ**waistline** *n* **1** measurement of the body round the waist: *a narrow/slim waistline.* **2** narrow part of a garment that fits at or just above or below the waist: *a dress with a high waistline.*

wait[1] /weɪt/ *v* **1** (a) [I, Ipr, It] ~ (**for sb/sth**) stay where one is, delay acting, etc for a specified time or until sb or sth comes or until sth happens: *'Have you been waiting long?' 'Yes, I've been waiting (for) twenty minutes.'* ○ *Tell him I can't see him now, he'll have to wait.* ○ *Wait for me, please.* ○ *We are waiting for the rain to stop.* ○ *You'll have to wait until the end of the month before I can pay you.* ○ (*infml*) *I was just waiting for* (ie expecting) *that (to happen).* ○ *The chairman is waiting to begin (the meeting).* ○ *I am waiting to hear the result.* ○ *I can't wait* (ie am impatient) *to read his latest novel.* (**b**) [Tn] wait and watch for (sth); await: *wait one's opportunity/chance to do sth* ○ *You will just have to wait your turn*, ie wait until your turn comes. ⇨ Usage. (**c**) [I] not be dealt with immediately; be postponed: *The matter can wait until the next meeting; it's not urgent.* **2** [Tn, Dn·pr] ~ **sth** (**for sb**) postpone (a meal) until sb arrives: *I shall be home late tonight, so don't wait dinner (for me).* **3** [I] stop a vehicle at the side of the road for a short time: *No Waiting*, ie as a warning that vehicles must not stop at the side of the road even for a short time. **4** (idm) **keep sb** ˈ**waiting** cause sb to wait or be delayed, eg because one is unpunctual: *I'm sorry to have kept you waiting.* ○ *He kept us waiting for ages while he packed his luggage.* **ready and waiting** ⇨ READY. **time and tide wait for no man** ⇨ TIME[1]. ˌ**wait and** ˈ**see** wait and find out what will happen before taking action; be patient: *We shall just have to wait and see; there's nothing we can do at the moment.* **wait at** ˈ**table** (*US* **wait on** ˈ**table**) (of a waiter or a servant in a private house) serve food and drink to people, clear away dishes, etc. **wait for the** ˈ**cat to jump/to see** ˈ**which way the** ˈ**cat jumps** (*infml*) delay taking action or a decision until it becomes clear how events will turn out. ˈ**wait for it** (*infml*) (used as a warning to sb not to act, speak, etc before the proper time to do so has come). **(play) a** ˈ**waiting game** (cause) a deliberate delay in taking action so that one may act more effectively later. **wait on sb hand and** ˈ**foot** serve sb by attending to all his needs: *He seemed to expect to be waited on hand and foot.* **what are we** ˈ**waiting for?** (*infml*) let us go ahead and do sth, esp sth that has been planned or discussed. **what are you** ˈ**waiting for?** (*infml ironic*) why don't you get on with the job, work, etc? **(just) you** ˈ**wait** (used when threatening sb that one will punish him or get one's revenge on him later) **5** (phr v) **wait about/around** stay in a place (usu idly or impatiently, eg because sb who is expected has not arrived). **wait behind** stay after other people have gone, esp to speak to sb privately: *Please wait behind after class today.* **wait in** stay at home, esp because sb is expected: *I waited in all day but they didn't arrive.* **wait on sb** (**a**) act as a servant for sb, esp by serving food and drink at a meal. (**b**) (*dated fml*) make a formal visit to sb to show respect. **wait up (for sb)** not go to bed (until sb comes home); stay up: *I shall be home very late tonight, so don't wait up (for me).*

▷ **waiter** (*fem* **waitress** /ˈweɪtrɪs/) *n* person employed to take customers' orders, bring food, etc in a restaurant, hotel dining-room, etc.

□ ˈ**waiting-list** *n* list of people who are waiting for service, treatment, etc that is not available now and who will receive it when it becomes available: *put sb on a waiting-list for theatre tickets* ○ *a hospital waiting-list*, eg for operations.

ˈ**waiting-room** *n* (**a**) room in a station where people can sit while they are waiting for trains. (**b**) room (eg in a doctor's or dentist's surgery) where people wait until they can be attended to.

NOTE ON USAGE: Compare **wait for** and **expect.** *I'm expecting him to arrive soon* means that I'm sure that he will. *I'm waiting for him to arrive* means that I thought he would come earlier but he is late. **Waiting** (for something) can be seen as an action: *I'll wait here until it's time to go.* ○ *I'm too nervous to read when I'm waiting to see the dentist.* **Expecting** can suggest that nothing can be done to change an event in the future: *I'm expecting to fail my exams.* ○ *The fall in profits had been expected.*

wait[2] /weɪt/ *n* **1** ~ (**for sth/sb**) act or time of waiting: *I was prepared for a wait.* ○ *We had a long wait for the bus.* **2** (idm) **lie in wait** ⇨ LIE[2].

waive /weɪv/ *v* [Tn] (*fml*) not insist on (sth) in a particular case; forego: *waive a claim, privilege, right, rule* ○ *We have decided to waive the age-limit for applicants in your case.*

▷ **waiver** /ˈweɪvə(r)/ *n* (*law*) (document that records the) waiving of a legal right, etc: *They were persuaded to sign a waiver of claims against the landlord.*

Wajda /ˈvɑːjdə/ Andrzej (1926-), Polish film director. He is best known for his trilogy of films about wartime and postwar Poland, *A Generation, Kanal* and *Ashes and Diamonds.* His more recent work includes *Man of Iron, Danton* (in French) and *Everything for Sale.*

wake[1] /weɪk/ *v* (*pt* **woke** /wəʊk/ *or, in archaic use,* **waked**, *pp* **woken** /ˈwəʊkən/ *or, in archaic use,* **waked**) **1** (**a**) [I, Ip, It] ~ (**up**) stop sleeping: *What time do you usually wake (up) in the morning?* ○ *She had just woken from a deep sleep.* ○ *I woke early this morning.* ○ *Wake up! It's eight o'clock.* ○ *I woke up in the night feeling cold.* ○ *She woke up with a start when the door slammed.* ○ *He woke (up) to find himself alone in the house.* (**b**) [Tn, Tn·p] ~ **sb (up)** cause sb to stop sleeping: *Try not to wake the baby (up).* ○ *I was woken (up) by a noise in the room.* Cf AWAKE[1], AWAKEN. **2** [Tn, Tn·p] ~ **sb/sth (up)** cause sb/sth to become active, alert, attentive, etc: *A cold shower will soon wake you up.* ○ *The incident woke memories of his past sufferings.* ○ *The audience needs waking up.* **3** [Tn] (*fml*) cause (sth) to re-echo; disturb with noise: *His echoing cry woke the mountain valley.* **4** (idm) **wake the** ˈ**dead** (of a noise) be unpleasantly loud: *They were making enough noise to wake the dead.* **one's** ˈ**waking hours** time when one is awake: *She spends all her waking hours worrying about her job.* **5** (phr v) **wake up to sth** become aware of sth; realize sth: *It's time you woke up to the fact that you're not very popular.* ○ *He hasn't yet woken up to the seriousness of the situation.*

▷ **wakeful** /-fl/ *adj* (**a**) unable to sleep. (**b**) alert; vigilant. (**c**) (of a night) with little or no sleep; sleepless: *a wakeful night spent in prayer.* **wakefully** /-fəlɪ/ *adv.* **wakefulness** *n* [U].

waken /ˈweɪkən/ *v* [I, Tn] (cause sb to) wake from sleep; awaken.

wake[2] /weɪk/ *n* (**a**) night spent keeping watch by a dead person's body before it is buried. (**b**) (esp in Ireland) gathering of people for this purpose, with food and drink provided for the mourners by the dead person's family.

wake[3] /weɪk/ *n* **1** track left on the surface of the water behind a moving ship: *the foaming white wake of the liner.* **2** (idm) **in the wake of sth** coming after or following sth: *Outbreaks of disease occurred in the wake of the drought.* ○ *The war brought many social changes in its wake.*

Waldorf salad /ˌwɔːldɔːf ˈsæləd/ salad made from chopped apples and celery, nuts and mayonnaise.

Wales /weɪlz/ country forming the western part of Britain; pop approx 2 800 000; capital Cardiff; unit of currency pound. Originally an independent nation, in 1277 it came under English rule, and in 1536 England and Wales formally became one country. ⇨ article. ⇨ map at UNITED KINGDOM. Cf WELSH.

walk[1] /wɔːk/ *v* **1** [I, Ipr, Ip, In/pr] (**a**) (of a person) move along at a moderate pace by lifting up and putting down each foot in turn, so that one foot is on the ground while the other is being lifted: *How old was the baby when she started to walk?* ○ *We walked slowly home.* ○ *He walked into the room.* ○ *walking up and down* ○ *They walked along the river.* ○ *I've walked ten miles today.* Cf RUN[1], TROT 2. (**b**) travel in this way and not ride, drive, be driven, etc: *'How did you get here?' 'I walked.'* ○ *I missed the bus and had to walk home.* (**c**) (often **go walking**) travel in this way for exercise or pleasure: *I like walking.* ○ *We are going walking in the Alps this summer.* (**d**) (of four-footed animals) move at the slowest pace, always having at least two feet on the ground. Cf GALLOP, TROT 1. **2** [Tn, Tn·pr, Tn·p] cause (sb/sth) to walk, esp by accompanying him/it: *Horses should be walked for a while after a race.* ○ *He's out walking the dog.* ○ *He walked the horse up the hill.* ○ *He walked her to her car.* ○ *He put his arm round me and walked me away.* ○ *I'll walk you home.* **3** [Tn] go along or over (sth) on foot: *walk the fields looking for wild flowers.* **4** [I] (*dated*) (of a ghost, etc) be seen moving about; appear: *It was the sort of night when phantoms might walk.* **5** (idm) **be on/walk the streets** ⇨ STREET. **run before one can walk** tackle difficult tasks before one has learnt the basic skills: *Don't try to run before you can walk.* **walk before one can** ˈ**run** learn the basic skills before trying to tackle more difficult tasks. **a walking** ˈ**dictionary, encycloˈpedia, etc** person who has a wide vocabulary or who seems to be very knowledgeable about a particular subject: *She's a walking textbook of medicine.* ˈ**walk it** (*infml*) win or succeed easily: *Don't worry about the match/exam; you'll walk it!* **walk one's** ˈ**legs off** (*infml*) walk until one is exhausted. **walk sb off his** ˈ**feet** (*infml*) tire sb by making him walk too far or too fast. **walk the** ˈ**plank** be sent to one's death by pirates by being forced to walk along a plank and to fall into the sea. **walk** ˈ**tall** feel proud and confident. **walk/tread a tightrope** ⇨ TIGHTROPE (TIGHT).

6 (phr v) **walk away from sb/sth** beat (an opponent) easily in a contest. **walk away from sth** survive (an accident) without serious injury: *Miraculously, she was able to walk away from the wreckage of the car.* **walk away/off with sth** (*infml*) (**a**) win (a prize) easily: *She walked away with two first prizes.* (**b**) steal sth: *Somebody has walked off with my pen.*

walk into sth (*infml*) (**a**) become caught in sth that one is not expecting, esp because one is not careful: *They set a trap for him and he walked right into it.* (**b**) be appointed to (a job) without having to make an effort: *She simply walked into a job at the bank as soon as she graduated.* **walk into sth/sb** strike against sth/sb while walking: *She wasn't looking where she was going and walked straight into me.*

walk out (*infml*) (of workers) go on strike suddenly. **walk out (of sth)** leave (a meeting, etc) suddenly and angrily. **walk out (with sb)** (*dated infml*) have a relationship with sb: *They were walking out for years before they got married.* **walk out on sb** (*infml*) abandon or desert sb: *He had a row with his wife and just walked out on her.*

walk over sb (*infml*) (**a**) thoroughly defeat sb in a competition: *The visiting team was too strong — they walked all over us.* (**b**) treat sb badly or unkindly: *You mustn't let him walk over you like that.*

walk up (usu imperative) come and see (a circus, show, etc): *Walk up! Walk up! The performance is about to begin.* **walk up (to sb/sth)** approach sb/sth: *A stranger walked up to me and shook my hand.* ○ *She walked up to the desk and asked to see the manager.*

▷ **walker** *n* **1** person who walks, esp for exercise

Wales

In some ways, Wales is the most 'foreign' of the four lands that make up the United Kingdom. The word 'Welsh' itself is derived from Old English 'wealh', the term used by the Anglo-Saxon invaders for the original Britons or Celts. The Welsh language is spoken by about two out of ten people in Wales. English people find it very difficult to spell and pronounce Welsh words, especially place names such as Llwchwr or Pwllheli. The Welsh name for Wales is 'Cymru', and that of the Welsh themselves is 'Cymry', meaning 'compatriot'.

Wales, although a small land, has considerable diversity. Its largest cities and main industrial centres are in the south, while the much more sparsely inhabited north is famous for its mountain landscapes, including Snowdonia.

Wales is often referred to as 'the principality', since the heir to the British throne, Prince Charles, has the title of Prince of Wales.

The chief industries of south Wales were for many years coal-mining and iron and steel production. In recent years, however, these have declined, and many coal-mines and steel mills have been closed. Even so, Wales still produces about a third of Britain's steel, and its former narrowly-based economy has been widened to include electronics and high technology industries. New factories have been built, many of them for Japanese and American companies. North Wales is predominantly rural and sheep farming, forestry and tourism are the most important economic activities.

Like other Celtic lands, Wales has a distinct cultural heritage that is reflected in the various annual eisteddfods. The most important of these is the Royal National Eisteddfod of Wales, an annual festival of music, singing, prose and poetry contests, all in Welsh. The winner of the poetry competition is ceremoniously crowned as the 'bard'. Titles and awards are judged by the Gorsedd ('court'), the body of bards and druids that assembles daily during the Eisteddfod. The Eisteddfod itself is held alternately in north and south Wales. Another eisteddfod, held annually at Llangollen in north Wales, is an international festival of folk dancing and music.

Choral singing is an art closely associated with the Welsh. There were formerly many miners' choirs in south Wales as well as the chapel choirs of the Nonconformist churches (mainly Methodists and Baptists). The Church of England has been disestablished in Wales (ie, deprived of its formal link with the state), since 1914. The Welsh also have a reputation for being good public speakers. The Welsh word 'hwyl' is a name for the gift of speaking with passion and eloquence.

Many Welsh are fiercely patriotic, and resent the presence or influence of the English (and the English language) in their land. Nationalists object in particular to the fact that so many holiday cottages in Wales are owned by the English, and have attempted to burn some of them down. The main official nationalist organization is the political party Plaid Cymru ('party of Wales'), founded in 1925 with the aim of gaining self-rule for Wales. In 1990 it had three members in the British parliament. Other nationalist movements are more extreme. One of the best known is Meibion Glyndwr ('sons of Glendower'), named after Owen Glendower (in Welsh, Owain Glyndwr), the Welsh chieftain who led a revolt against the rule in Wales of the English king Henry IV in the early 15th century.

The survival of the Welsh language is to some degree helped and encouraged by local radio and television stations, such as Radio Cymru and Sianel 4 Cymru ('Channel 4 Wales', usually called SC4) which broadcast in Welsh. Welsh is also used for official purposes, for example on government forms, is valid in the law courts, and is taught in most schools. All railway stations in Wales have their names in both Welsh and English, (for example 'Abertawe/Swansea'). A non-political organization founded in 1922 to protect the Welsh language is the Cwmni Urdd Gobaith Cymru ('Company of the Order of the Hope of Wales'), known simply as 'yr Urdd' ('the Order'). A more political, socialist association that actively campaigns for the retention of the Welsh language is Cymdeithas yr Iaith Gymraeg ('Welsh Language Society'). In 1988, the government set up the Welsh Language Board to draw up an official strategy for the preservation of the language. (Cf article at LANGUAGE.)

Wales and England are administered together for most purposes. They share the same legal and education systems. In this respect, Wales is unlike Scotland, which has its own system of local government, law and education. There is a Secretary of State for Wales, who is a Cabinet minister.

Wales's rich heritage, culture and language have encouraged the growth of tourism, which now ranks second to manufacturing industry. Many visitors to Wales are attracted by the sporting facilities, in particular the numerous yachting centres, both round the coast and on inland rivers, lakes and reservoirs. A new leisure park near Narberth, in south-west Wales, also draws many holiday-makers from southern England. Overseas visitors to Wales are fewer than they are to other parts of the British Isles, however, and many Welsh young people still have to look for jobs outside their native land, despite its attractions and revitalized industry.

or enjoyment. **2** framework that is used as a support by sb who cannot walk without one, eg a baby or a disabled person.

□ ˈ**walkabout** *n* **1** (in Australia) period of wandering in the bush by an Aboriginal: *go walkabout.* **2** informal stroll among a crowd by an important visitor, esp a royal person: *go on a walkabout.*

ˈ**walk-in** *adj* [attrib] **1** (*esp US*) (of a cupboard, wardrobe, etc) large enough to walk into: *a walk-in closet.* **2** (*US*) (of a flat) having its own entrance: *a walk-in apartment.*

ˈ**walking-tour** *n* holiday spent walking from place to place.

ˈ**walking papers** (*US*) dismissal from a job: *be given one's walking papers.*

ˈ**walking rein** = LEADING-REIN (LEADING).

ˈ**walking-stick** *n* (also **stick**) stick carried or used as a support when walking.

ˌ**walking ˈwounded** [pl] people who are injured but can still walk.

ˈ**Walkman** /-mən/ *n* (*pl* ~**s**) (*propr*) small cassette player with earphones that can be worn by sb walking about.

ˌ**walk-ˈon** *adj* [usu attrib] (of a part in a play) very small and without any words to say.

ˈ**walk-out** *n* sudden strike by workers.

ˈ**walk-over** *n* easy victory: *The match was a walk-over for the visiting team.*

ˈ**walk-up** *adj* [attrib] (*US*) (of a flat or block of flats) without a lift. — *n* building or flat without a lift.

ˈ**walkway** *n* passage or path for walking along.

walk[2] /wɔːk/ *n* **1** (**a**) [C] journey on foot, esp for pleasure or exercise: *go for a walk* ○ *have a pleasant walk across the fields* ○ *She took the dog for a walk.* (**b**) [sing] distance of this: *The station is ten minutes' walk from my house.* ○ *It's a short walk to the beach.* **2** [sing] (**a**) manner or style of walking; gait: *I recognized him at once by his walk.* (**b**) walking pace: *The horse slowed to a walk after its long gallop.* ○ *After running for ten minutes, he dropped into a walk,* ie began to walk. **3** [C] path or route for walking: *The path through the forest is one of my favourite walks.* ○ *Some of the walks in this area are only possible in dry weather.* ○ *The garden is well laid out, with many pleasant walks.* **4** (idm) **cock of the walk** ⇨ COCK[1]. **a walk of ˈlife** person's occupation, profession or rank: *They interview people from all walks of life.*

Walker Cup /ˌwɔːkə ˈkʌp/ **the Walker Cup** golf trophy played for every two years by amateur teams representing Britain and the USA.

walkie-talkie /ˌwɔːkɪ ˈtɔːkɪ/ *n* (*infml*) small portable radio transmitter and receiver.

wall /wɔːl/ *n* **1** (**a**) continuous upright solid structure of stone, brick, concrete, etc used to enclose, divide or protect sth (eg an area of land): *The old town on the hill had a wall right round it.* ○ *The fields were divided by stone walls.* ○ *The fruit trees grew against the garden wall.* (**b**) one of the vertical sides of a building or room: *The castle walls were very thick.* ○ *Hang the picture on the wall opposite the window.* ○ [attrib] *a wall light.* ⇨ illus at HOME. **2** (*fig*) thing similar to a wall in its appearance or effect: *The mountain rose up in a steep wall of rock.* ○ *The investigators were confronted by a wall of silence.* ○ *The tidal wave formed a terrifying wall of water.* **3** outer layer of a hollow structure, esp an organ or a cell of an animal or a plant: *the abdominal wall* ○ *the wall of an artery, a blood-vessel, etc.* **4** (idm) **bang, etc one's head against a brick wall** ⇨ HEAD[1]. **a fly on the wall** ⇨ FLY[1]. **have one's back to the wall** ⇨ BACK[1]. **a hole in the wall** ⇨ HOLE. ˌ**off the ˈwall** (*US sl*) (**a**) strange in a slightly mad way; bizarre, eccentric: [attrib] *off-the-wall humour.* (**b**) done without planning; impromptu. **to the ˈwall** to a difficult or desperate situation: *Several firms have gone to the wall* (ie been ruined) *recently.* ○ *drive/push sb to the wall,* ie defeat him. **up the ˈwall** (*infml*) furious or crazy: *That noise is driving/sending me up the wall.* ○ *I'll go up the wall if it doesn't stop soon.* ˌ**walls have ˈears** (*saying*) beware of eavesdroppers: *Be careful what you say; even the walls have ears!* **the writing on the wall** ⇨ WRITING.

▷ **wall** *v* **1** [Tn esp passive] surround (sth) with a wall or walls: *a walled city, garden, town.* **2** (phr v) **wall sth in/off** separate (and enclose) sth with a wall: *Part of the yard had been walled off.* **wall sth up** block up sth with a wall or bricks: *a walled-up door, fireplace, passage.*

□ ˈ**wallflower** *n* **1** common garden plant that has sweet-smelling (usu orange or brownish-red) flowers in spring. **2** (*infml*) person (esp a woman) who has no dancing partners at a dance and has to sit or stand around while others dance.

ˈ**wall-painting** *n* picture painted directly on the surface of a wall; fresco or mural.

ˈ**wallpaper** *n* [U] paper, usu with a coloured design, for covering the walls of a room. — *v* [I, Tn] put wallpaper on (the walls of a room).

ˌ**wall-to-ˈwall** *adj, adv* (of a floor-covering) that covers the whole floor of a room: *a ˌwall-to-wall ˈcarpet* ○ *a room carpeted wall-to-wall.*

wallaby /ˈwɒləbɪ/ *n* **1** [C] any of various types of small kangaroo. **2 the Wallabies** [pl] the Australian Rugby Union team.

Wallace[1] /ˈwɒlɪs/ Alfred Russell (1823-1913), British naturalist who independently developed a theory of evolution based on natural selection identical to that of Charles *Darwin. Darwin has since received most of the credit for the theory.

□ ˈ**Wallace's line** imaginary line dividing the sort of animals found in Asia from those found in Australia, indicating how long ago the two continents became separated.

Wallace[2] /ˈwɒlɪs/ (Richard Horatio) ·Edgar (1875-1932), English writer. He started his career as a journalist, but soon achieved success writing books, of which the most popular were thrillers (eg *The Four Just Men* and *The Ringer*).

Wallace[3] /ˈwɒlɪs/ William (c 1270-1305), Scottish national hero, who led Scottish resistance to the English invaders under *Edward I. He was eventually captured and executed by the English.

Wallace Collection /ˈwɒlɪs kəlekʃn/ **the Wallace Collection** museum in London containing a collection of French 18th-century paintings and furniture, English 18th-century portraits and medieval armour.

wallah /ˈwɒlə/ *n* (*infml*) (in India) person connected with a specified occupation or task: *bank wallahs.*

Waller /ˈwɒlə(r)/ Thomas Wright 'Fats' (1904-43), American jazz pianist and songwriter whose compositions include *Honeysuckle Rose* and *Ain't Misbehavin'.*

wallet /ˈwɒlɪt/ (*US* also ˈ**billfold**, ˈ**pocket-book**) *n* small flat folding case, usu made of leather, carried in the pocket and used esp for holding banknotes, documents, etc. Cf PURSE[1] 1.

wall-eyed /ˌwɔːl ˈaɪd/ *adj* having eyes that show an abnormal amount of white, esp because the irises turn outwards.

Wallis /ˈwɒlɪs/ Sir Barnes Neville (1887-1979), English inventor who designed the R100 airship, developed the 'bouncing' bomb used to destroy German dams in the Second World War, invented the swing-wing aircraft and worked on the Concorde supersonic airliner.

wallop /ˈwɒləp/ *v* [Tn, Tn·pr] (*infml*) **1** hit (sb/sth) hard; thrash: *If I ever catch the rascal I'll really wallop him!* ○ *She walloped the ball (for) miles.* **2** (in a contest, match, etc) defeat (sb) thoroughly: *walloped him at darts.*

▷ **wallop** *n* **1** [C] (*infml*) heavy resounding blow: *He crashed down on the floor with a wallop.* **2** [U] (*Brit sl*) beer.

walloping *adj* [attrib] (*infml*) very big: *He had to pay a walloping (great) fine.* — *n* (*infml*) **(a)** thrashing: *She threatened the children with a walloping.* **(b)** thorough defeat: *Our team got a terrible walloping yesterday.*

wallow /ˈwɒləʊ/ *v* [I, Ipr, Ip] ~ **(about/around) (in sth) 1** lie and roll about in mud, water, etc: *The children enjoyed watching the hippopotamus wallowing (about) in the mud.* ○ *The ship wallowed in* (ie was tossed about by) *the rough sea.* **2** take pleasure (in sth); indulge oneself: *wallow in a hot bath* ○ *wallowing in luxury* ○ *They're absolutely wallowing in money,* ie very rich. ○ *She seemed to be wallowing in her grief, instead of trying to recover from the disaster.*

▷ **wallow** *n* **1** act of wallowing. **2** place where animals go to wallow.

Wall Street /ˈwɔːl striːt/ **1** street in New York City where the New York Stock Exchange and other financial institutions are located: [attrib] *the Wall Street Journal.* ⇨ article at FINANCE. **2** (*fig*) the American money-market: *Share prices fell on Wall Street today.* ○ *Wall Street responded quickly to the news.*

wally /ˈwɒlɪ/ *n* (*Brit infml*) stupid or foolish person; twit: *Don't be such a wally!*

walnut /ˈwɔːlnʌt/ *n* **1** [C] nut containing an edible kernel with a wrinkled surface in a pair of boat-shaped shells. ⇨ illus at NUT. **2 (a)** [C] (also ˈ**walnut tree**) tree on which this nut grows. **(b)** [U] wood of this tree, used (esp as a veneer) in making furniture.

Walpole[1] /ˈwɔːlpəʊl/ Horace (1717-97), English writer best known for his Gothic novel *The Castle of Otranto.* He made his house, Strawberry Hill in Twickenham, into an imitation Gothic castle. He was the son of Sir Robert Walpole.

Walpole[2] /ˈwɔːlpəʊl/ Sir Robert (1676-1745), British Whig politician, prime minister 1715-17 and 1721-42. He is generally recognized as the first modern British prime minister. His periods in office were marked by national prosperity and a peaceful foreign policy, although Walpole himself was often accused of corruption. ⇨ App 2.

Walpurgis Night /vælˈpʊəgɪs naɪt/ night before May 1, when, according to German legend, witches used to gather on the Brocken, a peak in the Harz mountains.

walrus /ˈwɔːlrəs/ *n* large sea-animal living in the Arctic regions, similar to a seal but having two long tusks.

□ ˌ**walrus mouˈstache** (*infml*) long thick moustache that hangs down on each side of the mouth.

Walton[1] /ˈwɔːltən/ Izaak (1593-1683), English writer best known for *The Compleat Angler,* a book of advice on fishing which also includes songs and ballads, stories of country life, etc. He also wrote biographies.

Walton[2] /ˈwɔːltən/ Sir William (1902-83), English composer. He first achieved fame with *Façade,* a setting of the poems of Edith *Sitwell. Other works include two symphonies, violin and viola concertos, the oratorio *Belshazzar's Feast,* the opera *Troilus and Cressida,* and music for several films.

waltz /wɔːls; *US* wɔːlts/ *n* **(a)** ballroom dance for couples, with a graceful flowing melody in triple time. **(b)** music for this.

▷ **waltz** *v* **1** [I, Tn·pr] (cause sb to) dance a waltz: *She waltzes beautifully.* ○ *He waltzed her round the room.* **2** [Ipr, Ip] (*infml*) move in the specified direction gaily or casually or by dancing: *She waltzed up to us and announced that she was leaving.* ○ *He waltzes in and out as if the house belongs to him.* **3** (phr v) **waltz off with sth** (*infml*) **(a)** steal sth: *He's just waltzed off with my cigarette lighter!* **(b)** win sth easily: *She waltzed off with the school prizes for maths and science.*

□ **Waltzing Matilda** /ˌwɔːlsɪŋ məˈtɪldə/ Australian song about a tramp, often used as an unofficial Australian national anthem.

wampum /ˈwɒmpəm/ *n* [U] ornaments made of shells threaded on a string like beads, used formerly by N American Indians as money.

wan /wɒn/ *adj* **(-nner, -nnest)** (of a person, his appearance, etc) pale and looking ill or tired; pallid: *a wan smile,* ie a slight one from sb who is ill or tired or unhappy ○ (*fig*) *the wan light of a winter's morning.* ▷ **wanly** *adv*: *smile wanly.* **wanness** /ˈwɒnnɪs/ *n* [U].

wand /wɒnd/ *n* **1** slender stick or rod held in the hand, esp by a conjuror, fairy or magician when performing magic: *The fairy godmother waved her (magic) wand.* **2** = LIGHT PEN (LIGHT[1]).

wander /ˈwɒndə(r)/ *v* **1** [I, Ipr, Ip] **(a)** move around in an area or go from place to place without any special purpose or destination; roam: *wander through the countryside* ○ *enjoy wandering in a strange town* ○ *She was wandering aimlessly up and down the road.* ○ *We wandered around for hours looking for the house.* ○ (*fig*) *She was so weak that her pen kept wandering over the page as she wrote.* **(b)** go slowly or aimlessly in the specified direction: *They wandered back to work an hour later.* ○ *He wandered in to see me as if he had nothing else to do.* ○ *They wandered out into the darkness.* ○ (*fig*) *Her thoughts wandered back to her youth.* **2** [Tn] move aimlessly around in (a place); roam: *I've spent two years wandering the world.* ○ *The child was found wandering the streets alone.* **3** [I, Ipr, Ip] (of a road or river) follow a winding path or course; meander: *The road wanders (along) through the range of hills.* **4** [I, Ipr, Ip] ~ **(from/off sth)**; ~ **(away/off)** (of a person or an animal) leave the right place or way; stray from one's group: *The shepherd set out to look for the sheep that had wandered (away).* ○ *We seem to have wandered from the path.* ○ *The child wandered off and got lost.* ○ (*fig*) *Don't wander from the subject: stick to the point,* ie Don't digress. **5** [I] (of a person, his mind, etc) be inattentive, confused or delirious: *He realized his audience's attention was beginning to wander.* ○ *Her mind seemed to be wandering and she didn't recognize us.*

▷ **wander** *n* (*infml*) act of wandering: *She went for a little wander round the park.*

wanderer /ˈwɒndərə(r)/ *n* person or animal that wanders (WANDER 1).

wanderings /ˈwɒndərɪŋz/ *n* [pl] **1** journeys made from place to place: *After five years, he returned from his wanderings.* **2** confused speech during illness (esp a high fever).

□ **the** ˌ**Wandering** ˈ**Jew** (in medieval legend) Jew who was forced to wander around the Earth until the Day of Judgement because he insulted Christ.

wanderlust /ˈwɒndəlʌst/ *n* [U] strong desire to travel.

wane /weɪn/ *v* [I] **1** (of the moon) show a gradually decreasing area of brightness after being full. Cf WAX[2] 1. **2** gradually lose power or importance; become smaller or weaker or less impressive: *The power of the landowners waned during this period.* ○ *Her enthusiasm for the expedition was waning rapidly.* **3** (idm) **wax and wane** ⇨ WAX[2].

▷ **wane** *n* (idm) **on the** ˈ**wane** gradually decreasing; waning.

wangle /ˈwæŋgl/ *v* (*infml*) **1** [Tn, Tn·pr, Dn·n] ~ **sth (out of sb)** get or arrange sth that one wants by using trickery or clever persuasion: *I'd love to go to the match tomorrow — do you think you can wangle it?* ○ *She managed to wangle an invitation to the reception.* ○ *He was trying to wangle his way onto the committee.* ○ *I'll try to wangle a contribution out of him.* ○ *She's wangled an extra week's holiday for herself.* **2** (phr v) **wangle out of sth/doing sth** avoid having to do sth by scheming: *It's bound to be a boring party — let's try to wangle out of it/going.*

▷ **wangle** *n* act of wangling: *get sth by a wangle.*

wank /wæŋk/ *v* [I] (⚠ *Brit sl*) masturbate.

▷ **wank** *n* (⚠ *Brit sl*) act of masturbating.

wanker (⚠ *Brit sl*) **1** (*derog*) inefficient, lazy or stupid person. **2** person who masturbates.

wanna /ˈwɒnə/ *contracted form* (*infml esp US*) **1** want to: *I wanna hold your hand.* **2** want a: *You wanna cigarette?*

want[1] /wɒnt; *US* wɔːnt/ *v* **1** [Tn, Tt, Tnt] (no passive) [Tsg, Cn·n/a] have a desire for (sth); wish for: *They want a bigger flat.* ○ *Have you decided what you want?* ○ *The staff want a pay rise.* ○ *She wants to go to Italy.* ○ *She wants me to go with her.* ○ *I didn't want that to happen.* ○ *I want it (to be) done as quickly as possible.* ○ *I don't want you arriving late.* ○ *The people want him as their leader.* ⇨ Usage. **2** [Tn, Tg] require or need (sth): *We shall want more staff for the new office.* ○ *Let me know how many copies you want.* ○ (*infml*) *What that boy wants* (ie deserves) *is a good smack!* ○ *The plants want watering/want to be watered daily.* ○ *I'm sure you don't want reminding of the need for discretion.* **3** [Tt] (*infml*) should or ought to (do sth): *You want to be more careful.* ○ *They want to remember who they're speaking to!* **4** [Tn] (*fml*) not have enough of (sth); lack: *He wants the courage to speak the truth.* ○ *After the disaster there were many who wanted food and shelter.* **5** [Tn usu passive] require (sb) to be present; need (sb): *You will not be wanted this afternoon.* ○ *You are wanted immediately in the director's office.* ○ *He is wanted (for questioning) by the police,* eg because he is suspected of committing a crime. **6** [Tn] feel sexual desire for (sb). **7** [Tn] (used with *it*) fall short by (sth): *It still wants half an hour till midnight.* **8** (idm) **have/want it/things both ways** ⇨ BOTH. **not want to** ˈ**know (about sth)** deliberately avoid contact with or information about sb/sth which may cause inconvenience, trouble, etc; not care: *He was desperately in need of help but nobody seemed to want to know.* **waste not, want not** ⇨ WASTE². **9** (phr v) **want for sth** (esp in questions or negative sentances) suffer because of a lack of sth: *Those children want for nothing/never want for anything,* ie have everything they need. ○ *She didn't want for help from her friends.* **want ˈin/ˈout** (*infml*) want to come in/go out: *I think the dog wants in — I can hear it scratching at the door.* **want ˈout/out of sth** (*infml esp US*) no longer want to be involved in (a plan, project, etc).

NOTE ON USAGE: When expressing an offer or issuing an invitation, **like** is the most usual verb: *Would you like a cup of coffee?* ○ *Would you like to come to dinner with us next week?* **Care (for)** is more formal: *Would you care for another piece of cake?* ○ *Would you care to come for a walk with me?* **Want** is the most direct and informal: *Do you want a piece of chocolate?* ○ *We're going to the cinema tonight. Do you want to come with us?*

want² /wɒnt; *US* wɔ:nt/ *n* **1** [C usu *pl*] **(a)** desire for sth; requirement: *He is a man of few wants.* ○ *This book meets a long-felt want,* ie has been needed for a long time. **(b)** thing desired: *All their wants were provided by their host.* **2** [U, sing] ~ **of sth** lack or insufficiency of sth: *The refugees are suffering for want of food and medical supplies.* ○ *The plants died from want of water.* ○ *She decided to accept the offer for want of anything better.* ○ *She couldn't find anywhere to live, though not for want of trying,* ie not because she hadn't tried. **3** [U] state of being poor or in need; poverty: *live in want* ○ *Their health had suffered from years of want.* ○ *a policy aimed at fighting want and deprivation.* **4** (idm) **in want of sth** needing sth: *The house is in want of repair.*

□ **ˈwant ads** (*infml esp US*) = CLASSIFIED ADVERTISEMENTS (CLASSIFY).

wanting /ˈwɒntɪŋ; *US* ˈwɔ:n-/ *adj* [pred] **1** ~ **(in sth)** (*fml*) lacking in quality or quantity; deficient: *His behaviour was wanting in courtesy,* ie discourteous, rude. **2** (idm) **be found wanting** ⇨ FIND¹.

wanton /ˈwɒntən; *US* ˈwɔ:n-/ *adj* **1** [esp attrib] (of an action) done deliberately for no good reason; wilful: *wanton cruelty, damage, waste* ○ *the wanton destruction of a historic building.* **2** (*fml*) playful or capricious: *a wanton breeze* ○ *in a wanton mood.* **3** (of growth, etc) very abundant; luxuriant or wild: *The weeds grew in wanton profusion.* **4** (*dated fml*) not modest or chaste; licentious or immoral: *a wanton creature* ○ *wanton behaviour.*

▷ **wanton** *n* (*dated*) licentious or immoral person (esp a woman).

wantonly *adv*: *wantonly destructive.*

wantonness *n* [U].

wapiti /ˈwɒpɪtɪ/ *n* N American elk, resembing a red deer but larger.

war /wɔ:(r)/ *n* **1 (a)** [U] (state of) fighting between nations or groups within a nation using military force: *the horrors of war* ○ *the outbreak* (ie beginning) *of war* ○ *The border incident led to war between the two countries.* ○ *the art* (ie tactics and strategy) *of war* ○ *the fortunes of* (ie what may happen in) *war* ○ *The government wanted to avoid war at all costs.* ○ *civil war* ○ [attrib]: *a war correspondent,* ie a reporter who describes wars where they are happening. **(b)** [C] instance or period of such fighting: *during the Second World War* ○ *He had fought in two wars.* ○ *If a war breaks out, many other countries will be affected.* **2 (a)** [C, U] competition, conflict or hostility between people, groups, etc: *the class war* ○ *a trade war* ○ *There was a state of war between the rivals.* **(b)** [sing] ~ **(against sb/sth)** efforts made to eliminate disease, crime, etc: *a major step in the war against cancer* ○ *Little progress has been made in the war against drug traffickers.* **3** (idm) **at war** in a state of war: *The country has been at war with its neighbour for two years.* **carry the war into the enemy's camp** ⇨ CARRY. **declare war** ⇨ DECLARE. **go to war (against sb/sth)** start fighting a war (against sb/sth). **have been in the ˈwars** (*infml or joc*) show signs of being injured or badly treated. **make/wage war on sb/sth (a)** fight sb/sth with weapons. **(b)** try to eliminate sth: *wage war on crime, disease, poverty, etc.* **a war of ˈnerves** attempt to defeat an opponent by gradually destroying his morale, using threats, psychological pressures, etc. **a war of ˈwords** (campaign of) verbal abuse: *As the election approaches the war of words between the main political parties becomes increasingly intense.*

▷ **war** *v* **(-rr-)** [I] (*arch*) engage in a war or conflict: *warring tribes.*

□ **ˈwar bonnet** feathered head-dress worn by the warriors of certain N American Indian tribes.

ˈwar chest (*US*) fund of money collected to pay for a war or some other campaign.

ˈwar crime act that is against the international rules of war (eg torturing or killing prisoners of war): [attrib] *a war-crimes tribunal.*

ˈwar criminal person found guilty of war crimes.

ˈwar-cry *n* **(a)** word or phrase shouted as a signal in battle. **(b)** catchword used in a contest (eg by a political party); slogan.

ˈwar-dance *n* dance performed by the warriors of a tribe, eg before going into battle or to celebrate a victory.

warfare /ˈwɔ:feə(r)/ *n* [U] **(a)** (fighting a) war: *guerrilla, modern, nuclear warfare.* **(b)** (esp violent) conflict or struggle: *There is open warfare between the opponents of the plan and its supporters.*

ˈwar-game *n* **(a)** game in which models representing troops, ships, etc are moved about on maps, in order to test the players' tactical skill. **(b)** mock battle used as a training exercise.

ˈwar grave grave of a person killed in war.

ˈwarhead *n* explosive head of a missile or torpedo: *equipped with a nuclear warhead.*

ˈwar-horse *n* **1** (esp formerly) horse used in battle. **2** (*fig*) soldier, politician, etc who has fought in many campaigns.

warlike /ˈwɔ:laɪk/ *adj* fond of or skilled in fighting; aggressive: *a warlike people* ○ *a warlike appearance, mood, state.*

ˈwar-lord *n* (*dated or fml*) (chief) military commander.

ˈwar memorial monument built to honour people who have died in a war.

ˈwarmonger *n* (*derog*) person who tries to cause a war or who favours war.

the ˌWar of AˌmericanIndeˈpendence (also **the AˌmericanRevoˈlution**) war fought by American colonists (1775-83) to gain independence from Britain. Following battles at Lexington and Concord the colonists declared independence in 1776. In 1777 they beat the British at *Saratoga. They were supported by France and Spain, and the war virtually ended with the British surrender at Yorktown in 1781.

ˈwar-paint *n* [U] **(a)** paint put on the body before battle, eg by N American Indian warriors. **(b)** (*infml joc*) cosmetic make-up: *She never goes out to a party without putting her war-paint on!*

ˈwar-path *n* (idm) **(be/go) on the ˈwar-path** (*infml*) ready for a fight or a quarrel; hostile or angry: *Look out — the boss is on the war-path again!*

ˈwarship *n* ship for use in war.

the ˌWars of the ˈRoses English civil war (1455-85) between the supporters of two families, the House of Lancaster (whose symbol was a red rose) and the House of York (a white rose), to decide which would rule England. It ended when *Henry VII (of Lancaster) married Elizabeth (of York).

ˈwartime *n* [U] period of time when there is a war: *Special regulations were introduced in wartime.* ○ [attrib] *wartime rationing* ○ *the shortages of wartime Britain.*

ˈwar widow woman whose husband has been killed in a war.

ˈwar zone area in which a war takes place.

Warbeck /ˈwɔ:bek/ Perkin (1474-99), man who tried to claim the English Crown, pretending to be Richard, Duke of York, brother of *Edward V (who had actually been secretly murdered at the age of 10). He was arrested and eventually executed. Cf SIMNEL, LAMBERT.

warble /ˈwɔ:bl/ *v* **(a)** [I] (esp of a bird) sing in a continuous gentle trilling way: *larks warbling in the sky.* **(b)** [Tn] sing (a note, song, etc) in this way.

▷ **warble** *n* (usu *sing*) warbling sound: *the blackbird's warble.*

warbler /ˈwɔ:blə(r)/ *n* any of various types of bird that warble.

Ward /wɔ:d/ Mrs Humphry (1851-1920), English novelist whose books (eg *Robert Elsmere*) deal with social and religious themes. She was a niece of the poet Matthew *Arnold.

ward /wɔ:d/ *n* **1** separate part or room in a hospital for a particular group of patients: *a children's, maternity, surgical ward* ○ *a public/private ward.* **2** division of a city, etc that elects and is represented by a councillor in local government: *There are three candidates standing for election in this ward.* **3** person, esp a child, who is under the care of a guardian or the protection of a lawcourt: *She invested the money on behalf of her ward.* ○ *The child was made a ward of court.* **4** (usu *pl*) any one of the notches or projections in a key or lock (designed to prevent the lock being opened by any key except the right one). **5** (idm) **a ˌward in ˈchancery** (in Britain) person, usu a child, whose affairs are looked after by the Lord Chancellor (eg because of the death of the ward's parents).

▷ **ward** *v* (phr v) **ward sb/sth off** keep away (sb/sth that is dangerous or unpleasant); fend sb/sth off: *ward off blows, disease, danger, intruders.*

-ward *suff* (with *advs* forming *adjs*) in the direction of: *backward* ○ *eastward* ○ *homeward.* ▷ **-wards** (also *esp US* **-ward**) (forming *advs*): *onward(s)* ○ *forward(s).*

warden /ˈwɔ:dn/ *n* **1** person responsible for supervising sth: *a game warden* ○ *a traffic warden* ○ *the warden of a youth hostel.* **2** title of the heads of certain colleges and other institutions: *the Warden of Merton College, Oxford.* **3** (*US*) governor of a prison.

warder /ˈwɔ:də(r)/ *n* (*fem* **wardress** /ˈwɔ:drɪs/) (*Brit*) person who works as a guard in a prison; jailer.

Wardour Street /ˈwɔ:də stri:t/ street in Soho, London, where many film companies have their offices.

wardrobe /ˈwɔ:drəʊb/ *n* **1** place where clothes are stored, usu a large cupboard with shelves and a rail for hanging things on: *a built-in wardrobe,* ie one that forms part of the wall of a room. ⇨ illus at FURNITURE. **2** (usu *sing*) person's stock of clothes: *an extensive wardrobe of elegant dresses* ○ *buy a new winter wardrobe.* **3** stock of costumes worn by actors in a theatrical company.

□ **ˈwardrobe master, ˈwardrobe mistress** person responsible for looking after the costumes in a theatrical company.

wardroom /ˈwɔ:drʊm, -ru:m/ *n* place in a warship where all the commissioned officers except the commanding officer live and eat; mess-room.

ware /weə(r)/ *n* **1** [U] (esp in compounds) **(a)** manufactured goods (of the specified type): *ˈironware* ○ *ˈhardware* ○ *ˈsilverware.* **(b)** pottery or porcelain of a particular type or made for a particular purpose: *ˈearthenware* ○ *ˈovenware.* **2 wares** [pl] (*dated*) articles offered for sale (often not in a shop): *advertise, display, sell, peddle one's wares.*

□ **warehouse** /ˈweəhaʊs/ *n* **(a)** building where goods are stored before being sent to shops. **(b)** building where furniture is stored for its owners. — *v* [Tn] store (sth) in a warehouse: *the cost of warehousing goods.*

warfare ⇨ WAR.

Warhol /ˈwɔ:həʊl/ Andy (1930-87), American pop artist who achieved fame in the 1960s with large pictures of ordinary objects (eg soup tins) and portraits of film stars (eg Marilyn Monroe). He also made films, often with a controversially erotic content.

warily, wariness ⇨ WARY.

warlock /ˈwɔ:lɒk/ *n* (*arch*) magician or wizard, esp

an evil one.

warm[1] /wɔ:m/ *adj* (**-er, -est**) **1** (**a**) of or at a fairly high temperature, between cool and hot: *The weather is a bit warmer today.* ○ *gusts of warm air* ○ *Food for a baby should be warm, not hot.* (**b**) (of a person) having the normal body temperature, or a raised skin temperature (because of exercise, air temperature or excitement): *The patient must be kept warm.* ○ *Come and get warm by the fire.* ○ *I'm much too warm in here — please open the window.* ○ *have warm hands and feet.* (**c**) (of clothing) that keeps the body from becoming cold: *a warm pullover* ○ *Put on your warmest clothes before you go out in the snow.* (**d**) (of work, exercise, etc) causing a feeling of heat: *Sawing logs is warm work.* ○ *It was a warm climb to the summit.* Cf COLD[1], HOT. **2** showing enthusiasm; hearty: *warm applause, congratulations, thanks* ○ *a warm recommendation* ○ *give sb a warm welcome* ○ *a warm invitation to stay with sb* ○ *get a warm* (ie strongly welcoming or hostile) *reception.* **3** sympathetic or affectionate: *She is a warm kindly person.* ○ *He has a warm heart.* ○ *warm feelings of love and gratitude.* **4** (of colours, sounds, etc) pleasantly suggesting warmth: *The room was furnished in warm reds and browns.* ○ *The orchestra had a distinctively warm and mellow sound.* **5** (**a**) (of a scent in hunting) recently made and easily followed by the hounds; fresh. (**b**) [pred] (in a guessing game or game of hide-and-seek) near to the object, word, etc that is being looked for: *You're getting warm.* ○ *Am I getting warmer?* **6** (idm) **keep sb's ˈseat, etc warm (for him)** (*infml*) occupy a seat, post, etc temporarily so that it is available for sb later. **(look/feel) like death warmed up** ⇨ DEATH. **make it/things warm for sb** (*infml*) make things unpleasant or make trouble for sb; punish sb. **(as) warm as ˈtoast** (*infml*) very warm; pleasantly warm: *We lit the fire and were soon as warm as toast.*

▷ **warmly** *adv* in a warm manner: *warmly dressed* ○ *He thanked us all warmly.* ○ *I can warmly recommend it.*

warmth /wɔ:mθ/ *n* [U] (**a**) (also **warmness**) state of being warm: *the warmth of the climate.* (**b**) moderate heat: *Warmth is needed for the seeds to germinate.* (**c**) strength of feeling: *He was touched by the warmth of their welcome.* ○ *She denied the accusation with some warmth,* ie strenuously, forcefully.

□ **ˌwarm-ˈblooded** *adj* (**a**) (of animals) having a constant blood temperature (in the range 36°C-42°C); not cold-blooded like snakes, etc. (**b**) (of a person) having feelings, passions, etc that are easily roused; ardent.

ˌwarm ˈfront leading part of a moving mass of warm air. Cf COLD FRONT (COLD[1]).

ˌwarm-ˈhearted *adj* kind and sympathetic. **ˌwarm-ˈheartedness** *n* [U].

warm[2] /wɔ:m/ *v* **1** [I, Ip, Tn, Tn·p] ~ **(sth/sb) (up)** (cause sth/sb to) become warm or warmer: *a warming drink* ○ *The milk is warming (up) on the stove.* ○ *Please warm (up) the milk.* ○ *warm oneself/one's hands by the fire.* **2** (idm) **warm the ˈcockles (of sb's ˈheart)** make sb feel pleased or happy. **3** (phr v) **warm sth over** (*US*) (**a**) reheat (food); warm sth up. (**b**) bring out (old ideas, etc) without adding anything new. **warm to/towards sb** begin to like sb: *I warmed to her immediately.* ○ *He's not somebody one warms to easily.* **warm to/towards sth** become more interested in or enthusiastic about (a job, subject, task, etc); like sth more. **warm up** (**a**) prepare for athletic exercise, dancing, playing the piano, etc by practising gently beforehand. (**b**) (of a machine, engine, etc) run for a short time in order to reach the temperature at which it will operate efficiently. **warm (sb/sth) up** (cause sb/sth to) become more lively: *warm up an audience with a few jokes* ○ *The party soon warmed up.* **warm sth up** reheat (previously cooked food): *warmed-up stew.*

▷ **warmer** *n* (esp in compounds) thing that warms: *a foot-warmer.*

□ **ˈwarming-pan** *n* round metal pan with a lid and a long handle, formerly filled with hot coals and used to warm a bed.

ˈwarm-up *n* act or period of preparing for a game, performance, etc by practising gently.

warm[3] /wɔ:m/ *n* [sing] **1 the warm** warm atmosphere: *Come out of the cold street into the warm.* **2** act of warming: *She gave the sheets a warm by the fire before putting them on the bed.*

warn /wɔ:n/ *v* **1** (**a**) [Tn, Tn·pr, Dn·f, Dn·w] ~ **sb (of sth)** give sb notice of sth, esp possible danger or unpleasant consequences; inform sb in advance of what may happen: *'Mind the step,' she warned.* ○ *I tried to warn him, but he wouldn't listen.* ○ *She has been warned of the danger of driving the car in that state.* ○ *The police are warning (motorists) of possible delays.* ○ *If you warn me in advance, I will have your order ready for you.* ○ *They warned her that if she did it again she would be sent to prison.* ○ *I had been warned what to expect.* (**b**) [Tn·pr] ~ **sb about/against sb/sth;** ~ **sb against doing sth** put sb on his guard against sb/sth: *He warned us against pickpockets.* ○ *The police have warned shopkeepers about the forged banknotes.* ○ *The doctor warned us against overtiring the patient.* (**c**) [Dn·t] advise sb (not) to do sth: *They were warned not to climb the mountain in such bad weather.* ○ *She warned them to be careful.* **2** (phr v) **warn sb off (sth/doing sth)** give sb notice that he must go or stay away, eg from private property: *I had been warned off visiting her while she was still unwell.*

▷ **warning** *n* **1** [C] statement, event, etc that warns: *She has received a written warning about her conduct.* ○ *Her warnings were ignored.* ○ *a gale warning to shipping* ○ *Let that be a warning to you,* ie Let that (accident, misfortune, etc) teach you to be more careful in future. ○ *a warning of future difficulties* ○ [attrib] *warning lights, shots.* **2** [U] act of warning or state of being warned: *The attack occurred without (advance) warning,* ie unexpectedly. ○ *You should take warning from* (ie be warned by) *what happened to me.* ○ *The speaker sounded a note of warning,* ie spoke of possible danger.

warp[1] /wɔ:p/ *v* [I, Tn] **1** (cause sth to) become bent or twisted from the usual or natural shape, esp because of uneven shrinkage or expansion: *The damp wood began to warp.* ○ *The hot sun had warped the cover of the book.* **2** (*fig*) (cause sb/sth to) become biased, distorted or perverted: *His judgement was warped by self-interest.* ○ *a warped mind, sense of humour.*

▷ **warp** *n* (usu *sing*) warped condition: *a warp in his character* ○ *a time warp.*

warp[2] /wɔ:p/ *n* **the warp** [sing] (in weaving) the threads on a loom over and under which other threads (the *weft* or *woof*) are passed to make cloth. ⇨ illus at WEAVE.

warrant /ˈwɒrənt; *US* ˈwɔ:r-/ *n* **1** [C] ~ **(for sth)** (**a**) written order giving authority to do sth: *issue a warrant for sb's arrest* ○ *a death-/search-warrant* ○ *A warrant is out for his arrest/against him.* (**b**) voucher that entitles the holder to receive goods, money, services, etc: *a travel warrant* ○ *a warrant for dividends on shares.* **2** ~ **for sth/doing sth** [U] (*fml*) justification or authorization for (an action, etc): *He had no warrant for doing that/what he did.*

▷ **warrant** *v* **1** [Tn] (*fml*) be a warrant(2) for (sth); justify or deserve: *Nothing can warrant such severe punishment.* ○ *Her interference was not warranted.* ○ *The crisis warrants special measures.* **2** [usu passive: Tn, Cn·a, Cn·n, Cn·t] guarantee (sth) as genuine: *This material is warranted (to be) pure silk.* **3** (idm) **I('ll) warrant (you)** (*dated*) I assure or promise you: *The trouble isn't over yet, I'll warrant you.*

warrantee /ˌwɒrənˈti:; *US* ˌwɔ:r-/ *n* person to whom a warranty(1) is made.

warrantor /ˈwɒrəntɔ:(r); *US* ˈwɔ:r-/ *n* person who makes a warranty(1).

warranty /ˈwɒrəntɪ; *US* ˈwɔ:r-/ *n* **1** [C, U] (written or printed) guarantee, esp one given to the buyer of an article, promising to repair or replace it if necessary: *It is foolish to buy a car without a warranty.* ○ *The machine is still under warranty.* **2** [U] (*fml*) authority: *What warranty have you for doing this?*

□ **ˈwarrant-officer** *n* (**a**) (*Brit*) non-commissioned officer of the highest grade in the army, air force or marines. ⇨ App 4. (**b**) (*US*) non-commissioned officer of the highest grade in the army, air force, navy or marine corps. ⇨ App 4.

warren /ˈwɒrən; *US* ˈwɔ:rən/ *n* **1** area of land with many burrows in which rabbits live and breed. **2** (*fig*) (usu over-populated) building or district with many narrow passages, where it is difficult to find one's way: *lost in a warren of narrow streets.*

warrior /ˈwɒrɪə(r); *US* ˈwɔ:r-/ *n* **1** (*fml*) (esp formerly) person who fights in battle; soldier: [attrib] *a warrior nation,* ie fond of or skilled in fighting. **2** member of a tribe who fights for his tribe: *a Zulu warrior.*

Warsaw Pact /ˌwɔ:sɔ: ˈpækt/ **the Warsaw Pact** (treaty, signed in 1955, which set up an) alliance of E European countries (the USSR, E Germany, Poland, Hungary, Czechoslovakia, Romania and Bulgaria) for mutual defence and military aid.

wart /wɔ:t/ *n* **1** (**a**) small hard dry growth on the skin. (**b**) similar growth on a plant. **2** (idm) **ˌwarts and ˈall** (*infml*) without concealing blemishes or unattractive features: *You agreed to marry me, warts and all!*

▷ **warty** *adj* covered in warts.

□ **ˈwart-hog** *n* any of several types of African wild pig with two large tusks and wart-like growths on the face.

Warwick /ˈwɒrɪk/ Richard Neville, Earl of (1428-71), English statesman of the period of the *Wars of the Roses. His role in helping both the Yorkist *Edward IV and the Lancastrian *Henry VI to become king earned him the nickname 'Warwick the Kingmaker'.

Warwickshire /ˈwɒrɪkʃə(r)/ county of England, in the Midlands. It is now mainly agricultural, although it formerly contained the industrial centres of Birmingham and Coventry. *Shakespeare was born there. ⇨ map at App 1.

wary /ˈweərɪ/ *adj* (**-ier, -iest**) ~ **(of sb/sth)** looking out for possible danger or difficulty; cautious: *keep a wary eye on sb* ○ *She was wary of strangers.* ○ *be wary of giving offence.* ▷ **warily** /-rəlɪ/ *adv*: *They approached the stranger warily.* **wariness** *n* [U].

was ⇨ BE.

Wash /wɒʃ/ **the Wash** large shallow bay on the east coast of England, between Norfolk and Lincolnshire.

wash[1] /wɒʃ/ *n* **1** [C usu *sing*] act of cleaning or being cleaned with water: *He looks as if he needs a good* (ie thorough) *wash.* ○ *have a wash (and brush up),* ie wash oneself (and make oneself tidy, brush one's hair, etc) ○ *Please give the car a wash.* ○ *The colour has faded after only two washes.* ○ *a cold wash,* ie a wash in cold water. **2** (**a**) **the wash** [sing] process of laundering clothes: *All my shirts are in/have gone to the wash,* ie are being laundered. (**b**) [C usu *sing*] quantity of clothes, sheets, etc (to be) washed: *There is a large wash this week.* ○ *When does the wash come back from the laundry?* **3** [sing] (sound made by) disturbed water or air, eg behind a moving ship, aircraft, etc: *the wash of the waves against the side of the boat* ○ *the wash made by the steamer's propellers.* **4** [C] thin layer of water-colour painted on a surface. **5** [U] waste scraps of food mixed in liquid and given to pigs to eat; swill. **6** (idm) **come out in the ˈwash** (*infml*) (of mistakes, etc) come right or be put right eventually, without any harm being done.

□ **ˈwashboard** *n* board with ridges on it used (esp formerly) for rubbing clothes on when washing them.

ˈwash-day *n* (*dated*) day on which clothes are washed.

ˈwash-drawing *n* drawing done with a brush in a black or neutral water-colour.

wash[2] /wɒʃ; *US* wɔ:ʃ/ *v* **1** (**a**) [Tn, Cn·a] make (sb/sth) clean in water or some other liquid: *These clothes will have to be washed.* ○ *Go and wash yourself.* ○ *Have these glasses been washed?* ○ *The beach had been washed clean by the tide.* (**b**) [I] make oneself, clothes, one's face and hands, etc clean with water: *I had to wash and dress in a hurry.* ○ *They had to wash in cold water.* (**c**) [I] (of clothes, fabrics, etc) be able to be washed without losing colour, shrinking, etc: *This sweater washes well.* ○ *If a garment won't wash, it must be dry-cleaned.* **2** [Tn] (of the sea, a river, etc) flow past or against (sth): *The sea washes the base of the cliffs.* ○ *The garden wall is being washed by the flood water.* **3** (**a**) [Ipr, Ip] (of water) flow in the specified direction: *waves washing against the side of a boat* ○ *Water washed over the deck.* (**b**) [Tn·pr, Tn·p esp passive] (of water) move (sb/sth) by flowing in the specified direction: *debris washed along by the flood* ○ *The body was washed out to sea.* ○ *Pieces of the wreckage were washed ashore.* ○ *He was washed overboard in the storm.* **4** [Tn, Tn·p] ~ **sth** (**out**) (of water) form sth by flowing; scoop sth out: *The stream had washed (out) a channel in the sand.* **5** [Tn] pour water through gravel, etc in order to find (gold, etc): *washing ore.* **6** [Tn] cover (a surface) with a thin layer of water-paint. **7** [I, Ipr] (only in questions or negative sentences) ~ (**with sb**) (*infml*) be accepted or believed (by sb): *That excuse simply won't wash (with me).* **8** (idm) **wash one's dirty linen in ˈpublic** discuss one's personal (esp unpleasant) affairs or quarrels in public. **wash one's hands of sb/sth** refuse to be responsible for sb/sth (any longer): *I've washed my hands of the whole sordid business.* **9** (phr v) **wash sb/sth away** (of water) remove or carry sb/sth away to another place: *Her child was washed away in the flood.* ○ *footprints washed away by the rain.* ○ *The cliffs are being gradually washed away by the sea.*

wash sth down (**with sth**) (**a**) clean sth by using a stream or jet of water: *wash down the decks* ○ *wash down a car with a hose.* (**b**) drink sth after, or at the same time as, eating (food): *I had bread and cheese for lunch, washed down with beer.*

wash (**sth**) **off** (cause sth to) be removed from the surface of a material, etc by washing: *Those grease stains won't wash off.* ○ *Please wash that mud off (your boots) before you come in.*

wash out (of a dirty mark) be removed from a fabric by washing: *These ink stains won't wash out.*

wash sth out (**a**) wash sth or the inside of sth in order to remove dirt, etc: *wash out the empty bottles* ○ *If I wash your sports kit out now, it'll be dry by tomorrow morning.* (**b**) (of rain, etc) bring (a game) to an end or prevent it from starting: *The match was completely washed out.* ○ *Torrential rain washed out most of the weekend's events.*

wash over sb (*infml*) occur all around sb, or be expressed, without greatly affecting him: *The recent criticism she's had seems to have washed right over her.*

wash up (**a**) (*Brit*) wash the dishes, cutlery, etc after a meal. (**b**) (*US*) wash one's face and hands.

wash sth up (*Brit*) (**a**) wash (dishes, cutlery, etc) after a meal. (**b**) carry sth to shore: *The tide had washed up cargo from the wrecked ship.*

▷ **washable** /-əbl/ *adj* that can be washed without being spoiled: *washable clothes, fabrics, paint, surfaces.*

□ ˈ**wash-basin** (also ˈ**wash-hand-basin, basin,** *US* ˈ**wash-bowl**) *n* large bowl (usually fixed to a wall and fitted with taps) for washing one's hands, etc in.

ˈ**wash-cloth** *n* (*US*) = FACE-CLOTH (FACE[1]).

ˌ**washed** ˈ**out** (**a**) (of fabric or colour) faded by washing: *ˌwashed out blue ˈoveralls* ○ *a ˌwashed out ˌcotton ˈdress.* (**b**) (of a person, his appearance, etc) pale and tired; exhausted: *She looks washed out after her illness.*

ˌ**washed** ˈ**up** (*infml*) ruined or defeated, having failed: *Their marriage was washed up long before they separated.*

ˌ**washing-**ˈ**up** *n* [U] (**a**) task of washing dishes, etc after a meal: *do the washing-up.* (**b**) dishes, cutlery, glasses, etc to be washed up: *The washing-up had been left in the sink.* **washing-**ˈ**up liquid** liquid detergent for washing dishes, etc.

ˈ**wash-leather** *n* [C, U] (piece of) chamois leather, used for cleaning and polishing windows, etc.

ˈ**wash-out** *n* (*infml*) person, event, etc that is a complete failure: *The new manager is a wash-out.* ○ *The party was a total wash-out.*

ˈ**washroom** *n* (*US euph*) lavatory (esp in a public building). ⇨ Usage at TOILET.

ˈ**wash-stand** *n* (esp formerly, in houses without a piped supply of water to a bathroom or bedroom) special table that holds a basin and jug, for washing oneself in a bedroom.

ˈ**wash-tub** *n* large wooden tub used (esp formerly) for washing clothes.

washer /ˈwɒʃə(r); *US* ˈwɔː-/ *n* **1** small flat ring made of rubber, metal, plastic, etc placed between two surfaces (eg under a nut) to make a screw or joint tight, prevent leakage, etc. ⇨ illus at BOLT. **2** (*infml*) automatic machine for washing clothes.

washerwoman /ˈwɒʃəwʊmən/ *n* (*pl* **-women** /-wɪmɪn/) (*dated*) woman whose job is washing clothes.

washing /ˈwɒʃɪŋ; *US* ˈwɔː-/ *n* **1** [C, U] (act of) washing or being washed: *The sweater had shrunk after repeated washing(s).* ○ *Washing is a chore.* **2** [U] clothes being washed or to be washed: *hang the washing on the line to dry* ○ *put a load of washing in the washing-machine* ○ *Send one's (dirty) washing to the laundry.*

□ ˈ**washing-machine** *n* electric machine for washing clothes.

ˈ**washing-powder** *n* [U] soap or detergent in the form of powder for washing clothes.

ˈ**washing-soda** *n* [U] = SODIUM CARBONATE (SODIUM).

Washington[1] /ˈwɒʃɪŋtən/ (also ˌ**Washington, D**ˈ**C**) capital of the USA, situated in the District of Columbia, between Maryland and Virginia on the Potomac river. The site for the city was chosen by George Washington.

Washington[2] /ˈwɒʃɪŋtən/ state of the USA, on the north-west coast between Oregon and the Canadian border. Much of it is mountainous. Its economy is mainly agricultural, but there is also industry in Seattle and other cities. ⇨ map at App 1.

Washington[3] /ˈwɒʃɪŋtən/ George (1732-99), American soldier and statesman, first president of the USA 1789-97. He successfully led the American army (the 'Continental Army') against the British in the *War of American Independence. Afterwards he retired from public life, but in 1787 returned to become president of the commission in Philadelphia which drew up the US constitution. In 1789 he was elected president of the USA. He served two terms of office and is rightly called the father of his country. ⇨ App 2.

washy /ˈwɒʃɪ; *US* ˈwɔː-/ *adj* (*derog*) **1** (of colours) pale. **2** (of liquids) (too) watery; thin or weak: *washy coffee.* **3** lacking force, vigour or clarity: *washy encouragement, ideas, plans.* Cf WISHY-WASHY.

wasn't ⇨ BE.

wasp /wɒsp/ *n* any of several types of flying insect, the most common of which has black and yellow stripes, a narrow waist and a powerful sting in its tail.

▷ **waspish** *adj* (*derog*) making sharp comments or replies; irritable or snappish: *waspish remarks.* **waspishly** *adv.* **waspishness** *n* [U].

□ ˌ**wasp-**ˈ**waisted** *adj* (*dated*) (esp of a woman) having a very slender waist.

WASP (also **Wasp**) /wɒsp/ *abbr* (*esp US usu derog*) White Anglo-Saxon Protestant: *a typically Wasp attitude.*

wassail /ˈwɒseɪl/ *n* [U] (*arch*) merry-making (esp at Christmas) with eating and drinking. ▷ **wassail** *v* [I]: *go wassailing.*

wastage /ˈweɪstɪdʒ/ *n* [U] (**a**) amount that is wasted: *You must allow for five per cent wastage in transit.* (**b**) loss caused by waste: *The retailer has to absorb the cost of wastage.* ○ *natural wastage,* ie loss of employees because they retire or move to other jobs and not through redundancy.

waste[1] /weɪst/ *adj* [usu attrib] **1** (of land) that is not (fit to be) used; not inhabited or cultivated: *an area of waste ground.* **2** no longer useful and to be thrown away: *waste matter produced by the manufacturing process.* **3** (idm) **lay sth** ˈ**waste** (*fml*) destroy crops in (land, etc), esp during a war; ravage sth: *fields laid waste by the invading army.*

□ ˈ**wasteland** *n* (**a**) area of land that is not or cannot be used; barren or desolate land: *an industrial wasteland,* ie an area that has been spoilt by industrial development and is no longer used. (**b**) (*fig*) situation or life that is culturally or spiritually unproductive.

ˌ**waste-**ˈ**paper** *n* [U] paper that is thought to be spoilt or no longer useful; scrap paper. ˌ**waste-**ˈ**paper basket** (*Brit*) (*US* ˈ**waste-basket**, ˈ**waste-bin**) basket or other container for paper, etc that is to be thrown away.

ˈ**waste product** useless by-product of a physical or industrial process.

waste[2] /weɪst/ *v* **1** (**a**) [Tn, Tn·pr] ~ **sth** (**on sb/sth**) use sth extravagantly, needlessly or without an adequate result: *Hurry up, we're wasting time.* ○ *A dripping tap wastes water.* ○ *Don't waste food.* ○ *All our efforts were wasted.* ○ *I'm sorry you've had a wasted* (ie unnecessary, fruitless) *journey.* ○ *I'm not going to waste any more words on the subject.* ○ *She has wasted her money on things she doesn't need.* ○ (*fig*) *The humour is wasted on them,* ie They do not appreciate it. (**b**) [Tn usu passive] not make full use of (a person or his abilities): *She's wasted in her present job.* **2** [Tn esp passive] cause (sb/sth) to become weaker and thinner: *His body was wasted by long illness.* ○ *a wasting disease* ○ *limbs wasted by hunger.* **3** (idm) **lose/waste no time in doing sth** ⇨ TIME[1]. **waste one's** ˈ**breath** (**on sb/sth**) speak (about sb/sth) but not have any effect: *They won't listen, so don't waste your breath telling them.* ˌ**waste not,** ˈ**want not** (*saying*) if you never waste anything (esp food or money), you will always have it when you need it. **4** (phr v) **waste away** (of a person) grow unhealthily thin or weak.

▷ **waster** *n* (*derog*) (**a**) wasteful person. (**b**) = WASTREL.

waste[3] /weɪst/ *n* **1** [U, sing] (act of) wasting (WASTE[2] 1a) or being wasted: *a policy aimed at reducing waste* ○ *The waste of public money on the project was criticized.* ○ *It's a waste of time* (ie It's not worth) *doing that.* ○ *In his opinion, holidays are a waste of time and money.* **2** [U] material, food, etc that is no longer needed and is (to be) thrown away; refuse: *Dustbins are used for household waste.* ○ *regulations controlling the disposal of industrial waste* ○ *radioactive waste from nuclear power stations.* **3** [C] (**a**) (usu *pl*) large area of land that is not or cannot be inhabited or cultivated; desert: *the icy wastes of the Antarctic* ○ *the arid wastes of the Sahara.* (**b**) dreary scene: *the derelict waste of disused factories.* **4** (idm) **go/run to** ˈ**waste** be wasted: *What a pity to see all that food go to waste.*

▷ **wasteful** /-fl/ *adj* (**a**) causing waste: *wasteful habits, methods, processes.* (**b**) using more than is needed; extravagant: *wasteful luxury, expenditure, housekeeping.* **wastefully** /-fəlɪ/ *adv.* **wastefulness** *n* [U].

□ ˈ**waste-basket** (also ˈ**waste-bin**) *n* (*US*) = WASTE-PAPER BASKET (WASTE[1]).

ˈ**waste-pipe** *n* pipe that carries away water which has been used or is not needed, eg dirty water from a sink, bath, etc.

wastrel /ˈweɪstrəl/ (also **waster**) *n* (*fml*) lazy good-for-nothing person.

watch[1] /wɒtʃ/ *n* **1** [C] (**a**) (in a ship) period of duty (usu four hours) for part of the crew: *the middle watch,* ie midnight to 4 am ○ *the* ˈ*dog watches,* ie 4 pm to 6 pm and 6 pm to 8 pm. (**b**) part (usu half) of a ship's crew on duty during such a period. **2** [sing] (**a**) **the watch** (formerly) body of men employed to go through the streets, esp at night, in order to protect people and their property: *the constables of the watch* ○ *call out the watch.* (**b**) person or group of people employed to watch sb/sth: *The police put a watch on the suspect's house.* **3** [C usu *pl*] (*arch or fml*) period of time when one is awake during the night: *in the long watches of the night.* **4** (idm) **keep a close eye/watch on sb/sth** ⇨ CLOSE[1]. **keep** ˈ**watch** (**for sb/sth**) stay watching (for sb/sth): *post a guard to keep* ˈ*watch while the others sleep.* **on** ˈ**watch** on duty, eg as a member of

Water

Britain's water supply comes from a number of sources, both on the surface, such as mountain lakes, streams and rivers, and underground, such as wells and boreholes. Almost every home in the country is connected to the public water supply system.

Water is supplied to three-quarters of the population in England and Wales by ten independent water and sewage companies ('water authorities'). Each company serves a particular geographical region and is responsible not only for supplying water but also for removing and treating sewage and for preventing pollution in the different water sources. The remaining quarter are supplied by 29 private water companies operating within the areas of the regional companies. They are responsible for the supply and management of water only, not for sewage disposal.

Until 1989 the water authorities were state-owned companies, operating in the same regions as now. When they were privatized in that year, however, a new body, the National Rivers Authority (NRA), was set up to take over some of their responsibilities. The NRA now manages the rivers of England and Wales as sources of water supply, and includes in its functions the control of pollution in river and coastal waters, the drainage of riverside land, and the prevention of flooding. The management of water and sewage in Scotland remained unchanged, and is the responsibility of the nine regional and three island councils. The Central Scotland Water Development Board is also responsible for developing water resources and supplying water in bulk to five regional councils in central Scotland.

Before privatization, the water companies charged householders for their domestic water supply and sewage disposal according to the size and value of their property. Since privatization the companies are free to decide how to charge customers. As a result, many companies plan to meter the supply of water to homes, in the same way as gas and electricity are metered, in order to make a more accurate charge for the volume of water used. Businesses already have their water supply metered.

In some parts of the country the water supply is unusually hard, especially in regions where the soil is chalky or stony. This can cause problems, since calcium deposits build up and heavy scaling occurs in water pipes and taps and in kitchen utensils such as kettles. The degree of hardness of the water in an area, however, is outside the control of the regional authority, and has to be tackled by the consumer, mainly by using commercial water softeners. All water supplied to homes is of drinkable quality, but, increasingly, many people drink bottled mineral water because they prefer the taste and regard it as purer.

a ship's crew or as a guard. **(be) on (the) ˈwatch (for sb/sth)** (be) watching for sb/sth, esp possible danger: *Be on the watch for a sudden change in the patient's condition.* ○ *The police warned people to be on the watch for intruders.*

▷ **watchful** /-fl/ *adj* watching or observing closely; alert: *keep a watchful eye on sth.* **watchfully** /-fəlɪ/ *adv.* **watchfulness** *n* [U].

□ **ˈwatch-dog** *n* **(a)** dog that is kept to guard property, esp a house. **(b)** *(fig)* person, group, etc that acts as a guardian of people's rights, etc: [attrib] *a watch-dog committee.*

ˈwatchman /-mən/ *n* (*pl* **-men** /-mən/) person employed to guard a building (eg a bank, an office building or a factory), esp at night.

ˈwatch-night service religious service that takes place on the last night of the year.

ˈwatch-tower *n* high tower from which guards keep watch, eg in a forest to look for forest fires, or a fortified observation post.

watch[2] /wɒtʃ/ *v* **1 (a)** [I, Tn, Tw no passive, Tng, Tni no passive] look at (sb/sth); observe: *The students watched as the surgeon performed the operation.* ○ *He watched to see* (ie in order to see) *what would happen.* ○ *Watch me carefully.* ○ *Watch what I do and how I do it.* ○ *She had a feeling that she was being watched,* ie spied on. ○ *She watched the children crossing/as they crossed the road,* ie observed them as they did it (but not necessarily from start to finish). ○ *She watched the children cross the road,* ie observed the action from start to finish. **(b)** [Tn] look at (television, sport, etc) as an entertainment: *Are you going to play or will you just watch?* ○ *Do you watch football on television?* ○ *The match was watched by over twenty thousand people.* **2** [Ipr, Tn] ~ **(over) sb/sth** guard or protect sb/sth; keep an eye on sb/sth: *Could you watch (over) my clothes while I have a swim?* ○ *He felt that God was watching over him.* ○ *We'll have to watch the children in case they get too tired.* **3** [Ipr] ~ **for sth** look or wait attentively for sth: *They are watching for further developments.* ○ *You'll have to watch for the right moment.* **4** [Tn] *(infml)* be careful about (sb/sth), esp in order to keep him/it under control: *watch one's language, manners, tongue, etc* ○ *Watch yourself!* ie Be careful what you do or say, or you will be punished. ○ *watch every penny,* ie be very careful about what one spends ○ *Watch what you say about the project, they don't like criticism!* **5** [I, Ipr] ~ **(at sth)** *(esp arch)* remain awake: *watch all night at the bedside of a sick child.* **6** (idm) **mind/watch one's step** ⇨ STEP[2]. **watch the ˈclock** *(infml derog)* be careful not to work longer than the required time; think more about when one's work will finish than about the work itself. **ˈwatch it** *(infml)* (esp imperative) be careful. **watch this ˈspace** *(infml catchphrase)* wait for further developments to be announced. **watch the ˈtime** remain aware of what time it is (eg to avoid being late for sth). **watch the ˈworld go by** observe what is happening around one. **7** (phr v) **watch ˈout** be on one's guard; keep looking out for possible trouble, etc: *Watch out! There's a car coming.* **watch out for sb/sth** be alert so that one notices sb/sth; look out for sb/sth: *The staff were asked to watch out for forged banknotes.*

▷ **watcher** *n* person who looks at sth; observer.

□ **ˌwatching ˈbrief** brief of a lawyer who is present in court during a case in which his client is not directly concerned, in order to advise him and protect his interests.

watch[3] /wɒtʃ/ *n* small instrument showing the time, worn on the wrist or (esp formerly) carried in a pocket: *a pocket-watch* ○ *a wrist-watch* ○ *What time is it by your watch?/What does your watch say?* Cf CLOCK[1] 1.

□ **ˈwatchmaker** *n* person who makes and repairs watches and clocks.

ˈwatch-strap *(Brit)* (*US* **ˈwatch-band**) *n* strap for fastening a wrist-watch on one's wrist.

watchword /ˈwɒtʃwɜːd/ *n* **1** word or phrase that expresses briefly the principles of a party or group; slogan or catchphrase: *Our watchword is: 'Evolution, not revolution'.* **2** = PASSWORD (PASS[1]).

water[1] /ˈwɔːtə(r)/ *n* **1 (a)** [U] liquid without colour, smell or taste that falls as rain, is in lakes, rivers and seas, and is used for drinking, washing, etc: *Water is changed into steam by heat and into ice by cold.* ○ *Fish live in (the) water.* ○ *ˈdrinking water* ○ *ˈmineral water.* **(b)** [U] this liquid as supplied to homes, factories, etc in pipes: *The water was turned off for several hours a day during the drought.* ○ *The houses in this village are without water.* ○ *hot and cold running water,* ie a supply of hot and cold water piped to taps ○ [attrib] *water rationing, shortages.* **(c)** [sing] mass of this liquid, esp a lake, river or sea: *She fell in the water and drowned.* ○ *The flood water covered the whole area.* **(d)** [sing] surface of a lake, river, sea, etc: *float on the water* ○ *swim under the water* ○ *We could see fishes under the water.* **2** [U] (esp in compounds) preparation containing water or sth similar to water: *ˈrose-water* ○ *ˈlavender-water* ○ *ˈsoda-water.* **3 waters** [pl] **(a)** mass of water (in a lake, river, etc): *the (ˈhead-)waters of the Nile,* ie the lake from which it flows ○ *The waters of the lake flow out over a large waterfall.* ○ *the stormy waters of the Atlantic.* **(b)** sea near a particular country: *British (territorial) waters* ○ *in home/foreign waters.* **4** [U] state or level of the tide: *(at) high/low water.* **5** [sing] purity and brilliance of a precious stone: *a diamond of the first water,* ie highest quality. **6 waters** [pl] fluid that surrounds an unborn baby in the womb: *Her waters have broken* (ie The fluid has been released from the womb), *so she is about to give birth.* **7** (idm) **be in/get into hot water** ⇨ HOT. **blood is thicker than water** ⇨ BLOOD[1]. **bread and water** ⇨ BREAD. **by water** by boat, ship, barge, etc: *transported by water* ○ *You can reach the house by water.* **cast one's bread upon the waters** ⇨ CAST[1]. **hell or high water** ⇨ HELL. **fish in troubled waters** ⇨ FISH[2]. **a fish out of water** ⇨ FISH[1]. **go through fire and water** ⇨ FIRE[1]. **hold ˈwater** *(infml)* (of an argument, an excuse, a theory, etc) be capable of standing up to examination or testing; be valid. **in deep water** ⇨ DEEP[1]. **in smooth water** ⇨ SMOOTH[1]. **keep one's head above water** ⇨ HEAD[1]. **like a duck to water** ⇨ DUCK[1]. **like ˈwater** *(infml)* in great quantity; lavishly or recklessly: *spend money like water* ○ *The wine flowed like water at the party.* **a lot of/much water has flowed, etc under the ˈbridge** many things have happened (since an event, etc) and the situation is different now. **make ˈwater** (of a ship) have a leak: *We're making water* (ie Water is coming into the ship) *fast.* **make/pass ˈwater** *(fml)* urinate. **milk and water** ⇨ MILK[1]. **muddy the waters** ⇨ MUDDY (MUD). **of the first water** of the worst, most extreme, etc kind: *He's a scoundrel of the first water!* **pour/throw cold water on sth** ⇨ COLD[1]. **pour oil on troubled waters** ⇨ POUR. **still waters run deep** ⇨ STILL[1]. **take the ˈwaters** visit a spa in order to drink or bathe in the spring water there to improve one's health. **throw out the baby with the bath water** ⇨ BABY. **tread water** ⇨ TREAD. **under ˈwater (a)** in and covered by water: *swimming under water.* **(b)** flooded: *Several fields are under water after the heavy rain.* **(like) water off a ˈduck's ˈback** (esp of criticisms, etc) without any effect (on sb): *Their hints about his behaviour were (like) water off a duck's back.* **water under the ˈbridge** event, mistake, etc that has already occurred and cannot be altered, so there is no point in worrying about it: *Last year's dispute is (all) water under the bridge now.* **you can take a horse to water, but you can't make it drink** ⇨ HORSE.

▷ **waterless** *adj* (esp of an area of land) without water: *waterless deserts.*

□ **ˈwater-bed** *n* mattress for sleeping on, made of rubber or plastic and filled with water.

ˈwater-bird *n* any of several types of bird that swim or wade in (esp fresh) water. ⇨ illus at BIRD.

ˈwater-biscuit *n* thin crisp unsweetened biscuit,

usu eaten with butter and cheese.

ˌ**water-ˈboatman** *n* small beetle-like insect that lives in ponds and has long legs which it uses for swimming.

ˈ**water-borne** *adj* (**a**) (of goods) carried by water. (**b**) (of diseases) spread by the use of contaminated water.

ˈ**water-bottle** *n* (**a**) glass container for drinking-water, eg at table or in a bedroom. (**b**) (*US* **canteen**) metal flask for carrying drinking-water, used by a soldier, scout, etc.

ˈ**water-buffalo** *n* (*pl* unchanged or ~**es**) common domestic Indian buffalo.

ˈ**water-bus** *n* boat that carries passengers on a regular short route with stops, like a bus.

ˈ**water-butt** *n* = BUTT[1] 2.

ˈ**water-cannon** *n* machine that produces a powerful jet of water, used eg to disperse a crowd of rioters.

ˈ**water-closet** *n* (*abbr* **WC**) (*dated*) = LAVATORY.

ˈ**water-colour** (*US* **-color**) *n* **1** ˈ**water-colours** [pl] paints (to be) mixed with water and not oil. **2** [C] picture painted with such paints.

ˈ**water-cooled** *adj* cooled by water circulating round it: *a water-cooled engine, nuclear reactor*.

ˈ**watercourse** *n* (channel of a) stream, brook or man-made waterway.

ˈ**watercress** *n* [U] type of cress that grows in streams and pools, with strong-tasting peppery leaves used in salads.

ˈ**water-diviner** *n* = DIVINER (DIVINE[2]).

ˈ**waterfall** *n* stream or river that falls from a height, eg over rocks or a cliff.

ˈ**water-fowl** *n* (*pl* unchanged) (*usu pl*) bird that swims and lives near or on water, esp one of the types that are hunted for sport.

ˈ**waterfront** *n* street, part of a town, etc that is next to water (eg a harbour or the sea).

ˈ**water-hammer** *n* [U] knocking noise in a pipe when water is turned on or off.

ˈ**water-hole** *n* shallow depression in which water collects (esp in the bed of a river that is otherwise dry and to which animals go to drink).

ˈ**water-ice** *n* [C, U] (portion of) frozen water flavoured with fruit juice and sugar, served as a dessert.

ˈ**water-jump** *n* (in show-jumping, steeplechases, etc) place where a horse has to jump over water, eg a ditch or a fence with water beside it.

ˈ**water-level** *n* (**a**) surface of water in a reservoir, etc: *below the water-level*. (**b**) height of this: *raise the water-level*.

ˈ**water-lily** *n* any of several types of plant that grow in water, and have broad floating leaves and white, yellow, blue or red flowers.

ˈ**water-line** *n* line along which the surface of the water touches a ship's side: *the load water-line*, ie the water-line when the ship is loaded ○ *the light water-line*, ie the water-line when the ship is empty of cargo.

ˈ**waterlogged** /-lɒgd; *US* -lɔːgd/ *adj* (**a**) (of timber) so saturated with water or (of a ship) so full of water that it will barely float. (**b**) (of land) so saturated with water that it cannot hold any more; thoroughly soaked: *The match had to be abandoned because the pitch was waterlogged.*

ˈ**water-main** *n* main pipe in a water-supply system.

ˈ**waterman** /-mən/ *n* (*pl* **-men** /-mən/) boatman who ferries people or hires out his boat.

ˈ**watermark** *n* **1** manufacturer's design in some types of paper, which can be seen when the paper is held against the light. **2** mark that shows how high water (eg the tide or a river) has risen or how low it has fallen.

ˈ**water-meadow** *n* meadow that is fertile because it is periodically flooded by a stream.

ˈ**water-melon** *n* (**a**) [C, U] large smooth-skinned melon with juicy pink or red flesh and black seeds: *eating a slice of water-melon*. (**b**) [C] plant on which this grows.

ˈ**water-mill** *n* mill with machinery that is operated by water-power.

ˈ**water ouzel** = OUZEL 2.

ˈ**water-pistol** *n* toy gun that shoots a jet of water.

ˈ**water polo** game played by two teams of swimmers who try to throw a ball into a goal.

ˈ**water-power** *n* [U] power obtained from flowing or falling water, used to drive machinery or generate electric current.

ˈ**waterproof** *adj* that cannot be penetrated by water: *waterproof fabric*. — *n* garment made from waterproof fabric, esp a raincoat. — *v* [Tn] make (sth) waterproof.

ˈ**water-rat** *n* rat-like animal that swims in water and lives in a hole beside a river, lake, etc.

ˈ**water-rate** *n* (*Brit*) charge made for the use of water from a public water-supply.

ˈ**water-repellent** *adj* (esp of a fabric or garment) not letting in water; not easily wetted.

ˈ**watershed** *n* (**a**) line of high land where streams on one side flow into one river or sea and streams on the other side flow into a different river or sea. (**b**) (*fig*) turning-point in a course of events: *Her visit to India proved to be a watershed in her life.*

ˈ**waterside** *n* [sing] edge of a river, lake or sea: *stroll along the waterside* ○ [attrib] *a waterside housing development*.

ˈ**water-ski** *n* (*pl* **-skis**) (*usu pl*) either of a pair of flat boards on which a person stands in order to ski on water: *a pair of water-skis*. ˈ**water-skiing** *n* [U] sport of skiing on water while being towed along at speed by a fast motor boat.

ˈ**water-softener** *n* [C, U] device or substance that softens hard water.

ˈ**water-splash** *n* place where a road is crossed by a stream.

ˈ**waterspout** *n* funnel-shaped column of water between the sea and the clouds, formed when a whirlwind draws up a whirling mass of water.

ˈ**water-supply** *n* (usu *sing*) (**a**) system of providing and storing water. (**b**) amount of water stored for a town, district, building, etc.

ˈ**water-table** *n* level below which the ground is saturated with water: *The water-table has been lowered by drought.*

ˈ**watertight** *adj* **1** made or fastened so that water cannot get in or out: *a watertight compartment, joint, seal.* **2** (*fig*) (**a**) (of an excuse or alibi) impossible to disprove. (**b**) (of an agreement) drawn up so that there is no chance of anyone misunderstanding or avoiding any part of it.

ˈ**water-tower** *n* tower that holds a water-tank at a height that ensures enough pressure for distributing a water-supply.

ˈ**waterway** *n* route for travel by water (eg a canal or channel in a river where the water is deep enough for ships). ⇨ article at RIVER.

ˈ**water-wheel** *n* wheel turned by a flow of water, used to work machinery.

ˈ**water-wings** *n* [pl] pair of floats worn on the shoulders by a person who is learning to swim.

ˈ**waterworks** *n* **1** [sing or pl *v*] building with pumping machinery, etc for supplying water to a district. **2** [pl] (*infml euph*) (functioning of) the body's urinary system: *Are your waterworks all right?* **3** (idm) **turn on the** ˈ**waterworks** (*infml derog*) (start to) cry.

NOTE ON USAGE: When water is **heated** to 100 degrees Celsius, it **boils** and becomes **steam**. When steam touches a cold surface, it **condenses** and becomes water again. When water is **cooled** below 0 degrees Celsius, it **freezes** and becomes **ice**. If the temperature increases, the ice **melts**. When talking about **frozen** food or **icy** weather becoming warmer, we say it **thaws**. Frozen food **thaws** or **defrosts** when we take it out of the freezer.

water[2] /ˈwɔːtə(r)/ *v* **1** [Tn] pour or sprinkle water on (sth): *water a flowerbed, lawn, plant.* **2** [Tn] give water to (an animal) to drink: *water the horses.* **3** [Tn] add water to (a drink) to dilute it: *The owner of the pub was accused of watering the beer.* **4** [I] (of the eyes) become full of tears or (of the mouth) produce saliva: *The smoke made my eyes water.* ○ *The delicious smell from the kitchen made our mouths water.* **5** [Tn usu passive] (esp of rivers) flow through (an area of land) and provide it with water: *a country watered by numerous rivers.* **6** (phr v) **water sth down** (**a**) make (a liquid) weaker by adding water; dilute sth: *The milk had been watered down.* ○ *You have to water down the medicine before drinking it.* (**b**) weaken the effect of sth, eg by making the details less vivid: *The criticisms had been watered down so as not to offend anybody.* ○ *They gave the press a watered-down version of what really happened.*

□ ˌ**watered** ˈ**silk** silk fabric that has a glossy surface with irregular wavy markings on it.

watering-can /ˈwɔːtərɪŋ kæn/ *n* container with a long spout, used for watering plants.

watering-place /ˈwɔːtərɪŋ pleɪs/ *n* (**a**) pool where animals go to drink; water-hole. (**b**) (*dated esp Brit*) spa or seaside resort: *one of the favourite watering-places of the Victorians.*

Waterford crystal /ˌwɔːtəfəd ˈkrɪstl/ (also ˌ**Waterford** ˈ**glass**) [U] type of fine clear glass made in Waterford, a town in Ireland. It is used for drinking-glasses, bowls, vases, etc.

Watergate /ˈwɔːtəgeɪt/ US scandal resulting from an attempt in 1972 to steal information from the offices of the Democratic Party in the Watergate building, Washington, in order to help the campaign to re-elect the Republican President *Nixon. Nixon was accused of being involved, and eventually had to resign. The element *-gate* has come to be used in the USA as a suffix for naming similar scandals (eg *Irangate*, involving secret weapons sales to Iran).

Waterloo /ˌwɔːtəˈluː/ **1** village in Belgium, south of Brussels, where on 18 June 1815 *Napoleon's army was defeated by the British (under the Duke of *Wellington) and the Prussians. The battle ended Napoleon's attempt to return to power. **2** (idm) **meet one's Waterloo** ⇨ MEET[1].

watery /ˈwɔːtərɪ/ *adj* **1** (**a**) of or like water: *a watery consistency* ○ (*fig*) *a watery grave*, ie death by drowning. (**b**) (*usu derog*) containing or cooked in too much water: *watery coffee, soup, cabbage.* **2** (of colours) pale. **3** (**a**) full of moisture: *watery eyes* ○ *a watery* (ie weak and tearful) *smile.* (**b**) suggesting that there will be rain: *a watery moon, sun, sky.*

Watson[1] /ˈwɒtsn/ Doctor, character in the Sherlock *Holmes stories by Sir Arthur Conan *Doyle. Dr Watson is a friend of Holmes who accompanies and helps him in his investigations and later records them in writing.

Watson[2] /ˈwɒtsn/ James Dewey (1928-), American biologist who, with Francis *Crick, Maurice Wilkins and Rosalind Franklin, discovered the structure of the DNA molecule. He was awarded the Nobel prize for medicine in 1962 together with Crick and Wilkins.

Watt /wɒt/ James (1736-1819), Scottish inventor who developed the design of the steam-engine. He improved on earlier engines by cooling the used steam in a separate container, so that the cylinder remained hot and the engine was more efficient. This led to its widespread use in industry.

watt /wɒt/ *n* unit of electrical power: [attrib] *a 60-watt light-bulb.*

▷ **wattage** /ˈwɒtɪdʒ/ *n* [U] unit of power, esp electrical power: *a heater that runs on a very low wattage.*

□ ˌ**watt-**ˈ**hour** *n* unit of measurement of energy, that of one watt applied for one hour.

Watteau /ˈwɒtəʊ/ Jean Antoine (1684-1721), French rococo painter who introduced a type of subject-matter known as *fêtes galantes*: scenes of an imaginary pastoral world in which people pursue the pleasures of love.

wattle[1] /ˈwɒtl/ *n* **1** [U] structure of sticks or twigs woven under and over thicker upright sticks, used for fences, walls, etc. **2** [C, U] any of several types of Australian acacia with long pliant branches and golden flowers.

□ ˌ**wattle and** ˈ**daub** wattle[1](1) covered with mud or clay and used, esp formerly, as a building-material for walls and roofs.

wattle[2] /ˈwɒtl/ *n* red fleshy fold of skin that hangs down from the head or throat of a bird, eg a turkey.

Watts /wɒts/ George Frederick (1817-1904),

English painter and sculptor best known for his large allegorical pictures, biblical scenes and portraits.

Waugh /wɔː/ Evelyn Arthur St John (1903-66), English novelist who satirized English upper- and upper-middle-class life of the 1920s and 1930s in *Decline and Fall, Vile Bodies, Black Mischief* and *A Handful of Dust. Brideshead Revisited* is a more serious and complex study of an old Roman Catholic family, and the trilogy *Men at Arms, Officers and Gentlemen* and *Unconditional Surrender* is based on Waugh's experiences in the Second World War.

wave[1] /weɪv/ *v* **1** [I] (of a fixed object) move regularly and loosely to and fro or up and down: *a flag waving in the breeze* ○ *branches waving in the wind* ○ *a field of waving corn.* **2** (**a**) [I, Ipr] ~ (**at/to sb**) (of a person) move one's hand to and fro or up and down, eg in order to attract sb's attention: *He waved (to us) when he saw us.* ○ *They waved at us from across the room.* (**b**) [Tn, Tn·pr, Tn·p, Dpr·t] ~ **sth (at sb)**; ~ **sth about** cause (one's hand or sth held in one's hand) to move up and down or to and fro, eg in order to make a signal or give a greeting: *wave a magic wand* ○ *wave a hand, a flag, an umbrella (at sb)* ○ *He came out waving the document at the crowd.* ○ *wave one's arms (about) (in the air)* ○ *They waved to us to stay where we were.* (**c**) [Tn, Dn·n, Dn·pr] ~ **sth (to sb)** give (a greeting) (to sb) by waving one's hand: *They waved farewell.* ○ *wave sb goodbye/wave goodbye to sb.* **3** [I, Tn] (cause sth to) form a series of curves: *Her hair waves beautifully.* ○ *She has had her hair waved.* **4** (idm) **fly/show/wave the ˈflag** ⇨ FLAG[1]. **5** (phr v) **wave sb/sth along, away, on, etc** show that (a person or vehicle) should move in the specified direction, by waving one's hand: *She waved them away impatiently.* ○ *The policeman waved us on,* ie indicated that we should continue. **wave sth aside** dismiss (an objection, etc) as unimportant or irrelevant: *Their criticisms were waved aside.* **wave sth/sb down** signal to (a vehicle or its driver) to stop, by waving one's hand.

wave[2] /weɪv/ *n* **1** [C] (**a**) ridge of water, esp on the sea, between two hollows: *The storm whipped up huge waves.* (**b**) long ridge of water in the sea, etc that rises up in an arch and breaks on the shore: *waves crashing onto the beach.* ⇨ illus at SURF. (**c**) thing that is similar to this in appearance or movement, eg an advancing group of attackers: *the next wave of assault troops* ○ *It was not long before their peace was disturbed by the next wave of visitors.* **2 the waves** [pl] (*fml*) the sea. **3** [C] act or gesture of waving: *He greeted them with a wave.* ○ *The magician made the rabbit disappear with a wave of his wand.* **4** [C] (**a**) curve or arrangement of curves, like a wave or waves in the sea, eg in a line or in hair: *The child's hair grew in pretty waves.* ○ *Her hair has a natural wave.* (**b**) special treatment of the hair to give it these curves: *a permanent wave.* **5** [C] sudden, usu temporary, increase (and spread) of sth: *a wave of anger, enthusiasm, hysteria, sympathy, etc* ○ *a ˈcrime wave* ○ *a ˈheatwave.* **6** [C] (**a**) wave-like motion by which heat, light, sound, magnetism, electricity, etc is spread or carried: *radio waves.* (**b**) single curve in the course of this. **7** [C] (*physics*) means of energy transfer by some form of vibration: *sound waves* ○ *waves on a liquid surface.* **8** (idm) **in ˈwaves** in groups or at regular intervals: *The disturbances seem to occur in waves.* ○ *Invaders entered the country in waves.* **on the crest of a wave** ⇨ CREST.
▷ **wavelet** /ˈweɪvlɪt/ *n* small wave of water.
wavy *adj* (**-ier, -iest**) having curves like the waves of the sea: *a wavy line* ○ *wavy hair.* **wavily** *adv.* **waviness** *n* [U].

waveband /ˈweɪvbænd/ *n* = BAND 4.

wavelength /ˈweɪvleŋθ/ *n* **1** distance between the corresponding points in a sound wave or an electromagnetic wave. **2** length of the radio wave that a particular radio station uses to broadcast its programmes. **3** (idm) **on the same wavelength** ⇨ SAME[1].

waver /ˈweɪvə(r)/ *v* **1** [I] be or become weak or unsteady; falter: *His courage never wavered.* ○ *Her steady gaze did not waver.* ○ *They did not waver in their support for him.* **2** [I, Ipr] ~ (**between sth and sth**) hesitate, esp about making a decision or choice; dither: *While we were wavering, somebody else bought the house.* ○ *waver between two points of view.* **3** [I] (esp of light) move unsteadily; flicker.
▷ **waverer** /ˈweɪvərə(r)/ *n*: *The strength of his argument convinced the last few waverers.*
waveringly /ˈweɪvərɪŋlɪ/ *adv.*

wax[1] /wæks/ *n* [U] **1** (also ˈ**beeswax**) (**a**) soft sticky yellow substance produced by bees and used by them for making honeycombs. (**b**) this substance used, after being bleached and purified, for making candles, modelling, etc. **2** any of various soft sticky or oily substances that melt easily (obtained eg from petroleum), used for making candles, polish, etc: *paraffin wax* ○ *sealing wax* ○ [attrib] *a wax candle* ○ *wax polish.* **3** yellow substance like wax that is secreted in the ears.
▷ **wax** *v* [Tn] (**a**) polish (sth) with wax: *waxed floors, linoleum, wood.* (**b**) coat (sth) with wax: *waxed paper, thread.*
waxen /ˈwæksn/ *adj* (*fml*) smooth or pale like wax: *a waxen complexion.*
waxy *adj* having a surface or texture like wax: *waxy skin* ○ *waxy potatoes.* **waxiness** *n* [U].
□ ˈ**wax museum** (*US*) = WAXWORKS (WAXWORK b).
ˈ**waxwork** *n* (**a**) [C] object modelled in wax, esp the form of a human being with face and hands in wax, coloured and clothed to look lifelike. (**b**) ˈ**waxworks** [sing or pl *v*] place where lifelike wax models of famous people are shown to the public: *take the children to the waxworks.*

wax[2] /wæks/ *v* **1** [I] (of the moon) show a large bright area that gradually increases until the moon is full. Cf WANE 1. **2** [La] (*dated or rhet*) become; grow: *wax eloquent, lyrical, etc on the subject.* **3** (idm) ˌ**wax and ˈwane** increase and then decrease in strength or importance: *Throughout history empires have waxed and waned.*

way[1] /weɪ/ *n* **1** [C] (often in compounds) (**a**) place for walking, travelling, etc along; path, road, street, etc: *a way across the fields* ○ *a covered* (ie roofed) *way* ○ *across/over the way,* ie across/over the road ○ *a ˈhighway* ○ *the ˈhighways and ˈbyways,* ie main and minor roads ○ *a ˈwaterway* ○ *a ˈrailway.* (**b**) **Way** name of certain roads or streets: *The Appian Way.* **2** [C usu *sing*] (**a**) ~ (**from... to...**) route, road, etc (to be) taken in order to reach a place: *the best, quickest, right, shortest, etc way from A to B* ○ *Which way do you usually go to town?* ○ *find one's way home* ○ *tell sb the way* ○ *He asked me the way* (ie the best way) *to London.* ○ *the way down, in, out, up, etc* ○ (*fig*) *find a way out of one's difficulty* ○ (*fig*) *argue, bluff, talk, trick, etc one's way into, out of sth,* ie enter, escape, etc by arguing, etc ○ (*fig*) *fight, force, shout, etc one's way across, into, etc sth,* ie cross, enter, etc sth by fighting, etc. (**b**) route along which sb/sth is moving or would move if there was space: *cut a way though the undergrowth* ○ *We had to pick our way along the muddy track.* ○ *There was a lorry blocking the way.* ○ *Get out of my way!* (**c**) (in phrases after *which, this, that,* etc) (in a specified) direction: *'Which way did he go?' 'He went that way.'* ○ *Look this way, please.* ○ *Kindly step this way, ladies and gentlemen.* ○ *Look both ways* (ie to right and left) *before crossing the road.* ○ *They weren't looking our way,* ie towards us. ○ *Make sure that the sign's the right way up.* ○ *The arrow is pointing the wrong way.* ○ *If the tree falls that way, it will destroy the house.* ○ (*fig*) *Which way* (ie For which party) *will you vote?* **3** [C] (**a**) (usu *sing*) method, style or manner of doing sth: *What is the best way to clean this?* ○ *She showed them the way to do it.* ○ *the best, right, wrong, etc way to do sth* ○ *I like the way you've done your hair.* ○ *There are several ways of doing it.* ○ *a new way of storing information* ○ *You can see the way his mind works when you read his books.* ○ *She spoke in a kindly way.* (**b**) (after *my, his, her,* etc) course of action desired or chosen by sb: *She'll do it ˈher way whatever you suggest.* ○ *We all have our favourite ways of doing certain things.* ○ *I still think ˈmy way is better!* ○ *Try to find your ˈown way to express the idea.* (**c**) chosen, desired or habitual behaviour; custom or manner: *He has some rather odd ways.* ○ *Don't be offended, it's only his ˈway,* ie manner of behaving that has no special significance. ○ *It is not her ˈway to be selfish,* ie She is not selfish by nature. ○ *I don't like the way* (ie manner in which) *he looks at me.* ○ *It's disgraceful the way he treats his mother.* ○ *a fashionable way of dressing* ○ *They admired the way she dealt with the crisis.* **4** [sing] (esp after *long, little,* etc) distance (to be travelled) between two points: *It's a long way to London.* ○ *We are a long way from the coast.* ○ *There is quite a way still to go.* ○ *The roots go a long way down.* ○ (*fig*) *December is a long way off/away,* ie in the future, from now. ○ *Success is still a long way off.* ○ *better by a long way,* ie much better. **5** [sing] (*infml*) area near a place; neighbourhood: *He lives somewhere ˈLincoln way.* ○ *The crops are doing well down ˈour way,* ie in our part of the country. ○ *Please visit us next time you're over this way.* **6** [C] particular aspect of sth; respect: *Can I help you in any way?* ○ *She is in no way* (ie not at all) *to blame.* ○ *The changes are beneficial in some ways but not in others.* ○ *She helped us in every possible way.* **7** (idm) ˌ**all the ˈway** the whole distance. ˈ**be/be ˈborn/be ˈmade that way** (*infml*) (of a person) be as one is because of innate characteristics: *I'm afraid that's just the way he ˈis.* **be** ˌ**set in one's ˈways** be inflexible in one's habits, attitudes, etc. **both ˈways/each ˈway** (of money bet on a horse, race, etc) so that one will win money back if the horse, etc either wins or gains second or third place: *have £5 each way on the favourite* ○ *back the favourite both ways.* **by the ˈway** (**a**) by the roadside during a journey: *stopped for a picnic by the way.* (**b**) (used to introduce a comment or question that is only indirectly related, if at all, to the main subject of conversation): *Oh, by the way, there is a telephone message for you.* ○ *What did you say your name was, by the way?* **by way of** (**a**) (*fml*) by a route that includes (the place mentioned); via: *They are travelling to France by way of England.* (**b**) as a kind of (sth) or serving as (sth): *Let's eat out tonight, by way of a change.* ○ *What are you thinking of doing by way of a holiday this year?* ○ *By way of an introduction, I shall explain some of the historical background.* (**c**) with the intention of or for the purpose of (doing sth): *make enquiries by way of learning the facts of the case.* **change one's ways** ⇨ CHANGE. **come one's ˈway** occur or present itself to one: *An opportunity like that doesn't often come my way.* **cut both/two ˈways** (of an action, argument, etc) have an effect both for and against sth. **divide, split, etc, sth two, three, etc ˈways** share sth among two, three, etc people. **each way** ⇨ BOTH WAYS. **the error of one's/sb's ways** ⇨ ERROR. **feel one's way** ⇨ FEEL[1]. **find one's way; find its way to...** ⇨ FIND[1]. **get into/out of the way of (doing) sth** acquire/lose the habit of doing sth. **get/have one's own ˈway** get or do what one wants, often in spite of opposition: *She always gets her own way in the end.* **give ˈway** break or collapse: *The bridge gave way under the weight of the lorry.* ○ *Her legs suddenly gave way and she fell to the floor.* **give way (to sb/sth)** (**a**) allow sb/sth to be first; yield: *Give way to traffic coming from the right.* (**b**) let oneself be overcome (by sth): *give way to despair.* (**c**) make concessions (to sb/sth): *We must not give way to their demands.* **give way to sth** be replaced by sth: *The storm gave way to bright sunshine.* **go far/a long way** ⇨ FAR[2]. **go far/a long way to do sth/towards sth** ⇨ FAR[2]. **go out of one's ˈway (to do sth)** take particular care and trouble to do sth: *The shop assistant went out of his way to find what we needed.* **go one's own ˈway** act independently or as one chooses, esp against the advice of others: *Whatever you suggest, she will always go her own way.* **go one's way** (*dated*) depart. **go sb's way** (**a**) travel in the same direction as sb: *I'm going your way so I can give you a lift.* (**b**) (of events, etc) be favourable to sb: *Things certainly seem to be going our way.* **go the way of all ˈflesh** (*saying*) (live and) die as other people do; suffer the same changes, dangers, etc as other people. **the hard way** ⇨ HARD[1]. **have come**

a long way ⇨ LONG[1]. **have/want it/things ˈboth ways** ⇨ BOTH[1]. **have it/things/everything one's ˈown way** have what one wants, esp by imposing one's will on others: *All right, have it your own way — I'm tired of arguing.* **have a ˈway with one** have the power to attract or persuade others. **have a way with sb/sth** have a particular talent for dealing with sb/sth: *have a way with difficult children* ○ *have a way with motor bikes.* **in a bad ˈway** (a) very ill or in serious trouble. (b) (*infml*) obviously drunk. **in a ˈbig/ˈsmall way** on a large/small scale: *He's got himself into trouble in a big way.* ○ *She collects antiques in a small way.* **in a fair way to do sth** ⇨ FAIR[1]. **in the family way** ⇨ FAMILY. **ˌin more ways than ˈone** (used to draw attention to the fact that the statement made has more than one meaning): *He's a big man — in more ways than one.* **in a ˈway; in ˈone way; in ˈsome ways** to a certain extent but not entirely: *The changes are an improvement in one way.* **in the ordinary way** ⇨ ORDINARY. **in one's own sweet way** ⇨ SWEET[1]. **in the ˈway** causing inconvenience or an obstruction: *I'm afraid your car is in the way.* ○ *I left them alone, as I felt I was in the way.* **know one's way around** ⇨ KNOW. **lead the way** ⇨ LEAD[3]. **look the other ˈway** avoid seeing sb/sth, deliberately or by chance: *The usherette looked the other way so that the children could get into the cinema without paying.* **lose one's way** ⇨ LOSE. **make one's way (to/towards sth)** go: *I'll make my way home now.* ○ *make one's way* (ie succeed) *in life.* **make ˈway (for sb/sth)** allow (sb/sth) to pass. **mend one's ways** ⇨ MEND. **not know where/which way to look** ⇨ KNOW. **(there are) no two ways aˈbout it** (*saying*) there is only one correct or suitable way to act, speak or think with regard to sth. **ˌno ˈway** (*infml*) under no circumstances or by no means (will sth happen/be done): *Give up our tea break? No way!* ○ *No way will I go on working for that man.* **ˌone way and aˈnother** considering various aspects of the matter together: *She's been very successful, one way and another.* **ˌone way or aˈnother** by some means, methods, etc: *We must finish the job this week one way or another.* **on one's/the ˈway** in the process of going or coming: *I had better be on my way* (ie leave) *soon.* ○ *I'll buy some bread on the/my way home.* **on the ˈway** (*infml*) (of a baby) conceived but not yet born: *She has two children with another one on the way.* **on the way ˈout** (a) in the process of leaving: *I bumped into him on the way out.* (b) (*fig*) going out of fashion or favour; becoming obsolete. **the ˌother way ˈround** (a) reversed or inverted. (b) the opposite of what is expected or supposed: *I was accused of stealing money from her but in fact it was the other way round.* **out of harm's way** ⇨ HARM *n.* **ˌout of the ˈway** (a) far from a town or city; remote: [attrib] *a tiny ˌout-of-the-way ˈvillage in Cornwall.* (b) exceptional; uncommon: *He has done nothing out of the way yet.* **a/the parting of the ways** ⇨ PARTING. **pave the way for sth** ⇨ PAVE. **pay one's/its way** ⇨ PAY[2]. **point the way** ⇨ POINT[2]. **put sb in the way of (doing) sth** make it possible for sb to do sth or give sb an opportunity to do sth. **rub sb up the wrong way** ⇨ RUB[2]. **see one's way (clear) to doing sth** find that it is possible or convenient to do sth: *I can't see my way clear to finishing the work this year.* ○ *Could you see your way to lending me £10 for a couple of days?* **see which way the wind is blowing** see what is likely to happen. **show the way** ⇨ SHOW[2]. **(not) stand in sb's ˈway** (not) prevent sb from doing sth: *If you want to study medicine, we won't stand in your way.* **take the easy way out** ⇨ EASY. **ˌthat's the ˌway the ˌcookie ˈcrumbles** (*infml esp US*) that is the state of things and nothing can be done about it. **to ˈmy way of thinking** in my opinion. **under ˈway** having started and making progress: *The project is now well under way.* ○ *be/get under way*, ie (esp of a ship) move/start to move through the water. **wait for the cat to jump/to see which way the cat jumps** ⇨ WAIT[1]. **a/sb's way of ˈlife** normal pattern of social or working life of a person or group: *She adapted easily to the French way of life.* **the ˌway of the ˈworld** what many people do, how they behave, etc. **ˌways and ˈmeans** methods and resources for doing sth, esp providing money. **where there's a will, there's a way** ⇨ WILL[4]. **ˌwork one's ˈway (through college, etc)** have a paid job while one is a student: *She had to work her way through law school.* **work one's way through sth** read or do sth from beginning to end: *The board are still working their way through the application forms.* **ˌwork one's way ˈup** be promoted from a low grade to a high one: *He has worked his way up from junior clerk to managing director.*

□ ˈ**way-bill** *n* list of goods or passengers carried by a vehicle, with their destinations.

ˈ**wayfarer** /-feərə(r)/ *n* (*fml*) traveller, esp on foot.

ˈ**wayfaring** /-feərɪŋ/ *adj* [attrib] (*fml*) travelling: *a wayfaring man.*

ˈ**wayside** *n* (usu *sing*) **1** (land at the) side of a road or path: [attrib] *wayside flowers.* **2** (idm) **fall by the ˈwayside** (*euph*) fail to make progress in life; slip into dishonest ways.

way[2] /weɪ/ *adv* (*infml*) **1** (used with a *prep* or an *adv* and usu not negatively) very far: *She finished the race way ahead of the other runners.* ○ *The shot was way off target.* ○ *The price is way above what we can afford.* ○ *The initial estimate was way out*, ie very inaccurate. **2** (idm) ˈ**way back** a long time ago: *I first met him way back in the ˈfifties.*

□ ˌ**way-ˈout** *adj* (*infml*) exaggeratedly unusual or strange in style; eccentric or exotic: *ˌway-out ˈclothes, ˈfashions, iˈdeas, ˈmusic, ˈpoetry.*

waylay /ˌweɪˈleɪ/ *v* (*pt, pp* **waylaid** /-ˈleɪd/) [Tn] wait for and stop (sb who is passing), esp in order to rob him or to ask him for sth: *The patrol was waylaid by bandits.* ○ *He waylaid me with a request for a loan.*

-ways *suff* (with *ns* forming *adjs* and *advs*) in the specified direction: *lengthways* ○ *sideways.*

wayward /ˈweɪwəd/ *adj* not easily controlled or guided; childishly headstrong or capricious: *a wayward child* ○ *a wayward disposition.* ▷ **waywardness** *n* [U].

WC /ˌdʌblju: ˈsi:/ *abbr* **1** water-closet. ⇨ Usage at TOILET. **2** West Central: *London WC2B 4PH*, eg as a postal code.

WCC /ˌdʌblju: si: ˈsi:/ *abbr* World Council of Churches.

W/Cdr *abbr* Wing Commander: *W/Cdr (Bob) Hunt.*

we /wi:/ ⇨ Guide to Entries 5.2. *pers pron* (used as the subject of a *v*) **1** I and another or others; I and you: *We've moved to London.* ○ *We'd like to offer you a job.* ○ *Why don't we go and see it?* **2** (*fml*) (used instead of *I* by a king, queen or pope or by the writer of an editorial article in a newspaper, etc). Cf THE ROYAL WE (ROYAL). **3** (used when speaking to children, sick people, etc to indicate kindly superiority): *Now what are we doing over here?* ○ *And how are we feeling today?* Cf US.

WEA /ˌdʌblju: i: ˈeɪ/ *abbr* (*Brit*) Workers' Educational Association.

weak /wi:k/ *adj* (**-er, -est**) **1** (a) lacking strength or power; easily broken, bent or defeated: *She was still weak after her illness.* ○ *too weak to walk far* ○ *Her legs felt weak/She felt weak in the legs.* ○ *The supports were too weak for the weight of the load.* ○ *a weak barrier, defence, team* ○ *a weak chin/mouth*, ie suggesting or showing weakness of character ○ *identify the weak points in an argument*, ie those which may be attacked most easily. (b) (*commerce*) not financially sound or successful: *a weak currency, economy, market.* **2** not functioning properly; deficient: *weak eyes/sight* ○ *a weak heart* ○ *a weak stomach*, ie one that is easily upset by food. **3** not convincing or forceful: *weak arguments, evidence.* **4** not easily perceived; feeble or faint: *a weak light, signal, sound* ○ *a weak smile.* **5** (of liquids) containing a high proportion of water; dilute: *weak tea* ○ *a weak solution of salt and water.* **6** ~ (**at/in/on sth**) not achieving a high standard; deficient: *Her school report shows that she is weak at/in arithmetic and biology.* ○ *The book is weak on* (ie in its treatment of) *the medieval period.* **7** (*grammar*) (of verbs) forming the past tense, etc by the addition of a suffix (eg *walk, walked* or *waste, wasted*) and not by a change of vowel (eg *run, ran* or *come, came*). **8** (idm) ˌ**weak at the ˈknees** (*infml*) temporarily hardly able to stand because of emotion, fear, illness, etc: *The shock made me go all weak at the knees.* **the weaker ˈsex** (*dated sexist*) women in general. ˌ**weak in the ˈhead** (*infml*) stupid: *You must be weak in the head if you believe that.* **a weak ˈmoment** time when one is unusually easily persuaded or tempted: *In a weak moment, I agreed to pay for her holiday.*

▷ **the ˈweak** *n* [pl *v*] people who are poor, sick or powerless and are therefore easily exploited, infected, etc: *He argued that it was the role of governments to protect the weak.* ○ *the struggle of the weak against their oppressors.*

weaken /ˈwi:kən/ *v* **1** [I, Tn] (cause sb/sth to) become weak or weaker: *They watched her gradually weaken as the disease progressed.* ○ *The dollar has weakened in international currency trading.* ○ *Hunger and disease had weakened his constitution.* **2** [I] become less determined or certain about sth; waver: *They have not yet agreed to our requests but they are clearly weakening.*

weakling /ˈwi:klɪŋ/ *n* (*derog*) weak or feeble person or animal: *Don't be such a weakling!*

weakly *adv* in a weak manner: *smile weakly.*

weakness *n* **1** [U] state of being weak: *the weakness of a country's defences* ○ *weakness of character* ○ *New evidence revealed the weakness of the prosecution's case.* **2** [C] defect or fault, esp in a person's character: *We all have our weaknesses.* **3** [C usu *sing*] ~ **for sth/sb** special or foolish liking for sth/sb: *have a weakness for peanut butter, fast cars, tall women.*

□ ˈ**weak form** (*phonetics*) way of pronouncing certain common words in an unstressed position, with a shorter syllable and a different vowel sound, or by omitting a vowel sound or a consonant (eg /ən/ or /n/ for *and*, as in *bread and butter* /ˌbred n ˈbʌtə(r)/).

ˌ**weak-ˈkneed** *adj* (*fig*) (of a person) lacking determination or courage.

ˌ**weak-ˈminded** *adj* (a) lacking determination or resolution. (b) mentally deficient. **weak-mindedly** *adv.* **weak-mindedness** *n* [U].

weal /wi:l/ *n* raised mark on the skin made by hitting it with a stick, whip, etc.

wealth /welθ/ *n* **1** [U] (possession of a) large amount of money, property, etc; riches: *a man of great wealth* ○ *Nobody knew how she had acquired her wealth.* ○ *Wealth had not brought them happiness.* ○ *The country's wealth is based on trade.* **2** [sing] ~ **of sth** large amount or number of sth; abundance of sth: *a book with a wealth of illustrations* ○ *a wealth of opportunity.*

▷ **wealthy** *adj* (**-ier, -iest**) having wealth; rich. **wealthily** /-ɪlɪ/ *adv.*

wean /wi:n/ *v* **1** [Tn, Tn·pr] ~ **sb/sth (off sth) (on to sth)** gradually stop feeding (a baby or young animal) with its mother's milk and start feeding it with solid food. **2** (phr v) **wean sb (away) from sth/doing sth** cause sb to stop doing sth, esp gradually: *wean sb (away) from drugs, drinking, gambling, etc.*

weapon /ˈwepən/ *n* **1** thing designed or used for causing physical harm (eg a bomb, gun, knife, sword, etc): *They were carrying weapons.* ○ *armed with weapons* ○ *a deadly weapon.* **2** action or procedure used to defend oneself or get the better of sb in a struggle or contest: *Their ultimate weapon was the threat of an all-out strike.* ○ *Humour was his only weapon against their hostility.*

▷ **weaponry** /-rɪ/ *n* [U] weapons: *an arsenal of sophisticated weaponry.*

wear[1] /weə(r)/ *n* [U] **1** wearing or being worn as clothing: *a suit for everyday wear* ○ *Cotton is suitable for wear in summer.* **2** (esp in compounds) things for wearing; clothing: *ˈchildren's/ˈladies' wear* ○ *ˈmenswear* ○ *ˈunderwear* ○ *ˈfootwear* ○ *ˈsportswear.* **3** (damage or loss of quality caused by) use: *These shoes are showing (signs of) wear.* ○ *The carpet gets very heavy wear.* **4** capacity for continuing to be used: *There is still a lot of wear left*

Weather

The weather in Britain is very variable, not only from season to season, but from one day to the next. The fact that the weather is so unpredictable has made it a perennial topic of conversation, and when meeting or greeting someone, it is usual to make a comment on the weather. Typical informal remarks about the weather include such phrases as 'Better today, isn't it?' or 'Bit nippy this morning' or 'What a terrible day!'

Technically speaking, the climate of the British Isles is moderate and moist, with generally mild winters and cool summers. It owes its 'temperate' character to the influence of westerly and south-westerly winds blowing off the Atlantic and the warm waters of the Gulf Stream. The average midwinter temperature is in the range of 3° to 7°C (37° to 45°F) while that for midsummer is 11° to 17°C (52° to 63°F). However, some winter days can be as cold as –5°C (23°F) and there have been summer heatwaves with temperatures as high as 32°C (90°F), especially in the south and east, and even in parts of Scotland.

There are usually many days in the year when it rains. Because the prevailing wind in Britain is south-westerly, off the Atlantic, the wettest places are in the south and west, and the driest in the east, especially in East Anglia. Hilly and mountainous regions, too, attract more rain than low-lying areas.

In winter too there can be several days of snow, with the highest falls to be expected in north-east Scotland, and the lowest usually in the south-west of England. Only rarely, however, does enough snow fall for it to remain lying for long, since it usually melts in one of the series of mild, damp days that alternate in most winters with cold, dry spells. In fact, snow is a relative rarity, so that when it comes it can cause a surprising degree of disorganization to transport, with roads blocked, trains delayed, and even aircraft grounded.

In the 1980s there were unusual extremes of weather in Britain, with several hot, dry summers and mild winters without snow. The summer of 1989 was the sunniest so far this century, and that of 1990 the hottest. There have also been some record rainfalls. July 1988, for example, was the wettest in England since 1936, and there was considerable disruption to the major social and sporting events held that month, such as Wimbledon and the Open Golf Championship. In 1987 there were unusually severe storms that caused more deaths and greater destruction than any this century. Atmospheric problems such as 'global warming' or the 'greenhouse effect' have been suggested as possible causes for these unusual extremes of weather.

Many people listen regularly to a weather forecast on radio or television. The forecasts are provided by the Meteorological Office (informally called 'Met Office') through the London Weather Centre, and are presented by members of the Met Office staff, some of whom have become television personalities as a result. On radio, there are also regular shipping forecasts that give the weather conditions such as wind speed and visibility in all areas of the sea around Britain.

Most weather forecasts still include both Fahrenheit and Celsius temperatures, and for many older British people the Fahrenheit scale is still the most familiar one, especially in everyday speech. For example, 'It was in the eighties yesterday' means that it was hot, with a temperature of 27°C or more. On one hot day in August 1990, the only headline on the front page of *The Sun* newspaper was a huge '90°'.

There are a number of country sayings about the weather. For example, the appearance in the summer of green holly berries is said to foretell a hard winter, and 'Oak before ash, you'll get a splash; ash before oak, expect a soak' means that if the oak comes into leaf before the ash the summer will be dry, but if the ash leaves appear first it will be wet. Two other popular sayings are 'Red sky at night, shepherd's delight; red sky in the morning, shepherd's warning' (referring to the colour of the sunset or sunrise, as a sign of either good or bad weather), and 'Rain before seven, fine before eleven' (referring to the fact that overnight rain often clears up by mid-morning).

Some people keep a barometer on the wall and 'tap' it each morning to see which way the pointer moves. If it is 'up', better weather is promised; if it is 'down', unsettled weather is indicated, with rain, wind or, in winter, even snow. The usual wording on the barometer dial reads, clockwise from lower left: 'Stormy', 'Rain', 'Change', 'Fair', 'Set Fair', 'Very Dry'.

in that old coat. **5** (idm) ˌ**wear and** ˈ**tear** damage, deterioration, strain, etc caused by ordinary use: *The insurance policy does not cover damage caused by normal wear and tear.* **the worse for wear** ⇨ WORSE.

wear[2] /weə(r)/ *v* (*pt* **wore** /wɔ:(r)/, *pp* **worn** /wɔ:n/) **1** [Tn, Tn·pr, Cn·a] have (sth) on one's body, esp as clothing, as an ornament, etc: *wear a beard, coat, hat, ring, watch* ○ *Bowler hats are not often worn nowadays.* ○ *She was wearing sun-glasses.* ○ *She never wears green,* ie green clothes. ○ *He wore a gold chain round his neck.* ○ *She wears her hair long,* ie has long hair. ⇨ Usage. **2** [Tn] have (a certain look) on one's face: *He/His face wore a puzzled frown.* ○ (*fig*) *The house wore a neglected look.* **3** [Tn] (*infml*) (esp in questions and negative sentences) accept or tolerate (sth, esp sth that one does not approve of): *He wanted to sail the boat alone but his parents wouldn't wear it.* **4** [La, I, Tn, Tn·pr, Cn·a] (cause sth to) become damaged, useless or reduced by being used, rubbed, etc: *The sheets have worn thin in the middle.* ○ *The carpets are starting to wear.* ○ *That coat is starting to look worn.* ○ *The lettering on the gravestone was badly worn and almost illegible.* ○ *I have worn my socks into holes.* ○ *The stones had been worn smooth by the constant flow of water.* **5** [Tn·pr] make (a hole, groove, path, etc) in sth by constant rubbing, dripping, etc: *I've worn holes in my socks.* ○ *Look at the holes that have been worn in this rug.* ○ *The children have worn a path across the field where they walk each day to school.* ○ *The water had worn a channel in the rock.* **6** [I] endure or be capable of enduring continued use: *You should choose a fabric that will wear well,* ie last a long time. ○ (*fig*) *Despite her age she had worn well,* ie still looked quite young. **7** (idm) **wear one's** ˌ**heart on one's** ˈ**sleeve** allow one's emotions, esp one's love for sb, to be seen. **wear** ˈ**thin** begin to fail: *My patience is beginning to wear very thin.* ○ *Don't you think that joke's wearing a bit thin* (ie because we've heard it so many times)*?* **wear the** ˈ**pants**/ˈ**trousers** (*often derog*) (usu of a woman) be the dominant person in a relationship, esp a marriage: *It's quite clear who wears the trousers in that house!* **8** (phr v) **wear (sth) away** (cause sth to) become thin, damaged, weak, etc by constant use: *The inscription on the coin had worn away.* ○ *The steps had been worn away by the feet of thousands of visitors.* **wear (sth) down** (cause sth to) become gradually smaller, thinner, etc: *The tread on the tyres has (been) worn down to a dangerous level.* **wear sb/sth down** weaken sb/sth by constant attack, nervous strain, etc: *She was worn down by overwork.* ○ *The strategy was designed to wear down the enemy's resistance.* **wear (sth) off** (cause sth to) disappear or be removed gradually: *The dishwasher has worn the glaze off the china.* ○ *The novelty will soon wear off,* ie It is only attractive because it is new. ○ *The pain is slowly wearing off.* **wear on** (of time) pass, esp tediously: *As the evening wore on, she became more and more nervous.* ○ *His life was wearing on towards its close.* **wear (sth) out** (cause sth to) become useless, threadbare or exhausted through use: *I wore out two pairs of boots on the walking tour.* ○ *Her patience had/was at last worn out.* **wear sb out** cause sb to become exhausted; tire sb out: *They were worn out after a long day spent working in the fields.* ○ *Just listening to his silly chatter wears me out.*

▷ **wearable** /ˈweərəbl/ *adj* that can be, or is fit to be, worn: *a wardrobe full of clothes that are no longer wearable.*

wearer /ˈweərə(r)/ *n* person who is wearing sth: *These shoes will damage the wearer's feet.*

wearing /ˈweərɪŋ/ *adj* tiring: *I've had a wearing day.* ○ *The old lady finds shopping very wearing.*

NOTE ON USAGE: We **wear** clothes, including gloves and scarves, also belts, spectacles, even perfume on our bodies: *Do you have to wear a suit at work?* ○ *She was wearing her mother's coat.* ○ *Are you wearing aftershave?* We **carry** objects when we take them with us, especially in our hands or arms: *He wasn't wearing his raincoat, he was carrying it over his arm.* ○ *She always carries an umbrella in her briefcase.*

weary /ˈwɪərɪ/ *adj* (**-ier, -iest**) **1** (**a**) very tired, esp as a result of effort or endurance; exhausted: *weary in body and mind* ○ *They felt weary after all their hard work.* (**b**) ~ **of sth** no longer interested in or enthusiastic about sth; tired of sth: *The people are growing weary of the war.* ○ *I am weary of hearing about your problems.* **2** causing tiredness or boredom: *a weary journey, wait* ○ *the last weary mile of their climb.* **3** showing tiredness: *a weary sigh, smile.*

▷ **wearily** /ˈwɪərəlɪ/ *adv.*

weariness *n* [U].

wearisome /ˈwɪərɪsəm/ *adj* causing one to feel tired or bored: *wearisome complaints, duties, tasks.*

weary *v* **1** [Tn, Tn·pr] ~ **sb (with sth)** make sb feel annoyed or impatient: *It wearies me to have to explain everything in such detail.* ○ *She was wearied by the constant noise.* ○ *weary sb with requests.* **2** [Ip] ~ **of sb/sth** (*fml*) become dissatisfied with sb/sth: *She began to weary of her companions.* ○ *You will soon weary of living abroad.*

weasel /ˈwi:zl/ *n* small fierce animal with reddish-brown fur, that lives on rats, rabbits, birds' eggs, etc. Cf ERMINE, FERRET, STOAT. ⇨ illus at ANIMAL.

▷ **weasel** *v* (phr v) **weasel out (of sth)** (*infml derog esp US*) avoid fulfilling a promise, doing a duty, etc.

□ ˈ**weasel word** (*infml esp US*) word or expression that reduces the force of what one is saying, used when one wishes to avoid committing oneself to a definite statement.

weather[1] /ˈweðə(r)/ *n* **1** [U] condition of the atmosphere at a certain place and time, with reference to temperature and the presence of rain, sunshine, wind, etc: *cold, sunny, warm, wet, windy, etc weather* ○ *We had good weather on our holiday.* ○ *The weather is very changeable.* ○ *The success of the crop depends on the weather.* ○ *if the weather breaks/holds*, ie if the present good weather changes/continues ○ *We shall play the match tomorrow, weather permitting*, ie if the weather is fine. ⇨ article. Cf CLIMATE 1. **2** (idm) **in all weathers** in all kinds of weather, both good and bad. **keep a ˈweather eye open** be watchful and alert in order to avoid trouble. **make heavy weather of sth** ⇨ HEAVY. **under the ˈweather** (*infml*) feeling unwell or depressed: *be/feel/look under the weather* ○ *She's been a bit under the weather recently.*

▷ **weather** *adj* [attrib] windward: *on the weather side.*

□ **ˈweather-beaten** *adj* (esp of sb's skin) tanned, damaged, roughened, etc as a result of being exposed to the sun and wind: *the weather-beaten face of an old sailor.*

ˈweather-board *n* sloping board for keeping out rain and wind, esp one attached to the bottom of a door. **ˈweather-boarding** (*US* **ˈclapboard**) *n* [U] series of weather-boards with each one overlapping the one below, fixed to the outside wall of a building in order to protect it.

ˈweather-bound *adj* unable to make or continue a journey because of bad weather.

weather-chart, **ˈweather-map** *ns* diagram that shows details of the weather over a wide area.

ˈweathercock *n* weather-vane, often in the shape of a cockerel. ⇨ illus at CHURCH.

ˈweather forecast forecast of the weather for the next day or few days, esp one broadcast on radio or television.

ˈweatherman /-mæn/ *n* (*pl* **-men** /-men/) (*infml*) person who reports and forecasts the weather; meteorologist.

ˈweatherproof *adj* that can withstand exposure to the weather and keep out rain, snow, wind, etc: *a weatherproof shelter.*

ˈweather-vane *n* revolving pointer that can turn easily in the wind and is put in a high place, esp on top of a building, in order to show the direction of the wind.

weather[2] /ˈweðə(r)/ *v* **1** [Tn] dry or season (wood) by leaving it in the open air. **2** [I, Tn] (cause sth to) change shape or colour because of the action of the sun, rain, wind, etc: *Teak weathers to a greyish colour.* ○ *rocks weathered by wind and water.* **3** [Tn] come safely through (sth); survive: *weather a crisis, a storm, an upheaval.* **4** [Tn] (in sailing) pass on the windward side of (sth): *The ship weathered the cape.*

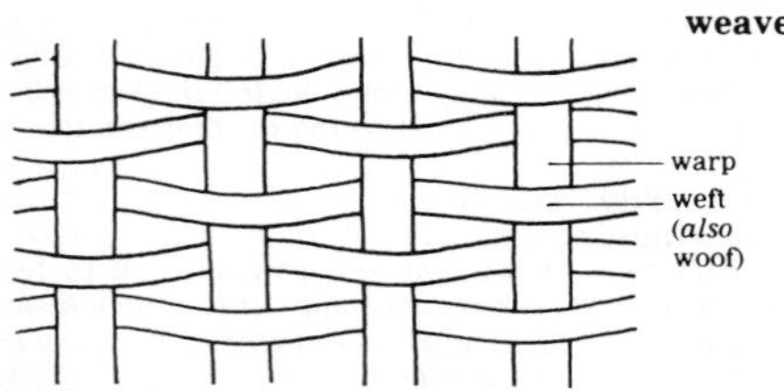

weave

weave /wi:v/ *v* (*pt* **wove** /wəʊv/ or in sense 4, **weaved**, *pp* **woven** /ˈwəʊvn/ or in sense 4, **weaved**) **1** (a) [Tn, Tn·pr] ~ **sth** (**from sth**) make (fabric, etc) by passing threads or strips crosswise over and under lengthwise ones, by hand or on a machine: *a tightly woven piece of cloth* ○ *cloth woven from silk and wool* ○ *weave a metre of tweed cloth* ○ *weave a basket from strips of willow.* (b) [I] work at a loom, making fabric, etc: *She had been taught to weave as a child.* ○ *The women earn their living by weaving.* (c) [Tn, Tn·pr, Tn·p] ~ **sth** (**into sth**) form fabric, etc out of (threads) by weaving: *weave woollen yarn into cloth* ○ *weave threads together.* **2** (a) [Tn·pr, Tn·p] ~ **sth** (**into sth**) twist (flowers, twigs, etc) together to make a garland, wreath, etc. (b) [Tn, Tn·pr] ~ **sth** (**out of/from sth**) make sth by twisting flowers, etc in this way: *weave a garland out of primroses.* **3** [Tn, Tn·pr] ~ **sth** (**into sth**) (*fig*) put (facts, events, etc) together into a story or a connected whole; compose: *weave a plot, a magic spell* ○ *weave one's ideas into a story.* **4** [Ipr, Ip, Tn·pr, Tn·p] move along by twisting and turning to avoid obstructions, etc: *weave (one's way) through a crowd* ○ *The road weaves through the range of hills.* ○ *weave in and out through the traffic.* **5** (idm) **get ˈweaving** (**on sth**) (*Brit infml*) start working (at sth) energetically or hurriedly: *The work must be finished this week, so we'd better get weaving!*

▷ **weave** *n* way in which material is woven; style of weaving: *a coarse, fine, loose, tight, etc weave* ○ *a diagonal weave.*

weaver *n* **1** person whose job is weaving cloth. **2** (also **ˈweaver-bird**) tropical bird that makes its nest by tightly weaving together leaves, grass, twigs, etc.

web /web/ *n* **1** network of fine threads spun by a spider or some other spinning creature: *a spider's web.* ⇨ illus at SPIDER. Cf COBWEB. **2** (*usu fig*) complex series or network: *a web of deceit, lies, intrigue, etc.* **3** piece of skin joining together the toes of some birds and animals that swim, eg ducks, geese, frogs, etc. **4** large roll of paper for printing on.

▷ **webbed** *adj* (of the foot of a bird or an animal) having the toes joined by webs.

□ **ˌweb-ˈfooted**, **ˌweb-ˈtoed** *adjs* (of a bird or an animal) having the toes joined by webs.

Webb[1] /web/ Beatrice (1858-1943), English socialist, who together with her husband Sidney Webb helped to found the London School of Economics and had a great influence on social reform in Britain. They wrote many books together, and on her own she wrote *My Apprenticeship* and *Our Partnership.*

Webb[2] /web/ Sidney James (1859-1947), English socialist who worked closely with his wife Beatrice in the area of social reform and wrote many books with her. He became a Labour Member of Parliament in 1922.

webbing /ˈwebɪŋ/ *n* [U] strong bands of woven fabric used in upholstery, for binding the edges of carpets and for making belts, etc.

Weber /ˈveɪbə(r)/ Carl Maria von (1786-1926), German composer whose romantic operas *Der Freischütz, Euryanthe* and *Oberon* established a tradition of operas in the German language that influenced *Wagner.

weber /ˈveɪbə(r)/ *n* unit of measurement of magnetic flux.

Webern /ˈveɪbən/ Anton (1883-1945), Austrian composer, a pupil of *Schoenberg, whose serial technique he developed in writing his characteristically short and concentrated pieces (eg a concerto for nine instruments).

Webster[1] /ˈwebstə(r)/ John (c 1578-c 1632), English playwright best known for *The White Devil* and *The Duchess of Malfi*, darkly powerful tragedies full of violent action. Though little is known about his life, his reputation is second only to that of Shakespeare among dramatists of the period.

Webster[2] /ˈwebstə(r)/ Noah (1758-1843), American lexicographer who in his *American Dictionary of the English Language* pioneered the recording of American usages. He standardized the American spelling of many words that differ from British English.

we'd /wi:d/ *contracted form* **1** we had ⇨ HAVE. **2** we would ⇨ WILL[1], WOULD[1].

wed /wed/ *v* (*pt, pp* **wedded** or **wed**) [I, Tn] (*dated or journalism*) (not in the continuous tenses) marry: *Rock star to wed top model*, eg as a headline.

▷ **wedded** *adj* [pred] ~ **to sth** (*fml*) **1** united or combined with sth: *beauty wedded to simplicity.* **2** unable to give sth up; devoted to sth: *He is wedded to his work.* ○ *She is wedded to her opinions and nothing will change her.*

Wed (also **Weds**) *abbr* Wednesday: *Wed 4 May.*

wedding /ˈwedɪŋ/ *n* **1** marriage ceremony (and the party which usually follows it): *There will be a wedding in the village church on Saturday.* ○ *We have been invited to their daughter's wedding.* ○ [attrib] *a wedding anniversary, dress, guest, invitation, present.* ⇨ article. Cf DIAMOND WEDDING (DIAMOND), GOLDEN WEDDING (GOLDEN), RUBY WEDDING (RUBY), SILVER WEDDING (SILVER), WHITE WEDDING (WHITE[1]). **2** (idm) **a shotgun wedding** ⇨ SHOTGUN (SHOT[1]).

□ **ˈwedding breakfast** special meal for the bride and bridegroom and their relatives, friends, etc after a marriage ceremony.

ˈwedding-cake *n* [C, U] iced cake, often with several tiers, that is cut up and eaten at a wedding, with pieces also being sent to absent friends.

ˈwedding-ring *n* ring that is placed on the bride's (and sometimes the groom's) finger during a marriage ceremony and worn afterwards to show that the wearer is married: *In Britain, wedding-rings are worn on the third finger of the left hand.*

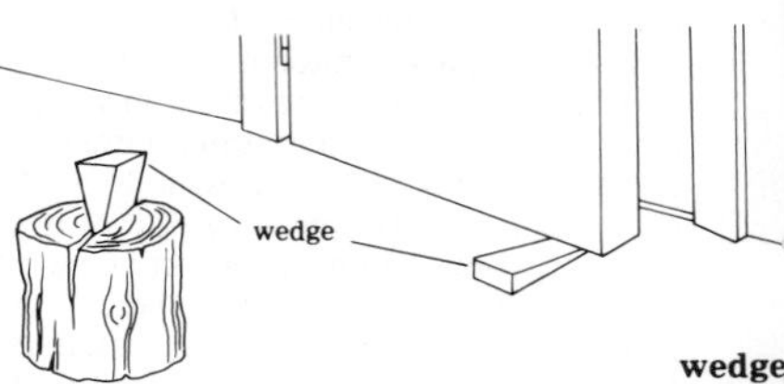

wedge

wedge /wedʒ/ *n* **1** (a) piece of wood or metal that is thick at one end and narrows at the other to a sharp edge, used eg to split wood or rock, to widen an opening or to keep things apart. (b) thing shaped like or used as a wedge: *a wedge of cake, cheese, etc*, ie a piece cut from a large round cake, cheese, etc. **2** (idm) **drive a wedge between A and B** ⇨ DRIVE[1]. **the thin end of the wedge** ⇨ THIN.

▷ **wedge** *v* **1** [Tn, Cn·a] fix (sth) firmly or force (sth) apart using a wedge: *The window doesn't stay closed unless you wedge it.* ○ *wedge a door open.* **2** [Tn·pr, Tn·p] pack or thrust (sth/sb/oneself) tightly into a space: *wedge packing material into the spaces round the vase.* ○ *I was so tightly wedged between two other passengers, I couldn't get off the bus.*

Wedgwood /ˈwedʒwʊd/ Josiah (1730-95), English potter who established a factory producing high-quality china, decorated mainly in classical style, at reasonable prices. One design in particular has become closely associated with the name Wedgwood: white embossed figures on a blue background.

▷ **Wedgwood** *n* [U] (*propr*) **1** china produced by the Wedgwood factory, esp with a white embossed design. **2** (also **ˌWedgwood ˈblue**) light blue colour characteristic of such china.

wedlock /ˈwedlɒk/ *n* [U] (*fml or law*) state of being married: *born out of wedlock*, ie illegitimate.

Wednesday /ˈwenzdɪ/ *n* [U, C] (*abbrs* **Wed**, **Weds**) the fourth day of the week, next after Tuesday.

For the uses of *Wednesday* see the examples at *Monday.*

wee[1] /wi:/ *adj* **1** (*esp Scot*) little: *the poor wee fellow.* **2** (*infml*) very small; tiny: *I'll have a wee drop of cream in my coffee.* ○ *I'm a wee bit worried about him.* ○ *We'll be a wee bit late, I'm afraid.*

wee[2] /wi:/ (also **wee-wee** /ˈwi:wi:/) *n* [C, U] (*infml*) (used esp by or when talking to young children) urine; urinating: *do (a) wee-wee.*

▷ **wee** (also **wee-wee**) *v* (*pt* (**wee-**)**weed**) [I] (used esp by or when talking to young children) urinate.

weed /wi:d/ *n* **1** (a) [C] wild plant growing where it is not wanted, esp among crops or garden plants: *The garden is overgrown with weeds.* ○ *She spent the afternoon pulling up the weeds in the flowerbeds.* (b) [U] any of several plants without flowers that grow in water and form a green, floating mass: *The pond is full of weed.* **2** [C] (*infml derog*) (a) thin weak-looking person. (b) person who has a weak character: *Don't be such a weed!* **3** (*infml*) (a) [C] (usu **the weed**) (*dated or joc*) tobacco or cigarettes: *I wish I could give up the weed*, ie stop smoking. (b) [U] marijuana.

Weddings

Although 'courting' in Britain is now a dated concept, most young couples spend some months getting to know each other before settling down to a life together. Some couples meet through one of the many computer dating 'agencies' that offer to find suitable partners, but couples may also meet at college, at work, in a club or society, or on holiday. Engagements to marry are often officially announced in newspapers, and may be celebrated with a party. Boy-friend and girl-friend become 'fiancé' and 'fiancée'. A typical announcement of an engagement in a local paper might be headed 'Mr J M Smith and Miss S J Brown' and read: 'The engagement is announced between John Martin, only son of Mr and Mrs B R Smith, of Marlborough, Wilts, and Susan Jane, younger daughter of Mr and Mrs W J Brown, of Oxford.'

After this announcement the next step is to decide the date and the type of wedding. The date will probably be fixed several months ahead. Weddings usually take place on a Saturday and traditionally spring, and especially Easter, is a popular time of year.

A religious wedding in the Church of England can be either by banns or by licence. If by banns, the announcement of the intended marriage is made in church during morning service on three successive Sundays in the parish (or parishes) where the fiancé and the fiancée live. A typical announcement might be 'I publish the banns of marriage between Peter James Black, bachelor, of this parish, and Deborah May White, spinster, of the parish of Littleton. If any of you know cause, or just impediment, why these two persons should not be joined together in holy matrimony, ye are to declare it. This is the first (second, etc) time of asking.'

Alternatively, a couple may be married without banns in any church or chapel licensed for marriage so long as one of the two has obtained a marriage licence from the bishop of the diocese, or they may choose to be married without religious ceremony in a registry office.

Many couples prefer a religious wedding, even when they are not regular churchgoers, because they want a 'white wedding', a ceremony in church, with the bride dressed in white, often with a veil and carrying flowers. The bride is normally taken to church by her father, who 'gives her away', while the bridegroom is accompanied by a 'best man'. The bride often has attendants, called bridesmaids, and sometimes small boys act as pages. After the marriage service, to which family and friends will have been invited, there is a reception, called a 'wedding breakfast', when traditionally the bride's parents are the hosts. It may be held at the bride's home or at a hotel. There will be drinks, a meal, and in due course speeches by the bride's father, the best man, and the bridegroom. There is also a wedding cake, a cake with white icing often made in two or three tiers. The bride is usually photographed cutting the cake. Photographs or videos of all stages of the ceremony are taken, including several in front of the church after the ceremony. After the reception, the couple usually leave for for a short holiday, called their 'honeymoon'. The car in which they drive away often has old tin cans or old boots and shoes tied to it and trailing behind it. (This is a sign that they are newly married and is regarded as a good luck symbol.)

A brief report of the wedding may appear in the local newspaper. A typical report might read: 'The ceremony at St Mary's Church was conducted by the Rev Hugh Baker. The bride was given away by her father and wore a dress of ivory silk and lace with a train and a short veil. She carried a bouquet of cream rose-buds and orchids. Attending the bride were Miss Clare Thomson, Miss Sally Parsons and Miss Emma Parsons. Best man was Mr David Gibbs. A reception was held at the Crown Hotel, Barnham. The couple will make their home in Cambridge.'

Many couples celebrate the anniversary of their wedding day each year and parties are often held to celebrate a silver wedding, after 25 years, and a golden wedding, after 50 years.

▷ **weed** *v* **1** [I, Tn] take out weeds from (the ground): *I've been busy weeding (in) the garden.* **2** (phr v) **weed sth/sb out** remove or get rid of (people or things that are not wanted) from amongst others that are valuable: *weed out the weakest saplings* ○ *weed out the herd*, ie get rid of inferior animals ○ *The new conductor started by weeding out the weaker players in the orchestra.*

weedy *adj* (**-ier**, **-iest**) (**a**) full of or overgrown with weeds (WEED 1a). (**b**) (*infml derog*) thin and weak-looking: *a weedy young man.*

□ **ˈweed-killer** *n* [C, U] substance that destroys weeds: *a systematic weed-killer.*

weeds /wi:dz/ *n* [pl] black clothes worn (esp by a widow) to show that one is mourning sb who has died.

week /wi:k/ *n* **1** (**a**) period of seven days, usu reckoned from midnight on Saturday: *last, next, this, etc week* ○ *What day of the week was 2 July last year?* ○ *early next week* ○ *at the end of last week* ○ *Sunday is the first day of the week.* ○ *He comes to see us once a week.* (**b**) any period of seven days: *a six weeks' holiday* ○ *a week ago today*, ie seven days ago ○ *three weeks ago yesterday*, ie twenty-two days ago ○ *They are going on holiday for two weeks.* ○ *I shall be away for no more than a week.* **2** (**a**) the six days apart from Sunday: *During the week, the road is very busy but there is very little traffic on Sundays.* (**b**) the five days other than Saturday and Sunday: *They live in London during the week and go to the country at the weekend.* ○ *They never have time to go to the cinema during the week.* (**c**) period in a week when one works: *a 35-hour week* ○ *The government is introducing a shorter working week.* ○ *How many lessons are there in the school week?* **3** (idm) **this day week** ⇨ DAY. **today, tomorrow, Monday, etc ˈweek** seven days after today, tomorrow, Monday, etc. **ˌweek after ˈweek** (*infml*) continuously for many weeks: *Week after week the drought continued.* **week ˌin, week ˈout** every week without exception: *Every Sunday, week in, week out, she writes to her parents.* **a ˌweek last ˈMonday, ˈyesterday, etc** seven days before last Monday, yesterday, etc: *It was a week yesterday (that) we heard the news.*

▷ **weekly** *adj, adv* (occurring, payable, published, etc) once a week or every week: *weekly payments* ○ *a weekly wage of £100* ○ *a weekly shopping trip* ○ *Wages are paid weekly.* ○ *The machine must be checked weekly.* — *n* newspaper or magazine that is published once a week.

□ **ˈweekday** /-deɪ/ *n* any day except Sunday: *The library is open on weekdays only.* ○ *Weekdays are always busy here.* ○ [attrib] *weekday opening times.*

ˌweekˈend (*US* **ˈweekend**) *n* (**a**) Saturday and Sunday: *The office is closed at the weekend.* ○ *He has to work (at) weekends.* (**b**) Saturday and Sunday or a slightly longer period as a holiday or rest: *a weekend in the country* ○ *spend the weekend at home* ○ [attrib] *a weekend house, visit.* — *v* [Ipr, Ip] (esp in the continuous tenses) make a weekend holiday or visit: *They're weekending at the seaside.*

weekender *n* person who spends the weekend away from home; weekend visitor: *Many of the cottages in the village are now owned by weekenders.*

weeny /ˈwi:nɪ/ *adj* (**-ier**, **-iest**) (*infml*) tiny. Cf TEENY.

weep /wi:p/ *v* (*pt, pp* **wept** /wept/) (*fml*) **1** (**a**) [I, Ipr, It] ~ (**for/over sb/sth**) shed tears; cry: *The sight made me want to weep.* ○ *weep for joy* ○ *a mother weeping over the death of her child* ○ *She wept to see him in such a state.* (**b**) [Tn] shed (tears): *weep tears of joy.* ⇨ Usage at CRY[1]. **2** [I] (esp of a wound) shed or ooze moisture, esp pus: *The cut is no longer weeping and is starting to heal.*

▷ **weep** *n* [sing] period of weeping: *A good weep would probably make you feel better.*

weeping *adj* [attrib] (of certain trees) having branches that droop: *a weeping birch, willow, etc.*

weepy *adj* (**-ier**, **-iest**) (**a**) inclined to weep; tearful: *She is still feeling weepy.* (**b**) (of a film, story, etc) tending to make one weep; sentimental: *a weepy ending.* — (also **weepie**) *n* sentimental or emotional film, book, etc.

weevil /ˈwi:vl/ *n* type of small beetle with a hard shell that feeds on grain, nuts and other seeds, and destroys crops.

wef /ˌdʌblju: i: ˈef/ *abbr* (*esp commerce*) with effect from: *wef 1 May 1986.*

weft /weft/ (also **woof**) *n* [sing] (in weaving) threads taken crosswise over and under the lengthwise threads of the warp. ⇨ illus at WEAVE.

weigh /weɪ/ *v* **1** [Tn] measure how heavy (sth) is by means of scales, a balance, etc: *He weighed himself on the bathroom scales.* ○ *The load must be weighed before it is put in the washing-machine.* ○ *He weighed the stone in his hand*, ie estimated how heavy it was by holding it. **2** [Ln] show a certain measure when put on scales, etc: *She weighs 60 kilos.* ○ *How much do you weigh?* ie How heavy are you? ○ *This piece of meat weighs four pounds.* **3** (**a**) [Tn, Tn·pr] ~ **sth** (**with/against sth**) consider carefully the relative value or importance of sth: *weigh one plan against another* ○ *weighing the pros and cons* ○ *weigh the advantages of the operation against the risks involved.* (**b**) [Tn, Tn·p] ~ **sth** (**up**) consider sth carefully: *weigh (up) the consequences of an action* ○ *weigh up one's chances of success.* **4** [Ipr] ~ (**with sb**) (**against sb/sth**) be considered important (by sb) when sb/sth is being judged: *His criminal record weighed heavily against him (with the jury).* ○ *Her past achievements weighed in her favour as a candidate.* **5** (idm) **weigh ˈanchor** raise the anchor of a ship at the start of a voyage, etc. **weigh the ˈevidence** consider the relative value of the evidence for and against sb/sth. **weigh a ˈton** (*infml*) be very heavy: *These cases weigh a ton — what have you got in them?* **weigh one's ˈwords** choose carefully words that express exactly what one means: *I must weigh my words to avoid any misunderstanding.* **6** (phr v) **weigh sb down** make sb feel anxious or depressed: *weighed down by worry and overwork* ○ *The responsibilities of the job are weighing her down.* **weigh sb/sth down** make sb/sth bend or sag: *The porter was weighed down by all the luggage.* ○ *The branches were weighed down with ripe apples.* **weigh in** (**at sth**) (of a jockey, boxer, etc) be weighed before a race, boxing match, etc: *He weighed in at several pounds below the limit.* **weigh in** (**with sth**) (*infml*) join in a discussion, an argument, etc by saying sth important or convincing; contribute confidently: *At that point, the chairman weighed in with a strong defence of company policy.* **weigh on sb/sth** make (sb/sb's mind, etc) anxious: *The responsibilities weigh (heavily) on him.* ○ *It's been weighing on my mind for days whether to tell her or not.* **weigh sth out** measure a quantity of sth by weight: *weigh out a kilo of tomatoes* ○ *Weigh out all the ingredients before you start making the cake.*

□ **ˈweighbridge** *n* weighing-machine with a platform set into the road, onto which vehicles can be driven to be weighed.

ˈweigh-in *n* (*pl* **-ins**) (usu *sing*) check on the weight of a boxer, jockey, etc, made just before a fight, race, etc.

ˈweighing-machine *n* machine for weighing people or things that are too heavy to be weighed on a simple balance.

ˈweighing-scale *n* balance used for weighing.

weight[1] /weɪt/ *n* **1** [U] degree of heaviness of a thing, esp as measured on a balance, weighing-machine, etc and expressed according to a particular system of measuring (eg kilos, tons, etc): *Bananas are usually sold by weight.* ○ *That man is twice my weight*, ie is twice as heavy as I am. ○ *Her weight has increased to 70 kilos.* ○ *The two boys are (of) the same weight.* ○ *He has grown both in height and weight.* ⇨ App 9, 10. **2** [U] quality of being heavy: *Lead is often used because of its weight.* ○ *The weight of the overcoat made it uncomfortable to wear.* **3** [U] (*physics*) force with which a body is drawn downwards by gravity. **4** [C, U] unit or system of units by which weight is measured and expressed: *tables of weights and measures* ○ *avoirdupois/troy weight.* ⇨ App 10. **5** [C] (**a**) piece of metal of a known heaviness, used with scales for weighing things: *a 2lb weight.* (**b**) heavy object, esp one used to bring or keep sth down: *a clock worked by weights* ○ *a ˈpaperweight*, ie for keeping papers in place ○ *The dressmaker put small weights in the hem of the dress.* ○ *The doctor said he must not lift heavy weights.* **6** [sing] ~ (**of sth**) (**a**) load to be supported: *The pillars have to support the weight of the roof.* ○ *The weight of the water from the burst pipe caused the ceiling to collapse.* (**b**) (*fig*) burden of responsibility or worry: *The full weight of decision-making falls on her.* **7** [U] (degree of) importance, seriousness or influence: *arguments of great weight* ○ *Recent events give added weight to their campaign.* ○ *The jury were convinced by the weight of the evidence against her.* **8** (idm) **be/take a load/weight off sb's mind** ⇨ MIND. **carry weight** ⇨ CARRY. **lose/take off ˈweight** (of a person) become less heavy; slim. **ˌover/ˌunder ˈweight** too heavy/not heavy enough. **pull one's weight** ⇨ PULL[2]. **put on weight** (of a person) become heavier; grow fat: *He's put on a lot of weight since he gave up smoking.* **take the ˈweight off one's feet** (*infml*) sit down. **throw one's weight about/around** (*infml*) behave in an aggressively arrogant way. **weight of ˈnumbers** combined weight, strength, influence, etc of a group which is larger than another: *They won the argument by sheer weight of numbers.* **worth one's/its weight in gold** ⇨ WORTH.

▷ **weightless** *adj* having no weight, or with no weight relative to one's/its surroundings because of the absence of gravity. **weightlessness** *n* [U]: *become accustomed to weightlessness in a spacecraft.*

weighty *adj* (**-ier, -iest**) **1** (**a**) having great weight; heavy. (**b**) burdensome. **2** showing or requiring serious thought; important or influential: *weighty arguments, decisions, matters.* **weightily** /-ɪlɪ/ *adv.* **weightiness** *n* [U].

□ **ˈweight-lifting** *n* [U] lifting heavy objects as a sport or as exercise. **ˈweight-lifter** *n* person who does weight-lifting.

ˈweight-watcher *n* one who tries to lose weight, esp by dieting.

weight[2] /weɪt/ *v* **1** (**a**) [Tn] attach a weight to (sth). (**b**) [Tn, Tn·pr, Tn·p] ~ **sth** (**down**) (**with sth**) hold sth down with a weight[1](5b) or weights: *The net is weighted to keep it below the surface of the water.* (**c**) [Tn, Tn·pr] ~ **sth** (**with sth**) make sth heavier: *The stick had been weighted with lead.* **2** [Tn] treat (a fabric) with a mineral substance to make it heavier: *weighted silk.* **3** [Tn·pr esp passive] plan or organize (sth) in a way that favours a particular person or group; bias: *a law weighted against/towards/in favour of those owning land.* **4** (phr v) **weight sb down** (**with sth**) burden sb: *She was weighted down with parcels.*

▷ **weighting** *n* [U] (*esp Brit*) extra pay or allowances given in special cases, eg to people working in cities because of the higher cost of living there: [attrib] *a London weighting allowance.*

Weill /vaɪl/ Kurt (1900-50), German composer who developed the idea of 'music theatre', operas with settings relevant to modern everyday life that can be performed with only a few musicians. His best-known works, with words by Bertolt *Brecht, include *The Threepenny Opera*, *The Rise and Fall of the City of Mahagonny* and *The Seven Deadly Sins*.

Weimar /ˈvaɪmɑː(r)/ city in eastern central Germany, where the German National Assembly met to establish the Weimar Republic in 1919.

□ **the ˌWeimar Reˈpublic** German republic 1919-33, whose constitution was drawn up at Weimar. It was overthrown by *Hitler.

weir /wɪə(r)/ *n* **1** wall or barrier built across a river in order to control or divert the flow of water. **2** fence made of stakes or branches put across a stream in order to make a pool where fish may be caught.

weird /wɪəd/ *adj* (**-er, -est**) **1** (frightening because it is) unnatural, uncanny or strange: *Weird shrieks were heard in the darkness.* **2** (*infml often derog*) unconventional, unusual or bizarre: *weird clothes, hairstyles, taste* ○ *I found some of her poems a bit weird.*

▷ **weirdly** *adv.*

weirdness *n* [U].

weirdo /ˈwɪədəʊ/ (*pl* ~**s** /-əʊz/) (also **weirdie** /ˈwɪədɪ/) *n* (*infml usu derog*) person who behaves, dresses, etc in a bizarre or an unconventional way; eccentric person.

welcome /ˈwelkəm/ *adj* **1** received with or giving pleasure: *a welcome change, relief, rest, sight, visitor* ○ *welcome news* ○ *Your offer of a loan is extremely welcome just now.* ○ *We had the feeling that we were not welcome at the meeting.* **2** [pred] ~ **to sth/to do sth** (**a**) freely permitted to take sth or to do sth: *You are welcome to use/to the use of my car any time.* ○ *She's welcome to stay here whenever she likes.* ○ *You are welcome to any books you would like to borrow.* (**b**) (*ironic*) freely permitted to have sth or to do sth because the speaker does not want to have it or to do it: *If anyone thinks he can do this job any better, he's welcome to it/to try!* ie I'll gladly let him do it. ○ *As far as I'm concerned, if it's my desk she wants, she's welcome to it!* **3** (idm) **make sb ˈwelcome** make sb feel that he is welcome; receive sb hospitably. **you're ˈwelcome** (used as a polite reply to thanks) there is no need to thank me.

▷ **welcome** *interj* (greeting used by a person who is already in a place to one who is arriving): *Welcome! Come in and meet my parents.* ○ *Welcome back/home!* ○ *Welcome on board!* ○ *Welcome to England!*

welcome *n* **1** greeting or reception, esp a kind or glad one; saying 'welcome': *an enthusiastic, a hearty, a warm, etc welcome* ○ *The victorious team were given a tumultuous welcome when they arrived home.* ○ *She was touched by the warmth of their welcome.* **2** (idm) **outstay/overstay one's ˈwelcome** stay too long as a guest, causing inconvenience or annoyance to one's host.

welcome *v* **1** [Tn, Tn·pr, Tn·p] greet (sb) on his arrival: *a welcoming smile* ○ *We were welcomed at the door by the children.* ○ *She welcomed the visitors warmly.* ○ *It is a pleasure to welcome you (back) on the show.* **2** [Tn] (**a**) show or feel pleasure or satisfaction at (sth): *The changes were welcomed by everybody.* ○ *We welcome the opportunity to express our gratitude.* (**b**) react to (sth) in the specified manner: *welcome the news with amazement, indifference, enthusiasm, etc* ○ *welcome a suggestion coldly, enthusiastically, warmly, etc.*

weld /weld/ *v* **1** (**a**) [Tn, Tn·pr] ~ **A and B** (**together**); ~ **A** (**on**)**to B** join (pieces of metal) by hammering or pressing (usu when the metal is softened by heat) or fuse them by using an oxy-acetylene flame or an electric arc: *weld the pieces of a broken axle* ○ *weld parts together* ○ *The car has had a new wing welded on.* (**b**) [Tn] make (sth) by joining pieces of metal in this way. (**c**) [I] (of iron, etc) be capable of being welded: *Some metals weld better than others.* **2** [Tn·pr] ~ **sb/sth into sth** (*fig*) unite (people or things) into an effective whole: *weld a bunch of untrained recruits into an efficient fighting force.* Cf FORGE[2] 1.

▷ **weld** *n* joint made by welding.

welder *n* person whose job is making welded joints (eg in a car factory).

welfare /ˈwelfeə(r)/ *n* [U] **1** good health, happiness, prosperity, etc of a person or group: *Parents are responsible for the welfare of their children.* ○ *the welfare of the nation* ○ *We are concerned about his welfare.* **2** care for the health, safety, etc of a particular group: *child/infant welfare* ○ [attrib] *a child welfare clinic.* **3** (*US*) (*Brit* **social security**) money paid by the State to those in need, eg because they are unemployed, disabled, etc. Cf SUPPLEMENTARY BENEFIT (SUPPLEMENTARY).

□ **ˌwelfare ˈstate** (often **the ˌWelfare ˈState**) (country that has a) system of ensuring the welfare of its citizens by means of social services (eg pensions, family allowances, free medical care, etc) provided by the State.

ˈwelfare work (**a**) organized efforts to ensure the welfare of a group of people (eg employees in a factory, the poor, the disabled, etc). (**b**) (*US*) social work. **ˈwelfare worker**.

well[1] /wel/ *n* **1** (**a**) shaft dug in the ground, usu lined with brick or stone, for obtaining water from an underground source: *dig/drive/sink a well* ○ *The villagers get their water from a well.* ○ [attrib] *well water.* (**b**) = OIL WELL (OIL). **2** enclosed space like the shaft of a well, eg one in a building from roof to basement that contains a staircase or lift. **3** (**a**) (*dated except in place-names*) spring or fountain: *Tunbridge Wells.* (**b**) ~ **of sth** (*dated fml fig*) source of sth: *a well of information.* **4** (*Brit*) (in a lawcourt) space in front of the judge where lawyers sit, separated from the rest of the court by a railing.

▷ **well** *v* **1** [Ipr, Ip] ~ (**out/up**) flow or rise like water from a well: *Blood was welling (out) from the wound.* ○ *Tears welled up in her eyes.* ○ *Anger was welling up in him.* **2** (phr v) **well over** overflow.

□ **ˈwell-head** (also **ˈwell-spring**) *n* source of a spring or fountain.

well[2] /wel/ *adj* (*compar* **better** /ˈbetə(r)/, *superl* **best** /best/) **1** [usu pred] in good health: *be, feel, get, look, etc well* ○ *Are you quite well?* ○ *Is she well enough to travel?* ○ *I'm better now, thank you.* ○ *He's not a well man.* ⇨ Usage at HEALTHY. **2** [pred] in a satisfactory state or position: (*saying*) *All's well that ends well.* ○ *We're very well where we are.* ○ *It seems that all is not well at home.* **3** [pred] advisable or desirable: *It would be well to start early.* **4** (idm) **ˌall very ˈwell** (**for sb**)... (*infml ironic*) (used to indicate that one is not happy, satisfied or in agreement with what sb has said or done): *It's all very well (for ˈyou) to suggest a skiing holiday, but I'm the one who will have to pay for it.* **ˌall well and ˈgood** (*infml*) satisfactory (though other things may not be satisfactory): *The job's done — that's all well and good — but what about the bonus we were promised?* **(just) as ˈwell (to do sth)** prudent or appropriate: *It would be (just) as well to phone and say we will be late.*

well[3] /wel/ *adv* (*compar* **better** /ˈbetə(r)/, *superl* **best** /best/) **1** (usu placed after the *v*, and after the direct object if the *v* is transitive) (**a**) in a good, right or satisfactory manner: *The children behaved well/were well-behaved.* ○ *She speaks English very well.* ○ *The conference was organized* *very well.* ○ *I can read well enough without glasses.* ○ *Well done, played, run, etc!* ie cries expressing admiration, congratulations, etc ○ *I hope everything is going well* (ie is satisfactory) *with you.* ○ *Things didn't go well for us at first, but everything is fine now.* ○ *Do these colours go well together* (ie harmonize with each other)*?* ○ *The plan didn't work out very well.* ○ *Investing in industry is money well spent.* Cf ILL[1] 1. **(b)** in a kind manner: *They treated me very well.* Cf ILL[1] 2. **(c)** thoroughly, completely or carefully: *Shake the mixture well.* ○ *Read the document well before you sign it.* ○ *The pan must be dried well before you put it away.* ○ *His shoes were always well polished.* ○ *She doesn't know him very well.* ○ *I'm well* (ie fully) *able to manage on my own.* **2** with praise or approval: *speak/think well of sb.* **3** (after *can, could, may, might*) justifiably, reasonably or probably: *You may well be right.* ○ *I might well consider it later.* ○ *I can't very well leave now.* ○ *I couldn't very well refuse to help them, could I?* ○ *'They've split up, you know.' 'I can well believe it.'* ○ *It may well be that the train is delayed.* **4** to a considerable extent or degree: *I don't know how old he is, but he looks well over/past forty.* ○ *She was driving at well over the speed limit.* ○ *lean well forward/back in one's chair* ○ *It was well worth waiting for.* ○ *Temperatures are well up in the forties.* **5** (idm) **as well (as sb/sth)** in addition (to sb/sth/doing sth): *Are they coming as well?* ○ *He grows flowers as well as vegetables.* ○ *She is a talented musician as well as being a photographer.* ⇨ Usage at ALSO. **augur well/ill for sb/sth** ⇨ AUGUR. **be ˌwell ˈout of sth** (*infml*) be fortunate that one is not involved in sth. **be well up in sth** be well informed about sth: *He's well up in all the latest developments in the industry.* **bloody well** ⇨ BLOODY[2]. **bode well/ill** ⇨ BODE. **deserve well/ill of sb** ⇨ DESERVE. **do oneself well** provide oneself with comforts, luxuries, etc. **do ˈwell (a)** be successful; prosper: *Simon is doing very well at school.* ○ *The business is doing well.* **(b)** (only in the continuous tenses) be making a good recovery from an illness, etc: *The patient is doing well.* ○ *Mother and baby are doing well.* **do well by sb** treat sb generously. **do ˈwell for oneself** become successful or prosperous. **do well out of sb/sth** make a profit out of or obtain money from sb/sth. **do well to do sth** (esp as a warning) act wisely or prudently in doing sth: *You would do well to remember who is paying the bill.* ○ *They would do well to concentrate more on their work.* ○ *You did well to sell when the price was high.* **fucking well** ⇨ FUCK. **jolly well** ⇨ JOLLY. **leave/let well aˈlone** not interfere with sth that is satisfactory or adequate: *Any changes would be very difficult to make so it's better to leave well alone.* **may/might (just) as well do sth** in the circumstances, no harm will come from doing sth: *Since nobody else wants the job, we might as well let him have it.* **one may/might as well be hanged/hung for a sheep as a lamb** ⇨ HANG[1]. **mean well** ⇨ MEAN[1]. **mean well by sb** ⇨ MEAN[1]. **pretty much/nearly/well** ⇨ PRETTY. **promise well** ⇨ PROMISE[2]. **speak well for sb/sth** ⇨ SPEAK. **stand well with sb** be in sb's favour. **ˌvery ˈwell** (used to indicate that one agrees or obeys, esp after sb else has persuaded, ordered or requested one to do sth): *Very well, doctor, I'll try to take more exercise.* ○ *Oh, very well, if you insist.* **ˌwell and ˈtruly** (*infml*) completely; decisively: *By that time we were well and truly lost.* **well aware of sth/that...** fully informed or conscious: *I'm well aware of the risks.* **ˈwell away (a)** having made good progress: *By the end of the month, we'll be well away.* **(b)** (*infml*) (beginning to be) drunk or hilarious. **well in (with sb)** (*infml*) regarded as a close friend (by sb); accepted: *She seems to be well in with the right people.* **well ˈoff** in a good position, esp financially: *His family is not very well off.* ○ *You don't need to look for another job — you're well off where you are.* **well off for sth** having plenty of sth: *We're well off for storage space in the new flat.* **wish sb/sth well/ill** ⇨ WISH.

□ (Compound *adjs* formed from *well-* + past participles are usu hyphenated when attributive but not hyphenated when predicative, except when the *adj* has acquired a restricted sense.)

ˌwell-adˈvised *adj* sensible; prudent: *You would be well advised to* (ie You ought to) *reconsider your decision.* ○ *a ˌwell-advised ˈmove.*

ˌwell-apˈpointed *adj* having all the necessary equipment, furniture, etc: *a ˌwell-appointed aˈpartment, hoˈtel, ˈoffice, etc.*

ˌwell-ˈbalanced *adj* (of a person) sensible and emotionally stable: *healthy, ˌwell-balanced ˈchildren* ○ *You need to be very well balanced to cope with the stress of a job like that.*

ˈwell-being *n* [U] state of being healthy, happy, etc: *have a sense of (physical/spiritual) well-being.*

ˌwell-ˈborn *adj* of an aristocratic or a socially superior family.

ˌwell-ˈbred *adj* having or showing good manners: *She was too well bred to show her disappointment.* Cf ILL-BRED (ILL[1]).

ˌwell-ˈbuilt *adj* (*usu approv*) (of a person) strong and muscular.

ˌwell-conˈnected *adj* friendly with or related to rich, influential or socially superior people.

ˌwell-disˈposed *adj* ~ **(towards sb/sth) (a)** sympathetic or friendly to (sb): *She seemed well disposed towards us.* **(b)** approving (a plan, etc); ready to help: *The committee are well disposed towards the idea.* Cf ILL-DISPOSED (ILL[1]).

ˌwell-ˈdone *adj* (of food, esp meat) cooked thoroughly or for a long time: *He prefers his steak well-done.*

ˌwell-ˈearned *adj* thoroughly deserved: *take a well-earned rest, holiday, etc.*

ˌwell-eˈstablished *adj* existing (and operating successfully) for a long time: *a ˌwell-established ˈfirm* ○ *ˌwell-established proˈcedures.*

ˌwell-ˈfed *adj* having good meals regularly: *The cat looked very sleek and well fed.*

ˌwell-ˈfounded *adj* based on facts; substantiated: *ˌwell-founded susˈpicions.*

ˌwell-ˈheeled *adj* (*infml*) rich: *a restaurant with many ˌwell-heeled ˈcustomers.*

ˌwell-inˈformed *adj* having (access to) knowledge or information: *ˌwell-informed oˈpinion, ˈquarters, ˈsources.*

ˌwell-inˈtentioned *adj* intended or intending to be helpful, useful, etc: *She reacted angrily to my ˌwell-intentioned reˈmarks.* ○ *He's well-intentioned but not very good at getting things done.*

ˌwell-ˈjudged *adj* done skilfully or appropriately.

ˌwell-ˈknown *adj* known to many people; familiar or famous.

ˌwell-ˈmade *adj* **(a)** (of an object) strongly constructed. **(b)** (of a person or an animal) strong and muscular; sturdy.

ˌwell-ˈmeaning *adj* acting with good intentions (but often not having the desired effect).

ˌwell-ˈmeant *adj* done, said, etc with good intentions but not having the desired effect.

ˌwell-ˈoiled *adj* (*sl*) drunk.

ˌwell-preˈserved *adj* **(a)** (of an old person) not showing many signs of old age; young-looking. **(b)** (of old things) in good condition: *a well-preserved Greek temple.*

ˌwell-ˈread *adj* having read many books, and therefore very knowledgeable.

ˌwell-ˈrounded *adj* **(a)** (of a person's body) pleasantly plump. **(b)** [usu attrib] wide and varied: *a ˌwell-rounded eduˈcation.*

ˌwell-ˈspoken *adj* speaking correctly or in a refined way.

ˌwell-ˈthought-of *adj* (of a person) respected, admired and liked: *He is well-thought-of in government circles.*

ˌwell-ˈthumbed *adj* (of a book, etc) having its pages marked or worn, because it has been read so often.

ˌwell-ˈtimed *adj* done, said, etc at the right time or at a suitable time: *Your remarks were certainly well timed.* ○ *a ˌwell-timed interˈvention.* Cf ILL-TIMED (ILL[1]).

ˌwell-to-ˈdo *adj* prosperous; wealthy.

ˌwell-ˈtried *adj* often used and therefore known to be reliable: *a ˌwell-tried ˈmethod, ˈremedy, etc.*

ˌwell-ˈtrodden *adj* (*often fig*) often walked upon: *Their argument proceeded along a well-trodden path,* ie followed a familiar course.

ˌwell-ˈturned *adj* (*fml*) expressed elegantly: *a ˌwell-turned ˈcompliment, ˈphrase, etc.*

ˌwell-ˈversed *adj* [pred] ~ **(in sth)** knowing a lot (about sth); experienced: *well-versed in the art of flattery.*

ˈwell-wisher *n* person who hopes that another will be happy, successful, healthy, etc: *They received many letters of sympathy from well-wishers.*

ˌwell-ˈworn *adj* **(a)** (of a phrase, etc) over-used (and therefore commonplace or trite). **(b)** very worn as a result of much use: *a ˌwell-worn old ˈcoat.*

well[4] /wel/ *interj* (esp in spoken English) **1** (used to express astonishment): *Well, who would have thought it?* ○ *Well, well (— I should never have guessed it)!* ○ *Well, you ˈdo surprise me!* **2** (used to express relief): *Well, thank goodness that's over!* ○ *Well, here we are at last!* **3** (also **oh well**) (used to express resignation): *Oh well, there's nothing we can do about it.* ○ *Well, it can't be helped.* **4** (also **very well**) (used to express agreement or understanding): *Very well, then, I'll accept your offer.* **5** (used when conceding a point in an argument, etc): *Well, you may be right.* **6** (used when resuming a conversation, etc or changing the subject after a pause): *Well, as I was saying, ...* ○ *Well, the next day...* ○ *Well, let's move on to the next item.* **7** (used to express hesitation, doubt, etc): *'Do you want to come?' 'Well — I'm not sure.'* **8** (idm) **well I ˈnever (ˈdid)!** (*infml*) (used as an exclamation of pleased or annoyed astonishment).

we'll /wi:l/ *contracted form* **1** we shall ⇨ SHALL. **2** we will ⇨ WILL[1].

Welles /welz/ (George) Orson (1915-85), American radio, theatre and film actor and director. His most famous film was *Citizen Kane*, which he starred in and directed. He was considered a brilliant but difficult and erratic man, who never fulfilled his genius.

Wellington[1] /ˈwelɪŋtən/ capital city of New Zealand, in the North Island.

Wellington[2] /ˈwelɪŋtən/ Arthur Wellesley, Ist Duke of (1769-1852), British soldier and statesman, known as the 'Iron Duke'. He successfully commanded the British armies in Spain during the *Peninsular War, and then defeated *Napoleon at the Battle of *Waterloo, bringing the Napoleonic Wars to an end. He later turned to politics, as a Conservative, and held several ministerial posts, including that of prime minister (1828-30 and 1834). ⇨ App 2.

wellington /ˈwelɪŋtən/ *n* (also **ˌwellington ˈboot**, *infml* **welly**) (*esp Brit*) waterproof rubber boot, usu reaching almost to the knee: *a pair of wellingtons/wellington boots.* ⇨ illus at BOOT.

wellnigh /ˌwelˈnaɪ/ *adv* (*fml or rhet*) almost: *The task is ˌwellnigh imˈpossible.* ○ *The party was wellnigh over by the time we arrived.*

Wells /welz/ H(erbert) G(eorge) (1866-1946), English novelist. He achieved early popularity with science-fiction stories such as *The Time Machine, The Invisible Man* and *The War of the Worlds*, later producing comic novels based on the lower-middle-class world of his youth (*Kipps* and *The History of Mr Polly*) and more serious fiction and non-fiction works dealing with political and historical as well as scientific issues (eg *Tono-Bungay, Outline of History* and *The Shape of Things to Come*).

Wells Fargo /ˌwelz ˈfɑ:gəʊ/ American company, founded in 1852, that carried mail by horse and stagecoach and by sea to and from the newly settled western part of the USA. The modern Wells Fargo & Co is principally a banking and financial services company.

welly /ˈwelɪ:/ *n* (*Brit infml*) = WELLINGTON: *a new pair of green wellies.*

Welsh /welʃ/ *adj* of Wales, its people or its language: *the Welsh coastline* ○ *Welsh poetry.*

▷ **Welsh** *n* **1** [U] Celtic language of Wales. ⇨ article at LANGUAGE. **2 the Welsh** [pl] the people of Wales.

□ **ˌWelsh ˈdresser** type of sideboard with

cupboards and drawers in the lower part and shelves in the upper part. ⇨ illus at FURNITURE.

Welshman /ˈwelʃmən/ (*pl* **-men** /-mən/, *fem* **Welshwoman** /-wʊmən/, *pl* **-women** /-wɪmɪn/) *n* native of Wales.

ˌ**Welsh** ˈ**rarebit** (also **rarebit**, ˌ**Welsh** ˈ**rabbit**) dish of melted cheese on toast.

welsh /welʃ/ *v* (*derog*) **1** [I, Ipr] ~ (**on sth**) avoid paying money owed, esp at gambling: *welsh on one's debts.* **2** [Ipr] ~ **on sb/sth** break one's promise to sb: *She welshed on (the bargain she made with) us.* ▷ **welsher** *n.*

welt /welt/ *n* **1** strip of leather round the edge of the upper(*n* 1) of a shoe, to which the sole is stitched. **2** mark left on the skin by a heavy blow, esp with a whip; weal.

welter /ˈweltə(r)/ *n* [sing] ~ **of sth/sb** disorderly mixture of things or people; general confusion: *a welter of unrelated facts* ○ *carried forward by the welter of surging bodies.*

▷ **welter** *v* [Ipr] ~ **in sth** (*arch*) lie soaking in (esp blood): *weltering in gore.*

welterweight /ˈweltəweɪt/ *n* boxer weighing between 61 and 67 kilograms, next above lightweight: *Throughout his career, he fought as a welterweight/at welterweight.* ○ [attrib] *a welterweight contest.*

Wembley /ˈwemblɪ/ (also ˌ**Wembley** ˈ**Stadium**) large sports stadium in north-west London, where important football matches are played.

wen /wen/ *n* harmless, usu permanent, tumour on the skin, esp on the head.

wench /wentʃ/ *n* (*arch or joc*) mature girl or young woman.

wend /wend/ *v* (idm) **wend one's way** (*arch or joc*) go: *It's time we were wending our way*, ie We must go.

Wenders /ˈvendəz/ Wim (1945-), German film director. His work, including *Paris, Texas* and *Wings of Desire*, shows characters lost in society and searching for a place in it.

Wendy house /ˈwendɪ haʊs/ (*esp Brit*) small houselike structure for children to play in.

Wensleydale /ˈwenzlɪdeɪl/ *n* [U] type of mild crumbly cheese originally made in N Yorkshire, England.

went *pt* of GO[1].

wept *pt, pp* of WEEP.

were ⇨ BE.

we're /wɪə(r)/ *contracted form* we are ⇨ BE.

weren't ⇨ BE.

werewolf /ˈwɪəwʊlf/ *n* (*pl* **-wolves** /-wʊlvz/) (in stories) person who changes, or is capable of changing, into a wolf, esp at the time of the full moon.

Wesker /ˈweskə(r)/ Arnold (1932-), English playwright whose work is based on English working-class life. His best-known plays are the so-called 'Wesker trilogy' (*Chicken Soup with Barley, Roots* and *I'm Talking about Jerusalem*) and *Chips with Everything*. Cf KITCHEN-SINK DRAMA (KITCHEN).

Wesley /ˈwezlɪ/ John (1703-91), English priest who founded the Methodist Church. Originally an Anglican, he was not allowed to preach his evangelical views within the Church of England, so he began to preach out of doors, riding over 8 000 miles a year to bring Methodism to people all over Britain. ▷ **Wesleyan** /ˈwezlɪən/ *n, adj* (member) of the Methodist Church founded by John Wesley: *a Wesleyan chapel.*

Wessex /ˈwesɪks/ former Anglo-Saxon kingdom, established in the 6th century AD in the area corresponding to modern Hampshire and gradually extended to most of southern England. Its name is used in the title of certain present-day regional authorities in central southern England, and Thomas *Hardy applied it to the area in which his novels were set (esp Dorset).

West /west/ Dame Rebecca (real name Cicily Isabel Fairfield, 1892-1983), English novelist, critic and feminist. Amongst her best-known works are *The Return of the Soldier* and *The Meaning of Treason.*

west /west/ *n* [sing] (*abbr* **W**) **1 the west** point on the horizon where the sun sets; one of the four main points of the compass: *The rain is coming from the west.* ○ *Bristol is in the west of England.* ○ *She lives to the west of* (ie further west than) *Glasgow.* Cf EAST, NORTH, SOUTH. **2 the West** (**a**) the non-Communist countries of Europe and N America. (**b**) Europe, contrasted with Oriental countries. **3 the West** the western side of the USA: *She's lived in the West* (eg California) *for ten years now.* **4** (idm) **go** ˈ**west** (*dated sl*) be destroyed, used up, ruined, etc: *There was a fire, and five years of research work went west.*

▷ **west** *adj* [attrib] **1** in or towards the west: *the west side of London.* **2** (of winds) blowing from the west. Cf WESTERLY.

west *adv* towards the west: *travel west* ○ *three miles west of here* ○ *The building faces west.*

westward /ˈwestwəd/ *adj* towards the west: *a westward journey.*

westwards (also **westward**) *adv*: *travel westward(s).* ⇨ Usage at FORWARD[2].

□ **the** ˌ**West** ˈ**Bank** area on the west bank of the River *Jordan, formerly (since 1948) part of Jordan but occupied by Israel in 1967. It is now disputed territory.

westbound /ˈwestbaʊnd/ *adj* travelling or leading towards the west: *westbound traffic* ○ *the westbound carriageway of the motorway.*

the ˈ**West Country** (*Brit*) the south-west region of Britain: [attrib] *a West-Country village.*

the ˌ**West** ˈ**End** (*Brit*) the area of London that includes most theatres, fashionable and expensive shops, etc: [attrib] *a* ˌ*West-End* ˈ*cinema.* Cf THE EAST END (EAST). ⇨ articles at LONDON, PERFORMING ARTS.

westerly /ˈwestəlɪ/ *adj* **1** [attrib] in or towards the west: *westerly shores* ○ *in a westerly direction.* **2** [usu attrib] (of winds) blowing from the west.

▷ **westerly** *n* wind blowing from the west: *a gale-force westerly.* — *adv* towards the west: *travel westerly.*

western /ˈwestən/ *adj* **1** [attrib] of or in the west: *western regions of the British Isles* ○ *the western United States.* **2** (also **Western**) [usu attrib] (characteristic) of the West: *the Western way of life* ○ *western attitudes, clothes, nations, philosophy.*

▷ **western** *n* film or book about the life of cowboys in the western part of the USA, esp during the time of the wars with the American Indians.

westerner *n* (**a**) native or inhabitant of the West: *a country in Asia visited by few westerners.* (**b**) native or inhabitant of the western part of a country, esp the USA.

westernize, -ise /-aɪz/ *v* [Tn] make (an Eastern country, person, etc) more like one in the West, esp in ways of living and thinking, institutions, etc: *The island became fully westernized after the war.*

westernization, -isation /ˌwestənaɪˈzeɪʃn; *US* -nɪˈz-/ *n* [U].

westernmost /-məʊst/ *adj* farthest west: *the westernmost tip of the island.*

Western Australia /ˌwestən ɒˈstreɪlɪə/ state of Australia, consisting of the western part of the country; capital Perth. It has large deposits of minerals. ⇨ map at App 1.

Western Isles /ˌwestən ˈaɪlz/ **the Western Isles** island area of Scotland, consisting of the Outer Hebrides (Barra, Harris, Lewis, North Uist and South Uist). Cf HEBRIDES. ⇨ map at App 1.

Western Sahara /səˈhɑːrə/ sparsely populated region in NW Africa on the Atlantic coast, part of the Sahara Desert. It is a Moroccan protectorate. The land is extremely arid. The economy is based on the raising of camels, goats and sheep and on recently discovered mineral resources including phosphates and iron. ⇨ map at ALGERIA.

Western Samoa /ˌwestən səˈməʊə/ country in the SW Pacific Ocean consisting of nine islands; pop approx 163 000; official languages English and Samoan; capital Apia; unit of currency tālā (dollar). Formerly a German colony, after the First World War it was administered by New Zealand, and in 1962 it became independent. Its main exports are copra, bananas and cocoa. ⇨ map at POLYNESIA.

West Glamorgan /ˌwest gləˈmɔːgən/ county of S Wales, created in 1974 from part of the former county of Glamorgan. ⇨ map at App 1.

West Indies /ˌwest ˈɪndɪz/ **the West Indies** chain of about 1 200 islands enclosing the Caribbean Sea, consisting of the *Bahamas, the Greater *Antilles (Jamaica, Puerto Rico, etc), the Lesser *Antilles (Barbados, Trinidad, etc), and the *Leeward and *Windward Islands. ⇨ map. ▷ ˌ**West** ˈ**Indian** /-ˈɪndɪən/ *adj, n*: *West Indian cricket.*

Westinghouse /ˈwestɪŋhaʊs/ George (1846-1914), American engineer, inventor and manufacturer who invented compressed-air brakes for trains, electrically controlled railway signals, etc, and founded a large company to make them.

West Midlands /ˌwest ˈmɪdləndz/ county of central England, formed in 1974 from parts of Warwickshire, Worcestershire and Staffordshire and including Birmingham. ⇨ map at App 1.

Westminster /ˈwestmɪnstə(r)/ borough of central London, containing the British parliament and many British government offices. The official name of the Houses of Parliament is the (New) Palace of Westminster: (*fig*) *The resignation sent shock waves through Westminster*, ie greatly surprised British politicians, civil servants, etc. ⇨ articles at PARLIAMENT, POLITICS.

□ ˌ**Westminster** ˈ**Abbey** church in Westminster, near the Houses of Parliament. The present building, begun in 1245, replaced an earlier church built by *Edward the Confessor. Most English kings and queens have been crowned there, and many famous British people are buried there. ⇨ illus at ARCHITECTURE, GOTHIC.

West Sussex /ˌwest ˈsʌsɪks/ county of southern England, formed in 1974 from the western part of *Sussex. ⇨ map at App 1.

West Virginia /ˌwest vəˈdʒɪnɪə/ state of the eastern USA, to the west of *Virginia. It contains

the West Indies

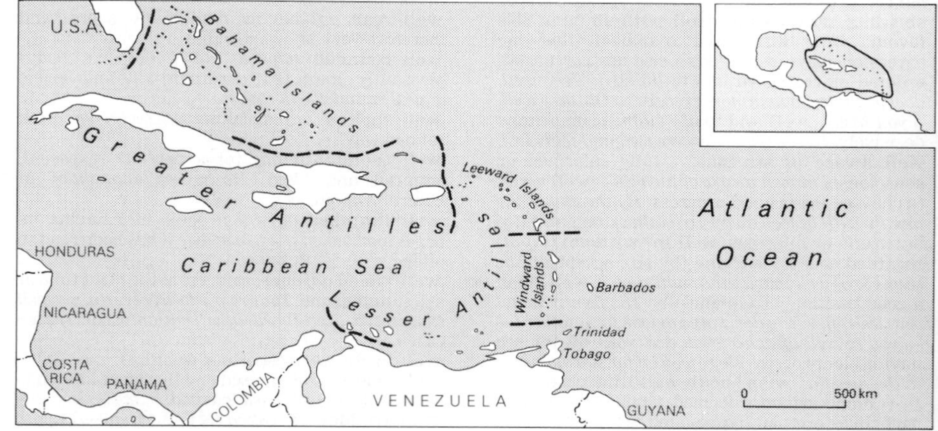

the *Allegheny mountains, from which it gets its nickname 'the Mountain State'. ⇨ map at App 1.

West Yorkshire /ˌwest ˈjɔːkʃə(r)/ county of northern England, formed in 1974 from parts of the former West Riding of Yorkshire. ⇨ map at App 1.

wet /wet/ *adj* (**-tter**, **-ttest**) **1** covered, soaked or moistened with liquid, esp water: *wet clothes, grass, roads* ○ *Her cheeks were wet with tears.* ○ *Did you get wet* (eg in the rain)? ○ *dripping/soaking/wringing* (ie thoroughly) *wet.* **2** (of weather, etc) rainy: *a wet day* ○ *the wet season* ○ *It was the wettest October for many years.* **3** (of ink, paint, plaster, etc) recently applied and not yet dry or set: *Be careful — the paint is still wet.* ○ *Don't walk on the wet cement.* **4** (*Brit infml derog*) (of a person) lacking purpose or spirit; ineffectual, indecisive or dull: *It was rather wet of you to say nothing when you had the chance.* **5** (of a country or region) where it is legal to buy or sell alcoholic drink. Cf DRY[1] 5. **6** (idm) **like a wet ˈrag** tired and bedraggled. **soaked/wet to the skin** ⇨ SKIN. **(still) ˌwet behind the ˈears** (*infml derog*) immature or inexperienced; nave. **a ˌwet ˈblanket** (*infml*) person who spoils other people's pleasure because he is gloomy, dull, pessimistic, etc: *He was such a wet blanket at the party that they never invited him again.* **ˌwet ˈthrough** thoroughly soaked: *We got wet through.* ○ *My overcoat is wet through.*

▷ **wet** *n* **1 the wet** [sing] wet weather; rain: *Come in out of the wet.* **2** [U] moisture. **3** [C] (*Brit derog*) **(a)** dull or feeble person. **(b)** politician who favours moderate rather than extreme policies: *Tory wets.*

wet *v* (**-tt-**; *pt, pp* **wet** or **wetted**) **1** [Tn] make (sth) wet; moisten (sth): *Wet the clay a bit more before you start to mould it.* **2** (idm) **wet the baby's ˈhead** (*infml*) celebrate the birth of a baby with a (usu alcoholic) drink. **wet the/one's ˈbed** (not passive; past tense usu *wet*) urinate when in bed (and asleep). **wet one's ˈwhistle** (*dated infml*) have a drink, esp an alcoholic one. **wetting** *n* (usu *sing*) instance of becoming or being made wet: *get a wetting in the heavy rain.*

wetly *adv*: *The leaves glistened wetly in the rain.* **wetness** *n* [U].

□ **ˈwetback** *n* (*US*) Mexican who enters the USA illegally, esp by swimming across the Rio Grande.

ˌwet ˈdock dock filled with water so that a ship can float in it.

ˌwet ˈdream erotic dream that causes an emission of semen.

ˈwet fish fresh uncooked fish for sale in a shop, etc.

ˈwetlands *n* [pl] marshy areas: *birds of the wetlands* ○ [attrib] *wetland birds.*

ˈwet-nurse *n* (esp formerly) woman employed to breast-feed another woman's baby.

ˈwet suit porous rubber garment worn by underwater swimmers, etc to keep warm.

wether /ˈweðə(r)/ *n* castrated ram.

we've /wiːv/ *contracted form* we have ⇨ HAVE.

whack /wæk; *US* hwæk/ *v* [Tn] (*infml*) strike or beat (sb/sth) vigorously.

▷ **whack** *n* **1** (sound of a) heavy blow: *heard a sudden whack* ○ *I'll give you such a whack!* **2** (*infml*) ~ **(at sth)** attempt: *I'm prepared to have a whack at it.* **3** (*infml*) share: *Have you all had a fair whack?* ○ *Some people are not doing their whack.* **4** (idm) **out of ˈwhack** (*infml esp US*) out of proper order, shape, etc; not working properly.

whacked *adj* [usu pred] (*infml*) (of a person) tired out; exhausted: *I'm absolutely whacked!*

whacking *n* (*infml*) beating: *That child deserves a whacking.* — *adj* (*infml*) big of its kind: *a whacking lie.* — *adv* (*infml*) very: *a whacking great bruise.*

whale /weɪl; *US* hweɪl/ *n* **1** any of several types of very large mammal that live in the sea, some of which are hunted for their oil and flesh. ⇨ illus. **2** (idm) **have a ˈwhale of a time** (*infml*) enjoy oneself very much; have a very good time: *The children had a whale of a time at the funfair.*

▷ **whale** *v* [I] (usu in the continuous tenses) hunt whales (and produce oil, etc from their carcasses).

whaler *n* **(a)** ship used for hunting whales. **(b)** person who hunts whales. **whaling** *n* [U] hunting whales: [attrib] *the whaling fleet.*

whale

5m

□ **ˈwhalebone** *n* [U] thin hard springy substance found in the upper jaw of some types of whale, used (esp formerly) for stiffening garments, eg corsets.

wham /wæm; *US* hwæm/ *interj, n* (*infml*) (imitation of the) sound of a sudden heavy blow: *Wham! The car hit the wall.* ○ *The door struck him in the face with a terrific wham.*

▷ **wham** *v* (**-mm-**) (*infml*) **(a)** [Ipr, Ip] strike sth/sb violently: *It whammed into the wall.* **(b)** [Tn, Tn·pr, Tn·p] strike (sth/sb) violently; move (sth) quickly, noisily or forcefully: *He whammed the ball into the back of the net.*

wharf /wɔːf; *US* hwɔːrf/ *n* (*pl* ~**s** or **-ves** /wɔːvz; *US* hwɔːrvz/) structure made of wood or stone at the water's edge, where ships may moor to load or unload cargo.

▷ **wharfage** /ˈwɔːfɪdʒ; *US* ˈhwɔːr-/ *n* [U] (money charged for the) use of a wharf.

wharfinger /ˈwɔːfɪndʒə(r); *US* ˈhwɔːr-/ *n* owner or manager of a wharf.

Wharton /ˈwɔːtn; *US* ˈhwɔːrtn/ Edith (1862-1937), American novelist, many of whose books satirize New York social life. They include *The House of Mirth* and *The Age of Innocence.*

what[1] /wɒt; *US* hwɒt/ *interrog det* (used to ask sb to specify one or more things, places, people, etc from an indefinite number): *What books have you got to read on the subject?* ○ *What time/date is it?* (Cf *Tell me what time it is.*) ○ *What experience has she had?* (Cf *Ask her what experience she has had.*) ○ *What woman are you thinking of?* ○ *Guess what famous person said this?* ⇨ Usage at WHICH.

▷ **what** *interrog pron* **1** (used to ask sb to specify one or more things, etc from an indefinite number): *What did you say?* ○ *What* (ie What job) *does he do?* ○ *What are you reading, sewing, thinking, etc?* ○ *What's the time/date?* ○ *What does it mean?* **2** (idm) **and ˈwhat not** (*infml*) and other things of the same type: *tools, machines and what not.* **get/give sb what ˈfor** (*infml*) be punished/punish sb severely: *I'll give her what for if she does that again.* **what for** for what purpose: *What is this tool for?* ○ (*infml*) *What did you do that for?* ie Why did you do that? **what if?** what would happen if?: *What if it rains when we can't get under shelter?* ○ *What if the rumour is true?* **what ˈof it?; so ˈwhat?** (*infml*) (used to admit that sth is true, but to question whether it is important or whether sb is going to do anything about it): *Yes, I wrote it. What of it?* **what's what** (*infml*) what things are useful, important, etc: *She certainly knows what's what.* **what with sth** (used to list various causes): *What with the weather and my bad leg, I haven't been out for weeks.*

□ **ˈwhat-d'you-call-him/-her/-it/-them** (also **ˈwhat's-his/-her/-its/-their-name**) *n* (used instead of a name that one cannot remember): *She's just gone out with old what-d'you-call-him.*

ˈwhatnot *n* **1** trivial, unknown or unspecified thing: *She'd put these whatnots in her hair as decoration.* **2** piece of furniture with shelves for small objects.

what[2] /wɒt; *US* hwɒt/ *det* the thing(s) or people) that: *What money I have will be yours when I die.* ○ *I spent what little time I had with my family.* ○ *What family and friends I still have live abroad.*

▷ **what** *pron* the thing(s) that: *What you say may well be true.* ○ *No one knows what will happen next.*

what[3] /wɒt; *US* hwɒt/ *det, adv* (used in exclamations): *What (awful) weather we're having!* ○ *What a lovely view!* ○ *What a terrible noise!* ○ *What big feet you've got!* ▷ **what** *interj* **1** (used to show disbelief or surprise): *'I've won a holiday in New York.' 'What?'* ○ *'It will cost £500.' 'What?'* **2** (*infml*) (used when one has not heard what sb has said): *What? Can you say that again?*

whatever /wɒtˈevə(r); *US* hwɒt-/ *det, pron* **1** any or every (thing): *We will be grateful for whatever amount you can afford.* ○ *You can eat whatever you like.* ○ *Whatever I have is yours.* **2** regardless of what: *Whatever nonsense the papers print, some people always believe it.* ○ *You are right, whatever opinions may be held by others.* ○ *Keep calm, whatever happens.* **3** (idm) **or whatˈever** (*infml*) or any other(s) of a similar type: *Take any sport — basketball, ice hockey, swimming or whatever.*

▷ **whatever** *interrog pron* (expressing surprise or bewilderment) what: *Whatever do you mean?* ○ *Whatever can it be?* ○ *You're going to keep snakes! Whatever next?*

whatever (also **whatsoever**) *adv* (used after *no* + *n*, *nothing*, *none*, etc for emphasis): *There can be no doubt whatever about it.* ○ *'Are there any signs of improvement?' 'None whatsoever.'*

wheat /wiːt; *US* hwiːt/ *n* [U] **1 (a)** grain from which flour (for bread, etc) is made: *a tonne of wheat* ○ [attrib] *wheat loaves.* **(b)** plant (genus *Triticum*) that produces this: *a field of wheat* ○ [attrib] *wheat farming.* ⇨ illus at CEREAL. **2** (idm) **separate the wheat from the chaff** ⇨ SEPARATE[2].

▷ **wheaten** /ˈwiːtn; *US* ˈhwiː-/ *adj* [usu attrib] made from wheat: *wheaten bread, cakes, flour.*

□ **ˈwheatcake** *n* (*US*) pancake made with whole wheat flour.

ˈwheat germ centre of the wheat grain, extracted during milling, which is a rich source of vitamins.

ˈwheatmeal *n* [U] wholemeal flour made from wheat.

wheatear /ˈwiːtɪə(r); *US* ˈhwiː-/ *n* small migratory bird of northern regions, esp one with a white belly and rump.

Wheatstone /ˈwiːtstən; *US* ˈhwiː-/ Sir Charles (1802-75), English physicist and inventor. He invented the kaleidoscope, the stereoscope and the concertina, but is best known for his electrical inventions, including the rheostat and the electric clock. He also helped to develop the electric telegraph.

□ **ˌWheatstone ˈbridge** apparatus for measuring electrical resistance, invented by Sir Charles Wheatstone.

wheedle /ˈwiːdl; *US* ˈhwiː-/ *v* (*derog*) **(a)** [I, Tn, Tn·pr] ~ **sth (out of sb)** obtain sth by being pleasant to or flattering sb: *a wheedling tone of voice* ○ *She wheedled the money out of her father.* ○ *He wheedled his way into the building*, ie got into it by wheedling. **(b)** [Tn·pr] ~ **sb into doing sth** persuade sb to do sth by being pleasant to or flattering him: *The children wheedled me into letting them go to the film.*

wheel /wiːl; *US* hwiːl/ *n* **1 (a)** disc or circular frame that turns on an axle, as on carts, cars, bicycles, etc or as part of a machine, etc: (*fig*) *keeping the wheels of government turning*, ie ensuring that it continues to operate. ⇨ illus at BICYCLE. **(b)** (esp in compounds) any of several types of machine of which a wheel is an essential part: *a potter's ˈwheel* ○ *a ˈspinning-wheel.* **2** (usu *sing*): = STEERING-WHEEL (STEER[1]): *The driver sat patiently behind the wheel.* ○ *He took* (ie grasped) *the wheel and steered the ship into port.* **3** circular movement, esp that of a line of soldiers pivoting on one end: *a left/right wheel.* **4** (idm) **at/behind the ˈwheel (of sth)** **(a)** steering (a vehicle or a ship): *Who was at the wheel when the car crashed?* **(b)** (*fig*) in control (of sth): *With her at the wheel, the company began to prosper.* **big wheel** ⇨ BIG. **oil the wheels** ⇨ OIL *v.* **put one's shoulder to the wheel** ⇨ SHOULDER. **put a spoke in sb's wheel** ⇨ SPOKE[1]. **ˌwheels within ˈwheels** situation in which a complicated or secret network of influences, motives, etc exists, making it difficult to understand fully.

▷ **wheel** *v* **1** [Tn, Tn·pr, Tn·p] **(a)** push or pull (a vehicle with wheels): *wheel a barrow (along the street).* **(b)** carry (sb/sth) in a vehicle with wheels:

wheel sb to the operating theatre on a trolley. **2** (**a**) [I, Ipr, Ip] move in a curve or circle: *birds wheeling (about) in the sky above us.* (**b**) [I, Ip] ~ (**round**/**around**) turn round and face the other way: *Left/Right wheel!* ie as an order given to soldiers ○ *They wheeled round in amazement.* **3** (idm) ˌ**wheel and** ˈ**deal** (*infml esp US*) negotiate or bargain in a clever, often dishonest, way: *There will be a lot of wheeling and dealing before an agreement is reached.*

-wheeled (forming compound *adjs*) having the specified number of wheels: *a* ˌ*sixteen-wheeled* ˈ*lorry.*

-wheeler (forming compound *ns*) vehicle with the specified number of wheels: *a* ˌ*three-*ˈ*wheeler.*

wheelie *n* (*sl*) act of riding a bicycle or motor cycle balancing on the back wheel, with the front wheel off the ground: *do a wheelie.*

wheelbarrow (also **barrow**)

□ ˈ**wheelbarrow** (also **barrow**) *n* open container for moving small loads in, with a wheel at one end, and two legs and two handles at the other.

ˈ**wheelbase** *n* (usu *sing*) distance between the front and rear axles of a motor vehicle.

ˈ**wheelchair** *n* chair with wheels, in which sb who is unable to walk can move himself or be pushed along: *She had polio as a child and spent the rest of her life in a wheelchair.*

ˈ**wheel-house** *n* small enclosed cabin on a ship where the pilot, etc stands at the wheel to steer.

ˈ**wheel-spin** *n* [U] turning of a vehicle's wheels without getting any grip, so that the vehicle does not move.

ˈ**wheelwright** *n* person who makes and repairs (esp wooden) wheels for carts, wagons, etc.

wheeler-dealer /ˌwi:lə ˈdi:lə(r); *US* ˌhwi:-/ *n* (*infml esp US*) person who is skilled at bargaining, often dishonestly.

wheeze /wi:z; *US* hwi:z/ *v* **1** [I] (**a**) breathe noisily, esp with a whistling sound in the chest (eg when suffering from asthma, bronchitis, etc). (**b**) (of a machine, pump, etc) make a similar sound. **2** [Tn] say, sing, etc (sth) while breathing noisily or with difficulty: *'I've got a sore throat,' he wheezed.*

▷ **wheeze** *n* **1** sound of wheezing: *He has a slight wheeze in his chest.* **2** (*dated Brit infml*) good idea, esp a joke or trick.

wheezy *adj* (**-ier, -iest**) making a wheezing sound: *a wheezy old man, pump* ○ *My cold's a lot better but I'm still a bit wheezy.* **wheezily** /-ɪlɪ/ *adv.* **wheeziness** *n* [U].

whelk /welk; *US* hwelk/ *n* any of several types of snail like sea animal with a spiral shell, esp one used as food.

whelp /welp; *US* hwelp/ *n* **1** young animal of the dog family; puppy or cub. **2** (*dated derog*) badly-behaved child or young man.

▷ **whelp** *v* [I] (*fml*) (of a female dog, wolf, etc) give birth.

when /wen; *US* hwen/ *interrog adv* at what time; on what occasion: *When can you come?* ○ *When did he die?* ○ *I don't know when he died.* ○ *When were you living in Spain?* ○ *Since when has he been missing?*

▷ **when** *rel adv* **1** (used after *time, day, month,* etc) at or on which: *Sunday is the day when very few people go to work.* ○ *There are times when I wonder why I do this job.* ○ *It was the sort of morning when everything goes wrong.* **2** at which time; on which occasion: *The Queen's last visit was in May, when she opened the new hospital.*

when *conj* **1** at or during the time that: *It was raining when we arrived.* ○ *When he saw her, he waved.* ○ *When visiting London I like to travel by bus.* **2** since; considering that: *How can they learn anything when they spend all their spare time watching television?*

whence /wens; *US* hwens/ *adv* (*arch or fml*) from where: *They have returned whence they came.*

whenever /wenˈevə(r); *US* hwen-/ *conj* **1** at any time, regardless of when: *I'll discuss it with you whenever you like.* **2** every time that; as often as: *Whenever she comes, she brings a friend.* ○ *The roof leaks whenever it rains.* **3** (idm) **or when**ˈ**ever** (*infml*) or at any time: *It's not urgent — we can do it next week or whenever.*

▷ **whenever** *interrog adv* (expressing surprise) when: *Whenever did you find time to do all that cooking?*

where /weə(r); *US* hweə(r)/ *interrog adv* in or to what place or position: *Where does he live?* ○ *Where does she come from?* ○ *I wonder where she comes from.* ○ *Where* (ie At what point) *did I go wrong in my calculation?* ○ *Where are you going for your holidays?* ○ *Where is all this leading?* ie What is the conclusion of what you are saying?

▷ **where** *rel adv* **1** (used after words or phrases that refer to a place) at, in, or to which (place): *the place where you last saw it* ○ *one of the few countries where people drive on the left.* **2** at which place: *We then moved to Paris, where we lived for six years.*

where *conj* (in) the place in which: *Put it where we can all see it.* ○ *Where food is hard to find, few birds remain throughout the year.* ○ (*fig*) *That's where you're wrong.*

□ ˈ**whereabouts** *interrog adv* in or near what place; where: *Whereabouts did you find it?* ○ *She won't tell me whereabouts she put it.* — *n* [sing or pl *v*] place where sb/sth is: *a person whose whereabouts is/are unknown.*

whereˈ**by** *rel adv* (*fml*) by which: *She devised a plan whereby they might escape.*

whereˈ**in** *rel adv* (*fml*) in which; in what; in what respect: *a dark forest wherein dangers lurk.*

whereuˈ**pon** *conj* after which; and then: *She laughed at him, whereupon he walked out.*

whereas /ˌweərˈæz; *US* ˌhweərˈæz/ *conj* **1** (*esp law*) taking into consideration the fact that. **2** (*fml*) but in contrast; while: *He earns £8 000 a year whereas she gets at least £20 000.*

wherever /ˌweərˈevə(r); *US* ˌhweər-/ *conj* **1** in any place, regardless of where: *Sit wherever you like.* ○ *I'll find him, wherever he is.* ○ *He comes from Boula, wherever that may be,* ie and I don't know where that is. **2** in all places that; everywhere: *Wherever she goes, there are crowds of people waiting to see her.* ○ *Wherever there is injustice, we try to help.* **3** (idm) **or wher**ˈ**ever** (*infml*) or any (other) place: *many foreign tourists from Spain, France or wherever.*

▷ **wherever** *interrog adv* (expressing surprise) where: *Wherever did you get that funny hat?*

wherewithal /ˈweəwɪðɔ:l; *US* ˈhweər-/ *n* **the wherewithal** [sing] (*rhet or joc*) the money needed for sth: *I'd like a new stereo, but I haven't got the wherewithal (to buy it).*

whet /wet; *US* hwet/ *v* (**-tt-**) [Tn] **1** (*fml*) sharpen (the blade of a knife, an axe, etc), esp by rubbing with a stone. **2** excite or stimulate (one's appetite, desire, interest, etc): *Reading travel brochures whets one's appetite for a holiday.*

□ ˈ**whetstone** *n* shaped stone used for sharpening tools, eg chisels, scythes, etc.

whether /ˈweðə(r); *US* ˈhweðər/ *conj* **1** (used before a clause or an infinitive expressing or implying alternatives) (**a**) (used as the object of *vs* like *know, doubt, wonder,* etc): *I don't know whether I will be able to come.* ○ *We'll be told tomorrow whether we should take the exam or not.* ○ *I asked him whether he had done all the work himself or whether he had had any assistance.* (Note that when there are two alternative clauses separated by *or, whether* is repeated.) ○ *We were wondering whether to go today or tomorrow.* Cf IF. (**b**) (after *adjs* and *preps*): *She was undecided (about) whether she should accept his offer.* ○ *He hesitated about whether to drive or take the train.* ○ *It all depends on whether she likes the boss or not.* (**c**) (used as the subject or complement of a sentence): *It's doubtful whether there'll be any seats left.* ○ *The question is whether to go to Munich or Vienna.* **2** (idm) **whether or not** (used to introduce two alternative possibilities): *Whether or not it rains/Whether it rains or not, we're playing football on Saturday.* ○ *Tell me whether or not you're interested.* ○ *They'll find out who did it, whether you tell them or not.* ⇨ Usage at IF.

whew (also **phew**) /fju:/ *interj* (used as the written form of any of various sounds made by breathing out strongly or whistling to express amazement, relief, exhaustion or dismay): *Whew! That car was going fast!* ○ *Whew! That was a lucky escape!*

whey /weɪ; *US* hweɪ/ *n* [U] watery liquid that remains after sour milk has formed curds.

which /wɪtʃ; *US* hwɪtʃ/ *interrog det* (used to ask sb to specify one or more people or things from a limited number): *Which way is quicker — by bus or by train?* ○ *Which Mr Smith do you mean — the one who teaches history or the one who teaches music?* ○ *Which languages did you study at school?* ○ *Ask him which platform the London train leaves from.* Cf. WHAT[1], ⇨ Usage.

▷ **which** *interrog pron* which person or thing (from a limited number): *Which is your favourite subject?* ○ *Which of the boys is tallest?* ○ *Here are the chairs. Tell me which are worth buying.* ○ *The twins are so much alike that I can't tell which is which,* ie can't distinguish one from the other.

which *rel det* (*fml*) (used to refer back to the preceding *n* or statement): *The questions were all on opera, about which subject I know nothing.* ○ *The postman comes at 6.30 in the morning, at which time* (ie when) *I am usually fast asleep.*

which *rel pron* (used to refer to sth previously mentioned): *Take the book which is lying on the table.* ○ *A house which overlooks the park will cost more.* ○ *Read the passage to which I referred in my talk.* ○ *His best film, which won several awards, was about the life of Gandhi.* ○ *His new car, for which he paid £7 000, has already had to be repaired.*

NOTE ON USAGE: Compare the use of **which** and **what** as determiners and pronouns in questions. **Which** refers to one or more members of a limited group: *Which car is yours/Which is your car? The Ford or the Volvo?* **What** is used when the group is not so limited: *What are your favourite books?* When we are referring to people, we often use **which** even if the choice is not restricted: *Which/What actors do you admire most?*

whichever /wɪtʃˈevə(r); *US* hwɪtʃ-/ *det, pron* **1** the person or thing which: *Take whichever hat suits you best.* ○ *We'll eat at whichever restaurant has a free table.* ○ *Whichever of you comes first will receive a prize.* **2** regardless of which: *Whichever you buy, there is a six-month guarantee.* ○ *It takes three hours, whichever route you take.*

▷ **whichever** *interrog det, interrog pron* (expressing surprise) which: *Whichever of these children is yours?*

whiff /wɪf; *US* hwɪf/ *n* ~ (**of sth**) (**a**) faint smell or puff of air or smoke: *catch a whiff of perfume, of cigar smoke* ○ *have a whiff of fresh air* ○ (*fig*) *a whiff* (ie a trace or hint) *of danger, scandal, suspicion.* (**b**) small amount breathed in: *a whiff of anaesthetic* ○ *He took a few whiffs,* ie of a cigar, pipe, etc. (**c**) (*infml euph*) bad smell: *There is an awful whiff coming from the dustbin.*

Whig /wɪg; *US* hwɪg/ *n* **1** member or supporter of a British political party between the late 17th and the mid 19th centuries which was in favour of the power of parliament (as against that of the king), supported the *Hanoverian kings (as against the deposed *Stuarts), and favoured a strong foreign policy and religious toleration. Whigs were mainly country landowners or rich merchants. They were in power for the first half of the 18th century. In the early 19th century they supported the constitutional reforms contained in the 1832 Reform Act, and in the middle of the century they gradually changed into the *Liberal Party. Cf TORY. **2** member of a US political party of 1834-56, succeeded by the *Republican Party. ⇨ article at POLITICS.

while[1] /waɪl; *US* hwaɪl/ *n* [sing] **1** (period of) time: *She worked in a bank for a while before studying law.* ○ *For a long while we had no news of him.* ○ *I'll be back in a little while*, ie soon. ○ *It took quite a while* (ie a long time) *to find a hotel.* ○ *We waited for three hours, all the while hoping that someone would come and fetch us.* **2** (idm) **once in a while** ⇨ ONCE. **worth sb's while** ⇨ WORTH.

▷ **while** *v* (phr v) **while sth away** pass (a period of time) in a leisurely way: *We whiled away the time at the airport reading magazines.* ○ *It's easy to while a few hours away in a museum.*

while[2] /waɪl; *US* hwaɪl/ (also **whilst** /waɪlst; *US* hwaɪlst/) *conj* **1 (a)** during the time that; when: *He fell asleep while (he was) doing his homework.* ○ *While I was in Madrid there was a carnival.* ○ *While (locked up) in prison, she wrote her first novel.* **(b)** at the same time as: *While Mary was writing a letter, the children were playing outside.* ○ *He listens to the radio while driving to work.* ○ *I lived in a hostel while I was a student.* **2** (used to show a contrast): *I drink black coffee while he prefers it with cream.* ○ *English is understood all over the world while Turkish is spoken by only a few people outside Turkey itself.* **3** (*fml*) although: *While I admit that there are problems, I don't agree that they cannot be solved.*

whim /wɪm; *US* hwɪm/ *n* sudden desire or idea, esp an unusual or unreasonable one; caprice: *It's only a passing whim*, ie one that will soon be forgotten. ○ *They seem ready to indulge* (ie satisfy) *his every whim.*

whimper /ˈwɪmpə(r); *US* ˈhwɪ-/ *v* **1** [I] (of a dog, person, etc) whine or cry softly, esp with fear or pain. **2** [Tn] say (sth) in this way: *'Please don't leave me alone,' he whimpered.* ⇨ Usage at CRY[1].

▷ **whimper** *n* whimpering cry; low sobbing sound.

whimsy /ˈwɪmzɪ; *US* ˈhwɪ-/ *n* **1** [U] odd or playful behaviour or humour: *His speech was full of whimsy.* ○ *'Why did you do it?' 'I don't know, pure whimsy.'* **2** [C] fanciful idea or desire; whim: *one of her bizarre whimsies.*

▷ **whimsical** /ˈwɪmzɪkl; *US* ˈhwɪ-/ *adj* full of whimsy; fanciful, playful or capricious: *a whimsical sense of humour* ○ *a whimsical story for children.* **whimsicality** /ˌwɪmzɪˈkælətɪ; *US* ˌhwɪ-/ *n* [U]. **whimsically** /-klɪ/ *adv.*

whin /wɪn; *US* hwɪn/ *n* [U] = GORSE.

whine /waɪn; *US* hwaɪn/ *n* (usu *sing*) **(a)** long high-pitched complaining cry, esp one made by a dog or child. **(b)** similar high-pitched (esp irritating) sound made by a siren, motor-cycle engine, etc: *the steady whine of a mechanical saw.*

▷ **whine** *v* **1** [I, It] make a whine: *a whining voice* ○ *The dog sat outside the door whining (to be let in).* **2 (a)** [I, Ipr] (*derog*) complain, esp about trivial things: *Do stop whining!* ○ *What is that child whining about now?* **(b)** [Tn] (*derog*) say (sth) in a pleading or complaining voice: *'I want to go home,' he whined.* **whiner** *n* animal or person that whines.

whinge /wɪndʒ; *US* hwɪndʒ/ *v* [I] (*infml derog*) complain or grumble, esp annoyingly in a whining voice. ▷ **whinger** *n.*

whinny /ˈwɪnɪ; *US* ˈhwɪ-/ *n* gentle neighing sound.

▷ **whinny** *v* (*pt, pp* **whinnied**) [I, Ipr] make this sound: *The horse whinnied with pleasure.*

whip

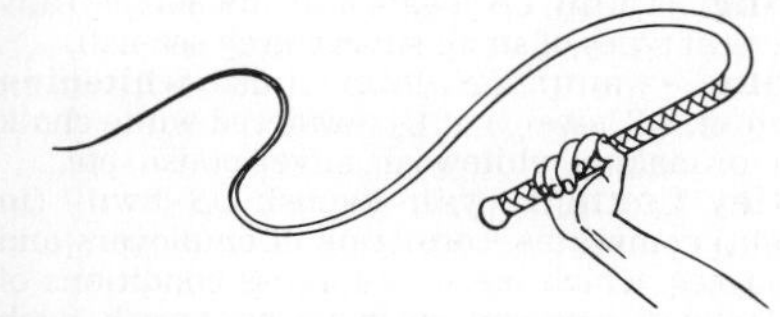

whip[1] /wɪp; *US* hwɪp/ *n* **1** [C] length of cord or strip of leather fastened to a handle, used esp for urging on an animal (esp a horse) or for striking a person or an animal as a punishment. Cf HORSEWHIP (HORSE). **2** [C] **(a)** (in Britain and the USA) official of a political party who has the authority to maintain discipline among its members, esp to make them attend and vote in important government debates: *the government chief whip.* **(b)** instructions given by this official: *a ˌthree-line* (ie very urgent) *ˈwhip.* **3** [C] = WHIPPER-IN. **4** [C, U] dish of whipped cream, eggs, etc with fruit or other flavouring: *caramel, chocolate, strawberry, etc whip.* **5** (idm) **a fair crack of the whip** ⇨ FAIR[1]. **get, have, hold, etc the ˈwhip hand (over sb)** be in a position where one has power or control (over sb): *Their opponents had the whip hand and it was useless to resist.*

▷ **whippy** *adj* flexible; springy: *a whippy cane.*

□ **ˈwhipcord** *n* [U] **1** type of strong, tightly twisted cord used for making whips, etc. **2** type of hard-wearing worsted fabric.

ˈwhiplash *n* lash of a whip. **ˈwhiplash injury** injury to the neck caused by a sudden jerk of the head (as in a collision).

whip[2] /wɪp; *US* hwɪp/ *v* (**-pp-**) **1** [Tn] strike (a person or an animal) with a whip, esp as a punishment: *The culprit will be whipped when he is found.* **2** [Tn, Tn·pr, Tn·p] ~ **sth (up) (into sth)** stir (eggs, cream, etc) rapidly with a fork or some other instrument in order to make a stiff light mass: *coffee with whipped cream* ○ *Whip the ingredients (up) into a smooth paste.* **3** [Tn] (*Brit infml*) steal (sth): *Who's whipped my umbrella?* **4** [Ipr, Ip, Tn·pr, Tn·p] (cause sb/sth to) move rapidly or suddenly in the direction specified: *The thief whipped round the corner and out of sight.* ○ *She whipped round just as he was about to attack her from behind.* ○ *The branch whipped back and hit me in the face.* ○ *The intruder whipped out a knife (from his pocket).* ○ *The wind whipped several slates off (the roof).* ○ *The star was whipped into a fast car and driven off.* **5** [Tn] **(a)** sew (a seam, piece of cloth, etc) with stitches that pass over the edge, esp in order to prevent fraying. **(b)** bind (a stitch, the end of a rope, etc) with a close tight covering of thread or string. **6** (phr v) **whip sb/sth on** drive sb to go faster, work harder, etc; make (an animal) go faster by striking it with a whip. **whip sth/sb up (a)** create (excitement, enthusiasm, etc) in people or cause (people) to be enthusiastic, etc; arouse: *They're trying to whip up support for their candidate.* ○ *The people were whipped up into a frenzy by the speaker.* **(b)** (*infml*) prepare (a meal, etc) very quickly: *I can easily whip you up some scrambled eggs.*

▷ **whipping** *n* [C, U] (instance of) being beaten with a whip as a punishment. **ˈwhipping-boy** *n* person who is regularly made to take the blame and punishment for the faults of others; scapegoat: *I am tired of being used as the whipping-boy for all the mistakes that are made in the office.* **ˈwhipping cream** cream that is suitable for whipping (WHIP[2] 2).

□ **ˈwhip-round** *n* (*Brit infml*) appeal for contributions from a group of people: *a whip-round for (a Christmas present for) the office cleaners.*

whipper-in /ˌwɪpər ˈɪn; *US* hw-/ *n* (*pl* ~**s-in**) (also **whip**) person responsible for controlling the hounds during a hunt.

whipper-snapper /ˈwɪpə snæpə(r); *US* ˈhwɪ-/ *n* (*dated infml derog*) young and unimportant person who behaves in a cheeky or over-confident way.

whippet /ˈwɪpɪt; *US* ˈhw-/ *n* small thin dog similar to a greyhound, often used for racing. ⇨ article at ANIMAL.

whirl /wɜːl; *US* hw-/ *v* **1** [I, Ipr, Ip, Tn, Tn·pr, Tn·p] (cause sb/sth to) move quickly round and round: *the whirling blades of the fan* ○ *The leaves whirled (round) as they fell.* ○ *The wind whirled (up) the fallen leaves.* ○ *She whirled the rope round and round (her head).* ○ *He whirled his partner round the dance floor.* **2** [Ipr, Ip, Tn·pr, Tn·p] (cause sb/sth to) move or travel rapidly (in the specified direction): *The houses whirled past us as the train gathered speed.* ○ *He whirled them away/off in his new sports car.* **3** [I] (of the brain, senses, etc) seem to go round and round, so that one feels confused or excited; reel: *I couldn't sleep: my mind was still whirling from all I had seen and heard.*

▷ **whirl** *n* [sing] **1** whirling movement: *the whirl of the propeller blades.* **2** rapid succession of activities: *an endless whirl of parties* ○ *the social whirl.* **3** state of confusion: *My mind is in a whirl.* **4** (idm) **give sth a ˈwhirl** (*infml*) try sth as an experiment, to see if it is suitable, pleasant, etc: *The job doesn't sound very exciting but I'll give it a whirl.*

□ **ˈwhirlpool** *n* place in a river or the sea where there are whirling currents; circular eddy.

ˈwhirlwind *n* **1** funnel-shaped column of swiftly circulating air: [attrib] (*fig*) *a whirlwind* (ie very rapid) *affair/courtship/romance.* **2** (idm) **reap the whirlwind** ⇨ REAP.

whirligig /ˈwɜːlɪgɪg; *US* ˈhw-/ *n* **1** any of several types of spinning or whirling toy, esp a top. **2** = ROUNDABOUT 1.

whirr (also *esp US* **whir**) /wɜː(r); *US* hw-/ *n* (usu *sing*) continuous rapid buzzing or vibrating sound: *the whirr of a fan, motor, propeller.*

▷ **whirr** (also *esp US* **whir**) *v* [I] make this sound: *The bird flew past, its wings whirring.*

whisk /wɪsk; *US* hw-/ *n* **1** device (usu made of coiled wire) for whipping eggs, cream, etc. ⇨ illus at KITCHEN. **2** small brush made from a bunch of grass, twigs, bristles, etc tied to a handle: *a ˈfly-whisk.* **3** quick light brushing movement (eg of a horse's tail).

▷ **whisk** *v* **1** [Tn] move (sth) quickly through the air with a light sweeping movement: *The horse whisked its tail angrily.* **2** [Tn] beat (eggs, etc) into a froth; whip. **3** (phr v) **whisk sth away/off** brush sth quickly and lightly away as if with a whisk: *whisk the flies away.* **whisk (sb/sth) away, off, etc** go or take (sb/sth) away quickly and suddenly: *The waiter whisked away the food before we had finished.* ○ *She (was) whisked up to the top floor in the lift.*

whisker /ˈwɪskə(r); *US* ˈhwɪ-/ *n* **1 whiskers** [pl] long hair growing on a man's face. Cf BEARD[1] a, MOUSTACHE 1. **2** [C] any of the long stiff hairs that grow near the mouth of a cat, rat, etc. **3** (idm) **be the cat's whiskers/pyjamas** ⇨ CAT[1]. **by a ˈwhisker** by a very small amount or margin: *She missed the first prize by a whisker.*

▷ **whiskered** /ˈwɪskəd; *US* ˈhw-/, **whiskery** /ˈwɪskərɪ; *US* ˈhw-/ *adjs* having whiskers.

whisky (*Brit*) (*US or Irish* **whiskey**) /ˈwɪskɪ; *US* ˈhwɪ-/ *n* **(a)** [U] strong alcoholic drink distilled from malted grain (esp barley or rye): *a bottle of whisky.* **(b)** [C] type of this: *This is a very good whisky.* **(c)** [C] glass of this: *Two whiskies, please.*

whisper /ˈwɪspə(r); *US* ˈhwɪ-/ *v* **1 (a)** [I] speak softly, using the breath but without vibrating the vocal cords: *Why are you whispering?* **(b)** [I, Ipr, Tn, Tn·pr, Tf, Dn·pr, Dpr·f, Dpr·t] ~ **(about sb/sth)**; ~ **sth (to sb)** talk or say sth in this way, esp privately or secretly: *Don't you know it's rude to whisper?* ○ *He whispered a word in my ear.* ○ *'I feel very afraid,' she whispered.* ○ *She whispered (to me) that she felt very afraid.* ○ *It is whispered* (ie There is a rumour) *that he is heavily in debt.* **2** [I] (of leaves, the wind, etc) make soft sounds; rustle: *The wind was whispering in the trees.*

▷ **whisper** *n* **1** whispering sound, speech or remark: *He spoke in a whisper.* **2** rumour: *I've heard whispers that the firm is likely to go bankrupt.*

□ **ˈwhispering campaign** attack made on sb's reputation by passing malicious statements about him from person to person.

whist /wɪst; *US* hwɪst/ *n* [U] card-game for two pairs of players, similar to bridge[2].

□ **ˈwhist drive** series of games of whist played by several sets of partners at different tables, with certain players moving after each round to the next table.

whistle /ˈwɪsl; *US* ˈhwɪ-/ *n* **1 (a)** clear shrill sound made by forcing breath through a small hole between partly closed lips: (*fig*) *the whistle of a steam engine.* **(b)** similar tuneful sound made by a bird: *the blackbird's whistle.* **2** instrument used to produce a clear shrill sound, esp as a signal: *The referee blew his whistle.* **3** (idm) **blow the whistle on sb/sth** ⇨ BLOW[1]. **clean as a whistle** ⇨ CLEAN[1]. **wet one's whistle** ⇨ WET *v*.

▷ **whistle** *v* **1** (**a**) [I, Ipr, Ip] make the sound of a whistle: *The boy was whistling (away) cheerfully.* ○ *A train whistled in the distance.* ○ *The wind whistled through a crack in the door.* (**b**) [Tn] produce (a tune) in this way: *He whistled a happy tune as he walked along.* (**c**) [Ipr, Tn·pr, Tn·p, Dn·pr, Dpr·t] make a signal to (sb/sth) in this way: *She whistled her dog back.* ○ *She whistled for her dog.* ○ *He whistled to his friend to keep hidden.* **2** [I, Ipr, Ip] move swiftly with a noise like a whistle: *A bullet whistled past his head.* **3** (idm) **whistle in the ˈdark** try to overcome one's fear in a frightening or dangerous situation. **4** (phr v) **whistle for sth** (*infml*) wish for or expect sth in vain: *If he wants his money now he'll have to whistle for it, I'm afraid.*

□ **ˈwhistle-stop** *n* (**a**) (*US*) small railway station where trains stop only when signalled to do so. (**b**) (*fig*) short stop made by a politician during an election campaign: [attrib] *on a whistle-stop tour of the country.*

ˌwhistling ˈkettle kettle with a whistle on its spout, sounded by the steam when the water in the kettle boils.

James Whistler: Nocturne in Blue and Gold; Old Battersea Bridge

Whistler /ˈwɪslə(r); *US* ˈhwɪs-/ James Abbott McNeill (1834-1903), American-born artist who lived mainly in England. He is best known for his landscapes, particularly views of the River Thames, which are concerned more with the relationship between muted colours and tones than with the representation of scenes. He also painted a famous portrait of his mother. He was greatly influenced by Oriental art. ⇨ illus.

Whit /wɪt; *US* hwɪt/ *n* [U, often attrib] = WHITSUN: *the Whit weekend.*

□ **ˌWhit ˈSunday** the seventh Sunday after Easter; Pentecost.

whit /wɪt; *US* hwɪt/ *n* [sing] (usu in negative sentences) the smallest amount: *I don't care a whit* (ie in the least) *whether she stays or not.* ○ *I've read the report but I'm no whit the wiser*, ie I don't understand it at all.

Whitaker's Almanack /ˌwɪtɪkəz ˈɔːlmənæk; *US* ˌhwɪtɪkəz ˈælmənæk/ British reference book, published every year, containing a wide range of information and statistics about Britain and other countries: *You're sure to find it in Whitaker('s Almanack).*

White[1] /waɪt; *US* hwaɪt/ Gilbert (1720-93), English clergyman and naturalist who wrote the *Natural History of Selborne*, observations of animal life around Selborne in Hampshire.

White[2] /waɪt; *US* hwaɪt/ Patrick Victor Martindale (1912-90), Australian novelist whose best-known work is *Voss*, the story of an expedition across Australia. Other books include *The Tree of Man* and *A Fringe of Leaves*. He was awarded the Nobel prize for literature in 1973.

white[1] /waɪt; *US* hwaɪt/ *adj* (**-r**, **-st**) **1** of the very palest colour, like fresh snow, common salt or milk: *walls painted white* ○ *strong white teeth* ○ *Her hair has turned white*, eg with age. ○ *I like my coffee white*, ie with milk or cream in it. Cf BLACK[1].

📖 White is traditionally worn by the bride at a wedding (called a 'white wedding'). In sport 'whites' refers to the clothes worn by cricketers (white shirt, trousers, boots), tennis players (white shirt, shorts or skirt, socks, shoes), or bowls players (white shirt or blouse, trousers or skirt, shoes).

2 of a pale-skinned race. **3** ~ (**with sth**) (of a person) pale as a result of emotion or illness: *He was white with fury.* **4** (idm) (**in**) **black and white** ⇨ BLACK[2]. **bleed sb white** ⇨ BLEED. **show the white feather** ⇨ SHOW[2]. (**as**) **ˌwhite as a ˈsheet** very pale, esp as a result of fear or shock: *She went as white as a sheet when she heard the news.* (**as**) **white as ˈsnow** very white: *an old man with hair as white as snow.* **a white elephant** possession that is useless and often expensive to maintain.

▷ **white** *v* [Tn] (idm) **a whited ˈsepulchre** (*fml*) person who seems to be good, but is really evil; hypocrite.

whiten /ˈwaɪtn; *US* ˈhwaɪ-/ *v* [I, Tn] (cause sth to) become white or whiter: *whiten one's tennis shoes.* **whiteness** *n* [U].

whitish *adj* tending towards white; fairly white: *a whitish blue* ○ *a whitish dress.*

□ **ˈwhite ant** = TERMITE.

ˈwhitebait *n* [U] young herrings, sprats or other small silvery white fish that are eaten whole as food.

ˈwhite cell, **ˌwhite ˈcorpuscle** any of the cells in the blood that fight infection; leucocyte. Cf RED CORPUSCLE (RED[1]).

ˌwhite ˈChristmas Christmas during which snow falls. Such Christmases are rare in Britain in the late 20th century.

ˌwhite ˈcoffee coffee with milk or cream added.

ˌwhite-ˈcollar *adj* [usu attrib] (of a job, worker, etc) not manual. Cf BLUE-COLLAR (BLUE[1]).

ˌwhite ˈdwarf small, very dense, faint star. Cf RED GIANT (RED[1]).

ˌwhite ˈensign flag flown by ships of the British navy. Cf RED ENSIGN (RED[1]).

ˌwhite ˈflag symbol of surrender.

ˌWhite ˈFriar member of the *Carmelite order of friars, who wear white clothes.

ˌwhite ˈgold pale metal consisting of gold mixed with another metal (eg platinum or nickel).

ˌwhite ˈheat high temperature at which metal looks white.

ˌwhite ˈhorses waves in the sea with white crests on them.

ˌwhite ˈhope (*infml*) person who is expected to bring success to a team, group, etc: *He was once the great white hope of the Labour Party.*

ˌwhite-ˈhot *adj* at white heat; extremely hot.

the ˈWhite House (**a**) the official residence (in Washington DC) of the President of the USA. (**b**) the US President and his advisers: *The White House has denied the report.*

ˌwhite ˈlead poisonous compound of lead carbonate, used as a pigment.

ˌwhite ˈlie harmless or trivial lie, esp one told in order to avoid hurting sb.

ˈwhite man (*fem* **ˈwhite woman**) member of a pale-skinned race; Caucasian: *remote areas where no white man had ever been.*

ˈwhite meat (**a**) poultry, veal or pork. (**b**) meat from the breast of a cooked chicken or other bird. Cf DARK MEAT (DARK[2]), RED MEAT (RED[2]).

ˌwhite ˈnoise noise that contains many frequencies with approximately equal energies.

ˈwhite-out *n* **1** weather condition in polar regions in which one cannot see clearly because of heavy cloud or fog and snow-covered ground. **2** heavy snowstorm; blizzard.

ˌWhite ˈPaper (*Brit*) report published by the government about its policy on a matter that is to be considered by Parliament. Cf GREEN PAPER (GREEN[1]).

ˌwhite ˈpepper pepper made by grinding peppercorns after the husks have been removed.

ˌwhite ˈsauce sauce made from butter, flour and milk: *Add cheese to the white sauce.*

ˌwhite ˈslave woman forced into becoming a prostitute, esp in a foreign country: [attrib] *the white-ˈslave trade/traffic.* **ˌwhite ˈslavery**.

ˌwhite ˈspirit (*esp Brit*) light petroleum used as a paint solvent or cleaning substance: *remove paint from the brushes with white spirit.*

ˌwhite ˈtie (man's white bow-tie worn as part of) full formal evening dress: [attrib] *Is it a white-tie affair?*

ˈwhitewash *n* **1** [U] powdered lime or chalk mixed with water, used for painting. **2** [C, U] (*fig*) (process of) hiding sb's errors, faults, etc: *The opposition dismissed the report as a whitewash.* — *v* [Tn] **1** put whitewash on (a wall, etc): *whitewash the outside of the cottage.* **2** try to make (sb, sb's reputation, etc) appear blameless by hiding errors, faults, etc.

ˌwhite ˈwedding wedding at which the bride wears a white dress, esp one that takes place in a church. ⇨ article at WEDDING.

ˌwhite ˈwine wine that is very pale yellow, amber or golden. Cf RED WINE (RED[1]), ROSÉ.

white[2] /waɪt; *US* hwaɪt/ *n* **1** [U] white colour or pigment: *Mix some more white in to make the paint paler.* **2** (**a**) [U] white clothes or material: *dressed all in white.* (**b**) **whites** [pl] white clothes, esp as worn for sports: *tennis whites* ○ *It's unwise to wash whites with coloureds*, ie coloured clothes. **3** [C, U] transparent substance that surrounds the yolk of an egg and becomes white when cooked: *Use the whites of two eggs/two egg whites.* ⇨ illus at EGG. **4** [C] white-skinned person; Caucasian. **5** [C] white part of the eye-ball: *The whites of her eyes are bloodshot.* **6** [C] white ball in snooker or billiards: *He potted the white by mistake.* **7** [sing] player with the white pieces in chess or draughts: *It's white's move.* **8** (idm) **black and white** ⇨ BLACK[2].

Whitehall /ˈwaɪthɔːl; *US* ˈhwaɪ-/ *n* (**a**) [U] street in London where there are many government offices: *Rumours are circulating in Whitehall.* (**b**) [Gp] the British government: *Whitehall is/are refusing to confirm the reports.*

□ **the ˌWhitehall ˈTheatre** theatre in the *West End of London, famous for a series of farces produced there in the 1950s and 1960s.

Whitehead /ˈwaɪthed; *US* ˈhwaɪt-/ Alfred North (1861-1947), English philosopher and mathematician, best known for the book *Principia Mathematica*, which he wrote with Bertrand *Russell. He helped to found mathematical logic.

White Sea /ˌwaɪt ˈsiː; *US* ˌhwaɪt/ **the White Sea** large inlet of the *Arctic Ocean on the north-west coast of Russia. The naval base of Archangel is on its shore.

whither /ˈwɪðə(r); *US* ˈhwɪ-/ *adv* (*arch or rhet*) to what place or state: *Whither goest thou?* ○ *Whither* (ie What is the likely future of) *the shipping industry?*

whiting[1] /ˈwaɪtɪŋ; *US* ˈhwaɪ-/ *n* (*pl* unchanged) any of several types of small silvery-grey sea-fish.

whiting[2] /ˈwaɪtɪŋ; *US* ˈhwaɪ-/ (also **whitening** /ˈwaɪtnɪŋ; *US* ˈhwaɪ-/) *n* [U] powdered white chalk used for making whitewash, silver polish, etc.

Whitley Council /ˌwɪtlɪ ˈkaʊnsl; *US* ˌhwɪt-/ (in Britain) committee, consisting of employers and employees, which meets to discuss conditions of employment, payment, etc in places of work. Such committees operate at national and local level.

whitlow /ˈwɪtləʊ; *US* ˈhwɪ-/ *n* small painfully inflamed place on a finger or toe, esp near a nail.

Whitman /ˈwɪtmən; *US* ˈhwɪt-/ Walt (1819-92), American poet whose work deals with issues such as freedom, friendship and sexuality. His best-known collection of poems is *Leaves of Grass*. Much of his verse was set to music by various composers in the early 20th century.

Whitsun /ˈwɪtsn; *US* ˈhwɪ-/ (also **Whit** /wɪt; *US* hwɪt/) *n* Whit Sunday and the days close to it.

□ ˈ**Whitsuntide** /-taɪd/ *n* = WHITSUN.

Whittington /ˈwɪtɪŋtən; *US* ˈhwɪt-/ Sir Richard (died 1423), Lord Mayor of London 1397-98, 1406-07, 1419-20. The story of how he came to London as a poor boy with his cat, and was about to leave when the church bells told him to stay, became the subject of a popular English pantomime called *Dick Whittington*.

Whittle /ˈwɪtl; *US* ˈhwɪtl/ Sir Frank (1907-), British engineer who invented the jet engine in 1930. He continued to work on its development, and the first jet aircraft using his engine flew in 1941.

whittle /ˈwɪtl; *US* ˈhwɪ-/ *v* **1** (**a**) [Ipr, Tn] ~ (**at**) **sth** cut thin slices or strips off (wood, etc). (**b**) [Tn, Tn·pr] ~ **A** (**from B**); ~ **B** (**into A**) make or shape (sth) by doing this: *whittling a tent-peg from a branch/a branch into a tent-peg.* **2** (phr v) **whittle sth away** gradually remove or decrease sth: *Inflation has whittled away their savings.* **whittle sth down** (**a**) make sth thinner by cutting off fine slices with a knife. (**b**) reduce the size of sth gradually: *The number of employees is being whittled down in order to reduce costs.*

whiz /wɪz; *US* hwɪz/ *v* (**-zz-**) [I, Ipr, Ip] (**a**) make a sound like that of an object moving very fast through the air: *A bullet whizzed past my ear.* (**b**) (*infml*) move very fast: *whizzing along (the motorway).*

NOTE ON USAGE: Compare **zoom**, **whiz**, **zip**, **shoot**, **dart**, and **nip. Zoom** and **whiz** are both informal and indicate the rapid noisy movement of a vehicle, etc. **Zoom** suggests a low engine noise; **whiz** suggests a high whistling sound: *The jet zoomed low over the houses, frightening everyone.* ○ *A bullet whizzed past my ear.* **Zip** also describes a vehicle moving fast but does not suggest noise. It can refer to people getting through a task or a process quickly: *These new trains really zip along.* ○ *We were lucky — we just zipped through customs.* **Shoot** and **dart** indicate the sudden rapid movement of a person, an animal or a thing: *A car suddenly shot out of a side road and nearly hit me.* ○ *The boy suddenly darted across the road in front of the bus.* **Nip** is informal, indicating someone hurrying somewhere for a short time and for a particular purpose: *I must nip round to the shops for some milk.*

whiz-kid /ˈwɪzkɪd; *US* ˈhwɪz-/ *n* (*infml sometimes derog*) person who becomes successful very quickly: *The new manager is a real whiz-kid.*

WHO /ˌdʌblju: eɪtʃ ˈəʊ/ *abbr* World Health Organization.

who /hu:/ *interrog pron* **1** (used as the subject of a *v* to ask about the name, identity or function of one or more people): *Who is the woman in the black hat?* ○ *I wonder who phoned this morning.* ○ *Who are the men in white coats?* ○ *Do you know who broke the window?* **2** (*infml*) (used as the object of a *v* or *prep*): *Who did you see at church?* ○ *Who are you phoning?* ○ *Who shall I give it to?* ○ *Who is the money for?* **3** (idm) **who am ˈI, are ˈyou, is ˈshe, etc, to do sth?** what right, authority, etc have I, etc to do sth: *Who are you to tell me I can't leave my bicycle here? It's not your house.* (**know, learn, etc**) **who's ˈwho** (be informed about) people's names, jobs, status, etc: *You'll soon find out who's who in this department.*

▷ **who** *rel pron* **1** (**a**) (in clauses which define the preceding *n*): *the man/men who wanted to meet you* ○ *The people who called yesterday want to buy the house.* (**b**) (in clauses which do not define the preceding *n*): *My wife, who is out at the moment, will phone you when she gets back.* ○ *Mrs Smith, who has a lot of teaching experience, will be joining us in the spring.* **2** (used as the object of a *v* or *prep*) (**a**) (in a defining clause, where it can be omitted): *The couple (who) we met on holiday have sent us a card.* ○ *The boy (who) I spoke to a moment ago is the son of my employer.* (**b**) (in a non-defining clause): *Mary, who we were talking about earlier, has just walked in.* ⇨ Usage at WHOM.

whoa /wəʊ/ *interj* (used as a command to a horse, etc to stop or stand still).

who'd /hu:d/ *contracted form* **1** who had ⇨ HAVE. **2** who would ⇨ WILL[1], WOULD[1].

whodunit (also **whodunnit**) /ˌhu:ˈdʌnɪt/ *n* (*infml*) detective story or play in which the person who does the crime is only revealed at the end: *her latest whodunit.*

whoever /hu:ˈevə(r)/ *pron* **1** the person who: *Whoever says that is a liar.* ○ *You're responsible to whoever is in charge of sales.* **2** regardless of who: *Whoever wants to speak to me on the phone, tell them I'm busy.* ○ *Tell whoever you like — it makes no difference to me.*

▷ **whoever** *interrog pron* (expressing surprise) who: *Whoever heard of such a thing!*

whole /həʊl/ *adj* **1** [attrib] entire; complete: *three whole days* ○ *We drank a whole bottle each.* ○ *The whole town was destroyed by the earthquake.* ○ (*infml*) *The whole country* (ie All the people in it) *mourned the death of the queen.* ○ *I've sold the whole lot,* ie everything. ○ *Let's forget the whole affair/matter/thing.* ○ *Tell me the whole truth.* ⇨ Usage at HALF[1]. **2** not broken, damaged or injured; intact: *After the party, there wasn't a glass left whole.* ○ *cook sth whole,* ie without cutting it up ○ *swallow sth whole,* ie without chewing it ○ (*fml*) *make sb whole,* ie well again (after injury or illness). **3** (idm) **go the whole hog** (*infml*) do sth thoroughly or completely: *They painted the kitchen and then decided to go the whole hog and decorate the other rooms as well.* **the whole bag of ˈtricks/ˈboiling/caˈboodle/sheˈbang/ˈshooting match** (*infml*) the whole collection of facts or things: *I just threw the whole caboodle in the back of the car.* ○ *They bought the house, the land, the stables — the whole shooting match.* **a whole lot** (**of sth**) (*infml*) a large number or amount: *a whole lot of reasons for not doing it* ○ *a whole lot of trouble.* **with all one's heart/one's whole heart** ⇨ HEART.

▷ **whole** *n* **1** [C] thing that is complete in itself: *Four quarters make a whole.* ○ *A whole is greater than any of its parts.* ⇨ Usage at HALF[1]. **2** [sing] ~ **of sth** all that there is of sth: *She spent the whole of the year in hospital.* **3** (idm) **as a ˈwhole** (**a**) as one thing or piece and not as separate parts: *Is the collection going to be divided up or sold as a whole?* (**b**) in general: *The population as a whole is/are in favour of the reform.* **on the whole** considering everything: *On the whole, I'm in favour of the proposal.*

wholeness *n* [U].

wholly /ˈhəʊllɪ/ *adv* completely; entirely: *not a wholly successful book* ○ *I'm not wholly convinced by your argument.*

□ ˈ**whole food**, ˈ**whole foods** food that has not been processed or refined and is free from artificial substances: [attrib] *a whole-food restaurant.*

ˌ**wholeˈhearted** *adj* without doubts or hesitation: *give ˌwholehearted supˈport.* ˌ**wholeˈheartedly** *adv*: *wholeheartedly in favour of the scheme.*

ˌ**whole ˈholiday** single whole day taken as a holiday, esp at a school.

ˈ**wholemeal** *n* [U] flour that is made from the whole grain of wheat, etc including the husk: [attrib] *wholemeal bread.*

ˌ**whole ˈnote** (*US*) = SEMIBREVE.

ˌ**whole ˈnumber** (*mathematics*) number that consists of one or more units, with no fractions; integer.

wholesale /ˈhəʊlseɪl/ *n* [U usu *attrib*] selling of goods (esp in large quantities) to shopkeepers for resale to the public: *the wholesale trade* ○ *wholesale prices.* Cf RETAIL.

▷ **wholesale** *adj, adv* (**a**) of, involving or engaged in wholesale as a method of trading: *We buy our supplies wholesale.* (**b**) (*often derog*) on a large scale: *the wholesale slaughter of innocent people.*

wholesale *v* [Tn] sell (goods) wholesale. **wholesaler** *n.*

wholesome /ˈhəʊlsəm/ *adj* (**a**) good for one's health or well-being: *plain but wholesome meals* ○ (*fig*) *wholesome advice.* (**b**) suggesting a healthy condition: *have a wholesome appearance.* ▷ **wholesomeness** *n* [U].

who'll /hu:l/ *contracted form* who will ⇨ WILL[1].

wholly ⇨ WHOLE.

whom /hu:m/ *interrog pron* (*fml*) (used as the object of a *v* or *prep*) which person or people: *Whom did they invite?* ○ *To whom should I refer the matter?* ○ *By whom was the order executed?*

▷ **whom** *rel pron* (*fml*) **1** (used as the object of a *v* or *prep* introducing a clause that describes a person): *The author whom you criticized in your review has written a letter in reply.* ○ *The person to whom this letter was addressed died three years ago.* **2** (used esp in formal written English as the object of a *v* or *prep* in a non-defining clause): *My parents, whom I'm sure you remember, passed away within a week of one another.* ○ *Her elder daughter, in whom she placed the greatest trust, failed to match her expectations.*

NOTE ON USAGE: **Whom** is rarely used in everyday language. **Who** is more common as the object form, especially in questions: *Who did you see at the party?* **Whom** is necessary after prepositions: *With whom did you go?* This use of preposition + **whom** is very formal and occurs especially in writing. In informal language we say: *Who did you go with?* In defining relative clauses **whom** is also unusual. The object pronoun is often omitted or replaced by **who** or **that:** *The students (whom/who/that) we examined last week were excellent.* In non-defining relative clauses **whom** or **who** (not **that**) is used and the pronoun cannot be omitted: *Our doctor, whom/who we all like very much, is leaving.* This construction is uncommon in spoken English.

whoop /hu:p, wu:p; *US* hwu:p/ *n* **1** loud cry, esp one expressing joy or excitement: *They opened the parcel with whoops of delight.* **2** harsh gasping sound made by sb with whooping cough.

▷ **whoop** *v* [I] **1** utter a loud (joyful or excited) cry: *whoop with joy.* **2** cough with a whoop(2). **3** (idm) ˌ**whoop it ˈup** /wu:p; *US* hwʊp/ (*infml*) take part in noisy celebrations: *After their victory they were whooping it up all night long.*

□ ˈ**whooping cough** infectious disease, esp of children, with gasping coughs and long rasping intakes of breath.

ˌ**whooping ˈcrane** large N American bird that makes a whooping sound (WHOOP 2). It is very rare.

whoopee /ˈwʊpi:; *US* ˈhwʊ-/ *interj* (expressing joy)

▷ **whoopee** *n* (idm) **make ˈwhoopee** (*dated infml*) rejoice or celebrate noisily.

whoops /wʊps/ (also **oops** /ʊps/) *interj* (*infml*) (**a**) (used when one has almost had an accident, broken sth, etc): *Whoops! I nearly dropped the tray.* (**b**) (used to express apology or regret when one has said something tactless, revealed a secret, etc).

whop /wɒp; *US* hwɒp/ *v* (**-pp-**) [Tn] (*infml esp US*) thrash or defeat (sb).

▷ **whopper** *n* (*infml*) (**a**) thing very big of its kind: *The fisherman had caught a whopper.* (**b**) big lie: *If she said that, she was telling a real whopper.*

whopping (*infml*) *adj* very big: *a whopping lie.* — *adv* (*infml*) very: *a whopping big hole in the ground.*

whore /hɔ:(r)/ *n* (*dated or derog*) (**a**) prostitute. (**b**) sexually immoral woman.

□ ˈ**whore-house** *n* (*dated or derog*) brothel.

who're /ˈhuə(r)/ *contracted form* who are ⇨ BE.

whorl /wɜ:l; *US* hw-/ *n* **1** one turn of a spiral. **2** complete circle formed by the ridges of a fingerprint. **3** ring of leaves, petals, etc round the stem of a plant.

whortleberry /ˈwɜ:tlberɪ; *US* ˈhwɜ:rtlberɪ/ *n* = BILBERRY.

who's /hu:z/ *contracted form* **1** who is ⇨ BE. **2** who has ⇨ HAVE.

whose /hu:z/ *interrog pron, interrog det* of whom:

Whose (house) is that? ○ *I wonder whose (book) this is.*

▷ **whose** *rel det* of whom; (less commonly); of which: *the boy whose father is in prison* ○ *the people whose house was broken into last week* ○ *the house whose door has a glass panel*, ie instead of *the house with a door with a glass panel*.

Who's Who /ˌhu:z ˈhu:/ (in Britain) book published every year giving biographical details of famous or distinguished living people.

who've /hu:v/ *contracted form* who have ⇨ HAVE.

why /waɪ; *US* hwaɪ/ *interrog adv* **1** for what reason or purpose: *Why were you late?* ○ *Why did you buy a spade?* ○ *Tell me why you did it.* ○ *Do you know why the door is locked?* **2** (used in front of a *v* to suggest that sth is unacceptable or unnecessary): *Why get upset just because you got a bad mark?* ○ *Why bother to write? We'll see him tomorrow.* **3** (idm) **why ever** (used to express surprise) why: *Why ever didn't you tell us before?* **why not** (used to make or agree to a suggestion): *Why not go now?* ○ *'Let's go to the cinema.' 'Why not?'*

▷ **why** *rel adv* (used esp after *reason*) for which (reason): *the reason why he left her* ○ *That is (the reason) why I came early.*

why *interj* (expressing surprise, impatience, etc): *Why, it's you!* ○ *Why, it's easy — a child could do it!*

why *n* (idm) **the whys and (the) wherefores** the reasons: *I don't need to hear all the whys and the wherefores, I just want to know what happened.*

WI *abbr* **1** (esp in addresses) West Indies. **2** /ˌdʌblju: ˈaɪ/ (*Brit infml*) Women's Institute.

wick /wɪk/ *n* **1** **(a)** length of thread in the centre of a candle, the top end of which is lit and burns as the wax melts. ⇨ illus at CANDLE. **(b)** flat or rounded length of woven material by which oil is drawn up to be burnt, in oil-lamps, oil-stoves and some types of cigarette lighters: *trim the wick of a lamp.* **2** (idm) **get on sb's ˈwick** (*Brit infml*) irritate sb continually.

wicked /ˈwɪkɪd/ *adj* **(-er, -est)** **1** (of a person or his actions) morally bad; sinful or evil: *That was very wicked of you.* ○ *a wicked deed, lie, plot* ○ (*fig*) *wicked* (ie very high) *prices* ○ *wicked* (ie very bad or unpleasant) *weather.* **2** intended to harm or capable of harming: *a wicked blow* ○ *a wicked-looking knife.* **3** mischievous: *a wicked sense of humour.*

▷ **the wicked** *n* [pl *v*] **1** wicked people. **2** (idm) **(there's) no peace, rest, etc for the ˈwicked** (*saying usu joc*) wrongdoers have (and must expect) a life full of fear, worry, etc.

wickedly *adv*: *The knife gleamed wickedly in the moonlight.*

wickedness *n* [U].

wicker /ˈwɪkə(r)/ *n* [U] twigs or canes woven together, esp to make baskets or furniture: [attrib] *a wicker chair.*

□ **ˈwickerwork** *n* [U] baskets, furniture, etc made of wicker: [attrib] *wickerwork chairs.*

wicket /ˈwɪkɪt/ *n* **1** small door or gate, esp one at the side of (or part of) a larger one. **2** **(a)** (in cricket) either of the two sets of three stumps (with cross-pieces called *bails* on), at which the ball is bowled and which is defended by the batsman: *take a wicket*, ie dismiss a batsman ○ *Surrey are four wickets down/have lost four wickets*, ie Four of their batsmen are out. ○ *We won by six wickets*, ie won with seven of our batsman not out. ⇨ illus at CRICKET. **(b)** stretch of ground between the two wickets: *a fast/slow wicket*, ie one on which the ball bounces at a quick/slow pace when bowled ○ (*fig infml*) *be on an easy, good, soft, sticky, etc wicket*, ie be in circumstances, a job, etc of the type specified. **3** (idm) **keep ˈwicket** act as a wicket-keeper. **leg before wicket** ⇨ LEG. **pitch wickets** ⇨ PITCH[2].

□ **ˈwicket-keeper** *n* (in cricket) player who stands behind the wicket in order to stop balls that the batsman misses, or to catch balls that the batsman hits, etc. ⇨ illus at CRICKET.

wide /waɪd/ *adj* **(-r, -st)** **1** **(a)** measuring much from side to side; not narrow: *a wide river* ○ *The gap in the fence was just wide enough for the sheep to get through.* ○ (*fig*) *a wide* (ie large) *selection.* Cf BROAD[1] 1. **(b)** having the specified width: *The garden is thirty feet wide.* ○ *a two-inch-wide ribbon.* **2** extending over a large area: *the whole wide world* ○ *a manager with wide experience of industry* ○ *The affair raises wider issues of national interest.* **3** fully open: *She stared at him with eyes wide.* **4** far from the point aimed at: *Her shot was wide (of the target).* **5** (idm) **be/fall wide of the ˈmark** be inaccurate or far from the point aimed at: *His guesses were all very wide of the mark.* **give sb/sth a wide ˈberth** remain at a safe distance from sb/sth: *He's so boring that I always try to give him a wide berth at parties.* **high, wide and handsome** ⇨ HIGH[1].

▷ **wide** *adv* **1** to the full extent; fully: *wide awake* ○ *with legs wide apart* ○ *Open your mouth wide.* **2** (idm) **cast one's net wide** ⇨ CAST[1]. **far and near/wide** ⇨ FAR. **wide ˈopen** (of a contest) with no competitor who is a certain winner. **wide open (to sth)** exposed (to attack, etc): *wide open to criticism.* **ˌwideaˈwake** *adj* (*infml approv*) alert: *a ˌwideawake young ˈwoman*, ie one who realizes what is going on, etc and is not easily deceived. **ˈwidespread** *adj* found or distributed over a large area: *widespread damage, confusion.*

wide *n* (in cricket) ball that is judged by the umpire to be bowled outside the batsman's reach.

-wide (forming *adjs* and *advs*) extending to the whole of sth: *a nationwide search* ○ *travelled worldwide.*

widely *adv* **1** to a large extent or degree: *differing widely in their opinions.* **2** over a large area: *widely scattered* ○ *It is widely known that....*

widen /ˈwaɪdn/ *v* [I, Tn] (cause sth to) become wider: *The road is being widened.* ○ *He wants to widen his knowledge of the industry.*

□ **ˌwide-angle ˈlens** camera lens that can give a wider field of vision than a standard lens.

ˈwide boy (*dated Brit infml derog*) person who is shrewd, unscrupulous and often dishonest, esp in business.

ˌwide-ˈeyed *adj* with eyes open widely in amazement or innocent surprise.

ˌwide-ˈranging *adj* covering a large area or many subjects: *ˌwide-ranging investiˈgations.*

widgeon /ˈwɪdʒən/ *n* (*pl* unchanged or **~s**) any of several types of wild duck.

widow /ˈwɪdəʊ/ *n* woman whose husband has died and who has not married again: *She has been a widow for ten years.* ○ *He married his brother's widow.*

▷ **widow** *v* [Tn esp passive] cause (sb) to become a widow or widower: *She was widowed at an early age.* ○ *Many people were widowed by the war.*

ˈwidowhood *n* [U] state or time of being a widow.

□ **ˌwidow's ˈmite** (*dated*) small amount of money given esp by a poor person.

ˌwidow's ˈpeak V-shaped area of hair growing down towards the centre of the forehead.

widower /ˈwɪdəʊə(r)/ *n* man whose wife has died and who has not married again.

width /wɪdθ, wɪtθ/ *n* **1** **(a)** [U, C] measurement from side to side: *10 metres in width* ○ *measure the width of the floor* ○ *The carpet is available in various widths.* ⇨ illus at DIMENSION. **(b)** [C] piece of material of a certain width: *Two widths of cloth were joined to make the curtain.* **2** [U] quality or state of being wide; wideness: *The river can be used by many ships because of its width.* ○ (*fig*) *width of experience, knowledge, mind.* **3** [C] distance between the sides of a swimming-pool: *She can swim two widths now.*

□ **ˈwidthways** *adv* along the width and not the length: *The fabric was folded widthways.*

wield /wi:ld/ *v* [Tn] hold in one's hand(s) and use (a weapon, tool, etc): *wield an axe, a sword, a tennis racket* ○ (*fig*) *wield authority, control, power, etc.*

wiener /ˈwi:nə(r)/ *n* (*US*) = FRANKFURTER.

Wiener schnitzel /ˌvi:nə ˈʃnɪtsl/ *n* /*US* ˈwi:nər ʃnɪtsl/ thin piece of veal coated in breadcrumbs and then fried.

wife /waɪf/ *n* (*pl* **wives** /waɪvz/) **1** married woman, esp when considered in relation to her husband: *the doctor's wife* ○ *She was a good wife and mother.* **2** (idm) **Caesar's wife** ⇨ CAESAR. **husband and wife** ⇨ HUSBAND. **an old wives' tale** ⇨ OLD. **all the world and his wife** ⇨ WORLD.

▷ **wifely** *adj* of, like or expected of a wife: *wifely duties, support, virtues.*

wig /wɪg/ *n* covering for the head made of real or artificial hair, worn to hide baldness, or in a lawcourt by barristers and judges, or by actors as part of a costume: *She disguised herself with a blonde wig and dark glasses.* ⇨ illus at DRESS. Cf TOUPEE.

wigging /ˈwɪgɪŋ/ *n* (usu *sing*) (*dated Brit infml*) lengthy rebuke; scolding: *get/give sb a good wigging.*

wiggle /ˈwɪgl/ *v* [I, Tn] (*infml*) (cause sth to) move from side to side with rapid short movements: *Stop wiggling and sit still!* ○ *The baby was wiggling its toes.* Cf WAG, WAGGLE.

▷ **wiggle** *n* (*infml*) wiggling movement.

wiggly /ˈwɪglɪ/ *adj* (*infml*) **(a)** moving with a wiggle: *a wiggly worm.* **(b)** not straight; wavy: *a wiggly line.*

Wightman Cup /ˌwaɪtmən ˈkʌp/ **the Wightman Cup** tennis trophy played for every year by women's teams representing Britain and the USA. The contest began in 1923.

wigwam /ˈwɪgwæm; *US* -wɑ:m/ *n* hut or tent made by fastening mats or animal skins over a framework of poles, esp as used formerly by N American Indians. Cf TEPEE.

Wilberforce /ˈwɪlbəfɔ:s/ William (1759-1833), English Member of Parliament who campaigned successfully to stop the trade in slaves and for the abolition of slavery throughout the British Empire.

wilco /ˈwɪlkəʊ/ *interj* (used in signalling, etc to confirm that a message has been received and orders will be carried out).

wild /waɪld/ *adj* **(-er, -est)** **1** [usu attrib] **(a)** (of animals, birds, etc) that normally live in natural conditions; not tame or domesticated: *a wild cat, giraffe, duck* ○ *filming wild animals.* ⇨ illus ANIMAL. **(b)** (of plants) growing in natural conditions; not cultivated: *wild flowers* ○ *wild roses, strawberries.* **2** [usu attrib] (of a person, tribe, etc) not civilized; savage. **3** (of scenery, an area of land, etc) not populated or cultivated; looking desolate: *a wild mountain region.* **4** tempestuous; stormy: *a wild night.* **5** out of control; undisciplined: *wild disorder* ○ *He led a wild life in his youth.* **6** full of strong unrestrained feeling; very angry, excited, passionate, etc: *wild laughter* ○ *The crowd went wild with delight.* ○ *It makes me wild* (ie very angry) *to see such cruelty.* ○ *She had a wild look on her face.* **7** [pred] ~ **(about sth/sb)** (*infml*) extremely enthusiastic (about sth/sb): *The children are wild about the new computer.* ○ *I can't say I'm wild about her new husband.* **8** not carefully aimed or planned; foolish or unreasonable: *a wild aim, guess, shot* ○ *a wild scheme.* **9** (idm) **beyond one's wildest ˈdreams** far more than one could ever have imagined or hoped for. **run ˈwild** (of an animal, plant, person, etc) grow or stray freely without any control: *Those boys have been allowed to run wild.* **sow one's wild oats** ⇨ SOW[2].

▷ **wild** *n* **(a)** **the wild** [sing] natural state or habitat: *animals living in the wild.* **(b)** **the wilds** [pl] (*sometimes derog*) remote (usu uncultivated) area where few people live: *the wilds of Australia* ○ *live out in the wilds*, ie far from towns, etc.

wildly *adv* **(a)** in a wild manner: *rushing wildly from room to room* ○ *talk wildly*, ie in an exaggerated or a very emotional way. **(b)** extremely: *a wildly exaggerated account.*

wildness *n* [U].

□ **ˈwild card** **1** (in card-games) playing-card that has been given the value of certain other cards. **2** player (eg at tennis) who is chosen to play in a tournament without having to qualify in the ordinary way.

ˈwildcat *adj* [attrib] (esp in business and finance) reckless or risky: *a wildcat scheme.* **ˌwildcat ˈstrike** sudden and unofficial strike by workers.

ˈwildfire *n* (idm) **spread like wildfire** ⇨ SPREAD.

ˈwildfowl *n* (*pl* unchanged) any of the types of birds that are shot or hunted as game, eg ducks,

geese, pheasants, quail, etc.
ˌwild-ˈgoose chase foolish or hopeless search, eg for sth or sb that does not exist or can only be found elsewhere: *The hoaxer had sent the police on a wild-goose chase.*
ˈwildlife *n* [U] wild animals, birds, etc: *the conservation of wildlife* ○ [attrib] *a wildlife sanctuary.*
the ˌWild ˈWest the western states of the USA during the period when they were being settled by Europeans and there was much lawlessness: *films about the Wild West.*

Oscar Wilde

Wilde /waɪld/ Oscar Fingal O'Flahertie Wills (1854-1900), Irish writer. His plays (eg *Lady Windermere's Fan, A Woman of No Importance* and *The Importance of Being Earnest)* are noted for their brilliantly witty lines and also their sharp social observation. He also wrote the novel *The Picture of Dorian Gray.* Wilde himself was famous for his flamboyant life-style. In 1895 he was sent to prison for homosexual offences. He described his imprisonment in the poem *The Ballad of Reading Gaol.* After his release he went to live in France, but soon died. ⇨ illus. ⇨ articles at HUMOUR, PERFORMING ARTS.

wildebeest /ˈwɪldɪbi:st/ *n (pl* unchanged or ~**s**) = GNU.

Wilder /ˈwaɪldə(r)/ Billy (1906-), Austrian-born American film writer and director. A highly versatile film maker, he is as at home with suspense (eg *Double Indemnity*) as he is with comedy (eg *Some Like It Hot*).

wilderness /ˈwɪldənɪs/ *n* (usu *sing*) **1** area of wild uncultivated land; desert: *the Arctic wilderness.* **2** ~ **(of sth)** area where plants, esp weeds, grow in an uncontrolled way: *The garden is turning into a wilderness.* ○ *(fig) a wilderness of old abandoned cars.* **3** (idm) **in the ˈwilderness** no longer in an important or influential (esp political) position: *After a few years in the wilderness he was reappointed to the Cabinet.*

wiles /waɪlz/ *n* [pl] trickery intended to deceive or attract sb: *All her wiles were not enough to persuade them to sell the property.*

wilful (*US* also **willful**) /ˈwɪlfl/ *adj* [usu attrib] (*derog*) **1** (of sth bad) done deliberately; intentional: *wilful disobedience, negligence, murder, waste.* **2** (of a person) determined to do as one wishes; headstrong or obstinate: *a wilful child.* ▷ **wilfully** /-fəlɪ/ *adv.* **wilfulness** *n* [U].

will[1] /wɪl/ *modal v* (*contracted form* **'ll** /l/; *neg* **will not**, *contracted form* **won't** /wəʊnt/; *pt* **would** /wəd; *strong form* wʊd/, *contracted form* **'d** /d/; *neg* **would not**, *contracted form* **wouldn't** /ˈwʊdnt/) **1 (a)** (indicating future predictions): *Next year will be the centenary of this firm.* ○ *He'll start school soon, won't he?* ○ *You'll be in time if you hurry.* ○ *How long will you be staying in Paris?* ○ *Fred said he'd soon be leaving.* ○ *If you phoned my secretary she'd give you an appointment.* ⇨ Usage 1 at SHALL. **(b)** (indicating present predictions): *That'll be the postman now!* ○ *They'll be home by this time.* **2 (a)** (indicating willingness or unwillingness): *He'll take you home — you only have to ask.* ○ *I'll check this letter for you, if you want.* ○ *We won't lend you any more money.* ○ *She wouldn't come to the zoo — she was frightened of the animals.* ○ *We said we would keep them.* ⇨ Usage 2 at SHALL. **(b)** (indicating requests): *Will you post this letter for me, please?* ○ *Will you (please) come in?* ○ *You'll water the plants while I'm away, won't you?* ○ *I asked him if he wouldn't mind calling later.* **3** (giving an order): *You will carry out these instructions and report back this afternoon.* ○ *Will you be quiet!* ⇨ Usage 3 at SHALL. **4 (a)** (describing general truths): *Oil will float on water.* ○ *Engines won't run without lubricants.* **(b)** (describing habits in the present or past): *She will listen to records, alone in her room, for hours.* ○ *He would spend hours in the bathroom or on the telephone.* **5** (insistence on the part of the subject): *He ˈwill comb his hair at the table, even though he knows I don't like it.* ○ *He ˈwould keep telling those dreadful stories.*

will[2] /wɪl/ *v* [I] (only used in the simple present tense; *3rd pers sing* **will**) **1** (*dated or fml*) wish: *Call it what you will, it's still a problem.* ○ *You're free to travel where you will in the country.* **2** (idm) **if you ˈwill** *(fml)* if you prefer to express it in these terms: *He became her senior adviser — her deputy, if you will.*

will[3] /wɪl/ *v* **1** [Tn, Tnt] try to make (sth) happen or to make (sb) do sth by using one's mental powers: *As a child he thought that his grandmother's death had happened because he had willed it.* ○ *The crowd were cheering their favourite on, willing her to win.* **2** [Tn, Tf] *(fml)* intend (sth); desire: *This happened because God willed it.* ○ *God wills that man should be happy.* **3** [Dn·n, Dn·pr] ~ **sth (to sb)** *(fml)* leave (property, etc) to sb by means of a will and testament: *Father willed me the house and my sister the income from the investments.* ○ *He willed most of his money to charities.*

will[4] /wɪl/ *n* **1** [U, sing] mental power by which a person can direct his thoughts and actions or influence those of others: *the freedom of the will* ○ *Man has (a) free will.* **2 (a)** [U, sing] (also **ˈwill-power** [U]) control that one can use over one's own impulses: *have a strong/weak will* ○ *He has no will of his own.* ○ *She shows great strength of will.* **(b)** [U, C] strong desire; determination: *Despite her injuries, she hasn't lost the will to live.* ○ *There was a clash of wills among committee members.* **3** [U] that which is desired (by sb): *try to do God's will* ○ *It is the will of Allah.* **4** (also **testament**) [C] legal document in which a person states how he wants his property and money to be disposed of after his death: *one's last will and testament.* **5** (idm) **against one's ˈwill** not according to one's wishes: *I was forced to sign the agreement against my will.* **at one's own sweet will** ⇨ SWEET[1]. **at ˈwill** wherever, whenever, etc one wishes: *The animals are allowed to wander at will in the park.* **of one's own free will** ⇨ FREE. **where there's a ˌwill there's a ˈway** (*saying*) a person with determination will find a way of doing sth. **with the best will in the world** ⇨ BEST[1]. **with a ˈwill** willingly and enthusiastically: *She started digging the garden with a will.*
▷ **-willed** (forming compound *adjs*) with a will of a specified kind: *strong-willed* ○ *weak-willed.*
□ **ˈwill-power** *n* [U] = WILL[4] 2a.

William I /ˈwɪlɪəm/ (also **William the Conqueror**) (c 1027-87), king of England 1066-87. As Duke of Normandy he claimed the English throne on the death of the childless *Edward the Confessor, stating that Edward had promised it to him. He invaded England, defeated *Harold at the Battle of *Hastings, and imposed Norman rule on England. ⇨ App 3.

William II /ˈwɪlɪəm/ (also **William Rufus**) (c 1056-1100), son of William I, king of England 1087-1100. His attempts to get money from the barons made him unpopular, though he was a good soldier and a shrewd ruler. He was killed, probably intentionally, while hunting in the *New Forest. He got his nickname '*Rufus*' (meaning 'red') because of the colour of his hair. ⇨ App 3.

William III /ˈwɪlɪəm/ (also **William of Orange**) (1650-1702), king of Great Britain and Ireland 1688-1702. Son of a Dutch prince, he was invited to become king of Britain by Protestant opponents of the Roman Catholic *James II. He invaded in 1688, and the following year was crowned together with his wife Mary, daughter of James II. In 1689-90 he defeated James's supporters in Scotland and Ireland. ⇨ App 3.

William IV /ˈwɪlɪəm/ (1765-1837), son of *George III, king of the United Kingdom 1830-37. The most significant action of his reign was his creation of 50 new Liberal peers to enable the 1832 *Reform Bill to be passed. ⇨ App 3.

William of Occam /ˌwɪlɪəm əv ˈɒkəm/ (c 1285-1349), English monk and philosopher. He was the last of the great scholastic philosophers. He said that Church and State should be separate, and that the Pope should not have temporal power. His ideas influenced *Luther. He proposed the principle — now known as 'Occam's razor' — that the fewest possible assumptions should be made in explaining sth.

Williams /ˈwɪlɪəmz/ Tennessee (real name Thomas Lanier Williams, 1911-83), American playwright. His plays, mainly set in the southern USA where he was born and brought up, include *A Streetcar Named Desire, Cat on a Hot Tin Roof, Suddenly Last Summer* and *The Night of the Iguana.* They deal largely with human sexual passion and its destructive effects. ⇨ article at PERFORMING ARTS.

willies /ˈwɪlɪz/ *n* **the willies** [pl] (*infml*) uneasy or nervous feeling: *Being alone in that gloomy house gave me the willies.*

willing /ˈwɪlɪŋ/ *adj* **1 (a)** ready or eager to help: *willing assistants.* **(b)** [pred] ~ **(to do sth)** having no objection (to doing sth); prepared: *Are you willing to accept responsibility?* **2** [attrib] done, given, etc readily or gladly: *willing co-operation, help, support, etc.* **3** (idm) **God willing** ⇨ GOD. **show willing** ⇨ SHOW[2]. **the spirit is willing** ⇨ SPIRIT. **a willing ˈhorse** person who works willingly (contrasted with sb who complains or resists): *She's the willing horse in the office and so gets given most of the work to do.* ▷ **willingly** *adv.* **willingness** *n* [U, sing]: *show (a) willingness to please.*

will-o'-the-wisp /ˌwɪl ə ðə ˈwɪsp/ *n* **1** bluish moving light that may be seen at night on marshy ground. **2** person or thing that is impossible to catch or reach: *You shouldn't hope to find perfect happiness — it's just a will-o'-the-wisp.*

willow /ˈwɪləʊ/ *n* **(a)** (also **ˈwillow-tree**) [C] any of various types of tree and shrub with thin flexible branches and long narrow leaves, usu growing near water: *a weeping willow.* ⇨ illus at TREE. **(b)** [U] its wood, used esp for making cricket bats.
▷ **willowy** *adj* (of a person) tall, lithe and slender: *a willowy young actress.*
□ **ˈwillow-pattern** *n* [U] traditional blue and white Chinese design that includes a picture of a willow-tree and a river, used esp on china plates, etc: [attrib] *a willow-pattern dinner service.*

willy /ˈwɪlɪ/ *n* (*Brit infml*) (used esp by or when speaking to young children) penis.

willy-nilly /ˌwɪlɪ ˈnɪlɪ/ *adv* whether one wants it or not; willingly or unwillingly: *They all had to take part, willy-nilly.*

Wilson[1] /ˈwɪlsn/ Sir Angus Frank Johnstone (1913-91), English writer, born in S Africa. His books, full of sharply humorous social observation, include *Hemlock and After,*

Anglo-Saxon Attitudes, The Old Men at the Zoo and several volumes of short stories.

Wilson[2] /ˈwɪlsn/ Edmund (1895-1972), American literary critic. His best-known work is *Axel's Castle*, a study of the symbolist movement.

Wilson[3] /ˈwɪlsn/ Thomas Woodrow (1856-1924), 28th president of the USA 1913-21. In a successful first term he introduced several administrative and financial reforms. He was then re-elected on the promise of keeping the USA out of the First World War, though circumstances soon forced America to enter it. Wilson proposed a progressive peace settlement afterwards, but his efforts were blocked. He was a Democrat.

wilt /wɪlt/ *v* (**a**) [I] (of a plant or flower) droop and wither: *The leaves are beginning to wilt.* ○ (*fig*) *spectators wilting* (ie becoming tired and weak) *in the heat.* (**b**) [Tn] cause (a plant or flower) to droop: *The plants were wilted by the heat.*

Wilton /ˈwɪltən/ *n* [C, U] type of carpet made out of cut loops of wool, originally made in the town of Wilton, in Wiltshire, England.

Wiltshire /ˈwɪltʃə(r)/ county of south-western England. ⇨ map at App 1.

wily /ˈwaɪlɪ/ *adj* (**-ier, -iest**) crafty or cunning; full of wiles: *as wily as a fox* ○ (*infml*) *a wily old bird*, ie a cunning person. ▷ **wiliness** *n* [U].

Wimbledon /ˈwɪmbldən/ **1** borough of south-west London. **2** annual international tennis championship, held at the All England Lawn Tennis and Croquet Club, in Wimbledon. ⇨ articles at SEASON, SPORT.

wimp /wɪmp/ *n* (*infml derog*) weak and timid person, esp a man: *Don't be such a wimp!*
▷ **wimpish** *adj* (*infml derog*) (behaving) like a wimp.

wimple /ˈwɪmpl/ *n* (**a**) head-dress made of linen or silk folded round the head and neck, worn by women in the Middle Ages. (**b**) similar linen head-dress worn by certain nuns.

win /wɪn/ *v* (**-nn-**; *pt, pp* **won** /wʌn/) **1** [I, Tn] be victorious in (a battle, contest, race, etc); do best: *Which team won?* ○ *She was determined to win (the race).* ○ *win a bet/wager.* **2** [Tn, Tn·pr] ~ **sth (from sb)** obtain or achieve sth as the result of a bet, competition, race, etc: *She won first prize (in the raffle).* ○ *The Conservatives won the seat* (ie in Parliament) *from Labour at the last election.* **3** (**a**) [Tn] obtain or reach (sth), esp as a result of hard work or perseverance: *They are trying to win support for their proposal.* (**b**) [Dn·n, Dn·pr] ~ **sth (for sb/sth)** cause (sb) to obtain or achieve sth: *Her performance won her much critical acclaim.* **4** (idm) **carry/win the day** ⇨ DAY. **gain/win sb's hand** ⇨ HAND[1]. **gain/win one's laurels** ⇨ LAUREL. **heads I win, tails you lose** ⇨ HEAD[1]. **lose/win by a neck** ⇨ NECK. **nothing venture, nothing gain/win** ⇨ VENTURE *v*. **win free** free oneself from a difficult position, etc by effort. **win (sth) ˌhands ˈdown** (*infml*) win easily, by a large margin: *The local team won (the match) hands down.* **win one's ˈspurs** (*fml*) achieve distinction or fame. **ˌwin or ˈlose** whether one succeeds or fails: *Win or lose, it should be a very good match.* **win/lose the toss** ⇨ TOSS *n*. **you, one, etc ˌcan't ˈwin** (*infml*) there is no way of achieving success or of pleasing people. **5** (phr v) **win sth/sb back** regain sth/sb after a struggle: *The party must try to win back the support it has lost.* ○ *He hoped to win her love back.* **win sb over/round (to sth)** gain sb's support or favour, esp by persuasion: *She's against the idea, but I'm sure I can win her over.* **win out/through** (*infml*) come successfully through a difficult period; achieve success eventually: *We are faced with a lot of problems but we'll win through in the end.*
▷ **win** *n* victory in a game, contest, etc: *Our team has had five wins and no losses this season.*

winner *n* **1** person, horse, etc that wins: *The winner was presented with a trophy.* **2** (*infml*) thing, idea, etc that is successful: *Their latest model is certain to be a winner.* **3** (idm) **pick a winner** ⇨ PICK[3].

winning *adj* **1** [attrib] that wins or has won: *the winning horse, number, ticket.* **2** [usu attrib] attractive or persuasive: *a winning smile* ○ *She has a winning way with her.* **ˈwinning-post** *n* post that marks the end of a race: *Her horse was first past the winning-post.*

winnings /ˈwɪnɪŋz/ *n* [pl] money that is won, esp by betting, gambling, etc: *collect one's winnings.*

wince /wɪns/ *v* [I, Ipr] ~ **(at sth)** show pain, distress or embarrassment by a slight involuntary movement, esp of the muscles in the face: *He winced as she stood on his injured foot.* ○ *I still wince at the memory of the stupid things I did.* ▷ **wince** *n* (usu *sing*).

winceyette /ˌwɪnsɪˈet/ *n* [U] soft fabric made from cotton, or from cotton and wool, used esp for making pyjamas, night-dresses, etc.

winch

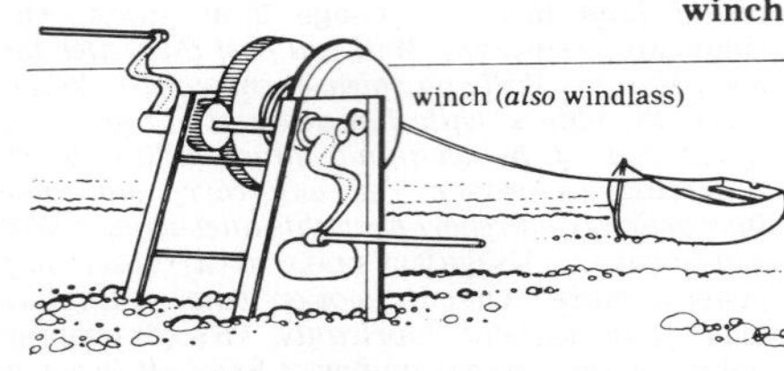

winch /wɪntʃ/ *n* machine for hoisting or pulling heavy objects by means of a rope or chain wound round a drum; windlass.
▷ **winch** *v* [Tn, Tn·pr, Tn·p] move (sb/sth) by using a winch: *winch a glider off the ground*, ie pull it along by means of a winch until it rises into the air ○ *The helicopter winched the survivor up* (eg out of the sea) *to safety.*

wind[1] /wɪnd/ *n* **1** [C, U] (also **the wind**) (used with *a* or in the plural when referring to the type of wind or its direction, etc; used with *much, little*, etc when referring to its strength, etc) air moving as a result of natural forces: *A gust of wind blew my hat off.* ○ *The day was very still, without a breath of wind.* ○ *a north wind*, ie one that blows from the north ○ *warm southerly winds* ○ *The wind has dropped* (ie is less strong) *now.* **2** [U] smell carried by the wind: *The deer have got our wind.* **3** [U] breath, esp as needed for continuous exercise or for sounding a musical instrument: *The runner had to stop and regain her wind*, ie wait until she could breathe more easily. **4** [U] air that has been swallowed with food or drink, or gas that forms in the stomach or intestines and causes discomfort; flatulence: *get a baby's wind up*, ie cause it to belch by stroking or patting its back. **5** [U] useless or boastful talk: *He's just full of wind, the pompous fool!* **6 the wind** [Gp, sing] (players of the) wind instruments in an orchestra: [attrib] *the wind section.* **7** (idm) **break ˈwind** (*euph*) expel air from the intestines through the anus. **the eye of the wind/wind's eye** ⇨ EYE[1]. **get one's second ˈwind** feel strong again after getting very tired: *I often feel sleepy after supper and then I get my second wind later in the evening.* **get wind of sth** hear a rumour that sth is happening; hear about sth secret: *Our competitors must not be allowed to get wind of our plans.* **get/have the ˈwind up (about sth)** (*infml*) become/be frightened. **in the ˈwind** about to happen: *They sensed that there was something in the wind.* **it's an ill wind** ⇨ ILL[2]. **like the ˈwind** very fast: *She goes like the wind on her new bicycle.* **put the wind up sb** (*infml*) cause sb to be frightened; alarm sb. **run/sail before the ˈwind** (*nautical*) sail with the wind behind the ship. **sail close/near to the wind** ⇨ SAIL[2]. **see which way the wind is blowing** ⇨ WAY[1]. **sound in wind and limb** ⇨ SOUND[1]. **a straw in the wind** ⇨ STRAW. **take the ˈwind out of sb's sails** (*infml*) cause sb to lose his confidence or pride: *Being beaten by a newcomer has really taken the wind out of his sails.* **throw, etc caution to the winds** ⇨ CAUTION. **to the four winds** (*rhet*) (blown, scattered, etc) in all directions. **a wind of ˈchange** influence that causes change; tendency to change: *There is a wind of change in the attitude of voters.*
▷ **windless** *adj* without wind: *a windless day.*

windward /-wəd/ *adj, adv* on or to the side from which the wind is blowing: *the windward side of the boat.* Cf LEE, LEEWARD. — *n* [U] side or direction from which the wind is blowing: *sail to windward* ○ *get to windward of sth*, ie place oneself on the windward side of sth, eg in order to avoid a bad smell.

windy *adj* (**-ier, -iest**) **1** (**a**) with much wind: *a windy day.* (**b**) exposed to (esp strong) winds: *a windy hillside.* **2** (*dated Brit infml*) nervous or frightened: *a bit windy about staying alone in the house.* **windily** /-ɪlɪ/ *adv*. **windiness** *n* [U].

□ **ˈwindbag** *n* (*infml derog*) person who talks a lot but says nothing important.

ˈwind-break *n* row of trees or a hedge, fence, etc that gives protection from the wind.

ˈwind-cheater (*US* **ˈwind-breaker**) *n* close-fitting jacket designed to protect the wearer from the wind.

ˈwindfall *n* **1** fruit, esp an apple, that has been blown off a tree by the wind. **2** (*fig*) unexpected piece of good fortune, esp a legacy.

ˈwind-gauge *n* = ANEMOMETER.

ˈwindhover /-hɒvə(r)/ *n* (*Brit dialect*) = KESTREL.

ˈwind instrument musical instrument (eg a flute or trumpet) in which sound is produced by a current of air, esp by the player's breath.

windmill

ˈwindmill *n* **1** mill worked by the action of wind on long projecting arms (*sails*) that turn on a central shaft. **2** (idm) **tilt at windmills** ⇨ TILT.

ˈwindpipe *n* passage from the throat to the bronchial tubes, through which air reaches the lungs. ⇨ illus at RESPIRE.

ˈwindscreen (*Brit*) (*US* **ˈwindshield**) *n* glass window in the front of a motor vehicle. ⇨ illus at CAR. **ˈwindscreen wiper** (*Brit*) (*US* **ˈwindshield wiper, wiper**) electrically operated blade with a rubber edge that wipes a windscreen clear of rain, snow, etc. ⇨ illus at CAR.

ˈwindshield (*US*) *n* (**a**) = WINDSCREEN. (**b**) glass or plastic screen that provides protection from the wind, eg at the front of a motorcycle.

ˈwind-sock (also **ˈwind-sleeve**) *n* canvas tube, open at both ends, that is flown at the top of a pole (eg on an airfield) to show the direction of the wind.

windsurfing

ˈwindsurfer *n* (*propr*) **1** board, similar to a surfboard, with a sail. **2** person who surfs on a windsurfer. **ˈwindsurf** *v* [I] (usu **go ˈwindsurfing**) surf on a windsurfer. **windsurfing** *n* [U] sport of surfing on a windsurfer.

ˈwind-swept *adj* (**a**) (of a place) exposed to strong winds: *a wind-swept hillside.* (**b**) (of a person's appearance) untidy after being blown about by the wind: *wind-swept hair*.

ˈwind-tunnel *n* device through which air can be blown at varying speeds past models to test the effect of wind or moving air on aircraft, buildings, etc.

wind[2] /wɪnd/ *v* [Tn] **1** cause (sb) to be out of breath: *We were winded by the steep climb.* ○ *The punch in the stomach completely winded me.* **2** help (a baby) to expel wind[1](4) from its stomach by patting or stroking its back. **3** detect the presence of (sb/sth) by smelling: *The hounds had winded the fox.*

wind[3] /waɪnd/ *v* (*pt, pp* **wound** /waʊnd/) **1** [I, Ipr, Ip, Tn·pr, Tn·p] (cause sth to) follow a curving, twisting or spiral course: *a winding road* ○ *The river winds down to the sea.* ○ *The staircase winds upwards round a central pillar.* ○ *She wound her way through the crowds.* **2** [Tn, Tn·pr, Tn·p] twist or coil (string, wool, yarn, etc) round and round on itself so that it forms a ball, or onto a reel, etc: *wind wool (up) into a ball* ○ *wind sewing thread onto a reel.* **3** [Tn·pr] (a) ~ **sth round sb/sth**; ~ **sb/sth in sth** fold sth round sb/sth closely; wrap sb/sth in sth: *wind a bandage round one's finger* ○ *wind a shawl round the baby/the baby in a shawl.* (b) ~ **itself round sb/sth** become twisted or entangled round sb/sth: *The film flew off the spool and wound itself round the projector.* **4** [Tn] turn (a handle, windlass, etc): *You operate the mechanism by winding this handle.* **5** [Tn, Tn·p] ~ **sth (up)** cause a mechanism (esp a clock or watch) to operate, eg by turning a key to tighten the spring: *Have you wound your watch?* **6** (phr v) **wind sth back, down, forward, in, off, on, up, etc** cause sth to move in the specified direction by turning a handle, spool, etc: *wind a tape back/forward/on* ○ *wind a car window down/up* ○ *wind a fishing line in.* **wind down** (a) (of a clock or watch) go slow and then stop. (b) (of a person) relax, esp after a period of stress or excitement: *This year has been frantically busy for us — I need a holiday just to wind down.* **wind up** (*infml*) (of a person) arrive finally in a place; end up: *We eventually wound up (staying) in a super little hotel by the sea.* ○ *I always said he would wind up in jail.* **wind (sth) up** finish (a speech, etc): *Before I wind up, there are two more things to be said.* ○ *If we all agree, let's wind up the discussion.* **wind sb up** cause sb to reach a high level of excitement or agitation: *He gets so wound up when he's arguing.* ○ (*infml*) *Are you deliberately winding me up* (ie annoying me)*?* **wind sth up** settle the affairs of and finally close (a business, company, etc): *wind up one's affairs.*

▷ **wind** *n* (a) bend or turn in a course, path, etc. (b) single turn made in winding (WIND[3] 5): *Give the clock another couple of winds.*

winder *n* lever or other instrument for winding (esp a clock, watch etc).

□ **ˈwinding-sheet** *n* = SHROUD.

ˈwind-up *n* (*infml*) deliberate attempt to annoy or provoke sb: [attrib] *a wind-up artist/merchant*, ie sb who does this.

windlass /ˈwɪndləs/ *n* device for pulling or lifting things (eg a bucket of water from a well) by means of a rope or chain that winds round a horizontal axle; winch. ⇨ illus at WINCH.

window /ˈwɪndəʊ/ *n* **1** (a) opening in the wall or roof of a building, car, etc to let in light (and often air), usu filled with glass in a frame: *Please open the window.* ○ *I saw them through the window.* ○ *He prefers to travel in a seat near the window.* ⇨ illus at HOME, ⇨ illus at CAR. (b) opening that resembles this: *There is a little window in the cassette case so that you can see the tape.* ○ *the window of an envelope*, ie the transparent part in which an address can be read. (c) piece of glass in the frame of a window: *The ball smashed a window.* (d) space behind the window of a shop where goods are displayed for sale: *I saw the vase in the window of an antique shop.* ○ [attrib] *a window display.* **2** (*computing*) one of the areas that a computer screen can be divided into in order to view more than one kind of information at one time. **3** (idm) **fly/go out of the ˈwindow** (*infml*) be no longer considered; disappear: *With the failure of the peace talks all hopes of a swift end to the war have flown out of the window.* **a window on the ˈworld** means of observing and learning about people, esp those of other countries: *International news broadcasts provide a window on the world.*

□ **ˈwindow-box** *n* long narrow box fixed outside a window, in which plants are grown.

ˈwindow-dressing *n* [U] (a) art or skill of arranging goods attractively in shop windows. (b) (*usu derog*) presentation of facts, etc in a way that creates a good (and often false) impression: *The company's support of scientific research is just window-dressing.*

ˈwindow-pane *n* pane of glass for or in a (section of a) window. ⇨ illus at HOME.

ˈwindow seat (a) seat beside a window (in an aircraft, a bus, etc). (b) backless seat fixed to a wall below a window in a room, often in an alcove.

ˈwindow shade (*US*) = BLIND[3].

ˈwindow-shopping *n* [U] looking at goods displayed in shop windows (usu without intending to buy anything): *go window-shopping*.

ˈwindow-sill (also **ˈwindow-ledge**) *n* ledge at the base of a window, either inside or outside. ⇨ illus at HOME.

Windsor /ˈwɪnzə(r)/ **1** town in Berkshire, England, to the west of London. **2** British royal house to which the royal family belongs. The name was adopted by *George V in 1917. After *Edward VIII gave up the throne, he took the title Duke of Windsor. ⇨ article at ROYAL FAMILY.

□ **ˌWindsor ˈCastle** castle in Windsor, begun by *William I. It is one of the British sovereign's official homes. ⇨ article at ARCHITECTURE.

ˈWindsor knot type of large knot used for tying a tie[1](1).

Windward Islands /ˈwɪndwəd aɪləndz/ **the Windward Islands** group of islands in the Caribbean Sea, including Dominica, Martinique, St Lucia, Barbados and Grenada. They are to the south of the *Leeward Islands. ⇨ map at WEST INDIES.

windy ⇨ WIND[1].

wine /waɪn/ *n* **1** [U, C] alcoholic drink made from the fermented juice of grapes: *red/rosé/white wine* ○ *dry/sweet wine* ○ *a barrel/bottle/carafe/glass of wine* ○ *a wine from a famous vineyard.* ⇨ article at DRINK. **2** [U, C] alcoholic drink made from plants or fruits other than grapes: *apple, cowslip, parsnip wine.* **3** [U] dark purplish red colour similar to that of red wine: [attrib] *a wine velvet evening dress.* **4** (idm) **ˌwine, ˌwomen and ˈsong** drinking, dancing, etc and enjoying oneself.

▷ **wine** *v* (idm) **ˌwine and ˈdine (sb)** entertain (sb) or be entertained with food and drink, esp lavishly: *Our hosts wined and dined us very well.* ○ *Too much wining and dining is making him fat.*

□ **ˈwine bar** place where a variety of wines is sold and drunk, sometimes with food.

ˈwine-cellar *n* (a) underground room where wine is stored. (b) (also **cellar**) wine stored in this: *He has an excellent wine-cellar.*

ˈwineglass *n* glass for drinking wine from. ⇨ illus at GLASS.

ˈwinepress *n* press[1](2) in which grapes are crushed for making wine.

wing /wɪŋ/ *n* **1** [C] (a) either of the pair of feathered limbs that a bird uses to fly. ⇨ illus at BIRD. (b) either of the similar projecting parts that an insect or a bat uses to fly. ⇨ illus at BUTTERFLY. (c) thing that is similar to this, eg the thin projection on the seeds of maple or sycamore trees. **2** [C] part that projects from the side of an aircraft and supports it in the air. ⇨ illus at AIRCRAFT. **3** [C] part of a building that projects from the main part: *the east/west wing of a house* ○ *build a new wing of a hospital.* **4** [C] (*Brit*) (*US* **fender**) projecting part of the bodywork of a motor vehicle above the wheel: *The nearside wing was damaged in the collision.* ○ [attrib] *a wing mirror.* ⇨ illus at CAR. **5** [C] either of the flanks of an army lined up for battle. **6** [C usu *sing*] part of an organization, esp a political party that holds certain views or has a particular function: *the radical wing of the Labour Party.* Cf LEFT-WING (LEFT[2]), RIGHT-WING (RIGHT[5]). **7** [C] (a) side part of the playing area in football, hockey, etc: *playing on the wing* ○ *kick the ball out to the wing.* (b) (also **winger**) (in football, hockey, etc) either of the forward players whose place is at the extreme end of the forward line: *the team's new left wing.* **8** (*Brit*) (a) [C] (in the Royal Air Force) unit of two or more squadrons. (b) **wings** [pl] (in the Royal Air Force) pilot's badge: *get one's wings.* **9 the wings** [pl] (in a theatre) area to the right and left of the stage that is hidden from the audience by curtains, scenery, etc: *She stood watching the performance from the wings.* ⇨ illus at THEATRE. **10** (idm) **clip sb's wings** ⇨ CLIP[2]. **(wait, etc) in the ˈwings** ready to do sth or to take over from sb: *He retires as chairman next year; his successor is already waiting in the wings.* **on the ˈwing** (while it is) flying: *photograph a bird on the wing.* **spread one's wings** ⇨ SPREAD. **take ˈwing** fly away. **under sb's/one's ˈwing** under sb's/one's protection: *She immediately took the new arrivals under her wing*, ie looked after them.

▷ **wing** *v* **1** [Ipr, Ip, Tn·pr, Tn·p] travel on wings; fly: *planes winging (their way) across the sky.* **2** [Tn] (a) wound (a bird) in the wing. (b) wound (sb) slightly, esp in an arm. **winged** *adj* (often forming compound *adjs*) having wings, esp of the specified number or type: *winged insects* ○ *delta-winged aircraft.*

winger *n* **1** (in football, hockey, etc) player who plays on the wing(7a). **2 -winger** (forming compound *ns*) (a) person who plays on the wing: *a ˌleft-/ˌright-ˈwinger.* (b) person on the left or right wing in politics or a political party: *She was active as a left-winger in the party.*

wingless *adj* (esp of insects) without wings.

□ **ˈwing case** hard covering which some insects have over each of their wings.

ˈwing-chair *n* armchair with a high back that has projecting pieces at each side.

ˌwing ˈcollar high stiff collar with its corners turned down.

ˈwing commander officer in the Royal Air Force between the ranks of squadron leader and group captain. ⇨ App 4.

ˌwing ˈforward = FLANKER (FLANK).

ˈwing-nut *n* nut with projections so that it can be turned by a thumb and a finger on a screw or bolt. ⇨ illus at BOLT[1].

ˈwing-span *n* distance between the end of one wing and the end of the other when the wings are fully stretched out: *a bird with a two-foot wing-span.*

wingding /ˈwɪŋdɪŋ/ *n* (*US infml*) wild festive party.

wink /wɪŋk/ *v* **1** [I, Ipr] ~ **(at sb)** close one eye very briefly, esp as a private signal to sb: *He winked at me to show that he was playing a joke on the others.* **2** [I] (of a light, star, etc) shine with a light that flickers or flashes quickly on and off: *We could see the lighthouse winking in the distance.* ○ *The car in front is winking — it's going to turn right.* **3** (idm) **easy as winking** ⇨ EASY. **4** (phr v) **wink at sth** (*dated*) pretend that one does not notice (bad behaviour, etc): *His wife has winked at his infidelity for years.*

▷ **wink** *n* **1** act of winking, esp as a signal: *give sb a meaningful wink.* **2** (idm) **(have/take) forty ˈwinks** short sleep, esp during the daytime. **a nod is as good as a wink** ⇨ NOD *n*. **not get/have a ˈwink of sleep; not sleep a ˈwink** not sleep at all: *The neighbours were having a party and we didn't get a wink of sleep all night.* **tip sb the wink** ⇨ TIP[3].

winker *n* (*Brit*) small light on a motor vehicle that flashes in order to indicate that it is going to change direction; indicator.

winkle /ˈwɪŋkl/ *n* = PERIWINKLE 2.

▷ **winkle** *v* (phr v) **winkle sb/sth out (of sth)** (*infml*) get sb/sth out (of a place) slowly and with difficulty: *The children were finally all winkled out of their hiding places.* **winkle sth out (of sb)** (*infml*) obtain information, etc from sb with difficulty: *She's very clever at winkling secrets out of people.*

□ **ˈwinkle-picker** *n* (usu *pl*) (*dated sl*) shoe with a long pointed toe: *a pair of winkle-pickers.*

winner, winning ⇨ WIN.

Winnie the Pooh /ˌwɪnɪ ðə ˈpuː/ bear that is the main character in a series of children's stories by A A *Milne.

winnow /ˈwɪnəʊ/ *v* (a) [Tn] blow a current of air through (grain) in order to remove the chaff. (b) [Tn·p, Tn·pr] ~ **sth away/out**; ~ **sth from sth** remove (the chaff) from grain in this way: *winnow the husks from the corn* ○ *(fig) winnow the truth from the mass of conflicting evidence.*

wino /ˈwaɪnəʊ/ *n* (*pl* ~**s**) (*infml*) person who is addicted to alcohol, esp to cheap wine; an alcoholic.

winsome /ˈwɪnsəm/ *adj* (*fml*) attractive and pleasant: *a winsome smile* ○ *She was a winsome creature.* ▷ **winsomely** *adv.* **winsomeness** *n* [U].

winter /ˈwɪntə(r)/ *n* [U, C] **1** the last and coldest season of the year, coming between autumn and spring, ie from December to February in the Northern hemisphere: *Many trees lose their leaves in winter.* ○ *The plants have survived the winter.* ○ *They worked on the building all through the winter.* ○ *They spend the winter(s) in a warmer climate.* ○ *She lived alone in the house for a whole winter.* ○ *He is going to retire next winter.* ○ *on a dark winter's night* ○ [attrib] *winter quarters*, ie (esp formerly) place where an army spends the winter during a campaign. **2** (idm) **in the dead of winter** ⇨ DEAD *n*.

▷ **winter** *v* [I] (*fml*) spend the winter: *It became fashionable for the rich to winter in the sun.* ○ *birds wintering in the south.*

winterize, -ise /ˈwɪntəraɪz/ *v* [Tn] (*esp US*) prepare (a house, car, etc) for winter weather.

wintry /ˈwɪntrɪ/ *adj* (**-ier, -iest**) of or like winter; cold, snowy, etc: *a wintry landscape* ○ *wintry light, weather* ○ *(fig) a wintry smile*, ie lacking warmth, unfriendly. **wintriness** *n* [U].

□ ˈ**wintergreen** *n* (a) [C, U] any of various small evergreen N American shrubs. (b) [U] substance, originally made from this plant but now usu made artificially, that is used medicinally or as a flavouring.

the ˌWinter ˈPalace palace in St Petersburg, USSR, in which the Russian tsars formerly lived. It was attacked during the 1917 revolution.

ˌ**winter ˈsports** sports that take place on snow or ice, eg skiing and skating.

ˈ**winter-time** *n* [U] period or season of winter: *The days are shorter in (the) winter-time.*

wipe /waɪp/ *v* **1** (a) [Tn, Tn·pr, Tn·p, Cn·a] ~ **sth (on sth)**; ~ **sth (down/over)** clean or dry sth by rubbing its surface with a cloth, piece of paper, etc: *wipe the dishes*, ie dry them after they have been washed ○ *wipe the table* ○ *Please wipe your feet*, ie remove the dirt from your shoes by wiping them on the doormat. ○ *wipe one's eyes*, ie to remove the tears ○ *wipe one's nose*, ie with a handkerchief ○ *wipe* (ie remove what has been recorded on) *a magnetic tape* ○ *wipe one's hands on a towel* ○ *wipe down the kitchen cupboards*, ie clean them with a cloth, etc from top to bottom ○ *wipe sth clean/dry.* (b) [Tn·pr] rub (a cloth, etc) over a surface: *wipe a damp sponge across one's face.* (c) [Tn·pr] put (a substance) onto a surface by rubbing: *Wipe the lotion onto your face.* **2** [Tn·pr, Tn·p] ~ **sth from/off sth**; ~ **sth away/off/up** clear or remove sth by wiping: *wipe (away) the tears from one's eyes* ○ *wipe the writing from the blackboard* ○ *wipe (up) the spilt milk off the floor* ○ *wipe a recording off (a tape)* ○ *(fig infml) Wipe that smile/grin/expression off your face!* ie Stop smiling, etc. **3** (idm) **wipe the ˈfloor with sb** (*infml*) defeat sb decisively in an argument, a competition, etc. **wipe sth off the ˌface of the ˈearth/off the ˈmap** utterly destroy sth. **wipe the ˈslate clean** forget past faults or offences; make a fresh start. **4** (phr v) **wipe sth out** (a) clean the inside of (a bowl, etc) by rubbing it with a cloth: *This vase wasn't wiped out properly before it was put away.* (b) remove or cancel sth: *wipe out one's debts*, ie by repaying them ○ *This year's losses have wiped out* (ie reduced to nothing) *last year's profits.* (c) destroy sth completely: *Whole villages were wiped out in the bombing raids.* ○ *The government is trying to wipe out drug trafficking.*

▷ **wipe** *n* act of wiping: *Please give the table mats a quick wipe.*

wiper *n* (a) thing that wipes or is used for wiping. (b) = WINDSCREEN WIPER (WIND[1]).

wire /ˈwaɪə(r)/ *n* **1** (a) [C, U] (piece or length of) metal that has been formed into a thin flexible thread-like rod: *a (coil of) copper wire* ○ *barbed ˈwire.* (b) [C, U] (piece or length of) wire used to carry electric current or signals: *ˈfuse wire* ○ *ˈtelephone wires.* (c) [U, sing] barrier, framework, fence, etc made from wire: *The hamster had got through the wire at the front of its cage.* **2** [C] (*infml esp US*) telegram: *send sb a wire.* **3** (idm) **get one's ˈwires crossed** (*infml*) be mistaken or confused about what sb is saying or has said: *We seem to have got our wires crossed. I thought you were coming yesterday.* **a live wire** ⇨ LIVE[1]. **pull (the) strings/wires** ⇨ PULL[2].

▷ **wire** *v* **1** (a) [Tn·pr, Tn·p] ~ **A (on) to B**; ~ **A and B together** fasten or join one thing to another with wire: *A handle had been wired (on) to the box.* ○ *The two pieces of wood were wired together.* (b) [Tn esp passive] put wire(s) in or on (sth), eg to strengthen it: *The fabric was displayed on a wired stand.* **2** [Tn, Tn·pr, Tn·p] ~ **sth (up)**; ~ **sth (for sth)** connect sth to a supply of electricity by means of wires: *The house is not wired for electricity yet.* ○ *The studio is being wired for sound.* ○ *As soon as the equipment is wired up, you can use it.* **3** (a) [Tn, Tf, Dn·f, Dpr·f, Dn·t, Dpr·t] (*infml esp US*) send (sb) a message by telegram: *He wired (to) his brother to send some money.* ○ *She wired (us) that she would be delayed.* (b) [Dn·n, Dn·pr] ~ **sth to sb** (*infml esp US*) send sth to sb by means of a telegram: *wire money to sb*, ie instruct a bank by telegram to give money to sb. **wiring** /ˈwaɪərɪŋ/ *n* [U] system of wires, esp for supplying electricity to a building: *The wiring is faulty and needs to be replaced.*

wiry /ˈwaɪərɪ/ *adj* (**-ier, -iest**) (a) (of a person) lean but strong. (b) tough and flexible, like wire: *wiry* (ie coarse and curly) *hair.* **wiriness** *n* [U].

□ ˈ**wire-cutter** *n* (esp *pl*) tool for cutting wire: *a pair of wire-cutters.*

ˌ**wire-ˈhaired** *adj* (esp of a dog) having stiff or wiry hair: *a ˌwire-haired ˈterrier.*

ˌ**wire ˈnetting** [U] netting made by weaving wires into a mesh, used for fences, etc.

ˈ**wire-tapping** *n* [U] practice of listening to other people's telephone conversations by making a secret connection to the telephone line.

ˌ**wire ˈwool** mass of fine wires, used for cleaning and polishing, often in the form of a small pad. Cf STEEL WOOL (STEEL).

ˈ**wire-worm** *n* any of several types of worm-like larva that destroy plants by eating them.

wireless /ˈwaɪəlɪs/ *n* (*dated*) **1** [U] radio communications: *broadcast by wireless.* **2** [C] (a) radio receiver or transmitter. (b) [C] = RADIO 2b.

Wisconsin /wɪsˈkɒnsɪn/ central northern state of the USA, bordering on Lakes Superior and Michigan. It is a major producer of dairy products. ⇨ map at App 1.

Wisden /ˈwɪzdən/ (also **Wisden's Cricketers' Almanack**) book published every year in Britain, giving cricket-match scores, cricket records, etc. It first appeared in 1864.

wisdom /ˈwɪzdəm/ *n* [U] **1** (a) experience and knowledge (shown in making decisions and judgements); quality of being wise: *She had acquired much wisdom during her long life.* (b) good judgement; advisability; common sense: *I question the wisdom of giving the child so much money.* ○ *Events were to prove the wisdom of their decision.* **2** (*fml*) wise thoughts, sayings, etc: *the wisdom of the ancients* ○ *the conventional/received wisdom*, ie the generally accepted view. **3** (idm) **wit and wisdom** ⇨ WIT.

□ ˈ**wisdom tooth** any of the four molars at the back of the mouth that appear when one is about 20 years old.

wise /waɪz/ *adj* (**-r, -st**) **1** (a) having or showing good judgement: *a wise choice, decision, precaution, friend* ○ *It was not very wise of you to sell the property.* ○ *I'm sure you're wise to wait a few days.* ○ *a wise nod of the head*, ie suggesting that one is wise. (b) having knowledge: *a wise old man.* **2** (idm) **be ˌwise after the eˈvent** be able to explain sth after it has happened but without having foreseen it: *We don't pay our financial analysts to be wise after the event!* **be/get wise to sth/sb** (*infml esp US*) be/become aware of sth or of sb's qualities or behaviour: *He thought he could fool me but I got wise to him.* **no/none the/not any the ˈwiser** knowing no more than before: *Even after listening to his explanation I'm none the wiser.* **penny wise pound foolish** ⇨ PENNY. **put sb ˈwise (to sth)** (*infml esp US*) inform sb about sth. **sadder but wiser** ⇨ SAD. **(as) ˌwise as an ˈowl** very wise. **a word to the wise** ⇨ WORD.

▷ **wise** *v* (phr v) **wise (sb) up (to sth)** (*infml esp US*) (cause sb to) become aware or informed of sth: *It's about time he wised up to the fact that people think his behaviour is ridiculous.*

wisely *adv.*

□ ˈ**wiseacre** *n* (*dated*) person who pretends to be wise; know-all.

ˈ**wisecrack** *n* (*infml*) smart or clever (often unkind) saying or remark. — *v* [I] make wisecracks.

ˈ**wise guy** (*infml derog*) person who speaks or behaves as if he knows more than other people.

-wise *suff* (with *ns* forming *adjs* and *advs*) **1** in the manner or direction of: *likewise* ○ *clockwise* ○ *anti-clockwise* ○ *lengthwise.* **2** (*infml*) with reference to; as far as sth is concerned: *businesswise* ○ *weatherwise* ○ *profitwise.*

wish /wɪʃ/ *v* **1** (a) [Ipr] ~ **for sth/sb** have or express a desire for sth/sb (esp sth/sb that is likely to be achieved or obtained only by good fortune): *It's no use wishing for things you can't have.* ○ *His wife is everything a man could wish for.* ○ *What more could one wish for?* ie Everything is perfect. (b) [Tf, Cn·a] (with *that* often omitted and the *that*-clause usu in the past tense) have as a desire that is unfulfilled or unlikely to be fulfilled: *I wish you hadn't told me all this.* ○ *She wished she had* (ie was sorry she had not) *stayed at home.* ○ *I wish I knew what was going to happen.* ○ *I wish he wouldn't go out every night.* ○ *I wish I were rich.* ○ *She began to wish the whole business finished.* ○ *He's dead and it's no use wishing him alive again.* (c) [Tn, Tt, Cn·t] (*fml*) demand or want (sth): *I'll do it if that's what you wish.* ○ *I wish to leave my property to my children.* ○ *She wishes to be alone.* ○ *I wish it to be clear that the decision is final.* ○ *Do you wish me to serve dinner now?* ⇨ Usage at HOPE. **2** [Dn·n] (a) say that one hopes sb will have sth: *They wished us a pleasant journey.* ○ *His colleagues wished him happiness on his retirement.* ○ *Wish me luck!* (b) say (sth) as a greeting: *wish sb good morning, goodbye, happy birthday, welcome, etc.* **3** [I] formulate (and express) a desire: *Do you wish when you see a shooting star?* **4** (idm) **(just) as you ˈwish** I am prepared to agree with you or to do what you want: *We can meet at my house or yours, just as you wish.* **wish sb/sth ˈwell/ˈill** hope that sb/sth does/does not have good fortune: *I wish him well in his new job.* ○ *She said she wished nobody ill.* **5** (phr v) **wish sth away** try to get rid of something by wishing it did not exist: *These problems can't be wished away, you know.* **wish sb/sth on sb** (*infml*) pass (an unwanted or unpleasant task, visitor, etc) on to sb: *It's not a job I'd wish on anybody.* ○ *I don't think we can wish the children on your parents while we're away.*

▷ **wish** *n* **1** (a) [C] ~ **(to do sth)**; ~ **(for sth)** (expression of a) desire or longing: *She expressed a wish to be alone.* ○ *He had no wish to intrude on their privacy.* ○ *If you had three wishes what would you choose?* ○ *Her wish came true*, ie She got what she wished for. ○ *You have deliberately acted against my wishes.* (b) **wishes** [pl ~**s**] ~ **(for sth)** (expression of) hopes for sb's happiness or welfare: *with best wishes*, eg at the end of a letter ○ *We all send our best wishes (for your recovery).* **2** [U] that which is wished for: *You will get your wish.* **3** (idm) **the ˌwish is ˌfather to the ˈthought** (*saying fml*) one thinks that sth is true or likely because one wants it to be so. **your wish is my comˈmand** (*fml or joc*) I am ready to do whatever you ask.

wishful /-fl/ *adj (fml)* having or expressing a wish: *wishful statements.* ˌ**wishful** ˈ**thinking** belief based on wishes and not on facts: *I think her condition is improving but it may just be wishful thinking on my part.*

□ ˈ**wishbone** *n* forked bone between the neck and the breast of a fowl (often pulled apart by two people, with the one who gets the larger part being allowed to make a wish).

wishy-washy /ˈwɪʃɪ wɒʃɪ; *US* -wɔːʃɪ/ *adj (usu derog)* weak or feeble in colour, characteristics, quality, etc: *a wishy-washy blue* ○ *a wishy-washy liberal,* ie one whose ideas are not clearly defined.

wisp /wɪsp/ *n* ~ **(of sth) 1 (a)** small separate bunch, bundle or twist (of sth): *a wisp of hair/hay/straw/grass.* **(b)** small streak or ribbon: *a wisp of smoke.* **2** small thin person: *a wisp of a girl.*

▷ **wispy** *adj* **(-ier, -iest)** like a wisp or in wisps; slight or straggly: *wispy hair, clouds* ○ *a wispy white beard.*

wistaria (also **wisteria**) /wɪˈstɪərɪə/ *n* [U] any of several types of climbing plant with a woody stem and long drooping clusters of pale purple or white flowers.

wistful /ˈwɪstfl/ *adj* full of or expressing sad or vague longing (esp for sth that is past or unobtainable): *wistful eyes* ○ *a wistful mood.* ▷ **wistfully** /-fəlɪ/ *adv*: *sighing wistfully* ○ *'If only I had known you then,' he said wistfully.* **wistfulness** *n* [U].

wit /wɪt/ *n* **1 (a)** [U] ability to combine words, ideas, etc so as to produce a clever type of humour: *have a ready wit* ○ *a journalist much admired for her wit* ○ *a literary style full of elegance and wit.* **(b)** [C] person who has or is famous for this; witty person: *a well-known wit and raconteur.* **2** [U] (also **wits** [pl]) quick understanding; intelligence: *He hadn't the wits/wit enough to realize the danger.* **3** (idm) **at one's wits'** ˈ**end** not knowing what to do or say because of worry or desperation: *I'm at my wits' end worrying about how to pay the bills.* **a battle of wits** ⇨ BATTLE. **collect/gather one's** ˈ**wits** become calm again after an unexpected shock, etc so that one can think clearly: *I needed time to gather my wits before seeing him again.* **frighten/scare sb out of his** ˈ**wits** ⇨ FRIGHTEN. **have/keep one's** ˈ**wits about one** be/remain alert and ready to act: *You need to keep your wits about you when you're dealing with a man like that.* **live by one's wits** ⇨ LIVE². **sharpen sb's wits** ⇨ SHARPEN (SHARP). **to** ˈ**wit** *(dated fml)* that is to say; namely: *He will leave at the end of term, to wit 30 July.* ˌ**wit and** ˈ**wisdom** combination of quick intelligence, good judgement and learning, esp in a writer or speaker.

▷ **witless** *adj* unintelligent or foolish; out of one's mind: *scare sb witless,* ie out of his wits.

-witted (forming compound adjs) having a certain type of intelligence: ˌ*dim-*ˈ*witted* ○ ˌ*quick-*ˈ*witted.*

witty *adj* **(-ier, -iest)** full of clever humour: *a witty speaker* ○ *witty comments.* **witticism** /ˈwɪtɪsɪzəm/ *n* witty remark. **wittily** /-ɪlɪ/ *adv.* **wittiness** *n* [U].

witch /wɪtʃ/ *n* **(a)** (esp formerly) woman thought to have evil magic powers (often portrayed in fairy stories wearing a black cloak and pointed hat and flying on a broomstick); sorceress. **(b)** *(fig)* fascinating or bewitching woman. **(c)** *(derog)* ugly old woman; hag.

▷ **witchery** /ˈwɪtʃərɪ/ *n* [U] *(fml)* **1** witchcraft. **2** bewitching power of beauty, eloquence, etc.

witching *adj* [attrib] *(dated fml)* bewitching: *the witching hour,* ie midnight, the time when witches are active.

□ ˈ**witchcraft** *n* [U] use of magic powers, esp evil ones; sorcery.

ˈ**witch-doctor** (also **medicine-man**) *n* (esp formerly in Africa) tribal doctor with supposed magic powers.

ˈ**witch-hazel** (also ˈ**wych-hazel**) *n* **1** [C] N American tree with yellow flowers. **2** [U] liquid obtained from the bark of this tree, used to treat bruises or sores on the skin.

ˈ**witch-hunt** *n* **(a)** search to find and destroy people thought to be witches. **(b)** *(fig usu derog)* investigation made in order to persecute people who hold unorthodox or unpopular views: *The crusade for sexual morality is turning into a witch-hunt.*

with /wɪð, wɪθ/ *prep* **1 (a)** in the company or presence of (sb/sth): *live with one's parents* ○ *go on holiday with a friend* ○ *spend time with the children* ○ *discuss the plans with an expert* ○ *I've got a client with me at the moment.* ○ *Put the dolls away with your other toys.* ○ *If you mix blue with yellow you get green.* ○ *Can I wear this tie with my blue shirt?* ○ *The money is on the table with the shopping-list.* **(b)** in the care, charge or possession of (sb): *I leave the baby with my mother every day.* ○ *I left a message for you with your secretary.* ○ *The keys are with reception.* **2** having or carrying (sth): *a girl with* (ie who has) *red hair* ○ *the man with the scar* ○ *a person with a knowledge of European markets* ○ *a coat with a belt* ○ *a house with a swimming-pool* ○ *the man with a wooden leg* ○ *the boy with a camera* ○ *He looked at her with a hurt expression.* **3 (a)** (indicating the tool or instrument used): *cut it with a knife* ○ *You can see it with a microscope.* ○ *He hit it with a hammer.* ○ *feed the baby with a spoon* ○ *sew with cotton thread* ○ *hold the door open with a stone* ○ *I can only move it with your help.* ○ *It was easy to translate with a dictionary.* **(b)** (indicating the material or item used): *fill the bowl with water* ○ *sprinkle the dish with salt* ○ *The lorry was loaded with timber.* ○ *The bag was stuffed with dirty clothes.* **4 (a)** agreeing with or supporting (sb/sth): *We've got all the nurses with us in our fight to stop closures.* ○ *She's going along with management on this issue.* ○ *I'm with you all the way!* **(b)** in opposition to (sth); against (sth): *fight, argue, quarrel, etc with sb* ○ *I had a row with Jane.* ○ *in competition with our rivals* ○ *play tennis with sb* ○ *at war with a neighbouring country.* **5** because of (sth); on account of (sth): *blush with embarrassment* ○ *tremble with fear* ○ *shaking with laughter* ○ *Her fingers were numb with cold.* **6** (indicating the manner, circumstances or condition in which sth is done or takes place): *I'll do it with pleasure.* ○ *I can lift 50 kilos with an effort.* ○ *She performed a somersault with ease,* ie easily. ○ *He acted with discretion,* ie discreetly. ○ *She sleeps with the light on.* ○ *He welcomed her with open arms.* ○ *Don't stand with your hands in your pockets.* ○ *With your permission, sir, I'd like to speak.* **7** in the same direction as (sth): *sail with the wind* ○ *swim with the tide* ○ *drift with the current* ○ *The shadow moves with the sun.* **8** because of and at the same rate as (sth): *The shadows lengthened with the approach of sunset.* ○ *Skill comes with experience.* ○ *Good wine will improve with age.* **9** in regard to, towards or concerning (sb/sth): *careful with the glasses* ○ *patient with your aunt* ○ *angry with my children* ○ *pleased with the result* ○ *inconsistent with an earlier statement* ○ *a problem with accommodation* ○ *What can he want with me?* ○ *What can one do with half a chess set?* **10** in the case of (sb/sth); as regards (sb/sth): *With Italians it's pronunciation that's the problem.* ○ *It's a very busy time with us at the moment.* **11** and also (sth); including (sth): *The meal with wine came to £12 each.* ○ *With preparation and marking a teacher works 12 hours a day* ○ *The week cost us over £500 but that was with skiing lessons.* **12** (as) an employee or client of (an organization): *I hear he's with ICI now.* ○ *She acted with a repertory company for three years.* ○ *We're with the same bank.* **13** (indicating separation from sth/sb): *I could never part with this ring.* ○ *Can we dispense with the formalities?* **14** considering (one fact in relation to another): *With only two days to go we can't afford to relax.* ○ *With no hope of a holiday life's very depressing.* ○ *She won't be able to help us, with all her family commitments.* **15** in spite of (sth); despite: *With all her faults he still liked her.* **16** (idm) **be with sb** *(infml)* be able to follow what sb is saying: *I'm afraid I'm not quite with you.* ˈ**with it** *(dated sl)* **(a)** knowledgeable about current fashions and ideas; alert: *Come on — get with it!* ○ *He's not very with it today.* **(b)** (of clothes and their wearers) fashionable: *She's more with it now than she was 20 years ago.* **with** ˈ**that** immediately after that: *He muttered a few words of apology and with that he left.*

withdraw /wɪðˈdrɔː, *also* wɪθˈd-/ *v* (*pt* **withdrew** /-ˈdruː/, *pp* **withdrawn** /-ˈdrɔːn/) **1** [Tn, Tn·pr] ~ **sb/sth (from sth) (a)** pull or take sb/sth back or away: *The general refused to withdraw his troops.* ○ *The old coins have been withdrawn from circulation.* ○ *The workers have threatened to withdraw their labour,* ie go on strike. **(b)** remove (money) from a bank account, etc: *She withdrew all her savings and left the country.* **2** [Tn] *(fml)* take back (a promise, an offer, a statement, etc); retract: *Unless the contract is signed immediately, I shall withdraw my offer.* ○ *I insist that you withdraw your offensive remarks immediately.* **3** [I, Ipr] ~ **(from sth)** go away from a place or from other people: *He talked to us for an hour and then withdrew.* ○ *withdraw into oneself,* ie become unresponsive or unsociable ○ *The troops had to withdraw to a less exposed position.*

▷ **withdrawal** /-ˈdrɔːəl/ *n* **1 (a)** [U] withdrawing or being withdrawn: *the withdrawal of supplies, support, troops* ○ *the withdrawal of a product from the market* ○ *(psychology) She is showing signs of withdrawal* (ie not wanting to communicate with other people) *and depression.* **(b)** [C] instance of this: *You are allowed to make two withdrawals a month from the account.* **2** [U] process of ceasing to take an addictive drug, often accompanied by unpleasant reactions: [attrib] *withdrawal symptoms.*

withdrawn *adj* (of a person) uncommunicative or unsociable: *He's become increasingly withdrawn since his wife's death.*

wither /ˈwɪðə(r)/ *v* **1** [I, Ip, Tn, Tn·p] ~ **(away)**; ~ **(sth) (up)** (cause sth to) become dry, shrivelled or dead: *The flowers will wither if you don't put them in water.* ○ *(fig) Their hopes gradually withered away.* ○ *limbs withered by disease and starvation.* **2** [Tn] subdue or overwhelm (sb) with scorn, etc: *She withered him with a glance.*

▷ **withering** /ˈwɪðərɪŋ/ *adj* (of a look, remark, etc) scornful or contemptuous: *withering sarcasm.* **witheringly** *adv.*

withers /ˈwɪðəz/ *n* [pl] highest part of the back of a horse, between the shoulder-blades. ⇨ illus at HORSE.

withhold /wɪðˈhəʊld, *also* wɪθˈh-/ *v* (*pt, pp* **withheld** /-ˈheld/) *(fml)* **(a)** [Tn, Tn·pr] ~ **sth (from sb/sth)** *(fml)* refuse to give sth; keep sth back: *withhold one's consent/permission* ○ *withhold information* ○ *The board has decided to withhold part of their grant money from certain students.* **(b)** [Tn] hold (sth) back; restrain: *We couldn't withhold our laughter.*

□ **with**ˈ**holding tax** (in the USA) tax that is deducted from an employee's pay before he or she receives it, and is paid directly to the government by the employer.

within /wɪˈðɪn/ *prep* **1 (a)** after not more than (the specified period of time): *She returned within an hour.* ○ *If you don't hear anything within seven days, phone again.* **(b)** ~ **sth (of sth)** not further than (the specified distance) (from sth): *a house within a mile of the station* ○ *The village has three pubs within a hundred metres (of each other).* **2** inside the range or limits of (sb/sth): *We are now within sight of* (ie able to see) *the shore.* ○ *There is a bell within the patient's reach,* ie which the patient can reach. ○ *He finds it hard to live within his income,* ie without spending more than he earns. ○ *I'd prefer you to keep this information within the family,* ie known only by members of the family. ○ *within the limits of my modest talents.* **3** *(fml)* inside (sth): *within the medieval walls of the city* ○ *Interview everyone living within the area shown on the map.*

▷ **within** *adv (fml)* inside: *Shop assistant required. Apply within.*

without /wɪˈðaʊt/ *prep* **1** not having, experiencing or showing (sth): *two days without food* ○ *three nights without sleep* ○ *You can't leave the country without a passport.* ○ *The letter had been posted without a stamp.* ○ *I've come out without any*

money. ○ *a bedroom without a private bath* ○ *a skirt without pockets* ○ *He acted without thought for himself.* ○ *She spoke without enthusiasm.* **2** in the absence of (sb/sth); not accompanied by (sb/sth): *He said he couldn't live without her.* ○ *I feel very lonely without my dog.* ○ *We can't reach a decision without our chairman.* ○ *Don't leave without me.* ○ *They were received without ceremony*, ie informally. **3** not using (sth): *How did you open the bottle without a bottle-opener?* ○ *She can't see to read without her glasses.* **4** (used with the *-ing* form to mean 'not'): *Try and do it without making any mistakes.* ○ *The party was organized without her knowing anything about it.* ○ *He walked past me without speaking.* ○ *I've often cheated in exams without being caught.* ○ *She entered the room without knocking.* **5** (*arch*) outside (sth): *without the city walls.* **6** (idm) **without so much as** ⇨ so[1].
▷ **without** *adv part* not having or showing sth: *We'll have one room with a bathroom and one room without.* ○ *If there's no sugar we'll have to manage without.*

withstand /wɪðˈstænd, *also* wɪθˈs-/ *v* (*pt, pp* **withstood** /-ˈstʊd/) [Tn] (*often fml*) endure (sth) without giving in, collapsing, wearing out, etc; resist: *withstand attacks, pressure, wind* ○ *shoes that will withstand hard wear.*

withy /ˈwɪðɪ/ *n* tough branch, esp of willow, that bends easily and is used for tying bundles.

witless ⇨ WIT.

witness /ˈwɪtnɪs/ *n* **1** [C] (**a**) (also ˈ**eye-witness**) person who sees an event take place (and is therefore able to describe it to others): *witnesses (at the scene) of the accident* ○ *I was a witness to their quarrel.* (**b**) person who gives evidence in a lawcourt after swearing to tell the truth: *a defence/prosecution witness* ○ *a witness for the defence/prosecution* ○ *The witness was cross-examined by the defending counsel.* (**c**) person who is present at an event, esp the signing of a document, in order to testify to the fact that it took place: *Will you act as witness to the agreement between us?* **2** [U, C usu *sing*] (*fml*) what is said about an event, etc, esp in a lawcourt; (thing that serves as) testimony or evidence: *give witness on behalf of an accused person* ○ *His ragged clothes were (a) witness to his poverty.* **3** (idm) **bear witness** ⇨ BEAR[2]. **call sb to witness (that...)** ⇨ CALL[2].
▷ **witness** *v* **1** [Tn] be present at (sth) and see it: *witness an accident, a murder, a quarrel* ○ *We were witnessing the most important scientific development of the century.* ○ (*fml*) *Weather forecasters are not always right: witness* (ie look at the example of) *their recent mistakes.* **2** [Tn] be a witness to the signing of (a document), esp by also signing the document oneself: *witness the signing of a contract* ○ *witness a signature, treaty, will.* **3** [Ipr] ~ **to sth** (*law or fml*) give evidence about sth in a lawcourt, etc: *witness* (ie testify) *to the truth of a statement.*
□ ˈ**witness-box** (*Brit*) (*US* ˈ**witness-stand**) *n* enclosure in a lawcourt in which a witness stands when giving evidence.

witter /ˈwɪtə(r)/ *v* [I, Ipr, Ip] ~ **(on) (about sth)** (*infml usu derog*) speak in a lengthy and annoying way about sth unimportant: *What are you wittering (on) about?*

Wittgenstein /ˈvɪtgənstaɪn/ Ludwig Josef Johann (1889-1951), Austrian-born philosopher who came to England in 1911. He studied under Bertrand *Russell and worked on theories of language. In his *Tractatus Logico-philosophicus* he put forward the view that language 'pictures' things by established conventions. He later changed his ideas, having come to think that usage is more important than convention.

witticism ⇨ WIT.

wittingly /ˈwɪtɪŋlɪ/ *adv* (esp in negative sentences) knowing what one does; intentionally: *I would never wittingly offend him.*

witty ⇨ WIT.

wives *pl* of WIFE.

wizard /ˈwɪzəd/ *n* **1** male witch (esp in fairy stories); magician. **2** person with extraordinary abilities; genius: *a financial wizard*, ie sb who is able to make money amazingly easily ○ *She's a wizard with computers.*
▷ **wizardry** /-drɪ/ *n* [U] (**a**) practice of magic. (**b**) extraordinary ability: *financial wizardry.*

wizened /ˈwɪznd/ *adj* having a dried-up wrinkled skin; shrivelled: *a wizened old woman* ○ *a face wizened with age* ○ *wizened apples.*

wk *abbr* **1** (*pl* **wks**) week. **2** work.

WO /ˌdʌblju: ˈəʊ/ *abbr* Warrant Officer.

woad /wəʊd/ *n* [U] (**a**) blue dye formerly obtained from a plant of the mustard family. (**b**) this plant (*Isatis tinctoria*).

wobble /ˈwɒbl/ *v* [I, Ipr, Ip, Tn, Tn·pr, Tn·p] ~ **(sth) (about/around)** (cause sth to) move from side to side unsteadily: *This table wobbles.* ○ *I was so terrified my legs were wobbling.* ○ *wobbling along the pavement in high-heeled boots* ○ (*fig*) *Her voice sometimes wobbles* (ie quivers, wavers) *on high notes.* ○ *Please don't wobble the desk (about) when I'm trying to write.*
▷ **wobble** *n* (usu *sing*) wobbling movement.
wobbly /ˈwɒblɪ/ *adj* (*infml*) tending to move unsteadily from side to side: *a wobbly tooth* ○ *a wobbly line*, ie not drawn straight ○ *wobbly jelly* ○ (*fig*) *He is still a bit wobbly (on his legs) after his illness.* **wobbliness** *n* [U].

Wodehouse /ˈwʊdhaʊs/ Sir P(elham) G(renville) (1881-1975), English humorous writer best known for his creation of the characters Bertie Wooster, a foolish upper-class young man, and his manservant *Jeeves. Other notable Wodehouse characters include Lord Emsworth, Psmith and Ukridge. He wrote over 120 books, as well as the words for many successful musical comedies in the USA (where he spent most of his life, becoming a US citizen in 1955).

wodge /wɒdʒ/ *n* ~ **(of sth)** (*Brit infml*) large piece or amount: *a thick wodge of cake* ○ *wodges of old newspapers.*

woe /wəʊ/ *n* (*dated or fml or joc*) **1** [U] great sorrow or distress: *a cry of woe* ○ *She needed someone to listen to her tale of woe*, ie the story of her misfortune. **2 woes** [pl] things that cause sorrow or distress; troubles or misfortunes: *She told him all her woes.* **3** (idm) **woe beˈtide sb** (*fml or joc*) there will be trouble for sb: *Woe betide anyone who arrives late!* ˌ**woe is ˈme!** *interj* (*arch or joc*) how unhappy I am.

woebegone /ˈwəʊbɪgɒn; *US* -gɔ:n/ *adj* (*fml*) looking unhappy: *a woebegone child, expression, face.*

woeful /ˈwəʊfl/ *adj* (*fml*) **1** full of woe; sad: *a woeful cry, look, sight.* **2** [usu attrib] undesirable or regrettable; very bad: *woeful ignorance.* ▷ **woefully** /-fəlɪ/ *adj*: *The preparations were woefully inadequate.*

wog /wɒg/ *n* (*Brit* ⚠ *sl offensive*) foreigner, esp a black or coloured one.

wok /wɒk/ *n* large pan shaped like a bowl, used for cooking (esp) Chinese food. ⇨ illus at PAN.

woke *pt* of WAKE[1].

woken *pp* of WAKE 1.

wolf

wolf /wʊlf/ *n* (*pl* **wolves** /wʊlvz/) **1** fierce wild animal of the dog family, usu hunting in packs. **2** (idm) **cry wolf** ⇨ CRY[1]. **keep the ˈwolf from the door** have enough money to avoid hunger and need: *Their wages are barely enough to keep the wolf from the door.* **a lone wolf** ⇨ LONE. **a wolf in ˈsheep's clothing** person who appears friendly or harmless but is really an enemy. **throw sb to the ˈwolves** leave sb to be roughly treated or criticized without trying to help or defend him.
▷ **wolf** *v* [Tn, Tn·p] ~ **sth (down)** (*infml*) eat sth quickly and greedily: *I wanted a biscuits but they'd wolfed the lot!* ○ *Don't wolf down your food.*
wolfish *adj* of or like a wolf: *a wolfish grin.*
□ ˈ**wolf-cub** *n* young wolf.
ˈ**wolfhound** *n* any of several types of very large dog originally bred for hunting wolves: *an Irish wolfhound.*
ˈ**wolf-whistle** *n* whistling sound made by a man to show that he finds a woman sexually attractive. — *v* [I, Ipr] ~ **(at sb)** make this sound.

Wolfe /wʊlf/ James (1727-59), British general who led the force which attacked and captured Quebec, thus effectively driving the French out of Canada. He died of wounds he received during the fighting.

wolfram /ˈwʊlfrəm/ *n* [U] (**a**) = TUNGSTEN. (**b**) tungsten ore.

Wollstonecraft /ˈwʊlstənkrɑ:ft; *US* -kræft/ Mary (1759-97), British feminist, who campaigned for equal educational opportunities for women. She was the mother of Mary *Shelley.

Wolsey /ˈwʊlzɪ/ Thomas (c 1474-1530), English cardinal who was *Henry VIII's chief adviser on foreign and domestic affairs in the early years of his reign. He became very powerful, but fell from favour when he was unable to gain the Pope's permission for Henry to divorce Catherine of Aragon so that he could marry Anne Boleyn. He built the palace of *Hampton Court, which he later gave to Henry.

wolverine /ˈwʊlvəri:n/ *n* fierce meat-eating animal of northern Europe, Asia and N America. It is the largest member of the weasel family.

woman /ˈwʊmən/ *n* (*pl* **women** /ˈwɪmɪn/) **1** [C] (**a**) adult female human being: *men, women and children* ○ *a single* (ie unmarried) *woman* ○ *It's more than a woman* (ie any woman) *can tolerate.* ([attrib] preferred to *lady* which is also used): *a* ˌ*woman* ˈ*driver* ○ ˌ*women* ˈ*drivers* ○ *I'd prefer a woman doctor to examine me.* ○ *a* ˈ*woman friend* ○ *a* ˈ*French woman.* (**b**) (as an offensive form of address): *Shut up, woman!* **2** [sing] (without *a* or *the*) female human beings in general; the female sex: *Woman has been portrayed by artists in many ways.* ⇨article. **3 the woman** [sing] the feminine side of a woman's character: *Newborn babies bring out the woman in her.* **4** (idm) **be twice the man/woman** ⇨ TWICE. **make an honest woman of sb** ⇨ HONEST. **a man/woman of parts** ⇨ PART[1]. **a man/woman of his/her word** ⇨ WORD. **a man/woman of the world** ⇨ WORLD. **wine, women and song** ⇨ WINE. **a woman of easy ˈvirtue** (*euph*) prostitute.
▷ **-woman** (with *ns* forming compound *ns*) woman concerned with: ˈ*chairwoman* ○ ˈ*horsewoman* ○ ˈ*sportswoman.* Cf -MAN (MAN[1]).
ˈ**womanhood** [U] state of being a woman: *grow to/reach womanhood.*
womanish *adj* (*derog*) (of a man) like a woman; suitable for women but not for men: *He has a rather womanish manner.*
womanize, -ise /-aɪz/ *v* [I] (*usu derog*) (of a man) have sexual affairs with numerous women. **womanizer, -iser** *n* man who does this.
womanly *adj* (*approv*) like a woman; feminine: *a womanly figure* ○ *womanly qualities, virtues.* **womanliness** *n* [U].
□ ˈ**womankind** *n* [U] (*fml*) female human beings in general: *the sufferings of womankind.*
ˌ**Women's ˈInstitute** (*abbr* **WI**) /ˌdʌblju: ˈaɪ/ world-wide organization that enables women in country areas to meet and take part in activities together. It originated in Canada in 1895.
ˌ**Women's Libeˈration** (also *infml* ˌ**Women's ˈLib** /lɪb/) freedom of women to enjoy the same social and economic rights as men. ˌ**Women's ˈLibber** (*infml*) person who campaigns for this ideal; feminist.
the ˈwomen's movement social and political movement that aims to achieve Women's Liberation by legislation and by changing people's attitudes. ⇨ article at PROTEST.

womb /wu:m/ *n* (*anatomy*) (in women and other female mammals) organ in which offspring is carried and nourished while it develops before birth; uterus. ⇨ illus at FEMALE.

wombat /ˈwɒmbæt/ *n* Australian wild animal similar to a small bear, the female of which carries its young in a pouch.

Women

The lives of women in Britain have changed dramatically in the course of the present century as many of the social, economic and political constraints have been removed. Women have gained equality with men in many fields. One of the main developments has been the increasing number of women in paid employment. This has come about not only because of recognition of the important contributions women can make, but also as a result of the altered nature of family life. The trend towards later marriage means that women usually work for some years before marrying and having children, and many women combine a job with raising a young family, although many find it difficult because of a shortage of child care provision. There is a degree of flexibility in some jobs and some employers provide help with child care for working mothers, but they are still in a minority. In Britain in the late 1980s about half of all married women of working age had a job or were looking for one. This is a higher proportion than anywhere else in Europe except Denmark.

Although there are now few jobs that cannot be taken on by women, there is still a noticeable difference in earnings between men and women, and there are certain areas of employment where women remain thinly represented. At the end of the 1980s, for example, women's average hourly earnings were about three-quarters those of men, and there is evidence to show that the gap is widening. Female manual workers in particular are paid significantly less than men. In the leading professions, too, women are represented by a proportion of less than one to five.

At present, the professions where women are most frequently found are those of pharmacists, opticians, veterinary surgeons, dentists, doctors and solicitors. Only one qualified engineer in 200 is a woman. Many professions are not geared to the career needs of women, and do not, for example, offer part-time work or provide 'career breaks' for women to have children. Nevertheless, women are now much more widely represented in the media (journalism, broadcasting, publishing) than they were, and in education many teachers are women.

The disparity between women's pay and men's is an injustice that has been combated in recent years, in many instances successfully. The Equal Pay Act of 1970 made it illegal for employers to pay a woman less than a man for the same or similar work or work of equal value. The Sex Discrimination Acts of 1975 and 1986 made it unlawful to discriminate in matters of employment or training on the grounds of sex. The Equal Opportunities Commission was set up in 1975 to enforce this legislation and to promote equality of opportunity. In 1988 a woman cook fought a four-year legal battle for 'equal pay for work of equal value' and won her case, so that her wages were raised to match those of male painters and insulation engineers in the company where she worked. In 1989, in a greater victory, several thousand women secretaries and typists at Lloyds Bank were granted pay rises to bring their wages to the same level as those of male senior messengers.

In the Church of England women were admitted for ordination as deacons in 1986, and the following year the General Synod voted to proceed with legislation to allow women to be ordained as priests. As a further development, two women were admitted as priests in the Church of Ireland, a member of the Anglican Communion, in 1990.

Real discrimination against women remains in some quarters, however. Women sentenced for criminal offences, for example, are more likely to be sent to prison than men, even though they represent only four per cent of the total prison population. In prison itself, too, women are often treated more harshly than men, especially if they do not conform to the popular image of 'woman as wife and mother'.

By contrast, educational opportunities for women are potentially now as good as they are for men. There is still resistance in some schools, however, to a provision for the education of girls in technical subjects, even in information technology, while many parents remain unconvinced that such subjects are 'useful' for their daughters. There is still a traditional division between subjects that are perceived as 'boys' subjects' such as science, mathematics and computer studies, and 'girls' subjects' such as English, foreign languages and home economics.

From the middle of the 19th century, women campaigned for equal voting rights with men, notably in the suffragette movement of the early 20th century. Only in 1918, however, were women over 30 given the vote, and full equality was not granted until 1928, when all British subjects over 21 were allowed to vote. Today, women are increasingly represented in Parliament. In 1990, of the total 650 members of Parliament (MPs), 43 were women. The number, though small compared to many other European countries, is twice what it was seven years earlier. In British society generally, women occupy key posts that only a short time ago would certainly have been held by men. The obvious example is Margaret Thatcher as Britain's first woman prime minister.

womenfolk /ˈwɪmɪnfəʊk/ *n* [pl] women, esp the women of a particular group, family, tribe, etc: *The dead soldiers were mourned by their womenfolk.* Cf MENFOLK.

won *pt, pp* of WIN.

wonder /ˈwʌndə(r)/ *n* **1** **(a)** [U] feeling of surprise mixed with admiration, bewilderment or disbelief: *The children watched the conjuror in silent wonder.* ○ *They were filled with wonder at the sight.* **(b)** [C] thing or event that causes this feeling: *the wonders of modern medicine* ○ *the seven wonders of the world* ○ [attrib] *a wonder drug*, ie one that has extremely good, almost miraculous, effects. **2** (idm) **a chinless wonder** ⇨ CHINLESS (CHIN). **do/work miracles/wonders (for sth)** ⇨ MIRACLE. **it's a wonder (that)...** it's surprising or puzzling (that)...: *It's a wonder (that) he continues to gamble when he always loses!* **a nine days' wonder** ⇨ DAY. **no/little/small ˈwonder (that...)** it is not/hardly surprising: *No wonder you were late!* ○ *Small wonder (that) he was so tired!* **ˌwonders will ˌnever ˈcease** (*saying esp ironic*) (expressing surprise and pleasure at sth, often sth trivial): *'I've washed the car for you.' 'Wonders will never cease!'*

▷ **wonder** *v* **1** [I, Ipr, It, Tf] ~ **(at sth)** (*fml*) feel great surprise, admiration, etc; marvel: *He could do nothing but stand and wonder.* ○ *We wondered at the speed with which it arrived.* ○ *I wonder* (ie am amazed) *(at the fact) that you weren't killed.* ○ *I wondered* (ie was surprised) *to hear her voice in the next room.* **2** **(a)** [I, Ipr] ~ **(about sth)** feel curious (about sth); ask oneself questions: *There has been no news for a week and he is beginning to wonder.* ○ *I was just wondering about that myself.* **(b)** [Tw] ask oneself: *I wonder who he is.* ○ *I wonder whether they will arrive on time.* ○ *wondered what time it was, where to go, how long it would last, why he had left.* **(c)** [Tw] (used as a polite way of introducing a request): *I wonder if/whether you could....* **3** (idm) **I ˌshouldn't ˈwonder** (*infml*) I should not be surprised (to discover): *It's paid for with stolen money, I shouldn't wonder.*

wonderful /-fl/ *adj* **(a)** causing wonder; very surprising: *It's wonderful that they managed to escape.* ○ *The child's skill is wonderful for his age.* **(b)** very good or admirable: *The weather is wonderful.* ○ *She is a wonderful mother.* ○ *a wonderful opportunity*. **wonderfully** /-fəlɪ/ *adv* **(a)** surprisingly: *She is wonderfully active for her age.* **(b)** extremely; admirably: *Their life together has been wonderfully happy.*

wonderingly /ˈwʌndrɪŋlɪ/ *adv*: *'Where did this come from?' she said wonderingly.*

wonderment *n* [U] pleasant amazement: *She gasped in wonderment at her good luck.*

wondrous /ˈwʌndrəs/ *adj* (*arch or fml*) wonderful: *a wondrous sight.* **wondrously** *adv.*

□ **ˈwonderland** /-lænd/ *n* (usu *sing*) land or place full of marvels or wonderful things.

wonky /ˈwɒŋkɪ/ *adj* **(-ier, -iest)** (*Brit infml*) unsteady or weak; wobbly: *a wonky chair* ○ *She still feels a bit wonky after her accident.*

wont /wəʊnt; *US* wɔːnt/ *adj* [pred] ~ **(to do sth)** (*dated or rhet*) in the habit of doing sth; accustomed to doing sth: *He was wont to give lengthy speeches.*

▷ **wont** *n* [sing] (*fml or rhet*) custom; habit: *She went for a walk after breakfast, as was her wont.*

wonted *adj* [attrib] (*fml or rhet*) usual, habitual: *with his wonted courtesy.*

won't *contracted form of* WILL NOT (WILL[1]).

woo /wuː/ *v* (*pt, pp* **wooed**) [Tn] **1** **(a)** try to obtain the support of (sb): *woo the voters.* **(b)** try to achieve or obtain (sth): *woo fame, fortune, success, etc.* **2** (*dated*) try to persuade (a woman) to marry one; court.

Wood /wʊd/ Sir Henry (1869-1944), English conductor who conducted the first promenade concerts (PROMENADE) and between 1895 and 1944 built them into a major feature of British musical life.

wood /wʊd/ *n* **1** **(a)** [U] hard fibrous substance in the trunk and branches of a tree, enclosed by the bark: *There are many kinds of wood growing in this forest.* **(b)** this substance, cut and used as building material, fuel, etc: *Tables are usually made of wood.* ○ *Put some more wood on the fire.* ○ [attrib] *a wood floor*, ie made of wood. **(c)** [C] particular type of this: *Pine is a soft wood and teak is a hard wood.* ○ *Oak is a good type of wood for making furniture.* **2** [C often *pl*] area of land (not as large as a forest) covered with growing trees: *a house in the middle of a wood* ○ *go for a walk in the wood(s).* **3** [C] (*sport*) = BOWL 2. **4** [C] golf-club with a wooden head. Cf IRON[1] 4. **5** (idm) **babes in the wood** ⇨ BABE. **dead wood** ⇨ DEAD. **from the ˈwood** from the cask or wooden barrel: *beer from the wood.* **neck of the woods** ⇨ NECK. **not see the ˌwood for the ˈtrees** not see or understand the main point, subject, etc because one is paying too much attention to details: *If you add too many notes to the* *text, the reader won't be able to see the wood for the trees.* ˌ**out of the ˈwood(s)** (*infml*) (usu with a negative) free from trouble or difficulties: *She's regained consciousness, but she's not out of the woods* (ie sure to recover) *yet.* **touch wood** ⇨ TOUCH².

▷ **wooded** *adj* (of land) covered with growing trees: *a wooded valley.*

wooden /ˈwʊdn/ *adj* **1** [esp attrib] made of wood: *wooden furniture, houses, toys.* **2** stiff and awkward (in one's manner): *She has a rather wooden manner.* ○ *a wooden smile, performance.* **woodenly** *adv* stiffly and awkwardly. **woodenness** *n* [U]. ˌ**wooden ˈspoon** = BOOBY PRIZE (BOOBY).

woody *adj* (**a**) wooded: *a woody hillside.* (**b**) of or like growing wood: *a plant with woody stems* ○ *a woody smell.*

□ ˈ**woodbine** *n* [U] (**a**) wild honeysuckle. (**b**) (*US*) = VIRGINIA CREEPER.

ˈ**wood-block** *n* (**a**) block of wood from which woodcuts are made. (**b**) any of many pieces of wood used in making a floor, often arranged in a pattern: [attrib] *a wood-block floor.*

ˈ**woodchuck** *n* (*US*) type of N American marmot; groundhog.

ˈ**woodcock** *n* (*pl* unchanged) (**a**) [C] type of brown game-bird found in woodland with a long straight bill, short legs and a short tail. (**b**) [U] its flesh eaten as food.

ˈ**woodcraft** *n* [U] knowledge of woodland conditions; skill in finding one's way in woods and forests, esp as used in hunting.

ˈ**woodcut** *n* print made from a design, drawing, etc cut in relief on a block of wood.

ˈ**woodcutter** *n* person who cuts down trees as an occupation.

ˈ**woodland** /-lənd/ *n* [U] land covered with trees; woods: [attrib] *woodland scenery.*

ˈ**wood lot** (*US*) area, eg on a farm, kept for growing trees.

ˈ**wood-louse** *n* (*pl* **-lice**) small wingless insect-like creature that lives in decaying wood, damp soil, etc.

ˈ**woodman** /-mən/ (also *esp US* ˈ**woodsman** /-zmən/) *n* (*pl* **-men**) forester; woodcutter.

ˈ**woodpecker** *n* bird that clings to the bark of trees and taps with its beak to find insects. ⇨ illus at BIRD.

ˈ**wood-pigeon** (also ˈ**ring-dove**) *n* type of large wild pigeon.

ˈ**wood-pulp** *n* [U] wood shredded and used for making paper.

ˈ**wood-shed** *n* shed where wood is stored (esp for fuel).

ˈ**woodwind** /-wɪnd/ *n* [Gp] (players of the) wind instruments of an orchestra which are (or were formerly) made of wood: [attrib] *a woodwind instrument* ○ *the woodwind section.* ⇨ illus at MUSIC.

ˈ**woodwork** *n* [U] **1** things made of wood, esp the wooden parts of a building, eg doors, stairs, etc: *The woodwork is painted white.* **2** skill or practice of making things from wood; carpentry.

ˈ**woodworm** *n* (**a**) [C] type of larva that bores through wood and eats it. (**b**) [U] holes caused by this: *This ladder is riddled with woodworm.*

woof¹ /wu:f/ *n* = WEFT.

woof² /wʊf/ *interj, n* (*infml*) (used to imitate the sound of the) bark of a dog.

▷ **woof** *v* [I] (*infml*) bark.

woofer /ˈwʊfə(r)/ *n* loudspeaker designed to reproduce low notes accurately. Cf TWEETER.

wool /wʊl/ *n* **1** (**a**) [U] fine soft hair that forms the coats of sheep, goats and some other animals (eg the llama and alpaca): *These goats are specially bred for their wool.* (**b**) [U] yarn, cloth, clothing, etc made from this: *a ball of knitting wool* ○ *a (type of) fine/heavy wool* ○ [attrib] *the* ˈ*wool trade* ○ *a wool* (ie woollen) *coat, blanket, etc.* **2** [U] substance that looks and feels like sheep's wool: *cotton wool* ○ *wire wool.* **3** (idm) **pull the wool over sb's eyes** ⇨ PULL².

▷ **woollen** (*US* **woolen**) /ˈwʊlən/ *adj* [usu attrib] (**a**) made wholly or partly of wool: *woollen cloth, blankets, socks, etc.* (**b**) of woollen fabrics: *woollen manufacturers, merchants, etc.* **woollens** (*US* **woolens**) *n* [pl] (esp knitted) woollen garments: *a special wash programme for woollens.*

woolly (*US* also **wooly**) /ˈwʊlɪ/ *adj* (**-ier**, **-iest**) **1** (**a**) covered with wool or wool-like hair: *woolly sheep* ○ *the dog's woolly coat.* (**b**) like or made of wool; woollen: *a woolly cotton fabric* ○ *a woolly hat.* **2** (also ˌ**woolly-ˈheaded**) (of a person or his mind, arguments, ideas, etc) not thinking clearly; not clearly expressed or thought out. — *n* (*infml*) woollen garment, esp a sweater: *wear one's winter woollies.* **woolliness** *n* [U].

□ ˈ**wool-gathering** *n* [U] (*infml*) absent-mindedness.

the ˈ**Woolsack** *n* seat without back or arms on which the Lord Chancellor sits in the British House of Lords. ⇨ article at PARLIAMENT.

Woolf /wʊlf/ Virginia (1882-1941), English novelist who was a pioneer of modernism in literature, developing the stream-of-consciousness (STREAM) technique. Her books include *The Voyage Out, Mrs Dalloway, To the Lighthouse, Orlando, The Waves* and *The Years.* She was a leading member of the *Bloomsbury Group. She often suffered from attacks of mental disturbance, and in 1941 she drowned herself. Her husband Leonard Sidney Woolf (1880-1969) was also a writer, and together they founded the Hogarth Press which published many of her books.

Woolworth /ˈwʊlwəθ/ Frank Winfield (1852-1919), American businessman who from 1879 onwards opened a chain of shops, in the USA and other countries, selling low-priced goods. In Britain, the shops are often informally called **Woollies** /ˈwʊlɪz/.

woozy /ˈwu:zɪ/ *adj* (**-ier**, **-iest**) (*infml*) (**a**) feeling dizzy or sick, eg as a result of drinking too much alcohol. (**b**) mentally confused; dazed.

wop /wɒp/ *n* (⚠ *sl offensive*) person from southern Europe, esp an Italian.

word /wɜ:d/ *n* **1** [C] (**a**) sound or combination of sounds that expresses a meaning and forms an independent unit of the grammar or vocabulary of a language: *The story is told in words and pictures.* ○ *The Latin word for 'table' is 'mensa'.* ○ *He couldn't put his feelings into words,* ie express them verbally. ○ *I have no words to* (ie cannot adequately) *express my gratitude.* (**b**) this represented as letters or symbols, usu with a space on either side: *That word is not spelled correctly.* ○ *The words in the dictionary are arranged in alphabetical order.* **2** (**a**) [C] anything said; remark or statement: *He didn't say a word about it.* ○ *I don't believe a word of his story.* ○ *a word/a few words of advice, sympathy, warning.* (**b**) **words** [pl] things that are said, contrasted with things that are done: *You must show your support by deeds, not words.* **3** [sing] (**a**) (without *a* or *the*) piece of news; message: *Please send (me)/leave word of your safe arrival/that you have arrived safely.* ○ *Word came that I was needed at home.* (**b**) **the word** rumour: *The word is that he's left the country.* **4** (usu **the word**) [sing] spoken command or signal: *Stay hidden until I give the word.* ○ *Their word is law,* ie their commands must be obeyed. **5 the Word** [sing] (also **the** ˌ**word of** ˈ**God**) (*Bible*) the Scriptures, esp the Gospels: *preach the Word* ○ *Hear the Word of God.* **6** (idm) **actions speak louder than words** ⇨ ACTION. **at the** ˌ**word of com**ˈ**mand** when the (military) order is given. **bandy words** ⇨ BANDY¹. **be as** ˌ**good as one's** ˈ**word** do what one has promised to do: *You'll find that she's as good as her word.* **be better than one's word** ⇨ BETTER¹. **be not the** ˈ**word for sth/ sb** (*infml*) be an inadequate description of sth/sb: *Unkind isn't the word for it! He treats the animals appallingly!* **breathe a word** ⇨ BREATHE. **by** ˌ**word of** ˈ**mouth** in spoken, not written, words: *He received the news by word of mouth.* **a dirty word** ⇨ DIRTY¹. **eat one's words** ⇨ EAT. **exchange words** ⇨ EXCHANGE². **famous last words** ⇨ FAMOUS. **fighting talk/words** ⇨ FIGHT¹. **(right) from the word** ˈ**go** (*infml*) right from the start: *She knew (right) from the word go that it was going to be difficult.* **(not) get a word in** ˈ**edgeways** (not) be able to interrupt sb who is very talkative. **give sb one's** ˈ**word (that...)/have sb's** ˈ**word for it (that...)** promise sb/be promised by sb (that...): *You have my word for it that the goods will arrive on time.* **go** ˌ**back on one's** ˈ**word** fail to fulfil a promise that one has made. **hang on sb's lips/ words/every word** ⇨ HANG¹. **(not) have a good word to** ˈ**say for sb/sth** (*infml*) (not) say anything at all favourable about sb/sth: *He doesn't have/ seldom has a good word to say for Britain.* **have, etc the last word** ⇨ LAST¹. **have a word in sb's** ˈ**ear** speak to sb in private/confidentially. **have a** ˈ**word (with sb) (about sth)** speak (to sb) (about sth), esp privately or confidentially: *Could we have a word before you go to the meeting?* **have** ˈ**words (with sb) (about sth)** quarrel (with sb) (about sth). **a household name/word** ⇨ HOUSEHOLD. **in a** ˈ**word** briefly: *In a word, I think he's a fool.* **in** ˈ**other words** expressed in a different way; that is to say. **(not) in so many** ˈ**words** (not) in exactly the same words as are claimed or reported to have been used. **in words of** ˈ**one syllable** using very simple language. **keep/break one's word** do/fail to do what one has promised. **one's last word** ⇨ LAST¹. **the last word** ⇨ LAST¹. **a man/woman of his/her** ˈ**word** person that does what he/she has promised to do. **mum's the word!** ⇨ MUM¹. **(upon) my** ˈ**word!** (*dated or fml*) (exclamation expressing surprise or consternation): *My word, you're back early!* **not to mince matters/words** ⇨ MINCE. **not a** ˈ**word (to sb) (about sth)** don't say anything; be silent!: *Not a word (to Mary) (about what I said)!* **a play on words** ⇨ PLAY¹. **put in/say a (good)** ˈ**word for sb** say sth in sb's favour in order to help him. **put** ˈ**words in sb's mouth** suggest that sb has said sth when he has not: *She accused the journalist of putting words in her mouth.* ˌ**say the** ˈ**word** (*infml*) give an order, a signal, etc: *If you want me to leave, you only have to say the word.* **swallow one's words** ⇨ SWALLOW². **take sb at his** ˈ**word** believe exactly what sb says or promises, without question. **take sb's** ˈ**word for it (that...)** accept sth on sb's authority: *I'll take your word for it that it won't happen again.* **take the** ˈ**words (right) out of sb's mouth** say just what sb else was about to say. **too funny, outrageous, sad, shocking, etc for** ˈ**words** so funny, etc that it cannot be expressed in words; extremely funny, etc. **a war of words** ⇨ WAR. **weigh one's words** ⇨ WEIGH. ˌ**without a** ˈ**word** without saying anything: *He left without a word.* ˌ**word for** ˈ**word** in exactly the same or (in translation) exactly equivalent words; verbatim: *He repeated what you said word for word.* ○ [attrib] *a* ˌ*word-for-word ac*ˈ*count, repe*ˈ*tition, trans*ˈ*lation.* **sb's** ˌ**word is as** ˌ**good as his** ˈ**bond** sb's promise can be relied upon completely. **one's** ˌ**word of** ˈ**honour** a solemn promise. **a** ˌ**word to the** ˈ**wise** an intelligent person can take a hint, draw his own conclusions, etc without a lot of explanation.

▷ **word** *v* [Tn esp passive] express (sth) in particular words; phrase (sth): *The advice wasn't very tactfully worded.* ○ *a carefully worded reminder* ○ *Be careful how you word your answer.*

wording *n* [sing] words used to express sth; way in which sth is expressed: *A different wording might make the meaning clearer.*

wordless *adj* (*fml*) not expressed in words: *wordless grief, sympathy.*

wordy *adj* (**-ier**, **-iest**) (*derog*) using or expressed in (too) many words; verbose: *a wordy expression of apology.* **wordily** /-ɪlɪ/ *adv.* **wordiness** *n* [U].

□ ˈ**word-blindness** *n* [U] = DYSLEXIA.

ˈ**word-game** *n* game (eg Scrabble) that involves the spelling, guessing, etc of words: *a dictionary for all word-game enthusiasts.*

ˌ**word-**ˈ**perfect** (*US* ˌ**letter-**ˈ**perfect**) *adj* able to say or recite sth from memory without making any mistakes.

ˈ**wordplay** *n* [U] use of words in a witty way, esp in making puns.

ˈ**word processor** device that records typed words, diagrams, etc and displays them on a visual display unit so that they can be corrected or edited and then automatically printed. Cf TYPEWRITER (TYPE[2]). ˈ**word processing** (practice of doing) work on a word processor: [attrib] *word-processing skills.*

Wordsworth /ˈwɜːdzwəθ; *US* -wɜːrθ/ William (1770-1850), English poet, generally regarded as the greatest of his time. He was born in the *Lake District, and it was his experience of the natural world in his youth (later described in his long autobiographical poem *The Prelude*) that shaped his poetry, which invokes a universal spirit pervading human beings and all of nature. With *Coleridge he created the English Romantic movement; together they published *Lyrical Ballads*, a collection of poems (including Wordsworth's 'Tintern Abbey') which attacked the poetical conventions of the 18th century. Wordsworth was living near Coleridge in Somerset at this period, but later returned to the Lake District, where he lived with his sister Dorothy Wordsworth (1771-1855), who kept a journal of their life. Here he produced *Poems in Two Volumes*, which includes 'Ode to Immortality' and 'The Daffodils'.

wore *pt* of WEAR[2].

work[1] /wɜːk/ *n* **1** [U] (**a**) use of bodily or mental power in order to do or make sth (esp as contrasted with rest or play or recreation): *His success was achieved by hard work.* ○ *The work of building the bridge took six months.* ○ *Years of research work have failed to produce a cure for the disease.* ○ *He never does a stroke of* (ie any) *work.* ○ *She was worn out with work.* (**b**) use of energy supplied by electricity, steam, etc to do or make sth: *Work done by machines has replaced manual labour.* ○ *The work of calculating wages can be done by a computer.* **2** [U] (**a**) task, etc that is to be done, not necessarily connected with a trade or an occupation: *There is plenty of work to be done in the garden.* ○ *I have some work for you to do.* ○ *You've done a good job of work.* (**b**) materials needed or used for this: *She took her work* (eg papers or sewing materials) *with her into the garden.* ○ *She often brings work* (eg files, documents) *home with her from the office.* ○ *His work was spread all over the floor.* **3** [U] (**a**) thing or things produced as a result of work: *an exhibition of the work of young sculptors* ○ *He was very proud of his work.* ○ *Is this all your own work?* ie Did you do it without help from others? ○ *The craftsmen sell their work to visitors.* ○ *She produced an excellent piece of work in the final examination.* (**b**) result of an action; what is done by sb: *The damage to the painting is the work of vandals.* ○ (*ironic*) *I hope you are pleased with your work — you've ruined everything!* **4** [U] (**a**) what a person does as an occupation, esp in order to earn money; employment: *It is difficult to find work in the present economic situation.* ○ *Many people are looking for work.* ○ *The accountant described his work to the sales staff.* ○ *unpaid/voluntary work* ○ [attrib] *work experience* ○ *work clothes.* (**b**) (not used with *the*) place where one does this: *He has to leave work early today.* ○ *She goes to/leaves for work at 8 o'clock.* ○ *What time do you arrive at/get to work in the morning?* ○ *Her friends from work came to see her in hospital.* ⇨ Usage. **5** (**a**) [C] piece of literary, musical or artistic composition; artistic creation: *Have you read her latest work?* ○ *a new work on* (ie book about) *Elizabethan poetry.* ○ *a new work by the composer of 'Cats'* ○ *He recognized the painting as an early work by Degas.* (**b**) **works** [pl] all the books written by a writer or the compositions of a composer: *the collected/complete works of Shakespeare* ○ *the works of Beethoven.* Cf OPUS 1. **6** [U] (*physics*) process of energy conversion in which an applied force moves. Cf JOULE. **7** [U] (in or forming compounds) (**a**) things made of or (the skill of) making things in the specified material: ˈ*wickerwork* ○ ˈ*woodwork* ○ ˈ*metalwork.* (**b**) things made or work done with the specified tool: ˈ*needlework* ○ ˈ*brushwork.* (**c**) ornamentation of a specified type: ˈ*latticework* ○ ˈ*paintwork* ○ ˈ*filigree work.* (**d**) structure of the specified type: ˈ*framework* ○ ˈ*network* ○ ˈ*bodywork.* **8 the works** [pl] moving parts of a machine, etc; mechanism: *the works of a clock* ○ *There's something wrong with the works.* **9 works** [pl] (esp in compounds) operations involving building or repair: ˈ*road-works* ○ ˌ*public* ˈ*works.* **10 works** [sing or pl *v*] (esp in compounds) place where industrial or manufacturing processes are carried out: *the engiˈneering works* ○ *a* ˈ*brick-works* ○ *The* ˈ*steel works is/are closed for the holidays.* ○ *There has been an accident at the works.* ⇨ Usage at FACTORY. **11 the works** [pl] (*infml*) everything: *She was wearing a tiara, a diamond necklace and a gold bracelet — the works!* **12** (idm) **all in a day's work** ⇨ DAY. **at** ˈ**work** (**a**) at the place where one works: *Please don't ring me at work.* ○ *I've left my bag at work.* (**b**) having an effect; operating: *She suspected that secret influences were at work.* **at work** (**on sth**) busy doing sth: *He is still at work on the restoration.* ○ *They were watching the artist at work.* **the devil makes work for idle hands** ⇨ DEVIL[1]. **dirty work** ⇨ DIRTY[1]. **get** (**down**) **to/go to/ set to** ˈ**work** (**on sth/to do sth**) begin; make a start. **give sb/sth the** ˈ**works** (*infml*) (**a**) give or tell sb everything. (**b**) give sb/sth the full or best possible treatment: *They gave the car the works and it looks like new.* (**c**) treat sb harshly or violently. **go/set about one's** ˈ**work** do/start to do one's work: *She went cheerfully about her work.* ˌ**good** ˈ**works** acts of charity. **gum up the works** ⇨ GUM[2]. **have one's** ˈ**work cut out** (**doing sth**) (*infml*) have sth difficult to do, esp in the available time: *You'll have your work cut out getting there by nine o'clock.* **in** ˈ**work/out of** ˈ**work** having/not having a paid job: *She had been out of work for a year.* ○ *He was looking forward to being in work again.* ○ [attrib] *an* ˌ*out-of-work* ˈ*actor.* **make hard work of sth** ⇨ HARD[1]. **make light work of sth** ⇨ LIGHT[3]. **make short work of sth/sb** ⇨ SHORT[1]. **many hands make light work** ⇨ HAND[1]. **a nasty piece of work** ⇨ NASTY. **nice work if you can get it** ⇨ NICE. **put/set sb to** ˈ**work** make sb start working on sth. **shoot the works** ⇨ SHOOT[1]. **a spanner in the works** ⇨ SPANNER. **the work of a** ˈ**moment,** ˈ**second, etc** thing that takes the specified (usu short) time to do: *It was the work of a few moments to hide the damage.*

□ ˈ**work-basket** *n* container for sewing materials, needlework, etc.

ˈ**work-bench** *n* table at which a mechanic, carpenter, etc works.

ˈ**workbook** *n* book that gives information on a subject and guidance for a student, with practice or exercises that he can do on his own.

ˈ**workday** *n* (also ˌ**working** ˈ**day**) (**a**) day on which one usu works: *Saturday is a workday for him.* (**b**) day that is not a Sunday or holiday.

ˈ**work ethic** belief that it is morally good to work hard.

ˈ**work-force** *n* [CGp] total number of workers employed (eg in a factory) or available for work: *Ten per cent of the work-force will be made redundant.*

ˈ**work-horse** *n* (**a**) horse that does work, eg pulling heavy loads. (**b**) (*fig*) person who is relied upon by others to do a lot of hard work: *He's a willing work-horse.*

ˈ**workhouse** (**a**) (*Brit*) (formerly) public institution where very poor people were sent to live and given work to do. (**b**) (*US*) prison to which people are sent to do a period of work as punishment.

ˈ**work-load** *n* amount of work (to be) done by sb: *have a heavy work-load* ○ *reduce/increase sb's work-load.*

ˈ**workman** /-mən/ *n* (*pl* **-men**) (**a**) man who is employed to do manual or mechanical work. (**b**) person who works in the specified way: *a good, neat, conscientious, etc workman* ○ *skilled/ unskilled workmen* ○ (*saying*) *A bad workman blames his tools.* ˈ**workmanlike** *adj* of or like a good workman; practical and skilful: *He did a very workmanlike job on it.* ○ *The team produced a very workmanlike performance.* ˈ**workmanship** *n* [U] (**a**) person's skill in working: *They admired her workmanship.* (**b**) quality of this as seen in sth that has been made: *Our new washing-machine keeps breaking down — it's entirely due to shoddy workmanship.*

ˌ**work of** ˈ**art** fine picture, poem, building, sculpture, etc: (*fig*) *The decoration on the cake was a work of art.*

ˈ**workpeople** *n* [pl] people who work in a business, factory, etc without any responsibility for its management; workers.

ˈ**workpiece** *n* thing (to be) worked on with a tool or machine.

ˈ**work-place** *n* place at which one works; office, factory, etc.

ˈ**work-room** *n* room in which work is done: *The watchmaker has a work-room at the back of his shop.*

ˈ**worksheet** *n* paper on which work that has been done or is in progress is recorded.

ˈ**workshop** *n* (**a**) room or building in which machines, etc are made or repaired. (**b**) period of discussion and practical work on a particular subject, when a group of people share their knowledge and experience: *a poetry workshop* ○ *a theatre workshop.*

ˈ**work-shy** *adj* (*derog*) not inclined to work (hard); lazy.

ˈ**work study** system of assessing people's work and working methods, intended to discover whether the work could be done more quickly or efficiently.

ˈ**work-table** *n* table on which work is done, esp one with drawers for eg sewing materials.

ˈ**work top** (also ˈ**work surface**) flat surface in a kitchen, on top of a cupboard, refrigerator, etc, used for preparing food, etc on.

NOTE ON USAGE: **Job** and **task** are countable nouns indicating a piece of work that a person does. **Job** is general and may be hard or easy, pleasant or unpleasant: *Some people tackle the difficult jobs first.* ○ *I've been given the enjoyable job of presenting the prizes.* It can also refer to a long-term occupation. A **task** is usually short-term and requires effort. It may not be voluntary: *The teacher gave the children holiday tasks.* It can also refer to long-term objectives: *the important tasks facing the new government.* **Work**, **labour** and **toil** are uncountable nouns indicating the activity needed to perform a job. **Work** is the most general: *This job will require a lot of hard work.* ○ *He's got a lot more work to do on the book.* **Labour** suggests physical effort: *He was sentenced to 10 years' hard labour.* ○ *Manual labour has become unpopular with young people.* **Toil** is formal and is used of hard, lengthy work: *workers exhausted by years of toil.*

work[2] /wɜːk/ *v* (*pt, pp* **worked** or, in archaic use, esp in sense 7, **wrought** /rɔːt/) **1** [I, Ipr, Ip] ~ (**away**) (**at/on sth**); ~ (**for sb/sth**); ~ (**under sb**) do work; engage in physical or mental activity: *Most people have to work in order to live,* ie to earn a living. ○ *She isn't working now,* eg because she is unemployed or retired. ○ *I've been working (away) (at my essay) all day.* ○ *The miners work (for) 38 hours per week.* ○ *He is working on a new novel.* ○ *She works for an engineering company.* ○ *I've worked under her* (ie with her as my boss) *for two years.* ○ *This craftsman works in leather,* ie makes leather goods, etc. **2** [Ipr, It] ~ **against/for sth** make efforts to defeat sth or to achieve sth: *work against reform* ○ *a statesman who works for peace* ○ *The committee is working to get the prisoners freed.* **3** (**a**) [I] (of a machine, device, etc) function; operate: *a lift, bell, switch that doesn't work* ○ *The gears work smoothly.* ○ *This machine works by electricity.* (**b**) [I, Ipr] ~ (**on sb/sth**) have the desired result or effect (on sb/sth): *Did the cleaning fluid work (on that stain)?* ie Did it remove it? ○ *My plan worked, and I got them to agree.* ○ *His charm doesn't work on me,* ie doesn't affect or impress me. **4** [Tn, Tn·pr] cause (oneself/sb/sth) to work; set (sth) in motion: *She works herself too hard.* ○ *Do you know how to work a lathe?* ○ *This machine is worked by electricity.* ○ *Don't work your employees to death.* **5** [Tn] manage or operate (sth) to gain benefit from it: *work a mine, an oil well* ○ *He works the North Wales area*, eg as a salesman. **6** [Tn] produce or obtain (sth) as a result of effort; effect: *work harm, mischief, havoc* ○ *work a cure, change, miracle*. **7** [Tn, Tn·pr] ~ **sth (into sth)** make or shape sth by hammering, kneading, pressing, etc: *work gold, iron, etc* ○ *work clay*, ie knead it with water ○ *work dough*, ie when making bread ○ *work the mixture into a paste* ○ *iron worked into ingots*. Cf WROUGHT. **8** [Tn, Tn·pr] ~ **sth (on sth)** make sth by stitching; embroider sth: *work (a design on) a cushion-cover* ○ *work one's initials on a handkerchief*. **9** [I] (of yeast) ferment. **10** [I] (of sb's features) move violently: twitch: *His lips worked as he tried to swallow the food.* ○ *Her face worked as she stared at him in terror.* **11** [Ipr, Ip, Tn·pr, Tn·p] (cause sth to) move, pass, etc into a new position, usu gradually or with an effort: *Rain has worked in through the roof.* ○ *The back of your shirt has worked out of your trousers.* ○ *Work the stick into the hole.* ○ *The story is too serious — can't you work a few jokes in?* **12** [La, Cn·a] (cause sth/sb to) become (free, loose, etc) through pressure, vibration, etc: *I was tied up, but managed to work (myself) free.* ○ *The screw worked (itself) loose.* ○ *There's a piece of wood jammed under the door — can you work it clear?* **13** (idm) **work it, things, etc** (*infml*) arrange matters: *Can you work it so that we get free tickets?* ○ *How did you work that?* (For other idioms containing **work** see entries for *ns*, etc, eg **work to rule** ⇨ RULE; **work one's way** ⇨ WAY[1].).

14 (phr v) **work around/round to sth/sb** gradually approach (a topic, subject, etc): *It was a long time before he worked around to what he really wanted to say.*

work sth off get rid of sth by work or activity: *work off a large bank loan* ○ *work off one's anger on sb* ○ *work off excess weight by regular exercise.*

work out (a) develop in a specified way; turn out: *How will things work out?* ○ *Things worked out quite well.* **(b)** train the body by heavy physical exercise: *I work out regularly to keep fit.* **(c)** be capable of being solved: *a sum, problem, etc that won't work out.* **work sb out** understand sb's nature: *I've never been able to work her out.* **work sth out (a)** calculate sth: *I've worked out your share of the expenses at £10.* **(b)** find the answer to sth; solve sth: *work out a problem, puzzle, coded message, etc* ○ *Can you work out what these squiggles mean?* **(c)** devise sth; plan sth: *a well worked-out scheme* ○ *The general worked out a new plan of attack.* **(d)** (usu passive) exhaust (a mine, etc) by taking out the ore, etc: *a worked-out silver mine.* **work out at sth** be equal to sth; have sth as a total: *The total works out at £10.* ○ *What does your share of the bonus work out at?*

work sb over (*sl*) beat sb all over, eg to make him give information: *He'd been worked over by the gang for giving information to the police.*

work round to sth/sb ⇨ WORK AROUND/ROUND TO STH/SB.

work to sth follow (a plan, etc): *Be careful with the money and work to a budget.* ○ *Journalists have to work to tight deadlines*, ie have little time in which to do their work.

work towards sth strive to reach or achieve sth: *We're working towards common objectives.*

work sth up (a) develop or improve sth gradually: *work up a business* ○ *working up custom for our products.* **(b)** increase sth in numbers or strength: *working up support for the party.* **work sb/oneself up (into sth)** rouse sb/oneself to a state of excitement: *work sb into a rage, frenzy, etc* ○ *Don't work yourself up/get worked up about something so trivial.* **work sth up into sth** bring sth to a more complete or more satisfactory state: *I'm working my notes up into a dissertation.* **work up to sth** develop to (a climax, etc): *The music worked up to a rousing finale.*

□ ˈ**work-in** *n* (usu *sing*) form of protest in which workers occupy and run a factory, etc which is due to be closed.

ˌ**working-ˈover** *n* (usu *sing*) (*sl*) physical beating of a person: *give sb a thorough working-over.*

ˈ**work-out** *n* period of intensive physical training: *a boxer who has a work-out in the gym every day.*

ˌ**work-to-ˈrule** *n* form of protest by workers, in which they adhere strictly to the rules made by their employers and refuse to work overtime, etc.

workable /ˈwɜːkəbl/ *adj* **1** that will work[2](3); practicable or feasible: *a workable compromise, plan, scheme.* **2** that can be or is worth working (WORK[2] 5): *The silver mine is no longer workable*, eg because it is flooded or because the ore is exhausted.

workaday /ˈwɜːkədeɪ/ *adj* [attrib] not unusual or especially interesting; ordinary, everyday or practical: *workaday concerns.*

workaholic /ˌwɜːkəˈhɒlɪk/ *n* (*derog or approv infml*) person who works obsessively and finds it difficult to stop.

worker /ˈwɜːkə(r)/ *n* **1 (a)** (often in compounds) person who works, esp one who does a particular type of work: *car, factory, office, rescue workers* ○ *The company provides houses for some of its workers.* **(b)** person who works in the specified way: *a good, hard, quick, slow, etc worker.* **(c)** (*infml*) person who works hard: *That girl is certainly a worker!* **2 (a)** employee, esp one who does manual or non-managerial work: *The workers in the factory are paid by the hour and the clerical staff are paid a monthly salary.* ○ *Workers are in dispute with management about the redundancies.* ○ [attrib] *worker participation in decision-making.* **(b)** member of the working class: *a workers' revolution.* **3** neuter or undeveloped female bee or ant that does the work of the hive or colony but cannot reproduce: [attrib] *a worker bee.* Cf DRONE[1] 1.

working /ˈwɜːkɪŋ/ *adj* [attrib] **1 (a)** engaged in work, esp manual labour; employed: *the working man*, ie manual workers in general ○ *The meeting must be held at a time convenient for working mothers.* ○ *The working population of the country* (ie The proportion of the population that works or is available for work) *is growing smaller.* **(b)** of, for or suitable for work: *My working hours are (from) 9 to 5.* ○ *She was still dressed in her working clothes.* ○ *The union has negotiated a 35-hour working week.* ○ *She had spent all her working life in the factory.* ○ *Working conditions in the industry have improved greatly.* ○ *a working breakfast/lunch*, ie one during which business is discussed ○ *He has a good working relationship with his boss.* **2** functioning or able to function: *a working model of a steam engine* ○ *The government has a working majority*, ie one that is sufficient to allow it to govern. **3** that is good enough as a basis for work, argument, etc and may be improved later; provisional: *a working definition, hypothesis, theory* ○ *She has a working knowledge of French.* **4** (idm) **in (full)** ˈ**working order** (esp of a machine) able to function properly; running smoothly.

▷ **working** *n* **1** [C] (part of a) mine or quarry that is being or has been worked (WORK[2] 5): *The boys went exploring in some disused workings*, eg the shafts of an old tin mine. **2 workings** [pl] ~**s (of sth)** (process involved in) the way a machine, an organization, a part of the body, etc operates: *the workings of the human mind* ○ *It was impossible to understand the workings of such a huge bureaucracy.*

□ ˌ**working** ˈ**capital** capital that is needed and used in running a business, and not invested in its buildings, equipment, etc.

the ˈ**working class** (also **the** ˈ**working classes**) social class whose members do manual or industrial work for wages: *His duty as a politician was to represent the interests of the working class.* ○ [attrib] *working-class attitudes, families, origins.*

ˌ**working** ˈ**day (a)** = WORKDAY (WORK[1]). **(b)** part of the day during which work is done: *The unions are campaigning for a shorter working day.*

ˌ**working men's** ˈ**club** (in Britain) club where working men come to meet each other socially, to enjoy games such as darts or to watch an entertainment (eg a comedy show or cabaret act).

ˈ**working party** group of people appointed (eg by a government department) to investigate sth and report or advise on it: *set up a working party to look into the matter.*

world /wɜːld/ *n* **1 the world** [sing] **(a)** everything that exists; the universe: *the creation of the world.* **(b)** the earth with all its countries and peoples: *a journey round the world* ○ *travel (all over) the world* ○ *The whole world would be affected by a nuclear war.* ○ *the rivers and oceans of the world* ○ *Pollution is one of the most important issues in the world today.* ○ *Which is the biggest city in the world?* ○ [attrib] *English is now a world language*, ie is used everywhere in the world. **(c)** particular section of the earth: *the eastern/western world* ○ *the ancient world* ○ *the Roman world*, ie the part of the earth that the Romans knew ○ *the New World*, ie America ○ *the Old World*, ie Europe, Asia and Africa ○ *the English-speaking world*, ie those parts where English is spoken as the first language. **2** [C] heavenly body that may be like the earth: *other worlds unknown to us beyond the stars.* **3** [C] time, state or scene of human existence: *this world and the next*, ie life on earth and existence after death ○ *the world to come*, ie existence after death ○ *It's a sad world where there is such suffering.* ○ *bring a child into/come into the world*, ie give birth to a child/be born. **4 the world** [sing] **(a)** human affairs; active life: *He showed no interest in the world around him.* ○ *know/see the world*, ie have experience of life ○ (*rhet*) *How goes the world with you?* ie How are your affairs going? **(b)** material or similar things and occupations (as contrasted with spiritual ones): *the temptations of the world* ○ *She decided to renounce the world and enter a convent.* **5 the world** [sing] **(a)** everybody (and everything): *He wanted to tell the news to the world.* ○ *The whole world seemed to be at the party.* ○ *She felt that the whole world was against her.* **(b)** fashionable or respectable society: *I don't care what the world thinks.* **6** [C] (often in compounds) people or things belonging to a certain class or sphere of activity, interest, etc: *the world of art, politics, sport* ○ *the animal/insect world* ○ *the racing, scientific, theatre world* ○ *The medical world is divided on this issue.* **7** (idm) **be** ˌ**all the** ˈ**world to sb** be very dear or very important to sb. **be not long for this world** ⇨ LONG[3]. **the best of both worlds** ⇨ BEST[3]. **a brave new world** ⇨ BRAVE. **come/go** ˈ**down**/ˈ**up in the world** become less/more important in society, successful in one's career, etc or poorer/richer: *They've come up in the world since I last met them.* **dead to the world** ⇨ DEAD. **the end of the world** ⇨ END[1]. **for all the world like sb/sth/as if...** (usu expressing surprise) very much or exactly like sb/sth or as if...: *She carried on with her work for all the world as if nothing had happened!* **(not) for (all) the** ˈ**world** whatever the inducement is or was: *I wouldn't sell that picture for all the world.* **how, what, where, who, etc on earth/in the world** ⇨ EARTH. **in the eyes of the world** ⇨ EYE[1]. **(be/live) in a world of one's** ˈ**own** live a life of fantasy without communicating with other people. **it's a small world** ⇨ SMALL. **the John** ˈ**Smiths, etc of this world** (*infml*) people like the person whose name is given: *'I hear Peter Brown's doing very well.' 'The Peter Browns of this world always do well!'* **a man/woman of the** ˈ**world** person with a lot of experience of life, public affairs, business, etc, esp one who is not easily surprised or shocked. **the next world** ⇨ NEXT. **on top of the world** ⇨ TOP[1]. ˌ**out of this** ˈ**world** (*infml*) absolutely wonderful, magnificent, beautiful, etc: *The meal was out of this world.* ○ *The scenery and costumes for the opera are out of this world.* **the** ˌ**outside** ˈ**world** people, places, activities, etc that are not those of an enclosed community, group, profession, etc: *working in a remote village cut off from the outside world.* **set the** ˈ**world on fire** (*infml*) be very successful and cause great excitement: *She does the job adequately but she's not going to set the world on fire!* **think the world of sb/sth** ⇨ THINK[1]. **watch the world go by** ⇨ WATCH[2]. **the way of the world** ⇨ WAY[1]. **what is the world** ˈ**coming to?** (used as an expression of disapproving surprise, shock, complaint, etc at changes in attitudes, behaviour, etc): *When I read the news these days I sometimes wonder what the world is coming to.* **a window on the world** ⇨ WINDOW. **with the best will in the world** ⇨ BEST[1]. **(all) the ˌworld and his ˈwife** (*infml*) large numbers of people, esp when assembled in a place as guests, holiday-makers, etc: *The world and his wife were in Brighton that day!* **the ˌworld, the ˌflesh and the ˈdevil** (*fml or rhet*) all that is not holy; all that tempts mankind to wickedness. **the ˌworld is one's ˈoyster** one is able to enjoy all the pleasures and opportunities that life has to offer: *She left school feeling that the world was her oyster.* **a/the ˈworld of difference, good, meaning, etc** (*infml*) a great deal of difference, etc: *There's a world of difference in the performance of the two cars.* ○ *That holiday did him the world of good.* **the (whole) world ˈover** in any place in the world; everywhere: *People are basically the same the world over.* **(think) the world owes one a ˈliving** (think that) one has a right to be provided for because one deserves it or simply because one exists: *It's no use thinking the world owes you a living, you know.* **(be) ˈworlds apart** completely different: *We're worlds apart in our political views.*

▷ **worldly** *adj* **(-ier, -iest)** **(a)** [attrib] of (the affairs of) the world, esp the pursuit of pleasure or material gain; not spiritual: *one's worldly goods*, ie property ○ *worldly concerns, distractions, preoccupations, etc.* **(b)** experienced in the affairs of life; sophisticated; practical: *a worldly person* ○ *a few words of worldly wisdom.* **worldliness** *n* [U].

ˌworldly-ˈwise *adj* [U] having or showing prudence and shrewdness in dealing with worldly matters.

□ **the ˌWorld ˈBank** international bank founded by the *United Nations in 1945 to encourage the economic development of the poorer countries of the world.

ˈworld-beater *n* person or thing that is better than all others: *She has enough talent as a player to be a world-beater.*

ˌworld-ˈclass *adj* as good as the best in the world: *a ˌworld-class ˈauthor, ˈfootballer* ○ *ˌworld-class ˈtennis.*

ˌWorld ˈCup any of various international sporting contests to decide the best national team in the world, esp the one for football held every four years.

ˌworld-ˈfamous *adj* known throughout the world: *a ˌworld-famous ˈfilm star.*

the ˌWorld ˈHealth Organization (*abbr* **WHO**) /ˌdʌblju: eɪtʃ ˈəʊ/ organization set up by the *United Nations in 1948 to improve health care and fight against disease throughout the world.

the ˌWorld ˈSeries annual US baseball championships, in which the winners of the two major leagues play each other.

ˌworld ˈpower *n* country that has major influence in international politics.

ˌworld ˈwar war that involves many important countries: *a treaty designed to prevent a world war.*

ˌWorld War ˈOne (also **the ˌFirst World ˈWar**) war (1914-18) between the 'Central Powers' (Germany, Austria-Hungary and their allies) and the 'Allies' (Britain, France, Russia, the USA — which joined in 1917 — and other nations). Most of it was fought in Europe: in NE France, where there was a long series of bloody battles between armies stationed in trenches, and in E Germany, Poland and Russia. The Germans agreed to stop fighting in 1918. A peace conference was held in Paris which laid the foundations for the various peace treaties, including the Treaty of Versailles, that ended the war. Over 10 million people were killed.

ˌWorld War ˈTwo (also **the ˌSecond World ˈWar**) war (1939-45) between the 'Axis Powers' (Germany, Italy and Japan and their allies) and the 'Allies' (Britain, the USA, the USSR and many other countries throughout the world). In Europe, *Hitler's Germany continued a series of conquests it had begun before the war (invading and occupying many countries, including France, the Netherlands and Norway), but it failed in its attempt to conquer the USSR. The Russians counter-attacked and eventually captured Berlin. Meanwhile, in 1944 the western Allies invaded Europe, advanced towards Germany, and in 1945 forced the Germans to surrender. In the Far East, Japan conquered territory in SE Asia and the Pacific, but the Allies gradually recaptured it, and Japan surrendered in 1945 after the USA dropped two atomic bombs on it. About 55 million people, including over 20 million Russians, were killed in the war, very many of them civilians.

ˈworld-weary *adj* bored with life or tired of living.

ˌworld-ˈwide *adj* found in or affecting the whole world: *world-wide economic trends* ○ *a ˌworld-wide ˈmarket.* — *adv* all over the world: *Our product is sold world-wide.*

worm

earthworm

worm /wɜ:m/ *n* **1** **(a)** [C] small long thin creeping animal with a soft rounded or flattened body and no backbone or limbs: *There are a lot of worms in the soil.* ○ *an ˈearthworm.* **(b)** [pl] worm that causes disease by living as a parasite in the intestines of a person or an animal: *The dog has worms.* **(c)** (esp in compounds) worm-like larva of an insect, esp in fruit or wood: *The apples are full of worms.* ○ *ˈwoodworm* ○ *ˈsilkworm.* **2** (usu *sing*) (*derog*) person considered weak and insignificant and who is not respected by others. **3** spiral part of a screw. **4** (idm) **a can of worms** ⇨ CAN[1]. **the early bird catches the worm** ⇨ EARLY. **the ˌworm will ˈturn** even a person who is normally quiet and does not complain will assert himself or rebel in an intolerable situation.

▷ **worm** *v* **1** [Tn] treat (an animal, usu a cat or a dog) in order to get rid of the worms living in its intestines: *We'll have to worm the dog*, ie by giving it medicine. **2** (phr v) **worm one's way/oneself along, through, etc** move in the specified direction by crawling or wriggling, esp slowly or with difficulty: *They had to worm their way through the narrow tunnel.* **worm one's way/oneself into sth** (*usu derog*) establish oneself in sb's affection, confidence, etc, esp in order to deceive: *She used flattery to worm her way/herself into his confidence.* **worm sth out (of sb)** obtain information (from sb) slowly and cunningly: *Eventually they wormed the truth out of her.*

wormy *adj* **1** containing many worms: *wormy soil.* **2** damaged by worms; wormeaten: *a wormy apple.*

□ **ˈworm-cast** *n* small tubular pile of earth that is pushed up to the surface of the ground by an earthworm.

ˈwormeaten *adj* full of worm-holes.

ˈworm-hole *n* hole left in wood, fruit, etc by a worm.

wormwood /ˈwɜ:mwʊd/ *n* [U] **1** woody plant with a bitter flavour, used in making some alcoholic drinks (eg absinthe) and medicines. **2** (experience that causes) intense bitterness, humiliation, shame, etc.

worn[1] *pp* of WEAR[2].

worn[2] /wɔ:n/ *adj* **1** damaged by use or wear: *These shoes are looking rather worn.* **2** (of a person) looking tired and exhausted: *She came back worn and worried.* **3** (idm) **worn, etc to a frazzle** ⇨ FRAZZLE.

□ **ˌworn-ˈout** *adj* **1** very worn and therefore no longer usable: *a ˌworn-out ˈcoat.* **2** [usu pred] (of a person) exhausted: *You look worn-out after your long journey.*

worrisome /ˈwʌrɪsəm/ *adj* (*dated*) causing worry; troublesome.

worry /ˈwʌrɪ/ *v* (*pt, pp* **worried**) **1** [I, Ipr] ~ **(about sb/sth)** be anxious (about sb, difficulties, the future, etc): *'Don't worry,' she said, putting an arm round his shoulder.* ○ *Don't worry if you can't finish it.* ○ *Your parents are worrying about you: do write to them.* ○ *There's nothing to worry about.* **2** [Tn, Tn·pr] ~ **sb/oneself (about sb/sth)** make sb/oneself anxious or troubled (about sb/sth): *What worries me is how he will manage now his wife's died.* ○ *I don't want to worry you, but...* ○ *She worried herself sick/She was worried sick about her missing son.* ○ *Many people are worried by the possibility of a nuclear accident.* ○ *It worries me that they haven't answered my letters.* **3** [Tn, Tn·pr] ~ **sb (with sth)** annoy or disturb sb; bother sb: *Don't worry her now; she's busy.* ○ *The noise doesn't seem to worry them.* **4** [Tn] (esp of a dog) seize (sth) with the teeth and shake or pull it about: *The dog was worrying a rat.* **5** (idm) **ˌnot to ˈworry** (*infml*) do not worry; let us not worry: *We've missed the train, but not to worry, there's another one in ten minutes.*

▷ **worried** *adj* ~ **(about sb/sth)**; ~ **(that...)** feeling or showing worry about sb/sth; anxious: *be worried about one's weight, one's job, one's husband* ○ *I was worried that you wouldn't come back.* ○ *There's no need to look so worried!* ○ *Worried relatives waited at the airport.* **worriedly** *adv.*

worrier *n* person who worries a lot: *Don't be such a worrier!*

worry *n* **1** [U] state of being worried; anxiety: *Worry and illness had made him prematurely old.* **2** [C] thing that causes one to worry; cause of anxiety: *He has a lot of financial worries at the moment.* ○ *Forget your worries and enjoy yourself!* **3** [C usu *sing*] thing that sb is responsible for: *Transport? That's your worry!*

worrying *adj* **1** causing worry: *worrying problems.* **2** full of worry: *It was a very worrying time for them.*

worse /wɜ:s/ *adj* (*comparative of* BAD[1]) **1** ~ **(than sth/doing sth)** of a less excellent or desirable kind: *The weather got worse during the day.* ○ *The interview was far/much worse than he had expected.* ○ *prevent an even worse tragedy* ○ *The economic crisis is getting worse and worse.* ○ *You are only making things worse.* Cf WORST. **2** [pred] in or into worse health: *If he gets any worse, we must phone for an ambulance.* Cf BETTER[1]. **3** (idm) **sb's bark is worse than his bite** ⇨ BARK[2]. **be none the ˈworse (for sth)** be unharmed (by sth): *The children were none the worse for their adventure.* **better/worse still** ⇨ STILL[2]. **be the worse for drink** be drunk. **a fate worse than death** ⇨ FATE. **make matters/things ˈworse** worsen a situation or condition that is already difficult or dangerous: *To make matters worse, he refused to apologize.* **so much the better/worse** ⇨ BETTER[3]. **the ˌworse for ˈwear** (*infml*) worn, damaged or tired: *Your copy of the dictionary is looking a bit the worse for wear.* ○ *Bill came home from the pub considerably the worse for wear*, ie drunk. **ˌworse ˈluck!** (*infml*) (as a comment on sth that has been mentioned) which is unfortunate or a pity: *I shall have to miss the party, worse luck!*

▷ **worse** *adv* **1** more badly: *He is behaving worse than ever.* Cf WORST *adv.* **2** more intensely (than before): *It's raining worse than ever.* **3** (idm) **be ˌworse ˈoff** be poorer, unhappier, less healthy, etc than before: *The increase in taxes means that we'll be £30 a month worse off.* ○ *I've only broken my arm; other patients are far worse off than me.*

worse *n* **1** [U] worse thing(s): *I'm afraid there is worse to come.* **2** (idm) **can/could do worse than do sth** be correct or sensible in doing sth: *If you want a safe investment, you could do a lot worse than put your money in the building society.* **a change for the better/worse** ⇨ CHANGE[2]. **for better or worse** ⇨ BETTER[3]. **go from ˌbad to ˈworse** (of unsatisfactory conditions, etc) become even worse: *Under the new management things have gone from bad to worse.*

worsen /ˈwɜ:sn/ *v* [I, Tn] (cause sth to) become worse: *The patient's condition worsened during the night.* ○ *the worsening economic situation* ○ *The drought had worsened their chances of survival.*

worship /ˈwɜ:ʃɪp/ *n* **1** [U] **(a)** reverence, respect or love for God or a god: *an act of worship* ○ *a place of worship*, eg a church, mosque or synagogue. **(b)** act or ceremony that shows this: *Morning worship begins at 11 o'clock.* ○ *a service of divine worship.* **2** [U] admiration, devotion or love felt for sb/sth: *hero-worship.* **3 his, your, etc Worship** [C] (*esp*

Brit) formal and polite form or address or way of referring to a magistrate or a mayor: *His Worship the Mayor of Chester* ○ *No, your Worship.*

▷ **worship** *v* (**-pp-**; *US* **-p-**) **1** (**a**) [Tn] give worship to (God). (**b**) [I] attend a church service: *the church where they had worshipped for years.* **2** [Tn] feel love and admiration for (sb/sth), esp to such an extent that one cannot see his/its faults; idolize: *She worshipped him and refused to listen to his critics.* ○ *worship success* ○ *He worships the ground she walks on,* ie feels intense love for her. **worshipper** (*US* **worshiper**) *n* person who worships.

worshipful /-fl/ *adj* **1** [attrib] showing or feeling reverence, respect and love. **2 Worshipful** (*fml esp Brit*) title used to address or refer to various distinguished people or bodies: *the Worshipful Company of Goldsmiths.*

worst /wɜːst/ *adj* (*superlative of* BAD[1]) **1** of the least excellent, desirable, suitable, etc kind: *It was the worst storm for years.* ○ *one of the worst cases of child abuse he'd ever seen* ○ *This is the worst essay I've read.* ○ *What you've told me confirms my worst fears,* ie proves they were right. Cf WORSE. **2** (idm) **one's ˌown worst ˈenemy** person whose own faults are worse than the bad things that have happened to him; the cause of one's own misfortunes: *With her indecisiveness, she is her own worst enemy.*

▷ **worst** *adv* most badly: *Bill played badly, James played worse, and I played worst of all!* ○ *Manufacturing industry was worst affected by the fuel shortage.* ○ *He is one of the worst dressed men I know.* Cf WORSE *adv*.

worst *n* **1 the worst** [sing] the most bad part, state, event, possibility, etc: *The worst of the storm is now over.* ○ *When they did not hear from her, they feared the worst.* ○ *I was prepared for the worst when I saw the wrecked car.* ○ *She was always optimistic, even when things were at their worst.* ○ *The worst of it is that I can't even be sure if they received my cheque.* **2** (idm) **at (the) ˈworst** if the worst happens: *At worst we'll have to sell the house so as to settle our debts.* **bring out the best/worst in sb** ⇨ BEST[3]. **do one's ˈworst** be as difficult, unpleasant, harmful, etc as possible: *We'll carry on as arranged and they can do their worst.* **get the ˈworst of it** be defeated: *The dog had been fighting and had obviously got the worst of it.* **if the ˌworst comes to the ˈworst** if circumstances become too difficult or dangerous; if the plan fails: *If the worst comes to the worst, we'll have to cancel our holiday plans.*

worst *v* [Tn] defeat (sb) in a fight or competition: *England were worsted in the replay.*

worsted /ˈwʊstɪd/ *n* [U] (**a**) fine twisted woollen yarn or thread. (**b**) cloth made from this: [attrib] *a worsted suit.* ⇨ illus at DRESS.

worth /wɜːθ/ *adj* [pred] **1** having a certain value: *Our house is worth about £60 000.* ○ *I paid only £3 000 for this used car but it's worth a lot more.* ○ *What's the old man worth?* ie What is the value of his possessions? ○ *This contract isn't worth the paper it's written on,* ie It is worthless. **2** (sometimes followed by the *-ing* form of a *v*) giving or likely to give a satisfactory or rewarding return for (doing sth): *The book is worth reading/It's worth reading the book.* ○ *He felt that his life was no longer worth living.* ○ *It's an idea that's worth considering.* ○ *It's such a small point that it's hardly worth troubling about.* ○ *It's not worth the effort/the trouble.* ○ *The scheme is well worth a try.* **3** (idm) **a bird in the hand is worth two in the bush** ⇨ BIRD. **for ˌall one is ˈworth** (*infml*) with all one's energy and effort: *The thief ran off down the road, so I chased him for all I was worth.* **for ˌwhat it's ˈworth** however much or little importance or value sth has: *And that's my opinion, for what it's worth.* **the game is not worth the candle** ⇨ GAME[1]. **not worth a ˈdamn, a ˈstraw, a ˈred cent, a tinker's ˈcuss, etc** (*infml*) worthless: *Their promises are not worth a damn.* **ˈworth it** certain or very likely to repay the money, effort or time given: *The new car cost a lot of money, but it's certainly worth it.* ○ *I don't bother to iron handkerchiefs — it's not worth it.* **ˌworth one's ˈsalt** deserving what one earns; doing one's job competently: *Any teacher worth his salt knows that.* **ˌworth one's/its ˌweight in ˈgold** extremely helpful, useful, etc; invaluable: *A reliable car is worth its weight in gold.* **ˌworth sb's ˈwhile** profitable or interesting to sb: *It would be (well) worth your while/You would find it (well) worth your while to come to the meeting.* ○ *They promised to make it worth her while* (ie pay or reward her) *if she would take part.*

▷ **worth** *n* [U] **1** ~ **of sth** (preceded by a *n* indicating amount, duration, etc) (**a**) amount of sth that a specified sum of money will buy: *The thieves stole £1 million worth of jewellery.* ○ *ten pounds' worth of petrol.* (**b**) amount of sth that will last for a specified length of time: *a day's worth of fuel* ○ *two weeks' worth of supplies.* **2** value or usefulness: *items of great, little, not much, etc worth* ○ *people of worth in the community.* **worthless** *adj* **1** having no value or usefulness: *worthless old rubbish* ○ *This contract is now worthless.* **2** (of a person) having bad qualities: *a worthless character.* **worthlessness** *n* [U].

□ **worthwhile** /wɜːθˈwaɪl/ *adj* important, interesting or rewarding enough to justify the time, money or effort that is spent: *It's worthwhile taking the trouble to explain a job fully to new employees.* ○ *Nursing is a very worthwhile career.*

worthy /ˈwɜːðɪ/ *adj* (**-ier**, **-iest**) **1** [pred] ~ **of sth/to do sth** deserving sth or to do sth: *Their efforts are worthy of your support.* ○ *a statment worthy of contempt* ○ *Her achievements are worthy of the highest praise.* ○ *She said she was not worthy to accept the honour they had offered her.* **2** [usu attrib] (**a**) (*approv*) deserving respect or consideration: *a worthy cause* ○ *a worthy record of achievements.* (**b**) (*usu joc*) (esp of a person) deserving respect or recognition: *the worthy citizens of the town.* **3** [pred] ~ **of sb/sth** (*usu approv*) (**a**) suitable for sth: *It was difficult to find words worthy of the occasion.* (**b**) typical of sb/sth: *It was a performance worthy of a master.*

▷ **worthily** /-ɪlɪ/ *adv*.

worthiness *n* [U].

worthy *n* (*esp joc*) person of importance or distinction: *One of the local worthies has been invited to the ceremony.*

-worthy (forming compounds *adjs*) deserving of or suitable for the thing specified: *noteworthy* ○ *roadworthy.*

would[1] /wəd; *strong form* wʊd/ *modal v* (*contracted form* **'d** /d/; *neg* **would not**, *contracted form* **wouldn't** /ˈwʊdnt/) **1** (**a**) (used to describe the consequence of an imagined event): *If he shaved his beard he would look much younger.* ○ *If you went to see him, he would be delighted.* ○ *I would think about it very carefully, if I were you.* (**b**) (used to describe a hypothetical action or event in the past): *If I had seen the advertisement I would have applied for the job.* ○ *If she hadn't gone back for the letter, she wouldn't have missed the bus.* (**c**) (used to describe a hypothetical action or event in the present): *She'd be a fool to accept,* ie if she accepted. ○ *Don't call her now — it would make us late.* ○ *It would be difficult to make an accurate forecast.* ○ *It would be a pity to miss the main film.* ○ *I would start from this end.* ○ *Would I be able to help?* **2** (**a**) (used in making polite requests): *Would you pay me in cash, please?* ○ *You wouldn't have the time to phone him now, would you?* (**b**) (used with *imagine, say, think,* etc to give tentative opinions): *I would imagine the operation will take about an hour.* **3** (**a**) (used in offers or invitations): *Would you like a sandwich?* ○ *Would they like to sit down?* ○ *Would she like to borrow my bicycle?* (**b**) (used with *like, love, hate, prefer, be glad/happy,* etc to express preferences): *I'd love a coffee.* ○ *I'd hate you to think I was criticizing you.* ○ *I'd be only too glad to help.* **4** (used when commenting on characteristic behaviour): *That's just what he ˈwould say,* ie what he might be expected to say. ○ *It ˈwould rain* (ie How typical it is of our weather that it should rain) *on the day we chose for a picnic!* **5** (used after *so that, in order that* to express purpose): *She burned the letters so that her husband would never read them.* ⇨ Usage 3 at MAY[1].

□ **ˈwould-be** *adj* [attrib] having the hope of becoming (the type of person specified): *a would-be artist, model, bride, etc.*

would[2] *pt* of WILL[1].

wound[1] /wuːnd/ *n* **1** (**a**) injury caused deliberately to part of the body by cutting, shooting, etc, esp as the result of an attack: *He died after receiving two bullet wounds in the head.* ○ *The wound was healing slowly.* (**b**) cut or tear done to the outer surface of a plant or tree. **2** ~ (**to sth**) hurt done to a person's feelings, reputation, etc: *deep psychological wounds* ○ *The defeat was a wound to his pride.* **3** (idm) **lick one's wounds** ⇨ LICK. **rub salt into the wound/sb's wounds** ⇨ RUB[1].

▷ **wound** *v* [Tn esp passive] **1** give a wound to (sb): *Ten soldiers were killed and thirty seriously wounded.* ○ *The guard was wounded in the leg.* **2** hurt (sb's feelings, reputation, etc): *He was/felt deeply wounded by their disloyalty.* ○ *wounding criticism.* **the wounded** *n* [pl *v*] wounded people: *The hospital was full of the sick and wounded.* ○ *Many of the wounded died on their way to hospital.*

NOTE ON USAGE: **Wound** and **injure** both indicate physical damage to the body. A person is **wounded** by a sharp instrument or bullet tearing the flesh. It is a deliberate action, often connected with battles and war. People are usually **injured** in an accident, eg with a machine or in sport. Compare *In a war there are many more wounded than killed* and *In the coach crash 10 people died and 18 were seriously injured.* **Hurt** may be as serious as **injure** or it may relate to a minor pain: *They were badly hurt in the accident.* ○ *I hurt my back lifting that box.*

wound[2] *pt, pp* of WIND[3].

wove *pt* of WEAVE.

woven *pp* of WEAVE.

wow[1] /waʊ/ *interj* (*infml*) (used to express astonishment or admiration): *Wow! That car certainly goes fast!*

▷ **wow** *n* [sing] (*sl*) very great success: *The new play at the National Theatre's a wow.*

wow *v* [Tn] (*sl esp US*) fill (sb) with admiration or enthusiasm; impress greatly: *The new musical wowed them on Broadway.*

wow[2] /waʊ/ *n* [U] variation in the pitch of sounds reproduced from a record or tape, resulting from changes in the speed of the motor. Cf FLUTTER *n* 3.

WP /ˌdʌbljuː ˈpiː/ *abbr* word processing; word processor: *typing a letter on the WP.*

wpb /ˌdʌbljuː piː ˈbiː/ *abbr* (*Brit infml*) waste-paper basket.

WPC /ˌdʌbljuː piː ˈsiː/ *abbr* (*Brit*) woman police constable: *WPC (Linda) Green.* Cf PC 2, PW.

wpm /dʌbljuː piː ˈem/ *abbr* words per minute: *60 wpm,* eg typing, taking shorthand, etc.

WPS /dʌbljuː piː ˈes/ *abbr* (*Brit*) woman police sergeant: *WPS (Jane) Bell.* Cf PS 1.

WRAC /dʌbljuː ɑːr eɪ ˈsiː/ *or, in informal use,* ræk/ *abbr* (*Brit*) Women's Royal Army Corps: *join the WRACs.* ⇨ article at ARMED FORCES.

wrack /ræk/ *n* [U] seaweed that grows on the shore or has been thrown onto it by the waves (and used as manure, etc).

WRAF /dʌbljuː ɑːr eɪ ˈef *or, in informal use,* ræf/ *abbr* (*Brit*) Women's Royal Air Force: *join the WRAF.* ⇨ article at ARMED FORCES.

wraith /reɪθ/ *n* ghostly image of a person seen shortly before or after his death; ghost: *a wraith-like figure,* ie a very thin pale person.

wrangle /ˈræŋgl/ *n* ~ (**with sb**) (**about/over sth**) noisy or angry argument or dispute (with sb) (about sth): *They were involved in a long legal wrangle (with the company) (over payment).*

▷ **wrangle** *v* [I, Ipr] ~ (**with sb**) (**about/over sth**) take part in a wrangle (with sb) (about sth): *The children were wrangling (with each other) over the new toy.*

wrangler /ˈræŋglə(r)/ *n* **1** person who wrangles. **2** (*US*) cowboy, esp one who looks after the horses which the cowboys use.

wrap /ræp/ *v* (**-pp-**) **1** [Tn, Tn·pr, Tn·p] ~ **sth** (**up**) (**in sth**) cover or enclose sth (in soft or flexible material): *I have wrapped (up) the parcels and they're ready to be posted.* ○ *The Christmas presents were wrapped (up) in tissue paper.* **2** (**a**) [Tn·pr] ~ **sth round/around sb/sth** wind or fold (a piece of material) round sb/sth as covering or protection: *Wrap a scarf round your neck.* ○ *He wrapped a clean rag around his ankle.* (**b**) [Tn·pr, Tn·p esp passive] ~ **sb/sth in sth** put sb/sth in (a piece of material) as a covering or protection: *The nurse carried in a baby wrapped (up) in a warm blanket.* **3** (idm) **be wrapped in sth** be thickly covered by sth so that nothing is visible: *The hills were wrapped in mist.* ○ (*fig*) *The events are wrapped in mystery.* **be wrapped up in sb/sth** have one's attention deeply occupied by sb/sth; be deeply involved in sb/sth: *They are completely wrapped up in their children.* ○ *She was so wrapped up in her work that she didn't realize how late it was.* **wrap sb up in cotton wool** (*infml*) protect sb too much from dangers or risks: *She keeps all her children wrapped up in cotton wool.* **4** (phr v) **wrap (it) up** (usu in the imperative) (*sl*) be quiet; shut up. **wrap (sb/oneself) up** put warm clothes on (sb/oneself): *Wrap up warm(ly)! It's very cold outside.* **wrap sth up** (*infml*) complete (a task, a discussion, an agreement, etc): *The salesman had already wrapped up a couple of deals by lunch-time.* **wrap sth up (in sth)** obscure (what one is saying) by using difficult or unnecessary words: *Why does he have to wrap it all up in such complicated language?*

▷ **wrap** *n* **1** outer garment, eg a scarf, shawl or cloak. **2** (idm) **under ˈwraps** (*infml*) secret or hidden: *The documents will stay/be kept under wraps for ten more years.*

wrapper *n* piece of material, usu paper, that covers sth such as a sweet, book, or newspaper that is posted: *Please put all your sweet wrappers in the bin.*

wrapping *n* (**a**) [C] thing used to cover or wrap up sth: *the wrappings round a mummy.* (**b**) [U] material used for covering or packing sth: *Put plenty of wrapping round the china when you pack it.* **ˈwrapping paper** strong or decorative paper for wrapping parcels or presents.

□ **ˈwrap-around** *adj* [attrib] **1** (also **ˈwrap-over**) (of a skirt) consisting of a single piece of material that is put on by wrapping it round the body and fastening it where the edges meet. **2** (of a part of a building, vehicle, etc) curving round a corner or an edge. **3** (of a cinema screen) wider than normal and curving towards the audience at the edges. — *n* [C, U] (*computing*) automatic moving of a word at the end of one line to the beginning of the next, eg in a word-processing program.

ˈwrap-over *adj* [attrib] = WRAP-AROUND 1.

wrath /rɒθ; *US* ræθ/ *n* [U] (*fml or dated*) extreme anger: *the wrath of God* ○ *The children's unruly behaviour incurred the headteacher's wrath.* ▷ **wrathful** /-fl/ *adj.* **wrathfully** /-fəlɪ/ *adv.*

wreak /ri:k/ *v* (*fml*) **1** [Tn, Tn·pr] ~ **sth (on sb)** carry out (revenge or vengeance) on sb; inflict sth: *wreak vengeance on one's enemy* ○ *wreak one's fury on sb.* **2** (idm) **play/wreak havoc with sth** ⇨ HAVOC.

wreath /ri:θ/ *n* (*pl* ~**s** /ri:ðz/) **1** (**a**) arrangement of flowers and leaves twisted or woven into a circle and placed on a grave, etc as a mark of respect for the dead: *to lay wreaths at the war memorial.* (**b**) circle of flowers or leaves worn as a mark of honour round sb's head or neck; garland: *a laurel wreath.* **2** ring or coil of smoke, cloud, etc: *wreaths of mist.*

wreathe /ri:ð/ *v* **1** [usu passive: Tn, Tn·pr] ~ **sth (in/with sth)** cover or surround sth (by sth): *The display was wreathed in/with laurel.* ○ *The hills were wreathed in mist.* ○ (*fig*) *Her face was wreathed in smiles,* ie she was smiling a lot. **2** [Tn·pr] ~ **oneself/sth round sb/sth** wind oneself, one's arms, etc round sb/sth: *The snake wreathed itself round the branch.* **3** [Ipr, Ip] (of smoke, mist, etc) move in rings or coils: *Smoke wreathed slowly upwards.*

wreck /rek/ *n* [C] **1** (**a**) vehicle, aeroplane, etc that has been badly damaged, esp in an accident: *The collision reduced the car to a useless wreck.* (**b**) ship that has been destroyed or badly damaged, esp in a storm: *Two wrecks block the entrance to the harbour.* **2** (usu *sing*) (*infml*) person whose physical or mental health has been seriously damaged: *The stroke left him a helpless wreck.* ○ *Worry about the business has turned her into a nervous wreck.*

▷ **wreck** *v* [Tn] destroy or ruin (sth): *The road was littered with wrecked cars.* ○ *Vandals completely wrecked the train.* ○ *They had been wrecked* (ie shipwrecked) *off the coast of Africa.* ○ (*fig*) *The weather wrecked all our plans.* **wrecker** *n* **1** (*derog*) person who deliberately spoils sth or prevents it from succeeding. **2** (*US*) person employed to knock down buildings or other structures or to break up motor vehicles. **3** (formerly) person who caused ships to crash onto rocks, in order to steal their cargo. **4** (*US*) vehicle used to tow away cars, lorries, etc that have broken down, been damaged, etc.

wreckage /ˈrekɪdʒ/ *n* [U] remains of sth that has been wrecked: *Wreckage of the aircraft was scattered over a wide area.* ○ (*fig*) *attempts to save something from the wreckage of his political career.*

Wren[1] /ren/ *n* (*Brit infml*) member of the Women's Royal Naval Service: *She's in the Wrens.* Cf WRNS.

Saint Paul's Cathedral, designed by Sir Christopher Wren

Wren[2] /ren/ Sir Christopher (1632-1723), English architect who designed the new *St Paul's Cathedral after the previous one had been destroyed in the Great Fire of London (1666). He designed several other London churches, many of which were destroyed in the Second World War. He was also a scientist, a mathematician, an astronomer and a founder-member of the *Royal Society. ⇨ illus. ⇨ article at ARCHITECTURE.

wren /ren/ *n* type of very small brown songbird with short wings.

wrench /rentʃ/ *v* **1** [Tn·pr, Tn·p, Cn·a] ~ **sth off (sth)**; ~ **sb/sth away** twist or pull sb/sth violently away from sth: *to wrench a door off its hinges* ○ *He wrenched his arm away.* ○ *He managed to wrench himself free.* **2** [Tn] injure (one's ankle, shoulder, etc) by twisting: *She must have wrenched her ankle when she fell.*

▷ **wrench** *n* **1** [C usu *sing*] sudden and violent twist or pull: *He pulled the handle off with a wrench.* ○ *She stumbled and gave her ankle a painful wrench,* ie twisted it by accident. **2** [sing] painful parting or separation: *Leaving home was a terrible wrench for him.* **3** [C] (*esp US*) = SPANNER.

wrest /rest/ *v* **1** [Tn·pr] ~ **sth from sb** take sth away from sb violently: *wrest the gun from his grasp.* **2** [Tn·pr] ~ **sth from sb/sth** obtain sth from sb/sth by a hard struggle: *wrest a confession from sb* ○ *Foreign investors are trying to wrest control of the firm from the family.*

wrestle /ˈresl/ *v* **1** (**a**) [I, Ipr] ~ **(with sb)** fight (esp as a sport) by grappling with sb and trying to throw him to the ground: *Can you wrestle?* ○ *The guards wrestled with the intruders.* (**b**) [Tn·pr] force (sb) to the ground by wrestling: *He wrestled*

wrestling

his opponent to the floor/ground. **2** [Ipr] ~ **with sth** struggle to deal with or overcome sth: *wrestle with a problem, a difficulty, one's conscience* ○ *The pilot was wrestling with the controls.*

▷ **wrestle** *n* **1** wrestling match. **2** ~ **(with sth)** hard struggle: *a wrestle with one's conscience.*

wrestler /ˈreslə(r)/ *n* person who takes part in the sport of wrestling.

wrestling /ˈreslɪŋ/ *n* [U] sport in which people wrestle: *watch (the) wrestling on television.*

wretch /retʃ/ *n* **1** very unfortunate or miserable person: *a poor half-starved wretch.* **2** evil or nasty person: *the despicable wretch who stole the old woman's money.* **3** (*infml derog esp joc*) rogue or rascal: *You wretch! You've taken the book I wanted.*

wretched /ˈretʃɪd/ *adj* **1** (**a**) very unhappy; miserable or pitiable: *the wretched survivors of the earthquake* ○ *His stomach-ache made him feel wretched* (ie ill) *all day.* (**b**) causing unhappiness or misery: *lead a wretched existence in the slums.* **2** of very poor quality; very bad: *wretched weather* ○ *The hotel food was absolutely wretched.* **3** [attrib] (*infml*) (used to express annoyance) damned: *The wretched car won't start!* ○ *It's that wretched cat again!* ▷ **wretchedly** *adv.* **wretchedness** *n* [U].

wriggle /ˈrɪgl/ *v* **1** [I, Ip, Tn, Tn·p] (cause sth to) make quick, short, twisting and turning movements: *Stop wriggling (about) and sit still!* ○ *I can't brush your hair if you keep wriggling all the time.* ○ *The baby was wriggling its toes.* **2** [La, Ipr, Ip, Tn·pr, Tn·p, Cn·a] move or make (one's way) in the specified direction with wriggling movements: *The thieves left her tied up with rope but she wriggled (herself) free.* ○ *The eel wriggled out of my fingers.* ○ *They managed to wriggle (their way) through the thick hedge.* ○ *He had to wriggle his way out.* **3** (phr v) **wriggle out of sth/doing sth** (*infml*) avoid (doing) an unpleasant task by being cunning or by making excuses: *It's your turn to take the dog for a walk — don't try to wriggle out of it.* ○ *She managed to wriggle out of answering all the questions.*

▷ **wriggle** *n* (usu *sing*) wriggling movement. **wriggly** /ˈrɪglɪ/ *adj.*

Kaufmann House, designed by Frank Lloyd Wright

Wright[1] /raɪt/ Frank Lloyd (1869-1959), American architect who developed the concept of 'organic'

the Wright brothers making their first flight, 17 December 1903

architecture, in which buildings appear to grow naturally out of the landscape they are situated in. His designs, with their long low lines, were very influential on American domestic architecture. ⇨ illus. ⇨ article at ARCHITECTURE.

Wright² /raɪt/ Orville (1871-1948) and Wilbur (1867-1912), American brothers who in 1903 were the first to make a controlled flight in a powered aircraft, near Kitty Hawk, in North Carolina. ⇨ illus.

wring /rɪŋ/ *v* (*pt, pp* **wrung** /rʌŋ/) **1** (**a**) [Tn, Tn·p] ~ **sth** (**out**) twist and squeeze sth in order to remove liquid from it: *He wrung the clothes (out) before putting them on the line to dry.* (**b**) [Tn·pr, Tn·p] ~ **sth out** (**of sth**) remove (a liquid) from sth in this way: *Wring the water out of your wet bathing costume.* **2** [Tn·pr] ~ **sth out of/from sb** extract or obtain sth from sb with effort or difficulty: *wring a confession from sb* ○ *They managed to wring a promise out of her.* **3** [Tn] squeeze (sb's hand) firmly and warmly when shaking hands as a greeting. **4** [Tn] twist (a bird's neck) in order to kill it. **5** [Tn] have a deep effect on (sb's heart or soul), causing sb to feel great sadness and pity: *The plight of the refugees really wrung my heart.* **6** (idm) ˌ**wring one's** ˈ**hands** squeeze and twist one's hands together as a sign of anxiety, sadness or despair: *It's no use just wringing our hands — we must do something to help.* ˌ**wring sb's** ˈ**neck** (*infml*) (used as an expression of anger or as a threat) strangle sb: *If I find the person who did this, I'll wring his neck!*

▷ **wring** *n* (usu *sing*) act of wringing clothes, etc: *Give the towels another wring.*

wringer /ˈrɪŋə(r)/ *n* device with a pair of rollers between which washed clothes, etc are passed so that water is squeezed out. Cf MANGLE².

wringing /ˈrɪŋɪŋ/ *adj* (also ˌ**wringing** ˈ**wet**) (of clothes, etc) so wet that a lot of water can be wrung out.

wrinkle /ˈrɪŋkl/ *n* **1** (usu *pl*) small fold or line in the skin, esp one of those on the face that are caused by age: *She's beginning to get wrinkles around her eyes.* **2** raised fold in a piece of material, eg paper or cloth; small crease: *She pressed her skirt to try to remove all the wrinkles.* **3** (*infml*) useful hint or suggestion; tip.

▷ **wrinkle** *v* **1** [I, Tn] (cause sth to) form wrinkles: *The paper has wrinkled where it got wet.* ○ *Too much sunbathing will wrinkle your skin.* **2** [Tn] draw up (the nose, forehead, etc) into lines or creases by tightening the muscles: *He wrinkled his brow, confused and worried by the strange events.* **wrinkled** /ˈrɪŋkld/ *adj* having or showing wrinkles: *his old wrinkled face* ○ *wrinkled socks.*

wrinkly /ˈrɪŋklɪ/ *adj* having or forming wrinkles: *an old apple with a wrinkly skin.*

wrist /rɪst/ *n* (**a**) part of the body between the hand and the forearm; joint on which the hand moves. ⇨ illus at HAND. (**b**) part of a garment that covers this.

▷ **wristy** *adj* using the wrists: *a wristy stroke.*

□ ˈ**wrist-watch** *n* watch attached to a strap or bracelet and worn on the wrist.

wristlet /ˈrɪstlɪt/ *n* band or bracelet worn round the wrist to strengthen or protect it or as an ornament.

writ /rɪt/ *n* formal legal written order to do or not to do sth, issued by a court of law or a person in authority: *serve sb with a writ* (ie deliver a writ to sb officially) *for libel.*

▷ **writ 1** (*arch*) *pp* of WRITE. **2** (idm) ˌ**writ** ˈ**large** (*fml or rhet*) (**a**) easily or clearly recognizable; very obvious: *Disappointment was writ large on the face of the loser.* (**b**) in an emphasized form: *This policy is liberalism writ large.*

write /raɪt/ *v* (*pt* **wrote** /rəʊt/, *pp* **written** /ˈrɪtn or, in archaic use/, **writ** /rɪt/) **1** [I, Ipr] make letters or other symbols on a surface (usu paper), esp with a pen or pencil: *The children are learning to read and write.* ○ *By the age of seven he could write beautifully.* ○ *Please write on both sides of the paper, and don't write in the margin.* ○ *You may write in biro or pencil.* **2** [Tn, Tn·pr] form (letters, symbols, words, messages, etc), esp on paper: *write capitals, Chinese characters, shorthand, etc* ○ *write one's name* ○ *write the answers in a book, on the blackboard, etc.* **3** [I] (of a pen, pencil, etc) be capable of being used for writing: *This pen won't write.* ○ *My new pen writes well.* **4** (**a**) [Tn, Dn·n, Dn·pr] ~ **sth** (**for sb/sth**) compose sth in written form (for sb/sth): *write a book, film script, poem, symphony, etc* ○ *Can you write me a story about your holiday?* ○ *He writes a weekly column for the local newspaper.* (**b**) [I, Ipr] ~ (**about/on sth**) work as an author or journalist by writing about sth or for a newspaper, etc: *He gave up his job in the factory in order to write*, ie earn a living by writing. ○ *She writes (about/on politics) for a weekly journal.* (**c**) [Tf, Tw] state in a book or magazine: *In his latest book, he writes that the theory has been disproved.* **5** (**a**) [I, Ipr, Tf, Tt, Dn·n, Dn·pr] ~ (**sth**) (**to sb**) write and send a letter (to sb): *Please write (to me) often while you're away.* ○ *He wrote that he would be coming home soon.* ○ *They wrote to thank us/he wrote thanking us for the present.* ○ *She wrote him a long letter/wrote a long letter to him.* (**b**) [Tn, Dn·f, Dn·w] (*esp US*) write a letter to (sb): *Write me when you get home.* ○ *He wrote me that he would be arriving on Wednesday.* **6** [Tn, Tn·p, Dn·n, Dn·pr] ~ **sth** (**out**) (**for sb**) fill or complete (a sheet of paper, a document, the spaces in a form) with writing: *She usually writes several pages when she makes her report.* ○ *He has written (out) 50 job applications.* ○ *I haven't any cash. I'll have to write you (out) a cheque.* ○ *In a day, a doctor may write (out) 30 prescriptions for patients.* **7** [Tn] record (data) in or on any computer storage device or medium. **8** (idm) **be written all over sb's** ˈ**face** (usu of a quality or emotion) be very obvious from the expression on sb's face: *Guilt was written all over his face.* **have sb written all** ˈ**over it** (*infml*) be obviously written, done, etc by the specified person. **nothing** (**much**) **to write** ˈ**home about** (*infml*) not outstanding or exceptional; ordinary: *The play was nothing (much) to write home about.* **9** (phr v) **write away** (**to sb/sth**) (**for sth**) ⇨ WRITE OFF away (TO SB sth) (FOR STH)).

write back (**to sb**) write and send a letter in reply to sb: *I wrote back (to him) immediately to thank them for the invitation.*

write sth down (**a**) put sth down in words on paper: *Write down the address before you forget it.* (**b**) (in accounting) reduce the nominal value of (stock, goods, etc): *the written-down value of the unsold stock.*

write in (**to sb/sth**) (**for sth**) write a letter to (an organization, a company, etc) to order sth, state an opinion, etc: *Thousands of people have written in to us for a free sample.* **write sth/sb in** (*US politics*) add (the name of a candidate) to a ballot paper if this does not include that name; vote for sb in this way. **write sth into sth** include sth as part of (a contract, an agreement, etc): *A penalty clause was written into the contract.*

write off/away (**to sb/sth**) (**for sth**) write to (an organization, a company, etc) to order sth or to ask for information about sth: *They wrote off (to the BBC) for the special booklet.* **write sth off** (**a**) recognize that sth is a loss or failure; cancel (a debt): *write off a debt, loss, etc* ○ *write off £5000 for depreciation of machinery.* (**b**) damage sth so badly that it is not worth repairing: *The driver escaped with minor injuries but the car was completely written off.* Cf WRITE-OFF. **write sb/sth off** regard sb/sth as a failure: *He lost this match, but don't write him off as a future champion.* ○ *It seemed that everyone had written off their marriage even before it had been given a proper chance.* **write sb/sth off as sth** regard sb/sth as unimportant, not worth listening to, etc: *It's easy to write him off as just an eccentric old bore.*

write sth out (**a**) write sth in full or in its final form: *write out a report, cheque, prescription, etc.* (**b**) copy sth: *Write out this word ten times so that you learn how to spell it.* **write sb out** (**of sth**) remove (a character) from a continuing drama series on radio or television: *After playing the part for over 20 years, she was eventually written out (of the series).*

write sth up (**a**) make a full written record of sth: *write up one's lecture notes, the minutes of a meeting, etc* ○ *write up one's diary*, ie bring it up to date. (**b**) write a review of (a play, etc) or an account of (an event), usu for a newspaper: *I'm writing up the film for the local paper.* Cf WRITE-UP.

▷ **written** *adj* (to be) expressed in writing, rather than in speech: *a written examination, request, message* ○ *a written confirmation, agreement, evidence.* **the** ˌ**written** ˈ**word** language expressed in writing.

□ ˈ**write-off** *n* thing, esp a vehicle, that is so badly damaged that it is not worth repairing: *After the accident, the car was a complete write-off.*

ˈ**write-up** *n* written or published account of an event, review of a play, etc: *His latest play got/was given an enthusiastic write-up in the local press.*

writer /ˈraɪtə(r)/ *n* **1** (**a**) person who writes or has written sth: *the writer of this letter.* (**b**) (with an *adj*) person who forms letters in a certain way when writing: *a neat, messy, etc writer.* **2** person whose job is to write books, stories, etc; author: *a short-story writer* ○ *a writer of poetry.*

□ ˌ**writer's** ˈ**block** state of mind sometimes experienced by writers when they feel unable to continue writing creatively.

ˌ**writer's** ˈ**cramp** pain or stiffness in the hand, caused by writing for a long time.

writhe /raɪð/ *v* **1** [I, Ip] (of sb or sb's body) twist or roll about, esp because of great pain: *the writhing coils of a snake* ○ *The patient was writhing (about) on the bed in agony.* **2** [I, Ipr] ~ (**at/under sth**); ~ (**with sth**) suffer mental agony (because of sth): *writhe under sb's insults* ○ *Her remarks made him writhe with shame.*

writing /ˈraɪtɪŋ/ *n* **1** [U] activity or occupation of writing (esp books): *She doesn't earn much from her writing.* ○ *Writing is a solitary pastime.* ○ [attrib] *writing materials*, eg pens, paper, ink ○ *a writing-pad.* **2** [U] written or printed words: *There is some writing on the other side of the page.* ○ *The writing on the stone was very faint.* **3** [U] style of written material: *He is admired for the elegance of his writing.* **4** [U] way in which a person forms letters when writing; handwriting: *I can never read your writing.* **5 writings** [pl] works of an author or on a subject: *the writings of Dickens* ○ *It is frequently mentioned in the poetic writings of the period.* **6** (idm) **in ˈwriting** in written form, esp in a document or contract: *You must get his agreement in writing.* **the ˌwriting (is) on the ˈwall** (there are) clear signs that warn of failure, disaster or defeat: *The writing is on the wall for the local football club: bankruptcy seems certain.*

□ **ˈwriting-desk** *n* desk with a flat or sloping surface and with drawers or compartments to keep writing materials in. ⇨ illus at FURNITURE. **ˈwriting-paper** *n* [U] (usu good-quality) paper cut into sheets of a suitable size for writing letters on.

written ⇨ WRITE.

WRNS /ˌdʌblju: ɑ:r en ˈes, *also* renz/ *abbr* (*Brit*) Women's Royal Naval Service: *join the WRNS.*

wrong /rɒŋ; *US* rɔ:ŋ/ *adj* **1** ~ (**to do sth**) not morally right; unjust: *It is wrong to steal.* ○ *You were wrong to take the car without permission.* ○ *He told me he had done nothing wrong.* Cf RIGHT[1] 1. **2** (**a**) not true or correct: *He did the sum but got the wrong answer/got the answer wrong.* ○ *Her estimate of the cost was completely wrong.* (**b**) [pred] (of a person) mistaken: *Am I wrong in thinking* (ie Do you agree) *that it is getting colder?* ○ *Can you prove that I am wrong?* ○ *That's where you're wrong.* ○ *Thousands of satisfied customers can't be wrong, so why don't you try our new washing-powder?* **3** [usu attrib] not required, suitable or the most desirable: *You're doing it the wrong way.* ○ *We discovered that we were on the wrong train.* ○ *The police arrested the wrong man.* ○ *We came the wrong way/took a wrong turning.* ○ *I'm afraid you've got the wrong number*, ie on the telephone. ○ *You're wearing your jumper the wrong way round*, ie The part that should be at the front is at the back. ○ *He's the wrong man for the job.* ○ *They live on the wrong side of town*, ie the part that is socially less desirable. ○ *I realized that I had said the wrong thing when I saw her reaction.* ○ *Their decision proved to be wrong.* **4** [pred] ~ (**with sb/sth**) (**a**) in a bad condition (and not working properly): *What's wrong* (ie What is the problem) *with the engine? It's making an awful noise.* ○ *There's something wrong with my eyes — I can't see properly.* (**b**) not as it should be: *Is anything wrong? You look ill.* ○ *What's wrong with you?* ○ *What's wrong with telling the truth?* ie How can it be criticized? **5** (idm) **back the wrong horse** ⇨ BACK[4]. **bark up the wrong tree** ⇨ BARK[2]. **be born on the wrong side of the blanket** ⇨ BORN. **catch sb on the wrong foot** ⇨ CATCH[1]. **do the right/wrong thing** ⇨ RIGHT[1]. **from/on the ˌwrong side of the ˈtracks** (*US*) living in an area (of a town, etc) which is regarded as socially inferior. **get on the right/wrong side of sb** ⇨ SIDE[1]. **get (hold of) the ˌwrong end of the ˈstick** (*infml*) misunderstand completely what has been said: *You've got the wrong end of the stick; he doesn't owe me money, I owe him!* **have got out of bed on the wrong side** ⇨ BED[1]. **hit/strike the right/wrong note** ⇨ NOTE[1]. **not far off/out/wrong** ⇨ FAR[2]. **on the right/wrong side of forty, fifty, etc** ⇨ SIDE[1]. **rub sb up the wrong way** ⇨ RUB[1]. **start off on the right/wrong foot** ⇨ START[2]. **ˌwrong side ˈout** turned, changed, etc so that the normally inner side is facing outwards: *You've got your sweater on wrong side out.*

▷ **wrong** *adv* (used after *vs*) **1** in a wrong manner or direction; mistakenly; with incorrect results: *You guessed wrong.* ○ *You've spelt my name wrong.* ○ *He played the tune all wrong.* Cf WRONGLY. **2** (idm) **get sb ˈwrong** (*infml*) misunderstand sb: *Please don't get me wrong, I'm not criticizing you.* **go ˈwrong** (**a**) make a mistake: *If you read the instructions, you'll see where you went wrong.* ○ *You can't go wrong* (ie You will surely succeed) *with our new carpet cleaner.* (**b**) (of a machine) stop working properly: *The television has gone wrong again.* (**c**) experience trouble: *Their marriage started to go wrong when he got a job abroad.* ○ *The experiment went disastrously wrong*, ie progressed in an unexpected way with very unpleasant results. **put a foot wrong** ⇨ FOOT[1].

wrong *n* **1** [U] what is wrong: *He doesn't know the difference between right and wrong.* ○ *She could do no wrong* (ie do nothing wrong) *in the opinion of her devoted followers.* **2** [C] (*fml*) unjust action; injustice: *They have done us a great wrong.* ○ *She complained of the wrongs she had suffered.* **3** (idm) **in the ˈwrong** in the position of being responsible for a mistake, an offence, a quarrel, etc: *He admitted that he was in the wrong*, ie that the fault was his. ○ *They tried to put me in the wrong*, ie to make it seem that the fault, error, etc was mine. **the rights and wrongs of sth** ⇨ RIGHT[3]. **ˌtwo ˌwrongs ˌdon't make a ˈright** (*saying*) you cannot justify a wrong action by saying that sb else has done sth similar or that sb has done sth wrong to you.

wrong *v* (*fml*) **1** [Tn usu passive] do wrong to (sb); treat (sb) unjustly or badly: *a wronged wife.* **2** [Tn] judge (sb) unfairly; attribute a bad motive to (sb) mistakenly: *You wrong me if you think I only did it for selfish reasons.*

wrongful /-fl/ *adj* [attrib] not fair, just or legal: *He sued his employer for wrongful dismissal.* **wrongfully** /-fəlɪ/ *adv*: *wrongfully arrested.*

wrongly *adv* (used esp before a past participle or a *v*) in a wrong manner; in the wrong way: *wrongly accused, addressed, informed* ○ *He imagines, wrongly, that she loves him.* ○ *Rightly or wrongly, she refused to accept the offer*, ie I don't know whether she was right or wrong to do so.

□ **wrongdoer** /ˈrɒŋdu:ə(r)/ *n* person who does sth immoral or illegal. **wrongdoing** /ˈrɒŋdu:ɪŋ/ *n* [U, C] wrong behaviour; wrong action: *such wrongdoing(s) should be punished.*

ˌwrong-ˈfoot *v* [Tn] (esp in sport) catch (sb) unprepared: *Her cleverly disguised lob completely wrong-footed her opponent.*

ˌwrong-ˈheaded *adj* (of a person) obstinately holding a wrong opinion or taking a wrong course of action.

wrote *pt* of WRITE.

wrought /rɔ:t/ *pt, pp* of WORK[2].

▷ **wrought** *adj* [attrib] **1** made or manufactured and decorated: *elaborately wrought carvings.* **2** (of metal) beaten out or shaped by hammering.

□ **ˌwrought ˈiron** tough form of iron made by forging or rolling: [attrib] *a ˌwrought-iron ˈbedstead, ˈgate, ˈrailing.* Cf CAST IRON (CAST[1]).

wrung *pt, pp* of WRING.

wry /raɪ/ *adj* (**wryer, wryest**) **1** [usu attrib] (of a person's face, features, etc) twisted into an expression of disappointment, disgust or mockery: *pull a wry face* ○ *a wry glance, grin, smile, etc.* **2** ironically humorous; slightly mocking: *She watched their fumbling efforts with wry amusement.* ▷ **wryly** *adv.* **wryness** *n* [U].

wt *abbr* weight: *net wt 454 gm*, eg on a jar of jam.

wunderkind /ˈvʊndəkɪnt/ *n* (*infml*) person who achieves great success while still young.

Wurlitzer /ˈwɜ:lɪtsə(r)/ *n* large electric organ of a type formerly used esp in cinemas, made by an American firm of the same name.

WWF *abbr* World Wide Fund for Nature.

WX /ˌdʌblju: ˈeks/ *abbr* (esp on clothing) women's extra large (size).

wych-elm /ˈwɪtʃ elm/ *n* type of elm tree with broad leaves and spreading branches.

wych-hazel = WITCH-HAZEL (WITCH).

Wyclif (also **Wycliffe**) /ˈwɪklɪf/ John (c 1329-84), English religious reformer. He campaigned against various abuses that were common in the Church of his time (eg the selling of pardons), and maintained that the authority of the Bible was greater than that of the Church. He organized the translation of the Bible into English, doing some of it himself. His followers were known as *Lollards.

Wyler /ˈwaɪlə(r)/ William (1902-81), American film director, born in Germany. Stylish and innovative, Wyler excelled at literary adaptations and contemporary drama, though he is best remembered for the epic *Ben Hur.*

Wyoming /waɪˈəʊmɪŋ/ state of the western central USA. The *Rocky Mountains run through it. It has large reserves of minerals. ⇨ map at App 1.

wyvern /ˈwaɪvən/ *n* (*heraldry*) mythical animal, a dragon with wings and two legs.

X, x

X, x /eks/ *n* (*pl* **X's**, **x's** /ˈeksɪz/) the twenty-fourth letter of the English alphabet: *'Xylophone' begins with (an) X/'X'.*

□ ˈ**X chromosome** (*biology*) chromosome that occurs as one of an identical pair in female cells to produce a female in the reproductive process, or singly combined with a single Y chromosome in male cells to produce a male. Cf Y CHROMOSOME (Y).

X (also **x**) *symb* **1** Roman numeral for 10. **2** (esp in letters, etc, indicating a kiss): *Love from Cathy XXX.* **3** (indicating a vote on a ballot-paper, etc): *James Blunt X.* **4** (indicating an error on corrected written work, etc). **5** (**a**) (*mathematics*) unknown quantity: $4x = x + x + x + x$. (**b**) (*fig*) unknown or unspecified person, number or influence: *Mr and Mrs X.* **6** (indicating a position marked eg on a map): *X marks the spot.* **7** (formerly used in Britain as a film classification, indicating that a film should not be shown to people under the age of 18 years): *a film with an X rating* ○ *an X-rated film* ○ *an X-certificate film.* **8** (also **Xt**) Christ (Greek *Christos*): *Xtian,* ie Christian ○ *Xmas,* ie Christmas.

Xavier /ˈzeɪvɪə(r), ˈzævɪə(r)/ Saint Francis (1506-52), Spanish Jesuit missionary. He converted many people in his journeys through India to Japan and died while on his way to China to continue his work there.

Xe *symb* xenon.

xenon /ˈzi:nɒn/ *n* [U] (*symb* **Xe**) chemical element, a colourless and odourless inert gas. ⇨ App 11.

xenophobia /ˌzenəˈfəʊbɪə/ *n* [U] intense dislike or fear of foreigners or strangers: *Excessive patriotism can lead to xenophobia.* ▷ **xenophobic** /-ˈfəʊbɪk/ *adj.*

Xenophon /ˈzenəfən/ (c 428-c 354BC), Greek soldier and writer. Banished from Athens for his anti-democratic views, he fought for the Spartans and Persians. The *Anabasis* records some of his military experiences. The teachings of his friend *Socrates appear in dialogues like the *Apologia*.

xerography /zɪəˈrɒgrəfɪ/ *n* [U] process used in photocopying, in which a copy of an original is made by dry powder adhering to the parts of the paper which have a slight electric charge. ▷ **xerographic** /zɪərəˈgræfɪk/ *adj.*

Xerox /ˈzɪərɒks/ *n* (*propr*) **1** process for producing photocopies without the use of wet materials: [attrib] *a Xerox machine.* Cf PHOTOCOPY, PHOTOSTAT. **2** photocopy made using this process: *make/take a couple of Xeroxes of the contract.*

▷ **xerox** *v* [I, Tn] produce copies of (documents, etc) using the Xerox or a similar process: *Could you xerox this letter please, Paula?*

Xhosa /ˈkɔ:sə/ *n* **1** [C] member of a Bantu people of Cape Province, S Africa. **2** [U] their language. ▷ **Xhosa** *adj.*

-xion ⇨ -ION.

XL /ˌeks ˈel/ *abbr* (esp on clothing) extra large.

Xmas /ˈkrɪsməs, ˈeksməs/ *n* [C, U] (*infml*) (used as a short form, esp in writing) Christmas: *A merry Xmas to all our readers!*

X-ray /ˈeks reɪ/ *n* **1** (usu *pl* except when used attributively) type of short-wave electromagnetic radiation that can penetrate solids and make it possible to see into or through them: *an X-ray machine,* ie one that emits X-rays ○ *an X-ray telescope,* ie one that can examine and measure the X-rays emitted by stars, etc ○ *X-ray therapy,* ie medical treatment using X-rays. **2** (**a**) (also **radiograph**) photograph made by X-rays, esp one showing bones or organs in the human body: *a chest X-ray* ○ *take an X-ray of sb's hand* ○ *The doctor doesn't think I've broken a bone but he's waiting to see the X-rays.* (**b**) (*infml*) medical examination using X-rays.

▷ **X-ray** *v* [Tn] (**a**) examine or photograph (sb/sth) using X-rays: *When his lungs were X-rayed the disease could be clearly seen.* (**b**) treat (sb/sth) medically using X-rays.

Xt = X *symb* 8.

xylem /ˈzaɪləm/ *n* [U] tissue in plants that transports water from the roots to other parts.

xylophone /ˈzaɪləfəʊn/ *n* musical instrument consisting of parallel wooden or metal bars mounted on a frame, which are of different lengths and so produce different notes when struck with small wooden hammers. ⇨ illus at MUSIC.

Y, y

Y, y /waɪ/ *n* (*pl* **Y's, y's** /waɪz/) the twenty-fifth letter of the English alphabet: *'Yak' begins with (a) Y/'Y'.*

□ **ˈY chromosome** (*biology*) chromosome that occurs singly and only in male cells, and produces a male after combining with an X chromosome during the reproductive process. Cf X CHROMOSOME (X).

ˈY-fronts *n* [pl] (*Brit propr*) men's underpants, with seams and an opening in the front sewn in the shape of an inverted Y: *a pair of Y-fronts.*

Y *abbr* **1** yen[1]. **2** /waɪ/ (*US infml*) = YMCA, YWCA.

Y /waɪ/ *symb* **1** (**a**) (also **y**) (*mathematics*) unknown quantity: *x = y + 2.* (**b**) (*fig*) second unknown or unspecified person, number or influence: *Mr X met Miss Y.* **2** (*chemistry*) yttrium.

-y[1] (also **-ey**) *suff* **1** (with *ns* forming *adjs*) full of; having the quality of: *dusty* ○ *icy* ○ *clayey.* **2** (with *vs* forming *adjs*) tending to: *runny* ○ *sticky.* ▷ **-ily** (forming *advs*). **-iness** (forming uncountable *ns*).

-y[2] *suff* **1** (with *vs* forming *ns*) action or process of: *inquiry* ○ *expiry.* **2** (also **-ie**) (with *ns* forming diminutives or pet names): *piggy* ○ *doggie* ○ *daddy* ○ *Susie.*

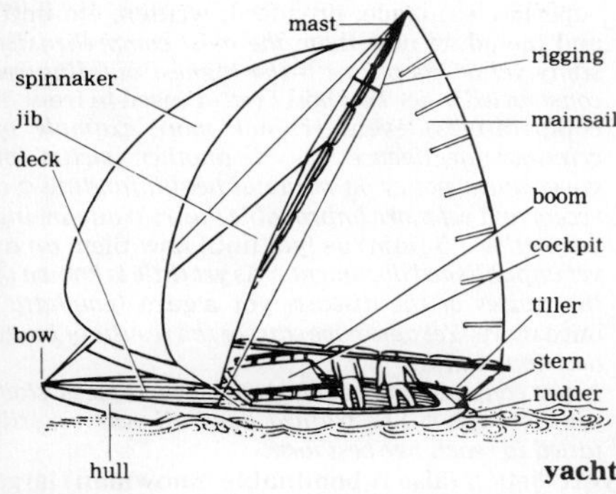

yacht

yacht /jɒt/ *n* **1** light sailing-boat, esp one built specifically for racing: [attrib] *a yacht race, club, crew* ○ *a sand yacht,* ie a yacht-like vehicle with wheels for use on sand. **2** large (usu power-driven) vessel used for private pleasure cruising. Cf DINGHY.

▷ **yacht** *v* [I] (usu in the continuous tenses) travel or race in a yacht, especially as a hobby: *I go yachting most weekends in the summer.* **yachting** *n* [U] art, practice or sport of sailing yachts: [attrib] *yachting equipment.*

□ **ˈyachtsman** /-smən/ *n* (*pl* **-smen** /-smən/, *fem* **ˈyachtswoman**) person who has yachting as a hobby: *a round-the-world yachtsman.*

yack /jæk/ *v* [I, Ipr, Ip] ~ (**away/on**) (**about sb/sth**) (*sl*) talk continuously and often noisily (usu about sth unimportant): *Joy kept yacking (on) about the wedding.*

▷ **yack** *n* (usu *sing*) (*sl*) persistent or trivial conversation; chatter: *having a good old yack with the neighbours.*

yackety-yack /ˌjækətɪ ˈjæk/ *n* [U] (*sl*) persistent chatter.

yahoo /jəˈhuː/ *n* (*pl* ~**s**) coarse brutish person: [attrib] *a yahoo attitude.*

yak /jæk/ *n* wild or domesticated ox of Central Asia, with long horns and hair.

Yale[1] /jeɪl/ *n* (also **ˈYale lock**) (*propr*) type of lock with revolving internal parts, commonly used for doors, etc: *have a Yale (lock) fitted* ○ [attrib] *a Yale key.*

Yale[2] /jeɪl/ university in New Haven, Connecticut. It is one of the oldest universities in the USA, founded in 1701. It moved to its present site in 1716, and was named in honour of Elihu Yale, who gave money for it. ⇨ article at POST-SCHOOL.

Yalta /ˈjæltə; *US* ˈjɔːltə/ town in the *Crimea, USSR, on the Black Sea. It is an important tourist resort and spa. In 1945, a conference held there between *Roosevelt, *Stalin and *Churchill produced the **Yalta Agreement**, which fixed European borders for the period following the Second World War.

yam /jæm/ *n* **1** (**a**) edible starchy tuber of a tropical climbing plant. (**b**) this plant. **2** (*US*) type of sweet potato.

yammer /ˈjæmə(r)/ *v* [I, Ipr, Ip] ~ (**on**) (**about sb/sth**) (*infml derog*) talk noisily and continuously; complain or speak in a whining, grumbling manner: *I do wish they'd stop yammering on about the size of the bill.*

yang /jæŋ/ *n* [U] (in Chinese philosophy) the active bright male principle of the universe. Cf YIN.

Yangtse /ˈjæŋtsɪ/ **the Yangtse** main river of China, 6 380 km (3 964 miles) long, the third longest river in the world. It rises in Tibet and flows through central China to the East China Sea.

Yank /jæŋk/ *n* (*infml*) = YANKEE.

yank /jæŋk/ *v* [I, Ipr, Tn, Tn·pr, Tn·p] (*infml*) pull (sth) with a sudden sharp tug (often in a specified direction): *She yanked (on) the rope and it broke.* ○ *yank the bedclothes off one's bed* ○ *yank out a tooth.*

▷ **yank** *n* sudden sharp tug: *The old chain only needed a couple of yanks before it snapped.*

Yankee /ˈjæŋkɪ/ (also **Yank**) *n* **1** (*Brit infml*) inhabitant of the United States of America; American: [attrib] *Yankee hospitality.* **2** (*US*) (**a**) inhabitant of any of the Northern states, esp those of New England. (**b**) Federal soldier in the American Civil War.

□ **ˌYankee ˈDoodle** traditional American patriotic song. Although originally sung by British troops during the *American War of Independence, a new version was adopted by the Americans and played at the British surrender at Yorktown.

yap /jæp/ *v* (**-pp-**) [I, Ipr] **1** ~ (**at sb/sth**) (esp of small dogs) utter short sharp barks: *yapping at the postman.* **2** (*sl*) talk noisily and foolishly: *Stop yapping!*

▷ **yap** *n* sound of yapping.

yard[1] /jɑːd/ *n* **1** (**a**) (usu unroofed) enclosed or partly enclosed space near or round a building or group of buildings, often paved. (**b**) (*US*) = BACKYARD (BACK[2]). **2** (usu in compounds) enclosure for a special purpose or business: *a ˈrailway yard/ˈmarshalling yard,* ie an area where trains are made up, and where coaches, wagons, etc are stored ○ *a ˈbuilder's yard.*

▷ **yard** *v* [Tn] place (cattle) inside a yard.

yard[2] /jɑːd/ *n* **1** (*abbr* **yd**) unit of length, equal to 3 feet (36 inches) or 0.9144 metre: *Can you still buy cloth by the yard in Britain?* ⇨ App 9, 10. **2** long pole-like piece of wood fastened to a mast for supporting and spreading a sail.

▷ **yardage** /ˈjɑːdɪdʒ/ *n* [C, U] size measured in yards or square yards: *a considerable yardage of canvas.*

□ **ˈyard-arm** *n* either end of a yard[2] (2) supporting a sail.

ˌyard of ˈale (**a**) ale or beer held in a deep slender drinking glass about a yard long. (**b**) this drinking glass.

yardstick /ˈjɑːdstɪk/ *n* ~ (**of sth**) standard of comparison: *Durability is one yardstick of quality.* ○ *We need a yardstick to measure our performance by.*

yarmulka /ˈjʌmʊlkə/ *n* skull-cap worn by Jewish men, esp at prayer.

yarn /jɑːn/ *n* **1** [U] fibres (esp of wool) that have been spun for knitting, weaving, etc. **2** [C] (*infml*) story; traveller's tale, esp one that is exaggerated or invented. **3** (idm) **spin a yarn** ⇨ SPIN.

▷ **yarn** *v* [I] (*infml*) tell yarns: *We stayed up yarning until midnight.*

yarrow /ˈjærəʊ/ *n* [C, U] plant with feathery leaves and small strong-smelling white or pinkish flowers in flat clusters: *hedgerows full of yarrow.*

yashmak /ˈjæʃmæk/ *n* veil covering most of the face, worn in public by Muslim women in certain countries.

yaw /jɔː/ *v* [I] (of a ship or aircraft, etc) turn unsteadily off a straight or correct course. Cf PITCH[3] 6, ROLL[2] 6.

▷ **yaw** *n* such a turn.

yawl /jɔːl/ *n* (*nautical*) **1** (**a**) sailing-boat with two masts, the second being a short one near the stern. (**b**) type of small fishing-boat. **2** ship's boat with four or six oars.

yawn /jɔːn/ *v* [I] **1** take (usu involuntarily) a deep breath with the mouth wide open, as when sleepy or bored. **2** (of large holes, etc) be wide open: *The deep crevasse yawned at their feet.* ○ *a yawning chasm* ○ (*fig*) *a yawning gap between the rich and poor in our society.*

▷ **yawn** *n* **1** act of yawning (YAWN *v* 1). **2** (usu *sing*) (*infml derog*) uninteresting or boring thing: *The meeting was one big yawn from start to finish.*

yaws /jɔːz/ *n* [sing or pl *v*] tropical skin disease causing raspberry-like swellings.

Yb *symb* ytterbium.

yd *abbr* (*pl* **yds**) yard (measurement): *12 yds of silk.* Cf FT, IN.

ye[1] /jiː/ *pers pron* (*arch*) (*pl of thou*) you.

ye[2] /jiː: *or pronounced as* **the**/ *det* (used in the names of pubs, shops, etc as if it were the old-fashioned spelling) the: *Ye Olde Bull and Bush,* eg on a pub sign.

yea /jeɪ/ *adv, n* (*arch*) yes. Cf NAY.

yeah /jeə/ *adv* (*infml*) **1** (casual pronunciation of) yes. **2** (idm) **ˌoh ˈyeah?** (used to show that one does not believe what has been said): *'I'm going to meet the Prime Minister.' 'Oh yeah? Very likely!'*

year /jɪə(r), *also* jɜː(r)/ *n* **1** [C] time taken by the earth to make one orbit round the sun, about $365\frac{1}{4}$ days. **2** [C] (also **ˈcalendar year**) period from 1 January to 31 December, ie 365 days (or 366 in a leap year) divided into 12 months: *in the year 1865* ○ *this year* ○ *the year after next* ○ *a good year for cheap vegetables,* ie a year in which vegetables are available cheaply. **3** [C] any period of 365 consecutive days: *It's just a year (today) since I arrived here.* ○ *I arrived a year ago (today).* ○ *She's worked there for ten years.* ○ *In a year's time they're getting married.* ○ [attrib] *a five-year forecast.* **4** [C] period of one year associated with sth, such as education or finance: *the ˌacademic ˈyear* ○ *the fiˌnancial/fiscal/ˌtax ˈyear* ○ [attrib] *first year students.* **5** [C usu *pl*] age; time of life: *twenty years old/of age* ○ *a seventy-year-old man* ○ *She looks young for her years/for a woman of her years,* ie looks younger than she is. ○ *He died in his sixtieth year,* ie at the age of 59. **6 years** [pl] (*infml*) a long time: *I've worked for this firm for years (and years).* ○ *It's years since we last met.* **7** (idm) **the age/years of discretion** ⇨ DISCRETION. **ˌall (the) year ˈround** throughout the year: *He swims in the sea all year round.* **donkey's years** ⇨ DONKEY. **man, woman, car, etc of the ˈyear** person or thing chosen as outstanding in a particular field in a particular year: *TV personality of the year.* **not/never in a**

hundred, etc ˈyears absolutely not/never. **old beyond one's years** ⇨ OLD. **put ˈyears on sb** make sb feel or appear older: *The shock put years on him.* **ring out the old year and ring in the new** ⇨ RING². **take ˈyears off sb** make sb feel or appear younger: *Giving up smoking has taken years off her.* **the turn of the year/century** ⇨ TURN². **year after ˈyear** continuously for many years: *She sent money year after year to help the poor.* **year by ˈyear** progressively each year: *Year by year their affection for each other grew stronger.* **the year ˈdot** (*infml*) a very long time ago: *I've been going there every summer since the year dot.* **year ˈin, year ˈout** every year without exception. **ˌyear of ˈgrace; ˌyear of our ˈLord** (*fml*) any specified year after the birth of Christ: *in the year of our Lord 1217*, ie 1217 AD.

▷ **yearly** *adj, adv* (occurring) every year or once a year: *a yearly conference/a conference held yearly.*

□ **ˈyear-book** *n* book issued once a year, giving information (reports, statistics, etc) about a particular subject.

ˌyear-ˈlong *adj* [attrib] continuing for or throughout a year: *a ˌyear-long ˈlecture tour.*

yearling /ˈjɪəlɪŋ/ *n* animal, esp a horse, between one and two years old: *a race for yearlings* ○ [attrib] *a yearling filly.*

yearn /jɜ:n/ *v* [I, Ipr, It] ~ **(for sb/sth)** desire strongly or with compassion or tenderness; be filled with longing: *a yearning desire* ○ *He yearned for his home and family.* ○ *She yearned to return to her native country.*

▷ **yearning** *n* [C, U] ~ **(for sb/sth)**; ~ **(to do sth)** strong desire; tender longing. **yearningly** *adv.*

yeast /ji:st/ *n* [C, U] (type of) fungous substance used in making of beer and wine, or to make bread rise²(10): *brewer's yeast* ○ *baker's yeast.*

▷ **yeasty** *adj* tasting or smelling strongly of yeast; frothy like yeast when it is developing. **yeastiness** *n* [U].

Yeats /jeɪts/ William Butler (1865-1939), Irish poet and playwright. He led the revival of Irish literature and his book of stories *The Celtic Twilight* gave its name to the movement inspired by Ireland's folklore. He was one of the founders of the *Abbey Theatre, and wrote several plays for it. Yeats was a nationalist and served as a member of the Irish Senate. He was awarded the Nobel prize for literature in 1923.

yell /jel/ *v* **1** [I, Ipr, Ip] ~ **(out) (at sb/sth)**; ~ **(out) (in/with sth)** utter a loud sharp cry or cries as of pain, excitement, etc: *Stop yelling, can't you!* ○ *She yelled (out) at her mischievous child.* ○ *yell out in anguish, terror, pain, etc* ○ *yell with fear, agony, laughter.* **2** [I, Ipr, Tn, Tn·pr, Tn·p] ~ **(at sb) (about/for sth)**; ~ **(out) sth (at sb/sth)** speak or say (sth) in a yelling voice: *She yelled at him about his constant drunkenness.* ○ *The crowd yelled (out) encouragement at the players.* ⇨ Usage at SHOUT.

▷ **yell** *n* **1** loud sharp cry of pain, excitement, etc: *a yell of terror* ○ *let out an ear-splitting yell.* **2** (*US*) particular type of shout or cheer used at a college to encourage a team, etc.

yellow /ˈjeləʊ/ *adj* **1** (a) of the colour of ripe lemons, egg yolks or gold, or of a colour similar to this. ⇨ illus at SPECTRUM. (b) (*often offensive*) having the light brown skin and complexion of certain eastern Asian peoples. **2** (also **ˈyellow-bellied**) (*infml derog*) cowardly: *I always suspected he was yellow.* **3** (idm) **a yellow ˈstreak** cowardice in sb's character.

▷ **yellow** *n* (a) [C, U] the colour yellow: *several different yellows* (ie shades of yellow) *in the paintbox.* (b) [U] yellow substance, material or covering; yellow clothes: *wearing yellow.*

yellow *v* [I, Tn] (cause sth to) become yellow: *yellowing autumn leaves* ○ *The manuscript had yellowed/was yellowed with age.*

yellowish, yellowy *adjs* rather yellow.

yellowness *n* [U].

□ **ˌyellow ˈcard** (in football, etc) card shown by the referee to a player that he is cautioning. Cf RED CARD (RED¹).

ˌyellow ˈfever [U] infectious tropical disease causing the skin to turn yellow.

ˌyellow ˈflag flag coloured yellow, displayed by a ship or hospital which is in quarantine.

ˌyellow ˈline yellow line painted at the side of a road to show restrictions on the parking of vehicles: *You can't park on a double yellow line.*

ˌyellow ˈpages (*Brit*) telephone directory, or section of one, listing companies according to the goods or services they offer. ⇨ article at TELEPHONE.

the yellow ˈpress (*infml derog*) newspapers that deliberately include sensational news items, etc in order to attract readers.

Yellow Book /ˈjeləʊ bʊk/ **the Yellow Book** British magazine dealing with literature and art that appeared 1894-97. Its contributors included Max *Beerbohm and Henry *James; *Beardsley was its first art editor. It became famous for the controversial writing it published.

yellowhammer /ˈjeləʊhæmə(r)/ *n* type of small bird, the male of which has a yellow head, neck and breast.

Yellowstone /ˈjeləstəʊn/ (in full **ˌYellowstone ˌNational ˈPark**) American national park in Wyoming and Montana, crossed by the Yellowstone River. It is famous for its mountain scenery, wildlife and geysers.

yelp /jelp/ *n* a short sharp cry (of pain, anger, excitement, etc): *The dog gave a yelp when I trod on its paw.*

▷ **yelp** *v* [I] utter such a cry.

Yemen Republic /ˈjemən/ **the Yemen Republic** country in the south-west of the Arabian peninsula; pop approx 12 300 000; official language Arabic; capital San'a; units of currency riyal (= 100 fils) and dinar (= 1000 fils). It became a unified country in 1990 after nearly thirty years of separation into the pro-Western north-west (North Yemen) and the Marxist south-east (South Yemen). Most of the population is concentrated in the high plateaus of the north-west. Most of the country is mountainous and agriculture is limited. Oil has been discovered in the north-west. Many Yemenis work in other Arab countries and the money they send home is an important part of the economy. ⇨ map at ARABIAN PENINSULA. ▷ **Yemeni** /-ɪ/ *n, adj.*

yen¹ /jen/ *n* (*pl* unchanged) unit of money in Japan.

yen² /jen/ *n* (usu *sing*) ~ **(for sth/to do sth)** (*infml*) longing or yearning: *I've always had a yen to visit Australia.*

yeoman /ˈjəʊmən/ *n* (*pl* **-men** /-mən/) (*Brit*) **1** (*esp arch*) farmer who owns and works his land: [attrib] *yeoman farmers.* **2** (formerly) servant in a royal or noble household.

▷ **yeomanry** /-rɪ/ *n* [Gp] (*Brit*) **1** country landowners. **2** (formerly) volunteer cavalry force raised from farmers, etc.

□ **ˌYeoman of the ˈGuard** member of the British sovereign's bodyguard, dressed in a red uniform dating from the Tudor period, similar to that of a Yeoman Warder.

ˌyeoman ˈservice (*esp rhet*) long and useful service; help, esp at a time of need: *retiring after 40 years' yeoman service to the company.*

ˌYeoman ˈWarder guard at the Tower of London, dressed in a red uniform dating from the Tudor period.

yes /jes/ *interj* **1** (a) (used to answer in the affirmative): *'Is this a painting by Picasso?' 'Yes, it is.'* ○ (*emphatic*) *'Don't you want to come with us?' 'Yes, of course I do.'* (b) (used to show that a statement is correct or that the speaker agrees): *'English is a difficult language.' 'Yes, but not as difficult as Chinese.'* ○ *'Isn't she sweet?' 'Yes, she is.'* (c) (used to agree with a request): *'Can I borrow this record?' 'Yes, of course.'* **2** (used to accept an invitation or offer): *'Coffee?' 'Yes, please.'* **3** (used to acknowledge one's presence in a group or to reply when one is called): *'Williams.' 'Yes, sir.'* ○ *'Waiter!' 'Yes, madam.'* **4** (used to ask what sb wants): *'Yes?' 'I'd like 2 tickets, please.'* Cf NO *interj.*

▷ **yes** *n* (*pl* **yeses** /ˈjesɪz/) answer that affirms, agrees, accepts, etc: *Can't you give me a straight* (ie direct) *yes or no?*

□ **yes-man** /ˈjesmæn/ *n* (*pl* **-men** /-men/) weak person who always agrees with his superior(s) in order to win favour or approval.

yesterday /ˈjestədɪ, -deɪ/ *adv* on the day just past; on the day before today: *He arrived only yesterday.* ○ *It was only yesterday that he arrived.* ○ *I can remember it as if it were yesterday.* ○ *Where were you yesterday morning/afternoon/evening?*

▷ **yesterday** *n* [U, C often *pl*] **1** the day before today: *Yesterday was Sunday.* ○ *Where's yesterday's (news)paper?* **2** the recent past: *dressed in yesterday's fashions* ○ *all our yesterdays.* **3** (idm) **be born yesterday** ⇨ BORN. **the day before yesterday** ⇨ DAY.

□ **ˌyesterday ˈweek** eight days ago: *I haven't seen him since yesterday week.*

yester-year /ˈjestə jɪə(r), *also* jɜ:(r)/ *n* [U] (*arch or rhet*) the recent past: *recalling holidays of yester-year.*

yet /jet/ *adv* **1** (a) (used in questions and negative sentences and after *vs* expressing uncertainty, usu in final position; in British English usu with the present or past perfect tense, in US English usu with the simple past) by this or that time; until now/then: *I haven't received a letter from him yet.* (Cf (*US*) *I didn't receive a letter from him yet.*) ○ *'Are you ready?' 'No, not yet.'* ○ *She was not yet sure if she could trust him.* ○ *I doubt if he has read it yet.* (b) now or in the immediate future: *Don't go yet.* ○ *You don't need to start yet.* ⇨ Usage at ALREADY. **2** (used with a *modal v*; formal if placed immediately after the *modal v*) at an indefinite time in the future: *We may win yet.* ○ *She may surprise us all yet.* ○ (*fml*) *We can yet reach our destination.* **3** (used after superlatives) made, produced, written, etc until and including now/then: *the most comprehensive study yet of his poetry* ○ *the highest building yet constructed* ○ *her best novel yet.* **4** (used in front of comparatives) even: *yet one more example of criminal negligence* ○ *yet another victim of government policy on national health funding* ○ *a recent and yet more improbable theory* ○ *advancing yet further.* **5** (idm) **as ˈyet** until now/then: *an as yet unpublished document* ○ *As yet little is known of the causes of the disease.* **yet aˈgain** (*emphatic*) once more: *Yet again we can see the results of hasty decision-making.*

▷ **yet** *conj* but at the same time; nevertheless: *slow yet thorough* ○ *She trained hard all year yet still failed to reach her best form.*

yeti /ˈjetɪ/ *n* (also **Aˌbominable ˈSnowman**) large hairy man-like or bear-like creature reported to live in the highest part of the Himalayas.

yew /ju:/ *n* (a) (also **ˈyew-tree**) [C] small evergreen tree with dark-green needle-like leaves and small red berries, often planted for garden hedges and in churchyards. ⇨ illus at TREE. (b) [U] wood of this tree.

YHA /ˌwaɪ eɪtʃ ˈeɪ/ *abbr* (*Brit*) Youth Hostels Association. ⇨ article at YOUTH MOVEMENT.

yid /jɪd/ *n* (⚠ *sl offensive*) Jew.

Yiddish /ˈjɪdɪʃ/ *adj, n* [U] (of the) international Jewish language, a form of old German with words borrowed from Hebrew and several modern languages, used by Jews in or from eastern or central Europe: *speak (in) Yiddish* ○ *a Yiddish speaker.* Cf HEBREW.

yield /ji:ld/ *v* **1** [Tn] bear, produce or provide (a natural product, a result or profit): *trees that no longer yield fruit* ○ *experiments yielding new insights* ○ *Building societies' investment accounts yield high interest.* **2** (a) [I, Ipr, Ip] ~ **(to sb/sth)** (*fml*) allow oneself to be overcome by pressure; cease opposition (to sb/sth): *The town was forced to yield after a long siege.* ○ *The government has not yielded to public opinion.* ○ *She yielded to temptation and had another chocolate.* (b) [I] be forced out of the usual or natural shape; bend or break under pressure: *Despite all our attempts to break it open, the lock would not yield.* ○ *The dam eventually yielded and collapsed under the weight of water.* **3** [Ipr] ~ **to sth** be replaced or superseded by sth: *Increasingly, farm land is yielding to property development.* ○ *The cinema has* *largely yielded to the home video.* **4** [Tn, Tn·pr, Tn·p] ~ **sb/sth (up) (to sb)** *(fml)* **(a)** reluctantly give control of sth (to sb); deliver sb/sth (to sb): *The terrorists have yielded two of their hostages (up) to the police.* **(b)** reveal sth; disclose sth: *The universe is slowly yielding up its secrets to scientists.* **5** [I, Ipr] ~ **(to sb/sth)** *(esp US)* (of traffic) allow other traffic to have right of way. **6** [I, Ipr] ~ **(to sb/sth)** *(fml)* admit that one is inferior (to sb/sth); concede: *I yield to no one in my admiration for* (ie am one of the greatest admirers of) *her work.*

▷ **yield** *n* [U, C] (amount of) that which is yielded or produced: *a good, high, poor, etc yield of wheat* ○ *What is the yield per acre?* ○ *the annual milk yield.*

yielding *adj* **(a)** that can bend and give[1](20); pliable rather than stiff: *a soft, yielding material.* **(b)** likely to accept the wishes of others; not obstinate; compliant: *a gentle, yielding personality* ○ *She is rarely yielding on such an issue.* **yieldingly** *adv.*

yin /jɪn/ *n* [U] (in Chinese philosophy) the passive dark female principle of the universe. Cf YANG.

yippee /ˈjɪpi:/ *interj* *(infml)* (used to express pleasure or excitement).

YMCA /ˌwaɪ em si: ˈeɪ/ (also *US infml* **Y**) *abbr* Young Men's Christian Association: *stay at the YMCA (hostel).* ⇨ article at VOLUNTARY.

yob /jɒb/ (also **yobbo** /ˈjɒbəʊ/) *n* (*pl* ~**s**) *(dated Brit sl)* aggressive, ill-tempered and ill-mannered young person; lout.

yodel (also **yodle**) /ˈjəʊdl/ *v* (**-ll-**; *US* **-l-**) [I, Tn] sing (a song) or utter a musical call, with frequent changes from the normal voice to high falsetto notes, in the traditional Swiss manner.

▷ **yodel** (also **yodle**) *n* yodelling song or call.

yodeller (*US* **yodeler**) *n.*

yoga /ˈjəʊɡə/ *n* [U] **(a)** Hindu philosophy that teaches control over the mind, senses and body in order to produce mystical experience and the union of the individual soul with the universal spirit. **(b)** system of exercises for the body and the control of breathing for those practising yoga or wanting to become fitter: [attrib] *yoga classes.*

▷ **yogi** /ˈjəʊɡɪ/ *n* (*pl* ~**s**) teacher of or expert in yoga.

yoghurt (also **ˈyogurt**, **ˈyoghourt**) /ˈjɒɡət; *US* ˈjəʊɡərt/ *n* [U, C] slightly sour thick liquid food, consisting of milk fermented by added bacteria and often flavoured with fruit, etc: *a breakfast of muesli and yoghurt* ○ *a carton of yoghurt* ○ *Two strawberry yoghurts, please.*

yoicks /jɔɪks/ *interj* (used in fox-hunting to encourage the hounds)

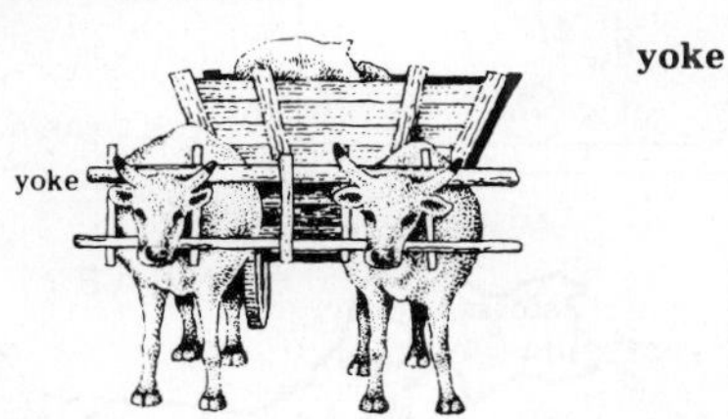

yoke

yoke /jəʊk/ *n* **1** [C] **(a)** shaped piece of wood fixed across the necks of two animals (esp oxen) pulling a cart, plough, etc. **(b)** (*pl* unchanged) two oxen working together: *five yoke of oxen.* **2** [C] object like a yoke in form or function, esp a piece of wood shaped to fit across a person's shoulders and support a pail at each end. **3** [C] (in dressmaking) part of a garment fitting round the shoulders or hips and from which the rest hangs. **4** [sing] ~ **(of sth/sb)** *(fml fig)* oppressive control; burdensome restraint: *throw off the yoke of slavery* ○ *under the yoke of a cruel master.*

▷ **yoke** *v* [Tn, Tn·pr, Tn·p] **1** ~ **sth (to sth)**; ~ **sth and sth (together)** put a yoke on (an animal): *yoke oxen to a plough* ○ *yoke oxen together.* **2** ~ **A (to/with B) (in sth)**; ~ **A and B (together) (in sth)** *(fml)* unite or form a bond between (people): *yoked to/with an unwilling partner* ○ *yoked (together) in marriage.*

yokel /ˈjəʊkl/ *n* *(joc or derog)* simple-minded country person; bumpkin.

yolk /jəʊk/ *n* [C, U] round yellow part in the middle of the white of an egg: *Beat up the yolks of three eggs.* ⇨ illus at EGG.

Yom Kippur /ˌjɒm ˈkɪpə(r), ˌjɒm kɪˈpʊə(r)/ (also **Day of Atonement**) the most important Jewish religious festival, when Jews eat no food and pray for their sins to be forgiven. It is on the tenth day of the New Year.

yomp /jɒmp/ *v* [I, Ipr, Ip] *(Brit army sl)* march with heavy equipment over difficult country: *yomping across moorland.*

yonder /ˈjɒndə(r)/ *det, adj, adv* *(arch or dialect)* (that is or that can be seen) over there: *Do you see yonder clump of trees* (ie that clump of trees over there)*?* ○ *Whose is that farm (over) yonder?*

yore /jɔ:(r)/ *n* (idm) **of yore** *(arch or rhet)* long ago: *in days of yore.*

York /jɔ:k/ **1** city in N Yorkshire. It was an important city in Roman and medieval times and has many historic buildings, including the cathedral, York Minster. **2** name of the English royal house descended from the first Duke of York, Edmund of Langley (1341-1402), 5th son of *Edward III. The House of York ruled England 1461-85 (*Edward IV, *Edward V, *Richard III) and was represented by a white rose in the *Wars of the Roses against the House of *Lancaster. ⇨ App 3.

▷ **Yorkist** *n* member or supporter of the House of York. — *adj.*

yorker /ˈjɔ:kə(r)/ *n* (in cricket) ball that is bowled so as to hit the ground just at the batsman's feet.

Yorkshire pudding /ˌjɔ:kʃə ˈpʊdɪŋ/ baked batter[2] often eaten with roast beef: *a large helping of Yorkshire pudding* ○ *four small Yorkshire puddings.*

Yorkshire terrier /ˌjɔ:kʃə ˈterɪə(r)/ small dog with shaggy brown and dark grey hair.

you /ju:/ *pers pron* **1** person or people being addressed. **(a)** (used as the subject or object of a *v* or after a *prep*; also used independently and after *be*): *You said you knew the way.* ○ *I thought she told you.* ○ *This is just between you and me,* ie not to be told to anyone else. ○ *I don't think that hair-style is you,* ie It doesn't suit your personality. ○ *Is there anyone among you who is a doctor?* **(b)** (used with *ns* and *adjs* to address sb directly): *You girls, stop talking!* ○ *You silly fool, you've lost us the game.* ○ *You angel, you've remembered my birthday.* **2** everyone; anyone: *You learn a language better if you visit the country where it's spoken.* ○ *Driving on the left is strange at first but you get used to it.* ○ *It's easier to cycle with the wind behind you.* ○ *Nobody wants to help you in this town.* **3** (idm) **ˈyou and ˌyours** you and your family and close friends: *a souvenir for you and yours to cherish.*

□ **you-all** /ˈju:ɔ:l/ *pers pron* *(esp southern US)* you (plural): *Have you-all brought swim-suits?*

you'd /ju:d/ *contracted form* **1** you had ⇨ HAVE. **2** you would ⇨ WILL[1], WOULD[1].

you'll /ju:l/ *contracted form* you will ⇨ WILL[1].

young /jʌŋ/ *adj* (**-nger** /-ŋɡə(r)/, **-ngest** /-ŋɡɪst/) **1** not far advanced in life, growth, development, etc; of recent birth or origin: *a young woman, animal, tree, nation.* Cf OLD 2. **2** still near its beginning: *The evening is still young.* **3 the younger** *(fml)* (used before or after a person's name, to distinguish that person from an older person with the same name): *the Younger Pitt/Pitt the Younger.* Cf ELDER[1] 2. **4** *(becoming dated)* **(a)** (used before a person's name to distinguish esp a son from his father): *Young Jones is just like his father.* **(b)** (used as a familiar or condescending form of address): *Now listen to me, (my) young man/lady!* **5** for, concerning or characteristic of youth or young people: *The young look is in fashion this year.* ○ *Those clothes she's wearing are much too young for her.* **6** [pred] ~ **in sth** having little practice or experience in sth: *young in crime.* **7** (idm) **not as/so young as one ˈused to be/(once) ˈwas** old or growing old and losing vigour, good health, etc: *I can't play squash twice a week: I'm not as young as I was, you know!* **not get any ˈyounger** become older: *Of course long walks tire you out — you're not getting any younger, you know.* **an old head on young shoulders** ⇨ OLD. **young and ˈold (aˈlike)** everyone, regardless of age: *This is a book for young and old (alike).* **ˌyoung at ˈheart** in spite of one's age, still feeling and behaving as one did when one was young. **the ˌyoung iˈdea** *(dated)* young people, esp schoolboys or schoolgirls and students. **one's young ˈlady/young ˈman** *(dated)* one's girl-friend/boy-friend: *When's your young man coming to dinner, then?* **you're only young ˈonce** *(saying)* young people should be allowed to enjoy themselves while they can, because they will have plenty to worry about when they get older. **a ˌyoung ˈTurk** *(infml)* young and enthusiastic person, eg in a company or political party, who wants to change existing methods, views, etc.

▷ **young** *n* [pl] **1** (of animals and birds) offspring; young ones: *The cat fought fiercely to defend its young,* ie its young kittens. **2 the young** young people considered as a group: *The young in our society need care and protection.* **3** (idm) **(be) with ˈyoung** (of animals) pregnant.

youngish *adj* fairly young; quite young: *a youngish President.*

youngster /-stə(r)/ *n* child; youth; young person: *How are the youngsters* (ie your children)*?*

□ **the ˌYoung Preˈtender** Charles Edward *Stuart.

your /jɔ:(r); *US* jʊər/ *possess det* **1** of or belonging to the person or people being addressed: *Excuse me, is this your seat?* ○ *Your hair's going grey.* ○ *You'll see the post office on your right.* ○ *Do you like your new job?* **2** *(often derog)* (used to refer to sth that the person being addressed is associated with): *These are your famous Oxford colleges* (ie the ones you talk about), *I suppose.* ○ *I don't think much of your English weather.* ○ *(ironic) You and your bright ideas!* **3** (also **Your**) (used when addressing royal people, important officials, etc): *Your Majesty* ○ *Your Excellency.*

▷ **yours** /jɔ:z; *US* jʊərz/ *possess pron* **1** of or belonging to you: *Is that book yours?* ○ *Is she a friend of yours?* **2** (usu **Yours**, *abbr* **yrs**) (used in ending a letter): *Yours sincerely* ○ *Yours faithfully* ○ *Yours truly.* ⇨ Usage below.

NOTE ON USAGE: **Yours faithfully**, **Yours sincerely**, *(esp US)* **Yours truly** are the commonest ways of ending formal and semi-formal letters. The correct style is to use **Yours faithfully** to end a letter which begins **Dear Sir/Madam** (ie when the name of the person being addressed is not known to the writer) and **Yours sincerely/truly** after **Dear Mr/Mrs/Miss/Ms Smith** (ie when the name is known but the person is not well known to the writer). In US English **Sincerely**, **Sincerely yours** and **Yours truly** are often used. If the writer knows the addressee personally, the first name is used and **With best wishes** may be added. More familiar still is the use of the first name and **Yours (ever)**.

Dear Madam, ... **Yours faithfully,** Jane Jones	Dear Mrs Brown, ... **Yours sincerely/truly,** Jane Jones
Dear Margaret, ... With best wishes, **Yours sincerely/truly,** Jane (Jones)	Dear Maggie, ... All the best, **Yours,** Jane

For further help with letter writing see Sample Texts 3a and 3b in Appendix 14.

you're /jʊə(r)/ (/jɔ:(r)/) *contracted form* you are ⇨ BE.

yourself /jɔ:ˈself; *US* jʊərˈself/ (*pl* **-selves** /-ˈselvz/) *reflex, emph pron* (only taking the main stress in sentences when used emphatically) **1** *(reflex)* (used when the person or people addressed

Youth Movements

Youth organizations have been popular in Britain since the 19th century. The Boy Scouts movement was founded by Robert Baden-Powell in 1908 and has since become a world-wide organization. Two years later, 'B-P', together with his sister Agnes, founded the Girl Guides. These were not Britain's earliest youth movements, however. The Sea Cadets and the Boys' Brigade began in the 19th century.

These organizations illustrate the extent to which military and religious influences helped to create the earliest British youth movements. The Scouts and Guides combine both these influences. The words 'Scout' and 'Guide' were actually selected by Baden-Powell from a military context.

Scouts and Guides today are still the leading youth organizations in Britain in terms of numbers: there are around 700 000 Scouts and slightly more Guides. The Scout Association has the aim of training boys to use their initiative, teaching them to use practical skills, and helping them to become useful members of society. It attaches importance to moral values such as loyalty and responsibility.

The organization is divided into four divisions according to age. The youngest are the Beavers, aged 6 to 8. Cubs are aged 8 to 11, and Scouts (formerly Boy Scouts) are 11 to 16. The senior group comprises the Venture Scouts, aged 16 to 20, and includes young women as well as men. Scouts are famous for their 'Gang Shows', entertainments staged locally in aid of charity, and for their annual 'Scout Job Week' when they carry out community service to raise funds.

The Girl Guides Association has similar aims but with greater emphasis on community service and activities such as camping, games and hiking. Its members are organized in the following groups: Rainbow Guides, aged under 7, Brownie Guides (or Brownies), aged 7 to 10, Guides, aged 10 to 14, and Ranger Guides (or Rangers), aged 14 to 18.

Many young people belong to a youth club, whose activities usually involve a mixture of sport and community service. Youth clubs operate under the overall guidance of the National Association of Youth Clubs, which is responsible for over 6 000 clubs in Britain with a total membership of about 700 000. Similar in style and organization are the 2 000 or so boys' clubs run by the National Association of Boys' Clubs. Young Farmers' Clubs (YFCs) are run to give young people practical experience in agriculture, home crafts and country life generally. YFCs have nearly 50 000 members. Both young people and adults belong to the popular Youth Hostels Association (YHA), which is an international organization.

The Sea Cadet Corps, the Army Cadet Force and the Air Training Corps are organizations for young people who are interested in joining one of the armed forces when they are older. Some boys' public schools have a Combined Cadet Force (CCF) where pupils can progress to a specific Naval, Army or Air Force section after basic military training.

Two of the leading religious organizations for young people are the Boys' Brigade, founded in 1883, currently with almost 150 000 members, and the Girls' Brigade, founded in 1965, with only about 1 300 members in Britain. Both are evangelical in outlook. The Boys' Brigade stresses the importance of 'Christian manliness' while the Girls' Brigade aims to improve the quality of life through 'self-control, reverence and a sense of responsibility'. More specifically evangelistic are the Covenantors, an association founded in 1906, which similarly uses the Bible as the basis of its Christian teaching to a membership of about 15 000 teenagers. The Scripture Union is a similar evangelical organization.

The Outward Bound Trust, founded in 1946, offers young people the chance to participate in adventurous activities such as sailing, canoeing, rock climbing and pot-holing.

Apart from youth movements such as these, there are a number of informal ways in which young people can form groups together or share an interest. These range from organizations like the many local clubs and social groups, or the national fan clubs for pop stars and pop groups, to less clearly defined groups, like skinheads, who adopt a distinctive life-style, their shaven heads and usually tattered clothing making a recognizable 'statement of identity'. The same is true of rockers, with their love of rock music, black clothes (often leather) and motor cycles. Seasonal rallies of rockers are still held, one of the best-known being the one attended by thousands every summer on the Isle of Wight.

The scouting movement in the USA is represented by the Boy Scouts of America, founded in 1910, and the Girl Scouts of the USA, founded in 1912 (originally as the American Girl Guides). Membership of the two organizations is about 5 million and 3 million respectively. There are also boys' clubs with over a million members and girls' clubs with more than 250 000 members.

cause(s) and is/are affected by an action): *Have you ˈhurt yourself?* **2** (*emph*) (used to emphasize the person or people addressed): *You yourself are one of the chief offenders.* ○ *You can try it out for yourˈselves.* ○ *Do it yourˈself — I haven't got time.* **3** (idm) **by yourˈself/yourˈselves** **(a)** alone: *How long were you by yourself in the classroom?* **(b)** without help: *Are you sure you did this exercise by yourself?*

youth /ju:θ/ *n* (*pl* ~**s** /ju:ðz/) **1** [U] period of being young, esp the time between childhood and maturity: *a wasted* (ie unprofitably spent) *youth* ○ *I often went there in my youth.* ○ *He painted scenes from his youth,* ie that reminded him of the time when he was young. Cf AGE[1] 2. **2** [U] (*fml*) state or quality of being young: *Her youth gives her an advantage over the other runners.* ○ *She is full of youth and vitality.* Cf AGE[1] 2. **3** [C] (*often derog*) young man (esp one in his teens): *As a youth he showed little promise.* ○ *The fight was started by some youths who had been drinking.* **4** (also **the youth**) [sing or pl *v*] young people considered as a group: *the youth of the country/the country's youth* ○ *The youth of today has/have greater opportunities than ever before.* ○ [attrib] *youth culture,* ie activities, interests, etc of young people. ⇨ article. **5** (idm) **the first/full flush of youth** ⇨ FLUSH[1].

▷ **youthful** /-fl/ *adj* having qualities typical of youth; young or seeming young: *a youthful managing director* ○ *a youthful appearance* ○ *She's a very youthful sixty-five.* **youthfully** /-fəlɪ/ *adv.* **youthfulness** *n* [U].

□ **ˈyouth club** club (usu provided by a church, a local authority or a voluntary organization) for young people's leisure and social activities. ⇨ article at CLUB.

ˈyouth hostel building in which cheap and simple food and accommodation is provided for (esp young) people on walking, riding or cycling holidays. **ˈyouth hostelling** staying in youth hostels: *go youth hostelling.*

you've /ju:v/ *contracted form* you have ⇨ HAVE.

yowl /jaʊl/ *n* loud wailing cry.

▷ **yowl** *v* [I] utter a yowl: *kept awake by cats yowling all night.*

Yo-Yo /ˈjəʊ jəʊ/ *n* (*pl* ~**s**) (*propr*) toy consisting of two thick discs of wood or plastic with a deep groove between, which can be made to rise and fall on an attached string when this is jerked with a finger: *The price of petrol is going up and down like a Yo-Yo.*

yr *abbr* **1** (*pl* **yrs**) year: *valid for 3 yrs* ○ *a race for 2-yr olds,* ie horses. **2** your.

yrs *abbr* yours: *yrs sincerely,* ie before a signature on a letter.

YTS /ˌwaɪ ti: ˈes/ *abbr* (*Brit*) Youth Training Scheme: *We've got a YTS girl helping us.* ⇨ article at EMPLOYMENT.

ytterbium /ɪˈtɜ:bɪəm/ *n* [U] (*symb* **Yb**) (*chemistry*) soft silvery metallic element. It has no known uses. ⇨ App 11.

yttrium /ˈɪtrɪəm/ *n* [U] (*symb* **Y**) (*chemistry*) silvery-grey metallic element. It is used in making superconductors. ⇨ App 11.

yucca /ˈjʌkə/ *n* tall plant with white bell-like flowers and stiff spiky leaves.

yuck /jʌk/ *interj* (*sl*) (used to express disgust, distaste, etc).

▷ **yucky** *adj* (**-ier**, **-iest**) (*sl*) nasty; disgusting: *yucky school dinners.*

Yugoslavia and its neighbours

Yugoslavia /ˌju:gəʊˈslɑ:vɪə/ former country in south-eastern Europe with a coast on the Adriatic Sea, a capital in Belgrade and a main language of Serbo-Croat. The country was created after World

War I from Serbia and Montenegro with Slav provinces of the Austro-Hungarian Empire, and became a federation of six republics in 1945. Its remarkable variety of races and religions held together until the late 1980s, when regional tension led to increasing dissent from federal government policies. Croatia and Slovenia seceded in 1991; the same year saw the start of widespread civil and inter-ethnic conflict which continued despite peacekeeping efforts of the United Nations and the European Community. By 1992 Bosnia-Herzegovina and Macedonia were also declaring independence. Serbia and Montenegro then announced themselves as joint legal successor to the former Yugoslav Republic. However, United Nations' economic and diplomatic sanctions imposed on Serbia left this successor internationally unrecognized after its exclusion from the General Assembly. ⇨ map. ▷ **Yugoslav** /ˈjuːɡəʊslɑːv/, **Yugoslavian** *ns, adjs*.

Yukon /ˈjuːkɒn/ **the Yukon** territory in north-western Canada. The discovery of gold in the *Klondike River in 1896 led to the *Gold Rush. ⇨ map at App 1.

yule /juːl/ (also **yule-tide** /ˈjuːl taɪd/) *n* (*arch*) festival of Christmas: [attrib] *Yule-tide greetings*, eg on a Chrismas card.

□ ˈ**yule-log** *n* large log of wood traditionally burnt on Christmas Eve.

yummy /ˈjʌmɪ/ *adj* (*infml*) (used esp by children in spoken English) tasty; delicious: *Chocolate cake for tea? How yummy!*

yum-yum /ˌjʌm ˈjʌm/ *interj* (*infml*) (used to express pleasure while eating, or when thinking about eating, pleasant food).

yuppie /ˈjʌpɪ/ *n* (*infml often derog*) young and ambitious professional person, esp one working in a city.

YWCA /ˌwaɪ dʌbljuː siː ˈeɪ/ (also *US infml* **Y**) *abbr* Young Women's Christian Association: *stay at the YWCA (hostel)*.

Z, z

Z, z /zed; *US* ziː/ *n* (*pl* **Z's, z's** /zedz; *US* ziːz/) **1** the twenty-sixth and last letter of the English alphabet; zed. **2** (idm) **from A to Z** ⇨ A, A¹.

zabaglione /ˌzæbælˈjəʊnɪ; *US* ˌzɑːblˈjəʊniː/ *n* [U] (*Italian*) sweet dish of egg yolks mixed with sugar and Marsala, heated and whisked till frothy.

Zaïre /zɑːˈɪə(r)/ country in central Africa, situated on the equator; pop approx 33 458 000; official language French; capital Kinshasa; unit of currency zaïre (= 100 makuta). Much of the country is covered in tropical forest, with savannah in the north. The River Zaïre, the second longest in Africa, crosses the country from the south-east to the coast, and has the world's largest hydroelectric power-station at its mouth. The main crops are cassava, maize and groundnuts, with coffee and wood for export. It has considerable mineral reserves including copper, gold and oil and is the world's largest producer of cobalt. Despite these assets it is one of the poorest countries in the world. ⇨ map (CENTRAL AFRICA).
▷ **Zaïrean** /-rɪən/ *n, adj.*

Zambezi /zæmˈbiːzɪ/ **the Zambezi** river of central Africa 2 655 km (1 650 miles) long. It rises in Angola, crosses into Zambia and forms the border between Zambia and Zimbabwe, flows through Mozambique and into the Indian Ocean.

Zambia /ˈzæmbɪə/ country in southern central Africa, a member of the Commonwealth; pop approx 8 780 000; official language English; capital Lusaka; unit of currency kwacha (= 100 ngwee). It consists of high plateaus with mountains in the east. Its agriculture is being developed, with maize, cassava, sunflowers and tobacco as the main crops. Zambia is a leading producer of copper and also has large reserves of cobalt, zinc and coal. President Kaunda, who had ruled since independence in 1964, was defeated in the elections of 1991. ⇨ map at NAMIBIA. ▷ **Zambian** *n, adj.*

ZANU /ˈzɑːnuː/ *abbr* Zimbabwe African National Union (an independence movement in Zimbabwe which later became the single national political party). Cf ZAPU.

zany /ˈzeɪnɪ/ *adj* (**-ier**, **-iest**) (*infml*) amusingly ridiculous; eccentric: *a zany haircut, life-style, personality.*
▷ **zanily** *adv.*
zaniness *n.*
zany *n* comical or eccentric person.

Zanzibar /ˈzænzɪbɑː(r), ˌzænzɪˈbɑː(r)/ island in the Indian Ocean off the coast of E Africa. It was an independent state (1963-64) before becoming part of *Tanzania. ▷ **Zanzibari** /zænzɪˈbɑːrɪ/ *n, adj.*

zap /zæp/ *v* (**-pp-**) (*infml*) **1** [Tn, Tn·pr] ~ **sb** (**with sth**) (**a**) kill sb, esp with a gun. (**b**) make sb unconscious with a hit, blow, etc; attack sb. **2** [Ipr, Ip] (**a**) move suddenly or quickly in the specified direction: *Have you seen him zapping around town on his new motor bike?* (**b**) use the fast-forward button on a remote control device to skip sections of a videotape or change television channels: *zap through the boring bits.*
▷ **zap** *n* [U] (*infml*) feeling of energy, liveliness, etc; vigour: *I really admire her — she's so full of zap!* Cf ZIP 2. **zappy** *adj* (*infml*) lively and energetic; amusing.

Central Africa

Zapata /səˈpɑːtə/ Emiliano (c 1877-1919), Mexican revolutionary. He led a fight for land reform for the Indians and controlled the south of the country before he was assassinated.

ZAPU /ˈzɑːpuː/ *abbr* Zimbabwe African People's Union (an independence movement in Zimbabwe and then a political party until 1987). Cf ZANU.

zeal /ziːl/ *n* [U] (*fml*) ~ (**for sth**) (usu intense) energy or enthusiasm; keenness: *show zeal for a cause* ○ *work with great zeal* ○ *revolutionary, religious zeal.*
▷ **zealous** /ˈzeləs/ *adj* full of zeal; eager: *zealous for liberty and freedom* ○ *zealous to succeed at work.*
zealously *adv.*

zealot /ˈzelət/ *n* (*sometimes derog*) person who is extremely enthusiastic about sth, esp religion or politics; fanatic.
▷ **zealotry** /-rɪ/ *n* [U] (*fml*) zealous attitude or behaviour.

zebra

zebra /ˈzebrə, ˈziːbrə/ *n* (*pl* unchanged or ~**s**) African wild animal of the horse family with a body covered by black (or dark brown) and white stripes. .

zebra crossing

□ ˌ**zebra ˈcrossing** (*Brit*) part of a road, marked with broad white stripes, where vehicles must stop if pedestrians wish to cross. ⇨ illus. Cf PEDESTRIAN CROSSING (PEDESTRIAN), PELICAN CROSSING (PELICAN).

Zechariah /ˌzekəˈraɪə/ book of the Old Testament containing the prophecies of Zechariah (6th century BC) and his call for the temple in Jerusalem to be rebuilt. ⇨ App 5.

zed /zed/ (*US* **zee** /ziː/) *n* the letter Z: *There are two zeds in 'puzzle'.*

Zeitgeist /ˈzaɪtgaɪst/ *n* (*German*) spirit of a particular period of history as shown by the ideas, beliefs, etc of the time.

Zen /zen/ *n* [U] Japanese form of Buddhism that stresses the importance of meditation more than the reading of religious writings: [attrib] *Zen Buddhism.*

zenith /ˈzenɪθ/ *n* **1** point in the heavens directly above an observer. Cf NADIR. **2** (*fig*) highest point (of power, prosperity, etc); peak: *reach the zenith of one's career, power, influence* ○ *At its zenith the Roman empire covered almost the whole of Europe.*

Zeno[1] /ˈzi:nəʊ/ (5th century BC), Greek philosopher. He is most famous for his mathematical paradoxes, such as that of Achilles and the tortoise: if Achilles races against the tortoise but starts the race after it, he can never overtake it, because by the time he reaches the point it has reached, it will have moved further forward.

Zeno[2] /ˈzi:nəʊ/ (3rd century BC) Greek philosopher, the founder of *Stoicism.

Zephaniah /ˌzefəˈnaɪə/ book of the Old Testament containing the prophecies of Zephaniah (7th century BC). ➪ App 5.

zephyr /ˈzefə(r)/ *n* (*dated or fml*) soft gentle breeze.

Zeppelin /ˈzepəlɪn/ *n* type of large airship used by the Germans in the First World War.

zero /ˈzɪərəʊ/ *pron, det* **1** 0; one less than one; nought: *Five, four, three, two, one, zero... We have lift-off!* **2** lowest point; nothing; nil: *Economic growth is at zero*, ie is not increasing. ○ *Prospects of success in the talks were put at zero.* **3** (**a**) point between plus (+) and minus (−) on a scale, esp on a thermometer: *The thermometer fell to zero last night.* (**b**) temperature, pressure, etc that corresponds to zero on a scale: *It was really cold last night — ten degrees below zero*, ie −10° C, ten degrees below the freezing point of water. ➪ Usage at NOUGHT. **4** (*infml esp US*) nothing at all; none: *Politics has zero interest for me*, ie I am not at all interested in it.
▷ **zero** *n* (*pl* ~**s**) the number 0.
zero *v* (phr v) **zero in on sb/sth 1** aim guns, etc at or find the range of (a particular target). **2** (*fig*) fix attention on sb/sth; focus on sb/sth: *zero in on the key issues for discussion.*
□ **zero ˈgrowth** no increase at all: *zero growth in industrial output, the economy, population.*
ˈ**zero-hour** *n* time when a military operation, an attack, etc is planned to start: *Zero-hour is 3.30 am.*
ˈ**zero-rated** *adj* (of goods, services, etc) on which no value added tax is charged.

zest /zest/ *n* [U, sing] **1** ~ (**for sth**) great enjoyment or excitement; gusto: *Her zest for life is as great as ever.* ○ *He entered into our plans with terrific zest.* **2** (quality of) having added interest, flavour, charm, etc: *The element of risk gave (an) added zest to the adventure.* **3** outer skin of oranges, lemons, etc, when used as a flavouring in cooking. Cf PEEL *n*, RIND, SKIN 4. ▷ **zestful** /-fəl/ *adj.* **zestfully** /-fəlɪ/ *adv.*

zeugma /ˈzju:gmə; *US* ˈzu:gmə/ *n* figure of speech in which a word is applied to two other words (eg one adjective to two nouns or one verb to two objects), when it can only be used naturally with one of them, as in *with weeping eyes and hearts.* Cf SYLLEPSIS.

Zeus /zju:s; *US* zu:s/ the supreme god of the ancient Greeks, corresponding to the Roman god Jupiter.

Ziegfeld /ˈzi:gfeld/ Florenz (1867-1932), American theatre manager. He produced the 'Ziegfeld Follies', shows combining magnificent scenery and attractive young women with comedy and variety acts.

ziggurat /ˈzɪgəræt/ *n* tower built in ancient *Mesopotamia and resembling a pyramid rising in steps. Ziggurats may have had a religious purpose and the one at *Babylon may have been the Tower of *Babel mentioned in the Bible.

zigzag /ˈzɪgzæg/ *adj* [attrib] (of a line, path, etc) turning right and left alternately at sharp angles: *a zigzag road, course, flash of lightning.*
▷ **zigzag** *n* line, path, etc forming a zigzag.
zigzag *v* (**-gg-**) [I, Ipr, Ip] go in a zigzag: *The narrow path zigzags up the cliff.* ➪ illus at PATTERN.

zilch /zɪltʃ/ *n* [U] (*sl esp US*) nothing; zero: *We've found out absolutely zilch.*

zillion /ˈzɪlɪən/ *n* (*infml esp US*) very large but indefinite number: [attrib] *She's a zillion times brainier than I am.*

Zimbabwe /zɪmˈbɑ:bwɪ/ country in SE Africa, a member of the Commonwealth; pop approx 8 878 000; official language English; capital Harare; unit of currency dollar (= 100 cents). Formerly called Rhodesia, it became independent in 1980. It took its new name from Zimbabwe, a now ruined settlement which was once the centre of a large pre-European civilization. It consists mainly of mountains and plateaus. The main crops are maize, millet and ground-nuts, with tobacco grown for export. Its mineral resources include gold, asbestos, nickel and coal. Its industry was developed largely during the period of illegal independence under the white minority (1965-80), when the United Nations applied trade sanctions. ➪ map at NAMIBIA. ▷ **Zimbabwean** *n, adj.*

zinc /zɪŋk/ *n* [U] (*symb* **Zn**) (*chemistry*) bluish-white metallic element used in alloys and to cover iron sheets, wire, etc as a protection against rust. ➪ App 11.

zing /zɪŋ/ *n* [U] (*infml*) liveliness; energy: *You need to put more zing into your playing.*

Zinnemann /ˈzɪnəmən/ Fred (1907-), Austrian-born American film director. Careful and well-meaning, his films, such as *High Noon* and *From Here to Eternity*, often denounced personal and political extremes.

Zion /ˈzaɪən/ *n* **1** the Jewish religion. **2** the Christian Church. **3** the kingdom of Heaven.

Zionism /ˈzaɪənɪzəm/ *n* [U] political movement concerned with the establishment and political and religious development of an independent Jewish state in what is now Israel.
▷ **Zionist** /ˈzaɪənɪst/ *n* person who supports Zionism.

zip(-fastener)
(also *esp US* zipper)

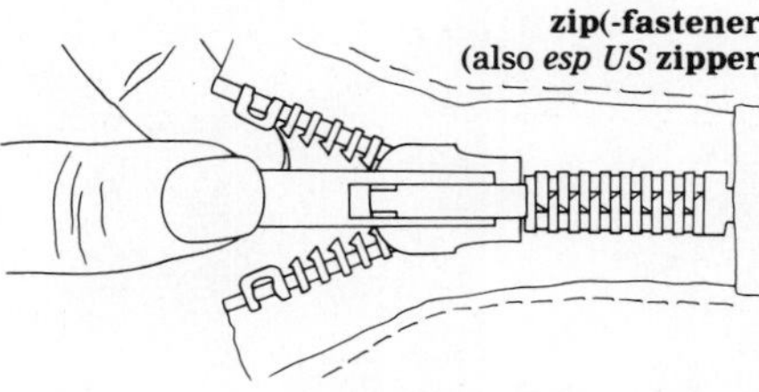

zip /zɪp/ *n* **1** (also *esp Brit* ˈ**zip-fastener**, *esp US* **zipper**) [C] device for bringing together or separating two rows of metal or plastic teeth by means of a sliding tab, used for fastening clothing, baggage, etc: *The zip on my anorak has got stuck.* **2** [U] (*infml*) vigour; energy. Cf ZAP *n*. **3** [sing] short sharp sound, eg of a bullet going through the air.
▷ **zip** *v* (**-pp-**) **1** [Tn, Tn·pr, Tn·p, Cn·a] fasten or unfasten (clothes, baggage, etc) with a zip(1): *She zipped her bag open.* **2** (phr v) **zip across, along, through, etc** move vigorously or quickly in the specified direction: *She's just zipped into town to buy some food.* ○ *After a slow beginning, the play fairly zips along in the second act.* ➪ Usage at WHIZ. **zip (sb/sth) up** fasten with a zip: *Will you zip me up, please?* ○ *The dress zips up at the back.*
zippy *adj* (**-ier, -iest**) (*infml*) full of zip; lively and energetic.

Zip code /ˈzɪp kəʊd/ (*US*) = POSTCODE (POST[2]).

zircon /ˈzɜ:kɒn/ *n* (**a**) [C] translucent bluish-white gem. (**b**) [U] zirconium silicate, the mineral from which this is cut.

zirconium /zɜ:ˈkəʊnɪəm/ *n* [U] (*symb* **Zr**) (*chemistry*) grey metallic element. It is used in some alloys and in the construction of nuclear reactors. ➪ App 11.

zit /zɪt/ *n* (*sl esp US*) spot or pimple, usu on the face.

zither /ˈzɪðə(r)/ *n* musical instrument with many strings on a box-like body, played by plucking with a plectrum and the fingers.

Zn *symb* zinc.

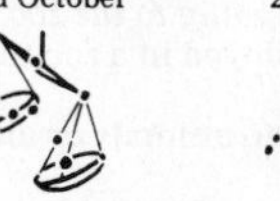

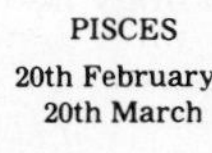

zodiac /ˈzəʊdɪæk/ *n* (**a**) **the zodiac** [sing] imaginary band in the sky containing the movements of the sun, the moon and the main planets, divided into 12 equal parts (the **signs of the zodiac**), named after 12 groups of stars. To an observer on earth, the position of the stars in the sky seems to be fixed, while the sun, moon and planets seem to rise in a different part of the sky according to the time of year. Ancient astronomers noted the way they seemed to move and believed that the planets and the constellations of the zodiac had an influence on human affairs. Astrology claimed eg that each sign affected a different part of the body and that this influence was altered by the presence of a particular planet, and doctors used to base their treatment on this. As the earth's axis changes gradually each year, the constellations are no longer in the same parts of the sky as they were when ancient astrologers divided up the zodiac. ➪ illus. (**b**) [C] (usu circular) diagram of these signs used in astrology to predict the future. Cf HOROSCOPE. ➪ article at SUPERSTITION. ▷ **zodiacal** /zəʊˈdaɪəkl/ *adj.*

NOTE ON USAGE: The **signs of the zodiac** are used in astrology and horoscopes (often called 'The Stars') in newspapers and magazines. People often refer to the signs and to the influence they are supposed to have on sb's personality and fate: *She was born under Gemini.* ○ *His birthday's on 19 October. He's (a) Libra/a Libran.* ○ *She is a typical Taurus/Taurean/has a typical Taurean personality.*

Zola /ˈzəʊlə/ Émile (1840-1902), French novelist. He is regarded as the founder of the naturalistic novel in France with works such as *Thérèse Raquin, L'Assommoir* and *Nana*. He was a social campaigner, famous for his defence of *Dreyfus.

zombie /ˈzɒmbɪ/ *n* **1** (in various African and Caribbean religions) dead body that has been brought to life again by witchcraft. **2** (*infml*) dull lifeless person who seems to act without thinking or not to be aware of what is happening around him; automaton.

zone /zəʊn/ *n* **1** area, band or stripe that is different from its surroundings in colour, texture, appearance, etc. **2** area or region with a particular feature or use: *the erogenous zones of the body* ○ *a nuclear-free, parking, war, time zone* ○ *industrial, residential, etc zones* ○ *smokeless zones*, ie urban areas in which only smokeless fuels may be used

in houses, factories, etc ○ *Danger zone — keep out!* **3** one of five parts (the ˈ**torrid zone**, **North** and **South** ˈ**temperate zones** and **North** and **South** ˈ**frigid zones**) that the earth's surface is divided into by imaginary lines parallel to the equator. **4** (*esp US*) area within which certain railway, postal, telephone, etc charges apply.
▷ **zonal** /ˈzəʊnl/ *adj* relating to or arranged in zones (ZONE 2).
zone *v* [Tn] **1** divide or mark (sth or a place) into zones (ZONE 2). **2** assign (sth) to a particular area. **zoning** *n* [U].

zonked /zɒŋkt/ *adj* [pred] ~ (**out**) (*sl*) **1** drugged or drunk. **2** very tired; exhausted: *I feel utterly zonked.*

zoo /zu:/ *n* (*pl* ~**s**) (also *fml* **zoological gardens**) place (eg a garden, park, etc) where living (esp wild) animals are kept for exhibition, study and breeding: *The children enjoy going to the zoo.*
□ ˈ**zoo-keeper** *n* person employed in a zoo to take care of the animals.

zoo- *comb form* of or relating to animals or animal life: *zoology.*

zoology /zəʊˈɒlədʒɪ/ *n* [U] scientific study of the structure, form and distribution of animals.
▷ **zoological** /ˌzəʊəˈlɒdʒɪkl/ *adj* of or relating to zoology. **zoologically** /-klɪ/ *adv.* ˌ**zoological** ˈ**gardens** (*fml*) = zoo.
zoologist /zəʊˈɒlədʒɪst/ *n* expert in or student of zoology. Cf BIOLOGY, BOTANY.

zoom /zu:m/ *v* **1** [I, Ipr, Ip] (of aircraft, cars, etc) move very quickly, esp with a buzzing or humming noise: *zooming along the motorway* ○ *The jet zoomed low over our heads.* ⇨ Usage at WHIZ. **2** [I, Ip] (*fig infml*) (of prices, costs, etc) rise sharply; soar: *Overnight trading caused share prices to zoom (up).* **3** (phr v) **zoom in** (**on sb/sth**)/**out** (of cameras) make the size of the object being photographed appear bigger/smaller by using a zoom lens.
▷ **zoom** *n* [sing] sound or act of zooming (ZOOM 1).
□ ˈ**zoom lens** camera lens that can be adjusted to make the object being photographed appear gradually bigger or smaller so that it seems to be getting steadily closer or more distant.

zoophyte /ˈzəʊəfaɪt/ *n* plant-like sea-animal, eg a sea anemone, coral, etc.

Zoroastrianism /ˌzɒrəʊˈæstrɪənɪzəm/ *n* [U] religion founded by the prophet Zarathustra (Greek name Zoroaster) in Persia during the 6th century BC. It believed in a supreme god, Ahura Mazda, who created twin spirits, one of whom chose truth and light, the other untruth and darkness. Later versions rename the god as Ormazd, who has an evil twin Ahriman. The religion survives today in parts of Iran and India. Cf PARSEE. ▷ **Zoroastrian** *adj, n.*

Zr *symb* zirconium.

zucchini /zʊˈki:nɪ/ *n* (*pl* unchanged or ~**s**) (*esp US*) = COURGETTE.

Zulu /ˈzu:lu:/ *n* **1** [C] member of a Bantu people of S Africa. **2** [U] their language.
▷ **Zulu** *adj* of the Zulu people or their language.

Zwingli /ˈzwɪŋglɪ/ Ulrich (1484-1531), Swiss Protestant reformer. Like *Luther, he opposed the power of the popes and stressed the authority of the Bible, but unlike Luther he viewed the eucharist as only symbolic. He had political control of the city of Zurich and was killed leading its forces against Catholic opponents.

zygote /ˈzaɪgəʊt/ *n* cell formed when two reproductive cells are united.

APPENDICES

APPENDIX 1

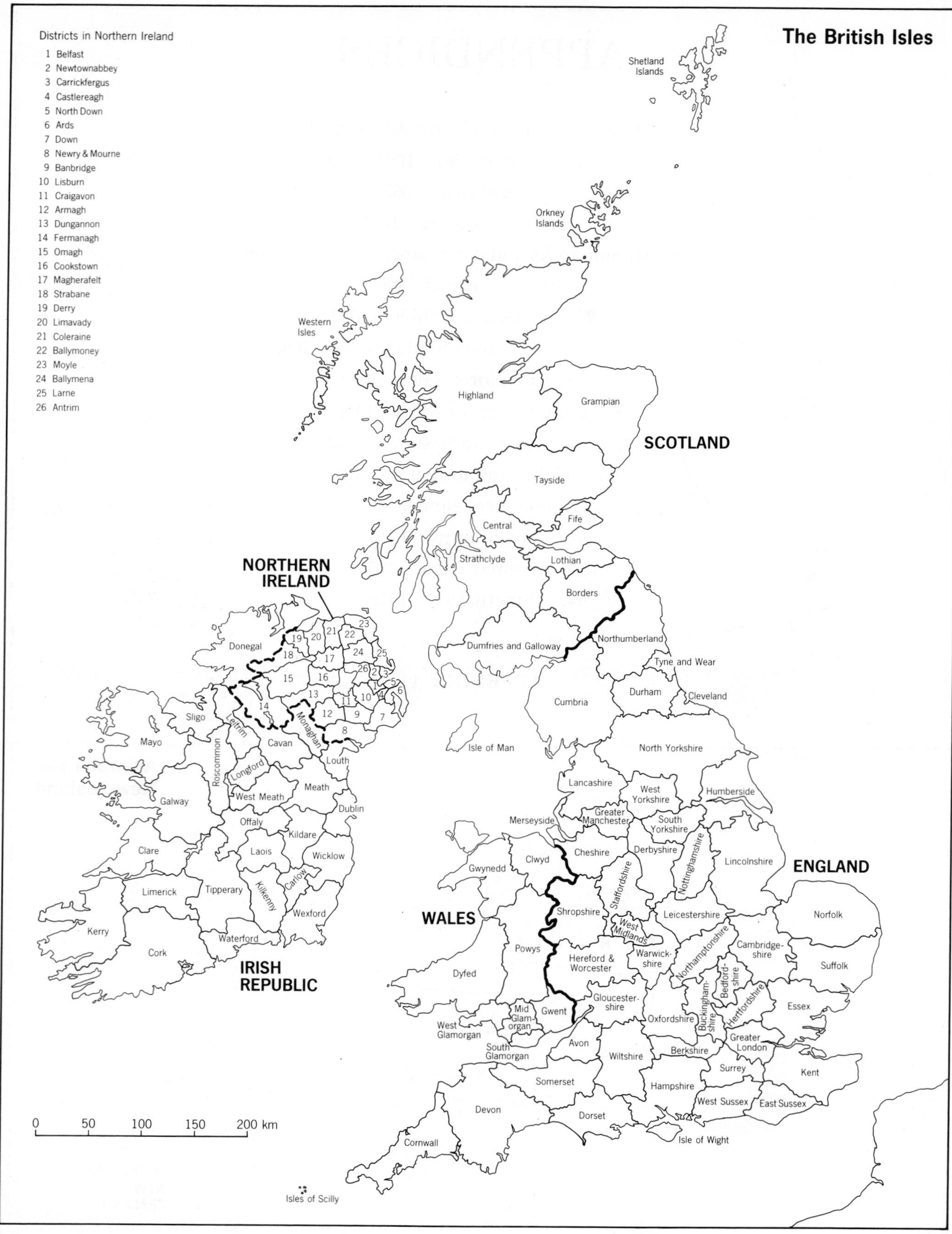
The British Isles
Districts in Northern Ireland
1 Belfast
2 Newtownabbey
3 Carrickfergus
4 Castlereagh
5 North Down
6 Ards
7 Down
8 Newry & Mourne
9 Banbridge
10 Lisburn
11 Craigavon
12 Armagh
13 Dungannon
14 Fermanagh
15 Omagh
16 Cookstown
17 Magherafelt
18 Strabane
19 Derry
20 Limavady
21 Coleraine
22 Ballymoney
23 Moyle
24 Ballymena
25 Larne
26 Antrim
Shetland Islands
Orkney Islands
Western Isles
Highland
Grampian
SCOTLAND
Tayside
Fife
Central
Strathclyde
Lothian
Borders
Dumfries and Galloway
Northumberland
Tyne and Wear
Durham
Cleveland
Cumbria
NORTHERN IRELAND
Donegal
Sligo
Mayo
Leitrim
Cavan
Monaghan
Louth
Roscommon
Longford
Meath
West Meath
Galway
Dublin
Offaly
Kildare
Laois
Wicklow
Clare
Carlow
Kilkenny
Limerick
Tipperary
Wexford
Kerry
Waterford
Cork
IRISH REPUBLIC
Isle of Man
North Yorkshire
Lancashire
West Yorkshire
Humberside
Merseyside
Greater Manchester
South Yorkshire
Cheshire
Derbyshire
Nottinghamshire
Lincolnshire
ENGLAND
Gwynedd
Clwyd
Staffordshire
Shropshire
West Midlands
Leicestershire
Norfolk
WALES
Powys
Hereford & Worcester
Warwick-shire
Northamptonshire
Cambridge-shire
Suffolk
Dyfed
Bedford-shire
Mid Glam-organ
Gwent
Gloucester-shire
Oxfordshire
Buckingham-shire
Hertfordshire
Essex
West Glamorgan
South Glamorgan
Avon
Wiltshire
Berkshire
Greater London
Surrey
Kent
Somerset
Hampshire
West Sussex
East Sussex
Devon
Dorset
Isle of Wight
Cornwall
Isles of Scilly
0 50 100 150 200 km

North America
ALASKA
0 500 km
YUKON
NORTHWEST TERRITORIES
CANADA
BRITISH COLUMBIA
ALBERTA
SASKATCHEWAN
MANITOBA
ONTARIO
QUEBEC
NEWFOUNDLAND
PRINCE EDWARD ISLAND
NEW BRUNSWICK
NOVA SCOTIA
WASHINGTON
OREGON
CALIFORNIA
NEVADA
IDAHO
MONTANA
WYOMING
UTAH
COLORADO
ARIZONA
NEW MEXICO
NORTH DAKOTA
SOUTH DAKOTA
NEBRASKA
KANSAS
OKLAHOMA
TEXAS
MINNESOTA
IOWA
MISSOURI
ARKANSAS
LOUISIANA
WISCONSIN
ILLINOIS
MICHIGAN
INDIANA
OHIO
KENTUCKY
TENNESSEE
MISSISSIPPI
ALABAMA
GEORGIA
FLORIDA
SOUTH CAROLINA
NORTH CAROLINA
VIRGINIA
WEST VIRGINIA
D.C.
MARYLAND
DELAWARE
NEW JERSEY
PENNSYLVANIA
NEW YORK
CONNECTICUT
RHODE ISLAND
MASSACHUSETTS
VERMONT
NEW HAMPSHIRE
MAINE
UNITED STATES
HAWAII
0 250 km
0 500 1000 km

APPENDIX 2

POLITICAL LEADERS

British Prime Ministers

[1721]–1742	Sir Robert Walpole *Whig*
1742–1743	Earl of Wilmington *Whig*
1743–1754	Henry Pelham *Whig*
1754–1756	Duke of Newcastle *Whig*
1756–1757	Duke of Devonshire *Whig*
1757–1762	Duke of Newcastle *Whig*
1762–1763	Earl of Bute *Tory*
1763–1765	George Grenville *Whig*
1765–1766	Marquis of Rockingham *Whig*
1766–1768	Earl of Chatham *Whig*
1768–1770	Duke of Grafton *Whig*
1770–1782	Lord North *Tory*
1782	Marquis of Rockingham *Whig*
1782–1783	Earl of Shelburne *Whig*
1783	Duke of Portland *coalition*
1783–1801	William Pitt *Tory*
1801–1804	Henry Addington *Tory*
1804–1806	William Pitt *Tory*
1806–1807	Lord William Grenville *Whig*
1807–1809	Duke of Portland *Tory*
1809–1812	Spencer Perceval *Tory*
1812–1827	Earl of Liverpool *Tory*
1827	George Canning *Tory*
1827–1828	Viscount Goderich *Tory*
1828–1830	Duke of Wellington *Tory*
1830–1834	Earl Grey *Whig*
1834	Viscount Melbourne *Whig*
1834	Duke of Wellington *Tory*
1834–1835	Sir Robert Peel *Conservative*
1835–1841	Viscount Melbourne *Whig*
1841–1846	Sir Robert Peel *Conservative*
1846–1852	Lord John Russell *Whig*
1852	Earl of Derby *Conservative*
1852–1855	Earl of Aberdeen *coalition*
1855–1858	Viscount Palmerston *Liberal*
1858–1859	Earl of Derby *Conservative*
1859–1865	Viscount Palmerston *Liberal*
1865–1866	Earl Russell *Liberal*
1866–1868	Earl of Derby *Conservative*
1868	Benjamin Disraeli *Conservative*
1868–1874	William Ewart Gladstone *Liberal*
1874–1880	Benjamin Disraeli *Conservative*
1880–1885	William Ewart Gladstone *Liberal*
1885–1886	Marquis of Salisbury *Conservative*
1886	William Ewart Gladstone *Liberal*
1886–1892	Marquis of Salisbury *Conservative*
1892–1894	William Ewart Gladstone *Liberal*
1894–1895	Earl of Rosebery *Liberal*
1895–1902	Marquis of Salisbury *Conservative*
1902–1905	Arthur James Balfour *Conservative*
1905–1908	Sir Henry Campbell-Bannerman *Liberal*
1908–1916	Herbert Henry Asquith *Liberal*
1916–1922	David Lloyd George *coalition*
1922–1923	Andrew Bonar Law *Conservative*
1923–1924	Stanley Baldwin *Conservative*
1924	James Ramsay MacDonald *Labour*
1924–1929	Stanley Baldwin *Conservative*
1929–1935	James Ramsay MacDonald *coalition*
1935–1937	Stanley Baldwin *coalition*
1937–1940	Neville Chamberlain *coalition*
1940–1945	Winston Spencer Churchill *coalition*
1945–1951	Clement Richard Attlee *Labour*
1951–1955	Sir Winston Spencer Churchill *Conservative*
1955–1957	Sir Anthony Eden *Conservative*
1957–1963	Harold Macmillan *Conservative*
1963–1964	Sir Alexander Douglas-Home *Conservative*
1964–1970	Harold Wilson *Labour*
1970–1974	Edward Heath *Conservative*
1974–1976	Harold Wilson *Labour*
1976–1979	James Callaghan *Labour*
1979–1990	Margaret Thatcher *Conservative*
1990–	John Major *Conservative*

Presidents of the United States of America

1	1789–1797	George Washington *Federalist*
2	1797–1801	John Adams *Federalist*
3	1801–1809	Thomas Jefferson *Democratic-Republican*
4	1809–1817	James Madison *Democratic-Republican*
5	1817–1825	James Monroe *Democratic-Republican*
6	1825–1829	John Quincy Adams *Independent*
7	1829–1837	Andrew Jackson *Democrat*
8	1837–1841	Martin Van Buren *Democrat*
9	1841	William H Harrison *Whig*
10	1841–1845	John Tyler *Whig, then Democrat*
11	1845–1849	James K Polk *Democrat*
12	1849–1850	Zachary Taylor *Whig*
13	1850–1853	Millard Fillmore *Whig*
14	1853–1857	Franklin Pierce *Democrat*
15	1857–1861	James Buchanan *Democrat*
16	1861–1865	Abraham Lincoln *Republican*
17	1865–1869	Andrew Johnson *Democrat*
18	1869–1877	Ulysses S Grant *Republican*
19	1877–1881	Rutherford B Hayes *Republican*
20	1881	James A Garfield *Republican*
21	1881–1885	Chester A Arthur *Republican*
22	1885–1889	Grover Cleveland *Democrat*
23	1889–1893	Benjamin Harrison *Republican*
24	1893–1897	Grover Cleveland *Democrat*
25	1897–1901	William McKinley *Republican*
26	1901–1909	Theodore Roosevelt *Republican*
27	1909–1913	William H Taft *Republican*
28	1913–1921	Woodrow Wilson *Democrat*
29	1921–1923	Warren G Harding *Republican*
30	1923–1929	Calvin Coolidge *Republican*
31	1929–1933	Herbert Hoover *Republican*
32	1933–1945	Franklin D Roosevelt *Democrat*
33	1945–1953	Harry S Truman *Democrat*
34	1953–1961	Dwight D Eisenhower *Republican*
35	1961–1963	John F Kennedy *Democrat*
36	1963–1969	Lyndon B Johnson *Democrat*
37	1969–1974	Richard M Nixon *Republican*
38	1974–1977	Gerald R Ford *Republican*
39	1977–1981	James Earl Carter *Democrat*
40	1981–1989	Ronald W Reagan *Republican*
41	1989–1993	George Bush *Republican*
42	1993–	William J Clinton *Democrat*

Prime Ministers of Canada

1867–1873	John A Macdonald
1873–1878	Alexander Mackenzie
1878–1891	John A Macdonald
1891–1892	John J C Abbott
1892–1894	John S D Thompson
1894–1896	Mackenzie Bowell
1896	Charles Tupper
1896–1911	Wilfrid Laurier
1911–1920	Robert L Borden
1920–1921	Arthur Meighen
1921–1926	W L Mackenzie King
1926	Arthur Meighen
1926–1930	W L Mackenzie King
1930–1935	Richard B Bennett
1935–1948	W L Mackenzie King
1948–1957	Louis Stephen St Laurent
1957–1963	John George Diefenbaker
1963–1968	Lester B Pearson
1968–1979	Pierre Elliott Trudeau
1979–1980	Joseph Clark
1980–1984	Pierre Elliott Trudeau
1984	John Turner
1984–1993	Brian Mulroney
1993	Kim Campbell
1993–	Jean Chrétien

Prime Ministers of Australia

1901–1903	Edmund Barton
1903–1904	Alfred Deakin
1904	John C Watson
1904–1905	George Houstoun Reid
1905–1908	Alfred Deakin
1908–1909	Andrew Fisher
1909–1910	Alfred Deakin
1910–1913	Andrew Fisher
1913–1914	Joseph Cook
1914–1915	Andrew Fisher
1915–1923	William M Hughes
1923–1929	Stanley M Bruce
1929–1931	James H Scullin
1932–1939	Joseph A Lyons
1939–1941	Robert Gordon Menzies
1941	Arthur William Fadden
1941–1945	John Curtin
1945–1949	Joseph Benedict Chifley
1949–1966	Robert Gordon Menzies
1966–1967	Harold Edward Holt
1968–1971	John Grey Gorton
1972–1975	Gough Whitlam
1975–1983	J Malcolm Fraser
1983–1991	Robert J L Hawke
1991–	Paul J Keating

Prime Ministers of New Zealand

1856	Henry Sewell
1856	William Fox
1856–1861	Edward William Stafford
1861–1862	William Fox
1862–1863	Alfred Domett
1863–1864	Frederick Whitaker
1864–1865	Frederick Aloysius Weld
1865–1869	Edward William Stafford
1869–1872	William Fox
1872	Edward William Stafford
1872–1873	George Marsden Waterhouse
1873	William Fox
1873–1875	Julius Vogel
1875–1876	Daniel Pollen
1876	Julius Vogel
1876–1877	Harry Albert Atkinson
1877–1879	George Grey
1879–1882	John Hall
1882–1883	Frederick Whitaker
1883–1884	Harry Albert Atkinson
1884	Robert Stout
1884	Harry Albert Atkinson
1884–1887	Robert Stout
1887–1891	Harry Albert Atkinson
1891–1893	John Ballance
1893–1906	Richard John Seddon
1906	William Hall-Jones
1906–1912	Joseph George Ward
1912	Thomas Mackenzie
1912–1925	William Ferguson Massey
1925	Francis Henry Dillon Bell
1925–1928	Joseph Gordon Coates
1928–1930	Joseph George Ward
1930–1935	George William Forbes
1935–1940	Michael J Savage
1940–1949	Peter Fraser
1949–1957	Sidney G Holland
1957–1960	Walter Nash
1960–1972	Keith J Holyoake
1972	John R Marshall
1972–1974	Norman Kirk
1974–1975	Wallace Rowling
1975–1984	Robert D Muldoon
1984–1989	Hon David Lange
1989–1990	Geoffrey Palmer
1990–	James B Bolger

APPENDIX 3

BRITISH MONARCHS AND KEY HISTORICAL EVENTS

55 BC		Roman invasion
43–410 AD		Roman occupation
c 450–600		Angles and Saxons conquer Britain, except for Cornwall, Scotland and Wales
865		Start of the Danish invasion

Saxon

871–899	Alfred the Great	King of Wessex
959–975	Edgar	
978–1016	Ethelred the Unready	

Danish line

1016–1035	Canute	by conquest
1037–1040	Harold I	
1040–1042	Hardicanute	

Saxon line

1042–1066	Edward the Confessor	
1066	Harold II	

House of Normandy

1066–1087	William I	Battle of Hastings, 1066 Norman Conquest of England Domesday Book, 1086
1087–1100	William II	
1100–1135	Henry I	
1135–1154	Stephen	

House of Plantagenet

1154–1189	Henry II	
1189–1199	Richard I	
1199–1216	John	John forced by the barons to accept Magna Carta
1216–1272	Henry III	Battle of Lewes, 1264 First parliament
1272–1307	Edward I	Conquest of Wales, 1284
1307–1327	Edward II	Battle of Bannockburn, 1314; Scottish independence secured
1327–1377	Edward III	100 Years War with France, 1340s to 1450s Black Death reaches Europe, 1348
1377–1399	Richard II	Peasants' Revolt, 1381

House of Lancaster

1399–1413	Henry IV	
1413–1422	Henry V	Battle of Agincourt, 1415
1422–1461	Henry VI	Wars of the Roses, 1455–85

House of York

1461–1483	Edward IV	William Caxton prints the first English text, 1474
1483	Edward V	
1483–1485	Richard III	Richard killed at the Battle of Bosworth, 1485

House of Tudor

1485–1509	Henry VII	Christopher Columbus's voyage to the West Indies, 1492
1509–1547	Henry VIII	Start of the Protestant Reformation with Luther, 1517
		Break from Rome
		Act of Union between Wales and England, 1535
		Dissolution of the Monasteries, 1536–39
1547–1553	Edward VI	
1553–1558	Mary I	Counter-Reformation; Cranmer and other Protestant bishops burnt at the stake
1558–1603	Elizabeth I	Drake sails round the world in the *Golden Hind*, 1577
		Defeat of the Spanish Armada, 1588
		Raleigh brings potatoes and tobacco back from America

House of Stuart

1603–1625	James I of England and VI of Scotland	30 Years War, 1618–48
		Guy Fawkes plots to blow up Parliament, 1605
1625–1649	Charles I	English Civil War, 1642–49
		Charles beheaded

Commonwealth (declared 1649)

1653–1658	Oliver Cromwell, Lord Protector	
1658–1659	Richard Cromwell	

House of Stuart

1660–1685	Charles II	Plague, 1665
		Great Fire of London, 1666
1685–1688	James II	Newton publishes his Laws of Motion, 1687
1688–1702	William III and Mary II (died 1694)	
1702–1714	Anne	Union of England and Scotland, 1707
		Scotland loses its Parliament

House of Hanover

1714–1727	George I	Walpole, first Prime Minister, 1721
1727–1760	George II	Beginning of the Industrial Revolution
		Seven Years War, 1756–63
1760–1820	George III	American War of Independence, 1775–81
		Union between Britain and Ireland, 1801
		Battle of Waterloo, 1815
		William Wilberforce's campaign against the slave trade results in its abolition, 1807
		Corn Laws, 1815
1820–1830	George IV	First railway, 1825
		Catholic Emancipation Act, 1826
1830–1837	William IV	Great Reform Act, 1832
1837–1901	Victoria	Invention of the electric telegraph, 1837
		Introduction of the penny post, 1840
		Irish potato famine, 1845–51
		Corn Laws repealed, 1846
		Reform Bill, 1867
		First Trades Union Congress, 1868
		Universal elementary education, 1870

House of Saxe-Coburg-Gotha

1901–1910	Edward VII	

House of Windsor

1910–1936	George V	National Insurance Act, 1911
		First World War, 1914–18
		Asquith displaced as prime minister by Lloyd George, 1916
		Electoral rights for women over 30, 1918
		Irish Free State formed, 1921
		League of Nations formed, 1919
		First television broadcast, 1926
		General strike, 1926
		Equal electoral rights for women, 1928
		Great Depression, 1929–33
1936	Edward VIII	King Edward abdicates
1936–1952	George VI	Second World War, 1939–45
		Normandy landings, 1944
		United Nations formed, 1945
		Republic of Ireland formed, 1949
1952–	Elizabeth II	Voting age lowered to 18, 1969
		Britain and Ireland join the European (Economic) Community, 1973

APPENDIX 4

MILITARY RANKS

Royal Navy (RN)

Admiral of the Fleet
Admiral (Adm)
Vice-Admiral (V-Adm)
Rear-Admiral (Rear-Adm)
Commodore (Cdre)
Captain (Capt)
Commander (Cdr)
Lieutenant-Commander (Lt-Cdr)
Lieutenant (Lt) /lefˈtenənt/
Sub-Lieutenant (Sub-Lt)
Acting Sub-Lieutenant (Act Sub-Lt)

Midshipman

Fleet Chief Petty Officer (FCPO)

Chief Petty Officer (CPO)

Petty Officer (PO)
Leading Seaman (LS)
Able Seaman (AB)
Ordinary Seaman (OD)
Junior Seaman (JS)

United States Navy (USN)

*Fleet Admiral
Admiral (ADM)
Vice Admiral (VADM)
Rear Admiral (RADM)
Commodore (CDRE)
Captain (CAPT)
Commander (CDR)
Lieutenant Commander (LCDR)
Lieutenant (LT) /luːˈtenənt/
Lieutenant Junior Grade (LTJG)
Ensign (ENS)
Chief Warrant Officer (CWO)
Midshipman

**Warrant Officer (WO 1)
Master Chief Petty Officer (MCPO)
Senior Chief Petty Officer (SCPO)
Chief Petty Officer (CPO)
Petty Officer 1st Class (PO1)
Petty Officer 2nd Class (PO2)
Petty Officer 3rd Class (PO3)
Seaman (SN)

Seaman Apprentice (SA)
Seaman Recruit (SR)

*Wartime rank only
**Rank discontinued 1976

Royal Air Force (RAF)

Marshal of the Royal Air Force
Air Chief Marshal (ACM)
Air Marshal (AM)
Air Vice Marshal (AVM)
Air Commodore (Air Cdre)
Group Captain (Gp Capt)
Wing Commander (Wing Cdr)
Squadron Leader (Sqn Ldr)
Flight Lieutenant (Flt Lt)
Flying Officer (FO)
Pilot Officer (PO)

Warrant Officer (WO)
Flight Sergeant (FS)

Chief Technician (Chf Tech)
Sergeant (Sgt)
Corporal (Cpl)
Junior Technician (Jnr Tech)
Senior Aircraftman (SAC)
Leading Aircraftman (LAC)
Aircraftman

United States Air Force (USAF)

General of the Air Force
General (GEN)
Lieutenant General (LTG)
Major General (MG)
Brigadier General (BG)
Colonel (COL)
Lieutenant Colonel (LTC)
Major (MAJ)
Captain (CAPT)
First Lieutenant (1 LT)
Second Lieutenant (2 LT)

Chief Warrant Officer (CW-3 and CW-4)
Warrant Officer (W-1 and W-2)
Chief Master Sergeant (CMSGT)
Senior Master Sergeant (SMSGT)
Master Sergeant (MSGT)
Technical Sergeant (TSGT)
Staff Sergeant (SSGT)
Sergeant (SGT)

Airman First Class (A1C)
Airman Basic (AB)

Note: USAF Warrant Officer ranks will be discontinued when those currrently on active duty are retired.

British Army

Field Marshal (FM)
General (Gen)
Lieutenant-General (Lt-Gen)
Major-General (Maj-Gen)
Brigadier (Brig)
Colonel (Col)
Lieutenant-Colonel (Lt-Col)
Major (Maj)
Captain (Capt)
Lieutenant (Lieut)
Second Lieutenant (2nd Lt)

Warrant Officer 1st Class (WO 1)

Warrant Officer 2nd Class (WO 2)

Staff Sergeant (S/Sgt)
or Colour Sergeant (C/Sgt)
Sergeant (Sgt)
Corporal (Cpl)
Lance Corporal (L/Cpl)
Private (Pte)

United States Army

General of the Army (GEN)
General (GEN)
Lieutenant General (LTG)
Major General (MG)
Brigadier General (BG)
Colonel (COL)
Lieutenant Colonel (LTC)
Major (MAJ)
Captain (CAPT)
First Lieutenant (1 LT)
Second Lieutenant (2 LT)
Chief Warrant Officer (CWO)
Warrant Officer (WO)
Command Sergeant Major (CSM)
Staff Sergeant Major (SSM)
1st Sergeant (1 SG)
Master Sergeant (MSG)
Sergeant 1st Class (SFC)
Staff Sergeant (SSG)

Sergeant (SGT)
Corporal (CPL)
Private First Class (P1C)
Private (PVT)

Note: Warrant Officers in the US Army are the equivalent of Commissioned Officers in the British Army, ie Second Lieutenant and above.
In the British and US Army the ranks of Corporal and above, to the rank of Second Lieutenant, are referred to as Non-Commissioned Officers (NCOs).

Royal Marines (RM)

General (Gen)
Lieutenant-General (Lt-Gen)
Major-General (Maj-Gen)
Brigadier (Brig)
Colonel (Col)
Lieutenant-Colonel (Lt-Col)
Major (Maj)
Captain (Capt)
Lieutenant (Lieut)
Acting-Lieutenant (Act-Lt)
Second Lieutenant (2nd Lt)

Warrant Officer 1st Class (WO 1)
Warrant Officer 2nd Class (WO 2)
Colour Sergeant (C/Sgt)

Sergeant (Sgt)

Corporal (Cpl)

Lance Corporal (L/Cpl)
Marine (Mne)
Junior Marine (J Mne)

United States Marine Corps (USMC)

General (GEN)
Lieutenant General (LTG)
Major General (MG)
Brigadier General (BG)
Colonel (COL)
Lieutenant Colonel (LTC)
Major (MAJ)
Captain (CPT)
First Lieutenant (1 LT)

Second Lieutenant (2 LT)

Sergeant Major (SGM)
Master Gunnery Sergeant (MGSGT)
First Sergeant (1 SGT)
Master Sergeant (MSGT)
Gunnery Sergeant (GSGT)
Staff Sergeant (SSGT)
Sergeant (SGT)
Corporal (CPL)
Lance-Corporal (L-CPL)
Private First Class (P1C)
Private (PVT)

APPENDIX 5

THE BOOKS OF THE BIBLE

The Old Testament

Genesis / ˈdʒenəsɪs /
Exodus / ˈeksədəs /
Leviticus / lɪˈvɪtɪkəs /
Numbers / ˈnʌmbəz /
Deuteronomy / ˌdju:təˈrɒnəmɪ; *US* ˌdu:- /
Joshua / ˈdʒɒʃʊə /
Judges / ˈdʒʌdʒɪz /
Ruth / ru:θ /
I Samuel / ˈsæmjʊəl /
II Samuel / sæmjʊəl /
I Kings / kɪŋz /
II Kings / kɪŋz /
I Chronicles / ˈkrɒnɪklz /
II Chronicles / ˈkrɒnɪklz /
Ezra / ˈezrə /
Nehemiah / ˌni:əˈmaɪə /
Esther / ˈestə(r) /
Job / dʒəʊb /
Psalms / sɑ:mz /
Proverbs / ˈprɒvɜ:bz /
Ecclesiastes / ɪˌkli:zɪˈæsti:z /
Song of Solomon / ˌsɒŋ əv ˈsɒləmən; *US* ˌsɔ:ŋ /
or Song of Songs
Isaiah / aɪˈzaɪə; *US* aɪˈzeɪə /
Jeremiah / ˌdʒerɪˈmaɪə /
Lamentations / ˌlæmənˈteɪʃnz /
Ezekiel / ɪˈzi:kɪəl /
Daniel / ˈdænɪəl /
Hosea / həʊˈzi:ə /
Joel / ˈdʒəʊəl /
Amos / ˈeɪmɒs; *US* -məs /
Obadiah / ˌəʊbəˈdaɪə /
Jonah / ˈdʒəʊnə /
Micah / ˈmaɪkə /
Nahum / ˈneɪhəm /
Habakkuk / ˈhæbəkək; *US* həˈbækək /
Zephaniah / ˌzefəˈnaɪə /
Haggai / ˈhægeɪaɪ; *US* ˈhægɪaɪ /
Zechariah / ˌzekəˈraɪə /
Malachi / ˈmæləkaɪ /

The Apocrypha / əˈpɒkrɪfə /

Tobit / ˈtəʊbɪt /
Judith / ˈdʒu:dɪθ /
Wisdom / ˈwɪzdəm /
Ecclesiasticus / ɪˌkli:zɪˈæstɪkəs /
Baruch / ˈbeərək /
I Maccabees / ˈmækəbi:z /
II Maccabees / ˈmækəbi:z /

The New Testament

St Matthew / ˈmæθju: /
St Mark / mɑ:k /
St Luke / lu:k /
St John / dʒɒn /
Acts / ækts /
Romans / ˈrəʊmənz /
I Corinthians / kəˈrɪnθɪənz /
II Corinthians / kəˈrɪnθɪənz /
Galatians / gəˈleɪʃnz /
Ephesians / ɪˈfi:ʒnz /
Philippians / fɪˈlɪpɪənz /
Colossians / kəˈlɒʃnz /
I Thessalonians / ˌθesəˈləʊnɪənz /
II Thessalonians / ˌθesəˈləʊnɪənz /
I Timothy / ˈtɪməθɪ /
II Timothy / ˈtɪməθɪ /
Titus / ˈtaɪtəs /
Philemon / fɪˈli:mən /
Hebrews / ˈhi:bru:z /
James / dʒeɪmz /
I Peter / ˈpi:tə(r) /
II Peter / ˈpi:tə(r) /
I John / dʒɒn /
II John / dʒɒn /
III John / dʒɒn /
Jude / dʒu:d /
Revelation / ˌrevəˈleɪʃn /
or Apocalypse / əˈpɒkəlɪps /

APPENDIX 6

THE WORKS OF WILLIAM SHAKESPEARE (1564–1616)

The lists below show the approximate date of composition of the plays and the date of the first printing of the poems.

Plays

1590–1591 King Henry VI, Part I
King Henry VI, Part II
King Henry VI, Part III
1592–1593 King Richard III
The Comedy of Errors
1593–1594 Titus Andronicus / ˌtaɪtəs ænˈdrɒnɪkəs /
The Taming of the Shrew
1594–1595 The Two Gentlemen of Verona / vəˈrəʊnə /
Love's Labour's Lost
Romeo and Juliet / ˌrəʊmɪəʊ ən ˈdʒu:lɪət /
1595–1596 King Richard II
A Midsummer Night's Dream
1596–1597 King John
The Merchant of Venice / ˈvenɪs /
1597–1598 King Henry IV, Part I
King Henry IV, Part II
1598–1600 Much Ado about Nothing
As You Like It
Twelfth Night, or What You Will
King Henry V
Julius Caesar / ˌdʒu:lɪəs ˈsi:zə(r) /
1600–1601 Hamlet, Prince of Denmark / ˈhæmlɪt /
The Merry Wives of Windsor / ˈwɪnzə(r) /
1601–1602 Troilus and Cressida / ˌtrɔɪləs n ˈkresɪdə /
All's Well that Ends Well
1604–1605 Measure for Measure
Othello, the Moor of Venice / əˈθeləʊ /
1605–1606 King Lear / lɪə(r) /
Macbeth / mækˈbeθ /
1606–1607 Antony and Cleopatra / ˌæntənɪ ən klɪəˈpætrə /
1607–1608 Coriolanus / ˌkɒrɪəˈleɪnəs; *US* ˌkɔ:r- /
Timon of Athens / ˌtaɪmən əv ˈæθɪnz /
1608–1610 Pericles, Prince of Tyre / ˈperɪkli:z /
Cymbeline / ˈsɪmbəli:n /
The Winter's Tale
1611–1612 The Tempest
1612–1613 King Henry VIII

Poems

1593 Venus and Adonis / ˌvi:nəs n əˈdəʊnɪs; *US* əˈdɒnɪs /
1594 The Rape of Lucrece / lu:ˈkri:s /
1601 The Phoenix and the Turtle
1609 Sonnets
1609 A Lover's Complaint

APPENDIX 7

COMMON FORENAMES

Note: Pet and short forms (which may sometimes be used as names in their own right) follow the name from which they are formed.

Female Names

Abigail / ˈæbɪgeɪl /
Ada / ˈeɪdə /
Agatha / ˈægəθə /; Aggie / ˈægɪ /
Agnes / ˈægnɪs /; Aggie / ˈægɪ /
Aileen ⇨ Eileen
Alexandra / ˌælɪgˈzɑːndrə; *US* -ˈzæn- /; Alex / ˈælɪks /
Alexis / əˈleksɪs /
Alice / ˈælɪs /
Alison / ˈælɪsn /
Amanda / əˈmændə /; Mandy / ˈmændɪ /
Amy / ˈeɪmɪ /
Angela / ˈændʒələ /; Angie / ˈændʒɪ /
Anita / əˈniːtə /
Ann, Anne / æn /; Annie / ˈænɪ /
Anna / ˈænə /
Annabel, Annabelle / ˈænəbel /
Anne, Annie ⇨ Ann
Annette / æˈnet /
Anthea / ˈænθɪə /
Antonia / ænˈtəʊnɪə /
Audrey / ˈɔːdrɪ /
Ava / ˈeɪvə /
Barbara, Barbra / ˈbɑːbrə /; Babs / bæbz /
Beatrice / ˈbɪətrɪs /
Becky ⇨ Rebecca
Belinda / bəˈlɪndə /
Bernadette / ˌbɜːnəˈdet /
Beryl / ˈberəl /
Bess, Bessie, Beth, Betsy, Bett, Betty ⇨ Elizabeth
Brenda / ˈbrendə /
Bridget, Bridgit, Brigid / ˈbrɪdʒɪt /; Bid / bɪd /
Candice / ˈkændɪs /
Carla / ˈkɑːlə /
Carol, Carole / ˈkærəl /
Caroline / ˈkærəlaɪn /; Carolyn / ˈkærəlɪn /; Carrie / ˈkærɪ /
Catherine, Cathy ⇨ Katherine
Cecilia / sɪˈsiːlɪə /
Cecily / ˈsesəlɪ /; Cicely / ˈsɪsəlɪ /
Celia / ˈsiːlɪə /
Charlene / ˈʃɑːliːn /
Charlotte / ˈʃɑːlət /
Cheryl / ˈtʃerəl /
Chloe / ˈkləʊɪ /
Christina / krɪˈstiːnə /; Tina / ˈtiːnə /
Christine / ˈkrɪstiːn /; Chris / krɪs /; Chrissie / ˈkrɪsɪ /
Cindy ⇨ Cynthia, Lucinda
Clare, Claire / kleə(r) /
Claudia / ˈklɔːdɪə /
Cleo, Clio / ˈkliːəʊ /
Constance / ˈkɒnstəns /; Connie / ˈkɒnɪ /
Cynthia / ˈsɪnθɪə /; Cindy / ˈsɪndɪ /
Daisy / ˈdeɪzɪ /
Daphne / ˈdæfnɪ /
Dawn / dɔːn /
Deborah / ˈdebərə /; Debbie, Debby / ˈdebɪ /; Deb / deb /
Deirdre / ˈdɪədrɪ /
Delia / ˈdiːlɪə /
Della / ˈdelə /
Denise / dəˈniːz /
Diana / daɪˈænə /; Diane / daɪˈæn /; Di / daɪ /
Dolly / ˈdɒlɪ /
Dora / ˈdɔːrə /
Doreen, Dorene / ˈdɔːriːn /
Doris / ˈdɒrɪs /
Dorothy / ˈdɒrəθɪ /; Dot / dɒt /; Dottie / ˈdɒtɪ /
Edith / ˈiːdɪθ /
Edna / ˈednə /
Eileen / ˈaɪliːn /; Aileen / ˈeɪliːn /
Elaine / ɪˈleɪn /
Eleanor / ˈelɪnə(r) /; Eleanora / ˌelɪˈnɔːrə /; Ellie / ˈelɪ /
Eliza / ɪˈlaɪzə /; Liza / ˈlaɪzə /; Lisa / ˈliːsə /
Elizabeth, Elisabeth / ɪˈlɪzəbəθ /; Liz / lɪz /; Lizzie, Lizzy / ˈlɪzɪ /; Libby / ˈlɪbɪ /; Beth / beθ /; Betsy / ˈbetsɪ /; Bett / bet /; Betty / ˈbetɪ /; Bess / bes /; Bessie / ˈbesɪ /
Ella / ˈelə /
Ellen / ˈelən /
Ellie ⇨ Eleanor
Elsie / ˈelsɪ /
Elspeth / ˈelspəθ / (*Scot*)
Emily / ˈeməlɪ /
Emma / ˈemə /
Erica / ˈerɪkə /
Ethel / ˈeθl /
Eunice / ˈjuːnɪs /
Eve / iːv /; Eva / ˈiːvə /
Evelyn / ˈiːvlɪn /
Fay / feɪ /
Felicity / fəˈlɪsətɪ /
Fiona / fɪˈəʊnə /
Flora / ˈflɔːrə /
Florence / ˈflɒrəns; *US* ˈflɔːr- /; Flo / fləʊ /; Florrie / ˈflɒrɪ /
Frances / ˈfrɑːnsɪs; *US* ˈfræn- /; Fran / fræn /; Frankie / ˈfræŋkɪ /
Freda / ˈfriːdə /
Georgia / ˈdʒɔːdʒɪə /; Georgie / ˈdʒɔːdʒɪ /; Georgina / dʒɔːˈdʒiːnə /
Geraldine / ˈdʒerəldiːn /
Germaine / dʒɜːˈmeɪn /
Gertrude / ˈgɜːtruːd /; Gertie / ˈgɜːtɪ /
Gillian / ˈdʒɪlɪən /; Jill, Gill / dʒɪl /; Jilly / ˈdʒɪlɪ /
Ginny ⇨ Virginia
Gladys / ˈglædɪs /
Glenda / ˈglendə /
Gloria / ˈglɔːrɪə /
Grace / greɪs /; Gracie / ˈgreɪsɪ /
Gwendoline / ˈgwendəlɪn /; Gwen / gwen /
Hannah / ˈhænə /
Harriet / ˈhærɪət /
Hazel / ˈheɪzl /
Heather / ˈheðə(r) /
Helen / ˈhelɪn /
Henrietta / ˌhenrɪˈetə /
Hilary / ˈhɪlərɪ /
Hilda / ˈhɪldə /
Ida / ˈaɪdə /
Ingrid / ˈɪŋgrɪd /
Irene / aɪˈriːnɪ; *US* ˈaɪriːn /
Iris / ˈaɪərɪs /
Isabel, (*esp Scot*) Isobel / ˈɪzəbel /
Isabella / ˌɪzəˈbelə /
Ivy / ˈaɪvɪ /
Jackie ⇨ Jacqueline
Jan ⇨ Janet, Janice
Jane / dʒeɪn /; Janey / ˈdʒeɪnɪ /
Janet / ˈdʒænɪt /; Janette / dʒəˈnet /; Jan / dʒæn /
Janice, Janis / ˈdʒænɪs /; Jan / dʒæn /
Jacqueline / ˈdʒækəlɪn /; Jackie / ˈdʒækɪ /
Jean / dʒiːn /; Jeanie / ˈdʒiːnɪ /
Jennifer / ˈdʒenɪfə(r) /; Jenny, Jennie / ˈdʒenɪ /
Jessica / ˈdʒesɪkə /; Jess / dʒes /; Jessie / ˈdʒesɪ /
Jill, Jilly ⇨ Gillian
Jo ⇨ Joanna, Josephine
Joan / dʒəʊn /
Joanna / dʒəʊˈænə /; Joanne / dʒəʊˈæn /; Jo / dʒəʊ /
Jocelyn / ˈdʒɒslɪn /
Josephine / ˈdʒəʊzəfiːn /; Jo / dʒəʊ /; Josie / ˈdʒəʊsɪ /
Jody / ˈdʒəʊdɪ /
Joyce / dʒɔɪs /
Judith / ˈdʒuːdɪθ /; Judy / ˈdʒuːdɪ /
Julia / ˈdʒuːlɪə /; Julie / ˈdʒuːlɪ /
Juliet / ˈdʒuːlɪət /
June / dʒuːn /
Karen, Karin / ˈkærən /
Katherine, Catherine, (*esp US*) -arine / ˈkæθrɪn /; Kathy, Cathy / ˈkæθɪ /; Kate / keɪt /; Katie, Katy / ˈkeɪtɪ /; Kay / keɪ /; Kitty / ˈkɪtɪ /
Kim / kɪm /
Kirsten / ˈkɜːstɪn /
Kitty ⇨ Katherine
Laura / ˈlɔːrə /
Lauretta, Loretta / ləˈretə /
Lesley / ˈlezlɪ /
Libby ⇨ Elizabeth
Lilian, Lillian / ˈlɪlɪən /
Lily / ˈlɪlɪ /
Linda / ˈlɪndə /
Lisa, Liza ⇨ Eliza
Livia / ˈlɪvɪə /
Liz, Lizzie, Lizzy ⇨ Elizabeth
Lois / ˈləʊɪs /
Lorna / ˈlɔːnə /
Louise / luːˈiːz /; Louisa / luːˈiːzə /
Lucia / ˈluːsɪə, *also* ˈluːʃə /
Lucinda / luːˈsɪndə /; Cindy / ˈsɪndɪ /
Lucy / ˈluːsɪ /
Lydia / ˈlɪdɪə /
Lyn(n) / lɪn /
Mabel / ˈmeɪbl /
Madeleine / ˈmædəlɪn /
Madge, Maggie ⇨ Margaret
Maisie / ˈmeɪzɪ /
Mandy ⇨ Amanda
Marcia / ˈmɑːsɪə, *also* ˈmɑːʃə /; Marcie / ˈmɑːsɪ /
Margaret / ˈmɑːgrɪt /; Madge / mædʒ /; Maggie / ˈmægɪ /; (*esp Scot*) Meg / meg /; Peg / peg /; Peggie, Peggy / ˈpegɪ /
Margery, Marjorie / ˈmɑːdʒərɪ /; Margie / ˈmɑːdʒɪ /
Marjorie ⇨ Margery
Marlene / ˈmɑːliːn /
Maria / məˈrɪə, *also* məˈraɪə /
Marian, Marion / ˈmærɪən /
Marie / məˈriː, *also* ˈmɑːrɪ /
Marilyn / ˈmærəlɪn /
Marion ⇨ Marian
Martha / ˈmɑːθə /
Martina / mɑːˈtiːnə /
Mary / ˈmeərɪ /
Maud / mɔːd /
Maureen / ˈmɔːriːn /
Mavis / ˈmeɪvɪs /
Meg ⇨ Margaret
Melanie / ˈmelənɪ /
Melinda / məˈlɪndə /
Michelle / mɪˈʃel /
Mildred / ˈmɪldrɪd /
Millicent / ˈmɪlɪsnt /; Millie, Milly / ˈmɪlɪ /
Miranda / mɪˈrændə /
Miriam / ˈmɪrɪəm /
Moira / ˈmɔɪrə /
Molly / ˈmɒlɪ /
Monica / ˈmɒnɪkə /
Muriel / ˈmjʊərɪəl /
Nadia / ˈnɑːdɪə /
Nancy / ˈnænsɪ /; Nan / næn /

Naomi / ˈneɪəmɪ /
Natalie / ˈnætəlɪ /
Natasha / nəˈtæʃə /
Nell / nel /; Nellie, Nelly / ˈnelɪ /
Nicola / ˈnɪkələ /; Nicky / ˈnɪkɪ /
Nora / ˈnɔːrə /
Norma / ˈnɔːmə /
Olive / ˈɒlɪv /
Olivia / əˈlɪvɪə /
Pamela / ˈpæmələ /; Pam / pæm /
Pat ⇨ Patricia
Patience / ˈpeɪʃns /
Patricia / pəˈtrɪʃə /; Pat / pæt /; Patti, Pattie, Patty / ˈpætɪ /; Tricia / ˈtrɪʃə /
Paula / ˈpɔːlə /
Pauline / ˈpɔːliːn /
Peg, Peggie, Peggy ⇨ Margaret
Penelope / pəˈneləpɪ /; Penny / ˈpenɪ /
Philippa / ˈfɪlɪpə /
Phoebe / ˈfiːbɪ /
Phyllis / ˈfɪlɪs /
Polly / ˈpɒlɪ / ; Poll / pɒl /
Priscilla / prɪˈsɪlə /; Cilla / ˈsɪlə /
Prudence / ˈpruːdns /; Pru, Prue / pruː /
Rachel / ˈreɪtʃl /
Rebecca / rɪˈbekə /; Becky / ˈbekɪ /
Rhoda / ˈrəʊdə /
Rita / ˈriːtə /
Roberta / rəˈbɜːtə /
Robin / ˈrɒbɪn /
Rosalie / ˈrəʊzəlɪ, *also* ˈrɒzəlɪ /
Rosalind / ˈrɒzəlɪnd /; Rosalyn / ˈrɒzəlɪn /
Rose / rəʊz /; Rosie / ˈrəʊzɪ /
Rosemary / ˈrəʊzmərɪ /; Rosie / ˈrəʊzɪ /
Ruth / ruːθ /
Sadie ⇨ Sarah
Sally / ˈsælɪ /; Sal / sæl /
Samantha / səˈmænθə /; Sam / sæm /
Sandra / ˈsɑːndrə; *US* ˈsæn- /; Sandy / ˈsændɪ /
Sandy ⇨ Alexandra, Sandra
Sarah, Sara / ˈseərə /; Sadie / ˈseɪdɪ /
Sharon / ˈʃærən /
Sheila, Shelagh / ˈʃiːlə /
Shirley / ˈʃɜːlɪ /
Sibyl ⇨ Sybil
Silvia, Sylvia / ˈsɪlvɪə /; Sylvie / ˈsɪlvɪ /
Sonia / ˈsɒnɪə, *also* ˈsəʊnɪə /
Sophia / səˈfaɪə /
Sophie, Sophy / ˈsəʊfɪ /
Stella / ˈstelə /
Stephanie / ˈstefənɪ /
Susan / ˈsuːzn /; Sue / suː /; Susie, Suzy / ˈsuːzɪ /
Susanna, Susannah / suːˈzænə /; Suzanne / suːˈzæn /; Susie, Suzy / ˈsuːzɪ /
Sybil, Sibyl / ˈsɪbəl /
Sylvia, Sylvie ⇨ Silvia
Teresa, Theresa / təˈriːzə /; Tess / tes /; Tessa / ˈtesə /; (*US*) Terri / ˈterɪ /
Thelma / ˈθelmə /
Tina ⇨ Christina
Toni / ˈtəʊnɪ / (*esp US*)
Tracy, Tracey / ˈtreɪsɪ /
Tricia ⇨ Patricia
Trudie, Trudy / ˈtruːdɪ /
Ursula / ˈɜːsjʊlə /
Valerie / ˈvælərɪ /; Val / væl /
Vanessa / vəˈnesə /
Vera / ˈvɪərə /
Veronica / vəˈrɒnɪkə /
Victoria / vɪkˈtɔːrɪə /; Vicki, Vickie, Vicky, Vikki / ˈvɪkɪ /
Viola / ˈvaɪələ /
Violet / ˈvaɪələt /
Virginia / vəˈdʒɪnɪə /; Ginny / ˈdʒɪnɪ /
Vivien, Vivienne / ˈvɪvɪən /; Viv / vɪv /
Wendy / ˈwendɪ /
Winifred / ˈwɪnɪfrɪd /; Winnie / ˈwɪnɪ /
Yvonne / ɪˈvɒn /
Zoe / ˈzəʊɪ /

Male Names

Abraham / ˈeɪbrəhæm /; Abe / eɪb /
Adam / ˈædəm /
Adrian / ˈeɪdrɪən /
Alan, Allan, Allen / ˈælən /; Al / æl /
Albert / ˈælbət /; Al / æl /; Bert / bɜːt /
Alexander / ˌælɪgˈzɑːndə(r); *US* -ˈzæn- /; Alec / ˈælɪk /; Alex / ˈælɪks /; Sandy / ˈsændɪ /
Alfred / ˈælfrɪd /; Alf / ælf /; Alfie / ˈælfɪ /
Andrew / ˈændruː /; Andy / ˈændɪ /
Alistair, Alisdair, Alas- / ˈælɪstə(r) / (*Scot*)
Allan, Allen ⇨ Alan
Alvin / ˈælvɪn /
Angus / ˈæŋgəs / (*Scot*)
Anthony, Antony / ˈæntənɪ /; Tony / ˈtəʊnɪ /
Archibald / ˈɑːtʃɪbɔːld /; Archie, Archy / ˈɑːtʃɪ /
Arnold / ˈɑːnəld /
Arthur / ˈɑːθə(r) /
Auberon / ˈɔːbərɒn /
Aubrey / ˈɔːbrɪ /
Barnaby / ˈbɑːnəbɪ /
Barry / ˈbærɪ /
Bartholomew / bɑːˈθɒləmjuː /
Basil / ˈbæzl /
Benjamin / ˈbendʒəmɪn /; Ben / ben /
Bernard / ˈbɜːnəd /; Bernie / ˈbɜːnɪ /
Bert ⇨ Albert, Gilbert, Herbert, Hubert
Bill, Billy ⇨ William
Bob, Bobby ⇨ Robert
Boris / ˈbɒrɪs /
Bradford / ˈbrædfəd /; Brad / bræd / (*esp US*)
Brendan / ˈbrendən / (*Irish*)
Brian, Bryan / ˈbraɪən /
Bruce / bruːs /
Bud / bʌd / (*US*)
Carl / kɑːl /
Cecil / ˈsesl; *US* ˈsiːsl /
Cedric / ˈsedrɪk /
Charles / tʃɑːlz /; Charlie / ˈtʃɑːlɪ /; Chas / tʃæz /; Chuck / tʃʌk / (*US*)
Christopher / ˈkrɪstəfə(r) /; Chris / krɪs /; Kit / kɪt /
Chuck ⇨ Charles
Clarence / ˈklærəns /
Clark / klɑːk / (*esp US*)
Claude, Claud / klɔːd /
Clement / ˈklemənt /
Clifford / ˈklɪfəd /; Cliff / klɪf /
Clint / klɪnt / (*esp US*)
Clive / klaɪv /
Clyde / klaɪd / (*esp US*)
Colin / ˈkɒlɪn /
Craig / kreɪg /
Curt / kɜːt /
Cyril / ˈsɪrəl /
Dale / deɪl / (*esp US*)
Daniel / ˈdænɪəl /; Dan / dæn /; Danny / ˈdænɪ /
Darrell / ˈdærəl /
Darren / ˈdærən / (*esp US*)
David / ˈdeɪvɪd /; Dave / deɪv /
Dean / diːn /
Dennis, Denis / ˈdenɪs /
Derek / ˈderɪk /
Dermot / ˈdɜːmɒt / (*Irish*)
Desmond / ˈdezmənd /; Des / dez /
Dick, Dickie, Dicky ⇨ Richard
Dirk / dɜːk /
Dominic / ˈdɒmɪnɪk /
Donald / ˈdɒnəld /; Don / dɒn /
Douglas / ˈdʌgləs /; Doug / dʌg /
Duane / duːˈeɪn /; Dwane / dweɪn / (*esp US*)
Dudley / ˈdʌdlɪ /; Dud / dʌd /
Duncan / ˈdʌŋkən /
Dustin / ˈdʌstɪn /
Dwight / dwaɪt / (*esp US*)
Eamonn, Eamon / ˈeɪmən / (*Irish*)
Ed, Eddie, Eddy ⇨ Edward
Edgar / ˈedgə(r) /
Edmund, Edmond / ˈedmənd /
Edward / ˈedwəd /; Ed / ed /; Eddie, Eddy / ˈedɪ /; Ted / ted /; Teddy / ˈtedɪ /; Ned / ned /; Neddy / ˈnedɪ /
Edwin / ˈedwɪn /
Elmer / ˈelmə(r) / (*US*)
Elroy / ˈelrɔɪ / (*US*)
Emlyn / ˈemlɪn / (*Welsh*)
Enoch / ˈiːnɒk /
Eric / ˈerɪk /
Ernest / ˈɜːnɪst /
Errol / ˈerəl /
Eugene / juːˈdʒiːn /; Gene / dʒiːn / (*US*)
Felix / ˈfiːlɪks /
Ferdinand / ˈfɜːdɪnænd /
Fergus / ˈfɜːgəs / (*Scot or Irish*)
Floyd / flɔɪd /
Francis / ˈfrɑːnsɪs; *US* ˈfræn- /; Frank / fræŋk /
Frank / fræŋk /; Frankie / ˈfræŋkɪ /
Frederick / ˈfredrɪk /; Fred / fred /; Freddie, Freddy / ˈfredɪ /
Gabriel / ˈgeɪbrɪəl /
Gareth / ˈgærəθ / (*esp Welsh*)
Gary / ˈgærɪ /
Gavin / ˈgævɪn /
Gene ⇨ Eugene
Geoffrey, Jeffrey / ˈdʒefrɪ /; Geoff, Jeff / dʒef /
George / dʒɔːdʒ /
Geraint / ˈgeraɪnt / (*Welsh*)
Gerald / ˈdʒerəld /; Gerry, Jerry / ˈdʒerɪ /
Gerard / ˈdʒerɑːd /
Gilbert / ˈgɪlbət /; Bert / bɜːt /
Giles / dʒaɪlz /
Glen / glen /
Godfrey / ˈgɒdfrɪ /
Gordon / ˈgɔːdn /
Graham, Grahame, Graeme / ˈgreɪəm /
Gregory / ˈgregərɪ /; Greg / greg /
Guy / gaɪ /
Hal, Hank ⇨ Henry
Harold / ˈhærəld /
Henry / ˈhenrɪ /; Harry / ˈhærɪ /; Hal / hæl /; Hank / hæŋk / (*US*)
Herbert / ˈhɜːbət /; Bert / bɜːt /; Herb / hɜːb /
Horace / ˈhɒrɪs; *US* ˈhɔːrəs /
Howard / ˈhaʊəd /
Hubert / ˈhjuːbət /; Bert / bɜːt /
Hugh / hjuː /
Hugo / ˈhjuːgəʊ /
Humphrey / ˈhʌmfrɪ /
Ian / ˈiːən /
Isaac / ˈaɪzək /
Ivan / ˈaɪvən /
Ivor / ˈaɪvə(r) /
Jack ⇨ John
Jacob / ˈdʒeɪkəb /; Jake / dʒeɪk /
Jake ⇨ Jacob, John
James / dʒeɪmz /; Jim / dʒɪm /; Jimmy / ˈdʒɪmɪ /; Jamie / ˈdʒeɪmɪ / (*Scot*)
Jason / ˈdʒeɪsn /
Jasper / ˈdʒæspə(r) /
Jed / dʒed / (*esp US*)
Jeff, Jeffrey ⇨ Geoffrey
Jeremy / ˈdʒerəmɪ /; Jerry / ˈdʒerɪ /
Jerome / dʒəˈrəʊm /
Jerry ⇨ Gerald, Jeremy
Jesse / ˈdʒesɪ / (*esp US*)
Jim, Jimmy ⇨ James
Jock ⇨ John
Joe ⇨ Joseph
John / dʒɒn /; Johnny / ˈdʒɒnɪ /; Jack / dʒæk /; Jake / dʒeɪk /; Jock / dʒɒk / (*Scot*)
Jonathan / ˈdʒɒnəθən /; Jon / dʒɒn /
Joseph / ˈdʒəʊzɪf /; Joe / dʒəʊ /
Julian / ˈdʒuːlɪən /
Justin / ˈdʒʌstɪn /
Keith / kiːθ /
Kenneth / ˈkenɪθ /; Ken / ken /; Kenny / ˈkenɪ /
Kevin / ˈkevɪn /; Kev / kev /
Kirk / kɜːk /
Kit ⇨ Christopher
Lance / lɑːns; *US* læns /
Laurence, Lawrence / ˈlɒrəns; *US* ˈlɔːr- /; Larry / ˈlærɪ /; Laurie / ˈlɒrɪ; *US* ˈlɔːrɪ /
Len, Lenny ⇨ Leonard
Leo / ˈliːəʊ /
Leonard / ˈlenəd /; Len / len /; Lenny / ˈlenɪ /
Leslie / ˈlezlɪ /; Les / lez /
Lester / ˈlestə(r) /
Lewis / ˈluːɪs /; Lew / luː /
Liam / ˈliːəm / (*Irish*)
Lionel / ˈlaɪənl /

Louis / ˈluːɪ; *US* ˈluːɪs /; Lou / luː / (*esp US*)
Luke / luːk /
Malcolm / ˈmælkəm /
Mark / mɑːk /
Martin / ˈmɑːtɪn; *US* ˈmɑːrtn /; Marty / ˈmɑːtɪ /
Matthew / ˈmæθjuː /; Matt / mæt /
Maurice, Morris / ˈmɒrɪs; *US* ˈmɔːrəs /
Max / mæks /
Mervyn / ˈmɜːvɪn /
Michael / ˈmaɪkl /; Mike / maɪk /; Mick / mɪk /; Micky, Mickey / ˈmɪkɪ /
Miles, Myles / maɪlz /
Mitchell / ˈmɪtʃl /; Mitch / mɪtʃ /
Morris ⇨ Maurice
Mort / mɔːt / (*US*)
Murray / ˈmʌrɪ / (*esp Scot*)
Myles ⇨ Miles
Nathan / ˈneɪθən /; Nat / næt /
Nathaniel / nəˈθænɪəl /; Nat / næt /
Neal ⇨ Neil
Ned, Neddy ⇨ Edward
Neil, Neal / niːl /
Nicholas, Nicolas / ˈnɪkələs; *US* ˈnɪkləs /; Nick / nɪk /; Nicky / ˈnɪkɪ /
Nigel / ˈnaɪdʒl /
Noel / ˈnəʊəl /
Norman / ˈnɔːmən /; Norm / nɔːm /
Oliver / ˈɒlɪvə(r) /; Ollie / ˈɒlɪ /
Oscar / ˈɒskə(r) /
Oswald / ˈɒzwəld /; Oz / ɒz /; Ozzie / ˈɒzɪ /
Owen / ˈəʊɪn / (*Welsh*)
Oz, Ozzie ⇨ Oswald

Patrick / ˈpætrɪk / (*esp Irish*); Pat / pæt /; Paddy / ˈpædɪ /
Paul / pɔːl /
Percy / ˈpɜːsɪ /
Peter / ˈpiːtə(r) /; Pete / piːt /
Philip / ˈfɪlɪp /; Phil / fɪl /
Quentin / ˈkwentɪn; *US* -tn /; Quintin / ˈkwɪntɪn; *US* -tn /
Ralph / rælf, *also, in British use,* reɪf /
Randolph, Randolf / ˈrændɒlf /; Randy / ˈrændɪ / (*esp US*)
Raphael / ˈræfeɪl /
Raymond / ˈreɪmənd /; Ray / reɪ /
Reginald / ˈredʒɪnəld /: Reg / redʒ /; Reggie / ˈredʒɪ /
Rex / reks /
Richard / ˈrɪtʃəd /; Dick / dɪk /; Dickie, Dicky / ˈdɪkɪ /; Rick / rɪk /; Ricky / ˈrɪkɪ /; Richie, Ritchie / ˈrɪtʃɪ /
Robert / ˈrɒbət /; Rob / rɒb /; Robbie / ˈrɒbɪ /; Bob / bɒb /; Bobby / ˈbɒbɪ /
Robin / ˈrɒbɪn /
Roderick / ˈrɒdrɪk /; Rod / rɒd /
Rodge ⇨ Roger
Rodney / ˈrɒdnɪ /; Rod / rɒd /
Roger / ˈrɒdʒə(r) /; Rodge / rɒdʒ /
Ronald / ˈrɒnəld /; Ron / rɒn /; Ronnie / ˈrɒnɪ /
Rory / ˈrɔːrɪ / (*Scot or Irish*)
Roy / rɔɪ /
Rudolph, Rudolf / ˈruːdɒlf /
Rufus / ˈruːfəs /
Rupert / ˈruːpət /
Russell / ˈrʌsl /; Russ / rʌs /

Samuel / ˈsæmjʊəl /; Sam / sæm /; Sammy / ˈsæmɪ /
Sandy ⇨ Alexander
Scott / skɒt /
Seamas, Seamus / ˈʃeɪməs / (*Irish*)
Sean / ʃɔːn / (*Irish or Scot*)
Sebastian / sɪˈbæstɪən /; Seb / seb /
Sidney, Sydney / ˈsɪdnɪ /; Sid / sɪd /
Simon / ˈsaɪmən /
Stanley / ˈstænlɪ /; Stan / stæn /
Stephen, Steven / ˈstiːvn /; Steve / stiːv /
Stewart, Stuart / ˈstjuːət; *US* ˈstuːərt /
Ted, Teddy ⇨ Edward
Terence / ˈterəns /; Terry / ˈterɪ /; Tel / tel /
Theodore / ˈθiːədɔː(r) /; Theo / ˈθiːəʊ /
Thomas / ˈtɒməs /; Tom / tɒm /; Tommy / ˈtɒmɪ /
Timothy / ˈtɪməθɪ /; Tim / tɪm /; Timmy / ˈtɪmɪ /
Toby / ˈtəʊbɪ /
Tom, Tommy ⇨ Thomas
Tony ⇨ Anthony
Trevor / ˈtrevə(r) /
Troy / trɔɪ /
Victor / ˈvɪktə(r) /; Vic / vɪk /
Vincent / ˈvɪnsnt /; Vince / vɪns /
Vivian / ˈvɪvɪən /; Viv / vɪv /
Walter / ˈwɔːltə(r), *also* ˈwɒltə(r) /; Wally / ˈwɒlɪ /
Warren / ˈwɒrən /
Wayne / weɪn /
Wilbur / ˈwɪlbə(r) / (*esp US*)
Wilfrid, Wilfred / ˈwɪlfrɪd /
William / ˈwɪlɪəm /; Bill / bɪl /; Billy / ˈbɪlɪ /; Will / wɪl /; Willy / ˈwɪlɪ /

APPENDIX 8

FAMILY RELATIONSHIPS

Jane's Family

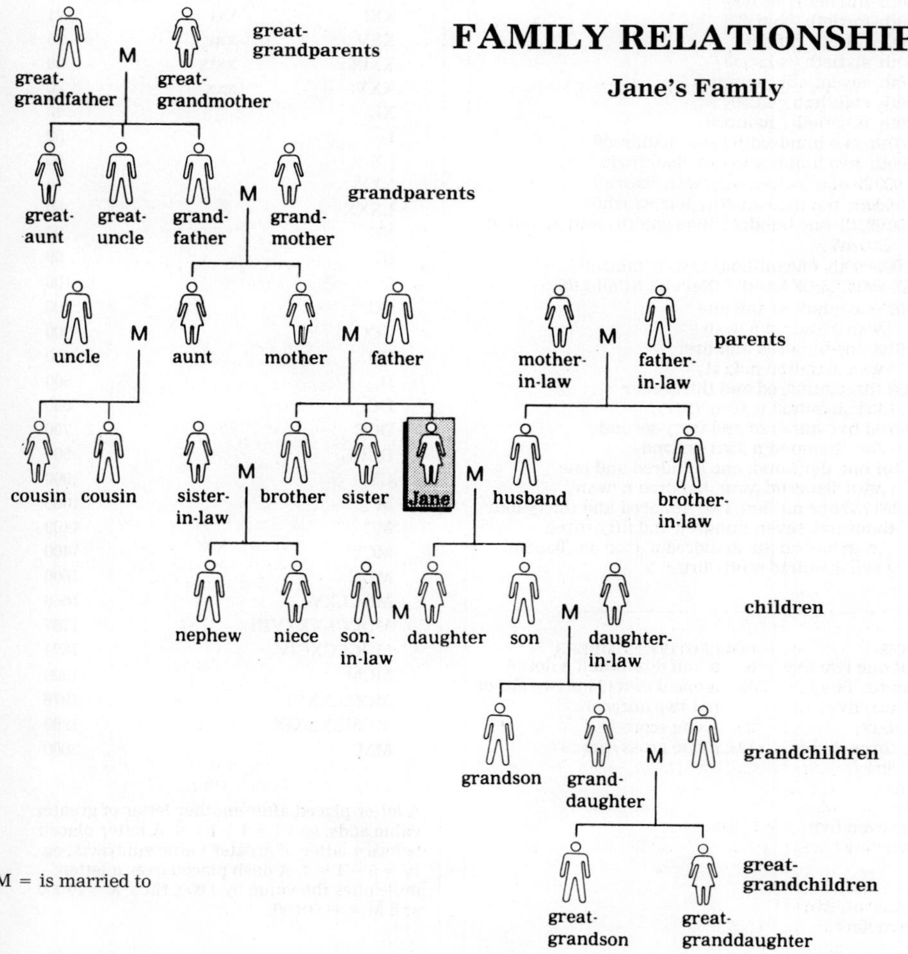

If Jane's husband dies or they get divorced, and Jane gets married a second time, her new husband will be the stepfather of her children and they will be his stepdaughter and stepson. If Jane and her second husband have a child, Jane's children will be the baby's half-brother and half-sister.

APPENDIX 9

NUMERICAL EXPRESSIONS

The following section gives help in the reading, speaking and writing of numbers and expressions which commonly contain numbers.

Numbers

CARDINAL

1 one / wʌn /
2 two / tuː /
3 three / θriː /
4 four / fɔː(r) /
5 five / faɪv /
6 six / sɪks /
7 seven / ˈsevn /
8 eight / eɪt /
9 nine / naɪn /
10 ten / ten /
11 eleven / ɪˈlevn /
12 twelve / twelv /
13 thirteen / ˌθɜːˈtiːn /
14 fourteen / ˌfɔːˈtiːn /
15 fifteen / ˌfɪfˈtiːn /
16 sixteen / ˌsɪkˈstiːn /
17 seventeen / ˌsevnˈtiːn /
18 eighteen / ˌeɪˈtiːn /
19 nineteen / ˌnaɪnˈtiːn /
20 twenty / ˈtwentɪ /
21 twenty-one / ˌtwentɪˈwʌn /
22 twenty-two / ˌtwentɪˈtuː /
23 twenty-three / ˌtwentɪˈθriː /
30 thirty / ˈθɜːtɪ /
40 forty / ˈfɔːtɪ /
50 fifty / ˈfɪftɪ /
60 sixty / ˈsɪkstɪ /
70 seventy / ˈsevntɪ /
80 eighty / ˈeɪtɪ /
90 ninety / ˈnaɪntɪ /
100 one hundred / wʌn ˈhʌndrəd /
200 two hundred / ˌtuː ˈhʌndrəd /
1 000 one thousand / wʌn ˈθaʊznd /
10 000 ten thousand / ˌten ˈθaʊznd /
100 000 one hundred thousand / wʌn ˌhʌndrəd ˈθaʊznd /
1 000 000 one million / wʌn ˈmɪlɪən /
1 000 000 000 one billion / wʌn ˈbɪlɪən /; (*dated esp Brit*) one thousand million(s) / wʌn ˌθaʊznd ˈmɪlɪən(z) /
1 000 000 000 000 one trillion / wʌn ˈtrɪlɪən /; (*dated esp Brit*) one billion / wʌn ˈbɪlɪən /
1 000 000 000 000 000 one quadrillion / wʌn kwɒˈdrɪlɪən / (*dated esp Brit*) one thousand billion(s) / wʌn ˌθaʊznd ˈbɪlɪən(z) /
1 000 000 000 000 000 000 one quintillion / wʌn kwɪnˈtɪlɪən /; (*dated esp Brit*) one trillion / wʌn ˈtrɪlɪən /

ORDINAL

1st first / fɜːst /
2nd second / ˈsekənd /
3rd third / θɜːd /
4th fourth / fɔːθ /
5th fifth / fɪfθ /
6th sixth / sɪksθ /
7th seventh / ˈsevənθ /
8th eighth / eɪtθ /
9th ninth / naɪnθ /
10th tenth / tenθ /
11th eleventh / ɪˈlevnθ /
12th twelfth / twelfθ /
13th thirteenth / ˌθɜːˈtiːnθ /
14th fourteenth / ˌfɔːˈtiːnθ /
15th fifteenth / ˌfɪfˈtiːnθ /
16th sixteenth / ˌsɪkˈstiːnθ /
17th seventeenth / ˌsevnˈtiːnθ /
18th eighteenth / ˌeɪˈtiːnθ /
19th nineteenth / ˌnaɪnˈtiːnθ /
20th twentieth / ˈtwentɪəθ /
21st twenty-first / ˌtwentɪˈfɜːst /
22nd twenty-second / ˌtwentɪˈsekənd /
23rd twenty-third / ˌtwentɪˈθɜːd /
30th thirtieth / ˈθɜːtɪəθ /
40th fortieth / ˈfɔːtɪəθ /
50th fiftieth / ˈfɪftɪəθ /
60th sixtieth / ˈsɪkstɪəθ /
70th seventieth / ˈsevntɪəθ /
80th eightieth / ˈeɪtɪəθ /
90th ninetieth / ˈnaɪntɪəθ /
100th one hundredth / wʌn ˈhʌndrədθ /
200th two hundredth / ˌtuː ˈhʌndrədθ /
1 000th one thousandth / wʌn ˈθaʊznθ /
10 000th ten thousandth / ˌten ˈθaʊznθ /
100 000th one hundred thousandth / wʌn ˌhʌndrəd ˈθaʊznθ /
1 000 000th one millionth / wʌn ˈmɪlɪənθ /

EXAMPLES OF MORE COMPLEX NUMBERS

101 one hundred and one / ˌwʌn ˌhʌndrəd n ˈwʌn /
101st one hundred and first / wʌn ˌhʌndrəd n ˈfɜːst /
334 three hundred and thirty-four / ˌθriː ˌhʌndrəd n ˌθɜːtɪ ˈfɔː(r) /
542nd five hundred and forty-second / ˌfaɪv ˌhʌndrəd n ˌfɔːtɪ ˈsekənd /
1 101 one thousand, one hundred and one / ˌwʌn ˈθaʊzənd ˌwʌn ˌhʌndrəd n ˈwʌn /
1 234 753 one million, two hundred and thirty-four thousand, seven hundred and fifty-three / ˌwʌn ˈmɪlɪən ˌtuː ˌhʌndrəd n ˌθɜːtɪ ˌfɔː ˈθaʊznd ˌsevn ˌhʌndrəd n fɪftɪ ˈθriː /

VULGAR FRACTIONS

$\frac{1}{8}$ an/one eighth / ən, wʌn ˈeɪtθ /
$\frac{1}{4}$ a/one quarter / ə, wʌn ˈkwɔːtə(r) /
$\frac{1}{3}$ a/one third / ə, wʌn ˈθɜːd /
$\frac{1}{2}$ a/one half / ə, wʌn ˈhɑːf; *US* ˈhæf /
$\frac{3}{4}$ three quarters / ˌθriː ˈkwɔːtəz /
$5\frac{1}{2}$ five and a half / ˌfaɪv ən ə ˈhɑːf; *US* ˈhæf /
$13\frac{3}{4}$ thirteen and three quarters / ˌθɜːtiːn ən θriː ˈkwɔːtəz /

DECIMAL FRACTIONS

0.125 (nought) point one two five / (ˌnɔːt) pɔɪnt ˌwʌn tuː ˈfaɪv /
0.25 (nought) point two five / (ˌnɔːt) pɔɪnt ˌtuː ˈfaɪv /
0.33 (nought) point three three / (ˌnɔːt) pɔɪnt θriː ˈθriː /
0.5 (nought) point five / (ˌnɔːt) pɔɪnt ˈfaɪv /
0.75 (nought) point seven five / (ˌnɔːt) pɔɪnt ˌsevn ˈfaɪv /
5.5 five point five / ˌfaɪv pɔɪnt ˈfaɪv /
13.75 thirteen point seven five / ˌθɜːtiːn pɔɪnt ˌsevn ˈfaɪv /

COLLECTIVE NUMBERS

6 a half dozen/half a dozen
12 a/one dozen (24 is two *dozen* not two *dozens*)
20 a/one score
144 a/one gross / grəʊs /

ROMAN		ARABIC
I	i	1
II	ii	2
III	iii	3
IV	iv	4
V	v	5
VI	vi	6
VII	vii	7
VIII	viii	8
IX	ix	9
X	x	10
XI	xi	11
XII	xii	12
XIII	xiii	13
XIV	xiv	14
XV	xv	15
XVI	xvi	16
XVII	xvii	17
XVIII	xviii	18
XIX	xix	19
XX	xx	20
XXI	xxi	21
XXV	xxv	25
XXIX	xxix	29
XXX	xxx	30
XL		40
L		50
LX		60
LXX		70
LXXX		80
XC		90
IC		99
C		100
CC		200
CCC		300
CD		400
D		500
DC		600
DCC		700
DCCC		800
CM		900
M		1000
MC		1100
MCD		1400
MDC		1600
MDCLXVI		1666
MDCCLXXXVIII		1788
MDCCCXCIV		1894
MCM		1900
MCMLXXVI		1976
MCMLXXXIX		1989
MM		2000

A letter placed after another letter of greater value adds, eg VI = 5 + 1 = 6. A letter placed before a letter of greater value subtracts, eg IV = 5 − 1 = 4. A dash placed over a letter multiplies the value by 1 000; thus $\overline{X}$ = 10 000 and $\overline{M}$ = 1 000 000.

Notes

1 In large numbers starting with *'one'* the indefinite article may be substituted in less formal use or when the number is not intended to be exact: *He's got over a thousand records.*

2 When saying ordinary numbers we can use *'zero'*, *'nought'* or *'o'* /əʊ/ for the number 0; *'zero'* is the most common US usage and the most technical or precise form; *'o'* is the least technical or precise. ⇨ Usage at NOUGHT.

3 A comma is sometimes used instead of a space to separate the thousands in numbers greater than 999: 1 000 / 1,000 10 000 / 10,000; 7 586 954 / 7,586,954.

4 Thousands may be spoken as hundreds, especially in informal use: *eleven hundred* (ie 1 100).

5 Long numbers (eg bank accounts, credit card numbers, etc) are spoken as separate digits grouped rhythmically in twos or threes: *o five four / eight six three / nine double six* (ie 054863966).

6 Names for numbers above *trillion* are rarely used. When larger numbers need to be expressed, eg in astronomy, this is usually done in terms of powers of ten, ie the number of zeros following the 10: *ten to the power fifteen / to the fifteenth (power)* (ie 10 000 000 000 000 000).

7 In the spoken forms of vulgar fractions, the versions *'and a half/quarter/third'* are preferred to *'and one half/quarter/third'* whether the measurement is approximate or precise. With more obviously precise fractions like $\frac{1}{8}$, $\frac{1}{16}$, *'and one eighth/sixteenth'* is normal. Complex fractions like $\frac{3}{462}$, $\frac{20}{83}$ are spoken as *'three over four-six-two; twenty over eighty-three'*, especially in mathematical expressions, eg *'twenty-two over seven'* for $\frac{22}{7}$ (π).

8 A point is used in writing decimal fractions (rather than a comma, as in continental Europe). The digits after the point are read by saying *'point'* and then each digit separately: *two hundred and seventy-three point two nine six* (ie 273.296). In decimal fractions less than one, the 'nought' (or 'zero') before the decimal point may be omitted: *(nought/zero) point seven five* (ie 0.75).

Mathematical Expressions

Where alternative ways of saying the expressions are given, the first is generally more formal or technical

+	plus / and
−	minus / take away
±	plus or minus
×	(is) multiplied by / times (*or, when giving dimensions*, by)
÷	(is) divided by
=	is equal to / equals
≠	is not equal to / does not equal
≃	is approximately equal to
≡	is equivalent to / is identical with
<	is less than
≮	is not less than
⩽	is less than or equal to
>	is more than
≯	is not more than
⩾	is more than or equal to
%	per cent
∞	infinity
∝	varies as / is proportional to
3:9: :4:12	three is to nine as four is to twelve
$\log_e$	natural logarithm *or* logarithm to the base e / iː /
√	(square) root
∛	cube root
x^2	x / eks / squared
x^3	x / eks / cubed
x^4	x / eks / to the power of four / to the fourth
π	pi / paɪ /
r	/ ɑː(r) / = radius of a circle
∫	the integral of
°	degree
′	minute (of an arc); foot *or* feet (unit of length)
″	second (of an arc); inch *or* inches (unit of length)

Numbers in Measurements

A: LINEAR MEASUREMENT

symb	*abbr*	*full word*
″	in	inch(es)
′	ft	foot/feet
	yd	yard
	ml (*US* mi)	mile(s)
	mm	millimetre(s)
	cm	centimetre(s)
	m	metre(s)
	km	kilometre(s)

Typical measurements

(i) Building

a piece of wood $\frac{1}{8}$″ thick
a piece of glass 7 mm thick

(ii) Rainfall

$1\frac{1}{2}$″ of rain in 24 hours
less than 600 mm of rain a year

(iii) Vital statistics

She's 36-24-38 (ie the circumference of her bust, waist and hips is 36, 24 and 38 inches respectively).

(iv) Clothing

He takes a $16\frac{1}{2}$ collar (ie his neck is $16\frac{1}{2}$ inches in circumference).

(v) Height of people

She's about 5 ft 6 in (tall).
The average height of the tribe is less than 1 m 20 cm.
Note: When referring to people, *'tall'* is used, not *'high'*, and measurements are given in feet and inches (but *not* yards) or metres and centimetres.

(vi) Height of objects

Maximum headroom 7′ $2\frac{1}{2}$″ or 2.2 m (ie passage is limited to vehicles of less than this height).
Ben Nevis is 4 406 ft high.
The road rises to 2 288 m above sea-level.

(vii) Dimensions

a baking dish measuring 9″ × 8″
A4 paper is 297 × 210 mm.
a room 16 feet (wide) by 25 feet (long)

(viii) Distance

about 100 yds down the road
a bridge 695 metres long
New York is 2 915 miles from Los Angeles by road.
The Amazon is more than 6 450 km long.

(ix) Speed

a speed limit of 30 mph
Sound travels at 331.7 metres per second.
Light travels 186 300 miles in a second.

B: AREA MEASUREMENT

abbr	*full word*	*symb*
sq in	square inch(es)	
sq ft	square foot/feet	
sq yd	square yard	
sq ml	square mile(s)	
	acre	
sq mm	square millimetre(s)	mm^2
sq cm	square centimetre(s)	cm^2
sq m	square metre(s)	m^2
sq km	square kilometre(s)	km^2
ha	hectare(s)	

Typical measurements

We require 5 000 sq ft of office space.
Light industrial lot (600 m²) for lease.
Dartmoor covers an area of more than 350 square miles in SW England.
Greater London is an administrative area of 1 610 sq km(s).
a house for sale with 10 acres of grounds
more than 500 hectares of orchard

C: VOLUME MEASUREMENT

abbr	*full word*
cu in	cubic inch(es)
cu ft	cubic foot/feet
cu yd	cubic yard

symb	*full word*
mm^3	cubic millimetre(s)
cc, cm^3	cubic centimetre(s)
m^3	cubic metre(s)

Typical measurements

a 1300 cc engine (ie the total capacity of the cylinders is 1 300 cubic centimetres)
You'll need 30 cubic feet of sand to mix with the cement.
a tunnelling machine capable of removing 400 m³ of earth an hour

D: LIQUID MEASUREMENT

abbr	*full name*
fl oz	fluid ounce(s)
pt	pint
qt	quart(s)
gall	gallon(s)
ml	millilitre(s)
cl	centilitre(s)
l	litre(s)

Typical measurements

Add 8 fl oz stock and bring to the boil.
The standard wine bottle contains 75 cl.
Three pints of bitter and half (a pint) of lager, please.
You'll need about five litres of paint for this room.
a car averaging 33 miles per gallon (ie that requires approximately 1 gallon of petrol to drive 33 miles)

E: WEIGHT MEASUREMENT

abbr	*full name*
oz	ounce(s)
lb	pound(s)
st	stone
	quarter
cwt	hundredweight
	ton
g/gm	gram(s)
kg	kilo(gram)(s)
	metric ton (tonne)

Typical measurements

Add 4 oz (100 gms) finely chopped ham.
Four pounds of potatoes and a pound of carrots, please.
(Brit) My brother weighs 12 stone eleven (pounds).
(US) My brother weighs 183 pounds.
Note: People's weight is usually measured in stone and pounds in Britain and in pounds only in the USA.
Maximum baggage allowance: 32 kg
half a hundredweight of gravel
a 10-ton lorry (ie a lorry that can carry a maximum load of ten tons)

Measurement of Temperature

Temperatures in Britain were traditionally measured by the Fahrenheit scale (°F). Although the Celsius or centigrade system (°C) is now officially in use, many people continue to refer informally to degrees Fahrenheit. The Fahrenheit scale is still used in the USA for non-scientific purposes.

The temperature will fall to minus five tonight. (−5°C)
They say we're going to have nine degrees of frost tonight. (23°F)
It must be ninety-five this afternoon. (95°F)
The normal temperature of the human body is 37°C.
She's ill in bed with a temperature of a hundred and two. (102°F)

Numbers in Measuring Time

A: AGE

He's 33 (years old).
The suspect is believed to be aged about twenty-seven.
a man in his thirties (ie between 30 and 39 years old)
He looks fortyish (ie about 40 years old).
She's in her early/middle/late teens (ie 13–15/15–17/17–19 years old).
'How old's your youngest child?'
'She's one year and three months/fifteen months (old).'
a two-week-old baby

B: TIME OF DAY

The twelve hour system is most widely used:

7.00	*seven o'clock; seven am/pm*
8.15	*eight fifteen; a quarter past eight* (*US* also *a quarter after eight*)
9.45	*nine forty-five; a quarter to ten* (*US* also *a quarter of ten*)
4.30	*four thirty*; (*esp Brit*) *half past four*; (*infml*) *half four*
5.10	*five ten; ten (minutes) past five*; (*US* also *ten after five*)
6.35	*six thirty-five; twenty-five (minutes) to seven*
8.03	*eight o three; three minutes past eight*
9.55	*nine fifty-five; five (minutes) to ten*; (*US* also *five of ten*)

The twenty-four hour clock is used in travel timetables, official communiqués, military communications, etc:

0700/07.00	
(ˌo) ˌseven ˈhundred (hours)	(7.00 am)
1030/10.30	
ˌten ˈthirty	(10.30 am)
1200/12.00	
ˌtwelve ˈhundred (hours)	(midday/noon)
1345/13.45	
ˌthirteen ˌforty-ˈfive	(1.45 pm)
1515/15.15	
ˌfifteen ˌfifˈteen	(3.15 pm)
1900/19.00	
ˌnineteen ˈhundred (hours)	(7.00 pm)
2250/22.50	
ˌtwenty-ˌtwo ˈfifty	(10.50 pm)
2305/23.05	
ˌtwenty-ˌthree ˌo ˈfive	(11.05 pm)
2400/24.00	
ˌtwenty-four ˈhundred (hours)	(midnight)
0000/00.00	
ˌo ˌo ˈdouble o	(midnight)

C: DURATION

symb	abbr	full word
"	sec	second
'	min	minute
	hr	hour

The car does 0 to 60 in 4.5 secs (ie it will accelerate from a stop to 60 miles per hour in four and a half seconds).

The winning runner completed the course in 2 mins 15 secs.

D: DATES

2000 BC/two thousand BC
AD 55/AD fifty-five
Queen Elizabeth I 1558–1603
Queen Elizabeth the First reigned from fifteen (hundred and) fifty-eight to sixteen (hundred and) three / sixteen o three.
(*Brit*) *3rd/3 January 1989: the third of January / January the third, nineteen eighty-nine.*
(*US*) *January 3, 1989: January third, nineteen eighty-nine.*
(*Brit*) 21.3.47; 21/3/47; (*US*) 3.21.47 = 21 March 1947

Numbers in Sport

A: SPORTS USING LINEAR MEASURE

(i) Athletics

He holds the world record for the fifteen hundred metres / the metric mile. (1 500 m)
She ran for her country in the women's two hundred metre hurdles. (200 m)
Our team was narrowly beaten in the four by four hundred metres relay. (4 × 400 m)
He won a bronze medal in the high jump, clearing a height of two point o five metres. (2.05 m)

(ii) Swimming

I swam for my school in the eight hundred metres free-style. (800 m)
She came second in the women's hundred metres backstroke. (100 m)

(iii) Horse-racing

The Derby is run over a distance of twelve furlongs/one mile four furlongs/one and a half miles/a mile and a half. (8 furlongs = 1 mile)
The winner of the 3.30 at Cheltenham was 'Never Say Die', a fourteen to one outsider; the favourite, 'Moonshine', was second at five to two; eleven ran (ie the race that started at 3.30 pm at Cheltenham race-track was won by a horse called 'Never Say Die', on which the odds were 14–1 against; the horse most favoured by betters, 'Moonshine', came second, at odds of 5–2 on; a total of eleven horses ran in the race).

B: SPORTS USING OTHER SCORING METHODS

(i) Tennis

Miss Smith won the first set six four / by six games to four (6-4). She dropped the second set seven six (7-6) after a tie-break, but won the deciding set six three (6-3). The scoring in the final game was fifteen love (15-0), fifteen all (15-15), fifteen thirty (15-30), thirty all (30-30), forty thirty (40-30), deuce (40-40), advantage Miss Smith, game to Miss Smith. Miss Smith won by two sets to one (2-1), six four, six seven, six three.

(ii) (Association) Football; Soccer

In the second half Watford scored twice to equalize (2-2), but five minutes from time (ie after 85 minutes of play), *Bryant scored from a penalty to give Arsenal a three two victory / victory by three goals to two (3-2). Tottenham, at home to Chelsea, were held to a goalless draw / drew nil nil (0-0).*

(iii) Rugby (football)

Wales beat Scotland sixteen six/by sixteen points to six (16-6). For Wales, Owen scored two tries (4 points each = 8 points). *Price converted the second try* (2 points) *and kicked two penalty goals* (3 points each = 6 points). *Scotland's score came from a penalty and a dropped goal* (3 points), *both kicked by Frazer.*

(iv) American football

In the third quarter, the Dallas quarterback threw a 67-yard pass for a touchdown (6 points). *The conversion* (1 point made by kicking a goal after a touchdown) *was good, giving them a seven point lead. In the final quarter, Miami ran the ball in from the six yard line to even the score (7-7), but ten seconds from the end Dallas kicked a 49-yard field goal* (3 points) *to win by ten points to seven.*

(v) Basketball

Our team was leading (by) twenty-seven (points) to twenty-two (27-22) at half-time but we gave away too many penalties in the second half, and our opponents won fifty-eight fifty-six (58-56).

(vi) Baseball

The Yankees scored in the third inning on a base hit to left field. A home run by the Red Sox at the bottom (ie second half) *of the fifth (inning) tied the game, until an error by Boston's third baseman gave New York a winning run late in the game.*
Final score: New York two, Boston one.

(vii) Golf

Palmer and Jackson share the lead on 75 at the end of the first round. Palmer was trailing until he birdied the 14th hole (ie completed it in one stroke less than par), *and then sank a 22-foot putt at the 16th. Jackson then failed to hole from 5 feet at the 18th.*

(viii) Cricket

England are 187 for three at tea (ie the team have scored 187 runs and three batsmen have been dismissed), *210 behind the New Zealand first innings total of 397 all out* (ie a score of 397 runs after 10 batsmen were dismissed). *Gatting is not out 42* (ie he has scored 42 runs and his innings will continue). *Broad was caught at the wicket four runs short of a century* (ie he scored 96 runs before being dismissed). *Hadlee finished the session with figures of 2 for 26* (ie this New Zealand bowler dismissed two England batsmen while 26 runs were scored from the balls he bowled).

Numbers in Using Money

A: BRITAIN

100 pence (100p) = 1 pound (£1)

symb	*full name*	*infml name*	*coin/note*
1p	a/one penny	one p	a penny
2p	two pence twopence /ˈtʌpəns/	two p	a twopenny piece
5p	five pence	five p	a fivepenny piece
10p	ten pence	ten p	a tenpenny piece
20p	twenty pence	twenty p	a twenty pence piece
50p	fifty pence	fifty p	a fifty pence piece
£1	a pound	a quid	a pound coin
£5	five pounds	five quid a fiver	a five pound note (*infml*) a fiver
£10	ten pounds	ten quid a tenner	a ten pound note (*infml*) a tenner
£20	twenty pounds	twenty quid	a twenty pound note
£3.82	three (pounds) eighty-two		

I paid ten pence each for them.
Coffee's 35p a cup.
Admission: £2 (adults), 50p (children)
It costs a couple of quid to get in, but only fifty p for the kids.
We'll have to charge you a ten pound refundable deposit.
A meal for two will set you back a good thirty pounds/thirty pounds odd/somewhere in the region of thirty pounds.

Notes

1) The penny symbol (*p* /piː/) is never used when writing a sum of money which begins with the pound sign: *£6.25*; *£106.00*; *£0.75*.
2) In informal use, the words *pound(s)* and *pence* are often omitted: *He charged me three fifty (£3.50). They're reduced from a hundred and fifteen ninety-five to ninety-nine ninety-five* (from £115.95 to £99.95).
3) In informal use, sums between £1100 and £1 900 may be spoken as hundreds: *This car's only twelve hundred quid* (ie £1 200).

B: USA AND CANADA

100 cents (¢) = 1 dollar ($)

symb	*full name*	*coin/note*
$0.01 / 1¢	one cent	a penny
$0.05 / 5¢	five cents	a nickel
$0.10 / 10¢	ten cents	a dime
$0.25 / 25¢	twenty-five cents	a quarter
$0.50 / 50¢	fifty cents	a half-dollar a fifty-cent piece
$1/$1.00	one dollar (*infml*) a buck	a dollar bill a one
$5	five dollars	a five (dollar bill)
$10	ten dollars	a ten (dollar bill)
$20	twenty dollars	a twenty (dollar bill)
$50	fifty dollars	a fifty (dollar bill)
$100	a/one hundred dollars	a hundred (dollar bill)
$3.82	three dollars (and) eight-two (cents)	

I bought it for a nickel.
You'll need a couple of quarters for the phone.
Coffee's eighty cents a cup.
They cost me a couple of bucks each.
Can you change this ten for a five and five ones?
I enclose a check for fifty dollars.

Notes

1) The cents symbol(¢) is never used when writing a sum of money which begins with the dollar sign: *$6.25; $106.00; $0.75.*
2) In informal use, the words *dollar(s)* and *cent(s)* are often omitted: *He charged me three fifty* ($3.50). *It's reduced from a hundred and fifteen ninety-five to ninety-nine ninety-five* (ie from $115.95 to $99.95).
3) Especially in informal use, sums between $1100 and $1 900 may be spoken as hundreds: *He earns less than sixteen hundred (dollars) a month.*
4) In informal and esp dated use, *ˌtwo ˈbits* = $0.25, *ˌfour ˈbits* = $0.50 and *ˌsix ˈbits* = $0.75. These expressions are not used in combinations: *I left two bits as a tip* but *I lent him a dollar twenty-five / one dollar and a quarter.*

Numbers in Telephoning

A: BRITAIN

Telephone numbers consist of a four-digit *national code* and/or the name of the *(telephone) exchange* followed by a three- to seven-digit number: *Oxford (0865) 56767.* The national code (also known as the *STD code*) is used when making a call outside the local area. Telephones in some large cities, eg London, have a two or three-digit national code followed by a seven-digit number: *071-246 8022.*

Both codes and numbers are spoken as a series of separate digits, 0 being pronounced /əʊ/: *ˌo ˌeight ˌsix ˈfive, ˌfive ˌsix ˌseven ˌsix ˈseven; ˌo ˌseven ˈone, ˌtwo ˌfour ˈsix, ˌeight ˌo ˌdouble ˈtwo.* When giving a telephone number on the phone, the exchange rather than the code is used: *Oxford five six seven six seven.*

B: USA AND CANADA

Telephone numbers consist of a three-digit *area code* followed by a seven-digit number. The area code is only used when dialling from one region to another (ie when *calling long distance/making a long-distance call*) and is often omitted when the number is spoken or written. If included, it is written in parentheses before the individual number, the first three digits of which are separated from the last four by a hyphen: *(202) 234-5678.* Both the area code and the prefix are spoken as a series of three separate numbers, 0 being pronounced /əʊ/, or said as *zero* or *nought*: *ˌtwo ˌo ˈtwo, ˌtwo ˌthree ˈfour.* The last four digits may be spoken either as separate numbers (*ˌfive ˈsix ˌseven ˈeight*) or as two sets of tens (*ˌfifty-ˈsix ˌseventy-ˈeight*). If the last four digits end in 00 or 000, they are usually treated as hundreds or thousands: *ˌfive ˌo ˈtwo, ˌfive ˌsix ˈhundred* (502-5600); *ˌfour ˌnine ˈnine, ˌfive ˈthousand* (499-5000).

Note

Business firms, etc often have a single telephone number from which callers may be connected to a three- or four-digit internal *extension (number)*: *Oxford 56767 Ext 429; (202) 234-5678 (x301).*

APPENDIX 10

WEIGHTS AND MEASURES

The Metric System

METRIC		GB & US
	length	
10 millimetres (mm)	= 1 centimetre (cm)	= 0.394 inch (in)
100 centimetres	= 1 metre (m)	= 39.4 inches or 1.094 yards (yd)
1000 metres	= 1 kilometre (km)	= 0.6214 mile or about ⅝ mile
	surface	
100 square metres (m²)	= 1 are (a)	= 0.025 acre
100 ares	= 1 hectare (ha)	= 2.471 acres
100 hectares	= 1 square kilometre (km²)	= 0.386 square mile
	weight	
10 milligrams (mg)	= 1 centigram (cg)	= 0.154 grain
100 centigrams	= 1 gram (g)	= 15.43 grains
1000 grams	= 1 kilogram (kg)	= 2.205 pounds
1000 kilograms	= 1 tonne	= 19.688 hundredweight
	capacity	
1000 millilitres (ml)	= 1 litre (l)	= 1.76 pints (2.1 US pints)
10 litres	= 1 decalitre (dl)	= 2.2 gallons (2.63 US gallons)

Avoirdupois Weight

GB & US		METRIC
	1 grain (gr)	= 0.065 gram (g)
437½ grains	= 1 ounce (oz)	= 28.35 grams
16 drams (dr)	= 1 ounce	= 28.35 grams
16 ounces	= 1 pound (lb)	= 0.454 kilogram (kg)
14 pounds	= 1 stone (st)	= 6.356 kilograms
2 stone	= 1 quarter	= 12.7 kilograms
4 quarters	= 1 hundredweight (cwt)	= 50.8 kilograms
112 pounds	= 1 hundredweight	= 50.8 kilograms
100 pounds	= 1 short hundredweight (US)	= 45.4 kilograms
20 hundredweight	= 1 ton	= 1016.04 kilograms
2000 pounds	= 1 short ton	= 0.907 tonne
2240 pounds	= 1 long ton	= 1.016 tonnes

Linear Measure

GB & US		METRIC
	1 inch (in)	= 25.4 millimetres (mm)
12 inches	= 1 foot (ft)	= 30.48 centimetres (cm)
3 feet	= 1 yard (yd)	= 0.914 metre (m)
5½ yards	= 1 rod, pole or perch	= 5.029 metres
22 yards	= 1 chain (ch)	= 20.17 metres
220 yards	= 1 furlong (fur)	= 201.17 metres
8 furlongs	= 1 mile	= 1.609 kilometres (km)
1760 yards	= 1 mile	= 1.609 kilometres
3 miles	= 1 league	= 4.828 kilometres

Square Measure

GB & US		METRIC
	1 square (sq) inch	= 6.452 sq centimetres
144 sq inches	= 1 sq foot	= 929.03 sq centimetres
9 sq feet	= 1 sq yard	= 0.836 sq metre
484 sq yards	= 1 sq chain	= 404.62 sq metres
4840 sq yards	= 1 acre	= 0.405 hectare
40 sq rods	= 1 rood	= 10.1168 ares
4 roods	= 1 acre	= 0.405 hectare
640 acres	= 1 sq mile	= 2.59 sq kilometres or 259 hectares

Cubic Measure

GB & US		METRIC
	1 cubic (cu) inch	= 16.39 cu centimetres
1728 cu inches	= 1 cu foot	= 0.028 cu metre
27 cu feet	= 1 cu yard	= 0.765 cu metre

Nautical Measure

used for measuring the depth and surface distance of seas, rivers, etc

GB & US		METRIC
6 feet	= 1 fathom	= 1.829 metres
608 feet (in the British Navy)	= 1 cable	= 185.31 metres
720 feet (in the US Navy)	= 1 cable	= 219.46 metres
6080 feet	= nautical (or sea) mile (1.151 statute miles)	= 1.852 kilometres
3 sea miles	= 1 sea league	= 5.55 kilometres
60 sea miles	= 1 degree (69.047 statute miles)	
360 degrees	= 1 circle	

The speed of one sea mile per hour is called a *knot.*

Measure of Capacity

	GB	US	METRIC
4 gills	= 1 pint (pt)	= 1.201 pints	= 0.568 litre
2 pints	= 1 quart (qt)	= 1.201 quarts	= 1.136 litres
4 quarts	= 1 gallon (gal)	= 1.201 gallons	= 4.546 litres

Circular or Angular Measure

60 seconds (″)	= 1 minute (′)	90 degrees	= 1 quadrant or right angle (∟)
60 minutes	= 1 degree (°)	360 degrees	= 1 circle or circumference

the diameter of a circle	= the straight line passing through its centre
the radius of a circle	= ½ × the diameter
the circumference of a circle	= 22/7 × the diameter

Time

60 seconds	= 1 minute (min)	4 weeks, or 28 days	= 1 lunar month (mth)
60 minutes	= 1 hour (hr)	52 weeks, 1 day; or 13 lunar months, 1 day	= 1 year (yr)
24 hours	= 1 day	365 days, 6 hours	= 1 (Julian) year
7 days	= 1 week (wk)		

Temperature Equivalents

	FAHRENHEIT (F)	CELSIUS OR CENTIGRADE (C)
Boiling-point	212°	100°
	194°	90°
	176°	80°
	158°	70°
	140°	60°
	122°	50°
	104°	40°
	86°	30°
	68°	20°
	50°	10°
Freezing-point	32°	0°
	14°	−10°
	0°	−17.8°
Absolute Zero	−459.67°	−273.15°

To convert Fahrenheit temperature into Celsius or centigrade: subtract 32 and multiply by 5/9 (five-ninths).
To convert Celsius or centigrade temperature into Fahrenheit: multiply by 9/5 (nine-fifths) and add 32.

APPENDIX 11

THE CHEMICAL ELEMENTS

element	*symbol*	*atomic number*
actinium	Ac	89
aluminium	Al	13
americium	Am	95
antimony	Sb	51
argon	Ar	18
arsenic	As	33
astatine	At	85
barium	Ba	56
berkelium	Bk	97
beryllium	Be	4
bismuth	Bi	83
boron	B	5
bromine	Br	35
cadmium	Cd	48
caesium	Cs	55
calcium	Ca	20
californium	Cf	98
carbon	C	6
cerium	Ce	58
chlorine	Cl	17
chromium	Cr	24
cobalt	Co	27
copper	Cu	29
curium	Cm	96
dysprosium	Dy	66
einsteinium	Es	99
erbium	Er	68
europium	Eu	63
fermium	Fm	100
fluorine	F	9
francium	Fr	87
gadolinium	Gd	64
gallium	Ga	31
germanium	Ge	32
gold	Au	79
hafnium	Hf	72
hahnium	Ha	105
helium	He	2
holmium	Ho	67
hydrogen	H	1
indium	In	49
iodine	I	53
iridium	Ir	77
iron	Fe	26
krypton	Kr	36
lanthanum	La	57
lawrencium	Lr	103
lead	Pb	82
lithium	Li	3
lutetium	Lu	71
magnesium	Mg	12
manganese	Mn	25
mendelevium	Md	101
mercury	Hg	80
molybdenum	Mo	42
neodymium	Nd	60
neon	Ne	10
neptunium	Np	93
nickel	Ni	28
niobium	Nb	41
nitrogen	N	7
nobelium	No	102
osmium	Os	76
oxygen	O	8
palladium	Pd	46
phosphorus	P	15
platinum	Pt	78
plutonium	Pu	94
polonium	Po	84
potassium	K	19
praseodymium	Pr	59
promethium	Pm	61
protactinium	Pa	91
radium	Ra	88
radon	Rn	86
rhenium	Re	75
rhodium	Rh	45
rubidium	Rb	37
ruthenium	Ru	44
rutherfordium	Rf	104
samarium	Sm	62
scandium	Sc	21
selenium	Se	34
silicon	Si	14
silver	Ag	47
sodium	Na	11
strontium	Sr	38
sulphur	S	16
tantalum	Ta	73
technetium	Tc	43
tellurium	Te	52
terbium	Tb	65
thallium	Tl	81
thorium	Th	90
thulium	Tm	69
tin	Sn	50
titanium	Ti	22
tungsten	W	74
uranium	U	92
vanadium	V	23
xenon	Xe	54
ytterbium	Yb	70
yttrium	Y	39
zinc	Zn	30
zirconium	Zr	40

APPENDIX 12

THE SI UNITS

The International System of Units (Système International d'Unités—SI) is an internationally agreed system of measurement that uses seven base units, with two supplementary units.
All other SI units are derived from the seven base units. In addition, multiples and sub-multiples (= fractions) of units are expressed by the use of approved affixes.

Base units

physical quantity	*name*	*symbol*
length	metre	m
mass	kilogram	kg
time	second	s
electric current	ampere	A
thermodynamic temperature	kelvin	K
luminous intensity	candela	cd
amount of substance	mole	mol

Supplementary units

physical quantity	*name*	*symbol*
plane angle	radian	rad
solid angle	steradian	sr

Affixes

multiple	*affix*	*symbol*	*sub-multiple*	*affix*	*symbol*
10	deca-	da	10^{-1}	deci-	d
10^2	hecto-	h	10^{-2}	centi-	c
10^3	kilo-	k	10^{-3}	milli-	m
10^6	mega-	M	10^{-6}	micro-	μ
10^9	giga-	G	10^{-9}	nano-	n
10^{12}	tera-	T	10^{-12}	pico-	p
10^{15}	peta-	P	10^{-15}	femto-	f
10^{18}	exa-	E	10^{-18}	atto-	a

APPENDIX 13

IRREGULAR VERBS

This appendix lists all the verbs with irregular forms that are included in the dictionary, except for those formed with a hyphenated prefix (eg *pre-set*, *re-lay*) and the modal verbs (eg *can*, *must*). Verbs shown in ordinary type (eg mishear) are 'derivative' verbs, with the same irregular forms as the 'base' verb which is shown in dark type (eg **hear**). Irregular forms that are only used in certain senses are marked with an asterisk, eg *abode. Full information on usage, pronunciation, etc will be found at the dictionary entries.

Infinitive	Past Tense	Past Participle
abide	abided, *abode	abided, *abode
arise	arose	arisen
awake	awoke	awoken
backbite	backbit	backbitten
backslide	backslid	backslid
be	was/were	been
bear	bore	borne
beat	beat	beaten
become	became	become
befall	befell	befallen
beget	begot, (*arch*) begat	begotten
begin	began	begun
behold	beheld	beheld
bend	bent	bent
beseech	besought, beseeched	besought, beseeched
beset	beset	beset
bespeak	bespoke	bespoke, bespoken
bestride	bestrode	bestridden
bet	bet, betted	bet, betted
bid	*bade, bid	*bidden, bid
bind	bound	bound
bite	bit	bitten
bleed	bled	bled
bless	blessed	blessed, blest
blow	blew	blown, *blowed
break	broke	broken
breed	bred	bred
bring	brought	brought
broadcast	broadcast	broadcast
browbeat	browbeat	browbeaten
build	built	built
burn	burnt, burned	burnt, burned
burst	burst	burst
bust	bust, busted	bust, busted
buy	bought	bought
cast	cast	cast
catch	caught	caught
chide	chided, chid	chided, chid, chidden
choose	chose	chosen
cleave[1]	cleaved, clove, cleft	cleaved, cloven, cleft
cleave[2]	cleaved, clave	cleaved
cling	clung	clung
come	came	come
cost	cost	cost
countersink	countersank	countersunk
creep	crept	crept
crow	crowed, (*arch*) crew	crowed
cut	cut	cut
deal	dealt	dealt
dig	dug	dug
dive	dived; (*US*) dove	dived
do[1,2]	did	done
draw	drew	drawn
dream	dreamt, dreamed	dreamt, dreamed
drink	drank	drunk
drive	drove	driven
dwell	dwelt	dwelt
eat	ate	eaten
fall	fell	fallen
feed	fed	fed
feel	felt	felt
fight	fought	fought
find	found	found
flee	fled	fled
fling	flung	flung
floodlight	floodlighted, floodlit	floodlighted, floodlit
fly	flew	flown
forbear	forbore	forborne
forbid	forbade, forbad	forbidden
forecast	forecast, forecasted	forecast, forecasted
foresee	foresaw	foreseen
foretell	foretold	foretold
forget	forgot	forgotten
forgive	forgave	forgiven
forsake	forsook	forsaken
forswear	forswore	forsworn
freeze	froze	frozen
gainsay	gainsaid	gainsaid
get	got	got; (*US*) gotten
gild	gilded, (*arch*) gilt	gilded, (*arch*) gilt
gird	girded, girt	girded, girt
give	gave	given
go	went	gone
grind	ground	ground
grow	grew	grown
hamstring	hamstringed, hamstrung	hamstringed, hamstrung
hang	hung, *hanged	hung, *hanged
have	had	had
hear	heard	heard
heave	heaved, hove	heaved, hove
hew	hewed	hewed, hewn
hide	hid	hidden
hit	hit	hit
hold	held	held
hurt	hurt	hurt
inlay	inlaid	inlaid
input	input, inputted	input, inputted
inset	inset	inset
interweave	interwove	interwoven
keep	kept	kept
ken	kenned, kent	kenned
kneel	knelt; (*esp US*) kneeled	knelt; (*esp US*) kneeled
knit	knitted, *knit	knitted, *knit
know	knew	known
lay	laid	laid
lead	led	led
lean	leant, leaned	leant, leaned
leap	leapt, leaped	leapt, leaped
learn	learnt, learned	learnt, learned
leave	left	left
lend	lent	lent
let	let	let
lie[2]	lay	lain
light	lighted, lit	lighted, lit
lose	lost	lost
make	made	made
mean	meant	meant
meet	met	met
miscast	miscast	miscast
misdeal	misdealt	misdealt
mishear	misheard	misheard
mishit	mishit	mishit
mislay	mislaid	mislaid
mislead	misled	misled
misread /ˌmɪsˈriːd/	misread /ˌmɪsˈred/	misread /ˌmɪsˈred/
misspell	misspelt, misspelled	misspelt, misspelled
misspend	misspent	misspent
mistake	mistook	mistaken
misunderstand	misunderstood	misunderstood
mow	mowed	mown, mowed
outbid	outbid	outbid
outdo	outdid	outdone
outfight	outfought	outfought
outgrow	outgrew	outgrown
output	output, outputted	output, outputted
outrun	outran	outrun
outsell	outsold	outsold
outshine	outshone	outshone
overbid	overbid	overbid
overcome	overcame	overcome
overdo	overdid	overdone
overdraw	overdrew	overdrawn

Infinitive	Past Tense	Past Participle
overeat	overate	overeaten
overfly	overflew	overflown
overhang	overhung	overhung
overhear	overheard	overheard
overlay	overlaid	overlaid
overpay	overpaid	overpaid
override	overrode	overridden
overrun	overran	overrun
oversee	oversaw	overseen
overshoot	overshot	overshot
oversleep	overslept	overslept
overtake	overtook	overtaken
overthrow	overthrew	overthrown
partake	partook	partaken
pay	paid	paid
plead	pleaded; (*US*) pled	pleaded; (*US*) pled
prepay	prepaid	prepaid
prove	proved	proved; (*US*) proven
put	put	put
quit	quit, quitted	quit, quitted
read /ri:d/	read /red/	read /red/
rebind	rebound	rebound
rebuild	rebuilt	rebuilt
recast	recast	recast
redo	redid	redone
rehear	reheard	reheard
remake	remade	remade
rend	rent	rent
repay	repaid	repaid
rerun	reran	rerun
resell	resold	resold
reset	reset	reset
resit	resat	resat
retake	retook	retaken
retell	retold	retold
rewrite	rewrote	rewritten
rid	rid	rid
ride	rode	ridden
ring	rang	rung
rise	rose	risen
run	ran	run
saw	sawed	sawn; (*US*) sawed
say	said	said
see	saw	seen
seek	sought	sought
sell	sold	sold
send	sent	sent
set	set	set
sew	sewed	sewn, sewed
shake	shook	shaken
shear	sheared	shorn, sheared
shed	shed	shed
shine	shone, *shined	shone, *shined
shit	shitted, shat	shitted, shat
shoe	shod	shod
shoot	shot	shot
show	showed	shown, showed
shrink	shrank, shrunk	shrunk
shrive	shrived, shrove	shrived, shriven
shut	shut	shut
sing	sang	sung
sink	sank	sunk
sit	sat	sat
slay	slew	slain
sleep	slept	slept
slide	slid	slid
sling	slung	slung
slink	slunk	slunk
slit	slit	slit
smell	smelt, smelled	smelt, smelled
smite	smote	smitten
sow	sowed	sown, sowed
speak	spoke	spoken
speed	sped, *speeded	sped, *speeded
spell	spelt, spelled	spelt, spelled
spend	spent	spent
spill	spilt, spilled	spilt, spilled
spin	spun, (*arch*) span	spun
spit	spat; (*esp US*) spit	spat; (*esp US*) spit
split	split	split
spoil	spoilt, spoiled	spoilt, spoiled
spotlight	spotlit, *spotlighted	spotlit, *spotlighted
spread	spread	spread
spring	sprang	sprung
stand	stood	stood
stave	staved, *stove	staved, *stove
steal	stole	stolen
stick	stuck	stuck
sting	stung	stung
stink	stank, stunk	stunk
strew	strewed	strewed, strewn
stride	strode	stridden
strike	struck	struck
string	strung	strung
strive	strove	striven
sublet	sublet	sublet
swear	swore	sworn
sweep	swept	swept
swell	swelled	swollen, swelled
swim	swam	swum
swing	swung	swung
take	took	taken
teach	taught	taught
tear	tore	torn
tell	told	told
think	thought	thought
thrive	thrived, throve	thrived, (*arch*) thriven
throw	threw	thrown
thrust	thrust	thrust
tread	trod	trodden, trod
unbend	unbent	unbent
underbid	underbid	underbid
undercut	undercut	undercut
undergo	underwent	undergone
underlie	underlay	underlain
underpay	underpaid	underpaid
undersell	undersold	undersold
understand	understood	understood
undertake	undertook	undertaken
underwrite	underwrote	underwritten
undo	undid	undone
unfreeze	unfroze	unfrozen
unsay	unsaid	unsaid
unwind	unwound	unwound
uphold	upheld	upheld
upset	upset	upset
wake	woke, (*arch*) waked	woken, (*arch*) waked
waylay	waylaid	waylaid
wear	wore	worn
weave	wove, *weaved	woven, *weaved
wed	wedded, wed	wedded, wed
weep	wept	wept
wet	wet, wetted	wet, wetted
win	won	won
wind[3] /waɪnd/	wound /waʊnd/	wound /waʊnd/
withdraw	withdrew	withdrawn
withhold	withheld	withheld
withstand	withstood	withstood
work	worked, *wrought	worked, *wrought
wring	wrung	wrung
write	wrote	written

APPENDIX 14
PUNCTUATION

Apostrophe (')

1 Used with 's' to indicate the possessive:
the dog's /dɒgz/ *bone* (singular noun)
the princess's /prɪnˈsesɪz/ *smile*
(singular noun ending in 's')
King Charles's /ˈtʃɑ:lzɪz/ *crown* OR
King Charles' /ˈtʃɑ:lzɪz/ *crown*
(proper noun ending in 's')
all the students' /ˈstju:dnts/ *books*
(plural noun)
the men's /menz/ *jackets* (irregular plural)

2 Used in contracted forms to indicate that letters or figures have been omitted:
I'm (= I am)
he's (= he is/has)
they'd (= they had/would)
the summer of '68 (= 1968)
(Note that apostrophes are not used with possessive determiners: *It's lost its top.*)

3 Sometimes used with 's' to form the plural of a letter, a figure or an abbreviation:
pronounce the r's more clearly
during the 1960's
all the MP's

Colon (:)

1 Used after a term describing a group or class or a linking phrase (eg *as follows, in the following manner*) to introduce a list of items:
His library consists of two books: the Bible and Shakespeare.
Proceed as follows: switch on the computer, insert a disk and press any key.

2 (*fml*) Used before a clause or phrase that illustrates or explains the main clause:
The garden had been neglected for a long time: it was overgrown and full of weeds.
(A semicolon or a full stop, but *not* a comma, may be used instead of a colon.)

3 ⇨ **Quotations** 2

Comma (,)

1 Used to separate the items in lists of words, phrases or clauses:
If you keep calm, take your time, concentrate and think ahead, you'll pass your driving test.
(Usually not used before *and*: *a bouquet of red, pink, yellow and white roses.*)

2 Often used between an adverbial clause or long phrase and the main clause:
When the sun is shining and the birds are singing, the world seems a happier place.
In the gales this autumn, many trees were blown down.

3 Used after a non-finite or verbless clause at the beginning of a sentence:
To be sure of getting there on time, she left an hour early.
Worn out by their experiences, the children soon fell asleep.

4 Used to separate an introductory or a transitional word or phrase (eg *therefore, however, by the way, for instance, on the contrary*) from the rest of the sentence:
Oh, so that's where it was!
As it happens, however, I never saw her again.
He is unreliable and should, for this reason alone, be dismissed.

5 Used before a dependent clause, etc that interrupts the sentence:
The fire, although it had been burning for several days, was still blazing fiercely.
You should, indeed you must, report this matter to the police.

6 Used before and after a non-defining relative clause or a phrase in apposition, giving additional information about the noun it follows:
The Pennine Hills, which are very popular with hikers, are situated between Lancashire and Yorkshire.
Mount Everest, the world's highest mountain, was first climbed in 1953.
(No commas are used around a clause that defines the noun it follows: *The hills that separate Lancashire from Yorkshire are called the Pennines.*)

7 Sometimes used to separate (especially long) main clauses linked by a conjunction (eg *and, as, but, for, or*):
He had been looking forward to our camping holiday all year, but unfortunately it rained every day.

8 Used to separate a question tag or similar word or phrase from the rest of the sentence:
It's quite expensive, isn't it?
You live in Bristol, right?

9 ⇨ **Conversation** 3, 4

10 ⇨ **Quotations** 1

Conversation

1 Normally a new paragraph is begun with each new speaker:
'You're sure of this?' I asked.
He nodded grimly.
'I'm certain.'

2 Quotation marks enclose all words and punctuation (but see 3, below):
'We must hope,' he replied wearily, 'that things will improve.'
(In British usage quotation marks are usually single: *'Help!'*; in US usage they are usually double: *"Help!"*. When dividing a long speech by one speaker into paragraphs, quotation marks are placed at the beginning of each paragraph and at the end of the speech, but not at the end of the intermediate paragraphs.)

3 Discourse markers (eg *he said, she told me, they complained*) are separated from the words spoken by commas unless a question mark or exclamation mark is used:
'That's all I know,' said Nick.
'That,' said Nick, 'is all I know.'
Nick said, 'That's all I know.'
'Why?' asked Nick.

4 Speech within speech is introduced by a comma and enclosed by **(a)** double quotation marks where single quotation marks are otherwise in use:
'When the judge said, "Not guilty", I could have hugged him.'
(b) single quotation marks where double quotation marks are otherwise in use:
"When the judge said, 'Not guilty', I could have hugged him."

5 Hesitant or interrupted speech is indicated by a dash or by three dots:
'Pass me – I mean, would you mind passing me the salt, please?'
His dying words were, 'The murderer was ...'

Dash (–)

(Cf **Hyphen**)

1 (*infml*) Used instead of a colon or semicolon to mark off a summary or conclusion of what has gone before:
Men were shouting, women were screaming, children were crying – it was chaos.
You've admitted that you lied to me – how can I trust you again?

2 (*infml*) Used singly or in pairs to separate extra information, an afterthought or a comment from the rest of the sentence:
He knew nothing at all about it – or so he said.
Winters in the Mediterranean – contrary to what many people think – can be very cold.

3 ⇨ **Conversation** 5
(In formal use, parentheses or commas replace dashes.)

Dots (...)

(also *esp US* **Ellipsis**)

1 ⇨ **Conversation** 5

2 ⇨ **Quotations** 3

Exclamation mark (!)

(*US* also **Exclamation point**)

Used at the end of a sentence or remark expressing great anger, surprise, joy or other strong emotion:
What wonderful news!
'Never!' she cried.
(In informal and especially in jocular use, more than one exclamation mark, or an exclamation mark and a question mark, are sometimes used: *'Your wife's just given birth to triplets.' 'Triplets!?'*)

Footnotes

Footnotes are indicated in the text by superscript numbers placed after the reference or quotation; the footnotes themselves appear either at the bottom of the page or at the end of the chapter or book:

For a more extended treatment of dialects, see the recent study by Frick[1]*, which one reviewer called 'a masterly analysis of this complex subject'*[2].

....

[1]Marjorie Frick, *English Dialects* (London: Faber and Faber, 1985).
[2]Peter Benson, 'Speaking in Tongues,' *Times Literary Supplement*, 11 April 1986.

Full stop (.)

(*US* **Period**)

1 Used to mark the end of a sentence that is not a direct question or an exclamation:
I knocked at the door. There was no reply.

2 Sometimes used, though not in this dictionary, in abbreviations:
Jan.; e.g.; a.m.

Hyphen (-)

(Cf **Dash**)

1 Used in compounds:
(a) Sometimes used to form a compound word from two other words:
hard-hearted; radio-telescope; fork-lift truck
(b) Used to form a compound from a prefix and a proper name:
pre-Raphaelite; pro-Soviet; anti-Nazi
(c) Used to form a compound from two other words that are separated by a preposition:
mother-in-law; mother-to-be; mother-of-pearl
(d) Used to vary the first element of a hyphenated compound:
common to both pre- and post-war Europe
(e) Used when forming attributive compounds from two or more proper names:
the Bush-Gorbachev summit
services on the London-Bahrain-Hong Kong route
(f) Used when writing out compound numbers between 21 and 99:
seventy-three; four hundred and thirty-one

2 (*esp Brit*) Sometimes used to separate a prefix ending in a vowel from a word beginning with the same vowel:
co-ordination; re-elect; pre-eminent

3 Used after the first section of a word that is divided between one line and the next:
... in order to avoid future mis-
takes of this kind.

4 Used between two numbers or dates to include everything that comes between these numbers or dates:
pp106-131
a study of the British economy, 1947-63

Italics

(In handwritten or typed text, and in the examples that follow, italics are indicated by underlining.)

1 Used to indicate stress or emphasis:
I'm not going to do it – you are.
... proposals which we cannot accept under any circumstances whatsoever.

2 Used for the titles of books, magazines, newspapers, plays, operas, films, paintings, etc:
Joyce's Ulysses
a letter in The Times / in today's Times
She has often sung the title-role in Tosca.

3 Used for foreign words or phrases that have not been naturalized into English and for the Latin names of plants and animals:
I had to renew my permesso di soggiorno, or residence permit.
'Tempus fugit,' (ie 'Time flies') as they say.
the English oak (Quercus robur)

Letters

➪ **Sample Texts** 3a, 3b

Parentheses ( )

(*Brit* also **Brackets**)

1 Used to separate extra information or an afterthought or a comment from the rest of the sentence:
Mount Robson (12 972 feet) is the highest mountain in the Canadian Rockies.
He thinks that modern music (ie anything written after 1900) is rubbish.

2 Used to enclose cross-references:
This moral ambiguity is a feature of Shakespeare's later works (see Chapter Eight).

3 Used to enclose numbers or letters in the text:
Our objectives are (1) to increase output, (2) to improve quality and (3) to maximize profits.
What you say is (a) untrue and (b) irrelevant.

4 ➪ **Square Brackets**

Question mark (?)

1 Used at the end of a direct question:
Where's the car?
You're leaving?
(Not used at the end of an indirect question: *He asked if I was leaving.*)

2 Used in parentheses to express doubt:
John Marston (?1575-1634)

Quotation marks (' ' " ")

(*Brit* also **Inverted commas**)

In British usage quotation marks are usually single: *'Help!'*. In US usage they are usually double: *"Help!"*.

1 Used to enclose all words and punctuation in direct speech:
'What on earth did you do that for?' he asked.
'I won't go,' she replied.
'Nonsense!'

2 Used to draw attention to a term that is unusual in the context (eg a technical or slang expression) or one that is being used for special effect (eg irony):
Next the dough is 'proved' to allow the yeast to start working.
He told me in no uncertain terms to 'get lost'.
Thousands were imprisoned in the name of 'national security'.

3 Used to enclose the titles of articles, short poems, radio and television programmes, etc:
Keats's 'Ode to Autumn'
I was watching 'Match of the Day'.

4 Used to enclose short quotations or sayings:
'Do you know the origin of the saying "A little learning is a dangerous thing"?'

5 ➪ **Conversation**, **Quotations**

Quotations

1 A short quotation is separated from its introduction by a comma and is enclosed in quotation-marks:
It was Disraeli who said, 'Little things affect little minds'.

2 A longer quotation is separated from its introduction by a colon and marked off from the rest of the text by indentation or spacing:
As Kenneth Morgan writes:
> *The truth was, perhaps, that Britain in the years from 1914 to 1983 had not changed all that fundamentally.*

Others, however, have challenged this view ...

3 A word or phrase omitted from a quotation is indicated by three dots; a word or phrase inserted into the quotation (eg to make the text grammatically correct) is enclosed in square brackets:
challenging Morgan's view that 'Britain in [these] years ... had not changed ...'

Semicolon (;)

1 Used instead of a comma to separate from each other parts of a sentence that already contain commas:
She wanted to be successful, whatever it might cost; to achieve her goal, whoever might suffer as a result.

2 (*fml*) Used to separate main clauses, especially those not joined by a conjunction:
The sun was already low in the sky; it would soon be dark.
He had never been to China; however, it had always been one of his ambitions.

Slash (/)

(*Brit* also **Oblique**) (*US* **Virgule**)

1 Used to separate alternative words or terms:
Take a mackintosh and/or an umbrella.
I certify that I am married/single/divorced (delete whichever does not apply).

2 Used to indicate the end of each line of poetry where several lines are run on:
Wordsworth's famous lines, 'I wandered lonely as a cloud / That floats on high o'er vales and hills ...'

Square brackets [ ]

(*US* **Brackets**)

1 Used to enclose editorial comments:
a notice reading 'Everything to be put away in it's [sic] *place after use'*
constant references in her diary to 'Mr G[*ladstone*]*'s visits'*

2 ➪ **Quotations** 3

Sample Texts

1

Serious and cultured speech and writing in America does not greatly differ from that used in Britain. However, during the 300 years in which American English has been developing, many new words or meanings have been added. There are also other differences: spelling (e.g. *color* = colour) and pronunciation, for instance. But these are of slight importance in comparison with the use of words and phrases which give American English its distinctive character.

This is only part of the picture, however. America is a vast country, and as Robert Burchfield has written, 'American English, as taught to foreigners, is ... not spoken by the majority of Americans.'

2

'But you said you loved me! "I'll never leave you, Sue, as long as I live." That's what you said, isn't it?'

Dave shrugged awkwardly.

'I don't remember exactly what I said,' he began, 'but ...'

'You liar!' Sue screamed, slapping his face. 'Lies, excuses, evasions – that's all I get from you. Well, I've had enough. You understand?'

'Look, I said I was sorry.'

Fixing him with a withering glare, Sue muttered, 'You *will* be sorry, Dave. I promise you that.'

3a

3 Willow Street
Frambleton
Suffolk
SF5 9PK

6 June 1989

The Director
Leisureland Hotels PLC
409 Piccadilly
London
WC2 4WW

Dear Sir

While staying in your hotel in Brighton recently, I mislaid a necklace which, although of little intrinsic value, was a great loss to me, as it belonged to my late mother. I mentioned the matter to the manager of the hotel concerned (Mr Perron), asking him to make enquiries. Several weeks later, I received a letter from him stating that the necklace had been found and asking me to 'call in at my convenience' to collect it.

Since then, I have written no fewer than four times to Mr Perron, explaining that it is not at all convenient for me to travel two hundred miles in order to collect the necklace in person, and asking him to post it to me. I have received no reply to any of these letters. May I ask you to contact Mr Perron and persuade him to send me my necklace as soon as possible?

Yours faithfully

Mary Burton

Mary Burton (Mrs)

3b

Willow St,
Frambleton

Friday

Dear Peter,

Sorry to trouble you, but I've got a bit of a problem with that necklace I lost. They've found it but don't want to send it back – they expect me to come and pick it up, if you please! I've written to their head office in London, but do you think there would be any chance of your picking it up for me next time you're in Brighton on business? If you can do it, phone me in advance so that I can authorize them to give it to you. You'd think it was the Crown Jewels, the way they're carrying on!

Best wishes,

Mary

NOUN AND ADJECTIVE CLASSES

C (**C**ountable noun) Refers to people or things that can be counted; singular form agrees with singular verb and plural form with plural verb: *a friend, a problem* ○ *these friends, those problems* ○ *A friend is coming to stay.* ○ *Your problem seems to be the same.* ○ *Not many friends were there.* ○ *Few problems were encountered.*

U (**U**ncountable noun) Refers to substances, qualities, etc that cannot be counted; not used with *a/an*; used in the singular form only, and with a singular verb: *butter, sympathy* ○ *much butter, little sympathy* ○ *This butter is expensive.* ○ *Not much sympathy was shown.*

CGp (**C**ountable **g**rou**p** noun) Refers to a collection of people or things; noun can be singular or plural; when singular, the noun can agree with a singular or plural verb: *She is on several committees.* ○ *The committee has/have elected a new chairwoman.* ○ *The Council meets/meet tomorrow.*

Gp (**G**rou**p** noun) Refers to a collection of people or things (and is usually a proper noun); used in the singular form only, but can agree with a singular or plural verb: *Whitehall is/are showing interest* ○ *The Kremlin has/have not yet reacted to the news.*

sing *v* (plural noun with **sing**ular **v**erb) *Dominoes is a relaxing game.* ○ *Measles is an infectious disease.* ○ *Physics is my best subject.*

pl *v* (singular noun with **pl**ural **v**erb) *More/Fewer police were on duty.* ○ *All the wounded have been treated.*

sing or pl *v* (plural noun with **sing**ular **or pl**ural **v**erb) *The barracks has/have been empty for some time.* ○ *The new steel works is/are going to create a lot of employment.*

pl (**pl**ural noun with **pl**ural verb) *These premises are unfurnished.* ○ *Our takings have increased.* Some nouns marked [pl] refer to garments, tools, etc, with two matching parts: *buy a pair of braces* ○ *another pair of trousers* ○ *I cut the wire with pliers.* ○ *These scissors are blunt.*

sing (**sing**ular noun with **sing**ular verb) Can be used with *a/an*: *Let me have a think.* ○ *An abundance of food was on display.*

attrib (**attrib**utive use) An adjective with this label can only be used *before* a noun: *sheer nonsense* ○ *a complete waste of time* ○ *an absolute disgrace.* A noun with this label can be used in front of another noun, to describe it: *a brick wall* ○ *a pottery jar* ○ *a silk blouse.*

pred (**pred**icative use) An adjective with this label can only be used after linking verbs (Ln, La) such as *be, seem, appear,* etc: *The house was ablaze.* ○ *This is tantamount to saying he is guilty.*

VERB PATTERN SCHEME

La (**L**inking verb + **a**djective)
*The soup **was delicious**.*

Ln (**L**inking verb + **n**oun)
*Frank **became** a **teacher**.*

I (**I**ntransitive verb)
*Frances is **reading**.*

Ipr (**I**ntransitive verb + **pr**epositional phrase)
*People are **complaining about** the traffic.*

Ip (**I**ntransitive verb + **p**article)
*The monkeys **chattered away**.*

In/pr (**I**ntransitive verb + **n**oun or **pr**epositional phrase
*The meeting **lasted** three **hours/for** three hours.*

It (**I**ntransitive verb + **t**o-infinitive)
*Jane **hesitated to phone** the office.*

Tn (**T**ransitive verb + **n**oun)
*A small boy **opened** the **door**.*

Tn·pr (**T**ransitive verb + **n**oun + **pr**epositional phrase)
*The accused **convinced** the **court of** his innocence.*

Tn·p (**T**ransitive verb + **n**oun + **p**article)
*The nurse **shook** the **medicine up**.*

Tf (**T**ransitive verb + **f**inite 'that' clause)
*Officials **believe that** a settlement is possible.*

Tw (**T**ransitive verb + **wh**-clause)
*We hadn't **decided what** we ought to do next/**what** to do next.*

Tt (**T**ransitive verb + **t**o-infinitive)
*Mary **hates to drive** in the rush-hour.*

Tnt (**T**ransitive verb + **n**oun + **t**o-infinitive)
*I **expect** the **parcel to arrive** tomorrow.*

Tg (**T**ransitive verb + -in**g** form of a verb)
*Peter **enjoys playing** football.*

Tsg (**T**ransitive verb + noun (+ **'s**) + -in**g** form of a verb)
*We **dread** Mary/**Mary's taking** over the business.*

Tng (**T**ransitive verb + **n**oun + -in**g** form of a verb)
*She **spotted** a **man waving** in the crowd.*

Tni (**T**ransitive verb + **n**oun + **i**nfinitive)
*We **watched** the **men unpack** the china.*

Cn·a (**C**omplex-transitive verb + **n**oun + **a**djective)
*The fridge **keeps** the **beer** cool.*

Cn·n (**C**omplex-transitive verb + **n**oun + **n**oun)
*The court **considered Smith** a trustworthy **witness**.*

Cn·n/a (**C**omplex-transitive verb + **n**oun + **as** + **n**oun or **a**djective)
*The police didn't **accept** the **story as** the **truth/as genuine**.*

Cn·t (**C**omplex-transitive verb + **n**oun + **t**o-infinitive)
*The thief **forced Jane to hand** over the money.*

Cn·g (**C**omplex-transitive verb + **n**oun + -in**g** form of a verb)
*The policeman **got the traffic moving**.*

Cn·i (**C**omplex-transitive verb + **n**oun + **i**nfinitive)
*Mother won't **let** the **children play** in the road.*

Dn·n (**D**ouble-transitive verb + **n**oun + **n**oun)
*Henri **taught** the **children French.***

Dn·pr (**D**ouble-transitive verb + **n**oun + **pr**epositional phrase)
*Henri **taught French to** the children.*

Dn·f (**D**ouble-transitive verb + **n**oun + **f**inite 'that' clause)
*Colleagues **told Paul that** the job wouldn't be easy.*

Dpr·f (**D**ouble-transitive verb + **pr**ep. phrase + **f**inite 'that' clause)
*Employers **announced to** journalists **that** the dispute had been settled.*

Dn·w (**D**ouble-transitive verb + **n**oun + **wh**-clause)
*The porter **reminded guests where** they should leave their luggage/**where** to leave their luggage.*

Dpr·w (**D**ouble-transitive verb + **pr**epositional phrase + **wh**-clause)
*You should **indicate to** the team **where** they are to assemble/**where** to assemble.*

Dn·t (**D**ouble-transitive verb + **n**oun + **t**o-infinitive)
*The director **warned** the **actors** not **to be** late.*

Dpr·t (**D**ouble-transitive verb + **pr**epositional phrase + **t**o-infinitive)
*Fred **signalled to** the waiter **to bring** another chair.*